INTERNATIONAL MONETARY FUND

Balance of
Payments Statistics

Part I: Country Tables

Yearbook 2008

BALANCE OF PAYMENTS STATISTICS YEARBOOK

Volume 59, Part 1: Country Tables, 2008
Prepared by the IMF Statistics Department
Adelheid Bürgi-Schmelz, Director, Statistics Department

For information related to this publication, please:
    fax the Statistics Department at (202) 623-6460,
    or write   Statistics Department
               International Monetary Fund
               Washington, D.C. 20431
    or e-mail your query to **StatisticsQuery@imf.org**
For copyright inquiries, please fax the Editorial Division at (202) 623-6579.
For purchases only, please contact Publication Services (see information below).

Balance of Payments Statistics Yearbook (BOPSY): Issued in three parts, this
annual publication contains balance of payments and international investment
position data. Part I provides detailed tables on balance of payments statistics for
approximately 174 countries and international investment position data for
116 countries. Part 2 presents tables of regional and world totals of major
balance of payments components. Part 3 contains description of methodologies,
compilation practices, and data sources used by reporting countries.

Cutoff date: August 25, 2008

Address orders to:
International Monetary Fund
Attention: Publication Services
Washington, D.C. 20431
U.S.A.
Telephone: (202) 623-7430
Telefax: (202) 623-7201
E-mail: publications@imf.org
Internet: http://www.imf.org

ISSN 0252-3035
ISBN 978-1-58906-753-0

CONTENTS

"Country" in this publication does not always refer to a territorial entity that is a state as understood by international law and practice; the term also covers the euro area, the Eastern Caribbean Currency Union, and some nonsovereign territorial entities, for which statistical data are provided internationally on a separate basis.

SELECTION OF STATISTICAL PUBLICATIONS

International Financial Statistics (IFS)
Acknowledged as a standard source of statistics on all aspects of international and domestic finance, *IFS* publishes, for most countries of the world, current data on exchange rates, international liquidity, international banking, money and banking, interest rates, prices, production, international transactions (including balance of payments and international investment position), government finance, and national accounts. Information is presented in tables for specific countries and in tables for area and world aggregates. *IFS* is published monthly and annually. *Price:* Subscription price is US$695 a year (US$445 to university faculty and students) for twelve monthly issues and the yearbook. Single copy price is US$89 for a monthly issue and US$145 for a yearbook issue.

Balance of Payments Statistics Yearbook (BOPSY)
Issued in three parts, this annual publication contains balance of payments and international investment position data. Part 1 provides detailed tables on balance of payments statistics for approximately 174 countries and international investment position data for 116 countries. Part 2 presents tables of regional and world totals of major balance of payments components. Part 3 contains descriptions of methodologies, compilation practices, and data sources used by reporting countries. *Price:* US$129.

Direction of Trade Statistics (DOTS)
Quarterly issues of this publication provide, for 158 countries, tables with current data (or estimates) on the value of imports from and exports to their most important trading partners. In addition, similar summary tables for the world, industrial countries, and developing countries are included. The yearbook provides, for the most recent seven years, detailed trade data by country for approximately 182 countries, the world, and major areas. *Price:* Subscription price is US$209 a year (US$179 to university faculty and students) for the quarterly issues and the yearbook. Price for a quarterly issue only is US$34, the yearbook only is US$92, and a guide only is US$12.50.

Government Finance Statistics Yearbook (GFSY)
This annual publication provides detailed data on transactions in revenue, expense, net acquisition of assets and liabilities, other economic flows, and balances of assets and liabilities of general government and its subsectors. The data are compiled according to the framework of the 2001 *Government Finance Statistics Manual,* which provides for several summary measures of government fiscal performance. *Price:* US$94.

CD-ROM Subscriptions
International Financial Statistics (IFS), Balance of Payments Statistics (BOPS), Direction of Trade Statistics (DOTS), and *Government Finance Statistics (GFS)* are available on CD-ROM by annual subscription. The CD-ROMs incorporate a Windows-based browser facility, as well as a flat file of the database in scientific notation. *Price of each subscription:* US$520 a year for single-user PC license (US$295 for university faculty and students). Network and redistribution licenses are negotiated on a case-by-case basis. Please contact Publication Services for information.

Subscription Packages

Combined Subscription Package
The combined subscription package includes all issues of *IFS, DOTS, BOPSY, GFSY,* and *Staff Papers,* the Fund's economic journal. *Combined subscription price:* US$1,195 a year (US$889 for university faculty and students). Expedited delivery available at additional cost; please inquire.

Combined Statistical Yearbook Subscription
This subscription comprises *BOPSY, GFSY, IFSY,* and *DOTSY* at a combined rate of US$415. Because of different publication dates of the four yearbooks, it may take up to one year to service an order. Expedited delivery available at additional cost; please inquire.

IFS on the Internet
The Statistics Department of the Fund is pleased to make available to subscribers the *International Financial Statistics (IFS)* database through an easy-to-use online service. The *IFS* database contains time series data beginning in 1948. The browser software provides a familiar and easy-to-use Windows interface for browsing the database, selecting series of interest, displaying the selected series in a spreadsheet format, and saving the selected series for transfer to other software systems, such as Microsoft Excel®. Single user license price for the *IFS Online Service* is $575, and $345 for academic users. Dependent on certain criteria, a range of scaled discounts is available. For full details of qualification for these discounts and online payment, please visit http://www.imfstatistics.org or email us directly at publications@imf.org.

Address orders to
Publication Services, IMF, Washington, DC 20431, USA
Telephone: (202) 623-7430   Telefax: (202) 623-7201   E-mail: publications@imf.org
Internet: http://www.imf.org

Note: Prices include the cost of delivery by surface mail. Expedited delivery is available for an additional charge.

INTRODUCTION[1]

Volume 59 of the *Balance of Payments Statistics Yearbook*, published by the International Monetary Fund (the Fund), contains balance of payments data that member countries have reported to the Fund. The Fund is grateful to these countries for their co-operation in providing these data. For some of these countries, some data have been supplemented by details Fund economists have derived from other sources.

The yearbook consists of three parts. Part 1 presents balance of payments and international investment position (IIP) data of individual countries. Part 2 contains regional and world totals for major components of the balance of payments. Part 3 provides technical descriptions for most reporting countries. Part 1 is separately bound, and Parts 2 and 3 are bound together.

This volume of the yearbook continues the features introduced in Volumes 46 through 58. As in Volume 46, balance of payments data are presented in accordance with the standard components of the fifth edition of the *Balance of Payments Manual (BPM5)*.[2] However, the standard components have changed with the publication of *Financial Derivatives, a Supplement to the Fifth Edition (1993) of the Balance of Payments Manual*, published in 2000 and amended in 2002. Thereafter, references to *BPM5* include the supplement and its addendum. In conformity with the recommendations in the addendum, this yearbook reflects the decision of the IMF Committee on Balance of Payments Statistics (BOPCOM) that the financial derivative transactions involving affiliated enterprises should be included in the financial derivatives component of the balance of payments statistics and the IIP. Similarly, as in Volume 47, IIP data also are presented in the *BPM5* format, and Part 3 of the yearbook publishes detailed reviews of the methodologies, compilation practices, and sources of data for most of the countries included in the volume.

The *BPM5*[3] introduced a number of methodological changes in the compilation of balance of payments data. Chapter I of the *BPM5* describes these changes in detail. Since Volume 46, a set of data codes has accompanied data presented in this yearbook under the standard components of the *BPM5*. These data codes were developed jointly by the Fund, the Organisation for Economic Cooperation and Development (OECD), and the Statistical Office of the European Union (Eurostat). An annex to this introduction explains the structure of the codes. In addition, beginning with Volume 46, the yearbook no longer presents quarterly balance of payments data for those countries that report quarterly balance of payments statistics to the Fund. Such quarterly data are published in the monthly Fund publication *International Financial Statistics (IFS)* and are available on the Balance of Payments Statistics CD-ROM, and on the Internet (BOP Online).

Data conversion work undertaken by the Fund staff has made possible the presentation in the *BPM5* format of both historical data from the Fund's database and more recent statistics reported by those member countries who are still compiling their data in the format of the fourth edition of the *Balance of Payments Manual (BPM4)*. In 1995, the Fund staff developed formulas to transform reported balance of payments data for each country in the Fund's database to approximate the *BPM5* methodology and presentation. Converted data for each reporting country were sent to the respective authorities for review, and their comments were incorporated in the new *BPM5* database. In 1996, the Fund staff, in collaboration with country authorities, completed a similar conversion of the *BPM4* IIP data into the *BPM5* presentation. In principle, the IIP of a country is a balance sheet of its stock of external financial assets and liabilities.

The technical descriptions of reporting countries' methodologies, compiling practices, and data sources, shown in Part 3 of the yearbook, are largely based on information that the countries provide to the Fund. The descriptions are intended to enhance users' understanding of the coverage, as well as of the limitations, of individual country data published in this yearbook. They are also designed to inform compilers of data sources and practices used by their counterparts in other countries.

The balance of this introduction is organized as follows:

- Section I describes essential features of the tables published in Part 1 of this volume of the yearbook. (Readers can find details on

---

[1]French and Spanish translations of this introduction appear after the annexes; data on individual countries follow immediately thereafter.

[2]Volume 1 of the yearbook, published in 1949, was based on the first edition of the Fund's *Balance of Payments Manual*, issued in 1948; Volumes 2-12 were compiled pursuant to the second edition of the manual, issued in 1950; Volumes 13-23 were based on the third edition of the manual, issued in 1961; and Volumes 24-29 were associated with that edition as well as the *Balance of Payments Manual: Supplement to Third Edition*, issued in 1973. Volumes 30-45 followed the guidance of the fourth edition of the manual, published in 1977.

[3]International Monetary Fund, *Balance of Payments Manual*, fifth edition, Washington, D.C., September 1993, and *Financial Derivatives, A Supplement to the Fifth Edition (1993) of the Balance of Payments Manual*, 2000.

coverage for Parts 2 and 3 in the separately bound publication.)

•　　　Section II offers information on the accessibility of the Fund's balance of payments data on CD-ROM and BOP Online.

•　　　There are six annexes. Annex I shows an analytic presentation of balance of payments components (and related data codes) arranged in a summary form. Annex II presents the standard components of the *BPM5* (and related data codes). Annex III explains the data coding scheme. Annex IV presents the standard components for IIP as shown in the *BPM5*. Annex V provides the conceptual framework of the balance of payments. Annex VI explains the coverage of major components of the balance of payments accounts, as set forth in the *BPM5*.

I. Part 1 of the Yearbook: Individual Country Data

Part 1 of the yearbook presents country pages alphabetically. "Country" in this publication does not always refer to a territorial entity that is a state as understood by international law and practice; the term also covers the euro area, the Eastern Caribbean Currency Union, and some nonsovereign territorial entities for which statistical data are provided internationally on a separate basis.

For most countries, balance of payments data are presented in two tables. Table 1 is an analytical summary of the more detailed data of Table 2. This table provides an array of balance of payments components to highlight the financing items (the reserves and related items). (See also Annex I.) Table 2 displays data in the standard components described in the *BPM5*. (See also Annex II.)

For countries for which IIP statistics are available, Table 3 presents those data. Tables 1, 2, and 3 present data for the years 2000–2007 for each country. Unless otherwise indicated, the tables report figures for calendar years.

Analytic Presentation

In the analytic presentation, shown in Table 1, balance of payments components are classified into five major data categories (groups A through E), which the Fund regards as useful for analyzing balance of payments developments uniformly. The selected groups, however, should not be considered to reflect the Fund's recommendation about the analytic approach appropriate for every country. Other analytical presentations could be arrayed by regrouping the standard components of Table 2 in other ways to take account of the special circumstances of a specific country or to serve particular analytical requirements.

Note that the figures shown in Tables 1 and 2 differ for some countries for balances of the current account, the capital account, and the financial account. This is because in Table 1 certain transactions under these accounts are excluded and reclassified as "exceptional financing" under reserves and related items. "Exceptional financing" refers to transactions undertaken by the authorities to finance balance of payments needs, including such items as external borrowing, payment arrears, and debt forgiveness. Exceptional financing does not include reserves.

Standard Presentation

The standard components of *BPM5*, shown in Table 2, list a more detailed classification of goods and services than appears in *BPM4*. The designated "capital and financial account" has separate components for the "capital" and the "financial account." Under the "financial account," components are classified by types of investment (i.e., direct investment, portfolio investment, financial derivatives,[4] other investment, and reserve assets), assets/liabilities, domestic sectors (monetary authorities, general government, banks, and other sectors), and original maturity.

International Investment Position

IIP data, as shown in Table 3, are arrayed in accordance with the standard components for IIP, as set forth in the *BPM5*. (See also Annex IV.)

Although the classification of the IIP components in Table 3 is consistent with that of the financial account of the balance of payments as shown in Table 2, there are several differences between the two tables. As mentioned earlier, IIP data reflect a country's external financial assets and liabilities at a specific point in time. Table 3, therefore, provides the basic presentation of the IIP components under two general categories, namely, assets and liabilities, as opposed to the functional types of investment (direct investment, portfolio investment, financial derivatives, other investment, and reserve assets) shown in Table 2. Also, the data in Table 3 reflect a country's IIP at the end of the reporting period, as opposed to transactions during the period shown in Table 2. Furthermore, unlike Table 2, which shows the value of financial transactions over a period, the

---

[4]Owing to the unique nature of financial derivatives, and the manner in which some institutions record transactions, some countries can provide only net transactions data. While such net data could be included under assets, in this yearbook it has been decided to include these net transactions, and net positions when reported, under liabilities. The reason is that one common source of demand for these instruments is from entities that are hedging cash flows associated with debt liabilities.

Box. International Investment Position

IIP statements for reporting countries are shown as Table 3 in the country pages. A country's IIP statement should be read in conjunction with the notes included in Part 3—Methodologies, Compilation Practices, and Data Sources—for that particular country. As countries collect more IIP data, the coverage of the IIP will be expanded in subsequent volumes of the yearbook.

Readers may refer to Chapter XXIII of the *BPM5* for a full discussion of the concept of international investment position.

External debt is not a separate component of the IIP but can be derived by summing up the non-equity liability components of the IIP (i.e., all recorded liabilities other than equity securities, direct investment equity capital [including reinvested earnings], and financial derivatives). Such a view is in general concordance with the core definition of gross external debt in the *External Debt Statistics: Guide for Compilers and Users*, prepared by the Inter-Agency Task Force on Finance Statistics. The Task Force was chaired by the IMF, and the work on the Guide involved representatives from the Bank for International Settlements, the Commonwealth Secretariat, the European Central Bank, Eurostat, the IMF, the OECD, the Paris Club Secretariat, the United Nations Conference on Trade and Development, and the World Bank.

Key Components [1]

A. Assets

1. Direct investment
    1.1 Equity capital and
        reinvested earnings
    1.2 Other capital[2]

2. Portfolio investment
    2.1 Equity securities
    2.2 Debt securities[4]

3. Financial derivatives
    3.1 Monetary authorities
    3.2 General government
    3.3 Banks
    3.4 Other sectors

4. Other investment
    4.1 Trade credits
    4.2 Loans
    4.3 Currency and deposits
    4.4 Other assets

5. Reserve assets
    5.1 Monetary gold
    5.2 SDRs
    5.3 Reserve position in the Fund
    5.4 Foreign exchange
    5.5 Other claims

B. Liabilities

1. Direct investment
    1.1 Equity capital and
        reinvested earnings
    1.2 Other capital[3]

2. Portfolio investment
    2.1 Equity securities
    2.2 Debt securities[3,4]

3. Financial derivatives
    3.1 Monetary authorities
    3.2 General government
    3.3 Banks
    3.4 Other sectors

4. Other investment
    4.1 Trade credits[3]
    4.2 Loans[3]
    4.3 Currency and deposits[3]
    4.4 Other liabilities[3]

---

[1] Not all components are shown, such as those broken down by sector (monetary authorities, general government, banks, and other) and, in some cases, by maturity. If a country reports IIP data with major subcomponents missing, totals may not be published.

[2] Liabilities to affiliated enterprises, a component of other capital, are included in external debt.

[3] Liabilities to direct investors, a component of other capital, are included in external debt.

[4] Includes bonds, notes, and money market instruments.

valuation of a country's IIP shown in Table 3 reflects the value of financial transactions, valuation changes, and other adjustments at the end of the reporting period. The net IIP shown in Table 3 is derived by taking the difference between the value of reported external financial assets and that of reported external financial liabilities.

Data Codes

Tables 1, 2, and 3 show codes for each data category and component. As mentioned earlier, these codes were developed jointly by the Fund, the OECD, and Eurostat and are intended to facilitate international data reporting. The codes are designed for the standard components of balance of payments and international investment position data as defined in the *BPM5*, as well as for the OECD/Eurostat components for trade in services.

There are six digits/characters for each code shown in the yearbook. The first digit designates credit/debit/net, with the number "2" assigned to credit, "3" to debit, and "4" to net (the difference between credit and debit). The next three digits are used to classify balance of payments components. For example the current account is coded 993, the capital account, 994, and the financial account, 995. Readers may refer to Annex III for details of the coding scheme.

The fifth and sixth digits/characters of the code shown in the yearbook denote special features about specific data components. For example, in Table 1, the fifth character Z indicates that the component excludes exceptional financing; W is used to show where exceptional financing and use of Fund credit and loans from the Fund are excluded. Letters A, B, C, and D in Table 1 differentiate the various domestic sectors. In Table 2, the letters A, B, and C indicate nonstandard subcomponents, such as those for transportation (viz., passenger, freight, and other).

Credits and Debits

In Tables 1 and 2, the transactions data are shown as gross credit or gross debit entries in the current and capital accounts. In the financial account, they are shown as net credit or net debit entries (to reflect net changes in liabilities and net changes in assets). Credit entries, gross or net, are positive (but without a plus sign), and debit entries, gross or net, are negative (with a minus sign). Thus, decreases in assets and increases in liabilities (credits) are shown as positive, and increases in assets and decreases in liabilities (debits) are shown as negative.

Nil, Unavailable Entries, or Confidential Data

It is often difficult to discern in data reported by countries whether missing numbers are not available, zero or insignificant, or confidential. In the yearbook tables, dots (....) indicate that data are either not available, zero or insignificant, or confidential. In cases where data for one or more given subcomponent cannot be revealed due to confidentiality reasons, the nondisclosed value(s) will be added to a generic subcomponent (such as "other") within the relevant data component, so that the totals are not changed.

A Note on the Components of *Income* and *Other Investment*

In Table 2, Standard Presentation, the data reported by certain countries under "income" and "other investment" are at a level of aggregation that does not allow all the individual components within this category to be separately identified. In these cases, therefore, the aggregate data for certain subcategories cannot be derived by summing the components for these subcategories. The same principle applies to "other investment" shown in Table 3, International Investment Position.

Previously, in Volumes 46 through 49, the tables showed data for "other investment" (assets and liabilities) under "long-term" and "short-term." Beginning with volume 50, tables now show the data for "other investment" (assets and liabilities) for monetary authorities, general government, banks, and other sectors as totals (of long- and short-term financing) and as "of which: short-term." (For "loans, monetary authorities," tables show the data as totals, as "of which: use of Fund credit and loans from the Fund," and as "of which: short-term.") However, in Annex II, the Standard Presentation has not been modified.

Rounding of Figures

Most data in the tables are expressed in units of one million; users should not assume that any table showing smaller units necessarily contains more accurate figures. The unit is chosen to present the figures conveniently. Because of the calculation routines used, there may be rounding differences between an aggregate and the sum of its components.

Currency Conversion

Most of the balance of payments data reported to the Fund are expressed in national currencies or in U.S. dollars, although some countries report certain data in SDRs. To ease comparisons among countries, all balance of payments statements published in the yearbook are expressed in U.S. dollars. In addition, all countries' reported data on transactions with the Fund and transactions in SDRs are replaced with data obtained from the Fund records, which are kept in SDRs. This information is, in turn, converted to U.S. dollars.

For countries that do not report in U.S. dollars, balance of payments data are converted using the country conversion rates shown at the bottom of Table 1. These rates are normally the average exchange rates for a country for the relevant period taken from the *IFS*. For example, the *IFS* pages for the Euro Area contain line "rf," giving average rates for euros per U.S. dollar. Conversions of transactions data from SDRs into U.S. dollars are made at the rates shown in line "sb" of the *IFS* pages for the United States. For countries reporting quarterly data in national currencies, annual U.S. dollar totals are obtained by aggregating the quarterly U.S. dollar figures.

For countries that do not report IIP data in U.S. dollars, data are converted using the country conversion rates shown at the bottom of Table 3. These rates are normally the end-of- period exchange rates for a country (line "ae") for the relevant period taken from *IFS*.

Readers may find more information on the exchange rates that are used in the introduction to *IFS*, Section 1.

II. CD-ROM and Internet Versions

Statistics published in the yearbook are also available on CD-ROM and on the Internet (Balance of Payments Statistics Online—BOP online). In this electronic version, the number of countries and time series covered is slightly larger than that appearing in the printed version of the yearbook, as is the number of periods for which data observations of time series are given. Also, quarterly data reported by countries are available, and updates and revisions of the data are included as they become available. Inquiries about the CD-ROM and BOP Online should be addressed to:

> Publication Services
> International Monetary Fund
> Washington, D.C. 20431, U.S.A.
> Telephone (202) 623-7430
> Telefax   (202) 623-7201
> E-mail   publications@imf.org
> Internet   http://www.imf.org

ANNEX I. ANALYTIC PRESENTATION

---

[1]Excludes components that have been classified in the categories of Group E.

ANNEX II. STANDARD PRESENTATION

Data Codes

Other services, credit	2 200 BA
Communications	2 245 ..
Construction	2 249 ..
Insurance	2 253 ..
Financial	2 260 ..
Computer and information	2 262 ..
Royalties and license fees	2 266 ..
Other business services	2 268 ..
Personal, cultural, and recreational	2 287 ..
Government, n.i.e.	2 291 ..
Other services, debit	3 200 BA
Communications	3 245 ..
Construction	3 249 ..
Insurance	3 253 ..
Financial	3 260 ..
Computer and information	3 262 ..
Royalties and license fees	3 266 ..
Other business services	3 268 ..
Personal, cultural, and recreational	3 287 ..
Government, n.i.e.	3 291 ..
C. INCOME	4 300 ..
Total Credit	2 300 ..
Total Debit	3 300 ..
Compensation of employees, credit	2 310 ..
Compensation of employees, debit	3 310 ..
Investment income, credit	2 320 ..
Direct investment income	2 330 ..
Dividends and distributed branch profits	2 332 ..
Reinvested earnings and undistributed branch profits	2 333 ..
Income on debt (interest)	2 334 ..
Portfolio investment income	2 339 ..
Income on equity	2 340 ..
Income on bonds and notes	2 350 ..
Income on money market instruments	2 360 ..
Other investment income	2 370 ..
Investment income, debit	3 320 ..
Direct investment income	3 330 ..
Dividends and distributed branch profits	3 332 ..
Reinvested earnings and undistributed branch profits	3 333 ..
Income on debt (interest)	3 334 ..
Portfolio investment income	3 339 ..
Income on equity	3 340 ..
Income on bonds and notes	3 350 ..
Income on money market instruments	3 360 ..
Other investment income	3 370 ..
D. CURRENT TRANSFERS	4 379 ..
Credit	2 379 ..
General government	2 380 ..
Other sectors	2 390 ..
Workers' remittances	2 391 ..
Other current transfers	2 392 ..

	Data Codes
Debit	3 379 ..
General government	3 380 ..
Other sectors	3 390 ..
Workers' remittances	3 391 ..
Other current transfers	3 392 ..
CAPITAL AND FINANCIAL ACCOUNT	4 996 ..
CAPITAL ACCOUNT	4 994 ..
Total Credit	2 994 ..
Total Debit	3 994 ..
Capital transfers, credit	2 400 ..
General government	2 401 ..
Debt forgiveness	2 402 ..
Other capital transfers	2 410 ..
Other sectors	2 430 ..
Migrants' transfers	2 431 ..
Debt forgiveness	2 432 ..
Other capital transfers	2 440 ..
Capital transfers, debit	3 400 ..
General government	3 401 ..
Debt forgiveness	3 402 ..
Other capital transfers	3 410 ..
Other sectors	3 430 ..
Migrants' transfers	3 431 ..
Debt forgiveness	3 432 ..
Other capital transfers	3 440 ..
Nonproduced nonfinancial assets, credit	2 480 ..
Nonproduced nonfinancial assets, debit	3 480 ..
FINANCIAL ACCOUNT	4 995 ..
A. **DIRECT INVESTMENT**	4 500 ..
Direct investment abroad	4 505 ..
Equity capital	4 510 ..
Claims on affiliated enterprises	4 515 ..
Liabilities to affiliated enterprises	4 520 ..
Reinvested earnings	4 525 ..
Other capital	4 530 ..
Claims on affiliated enterprises	4 535 ..
Liabilities to affiliated enterprises	4 540 ..
Direct investment in reporting economy	4 555 ..
Equity capital	4 560 ..
Claims on direct investors	4 565 ..
Liabilities to direct investors	4 570 ..
Reinvested earnings	4 575 ..
Other capital	4 580 ..
Claims on direct investors	4 585 ..
Liabilities to direct investors	4 590 ..

Data Codes

B.	**PORTFOLIO INVESTMENT**	4 600 ..
	Assets	4 602 ..
	Equity securities	4 610 ..
	Monetary authorities	4 611 ..
	General government	4 612 ..
	Banks	4 613 ..
	Other sectors	4 614 ..
	Debt securities	4 619 ..
	Bonds and notes	4 620 ..
	Monetary authorities	4 621 ..
	General government	4 622 ..
	Banks	4 623 ..
	Other sectors	4 624 ..
	Money market instruments	4 630 ..
	Monetary authorities	4 631 ..
	General government	4 632 ..
	Banks	4 633 ..
	Other sectors	4 634 ..
	Liabilities	4 652 ..
	Equity securities	4 660 ..
	Banks	4 663 ..
	Other sectors	4 664 ..
	Debt securities	4 669 ..
	Bonds and notes	4 670 ..
	Monetary authorities	4 671 ..
	General government	4 672 ..
	Banks	4 673 ..
	Other sectors	4 674 ..
	Money market instruments	4 680 ..
	Monetary authorities	4 681 ..
	General government	4 682 ..
	Banks	4 683 ..
	Other sectors	4 684 ..
C.	**FINANCIAL DERIVATIVES**	4 910 ..
	Monetary authorities	4 911 ..
	General government	4 912 ..
	Banks	4 913 ..
	Other sectors	4 914 ..
	Assets	4 900 ..
	Monetary authorities	4 901 ..
	General government	4 902 ..
	Banks	4 903 ..
	Other sectors	4 904 ..
	Liabilities	4 905 ..
	Monetary authorities	4 906 ..
	General government	4 907 ..
	Banks	4 908 ..
	Other sectors	4 909 ..
D.	**OTHER INVESTMENT**	4 700 ..
	Assets	4 703 ..
	Trade credits	4 706 ..
	General government	4 707 ..
	of which: short-term	4 709 ..
	Other sectors	4 710 ..
	of which: short-term	4 712 ..

	Data Codes
Loans	4 714 ..
Monetary authorities	4 715 ..
of which: short-term	4 718 ..
General government	4 719 ..
of which: short-term	4 721 ..
Banks	4 722 ..
of which: short-term	4 724 ..
Other sectors	4 725 ..
of which: short-term	4 727 ..
Currency and deposits	4 730 ..
Monetary authorities	4 731 ..
General government	4 732 ..
Banks	4 733 ..
Other sectors	4 734 ..
Other assets	4 736 ..
Monetary authorities	4 737 ..
of which: short-term	4 739 ..
General government	4 740 ..
of which: short-term	4 742 ..
Banks	4 743 ..
of which: short-term	4 745 ..
Other sectors	4 746 ..
of which: short-term	4 748 ..
Liabilities	4 753 ..
Trade credits	4 756 ..
General government	4 757 ..
of which: short-term	4 759 ..
Other sectors	4 760 ..
of which: short-term	4 762 ..
Loans	4 764 ..
Monetary authorities	4 765 ..
of which: Use of Fund credit and loans from the Fund	4 766 ..
of which: short-term	4 768 ..
General government	4 769 ..
of which: short-term	4 771 ..
Banks	4 772 ..
of which: short-term	4 774 ..
Other sectors	4 775 ..
of which: short-term	4 777 ..
Currency and deposits	4 780 ..
Monetary authorities	4 781 ..
General government	4 782 ..
Banks	4 783 ..
Other sectors	4 784 ..
Other liabilities	4 786 ..
Monetary authorities	4 787 ..
of which: short-term	4 789 ..
General government	4 790 ..
of which: short-term	4 792 ..
Banks	4 793 ..
of which: short-term	4 795 ..
Other sectors	4 796 ..
of which: short-term	4 798 ..
E. RESERVE ASSETS	4 802 ..
Monetary gold	4 812 ..
SDRs	4 811 ..
Reserve position in the Fund	4 810 ..
Foreign exchange	4 803 ..
Other claims	4 813 ..
NET ERRORS AND OMISSIONS	4 998 ..

ANNEX III. IMF/OECD/Eurostat Coding System for Balance of Payments, International Investment Position, and Trade In Services[1]

This coding system incorporates all the standard components and supplementary information lines of the fifth edition of the *Balance of Payments Manual,* as well as the components and memorandum items of the OECD-Eurostat classification for international trade in services.

The code consists of three components or sections as follows:

<position>   one decimal digit (selected from the range of 1 to 8) that describes the position of the subject in the international investment position (IIP)/balance of payments (BOP) accounts;

<BOP topic>   three decimal digits (selected from the range of integers from 100 to 998) that identify all the BOP, trade-in-services, and selected supplementary information components; and

<tag>   a user-defined component that may be of any length.

The complete code would take the form <position><topic><tag>. However, the tag component is optional. In contrast, the position and the topic components of the code are always required. Thus, a common implementation of the code will take the form <position><topic>.

The first section of the code describes the position in the IIP and BOP accounts and is defined as follows:

Code	Position in IIP/BOP Accounts
1	stock at the beginning of the period
2	credit flows
3	debit flows
4	net flows
5	price valuation adjustment
6	exchange rate valuation adjustment
7	other adjustments
8	stock at the end of the period
0	other

The first digit of the topic component identifies the section of the balance of payments as follows:

Code	Section of the accounts
1	goods
2	services
3	income and current transfers
4	capital account
5	direct investment
6	portfolio investment
7	other investment
8	reserves
9	aggregates, financial derivatives and supplementary information

The second and third digits of the component are generally sequential counts of the components with some gaps to allow for the possibility of additional codes being included at a later time. In addition, with the exception of the direct investment accounts, the second digit of the topic component takes the numbers 0, 1, 2, 3, or 4 for assets and 5, 6, 7, 8, or 9 for liabilities in the financial accounts.

Examples of data codes for "Other Investment" of the financial account are shown below.

Topic	Single Field			Multiple Field		
	Credit	Debit	Net	Credit	Debit	Net
Other investment	2700	3700	4700	2700	3700	4700
Liabilities	2750	3750	4750	2750	3750	4750
Loans	2762	3762	4762	2762	3762	4762
General govt.	2767	3767	4767	2767	3767	4767
Long-term	2768	3768	4768	2768	3768	4768
Short-term	2769	3769	4769	2769	3769	4769
Banks	2770	3770	4770	2770	3770	4770
Long-term	2771	3771	4771	2771	3771	4771
Short-term	2772	3772	4772	2772	3772	4772
Other sectors	2773	3773	4773	2773	3773	4773
Long-term	2774	3774	4774	2774	3774	4774
Short-term	2775	3775	4775	2775	3775	4775

When considering credits and debits for loans, the language that is commonly used is drawings and repayments. The *BPM5* recommends reporting of all drawings and repayments for long-term loans as a supplementary classification. Most other financial account items are presently collected by the Fund on a net basis. Nevertheless, the coding system provides for the identification of all flows on a credit, debit, and net basis.

---

[1] This is adopted from International Monetary Fund, "Balance of Payments Codes for Standard Components and Additional Items," Washington, D.C., March 3, 1995.

ANNEX IV. STANDARD COMPONENTS OF INTERNATIONAL INVESTMENT POSITION

Data Codes

A. ASSETS	8 995 C
Direct investment abroad	8 505 ..
Equity capital and reinvested earnings	8 506 ..
Claims on affiliated enterprises	8 507 ..
Liabilities to affiliated enterprises	8 508 ..
Other capital	8 530 ..
Claims on affiliated enterprises	8 535 ..
Liabilities to affiliated enterprises	8 540 ..
Portfolio investment	8 602 ..
Equity securities	8 610 ..
Monetary authorities	8 611 ..
General government	8 612 ..
Banks	8 613 ..
Other sectors	8 614 ..
Debt securities	8 619 ..
Bonds and notes	8 620 ..
Monetary authorities	8 621 ..
General government	8 622 ..
Banks	8 623 ..
Other sectors	8 624 ..
Money market instruments	8 630 ..
Monetary authorities	8 631 ..
General government	8 632 ..
Banks	8 633 ..
Other sectors	8 634 ..
Financial derivatives	8 900 ..
Monetary authorities	8 901 ..
General government	8 902 ..
Banks	8 903 ..
Other sectors	8 904 ..
Other investment	8 703 ..
Trade credits	8 706 ..
General government	8 707 ..
of which: short-term	8 709 ..
Other sectors	8 710 ..
of which: short-term	8 712 ..
Loans	8 714 ..
Monetary authorities	8 715 ..
of which: short-term	8 718 ..
General government	8 719 ..
of which: short-term	8 721 ..
Banks	8 722 ..
of which: short-term	8 724 ..
Other sectors	8 725 ..
of which: short-term	8 727 ..
Currency and deposits	8 730 ..
Monetary authorities	8 731 ..
General government	8 732 ..
Banks	8 733 ..
Other sectors	8 734 ..

	Data Codes
Other assets	8 736 ..
Monetary authorities	8 737 ..
of which: short-term	8 739 ..
General government	8 740 ..
of which: short-term	8 742 ..
Banks	8 743 ..
of which: short-term	8 745 ..
Other sectors	8 746 ..
of which: short-term	8 748 ..
Reserve assets	8 802 ..
Monetary gold	8 812 ..
SDRs	8 811 ..
Reserve position in the Fund	8 810 ..
Foreign exchange	8 803 ..
Other claims	8 813 ..
B. LIABILITIES	8 995 D .
Direct investment in reporting economy	8 555 ..
Equity capital and reinvested earnings	8 556 ..
Claims on direct investors	8 557 ..
Liabilities to direct investors	8 558 ..
Other capital	8 580 ..
Claims on direct investors	8 585 ..
Liabilities to direct investors	8 590 ..
Portfolio investment	8 652 ..
Equity securities	8 660 ..
Banks	8 663 ..
Other sectors	8 664 ..
Debt securities	8 669 ..
Bonds and notes	8 670 ..
Monetary authorities	8 671 ..
General government	8 672 ..
Banks	8 673 ..
Other sectors	8 674 ..
Money market instruments	8 680 ..
Monetary authorities	8 681 ..
General government	8 682 ..
Banks	8 683 ..
Other sectors	8 684 ..
Financial derivatives	8 905 ..
Monetary authorities	8 906 ..
General government	8 907 ..
Banks	8 908 ..
Other sectors	8 909 ..
Other investment	8 753 ..
Trade credits	8 756 ..
General government	8 757 ..
of which: short-term	8 759 ..
Other sectors	8 760 ..
of which: short-term	8 762 ..

Data Codes

	Data Codes
Loans	8 764 ..
Monetary authorities	8 765 ..
of which: Use of Fund credit and loans from the Fund	8 766 ..
of which: short-term	8 768 ..
General government	8 769 ..
of which: short-term	8 771 ..
Banks	8 772 ..
of which: short-term	8 774 ..
Other sectors	8 775 ..
of which: short-term	8 777 ..
Currency and deposits	8 780 ..
Monetary authorities	8 781 ..
General government	8 782 ..
Banks	8 783 ..
Other sectors	8 784 ..
Other liabilities	8 786 ..
Monetary authorities	8 787 ..
of which: short-term	8 789 ..
General government	8 790 ..
of which: short-term	8 792 ..
Banks	8 793 ..
of which: short-term	8 795 ..
Other sectors	8 796 ..
of which: short-term	8 798 ..
NET INTERNATIONAL INVESTMENT POSITION	8 995 ..
Conversion rates (end of period)	0 102 ..

This annex is reproduced from Chapter II of the BPM5. Please note that paragraph and page numbers cited in this annex refer to those that appear in the BPM5.

Definitions

12. Part one of this *Manual* deals with the conceptual framework of balance of payments accounts and the international investment position. Part one covers their relationship to national accounts; to concepts of residence, valuation, and time of recording; and to the unit of account and conversion.

13. The balance of payments is a statistical statement that systematically summarizes, for a specific time period, the economic transactions of an economy with the rest of the world. Transactions, for the most part between residents and nonresidents,[1] consist of those involving goods, services, and income; those involving financial claims on, and liabilities to, the rest of the world; and those (such as gifts) classified as transfers, which involve offsetting entries to balance—in an accounting sense—one-sided transactions. (See paragraph 28.)[2] A transaction itself is defined as an economic flow that reflects the creation, transformation, exchange, transfer, or extinction of economic value and involves changes in ownership of goods and/or financial assets, the provision of services, or the provision of labor and capital.

14. Closely related to the flow-oriented balance of payments framework is the stock-oriented international investment position. Compiled at a specified date such as year end, this investment position is a statistical statement of (i) the value and composition of the stock of an economy's financial assets or the economy's claims on the rest of the world, and (ii) the value and composition of the stock of an economy's liabilities to the rest of the world. In some instances, it may be of analytic interest to compute the difference between the two sides of the balance sheet. The calculation would provide a measure of the net position, and the measure would be equivalent to that portion of an economy's net worth attributable to, or derived from, its relationship with the rest of the world. A change in stocks during any defined period can be attributable to transactions (flows); to valuation changes reflecting changes in exchange rates, prices, etc.; or to other adjustments (e.g., uncompensated seizures). By contrast, balance of payments accounts reflect only transactions.

---

[1]The exceptions to the resident/nonresident basis of the balance of payments are the exchange of transferable foreign financial assets between resident sectors and, to a lesser extent, the exchange of transferable foreign financial liabilities between nonresidents. (See paragraph 318.)

[2]The definitions and classifications of international accounts presented in this *Manual* are intended to facilitate reporting of data on international transactions to the Fund. These definitions and classifications do not purport to give effect to, or interpret, various provisions (which pertain to the legal characterization of official action or inaction in relation to such transactions) of the *Articles of Agreement of the International Monetary Fund.*

Principles and Concepts

15. The remainder of this chapter deals with the conceptual framework of international accounts, that is, the set of underlying principles and conventions that ensure the systematized and coherent recording of international transactions and stocks of foreign assets and liabilities. Relevant aspects of these principles, together with practical considerations and limitations, will be thoroughly discussed in subsequent chapters.

Double Entry System

16. The basic convention applied in constructing a balance of payments statement is that every recorded transaction is represented by two entries with equal values. One of these entries is designated a credit with a positive arithmetic sign; the other is designated a debit with a negative sign. In principle, the sum of all credit entries is identical to the sum of all the debit entries, and the net balance of all entries in the statement is zero.

17. In practice, however, the accounts frequently do not balance. Data for balance of payments estimates often are derived independently from different sources; as a result, there may be a summary net credit or net debit (i.e., net errors and omissions in the accounts). A separate entry, equal to that amount with the sign reversed, is then made to balance the accounts. Because inaccurate or missing estimates may be offsetting, the size of the net residual cannot be taken as an indicator of the relative accuracy of the balance of payments statement. Nonetheless, a large, persistent residual that is not reversed should cause concern. Such a residual impedes analysis or interpretation of estimates and diminishes the credibility of both. A large net residual may also have implications for interpretation of the investment position statement. (See the discussion in Chapter XXIII.)

18. Most entries in the balance of payments refer to transactions in which economic values are provided or received in exchange for other economic values; those values consist of real resources (goods, services, and income) and financial items. Therefore, the offsetting credit and debit entries called for by the recording system are often the result of equal amounts having been entered for the two items exchanged. When items are given away rather than exchanged, or when a recording is one-sided for other reasons, special types of entries—referred to as *transfers*—are made as the required offsets. (The various kinds of entries that may be made in the balance of payments are discussed in paragraphs 26 through 31.)

19. Under the conventions of the system, a compiling economy records credit entries (i) for real resources denoting exports and (ii) for financial items reflecting reductions in an economy's foreign assets or increases in an economy's foreign liabilities. Conversely, a compiling economy records debit entries (i) for real resources denoting imports and (ii) for financial items reflecting increases in assets or decreases in liabilities. In other words, for assets—whether real or financial—a positive figure (credit) represents a decrease in holdings, and a negative figure (debit) represents an increase. In contrast, for liabilities, a positive figure shows an increase, and a negative figure shows a decrease. Transfers are shown as credits when the entries to which they provide the offsets are debits and as debits when those entries are credits.

20. The content or coverage of a balance of payments statement depends somewhat on whether transactions are treated on a gross or on a net basis. The recommendations in this *Manual* specify which transactions should be recorded gross or net. The recommendations are appropriately reflected in the list of standard components and in suggested supplementary presentations.

Concepts of Economic Territory, Residence, and Center of Economic Interest

21. Identical concepts of economic territory, residence, and center of economic interest are used in this *Manual* and in the *SNA*. (These concepts are discussed fully in Chapter IV.) Economic territory may not be identical with boundaries recognized for political purposes. A country's economic territory consists of a geographic territory administered by a government; within this geographic territory, persons, goods, and capital circulate freely. For maritime countries, geographic territory includes any islands subject to the same fiscal and monetary authorities as the mainland.

22. An institutional unit has a center of economic interest and is a resident unit of a country when, from some location (dwelling, place of production, or other premises) within the economic territory of the country, the unit engages and intends to continue engaging (indefinitely or for a finite period) in economic activities and transactions on a significant scale. (One year or more may be used as a guideline but not as an inflexible rule.)

Principles for Valuation and Time of Recording

23. A uniform basis of valuation for the international accounts (both real resources and financial claims and liabilities) is necessary for compiling, on a consistent basis, any aggregate of individual transactions and an asset/liability position consistent with such transactions. This *Manual* generally uses, as the basis of transaction valuations, actual market prices agreed upon by transactors. (This practice is consistent with that of the *SNA*.) Conceptually, all stocks of assets and liabilities are valued at market prices prevailing at the time to which the international investment position relates. A full exposition of valuation principles; recommended practices; limitations; and the valuation of transfers, financial items, and stocks of assets and liabilities appears in Chapter V. (The exposition includes cases in which conditions may not allow for the existence or assumption of market prices.)

24. In the *Manual* and the *SNA*, the principle of accrual accounting governs the *time of recording* for transactions. Therefore, transactions are recorded when economic value

is created, transformed, exchanged, transferred, or extinguished. Claims and liabilities arise when there is a change in ownership. The change may be legal or physical (economic). In practice, when a change in ownership is not obvious, the change may be proxied by the time that parties to a transaction record it in their books or accounts. (The recommended timing and conventions for various balance of payments entries, together with exceptions to and departures from the change of ownership principle, are covered in Chapter VI.)

Concept and Types of Transactions

25. Broadly speaking, changes in economic relationships registered by the balance of payments stem primarily from dealings between two parties. These parties are, with one exception (see footnote 1), a resident and a nonresident, and all dealings of this kind are covered in the balance of payments. Recommendations for specific entries are embodied in the list of standard components (see Chapter VIII) and are spelled out in detail from Chapter IX onward.

26. Despite the connotation, the balance of payments is not concerned with *payments*, as that term is generally understood, but with *transactions*. A number of international transactions that are of interest in a balance of payments context may not involve the payment of money, and some are not paid for in any sense. The inclusion of these transactions, in addition to those matched by actual payments, constitutes a principal difference between a balance of payments statement and a record of foreign payments.

Exchanges

27. The most numerous and important transactions found in the balance of payments may be characterized as *exchanges*. A transactor (economic entity) provides an economic value to another transactor and receives in return an equal value. The economic values provided by one economy to another may be categorized broadly as real resources (goods, services, income) and financial items. The parties that engage in the exchange are residents of different economies, except in the case of an exchange of foreign financial items between resident sectors. The provision of a financial item may involve not only a change in the ownership of an existing claim or liability but also the creation of a new claim or liability or the cancellation of existing ones. Moreover, the terms of a contract pertaining to a financial item (e.g., contractual maturity) may be altered by agreement between the parties. Such a case is equivalent to fulfillment of the original contract and replacement by a contract with different terms. All exchanges of these kinds are covered in the balance of payments.

Transfers

28. Transactions involving *transfers* differ from exchanges in that one transactor provides an economic value to another transactor but does not receive a quid pro quo on which, according to the conventions and rules adopted for the system, economic value is placed. This absence of value on one side is represented by an entry referred to as a *transfer*. Such transfers (economic value provided and received without a quid pro quo) are shown in the balance of payments. **Current transfers** are included in the **current account** (see Chapter XV) and *capital transfers* appear in the **capital account**. (See Chapter XVII.)

Migration

29. Because an economy is defined in terms of the economic entities associated with its territory, the scope of an economy is likely to be affected by changes in entities associated with the economy.

30. Migration occurs when the residence of an individual changes from one economy to another because the person moves his or her abode. Certain movable, tangible assets owned by the migrant are, in effect, imported into the new economy. The migrant's immovable assets and certain movable, tangible assets located in the old economy become claims of the new economy on the old economy. The migrant's claims on, or liabilities to, residents of an economy other than the new economy become foreign claims or liabilities of the new economy. The migrant's claims on, or liabilities to, residents of the new economy cease to be claims on, or liabilities to, the rest of the world for any economy. The net sum of all these shifts is equal to the net worth of the migrant, and his or her net worth must also be recorded as an offset if the other shifts are recorded. These entries are made in the balance of payments where the offset is conventionally included with transfers.

Other imputed transactions

31. In some instances, transactions may be imputed and entries may be made in balance of payments accounts when no actual flow occurs. Attribution of reinvested earnings to foreign direct investors is an example. The earnings of a foreign subsidiary or branch include earnings attributable to a direct investor. The earnings, whether distributed or reinvested in the enterprise, are proportionate to the direct investor's equity share in the enterprise. Reinvested earnings are recorded as part of direct investment income. An offset-

ting entry, with opposite sign, is made in the *financial account*, under direct investment, reinvested earnings, to reflect the direct investor's increased investment in the foreign subsidiary or branch. (Reinvested earnings are discussed in Chapters XIV and XVIII.)

Changes Other Than Transactions

Reclassification of claims and liabilities

32. The classification of financial items in the *Manual* reflects characteristics designed to reveal the motivation of creditor or debtor. Changes in motivation affect the characteristics, and financial items are subject to reclassification in accordance with such changes. A case in point is the distinction drawn between *direct investment* and other types of investment. For example, several independent holders of *portfolio investment* (in the form of corporate equities issued by a single enterprise abroad) may form an associated group to have a lasting, effective voice in the management of the enterprise. Their holdings will then meet the criteria for *direct investment*, and the change in the status of the investment could be recorded as a reclassification. Such a reclassification would be reflected, at the end of the period during which it occurred, in the international investment position but not in the balance of payments. Similarly, claims on nonresidents can come under, or be released from, the control of resident monetary authorities. In such cases, there are reclassifications between *reserve assets* and assets other than reserves.

Valuation changes

33. The values of real resources and financial items are constantly subject to change stemming from either or both of two causes: (i) The price at which transactions in a certain type of item customarily take place may undergo alteration in terms of the currency in which that price is quoted. (ii) The exchange rate for the currency in which the price is quoted may change in relation to the unit of account that is being used. Valuation changes are not included in the balance of payments but are included in the international investment position.

ANNEX VI. CLASSIFICATION AND STANDARD COMPONENTS OF THE BALANCE OF PAYMENTS

This annex is reproduced from Chapter VIII of the BPM5. Please note that paragraph and page numbers cited in this annex refer to those that appear in the BPM5.

Structure and Classification

139. Part two of this *Manual* deals with the structure and classification of balance of payments accounts and the international investment position. Part two encompasses the standard components of both sets of accounts and contains discussions and elaboration of the **current account**, the **capital and financial account**, selected supplementary information, and the international investment position.

140. Balance of payments statistics must be arranged within a coherent structure to facilitate their utilization and adaptation for multiple purposes—policy formulation, analytical studies, projections, bilateral comparisons of particular components or total transactions, regional and global aggregations, etc. (See paragraph 7.)

141. The standard classification and the list of components reflect conceptual and practical considerations, take into account views expressed by national balance of payments experts, and are in general concordance with the *SNA* and with harmonization of the expanded classification of international transactions in services with the Central Product Classification (CPC). (See Appendix III.)

142. The scheme also reflects efforts to link the structure of the **capital account** to income accounts and to the international investment position classification. The scheme is designed as a flexible framework to be used by many countries in the long-term development of external statistics. Some countries may not be able to provide data for many items; other countries may be able to provide additional data.

Standard Components

143. The determination of standard components (see list at end of this chapter) is based on a number of considerations. Those that have been given the greatest weight are:

The item should exhibit distinctive behavior. The economic factor or factors that influence the item should be different from those that influence other items, or the item should respond differently to the same factor or combination. This response to economic influences is what the balance of payments purports to make evident.

The item should be important for a number of countries. Importance may be defined as a function of behavior (unusual variability, for example) or as absolute size.

It should be possible to collect statistics for the item without undue difficulty. However, the desirability of collection should be evaluated according to the two previous criteria.

The item should be needed on a separate basis for other purposes, such as incorporation into, or reconciliation with, the national accounts. The list of standard components should not be unduly long. A large number of countries, including many that are statistically less advanced, are asked to report uniformly on the components.

To the extent practicable, standard components should be in concordance with, and apply to, other IMF statistical systems, the *SNA*, and, for **services** in particular, the CPC.

144. The list of standard components carries no implication that recommendations made in this *Manual* are intended to inhibit countries from compiling and publishing additional data of national importance. IMF requests for information will not be limited to standard components when further details are needed to understand the circumstances of particular countries or to analyze new developments. Supplementary information can also be most useful for verifying and reconciling the statistics of partner countries and, for example, analyzing exceptional financing transactions. (See the table entitled *Selected Supplementary Information* at the end of this chapter.) IMF staff will, from time to time, consult with countries to decide on the reporting of additional details.

145. Few countries are likely to have significant information to report for every standard component. Furthermore, several components may be available only in combination, or a minor component may be grouped with one that is more significant. The standard components should nevertheless be reported to the IMF as completely and accurately as possible. National compilers are in better positions than IMF staff to make estimates and adjustments for those components that do not exactly correspond to the basic series of the compiling economy.

Net Errors and Omissions

146. Application of the principles recommended in this *Manual* should result in a consistent body of positive and negative entries with a net (conceptual) total of zero. In practice, however, when all actual entries are totaled, the resulting balance will almost inevitably show a net credit or a net debit. That balance is the result of errors and omissions in compilation of statements. Some of the errors and omissions may be related to recommendations for practical approximation to principles.

147. In balance of payments statements, the standard practice is to show separately an item for net errors and omissions. Labeled by some compilers as a balancing item or statistical discrepancy, that item is intended as an offset to the overstatement or understatement of the recorded components. Thus, if the balance of those components is a credit, the item for net errors and omissions will be shown as a debit of equal value, and vice versa.

148. Some of the errors and omissions that occur in the course of compilation usually offset one another. Therefore, the size of the residual item does not necessarily provide any indication of the overall accuracy of the statement. Nonetheless, interpretation of the statement is hampered by a large net residual.

Major Classifications

149. The standard components, which are listed at the end of this chapter, are comprised of two main groups of accounts:

> The **current account** refers to *goods and services, income,* and *current transfers*.
>
> The **capital and financial account** refers to (i) *capital transfers* and *acquisition/disposal of nonproduced, nonfinancial assets* and (ii) financial assets and liabilities.

This arrangement is based on common historical usage in most countries and on a major change introduced in this *Manual*. The former capital account has been relabeled **capital and financial account**. Reflecting harmonization with the *SNA*, this change introduces that system's distinction between *capital transfers* and **current transfers** in balance of payments accounts and concordance of the account with *SNA* capital and financial accounts.

150. Current account entries for most items in the list of standard components should show gross debits and credits. Most **capital and financial account** entries should be made on a net basis; that is, each component is shown only as a credit or a debit. (The recommended treatments for specific items and exceptions are discussed in appropriate chapters.) Inflows of real resources, increases in financial assets, and decreases in liabilities should be shown as debits; outflows of real resources, decreases in financial assets, and increases in liabilities should be shown as credits. Transfers, both in sections 1.C and 2.A, should be numerically equal with opposite sign to the entries for which they provide offsets.

Detailed Classifications

151. The following classifications of standard components have been developed in accordance with the criteria set out in paragraph 143. The structure and characteristics of the **current account** and the **capital and financial account** and significant changes from the fourth to the fifth edition of the *Manual* are discussed in chapters IX and XVI, respectively. The standard components of the **current account** are described fully in chapters X through XV, and those of the **capital and financial account** are covered in chapters XVII through XXI, and in *Financial Derivatives, A Supplement to the Fifth Edition (1993) of the Balance of Payments Manual,* 2000.

Current Account (1.)

152. Covered in the **current account** are all transactions (other than those in financial items) that involve economic values and occur between resident and nonresident entities. Also covered are offsets to current economic values provided or acquired without a quid pro quo. Specifically, the major classifications are **goods and services, income,** and **current transfers**.

Goods and services (1.A.)

Goods (1.A.a.)

153. *General merchandise* covers most movable goods that are exported to, or imported from, nonresidents by residents and that, with a few specified exceptions, undergo changes in ownership (actual or imputed).

154. *Goods for processing* cover exports (or imports, in the compiling economy) of goods crossing the frontier for processing abroad and subsequent reimport (or export, in the compiling economy) of the goods, which are valued on a gross basis before and after processing. This item is an exception to the change of ownership principle.

155. *Repairs on goods* cover repair activity on goods provided to or received from nonresidents on ships, aircraft, etc. Although the physical movement of these goods is similar to that described in paragraph 154, the repairs are valued at the prices (fees paid or received) of the repairs and not at the gross values of the goods before and after repairs are made.

156. *Goods procured in ports by carriers* cover all goods (such as fuels, provisions, stores, and supplies) that resident/nonresident carriers—air, shipping, etc.—procure abroad (in the compiling economy). The classification does not cover the provision of auxiliary services (towing, maintenance, etc.), which are covered under *transportation*.

157. *Nonmonetary gold* covers exports and imports of all gold that is not held as a reserve asset (monetary gold) by the authorities. *Nonmonetary gold* is treated the same as any other commodity and is subdivided, when feasible, into gold held as a store of value and other (industrial) gold.

Services (1.A.b.)

158. *Transportation* covers most of the services, performed by residents for nonresidents and vice versa, that were included in shipment and other transportation in the fourth edition of the *Manual*. However, freight insurance is now included with *insurance services* rather than with *transportation*. *Transportation* includes freight and passenger transportation by all modes of transportation and other distributive and auxiliary services, including rentals of transportation equipment with crew. Certain exceptions are noted in chapters X, XI, and XIII.

159. *Travel* covers goods and services—including those related to health and education—acquired from an economy by nonresident travelers (including excursionists) for business purposes and personal use during their visits (of less than one year) in that economy. *Travel* excludes international passenger services, which are included in *transportation*. Students and medical patients are treated as travelers, regardless of their length of stay. Certain others—military and embassy personnel and nonresident workers—are not regarded as travelers. However, expenditures by nonresident workers are included in *travel*, while those of military and embassy personnel are included in *government services, n.i.e.* These cases are noted in chapters XII and XIII.

160. *Communications services* cover communications transactions between residents and nonresidents. Such services comprise postal, courier, and telecommunications services (transmission of sound, images, and other information by various modes and associated maintenance provided by/for residents by/for nonresidents).

161. *Construction services* cover construction and installation project work that is, on a temporary basis, performed abroad/in the compiling economy or in extraterritorial enclaves by resident/nonresident enterprises and their personnel. Such work does not include that undertaken by a foreign affiliate of a resident enterprise or by an unincorporated site office that, if it meets certain criteria, is equivalent to a foreign affiliate. Such residency aspects are covered in chapters IV and XIII.

162. *Insurance services* cover the provision of insurance to nonresidents by resident insurance enterprises and vice versa. This item comprises services provided for freight insurance (on goods exported and imported), services provided for other types of direct insurance (including life and non-life), and services provided for reinsurance. (For the method of calculating the value of insurance services, see paragraphs 256 and 257.)

163. *Financial services* (other than those related to insurance enterprises and pension funds) cover financial intermediation services and auxiliary services conducted between residents and nonresidents. Included are commissions and fees for letters of credit, lines of credit, financial leasing services, foreign exchange transactions, consumer and business credit services, brokerage services, underwriting services, arrangements for various forms of hedging instruments, etc. Auxiliary services include financial market operational and regulatory services, security custody services, etc.

164. *Computer and information services* cover resident/nonresident transactions related to hardware consultancy, software implementation, information services (data processing, database, news agency), and maintenance and repair of computers and related equipment.

165. *Royalties and license fees* cover receipts (exports) and payments (imports) of residents and nonresidents for: (i) the authorized use of intangible nonproduced, nonfinancial assets and proprietary rights such as trademarks, copyrights, patents, processes, techniques, designs, manufacturing rights, franchises,

etc. and (ii) the use, through licensing agreements, of produced originals or prototypes, such as manuscripts, films, etc.

166. *Other business services* provided by residents to nonresidents and vice versa cover merchanting and other trade-related services; operational leasing services; and miscellaneous business, professional, and technical services. (See the table on *Selected Supplementary Information* following this chapter and paragraphs 261 through 264 for details.)

167. *Personal, cultural, and recreational services* cover (i) audiovisual and related services and (ii) other cultural services provided by residents to nonresidents and vice versa. Included under (i) are services associated with the production of motion pictures on films or video tape, radio and television programs, and musical recordings. (Examples of these services are rentals and fees received by actors, producers, etc. for productions and for distribution rights sold to the media.) Included under (ii) are other personal, cultural, and recreational services, such as those associated with libraries, museums, and other cultural and sporting activities.

168. *Government services, n.i.e.* cover all services (such as expenditures of embassies and consulates) associated with government sectors or international and regional organizations and not classified under other items.

Income (1.B.)

169. *Compensation of employees* covers wages, salaries, and other benefits, in cash or in kind, and includes those of border, seasonal, and other nonresident workers (e.g., local staff of embassies).

170. *Investment income* covers receipts and payments of income associated, respectively, with holdings of external financial assets by residents and with liabilities to nonresidents. *Investment income* consists of direct investment income, portfolio investment income, and other investment income. The direct investment component is broken down into income on equity (dividends, branch profits, and reinvested earnings) and income on debt (interest); portfolio investment income is broken down into income on equity (dividends) and income on debt (interest); other investment income covers interest earned on other capital (loans, etc.) and, in principle, imputed income to households from net equity in life insurance reserves and in pension funds.

Current transfers (1.C.)

171. *Current transfers* are distinguished from *capital transfers*, which are included in the **capital and financial account** in accordance with the *SNA* treatment of transfers. Transfers are the offsets to changes, which take place between residents and nonresidents, in ownership of real resources or financial items and, whether the changes are voluntary or compulsory, do not involve a quid pro quo in economic value. ***Current transfers*** consist of all transfers that **do not involve** (i) transfers of ownership of fixed assets; (ii) transfers of funds linked to, or conditioned upon, acquisition or disposal of fixed assets; (iii) forgiveness, without any counterparts being received in return, of liabilities by creditors. All of these are *capital transfers*. **Current transfers** include those of general government (e.g., current international cooperation between different governments, payments of current taxes on income and wealth, etc.) and other transfers (e.g., workers' remittances, premiums—less service charges, and claims on non-life insurance). A full discussion of the distinction between **current transfers** and *capital transfers* appears in Chapter XV; see also paragraphs 175 and 344.

Capital and Financial Account (2.)

172. The **capital and financial account** has two major components—the ***capital account*** and the ***financial account***—that are in concordance with those same accounts in the *SNA*. Assets represent claims on nonresidents, and liabilities represent indebtedness to nonresidents. The two parties to a transaction in assets or liabilities are usually a resident and a nonresident but, in some instances, both parties may both be residents or nonresidents. (See paragraph 318.)

173. All valuation and other changes in foreign assets and liabilities, which do not reflect transactions (see paragraph 310), are excluded from the **capital and financial account** but are reflected in the international investment position. Supplementary statements identify certain items that are of analytical interest and that affect various accounts. Examples of such items are liabilities constituting foreign authorities' reserves and exceptional financing transactions, which are discussed in Chapter XXII.

174. Classification of the ***financial account*** and the income components of the **current account** are interrelated and must be consistent to facilitate analysis, to form an effective link between the balance of payments and the international investment position, and to be compatible with the *SNA* and other IMF statistical systems.

Capital account (2.A.)

175. The major components of the ***capital account*** are *capital transfers* and *acquisition/disposal of nonproduced, nonfinancial assets*. *Capital transfers* consist of those involving transfers of ownership of fixed assets; transfers of funds linked to, or conditional upon, acquisition or disposal of fixed assets; or cancellation, without any counterparts being received in return, of liabilities by creditors. *Capital transfers* include two components: (i) general government, subdivided into debt forgiveness and other, and (ii) other, subdivided into migrants' transfers, debt forgiveness, and other

transfers. (See Chapter XV for discussion of the distinction between *capital transfers* and **current transfers**. *Acquisition/disposal of nonproduced, nonfinancial assets largely covers intangibles, such as patented entities, leases or other transferable contracts, goodwill, etc. This item does not cover land in a specific economic territory but may include the purchase or sale of land by a foreign embassy.* (See paragraph 312.)

Financial account (2.B.)

176. The classification of standard components in the ***financial account*** is based on these criteria:

All components are classified according to type of investment or by functional breakdown (*direct investment, portfolio investment, financial derivatives, other investment, reserve assets*).

For the category of *direct investment*, there are directional distinctions (abroad or in the reporting economy) and for the equity capital, other capital.

For the categories of *portfolio investment, financial derivatives,* and *other investment*, there are the customary asset/liability distinctions.

Particularly significant for *portfolio investment* and *other investment* is the distinction by type of instrument (equity or debt securities, trade credits, loans, currency and deposits, other assets or liabilities). In this *Manual*, traditional and new money market and other financial instruments are included in *portfolio investment*.

For *portfolio investment, financial derivatives,* and *other investment*, there are distinctions by sector of the domestic creditor for assets or by sector of the domestic debtor for liabilities. These distinctions serve to facilitate links with the income accounts, the international investment position, the *SNA*, and other statistical systems.

The traditional distinction, which is based on original contractual maturity of more than one year or one year or less, between long- and short-term assets and liabilities applies only to *other investment*. In recent years, the significance of this distinction has clearly diminished for many domestic and international transactions. Consequently, the long- and short-term distinction is accorded less importance in the *SNA* and in this *Manual* than in previous editions. However, because the maturity factor remains important for specific purposes—analysis of external debt, for example—it is retained in the *Manual* for *other investment*.

177. *Direct investment*—reflecting the lasting interest of a resident entity in one economy (direct investor) in an entity resident in another economy (direct investment enterprise)—covers all transactions between direct investors and direct investment enterprises. That is, *direct investment* covers the initial transaction between the two and all subsequent transactions between them and among affiliated enterprises, both incorporated and unincorporated. Direct investment transactions occurring abroad and in the reporting economy are subclassified into equity capital, reinvested earnings, other capital (intercompany debt transactions). For equity capital and other capital, claims on and liabilities to affiliated enterprises and to direct investors are distinguished. Transactions between affiliated banks and between other affiliated financial intermediaries are limited to equity and permanent debt capital. (See paragraph 372 of the fifth edition of the *Balance of Payments Manual.*)

178. *Portfolio investment* covers transactions in equity securities and debt securities; the latter are subclassified, into bonds and notes and money market instruments. Various new financial instruments, other than financial derivatives, are covered under appropriate instrument classifications. (Transactions covered under *direct investment* and *reserve assets* are excluded.)

179. The *financial derivatives* category covers financial instruments that are linked to other specific financial instruments, indicators, or commodities and through which specific financial risks (such as interest rate risk, foreign exchange risk, equity and commodity price risks, credit risk. etc.) can, in their own right, be traded in financial markets. Transactions in financial derivatives should be treated as separate transactions rather than as integral parts of the values of the underlying transactions to which they are linked.

180. *Other investment* covers short- and long-term trade credits; loans (including use of Fund credit, loans from the Fund, and loans associated with financial leases); currency and deposits (transferable and other—such as savings and term deposits, savings and loan shares, shares in credit unions, etc.); and other accounts receivable and payable. (Transactions covered under *direct investment* are excluded.)

181. *Reserve assets* cover transactions in those assets that are considered, by the monetary authorities of an economy, to be available for use in meeting balance of payments and, in some instances, other needs. Such availability is not closely linked in principle to formal criteria such as ownership or currency of denomination. The items covered are monetary gold, SDRs, reserve position in the Fund, foreign exchange assets (currency, deposits, and securities), and other claims.

182. Coverage and identification of *reserve asset* components are linked to an analytic concept, are in part judgmental, and are not always amenable to application of objective, formal criteria or clear rankings as to conditionality and other considerations. In contrast to the treatment in the fourth edition of the *Manual*, valuation changes in *reserve assets* are excluded, along with counterparts to such changes, in the fifth edition. Also excluded are the allocation/cancellation of SDRs, the monetization/demonetization of gold, and counterpart entries. These changes, which do not constitute transactions, are reflected in the international investment position.

INTRODUCTION

Le volume 59 du *Balance of Payments Statistics Yearbook* (Annuaire de statistiques de balance des paiements) (l'annuaire), publié par le Fonds monétaire international (FMI), présente les données de balance des paiements que lui ont communiqué ses pays membres. Le FMI est reconnaissant à ces derniers d'avoir collaboré au présent ouvrage en lui fournissant ces informations. Pour certains pays, les données sont parfois complétées par des renseignements que les économistes ont tirées d'autres sources.

Le présent volume de l'annuaire se compose de trois parties. La première présente les données de la balance des paiements et de la position extérieure globale (PEG) pour les divers pays. La deuxième contient des totaux régionaux et mondiaux pour les principales composantes de la balance des paiements. La troisième partie fournit une description technique des méthodes de la plupart des pays qui ont communiqué les données. La première partie constitue une publication distincte, et les deuxième et troisième parties sont reliées ensemble.

Les caractéristiques introduites dans les volumes 46 à 58 sont conservées dans le présent ouvrage. Comme dans le volume 46, les données de balance des paiements sont présentées conformément à la classification des composantes types adoptées dans la cinquième édition du *Manuel de la balance des paiements (MBP5)*[1]. Il convient toutefois de noter que les composantes types ont été modifiées par suite de la publication, en 2000, puis de la modification en 2002, de l'ouvrage intitulé «*Dérivés financiers — Supplément à la cinquième édition (1993) du Manuel de la balance des paiements*» (le Supplément). À compter de cette date, toute référence au *MBP5* renvoie également au Supplément et à son addendum. Conformément aux recommandations formulées dans l'addendum, le présent annuaire rend compte de la décision prise par le Comité d'experts de la balance des paiements créé sous les auspices du FMI (Comité d'experts) qui préconise d'inclure les trans

actions sur dérivés financiers effectuées par les entreprises apparentées dans la composante dérivés financiers de la balance des paiements et de la position extérieure globale (PEG). Parallèlement, comme pour le volume 47, les données sur la PEG sont elles aussi présentées conformément au *MBP5*, et la troisième partie de l'annuaire présente une analyse détaillée des méthodologies, méthodes de calcul et sources de données utilisées par la plupart des pays compris dans l'annuaire. Le *MBP5*[2] apporte un certain nombre de changements à la méthodologie utilisée pour l'établissement des données de balance des paiements. Ces changements sont décrits en détail au chapitre I du *MBP5*. Depuis la publication du volume 46, une série de codes accompagne les données présentées dans le présent Annuaire conformément à la classification des composantes types du *MBP5*. Ces codes ont été mis au point conjointement par le FMI, l'Organisation de coopération et de développement économiques (OCDE) et l'Office statistique de l'Union européenne (Eurostat). La structure de ces codes est décrite en annexe. En outre, à partir du volume 46, l'annuaire ne présente plus de données trimestrielles de balance des paiements pour les pays qui communiquent ce type de statistiques au FMI. Ces données trimestrielles sont publiées dans l'édition mensuelle de *Statistiques financières internationales (SFI)*, et sont également disponibles sur le CD-ROM de balance des paiements ainsi que sur la version Internet en ligne (BOP Online).

La conversion des données par les services du FMI a permis de présenter, selon la classification retenue dans le *MBP5*, les statistiques de la base de données du FMI qui se rapportent à des périodes antérieures, ainsi que les données communiquées pour des périodes plus récentes par les pays membres qui continuent à suivre les recommandations de la quatrième édition du *Manuel de la balance des paiements*. En 1995, les services du FMI ont mis au point des formules de conversion permettant de mettre sous une forme à peu près conforme à la méthodologie et à la présentation retenues dans la cinquième édition les données de balance des paiements reçues de chaque pays et figurant dans la base de données du FMI. Une fois converties, les données ont été soumises à l'examen des autorités des pays en question, et les observations formulées ont été incorporées dans la nouvelle base de données du *MBP5*. En 1996, avec la collaboration des autorités nationales, les services du FMI ont procédé d'une manière analogue pour présenter conformément au *MBP5* les données sur la PEG établies selon les recommandations de la quatrième édition. En principe, la PEG d'un pays est un relevé du stock de ses avoirs et engagements financiers extérieurs.

---

[1]Le volume 1 de l'annuaire, paru en 1949, était fondé sur la première édition du Manuel de la balance des paiements du FMI, publiée en 1948; les volumes 2 à 12, sur la deuxième édition du Manuel, publiée en 1950; les volumes 13 à 23, sur la troisième édition du Manuel, publiée en 1961; et les volumes 24 à 29, sur la troisième édition, ainsi que sur le Manuel de la balance des paiements : supplément à la troisième édition, paru en 1973. Les volumes 30 à 45 ont été établis sur la base des directives de la quatrième édition du Manuel, publiée en 1977.

[2]Fonds monétaire international, Manuel de la balance des paiements, cinquième édition, Washington, Septembre 1993, et Dérivés financiers — Supplément à la cinquième édition (1993) du Manuel de la balance des paiements, Washington, 2000.

La troisième partie présente une description technique des méthodologies, méthodes de calcul et sources de données qui se fonde en grande partie sur les renseignements que les pays transmettent au FMI. Les descriptions ont pour but de mieux renseigner les utilisateurs sur la couverture et les limitations des données publiées pour les différents pays dans cet annuaire, de même que les statisticiens sur les sources de données et méthodes utilisées par leurs homologues étrangers.

Le reste de la présente introduction s'articule comme suit :

• La section I décrit les caractéristiques fondamentales des tableaux publiés dans la première partie du présent volume de l'annuaire. (Les lecteurs trouveront dans les deuxième et troisième parties des précisions sur le champ d'application des données.)

• La section II donne des indications sur l'abonnement aux données de balance des paiements du FMI sur disques optiques compacts (CD-ROM et BOP Online).

• Il y a six annexes. L'annexe I contient une présentation analytique des composantes de la balance des paiements (accompagnées des codes correspondants) sous forme résumée. L'annexe II présente les composantes types définies dans le *MBP5* (et les codes correspondants). L'annexe III explique le système de codage des données. L'annexe IV présente les composantes types de la PEG, telles qu'elles ressortent du *MBP5*. L'annexe V est consacrée au cadre conceptuel de la balance des paiements. L'annexe VI décrit le champ couvert par les principales composantes de la balance des paiements, telles qu'elles sont définies dans le *MBP5*.

I. Première partie de l'annuaire : données relatives aux pays

La première partie de l'annuaire présente les pages consacrées aux divers pays suivant un ordre alphabétique. Il convient de noter toutefois que, dans la présente publication, le terme «pays» ne désigne pas toujours une entité territoriale constituant un État tel qu'il est défini selon l'usage et le droit internationaux; ce terme recouvre également la zone euro, l'Union monétaire des Caraïbes orientales et certaines entités territoriales qui ne sont pas des États souverains mais sur lesquelles des données statistiques sont disponibles séparément au niveau international.

Pour la plupart des pays, les données de balance des paiements se présentent sous la forme de deux tableaux. Le tableau 1 constitue un résumé analy-

tique des données plus détaillées contenues au tableau 2, et présente toute une série de composantes de la balance des paiements de manière à mettre en relief les postes de financement (réserves et postes apparentés). (Voir aussi l'annexe I). Le tableau 2 présente des données correspondant aux composantes types décrites dans le *MBP5*. (Voir aussi l'annexe II). Dans le cas des pays pour lesquels on dispose de statistiques sur la PEG, ces dernières figurent au tableau 3. Les tableaux 1, 2 et 3 présentent, pour chaque pays, des données pour les années 2000 à 2007. Sauf indication contraire, les chiffres portent sur l'année civile.

Présentation analytique

Dans la présentation analytique, qui fait l'objet du tableau 1, les composantes de la balance des paiements sont réparties entre cinq grandes catégories (groupes A à E), que le FMI juge utiles à une analyse homogène de l'évolution de la balance des paiements. Cependant, le choix des groupes ne saurait être considéré comme découlant de la recommandation du FMI quant à l'approche analytique à retenir pour chaque pays. Il existe d'autres types de présentation analytique, qui consisteraient à regrouper les composantes types du tableau 2 d'une manière différente, soit pour tenir compte de la situation particulière d'un pays donné, soit pour répondre à des besoins analytiques précis.

Il convient de noter que les données présentées au tableau 1 sur le solde du compte des transactions courantes, du compte de capital et du compte d'opérations financières de certains pays ne concordent pas avec les données correspondantes du tableau 2. Cela tient au fait que, dans le tableau 1, certaines transactions relevant de ces comptes en sont exclues et sont reclassées en tant que «financement exceptionnel» à la rubrique des réserves et postes apparentés. Le «financement exceptionnel» se rapporte aux transactions que les autorités effectuent pour répondre aux besoins de financement de la balance des paiements et prend notamment la forme d'emprunts extérieurs, d'arriérés de paiements et de remises de dette. Le financement exceptionnel ne comprend pas les réserves.

Présentation type

Comme le montre le tableau 2, la liste des composantes types du *MBP5* présentée au tableau 2 fait apparaître une classification plus détaillée des biens et services que celle qui figure dans la quatrième édition. Le compte dénommé «compte de capital et d'opérations financières» comporte deux volets distincts, qui sont le «compte de capital» et le «compte d'opérations financières». Les composantes du «compte d'opérations financières»

Encadré – Position extérieure globale

Les relevés de la PEG des pays déclarants font l'objet du tableau 3 aux pages par pays. Il convient, pour chaque pays donné, de lire le relevé de la PEG en consultant simultanément les notes de la troisième partie — Méthodologies, méthodes de calcul et sources de données — qui se rapportent au pays concerné. Au fur et à mesure que les pays recueilleront davantage de données pour la PEG, la couverture des données de la PEG sera élargie dans les éditions ultérieures de l'Annuaire.

Voir le chapitre XXIII du *MBP5* pour une étude exhaustive du concept de position extérieure globale.

La dette extérieure ne constitue pas une composante distincte de la PEG, mais elle peut être calculée par addition des composantes de la PEG autres que le capital social (c'est-à-dire tous les engagements autres que les titres de participation, le capital social correspondant à des investissements directs [y compris les bénéfices réinvestis] et les dérivés financiers). Cette conception cadre dans l'ensemble avec la définition de référence de la dette extérieure brute qui est retenue dans l'ouvrage intitulé Statistiques de la dette extérieure : Guide du statisticien et de l'utilisateur (External Debt Statistics : Guide for Compilers and Users), mis au point par l'Équipe spéciale interinstitutions des statistiques financières. L'Équipe spéciale était présidée par le FMI et des représentants de la Banque centrale européenne, de la Banque mondiale, de la Banque des Règlements internationaux, de la CNUCED, d'Eurostat, du FMI, de l'OCDE, du Secrétariat du Club de Paris et du Secrétariat du Commonwealth ont pris part aux travaux du Guide.

Position extérieure globale : composantes types[1]

A. Avoirs

1. Investissements directs
    1.1 Capital social et
        bénéfices réinvestis
    1.2 Autres capitaux[2]

2. Investissements de portefeuille
    2.1 Titres de participation
    2.2 Titres de créance[4]

3. Dérivés financiers
    3.1 Autorités monétaires
    3.2 Administrations publiques
    3.3 Banques
    3.4 Autres secteurs

4. Autres investissements
    4.1 Crédits commerciaux
    4.2 Prêts
    4.3 Monnaie fiduciaire et dépôts
    4.4 Autres avoirs

5. Avoirs de réserve
    5.1 Or monétaire
    5.2 Droits de tirage spéciaux
    5.3 Position de réserve au FMI
    5.4 Devises étrangères
    5.5 Autres créances

B. Engagements

1. Investissements directs
    1.1 Capital social et
        bénéfices réinvestis
    1.2 Autres capitaux[3]

2. Investissements de portefeuille
    2.1 Titres de participation
    2.2 Titres d'engagement[3,4]

3. Dérivés financiers
    3.1 Autorités monétaires
    3.2 Administrations publiques
    3.3 Banques
    3.4 Autres secteurs

4. Autres investissements
    4.1 Crédits commerciaux[3]
    4.2 Prêts[3]
    4.3 Monnaie fiduciaire et dépôts[3]
    4.4 Autres engagements[3]

[1] Les composantes ne sont pas toutes présentées, comme par exemple celles qui sont ventilées par secteur (autorités monétaires, administrations publiques, banques, autres secteurs) ou, dans certains cas, par échéance. Si un pays fournit des données de PEG dont des composantes majeures sont manquantes, les totaux peuvent ne pas être publiés.

[2] Les passifs à l'égard des entreprises apparentées, qui entrent dans la composition des «Autres capitaux», sont inclus dans la dette extérieure.

[3] Les passifs envers les investisseurs directs, qui entrent dans la composition des «Autres capitaux», sont inclus dans la dette extérieure.

[4] Ce poste comprend les obligations, les effets et les instruments du marché monétaire.

sont classées selon plusieurs critères : type d'investissement (c'est-à-dire investissements directs, investissements de portefeuille, dérivés financiers[3], autres investissements et avoirs de réserve), avoirs et engagements, secteurs intérieurs (autorités monétaires, administrations publiques, banques et autres secteurs) et échéances initiales (long terme et court terme).

Position extérieure globale

Comme le montre le tableau 3, les données de la PEG sont disposées conformément à la classification des composantes types de la PEG retenue dans le *MBP5*. (Voir aussi l'annexe IV.)

La classification des composantes de la PEG présentée au tableau 3 correspond à celle des composantes du compte d'opérations financières de la balance des paiements figurant au tableau 2, mais plusieurs différences apparaissent toutefois entre les deux tableaux. Comme indiqué précédemment, la PEG est un relevé des avoirs et engagements extérieurs d'un pays à un moment précis. Par conséquent, au tableau 3, la présentation de base des composantes de la PEG comporte deux catégories générales, celles des avoirs et des engagements, par opposition à la classification fonctionnelle des investissements retenue au tableau 2 (investissements directs, investissements de portefeuille, dérivés financiers, autres investissements et avoirs de réserve). En outre, le tableau 3 présente la PEG d'un pays à la fin de la période considérée, alors que le tableau 2 retrace les transactions effectuées pendant cette période. Par ailleurs, contrairement au tableau 2, qui indique la valeur des transactions financières pendant une période, le tableau 3 présente de la PEG d'un pays une évaluation qui reflète les transactions financières, réévaluations et autres ajustements opérés à la fin de la période considérée. La PEG nette indiquée au tableau 3 est égale à la différence entre la valeur des avoirs financiers extérieurs recensés et celle des engagements financiers extérieurs recensés.

Codage des données

Aux tableaux 1, 2 et 3, chaque catégorie de données et chaque composante s'accompagnent d'un code. Comme indiqué plus haut, ces codes ont été établis conjointement par le FMI, l'OCDE et Eurostat en vue de faciliter la communication des statistiques au niveau international. Les codes s'appliquent aux composantes types de la balance des paiements et de

la position extérieure globale, telles qu'elles sont définies dans le *MBP5*, ainsi qu'aux composantes de la classification OCDE/Eurostat pour le commerce des services.

Chaque code figurant dans l'annuaire est un code alphanumérique à six composantes. Le chiffre placé en première position indique s'il s'agit d'un crédit, d'un débit ou d'un solde; le chiffre «2» désigne un crédit, «3» un débit et «4» un solde (différence entre crédit et débit). Les trois chiffres suivants correspondent au code attribué à la composante de la balance des paiements. Par exemple, le compte des transactions courantes a pour code 993, le compte de capital, 994, et le compte d'opérations financières, 995. Pour plus de précisions sur le système de codage, les lecteurs pourront se référer à l'annexe III.

Les cinquième et sixième chiffres ou lettres du code figurant dans l'annuaire signalent l'existence de caractéristiques particulières à certaines composantes. Par exemple, dans le tableau 1, la lettre Z, placée en cinquième position, indique que la composante exclut le financement exceptionnel; W signifie que, outre le financement exceptionnel, les données excluent l'utilisation des crédits et les prêts du FMI. Au tableau 1, les lettres A, B, C et D différencient les divers secteurs intérieurs. Au tableau 2, les lettres A, B et C servent à indiquer qu'il ne s'agit pas de sous-composantes types, comme c'est le cas, par exemple, pour les postes ayant trait aux transports (passagers, fret et autres).

Écritures passées au crédit et au débit

Aux tableaux 1 et 2, les données sur les transactions sont présentées sous forme de chiffres bruts inscrits au crédit ou au débit du compte des transactions courantes et du compte de capital. Au compte d'opérations financières, les données sont présentées en chiffres nets au crédit ou au débit (pour rendre compte des variations nettes des passifs et des actifs). Les montants inscrits au crédit, qu'ils soient bruts ou nets, sont positifs (mais ne sont pas accompagnés du signe plus) et les montants portés au débit, bruts ou nets, sont négatifs (ils sont affectés du signe moins). En conséquence, la diminution des avoirs et l'augmentation des engagements (crédit) sont indiquées par des chiffres positifs, et l'accroissement des avoirs et la diminution des engagements (débit), par des chiffres négatifs.

Montants nuls, non disponibles, ou données confidentielles

Lorsqu'il manque des chiffres dans les statistiques communiquées par les pays, il est souvent difficile de savoir si ces données font défaut parce qu'elles ne sont pas disponibles, ou parce qu'il s'agit de montants nuls ou négligeables, ou confidentiels. Dans les tableaux de l'annuaire, le symbole (....) indique que les données ne sont pas disponibles, ou que les mon-

---

[3]Compte tenu du caractère spécifique des dérivés financiers et de la manière dont certaines institutions comptabilisent les transactions, certains pays ne peuvent communiquer que des chiffres nets. Bien qu'il soit possible de classer ces transactions nettes parmi les actifs, il a été décidé dans le présent annuaire de les classer parmi les passifs, tout comme les positions nettes lorsqu'elles sont communiquées, parce que la demande de ces instruments émane habituellement d'entités qui couvrent des flux monétaires liés à des opérations d'endettement.

tants sont nuls ou négligeables, ou que les données sont confidentielles. Au cas ou les données pour une ou plusieurs sous-composantes ne peuvent être publiées pour des raisons de confidentialité, les valeurs non déclarées seront ajoutées à une sous-composante générique (telle que "autres") au sein de la composante correspondante afin que les totaux ne soient pas modifiés.

Note sur les composantes du *Revenu* et des *Autres investissements*

Au tableau 2, Standard Presentation (Présentation type), les chiffres que certains pays communiquent pour les postes "Income" (Revenu) et "Other Investment" (Autres investissements) présentent un niveau d'agrégation qui ne permet pas d'identifier séparément chaque composante de la catégorie intéressée. En pareil cas, il n'est donc pas possible de faire la somme des composantes de certaines sous-catégories pour calculer le total agrégé de ces mêmes sous-catégories. Il en va de même pour le poste "Other Investment" (Autres investissements) du tableau 3, International Investment Position (Position extérieure globale).

Auparavant, dans les volumes 46 à 49, les données concernant les «Autres investissements» (avoirs et engagements) étaient ventilées sous les rubriques «long terme» et «court terme». Depuis la publication du volume 50, les tableaux présentent dorénavant les chiffres des «autres investissements» (actifs et passifs) pour les autorités monétaires, les administrations publiques, les banques et les autres secteurs sous forme de totaux (du financement à long terme et du financement à court terme), avec une rubrique «dont : court terme». (Au poste «prêts, autorités monétaires», les chiffrent sont présentés sous forme de totaux, avec une rubrique «dont : utilisation des crédits et des prêts du FMI» et une rubrique «dont : court terme»). La présentation type n'a toutefois pas été modifiée à l'annexe II.

Présentation de chiffres arrondis

La plupart des chiffres des tableaux sont exprimés en millions; les utilisateurs ne doivent pas présumer qu'un tableau présentant des chiffres exprimés en unités plus petites fournit nécessairement des données plus exactes. L'unité est choisie pour des raisons de commodité. Compte tenu des pratiques couramment utilisées pour le calcul, il peut exister un écart, dû au fait que les chiffres ont été arrondis, entre le total indiqué et la somme de ses composantes.

Méthodes de conversion

La plupart des données de balance des paiements communiquées au FMI sont exprimées en monnaie nationale ou en dollars E.U., bien que quelques pays fournissent certaines données en DTS. Pour faciliter les comparaisons entre pays, tous les états de ba-lance des paiements publiés dans l'annuaire sont exprimés en dollars E.U. En outre, dans tous les cas, les données que les pays communiquent sur leurs transactions avec le FMI et sur leurs transactions en DTS sont remplacées par des données tirées des registres du FMI, qui sont exprimées en DTS; celles-ci sont à leur tour converties en dollars E.U.

Pour les pays qui communiquent des données de la balance des paiments exprimées en unités autres que le dollar E.U., les chiffres sont convertis à l'aide des taux de conversion figurant au bas du tableau 1. Ces taux de conversion sont normalement les taux de change moyens de la monnaie du pays pour la période considérée publiés dans *SFI*. Par exemple, les pages consacrées à la zone euro dans *SFI* comportent la ligne «rf», qui présente le taux moyen du dollar en euros. Les données de flux exprimées en DTS sont converties en dollars E.U. à l'aide des taux indiqués à la ligne «sb» de la page consacrée aux États-Unis dans *SFI*. Pour les pays qui transmettent des données trimestrielles exprimées en monnaie nationale, le total annuel en dollars E.U. est égal à la somme des données trimestrielles en dollars E.U.

Pour les pays qui communiquent des données de position extérieure globale dans des unités autres que le dollar EU, les chiffres sont convertis à partir des taux de conversion figurant au bas du tableau 3. Ces taux sont normalement les taux de change en vigueur en fin de période (ligne "ae"), pour la période considérée, publiés dans SFI.

Les lecteurs trouveront à la section 1 de l'introduction de *International Financial Statistics (IFS)* de plus amples renseignements sur les taux de change retenus.

II. Versions CD-ROM et Internet

Les statistiques publiées dans l'annuaire sont également disponibles sur CD-ROM et sur l'Internet (Balance of Payments Statistics Online—BOP Online). Dans cette version électronique, le nombre de pays et de séries chronologiques est légèrement supérieur à celui de la version imprimée de l'annuaire; il en est de même pour le nombre de périodes auxquelles se rapportent les séries chronologiques. Elle contient également les données trimestrielles communiquées par les pays, et fournit en outre les révisions et les mises à jour dès que les données actualisées sont disponibles. Les demandes de renseignements concernant les CD-ROM et BOP Online doivent être adressées à :

Publication Services
International Monetary Fund
Washington, DC 20431, U.S.A.
Téléphone : (202) 623–7430
Télécopie : (202) 623–7201
Messagerie électronique : publications@imf.org
Internet : http://www.imf.org

ANNEXE I. PRÉSENTATION ANALYTIQUE

	Codes
A. COMPTE DES TRANSACTIONS COURANTES[1]	4 993 Z .
Biens : exportations, f.à.b.	2 100 ..
Biens : importations, f.à.b.	3 100 ..
Solde au titre des biens	4 100 ..
Services : crédit	2 200 ..
Services : débit	3 200 ..
Solde au titre des biens et services	4 991 ..
Revenus : crédit	2 300 ..
Revenus : débit	3 300 ..
Solde au titre des biens, services et revenus	4 992 ..
Transferts courants : crédit	2 379 Z .
Transferts courants : débit	3 379 ..
B. COMPTE DE CAPITAL[1]	4 994 Z .
Compte de capital : crédit	2 994 Z .
Compte de capital : débit	3 994 ..
Total, groupes A plus B	4 981 ..
C. COMPTE D'OPÉRATIONS FINANCIÈRES[1]	4 995W .
Investissements directs à l'étranger	4 505 ..
Investissements directs dans l'économie	4 555 Z .
Investissements de portefeuille : avoirs	4 602 ..
Titres de participation	4 610 ..
Titres de créance	4 619 ..
Investissements de portefeuille : engagements	4 652 Z .
Titres de participation	4 660 ..
Titres d'engagement	4 669 Z .
Dérivés financiers	4 910 ..
Dérivés financiers (actifs)	4 900 ..
Dérivés financiers (passifs)	4 905 ..
Autres investissements : avoirs	4 703 ..
Autorités monétaires	4 701 ..
Administrations publiques	4 704 ..
Banques	4 705 ..
Autres secteurs	4 728 ..
Autres investissements : engagements	4 753W .
Autorités monétaires	4 753WA
Administrations publiques	4 753 ZB
Banques	4 753 ZC
Autres secteurs	4 753 ZD
Total, groupes A à C inclus	4 983 ..
D. ERREURS ET OMISSIONS NETTES	4 998 ..
Total, groupes A à D inclus	4 984 ..
E. RÉSERVES ET POSTES APPARENTÉS	4 802.A.
Avoirs de réserve	4 802 ..
Utilisation des crédits et prêts du FMI	4 766 ..
Financements exceptionnels	4 920 ..
TAUX DE CONVERSION : MONTANT D'UNITÉS MONÉTAIRES POUR UN DOLLAR E.U.	0 101 ..

---

[1]Non compris les composantes qui font partie des catégories du groupe E.

ANNEXE II. COMPOSANTES TYPES

	Codes
Autres services, crédit	2 200 BA
Services de communication	2 245
Services de bâtiment et travaux publics	2 249
Services d'assurance	2 253
Services financiers	2 260
Services d'informatique et d'information	2 262
Redevances et droits de licence	2 266
Autres services aux entreprises	2 268
Services personnels, culturels et relatifs aux loisirs	2 287
Services fournis ou reçus par les administrations publiques, n.c.a.	2 291
Autres services, débit	3 200 BA
Services de communication	3 245
Services de bâtiment et travaux publics	3 249
Services d'assurance	3 253
Services financiers	3 260
Services d'informatique et d'information	3 262
Redevances et droits de licence	3 266
Autres services aux entreprises	3 268
Services personnels, culturels et relatifs aux loisirs	3 287
Services fournis ou reçus par les administrations publiques, n.c.a.	3 291
C. REVENUS	4 300
Total, crédit	2 300
Total, débit	3 300
Rémunération des salariés, crédit	2 310
Rémunération des salariés, débit	3 310
Revenu des investissements, crédit	2 320
Revenu des investissements directs	2 330
Dividendes et bénéfices distribués des succursales	2 332
Bénéfices réinvestis et bénéfices non distribués des succursales	2 333
Revenu des titres de créance (intérêts)	2 334
Revenu des investissements de portefeuille	2 339
Revenu des titres de participation	2 340
Revenu des obligations et autres titres d'emprunt	2 350
Revenu des instruments du marché monétaire	2 360
Revenu des autres investissements	2 370
Revenu des investissements, débit	3 320
Revenu des investissements directs	3 330
Dividendes et bénéfices distribués des succursales	3 332
Bénéfices réinvestis et bénéfices non distribués des succursales	3 333
Revenu des titres de créance (intérêts)	3 334
Revenu des investissements de portefeuille	3 339
Revenu des titres de participation	3 340
Revenu des obligations et autres titres d'emprunt	3 350
Revenu des instruments du marché monétaire	3 360
Revenu des autres investissements	3 370
D. TRANSFERTS COURANTS	4 379
Crédit	2 379
Administrations publiques	2 380
Autres secteurs	2 390
Envois de fonds des travailleurs	2 391
Autres transferts courants	2 392

		Codes
B.	**INVESTISSEMENTS DE PORTEFEUILLE**	4 600 . .
	Avoirs	4 602 . .
	Titres de participation	4 610 . .
	Autorités monétaires	4 611 . .
	Administrations publiques	4 612 . .
	Banques	4 613 . .
	Autres secteurs	4 614 . .
	Titres de créance	4 619 . .
	Obligations et autres titres d'emprunt	4 620 . .
	Autorités monétaires	4 621 . .
	Administrations publiques	4 622 . .
	Banques	4 623 . .
	Autres secteurs	4 624 . .
	Instruments du marché monétaire	4 630 . .
	Autorités monétaires	4 631 . .
	Administrations publiques	4 632 . .
	Banques	4 633 . .
	Autres secteurs	4 634 . .
	Engagements	4 652 . .
	Titres de participation	4 660 . .
	Banques	4 663 . .
	Autres secteurs	4 664 . .
	Titres d'engagement	4 669 . .
	Obligations et autres titres d'emprunt	4 670 . .
	Autorités monétaires	4 671 . .
	Administrations publiques	4 672 . .
	Banques	4 673 . .
	Autres secteurs	4 674 . .
	Instruments du marché monétaire	4 680 . .
	Autorités monétaires	4 681 . .
	Administrations publiques	4 682 . .
	Banques	4 683 . .
	Autres secteurs	4 684 . .
C.	**DÉRIVÉS FINANCIERS**	4 910 . .
	Autorités monétaires	4 911 . .
	Administrations publiques	4 912 . .
	Banques	4 913 . .
	Autres secteurs	4 914 . .
	Avoirs	4 900 . .
	Autorités monétaires	4 901 . .
	Administrations publiques	4 902 . .
	Banques	4 903 . .
	Autres secteurs	4 904 . .
	Engagements	4 905 . .
	Autorités monétaires	4 906 . .
	Administrations publiques	4 907 . .
	Banques	4 908 . .
	Autres secteurs	4 909 . .
D.	**AUTRES INVESTISSEMENTS**	4 700 . .
	Avoirs	4 703 . .
	Crédits commerciaux	4 706 . .
	Administrations publiques	4 707 . .
	dont : court terme	4 709 . .
	Autres secteurs	4 710 . .
	dont : court terme	4 712 . .

Annexe III. Système de codage FMI/OCDE/Eurostat applicable à la balance des paiements, à la position extérieure globale et au commerce international de services[1]

Le système de codage examiné ici s'applique à toutes les composantes types et aux postes complémentaires définis dans la cinquième édition du *Manuel de la balance des paiements*; il s'applique également aux composantes et postes pour mémoire de la classification OCDE-Eurostat des données sur le commerce international de services.

Le code a trois composantes ou sections, qui sont :

<position> un nombre à un chiffre (compris entre 1 et 8) décrivant la position du poste dans les comptes de la position extérieure globale (PEG) ou de la balance des paiements (BP);

<sujet> un nombre à trois chiffres (choisi parmi les nombres entiers compris entre 100 et 998) permettant d'identifier toutes les composantes de la balance des paiements et de la classification du commerce international des services et certains postes complémentaires;

<sous-code> une composante définie par l'utilisateur et de longueur illimitée.

Le code complet comprendrait ces trois éléments dans l'ordre suivant : <position><sujet><sous-code>. Cependant, le sous-code est fa-cultatif, contrairement au code de la position et au code du sujet. En conséquence, le code comportera, sous sa forme couramment utilisée, les composantes suivantes : <position><sujet>.

La première composante du code indique la position du poste dans les comptes de la position extérieure globale (PEG) et de la balance des paiements (BP); elle est définie comme suit :

Code	Position dans les comptes de la PEG et de la BP
1	Stock au début de la période
2	Flux, crédit
3	Flux, débit
4	Flux nets
5	Ajustement de la valeur en fonction des variations du prix
6	Ajustement de la valeur en fonction des variations du taux de change
7	Autres ajustements
8	Stock à la fin de la période
0	Autres

Le premier chiffre de la composante indicative du sujet correspond à la rubrique de la balance des paiements, c'est-à-dire :

Code	Rubrique de la BP
1	Biens
2	Services
3	Revenus et transferts courants
4	Compte de capital
5	Investissements directs
6	Investissements de portefeuille
7	Autres investissements
8	Avoirs de réserve
9	Principaux agrégats, dérivés financiers et détails complémentaires

Les deuxième et troisième chiffres de la composante sont généralement attribués dans un ordre consécutif et sont séparés par des espaces permettant l'inclusion ultérieure de codes additionnels, le cas échéant. En outre, dans le compte d'opérations financières, à l'exception des comptes des investissements directs, le deuxième chiffre de cette composante est 0, 1, 2, 3 ou 4 pour les avoirs et 5, 6, 7, 8 ou 9 pour les engagements.

Un exemple des codes appliqués aux «Autres investissements» dans le compte d'opérations financières est donné ci-après.

Sujet	Champ unique			Champ multiple		
	Crédit	Débit	Net	Crédit	Débit	Net
Autres investissements	2700	3700	4700	2700	3700	4700
Engagements	2750	3750	4750	2750	3750	4750
Prêts	2762	3762	4762	2762	3762	4762
Administrations publiques	2767	3767	4767	2767	3767	4767
Long terme	2768	3768	4768	2768	3768	4768
Court terme	2769	3769	4769	2769	3769	4769
Banques	2770	3770	4770	2770	3770	4770
Long terme	2771	3771	4771	2771	3771	4771
Court terme	2772	3772	4772	2772	3772	4772
Autres secteurs	2773	3773	4773	2773	3773	4773
Long terme	2774	3774	4774	2774	3774	4774
Court terme	2775	3775	4775	2775	3775	4775

Pour les prêts, les écritures passées au crédit et au débit servent à comptabiliser les transactions communément dénommées tirages et remboursements. La cinquième édition du *Manuel* recommande de classer tous les tirages sur prêts à long terme et tous les remboursements de ces prêts parmi les postes complémentaires. À l'heure actuelle, le FMI recueille des données nettes sur la plupart des autres postes du compte d'opérations financières. Néanmoins, le système de codage permet d'identifier tous les flux, qu'il s'agisse de transactions nettes ou de transactions inscrites au crédit ou au débit.

[1] Tiré de l'ouvrage du FMI intitulé «Balance des paiements : codes utilisés pour les composantes types et les postes complémentaires», Washington, DC, 3 mars 1995.

Annexe IV. Position extérieure globale : composantes types

	Codes
A. AVOIRS	8 995 C.
Investissements directs à l'étranger	8 505 ..
Capital social et bénéfices réinvestis	8 506 ..
Créances sur les entreprises apparentées	8 507 ..
Engagements envers les entreprises apparentées	8 508 ..
Autres capitaux	8 530 ..
Créances sur les entreprises apparentées	8 535 ..
Engagements envers les entreprises apparentées	8 540 ..
Investissements de portefeuille	8 602 ..
Titres de participation	8 610 ..
Autorités monétaires	8 611 ..
Administrations publiques	8 612 ..
Banques	8 613 ..
Autres secteurs	8 614 ..
Titres de créances	8 619 ..
Obligations et autres titres d'emprunt	8 620 ..
Autorités monétaires	8 621 ..
Administrations publiques	8 622 ..
Banques	8 623 ..
Autres secteurs	8 624 ..
Instruments du marché monétaire	8 630 ..
Autorités monétaires	8 631 ..
Administrations publiques	8 632 ..
Banques	8 633 ..
Autres secteurs	8 634 ..
Dérivés financiers	8 900 ..
Autorités monétaires	8 901 ..
Administrations publiques	8 902 ..
Banques	8 903 ..
Autres secteurs	8 904 ..
Autres investissements	8 703 ..
Crédits commerciaux	8 706 ..
Administrations publiques	8 707 ..
dont : court terme	8 709 ..
Autres secteurs	8 710 ..
dont : court terme	8 712 ..
Prêts	8 714 ..
Autorités monétaires	8 715 ..
dont : court terme	8 718 ..
Administrations publiques	8 719 ..
dont : court terme	8 721 ..
Banques	8 722 ..
dont : court terme	8 724 ..
Autres secteurs	8 725 ..
dont : court terme	8 727 ..
Monnaie fiduciaire et dépôts	8 730 ..
Autorités monétaires	8 731 ..
Administrations publiques	8 732 ..
Banques	8 733 ..
Autres secteurs	8 734 ..

	Codes
Autres avoirs	8 736 ..
Autorités monétaires	8 737 ..
dont : court terme	8 739 ..
Administrations publiques	8 740 ..
dont : court terme	8 742 ..
Banques	8 743 ..
dont : court terme	8 745 ..
Autres secteurs	8 746 ..
dont : court terme	8 748 ..
Avoirs de réserve	8 802 ..
Or monétaire	8 812 ..
DTS	8 811 ..
Position de réserve au FMI	8 810 ..
Devises étrangères	8 803 ..
Autres créances	8 813 ..
B. ENGAGEMENTS	8 995 D.
Investissements directs de l'étranger dans l'économie	8 555 ..
Capital social et bénéfices réinvestis	8 556 ..
Créances sur les investisseurs directs	8 557 ..
Engagements envers les investisseurs directs	8 558 ..
Autres capitaux	8 580 ..
Créances sur les investisseurs directs	8 585 ..
Engagements envers les investisseurs directs	8 590 ..
Investissements de portefeuille	8 652 ..
Titres de participation	8 660 ..
Banques	8 663 ..
Autres secteurs	8 664 ..
Titres d'engagement	8 669 ..
Obligations et autres titres d'emprunt	8 670 ..
Autorités monétaires	8 671 ..
Administrations publiques	8 672 ..
Banques	8 673 ..
Autres secteurs	8 674 ..
Instruments du marché monétaire	8 680 ..
Autorités monétaires	8 681 ..
Administrations publiques	8 682 ..
Banques	8 683 ..
Autres secteurs	8 684 ..
Dérivés financiers	8 905 ..
Autorités monétaires	8 906 ..
Administrations publiques	8 907 ..
Banques	8 908 ..
Autres secteurs	8 909 ..
Autres investissements	8 753 ..
Crédits commerciaux	8 756 ..
Administrations publiques	8 757 ..
dont : court terme	8 759 ..
Autres secteurs	8 760 ..
dont : court terme	8 762 ..

	Codes
Prêts	8 764 ..
Autorités monétaires	8 765 ..
dont : utilisation des crédits et des prêts du FMI	8 766 ..
dont : court terme	8 768 ..
Administrations publiques	8 769 ..
dont : court terme	8 771 ..
Banques	8 772 ..
dont : court terme	8 774 ..
Autres secteurs	8 775 ..
dont : court terme	8 777 ..
Monnaie fiduciaire et dépôts	8 780 ..
Autorités monétaires	8 781 ..
Administrations publiques	8 782 ..
Banques	8 783 ..
Autres secteurs	8 784 ..
Autres engagements	8 786 ..
Autorités monétaires	8 787 ..
dont : court terme	8 789 ..
Administrations publiques	8 790 ..
dont : court terme	8 792 ..
Banques	8 793 ..
dont : court terme	8 795 ..
Autres secteurs	8 796 ..
dont : court terme	8 798 ..
POSITION EXTÉRIEURE GLOBALE NETTE	8 995 ..
Taux de conversion (fin de période)	0 102 ..

Annexe V. Cadre conceptuel de la balance des paiements et de la position extérieure globale

La présente annexe reprend le texte du chapitre II de la cinquième édition du Manuel. *Il convient de noter que les numéros de paragraphe et page cités dans cette annexe sont ceux du* Manuel.

Définitions

12. La première partie du présent *Manuel* décrit le cadre conceptuel de la balance des paiements et de la position extérieure globale. Elle traite de leur relation avec la comptabilité nationale, du concept de résidence, des principes d'évaluation et de chronologie, enfin des notions d'unité de compte et de conversion.

13. La balance des paiements est un état statistique où sont systématiquement résumées, pour une période donnée, les transactions économiques d'une économie avec le reste du monde. Les transactions, pour la plupart entre résidents et non-résidents[1], sont celles qui portent sur les biens, services et revenus; celles qui font naître des créances financières sur le reste du monde ou des engagements financiers envers celui-ci; et celles qui, telles les donations, sont considérées comme des transferts, pour lesquels il y a lieu de passer des contre-écritures de manière à solder — au sens comptable du terme — les transactions à sens unique (voir paragraphe 28)[2]. Une transaction se définit comme un flux économique découlant de la création, de la transformation, de l'échange, du transfert ou de l'extinction d'une valeur économique et faisant intervenir le transfert de propriété de biens ou d'actifs financiers, la prestation de services ou la fourniture de travail et de capital.

14. De même que la balance des paiements retrace des flux, la position extérieure globale est un relevé de stocks. C'est un état statistique qui présente, à une date donnée, par exemple en fin d'année, i) la valeur et la composition du stock des actifs financiers d'une économie ou de ses créances sur le reste du monde, ainsi que ii) la valeur et la composition du stock de ses engagements envers le reste du monde. Dans certains cas, il peut être utile, pour les besoins de l'analyse, de calculer la différence entre avoirs et engagements extérieurs de ce bilan pour évaluer la position nette de l'économie, qui équivaut à la partie de la valeur nette de son patrimoine attribuable à ses relations avec le reste du monde ou en résultant. Une variation des stocks pendant une période définie peut être attribuable soit à des transactions (flux), soit à des réévaluations (qui rendent compte des variations des taux de change, des prix, etc.), soit à d'autres ajustements (des confiscations sans dédommagement, par exemple). Au contraire, la balance des paiements n'enregistre que des transactions.

[1]Sauf dans le cas d'échanges d'avoirs financiers extérieurs transférables entre secteurs résidents et, dans une moindre mesure, d'engagements financiers extérieurs entre non-résidents (voir paragraphe 318).

[2]Les définitions et classifications des comptes internationaux contenues dans le présent *Manuel* visent à faciliter la communication au FMI des données sur les transactions internationales, et non à donner effet ou à interpréter les diverses dispositions des statuts du Fonds monétaire international qui ont trait aux aspects juridiques de l'action (ou du manque d'action) officielle concernant ces transactions.

Principes et concepts

15. Le reste du présent chapitre est consacré au cadre conceptuel des comptes internationaux — c'est-à-dire l'ensemble de conventions et principes sous-jacents qui assurent l'enregistrement systématisé et cohérent des transactions internationales et des stocks d'avoirs et engagements extérieurs. Les aspects pertinents de ces principes, ainsi que les considérations et contraintes pratiques qui s'y rapportent, seront examinés en détail dans les chapitres suivants.

Système d'enregistrement en partie double

16. La convention de base à respecter pour l'établissement d'un état de balance des paiements est que toute transaction enregistrée doit donner lieu à deux inscriptions de montants égaux. L'un de ces montants est inscrit en crédit et est affecté du signe plus, tandis que l'autre est inscrit en débit et affecté du signe moins. En théorie, donc, la somme des montants inscrits en crédit est censée être identique à celle des montants inscrits en débit et le solde de toutes les inscriptions est égal à zéro.

17. Dans la pratique, toutefois, il arrive fréquemment que les comptes ne s'équilibrent pas. Les données servant à établir les estimations pour la balance des paiements sont souvent obtenues séparément de sources différentes. C'est pourquoi le solde peut être un crédit net ou un débit net, qui correspond au montant net des erreurs et omissions. Une écriture distincte, de montant égal mais de signe contraire, doit alors être passée pour équilibrer les comptes. Comme les estimations erronées ou manquantes peuvent s'annuler, on ne peut juger du degré d'exactitude de l'état de balance des paiements d'après le montant de la différence entre la somme des crédits et celle des débits. Néanmoins, il y a lieu de s'inquiéter lorsqu'il subsiste une différence non négligeable qui n'est pas corrigée, car cela gêne l'analyse ou l'interprétation des estimations et en mine la crédibilité (il peut en aller de même pour l'interprétation de l'état de la position extérieure globale dont il sera question au chapitre XXIII).

18. La plupart des inscriptions à la balance des paiements se rapportent à des transactions dans lesquelles des valeurs économiques sont fournies ou reçues en échange d'autres valeurs économiques; ces valeurs sont soit des ressources réelles (biens, services et revenus), soit des actifs financiers. Les écritures compensatoires en crédit et en débit que requiert le système d'enregistrement résultent donc souvent de l'inscription de montants égaux pour les deux éléments échangés. Dans le cas où il y a don, et non échange, ou quand, pour d'autres raisons, la transaction donne lieu à un enregistrement unique, et non à deux enregistrements, une écriture — dénommée *transfert* — spécifiquement conçue pour assurer la compensation nécessaire doit être passée. (Les diverses sortes d'inscriptions qui peuvent être faites à la balance des paiements sont décrites aux paragraphes 26 à 31.)

19. Par convention de ce système, les inscriptions effectuées en crédit par l'économie qui établit sa balance des paiements reflètent i) des exportations lorsqu'il s'agit de ressources réelles et ii) soit une diminution des avoirs extérieurs de l'économie, soit une augmentation de ses engagements extérieurs, lorsqu'il s'agit d'actifs financiers. Parallèlement, les inscriptions faites en débit par l'économie qui établit les données reflètent i) des importations lorsqu'il s'agit de ressources réelles et ii) soit une augmentation des avoirs, soit une diminution des engagements lorsqu'il s'agit d'actifs financiers. En d'autres termes, pour les avoirs — qu'ils soient réels ou financiers —, un chiffre positif (crédit) dénote une baisse, tandis qu'un chiffre négatif (débit) correspond à une hausse. Par contre, pour les engagements, un chiffre positif indique une augmentation et un chiffre négatif une diminution. Les transferts sont portés au crédit lorsque les inscriptions qu'ils compensent sont faites en débit et ils sont portés au débit lorsque ces inscriptions sont effectuées en crédit.

20. La teneur ou la composition d'un état de balance des paiements varie quelque peu selon que les transactions sont enre-gistrées sur une base brute ou sur une base nette; les recommandations énoncées dans le présent *Manuel* indiquent quelles transactions sont à enregistrer sur une base brute et lesquelles sont à comptabiliser sur une base nette. Les inscriptions qu'il est recommandé d'effectuer sont énumérées dans la liste des composantes types de la balance des paiements et des renseignements complémentaires qui peuvent être présentés séparément.

Concepts de territoire économique, de résidence et de pôle d'intérêt économique

21. Les concepts de territoire économique, de résidence et de pôle d'intérêt économique utilisés dans le présent *Manuel* sont identiques à ceux qui ont été adoptés dans le *SCN* et seront exa-minés en détail au chapitre IV. Le territoire économique ne corres-pond pas forcément à la zone délimitée par les frontières reconnues sur le plan politique. Il recouvre un territoire géographique admi-nistré par un gouvernement. À l'intérieur de ce territoire géographique circulent librement des personnes, des biens et des ca-pitaux. Dans le cas de pays maritimes, le territoire géographique comprend toutes les îles régies par les mêmes autorités fiscales et monétaires que le territoire principal.

22. Une unité institutionnelle a son pôle d'intérêt économique dans un pays et est résidente dudit pays lorsqu'il existe, sur le territoire économique de celui-ci, un endroit (domicile, lieu de production ou locaux à autre usage) auquel ou à partir duquel elle exerce et a l'intention de continuer à exercer des activités économiques et effectue ou a l'intention de continuer à effectuer des transactions sur une grande échelle, que ce soit pendant une période de temps indéfinie ou déterminée — en principe d'un an au moins, mais c'est là un critère indicatif et non une règle absolue.

Principes d'évaluation et de chronologie

23. Il est nécessaire d'utiliser une base d'évaluation uniforme pour l'ensemble des transactions internationales (qu'elles portent sur des ressources réelles ou sur des créances et engagements financiers) afin de pouvoir établir de façon systématique et cohérente la somme des transactions individuelles et une position des avoirs et des

engagements qui corresponde bien à ces transactions. La base d'évaluation des transactions retenue dans le présent *Manuel* — comme dans le *SCN* — est généralement le prix de marché effectif convenu entre les agents. En théorie, tous les stocks d'avoirs et engagements doivent être évalués aux prix en vigueur sur le marché à la date à laquelle se rapporte la position extérieure globale. Les principes d'évaluation, les pratiques recommandées et leurs limites sont décrits au chapitre V, de même que la méthode d'évaluation des transferts, des actifs financiers et des stocks d'avoirs et engagements. (On y traitera aussi des cas où un prix de marché ne peut ni exister, ni être présumé.)

24. Dans le *Manuel* comme dans le *SCN*, c'est le principe de la comptabilité sur la base des faits générateurs (des droits constatés) qui régit le *moment de l'enregistrement* des transactions. Elles sont donc enregistrées au moment où une valeur économique est créée, transformée, échangée, transférée ou éteinte. Des créances et des engagements se créent lorsqu'il y a transfert de propriété. Le transfert peut être soit juridique, soit matériel (économique). Dans la pratique, lorsque le transfert de propriété n'est pas manifeste, on peut considérer comme une approximation raisonnable de cette date celle à laquelle les parties à une transaction l'enregistrent dans leurs livres ou dans leurs comptes. (Les principes de chronologie et les conventions qu'il est recommandé de respecter pour les diverses inscriptions à la balance des paiements, ainsi que les cas où il est possible de faire exception à la règle du transfert de propriété ou de s'en écarter, sont traités au chapitre VI.)

Le concept et les différents types de transactions

25. En général, les modifications des rapports économiques qu'enregistre la balance des paiements résultent principalement de la relation qui se noue entre deux parties, c'est-à-dire, à une exception près (voir la note 1), entre un résident et un non-résident, et toutes les transactions de cet ordre sont comptabilisées à la balance des paiements. Les inscriptions spécifiques qu'il est recommandé d'effectuer sont celles qui figurent dans la liste des composantes types (voir le chapitre VIII) et elles sont décrites en détail dans les chapitres IX et suivants.

26. En dépit de son appellation, la balance des paiements ne rend pas compte des *paiements*, au sens usuel du terme, mais des *transactions*. Un certain nombre de transactions internationales qui ont leur place à la balance des paiements peuvent ne pas donner lieu à un paiement moné-taire et certaines ne comportent même aucun type de paiement. L'enregistrement de ces transactions, en plus de celles qui ont un paiement pour contrepartie, constitue la principale différence entre un état de balance des paiements et un relevé des paiements extérieurs.

Échanges

27. Parmi les transactions qui figurent à la balance des paiements, les plus nombreuses et les plus importantes sont celles qui peuvent être dénommées *échanges*. Un agent économique (entité économique) fournit une valeur économique à un autre et reçoit en échange une valeur égale. Les valeurs économiques fournies par une économie à une autre appartiennent à deux grandes catégories : les ressources réelles (biens, services, revenus), d'une part, et les instruments financiers, d'autre part. Les deux parties à l'échange sont des résidents d'économies différentes, sauf lorsqu'il s'agit d'échanges d'actifs financiers extérieurs entre secteurs résidents. Il se peut que la fourniture d'un instrument financier fasse intervenir non seulement le transfert de propriété d'une créance ou d'un engagement existant, mais aussi la création d'un nouvel avoir ou engagement ou l'annulation d'un avoir ou engagement existant. En outre, les modalités d'un contrat afférent à un instrument financier (par exemple son échéance) peuvent être modifiées par accord entre les parties; on considère dans ce cas que le contrat initial a été exécuté et est remplacé par un autre, assorti de modalités différentes. Tous les échanges de cet ordre doivent être enregistrés à la balance des paiements.

Transferts

28. Les transactions donnant lieu à un *transfert* diffèrent des échanges en ce qu'un agent économique fournit une valeur économique à un autre agent économique sans en recevoir une contrepartie qui, d'après les conventions et règles adoptées aux fins de ce système, a une valeur économique. La valeur qui fait défaut d'un côté de la transaction est représentée par une inscription dénommée *transfert*. Les transferts (valeurs économiques fournies et reçues sans réciprocité) doivent figurer à la balance des paiements. Les **transferts courants** figurent au **compte des transactions courantes** (voir le chapitre XV), tandis que les *transferts de capital* sont classés dans le **compte de capital** (voir le chapitre XVII).

Migration

29. Comme une économie se définit en fonction des entités économiques qui sont associées à son territoire, il est probable que toute modification touchant ces entités influera sur le champ que recouvre l'économie.

30. Il y a migration lorsqu'un particulier devient résident d'une nouvelle économie parce qu'il y transfère son lieu d'habitation principal. Certains avoirs mobiliers corporels appartenant au migrant sont effectivement importés dans la nouvelle économie; les avoirs immobiliers du migrant et certains de ses avoirs mobiliers corporels qui sont situés sur le territoire de l'ancienne économie deviennent des créances de la nouvelle économie sur l'ancienne; les créances du migrant sur les résidents d'une économie autre que la nouvelle ou ses engagements envers ceux-ci deviennent des créances ou engagements extérieurs de la nouvelle économie; et les créances du migrant sur les résidents de la nouvelle économie ou ses engagements envers ceux-ci cessent d'être des créances d'une économie, quelle qu'elle soit, sur le reste du monde, ou des engagements de cette économie envers celui-ci. La somme nette de tous ces changements est égale à la valeur nette du patrimoine du migrant, qui doit être inscrite en contrepartie si les autres chan-gements sont enregistrés; ces inscriptions doivent être effectuées à la balance des paiements, où, par convention, la contre-écriture est passée sous la rubrique des transferts.

Autres transactions imputées

31. Dans quelques autres cas, des transactions peuvent être imputées et des inscriptions faites à la balance des paiements sans que des flux aient été effectivement engendrés. L'attribution des bénéfices réinvestis aux investisseurs directs étrangers en constitue un exemple. Les bénéfices d'une filiale ou succursale étrangère comprennent les bénéfices attribuables à l'investisseur direct. Ces bénéfices, qu'ils soient distribués ou réinvestis dans l'entreprise, sont proportionnels à sa participation au capital de l'entreprise. Les bénéfices réinvestis sont classés parmi les revenus des investissements directs. Un montant affecté du signe contraire est inscrit en contrepartie au poste investissement direct du *compte d'opérations financières* et représente l'augmentation de la participation des investisseurs directs étrangers au capital de la filiale ou succursale étrangère. (Les bénéfices réinvestis sont traités aux chapitres XIV et XVIII.)

Modifications non dues aux transactions

Reclassement des créances et engagements

32. Dans le *Manuel*, la classification des actifs financiers est établie en fonction de caractéristiques choisies de manière à révéler les intentions du créancier ou du débiteur. Les changements d'intentions influent sur les caractéristiques retenues, et il y a lieu de reclasser les actifs financiers en conséquence. L'un des cas ty-piques est celui de la distinction qui est faite entre les *investissements directs* et les autres catégories d'opérations financières. Par exemple, plusieurs détenteurs indépendants d'*investissements de portefeuille* (sous forme d'actions émises par une même entreprise à l'étranger) peuvent s'associer de manière à avoir, de façon durable, un pouvoir de décision effectif dans la gestion de l'entreprise. Leurs avoirs répondront alors à la définition de l'*investissement direct*, et la modification de la nature de l'investissement pourrait être assimilée à un reclassement. Ce reclassement se reflétera, à la fin de la période pendant laquelle il aura eu lieu, dans la position extérieure globale, mais non dans la balance des paiements. De même, les créances sur les non-résidents peuvent être soumises, ou cesser d'être assujetties, au contrôle des autorités monétaires résidentes. En pareil cas, il y aura reclassement entre les *actifs de réserve* et les actifs autres que les réserves.

Réévaluations

33. La valeur des ressources réelles et des actifs financiers est constamment sujette à variation. Cette variation peut être due à l'une ou à l'autre des causes suivantes, ou aux deux à la fois : i) le prix auquel les transactions sur une certaine sorte d'avoirs s'effectuent habituellement peut subir des variations qui sont liées à la monnaie dans laquelle le prix est exprimé; ii) le taux de change de la monnaie dans laquelle le prix est exprimé peut varier par rapport à l'unité de compte utilisée. Les réévaluations ne doivent pas être reportées à la balance des paiements, mais doivent figurer dans la position extérieure globale.

ANNEXE VI. CLASSIFICATION ET COMPOSANTES TYPES DE LA BALANCE DES PAIEMENTS

La présente annexe reprend le texte du chapitre VIII de la cinquième édition du Manuel. *Il convient de noter que les numéros de paragraphe et de page cités dans cette annexe sont ceux du* Manuel.

Structure et classification

139. La deuxième partie de ce *Manuel* a trait à la structure et à la classification des comptes de la balance des paiements et de la position extérieure globale. À l'examen des composantes types de ces deux séries de comptes succéderont l'analyse et la description détaillée du ***compte des transactions courantes***, du ***compte de capital et d'opérations financières***, des renseignements complémentaires qui peuvent être requis sur certains postes et de la position extérieure globale.

140. Il importe d'ordonner les statistiques de la balance des paiements selon une structure cohérente afin d'en faciliter l'utilisation et l'adaptation à des fins multiples : élaboration de politiques, études analytiques, projections, comparaisons bilatérales de telle ou telle composante ou de l'ensemble des transactions, agrégations régionales ou mondiales, etc. (Voir paragraphe 7.)

141. La classification et la liste des composantes types reposent sur des considérations théoriques et pratiques qui tiennent compte des opinions exprimées par les experts nationaux de la balance des paiements; elles concordent en général avec les définitions que donne le *SCN*. La classification élargie des transactions internationales au titre des services est conforme aux principes de la Classification centrale des produits (CCP). (Voir l'appendice III.)

142. Le système de classification est aussi le résultat d'efforts entrepris pour rattacher la structure du ***compte de capital*** aux comptes de revenu et à la classification de la position extérieure globale. Il a été conçu de manière à offrir un cadre flexible pouvant être utilisé par de nombreux pays pour développer au fil des années leurs statistiques extérieures. Certains pays ne sont peut-être pas en mesure de communiquer des chiffres pour de nombreux postes. D'autres sont peut-être en mesure de fournir des données supplémentaires.

Composantes types

143. Le choix des composantes types (dont la liste figure à la fin du présent chapitre) est fonction d'un certain nombre de considérations; celles qui suivent ont été jugées primordiales.

> Le poste doit manifester un comportement distinct. Il doit être influencé par un facteur économique ou un ensemble de facteurs différents de ceux qui influent sur les autres postes, ou réagir différemment au même facteur ou ensemble de facteurs. C'est cette réaction aux facteurs économiques que la balance des paiements cherche à mettre en évidence.

> Le poste doit revêtir de l'importance pour plusieurs pays; cette importance peut être fonction soit de son

comportement (par exemple une variabilité exceptionnelle), soit de son ordre de grandeur.

> Les données relatives à ce poste ne doivent pas être excessivement difficiles à obtenir. L'utilité qu'il présente doit cependant être évaluée à la lumière des deux considérations qui précèdent.

> Le poste doit être utilisable séparément à d'autres fins, par exemple pouvoir être incorporé dans la comptabilité nationale ou servir au rapprochement avec cette dernière. La liste des composantes types ne doit pas être trop longue. En effet, un très grand nombre de pays, dont beaucoup ne disposent pas d'un système statistique très développé, sont censés utiliser les mêmes catégories lorsqu'ils communiquent leurs données.

> Dans la mesure du possible, les composantes types doivent être conformes et applicables aux autres systèmes statistiques du FMI et au *SCN* et concorder, pour les *services* en particulier, avec la CCP.

144. La liste type n'implique nullement que les recommandations formulées dans ce *Manuel* empêchent les pays d'établir et de publier d'autres données qu'ils jugent importantes. En fait, lorsque de plus amples détails sont nécessaires pour comprendre les circonstances particulières à tel ou tel pays ou pour analyser les situations nouvelles, les demandes de renseignements que le FMI adresse à ses pays membres ne se limitent pas aux composantes types. Des renseignements complémentaires peuvent être aussi très utiles pour vérifier et rapprocher les statistiques de pays partenaires, et, par exemple, pour analyser les financements exceptionnels. (Voir, à la fin du chapitre, le tableau intitulé *Renseignements complémentaires qui peuvent être requis sur certains postes*.) De temps en temps, les services du FMI tiennent des consultations avec les pays membres afin de déterminer avec eux quelles données complémentaires ils devraient lui communiquer.

145. Rares sont les pays qui ont des renseignements significatifs à communiquer pour chacune des composantes types. Il se peut aussi que certaines des composantes n'existent que regroupées ou qu'une composante mineure soit incluse dans une composante plus importante. Les composantes types doivent néanmoins être communiquées au FMI de manière aussi complète et exacte que possible. Les statisticiens nationaux sont incontestablement mieux placés que les services du FMI pour estimer et ajuster les composantes qui ne correspondent pas exactement aux séries de base de l'économie établissant ses statistiques.

Erreurs et omissions nettes

146. L'application des principes recommandés dans le présent *Manuel* devrait donner un ensemble cohérent d'inscriptions positives et négatives dont la somme est (en principe) égale à zéro. Or, en pratique, si l'on additionne toutes les inscriptions effectuées, on obtient presque inévitablement un crédit net ou un débit net. Ce solde est le résultat d'erreurs et d'omissions dont certaines peuvent être liées aux méthodes d'approximation recommandées pour la mise en pratique des principes.

147. La balance des paiements comprend normalement un poste distinct réservé aux erreurs et omissions nettes, appelé par certains statisticiens «solde» ou «écart statistique». Ce poste vise à compenser la surévaluation ou la sous-évaluation des composantes enregistrées. Ainsi donc, si ces composantes se soldent par un crédit, le poste des erreurs et omissions nettes constituera un débit de valeur égale et vice versa.

148. Certaines erreurs et omissions qui se produisent au cours de l'établissement des données se neutralisent habituellement. C'est pourquoi le montant du solde ne renseigne pas nécessairement sur la précision globale du relevé. Cependant, l'interprétation du relevé devient difficile si ce solde est considérable.

Classification générale

149. Les composantes types, dont la liste est donnée à la fin du présent chapitre, sont réparties en deux principales sections :

> Le compte des transactions courantes, qui se subdivise en : *biens et services*, *revenus* et *transferts courants*.
>
> Le **compte de capital et d'opérations financières**, qui enregistre i) les *transferts de capital* et les *acquisitions ou cessions d'actifs non financiers non produits*, et ii) les opérations portant sur des avoirs et engagements financiers.

Cette répartition correspond à la pratique suivie par la plupart des pays depuis de longues années et dénote un changement important apporté dans le présent *Manuel*. L'ancien compte des mouvements de capitaux a été rebaptisé **compte de capital et d'opérations financières**. Dicté par un souci d'harmonisation avec le *SCN*, ce changement consiste à adopter pour la balance des paiements la distinction que le *SCN* établit entre les *transferts de capital* et les *transferts courants* et à faire concorder le nouveau compte avec le compte de capital et le compte financier du *SCN*.

150. Les inscriptions à la plupart des rubriques du **compte des transactions courantes** doivent faire apparaître les crédits ou débits bruts. La plupart des inscriptions au **compte de capital et d'opérations financières** doivent être effectuées sur une base nette, c'est-à-dire que chaque composante ne doit y figurer que comme un crédit ou un débit (le mode de traitement recommandé pour certains postes spécifiques et les exceptions seront examinés dans les chapitres correspondants). Les entrées de ressources réelles et les augmentations d'avoirs financiers (ou diminutions d'engagements) seront enregistrées au débit; les sorties de ressources réelles et les diminu-

tions d'avoirs financiers (ou augmentations d'engagements) seront enregistrées au crédit. Les transferts, dans les sections 1.C et 2.A, doivent avoir la même valeur numérique, mais affectée du signe opposé, que les inscriptions dont ils sont la contre-écriture.

Classification détaillée

151. La classification des composantes types qui suit a été mise au point conformément aux critères exposés au paragraphe 143. La structure et les caractéristiques du **compte des transactions courantes** et du **compte de capital et d'opérations financières**, sensiblement modifiées par rapport à la quatrième édition du *Manuel*, sont exposées aux chapitres IX et XVI, respectivement. Les composantes types du **compte des transactions courantes** sont décrites en détail aux chapitres X à XV, celles du **compte de capital et d'opérations financières** aux chapitres XVII à XXI et dans *Dérivés financiers — Supplément à la cinquième édition (1993) du Manuel de la balance des paiements*, Washington, 2000.

Transactions courantes (1.)

152. Sont incluses dans le **compte des transactions courantes** toutes les transactions portant sur des valeurs économiques (autres que des actifs financiers) entre entités résidentes et non résidentes. On y inscrit aussi les contreparties des valeurs économiques courantes qui sont fournies ou acquises sans réciprocité. Les grandes subdivisions (postes) sont les *biens et services*, les *revenus* et les *transferts courants*.

Biens et services (1.A)
Biens (1.A.a.)

153. La rubrique *marchandises générales* recouvre la plupart des biens meubles que les résidents exportent à destination de non-résidents ou qu'ils importent en provenance de non-résidents et qui, à quelques exceptions près, font l'objet d'un transfert de propriété (effectif ou présumé).

154. La rubrique *biens importés ou exportés pour transformation* recouvre les exportations (ou importations dans l'économie établissant sa balance des paiements) de biens franchissant une frontière pour faire l'objet à l'étranger d'une transformation, suivie d'une réimportation (ou exportation) des biens, dont la valeur est établie sur une base brute avant et après la transformation. Cette rubrique fait exception au principe du transfert de propriété.

155. La rubrique *réparations de biens* recouvre les travaux de réparation de biens — bateaux, avions, etc. — fournis à des non-résidents ou reçus de non-résidents. Bien que le mouvement physique de ces biens soit analogue à celui qui est décrit au paragraphe 154, la valeur de la réparation correspond à son prix (c'est-à-dire au montant payé ou reçu pour cette réparation) et non à la valeur brute des biens avant et après la réparation.

156. La rubrique *achats de biens dans les ports par les transporteurs* recouvre tous les biens, tels que carburants, vivres, approvisionnements et fournitures, que les transporteurs résidents ou non résidents — aériens ou maritimes, par exemple — ont achetés à l'étranger (ou dans l'économie établissant sa balance des paiements). Cette rubrique n'enregistre pas les services auxiliaires fournis (remorquage, entretien, etc.), qui sont inclus dans les services de *transports*.

157. La rubrique *or non monétaire* recouvre les exportations et importations de tout or non détenu sous la forme d'avoir de réserve (or monétaire) par les autorités. L'*or non monétaire* est traité comme n'importe quel autre produit et se décompose, lorsque cela est possible, en or détenu à titre de réserve de valeur et or détenu à d'autres fins (industrielles).

Services (1.A.b.)

158. La rubrique *transports* recouvre la plupart des services fournis par les résidents aux non-résidents et vice versa, qui étaient précédemment classés aux rubriques *expéditions* et *autres transports* dans la quatrième édition du *Manuel*. Cependant, l'assurance du fret ne figure pas ici, mais à la rubrique des *services d'assu-rance*. Sous la rubrique *transports*, on enregistre le transport de marchandises et de passagers, quel qu'en soit le mode, ainsi que les autres services de distribution et services auxiliaires, y compris l'affrètement de véhicules de transport avec leur équipage. Certaines exceptions sont signalées aux chapitres X, XI et XIII.

159. La rubrique *voyages* recouvre les biens et les services acquis dans une économie par les voyageurs non résidents (y compris les excursionnistes), à des fins professionnelles ou personnelles — notamment pour des raisons de santé ou à titre éducatif —, au cours de leur séjour (de moins d'un an) sur le territoire de cette économie. Cette rubrique exclut les services internationaux fournis aux passagers, qui sont inclus dans les *transports*. Les étudiants et les personnes en traitement médical sont consi-dérés comme étant des voyageurs, quelle que soit la durée de leur séjour, contrairement à certaines autres catégories — militaires, personnel des ambassades et travailleurs non résidents. Les dépenses des travailleurs non résidents sont toutefois comprises dans les *voyages*, tandis que celles des militaires et du personnel des ambassades sont incluses dans les *services fournis ou reçus par les administrations publiques, n.c.a.* Ces cas sont signalés aux chapitres XII et XIII.

160. La rubrique *services de communication* recouvre les opérations de communication entre résidents et non-résidents. Ce sont les services postaux (y compris les messageries) et les services de télécommunication (transmission du son, des images et d'autres types d'information par divers moyens et entretien des installations correspondantes, assuré par des résidents pour le compte de non-résidents et vice versa).

161. La rubrique *services de bâtiment et travaux publics (BTP)* recouvre les travaux de construction et d'installation effectués à l'étranger (ou dans l'économie qui établit sa balance des paiements) ou dans les enclaves extraterritoriales, à titre temporaire, par les entreprises résidentes (ou non résidentes) et leur personnel mais qui ne sont effectués ni par une entreprise étrangère apparentée à une entreprise résidente, ni par un bureau sur place non constitué en société qui, dans certaines conditions, équivaut à une entreprise étrangère apparentée. Ces aspects de la résidence sont traités aux chapitres IV et XIII.

162. La rubrique *services d'assurance* recouvre les assurances fournies aux non-résidents par des compagnies d'assurances résidentes et vice versa. On entend par là l'assurance du fret (pour les biens exportés ou importés) et les autres types d'assurance directe (notamment l'assurance-vie et autres formes d'assurances), ainsi que la réassurance. (Pour la méthode de calcul de la valeur des services d'assurance, voir paragraphes 256 et 257.)

163. La rubrique *services financiers* (autres que ceux qui sont offerts par les compagnies d'assurances et les caisses de retraite) recouvre les services d'intermédiation financière et les services auxiliaires entre résidents et non-résidents. Sont inclus les commissions et les frais ayant trait aux services suivants : lettres de crédit, lignes de crédit, crédit-bail, opérations de change, services de crédit aux consommateurs et aux entreprises, opérations de courtage, souscriptions de titres, différentes formes de couverture des opérations à terme, etc. Les services auxiliaires se rapportent à l'administration et à la réglementation des marchés financiers, à la garde de titres, etc.

164. La rubrique *services d'informatique et d'information* recouvre les transactions entre résidents et non-résidents concernant le conseil en matériel, l'installation de logiciels, les services d'information (traitement de données, banques de données, agences de presse) et l'entretien et la réparation des ordinateurs et du matériel connexe.

165. La rubrique *redevances et droits de licence* recouvre les recettes (exportations) et paiements (importations) des résidents et non-résidents se rapportant à i) l'exploitation d'actifs incorporels non financiers non produits et de droits de propriété — marques, droits d'auteur, brevets, procédés, techniques, dessins, licences de fabrication, franchises, etc. — et à ii) l'utilisation, dans le cadre d'accords de licence, de brevets, d'oeuvres originales ou de prototypes, tels que les manuscrits, films, etc.

166. La rubrique *autres services aux entreprises* recouvre les services fournis par des résidents à des non-résidents et vice versa : le négoce international et les autres services liés au commerce, la location-exploitation et divers services aux entreprises, spécialisés et techniques. (Voir, à la fin du chapitre, le tableau des *Renseignements complémentaires qui peuvent être requis sur certains postes*, et les paragraphes 261 à 264 pour de plus amples détails.)

167. La rubrique *services personnels, culturels et relatifs aux loisirs* recouvre i) les services audio-visuels et connexes et ii) les autres services culturels fournis par des résidents à des non-résidents et vice versa. Sont compris dans la catégorie i) les services qui ont trait à la production de films cinématographiques (films ou bandes vidéo), d'émissions de radio ou de télévision et d'enre-gistrements musicaux, par exemple les droits de location, les redevances perçues par les acteurs, producteurs etc., pour les productions et pour les droits de distribution cédés aux médias. Dans la catégorie ii) figurent les autres services personnels, culturels et relatifs aux loisirs tels que ceux qui ont associés aux bibliothèques, musées et autres activités culturelles ou sportives.

168. La rubrique *services fournis ou reçus par les administrations publiques, n.c.a.* recouvre tous les services (auxquels corres-pondent par exemple les dépenses des ambassades et consulats) fournis ou reçus par le secteur public ou les organisations internationales ou régionales et non classés ailleurs.

Revenus (1.B.)

169. La rubrique *rémunération des salariés* recouvre les salaires, traitements et autres émoluments versés, en espèces ou en nature, aux travailleurs frontaliers, saisonniers et autres travailleurs non résidents, (par exemple le personnel local des ambassades).

170. La rubrique *revenus des investissements* recouvre les recettes et paiements se rapportant respectivement à la détention d'avoirs financiers extérieurs par les résidents et aux engagements envers les non-résidents. Cela comprend les revenus des investissements directs, les revenus des investissements de portefeuille et les autres revenus d'investissement. La composante investissements directs se subdivise en revenus des participations au capital (dividendes, bénéfices des succursales et bénéfices réinvestis) et en revenus des titres de créance (intérêts); les revenus des investissements de portefeuille se subdivisent en revenus des participations au capital (dividendes) et en revenus des titres de créance (intérêts); les autres revenus d'investissement recouvrent les intérêts provenant d'autres opérations financières (prêts, etc.) et, en principe, les droits nets des ménages sur les réserves techniques d'assurance-vie et les réserves des caisses de retraite.

Transferts courants (1.C.)

171. À l'instar du *SCN*, le *Manuel* distingue les **transferts courants** des *transferts de capital* (ces derniers sont enregistrés au **compte de capital et** **d'opérations financières**). Les transferts sont la contrepartie des transferts de propriété, volontaires ou forcés, de ressources réelles ou d'actifs financiers entre résidents et non-résidents, qui ne reçoivent pas en échange une valeur économique. Les ***transferts courants*** sont tous ceux qui **ne font pas intervenir** i) le transfert de propriété d'un actif fixe, ii) le transfert de fonds lié ou subordonné à l'acquisition ou à la cession d'un actif fixe, ni iii) la remise, sans contrepartie, d'une dette par un créancier (toutes ces opérations sont des *transferts de capital*). Les ***transferts courants*** comprennent ceux des administrations publiques — par exemple la coopération internationale courante (entre des administrations publiques appartenant à différentes économies), les paiements des impôts courants sur le revenu et sur la fortune, etc. — et les autres transferts, tels que les envois de fonds des travailleurs, les primes (moins les commissions de service) et les indemnités au titre des assurances autres que l'assu-rance-vie, etc. La distinction entre les ***transferts courants*** et les *transferts de capital* fait l'objet d'un examen approfondi au chapitre XV (voir également les paragraphes 175 et 344).

Le compte de capital et d'opérations financières (2.)

172. Le **compte de capital et d'opérations financières** a deux principales composantes — le ***compte de capital*** correspond au compte de capital du *SCN* et le ***compte d'opérations financières*** au compte financier du *SCN*. Les avoirs (ou actifs) sont des créances sur les non-résidents et les engagements (ou passifs) des dettes envers les non-résidents. Les deux parties à une transaction portant sur des avoirs ou des engagements sont en général un résident et un non-résident mais, dans certains cas, il peut s'agir de deux résidents ou de deux non-résidents. (Voir paragraphe 318.)

173. Toutes les réévaluations et toutes les autres variations d'actifs et de passifs extérieurs qui ne sont pas dues à des transactions (voir paragraphe 310) sont exclues du **compte de capital et d'opérations financières** mais apparaissent dans la position extérieure globale. Des relevés complémentaires identifient certains postes qui présentent un intérêt pour l'analyse et qui relèvent de plusieurs comptes. C'est le cas, par exemple, des engagements qui constituent des réserves pour les autorités étrangères et des financements exceptionnels, dont il est question au chapitre XXII.

174. La classification des ***opérations financières*** et celle des composantes des revenus dans les **transactions courantes** sont liées et doivent être cohérentes pour faciliter l'analyse, permettre le rapprochement effectif entre la balance des paiements et la position extérieure globale, et assurer la compatibilité avec le *SCN* et avec les autres systèmes statistiques du FMI.

Compte de capital (2.A.)

175. Les grandes subdivisions du **compte de capital** sont les *transferts de capital* et les *acquisitions et cessions d'actifs non financiers non produits*. Les *transferts de capital* sont ceux qui font intervenir le transfert de propriété d'un actif fixe; le transfert de fonds lié ou subordonné à l'acquisition ou à la cession d'un actif fixe; ou la remise, sans contrepartie, d'une dette par un créancier. Ils se subdivisent en deux catégories : i) les transferts des adminis-trations publiques, qui se décomposent en remises de dettes et autres transferts et ii) les autres transferts, qui se subdivisent en transferts des migrants, remises de dettes et autres transferts. (Voir le chapitre XV, qui traite de la distinction entre les *transferts de capital* et les **transferts courants**). Les *acquisitions et cessions d'actifs non financiers non produits* se rapportent généralement aux avoirs incorporels tels que les brevets, les contrats de location et autres contrats transférables, la marque, etc. Ce poste ne recouvre pas les propriétés non bâties situées sur le territoire d'une économie donnée mais peut inclure l'achat (ou la vente) de terrains par une ambassade étrangère. (Voir paragraphe 312.)

Compte d'opérations financières (2.B.)

176. La classification des composantes types comprises sous ce poste est fondée sur les critères suivants :

La nature des investissements ou leur ventilation fonctionnelle (*investissements directs, investissements de portefeuille, dérivés financiers, autres investissements* et *avoirs de réserve*).

Dans le cas des *investissements directs*, la distinction en fonction du sens des mouvements de capitaux — entre l'étranger et l'économie qui établit sa balance des paiements — étant entendu que, dans chaque sous-catégorie, les avoirs sont distingués des engagements.

Pour ce qui est des *investissements de portefeuille*, des *dérivés financiers* et des *autres investissements*, la distinction traditionnelle entre avoirs et engagements.

La nature de l'instrument est particulièrement importante pour les *investissements de portefeuille* et les *autres investissements* (titres de participation ou d'engagement, crédits commerciaux, prêts, monnaie et dépôts, autres avoirs ou engagements). Le présent *Manuel* regroupe dans les *investissements de portefeuille* les instruments du marché monétaire, ainsi que les autres instruments financiers, tant traditionnels que nouveaux.

Pour ce qui est des *investissements de portefeuille*, des *dérivés financiers,* et des *autres investissements*, on distingue le secteur dont relève le créancier intérieur en ce qui concerne les avoirs et le secteur dont relève le débiteur intérieur en ce qui concerne les engagements. Cette distinc-tion facilite les rapprochements avec les comptes de revenu et la position extérieure globale ainsi qu'avec le *SCN* et les autres systèmes statistiques;

La distinction habituelle entre les avoirs et engagements à long et à court terme, le long terme étant défini par une échéance contractuelle initiale de plus d'un an et le court terme par une échéance ne dépassant pas un an, n'est faite que pour les *autres investissements*. Depuis quelques années, cette distinction a perdu à l'évidence beaucoup de son utilité pour de nombreuses transactions, intérieures ou internationales. C'est pourquoi la différenciation du long et du court terme a moins d'importance dans le présent *Manuel* — et dans le *SCN* — que dans les éditions précédentes. Cependant, parce qu'elle est importante à certains égards, par exemple pour l'analyse de la dette extérieure, elle est retenue dans le présent *Manuel* pour les *autres investissements*.

177. La rubrique *investissements directs* — lesquels témoignent d'un intérêt durable de la part d'une entité résidente d'une économie (l'investisseur direct) pour une entité résidente d'une autre économie (l'entreprise d'investissement direct) — recouvre toutes les transactions entre les investisseurs directs et les entreprises d'investissement direct. Les *investissements directs* recouvrent donc la transaction initiale entre les uns et les autres et toutes les transactions ultérieures entre eux, ainsi que les transactions entre les entreprises apparentées, constituées ou non en sociétés. Les opérations d'investissement direct effectuées à l'étranger et dans l'économie déclarante se décomposent en capital social, bénéfices réinvestis, autres opérations en capital (transactions liées aux dettes entre entreprises d'un même groupe). En ce qui concerne le capital social et les autres capitaux, les créances et les engagements à l'égard des entreprises affiliées et à l'égard des investisseurs directs sont ventilés séparément. Les transactions entre banques apparentées et entre autres intermédiaires financiers apparentés se limitent aux transactions portant sur des titres de participation (capital social) et des dettes/créances permanentes. (Voir paragraphe 372 de la cinquième édition du *Manuel de la balance des paiements*).

178. Les investissements de portefeuille comprennent les titres de participation et les titres de créance; ces derniers se subdivisent en obligations et autres titres d'emprunt, et instruments du marché monétaire. Divers nouveaux instruments financiers, autres que les dérivés financiers, sont classés dans les catégories d'instruments appropriées. (Les opérations classées parmi les investissements directs et les avoirs de réserve sont exclues.)

179. La catégorie des *dérivés financiers* recouvre les instruments financiers qui sont liés à un autre instrument ou indicateur financier ou produit de base spécifique et par le biais desquels des risques financiers spécifiques (de taux d'intérêt, de taux de change, de participation ou de prix des produits de base, de crédit, etc.) peuvent être négociés en tant que tels sur les marchés financiers. Les opérations sur dérivés financiers doivent être traitées en tant qu'opérations distinctes et non comme faisant partie intégrante de la valeur des opérations sous-jacentes auxquelles elles sont liées.

180. La rubrique *autres investissements* recouvre les crédits commerciaux et les prêts à court et à long terme (y compris l'uti-lisation des crédits et des prêts du FMI, ainsi que les prêts/emprunts au titre de la location-vente; la monnaie fiduciaire et les dépôts (transférables et autres, tels que les dépôts d'épargne et les dépôts à terme, les parts des associations d'épargne et de prêt, des associations de crédit mutuel, etc.); et d'autres comptes à payer et à recevoir. (Les transactions classées parmi les *investissements directs* sont exclues de la présente rubrique.)

181. La rubrique *avoirs de réserve* recouvre les transactions portant sur les avoirs dont les autorités monétaires d'une économie considèrent qu'elles disposent pour répondre aux besoins de financement de la balance des paiements et, dans certains cas, à d'autres besoins; en principe, cette disponibilité n'est pas étroitement liée à des critères formels tels que la propriété des avoirs ou la monnaie dans laquelle ils sont libellés. Les rubriques incluses sous ce poste sont l'or monétaire, les DTS, la position de réserve au FMI, les avoirs en devises (monnaie fiduciaire et dépôts, et valeurs mobilières) et les autres créances.

182. Le champ couvert par les composantes des *avoirs de réserve* et leur définition répondent aux besoins de l'analyse, comportent un élément d'appréciation et ne se prêtent pas toujours à l'application de critères objectifs formels ou de systèmes de classement précis fondés sur la conditionnalité ou sur d'autres facteurs. Contrairement à la quatrième édition du *Manuel*, la cinquième édition prescrit d'exclure de ce poste les réévaluations des *avoirs de réserve*, ainsi que leurs contreparties. Sont aussi exclues les allocations ou annulations de DTS, la monétisation ou la démonétisation de l'or et les inscriptions de contrepartie. Ces variations, qui ne sont pas des transactions, apparaissent dans la position extérieure globale.

INTRODUCCIÓN

El volumen 59 de *Balance of Payments Statistics Year-book* (anuario) que publica el Fondo Monetario Internacional (FMI) presenta las estadísticas de balanza de pagos declaradas por los países miembros al FMI. El FMI agradece a los países miembros su cooperación en la declaración de estos datos. En el caso de algunos países, esta información se complementa con detalles que los economistas de la institución obtienen de diferentes fuentes.

El anuario consta de tres partes. En la parte 1 se presentan datos de balanza de pagos y datos sobre la posición de inversión internacional de cada país. En la parte 2 figuran los totales regionales y mundiales de los componentes principales de la balanza de pagos. En la parte 3 se presentan descripciones técnicas sobre la mayoría de países declarantes. La parte 1 se publica en un tomo separado y las partes 2 y 3 en un mismo tomo.

En este volumen del anuario se mantienen las características introducidas en los volúmenes 46 al 58 inclusive. Como en el volumen 46, los datos de balanza de pagos se desglosan conforme a los componentes normalizados de la quinta edición del *Manual de Balanza de Pagos (Manual)*[1]. No obstante, se han modificado los componentes normalizados tras la publicación de *Instrumentos financieros derivados: Suplemento a la quinta edición (1993) del* Manual de Balanza de Pagos, en 2000 y las modificaciones de dicha publicación en 2002. Por consiguiente, las referencias a la quinta edición del *Manual* incluyen el suplemento y el apéndice. De conformidad con las recomendaciones del suplemento y el apéndice, el presente anuario refleja la decisión del Comité del FMI de Estadísticas de Balanza de Pagos en el sentido de que las transacciones de instrumentos financieros derivados relacionadas con empresas afiliadas deben incluirse en el componente correspondiente a los instrumentos financieros derivados de las estadísticas de balanza de pagos y de la posición de inversión in

ternacional. Además, como en el volumen 47, se incluyen los datos sobre la posición de inversión internacional en el formato de la quinta edición del *Manual*, y en la parte 3 del anuario, se publican descripciones detalladas de las metodologías, los procedimientos de compilación y las fuentes de datos que se utilizan en la mayoría de los países incluidos en el presente volumen. En el *Manual*[2], se introducen varios cambios metodológicos en la compilación de los datos de balanza de pagos, cambios que se describen con detalle en el capítulo I del *Manual*. A partir del volumen 46, en este anuario los datos presentados conforme a los componentes normalizados del *Manual* están acompañados de una lista de códigos, preparada conjuntamente por el FMI, la Organización de Cooperación y Desarrollo Económicos (OCDE) y la Oficina Estadística de las Comunidades Europeas (Eurostat). La estructura de estos códigos se explica en un anexo de esta introducción. Además, a partir del volumen 46, no se presentan datos trimestrales de balanza de pagos en el caso de los países que declaran estadísticas trimestrales de balanza de pagos al FMI. Estos datos trimestrales se publican en las ediciones mensuales de la publicación del FMI *International financial statistics (IFS)* y también se presentan en el CD-ROM y en Internet (Balanza de Pagos en Línea).

La conversión de los datos realizada por el personal del FMI ha permitido presentar en el formato de la quinta edición los datos históricos extraídos de la base de datos del FMI, así como los datos más recientes declarados por los países miembros en el formato de la cuarta edición del *Manual de Balanza de Pagos*. En 1995, el personal del FMI elaboró fórmulas para transformar la información de balanza de pagos de cada país incluida en la base de datos del FMI a fin de adaptarla a la metodología y presentación que se establecen en la quinta edición. Seguidamente se enviaron los datos convertidos a las autoridades de los respectivos países para su revisión y se incorporaron los comentarios recibidos a la nueva base de datos. En 1996, el personal del FMI, en colaboración con las autoridades de los países, convirtió en forma similar los datos sobre la posición de inversión internacional declarados en el formato de la cuarta edición a la presentación de la quinta edición. En principio, la posición de inversión internacional de un país es un balance general de las tenencias de activos y pasivos financieros frente al exterior.

En la parte 3 del anuario se incluyen las descripciones técnicas de la metodología, los procedimientos de compilación y las fuentes de datos que utilizan los países que declaran datos. Las descripciones se basan en gran medida en la información que los

---

[1]El volumen 1 del anuario, publicado en 1949, se basó en la primera edición del Manual de Balanza de Pagos del FMI, publicado en 1948; los volúmenes 2–12 se basaron en la segunda edición del manual, publicada en 1950; los volúmenes 13–23 se basaron en la tercera edición, publicada en 1961, y los volúmenes 24–29 se basaron en esa edición así como en el Ma-nual de Balanza de Pagos: Suplemento a la tercera edición, que apareció en 1973. Desde el volumen 30 al 45, las presentaciones siguieron las recomendaciones de la cuarta edición del manual, publicada en 1977.

[2]Fondo Monetario Internacional, *Manual de Balanza de Pagos*, quinta edición, Washington, septiembre de 1993, e *Instrumentos financieros derivados: Suplemento a la quinta edición (1993) del* Manual de Balanza de Pagos, 2000.

países suministran al FMI. Se incluyen estas descripciones para que los usuarios comprendan mejor la cobertura de los datos de los distintos países publicados en el anuario, así como sus limitaciones, y para informar a los compiladores sobre las fuentes de datos y los métodos utilizados por los compiladores de otros países.

El resto de esta introducción se ha organizado de la siguiente manera:

- En la sección I se describen las características básicas de los cuadros que se publican en la parte 1 del anuario. (Pueden consultarse los detalles sobre cobertura de los datos de las partes 2 y 3 en el segundo tomo.)

- La sección II contiene información sobre la manera de acceder a la información del FMI sobre balanza de pagos en CD-ROM y en Internet (Balanza de Pagos en Línea).

- Se han incluido seis anexos. En el anexo I se incluye una presentación analítica sucinta de los componentes de la balanza de pagos (y los códigos correspondientes). En el anexo II se presentan los componentes normalizados (con sus respectivos códigos) de la quinta edición del *Manual*. En el anexo III se explica el sistema de codificación empleado. En el anexo IV se presentan los componentes normalizados de la posición de inversión internacional que figuran en la quinta edición del *Manual*. En el anexo V se describe el marco conceptual de la balanza de pagos y, en el anexo VI, se explica la cobertura de los componentes principales de las cuentas de la balanza de pagos conforme a las directrices establecidas en la quinta edición del *Manual*.

I. Parte 1 del anuario: Datos de cada país

En la parte 1 del anuario se presentan las páginas de países en orden alfabético. Debe hacerse la salvedad de que el término "país", según se emplea en esta publicación, no siempre se refiere a una entidad territorial que constituya un Estado conforme al derecho y la práctica internacionales; el término también abarca la zona del euro, la Unión Monetaria del Caribe Oriental y ciertas entidades territoriales que no son Estados soberanos, sobre las cuales también se facilitan datos estadísticos a nivel internacional en forma separada.

Los datos de balanza de pagos de la mayoría de los países se presentan en dos cuadros. El cuadro 1 es un resumen analítico de los datos más detallados que se presentan en el cuadro 2. En el cuadro 1 se presentan los componentes de la balanza de pagos que están ordenados de tal manera que se destacan las partidas de financiamiento (reservas y partidas conexas). (Véase también el anexo I.) El cuadro 2 presenta los datos correspondientes a los compo-

nentes normalizados que se describen en la quinta edición del *Manual*. (Véase también el anexo II.) En el caso de los países sobre los que se dispone de información relativa a la posición de inversión internacional, los datos se presentan en el cuadro 3. En los cuadros 1, 2 y 3, los datos corresponden al período 2000–2007 para cada país. Los datos que figuran en los cuadros se declaran en base a los años calendario, salvo indicación contraria.

Presentación analítica

En la presentación analítica, que figura en el cuadro 1, los componentes de la balanza de pagos se clasifican en cinco categorías principales de datos (grupos A a E) que el FMI considera útiles para analizar de manera uniforme la evolución de la balanza de pagos. No obstante, no debe interpretarse que esta división en grupos refleja una recomendación del FMI sobre el enfoque analítico más apropiado para todos los países. Los componentes normalizados del cuadro 2 podrían agruparse conforme a una presentación analítica diferente en función de las circunstancias especiales de determinado país o de ciertos requisitos analíticos.

Obsérvese que las cifras que aparecen en los cuadros 1 y 2 en lo que respecta a los saldos de la cuenta corriente, la cuenta de capital y la cuenta financiera difieren en el caso de algunos países. Esto se debe a que en el cuadro 1 se excluyen ciertas transacciones que se clasifican en estas cuentas porque han sido reclasificadas como "financiamiento excepcional" en reservas y partidas conexas. El "financiamiento excepcional" se refiere a las transacciones efectuadas por las autoridades para financiar su balanza de pagos, e incluye la obtención de recursos en préstamo del exterior, los atrasos en los pagos y la condonación de deudas, pero no incluye las reservas.

Presentación normalizada

Los componentes normalizados conforme a la quinta edición del *Manual*, que figuran en el cuadro 2, ofrecen una clasificación más detallada de los bienes y servicios que en la cuarta edición. La llamada "cuenta de capital y financiera" agrupa diferentes componentes bajo la "cuenta de capital" y la "cuenta financiera". En esta última se clasifican los componentes según la clase de inversión (es decir, inversión directa, inversión de cartera, instrumentos financieros derivados[3], otra inversión y activos de reserva),

---

[3] Debido a la naturaleza única de los instrumentos financieros derivados, y a la forma en que algunas instituciones registran las transacciones, algunos países sólo pueden declarar datos en cifras netas. Si bien estos datos en cifras netas podrían incluirse en la categoría de activos, en el presente anuario estas transacciones se incluyen en cifras netas, y las posiciones en cifras netas cuando se declaran, en la categoría de pasivos, porque las entidades que negocian con flujos de efectivo relacionados con obligaciones de deuda son las que generan mayor demanda de estos instrumentos.

Recuadro. Posición de inversión internacional

Las declaraciones de la posición de inversión internacional de los países declarantes figuran como cuadro 3 en las páginas de países. Las declaraciones sobre la posición de inversión internacional de algunos países deben interpretarse teniendo en cuenta las notas que figuran en la parte 3 en la que se presentan las metodologías, los procedimientos de compilación y las fuentes de datos que utilizan estos países. A medida que los países sigan recopilando datos más completos, se publicará una presentación más extensa de los datos sobre la posición de inversión internacional en volúmenes subsiguientes del anuario.

Véase el capítulo XXIII de la quinta edición del *Manual* en el que se presenta un análisis detallado del concepto de posición de inversión internacional.

Deuda externa no es un componente aparte de la posición de inversión internacional sino que se deriva mediante la suma de los componentes del pasivo de la posición de inversión internacional que no corresponden a capital (es decir, todos los pasivos registrados que no sean títulos de participación en el capital, ni acciones y otras participaciones de capital mediante inversión directa, incluidas las utilidades reinvertidas, y los instrumentos financieros derivados). Esta opinión concuerda, en general, con la definición básica de la deuda externa bruta adoptada en la publicación *Estadísticas de la deuda externa: Guía para compiladores y usuarios (Guía)* realizada por el Grupo de tareas interinstitucional sobre estadísticas financieras. Este grupo de tareas, que se reunió bajo la presidencia del FMI, se encargó de la elaboración de la *Guía* en la que participaron representantes del Banco de Pagos Internacionales (BPI), la Secretaría del Commonwealth, el Banco Central Europeo, Eurostat, el FMI, la OCDE, la Secretaría del Club de París, la Conferencia de las Naciones Unidas sobre Comercio y Desarrollo (UNCTAD) y el Banco Mundial.

Posición de inversión internacional: Componentes clave[1]

A. Activos

1. Inversión directa
    1.1 Acciones y otras participaciones de capital y utilidades reinvertidas
    1.2 Otro capital[2]

2. Inversión de cartera
    2.1 Títulos de participación en el capital
    2.2 Títulos de deuda[4]

3. Instrumentos financieros derivados
    3.1 Autoridades monetarias
    3.2 Gobierno general
    3.3 Bancos
    3.4 Otros sectores

4. Otra inversión
    4.1 Créditos comerciales
    4.2 Préstamos
    4.3 Moneda y depósitos
    4.4 Otros activos

5. Activos de reserva
    5.1 Oro monetario
    5.2 Derechos especiales de giro
    5.3 Posición de reserva en el FMI
    5.4 Divisas
    5.5 AOtros activos

B. Pasivos

1. Inversión directa
    1.1 Acciones y otras participaciones de capital y utilidades reinvertidas
    1.2 Otro capital[3]

2. Inversión de cartera
    2.1 Títulos de participación en el capital
    2.2 Títulos de deuda[3,4]

3. Instrumentos financieros derivados
    3.1 Autoridades monetarias
    3.2 Gobierno general
    3.3 Bancos
    3.4 Otros sectores

4. Otra inversión
    4.1 Créditos comerciales[3]
    4.2 Préstamos [3]
    4.3 Moneda y depósitos[3]
    4.4 Otros pasivos[3]

---

[1] No se indican todos los componentes, por ejemplo, los que están desglosados por sectores (autoridades monetarias, gobierno general, bancos y otros) y, en algunos casos, por vencimientos. Un país que reporte datos de la PII omitiendo los principales subcomponentes, los totales podrían no ser publicados.

[2] Los pasivos frente a empresas filiales, componentes de otro capital, se incluyen en la deuda externa.

[3] Los pasivos frente a inversionistas directos, componentes de otro capital, se incluyen en la deuda externa.

[4] Incluye bonos, pagarés e instrumentos del mercado de dinero.

activos/pasivos, sectores internos (autoridades monetarias, gobierno general, bancos y otros sectores) y vencimiento original.

Posición de inversión internacional

Los datos sobre la posición de inversión internacional, que figuran en el cuadro 3, se agrupan conforme a los componentes normalizados de la posición de inversión internacional que se establecen en la quinta edición del *Manual*. (Véase también el anexo IV.)

La clasificación de los componentes de la posición de inversión internacional en el cuadro 3 coincide con la de la cuenta financiera de la balanza de pagos que figura en el cuadro 2. Sin embargo, hay varias diferencias entre los dos cuadros. Como se mencionó anteriormente, los datos sobre la posición de inversión internacional reflejan los activos y pasivos financieros de un país frente al exterior en un momento determinado. Por lo tanto, en el cuadro 3 los componentes de la posición de inversión internacional se agrupan en la presentación básica en dos categorías generales, a saber, activos y pasivos, a diferencia de la clasificación funcional de la inversión (es decir, inversión directa, inversión de cartera, instrumentos financieros derivados, otra inversión y activos de reserva) que figura en el cuadro 2. Además, los datos del cuadro 3 reflejan la posición de inversión internacional de un país al final del período de declaración de datos, a diferencia de las transacciones que tuvieron lugar durante el período, que se presentan en el cuadro 2. Asimismo, a diferencia del cuadro 2, en el que se indica el valor de las transacciones a lo largo de un período, la valoración de la posición de inversión internacional de un país, que se presenta en el cuadro 3, refleja el valor de las transacciones financieras, las variaciones por valoración y otros ajustes al final del período de declaración. La posición de inversión internacional neta, que figura en el cuadro 3, se calcula como diferencia entre el valor de los activos financieros externos declarados y el de los pasivos financieros externos declarados.

Códigos de datos

En los cuadros 1, 2 y 3 se indican los códigos de cada categoría y componente. Como se señaló anteriormente, los códigos fueron elaborados conjuntamente por el FMI, la OCDE y Eurostat, a efectos de facilitar la declaración de datos a nivel internacional. Los códigos corresponden a los componentes normalizados de la balanza de pagos y de la posición de inversión internacional según se definen en la quinta edición del *Manual*, así como a los componentes de la clasificación conjunta OCDE/Eurostat para el comercio de servicios.

Cada uno de los códigos que figuran en el anuario está formado por seis dígitos/caracteres. El primer dígito indica si se trata de un crédito, un débito o del valor neto (el número "2" corresponde a un crédito, el "3" a un débito y el "4" al valor neto, es decir, la diferencia entre créditos y débitos). Los tres dígitos siguientes se utilizan para clasificar los componentes de la balanza de pagos. Por ejemplo, para la cuenta corriente se utiliza el código 993, para la cuenta de capital 994 y para la cuenta financiera 995. Los detalles del sistema de codificación figuran en el anexo III.

Los dígitos/caracteres que ocupan los lugares quinto y sexto de los códigos que figuran en el anuario se reservan para indicar características especiales de ciertos componentes específicos. Por ejemplo, en el cuadro 1, la Z del quinto carácter señala que se excluye de ese componente el financiamiento excepcional; la W indica que se excluyen esta misma partida y el uso del crédito del FMI y préstamos del FMI. Las letras A, B, C y D del cuadro 1 indican los distintos sectores internos. En el cuadro 2, las letras A, B y C se refieren a subcomponentes no normalizados, como los de transportes (pasajeros, fletes y otros).

Créditos y débitos

En los cuadros 1 y 2, los datos sobre transacciones figuran como asientos de crédito bruto o débito bruto en la cuenta corriente y la cuenta de capital. En la cuenta financiera se presentan como asientos de crédito neto o débito neto (para reflejar variaciones netas de los pasivos y de los activos) en la cuenta financiera. Los asientos de crédito, bruto o neto, representan valores positivos (aunque no se indica el signo) y los asientos de débito, bruto o neto, son negativos (y sí se indica el signo). Por lo tanto, toda disminución de los activos y todo aumento de los pasivos (crédito) figuran como valores positivos y todo aumento de los activos y toda disminución de los pasivos (débito) aparecen con signo negativo.

Asientos nulos, carencia de datos, o datos confidenciales

Con frecuencia es difícil discernir en la información declarada por los países si faltan cifras porque no se dispone de datos, porque el valor de esa partida es cero o insignificante, o porque son datos confidenciales. La inclusión de tres puntos (....) en los cuadros del anuario significa cualquiera de las dos posibilidades: bien que no se dispone de datos o bien que el valor es cero o insignificante, o confidencial. En caso que datos para uno o mas subcomponentes no pueda ser revelado debido, a razones de confidencialidad, el valor(s) no mostrado se adicionara a un subcomponente generico.

Nota sobre los componentes de renta y otra inversión

En el cuadro 2 relativo a la presentación normalizada, los datos declarados por algunos países en las categorías de "renta" y "otra inversión" presentan un grado de agregación que no permite identificar por separado cada uno de los componentes que figuran en esta categoría. Por consiguiente, en estos casos, los datos agregados de ciertas subcategorías no pueden obtenerse sumando los componentes de estas sub-categorías. Lo mismo ocurre en el caso de los datos relativos a "otra inversión" que figuran en el cuadro 3 relativo a la posición de inversión internacional.

Anteriormente, en los volúmenes 46 al 49, en los cuadros se presentaban los datos correspondientes a "otra inversión" (activos y pasivos) desglosados en "a largo plazo" y "a corto plazo". Desde el Volumen 50, en los cuadros se presentan los datos correspondientes a "otra inversión" (activos y pasivos) de las autoridades monetarias, el gobierno general, los bancos y otros sectores en cifras totales (del financiamiento a largo plazo y a corto plazo) y en partidas "de los cuales: a corto plazo". (En el caso de los préstamos, autoridades monetarias, los datos se indican en cifras totales, desglosados en "de los cuales: uso del crédito del FMI y préstamos del FMI" y "de los cuales: a corto plazo".) Sin embargo, en el Anexo II, no se ha modificado la presentación normalizada.

Redondeo de las cifras

La mayor parte de las cifras de los cuadros se expresan en unidades de un millón; no debe suponerse que los cuadros que incluyen unidades más pequeñas representan, necesariamente, cifras más exactas. La unidad se elige con el fin de presentar las cifras de una manera práctica. Debido al redondeo en el cálculo de las cifras, puede haber diferencias entre un total y la suma de sus componentes.

Conversión de monedas

La mayoría de los datos de balanza de pagos declarados al FMI se expresan en unidades de moneda nacional o en dólares de EE.UU., pero algunos países declaran ciertos datos en DEG. Para facilitar la comparación de datos entre los países, todos los estados de balanza de pagos publicados en el anuario se expresan en dólares de EE.UU. Además, los datos sobre transacciones con el FMI y sobre transacciones en DEG declarados por todos los países se remplazan por los datos que figuran en los registros del FMI, expresados en DEG. Esta información se convierte, a su vez, a dólares de EE.UU.

En el caso de los países que no declaran sus estadísticas en dólares de EE.UU., los datos se convierten utilizando el tipo de cambio que figura al pie

del cuadro 1 para cada país, que normalmente es el tipo promedio vigente en el país en el período correspondiente y se obtiene de *IFS*. Por ejemplo, en las páginas de *IFS* correspondientes a la zona del euro figura la línea "rf", en la que se indica el tipo de cambio promedio del euro frente al dólar de EE.UU. La conversión de los datos sobre transacciones de DEG a dólares de EE.UU. se efectúa a los tipos de cambio que se indican en la línea "sb" de las páginas de *IFS* correspondientes a Estados Unidos. En lo que respecta a los países que declaran datos trimestrales en unidades de moneda nacional, los totales anuales en dólares de EE.UU. se obtienen sumando los montos trimestrales en dólares de EE.UU.

En el caso de los países que no declaran datos sobre posición de inversión internacional en dólares de EE.UU., los datos se convierten utilizando las tasas de conversión para el país que figuran en la parte inferior del cuadro 3. Estas tasas son normalmente las del fin del período basado en los datos de IFS pertinente para el país (linea "ae").

En la introducción de *IFS*, sección 1, se presenta mayor información sobre los tipos de cambio empleados.

II. Versiones en CD-ROM e Internet

Las estadísticas publicadas en el anuario también se presentan en CD-ROM y en Internet, (Estadísticas de Balanza de Pagos en Línea). En esta versión electrónica, el número de países y las series cronológicas son ligeramente mayores que en la versión impresa del anuario, así como el número de períodos sobre los cuales se incluyen observaciones estadísticas en las series cronológicas. También se incluyen los datos trimestrales declarados por los países y los datos actualizados y corregidos a medida que se dispone de los mismos. Para mayor información sobre el CD-ROM y Estadísticas de Balanza de Pagos en Línea, sírvase dirigirse a:

Publication Services
International Monetary Fund
Washington, D.C. 20431, EE.UU.
Teléfono: (202) 623–7430
Fax: (202) 623–7201
Correo electrónico: publications@imf.org
Internet: http://www.imf.org

Anexo I. Presentación Analítica

¹Excluidos los componentes que se han clasificado en las categorías del Grupo E

ANEXO II. PRESENTACIÓN NORMALIZADA

	Códigos
Otros servicios, crédito	2 200 BA
Comunicaciones	2 245 ..
Construcción	2 249 ..
Seguros	2 253 ..
Financieros	2 260 ..
Informática e información	2 262 ..
Regalías y derechos de licencia	2 266 ..
Otros servicios empresariales	2 268 ..
Personales, culturales y recreativos	2 287 ..
Servicios del gobierno, n.i.o.p.	2 291 ..
Otros servicios, débito	3 200 BA
Comunicaciones	3 245 ..
Construcción	3 249 ..
Seguros	3 253 ..
Financieros	3 260 ..
Informática e información	3 262 ..
Regalías y derechos de licencia	3 266 ..
Otros servicios empresariales	3 268 ..
Personales, culturales y recreativos	3 287 ..
Servicios del gobierno, n.i.o.p.	3 291 ..
C. RENTA	4 300 ..
Crédito total	2 300 ..
Débito total	3 300 ..
Remuneración de empleados, crédito	2 310 ..
Remuneración de empleados, débito	3 310 ..
Renta de la inversión, crédito	2 320 ..
Renta de la inversión directa	2 330 ..
Dividendos y utilidades distribuidas de sucursales	2 332 ..
Utilidades reinvertidas y utilidades no distribuidas de sucursales	2 333 ..
Renta procedente de la deuda (intereses)	2 334 ..
Renta de la inversión de cartera	2 339 ..
Renta procedente de acciones y otras participaciones de capital	2 340 ..
Renta procedente de bonos y pagarés	2 350 ..
Renta procedente de instrumentos del mercado monetario	2 360 ..
Renta de otra inversión	2 370 ..
Renta de la inversión, débito	3 320 ..
Renta de la inversión directa	3 330 ..
Dividendos y utilidades distribuidas de sucursales	3 332 ..
Utilidades reinvertidas y utilidades no distribuidas de sucursales	3 333 ..
Renta procedente de la deuda (intereses)	3 334 ..
Renta de la inversión de cartera	3 339 ..
Renta procedente de acciones y otras participaciones de capital	3 340 ..
Renta procedente de bonos y pagarés	3 350 ..
Renta procedente de instrumentos del mercado monetario	3 360 ..
Renta de otra inversión	3 370 ..
D. TRANSFERENCIAS CORRIENTES	4 379 ..
Crédito	2 379 ..
Gobierno general	2 380 ..
Otros sectores	2 390 ..
Remesas de trabajadores	2 391 ..
Otras transferencias corrientes	2 392 ..

		Códigos
B.	**INVERSIÓN DE CARTERA**	4 600 ..
	Activos	4 602 ..
	Títulos de participación en el capital	4 610 ..
	Autoridades monetarias	4 611 ..
	Gobierno general	4 612 ..
	Bancos	4 613 ..
	Otros sectores	4 614 ..
	Títulos de deuda	4 619 ..
	Bonos y pagarés	4 620 ..
	Autoridades monetarias	4 621 ..
	Gobierno general	4 622 ..
	Bancos	4 623 ..
	Otros sectores	4 624 ..
	Instrumentos del mercado monetario	4 630 ..
	Autoridades monetarias	4 631 ..
	Gobierno general	4 632 ..
	Bancos	4 633 ..
	Otros sectores	4 634 ..
	Pasivos	4 652 ..
	Títulos de participación en el capital	4 660 ..
	Bancos	4 663 ..
	Otros sectores	4 664 ..
	Títulos de deuda	4 669 ..
	Bonos y pagarés	4 670 ..
	Autoridades monetarias	4 671 ..
	Gobierno general	4 672 ..
	Bancos	4 673 ..
	Otros sectores	4 674 ..
	Instrumentos del mercado monetario	4 680 ..
	Autoridades monetarias	4 681 ..
	Gobierno general	4 682 ..
	Bancos	4 683 ..
	Otros sectores	4 684 ..
C.	**INSTRUMENTOS FINANCIEROS DERIVADOS**	4 910 ..
	Autoridades monetarias	4 911 ..
	Gobierno general	4 912 ..
	Bancos	4 913 ..
	Otros sectores	4 914 ..
	Activos	4 900 ..
	Autoridades monetarias	4 901 ..
	Gobierno general	4 902 ..
	Bancos	4 903 ..
	Otros sectores	4 904 ..
	Pasivos	4 905 ..
	Autoridades monetarias	4 906 ..
	Gobierno general	4 907 ..
	Bancos	4 908 ..
	Otros sectores	4 909 ..
D.	**OTRA INVERSIÓN**	4 700 ..
	Activos	4 703 ..
	Créditos comerciales	4 706 ..
	Gobierno general	4 707 ..
	de la cual: a corto plazo	4 709 ..
	Otros sectores	4 710 ..
	de la cual: a corto plazo	4 712 ..

Anexo III. Sistema de codificación FMI/OCDE/Eurostat para la balanza de pagos, la posición de inversión internacional y el comercio de servicios[1]

Este sistema de codificación incorpora todos los componentes normalizados y las líneas de información suplementaria de la quinta edición del *Manual de Balanza de Pagos*, así como los componentes y partidas informativas de la clasificación OCDE/Eurostat para el comercio internacional de servicios.

El código consta de tres partes:

\<posición\>	Un dígito (del 1 al 8) que describe la posición de la partida en las cuentas de la posición de inversión internacional o de la balanza de pagos.
\<tema\>	Tres dígitos (del 100 al 998) que identifican todos los componentes de la balanza de pagos, del comercio de servicios y de información suplementaria seleccionada.
\<sufijo\>	Serie de caracteres definidos por el usuario; puede ser de cualquier longitud.

El código completo deberá tener la siguiente configuración: \<posición\>\<tema\>\<sufijo\>, aunque el sufijo es optativo. Los dígitos de posición y tema, en cambio, son obligatorios. Por esa razón, en la mayoría de los casos, la configuración del código es \<posición\>\<tema\>.

El primer dígito del código describe la posición de la partida en las cuentas de la posición de inversión internacional y de la balanza de pagos, a saber:

Código	Posición en las cuentas de la posición de inversión internacional y la balanza de pagos
1	Posición al comienzo del período
2	Flujos de crédito
3	Flujos de débito
4	Flujos netos
5	Ajuste por variaciones de precios
6	Ajuste por variaciones de tipos de cambio
7	Otros ajustes
8	Posición al final del período
0	Otros

El primer dígito del tema identifica la sección de la balanza de pagos, a saber:

Código	Sección de las cuentas
1	Bienes
2	Servicios
3	Renta y transferencias corrientes
4	Cuenta de capital
5	Inversión directa
6	Inversión de cartera
7	Otra inversión
8	Activos de reserva
9	Agregados principales, instrumentos financieros e información suplementaria

El segundo y tercer dígito del tema corresponden al orden consecutivo de los componentes con interrupciones para poder incluir códigos adicionales posteriormente. Además, en la cuenta financiera, salvo las cuentas de inversión directa, el segundo dígito del tema puede ser 0, 1, 2, 3 ó 4 en el caso de los activos y 5, 6, 7, 8 ó 9 en el caso de los pasivos.

A continuación se presentan ejemplos de códigos para "Otra inversión" en la cuenta financiera.

Tema	Campo único			Campo múltiple		
	Crédito	Débito	Neto	Crédito	Débito	Neto
Otra inversión	2700	3700	4700	2700	3700	4700
Pasivos	2750	3750	4750	2750	3750	4750
Préstamos	2762	3762	4762	2762	3762	4762
Gobierno general	2767	3767	4767	2767	3767	4767
A largo plazo	2768	3768	4768	2768	3768	4768
A corto plazo	2769	3769	4769	2769	3769	4769
Bancos	2770	3770	4770	2770	3770	4770
A largo plazo	2771	3771	4771	2771	3771	4771
A corto plazo	2772	3772	4772	2772	3772	4772
Otros sectores	2773	3773	4773	2773	3773	4773
A largo plazo	2774	3774	4774	2774	3774	4774
A corto plazo	2775	3775	4775	2775	3775	4775

Tratándose de créditos y débitos correspondientes a préstamos, los términos que se emplean comúnmente son giros y rembolsos. La quinta edición del *Manual* recomienda declarar todos los giros y rembolsos de los préstamos a largo plazo en una clasificación suplementaria. Actualmente, el FMI recopila la mayoría de las demás partidas de la cuenta financiera en cifras netas. No obstante, el sistema de co-dificación permite identificar todos los flujos como créditos, débitos o flujos netos.

---

[1] Adoptado de "Balance of Payments Codes for Standard Components and Additional Items", FMI, Washington, 3 de marzo de 1995.

ANEXO IV. POSICIÓN DE INVERSIÓN INTERNACIONAL
COMPONENTES NORMALIZADOS

	Códigos
A. ACTIVOS	8 995 C
Inversión directa en el extranjero	8 505
Acciones y otras participaciones de capital y utilidades reinvertidas	8 506
Activos frente a empresas filiales	8 507
Pasivos frente a empresas filiales	8 508
Otro capital	8 530
Activos frente a empresas filiales	8 535
Pasivos frente a empresas filiales	8 540
Inversión de cartera	8 602
Títulos de participación en el capital	8 610
Autoridades monetarias	8 611
Gobierno general	8 612
Bancos	8 613
Otros sectores	8 614
Títulos de deuda	8 619
Bonos y pagarés	8 620
Autoridades monetarias	8 621
Gobierno general	8 622
Bancos	8 623
Otros sectores	8 624
Instrumentos del mercado monetario	8 630
Autoridades monetarias	8 631
Gobierno general	8 632
Bancos	8 633
Otros sectores	8 634
Instrumentos financieros derivados	8 900
Autoridades monetarias	8 901
Gobierno general	8 902
Bancos	8 903
Otros sectores	8 904
Otra inversión	8 703
Créditos comerciales	8 706
Gobierno general	8 707
de la cual: a corto plazo	8 709
Otros sectores	8 710
de la cual: a corto plazo	8 712
Préstamos	8 714
Autoridades monetarias	8 715
de la cual: a corto plazo	8 718
Gobierno general	8 719
de la cual: a corto plazo	8 721
Bancos	8 722
de la cual: a corto plazo	8 724
Otros sectores	8 725
de la cual: a corto plazo	8 727
Moneda y depósitos	8 730
Autoridades monetarias	8 731
Gobierno general	8 732
Bancos	8 733
Otros sectores	8 734

	Códigos
Otros activos	8 736 ..
Autoridades monetarias	8 737 ..
de la cual: a corto plazo	8 739 ..
Gobierno general	8 740 ..
de la cual: a corto plazo	8 742 ..
Bancos	8 743 ..
de la cual: a corto plazo	8 745 ..
Otros sectores	8 746 ..
de la cual: a corto plazo	8 748 ..
Activos de reserva	8 802 ..
Oro monetario	8 812 ..
Derechos especiales de giro	8 811 ..
Posición de reserva en el FMI	8 810 ..
Divisas	8 803 ..
Otros activos	8 813 ..
B. PASIVOS	8 995 D .
Inversión directa en la economía declarante	8 555 ..
Acciones y otras participaciones de capital y utilidades reinvertidas	8 556 ..
Activos frente a inversionistas directos	8 557 ..
Pasivos frente a inversionistas directos	8 558 ..
Otro capital	8 580 ..
Activos frente a inversionistas directos	8 585 ..
Pasivos frente a inversionistas directos	8 590 ..
Inversión de cartera	8 652 ..
Títulos de participación en el capital	8 660 ..
Bancos	8 663 ..
Otros sectores	8 664 ..
Títulos de deuda	8 669 ..
Bonos y pagarés	8 670 ..
Autoridades monetarias	8 671 ..
Gobierno general	8 672 ..
Bancos	8 673 ..
Otros sectores	8 674 ..
Instrumentos del mercado monetario	8 680 ..
Autoridades monetarias	8 681 ..
Gobierno general	8 682 ..
Bancos	8 683 ..
Otros sectores	8 684 ..
Instrumentos financieros derivados	8 905 ..
Autoridades monetarias	8 906 ..
Gobierno general	8 907 ..
Bancos	8 908 ..
Otros sectores	8 909 ..
Otra inversión	8 753 ..
Créditos comerciales	8 756 ..
Gobierno general	8 757 ..
de la cual: a corto plazo	8 759 ..
Otros sectores	8 760 ..
de la cual: a corto plazo	8 762 ..

	Códigos
Préstamos	8 764 ..
Autoridades monetarias	8 765 ..
de la cual: uso del crédito del FMI y préstamos del FMI	8 766 ..
de la cual: a corto plazo	8 768 ..
Gobierno general	8 769 ..
de la cual: a corto plazo	8 771 ..
Bancos	8 772 ..
de la cual: a corto plazo	8 774 ..
Otros sectores	8 775 ..
de la cual: a corto plazo	8 777 ..
Moneda y depósitos	8 780 ..
Autoridades monetarias	8 781 ..
Gobierno general	8 782 ..
Bancos	8 783 ..
Otros sectores	8 784 ..
Otros pasivos	8 786 ..
Autoridades monetarias	8 787 ..
de la cual: a corto plazo	8 789 ..
Gobierno general	8 790 ..
de la cual: a corto plazo	8 792 ..
Bancos	8 793 ..
de la cual: a corto plazo	8 795 ..
Otros sectores	8 796 ..
de la cual: a corto plazo	8 798 ..
POSICIÓN DE INVERSIÓN INTERNACIONAL NETA	8 995 ..
Tipos de conversión (fin de período)	0 102 ..

Anexo V. Marco conceptual de la balanza de pagos y de la posición de inversión internacional

Este anexo es la reproducción del capítulo II del Manual de Balanza de Pagos, 5a. edición. *Los párrafos y los números de página citados en este anexo corresponden a los del* Manual.

Definiciones

12. La primera parte de este *Manual* abarca el marco conceptual de las cuentas de la balanza de pagos y de la posición de inversión internacional, examinándose su relación con las cuentas nacionales y con los conceptos de residencia, valoración, momento de re-gistro, unidad de cuenta y conversión.

13. La balanza de pagos es un estado estadístico que resume sistemáticamente, para un período específico dado, las transacciones económicas entre una economía y el resto del mundo. Las transacciones, que en su mayoría tienen lugar entre residentes y no residentes[1], comprenden las que se refieren a bienes, servicios y renta, las que entrañan activos y pasivos financieros frente al resto del mundo y las que se clasifican como transferencias (como los regalos), en las que se efectúan asientos compensatorios para equilibrar —desde el punto de vista contable— las transacciones unilaterales (véase el párrafo 28)[2]. Una transacción en sí se define como un flujo económico que refleja la creación, transformación, intercambio, transferencia o extinción de un valor económico y entraña traspasos de propiedad de bienes y/o activos financieros, la prestación de servicios o el suministro de mano de obra y capital.

14. En estrecha relación con el marco de la balanza de pagos, basado en los flujos, se encuentra la posición de inversión internacional, definida por las tenencias de recursos financieros. Esta última, que corresponde a una fecha específica como el fin del año, es un estado estadístico que representa i) el valor y la composición de las tenencias de activos financieros de una economía, o de los créditos adquiridos por una economía frente al resto del mundo, y ii) el valor y la composición de las tenencias de pasivos de una economía a favor del resto del mundo. En algunos casos, puede ser de interés analítico calcular la diferencia entre los dos lados del balance para tener una medida de la posición neta. Dicha medida sería equivalente a la porción del patrimonio de una economía atribuible a su relación con el resto del mundo, o derivado de ella. Toda variación de las tenencias en cualquier período definido puede atribuirse a transacciones (flujos), a variaciones de valoración debidas a fluctuaciones del tipo de cambio, precios, etc., o a otros ajustes (por ejemplo, confiscaciones sin indemnización). En cambio, las cuentas de la balanza de pagos sólo reflejan transacciones.

Criterios y conceptos

15. El resto de este capítulo se refiere al marco conceptual de las cuentas internacionales, vale decir, al conjunto de criterios y convenciones básicos que permite el registro sistematizado y coherente de las transacciones internacionales y de las tenencias de activos y pasivos sobre el exterior. En los capítulos subsiguientes se analizarán detenidamente los aspectos sobresalientes de estos criterios, así como sus consideraciones y limitaciones prácticas.

Método de contabilidad por partida doble

16. El criterio básico aplicado a la preparación del estado de balanza de pagos es que toda transacción registrada está representada por dos asientos de igual valor. Uno de ellos se denomina crédito y tiene signo aritmético positivo. El otro se llama débito y tiene signo negativo. En principio, la suma de todos los asientos de crédito es igual a la suma de todos los asientos de débito y el saldo neto de la totalidad de los asientos del estado es igual a cero.

17. En la práctica, sin embargo, las cuentas no suelen estar en equilibrio. A menudo, los datos empleados para estimar la balanza de pagos suelen derivarse en forma independiente de diferentes fuentes; en consecuencia, puede haber un crédito neto o débito neto agregado (es decir, errores y omisiones netos en las cuentas). Para equilibrar las cuentas, se deberá efectuar un asiento separado por un monto equivalente pero de signo contrario. Debe observarse que, como hay estimaciones imprecisas o faltantes de signo contrario que suelen compensarse mutuamente, la magnitud del residuo neto no es indicativa de la exactitud relativa del estado de balanza de pagos. No obstante, la existencia de un residuo significativo y persistente que no se corrige debe ser motivo de preocupación, porque esta situación impide el análisis o la interpretación de las estimaciones y les resta credibilidad. Por otra parte, un residuo neto elevado también puede afectar a la interpretación del estado de la posición de inversión internacional. (Véase la explicación en el capítulo XXIII.)

18. La mayoría de los asientos de la balanza de pagos se refieren a transacciones en las que se entregan o reciben valores económicos a cambio de otros. Dichos valores comprenden recursos reales (bienes, servicios y renta) y financieros. Así, los asientos compensatorios de crédito y débito que exige el método de re-gistro suelen resultar del hecho de que se han anotado montos iguales para los dos recursos que se han intercambiado. Si en vez de ser intercambiados se ceden gratuitamente, o si el registro es unilateral por otras razones, se efectúan asientos especiales —llamados transferencias—para saldarlos. En los párrafos 26 a 31 se describen las distintas clases de asientos que pueden figurar en la balanza de pagos.

---

[1]En la balanza de pagos, las únicas transacciones que no se efectúan entre residentes y no residentes son el intercambio de activos financieros sobre el exterior transferibles entre sectores residentes y, en menor medida, el intercambio de pasivos financieros sobre el exterior transferibles entre no residentes. (Véase el párrafo 318.)

[2]Cabe destacar que las definiciones y clasificaciones de las cuentas internacionales que se presentan en este Manual tienen por objeto facilitar a los países miembros la tarea de declarar al FMI la información sobre transacciones internacionales y no pretenden hacer efectivas ni interpretar las disposiciones del Convenio Constitutivo del Fondo Monetario Internacional que se refieren al carácter jurídico de la acción (o falta de acción) oficial en relación con dichas transacciones.

19. Conforme a las convenciones del método contable, una economía compiladora registra asientos de crédito i) para los recursos reales que denotan exportaciones y ii) para los recursos financieros que indican reducciones de sus activos sobre el exterior o aumentos de sus pasivos sobre el exterior. A su vez, registra asientos de débito i) para los recursos reales que denotan importaciones y ii) para los recursos financieros que indican aumentos de los activos o disminuciones de los pasivos. En otras palabras, en los activos —reales o financieros— una cifra con signo positivo (crédito) representa una disminución de las tenencias y una cifra con signo negativo (débito) indica un incremento. En cambio, en los pasivos, una cifra con signo positivo significa un aumento, y una cifra con signo negativo, una disminución. Las transferencias aparecen como créditos si compensan asientos de débito, y como débitos si saldan asientos de crédito.

20. El contenido o la cobertura del estado de balanza de pagos depende, en cierto modo, de que las transacciones sean tratadas en base a valores brutos o netos. Las recomendaciones de este *Ma-nual* especifican cuáles deberán registrarse en valores brutos y cuáles en valores netos, como se refleja en la lista de componentes normalizados y en las presentaciones suplementarias sugeridas.

Conceptos de territorio económico, residencia y centro de interés económico

21. Los conceptos de territorio económico, residencia y centro de interés económico que se utilizan en este *Manual* son idénticos a los del *SCN* y se describen detalladamente en el capítulo IV. El territorio económico puede no coincidir con las fronteras políticas reconocidas. El territorio económico de un país comprende el terri-torio geográfico administrado por un gobierno dentro del cual circulan libremente personas, bienes y capital. En el caso de países marítimos, incluye también las islas que están sujetas a las mismas autoridades fiscales y monetarias que el territorio continental.

22. Una unidad institucional tiene un centro de interés económico y es residente de un país cuando desde algún lugar (vivienda, planta de producción u otro establecimiento), ubicado dentro del territorio económico del país, dicha unidad realiza e intenta seguir realizando (indefinidamente o durante un período finito) actividades económicas y transacciones en gran escala. (Se sugiere emplear un año o más como referencia, aunque no se trata de una regla inflexible.)

Criterios de valoración y momento de registro

23. Para compilar de manera uniforme cualquier agregado de transacciones individuales y registrar la posición de los activos y pasivos que les corresponden, es necesario contar con una base uniforme de valoración de las cuentas internacionales (tanto los recursos reales como los activos y pasivos financieros). En general, en este *Manual* se utiliza como base para la valoración de las transacciones el precio efectivo de mercado acordado por las partes que intervienen

en la transacción. (Este criterio coincide con el adoptado en el *SCN*.) Desde el punto de vista conceptual, todas las tenencias de activos y pasivos deberán valorarse de acuerdo a los precios de mercado vigentes en el momento al cual se refiere la posición de inversión internacional. En el capítulo V se presenta una exposición completa de los criterios de valoración, las prácticas recomendadas, las limitaciones y la valoración de transferencias, recursos financieros y tenencias de activos y pasivos. (Se incluyen también casos en que no existe un precio de mercado o no es posible suponerlo.)

24. En el *Manual* y en el *SCN*, el criterio que se aplica con res-pecto al *momento de registro* de las transacciones es el de contabilidad en valores devengados. Por lo tanto, las transacciones deben registrarse con referencia al momento en que se crea, transforma, intercambia, transfiere o extingue un valor económico. Se crean activos y pasivos cuando tiene lugar un traspaso de propiedad, ya sea de índole legal o física (económica). En la práctica, cuando no sea evidente el traspaso de propiedad, el momento en que éste ocurre puede determinarse de una forma aproximada utilizando la fecha en que las partes de una transacción la registran en sus libros o en sus cuentas. (El capítulo VI trata sobre los momentos de registro y convenciones recomendados para diferentes asientos de la balanza de pagos, e incluye excepciones y desviaciones del criterio de traspaso de propiedad.)

Concepto y clase de transacción

25. En general, las variaciones de las relaciones económicas que se registran en la balanza de pagos provienen básicamente de las transacciones realizadas entre dos partes. Dichas partes son, con una excepción (véase la nota 1), un residente y un no residente, y todas las transacciones de esta clase aparecen en la balanza de pagos. Las recomendaciones sobre los asientos específicos necesarios se hallan incorporadas en la lista de componentes normalizados (véase el capítulo VIII) y se detallan a partir del capítulo IX.

26. A pesar de su nombre, la balanza de pagos no se refiere a *pagos* en su acepción común, sino a *transacciones*. Algunas transacciones internacionales que revisten interés a efectos de la balanza de pagos pueden no entrañar un pago en efectivo y algunas no se pagan en ningún sentido. La inclusión de estas transacciones, además de las que tienen como contrapartida un pago, constituye la diferencia principal entre un estado de balanza de pagos y un registro de pagos externos.

Intercambios

27. Las transacciones más comunes e importantes de la balanza de pagos pueden caracterizarse como *intercambios*. Una parte (entidad económica) suministra un valor económico a otra y recibe a cambio un valor igual. Los valores económicos suministrados por una economía a otra pueden clasificarse en términos generales como recursos reales (bienes, servicios, renta) y recursos financieros. Las partes que intervienen en la transacción son residentes de distintas economías, salvo en el caso de intercambio de recursos financieros externos entre sectores residentes. El sumi-nistro de un recurso financiero puede suponer no sólo un traspaso de propiedad de un activo o de un pasivo existente sino también la creación de uno nuevo o la cancelación de uno existente. Es más, las condiciones de un contrato relativo a un recurso financiero (por ejemplo, el plazo de vencimiento contractual) pueden modificarse por acuerdo entre las partes, en cuyo caso se da por cumplido el primer contrato y se considera que éste ha sido remplazado por otro con condiciones distintas. Todos estos intercambios se deberán incluir en la balanza de pagos.

Transferencias

28. Las transacciones que comprenden *transferencias* difieren de los intercambios porque una de las partes entrega un valor económico a la otra sin recibir un quid pro quo que, según las normas y reglas adoptadas en el sistema, tiene valor económico. Esta ausencia de valor por un lado de la transacción está representado por un asiento denominado *transferencia*. Las transferencias de esta clase (valores económicos suministrados y recibidos sin quid pro quo) se registran en la balanza de pagos. Las **transferencias corrientes** se incluyen en la **cuenta corriente** (véase el capítulo XV), en tanto que las *transferencias de capital* aparecen en la **cuenta de capital** (véase el capítulo XVII).

Migración

29. Como una economía se define en función de las entidades económicas vinculadas a su territorio, su ámbito posiblemente se vea afectado por los cambios que tengan lugar en las entidades vinculadas a ella.

30. Se produce una migración cuando la residencia de una persona se traslada de una economía a otra por haber cambiado su domicilio. Ciertos bienes muebles del emigrante se importan, de hecho, a la nueva economía. Sus bienes inmuebles y ciertos bienes muebles que se encuentran en la economía anterior se transforman en activos de la nueva economía frente a la anterior. Sus activos o pasivos frente a residentes de otra economía distinta de la nueva pasan a ser activos o pasivos sobre el exterior de la nueva economía. Sus activos o pasivos frente a residentes de la nueva economía dejan de ser activos o pasivos de una economía frente al resto del mundo. La suma neta de todas estas variaciones es igual al patrimonio del emigrante, que también debe registrarse como asiento compensatorio, si se registran los demás cambios. Estos asientos se efectúan en la balanza de pagos donde, por norma, se incluyen en las transferencias.

Otras transacciones imputadas

31. En algunos casos, las transacciones pueden ser imputadas y pueden efectuarse asientos en las cuentas de la balanza de pagos cuando no exista un flujo efectivo. Cabe citar como ejemplo la atribución de las utilidades reinvertidas a inversionistas directos extranjeros. Las utilidades de una filial o sucursal extranjera incluyen utilidades atribuibles a un inversionista directo residente. Dichas utilidades, independientemente de que se hayan distribuido o reinvertido en la empresa, son proporcionales a la participación del inversionista directo residente en el capital de la empresa. Las utilidades reinvertidas se registran como parte de la renta de la inversión directa. Se efectúa un asiento compensatorio, con signo contrario, en el rubro inversión directa de la *cuenta financiera* para reflejar el hecho de que aumentó la inversión del inversionista directo extranjero en la filial o sucursal extranjera. (En los capítulos XIV y XVIII se trata el tema de las utilidades reinvertidas.)

Otras variaciones que no entrañan transacciones

Reclasificación de activos y pasivos

32. En este *Manual*, la clasificación de los recursos financieros se basa en características que revelan los motivos del acreedor o del deudor. Si cambian los motivos, varían también dichas características, de modo que los recursos financieros quedan sujetos a reclasificación en función de dichos cambios. Cabe destacar la diferencia que se establece entre la *inversión directa* y otras clases de inversión. Por ejemplo, varios tenedores independientes de *inversiones de cartera* (en forma de acciones y otras participaciones de capital social emitidas por una sola empresa en el extranjero) pueden asociarse para adquirir una participación efectiva duradera en la dirección de la empresa. Sus tenencias reúnen así las condiciones de una *inversión directa* y el cambio de situación de la inversión puede registrarse como reclasificación. Dicha reclasificación se reflejará, al final del período en el que tuvo lugar, en la posición de inversión internacional, pero no en la balanza de pagos. Análogamente, ciertos activos frente a no residentes pueden pasar al control de las autoridades monetarias residentes o quedar fuera de su control, lo cual da lugar a una reclasificación entre *activos de reserva* y activos que no constituyen reservas.

Variaciones de valoración

33. El valor de los recursos reales y financieros está sujeto a constantes cambios, que pueden atribuirse a una de las dos, o a las dos, causas siguientes: i) el precio habitual al que se efectúan transacciones de ciertos tipos de recursos puede variar en relación con la moneda en que se cotiza dicho precio; ii) el tipo de cambio de la moneda en que se cotiza el precio puede variar en relación con la unidad de cuenta utilizada. Las variaciones de valoración no se registran en la balanza de pagos, pero sí en la posición de inversión internacional.

ANEXO VI. CLASIFICACIÓN Y COMPONENTES NORMALIZADOS DE LA BALANZA DE PAGOS

Este anexo es la reproducción del capítulo VIII del Manual de Balanza de Pagos, *5ª edición. Los párrafos y los números de página citados en este anexo corresponden a los del* Manual.

Estructura y clasificación

139. En la segunda parte de este *Manual* se definen la estructura y la clasificación de las cuentas de la balanza de pagos y de la posición de inversión internacional. Abarca, asimismo, los componentes normalizados de ambos grupos de cuentas; se examina y explica la forma de preparar la **cuenta corriente**, la **cuenta de capital y financiera**, la información suplementaria seleccionada y la posición de inversión internacional.

140. Las estadísticas de balanza de pagos deben organizarse dentro de una estructura coherente para facilitar su utilización y adaptación para diferentes fines, tales como formulación de la política económica, estudios analíticos, proyecciones, comparaciones bilaterales de componentes específicos o transacciones totales, agregados regionales y mundiales, etc. (Véase el párrafo 7.)

141. La clasificación y la lista de componentes normalizados reflejan consideraciones de índole conceptual y práctica, toman en cuenta opiniones expresadas por expertos nacionales en balanza de pagos y, en general, concuerdan con el *SCN* y con la armonización entre la nueva clasificación de las transacciones internacionales de servicios y la Clasificación Central de Productos (CCP). (Véase el apéndice III.)

142. Se ha hecho todo lo posible para vincular la estructura de la **cuenta de capital** a las cuentas de renta y a la clasificación de la posición de inversión internacional. El objetivo es que muchos países puedan utilizarla como marco flexible para desarrollar a largo plazo sus estadísticas del sector externo. Si bien puede ocurrir que algunos países no puedan proporcionar datos para muchas partidas, este marco permitirá a otros países declarar da-tos adicionales.

Componentes normalizados

143. La determinación de los componentes normalizados (véase la lista al final de este capítulo) depende de una serie de factores, considerándose los más importantes los siguientes:

La partida debe exhibir un comportamiento característico, que indique que influyen en ella un factor o una combinación de factores económicos distintos de los que influyen en las demás partidas o que responde de dife-rente manera ante el mismo factor o combinación de factores. En la balanza de pagos se trata precisamente de poner de manifiesto esta respuesta ante las influencias económicas.

La partida debe ser importante para una serie de países, ya sea en función de su comportamiento (por ejemplo, varia-bilidad excepcional) o de su valor absoluto.

Deberá ser posible obtener los datos estadísticos de la partida sin demasiada dificultad, aunque cabe tener en cuenta la conveniencia de recopilarlos en razón de las dos pri-meras consideraciones citadas.

La partida deberá también ser necesaria para otros fines, por ejemplo, para incluirla en las cuentas nacionales o conciliarla con éstas. La lista de componentes normalizados no debe ser demasiado larga, dado el gran número de países, entre ellos muchos con sistemas estadísticos menos adelantados, a los cuales se solicita que presenten esos datos de manera uniforme.

En la medida en que sea posible, los componentes norma-lizados deberán ser compatibles con otros sistemas estadísticos del FMI, el *SCN* y, en el caso específico de los *servicios*, con la CCP.

144. La presentación de una lista de componentes normalizados no significa que las recomendaciones formuladas en este *Manual* tengan por objeto disuadir a los países de compilar y publicar otros datos de importancia nacional. Si se requieren mayores datos para comprender las circunstancias que rodean a determinados países o para analizar nuevas situaciones que puedan surgir, la información que solicite el FMI a los países miembros no se limitará a la lista de componentes normalizados. La información suplementaria también puede ser sumamente útil para verificar y conciliar las estadísticas de países que comercian entre sí y, por ejemplo, para analizar transacciones de financiamiento excepcional. (Véase el cuadro *Información suplementaria seleccionada* al final de este capítulo.) El personal del FMI consultará periódicamente con los países para decidir qué otros datos deberán presentar.

145. Es probable que sean pocos los países que cuentan con información significativa sobre todos los componentes normalizados. Tal vez los datos sobre varios de los componentes sólo puedan obtenerse en combinación con otros, o quizás un componente de menor importancia esté agrupado con otro más importante. No obstante, los componentes normalizados deberán declararse al FMI de la manera más completa y exacta que sea posible. En este sentido, los compiladores nacionales se encuentran en mejores condiciones que el personal del FMI para estimar y ajustar los componentes que no correspondan exactamente a los datos básicos de la economía declarante.

Errores y omisiones netos

146. Al aplicar los criterios recomendados en este *Manual*, se obtiene un conjunto coherente de asientos con signo positivo y negativo cuyo total neto es teóricamente igual a cero. En la práctica, sin embargo, una vez sumados todos los asientos, la balanza de pagos casi siempre arroja un crédito neto o un débito neto. Este saldo se debe a errores y omisiones en la compilación de las estadísticas, algunos de los cuales pueden tener relación con recomendaciones para una aproximación práctica a los criterios establecidos.

147. Por regla general, en el estado de balanza de pagos se presenta una partida separada de errores y omisiones netos, que algunos compiladores denominan partida equilibradora o discre-pancia estadística, para compensar toda sobrestimación o subestimación de los componentes registra-dos. Así, si el saldo de estos componentes refleja un crédito, la partida de errores y omisiones netos aparece como un débito de igual valor, y viceversa.

148. Como algunos de los errores y omisiones que se producen al compilar los datos suelen compensarse entre sí, la magnitud de la partida residual no es necesariamente un indicio de la exactitud global del estado. Aun así, cuando el residuo neto es grande, es difícil interpretar un estado.

Clasificaciones principales

149. Los componentes normalizados, cuya lista figura al final de este capítulo, se clasifican en dos grupos principales de cuentas:

La **cuenta corriente**, que comprende *bienes y servicios, renta* y *transferencias corrientes*.

La **cuenta de capital y financiera**, que se refiere a i) *transferencias de capital y adquisición/enajenación de activos no financieros no producidos* y ii) activos y pasivos financieros.

Esta presentación general refleja el uso común adoptado en la mayoría de los países en el transcurso de los años y un importante cambio que se introduce en este *Manual*. La cuenta de capital se denomina ahora **cuenta de capital y financiera**. A efectos de mantener la uniformidad con el *SCN*, se hace la distinción entre *transferencias de capital* y **transferencias corrientes** en las cuentas de la balanza de pagos, y se procura la concordancia con la cuenta de capital y la cuenta financiera del *SCN*.

150. Los asientos de la mayoría de las partidas de la lista de componentes normalizados de la **cuenta corriente** deberán mostrar créditos y débitos en cifras brutas. La mayoría de los asientos de la **cuenta de capital y financiera** deberán registrarse en cifras netas, es decir, cada componente se indicará únicamente como un crédito o como un débito. (Los tratamientos recomendados para determinadas partidas y las excepciones se describen en los capítulos correspondientes.) Las entradas de recursos reales, los aumentos de activos financieros y las disminuciones de pasivos deberán aparecer como débitos, en tanto que las salidas de recursos reales, las disminuciones de activos financieros y los aumentos de pasivos deberán figurar como créditos. Las transferencias de las secciones 1.C. y 2.A. deben ser numéricamente iguales, pero con signo contrario, a los asientos que saldan.

Clasificaciones detalladas

151. De acuerdo con los criterios establecidos en el párrafo 143, se han determinado las siguientes clasificaciones de los componentes normalizados. En los capítulos IX y XVI, respectivamente, se analizan la estructura y las características de la **cuenta corriente** y de la **cuenta de capital y financiera**, mencionándose los cambios significativos con respecto a la cuarta edición. En los capítulos X al XV se describen detalladamente los componentes normalizados de la **cuenta corriente**, y en los capítulos XVII al XXI, los de la **cuenta de capital y financiera** e *Instrumentos financieros derivados: Suplemento a la quinta edición (1993) del* Manual de Balanza de Pagos, 2000.

Cuenta corriente (1.)

152. En la **cuenta corriente** se registran todas las transacciones en valores económicos, salvo recursos financieros, que tienen lugar entre entidades residentes y no residentes; asimismo se re-gistran los asientos compensatorios de los valores económicos co-rrientes que se suministren o adquieran sin un quid pro quo. Con-cretamente, las clasificaciones principales son *bienes y servicios, renta* y *transferencias corrientes*.

Bienes y servicios (1.A.)

Bienes (1.A.a.)

153. *Mercancías generales* comprende la mayoría de los bienes muebles que los residentes exportan a no residentes, o importan de ellos, dando lugar, salvo algunas excepciones especificadas, a un traspaso de propiedad (efectivo o imputado).

154. *Bienes para transformación* comprende la exportación (o importación, en la economía compiladora) de bienes que cruzan la frontera para ser transformados en el extranjero y la reimportación (o exportación, en la economía compiladora) subsiguiente de dichos bienes, valorados en cifras brutas antes y después de su transformación. Esta partida constituye una excepción al criterio de traspaso de propiedad.

155. *Reparaciones de bienes* comprende las reparaciones de bienes efectuadas para no residentes o recibidas de ellos en embarcaciones, aeronaves, etc. Si bien el movimiento físico de estos bienes es similar al descrito en el párrafo 154, las reparaciones deben valorarse según el precio (derechos pagados o recibidos) de las mismas y no según el valor bruto de los bienes antes y después de las reparaciones.

156. *Bienes adquiridos en puerto por medios de transporte* comprende todos los bienes (como combustibles, víveres, pertrechos y suministros) que las empresas residentes/no residentes de transporte —aéreo, marítimo, etc.— adquieren en el extranjero/en la economía compiladora. Esta clasificación no cubre los servicios auxiliares prestados (remolque, mantenimiento, etc.), que se clasifican en la categoría *transportes*.

157. *Oro no monetario* comprende las exportaciones e importaciones de todo el oro que no esté en poder de las autoridades como activo de reserva (oro monetario). El *oro no monetario* se trata como cualquier otra mercancía y se subdivide, toda vez que sea posible, en oro que se mantiene como reserva de valor y oro para otros usos (industrial).

Servicios (1.A.b.)

158. *Transportes* abarca la mayoría de los servicios prestados por residentes a no residentes, y viceversa, que se incluían en las partidas embarques y otros transportes en la cuarta edición del *Manual*. En esta edición se excluye el seguro de fletes, que ahora forma parte de *servicios de seguros*. *Transportes* incluye el transporte de carga y de pasajeros por todos los medios, así como otros servicios de distribución y auxiliares, incluido el arrendamiento de equipo de transporte tripulado, con ciertas excepciones indicadas en los capítulos X, XI y XIII.

159. *Viajes* comprende bienes y servicios —incluidos los relacionados con salud y educación— adquiridos en una economía por viajeros no residentes (incluidos los excursionistas) para fines de negocios y para uso personal durante su estancia (inferior a un año) en esa economía. En *viajes* no se incluyen los servicios de transporte internacional de pasajeros, que forman parte de *transportes*. Los estudiantes y las personas que están bajo tratamiento médico se tratan como viajeros, independientemente de la duración de su estancia, en tanto que otros individuos —personal militar y de embajadas y trabajadores no residentes— no se consideran viajeros. No obstante, los gastos incurridos por los trabajadores no residentes se incluyen en *viajes*, mientras que los del personal militar y de embajadas se incluyen en *servicios del gobierno, n.i.o.p.* Estos casos se tratan en los capítulos XII y XIII.

160. *Servicios de comunicaciones* abarca las transacciones de comunicaciones entre residentes y no residentes, incluidos los servicios postales, de mensajería y de telecomunicaciones (transmisión de sonido, imagen y otra información por diferentes medios, así como el mantenimiento pertinente proporcionado por residentes a no residentes y viceversa).

161. *Servicios de construcción* incluye las obras de proyectos de construcción e instalación realizadas, con carácter temporal, en el extranjero/en la economía compiladora o en enclaves extraterritoriales por empresas residentes/no residentes y su personal. En este concepto no se incluyen las obras realizadas por una filial extranjera de una empresa residente o una oficina local no constituida en sociedad que sea equivalente siempre y cuando satisfaga ciertos criterios a una filial extranjera. En los capítulos IV y XIII se explica lo relativo a la residencia de esta clase de empresas.

162. *Servicios de seguros* comprende la contratación de seguros de no residentes con aseguradoras residentes y viceversa, incluidos los seguros de fletes (de bienes exportados e importados), los servicios correspondientes a otras clases de seguros directos (de vida y otros) y los servicios correspondientes a reaseguros. (En los pá-rrafos 256 y 257 se describe el método que se emplea para calcular el valor de los servicios de seguros.)

163. *Servicios financieros* (salvo los relacionados con las empresas aseguradoras y las cajas de pensiones) abarca los servicios de intermediación financiera y los servicios auxiliares entre residentes y no residentes. Se incluyen las comisiones y derechos relacionados con cartas de crédito, líneas de crédito, arrendamiento financiero, transacciones en divisas, crédito al consumidor y a las empresas, corretaje, colocación y suscripción de valores, instrumentos de coberturas de riesgo de diferentes clases, etc. En los servicios auxi-liares se incluyen los servicios de operación y reglamentación de los mercados financieros, servicios de custodia de valores, etc.

164. *Servicios de informática y de información* abarca las transacciones entre residentes y no residentes relacionadas con el asesoramiento en soporte técnico (*hardware*), aplicación de soporte lógico (*software*), servicios de información (procesamiento de datos, bases de datos, agencias noticiosas), y mantenimiento y reparación de computadores y equipo conexo.

165. *Regalías y derechos de licencia* comprende ingresos (exportación) y pagos (importación) de residentes y no residentes por: i) el uso autorizado de activos intangibles no financieros no producidos y derechos de propiedad como marcas registradas, derechos de autor, patentes, procesos, técnicas, diseños, derechos de fabricación, concesiones, etc., y ii) el uso, mediante convenios de licencia, de originales o prototipos producidos, como manuscritos, películas, etc.

166. *Otros servicios empresariales* prestados por residentes a no residentes y viceversa se refiere a servicios de compraventa y otros servicios relacionados con el comercio, servicios de arrendamiento de explotación y servicios empresariales, profesionales y técnicos varios. (Para información más detallada, véase el cuadro *Información suplementaria seleccionada* al final de este capítulo y los párrafos 261 a 264.)

167. *Servicios personales, culturales y recreativos* abarca i) servicios audiovisuales y conexos y ii) otros servicios culturales prestados por residentes a no residentes y viceversa. En el inciso i) se incluyen servicios relacionados con la producción de películas cinematográficas o videocintas, programas de radio y televisión y grabaciones musicales. (Ejemplos de estos servicios son los alqui-leres y honorarios percibidos por artistas, productores, etc. por sus producciones y por la venta de derechos de distribución a los medios de comunicación.) En el inciso ii) se incluyen otros servicios personales, culturales y recreativos, como los relacionados con bibliotecas, museos y otras actividades culturales y deportivas.

168. *Servicios del gobierno, n.i.o.p.* incluye todos los servicios (como los gastos incurridos por embajadas y consulados) relacionados con sectores gubernamentales u organismos internacionales y regionales y no clasificados en otras partidas.

Renta (1.B.)

169. *Remuneración de empleados* abarca los salarios, sueldos y otras prestaciones, en efectivo o en especie, incluidos los de los trabajadores fronterizos, de temporada y otros no residentes (por ejemplo, personal local de embajadas).

170. *Renta de la inversión* comprende los ingresos y pagos de la renta derivados, respectivamente, de las tenencias de activos financieros de residentes frente al exterior y de pasivos frente a no residentes, y se divide en renta de la inversión directa, renta de la inversión de cartera y renta de otra inversión. El componente inversión directa se desglosa en renta procedente de acciones y otras participaciones de capital (dividendos, utilidades de sucursales y utilidades reinvertidas) y en renta procedente de la deuda (intereses); la renta de la inversión de cartera se desglosa también en renta procedente de acciones y otras participaciones de capital (dividendos) y renta procedente de la deuda (intereses); en renta de otra inversión se registran los intereses devengados por otra inversión (préstamos, etc.) y, en principio, la renta imputada a las unidades familiares procedente de su parti-cipación neta de capital en las reservas de los seguros de vida y en las cajas de pensiones.

Transferencias corrientes (1.C.)

171. Las ***transferencias corrientes*** se distinguen de las *transfe-rencias de capital*, que se incluyen en la **cuenta de capital y financiera** para guardar la uniformidad con el tratamiento de las transferencias que hace el *SCN*. Las transferencias son los asientos compensatorios de los traspasos de propiedad de recursos reales o financieros entre residentes y no residentes, ya sea en forma voluntaria u obligatoria, que no entrañan un quid pro quo en valor económico. Las ***transferencias corrientes*** comprenden todas aque-llas en las que **no tiene lugar**: i) un ***traspaso*** de propiedad de activos fijos; ii) un traspaso de fondos vinculados o condicionados a la adquisición o enajenación de activos fijos; iii) una condonación de un pasivo por parte de un acreedor, sin que se reciba a cambio una contrapartida. Todas éstas son *transferencias de capital*. En las ***transferencias corrientes*** se distinguen las del gobierno general (por ejemplo, cooperación internacional corriente entre diferentes go-biernos, pagos de impuestos corrientes sobre la renta y el patrimonio, etc.) y otras transferencias (por ejemplo, remesas de trabajadores, primas —menos cargos por servicio— e indemnizaciones de seguros excepto los de vida). En el capítulo XV se examina en forma detallada la distinción entre ***transferencias corrientes*** y *transferencias de capital*; véanse también los párrafos 175 y 344.

Cuenta de capital y financiera (2.)

172. Esta cuenta tiene dos componentes principales —la **cuenta de capital** y la **cuenta financiera**— coin-cidiendo así con la clasificación adoptada en el *SCN*. Los activos representan créditos frente a no residentes y los pasivos representan deudas contraídas con no residentes. Las dos partes de una transacción de activos o pasivos son, generalmente, un residente y un no residente pero, en algunos casos, ambas partes pueden ser residentes o bien no residentes. (Véase el párrafo 318.)

173. Todas las variaciones de valoración y de otra índole de los activos y pasivos frente al exterior que no reflejen transacciones (véase el párrafo 310) se excluyen de la **cuenta de capital y financiera** pero figuran en la posición de inversión internacional. Los estados suplementarios identifican ciertas partidas que tienen interés analítico y que afectan a varias cuentas, como los pasivos que constituyen reservas de autoridades extranjeras y las transacciones de financiamiento excepcional, que se describen en el capítulo XXII.

174. La clasificación de la **cuenta financiera** y de los componentes de renta de la **cuenta corriente** están interrelacionadas y deben ser coherentes para facilitar el análisis, permitir una vinculación eficaz de la balanza de pagos con la posición de inversión internacional y mantener la compatibilidad con el *SCN* y con otros sistemas estadísticos del FMI.

Cuenta de capital (2.A.)

175. Los componentes principales de la **cuenta de capital** son las *transferencias de capital* y la *adquisición/enajenación de activos no financieros no producidos*. Las *transferencias de capital* son aquéllas en las que tiene lugar un traspaso de propiedad de un activo fijo, un traspaso de fondos vinculado o condicionado a la adquisición o enajenación de un activo fijo, o la cancelación de un pasivo por parte de un acreedor sin que se reciba a cambio una contrapartida. Las *transferencias de capital* se dividen en: i) las del gobierno general, que a su vez se subdividen en condonación de deudas y otras y ii) las de otros sectores, haciéndose el desglose en transferencias de emigrantes, condonación de deudas y otras. (Véase el capítulo XV, donde se explica la diferencia entre las *transferencias de capital* y las ***transferencias corrientes*.**) La *adquisición/enajenación de activos no financieros no producidos* abarca, en general, los factores intangibles, como las patentes, arrendamientos u otros contratos transferibles, el buen nombre, etc. En esta partida no se incluyen las tierras situadas en un territorio económico específico, pero puede incluirse la compra o venta de tierras por una embajada. (Véase el párrafo 312.)

Cuenta financiera (2.B.)

176. La clasificación de los componentes normalizados de la cuenta financiera se basa en los siguientes criterios:

Todos los componentes se clasifican según la clase de inversión o haciéndose un desglose funcional (*inversión directa, inversión de cartera, instrumentos financieros derivados, otra inversión, activos de reserva*).

Para la categoría *inversión directa*, se hace la distinción según la dirección (en el extranjero o en la economía declarante); para los componentes acciones y otras participaciones de capital, otro capital.

En *inversión de cartera, instrumentos financieros derivados* y *otra inversión* se hace la distinción habitual entre activos y pasivos.

Cobra particular importancia en *inversión de cartera* y *otra inversión* la distinción por clases de instrumentos (títulos de participación en el capital, títulos de deuda, créditos comerciales, préstamos, moneda y depósitos, otros activos o pasivos). En este *Manual*, se incluyen en *inversión de cartera* los instrumentos tradicionales y nuevos del mercado monetario y otros instrumentos financieros básicos.

La distinción tradicional entre activos y pasivos a largo y a corto plazo, basada en un plazo contractual original de más de un año o de un año o menos, se efectúa solamente en *otra inversión*. En los últimos años, este desglose ha perdido importancia para muchas transacciones internas e internacionales. En consecuencia, tanto en el *SCN* como en este *Manual*, se da menos importancia a la diferencia entre largo y corto plazo que en ediciones previas. Sin embargo, debido a que el vencimiento sigue siendo importante para fines específicos —el análisis de la deuda externa, por ejemplo—, esta distinción se mantiene en el *Manual* para *otra inversión*.

177. *Inversión directa*, categoría que refleja el interés duradero de una entidad residente de una economía (inversionista directo) en una entidad residente de otra economía (empresa de inversión directa), abarca todas las transacciones entre inversionistas directos y empresas de inversión directa. Es decir, la *inversión directa* abarca la transacción inicial entre las dos partes y todas las transacciones subsiguientes que tienen lugar entre ellas y entre empresas filiales, constituidas o no en sociedad. Las transacciones de inversión directa (en el extranjero y en la economía declarante) se subclasifican en acciones y otras participaciones de capital, utilidades reinvertidas y otro capital (transacciones entre empresas afiliadas). En el caso de las acciones y otras participaciones de capital y otro capital, se hace la distinción entre activos y pasivos frente a empresas filiales y frente a inversionistas directos. Las transacciones entre bancos filiales y entre otros intermediarios financieros filiales se limitan al capital en acciones y al que está relacionado con la deuda permanente. (Véase el párrafo 372 de la quinta edición del *Manual de Balanza de Pagos*.)

178. *Inversión de cartera* comprende las transacciones en títulos de participación en el capital y títulos de deuda. Los títulos de deuda están subdivididos en bonos y pagarés e instrumentos del mercado monetario. Se incluyen, asimismo, varios instrumentos financieros nuevos, además de los derivados financieros, en las clasificaciones de instrumentos pertinentes.(Se excluyen las transacciones clasificadas como *inversión directa* y *activos de reserva*.)

179. La categoría de instrumentos financieros derivados abarca los instrumentos financieros vinculados a otros instrumentos financieros específicos o indicadores o productos primarios, a través de los cuales pueden negociarse en los mercados financieros, por derecho propio, riesgos financieros específicos (como riesgos de variaciones de tasas de interés, riesgo cambiario, riesgos de variaciones de las cotizaciones bursátiles y de los precios de los productos primarios, riesgo de crédito, etc.). Las transacciones de instrumentos financieros derivados deberán tratarse por separado y no como parte integral del valor de las transacciones a las que estén vinculadas.

180. *Otra inversión* incluye créditos comerciales a corto y largo plazo; préstamos (entre ellos, el uso de crédito del FMI, préstamos del FMI y préstamos relacionados con arrendamientos financieros); moneda y depósitos (transferibles y otros, como depósitos de ahorro y a plazo, acciones de asociaciones de ahorro y préstamo, acciones de cooperativas de crédito, etc.); otras cuentas por cobrar y por pagar. (Se excluyen las transacciones clasificadas como *inversión directa*.)

181. *Activos de reserva* comprende las transacciones de aque-llos activos que las autoridades monetarias de una economía consideran disponibles para atender necesidades de financiamiento de la balanza de pagos y, en algunos casos, otras necesidades. Tal disponibilidad, en principio, no guarda estrecha relación con criterios formales tales como los de propiedad o moneda de denominación. Esta categoría se divide en oro monetario, DEG, posición de reserva en el FMI, activos en divisas (moneda, depósitos y va-lores) y otros activos.

182. La cobertura e identificación de los componentes de los *activos de reserva* están relacionadas con un concepto analítico, son en parte resultado de una decisión razonada y no siempre se prestan a la aplicación de criterios objetivos y formales ni a clasificaciones bien delimitadas respecto a la condicionalidad y otras consideraciones. A diferencia de la cuarta edición del *Manual*, en la quinta edición se excluyen las variaciones de valoración de los *activos de reserva* y sus contrapartidas. También se excluyen la asignación y cancelación de DEG, la monetización y desmonetización del oro y los asientos de contrapartida. Estas variaciones, que no constituyen transacciones, figuran en la posición de inversión internacional.

COUNTRY TABLES

Table 1. ANALYTIC PRESENTATION, 2000–2007

(Millions of U.S. dollars)

	Code	2000	2001	2002	2003	2004	2005	2006	2007
A. Current Account[1]	4 993 Z.	**−156.3**	**−217.3**	**−407.5**	**−406.8**	**−357.9**	**−571.5**	**−670.9**	**−831.0**
Goods: exports f.o.b.	2 100 ..	255.7	304.5	330.2	447.2	603.3	656.3	792.9	786.3
Goods: imports f.o.b.	3 100 ..	−1,070.0	−1,331.6	−1,485.4	−1,783.5	−2,194.9	−2,477.6	−2,915.6	−2,890.4
Balance on Goods	4 100 ..	*−814.3*	*−1,027.1*	*−1,155.1*	*−1,336.3*	*−1,591.6*	*−1,821.3*	*−2,122.7*	*−2,104.0*
Services: credit	2 200 ..	447.8	534.3	585.0	719.7	1,003.5	1,164.6	1,504.0	1,415.0
Services: debit	3 200 ..	−429.3	−444.1	−590.2	−802.6	−1,054.8	−1,382.9	−1,584.8	−1,402.0
Balance on Goods and Services	4 991 ..	*−795.8*	*−936.9*	*−1,160.3*	*−1,419.2*	*−1,642.9*	*−2,039.6*	*−2,203.5*	*−2,091.0*
Income: credit	2 300 ..	115.9	162.5	148.3	194.8	203.7	226.7	332.1	278.6
Income: debit	3 300 ..	−9.3	−13.5	−20.6	−24.4	−28.3	−52.6	−69.1	−61.5
Balance on Goods, Services, and Income	4 992 ..	*−689.2*	*−787.9*	*−1,032.6*	*−1,248.8*	*−1,467.5*	*−1,865.5*	*−1,940.5*	*−1,873.9*
Current transfers: credit	2 379 Z.	629.0	647.5	683.7	924.2	1,200.2	1,519.2	1,426.3	1,219.8
Current transfers: debit	3 379 ..	−96.1	−76.9	−58.6	−82.3	−90.6	−225.1	−156.7	−176.9
B. Capital Account[1]	4 994 Z.	**78.0**	**117.7**	**121.2**	**157.0**	**132.4**	**122.9**	**179.8**	**90.1**
Capital account: credit	2 994 Z.	78.0	117.7	121.2	157.0	132.4	122.9	179.8	90.1
Capital account: debit	3 994 ..	....	....	....	....	....	....	....	....
Total, Groups A Plus B	4 981 ..	*−78.3*	*−99.6*	*−286.3*	*−249.9*	*−225.5*	*−448.6*	*−491.1*	*−741.0*
C. Financial Account[1]	4 995 W.	**188.4**	**110.0**	**213.4**	**200.6**	**396.3**	**392.6**	**523.4**	**743.6**
Direct investment abroad	4 505 ..	....	....	....	....	−13.6	−4.1	−10.6	−11.0
Direct investment in Albania	4 555 Z.	143.0	207.3	135.0	178.0	341.3	262.5	325.3	476.7
Portfolio investment assets	4 602 ..	−25.0	−23.5	−36.8	−22.5	−3.6	−5.7	34.2	18.5
Equity securities	4 610 ..	....	....	....	....	....	....	....	....
Debt securities	4 619 ..	−25.0	−23.5	−36.8	−22.5	−3.6	−5.7	34.2	18.5
Portfolio investment liabilities	4 652 Z.	....	....	....	....	....	....	....	....
Equity securities	4 660 ..	....	....	....	....	....	....	....	....
Debt securities	4 669 Z.	....	....	....	....	....	....	....	....
Financial derivatives	4 910 ..	....	....	....	....	....	....	....	....
Financial derivatives assets	4 900 ..	....	....	....	....	....	....	....	....
Financial derivatives liabilities	4 905 ..	....	....	....	....	....	....	....	....
Other investment assets	4 703 ..	−40.2	−197.2	−2.7	−71.6	−113.8	6.6	−210.7	−64.2
Monetary authorities	4 701 ..	....	−1.8	2.2	.3	....	....	−.6	−4.2
General government	4 704 ..	....	....	....	....	....	....	....	....
Banks	4 705 ..	−2.5	−132.3	42.2	−45.3	−112.1	8.5	−212.5	−61.1
Other sectors	4 728 ..	−37.7	−63.1	−47.1	−26.7	−1.7	−1.9	2.4	1.1
Other investment liabilities	4 753 W.	110.6	123.4	118.0	116.7	186.1	133.2	385.2	323.6
Monetary authorities	4 753 WA	−.2	−.3	.5	−1.0	−1.2	−1.5	−1.3	−.7
General government	4 753 ZB	90.8	86.1	118.2	96.6	106.4	50.4	51.9	56.5
Banks	4 753 ZC	5.2	42.1	10.9	19.8	.3	20.7	244.1	226.4
Other sectors	4 753 ZD	14.8	−4.5	−11.6	1.4	80.6	63.6	90.5	41.3
Total, Groups A Through C	4 983 ..	*110.1*	*10.4*	*−72.9*	*−49.2*	*170.8*	*−56.0*	*32.2*	*2.6*
D. Net Errors and Omissions	4 998 ..	**9.8**	**136.3**	**108.5**	**147.4**	**115.3**	**203.8**	**237.0**	**150.8**
Total, Groups A Through D	4 984 ..	*119.9*	*146.7*	*35.6*	*98.1*	*286.1*	*147.8*	*269.2*	*153.4*
E. Reserves and Related Items	4 802 A.	**−119.9**	**−146.7**	**−35.6**	**−98.1**	**−286.1**	**−147.8**	**−269.2**	**−153.4**
Reserve assets	4 802 ..	−132.0	−145.1	−28.6	−99.6	−288.4	−150.7	−265.1	−146.5
Use of Fund credit and loans	4 766 ..	12.1	−1.6	−8.5	1.5	2.4	3.0	−4.1	−7.0
Exceptional financing	4 920 ..	....	....	1.5	....	....	....	....	.1
Conversion rates: leks per U.S. dollar	0 101 ..	**143.71**	**143.48**	**140.15**	**121.86**	**102.78**	**99.87**	**98.10**	**90.43**

[1] Excludes components that have been classified in the categories of Group E.

Table 2. STANDARD PRESENTATION, 2000–2007

(Millions of U.S. dollars)

	Code	2000	2001	2002	2003	2004	2005	2006	2007
CURRENT ACCOUNT	4 993	−156.3	−217.3	−407.5	−406.8	−357.9	−571.5	−670.9	−831.0
A. GOODS	4 100	−814.3	−1,027.1	−1,155.1	−1,336.3	−1,591.6	−1,821.3	−2,122.7	−2,104.0
Credit	2 100	255.7	304.5	330.2	447.2	603.3	656.3	792.9	786.3
General merchandise: exports f.o.b.	2 110	95.2	109.5	85.2	100.7	149.0	194.1	233.1	261.8
Goods for processing: exports f.o.b.	2 150	160.5	195.0	245.1	346.5	454.3	462.2	559.8	524.5
Repairs on goods	2 160	....	....	....	....	....	....	....	....
Goods procured in ports by carriers	2 170	....	....	....	....	....	....	....	....
Nonmonetary gold	2 180	....	....	....	....	....	....	....	....
Debit	3 100	−1,070.0	−1,331.6	−1,485.4	−1,783.5	−2,194.9	−2,477.6	−2,915.6	−2,890.4
General merchandise: imports f.o.b.	3 110	−921.0	−1,151.0	−1,237.3	−1,463.3	−1,837.9	−2,117.5	−2,499.8	−2,484.8
Goods for processing: imports f.o.b.	3 150	−149.0	−180.6	−248.1	−320.1	−357.0	−360.1	−415.8	−405.6
Repairs on goods	3 160	....	....	....	....	....	....	....	....
Goods procured in ports by carriers	3 170	....	....	....	....	....	....	....	....
Nonmonetary gold	3 180	....	....	....	....	....	....	....	....
B. SERVICES	4 200	18.5	90.2	−5.2	−82.9	−51.4	−218.3	−80.8	13.0
Total credit	2 200	*447.8*	*534.3*	*585.0*	*719.7*	*1,003.5*	*1,164.6*	*1,504.0*	*1,415.0*
Total debit	3 200	*−429.3*	*−444.1*	*−590.2*	*−802.6*	*−1,054.8*	*−1,382.9*	*−1,584.8*	*−1,402.0*
Transportation services, credit	2 205	17.2	15.4	18.9	68.8	98.2	126.1	163.2	115.2
Passenger	2 850	*9.4*	*5.4*	*4.6*	*15.4*	*21.1*	*26.4*	*44.5*	*53.2*
Freight	2 851	*7.7*	*9.2*	*9.9*	*51.8*	*64.8*	*72.7*	*86.0*	*45.9*
Other	2 852	*.1*	*.8*	*4.3*	*1.6*	*12.2*	*27.0*	*32.7*	*16.1*
Sea transport, passenger	2 207	....	2.2	1.9	6.1	8.5	10.6	17.8	21.3
Sea transport, freight	2 208	....	8.3	8.9	46.6	58.4	65.4	77.4	41.4
Sea transport, other	2 209	....	....	2.2	.8	6.1	13.5	16.4	8.0
Air transport, passenger	2 211	....	3.2	2.8	9.2	12.7	15.8	26.7	31.9
Air transport, freight	2 212	....	.9	1.0	5.2	6.5	7.3	8.6	4.6
Air transport, other	2 213	....	....	2.2	.8	6.1	13.5	16.4	8.0
Other transport, passenger	2 215	....	....	....	....	....	....	....	....
Other transport, freight	2 216	....	....	....	....	....	....	....	....
Other transport, other	2 217	....	....	....	....	....	....	....	....
Transportation services, debit	3 205	−93.9	−107.0	−127.7	−156.3	−204.1	−226.6	−250.0	−178.4
Passenger	3 850	*−18.0*	*−12.1*	*−21.2*	*−18.2*	*−26.5*	*−21.5*	*−24.1*	*−17.2*
Freight	3 851	*−75.9*	*−94.1*	*−105.1*	*−124.4*	*−154.6*	*−173.8*	*−205.1*	*−146.3*
Other	3 852	....	*−.8*	*−1.4*	*−13.8*	*−23.0*	*−31.2*	*−20.8*	*−14.9*
Sea transport, passenger	3 207	....	−4.9	−8.5	−7.3	−10.6	−8.6	−9.7	−6.9
Sea transport, freight	3 208	....	−84.8	−94.6	−111.9	−139.1	−156.4	−184.6	−131.7
Sea transport, other	3 209	....	−.4	−.7	−6.9	−11.5	−15.6	−10.4	−7.5
Air transport, passenger	3 211	....	−7.2	−12.7	−10.9	−15.9	−12.9	−14.5	−10.3
Air transport, freight	3 212	....	−9.3	−10.5	−12.4	−15.5	−17.4	−20.5	−14.6
Air transport, other	3 213	....	−.4	−.7	−6.9	−11.5	−15.6	−10.4	−7.5
Other transport, passenger	3 215	....	....	....	....	....	....	....	....
Other transport, freight	3 216	....	....	....	....	....	....	....	....
Other transport, other	3 217	....	....	....	....	....	....	....	....
Travel, credit	2 236	389.4	446.4	486.9	522.1	735.3	853.9	1,012.1	1,001.5
Business travel	2 237	389.4	446.4	234.9	212.4	332.4	211.5	233.9	184.1
Personal travel	2 240	....	....	252.0	309.7	402.9	642.4	778.2	817.5
Travel, debit	3 236	−272.2	−257.4	−365.5	−489.1	−641.5	−786.1	−964.6	−922.6
Business travel	3 237	−90.7	−85.8	−172.1	−170.8	−217.9	−167.9	−191.8	−237.4
Personal travel	3 240	−181.5	−171.6	−193.4	−318.2	−423.6	−618.3	−772.8	−685.1
Other services, credit	2 200 BA	41.2	72.5	79.3	128.8	169.9	184.6	328.6	298.3
Communications	2 245	19.1	31.5	32.6	48.1	75.1	71.4	52.8	49.5
Construction	2 249	....	....	....	3.3	3.4	2.7	2.3	5.6
Insurance	2 253	....	1.2	1.0	3.1	6.5	5.7	3.6	5.0
Financial	2 260	.9	.5	9.9	20.6	10.9	16.0	25.8	30.6
Computer and information	2 262	2.2	....	.6	1.2	.6	3.1	1.3	2.0
Royalties and licence fees	2 266	....	....	....	5.3	15.4	.5	.7	5.3
Other business services	2 268	....	....	....	17.5	43.9	56.6	161.0	134.5
Personal, cultural, and recreational	2 287	....	....	2.5	4.5	7.8	18.1	58.3	49.6
Government, n.i.e.	2 291	19.0	39.3	32.8	25.1	6.3	10.4	22.9	16.1
Other services, debit	3 200 BA	−63.2	−79.7	−97.0	−157.3	−209.2	−370.2	−370.2	−301.0
Communications	3 245	−12.1	−14.1	−10.1	−21.2	−20.9	−14.6	−7.4	−4.3
Construction	3 249	....	....	....	−1.8	−.7	−1.6	−2.0	−20.2
Insurance	3 253	−33.3	−43.2	−49.2	−21.1	−26.1	−30.5	−35.9	−47.5
Financial	3 260	−.8	....	−1.2	−5.3	−5.4	−17.4	−20.2	−18.3
Computer and information	3 262	−.8	....	−1.0	−1.8	−1.6	−3.4	−3.4	−11.1
Royalties and licence fees	3 266	....	....	....	−8.4	−4.9	−4.2	−6.8	−8.4
Other business services	3 268	....	....	....	−20.9	−55.7	−129.2	−149.0	−128.5
Personal, cultural, and recreational	3 287	....	....	−6.6	−8.2	−30.4	−104.0	−112.9	−51.9
Government, n.i.e.	3 291	−16.2	−22.4	−29.0	−68.6	−63.4	−65.2	−32.6	−10.8

Table 2 (Continued). STANDARD PRESENTATION, 2000–2007

(Millions of U.S. dollars)

	Code	2000	2001	2002	2003	2004	2005	2006	2007
C. INCOME	4 300 ..	**106.6**	**149.0**	**127.7**	**170.4**	**175.4**	**174.1**	**263.0**	**217.1**
Total credit	2 300 ..	*115.9*	*162.5*	*148.3*	*194.8*	*203.7*	*226.7*	*332.1*	*278.6*
Total debit	3 300 ..	*–9.3*	*–13.5*	*–20.6*	*–24.4*	*–28.3*	*–52.6*	*–69.1*	*–61.5*
Compensation of employees, credit	2 310 ..	**67.0**	**84.4**	**90.1**	**110.6**	**132.3**	**129.0**	**183.9**	**119.2**
Compensation of employees, debit	3 310 ..	....	....	....	**–4.1**	**–4.9**	**–6.5**	**–26.5**	**–7.0**
Investment income, credit	2 320 ..	**48.9**	**78.1**	**58.1**	**84.1**	**71.4**	**97.7**	**148.2**	**159.5**
Direct investment income	2 330 ..	....	....	....	....	....	.4	13.3	13.7
Dividends and distributed branch profits	2 332 ..	....	....	....	....	....	.4	13.3	13.7
Reinvested earnings and undistributed branch profits	2 333 ..	....	....	....	....	....	....	....	....
Income on debt (interest)	2 334 ..	....	....	....	....	....	....	....	....
Portfolio investment income	2 339 ..	....	3.0	20.3	31.2	25.8	37.0	51.4	64.4
Income on equity	2 340 ..	....	....	....	....	....	7.9	22.4	13.7
Income on bonds and notes	2 350 ..	....	3.0	20.3	31.2	25.8	29.2	29.0	50.7
Income on money market instruments	2 360 ..	....	....	....	....	....	....	....	....
Other investment income	2 370 ..	48.9	75.1	37.8	53.0	45.7	60.2	83.6	81.4
Investment income, debit	3 320 ..	**–9.3**	**–13.5**	**–20.6**	**–20.2**	**–23.5**	**–46.1**	**–42.6**	**–54.5**
Direct investment income	3 330 ..	–.1	–.1	–.6	–1.0	–.2	–2.1	–4.6	–6.1
Dividends and distributed branch profits	3 332 ..	–.1	–.1	–.6	–1.0	–.2	–2.1	–4.6	–6.1
Reinvested earnings and undistributed branch profits	3 333 ..	....	....	....	....	....	....	....	....
Income on debt (interest)	3 334 ..	....	....	....	....	....	....	....	....
Portfolio investment income	3 339 ..	....	....	....	....	....	–11.3	–1.9	–5.9
Income on equity	3 340 ..	....	....	....	....	....	–10.8	–1.2	–1.1
Income on bonds and notes	3 350 ..	....	....	....	....	....	–.4	–.8	–4.8
Income on money market instruments	3 360 ..	....	....	....	....	....	....	....	....
Other investment income	3 370 ..	–9.2	–13.4	–20.0	–19.3	–23.3	–32.7	–36.1	–42.5
D. CURRENT TRANSFERS	4 379 ..	**532.9**	**570.6**	**625.1**	**841.9**	**1,109.6**	**1,294.0**	**1,269.6**	**1,042.9**
Credit	2 379 ..	**629.0**	**647.5**	**683.7**	**924.2**	**1,200.2**	**1,519.2**	**1,426.3**	**1,219.8**
General government	2 380 ..	97.2	32.4	39.9	61.1	75.7	80.2	62.3	60.5
Other sectors	2 390 ..	531.8	615.1	643.8	863.1	1,124.5	1,439.0	1,364.1	1,159.2
Workers' remittances	2 391 ..	530.8	614.9	643.4	778.1	1,028.3	1,160.7	1,175.6	951.7
Other current transfers	2 392 ..	1.0	.2	.3	85.0	96.1	278.3	188.5	207.5
Debit	3 379 ..	**–96.1**	**–76.9**	**–58.6**	**–82.3**	**–90.6**	**–225.1**	**–156.7**	**–176.9**
General government	3 380 ..	–2.8	–4.4	–1.7	–.9	....	–4.7	–9.5	–.4
Other sectors	3 390 ..	–93.3	–72.5	–56.9	–81.4	–90.6	–220.5	–147.3	–176.5
Workers' remittances	3 391 ..	....	....	....	....	....	....	....	....
Other current transfers	3 392 ..	–93.3	–72.5	–56.9	–81.4	–90.6	–220.5	–147.2	–176.5
CAPITAL AND FINANCIAL ACCOUNT	4 996 ..	**146.5**	**81.0**	**299.1**	**259.5**	**242.6**	**367.7**	**433.9**	**680.2**
CAPITAL ACCOUNT	4 994 ..	**78.0**	**117.7**	**121.2**	**157.0**	**132.4**	**122.9**	**179.8**	**90.1**
Total credit	2 994 ..	*78.0*	*117.7*	*121.2*	*157.0*	*132.4*	*122.9*	*179.8*	*90.1*
Total debit	3 994 ..	....	....	....	....	....	....	....	....
Capital transfers, credit	2 400 ..	**78.0**	**117.7**	**121.2**	**157.0**	**132.4**	**122.9**	**179.8**	**90.1**
General government	2 401 ..	78.0	117.7	121.2	157.0	132.4	122.9	179.8	90.1
Debt forgiveness	2 402 ..	....	9.4	.4	....	....	....	....	....
Other capital transfers	2 410 ..	78.0	108.3	120.8	157.0	132.4	122.9	179.8	90.1
Other sectors	2 430 ..	....	....	....	....	....	....	....	....
Migrants' transfers	2 431 ..	....	....	....	....	....	....	....	....
Debt forgiveness	2 432 ..	....	....	....	....	....	....	....	....
Other capital transfers	2 440 ..	....	....	....	....	....	....	....	....
Capital transfers, debit	3 400 ..	....	....	....	....	....	....	....	....
General government	3 401 ..	....	....	....	....	....	....	....	....
Debt forgiveness	3 402 ..	....	....	....	....	....	....	....	....
Other capital transfers	3 410 ..	....	....	....	....	....	....	....	....
Other sectors	3 430 ..	....	....	....	....	....	....	....	....
Migrants' transfers	3 431 ..	....	....	....	....	....	....	....	....
Debt forgiveness	3 432 ..	....	....	....	....	....	....	....	....
Other capital transfers	3 440 ..	....	....	....	....	....	....	....	....
Nonproduced nonfinancial assets, credit	2 480 ..	....	....	....	....	....	....	....	....
Nonproduced nonfinancial assets, debit	3 480 ..	....	....	....	....	....	....	....	....

Table 2 (Continued). STANDARD PRESENTATION, 2000–2007

(Millions of U.S. dollars)

	Code	2000	2001	2002	2003	2004	2005	2006	2007
FINANCIAL ACCOUNT..	4 995 ..	**68.5**	**−36.7**	**177.8**	**102.5**	**110.2**	**244.8**	**254.1**	**590.1**
A. DIRECT INVESTMENT..	4 500 ..	**143.0**	**207.3**	**135.0**	**178.0**	**327.7**	**258.4**	**314.6**	**465.7**
Direct investment abroad.............................	4 505 ..	....	....	....	....	−13.6	−4.1	−10.6	−11.0
Equity capital...	4 510 ..	....	....	....	....	−13.6	−4.1	−10.6	−10.8
Claims on affiliated enterprises....................	4 515 ..	....	....	....	....	−13.6	−4.1	−10.5	....
Liabilities to affiliated enterprises...............	4 520 ..	....	....	....	....	....	....	−.1	−10.8
Reinvested earnings......................................	4 525 ..	....	....	....	....	....	....	....	....
Other capital...	4 530 ..	....	....	....	....	....	....	....	−.2
Claims on affiliated enterprises....................	4 535 ..	....	....	....	....	....	....	....	....
Liabilities to affiliated enterprises...............	4 540 ..	....	....	....	....	....	....	....	−.2
Direct investment in Albania............................	4 555 ..	**143.0**	**207.3**	**135.0**	**178.0**	**341.3**	**262.5**	**325.3**	**476.7**
Equity capital...	4 560 ..	143.0	207.3	135.0	178.0	341.3	262.5	75.8	340.0
Claims on direct investors............................	4 565 ..	....	....	....	....	....	....	....	....
Liabilities to direct investors.......................	4 570 ..	143.0	207.3	135.0	178.0	341.3	262.5	75.8	340.0
Reinvested earnings......................................	4 575 ..	....	....	....	....	....	....	....	....
Other capital...	4 580 ..	....	....	....	....	....	....	249.5	136.6
Claims on direct investors............................	4 585 ..	....	....	....	....	....	....	....	....
Liabilities to direct investors.......................	4 590 ..	....	....	....	....	....	....	249.5	136.6
B. PORTFOLIO INVESTMENT..............................	4 600 ..	**−25.0**	**−23.5**	**−36.8**	**−22.5**	**−3.6**	**−5.7**	**34.2**	**18.5**
Assets...	4 602 ..	**−25.0**	**−23.5**	**−36.8**	**−22.5**	**−3.6**	**−5.7**	**34.2**	**18.5**
Equity securities...	4 610 ..	....	....	....	....	....	....	....	....
Monetary authorities....................................	4 611 ..	....	....	....	....	....	....	....	....
General government......................................	4 612 ..	....	....	....	....	....	....	....	....
Banks...	4 613 ..	....	....	....	....	....	....	....	....
Other sectors..	4 614 ..	....	....	....	....	....	....	....	....
Debt securities...	4 619 ..	−25.0	−23.5	−36.8	−22.5	−3.6	−5.7	34.2	18.5
Bonds and notes...	4 620 ..	−25.0	−23.5	−36.8	−22.5	−3.6	−5.7	34.2	18.5
Monetary authorities....................................	4 621 ..	....	....	....	....	....	....	....	....
General government......................................	4 622 ..	....	....	....	....	....	....	....	....
Banks...	4 623 ..	−25.0	−23.5	−36.8	−22.5	−3.6	−5.7	34.2	18.5
Other sectors..	4 624 ..	....	....	....	....	....	....	....	....
Money market instruments...........................	4 630 ..	....	....	....	....	....	....	....	....
Monetary authorities....................................	4 631 ..	....	....	....	....	....	....	....	....
General government......................................	4 632 ..	....	....	....	....	....	....	....	....
Banks...	4 633 ..	....	....	....	....	....	....	....	....
Other sectors..	4 634 ..	....	....	....	....	....	....	....	....
Liabilities...	4 652 ..	....	....	....	....	....	....	....	....
Equity securities...	4 660 ..	....	....	....	....	....	....	....	....
Banks...	4 663 ..	....	....	....	....	....	....	....	....
Other sectors..	4 664 ..	....	....	....	....	....	....	....	....
Debt securities...	4 669 ..	....	....	....	....	....	....	....	....
Bonds and notes...	4 670 ..	....	....	....	....	....	....	....	....
Monetary authorities....................................	4 671 ..	....	....	....	....	....	....	....	....
General government......................................	4 672 ..	....	....	....	....	....	....	....	....
Banks...	4 673 ..	....	....	....	....	....	....	....	....
Other sectors..	4 674 ..	....	....	....	....	....	....	....	....
Money market instruments...........................	4 680 ..	....	....	....	....	....	....	....	....
Monetary authorities....................................	4 681 ..	....	....	....	....	....	....	....	....
General government......................................	4 682 ..	....	....	....	....	....	....	....	....
Banks...	4 683 ..	....	....	....	....	....	....	....	....
Other sectors..	4 684 ..	....	....	....	....	....	....	....	....
C. FINANCIAL DERIVATIVES...............................	4 910 ..	....	....	....	....	....	....	....	....
Monetary authorities....................................	4 911 ..	....	....	....	....	....	....	....	....
General government......................................	4 912 ..	....	....	....	....	....	....	....	....
Banks...	4 913 ..	....	....	....	....	....	....	....	....
Other sectors..	4 914 ..	....	....	....	....	....	....	....	....
Assets...	4 900 ..	....	....	....	....	....	....	....	....
Monetary authorities....................................	4 901 ..	....	....	....	....	....	....	....	....
General government......................................	4 902 ..	....	....	....	....	....	....	....	....
Banks...	4 903 ..	....	....	....	....	....	....	....	....
Other sectors..	4 904 ..	....	....	....	....	....	....	....	....
Liabilities...	4 905 ..	....	....	....	....	....	....	....	....
Monetary authorities....................................	4 906 ..	....	....	....	....	....	....	....	....
General government......................................	4 907 ..	....	....	....	....	....	....	....	....
Banks...	4 908 ..	....	....	....	....	....	....	....	....
Other sectors..	4 909 ..	....	....	....	....	....	....	....	....

2008, International Monetary Fund: *Balance of Payments Statistics Yearbook*

Table 2 (Concluded). STANDARD PRESENTATION, 2000–2007

(Millions of U.S. dollars)

	Code	2000	2001	2002	2003	2004	2005	2006	2007
D. OTHER INVESTMENT	4 700 ..	**82.5**	**−75.4**	**108.2**	**46.6**	**74.6**	**142.8**	**170.4**	**252.5**
Assets	4 703 ..	**−40.2**	**−197.2**	**−2.7**	**−71.6**	**−113.8**	**6.6**	**−210.7**	**−64.2**
Trade credits	4 706 ..	....	....	....	....	....	....	....	....
General government	4 707 ..	....	....	....	....	....	....	....	....
of which: Short-term	4 709 ..	....	....	....	....	....	....	....	....
Other sectors	4 710 ..	....	....	....	....	....	....	....	....
of which: Short-term	4 712 ..	....	....	....	....	....	....	....	....
Loans	4 714 ..	....	−17.1	....	....	....	....	....	....
Monetary authorities	4 715 ..	....	....	....	....	....	....	....	....
of which: Short-term	4 718 ..	....	....	....	....	....	....	....	....
General government	4 719 ..	....	....	....	....	....	....	....	....
of which: Short-term	4 721 ..	....	....	....	....	....	....	....	....
Banks	4 722 ..	....	....	....	....	....	....	....	....
of which: Short-term	4 724 ..	....	....	....	....	....	....	....	....
Other sectors	4 725 ..	....	−17.1	....	....	....	....	....	....
of which: Short-term	4 727 ..	....	*−17.1*	....	....	....	....	....	....
Currency and deposits	4 730 ..	−40.2	−180.1	−2.7	−70.4	−110.5	63.2	−219.9	−74.8
Monetary authorities	4 731 ..	....	−1.8	2.2	.3	....	....	−.6	−4.2
General government	4 732 ..	....	....	....	....	....	....	....	....
Banks	4 733 ..	−2.5	−132.3	42.2	−44.0	−108.7	65.2	−225.2	−70.6
Other sectors	4 734 ..	−37.7	−46.0	−47.1	−26.7	−1.7	−1.9	5.9	....
Other assets	4 736 ..	....	....	....	−1.3	−3.4	−56.6	9.2	10.7
Monetary authorities	4 737 ..	....	....	....	....	....	....	....	....
of which: Short-term	4 739 ..	....	....	....	....	....	....	....	....
General government	4 740 ..	....	....	....	....	....	....	....	....
of which: Short-term	4 742 ..	....	....	....	....	....	....	....	....
Banks	4 743 ..	....	....	....	−1.3	−3.4	−56.6	12.7	9.5
of which: Short-term	4 745 ..	....	....	....	*−1.3*	*−3.4*	*−56.6*	*12.7*	*9.5*
Other sectors	4 746 ..	....	....	....	....	....	....	−3.5	1.1
of which: Short-term	4 748 ..	....	....	....	....	....	....	*−3.5*	*1.1*
Liabilities	4 753 ..	**122.7**	**121.8**	**110.9**	**118.2**	**188.4**	**136.2**	**381.1**	**316.7**
Trade credits	4 756 ..	22.6	−2.9	6.8	11.1	23.1	9.6	9.7	13.5
General government	4 757 ..	....	....	....	....	....	....	....	....
of which: Short-term	4 759 ..	....	....	....	....	....	....	....	....
Other sectors	4 760 ..	22.6	−2.9	6.8	11.1	23.1	9.6	9.7	13.5
of which: Short-term	4 762 ..	*22.6*	*−2.9*	*6.8*	*11.1*	*23.1*	*9.6*	*9.7*	*13.5*
Loans	4 764 ..	101.4	82.6	113.8	118.9	193.2	134.0	124.6	76.1
Monetary authorities	4 765 ..	11.9	−1.9	−8.0	.5	1.2	1.5	−5.4	−7.7
of which: Use of Fund credit and loans from the Fund	4 766 ..	*12.1*	*−1.6*	*−8.5*	*1.5*	*2.4*	*3.0*	*−4.1*	*−7.0*
of which: Short-term	4 768 ..	....	....	....	....	....	....	....	....
General government	4 769 ..	90.8	86.1	118.2	96.6	106.4	50.4	51.9	56.3
of which: Short-term	4 771 ..	....	....	....	....	....	....	....	....
Banks	4 772 ..	....	....	....	....	....	....	−.7	−.3
of which: Short-term	4 774 ..	....	....	....	....	....	....	....	....
Other sectors	4 775 ..	−1.3	−1.6	3.7	21.8	85.7	82.1	78.8	27.8
of which: Short-term	4 777 ..	....	....	....	....	....	....	....	....
Currency and deposits	4 780 ..	5.2	42.1	8.3	19.7	3.4	−36.9	163.6	103.8
Monetary authorities	4 781 ..	....	....	....	....	....	....	....	....
General government	4 782 ..	....	....	....	....	....	....	....	....
Banks	4 783 ..	5.2	42.1	8.3	19.7	3.4	−36.9	163.6	103.8
Other sectors	4 784 ..	....	....	....	....	....	....	....	....
Other liabilities	4 786 ..	−6.5	....	−18.0	−31.4	−31.4	29.5	83.3	123.2
Monetary authorities	4 787 ..	....	....	.1	....	....	....	....	....
of which: Short-term	4 789 ..	....	....	*.1*	....	....	....	....	....
General government	4 790 ..	....	....	1.4	....	....	....	....	.2
of which: Short-term	4 792 ..	....	....	*1.4*	....	....	....	....	*.2*
Banks	4 793 ..	....	....	2.6	.1	−3.1	57.5	81.2	122.9
of which: Short-term	4 795 ..	....	....	*2.6*	*.1*	*−3.1*	*57.5*	*81.2*	*122.9*
Other sectors	4 796 ..	−6.5	....	−22.0	−31.5	−28.3	−28.1	2.1	.1
of which: Short-term	4 798 ..	*−6.5*	....	*−22.0*	*−31.5*	*−28.3*	*−28.1*	*2.1*	*.1*
E. RESERVE ASSETS	4 802 ..	**−132.0**	**−145.1**	**−28.6**	**−99.6**	**−288.4**	**−150.7**	**−265.1**	**−146.5**
Monetary gold	4 812 ..	....	....	....	....	....	....	....	....
Special drawing rights	4 811 ..	−3.5	−8.4	6.4	−1.2	−5.8	82.1	4.2	7.4
Reserve position in the Fund	4 810 ..	....	....	....	....	....	....	....	....
Foreign exchange	4 803 ..	−128.5	−136.7	−35.0	−98.4	−282.7	−232.8	−269.3	−153.9
Other claims	4 813 ..	....	....	....	....	....	....	....	....
NET ERRORS AND OMISSIONS	4 998 ..	**9.8**	**136.3**	**108.5**	**147.4**	**115.3**	**203.8**	**237.0**	**150.8**

Table 1. ANALYTIC PRESENTATION, 2000–2007

(Millions of U.S. dollars)

	Code	2000	2001	2002	2003	2004	2005	2006	2007
A. Current Account[1].....................................	4 993 Z.	**795.7**	**−1,430.9**	**−150.1**	**−719.6**	**686.2**	**5,137.9**	**10,689.8**	**9,402.1**
Goods: exports f.o.b..............................	2 100 ..	7,920.7	6,534.3	8,327.9	9,508.2	13,475.0	24,109.4	31,862.2	44,396.2
Goods: imports f.o.b..............................	3 100 ..	−3,039.5	−3,179.2	−3,760.1	−5,480.1	−5,831.8	−8,353.2	−8,777.6	−13,661.5
Balance on Goods................................	4 100 ..	*4,881.2*	*3,355.1*	*4,567.8*	*4,028.1*	*7,643.2*	*15,756.2*	*23,084.6*	*30,734.7*
Services: credit....................................	2 200 ..	267.3	202.5	206.8	201.1	322.8	176.8	1,484.2	310.7
Services: debit.....................................	3 200 ..	−2,699.5	−3,518.1	−3,322.0	−3,321.1	−4,802.7	−6,791.0	−7,511.2	−12,643.3
Balance on Goods and Services........................	4 991 ..	*2,449.0*	*39.5*	*1,452.6*	*908.0*	*3,163.3*	*9,142.0*	*17,057.7*	*18,402.2*
Income: credit.....................................	2 300 ..	34.4	23.0	17.7	12.3	33.0	25.8	145.0	33.0
Income: debit......................................	3 300 ..	−1,715.2	−1,584.0	−1,652.3	−1,738.7	−2,516.6	−4,056.6	−6,322.9	−8,811.1
Balance on Goods, Services, and Income........................	4 992 ..	*768.2*	*−1,521.5*	*−182.1*	*−818.5*	*679.6*	*5,111.1*	*10,879.8*	*9,624.0*
Current transfers: credit...........................	2 379 Z.	123.5	208.3	142.3	186.2	124.4	172.5	59.5	45.7
Current transfers: debit............................	3 379 ..	−96.0	−117.8	−110.3	−87.3	−117.9	−145.8	−249.5	−267.6
B. Capital Account[1].....................................	4 994 Z.	**18.3**	**3.9**	....	....	....	....	....	**6.9**
Capital account: credit............................	2 994 Z.	18.3	3.9	....	....	....	....	....	6.9
Capital account: debit.............................	3 994 ..	....	....	....	....	....	....	....	....
Total, Groups A Plus B........................	4 981 ..	*814.0*	*−1,427.0*	*−150.1*	*−719.6*	*686.2*	*5,137.9*	*10,689.8*	*9,409.0*
C. Financial Account[1].....................................	4 995 W.	**−445.6**	**950.0**	**−356.7**	**1,370.5**	**−623.2**	**−3,115.2**	**−5,601.2**	**−11,910.0**
Direct investment abroad........................	4 505 ..	....	....	−28.7	−23.6	−35.2	−219.4	−190.6	−911.8
Direct investment in Angola.....................	4 555 Z.	878.6	2,145.5	1,672.1	3,504.7	1,449.2	−1,303.8	−37.7	−893.3
Portfolio investment assets.....................	4 602 ..	....	....	....	1.0	−2.7	−1,267.0	−1,439.5	−2,015.4
Equity securities.............................	4 610 ..	....	....	....	....	−3.3	−1,264.0	−1,491.0	−1,965.9
Debt securities..............................	4 619 ..	....	....	....	1.0	.6	−3.0	51.5	−49.6
Portfolio investment liabilities.................	4 652 Z.	....	....	....	....	....	....	....	....
Equity securities.............................	4 660 ..	....	....	....	....	....	....	....	....
Debt securities..............................	4 669 Z.	....	....	....	....	....	....	....	....
Financial derivatives............................	4 910 ..	....	....	....	....	....	....	....	....
Financial derivatives assets.....................	4 900 ..	....	....	....	....	....	....	....	....
Financial derivatives liabilities.................	4 905 ..	....	....	....	....	....	....	....	....
Other investment assets........................	4 703 ..	−702.1	−516.6	−1,321.0	120.0	−1,951.5	−1,850.1	−1,633.1	−4,854.9
Monetary authorities..........................	4 701 ..	....	....	....	....	....	....	....	....
General government..........................	4 704 ..	....	....	....	....	....	....	....	....
Banks......................................	4 705 ..	....	....	−1,112.6	75.0	−68.2	−371.0	−1,444.3	42.2
Other sectors................................	4 728 ..	−702.1	−516.6	−208.4	45.0	−1,883.3	−1,479.1	−188.7	−4,897.1
Other investment liabilities.....................	4 753 W.	−622.1	−678.9	−679.1	−2,231.5	−83.0	1,525.1	−2,300.3	−3,234.5
Monetary authorities..........................	4 753 WA	17.3	−62.0	−142.7	−38.0	−2.2	.1	10.0	....
General government..........................	4 753 ZB	−665.3	−483.1	−352.0	309.5	−161.1	−1,141.7	−2,186.6	−521.9
Banks......................................	4 753 ZC	....	....	52.1	−10.5	18.4	29.7	133.9	506.4
Other sectors................................	4 753 ZD	25.9	−133.8	−236.6	−2,492.5	61.9	2,637.0	−257.7	−3,219.0
Total, Groups A Through C........................	4 983 ..	*368.4*	*−477.0*	*−506.8*	*651.0*	*62.9*	*2,022.7*	*5,088.6*	*−2,501.0*
D. Net Errors and Omissions.................................	4 998 ..	**−50.6**	**−308.6**	**150.5**	**−388.2**	**277.3**	**−377.9**	**289.8**	**−461.7**
Total, Groups A Through D........................	4 984 ..	*317.8*	*−785.6*	*−356.3*	*262.8*	*340.3*	*1,644.9*	*5,378.4*	*−2,962.7*
E. Reserves and Related Items.................................	4 802 A.	**−317.8**	**785.6**	**356.3**	**−262.8**	**−340.3**	**−1,644.9**	**−5,378.4**	**2,962.7**
Reserve assets..................................	4 802 ..	−631.3	466.3	356.3	−262.8	−780.3	−1,817.3	−5,401.7	−3,019.1
Use of Fund credit and loans....................	4 766 ..	....	....	....	....	....	....	....	....
Exceptional financing............................	4 920 ..	313.4	319.3	....	....	440.0	172.4	23.3	5,981.8
Conversion rates: kwanzas per U.S. dollar.............	0 101 ..	**10.041**	**22.058**	**43.530**	**74.606**	**83.541**	**87.159**	**80.368**	**76.706**

---

[1] Excludes components that have been classified in the categories of Group E.

Table 2. STANDARD PRESENTATION, 2000–2007

(Millions of U.S. dollars)

	Code	2000	2001	2002	2003	2004	2005	2006	2007
CURRENT ACCOUNT....................................	4 993 ..	**795.7**	**−1,430.9**	**−150.1**	**−719.6**	**686.2**	**5,137.9**	**10,689.8**	**9,402.1**
A. GOODS....................................	4 100 ..	**4,881.2**	**3,355.1**	**4,567.8**	**4,028.1**	**7,643.2**	**15,756.2**	**23,084.6**	**30,734.7**
Credit....................................	2 100 ..	**7,920.7**	**6,534.3**	**8,327.9**	**9,508.2**	**13,475.0**	**24,109.4**	**31,862.2**	**44,396.2**
General merchandise: exports f.o.b........	2 110 ..	7,920.7	6,534.3	8,327.9	9,508.2	13,475.0	24,109.4	31,862.2	44,396.2
Goods for processing: exports f.o.b........	2 150 ..	....	....	....	....	....	....	....	....
Repairs on goods....................................	2 160 ..	....	....	....	....	....	....	....	....
Goods procured in ports by carriers........	2 170 ..	....	....	....	....	....	....	....	....
Nonmonetary gold....................................	2 180 ..	....	....	....	....	....	....	....	....
Debit....................................	3 100 ..	**−3,039.5**	**−3,179.2**	**−3,760.1**	**−5,480.1**	**−5,831.8**	**−8,353.2**	**−8,777.6**	**−13,661.5**
General merchandise: imports f.o.b........	3 110 ..	−3,039.5	−3,179.2	−3,760.1	−5,480.1	−5,831.8	−8,353.2	−8,777.6	−13,661.5
Goods for processing: imports f.o.b........	3 150 ..	....	....	....	....	....	....	....	....
Repairs on goods....................................	3 160 ..	....	....	....	....	....	....	....	....
Goods procured in ports by carriers........	3 170 ..	....	....	....	....	....	....	....	....
Nonmonetary gold....................................	3 180 ..	....	....	....	....	....	....	....	....
B. SERVICES....................................	4 200 ..	**−2,432.2**	**−3,315.6**	**−3,115.2**	**−3,120.0**	**−4,480.0**	**−6,614.1**	**−6,027.0**	**−12,332.5**
Total credit....................................	2 200 ..	*267.3*	*202.5*	*206.8*	*201.1*	*322.8*	*176.8*	*1,484.2*	*310.7*
Total debit....................................	3 200 ..	*−2,699.5*	*−3,518.1*	*−3,322.0*	*−3,321.1*	*−4,802.7*	*−6,791.0*	*−7,511.2*	*−12,643.3*
Transportation services, credit........	2 205 ..	**16.1**	**13.5**	**16.8**	**15.8**	**17.7**	**18.1**	**20.2**	**16.7**
Passenger....................................	2 850 ..	*16.1*	*13.5*	*13.9*	*13.7*	*16.0*	*15.4*	*15.7*	*11.1*
Freight....................................	2 851 ..	....	....	....	....	....	*.7*	*.6*	*.4*
Other....................................	2 852 ..	....	....	*2.8*	*2.1*	*1.7*	*2.0*	*3.9*	*5.3*
Sea transport, passenger....................	2 207 ..	....	....	....	....	....	....	....	....
Sea transport, freight....................	2 208 ..	....	....	....	....	....	....	....	....
Sea transport, other....................	2 209 ..	....	....	....	....	....	....	....	....
Air transport, passenger....................	2 211 ..	....	....	13.9	13.7	16.0	15.4	15.7	11.1
Air transport, freight....................	2 212 ..	....	....	....	....	....	.7	.6	.4
Air transport, other....................	2 213 ..	....	....	2.8	2.1	1.7	2.0	3.9	5.3
Other transport, passenger....................	2 215 ..	....	....	....	....	....	....	....	....
Other transport, freight....................	2 216 ..	....	....	....	....	....	....	....	....
Other transport, other....................	2 217 ..	....	....	....	....	....	....	....	....
Transportation services, debit........	3 205 ..	**−311.3**	**−392.5**	**−476.8**	**−758.6**	**−877.4**	**−1,320.2**	**−1,626.7**	**−2,505.0**
Passenger....................................	3 850 ..	*−10.0*	*−13.6*	*−33.5*	*−36.6*	*−47.0*	*−61.0*	*−245.2*	*−261.5*
Freight....................................	3 851 ..	*−211.2*	*−288.0*	*−422.2*	*−695.6*	*−795.0*	*−1,217.7*	*−1,331.9*	*−2,187.2*
Other....................................	3 852 ..	*−90.1*	*−90.9*	*−21.1*	*−26.5*	*−35.5*	*−41.6*	*−49.7*	*−56.3*
Sea transport, passenger....................	3 207 ..	....	....	....	....	....	....	....	....
Sea transport, freight....................	3 208 ..	....	....	−420.5	−695.6	−786.5	−1,216.0	−1,330.3	−2,185.2
Sea transport, other....................	3 209 ..	....	....	....	....	....	....	....	....
Air transport, passenger....................	3 211 ..	....	....	−33.5	−36.6	−47.0	−61.0	−245.2	−261.5
Air transport, freight....................	3 212 ..	....	....	−1.7	....	−8.5	−1.7	−1.6	−2.0
Air transport, other....................	3 213 ..	....	....	−21.1	−26.5	−35.5	−41.6	−49.7	−56.3
Other transport, passenger....................	3 215 ..	....	....	....	....	....	....	....	....
Other transport, freight....................	3 216 ..	....	....	....	....	....	....	....	....
Other transport, other....................	3 217 ..	....	....	....	....	....	....	....	....
Travel, credit....................................	2 236 ..	....	....	**36.9**	**49.0**	**65.8**	**88.3**	**74.9**	**224.9**
Business travel....................................	2 237 ..	....	....	36.9	49.0	65.8	88.3	74.9	160.8
Personal travel....................................	2 240 ..	....	....	....	....	....	....	....	64.1
Travel, debit....................................	3 236 ..	**−136.3**	**−66.4**	**−19.4**	**−12.1**	**−38.8**	**−74.0**	**−147.7**	**−211.9**
Business travel....................................	3 237 ..	....	....	−16.6	−12.1	−38.2	−24.1	−29.3	−102.4
Personal travel....................................	3 240 ..	....	....	−2.8	....	−.6	−49.9	−118.4	−109.5
Other services, credit....................	2 200 BA	**251.2**	**189.0**	**153.1**	**136.3**	**239.3**	**70.5**	**1,389.1**	**69.0**
Communications....................................	2 245 ..	....	....	....	....	....	14.0	10.7	....
Construction....................................	2 249 ..	....	....	....	....	....	....	....	....
Insurance....................................	2 253 ..	35.3	27.7	....	−.3	....	....	....	....
Financial....................................	2 260 ..	....	....	....	....	....	....	....	....
Computer and information....................	2 262 ..	....	....	....	....	....	....	....	....
Royalties and licence fees....................	2 266 ..	15.8	4.4	....	....	226.8	49.4	1,339.6	12.0
Other business services....................	2 268 ..	200.1	156.9	151.9	135.5	9.6	2.5	32.4	47.9
Personal, cultural, and recreational........	2 287 ..	....	....	1.2	1.1	2.9	4.6	6.4	9.1
Government, n.i.e....................................	2 291 ..	....	....	....	....	....	....	....	....
Other services, debit....................	3 200 BA	**−2,251.8**	**−3,059.3**	**−2,825.8**	**−2,550.4**	**−3,886.4**	**−5,396.7**	**−5,736.7**	**−9,926.4**
Communications....................................	3 245 ..	....	....	−7.7	−9.1	−16.9	−23.3	−19.0	−48.2
Construction....................................	3 249 ..	....	....	−555.3	−149.9	−866.4	−1,323.2	−1,475.7	−2,633.7
Insurance....................................	3 253 ..	−63.1	−93.1	−94.2	−157.5	−174.4	−103.5	−296.9	−414.2
Financial....................................	3 260 ..	....	....	−33.7	−9.4	−59.0	−16.2	−123.5	−154.1
Computer and information....................	3 262 ..	....	....	−.9	−1.9	−7.7	−17.8	−11.8	−23.3
Royalties and licence fees....................	3 266 ..	−5.6	−.4	....	....	−2.5	−3.4	−1.4	−1.2
Other business services....................	3 268 ..	−1,754.3	−2,623.3	−1,562.9	−1,665.1	−2,212.8	−3,264.6	−3,092.5	−5,519.7
Personal, cultural, and recreational........	3 287 ..	....	....	−15.0	−10.8	−28.5	−44.9	−64.7	−99.1
Government, n.i.e....................................	3 291 ..	−428.8	−342.4	−556.1	−546.8	−518.2	−599.8	−651.2	−1,032.9

Table 2 (Continued). STANDARD PRESENTATION, 2000–2007

(Millions of U.S. dollars)

	Code	2000	2001	2002	2003	2004	2005	2006	2007
C. INCOME	4 300	**−1,680.9**	**−1,561.0**	**−1,634.7**	**−1,726.5**	**−2,483.6**	**−4,030.9**	**−6,177.9**	**−8,778.2**
Total credit	2 300	*34.4*	*23.0*	*17.7*	*12.3*	*33.0*	*25.8*	*145.0*	*33.0*
Total debit	3 300	*−1,715.2*	*−1,584.0*	*−1,652.3*	*−1,738.7*	*−2,516.6*	*−4,056.6*	*−6,322.9*	*−8,811.1*
Compensation of employees, credit	2 310	....	....	....	....	....	....	....	....
Compensation of employees, debit	3 310	−189.9	−117.8	−123.3	−141.9	−178.6	−97.7	−240.8	−374.4
Investment income, credit	2 320	34.4	23.0	17.7	12.3	33.0	25.8	145.0	33.0
Direct investment income	2 330	....	....	....	....	....	17.9	....	....
Dividends and distributed branch profits	2 332	....	....	....	....	....	....	....	....
Reinvested earnings and undistributed branch profits	2 333	....	....	....	....	....	17.9	....	....
Income on debt (interest)	2 334	....	....	....	....	....	....	....	....
Portfolio investment income	2 339	....	....	....	....	....	....	....	....
Income on equity	2 340	....	....	....	....	....	....	....	....
Income on bonds and notes	2 350	....	....	....	....	....	....	....	....
Income on money market instruments	2 360	....	....	....	....	....	....	....	....
Other investment income	2 370	34.4	23.0	17.7	12.3	33.0	7.9	145.0	33.0
Investment income, debit	3 320	**−1,525.4**	**−1,466.1**	**−1,529.0**	**−1,596.8**	**−2,338.1**	**−3,958.9**	**−6,082.2**	**−8,436.7**
Direct investment income	3 330	−928.6	−927.1	−1,100.3	−1,263.9	−1,950.2	−3,405.9	−5,278.4	−7,268.2
Dividends and distributed branch profits	3 332	−928.6	−927.1	−493.3	−574.4	−896.0	−2,264.2	−2,361.3	−4,025.5
Reinvested earnings and undistributed branch profits	3 333	....	....	−583.1	−679.6	−1,052.9	−1,139.7	−2,915.7	−3,242.7
Income on debt (interest)	3 334	....	....	−23.9	−9.9	−1.3	−1.9	−1.4	....
Portfolio investment income	3 339	....	....	....	....	....	....	....	....
Income on equity	3 340	....	....	....	....	....	....	....	....
Income on bonds and notes	3 350	....	....	....	....	....	....	....	....
Income on money market instruments	3 360	....	....	....	....	....	....	....	....
Other investment income	3 370	−596.7	−539.0	−428.8	−332.9	−387.9	−553.1	−803.7	−1,168.5
D. CURRENT TRANSFERS	4 379	**27.5**	**90.6**	**32.0**	**98.9**	**6.5**	**26.8**	**−190.0**	**−221.9**
Credit	2 379	**123.5**	**208.3**	**142.3**	**186.2**	**124.4**	**172.5**	**59.5**	**45.7**
General government	2 380	9.0	115.2	142.3	186.2	124.4	172.5	59.5	45.7
Other sectors	2 390	114.5	93.1	....	....	....	....	....	....
Workers' remittances	2 391	....	....	....	....	....	....	....	....
Other current transfers	2 392	114.5	93.1	....	....	....	....	....	....
Debit	3 379	**−96.0**	**−117.8**	**−110.3**	**−87.3**	**−117.9**	**−145.8**	**−249.5**	**−267.6**
General government	3 380	−4.7	−9.9	−7.0	....	....	−28.4	−35.8	−37.7
Other sectors	3 390	−91.2	−107.9	−103.3	−87.3	−117.9	−117.3	−213.7	−229.9
Workers' remittances	3 391	−76.4	−98.2	−100.2	−87.9	−117.5	−117.2	−171.9	−228.3
Other current transfers	3 392	−14.8	−9.7	−3.1	.6	−.4	−.1	−41.8	−1.7
CAPITAL AND FINANCIAL ACCOUNT	4 996	**−745.1**	**1,739.5**	**−.4**	**1,107.7**	**−963.5**	**−4,760.0**	**−10,979.6**	**−8,940.4**
CAPITAL ACCOUNT	4 994	**18.3**	**3.9**	....	....	**440.0**	**172.4**	**23.3**	**7.2**
Total credit	2 994	*18.3*	*3.9*	....	....	*440.0*	*172.4*	*23.3*	*7.2*
Total debit	3 994	....	....	....	....	....	....	....	....
Capital transfers, credit	2 400	**18.3**	**3.9**	....	....	**440.0**	**172.4**	**23.3**	**7.2**
General government	2 401	18.3	3.9	....	....	440.0	172.4	23.3	7.2
Debt forgiveness	2 402	18.2	3.9	....	....	440.0	172.4	23.3	.3
Other capital transfers	2 410	.2	....	....	....	....	....	....	6.9
Other sectors	2 430	....	....	....	....	....	....	....	....
Migrants' transfers	2 431	....	....	....	....	....	....	....	....
Debt forgiveness	2 432	....	....	....	....	....	....	....	....
Other capital transfers	2 440	....	....	....	....	....	....	....	....
Capital transfers, debit	3 400	....	....	....	....	....	....	....	....
General government	3 401	....	....	....	....	....	....	....	....
Debt forgiveness	3 402	....	....	....	....	....	....	....	....
Other capital transfers	3 410	....	....	....	....	....	....	....	....
Other sectors	3 430	....	....	....	....	....	....	....	....
Migrants' transfers	3 431	....	....	....	....	....	....	....	....
Debt forgiveness	3 432	....	....	....	....	....	....	....	....
Other capital transfers	3 440	....	....	....	....	....	....	....	....
Nonproduced nonfinancial assets, credit	2 480	....	....	....	....	....	....	....	....
Nonproduced nonfinancial assets, debit	3 480	....	....	....	....	....	....	....	....

Table 2 (Continued). STANDARD PRESENTATION, 2000–2007

(Millions of U.S. dollars)

	Code	2000	2001	2002	2003	2004	2005	2006	2007
FINANCIAL ACCOUNT	4 995 ..	**−763.4**	**1,735.6**	**−.4**	**1,107.7**	**−1,403.5**	**−4,932.5**	**−11,002.9**	**−8,947.5**
A. DIRECT INVESTMENT	4 500 ..	**878.6**	**2,145.5**	**1,643.4**	**3,481.1**	**1,414.0**	**−1,523.2**	**−228.3**	**−1,805.1**
Direct investment abroad	4 505 ..	....	....	**−28.7**	**−23.6**	**−35.2**	**−219.4**	**−190.6**	**−911.8**
Equity capital	4 510 ..	....	....	....	....	....	....	....	−80.5
Claims on affiliated enterprises	4 515 ..	....	....	....	....	....	....	....	−80.5
Liabilities to affiliated enterprises	4 520 ..	....	....	....	....	....	....	....	....
Reinvested earnings	4 525 ..	....	....	....	....	....	−17.9		
Other capital	4 530 ..	....	....	−28.7	−23.6	−35.2	−201.5	−190.6	−831.3
Claims on affiliated enterprises	4 535 ..	....	....	−28.7	−23.6	−.3	−.5	3.5	−4.1
Liabilities to affiliated enterprises	4 540 ..	....	....	....	....	−34.9	−201.0	−194.1	−827.3
Direct investment in Angola	4 555 ..	**878.6**	**2,145.5**	**1,672.1**	**3,504.7**	**1,449.2**	**−1,303.8**	**−37.7**	**−893.3**
Equity capital	4 560 ..	....	....	....	....	−748.0	....	....	....
Claims on direct investors	4 565 ..	....	....	....	....	−748.0	....	....	....
Liabilities to direct investors	4 570 ..	....	....	....	....	....	....	....	....
Reinvested earnings	4 575 ..	....	....	583.1	679.6	1,052.9	1,139.7	2,915.7	3,242.7
Other capital	4 580 ..	878.6	2,145.5	1,089.0	2,825.1	1,144.3	−2,443.6	−2,953.5	−4,136.1
Claims on direct investors	4 585 ..	....	....	−71.4	−72.3	....	....	....	....
Liabilities to direct investors	4 590 ..	....	....	1,160.4	2,897.4	1,144.3	−2,443.6	−2,953.5	−4,136.1
B. PORTFOLIO INVESTMENT	4 600 ..	....	....	....	**1.0**	**−2.7**	**−1,267.0**	**−1,439.5**	**−2,015.4**
Assets	4 602 ..	....	....	....	1.0	−2.7	−1,267.0	−1,439.5	−2,015.4
Equity securities	4 610 ..	....	....	....	....	−3.3	−1,264.0	−1,491.0	−1,965.9
Monetary authorities	4 611 ..	....	....	....	....	....	....	....	....
General government	4 612 ..	....	....	....	....	....	....	....	....
Banks	4 613 ..	....	....	....	....	....	....	....	....
Other sectors	4 614 ..	....	....	....	....	−3.3	−1,264.0	−1,491.0	−1,965.9
Debt securities	4 619 ..	....	....	....	1.0	.6	−3.0	51.5	−49.6
Bonds and notes	4 620 ..	....	....	....	....	.6	−3.0	51.5	−49.6
Monetary authorities	4 621 ..	....	....	....	....	....	....	....	....
General government	4 622 ..	....	....	....	....	....	....	....	....
Banks	4 623 ..	....	....	....	....	.6	−3.0	51.5	−49.6
Other sectors	4 624 ..	....	....	....	....	....	....	....	....
Money market instruments	4 630 ..	....	....	....	1.0	....	....	....	....
Monetary authorities	4 631 ..	....	....	....	....	....	....	....	....
General government	4 632 ..	....	....	....	....	....	....	....	....
Banks	4 633 ..	....	....	....	1.0	....	....	....	....
Other sectors	4 634 ..	....	....	....	....	....	....	....	....
Liabilities	4 652 ..	....	....	....	....	....	....	....	....
Equity securities	4 660 ..	....	....	....	....	....	....	....	....
Banks	4 663 ..	....	....	....	....	....	....	....	....
Other sectors	4 664 ..	....	....	....	....	....	....	....	....
Debt securities	4 669 ..	....	....	....	....	....	....	....	....
Bonds and notes	4 670 ..	....	....	....	....	....	....	....	....
Monetary authorities	4 671 ..	....	....	....	....	....	....	....	....
General government	4 672 ..	....	....	....	....	....	....	....	....
Banks	4 673 ..	....	....	....	....	....	....	....	....
Other sectors	4 674 ..	....	....	....	....	....	....	....	....
Money market instruments	4 680 ..	....	....	....	....	....	....	....	....
Monetary authorities	4 681 ..	....	....	....	....	....	....	....	....
General government	4 682 ..	....	....	....	....	....	....	....	....
Banks	4 683 ..	....	....	....	....	....	....	....	....
Other sectors	4 684 ..	....	....	....	....	....	....	....	....
C. FINANCIAL DERIVATIVES	4 910 ..	....	....	....	....	....	....	....	....
Monetary authorities	4 911 ..	....	....	....	....	....	....	....	....
General government	4 912 ..	....	....	....	....	....	....	....	....
Banks	4 913 ..	....	....	....	....	....	....	....	....
Other sectors	4 914 ..	....	....	....	....	....	....	....	....
Assets	4 900 ..	....	....	....	....	....	....	....	....
Monetary authorities	4 901 ..	....	....	....	....	....	....	....	....
General government	4 902 ..	....	....	....	....	....	....	....	....
Banks	4 903 ..	....	....	....	....	....	....	....	....
Other sectors	4 904 ..	....	....	....	....	....	....	....	....
Liabilities	4 905 ..	....	....	....	....	....	....	....	....
Monetary authorities	4 906 ..	....	....	....	....	....	....	....	....
General government	4 907 ..	....	....	....	....	....	....	....	....
Banks	4 908 ..	....	....	....	....	....	....	....	....
Other sectors	4 909 ..	....	....	....	....	....	....	....	....

Table 2 (Concluded). STANDARD PRESENTATION, 2000–2007

(Millions of U.S. dollars)

	Code	2000	2001	2002	2003	2004	2005	2006	2007
D. OTHER INVESTMENT	4 700 ..	−1,010.8	−876.2	−2,000.1	−2,111.5	−2,034.6	−324.9	−3,933.4	−2,107.9
Assets	4 703 ..	−702.1	−516.6	−1,321.0	120.0	−1,951.5	−1,850.1	−1,633.1	−4,854.9
Trade credits	4 706 ..	....	....	−207.7	45.0	−251.1	−1,366.1	138.3	−2,751.7
General government	4 707 ..	....	....	....	....	....	....	....	....
of which: Short-term	4 709 ..	....	....	....	....	....	....	....	....
Other sectors	4 710 ..	....	....	−207.7	45.0	−251.1	−1,366.1	138.3	−2,751.7
of which: Short-term	4 712 ..	....	....	−275.0	45.0	−251.1	−1,366.1	138.3	−2,751.7
Loans	4 714 ..	−501.4	−334.2	7.4	−12.6	−.1	9.2	−7.0	7.1
Monetary authorities	4 715 ..	....	....	....	....	....	....	....	....
of which: Short-term	4 718 ..	....	....	....	....	....	....	....	....
General government	4 719 ..	....	....	....	....	....	....	....	....
of which: Short-term	4 721 ..	....	....	....	....	....	....	....	....
Banks	4 722 ..	....	....	8.1	−12.6	−.1	9.2	−7.0	7.1
of which: Short-term	4 724 ..	....	....	−4.7	−12.6	−.1	9.2	−7.0	7.1
Other sectors	4 725 ..	−501.4	−334.2	−.7	....	....	....	....	....
of which: Short-term	4 727 ..	−501.4	−334.2	−.7	....	....	....	....	....
Currency and deposits	4 730 ..	−200.7	−182.4	−1,098.6	100.6	−1,679.1	−511.4	−1,783.5	−2,107.9
Monetary authorities	4 731 ..	....	....	....	....	....	....	....	....
General government	4 732 ..	....	....	....	....	....	....	....	....
Banks	4 733 ..	....	....	−1,098.6	100.6	−46.9	−398.4	−1,456.5	37.6
Other sectors	4 734 ..	−200.7	−182.4	....	....	−1,632.2	−113.0	−327.0	−2,145.5
Other assets	4 736 ..	....	....	−22.1	−13.0	−21.1	18.2	19.2	−2.5
Monetary authorities	4 737 ..	....	....	....	....	....	....	....	....
of which: Short-term	4 739 ..	....	....	....	....	....	....	....	....
General government	4 740 ..	....	....	....	....	....	....	....	....
of which: Short-term	4 742 ..	....	....	....	....	....	....	....	....
Banks	4 743 ..	....	....	−22.1	−13.0	−21.1	18.2	19.2	−2.5
of which: Short-term	4 745 ..	....	....	−22.1	−13.0	−21.1	18.2	19.2	−2.5
Other sectors	4 746 ..	....	....	....	....	....	....	....	....
of which: Short-term	4 748 ..	....	....	....	....	....	....	....	....
Liabilities	4 753 ..	−308.7	−359.6	−679.1	−2,231.5	−83.0	1,525.1	−2,300.3	2,747.0
Trade credits	4 756 ..	....	....	2.4	....	....	−6.8	406.9	−198.1
General government	4 757 ..	....	....	....	....	....	....	....	....
of which: Short-term	4 759 ..	....	....	....	....	....	....	....	....
Other sectors	4 760 ..	....	....	2.4	....	....	−6.8	406.9	−198.1
of which: Short-term	4 762 ..	....	....	2.4	....	....	−6.8	406.9	−198.1
Loans	4 764 ..	−490.0	−639.2	−421.3	−2,290.2	−80.8	1,484.7	−2,747.1	2,532.1
Monetary authorities	4 765 ..	27.6	−62.0	−142.7	−38.0	−2.2	.1	10.0	....
of which: Use of Fund credit and loans from the Fund..	4 766 ..								
of which: Short-term	4 768 ..	17.3	−62.0	−150.1	−40.3	1.8	.1	3.6	....
General government	4 769 ..	−473.7	−443.5	−352.0	309.5	−161.1	−1,141.7	−2,186.6	1,425.8
of which: Short-term	4 771 ..	.4	1.4	246.7	−91.7	−1,151.5	104.0	−1,180.8	....
Banks	4 772 ..	....	....	55.3	−2.1	20.6	−17.5	94.1	94.7
of which: Short-term	4 774 ..	....	....	55.3	−1.2	20.6	−17.5	22.1	7.4
Other sectors	4 775 ..	−43.9	−133.8	18.0	−2,559.5	61.9	2,643.8	−664.6	1,011.5
of which: Short-term	4 777 ..	56.4	56.1	163.8	−1,913.6	17.4	6.5	−377.0	....
Currency and deposits	4 780 ..	....	....	−267.4	75.0	.4	42.7	44.4	519.1
Monetary authorities	4 781 ..	....	....	....	....	....	....	....	....
General government	4 782 ..	....	....	....	....	....	....	....	....
Banks	4 783 ..	....	....	−10.4	8.0	.4	42.7	44.4	519.1
Other sectors	4 784 ..	....	....	−257.0	67.0	....	....	....	....
Other liabilities	4 786 ..	181.3	279.6	7.2	−16.4	−2.6	4.5	−4.5	−106.1
Monetary authorities	4 787 ..	−141.6	17.1	....	....	....	....	....	....
of which: Short-term	4 789 ..	−141.6	17.1	....	....	....	....	....	....
General government	4 790 ..	253.1	262.5	....	....	....	....	....	−26.3
of which: Short-term	4 792 ..	253.1	262.5	....	....	....	....	....	−26.3
Banks	4 793 ..	....	....	7.2	−16.4	−2.6	4.5	−4.5	2.9
of which: Short-term	4 795 ..	....	....	7.2	−16.4	−2.6	4.5	−4.5	2.9
Other sectors	4 796 ..	69.8	....	....	....	....	....	....	−82.8
of which: Short-term	4 798 ..	69.8	....	....	....	....	....	....	−82.8
E. RESERVE ASSETS	4 802 ..	−631.3	466.3	356.3	−262.8	−780.3	−1,817.3	−5,401.7	−3,019.1
Monetary gold	4 812 ..	....	....	....	....	....	....	....	....
Special drawing rights	4 811 ..	....	....	....	....	....	....	....	....
Reserve position in the Fund	4 810 ..	....	....	....	....	....	....	....	....
Foreign exchange	4 803 ..	−631.3	466.4	356.3	−262.8	−780.2	−1,817.3	−5,401.7	−3,019.0
Other claims	4 813 ..	....	....	....	....	....	....	....	....
NET ERRORS AND OMISSIONS	4 998 ..	−50.6	−308.6	150.5	−388.2	277.3	−377.9	289.8	−461.7

Table 3. INTERNATIONAL INVESTMENT POSITION (End-period stocks), 2000–2007

(Millions of U.S. dollars)

	Code	2000	2001	2002	2003	2004	2005	2006	2007
ASSETS............	8 995 C.	....	....	....	2,934.4	5,771.6	9,414.4	18,217.5	25,846.1
Direct investment abroad............	8 505 ..	....	....	....	23.6	23.9	24.4	215.0	1,126.8
Equity capital and reinvested earnings............	8 506 ..	....	....	....	....	....	....	....	....
Claims on affiliated enterprises............	8 507 ..	....	....	....	....	....	....	....	....
Liabilities to affiliated enterprises............	8 508 ..	....	....	....	....	....	....	....	....
Other capital............	8 530 ..	....	....	....	....	....	....	....	....
Claims on affiliated enterprises............	8 535 ..	....	....	....	....	....	....	....	....
Liabilities to affiliated enterprisess............	8 540 ..	....	....	....	....	....	....	....	....
Portfolio investment............	8 602 ..	....	....	....	50.4	49.8	1,316.8	2,756.3	4,771.7
Equity securities............	8 610 ..	....	....	....	....	....	....	....	....
Monetary authorities............	8 611 ..	....	....	....	....	....	....	....	....
General government............	8 612 ..	....	....	....	....	....	....	....	....
Banks............	8 613 ..	....	....	....	....	....	....	....	....
Other sectors............	8 614 ..	....	....	....	....	....	....	....	....
Debt securities............	8 619 ..	....	....	....	....	....	....	....	....
Bonds and notes............	8 620 ..	....	....	....	....	....	....	....	....
Monetary authorities............	8 621 ..	....	....	....	....	....	....	....	....
General government............	8 622 ..	....	....	....	....	....	....	....	....
Banks............	8 623 ..	....	....	....	....	....	....	....	....
Other sectors............	8 624 ..	....	....	....	....	....	....	....	....
Money market instruments............	8 630 ..	....	....	....	....	....	....	....	....
Monetary authorities............	8 631 ..	....	....	....	....	....	....	....	....
General government............	8 632 ..	....	....	....	....	....	....	....	....
Banks............	8 633 ..	....	....	....	....	....	....	....	....
Other sectors............	8 634 ..	....	....	....	....	....	....	....	....
Financial derivatives............	8 900 ..	....	....	....	....	....	....	....	....
Monetary authorities............	8 901 ..	....	....	....	....	....	....	....	....
General government............	8 902 ..	....	....	....	....	....	....	....	....
Banks............	8 903 ..	....	....	....	....	....	....	....	....
Other sectors............	8 904 ..	....	....	....	....	....	....	....	....
Other investment............	8 703 ..	....	....	....	2,226.4	4,318.3	4,876.3	6,647.6	8,750.8
Trade credits............	8 706 ..	....	....	....	....	....	....	....	....
General government............	8 707 ..	....	....	....	....	....	....	....	....
of which: Short-term............	8 709 ..	....	....	....	....	....	....	....	....
Other sectors............	8 710 ..	....	....	....	....	....	....	....	....
of which: Short-term............	8 712 ..	....	....	....	....	....	....	....	....
Loans............	8 714 ..	....	....	....	14.3	14.4	5.2	12.2	5.1
Monetary authorities............	8 715 ..	....	....	....	....	....	....	....	....
of which: Short-term............	8 718 ..	....	....	....	....	....	....	....	....
General government............	8 719 ..	....	....	....	....	....	....	....	....
of which: Short-term............	8 721 ..	....	....	....	....	....	....	....	....
Banks............	8 722 ..	....	....	....	14.3	14.4	5.2	12.2	5.1
of which: Short-term............	8 724 ..	....	....	....	....	....	....	....	....
Other sectors............	8 725 ..	....	....	....	....	....	....	....	....
of which: Short-term............	8 727 ..	....	....	....	....	....	....	....	....
Currency and deposits............	8 730 ..	....	....	....	2,185.2	4,250.2	4,835.6	6,619.1	8,726.9
Monetary authorities............	8 731 ..	....	....	....	....	....	....	....	....
General government............	8 732 ..	....	....	....	....	....	....	....	....
Banks............	8 733 ..	....	....	....	1,172.2	1,216.0	1,614.4	3,070.9	3,033.3
Other sectors............	8 734 ..	....	....	....	1,013.0	3,034.2	3,221.2	3,548.2	5,693.6
Other assets............	8 736 ..	....	....	....	26.9	53.7	35.5	16.3	18.8
Monetary authorities............	8 737 ..	....	....	....	....	....	....	....	....
of which: Short-term............	8 739 ..	....	....	....	....	....	....	....	....
General government............	8 740 ..	....	....	....	....	....	....	....	....
of which: Short-term............	8 742 ..	....	....	....	....	....	....	....	....
Banks............	8 743 ..	....	....	....	26.9	53.7	35.5	16.3	18.8
of which: Short-term............	8 745 ..	....	....	....	....	....	....	....	....
Other sectors............	8 746 ..	....	....	....	....	....	....	....	....
of which: Short-term............	8 748 ..	....	....	....	....	....	....	....	....
Reserve assets............	8 802 ..	....	....	....	634.0	1,379.6	3,196.9	8,598.6	11,196.8
Monetary gold............	8 812 ..	....	....	....	....	....	....	....	....
Special drawing rights............	8 811 ..	.2	.2	.2	.2	.2	.2	.2	.3
Reserve position in the Fund............	8 810 ..	....	....	....	....	....	....	....	....
Foreign exchange............	8 803 ..	....	....	....	633.8	1,379.4	3,196.6	8,598.4	11,196.5
Other claims............	8 813 ..	....	....	....	....	....	....	....	....

Table 3 (Concluded). INTERNATIONAL INVESTMENT POSITION (End-period stocks), 2000–2007

(Millions of U.S. dollars)

	Code	2000	2001	2002	2003	2004	2005	2006	2007
LIABILITIES..	8 995 D.	....	....	....	**20,518.8**	**22,542.0**	**22,487.4**	**20,350.2**	**21,948.7**
Direct investment in Angola......................	8 555 ..	....	....	....	**11,987.5**	**13,436.7**	**12,132.9**	**12,170.6**	**11,201.8**
Equity capital and reinvested earnings...............	8 556 ..	....	....	....	....	....	....	....	....
Claims on direct investors........................	8 557 ..	....	....	....	....	....	....	....	....
Liabilities to direct investors....................	8 558 ..	....	....	....	....	....	....	....	....
Other capital..	8 580 ..	....	....	....	....	....	....	....	....
Claims on direct investors........................	8 585 ..	....	....	....	....	....	....	....	....
Liabilities to direct investors....................	8 590 ..	....	....	....	....	....	....	....	....
Portfolio investment............................	8 652 ..	....	....	....	....	....	....		....
Equity securities....................................	8 660 ..	....	....	....	....	....	....	....	....
Banks..	8 663 ..	....	....	....	....	....	....	....	....
Other sectors....................................	8 664 ..	....	....	....	....	....	....	....	....
Debt securities......................................	8 669 ..	....	....	....	....	....	....	....	....
Bonds and notes..................................	8 670 ..	....	....	....	....	....	....	....	....
Monetary authorities...........................	8 671 ..	....	....	....	....	....	....	....	....
General government.............................	8 672 ..	....	....	....	....	....	....	....	....
Banks...	8 673 ..	....	....	....	....	....	....	....	....
Other sectors.................................	8 674 ..	....	....	....	....	....	....	....	....
Money market instruments.........................	8 680 ..	....	....	....	....	....	....	....	....
Monetary authorities...........................	8 681 ..	....	....	....	....	....	....	....	....
General government.............................	8 682 ..	....	....	....	....	....	....	....	....
Banks...	8 683 ..	....	....	....	....	....	....	....	....
Other sectors.................................	8 684 ..	....	....	....	....	....	....	....	....
Financial derivatives...........................	8 905 ..	....	....	....	....	....	....		....
Monetary authorities................................	8 906 ..	....	....	....	....	....	....	....	....
General government..................................	8 907 ..	....	....	....	....	....	....	....	....
Banks...	8 908 ..	....	....	....	....	....	....	....	....
Other sectors.......................................	8 909 ..	....	....	....	....	....	....	....	....
Other investment...............................	8 753 ..	....	....	....	**8,531.3**	**9,105.3**	**10,354.6**	**8,179.6**	**10,746.9**
Trade credits..	8 756 ..	....	....	....	....	....	....	406.9	208.8
General government...............................	8 757 ..	....	....	....	....	....	....	....	....
of which: Short-term...........................	8 759 ..	....	....	....	....	....	....	....	....
Other sectors....................................	8 760 ..	....	....	....	....	....	....	406.9	208.8
of which: Short-term...........................	8 762 ..	....	....	....	....	....	....	....	....
Loans..	8 764 ..	....	....	....	8,512.6	9,088.9	10,292.4	7,670.7	9,122.9
Monetary authorities.............................	8 765 ..	....	....	....	22.0	7.1	7.2	17.3	12.0
General government ns from the Fund...........	8 766 ..	....	....	....	....	....	....	....	....
of which: Short-term.........................	8 768 ..	....	....	....	....	....	....	....	....
General government..............................	8 769 ..	....	....	....	6,974.4	7,477.0	6,104.5	4,056.9	4,595.9
of which: Short-term.........................	8 771 ..	....	....	....	....	....	....	....	....
Banks...	8 772 ..	....	....	....	72.1	92.8	75.2	187.9	293.0
of which: Short-term.........................	8 774 ..	....	....	....	....	....	....	....	....
Other sectors...................................	8 775 ..	....	....	....	1,444.1	1,512.0	4,105.5	3,408.7	4,222.0
of which: Short-term.........................	8 777 ..	....	....	....	....	....	....	....	....
Currency and deposits................................	8 780 ..	....	....	....	15.9	16.3	57.5	101.8	620.9
Monetary authorities.............................	8 781 ..	....	....	....	....	....	....	....	....
General government..............................	8 782 ..	....	....	....	....	....	....	....	....
Banks...	8 783 ..	....	....	....	15.9	16.3	57.5	101.8	620.9
Other sectors...................................	8 784 ..	....	....	....	....	....	....	....	....
Other liabilities....................................	8 786 ..	....	....	....	2.7	.1	4.6	.2	794.3
Monetary authorities.............................	8 787 ..	....	....	....	....	....	....	....	....
of which: Short-term..........................	8 789 ..	....	....	....	....	....	....	....	....
General government..............................	8 790 ..	....	....	....	....	....	....	....	709.0
of which: Short-term.........................	8 792 ..	....	....	....	....	....	....	....	....
Banks...	8 793 ..	....	....	....	2.7	.1	4.6	.2	16.6
of which: Short-term.........................	8 795 ..	....	....	....	....	....	....	....	....
Other sectors...................................	8 796 ..	....	....	....	....	....	....	....	68.7
of which: Short-term.........................	8 798 ..	....	....	....	....	....	....	....	....
NET INTERNATIONAL INVESTMENT POSITION........	8 995 ..	....	....	....	**−17,584.4**	**−16,770.4**	**−13,073.0**	**−2,132.7**	**3,897.4**
Conversion rates: kwanzas per U.S. dollar (end of period)..	0 102 ..	**16.818**	**31.949**	**58.666**	**79.081**	**85.988**	**80.780**	**80.264**	**75.023**

Table 1. ANALYTIC PRESENTATION, 2000–2007

(Millions of U.S. dollars)

	Code	2000	2001	2002	2003	2004	2005	2006	2007
A. Current Account[1]............................	4 993 Z.	**−60.97**	**−39.88**	**−35.89**	**−39.87**	**−47.40**	**−51.91**	**−172.19**	**−254.76**
Goods: exports f.o.b.	2 100 ..	4.44	3.56	4.38	4.26	6.02	15.02	12.27	13.74
Goods: imports f.o.b.	3 100 ..	−83.29	−68.50	−61.63	−67.60	−90.18	−114.29	−215.64	−280.32
Balance on Goods	4 100 ..	*−78.85*	*−64.93*	*−57.25*	*−63.34*	*−84.16*	*−99.28*	*−203.36*	*−266.58*
Services: credit	2 200 ..	64.93	70.41	65.54	72.70	77.90	98.69	123.88	138.14
Services: debit	3 200 ..	−40.86	−39.11	−38.66	−43.51	−46.56	−56.27	−100.66	−130.61
Balance on Goods and Services	4 991 ..	*−54.79*	*−33.64*	*−30.37*	*−34.15*	*−52.82*	*−56.85*	*−180.15*	*−259.06*
Income: credit	2 300 ..	3.97	1.86	1.56	1.87	7.66	11.68	14.98	17.04
Income: debit	3 300 ..	−13.16	−9.37	−7.96	−7.81	−6.88	−7.71	−7.18	−7.77
Balance on Goods, Services, and Income	4 992 ..	*−63.98*	*−41.14*	*−36.78*	*−40.09*	*−52.05*	*−52.88*	*−172.34*	*−249.78*
Current transfers: credit	2 379 Z.	11.15	9.83	9.25	10.40	14.37	10.74	14.34	11.44
Current transfers: debit	3 379 ..	−8.14	−8.57	−8.36	−10.17	−9.71	−9.77	−14.19	−16.42
B. Capital Account[1]............................	4 994 Z.	**9.75**	**8.81**	**8.00**	**7.83**	**8.19**	**12.81**	**17.88**	**13.42**
Capital account: credit	2 994 Z.	11.10	10.11	9.33	9.20	9.57	14.19	19.28	15.08
Capital account: debit	3 994 ..	−1.35	−1.30	−1.32	−1.38	−1.38	−1.38	−1.40	−1.66
Total, Groups A Plus B	4 981 ..	*−51.22*	*−31.07*	*−27.89*	*−32.04*	*−39.20*	*−39.09*	*−154.31*	*−241.33*
C. Financial Account[1]..........................	4 995 W.	**44.59**	**20.29**	**17.96**	**45.91**	**42.24**	**47.25**	**154.67**	**245.87**
Direct investment abroad	4 505 ..	....	....	....	....	....	....	....	....
Direct investment in Anguilla	4 555 Z.	39.71	29.62	33.24	29.39	86.73	117.31	163.97	217.07
Portfolio investment assets	4 602 ..	....	....	....	....	....	....	−.18	....
Equity securities	4 610 ..	....	....	....	....	....	....	....	....
Debt securities	4 619 ..	....	....	....	....	....	....	....	....
Portfolio investment liabilities	4 652 Z.	....	1.15	.01	−.22	1.17	.59	3.69	3.78
Equity securities	4 660 ..	....	....	....	....	....	....	....	....
Debt securities	4 669 Z.	....	....	....	....	....	....	....	....
Financial derivatives	4 910 ..	....	....	....	....	....	....	....	....
Financial derivatives assets	4 900 ..	....	....	....	....	....	....	....	....
Financial derivatives liabilities	4 905 ..	....	....	....	....	....	....	....	....
Other investment assets	4 703 ..	6.94	8.06	5.41	30.71	18.19	2.92	3.29	54.56
Monetary authorities	4 701 ..	....	....	....	....	....	....	....	....
General government	4 704 ..	....	....	....	....	....	....	....	....
Banks	4 705 ..	....	....	....	....	....	....	....	....
Other sectors	4 728 ..	....	....	....	....	....	....	....	....
Other investment liabilities	4 753 W.	−2.06	−18.54	−20.70	−13.97	−63.85	−73.57	−16.10	−29.54
Monetary authorities	4 753 WA	....	....	....	....	....	....	....	....
General government	4 753 ZB	....	....	....	....	....	....	....	....
Banks	4 753 ZC	....	....	....	....	....	....	....	....
Other sectors	4 753 ZD	....	....	....	....	....	....	....	....
Total, Groups A Through C	4 983 ..	*−6.62*	*−10.78*	*−9.93*	*13.87*	*3.03*	*8.15*	*.37*	*4.53*
D. Net Errors and Omissions..................	4 998 ..	**7.01**	**14.68**	**11.94**	**−6.79**	**−2.06**	**−2.70**	**1.75**	**−1.49**
Total, Groups A Through D	4 984 ..	*.39*	*3.89*	*2.01*	*7.08*	*.97*	*5.45*	*2.12*	*3.05*
E. Reserves and Related Items..............	4 802 A.	**−.39**	**−3.89**	**−2.01**	**−7.08**	**−.97**	**−5.45**	**−2.12**	**−3.05**
Reserve assets	4 802 ..	−.39	−3.89	−2.01	−7.08	−.97	−5.45	−2.12	−3.05
Use of Fund credit and loans	4 766 ..	....	....	....	....	....	....	....	....
Exceptional financing	4 920 ..	....	....	....	....	....	....	....	....
Conversion rates: Eastern Caribbean dollars per U.S. dollar..............	0 101 ..	**2.7000**	**2.7000**	**2.7000**	**2.7000**	**2.7000**	**2.7000**	**2.7000**	**2.7000**

[1] Excludes components that have been classified in the categories of Group E.

Table 2. STANDARD PRESENTATION, 2000–2007

(Millions of U.S. dollars)

	Code	2000	2001	2002	2003	2004	2005	2006	2007
CURRENT ACCOUNT	4 993	−60.97	−39.88	−35.89	−39.87	−47.40	−51.91	−172.19	−254.76
A. GOODS	4 100	−78.85	−64.93	−57.25	−63.34	−84.16	−99.28	−203.36	−266.58
Credit	2 100	4.44	3.56	4.38	4.26	6.02	15.02	12.27	13.74
General merchandise: exports f.o.b.	2 110	4.42	3.53	4.36	4.25	5.75	14.74	12.25	13.71
Goods for processing: exports f.o.b.	2 150	....	....	....	....	....	....	....	....
Repairs on goods	2 160	.01	.03	.02	....	....	....	....	....
Goods procured in ports by carriers	2 170	....	.01	.01	.01	.27	.27	.02	.02
Nonmonetary gold	2 180	....	....	....	....	....	....	....	....
Debit	3 100	−83.29	−68.50	−61.63	−67.60	−90.18	−114.29	−215.64	−280.32
General merchandise: imports f.o.b.	3 110	−83.17	−68.38	−61.51	−67.56	−90.15	−114.26	−215.59	−280.27
Goods for processing: imports f.o.b.	3 150	....	....	....	....	....	....	....	....
Repairs on goods	3 160	....	....	....	....	....	....	....	....
Goods procured in ports by carriers	3 170	−.11	−.12	−.12	−.04	−.04	−.04	−.04	−.05
Nonmonetary gold	3 180	....	....	....	....	....	....	....	....
B. SERVICES	4 200	24.07	31.30	26.88	29.20	31.34	42.42	23.22	7.52
Total credit	2 200	*64.93*	*70.41*	*65.54*	*72.70*	*77.90*	*98.69*	*123.88*	*138.14*
Total debit	3 200	*−40.86*	*−39.11*	*−38.66*	*−43.51*	*−46.56*	*−56.27*	*−100.66*	*−130.61*
Transportation services, credit	2 205	1.69	1.78	1.69	1.52	1.80	1.91	2.39	2.45
Passenger	2 850	....	....	....	....	....	....	....	....
Freight	2 851	....	....	....	....	....	....	....	....
Other	2 852	....	....	....	....	....	....	....	....
Sea transport, passenger	2 207	....	....	....	....	....	....	....	....
Sea transport, freight	2 208	....	....	....	....	....	....	....	....
Sea transport, other	2 209	....	....	....	....	....	....	....	....
Air transport, passenger	2 211	....	....	....	....	....	....	....	....
Air transport, freight	2 212	....	....	....	....	....	....	....	....
Air transport, other	2 213	....	....	....	....	....	....	....	....
Other transport, passenger	2 215	....	....	....	....	....	....	....	....
Other transport, freight	2 216	....	....	....	....	....	....	....	....
Other transport, other	2 217	....	....	....	....	....	....	....	....
Transportation services, debit	3 205	−14.27	−12.36	−10.49	−11.30	−13.23	−16.38	−29.24	−37.44
Passenger	3 850	....	....	....	....	....	....	....	....
Freight	3 851	....	....	....	....	....	....	....	....
Other	3 852	....	....	....	....	....	....	....	....
Sea transport, passenger	3 207	....	....	....	....	....	....	....	....
Sea transport, freight	3 208	....	....	....	....	....	....	....	....
Sea transport, other	3 209	....	....	....	....	....	....	....	....
Air transport, passenger	3 211	....	....	....	....	....	....	....	....
Air transport, freight	3 212	....	....	....	....	....	....	....	....
Air transport, other	3 213	....	....	....	....	....	....	....	....
Other transport, passenger	3 215	....	....	....	....	....	....	....	....
Other transport, freight	3 216	....	....	....	....	....	....	....	....
Other transport, other	3 217	....	....	....	....	....	....	....	....
Travel, credit	2 236	56.34	61.71	56.89	64.42	69.23	86.03	107.40	119.33
Business travel	2 237	....	....	....	....	....	....	....	....
Personal travel	2 240	....	....	....	....	....	....	....	....
Travel, debit	3 236	−8.64	−8.73	−8.34	−8.88	−9.05	−9.79	−12.58	−14.84
Business travel	3 237	....	....	....	....	....	....	....	....
Personal travel	3 240	....	....	....	....	....	....	....	....
Other services, credit	2 200 BA	6.90	6.92	6.96	6.76	6.87	10.74	14.10	16.37
Communications	2 245	1.63	1.52	1.78	1.18	1.10	1.21	1.28	1.51
Construction	2 249	....	....	....	....	....	....	....	....
Insurance	2 253	.43	.57	.56	1.06	1.13	.99	1.31	1.54
Financial	2 260	....	....	....	....	....	....	....	....
Computer and information	2 262	....	....	....	....	....	....	....	....
Royalties and licence fees	2 266	....	....	....	....	....	....	....	....
Other business services	2 268	3.27	3.67	3.39	3.21	3.44	7.10	9.86	11.63
Personal, cultural, and recreational	2 287	....	....	....	....	....	....	....	....
Government, n.i.e.	2 291	1.57	1.15	1.24	1.31	1.20	1.44	1.65	1.69
Other services, debit	3 200 BA	−17.96	−18.03	−19.84	−23.32	−24.28	−30.10	−58.85	−78.34
Communications	3 245	−1.79	−1.19	−1.20	−.92	−.78	−1.85	−1.94	−1.98
Construction	3 249	....	−.04	−1.64	−2.86	−5.48	−4.26	−28.27	−42.20
Insurance	3 253	−2.02	−1.75	−1.56	−2.05	−2.95	−3.06	−5.40	−6.96
Financial	3 260	....	....	....	....	....	....	....	....
Computer and information	3 262	....	....	....	....	....	−.07	−.09	....
Royalties and licence fees	3 266	....	....	−.22	−.21	−.23	−.39	−.40	−.47
Other business services	3 268	−12.70	−12.86	−12.41	−14.83	−13.19	−20.16	−21.94	−25.87
Personal, cultural, and recreational	3 287	....	....	....	....	....	....	....	....
Government, n.i.e.	3 291	−1.44	−2.20	−2.80	−2.44	−1.66	−.32	−.82	−.84

Table 2 (Continued). STANDARD PRESENTATION, 2000–2007

(Millions of U.S. dollars)

	Code	2000	2001	2002	2003	2004	2005	2006	2007
C. INCOME	4 300	**−9.19**	**−7.51**	**−6.40**	**−5.95**	**.77**	**3.97**	**7.80**	**9.28**
Total credit	2 300	*3.97*	*1.86*	*1.56*	*1.87*	*7.66*	*11.68*	*14.98*	*17.04*
Total debit	3 300	*−13.16*	*−9.37*	*−7.96*	*−7.81*	*−6.88*	*−7.71*	*−7.18*	*−7.77*
Compensation of employees, credit	2 310	....	....	.23	.48	3.83	2.98	3.71	3.80
Compensation of employees, debit	3 310	....	....	....	....	....	....	....	....
Investment income, credit	2 320	**3.97**	**1.86**	**1.33**	**1.38**	**3.82**	**8.70**	**11.28**	**13.25**
Direct investment income	2 330	.02	....	....	....	....	....	....	....
Dividends and distributed branch profits	2 332	....	....	....	....	....	....	....	....
Reinvested earnings and undistributed branch profits	2 333	....	....	....	....	....	....	....	....
Income on debt (interest)	2 334	.02	....	....	....	....	....	....	....
Portfolio investment income	2 339	.22	.38	.10	.17	.71	.87	2.09	2.47
Income on equity	2 340	.22	.38	.10	.17	.71	.87	2.09	2.47
Income on bonds and notes	2 350	....	....	....	....	....	....	....	....
Income on money market instruments	2 360	....	....	....	....	....	....	....	....
Other investment income	2 370	3.72	1.49	1.23	1.21	3.11	7.84	9.18	10.77
Investment income, debit	3 320	**−13.16**	**−9.37**	**−7.96**	**−7.81**	**−6.88**	**−7.71**	**−7.18**	**−7.77**
Direct investment income	3 330	−10.04	−8.01	−6.83	−6.47	−4.57	−4.46	−4.17	−4.37
Dividends and distributed branch profits	3 332	−4.03	−4.91	−2.92	−1.24	−1.74	−2.75	−.51	−.60
Reinvested earnings and undistributed branch profits	3 333	−5.80	−2.94	−3.72	−5.06	−2.66	−1.60	−3.56	−3.65
Income on debt (interest)	3 334	−.21	−.16	−.19	−.17	−.17	−.11	−.11	−.12
Portfolio investment income	3 339	....	....	....	....	....	....	....	....
Income on equity	3 340	....	....	....	....	....	....	....	....
Income on bonds and notes	3 350	....	....	....	....	....	....	....	....
Income on money market instruments	3 360	....	....	....	....	....	....	....	....
Other investment income	3 370	−3.12	−1.36	−1.13	−1.35	−2.31	−3.25	−3.01	−3.40
D. CURRENT TRANSFERS	4 379	**3.01**	**1.27**	**.89**	**.23**	**4.65**	**.97**	**.15**	**−4.97**
Credit	2 379	**11.15**	**9.83**	**9.25**	**10.40**	**14.37**	**10.74**	**14.34**	**11.44**
General government	2 380	2.09	3.19	3.18	4.33	7.94	3.90	7.08	4.00
Other sectors	2 390	9.06	6.65	6.07	6.07	6.42	6.84	7.26	7.44
Workers' remittances	2 391	5.74	5.79	5.89	6.02	6.22	6.39	6.59	6.75
Other current transfers	2 392	3.32	.86	.18	.06	.20	.45	.67	.69
Debit	3 379	**−8.14**	**−8.57**	**−8.36**	**−10.17**	**−9.71**	**−9.77**	**−14.19**	**−16.42**
General government	3 380	−.56	−.63	−.79	−.63	−.63	−.48	−.75	−.57
Other sectors	3 390	−7.58	−7.94	−7.57	−9.54	−9.09	−9.29	−13.44	−15.85
Workers' remittances	3 391	−7.57	−7.93	−6.43	−6.54	−6.87	−7.22	−10.82	−12.77
Other current transfers	3 392	−.01	−.01	−1.15	−3.00	−2.22	−2.08	−2.62	−3.09
CAPITAL AND FINANCIAL ACCOUNT	4 996	**53.96**	**25.20**	**23.94**	**46.66**	**49.46**	**54.61**	**170.44**	**256.24**
CAPITAL ACCOUNT	4 994	**9.75**	**8.81**	**8.00**	**7.83**	**8.19**	**12.81**	**17.88**	**13.42**
Total credit	2 994	*11.10*	*10.11*	*9.33*	*9.20*	*9.57*	*14.19*	*19.28*	*15.08*
Total debit	3 994	*−1.35*	*−1.30*	*−1.32*	*−1.38*	*−1.38*	*−1.38*	*−1.40*	*−1.66*
Capital transfers, credit	2 400	**11.10**	**10.11**	**9.33**	**9.20**	**9.57**	**14.19**	**19.28**	**15.08**
General government	2 401	3.63	2.29	1.50	1.23	1.20	1.64	5.48	.93
Debt forgiveness	2 402	....	....	....	....	....	....	....	....
Other capital transfers	2 410	3.63	2.29	1.50	1.23	1.20	1.64	5.48	.93
Other sectors	2 430	7.47	7.83	7.83	7.97	8.37	12.55	13.81	14.15
Migrants' transfers	2 431	7.47	7.83	7.83	7.97	8.37	12.55	13.81	14.15
Debt forgiveness	2 432	....	....	....	....	....	....	....	....
Other capital transfers	2 440	....	....	....	....	....	....	....	....
Capital transfers, debit	3 400	**−1.35**	**−1.30**	**−1.32**	**−1.38**	**−1.38**	**−1.38**	**−1.40**	**−1.66**
General government	3 401	....	....	....	....	....	....	....	....
Debt forgiveness	3 402	....	....	....	....	....	....	....	....
Other capital transfers	3 410	....	....	....	....	....	....	....	....
Other sectors	3 430	−1.35	−1.30	−1.32	−1.38	−1.38	−1.38	−1.40	−1.66
Migrants' transfers	3 431	−1.35	−1.30	−1.32	−1.38	−1.38	−1.38	−1.40	−1.66
Debt forgiveness	3 432	....	....	....	....	....	....	....	....
Other capital transfers	3 440	....	....	....	....	....	....	....	....
Nonproduced nonfinancial assets, credit	2 480	....	....	....	....	....	....	....	....
Nonproduced nonfinancial assets, debit	3 480	....	....	....	....	....	....	....	....

Table 2 (Continued). STANDARD PRESENTATION, 2000–2007

(Millions of U.S. dollars)

	Code	2000	2001	2002	2003	2004	2005	2006	2007
FINANCIAL ACCOUNT...	4 995 ..	**44.21**	**16.39**	**15.94**	**38.83**	**41.27**	**41.80**	**152.56**	**242.82**
A. DIRECT INVESTMENT.......................................	4 500 ..	**39.71**	**29.62**	**33.24**	**29.39**	**86.73**	**117.31**	**163.97**	**217.07**
Direct investment abroad...................................	4 505 ..	....	....	....	....	....	....	....	....
Equity capital...	4 510 ..	....	....	....	....	....	....	....	....
Claims on affiliated enterprises.....................	4 515 ..	....	....	....	....	....	....	....	....
Liabilities to affiliated enterprises.................	4 520 ..	....	....	....	....	....	....	....	....
Reinvested earnings.......................................	4 525 ..	....	....	....	....	....	....	....	....
Other capital..	4 530 ..	....	....	....	....	....	....	....	....
Claims on affiliated enterprises.....................	4 535 ..	....	....	....	....	....	....	....	....
Liabilities to affiliated enterprises.................	4 540 ..	....	....	....	....	....	....	....	....
Direct investment in Anguilla...........................	4 555 ..	**39.71**	**29.62**	**33.24**	**29.39**	**86.73**	**117.31**	**163.97**	**217.07**
Equity capital...	4 560 ..	35.31	23.22	19.41	6.34	21.47	89.93	94.22	140.68
Claims on direct investors...........................	4 565 ..	....	....	....	....	....	....	....	....
Liabilities to direct investors.......................	4 570 ..	35.31	23.22	19.41	6.34	21.47	89.93	94.22	140.68
Reinvested earnings.......................................	4 575 ..	5.80	2.94	3.72	5.06	2.66	1.60	3.56	3.65
Other capital..	4 580 ..	−1.39	3.46	10.11	17.99	62.59	25.77	66.19	72.74
Claims on direct investors...........................	4 585 ..	....	....	....	....	....	....	....	....
Liabilities to direct investors.......................	4 590 ..	−1.39	3.46	10.11	17.99	62.59	25.77	66.19	72.74
B. PORTFOLIO INVESTMENT................................	4 600 ..	....	**1.15**	**.01**	**−.22**	**1.17**	**.59**	**3.51**	**3.78**
Assets...	4 602 ..	....	....	....	....	....	....	−.18	....
Equity securities...	4 610 ..	....	....	....	....	....	....	....	....
Monetary authorities..................................	4 611 ..	....	....	....	....	....	....	....	....
General government...................................	4 612 ..	....	....	....	....	....	....	....	....
Banks..	4 613 ..	....	....	....	....	....	....	....	....
Other sectors..	4 614 ..	....	....	....	....	....	....	....	....
Debt securities..	4 619 ..	....	....	....	....	....	....	....	....
Bonds and notes..	4 620 ..	....	....	....	....	....	....	....	....
Monetary authorities.................................	4 621 ..	....	....	....	....	....	....	....	....
General government..................................	4 622 ..	....	....	....	....	....	....	....	....
Banks...	4 623 ..	....	....	....	....	....	....	....	....
Other sectors...	4 624 ..	....	....	....	....	....	....	....	....
Money market instruments...........................	4 630 ..	....	....	....	....	....	....	....	....
Monetary authorities.................................	4 631 ..	....	....	....	....	....	....	....	....
General government..................................	4 632 ..	....	....	....	....	....	....	....	....
Banks...	4 633 ..	....	....	....	....	....	....	....	....
Other sectors...	4 634 ..	....	....	....	....	....	....	....	....
Liabilities...	4 652 ..	....	**1.15**	**.01**	**−.22**	**1.17**	**.59**	**3.69**	**3.78**
Equity securities...	4 660 ..	....	....	....	....	....	....	....	....
Banks..	4 663 ..	....	....	....	....	....	....	....	....
Other sectors..	4 664 ..	....	....	....	....	....	....	....	....
Debt securities..	4 669 ..	....	....	....	....	....	....	....	....
Bonds and notes..	4 670 ..	....	....	....	....	....	....	....	....
Monetary authorities.................................	4 671 ..	....	....	....	....	....	....	....	....
General government..................................	4 672 ..	....	....	....	....	....	....	....	....
Banks...	4 673 ..	....	....	....	....	....	....	....	....
Other sectors...	4 674 ..	....	....	....	....	....	....	....	....
Money market instruments...........................	4 680 ..	....	....	....	....	....	....	....	....
Monetary authorities.................................	4 681 ..	....	....	....	....	....	....	....	....
General government..................................	4 682 ..	....	....	....	....	....	....	....	....
Banks...	4 683 ..	....	....	....	....	....	....	....	....
Other sectors...	4 684 ..	....	....	....	....	....	....	....	....
C. FINANCIAL DERIVATIVES................................	4 910 ..	....	....	....	....	....	....	....	....
Monetary authorities.....................................	4 911 ..	....	....	....	....	....	....	....	....
General government......................................	4 912 ..	....	....	....	....	....	....	....	....
Banks..	4 913 ..	....	....	....	....	....	....	....	....
Other sectors...	4 914 ..	....	....	....	....	....	....	....	....
Assets...	4 900 ..	....	....	....	....	....	....	....	....
Monetary authorities.....................................	4 901 ..	....	....	....	....	....	....	....	....
General government......................................	4 902 ..	....	....	....	....	....	....	....	....
Banks..	4 903 ..	....	....	....	....	....	....	....	....
Other sectors...	4 904 ..	....	....	....	....	....	....	....	....
Liabilities...	4 905 ..	....	....	....	....	....	....	....	....
Monetary authorities.....................................	4 906 ..	....	....	....	....	....	....	....	....
General government......................................	4 907 ..	....	....	....	....	....	....	....	....
Banks..	4 908 ..	....	....	....	....	....	....	....	....
Other sectors...	4 909 ..	....	....	....	....	....	....	....	....

Table 2 (Concluded). STANDARD PRESENTATION, 2000–2007

(Millions of U.S. dollars)

	Code	2000	2001	2002	2003	2004	2005	2006	2007
D. OTHER INVESTMENT....................................	4 700 ..	**4.88**	**−10.48**	**−15.29**	**16.74**	**−45.66**	**−70.65**	**−12.81**	**25.02**
Assets..	4 703 ..	**6.94**	**8.06**	**5.41**	**30.71**	**18.19**	**2.92**	**3.29**	**54.56**
Trade credits..	4 706 ..	....	....	....	....	....	....	....	....
General government........................	4 707 ..	....	....	....	....	....	....	....	....
of which: Short-term.................	4 709 ..	....	....	....	....	....	....	....	....
Other sectors...............................	4 710 ..	....	....	....	....	....	....	....	....
of which: Short-term.................	4 712 ..	....	....	....	....	....	....	....	....
Loans..	4 714 ..	....	....	....	....	....	....	....	....
Monetary authorities......................	4 715 ..	....	....	....	....	....	....	....	....
of which: Short-term.................	4 718 ..	....	....	....	....	....	....	....	....
General government........................	4 719 ..	....	....	....	....	....	....	....	....
of which: Short-term.................	4 721 ..	....	....	....	....	....	....	....	....
Banks..	4 722 ..	....	....	....	....	....	....	....	....
of which: Short-term.................	4 724 ..	....	....	....	....	....	....	....	....
Other sectors...............................	4 725 ..	....	....	....	....	....	....	....	....
of which: Short-term.................	4 727 ..	....	....	....	....	....	....	....	....
Currency and deposits.........................	4 730 ..	....	....	....	....	....	....	....	....
Monetary authorities......................	4 731 ..	....	....	....	....	....	....	....	....
General government........................	4 732 ..	....	....	....	....	....	....	....	....
Banks..	4 733 ..	....	....	....	....	....	....	....	....
Other sectors...............................	4 734 ..	....	....	....	....	....	....	....	....
Other assets.....................................	4 736 ..	....	....	....	....	....	....	....	....
Monetary authorities......................	4 737 ..	....	....	....	....	....	....	....	....
of which: Short-term.................	4 739 ..	....	....	....	....	....	....	....	....
General government........................	4 740 ..	....	....	....	....	....	....	....	....
of which: Short-term.................	4 742 ..	....	....	....	....	....	....	....	....
Banks..	4 743 ..	....	....	....	....	....	....	....	....
of which: Short-term.................	4 745 ..	....	....	....	....	....	....	....	....
Other sectors...............................	4 746 ..	....	....	....	....	....	....	....	....
of which: Short-term.................	4 748 ..	....	....	....	....	....	....	....	....
Liabilities..	4 753 ..	**−2.06**	**−18.54**	**−20.70**	**−13.97**	**−63.85**	**−73.57**	**−16.10**	**−29.54**
Trade credits..	4 756 ..	....	....	....	....	....	....	....	....
General government........................	4 757 ..	....	....	....	....	....	....	....	....
of which: Short-term.................	4 759 ..	....	....	....	....	....	....	....	....
Other sectors...............................	4 760 ..	....	....	....	....	....	....	....	....
of which: Short-term.................	4 762 ..	....	....	....	....	....	....	....	....
Loans..	4 764 ..	....	....	....	....	....	....	....	....
Monetary authorities......................	4 765 ..	....	....	....	....	....	....	....	....
of which: Use of Fund credit and loans from the Fund..	4 766 ..	....	....	....	....	....	....	....	....
of which: Short-term.................	4 768 ..	....	....	....	....	....	....	....	....
General government........................	4 769 ..	....	....	....	....	....	....	....	....
of which: Short-term.................	4 771 ..	....	....	....	....	....	....	....	....
Banks..	4 772 ..	....	....	....	....	....	....	....	....
of which: Short-term.................	4 774 ..	....	....	....	....	....	....	....	....
Other sectors...............................	4 775 ..	....	....	....	....	....	....	....	....
of which: Short-term.................	4 777 ..	....	....	....	....	....	....	....	....
Currency and deposits.........................	4 780 ..	....	....	....	....	....	....	....	....
Monetary authorities......................	4 781 ..	....	....	....	....	....	....	....	....
General government........................	4 782 ..	....	....	....	....	....	....	....	....
Banks..	4 783 ..	....	....	....	....	....	....	....	....
Other sectors...............................	4 784 ..	....	....	....	....	....	....	....	....
Other liabilities.................................	4 786 ..	....	....	....	....	....	....	....	....
Monetary authorities......................	4 787 ..	....	....	....	....	....	....	....	....
of which: Short-term.................	4 789 ..	....	....	....	....	....	....	....	....
General government........................	4 790 ..	....	....	....	....	....	....	....	....
of which: Short-term.................	4 792 ..	....	....	....	....	....	....	....	....
Banks..	4 793 ..	....	....	....	....	....	....	....	....
of which: Short-term.................	4 795 ..	....	....	....	....	....	....	....	....
Other sectors...............................	4 796 ..	....	....	....	....	....	....	....	....
of which: Short-term.................	4 798 ..	....	....	....	....	....	....	....	....
E. RESERVE ASSETS....................................	4 802 ..	**−.39**	**−3.89**	**−2.01**	**−7.08**	**−.97**	**−5.45**	**−2.12**	**−3.05**
Monetary gold.......................................	4 812 ..	....	....	....	....	....	....	....	....
Special drawing rights...........................	4 811 ..	....	....	....	....	....	....	....	....
Reserve position in the Fund....................	4 810 ..	....	....	....	....	....	....	....	....
Foreign exchange.................................	4 803 ..	−.39	−3.89	−2.01	−7.08	−.97	−5.45	−2.12	−3.05
Other claims.......................................	4 813 ..	....	....	....	....	....	....	....	....
NET ERRORS AND OMISSIONS............................	4 998 ..	**7.01**	**14.68**	**11.94**	**−6.79**	**−2.06**	**−2.70**	**1.75**	**−1.49**

Table 1. ANALYTIC PRESENTATION, 2000–2007

(Millions of U.S. dollars)

	Code	2000	2001	2002	2003	2004	2005	2006	2007
A. Current Account[1].................	4 993 Z.	**−66.77**	**−56.89**	**−82.41**	**−97.56**	**−95.73**	**−171.33**	**−309.09**	**−401.72**
Goods: exports f.o.b...................	2 100 ..	52.36	44.66	33.65	44.73	57.13	82.52	74.03	83.13
Goods: imports f.o.b...................	3 100 ..	−342.39	−317.50	−302.99	−352.28	−402.36	−455.35	−559.70	−653.07
Balance on Goods.....................	4 100 ..	*−290.03*	*−272.84*	*−269.35*	*−307.56*	*−345.23*	*−372.83*	*−485.67*	*−569.94*
Services: credit..........................	2 200 ..	414.50	400.68	394.22	417.91	476.84	462.53	477.44	497.57
Services: debit...........................	3 200 ..	−156.07	−169.07	−171.45	−182.47	−189.98	−226.63	−258.71	−294.16
Balance on Goods and Services.........	4 991 ..	*−31.60*	*−41.24*	*−46.57*	*−72.11*	*−58.37*	*−136.93*	*−266.95*	*−366.53*
Income: credit...........................	2 300 ..	15.52	18.68	8.09	8.61	11.54	17.96	26.71	31.04
Income: debit............................	3 300 ..	−60.04	−43.47	−49.54	−47.31	−57.25	−60.36	−90.78	−86.84
Balance on Goods, Services, and Income.........	4 992 ..	*−76.12*	*−66.03*	*−88.02*	*−110.81*	*−104.08*	*−179.33*	*−331.02*	*−422.32*
Current transfers: credit...............	2 379 Z.	18.43	22.52	22.97	29.46	25.10	26.17	41.08	42.11
Current transfers: debit...............	3 379 ..	−9.09	−13.39	−17.36	−16.21	−16.75	−18.17	−19.15	−21.51
B. Capital Account[1].................	4 994 Z.	**39.33**	**11.93**	**13.92**	**10.19**	**21.30**	**214.33**	**31.57**	**11.11**
Capital account: credit...............	2 994 Z.	39.33	11.93	13.92	10.19	21.30	214.33	31.57	11.11
Capital account: debit...............	3 994 ..	....	....	....	....	....	....	....	....
Total, Groups A Plus B.................	4 981 ..	*−27.45*	*−44.96*	*−68.48*	*−87.37*	*−74.43*	*42.99*	*−277.51*	*−390.61*
C. Financial Account[1].................	4 995 W.	**42.07**	**60.16**	**101.54**	**100.02**	**99.46**	**−31.94**	**295.53**	**395.20**
Direct investment abroad...............	4 505 ..	....	....	....	....	....	....	....	....
Direct investment in Antigua & Barbuda........	4 555 Z.	43.12	98.45	65.87	166.32	80.37	213.56	374.38	390.95
Portfolio investment assets...............	4 602 ..	−.01	−.05	−2.92	−.03	−1.38	.47	....	....
Equity securities.......................	4 610 ..	....	....	....	....	....	....	....	....
Debt securities........................	4 619 ..	....	....	....	....	....	....	....	....
Portfolio investment liabilities...............	4 652 Z.	2.35	−2.46	.75	2.67	13.48	10.06	24.78	−6.02
Equity securities.......................	4 660 ..	....	....	....	....	....	....	....	....
Debt securities........................	4 669 Z.	....	....	....	....	....	....	....	....
Financial derivatives...................	4 910 ..	....	....	....	....	....	....	....	....
Financial derivatives assets...............	4 900 ..	....	....	....	....	....	....	....	....
Financial derivatives liabilities...............	4 905 ..	....	....	....	....	....	....	....	....
Other investment assets...............	4 703 ..	86.71	53.83	80.09	85.38	80.67	60.10	74.12	88.27
Monetary authorities...................	4 701 ..	....	....	....	....	....	....	....	....
General government...................	4 704 ..	....	....	....	....	....	....	....	....
Banks..................................	4 705 ..	....	....	....	....	....	....	....	....
Other sectors........................	4 728 ..	....	....	....	....	....	....	....	....
Other investment liabilities...............	4 753 W.	−90.10	−89.62	−42.24	−154.32	−73.68	−316.12	−177.75	−78.00
Monetary authorities...................	4 753 WA	....	....	....	....	....	....	....	....
General government...................	4 753 ZB	....	....	....	....	....	....	....	....
Banks..................................	4 753 ZC	....	....	....	....	....	....	....	....
Other sectors........................	4 753 ZD	....	....	....	....	....	....	....	....
Total, Groups A Through C.................	4 983 ..	*14.62*	*15.19*	*33.06*	*12.65*	*25.03*	*11.06*	*18.01*	*4.59*
D. Net Errors and Omissions...................	4 998 ..	**−20.78**	**.80**	**−25.33**	**13.50**	**−18.61**	**−3.82**	**−2.76**	**−3.76**
Total, Groups A Through D.................	4 984 ..	*−6.16*	*16.00*	*7.73*	*26.15*	*6.42*	*7.24*	*15.26*	*.83*
E. Reserves and Related Items...................	4 802 A.	**6.16**	**−16.00**	**−7.73**	**−26.15**	**−6.42**	**−7.24**	**−15.26**	**−.83**
Reserve assets........................	4 802 ..	6.16	−16.00	−7.73	−26.15	−6.42	−7.24	−15.26	−.83
Use of Fund credit and loans...............	4 766 ..	....	....	....	....	....	....	....	....
Exceptional financing...................	4 920 ..	....	....	....	....	....	....	....	....
Conversion rates: Eastern Caribbean dollars per U.S. dollar...................	0 101 ..	2.7000	2.7000	2.7000	2.7000	2.7000	2.7000	2.7000	2.7000

[1] Excludes components that have been classified in the categories of Group E.

Table 2. STANDARD PRESENTATION, 2000–2007

(Millions of U.S. dollars)

	Code	2000	2001	2002	2003	2004	2005	2006	2007
CURRENT ACCOUNT...	4 993 ..	**−66.77**	**−56.89**	**−82.41**	**−97.56**	**−95.73**	**−171.33**	**−309.09**	**−401.72**
A. GOODS...	4 100 ..	**−290.03**	**−272.84**	**−269.35**	**−307.56**	**−345.23**	**−372.83**	**−485.67**	**−569.94**
Credit...	2 100 ..	**52.36**	**44.66**	**33.65**	**44.73**	**57.13**	**82.52**	**74.03**	**83.13**
General merchandise: exports f.o.b..........................	2 110 ..	23.77	20.53	11.57	18.30	21.42	35.24	23.30	26.16
Goods for processing: exports f.o.b..........................	2 150 ..	....	....	....	....	....	....	....	....
Repairs on goods...	2 160 ..	.01	.01	.01	....	.07	.07	.03	.04
Goods procured in ports by carriers..........................	2 170 ..	28.58	24.12	22.07	26.42	35.64	47.22	50.70	56.93
Nonmonetary gold..	2 180 ..	....	....	....	....	....	....	....	....
Debit...	3 100 ..	**−342.39**	**−317.50**	**−302.99**	**−352.28**	**−402.36**	**−455.35**	**−559.70**	**−653.07**
General merchandise: imports f.o.b..........................	3 110 ..	−338.29	−310.09	−295.85	−344.36	−393.56	−444.36	−547.86	−639.77
Goods for processing: imports f.o.b..........................	3 150 ..	....	....	....	....	....	....	....	....
Repairs on goods...	3 160 ..	....	....	....	....	....	....	....	....
Goods procured in ports by carriers..........................	3 170 ..	−4.10	−7.41	−7.14	−7.92	−8.80	−11.00	−11.84	−13.30
Nonmonetary gold..	3 180 ..	....	....	....	....	....	....	....	....
B. SERVICES..	4 200 ..	**258.43**	**231.60**	**222.77**	**235.45**	**286.86**	**235.90**	**218.73**	**203.41**
Total credit	2 200 ..	*414.50*	*400.68*	*394.22*	*417.91*	*476.84*	*462.53*	*477.44*	*497.57*
Total debit	3 200 ..	*−156.07*	*−169.07*	*−171.45*	*−182.47*	*−189.98*	*−226.63*	*−258.71*	*−294.16*
Transportation services, credit.........................	2 205 ..	**65.72**	**74.06**	**76.17**	**74.60**	**79.75**	**84.63**	**80.15**	**82.15**
Passenger...	2 850 ..	....	....	....	....	....	....	....	....
Freight..	2 851 ..	....	....	....	....	....	....	....	....
Other..	2 852 ..	....	....	....	....	....	....	....	....
Sea transport, passenger.......................................	2 207 ..	....	....	....	....	....	....	....	....
Sea transport, freight...	2 208 ..	....	....	....	....	....	....	....	....
Sea transport, other...	2 209 ..	....	....	....	....	....	....	....	....
Air transport, passenger...	2 211 ..	....	....	....	....	....	....	....	....
Air transport, freight...	2 212 ..	....	....	....	....	....	....	....	....
Air transport, other...	2 213 ..	....	....	....	....	....	....	....	....
Other transport, passenger.....................................	2 215 ..	....	....	....	....	....	....	....	....
Other transport, freight...	2 216 ..	....	....	....	....	....	....	....	....
Other transport, other...	2 217 ..	....	....	....	....	....	....	....	....
Transportation services, debit...........................	3 205 ..	**−56.52**	**−57.37**	**−56.43**	**−61.39**	**−66.09**	**−78.02**	**−87.85**	**−101.44**
Passenger...	3 850 ..	....	....	....	....	....	....	....	....
Freight..	3 851 ..	....	....	....	....	....	....	....	....
Other..	3 852 ..	....	....	....	....	....	....	....	....
Sea transport, passenger.......................................	3 207 ..	....	....	....	....	....	....	....	....
Sea transport, freight...	3 208 ..	....	....	....	....	....	....	....	....
Sea transport, other...	3 209 ..	....	....	....	....	....	....	....	....
Air transport, passenger...	3 211 ..	....	....	....	....	....	....	....	....
Air transport, freight...	3 212 ..	....	....	....	....	....	....	....	....
Air transport, other...	3 213 ..	....	....	....	....	....	....	....	....
Other transport, passenger.....................................	3 215 ..	....	....	....	....	....	....	....	....
Other transport, freight...	3 216 ..	....	....	....	....	....	....	....	....
Other transport, other...	3 217 ..	....	....	....	....	....	....	....	....
Travel, credit..	2 236 ..	**290.54**	**272.07**	**273.77**	**299.82**	**337.32**	**309.45**	**326.75**	**337.77**
Business travel...	2 237 ..	....	....	....	....	....	....	....	....
Personal travel...	2 240 ..	....	....	....	....	....	....	....	....
Travel, debit..	3 236 ..	**−30.70**	**−31.55**	**−33.09**	**−34.82**	**−37.50**	**−40.05**	**−45.34**	**−50.91**
Business travel...	3 237 ..	....	....	....	....	....	....	....	....
Personal travel...	3 240 ..	....	....	....	....	....	....	....	....
Other services, credit.......................................	2 200 BA	**58.25**	**54.55**	**44.27**	**43.50**	**59.78**	**68.45**	**70.54**	**77.65**
Communications...	2 245 ..	18.33	15.89	9.88	8.83	8.06	8.06	8.06	9.05
Construction...	2 249 ..	....	....	....	....	....	....	....	....
Insurance...	2 253 ..	15.91	11.98	8.89	5.69	13 85	15.50	10.98	12.33
Financial..	2 260 ..	....	....	....	....	....	....	....	....
Computer and information..	2 262 ..	....	....	....	....	....	....	....	....
Royalties and licence fees.......................................	2 266 ..	....	....	....	....	....	....	....	....
Other business services..	2 268 ..	15.11	18.88	20.21	23.77	31.47	36.45	39.53	44.00
Personal, cultural, and recreational..........................	2 287 ..	....	....	....	....	....	....	....	....
Government, n.i.e...	2 291 ..	8.89	7.80	5.29	5.21	6.40	8.43	11.97	12.27
Other services, debit...	3 200 BA	**−68.85**	**−80.16**	**−81.92**	**−86.25**	**−86.39**	**−108.55**	**−125.52**	**−141.80**
Communications...	3 245 ..	−13.48	−7.00	−5.97	−5.29	−5.03	−5.03	−5.03	−5.15
Construction...	3 249 ..	−2.33	−2.37	−3.43	−3.47	−1.44	−17.08	−25.09	−29.36
Insurance...	3 253 ..	−15.69	−27.79	−30.76	−31.18	−31.63	−36.48	−44.89	−50.84
Financial..	3 260 ..	....	....	....	....	....	....	....	....
Computer and information..	3 262 ..	....	....	....	−.02	....	....	....	....
Royalties and licence fees.......................................	3 266 ..	−.29	−.47	−.51	−.51	−.53	−.58	−.77	−.86
Other business services..	3 268 ..	−27.56	−32.93	−33.07	−37.63	−39.69	−40.44	−40.34	−45.30
Personal, cultural, and recreational..........................	3 287 ..	....	....	....	....	....	....	....	....
Government, n.i.e...	3 291 ..	−9.50	−9.60	−8.18	−8.14	−8.08	−8.95	−9.40	−10.28

Table 2 (Continued). STANDARD PRESENTATION, 2000–2007

(Millions of U.S. dollars)

	Code	2000	2001	2002	2003	2004	2005	2006	2007
C. INCOME	4 300 ..	**−44.52**	**−24.79**	**−41.45**	**−38.70**	**−45.71**	**−42.40**	**−64.07**	**−55.79**
Total credit	2 300 ..	*15.52*	*18.68*	*8.09*	*8.61*	*11.54*	*17.96*	*26.71*	*31.04*
Total debit	3 300 ..	*−60.04*	*−43.47*	*−49.54*	*−47.31*	*−57.25*	*−60.36*	*−90.78*	*−86.84*
Compensation of employees, credit	2 310 ..	**6.65**	**12.99**	**3.32**	**5.22**	**6.16**	**6.56**	**7.22**	**7.40**
Compensation of employees, debit	3 310 ..	....	....	....	....	....	....	....	....
Investment income, credit	2 320 ..	**8.87**	**5.70**	**4.77**	**3.39**	**5.38**	**11.40**	**19.49**	**23.65**
Direct investment income	2 330 ..	....	....	....	....	....	....	....	....
Dividends and distributed branch profits	2 332 ..	....	....	....	....	....	....	....	....
Reinvested earnings and undistributed branch profits	2 333 ..	....	....	....	....	....	....	....	....
Income on debt (interest)	2 334 ..	....	....	....	....	....	....	....	....
Portfolio investment income	2 339 ..	1.19	1.19	.72	.69	.05	.08	1.50	1.54
Income on equity	2 340 ..	1.19	1.19	.72	.69	.05	.08	1.50	1.54
Income on bonds and notes	2 350 ..	....	....	....	....	....	....	....	....
Income on money market instruments	2 360 ..	....	....	....	....	....	....	....	....
Other investment income	2 370 ..	7.68	4.51	4.06	2.70	5.33	11.32	17.99	22.11
Investment income, debit	3 320 ..	**−60.04**	**−43.47**	**−49.54**	**−47.31**	**−57.25**	**−60.36**	**−90.78**	**−86.84**
Direct investment income	3 330 ..	−22.25	−26.22	−24.13	−23.88	−24.68	−30.69	−41.55	−46.66
Dividends and distributed branch profits	3 332 ..	−13.90	−10.84	−12.31	−11.60	−11.04	−15.57	−29.69	−33.34
Reinvested earnings and undistributed branch profits	3 333 ..	−7.48	−11.73	−8.33	−9.00	−11.27	−12.86	−8.59	−9.65
Income on debt (interest)	3 334 ..	−.87	−3.65	−3.49	−3.27	−2.37	−2.26	−3.27	−3.68
Portfolio investment income	3 339 ..	....	....	....	....	....	....	−2.64	−2.27
Income on equity	3 340 ..	....	....	....	....	....	....	−2.64	−2.27
Income on bonds and notes	3 350 ..	....	....	....	....	....	....	....	....
Income on money market instruments	3 360 ..	....	....	....	....	....	....	....	....
Other investment income	3 370 ..	−37.80	−17.25	−25.40	−23.43	−32.57	−29.67	−46.58	−37.91
D. CURRENT TRANSFERS	4 379 ..	**9.35**	**9.13**	**5.61**	**13.25**	**8.35**	**8.00**	**21.93**	**20.60**
Credit	2 379 ..	**18.43**	**22.52**	**22.97**	**29.46**	**25.10**	**26.17**	**41.08**	**42.11**
General government	2 380 ..	3.67	4.55	3.43	4.70	4.24	5.01	7.22	7.40
Other sectors	2 390 ..	14.76	17.97	19.54	24.76	20.86	21.15	33.86	34.71
Workers' remittances	2 391 ..	10.69	10.69	10.93	11.16	11.45	11.74	12.11	12.41
Other current transfers	2 392 ..	4.07	7.28	8.62	13.60	9.42	9.41	21.75	22.30
Debit	3 379 ..	**−9.09**	**−13.39**	**−17.36**	**−16.21**	**−16.75**	**−18.17**	**−19.15**	**−21.51**
General government	3 380 ..	−1.27	−3.82	−4.06	−3.56	−3.59	−4.22	−5.27	−5.92
Other sectors	3 390 ..	−7.81	−9.56	−13.30	−12.65	−13.17	−13.95	−13.88	−15.59
Workers' remittances	3 391 ..	−1.56	−1.56	−1.41	−1.49	−1.57	−1.67	−1.84	−2.06
Other current transfers	3 392 ..	−6.25	−8.00	−11.89	−11.16	−11.60	−12.28	−12.04	−13.52
CAPITAL AND FINANCIAL ACCOUNT	4 996 ..	**87.56**	**56.09**	**107.74**	**84.06**	**114.34**	**175.15**	**311.84**	**405.48**
CAPITAL ACCOUNT	4 994 ..	**39.33**	**11.93**	**13.92**	**10.19**	**21.30**	**214.33**	**31.57**	**11.11**
Total credit	2 994 ..	*39.33*	*11.93*	*13.92*	*10.19*	*21.30*	*214.33*	*31.57*	*11.11*
Total debit	3 994 ..	....	....	....	....	....	....	....	....
Capital transfers, credit	2 400 ..	**38.36**	**11.93**	**13.92**	**10.19**	**21.30**	**214.33**	**31.57**	**11.11**
General government	2 401 ..	35.03	8.60	10.59	6.86	17.97	210.62	27.87	7.41
Debt forgiveness	2 402 ..	32.37	4.81	....	....	15.65	202.69	....	....
Other capital transfers	2 410 ..	2.66	3.78	10.59	6.86	2.32	7.94	27.87	7.41
Other sectors	2 430 ..	3.33	3.33	3.33	3.33	3.33	3.70	3.70	3.70
Migrants' transfers	2 431 ..	3.33	3.33	3.33	3.33	3.33	3.70	3.70	3.70
Debt forgiveness	2 432 ..	....	....	....	....	....	....	....	....
Other capital transfers	2 440 ..	....	....	....	....	....	....	....	....
Capital transfers, debit	3 400 ..	....	....	....	....	....	....	....	....
General government	3 401 ..	....	....	....	....	....	....	....	....
Debt forgiveness	3 402 ..	....	....	....	....	....	....	....	....
Other capital transfers	3 410 ..	....	....	....	....	....	....	....	....
Other sectors	3 430 ..	....	....	....	....	....	....	....	....
Migrants' transfers	3 431 ..	....	....	....	....	....	....	....	....
Debt forgiveness	3 432 ..	....	....	....	....	....	....	....	....
Other capital transfers	3 440 ..	....	....	....	....	....	....	....	....
Nonproduced nonfinancial assets, credit	2 480 ..	**.96**	....	....	....	....	....	....	....
Nonproduced nonfinancial assets, debit	3 480 ..	....	....	....	....	....	....	....	....

Table 2 (Continued). STANDARD PRESENTATION, 2000–2007

(Millions of U.S. dollars)

	Code	2000	2001	2002	2003	2004	2005	2006	2007
FINANCIAL ACCOUNT	4 995	**48.23**	**44.16**	**93.82**	**73.87**	**93.04**	**−39.17**	**280.27**	**394.37**
A. DIRECT INVESTMENT	4 500	**43.12**	**98.45**	**65.87**	**166.32**	**80.37**	**213.56**	**374.38**	**390.95**
Direct investment abroad	4 505	....	....	....	....	....	....	....	....
Equity capital	4 510	....	....	....	....	....	....	....	....
Claims on affiliated enterprises	4 515	....	....	....	....	....	....	....	....
Liabilities to affiliated enterprises	4 520	....	....	....	....	....	....	....	....
Reinvested earnings	4 525	....	....	....	....	....	....	....	....
Other capital	4 530	....	....	....	....	....	....	....	....
Claims on affiliated enterprises	4 535	....	....	....	....	....	....	....	....
Liabilities to affiliated enterprises	4 540	....	....	....	....	....	....	....	....
Direct investment in Antigua & Barbuda	4 555	**43.12**	**98.45**	**65.87**	**166.32**	**80.37**	**213.56**	**374.38**	**390.95**
Equity capital	4 560	18.33	23.71	34.26	34.74	14.37	170.81	287.93	293.60
Claims on direct investors	4 565	....	....	....	....	....	....	....	....
Liabilities to direct investors	4 570	18.33	23.71	34.26	34.74	14.37	170.81	287.93	293.60
Reinvested earnings	4 575	7.48	11.73	8.33	9.00	11.27	12.86	8.59	9.65
Other capital	4 580	17.30	63.02	23.28	122.57	54.73	29.88	77.85	87.70
Claims on direct investors	4 585	....	....	....	....	....	....	....	....
Liabilities to direct investors	4 590	17.30	63.02	23.28	122.57	54.73	29.88	77.85	87.70
B. PORTFOLIO INVESTMENT	4 600	**2.34**	**−2.50**	**−2.17**	**2.64**	**12.10**	**10.53**	**24.78**	**−6.01**
Assets	4 602	**−.01**	**−.05**	**−2.92**	**−.03**	**−1.38**	**.47**	....	....
Equity securities	4 610	....	....	....	....	....	....	....	....
Monetary authorities	4 611	....	....	....	....	....	....	....	....
General government	4 612	....	....	....	....	....	....	....	....
Banks	4 613	....	....	....	....	....	....	....	....
Other sectors	4 614	....	....	....	....	....	....	....	....
Debt securities	4 619	....	....	....	....	....	....	....	....
Bonds and notes	4 620	....	....	....	....	....	....	....	....
Monetary authorities	4 621	....	....	....	....	....	....	....	....
General government	4 622	....	....	....	....	....	....	....	....
Banks	4 623	....	....	....	....	....	....	....	....
Other sectors	4 624	....	....	....	....	....	....	....	....
Money market instruments	4 630	....	....	....	....	....	....	....	....
Monetary authorities	4 631	....	....	....	....	....	....	....	....
General government	4 632	....	....	....	....	....	....	....	....
Banks	4 633	....	....	....	....	....	....	....	....
Other sectors	4 634	....	....	....	....	....	....	....	....
Liabilities	4 652	**2.35**	**−2.46**	**.75**	**2.67**	**13.48**	**10.06**	**24.78**	**−6.01**
Equity securities	4 660	....	....	....	....	....	....	....	....
Banks	4 663	....	....	....	....	....	....	....	....
Other sectors	4 664	....	....	....	....	....	....	....	....
Debt securities	4 669	....	....	....	....	....	....	....	....
Bonds and notes	4 670	....	....	....	....	....	....	....	....
Monetary authorities	4 671	....	....	....	....	....	....	....	....
General government	4 672	....	....	....	....	....	....	....	....
Banks	4 673	....	....	....	....	....	....	....	....
Other sectors	4 674	....	....	....	....	....	....	....	....
Money market instruments	4 680	....	....	....	....	....	....	....	....
Monetary authorities	4 681	....	....	....	....	....	....	....	....
General government	4 682	....	....	....	....	....	....	....	....
Banks	4 683	....	....	....	....	....	....	....	....
Other sectors	4 684	....	....	....	....	....	....	....	....
C. FINANCIAL DERIVATIVES	4 910	....	....	....	....	....	....	....	....
Monetary authorities	4 911	....	....	....	....	....	....	....	....
General government	4 912	....	....	....	....	....	....	....	....
Banks	4 913	....	....	....	....	....	....	....	....
Other sectors	4 914	....	....	....	....	....	....	....	....
Assets	4 900	....	....	....	....	....	....	....	....
Monetary authorities	4 901	....	....	....	....	....	....	....	....
General government	4 902	....	....	....	....	....	....	....	....
Banks	4 903	....	....	....	....	....	....	....	....
Other sectors	4 904	....	....	....	....	....	....	....	....
Liabilities	4 905	....	....	....	....	....	....	....	....
Monetary authorities	4 906	....	....	....	....	....	....	....	....
General government	4 907	....	....	....	....	....	....	....	....
Banks	4 908	....	....	....	....	....	....	....	....
Other sectors	4 909	....	....	....	....	....	....	....	....

Table 2 (Concluded). STANDARD PRESENTATION, 2000–2007

(Millions of U.S. dollars)

	Code	2000	2001	2002	2003	2004	2005	2006	2007
D. OTHER INVESTMENT	4 700 ..	−3.39	−35.79	37.85	−68.94	6.99	−256.02	−103.63	10.27
Assets	4 703 ..	86.71	53.83	80.09	85.38	80.67	60.10	74.12	88.27
Trade credits	4 706 ..	....	....	....	....	....	....	....	....
General government	4 707 ..	....	....	....	....	....	....	....	....
of which: Short-term	4 709 ..	....	....	....	....	....	....	....	....
Other sectors	4 710 ..	....	....	....	....	....	....	....	....
of which: Short-term	4 712 ..	....	....	....	....	....	....	....	....
Loans	4 714 ..	....	....	....	....	....	....	....	....
Monetary authorities	4 715 ..	....	....	....	....	....	....	....	....
of which: Short-term	4 718 ..	....	....	....	....	....	....	....	....
General government	4 719 ..	....	....	....	....	....	....	....	....
of which: Short-term	4 721 ..	....	....	....	....	....	....	....	....
Banks	4 722 ..	....	....	....	....	....	....	....	....
of which: Short-term	4 724 ..	....	....	....	....	....	....	....	....
Other sectors	4 725 ..	....	....	....	....	....	....	....	....
of which: Short-term	4 727 ..	....	....	....	....	....	....	....	....
Currency and deposits	4 730 ..	....	....	....	....	....	....	....	....
Monetary authorities	4 731 ..	....	....	....	....	....	....	....	....
General government	4 732 ..	....	....	....	....	....	....	....	....
Banks	4 733 ..	....	....	....	....	....	....	....	....
Other sectors	4 734 ..	....	....	....	....	....	....	....	....
Other assets	4 736 ..	....	....	....	....	....	....	....	....
Monetary authorities	4 737 ..	....	....	....	....	....	....	....	....
of which: Short-term	4 739 ..	....	....	....	....	....	....	....	....
General government	4 740 ..	....	....	....	....	....	....	....	....
of which: Short-term	4 742 ..	....	....	....	....	....	....	....	....
Banks	4 743 ..	....	....	....	....	....	....	....	....
of which: Short-term	4 745 ..	....	....	....	....	....	....	....	....
Other sectors	4 746 ..	....	....	....	....	....	....	....	....
of which: Short-term	4 748 ..	....	....	....	....	....	....	....	....
Liabilities	4 753 ..	−90.10	−89.62	−42.24	−154.32	−73.68	−316.12	−177.75	−78.00
Trade credits	4 756 ..	....	....	....	....	....	....	....	....
General government	4 757 ..	....	....	....	....	....	....	....	....
of which: Short-term	4 759 ..	....	....	....	....	....	....	....	....
Other sectors	4 760 ..	....	....	....	....	....	....	....	....
of which: Short-term	4 762 ..	....	....	....	....	....	....	....	....
Loans	4 764 ..	....	....	....	....	....	....	....	....
Monetary authorities	4 765 ..	....	....	....	....	....	....	....	....
of which: Use of Fund credit and loans from the Fund	4 766 ..	....	....	....	....	....	....	....	....
of which: Short-term	4 768 ..	....	....	....	....	....	....	....	....
General government	4 769 ..	....	....	....	....	....	....	....	....
of which: Short-term	4 771 ..	....	....	....	....	....	....	....	....
Banks	4 772 ..	....	....	....	....	....	....	....	....
of which: Short-term	4 774 ..	....	....	....	....	....	....	....	....
Other sectors	4 775 ..	....	....	....	....	....	....	....	....
of which: Short-term	4 777 ..	....	....	....	....	....	....	....	....
Currency and deposits	4 780 ..	....	....	....	....	....	....	....	....
Monetary authorities	4 781 ..	....	....	....	....	....	....	....	....
General government	4 782 ..	....	....	....	....	....	....	....	....
Banks	4 783 ..	....	....	....	....	....	....	....	....
Other sectors	4 784 ..	....	....	....	....	....	....	....	....
Other liabilities	4 786 ..	....	....	....	....	....	....	....	....
Monetary authorities	4 787 ..	....	....	....	....	....	....	....	....
of which: Short-term	4 789 ..	....	....	....	....	....	....	....	....
General government	4 790 ..	....	....	....	....	....	....	....	....
of which: Short-term	4 792 ..	....	....	....	....	....	....	....	....
Banks	4 793 ..	....	....	....	....	....	....	....	....
of which: Short-term	4 795 ..	....	....	....	....	....	....	....	....
Other sectors	4 796 ..	....	....	....	....	....	....	....	....
of which: Short-term	4 798 ..	....	....	....	....	....	....	....	....
E. RESERVE ASSETS	4 802 ..	6.16	−16.00	−7.73	−26.15	−6.42	−7.24	−15.26	−.83
Monetary gold	4 812 ..	....	....	....	....	....	....	....	....
Special drawing rights	4 811 ..	....	....	....	....	....	....	....	....
Reserve position in the Fund	4 810 ..	....	....	....	−.01	....	....	....	....
Foreign exchange	4 803 ..	6.17	−16.17	−7.92	−26.11	−6.37	−7.18	−15.31	−1.21
Other claims	4 813 ..	−.01	.17	.20	−.03	−.05	−.05	.05	.38
NET ERRORS AND OMISSIONS	4 998 ..	−20.78	.80	−25.33	13.50	−18.61	−3.82	−2.76	−3.76

Table 1. ANALYTIC PRESENTATION, 2000–2007

(Millions of U.S. dollars)

	Code	2000	2001	2002	2003	2004	2005	2006	2007
A. Current Account[1]	4 993 Z.	**−8,981**	**−3,780**	**8,767**	**8,140**	**3,213**	**5,265**	**7,712**	**7,113**
Goods: exports f.o.b.	2 100 ..	26,341	26,543	25,651	29,939	34,576	40,387	46,546	55,780
Goods: imports f.o.b.	3 100 ..	−23,889	−19,158	−8,473	−13,134	−21,311	−27,300	−32,588	−42,525
Balance on Goods	4 100 ..	*2,452*	*7,385*	*17,178*	*16,805*	*13,265*	*13,087*	*13,958*	*13,255*
Services: credit	2 200 ..	4,936	4,627	3,495	4,500	5,288	6,637	8,001	10,320
Services: debit	3 200 ..	−9,219	−8,490	−4,956	−5,693	−6,619	−7,639	−8,532	−10,846
Balance on Goods and Services	4 991 ..	*−1,832*	*3,522*	*15,717*	*15,611*	*11,934*	*12,085*	*13,427*	*12,729*
Income: credit	2 300 ..	7,420	5,358	3,039	3,104	3,721	4,313	5,674	6,637
Income: debit	3 300 ..	−14,968	−13,085	−10,530	−11,080	−13,003	−11,617	−11,834	−12,568
Balance on Goods, Services, and Income	4 992 ..	*−9,380*	*−4,205*	*8,227*	*7,636*	*2,652*	*4,781*	*7,267*	*6,798*
Current transfers: credit	2 379 Z.	792	856	818	942	1,110	1,226	1,409	1,583
Current transfers: debit	3 379 ..	−393	−431	−278	−438	−549	−742	−964	−1,268
B. Capital Account[1]	4 994 Z.	**106**	**157**	**406**	**39**	**196**	**89**	**97**	**112**
Capital account: credit	2 994 Z.	121	165	410	46	201	93	107	132
Capital account: debit	3 994 ..	−15	−8	−4	−7	−4	−4	−9	−20
Total, Groups A Plus B	4 981 ..	*−8,875*	*−3,624*	*9,173*	*8,179*	*3,409*	*5,354*	*7,809*	*7,224*
C. Financial Account[1]	4 995 W.	**7,853**	**−14,971**	**−20,685**	**−15,860**	**−10,949**	**1,898**	**5,145**	**4,103**
Direct investment abroad	4 505 ..	−901	−161	627	−774	−676	−1,311	−2,438	−1,465
Direct investment in Argentina	4 555 Z.	10,418	2,166	2,149	1,652	4,125	5,265	5,537	6,462
Portfolio investment assets	4 602 ..	−1,252	212	477	−95	−77	1,368	−1	−2
Equity securities	4 610 ..	−1,455	−931	13	−34	−72	−4	6	13
Debt securities	4 619 ..	203	1,143	464	−61	−5	1,373	−7	−14
Portfolio investment liabilities	4 652 Z.	−1,331	−9,715	−5,117	−7,663	−9,339	−1,731	7,921	7,098
Equity securities	4 660 ..	−3,227	31	−116	65	−86	−48	707	1,785
Debt securities	4 669 Z.	1,896	−9,746	−5,001	−7,728	−9,253	−1,683	7,215	5,313
Financial derivatives	4 910 ..	. . . .	. . . .	. . . .	. . . .	. . . .	. . . .	−127	−565
Financial derivatives assets	4 900 ..	. . . .	. . . .	. . . .	. . . .	. . . .	. . . .	. . . .	. . . .
Financial derivatives liabilities	4 905 ..	. . . .	. . . .	. . . .	. . . .	. . . .	. . . .	−127	−565
Other investment assets	4 703 ..	−1,368	−1,907	−8,896	−4,400	−2,347	1,956	−4,527	−11,696
Monetary authorities	4 701 ..	. . . .	. . . .	. . . .	. . . .	. . . .	. . . .	. . . .	. . . .
General government	4 704 ..	1,056	232	307	−74	−191	−59	−346	−427
Banks	4 705 ..	−2,348	8,960	1,896	447	240	−129	−505	−1,272
Other sectors	4 728 ..	−76	−11,099	−11,099	−4,773	−2,395	2,143	−3,676	−9,997
Other investment liabilities	4 753 W.	2,287	−5,566	−9,924	−4,580	−2,636	−3,649	−1,221	4,271
Monetary authorities	4 753 WA	−16	1,130	−340	−633	54	−10	−1,172	−198
General government	4 753 ZB	440	1,007	−2,509	−98	−1,054	−1,374	−1,439	1
Banks	4 753 ZC	898	−6,775	−2,178	−2,917	−916	−1,304	−31	952
Other sectors	4 753 ZD	964	−928	−4,897	−932	−719	−961	1,421	3,515
Total, Groups A Through C	4 983 ..	*−1,022*	*−18,595*	*−11,513*	*−7,680*	*−7,540*	*7,251*	*12,955*	*11,328*
D. Net Errors and Omissions	4 998 ..	**−154**	**−2,810**	**−1,890**	**−1,397**	**547**	**393**	**1,293**	**248**
Total, Groups A Through D	4 984 ..	*−1,176*	*−21,405*	*−13,402*	*−9,077*	*−6,993*	*7,644*	*14,247*	*11,576*
E. Reserves and Related Items	4 802 A.	**1,176**	**21,405**	**13,402**	**9,077**	**6,993**	**−7,644**	**−14,247**	**−11,576**
Reserve assets	4 802 ..	403	12,070	4,526	−3,497	−5,283	−9,088	−3,468	−13,075
Use of Fund credit and loans	4 766 ..	773	9,335	−739	−151	−2,038	−3,582	−9,630	. . . .
Exceptional financing	4 920 ..	. . . .	. . . .	9,616	12,725	14,314	5,026	−1,149	1,499
Conversion rates: Argentine pesos per U.S. dollar	0 101 ..	.99950	.99950	3.06326	2.90063	2.92330	2.90366	3.05431	3.09565

[1] Excludes components that have been classified in the categories of Group E.

Table 2. STANDARD PRESENTATION, 2000–2007

(Millions of U.S. dollars)

	Code	2000	2001	2002	2003	2004	2005	2006	2007
CURRENT ACCOUNT	4 993	**−8,981**	**−3,780**	**8,767**	**8,140**	**3,213**	**5,265**	**7,712**	**7,113**
A. GOODS	4 100	**2,452**	**7,385**	**17,178**	**16,805**	**13,265**	**13,087**	**13,958**	**13,255**
Credit	2 100	**26,341**	**26,543**	**25,651**	**29,939**	**34,576**	**40,387**	**46,546**	**55,780**
General merchandise: exports f.o.b.	2 110	25,925	26,139	25,287	29,500	34,069	39,636	45,249	54,617
Goods for processing: exports f.o.b.	2 150	....	....	....	....	....	....	....	....
Repairs on goods	2 160	....	....	....	....	....	....	....	....
Goods procured in ports by carriers	2 170	319	305	253	328	372	608	750	875
Nonmonetary gold	2 180	96	99	111	111	135	143	547	287
Debit	3 100	**−23,889**	**−19,158**	**−8,473**	**−13,134**	**−21,311**	**−27,300**	**−32,588**	**−42,525**
General merchandise: imports f.o.b.	3 110	−23,771	−19,107	−8,412	−13,055	−21,218	−27,162	−32,443	−42,358
Goods for processing: imports f.o.b.	3 150	....	....	....	....	....	....	....	....
Repairs on goods	3 160	....	....	....	....	....	....	....	....
Goods procured in ports by carriers	3 170	−118	−50	−61	−80	−94	−138	−145	−167
Nonmonetary gold	3 180	....	....	....	....	....	....	....	....
B. SERVICES	4 200	**−4,284**	**−3,863**	**−1,460**	**−1,193**	**−1,331**	**−1,002**	**−531**	**−526**
Total credit	2 200	*4,936*	*4,627*	*3,495*	*4,500*	*5,288*	*6,637*	*8,001*	*10,320*
Total debit	3 200	*−9,219*	*−8,490*	*−4,956*	*−5,693*	*−6,619*	*−7,639*	*−8,532*	*−10,846*
Transportation services, credit	2 205	**1,145**	**893**	**755**	**932**	**1,140**	**1,264**	**1,386**	**1,673**
Passenger	2 850	*291*	*114*	*181*	*300*	*425*	*480*	*555*	*670*
Freight	2 851	*226*	*219*	*216*	*224*	*256*	*237*	*246*	*301*
Other	2 852	*629*	*560*	*358*	*408*	*459*	*547*	*585*	*702*
Sea transport, passenger	2 207	9	7	5	4	3	....	....	....
Sea transport, freight	2 208	136	133	121	106	90	55	44	49
Sea transport, other	2 209	282	279	242	280	299	348	386	466
Air transport, passenger	2 211	268	93	168	287	410	463	533	643
Air transport, freight	2 212	9	5	5	8	10	10	9	9
Air transport, other	2 213	345	279	116	128	160	198	199	236
Other transport, passenger	2 215	14	14	7	9	12	17	23	27
Other transport, freight	2 216	81	81	90	110	156	172	193	243
Other transport, other	2 217	2	2	....	....	....	....	....	....
Transportation services, debit	3 205	**−2,413**	**−2,104**	**−929**	**−1,126**	**−1,600**	**−1,968**	**−2,286**	**−3,029**
Passenger	3 850	*−1,035*	*−995*	*−416*	*−486*	*−604*	*−774*	*−947*	*−1,149*
Freight	3 851	*−1,090*	*−911*	*−381*	*−529*	*−869*	*−1,078*	*−1,196*	*−1,713*
Other	3 852	*−288*	*−198*	*−132*	*−111*	*−127*	*−116*	*−143*	*−166*
Sea transport, passenger	3 207	−42	−39	−20	−17	−26	−41	−41	−52
Sea transport, freight	3 208	−715	−594	−242	−337	−550	−729	−809	−1,242
Sea transport, other	3 209	−47	−45	−38	−17	−16	−11	−8	−10
Air transport, passenger	3 211	−974	−938	−388	−461	−569	−723	−897	−1,088
Air transport, freight	3 212	−225	−169	−73	−104	−177	−191	−200	−242
Air transport, other	3 213	−240	−152	−94	−94	−111	−105	−135	−156
Other transport, passenger	3 215	−19	−19	−8	−8	−10	−10	−10	−10
Other transport, freight	3 216	−150	−148	−66	−88	−142	−158	−187	−229
Other transport, other	3 217	−1	....	....	....	....	....	....	....
Travel, credit	2 236	**2,904**	**2,642**	**1,535**	**2,006**	**2,235**	**2,729**	**3,344**	**4,314**
Business travel	2 237	1,010	866	477	669	445	504	520	684
Personal travel	2 240	1,893	1,776	1,058	1,337	1,790	2,226	2,824	3,629
Travel, debit	3 236	**−4,425**	**−3,893**	**−2,328**	**−2,511**	**−2,604**	**−2,790**	**−3,099**	**−3,921**
Business travel	3 237	−1,046	−863	−529	−598	−936	−1,030	−1,120	−1,515
Personal travel	3 240	−3,379	−3,030	−1,798	−1,914	−1,669	−1,760	−1,979	−2,405
Other services, credit	2 200 BA	**887**	**1,092**	**1,205**	**1,562**	**1,913**	**2,644**	**3,271**	**4,333**
Communications	2 245	175	187	150	146	162	210	273	314
Construction	2 249	7	....	16	41	61	46	20	38
Insurance	2 253	12	....	....	....	....	....	....	....
Financial	2 260	6	4	1	1	2	4	6	9
Computer and information	2 262	147	189	127	166	193	237	362	506
Royalties and licence fees	2 266	37	47	33	51	61	51	70	86
Other business services	2 268	324	471	715	953	1,194	1,778	2,157	2,957
Personal, cultural, and recreational	2 287	18	38	95	122	153	203	257	293
Government, n.i.e.	2 291	160	158	67	81	86	115	124	130
Other services, debit	3 200 BA	**−2,382**	**−2,493**	**−1,699**	**−2,056**	**−2,415**	**−2,881**	**−3,147**	**−3,897**
Communications	3 245	−205	−239	−224	−228	−223	−269	−309	−362
Construction	3 249	....	....	−8	−37	−31	−2	−1	−17
Insurance	3 253	−200	−219	−52	−149	−158	−230	−283	−373
Financial	3 260	−170	−185	−50	−113	−105	−210	−78	−86
Computer and information	3 262	−149	−192	−131	−139	−160	−195	−226	−291
Royalties and licence fees	3 266	−580	−564	−351	−403	−521	−655	−803	−1,037
Other business services	3 268	−648	−639	−608	−648	−827	−894	−996	−1,222
Personal, cultural, and recreational	3 287	−171	−228	−96	−108	−143	−165	−170	−204
Government, n.i.e.	3 291	−260	−228	−180	−231	−246	−262	−281	−307

Table 2 (Continued). STANDARD PRESENTATION, 2000–2007

(Millions of U.S. dollars)

	Code	2000	2001	2002	2003	2004	2005	2006	2007
C. INCOME	4 300	**−7,548**	**−7,727**	**−7,491**	**−7,976**	**−9,282**	**−7,304**	**−6,161**	**−5,931**
Total credit	2 300	*7,420*	*5,358*	*3,039*	*3,104*	*3,721*	*4,313*	*5,674*	*6,637*
Total debit	3 300	*−14,968*	*−13,085*	*−10,530*	*−11,080*	*−13,003*	*−11,617*	*−11,834*	*−12,568*
Compensation of employees, credit	2 310	**36**	**34**	**36**	**38**	**42**	**51**	**56**	**63**
Compensation of employees, debit	3 310	**−28**	**−30**	**−60**	**−63**	**−81**	**−102**	**−114**	**−138**
Investment income, credit	2 320	**7,384**	**5,324**	**3,004**	**3,066**	**3,679**	**4,262**	**5,618**	**6,573**
Direct investment income	2 330	978	634	349	450	859	1,020	1,635	1,483
Dividends and distributed branch profits	2 332	425	324	−21	148	217	277	310	353
Reinvested earnings and undistributed branch profits	2 333	553	310	370	302	643	744	1,325	1,130
Income on debt (interest)	2 334	....	....	....	....	....	....	....	....
Portfolio investment income	2 339	216	263	91	99	173	122	382	954
Income on equity	2 340	....	1	1	1	2	2	2	2
Income on bonds and notes	2 350	216	262	90	97	171	120	380	951
Income on money market instruments	2 360	....	....	....	....	....	....	....	....
Other investment income	2 370	6,189	4,427	2,563	2,518	2,647	3,120	3,601	4,136
Investment income, debit	3 320	**−14,940**	**−13,055**	**−10,469**	**−11,017**	**−12,922**	**−11,515**	**−11,720**	**−12,430**
Direct investment income	3 330	−3,086	−1,397	−854	−1,626	−3,712	−5,456	−7,112	−7,283
Dividends and distributed branch profits	3 332	−2,211	−4,077	−1,038	−1,865	−3,066	−3,755	−3,446	−4,645
Reinvested earnings and undistributed branch profits	3 333	−261	3,306	924	808	−71	−1,156	−3,108	−2,050
Income on debt (interest)	3 334	−614	−626	−740	−568	−575	−545	−558	−588
Portfolio investment income	3 339	−7,344	−6,963	−5,809	−6,181	−6,541	−3,396	−2,423	−2,696
Income on equity	3 340	−115	−122	−7	−27	−11	−6	−23	−33
Income on bonds and notes	3 350	−7,228	−6,841	−5,802	−6,154	−6,530	−3,390	−2,400	−2,662
Income on money market instruments	3 360	....	....	....	....	....	....	....	....
Other investment income	3 370	−4,510	−4,695	−3,807	−3,209	−2,668	−2,663	−2,185	−2,451
D. CURRENT TRANSFERS	4 379	**399**	**424**	**540**	**504**	**561**	**484**	**446**	**315**
Credit	2 379	**792**	**856**	**818**	**942**	**1,110**	**1,226**	**1,409**	**1,583**
General government	2 380	359	352	232	255	315	358	430	542
Other sectors	2 390	433	504	586	687	795	868	979	1,041
Workers' remittances	2 391	50	156	171	236	270	381	486	541
Other current transfers	2 392	383	348	415	451	525	486	494	500
Debit	3 379	**−393**	**−431**	**−278**	**−438**	**−549**	**−742**	**−964**	**−1,268**
General government	3 380	−49	−55	−27	−71	−86	−84	−107	−118
Other sectors	3 390	−344	−376	−251	−366	−462	−659	−856	−1,150
Workers' remittances	3 391	−240	−226	−59	−117	−154	−212	−252	−334
Other current transfers	3 392	−105	−150	−191	−249	−309	−447	−604	−816
CAPITAL AND FINANCIAL ACCOUNT	4 996	**9,135**	**6,590**	**−6,877**	**−6,743**	**−3,760**	**−5,658**	**−9,005**	**−7,361**
CAPITAL ACCOUNT	4 994	**106**	**157**	**406**	**39**	**196**	**89**	**97**	**112**
Total credit	2 994	*121*	*165*	*410*	*46*	*201*	*93*	*107*	*132*
Total debit	3 994	*−15*	*−8*	*−4*	*−7*	*−4*	*−4*	*−9*	*−20*
Capital transfers, credit	2 400	....	....	....	....	**149**	....	**35**	....
General government	2 401	....	....	....	....	....	....	....	....
Debt forgiveness	2 402	....	....	....	....	....	....	....	....
Other capital transfers	2 410	....	....	....	....	....	....	....	....
Other sectors	2 430	....	....	....	....	149	....	35	....
Migrants' transfers	2 431	....	....	....	....	....	....	....	....
Debt forgiveness	2 432	....	....	....	....	149	....	35	....
Other capital transfers	2 440	....	....	....	....	....	....	....	....
Capital transfers, debit	3 400	....	....	....	....	....	....	....	....
General government	3 401	....	....	....	....	....	....	....	....
Debt forgiveness	3 402	....	....	....	....	....	....	....	....
Other capital transfers	3 410	....	....	....	....	....	....	....	....
Other sectors	3 430	....	....	....	....	....	....	....	....
Migrants' transfers	3 431	....	....	....	....	....	....	....	....
Debt forgiveness	3 432	....	....	....	....	....	....	....	....
Other capital transfers	3 440	....	....	....	....	....	....	....	....
Nonproduced nonfinancial assets, credit	2 480	**121**	**165**	**410**	**46**	**52**	**93**	**72**	**132**
Nonproduced nonfinancial assets, debit	3 480	**−15**	**−8**	**−4**	**−7**	**−4**	**−4**	**−9**	**−20**

Table 2 (Continued). STANDARD PRESENTATION, 2000–2007

(Millions of U.S. dollars)

	Code	2000	2001	2002	2003	2004	2005	2006	2007
FINANCIAL ACCOUNT	4 995	9,029	6,434	−7,283	−6,782	−3,956	−5,747	−9,102	−7,472
A. DIRECT INVESTMENT	4 500	9,517	2,005	2,776	878	3,449	3,954	3,100	4,997
Direct investment abroad	4 505	−901	−161	627	−774	−676	−1,311	−2,438	−1,465
Equity capital	4 510	−166	193	1,111	−228	−44	−567	−1,113	−335
Claims on affiliated enterprises	4 515	−166	193	1,111	−228	−44	−567	−1,113	−335
Liabilities to affiliated enterprises	4 520	....	....	....	....	....	....	....	....
Reinvested earnings	4 525	−553	−310	−370	−302	−643	−744	−1,325	−1,130
Other capital	4 530	−182	−43	−113	−243	11	....	....	....
Claims on affiliated enterprises	4 535	−182	−43	−113	−243	11	....	....	....
Liabilities to affiliated enterprises	4 540	....	....	....	....	....	....	....	....
Direct investment in Argentina	4 555	10,418	2,166	2,149	1,652	4,125	5,265	5,537	6,462
Equity capital	4 560	9,070	4,472	6,066	2,975	3,025	4,590	2,166	2,572
Claims on direct investors	4 565	....	....	....	....	....	....	....	....
Liabilities to direct investors	4 570	9,070	4,472	6,066	2,975	3,025	4,590	2,166	2,572
Reinvested earnings	4 575	261	−3,306	−924	−808	71	1,156	3,108	2,050
Other capital	4 580	1,088	1,000	−2,992	−515	1,029	−481	263	1,841
Claims on direct investors	4 585	....	....	....	....	....	....	....	....
Liabilities to direct investors	4 590	1,088	1,000	−2,992	−515	1,029	−481	263	1,841
B. PORTFOLIO INVESTMENT	4 600	−2,584	−9,503	−4,640	−7,758	−9,416	−387	7,823	7,069
Assets	4 602	−1,252	212	477	−95	−77	1,368	−1	−2
Equity securities	4 610	−1,455	−931	13	−34	−72	−4	6	13
Monetary authorities	4 611	....	....	....	....	....	....	....	....
General government	4 612	....	....	....	....	....	....	....	....
Banks	4 613	−12	−35	13	−34	−72	−4	6	13
Other sectors	4 614	−1,443	−896	....	....	....	....	....	....
Debt securities	4 619	203	1,143	464	−61	−5	1,373	−7	−14
Bonds and notes	4 620	203	1,143	464	−61	−5	1,373	−7	−14
Monetary authorities	4 621	....	....	....	....	....	....	....	....
General government	4 622	1,122	360	367	−63	−68	1,373	−7	−8
Banks	4 623	−88	1,348	96	1	64	....	....	−6
Other sectors	4 624	−831	−565	....	....	....	....	....	....
Money market instruments	4 630	....	....	....	....	....	....	....	....
Monetary authorities	4 631	....	....	....	....	....	....	....	....
General government	4 632	....	....	....	....	....	....	....	....
Banks	4 633	....	....	....	....	....	....	....	....
Other sectors	4 634	....	....	....	....	....	....	....	....
Liabilities	4 652	−1,331	−9,715	−5,117	−7,663	−9,339	−1,755	7,824	7,070
Equity securities	4 660	−3,227	31	−116	65	−86	−48	707	1,785
Banks	4 663	−274	36	−72	28	−45	−13	439	151
Other sectors	4 664	−2,953	−5	−44	38	−41	−35	267	1,634
Debt securities	4 669	1,896	−9,746	−5,001	−7,728	−9,253	−1,707	7,118	5,285
Bonds and notes	4 670	1,896	−9,746	−5,001	−7,728	−9,253	−1,707	7,118	5,285
Monetary authorities	4 671	....	....	....	....	....	−24	−97	−27
General government	4 672	2,633	−7,480	−3,826	−5,463	−8,172	−139	7,639	6,007
Banks	4 673	250	−1,278	−1,208	−978	455	−514	69	−160
Other sectors	4 674	−987	−988	32	−1,287	−1,536	−1,031	−492	−534
Money market instruments	4 680	....	....	....	....	....	....	....	....
Monetary authorities	4 681	....	....	....	....	....	....	....	....
General government	4 682	....	....	....	....	....	....	....	....
Banks	4 683	....	....	....	....	....	....	....	....
Other sectors	4 684	....	....	....	....	....	....	....	....
C. FINANCIAL DERIVATIVES	4 910	....	....	....	....	....	....	−127	−565
Monetary authorities	4 911	....	....	....	....	....	....	−243	−535
General government	4 912	....	....	....	....	....	....	116	−30
Banks	4 913	....	....	....	....	....	....	....	....
Other sectors	4 914	....	....	....	....	....	....	....	....
Assets	4 900	....	....	....	....	....	....	....	....
Monetary authorities	4 901	....	....	....	....	....	....	....	....
General government	4 902	....	....	....	....	....	....	....	....
Banks	4 903	....	....	....	....	....	....	....	....
Other sectors	4 904	....	....	....	....	....	....	−127	−565
Liabilities	4 905	....	....	....	....	....	....	−127	−565
Monetary authorities	4 906	....	....	....	....	....	....	−243	−535
General government	4 907	....	....	....	....	....	....	116	−30
Banks	4 908	....	....	....	....	....	....	....	....
Other sectors	4 909	....	....	....	....	....	....	....	....

Table 2 (Concluded). STANDARD PRESENTATION, 2000–2007

(Millions of U.S. dollars)

	Code	2000	2001	2002	2003	2004	2005	2006	2007
D. OTHER INVESTMENT	4 700	**1,692**	**1,862**	**−9,945**	**3,595**	**7,294**	**−225**	**−16,431**	**−5,899**
Assets	4 703	−1,368	−1,907	−8,896	−4,400	−2,347	1,956	−4,527	−11,696
Trade credits	4 706	−657	199	....	....	....	....	....	....
General government	4 707	....	....	....	....	....	....	....	....
of which: Short-term	4 709	....	....	....	....	....	....	....	....
Other sectors	4 710	−657	199	....	....	....	....	....	....
of which: Short-term	4 712	*−657*	*199*	....	....	....	....	....	....
Loans	4 714	−2,199	4,879	1,203	838	−456	85	−346	−1,004
Monetary authorities	4 715	....	....	....	....	....	....	....	....
of which: Short-term	4 718	....	....	....	....	....	....	....	....
General government	4 719	−30	7	42	−40	−102	−95	−128	−194
of which: Short-term	4 721	....	....	....	....	....	....	....	....
Banks	4 722	−2,169	4,872	1,160	877	−354	180	−218	−810
of which: Short-term	4 724	*−2,169*	*4,872*	*1,160*	*877*	*−354*	*180*	*−218*	*−810*
Other sectors	4 725	....	....	....	....	....	....	....	....
of which: Short-term	4 727	....	....	....	....	....	....	....	....
Currency and deposits	4 730	1,488	−6,984	1,000	−419	562	−236	−406	−642
Monetary authorities	4 731	....	....	....	....	....	....	....	....
General government	4 732	1,086	226	265	11	−31	72	−120	−180
Banks	4 733	−179	4,088	735	−430	594	−309	−287	−462
Other sectors	4 734	581	−11,298	....	....	....	....	....	....
Other assets	4 736	....	−1	−11,099	−4,819	−2,453	2,107	−3,775	−10,050
Monetary authorities	4 737	....	....	....	....	....	....	....	....
of which: Short-term	4 739	....	....	....	....	....	....	....	....
General government	4 740	....	−1	....	−46	−58	−36	−99	−53
of which: Short-term	4 742	....	....	....	....	....	....	....	....
Banks	4 743	....	....	....	....	....	....	....	....
of which: Short-term	4 745	....	....	....	....	....	....	....	....
Other sectors	4 746	....	....	−11,099	−4,773	−2,395	2,143	−3,676	−9,997
of which: Short-term	4 748	....	....	....	....	....	....	....	....
Liabilities	4 753	**3,060**	**3,769**	**−1,048**	**7,995**	**9,640**	**−2,181**	**−11,904**	**5,797**
Trade credits	4 756	−64	−139	−372	810	1,144	571	1,547	2,309
General government	4 757	....	....	....	....	....	....	....	....
of which: Short-term	4 759	....	....	....	....	....	....	....	....
Other sectors	4 760	−64	−139	−372	810	1,144	571	1,547	2,309
of which: Short-term	4 762	*−64*	*−139*	*−372*	*810*	*1,144*	*571*	*1,547*	*2,309*
Loans	4 764	527	9,736	−8,465	−5,182	−6,391	−7,457	−12,048	2,580
Monetary authorities	4 765	767	10,327	−1,116	−774	−2,038	−2,882	−10,330	1,520
of which: Use of Fund credit and loans from the Fund	4 766	*773*	*9,335*	*−739*	*−151*	*−2,038*	*−3,582*	*−9,630*	....
of which: Short-term	4 768	....	....	....	....	....	*700*	*−700*	*1,520*
General government	4 769	361	792	−2,492	−87	−1,263	−1,460	−1,424	9
of which: Short-term	4 771	....	....	....	....	....	....	....	....
Banks	4 772	−1,480	−867	−290	−2,579	−1,227	−1,583	−168	−155
of which: Short-term	4 774	*−1,447*	*−905*	*14*	*−2,519*	*−1,375*	*−1,571*	*−174*	*11*
Other sectors	4 775	878	−515	−4,568	−1,742	−1,863	−1,532	−126	1,206
of which: Short-term	4 777	....	....	....	....	....	....	....	....
Currency and deposits	4 780	1,158	−2,568	−922	−31	17	80	279	194
Monetary authorities	4 781	....	....	....	....	....	....	....	....
General government	4 782	....	....	....	....	....	....	....	....
Banks	4 783	1,158	−2,568	−922	−31	17	80	279	194
Other sectors	4 784	....	....	....	....	....	....	....	....
Other liabilities	4 786	1,439	−3,261	8,711	12,398	14,870	4,625	−1,681	713
Monetary authorities	4 787	−10	138	163	−135	54	−10	−72	2
of which: Short-term	4 789	*−7*	*145*	*162*	*−136*	*53*	*−11*	*−73*	*1*
General government	4 790	79	215	8,100	11,447	15,500	4,588	−877	−57
of which: Short-term	4 792	*79*	*215*	*8,100*	*11,447*	*15,500*	*4,588*	*−877*	*−57*
Banks	4 793	1,221	−3,341	−320	466	−941	80	−141	913
of which: Short-term	4 795	*1,221*	*−3,341*	*−320*	*466*	*−941*	*80*	*−141*	*913*
Other sectors	4 796	150	−273	769	621	257	−33	−591	−144
of which: Short-term	4 798	*150*	*−273*	*769*	*621*	*257*	*−33*	*−591*	*−144*
E. RESERVE ASSETS	4 802	**403**	**12,070**	**4,526**	**−3,497**	**−5,283**	**−9,088**	**−3,468**	**−13,075**
Monetary gold	4 812	111	4	....	−1	−765	−139	−207	−353
Special drawing rights	4 811	−603	705	−79	−824	168	−3,794	4,022	....
Reserve position in the Fund	4 810	....	....	....	....	....	....	....	....
Foreign exchange	4 803	895	11,361	4,606	−2,673	−4,685	−5,155	−6,928	−12,784
Other claims	4 813	....	....	....	....	....	....	−355	62
NET ERRORS AND OMISSIONS	4 998	**−154**	**−2,810**	**−1,890**	**−1,397**	**547**	**393**	**1,293**	**248**

Table 3. INTERNATIONAL INVESTMENT POSITION (End-period stocks), 2000–2007

(Millions of U.S. dollars)

	Code	2000	2001	2002	2003	2004	2005	2006	2007
ASSETS..	8 995 C.	**152,946**	**131,807**	**131,376**	**144,822**	**154,576**	**165,794**	**177,610**	**205,056**
Direct investment abroad................................	8 505 ..	**21,141**	**21,283**	**20,618**	**21,500**	**21,804**	**23,340**	**25,577**	**26,820**
Equity capital and reinvested earnings............................	8 506 ..	21,141	21,283	20,618	21,500	21,804	23,340	25,577	26,820
Claims on affiliated enterprises............................	8 507 ..	21,141	21,283	20,618	21,500	....	....	....	....
Liabilities to affiliated enterprises............................	8 508 ..	....	....	....	....	....	....	....	....
Other capital..............................	8 530 ..	....	....	....	....	....	....	....	....
Claims on affiliated enterprises............................	8 535 ..	....	....	....	....	....	....	....	....
Liabilities to affiliated enterprises............................	8 540 ..	....	....	....	....	....	....	....	....
Portfolio investment............................	8 602 ..	**35,190**	**1,225**	**843**	**939**	**1,016**	**192**	**192**	**195**
Equity securities..............................	8 610 ..	43	43	30	64	73	77	70	58
Monetary authorities............................	8 611 ..	....	....	....	....	....	....	....	....
General government............................	8 612 ..	....	....	....	....	....	....	....	....
Banks..............................	8 613 ..	43	43	30	64	73	77	70	58
Other sectors..............................	8 614 ..	....	....	....	....	....	....	....	....
Debt securities..............................	8 619 ..	35,147	1,182	813	875	943	115	122	137
Bonds and notes..............................	8 620 ..	35,147	1,182	813	875	943	115	122	137
Monetary authorities............................	8 621 ..	....	....	....	....	....	....	....	....
General government............................	8 622 ..	1,782	1,082	811	874	942	114	121	129
Banks..............................	8 623 ..	1,413	100	3	1	1	1	1	8
Other sectors..............................	8 624 ..	31,952	....	....	....	....	....	....	....
Money market instruments............................	8 630 ..	....	....	....	....	....	....	....	....
Monetary authorities............................	8 631 ..	....	....	....	....	....	....	....	....
General government............................	8 632 ..	....	....	....	....	....	....	....	....
Banks..............................	8 633 ..	....	....	....	....	....	....	....	....
Other sectors..............................	8 634 ..	....	....	....	....	....	....	....	....
Financial derivatives............................	8 900 ..	....	....	....	....	....	....	....	....
Monetary authorities............................	8 901 ..	....	....	....	....	....	....	....	....
General government............................	8 902 ..	....	....	....	....	....	....	....	....
Banks..............................	8 903 ..	....	....	....	....	....	....	....	....
Other sectors..............................	8 904 ..	....	....	....	....	....	....	....	....
Other investment............................	8 703 ..	**68,965**	**94,376**	**99,346**	**107,256**	**111,232**	**109,749**	**119,322**	**131,869**
Trade credits..............................	8 706 ..	3,400	3,201	3,994	4,830	4,934	2,761	2,997	3,066
General government............................	8 707 ..	....	....	....	....	....	....	....	....
of which: Short-term............................	8 709 ..	....	....	....	....	....	....	....	....
Other sectors..............................	8 710 ..	3,400	3,201	3,994	4,830	4,934	2,761	2,997	3,066
of which: Short-term............................	8 712 ..	*3,400*	*3,201*	*3,994*	*4,830*	*4,934*	*2,761*	*2,997*	*3,066*
Loans..............................	8 714 ..	....	....	....	....	....	....	....	....
Monetary authorities............................	8 715 ..	....	....	....	....	....	....	....	....
of which: Short-term............................	8 718 ..	....	....	....	....	....	....	....	....
General government............................	8 719 ..	....	....	....	....	....	....	....	....
of which: Short-term............................	8 721 ..	....	....	....	....	....	....	....	....
Banks..............................	8 722 ..	....	....	....	....	....	....	....	....
of which: Short-term............................	8 724 ..	....	....	....	....	....	....	....	....
Other sectors..............................	8 725 ..	....	....	....	....	....	....	....	....
of which: Short-term............................	8 727 ..	....	....	....	....	....	....	....	....
Currency and deposits............................	8 730 ..	50,012	1,837	1,016	1,446	841	1,149	1,436	1,898
Monetary authorities............................	8 731 ..	....	....	....	....	....	....	....	....
General government............................	8 732 ..	....	....	....	....	....	....	....	....
Banks..............................	8 733 ..	5,926	1,837	1,016	1,446	841	1,149	1,436	1,898
Other sectors..............................	8 734 ..	44,086	....	....	....	....	....	....	....
Other assets..............................	8 736 ..	15,553	89,338	94,335	100,979	105,458	105,839	114,889	126,904
Monetary authorities............................	8 737 ..	....	....	....	....	....	....	....	....
of which: Short-term............................	8 739 ..	....	....	....	....	....	....	....	....
General government............................	8 740 ..	6,384	6,613	6,113	6,334	6,745	7,050	7,507	8,594
of which: Short-term............................	8 742 ..	....	....	....	....	....	....	....	....
Banks..............................	8 743 ..	9,170	4,051	2,125	1,247	1,601	1,421	1,639	2,449
of which: Short-term............................	8 745 ..	....	....	....	....	....	....	....	....
Other sectors..............................	8 746 ..	....	78,674	86,097	93,398	97,112	97,368	105,742	115,862
of which: Short-term............................	8 748 ..	....	....	....	....	....	....	....	....
Reserve assets............................	8 802 ..	**27,651**	**14,923**	**10,570**	**15,128**	**20,523**	**32,513**	**32,520**	**46,173**
Monetary gold..............................	8 812 ..	7	3	3	4	769	908	1,115	1,468
Special drawing rights............................	8 811 ..	733	11	94	1,008	877	4,437	482	507
Reserve position in the Fund............................	8 810 ..	....	....	....	....	....	....	....	....
Foreign exchange..............................	8 803 ..	26,908	14,915	10,491	14,149	18,881	27,178	30,914	44,030
Other claims..............................	8 813 ..	3	−5	−18	−34	−4	−10	8	169

Table 3 (Concluded). INTERNATIONAL INVESTMENT POSITION (End-period stocks), 2000–2007

(Millions of U.S. dollars)

	Code	2000	2001	2002	2003	2004	2005	2006	2007
LIABILITIES	8 995 D.	**213,540**	**190,722**	**133,701**	**145,583**	**151,541**	**143,817**	**155,633**	**168,235**
Direct investment in Argentina	8 555 ..	**67,769**	**79,504**	**43,146**	**48,262**	**52,507**	**55,139**	**59,753**	**66,008**
Equity capital and reinvested earnings	8 556 ..	59,415	59,565	27,100	33,456	36,897	40,694	45,776	49,779
Claims on direct investors	8 557 ..	....	....	....	....			....	....
Liabilities to direct investors	8 558 ..	59,415	59,565	27,100	33,456	....	....	....	....
Other capital	8 580 ..	8,354	19,938	16,046	14,806	15,610	14,445	13,977	16,228
Claims on direct investors	8 585 ..	....	....	....	....				
Liabilities to direct investors	8 590 ..	....	....	....	....	15,610	14,445	13,977	16,228
Portfolio investment	8 652 ..	**78,437**	**34,265**	**21,794**	**30,456**	**36,122**	**33,794**	**46,296**	**49,432**
Equity securities	8 660 ..	3,636	2,206	862	2,127	2,371	2,497	4,787	6,786
Banks	8 663 ..	994	365	165	529	658	622	1,560	1,377
Other sectors	8 664 ..	2,642	1,841	697	1,598	1,713	1,875	3,227	5,409
Debt securities	8 669 ..	74,802	32,059	20,932	28,329	33,751	31,297	41,509	42,647
Bonds and notes	8 670 ..	74,802	32,059	20,932	28,329	33,751	31,297	41,509	42,647
Monetary authorities	8 671 ..	....	....	....	....	....	97	872	2,239
General government	8 672 ..	52,011	22,558	13,109	18,455	22,569	19,831	28,902	29,804
Banks	8 673 ..	6,492	2,660	1,373	1,376	1,858	2,165	2,474	1,812
Other sectors	8 674 ..	16,298	6,840	6,451	8,497	9,324	9,205	9,261	8,792
Money market instruments	8 680 ..	....	....	....	....	....	....	....	....
Monetary authorities	8 681 ..	....	....	....	....	....	....	....	....
General government	8 682 ..	....	....	....	....	....	....	....	....
Banks	8 683 ..	....	....	....	....	....	....	....	....
Other sectors	8 684 ..	....	....	....	....	....	....	....	....
Financial derivatives	8 905 ..	....	....	....	....	....	**1,832**	**5,323**	**4,641**
Monetary authorities	8 906 ..	....	....	....	....	....	....	....	....
General government	8 907 ..	....	....	....	....	....	1,832	5,323	4,641
Banks	8 908 ..	....	....	....	....	....	....	....	....
Other sectors	8 909 ..	....	....	....	....	....	....	....	....
Other investment	8 753 ..	**67,333**	**76,953**	**68,761**	**66,865**	**62,913**	**53,052**	**44,262**	**48,154**
Trade credits	8 756 ..	2,596	7,348	6,657	6,902	7,649	7,349	8,481	11,955
General government	8 757 ..	284	291	220	181	108	42	34	49
of which: Short-term	8 759 ..	....	....	....	....	....	....	....	....
Other sectors	8 760 ..	2,312	7,056	6,438	6,721	7,541	7,307	8,447	11,906
of which: Short-term	8 762 ..	*1,595*	*5,081*	*1,931*	*5,646*	*5,128*	*3,434*	*4,378*	*5,596*
Loans	8 764 ..	60,949	68,385	60,139	57,049	51,979	41,155	29,871	29,840
Monetary authorities	8 765 ..	5,067	13,980	14,340	15,512	14,091	9,513	....	....
of which: Use of Fund credit and loans from the Fund	8 766 ..	*5,056*	*13,976*	*14,340*	*15,523*	*14,091*	*9,513*		
of which: Short-term	8 768 ..	....	....	....	....	....	....	....	....
General government	8 769 ..	22,647	23,257	21,389	21,920	21,180	18,234	17,059	17,179
of which: Short-term	8 771 ..	....	....	....	....	....	....	....	....
Banks	8 772 ..	14,389	10,181	8,314	5,428	4,122	2,760	2,451	3,209
of which: Short-term	8 774 ..	*5,036*	*2,443*	*2,827*	*2,985*	*1,113*	*580*	*564*	*834*
Other sectors	8 775 ..	18,846	20,967	16,097	14,189	12,586	10,648	10,361	9,452
of which: Short-term	8 777 ..	*3,958*	*5,451*	*5,312*	*6,527*	*6,419*	*3,727*	*3,150*	*4,064*
Currency and deposits	8 780 ..	3,788	1,221	150	119	136	217	495	689
Monetary authorities	8 781 ..	....	....	....	....	....	....	....	....
General government	8 782 ..	....	....	....	....	....	....	....	....
Banks	8 783 ..	3,788	1,221	150	119	136	217	495	689
Other sectors	8 784 ..	....	....	....	....	....	....	....	....
Other liabilities	8 786 ..	....	....	1,814	2,795	3,148	4,331	5,415	5,669
Monetary authorities	8 787 ..	....	....	126	....	....	....	....	....
of which: Short-term	8 789 ..	....	....	*126*	....	....	....	....	....
General government	8 790 ..	....	....	1,427	1,742	3,022	4,271	5,354	5,608
of which: Short-term	8 792 ..	....	....	*1,427*	*1,742*	*3,022*	*4,271*	*5,354*	*5,608*
Banks	8 793 ..	....	....	261	1,054	127	61	61	61
of which: Short-term	8 795 ..	....	....	*261*	*1,054*	*127*	*61*	*61*	*61*
Other sectors	8 796 ..	....	....	....	....	....	....	....	....
of which: Short-term	8 798 ..	....	....	....	....	....	....	....	....
NET INTERNATIONAL INVESTMENT POSITION	8 995 ..	**−60,594**	**−58,914**	**−2,325**	**−761**	**3,034**	**21,977**	**21,977**	**36,821**
Conversion rates: Argentine pesos per U.S. dollar (end of period)	0 102 ..	.99950	.99950	3.32000	2.90500	2.95900	3.01200	3.04200	3.12900

Table 1. ANALYTIC PRESENTATION, 2000–2007

(Millions of U.S. dollars)

	Code	2000	2001	2002	2003	2004	2005	2006	2007
A. Current Account[1]	4 993 Z.	−278.37	−199.56	−147.88	−189.44	−19.63	−51.71	−117.13	−589.65
Goods: exports f.o.b.	2 100 ..	309.91	353.11	513.78	696.13	738.31	1,004.85	1,025.45	1,196.64
Goods: imports f.o.b.	3 100 ..	−773.43	−773.33	−882.54	−1,130.21	−1,196.26	−1,592.78	−1,921.30	−2,796.90
Balance on Goods	4 100 ..	*−463.52*	*−420.22*	*−368.76*	*−434.08*	*−457.95*	*−587.93*	*−895.86*	*−1,600.26*
Services: credit	2 200 ..	136.93	186.53	183.83	207.36	332.60	411.09	484.74	580.02
Services: debit	3 200 ..	−192.75	−204.30	−224.52	−275.70	−431.53	−531.05	−615.13	−792.56
Balance on Goods and Services	4 991 ..	*−519.33*	*−438.00*	*−409.45*	*−502.42*	*−556.89*	*−707.89*	*−1,026.25*	*−1,812.80*
Income: credit	2 300 ..	103.74	103.75	136.57	165.97	397.46	457.51	624.26	810.74
Income: debit	3 300 ..	−50.84	−39.29	−48.36	−71.48	−290.04	−324.99	−409.09	−532.35
Balance on Goods, Services, and Income	4 992 ..	*−466.43*	*−373.54*	*−321.23*	*−407.93*	*−449.47*	*−575.37*	*−811.08*	*−1,534.40*
Current transfers: credit	2 379 Z.	208.52	200.79	199.68	245.01	514.82	603.52	791.67	1,024.77
Current transfers: debit	3 379 ..	−20.46	−26.81	−26.33	−26.53	−84.98	−79.86	−97.71	−80.02
B. Capital Account[1]	4 994 Z.	28.31	30.12	68.06	89.94	41.34	73.25	86.38	142.76
Capital account: credit	2 994 Z.	29.49	32.57	70.18	92.14	47.23	76.06	91.94	160.12
Capital account: debit	3 994 ..	−1.18	−2.45	−2.12	−2.20	−5.89	−2.81	−5.56	−17.36
Total, Groups A Plus B	4 981 ..	*−250.06*	*−169.44*	*−79.83*	*−99.51*	*21.71*	*21.54*	*−30.74*	*−446.89*
C. Financial Account[1]	4 995 W.	249.89	175.14	147.41	174.45	16.62	162.73	434.12	1,008.44
Direct investment abroad	4 505 ..	. . . .	. . . .	. . . .	−.36	−2.25	−6.72	−3.08	2.14
Direct investment in Armenia	4 555 Z.	104.19	69.87	110.74	120.87	247.86	239.38	453.17	698.81
Portfolio investment assets	4 602 ..	−19.10	−5.75	3.38	.05	−.48	−2.72	−.18	.53
Equity securities	4 610 ..	−3.01	−.52	−.86	.05	−.11	−.20	.41	−.13
Debt securities	4 619 ..	−16.09	−5.23	4.24	. . . .	−.37	−2.52	−.59	.67
Portfolio investment liabilities	4 652 Z.	.25	.04	−1.85	.21	−2.39	1.13	9.40	−9.74
Equity securities	4 660 ..	.40	.49	−.41	.05	1.37	1.33	−.60	.18
Debt securities	4 669 Z.	−.15	−.45	−1.44	.16	−3.77	−.20	10.00	−9.92
Financial derivatives	4 910 ..	. . . .	. . . .	. . . .	. . . .	. . . .	. . . .	. . . .	. . . .
Financial derivatives assets	4 900 ..	. . . .	. . . .	. . . .	. . . .	. . . .	. . . .	. . . .	. . . .
Financial derivatives liabilities	4 905 ..	. . . .	. . . .	. . . .	. . . .	. . . .	. . . .	. . . .	. . . .
Other investment assets	4 703 ..	−9.48	−18.34	−88.53	−63.59	−315.80	−170.65	−175.67	−257.81
Monetary authorities	4 701 ..	−.10	.03	−.46	−.10	−1.46	2.55	.70	−.04
General government	4 704 ..	11.33	12.76	−6.80	2.18	−19.89	−58.71	84.24	−2.18
Banks	4 705 ..	−14.11	−19.69	−38.21	−52.71	−62.90	42.10	−7.68	−18.59
Other sectors	4 728 ..	−6.60	−11.43	−43.07	−12.95	−231.56	−156.59	−252.94	−236.99
Other investment liabilities	4 753 W.	174.03	129.32	123.68	117.27	89.69	102.31	150.48	574.51
Monetary authorities	4 753 WA	1.59	3.97	4.56	.24	5.25	.87	−.55	9.31
General government	4 753 ZB	44.28	62.31	45.14	24.68	38.46	36.05	68.67	181.11
Banks	4 753 ZC	8.78	−3.70	2.67	10.51	32.85	24.16	34.05	331.67
Other sectors	4 753 ZD	119.38	66.74	71.31	81.84	13.13	41.23	48.32	52.42
Total, Groups A Through C	4 983 ..	*−.18*	*5.70*	*67.59*	*74.95*	*38.33*	*184.27*	*403.38*	*561.55*
D. Net Errors and Omissions	4 998 ..	17.09	11.02	−4.39	−1.56	−5.53	2.37	−16.12	−1.90
Total, Groups A Through D	4 984 ..	*16.91*	*16.72*	*63.20*	*73.39*	*32.81*	*186.64*	*387.26*	*559.65*
E. Reserves and Related Items	4 802 A.	−16.91	−16.72	−63.20	−73.39	−32.81	−186.64	−387.26	−559.65
Reserve assets	4 802 ..	−19.75	−20.06	−82.25	−47.36	−26.40	−161.89	−365.90	−546.13
Use of Fund credit and loans	4 766 ..	−15.91	3.35	8.07	1.78	−6.41	−24.75	−21.36	−13.52
Exceptional financing	4 920 ..	18.76	. . . .	10.97	−27.81	. . . .	. . . .	. . . .	. . . .
Conversion rates: drams per U.S. dollar	0 101 ..	539.53	555.08	573.35	578.76	533.45	457.69	416.04	342.08

[1] Excludes components that have been classified in the categories of Group E.

Table 2. STANDARD PRESENTATION, 2000–2007

(Millions of U.S. dollars)

	Code	2000	2001	2002	2003	2004	2005	2006	2007
CURRENT ACCOUNT	4 993 ..	−278.37	−199.56	−147.88	−189.44	−19.63	−51.71	−117.13	−589.65
A. GOODS	4 100 ..	−463.52	−420.22	−368.76	−434.08	−457.95	−587.93	−895.86	−1,600.26
Credit	2 100 ..	309.91	353.11	513.78	696.13	738.31	1,004.85	1,025.45	1,196.64
General merchandise: exports f.o.b.	2 110 ..	300.49	341.83	505.16	685.60	722.91	973.92	991.95	1,162.55
Goods for processing: exports f.o.b.	2 150 ..	5.45	3.01	1.35	1.03	1.30	1.29	1.33	1.88
Repairs on goods	2 160 ..	....	....	....	....	....	....	....	....
Goods procured in ports by carriers	2 170 ..	3.97	8.27	7.27	9.50	14.10	29.65	32.17	32.21
Nonmonetary gold	2 180 ..	....	....	....	....	....	....	....	....
Debit	3 100 ..	−773.43	−773.33	−882.54	−1,130.21	−1,196.26	−1,592.78	−1,921.30	−2,796.90
General merchandise: imports f.o.b.	3 110 ..	−759.47	−753.89	−863.58	−1,115.86	−1,173.06	−1,556.11	−1,883.73	−2,755.97
Goods for processing: imports f.o.b.	3 150 ..	−3.54	−1.80	−1.06	−.89	−.92	−.93	−.84	−.87
Repairs on goods	3 160 ..	....	....	....	....	....	....	....	....
Goods procured in ports by carriers	3 170 ..	−10.42	−17.64	−17.91	−13.46	−22.29	−35.75	−36.73	−40.06
Nonmonetary gold	3 180 ..	....	....	....	....	....	....	....	....
B. SERVICES	4 200 ..	−55.81	−17.78	−40.69	−68.34	−98.93	−119.96	−130.39	−212.54
Total credit	*2 200* ..	*136.93*	*186.53*	*183.83*	*207.36*	*332.60*	*411.09*	*484.74*	*580.02*
Total debit	*3 200* ..	*−192.75*	*−204.30*	*−224.52*	*−275.70*	*−431.53*	*−531.05*	*−615.13*	*−792.56*
Transportation services, credit	2 205 ..	63.95	71.17	64.29	73.00	73.56	92.16	102.31	132.97
Passenger	*2 850* ..	*13.57*	*16.13*	*18.49*	*17.24*	*16.89*	*19.54*	*35.60*	*38.29*
Freight	*2 851* ..	*42.79*	*46.94*	*37.00*	*46.21*	*43.21*	*58.02*	*59.19*	*83.31*
Other	*2 852* ..	*7.59*	*8.10*	*8.80*	*9.55*	*13.46*	*14.59*	*7.52*	*11.38*
Sea transport, passenger	2 207 ..	....	....	....	....	....	....	....	....
Sea transport, freight	2 208 ..	....	....	....	....	....	....	....	....
Sea transport, other	2 209 ..	....	....	....	....	....	....	....	....
Air transport, passenger	2 211 ..	10.85	13.52	15.96	14.18	12.99	15.18	30.32	31.98
Air transport, freight	2 212 ..	1.73	1.61	1.22	1.31	.75	.80	.88	.80
Air transport, other	2 213 ..	7.59	8.10	8.75	9.49	13.38	14.34	6.59	9.37
Other transport, passenger	2 215 ..	2.72	2.61	2.53	3.06	3.89	4.36	5.28	6.31
Other transport, freight	2 216 ..	41.06	45.33	35.77	44.90	42.46	57.22	58.30	82.51
Other transport, other	2 217 ..	....	....	.05	.07	.08	.25	.92	2.01
Transportation services, debit	3 205 ..	−115.95	−120.58	−129.91	−151.33	−178.66	−211.56	−231.90	−361.30
Passenger	*3 850* ..	*−15.56*	*−19.30*	*−31.12*	*−29.98*	*−37.26*	*−48.13*	*−34.57*	*−51.26*
Freight	*3 851* ..	*−82.54*	*−82.63*	*−87.16*	*−116.57*	*−118.28*	*−147.18*	*−183.93*	*−267.80*
Other	*3 852* ..	*−17.85*	*−18.66*	*−11.63*	*−4.78*	*−23.11*	*−16.25*	*−13.40*	*−42.23*
Sea transport, passenger	3 207 ..	....	....	....	....	....	....	....	....
Sea transport, freight	3 208 ..	−11.10	−10.04	−11.50	−14.81	−24.31	−33.44	−36.65	−54.57
Sea transport, other	3 209 ..	....	....	....	....	....	....	....	....
Air transport, passenger	3 211 ..	−12.04	−15.75	−26.22	−24.59	−30.85	−36.18	−26.79	−42.78
Air transport, freight	3 212 ..	−.65	−.61	−.99	−1.26	−1.38	−1.36	−4.45	−1.09
Air transport, other	3 213 ..	−17.85	−18.66	−11.56	−4.57	−22.40	−14.26	−10.21	−37.04
Other transport, passenger	3 215 ..	−3.52	−3.55	−4.90	−5.40	−6.42	−11.95	−7.78	−8.48
Other transport, freight	3 216 ..	−70.79	−71.97	−74.67	−100.50	−92.59	−112.38	−142.82	−212.14
Other transport, other	3 217 ..	....	....	−.07	−.21	−.71	−1.99	−3.20	−5.19
Travel, credit	2 236 ..	37.76	64.88	63.27	72.69	171.45	219.97	270.73	304.90
Business travel	2 237 ..	14.35	33.41	25.73	35.06	60.01	98.99	111.00	108.90
Personal travel	2 240 ..	23.41	31.47	37.54	37.64	111.44	120.99	159.73	195.99
Travel, debit	3 236 ..	−39.68	−39.73	−53.90	−67.00	−178.85	−236.34	−286.04	−294.32
Business travel	3 237 ..	−27.71	−25.16	−26.18	−33.58	−77.24	−126.49	−134.73	−95.84
Personal travel	3 240 ..	−11.97	−14.57	−27.72	−33.42	−101.61	−109.85	−151.31	−198.48
Other services, credit	2 200 BA	35.22	50.48	56.27	61.66	87.59	98.95	111.70	142.15
Communications	2 245 ..	15.84	22.69	17.71	16.70	23.75	28.19	22.88	41.35
Construction	2 249 ..	....	.67	6.22	7.91	11.95	10.56	9.94	11.16
Insurance	2 253 ..	3.00	3.53	5.44	7.42	9.24	11.89	14.77	14.67
Financial	2 260 ..	1.38	.88	1.27	1.58	2.70	3.23	3.60	4.14
Computer and information	2 262 ..	1.97	8.35	9.85	11.01	17.64	22.45	33.03	43.61
Royalties and licence fees	2 266 ..	....	....	....	....	....	....	....	....
Other business services	2 268 ..	5.60	5.56	6.01	6.72	9.15	9.53	12.44	12.14
Personal, cultural, and recreational	2 287 ..	.78	1.70	2.04	2.28	4.93	4.78	5.42	5.87
Government, n.i.e.	2 291 ..	6.65	7.11	7.73	8.04	8.23	8.34	9.61	9.20
Other services, debit	3 200 BA	−37.12	−43.99	−40.71	−57.37	−74.03	−83.15	−97.19	−136.95
Communications	3 245 ..	−8.70	−13.94	−11.17	−10.95	−12.86	−13.90	−16.51	−17.17
Construction	3 249 ..	....	−.78	−2.87	−3.08	−3.32	−2.77	−3.21	−3.75
Insurance	3 253 ..	−10.20	−10.36	−11.09	−15.36	−18.37	−23.70	−28.68	−48.94
Financial	3 260 ..	−1.16	−.41	−.26	−1.06	−2.16	−1.89	−2.65	−4.99
Computer and information	3 262 ..	....	....	−.75	−.78	−1.42	−1.52	−2.61	−3.87
Royalties and licence fees	3 266 ..	....	....	....	....	....	....	....	....
Other business services	3 268 ..	−.46	−1.53	−2.06	−8.81	−17.06	−18.30	−21.24	−29.68
Personal, cultural, and recreational	3 287 ..	−.75	−4.55	−4.65	−5.17	−6.06	−6.66	−7.32	−7.97
Government, n.i.e.	3 291 ..	−15.85	−12.42	−7.86	−12.18	−12.78	−14.41	−14.97	−20.58

Table 2 (Continued). STANDARD PRESENTATION, 2000–2007

(Millions of U.S. dollars)

	Code	2000	2001	2002	2003	2004	2005	2006	2007
C. INCOME	4 300	**52.90**	**64.46**	**88.21**	**94.49**	**107.41**	**132.52**	**215.17**	**278.40**
Total credit	2 300	*103.74*	*103.75*	*136.57*	*165.97*	*397.46*	*457.51*	*624.26*	*810.74*
Total debit	3 300	*–50.84*	*–39.29*	*–48.36*	*–71.48*	*–290.04*	*–324.99*	*–409.09*	*–532.35*
Compensation of employees, credit	2 310	**78.16**	**84.23**	**120.81**	**152.87**	**381.81**	**428.75**	**575.95**	**742.67**
Compensation of employees, debit	3 310	**–1.21**	**–11.71**	**–15.37**	**–19.12**	**–122.29**	**–132.99**	**–129.63**	**–166.08**
Investment income, credit	2 320	**25.58**	**19.52**	**15.76**	**13.10**	**15.65**	**28.76**	**48.30**	**68.08**
Direct investment income	2 330	....	....	....	....	....	.43	1.41	1.01
Dividends and distributed branch profits	2 332	....	....	....	....	....	....	.72	....
Reinvested earnings and undistributed branch profits	2 333	....	....	....	....	....	.43	.69	1.01
Income on debt (interest)	2 334	....	....	....	....	....	....	....	....
Portfolio investment income	2 339	1.99	1.30	1.70	1.80	3.41	6.95	8.64	14.81
Income on equity	2 340	....	....	....	....	....	....	....	....
Income on bonds and notes	2 350	....	....	....	....	....	6.91	8.60	14.77
Income on money market instruments	2 360	1.99	1.30	1.70	1.80	3.41	.04	.04	.03
Other investment income	2 370	23.59	18.21	14.06	11.30	12.24	21.38	38.26	52.25
Investment income, debit	3 320	**–49.63**	**–27.59**	**–32.98**	**–52.35**	**–167.75**	**–192.00**	**–279.46**	**–366.26**
Direct investment income	3 330	–22.02	–3.58	–13.03	–34.81	–146.53	–169.91	–244.37	–332.22
Dividends and distributed branch profits	3 332	....	....	–5.58	–7.64	–38.93	–14.19	–49.26	–81.02
Reinvested earnings and undistributed branch profits	3 333	–22.02	–3.58	–7.45	–27.17	–107.60	–155.24	–193.90	–250.22
Income on debt (interest)	3 334	....	....	....	....	....	–.47	–1.22	–.98
Portfolio investment income	3 339	–1.21	–1.33	–.77	–.45	–.22	–.58	–.85	–1.21
Income on equity	3 340	....	....	....	....	....	....	–.30	–.37
Income on bonds and notes	3 350	....	–.15	–.04	–.05	–.05	–.31	–.54	–.83
Income on money market instruments	3 360	–1.21	–1.18	–.73	–.40	–.17	–.27	....	....
Other investment income	3 370	–26.40	–22.68	–19.18	–17.10	–21.00	–21.52	–34.24	–32.83
D. CURRENT TRANSFERS	4 379	**188.06**	**173.99**	**173.35**	**218.48**	**429.84**	**523.66**	**693.95**	**944.76**
Credit	2 379	**208.52**	**200.79**	**199.68**	**245.01**	**514.82**	**603.52**	**791.67**	**1,024.77**
General government	2 380	104.52	75.77	56.59	62.03	62.96	68.49	81.95	97.22
Other sectors	2 390	104.00	125.02	143.09	182.99	451.86	535.02	709.71	927.55
Workers' remittances	2 391	9.31	10.16	10.17	9.32	42.54	57.99	74.38	94.37
Other current transfers	2 392	94.69	114.86	132.92	173.66	409.32	477.03	635.33	833.19
Debit	3 379	**–20.46**	**–26.81**	**–26.33**	**–26.53**	**–84.98**	**–79.86**	**–97.71**	**–80.02**
General government	3 380	–2.01	–3.88	–1.89	–1.84	–2.01	–2.42	–2.00	–2.76
Other sectors	3 390	–18.45	–22.93	–24.44	–24.69	–82.98	–77.44	–95.71	–77.25
Workers' remittances	3 391	–2.31	–6.38	–6.56	–5.59	–10.02	–16.04	–18.53	–5.32
Other current transfers	3 392	–16.14	–16.55	–17.88	–19.11	–72.95	–61.40	–77.18	–71.93
CAPITAL AND FINANCIAL ACCOUNT	4 996	**261.28**	**188.54**	**152.27**	**191.01**	**25.16**	**49.35**	**133.25**	**591.55**
CAPITAL ACCOUNT	4 994	**28.31**	**30.12**	**68.06**	**89.94**	**41.34**	**73.25**	**86.38**	**142.76**
Total credit	2 994	*29.49*	*32.57*	*70.18*	*92.14*	*47.23*	*76.06*	*91.94*	*160.12*
Total debit	3 994	*–1.18*	*–2.45*	*–2.12*	*–2.20*	*–5.89*	*–2.81*	*–5.56*	*–17.36*
Capital transfers, credit	2 400	**29.49**	**32.57**	**70.18**	**92.14**	**47.23**	**76.06**	**91.94**	**160.12**
General government	2 401	29.49	32.57	70.18	86.63	13.08	18.03	24.51	62.42
Debt forgiveness	2 402	....	....	....	....	....	....	....	....
Other capital transfers	2 410	29.49	32.57	70.18	86.63	13.08	18.03	24.51	62.42
Other sectors	2 430	....	....	....	5.52	34.15	58.03	67.43	97.70
Migrants' transfers	2 431	....	....	....	5.52	10.21	11.32	7.81	8.83
Debt forgiveness	2 432	....	....	....	....	....	....	....	....
Other capital transfers	2 440	....	....	....	....	23.95	46.71	59.62	88.87
Capital transfers, debit	3 400	**–1.18**	**–2.45**	**–2.12**	**–2.20**	**–5.89**	**–2.81**	**–5.56**	**–17.36**
General government	3 401	....	....	....	....	....	....	....	....
Debt forgiveness	3 402	....	....	....	....	....	....	....	....
Other capital transfers	3 410	....	....	....	....	....	....	....	....
Other sectors	3 430	–1.18	–2.45	–2.12	–2.20	–5.89	–2.81	–5.56	–17.36
Migrants' transfers	3 431	–1.18	–2.45	–2.12	–2.20	–5.89	–2.81	–5.56	–4.73
Debt forgiveness	3 432	....	....	....	....	....	....	....	....
Other capital transfers	3 440	....	....	....	....	....	....	....	–12.63
Nonproduced nonfinancial assets, credit	2 480	....	....	....	....	....	....	....	....
Nonproduced nonfinancial assets, debit	3 480	....	....	....	....	....	....	....	....

Table 2 (Continued). STANDARD PRESENTATION, 2000–2007

(Millions of U.S. dollars)

	Code	2000	2001	2002	2003	2004	2005	2006	2007
FINANCIAL ACCOUNT	4 995 ..	**232.97**	**158.42**	**84.21**	**101.07**	**−16.19**	**−23.90**	**46.86**	**448.79**
A. DIRECT INVESTMENT	4 500 ..	**104.19**	**69.87**	**110.74**	**120.51**	**245.61**	**232.66**	**450.09**	**700.95**
Direct investment abroad	4 505 ..	....	....	....	−.36	−2.25	−6.72	−3.08	2.14
Equity capital	4 510 ..	....	....	....	−.36	−2.25	−6.29	−2.39	3.15
Claims on affiliated enterprises	4 515 ..	....	....	....	−.36	−2.25	−6.29	−2.39	3.15
Liabilities to affiliated enterprises	4 520 ..	....	....	....	....	....	....	....	....
Reinvested earnings	4 525 ..	....	....	....	....	....	−.43	−.69	−1.01
Other capital	4 530 ..	....	....	....	....	....	....	....	....
Claims on affiliated enterprises	4 535 ..	....	....	....	....	....	....	....	....
Liabilities to affiliated enterprises	4 540 ..	....	....	....	....	....	....	....	....
Direct investment in Armenia	4 555 ..	104.19	69.87	110.74	120.87	247.86	239.38	453.17	698.81
Equity capital	4 560 ..	68.47	60.80	98.42	75.20	117.63	74.06	216.73	207.45
Claims on direct investors	4 565 ..	....	....	....	....	....	....	....	....
Liabilities to direct investors	4 570 ..	68.47	60.80	98.42	75.20	117.63	74.06	216.73	207.45
Reinvested earnings	4 575 ..	22.02	3.58	7.45	27.17	107.60	155.24	193.90	250.22
Other capital	4 580 ..	13.70	5.50	4.86	18.51	22.63	10.08	42.54	241.14
Claims on direct investors	4 585 ..	....	....	....	....	....	....	....	....
Liabilities to direct investors	4 590 ..	13.70	5.50	4.86	18.51	22.63	10.08	42.54	241.14
B. PORTFOLIO INVESTMENT	4 600 ..	**−18.85**	**−5.71**	**1.53**	**.26**	**−2.88**	**−1.59**	**9.22**	**−9.21**
Assets	4 602 ..	**−19.10**	**−5.75**	**3.38**	**.05**	**−.48**	**−2.72**	**−.18**	**.53**
Equity securities	4 610 ..	−3.01	−.52	−.86	.05	−.11	−.20	.41	−.13
Monetary authorities	4 611 ..	....	....	....	....	....	....	....	....
General government	4 612 ..	....	....	....	....	....	....	....	....
Banks	4 613 ..	−.41	.21	−.31	.05	−.01	−.10	.41	−.13
Other sectors	4 614 ..	−2.60	−.73	−.55	....	−.10	−.10	....	....
Debt securities	4 619 ..	−16.09	−5.23	4.24	....	−.37	−2.52	−.59	.67
Bonds and notes	4 620 ..	−16.09	−5.23	−.04	.02	.01	−2.40	−.83	.95
Monetary authorities	4 621 ..	....	....	....	....	....	....	....	....
General government	4 622 ..	....	....	....	....	....	....	....	....
Banks	4 623 ..	−16.09	−5.23	−.04	.02	.01	−2.40	−.83	.95
Other sectors	4 624 ..	....	....	....	....	....	....	....	....
Money market instruments	4 630 ..	....	....	4.28	−.02	−.38	−.12	.24	−.28
Monetary authorities	4 631 ..	....	....	....	....	....	....	....	....
General government	4 632 ..	....	....	....	....	....	....	....	....
Banks	4 633 ..	....	....	4.28	−.02	−.38	−.12	.24	−.28
Other sectors	4 634 ..	....	....	....	....	....	....	....	....
Liabilities	4 652 ..	**.25**	**.04**	**−1.85**	**.21**	**−2.39**	**1.13**	**9.40**	**−9.74**
Equity securities	4 660 ..	.40	.49	−.41	.05	1.37	1.33	−.60	.18
Banks	4 663 ..	.20	.49	−.41	.05	1.37	1.33	−.60	.18
Other sectors	4 664 ..	.20	....	....	....	....	....	....	....
Debt securities	4 669 ..	−.15	−.45	−1.44	.16	−3.77	−.20	10.00	−9.92
Bonds and notes	4 670 ..	....	.13	.02	.37	−.62	....	....	−10.00
Monetary authorities	4 671 ..	....	....	....	....	....	....	....	....
General government	4 672 ..	....	.13	.02	.37	−.62	....	....	....
Banks	4 673 ..	....	....	....	....	....	....	....	−10.00
Other sectors	4 674 ..	....	....	....	....	....	....	....	....
Money market instruments	4 680 ..	−.15	−.58	−1.46	−.21	−3.15	−.20	10.00	.08
Monetary authorities	4 681 ..	....	....	....	....	....	....	....	....
General government	4 682 ..	−.15	−.58	−1.30	....	−3.11	−.20	....	....
Banks	4 683 ..	....	....	−.16	−.21	−.04	....	10.00	.08
Other sectors	4 684 ..	....	....	....	....	....	....	....	....
C. FINANCIAL DERIVATIVES	4 910 ..	....	....	....	....	....	....	....	....
Monetary authorities	4 911 ..	....	....	....	....	....	....	....	....
General government	4 912 ..	....	....	....	....	....	....	....	....
Banks	4 913 ..	....	....	....	....	....	....	....	....
Other sectors	4 914 ..	....	....	....	....	....	....	....	....
Assets	4 900 ..	....	....	....	....	....	....	....	....
Monetary authorities	4 901 ..	....	....	....	....	....	....	....	....
General government	4 902 ..	....	....	....	....	....	....	....	....
Banks	4 903 ..	....	....	....	....	....	....	....	....
Other sectors	4 904 ..	....	....	....	....	....	....	....	....
Liabilities	4 905 ..	....	....	....	....	....	....	....	....
Monetary authorities	4 906 ..	....	....	....	....	....	....	....	....
General government	4 907 ..	....	....	....	....	....	....	....	....
Banks	4 908 ..	....	....	....	....	....	....	....	....
Other sectors	4 909 ..	....	....	....	....	....	....	....	....

Table 2 (Concluded). STANDARD PRESENTATION, 2000–2007

(Millions of U.S. dollars)

	Code	2000	2001	2002	2003	2004	2005	2006	2007
D. OTHER INVESTMENT	4 700 ..	**167.39**	**114.33**	**54.19**	**27.66**	**−232.52**	**−93.09**	**−46.55**	**303.18**
Assets	4 703 ..	**−9.48**	**−18.34**	**−88.53**	**−63.59**	**−315.80**	**−170.65**	**−175.67**	**−257.81**
Trade credits	4 706 ..	−21.81	−22.34	−35.08	−23.36	−22.05	−24.35	−23.25	−22.05
General government	4 707 ..	....	....	....	....	....	....	....	....
of which: Short-term	4 709 ..	....	....	....	....	....	....	....	....
Other sectors	4 710 ..	−21.81	−22.34	−35.08	−23.36	−22.05	−24.35	−23.25	−22.05
of which: Short-term	4 712 ..	*−21.81*	*−22.34*	*−35.08*	*−23.36*	*−22.05*	*−24.35*	*−23.25*	*−22.05*
Loans	4 714 ..	−4.55	5.21	−12.82	4.17	−19.93	1.13	−4.09	8.95
Monetary authorities	4 715 ..	....	....	....	....	....	....	....	....
of which: Short-term	4 718 ..	....	....	....	....	....	....	....	....
General government	4 719 ..	....	....	....	....	....	1.35	.83	.15
of which: Short-term	4 721 ..	....	....	....	....	....	....	....	....
Banks	4 722 ..	−4.55	5.21	−12.82	4.17	−.78	−7.87	3.84	6.79
of which: Short-term	4 724 ..	*−4.55*	*5.21*	*−12.79*	*8.11*	*−1.07*	*−8.62*	*4.50*	*6.98*
Other sectors	4 725 ..	....	....	....	....	−19.15	7.65	−8.75	2.00
of which: Short-term	4 727 ..	....	....	....	....	*−4.15*	*14.15*	*−8.00*	*3.00*
Currency and deposits	4 730 ..	17.89	−1.55	−39.29	−45.79	−270.68	−145.18	−148.36	−228.72
Monetary authorities	4 731 ..	−.08	.08	−.02	−.02	−.04	−.04	.12	....
General government	4 732 ..	11.33	12.76	−6.80	2.18	−19.89	−57.45	85.56	....
Banks	4 733 ..	−8.57	−25.30	−24.48	−58.36	−60.40	52.20	−13.10	−11.70
Other sectors	4 734 ..	15.21	10.91	−7.99	10.41	−190.35	−139.89	−220.94	−217.01
Other assets	4 736 ..	−1.01	.34	−1.35	1.39	−3.13	−2.25	.02	−15.99
Monetary authorities	4 737 ..	−.02	−.06	−.44	−.08	−1.42	2.59	.58	−.04
of which: Short-term	4 739 ..	*−.02*	*−.06*	*−.44*	*−.08*	*−1.42*	*2.59*	*.58*	*−.04*
General government	4 740 ..	....	....	....	....	....	−2.61	−2.14	−2.33
of which: Short-term	4 742 ..	....	....	....	....	....	*−2.61*	*−2.14*	*−2.33*
Banks	4 743 ..	−.99	.40	−.91	1.47	−1.72	−2.23	1.58	−13.68
of which: Short-term	4 745 ..	*−.99*	*.40*	*−.91*	*1.47*	*−1.72*	*−2.23*	*1.58*	*−13.68*
Other sectors	4 746 ..	....	....	....	....	....	....	....	.07
of which: Short-term	4 748 ..	....	....	....	....	....	....	....	*−.08*
Liabilities	4 753 ..	**176.87**	**132.66**	**142.72**	**91.24**	**83.28**	**77.57**	**129.13**	**560.99**
Trade credits	4 756 ..	92.19	47.90	19.95	46.15	23.76	−10.62	−39.45	−80.49
General government	4 757 ..	....	....	....	....	....	....	....	....
of which: Short-term	4 759 ..	....	....	....	....	....	....	....	....
Other sectors	4 760 ..	92.19	47.90	19.95	46.15	23.76	−10.62	−39.45	−80.49
of which: Short-term	4 762 ..	*59.20*	*43.55*	*24.90*	*34.94*	*17.74*	*−2.14*	*−.42*	*−63.72*
Loans	4 764 ..	59.74	78.27	59.58	57.46	43.73	93.52	179.67	538.66
Monetary authorities	4 765 ..	−14.37	7.16	12.62	1.78	−.83	−24.75	−21.36	−4.92
of which: Use of Fund credit and loans from the Fund..	4 766 ..	*−15.91*	*3.35*	*8.07*	*1.78*	*−6.41*	*−24.75*	*−21.36*	*−13.52*
of which: Short-term	4 768 ..	....	....	....	....	....	....	....	....
General government	4 769 ..	44.28	64.24	45.14	24.68	38.46	36.05	68.67	181.11
of which: Short-term	4 771 ..	....	....	....	....	....	....	....	....
Banks	4 772 ..	2.64	−11.27	−8.39	−1.14	7.76	15.66	38.90	243.58
of which: Short-term	4 774 ..	*2.64*	....	*.14*	*2.09*	*−1.14*	*−1.42*	*17.80*	*107.37*
Other sectors	4 775 ..	27.19	18.15	10.21	32.14	−1.67	66.56	93.46	118.88
of which: Short-term	4 777 ..	*.31*	....	*3.83*	*20.02*	*5.46*	*6.06*	*37.89*	*24.13*
Currency and deposits	4 780 ..	5.42	7.71	9.74	12.07	17.74	12.23	−2.43	76.32
Monetary authorities	4 781 ..	....	....	.01	.03	−.06	.88	−.50	.55
General government	4 782 ..	....	....	....	....	....	....	....	....
Banks	4 783 ..	5.42	7.71	9.73	12.04	17.79	11.16	−1.93	75.78
Other sectors	4 784 ..	....	....	....	....	....	.19	....	....
Other liabilities	4 786 ..	19.53	−1.20	53.44	−24.43	−1.94	−17.57	−8.66	26.50
Monetary authorities	4 787 ..	.05	.16	....	.21	−.28	....	−.05	.17
of which: Short-term	4 789 ..	....	....	....	....	−.28	....	−.05	.17
General government	4 790 ..	18.76	−1.93	10.97	−27.81	....	....	....	....
of which: Short-term	4 792 ..	*18.76*	*−1.93*	*10.97*	*−27.81*	....	....	....	....
Banks	4 793 ..	.72	−.13	1.33	−.39	7.29	−2.66	−2.92	12.31
of which: Short-term	4 795 ..	*.72*	*−.13*	*1.33*	*−.39*	*7.29*	*−2.66*	*−2.92*	*12.31*
Other sectors	4 796 ..	....	.70	41.14	3.56	−8.95	−14.90	−5.69	14.02
of which: Short-term	4 798 ..	....	*.08*	*23.77*	*2.45*	*−6.95*	*.49*	*−2.74*	*11.79*
E. RESERVE ASSETS	4 802 ..	**−19.75**	**−20.06**	**−82.25**	**−47.36**	**−26.40**	**−161.89**	**−365.90**	**−546.13**
Monetary gold	4 812 ..	.36	−.10	.03	15.68	....	....	....	....
Special drawing rights	4 811 ..	17.42	10.64	−18.81	12.81	7.30	1.07	−3.16	4.69
Reserve position in the Fund	4 810 ..	....	....	....	....	....	....	....	....
Foreign exchange	4 803 ..	−37.72	−30.61	−63.46	−75.85	−33.61	−163.07	−363.05	−547.44
Other claims	4 813 ..	.19	.01	....	−.01	−.09	.11	.31	−3.37
NET ERRORS AND OMISSIONS	4 998 ..	**17.09**	**11.02**	**−4.39**	**−1.56**	**−5.53**	**2.37**	**−16.12**	**−1.90**

Table 3. INTERNATIONAL INVESTMENT POSITION (End-period stocks), 2000–2007

(Millions of U.S. dollars)

	Code	2000	2001	2002	2003	2004	2005	2006	2007
ASSETS	8 995 C.	**529.43**	**544.13**	**685.02**	**786.85**	**1,141.46**	**1,427.93**	**1,982.46**	**2,822.64**
Direct investment abroad	8 505 ..	.01	.02	.36	.39	2.67	10.27	15.54	14.34
Equity capital and reinvested earnings	8 506 ..	.01	.02	.36	.39	2.67	10.27	15.54	14.34
Claims on affiliated enterprises	8 507 ..	.01	.02	.36	.39	2.67	10.27	15.54	14.34
Liabilities to affiliated enterprises	8 508 ..	....	....	....	....	....	....	....	....
Other capital	8 530 ..	....	....	....	....	....	....	....	....
Claims on affiliated enterprises	8 535 ..	....	....	....	....	....	....	....	....
Liabilities to affiliated enterprises	8 540 ..	....	....	....	....	....	....	....	....
Portfolio investment	8 602 ..	**19.27**	**8.90**	**4.51**	**4.45**	**4.62**	**5.94**	**5.26**	**4.89**
Equity securities	8 610 ..	3.09	3.60	4.46	4.39	4.49	3.29	2.04	2.17
Monetary authorities	8 611 ..	....	....	....	....	....	....	....	....
General government	8 612 ..	....	....	....	....	....	....	....	....
Banks	8 613 ..	.42	.20	.51	.45	.47	.58	.22	.36
Other sectors	8 614 ..	2.67	3.41	3.96	3.94	4.02	2.71	1.82	1.82
Debt securities	8 619 ..	16.18	5.30	.04	.06	.13	2.64	3.22	2.71
Bonds and notes	8 620 ..	16.11	5.24	.05	....	.01	2.41	3.22	2.32
Monetary authorities	8 621 ..	.01	....	....	....	....	....	....	....
General government	8 622 ..	....	....	....	....	....	....	....	....
Banks	8 623 ..	16.10	5.24	.06	....	.01	2.41	3.22	2.32
Other sectors	8 624 ..	....	....	....	....	....	....	....	....
Money market instruments	8 630 ..	.07	.06	−.01	.06	.12	.24	....	.40
Monetary authorities	8 631 ..	....	....	....	....	....	....	....	....
General government	8 632 ..	....	....	....	....	....	....	....	....
Banks	8 633 ..	.07	.06	....	.07	.12	.24	−.01	.30
Other sectors	8 634 ..	....	....	....	....	....	....	....	.09
Financial derivatives	8 900 ..	....	....	**−.01**	....	**−.01**	**.01**	**.01**	....
Monetary authorities	8 901 ..	....	....	....	....	....	....	....	....
General government	8 902 ..	....	....	....	....	....	....	....	....
Banks	8 903 ..	....	....	....	....	....	....	....	....
Other sectors	8 904 ..	....	....	....	....	....	....	....	....
Other investment	8 703 ..	**196.02**	**204.06**	**247.98**	**277.95**	**584.23**	**737.96**	**889.73**	**1,144.33**
Trade credits	8 706 ..	40.61	61.03	68.09	65.98	73.10	85.08	72.07	76.00
General government	8 707 ..	....	....	....	....	....	....	....	....
of which: Short-term	8 709 ..	....	....	....	....	....	....	....	....
Other sectors	8 710 ..	40.61	61.03	68.09	65.98	73.10	85.08	72.07	76.00
of which: Short-term	8 712 ..	*40.61*	*61.03*	*68.09*	*65.98*	*73.10*	*85.08*	*72.07*	*76.00*
Loans	8 714 ..	26.14	20.89	33.45	29.22	49.83	48.84	52.50	44.84
Monetary authorities	8 715 ..	....	....	....	....	....	....	....	....
of which: Short-term	8 718 ..	....	....	....	....	....	....	....	....
General government	8 719 ..	19.59	19.59	19.59	19.59	19.59	18.49	17.66	17.51
of which: Short-term	8 721 ..	....	....	....	....	....	....	....	....
Banks	8 722 ..	6.55	1.30	13.86	9.63	10.93	18.80	15.94	10.40
of which: Short-term	8 724 ..	*6.55*	*1.30*	*13.63*	*5.57*	*6.97*	*15.55*	*11.96*	*5.98*
Other sectors	8 725 ..	....	....	....	....	19.31	11.56	18.90	16.94
of which: Short-term	8 727 ..	....	....	....	....	*4.15*	*−10.05*	*−2.87*	*−5.87*
Currency and deposits	8 730 ..	128.10	121.89	144.09	180.84	455.94	596.42	756.50	997.09
Monetary authorities	8 731 ..	.09	.01	.02	.03	.08	.12	....	....
General government	8 732 ..	16.37	3.60	10.40	8.21	28.10	85.56	....	....
Banks	8 733 ..	75.70	97.13	115.71	169.82	234.63	177.92	194.95	215.15
Other sectors	8 734 ..	35.94	21.15	17.96	2.78	193.13	332.82	561.55	781.94
Other assets	8 736 ..	1.17	.25	2.35	1.92	5.36	7.61	8.66	26.39
Monetary authorities	8 737 ..	.05	.16	.60	.68	2.41	.01	.46	.68
of which: Short-term	8 739 ..	*.03*	*.16*	*.60*	*.68*	*2.41*	*.01*	*.46*	*.68*
General government	8 740 ..	....	....	....	....	....	2.61	4.75	7.08
of which: Short-term	8 742 ..	....	....	....	....	....	*2.61*	*4.75*	*7.08*
Banks	8 743 ..	1.12	.09	1.75	1.23	2.96	4.99	3.45	17.59
of which: Short-term	8 745 ..	*1.12*	*.09*	*1.75*	*1.23*	*2.96*	*4.99*	*3.45*	*17.59*
Other sectors	8 746 ..	....	....	....	....	....	....	....	1.04
of which: Short-term	8 748 ..	....	....	....	....	....	....	....	*1.04*
Reserve assets	8 802 ..	**314.13**	**331.15**	**432.18**	**504.06**	**549.96**	**673.76**	**1,071.92**	**1,659.09**
Monetary gold	8 812 ..	....	12.45	15.68	....	....	....	....	....
Special drawing rights	8 811 ..	21.55	10.24	30.10	18.83	11.96	10.18	13.96	9.60
Reserve position in the Fund	8 810 ..	....	....	....	....	....	....	....	....
Foreign exchange	8 803 ..	292.57	308.46	386.39	485.22	537.89	663.58	1,057.95	1,647.20
Other claims	8 813 ..	.01	....	....	.01	.11	....	....	2.29

Table 3 (Concluded). INTERNATIONAL INVESTMENT POSITION (End-period stocks), 2000–2007

(Millions of U.S. dollars)

	Code	2000	2001	2002	2003	2004	2005	2006	2007
LIABILITIES	8 995 D.	**1,829.71**	**1,978.23**	**2,197.46**	**2,363.90**	**2,703.32**	**2,899.76**	**3,528.98**	**4,912.35**
Direct investment in Armenia	8 555 ..	**513.09**	**579.84**	**684.48**	**793.38**	**1,037.93**	**1,298.29**	**1,774.37**	**2,485.77**
Equity capital and reinvested earnings	8 556 ..	350.21	416.91	513.81	605.39	830.45	1,070.11	1,503.53	1,986.93
Claims on direct investors	8 557 ..	....	....	....	....	....	....	....	....
Liabilities to direct investors	8 558 ..	350.21	416.91	513.81	605.39	830.45	1,070.11	1,503.53	1,986.93
Other capital	8 580 ..	162.88	162.94	170.67	187.99	207.48	228.17	270.84	498.83
Claims on direct investors	8 585 ..	....	....	....	....	....	....	....	....
Liabilities to direct investors	8 590 ..	162.88	162.94	170.67	187.99	207.48	228.17	270.84	498.83
Portfolio investment	8 652 ..	**4.79**	**5.93**	**5.83**	**6.38**	**4.87**	**5.47**	**15.96**	**9.36**
Equity securities	8 660 ..	1.09	1.55	2.93	2.95	4.84	5.48	5.97	9.27
Banks	8 663 ..	.89	1.35	2.73	2.75	4.68	5.32	5.81	9.17
Other sectors	8 664 ..	.20	.20	.20	.20	.16	.16	.16	.11
Debt securities	8 669 ..	3.70	4.38	2.90	3.43	.03	−.01	9.99	.08
Bonds and notes	8 670 ..	−.14	.19	.04	.41	−.15	−.01	10.00	....
Monetary authorities	8 671 ..	....	....	....	....	....	....	....	....
General government	8 672 ..	....	.33	.18	.55	....	....	....	....
Banks	8 673 ..	....	....	....	....	....	....	10.00	....
Other sectors	8 674 ..	−.14	−.14	−.14	−.14	−.14	....	....	....
Money market instruments	8 680 ..	3.84	4.18	2.86	3.02	.18	....	....	.08
Monetary authorities	8 681 ..	....	....	....	....	....	....	....	....
General government	8 682 ..	3.84	4.18	2.86	2.99	.18	....	....	....
Banks	8 683 ..	....	....	....	.04	....	....	....	.08
Other sectors	8 684 ..	....	....	....	....	....	....	....	....
Financial derivatives	8 905 ..	....	....	....	....	....	....	....	....
Monetary authorities	8 906 ..	....	....	....	....	....	....	....	....
General government	8 907 ..	....	....	....	....	....	....	....	....
Banks	8 908 ..	....	....	....	....	....	....	....	....
Other sectors	8 909 ..	....	....	....	....	....	....	....	....
Other investment	8 753 ..	**1,311.83**	**1,392.46**	**1,507.15**	**1,564.14**	**1,660.51**	**1,596.00**	**1,738.65**	**2,417.23**
Trade credits	8 756 ..	268.52	269.56	234.97	229.68	208.58	161.92	93.74	7.33
General government	8 758 ..	....	....	....	....	....	....	....	....
of which: Short-term	8 759 ..	....	....	....	....	....	....	....	....
Other sectors	8 760 ..	268.52	269.56	234.97	229.68	208.58	161.92	93.74	7.33
of which: Short-term	8 762 ..	*192.22*	*195.00*	*174.99*	*162.77*	*137.99*	*113.59*	*80.82*	*7.44*
Loans	8 764 ..	932.32	1,005.18	1,111.72	1,194.25	1,294.23	1,290.17	1,516.10	2,165.45
Monetary authorities	8 765 ..	178.32	178.92	207.54	229.86	240.45	196.23	185.79	191.68
of which: Use of Fund credit and loans from the Fund	8 766 ..	*175.45*	*172.61*	*194.80*	*214.64*	*217.63*	*176.40*	*163.67*	*157.90*
of which: Short-term	8 768 ..	....	....	....	....	....	....	....	....
General government	8 769 ..	675.48	740.87	825.36	860.23	942.49	903.15	1,021.20	1,259.79
of which: Short-term	8 771 ..	....	....	....	....	....	....	....	....
Banks	8 772 ..	42.02	30.73	19.35	14.58	22.23	37.88	83.85	333.90
of which: Short-term	8 774 ..	*42.02*	*42.00*	*5.90*	*4.35*	*3.09*	*1.67*	*29.55*	*137.45*
Other sectors	8 775 ..	36.50	54.65	59.46	89.59	89.06	152.92	225.27	380.08
of which: Short-term	8 777 ..	*6.17*	*6.17*	*9.98*	*29.97*	*35.72*	*40.47*	*76.76*	*107.17*
Currency and deposits	8 780 ..	76.41	83.58	74.06	78.75	98.25	109.50	108.26	194.93
Monetary authorities	8 781 ..	....	....	.01	.03	.01	.88	.59	1.22
General government	8 782 ..	....	....	....	....	....	....	....	....
Banks	8 783 ..	76.26	83.43	73.90	78.57	98.25	108.43	107.48	193.72
Other sectors	8 784 ..	.15	.15	.15	.15	....	.19	.19	....
Other liabilities	8 786 ..	34.58	34.15	86.40	61.45	59.44	34.41	20.55	49.52
Monetary authorities	8 787 ..	.03	.20	.14	.54	.10	.12	.17	.38
of which: Short-term	8 789 ..	....	*.20*	*.14*	*.36*	*.28*	*.30*	*.35*	*.38*
General government	8 790 ..	18.75	16.84	27.80	....	....	....	....	....
of which: Short-term	8 792 ..	*18.75*	*16.84*	*27.80*	....	....	....	....	....
Banks	8 793 ..	.20	.81	1.57	1.48	8.87	6.08	3.51	16.01
of which: Short-term	8 795 ..	*.20*	*.81*	*1.57*	*1.48*	*8.87*	*6.08*	*3.51*	*16.01*
Other sectors	8 796 ..	15.60	16.30	56.89	59.44	50.48	28.21	16.87	33.13
of which: Short-term	8 798 ..	*3.93*	*4.02*	*27.58*	*29.67*	*22.72*	*17.19*	*13.66*	*28.64*
NET INTERNATIONAL INVESTMENT POSITION	8 995 ..	**−1,300.29**	**−1,434.10**	**−1,512.44**	**−1,577.04**	**−1,561.85**	**−1,471.83**	**−1,546.52**	**−2,089.71**
Conversion rates: drams per U.S. dollar (end of period)	0 102 ..	**552.18**	**561.81**	**584.89**	**566.00**	**485.84**	**450.19**	**363.50**	**304.22**

Table 1. ANALYTIC PRESENTATION, 2000–2007

(Millions of U.S. dollars)

	Code	2000	2001	2002	2003	2004	2005	2006	2007
A. Current Account[1]	4 993 Z.	**201.8**	**313.5**	**−338.2**	**−163.1**	**−6.6**	**−197.7**	**−43.3**	**214.9**
Goods: exports f.o.b.	2 100 ..	2,523.5	2,423.1	1,487.9	2,051.9	2,723.5	3,483.3	3,668.9	2,690.8
Goods: imports f.o.b.	3 100 ..	−2,583.2	−2,371.6	−2,024.2	−2,400.4	−3,004.3	−3,460.2	−3,790.1	−2,850.3
Balance on Goods	4 100 ..	*−59.7*	*51.4*	*−536.3*	*−348.5*	*−280.8*	*23.1*	*−121.2*	*−159.4*
Services: credit	2 200 ..	1,008.2	988.1	1,000.7	1,047.3	1,248.0	1,304.0	1,323.5	1,492.1
Services: debit	3 200 ..	−643.9	−613.3	−605.6	−726.8	−793.9	−916.8	−1,002.0	−941.4
Balance on Goods and Services	4 991 ..	*304.6*	*426.3*	*−141.2*	*−27.9*	*173.4*	*410.4*	*200.3*	*391.3*
Income: credit	2 300 ..	53.0	49.8	32.2	32.1	35.0	41.6	61.0	79.3
Income: debit	3 300 ..	−79.7	−104.8	−164.6	−82.1	−111.1	−525.8	−183.2	−157.0
Balance on Goods, Services, and Income	4 992 ..	*277.9*	*371.3*	*−273.6*	*−77.9*	*97.2*	*−73.8*	*78.1*	*313.7*
Current transfers: credit	2 379 Z.	39.5	42.1	40.8	41.4	44.8	53.3	55.3	57.8
Current transfers: debit	3 379 ..	−115.6	−99.9	−105.3	−126.5	−148.7	−177.2	−176.6	−156.6
B. Capital Account[1]	4 994 Z.	**11.2**	**−1.0**	**21.3**	**100.5**	**18.8**	**18.7**	**−14.1**	**18.2**
Capital account: credit	2 994 Z.	16.3	9.0	28.5	123.0	30.9	26.9	29.5	27.4
Capital account: debit	3 994 ..	−5.0	−10.0	−7.2	−22.5	−12.0	−8.2	−43.6	−9.1
Total, Groups A Plus B	4 981 ..	*213.1*	*312.5*	*−316.9*	*−62.6*	*12.2*	*−179.0*	*−57.4*	*233.1*
C. Financial Account[1]	4 995 W.	**−240.7**	**−223.5**	**347.9**	**3.3**	**−15.8**	**154.7**	**111.4**	**−196.9**
Direct investment abroad	4 505 ..	.2	5.0	6.2	3.1	10.1	8.8	13.5	−29.3
Direct investment in Aruba	4 555 Z.	−120.2	−262.9	337.1	157.9	152.7	119.0	609.7	−116.2
Portfolio investment assets	4 602 ..	−48.7	39.8	6.9	−31.2	−34.4	−18.2	−84.3	−320.7
Equity securities	4 610 ..	−45.6	5.9	−5.0	−19.6	−26.3	−3.5	−75.7	−36.6
Debt securities	4 619 ..	−3.1	33.9	11.9	−11.6	−8.1	−14.7	−8.6	−284.0
Portfolio investment liabilities	4 652 Z.	41.0	17.2	56.8	66.4	60.6	21.2	40.5	85.5
Equity securities	4 660 ..	....	....	....	....	....	....	....	....
Debt securities	4 669 Z.	41.0	17.2	56.8	66.4	60.6	21.2	40.5	85.5
Financial derivatives	4 910 ..	....	....	.1	....	....	.8	−2.7	−1.0
Financial derivatives assets	4 900 ..	....	....	....	....	....	.8	−2.7	−1.0
Financial derivatives liabilities	4 905 ..	....	....	.1	....	....	....	....	....
Other investment assets	4 703 ..	−27.7	3.0	−59.8	−83.3	−103.0	51.7	−424.3	198.9
Monetary authorities	4 701 ..	....	....	....	....	....	....	....	....
General government	4 704 ..	....	....	....	.2	....	....	....	....
Banks	4 705 ..	−15.5	−11.0	8.2	−73.9	48.7	−7.8	−2.5	−52.5
Other sectors	4 728 ..	−12.3	14.0	−68.0	−9.7	−151.7	59.5	−421.8	251.4
Other investment liabilities	4 753 W.	−85.3	−25.6	.8	−109.7	−101.8	−28.7	−41.1	−14.2
Monetary authorities	4 753 WA	....	....	....	....	....	....	....	....
General government	4 753 ZB	−21.6	−1.6	−1.4	−160.1	−13.0	−3.2	−13.7	−12.7
Banks	4 753 ZC	27.7	6.5	23.6	78.0	−51.5	8.2	29.9	47.5
Other sectors	4 753 ZD	−91.4	−30.6	−21.3	−27.6	−37.3	−33.7	−57.2	−49.0
Total, Groups A Through C	4 983 ..	*−27.7*	*89.0*	*31.0*	*−59.3*	*−3.6*	*−24.4*	*54.0*	*36.2*
D. Net Errors and Omissions	4 998 ..	**12.7**	**−6.2**	**9.2**	**22.9**	**5.1**	**2.2**	**1.1**	**7.0**
Total, Groups A Through D	4 984 ..	*−15.0*	*82.8*	*40.2*	*−36.4*	*1.6*	*−22.2*	*55.1*	*43.2*
E. Reserves and Related Items	4 802 A.	**15.0**	**−82.8**	**−40.2**	**36.4**	**−1.6**	**22.2**	**−55.1**	**−43.2**
Reserve assets	4 802 ..	15.0	−82.8	−40.2	36.4	−1.6	22.2	−55.1	−43.2
Use of Fund credit and loans	4 766 ..	....	....	....	....	....	....	....	....
Exceptional financing	4 920 ..	....	....	....	....	....	....	....	....
Conversion rates: florins per U.S. dollar	0 101 ..	**1.7900**	**1.7900**	**1.7900**	**1.7900**	**1.7900**	**1.7900**	**1.7900**	**1.7900**

[1] Excludes components that have been classified in the categories of Group E.

Table 2. STANDARD PRESENTATION, 2000–2007

(Millions of U.S. dollars)

	Code	2000	2001	2002	2003	2004	2005	2006	2007
CURRENT ACCOUNT...................................	4 993	**201.8**	**313.5**	**−338.2**	**−163.1**	**−6.6**	**−197.7**	**−43.3**	**214.9**
A. GOODS...................................	4 100	**−59.7**	**51.4**	**−536.3**	**−348.5**	**−280.8**	**23.1**	**−121.2**	**−159.4**
Credit....................................	2 100	**2,523.5**	**2,423.1**	**1,487.9**	**2,051.9**	**2,723.5**	**3,483.3**	**3,668.9**	**2,690.8**
General merchandise: exports f.o.b...............	2 110	96.9	104.7	80.9	60.7	54.0	58.6	75.8	71.9
Goods for processing: exports f.o.b...............	2 150	2,288.3	2,231.2	1,264.1	1,892.5	2,516.5	3,311.7	3,504.1	2,548.6
Repairs on goods....................................	2 160	.5	....	....	....	....	....	....	....
Goods procured in ports by carriers...............	2 170	137.8	87.1	142.9	98.8	152.9	113.0	89.0	70.4
Nonmonetary gold....................................	2 180	....	....	....	....	....	....	....	....
Debit....................................	3 100	**−2,583.2**	**−2,371.6**	**−2,024.2**	**−2,400.4**	**−3,004.3**	**−3,460.2**	**−3,790.1**	**−2,850.3**
General merchandise: imports f.o.b...............	3 110	−846.3	−974.4	−981.1	−1,066.1	−939.2	−1,090.6	−1,189.5	−1,141.4
Goods for processing: imports f.o.b...............	3 150	−1,720.1	−1,396.5	−1,042.7	−1,334.3	−2,065.0	−2,369.5	−2,600.4	−1,708.2
Repairs on goods....................................	3 160	−3.4	−.6	−.4	....	−.1	....	−.1	....
Goods procured in ports by carriers...............	3 170	−13.3	....	....	....	....	....	....	−.7
Nonmonetary gold....................................	3 180	....	....	....	....	....	....	....	....
B. SERVICES...................................	4 200	**364.3**	**374.8**	**395.1**	**320.5**	**454.1**	**387.3**	**321.5**	**550.8**
Total credit...................................	2 200	*1,008.2*	*988.1*	*1,000.7*	*1,047.3*	*1,248.0*	*1,304.0*	*1,323.5*	*1,492.1*
Total debit...................................	3 200	*−643.9*	*−613.3*	*−605.6*	*−726.8*	*−793.9*	*−916.8*	*−1,002.0*	*−941.4*
Transportation services, credit...............	2 205	**78.5**	**47.9**	**32.6**	**35.5**	**49.0**	**52.9**	**47.1**	**48.6**
Passenger....................................	2 850	*36.4*	*3.5*	*.9*	*.1*	....	....	....	*.3*
Freight....................................	2 851	....	....	....	....	....	....	....	....
Other....................................	2 852	*42.1*	*44.4*	*31.7*	*35.4*	*49.0*	*52.8*	*47.1*	*48.3*
Sea transport, passenger...............	2 207	....	....	....	....	....	....	....	....
Sea transport, freight...............	2 208	....	....	....	....	....	....	....	....
Sea transport, other...............	2 209	....	....	....	....	....	....	....	....
Air transport, passenger...............	2 211	....	....	....	....	....	....	....	....
Air transport, freight...............	2 212	....	....	....	....	....	....	....	....
Air transport, other...............	2 213	....	....	....	....	....	....	....	....
Other transport, passenger...............	2 215	....	....	....	....	....	....	....	....
Other transport, freight...............	2 216	....	....	....	....	....	....	....	....
Other transport, other...............	2 217	....	....	....	....	....	....	....	....
Transportation services, debit...............	3 205	**−281.5**	**−264.9**	**−218.7**	**−266.3**	**−331.6**	**−371.1**	**−402.8**	**−304.4**
Passenger....................................	3 850	*−16.6*	*−21.1*	*−12.6*	*−24.8*	*−30.1*	*−24.1*	*−22.6*	*−18.6*
Freight....................................	3 851	*−258.3*	*−237.2*	*−202.6*	*−240.4*	*−301.0*	*−346.7*	*−380.0*	*−285.8*
Other....................................	3 852	*−6.5*	*−6.6*	*−3.5*	*−1.1*	*−.5*	*−.3*	*−.2*	*−.1*
Sea transport, passenger...............	3 207	....	....	....	....	....	....	....	....
Sea transport, freight...............	3 208	....	....	....	....	....	....	....	....
Sea transport, other...............	3 209	....	....	....	....	....	....	....	....
Air transport, passenger...............	3 211	....	....	....	....	....	....	....	....
Air transport, freight...............	3 212	....	....	....	....	....	....	....	....
Air transport, other...............	3 213	....	....	....	....	....	....	....	....
Other transport, passenger...............	3 215	....	....	....	....	....	....	....	....
Other transport, freight...............	3 216	....	....	....	....	....	....	....	....
Other transport, other...............	3 217	....	....	....	....	....	....	....	....
Travel, credit...............	2 236	**814.3**	**822.2**	**834.2**	**859.0**	**1,056.0**	**1,093.7**	**1,080.9**	**1,256.8**
Business travel....................................	2 237	....	....	....	....	....	....	....	....
Personal travel....................................	2 240	....	....	....	....	....	....	....	....
Travel, debit...............	3 236	**−146.6**	**−135.1**	**−159.3**	**−188.6**	**−218.3**	**−217.6**	**−234.0**	**−282.2**
Business travel....................................	3 237	....	....	....	....	....	....	....	....
Personal travel....................................	3 240	....	....	....	....	....	....	....	....
Other services, credit...............	2 200 BA	**115.4**	**118.0**	**133.9**	**152.8**	**143.0**	**157.5**	**195.4**	**186.8**
Communications...............	2 245	10.5	5.7	13.1	10.4	13.5	10.4	14.5	15.0
Construction...............	2 249	1.9	3.5	1.1	.1	....	.1	1.6	4.3
Insurance...............	2 253	.6	.4	.1	.3	.1	.1	.2	.8
Financial...............	2 260	5.9	2.6	1.9	3.1	3.0	5.5	5.1	5.0
Computer and information...............	2 262	.4	.3	.1	.2	....	.1	.3	.4
Royalties and licence fees...............	2 266	....	....	....	.2	....	....	.1	....
Other business services...............	2 268	79.3	92.3	99.9	124.2	110.7	124.5	154.3	142.7
Personal, cultural, and recreational...............	2 287	....	....	....	....	....	....	....	....
Government, n.i.e...............	2 291	16.8	13.2	17.6	14.2	15.7	16.8	19.4	18.7
Other services, debit...............	3 200 BA	**−215.8**	**−213.3**	**−227.6**	**−271.9**	**−243.9**	**−328.1**	**−365.2**	**−354.7**
Communications...............	3 245	−18.9	−20.2	−29.6	−21.7	−19.4	−19.1	−22.6	−27.4
Construction...............	3 249	−20.1	−15.2	−14.8	−25.8	−25.1	−26.1	−46.7	−41.7
Insurance...............	3 253	−2.7	−.9	−.3	−.2	−.2	−.3	−.3	−1.6
Financial...............	3 260	−8.6	−10.4	−8.2	−7.0	−7.9	−12.0	−13.3	−13.4
Computer and information...............	3 262	−5.6	−6.2	−5.5	−12.5	−5.9	−17.4	−16.0	−12.1
Royalties and licence fees...............	3 266	−.4	−1.4	−3.4	−4.2	−4.5	−7.2	−10.3	−9.6
Other business services...............	3 268	−136.5	−135.7	−134.8	−164.3	−148.6	−218.3	−222.6	−214.3
Personal, cultural, and recreational...............	3 287	....	....	....	....	....	....	....	....
Government, n.i.e...............	3 291	−22.9	−23.3	−31.1	−36.1	−32.3	−27.8	−33.5	−34.4

Table 2 (Continued). STANDARD PRESENTATION, 2000–2007

(Millions of U.S. dollars)

	Code	2000	2001	2002	2003	2004	2005	2006	2007
C. INCOME	4 300	−26.7	−55.0	−132.4	−50.0	−76.1	−484.2	−122.2	−77.7
Total credit	2 300	*53.0*	*49.8*	*32.2*	*32.1*	*35.0*	*41.6*	*61.0*	*79.3*
Total debit	3 300	*−79.7*	*−104.8*	*−164.6*	*−82.1*	*−111.1*	*−525.8*	*−183.2*	*−157.0*
Compensation of employees, credit	2 310	.1	.5	.5	.3	.6	.8	.6	3.5
Compensation of employees, debit	3 310	−.3	−.6	−.6	−.8	−1.0	−2.6	−8.9	−9.1
Investment income, credit	2 320	53.0	49.4	31.7	31.8	34.4	40.8	60.4	75.9
Direct investment income	2 330	.6	1.8	1.0	.6	2.2	3.5	15.8	14.8
Dividends and distributed branch profits	2 332	....	....	....	....	....	....	....	....
Reinvested earnings and undistributed branch profits	2 333	....	....	....	....	....	....	....	....
Income on debt (interest)	2 334	....	....	....	....	....	....	....	....
Portfolio investment income	2 339	20.6	23.3	17.6	17.0	20.0	20.5	23.9	34.6
Income on equity	2 340	2.5	3.3	1.8	2.5	4.5	4.7	4.8	12.0
Income on bonds and notes	2 350	....	....	....	....	....	....	....	....
Income on money market instruments	2 360	....	....	....	....	....	....	....	....
Other investment income	2 370	31.7	24.3	13.2	14.2	12.2	16.7	20.7	26.4
Investment income, debit	3 320	−79.5	−104.3	−164.0	−81.3	−110.1	−523.2	−174.3	−147.9
Direct investment income	3 330	−29.1	−51.0	−109.7	−30.6	−45.9	−455.0	−104.5	−83.9
Dividends and distributed branch profits	3 332	....	....	....	....	....	....	....	....
Reinvested earnings and undistributed branch profits	3 333	....	....	....	....	....	....	....	....
Income on debt (interest)	3 334	....	....	....	....	....	....	....	....
Portfolio investment income	3 339	−10.5	−14.0	−16.0	−21.2	−28.3	−32.6	−36.0	−32.1
Income on equity	3 340	....	....	−.1	....	−.7	−.1	−.5	....
Income on bonds and notes	3 350	....	....	....	....	....	....	....	....
Income on money market instruments	3 360	....	....	....	....	....	....	....	....
Other investment income	3 370	−39.9	−39.3	−38.3	−29.5	−35.9	−35.6	−33.9	−31.9
D. CURRENT TRANSFERS	4 379	−76.1	−57.8	−64.5	−85.1	−103.9	−123.9	−121.4	−98.8
Credit	2 379	39.5	42.1	40.8	41.4	44.8	53.3	55.3	57.8
General government	2 380	12.6	17.6	14.2	13.6	15.5	18.2	15.2	14.1
Other sectors	2 390	26.9	24.5	26.5	27.8	29.3	35.1	40.1	43.7
Workers' remittances	2 391	1.0	.9	.9	.6	1.1	2.2	....	.4
Other current transfers	2 392	25.8	23.6	25.7	27.2	28.2	32.9	40.1	43.2
Debit	3 379	−115.6	−99.9	−105.3	−126.5	−148.7	−177.2	−176.6	−156.6
General government	3 380	−7.5	−6.0	−7.4	−7.9	−5.1	−11.5	−8.5	−9.0
Other sectors	3 390	−108.1	−93.8	−97.9	−118.7	−143.6	−165.7	−168.2	−147.5
Workers' remittances	3 391	−43.5	−38.4	−45.0	−46.6	−47.9	−58.7	−62.7	−62.0
Other current transfers	3 392	−64.7	−55.4	−53.0	−72.1	−95.7	−107.0	−105.5	−85.5
CAPITAL AND FINANCIAL ACCOUNT	4 996	−214.5	−307.3	329.0	140.1	1.5	195.5	42.1	−221.8
CAPITAL ACCOUNT	4 994	11.2	−1.0	21.3	100.5	18.8	18.7	−14.1	18.2
Total credit	2 994	*16.3*	*9.0*	*28.5*	*123.0*	*30.9*	*26.9*	*29.5*	*27.4*
Total debit	3 994	*−5.0*	*−10.0*	*−7.2*	*−22.5*	*−12.0*	*−8.2*	*−43.6*	*−9.1*
Capital transfers, credit	2 400	16.3	8.4	28.5	122.7	30.9	26.9	29.5	27.4
General government	2 401	9.5	....	20.9	112.9	17.3	15.9	18.5	18.7
Debt forgiveness	2 402	....	....	....	95.9	....	....	....	....
Other capital transfers	2 410	9.5	....	20.9	17.0	17.3	15.9	18.5	18.7
Other sectors	2 430	6.8	8.4	7.6	9.8	13.6	10.9	11.0	8.7
Migrants' transfers	2 431	6.8	8.4	7.6	9.8	13.6	10.8	11.0	8.7
Debt forgiveness	2 432	....	....	....	....	....	.1	....	....
Other capital transfers	2 440	....	....	....	....	....	....	....	....
Capital transfers, debit	3 400	−5.0	−10.0	−5.9	−22.5	−11.9	−8.2	−8.3	−9.1
General government	3 401	....	....	....	−10.0	....	....	....	....
Debt forgiveness	3 402	....	....	....	....	....	....	....	....
Other capital transfers	3 410	....	....	....	−10.0	....	....	....	....
Other sectors	3 430	−5.0	−10.0	−5.9	−12.5	−11.9	−8.2	−8.3	−9.1
Migrants' transfers	3 431	−5.0	−10.0	−5.9	−12.5	−11.9	−8.2	−8.3	−9.1
Debt forgiveness	3 432	....	....	....	....	....	....	....	....
Other capital transfers	3 440	....	....	....	....	....	....	....	....
Nonproduced nonfinancial assets, credit	2 480	....	.6	....	.3	....	....	....	....
Nonproduced nonfinancial assets, debit	3 480	....	....	−1.3	....	−.1	....	−35.2	....

Table 2 (Continued). STANDARD PRESENTATION, 2000–2007

(Millions of U.S. dollars)

	Code	2000	2001	2002	2003	2004	2005	2006	2007
FINANCIAL ACCOUNT	4 995	**−225.8**	**−306.3**	**307.7**	**39.6**	**−17.4**	**176.8**	**56.2**	**−240.1**
A. DIRECT INVESTMENT	4 500	**−120.0**	**−257.9**	**343.2**	**161.0**	**162.8**	**127.8**	**623.2**	**−145.5**
Direct investment abroad	4 505	**.2**	**5.0**	**6.2**	**3.1**	**10.1**	**8.8**	**13.5**	**−29.3**
Equity capital	4 510	−5.1	−.7	−1.4	−4.2	−.1	.7	1.0	1.7
Claims on affiliated enterprises	4 515	....	....	....	....	....	....	....	....
Liabilities to affiliated enterprises	4 520	....	....	....	....	....	....	....	....
Reinvested earnings	4 525	....	....	....	....	....	....	....	....
Other capital	4 530	5.3	5.7	7.6	7.3	10.1	8.0	12.5	−31.0
Claims on affiliated enterprises	4 535	....	....	....	....	....	....	....	....
Liabilities to affiliated enterprises	4 540	....	....	....	....	....	....	....	....
Direct investment in Aruba	4 555	**−120.2**	**−262.9**	**337.1**	**157.9**	**152.7**	**119.0**	**609.7**	**−116.2**
Equity capital	4 560	56.1	−2.7	17.0	21.8	−.7	26.6	183.2	1.8
Claims on direct investors	4 565	....	....	....	....	....	....	....	....
Liabilities to direct investors	4 570	....	....	....	....	....	....	....	....
Reinvested earnings	4 575	....	....	....	....	....	....	....	....
Other capital	4 580	−176.3	−260.2	320.0	136.0	153.4	92.4	426.6	−117.9
Claims on direct investors	4 585	....	....	....	....	....	....	....	....
Liabilities to direct investors	4 590	....	....	....	....	....	92.4	....	....
B. PORTFOLIO INVESTMENT	4 600	**−7.7**	**57.0**	**63.6**	**35.2**	**26.3**	**3.0**	**−43.8**	**−235.2**
Assets	4 602	**−48.7**	**39.8**	**6.9**	**−31.2**	**−34.4**	**−18.2**	**−84.3**	**−320.7**
Equity securities	4 610	−45.6	5.9	−5.0	−19.6	−26.3	−3.5	−75.7	−36.6
Monetary authorities	4 611	....	....	....	....	....	....	....	....
General government	4 612	....	....	....	....	....	....	....	....
Banks	4 613	....	....	....	....	....	....	....	....
Other sectors	4 614	−45.6	5.9	−5.0	−19.6	−26.3	−3.5	−75.7	−36.6
Debt securities	4 619	−3.1	33.9	11.9	−11.6	−8.1	−14.7	−8.6	−284.0
Bonds and notes	4 620	−1.3	34.7	11.0	−1.5	−4.6	−8.0	.6	22.7
Monetary authorities	4 621	....	....	....	....	....	....	....	....
General government	4 622	....	....	....	....	....	....	....	....
Banks	4 623	−1.1	14.8	−11.6	−6.5	−6.6	10.9	−3.6	17.8
Other sectors	4 624	−.2	19.9	22.6	5.0	2.0	−18.9	4.1	4.9
Money market instruments	4 630	−1.8	−.7	.9	−10.1	−3.4	−6.7	−9.2	−306.7
Monetary authorities	4 631	....	....	....	....	....	....	....	....
General government	4 632	....	....	....	....	....	....	....	....
Banks	4 633	....	....	....	....	....	....	....	....
Other sectors	4 634	−1.8	−.7	.9	−10.1	−3.4	−6.7	−9.2	−306.7
Liabilities	4 652	**41.0**	**17.2**	**56.8**	**66.4**	**60.6**	**21.2**	**40.5**	**85.5**
Equity securities	4 660	....	....	....	....	....	....	....	....
Banks	4 663	....	....	....	....	....	....	....	....
Other sectors	4 664	....	....	....	....	....	....	....	....
Debt securities	4 669	41.0	17.2	56.8	66.4	60.6	21.2	40.5	85.5
Bonds and notes	4 670	40.0	18.2	56.8	64.9	59.9	23.4	40.5	85.5
Monetary authorities	4 671	....	....	....	....	....	....	....	....
General government	4 672	40.1	24.2	61.0	46.5	66.8	30.4	46.4	29.4
Banks	4 673	....	....	....	....	....	....	....	....
Other sectors	4 674	....	−6.0	−4.2	18.4	−6.8	−7.0	−5.9	56.1
Money market instruments	4 680	1.0	−1.0	....	1.5	.7	−2.1	....	....
Monetary authorities	4 681	....	....	....	....	....	....	....	....
General government	4 682	1.0	−1.0	....	1.5	....	....	....	....
Banks	4 683	....	....	....	....	....	....	....	....
Other sectors	4 684	....	....	....	....	.7	−2.1	....	....
C. FINANCIAL DERIVATIVES	4 910	....	....	**.1**	....	....	**.8**	**−2.7**	**−1.0**
Monetary authorities	4 911	....	....	....	....	....	....	....	....
General government	4 912	....	....	....	....	....	....	....	....
Banks	4 913	....	....	....	....	....	....	−.7	−.3
Other sectors	4 914	....	....	.1	....	....	.8	−2.0	−.7
Assets	4 900	....	....	....	....	....	**.8**	**−2.7**	**−1.0**
Monetary authorities	4 901	....	....	....	....	....	....	....	....
General government	4 902	....	....	....	....	....	....	....	....
Banks	4 903	....	....	....	....	....	....	−.7	−.3
Other sectors	4 904	....	....	....	....	....	.8	−2.0	−.7
Liabilities	4 905	....	....	**.1**	....	....	....	....	....
Monetary authorities	4 906	....	....	....	....	....	....	....	....
General government	4 907	....	....	....	....	....	....	....	....
Banks	4 908	....	....	....	....	....	....	....	....
Other sectors	4 909	....	....	.1	....	....	....	....	....

Table 2 (Concluded). STANDARD PRESENTATION, 2000–2007

(Millions of U.S. dollars)

	Code	2000	2001	2002	2003	2004	2005	2006	2007
D. OTHER INVESTMENT	4 700	**−113.0**	**−22.7**	**−59.0**	**−192.9**	**−204.8**	**23.0**	**−465.4**	**184.7**
Assets	4 703	**−27.7**	**3.0**	**−59.8**	**−83.3**	**−103.0**	**51.7**	**−424.3**	**198.9**
Trade credits	4 706	....	....	....	....	....	....	....	....
General government	4 707	....	....	....	....	....	....	....	....
of which: Short-term	4 709	....	....	....	....	....	....	....	....
Other sectors	4 710	....	....	....	....	....	....	....	....
of which: Short-term	4 712	....	....	....	....	....	....	....	....
Loans	4 714	−6.3	28.7	11.9	−12.5	4.4	7.9	19.2	1.3
Monetary authorities	4 715	....	....	....	....	....	....	....	....
of which: Short-term	4 718	....	....	....	....	....	....	....	....
General government	4 719	....	....	....	....	....	....	....	....
of which: Short-term	4 721	....	....	....	....	....	....	....	....
Banks	4 722	−14.5	9.9	12.5	−7.9	5.1	11.4	16.8	−4.5
of which: Short-term	4 724	....	....	....	....	....	....	....	....
Other sectors	4 725	8.3	18.8	−.6	−4.6	−.8	−3.5	2.3	5.8
of which: Short-term	4 727	....	....	....	....	....	....	....	....
Currency and deposits	4 730	−24.3	−20.7	−59.2	−81.3	−98.5	46.1	−443.3	203.8
Monetary authorities	4 731	....	....	....	....	....	....	....	....
General government	4 732	....	....	....	.2	....	....	....	....
Banks	4 733	−6.0	−22.2	5.1	−79.8	47.7	−18.4	−22.1	−45.0
Other sectors	4 734	−18.3	1.5	−64.4	−1.7	−146.3	64.5	−421.2	248.8
Other assets	4 736	2.8	−5.0	−12.5	10.5	−8.8	−2.3	−.2	−6.2
Monetary authorities	4 737	....	....	....	....	....	....	....	....
of which: Short-term	4 739	....	....	....	....	....	....	....	....
General government	4 740	....	....	....	....	....	....	....	....
of which: Short-term	4 742	....	....	....	....	....	....	....	....
Banks	4 743	5.1	1.3	−9.4	13.9	−4.1	−.8	2.8	−3.0
of which: Short-term	4 745	....	....	....	....	....	....	....	....
Other sectors	4 746	−2.3	−6.3	−3.1	−3.4	−4.7	−1.5	−3.0	−3.2
of which: Short-term	4 748	....	....	....	....	....	....	....	....
Liabilities	4 753	**−85.3**	**−25.6**	**.8**	**−109.7**	**−101.8**	**−28.7**	**−41.1**	**−14.2**
Trade credits	4 756	....	....	....	....	....	....	....	....
General government	4 757	....	....	....	....	....	....	....	....
of which: Short-term	4 759	....	....	....	....	....	....	....	....
Other sectors	4 760	....	....	....	....	....	....	....	....
of which: Short-term	4 762	....	....	....	....	....	....	....	....
Loans	4 764	−136.9	−46.0	−32.6	28.6	−33.7	−25.6	−52.4	−55.8
Monetary authorities	4 765	....	....	....	....	....	....	....	....
of which: Use of Fund credit and loans from the Fund	4 766	....	....	....	....	....	....	....	....
of which: Short-term	4 768	....	....	....	....	....	....	....	....
General government	4 769	−42.0	−21.9	−21.7	45.8	−13.0	−3.2	−13.7	−12.7
of which: Short-term	4 771	....	....	....	....	....	....	....	....
Banks	4 772	....	−3.0	4.5	....	1.7	....	....	−2.8
of which: Short-term	4 774	....	....	....	....	....	....	....	....
Other sectors	4 775	−95.0	−21.1	−15.4	−17.2	−22.5	−22.5	−38.7	−40.3
of which: Short-term	4 777	....	....	....	....	....	....	....	....
Currency and deposits	4 780	29.5	18.1	−4.4	49.2	−25.6	1.9	23.2	54.5
Monetary authorities	4 781	....	....	....	....	....	....	....	....
General government	4 782	....	....	....	....	....	....	....	....
Banks	4 783	29.5	18.1	−4.4	49.2	−25.6	1.9	23.2	54.5
Other sectors	4 784	....	....	....	....	....	....	....	....
Other liabilities	4 786	22.1	2.3	37.9	−187.5	−42.5	−5.0	−11.9	−12.8
Monetary authorities	4 787	....	....	....	....	....	....	....	....
of which: Short-term	4 789	....	....	....	....	....	....	....	....
General government	4 790	20.3	20.3	20.3	−205.9	....	....	....	....
of which: Short-term	4 792	....	....	....	....	....	....	....	....
Banks	4 793	−1.8	−8.5	23.5	28.8	−27.7	6.3	6.6	−4.1
of which: Short-term	4 795	....	....	....	....	....	....	....	....
Other sectors	4 796	3.6	−9.5	−5.9	−10.4	−14.9	−11.2	−18.5	−8.7
of which: Short-term	4 798	....	....	....	....	....	....	....	....
E. RESERVE ASSETS	4 802	**15.0**	**−82.8**	**−40.2**	**36.4**	**−1.6**	**22.2**	**−55.1**	**−43.2**
Monetary gold	4 812	....	....	....	....	....	....	....	....
Special drawing rights	4 811	....	....	....	....	....	....	....	....
Reserve position in the Fund	4 810	....	....	....	....	....	....	....	....
Foreign exchange	4 803	15.0	−82.8	−40.2	36.4	−1.6	22.2	−55.1	−43.2
Other claims	4 813	....	....	....	....	....	....	....	....
NET ERRORS AND OMISSIONS	4 998	**12.7**	**−6.2**	**9.2**	**22.9**	**5.1**	**2.2**	**1.1**	**7.0**

Table 3. INTERNATIONAL INVESTMENT POSITION (End-period stocks), 2000–2007

(Millions of U.S. dollars)

	Code	2000	2001	2002	2003	2004	2005	2006	2007
ASSETS..	8 995 C.	1,272.5	1,339.9	1,348.8	1,471.0	1,684.1	1,623.3	2,234.4	2,407.7
Direct investment abroad...........................	8 505 ..	373.8	368.8	362.7	359.5	349.5	340.7	327.2	356.6
Equity capital and reinvested earnings........................	8 506 ..	....	....	....	....	....	....	....	....
Claims on affiliated enterprises.........................	8 507 ..	....	....	....	....	....	....	....	....
Liabilities to affiliated enterprises......................	8 508 ..	....	....	....	....	....	....	....	....
Other capital........................	8 530 ..	....	....	....	....	....	....	....	....
Claims on affiliated enterprises.........................	8 535 ..	....	....	....	....	....	....	....	....
Liabilities to affiliated enterprises......................	8 540 ..	....	....	....	....	....	....	....	....
Portfolio investment.................................	8 602 ..	300.2	303.3	281.4	344.6	382.5	404.3	502.8	809.6
Equity securities............................	8 610 ..	182.8	193.3	174.3	236.4	261.0	275.4	339.1	365.0
Monetary authorities...........................	8 611 ..	....	....	....	....	....	....	....	....
General government...........................	8 612 ..	....	....	....	....	....	....	....	....
Banks..........................	8 613 ..	....	....	....	....	....	....	....	....
Other sectors..........................	8 614 ..	182.8	193.3	174.3	236.4	261.0	275.4	339.1	365.0
Debt securities............................	8 619 ..	117.4	110.0	107.1	108.2	121.5	129.0	163.7	444.6
Bonds and notes...........................	8 620 ..	106.2	98.7	93.9	89.3	83.5	103.0	95.8	115.9
Monetary authorities.........................	8 621 ..	....	....	....	....	....	....	....	....
General government.........................	8 622 ..	....	....	....	....	....	....	....	....
Banks.........................	8 623 ..	15.8	1.8	5.7	15.5	12.7	8.7	2.8	....
Other sectors.........................	8 624 ..	90.4	96.9	88.1	73.8	70.9	94.3	93.0	115.9
Money market instruments.........................	8 630 ..	11.1	11.3	13.3	18.9	38.0	26.0	67.9	328.6
Monetary authorities.........................	8 631 ..	....	....	....	....	....	....	....	....
General government.........................	8 632 ..	....	....	....	....	....	....	....	....
Banks.........................	8 633 ..	2.8	2.0	9.7	6.4	15.9	9.0	18.4	3.4
Other sectors.........................	8 634 ..	8.3	9.3	3.5	12.6	22.1	17.0	49.5	325.2
Financial derivatives...........................	8 900 ..	....	....	....	....	....	.8	−2.7	−1.0
Monetary authorities............................	8 901 ..	....	....	....	....	....	....	....	....
General government............................	8 902 ..	....	....	....	....	....	....	....	....
Banks............................	8 903 ..	....	....	....	....	....	.8	−2.7	−1.0
Other sectors............................	8 904 ..	....	....	....	....	....	....	....	....
Other investment.................................	8 703 ..	362.6	343.3	326.9	425.3	608.1	546.9	998.6	777.4
Trade credits........................	8 706 ..	....	....	....	....	....	....	....	....
General government........................	8 707 ..	....	....	....	....	....	....	....	....
of which: Short-term........................	8 709 ..	....	....	....	....	....	....	....	....
Other sectors........................	8 710 ..	....	....	....	....	....	....	....	....
of which: Short-term........................	8 712 ..	....	....	....	....	....	....	....	....
Loans........................	8 714 ..	109.5	94.7	80.4	96.8	90.8	73.3	57.3	62.2
Monetary authorities........................	8 715 ..	....	....	....	....	....	....	....	....
of which: Short-term........................	8 718 ..	....	....	....	....	....	....	....	....
General government........................	8 719 ..	....	....	....	....	....	....	....	....
of which: Short-term........................	8 721 ..	....	....	....	....	....	....	....	....
Banks........................	8 722 ..	89.5	79.7	67.2	75.0	69.9	58.5	41.7	46.1
of which: Short-term........................	8 724 ..	*28.4*	*20.6*	*25.5*	*36.2*	*29.5*	*20.6*	*12.3*	*14.5*
Other sectors........................	8 725 ..	20.0	15.0	13.2	21.8	20.9	14.8	15.7	16.0
of which: Short-term........................	8 727 ..	*7.6*	*3.3*	*.3*	*1.9*	*1.7*	*3.6*	*3.5*	*1.5*
Currency and deposits........................	8 730 ..	238.3	235.1	222.2	319.5	504.0	459.6	930.1	699.5
Monetary authorities........................	8 731 ..	....	....	....	....	....	....	....	....
General government........................	8 732 ..	....	....	....	....	....	....	....	....
Banks........................	8 733 ..	173.6	195.8	190.7	270.5	222.8	241.2	263.3	306.9
Other sectors........................	8 734 ..	64.7	39.3	31.5	49.0	281.2	218.4	666.8	392.6
Other assets........................	8 736 ..	14.7	13.5	24.3	9.1	13.2	14.0	11.2	15.8
Monetary authorities........................	8 737 ..	....	....	....	....	....	....	....	....
of which: Short-term........................	8 739 ..	....	....	....	....	....	....	....	....
General government........................	8 740 ..	....	....	....	....	....	....	....	....
of which: Short-term........................	8 742 ..	....	....	....	....	....	....	....	....
Banks........................	8 743 ..	14.7	13.5	22.9	9.1	13.2	14.0	11.2	15.6
of which: Short-term........................	8 745 ..	*11.5*	*10.1*	*20.3*	*3.7*	*7.8*	*8.6*	*5.7*	*10.2*
Other sectors........................	8 746 ..	....	....	1.4	....	....	....	....	.2
of which: Short-term........................	8 748 ..	....	....	*1.4*	....	....	....	....	....
Reserve assets...........................	8 802 ..	235.8	324.4	377.8	341.6	344.1	330.5	408.4	465.0
Monetary gold........................	8 812 ..	22.9	30.7	38.1	46.4	48.7	57.0	70.6	92.9
Special drawing rights........................	8 811 ..	....	....	....	....	....	....	....	....
Reserve position in the Fund........................	8 810 ..	....	....	....	....	....	....	....	....
Foreign exchange........................	8 803 ..	210.2	291.4	338.2	293.7	294.0	271.5	335.6	369.7
Other claims........................	8 813 ..	2.8	2.3	1.5	1.5	1.4	2.0	2.3	2.4

Table 3 (Concluded). INTERNATIONAL INVESTMENT POSITION (End-period stocks), 2000–2007

(Millions of U.S. dollars)

	Code	2000	2001	2002	2003	2004	2005	2006	2007
LIABILITIES..	8 995 D.	**1,796.8**	**1,676.2**	**2,147.1**	**2,356.8**	**2,450.2**	**2,536.0**	**3,215.8**	**3,224.4**
Direct investment in Aruba............................	8 555 ..	**760.4**	**511.7**	**849.8**	**1,024.5**	**1,196.9**	**1,315.2**	**1,944.5**	**1,846.1**
Equity capital and reinvested earnings..................	8 556 ..	....	....	....	....	....	....	....	....
Claims on direct investors..........................	8 557 ..	....	....	....	....	....	....	....	....
Liabilities to direct investors.......................	8 558 ..	....	....	....	....	....	....	....	....
Other capital....................................	8 580 ..	....	....	....	....	....	....	....	....
Claims on direct investors..........................	8 585 ..	....	....	....	....	....	....	....	....
Liabilities to direct investors.......................	8 590 ..	....	....	....	....	....	....	....	....
Portfolio investment........................	8 652 ..	**93.2**	**193.4**	**251.2**	**317.2**	**379.2**	**403.1**	**438.9**	**524.0**
Equity securities..................................	8 660 ..	....	....	....	....	....	....	....	....
Banks..	8 663 ..	....	....	....	....	....	....	....	....
Other sectors.................................	8 664 ..	....	....	....	....	....	....	....	....
Debt securities...................................	8 669 ..	93.2	193.4	251.2	317.2	379.2	403.1	438.9	524.0
Bonds and notes...............................	8 670 ..	93.2	193.4	251.2	317.2	379.2	403.1	438.9	524.0
Monetary authorities..........................	8 671 ..	....	....	....	....	....	....	....	....
General government..........................	8 672 ..	87.0	110.2	171.2	219.2	286.0	316.4	362.8	392.3
Banks......................................	8 673 ..	....	....	....	....	....	....	....	....
Other sectors...............................	8 674 ..	6.1	83.2	80.0	98.0	93.2	86.7	76.0	131.7
Money market instruments.......................	8 680 ..	....	....	....	....	....	....	....	....
Monetary authorities..........................	8 681 ..	....	....	....	....	....	....	....	....
General government..........................	8 682 ..	....	....	....	....	....	....	....	....
Banks......................................	8 683 ..	....	....	....	....	....	....	....	....
Other sectors...............................	8 684 ..	....	....	....	....	....	....	....	....
Financial derivatives........................	8 905 ..	....	....	....	....	....	....	....	....
Monetary authorities.............................	8 906 ..	....	....	....	....	....	....	....	....
General government..............................	8 907 ..	....	....	....	....	....	....	....	....
Banks...	8 908 ..	....	....	....	....	....	....	....	....
Other sectors....................................	8 909 ..	....	....	....	....	....	....	....	....
Other investment........................	8 753 ..	**943.2**	**971.1**	**1,046.0**	**1,015.1**	**874.2**	**817.7**	**832.4**	**854.4**
Trade credits.....................................	8 756 ..	....	....	....	....	....	....	....	....
General government..............................	8 757 ..	....	....	....	....	....	....	....	....
of which: Short-term..........................	8 759 ..	....	....	....	....	....	....	....	....
Other sectors..................................	8 760 ..	....	....	....	....	....	....	....	....
of which: Short-term..........................	8 762 ..	....	....	....	....	....	....	....	....
Loans..	8 764 ..	707.5	708.3	745.0	686.4	569.9	500.8	491.1	445.3
Monetary authorities.............................	8 765 ..	....	....	....	....	....	....	....	....
of which: Use of Fund credit and loans from the Fund....	8 766 ..	....	....	....	....	....	....	....	....
of which: Short-term..........................	8 768 ..	....	....	....	....	....	....	....	....
General government..............................	8 769 ..	317.9	310.4	328.0	185.4	181.2	162.3	158.8	156.4
of which: Short-term..........................	8 771 ..	....	....	....	....	....	....	....	....
Banks..	8 772 ..	14.3	2.3	4.5	58.7	27.5	31.6	40.4	33.5
of which: Short-term..........................	8 774 ..	*9.6*	*.6*	....	*54.2*	*21.3*	*6.4*	*15.2*	*11.1*
Other sectors..................................	8 775 ..	375.3	395.6	412.4	442.4	361.2	306.9	291.9	255.5
of which: Short-term..........................	8 777 ..	....	....	....	....	....	....	....	....
Currency and deposits.............................	8 780 ..	203.2	221.4	220.3	266.3	240.1	242.7	274.0	321.3
Monetary authorities.............................	8 781 ..	1.3	1.4	4.7	1.5	.8	1.7	9.6	2.5
General government..............................	8 782 ..	....	....	....	....	....	....	....	....
Banks..	8 783 ..	201.9	220.0	215.5	264.8	239.2	241.1	264.4	318.8
Other sectors..................................	8 784 ..	....	....	....	....	....	....	....	....
Other liabilities..................................	8 786 ..	32.6	41.4	80.8	62.4	64.2	74.1	67.3	87.8
Monetary authorities.............................	8 787 ..	15.9	21.6	31.6	34.9	36.4	44.2	59.2	79.7
of which: Short-term..........................	8 789 ..	....	....	....	....	....	....	....	....
General government..............................	8 790 ..	....	....	....	....	....	....	....	....
of which: Short-term..........................	8 792 ..	....	....	....	....	....	....	....	....
Banks..	8 793 ..	2.7	3.1	27.2	1.8	7.1	9.2	7.1	7.1
of which: Short-term..........................	8 795 ..	*2.7*	*3.1*	*27.2*	*1.8*	*7.1*	*9.2*	*7.1*	*7.1*
Other sectors..................................	8 796 ..	14.0	16.7	22.0	25.7	20.6	20.7	1.1	1.0
of which: Short-term..........................	8 798 ..	*14.0*	*16.7*	*22.0*	*25.7*	*20.6*	*20.7*	*1.1*	*1.0*
NET INTERNATIONAL INVESTMENT POSITION........	8 995 ..	**−524.4**	**−336.3**	**−798.2**	**−885.8**	**−766.1**	**−912.7**	**−981.4**	**−816.8**
Conversion rates: florins per U.S. dollar (end of period)..	0 102 ..	**1.7900**	**1.7900**	**1.7900**	**1.7900**	**1.7900**	**1.7900**	**1.7900**	**1.7900**

Table 1. ANALYTIC PRESENTATION, 2000–2007

(Millions of U.S. dollars)

	Code	2000	2001	2002	2003	2004	2005	2006	2007
A. Current Account[1]	4 993 Z.	**−14,763**	**−7,411**	**−15,809**	**−28,684**	**−38,854**	**−41,032**	**−41,504**	**−56,783**
Goods: exports f.o.b.	2 100 ..	64,004	63,626	65,014	70,522	87,166	107,011	124,913	142,133
Goods: imports f.o.b.	3 100 ..	−68,866	−61,890	−70,527	−85,861	−105,230	−120,383	−134,509	−160,047
Balance on Goods	4 100 ..	*−4,862*	*1,737*	*−5,514*	*−15,339*	*−18,064*	*−13,372*	*−9,596*	*−17,914*
Services: credit	2 200 ..	19,894	18,092	19,594	23,747	28,485	31,047	33,088	40,449
Services: debit	3 200 ..	−18,934	−17,351	−18,388	−21,940	−27,943	−30,505	−32,219	−38,899
Balance on Goods and Services	4 991 ..	*−3,901*	*2,478*	*−4,308*	*−13,532*	*−17,521*	*−12,830*	*−8,727*	*−16,364*
Income: credit	2 300 ..	8,977	8,200	8,522	10,487	14,311	16,445	21,748	29,513
Income: debit	3 300 ..	−19,791	−18,132	−19,974	−25,456	−35,327	−44,166	−54,131	−69,685
Balance on Goods, Services, and Income	4 992 ..	*−14,715*	*−7,454*	*−15,760*	*−28,501*	*−38,537*	*−40,552*	*−41,110*	*−56,536*
Current transfers: credit	2 379 Z.	2,622	2,296	2,373	2,743	3,114	3,333	3,698	4,413
Current transfers: debit	3 379 ..	−2,669	−2,254	−2,422	−2,926	−3,431	−3,813	−4,092	−4,661
B. Capital Account[1]	4 994 Z.	**615**	**645**	**583**	**889**	**1,076**	**1,252**	**1,737**	**1,722**
Capital account: credit	2 994 Z.	1,406	1,320	1,298	1,664	1,979	2,009	2,467	2,640
Capital account: debit	3 994 ..	−791	−675	−715	−775	−904	−757	−731	−918
Total, Groups A Plus B	4 981 ..	*−14,148*	*−6,767*	*−15,226*	*−27,795*	*−37,778*	*−39,780*	*−39,767*	*−55,061*
C. Financial Account[1]	4 995 W.	**12,953**	**8,155**	**16,249**	**34,694**	**39,373**	**47,617**	**49,901**	**20,166**
Direct investment abroad	4 505 ..	−3,275	−11,967	−7,793	−17,216	−11,055	33,940	−23,933	−24,967
Direct investment in Australia	4 555 Z.	13,618	8,261	16,992	8,024	36,827	−35,601	26,415	23,026
Portfolio investment assets	4 602 ..	−10,919	−10,053	−16,820	−8,168	−24,579	−21,271	−43,866	−48,298
Equity securities	4 610 ..	−7,346	−4,936	−11,854	−3,419	−11,071	−8,383	−22,156	−33,147
Debt securities	4 619 ..	−3,573	−5,117	−4,966	−4,749	−13,509	−12,888	−21,710	−15,152
Portfolio investment liabilities	4 652 Z.	14,874	16,237	17,126	49,389	40,018	58,979	97,180	50,574
Equity securities	4 660 ..	−726	7,159	283	12,209	−25,221	8,127	13,933	11,908
Debt securities	4 669 Z.	15,601	9,078	16,843	37,180	65,239	50,852	83,248	38,666
Financial derivatives	4 910 ..	−874	461	−316	−520	250	−38	2,452	−10,793
Financial derivatives assets	4 900 ..	−1,165	2,215	2,015	7,910	19,397	16,498	13,378	12,634
Financial derivatives liabilities	4 905 ..	291	−1,754	−2,331	−8,430	−19,147	−16,536	−10,925	−23,427
Other investment assets	4 703 ..	−4,887	834	−3,708	−4,603	−5,844	−3,188	−16,736	−8,178
Monetary authorities	4 701 ..	133	275	411	110	....	....	....	....
General government	4 704 ..	−22	−153	−85	−104	−147	−274	−549	−241
Banks	4 705 ..	−1,745	−2,616	−3,593	−4,823	−6,241	−1,457	−16,566	−6,558
Other sectors	4 728 ..	−3,253	3,328	−441	214	544	−1,457	379	−1,379
Other investment liabilities	4 753 W.	4,416	4,382	10,767	7,788	3,757	14,796	8,389	38,801
Monetary authorities	4 753 WA	−70	3	7	37	7	10	18	230
General government	4 753 ZB	75	−125	....	....	−27	....	....	....
Banks	4 753 ZC	4,924	3,536	10,178	9,455	670	1,668	5,899	50,516
Other sectors	4 753 ZD	−514	969	582	−1,704	3,108	13,118	2,472	−11,945
Total, Groups A Through C	4 983 ..	*−1,194*	*1,389*	*1,023*	*6,899*	*1,595*	*7,837*	*10,134*	*−34,895*
D. Net Errors and Omissions	4 998 ..	**−171**	**−293**	**−900**	**−22**	**−429**	**−581**	**−412**	**−253**
Total, Groups A Through D	4 984 ..	*−1,365*	*1,096*	*122*	*6,877*	*1,166*	*7,256*	*9,722*	*−35,148*
E. Reserves and Related Items	4 802 A.	**1,365**	**−1,096**	**−122**	**−6,877**	**−1,166**	**−7,256**	**−9,722**	**35,148**
Reserve assets	4 802 ..	1,365	−1,096	−122	−6,877	−1,166	−7,256	−9,722	35,148
Use of Fund credit and loans	4 766 ..	....	....	....	....	....	....	....	....
Exceptional financing	4 920 ..	....	....	....	....	....	....	....	....
Conversion rates: Australian dollars per U.S. dollar	0 101 ..	1.7248	1.9334	1.8406	1.5419	1.3598	1.3095	1.3280	1.1951

[1] Excludes components that have been classified in the categories of Group E.

Table 2. STANDARD PRESENTATION, 2000–2007

(Millions of U.S. dollars)

	Code	2000	2001	2002	2003	2004	2005	2006	2007
CURRENT ACCOUNT	4 993	−14,763	−7,411	−15,809	−28,684	−38,854	−41,032	−41,504	−56,783
A. GOODS	4 100	−4,862	1,737	−5,514	−15,339	−18,064	−13,372	−9,596	−17,914
Credit	2 100	64,004	63,626	65,014	70,522	87,166	107,011	124,913	142,133
General merchandise: exports f.o.b.	2 110	59,844	59,615	60,648	64,896	81,460	100,692	115,415	130,879
Goods for processing: exports f.o.b.	2 150	88	42	47	67	105	137	387	300
Repairs on goods	2 160	33	31	29	50	40	64	54	81
Goods procured in ports by carriers	2 170	528	477	480	503	685	925	1,100	1,171
Nonmonetary gold	2 180	3,511	3,462	3,810	5,007	4,875	5,193	7,956	9,703
Debit	3 100	−68,866	−61,890	−70,527	−85,861	−105,230	−120,383	−134,509	−160,047
General merchandise: imports f.o.b.	3 110	−67,360	−60,063	−68,489	−83,217	−102,370	−116,938	−128,646	−153,218
Goods for processing: imports f.o.b.	3 150	−63	−31	−33	−48	−126	−130	−507	−186
Repairs on goods	3 160	−63	−116	−139	−157	−125	−135	−82	−111
Goods procured in ports by carriers	3 170	−470	−536	−440	−533	−689	−936	−1,134	−1,185
Nonmonetary gold	3 180	−909	−1,144	−1,426	−1,907	−1,920	−2,244	−4,140	−5,348
B. SERVICES	4 200	961	741	1,206	1,807	543	542	869	1,550
Total credit	2 200	*19,894*	*18,092*	*19,594*	*23,747*	*28,485*	*31,047*	*33,088*	*40,449*
Total debit	3 200	*−18,934*	*−17,351*	*−18,388*	*−21,940*	*−27,943*	*−30,505*	*−32,219*	*−38,899*
Transportation services, credit	2 205	4,314	4,087	4,131	4,722	5,792	6,170	6,358	7,229
Passenger	2 850	*3,727*	*3,580*	*3,653*	*4,209*	*5,239*	*5,698*	*5,875*	*6,728*
Freight	2 851	*587*	*507*	*478*	*513*	*553*	*472*	*483*	*501*
Other	2 852	....	....	....	....	....	....	....	....
Sea transport, passenger	2 207	....	....	....	....	....	....	....	....
Sea transport, freight	2 208	....	....	....	....	....	....	....	....
Sea transport, other	2 209	....	....	....	....	....	....	....	....
Air transport, passenger	2 211	....	....	....	....	....	....	....	....
Air transport, freight	2 212	....	....	....	....	....	....	....	....
Air transport, other	2 213	....	....	....	....	....	....	....	....
Other transport, passenger	2 215	....	....	....	....	....	....	....	....
Other transport, freight	2 216	....	....	....	....	....	....	....	....
Other transport, other	2 217	....	....	....	....	....	....	....	....
Transportation services, debit	3 205	−6,292	−5,750	−5,990	−7,231	−9,681	−10,759	−11,334	−13,100
Passenger	3 850	*−2,393*	*−2,193*	*−2,422*	*−2,865*	*−3,982*	*−4,340*	*−4,703*	*−5,591*
Freight	3 851	*−3,343*	*−3,031*	*−3,051*	*−3,845*	*−5,082*	*−5,781*	*−6,023*	*−6,857*
Other	3 852	*−556*	*−526*	*−517*	*−520*	*−617*	*−637*	*−608*	*−652*
Sea transport, passenger	3 207	....	....	....	....	....	....	....	....
Sea transport, freight	3 208	....	....	....	....	....	....	....	....
Sea transport, other	3 209	....	....	....	....	....	....	....	....
Air transport, passenger	3 211	....	....	....	....	....	....	....	....
Air transport, freight	3 212	....	....	....	....	....	....	....	....
Air transport, other	3 213	....	....	....	....	....	....	....	....
Other transport, passenger	3 215	....	....	....	....	....	....	....	....
Other transport, freight	3 216	....	....	....	....	....	....	....	....
Other transport, other	3 217	....	....	....	....	....	....	....	....
Travel, credit	2 236	9,289	9,224	9,971	12,438	15,214	16,868	17,854	22,337
Business travel	2 237	899	809	943	1,093	1,313	1,446	1,721	2,126
Personal travel	2 240	8,390	8,415	9,028	11,345	13,901	15,423	16,133	20,211
Travel, debit	3 236	−6,387	−5,860	−6,072	−7,270	−10,241	−11,253	−11,690	−14,253
Business travel	3 237	−1,528	−1,219	−1,271	−1,500	−1,830	−1,864	−1,951	−2,233
Personal travel	3 240	−4,859	−4,641	−4,801	−5,770	−8,412	−9,389	−9,739	−12,020
Other services, credit	2 200 BA	6,291	4,781	5,492	6,587	7,480	8,009	8,876	10,883
Communications	2 245	889	525	541	627	601	625	646	567
Construction	2 249	28	53	68	63	78	95	98	111
Insurance	2 253	437	351	366	441	505	530	530	599
Financial	2 260	524	488	530	652	740	764	756	856
Computer and information	2 262	494	457	640	769	939	886	1,060	1,276
Royalties and licence fees	2 266	372	316	324	430	517	552	621	734
Other business services	2 268	2,006	1,891	2,172	2,615	3,035	3,451	4,013	5,540
Personal, cultural, and recreational	2 287	1,058	297	419	469	421	438	502	490
Government, n.i.e.	2 291	482	403	433	521	644	668	650	710
Other services, debit	3 200 BA	−6,255	−5,740	−6,326	−7,440	−8,020	−8,493	−9,195	−11,545
Communications	3 245	−1,120	−865	−862	−797	−682	−625	−643	−644
Construction	3 249	....	....	....	....	....	....	....	....
Insurance	3 253	−525	−442	−465	−563	−643	−677	−678	−768
Financial	3 260	−348	−311	−324	−365	−399	−408	−452	−512
Computer and information	3 262	−514	−446	−543	−696	−782	−802	−935	−1,219
Royalties and licence fees	3 266	−1,160	−1,001	−1,185	−1,503	−1,743	−2,005	−2,190	−2,962
Other business services	3 268	−1,701	−1,913	−2,050	−2,427	−2,423	−2,607	−2,827	−3,786
Personal, cultural, and recreational	3 287	−509	−432	−531	−625	−781	−774	−851	−942
Government, n.i.e.	3 291	−379	−330	−365	−465	−566	−596	−619	−711

Table 2 (Continued). STANDARD PRESENTATION, 2000–2007

(Millions of U.S. dollars)

	Code	2000	2001	2002	2003	2004	2005	2006	2007
C. INCOME	4 300	**−10,814**	**−9,932**	**−11,452**	**−14,969**	**−21,015**	**−27,721**	**−32,383**	**−40,172**
Total credit	2 300	*8,977*	*8,200*	*8,522*	*10,487*	*14,311*	*16,445*	*21,748*	*29,513*
Total debit	3 300	*−19,791*	*−18,132*	*−19,974*	*−25,456*	*−35,327*	*−44,166*	*−54,131*	*−69,685*
Compensation of employees, credit	2 310	**504**	**472**	**479**	**695**	**868**	**982**	**1,018**	**1,247**
Compensation of employees, debit	3 310	**−578**	**−599**	**−734**	**−1,192**	**−1,530**	**−1,686**	**−2,190**	**−2,760**
Investment income, credit	2 320	**8,473**	**7,727**	**8,043**	**9,792**	**13,444**	**15,463**	**20,730**	**28,267**
Direct investment income	2 330	5,468	4,701	4,859	6,054	8,273	9,058	11,800	17,027
Dividends and distributed branch profits	2 332	2,457	1,300	1,664	1,499	1,529	1,979	3,490	4,091
Reinvested earnings and undistributed branch profits	2 333	3,098	3,420	3,179	4,466	6,662	7,084	8,394	12,946
Income on debt (interest)	2 334	−87	−19	16	90	83	−5	−84	−10
Portfolio investment income	2 339	1,847	2,053	2,327	2,874	3,884	4,728	6,264	7,853
Income on equity	2 340	594	746	807	1,154	1,558	1,738	2,153	2,722
Income on bonds and notes	2 350	1,253	1,307	1,520	1,720	2,327	2,990	4,111	5,130
Income on money market instruments	2 360	....	....	....	....	....	....	....	....
Other investment income	2 370	1,158	973	858	864	1,286	1,677	2,666	3,387
Investment income, debit	3 320	**−19,213**	**−17,533**	**−19,241**	**−24,264**	**−33,796**	**−42,480**	**−51,941**	**−66,925**
Direct investment income	3 330	−7,290	−6,719	−8,383	−12,301	−16,956	−21,893	−24,185	−32,413
Dividends and distributed branch profits	3 332	−2,933	−3,716	−3,529	−5,301	−6,102	−7,462	−10,008	−11,085
Reinvested earnings and undistributed branch profits	3 333	−3,875	−2,462	−4,151	−6,119	−9,649	−13,465	−12,747	−18,581
Income on debt (interest)	3 334	−482	−542	−703	−881	−1,204	−966	−1,430	−2,748
Portfolio investment income	3 339	−9,771	−8,852	−9,146	−10,504	−15,211	−18,236	−24,186	−30,268
Income on equity	3 340	−1,737	−1,805	−2,117	−2,695	−3,903	−4,720	−6,158	−7,390
Income on bonds and notes	3 350	−6,621	−5,694	−6,087	−7,042	−10,508	−12,615	−15,854	−19,550
Income on money market instruments	3 360	−1,413	−1,353	−942	−767	−800	−901	−2,174	−3,327
Other investment income	3 370	−2,153	−1,961	−1,711	−1,459	−1,629	−2,351	−3,570	−4,244
D. CURRENT TRANSFERS	4 379	**−47**	**42**	**−49**	**−183**	**−317**	**−480**	**−394**	**−248**
Credit	2 379	**2,622**	**2,296**	**2,373**	**2,743**	**3,114**	**3,333**	**3,698**	**4,413**
General government	2 380	686	694	688	721	817	938	1,316	1,736
Other sectors	2 390	1,936	1,602	1,684	2,022	2,297	2,395	2,382	2,677
Workers' remittances	2 391	....	....	....	....	....	....	....	....
Other current transfers	2 392	1,936	1,602	1,684	2,022	2,297	2,395	2,382	2,677
Debit	3 379	**−2,669**	**−2,254**	**−2,422**	**−2,926**	**−3,431**	**−3,813**	**−4,092**	**−4,661**
General government	3 380	−991	−675	−481	−558	−629	−643	−658	−764
Other sectors	3 390	−1,678	−1,579	−1,941	−2,368	−2,802	−3,170	−3,434	−3,897
Workers' remittances	3 391	....	....	....	....	....	....	....	....
Other current transfers	3 392	−1,678	−1,579	−1,941	−2,368	−2,802	−3,170	−3,434	−3,897
CAPITAL AND FINANCIAL ACCOUNT	4 996	**14,933**	**7,704**	**16,710**	**28,706**	**39,283**	**41,613**	**41,916**	**57,036**
CAPITAL ACCOUNT	4 994	**615**	**645**	**583**	**889**	**1,076**	**1,252**	**1,737**	**1,722**
Total credit	2 994	*1,406*	*1,320*	*1,298*	*1,664*	*1,979*	*2,009*	*2,467*	*2,640*
Total debit	3 994	*−791*	*−675*	*−715*	*−775*	*−904*	*−757*	*−731*	*−918*
Capital transfers, credit	2 400	**1,399**	**1,311**	**1,294**	**1,631**	**1,969**	**2,008**	**2,112**	**2,615**
General government	2 401	....	....	....	....	....	....	....	....
Debt forgiveness	2 402	....	....	....	....	....	....	....	....
Other capital transfers	2 410	....	....	....	....	....	....	....	....
Other sectors	2 430	1,399	1,311	1,294	1,631	1,969	2,008	2,112	2,615
Migrants' transfers	2 431	1,399	1,311	1,294	1,631	1,969	2,008	2,112	2,615
Debt forgiveness	2 432	....	....	....	....	....	....	....	....
Other capital transfers	2 440	....	....	....	....	....	....	....	....
Capital transfers, debit	3 400	**−728**	**−631**	**−596**	**−715**	**−844**	**−799**	**−729**	**−915**
General government	3 401	−253	−170	−111	−127	−121	−111	−105	−116
Debt forgiveness	3 402	....	....	....	....	....	....	....	....
Other capital transfers	3 410	−253	−170	−111	−127	−121	−111	−105	−116
Other sectors	3 430	−475	−460	−485	−587	−723	−689	−625	−799
Migrants' transfers	3 431	−475	−460	−485	−587	−723	−689	−625	−799
Debt forgiveness	3 432	....	....	....	....	....	....	....	....
Other capital transfers	3 440	....	....	....	....	....	....	....	....
Nonproduced nonfinancial assets, credit	2 480	**6**	**9**	**4**	**33**	**10**	**2**	**355**	**25**
Nonproduced nonfinancial assets, debit	3 480	**−63**	**−44**	**−118**	**−61**	**−60**	**42**	**−1**	**−3**

Table 2 (Continued). STANDARD PRESENTATION, 2000–2007

(Millions of U.S. dollars)

	Code	2000	2001	2002	2003	2004	2005	2006	2007
FINANCIAL ACCOUNT	4 995	14,318	7,060	16,127	27,817	38,208	40,361	40,179	55,314
A. DIRECT INVESTMENT	4 500	10,343	−3,706	9,199	−9,192	25,771	−1,661	2,482	−1,941
Direct investment abroad	4 505	−3,275	−11,967	−7,793	−17,216	−11,055	33,940	−23,933	−24,967
Equity capital	4 510	−550	−7,611	−3,098	−13,298	−2,832	43,388	−10,340	−10,912
Claims on affiliated enterprises	4 515	....	....	....	....	....	....	....	....
Liabilities to affiliated enterprises	4 520	....	....	....	....	....	....	....	....
Reinvested earnings	4 525	−3,098	−3,420	−3,179	−4,466	−6,662	−7,084	−8,394	−12,946
Other capital	4 530	373	−936	−1,517	548	−1,562	−2,364	−5,199	−1,109
Claims on affiliated enterprises	4 535	−943	−1,088	−2,269	−802	−1,641	−497	−7,562	−566
Liabilities to affiliated enterprises	4 540	1,317	152	753	1,350	79	−1,866	2,363	−543
Direct investment in Australia	4 555	13,618	8,261	16,992	8,024	36,827	−35,601	26,415	23,026
Equity capital	4 560	3,631	8,769	2,030	2,401	26,043	−50,570	5,037	1,522
Claims on direct investors	4 565	....	....	....	....	....	....	....	....
Liabilities to direct investors	4 570	....	....	....	....	....	....	....	....
Reinvested earnings	4 575	3,875	2,462	4,151	6,119	9,649	13,465	12,747	18,581
Other capital	4 580	6,112	−2,969	10,811	−496	1,134	1,504	8,631	2,922
Claims on direct investors	4 585	−623	−2,408	190	−1,949	−676	−776	−1,651	−3,722
Liabilities to direct investors	4 590	6,735	−561	10,621	1,452	1,810	2,280	10,282	6,644
B. PORTFOLIO INVESTMENT	4 600	3,955	6,184	307	41,222	15,439	37,707	53,314	2,276
Assets	4 602	−10,919	−10,053	−16,820	−8,168	−24,579	−21,271	−43,866	−48,298
Equity securities	4 610	−7,346	−4,936	−11,854	−3,419	−11,071	−8,383	−22,156	−33,147
Monetary authorities	4 611	....	....	....	....	....	....	....	....
General government	4 612	....	....	....	....	....	....	....	....
Banks	4 613	1	....	−57	19	....	....	....	....
Other sectors	4 614	−7,347	−4,936	−11,796	−3,437	....	....	....	....
Debt securities	4 619	−3,573	−5,117	−4,966	−4,749	−13,509	−12,888	−21,710	−15,152
Bonds and notes	4 620	−3,360	−5,162	−4,234	−5,073	−11,884	−14,087	−19,676	−16,272
Monetary authorities	4 621	....	....	....	....	....	....	....	....
General government	4 622	....	....	....	....	....	....	....	....
Banks	4 623	−111	−454	−1,346	−1,807	−2,770	2,359	−3,743	−4,135
Other sectors	4 624	−3,250	−4,708	−2,888	−3,265	−9,113	−16,446	−15,933	−12,137
Money market instruments	4 630	−212	45	−732	323	−1,625	1,199	−2,034	1,121
Monetary authorities	4 631	....	....	....	....	....	....	....	....
General government	4 632	....	....	....	....	....	....	....	....
Banks	4 633	−125	−257	−751	411	−1,541	1,421	−1,223	314
Other sectors	4 634	−88	303	19	−88	−84	−222	−811	807
Liabilities	4 652	14,874	16,237	17,126	49,389	40,018	58,979	97,180	50,574
Equity securities	4 660	−726	7,159	283	12,209	−25,221	8,127	13,933	11,908
Banks	4 663	2,794	1,336	−2,930	1,207	505	622	−2,117	468
Other sectors	4 664	−3,520	5,823	3,213	11,002	−25,727	7,505	16,050	11,440
Debt securities	4 669	15,601	9,078	16,843	37,180	65,239	50,852	83,248	38,666
Bonds and notes	4 670	7,221	13,292	14,627	36,913	61,678	38,449	57,043	48,119
Monetary authorities	4 671	....	....	....	....	....	....	....	....
General government	4 672	−4,020	−529	140	2,623	4,374	3,363	−215	7,734
Banks	4 673	6,100	8,180	7,307	18,549	35,976	21,695	34,080	14,082
Other sectors	4 674	5,140	5,641	7,179	15,742	21,328	13,390	23,179	26,303
Money market instruments	4 680	8,380	−4,214	2,216	267	3,561	12,403	26,204	−9,453
Monetary authorities	4 681	....	....	....	....	....	....	....	....
General government	4 682	−11	362	43	−592	....	....	....	....
Banks	4 683	4,272	−968	1,358	3,148	4,332	10,294	21,890	−11,823
Other sectors	4 684	4,119	−3,608	816	−2,290	−770	2,109	4,315	2,371
C. FINANCIAL DERIVATIVES	4 910	−874	461	−316	−520	250	−38	2,452	−10,793
Monetary authorities	4 911	....	....	....	....	....	....	....	....
General government	4 912	....	....	....	....	....	....	....	....
Banks	4 913	−606	594	−893	−1,692	−974	−52	−1,187	−9,769
Other sectors	4 914	−268	−133	577	1,173	1,224	14	3,639	−1,024
Assets	4 900	−1,165	2,215	2,015	7,910	19,397	16,498	13,378	12,634
Monetary authorities	4 901	....	....	....	....	....	....	....	....
General government	4 902	....	....	....	....	....	....	....	....
Banks	4 903	−1,036	2,497	1,700	6,004	17,819	15,925	8,938	12,239
Other sectors	4 904	−130	−282	314	1,905	1,579	572	4,440	395
Liabilities	4 905	291	−1,754	−2,331	−8,430	−19,147	−16,536	−10,925	−23,427
Monetary authorities	4 906	....	....	....	....	....	....	....	....
General government	4 907	....	....	....	....	....	....	....	....
Banks	4 908	429	−1,903	−2,593	−7,697	−18,793	−15,978	−10,125	−22,008
Other sectors	4 909	−138	148	262	−733	−355	−558	−800	−1,419

Table 2 (Concluded). STANDARD PRESENTATION, 2000–2007

(Millions of U.S. dollars)

	Code	2000	2001	2002	2003	2004	2005	2006	2007
D. OTHER INVESTMENT	4 700 ..	**−471**	**5,216**	**7,060**	**3,185**	**−2,087**	**11,608**	**−8,347**	**30,623**
Assets	4 703 ..	**−4,887**	**834**	**−3,708**	**−4,603**	**−5,844**	**−3,188**	**−16,736**	**−8,178**
Trade credits	4 706 ..	610	−137	−130	481	−645	−1,501	−929	−520
General government	4 707 ..	153	−153	−85	−104	−147	−274	−549	−241
of which: Short-term	4 709 ..	....	....	....	....	....	....	....	....
Other sectors	4 710 ..	456	16	−45	584	−498	−1,227	−380	−280
of which: Short-term	4 712 ..	424	17	99	463	−479	....	....	....
Loans	4 714 ..	48	−2,025	−1,811	−3,209	−4,591	−4,604	−16,721	7,333
Monetary authorities	4 715 ..	133	275	411	110	....	....	....	....
of which: Short-term	4 718 ..	....	....	....	....	....	....	....	....
General government	4 719 ..	....	....	....	....	....	....	....	....
of which: Short-term	4 721 ..	....	....	....	....	....	....	....	....
Banks	4 722 ..	−150	−2,499	−1,404	−3,207	−5,188	−4,697	−17,634	7,055
of which: Short-term	4 724 ..	1,253	−238	386	−1,547	244	−3,118	−11,365	−3,463
Other sectors	4 725 ..	64	199	−818	−113	597	94	913	278
of which: Short-term	4 727 ..	−36	73	−390	−165	....	....	....	....
Currency and deposits	4 730 ..	−5,095	3,494	−2,049	−1,368	−907	2,974	1,296	−13,249
Monetary authorities	4 731 ..	....	....	....	....	....	....	....	....
General government	4 732 ..	....	....	....	....	....	....	....	....
Banks	4 733 ..	−1,590	−120	−2,121	−928	−1,214	3,315	1,427	−12,001
Other sectors	4 734 ..	−3,505	3,614	73	−440	307	−341	−131	−1,249
Other assets	4 736 ..	−449	−497	282	−506	299	−57	−383	−1,741
Monetary authorities	4 737 ..	....	....	....	....	....	....	....	....
of which: Short-term	4 739 ..	....	....	....	....	....	....	....	....
General government	4 740 ..	−175	....	....	....	....	....	....	....
of which: Short-term	4 742 ..	....	....	....	....	....	....	....	....
Banks	4 743 ..	−5	4	−68	−688	161	−74	−359	−1,613
of which: Short-term	4 745 ..	−3	4	−68	−654	....	....	....	....
Other sectors	4 746 ..	−269	−501	350	182	138	17	−23	−128
of which: Short-term	4 748 ..	−268	−510	356	172	306	43	−9	−83
Liabilities	4 753 ..	**4,416**	**4,382**	**10,767**	**7,788**	**3,757**	**14,796**	**8,389**	**38,801**
Trade credits	4 756 ..	176	−162	520	−707	−11	−10	348	−352
General government	4 757 ..	....	....	....	....	....	....	....	....
of which: Short-term	4 759 ..	....	....	....	....	....	....	....	....
Other sectors	4 760 ..	176	−162	520	−707	−11	−10	348	−352
of which: Short-term	4 762 ..	70	−11	508	−692	23	−33	....	....
Loans	4 764 ..	236	672	8,195	−1,806	7,027	9,046	7,803	19,997
Monetary authorities	4 765 ..	....	....	....	....	....	....	....	....
of which: Use of Fund credit and loans from the Fund..	4 766 ..	....	....	....	....	....	....	....	....
of which: Short-term	4 768 ..	....	....	....	....	....	....	....	....
General government	4 769 ..	....	1	....	....	−27	....	....	....
of which: Short-term	4 771 ..	....	....	....	....	....	....	....	....
Banks	4 772 ..	613	−304	7,803	−1,092	3,610	−4,556	4,997	30,877
of which: Short-term	4 774 ..	1,457	−242	5,739	−2,733	4,415	−1,925	2,564	27,993
Other sectors	4 775 ..	−378	975	392	−714	3,444	13,602	2,806	−10,880
of which: Short-term	4 777 ..	−700	1,414	1,146	−533	4,307	2,580	547	−12,959
Currency and deposits	4 780 ..	3,903	3,870	2,765	10,314	−3,747	5,697	1,759	16,416
Monetary authorities	4 781 ..	−70	3	7	37	7	10	18	230
General government	4 782 ..	....	....	....	....	....	....	....	....
Banks	4 783 ..	3,973	3,867	2,758	10,277	−3,754	5,687	1,741	16,186
Other sectors	4 784 ..	....	....	....	....	....	....	....	....
Other liabilities	4 786 ..	101	3	−713	−13	488	63	−1,521	2,741
Monetary authorities	4 787 ..	....	....	....	....	....	....	....	....
of which: Short-term	4 789 ..	....	....	....	....	....	....	....	....
General government	4 790 ..	75	−125	....	....	....	....	....	....
of which: Short-term	4 792 ..	....	....	....	....	....	....	....	....
Banks	4 793 ..	338	−28	−383	270	814	537	−839	3,453
of which: Short-term	4 795 ..	340	−28	−383	270	814	537	−900	3,453
Other sectors	4 796 ..	−312	156	−330	−283	−325	−474	−682	−712
of which: Short-term	4 798 ..	−321	171	−334	−279	....	....	....	....
E. RESERVE ASSETS	4 802 ..	**1,365**	**−1,096**	**−122**	**−6,877**	**−1,166**	**−7,256**	**−9,722**	**35,148**
Monetary gold	4 812 ..	....	....	....	....	....	....	....	....
Special drawing rights	4 811 ..	−25	−19	−17	−20	−17	−14	4	17
Reserve position in the Fund	4 810 ..	315	−216	−394	63	418	813	377	106
Foreign exchange	4 803 ..	1,075	−861	289	−6,920	−1,567	−8,055	−10,102	35,026
Other claims	4 813 ..	....	....	....	....	....	....	....	....
NET ERRORS AND OMISSIONS	4 998 ..	**−171**	**−293**	**−900**	**−22**	**−429**	**−581**	**−412**	**−253**

Table 3. INTERNATIONAL INVESTMENT POSITION (End-period stocks), 2000–2007

(Millions of U.S. dollars)

	Code	2000	2001	2002	2003	2004	2005	2006	2007
ASSETS	8 995 C.	231,688	258,480	287,650	415,442	513,502	501,939	660,497	779,655
Direct investment abroad	8 505 ..	85,385	109,602	114,888	161,948	204,347	178,481	227,531	280,579
Equity capital and reinvested earnings	8 506 ..	87,127	110,627	114,482	162,278	202,968	174,516	217,687	267,713
Claims on affiliated enterprises	8 507 ..	....	....	....	....	....	....	....	....
Liabilities to affiliated enterprises	8 508 ..	....	....	....	....	....	....	....	....
Other capital	8 530 ..	−1,742	−1,024	407	−330	1,379	3,965	9,844	12,866
Claims on affiliated enterprises	8 535 ..	3,966	4,568	7,119	9,491	11,577	11,864	20,674	24,694
Liabilities to affiliated enterprises	8 540 ..	−5,708	−5,593	−6,713	−9,821	−10,199	−7,899	−10,830	−11,828
Portfolio investment	8 602 ..	75,990	79,667	92,005	129,982	167,066	187,209	249,684	315,546
Equity securities	8 610 ..	59,024	59,889	65,308	92,613	114,438	126,870	164,800	210,223
Monetary authorities	8 611 ..	....	....	....	....	....	....	....	....
General government	8 612 ..	....	....	....	....	....	....	....	....
Banks	8 613 ..	....	....	59	190	....	....	....	....
Other sectors	8 614 ..	59,024	59,889	65,249	92,423	....	....	....	....
Debt securities	8 619 ..	16,966	19,778	26,696	37,369	52,628	60,339	84,884	105,323
Bonds and notes	8 620 ..	15,343	18,708	24,732	35,527	48,916	57,967	80,731	101,209
Monetary authorities	8 621 ..	....	....	....	....	....	....	−1	−1
General government	8 622 ..	....	....	....	....	....	....	....	....
Banks	8 623 ..	721	1,077	2,727	5,539	8,602	5,408	9,203	13,689
Other sectors	8 624 ..	14,622	17,632	22,005	29,988	40,314	52,559	71,529	87,521
Money market instruments	8 630 ..	1,623	1,070	1,964	1,842	3,712	2,373	4,154	4,114
Monetary authorities	8 631 ..	....	....	....	....	....	....	−1	−1
General government	8 632 ..	....	....	....	....	....	....	....	....
Banks	8 633 ..	612	733	1,564	1,481	3,154	1,635	2,800	2,353
Other sectors	8 634 ..	1,011	336	400	361	558	738	1,355	1,762
Financial derivatives	8 900 ..	12,593	14,780	19,576	33,139	38,960	27,696	41,156	52,952
Monetary authorities	8 901 ..	....	....	....	....	....	....	....	....
General government	8 902 ..	....	....	....	....	....	....	....	....
Banks	8 903 ..	11,164	12,505	17,372	31,901	36,119	24,802	40,124	51,909
Other sectors	8 904 ..	1,429	2,275	2,204	1,238	2,841	2,894	1,033	1,043
Other investment	8 703 ..	38,903	35,767	39,614	57,116	66,202	65,296	87,045	103,670
Trade credits	8 706 ..	5,229	5,089	1,955	6,049	7,101	8,093	9,121	10,171
General government	8 707 ..	1,585	1,723	1,811	2,111	2,225	2,401	3,063	3,198
of which: Short-term	8 709 ..	....	....	....	....	....	....	....	....
Other sectors	8 710 ..	3,644	3,366	143	3,938	4,876	5,693	6,057	6,973
of which: Short-term	8 712 ..	*3,642*	*3,363*	....	*3,917*	*4,834*	....	....	....
Loans	8 714 ..	21,080	21,651	25,800	33,983	40,471	42,563	63,054	61,911
Monetary authorities	8 715 ..	875	536	273	....	....	....	....	....
of which: Short-term	8 718 ..	....	....	*136*	....	....	....	....	....
General government	8 719 ..	....	....	....	....	....	....	....	....
of which: Short-term	8 721 ..	....	....	....	....	....	....	....	....
Banks	8 722 ..	17,622	18,737	22,150	30,286	37,323	39,628	60,946	59,979
of which: Short-term	8 724 ..	*9,153*	*8,480*	*9,095*	*12,482*	*12,998*	*15,328*	*28,026*	*34,139*
Other sectors	8 725 ..	2,583	2,378	3,377	3,697	3,147	2,936	2,108	1,932
of which: Short-term	8 727 ..	*141*	*70*	*487*	*701*	....	....	....	....
Currency and deposits	8 730 ..	8,785	4,904	7,420	11,024	12,720	9,251	8,693	23,138
Monetary authorities	8 731 ..	....	....	....	....	....	....	....	....
General government	8 732 ..	....	....	....	....	....	....	....	....
Banks	8 733 ..	3,402	3,285	5,830	8,751	10,682	6,929	5,985	19,100
Other sectors	8 734 ..	5,383	1,619	1,590	2,273	2,037	2,322	2,709	4,038
Other assets	8 736 ..	3,808	4,122	4,440	6,061	5,911	5,388	6,178	8,450
Monetary authorities	8 737 ..	....	....	136	....	....	....	....	....
of which: Short-term	8 739 ..	....	....	....	....	....	....	....	....
General government	8 740 ..	2,638	2,431	2,696	3,572	3,710	3,494	3,768	4,198
of which: Short-term	8 742 ..	....	....	....	....	....	....	....	....
Banks	8 743 ..	158	138	240	1,037	942	960	1,454	3,435
of which: Short-term	8 745 ..	*158*	*138*	*240*	*999*	....	....	....	....
Other sectors	8 746 ..	1,012	1,553	1,367	1,453	1,260	934	956	817
of which: Short-term	8 748 ..	*998*	*1,549*	*1,355*	*1,448*	*1,084*	*787*	*781*	*576*
Reserve assets	8 802 ..	18,817	18,664	21,567	33,258	36,927	43,257	55,080	26,908
Monetary gold	8 812 ..	699	709	878	1,070	1,123	1,316	1,631	2,140
Special drawing rights	8 811 ..	94	109	136	170	195	193	200	193
Reserve position in the Fund	8 810 ..	1,243	1,412	1,934	2,053	1,706	776	428	339
Foreign exchange	8 803 ..	16,782	16,434	18,618	29,966	33,903	40,972	52,822	24,237
Other claims	8 813 ..	....	....	....	....	....	....	....	....

Table 3 (Concluded). INTERNATIONAL INVESTMENT POSITION (End-period stocks), 2000–2007

(Millions of U.S. dollars)

	Code	2000	2001	2002	2003	2004	2005	2006	2007
LIABILITIES	8 995 D.	428,585	433,878	513,216	741,249	889,588	891,451	1,138,776	1,429,242
Direct investment in Australia	8 555 ..	111,138	111,739	141,136	199,340	261,552	207,952	249,963	314,960
Equity capital and reinvested earnings	8 556 ..	92,434	97,597	114,128	165,779	225,358	171,650	203,071	260,470
Claims on direct investors	8 557 ..	....	....	....	....	....	....	....	....
Liabilities to direct investors	8 558 ..	....	....	....	....	....	....	....	....
Other capital	8 580 ..	18,704	14,142	27,008	33,562	36,193	36,302	46,892	54,489
Claims on direct investors	8 585 ..	−4,641	−6,894	−7,157	−11,706	−12,662	−12,648	−15,618	−21,129
Liabilities to direct investors	8 590 ..	23,345	21,036	34,165	45,268	48,855	48,950	62,510	75,618
Portfolio investment	8 652 ..	241,859	247,051	273,147	401,381	482,548	537,752	714,026	878,537
Equity securities	8 660 ..	84,902	89,081	87,308	138,854	146,415	176,266	244,206	329,317
Banks	8 663 ..	19,259	22,039	20,231	29,607	35,001	40,324	48,132	55,823
Other sectors	8 664 ..	65,642	67,042	67,077	109,247	111,413	135,942	196,074	273,494
Debt securities	8 669 ..	156,958	157,969	185,839	262,526	336,134	361,486	469,820	549,220
Bonds and notes	8 670 ..	113,253	119,645	141,850	208,749	276,443	293,280	367,160	446,689
Monetary authorities	8 671 ..	....	....	....	....	....	....	....	....
General government	8 672 ..	13,066	11,324	12,908	18,998	23,874	25,315	25,879	34,743
Banks	8 673 ..	48,119	53,799	63,115	91,174	129,049	140,666	187,161	222,490
Other sectors	8 674 ..	52,068	54,522	65,826	98,577	123,520	127,299	154,120	189,456
Money market instruments	8 680 ..	43,705	38,324	43,989	53,777	59,691	68,206	102,660	102,531
Monetary authorities	8 681 ..	....	....	....	....	....	....	....	....
General government	8 682 ..	125	465	552	....	....	....	....	....
Banks	8 683 ..	34,517	32,378	36,816	49,076	55,748	62,425	92,549	89,988
Other sectors	8 684 ..	9,063	5,482	6,621	4,702	3,943	5,781	10,111	12,543
Financial derivatives	8 905 ..	13,318	12,900	20,919	36,584	37,712	27,899	43,960	52,582
Monetary authorities	8 906 ..	....	....	....	....	....	....	....	....
General government	8 907 ..	....	....	....	....	....	....	....	....
Banks	8 908 ..	11,313	11,278	19,012	35,031	36,094	26,137	41,339	49,035
Other sectors	8 909 ..	2,005	1,623	1,907	1,553	1,618	1,762	2,621	3,547
Other investment	8 753 ..	62,270	62,189	78,014	103,944	107,776	117,848	130,826	183,163
Trade credits	8 756 ..	2,004	1,447	2,165	1,852	2,229	2,035	2,560	2,472
General government	8 757 ..	....	....	....	....	....	....	....	....
of which: Short-term	8 759 ..	....	....	....	....	....	....	....	....
Other sectors	8 760 ..	2,004	1,447	2,165	1,852	2,229	2,035	2,560	2,472
of which: Short-term	8 762 ..	1,819	1,413	2,124	1,823	2,198	1,975	....	....
Loans	8 764 ..	30,047	28,708	39,670	46,073	53,030	59,604	68,971	98,841
Monetary authorities	8 765 ..	....	....	....	....	....	....	....	....
of which: Use of Fund credit and loans from the Fund	8 766 ..	....	....	....	....	....	....	....	....
of which: Short-term	8 768 ..	....	....	....	....	....	....	....	....
General government	8 769 ..	30	23	25	29	....	....	....	....
of which: Short-term	8 771 ..	....	....	25	29	....	....	....	....
Banks	8 772 ..	20,419	18,967	28,571	33,713	37,142	31,132	36,173	72,788
of which: Short-term	8 774 ..	18,150	16,410	23,711	25,626	29,786	26,547	28,722	58,748
Other sectors	8 775 ..	9,597	9,719	11,074	12,332	15,888	28,473	32,798	26,054
of which: Short-term	8 777 ..	2,302	3,627	5,207	5,143	9,578	11,878	13,989	2,699
Currency and deposits	8 780 ..	27,306	29,574	34,204	53,423	49,279	52,902	57,174	76,444
Monetary authorities	8 781 ..	18	19	28	81	91	93	119	373
General government	8 782 ..	....	....	....	....	....	....	....	....
Banks	8 783 ..	27,288	29,555	34,175	53,342	49,188	52,809	57,054	76,071
Other sectors	8 784 ..	....	....	....	....	....	....	....	....
Other liabilities	8 786 ..	2,912	2,459	1,975	2,596	3,238	3,308	2,121	5,406
Monetary authorities	8 787 ..	....	....	....	....	....	....	....	....
of which: Short-term	8 789 ..	....	....	....	....	....	....	....	....
General government	8 790 ..	179	41	45	60	62	59	63	71
of which: Short-term	8 792 ..	....	....	....	....	....	....	....	....
Banks	8 793 ..	460	458	99	462	1,330	1,921	1,579	5,293
of which: Short-term	8 795 ..	460	458	99	462	1,330	1,921	1,514	5,229
Other sectors	8 796 ..	2,273	1,960	1,831	2,074	1,846	1,328	480	42
of which: Short-term	8 798 ..	2,255	1,960	1,825	2,061	....	....	....	....
NET INTERNATIONAL INVESTMENT POSITION	8 995 ..	−196,897	−175,398	−225,567	−325,807	−376,087	−389,513	−478,279	−649,587
Conversion rates: Australian dollars per U.S. dollar (end of period)	0 102 ..	1.8051	1.9585	1.7662	1.3333	1.2837	1.3630	1.2637	1.1343

Table 1. ANALYTIC PRESENTATION, 2000–2007
(Millions of U.S. dollars)

	Code	2000	2001	2002	2003	2004	2005	2006	2007
A. Current Account¹	4 993 Z.	**−1,339**	**−1,512**	**5,464**	**4,186**	**6,074**	**6,245**	**7,807**	**12,031**
Goods: exports f.o.b.	2 100 ..	64,685	66,900	73,667	88,105	109,875	119,228	133,844	162,147
Goods: imports f.o.b.	3 100 ..	−68,662	−70,140	−72,375	−89,799	−110,905	−120,977	−133,419	−160,302
Balance on Goods	4 100 ..	*−3,978*	*−3,240*	*1,293*	*−1,694*	*−1,029*	*−1,750*	*426*	*1,846*
Services: credit	2 200 ..	23,092	23,978	25,861	32,455	37,945	42,589	46,112	55,736
Services: debit	3 200 ..	−16,462	−17,555	−18,727	−23,738	−27,986	−30,730	−33,514	−39,033
Balance on Goods and Services	4 991 ..	*2,653*	*3,184*	*8,427*	*7,023*	*8,930*	*10,109*	*13,024*	*18,549*
Income: credit	2 300 ..	12,405	12,343	14,168	16,514	20,193	25,914	28,027	37,858
Income: debit	3 300 ..	−14,664	−15,324	−15,630	−17,611	−21,403	−27,957	−31,701	−43,023
Balance on Goods, Services, and Income	4 992 ..	*393*	*203*	*6,965*	*5,926*	*7,720*	*8,066*	*9,350*	*13,383*
Current transfers: credit	2 379 Z.	2,051	2,065	2,356	2,954	3,449	3,949	4,290	5,050
Current transfers: debit	3 379 ..	−3,783	−3,779	−3,857	−4,693	−5,096	−5,770	−5,833	−6,402
B. Capital Account¹	4 994 Z.	**−432**	**−528**	**−379**	**8**	**−342**	**−237**	**−1,009**	**−90**
Capital account: credit	2 994 Z.	529	483	1,012	897	764	739	586	664
Capital account: debit	3 994 ..	−961	−1,011	−1,391	−888	−1,105	−976	−1,595	−754
Total, Groups A Plus B	4 981 ..	*−1,771*	*−2,040*	*5,085*	*4,194*	*5,732*	*6,008*	*6,799*	*11,941*
C. Financial Account¹	4 995 W.	**3,382**	**1,772**	**−4,021**	**−2,515**	**−2,823**	**−917**	**−6,862**	**−6,045**
Direct investment abroad	4 505 ..	−5,598	−3,132	−5,744	−7,143	−8,425	−81,842	−5,527	−31,453
Direct investment in Austria	4 555 Z.	8,525	5,906	318	7,098	3,892	81,648	2,477	30,717
Portfolio investment assets	4 602 ..	−27,143	−10,955	−22,992	−18,654	−33,024	−44,004	−32,900	−18,383
Equity securities	4 610 ..	−15,387	35	−3,062	−2,762	−4,067	−5,690	−8,420	−1,335
Debt securities	4 619 ..	−11,756	−10,990	−19,930	−15,893	−28,957	−38,314	−24,480	−17,048
Portfolio investment liabilities	4 652 Z.	30,362	16,699	18,790	23,440	31,695	30,525	47,725	46,590
Equity securities	4 660 ..	3,436	−4,538	2,772	2,431	6,926	5,999	10,550	3,684
Debt securities	4 669 Z.	26,926	21,237	16,018	21,009	24,769	24,526	37,176	42,907
Financial derivatives	4 910 ..	−187	−48	−487	−742	−669	153	−1,029	−3,031
Financial derivatives assets	4 900 ..	−441	−143	−495	−666	144	283	....	....
Financial derivatives liabilities	4 905 ..	254	95	8	−77	−813	−129	−1,029	−3,031
Other investment assets	4 703 ..	−16,372	−8,727	11,902	−16,648	−21,440	−30,098	−68,095	−47,925
Monetary authorities	4 701 ..	1,761	538	−139	362	−147	−29	....	....
General government	4 704 ..	−1,002	−284	775	−243	−541	−135	....	....
Banks	4 705 ..	−13,592	−6,790	12,057	−12,756	−16,666	−27,618	....	....
Other sectors	4 728 ..	−3,538	−2,191	−791	−4,011	−4,086	−2,317	....	....
Other investment liabilities	4 753 W.	13,795	2,028	−5,808	10,135	25,147	42,701	50,485	17,441
Monetary authorities	4 753 WA	−647	−6,129	−1,442	960	12,470	8,774	....	....
General government	4 753 ZB	157	1,417	−392	53	1,420	5,032	986	535
Banks	4 753 ZC	11,719	5,811	−9,146	7,500	9,372	25,852	....	....
Other sectors	4 753 ZD	2,566	929	5,173	1,621	1,884	3,042	....	....
Total, Groups A Through C	4 983 ..	*1,611*	*−268*	*1,064*	*1,679*	*2,909*	*5,091*	*−64*	*5,896*
D. Net Errors and Omissions	4 998 ..	**−2,356**	**−1,620**	**−2,786**	**−3,703**	**−4,758**	**−5,841**	**−797**	**−3,371**
Total, Groups A Through D	4 984 ..	*−745*	*−1,888*	*−1,723*	*−2,023*	*−1,849*	*−750*	*−861*	*2,525*
E. Reserves and Related Items	4 802 A.	**745**	**1,888**	**1,723**	**2,023**	**1,849**	**750**	**861**	**−2,525**
Reserve assets	4 802 ..	745	1,888	1,723	2,023	1,849	750	861	−2,525
Use of Fund credit and loans	4 766 ..	....	....	....	....	....	....	....	....
Exceptional financing	4 920 ..	....	....	....	....	....	....	....	....
Conversion rates: euros per U.S. dollar	0 103 ..	**1.0854**	**1.1175**	**1.0626**	**.8860**	**.8054**	**.8041**	**.7971**	**.7306**

¹ Excludes components that have been classified in the categories of Group E.

Table 2. STANDARD PRESENTATION, 2000–2007

(Millions of U.S. dollars)

	Code	2000	2001	2002	2003	2004	2005	2006	2007
CURRENT ACCOUNT...........................	4 993 ..	−1,339	−1,512	5,464	4,186	6,074	6,245	7,807	12,031
A. GOODS............................	4 100 ..	−3,978	−3,240	1,293	−1,694	−1,029	−1,750	426	1,846
Credit................................	2 100 ..	64,685	66,900	73,667	88,105	109,875	119,228	133,844	162,147
General merchandise: exports f.o.b.	2 110 ..	61,197	63,781	70,195	83,653	102,648	111,320	133,844	162,147
Goods for processing: exports f.o.b.	2 150 ..	2,471	2,414	2,553	3,096	3,679	3,375	....	....
Repairs on goods..................................	2 160 ..	887	632	798	1,205	3,400	4,276	....	....
Goods procured in ports by carriers........	2 170 ..	....	21	18	38	39	96	....	....
Nonmonetary gold................................	2 180 ..	129	53	103	113	110	160	....	....
Debit................................	3 100 ..	−68,662	−70,140	−72,375	−89,799	−110,905	−120,977	−133,419	−160,302
General merchandise: imports f.o.b.	3 110 ..	−65,497	−66,925	−69,428	−85,163	−103,964	−113,119	−133,419	−160,302
Goods for processing: imports f.o.b.	3 150 ..	−2,417	−2,565	−2,595	−3,319	−3,638	−3,365	....	....
Repairs on goods..................................	3 160 ..	−745	−643	−331	−1,273	−3,277	−4,468	....	....
Goods procured in ports by carriers........	3 170 ..	....	....	....	....	....	....	....	....
Nonmonetary gold................................	3 180 ..	−4	−6	−21	−44	−26	−25	....	....
B. SERVICES............................	4 200 ..	6,630	6,424	7,134	8,717	9,959	11,859	12,598	16,703
Total credit..................................	2 200 ..	23,092	23,978	25,861	32,455	37,945	42,589	46,112	55,736
Total debit..................................	3 200 ..	−16,462	−17,555	−18,727	−23,738	−27,986	−30,730	−33,514	−39,033
Transportation services, credit........................	2 205 ..	4,208	4,649	5,259	6,544	8,169	8,969	10,291	11,981
Passenger..................................	2 850 ..	1,483	1,563	1,531	1,821	2,101	2,228	2,376	2,538
Freight..................................	2 851 ..	2,325	2,657	3,226	4,051	5,279	5,846	6,849	8,171
Other..................................	2 852 ..	400	428	501	672	789	895	1,066	1,273
Sea transport, passenger......................	2 207 ..	4	8	9	7	6	9	16	12
Sea transport, freight..........................	2 208 ..	156	188	222	289	369	437	545	657
Sea transport, other............................	2 209 ..	11	11	6	13	31	29	23	18
Air transport, passenger......................	2 211 ..	1,323	1,390	1,351	1,636	1,924	2,023	2,146	2,313
Air transport, freight..........................	2 212 ..	229	219	244	267	340	351	367	406
Air transport, other............................	2 213 ..	178	215	235	289	346	378	409	482
Other transport, passenger..................	2 215 ..	157	165	172	178	171	196	214	213
Other transport, freight......................	2 216 ..	1,940	2,251	2,760	3,494	4,569	5,059	5,936	7,108
Other transport, other........................	2 217 ..	211	202	261	371	412	489	634	773
Transportation services, debit........................	3 205 ..	−3,749	−4,140	−4,451	−5,639	−7,588	−8,661	−10,201	−11,938
Passenger..................................	3 850 ..	−769	−829	−842	−1,138	−1,575	−1,761	−2,093	−2,273
Freight..................................	3 851 ..	−2,599	−2,874	−3,148	−3,979	−5,391	−6,230	−7,214	−8,763
Other..................................	3 852 ..	−380	−437	−461	−522	−622	−669	−895	−902
Sea transport, passenger......................	3 207 ..	−9	−7	−10	−14	−16	−17	−16	−18
Sea transport, freight..........................	3 208 ..	−368	−495	−513	−606	−796	−953	−1,141	−1,355
Sea transport, other............................	3 209 ..	−55	−76	−68	−64	−81	−72	−58	−45
Air transport, passenger......................	3 211 ..	−694	−756	−754	−1,009	−1,411	−1,580	−1,919	−2,089
Air transport, freight..........................	3 212 ..	−377	−389	−432	−476	−568	−545	−486	−521
Air transport, other............................	3 213 ..	−244	−268	−278	−325	−396	−447	−638	−625
Other transport, passenger..................	3 215 ..	−66	−66	−77	−116	−148	−164	−157	−166
Other transport, freight......................	3 216 ..	−1,854	−1,989	−2,203	−2,897	−4,028	−4,732	−5,586	−6,887
Other transport, other........................	3 217 ..	−82	−92	−116	−132	−145	−150	−199	−232
Travel, credit..............................	2 236 ..	9,899	9,948	10,803	13,307	15,150	16,243	16,510	18,754
Business travel..................................	2 237 ..	1,588	1,579	1,717	2,112	2,487	2,881	3,053	3,529
Personal travel..................................	2 240 ..	8,311	8,370	9,086	11,195	12,663	13,362	13,458	15,225
Travel, debit..............................	3 236 ..	−6,232	−6,579	−6,901	−8,623	−9,237	−9,316	−9,626	−10,566
Business travel..................................	3 237 ..	−1,397	−1,504	−1,535	−1,830	−2,029	−1,957	−1,958	−2,170
Personal travel..................................	3 240 ..	−4,834	−5,075	−5,366	−6,793	−7,208	−7,359	−7,669	−8,397
Other services, credit............................	2 200 BA	8,985	9,381	9,799	12,604	14,626	17,377	19,312	25,001
Communications..................................	2 245 ..	478	565	648	684	672	1,010	1,416	1,663
Construction......................................	2 249 ..	586	696	649	1,043	1,174	985	969	1,385
Insurance..	2 253 ..	670	339	463	647	775	797	756	1,328
Financial..	2 260 ..	1,054	587	506	429	524	913	804	1,485
Computer and information....................	2 262 ..	296	329	420	657	899	1,234	1,503	1,871
Royalties and licence fees....................	2 266 ..	161	138	243	347	372	391	540	757
Other business services........................	2 268 ..	5,384	6,341	6,439	8,254	9,618	11,423	12,635	15,727
Personal, cultural, and recreational........	2 287 ..	129	142	137	177	219	236	251	260
Government, n.i.e.	2 291 ..	228	244	295	365	373	388	437	525
Other services, debit............................	3 200 BA	−6,482	−6,836	−7,376	−9,475	−11,161	−12,753	−13,687	−16,528
Communications..................................	3 245 ..	−431	−487	−445	−624	−664	−824	−1,132	−1,314
Construction......................................	3 249 ..	−311	−487	−553	−942	−1,000	−840	−773	−1,226
Insurance..	3 253 ..	−85	−200	−116	−534	−660	−913	−1,105	−1,822
Financial..	3 260 ..	−996	−652	−563	−420	−337	−745	−613	−735
Computer and information....................	3 262 ..	−374	−401	−506	−667	−857	−949	−1,080	−1,422
Royalties and licence fees....................	3 266 ..	−566	−757	−1,057	−1,118	−1,249	−1,334	−1,328	−1,471
Other business services........................	3 268 ..	−3,431	−3,540	−3,754	−4,610	−5,614	−6,314	−6,799	−7,598
Personal, cultural, and recreational........	3 287 ..	−209	−248	−298	−467	−693	−728	−750	−815
Government, n.i.e.	3 291 ..	−79	−64	−82	−93	−88	−106	−107	−124

Table 2 (Continued). STANDARD PRESENTATION, 2000–2007

(Millions of U.S. dollars)

	Code	2000	2001	2002	2003	2004	2005	2006	2007
C. INCOME	4 300	**−2,259**	**−2,981**	**−1,461**	**−1,097**	**−1,210**	**−2,043**	**−3,674**	**−5,166**
Total credit	2 300	*12,405*	*12,343*	*14,168*	*16,514*	*20,193*	*25,914*	*28,027*	*37,858*
Total debit	3 300	*−14,664*	*−15,324*	*−15,630*	*−17,611*	*−21,403*	*−27,957*	*−31,701*	*−43,023*
Compensation of employees, credit	2 310	**1,325**	**1,265**	**1,332**	**1,608**	**1,865**	**1,917**	**1,880**	**2,104**
Compensation of employees, debit	3 310	**−590**	**−639**	**−687**	**−856**	**−1,121**	**−1,316**	**−1,406**	**−1,669**
Investment income, credit	2 320	**11,080**	**11,078**	**12,836**	**14,906**	**18,328**	**23,997**	**26,147**	**35,753**
Direct investment income	2 330	1,278	1,196	2,630	3,494	5,214	8,770	8,541	11,572
Dividends and distributed branch profits	2 332	1,103	999	1,084	1,886	2,429	4,893	4,151	4,080
Reinvested earnings and undistributed branch profits	2 333	115	128	1,488	1,537	2,736	3,811	3,368	6,334
Income on debt (interest)	2 334	60	70	58	71	50	66	1,022	1,158
Portfolio investment income	2 339	4,399	4,345	5,232	6,641	8,049	9,425	11,145	14,512
Income on equity	2 340	393	148	346	486	637	798	....	....
Income on bonds and notes	2 350	3,916	4,109	4,805	6,060	7,302	8,450	....	....
Income on money market instruments	2 360	90	88	81	94	110	177	....	....
Other investment income	2 370	5,402	5,537	4,974	4,771	5,064	5,802	6,461	9,670
Investment income, debit	3 320	**−14,074**	**−14,684**	**−14,943**	**−16,755**	**−20,282**	**−26,641**	**−30,295**	**−41,354**
Direct investment income	3 330	−2,599	−2,744	−3,529	−3,731	−5,006	−9,233	−9,278	−11,467
Dividends and distributed branch profits	3 332	−1,694	−1,506	−1,746	−2,805	−3,363	−5,070	−5,555	−2,859
Reinvested earnings and undistributed branch profits	3 333	−900	−1,235	−1,781	−902	−1,618	−4,147	−2,642	−7,235
Income on debt (interest)	3 334	−5	−3	−3	−24	−25	−16	−1,080	−1,373
Portfolio investment income	3 339	−6,774	−7,419	−8,295	−9,792	−11,353	−12,178	−13,929	−18,584
Income on equity	3 340	−228	−258	−297	−352	−536	−740	....	....
Income on bonds and notes	3 350	−6,225	−6,891	−7,828	−9,242	−10,684	−11,204	....	....
Income on money market instruments	3 360	−321	−270	−170	−198	−132	−234	....	....
Other investment income	3 370	−4,701	−4,522	−3,118	−3,232	−3,922	−5,230	−7,088	−11,304
D. CURRENT TRANSFERS	4 379	**−1,732**	**−1,714**	**−1,502**	**−1,740**	**−1,646**	**−1,821**	**−1,543**	**−1,352**
Credit	2 379	**2,051**	**2,065**	**2,356**	**2,954**	**3,449**	**3,949**	**4,290**	**5,050**
General government	2 380	412	432	531	687	776	880	883	940
Other sectors	2 390	1,639	1,633	1,824	2,267	2,674	3,069	3,407	4,110
Workers' remittances	2 391	254	254	276	340	383	398	418	467
Other current transfers	2 392	1,385	1,379	1,548	1,926	2,291	2,672	2,990	3,643
Debit	3 379	**−3,783**	**−3,779**	**−3,857**	**−4,693**	**−5,096**	**−5,770**	**−5,833**	**−6,402**
General government	3 380	−1,619	−1,827	−1,892	−2,444	−2,896	−3,291	−3,273	−3,487
Other sectors	3 390	−2,164	−1,952	−1,966	−2,249	−2,200	−2,479	−2,560	−2,915
Workers' remittances	3 391	−513	−522	−570	−694	−789	−804	−839	−959
Other current transfers	3 392	−1,651	−1,430	−1,395	−1,555	−1,411	−1,675	−1,721	−1,956
CAPITAL AND FINANCIAL ACCOUNT	4 996	**3,695**	**3,132**	**−2,677**	**−483**	**−1,316**	**−404**	**−7,010**	**−8,660**
CAPITAL ACCOUNT	4 994	**−432**	**−528**	**−379**	**8**	**−342**	**−237**	**−1,009**	**−90**
Total credit	2 994	*529*	*483*	*1,012*	*897*	*764*	*739*	*586*	*664*
Total debit	3 994	*−961*	*−1,011*	*−1,391*	*−888*	*−1,105*	*−976*	*−1,595*	*−754*
Capital transfers, credit	2 400	**488**	**435**	**968**	**857**	**577**	**684**	**487**	**548**
General government	2 401	151	57	210	135	145	175	125	170
Debt forgiveness	2 402	....	....	....	....	....	....	....	....
Other capital transfers	2 410	151	57	210	135	145	175	125	170
Other sectors	2 430	337	378	758	722	432	509	361	378
Migrants' transfers	2 431	225	255	377	548	273	294	341	373
Debt forgiveness	2 432	8	14	228	44	35	66	....	....
Other capital transfers	2 440	103	109	153	131	125	149	20	5
Capital transfers, debit	3 400	**−894**	**−923**	**−1,349**	**−878**	**−916**	**−906**	**−1,323**	**−451**
General government	3 401	−8	−152	−168	−50	−37	−3	−879	....
Debt forgiveness	3 402	....	....	....	....	....	....	−575	....
Other capital transfers	3 410	−8	−152	−168	−50	−37	−3	−304	....
Other sectors	3 430	−886	−771	−1,180	−828	−879	−903	−443	−451
Migrants' transfers	3 431	−195	−261	−260	−324	−317	−447	−330	−356
Debt forgiveness	3 432	−481	−404	−737	−380	−418	−313	−104	−94
Other capital transfers	3 440	−210	−107	−183	−124	−144	−143	−9	....
Nonproduced nonfinancial assets, credit	2 480	**41**	**48**	**45**	**39**	**186**	**55**	**99**	**116**
Nonproduced nonfinancial assets, debit	3 480	**−66**	**−88**	**−42**	**−10**	**−189**	**−70**	**−272**	**−303**

Table 2 (Continued). STANDARD PRESENTATION, 2000–2007

(Millions of U.S. dollars)

	Code	2000	2001	2002	2003	2004	2005	2006	2007
FINANCIAL ACCOUNT	4 995	4,127	3,660	−2,298	−491	−974	−168	−6,002	−8,570
A. DIRECT INVESTMENT	4 500	2,927	2,774	−5,426	−45	−4,533	−194	−3,050	−736
Direct investment abroad	4 505	−5,598	−3,132	−5,744	−7,143	−8,425	−81,842	−5,527	−31,453
Equity capital	4 510	−4,819	−2,928	−4,036	−4,925	−6,062	−76,979	−1,573	−27,236
Claims on affiliated enterprises	4 515	....	....	....	....	....	....	....	....
Liabilities to affiliated enterprises	4 520	....	....	....	....	....	....	....	....
Reinvested earnings	4 525	−115	−128	−1,488	−1,537	−2,736	−3,811	−3,368	−6,334
Other capital	4 530	−664	−77	−220	−681	373	−1,052	−586	2,117
Claims on affiliated enterprises	4 535	−683	−89	−269	−612	375	−726	−701	595
Liabilities to affiliated enterprises	4 540	19	12	49	−70	−2	−327	115	1,522
Direct investment in Austria	4 555	8,525	5,906	318	7,098	3,892	81,648	2,477	30,717
Equity capital	4 560	7,476	3,817	−402	3,139	1,876	79,299	−2,881	4,121
Claims on direct investors	4 565	....	....	....	....	....	....	....	....
Liabilities to direct investors	4 570	....	....	....	....	....	....	....	....
Reinvested earnings	4 575	900	1,235	1,781	902	1,618	4,147	2,642	7,235
Other capital	4 580	149	854	−1,061	3,058	398	−1,798	2,716	19,360
Claims on direct investors	4 585	90	−195	−643	641	2	34	−171	−311
Liabilities to direct investors	4 590	59	1,049	−418	2,417	396	−1,832	2,887	19,671
B. PORTFOLIO INVESTMENT	4 600	3,218	5,744	−4,203	4,786	−1,329	−13,479	14,826	28,208
Assets	4 602	−27,143	−10,955	−22,992	−18,654	−33,024	−44,004	−32,900	−18,383
Equity securities	4 610	−15,387	35	−3,062	−2,762	−4,067	−5,690	−8,420	−1,335
Monetary authorities	4 611	−75	207	4	−99	−186	−176	....	....
General government	4 612	−78	−60	24	2	−41	−33	....	....
Banks	4 613	103	−1	199	−138	−414	−543	....	....
Other sectors	4 614	−15,336	−111	−3,289	−2,526	−3,426	−4,938	....	....
Debt securities	4 619	−11,756	−10,990	−19,930	−15,893	−28,957	−38,314	−24,480	−17,048
Bonds and notes	4 620	−10,906	−11,206	−16,136	−19,880	−27,639	−37,552	−26,706	−16,362
Monetary authorities	4 621	−395	−272	71	−2,122	1,074	−982	....	....
General government	4 622	−387	−354	1	209	−85	32	....	....
Banks	4 623	−4,313	−5,190	−7,146	−7,375	−17,763	−17,179	....	....
Other sectors	4 624	−5,810	−5,390	−9,062	−10,592	−10,864	−19,423	....	....
Money market instruments	4 630	−850	216	−3,794	3,987	−1,318	−761	2,226	−686
Monetary authorities	4 631	345	195	−1,554	1,837	−1,676	772	....	....
General government	4 632	−1,552	126	−1,212	1,521	818	−1,008	....	....
Banks	4 633	81	15	−1,094	610	−614	244	....	....
Other sectors	4 634	276	−120	66	20	153	−769	....	....
Liabilities	4 652	30,362	16,699	18,790	23,440	31,695	30,525	47,725	46,590
Equity securities	4 660	3,436	−4,538	2,772	2,431	6,926	5,999	10,550	3,684
Banks	4 663	476	115	595	1,390	437	−2,832	....	....
Other sectors	4 664	2,960	−4,652	2,177	1,040	6,489	8,831	....	....
Debt securities	4 669	26,926	21,237	16,018	21,009	24,769	24,526	37,176	42,907
Bonds and notes	4 670	25,032	23,572	17,330	20,263	23,167	23,193	29,208	40,016
Monetary authorities	4 671	....	....	....	....	....	....	....	....
General government	4 672	11,125	9,214	10,390	10,701	8,184	5,618	....	....
Banks	4 673	12,965	9,975	5,810	5,549	11,290	12,899	....	....
Other sectors	4 674	943	4,383	1,129	4,013	3,693	4,676	....	....
Money market instruments	4 680	1,894	−2,335	−1,312	746	1,601	1,333	7,967	2,890
Monetary authorities	4 681	....	....	....	....	....	....	....	....
General government	4 682	−202	−446	−847	265	320	224	....	....
Banks	4 683	2,330	−1,678	−231	452	1,306	1,170	....	....
Other sectors	4 684	−235	−210	−234	29	−24	−61	....	....
C. FINANCIAL DERIVATIVES	4 910	−187	−48	−487	−742	−669	153	−1,029	−3,031
Monetary authorities	4 911	2	−37	4	−23	12	8	....	....
General government	4 912	235	312	−136	449	1,124	1,584	....	....
Banks	4 913	−86	−1,019	488	−620	−1,062	−1,215	....	....
Other sectors	4 914	−338	696	−842	−548	−743	−223	−1,029	−3,031
Assets	4 900	−441	−143	−495	−666	144	283	....	....
Monetary authorities	4 901	2	−37	4	−23	12	8	....	....
General government	4 902	235	312	−136	449	1,124	1,584	....	....
Banks	4 903	−361	−1,169	494	−546	−234	−1,052	....	....
Other sectors	4 904	−317	751	−856	−545	−759	−257	....	....
Liabilities	4 905	254	95	8	−77	−813	−129	−1,029	−3,031
Monetary authorities	4 906	....	....	....	....	....	....	....	....
General government	4 907	....	....	....	....	....	....	....	....
Banks	4 908	275	150	−6	−75	−828	−163	....	....
Other sectors	4 909	−21	−55	14	−2	15	34	−1,029	−3,031

Table 2 (Concluded). STANDARD PRESENTATION, 2000–2007

(Millions of U.S. dollars)

	Code	2000	2001	2002	2003	2004	2005	2006	2007
D. OTHER INVESTMENT	4 700	−2,577	−6,699	6,094	−6,513	3,707	12,602	−17,610	−30,485
Assets	4 703	−16,372	−8,727	11,902	−16,648	−21,440	−30,098	−68,095	−47,925
Trade credits	4 706	−2,046	264	108	52	−490	−728	−1,720	−415
General government	4 707	....	....	....	....	−647	−99	....	....
of which: Short-term	4 709	....	....	....	....	....	....	....	....
Other sectors	4 710	−2,046	264	108	52	157	−629	....	....
of which: Short-term	4 712	−2,046	264	108	52	157	−629	....	....
Loans	4 714	−9,302	−7,535	−3,051	−14,568	−8,104	−15,237	−17,303	−35,720
Monetary authorities	4 715	820	93	....	....	....	−1	....	....
of which: Short-term	4 718	820	93	....	....	....	−1	....	....
General government	4 719	16	14	−9	30	7	−4	....	....
of which: Short-term	4 721	4	4	−4	....	11	....	....	....
Banks	4 722	−8,519	−6,214	−2,166	−12,973	−5,916	−14,212	....	....
of which: Short-term	4 724	−4,006	−879	2,451	−894	6,017	−6,272	....	....
Other sectors	4 725	−1,618	−1,428	−877	−1,625	−2,194	−1,021	....	....
of which: Short-term	4 727	−1,071	−145	−344	−1,327	−516	−353	....	....
Currency and deposits	4 730	−4,985	−790	14,506	−2,089	−12,002	−13,670	−48,879	−11,035
Monetary authorities	4 731	941	446	−139	362	−150	−28	....	....
General government	4 732	−917	−223	811	−192	192	78	....	....
Banks	4 733	−5,373	−8	14,077	−147	−10,685	−13,283	....	....
Other sectors	4 734	364	−1,005	−244	−2,112	−1,359	−438	....	....
Other assets	4 736	−39	−666	340	−43	−844	−464	−193	−755
Monetary authorities	4 737	....	....	....	....	3	....	....	....
of which: Short-term	4 739	....	....	....	....	....	....	....	....
General government	4 740	−101	−75	−28	−82	−93	−111	....	....
of which: Short-term	4 742	−63	....	....	....	....	....	....	....
Banks	4 743	300	−568	146	364	−64	−123	....	....
of which: Short-term	4 745	206	−553	121	385	−30	−91	....	....
Other sectors	4 746	−238	−22	222	−326	−689	−230	....	....
of which: Short-term	4 748	−31	36	314	−185	−121	118	....	....
Liabilities	4 753	13,795	2,028	−5,808	10,135	25,147	42,701	50,485	17,441
Trade credits	4 756	454	−637	−297	171	507	117	1,071	136
General government	4 757	....	....	....	....	....	....	....	....
of which: Short-term	4 759	....	....	....	....	....	....	....	....
Other sectors	4 760	454	−637	−297	171	507	117	....	....
of which: Short-term	4 762	454	−637	−297	171	507	117	....	....
Loans	4 764	2,289	2,931	5,189	940	2,545	7,431	18,695	−9,071
Monetary authorities	4 765	....	....	....	....	....	....	....	....
of which: Use of Fund credit and loans from the Fund	4 766	....	....	....	....	....	....	....	....
of which: Short-term	4 768	....	....	....	....	....	....	....	....
General government	4 769	−115	1,332	−202	−256	1,641	5,074	986	535
of which: Short-term	4 771	3	54	....	....	−1	−1	....	....
Banks	4 772	....	....	....	....	....	....	....	....
of which: Short-term	4 774	....	....	....	....	....	....	....	....
Other sectors	4 775	2,404	1,599	5,390	1,196	904	2,358	....	....
of which: Short-term	4 777	1,464	523	1,485	260	736	1,414	....	....
Currency and deposits	4 780	10,886	−296	−10,579	8,200	21,803	34,252	29,954	24,758
Monetary authorities	4 781	−647	−6,129	−1,442	960	12,470	8,774	....	....
General government	4 782	....	....	....	....	....	....	....	....
Banks	4 783	11,533	5,832	−9,136	7,240	9,332	25,478	....	....
Other sectors	4 784	....	....	....	....	....	....	....	....
Other liabilities	4 786	165	31	−122	824	292	901	765	1,617
Monetary authorities	4 787	....	....	....	....	....	....	....	....
of which: Short-term	4 789	....	....	....	....	....	....	....	....
General government	4 790	272	85	−191	310	−221	−41	....	....
of which: Short-term	4 792	272	85	−191	310	−221	−41	....	....
Banks	4 793	186	−21	−10	260	40	374	....	....
of which: Short-term	4 795	194	−84	−9	249	8	253	....	....
Other sectors	4 796	−292	−33	79	254	473	568	....	....
of which: Short-term	4 798	−184	−63	39	54	−43	50	....	....
E. RESERVE ASSETS	4 802	745	1,888	1,723	2,023	1,849	750	861	−2,525
Monetary gold	4 812	253	254	285	....	140	70	219	187
Special drawing rights	4 811	4	−105	62	20	28	1	−36	−32
Reserve position in the Fund	4 810	221	−166	−55	−90	251	477	163	61
Foreign exchange	4 803	267	1,905	1,431	2,095	1,430	202	515	−2,741
Other claims	4 813	....	....	....	−2	1	....	....	....
NET ERRORS AND OMISSIONS	4 998	−2,356	−1,620	−2,786	−3,703	−4,758	−5,841	−797	−3,371

Table 3. INTERNATIONAL INVESTMENT POSITION (End-period stocks), 2000–2007

(Millions of U.S. dollars)

	Code	2000	2001	2002	2003	2004	2005	2006	2007
ASSETS	8 995 C.	**261,554**	**267,909**	**335,379**	**443,661**	**548,839**	**650,836**	**853,539**	**1,055,913**
Direct investment abroad	8 505 ..	**26,262**	**29,934**	**44,076**	**58,295**	**70,997**	**149,146**	**184,116**	**240,885**
Equity capital and reinvested earnings	8 506 ..	23,653	27,148	39,299	54,918	67,809	139,611	175,597	234,597
Claims on affiliated enterprises	8 507 ..	....	....	....	....	....	....	....	....
Liabilities to affiliated enterprises	8 508 ..	....	....	....	....	....	....	....	....
Other capital	8 530 ..	2,609	2,786	4,777	3,377	3,187	9,535	8,519	6,289
Claims on affiliated enterprises	8 535 ..	....	....	5,164	4,117	4,153	....	....	....
Liabilities to affiliated enterprises	8 540 ..	....	....	−387	−740	....	....	....	....
Portfolio investment	8 602 ..	**115,680**	**112,458**	**152,484**	**207,035**	**264,539**	**284,173**	**352,401**	**405,027**
Equity securities	8 610 ..	42,698	31,190	30,047	44,149	54,935	63,566	87,890	100,078
Monetary authorities	8 611 ..	1,347	999	1,425	1,839	2,194	2,072	2,322	2,690
General government	8 612 ..	56	91	50	57	95	125	171	208
Banks	8 613 ..	1,908	1,817	1,704	2,229	2,818	3,469	4,481	4,481
Other sectors	8 614 ..	39,388	28,283	26,869	40,024	49,827	57,900	80,915	92,697
Debt securities	8 619 ..	72,982	81,268	122,437	162,885	209,604	220,607	264,511	304,950
Bonds and notes	8 620 ..	71,377	80,288	116,358	159,650	204,408	216,173	261,190	298,910
Monetary authorities	8 621 ..	2,784	3,006	5,674	9,073	7,972	7,517	8,380	12,144
General government	8 622 ..	153	548	582	448	569	448	743	726
Banks	8 623 ..	26,851	30,715	43,799	59,716	84,584	91,075	115,493	136,675
Other sectors	8 624 ..	41,589	46,019	66,303	90,412	111,282	117,132	136,574	149,364
Money market instruments	8 630 ..	1,605	980	6,079	3,236	5,196	4,434	3,321	6,040
Monetary authorities	8 631 ..	629	232	2,522	951	2,700	1,606	64	698
General government	8 632 ..	222	....	1,612	414	7	....	....	....
Banks	8 633 ..	393	355	1,566	1,282	2,095	1,686	1,504	3,000
Other sectors	8 634 ..	361	392	379	589	395	1,143	1,752	2,342
Financial derivatives	8 900 ..	....	....	....	....	....	....	**4,632**	**7,297**
Monetary authorities	8 901 ..	....	....	....	....	....	....	4	3
General government	8 902 ..	....	....	....	....	....	....	....	1,151
Banks	8 903 ..	....	....	....	....	....	....	4,476	6,065
Other sectors	8 904 ..	....	....	....	....	....	....	152	78
Other investment	8 703 ..	**101,985**	**109,906**	**125,638**	**165,602**	**201,115**	**205,685**	**299,479**	**384,484**
Trade credits	8 706 ..	5,482	4,920	5,753	6,912	7,994	7,675	10,701	12,129
General government	8 707 ..	....	....	....	....	....	....	....	....
of which: Short-term	8 709 ..	....	....	....	....	....	....	....	....
Other sectors	8 710 ..	5,482	4,920	5,753	6,912	7,994	7,675	10,701	12,129
of which: Short-term	8 712 ..	*5,482*	*4,920*	....	....	....	....	....	....
Loans	8 714 ..	54,634	59,738	74,786	101,343	81,990	86,122	113,912	163,172
Monetary authorities	8 715 ..	93	....	....	....	....	3	....	....
of which: Short-term	8 718 ..	*93*	....	....	....	....	....	....	....
General government	8 719 ..	20	9	85	82	78	19	21	23
of which: Short-term	8 721 ..	....	*−6*	....	....	....	....	....	....
Banks	8 722 ..	46,211	50,548	62,664	85,604	62,614	68,374	88,685	126,854
of which: Short-term	8 724 ..	*13,431*	*15,503*	*16,000*	*20,238*	*9,531*	*14,312*	*19,257*	*27,923*
Other sectors	8 725 ..	8,310	9,181	12,036	15,657	19,299	17,726	25,206	36,294
of which: Short-term	8 727 ..	*4,698*	*4,464*	....	....	....	....	....	....
Currency and deposits	8 730 ..	35,965	39,387	38,528	49,443	101,937	107,775	169,243	202,423
Monetary authorities	8 731 ..	2,180	1,660	2,096	2,023	2,327	2,144	3,091	2,411
General government	8 732 ..	1,265	1,453	747	1,106	1,302	683	263	1,575
Banks	8 733 ..	32,009	34,432	33,172	40,849	90,865	102,297	145,483	194,527
Other sectors	8 734 ..	512	1,842	2,513	5,464	7,444	2,652	20,406	3,910
Other assets	8 736 ..	5,904	5,861	6,571	7,904	9,193	4,113	5,623	6,760
Monetary authorities	8 737 ..	110	104	124	149	159	137	153	173
of which: Short-term	8 739 ..	....	....	....	....	....	....	....	....
General government	8 740 ..	1,568	1,472	1,718	2,158	2,428	2,052	2,024	1,900
of which: Short-term	8 742 ..	....	*30*	....	....	....	....	....	....
Banks	8 743 ..	2,677	3,013	3,516	3,886	4,247	1,834	1,811	2,476
of which: Short-term	8 745 ..	....	*2,920*	....	....	....	....	....	....
Other sectors	8 746 ..	1,548	1,272	1,213	1,710	2,359	89	1,635	2,211
of which: Short-term	8 748 ..	....	*135*	....	....	....	....	....	....
Reserve assets	8 802 ..	**17,627**	**15,611**	**13,181**	**12,729**	**12,188**	**11,832**	**12,911**	**18,219**
Monetary gold	8 812 ..	3,308	3,102	3,498	4,259	4,330	4,989	5,901	7,530
Special drawing rights	8 811 ..	134	233	185	181	160	147	190	233
Reserve position in the Fund	8 810 ..	692	833	959	1,145	935	394	247	195
Foreign exchange	8 803 ..	13,492	11,444	8,540	7,144	6,763	6,302	6,573	10,261
Other claims	8 813 ..	....	....	....	....	....	....	....	....

Table 3 (Concluded). INTERNATIONAL INVESTMENT POSITION (End-period stocks), 2000–2007

(Millions of U.S. dollars)

	Code	2000	2001	2002	2003	2004	2005	2006	2007
LIABILITIES	8 995 D.	**299,033**	**315,205**	**379,038**	**480,881**	**610,289**	**711,981**	**923,406**	**1,115,862**
Direct investment in Austria	8 555 ..	**31,280**	**35,164**	**44,618**	**56,529**	**65,842**	**157,301**	**192,199**	**247,868**
Equity capital and reinvested earnings	8 556 ..	29,841	31,860	40,778	49,901	58,863	148,271	180,770	215,453
Claims on direct investors	8 557 ..	....	....	....	....	....	....	....	....
Liabilities to direct investors	8 558 ..	....	....	....	....	....	....	....	....
Other capital	8 580 ..	1,439	3,304	3,840	6,628	6,978	9,030	11,429	32,415
Claims on direct investors	8 585 ..	....	....	−2,201	−2,140	−2,307	....	....	....
Liabilities to direct investors	8 590 ..	....	....	6,042	8,768				
Portfolio investment	8 652 ..	**161,082**	**171,393**	**218,273**	**281,670**	**348,127**	**350,616**	**447,308**	**534,296**
Equity securities	8 660 ..	19,569	14,920	17,235	26,470	45,181	59,237	92,957	105,118
Banks	8 663 ..	2,793	1,335	2,002	5,459	9,536	7,517	13,970	13,022
Other sectors	8 664 ..	16,776	13,585	15,234	21,011	35,645	51,720	78,987	92,096
Debt securities	8 669 ..	141,512	156,473	201,037	255,201	302,946	291,379	354,351	429,179
Bonds and notes	8 670 ..	132,689	149,636	194,972	247,486	293,229	280,804	336,306	408,063
Monetary authorities	8 671 ..	....	....	....	....	....	....	....	....
General government	8 672 ..	66,531	72,945	100,692	129,146	149,902	137,275	156,711	180,487
Banks	8 673 ..	54,248	60,035	73,442	89,921	108,405	118,005	152,011	192,376
Other sectors	8 674 ..	11,910	16,657	20,838	28,420	34,922	25,524	27,584	35,199
Money market instruments	8 680 ..	8,823	6,837	6,065	7,714	9,717	10,575	18,045	21,116
Monetary authorities	8 681 ..	....	....	....	....	....	....	....	....
General government	8 682 ..	1,801	1,271	427	788	1,143	1,174	1,087	1,096
Banks	8 683 ..	6,781	5,392	5,617	6,858	8,505	9,326	16,839	19,846
Other sectors	8 684 ..	240	174	21	68	69	76	120	174
Financial derivatives	8 905 ..	....	....	....	....	....	....	**4,651**	**8,422**
Monetary authorities	8 906 ..	....	....	....	....	....	....	....	....
General government	8 907 ..	....	....	....	....	....	....	1,221	1,556
Banks	8 908 ..	....	....	....	....	....	....	3,331	6,699
Other sectors	8 909 ..	....	....	....	....	....	....	99	167
Other investment	8 753 ..	**106,672**	**108,648**	**116,147**	**142,681**	**196,321**	**204,063**	**279,248**	**325,276**
Trade credits	8 756 ..	3,734	2,910	3,127	3,936	4,801	4,510	7,973	10,091
General government	8 757 ..	....	....	....	....	....	....	....	....
of which: Short-term	8 759 ..	....	....	....	....	....	....	....	....
Other sectors	8 760 ..	3,734	2,910	3,127	3,936	4,801	4,510	7,973	10,091
of which: Short-term	8 762 ..	*3,734*	*2,910*	....	....	....	....	....	....
Loans	8 764 ..	16,031	17,675	31,299	38,981	45,007	29,495	53,895	49,253
Monetary authorities	8 765 ..	958	1,017	699	566	....	....	....	....
of which: Use of Fund credit and loans from the Fund	8 766 ..	....	....	....	....	....	....	....	....
of which: Short-term	8 768 ..	*90*	*208*	....	....	....	....	....	....
General government	8 769 ..	2,510	3,282	3,468	3,741	5,786	10,000	12,108	14,083
of which: Short-term	8 771 ..	....	*63*	....	....	....	....	....	....
Banks	8 772 ..	5,545	4,953	11,883	15,236	16,424	....	....	....
of which: Short-term	8 774 ..	*2,494*	*1,802*	*2,234*	*5,072*	*6,422*	....	....	....
Other sectors	8 775 ..	7,018	8,425	15,249	19,439	22,797	19,495	41,787	35,171
of which: Short-term	8 777 ..	*2,634*	*3,091*	....	....	....	....	....	....
Currency and deposits	8 780 ..	83,441	84,478	78,014	94,880	141,530	167,503	213,096	258,437
Monetary authorities	8 781 ..	4,681	−1,579	−2,995	−1,934	12,262	18,533	28,544	38,424
General government	8 782 ..	....	....	....	....	....	....	....	....
Banks	8 783 ..	78,760	86,056	81,010	96,814	129,267	148,970	184,552	220,013
Other sectors	8 784 ..	....	....	....	....	....	....	....	....
Other liabilities	8 786 ..	3,467	3,585	3,707	4,884	4,983	2,555	4,283	7,494
Monetary authorities	8 787 ..	....	....	....	....	....	....	....	....
of which: Short-term	8 789 ..	....	....	....	....	....	....	....	....
General government	8 790 ..	902	1,037	970	1,450	1,249	1,721	1,617	2,867
of which: Short-term	8 792 ..	....	*653*	....	....	....	....	....	....
Banks	8 793 ..	601	589	644	980	1,187	....	....	....
of which: Short-term	8 795 ..	....	*308*	....	....	....	....	....	....
Other sectors	8 796 ..	1,963	1,960	2,093	2,454	2,547	835	2,666	4,627
of which: Short-term	8 798 ..	....	*20*	....	....	....	....	....	....
NET INTERNATIONAL INVESTMENT POSITION	8 995 ..	**−37,480**	**−47,297**	**−43,659**	**−37,220**	**−61,450**	**−61,144**	**−69,867**	**−59,949**
Conversion rates: euros per U.S. dollar (end of period)	0 104 ..	**1.0747**	**1.1347**	**.9536**	**.7918**	**.7342**	**.8477**	**.7593**	**.6793**

Table 1. ANALYTIC PRESENTATION, 2000–2007

(Millions of U.S. dollars)

	Code	2000	2001	2002	2003	2004	2005	2006	2007
A. Current Account[1]	4 993 Z.	−167.8	−51.8	−768.4	−2,020.9	−2,589.2	167.3	3,707.6	9,018.9
Goods: exports f.o.b.	2 100 ..	1,858.3	2,078.9	2,304.9	2,624.6	3,743.0	7,649.0	13,014.6	21,269.3
Goods: imports f.o.b.	3 100 ..	−1,539.0	−1,465.1	−1,823.3	−2,723.1	−3,581.7	−4,349.9	−5,269.3	−6,045.0
Balance on Goods	4 100 ..	*319.3*	*613.9*	*481.6*	*−98.5*	*161.3*	*3,299.1*	*7,745.3*	*15,224.3*
Services: credit	2 200 ..	259.8	289.8	362.1	432.0	492.0	683.0	939.9	1,247.5
Services: debit	3 200 ..	−484.5	−664.9	−1,297.7	−2,046.5	−2,730.4	−2,653.0	−2,863.2	−3,378.6
Balance on Goods and Services	4 991 ..	*94.6*	*238.8*	*−454.0*	*−1,713.0*	*−2,077.1*	*1,329.1*	*5,821.9*	*13,093.3*
Income: credit	2 300 ..	55.9	41.5	37.1	52.6	65.3	201.8	280.0	327.8
Income: debit	3 300 ..	−391.4	−408.7	−421.8	−494.7	−765.9	−1,847.4	−2,960.6	−5,407.2
Balance on Goods, Services, and Income	4 992 ..	*−240.9*	*−128.4*	*−838.7*	*−2,155.0*	*−2,777.7*	*−316.6*	*3,141.3*	*8,013.9*
Current transfers: credit	2 379 Z.	135.0	176.5	228.2	225.1	262.6	626.2	748.2	1,313.4
Current transfers: debit	3 379 ..	−62.0	−99.9	−157.9	−90.9	−74.1	−142.3	−182.0	−308.4
B. Capital Account[1]	4 994 Z.	....	....	−28.7	−23.1	−4.1	40.9	−3.8	−2.8
Capital account: credit	2 994 Z.	....	....	18.4	15.0	24.0	70.2	25.0	28.0
Capital account: debit	3 994 ..	....	....	−47.1	−38.1	−28.1	−29.3	−28.9	−30.8
Total, Groups A Plus B	4 981 ..	*−167.8*	*−51.8*	*−797.1*	*−2,044.0*	*−2,593.4*	*208.2*	*3,703.8*	*9,016.1*
C. Financial Account[1]	4 995 W.	493.4	126.0	918.0	2,279.7	2,960.2	78.0	−2,105.3	−6,874.1
Direct investment abroad	4 505 ..	−.8	....	−325.6	−933.3	−1,204.8	−1,220.8	−705.5	−285.6
Direct investment in Azerbaijan	4 555 Z.	129.9	226.5	1,392.4	3,285.0	3,556.1	1,679.9	−584.0	−4,748.9
Portfolio investment assets	4 602 ..	....	....	−.4	....	−18.1	−47.8	−34.4	−110.9
Equity securities	4 610 ..	....	....			1.9	....	−3.1	−11.9
Debt securities	4 619 ..	....	....	−.4	....	−20.0	−47.8	−31.3	−99.0
Portfolio investment liabilities	4 652 Z.	....	....	....	....	....	78.3	22.3	84.5
Equity securities	4 660 ..	....	....	....	....	....	....	.8	2.0
Debt securities	4 669 Z.	....	....	....	....	....	78.3	21.6	82.5
Financial derivatives	4 910 ..	....	....	....	....	....	....	....	....
Financial derivatives assets	4 900 ..	....	....	....	....	....	....	....	....
Financial derivatives liabilities	4 905 ..	....	....	....	....	....	....	....	....
Other investment assets	4 703 ..	−114.2	−394.0	−302.9	−169.2	−360.4	−1,365.3	−1,416.7	−2,687.8
Monetary authorities	4 701 ..	....	....	....	....	1.8	....	....	....
General government	4 704 ..	....	−220.5	−200.7	−109.4	−123.5	−475.7	−408.7	−1,153.6
Banks	4 705 ..	7.1	−77.7	−18.3	−16.7	20.1	−83.7	−58.5	−246.9
Other sectors	4 728 ..	−121.2	−95.8	−83.9	−43.2	−258.8	−806.0	−949.5	−1,287.2
Other investment liabilities	4 753 W.	478.4	293.5	154.4	97.2	987.4	953.7	612.9	874.6
Monetary authorities	4 753 WA	....	....	30.3	34.4	....	−1.0	16.9	−1.4
General government	4 753 ZB	246.2	138.6	17.2	32.4	34.8	37.5	80.5	139.1
Banks	4 753 ZC	−22.9	3.0	16.9	−.2	−16.4	46.7	336.1	742.2
Other sectors	4 753 ZD	255.0	151.9	90.0	30.5	969.0	870.4	179.5	−5.2
Total, Groups A Through C	4 983 ..	*325.6*	*74.3*	*120.9*	*235.7*	*366.9*	*286.2*	*1,598.4*	*2,142.0*
D. Net Errors and Omissions	4 998 ..	....	−.9	−86.7	−111.8	−49.9	−125.7	−255.9	−360.6
Total, Groups A Through D	4 984 ..	*325.6*	*73.4*	*34.2*	*123.8*	*317.0*	*160.5*	*1,342.6*	*1,781.3*
E. Reserves and Related Items	4 802 A.	−325.6	−73.4	−34.2	−123.8	−317.0	−160.5	−1,342.6	−1,781.3
Reserve assets	4 802 ..	−274.2	−44.1	5.0	−82.0	−257.2	−132.0	−1,305.5	−1,744.8
Use of Fund credit and loans	4 766 ..	−51.4	−29.3	−39.2	−41.8	−59.8	−28.5	−37.1	−36.5
Exceptional financing	4 920 ..	....	....	....	....	....	....	....	....
Conversion rates: manat per U.S. dollar	0 101 ..	.8948	.9313	.9722	.9821	.9827	.9454	.8934	.8581

[1] Excludes components that have been classified in the categories of Group E.

Table 2. STANDARD PRESENTATION, 2000–2007

(Millions of U.S. dollars)

	Code	2000	2001	2002	2003	2004	2005	2006	2007
CURRENT ACCOUNT	4 993	−167.8	−51.8	−768.4	−2,020.9	−2,589.2	167.3	3,707.6	9,018.9
A. GOODS	4 100	319.3	613.9	481.6	−98.5	161.3	3,299.1	7,745.3	15,224.3
Credit	2 100	1,858.3	2,078.9	2,304.9	2,624.6	3,743.0	7,649.0	13,014.6	21,269.3
General merchandise: exports f.o.b.	2 110	1,858.3	2,077.2	2,261.4	2,529.9	3,538.1	7,383.0	12,729.3	20,822.0
Goods for processing: exports f.o.b.	2 150	....	....	9.4	12.1	151.1	241.7	248.5	340.0
Repairs on goods	2 160	....	....	....	1.5	5.0	9.2	11.7	27.6
Goods procured in ports by carriers	2 170	....	1.7	34.1	81.2	48.8	15.1	25.1	79.7
Nonmonetary gold	2 180	....	....	....	....	....	....	....	....
Debit	3 100	−1,539.0	−1,465.1	−1,823.3	−2,723.1	−3,581.7	−4,349.9	−5,269.3	−6,045.0
General merchandise: imports f.o.b.	3 110	−1,539.0	−1,455.5	−1,798.0	−2,701.3	−3,459.7	−4,146.4	−4,948.7	−5,866.2
Goods for processing: imports f.o.b.	3 150	....	....	−20.5	−18.6	−112.0	−193.3	−236.9	−159.1
Repairs on goods	3 160	....	....	....	−.5	−5.4	−5.0	−78.6	−9.2
Goods procured in ports by carriers	3 170	....	−9.6	−4.9	−2.7	−4.6	−5.2	−5.2	−10.5
Nonmonetary gold	3 180	....	....	....	....	....	....	....	....
B. SERVICES	4 200	−224.7	−375.0	−935.6	−1,614.5	−2,238.4	−1,970.0	−1,923.4	−2,131.0
Total credit	2 200	*259.8*	*289.8*	*362.1*	*432.0*	*492.0*	*683.0*	*939.9*	*1,247.5*
Total debit	3 200	*−484.5*	*−664.9*	*−1,297.7*	*−2,046.5*	*−2,730.4*	*−2,653.0*	*−2,863.2*	*−3,378.6*
Transportation services, credit	2 205	119.3	161.7	212.1	198.2	205.7	239.2	407.7	604.7
Passenger	2 850	*5.2*	*14.3*	*12.3*	*11.6*	*14.0*	*21.8*	*83.9*	*139.4*
Freight	2 851	*88.5*	*125.8*	*173.3*	*144.7*	*112.1*	*143.8*	*208.9*	*320.9*
Other	2 852	*25.6*	*21.6*	*26.5*	*41.9*	*79.6*	*73.6*	*114.8*	*144.3*
Sea transport, passenger	2 207	....	....	....	....	....	....	2.8	.4
Sea transport, freight	2 208	....	....	....	....	....	....	57.0	72.7
Sea transport, other	2 209	....	....	....	....	....	....	29.8	41.6
Air transport, passenger	2 211	....	....	....	....	....	....	78.6	127.4
Air transport, freight	2 212	....	....	....	....	....	....	29.8	58.6
Air transport, other	2 213	....	....	....	....	....	....	82.2	98.1
Other transport, passenger	2 215	....	....	....	....	....	....	2.6	11.7
Other transport, freight	2 216	....	....	....	....	....	....	122.1	189.7
Other transport, other	2 217	....	....	....	....	....	....	2.8	4.6
Transportation services, debit	3 205	−144.1	−156.6	−173.3	−190.0	−289.4	−378.9	−509.2	−547.6
Passenger	3 850	*−6.4*	*−9.9*	*−4.9*	*−8.8*	*−13.6*	*−24.0*	*−54.9*	*−116.8*
Freight	3 851	*−101.2*	*−118.4*	*−132.3*	*−140.7*	*−206.3*	*−270.1*	*−361.4*	*−340.1*
Other	3 852	*−36.5*	*−28.4*	*−36.0*	*−40.5*	*−69.5*	*−84.9*	*−92.9*	*−90.7*
Sea transport, passenger	3 207	....	....	....	....	....	....		−.2
Sea transport, freight	3 208	....	....	....	....	....	....	−73.5	−12.0
Sea transport, other	3 209	....	....	....	....	....	....	−25.4	−32.4
Air transport, passenger	3 211	....	....	....	....	....	....	−54.6	−115.7
Air transport, freight	3 212	....	....	....	....	....	....	−46.6	−39.7
Air transport, other	3 213	....	....	....	....	....	....	−57.4	−37.4
Other transport, passenger	3 215	....	....	....	....	....	....	−.3	−.9
Other transport, freight	3 216	....	....	....	....	....	....	−241.3	−288.4
Other transport, other	3 217	....	....	....	....	....	....	−10.0	−20.9
Travel, credit	2 236	63.1	42.6	51.1	57.7	65.3	77.7	116.9	177.8
Business travel	2 237	32.7	20.8	14.1	6.1	11.3	16.3	29.7	59.0
Personal travel	2 240	30.4	21.7	36.9	51.6	54.0	61.3	87.3	118.7
Travel, debit	3 236	−131.6	−108.9	−105.5	−111.4	−126.2	−164.0	−201.4	−263.6
Business travel	3 237	−17.5	−12.9	−10.5	−10.9	−15.5	−18.5	−22.2	−18.2
Personal travel	3 240	−114.2	−96.0	−94.9	−100.5	−110.7	−145.5	−179.2	−245.4
Other services, credit	2 200 BA	77.4	85.6	99.0	176.0	221.1	366.1	415.2	465.1
Communications	2 245	16.1	14.0	22.6	22.4	36.5	35.6	31.0	34.0
Construction	2 249	5.1	6.8	7.3	3.8	9.8	9.4	45.8	45.8
Insurance	2 253	....	....	....	4.5	7.5	7.8	13.7	7.8
Financial	2 260	....	....	....	....	....	.1	1.4	.1
Computer and information	2 262	....	....	....	....	....	.1	2.7	4.2
Royalties and licence fees	2 266	....	....	....	....	....	....	.1	....
Other business services	2 268	30.9	30.8	27.8	102.5	126.1	251.7	219.2	294.3
Personal, cultural, and recreational	2 287	....	....	....	2.5	2.6	3.0	3.0	3.2
Government, n.i.e.	2 291	25.3	34.0	41.3	40.4	38.5	58.3	98.4	75.6
Other services, debit	3 200 BA	−208.8	−399.3	−1,019.0	−1,745.1	−2,314.9	−2,110.1	−2,152.7	−2,567.4
Communications	3 245	−6.8	−6.8	−16.2	−12.7	−16.5	−12.2	−10.8	−10.4
Construction	3 249	−90.8	−186.8	−566.9	−1,023.2	−1,373.6	−1,498.8	−1,300.3	−1,471.1
Insurance	3 253	....	−11.7	−13.3	−24.4	−31.6	−40.6	−70.9	−66.5
Financial	3 260	....	....	....	−.1	−5.2	−10.4	−48.0	−121.7
Computer and information	3 262	....	....	....	....	....	−.3	−7.3	−8.3
Royalties and licence fees	3 266	....	....	−2.1	−.1	....	....	−1.3	−4.7
Other business services	3 268	−102.0	−179.5	−406.0	−660.0	−854.8	−514.9	−629.7	−825.2
Personal, cultural, and recreational	3 287	....	....	....	−5.1	−5.0	−5.0	−5.0	−5.4
Government, n.i.e.	3 291	−9.3	−14.6	−14.5	−19.4	−28.2	−27.9	−79.4	−54.1

Table 2 (Continued). STANDARD PRESENTATION, 2000–2007

(Millions of U.S. dollars)

	Code	2000	2001	2002	2003	2004	2005	2006	2007
C. INCOME	4 300	−335.5	−367.2	−384.7	−442.0	−700.6	−1,645.6	−2,680.6	−5,079.4
Total credit	2 300	*55.9*	*41.5*	*37.1*	*52.6*	*65.3*	*201.8*	*280.0*	*327.8*
Total debit	3 300	*−391.4*	*−408.7*	*−421.8*	*−494.7*	*−765.9*	*−1,847.4*	*−2,960.6*	*−5,407.2*
Compensation of employees, credit	2 310	....	....	....	1.8	12.3	133.0	127.9	75.6
Compensation of employees, debit	3 310	−47.4	−47.3	−38.9	−53.6	−107.6	−112.2	−124.9	−131.1
Investment income, credit	2 320	55.9	41.5	37.1	50.8	53.1	68.8	152.1	252.2
Direct investment income	2 330	....	....	....	.2	....	.4	.5	.1
Dividends and distributed branch profits	2 332	....	....	....	.2	....	....	....	.1
Reinvested earnings and undistributed branch profits	2 333	....	....	....	....	....	....	....	....
Income on debt (interest)	2 334	....	....	....	....	....	....	....	....
Portfolio investment income	2 339	....	....	....	....	....	....	2.0	6.5
Income on equity	2 340	....	....	....	....	....	....	....	....
Income on bonds and notes	2 350	....	....	....	....	....	....	2.0	6.5
Income on money market instruments	2 360	....	....	....	....	....	....	....	....
Other investment income	2 370	55.9	41.5	37.1	50.6	53.1	68.4	149.6	245.6
Investment income, debit	3 320	−344.0	−361.4	−382.9	−441.1	−658.4	−1,735.2	−2,835.7	−5,276.1
Direct investment income	3 330	−317.2	−329.2	−356.3	−422.3	−581.2	−1,581.7	−2,624.4	−4,995.3
Dividends and distributed branch profits	3 332	....	....	....	....	....	....	−2,493.0	−4,920.9
Reinvested earnings and undistributed branch profits	3 333	....	....	....	....	....	....	−131.3	−74.4
Income on debt (interest)	3 334	....	....	....	....	....	....	....	....
Portfolio investment income	3 339	....	....	....	....	....	....	....	−4.2
Income on equity	3 340	....	....	....	....	....	....	....	....
Income on bonds and notes	3 350	....	....	....	....	....	....	....	−4.2
Income on money market instruments	3 360	....	....	....	....	....	....	....	....
Other investment income	3 370	−26.7	−32.2	−26.6	−18.8	−77.2	−153.5	−211.4	−276.6
D. CURRENT TRANSFERS	4 379	73.1	76.6	70.4	134.1	188.5	483.9	566.3	1,005.0
Credit	2 379	135.0	176.5	228.2	225.1	262.6	626.2	748.2	1,313.4
General government	2 380	65.7	66.3	60.4	62.6	63.3	122.3	69.2	103.2
Other sectors	2 390	69.3	110.2	167.8	162.4	199.3	503.9	679.0	1,210.2
Workers' remittances	2 391	57.1	104.1	163.3	154.1	191.3	490.2	662.3	1,192.1
Other current transfers	2 392	12.2	6.1	4.5	8.3	8.0	13.6	16.7	18.1
Debit	3 379	−62.0	−99.9	−157.9	−90.9	−74.1	−142.3	−182.0	−308.4
General government	3 380	−3.3	−2.6	−5.3	−6.0	−5.8	−7.3	−7.2	−9.0
Other sectors	3 390	−58.6	−97.3	−152.6	−84.9	−68.3	−135.0	−174.8	−299.4
Workers' remittances	3 391	−53.6	−94.6	−149.0	−77.7	−64.7	−127.2	−149.5	−273.4
Other current transfers	3 392	−5.0	−2.7	−3.6	−7.2	−3.5	−7.9	−25.3	−26.0
CAPITAL AND FINANCIAL ACCOUNT	4 996	167.8	52.6	855.0	2,132.7	2,639.1	−41.6	−3,451.7	−8,658.2
CAPITAL ACCOUNT	4 994	....	....	−28.7	−23.1	−4.1	40.9	−3.8	−2.8
Total credit	2 994	....	....	*18.4*	*15.0*	*24.0*	*70.2*	*25.0*	*28.0*
Total debit	3 994	....	....	*−47.1*	*−38.1*	*−28.1*	*−29.3*	*−28.9*	*−30.8*
Capital transfers, credit	2 400	....	....	18.4	15.0	24.0	70.2	22.3	19.5
General government	2 401	....	....	....	....	....	....	....	....
Debt forgiveness	2 402	....	....	....	....	....	....	....	....
Other capital transfers	2 410	....	....	....	....	....	....	....	....
Other sectors	2 430	....	....	18.4	15.0	24.0	70.2	22.3	19.5
Migrants' transfers	2 431	....	....	18.4	15.0	24.0	70.2	22.3	19.5
Debt forgiveness	2 432	....	....	....	....	....	....	....	....
Other capital transfers	2 440	....	....	....	....	....	....	....	....
Capital transfers, debit	3 400	....	....	−47.1	−38.1	−28.1	−29.3	−26.6	−30.8
General government	3 401	....	....	−.3	−.1	−.1	−.1	−.1	....
Debt forgiveness	3 402	....	....	....	....	....	....	....	....
Other capital transfers	3 410	....	....	−.3	....	....	....	....	....
Other sectors	3 430	....	....	−46.8	−38.0	−28.0	−29.2	−26.4	−30.8
Migrants' transfers	3 431	....	....	−46.8	−38.0	−28.0	−29.2	−26.4	−30.8
Debt forgiveness	3 432	....	....	....	....	....	....	....	....
Other capital transfers	3 440	....	....	....	....	....	....	....	....
Nonproduced nonfinancial assets, credit	2 480	....	....	....	....	....	....	2.7	8.5
Nonproduced nonfinancial assets, debit	3 480	....	....	....	....	....	....	−2.3	....

Table 2 (Continued). STANDARD PRESENTATION, 2000–2007

(Millions of U.S. dollars)

	Code	2000	2001	2002	2003	2004	2005	2006	2007
FINANCIAL ACCOUNT	4 995 ..	**167.8**	**52.6**	**883.8**	**2,155.8**	**2,643.2**	**−82.5**	**−3,447.9**	**−8,655.4**
A. DIRECT INVESTMENT	4 500 ..	**129.2**	**226.5**	**1,066.8**	**2,351.7**	**2,351.3**	**459.2**	**−1,289.5**	**−5,034.5**
Direct investment abroad	4 505 ..	**−.8**	....	**−325.6**	**−933.3**	**−1,204.8**	**−1,220.8**	**−705.5**	**−285.6**
Equity capital	4 510 ..	....	....	−325.6	−933.3	−1,204.8	−1,220.8	−705.5	−516.0
Claims on affiliated enterprises	4 515 ..	....	....	−325.6	−933.3	−1,204.8	−1,220.8	−705.5	−516.9
Liabilities to affiliated enterprises	4 520 ..	....	....	....	....	....	....	....	.9
Reinvested earnings	4 525 ..	....	....	....	....	....	....	....	....
Other capital	4 530 ..	....	....	....	....	....	....	....	230.4
Claims on affiliated enterprises	4 535 ..	....	....	....	....	....	....	....	....
Liabilities to affiliated enterprises	4 540 ..	....	....	....	....	....	....	....	....
Direct investment in Azerbaijan	4 555 ..	**129.9**	**226.5**	**1,392.4**	**3,285.0**	**3,556.1**	**1,679.9**	**−584.0**	**−4,748.9**
Equity capital	4 560 ..	129.9	226.5	1,392.4	3,285.0	3,556.1	1,679.9	−897.2	−5,101.2
Claims on direct investors	4 565 ..	....	−593.1	−632.1	−722.3	−1,163.0	−2,796.5	−5,069.4	−9,105.1
Liabilities to direct investors	4 570 ..	....	819.6	2,024.6	4,007.3	4,719.1	4,476.4	4,172.1	4,003.9
Reinvested earnings	4 575 ..	....	....	....	....	....	....	131.3	74.4
Other capital	4 580 ..	....	....	....	....	....	....	182.0	277.9
Claims on direct investors	4 585 ..	....	....	....	....	....	....	−.6	−3.1
Liabilities to direct investors	4 590 ..	....	....	....	....	....	....	182.5	281.0
B. PORTFOLIO INVESTMENT	4 600 ..	....	....	**−.4**	....	**−18.1**	**30.5**	**−12.0**	**−26.4**
Assets	4 602 ..	....	....	**−.4**	....	**−18.1**	**−47.8**	**−34.4**	**−110.9**
Equity securities	4 610 ..	....	....	....	....	1.9	....	−3.1	−11.9
Monetary authorities	4 611 ..	....	....	....	....	....	....	....	....
General government	4 612 ..	....	....	....	....	....	....	−3.0	....
Banks	4 613 ..	....	....	....	....	1.9	....	....	....
Other sectors	4 614 ..	....	....	....	....	....	....	−.1	−11.9
Debt securities	4 619 ..	....	....	−.4	....	−20.0	−47.8	−31.3	−99.0
Bonds and notes	4 620 ..	....	....	−.4	....	−20.0	−47.8	−31.3	−99.0
Monetary authorities	4 621 ..	....	....	....	....	....	....	....	....
General government	4 622 ..	....	....	....	....	....	....	....	−2.7
Banks	4 623 ..	....	....	−.4	....	−19.8	....	−31.3	−28.6
Other sectors	4 624 ..	....	....	....	....	−.2	....	....	−67.7
Money market instruments	4 630 ..	....	....	....	....	....	....	....	....
Monetary authorities	4 631 ..	....	....	....	....	....	....	....	....
General government	4 632 ..	....	....	....	....	....	....	....	....
Banks	4 633 ..	....	....	....	....	....	....	....	....
Other sectors	4 634 ..	....	....	....	....	....	....	....	....
Liabilities	4 652 ..	....	....	....	....	....	**78.3**	**22.3**	**84.5**
Equity securities	4 660 ..	....	....	....	....	....	....	.8	2.0
Banks	4 663 ..	....	....	....	....	....	....	.8	....
Other sectors	4 664 ..	....	....	....	....	....	....	....	2.0
Debt securities	4 669 ..	....	....	....	....	....	78.3	21.6	82.5
Bonds and notes	4 670 ..	....	....	....	....	....	78.3	21.6	82.5
Monetary authorities	4 671 ..	....	....	....	....	....	....	....	....
General government	4 672 ..	....	....	....	....	....	....	....	62.0
Banks	4 673 ..	....	....	....	....	....	78.3	32.1	14.0
Other sectors	4 674 ..	....	....	....	....	....	....	−10.5	6.6
Money market instruments	4 680 ..	....	....	....	....	....	....	....	....
Monetary authorities	4 681 ..	....	....	....	....	....	....	....	....
General government	4 682 ..	....	....	....	....	....	....	....	....
Banks	4 683 ..	....	....	....	....	....	....	....	....
Other sectors	4 684 ..	....	....	....	....	....	....	....	....
C. FINANCIAL DERIVATIVES	4 910 ..	....	....	....	....	....	....	....	....
Monetary authorities	4 911 ..	....	....	....	....	....	....	....	....
General government	4 912 ..	....	....	....	....	....	....	....	....
Banks	4 913 ..	....	....	....	....	....	....	....	....
Other sectors	4 914 ..	....	....	....	....	....	....	....	....
Assets	4 900 ..	....	....	....	....	....	....	....	....
Monetary authorities	4 901 ..	....	....	....	....	....	....	....	....
General government	4 902 ..	....	....	....	....	....	....	....	....
Banks	4 903 ..	....	....	....	....	....	....	....	....
Other sectors	4 904 ..	....	....	....	....	....	....	....	....
Liabilities	4 905 ..	....	....	....	....	....	....	....	....
Monetary authorities	4 906 ..	....	....	....	....	....	....	....	....
General government	4 907 ..	....	....	....	....	....	....	....	....
Banks	4 908 ..	....	....	....	....	....	....	....	....
Other sectors	4 909 ..	....	....	....	....	....	....	....	....

Table 2 (Concluded). STANDARD PRESENTATION, 2000–2007

(Millions of U.S. dollars)

	Code	2000	2001	2002	2003	2004	2005	2006	2007
D. OTHER INVESTMENT	4 700 ..	**312.8**	**−129.8**	**−187.7**	**−113.9**	**567.2**	**−440.2**	**−840.9**	**−1,849.7**
Assets	4 703 ..	**−114.2**	**−394.0**	**−302.9**	**−169.2**	**−360.4**	**−1,365.3**	**−1,416.7**	**−2,687.8**
Trade credits	4 706 ..	−119.9	−93.2	−83.9	−42.9	−57.9	−766.4	−948.5	−1,257.2
General government	4 707 ..	....	....	....	....	....	....	....	....
of which: Short-term	4 709 ..	....	....	....	....	....	....	....	....
Other sectors	4 710 ..	−119.9	−93.2	−83.9	−42.9	−57.9	−766.4	−948.5	−1,257.2
of which: Short-term	4 712 ..	....	−93.2	−83.9	−42.9	−57.9	−766.4	−948.5	−1,257.2
Loans	4 714 ..	....	....	.3	.2	....	−12.6	−42.0	−142.3
Monetary authorities	4 715 ..	....	....	....	....	....	....	....	....
of which: Short-term	4 718 ..	....	....	....	....	....	....	....	....
General government	4 719 ..	....	....	....	....	....	....	2.1	....
of which: Short-term	4 721 ..	....	....	....	....	....	....	....	....
Banks	4 722 ..	....	....	.3	....	....	−9.5	−43.0	−112.3
of which: Short-term	4 724 ..	....	....	....	....	....	....	....	....
Other sectors	4 725 ..	....	....	....	.2	....	−3.1	−1.1	−30.0
of which: Short-term	4 727 ..	....	....	....	.2	....	....	−1.1	....
Currency and deposits	4 730 ..	7.1	−298.2	−219.3	−138.3	−307.8	−549.9	−426.3	−1,288.2
Monetary authorities	4 731 ..	....	....	....	....	....	....	....	....
General government	4 732 ..	....	−220.5	−200.7	−123.4	−127.0	−475.7	−410.8	−1,153.6
Banks	4 733 ..	7.1	−77.7	−18.6	−14.9	20.1	−74.2	−15.5	−134.6
Other sectors	4 734 ..	....	....	....	....	−200.9	....	....	....
Other assets	4 736 ..	−1.4	−2.6	....	11.8	5.3	−36.4	....	....
Monetary authorities	4 737 ..	....	....	....	....	1.8	....	....	....
of which: Short-term	4 739 ..	....	....	....	....	1.8	....	....	....
General government	4 740 ..	....	....	....	14.0	3.5	....	....	....
of which: Short-term	4 742 ..	....	....	....	....	....	....	....	....
Banks	4 743 ..	....	....	....	−1.8	....	....	....	....
of which: Short-term	4 745 ..	....	....	....	−1.8	....	....	....	....
Other sectors	4 746 ..	−1.4	−2.6	....	−.5	....	−36.4	....	....
of which: Short-term	4 748 ..	....	−2.6	....	−.5	....	....	....	....
Liabilities	4 753 ..	**427.0**	**264.3**	**115.1**	**55.4**	**927.7**	**925.1**	**575.9**	**838.1**
Trade credits	4 756 ..	33.5	74.5	−57.4	−169.9	−89.9	−97.4	−302.2	163.1
General government	4 757 ..	....	....	....	....	....	....	....	....
of which: Short-term	4 759 ..	....	....	....	....	....	....	....	....
Other sectors	4 760 ..	33.5	74.5	−57.4	−169.9	−89.9	−97.4	−302.2	163.1
of which: Short-term	4 762 ..	....	74.5	−57.4	−169.9	−89.9	−97.4	−302.2	163.1
Loans	4 764 ..	203.4	104.1	138.7	210.3	1,038.1	1,179.6	701.4	597.9
Monetary authorities	4 765 ..	−51.4	−29.3	−9.0	−7.4	−59.8	−29.5	−20.2	−37.9
of which: Use of Fund credit and loans from the Fund..	4 766 ..	−51.4	−29.3	−39.2	−41.8	−59.8	−28.5	−37.1	−36.5
of which: Short-term	4 768 ..	....	....	....	....	....	....	....	....
General government	4 769 ..	246.2	138.6	17.2	32.4	34.8	37.5	80.5	139.1
of which: Short-term	4 771 ..	....	−46.7	....	....	....	....	....	....
Banks	4 772 ..	−.3	5.2	−1.1	−.2	4.1	31.9	159.4	665.1
of which: Short-term	4 774 ..	....	−1.7	....	....	....	....	....	....
Other sectors	4 775 ..	8.9	−10.5	131.5	185.5	1,058.9	1,139.7	481.8	−168.3
of which: Short-term	4 777 ..	....	−20.8	....	....	....	....	....	....
Currency and deposits	4 780 ..	−22.6	−2.2	18.0	....	−20.5	14.8	176.7	77.1
Monetary authorities	4 781 ..	....	....	....	....	....	....	....	....
General government	4 782 ..	....	....	....	....	....	....	....	....
Banks	4 783 ..	−22.6	−2.2	18.0	....	−20.5	14.8	176.7	77.1
Other sectors	4 784 ..	....	....	....	....	....	....	....	....
Other liabilities	4 786 ..	212.6	87.8	15.8	15.0	....	−171.9	....	....
Monetary authorities	4 787 ..	....	....	....	....	....	....	....	....
of which: Short-term	4 789 ..	....	....	....	....	....	....	....	....
General government	4 790 ..	....	....	....	....	....	....	....	....
of which: Short-term	4 792 ..	....	....	....	....	....	....	....	....
Banks	4 793 ..	....	....	....	....	....	....	....	....
of which: Short-term	4 795 ..	....	....	....	....	....	....	....	....
Other sectors	4 796 ..	212.6	87.8	15.8	15.0	....	−171.9	....	....
of which: Short-term	4 798 ..	....	87.8	15.8	15.0	....	−171.9	....	....
E. RESERVE ASSETS	4 802 ..	**−274.2**	**−44.1**	**5.0**	**−82.0**	**−257.2**	**−132.0**	**−1,305.5**	**−1,744.8**
Monetary gold	4 812 ..	....	....	....	−17.0	3.6	−.4	−1.4	5.5
Special drawing rights	4 811 ..	.1	4.1	2.3	....	....	....	....	−.1
Reserve position in the Fund	4 810 ..	....	....	....	....	....	....	....	....
Foreign exchange	4 803 ..	−274.2	−48.2	2.7	−65.0	−260.8	−131.6	−1,304.2	−1,750.2
Other claims	4 813 ..	....	....	....	....	....	....	....	....
NET ERRORS AND OMISSIONS	4 998 ..	....	**−.9**	**−86.7**	**−111.8**	**−49.9**	**−125.7**	**−255.9**	**−360.6**

Table 3. INTERNATIONAL INVESTMENT POSITION (End-period stocks), 2000–2007

(Millions of U.S. dollars)

	Code	2000	2001	2002	2003	2004	2005	2006	2007
ASSETS	8 995 C.	....	....	2,000.9	3,154.6	4,937.3	7,456.4	10,180.5	14,187.4
Direct investment abroad	8 505 ..	.8	.8	326.4	1,259.7	2,464.5	3,685.3	4,390.8	4,676.4
Equity capital and reinvested earnings	8 506 ..	....	.8	326.4	1,259.7	2,464.5	3,685.3	4,390.8	4,910.5
Claims on affiliated enterprises	8 507 ..	....	.8	326.4	1,259.7	2,464.5	3,685.3	4,390.8	4,910.5
Liabilities to affiliated enterprises	8 508 ..	....	....	....	....	....	....	....	....
Other capital	8 530 ..	....	....	....	....	....	....	....	−234.1
Claims on affiliated enterprises	8 535 ..	....	....	....	....	....	....	....	....
Liabilities to affiliated enterprises	8 540 ..	....	....	....	....	....	....	....	−234.1
Portfolio investment	8 602 ..	....	....	.4	.4	20.4	84.6	119.0	229.9
Equity securities	8 610 ..	....	....	....	....	....	....	....	....
Monetary authorities	8 611 ..	....	....	....	....	....	....	....	....
General government	8 612 ..	....	....	....	....	....	....	....	....
Banks	8 613 ..	....	....	....	....	....	....	....	....
Other sectors	8 614 ..	....	....	....	....	....	....	....	....
Debt securities	8 619 ..	....	....	.4	.4	20.4	84.6	119.0	229.9
Bonds and notes	8 620 ..	....	....	.4	.4	20.4	84.6	119.0	229.9
Monetary authorities	8 621 ..	....	....	....	....	....	....	....	....
General government	8 622 ..	....	....	....	....	....	....	....	....
Banks	8 623 ..	....	....	.4	.4	20.4	84.6	119.0	229.9
Other sectors	8 624 ..	....	....	....	....	....	....	....	....
Money market instruments	8 630 ..	....	....	....	....	....	....	....	....
Monetary authorities	8 631 ..	....	....	....	....	....	....	....	....
General government	8 632 ..	....	....	....	....	....	....	....	....
Banks	8 633 ..	....	....	....	....	....	....	....	....
Other sectors	8 634 ..	....	....	....	....	....	....	....	....
Financial derivatives	8 900 ..	....	....	....	....	....	....	....	....
Monetary authorities	8 901 ..	....	....	....	....	....	....	....	....
General government	8 902 ..	....	....	....	....	....	....	....	....
Banks	8 903 ..	....	....	....	....	....	....	....	....
Other sectors	8 904 ..	....	....	....	....	....	....	....	....
Other investment	8 703 ..	162.5	734.3	953.6	1,091.7	1,376.4	2,508.8	3,170.4	5,008.0
Trade credits	8 706 ..	....	....	....	....	....	824.3	948.5	1,257.2
General government	8 707 ..	....	....	....	....	....	....	....	....
of which: Short-term	8 709 ..	....	....	....	....	....	....	....	....
Other sectors	8 710 ..	....	....	....	....	....	824.3	948.5	1,257.2
of which: Short-term	8 712 ..	....	....	....	....	....	*824.3*	*948.5*	*1,257.2*
Loans	8 714 ..	....	....	....	....	....	15.3	62.5	219.3
Monetary authorities	8 715 ..	....	....	....	....	....	....	....	....
of which: Short-term	8 718 ..	....	....	....	....	....	....	....	....
General government	8 719 ..	....	....	....	....	....	....	....	14.5
of which: Short-term	8 721 ..	....	....	....	....	....	....	....	....
Banks	8 722 ..	....	....	....	....	....	12.2	58.3	170.6
of which: Short-term	8 724 ..	....	....	....	....	....	....	....	....
Other sectors	8 725 ..	....	....	....	....	....	3.1	4.2	34.2
of which: Short-term	8 727 ..	....	....	....	....	....	*3.1*	....	....
Currency and deposits	8 730 ..	113.0	682.2	901.5	1,039.4	1,376.4	1,669.2	2,159.4	3,531.5
Monetary authorities	8 731 ..	....	....	....	....	....	....	....	....
General government	8 732 ..	....	491.5	692.2	815.6	971.8	1,394.0	1,868.7	3,106.2
Banks	8 733 ..	....	190.7	209.3	223.8	203.7	275.2	290.7	425.3
Other sectors	8 734 ..	....	....	....	....	200.9	....	....	....
Other assets	8 736 ..	49.5	52.1	52.1	52.3	....	....	....	....
Monetary authorities	8 737 ..	....	....	....	....	....	....	....	....
of which: Short-term	8 739 ..	....	....	....	....	....	....	....	....
General government	8 740 ..	....	....	....	....	....	....	....	....
of which: Short-term	8 742 ..	....	....	....	....	....	....	....	....
Banks	8 743 ..	....	....	....	....	....	....	....	....
of which: Short-term	8 745 ..	....	....	....	....	....	....	....	....
Other sectors	8 746 ..	....	52.1	52.1	52.3	....	....	....	....
of which: Short-term	8 748 ..	....	*52.1*	*52.1*	*52.3*	....	....	....	....
Reserve assets	8 802 ..	950.8	725.4	720.5	802.8	1,076.0	1,177.7	2,500.3	4,273.1
Monetary gold	8 812 ..	....	....	....	....	....	....	....	....
Special drawing rights	8 811 ..	6.6	2.5	.7	18.0	14.5	13.9	15.4	10.1
Reserve position in the Fund	8 810 ..	....	....	....	....	....	....	....	.1
Foreign exchange	8 803 ..	944.2	722.9	719.8	784.8	1,061.5	1,163.8	2,484.9	4,262.9
Other claims	8 813 ..	....	....	....	....	....	....	....	....

Azerbaijan, Republic of   912

Table 3 (Concluded). INTERNATIONAL INVESTMENT POSITION (End-period stocks), 2000–2007

(Millions of U.S. dollars)

	Code	2000	2001	2002	2003	2004	2005	2006	2007
LIABILITIES	8 995 D.	....	....	7,279.3	10,903.6	14,395.4	16,805.1	17,247.0	13,555.6
Direct investment in Azerbaijan	8 555	3,735.2	3,961.7	5,354.1	8,639.1	11,482.4	12,757.5	11,346.5	6,597.6
Equity capital and reinvested earnings	8 556	....	3,961.7	5,354.1	8,639.1	11,482.4	12,757.5	11,346.5	6,597.6
Claims on direct investors	8 557	....	−1,641.3	−2,273.4	−2,995.8	−4,158.8	−7,360.1	−13,257.0	−22,365.3
Liabilities to direct investors	8 558	....	5,603.0	7,627.5	11,634.9	15,641.2	20,117.6	24,603.5	28,962.9
Other capital	8 580	....	....	....	....	....	....	....	....
Claims on direct investors	8 585	....	....	....	....	....	....	....	....
Liabilities to direct investors	8 590	....	....	....	....	....	....	....	....
Portfolio investment	8 652	....	....	....	....	....	97.1	119.4	203.9
Equity securities	8 660	....	....	....	....	....	....	....	....
Banks	8 663	....	....	....	....	....	....	....	....
Other sectors	8 664	....	....	....	....	....	....	....	....
Debt securities	8 669	....	....	....	....	....	97.1	119.4	203.9
Bonds and notes	8 670	....	....	....	....	....	97.1	119.4	203.9
Monetary authorities	8 671	....	....	....	....	....	....	....	....
General government	8 672	....	....	....	....	....	....	....	....
Banks	8 673	....	....	....	....	....	97.1	119.4	203.9
Other sectors	8 674	....	....	....	....	....	....	....	....
Money market instruments	8 680	....	....	....	....	....	....	....	....
Monetary authorities	8 681	....	....	....	....	....	....	....	....
General government	8 682	....	....	....	....	....	....	....	....
Banks	8 683	....	....	....	....	....	....	....	....
Other sectors	8 684	....	....	....	....	....	....	....	....
Financial derivatives	8 905	....	....	....	....	....	....	....	....
Monetary authorities	8 906	....	....	....	....	....	....	....	....
General government	8 907	....	....	....	....	....	....	....	....
Banks	8 908	....	....	....	....	....	....	....	....
Other sectors	8 909	....	....	....	....	....	....	....	....
Other investment	8 753	1,463.6	1,723.4	1,925.2	2,264.5	2,913.0	3,950.5	5,781.1	6,754.1
Trade credits	8 756	....	....	....	....	....	....	....	163.1
General government	8 757	....	....	....	....	....	....	....	....
of which: Short-term	8 759	....	....	....	....	....	....	....	....
Other sectors	8 760	....	....	....	....	....	....	....	163.1
of which: Short-term	8 762	....	....	....	....	....	....	....	163.1
Loans	8 764	1,061.5	1,235.7	1,403.7	1,730.5	2,825.4	3,889.3	5,543.2	6,276.0
Monetary authorities	8 765	519.5	446.9	453.9	476.9	455.0	392.2	393.3	375.0
of which: Use of Fund credit and loans from the Fund	8 766	335.8	295.2	278.8	259.3	208.4	163.6	134.2	103.0
of which: Short-term	8 768	....	....	....	....	....	....	....	....
General government	8 769	525.9	56.8	87.3	131.4	237.0	351.9	1,007.1	1,210.4
of which: Short-term	8 771	....	....	....	....	....	....	....	....
Banks	8 772	.4	5.6	4.6	4.4	8.5	40.4	258.0	923.1
of which: Short-term	8 774	....	5.6	4.6	4.4	....	....	....	....
Other sectors	8 775	15.7	726.4	857.9	1,117.8	2,124.9	3,104.8	3,884.8	3,767.5
of which: Short-term	8 777	....	....	....	....	....	....	....	....
Currency and deposits	8 780	94.8	92.6	110.6	108.1	87.6	61.2	237.9	315.0
Monetary authorities	8 781	....	....	....	....	....	....	....	....
General government	8 782	....	....	....	....	....	....	....	....
Banks	8 783	....	92.6	110.6	108.1	87.6	61.2	237.9	315.0
Other sectors	8 784	....	....	....	....	....	....	....	....
Other liabilities	8 786	307.3	395.1	410.9	425.9	....	....	....	....
Monetary authorities	8 787	....	....	....	....	....	....	....	....
of which: Short-term	8 789	....	....	....	....	....	....	....	....
General government	8 790	....	....	....	....	....	....	....	....
of which: Short-term	8 792	....	....	....	....	....	....	....	....
Banks	8 793	....	....	....	....	....	....	....	....
of which: Short-term	8 795	....	....	....	....	....	....	....	....
Other sectors	8 796	....	395.1	410.9	425.9	....	....	....	....
of which: Short-term	8 798	....	395.1	410.9	425.9	....	....	....	....
NET INTERNATIONAL INVESTMENT POSITION	8 995	....	....	−5,278.4	−7,748.9	−9,458.0	−9,348.7	−7,066.5	631.8
Conversion rates: manat per U.S. dollar (end of period)	0 102	.9130	.9550	.9786	.9846	.9806	.9186	.8714	.8453

Table 1. ANALYTIC PRESENTATION, 2000–2007

(Millions of U.S. dollars)

	Code	2000	2001	2002	2003	2004	2005	2006	2007
A. Current Account[1]...............	4 993 Z.	**−632.9**	**−645.0**	**−423.3**	**−473.5**	**−307.1**	**−700.6**	**−1,408.0**	**−1,317.2**
Goods: exports f.o.b...............	2 100 ..	464.8	416.9	422.1	426.5	477.5	549.1	703.5	801.9
Goods: imports f.o.b...............	3 100 ..	−1,983.1	−1,804.2	−1,749.0	−1,758.6	−1,906.8	−2,377.4	−2,768.4	−2,957.8
Balance on Goods...............	4 100 ..	*−1,518.3*	*−1,387.3*	*−1,327.0*	*−1,332.0*	*−1,429.4*	*−1,828.3*	*−2,064.8*	*−2,155.9*
Services: credit...............	2 200 ..	1,973.2	1,804.4	2,061.8	2,054.7	2,244.1	2,510.9	2,433.6	2,598.2
Services: debit...............	3 200 ..	−1,025.7	−973.2	−1,016.1	−1,092.4	−1,231.3	−1,286.4	−1,610.9	−1,579.6
Balance on Goods and Services...............	4 991 ..	*−570.8*	*−556.1*	*−281.3*	*−369.8*	*−416.6*	*−603.8*	*−1,242.1*	*−1,137.4*
Income: credit...............	2 300 ..	316.9	184.5	107.7	79.1	79.7	97.0	119.4	121.3
Income: debit...............	3 300 ..	−457.1	−383.4	−292.1	−231.6	−221.1	−279.1	−337.4	−352.9
Balance on Goods, Services, and Income...............	4 992 ..	*−711.0*	*−755.0*	*−465.7*	*−522.2*	*−557.9*	*−785.9*	*−1,460.1*	*−1,369.0*
Current transfers: credit...............	2 379 Z.	88.5	120.9	55.4	59.8	264.7	103.3	66.4	71.0
Current transfers: debit...............	3 379 ..	−10.5	−10.9	−13.0	−11.1	−13.9	−18.1	−14.3	−19.2
B. Capital Account[1]...............	4 994 Z.	**−16.4**	**−21.3**	**−24.5**	**−37.4**	**−47.9**	**−60.4**	**−63.5**	**−75.7**
Capital account: credit...............	2 994 Z.	....	....	....	....	....	....	....	....
Capital account: debit...............	3 994 ..	−16.4	−21.3	−24.5	−37.4	−47.9	−60.4	−63.5	−75.7
Total, Groups A Plus B...............	4 981 ..	*−649.4*	*−666.3*	*−447.8*	*−510.9*	*−355.0*	*−761.1*	*−1,471.6*	*−1,392.9*
C. Financial Account[1]...............	4 995 W.	**429.9**	**264.6**	**405.0**	**535.5**	**358.5**	**822.1**	**1,280.2**	**1,030.6**
Direct investment abroad...............	4 505 ..	....	....	....	....	....	....	....	....
Direct investment in The Bahamas...............	4 555 Z.	250.3	102.4	152.8	190.2	273.6	563.4	706.4	713.3
Portfolio investment assets...............	4 602 ..	....	....	....	....	....	....	−18.8	−7.2
Equity securities...............	4 610 ..	....	....	....	....	....	....		−4.1
Debt securities...............	4 619 ..	....	....	....	....	....	....	−18.8	−3.1
Portfolio investment liabilities...............	4 652 Z.	....	....	....	....	....	....	....	....
Equity securities...............	4 660 ..	....	....	....	....	....	....	....	....
Debt securities...............	4 669 Z.	....	....	....	....	....	....	....	....
Financial derivatives...............	4 910 ..	....	....	....	....	....	....	....	....
Financial derivatives assets...............	4 900 ..	....	....	....	....	....	....	....	....
Financial derivatives liabilities...............	4 905 ..	....	....	....	....	....	....	....	....
Other investment assets...............	4 703 ..	−19,067.2	−25,411.7	−32,840.8	46,576.8	19,293.4	−11,064.2	−9,016.7	−15,801.8
Monetary authorities...............	4 701 ..	....	....	....	....	....	....	....	....
General government...............	4 704 ..	....	....	....	....	....	....	....	....
Banks...............	4 705 ..	−19,067.2	−25,411.7	−32,840.8	46,576.8	19,293.4	−11,064.2	−9,016.7	−15,801.8
Other sectors...............	4 728 ..	....	....	....	....	....	....	....	....
Other investment liabilities...............	4 753 W.	19,246.9	25,573.9	33,093.1	−46,231.5	−19,208.5	11,322.9	9,609.3	16,126.3
Monetary authorities...............	4 753 WA	....	....	....	....	....	....	....	....
General government...............	4 753 ZB	−11.2	−22.0	−35.1	52.6	−20.6	−8.5	−3.5	−6.4
Banks...............	4 753 ZC	19,039.1	25,532.1	33,024.4	−46,679.2	−19,358.0	11,111.7	9,159.8	15,715.2
Other sectors...............	4 753 ZD	218.9	63.8	103.8	395.1	170.1	219.7	453.0	417.4
Total, Groups A Through C...............	4 983 ..	*−219.4*	*−401.7*	*−42.8*	*24.6*	*3.5*	*61.1*	*−191.4*	*−362.3*
D. Net Errors and Omissions...............	4 998 ..	**158.4**	**370.8**	**102.9**	**85.5**	**179.8**	**−149.2**	**111.9**	**316.0**
Total, Groups A Through D...............	4 984 ..	*−61.0*	*−30.9*	*60.1*	*110.1*	*183.3*	*−88.1*	*−79.5*	*−46.3*
E. Reserves and Related Items...............	4 802 A.	**61.0**	**30.9**	**−60.1**	**−110.1**	**−183.3**	**88.1**	**79.5**	**46.3**
Reserve assets...............	4 802 ..	61.0	29.9	−60.1	−110.1	−183.3	88.1	79.5	46.3
Use of Fund credit and loans...............	4 766 ..	....	....	....	....	....	....	....	....
Exceptional financing...............	4 920 ..	....	1.0	....	....	....	....	....	....
Conversion rates: Bahamian dollars per U.S. dollar...............	0 101 ..	**1.0000**	**1.0000**	**1.0000**	**1.0000**	**1.0000**	**1.0000**	**1.0000**	**1.0000**

[1] Excludes components that have been classified in the categories of Group E.

Table 2. STANDARD PRESENTATION, 2000–2007

(Millions of U.S. dollars)

	Code	2000	2001	2002	2003	2004	2005	2006	2007
CURRENT ACCOUNT	4 993	−632.9	−645.0	−423.3	−473.5	−307.1	−700.6	−1,408.0	−1,317.2
A. GOODS	4 100	−1,518.3	−1,387.3	−1,327.0	−1,332.0	−1,429.4	−1,828.3	−2,064.8	−2,155.9
Credit	2 100	464.8	416.9	422.1	426.5	477.5	549.1	703.5	801.9
General merchandise: exports f.o.b.	2 110	360.8	300.9	298.2	340.4	363.6	388.1	454.4	502.5
Goods for processing: exports f.o.b.	2 150	....	....	....	....	....	....	....	....
Repairs on goods	2 160	....	....	....	....	....	....	....	....
Goods procured in ports by carriers	2 170	104.0	116.0	123.9	86.2	113.9	161.0	249.1	299.4
Nonmonetary gold	2 180	....	....	....	....	....	....	....	....
Debit	3 100	−1,983.1	−1,804.2	−1,749.0	−1,758.6	−1,906.8	−2,377.4	−2,768.4	−2,957.8
General merchandise: imports f.o.b.	3 110	−1,981.6	−1,800.7	−1,745.8	−1,755.5	−1,903.6	−2,374.3	−2,765.2	−2,949.6
Goods for processing: imports f.o.b.	3 150	....	....	....	....	....	....	....	....
Repairs on goods	3 160	....	....	....	....	....	....	....	....
Goods procured in ports by carriers	3 170	−1.5	−3.5	−3.2	−3.1	−3.2	−3.1	−3.2	−8.3
Nonmonetary gold	3 180	....	....	....	....	....	....	....	....
B. SERVICES	4 200	947.5	831.2	1,045.6	962.2	1,012.8	1,224.5	822.7	1,018.6
Total credit	2 200	*1,973.2*	*1,804.4*	*2,061.8*	*2,054.7*	*2,244.1*	*2,510.9*	*2,433.6*	*2,598.2*
Total debit	3 200	*−1,025.7*	*−973.2*	*−1,016.1*	*−1,092.4*	*−1,231.3*	*−1,286.4*	*−1,610.9*	*−1,579.6*
Transportation services, credit	2 205	54.4	50.1	57.5	56.7	55.3	55.6	57.4	57.5
Passenger	2 850	*15.2*	*16.9*	*12.9*	*13.0*	*13.0*	*9.7*	*9.8*	*10.7*
Freight	2 851	....	....	....	....	....	....	....	....
Other	2 852	*39.2*	*33.2*	*44.6*	*43.7*	*42.3*	*45.9*	*47.6*	*46.8*
Sea transport, passenger	2 207	....	....	....	....	....	....	....	....
Sea transport, freight	2 208	....	....	....	....	....	....	....	....
Sea transport, other	2 209	26.3	20.1	31.0	31.7	26.8	26.9	31.4	31.4
Air transport, passenger	2 211	15.2	16.9	12.9	13.0	13.0	9.7	9.8	10.7
Air transport, freight	2 212	....	....	....	....	....	....	....	....
Air transport, other	2 213	12.9	13.1	13.5	12.1	15.5	19.0	16.2	15.5
Other transport, passenger	2 215	....	....	....	....	....	....	....	....
Other transport, freight	2 216	....	....	....	....	....	....	....	....
Other transport, other	2 217	....	....	....	....	....	....	....	....
Transportation services, debit	3 205	−249.0	−254.6	−236.4	−244.2	−304.6	−366.4	−358.5	−373.3
Passenger	3 850	*−86.6*	*−86.1*	*−93.9*	*−98.9*	*−153.0*	*−183.7*	*−156.1*	*−161.2*
Freight	3 851	*−153.5*	*−137.6*	*−131.1*	*−132.4*	*−138.4*	*−166.5*	*−185.2*	*−193.3*
Other	3 852	*−8.9*	*−30.9*	*−11.4*	*−12.9*	*−13.2*	*−16.2*	*−17.3*	*−18.7*
Sea transport, passenger	3 207	−4.0	....	....	....	....	....	....	....
Sea transport, freight	3 208	−122.8	−110.2	−104.9	−105.9	−110.7	−133.1	−148.1	−154.7
Sea transport, other	3 209	−1.4	−1.2	−1.5	−2.2	−2.6	−3.0	−4.1	−4.5
Air transport, passenger	3 211	−82.6	−86.1	−93.9	−98.9	−153.0	−183.7	−156.1	−161.2
Air transport, freight	3 212	−30.7	−27.4	−26.2	−26.5	−27.7	−33.4	−37.0	−38.7
Air transport, other	3 213	−7.5	−29.7	−9.9	−10.6	−10.6	−13.2	−13.2	−14.2
Other transport, passenger	3 215	....	....	....	....	....	....	....	....
Other transport, freight	3 216	....	....	....	....	....	....	....	....
Other transport, other	3 217	....	....	....	....	....	....	....	....
Travel, credit	2 236	1,738.0	1,647.7	1,759.8	1,757.4	1,884.5	2,070.5	2,056.4	2,187.2
Business travel	2 237	....	....	....	....	....	....	....	....
Personal travel	2 240	1,738.0	1,647.7	1,759.8	1,757.4	1,884.5	2,070.5	2,056.4	2,187.2
Travel, debit	3 236	−260.9	−255.5	−243.9	−304.7	−315.6	−344.3	−385.2	−377.4
Business travel	3 237	−40.9	−42.6	−38.2	−46.6	−39.5	−38.9	−52.9	−39.2
Personal travel	3 240	−220.0	−212.9	−205.7	−258.1	−276.1	−305.4	−332.3	−338.3
Other services, credit	2 200 BA	180.8	106.6	244.5	240.6	304.3	384.8	319.8	353.4
Communications	2 245	....	....	....	....	....	....	....	....
Construction	2 249	....	....	....	....	....	....	....	....
Insurance	2 253	....	....	....	....	....	....	....	....
Financial	2 260	....	....	....	....	....	....	....	....
Computer and information	2 262	....	....	....	....	....	....	....	....
Royalties and licence fees	2 266	....	....	....	....	....	....	....	....
Other business services	2 268	153.4	78.3	218.1	214.1	271.0	333.6	289.3	321.7
Personal, cultural, and recreational	2 287	....	....	....	....	....	....	....	....
Government, n.i.e.	2 291	27.4	28.3	26.3	26.5	33.3	51.2	30.4	31.7
Other services, debit	3 200 BA	−515.8	−463.1	−535.8	−543.6	−611.1	−575.7	−867.1	−828.9
Communications	3 245	−1.2	−1.2	−1.0	−1.0	−1.0	−1.0	−1.0	−1.0
Construction	3 249	−101.5	−33.0	−55.2	−37.8	−23.2	−40.7	−214.4	−176.2
Insurance	3 253	−74.1	−83.5	−92.7	−105.7	−81.6	−96.9	−120.7	−107.0
Financial	3 260	....	....	....	....	....	....	....	....
Computer and information	3 262	....	....	....	....	....	....	....	....
Royalties and licence fees	3 266	−14.2	−13.2	−13.7	−14.6	−18.5	−16.1	−17.7	−19.7
Other business services	3 268	−265.9	−253.3	−284.2	−298.7	−422.3	−341.3	−410.0	−445.3
Personal, cultural, and recreational	3 287	−2.0	−2.0	−2.0	−2.0	−2.0	−2.0	−2.0	−2.0
Government, n.i.e.	3 291	−56.9	−76.9	−87.1	−83.8	−62.5	−77.8	−101.3	−77.7

Table 2 (Continued). STANDARD PRESENTATION, 2000–2007

(Millions of U.S. dollars)

	Code	2000	2001	2002	2003	2004	2005	2006	2007
C. INCOME	4 300	−140.2	−198.9	−184.3	−152.4	−141.3	−182.1	−218.0	−231.6
Total credit	2 300	*316.9*	*184.5*	*107.7*	*79.1*	*79.7*	*97.0*	*119.4*	*121.3*
Total debit	3 300	*−457.1*	*−383.4*	*−292.1*	*−231.6*	*−221.1*	*−279.1*	*−337.4*	*−352.9*
Compensation of employees, credit	2 310	....	....	....	....	....	....	....	....
Compensation of employees, debit	3 310	−51.0	−48.5	−49.8	−56.3	−63.3	−73.2	−92.8	−84.7
Investment income, credit	2 320	316.9	184.5	107.7	79.1	79.7	97.0	119.4	121.3
Direct investment income	2 330	....	....	....	....	....	....	....	....
Dividends and distributed branch profits	2 332	....	....	....	....	....	....	....	....
Reinvested earnings and undistributed branch profits	2 333	....	....	....	....	....	....	....	....
Income on debt (interest)	2 334	....	....	....	....	....	....	....	....
Portfolio investment income	2 339	....	....	....	....	....	....	....	....
Income on equity	2 340	....	....	....	....	....	....	....	....
Income on bonds and notes	2 350	....	....	....	....	....	....	....	....
Income on money market instruments	2 360	....	....	....	....	....	....	....	....
Other investment income	2 370	316.9	184.5	107.7	79.1	79.7	97.0	119.4	121.3
Investment income, debit	3 320	−406.1	−334.9	−242.3	−175.3	−157.8	−205.9	−244.6	−268.2
Direct investment income	3 330	....	....	....	....	....	....	....	....
Dividends and distributed branch profits	3 332	....	....	....	....	....	....	....	....
Reinvested earnings and undistributed branch profits	3 333	....	....	....	....	....	....	....	....
Income on debt (interest)	3 334	....	....	....	....	....	....	....	....
Portfolio investment income	3 339	....	....	....	....	....	....	....	....
Income on equity	3 340	....	....	....	....	....	....	....	....
Income on bonds and notes	3 350	....	....	....	....	....	....	....	....
Income on money market instruments	3 360	....	....	....	....	....	....	....	....
Other investment income	3 370	−406.1	−334.9	−242.3	−175.3	−157.8	−205.9	−244.6	−268.2
D. CURRENT TRANSFERS	4 379	78.0	110.0	42.4	48.7	250.8	85.2	52.0	51.8
Credit	2 379	88.5	120.9	55.4	59.8	264.7	103.3	66.4	71.0
General government	2 380	52.6	51.5	54.2	58.6	65.5	66.3	65.2	69.8
Other sectors	2 390	35.8	69.5	1.2	1.2	199.2	37.0	1.2	1.2
Workers' remittances	2 391	....	....	....	....	....	....	....	....
Other current transfers	2 392	35.8	69.5	1.2	1.2	199.2	37.0	1.2	1.2
Debit	3 379	−10.5	−10.9	−13.0	−11.1	−13.9	−18.1	−14.3	−19.2
General government	3 380	−5.3	−5.8	−5.2	−4.6	−5.8	−7.3	−6.8	−8.9
Other sectors	3 390	−5.2	−5.1	−7.8	−6.5	−8.1	−10.8	−7.5	−10.3
Workers' remittances	3 391	−5.2	−5.1	−7.8	−6.5	−8.1	−10.8	−7.5	−10.3
Other current transfers	3 392	....	....	....	....	....	....	....	....
CAPITAL AND FINANCIAL ACCOUNT	4 996	474.5	274.2	320.4	388.0	127.3	849.8	1,296.2	1,001.1
CAPITAL ACCOUNT	4 994	−16.4	−21.3	−24.5	−37.4	−47.9	−60.4	−63.5	−75.7
Total credit	2 994	....	....	....	....	....	....	....	....
Total debit	3 994	*−16.4*	*−21.3*	*−24.5*	*−37.4*	*−47.9*	*−60.4*	*−63.5*	*−75.7*
Capital transfers, credit	2 400	....	....	....	....	....	....	....	....
General government	2 401	....	....	....	....	....	....	....	....
Debt forgiveness	2 402	....	....	....	....	....	....	....	....
Other capital transfers	2 410	....	....	....	....	....	....	....	....
Other sectors	2 430	....	....	....	....	....	....	....	....
Migrants' transfers	2 431	....	....	....	....	....	....	....	....
Debt forgiveness	2 432	....	....	....	....	....	....	....	....
Other capital transfers	2 440	....	....	....	....	....	....	....	....
Capital transfers, debit	3 400	−16.4	−21.3	−24.5	−37.4	−47.9	−60.4	−63.5	−75.7
General government	3 401	....	....	....	....	....	....	....	....
Debt forgiveness	3 402	....	....	....	....	....	....	....	....
Other capital transfers	3 410	....	....	....	....	....	....	....	....
Other sectors	3 430	−16.4	−21.3	−24.5	−37.4	−47.9	−60.4	−63.5	−75.7
Migrants' transfers	3 431	−16.4	−21.3	−24.5	−37.4	−47.9	−60.4	−63.5	−75.7
Debt forgiveness	3 432	....	....	....	....	....	....	....	....
Other capital transfers	3 440	....	....	....	....	....	....	....	....
Nonproduced nonfinancial assets, credit	2 480	....	....	....	....	....	....	....	....
Nonproduced nonfinancial assets, debit	3 480	....	....	....	....	....	....	....	....

Table 2 (Continued). STANDARD PRESENTATION, 2000–2007

(Millions of U.S. dollars)

	Code	2000	2001	2002	2003	2004	2005	2006	2007
FINANCIAL ACCOUNT....................................	4 995 ..	**490.9**	**295.5**	**344.9**	**425.4**	**175.2**	**910.3**	**1,359.7**	**1,076.9**
A. DIRECT INVESTMENT................................	4 500 ..	**250.3**	**102.4**	**152.8**	**190.2**	**273.6**	**563.4**	**706.4**	**713.3**
Direct investment abroad..............................	4 505 ..	....	....	....	....	....	....	....	....
Equity capital...	4 510 ..	....	....	....	....	....	....	....	....
Claims on affiliated enterprises....................	4 515 ..	....	....	....	....	....	....	....	....
Liabilities to affiliated enterprises...............	4 520 ..	....	....	....	....	....	....	....	....
Reinvested earnings......................................	4 525 ..	....	....	....	....	....	....	....	....
Other capital..	4 530 ..	....	....	....	....	....	....	....	....
Claims on affiliated enterprises....................	4 535 ..	....	....	....	....	....	....	....	....
Liabilities to affiliated enterprises...............	4 540 ..	....	....	....	....	....	....	....	....
Direct investment in The Bahamas...................	4 555 ..	250.3	102.4	152.8	190.2	273.6	563.4	706.4	713.3
Equity capital...	4 560 ..	106.2	38.2	51.2	44.7	90.2	219.8	233.9	356.0
Claims on direct investors............................	4 565 ..	....	....	....	....	....	....	....	....
Liabilities to direct investors.......................	4 570 ..	106.2	38.2	51.2	44.7	90.2	219.8	233.9	356.0
Reinvested earnings......................................	4 575 ..	....	....	....	....	....	....	....	....
Other capital..	4 580 ..	144.0	64.2	101.6	145.5	183.4	343.6	472.5	357.4
Claims on direct investors............................	4 585 ..	....	....	....	....	....	....	....	....
Liabilities to direct investors.......................	4 590 ..	144.0	64.2	101.6	145.5	183.4	343.6	472.5	357.4
B. PORTFOLIO INVESTMENT..........................	4 600 ..	....	....	....	....	....	....	**−18.8**	**−7.2**
Assets..	4 602 ..	....	....	....	....	....	....	**−18.8**	**−7.2**
Equity securities...	4 610 ..	....	....	....	....	....	....	....	−4.1
Monetary authorities.....................................	4 611 ..	....	....	....	....	....	....	....	....
General government......................................	4 612 ..	....	....	....	....	....	....	....	....
Banks...	4 613 ..	....	....	....	....	....	....	....	....
Other sectors..	4 614 ..	....	....	....	....	....	....	....	−4.1
Debt securities..	4 619 ..	....	....	....	....	....	....	−18.8	−3.1
Bonds and notes...	4 620 ..	....	....	....	....	....	....	−18.8	−3.1
Monetary authorities.................................	4 621 ..	....	....	....	....	....	....	....	....
General government..................................	4 622 ..	....	....	....	....	....	....	....	....
Banks...	4 623 ..	....	....	....	....	....	....	....	....
Other sectors..	4 624 ..	....	....	....	....	....	....	−18.8	−3.1
Money market instruments............................	4 630 ..	....	....	....	....	....	....	....	....
Monetary authorities.................................	4 631 ..	....	....	....	....	....	....	....	....
General government..................................	4 632 ..	....	....	....	....	....	....	....	....
Banks...	4 633 ..	....	....	....	....	....	....	....	....
Other sectors..	4 634 ..	....	....	....	....	....	....	....	....
Liabilities..	4 652 ..	....	....	....	....	....	....	....	....
Equity securities...	4 660 ..	....	....	....	....	....	....	....	....
Banks...	4 663 ..	....	....	....	....	....	....	....	....
Other sectors..	4 664 ..	....	....	....	....	....	....	....	....
Debt securities..	4 669 ..	....	....	....	....	....	....	....	....
Bonds and notes...	4 670 ..	....	....	....	....	....	....	....	....
Monetary authorities.................................	4 671 ..	....	....	....	....	....	....	....	....
General government..................................	4 672 ..	....	....	....	....	....	....	....	....
Banks...	4 673 ..	....	....	....	....	....	....	....	....
Other sectors..	4 674 ..	....	....	....	....	....	....	....	....
Money market instruments............................	4 680 ..	....	....	....	....	....	....	....	....
Monetary authorities.................................	4 681 ..	....	....	....	....	....	....	....	....
General government..................................	4 682 ..	....	....	....	....	....	....	....	....
Banks...	4 683 ..	....	....	....	....	....	....	....	....
Other sectors..	4 684 ..	....	....	....	....	....	....	....	....
C. FINANCIAL DERIVATIVES..........................	4 910 ..	....	....	....	....	....	....	....	....
Monetary authorities.....................................	4 911 ..	....	....	....	....	....	....	....	....
General government......................................	4 912 ..	....	....	....	....	....	....	....	....
Banks...	4 913 ..	....	....	....	....	....	....	....	....
Other sectors..	4 914 ..	....	....	....	....	....	....	....	....
Assets..	4 900 ..	....	102.4	....	190.2	273.6	563.4	....	....
Monetary authorities.....................................	4 901 ..	....	....	....	....	....	....	....	....
General government......................................	4 902 ..	....	....	....	....	....	....	....	....
Banks...	4 903 ..	....	....	....	....	....	....	....	....
Other sectors..	4 904 ..	....	....	....	....	....	....	....	....
Liabilities..	4 905 ..	....	....	....	....	183.4	....	....	....
Monetary authorities.....................................	4 906 ..	....	....	....	....	....	....	....	....
General government......................................	4 907 ..	....	....	....	....	....	....	....	....
Banks...	4 908 ..	....	....	....	....	....	....	....	....
Other sectors..	4 909 ..	....	....	....	....	....	....	....	....

Table 2 (Concluded). STANDARD PRESENTATION, 2000–2007

(Millions of U.S. dollars)

	Code	2000	2001	2002	2003	2004	2005	2006	2007
D. OTHER INVESTMENT..	4 700 ..	179.7	163.3	252.3	345.3	84.9	258.7	592.6	324.5
Assets...	4 703 ..	−19,067.2	−25,411.7	−32,840.8	46,576.8	19,293.4	−11,064.2	−9,016.7	−15,801.8
Trade credits...	4 706 ..	....	....	....	....	....	....	....	....
General government..............................	4 707 ..	....	....	....	....	....	....	....	....
of which: Short-term.........................	4 709 ..	....	....	....	....	....	....	....	....
Other sectors.......................................	4 710 ..	....	....	....	....	....	....	....	....
of which: Short-term.........................	4 712 ..	....	....	....	....	....	....	....	....
Loans...	4 714 ..	....	....	....	....	....	....	....	....
Monetary authorities............................	4 715 ..	....	....	....	....	....	....	....	....
of which: Short-term.........................	4 718 ..	....	....	....	....	....	....	....	....
General government..............................	4 719 ..	....	....	....	....	....	....	....	....
of which: Short-term.........................	4 721 ..	....	....	....	....	....	....	....	....
Banks...	4 722 ..	....	....	....	....	....	....	....	....
of which: Short-term.........................	4 724 ..	....	....	....	....	....	....	....	....
Other sectors.......................................	4 725 ..	....	....	....	....	....	....	....	....
of which: Short-term.........................	4 727 ..	....	....	....	....	....	....	....	....
Currency and deposits.............................	4 730 ..	−19,067.2	−25,411.7	−32,840.8	46,576.8	19,293.4	−11,064.2	−9,016.7	−15,801.8
Monetary authorities............................	4 731 ..	....	....	....	....	....	....	....	....
General government..............................	4 732 ..	....	....	....	....	....	....	....	....
Banks...	4 733 ..	−19,067.2	−25,411.7	−32,840.8	46,576.8	19,293.4	−11,064.2	−9,016.7	−15,801.8
Other sectors.......................................	4 734 ..	....	....	....	....	....	....	....	....
Other assets...	4 736 ..	....	....	....	....	....	....	....	....
Monetary authorities............................	4 737 ..	....	....	....	....	....	....	....	....
of which: Short-term.........................	4 739 ..	....	....	....	....	....	....	....	....
General government..............................	4 740 ..	....	....	....	....	....	....	....	....
of which: Short-term.........................	4 742 ..	....	....	....	....	....	....	....	....
Banks...	4 743 ..	....	....	....	....	....	....	....	....
of which: Short-term.........................	4 745 ..	....	....	....	....	....	....	....	....
Other sectors.......................................	4 746 ..	....	....	....	....	....	....	....	....
of which: Short-term.........................	4 748 ..	....	....	....	....	....	....	....	....
Liabilities...	4 753 ..	19,246.9	25,574.9	33,093.1	−46,231.5	−19,208.5	11,322.9	9,609.3	16,126.3
Trade credits...	4 756 ..	....	....	....	....	....	....	....	....
General government..............................	4 757 ..	....	....	....	....	....	....	....	....
of which: Short-term.........................	4 759 ..	....	....	....	....	....	....	....	....
Other sectors.......................................	4 760 ..	....	....	....	....	....	....	....	....
of which: Short-term.........................	4 762 ..	....	....	....	....	....	....	....	....
Loans...	4 764 ..	207.7	42.8	68.7	447.7	149.5	211.3	449.5	411.0
Monetary authorities............................	4 765 ..	....	....	....	....	....	....	....	....
of which: Use of Fund credit and loans from the Fund..	4 766 ..	....	....	....	....	....	....	....	....
of which: Short-term.........................	4 768 ..	....	....	....	....	....	....	....	....
General government..............................	4 769 ..	−11.2	−22.0	−35.1	52.6	−20.6	−8.5	−3.5	−6.4
of which: Short-term.........................	4 771 ..	....	....	....	....	....	....	....	....
Banks...	4 772 ..	....	1.0	....	....	....	....	....	....
of which: Short-term.........................	4 774 ..	....	1.0	....	....	....	....	....	....
Other sectors.......................................	4 775 ..	218.9	63.8	103.8	395.1	170.1	219.7	453.0	417.4
of which: Short-term.........................	4 777 ..	....	....	....	....	....	....	....	....
Currency and deposits.............................	4 780 ..	19,039.1	25,532.1	33,024.4	−46,679.2	−19,358.0	11,111.7	9,159.8	15,715.2
Monetary authorities............................	4 781 ..	....	....	....	....	....	....	....	....
General government..............................	4 782 ..	....	....	....	....	....	....	....	....
Banks...	4 783 ..	19,039.1	25,532.1	33,024.4	−46,679.2	−19,358.0	11,111.7	9,159.8	15,715.2
Other sectors.......................................	4 784 ..	....	....	....	....	....	....	....	....
Other liabilities.......................................	4 786 ..	....	....	....	....	....	....	....	....
Monetary authorities............................	4 787 ..	....	....	....	....	....	....	....	....
of which: Short-term.........................	4 789 ..	....	....	....	....	....	....	....	....
General government..............................	4 790 ..	....	....	....	....	....	....	....	....
of which: Short-term.........................	4 792 ..	....	....	....	....	....	....	....	....
Banks...	4 793 ..	....	....	....	....	....	....	....	....
of which: Short-term.........................	4 795 ..	....	....	....	....	....	....	....	....
Other sectors.......................................	4 796 ..	....	....	....	....	....	....	....	....
of which: Short-term.........................	4 798 ..	....	....	....	....	....	....	....	....
E. RESERVE ASSETS.......................................	4 802 ..	61.0	29.9	−60.1	−110.1	−183.3	88.1	79.5	46.3
Monetary gold...	4 812 ..	....	....	....	....	....	....	....	....
Special drawing rights................................	4 811 ..	−.1	....	....	.1	....	....	....	−.1
Reserve position in the Fund.........................	4 810 ..	....	....	....	....	....	....	....	....
Foreign exchange.......................................	4 803 ..	61.1	29.9	−60.1	−110.2	−183.2	88.1	79.5	46.3
Other claims..	4 813 ..	....	....	....	....	....	....	....	....
NET ERRORS AND OMISSIONS............................	4 998 ..	158.4	370.8	102.9	85.5	179.8	−149.2	111.9	316.0

Table 1. ANALYTIC PRESENTATION, 2000–2007

(Millions of U.S. dollars)

	Code	2000	2001	2002	2003	2004	2005	2006	2007
A. Current Account¹	4 993 Z.	**830.2**	**225.9**	**−49.6**	**200.4**	**471.6**	**1,474.2**	**2,187.5**	**2,906.5**
Goods: exports f.o.b.	2 100 ..	6,242.7	5,656.0	5,888.1	6,720.6	7,660.3	10,348.7	12,339.8	13,790.2
Goods: imports f.o.b.	3 100 ..	−4,375.3	−4,029.1	−4,678.5	−5,298.4	−6,922.6	−8,870.7	−9,953.8	−10,925.4
Balance on Goods	4 100 ..	*1,867.4*	*1,626.9*	*1,209.6*	*1,422.2*	*737.7*	*1,477.9*	*2,386.0*	*2,864.8*
Services: credit	2 200 ..	933.5	950.4	1,068.0	1,260.1	2,676.4	3,048.3	3,322.4	3,524.2
Services: debit	3 200 ..	−756.8	−765.7	−945.4	−906.7	−1,247.8	−1,416.2	−1,605.2	−1,700.9
Balance on Goods and Services	4 991 ..	*2,044.1*	*1,811.6*	*1,332.2*	*1,775.6*	*2,166.3*	*3,110.0*	*4,103.2*	*4,688.0*
Income: credit	2 300 ..	6,327.9	3,794.4	1,678.9	1,266.6	2,544.3	5,015.8	7,633.7	10,373.6
Income: debit	3 300 ..	−6,551.5	−4,115.9	−2,203.8	−1,759.6	−3,119.1	−5,428.1	−8,018.6	−10,672.3
Balance on Goods, Services, and Income	4 992 ..	*1,820.4*	*1,490.0*	*807.2*	*1,282.6*	*1,591.5*	*2,697.6*	*3,718.3*	*4,389.3*
Current transfers: credit	2 379 Z.	22.4	22.9	14.7	....	....	....	....	....
Current transfers: debit	3 379 ..	−1,012.7	−1,286.9	−871.5	−1,082.2	−1,119.9	−1,223.4	−1,530.8	−1,482.8
B. Capital Account¹	4 994 Z.	**50.0**	**100.0**	**101.6**	**50.0**	**50.0**	**50.0**	**75.0**	**50.0**
Capital account: credit	2 994 Z.	50.0	100.0	101.6	50.0	50.0	50.0	75.0	50.0
Capital account: debit	3 994 ..	....	....	....	....	....	....	....	....
Total, Groups A Plus B	4 981 ..	*880.2*	*325.9*	*52.0*	*250.4*	*521.6*	*1,524.2*	*2,262.5*	*2,956.5*
C. Financial Account¹	4 995 W.	**−29.8**	**−417.1**	**−1,234.1**	**493.1**	**−390.8**	**−1,380.0**	**−1,451.7**	**−1,551.9**
Direct investment abroad	4 505 ..	−9.6	−216.0	−190.0	−741.4	−1,035.6	−1,135.4	−980.1	−1,669.1
Direct investment in Bahrain	4 555 Z.	363.6	80.4	217.0	516.7	865.3	1,048.6	2,914.9	1,756.0
Portfolio investment assets	4 602 ..	−88.3	−1,448.0	−5,140.0	−3,095.7	−3,892.6	−7,036.2	−10,527.4	−9,890.1
Equity securities	4 610 ..	−161.1	−389.0	−1,143.5	−489.0	−1,999.0	−2,219.7	−2,200.7	−3,368.1
Debt securities	4 619 ..	72.8	−1,059.0	−3,996.5	−2,606.7	−1,893.6	−4,816.5	−8,326.7	−6,522.0
Portfolio investment liabilities	4 652 Z.	282.5	−30.7	915.2	688.4	387.7	2,421.9	1,696.1	1,330.2
Equity securities	4 660 ..	....	1.2	366.0	238.5	20.9	1,801.1	133.8	138.8
Debt securities	4 669 Z.	282.5	−31.9	549.2	449.9	366.8	620.8	1,562.3	1,191.5
Financial derivatives	4 910 ..	....	....	....	....	....	....	....	....
Financial derivatives assets	4 900 ..	....	....	....	....	....	....	....	....
Financial derivatives liabilities	4 905 ..	....	....	....	....	....	....	....	....
Other investment assets	4 703 ..	−3,833.9	5,623.2	33,425.4	−20,786.6	−9,779.9	−11,562.4	−30,234.9	−38,504.7
Monetary authorities	4 701 ..	....	....	....	....	....	....	....	....
General government	4 704 ..	−5.9	−6.9	−7.2	−10.4	−5.1	−4.5	−11.4	−10.6
Banks	4 705 ..	−3,828.0	5,629.1	33,427.2	−20,777.7	−9,777.2	−11,562.2	−30,226.6	−38,497.3
Other sectors	4 728 ..	....	1.0	5.3	1.6	2.3	4.3	3.2	3.2
Other investment liabilities	4 753 W.	3,255.8	−4,426.0	−30,461.7	23,911.6	13,064.3	14,883.6	35,679.6	45,425.8
Monetary authorities	4 753 WA	....	....	....	....	....	....	....	....
General government	4 753 ZB	59.1	34.6	102.7	168.5	24.7	39.7	22.7	46.3
Banks	4 753 ZC	3,249.2	−4,289.7	−29,734.7	23,793.4	13,004.7	14,797.4	35,612.7	45,332.2
Other sectors	4 753 ZD	−52.4	−170.9	−829.7	−50.3	35.0	46.5	44.1	47.3
Total, Groups A Through C	4 983 ..	*850.4*	*−91.2*	*−1,182.2*	*743.5*	*130.7*	*144.2*	*810.9*	*1,404.6*
D. Net Errors and Omissions	4 998 ..	**−650.3**	**214.7**	**1,216.9**	**−699.8**	**27.2**	**149.9**	**11.1**	**10.1**
Total, Groups A Through D	4 984 ..	*200.1*	*123.5*	*34.8*	*43.7*	*157.9*	*294.2*	*822.0*	*1,414.7*
E. Reserves and Related Items	4 802 A.	**−200.1**	**−123.5**	**−34.8**	**−43.7**	**−157.9**	**−294.2**	**−822.0**	**−1,414.7**
Reserve assets	4 802 ..	−200.1	−123.5	−34.8	−43.7	−157.9	−294.2	−822.0	−1,414.7
Use of Fund credit and loans	4 766 ..	....	....	....	....	....	....	....	....
Exceptional financing	4 920 ..	....	....	....	....	....	....	....	....
Conversion rates: Bahrain dinar per U.S. dollar	0 101 ..	**.3760**	**.3760**	**.3760**	**.3760**	**.3760**	**.3760**	**.3760**	**.3760**

¹ Excludes components that have been classified in the categories of Group E.

Table 2. STANDARD PRESENTATION, 2000–2007

(Millions of U.S. dollars)

	Code	2000	2001	2002	2003	2004	2005	2006	2007
CURRENT ACCOUNT	4 993 ..	**830.2**	**225.9**	**−49.6**	**200.4**	**471.6**	**1,474.2**	**2,187.5**	**2,906.5**
A. GOODS	4 100 ..	**1,867.4**	**1,626.9**	**1,209.6**	**1,422.2**	**737.7**	**1,477.9**	**2,386.0**	**2,864.8**
Credit	2 100 ..	**6,242.7**	**5,656.0**	**5,888.1**	**6,720.6**	**7,660.3**	**10,348.7**	**12,339.8**	**13,790.2**
General merchandise: exports f.o.b.	2 110 ..	6,194.9	5,575.8	5,795.2	6,631.4	7,558.2	10,242.0	12,200.0	13,633.5
Goods for processing: exports f.o.b.	2 150 ..	....	....	....	....	....	....	....	....
Repairs on goods	2 160 ..	47.7	80.2	92.9	89.2	102.1	106.6	139.8	156.6
Goods procured in ports by carriers	2 170 ..	....	....	....	....	....	....	....	....
Nonmonetary gold	2 180 ..	....	....	....	....	....	....	....	....
Debit	3 100 ..	**−4,375.3**	**−4,029.1**	**−4,678.5**	**−5,298.4**	**−6,922.6**	**−8,870.7**	**−9,953.8**	**−10,925.4**
General merchandise: imports f.o.b.	3 110 ..	−4,375.3	−4,029.1	−4,678.5	−5,298.4	−6,922.6	−8,870.7	−9,953.8	−10,925.4
Goods for processing: imports f.o.b.	3 150 ..	....	....	....	....	....	....	....	....
Repairs on goods	3 160 ..	....	....	....	....	....	....	....	....
Goods procured in ports by carriers	3 170 ..	....	....	....	....	....	....	....	....
Nonmonetary gold	3 180 ..	....	....	....	....	....	....	....	....
B. SERVICES	4 200 ..	**176.7**	**184.6**	**122.6**	**353.4**	**1,428.6**	**1,632.0**	**1,717.2**	**1,823.3**
Total credit	2 200 ..	*933.5*	*950.4*	*1,068.0*	*1,260.1*	*2,676.4*	*3,048.3*	*3,322.4*	*3,524.2*
Total debit	3 200 ..	*−756.8*	*−765.7*	*−945.4*	*−906.7*	*−1,247.8*	*−1,416.2*	*−1,605.2*	*−1,700.9*
Transportation services, credit	2 205 ..	**281.4**	**255.9**	**244.7**	**486.4**	**640.4**	**683.0**	**737.5**	**749.2**
Passenger	2 850 ..	*281.4*	*255.9*	*244.7*	*486.4*	*640.4*	*683.0*	*737.5*	*749.2*
Freight	2 851 ..	....	....	....	....	....	....	....	....
Other	2 852 ..	....	....	....	....	....	....	....	....
Sea transport, passenger	2 207 ..	....	....	....	....	....	....	....	....
Sea transport, freight	2 208 ..	....	....	....	....	....	....	....	....
Sea transport, other	2 209 ..	....	....	....	....	....	....	....	....
Air transport, passenger	2 211 ..	281.4	255.9	244.7	486.4	640.4	683.0	737.5	749.2
Air transport, freight	2 212 ..	....	....	....	....	....	....	....	....
Air transport, other	2 213 ..	....	....	....	....	....	....	....	....
Other transport, passenger	2 215 ..	....	....	....	....	....	....	....	....
Other transport, freight	2 216 ..	....	....	....	....	....	....	....	....
Other transport, other	2 217 ..	....	....	....	....	....	....	....	....
Transportation services, debit	3 205 ..	**−433.7**	**−421.7**	**−470.6**	**−442.8**	**−557.0**	**−630.2**	**−689.3**	**−698.4**
Passenger	3 850 ..	*−201.3*	*−172.6*	*−170.0*	*−119.7*	*−141.2*	*−160.1*	*−184.0*	*−192.3*
Freight	3 851 ..	*−232.4*	*−249.1*	*−300.6*	*−323.2*	*−415.7*	*−470.1*	*−505.2*	*−506.1*
Other	3 852 ..	....	....	....	....	....	....	....	....
Sea transport, passenger	3 207 ..	....	....	....	....	....	....	....	....
Sea transport, freight	3 208 ..	−232.4	−249.1	−300.6	−323.2	−415.7	−470.1	−505.2	−506.1
Sea transport, other	3 209 ..	....	....	....	....	....	....	....	....
Air transport, passenger	3 211 ..	−201.3	−172.6	−170.0	−119.7	−141.2	−160.1	−184.0	−192.3
Air transport, freight	3 212 ..	....	....	....	....	....	....	....	....
Air transport, other	3 213 ..	....	....	....	....	....	....	....	....
Other transport, passenger	3 215 ..	....	....	....	....	....	....	....	....
Other transport, freight	3 216 ..	....	....	....	....	....	....	....	....
Other transport, other	3 217 ..	....	....	....	....	....	....	....	....
Travel, credit	2 236 ..	**572.9**	**630.1**	**740.5**	**720.0**	**864.2**	**919.8**	**1,047.7**	**1,105.1**
Business travel	2 237 ..	....	....	....	....	....	....	....	....
Personal travel	2 240 ..	....	....	....	....	....	....	....	....
Travel, debit	3 236 ..	**−223.5**	**−249.9**	**−379.9**	**−371.8**	**−386.8**	**−413.8**	**−455.3**	**−478.7**
Business travel	3 237 ..	....	....	....	....	....	....	....	....
Personal travel	3 240 ..	....	....	....	....	....	....	....	....
Other services, credit	2 200 BA ..	**79.2**	**64.4**	**82.8**	**53.6**	**1,171.8**	**1,445.5**	**1,537.2**	**1,669.9**
Communications	2 245 ..	....	....	....	....	632.4	637.5	634.3	666.5
Construction	2 249 ..	....	....	....	....	....	....	....	....
Insurance	2 253 ..	....	....	....	....	394.9	655.1	732.7	819.1
Financial	2 260 ..	....	....	....	....	....	....	....	....
Computer and information	2 262 ..	....	....	....	....	....	....	....	....
Royalties and licence fees	2 266 ..	....	....	....	....	....	....	....	....
Other business services	2 268 ..	79.2	64.4	82.8	53.6	144.4	152.9	170.2	184.3
Personal, cultural, and recreational	2 287 ..	....	....	....	....	....	....	....	....
Government, n.i.e.	2 291 ..	....	....	....	....	....	....	....	....
Other services, debit	3 200 BA ..	**−99.5**	**−94.2**	**−94.9**	**−92.0**	**−304.0**	**−372.2**	**−460.7**	**−523.8**
Communications	3 245 ..	....	....	....	....	−5.3	−11.2	−16.2	−23.7
Construction	3 249 ..	....	....	....	....	....	....	....	....
Insurance	3 253 ..	−25.8	−27.7	−33.4	−35.9	−177.3	−234.1	−305.6	−352.0
Financial	3 260 ..	....	....	....	....	....	....	....	....
Computer and information	3 262 ..	....	....	....	....	....	....	....	....
Royalties and licence fees	3 266 ..	....	....	....	....	....	....	....	....
Other business services	3 268 ..	−73.7	−66.5	−61.5	−56.1	−121.4	−126.9	−138.8	−148.1
Personal, cultural, and recreational	3 287 ..	....	....	....	....	....	....	....	....
Government, n.i.e.	3 291 ..	....	....	....	....	....	....	....	....

Table 2 (Continued). STANDARD PRESENTATION, 2000–2007

(Millions of U.S. dollars)

	Code	2000	2001	2002	2003	2004	2005	2006	2007
C. INCOME	4 300 ..	**−223.6**	**−321.6**	**−524.9**	**−493.0**	**−574.8**	**−412.4**	**−384.9**	**−298.7**
Total credit	2 300 ..	*6,327.9*	*3,794.4*	*1,678.9*	*1,266.6*	*2,544.3*	*5,015.8*	*7,633.7*	*10,373.6*
Total debit	3 300 ..	*−6,551.5*	*−4,115.9*	*−2,203.8*	*−1,759.6*	*−3,119.1*	*−5,428.1*	*−8,018.6*	*−10,672.3*
Compensation of employees, credit	2 310 ..	....	....	....	....	....	....	....	....
Compensation of employees, debit	3 310 ..	....	....	....	....	....	....	....	....
Investment income, credit	2 320 ..	**6,327.9**	**3,794.4**	**1,678.9**	**1,266.6**	**2,544.3**	**5,015.8**	**7,633.7**	**10,373.6**
Direct investment income	2 330 ..	208.9	208.8	234.7	257.5	346.5	470.8	607.0	724.6
Dividends and distributed branch profits	2 332 ..	83.5	83.5	93.9	103.0	138.6	188.3	242.8	289.9
Reinvested earnings and undistributed branch profits	2 333 ..	125.3	125.3	140.8	154.5	207.9	282.5	364.2	434.8
Income on debt (interest)	2 334 ..	....	....	....	....	....	....	....	....
Portfolio investment income	2 339 ..	824.7	501.6	299.6	254.9	515.1	1,120.1	1,754.9	2,297.1
Income on equity	2 340 ..	114.2	74.9	53.1	47.4	73.8	191.1	296.0	401.1
Income on bonds and notes	2 350 ..	710.5	426.7	246.4	207.5	441.3	929.0	1,458.8	1,896.1
Income on money market instruments	2 360 ..	....	....	....	....	....	....	....	....
Other investment income	2 370 ..	5,294.4	3,084.0	1,144.6	754.1	1,682.7	3,424.9	5,271.8	7,351.8
Investment income, debit	3 320 ..	**−6,551.5**	**−4,115.9**	**−2,203.8**	**−1,759.6**	**−3,119.1**	**−5,428.1**	**−8,018.6**	**−10,672.3**
Direct investment income	3 330 ..	−880.9	−922.2	−934.3	−943.9	−1,006.0	−1,158.0	−1,445.7	−1,914.9
Dividends and distributed branch profits	3 332 ..	−357.1	−372.3	−377.4	−379.0	−393.1	−453.3	−640.3	−826.4
Reinvested earnings and undistributed branch profits	3 333 ..	−523.8	−549.8	−556.9	−564.9	−612.9	−704.6	−805.4	−1,088.5
Income on debt (interest)	3 334 ..	....	....	....	....	....	....	....	....
Portfolio investment income	3 339 ..	−29.3	−21.7	−14.9	−13.2	−48.9	−92.5	−164.3	−242.8
Income on equity	3 340 ..	....	....	....	....	....	....	....	....
Income on bonds and notes	3 350 ..	−29.3	−21.7	−14.9	−13.2	−48.9	−92.5	−164.3	−242.8
Income on money market instruments	3 360 ..	....	....	....	....	....	....	....	....
Other investment income	3 370 ..	−5,641.3	−3,172.1	−1,254.6	−802.5	−2,064.1	−4,177.6	−6,408.6	−8,514.6
D. CURRENT TRANSFERS	4 379 ..	**−990.3**	**−1,264.0**	**−856.8**	**−1,082.2**	**−1,119.9**	**−1,223.4**	**−1,530.8**	**−1,482.8**
Credit	2 379 ..	**22.4**	**22.9**	**14.7**	....	....	....	....	....
General government	2 380 ..	....	....	....	....	....	....	....	....
Other sectors	2 390 ..	22.4	22.9	14.7	....	....	....	....	....
Workers' remittances	2 391 ..	....	....	....	....	....	....	....	....
Other current transfers	2 392 ..	22.4	22.9	14.7	....	....	....	....	....
Debit	3 379 ..	**−1,012.7**	**−1,286.9**	**−871.5**	**−1,082.2**	**−1,119.9**	**−1,223.4**	**−1,530.8**	**−1,482.8**
General government	3 380 ..	....	....	....	....	....	....	....	....
Other sectors	3 390 ..	−1,012.7	−1,286.9	−871.5	−1,082.2	−1,119.9	−1,223.4	−1,530.8	−1,482.8
Workers' remittances	3 391 ..	−1,012.7	−1,286.9	−871.5	−1,082.2	−1,119.9	−1,223.4	−1,530.8	−1,482.8
Other current transfers	3 392 ..	....	....	....	....	....	....	....	....
CAPITAL AND FINANCIAL ACCOUNT	4 996 ..	**−179.9**	**−440.6**	**−1,167.3**	**499.4**	**−498.8**	**−1,624.1**	**−2,198.6**	**−2,916.6**
CAPITAL ACCOUNT	4 994 ..	**50.0**	**100.0**	**101.6**	**50.0**	**50.0**	**50.0**	**75.0**	**50.0**
Total credit	2 994 ..	*50.0*	*100.0*	*101.6*	*50.0*	*50.0*	*50.0*	*75.0*	*50.0*
Total debit	3 994 ..	....	....	....	....	....	....	....	....
Capital transfers, credit	2 400 ..	**50.0**	**100.0**	**101.6**	**50.0**	**50.0**	**50.0**	**75.0**	**50.0**
General government	2 401 ..	50.0	100.0	101.6	50.0	50.0	50.0	75.0	50.0
Debt forgiveness	2 402 ..	....	....	....	....	....	....	....	....
Other capital transfers	2 410 ..	50.0	100.0	101.6	50.0	50.0	50.0	75.0	50.0
Other sectors	2 430 ..	....	....	....	....	....	....	....	....
Migrants' transfers	2 431 ..	....	....	....	....	....	....	....	....
Debt forgiveness	2 432 ..	....	....	....	....	....	....	....	....
Other capital transfers	2 440 ..	....	....	....	....	....	....	....	....
Capital transfers, debit	3 400 ..	....	....	....	....	....	....	....	....
General government	3 401 ..	....	....	....	....	....	....	....	....
Debt forgiveness	3 402 ..	....	....	....	....	....	....	....	....
Other capital transfers	3 410 ..	....	....	....	....	....	....	....	....
Other sectors	3 430 ..	....	....	....	....	....	....	....	....
Migrants' transfers	3 431 ..	....	....	....	....	....	....	....	....
Debt forgiveness	3 432 ..	....	....	....	....	....	....	....	....
Other capital transfers	3 440 ..	....	....	....	....	....	....	....	....
Nonproduced nonfinancial assets, credit	2 480 ..	....	....	....	....	....	....	....	....
Nonproduced nonfinancial assets, debit	3 480 ..	....	....	....	....	....	....	....	....

Table 2 (Continued). STANDARD PRESENTATION, 2000–2007

(Millions of U.S. dollars)

	Code	2000	2001	2002	2003	2004	2005	2006	2007
FINANCIAL ACCOUNT	4 995 ..	−229.9	−540.6	−1,268.9	449.4	−548.8	−1,674.1	−2,273.6	−2,966.6
A. DIRECT INVESTMENT	4 500 ..	354.0	−135.6	27.0	−224.7	−170.3	−86.8	1,934.9	86.9
Direct investment abroad	4 505 ..	−9.6	−216.0	−190.0	−741.4	−1,035.6	−1,135.4	−980.1	−1,669.1
Equity capital	4 510 ..	115.8	−90.7	−49.2	−586.8	−827.7	−852.9	−615.8	−1,234.4
Claims on affiliated enterprises	4 515 ..	115.8	−90.7	−49.2	−586.8	−827.7	−852.9	−615.8	−1,234.4
Liabilities to affiliated enterprises	4 520 ..	....	....	....	....	....	....	....	....
Reinvested earnings	4 525 ..	−125.3	−125.3	−140.8	−154.5	−207.9	−282.5	−364.2	−434.8
Other capital	4 530 ..	....	....	....	....	....	....	....	....
Claims on affiliated enterprises	4 535 ..	....	....	....	....	....	....	....	....
Liabilities to affiliated enterprises	4 540 ..	....	....	....	....	....	....	....	....
Direct investment in Bahrain	4 555 ..	363.6	80.4	217.0	516.7	865.3	1,048.6	2,914.9	1,756.0
Equity capital	4 560 ..	−160.2	−469.5	−339.9	−48.2	252.4	344.0	2,109.5	667.5
Claims on direct investors	4 565 ..	....	....	....	....	....	....	....	....
Liabilities to direct investors	4 570 ..	−160.2	−469.5	−339.9	−48.2	252.4	344.0	2,109.5	667.5
Reinvested earnings	4 575 ..	523.8	549.8	556.9	564.9	612.9	704.6	805.4	1,088.5
Other capital	4 580 ..	....	....	....	....	....	....	....	....
Claims on direct investors	4 585 ..	....	....	....	....	....	....	....	....
Liabilities to direct investors	4 590 ..	....	....	....	....	....	....	....	....
B. PORTFOLIO INVESTMENT	4 600 ..	194.2	−1,478.7	−4,224.8	−2,407.3	−3,504.9	−4,614.3	−8,831.2	−8,559.9
Assets	4 602 ..	−88.3	−1,448.0	−5,140.0	−3,095.7	−3,892.6	−7,036.2	−10,527.4	−9,890.1
Equity securities	4 610 ..	−161.1	−389.0	−1,143.5	−489.0	−1,999.0	−2,219.7	−2,200.7	−3,368.1
Monetary authorities	4 611 ..	....	....	....	....	....	....	....	....
General government	4 612 ..	....	....	....	....	....	....	....	....
Banks	4 613 ..	−150.4	−299.9	−469.6	−301.8	−1,668.6	−1,103.7	−1,342.0	−2,183.6
Other sectors	4 614 ..	−10.6	−89.1	−673.9	−187.2	−330.4	−1,116.0	−858.6	−1,184.5
Debt securities	4 619 ..	72.8	−1,059.0	−3,996.5	−2,606.7	−1,893.6	−4,816.5	−8,326.7	−6,522.0
Bonds and notes	4 620 ..	72.8	−1,059.0	−3,996.5	−2,606.7	−1,893.6	−4,816.5	−8,326.7	−6,522.0
Monetary authorities	4 621 ..	....	....	....	....	....	....	....	....
General government	4 622 ..	....	....	....	....	....	....	....	....
Banks	4 623 ..	66.7	−1,036.2	−3,859.4	−2,559.9	−1,812.3	−4,538.8	−8,113.1	−6,226.9
Other sectors	4 624 ..	6.1	−22.8	−137.1	−46.8	−81.3	−277.7	−213.6	−295.1
Money market instruments	4 630 ..	....	....	....	....	....	....	....	....
Monetary authorities	4 631 ..	....	....	....	....	....	....	....	....
General government	4 632 ..	....	....	....	....	....	....	....	....
Banks	4 633 ..	....	....	....	....	....	....	....	....
Other sectors	4 634 ..	....	....	....	....	....	....	....	....
Liabilities	4 652 ..	282.5	−30.7	915.2	688.4	387.7	2,421.9	1,696.1	1,330.2
Equity securities	4 660 ..	....	1.2	366.0	238.5	20.9	1,801.1	133.8	138.8
Banks	4 663 ..	....	....	....	....	....	....	....	....
Other sectors	4 664 ..	....	1.2	366.0	238.5	20.9	1,801.1	133.8	138.8
Debt securities	4 669 ..	282.5	−31.9	549.2	449.9	366.8	620.8	1,562.3	1,191.5
Bonds and notes	4 670 ..	282.5	−31.9	549.2	449.9	366.8	620.8	1,562.3	1,191.5
Monetary authorities	4 671 ..	....	....	....	....	....	....	....	....
General government	4 672 ..	....	....	....	500.0	....	....	....	....
Banks	4 673 ..	282.5	−31.9	549.2	−50.1	366.8	620.8	1,562.3	1,191.5
Other sectors	4 674 ..	....	....	....	....	....	....	....	....
Money market instruments	4 680 ..	....	....	....	....	....	....	....	....
Monetary authorities	4 681 ..	....	....	....	....	....	....	....	....
General government	4 682 ..	....	....	....	....	....	....	....	....
Banks	4 683 ..	....	....	....	....	....	....	....	....
Other sectors	4 684 ..	....	....	....	....	....	....	....	....
C. FINANCIAL DERIVATIVES	4 910 ..	....	....	....	....	....	....	....	....
Monetary authorities	4 911 ..	....	....	....	....	....	....	....	....
General government	4 912 ..	....	....	....	....	....	....	....	....
Banks	4 913 ..	....	....	....	....	....	....	....	....
Other sectors	4 914 ..	....	....	....	....	....	....	....	....
Assets	4 900 ..	....	....	....	....	....	....	....	....
Monetary authorities	4 901 ..	....	....	....	....	....	....	....	....
General government	4 902 ..	....	....	....	....	....	....	....	....
Banks	4 903 ..	....	....	....	....	....	....	....	....
Other sectors	4 904 ..	....	....	....	....	....	....	....	....
Liabilities	4 905 ..	....	....	....	....	....	....	....	....
Monetary authorities	4 906 ..	....	....	....	....	....	....	....	....
General government	4 907 ..	....	....	....	....	....	....	....	....
Banks	4 908 ..	....	....	....	....	....	....	....	....
Other sectors	4 909 ..	....	....	....	....	....	....	....	....

Table 2 (Concluded). STANDARD PRESENTATION, 2000–2007

(Millions of U.S. dollars)

	Code	2000	2001	2002	2003	2004	2005	2006	2007
D. OTHER INVESTMENT	4 700	−578.0	1,197.1	2,963.7	3,125.0	3,284.4	3,321.2	5,444.7	6,921.0
Assets	4 703	−3,833.9	5,623.2	33,425.4	−20,786.6	−9,779.9	−11,562.4	−30,234.9	−38,504.7
Trade credits	4 706	....	....	....	....	....	....	....	....
General government	4 707	....	....	....	....	....	....	....	....
of which: Short-term	4 709	....	....	....	....	....	....	....	....
Other sectors	4 710	....	....	....	....	....	....	....	....
of which: Short-term	4 712	....	....	....	....	....	....	....	....
Loans	4 714	−1,258.1	1,954.2	−290.6	−2,854.0	−3,798.1	−8,409.7	−15,644.6	−24,544.4
Monetary authorities	4 715	....	....	....	....	....	....	....	....
of which: Short-term	4 718	....	....	....	....	....	....	....	....
General government	4 719	....	....	....	....	....	....	....	....
of which: Short-term	4 721	....	....	....	....	....	....	....	....
Banks	4 722	−1,258.1	1,954.2	−290.6	−2,854.0	−3,798.1	−8,409.7	−15,644.6	−24,544.4
of which: Short-term	4 724	....	....	....	....	....	....	....	....
Other sectors	4 725	....	....	....	....	....	....	....	....
of which: Short-term	4 727	....	....	....	....	....	....	....	....
Currency and deposits	4 730	−2,569.9	3,674.9	33,717.8	−17,923.7	−5,979.1	−3,152.5	−14,582.0	−13,952.9
Monetary authorities	4 731	....	....	....	....	....	....	....	....
General government	4 732	....	....	....	....	....	....	....	....
Banks	4 733	−2,569.9	3,674.9	33,717.8	−17,923.7	−5,979.1	−3,152.5	−14,582.0	−13,952.9
Other sectors	4 734	....	....	....	....	....	....	....	....
Other assets	4 736	−5.9	−6.0	−1.8	−8.8	−2.7	−.3	−8.2	−7.4
Monetary authorities	4 737	....	....	....	....	....	....	....	....
of which: Short-term	4 739	....	....	....	....	....	....	....	....
General government	4 740	−5.9	−6.9	−7.2	−10.4	−5.1	−4.5	−11.4	−10.6
of which: Short-term	4 742	....	....	....	....	....	....	....	....
Banks	4 743	....	....	....	....	....	....	....	....
of which: Short-term	4 745	....	....	....	....	....	....	....	....
Other sectors	4 746	....	1.0	5.3	1.6	2.3	4.3	3.2	3.2
of which: Short-term	4 748	....	....	....	....	....	....	....	....
Liabilities	4 753	3,255.8	−4,426.0	−30,461.7	23,911.6	13,064.3	14,883.6	35,679.6	45,425.8
Trade credits	4 756	....	....	.8	1.0	3.1	−11.3	−5.6	−7.7
General government	4 757	....	....	....	....	....	....	....	....
of which: Short-term	4 759	....	....	....	....	....	....	....	....
Other sectors	4 760	....	....	.8	1.0	3.1	−11.3	−5.6	−7.7
of which: Short-term	4 762	....	....	....	....	....	....	....	....
Loans	4 764	6.6	−136.7	−726.1	117.4	57.2	97.9	80.9	109.8
Monetary authorities	4 765	....	....	....	....	....	....	....	....
of which: Use of Fund credit and loans from the Fund	4 766	....	....	....	....	....	....	....	....
of which: Short-term	4 768	....	....	....	....	....	....	....	....
General government	4 769	59.1	34.6	102.7	168.5	24.7	39.7	22.7	46.3
of which: Short-term	4 771	....	....	....	....	....	....	....	....
Banks	4 772	....	....	....	....	....	....	....	....
of which: Short-term	4 774	....	....	....	....	....	....	....	....
Other sectors	4 775	−52.4	−171.2	−828.8	−51.1	32.4	58.2	58.2	63.6
of which: Short-term	4 777	....	....	....	....	....	....	....	....
Currency and deposits	4 780	3,249.2	−4,289.7	−29,734.7	23,793.4	13,004.7	14,797.4	35,612.7	45,332.2
Monetary authorities	4 781	....	....	....	....	....	....	....	....
General government	4 782	....	....	....	....	....	....	....	....
Banks	4 783	3,249.2	−4,289.7	−29,734.7	23,793.4	13,004.7	14,797.4	35,612.7	45,332.2
Other sectors	4 784	....	....	....	....	....	....	....	....
Other liabilities	4 786	....	.4	−1.6	−.3	−.6	−.5	−8.5	−8.5
Monetary authorities	4 787	....	....	....	....	....	....	....	....
of which: Short-term	4 789	....	....	....	....	....	....	....	....
General government	4 790	....	....	....	....	....	....	....	....
of which: Short-term	4 792	....	....	....	....	....	....	....	....
Banks	4 793	....	....	....	....	....	....	....	....
of which: Short-term	4 795	....	....	....	....	....	....	....	....
Other sectors	4 796	....	.4	−1.6	−.3	−.6	−.5	−8.5	−8.5
of which: Short-term	4 798	....	....	....	....	....	....	....	....
E. RESERVE ASSETS	4 802	−200.1	−123.5	−34.8	−43.7	−157.9	−294.2	−822.0	−1,414.7
Monetary gold	4 812	....	....	....	....	....	....	....	....
Special drawing rights	4 811	−1.4	.2	.1	.1	.1	−1.6	−3.1	−4.1
Reserve position in the Fund	4 810	−3.3	−3.0	−1.9	−1.5	−1.7	−.5	....	....
Foreign exchange	4 803	−194.9	−121.5	−33.0	−42.3	−156.4	−292.0	−818.9	−1,410.6
Other claims	4 813	−.5	.8	....	....	....	....	....	....
NET ERRORS AND OMISSIONS	4 998	−650.3	214.7	1,216.9	−699.8	27.2	149.9	11.1	10.1

Table 3. INTERNATIONAL INVESTMENT POSITION (End-period stocks), 2000–2007

(Millions of U.S. dollars)

	Code	2000	2001	2002	2003	2004	2005	2006	2007
ASSETS	8 995 C.	97,291.7	93,445.9	65,134.5	89,800.2	104,666.0	124,680.7	167,262.9	218,712.8
Direct investment abroad	8 505 ..	1,752.1	1,968.1	2,158.1	2,899.5	3,935.1	5,070.5	6,050.5	7,719.7
Equity capital and reinvested earnings	8 506 ..	1,752.1	1,968.1	2,158.1	2,899.5	3,935.1	5,070.5	6,050.5	7,719.7
Claims on affiliated enterprises	8 507 ..	1,752.1	1,968.1	2,158.1	2,899.5	3,935.1	5,070.5	6,050.5	7,719.7
Liabilities to affiliated enterprises	8 508 ..	....	....	....	....	....	....	....	....
Other capital	8 530 ..	....	....	....	....	....	....	....	....
Claims on affiliated enterprises	8 535 ..	....	....	....	....	....	....	....	....
Liabilities to affiliated enterprises	8 540 ..	....	....	....	....	....	....	....	....
Portfolio investment	8 602 ..	12,719.2	14,167.2	19,307.2	22,402.9	26,295.5	33,331.7	43,883.0	53,749.1
Equity securities	8 610 ..	1,840.2	2,229.2	3,372.7	3,861.7	5,860.7	8,080.4	10,281.1	13,649.2
Monetary authorities	8 611 ..								
General government	8 612 ..	....	....	....	....	....	....	....	....
Banks	8 613 ..	1,290.0	1,589.9	2,059.5	2,361.3	4,029.9	5,133.6	6,475.6	8,659.2
Other sectors	8 614 ..	550.2	639.3	1,313.2	1,500.4	1,830.8	2,946.9	3,805.5	4,990.0
Debt securities	8 619 ..	10,879.0	11,938.0	15,934.5	18,541.2	20,434.8	25,251.2	33,601.9	40,099.9
Bonds and notes	8 620 ..	10,879.0	11,938.0	15,934.5	18,541.2	20,434.8	25,251.2	33,601.9	40,099.9
Monetary authorities	8 621 ..	....	....	....	....	....	....	....	....
General government	8 622 ..	....	....	....	....	....	....	....	....
Banks	8 623 ..	10,741.4	11,777.6	15,637.0	18,196.9	20,009.2	24,548.0	32,685.1	38,888.0
Other sectors	8 624 ..	137.6	160.4	297.5	344.3	425.5	703.2	916.8	1,211.9
Money market instruments	8 630 ..	....	....	....	....	....	....	....	....
Monetary authorities	8 631 ..	....	....	....	....	....	....	....	....
General government	8 632 ..	....	....	....	....	....	....	....	....
Banks	8 633 ..	....	....	....	....	....	....	....	....
Other sectors	8 634 ..	....	....	....	....	....	....	....	....
Financial derivatives	8 900 ..	....	....	....	....	....	....	....	....
Monetary authorities	8 901 ..	....	....	....	....	....	....	....	....
General government	8 902 ..	....	....	....	....	....	....	....	....
Banks	8 903 ..	....	....	....	....	....	....	....	....
Other sectors	8 904 ..	....	....	....	....	....	....	....	....
Other investment	8 703 ..	81,245.7	75,615.6	42,183.1	62,959.2	72,734.1	84,291.9	114,515.3	153,009.4
Trade credits	8 706 ..	....	....	....	....	....	....	....	....
General government	8 707 ..	....	....	....	....	....	....	....	....
of which: Short-term	8 709 ..	....	....	....	....	....	....	....	....
Other sectors	8 710 ..	....	....	....	....	....	....	....	....
of which: Short-term	8 712 ..	....	....	....	....	....	....	....	....
Loans	8 714 ..	17,134.2	15,180.0	15,470.5	18,324.5	22,122.6	30,532.3	46,176.9	70,721.2
Monetary authorities	8 715 ..	....	....	....	....	....	....	....	....
of which: Short-term	8 718 ..	....	....	....	....	....	....	....	....
General government	8 719 ..	....	....	....	....	....	....	....	....
of which: Short-term	8 721 ..	....	....	....	....	....	....	....	....
Banks	8 722 ..	17,134.2	15,180.0	15,470.5	18,324.5	22,122.6	30,532.3	46,176.9	70,721.2
of which: Short-term	8 724 ..	....	....	....	....	....	....	....	....
Other sectors	8 725 ..	....	....	....	....	....	....	....	....
of which: Short-term	8 727 ..	....	....	....	....	....	....	....	....
Currency and deposits	8 730 ..	64,085.9	60,411.0	26,693.2	44,616.9	50,596.0	53,748.5	68,330.5	82,283.3
Monetary authorities	8 731 ..	....	....	....	....	....	....	....	....
General government	8 732 ..	....	....	....	....	....	....	....	....
Banks	8 733 ..	64,085.9	60,411.0	26,693.2	44,616.9	50,596.0	53,748.5	68,330.5	82,283.3
Other sectors	8 734 ..	....	....	....	....	....	....	....	....
Other assets	8 736 ..	25.7	24.7	19.4	17.8	15.4	11.2	8.0	4.8
Monetary authorities	8 737 ..	....	....	....	....	....	....	....	....
of which: Short-term	8 739 ..	....	....	....	....	....	....	....	....
General government	8 740 ..	....	....	....	....	....	....	....	....
of which: Short-term	8 742 ..	....	....	....	....	....	....	....	....
Banks	8 743 ..	....	....	....	....	....	....	....	....
of which: Short-term	8 745 ..	....	....	....	....	....	....	....	....
Other sectors	8 746 ..	25.7	24.7	19.4	17.8	15.4	11.2	8.0	4.8
of which: Short-term	8 748 ..	....	....	....	....	....	....	....	....
Reserve assets	8 802 ..	1,574.7	1,695.1	1,486.1	1,538.6	1,701.4	1,986.6	2,814.1	4,234.6
Monetary gold	8 812 ..	6.6	6.6	6.6	6.6	6.6	6.6	6.6	6.6
Special drawing rights	8 811 ..	1.3	1.1	1.1	1.0	.9	2.4	5.7	10.2
Reserve position in the Fund	8 810 ..	84.5	84.4	93.3	103.6	110.0	101.8	107.1	112.5
Foreign exchange	8 803 ..	1,230.6	1,352.1	1,385.1	1,427.4	1,583.8	1,875.8	2,694.7	4,105.3
Other claims	8 813 ..	251.6	250.8	....	....	....	....	....	....

Table 3 (Concluded). INTERNATIONAL INVESTMENT POSITION (End-period stocks), 2000–2007

(Millions of U.S. dollars)

	Code	2000	2001	2002	2003	2004	2005	2006	2007
LIABILITIES...........................	8 995 D.	**92,136.4**	**87,929.8**	**59,426.0**	**84,599.9**	**98,670.6**	**116,845.5**	**157,067.8**	**205,545.3**
Direct investment in Bahrain...........	8 555 ..	**5,905.8**	**5,986.1**	**6,203.1**	**6,719.8**	**7,354.0**	**8,276.1**	**11,190.7**	**12,947.0**
Equity capital and reinvested earnings...........	8 556 ..	5,905.8	5,986.1	6,203.1	6,719.8	7,354.0	8,276.1	11,190.7	12,947.0
Claims on direct investors..................	8 557 ..	....	....	....	....	....	....	....	....
Liabilities to direct investors..............	8 558 ..	5,905.8	5,986.1	6,203.1	6,719.8	7,354.0	8,276.1	11,190.7	12,947.0
Other capital........................	8 580 ..	....	....	....	....	....	....	....	....
Claims on direct investors..................	8 585 ..	....	....	....	....	....	....	....	....
Liabilities to direct investors..............	8 590 ..	....	....	....	....	....	....	....	....
Portfolio investment........................	8 652 ..	**615.9**	**585.3**	**1,500.5**	**2,188.9**	**2,576.6**	**4,998.4**	**6,694.6**	**8,024.8**
Equity securities........................	8 660 ..	25.8	27.1	393.0	631.5	652.4	2,453.5	2,587.3	2,726.1
Banks..............................	8 663 ..	....	....	....	....	....	....	....	....
Other sectors........................	8 664 ..	25.8	27.1	393.0	631.5	652.4	2,453.5	2,587.3	2,726.1
Debt securities........................	8 669 ..	590.1	558.2	1,107.4	1,557.4	1,924.2	2,545.0	4,107.3	5,298.7
Bonds and notes......................	8 670 ..	590.1	558.2	1,107.4	1,557.4	1,924.2	2,545.0	4,107.3	5,298.7
Monetary authorities...	8 671 ..	....	....	....	....	....	....	....	....
General government..................	8 672 ..	....	....	....	500.0	500.0	500.0	500.0	500.0
Banks..........................	8 673 ..	590.1	558.2	1,107.4	1,057.4	1,424.2	2,045.0	3,607.3	4,798.7
Other sectors......................	8 674 ..	....	....	....	....	....	....	....	....
Money market instruments..............	8 680 ..	....	....	....	....	....	....	....	....
Monetary authorities..................	8 681 ..	....	....	....	....	....	....	....	....
General government..................	8 682 ..	....	....	....	....	....	....	....	....
Banks..........................	8 683 ..	....	....	....	....	....	....	....	....
Other sectors......................	8 684 ..	....	....	....	....	....	....	....	....
Financial derivatives......................	8 905 ..	....	....	....	....	....	....	....	....
Monetary authorities......................	8 906 ..	....	....	....	....	....	....	....	....
General government......................	8 907 ..	....	....	....	....	....	....	....	....
Banks..............................	8 908 ..	....	....	....	....	....	....	....	....
Other sectors........................	8 909 ..	....	....	....	....	....	....	....	....
Other investment........................	8 753 ..	**85,614.7**	**81,358.4**	**51,722.4**	**75,691.2**	**88,740.0**	**103,570.9**	**139,182.5**	**184,573.4**
Trade credits........................	8 756 ..	3.6	3.6	4.3	5.4	8.5	−2.7	−8.2	.5
General government..................	8 757 ..	....	....	....	....	....	....	....	....
of which: Short-term..................	8 759 ..	....	....	....	....	....	....	....	....
Other sectors........................	8 760 ..	3.6	3.6	4.3	5.4	8.5	−2.7	−8.2	.5
of which: Short-term..................	8 762 ..	....	....	....	....	....	....	....	....
Loans..............................	8 764 ..	345.8	378.8	478.3	653.0	694.7	739.9	752.4	811.5
Monetary authorities..................	8 765 ..	....	....	....	....	....	....	....	....
of which: Use of Fund credit and loans from the Fund....	8 766 ..	....	....	....	....	....	....	....	....
of which: Short-term..................	8 768 ..	....	....	....	....	....	....	....	....
General government..................	8 769 ..	345.8	378.8	478.3	653.0	694.7	739.9	752.4	811.5
of which: Short-term..................	8 771 ..	....	....	....	....	....	....	....	....
Banks..........................	8 772 ..	....	....	....	....	....	....	....	....
of which: Short-term..................	8 774 ..	....	....	....	....	....	....	....	....
Other sectors......................	8 775 ..	....	....	....	....	....	....	....	....
of which: Short-term..................	8 777 ..	....	....	....	....	....	....	....	....
Currency and deposits..................	8 780 ..	85,256.0	80,966.3	51,231.6	75,025.0	88,029.6	102,827.0	138,440.2	183,771.8
Monetary authorities..................	8 781 ..	....	....	....	....	....	....	....	....
General government..................	8 782 ..	....	....	....	....	....	....	....	....
Banks..........................	8 783 ..	85,256.0	80,966.3	51,231.6	75,025.0	88,029.6	102,827.0	138,440.2	183,771.8
Other sectors......................	8 784 ..	....	....	....	....	....	....	....	....
Other liabilities......................	8 786 ..	9.4	9.7	8.1	7.8	7.2	6.6	−1.9	−10.4
Monetary authorities..................	8 787 ..	....	....	....	....	....	....	....	....
of which: Short-term..................	8 789 ..	....	....	....	....	....	....	....	....
General government..................	8 790 ..	....	....	....	....	....	....	....	....
of which: Short-term..................	8 792 ..	....	....	....	....	....	....	....	....
Banks..........................	8 793 ..	....	....	....	....	....	....	....	....
of which: Short-term..................	8 795 ..	....	....	....	....	....	....	....	....
Other sectors......................	8 796 ..	9.4	9.7	8.1	7.8	7.2	6.6	−1.9	−10.4
of which: Short-term..	8 798 ..	....	....	....	....	....	....	....	....
NET INTERNATIONAL INVESTMENT POSITION........	8 995 ..	**5,155.2**	**5,516.2**	**5,708.5**	**5,200.3**	**5,995.4**	**7,835.2**	**10,195.1**	**13,167.5**
Conversion rates: Bahrain dinar per U.S. dollar (end of period)...........	0 102 ..	.3760	.3760	.3760	.3760	.3760	.3760	.3760	.3760

Table 1. ANALYTIC PRESENTATION, 2000–2007

(Millions of U.S. dollars)

	Code	2000	2001	2002	2003	2004	2005	2006	2007
A. Current Account[1]	4 993 Z.	**−305.8**	**−535.4**	**739.3**	**131.6**	**−278.7**	**−176.2**	**1,196.1**	**856.9**
Goods: exports f.o.b.	2 100 ..	6,399.2	6,084.7	6,102.4	7,050.1	8,150.7	9,302.5	11,553.7	12,474.3
Goods: imports f.o.b.	3 100 ..	−8,052.9	−8,133.4	−7,780.1	−9,492.0	−11,157.1	−12,501.6	−14,443.4	−16,669.2
Balance on Goods	4 100 ..	*−1,653.7*	*−2,048.7*	*−1,677.8*	*−2,441.9*	*−3,006.5*	*−3,199.1*	*−2,889.7*	*−4,194.9*
Services: credit	2 200 ..	815.1	752.2	848.7	1,011.7	1,083.0	1,249.0	1,333.8	1,616.8
Services: debit	3 200 ..	−1,620.2	−1,521.5	−1,405.7	−1,711.5	−1,931.4	−2,206.7	−2,340.5	−2,884.0
Balance on Goods and Services	4 991 ..	*−2,458.9*	*−2,818.0*	*−2,234.8*	*−3,141.7*	*−3,854.9*	*−4,156.8*	*−3,896.3*	*−5,462.0*
Income: credit	2 300 ..	78.4	76.6	56.8	56.5	102.6	116.6	177.4	244.1
Income: debit	3 300 ..	−344.8	−361.9	−322.0	−361.3	−473.9	−910.2	−1,018.1	−1,212.0
Balance on Goods, Services, and Income	4 992 ..	*−2,725.3*	*−3,103.3*	*−2,500.1*	*−3,446.4*	*−4,226.2*	*−4,950.4*	*−4,737.0*	*−6,430.0*
Current transfers: credit	2 379 Z.	2,426.5	2,572.8	3,245.4	3,586.2	3,960.4	4,785.0	5,941.3	7,296.6
Current transfers: debit	3 379 ..	−7.0	−4.9	−6.0	−8.2	−12.9	−10.8	−8.2	−9.8
B. Capital Account[1]	4 994 Z.	**248.7**	**235.4**	**363.7**	**386.7**	**142.1**	**261.7**	**152.5**	**700.7**
Capital account: credit	2 994 Z.	248.7	235.4	363.7	386.7	142.1	261.7	152.5	700.7
Capital account: debit	3 994 ..	....	....	....	....	....	....	....	....
Total, Groups A Plus B	4 981 ..	*−57.1*	*−300.0*	*1,102.9*	*518.4*	*−136.6*	*85.5*	*1,348.6*	*1,557.5*
C. Financial Account[1]	4 995 W.	**−256.0**	**262.1**	**−256.2**	**289.0**	**665.0**	**142.4**	**120.2**	**735.1**
Direct investment abroad	4 505 ..	....	....	−2.7	−2.8	−4.1	−1.9	....	....
Direct investment in Bangladesh	4 555 Z.	280.4	78.5	52.3	268.3	448.9	813.3	697.2	652.8
Portfolio investment assets	4 602 ..	....	.1	−1.2	....	....	−.1	−2.6	−12.9
Equity securities	4 610 ..	....	−.2	−1.2	....	....	−.1	−2.6	−12.9
Debt securities	4 619 ..	....	.3	....	....	....	....	....	....
Portfolio investment liabilities	4 652 Z.	1.3	−3.5	−1.4	1.6	4.3	19.5	30.8	153.9
Equity securities	4 660 ..	1.2	−3.5	−1.4	1.6	4.3	19.5	30.8	153.4
Debt securities	4 669 Z.	.1	....	....	....	....	....	....	.5
Financial derivatives	4 910 ..	....	....	....	....	....	....	....	....
Financial derivatives assets	4 900 ..	....	....	....	....	....	....	....	....
Financial derivatives liabilities	4 905 ..	....	....	....	....	....	....	....	....
Other investment assets	4 703 ..	−1,246.8	−433.8	−560.4	−693.6	−495.1	−865.3	−1,352.8	−952.8
Monetary authorities	4 701 ..	....	....	....	....	....	....	....	....
General government	4 704 ..	....	....	....	....	....	....	....	....
Banks	4 705 ..	−315.7	151.7	143.7	136.2	−7.9	−61.8	−90.6	−14.6
Other sectors	4 728 ..	−931.0	−585.5	−704.0	−829.8	−487.2	−803.5	−1,262.2	−938.2
Other investment liabilities	4 753 W.	709.1	620.7	257.1	715.5	711.0	176.8	747.6	894.1
Monetary authorities	4 753 WA	35.2	132.7	−99.9	37.9	55.1	−50.6	58.9	122.2
General government	4 753 ZB	537.9	413.7	138.2	728.2	664.9	73.0	602.4	828.6
Banks	4 753 ZC	105.7	29.0	58.4	−188.4	−35.4	96.5	72.3	−79.8
Other sectors	4 753 ZD	30.4	45.3	160.4	137.9	26.4	57.9	14.0	23.1
Total, Groups A Through C	4 983 ..	*−313.1*	*−38.0*	*846.7*	*807.4*	*528.5*	*227.9*	*1,468.8*	*2,292.7*
D. Net Errors and Omissions	4 998 ..	**282.4**	**−106.0**	**−349.3**	**81.1**	**−25.0**	**−643.9**	**−603.5**	**−919.9**
Total, Groups A Through D	4 984 ..	*−30.7*	*−143.9*	*497.4*	*888.5*	*503.4*	*−416.1*	*865.3*	*1,372.8*
E. Reserves and Related Items	4 802 A.	**30.7**	**143.9**	**−497.4**	**−888.5**	**−503.4**	**416.1**	**−865.3**	**−1,372.8**
Reserve assets	4 802 ..	121.0	207.9	−411.8	−886.3	−649.8	318.6	−1,012.0	−1,372.8
Use of Fund credit and loans	4 766 ..	−90.3	−64.0	−85.6	−2.2	146.3	97.5	146.7	....
Exceptional financing	4 920 ..	....	....	....	....	....	....	....	....
Conversion rates: taka per U.S. dollar	0 101 ..	**52.142**	**55.807**	**57.888**	**58.150**	**59.513**	**64.327**	**68.933**	**68.875**

[1] Excludes components that have been classified in the categories of Group E.

Table 2. STANDARD PRESENTATION, 2000–2007

(Millions of U.S. dollars)

	Code	2000	2001	2002	2003	2004	2005	2006	2007
CURRENT ACCOUNT........................	4 993 ..	**−305.8**	**−535.4**	**739.3**	**131.6**	**−278.7**	**−176.2**	**1,196.1**	**856.9**
A. GOODS............................	4 100 ..	**−1,653.7**	**−2,048.7**	**−1,677.8**	**−2,441.9**	**−3,006.5**	**−3,199.1**	**−2,889.7**	**−4,194.9**
Credit............................	2 100 ..	**6,399.2**	**6,084.7**	**6,102.4**	**7,050.1**	**8,150.7**	**9,302.5**	**11,553.7**	**12,474.3**
General merchandise: exports f.o.b............	2 110 ..	6,392.7	6,078.7	5,981.0	6,804.2	7,966.5	9,038.8	11,200.9	12,098.1
Goods for processing: exports f.o.b...........	2 150 ..	....	....	112.3	234.5	171.7	246.7	317.9	332.6
Repairs on goods.............................	2 160 ..	.7	1.1	1.1	1.3	1.2	1.3	2.0	4.3
Goods procured in ports by carriers..........	2 170 ..	5.7	5.0	8.0	10.1	11.3	15.7	32.9	39.2
Nonmonetary gold.............................	2 180 ..	....	....	....	....	....	....	....	....
Debit............................	3 100 ..	**−8,052.9**	**−8,133.4**	**−7,780.1**	**−9,492.0**	**−11,157.1**	**−12,501.6**	**−14,443.4**	**−16,669.2**
General merchandise: imports f.o.b............	3 110 ..	−8,023.0	−8,109.3	−7,706.3	−9,340.7	−11,013.8	−12,345.9	−14,242.8	−16,469.4
Goods for processing: imports f.o.b...........	3 150 ..	....	....	−64.2	−133.5	−115.8	−131.3	−143.0	−184.0
Repairs on goods.............................	3 160 ..	−27.5	−16.7	−6.5	−5.5	−20.1	−26.5	−54.7	−15.4
Goods procured in ports by carriers..........	3 170 ..	−2.4	−7.5	−3.1	−12.2	−7.5	2.2	−2.9	−.4
Nonmonetary gold.............................	3 180 ..	....	....	....	....	....	....	....	....
B. SERVICES............................	4 200 ..	**−805.1**	**−769.3**	**−557.1**	**−699.8**	**−848.4**	**−957.7**	**−1,006.6**	**−1,267.1**
Total credit............................	2 200 ..	*815.1*	*752.2*	*848.7*	*1,011.7*	*1,083.0*	*1,249.0*	*1,333.8*	*1,616.8*
Total debit............................	3 200 ..	*−1,620.2*	*−1,521.5*	*−1,405.7*	*−1,711.5*	*−1,931.4*	*−2,206.7*	*−2,340.5*	*−2,884.0*
Transportation services, credit............	2 205 ..	**91.4**	**72.1**	**91.6**	**71.9**	**77.4**	**113.0**	**88.7**	**80.0**
Passenger............................	2 850 ..	....	....	*1.6*	*1.7*	*8.6*	*8.5*	*.2*	....
Freight............................	2 851 ..	*10.0*	*2.0*	*13.3*	*7.9*	*10.5*	*24.5*	*18.9*	*16.1*
Other............................	2 852 ..	*81.4*	*70.1*	*76.7*	*62.3*	*58.3*	*80.0*	*69.6*	*63.8*
Sea transport, passenger.....................	2 207 ..	....	....	....	....	....	....	....	....
Sea transport, freight.......................	2 208 ..	5.5	1.5	7.3	3.3	9.2	24.5	18.9	16.1
Sea transport, other.........................	2 209 ..	61.9	59.7	57.6	54.1	55.7	77.0	65.5	61.9
Air transport, passenger.....................	2 211 ..	....	....	1.6	1.7	8.6	8.5	.2	....
Air transport, freight.......................	2 212 ..	4.5	.5	6.1	4.6	1.3	....	....	.1
Air transport, other.........................	2 213 ..	19.1	10.4	19.1	8.2	2.7	3.0	4.0	1.9
Other transport, passenger...................	2 215 ..	....	....	....	....	....	....	....	....
Other transport, freight.....................	2 216 ..	....	....	....	....	....	....	....	....
Other transport, other.......................	2 217 ..	.3	....	....	....	....	....	....	....
Transportation services, debit.............	3 205 ..	**−1,012.8**	**−1,032.1**	**−1,006.3**	**−1,203.5**	**−1,418.2**	**−1,544.7**	**−1,607.5**	**−2,102.3**
Passenger............................	3 850 ..	*−181.3*	*−175.9*	*−196.4*	*−223.9*	*−281.3*	*−239.4*	*−303.5*	*−374.2*
Freight............................	3 851 ..	*−822.7*	*−833.7*	*−781.9*	*−949.3*	*−1,127.6*	*−1,304.9*	*−1,303.9*	*−1,727.7*
Other............................	3 852 ..	*−8.7*	*−22.5*	*−28.0*	*−30.3*	*−9.2*	*−.4*	*−.1*	*−.5*
Sea transport, passenger.....................	3 207 ..	....	....	....	....	....	....	....	....
Sea transport, freight.......................	3 208 ..	−822.7	−833.7	−781.4	−949.3	−1,127.5	−1,286.9	−1,276.1	−1,697.6
Sea transport, other.........................	3 209 ..	−3.3	−1.3	−4.0	−2.8	−1.0	−.4	−.1	−.1
Air transport, passenger.....................	3 211 ..	−181.3	−175.9	−196.4	−223.9	−281.3	−239.4	−303.5	−374.2
Air transport, freight.......................	3 212 ..	−.1	....	−.5	....	−.2	−18.0	−27.8	−30.1
Air transport, other.........................	3 213 ..	−5.4	−21.2	−24.0	−27.5	−8.2	....	....	−.4
Other transport, passenger...................	3 215 ..	....	....	....	....	....	....	....	....
Other transport, freight.....................	3 216 ..	....	....	....	....	....	....	....	....
Other transport, other.......................	3 217 ..	....	....	....	....	....	....	....	....
Travel, credit............................	2 236 ..	**50.4**	**47.6**	**57.2**	**56.9**	**66.9**	**70.0**	**80.3**	**76.4**
Business travel..............................	2 237 ..	2.6	1.5	1.5	.9	1.5	2.1	1.8	1.8
Personal travel..............................	2 240 ..	47.8	46.1	55.7	56.0	65.4	67.9	78.6	74.6
Travel, debit............................	3 236 ..	**−289.9**	**−165.4**	**−113.0**	**−164.9**	**−160.7**	**−136.3**	**−139.6**	**−155.8**
Business travel..............................	3 237 ..	−33.0	−29.9	−25.2	−26.0	−29.2	−24.3	−25.8	−24.4
Personal travel..............................	3 240 ..	−256.9	−135.5	−87.8	−138.9	−131.6	−112.0	−113.8	−131.3
Other services, credit.....................	2 200 BA	**673.3**	**632.5**	**699.9**	**882.9**	**938.7**	**1,066.0**	**1,164.8**	**1,460.5**
Communications..............................	2 245 ..	21.5	10.8	36.2	71.5	55.7	23.9	62.4	76.5
Construction................................	2 249 ..	.2	....	.3	2.8	2.4	14.2	22.4	29.9
Insurance...................................	2 253 ..	3.5	1.7	3.9	3.8	3.9	5.0	8.0	10.6
Financial...................................	2 260 ..	13.1	9.9	11.4	28.5	15.1	18.0	26.2	20.6
Computer and information....................	2 262 ..	3.2	2.5	3.1	5.1	10.2	18.7	31.2	16.0
Royalties and licence fees..................	2 266 ..	.1	.1	.1	.3	.1	.3	.3	....
Other business services.....................	2 268 ..	99.3	98.0	101.5	152.9	187.9	210.0	280.5	374.2
Personal, cultural, and recreational........	2 287 ..	.5	.4	.2	4.0	.5	1.1	2.6	1.2
Government, n.i.e............................	2 291 ..	531.9	509.0	543.2	614.0	662.8	774.8	731.3	931.4
Other services, debit......................	3 200 BA	**−317.5**	**−324.1**	**−286.5**	**−343.1**	**−352.5**	**−525.7**	**−593.3**	**−625.9**
Communications..............................	3 245 ..	−7.4	−5.6	−6.8	−9.7	−12.2	−20.6	−11.9	−23.9
Construction................................	3 249 ..	−2.1	−3.2	−7.8	−7.4	−.7	−1.1	−1.4	−.3
Insurance...................................	3 253 ..	−91.1	−97.6	−93.2	−114.3	−135.1	−150.6	−175.0	−201.9
Financial...................................	3 260 ..	−30.8	−16.0	−10.2	−7.7	−8.8	−13.3	−20.3	−21.7
Computer and information....................	3 262 ..	−1.5	−1.2	−.8	−1.0	−1.5	−4.3	−2.6	−3.9
Royalties and licence fees..................	3 266 ..	−4.4	−5.5	−3.1	−3.7	−5.1	−2.7	−5.2	−7.7
Other business services.....................	3 268 ..	−83.3	−96.7	−76.1	−82.6	−92.7	−137.7	−147.4	−155.7
Personal, cultural, and recreational........	3 287 ..	−.1	....	−.7	−.2	−.1	....	−.4	−.2
Government, n.i.e............................	3 291 ..	−96.9	−98.2	−87.8	−116.5	−96.1	−195.3	−229.1	−210.5

Table 2 (Continued). STANDARD PRESENTATION, 2000–2007

(Millions of U.S. dollars)

	Code	2000	2001	2002	2003	2004	2005	2006	2007
C. INCOME	4 300	**−266.5**	**−285.3**	**−265.2**	**−304.8**	**−371.3**	**−793.6**	**−840.7**	**−967.9**
Total credit	2 300	*78.4*	*76.6*	*56.8*	*56.5*	*102.6*	*116.6*	*177.4*	*244.1*
Total debit	3 300	*−344.8*	*−361.9*	*−322.0*	*−361.3*	*−473.9*	*−910.2*	*−1,018.1*	*−1,212.0*
Compensation of employees, credit	2 310	**9.4**	**10.4**	**10.4**	**11.7**	**11.6**	**12.1**	**9.9**	**9.2**
Compensation of employees, debit	3 310	**−1.8**	**−1.8**	**−2.9**	**−2.9**	**−3.1**	**−2.9**	**−1.5**	**−.8**
Investment income, credit	2 320	**68.9**	**66.2**	**46.4**	**44.8**	**90.9**	**104.5**	**167.6**	**234.9**
Direct investment income	2 330	1.8	1.8	1.4	2.7	3.0	2.1	10.7	12.2
Dividends and distributed branch profits	2 332	1.8	1.8	1.4	1.7	1.0	2.1	10.7	12.2
Reinvested earnings and undistributed branch profits	2 333	....	....	....	1.1	2.0	....	....	....
Income on debt (interest)	2 334	....	....	....	....	....	....	....	....
Portfolio investment income	2 339	....	....	....	....	.1	....	....	.3
Income on equity	2 340	....	....	....	....	.1	....	....	.3
Income on bonds and notes	2 350	....	....	....	....	....	....	....	....
Income on money market instruments	2 360	....	....	....	....	....	....	....	....
Other investment income	2 370	67.1	64.4	45.0	42.1	87.9	102.4	156.9	222.3
Investment income, debit	3 320	**−343.0**	**−360.1**	**−319.1**	**−358.4**	**−470.8**	**−907.3**	**−1,016.6**	**−1,211.2**
Direct investment income	3 330	−149.0	−175.2	−128.7	−177.7	−246.7	−661.4	−764.9	−903.3
Dividends and distributed branch profits	3 332	−149.0	−175.2	−128.1	−95.2	−77.7	−418.6	−460.6	−697.8
Reinvested earnings and undistributed branch profits	3 333	....	....	....	−82.5	−168.2	−242.8	−304.2	−205.5
Income on debt (interest)	3 334	....	....	−.6	....	−.7	....	....	....
Portfolio investment income	3 339	−.8	−.8	−.6	−.1	−.9	−.7	−1.0	−1.1
Income on equity	3 340	−.8	−.8	−.6	−.1	−.9	−.7	−1.0	−1.1
Income on bonds and notes	3 350	....	....	....	....	....	....	....	....
Income on money market instruments	3 360	....	....	....	....	....	....	....	....
Other investment income	3 370	−193.3	−184.0	−189.8	−180.7	−223.3	−245.3	−250.7	−306.8
D. CURRENT TRANSFERS	4 379	**2,419.5**	**2,567.9**	**3,239.3**	**3,578.1**	**3,947.5**	**4,774.2**	**5,933.1**	**7,286.8**
Credit	2 379	**2,426.5**	**2,572.8**	**3,245.4**	**3,586.2**	**3,960.4**	**4,785.0**	**5,941.3**	**7,296.6**
General government	2 380	212.0	243.1	134.9	69.5	23.7	37.8	11.6	167.6
Other sectors	2 390	2,214.5	2,329.6	3,110.5	3,516.7	3,936.7	4,747.1	5,929.6	7,129.0
Workers' remittances	2 391	1,958.1	2,094.1	2,847.7	3,180.0	3,572.2	4,302.4	5,417.7	6,553.1
Other current transfers	2 392	256.4	235.5	262.8	336.7	364.5	444.7	512.0	575.9
Debit	3 379	**−7.0**	**−4.9**	**−6.0**	**−8.2**	**−12.9**	**−10.8**	**−8.2**	**−9.8**
General government	3 380	−.7	−.5	−.6	−.6	−1.0	−1.0	−.8	−1.6
Other sectors	3 390	−6.2	−4.4	−5.5	−7.6	−11.9	−9.8	−7.4	−8.2
Workers' remittances	3 391	−2.6	−1.9	−2.8	−4.2	−4.7	−2.6	−1.8	−2.1
Other current transfers	3 392	−3.7	−2.5	−2.7	−3.4	−7.3	−7.2	−5.6	−6.1
CAPITAL AND FINANCIAL ACCOUNT	4 996	**23.5**	**641.4**	**−389.9**	**−212.8**	**303.7**	**820.2**	**−592.5**	**63.0**
CAPITAL ACCOUNT	4 994	**248.7**	**235.4**	**363.7**	**386.7**	**142.1**	**261.7**	**152.5**	**700.7**
Total credit	2 994	*248.7*	*235.4*	*363.7*	*386.7*	*142.1*	*261.7*	*152.5*	*700.7*
Total debit	3 994	....	....	....	....	....	....	....	....
Capital transfers, credit	2 400	**248.7**	**235.4**	**363.7**	**386.7**	**142.1**	**261.7**	**152.5**	**700.7**
General government	2 401	248.6	235.4	363.7	386.7	142.1	261.7	152.5	700.7
Debt forgiveness	2 402	....	....	99.1	86.0	....	....	....	....
Other capital transfers	2 410	248.6	235.4	264.5	300.7	142.1	261.7	152.5	700.7
Other sectors	2 430	.1	....	....	....	....	....	....	....
Migrants' transfers	2 431	....	....	....	....	....	....	....	....
Debt forgiveness	2 432	....	....	....	....	....	....	....	....
Other capital transfers	2 440	.1	....	....	....	....	....	....	....
Capital transfers, debit	3 400	....	....	....	....	....	....	....	....
General government	3 401	....	....	....	....	....	....	....	....
Debt forgiveness	3 402	....	....	....	....	....	....	....	....
Other capital transfers	3 410	....	....	....	....	....	....	....	....
Other sectors	3 430	....	....	....	....	....	....	....	....
Migrants' transfers	3 431	....	....	....	....	....	....	....	....
Debt forgiveness	3 432	....	....	....	....	....	....	....	....
Other capital transfers	3 440	....	....	....	....	....	....	....	....
Nonproduced nonfinancial assets, credit	2 480	....	....	....	....	....	....	....	....
Nonproduced nonfinancial assets, debit	3 480	....	....	....	....	....	....	....	....

Table 2 (Continued). STANDARD PRESENTATION, 2000–2007

(Millions of U.S. dollars)

	Code	2000	2001	2002	2003	2004	2005	2006	2007
FINANCIAL ACCOUNT	4 995 ..	**−225.2**	**406.0**	**−753.6**	**−599.5**	**161.6**	**558.4**	**−745.1**	**−637.7**
A. DIRECT INVESTMENT	4 500 ..	**280.4**	**78.5**	**49.7**	**265.5**	**444.8**	**811.4**	**697.2**	**652.8**
Direct investment abroad	4 505 ..	....	....	−2.7	−2.8	−4.1	−1.9	....	....
Equity capital	4 510 ..	....	....	−2.7	−1.7	−2.1	−1.9	....	....
Claims on affiliated enterprises	4 515 ..	....	....	−2.6	−1.7	−2.1	....	....	....
Liabilities to affiliated enterprises	4 520 ..	....	....	....	....	....	....	....	....
Reinvested earnings	4 525 ..	....	....	....	−1.1	−2.0	....	....	....
Other capital	4 530 ..	....	....	....	....	....	....	....	....
Claims on affiliated enterprises	4 535 ..	....	....	....	....	....	....	....	....
Liabilities to affiliated enterprises	4 540 ..	....	....	....	....	....	....	....	....
Direct investment in Bangladesh	4 555 ..	**280.4**	**78.5**	**52.3**	**268.3**	**448.9**	**813.3**	**697.2**	**652.8**
Equity capital	4 560 ..	278.9	77.5	45.8	138.4	183.9	417.8	361.2	347.8
Claims on direct investors	4 565 ..	....	....	....	....	....	....	....	....
Liabilities to direct investors	4 570 ..	278.9	77.5	45.8	138.4	183.9	417.8	361.2	347.8
Reinvested earnings	4 575 ..	....	....	....	82.5	168.2	242.8	304.2	205.5
Other capital	4 580 ..	1.5	1.1	6.6	47.4	96.7	152.8	31.8	99.5
Claims on direct investors	4 585 ..	....	....	....	....	....	....	....	....
Liabilities to direct investors	4 590 ..	1.5	1.1	6.6	47.4	96.7	152.8	31.8	99.5
B. PORTFOLIO INVESTMENT	4 600 ..	**1.3**	**−3.4**	**−2.6**	**1.6**	**4.3**	**19.4**	**28.2**	**141.0**
Assets	4 602 ..	....	.1	−1.2	....	....	−.1	−2.6	−12.9
Equity securities	4 610 ..	....	−.2	−1.2	....	....	−.1	−2.6	−12.9
Monetary authorities	4 611 ..	....	....	....	....	....	....	....	....
General government	4 612 ..	....	....	....	....	....	....	....	....
Banks	4 613 ..	....	....	....	....	....	....	....	....
Other sectors	4 614 ..	....	−.2	....	....	....	−.1	−2.6	−12.9
Debt securities	4 619 ..	....	.3	....	....	....	....	....	....
Bonds and notes	4 620 ..	....	....	....	....	....	....	....	....
Monetary authorities	4 621 ..	....	....	....	....	....	....	....	....
General government	4 622 ..	....	....	....	....	....	....	....	....
Banks	4 623 ..	....	....	....	....	....	....	....	....
Other sectors	4 624 ..	....	....	....	....	....	....	....	....
Money market instruments	4 630 ..	....	....	....	....	....	....	....	....
Monetary authorities	4 631 ..	....	....	....	....	....	....	....	....
General government	4 632 ..	....	....	....	....	....	....	....	....
Banks	4 633 ..	....	....	....	....	....	....	....	....
Other sectors	4 634 ..	....	....	....	....	....	....	....	....
Liabilities	4 652 ..	**1.3**	**−3.5**	**−1.4**	**1.6**	**4.3**	**19.5**	**30.8**	**153.9**
Equity securities	4 660 ..	1.2	−3.5	−1.4	1.6	4.3	19.5	30.8	153.4
Banks	4 663 ..	....	....	....	....	....	....	3.6	29.9
Other sectors	4 664 ..	1.2	−3.5	−1.4	1.6	4.3	19.5	27.2	123.4
Debt securities	4 669 ..	.1	....	....	....	....	....	....	.5
Bonds and notes	4 670 ..	.1	....	....	....	....	....	....	.5
Monetary authorities	4 671 ..	....	....	....	....	....	....	....	....
General government	4 672 ..	....	....	....	....	....	....	....	....
Banks	4 673 ..	.1	....	....	....	....	....	....	....
Other sectors	4 674 ..	....	....	....	....	....	....	....	.5
Money market instruments	4 680 ..	....	....	....	....	....	....	....	....
Monetary authorities	4 681 ..	....	....	....	....	....	....	....	....
General government	4 682 ..	....	....	....	....	....	....	....	....
Banks	4 683 ..	....	....	....	....	....	....	....	....
Other sectors	4 684 ..	....	....	....	....	....	....	....	....
C. FINANCIAL DERIVATIVES	4 910 ..	....	....	....	....	....	....	....	....
Monetary authorities	4 911 ..	....	....	....	....	....	....	....	....
General government	4 912 ..	....	....	....	....	....	....	....	....
Banks	4 913 ..	....	....	....	....	....	....	....	....
Other sectors	4 914 ..	....	....	....	....	....	....	....	....
Assets	4 900 ..	....	....	....	....	....	....	....	....
Monetary authorities	4 901 ..	....	....	....	....	....	....	....	....
General government	4 902 ..	....	....	....	....	....	....	....	....
Banks	4 903 ..	....	....	....	....	....	....	....	....
Other sectors	4 904 ..	....	....	....	....	....	....	....	....
Liabilities	4 905 ..	....	....	....	....	....	....	....	....
Monetary authorities	4 906 ..	....	....	....	....	....	....	....	....
General government	4 907 ..	....	....	....	....	....	....	....	....
Banks	4 908 ..	....	....	....	....	....	....	....	....
Other sectors	4 909 ..	....	....	....	....	....	....	....	....

Table 2 (Concluded). STANDARD PRESENTATION, 2000–2007

(Millions of U.S. dollars)

	Code	2000	2001	2002	2003	2004	2005	2006	2007
D. OTHER INVESTMENT	4 700 ..	−627.9	122.9	−388.9	19.7	362.2	−590.9	−458.5	−58.7
Assets	4 703 ..	−1,246.8	−433.8	−560.4	−693.6	−495.1	−865.3	−1,352.8	−952.8
Trade credits	4 706 ..	−935.7	−585.9	−657.3	−713.5	−310.1	−621.3	−842.4	−392.9
General government	4 707 ..	....	....	....	....	....	....	....	....
of which: Short-term	4 709 ..	....	....	....	....	....	....	....	....
Other sectors	4 710 ..	−935.7	−585.9	−657.3	−713.5	−310.1	−621.3	−842.4	−392.9
of which: Short-term	4 712 ..	−935.7	−585.9	−657.3	−713.5	−310.1	−621.3	−842.4	−413.2
Loans	4 714 ..	−27.1	31.0	−13.9	....	....	....	....	....
Monetary authorities	4 715 ..	....	....	....	....	....	....	....	....
of which: Short-term	4 718 ..	....	....	....	....	....	....	....	....
General government	4 719 ..	....	....	....	....	....	....	....	....
of which: Short-term	4 721 ..	....	....	....	....	....	....	....	....
Banks	4 722 ..	−31.8	30.6	−13.9	....	....	....	....	....
of which: Short-term	4 724 ..	−31.8	30.6	−13.9	....	....	....	....	....
Other sectors	4 725 ..	4.7	.4	....	....	....	....	....	....
of which: Short-term	4 727 ..	....	.3	....	....	....	....	....	....
Currency and deposits	4 730 ..	−284.0	121.2	157.6	136.2	−7.9	−61.8	−90.6	−14.6
Monetary authorities	4 731 ..	....	....	....	....	....	....	....	....
General government	4 732 ..	....	....	....	....	....	....	....	....
Banks	4 733 ..	−284.0	121.2	157.6	136.2	−7.9	−61.8	−90.6	−14.6
Other sectors	4 734 ..	....	....	....	....	....	....	....	....
Other assets	4 736 ..	....	....	−46.7	−116.3	−177.0	−182.1	−419.8	−545.3
Monetary authorities	4 737 ..	....	....	....	....	....	....	....	....
of which: Short-term	4 739 ..	....	....	....	....	....	....	....	....
General government	4 740 ..	....	....	....	....	....	....	....	....
of which: Short-term	4 742 ..	....	....	....	....	....	....	....	....
Banks	4 743 ..	....	....	....	....	....	....	....	....
of which: Short-term	4 745 ..	....	....	....	....	....	....	....	....
Other sectors	4 746 ..	....	....	−46.7	−116.3	−177.0	−182.1	−419.8	−545.3
of which: Short-term	4 748 ..	....	....	−41.6	−95.1	−123.0	−157.4	−123.7	−429.6
Liabilities	4 753 ..	618.9	556.7	171.5	713.3	857.4	274.4	894.3	894.1
Trade credits	4 756 ..	....	....	140.3	147.4	63.7	78.7	18.8	....
General government	4 757 ..	....	....	....	....	....	....	....	....
of which: Short-term	4 759 ..	....	....	....	....	....	....	....	....
Other sectors	4 760 ..	....	....	140.3	147.4	63.7	78.7	18.8	....
of which: Short-term	4 762 ..	....	....	140.3	147.4	63.7	78.7	18.8	....
Loans	4 764 ..	477.4	320.8	155.7	722.6	777.6	157.1	748.3	814.6
Monetary authorities	4 765 ..	−90.3	−64.0	−85.6	−2.2	146.3	97.5	146.7	....
of which: Use of Fund credit and loans from the Fund	4 766 ..	−90.3	−64.0	−85.6	−2.2	146.3	97.5	146.7	....
of which: Short-term	4 768 ..	....	....	....	....	....	....	....	....
General government	4 769 ..	537.9	413.7	138.2	728.2	664.9	73.0	602.4	828.6
of which: Short-term	4 771 ..	....	....	−127.9	222.1	173.9	−209.8	296.7	188.6
Banks	4 772 ..	−.6	−74.3	83.0	6.1	3.7	7.4	3.9	−37.1
of which: Short-term	4 774 ..	−.2	−73.6	86.6	....	....	....	....	−34.1
Other sectors	4 775 ..	30.4	45.3	20.0	−9.5	−37.3	−20.9	−4.7	23.1
of which: Short-term	4 777 ..	15.9	46.9	33.8	....	....	....	....	....
Currency and deposits	4 780 ..	104.4	103.2	−24.7	−195.7	−39.1	89.1	68.4	−42.8
Monetary authorities	4 781 ..	−2.0	....	....	−1.2	....	....	....	....
General government	4 782 ..	....	....	....	....	....	....	....	....
Banks	4 783 ..	106.3	103.2	−24.6	−194.5	−39.1	89.1	68.4	−42.8
Other sectors	4 784 ..	....	....	....	....	....	....	....	....
Other liabilities	4 786 ..	37.1	132.7	−99.9	39.1	55.1	−50.6	58.9	122.2
Monetary authorities	4 787 ..	37.1	132.7	−99.9	39.1	55.1	−50.6	58.9	122.2
of which: Short-term	4 789 ..	37.1	132.7	−99.9	39.1	55.1	−50.6	58.9	122.2
General government	4 790 ..	....	....	....	....	....	....	....	....
of which: Short-term	4 792 ..	....	....	....	....	....	....	....	....
Banks	4 793 ..	....	....	....	....	....	....	....	....
of which: Short-term	4 795 ..	....	....	....	....	....	....	....	....
Other sectors	4 796 ..	....	....	....	....	....	....	....	....
of which: Short-term	4 798 ..	....	....	....	....	....	....	....	....
E. RESERVE ASSETS	4 802 ..	121.0	207.9	−411.8	−886.3	−649.8	318.6	−1,012.0	−1,372.8
Monetary gold	4 812 ..	1.8	−1.3	−2.8	....	....	....	....	....
Special drawing rights	4 811 ..	−.3	−1.1	−.6	−.6	2.0	.2	−.4	.6
Reserve position in the Fund	4 810 ..	....	....	....	....	....	....	....	....
Foreign exchange	4 803 ..	119.5	210.3	−408.5	−885.7	−651.8	318.3	−1,011.6	−1,373.3
Other claims	4 813 ..	....	....	....	....	....	....	....	....
NET ERRORS AND OMISSIONS	4 998 ..	282.4	−106.0	−349.3	81.1	−25.0	−643.9	−603.5	−919.9

Table 3. INTERNATIONAL INVESTMENT POSITION (End-period stocks), 2000–2007

(Millions of U.S. dollars)

	Code	2000	2001	2002	2003	2004	2005	2006	2007
ASSETS	8 995 C.	**2,783.6**	**2,082.8**	**2,693.8**	**3,452.1**	**4,100.7**	**3,779.6**	**5,026.8**	**6,390.0**
Direct investment abroad	8 505 ..	**68.3**	**85.3**	**88.3**	**95.5**	**94.7**	**93.9**	**97.2**	**105.7**
Equity capital and reinvested earnings	8 506 ..	32.2	51.4	55.7	63.4	61.3	60.2	62.3	67.8
Claims on affiliated enterprises	8 507 ..	32.2	51.4	55.7	63.4	61.3	60.2	62.3	67.8
Liabilities to affiliated enterprises	8 508 ..	....	....	....	....	....	....	....	....
Other capital	8 530 ..	36.0	33.9	32.6	32.1	33.4	33.6	34.8	37.9
Claims on affiliated enterprises	8 535 ..	36.0	33.9	32.6	32.1	33.4	33.6	34.8	37.9
Liabilities to affiliated enterprises	8 540 ..	....	....	....	....	....	....	....	....
Portfolio investment	8 602 ..	**.6**	**.7**	**26.0**	**28.3**	**26.9**	**25.3**	**26.6**	**27.3**
Equity securities	8 610 ..	.6	.7	26.0	28.3	26.9	25.3	26.6	27.3
Monetary authorities	8 611 ..	....	....	....	....	....	....	....	....
General government	8 612 ..	....	....	....	....	....	....	....	....
Banks	8 613 ..	....	....	25.0	27.3	26.5	25.1	26.4	27.1
Other sectors	8 614 ..	.6	.7	1.0	1.0	.4	.2	.2	.2
Debt securities	8 619 ..	....	....	....	....	....	....	....	....
Bonds and notes	8 620 ..	....	....	....	....	....	....	....	....
Monetary authorities	8 621 ..	....	....	....	....	....	....	....	....
General government	8 622 ..	....	....	....	....	....	....	....	....
Banks	8 623 ..	....	....	....	....	....	....	....	....
Other sectors	8 624 ..	....	....	....	....	....	....	....	....
Money market instruments	8 630 ..	....	....	....	....	....	....	....	....
Monetary authorities	8 631 ..	....	....	....	....	....	....	....	....
General government	8 632 ..	....	....	....	....	....	....	....	....
Banks	8 633 ..	....	....	....	....	....	....	....	....
Other sectors	8 634 ..	....	....	....	....	....	....	....	....
Financial derivatives	8 900 ..	**....**	**....**	**....**	**....**	**....**	**....**	**....**	**....**
Monetary authorities	8 901 ..	....	....	....	....	....	....	....	....
General government	8 902 ..	....	....	....	....	....	....	....	....
Banks	8 903 ..	....	....	....	....	....	....	....	....
Other sectors	8 904 ..	....	....	....	....	....	....	....	....
Other investment	8 703 ..	**1,203.4**	**691.1**	**896.2**	**750.5**	**806.6**	**893.1**	**1,097.5**	**1,073.6**
Trade credits	8 706 ..	....	....	....	....	....	....	....	....
General government	8 707 ..	....	....	....	....	....	....	....	....
of which: Short-term	8 709 ..	....	....	....	....	....	....	....	....
Other sectors	8 710 ..	....	....	....	....	....	....	....	....
of which: Short-term	8 712 ..	....	....	....	....	....	....	....	....
Loans	8 714 ..	....	....	347.8	389.4	436.3	457.3	573.6	534.5
Monetary authorities	8 715 ..	....	....	....	....	....	....	....	....
of which: Short-term	8 718 ..	....	....	....	....	....	....	....	....
General government	8 719 ..	....	....	....	....	....	....	....	....
of which: Short-term	8 721 ..	....	....	....	....	....	....	....	....
Banks	8 722 ..	....	....	347.8	389.4	436.3	457.3	573.6	534.5
of which: Short-term	8 724 ..	....	....	*347.8*	*389.4*	*436.3*	*457.3*	*573.6*	*534.5*
Other sectors	8 725 ..	....	....	....	....	....	....	....	....
of which: Short-term	8 727 ..	....	....	....	....	....	....	....	....
Currency and deposits	8 730 ..	1,203.4	691.1	543.4	356.1	364.5	429.8	517.9	532.0
Monetary authorities	8 731 ..	....	....	....	....	....	....	....	....
General government	8 732 ..	....	....	....	....	....	....	....	....
Banks	8 733 ..	1,203.4	691.1	543.4	356.1	364.5	429.8	517.9	532.0
Other sectors	8 734 ..	....	....	....	....	....	....	....	....
Other assets	8 736 ..	....	....	5.0	5.0	5.9	6.1	6.1	7.0
Monetary authorities	8 737 ..	....	....	5.0	5.0	5.9	6.1	6.1	7.0
of which: Short-term	8 739 ..	....	....	....	....	....	....	....	....
General government	8 740 ..	....	....	....	....	....	....	....	....
of which: Short-term	8 742 ..	....	....	....	....	....	....	....	....
Banks	8 743 ..	....	....	....	....	....	....	....	....
of which: Short-term	8 745 ..	....	....	....	....	....	....	....	....
Other sectors	8 746 ..	....	....	....	....	....	....	....	....
of which: Short-term	8 748 ..	....	....	....	....	....	....	....	....
Reserve assets	8 802 ..	**1,511.4**	**1,305.7**	**1,683.2**	**2,577.8**	**3,172.4**	**2,767.2**	**3,805.6**	**5,183.4**
Monetary gold	8 812 ..	29.6	30.6	....	....	....	....	....	....
Special drawing rights	8 811 ..	.4	1.2	2.2	3.2	1.2	.9	1.3	.8
Reserve position in the Fund	8 810 ..	.2	.2	.3	.3	.3	.3	.4	.4
Foreign exchange	8 803 ..	1,481.1	1,273.6	1,680.7	2,574.3	3,170.8	2,766.0	3,803.9	5,182.2
Other claims	8 813 ..	....	....	....	....	....	....	....	....

Table 3 (Concluded). INTERNATIONAL INVESTMENT POSITION (End-period stocks), 2000–2007

(Millions of U.S. dollars)

	Code	2000	2001	2002	2003	2004	2005	2006	2007
LIABILITIES	8 995 D.	**18,100.8**	**17,813.1**	**20,324.9**	**21,484.3**	**22,551.5**	**23,650.9**	**25,717.7**	**27,372.6**
Direct investment in Bangladesh	8 555 ..	**2,202.0**	**2,246.3**	**2,524.5**	**2,973.1**	**2,830.1**	**3,701.8**	**4,247.7**	**4,248.5**
Equity capital and reinvested earnings	8 556 ..	1,685.9	1,820.1	2,022.8	2,465.9	2,573.0	3,181.2	3,870.6	3,971.2
Claims on direct investors	8 557 ..	....	....	....	....	....	....	....	....
Liabilities to direct investors	8 558 ..	1,685.9	1,820.1	2,022.8	2,465.9	2,573.0	3,181.2	3,870.6	3,971.2
Other capital	8 580 ..	516.1	426.2	501.7	507.2	257.2	520.6	377.1	277.3
Claims on direct investors	8 585 ..	−76.5	−68.2	−47.6	−45.1	−41.8	−51.5	−81.7	−87.6
Liabilities to direct investors	8 590 ..	592.5	494.3	549.4	552.3	299.0	572.1	458.7	364.9
Portfolio investment	8 652 ..	**22.2**	**17.2**	**16.7**	**36.0**	**87.2**	**81.7**	**105.4**	**416.1**
Equity securities	8 660 ..	19.8	15.2	14.7	34.0	85.3	81.6	105.4	416.1
Banks	8 663 ..	....	....	.2	.4	1.6	2.3	10.4	260.6
Other sectors	8 664 ..	19.8	15.2	14.5	33.6	83.7	79.3	94.9	155.5
Debt securities	8 669 ..	2.4	2.0	2.0	2.0	1.9	....	....	....
Bonds and notes	8 670 ..	2.4	2.0	2.0	2.0	1.9	....	....	....
Monetary authorities	8 671 ..	....	....	....	....	....	....	....	....
General government	8 672 ..	....	....	....	....	....	....	....	....
Banks	8 673 ..	....	....	....	....	....	....	....	....
Other sectors	8 674 ..	2.4	2.0	2.0	2.0	1.9	....	....	....
Money market instruments	8 680 ..	....	....	....	....	....	....	....	....
Monetary authorities	8 681 ..	....	....	....	....	....	....	....	....
General government	8 682 ..	....	....	....	....	....	....	....	....
Banks	8 683 ..	....	....	....	....	....	....	....	....
Other sectors	8 684 ..	....	....	....	....	....	....	....	....
Financial derivatives	8 905 ..	....	....	....	....	....	....	....	....
Monetary authorities	8 906 ..	....	....	....	....	....	....	....	....
General government	8 907 ..	....	....	....	....	....	....	....	....
Banks	8 908 ..	....	....	....	....	....	....	....	....
Other sectors	8 909 ..	....	....	....	....	....	....	....	....
Other investment	8 753 ..	**15,876.7**	**15,549.6**	**17,783.7**	**18,475.2**	**19,634.2**	**19,867.4**	**21,364.6**	**22,708.0**
Trade credits	8 756 ..	....	....	....	....	....	....	....	....
General government	8 757 ..	....	....	....	....	....	....	....	....
of which: Short-term	8 759 ..	....	....	....	....	....	....	....	....
Other sectors	8 760 ..	....	....	....	....	....	....	....	....
of which: Short-term	8 762 ..	....	....	....	....	....	....	....	....
Loans	8 764 ..	15,307.0	15,074.7	17,269.9	17,978.0	19,116.3	19,341.7	20,674.2	21,888.1
Monetary authorities	8 765 ..	219.6	148.6	70.6	73.6	230.6	308.4	476.5	500.5
of which: Use of Fund credit and loans from the Fund	8 766 ..	*219.6*	*148.6*	*70.6*	*73.6*	*230.6*	*308.4*	*476.5*	*500.5*
of which: Short-term	8 768 ..	....	....	....	....	....	....	....	....
General government	8 769 ..	15,087.4	14,926.1	16,205.5	17,139.5	18,186.3	18,260.8	19,176.3	19,568.3
of which: Short-term	8 771 ..	....	....	....	....	....	....	....	....
Banks	8 772 ..	....	....	340.0	210.5	171.0	196.7	235.5	160.0
of which: Short-term	8 774 ..	....	....	*292.4*	*158.6*	*125.0*	*144.8*	*178.1*	*96.1*
Other sectors	8 775 ..	....	....	653.8	554.4	528.3	575.8	785.9	1,659.3
of which: Short-term	8 777 ..	....	....	....	....	....	....	....	*552.0*
Currency and deposits	8 780 ..	569.7	475.0	327.5	270.7	210.4	261.6	362.0	369.9
Monetary authorities	8 781 ..	....	....	....	....	....	....	....	....
General government	8 782 ..	....	....	....	....	....	....	....	....
Banks	8 783 ..	569.7	475.0	327.5	270.7	210.4	261.6	362.0	369.9
Other sectors	8 784 ..	....	....	....	....	....	....	....	....
Other liabilities	8 786 ..	....	....	186.3	226.6	307.5	264.1	328.4	449.9
Monetary authorities	8 787 ..	....	....	186.3	226.6	307.5	264.1	328.4	449.9
of which: Short-term	8 789 ..	....	....	*186.3*	*226.6*	*307.5*	*264.1*	*328.4*	*449.9*
General government	8 790 ..	....	....	....	....	....	....	....	....
of which: Short-term	8 792 ..	....	....	....	....	....	....	....	....
Banks	8 793 ..	....	....	....	....	....	....	....	....
of which: Short-term	8 795 ..	....	....	....	....	....	....	....	....
Other sectors	8 796 ..	....	....	....	....	....	....	....	....
of which: Short-term	8 798 ..	....	....	....	....	....	....	....	....
NET INTERNATIONAL INVESTMENT POSITION	8 995 ..	−15,317.2	−15,730.3	−17,631.2	−18,032.2	−18,450.8	−19,871.3	−20,690.9	−20,982.7
Conversion rates: taka per U.S. dollar (end of period)	0 102 ..	54.000	57.000	57.900	58.782	60.742	66.210	69.065	68.576

2008, International Monetary Fund: *Balance of Payments Statistics Yearbook*

Table 1. ANALYTIC PRESENTATION, 2000–2007

(Millions of U.S. dollars)

	Code	2000	2001	2002	2003	2004	2005	2006	2007
A. Current Account[1]................................	4 993 Z.	**−145.5**	**−111.1**	**−168.1**	**−169.7**	**−337.2**	**−386.7**	....	....
Goods: exports f.o.b................................	2 100 ..	286.4	271.2	253.0	264.2	293.1	378.6	....	....
Goods: imports f.o.b................................	3 100 ..	−1,030.3	−952.3	−955.0	−1,065.6	−1,264.1	−1,464.2	....	....
Balance on Goods..................................	4 100 ..	*−743.9*	*−681.1*	*−702.0*	*−801.4*	*−971.1*	*−1,085.6*	....	....
Services: credit......................................	2 200 ..	1,090.2	1,068.5	1,041.3	1,165.5	1,224.0	1,457.4	....	....
Services: debit......................................	3 200 ..	−487.4	−498.5	−491.4	−518.9	−555.7	−679.7	....	....
Balance on Goods and Services..........	4 991 ..	*−141.1*	*−111.1*	*−152.0*	*−154.8*	*−302.8*	*−307.9*	....	....
Income: credit......................................	2 300 ..	70.2	73.0	72.2	75.1	75.3	85.0	....	....
Income: debit.......................................	3 300 ..	−152.5	−166.4	−174.0	−182.1	−197.3	−257.0	....	....
Balance on Goods, Services, and Income........................	4 992 ..	*−223.4*	*−204.5*	*−253.8*	*−261.8*	*−424.8*	*−479.9*	....	....
Current transfers: credit.......................	2 379 Z.	108.9	125.6	120.1	126.5	125.8	160.4	....	....
Current transfers: debit........................	3 379 ..	−31.0	−32.3	−34.3	−34.5	−38.2	−67.2	....	....
B. Capital Account[1]................................	4 994 Z.	**1.8**	**1.3**	....	....	....	....	....	....
Capital account: credit.........................	2 994 Z.	1.8	1.3	....	....	....	....	....	....
Capital account: debit..........................	3 994 ..	....	....	....	....	....	....	....	....
Total, Groups A Plus B.........................	4 981 ..	*−143.7*	*−109.9*	*−168.1*	*−169.7*	*−337.2*	*−386.7*	....	....
C. Financial Account[1]............................	4 995 W.	**289.2**	**284.8**	**118.6**	**202.6**	**134.5**	**391.2**	....	....
Direct investment abroad......................	4 505 ..	−1.1	−1.1	−.5	−.5	−3.9	−9.2	....	....
Direct investment in Barbados..............	4 555 Z.	19.4	18.6	17.4	58.3	−12.1	62.0	....	....
Portfolio investment assets..................	4 602 ..	−29.2	−30.5	−24.8	−23.0	−58.5	−76.4	....	....
Equity securities...............................	4 610 ..	−14.2	−14.8	−21.2	−23.2	−44.7	−53.2	....	....
Debt securities.................................	4 619 ..	−15.0	−15.7	−3.6	.2	−13.8	−23.2	....	....
Portfolio investment liabilities..............	4 652 Z.	100.3	150.2	−8.9	84.3	−9.7	98.3	....	....
Equity securities...............................	4 660 ..	....	....	1.1	94.7	.3	−4.8	....	....
Debt securities.................................	4 669 Z.	100.3	150.2	−10.0	−10.4	−10.0	103.1	....	....
Financial derivatives...........................	4 910 ..	....	....	....	....	....	6.6	....	....
Financial derivatives assets.................	4 900 ..	....	....	....	....	....	1.6	....	....
Financial derivatives liabilities.............	4 905 ..	....	....	....	....	....	5.0	....	....
Other investment assets......................	4 703 ..	52.9	−56.7	−180.7	−82.9	30.1	−238.5	....	....
Monetary authorities.........................	4 701 ..	....	....	....	....	....	....	....	....
General government..........................	4 704 ..	−4.3	−5.4	−5.4	−4.3	−4.7	−.2	....	....
Banks..	4 705 ..	66.9	−83.1	−201.3	−87.9	−26.0	−155.1	....	....
Other sectors...................................	4 728 ..	−9.7	31.8	26.1	9.3	60.8	−83.3	....	....
Other investment liabilities..................	4 753 W.	146.9	204.4	315.9	166.5	188.6	548.5	....	....
Monetary authorities.........................	4 753 WA	....	....	....	....	....	....	....	....
General government..........................	4 753 ZB	18.6	11.5	−2.2	4.8	−23.2	−6.8	....	....
Banks..	4 753 ZC	−77.0	67.9	167.0	−41.1	49.2	247.2	....	....
Other sectors...................................	4 753 ZD	205.2	125.0	151.1	202.8	162.6	308.0	....	....
Total, Groups A Through C..................	4 983 ..	*145.5*	*175.0*	*−49.5*	*32.9*	*−202.7*	*4.5*	....	....
D. Net Errors and Omissions...................	4 998 ..	**32.1**	**47.4**	**25.1**	**34.4**	**45.4**	**17.8**	....	....
Total, Groups A Through D..................	4 984 ..	*177.6*	*222.4*	*−24.4*	*67.3*	*−157.3*	*22.3*	....	....
E. Reserves and Related Items...............	4 802 A.	**−177.6**	**−222.4**	**24.4**	**−67.3**	**157.3**	**−22.3**	....	....
Reserve assets......................................	4 802 ..	−178.1	−222.9	23.9	−67.9	156.7	−23.9	....	....
Use of Fund credit and loans...............	4 766 ..	....	....	....	....	....	....	....	....
Exceptional financing...........................	4 920 ..	.5	.6	.5	.6	.6	1.7	....	....
Conversion rates: Barbados dollars per U.S. dollar...............	0 101 ..	**2.0000**	**2.0000**	**2.0000**	**2.0000**	**2.0000**	**2.0000**	**2.0000**	**2.0000**

[1] Excludes components that have been classified in the categories of Group E.

Table 2. STANDARD PRESENTATION, 2000–2007

(Millions of U.S. dollars)

	Code	2000	2001	2002	2003	2004	2005	2006	2007
CURRENT ACCOUNT............	4 993 ..	−145.0	−110.6	−167.6	−169.1	−336.6	−385.0	....	....
A. GOODS............	4 100 ..	−743.9	−681.1	−702.0	−801.4	−971.1	−1,085.6	....	....
Credit............	2 100 ..	286.4	271.2	253.0	264.2	293.1	378.6	....	....
General merchandise: exports f.o.b............	2 110 ..	229.1	219.9	203.1	210.3	233.0	320.7	....	....
Goods for processing: exports f.o.b............	2 150 ..	11.5	9.6	9.5	12.0	14.8	17.1	....	....
Repairs on goods............	2 160 ..	.7	.4	.1	.1	....	....	....	....
Goods procured in ports by carriers............	2 170 ..	45.1	41.4	40.4	41.9	45.3	40.8	....	....
Nonmonetary gold............	2 180 ..	....	....	....	....	....	....	....	....
Debit............	3 100 ..	−1,030.3	−952.3	−955.0	−1,065.6	−1,264.1	−1,464.2	....	....
General merchandise: imports f.o.b............	3 110 ..	−1,029.7	−951.7	−954.8	−1,065.5	−1,260.1	−1,431.5	....	....
Goods for processing: imports f.o.b............	3 150 ..	....	−.1	....	....	−3.9	−32.7	....	....
Repairs on goods............	3 160 ..	....	....	−.1	....	−.1	−.1	....	....
Goods procured in ports by carriers............	3 170 ..	−.6	−.6	−.1	−.1	−.1	....	....	....
Nonmonetary gold............	3 180 ..	....	....	....	....	....	....	....	....
B. SERVICES............	4 200 ..	602.9	570.0	550.0	646.6	668.3	777.6	....	....
Total credit............	2 200 ..	*1,090.2*	*1,068.5*	*1,041.3*	*1,165.5*	*1,224.0*	*1,457.4*	....	....
Total debit............	3 200 ..	*−487.4*	*−498.5*	*−491.4*	*−518.9*	*−555.7*	*−679.7*	....	....
Transportation services, credit............	2 205 ..	24.8	22.4	21.0	23.2	35.7	25.4	....	....
Passenger............	2 850 ..	*10.5*	*9.3*	*8.3*	*8.6*	*8.5*	*7.6*	....	....
Freight............	2 851 ..	*4.6*	*4.3*	*4.0*	*4.6*	*4.8*	*5.9*	....	....
Other............	2 852 ..	*9.7*	*8.8*	*8.8*	*10.1*	*22.4*	*11.9*	....	....
Sea transport, passenger............	2 207 ..	4.6	4.3	3.5	3.6	3.8	3.4	....	....
Sea transport, freight............	2 208 ..	....	....	....	....	....	....	....	....
Sea transport, other............	2 209 ..	....	....	....	.1	1.8	3.9	....	....
Air transport, passenger............	2 211 ..	.8	.8	.8	.8	.5	.5	....	....
Air transport, freight............	2 212 ..	....	....	....	....	....	....	....	....
Air transport, other............	2 213 ..	3.5	3.2	2.8	3.0	3.1	3.5	....	....
Other transport, passenger............	2 215 ..	5.2	4.3	4.0	4.3	4.3	3.8	....	....
Other transport, freight............	2 216 ..	4.6	4.3	4.0	4.6	4.8	5.9	....	....
Other transport, other............	2 217 ..	6.2	5.7	6.0	7.0	17.6	4.6	....	....
Transportation services, debit............	3 205 ..	−163.5	−156.0	−155.3	−169.8	−197.5	−218.3	....	....
Passenger............	3 850 ..	*−46.7*	*−47.8*	*−47.0*	*−49.1*	*−55.0*	*−56.6*	....	....
Freight............	3 851 ..	*−115.6*	*−106.9*	*−107.1*	*−119.5*	*−141.3*	*−160.5*	....	....
Other............	3 852 ..	*−1.2*	*−1.3*	*−1.3*	*−1.2*	*−1.2*	*−1.3*	....	....
Sea transport, passenger............	3 207 ..	−.1	−.1	....	−.1	−.1	....	....	....
Sea transport, freight............	3 208 ..	−92.5	−85.5	−85.7	−95.6	−113.1	−128.4	....	....
Sea transport, other............	3 209 ..	−.1	−.2	....	....	....	....	....	....
Air transport, passenger............	3 211 ..	−46.7	−47.8	−47.0	−49.0	−54.9	−56.6	....	....
Air transport, freight............	3 212 ..	−23.1	−21.4	−21.4	−23.9	−28.3	−32.1	....	....
Air transport, other............	3 213 ..	−1.1	−1.2	−1.2	−.7	−.7	−.7	....	....
Other transport, passenger............	3 215 ..	....	....	....	....	....	....	....	....
Other transport, freight............	3 216 ..	....	....	....	....	....	....	....	....
Other transport, other............	3 217 ..	....	....	−.1	−.6	−.6	−.7	....	....
Travel, credit............	2 236 ..	723.0	697.2	657.9	757.8	775.5	896.8	....	....
Business travel............	2 237 ..	3.8	2.5	2.3	2.9	3.3	3.0	....	....
Personal travel............	2 240 ..	719.2	694.7	655.6	755.0	772.3	893.8	....	....
Travel, debit............	3 236 ..	−94.1	−100.9	−99.0	−104.5	−107.8	−95.7	....	....
Business travel............	3 237 ..	−32.7	−33.7	−32.0	−32.6	−32.6	−27.4	....	....
Personal travel............	3 240 ..	−61.4	−67.2	−67.0	−71.9	−75.2	−68.3	....	....
Other services, credit............	2 200 BA ..	342.5	349.0	362.4	384.5	412.8	535.3	....	....
Communications............	2 245 ..	27.8	29.4	30.9	32.2	32.3	32.5	....	....
Construction............	2 249 ..	2.8	2.9	3.1	3.6	3.8	3.6	....	....
Insurance............	2 253 ..	79.5	84.9	87.3	90.1	91.0	143.3	....	....
Financial............	2 260 ..	75.2	71.0	70.0	73.6	79.7	117.1	....	....
Computer and information............	2 262 ..	17.4	17.5	17.6	18.1	19.9	22.7	....	....
Royalties and licence fees............	2 266 ..	.3	.3	.5	.9	2.3	1.7	....	....
Other business services............	2 268 ..	104.5	106.7	114.6	123.7	141.3	167.4	....	....
Personal, cultural, and recreational............	2 287 ..	.3	.4	.5	.8	....	.3	....	....
Government, n.i.e............	2 291 ..	34.9	36.1	38.0	41.8	42.6	46.9	....	....
Other services, debit............	3 200 BA ..	−229.8	−241.7	−237.1	−244.7	−250.5	−365.7	....	....
Communications............	3 245 ..	−7.9	−9.4	−9.7	−11.2	−12.5	−11.8	....	....
Construction............	3 249 ..	−2.1	−2.2	−2.3	−3.0	−3.0	−3.4	....	....
Insurance............	3 253 ..	−109.5	−117.4	−119.1	−123.1	−121.1	−194.2	....	....
Financial............	3 260 ..	−5.1	−5.2	−5.8	−5.3	−5.5	−5.8	....	....
Computer and information............	3 262 ..	−5.2	−5.5	−5.7	−6.9	−7.3	−8.2	....	....
Royalties and licence fees............	3 266 ..	−23.7	−24.3	−24.6	−25.0	−20.0	−29.1	....	....
Other business services............	3 268 ..	−48.9	−49.9	−44.2	−43.4	−43.9	−69.3	....	....
Personal, cultural, and recreational............	3 287 ..	−.2	−.3	....	−.1	−1.4	−.2	....	....
Government, n.i.e............	3 291 ..	−27.4	−27.7	−25.8	−26.9	−36.0	−44.0	....	....

Table 2 (Continued). STANDARD PRESENTATION, 2000–2007

(Millions of U.S. dollars)

	Code	2000	2001	2002	2003	2004	2005	2006	2007
C. INCOME	4 300	**−82.3**	**−93.4**	**−101.8**	**−107.0**	**−122.0**	**−172.0**	....	....
Total credit	2 300	*70.2*	*73.0*	*72.2*	*75.1*	*75.3*	*85.0*	....	....
Total debit	3 300	*−152.5*	*−166.4*	*−174.0*	*−182.1*	*−197.3*	*−257.0*	....	....
Compensation of employees, credit	2 310	**15.8**	**16.2**	**15.9**	**16.5**	**9.3**	**9.3**	....	....
Compensation of employees, debit	3 310	**−2.2**	**−2.2**	**−2.5**	**−3.0**	**−2.5**	**−3.3**	....	....
Investment income, credit	2 320	**54.4**	**56.8**	**56.3**	**58.6**	**66.0**	**75.7**	....	....
Direct investment income	2 330	5.8	5.9	5.8	6.1	20.4	26.9	....	....
Dividends and distributed branch profits	2 332	5.1	5.3	5.1	5.4	18.2	23.3	....	....
Reinvested earnings and undistributed branch profits	2 333	.7	.6	.7	.7	1.7	3.6	....	....
Income on debt (interest)	2 334	....	....	....	....	.5	....	....	....
Portfolio investment income	2 339	48.2	50.7	50.3	52.3	45.6	48.5	....	....
Income on equity	2 340	15.7	16.7	16.6	17.8	17.8	21.1	....	....
Income on bonds and notes	2 350	32.5	34.0	33.7	34.5	27.8	27.5	....	....
Income on money market instruments	2 360	....	....	....	....	....	....	....	....
Other investment income	2 370	.5	.3	.3	.3	....	.3	....	....
Investment income, debit	3 320	**−150.3**	**−164.2**	**−171.5**	**−179.1**	**−194.8**	**−253.7**	....	....
Direct investment income	3 330	−17.0	−18.4	−18.9	−20.9	−76.1	−81.5	....	....
Dividends and distributed branch profits	3 332	−5.6	−7.9	−8.6	−9.6	−62.7	−45.0	....	....
Reinvested earnings and undistributed branch profits	3 333	−11.4	−10.5	−10.3	−11.3	−13.5	−22.3	....	....
Income on debt (interest)	3 334	....	....	....	....	....	−14.3	....	....
Portfolio investment income	3 339	−131.2	−143.7	−150.5	−156.6	−118.7	−171.9	....	....
Income on equity	3 340	−39.3	−44.3	−45.1	−46.6	−46.6	−48.5	....	....
Income on bonds and notes	3 350	−91.9	−99.4	−105.4	−110.0	−72.1	−123.5	....	....
Income on money market instruments	3 360	....	....	....	....	....	....	....	....
Other investment income	3 370	−2.2	−2.2	−2.2	−1.6	....	−.3	....	....
D. CURRENT TRANSFERS	4 379	**78.4**	**93.9**	**86.3**	**92.7**	**88.2**	**94.9**	....	....
Credit	2 379	**109.4**	**126.2**	**120.6**	**127.1**	**126.3**	**162.1**	....	....
General government	2 380	3.4	3.6	3.2	3.3	.7	6.0	....	....
Other sectors	2 390	106.0	122.6	117.4	123.8	125.6	156.1	....	....
Workers' remittances	2 391	84.2	100.2	93.3	96.9	100.0	130.7	....	....
Other current transfers	2 392	21.9	22.4	24.2	26.9	25.6	25.4	....	....
Debit	3 379	**−31.0**	**−32.3**	**−34.3**	**−34.5**	**−38.2**	**−67.2**	....	....
General government	3 380	−6.1	−6.1	−8.7	−7.9	−10.9	−8.9	....	....
Other sectors	3 390	−25.0	−26.2	−25.6	−26.6	−27.3	−58.3	....	....
Workers' remittances	3 391	−14.3	−15.4	−14.9	−15.8	−15.8	−37.0	....	....
Other current transfers	3 392	−10.7	−10.8	−10.8	−10.9	−11.5	−21.3	....	....
CAPITAL AND FINANCIAL ACCOUNT	4 996	**112.9**	**63.1**	**142.5**	**134.7**	**291.2**	**367.3**	....	....
CAPITAL ACCOUNT	4 994	**1.8**	**1.3**	....	....	....	....	....	....
Total credit	2 994	*1.8*	*1.3*	....	....	....	....	....	....
Total debit	3 994	....	....	....	....	....	....	....	....
Capital transfers, credit	2 400	**1.8**	**1.3**	....	....	....	....	....	....
General government	2 401	....	....	....	....	....	....	....	....
Debt forgiveness	2 402	....	....	....	....	....	....	....	....
Other capital transfers	2 410	....	....	....	....	....	....	....	....
Other sectors	2 430	1.8	1.3	....	....	....	....	....	....
Migrants' transfers	2 431	1.8	1.3	....	....	....	....	....	....
Debt forgiveness	2 432	....	....	....	....	....	....	....	....
Other capital transfers	2 440	....	....	....	....	....	....	....	....
Capital transfers, debit	3 400	....	....	....	....	....	....	....	....
General government	3 401	....	....	....	....	....	....	....	....
Debt forgiveness	3 402	....	....	....	....	....	....	....	....
Other capital transfers	3 410	....	....	....	....	....	....	....	....
Other sectors	3 430	....	....	....	....	....	....	....	....
Migrants' transfers	3 431	....	....	....	....	....	....	....	....
Debt forgiveness	3 432	....	....	....	....	....	....	....	....
Other capital transfers	3 440	....	....	....	....	....	....	....	....
Nonproduced nonfinancial assets, credit	2 480	....	....	....	....	....	....	....	....
Nonproduced nonfinancial assets, debit	3 480	....	....	....	....	....	....	....	....

Table 2 (Continued). STANDARD PRESENTATION, 2000–2007

(Millions of U.S. dollars)

	Code	2000	2001	2002	2003	2004	2005	2006	2007
FINANCIAL ACCOUNT...	4 995 ..	111.1	61.9	142.5	134.7	291.2	367.3	....	....
A. DIRECT INVESTMENT.....................................	4 500 ..	18.4	17.5	17.0	57.8	−16.0	52.8	....	....
Direct investment abroad.................................	4 505 ..	−1.1	−1.1	−.5	−.5	−3.9	−9.2	....	....
Equity capital...	4 510 ..	−.1	−.1	....	−.1	−.3	−.5	....	....
Claims on affiliated enterprises............................	4 515 ..	....	....	....	....	....	....	....	....
Liabilities to affiliated enterprises.......................	4 520 ..	....	....	....	....	....	....	....	....
Reinvested earnings...	4 525 ..	−.7	−.6	−.7	−.7	−1.7	−3.6	....	....
Other capital..	4 530 ..	−.3	−.5	.3	.3	−2.0	−5.1	....	....
Claims on affiliated enterprises............................	4 535 ..	....	....	....	....	....	....	....	....
Liabilities to affiliated enterprises.......................	4 540 ..	....	....	....	....	....	....	....	....
Direct investment in Barbados..........................	4 555 ..	19.4	18.6	17.4	58.3	−12.1	62.0	....	....
Equity capital...	4 560 ..	4.6	4.7	4.3	21.5	−25.6	4.4	....	....
Claims on direct investors...................................	4 565 ..	....	....	....	....	....	....	....	....
Liabilities to direct investors..............................	4 570 ..	....	....	....	....	....	4.4	....	....
Reinvested earnings...	4 575 ..	11.4	10.5	10.3	11.3	13.5	22.3	....	....
Other capital..	4 580 ..	3.5	3.4	2.9	25.5	....	35.3	....	....
Claims on direct investors...................................	4 585 ..	....	....	....	....	....	....	....	....
Liabilities to direct investors..............................	4 590 ..	....	....	....	....	....	....	....	....
B. PORTFOLIO INVESTMENT...............................	4 600 ..	71.1	119.7	−33.6	61.3	−68.2	21.9	....	....
Assets..	4 602 ..	−29.2	−30.5	−24.8	−23.0	−58.5	−76.4	....	....
Equity securities..	4 610 ..	−14.2	−14.8	−21.2	−23.2	−44.7	−53.2	....	....
Monetary authorities..	4 611 ..	....	....	....	....	....	....	....	....
General government...	4 612 ..	−.3	....	−.2	−.2	−3.2	....	....	....
Banks..	4 613 ..	....	....	....	....	....	....	....	....
Other sectors..	4 614 ..	−13.9	−14.8	−21.0	−23.1	−41.5	−53.2	....	....
Debt securities..	4 619 ..	−15.0	−15.7	−3.6	.2	−13.8	−23.2	....	....
Bonds and notes...	4 620 ..	−10.8	−11.4	.4	.2	−19.5	−16.7	....	....
Monetary authorities..	4 621 ..	....	....	....	....	....	....	....	....
General government...	4 622 ..	−8.4	−8.5	.3	....	−22.9	6.6	....	....
Banks..	4 623 ..	....	....	....	....	....	....	....	....
Other sectors..	4 624 ..	−2.4	−2.9	.1	.2	3.4	−23.2	....	....
Money market instruments................................	4 630 ..	−4.3	−4.4	−4.0	.1	5.7	−6.6	....	....
Monetary authorities..	4 631 ..	....	....	....	....	....	....	....	....
General government...	4 632 ..	....	....	....	....	....	....	....	....
Banks..	4 633 ..	....	....	....	....	....	....	....	....
Other sectors..	4 634 ..	−4.3	−4.4	−4.0	.1	5.7	−6.6	....	....
Liabilities..	4 652 ..	100.3	150.2	−8.9	84.3	−9.7	98.3	....	....
Equity securities..	4 660 ..	....	....	1.1	94.7	.3	−4.8	....	....
Banks..	4 663 ..	....	....	....	....	....	....	....	....
Other sectors..	4 664 ..	....	....	1.1	94.7	.3	−4.8	....	....
Debt securities..	4 669 ..	100.3	150.2	−10.0	−10.4	−10.0	103.1	....	....
Bonds and notes...	4 670 ..	100.0	150.0	−10.0	−10.0	−10.0	102.8	....	....
Monetary authorities..	4 671 ..	....	....	....	....	....	....	....	....
General government...	4 672 ..	100.0	150.0	−10.0	−10.0	−10.0	102.8	....	....
Banks..	4 673 ..	....	....	....	....	....	....	....	....
Other sectors..	4 674 ..	....	....	....	....	....	....	....	....
Money market instruments................................	4 680 ..	.3	.2	.1	−.4	....	.3	....	....
Monetary authorities..	4 681 ..	....	....	....	....	....	....	....	....
General government...	4 682 ..	....	....	....	....	....	....	....	....
Banks..	4 683 ..	....	....	....	....	....	....	....	....
Other sectors..	4 684 ..	.3	.2	.1	−.4	....	.3	....	....
C. FINANCIAL DERIVATIVES................................	4 910 ..	....	....	....	....	....	6.6	....	....
Monetary authorities..	4 911 ..	....	....	....	....	....	....	....	....
General government...	4 912 ..	....	....	....	....	....	....	....	....
Banks..	4 913 ..	....	....	....	....	....	....	....	....
Other sectors..	4 914 ..	....	....	....	....	....	6.6	....	....
Assets..	4 900 ..	....	....	....	....	....	1.6	....	....
Monetary authorities..	4 901 ..	....	....	....	....	....	....	....	....
General government...	4 902 ..	....	....	....	....	....	....	....	....
Banks..	4 903 ..	....	....	....	....	....	....	....	....
Other sectors..	4 904 ..	....	....	....	....	....	1.6	....	....
Liabilities..	4 905 ..	....	....	....	....	....	5.0	....	....
Monetary authorities..	4 906 ..	....	....	....	....	....	....	....	....
General government...	4 907 ..	....	....	....	....	....	....	....	....
Banks..	4 908 ..	....	....	....	....	....	....	....	....
Other sectors..	4 909 ..	....	....	....	....	....	5.0	....	....

2008, International Monetary Fund: *Balance of Payments Statistics Yearbook*

Table 2 (Concluded). STANDARD PRESENTATION, 2000–2007

(Millions of U.S. dollars)

	Code	2000	2001	2002	2003	2004	2005	2006	2007
D. OTHER INVESTMENT	4 700 ..	**199.8**	**147.7**	**135.2**	**83.6**	**218.7**	**310.0**	....	....
Assets	4 703 ..	**52.9**	**−56.7**	**−180.7**	**−82.9**	**30.1**	**−238.5**	....	....
Trade credits	4 706 ..	−7.1	27.6	21.0	.5	39.5	−101.2	....	....
General government	4 707 ..	....	....	....	....	....	....	....	....
of which: Short-term	4 709 ..	....	....	....	....	....	....	....	....
Other sectors	4 710 ..	−7.1	27.6	21.0	.5	39.5	−101.2	....	....
of which: Short-term	4 712 ..	*−1.9*	*22.5*	*7.8*	*−10.3*	*28.5*	*−81.8*	....	....
Loans	4 714 ..	−5.8	−1.9	−2.1	−1.3	−2.0	−6.2	....	....
Monetary authorities	4 715 ..	....	....	....	....	....	....	....	....
of which: Short-term	4 718 ..	....	....	....	....	....	....	....	....
General government	4 719 ..	−.7	−.7	−.7	−.7	.7	−.2	....	....
of which: Short-term	4 721 ..	*−.7*	*−.7*	*−.7*	*−.7*	*.7*	*−.2*	....	....
Banks	4 722 ..	....	....	....	....	....	....	....	....
of which: Short-term	4 724 ..	....	....	....	....	....	....	....	....
Other sectors	4 725 ..	−5.2	−1.2	−1.4	−.7	−2.7	−6.0	....	....
of which: Short-term	4 727 ..	....	....	....	....	....	....	....	....
Currency and deposits	4 730 ..	−9.7	−9.8	−2.5	−5.4	−3.8	−20.0	....	....
Monetary authorities	4 731 ..	....	....	....	....	....	....	....	....
General government	4 732 ..	....	....	....	....	....	....	....	....
Banks	4 733 ..	−9.7	−9.8	−2.5	−5.4	−3.8	−20.0	....	....
Other sectors	4 734 ..	....	....	....	....	....	....	....	....
Other assets	4 736 ..	75.4	−72.7	−197.1	−76.8	−3.6	−111.2	....	....
Monetary authorities	4 737 ..	....	....	....	....	....	....	....	....
of which: Short-term	4 739 ..	....	....	....	....	....	....	....	....
General government	4 740 ..	−3.6	−4.8	−4.8	−3.6	−5.4	....	....	....
of which: Short-term	4 742 ..	*−3.5*	*−3.7*	*−2.2*	*−2.0*	*−2.0*	....	....	....
Banks	4 743 ..	76.5	−73.3	−198.8	−82.6	−22.2	−135.1	....	....
of which: Short-term	4 745 ..	....	....	....	....	....	....	....	....
Other sectors	4 746 ..	2.5	5.4	6.5	9.4	24.0	23.9	....	....
of which: Short-term	4 748 ..	*1.4*	*4.3*	*6.5*	*8.2*	*20.7*	*25.8*	....	....
Liabilities	4 753 ..	**146.9**	**204.4**	**315.9**	**166.5**	**188.6**	**548.5**	....	....
Trade credits	4 756 ..	38.6	−13.5	40.7	79.5	156.0	298.1	....	....
General government	4 757 ..	2.9	5.1	−1.1	.9	−1.8	−1.2	....	....
of which: Short-term	4 759 ..	....	....	....	....	....	....	....	....
Other sectors	4 760 ..	35.7	−18.6	41.8	78.6	157.7	299.3	....	....
of which: Short-term	4 762 ..	*26.3*	*−25.8*	*34.5*	*64.7*	*99.8*	*225.3*	....	....
Loans	4 764 ..	147.3	96.6	38.9	51.5	−79.7	4.1	....	....
Monetary authorities	4 765 ..	....	....	....	....	....	....	....	....
of which: Use of Fund credit and loans from the Fund	4 766 ..	....	....	....	....	....	....	....	....
of which: Short-term	4 768 ..	....	....	....	....	....	....	....	....
General government	4 769 ..	15.7	6.4	−1.1	3.9	−21.5	−5.6	....	....
of which: Short-term	4 771 ..	....	....	....	....	....	....	....	....
Banks	4 772 ..	....	....	....	....	....	....	....	....
of which: Short-term	4 774 ..	....	....	....	....	....	....	....	....
Other sectors	4 775 ..	131.6	90.2	40.0	47.6	−58.3	9.7	....	....
of which: Short-term	4 777 ..	....	....	....	....	....	....	....	....
Currency and deposits	4 780 ..	....	....	....	....	....	....	....	....
Monetary authorities	4 781 ..	....	....	....	....	....	....	....	....
General government	4 782 ..	....	....	....	....	....	....	....	....
Banks	4 783 ..	....	....	....	....	....	....	....	....
Other sectors	4 784 ..	....	....	....	....	....	....	....	....
Other liabilities	4 786 ..	−39.0	121.3	236.3	35.5	112.3	246.3	....	....
Monetary authorities	4 787 ..	....	....	....	....	....	....	....	....
of which: Short-term	4 789 ..	....	....	....	....	....	....	....	....
General government	4 790 ..	....	....	....	....	....	....	....	....
of which: Short-term	4 792 ..	....	....	....	....	....	....	....	....
Banks	4 793 ..	−77.0	67.9	167.0	−41.1	49.2	247.2	....	....
of which: Short-term	4 795 ..	....	....	....	....	....	....	....	....
Other sectors	4 796 ..	38.0	53.4	69.3	76.6	63.1	−1.0	....	....
of which: Short-term	4 798 ..	*10.4*	*18.5*	*27.8*	*29.6*	*33.0*	*−3.4*	....	....
E. RESERVE ASSETS	4 802 ..	**−178.1**	**−222.9**	**23.9**	**−67.9**	**156.7**	**−23.9**	....	....
Monetary gold	4 812 ..	....	....	....	....	....	....	....	....
Special drawing rights	4 811 ..	....	....	....	.1	....	....	....	....
Reserve position in the Fund	4 810 ..	....	−.1	−.2	−.2	−.2	−.2	....	....
Foreign exchange	4 803 ..	−155.4	−193.2	53.5	−36.4	165.9	−29.1	....	....
Other claims	4 813 ..	−22.8	−29.7	−29.4	−31.4	−8.9	5.4	....	....
NET ERRORS AND OMISSIONS	4 998 ..	**32.1**	**47.4**	**25.1**	**34.4**	**45.4**	**17.8**	....	....

Table 1. ANALYTIC PRESENTATION, 2000–2007

(Millions of U.S. dollars)

	Code	2000	2001	2002	2003	2004	2005	2006	2007
A. Current Account[1]................................	4 993 Z.	**−338.4**	**−400.8**	**−333.8**	**−426.2**	**−1,193.3**	**435.5**	**−1,447.4**	**−3,059.9**
Goods: exports f.o.b................................	2 100 ..	6,640.5	7,334.1	7,964.7	10,076.1	13,942.2	16,108.8	19,834.7	24,328.9
Goods: imports f.o.b................................	3 100 ..	−7,551.6	−8,188.3	−8,944.7	−11,397.3	−16,214.0	−16,746.4	−22,103.7	−28,399.9
Balance on Goods................................	4 100 ..	*−911.1*	*−854.2*	*−980.0*	*−1,321.2*	*−2,271.8*	*−637.6*	*−2,269.0*	*−4,071.0*
Services: credit................................	2 200 ..	1,000.3	1,142.3	1,340.8	1,499.9	1,746.9	2,072.7	2,396.5	3,254.1
Services: debit................................	3 200 ..	−535.6	−793.8	−842.3	−841.2	−970.4	−1,093.3	−1,658.0	−2,020.8
Balance on Goods and Services................	4 991 ..	*−446.4*	*−505.7*	*−481.5*	*−662.5*	*−1,495.3*	*341.8*	*−1,530.5*	*−2,837.7*
Income: credit................................	2 300 ..	25.7	27.0	45.4	126.3	157.6	168.4	246.6	275.5
Income: debit................................	3 300 ..	−72.4	−75.9	−96.6	−112.1	−158.5	−239.4	−367.4	−686.6
Balance on Goods, Services, and Income......	4 992 ..	*−493.1*	*−554.6*	*−532.7*	*−648.3*	*−1,496.2*	*270.8*	*−1,651.3*	*−3,248.8*
Current transfers: credit........................	2 379 Z.	177.1	202.4	260.4	291.7	390.6	266.8	316.6	348.4
Current transfers: debit........................	3 379 ..	−22.4	−48.6	−61.5	−69.6	−87.7	−102.1	−112.7	−159.5
B. Capital Account[1]................................	4 994 Z.	**69.4**	**56.3**	**52.7**	**68.9**	**49.3**	**40.5**	**74.3**	**92.2**
Capital account: credit........................	2 994 Z.	125.6	132.3	119.8	133.2	130.4	134.7	165.0	199.9
Capital account: debit[1]........................	3 994 ..	−56.2	−76.0	−67.1	−64.3	−81.1	−94.2	−90.7	−107.7
Total, Groups A Plus B........................	4 981 ..	*−269.0*	*−344.5*	*−281.1*	*−357.3*	*−1,144.0*	*476.0*	*−1,373.1*	*−2,967.7*
C. Financial Account[1]................................	4 995 W.	**140.7**	**332.3**	**753.1**	**428.9**	**1,151.7**	**−64.9**	**1,690.9**	**5,199.5**
Direct investment abroad........................	4 505 ..	−.2	−.3	206.2	−1.5	−1.3	−2.5	−3.0	−15.2
Direct investment in Belarus....................	4 555 Z.	118.8	95.8	247.1	171.8	163.8	305.0	354.0	1,785.2
Portfolio investment assets....................	4 602 ..	−5.7	25.5	−2.4	.8	3.2	−2.9	−1.7	−41.2
Equity securities........................	4 610 ..	.5	.7	6.9	−1.1	.6	....	−5.6	−5.8
Debt securities........................	4 619 ..	−6.2	24.8	−9.3	1.9	2.6	−2.9	3.9	−35.4
Portfolio investment liabilities................	4 652 Z.	50.1	−45.4	−6.7	5.3	59.6	−38.6	−24.7	2.4
Equity securities........................	4 660 ..	.5	2.5	.7	3.3	.5	.6	−1.2	4.5
Debt securities........................	4 669 Z.	49.6	−47.9	−7.4	2.0	59.1	−39.2	−23.5	−2.1
Financial derivatives........................	4 910 ..	....	....	....	....	....	−.2	−12.9	....
Financial derivatives assets....................	4 900 ..	....	....	....	....	....	1.6	.1	....
Financial derivatives liabilities................	4 905 ..	....	....	....	....	....	−1.8	−13.0	....
Other investment assets........................	4 703 ..	41.7	−139.2	−421.0	18.4	−151.4	−492.1	−165.7	−1,931.7
Monetary authorities........................	4 701 ..	−.2	−99.3	−215.1	−10.0	231.5	72.8	−15.4	−185.4
General government........................	4 704 ..	....	....	....	....	....	....	....	−7.3
Banks........................	4 705 ..	8.4	17.5	19.1	−61.1	−120.5	−232.5	257.7	−775.3
Other sectors........................	4 728 ..	33.5	−57.4	−225.0	89.5	−262.4	−332.4	−408.0	−963.7
Other investment liabilities....................	4 753 W.	−64.0	395.9	729.9	234.1	1,077.8	166.4	1,544.9	5,400.0
Monetary authorities........................	4 753 WA	−21.2	88.6	109.1	13.4	−194.9	−65.7	....	589.9
General government........................	4 753 ZB	−37.2	44.9	9.3	−43.2	122.1	116.5	3.4	1,419.9
Banks........................	4 753 ZC	2.0	80.2	88.6	118.4	218.8	214.4	534.5	1,075.1
Other sectors........................	4 753 ZD	−7.6	182.2	522.9	145.5	931.8	−98.8	1,007.0	2,315.1
Total, Groups A Through C....................	4 983 ..	*−128.3*	*−12.2*	*472.0*	*71.6*	*7.7*	*411.1*	*317.8*	*2,231.8*
D. Net Errors and Omissions....................	4 998 ..	**254.2**	**−1.0**	**−288.8**	**−13.2**	**270.3**	**108.9**	**−301.6**	**504.7**
Total, Groups A Through D....................	4 984 ..	*125.9*	*−13.2*	*183.2*	*58.4*	*278.0*	*520.0*	*16.2*	*2,736.5*
E. Reserves and Related Items................	4 802 A.	**−125.9**	**13.2**	**−183.2**	**−58.4**	**−278.0**	**−520.0**	**−16.2**	**−2,736.5**
Reserve assets........................	4 802 ..	−75.7	5.2	−100.9	13.8	−255.8	−539.2	1.4	−2,778.1
Use of Fund credit and loans....................	4 766 ..	−55.8	−29.8	−30.2	−32.3	−17.3	−8.9	....	....
Exceptional financing........................	4 920 ..	5.6	37.8	−52.2	−40.0	−4.9	28.1	−17.6	41.6
Conversion rates: rubels per U.S. dollar............	0 101 ..	**876.8**	**1,390.0**	**1,790.9**	**2,051.3**	**2,160.3**	**2,153.8**	**2,144.6**	**2,146.1**

[1] Excludes components that have been classified in the categories of Group E.

Table 2. STANDARD PRESENTATION, 2000–2007

(Millions of U.S. dollars)

	Code	2000	2001	2002	2003	2004	2005	2006	2007
CURRENT ACCOUNT	4 993 ..	−338.4	−400.8	−333.8	−426.2	−1,193.3	435.5	−1,447.4	−3,059.9
A. GOODS	4 100 ..	−911.1	−854.2	−980.0	−1,321.2	−2,271.8	−637.6	−2,269.0	−4,071.0
Credit	2 100 ..	6,640.5	7,334.1	7,964.7	10,076.1	13,942.2	16,108.8	19,834.7	24,328.9
General merchandise: exports f.o.b.	2 110 ..	6,054.8	6,695.1	7,258.0	9,177.7	13,009.3	15,197.9	18,876.7	23,247.6
Goods for processing: exports f.o.b.	2 150 ..	572.6	628.3	689.3	830.5	873.9	821.6	870.9	984.1
Repairs on goods	2 160 ..	12.2	8.7	12.9	59.8	46.1	65.6	45.0	38.3
Goods procured in ports by carriers	2 170 ..	.9	2.0	4.5	8.1	12.9	23.7	42.1	58.9
Nonmonetary gold	2 180 ..	....	....	....	....	....	....	....	....
Debit	3 100 ..	−7,551.6	−8,188.3	−8,944.7	−11,397.3	−16,214.0	−16,746.4	−22,103.7	−28,399.9
General merchandise: imports f.o.b.	3 110 ..	−7,103.1	−7,698.4	−8,249.8	−10,727.8	−15,484.5	−16,052.2	−21,336.0	−27,556.1
Goods for processing: imports f.o.b.	3 150 ..	−422.7	−464.3	−666.4	−621.4	−670.3	−624.2	−679.8	−729.2
Repairs on goods	3 160 ..	−16.7	−8.2	−11.0	−25.6	−27.9	−22.7	−23.2	−32.7
Goods procured in ports by carriers	3 170 ..	−9.1	−17.4	−17.5	−22.5	−31.3	−47.3	−64.7	−81.9
Nonmonetary gold	3 180 ..	....	....	....	....	....	....	....	....
B. SERVICES	4 200 ..	464.7	348.5	498.5	658.7	776.5	979.4	738.5	1,233.3
Total credit	2 200 ..	*1,000.3*	*1,142.3*	*1,340.8*	*1,499.9*	*1,746.9*	*2,072.7*	*2,396.5*	*3,254.1*
Total debit	3 200 ..	*−535.6*	*−793.8*	*−842.3*	*−841.2*	*−970.4*	*−1,093.3*	*−1,658.0*	*−2,020.8*
Transportation services, credit	2 205 ..	583.6	628.0	710.2	856.3	1,025.5	1,337.5	1,710.2	2,344.7
Passenger	2 850 ..	*94.5*	*60.6*	*60.7*	*71.8*	*92.4*	*92.5*	*115.3*	*155.4*
Freight	2 851 ..	*457.5*	*516.9*	*597.2*	*728.2*	*855.1*	*1,147.5*	*1,460.5*	*2,021.3*
Other	2 852 ..	*31.6*	*50.5*	*52.3*	*56.3*	*78.0*	*97.5*	*134.4*	*168.0*
Sea transport, passenger	2 207 ..	....	....	....	....	....	....	....	....
Sea transport, freight	2 208 ..	....	....	....	....	2.2	4.7	147.1	325.9
Sea transport, other	2 209 ..	....	....	.3	1.1	4.5	3.6	....	.1
Air transport, passenger	2 211 ..	24.7	23.8	23.6	31.8	44.7	37.9	44.6	64.3
Air transport, freight	2 212 ..	8.7	10.1	10.4	9.6	10.6	13.1	21.5	18.2
Air transport, other	2 213 ..	18.5	15.6	23.8	26.6	37.7	48.8	52.2	66.6
Other transport, passenger	2 215 ..	69.8	36.8	37.1	40.0	47.7	54.6	70.7	91.1
Other transport, freight	2 216 ..	448.8	506.8	586.8	718.6	842.3	1,129.7	1,291.9	1,677.2
Other transport, other	2 217 ..	13.1	34.9	28.2	28.6	35.8	45.1	82.2	101.3
Transportation services, debit	3 205 ..	−109.5	−124.7	−136.1	−191.0	−248.6	−308.8	−677.5	−896.8
Passenger	3 850 ..	*−31.1*	*−32.1*	*−33.5*	*−36.9*	*−50.1*	*−68.3*	*−88.6*	*−118.0*
Freight	3 851 ..	*−55.1*	*−57.4*	*−66.4*	*−94.5*	*−135.1*	*−183.7*	*−489.9*	*−664.1*
Other	3 852 ..	*−23.3*	*−35.2*	*−36.2*	*−59.6*	*−63.4*	*−56.8*	*−99.0*	*−114.7*
Sea transport, passenger	3 207 ..	....	....	....	....	....	....	....	....
Sea transport, freight	3 208 ..	−3.1	−3.4	−3.2	−4.7	−6.6	−15.1	−130.6	−300.6
Sea transport, other	3 209 ..	....	....	−13.3	−33.8	−34.6	−20.6	−22.7	−38.3
Air transport, passenger	3 211 ..	−12.2	−14.5	−15.1	−17.3	−24.4	−29.9	−35.8	−49.1
Air transport, freight	3 212 ..	−2.4	−1.7	−3.1	−3.1	−2.6	−2.5	−3.6	−4.9
Air transport, other	3 213 ..	−16.3	−17.0	−9.3	−9.7	−11.8	−13.4	−18.8	−26.0
Other transport, passenger	3 215 ..	−18.9	−17.6	−18.4	−19.6	−25.7	−38.4	−52.8	−68.9
Other transport, freight	3 216 ..	−49.6	−52.3	−60.1	−86.7	−125.9	−166.1	−355.7	−358.6
Other transport, other	3 217 ..	−7.0	−18.2	−13.6	−16.1	−17.0	−22.8	−57.5	−50.4
Travel, credit	2 236 ..	93.2	211.4	233.5	266.9	270.0	253.1	286.3	324.4
Business travel	2 237 ..	28.1	83.3	89.0	107.4	112.7	104.9	110.9	119.3
Personal travel	2 240 ..	65.1	128.1	144.5	159.5	157.3	148.2	175.4	205.1
Travel, debit	3 236 ..	−216.2	−453.7	−492.8	−399.3	−449.9	−447.6	−586.4	−605.5
Business travel	3 237 ..	−103.7	−137.6	−140.7	−105.9	−110.2	−97.9	−127.3	−133.6
Personal travel	3 240 ..	−112.5	−316.1	−352.1	−293.4	−339.7	−349.7	−459.1	−471.9
Other services, credit	2 200 BA	323.5	302.9	397.1	376.7	451.4	482.1	400.0	585.0
Communications	2 245 ..	50.0	54.0	60.7	70.3	82.4	94.0	105.5	124.2
Construction	2 249 ..	42.0	46.3	55.1	60.3	79.9	60.1	47.7	81.2
Insurance	2 253 ..	3.6	3.2	3.8	1.0	1.3	1.2	....	5.5
Financial	2 260 ..	2.1	3.7	2.6	1.5	2.6	2.8	5.3	6.4
Computer and information	2 262 ..	4.5	6.7	12.3	17.4	17.5	26.4	49.4	95.5
Royalties and licence fees	2 266 ..	.9	.5	.8	1.4	1.7	3.1	5.9	6.9
Other business services	2 268 ..	206.9	168.6	235.9	200.2	242.6	274.7	165.1	238.6
Personal, cultural, and recreational	2 287 ..	1.9	1.3	1.6	1.8	2.5	2.4	4.9	7.7
Government, n.i.e.	2 291 ..	11.6	18.6	24.3	22.8	20.9	17.4	16.2	19.0
Other services, debit	3 200 BA	−209.9	−215.4	−213.4	−250.9	−271.9	−336.9	−394.1	−518.5
Communications	3 245 ..	−40.4	−46.7	−52.2	−63.8	−65.4	−71.7	−73.7	−76.5
Construction	3 249 ..	−11.0	−15.8	−21.7	−28.0	−17.7	−19.9	−27.4	−47.1
Insurance	3 253 ..	−10.7	−12.2	−11.4	−2.4	−4.0	−5.3	....	−6.4
Financial	3 260 ..	−3.2	−3.6	−3.5	−4.9	−12.4	−18.4	−30.1	−52.0
Computer and information	3 262 ..	−4.4	−5.8	−9.6	−7.0	−13.6	−12.5	−21.2	−19.3
Royalties and licence fees	3 266 ..	−2.7	−3.8	−3.2	−5.5	−9.1	−19.5	−50.5	−68.5
Other business services	3 268 ..	−123.3	−111.5	−92.3	−113.3	−115.0	−141.7	−155.4	−205.8
Personal, cultural, and recreational	3 287 ..	−3.0	−4.1	−3.6	−5.2	−6.8	−11.1	−15.5	−20.8
Government, n.i.e.	3 291 ..	−11.2	−11.9	−15.9	−20.8	−27.9	−36.8	−20.3	−22.1

Table 2 (Continued). STANDARD PRESENTATION, 2000–2007

(Millions of U.S. dollars)

	Code	2000	2001	2002	2003	2004	2005	2006	2007
C. INCOME	4 300	**−46.7**	**−48.9**	**−51.2**	**14.2**	**−.9**	**−71.0**	**−120.8**	**−411.1**
Total credit	2 300	*25.7*	*27.0*	*45.4*	*126.3*	*157.6*	*168.4*	*246.6*	*275.5*
Total debit	3 300	*−72.4*	*−75.9*	*−96.6*	*−112.1*	*−158.5*	*−239.4*	*−367.4*	*−686.6*
Compensation of employees, credit	2 310	**13.6**	**16.9**	**20.5**	**89.2**	**126.3**	**120.1**	**175.4**	**156.6**
Compensation of employees, debit	3 310	**−2.2**	**−.7**	**−.6**	**−.7**	**−.5**	**−.3**	**−2.5**	**−5.0**
Investment income, credit	2 320	**12.1**	**10.1**	**24.9**	**37.1**	**31.3**	**48.3**	**71.2**	**118.9**
Direct investment income	2 330	.1	.4	1.6	1.1	1.0	1.3	1.0	1.9
Dividends and distributed branch profits	2 332	.1	.4	1.6	1.1	1.0	1.3	1.0	1.8
Reinvested earnings and undistributed branch profits	2 333	....	....	....	....	....	....	....	.1
Income on debt (interest)	2 334	....	....	....	....	....	....	....	....
Portfolio investment income	2 339	.5	.3	2.5	.5	.8	.7	1.6	.9
Income on equity	2 340	....	....	.2	.5	.7	.6	1.3	.9
Income on bonds and notes	2 350	.5	.3	2.3	....	....	....	.3	....
Income on money market instruments	2 360	....	....	....	....	.1	.1	....	....
Other investment income	2 370	11.5	9.4	20.8	35.5	29.5	46.3	68.6	116.1
Investment income, debit	3 320	**−70.2**	**−75.2**	**−96.0**	**−111.4**	**−158.0**	**−239.1**	**−364.9**	**−681.6**
Direct investment income	3 330	−4.6	−13.3	−26.8	−37.5	−75.7	−134.9	−236.3	−434.8
Dividends and distributed branch profits	3 332	−4.2	−13.2	−23.9	−25.2	−52.1	−91.6	−166.3	−234.0
Reinvested earnings and undistributed branch profits	3 333	−.4	−.1	−2.9	−12.3	−23.6	−32.6	−58.4	−185.2
Income on debt (interest)	3 334	....	....	....	....	....	−10.7	−11.6	−15.6
Portfolio investment income	3 339	−1.0	−.5	−1.0	−1.1	−2.2	−4.0	−1.8	−4.0
Income on equity	3 340	....	−.2	−.2	−1.0	−2.2	−4.0	−1.7	−4.0
Income on bonds and notes	3 350	−1.0	−.3	−.8	−.1	....	....	−.1	....
Income on money market instruments	3 360	....	....	....	....	....	....	....	....
Other investment income	3 370	−64.6	−61.4	−68.2	−72.8	−80.1	−100.2	−126.8	−242.8
D. CURRENT TRANSFERS	4 379	**154.7**	**153.8**	**198.9**	**222.1**	**302.9**	**164.7**	**203.9**	**188.9**
Credit	2 379	**177.1**	**202.4**	**260.4**	**291.7**	**390.6**	**266.8**	**316.6**	**348.4**
General government	2 380	57.3	80.8	73.4	60.8	58.2	59.1	100.5	112.9
Other sectors	2 390	119.8	121.6	187.0	230.9	332.4	207.7	216.1	235.5
Workers' remittances	2 391	....	....	....	....	....	....	....	....
Other current transfers	2 392	119.8	121.6	187.0	230.9	332.4	207.7	216.1	235.5
Debit	3 379	**−22.4**	**−48.6**	**−61.5**	**−69.6**	**−87.7**	**−102.1**	**−112.7**	**−159.5**
General government	3 380	−10.4	−14.4	−11.1	−25.5	−17.0	−15.0	−7.3	−10.4
Other sectors	3 390	−12.0	−34.2	−50.4	−44.1	−70.7	−87.1	−105.4	−149.1
Workers' remittances	3 391	....	....	....	....	....	....	....	....
Other current transfers	3 392	−12.0	−34.2	−50.4	−44.1	−70.7	−87.1	−105.4	−149.1
CAPITAL AND FINANCIAL ACCOUNT	4 996	**84.2**	**401.8**	**622.6**	**439.4**	**923.0**	**−544.4**	**1,749.0**	**2,555.2**
CAPITAL ACCOUNT	4 994	**69.4**	**56.3**	**52.7**	**68.9**	**49.3**	**40.5**	**74.3**	**92.2**
Total credit	2 994	*125.6*	*132.3*	*119.8*	*133.2*	*130.4*	*134.7*	*165.0*	*199.9*
Total debit	3 994	*−56.2*	*−76.0*	*−67.1*	*−64.3*	*−81.1*	*−94.2*	*−90.7*	*−107.7*
Capital transfers, credit	2 400	**125.6**	**132.3**	**119.8**	**133.2**	**130.4**	**134.5**	**164.5**	**197.7**
General government	2 401	....	....	....	....	....	....	....	....
Debt forgiveness	2 402	....	....	....	....	....	....	....	....
Other capital transfers	2 410	....	....	....	....	....	....	....	....
Other sectors	2 430	125.6	132.3	119.8	133.2	130.4	134.5	164.5	197.7
Migrants' transfers	2 431	125.6	132.3	119.8	133.2	130.4	134.5	164.4	197.6
Debt forgiveness	2 432	....	....	....	....	....	....	....	....
Other capital transfers	2 440	....	....	....	....	....	....	.1	.1
Capital transfers, debit	3 400	**−56.2**	**−76.0**	**−67.1**	**−64.3**	**−81.1**	**−94.2**	**−90.2**	**−104.2**
General government	3 401	....	....	....	....	....	....	....	....
Debt forgiveness	3 402	....	....	....	....	....	....	....	....
Other capital transfers	3 410	....	....	....	....	....	....	....	....
Other sectors	3 430	−56.2	−76.0	−67.1	−64.3	−81.1	−94.2	−90.2	−104.2
Migrants' transfers	3 431	−56.2	−76.0	−67.1	−64.3	−81.1	−94.2	−90.2	−104.2
Debt forgiveness	3 432	....	....	....	....	....	....	....	....
Other capital transfers	3 440	....	....	....	....	....	....	....	....
Nonproduced nonfinancial assets, credit	2 480	....	....	....	....	....	.2	.5	2.2
Nonproduced nonfinancial assets, debit	3 480	....	....	....	....	....	....	−.5	−3.5

Table 2 (Continued). STANDARD PRESENTATION, 2000–2007

(Millions of U.S. dollars)

	Code	2000	2001	2002	2003	2004	2005	2006	2007
FINANCIAL ACCOUNT	4 995	**14.8**	**345.5**	**569.9**	**370.5**	**873.7**	**−584.9**	**1,674.7**	**2,463.0**
A. DIRECT INVESTMENT	4 500	**118.6**	**95.5**	**453.3**	**170.3**	**162.5**	**302.5**	**351.0**	**1,770.0**
Direct investment abroad	4 505	−.2	−.3	206.2	−1.5	−1.3	−2.5	−3.0	−15.2
Equity capital	4 510	−.2	−.3	206.8	−1.3	−1.3	−2.9	−2.4	−13.5
Claims on affiliated enterprises	4 515	−.2	−.3	206.8	−1.3	−1.3	−2.9	−2.4	−13.5
Liabilities to affiliated enterprises	4 520	....	....	....	....	....	....	....	....
Reinvested earnings	4 525	....	....	....	....	....	....	....	−.1
Other capital	4 530	....	....	−.6	−.2	....	.4	−.6	−1.6
Claims on affiliated enterprises	4 535	....	....	−.6	−.2	....	.4	−.6	−1.6
Liabilities to affiliated enterprises	4 540	....	....	....	....	....	....	....	....
Direct investment in Belarus	4 555	**118.8**	**95.8**	**247.1**	**171.8**	**163.8**	**305.0**	**354.0**	**1,785.2**
Equity capital	4 560	115.2	89.8	118.7	136.1	120.3	281.1	304.9	1,438.5
Claims on direct investors	4 565	....	....	....	....	....	....	....	....
Liabilities to direct investors	4 570	115.2	89.8	118.7	136.1	120.3	281.1	304.9	1,438.5
Reinvested earnings	4 575	.4	.1	2.9	12.3	23.6	32.6	58.4	185.2
Other capital	4 580	3.2	5.9	125.5	23.4	19.9	−8.7	−9.3	161.5
Claims on direct investors	4 585	....	....	....	....	....	....	....	....
Liabilities to direct investors	4 590	3.2	5.9	125.5	23.4	19.9	−8.7	−9.3	161.5
B. PORTFOLIO INVESTMENT	4 600	**44.4**	**−19.9**	**−9.1**	**6.1**	**62.8**	**−41.5**	**−26.4**	**−38.8**
Assets	4 602	**−5.7**	**25.5**	**−2.4**	**.8**	**3.2**	**−2.9**	**−1.7**	**−41.2**
Equity securities	4 610	.5	.7	6.9	−1.1	.6	....	−5.6	−5.8
Monetary authorities	4 611	....	....	....	....	....	....	....	....
General government	4 612	....	....	....	....	....	....	....	....
Banks	4 613	−.1	.2	6.8	....	.5	....	−1.2	−.5
Other sectors	4 614	.6	.5	.1	−1.1	.1	....	−4.4	−5.3
Debt securities	4 619	−6.2	24.8	−9.3	1.9	2.6	−2.9	3.9	−35.4
Bonds and notes	4 620	−6.2	24.8	−9.3	....	....	....	....	....
Monetary authorities	4 621	....	....	....	....	....	....	....	....
General government	4 622	....	....	....	....	....	....	....	....
Banks	4 623	−7.0	22.0	−3.6	....	....	....	....	....
Other sectors	4 624	.8	2.8	−5.7	....	....	....	....	....
Money market instruments	4 630	....	....	....	1.9	2.6	−2.9	3.9	−35.4
Monetary authorities	4 631	....	....	....	....	....	....	....	....
General government	4 632	....	....	....	....	....	....	....	....
Banks	4 633	....	....	....	2.1	6.1	−2.4	7.5	−29.2
Other sectors	4 634	....	....	....	−.2	−3.5	−.5	−3.6	−6.2
Liabilities	4 652	**50.1**	**−45.4**	**−6.7**	**5.3**	**59.6**	**−38.6**	**−24.7**	**2.4**
Equity securities	4 660	.5	2.5	.7	3.3	.5	.6	−1.2	4.5
Banks	4 663	.1	−.4	.3	2.6	....	1.1	−1.3	3.6
Other sectors	4 664	.4	2.9	.4	.7	.5	−.5	.1	.9
Debt securities	4 669	49.6	−47.9	−7.4	2.0	59.1	−39.2	−23.5	−2.1
Bonds and notes	4 670	49.6	−47.9	−7.4	.1	4.1	−4.0	−1.6	−.8
Monetary authorities	4 671	50.0	−48.9	5.0	....	....	....	....	....
General government	4 672	.6	−2.5	−3.7	.1	3.8	−1.3	−1.6	−.5
Banks	4 673	1.4	4.0	−8.0	....	.1	....	....	....
Other sectors	4 674	−2.4	−.5	−.7	....	.2	−2.7	....	−.3
Money market instruments	4 680	....	....	....	1.9	55.0	−35.2	−21.9	−1.3
Monetary authorities	4 681	....	....	....	−1.0	−5.1	.1	....	....
General government	4 682	....	....	....	2.1	51.7	−31.9	−21.9	−1.2
Banks	4 683	....	....	....	.8	4.5	−3.4	....	....
Other sectors	4 684	....	....	....	....	3.9	....	....	−.1
C. FINANCIAL DERIVATIVES	4 910	....	....	....	....	....	**−.2**	**−12.9**	....
Monetary authorities	4 911	....	....	....	....	....	−.2	−12.9	....
General government	4 912	....	....	....	....	....	....	....	....
Banks	4 913	....	....	....	....	....	....	....	....
Other sectors	4 914	....	....	....	....	....	....	....	....
Assets	4 900	....	....	....	....	....	**1.6**	**.1**	....
Monetary authorities	4 901	....	....	....	....	....	1.6	.1	....
General government	4 902	....	....	....	....	....	....	....	....
Banks	4 903	....	....	....	....	....	....	....	....
Other sectors	4 904	....	....	....	....	....	....	....	....
Liabilities	4 905	....	....	....	....	....	**−1.8**	**−13.0**	....
Monetary authorities	4 906	....	....	....	....	....	−1.8	−13.0	....
General government	4 907	....	....	....	....	....	....	....	....
Banks	4 908	....	....	....	....	....	....	....	....
Other sectors	4 909	....	....	....	....	....	....	....	....

Table 2 (Concluded). STANDARD PRESENTATION, 2000–2007

(Millions of U.S. dollars)

	Code	2000	2001	2002	2003	2004	2005	2006	2007
D. OTHER INVESTMENT	4 700 ..	**−72.5**	**264.7**	**226.5**	**180.2**	**904.2**	**−306.5**	**1,361.6**	**3,509.9**
Assets	4 703 ..	41.7	−139.2	−421.0	18.4	−151.4	−492.1	−165.7	−1,931.7
Trade credits	4 706 ..	55.8	−36.5	−236.8	119.3	−261.8	−300.6	−410.0	−806.9
General government	4 707 ..	....	....	....	....	....	....	....	....
of which: Short-term	4 709 ..	....	....	....	....	....	....	....	....
Other sectors	4 710 ..	55.8	−36.5	−236.8	119.3	−261.8	−300.6	−410.0	−806.9
of which: Short-term	4 712 ..	*55.8*	*−36.5*	*−236.8*	*119.3*	*−261.8*	*−300.6*	*−410.0*	*−806.9*
Loans	4 714 ..	1.6	−21.2	−35.2	12.6	6.0	6.8	−43.5	−174.0
Monetary authorities	4 715 ..	....	−20.0	−34.5	14.7	15.0	−5.0	....	....
of which: Short-term	4 718 ..	....	*−20.0*	*−9.5*	*14.7*	*15.0*	....	....	....
General government	4 719 ..	....	....	....	....	....	....	....	....
of which: Short-term	4 721 ..	....	....	....	....	....	....	....	....
Banks	4 722 ..	1.0	−1.7	−2.3	−2.1	−9.2	13.2	−24.6	−71.1
of which: Short-term	4 724 ..	*1.0*	*−1.8*	*−2.3*	*−1.9*	*−8.6*	*12.5*	*−21.8*	*−69.6*
Other sectors	4 725 ..	.6	.5	1.6	....	.2	−1.4	−18.9	−102.9
of which: Short-term	4 727 ..	....	....	....	....	....	*−1.2*	*−17.6*	*−104.1*
Currency and deposits	4 730 ..	9.8	−64.6	−145.2	−58.0	133.9	−189.5	258.9	−785.7
Monetary authorities	4 731 ..	.3	−79.7	−159.4	17.0	245.5	22.0	−15.5	−185.4
General government	4 732 ..	....	....	....	....	....	....	....	....
Banks	4 733 ..	9.1	19.2	13.5	−59.8	−112.6	−213.9	278.7	−595.8
Other sectors	4 734 ..	.4	−4.1	.7	−15.2	1.0	2.4	−4.3	−4.5
Other assets	4 736 ..	−25.5	−16.9	−3.8	−55.5	−29.5	−8.8	28.9	−165.1
Monetary authorities	4 737 ..	−.5	.4	−21.2	−41.7	−29.0	55.8	.1	....
of which: Short-term	4 739 ..	*−.5*	*.4*	*−21.2*	*−41.7*	*−29.0*	*55.8*	*.1*	....
General government	4 740 ..	....	....	....	....	....	....	....	−7.3
of which: Short-term	4 742 ..	....	....	....	....	....	....	....	*−1.5*
Banks	4 743 ..	−1.7	....	7.9	.8	1.3	−31.8	3.6	−108.4
of which: Short-term	4 745 ..	*−1.7*	....	*7.9*	*.8*	*1.3*	*−31.8*	*3.6*	*−108.4*
Other sectors	4 746 ..	−23.3	−17.3	9.5	−14.6	−1.8	−32.8	25.2	−49.4
of which: Short-term	4 748 ..	*−23.3*	*−17.3*	*9.5*	*−14.6*	*−1.8*	*−32.8*	*25.2*	*−49.4*
Liabilities	4 753 ..	**−114.2**	**403.9**	**647.5**	**161.8**	**1,055.6**	**185.6**	**1,527.3**	**5,441.6**
Trade credits	4 756 ..	−125.5	−19.1	350.9	63.4	852.6	−245.1	567.5	1,497.1
General government	4 757 ..	....	....	....	....	....	....	....	....
of which: Short-term	4 759 ..	....	....	....	....	....	....	....	....
Other sectors	4 760 ..	−125.5	−19.1	350.9	63.4	852.6	−245.1	567.5	1,497.1
of which: Short-term	4 762 ..	*−125.5*	*−19.1*	*350.9*	*63.4*	*852.6*	*−245.1*	*567.5*	*1,497.1*
Loans	4 764 ..	50.4	323.7	316.8	59.7	191.7	299.1	1,171.2	3,714.6
Monetary authorities	4 765 ..	−55.8	38.6	58.5	−19.9	−183.8	−61.8	....	440.0
of which: Use of Fund credit and loans from the Fund	4 766 ..	*−55.8*	*−29.8*	*−30.2*	*−32.3*	*−17.3*	*−8.9*	....	....
of which: Short-term	4 768 ..	....	....	*5.1*	*−5.1*	....	....	....	*200.0*
General government	4 769 ..	−37.2	44.9	9.3	−43.2	122.1	116.5	3.4	1,419.9
of which: Short-term	4 771 ..	....	....	....	....	....	*32.0*	*53.6*	*−95.7*
Banks	4 772 ..	25.5	38.9	77.0	40.7	174.2	98.1	728.3	1,036.7
of which: Short-term	4 774 ..	*25.5*	*38.9*	*77.0*	*40.7*	*174.2*	*98.1*	*452.3*	*671.9*
Other sectors	4 775 ..	117.9	201.3	172.0	82.1	79.2	146.3	439.5	818.0
of which: Short-term	4 777 ..	*22.1*	*18.0*	*5.7*	*84.7*	*116.6*	*111.6*	*177.8*	*438.2*
Currency and deposits	4 780 ..	−44.7	61.5	32.0	78.7	16.2	103.5	−226.7	172.8
Monetary authorities	4 781 ..	−21.2	20.2	20.4	1.0	−28.4	−12.8	....	144.6
General government	4 782 ..	....	....	....	....	....	....	....	....
Banks	4 783 ..	−23.5	41.3	11.6	77.7	44.6	116.3	−226.7	28.2
Other sectors	4 784 ..	....	....	....	....	....	....	....	....
Other liabilities	4 786 ..	5.6	37.8	−52.2	−40.0	−4.9	28.1	15.3	57.1
Monetary authorities	4 787 ..	....	....	....	....	....	....	....	5.3
of which: Short-term	4 789 ..	....	....	....	....	....	....	....	*5.3*
General government	4 790 ..	9.4	−38.0	−3.4	21.0	−20.8	−.5	....	....
of which: Short-term	4 792 ..	*9.4*	*−38.0*	*−3.4*	*21.0*	*−20.8*	*−.5*	....	....
Banks	4 793 ..	−.1	1.2	2.2	.3	.8	5.5	32.9	10.2
of which: Short-term	4 795 ..	*−.1*	*1.2*	*2.2*	*.3*	*.8*	*5.5*	*32.9*	*10.2*
Other sectors	4 796 ..	−3.7	74.6	−51.0	−61.3	15.1	23.1	−17.6	41.6
of which: Short-term	4 798 ..	*−3.7*	*74.6*	*−51.0*	*−61.3*	*15.1*	*23.1*	*−17.6*	*41.6*
E. RESERVE ASSETS	4 802 ..	**−75.7**	**5.2**	**−100.9**	**13.8**	**−255.8**	**−539.2**	**1.4**	**−2,778.1**
Monetary gold	4 812 ..	−13.6	....	7.6	35.7	−35.9	−90.4	−80.1	34.8
Special drawing rights	4 811 ..	−.2	−.2	.1	.2	....	....	....	....
Reserve position in the Fund	4 810 ..	....	....	....	....	....	....	....	....
Foreign exchange	4 803 ..	−61.7	9.5	−111.3	−22.1	−220.4	−448.2	81.9	−2,728.8
Other claims	4 813 ..	−.2	−4.1	2.7	....	.5	−.6	−.4	−84.1
NET ERRORS AND OMISSIONS	4 998 ..	**254.2**	**−1.0**	**−288.8**	**−13.2**	**270.3**	**108.9**	**−301.6**	**504.7**

Belarus   913

Table 3. INTERNATIONAL INVESTMENT POSITION (End-period stocks), 2000–2007

(Millions of U.S. dollars)

	Code	2000	2001	2002	2003	2004	2005	2006	2007
ASSETS	8 995 C.	1,015.2	1,266.7	1,771.0	1,811.4	2,240.7	3,289.1	3,583.4	8,576.6
Direct investment abroad	8 505 ..	23.8	20.1	3.7	6.2	8.2	13.9	18.5	34.4
Equity capital and reinvested earnings	8 506 ..	23.8	19.7	2.8	5.2	7.1	12.4	16.6	24.7
Claims on affiliated enterprises	8 507 ..	23.8	19.7	2.8	5.2	7.1	12.4	16.6	24.7
Liabilities to affiliated enterprises	8 508 ..	....	....	....	....	....	....	....	....
Other capital	8 530 ..	....	.4	.9	1.0	1.1	1.5	1.9	9.7
Claims on affiliated enterprises	8 535 ..	....	.4	.9	1.0	1.1	1.5	1.9	9.7
Liabilities to affiliated enterprises	8 540 ..	....	....	....	....	....	....	....	....
Portfolio investment	8 602 ..	57.5	31.6	16.3	16.3	9.1	21.3	23.0	62.2
Equity securities	8 610 ..	9.3	8.3	.8	1.8	.3	.3	5.9	12.5
Monetary authorities	8 611 ..	.1	.1	....	....	....	....	....	....
General government	8 612 ..	....	....	....	....	....	....	....	....
Banks	8 613 ..	7.8	7.3	.6	.5	.1	.1	1.3	2.1
Other sectors	8 614 ..	1.4	.9	.2	1.3	.2	.2	4.6	10.4
Debt securities	8 619 ..	48.2	23.3	15.5	14.5	8.8	21.0	17.1	49.7
Bonds and notes	8 620 ..	....	....	....	....	....	....	....	....
Monetary authorities	8 621 ..	....	....	....	....	....	....	....	....
General government	8 622 ..	....	....	....	....	....	....	....	....
Banks	8 623 ..	....	....	....	....	....	....	....	....
Other sectors	8 624 ..	....	....	....	....	....	....	....	....
Money market instruments	8 630 ..	48.2	23.3	15.5	14.5	8.8	21.0	17.1	49.7
Monetary authorities	8 631 ..	....	....	....	....	....	....	....	....
General government	8 632 ..	....	....	....	....	....	....	....	....
Banks	8 633 ..	34.0	11.9	15.5	14.3	8.6	20.3	13.1	42.5
Other sectors	8 634 ..	14.2	11.4	....	.2	.2	.7	4.0	7.2
Financial derivatives	8 900 ..	....	....	....	....	2.0	....	....	....
Monetary authorities	8 901 ..	....	....	....	....	2.0	....	....	....
General government	8 902 ..	....	....	....	....	....	....	....	....
Banks	8 903 ..	....	....	....	....	....	....	....	....
Other sectors	8 904 ..	....	....	....	....	....	....	....	....
Other investment	8 703 ..	577.1	855.6	1,273.2	1,289.9	1,451.2	1,957.3	2,158.9	4,297.8
Trade credits	8 706 ..	245.8	371.8	608.6	431.9	687.8	988.5	1,398.5	2,205.4
General government	8 707 ..	....	....	....	....	....	....	....	....
of which: Short-term	8 709 ..	....	....	....	....	....	....	....	....
Other sectors	8 710 ..	245.8	371.8	608.6	431.9	687.8	988.5	1,398.5	2,205.4
of which: Short-term	8 712 ..	*245.8*	*371.8*	*608.6*	*431.9*	*687.8*	*988.5*	*1,398.5*	*2,205.4*
Loans	8 714 ..	8.1	29.0	63.9	51.7	47.4	40.5	90.0	257.9
Monetary authorities	8 715 ..	....	20.0	54.2	40.0	25.0	30.0	30.0	30.0
of which: Short-term	8 718 ..	....	*20.0*	*29.2*	*15.0*	....	....	....	....
General government	8 719 ..	....	....	....	....	....	....	....	....
of which: Short-term	8 721 ..	....	....	....	....	....	....	....	....
Banks	8 722 ..	5.8	7.2	9.5	11.5	20.8	7.6	32.6	105.1
of which: Short-term	8 724 ..	*5.7*	*7.2*	*9.5*	*11.3*	*19.9*	*7.3*	*29.6*	*100.5*
Other sectors	8 725 ..	2.3	1.8	.2	.2	1.6	2.9	27.4	122.8
of which: Short-term	8 727 ..	....	....	....	....	*1.2*	*2.4*	*22.8*	*120.3*
Currency and deposits	8 730 ..	276.7	372.1	518.4	599.6	468.7	734.8	504.6	1,502.4
Monetary authorities	8 731 ..	1.6	114.7	276.0	277.1	38.3	96.3	132.8	522.1
General government	8 732 ..	....	....	....	....	....	....	....	....
Banks	8 733 ..	271.5	250.0	234.9	297.8	413.8	624.8	352.8	954.9
Other sectors	8 734 ..	3.6	7.4	7.5	24.7	16.6	13.7	19.0	25.4
Other assets	8 736 ..	46.5	82.7	82.3	206.7	247.3	193.5	165.8	332.1
Monetary authorities	8 737 ..	.6	13.7	30.8	84.0	118.3	.2	.1	.3
of which: Short-term	8 739 ..	*.6*	*13.7*	*30.8*	*84.0*	*118.3*	*.2*	*.1*	*.3*
General government	8 740 ..	....	....	....	....	....	....	....	7.3
of which: Short-term	8 742 ..	....	....	....	....	....	....	....	*1.5*
Banks	8 743 ..	11.6	11.4	3.4	2.6	1.2	32.8	30.5	139.9
of which: Short-term	8 745 ..	*11.6*	*11.4*	*3.4*	*2.6*	*1.2*	*32.8*	*30.5*	*139.9*
Other sectors	8 746 ..	34.3	57.6	48.1	120.1	127.8	160.5	135.2	184.6
of which: Short-term	8 748 ..	*34.3*	*57.6*	*48.1*	*120.1*	*127.8*	*160.5*	*135.2*	*184.6*
Reserve assets	8 802 ..	356.8	359.4	477.8	499.0	770.2	1,296.6	1,383.0	4,182.2
Monetary gold	8 812 ..	6.3	55.7	60.4	37.4	79.4	190.0	314.4	230.0
Special drawing rights	8 811 ..	.2	.4	.3	....	....	....	....	....
Reserve position in the Fund	8 810 ..	....	....	....	....	....	....	....	....
Foreign exchange	8 803 ..	350.0	300.1	416.4	460.7	690.4	1,105.6	1,067.2	3,866.1
Other claims	8 813 ..	.3	3.2	.7	.8	.4	.9	1.3	86.0

Table 3 (Concluded). INTERNATIONAL INVESTMENT POSITION (End-period stocks), 2000–2007

(Millions of U.S. dollars)

	Code	2000	2001	2002	2003	2004	2005	2006	2007
LIABILITIES	8 995 D.	**3,436.8**	**4,415.9**	**5,378.4**	**5,819.2**	**6,697.9**	**7,184.9**	**9,200.6**	**16,523.1**
Direct investment in Belarus	8 555 ..	**1,305.5**	**1,397.2**	**1,645.9**	**1,898.6**	**2,057.0**	**2,382.8**	**2,734.3**	**4,508.2**
Equity capital and reinvested earnings	8 556 ..	1,305.5	1,397.2	1,446.4	1,605.6	1,718.8	2,030.9	2,337.9	4,006.4
Claims on direct investors	8 557 ..	....	....	....	....	....	....	....	....
Liabilities to direct investors	8 558 ..	1,305.5	1,397.2	1,446.4	1,605.6	1,718.8	2,030.9	2,337.9	4,006.4
Other capital	8 580 ..	....	....	199.5	293.0	338.2	351.9	396.4	501.8
Claims on direct investors	8 585 ..	....	....	....	....	....	....	....	....
Liabilities to direct investors	8 590 ..	....	....	199.5	293.0	338.2	351.9	396.4	501.8
Portfolio investment	8 652 ..	**78.6**	**36.1**	**20.3**	**24.9**	**87.8**	**50.7**	**27.2**	**30.0**
Equity securities	8 660 ..	8.8	11.4	9.8	11.7	16.9	18.7	18.6	23.2
Banks	8 663 ..	7.3	6.9	7.2	9.7	9.8	10.9	9.6	13.2
Other sectors	8 664 ..	1.5	4.5	2.6	2.0	7.1	7.8	9.0	10.0
Debt securities	8 669 ..	69.8	24.7	10.5	13.2	70.9	32.0	8.6	6.8
Bonds and notes	8 670 ..	....	....	....	....	....	....	....	....
Monetary authorities	8 671 ..	....	....	....	....	....	....	....	....
General government	8 672 ..	....	....	....	....	....	....	....	....
Banks	8 673 ..	....	....	....	....	....	....	....	....
Other sectors	8 674 ..	....	....	....	....	....	....	....	....
Money market instruments	8 680 ..	69.8	24.7	10.5	13.2	70.9	32.0	8.6	6.8
Monetary authorities	8 681 ..	50.0	1.1	6.1	5.1	....	.1	.1	.1
General government	8 682 ..	....	.2	.9	3.0	58.5	25.7	2.3	.6
Banks	8 683 ..	7.4	11.5	3.5	5.1	9.7	6.2	6.1	6.1
Other sectors	8 684 ..	12.4	11.9	....	....	2.7	....	.1	....
Financial derivatives	8 905 ..	....	....	....	....	**3.7**	**7.1**	....	....
Monetary authorities	8 906 ..	....	....	....	....	3.7	7.1	....	....
General government	8 907 ..	....	....	....	....	....	....	....	....
Banks	8 908 ..	....	....	....	....	....	....	....	....
Other sectors	8 909 ..	....	....	....	....	....	....	....	....
Other investment	8 753 ..	**2,052.7**	**2,982.6**	**3,712.2**	**3,895.7**	**4,549.4**	**4,744.3**	**6,439.1**	**11,984.9**
Trade credits	8 756 ..	494.6	980.5	1,331.3	1,259.5	2,161.7	1,966.2	2,533.7	4,030.9
General government	8 757 ..	....	....	....	....	....	....	....	....
of which: Short-term	8 759 ..	....	....	....	....	....	....	....	....
Other sectors	8 760 ..	494.6	980.5	1,331.3	1,259.5	2,161.7	1,966.2	2,533.7	4,030.9
of which: Short-term	8 762 ..	*494.6*	*980.5*	*1,331.3*	*1,259.5*	*2,161.7*	*1,966.2*	*2,533.7*	*4,030.9*
Loans	8 764 ..	1,051.0	1,347.1	1,751.2	1,842.2	1,631.5	1,942.6	3,278.4	7,089.2
Monetary authorities	8 765 ..	142.1	174.4	241.0	238.8	63.5	....	....	440.0
of which: Use of Fund credit and loans from the Fund	8 766 ..	*114.2*	*80.8*	*55.6*	*26.0*	*9.1*	....	....	....
of which: Short-term	8 768 ..	....	....	*5.1*	....	....	....	....	*200.0*
General government	8 769 ..	302.8	349.5	361.2	319.4	433.1	581.1	586.7	2,035.7
of which: Short-term	8 771 ..	....	....	....	....	....	*32.0*	*85.6*	....
Banks	8 772 ..	62.4	99.5	176.2	216.8	390.9	595.4	1,324.8	2,368.3
of which: Short-term	8 774 ..	*62.4*	*99.5*	*176.2*	*216.8*	*390.9*	*149.8*	*603.2*	*1,281.9*
Other sectors	8 775 ..	543.7	723.7	972.8	1,067.2	744.0	766.1	1,366.9	2,245.2
of which: Short-term	8 777 ..	*90.9*	*105.5*	*130.5*	*187.8*	*122.5*	*283.0*	*523.7*	*977.8*
Currency and deposits	8 780 ..	51.0	106.8	133.5	215.7	233.0	336.2	110.6	289.4
Monetary authorities	8 781 ..	.3	20.4	40.8	41.8	13.4	.6	.6	150.8
General government	8 782 ..	....	....	....	....	....	....	....	....
Banks	8 783 ..	50.7	86.4	92.7	173.9	219.6	335.6	110.0	138.6
Other sectors	8 784 ..	....	....	....	....	....	....	....	....
Other liabilities	8 786 ..	456.1	548.2	496.2	578.3	523.2	499.3	516.4	575.4
Monetary authorities	8 787 ..	....	....	....	....	....	....	....	5.3
of which: Short-term	8 789 ..	....	....	....	....	....	....	....	*5.3*
General government	8 790 ..	43.2	3.8	.5	21.5	.5	....	....	....
of which: Short-term	8 792 ..	*43.2*	*3.8*	*.5*	*21.5*	*.5*	....	....	....
Banks	8 793 ..	1.0	2.2	4.5	4.9	5.6	11.1	45.8	57.8
of which: Short-term	8 795 ..	*1.0*	*2.2*	*4.5*	*4.9*	*5.6*	*11.1*	*45.8*	*57.8*
Other sectors	8 796 ..	411.9	542.2	491.2	551.9	517.1	488.2	470.6	512.3
of which: Short-term	8 798 ..	*411.9*	*542.2*	*491.2*	*551.9*	*517.1*	*488.2*	*470.6*	*512.3*
NET INTERNATIONAL INVESTMENT POSITION	8 995 ..	**−2,421.6**	**−3,149.1**	**−3,607.4**	**−4,007.9**	**−4,457.1**	**−3,895.8**	**−5,617.2**	**−7,946.5**
Conversion rates: rubels per U.S. dollar (end of period)	0 102 ..	**1,180.0**	**1,580.0**	**1,920.0**	**2,156.0**	**2,170.0**	**2,152.0**	**2,140.0**	**2,150.0**

Table 1. ANALYTIC PRESENTATION, 2000–2007

(Millions of U.S. dollars)

	Code	2000	2001	2002	2003	2004	2005	2006	2007
A. Current Account[1]	4 993 Z.	**11,381**	**9,392**	....	....	....	....	....	....
Goods: exports f.o.b.	2 100 ..	164,677	163,498	....	....	....	....	....	....
Goods: imports f.o.b.	3 100 ..	−162,086	−159,790	....	....	....	....	....	....
Balance on Goods	4 100 ..	*2,591*	*3,707*	....	....	....	....	....	....
Services: credit	2 200 ..	49,789	50,314	....	....	....	....	....	....
Services: debit	3 200 ..	−41,868	−43,316	....	....	....	....	....	....
Balance on Goods and Services	4 991 ..	*10,512*	*10,705*	....	....	....	....	....	....
Income: credit	2 300 ..	75,673	78,906	....	....	....	....	....	....
Income: debit	3 300 ..	−70,625	−75,999	....	....	....	....	....	....
Balance on Goods, Services, and Income	4 992 ..	*15,560*	*13,612*	....	....	....	....	....	....
Current transfers: credit	2 379 Z.	7,014	7,316	....	....	....	....	....	....
Current transfers: debit	3 379 ..	−11,193	−11,535	....	....	....	....	....	....
B. Capital Account[1]	4 994 Z.	**−213**	**26**	....	....	....	....	....	....
Capital account: credit	2 994 Z.	222	480	....	....	....	....	....	....
Capital account: debit	3 994 ..	−436	−454	....	....	....	....	....	....
Total, Groups A Plus B	4 981 ..	*11,168*	*9,418*	....	....	....	....	....	....
C. Financial Account[1]	4 995 W.	**−9,233**	**−7,978**	....	....	....	....	....	....
Direct investment abroad	4 505 ..	−207,472	−86,091	....	....	....	....	....	....
Direct investment in Belgium-Luxembourg	4 555 Z.	214,941	73,635	....	....	....	....	....	....
Portfolio investment assets	4 602 ..	−122,814	−125,068	....	....	....	....	....	....
Equity securities	4 610 ..	−103,290	−57,427	....	....	....	....	....	....
Debt securities	4 619 ..	−19,524	−67,642	....	....	....	....	....	....
Portfolio investment liabilities	4 652 Z.	132,547	140,588	....	....	....	....	....	....
Equity securities	4 660 ..	82,908	97,662	....	....	....	....	....	....
Debt securities	4 669 Z.	49,639	42,926	....	....	....	....	....	....
Financial derivatives	4 910 ..	−2,401	−4,147	....	....	....	....	....	....
Financial derivatives assets	4 900 ..	−3,653	−5,089	....	....	....	....	....	....
Financial derivatives liabilities	4 905 ..	1,252	942	....	....	....	....	....	....
Other investment assets	4 703 ..	−39,033	−70,053	....	....	....	....	....	....
Monetary authorities	4 701 ..	−342	13	....	....	....	....	....	....
General government	4 704 ..	−236	−137	....	....	....	....	....	....
Banks	4 705 ..	−22,296	−58,086	....	....	....	....	....	....
Other sectors	4 728 ..	−16,159	−11,843	....	....	....	....	....	....
Other investment liabilities	4 753 W.	14,999	63,158	....	....	....	....	....	....
Monetary authorities	4 753 WA	−1,386	−3,903	....	....	....	....	....	....
General government	4 753 ZB	−1,279	415	....	....	....	....	....	....
Banks	4 753 ZC	7,139	67,159	....	....	....	....	....	....
Other sectors	4 753 ZD	10,524	−513	....	....	....	....	....	....
Total, Groups A Through C	4 983 ..	*1,935*	*1,440*	....	....	....	....	....	....
D. Net Errors and Omissions	4 998 ..	**−2,894**	**3**	....	....	....	....	....	....
Total, Groups A Through D	4 984 ..	*−959*	*1,442*	....	....	....	....	....	....
E. Reserves and Related Items	4 802 A.	**959**	**−1,442**	....	....	....	....	....	....
Reserve assets	4 802 ..	959	−1,442	....	....	....	....	....	....
Use of Fund credit and loans	4 766 ..	....	....	....	....	....	....	....	....
Exceptional financing	4 920 ..	....	....	....	....	....	....	....	....
Conversion rates: euros per U.S. dollar	0 103 ..	1.08540	1.11751	1.06255	.88603	.80537	.80412	.79714	.73064

[1] Excludes components that have been classified in the categories of Group E.

Table 2. STANDARD PRESENTATION, 2000–2007

(Millions of U.S. dollars)

	Code	2000	2001	2002	2003	2004	2005	2006	2007
CURRENT ACCOUNT	4 993	11,381	9,392	....	....	....	....	....	....
A. GOODS	4 100	2,591	3,707	....	....	....	....	....	....
Credit	2 100	164,677	163,498	....	....	....	....	....	....
General merchandise: exports f.o.b.	2 110	149,435	146,625	....	....	....	....	....	....
Goods for processing: exports f.o.b.	2 150	12,973	14,607	....	....	....	....	....	....
Repairs on goods	2 160	372	380	....	....	....	....	....	....
Goods procured in ports by carriers	2 170	1,293	1,332	....	....	....	....	....	....
Nonmonetary gold	2 180	605	554	....	....	....	....	....	....
Debit	3 100	−162,086	−159,790	....	....	....	....	....	....
General merchandise: imports f.o.b.	3 110	−148,952	−145,147	....	....	....	....	....	....
Goods for processing: imports f.o.b.	3 150	−11,589	−13,307	....	....	....	....	....	....
Repairs on goods	3 160	−396	−349	....	....	....	....	....	....
Goods procured in ports by carriers	3 170	−642	−570	....	....	....	....	....	....
Nonmonetary gold	3 180	−508	−417	....	....	....	....	....	....
B. SERVICES	4 200	7,921	6,998	....	....	....	....	....	....
Total credit	2 200	*49,789*	*50,314*	....	....	....	....	....	....
Total debit	3 200	*−41,868*	*−43,316*	....	....	....	....	....	....
Transportation services, credit	2 205	10,665	10,178	....	....	....	....	....	....
Passenger	2 850	*1,693*	*1,425*	....	....	....	....	....	....
Freight	2 851	*7,736*	*7,622*	....	....	....	....	....	....
Other	2 852	*1,236*	*1,131*	....	....	....	....	....	....
Sea transport, passenger	2 207	11	9	....	....	....	....	....	....
Sea transport, freight	2 208	3,912	3,833	....	....	....	....	....	....
Sea transport, other	2 209	710	631	....	....	....	....	....	....
Air transport, passenger	2 211	1,603	1,329	....	....	....	....	....	....
Air transport, freight	2 212	797	922	....	....	....	....	....	....
Air transport, other	2 213	269	165	....	....	....	....	....	....
Other transport, passenger	2 215	79	87	....	....	....	....	....	....
Other transport, freight	2 216	3,027	2,866	....	....	....	....	....	....
Other transport, other	2 217	257	335	....	....	....	....	....	....
Transportation services, debit	3 205	−8,386	−8,368	....	....	....	....	....	....
Passenger	3 850	*−1,225*	*−1,111*	....	....	....	....	....	....
Freight	3 851	*−6,472*	*−6,593*	....	....	....	....	....	....
Other	3 852	*−689*	*−663*	....	....	....	....	....	....
Sea transport, passenger	3 207	−7	−10	....	....	....	....	....	....
Sea transport, freight	3 208	−3,592	−3,644	....	....	....	....	....	....
Sea transport, other	3 209	−182	−175	....	....	....	....	....	....
Air transport, passenger	3 211	−1,151	−1,031	....	....	....	....	....	....
Air transport, freight	3 212	−563	−588	....	....	....	....	....	....
Air transport, other	3 213	−437	−385	....	....	....	....	....	....
Other transport, passenger	3 215	−67	−71	....	....	....	....	....	....
Other transport, freight	3 216	−2,316	−2,361	....	....	....	....	....	....
Other transport, other	3 217	−70	−103	....	....	....	....	....	....
Travel, credit	2 236	7,447	7,613	....	....	....	....	....	....
Business travel	2 237	2,924	3,360	....	....	....	....	....	....
Personal travel	2 240	4,523	4,253	....	....	....	....	....	....
Travel, debit	3 236	−10,182	−10,569	....	....	....	....	....	....
Business travel	3 237	−3,513	−4,042	....	....	....	....	....	....
Personal travel	3 240	−6,669	−6,527	....	....	....	....	....	....
Other services, credit	2 200 BA	31,676	32,523	....	....	....	....	....	....
Communications	2 245	1,894	2,056	....	....	....	....	....	....
Construction	2 249	924	893	....	....	....	....	....	....
Insurance	2 253	1,068	1,031	....	....	....	....	....	....
Financial	2 260	13,122	12,587	....	....	....	....	....	....
Computer and information	2 262	1,786	1,916	....	....	....	....	....	....
Royalties and licence fees	2 266	779	887	....	....	....	....	....	....
Other business services	2 268	10,243	11,207	....	....	....	....	....	....
Personal, cultural, and recreational	2 287	628	602	....	....	....	....	....	....
Government, n.i.e.	2 291	1,232	1,343	....	....	....	....	....	....
Other services, debit	3 200 BA	−23,300	−24,379	....	....	....	....	....	....
Communications	3 245	−988	−1,188	....	....	....	....	....	....
Construction	3 249	−609	−585	....	....	....	....	....	....
Insurance	3 253	−868	−859	....	....	....	....	....	....
Financial	3 260	−7,904	−7,314	....	....	....	....	....	....
Computer and information	3 262	−1,322	−1,475	....	....	....	....	....	....
Royalties and licence fees	3 266	−918	−1,246	....	....	....	....	....	....
Other business services	3 268	−9,440	−10,494	....	....	....	....	....	....
Personal, cultural, and recreational	3 287	−826	−757	....	....	....	....	....	....
Government, n.i.e.	3 291	−424	−460	....	....	....	....	....	....

Belgium-Luxembourg 126

Table 2 (Continued). STANDARD PRESENTATION, 2000–2007

(Millions of U.S. dollars)

	Code	2000	2001	2002	2003	2004	2005	2006	2007
C. INCOME	4 300	**5,048**	**2,907**	....	....	....	....	....	....
Total credit	2 300	*75,673*	*78,906*	....	....	....	....	....	....
Total debit	3 300	*−70,625*	*−75,999*	....	....	....	....	....	....
Compensation of employees, credit	2 310	**3,720**	**3,662**	....	....	....	....	....	....
Compensation of employees, debit	3 310	**−2,932**	**−3,273**	....	....	....	....	....	....
Investment income, credit	2 320	**71,954**	**75,244**	....	....	....	....	....	....
Direct investment income	2 330	5,138	6,909	....	....	....	....	....	....
Dividends and distributed branch profits	2 332	2,431	2,795	....	....	....	....	....	....
Reinvested earnings and undistributed branch profits	2 333	184	38	....	....	....	....	....	....
Income on debt (interest)	2 334	2,523	4,075	....	....	....	....	....	....
Portfolio investment income	2 339	34,143	35,678	....	....	....	....	....	....
Income on equity	2 340	5,040	5,235	....	....	....	....	....	....
Income on bonds and notes	2 350	26,298	26,980	....	....	....	....	....	....
Income on money market instruments	2 360	2,805	3,462	....	....	....	....	....	....
Other investment income	2 370	32,673	32,658	....	....	....	....	....	....
Investment income, debit	3 320	**−67,693**	**−72,726**	....	....	....	....	....	....
Direct investment income	3 330	−11,488	−13,739	....	....	....	....	....	....
Dividends and distributed branch profits	3 332	−6,118	−7,782	....	....	....	....	....	....
Reinvested earnings and undistributed branch profits	3 333	−3,197	−3,498	....	....	....	....	....	....
Income on debt (interest)	3 334	−2,173	−2,459	....	....	....	....	....	....
Portfolio investment income	3 339	−24,102	−26,769	....	....	....	....	....	....
Income on equity	3 340	−17,379	−18,236	....	....	....	....	....	....
Income on bonds and notes	3 350	−5,330	−6,713	....	....	....	....	....	....
Income on money market instruments	3 360	−1,393	−1,820	....	....	....	....	....	....
Other investment income	3 370	−32,103	−32,219	....	....	....	....	....	....
D. CURRENT TRANSFERS	4 379	**−4,179**	**−4,220**	....	....	....	....	....	....
Credit	2 379	**7,014**	**7,316**	....	....	....	....	....	....
General government	2 380	1,987	2,099	....	....	....	....	....	....
Other sectors	2 390	5,027	5,217	....	....	....	....	....	....
Workers' remittances	2 391	101	91	....	....	....	....	....	....
Other current transfers	2 392	4,926	5,125	....	....	....	....	....	....
Debit	3 379	**−11,193**	**−11,535**	....	....	....	....	....	....
General government	3 380	−5,080	−5,327	....	....	....	....	....	....
Other sectors	3 390	−6,113	−6,209	....	....	....	....	....	....
Workers' remittances	3 391	−431	−364	....	....	....	....	....	....
Other current transfers	3 392	−5,682	−5,845	....	....	....	....	....	....
CAPITAL AND FINANCIAL ACCOUNT	4 996	**−8,487**	**−9,395**	....	....	....	....	....	....
CAPITAL ACCOUNT	4 994	**−213**	**26**	....	....	....	....	....	....
Total credit	2 994	*222*	*480*	....	....	....	....	....	....
Total debit	3 994	*−436*	*−454*	....	....	....	....	....	....
Capital transfers, credit	2 400	**214**	**218**	....	....	....	....	....	....
General government	2 401	1	1	....	....	....	....	....	....
Debt forgiveness	2 402	....	....	....	....	....	....	....	....
Other capital transfers	2 410	1	1	....	....	....	....	....	....
Other sectors	2 430	213	217	....	....	....	....	....	....
Migrants' transfers	2 431	184	180	....	....	....	....	....	....
Debt forgiveness	2 432	....	....	....	....	....	....	....	....
Other capital transfers	2 440	29	37	....	....	....	....	....	....
Capital transfers, debit	3 400	**−344**	**−357**	....	....	....	....	....	....
General government	3 401	−84	−71	....	....	....	....	....	....
Debt forgiveness	3 402	....	....	....	....	....	....	....	....
Other capital transfers	3 410	−84	−71	....	....	....	....	....	....
Other sectors	3 430	−260	−286	....	....	....	....	....	....
Migrants' transfers	3 431	−225	−269	....	....	....	....	....	....
Debt forgiveness	3 432	....	....	....	....	....	....	....	....
Other capital transfers	3 440	−35	−17	....	....	....	....	....	....
Nonproduced nonfinancial assets, credit	2 480	**8**	**262**	....	....	....	....	....	....
Nonproduced nonfinancial assets, debit	3 480	**−91**	**−97**	....	....	....	....	....	....

Table 2 (Continued). STANDARD PRESENTATION, 2000–2007

(Millions of U.S. dollars)

	Code	2000	2001	2002	2003	2004	2005	2006	2007
FINANCIAL ACCOUNT	4 995	−8,274	−9,420	....	....	....	....	....	....
A. DIRECT INVESTMENT	4 500	7,469	−12,456	....	....	....	....	....	....
Direct investment abroad	4 505	−207,472	−86,091	....	....	....	....	....	....
Equity capital	4 510	−142,280	−47,843	....	....	....	....	....	....
Claims on affiliated enterprises	4 515	....	....	....	....	....	....	....	....
Liabilities to affiliated enterprises	4 520	....	....	....	....	....	....	....	....
Reinvested earnings	4 525	−184	−38	....	....	....	....	....	....
Other capital	4 530	−65,008	−38,210	....	....	....	....	....	....
Claims on affiliated enterprises	4 535	....	....	....	....	....	....	....	....
Liabilities to affiliated enterprises	4 540	....	....	....	....	....	....	....	....
Direct investment in Belgium-Luxembourg	4 555	214,941	73,635	....	....	....	....	....	....
Equity capital	4 560	163,774	63,767	....	....	....	....	....	....
Claims on direct investors	4 565	....	....	....	....	....	....	....	....
Liabilities to direct investors	4 570	....	....	....	....	....	....	....	....
Reinvested earnings	4 575	3,197	3,498	....	....	....	....	....	....
Other capital	4 580	47,970	6,371	....	....	....	....	....	....
Claims on direct investors	4 585	....	....	....	....	....	....	....	....
Liabilities to direct investors	4 590	....	....	....	....	....	....	....	....
B. PORTFOLIO INVESTMENT	4 600	9,733	15,519	....	....	....	....	....	....
Assets	4 602	−122,814	−125,068	....	....	....	....	....	....
Equity securities	4 610	−103,290	−57,427	....	....	....	....	....	....
Monetary authorities	4 611	....	....	....	....	....	....	....	....
General government	4 612	....	....	....	....	....	....	....	....
Banks	4 613	−1,164	756	....	....	....	....	....	....
Other sectors	4 614	−102,125	−58,183	....	....	....	....	....	....
Debt securities	4 619	−19,524	−67,642	....	....	....	....	....	....
Bonds and notes	4 620	−48,020	−75,830	....	....	....	....	....	....
Monetary authorities	4 621	143	−413	....	....	....	....	....	....
General government	4 622	....	....	....	....	....	....	....	....
Banks	4 623	−19,303	−61,541	....	....	....	....	....	....
Other sectors	4 624	−28,860	−13,876	....	....	....	....	....	....
Money market instruments	4 630	28,496	8,189	....	....	....	....	....	....
Monetary authorities	4 631	....	....	....	....	....	....	....	....
General government	4 632	....	....	....	....	....	....	....	....
Banks	4 633	20,121	694	....	....	....	....	....	....
Other sectors	4 634	8,375	7,495	....	....	....	....	....	....
Liabilities	4 652	132,547	140,588	....	....	....	....	....	....
Equity securities	4 660	82,908	97,662	....	....	....	....	....	....
Banks	4 663	....	....	....	....	....	....	....	....
Other sectors	4 664	....	....	....	....	....	....	....	....
Debt securities	4 669	49,639	42,926	....	....	....	....	....	....
Bonds and notes	4 670	55,573	14,328	....	....	....	....	....	....
Monetary authorities	4 671	....	....	....	....	....	....	....	....
General government	4 672	24,792	8,671	....	....	....	....	....	....
Banks	4 673	973	959	....	....	....	....	....	....
Other sectors	4 674	29,808	4,698	....	....	....	....	....	....
Money market instruments	4 680	−5,934	28,598	....	....	....	....	....	....
Monetary authorities	4 681	....	....	....	....	....	....	....	....
General government	4 682	−1,899	−1,163	....	....	....	....	....	....
Banks	4 683	−1,537	7,206	....	....	....	....	....	....
Other sectors	4 684	−2,498	22,556	....	....	....	....	....	....
C. FINANCIAL DERIVATIVES	4 910	−2,401	−4,147	....	....	....	....	....	....
Monetary authorities	4 911	....	....	....	....	....	....	....	....
General government	4 912	70	−642	....	....	....	....	....	....
Banks	4 913	−692	−449	....	....	....	....	....	....
Other sectors	4 914	−1,779	−3,056	....	....	....	....	....	....
Assets	4 900	−3,653	−5,089	....	....	....	....	....	....
Monetary authorities	4 901	....	....	....	....	....	....	....	....
General government	4 902	70	−642	....	....	....	....	....	....
Banks	4 903	−692	−449	....	....	....	....	....	....
Other sectors	4 904	−3,031	−3,998	....	....	....	....	....	....
Liabilities	4 905	1,252	942	....	....	....	....	....	....
Monetary authorities	4 906	....	....	....	....	....	....	....	....
General government	4 907	....	....	....	....	....	....	....	....
Banks	4 908	....	....	....	....	....	....	....	....
Other sectors	4 909	1,252	942	....	....	....	....	....	....

Table 2 (Concluded). STANDARD PRESENTATION, 2000–2007

(Millions of U.S. dollars)

	Code	2000	2001	2002	2003	2004	2005	2006	2007
D. OTHER INVESTMENT	4 700	−24,034	−6,895	....	....	....	....	....	....
Assets	4 703	−39,033	−70,053	....	....	....	....	....	....
Trade credits	4 706	−2,002	431	....	....	....	....	....	....
General government	4 707	....	....	....	....	....	....	....	....
of which: Short-term	4 709	....	....	....	....	....	....	....	....
Other sectors	4 710	−2,002	431	....	....	....	....	....	....
of which: Short-term	4 712	....	....	....	....	....	....	....	....
Loans	4 714	−1,632	−398	....	....	....	....	....	....
Monetary authorities	4 715	....	....	....	....	....	....	....	....
of which: Short-term	4 718	....	....	....	....	....	....	....	....
General government	4 719	15	−2	....	....	....	....	....	....
of which: Short-term	4 721	−1	−6	....	....	....	....	....	....
Banks	4 722	−1,505	661	....	....	....	....	....	....
of which: Short-term	4 724	61	−52	....	....	....	....	....	....
Other sectors	4 725	−142	−1,057	....	....	....	....	....	....
of which: Short-term	4 727	....	....	....	....	....	....	....	....
Currency and deposits	4 730	−36,402	−70,923	....	....	....	....	....	....
Monetary authorities	4 731	−342	13	....	....	....	....	....	....
General government	4 732	−237	25	....	....	....	....	....	....
Banks	4 733	−20,791	−58,747	....	....	....	....	....	....
Other sectors	4 734	−15,032	−12,214	....	....	....	....	....	....
Other assets	4 736	1,002	837	....	....	....	....	....	....
Monetary authorities	4 737	....	....	....	....	....	....	....	....
of which: Short-term	4 739	....	....	....	....	....	....	....	....
General government	4 740	−15	−160	....	....	....	....	....	....
of which: Short-term	4 742	....	....	....	....	....	....	....	....
Banks	4 743	....	....	....	....	....	....	....	....
of which: Short-term	4 745	....	....	....	....	....	....	....	....
Other sectors	4 746	1,017	997	....	....	....	....	....	....
of which: Short-term	4 748	....	....	....	....	....	....	....	....
Liabilities	4 753	**14,999**	**63,158**	....	....	....	....	....	....
Trade credits	4 756	893	−313	....	....	....	....	....	....
General government	4 757	....	....	....	....	....	....	....	....
of which: Short-term	4 759	....	....	....	....	....	....	....	....
Other sectors	4 760	893	−313	....	....	....	....	....	....
of which: Short-term	4 762	....	....	....	....	....	....	....	....
Loans	4 764	10,857	3,791	....	....	....	....	....	....
Monetary authorities	4 765	....	....	....	....	....	....	....	....
of which: Use of Fund credit and loans from the Fund	4 766	....	....	....	....	....	....	....	....
of which: Short-term	4 768	....	....	....	....	....	....	....	....
General government	4 769	−1,279	415	....	....	....	....	....	....
of which: Short-term	4 771	−1,337	221	....	....	....	....	....	....
Banks	4 772	4,044	6,468	....	....	....	....	....	....
of which: Short-term	4 774	....	....	....	....	....	....	....	....
Other sectors	4 775	8,092	−3,092	....	....	....	....	....	....
of which: Short-term	4 777	5,561	−3,248	....	....	....	....	....	....
Currency and deposits	4 780	1,709	56,788	....	....	....	....	....	....
Monetary authorities	4 781	−1,386	−3,903	....	....	....	....	....	....
General government	4 782	....	....	....	....	....	....	....	....
Banks	4 783	3,095	60,691	....	....	....	....	....	....
Other sectors	4 784	....	....	....	....	....	....	....	....
Other liabilities	4 786	1,539	2,893	....	....	....	....	....	....
Monetary authorities	4 787	....	....	....	....	....	....	....	....
of which: Short-term	4 789	....	....	....	....	....	....	....	....
General government	4 790	....	....	....	....	....	....	....	....
of which: Short-term	4 792	....	....	....	....	....	....	....	....
Banks	4 793	....	....	....	....	....	....	....	....
of which: Short-term	4 795	....	....	....	....	....	....	....	....
Other sectors	4 796	1,539	2,893	....	....	....	....	....	....
of which: Short-term	4 798	897	2,285	....	....	....	....	....	....
E. RESERVE ASSETS	4 802	**959**	**−1,442**	....	....	....	....	....	....
Monetary gold	4 812	....	....	....	....	....	....	....	....
Special drawing rights	4 811	−53	−183	....	....	....	....	....	....
Reserve position in the Fund	4 810	483	−451	....	....	....	....	....	....
Foreign exchange	4 803	528	−808	....	....	....	....	....	....
Other claims	4 813	....	....	....	....	....	....	....	....
NET ERRORS AND OMISSIONS	4 998	**−2,894**	**3**	....	....	....	....	....	....

Table 1. ANALYTIC PRESENTATION, 2000–2007

(Millions of U.S. dollars)

	Code	2000	2001	2002	2003	2004	2005	2006	2007
A. Current Account[1]	4 993 Z.	....	....	**11,611**	**12,906**	**12,537**	**9,945**	**8,035**	**7,216**
Goods: exports f.o.b.	2 100 ..	....	....	169,166	204,962	245,426	263,056	281,135	323,708
Goods: imports f.o.b.	3 100 ..	....	....	−159,648	−194,003	−235,718	−257,137	−277,778	−322,023
Balance on Goods	4 100 ..	....	....	*9,518*	*10,959*	*9,708*	*5,919*	*3,357*	*1,685*
Services: credit	2 200 ..	....	....	37,822	44,708	52,708	56,144	59,516	79,113
Services: debit	3 200 ..	....	....	−35,863	−42,862	−49,023	−51,172	−53,250	−72,578
Balance on Goods and Services	4 991 ..	....	....	*11,477*	*12,804*	*13,392*	*10,891*	*9,623*	*8,220*
Income: credit	2 300 ..	....	....	36,372	40,213	48,891	59,028	74,277	98,581
Income: debit	3 300 ..	....	....	−31,897	−33,732	−43,269	−53,604	−69,324	−92,765
Balance on Goods, Services, and Income	4 992 ..	....	....	*15,952*	*19,286*	*19,014*	*16,314*	*14,576*	*14,036*
Current transfers: credit	2 379 Z.	....	....	5,275	6,515	7,949	9,355	8,812	8,681
Current transfers: debit	3 379 ..	....	....	−9,616	−12,894	−14,427	−15,724	−15,353	−15,500
B. Capital Account[1]	4 994 Z.	....	....	**−585**	**−1,021**	**−497**	**−894**	**−405**	**−1,499**
Capital account: credit	2 994 Z.	....	....	219	267	399	399	984	536
Capital account: debit	3 994 ..	....	....	−803	−1,288	−896	−1,293	−1,389	−2,035
Total, Groups A Plus B	4 981 ..	....	....	*11,027*	*11,886*	*12,039*	*9,051*	*7,630*	*5,718*
C. Financial Account[1]	4 995 W.	....	....	**−6,483**	**−12,518**	**−10,660**	**−8,929**	**−9,116**	**−6,634**
Direct investment abroad	4 505 ..	....	....	−8,902	−39,043	−34,682	−30,433	−49,657	−55,073
Direct investment in Belgium	4 555 Z.	....	....	18,081	34,544	44,415	34,040	56,744	72,195
Portfolio investment assets	4 602 ..	....	....	−5,707	−6,046	−35,558	−43,491	−26,529	−80,503
Equity securities	4 610 ..	....	....	−3,551	−5,508	−8,037	−20,449	−19,980	−20,401
Debt securities	4 619 ..	....	....	−2,156	−538	−27,520	−23,043	−6,548	−60,102
Portfolio investment liabilities	4 652 Z.	....	....	20,149	6,628	5,070	−1,215	17,348	36,694
Equity securities	4 660 ..	....	....	−467	3,182	4,092	5,712	4,588	3,360
Debt securities	4 669 Z.	....	....	20,616	3,446	978	−6,927	12,760	33,334
Financial derivatives	4 910 ..	....	....	−1,934	−3,626	−5,586	−5,448	3,372	1,434
Financial derivatives assets	4 900 ..	....	....	−3,851	−7,195	−8,648	−9,647	−1,497	1,217
Financial derivatives liabilities	4 905 ..	....	....	1,917	3,570	3,063	4,199	4,870	216
Other investment assets	4 703 ..	....	....	−43,583	−75,625	−64,685	−87,399	−91,915	−162,433
Monetary authorities	4 701 ..	....	....	186	−107	−853	−130	242	−840
General government	4 704 ..	....	....	−1	878	−403	19	−297	1,300
Banks	4 705 ..	....	....	−40,292	−69,263	−64,840	−92,342	−80,317	−148,885
Other sectors	4 728 ..	....	....	−3,475	−7,133	1,412	5,055	−9,758	−14,009
Other investment liabilities	4 753 W.	....	....	15,413	70,649	80,365	125,017	81,520	181,053
Monetary authorities	4 753 WA	....	....	6,695	6,663	15,366	5,639	13,562	25,081
General government	4 753 ZB	....	....	−1,200	−632	−786	−296	−2,736	−3
Banks	4 753 ZC	....	....	6,681	57,497	57,694	119,771	64,658	147,477
Other sectors	4 753 ZD	....	....	3,238	7,121	8,092	−97	4,986	8,499
Total, Groups A Through C	4 983 ..	....	....	*4,544*	*−632*	*1,379*	*122*	*−1,486*	*−916*
D. Net Errors and Omissions	4 998 Z.	....	....	**−4,579**	**−1,093**	**−2,103**	**−2,298**	**1,641**	**2,142**
Total, Groups A Through D	4 984 ..	....	....	*−35*	*−1,725*	*−723*	*−2,176*	*156*	*1,226*
E. Reserves and Related Items	4 802 A.	....	....	**35**	**1,725**	**723**	**2,176**	**−156**	**−1,226**
Reserve assets	4 802 ..	....	....	35	1,725	723	2,176	−156	−1,226
Use of Fund credit and loans	4 766 ..	....	....	....	....	....	....	....	....
Exceptional financing	4 920 ..	....	....	....	....	....	....	....	....
Conversion rates: euros per U.S. dollar	0 103 ..	1.08540	1.11751	1.06255	.88603	.80537	.80412	.79714	.73064

[1] Excludes components that have been classified in the categories of Group E.

Table 2. STANDARD PRESENTATION, 2000–2007

(Millions of U.S. dollars)

	Code	2000	2001	2002	2003	2004	2005	2006	2007
CURRENT ACCOUNT	4 993	....	....	11,611	12,906	12,537	9,945	8,035	7,216
A. GOODS	4 100	....	....	9,518	10,959	9,708	5,919	3,357	1,685
Credit	2 100	....	....	169,166	204,962	245,426	263,056	281,135	323,708
General merchandise: exports f.o.b.	2 110	....	....	154,088	189,041	228,464	246,322	263,033	302,360
Goods for processing: exports f.o.b.	2 150	....	....	13,713	14,325	14,946	14,379	15,219	18,870
Repairs on goods	2 160	....	....	276	247	279	386	404	623
Goods procured in ports by carriers	2 170	....	....	989	1,287	1,646	1,777	2,012	1,733
Nonmonetary gold	2 180	....	....	100	62	92	192	467	121
Debit	3 100	....	....	−159,648	−194,003	−235,718	−257,137	−277,778	−322,023
General merchandise: imports f.o.b.	3 110	....	....	−146,273	−180,328	−221,185	−243,055	−262,608	−305,540
Goods for processing: imports f.o.b.	3 150	....	....	−12,637	−12,823	−13,562	−12,881	−13,547	−14,758
Repairs on goods	3 160	....	....	−231	−190	−211	−259	−307	−311
Goods procured in ports by carriers	3 170	....	....	−377	−475	−529	−625	−767	−1,211
Nonmonetary gold	3 180	....	....	−129	−187	−231	−317	−550	−203
B. SERVICES	4 200	....	....	1,959	1,846	3,685	4,972	6,266	6,535
Total credit	2 200	....	....	*37,822*	*44,708*	*52,708*	*56,144*	*59,516*	*79,113*
Total debit	3 200	....	....	*−35,863*	*−42,862*	*−49,023*	*−51,172*	*−53,250*	*−72,578*
Transportation services, credit	2 205	....	....	8,637	9,949	13,048	13,872	15,664	24,847
Passenger	2 850	....	....	*663*	*655*	*881*	*1,036*	*1,314*	*1,278*
Freight	2 851	....	....	*6,220*	*6,836*	*9,235*	*9,551*	*10,327*	*14,890*
Other	2 852	....	....	*1,754*	*2,458*	*2,931*	*3,285*	*4,022*	*8,680*
Sea transport, passenger	2 207	....	....	7	4	3	6	4	1
Sea transport, freight	2 208	....	....	3,466	3,625	5,257	5,244	5,541	9,157
Sea transport, other	2 209	....	....	879	1,099	1,448	1,850	2,201	3,595
Air transport, passenger	2 211	....	....	596	569	791	907	1,172	1,261
Air transport, freight	2 212	....	....	336	375	490	541	588	1,391
Air transport, other	2 213	....	....	329	592	673	529	432	988
Other transport, passenger	2 215	....	....	60	82	88	123	138	15
Other transport, freight	2 216	....	....	2,418	2,836	3,488	3,766	4,198	4,342
Other transport, other	2 217	....	....	545	767	811	907	1,389	4,096
Transportation services, debit	3 205	....	....	−7,713	−9,036	−11,065	−12,265	−13,041	−20,411
Passenger	3 850	....	....	*−1,085*	*−1,192*	*−1,500*	*−1,823*	*−2,317*	*−1,827*
Freight	3 851	....	....	*−5,765*	*−6,631*	*−8,165*	*−8,702*	*−8,932*	*−12,599*
Other	3 852	....	....	*−863*	*−1,213*	*−1,400*	*−1,740*	*−1,792*	*−5,985*
Sea transport, passenger	3 207	....	....	−22	−27	−28	−40	−30	−7
Sea transport, freight	3 208	....	....	−3,461	−4,117	−5,124	−5,244	−5,183	−6,488
Sea transport, other	3 209	....	....	−259	−334	−401	−629	−776	−1,876
Air transport, passenger	3 211	....	....	−1,000	−1,093	−1,375	−1,659	−2,162	−1,804
Air transport, freight	3 212	....	....	−456	−370	−458	−736	−906	−1,915
Air transport, other	3 213	....	....	−376	−588	−775	−883	−721	−515
Other transport, passenger	3 215	....	....	−62	−72	−97	−124	−124	−17
Other transport, freight	3 216	....	....	−1,848	−2,144	−2,583	−2,723	−2,842	−4,196
Other transport, other	3 217	....	....	−228	−291	−225	−228	−295	−3,594
Travel, credit	2 236	....	....	6,935	8,193	9,208	9,845	10,311	10,898
Business travel	2 237	....	....	1,294	1,467	1,676	1,773	1,936	2,208
Personal travel	2 240	....	....	5,641	6,726	7,533	8,071	8,375	8,690
Travel, debit	3 236	....	....	−10,185	−12,210	−13,956	−14,948	−15,574	−17,268
Business travel	3 237	....	....	−1,178	−1,394	−2,394	−2,129	−2,292	−2,559
Personal travel	3 240	....	....	−9,008	−10,816	−11,562	−12,819	−13,281	−14,708
Other services, credit	2 200 BA	....	....	22,250	26,566	30,452	32,427	33,541	43,368
Communications	2 245	....	....	1,714	1,861	2,230	2,206	2,028	3,859
Construction	2 249	....	....	1,318	1,966	1,889	1,907	2,228	1,085
Insurance	2 253	....	....	499	743	854	829	933	1,000
Financial	2 260	....	....	2,215	2,544	2,976	3,395	3,613	3,690
Computer and information	2 262	....	....	1,774	2,132	2,441	2,581	2,869	3,009
Royalties and licence fees	2 266	....	....	649	882	1,021	1,360	1,544	1,640
Other business services	2 268	....	....	12,257	14,714	16,500	17,577	17,462	26,482
Personal, cultural, and recreational	2 287	....	....	289	368	454	518	558	366
Government, n.i.e.	2 291	....	....	1,537	1,356	2,087	2,052	2,307	2,238
Other services, debit	3 200 BA	....	....	−17,964	−21,616	−24,003	−23,958	−24,635	−34,900
Communications	3 245	....	....	−1,298	−1,453	−1,598	−1,321	−1,593	−3,125
Construction	3 249	....	....	−729	−983	−1,123	−849	−939	−798
Insurance	3 253	....	....	−449	−643	−619	−511	−551	−722
Financial	3 260	....	....	−2,299	−2,693	−3,214	−3,506	−3,451	−2,717
Computer and information	3 262	....	....	−1,395	−1,606	−2,003	−1,867	−1,985	−2,274
Royalties and licence fees	3 266	....	....	−741	−984	−1,036	−1,050	−1,075	−1,867
Other business services	3 268	....	....	−10,100	−12,111	−13,152	−13,621	−13,680	−22,689
Personal, cultural, and recreational	3 287	....	....	−380	−443	−494	−470	−498	−512
Government, n.i.e.	3 291	....	....	−575	−699	−764	−764	−863	−195

Table 2 (Continued). STANDARD PRESENTATION, 2000–2007

(Millions of U.S. dollars)

	Code	2000	2001	2002	2003	2004	2005	2006	2007
C. INCOME	4 300	....	....	**4,475**	**6,481**	**5,622**	**5,424**	**4,953**	**5,816**
Total credit	2 300	....	....	*36,372*	*40,213*	*48,891*	*59,028*	*74,277*	*98,581*
Total debit	3 300	....	....	*−31,897*	*−33,732*	*−43,269*	*−53,604*	*−69,324*	*−92,765*
Compensation of employees, credit	2 310	....	....	**4,490**	**5,754**	**6,536**	**6,868**	**7,239**	**8,448**
Compensation of employees, debit	3 310	....	....	**−1,363**	**−1,763**	**−1,997**	**−2,012**	**−2,134**	**−2,715**
Investment income, credit	2 320	....	....	**31,881**	**34,459**	**42,355**	**52,160**	**67,038**	**90,133**
Direct investment income	2 330	....	....	8,332	9,189	13,862	17,287	25,321	31,825
Dividends and distributed branch profits	2 332	....	....	4,326	4,120	4,693	6,226	8,908	11,117
Reinvested earnings and undistributed branch profits	2 333	....	....	793	1,610	3,814	4,659	8,576	9,397
Income on debt (interest)	2 334	....	....	3,213	3,459	5,354	6,402	7,837	11,311
Portfolio investment income	2 339	....	....	16,210	18,775	19,759	22,468	23,616	26,988
Income on equity	2 340	....	....	3,392	3,622	4,025	4,966	5,635	6,504
Income on bonds and notes	2 350	....	....	12,472	14,888	15,485	17,238	17,715	19,798
Income on money market instruments	2 360	....	....	346	266	249	264	266	685
Other investment income	2 370	....	....	7,340	6,495	8,734	12,405	18,101	31,320
Investment income, debit	3 320	....	....	**−30,534**	**−31,969**	**−41,272**	**−51,593**	**−67,191**	**−90,050**
Direct investment income	3 330	....	....	−12,653	−12,090	−17,260	−22,522	−30,804	−36,187
Dividends and distributed branch profits	3 332	....	....	−8,714	−9,961	−11,105	−14,210	−15,742	−19,408
Reinvested earnings and undistributed branch profits	3 333	....	....	−1,593	569	−3,711	−5,078	−11,247	−12,441
Income on debt (interest)	3 334	....	....	−2,345	−2,698	−2,445	−3,234	−3,815	−4,338
Portfolio investment income	3 339	....	....	−7,697	−10,116	−11,452	−12,261	−12,840	−16,403
Income on equity	3 340	....	....	−674	−730	−884	−1,245	−1,593	−2,352
Income on bonds and notes	3 350	....	....	−5,906	−8,242	−9,051	−9,395	−9,213	−11,597
Income on money market instruments	3 360	....	....	−1,116	−1,143	−1,517	−1,620	−2,034	−2,453
Other investment income	3 370	....	....	−10,185	−9,763	−12,560	−16,810	−23,547	−37,460
D. CURRENT TRANSFERS	4 379	....	....	**−4,341**	**−6,379**	**−6,478**	**−6,369**	**−6,541**	**−6,819**
Credit	2 379	....	....	5,275	6,515	7,949	9,355	8,812	8,681
General government	2 380	....	....	1,586	1,905	2,513	3,297	3,010	2,934
Other sectors	2 390	....	....	3,689	4,610	5,436	6,058	5,802	5,747
Workers' remittances	2 391	....	....	40	20	19	20	27	114
Other current transfers	2 392	....	....	3,649	4,590	5,418	6,038	5,775	5,633
Debit	3 379	....	....	**−9,616**	**−12,894**	**−14,427**	**−15,724**	**−15,353**	**−15,500**
General government	3 380	....	....	−5,101	−6,505	−7,278	−8,017	−8,325	−8,826
Other sectors	3 390	....	....	−4,515	−6,389	−7,148	−7,707	−7,027	−6,674
Workers' remittances	3 391	....	....	−264	−333	−343	−416	−429	−477
Other current transfers	3 392	....	....	−4,251	−6,056	−6,805	−7,292	−6,598	−6,197
CAPITAL AND FINANCIAL ACCOUNT	4 996	....	....	**−7,033**	**−11,814**	**−10,434**	**−7,648**	**−9,676**	**−9,358**
CAPITAL ACCOUNT	4 994	....	....	**−585**	**−1,021**	**−497**	**−894**	**−405**	**−1,499**
Total credit	2 994	....	....	*219*	*267*	*399*	*399*	*984*	*536*
Total debit	3 994	....	....	*−803*	*−1,288*	*−896*	*−1,293*	*−1,389*	*−2,035*
Capital transfers, credit	2 400	....	....	**172**	**241**	**342**	**391**	**226**	**299**
General government	2 401	....	....	2	....	6	4	....	299
Debt forgiveness	2 402	....	....	....	....	....	....	....	....
Other capital transfers	2 410	....	....	2	....	6	4	....	299
Other sectors	2 430	....	....	170	241	336	388	226	....
Migrants' transfers	2 431	....	....	144	216	308	354	222	....
Debt forgiveness	2 432	....	....	....	....	....	....	....	....
Other capital transfers	2 440	....	....	26	25	28	33	4	....
Capital transfers, debit	3 400	....	....	**−679**	**−1,104**	**−655**	**−1,024**	**−721**	**−657**
General government	3 401	....	....	−83	−131	−160	−201	−208	−554
Debt forgiveness	3 402	....	....	−34	....	−20	−25	−50	−115
Other capital transfers	3 410	....	....	−49	−131	−140	−176	−158	−439
Other sectors	3 430	....	....	−596	−973	−495	−824	−512	−103
Migrants' transfers	3 431	....	....	−218	−233	−277	−327	−136	....
Debt forgiveness	3 432	....	....	−151	−714	−185	−449	−357	−103
Other capital transfers	3 440	....	....	−226	−26	−34	−48	−20	....
Nonproduced nonfinancial assets, credit	2 480	....	....	**47**	**26**	**57**	**7**	**758**	**238**
Nonproduced nonfinancial assets, debit	3 480	....	....	**−125**	**−184**	**−241**	**−268**	**−668**	**−1,378**

Table 2 (Continued). STANDARD PRESENTATION, 2000–2007

(Millions of U.S. dollars)

	Code	2000	2001	2002	2003	2004	2005	2006	2007
FINANCIAL ACCOUNT	4 995	....	....	**−6,448**	**−10,793**	**−9,937**	**−6,753**	**−9,271**	**−7,860**
A. DIRECT INVESTMENT	4 500	....	....	**9,178**	**−4,499**	**9,733**	**3,607**	**7,087**	**17,122**
Direct investment abroad	4 505	....	....	**−8,902**	**−39,043**	**−34,682**	**−30,433**	**−49,657**	**−55,073**
Equity capital	4 510	....	....	....	−14,392	−17,428	−21,001	−16,778	−34,868
Claims on affiliated enterprises	4 515	....	....	....	....	....	....	....	....
Liabilities to affiliated enterprises	4 520	....	....	....	....	....	....	....	....
Reinvested earnings	4 525	....	....	−793	−1,610	−3,814	−4,659	−8,576	−9,397
Other capital	4 530	....	....	−8,109	−23,041	−13,439	−4,773	−24,302	−10,808
Claims on affiliated enterprises	4 535	....	....	....	....	....	....	....	....
Liabilities to affiliated enterprises	4 540	....	....	....	....	....	....	....	....
Direct investment in Belgium	4 555	....	....	**18,081**	**34,544**	**44,415**	**34,040**	**56,744**	**72,195**
Equity capital	4 560	....	....	8,788	26,653	32,590	30,357	53,791	33,757
Claims on direct investors	4 565	....	....	....	....	....	....	....	....
Liabilities to direct investors	4 570	....	....	....	....	....	....	....	....
Reinvested earnings	4 575	....	....	1,593	−569	3,711	5,078	11,247	12,438
Other capital	4 580	....	....	7,699	8,460	8,114	−1,395	−8,295	26,000
Claims on direct investors	4 585	....	....	....	....	....	....	....	....
Liabilities to direct investors	4 590	....	....	....	....	....	....	....	....
B. PORTFOLIO INVESTMENT	4 600	....	....	**14,442**	**582**	**−30,488**	**−44,706**	**−9,181**	**−43,809**
Assets	4 602	....	....	**−5,707**	**−6,046**	**−35,558**	**−43,491**	**−26,529**	**−80,503**
Equity securities	4 610	....	....	−3,551	−5,508	−8,037	−20,449	−19,980	−20,401
Monetary authorities	4 611	....	....	....	....	....	....	....	....
General government	4 612	....	....	....	....	....	....	....	−1,504
Banks	4 613	....	....	164	−707	467	−974	−900	−2,690
Other sectors	4 614	....	....	−3,715	−4,801	−8,504	−19,475	−19,081	−16,207
Debt securities	4 619	....	....	−2,156	−538	−27,520	−23,043	−6,548	−60,102
Bonds and notes	4 620	....	....	1,112	−6,123	−28,319	−28,680	−14,411	−52,128
Monetary authorities	4 621	....	....	−129	−888	−872	55	−52	−11,516
General government	4 622	....	....	....	....	....	....	....	....
Banks	4 623	....	....	5,898	−12,248	−21,297	−19,118	3,912	4,679
Other sectors	4 624	....	....	−4,657	7,013	−6,150	−9,617	−18,271	−45,290
Money market instruments	4 630	....	....	−3,268	5,585	799	5,638	7,863	−7,974
Monetary authorities	4 631	....	....	....	....	....	....	....	....
General government	4 632	....	....	....	....	....	....	....	....
Banks	4 633	....	....	−1,744	819	−241	2,302	2,837	−6,028
Other sectors	4 634	....	....	−1,524	4,766	1,040	3,336	5,026	−1,946
Liabilities	4 652	....	....	**20,149**	**6,628**	**5,070**	**−1,215**	**17,348**	**36,694**
Equity securities	4 660	....	....	−467	3,182	4,092	5,712	4,588	3,360
Banks	4 663	....	....	....	−126	141	−31	1,295	....
Other sectors	4 664	....	....	....	3,307	3,951	5,742	3,293	3,360
Debt securities	4 669	....	....	20,616	3,446	978	−6,927	12,760	33,334
Bonds and notes	4 670	....	....	11,339	9,592	−2,144	−1,450	13,847	26,871
Monetary authorities	4 671	....	....	....	....	....	....	....	....
General government	4 672	....	....	13,872	10,279	−1,946	−498	6,733	20,659
Banks	4 673	....	....	−829	−922	−430	266	2,102	3,821
Other sectors	4 674	....	....	−1,703	235	231	−1,218	5,013	2,390
Money market instruments	4 680	....	....	9,277	−6,146	3,122	−5,476	−1,087	6,464
Monetary authorities	4 681	....	....	....	....	....	....	....	....
General government	4 682	....	....	1,154	256	3,929	−659	1,357	3,898
Banks	4 683	....	....	−1,122	−453	2,066	−2,035	−116	2,419
Other sectors	4 684	....	....	9,244	−5,948	−2,874	−2,782	−2,328	146
C. FINANCIAL DERIVATIVES	4 910	....	....	**−1,934**	**−3,626**	**−5,586**	**−5,448**	**3,372**	**1,434**
Monetary authorities	4 911	....	....	....	....	....	....	....	....
General government	4 912	....	....	−1,065	890	16	−551	−342	287
Banks	4 913	....	....	207	−1,774	−2,579	−4,909	1,160	−555
Other sectors	4 914	....	....	−1,077	−2,742	−3,023	12	2,555	1,701
Assets	4 900	....	....	**−3,851**	**−7,195**	**−8,648**	**−9,647**	**−1,497**	**1,217**
Monetary authorities	4 901	....	....	....	....	....	....	....	....
General government	4 902	....	....	−1,065	890	16	−551	−342	71
Banks	4 903	....	....	207	−1,774	−2,579	−4,909	1,160	−555
Other sectors	4 904	....	....	−2,994	−6,312	−6,085	−4,188	−2,315	1,701
Liabilities	4 905	....	....	**1,917**	**3,570**	**3,063**	**4,199**	**4,870**	**216**
Monetary authorities	4 906	....	....	....	....	....	....	....	....
General government	4 907	....	....	....	....	....	....	....	216
Banks	4 908	....	....	....	....	....	....	....	....
Other sectors	4 909	....	....	1,917	3,570	3,063	4,199	4,870	....

Table 2 (Concluded). STANDARD PRESENTATION, 2000–2007

(Millions of U.S. dollars)

	Code	2000	2001	2002	2003	2004	2005	2006	2007
D. OTHER INVESTMENT	4 700 ..	....	....	**−28,169**	**−4,976**	**15,680**	**37,619**	**−10,394**	**18,620**
Assets	4 703 ..	....	....	**−43,583**	**−75,625**	**−64,685**	**−87,399**	**−91,915**	**−162,433**
Trade credits	4 706 ..	....	....	−56	−352	−1,110	−1,930	−1,784	−1,212
General government	4 707 ..	....	....	....	....	....	....	....	....
of which: Short-term	4 709 ..	....	....	....	....	....	....	....	....
Other sectors	4 710 ..	....	....	−56	−352	−1,110	−1,930	....	−1,212
of which: Short-term	4 712 ..	....	....	....	....	....	....	....	....
Loans	4 714 ..	....	....	−755	−2,435	−6,332	−32,894	−11,635	−4,686
Monetary authorities	4 715 ..	....	....	....	....	....	....	....	....
of which: Short-term	4 718 ..	....	....	....	....	....	....	....	....
General government	4 719 ..	....	....	46	22	−629	58	64	127
of which: Short-term	4 721 ..	....	....	*1*	....	....	*11*	....	....
Banks	4 722 ..	....	....	−744	−2,414	−5,512	−32,522	−9,036	1,644
of which: Short-term	4 724 ..	....	....	*118*	*−40*	*82*	*9*	*37*	*27*
Other sectors	4 725 ..	....	....	−56	−43	−191	−430	−2,663	−6,457
of which: Short-term	4 727 ..	....	....	....	....	....	....	....	....
Currency and deposits	4 730 ..	....	....	−42,564	−72,754	−56,988	−52,702	−78,419	−153,421
Monetary authorities	4 731 ..	....	....	186	−107	−529	−83	242	−834
General government	4 732 ..	....	....	42	897	355	186	127	446
Banks	4 733 ..	....	....	−39,548	−66,849	−59,328	−59,820	−71,281	−144,423
Other sectors	4 734 ..	....	....	−3,243	−6,695	2,515	7,016	−7,507	−8,611
Other assets	4 736 ..	....	....	−208	−84	−254	127	−77	−3,113
Monetary authorities	4 737 ..	....	....	....	....	−324	−48	....	−7
of which: Short-term	4 739 ..	....	....	....	....	....	....	....	....
General government	4 740 ..	....	....	−89	−41	−129	−224	−488	727
of which: Short-term	4 742 ..	....	....	....	....	....	....	....	....
Banks	4 743 ..	....	....	....	....	....	....	....	−6,105
of which: Short-term	4 745 ..	....	....	....	....	....	....	....	*−6,614*
Other sectors	4 746 ..	....	....	−119	−43	198	399	412	2,271
of which: Short-term	4 748 ..	....	....	....	....	....	....	....	*2,262*
Liabilities	4 753 ..	....	....	**15,413**	**70,649**	**80,365**	**125,017**	**81,520**	**181,053**
Trade credits	4 756 ..	....	....	734	610	691	1,150	1,050	2,975
General government	4 757 ..	....	....	....	....	....	....	....	....
of which: Short-term	4 759 ..	....	....	....	....	....	....	....	....
Other sectors	4 760 ..	....	....	734	610	691	1,150	....	2,975
of which: Short-term	4 762 ..	....	....	....	....	....	....	....	*2,975*
Loans	4 764 ..	....	....	976	4,771	2,116	1,793	17,078	16,248
Monetary authorities	4 765 ..	....	....	....	....	....	....	....	....
of which: Use of Fund credit and loans from the Fund	4 766 ..	....	....	....	....	....	....	....	....
of which: Short-term	4 768 ..	....	....	....	....	....	....	....	....
General government	4 769 ..	....	....	−1,200	−632	−786	−296	−2,736	−492
of which: Short-term	4 771 ..	....	....	*−822*	*−406*	*−585*	*131*	*−2,537*	*−238*
Banks	4 772 ..	....	....	2,518	2,072	−143	1,948	15,127	10,670
of which: Short-term	4 774 ..	....	....	....	....	....	....	....	....
Other sectors	4 775 ..	....	....	−341	3,330	3,045	140	4,686	6,070
of which: Short-term	4 777 ..	....	....	*−518*	*623*	*725*	*182*	*2,372*	*3,073*
Currency and deposits	4 780 ..	....	....	10,858	62,088	73,202	123,461	63,093	151,859
Monetary authorities	4 781 ..	....	....	6,695	6,663	15,366	5,639	13,562	25,079
General government	4 782 ..	....	....	....	....	....	....	....	....
Banks	4 783 ..	....	....	4,164	55,425	57,836	117,823	49,531	126,780
Other sectors	4 784 ..	....	....	....	....	....	....	....	....
Other liabilities	4 786 ..	....	....	2,845	3,180	4,356	−1,388	299	9,972
Monetary authorities	4 787 ..	....	....	....	....	....	....	....	1
of which: Short-term	4 789 ..	....	....	....	....	....	....	....	*1*
General government	4 790 ..	....	....	....	....	....	....	....	489
of which: Short-term	4 792 ..	....	....	....	....	....	....	....	*489*
Banks	4 793 ..	....	....	....	....	....	....	....	10,027
of which: Short-term	4 795 ..	....	....	....	....	....	....	....	*9,595*
Other sectors	4 796 ..	....	....	2,845	3,180	4,356	−1,388	299	−546
of which: Short-term	4 798 ..	....	....	*2,755*	*2,922*	*4,016*	*−1,496*	....	*−555*
E. RESERVE ASSETS	4 802 ..	....	....	**35**	**1,725**	**723**	**2,176**	**−156**	**−1,226**
Monetary gold	4 812 ..	....	....	1	1	2	417	....	3
Special drawing rights	4 811 ..	....	....	−42	−37	314	10	−214	−36
Reserve position in the fund	4 810 ..	....	....	−168	−69	495	1,027	534	167
Foreign exchange	4 803 ..	....	....	243	1,830	−89	721	−476	−1,360
Other claims	4 813 ..	....	....	....	....	....	....	....	....
NET ERRORS AND OMISSIONS	4 998 ..	....	....	**−4,579**	**−1,093**	**−2,103**	**−2,298**	**1,641**	**2,142**

Table 3. INTERNATIONAL INVESTMENT POSITION (End-period stocks), 2000–2007

(Millions of U.S. dollars)

	Code	2000	2001	2002	2003	2004	2005	2006	2007
ASSETS	8 995 C.	**757,673**	**771,750**	**919,531**	**1,243,816**	**1,500,462**	**1,557,568**	**1,892,379**	**2,407,100**
Direct investment abroad	8 505 ..	**179,773**	**181,459**	**223,940**	**313,938**	**369,230**	**378,158**	**481,356**	**592,974**
Equity capital and reinvested earnings	8 506 ..	112,218	100,544	122,438	170,645	203,559	225,815	290,647	360,737
Claims on affiliated enterprises	8 507 ..	....	....	....	....	....	....	....	....
Liabilities to affiliated enterprises	8 508 ..	....	....	....	....	....	....	....	....
Other capital	8 530 ..	67,554	80,915	101,503	143,292	165,671	152,343	190,708	232,237
Claims on affiliated enterprises	8 535 ..	....	....	....	....	....	....	....	....
Liabilities to affiliated enterprises	8 540 ..	....	....	....	....	....	....	....	....
Portfolio investment	8 602 ..	**297,202**	**320,225**	**351,786**	**455,923**	**534,074**	**554,645**	**643,194**	**828,464**
Equity securities	8 610 ..	124,687	110,226	104,971	146,643	172,164	204,560	248,210	317,261
Monetary authorities	8 611 ..	....	....	....	....	....	....	....	....
General government	8 612 ..	558	616	696	743	836	751	944	2,601
Banks	8 613 ..	1,954	2,156	2,357	3,519	3,281	3,828	5,128	8,392
Other sectors	8 614 ..	122,175	107,454	101,917	142,382	168,046	199,980	242,137	306,267
Debt securities	8 619 ..	172,515	209,999	246,816	309,280	361,910	350,085	394,984	511,203
Bonds and notes	8 620 ..	165,908	205,537	234,517	296,233	347,391	343,071	374,867	493,070
Monetary authorities	8 621 ..	2,233	2,515	2,997	4,489	5,793	4,952	5,458	19,126
General government	8 622 ..	93	44	....	....	....	88	43	50
Banks	8 623 ..	80,116	112,145	123,301	158,402	193,365	186,113	202,502	205,719
Other sectors	8 624 ..	83,466	90,832	108,218	133,342	148,233	151,917	166,864	268,175
Money market instruments	8 630 ..	6,607	4,462	12,299	13,047	14,519	7,014	20,117	18,133
Monetary authorities	8 631 ..	....	....	....	....	....	....	....	....
General government	8 632 ..	....	....	2	1	....	6	....	....
Banks	8 633 ..	6,607	4,462	6,942	7,313	8,081	5,034	2,490	8,740
Other sectors	8 634 ..	....	....	5,355	5,733	6,437	1,975	17,627	9,393
Financial derivatives	8 900 ..	**4,187**	**6,564**	**476**	**611**	**1,667**	**3,635**	**10,561**	**21,098**
Monetary authorities	8 901 ..	....	....	....	....	131			
General government	8 902 ..	....	....	....	....	....	365	71	....
Banks	8 903 ..	....	−1,870	19	1	672	2,136	8,985	19,383
Other sectors	8 904 ..	4,187	8,434	457	610	865	1,134	1,505	1,715
Other investment	8 703 ..	**264,269**	**249,933**	**328,630**	**458,896**	**581,502**	**609,135**	**743,832**	**948,059**
Trade credits	8 706 ..	6,607	5,613	6,870	9,387	11,466	11,447	12,673	9,778
General government	8 707 ..	....	....	....	....	....	....	....	....
of which: Short-term	8 709 ..	....	....	....	....	....	....	....	....
Other sectors	8 710 ..	6,607	5,613	6,870	9,387	11,466	11,447	12,673	9,778
of which: Short-term	8 712 ..	....	....	....	....	....	....	....	....
Loans	8 714 ..	167,118	175,270	235,817	340,061	430,462	480,901	604,403	803,170
Monetary authorities	8 715 ..	372	368	253	418	349	621	391	1,123
of which: Short-term	8 718 ..	*372*	*368*	*253*	*418*	*349*	*621*	*391*	*1,123*
General government	8 719 ..	5,025	4,815	405	650	753	1,532	1,636	1,665
of which: Short-term	8 721 ..	*372*	*376*	....	....	....	....	....	....
Banks	8 722 ..	161,349	169,759	234,895	338,483	428,455	477,548	598,247	791,417
of which: Short-term	8 724 ..	*143,297*	*152,470*	*212,794*	*310,756*	*392,715*	*414,443*	*519,979*	*709,707*
Other sectors	8 725 ..	372	329	264	510	904	1,200	4,129	8,965
of which: Short-term	8 727 ..	....	....	....	....	....	....	....	....
Currency and deposits	8 730 ..	70,532	75,980	61,911	77,037	96,467	66,523	72,199	82,741
Monetary authorities	8 731 ..	....	....	....	....	....	....	....	....
General government	8 732 ..	....	....	....	....	....	....	....	....
Banks	8 733 ..	....	56	52	....	....	851	948	1,265
Other sectors	8 734 ..	70,532	75,925	61,859	77,037	96,467	65,673	71,251	81,476
Other assets	8 736 ..	20,013	−6,931	24,032	32,411	43,108	50,263	54,557	52,370
Monetary authorities	8 737 ..	1,489	1,389	1,653	1,990	2,129	1,843	2,057	2,307
of which: Short-term	8 739 ..	....	....	....	....	....	....	....	....
General government	8 740 ..	....	....	....	183	....	130	884	240
of which: Short-term	8 742 ..	....	....	....	....	....	....	....	....
Banks	8 743 ..	1,496	2,319	21,331	28,974	37,083	45,192	48,672	48,520
of which: Short-term	8 745 ..	....	....	....	....	....	....	....	....
Other sectors	8 746 ..	17,028	−10,638	1,049	1,263	3,896	3,099	2,943	1,303
of which: Short-term	8 748 ..	....	....	....	....	....	....	....	....
Reserve assets	8 802 ..	**12,242**	**13,569**	**14,698**	**14,449**	**13,988**	**11,996**	**13,436**	**16,505**
Monetary gold	8 812 ..	2,233	2,303	2,843	3,459	3,629	3,755	4,653	6,121
Special drawing rights	8 811 ..	307	472	554	645	350	314	545	609
Reserve position in the Fund	8 810 ..	1,699	2,051	2,392	2,693	2,296	1,112	620	477
Foreign exchange	8 803 ..	8,002	8,743	8,909	7,651	7,714	6,815	7,619	9,298
Other claims	8 813 ..	....	....	....	....	....	....	....	....

Table 3 (Concluded). INTERNATIONAL INVESTMENT POSITION (End-period stocks), 2000–2007

(Millions of U.S. dollars)

	Code	2000	2001	2002	2003	2004	2005	2006	2007
LIABILITIES	8 995 D.	**615,340**	**653,214**	**815,099**	**1,116,151**	**1,387,972**	**1,437,556**	**1,772,170**	**2,266,379**
Direct investment in Belgium	8 555	**195,219**	**203,537**	**255,745**	**357,137**	**471,071**	**478,183**	**618,650**	**747,463**
Equity capital and reinvested earnings	8 556	155,021	169,627	202,995	287,840	387,166	406,455	549,365	632,872
Claims on direct investors	8 557	....	....	....	....	....	....	....	....
Liabilities to direct investors	8 558	....	....	....	....	....	....	....	....
Other capital	8 580	40,198	33,910	52,751	69,297	83,905	71,728	69,285	114,591
Claims on direct investors	8 585	....	....	....	....	....	....	....	....
Liabilities to direct investors	8 590	....	....	....	....	....	....	....	....
Portfolio investment	8 652	**126,455**	**127,152**	**167,594**	**223,877**	**259,902**	**244,761**	**285,082**	**394,458**
Equity securities	8 660	14,237	15,663	18,060	27,885	44,251	43,015	57,769	72,897
Banks	8 663	3,071	2,919	....	....	....	....	....	....
Other sectors	8 664	11,166	12,744	18,060	27,885	44,251	43,015	57,769	72,897
Debt securities	8 669	112,218	111,489	149,534	195,992	215,652	201,745	227,313	321,561
Bonds and notes	8 670	85,978	88,817	121,731	158,514	170,333	156,350	174,542	256,636
Monetary authorities	8 671	....	....	....	....	....	....	....	....
General government	8 672	77,976	82,017	111,476	137,760	149,000	135,673	149,458	211,703
Banks	8 673	4,187	4,346	4,910	4,885	3,851	3,379	5,901	10,453
Other sectors	8 674	3,815	2,454	5,345	15,868	17,483	17,299	19,182	34,480
Money market instruments	8 680	26,240	22,671	27,803	37,478	45,318	45,395	52,771	64,925
Monetary authorities	8 681	....	....	....	....	....	....	....	....
General government	8 682	12,003	11,757	12,396	18,152	23,540	23,162	28,105	35,938
Banks	8 683	3,722	1,612	7,026	6,200	8,213	5,303	5,783	12,516
Other sectors	8 684	10,515	9,303	8,381	13,126	13,565	16,930	18,883	16,471
Financial derivatives	8 905	**4,746**	**4,421**	**....**	**....**	**16**	**3,381**	**9,776**	**22,221**
Monetary authorities	8 906	....	....	....	....	....	....	....	....
General government	8 907	....	....	....	....	....	....	....	240
Banks	8 908	1,024	....	....	....	16	3,329	9,343	21,660
Other sectors	8 909	3,722	4,421	....	....	....	52	433	321
Other investment	8 753	**288,920**	**318,103**	**391,760**	**535,137**	**656,982**	**711,232**	**858,662**	**1,102,236**
Trade credits	8 756	3,722	2,978	4,381	5,982	6,396	6,748	7,448	10,265
General government	8 757	....	....	....	....	....	....	....	....
of which: Short-term	8 759	....	....	....	....	....	....	....	....
Other sectors	8 760	3,722	2,978	4,381	5,982	6,396	6,748	7,448	10,265
of which: Short-term	8 762	....	....	....	....	....	....	....	....
Loans	8 764	202,105	219,623	239,078	338,763	389,984	431,653	553,532	682,657
Monetary authorities	8 765	....	....	....	....	....	....	....	....
of which: Use of Fund credit and loans from the Fund	8 766	....	....	....	....	....	....	....	....
of which: Short-term	8 768	....	....	....	....	....	....	....	....
General government	8 769	651	888	807	681	734	3,950	4,394	4,357
of which: Short-term	8 771	*558*	*653*	*315*	....	....	*190*	*287*	*40*
Banks	8 772	174,097	190,847	215,390	299,994	354,414	401,473	515,421	637,569
of which: Short-term	8 774	*160,046*	*176,479*	*199,265*	*279,694*	*334,261*	*384,181*	*492,052*	*617,667*
Other sectors	8 775	27,357	27,887	22,881	38,088	34,836	26,231	33,718	40,730
of which: Short-term	8 777	*11,910*	*12,757*	*10,367*	*14,151*	*12,704*	*10,410*	*14,052*	*17,224*
Currency and deposits	8 780	60,110	62,434	122,678	156,088	205,373	218,911	240,371	336,213
Monetary authorities	8 781	7,165	6,274	14,649	24,266	42,799	42,790	61,235	93,684
General government	8 782	....	....	....	....	....	....	....	....
Banks	8 783	52,945	56,160	106,998	131,822	162,575	176,121	179,136	242,528
Other sectors	8 784	....	....	1,031	....	....	....	....	....
Other liabilities	8 786	22,983	33,069	25,622	34,304	55,228	53,919	57,311	73,102
Monetary authorities	8 787	....	....	....	....	....	....	1	3
of which: Short-term	8 789	....	....	....	....	....	....	*1*	*3*
General government	8 790	....	....	3,587	4,103	4,360	3,100	3,220	4,063
of which: Short-term	8 792	....	....	....	....	....	....	....	....
Banks	8 793	18,889	29,084	20,987	29,854	40,636	44,515	46,923	61,765
of which: Short-term	8 795	....	....	....	....	....	....	....	....
Other sectors	8 796	4,094	3,985	1,049	347	10,232	6,304	7,166	7,271
of which: Short-term	8 798	....	....	....	....	....	....	....	....
NET INTERNATIONAL INVESTMENT POSITION	8 995	**142,333**	**118,535**	**104,432**	**127,665**	**112,490**	**120,012**	**120,209**	**140,721**
Conversion rates: euros per U.S. dollar (end of period)	0 104	**1.07469**	**1.13469**	**.95356**	**.79177**	**.73416**	**.84767**	**.75930**	**.67930**

Table 1. ANALYTIC PRESENTATION, 2000–2007

(Millions of U.S. dollars)

	Code	2000	2001	2002	2003	2004	2005	2006	2007
A. Current Account[1].....................	4 993 Z.	**−161.6**	**−190.4**	**−165.3**	**−184.3**	**−154.9**	**−151.2**	**−16.2**	**−42.6**
Goods: exports f.o.b..............	2 100 ..	281.8	269.1	309.7	315.5	308.4	325.2	427.1	428.5
Goods: imports f.o.b..............	3 100 ..	−478.4	−478.1	−496.9	−522.3	−480.7	−556.2	−611.9	−642.0
Balance on Goods...............	4 100 ..	*−196.6*	*−209.0*	*−187.2*	*−206.8*	*−172.3*	*−231.0*	*−184.8*	*−213.5*
Services: credit....................	2 200 ..	152.7	166.3	175.9	212.1	235.3	301.8	373.8	398.1
Services: debit.....................	3 200 ..	−122.6	−120.2	−129.8	−141.0	−147.1	−158.8	−150.2	−166.5
Balance on Goods and Services......	4 991 ..	*−166.6*	*−162.8*	*−141.2*	*−135.7*	*−84.1*	*−88.0*	*38.9*	*18.1*
Income: credit.....................	2 300 ..	6.9	8.6	4.2	5.5	4.3	6.8	10.0	7.0
Income: debit......................	3 300 ..	−59.8	−75.7	−71.7	−95.0	−121.1	−121.2	−139.0	−161.1
Balance on Goods, Services, and Income.......	4 992 ..	*−219.5*	*−229.9*	*−208.6*	*−225.2*	*−200.8*	*−202.4*	*−90.2*	*−136.0*
Current transfers: credit.......	2 379 Z.	61.1	53.8	58.8	59.1	60.8	68.4	92.2	136.6
Current transfers: debit........	3 379 ..	−3.2	−14.2	−15.5	−18.3	−14.9	−17.1	−18.2	−43.2
B. Capital Account[1]..................	4 994 Z.	**−2.5**	**6.0**	**14.2**	**4.2**	**9.8**	**3.0**	**9.1**	**4.1**
Capital account: credit..........	2 994 Z.	1.6	7.3	15.3	5.1	10.6	3.9	10.2	5.1
Capital account: debit...........	3 994 ..	−4.1	−1.3	−1.1	−.9	−.8	−1.0	−1.1	−1.0
Total, Groups A Plus B..........	4 981 ..	*−164.1*	*−184.3*	*−151.1*	*−180.1*	*−145.1*	*−148.3*	*−7.0*	*−38.5*
C. Financial Account[1]..............	4 995 W.	**205.1**	**164.6**	**151.5**	**204.3**	**117.4**	**144.3**	**69.1**	**70.5**
Direct investment abroad........	4 505 ..	....	....	....	−.4	−.1	−1.0	−.6	−1.0
Direct investment in Belize......	4 555 Z.	23.3	61.2	25.4	−10.9	111.5	126.9	103.8	112.3
Portfolio investment assets.......	4 602 ..	....	....	....	−.2	−.2	−.2	−.3	−.4
Equity securities...............	4 610 ..	....	....	....	−.2	−.2	−.2	−.3	−.4
Debt securities................	4 619 ..	....	....	....	....	....	....	....	....
Portfolio investment liabilities....	4 652 Z.	113.1	−19.4	124.0	79.4	76.9	18.1	−21.4	79.1
Equity securities...............	4 660 ..	....	....	....	....	....	....	4.0	....
Debt securities................	4 669 Z.	113.1	−19.4	124.0	79.4	76.9	18.1	−25.4	79.1
Financial derivatives............	4 910 ..	....	....	.8	.7	.5	−5.3	....	....
Financial derivatives assets......	4 900 ..	....	....	.8	.7	.5	.3	....	....
Financial derivatives liabilities....	4 905 ..	....	....	....	....	....	−5.6	....	....
Other investment assets.........	4 703 ..	−50.6	1.3	7.3	−9.9	−4.4	−39.1	−13.6	4.7
Monetary authorities..........	4 701 ..	....	....	....	....	....	−30.6	12.1	18.5
General government............	4 704 ..	−11.1	....	....	....	....	.1	3.4	−1.9
Banks........................	4 705 ..	−26.2	2.5	10.1	−2.6	−5.3	−9.2	−16.4	−11.4
Other sectors.................	4 728 ..	−13.3	−1.1	−2.8	−7.3	.9	.6	−12.8	−.5
Other investment liabilities......	4 753 W.	119.2	121.5	−6.1	145.6	−66.8	45.0	1.1	−124.3
Monetary authorities..........	4 753 WA	41.8	−1.9	−33.0	−2.6	−4.0	−1.3	−.2	....
General government............	4 753 ZB	56.8	116.4	−2.5	76.4	−53.0	45.1	32.0	−87.9
Banks........................	4 753 ZC	15.5	11.6	−1.4	28.5	.4	3.2	−32.3	−29.3
Other sectors.................	4 753 ZD	5.1	−4.7	30.8	43.3	−10.2	−2.1	1.5	−7.1
Total, Groups A Through C........	4 983 ..	*41.0*	*−19.7*	*.4*	*24.2*	*−27.7*	*−3.9*	*62.1*	*32.0*
D. Net Errors and Omissions.................	4 998 ..	**10.7**	**8.6**	**−8.6**	**−35.0**	**−3.7**	**−7.6**	**−12.7**	**−9.5**
Total, Groups A Through D........	4 984 ..	*51.6*	*−11.1*	*−8.2*	*−10.8*	*−31.4*	*−11.5*	*49.3*	*22.4*
E. Reserves and Related Items..............	4 802 A.	**−51.6**	**11.1**	**8.2**	**10.8**	**31.4**	**11.5**	**−49.3**	**−22.4**
Reserve assets...................	4 802 ..	−51.9	2.5	6.0	30.8	31.4	11.5	−49.3	−22.4
Use of Fund credit and loans.....	4 766 ..	....	....	....	....	....	....	....	....
Exceptional financing............	4 920 ..	.3	8.6	2.2	−20.0	....	....	....	....
Conversion rates: Belize dollars per U.S. dollar.....	0 101 ..	**2.0000**	**2.0000**	**2.0000**	**2.0000**	**2.0000**	**2.0000**	**2.0000**	**2.0000**

[1] Excludes components that have been classified in the categories of Group E.

Table 2. STANDARD PRESENTATION, 2000–2007

(Millions of U.S. dollars)

	Code	2000	2001	2002	2003	2004	2005	2006	2007
CURRENT ACCOUNT	4 993 ..	**−161.6**	**−190.4**	**−165.3**	**−184.3**	**−154.9**	**−151.2**	**−16.2**	**−42.6**
A. GOODS	4 100 ..	**−196.6**	**−209.0**	**−187.2**	**−206.8**	**−172.3**	**−231.0**	**−184.8**	**−213.5**
Credit	2 100 ..	**281.8**	**269.1**	**309.7**	**315.5**	**308.4**	**325.2**	**427.1**	**428.5**
General merchandise: exports f.o.b.	2 110 ..	256.9	249.2	291.1	294.7	285.3	301.4	401.2	409.9
Goods for processing: exports f.o.b.	2 150 ..	19.9	15.2	14.9	15.4	18.6	17.3	18.3	9.4
Repairs on goods	2 160 ..	....	....	....	....	....	....	....	....
Goods procured in ports by carriers	2 170 ..	5.0	4.7	3.7	5.3	4.5	6.5	7.7	9.1
Nonmonetary gold	2 180 ..	....	....	....	....	....	....	....	....
Debit	3 100 ..	**−478.4**	**−478.1**	**−496.9**	**−522.3**	**−480.7**	**−556.2**	**−611.9**	**−642.0**
General merchandise: imports f.o.b.	3 110 ..	−467.7	−468.0	−490.5	−510.5	−465.1	−544.2	−597.9	−634.7
Goods for processing: imports f.o.b.	3 150 ..	−10.8	−10.0	−6.4	−11.9	−15.6	−12.0	−14.1	−7.3
Repairs on goods	3 160 ..	....	....	....	....	....	....	....	....
Goods procured in ports by carriers	3 170 ..	....	....	....	....	....	....	....	....
Nonmonetary gold	3 180 ..	....	....	....	....	....	....	....	....
B. SERVICES	4 200 ..	**30.1**	**46.1**	**46.0**	**71.1**	**88.2**	**143.0**	**223.7**	**231.6**
Total credit	2 200 ..	*152.7*	*166.3*	*175.9*	*212.1*	*235.3*	*301.8*	*373.8*	*398.1*
Total debit	3 200 ..	*−122.6*	*−120.2*	*−129.8*	*−141.0*	*−147.1*	*−158.8*	*−150.2*	*−166.5*
Transportation services, credit	2 205 ..	**10.8**	**11.8**	**18.1**	**22.1**	**27.4**	**29.7**	**28.5**	**29.9**
Passenger	2 850 ..	....	....	....	....	....	....	....	....
Freight	2 851 ..	....	....	....	....	....	....	....	....
Other	2 852 ..	*10.8*	*11.8*	*18.1*	*22.1*	*27.4*	*29.7*	*28.5*	*29.9*
Sea transport, passenger	2 207 ..	....	....	....	....	....	....	....	....
Sea transport, freight	2 208 ..	....	....	....	....	....	....	....	....
Sea transport, other	2 209 ..	8.2	8.1	14.8	18.8	22.1	24.1	21.9	23.3
Air transport, passenger	2 211 ..	....	....	....	....	....	....	....	....
Air transport, freight	2 212 ..	....	....	....	....	....	....	....	....
Air transport, other	2 213 ..	2.6	3.7	3.3	3.4	5.3	5.7	6.6	6.6
Other transport, passenger	2 215 ..	....	....	....	....	....	....	....	....
Other transport, freight	2 216 ..	....	....	....	....	....	....	....	....
Other transport, other	2 217 ..	....	....	....	....	....	....	....	....
Transportation services, debit	3 205 ..	**−36.9**	**−35.8**	**−37.8**	**−39.7**	**−44.6**	**−50.1**	**−54.6**	**−56.9**
Passenger	3 850 ..	*−3.8*	*−2.9*	*−3.8*	*−4.1*	*−3.7*	*−3.1*	*−2.3*	*−2.6*
Freight	3 851 ..	*−33.0*	*−33.0*	*−34.0*	*−35.6*	*−40.9*	*−47.0*	*−52.2*	*−54.3*
Other	3 852 ..	....	....	....	....	....	....	....	....
Sea transport, passenger	3 207 ..	....	....	....	....	....	....	....	....
Sea transport, freight	3 208 ..	−33.0	−33.0	−34.0	−35.6	−40.9	−47.0	−52.2	−54.3
Sea transport, other	3 209 ..	....	....	....	....	....	....	....	....
Air transport, passenger	3 211 ..	−3.8	−2.9	−3.8	−4.1	−3.7	−3.1	−2.3	−2.6
Air transport, freight	3 212 ..	....	....	....	....	....	....	....	....
Air transport, other	3 213 ..	....	....	....	....	....	....	....	....
Other transport, passenger	3 215 ..	....	....	....	....	....	....	....	....
Other transport, freight	3 216 ..	....	....	....	....	....	....	....	....
Other transport, other	3 217 ..	....	....	....	....	....	....	....	....
Travel, credit	2 236 ..	**110.7**	**111.1**	**121.5**	**149.7**	**168.1**	**213.6**	**271.0**	**290.6**
Business travel	2 237 ..	7.1	6.9	7.7	8.3	8.8	10.3	18.8	17.1
Personal travel	2 240 ..	103.6	104.2	113.8	141.4	159.3	203.3	252.2	273.5
Travel, debit	3 236 ..	**−40.5**	**−41.9**	**−44.0**	**−45.8**	**−42.6**	**−41.6**	**−41.1**	**−42.7**
Business travel	3 237 ..	−3.5	−3.6	−3.6	−3.4	−2.9	−2.5	−2.0	−2.0
Personal travel	3 240 ..	−36.9	−38.3	−40.3	−42.4	−39.7	−39.2	−39.1	−40.8
Other services, credit	2 200 BA	**31.2**	**43.4**	**36.3**	**40.3**	**39.9**	**58.4**	**74.3**	**77.6**
Communications	2 245 ..	7.2	6.1	4.8	6.1	5.7	8.0	9.1	12.6
Construction	2 249 ..	....	....	....	....	....	1.6	3.6	....
Insurance	2 253 ..	....	.1	.1	.1	.1	.1	.1	.1
Financial	2 260 ..	....	.5	....	.5	.5	.7	.7	.7
Computer and information	2 262 ..	....	....	....	....	....	....	....	....
Royalties and licence fees	2 266 ..	....	....	....	....	....	....	....	....
Other business services	2 268 ..	6.3	13.6	16.3	17.5	21.7	30.3	36.9	37.0
Personal, cultural, and recreational	2 287 ..	....	....	....	....	....	....	....	....
Government, n.i.e.	2 291 ..	17.8	23.1	15.1	16.1	11.9	17.8	23.8	27.2
Other services, debit	3 200 BA	**−45.2**	**−42.4**	**−48.1**	**−55.5**	**−59.9**	**−67.0**	**−54.5**	**−66.9**
Communications	3 245 ..	−4.1	−2.6	−1.0	−1.3	−1.4	−1.8	−2.0	−2.5
Construction	3 249 ..	....	....	....	....	....	....	....	....
Insurance	3 253 ..	−10.2	−11.3	−13.6	−18.8	−18.5	−28.3	−24.1	−32.3
Financial	3 260 ..	−1.3	−1.9	−7.0	−7.6	−13.7	−6.6	−2.1	−8.6
Computer and information	3 262 ..	−.5	−.6	−.4	−.6	−.4	−.5	−.4	−.8
Royalties and licence fees	3 266 ..	−2.9	−2.2	−.3	−.2	−.4	−.4	−.4	−.9
Other business services	3 268 ..	−19.2	−14.3	−17.3	−13.2	−16.9	−17.7	−16.5	−12.2
Personal, cultural, and recreational	3 287 ..	....	....	....	−.1	−.4	−.2	−.3	−.4
Government, n.i.e.	3 291 ..	−6.9	−9.5	−8.4	−13.7	−8.2	−11.6	−8.9	−9.2

Table 2 (Continued). STANDARD PRESENTATION, 2000–2007

(Millions of U.S. dollars)

	Code	2000	2001	2002	2003	2004	2005	2006	2007
C. INCOME	4 300	**−52.9**	**−67.0**	**−67.5**	**−89.5**	**−116.7**	**−114.4**	**−129.0**	**−154.1**
Total credit	2 300	*6.9*	*8.6*	*4.2*	*5.5*	*4.3*	*6.8*	*10.0*	*7.0*
Total debit	3 300	*−59.8*	*−75.7*	*−71.7*	*−95.0*	*−121.1*	*−121.2*	*−139.0*	*−161.1*
Compensation of employees, credit	2 310	**2.0**	**2.0**	**1.9**	**2.5**	**2.4**	**3.8**	**6.0**	**2.4**
Compensation of employees, debit	3 310	**−5.6**	**−4.7**	**−4.2**	**−5.4**	**−6.2**	**−5.9**	**−5.7**	**−5.2**
Investment income, credit	2 320	**4.9**	**6.6**	**2.4**	**3.0**	**1.9**	**3.0**	**4.1**	**4.6**
Direct investment income	2 330	....	.3	.3	.4	.4	.5	.5	.5
Dividends and distributed branch profits	2 332	....	.3	.3	.4	.4	.5	.5	.5
Reinvested earnings and undistributed branch profits	2 333	....	....	....	....	....	....	....	....
Income on debt (interest)	2 334	....	....	....	....	....	....	....	....
Portfolio investment income	2 339	....	....	....	....	....	....	....	....
Income on equity	2 340	....	....	....	....	....	....	....	....
Income on bonds and notes	2 350	....	....	....	....	....	....	....	....
Income on money market instruments	2 360	....	....	....	....	....	....	....	....
Other investment income	2 370	4.8	6.3	2.1	2.6	1.5	2.5	3.5	4.1
Investment income, debit	3 320	**−54.2**	**−71.0**	**−67.5**	**−89.5**	**−114.9**	**−115.3**	**−133.4**	**−155.9**
Direct investment income	3 330	−30.5	−33.3	−33.0	−31.0	−42.4	−34.9	−55.3	−83.6
Dividends and distributed branch profits	3 332	−19.5	−20.0	−23.8	−18.3	−21.7	−16.3	−30.0	−53.6
Reinvested earnings and undistributed branch profits	3 333	−11.1	−13.3	−9.3	−12.1	−20.7	−18.6	−25.2	−30.0
Income on debt (interest)	3 334	....	....	....	−.5	....	....	−.1	....
Portfolio investment income	3 339	−4.2	−11.1	−9.7	−30.5	−36.6	−50.3	−39.0	−36.8
Income on equity	3 340	....	....	....	....	....	....	....	....
Income on bonds and notes	3 350	−4.2	−11.1	−9.7	−26.8	−33.1	−47.2	−36.2	−34.4
Income on money market instruments	3 360	....	....	....	−3.7	−3.4	−3.1	−2.8	−2.4
Other investment income	3 370	−19.5	−26.6	−24.8	−28.1	−35.9	−30.1	−39.1	−35.5
D. CURRENT TRANSFERS	4 379	**57.9**	**39.5**	**43.3**	**40.9**	**45.9**	**51.2**	**74.0**	**93.4**
Credit	2 379	**61.1**	**53.8**	**58.8**	**59.1**	**60.8**	**68.4**	**92.2**	**136.6**
General government	2 380	8.5	2.8	10.1	.8	10.4	5.5	10.9	41.0
Other sectors	2 390	52.6	50.9	48.7	58.3	50.4	62.8	81.2	95.6
Workers' remittances	2 391	22.8	26.4	24.9	29.7	31.2	40.9	57.8	70.8
Other current transfers	2 392	29.7	24.5	23.8	28.6	19.2	21.9	23.4	24.8
Debit	3 379	**−3.2**	**−14.2**	**−15.5**	**−18.3**	**−14.9**	**−17.1**	**−18.2**	**−43.2**
General government	3 380	−2.1	−2.5	−2.7	−3.2	−2.3	−2.4	−2.4	−25.2
Other sectors	3 390	−1.0	−11.7	−12.8	−15.1	−12.6	−14.8	−15.8	−18.0
Workers' remittances	3 391	−.9	−11.4	−12.4	−14.3	−11.8	−13.5	−14.9	−16.2
Other current transfers	3 392	−.2	−.4	−.4	−.8	−.8	−1.3	−.8	−1.8
CAPITAL AND FINANCIAL ACCOUNT	4 996	**150.9**	**181.7**	**173.9**	**219.3**	**158.7**	**158.8**	**28.9**	**52.2**
CAPITAL ACCOUNT	4 994	**−2.2**	**14.6**	**16.4**	**6.6**	**9.8**	**3.0**	**9.1**	**4.1**
Total credit	2 994	*1.9*	*15.9*	*17.5*	*7.5*	*10.6*	*3.9*	*10.2*	*5.1*
Total debit	3 994	*−4.1*	*−1.3*	*−1.1*	*−.9*	*−.8*	*−1.0*	*−1.1*	*−1.0*
Capital transfers, credit	2 400	**1.9**	**15.9**	**17.5**	**7.5**	**10.6**	**3.9**	**10.2**	**5.1**
General government	2 401	.3	13.8	8.0	5.8	9.3	2.6	8.0	3.3
Debt forgiveness	2 402	.3	8.6	2.2	2.4	3.0	.7	4.6	....
Other capital transfers	2 410	....	5.2	5.7	3.4	6.3	1.9	3.5	3.3
Other sectors	2 430	1.6	2.1	9.6	1.7	1.3	1.4	2.2	1.8
Migrants' transfers	2 431	1.6	2.1	1.6	1.7	1.3	1.4	1.7	1.7
Debt forgiveness	2 432	....	....	8.0	....	....	....	....	....
Other capital transfers	2 440	....	....	....	....	....	....	.5	.1
Capital transfers, debit	3 400	**−4.1**	**−1.3**	**−1.1**	**−.9**	**−.8**	**−1.0**	**−1.1**	**−1.0**
General government	3 401	....	....	....	....	....	....	....	....
Debt forgiveness	3 402	....	....	....	....	....	....	....	....
Other capital transfers	3 410	....	....	....	....	....	....	....	....
Other sectors	3 430	−4.1	−1.3	−1.1	−.9	−.8	−1.0	−1.1	−1.0
Migrants' transfers	3 431	−4.1	−1.3	−1.1	−.9	−.8	−1.0	−1.1	−1.0
Debt forgiveness	3 432	....	....	....	....	....	....	....	....
Other capital transfers	3 440	....	....	....	....	....	....	....	....
Nonproduced nonfinancial assets, credit	2 480	....	....	....	....	....	....	....	....
Nonproduced nonfinancial assets, debit	3 480	....	....	....	....	....	....	....	....

Table 2 (Continued). STANDARD PRESENTATION, 2000–2007

(Millions of U.S. dollars)

	Code	2000	2001	2002	2003	2004	2005	2006	2007
FINANCIAL ACCOUNT	4 995	**153.2**	**167.1**	**157.5**	**212.7**	**148.8**	**155.8**	**19.8**	**48.1**
A. DIRECT INVESTMENT	4 500	**23.3**	**61.2**	**25.4**	**−11.3**	**111.4**	**125.9**	**103.3**	**111.3**
Direct investment abroad	4 505	....	....	....	−.4	−.1	−1.0	−.6	−1.0
Equity capital	4 510	....	....	....	−.4	−.1	−1.0	−.6	−1.0
Claims on affiliated enterprises	4 515	....	....	....	−.4	−.1	−1.0	−.6	−1.0
Liabilities to affiliated enterprises	4 520	....	....	....	....	....	....	....	....
Reinvested earnings	4 525	....	....	....	....	....	....	....	....
Other capital	4 530	....	....	....	....	....	....	....	....
Claims on affiliated enterprises	4 535	....	....	....	....	....	....	....	....
Liabilities to affiliated enterprises	4 540	....	....	....	....	....	....	....	....
Direct investment in Belize	4 555	**23.3**	**61.2**	**25.4**	**−10.9**	**111.5**	**126.9**	**103.8**	**112.3**
Equity capital	4 560	7.3	47.9	16.1	−34.2	77.3	87.7	93.3	67.4
Claims on direct investors	4 565	−6.2	....	−.1	....	....	....	....	....
Liabilities to direct investors	4 570	13.5	47.9	16.2	−34.2	77.3	87.7	93.3	67.4
Reinvested earnings	4 575	11.1	13.3	9.3	12.1	20.7	18.6	25.2	30.0
Other capital	4 580	5.0	....	....	11.1	13.5	20.7	−14.7	14.9
Claims on direct investors	4 585	....	....	....	....	....	....	....	....
Liabilities to direct investors	4 590	5.0	....	....	11.1	13.5	20.7	−14.7	14.9
B. PORTFOLIO INVESTMENT	4 600	**113.1**	**−19.4**	**124.0**	**79.2**	**76.6**	**17.8**	**−21.6**	**78.7**
Assets	4 602	....	....	....	−.2	−.2	−.2	−.3	−.4
Equity securities	4 610	....	....	....	−.2	−.2	−.2	−.3	−.4
Monetary authorities	4 611	....	....	....	....	....	....	....	....
General government	4 612	....	....	....	....	....	....	....	....
Banks	4 613	....	....	....	....	....	....	....	....
Other sectors	4 614	....	....	....	−.2	−.2	−.2	−.3	−.4
Debt securities	4 619	....	....	....	....	....	....	....	....
Bonds and notes	4 620	....	....	....	....	....	....	....	....
Monetary authorities	4 621	....	....	....	....	....	....	....	....
General government	4 622	....	....	....	....	....	....	....	....
Banks	4 623	....	....	....	....	....	....	....	....
Other sectors	4 624	....	....	....	....	....	....	....	....
Money market instruments	4 630	....	....	....	....	....	....	....	....
Monetary authorities	4 631	....	....	....	....	....	....	....	....
General government	4 632	....	....	....	....	....	....	....	....
Banks	4 633	....	....	....	....	....	....	....	....
Other sectors	4 634	....	....	....	....	....	....	....	....
Liabilities	4 652	**113.1**	**−19.4**	**124.0**	**79.4**	**76.9**	**18.1**	**−21.4**	**79.1**
Equity securities	4 660	....	....	....	....	....	....	4.0	....
Banks	4 663	....	....	....	....	....	....	....	....
Other sectors	4 664	....	....	....	....	....	....	4.0	....
Debt securities	4 669	113.1	−19.4	124.0	79.4	76.9	18.1	−25.4	79.1
Bonds and notes	4 670	83.3	−7.8	118.4	92.9	144.7	21.7	−21.4	83.4
Monetary authorities	4 671	−3.0	−3.0	−3.0	−3.0	....	....	....	....
General government	4 672	86.3	−4.8	121.4	95.9	144.7	21.7	−21.4	83.4
Banks	4 673	....	....	....	....	....	....	....	....
Other sectors	4 674	....	....	....	....	....	....	....	....
Money market instruments	4 680	29.8	−11.6	5.7	−13.6	−67.8	−3.6	−4.0	−4.3
Monetary authorities	4 681	....	....	....	....	....	....	....	....
General government	4 682	29.8	−11.6	5.7	−13.6	−67.8	−3.6	−4.0	−4.3
Banks	4 683	....	....	....	....	....	....	....	....
Other sectors	4 684	....	....	....	....	....	....	....	....
C. FINANCIAL DERIVATIVES	4 910	....	....	.8	.7	.5	−5.3	....	....
Monetary authorities	4 911	....	....	....	....	....	....	....	....
General government	4 912	....	....	.8	.7	.5	−5.3	....	....
Banks	4 913	....	....	....	....	....	....	....	....
Other sectors	4 914	....	....	....	....	....	....	....	....
Assets	4 900	....	....	.8	.7	.5	.3	....	....
Monetary authorities	4 901	....	....	....	....	....	....	....	....
General government	4 902	....	....	.8	.7	.5	.3	....	....
Banks	4 903	....	....	....	....	....	....	....	....
Other sectors	4 904	....	....	....	....	....	....	....	....
Liabilities	4 905	....	....	....	....	....	−5.6	....	....
Monetary authorities	4 906	....	....	....	....	....	....	....	....
General government	4 907	....	....	....	....	....	−5.6	....	....
Banks	4 908	....	....	....	....	....	....	....	....
Other sectors	4 909	....	....	....	....	....	....	....	....

Table 2 (Concluded). STANDARD PRESENTATION, 2000–2007

(Millions of U.S. dollars)

	Code	2000	2001	2002	2003	2004	2005	2006	2007
D. OTHER INVESTMENT	4 700	**68.6**	**122.8**	**1.2**	**113.2**	**−71.2**	**5.9**	**−12.6**	**−119.6**
Assets	4 703	**−50.6**	**1.3**	**7.3**	**−9.9**	**−4.4**	**−39.1**	**−13.6**	**4.7**
Trade credits	4 706	−2.0	−1.9	−3.5	−.2	−.1	−.3	−1.2	−1.3
General government	4 707	....	....	....	....	....	....	....	....
of which: Short-term	4 709	....	....	....	....	....	....	....	....
Other sectors	4 710	−2.0	−1.9	−3.5	−.2	−.1	−.3	−1.2	−1.3
of which: Short-term	4 712	*−2.0*	*−1.9*	*−3.5*	*−.2*	*−.1*	*−.3*	*−1.2*	*−1.3*
Loans	4 714	....	....	....	....	....	....	....	....
Monetary authorities	4 715	....	....	....	....	....	....	....	....
of which: Short-term	4 718	....	....	....	....	....	....	....	....
General government	4 719	....	....	....	....	....	....	....	....
of which: Short-term	4 721	....	....	....	....	....	....	....	....
Banks	4 722	....	....	....	....	....	....	....	....
of which: Short-term	4 724	....	....	....	....	....	....	....	....
Other sectors	4 725	....	....	....	....	....	....	....	....
of which: Short-term	4 727	....	....	....	....	....	....	....	....
Currency and deposits	4 730	−48.6	3.3	10.8	−9.8	−4.3	−38.8	−10.9	7.9
Monetary authorities	4 731	....	....	....	....	....	−30.6	12.1	18.5
General government	4 732	−11.1	....	....	....	....	.1	5.0	....
Banks	4 733	−26.2	2.5	10.1	−2.6	−5.3	−9.2	−16.4	−11.4
Other sectors	4 734	−11.3	.8	.7	−7.2	1.0	.9	−11.6	.8
Other assets	4 736	....	....	....	....	....	....	−1.6	−1.9
Monetary authorities	4 737	....	....	....	....	....	....	....	....
of which: Short-term	4 739	....	....	....	....	....	....	....	....
General government	4 740	....	....	....	....	....	....	−1.6	−1.9
of which: Short-term	4 742	....	....	....	....	....	....	....	....
Banks	4 743	....	....	....	....	....	....	....	....
of which: Short-term	4 745	....	....	....	....	....	....	....	....
Other sectors	4 746	....	....	....	....	....	....	....	....
of which: Short-term	4 748	....	....	....	....	....	....	....	....
Liabilities	4 753	**119.2**	**121.5**	**−6.1**	**123.2**	**−66.8**	**45.0**	**1.1**	**−124.3**
Trade credits	4 756	4.0	3.0	1.1	4.9	2.6	−1.3	−.2	1.6
General government	4 757	....	....	....	....	....	....	....	....
of which: Short-term	4 759	....	....	....	....	....	....	....	....
Other sectors	4 760	4.0	3.0	1.1	4.9	2.6	−1.3	−.2	1.6
of which: Short-term	4 762	*4.0*	*3.0*	*1.1*	*4.9*	*2.6*	*−1.3*	*−.2*	*1.6*
Loans	4 764	113.5	124.3	−2.5	125.8	−72.3	47.7	62.1	−123.0
Monetary authorities	4 765	42.0	−2.5	−34.5	−2.5	−2.5	−1.3	....	....
of which: Use of Fund credit and loans from the Fund..	4 766	....	....	....	....	....	....	....	....
of which: Short-term	4 768	....	....	....	....	....	....	....	....
General government	4 769	57.5	116.4	−2.5	51.5	−52.7	43.7	34.8	−87.9
of which: Short-term	4 771	....	....	....	*80.0*	*−79.0*	....	....	....
Banks	4 772	2.4	9.8	−3.8	33.3	−7.0	2.1	23.2	−29.5
of which: Short-term	4 774	*2.4*	*9.8*	*−3.8*	*33.3*	*−7.0*	*2.1*	*23.2*	*−29.5*
Other sectors	4 775	11.6	.6	38.3	43.5	−10.2	3.1	4.1	−5.6
of which: Short-term	4 777	*−.3*	*−3.0*	*−2.9*	*−.2*	....	....	*−.2*	*−1.4*
Currency and deposits	4 780	8.3	−3.8	−2.7	−7.1	3.7	−.6	−60.8	−2.9
Monetary authorities	4 781	−.2	.6	1.5	−.1	−1.5	....	−.2	....
General government	4 782	−.7	....	....	2.4	−.3	1.4	−2.8	....
Banks	4 783	13.1	1.8	2.4	−4.8	7.3	1.1	−55.5	.3
Other sectors	4 784	−3.9	−6.3	−6.6	−4.7	−1.9	−3.1	−2.4	−3.1
Other liabilities	4 786	−6.6	−1.9	−2.0	−.4	−.7	−.8	....	−.1
Monetary authorities	4 787	....	....	....	....	....	....	....	....
of which: Short-term	4 789	....	....	....	....	....	....	....	....
General government	4 790	....	....	....	....	....	....	....	....
of which: Short-term	4 792	....	....	....	....	....	....	....	....
Banks	4 793	....	....	....	....	....	....	....	....
of which: Short-term	4 795	....	....	....	....	....	....	....	....
Other sectors	4 796	−6.6	−1.9	−2.0	−.4	−.7	−.8	....	−.1
of which: Short-term	4 798	*−6.6*	*−1.9*	*−2.0*	*−.4*	*−.7*	*−.8*	....	*−.1*
E. RESERVE ASSETS	4 802	**−51.9**	**2.5**	**6.0**	**30.8**	**31.4**	**11.5**	**−49.3**	**−22.4**
Monetary gold	4 812	....	....	....	....	....	....	....	....
Special drawing rights	4 811	−.2	−.2	−.1	−.1	−.1	−.2	−.3	−.3
Reserve position in the Fund	4 810	....	....	....	....	....	....	....	....
Foreign exchange	4 803	−51.8	2.7	6.1	30.9	31.5	12.0	−48.8	−21.5
Other claims	4 813	.1	....	.1	.1	.1	−.3	−.2	−.6
NET ERRORS AND OMISSIONS	4 998	**10.7**	**8.6**	**−8.6**	**−35.0**	**−3.7**	**−7.6**	**−12.7**	**−9.5**

Table 1. ANALYTIC PRESENTATION, 2000–2007

(Millions of U.S. dollars)

	Code	2000	2001	2002	2003	2004	2005	2006	2007
A. Current Account[1]............................	4 993 Z.	−111.0	−160.5	−238.9	−348.6	−316.5	−270.3	−327.3	....
Goods: exports f.o.b..................................	2 100 ..	392.4	373.5	447.8	540.8	568.6	578.3	735.5	....
Goods: imports f.o.b..................................	3 100 ..	−516.1	−553.0	−678.9	−818.7	−842.0	−865.7	−1,045.8	....
Balance on Goods..................................	4 100 ..	*−123.7*	*−179.5*	*−231.1*	*−277.9*	*−273.5*	*−287.4*	*−310.3*	....
Services: credit..	2 200 ..	136.1	147.1	152.2	172.3	215.6	193.8	217.1	....
Services: debit..	3 200 ..	−191.7	−191.9	−208.8	−253.9	−287.1	−279.1	−352.2	....
Balance on Goods and Services........................	4 991 ..	*−179.4*	*−224.3*	*−287.7*	*−359.5*	*−345.0*	*−372.7*	*−445.4*	....
Income: credit..	2 300 ..	23.5	22.4	20.8	22.8	22.9	25.4	23.8	....
Income: debit..	3 300 ..	−35.7	−35.8	−46.6	−60.9	−59.9	−43.2	−54.0	....
Balance on Goods, Services, and Income................	4 992 ..	*−191.6*	*−237.7*	*−313.5*	*−397.6*	*−382.0*	*−390.5*	*−475.6*	....
Current transfers: credit............................	2 379 Z.	91.3	87.3	93.2	56.6	73.4	152.8	205.5	....
Current transfers: debit............................	3 379 ..	−10.7	−10.0	−18.6	−7.5	−7.9	−32.6	−57.2	....
B. Capital Account[1]............................	4 994 Z.	**73.3**	**48.6**	**37.6**	**34.4**	**51.6**	**99.0**	**82.9**	....
Capital account: credit............................	2 994 Z.	73.4	48.6	37.6	34.9	52.2	105.3	89.0	....
Capital account: debit............................	3 994 ..	−.1	....	....	−.5	−.6	−6.3	−6.1	....
Total, Groups A Plus B............................	4 981 ..	*−37.7*	*−111.9*	*−201.3*	*−314.1*	*−264.9*	*−171.3*	*−244.4*	....
C. Financial Account[1]............................	4 995 W.	**10.8**	**39.6**	**−61.4**	**32.1**	**−28.1**	**105.2**	**−900.8**	....
Direct investment abroad............................	4 505 ..	−3.6	−2.3	−1.4	−.3	1.3	.4	1.7	....
Direct investment in Benin........................	4 555 Z.	59.7	43.9	13.5	44.7	63.8	53.0	53.2	....
Portfolio investment assets........................	4 602 ..	5.7	3.1	−3.6	−7.2	2.5	14.7	6.0	....
Equity securities..................................	4 610 ..	.9	−1.1	5.6	.3	.5	1.4	.3	....
Debt securities....................................	4 619 ..	4.7	4.2	−9.2	−7.5	2.0	13.3	5.7	....
Portfolio investment liabilities....................	4 652 Z.	.1	−.4	1.5	−.4	−2.9	2.3	.3	....
Equity securities..................................	4 660 ..	.1	−.4	1.5	−.4	−2.9	2.3	.3	....
Debt securities....................................	4 669 Z.	....	....	....	....	....	....	....	....
Financial derivatives..............................	4 910 ..	....	−.2	.1	−.2	−.5	−.3	....	....
Financial derivatives assets........................	4 900 ..	....	−.2	.1	−.2	−.5	−.3	....	....
Financial derivatives liabilities....................	4 905 ..	....	....	....	....	....	....	....	....
Other investment assets............................	4 703 ..	25.1	−34.4	−81.8	25.7	−19.3	6.7	−51.4	....
Monetary authorities..............................	4 701 ..	....	....	....	....	....	....	....	....
General government..............................	4 704 ..	....	....	−.1	.1	−.3	.2	−.3	....
Banks..	4 705 ..	1.8	−46.6	−.5	22.6	−32.4	1.1	−72.7	....
Other sectors....................................	4 728 ..	23.4	12.2	−81.8	3.1	13.4	5.4	21.5	....
Other investment liabilities........................	4 753 W.	−76.2	29.9	10.2	−30.2	−73.0	28.4	−910.7	....
Monetary authorities..............................	4 753 WA	−1.4	.8	−.8	4.5	18.4	−7.1	5.6	....
General government..............................	4 753 ZB	−49.2	−30.9	−46.8	−46.2	−40.2	−34.3	−1,026.7	....
Banks..	4 753 ZC	−21.0	12.7	−.9	32.4	.4	18.8	4.2	....
Other sectors....................................	4 753 ZD	−4.7	47.4	58.7	−20.9	−51.7	51.0	106.2	....
Total, Groups A Through C........................	4 983 ..	*−27.0*	*−72.3*	*−262.6*	*−282.0*	*−293.0*	*−66.1*	*−1,145.3*	....
D. Net Errors and Omissions......................	4 998 ..	**6.7**	**3.6**	**2.1**	**182.0**	**−10.1**	**8.8**	**28.0**	....
Total, Groups A Through D........................	4 984 ..	*−20.3*	*−68.7*	*−260.5*	*−100.0*	*−303.1*	*−57.3*	*−1,117.3*	....
E. Reserves and Related Items....................	4 802 A.	**20.3**	**68.7**	**260.5**	**100.0**	**303.1**	**57.3**	**1,117.3**	....
Reserve assets..	4 802 ..	−87.3	−147.4	88.8	−6.2	126.9	−111.7	−171.5	....
Use of Fund credit and loans........................	4 766 ..	−3.6	−4.1	−9.2	−6.6	−10.6	−7.6	−50.8	....
Exceptional financing..............................	4 920 ..	111.2	220.2	180.9	112.8	186.9	176.6	1,339.7	....
Conversion rates: CFA francs per U.S. dollar..........	0 101 ..	**711.98**	**733.04**	**696.99**	**581.20**	**528.28**	**527.47**	**522.89**	**479.27**

[1] Excludes components that have been classified in the categories of Group E.

Table 2. STANDARD PRESENTATION, 2000–2007

(Millions of U.S. dollars)

	Code	2000	2001	2002	2003	2004	2005	2006	2007
CURRENT ACCOUNT	4 993	−80.6	−74.9	−156.2	−331.2	−288.5	−226.1	−217.0	....
A. GOODS	4 100	−123.7	−179.5	−231.1	−277.9	−273.5	−287.4	−310.3	....
Credit	2 100	392.4	373.5	447.8	540.8	568.6	578.3	735.5	....
General merchandise: exports f.o.b.	2 110	384.4	367.4	442.3	532.1	555.9	563.1	722.7	....
Goods for processing: exports f.o.b.	2 150	....	....	....	....	....	....	....	....
Repairs on goods	2 160	....	....	....	....	....	....	....	....
Goods procured in ports by carriers	2 170	8.0	6.1	5.6	8.8	12.7	15.2	12.8	....
Nonmonetary gold	2 180	....	....	....	....	....	....	....	....
Debit	3 100	−516.1	−553.0	−678.9	−818.7	−842.0	−865.7	−1,045.8	....
General merchandise: imports f.o.b.	3 110	−514.8	−552.8	−678.0	−818.5	−839.3	−863.4	−1,041.9	....
Goods for processing: imports f.o.b.	3 150	....	....	....	....	....	....	....	....
Repairs on goods	3 160	−1.3	−.2	−.9	−.2	−2.3	−2.3	−3.8	....
Goods procured in ports by carriers	3 170	....	....	....	....	−.5	....	−.1	....
Nonmonetary gold	3 180	....	....	....	....	....	....	....	....
B. SERVICES	4 200	−55.6	−44.8	−56.6	−81.6	−71.5	−85.3	−135.2	....
Total credit	2 200	*136.1*	*147.1*	*152.2*	*172.3*	*215.6*	*193.8*	*217.1*	....
Total debit	3 200	*−191.7*	*−191.9*	*−208.8*	*−253.9*	*−287.1*	*−279.1*	*−352.2*	....
Transportation services, credit	2 205	18.1	19.6	12.8	14.4	33.7	32.8	29.2	....
Passenger	2 850	*.4*	*.5*	*1.5*	*1.9*	*2.9*	*4.7*	*5.6*	....
Freight	2 851	*11.9*	*13.0*	*5.8*	*6.0*	*8.1*	*8.4*	*.2*	....
Other	2 852	*5.8*	*6.0*	*5.5*	*6.4*	*22.7*	*19.7*	*23.4*	....
Sea transport, passenger	2 207	....	....	....	....	....	....	....	....
Sea transport, freight	2 208	1.3	....	....	....	....	....	....	....
Sea transport, other	2 209	5.4	5.4	4.5	5.2	21.0	19.7	15.1	....
Air transport, passenger	2 211	....	....	....	.1	.5	2.2	5.4	....
Air transport, freight	2 212	....	....	....	....	....	....	.1	....
Air transport, other	2 213	.3	.7	1.0	1.2	1.6	....	3.0	....
Other transport, passenger	2 215	.4	.5	1.5	1.8	2.4	2.5	.2	....
Other transport, freight	2 216	10.6	13.0	5.8	6.0	8.1	8.4	.1	....
Other transport, other	2 217	....	....	....	....	....	....	5.3	....
Transportation services, debit	3 205	−125.6	−126.0	−141.5	−170.6	−173.3	−174.2	−216.8	....
Passenger	3 850	*−38.3*	*−30.7*	*−29.3*	*−32.1*	*−30.0*	*−30.5*	*−36.9*	....
Freight	3 851	*−83.2*	*−89.8*	*−110.0*	*−134.7*	*−135.9*	*−136.8*	*−168.5*	....
Other	3 852	*−4.2*	*−5.5*	*−2.2*	*−3.9*	*−7.4*	*−6.9*	*−11.4*	....
Sea transport, passenger	3 207	....	....	....	....	....	....	....	....
Sea transport, freight	3 208	−64.0	−71.0	−86.0	−104.3	−105.2	−105.9	−126.8	....
Sea transport, other	3 209	−3.1	−3.0	−1.4	−2.6	−5.7	−5.4	−9.6	....
Air transport, passenger	3 211	−34.9	−29.6	−28.0	−30.8	−28.6	−28.9	−36.9	....
Air transport, freight	3 212	−16.0	−17.8	−21.5	−26.1	−26.3	−26.4	−31.8	....
Air transport, other	3 213	−1.1	−1.1	−.8	−1.2	−1.7	−1.5	−1.8	....
Other transport, passenger	3 215	−3.4	−1.1	−1.2	−1.3	−1.4	−1.6	....	....
Other transport, freight	3 216	−3.2	−1.0	−2.4	−4.3	−4.4	−4.5	−9.9	....
Other transport, other	3 217	....	−1.3	....	....	....	....	....	....
Travel, credit	2 236	76.8	84.6	92.9	106.4	118.5	103.4	116.3	....
Business travel	2 237	25.1	24.9	30.4	29.8	39.9	38.1	44.2	....
Personal travel	2 240	51.7	59.6	62.5	76.6	78.6	65.3	72.0	....
Travel, debit	3 236	−12.3	−17.3	−19.6	−21.2	−29.1	−26.9	−34.2	....
Business travel	3 237	−4.2	−7.7	−8.3	−6.8	−11.5	−10.2	−16.8	....
Personal travel	3 240	−8.1	−9.6	−11.3	−14.4	−17.6	−16.6	−17.5	....
Other services, credit	2 200 BA	41.1	43.0	46.5	51.6	63.5	57.6	71.6	....
Communications	2 245	4.2	3.7	5.6	4.2	5.2	5.4	11.2	....
Construction	2 249	.1	.7	.3	....	2.7	.1	.1	....
Insurance	2 253	.4	.5	.7	.2	2.3	1.2	.6	....
Financial	2 260	2.6	2.6	3.2	.6	.8	2.9	4.2	....
Computer and information	2 262	....	....	....	....	....	....	.6	....
Royalties and licence fees	2 266	....	....	....	.1	....	....	....	....
Other business services	2 268	24.2	21.7	25.1	36.8	40.8	33.5	34.3	....
Personal, cultural, and recreational	2 287	....	....	....	....	....	....	....	....
Government, n.i.e.	2 291	9.8	13.8	11.6	9.6	11.7	14.6	20.6	....
Other services, debit	3 200 BA	−53.8	−48.6	−47.7	−62.1	−84.8	−78.0	−101.2	....
Communications	3 245	−4.0	−2.4	−4.6	−6.7	−14.3	−16.4	−17.2	....
Construction	3 249	−13.1	−2.8	−.2	....	−1.8	−.1	−10.4	....
Insurance	3 253	−15.5	−16.9	−20.9	−29.4	−27.4	−27.3	−31.6	....
Financial	3 260	−1.8	−2.1	−1.9	−3.1	−3.5	−2.8	−2.3	....
Computer and information	3 262	−.7	−.7	−1.6	−1.3	−1.8	−3.1	−4.4	....
Royalties and licence fees	3 266	−.4	−.7	−.8	−1.9	−2.3	−1.9	−1.6	....
Other business services	3 268	−13.0	−16.6	−11.8	−9.3	−19.9	−14.5	−23.5	....
Personal, cultural, and recreational	3 287	−.1	−.1	....	....	−.1	−.1	−.2	....
Government, n.i.e.	3 291	−5.3	−6.3	−5.8	−10.1	−13.7	−11.9	−10.0	....

Table 2 (Continued). STANDARD PRESENTATION, 2000–2007

(Millions of U.S. dollars)

	Code	2000	2001	2002	2003	2004	2005	2006	2007
C. INCOME	4 300	**−12.3**	**−13.4**	**−25.8**	**−38.1**	**−37.0**	**−17.8**	**−30.2**	....
Total credit	2 300	*23.5*	*22.4*	*20.8*	*22.8*	*22.9*	*25.4*	*23.8*	....
Total debit	3 300	*−35.7*	*−35.8*	*−46.6*	*−60.9*	*−59.9*	*−43.2*	*−54.0*	....
Compensation of employees, credit	2 310	**5.2**	**5.2**	**5.8**	**5.8**	**8.9**	**9.8**	**9.3**	....
Compensation of employees, debit	3 310	**−2.3**	**−3.0**	**−1.4**	**−1.4**	**−2.8**	**−3.0**	**−8.7**	....
Investment income, credit	2 320	**18.3**	**17.2**	**15.0**	**16.9**	**14.0**	**15.6**	**14.5**	....
Direct investment income	2 330	.3	.5	.3	.9	.8	−.3	1.1	....
Dividends and distributed branch profits	2 332	....	....	.1	.3	.5	....	1.7	....
Reinvested earnings and undistributed branch profits	2 333	.2	.4	....	.2	....	−.9	−1.1	....
Income on debt (interest)	2 334	....	....	.2	.5	.3	.6	.5	....
Portfolio investment income	2 339	3.4	3.4	3.0	3.9	5.6	5.6	3.9	....
Income on equity	2 340	.1	.1	.1	.1	.2	1.0	.1	....
Income on bonds and notes	2 350	2.5	2.7	2.3	3.2	4.9	3.9	3.3	....
Income on money market instruments	2 360	.9	.7	.6	.7	.5	.7	.5	....
Other investment income	2 370	14.6	13.3	11.7	12.1	7.5	10.4	9.6	....
Investment income, debit	3 320	**−33.4**	**−32.8**	**−45.2**	**−59.5**	**−57.1**	**−40.1**	**−45.4**	....
Direct investment income	3 330	.8	−.2	−12.7	−22.4	−13.5	−9.0	−14.8	....
Dividends and distributed branch profits	3 332	−2.8	−3.0	−5.7	−8.1	−5.2	−7.0	−11.7	....
Reinvested earnings and undistributed branch profits	3 333	4.6	3.8	−6.1	−13.3	−6.6	.7	−3.1	....
Income on debt (interest)	3 334	−1.0	−1.0	−.9	−1.1	−1.7	−2.7	....	....
Portfolio investment income	3 339	−5.4	−7.0	−10.1	−7.2	−17.6	−8.4	−8.5	....
Income on equity	3 340	−1.6	−2.6	−2.4	−2.1	−7.8	−1.5	−1.7	....
Income on bonds and notes	3 350	−3.7	−4.5	−7.7	−5.1	−9.5	−6.9	−6.8	....
Income on money market instruments	3 360	....	....	....	....	−.3	....	....	....
Other investment income	3 370	−28.8	−25.5	−22.5	−29.9	−26.0	−22.7	−22.0	....
D. CURRENT TRANSFERS	4 379	**111.0**	**162.8**	**157.3**	**66.4**	**93.5**	**164.4**	**258.6**	....
Credit	2 379	**121.7**	**172.8**	**175.9**	**73.9**	**101.4**	**197.0**	**315.8**	....
General government	2 380	30.4	85.5	82.7	17.4	28.0	44.2	110.3	....
Other sectors	2 390	91.3	87.3	93.2	56.6	73.4	152.8	205.5	....
Workers' remittances	2 391	80.5	77.8	70.0	49.5	54.1	137.1	186.2	....
Other current transfers	2 392	10.8	9.5	23.3	7.1	19.3	15.7	19.3	....
Debit	3 379	**−10.7**	**−10.0**	**−18.6**	**−7.5**	**−7.9**	**−32.6**	**−57.2**	....
General government	3 380	−2.9	−1.9	−4.7	−2.3	−2.9	−.5	−3.2	....
Other sectors	3 390	−7.7	−8.1	−13.9	−5.3	−5.0	−32.2	−54.0	....
Workers' remittances	3 391	−6.6	−7.3	−5.2	−3.9	−2.9	−30.5	−52.1	....
Other current transfers	3 392	−1.2	−.8	−8.7	−1.4	−2.2	−1.7	−1.9	....
CAPITAL AND FINANCIAL ACCOUNT	4 996	**73.9**	**71.4**	**154.1**	**149.2**	**298.6**	**217.3**	**189.0**	....
CAPITAL ACCOUNT	4 994	**73.3**	**70.0**	**63.2**	**63.6**	**80.4**	**121.9**	**1,154.8**	....
Total credit	2 994	*73.4*	*70.0*	*63.2*	*64.1*	*81.1*	*128.2*	*1,160.9*	....
Total debit	3 994	*−.1*	....	....	*−.5*	*−.6*	*−6.3*	*−6.1*	....
Capital transfers, credit	2 400	**73.4**	**70.0**	**63.2**	**64.1**	**81.1**	**128.2**	**1,160.9**	....
General government	2 401	68.6	64.6	57.7	61.3	74.8	98.1	1,127.7	....
Debt forgiveness	2 402	23.2	21.4	25.5	29.2	28.9	22.8	1,071.9	....
Other capital transfers	2 410	45.4	43.3	32.2	32.1	45.9	75.3	55.8	....
Other sectors	2 430	4.8	5.3	5.4	2.8	6.3	30.1	33.2	....
Migrants' transfers	2 431	1.4	.6	.5	.1	....	25.8	28.5	....
Debt forgiveness	2 432	....	....	....	....	....	....	....	....
Other capital transfers	2 440	3.4	4.7	4.9	2.7	6.3	4.2	4.6	....
Capital transfers, debit	3 400	....	....	....	**−.4**	**−.6**	**−6.3**	**−6.1**	....
General government	3 401	....	....	....	....	....	....	....	....
Debt forgiveness	3 402	....	....	....	....	....	....	....	....
Other capital transfers	3 410	....	....	....	....	....	....	....	....
Other sectors	3 430	....	....	....	−.4	−.6	−6.3	−6.1	....
Migrants' transfers	3 431	....	....	....	−.4	−.6	−6.3	−6.1	....
Debt forgiveness	3 432	....	....	....	....	....	....	....	....
Other capital transfers	3 440	....	....	....	....	....	....	....	....
Nonproduced nonfinancial assets, credit	2 480	....	....	....	....	....	....	....	....
Nonproduced nonfinancial assets, debit	3 480	**−.1**	....	....	....	....	....	....	....

Table 2 (Continued). STANDARD PRESENTATION, 2000–2007

(Millions of U.S. dollars)

	Code	2000	2001	2002	2003	2004	2005	2006	2007
FINANCIAL ACCOUNT	4 995 ..	.6	1.4	90.9	85.6	218.2	95.4	−965.8	....
A. DIRECT INVESTMENT	4 500 ..	56.2	41.6	12.2	44.4	65.2	53.4	54.9	....
Direct investment abroad	4 505 ..	−3.6	−2.3	−1.4	−.3	1.3	.4	1.7	....
Equity capital	4 510 ..	....	−.9	−1.7	−1.9	−.8	7.8	....	....
Claims on affiliated enterprises	4 515 ..	....	....	.1	....	1.5	8.9	3.2	....
Liabilities to affiliated enterprises	4 520 ..	....	−.9	−1.8	−1.9	−2.3	−1.1	−3.2	....
Reinvested earnings	4 525 ..	−.2	−.4	....	−.2	....	.9	1.1	....
Other capital	4 530 ..	−3.4	−.9	.3	1.7	2.1	−8.3	.7	....
Claims on affiliated enterprises	4 535 ..	−4.0	−2.7	−.1	1.9	8.0	2.3	4.5	....
Liabilities to affiliated enterprises	4 540 ..	.6	1.8	.4	−.2	−5.9	−10.6	−3.8	....
Direct investment in Benin	4 555 ..	59.7	43.9	13.5	44.7	63.8	53.0	53.2	....
Equity capital	4 560 ..	73.5	18.7	21.8	28.6	71.2	23.9	14.6	....
Claims on direct investors	4 565 ..	70.2	30.7	33.7	34.7	92.7	52.6	65.8	....
Liabilities to direct investors	4 570 ..	3.3	−12.0	−11.9	−6.1	−21.5	−28.7	−51.2	....
Reinvested earnings	4 575 ..	−4.6	−3.8	6.1	13.3	6.6	−.7	3.1	....
Other capital	4 580 ..	−9.2	28.9	−14.4	2.8	−14.0	29.9	35.5	....
Claims on direct investors	4 585 ..	3.0	−2.7	−2.3	−2.6	3.7	−2.5	35.9	....
Liabilities to direct investors	4 590 ..	−12.2	31.6	−12.1	5.4	−17.7	32.4	−.4	....
B. PORTFOLIO INVESTMENT	4 600 ..	3.2	−1.3	−1.4	−8.2	−.7	16.7	14.6	....
Assets	4 602 ..	5.7	3.1	−3.6	−7.2	2.5	14.7	6.0	....
Equity securities	4 610 ..	.9	−1.1	5.6	.3	.5	1.4	.3	....
Monetary authorities	4 611 ..	....	....	....	....	....	....	....	....
General government	4 612 ..	....	....	....	....	....	....	....	....
Banks	4 613 ..	3.0	....	....	.5	4.1	....	.3	....
Other sectors	4 614 ..	−2.1	−1.1	5.6	−.2	−3.6	1.4	....	....
Debt securities	4 619 ..	4.7	4.2	−9.2	−7.5	2.0	13.3	5.7	....
Bonds and notes	4 620 ..	−9.4	−.8	−4.7	−8.8	−.6	7.2	2.0	....
Monetary authorities	4 621 ..	....	....	....	....	....	....	....	....
General government	4 622 ..	....	....	....	....	....	....	....	....
Banks	4 623 ..	−8.1	1.6	....	−7.6	.9	7.9	6.4	....
Other sectors	4 624 ..	−1.3	−2.4	−4.7	−1.1	−1.5	−.7	−4.3	....
Money market instruments	4 630 ..	14.2	5.0	−4.5	1.3	2.7	6.1	3.7	....
Monetary authorities	4 631 ..	....	....	....	....	....	....	....	....
General government	4 632 ..	....	....	....	....	....	....	....	....
Banks	4 633 ..	12.1	4.0	−4.1	1.5	2.7	4.7	3.7	....
Other sectors	4 634 ..	2.1	1.0	−.4	−.2	....	1.4	....	....
Liabilities	4 652 ..	−2.4	−4.4	2.2	−.9	−3.2	2.0	8.5	....
Equity securities	4 660 ..	.1	−.4	1.5	−.4	−2.9	2.3	.3	....
Banks	4 663 ..	−1.0	−.6	.7	−.6	−2.9	.2	−1.1	....
Other sectors	4 664 ..	1.1	.3	.8	.2	....	2.1	1.4	....
Debt securities	4 669 ..	−2.5	−4.1	.7	−.6	−.3	−.3	8.3	....
Bonds and notes	4 670 ..	−2.9	−3.7	−.7	−.6	−.3	−.3	8.3	....
Monetary authorities	4 671 ..	....	....	....	....	....	....	....	....
General government	4 672 ..	−.2	−.1	−.1	−.3	....	....	....	....
Banks	4 673 ..	−.6	−.6	.8	−.3	−.8	−.3	−.5	....
Other sectors	4 674 ..	−2.1	−3.0	−1.4	....	.5	−.1	8.8	....
Money market instruments	4 680 ..	.4	−.4	1.4	....	....	....	....	....
Monetary authorities	4 681 ..	....	....	....	....	....	....	....	....
General government	4 682 ..	....	....	....	....	....	....	....	....
Banks	4 683 ..	....	....	.7	....	....	....	....	....
Other sectors	4 684 ..	.4	−.4	.7	....	....	....	....	....
C. FINANCIAL DERIVATIVES	4 910 ..	....	−.2	.1	−.2	−.5	−.3	....	....
Monetary authorities	4 911 ..	....	....	....	....	....	....	....	....
General government	4 912 ..	....	....	....	....	....	....	....	....
Banks	4 913 ..	....	....	....	....	....	....	....	....
Other sectors	4 914 ..	....	−.2	.1	−.2	−.5	−.3	....	....
Assets	4 900 ..	....	−.2	.1	−.2	−.5	−.3	....	....
Monetary authorities	4 901 ..	....	....	....	....	....	....	....	....
General government	4 902 ..	....	....	....	....	....	....	....	....
Banks	4 903 ..	....	....	....	....	....	....	....	....
Other sectors	4 904 ..	....	−.2	.1	−.2	−.5	−.3	....	....
Liabilities	4 905 ..	....	....	....	....	....	....	....	....
Monetary authorities	4 906 ..	....	....	....	....	....	....	....	....
General government	4 907 ..	....	....	....	....	....	....	....	....
Banks	4 908 ..	....	....	....	....	....	....	....	....
Other sectors	4 909 ..	....	....	....	....	....	....	....	....

Table 2 (Concluded). STANDARD PRESENTATION, 2000–2007

(Millions of U.S. dollars)

	Code	2000	2001	2002	2003	2004	2005	2006	2007
D. OTHER INVESTMENT	4 700	**28.5**	**108.8**	**–8.8**	**55.8**	**27.3**	**137.3**	**–863.8**	....
Assets	4 703	**25.1**	**–34.4**	**–81.8**	**25.7**	**–19.3**	**6.7**	**–51.4**	....
Trade credits	4 706	13.6	–8.3	–55.8	–2.0	12.4	–3.3	17.2	....
General government	4 707	....	....	....	....	....	....	....	....
of which: Short-term	4 709	....	....	....	....	....	....	....	....
Other sectors	4 710	13.6	–8.3	–55.8	–2.0	12.4	–3.3	17.2	....
of which: Short-term	4 712	13.6	–8.3	–55.8	–2.0	12.4	–3.3		....
Loans	4 714	–6.7	–35.2	–3.4	20.8	–22.9	8.6	–32.7	....
Monetary authorities	4 715	....	....	....	....	....	....	....	....
of which: Short-term	4 718	....	....	....	....	....	....	....	....
General government	4 719	....	....	....	....	....	....	....	....
of which: Short-term	4 721	....	....	....	....	....	....	....	....
Banks	4 722	–6.7	–35.2	–3.4	20.8	–22.9	8.6	–32.5	....
of which: Short-term	4 724	.8	–30.1	6.0	20.8	10.0	–8.1	–40.4	....
Other sectors	4 725	....	....	....	....	....	....	–.2	....
of which: Short-term	4 727	....	....	....	....	....	....	....	....
Currency and deposits	4 730	15.6	15.3	4.8	–.6	–1.1	–8.3	–40.5	....
Monetary authorities	4 731	....	....	....	....	....	....	....	....
General government	4 732	....	....	–.1	.1	–.3	....	–.1	....
Banks	4 733	12.7	–12.3	4.6	1.8	–6.0	–10.2	–39.5	....
Other sectors	4 734	2.9	27.5	.2	–2.5	5.2	1.9	–.8	....
Other assets	4 736	2.6	–6.2	–27.4	7.5	–7.8	9.6	4.7	....
Monetary authorities	4 737	....	....	....	....	....	....	....	....
of which: Short-term	4 739	....	....	....	....	....	....	....	....
General government	4 740	....	....	–.1	....	....	.2	–.2	....
of which: Short-term	4 742	....	....	–.1	....	....	.2	....	....
Banks	4 743	–4.2	.9	–1.7	....	–3.6	2.7	–.6	....
of which: Short-term	4 745	–4.2	.9	–1.7	....	–3.6	2.7	–.6	....
Other sectors	4 746	6.8	–7.0	–25.6	7.6	–4.2	6.8	5.4	....
of which: Short-term	4 748	9.0	–2.3	–5.8	–5.7	–4.2	6.8	42.6	....
Liabilities	4 753	**3.4**	**143.2**	**73.0**	**30.0**	**46.7**	**130.6**	**–812.4**	....
Trade credits	4 756	–15.9	35.9	46.1	–26.5	–34.6	35.6	95.5	....
General government	4 757	....	....	....	....	....	....	....	....
of which: Short-term	4 759	....	....	....	....	....	....	....	....
Other sectors	4 760	–15.9	35.9	46.1	–26.5	–34.6	35.6	95.5	....
of which: Short-term	4 762	....	....	....	....	....	....	....	....
Loans	4 764	–9.1	92.7	22.3	11.8	65.3	76.1	–928.0	....
Monetary authorities	4 765	–3.6	–4.1	–9.2	–6.6	–10.6	–7.6	–50.8	....
of which: Use of Fund credit and loans from the Fund	4 766	–3.6	–4.1	–9.2	–6.6	–10.6	–7.6	–50.8	....
of which: Short-term	4 768	....	....	....	....	....	....	....	....
General government	4 769	24.4	83.7	22.9	19.0	75.3	66.0	–901.4	....
of which: Short-term	4 771	–4.5	....	....	....	....	....	....	....
Banks	4 772	9.9	–.1	1.6	.3	9.9	2.2	21.5	....
of which: Short-term	4 774	5.8	1.9	.8	–1.6	....	....	13.5	....
Other sectors	4 775	–39.7	13.2	7.0	–.9	–9.2	15.5	2.8	....
of which: Short-term	4 777	–43.4	4.3	....	....	–6.5	17.5	7.2	....
Currency and deposits	4 780	–19.9	13.6	–.4	34.7	4.9	22.0	5.5	....
Monetary authorities	4 781	1.1	–2.0	.3	.7	3.7	2.2	1.3	....
General government	4 782	....	....	....	....	....	....	....	....
Banks	4 783	–21.0	15.6	–.7	34.0	1.3	19.8	4.2	....
Other sectors	4 784	....	....	....	....	....	....	....	....
Other liabilities	4 786	48.3	1.1	5.0	10.1	11.0	–3.1	14.7	....
Monetary authorities	4 787	–2.4	2.8	–1.2	3.8	14.8	–9.3	4.3	....
of which: Short-term	4 789	....	....	....	....	....	....	....	....
General government	4 790	....	....	....	....	....	....	....	....
of which: Short-term	4 792	....	....	....	....	....	....	....	....
Banks	4 793	–.2	....	.6	–.2	–.3	.6	1.1	....
of which: Short-term	4 795	–.2	....	.6	–.2	–.3	.6	1.1	....
Other sectors	4 796	50.9	–1.7	5.6	6.4	–3.5	5.6	9.2	....
of which: Short-term	4 798	50.9	–1.7	5.6	6.4	–3.5	5.6	....	....
E. RESERVE ASSETS	4 802	**–87.3**	**–147.4**	**88.8**	**–6.2**	**126.9**	**–111.7**	**–171.5**	....
Monetary gold	4 812	....	....	....	....	....	....	....	....
Special drawing rights	4 811	.1	–.3	.3	–.1	.2	–.2	.1	....
Reserve position in the Fund	4 810	....	....	....	....	....	....	....	....
Foreign exchange	4 803	–87.4	–147.1	88.5	–6.2	126.7	–111.5	–171.6	....
Other claims	4 813	....	....	....	....	....	....	....	....
NET ERRORS AND OMISSIONS	4 998	**6.7**	**3.6**	**2.1**	**182.0**	**–10.1**	**8.8**	**28.0**	....

Table 3. INTERNATIONAL INVESTMENT POSITION (End-period stocks), 2000–2007

(Millions of U.S. dollars)

	Code	2000	2001	2002	2003	2004	2005	2006	2007
ASSETS..	8 995 C.	737.4	936.7	1,089.0	1,224.0	1,147.1	1,093.8	1,499.4	....
Direct investment abroad.....................	8 505 ..	10.5	12.6	16.2	19.7	9.3	19.6	14.5	....
Equity capital and reinvested earnings............	8 506 ..	6.5	7.9	11.1	15.6	18.1	16.2	15.7	....
Claims on affiliated enterprises..............	8 507 ..	6.5	7.9	11.1	15.6	18.1	16.2	15.7	....
Liabilities to affiliated enterprises..........	8 508 ..	....	....	....	....	....	....	....	....
Other capital...........................	8 530 ..	4.0	4.7	5.1	4.1	−8.8	3.4	−1.2	....
Claims on affiliated enterprises..............	8 535 ..	4.0	4.7	5.1	4.1		3.4	−1.2	....
Liabilities to affiliated enterprises..........	8 540 ..	....	....	....	....	−8.8			....
Portfolio investment........................	8 602 ..	67.6	65.0	83.4	95.5	114.6	99.5	102.1	....
Equity securities.........................	8 610 ..	3.2	3.2	1.7	1.4	4.5	1.6	.8	....
Monetary authorities....................	8 611 ..	....	....	....	....	....	....	....	....
General government.....................	8 612 ..	....	....	....	....	....	....	....	....
Banks...............................	8 613 ..	.5	.4	.6	1.0	.3	.1	.1	....
Other sectors.........................	8 614 ..	2.7	2.8	1.1	.5	4.2	1.5	.7	....
Debt securities..........................	8 619 ..	64.4	61.8	81.7	94.1	110.1	98.0	101.3	....
Bonds and notes.......................	8 620 ..	46.2	48.5	61.0	74.4	98.4	91.3	90.6	....
Monetary authorities.................	8 621 ..	....	....	....	....	....	....	....	....
General government..................	8 622 ..	....	....	....	....	....	....	....	....
Banks..............................	8 623 ..	43.3	40.2	47.8	65.6	71.7	51.6	44.4	....
Other sectors........................	8 624 ..	2.8	8.3	13.2	8.8	26.7	39.7	46.2	....
Money market instruments................	8 630 ..	18.3	13.3	20.7	19.7	11.8	6.7	10.7	....
Monetary authorities.................	8 631 ..	....	....	....	....	....	....	....	....
General government..................	8 632 ..	....	....	....	....	....	....	....	....
Banks..............................	8 633 ..	16.2	10.7	18.1	19.7	11.8	5.3	10.7	....
Other sectors........................	8 634 ..	2.1	2.6	2.6	....	....	1.4	....	....
Financial derivatives.......................	8 900 ..	....	.2	.3	.5	1.1	1.1	.1	....
Monetary authorities......................	8 901 ..	....	....	....	....	....	....	....	....
General government......................	8 902 ..	....	....	....	....	....	....	....	....
Banks..................................	8 903 ..	....	....	....	....	....	....	....	....
Other sectors...........................	8 904 ..	....	.2	.3	.5	1.1	1.1	.1	....
Other investment..........................	8 703 ..	200.5	279.1	398.5	390.3	387.2	317.5	470.5	....
Trade credits............................	8 706 ..	30.5	38.5	105.3	119.4	93.8	68.7	81.2	....
General government.....................	8 707 ..	....	....	....	....	....	....	....	....
of which: Short-term..................	8 709 ..	....	....	....	....	....	....	....	....
Other sectors.........................	8 710 ..	30.5	38.5	105.3	119.4	93.8	68.7	81.2	....
of which: Short-term..................	8 712 ..	*30.5*	*38.5*	*105.3*	*119.4*	*93.8*	*68.7*	*81.2*	....
Loans.................................	8 714 ..	69.4	100.2	115.3	115.4	136.2	109.3	156.4	....
Monetary authorities....................	8 715 ..	....	....	....	....	....	....	....	....
of which: Short-term..................	8 718 ..	....	....	....	....	....	....	....	....
General government.....................	8 719 ..	....	....	....	....	....	....	....	....
of which: Short-term..................	8 721 ..	....	....	....	....	....	....	....	....
Banks...............................	8 722 ..	69.4	100.2	115.3	115.4	136.2	109.3	156.2	....
of which: Short-term..................	8 724 ..	*56.4*	*82.8*	*83.5*	*77.2*	*58.9*	*58.3*	*112.9*	....
Other sectors.........................	8 725 ..	....	....	....	....	....	....	.2	....
of which: Short-term..................	8 727 ..	....	....	....	....	....	....	.2	....
Currency and deposits....................	8 730 ..	90.5	106.6	114.2	135.2	142.6	129.3	185.0	....
Monetary authorities....................	8 731 ..	....	....	....	....	....	....	....	....
General government.....................	8 732 ..	....	....	.1	....	.3	.2	.3	....
Banks...............................	8 733 ..	79.3	87.2	98.6	116.8	132.5	124.5	180.5	....
Other sectors.........................	8 734 ..	11.2	19.4	15.6	18.4	9.8	4.6	4.2	....
Other assets...........................	8 736 ..	10.0	33.8	63.6	20.3	14.5	10.2	48.0	....
Monetary authorities....................	8 737 ..	....	....	....	....	....	....	....	....
of which: Short-term..................	8 739 ..	....	....	....	....	....	....	....	....
General government.....................	8 740 ..	.1	.1	.2	.3	.3	.1	.3	....
of which: Short-term..................	8 742 ..	*.1*	*.1*	*.2*	*.3*	*.3*	*.1*	*.3*	....
Banks...............................	8 743 ..	6.5	.3	1.9	....	3.9	.9	1.6	....
of which: Short-term..................	8 745 ..	*6.5*	*.3*	*1.9*	....	*3.9*	*.9*	*1.6*	....
Other sectors.........................	8 746 ..	3.4	33.3	61.5	20.0	10.3	9.2	46.1	....
of which: Short-term..................	8 748 ..	*3.4*	*33.3*	*61.5*	*20.0*	*10.3*	*9.2*	*46.1*	....
Reserve assets...........................	8 802 ..	458.8	579.7	590.6	717.9	634.9	656.0	912.2	....
Monetary gold...........................	8 812 ..	....	....	....	....	....	....	....	....
Special drawing rights.....................	8 811 ..	.1	.4	.1	.2	....	.2	.1	.1
Reserve position in the Fund................	8 810 ..	2.9	2.7	3.0	3.3	3.4	3.1	3.3	3.5
Foreign exchange.........................	8 803 ..	455.8	576.6	587.5	714.4	631.5	652.7	908.9	....
Other claims............................	8 813 ..	....	....	....	....	....	....	....	....

Table 3 (Concluded). INTERNATIONAL INVESTMENT POSITION (End-period stocks), 2000–2007

(Millions of U.S. dollars)

	Code	2000	2001	2002	2003	2004	2005	2006	2007
LIABILITIES	8 995 D.	**1,842.2**	**1,884.0**	**2,126.2**	**2,253.6**	**2,622.7**	**2,460.3**	**2,112.2**	....
Direct investment in Benin	8 555 ..	**213.2**	**149.0**	**190.9**	**231.2**	**269.0**	**284.3**	**384.5**	....
Equity capital and reinvested earnings	8 556 ..	136.5	75.4	107.9	132.1	194.6	182.4	210.1	....
Claims on direct investors	8 557 ..	....	....	....	....	....	....	....	....
Liabilities to direct investors	8 558 ..	136.5	75.4	107.9	132.1	194.6	182.4	210.1	....
Other capital	8 580 ..	76.7	73.5	83.0	99.1	74.4	102.0	174.4	....
Claims on direct investors	8 585 ..	....	....	....	....	....	....	....	....
Liabilities to direct investors	8 590 ..	76.7	73.5	83.0	99.1	74.4	102.0	174.4	....
Portfolio investment	8 652 ..	**16.3**	**11.4**	**16.9**	**15.9**	**13.6**	**14.0**	**33.8**	....
Equity securities	8 660 ..	6.1	4.7	10.7	11.1	8.8	12.3	12.9	....
Banks	8 663 ..	4.1	3.3	8.6	9.7	7.3	9.0	9.8	....
Other sectors	8 664 ..	1.9	1.4	2.0	1.4	1.5	3.3	3.2	....
Debt securities	8 669 ..	10.2	6.6	6.3	4.7	4.8	1.7	20.9	....
Bonds and notes	8 670 ..	9.8	6.6	5.5	4.7	3.2	1.7	20.9	....
Monetary authorities	8 671 ..	....	....	....	....	....	....	....	....
General government	8 672 ..	....	....	....	....	....	....	....	....
Banks	8 673 ..	1.8	1.2	2.1	2.2	....	1.1	.6	....
Other sectors	8 674 ..	8.0	5.5	3.4	2.5	3.2	.7	20.2	....
Money market instruments	8 680 ..	.4	....	.8	....	1.5	....	....	....
Monetary authorities	8 681 ..	....	....	....	....	....	....	....	....
General government	8 682 ..	....	....	....	....	....	....	....	....
Banks	8 683 ..	.4	....	.8	....	1.5	....	....	....
Other sectors	8 684 ..	....	....	....	....	....	....	....	....
Financial derivatives	8 905 ..	....	....	**.3**	....	....	....	....	....
Monetary authorities	8 906 ..	....	....	....	....	....	....	....	....
General government	8 907 ..	....	....	....	....	....	....	....	....
Banks	8 908 ..	....	....	.3	....	....	....	....	....
Other sectors	8 909 ..	....	....	....	....	....	....	....	....
Other investment	8 753 ..	**1,612.7**	**1,723.6**	**1,918.0**	**2,006.5**	**2,340.1**	**2,161.9**	**1,693.9**	....
Trade credits	8 756 ..	38.0	86.8	143.7	105.8	229.6	228.5	343.0	....
General government	8 757 ..	....	....	....	....	....	....	....	....
of which: Short-term	8 759 ..	....	....	....	....	....	....	....	....
Other sectors	8 760 ..	38.0	86.8	143.7	105.8	229.6	228.5	343.0	....
of which: Short-term	8 762 ..	*38.0*	*86.8*	*143.7*	*105.8*	*229.6*	*228.5*	*343.0*	....
Loans	8 764 ..	1,446.8	1,493.3	1,660.9	1,727.9	1,871.6	1,763.4	1,144.9	....
Monetary authorities	8 765 ..	83.9	76.8	73.3	73.1	65.3	52.8	2.6	....
of which: Use of Fund credit and loans from the Fund	8 766 ..	*83.9*	*76.8*	*73.3*	*73.1*	*65.3*	*52.8*	*2.6*	*4.2*
of which: Short-term	8 768 ..	....	....	....	....	....	....	....	....
General government	8 769 ..	1,291.5	1,310.0	1,470.6	1,585.0	1,696.1	1,653.6	1,043.6	....
of which: Short-term	8 771 ..	....	....	....	....	....	....	....	....
Banks	8 772 ..	12.8	12.0	16.0	19.6	32.0	29.8	55.8	....
of which: Short-term	8 774 ..	*9.5*	*10.8*	*13.8*	*14.8*	*27.7*	*27.1*	*44.5*	....
Other sectors	8 775 ..	58.6	94.4	101.0	50.2	78.2	27.3	42.9	....
of which: Short-term	8 777 ..	*36.3*	*57.7*	*66.2*	*32.1*	*58.7*	....	....	....
Currency and deposits	8 780 ..	64.6	80.7	88.6	132.5	145.5	149.6	176.5	....
Monetary authorities	8 781 ..	6.7	4.0	1.4	2.0	6.0	7.3	9.4	....
General government	8 782 ..	....	....	....	....	....	....	....	....
Banks	8 783 ..	57.9	76.7	87.2	130.5	139.5	142.3	167.1	....
Other sectors	8 784 ..	....	....	....	....	....	....	....	....
Other liabilities	8 786 ..	63.3	62.8	24.8	40.4	93.4	20.4	29.4	....
Monetary authorities	8 787 ..	−1.4	1.4	.4	4.8	21.4	9.7	15.3	....
of which: Short-term	8 789 ..	....	....	....	....	....	....	....	....
General government	8 790 ..	....	....	....	....	....	....	....	....
of which: Short-term	8 792 ..	....	....	....	....	....	....	....	....
Banks	8 793 ..	....	....	....	....	....	....	....	....
of which: Short-term	8 795 ..	....	....	....	....	....	....	....	....
Other sectors	8 796 ..	64.7	61.3	24.4	35.6	72.0	10.8	14.1	....
of which: Short-term	8 798 ..	....	....	....	....	....	....	....	....
NET INTERNATIONAL INVESTMENT POSITION	8 995 ..	**−1,104.8**	**−947.3**	**−1,037.1**	**−1,029.6**	**−1,475.6**	**−1,366.5**	**−612.8**	....
Conversion rates: CFA francs per U.S. dollar (end of period)	0 102 ..	704.95	744.31	625.50	519.36	481.58	556.04	498.07	445.59

Table 1. ANALYTIC PRESENTATION, 2000–2007

(Millions of U.S. dollars)

	Code	2000	2001	2002	2003	2004	2005	2006	2007
A. Current Account[1]............................	4 993 Z.	**−446.3**	**−274.0**	**−351.9**	**75.6**	**337.5**	**622.4**	**1,317.5**	**1,799.6**
Goods: exports f.o.b..........................	2 100 ..	1,246.1	1,284.8	1,298.7	1,597.8	2,146.0	2,791.1	3,874.5	4,490.4
Goods: imports f.o.b..........................	3 100 ..	−1,610.2	−1,580.0	−1,638.7	−1,497.4	−1,724.7	−2,182.6	−2,632.1	−3,249.2
Balance on Goods........................	4 100 ..	*−364.1*	*−295.2*	*−340.0*	*100.5*	*421.3*	*608.5*	*1,242.4*	*1,241.2*
Services: credit................................	2 200 ..	224.0	235.9	256.6	363.9	416.4	488.8	476.6	468.4
Services: debit................................	3 200 ..	−467.7	−399.4	−433.3	−551.2	−606.7	−682.5	−826.6	−828.5
Balance on Goods and Services........*	4 991 ..	*−607.8*	*−458.7*	*−516.7*	*−86.9*	*231.1*	*414.8*	*892.5*	*881.2*
Income: credit................................	2 300 ..	139.7	121.2	103.2	71.1	76.0	121.2	235.4	369.8
Income: debit................................	3 300 ..	−365.0	−332.5	−307.9	−373.7	−460.6	−497.6	−632.7	−542.7
Balance on Goods, Services, and Income......	4 992 ..	*−833.1*	*−670.1*	*−721.4*	*−389.5*	*−153.6*	*38.4*	*495.2*	*708.3*
Current transfers: credit....................	2 379 Z.	420.0	431.6	407.8	510.9	542.6	648.7	895.1	1,163.2
Current transfers: debit....................	3 379 ..	−33.2	−35.5	−38.4	−45.7	−51.5	−64.7	−72.9	−72.0
B. Capital Account[1]............................	4 994 Z.	....	....	....	....	....	8.7	1,813.2	1,180.2
Capital account: credit....................	2 994 Z.	....	....	....	....	....	8.7	1,813.2	1,180.2
Capital account: debit....................	3 994 ..	....	....	....	....	....	....	....	....
Total, Groups A Plus B..................	4 981 ..	*−446.3*	*−274.0*	*−351.9*	*75.6*	*337.5*	*631.1*	*3,130.7*	*2,979.7*
C. Financial Account[1]........................	4 995 W.	**461.8**	**440.7**	**649.0**	**36.3**	**360.5**	**180.6**	**−1,588.6**	**−1,034.3**
Direct investment abroad..................	4 505 ..	−2.8	−2.5	−2.5	−2.8	−2.8	−3.0	−3.0	−3.0
Direct investment in Bolivia..............	4 555 Z.	736.4	705.8	676.6	197.4	65.4	−238.6	280.8	204.2
Portfolio investment assets..............	4 602 ..	55.4	−23.0	−19.3	−68.2	−35.4	−153.4	25.1	−24.5
Equity securities........................	4 610 ..	....	....	....	....	1.2	....	....	....
Debt securities..........................	4 619 ..	55.4	−23.0	−19.3	−68.2	−36.6	−153.4	25.1	−24.5
Portfolio investment liabilities..........	4 652 Z.	....	....	....	....	....	....	....	....
Equity securities........................	4 660 ..	....	....	....	....	....	....	....	....
Debt securities..........................	4 669 Z.	....	....	....	....	....	....	....	....
Financial derivatives......................	4 910 ..	....	....	....	....	....	....	....	....
Financial derivatives assets..............	4 900 ..	....	....	....	....	....	....	....	....
Financial derivatives liabilities..........	4 905 ..	....	....	....	....	....	....	....	....
Other investment assets..................	4 703 ..	−146.1	−166.7	−193.4	−462.9	94.3	123.8	−262.4	17.8
Monetary authorities....................	4 701 ..	−1.2	....	....	....	....	....	....	....
General government....................	4 704 ..	−7.9	−15.7	−17.1	−17.7	−15.7	−12.1	1.5	−14.5
Banks....................................	4 705 ..	−94.4	−157.0	49.8	46.3	5.6	−131.7	−105.2	137.2
Other sectors..........................	4 728 ..	−42.6	6.1	−226.1	−491.5	104.4	267.6	−158.7	−104.9
Other investment liabilities..............	4 753 W.	−181.1	−72.9	187.7	372.7	239.0	451.8	−1,629.1	−1,228.8
Monetary authorities....................	4 753 WA	−23.7	−20.3	−18.1	−2.8	.1	.9	1.2	....
General government....................	4 753 ZB	131.4	226.1	310.3	280.1	200.8	132.4	−1,632.5	−1,132.7
Banks....................................	4 753 ZC	−280.1	−247.7	−35.5	−80.9	20.1	−1.9	−20.5	−57.8
Other sectors..........................	4 753 ZD	−8.7	−31.0	−69.0	176.4	18.0	320.5	22.7	−38.3
Total, Groups A Through C............	4 983 ..	*15.4*	*166.7*	*297.1*	*111.9*	*698.0*	*811.7*	*1,542.1*	*1,945.4*
D. Net Errors and Omissions................	4 998 ..	**−54.8**	**−202.7**	**−639.8**	**−173.5**	**−625.4**	**−374.5**	**−103.3**	**−80.4**
Total, Groups A Through D............	4 984 ..	*−39.4*	*−36.0*	*−342.7*	*−61.6*	*72.6*	*437.2*	*1,438.8*	*1,865.1*
E. Reserves and Related Items............	4 802 A.	**39.4**	**36.0**	**342.7**	**61.6**	**−72.6**	**−437.2**	**−1,438.8**	**−1,865.1**
Reserve assets............................	4 802 ..	38.8	32.5	303.0	−152.0	−157.2	−463.4	−1,286.3	−1,937.7
Use of Fund credit and loans..............	4 766 ..	−14.5	−5.3	−27.7	60.0	14.3	−39.2	−232.9	−14.6
Exceptional financing......................	4 920 ..	15.1	8.8	67.3	153.5	70.3	65.3	80.4	87.3
Conversion rates: bolivianos per U.S. dollar..........	0 101 ..	**6.1835**	**6.6069**	**7.1700**	**7.6592**	**7.9363**	**8.0661**	**8.0116**	**7.8512**

[1] Excludes components that have been classified in the categories of Group E.

Table 2. STANDARD PRESENTATION, 2000–2007

(Millions of U.S. dollars)

	Code	2000	2001	2002	2003	2004	2005	2006	2007
CURRENT ACCOUNT	4 993	**−446.3**	**−274.0**	**−351.9**	**75.6**	**337.5**	**622.4**	**1,317.5**	**1,799.6**
A. GOODS	4 100	**−364.1**	**−295.2**	**−340.0**	**100.5**	**421.3**	**608.5**	**1,242.4**	**1,241.2**
Credit	2 100	**1,246.1**	**1,284.8**	**1,298.7**	**1,597.8**	**2,146.0**	**2,791.1**	**3,874.5**	**4,490.4**
General merchandise: exports f.o.b.	2 110	1,039.2	1,092.7	1,082.8	1,406.7	2,002.7	2,528.8	3,518.2	4,122.9
Goods for processing: exports f.o.b.	2 150	98.4	86.5	112.1	96.1	94.9	159.2	187.9	194.4
Repairs on goods	2 160	8.6	9.6	2.3	8.8	6.6	9.2	22.9	24.6
Goods procured in ports by carriers	2 170	11.9	9.8	11.9	14.4	8.1	16.2	19.4	25.5
Nonmonetary gold	2 180	88.0	86.2	89.7	71.8	33.7	77.8	126.1	123.0
Debit	3 100	**−1,610.2**	**−1,580.0**	**−1,638.7**	**−1,497.4**	**−1,724.7**	**−2,182.6**	**−2,632.1**	**−3,249.2**
General merchandise: imports f.o.b.	3 110	−1,610.2	−1,580.0	−1,638.7	−1,497.4	−1,724.7	−2,182.6	−2,632.1	−3,249.2
Goods for processing: imports f.o.b.	3 150	....	....	....	....	....	....	....	....
Repairs on goods	3 160	....	....	....	....	....	....	....	....
Goods procured in ports by carriers	3 170	....	....	....	....	....	....	....	....
Nonmonetary gold	3 180	....	....	....	....	....	....	....	....
B. SERVICES	4 200	**−243.7**	**−163.5**	**−176.7**	**−187.4**	**−190.3**	**−193.7**	**−350.0**	**−360.1**
Total credit	2 200	*224.0*	*235.9*	*256.6*	*363.9*	*416.4*	*488.8*	*476.6*	*468.4*
Total debit	3 200	*−467.7*	*−399.4*	*−433.3*	*−551.2*	*−606.7*	*−682.5*	*−826.6*	*−828.5*
Transportation services, credit	2 205	**50.1**	**67.2**	**62.4**	**100.9**	**116.9**	**143.2**	**111.4**	**60.1**
Passenger	2 850	*32.8*	*42.8*	*43.3*	*77.0*	*91.4*	*106.0*	*86.0*	*35.3*
Freight	2 851	*4.3*	*9.8*	*7.1*	*7.9*	*8.4*	*13.3*	*8.9*	*11.9*
Other	2 852	*13.0*	*14.5*	*12.0*	*16.0*	*17.1*	*23.9*	*16.5*	*12.9*
Sea transport, passenger	2 207	....	....	....	....	....	....	....	....
Sea transport, freight	2 208	....	....	....	....	....	....	....	....
Sea transport, other	2 209	....	....	....	....	....	....	....	....
Air transport, passenger	2 211	30.0	41.1	40.6	74.4	88.6	102.7	82.8	30.0
Air transport, freight	2 212	1.9	1.9	1.1	1.4	1.9	4.0	.6	....
Air transport, other	2 213	12.6	14.0	11.7	15.8	17.0	23.8	16.4	12.7
Other transport, passenger	2 215	2.8	1.7	2.6	2.6	2.8	3.2	3.2	5.4
Other transport, freight	2 216	2.4	7.9	6.1	6.5	6.5	9.2	8.3	11.9
Other transport, other	2 217	.4	.6	.3	.2	.1	.1	.2	.1
Transportation services, debit	3 205	**−269.7**	**−186.6**	**−169.5**	**−187.5**	**−195.6**	**−233.7**	**−274.0**	**−287.9**
Passenger	3 850	*−38.6*	*−30.7*	*−33.9*	*−58.9*	*−68.1*	*−70.7*	*−87.1*	*−75.9*
Freight	3 851	*−176.3*	*−110.1*	*−100.7*	*−84.3*	*−95.2*	*−121.1*	*−137.0*	*−158.9*
Other	3 852	*−54.8*	*−45.9*	*−34.8*	*−44.3*	*−32.3*	*−41.8*	*−50.0*	*−53.2*
Sea transport, passenger	3 207	....	....	....	....	....	....	....	....
Sea transport, freight	3 208	−173.3	−106.0	−97.8	−59.7	−40.1	−43.9	−46.6	−65.6
Sea transport, other	3 209	−30.0	−12.8	−18.8	−13.9	−2.6	−2.1	−4.6	−5.1
Air transport, passenger	3 211	−35.7	−28.4	−31.7	−56.1	−65.2	−68.8	−82.3	−66.8
Air transport, freight	3 212	−.6	−1.5	−.8	−4.1	−9.7	−7.0	−7.5	−10.2
Air transport, other	3 213	−24.4	−32.2	−14.2	−26.0	−25.5	−35.3	−36.8	−40.0
Other transport, passenger	3 215	−2.9	−2.2	−2.2	−2.8	−2.9	−2.0	−4.8	−9.0
Other transport, freight	3 216	−2.4	−2.6	−2.1	−20.5	−45.4	−70.2	−82.8	−83.1
Other transport, other	3 217	−.4	−.9	−1.8	−4.4	−4.2	−4.5	−8.6	−8.0
Travel, credit	2 236	**68.4**	**75.7**	**100.5**	**166.5**	**191.6**	**238.6**	**244.1**	**259.1**
Business travel	2 237	20.8	24.2	28.5	40.1	48.4	68.4	65.0	74.4
Personal travel	2 240	47.6	51.5	72.0	126.4	143.2	170.2	179.1	184.7
Travel, debit	3 236	**−77.2**	**−83.1**	**−80.0**	**−138.5**	**−164.4**	**−186.4**	**−272.6**	**−249.1**
Business travel	3 237	−17.8	−20.0	−26.1	−44.3	−51.0	−46.7	−83.0	−76.1
Personal travel	3 240	−59.4	−63.1	−53.9	−94.2	−113.4	−139.7	−189.5	−173.0
Other services, credit	2 200 BA	**105.5**	**93.0**	**93.7**	**96.5**	**107.9**	**107.0**	**121.1**	**149.2**
Communications	2 245	35.3	31.8	24.6	26.9	33.3	36.7	42.9	58.0
Construction	2 249	....	....	....	.3	.4	.4	.4	.4
Insurance	2 253	41.2	35.4	33.5	37.6	41.5	35.4	40.0	46.8
Financial	2 260	4.5	3.6	10.3	5.6	6.0	7.0	9.2	11.5
Computer and information	2 262	.4	.4	.4	.4	.4	.4	.4	.5
Royalties and licence fees	2 266	1.6	1.6	1.8	1.7	1.8	1.9	1.8	2.0
Other business services	2 268	4.7	4.8	7.3	7.5	7.4	7.6	10.4	13.0
Personal, cultural, and recreational	2 287	1.0	.9	.9	1.2	1.3	1.4	1.2	1.3
Government, n.i.e.	2 291	16.8	14.5	15.0	15.4	15.7	16.2	14.9	15.6
Other services, debit	3 200 BA	**−120.8**	**−129.7**	**−183.9**	**−225.2**	**−246.7**	**−262.5**	**−280.0**	**−291.4**
Communications	3 245	−13.9	−9.3	−8.2	−12.6	−13.2	−13.1	−13.3	−18.2
Construction	3 249	....	....	....	−5.0	−6.2	−7.4	−10.0	−15.6
Insurance	3 253	−61.7	−74.6	−102.7	−106.2	−116.8	−120.7	−120.0	−109.8
Financial	3 260	−3.1	−2.5	−2.3	−2.2	−1.7	−1.9	−2.0	−2.1
Computer and information	3 262	−4.2	−4.5	−5.3	−8.0	−9.5	−10.9	−13.1	−15.7
Royalties and licence fees	3 266	−5.0	−5.3	−5.7	−8.0	−9.7	−11.2	−14.4	−16.2
Other business services	3 268	−13.7	−14.4	−41.4	−61.7	−67.1	−72.6	−81.4	−85.7
Personal, cultural, and recreational	3 287	−2.0	−2.1	−2.3	−4.5	−5.4	−6.0	−7.6	−9.4
Government, n.i.e.	3 291	−17.2	−17.0	−15.9	−17.2	−17.2	−18.7	−18.3	−18.8

Table 2 (Continued). STANDARD PRESENTATION, 2000–2007

(Millions of U.S. dollars)

	Code	2000	2001	2002	2003	2004	2005	2006	2007
C. INCOME	4 300	**−225.3**	**−211.3**	**−204.7**	**−302.6**	**−384.7**	**−376.4**	**−397.2**	**−172.9**
Total credit	2 300	*139.7*	*121.2*	*103.2*	*71.1*	*76.0*	*121.2*	*235.4*	*369.8*
Total debit	3 300	*−365.0*	*−332.5*	*−307.9*	*−373.7*	*−460.6*	*−497.6*	*−632.7*	*−542.7*
Compensation of employees, credit	2 310	**25.8**	**28.1**	**29.9**	**31.5**	**32.3**	**33.5**	**33.5**	**33.5**
Compensation of employees, debit	3 310	**−5.8**	**−6.2**	**−6.8**	**−7.2**	**−7.4**	**−7.4**	**−7.4**	**−7.4**
Investment income, credit	2 320	**113.9**	**93.1**	**73.3**	**39.6**	**43.7**	**87.7**	**202.0**	**336.3**
Direct investment income	2 330	3.2	3.0	3.0	3.2	2.8	3.0	3.0	3.0
Dividends and distributed branch profits	2 332	.4	.4	.4	.4	....	....	....	....
Reinvested earnings and undistributed branch profits	2 333	2.8	2.6	2.6	2.8	2.8	3.0	3.0	3.0
Income on debt (interest)	2 334	....	....	....	....	....	....	....	....
Portfolio investment income	2 339	110.7	90.1	70.3	36.4	40.9	84.7	199.0	333.3
Income on equity	2 340	....	....	....	....	....	....	....	....
Income on bonds and notes	2 350	14.4	25.1	23.7	5.3	5.0	18.3	....	....
Income on money market instruments	2 360	96.3	65.0	46.6	31.1	35.9	66.5	199.0	333.3
Other investment income	2 370	....	....	....	....	....	....	....	....
Investment income, debit	3 320	**−359.2**	**−326.3**	**−301.1**	**−366.5**	**−453.2**	**−490.2**	**−625.3**	**−535.3**
Direct investment income	3 330	−148.4	−167.6	−183.3	−233.6	−291.9	−270.7	−391.5	−327.4
Dividends and distributed branch profits	3 332	−86.0	−60.8	−98.4	−81.1	−200.4	−177.0	−49.8	−67.5
Reinvested earnings and undistributed branch profits	3 333	−62.4	−89.5	−43.4	−96.9	−38.5	−30.3	−266.1	−180.4
Income on debt (interest)	3 334	....	−17.3	−41.5	−55.7	−52.9	−63.4	−75.6	−79.5
Portfolio investment income	3 339	....	....	....	....	....	....	....	....
Income on equity	3 340	....	....	....	....	....	....	....	....
Income on bonds and notes	3 350	....	....	....	....	....	....	....	....
Income on money market instruments	3 360	....	....	....	....	....	....	....	....
Other investment income	3 370	−210.8	−158.7	−117.8	−132.9	−161.3	−219.5	−233.8	−207.9
D. CURRENT TRANSFERS	4 379	**386.8**	**396.1**	**369.4**	**465.1**	**491.1**	**584.0**	**822.3**	**1,091.3**
Credit	2 379	**420.0**	**431.6**	**407.8**	**510.9**	**542.6**	**648.7**	**895.1**	**1,163.2**
General government	2 380	243.8	260.0	261.5	351.6	327.9	309.2	297.4	216.1
Other sectors	2 390	176.2	171.6	146.3	159.2	214.8	339.5	597.8	947.1
Workers' remittances	2 391	101.1	107.2	83.0	126.7	178.3	303.5	569.5	883.8
Other current transfers	2 392	75.1	64.4	63.3	32.6	36.5	36.0	28.3	63.3
Debit	3 379	**−33.2**	**−35.5**	**−38.4**	**−45.7**	**−51.5**	**−64.7**	**−72.9**	**−72.0**
General government	3 380	−2.0	−5.3	−4.3	−5.4	−5.4	−2.2	−3.3	−2.5
Other sectors	3 390	−31.2	−30.2	−34.1	−40.4	−46.2	−62.5	−69.6	−69.5
Workers' remittances	3 391	−31.2	−30.2	−31.1	−38.6	−43.2	−59.3	−65.8	−64.8
Other current transfers	3 392	....	....	−3.0	−1.8	−3.0	−3.1	−3.8	−4.7
CAPITAL AND FINANCIAL ACCOUNT	4 996	**501.2**	**476.7**	**991.7**	**97.9**	**287.9**	**−248.0**	**−1,214.2**	**−1,719.2**
CAPITAL ACCOUNT	4 994	....	....	....	**7.0**	**8.0**	**8.7**	**1,813.2**	**1,180.2**
Total credit	2 994	....	....	....	*7.0*	*8.0*	*8.7*	*1,813.2*	*1,180.2*
Total debit	3 994	....	....	....	....	....	....	....	....
Capital transfers, credit	2 400	....	....	....	**7.0**	**8.0**	**8.7**	**1,813.2**	**1,180.2**
General government	2 401	....	....	....	7.0	8.0	....	1,804.3	1,171.0
Debt forgiveness	2 402	....	....	....	7.0	8.0	....	1,804.3	1,171.0
Other capital transfers	2 410	....	....	....	....	....	....	....	....
Other sectors	2 430	....	....	....	....	....	8.7	8.9	9.2
Migrants' transfers	2 431	....	....	....	....	....	8.7	8.9	9.2
Debt forgiveness	2 432	....	....	....	....	....	....	....	....
Other capital transfers	2 440	....	....	....	....	....	....	....	....
Capital transfers, debit	3 400	....	....	....	....	....	....	....	....
General government	3 401	....	....	....	....	....	....	....	....
Debt forgiveness	3 402	....	....	....	....	....	....	....	....
Other capital transfers	3 410	....	....	....	....	....	....	....	....
Other sectors	3 430	....	....	....	....	....	....	....	....
Migrants' transfers	3 431	....	....	....	....	....	....	....	....
Debt forgiveness	3 432	....	....	....	....	....	....	....	....
Other capital transfers	3 440	....	....	....	....	....	....	....	....
Nonproduced nonfinancial assets, credit	2 480	....	....	....	....	....	....	....	....
Nonproduced nonfinancial assets, debit	3 480	....	....	....	....	....	....	....	....

Table 2 (Continued). STANDARD PRESENTATION, 2000–2007

(Millions of U.S. dollars)

	Code	2000	2001	2002	2003	2004	2005	2006	2007
FINANCIAL ACCOUNT	4 995	**501.2**	**476.7**	**991.7**	**90.9**	**279.9**	**−256.6**	**−3,027.4**	**−2,899.4**
A. DIRECT INVESTMENT	4 500	**733.6**	**703.3**	**674.1**	**194.6**	**62.6**	**−241.6**	**277.8**	**201.2**
Direct investment abroad	4 505	**−2.8**	**−2.5**	**−2.5**	**−2.8**	**−2.8**	**−3.0**	**−3.0**	**−3.0**
Equity capital	4 510	....	....	....	....	....	....	....	....
Claims on affiliated enterprises	4 515	....	....	....	....	....	....	....	....
Liabilities to affiliated enterprises	4 520	....	....	....	....	....	....	....	....
Reinvested earnings	4 525	−2.8	−2.5	−2.5	−2.8	−2.8	−3.0	−3.0	−3.0
Other capital	4 530	....	....	....	....	....	....	....	....
Claims on affiliated enterprises	4 535	....	....	....	....	....	....	....	....
Liabilities to affiliated enterprises	4 540	....	....	....	....	....	....	....	....
Direct investment in Bolivia	4 555	**736.4**	**705.8**	**676.6**	**197.4**	**65.4**	**−238.6**	**280.8**	**204.2**
Equity capital	4 560	353.8	355.6	121.7	24.7	37.9	−121.6	−40.8	−135.7
Claims on direct investors	4 565	....	....	....	....	....	....	....	....
Liabilities to direct investors	4 570	353.8	355.6	121.7	24.7	37.9	−121.6	−40.8	−135.7
Reinvested earnings	4 575	62.4	89.5	43.4	96.9	38.5	30.3	266.1	180.4
Other capital	4 580	320.2	260.7	511.5	75.8	−11.0	−147.3	55.5	159.6
Claims on direct investors	4 585	....	....	....	....	....	....	....	....
Liabilities to direct investors	4 590	320.2	260.7	511.5	75.8	−11.0	−147.3	55.5	159.6
B. PORTFOLIO INVESTMENT	4 600	**55.4**	**−23.0**	**−19.3**	**−68.2**	**−35.4**	**−153.4**	**25.1**	**−24.5**
Assets	4 602	**55.4**	**−23.0**	**−19.3**	**−68.2**	**−35.4**	**−153.4**	**25.1**	**−24.5**
Equity securities	4 610	....	....	....	....	1.2	....	....	....
Monetary authorities	4 611	....	....	....	....	....	....	....	....
General government	4 612	....	....	....	....	....	....	....	....
Banks	4 613	....	....	....	....	....	....	....	....
Other sectors	4 614	....	....	....	....	1.2	....	....	....
Debt securities	4 619	55.4	−23.0	−19.3	−68.2	−36.6	−153.4	25.1	−24.5
Bonds and notes	4 620	....	....	....	....	....	....	....	....
Monetary authorities	4 621	....	....	....	....	....	....	....	....
General government	4 622	....	....	....	....	....	....	....	....
Banks	4 623	....	....	....	....	....	....	....	....
Other sectors	4 624	....	....	....	....	....	....	....	....
Money market instruments	4 630	55.4	−23.0	−19.3	−68.2	−36.6	−153.4	25.1	−24.5
Monetary authorities	4 631	....	....	....	....	....	....	....	....
General government	4 632	....	....	....	....	....	....	....	....
Banks	4 633	13.4	15.0	40.2	6.9	17.7	−84.0	28.5	−10.2
Other sectors	4 634	42.1	−38.0	−59.5	−75.1	−54.3	−69.5	−3.4	−14.3
Liabilities	4 652	....	....	....	....	....	....	....	....
Equity securities	4 660	....	....	....	....	....	....	....	....
Banks	4 663	....	....	....	....	....	....	....	....
Other sectors	4 664	....	....	....	....	....	....	....	....
Debt securities	4 669	....	....	....	....	....	....	....	....
Bonds and notes	4 670	....	....	....	....	....	....	....	....
Monetary authorities	4 671	....	....	....	....	....	....	....	....
General government	4 672	....	....	....	....	....	....	....	....
Banks	4 673	....	....	....	....	....	....	....	....
Other sectors	4 674	....	....	....	....	....	....	....	....
Money market instruments	4 680	....	....	....	....	....	....	....	....
Monetary authorities	4 681	....	....	....	....	....	....	....	....
General government	4 682	....	....	....	....	....	....	....	....
Banks	4 683	....	....	....	....	....	....	....	....
Other sectors	4 684	....	....	....	....	....	....	....	....
C. FINANCIAL DERIVATIVES	4 910	....	....	....	....	....	....	....	....
Monetary authorities	4 911	....	....	....	....	....	....	....	....
General government	4 912	....	....	....	....	....	....	....	....
Banks	4 913	....	....	....	....	....	....	....	....
Other sectors	4 914	....	....	....	....	....	....	....	....
Assets	4 900	....	....	....	....	....	....	....	....
Monetary authorities	4 901	....	....	....	....	....	....	....	....
General government	4 902	....	....	....	....	....	....	....	....
Banks	4 903	....	....	....	....	....	....	....	....
Other sectors	4 904	....	....	....	....	....	....	....	....
Liabilities	4 905	....	....	....	....	....	....	....	....
Monetary authorities	4 906	....	....	....	....	....	....	....	....
General government	4 907	....	....	....	....	....	....	....	....
Banks	4 908	....	....	....	....	....	....	....	....
Other sectors	4 909	....	....	....	....	....	....	....	....

Table 2 (Concluded). STANDARD PRESENTATION, 2000–2007

(Millions of U.S. dollars)

	Code	2000	2001	2002	2003	2004	2005	2006	2007
D. OTHER INVESTMENT	4 700 ..	**−326.6**	**−236.1**	**33.9**	**116.5**	**409.8**	**601.8**	**−2,043.9**	**−1,138.3**
Assets	4 703 ..	**−146.1**	**−166.7**	**−193.4**	**−462.9**	**94.3**	**123.8**	**−262.4**	**17.8**
Trade credits	4 706 ..	....	....	....	....	....	....	....	....
General government	4 707 ..	....	....	....	....	....	....	....	....
of which: Short-term	4 709 ..	....	....	....	....	....	....	....	....
Other sectors	4 710 ..	....	....	....	....	....	....	....	....
of which: Short-term	4 712 ..	....	....	....	....	....	....	....	....
Loans	4 714 ..	....	....	....	....	....	....	....	....
Monetary authorities	4 715 ..	....	....	....	....	....	....	....	....
of which: Short-term	4 718 ..	....	....	....	....	....	....	....	....
General government	4 719 ..	....	....	....	....	....	....	....	....
of which: Short-term	4 721 ..	....	....	....	....	....	....	....	....
Banks	4 722 ..	....	....	....	....	....	....	....	....
of which: Short-term	4 724 ..	....	....	....	....	....	....	....	....
Other sectors	4 725 ..	....	....	....	....	....	....	....	....
of which: Short-term	4 727 ..	....	....	....	....	....	....	....	....
Currency and deposits	4 730 ..	−139.4	−151.1	−175.7	−442.7	110.6	141.3	−261.4	34.2
Monetary authorities	4 731 ..	....	....	....	....	....	....	....	....
General government	4 732 ..	....	....	....	....	....	....	....	....
Banks	4 733 ..	−94.4	−157.0	49.8	46.3	5.6	−131.7	−105.2	137.2
Other sectors	4 734 ..	−45.0	5.9	−225.5	−489.0	105.0	273.0	−156.2	−103.0
Other assets	4 736 ..	−6.7	−15.5	−17.7	−20.2	−16.3	−17.5	−1.0	−16.4
Monetary authorities	4 737 ..	−1.2	....	....	....	....	....	....	....
of which: Short-term	4 739 ..	....	....	....	....	....	....	....	....
General government	4 740 ..	−7.9	−15.7	−17.1	−17.7	−15.7	−12.1	1.5	−14.5
of which: Short-term	4 742 ..	....	....	....	....	....	....	....	....
Banks	4 743 ..	....	....	....	....	....	....	....	....
of which: Short-term	4 745 ..	....	....	....	....	....	....	....	....
Other sectors	4 746 ..	2.4	.2	−.6	−2.5	−.6	−5.4	−2.5	−1.9
of which: Short-term	4 748 ..	*2.4*	*.2*	*−.6*	*−2.5*	*−.6*	*−5.4*	*−2.5*	*−1.9*
Liabilities	4 753 ..	**−180.5**	**−69.5**	**227.4**	**579.3**	**315.6**	**478.0**	**−1,781.5**	**−1,156.2**
Trade credits	4 756 ..	....	....	....	....	....	....	....	....
General government	4 757 ..	....	....	....	....	....	....	....	....
of which: Short-term	4 759 ..	....	....	....	....	....	....	....	....
Other sectors	4 760 ..	....	....	....	....	....	....	....	....
of which: Short-term	4 762 ..	....	....	....	....	....	....	....	....
Loans	4 764 ..	−182.3	−73.3	226.7	579.2	313.6	476.4	−1,783.4	−1,156.2
Monetary authorities	4 765 ..	−40.0	−29.5	−46.4	57.2	12.4	−39.9	−233.6	−14.6
of which: Use of Fund credit and loans from the Fund	4 766 ..	*−14.5*	*−5.3*	*−27.7*	*60.0*	*14.3*	*−39.2*	*−232.9*	*−14.6*
of which: Short-term	4 768 ..	....	....	....	....	....	....	....	....
General government	4 769 ..	146.5	234.8	377.6	426.6	263.1	197.7	−1,552.1	−1,045.5
of which: Short-term	4 771 ..	....	....	*25.0*	....	*−25.0*	*5.5*	*22.0*	*17.0*
Banks	4 772 ..	−280.1	−247.7	−35.5	−80.9	20.1	−1.9	−20.5	−57.8
of which: Short-term	4 774 ..	*−186.6*	*−215.5*	*13.8*	*−60.2*	*5.0*	*−19.1*	*−6.5*	*5.7*
Other sectors	4 775 ..	−8.7	−31.0	−69.0	176.4	18.0	320.5	22.7	−38.3
of which: Short-term	4 777 ..	*6.0*	*16.1*	*−23.6*	*44.1*	*−39.6*	*−60.3*	*22.0*	*−26.8*
Currency and deposits	4 780 ..	1.9	2.5	1.0	....	....	....	....	....
Monetary authorities	4 781 ..	1.9	2.5	1.0	....	....	....	....	....
General government	4 782 ..	....	....	....	....	....	....	....	....
Banks	4 783 ..	....	....	....	....	....	....	....	....
Other sectors	4 784 ..	....	....	....	....	....	....	....	....
Other liabilities	4 786 ..	....	1.4	−.3	.1	2.0	1.6	1.9	....
Monetary authorities	4 787 ..	....	1.4	−.3	.1	2.0	1.6	1.9	....
of which: Short-term	4 789 ..	....	*1.4*	*−.3*	*.1*	*2.0*	*1.6*	*1.9*	....
General government	4 790 ..	....	....	....	....	....	....	....	....
of which: Short-term	4 792 ..	....	....	....	....	....	....	....	....
Banks	4 793 ..	....	....	....	....	....	....	....	....
of which: Short-term	4 795 ..	....	....	....	....	....	....	....	....
Other sectors	4 796 ..	....	....	....	....	....	....	....	....
of which: Short-term	4 798 ..	....	....	....	....	....	....	....	....
E. RESERVE ASSETS	4 802 ..	**38.8**	**32.5**	**303.0**	**−152.0**	**−157.2**	**−463.4**	**−1,286.3**	**−1,937.7**
Monetary gold	4 812 ..	1.0	....	1.2	....	−.1	....	.2	−.2
Special drawing rights	4 811 ..	....	....	....	.3	.9	−.3	....	−.1
Reserve position in the Fund	4 810 ..	....	....	....	....	....	....	....	....
Foreign exchange	4 803 ..	46.0	44.8	309.0	−142.1	−154.0	−459.3	−1,284.5	−1,936.4
Other claims	4 813 ..	−8.2	−12.2	−7.1	−10.2	−3.9	−3.8	−2.0	−1.0
NET ERRORS AND OMISSIONS	4 998 ..	**−54.8**	**−202.7**	**−639.8**	**−173.5**	**−625.4**	**−374.5**	**−103.3**	**−80.4**

Table 3. INTERNATIONAL INVESTMENT POSITION (End-period stocks), 2000–2007

(Millions of U.S. dollars)

	Code	2000	2001	2002	2003	2004	2005	2006	2007
ASSETS	8 995 C.	**2,659.5**	**2,834.7**	**2,760.8**	**2,984.9**	**3,110.4**	**3,990.4**	**6,196.9**	**8,569.5**
Direct investment abroad	8 505 ..	**29.4**	**31.9**	**34.4**	**83.4**	**84.2**	**87.2**	**90.2**	**94.2**
Equity capital and reinvested earnings	8 506 ..	29.4	31.9	34.4	24.2	26.1	29.1	32.1	36.1
Claims on affiliated enterprises	8 507 ..	29.4	31.9	34.4	24.2	26.1	29.1	32.1	36.1
Liabilities to affiliated enterprises	8 508 ..	....	....	....	....	....	....	....	....
Other capital	8 530 ..	....	....	....	59.2	58.1	58.1	58.1	58.1
Claims on affiliated enterprises	8 535 ..	....	....	....	59.2	58.1	58.1	58.1	58.1
Liabilities to affiliated enterprises	8 540 ..	....	....	....	....	....	....	....	....
Portfolio investment	8 602 ..	**662.9**	**685.9**	**837.0**	**398.4**	**433.8**	**587.2**	**562.2**	**586.7**
Equity securities	8 610 ..	....	....	....	....	....	....	....	....
Monetary authorities	8 611 ..	....	....	....	....	....	....	....	....
General government	8 612 ..	....	....	....	....	....	....	....	....
Banks	8 613 ..	....	....	....	....	....	....	....	....
Other sectors	8 614 ..	....	....	....	....	....	....	....	....
Debt securities	8 619 ..	662.9	685.9	837.0	398.4	433.8	587.2	562.2	586.7
Bonds and notes	8 620 ..	....	....	....	....	....	....	....	....
Monetary authorities	8 621 ..	....	....	....	....	....	....	....	....
General government	8 622 ..	....	....	....	....	....	....	....	....
Banks	8 623 ..	....	....	....	....	....	....	....	....
Other sectors	8 624 ..	....	....	....	....	....	....	....	....
Money market instruments	8 630 ..	662.9	685.9	837.0	398.4	433.8	587.2	562.2	586.7
Monetary authorities	8 631 ..	....	....	....	....	....	....	....	....
General government	8 632 ..	....	....	....	....	....	....	....	....
Banks	8 633 ..	273.6	258.6	218.4	211.5	193.8	277.8	249.2	259.4
Other sectors	8 634 ..	389.3	427.3	618.6	186.9	240.0	309.5	312.9	327.2
Financial derivatives	8 900 ..	....	....	....	....	....	....	....	....
Monetary authorities	8 901 ..	....	....	....	....	....	....	....	....
General government	8 902 ..	....	....	....	....	....	....	....	....
Banks	8 903 ..	....	....	....	....	....	....	....	....
Other sectors	8 904 ..	....	....	....	....	....	....	....	....
Other investment	8 703 ..	**662.3**	**831.9**	**840.6**	**1,250.2**	**1,160.6**	**1,356.6**	**2,352.2**	**2,569.6**
Trade credits	8 706 ..	....	....	....	....	....	....	....	....
General government	8 707 ..	....	....	....	....	....	....	....	....
of which: Short-term	8 709 ..	....	....	....	....	....	....	....	....
Other sectors	8 710 ..	....	....	....	....	....	....	....	....
of which: Short-term	8 712 ..	....	....	....	....	....	....	....	....
Loans	8 714 ..	....	....	....	....	....	....	....	....
Monetary authorities	8 715 ..	....	....	....	....	....	....	....	....
of which: Short-term	8 718 ..	....	....	....	....	....	....	....	....
General government	8 719 ..	....	....	....	....	....	....	....	....
of which: Short-term	8 721 ..	....	....	....	....	....	....	....	....
Banks	8 722 ..	....	....	....	....	....	....	....	....
of which: Short-term	8 724 ..	....	....	....	....	....	....	....	....
Other sectors	8 725 ..	....	....	....	....	....	....	....	....
of which: Short-term	8 727 ..	....	....	....	....	....	....	....	....
Currency and deposits	8 730 ..	460.7	611.7	594.9	968.6	858.0	1,024.7	1,849.9	2,046.7
Monetary authorities	8 731 ..	....	....	....	....	....	....	....	....
General government	8 732 ..	....	....	....	....	....	....	....	....
Banks	8 733 ..	271.7	428.7	378.9	332.6	327.0	458.7	563.9	426.7
Other sectors	8 734 ..	189.0	183.0	216.0	636.0	531.0	566.0	1,286.0	1,620.0
Other assets	8 736 ..	201.6	220.2	245.7	281.6	302.6	331.9	502.3	522.9
Monetary authorities	8 737 ..	123.7	124.9	134.3	152.1	164.4	170.4	331.8	343.7
of which: Short-term	8 739 ..	....	....	....	....	....	....	....	....
General government	8 740 ..	74.0	88.5	103.9	119.7	127.6	145.6	152.1	158.8
of which: Short-term	8 742 ..	....	....	....	....	....	....	....	....
Banks	8 743 ..	....	....	....	....	....	....	....	....
of which: Short-term	8 745 ..	....	....	....	....	....	....	....	....
Other sectors	8 746 ..	3.9	6.8	7.4	9.9	10.5	15.9	18.4	20.4
of which: Short-term	8 748 ..	*3.9*	*6.8*	*7.4*	*9.9*	*10.5*	*15.9*	*18.4*	*20.4*
Reserve assets	8 802 ..	**1,304.9**	**1,285.0**	**1,048.8**	**1,252.9**	**1,431.9**	**1,959.3**	**3,192.4**	**5,319.1**
Monetary gold	8 812 ..	244.8	259.6	316.4	379.4	399.4	470.6	577.6	764.3
Special drawing rights	8 811 ..	35.6	34.3	37.2	40.3	41.2	38.2	40.2	42.3
Reserve position in the Fund	8 810 ..	11.6	11.2	12.1	13.2	13.8	12.7	13.4	14.0
Foreign exchange	8 803 ..	869.3	825.3	521.2	663.3	817.3	1,276.7	2,561.2	4,497.7
Other claims	8 813 ..	143.7	154.6	161.9	156.7	160.1	161.1	....	.7

Table 3 (Concluded). INTERNATIONAL INVESTMENT POSITION (End-period stocks), 2000–2007

(Millions of U.S. dollars)

	Code	2000	2001	2002	2003	2004	2005	2006	2007
LIABILITIES	8 995 D.	**10,662.6**	**11,259.5**	**11,805.2**	**10,956.9**	**10,905.5**	**11,209.1**	**9,820.7**	**8,869.2**
Direct investment in Bolivia	8 555 ..	**5,187.7**	**5,893.5**	**6,570.0**	**4,782.0**	**4,816.6**	**4,904.5**	**5,118.9**	**5,323.1**
Equity capital and reinvested earnings	8 556 ..	3,944.9	4,390.0	4,555.1	3,284.0	3,360.4	3,506.4	3,635.2	3,679.8
Claims on direct investors	8 557 ..	....	....	....	....	....	....	....	....
Liabilities to direct investors	8 558 ..	3,944.9	4,390.0	4,555.1	3,284.0	3,360.4	3,506.4	3,635.2	3,679.8
Other capital	8 580 ..	1,242.8	1,503.5	2,015.0	1,498.0	1,456.2	1,398.1	1,483.7	1,643.3
Claims on direct investors	8 585 ..	....	....	....	−175.0	−205.9	−209.7	....	....
Liabilities to direct investors	8 590 ..	1,242.8	1,503.5	2,015.0	1,673.0	1,662.1	1,607.8	1,483.7	1,643.3
Portfolio investment	8 652 ..	**....**	**....**	**....**	**48.2**	**41.8**	**41.8**	**41.8**	**41.8**
Equity securities	8 660 ..	....	....	....	46.8	40.9	40.9	40.9	40.9
Banks	8 663 ..	....	....	....	10.5	8.5	9.0	9.2	9.3
Other sectors	8 664 ..	....	....	....	36.3	32.5	31.9	31.8	31.6
Debt securities	8 669 ..	....	....	....	1.4	.9	.9	.9	.9
Bonds and notes	8 670 ..	....	....	....	....	....	....	....	....
Monetary authorities	8 671 ..	....	....	....	....	....	....	....	....
General government	8 672 ..	....	....	....	....	....	....	....	....
Banks	8 673 ..	....	....	....	....	....	....	....	....
Other sectors	8 674 ..	....	....	....	....	....	....	....	....
Money market instruments	8 680 ..	....	....	....	1.4	.9	.9	.9	.9
Monetary authorities	8 681 ..	....	....	....	....	....	....	....	....
General government	8 682 ..	....	....	....	....	....	....	....	....
Banks	8 683 ..	....	....	....	....	....	....	....	....
Other sectors	8 684 ..	....	....	....	1.4	.9	.9	.9	.9
Financial derivatives	8 905 ..	**....**	**....**	**....**	**....**	**....**	**....**	**....**	**....**
Monetary authorities	8 906 ..	....	....	....	....	....	....	....	....
General government	8 907 ..	....	....	....	....	....	....	....	....
Banks	8 908 ..	....	....	....	....	....	....	....	....
Other sectors	8 909 ..	....	....	....	....	....	....	....	....
Other investment	8 753 ..	**5,474.9**	**5,366.0**	**5,235.2**	**6,126.7**	**6,047.2**	**6,262.8**	**4,660.0**	**3,504.4**
Trade credits	8 756 ..	....	....	....	....	....	....	....	....
General government	8 757 ..	....	....	....	....	....	....	....	....
of which: Short-term	8 759 ..	....	....	....	....	....	....	....	....
Other sectors	8 760 ..	....	....	....	....	....	....	....	....
of which: Short-term	8 762 ..	....	....	....	....	....	....	....	....
Loans	8 764 ..	5,449.6	5,337.7	5,206.2	6,071.7	5,986.2	6,225.3	4,619.0	3,459.9
Monetary authorities	8 765 ..	572.5	313.3	305.6	395.0	321.2	257.1	27.3	....
of which: Use of Fund credit and loans from the Fund	8 766 ..	*219.9*	*207.2*	*195.3*	*278.7*	*307.0*	*243.8*	*14.5*	*....*
of which: Short-term	8 768 ..	....	....	....	....	....	....	....	....
General government	8 769 ..	3,434.5	3,774.3	3,773.7	4,455.2	4,409.5	4,408.1	2,975.8	2,123.0
of which: Short-term	8 771 ..	*....*	*....*	*25.0*	*25.0*	*....*	*5.3*	*27.2*	*59.2*
Banks	8 772 ..	579.5	397.3	401.0	306.4	318.5	312.5	291.5	139.0
of which: Short-term	8 774 ..	*292.9*	*77.4*	*91.3*	*31.1*	*36.0*	*17.0*	*10.4*	*16.1*
Other sectors	8 775 ..	863.2	852.9	725.8	915.2	937.1	1,247.5	1,324.4	1,197.9
of which: Short-term	8 777 ..	*173.3*	*210.7*	*212.3*	*276.0*	*236.4*	*160.3*	*188.3*	*149.2*
Currency and deposits	8 780 ..	....	....	....	....	....	....	....	....
Monetary authorities	8 781 ..	....	....	....	....	....	....	....	....
General government	8 782 ..	....	....	....	....	....	....	....	....
Banks	8 783 ..	....	....	....	....	....	....	....	....
Other sectors	8 784 ..	....	....	....	....	....	....	....	....
Other liabilities	8 786 ..	25.2	28.3	29.0	55.0	60.9	37.6	41.0	44.4
Monetary authorities	8 787 ..	25.2	28.3	29.0	29.2	35.1	37.6	41.0	44.4
of which: Short-term	8 789 ..	....	....	....	....	....	....	....	....
General government	8 790 ..	....	....	....	....	....	....	....	....
of which: Short-term	8 792 ..	....	....	....	....	....	....	....	....
Banks	8 793 ..	....	....	....	....	....	....	....	....
of which: Short-term	8 795 ..	....	....	....	....	....	....	....	....
Other sectors	8 796 ..	....	....	....	25.9	25.9	....	....	....
of which: Short-term	8 798 ..	....	....	....	....	....	....	....	....
NET INTERNATIONAL INVESTMENT POSITION	8 995 ..	−8,003.1	−8,424.8	−9,044.4	−7,972.0	−7,795.1	−7,218.7	−3,623.7	−299.7
Conversion rates: bolivianos per U.S. dollar (end of period)	0 102 ..	6.3900	6.8200	7.4900	7.8300	8.0500	8.0400	7.9800	7.6200

Table 1. ANALYTIC PRESENTATION, 2000–2007

(Millions of U.S. dollars)

	Code	2000	2001	2002	2003	2004	2005	2006	2007
A. Current Account[1]	4 993 Z.	**−395.7**	**−742.8**	**−1,190.7**	**−1,631.0**	**−1,639.3**	**−1,844.4**	**−973.4**	**−1,930.3**
Goods: exports f.o.b.	2 100 ..	1,129.8	1,134.2	1,109.7	1,477.5	2,086.7	2,555.3	3,381.4	4,243.3
Goods: imports f.o.b.	3 100 ..	−3,894.2	−4,092.0	−4,449.4	−5,636.8	−6,656.4	−7,454.2	−7,679.5	−9,947.2
Balance on Goods	4 100 ..	*−2,764.4*	*−2,957.8*	*−3,339.7*	*−4,159.3*	*−4,569.7*	*−4,898.9*	*−4,298.1*	*−5,703.9*
Services: credit	2 200 ..	450.0	496.8	524.2	721.0	863.5	989.0	1,161.3	1,364.5
Services: debit	3 200 ..	−263.1	−269.1	−305.1	−383.6	−432.2	−435.6	−487.8	−566.9
Balance on Goods and Services	4 991 ..	*−2,577.5*	*−2,730.1*	*−3,120.6*	*−3,821.9*	*−4,138.4*	*−4,345.5*	*−3,624.6*	*−4,906.3*
Income: credit	2 300 ..	666.8	625.5	605.5	653.9	674.6	682.3	732.6	895.2
Income: debit	3 300 ..	−76.4	−93.1	−97.4	−120.6	−170.1	−212.8	−315.8	−494.8
Balance on Goods, Services, and Income	4 992 ..	*−1,987.2*	*−2,197.7*	*−2,612.6*	*−3,288.6*	*−3,633.9*	*−3,876.0*	*−3,207.8*	*−4,506.0*
Current transfers: credit	2 379 Z.	1,666.8	1,527.7	1,523.9	1,780.8	2,204.2	2,171.9	2,399.1	2,775.2
Current transfers: debit	3 379 ..	−75.4	−72.9	−101.9	−123.2	−209.6	−140.3	−164.7	−199.5
B. Capital Account[1]	4 994 Z.	**546.4**	**399.7**	**412.4**	**465.6**	**300.8**	**281.3**	**294.1**	**309.1**
Capital account: credit	2 994 Z.	546.4	399.7	412.4	465.6	300.8	281.3	294.1	309.1
Capital account: debit	3 994 ..	....	....	....	....	....	....	....	....
Total, Groups A Plus B	4 981 ..	*150.7*	*−343.2*	*−778.3*	*−1,165.4*	*−1,338.5*	*−1,563.1*	*−679.3*	*−1,621.2*
C. Financial Account[1]	4 995 W.	**83.6**	**995.3**	**551.7**	**1,055.9**	**1,388.9**	**1,827.9**	**1,242.8**	**2,177.4**
Direct investment abroad	4 505 ..	....	....	....	....	−1.6	−.4	−4.1	−24.7
Direct investment in Bosnia and Herzegovina	4 555 Z.	146.1	118.5	267.8	381.8	709.8	607.8	722.5	2,111.3
Portfolio investment assets	4 602 ..	....	....	....	....	−2.8	2.6	−.4	−.8
Equity securities	4 610 ..	....	....	....	....	....	....	....	....
Debt securities	4 619 ..	....	....	....	....	−2.8	2.6	−.4	−.8
Portfolio investment liabilities	4 652 Z.	....	....	....	....	....	....	....	....
Equity securities	4 660 ..	....	....	....	....	....	....	....	....
Debt securities	4 669 Z.	....	....	....	....	....	....	....	....
Financial derivatives	4 910 ..	....	....	....	....	....	....	....	....
Financial derivatives assets	4 900 ..	....	....	....	....	....	....	....	....
Financial derivatives liabilities	4 905 ..	....	....	....	....	....	....	....	....
Other investment assets	4 703 ..	−675.0	648.9	−155.0	101.0	296.4	305.1	28.9	−995.1
Monetary authorities	4 701 ..	....	....	....	....	....	....	....	....
General government	4 704 ..	....	....	....	....	....	....	....	....
Banks	4 705 ..	−91.6	−185.3	−49.1	−56.8	−225.8	−126.0	−150.4	−834.9
Other sectors	4 728 ..	−583.4	834.1	−105.9	157.8	522.2	431.0	179.3	−160.2
Other investment liabilities	4 753 W.	612.5	227.9	438.9	573.2	387.0	912.9	495.9	1,086.7
Monetary authorities	4 753 WA	1.3	13.6	−13.4	−.1	....	....	....	....
General government	4 753 ZB	75.9	66.9	101.9	33.2	99.3	59.8	5.7	58.4
Banks	4 753 ZC	308.6	−20.1	130.8	382.4	6.5	395.3	197.8	634.4
Other sectors	4 753 ZD	226.7	167.6	219.6	157.7	281.3	457.7	292.5	394.0
Total, Groups A Through C	4 983 ..	*234.3*	*652.1*	*−226.6*	*−109.4*	*50.4*	*264.8*	*563.4*	*556.2*
D. Net Errors and Omissions	4 998 ..	**−173.3**	**99.6**	**98.0**	**323.2**	**408.8**	**226.6**	**197.3**	**249.9**
Total, Groups A Through D	4 984 ..	*61.0*	*751.7*	*−128.5*	*213.7*	*459.2*	*491.4*	*760.8*	*806.1*
E. Reserves and Related Items	4 802 A.	**−61.0**	**−751.7**	**128.5**	**−213.7**	**−459.2**	**−491.4**	**−760.8**	**−806.1**
Reserve assets	4 802 ..	−76.5	−761.6	109.6	−196.6	−433.0	−461.4	−789.6	−876.1
Use of Fund credit and loans	4 766 ..	15.5	9.9	19.0	−17.1	−29.7	−39.4	−44.1	−18.3
Exceptional financing	4 920 ..	....	....	....	....	3.5	9.3	72.9	88.3
Conversion rates: convertible marka per U.S. dollar	0 101 ..	**2.1229**	**2.1857**	**2.0782**	**1.7329**	**1.5752**	**1.5727**	**1.5591**	**1.4290**

[1] Excludes components that have been classified in the categories of Group E.

Table 2. STANDARD PRESENTATION, 2000–2007

(Millions of U.S. dollars)

	Code	2000	2001	2002	2003	2004	2005	2006	2007
CURRENT ACCOUNT..................................	4 993 ..	**−395.7**	**−742.8**	**−1,190.7**	**−1,631.0**	**−1,639.3**	**−1,844.4**	**−973.4**	**−1,930.3**
A. GOODS...	4 100 ..	**−2,764.4**	**−2,957.8**	**−3,339.7**	**−4,159.3**	**−4,569.7**	**−4,898.9**	**−4,298.1**	**−5,703.9**
Credit...	2 100 ..	**1,129.8**	**1,134.2**	**1,109.7**	**1,477.5**	**2,086.7**	**2,555.3**	**3,381.4**	**4,243.3**
General merchandise: exports f.o.b...............	2 110 ..	1,129.8	1,134.2	1,109.7	1,477.5	2,086.7	2,555.3	3,381.4	4,243.3
Goods for processing: exports f.o.b...............	2 150 ..	....	....	....	....	....	....	....	....
Repairs on goods....................................	2 160 ..	....	....	....	....	....	....	....	....
Goods procured in ports by carriers.............	2 170 ..	....	....	....	....	....	....	....	....
Nonmonetary gold..................................	2 180 ..	....	....	....	....	....	....	....	....
Debit..	3 100 ..	**−3,894.2**	**−4,092.0**	**−4,449.4**	**−5,636.8**	**−6,656.4**	**−7,454.2**	**−7,679.5**	**−9,947.2**
General merchandise: imports f.o.b..............	3 110 ..	−3,894.2	−4,092.0	−4,449.4	−5,636.8	−6,656.4	−7,454.2	−7,679.5	−9,947.2
Goods for processing: imports f.o.b..............	3 150 ..	....	....	....	....	....	....	....	....
Repairs on goods....................................	3 160 ..	....	....	....	....	....	....	....	....
Goods procured in ports by carriers.............	3 170 ..	....	....	....	....	....	....	....	....
Nonmonetary gold..................................	3 180 ..	....	....	....	....	....	....	....	....
B. SERVICES...	4 200 ..	**186.8**	**227.7**	**219.0**	**337.4**	**431.3**	**553.4**	**673.4**	**797.6**
Total credit..	2 200 ..	*450.0*	*496.8*	*524.2*	*721.0*	*863.5*	*989.0*	*1,161.3*	*1,364.5*
Total debit..	3 200 ..	*−263.1*	*−269.1*	*−305.1*	*−383.6*	*−432.2*	*−435.6*	*−487.8*	*−566.9*
Transportation services, credit..............	2 205 ..	**26.7**	**28.0**	**32.3**	**44.3**	**51.4**	**108.0**	**128.3**	**166.5**
Passenger...	2 850 ..	*13.1*	*14.4*	*19.0*	*26.5*	*26.4*	*38.1*	*51.2*	*69.8*
Freight...	2 851 ..	*13.6*	*13.6*	*13.3*	*17.7*	*25.0*	*69.9*	*77.1*	*96.7*
Other..	2 852 ..	....	....	....	....	....	....	....	....
Sea transport, passenger........................	2 207 ..	....	....	....	....	....	....	....	....
Sea transport, freight............................	2 208 ..	....	....	....	....	....	....	....	....
Sea transport, other.............................	2 209 ..	....	....	....	....	....	....	....	....
Air transport, passenger........................	2 211 ..	9.8	10.6	14.4	20.1	16.9	27.5	37.4	52.4
Air transport, freight.............................	2 212 ..	....	....	....	....	....	....	....	....
Air transport, other..............................	2 213 ..	....	....	....	....	....	....	....	....
Other transport, passenger.....................	2 215 ..	3.3	3.8	4.6	6.5	9.5	10.5	13.8	17.4
Other transport, freight.........................	2 216 ..	13.6	13.6	13.3	17.7	25.0	69.9	77.1	96.7
Other transport, other..........................	2 217 ..	....	....	....	....	....	....	....	....
Transportation services, debit..............	3 205 ..	**−123.5**	**−118.8**	**−134.0**	**−168.5**	**−195.3**	**−199.5**	**−208.8**	**−242.5**
Passenger...	3 850 ..	*−18.7*	*−22.1*	*−26.8*	*−39.3*	*−44.8*	*−36.4*	*−39.0*	*−51.5*
Freight...	3 851 ..	*−104.7*	*−96.7*	*−107.2*	*−129.2*	*−150.5*	*−163.1*	*−169.8*	*−191.0*
Other..	3 852 ..	....	....	....	....	....	....	....	....
Sea transport, passenger........................	3 207 ..	....	....	....	....	....	....	....	....
Sea transport, freight............................	3 208 ..	....	....	....	....	....	....	....	....
Sea transport, other.............................	3 209 ..	....	....	....	....	....	....	....	....
Air transport, passenger........................	3 211 ..	−16.8	−19.8	−24.0	−35.5	−40.0	−31.6	−33.2	−44.8
Air transport, freight.............................	3 212 ..	....	....	....	....	....	....	....	....
Air transport, other..............................	3 213 ..	....	....	....	....	....	....	....	....
Other transport, passenger.....................	3 215 ..	−2.0	−2.3	−2.8	−3.8	−4.9	−4.7	−5.8	−6.7
Other transport, freight.........................	3 216 ..	−104.7	−96.7	−107.2	−129.2	−150.5	−163.1	−169.8	−191.0
Other transport, other..........................	3 217 ..	....	....	....	....	....	....	....	....
Travel, credit...................................	2 236 ..	**232.9**	**265.0**	**287.9**	**377.3**	**481.2**	**518.6**	**606.9**	**729.1**
Business travel.....................................	2 237 ..	16.7	26.4	28.2	36.2	43.8	44.9	44.7	48.8
Personal travel.....................................	2 240 ..	216.2	238.5	259.7	341.1	437.3	473.7	562.2	680.3
Travel, debit....................................	3 236 ..	**−72.9**	**−74.1**	**−85.4**	**−106.1**	**−117.1**	**−122.5**	**−162.7**	**−194.8**
Business travel.....................................	3 237 ..	−22.6	−23.3	−27.3	−31.5	−34.2	−32.1	−33.9	−41.1
Personal travel.....................................	3 240 ..	−50.3	−50.8	−58.1	−74.6	−82.9	−90.4	−128.8	−153.7
Other services, credit.........................	2 200 BA	**190.4**	**203.8**	**204.0**	**299.4**	**331.0**	**362.4**	**426.1**	**468.9**
Communications..................................	2 245 ..	36.6	46.2	60.5	91.7	104.1	118.7	123.3	129.1
Construction.......................................	2 249 ..	72.6	78.3	60.6	112.3	130.3	149.6	205.2	221.5
Insurance...	2 253 ..	4.7	4.8	4.7	6.2	9.4	5.1	8.2	10.2
Financial..	2 260 ..	11.5	12.6	15.1	19.0	21.7	23.7	31.7	36.3
Computer and information......................	2 262 ..	....	....	....	....	....	....	....	....
Royalties and licence fees.......................	2 266 ..	....	....	....	....	....	....	....	....
Other business services..........................	2 268 ..	62.9	60.1	61.5	68.3	63.2	63.0	55.2	68.3
Personal, cultural, and recreational............	2 287 ..	....	....	....	....	....	....	....	....
Government, n.i.e.................................	2 291 ..	2.0	1.8	1.7	1.9	2.2	2.3	2.4	3.4
Other services, debit..........................	3 200 BA	**−66.7**	**−76.2**	**−85.7**	**−109.0**	**−119.8**	**−113.6**	**−116.3**	**−129.7**
Communications..................................	3 245 ..	−26.7	−29.8	−34.2	−47.2	−46.8	−59.7	−56.2	−58.3
Construction.......................................	3 249 ..	−8.5	−9.3	−7.6	−9.2	−10.5	−8.7	−9.2	−10.8
Insurance...	3 253 ..	−16.6	−22.3	−28.3	−37.2	−44.2	−22.6	−24.2	−27.0
Financial..	3 260 ..	−7.9	−7.9	−8.5	−6.3	−8.6	−11.8	−12.3	−16.9
Computer and information......................	3 262 ..	....	....	....	....	....	....	....	....
Royalties and licence fees.......................	3 266 ..	....	....	....	....	....	....	....	....
Other business services..........................	3 268 ..	....	....	....	....	....	....	....	....
Personal, cultural, and recreational............	3 287 ..	....	....	....	....	....	....	....	....
Government, n.i.e.................................	3 291 ..	−7.0	−6.9	−7.2	−9.1	−9.8	−10.7	−14.5	−16.6

Table 2 (Continued). STANDARD PRESENTATION, 2000–2007

(Millions of U.S. dollars)

	Code	2000	2001	2002	2003	2004	2005	2006	2007
C. INCOME............	4 300 ..	**590.4**	**532.4**	**508.0**	**533.3**	**504.5**	**469.5**	**416.8**	**400.3**
Total credit............	2 300 ..	*666.8*	*625.5*	*605.5*	*653.9*	*674.6*	*682.3*	*732.6*	*895.2*
Total debit............	3 300 ..	*–76.4*	*–93.1*	*–97.4*	*–120.6*	*–170.1*	*–212.8*	*–315.8*	*–494.8*
Compensation of employees, credit............	2 310 ..	**631.2**	**581.2**	**540.1**	**594.6**	**579.2**	**570.4**	**560.0**	**596.4**
Compensation of employees, debit............	3 310 ..	**–2.4**	**–5.8**	**–7.4**	**–10.5**	**–13.3**	**–12.3**	**–13.6**	**–15.1**
Investment income, credit............	2 320 ..	**35.6**	**44.2**	**65.4**	**59.3**	**95.4**	**111.9**	**172.5**	**298.7**
Direct investment income............	2 330 ..	....	....	....	....	....	....	....	1.5
Dividends and distributed branch profits............	2 332 ..	....	....	....	....	....	....	....	....
Reinvested earnings and undistributed branch profits.....	2 333 ..	....	....	....	....	....	....	....	1.5
Income on debt (interest)............	2 334 ..	....	....	....	....	....	....	....	....
Portfolio investment income............	2 339 ..	....	....	....	....	....	....	....	....
Income on equity............	2 340 ..	....	....	....	....	....	....	....	....
Income on bonds and notes............	2 350 ..	....	....	....	....	....	....	....	....
Income on money market instruments............	2 360 ..	....	....	....	....	....	....	....	....
Other investment income............	2 370 ..	35.6	44.2	65.4	59.3	95.4	111.9	172.5	297.2
Investment income, debit............	3 320 ..	**–74.1**	**–87.3**	**–90.0**	**–110.1**	**–156.8**	**–200.5**	**–302.2**	**–479.7**
Direct investment income............	3 330 ..	....	–2.1	–4.7	–10.0	–59.0	–96.9	–179.7	–304.2
Dividends and distributed branch profits............	3 332 ..	....	....	....	....	–10.3	–24.3	–24.6	–31.8
Reinvested earnings and undistributed branch profits.....	3 333 ..	....	....	....	....	–32.4	–33.0	–100.5	–182.5
Income on debt (interest)............	3 334 ..	....	....	....	....	–16.3	–39.6	–54.6	–89.9
Portfolio investment income............	3 339 ..	....	....	....	....	....	....	....	....
Income on equity............	3 340 ..	....	....	....	....	....	....	....	....
Income on bonds and notes............	3 350 ..	....	....	....	....	....	....	....	....
Income on money market instruments............	3 360 ..	....	....	....	....	....	....	....	....
Other investment income............	3 370 ..	–74.1	–85.1	–85.4	–100.1	–97.8	–103.7	–122.5	–175.5
D. CURRENT TRANSFERS............	4 379 ..	**1,591.5**	**1,454.8**	**1,421.9**	**1,657.6**	**1,994.6**	**2,031.6**	**2,234.4**	**2,575.7**
Credit............	2 379 ..	**1,666.8**	**1,527.7**	**1,523.9**	**1,780.8**	**2,204.2**	**2,171.9**	**2,399.1**	**2,775.2**
General government............	2 380 ..	311.8	402.4	328.5	338.0	323.3	312.0	297.7	270.3
Other sectors............	2 390 ..	1,355.0	1,125.4	1,195.3	1,442.7	1,880.9	1,859.9	2,101.4	2,504.9
Workers' remittances............	2 391 ..	949.8	918.8	955.6	1,143.5	1,474.0	1,467.3	1,588.9	1,909.8
Other current transfers............	2 392 ..	405.2	206.6	239.7	299.3	406.9	392.5	512.5	595.1
Debit............	3 379 ..	**–75.4**	**–72.9**	**–101.9**	**–123.2**	**–209.6**	**–140.3**	**–164.7**	**–199.5**
General government............	3 380 ..	....	....	....	....	....	....	....	....
Other sectors............	3 390 ..	–75.4	–72.9	–101.9	–123.2	–209.6	–140.3	–164.7	–199.5
Workers' remittances............	3 391 ..	....	–5.0	–6.6	–9.5	–48.7	–27.7	–40.9	–50.2
Other current transfers............	3 392 ..	–75.4	–67.9	–95.3	–113.7	–160.9	–112.5	–123.8	–149.3
CAPITAL AND FINANCIAL ACCOUNT............	4 996 ..	**569.0**	**643.3**	**1,092.6**	**1,307.9**	**1,230.5**	**1,617.8**	**776.1**	**1,680.5**
CAPITAL ACCOUNT............	4 994 ..	**546.4**	**399.7**	**412.4**	**465.6**	**300.8**	**281.3**	**294.1**	**309.1**
Total credit............	2 994 ..	*546.4*	*399.7*	*412.4*	*465.6*	*300.8*	*281.3*	*294.1*	*309.1*
Total debit............	3 994 ..	....	....	....	....	....	....	....	....
Capital transfers, credit............	2 400 ..	**546.4**	**399.7**	**412.4**	**465.6**	**300.8**	**281.3**	**294.1**	**309.1**
General government............	2 401 ..	368.1	203.1	171.2	180.8	151.0	156.1	148.7	146.1
Debt forgiveness............	2 402 ..	....	....	....	....	....	....	....	....
Other capital transfers............	2 410 ..	368.1	203.1	171.2	180.8	151.0	156.1	148.7	146.1
Other sectors............	2 430 ..	178.3	196.6	241.1	284.8	149.8	125.1	145.4	162.9
Migrants' transfers............	2 431 ..	26.3	24.9	30.0	10.9	18.8	4.9	7.9	13.5
Debt forgiveness............	2 432 ..	....	....	....	....	....	....	....	....
Other capital transfers............	2 440 ..	152.0	171.7	211.1	273.9	131.0	120.3	137.5	149.5
Capital transfers, debit............	3 400 ..	....	....	....	....	....	....	....	....
General government............	3 401 ..	....	....	....	....	....	....	....	....
Debt forgiveness............	3 402 ..	....	....	....	....	....	....	....	....
Other capital transfers............	3 410 ..	....	....	....	....	....	....	....	....
Other sectors............	3 430 ..	....	....	....	....	....	....	....	....
Migrants' transfers............	3 431 ..	....	....	....	....	....	....	....	....
Debt forgiveness............	3 432 ..	....	....	....	....	....	....	....	....
Other capital transfers............	3 440 ..	....	....	....	....	....	....	....	....
Nonproduced nonfinancial assets, credit............	2 480 ..	....	....	....	....	....	....	....	....
Nonproduced nonfinancial assets, debit............	3 480 ..	....	....	....	....	....	....	....	....

Table 2 (Continued). STANDARD PRESENTATION, 2000–2007

(Millions of U.S. dollars)

	Code	2000	2001	2002	2003	2004	2005	2006	2007
FINANCIAL ACCOUNT	4 995	22.6	243.6	680.3	842.2	929.7	1,336.5	482.0	1,371.4
A. DIRECT INVESTMENT	4 500	146.1	118.5	267.8	381.8	708.3	607.4	718.4	2,086.6
Direct investment abroad	4 505	....	....	....	....	−1.6	−.4	−4.1	−24.7
Equity capital	4 510	....	....	....	....	−.7	.7	−2.7	−16.8
Claims on affiliated enterprises	4 515	....	....	....	....	−.7	.7	−2.7	−16.8
Liabilities to affiliated enterprises	4 520	....	....	....	....	....	....	....	
Reinvested earnings	4 525	....	....	....	....	....	....	....	−1.5
Other capital	4 530	....	....	....	....	−.9	−1.2	−1.3	−6.4
Claims on affiliated enterprises	4 535	....	....	....	....	−.9	−1.2	−1.3	−6.4
Liabilities to affiliated enterprises	4 540	....	....	....	....	....	....	....	....
Direct investment in Bosnia and Herzegovina	4 555	146.1	118.5	267.8	381.8	709.8	607.8	722.5	2,111.3
Equity capital	4 560	146.1	118.5	267.8	381.8	429.0	281.1	334.2	1,567.7
Claims on direct investors	4 565	....	....	....	....	−98.4		....	
Liabilities to direct investors	4 570	146.1	118.5	267.8	381.8	527.4	281.1	334.2	1,567.7
Reinvested earnings	4 575	....	....	....	....	32.4	33.0	100.5	182.5
Other capital	4 580	....	....	....	....	248.5	293.8	287.7	361.1
Claims on direct investors	4 585	....	....	....	....	−81.3	−16.0	−14.8	−21.4
Liabilities to direct investors	4 590	....	....	....	....	329.8	309.8	302.5	382.5
B. PORTFOLIO INVESTMENT	4 600	....	....	....	....	−2.8	2.6	−.4	−.8
Assets	4 602	....	....	....	....	−2.8	2.6	−.4	−.8
Equity securities	4 610	....	....	....	....	....	....	....	....
Monetary authorities	4 611	....	....	....	....	....	....	....	....
General government	4 612	....	....	....	....	....	....	....	....
Banks	4 613	....	....	....	....	....	....	....	....
Other sectors	4 614	....	....	....	....	....	....	....	....
Debt securities	4 619	....	....	....	....	−2.8	2.6	−.4	−.8
Bonds and notes	4 620	....	....	....	....	−1.8	2.5	−.5	−2.1
Monetary authorities	4 621	....	....	....	....	....	....	....	....
General government	4 622	....	....	....	....	....	....	....	....
Banks	4 623	....	....	....	....	−1.8	2.5	−.5	−2.1
Other sectors	4 624	....	....	....	....	....	....	....	....
Money market instruments	4 630	....	....	....	....	−1.0	....	.1	1.3
Monetary authorities	4 631	....	....	....	....	....	....	....	....
General government	4 632	....	....	....	....	....	....	....	....
Banks	4 633	....	....	....	....	−1.0	....	.1	1.3
Other sectors	4 634	....	....	....	....	....	....	....	....
Liabilities	4 652	....	....	....	....	....	....	....	....
Equity securities	4 660	....	....	....	....	....	....	....	....
Banks	4 663	....	....	....	....	....	....	....	....
Other sectors	4 664	....	....	....	....	....	....	....	....
Debt securities	4 669	....	....	....	....	....	....	....	....
Bonds and notes	4 670	....	....	....	....	....	....	....	....
Monetary authorities	4 671	....	....	....	....	....	....	....	....
General government	4 672	....	....	....	....	....	....	....	....
Banks	4 673	....	....	....	....	....	....	....	....
Other sectors	4 674	....	....	....	....	....	....	....	....
Money market instruments	4 680	....	....	....	....	....	....	....	....
Monetary authorities	4 681	....	....	....	....	....	....	....	....
General government	4 682	....	....	....	....	....	....	....	....
Banks	4 683	....	....	....	....	....	....	....	....
Other sectors	4 684	....	....	....	....	....	....	....	....
C. FINANCIAL DERIVATIVES	4 910	....	....	....	....	....	....	....	....
Monetary authorities	4 911	....	....	....	....	....	....	....	....
General government	4 912	....	....	....	....	....	....	....	....
Banks	4 913	....	....	....	....	....	....	....	....
Other sectors	4 914	....	....	....	....	....	....	....	....
Assets	4 900	....	....	....	....	....	....	....	....
Monetary authorities	4 901	....	....	....	....	....	....	....	....
General government	4 902	....	....	....	....	....	....	....	....
Banks	4 903	....	....	....	....	....	....	....	....
Other sectors	4 904	....	....	....	....	....	....	....	....
Liabilities	4 905	....	....	....	....	....	....	....	....
Monetary authorities	4 906	....	....	....	....	....	....	....	....
General government	4 907	....	....	....	....	....	....	....	....
Banks	4 908	....	....	....	....	....	....	....	....
Other sectors	4 909	....	....	....	....	....	....	....	....

Table 2 (Concluded). STANDARD PRESENTATION, 2000–2007

(Millions of U.S. dollars)

	Code	2000	2001	2002	2003	2004	2005	2006	2007
D. OTHER INVESTMENT...............................	4 700 ..	**−47.0**	**886.7**	**302.9**	**657.1**	**657.3**	**1,187.9**	**553.6**	**161.7**
Assets...	4 703 ..	**−675.0**	**648.9**	**−155.0**	**101.0**	**296.4**	**305.1**	**28.9**	**−995.1**
Trade credits................................	4 706 ..	−4.3	.7	−9.3	−20.6	−35.6	−157.7	−145.6	−67.0
General government...................	4 707 ..	....	....	....	....	....	....	....	....
of which: Short-term...............	4 709 ..	....	....	....	....	....	....	....	....
Other sectors............................	4 710 ..	−4.3	.7	−9.3	−20.6	−35.6	−157.7	−145.6	−67.0
of which: Short-term...............	4 712 ..	*−4.3*	*.7*	*−9.3*	*−20.6*	*−35.6*	*−157.7*	*−145.6*	*−67.0*
Loans..	4 714 ..	....	....	....	....	....	....	....	....
Monetary authorities.................	4 715 ..	....	....	....	....	....	....	....	....
of which: Short-term...............	4 718 ..	....	....	....	....	....	....	....	....
General government...................	4 719 ..	....	....	....	....	....	....	....	....
of which: Short-term...............	4 721 ..	....	....	....	....	....	....	....	....
Banks......................................	4 722 ..	....	....	....	....	....	....	....	....
of which: Short-term...............	4 724 ..	....	....	....	....	....	....	....	....
Other sectors............................	4 725 ..	....	....	....	....	....	....	....	....
of which: Short-term...............	4 727 ..	....	....	....	....	....	....	....	....
Currency and deposits.....................	4 730 ..	−672.3	680.3	−149.2	100.2	361.6	475.0	195.7	−889.5
Monetary authorities.................	4 731 ..	....	....	....	....	....	....	....	....
General government...................	4 732 ..	....	....	....	....	....	....	....	....
Banks......................................	4 733 ..	−93.2	−153.2	−52.6	−78.3	−195.2	−117.7	−128.2	−801.7
Other sectors............................	4 734 ..	−579.1	833.4	−96.6	178.4	556.8	592.7	323.9	−87.8
Other assets.................................	4 736 ..	1.5	−32.1	3.5	21.4	−29.6	−12.2	−21.2	−38.5
Monetary authorities.................	4 737 ..	....	....	....	....	....	....	....	....
of which: Short-term...............	4 739 ..	....	....	....	....	....	....	....	....
General government...................	4 740 ..	....	....	....	....	....	....	....	....
of which: Short-term...............	4 742 ..	....	....	....	....	....	....	....	....
Banks......................................	4 743 ..	1.5	−32.1	3.5	21.4	−30.6	−8.2	−22.2	−33.2
of which: Short-term...............	4 745 ..	*−2.9*	*−33.3*	*3.2*	*24.4*	*−31.7*	*−.7*	*−10.6*	*−7.5*
Other sectors............................	4 746 ..	....	....	....	....	1.0	−4.0	1.0	−5.3
of which: Short-term...............	4 748 ..	....	....	....	....	*1.0*	*−4.0*	*1.0*	*−5.3*
Liabilities..................................	4 753 ..	**628.0**	**237.9**	**457.9**	**556.1**	**360.8**	**882.8**	**524.7**	**1,156.8**
Trade credits................................	4 756 ..	11.1	92.8	49.8	70.5	118.7	246.9	221.4	268.2
General government...................	4 757 ..	....	....	....	....	....	....	....	....
of which: Short-term...............	4 759 ..	....	....	....	....	....	....	....	....
Other sectors............................	4 760 ..	11.1	92.8	49.8	70.5	118.7	246.9	221.4	268.2
of which: Short-term...............	4 762 ..	*11.1*	*92.8*	*49.8*	*70.5*	*118.7*	*246.9*	*221.4*	*268.2*
Loans..	4 764 ..	583.4	107.6	273.1	260.5	−37.8	337.9	162.3	498.3
Monetary authorities.................	4 765 ..	15.5	9.9	19.0	−17.1	−29.7	−39.4	−44.1	−18.3
of which: Use of Fund credit and loans from the Fund..	4 766 ..	*15.5*	*9.9*	*19.0*	*−17.1*	*−29.7*	*−39.4*	*−44.1*	*−18.3*
of which: Short-term...............	4 768 ..	....	....	....	....	....	....	....	....
General government...................	4 769 ..	75.9	66.9	101.9	33.2	99.3	59.8	5.7	58.4
of which: Short-term...............	4 771 ..	....	....	....	....	....	....	....	....
Banks......................................	4 772 ..	276.5	−44.0	−17.5	157.2	−260.0	57.0	57.7	216.2
of which: Short-term...............	4 774 ..	*1.7*	*5.6*	*−3.9*	*−6.8*	*−1.4*	*−13.0*	*3.8*	*−5.1*
Other sectors............................	4 775 ..	215.6	74.8	169.8	87.2	152.6	260.5	143.0	241.9
of which: Short-term...............	4 777 ..	....	....	....	....	*−1.4*	*1.1*	*14.5*	*70.0*
Currency and deposits.....................	4 780 ..	30.5	24.8	149.6	222.5	259.3	341.0	139.3	406.3
Monetary authorities.................	4 781 ..	.6	13.6	−13.4	−.1	....	....	....	....
General government...................	4 782 ..	....	....	....	....	....	....	....	....
Banks......................................	4 783 ..	29.9	11.1	163.0	222.5	259.3	340.9	139.3	406.4
Other sectors............................	4 784 ..	....	....	....	....	....	....	....	....
Other liabilities............................	4 786 ..	2.9	12.8	−14.7	2.7	20.6	−42.9	1.8	−16.0
Monetary authorities.................	4 787 ..	.6	....	....	....	....	....	....	....
of which: Short-term...............	4 789 ..	....	....	....	....	....	....	....	....
General government...................	4 790 ..	....	....	....	....	....	....	....	....
of which: Short-term...............	4 792 ..	....	....	....	....	....	....	....	....
Banks......................................	4 793 ..	2.3	12.8	−14.7	2.7	7.2	−2.6	.7	11.8
of which: Short-term...............	4 795 ..	*2.4*	*12.7*	*−14.6*	*2.7*	*7.2*	*−2.4*	*.6*	*10.0*
Other sectors............................	4 796 ..	....	....	....	....	13.5	−40.3	1.0	−27.8
of which: Short-term...............	4 798 ..	....	....	....	....	*13.5*	*−40.3*	*1.0*	*−27.8*
E. RESERVE ASSETS............................	4 802 ..	**−76.5**	**−761.6**	**109.6**	**−196.6**	**−433.0**	**−461.4**	**−789.6**	**−876.1**
Monetary gold.............................	4 812 ..	....	....	....	....	....	....	....	....
Special drawing rights....................	4 811 ..	−3.2	4.3	3.1	....	2.9	.1	....	.1
Reserve position in the Fund............	4 810 ..	....	....	....	....	....	....	....	....
Foreign exchange..........................	4 803 ..	−73.3	−765.9	106.5	−196.7	−429.6	−458.6	−774.9	−855.6
Other claims................................	4 813 ..	....	....	....	....	−6.4	−2.9	−14.7	−20.6
NET ERRORS AND OMISSIONS............................	4 998 ..	**−173.3**	**99.6**	**98.0**	**323.2**	**408.8**	**226.6**	**197.3**	**249.9**

Table 1. ANALYTIC PRESENTATION, 2000–2007

(Millions of U.S. dollars)

	Code	2000	2001	2002	2003	2004	2005	2006	2007
A. Current Account[1]	4 993 Z.	**545.2**	**597.7**	**156.7**	**462.2**	**308.9**	**1,597.1**	**1,939.8**	**2,434.2**
Goods: exports f.o.b.	2 100 ..	2,675.4	2,314.5	2,318.6	3,024.3	3,695.9	4,443.5	4,520.8	5,157.9
Goods: imports f.o.b.	3 100 ..	−1,773.2	−1,604.1	−1,642.3	−2,127.2	−2,864.0	−2,686.0	−2,616.5	−3,447.1
Balance on Goods	4 100 ..	*902.1*	*710.4*	*676.3*	*897.2*	*831.9*	*1,757.5*	*1,904.3*	*1,710.8*
Services: credit	2 200 ..	324.8	340.3	489.6	643.2	779.9	854.2	771.0	934.5
Services: debit	3 200 ..	−547.5	−513.3	−509.7	−652.4	−792.9	−856.9	−834.8	−970.2
Balance on Goods and Services	4 991 ..	*679.4*	*537.3*	*656.2*	*887.9*	*819.0*	*1,754.7*	*1,840.5*	*1,675.2*
Income: credit	2 300 ..	378.1	358.4	268.4	382.6	217.3	456.0	529.1	473.2
Income: debit	3 300 ..	−729.5	−495.4	−980.2	−1,098.4	−1,253.5	−1,291.9	−1,301.3	−819.3
Balance on Goods, Services, and Income	4 992 ..	*328.1*	*400.3*	*−55.7*	*172.2*	*−217.2*	*918.8*	*1,068.4*	*1,329.1*
Current transfers: credit	2 379 Z.	426.1	383.0	400.4	538.3	743.0	896.1	1,073.4	1,368.2
Current transfers: debit	3 379 ..	−209.0	−185.5	−188.1	−248.2	−216.8	−217.7	−202.0	−263.1
B. Capital Account[1]	4 994 Z.	**38.1**	**5.8**	**15.7**	**22.5**	**31.8**	**31.5**	**24.4**	**89.4**
Capital account: credit	2 994 Z.	51.5	18.7	29.7	42.5	53.0	53.2	45.1	110.4
Capital account: debit	3 994 ..	−13.3	−12.9	−14.0	−20.0	−21.2	−21.7	−20.7	−21.1
Total, Groups A Plus B	4 981 ..	*583.3*	*603.5*	*172.4*	*484.7*	*340.7*	*1,628.6*	*1,964.2*	*2,523.5*
C. Financial Account[1]	4 995 W.	**−214.0**	**−509.4**	**−217.3**	**−378.8**	**−275.6**	**53.9**	**−66.8**	**−665.3**
Direct investment abroad	4 505 ..	−2.3	−370.9	−42.9	−206.1	−29.2	55.9	49.8	−3.7
Direct investment in Botswana	4 555 Z.	57.2	22.1	403.4	418.0	391.0	278.6	486.4	−28.6
Portfolio investment assets	4 602 ..	−34.1	−68.4	−420.2	−587.3	−437.9	−404.5	−593.0	−475.3
Equity securities	4 610 ..	−3.4	−5.8	−325.5	−451.6	−415.1	−289.4	−561.4	−410.7
Debt securities	4 619 ..	−30.7	−62.6	−94.8	−135.7	−22.9	−115.0	−31.6	−64.6
Portfolio investment liabilities	4 652 Z.	−5.9	6.0	7.1	66.8	−29.2	16.2	36.0	13.7
Equity securities	4 660 ..	−5.9	6.0	7.1	10.2	.6	61.6	35.9	9.4
Debt securities	4 669 Z.	....	....	....	56.6	−29.8	−45.4	.2	4.3
Financial derivatives	4 910 ..	−3.0	....	....	....	....	....	....	....
Financial derivatives assets	4 900 ..	....	....	....	....	....	....	....	....
Financial derivatives liabilities	4 905 ..	−3.0	....	....	....	....	....	....	....
Other investment assets	4 703 ..	−263.6	−152.7	−221.1	−220.7	−85.8	−152.2	−278.2	−140.5
Monetary authorities	4 701 ..	....	....	....	....	....	....	....	....
General government	4 704 ..	−90.4	−52.6	−80.8	−72.5	−122.0	....	....	....
Banks	4 705 ..	−135.0	−78.5	−112.9	−124.0	62.0	−36.6	−148.7	−144.3
Other sectors	4 728 ..	−38.3	−21.6	−27.3	−24.2	−25.8	−115.6	−129.5	3.9
Other investment liabilities	4 753 W.	37.7	54.4	56.3	150.5	−84.4	259.9	232.1	−31.0
Monetary authorities	4 753 WA	....	....	....	....	....	....	....	....
General government	4 753 ZB	−22.5	−21.1	−23.1	−13.5	−11.8	−.2	−31.1	−11.3
Banks	4 753 ZC	1.4	7.2	7.6	37.6	−2.2	202.9	10.6	−31.1
Other sectors	4 753 ZD	58.9	68.3	71.9	126.4	−70.5	57.2	252.6	11.5
Total, Groups A Through C	4 983 ..	*369.3*	*94.1*	*−45.0*	*105.9*	*65.2*	*1,682.5*	*1,897.3*	*1,858.2*
D. Net Errors and Omissions	4 998 ..	**−1.9**	**75.8**	**105.6**	**65.5**	**−122.0**	**−319.0**	**−141.7**	**−123.9**
Total, Groups A Through D	4 984 ..	*367.4*	*170.0*	*60.6*	*171.5*	*−56.9*	*1,363.5*	*1,755.6*	*1,734.3*
E. Reserves and Related Items	4 802 A.	**−367.4**	**−170.0**	**−60.6**	**−171.5**	**56.9**	**−1,363.5**	**−1,755.6**	**−1,734.3**
Reserve assets	4 802 ..	−367.4	−170.0	−60.6	−171.5	56.9	−1,363.5	−1,755.6	−1,734.3
Use of Fund credit and loans	4 766 ..	....	....	....	....	....	....	....	....
Exceptional financing	4 920 ..	....	....	....	....	....	....	....	....
Conversion rates: pula per U.S. dollar	0 101 ..	**5.1018**	**5.8412**	**6.3278**	**4.9499**	**4.6929**	**5.1104**	**5.8366**	**6.1388**

[1] Excludes components that have been classified in the categories of Group E.

Table 2. STANDARD PRESENTATION, 2000–2007

(Millions of U.S. dollars)

	Code	2000	2001	2002	2003	2004	2005	2006	2007
CURRENT ACCOUNT...	4 993 ..	**545.2**	**597.7**	**156.7**	**462.2**	**308.9**	**1,597.1**	**1,939.8**	**2,434.2**
A. GOODS..	4 100 ..	**902.1**	**710.4**	**676.3**	**897.2**	**831.9**	**1,757.5**	**1,904.3**	**1,710.8**
Credit..	2 100 ..	**2,675.4**	**2,314.5**	**2,318.6**	**3,024.3**	**3,695.9**	**4,443.5**	**4,520.8**	**5,157.9**
General merchandise: exports f.o.b.	2 110 ..	2,675.4	2,314.5	2,318.6	3,024.3	3,695.9	4,442.4	4,520.2	5,157.9
Goods for processing: exports f.o.b.	2 150 ..	....	....	....	....	....	....	....	....
Repairs on goods..	2 160 ..	....	....	....	....	....	1.1	.3	....
Goods procured in ports by carriers..................	2 170 ..	....	....	....	....	....	....	.3	....
Nonmonetary gold..	2 180 ..	....	....	....	....	....	....	....	....
Debit..	3 100 ..	**−1,773.2**	**−1,604.1**	**−1,642.3**	**−2,127.2**	**−2,864.0**	**−2,686.0**	**−2,616.5**	**−3,447.1**
General merchandise: imports f.o.b.	3 110 ..	−1,773.2	−1,604.1	−1,642.3	−2,127.2	−2,864.0	−2,683.2	−2,614.5	−3,444.4
Goods for processing: imports f.o.b.	3 150 ..	....	....	....	....	....	....	....	....
Repairs on goods..	3 160 ..	....	....	....	....	....	−2.5	−2.0	−2.7
Goods procured in ports by carriers..................	3 170 ..	....	....	....	....	....	−.3	....	....
Nonmonetary gold..	3 180 ..	....	....	....	....	....	....	....	....
B. SERVICES...	4 200 ..	**−222.7**	**−173.0**	**−20.1**	**−9.3**	**−12.9**	**−2.7**	**−63.8**	**−35.6**
Total credit..	2 200 ..	*324.8*	*340.3*	*489.6*	*643.2*	*779.9*	*854.2*	*771.0*	*934.5*
Total debit...	3 200 ..	*−547.5*	*−513.3*	*−509.7*	*−652.4*	*−792.9*	*−856.9*	*−834.8*	*−970.2*
Transportation services, credit.........................	2 205 ..	**51.9**	**52.7**	**55.4**	**69.1**	**83.0**	**85.0**	**81.2**	**83.0**
Passenger...	2 850 ..	*4.8*	*4.8*	*5.1*	*1.8*	*1.0*	*.8*	*2.2*	*2.8*
Freight...	2 851 ..	*15.8*	*15.8*	*16.6*	*24.1*	*31.5*	*33.1*	*27.5*	*47.5*
Other...	2 852 ..	*31.2*	*32.1*	*33.8*	*43.1*	*50.5*	*51.1*	*51.5*	*32.7*
Sea transport, passenger..................................	2 207 ..	....	....	....	....	....	....	....	....
Sea transport, freight.......................................	2 208 ..	....	....	....	....	....	....	....	....
Sea transport, other...	2 209 ..	....	....	....	....	....	....	....	....
Air transport, passenger...................................	2 211 ..	....	....	....	1.8	1.0	.8	2.2	2.4
Air transport, freight..	2 212 ..	....	....	....	....	....	....	....	....
Air transport, other..	2 213 ..	....	....	....	....	....	....	....	....
Other transport, passenger..............................	2 215 ..	....	....	....	....	....	....	....	.3
Other transport, freight....................................	2 216 ..	....	....	....	24.1	31.5	33.1	27.5	47.5
Other transport, other......................................	2 217 ..	....	....	....	43.1	50.5	51.1	51.5	32.7
Transportation services, debit..........................	3 205 ..	**−225.9**	**−205.9**	**−213.3**	**−248.1**	**−291.1**	**−340.1**	**−322.0**	**−399.0**
Passenger...	3 850 ..	*−10.9*	*−10.6*	*−13.4*	*−4.6*	*−4.3*	*−19.4*	*−7.6*	*−2.8*
Freight...	3 851 ..	*−206.1*	*−186.4*	*−191.0*	*−243.5*	*−286.9*	*−320.7*	*−314.4*	*−396.2*
Other...	3 852 ..	*−8.9*	*−8.8*	*−9.0*	....	....	....	....	....
Sea transport, passenger..................................	3 207 ..	....	....	....	....	....	....	....	....
Sea transport, freight.......................................	3 208 ..	....	....	....	....	....	....	....	....
Sea transport, other...	3 209 ..	....	....	....	....	....	....	....	....
Air transport, passenger...................................	3 211 ..	....	....	....	−3.8	....	−.4	−3.1	−1.5
Air transport, freight..	3 212 ..	....	....	....	−31.4	−24.1	−22.6	−51.5	−52.7
Air transport, other..	3 213 ..	....	....	....	....	....	....	....	....
Other transport, passenger..............................	3 215 ..	....	....	....	−.9	−4.3	−19.0	−4.5	−1.4
Other transport, freight....................................	3 216 ..	....	....	....	−212.1	−262.8	−298.1	−262.8	−343.5
Other transport, other......................................	3 217 ..	....	....	....	....	....	....	....	....
Travel, credit...	2 236 ..	**222.2**	**230.2**	**319.1**	**456.7**	**581.0**	**560.0**	**537.2**	**546.1**
Business travel..	2 237 ..	33.2	30.0	136.7	160.5	192.2	196.7	188.0	196.7
Personal travel..	2 240 ..	189.0	200.2	182.4	296.2	388.7	363.4	349.2	349.4
Travel, debit..	3 236 ..	**−197.7**	**−204.3**	**−183.8**	**−229.5**	**−276.1**	**−282.5**	**−276.5**	**−278.1**
Business travel..	3 237 ..	−47.5	−49.0	−44.1	−55.1	−66.3	−67.8	−66.4	−67.6
Personal travel..	3 240 ..	−150.3	−155.3	−139.7	−174.4	−209.9	−214.7	−210.2	−210.5
Other services, credit......................................	2 200 BA	**50.7**	**57.4**	**115.0**	**117.5**	**115.9**	**209.1**	**152.5**	**305.4**
Communications..	2 245 ..	.4	5.4	9.7	8.3	7.9	21.8	16.1	57.2
Construction..	2 249 ..	.8	7.3	8.1	8.7	8.4	13.9	8.1	12.4
Insurance..	2 253 ..	6.6	8.1	7.9	33.8	48.5	70.3	19.6	26.1
Financial...	2 260 ..	4.1	2.8	1.4	1.9	3.7	5.2	2.4	7.8
Computer and information................................	2 262 ..	....	.4	1.7	1.4	.4	1.2	1.4	6.0
Royalties and licence fees................................	2 266 ..	....	....	.5	3.4	5.4	.5	.3	.2
Other business services...................................	2 268 ..	19.7	19.3	35.3	42.5	36.1	83.9	104.6	182.9
Personal, cultural, and recreational...................	2 287 ..	....	....	....	....	....	....	....	....
Government, n.i.e...	2 291 ..	19.0	14.2	50.4	17.6	5.5	12.4	....	12.8
Other services, debit.......................................	3 200 BA	**−123.9**	**−103.2**	**−112.6**	**−174.8**	**−225.6**	**−234.3**	**−236.2**	**−293.1**
Communications..	3 245 ..	−10.6	−4.2	−6.1	−14.3	−21.4	−36.7	−14.4	−46.9
Construction..	3 249 ..	−2.0	−7.8	−7.7	−8.2	−10.7	−10.4	−16.9	−9.6
Insurance..	3 253 ..	−18.3	−13.5	−14.2	−21.5	−41.0	−27.7	−27.6	−39.9
Financial...	3 260 ..	−2.8	−3.1	−3.2	−5.5	−5.7	−3.0	−1.9	−2.2
Computer and information................................	3 262 ..	−2.6	−4.3	−3.8	−6.1	−7.2	−9.0	−4.3	−7.2
Royalties and licence fees................................	3 266 ..	−5.8	−8.7	−8.4	−11.8	−11.0	−12.3	−7.3	−11.4
Other business services...................................	3 268 ..	−72.6	−60.6	−67.3	−106.4	−119.2	−117.9	−162.8	−175.4
Personal, cultural, and recreational...................	3 287 ..	....	....	....	....	....	....	....	....
Government, n.i.e...	3 291 ..	−9.3	−.9	−1.8	−.9	−9.4	−17.2	−1.0	−.5

Table 2 (Continued). STANDARD PRESENTATION, 2000–2007

(Millions of U.S. dollars)

	Code	2000	2001	2002	2003	2004	2005	2006	2007
C. INCOME	4 300	**−351.3**	**−137.1**	**−711.8**	**−715.8**	**−1,036.2**	**−835.9**	**−772.2**	**−346.1**
Total credit	2 300	*378.1*	*358.4*	*268.4*	*382.6*	*217.3*	*456.0*	*529.1*	*473.2*
Total debit	3 300	*−729.5*	*−495.4*	*−980.2*	*−1,098.4*	*−1,253.5*	*−1,291.9*	*−1,301.3*	*−819.3*
Compensation of employees, credit	2 310	**18.2**	**18.1**	**19.1**	**27.3**	**29.5**	**29.5**	**25.5**	**48.3**
Compensation of employees, debit	3 310	**−54.9**	**−54.7**	**−57.6**	**−82.4**	**−89.0**	**−91.1**	**−87.1**	**−88.5**
Investment income, credit	2 320	**359.9**	**340.2**	**249.3**	**355.3**	**187.8**	**426.4**	**503.5**	**424.8**
Direct investment income	2 330	25.2	36.3	26.8	117.4	.3	194.4	150.0	38.2
Dividends and distributed branch profits	2 332	13.6	18.3	23.3	112.6	.1	194.3	149.9	37.8
Reinvested earnings and undistributed branch profits	2 333	4.5	12.0	....	4.7	.2	....	.2	.4
Income on debt (interest)	2 334	7.1	6.1	3.4	....	.1	....	....	....
Portfolio investment income	2 339	317.5	314.0	208.6	238.0	209.2	232.1	353.5	386.7
Income on equity	2 340	312.4	310.5	204.9	176.0	188.8	211.1	285.1	381.3
Income on bonds and notes	2 350	5.1	3.5	3.7	....	....	....	....	....
Income on money market instruments	2 360	....	....	....	61.9	20.4	20.9	68.4	5.3
Other investment income	2 370	17.3	−10.1	13.9	....	−21.7	....	....	....
Investment income, debit	3 320	**−674.6**	**−440.8**	**−922.6**	**−1,016.0**	**−1,164.5**	**−1,200.9**	**−1,214.2**	**−730.8**
Direct investment income	3 330	−657.9	−343.7	−909.0	−1,003.5	−1,092.3	−1,065.7	−1,042.5	−631.8
Dividends and distributed branch profits	3 332	−599.4	−381.6	−559.1	−651.0	−732.3	−851.5	−778.2	−591.7
Reinvested earnings and undistributed branch profits	3 333	−4.1	100.4	−342.1	−352.6	−357.0	−213.8	−264.4	−40.0
Income on debt (interest)	3 334	−54.4	−62.5	−7.8	....	−2.9	−.4	....	−.1
Portfolio investment income	3 339	−.1	−18.2	−.1	....	−22.8	−89.2	−58.0	−37.6
Income on equity	3 340	−.1	−.1	−.1	....	....	....	....	....
Income on bonds and notes	3 350	....	−18.1	....	....	....	−68.3	−58.0	−37.6
Income on money market instruments	3 360	....	....	....	....	−22.8	−20.9	....	....
Other investment income	3 370	−16.6	−78.8	−13.6	−12.5	−49.4	−46.0	−113.6	−61.4
D. CURRENT TRANSFERS	4 379	**217.1**	**197.5**	**212.3**	**290.1**	**526.1**	**678.3**	**871.4**	**1,105.1**
Credit	2 379	**426.1**	**383.0**	**400.4**	**538.3**	**743.0**	**896.1**	**1,073.4**	**1,368.2**
General government	2 380	412.7	366.3	381.2	510.8	662.5	794.4	955.9	1,272.0
Other sectors	2 390	13.4	16.7	19.2	27.5	80.5	101.7	117.5	96.1
Workers' remittances	2 391	.4	.4	....	....	50.8	82.4	78.7	80.0
Other current transfers	2 392	13.1	16.3	19.2	27.5	29.7	19.3	38.8	16.1
Debit	3 379	**−209.0**	**−185.5**	**−188.1**	**−248.2**	**−216.8**	**−217.7**	**−202.0**	**−263.1**
General government	3 380	−127.9	−111.1	−116.0	−145.1	−206.6	−207.3	−192.0	−253.0
Other sectors	3 390	−81.1	−74.4	−72.1	−103.2	−10.2	−10.4	−10.0	−10.2
Workers' remittances	3 391	−79.0	−71.7	−72.1	−103.2	−10.2	−10.4	−10.0	−10.2
Other current transfers	3 392	−2.0	−2.6	....	....	....	....	....	....
CAPITAL AND FINANCIAL ACCOUNT	4 996	**−543.3**	**−673.5**	**−262.3**	**−527.8**	**−186.9**	**−1,278.1**	**−1,798.1**	**−2,310.3**
CAPITAL ACCOUNT	4 994	**38.1**	**5.8**	**15.7**	**22.5**	**31.8**	**31.5**	**24.4**	**89.4**
Total credit	2 994	*51.5*	*18.7*	*29.7*	*42.5*	*53.0*	*53.2*	*45.1*	*110.4*
Total debit	3 994	*−13.3*	*−12.9*	*−14.0*	*−20.0*	*−21.2*	*−21.7*	*−20.7*	*−21.1*
Capital transfers, credit	2 400	**51.5**	**18.7**	**29.7**	**42.5**	**53.0**	**53.2**	**45.1**	**110.4**
General government	2 401	43.7	11.2	21.6	30.9	40.1	40.0	32.6	97.7
Debt forgiveness	2 402	....	....	....	....	....	....	....	....
Other capital transfers	2 410	43.7	11.2	21.6	30.9	40.1	40.0	32.6	97.7
Other sectors	2 430	7.7	7.4	8.1	11.6	12.8	13.1	12.6	12.8
Migrants' transfers	2 431	7.7	7.4	8.1	11.6	12.8	13.1	12.6	12.8
Debt forgiveness	2 432	....	....	....	....	....	....	....	....
Other capital transfers	2 440	....	....	....	....	....	....	....	....
Capital transfers, debit	3 400	**−13.3**	**−12.9**	**−14.0**	**−20.0**	**−21.2**	**−21.7**	**−20.7**	**−21.1**
General government	3 401	....	....	....	....	....	....	....	....
Debt forgiveness	3 402	....	....	....	....	....	....	....	....
Other capital transfers	3 410	....	....	....	....	....	....	....	....
Other sectors	3 430	−13.3	−12.9	−14.0	−20.0	−21.2	−21.7	−20.7	−21.1
Migrants' transfers	3 431	−13.3	−12.9	−14.0	−20.0	−21.2	−21.7	−20.7	−21.1
Debt forgiveness	3 432	....	....	....	....	....	....	....	....
Other capital transfers	3 440	....	....	....	....	....	....	....	....
Nonproduced nonfinancial assets, credit	2 480	....	....	....	....	....	....	....	....
Nonproduced nonfinancial assets, debit	3 480	....	....	....	....	....	....	....	....

Table 2 (Continued). STANDARD PRESENTATION, 2000–2007

(Millions of U.S. dollars)

	Code	2000	2001	2002	2003	2004	2005	2006	2007
FINANCIAL ACCOUNT................................	4 995 ..	**−581.4**	**−679.3**	**−278.0**	**−550.2**	**−218.7**	**−1,309.6**	**−1,822.5**	**−2,399.7**
A. DIRECT INVESTMENT..........................	4 500 ..	**54.9**	**−348.8**	**360.5**	**211.9**	**361.8**	**334.5**	**536.1**	**−32.3**
Direct investment abroad..................	4 505 ..	**−2.3**	**−370.9**	**−42.9**	**−206.1**	**−29.2**	**55.9**	**49.8**	**−3.7**
Equity capital...............................	4 510 ..	....	−375.3	−37.1	−201.5	−40.0	52.2	29.0	−1.0
Claims on affiliated enterprises..........	4 515 ..	....	−375.3	−37.1	−201.5	−40.0	52.2	29.0	−1.0
Liabilities to affiliated enterprises.......	4 520 ..	....	....	....	....	....	....	....	....
Reinvested earnings......................	4 525 ..	−4.5	−12.0	....	−4.7	−.2	....	−.2	−.4
Other capital.............................	4 530 ..	2.2	16.3	−5.8	.2	11.0	3.7	21.0	−2.4
Claims on affiliated enterprises..........	4 535 ..	2.2	16.3	−5.8	.2	11.0	3.7	21.0	−2.4
Liabilities to affiliated enterprises.......	4 540 ..	....	....	....	....	....	....	....	....
Direct investment in Botswana..........	4 555 ..	**57.2**	**22.1**	**403.4**	**418.0**	**391.0**	**278.6**	**486.4**	**−28.6**
Equity capital.............................	4 560 ..	6.2	60.1	56.8	65.3	31.8	−3.4	226.3	32.7
Claims on direct investors..............	4 565 ..	....	....	....	....	....	....	....	....
Liabilities to direct investors...........	4 570 ..	6.2	60.1	56.8	65.3	31.8	−3.4	226.3	32.7
Reinvested earnings......................	4 575 ..	4.1	−100.4	342.1	352.6	357.0	213.8	264.4	40.0
Other capital.............................	4 580 ..	46.9	62.5	4.6	.1	2.2	68.2	−4.3	−101.3
Claims on direct investors..............	4 585 ..	....	....	....	....	....	....	....	....
Liabilities to direct investors...........	4 590 ..	46.9	62.5	4.6	.1	2.2	68.2	−4.3	−101.3
B. PORTFOLIO INVESTMENT.....................	4 600 ..	**−40.0**	**−62.3**	**−413.1**	**−520.5**	**−467.1**	**−388.2**	**−556.9**	**−461.6**
Assets...	4 602 ..	**−34.1**	**−68.4**	**−420.2**	**−587.3**	**−437.9**	**−404.5**	**−593.0**	**−475.3**
Equity securities..........................	4 610 ..	−3.4	−5.8	−325.5	−451.6	−415.1	−289.4	−561.4	−410.7
Monetary authorities....................	4 611 ..	....	....	....	....	....	....	....	....
General government....................	4 612 ..	....	....	....	....	....	....	....	....
Banks...................................	4 613 ..	....	....	....	....	....	....	....	....
Other sectors...........................	4 614 ..	−3.4	−5.8	−325.5	−451.6	−415.1	−289.4	−561.4	−410.7
Debt securities...........................	4 619 ..	−30.7	−62.6	−94.8	−135.7	−22.9	−115.0	−31.6	−64.6
Bonds and notes........................	4 620 ..	−23.6	....	....	....	....	....	....	....
Monetary authorities..................	4 621 ..	....	....	....	....	....	....	....	....
General government..................	4 622 ..	....	....	....	....	....	....	....	....
Banks.................................	4 623 ..	....	....	....	....	....	....	....	....
Other sectors.........................	4 624 ..	−23.6	....	....	....	....	....	....	....
Money market instruments.............	4 630 ..	−7.1	....	....	−135.7	−22.9	−115.0	−31.6	−64.6
Monetary authorities..................	4 631 ..	....	....	....	....	....	....	....	....
General government..................	4 632 ..	....	....	....	....	....	....	....	....
Banks.................................	4 633 ..	....	....	....	....	....	....	....	....
Other sectors.........................	4 634 ..	−7.1	....	....	−135.7	−22.9	−115.0	−31.6	−64.6
Liabilities...................................	4 652 ..	**−5.9**	**6.0**	**7.1**	**66.8**	**−29.2**	**16.2**	**36.0**	**13.7**
Equity securities..........................	4 660 ..	−5.9	6.0	7.1	10.2	.6	61.6	35.9	9.4
Banks...................................	4 663 ..	....	....	....	....	....	....	....	....
Other sectors...........................	4 664 ..	−5.9	6.0	7.1	10.2	.6	61.6	35.9	9.4
Debt securities...........................	4 669 ..	....	....	....	56.6	−29.8	−45.4	.2	4.3
Bonds and notes........................	4 670 ..	....	....	....	56.6	−29.8	−45.4	.2	4.3
Monetary authorities..................	4 671 ..	....	....	....	....	....	....	....	....
General government..................	4 672 ..	....	....	....	56.6	−29.8	−45.4	.2	4.3
Banks.................................	4 673 ..	....	....	....	....	....	....	....	....
Other sectors.........................	4 674 ..	....	....	....	....	....	....	....	....
Money market instruments.............	4 680 ..	....	....	....	....	....	....	....	....
Monetary authorities..................	4 681 ..	....	....	....	....	....	....	....	....
General government..................	4 682 ..	....	....	....	....	....	....	....	....
Banks.................................	4 683 ..	....	....	....	....	....	....	....	....
Other sectors.........................	4 684 ..	....	....	....	....	....	....	....	....
C. FINANCIAL DERIVATIVES......................	4 910 ..	**−3.0**	....	....	....	....	....	....	....
Monetary authorities......................	4 911 ..	....	....	....	....	....	....	....	....
General government.......................	4 912 ..	....	....	....	....	....	....	....	....
Banks.....................................	4 913 ..	−3.0	....	....	....	....	....	....	....
Other sectors.............................	4 914 ..	....	....	....	....	....	....	....	....
Assets...	4 900 ..	....	....	....	....	....	....	....	....
Monetary authorities......................	4 901 ..	....	....	....	....	....	....	....	....
General government.......................	4 902 ..	....	....	....	....	....	....	....	....
Banks.....................................	4 903 ..	....	....	....	....	....	....	....	....
Other sectors.............................	4 904 ..	....	....	....	....	....	....	....	....
Liabilities...................................	4 905 ..	**−3.0**	....	....	....	....	....	....	....
Monetary authorities......................	4 906 ..	....	....	....	....	....	....	....	....
General government.......................	4 907 ..	....	....	....	....	....	....	....	....
Banks.....................................	4 908 ..	−3.0	....	....	....	....	....	....	....
Other sectors.............................	4 909 ..	....	....	....	....	....	....	....	....

Table 2 (Concluded). STANDARD PRESENTATION, 2000–2007

(Millions of U.S. dollars)

	Code	2000	2001	2002	2003	2004	2005	2006	2007
D. OTHER INVESTMENT	4 700 ..	−225.9	−98.2	−164.7	−70.2	−170.2	107.7	−46.1	−171.5
Assets	4 703 ..	−263.6	−152.7	−221.1	−220.7	−85.8	−152.2	−278.2	−140.5
Trade credits	4 706 ..	−5.1	−15.0	−1.3	−17.3	−21.6	−95.0	−91.3	2.5
General government	4 707 ..	....	....	....	....	....	....	....	....
of which: Short-term	4 709 ..	....	....	....	....	....	....	....	....
Other sectors	4 710 ..	−5.1	−15.0	−1.3	−17.3	−21.6	−95.0	−91.3	2.5
of which: Short-term	4 712 ..	*−5.1*	*−15.0*	*−1.3*	*−17.3*	*−21.6*	*−95.0*	*−91.3*	*2.5*
Loans	4 714 ..	−3.7	−.6	−.1	−5.8	−4.2	−20.5	−38.2	1.4
Monetary authorities	4 715 ..	....	....	....	....	....	....	....	....
of which: Short-term	4 718 ..	....	....	....	....	....	....	....	....
General government	4 719 ..	....	....	....	....	....	....	....	....
of which: Short-term	4 721 ..	....	....	....	....	....	....	....	....
Banks	4 722 ..	....	....	....	....	....	....	....	....
of which: Short-term	4 724 ..	....	....	....	....	....	....	....	....
Other sectors	4 725 ..	−3.7	−.6	−.1	−5.8	−4.2	−20.5	−38.2	1.4
of which: Short-term	4 727 ..	*−3.7*	*−.6*	*−.1*					
Currency and deposits	4 730 ..	−164.1	−84.4	−138.9	−124.0	62.0	−36.6	−148.7	−144.3
Monetary authorities	4 731 ..	....	....	....	....	....	....	....	....
General government	4 732 ..	....	....	....	....	....	....	....	....
Banks	4 733 ..	−135.0	−78.5	−112.9	−124.0	62.0	−36.6	−148.7	−144.3
Other sectors	4 734 ..	−29.1	−5.9	−26.0	....	....	....	....	....
Other assets	4 736 ..	−90.7	−52.6	−80.8	−73.7	−122.0	....	....	....
Monetary authorities	4 737 ..	....	....	....	....	....	....	....	....
of which: Short-term	4 739 ..	....	....	....	....	....	....	....	....
General government	4 740 ..	−90.4	−52.6	−80.8	−72.5	−122.0	....	....	....
of which: Short-term	4 742 ..	....	....	....	....	....	....	....	....
Banks	4 743 ..	....	....	....	....	....	....	....	....
of which: Short-term	4 745 ..	....	....	....	....	....	....	....	....
Other sectors	4 746 ..	−.4	....	....	−1.2	....	....	....	....
of which: Short-term	4 748 ..	*−.4*	....	....	....	....	....	....	....
Liabilities	4 753 ..	37.7	54.4	56.3	150.5	−84.4	259.9	232.1	−31.0
Trade credits	4 756 ..	−1.9	11.6	1.9	8.3	13.2	9.2	....	17.4
General government	4 757 ..	....	....	....	8.3	13.2	9.2	....	17.4
of which: Short-term	4 759 ..	....	....	....	*8.3*	*13.2*	*9.2*	....	*−11.3*
Other sectors	4 760 ..	−1.9	11.6	1.9	....	....	....	....	....
of which: Short-term	4 762 ..	*−1.9*	*11.6*	*1.9*	....	....	....	....	....
Loans	4 764 ..	−20.5	−10.9	−23.1	−21.8	−24.9	−9.4	−31.1	−28.7
Monetary authorities	4 765 ..	....	....	....	....	....	....	....	....
of which: Use of Fund credit and loans from the Fund	4 766 ..	....	....	....	....	....	....	....	....
of which: Short-term	4 768 ..	....	....	....	....	....	....	....	....
General government	4 769 ..	−22.5	−21.1	−23.1	−21.8	−24.9	−9.4	−31.1	−28.7
of which: Short-term	4 771 ..	....	....	....	....	....	....	....	....
Banks	4 772 ..	....	....	....	....	....	....	....	....
of which: Short-term	4 774 ..	....	....	....	....	....	....	....	....
Other sectors	4 775 ..	2.0	10.1	....	....	....	....	....	....
of which: Short-term	4 777 ..	....	*5.5*	....	....	....	....	....	....
Currency and deposits	4 780 ..	1.4	7.2	7.6	32.4	−2.2	202.9	10.6	−31.1
Monetary authorities	4 781 ..	....	....	....	....	....	....	....	....
General government	4 782 ..	....	....	....	....	....	....	....	....
Banks	4 783 ..	1.4	7.2	7.6	32.4	−2.2	202.9	10.6	−31.1
Other sectors	4 784 ..	....	....	....	....	....	....	....	....
Other liabilities	4 786 ..	58.8	46.5	69.9	131.6	−70.5	57.2	252.6	11.5
Monetary authorities	4 787 ..	....	....	....	....	....	....	....	....
of which: Short-term	4 789 ..	....	....	....	....	....	....	....	....
General government	4 790 ..	....	....	....	....	....	....	....	....
of which: Short-term	4 792 ..	....	....	....	....	....	....	....	....
Banks	4 793 ..	....	....	....	5.2	....	....	....	....
of which: Short-term	4 795 ..	....	....	....	*5.2*	....	....	....	....
Other sectors	4 796 ..	58.8	46.5	69.9	126.4	−70.5	57.2	252.6	11.5
of which: Short-term	4 798 ..	....	....	....	*126.4*	*−70.5*	*57.2*	*252.6*	*11.5*
E. RESERVE ASSETS	4 802 ..	−367.4	−170.0	−60.6	−171.5	56.9	−1,363.5	−1,755.6	−1,734.3
Monetary gold	4 812 ..	....	....	....	....	....	....	....	....
Special drawing rights	4 811 ..	−2.4	−2.1	−1.4	−1.2	−1.3	−1.7	−2.0	−2.3
Reserve position in the Fund	4 810 ..	6.4	−5.9	−2.1	−9.1	14.7	19.0	1.7	2.7
Foreign exchange	4 803 ..	−371.5	−162.0	1,774.7	1,254.3	−128.4	−2,041.2	−2,288.1	−1,710.2
Other claims	4 813 ..	....	....	−1,831.8	−1,415.4	172.0	660.3	532.7	−24.5
NET ERRORS AND OMISSIONS	4 998 ..	−1.9	75.8	105.6	65.5	−122.0	−319.0	−141.7	−123.9

Table 3. INTERNATIONAL INVESTMENT POSITION (End-period stocks), 2000–2007

(Millions of U.S. dollars)

	Code	2000	2001	2002	2003	2004	2005	2006	2007
ASSETS..	8 995 C.	**7,391.7**	**7,390.1**	**7,633.9**	**8,828.4**	**9,149.6**	**10,153.7**	**12,637.8**	**14,902.2**
Direct investment abroad..........................	8 505 ..	**516.6**	**865.8**	**1,023.7**	**1,446.6**	**950.1**	**796.0**	**757.9**	**914.0**
Equity capital and reinvested earnings............	8 506 ..	505.9	861.0	1,014.5	1,446.1	941.9	776.7	732.2	885.8
Claims on affiliated enterprises................	8 507 ..	505.9	861.0	1,014.5	1,446.1	941.9	776.7	732.2	885.8
Liabilities to affiliated enterprises..............	8 508 ..	....	....	....	....	....	....	....	....
Other capital..	8 530 ..	10.6	4.8	9.2	.6	8.2	19.3	25.7	28.2
Claims on affiliated enterprises................	8 535 ..	....	....	....	.6	8.2	19.3	25.7	28.2
Liabilities to affiliated enterprises..............	8 540 ..	....	....	....	....	....	....	....	....
Portfolio investment................................	8 602 ..	**226.1**	**296.8**	**755.8**	**1,583.0**	**2,093.5**	**2,607.3**	**3,119.1**	**3,480.0**
Equity securities.......................................	8 610 ..	129.7	197.7	430.4	1,013.5	1,485.4	1,819.4	2,368.5	2,798.2
Monetary authorities..............................	8 611 ..	....	....	....	....	....	....	....	....
General government..............................	8 612 ..	....	....	....	....	....	....	....	....
Banks..	8 613 ..	....	....	....	....	....	....	....	....
Other sectors.......................................	8 614 ..	129.7	197.7	430.4	1,013.5	1,485.4	1,819.4	2,368.5	2,798.2
Debt securities...	8 619 ..	96.4	99.1	325.3	569.5	608.2	787.8	750.6	681.8
Bonds and notes...................................	8 620 ..	96.5	99.1	325.3	569.5	608.2	787.8	750.6	681.8
Monetary authorities..........................	8 621 ..	....	....	....	....	....	....	....	....
General government..........................	8 622 ..	....	....	....	....	....	....	....	....
Banks..	8 623 ..	....	....	....	....	....	....	....	....
Other sectors...................................	8 624 ..	96.5	99.1	325.3	569.5	608.2	787.8	750.6	681.8
Money market instruments.......................	8 630 ..	....	....	....	....	....	....	....	....
Monetary authorities..........................	8 631 ..	....	....	....	....	....	....	....	....
General government..........................	8 632 ..	....	....	....	....	....	....	....	....
Banks..	8 633 ..	....	....	....	....	....	....	....	....
Other sectors...................................	8 634 ..	....	....	....	....	....	....	....	....
Financial derivatives...............................	8 900 ..	....	....	....	....	....	....	....	....
Monetary authorities...............................	8 901 ..	....	....	....	....	....	....	....	....
General government................................	8 902 ..	....	....	....	....	....	....	....	....
Banks...	8 903 ..	....	....	....	....	....	....	....	....
Other sectors..	8 904 ..	....	....	....	....	....	....	....	....
Other investment...................................	8 703 ..	**330.8**	**330.2**	**380.5**	**459.0**	**451.7**	**472.2**	**712.1**	**764.9**
Trade credits...	8 706 ..	17.1	12.9	18.0	45.4	83.8	114.4	138.1	71.3
General government..............................	8 707 ..	....	....	....	....	....	....	....	....
of which: Short-term........................	8 709 ..	....	....	....	....	....	....	....	....
Other sectors.......................................	8 710 ..	17.1	12.9	18.0	45.4	83.8	114.4	138.1	71.3
of which: Short-term........................	8 712 ..	*17.1*	*12.9*	*18.0*	*45.4*	*83.8*	*114.4*	*138.1*	*71.3*
Loans...	8 714 ..	....	3.8	.6	....	1.7	45.1	41.3	11.1
Monetary authorities..............................	8 715 ..	....	....	....	....	....	....	....	....
of which: Short-term........................	8 718 ..	....	....	....	....	....	....	....	....
General government..............................	8 719 ..	....	....	....	....	....	....	....	....
of which: Short-term........................	8 721 ..	....	....	....	....	....	....	....	....
Banks..	8 722 ..	....	....	....	....	....	....	....	....
of which: Short-term........................	8 724 ..	....	....	....	....	....	....	....	....
Other sectors.......................................	8 725 ..	....	3.8	.6	....	1.7	45.1	41.3	11.1
of which: Short-term........................	8 727 ..	....	*3.8*	*.6*	....	*1.7*	*45.1*	*41.3*	*11.1*
Currency and deposits...............................	8 730 ..	313.6	313.5	361.9	413.6	366.1	312.7	532.7	682.5
Monetary authorities..............................	8 731 ..	....	....	....	....	....	....	....	....
General government..............................	8 732 ..	....	....	....	....	....	....	....	....
Banks..	8 733 ..	250.9	274.3	361.9	413.6	366.1	312.7	532.7	682.5
Other sectors.......................................	8 734 ..	62.6	39.1	....	....	....	....	....	....
Other assets..	8 736 ..	.1	....	....	....	....	....	....	....
Monetary authorities..............................	8 737 ..	....	....	....	....	....	....	....	....
of which: Short-term........................	8 739 ..	....	....	....	....	....	....	....	....
General government..............................	8 740 ..	....	....	....	....	....	....	....	....
of which: Short-term........................	8 742 ..	....	....	....	....	....	....	....	....
Banks..	8 743 ..	....	....	....	....	....	....	....	....
of which: Short-term........................	8 745 ..	....	....	....	....	....	....	....	....
Other sectors.......................................	8 746 ..	.1	....	....	....	....	....	....	....
of which: Short-term........................	8 748 ..	*.1*	....	....	....	....	....	....	....
Reserve assets.......................................	8 802 ..	**6,318.2**	**5,897.2**	**5,473.9**	**5,339.8**	**5,654.2**	**6,278.2**	**8,048.7**	**9,743.2**
Monetary gold...	8 812 ..	....	....	....	....	....	....	....	....
Special drawing rights...............................	8 811 ..	38.9	39.6	44.4	49.8	53.5	50.8	55.5	60.7
Reserve position in the Fund......................	8 810 ..	23.1	28.0	32.4	45.0	31.8	10.6	9.4	7.0
Foreign exchange.....................................	8 803 ..	6,256.2	5,829.6	5,397.2	5,244.9	5,568.9	6,216.8	7,983.8	9,675.5
Other claims..	8 813 ..	....	....	....	....	....	....	....	....

Table 3 (Concluded). INTERNATIONAL INVESTMENT POSITION (End-period stocks), 2000–2007

(Millions of U.S. dollars)

	Code	2000	2001	2002	2003	2004	2005	2006	2007
LIABILITIES	8 995 D.	3,056.6	2,338.7	1,987.2	2,492.2	2,197.8	2,183.6	2,619.0	2,591.9
Direct investment in Botswana	8 555 ..	1,826.6	1,388.5	854.1	1,280.2	982.1	759.7	1,140.4	1,149.2
Equity capital and reinvested earnings	8 556 ..	665.3	574.0	807.0	1,192.8	926.6	644.4	1,067.5	1,136.3
Claims on direct investors	8 557 ..	....	....	....	....	....	....	....	....
Liabilities to direct investors	8 558 ..	665.3	574.0	807.0	1,192.8	926.6	644.4	1,067.5	1,136.3
Other capital	8 580 ..	1,161.3	814.5	47.1	87.3	55.5	115.2	72.9	13.0
Claims on direct investors	8 585 ..	....	....	....	....	....	....	....	....
Liabilities to direct investors	8 590 ..	1,161.3	814.5	47.1	87.3	55.5	115.2	72.9	13.0
Portfolio investment	8 652 ..	13.4	15.4	23.5	86.7	123.9	116.1	141.0	187.6
Equity securities	8 660 ..	12.7	14.8	23.5	86.7	69.7	116.1	140.8	187.6
Banks	8 663 ..	....	....	....	....	....	....	....	....
Other sectors	8 664 ..	12.7	14.8	23.5	86.7	69.7	116.1	140.8	187.6
Debt securities	8 669 ..	.7	.5	....	....	54.3	....	.2	....
Bonds and notes	8 670 ..	.7	.5	....	....	54.3	....	.2	....
Monetary authorities	8 671 ..	....	....	....	....	....	....	....	....
General government	8 672 ..	....	....	....	....	54.3	....	....	....
Banks	8 673 ..	....	....	....	....	....	....	....	....
Other sectors	8 674 ..	.7	.5	....	....	....	....	.2	....
Money market instruments	8 680 ..	....	....	....	....	....	....	....	....
Monetary authorities	8 681 ..	....	....	....	....	....	....	....	....
General government	8 682 ..	....	....	....	....	....	....	....	....
Banks	8 683 ..	....	....	....	....	....	....	....	....
Other sectors	8 684 ..	....	....	....	....	....	....	....	....
Financial derivatives	8 905 ..	....	....	....	....	....	....	....	....
Monetary authorities	8 906 ..	....	....	....	....	....	....	....	....
General government	8 907 ..	....	....	....	....	....	....	....	....
Banks	8 908 ..	....	....	....	....	....	....	....	....
Other sectors	8 909 ..	....	....	....	....	....	....	....	....
Other investment	8 753 ..	1,216.5	934.9	1,109.7	1,125.3	1,091.8	1,307.9	1,337.6	1,255.0
Trade credits	8 756 ..	71.9	51.9	52.1	89.3	179.1	151.1	275.9	161.3
General government	8 757 ..	....	....	....	....	10.0	9.6	8.4	5.9
of which: Short-term	8 759 ..	....	....	....	....	....	....	....	....
Other sectors	8 760 ..	71.9	51.9	52.1	89.3	169.1	141.5	267.5	155.4
of which: Short-term	8 762 ..	*71.9*	*51.9*	*52.1*	*89.3*	*169.1*	*141.5*	*267.5*	*155.4*
Loans	8 764 ..	927.0	627.0	746.8	639.1	569.6	569.1	525.4	728.5
Monetary authorities	8 765 ..	....	....	....	....	....	....	....	....
of which: Use of Fund credit and loans from the Fund	8 766 ..	....	....	....	....	....	....	....	....
of which: Short-term	8 768 ..	....	....	....	....	....	....	....	....
General government	8 769 ..	419.3	314.8	467.1	493.8	464.7	397.1	347.0	317.4
of which: Short-term	8 771 ..	....	....	....	....	....	....	....	....
Banks	8 772 ..	....	....	....	....	....	....	....	....
of which: Short-term	8 774 ..	....	....	....	....	....	....	....	....
Other sectors	8 775 ..	507.7	312.3	279.7	145.2	105.0	171.9	178.4	411.1
of which: Short-term	8 777 ..	*4.5*	....	....	....	....	....	....	....
Currency and deposits	8 780 ..	25.3	25.5	31.1	....	34.5	213.1	197.0	36.9
Monetary authorities	8 781 ..	....	....	....	....	....	....	....	....
General government	8 782 ..	....	....	....	....	....	....	....	....
Banks	8 783 ..	25.3	25.5	31.1	....	34.5	213.1	197.0	36.9
Other sectors	8 784 ..	....	....	....	....	....	....	....	....
Other liabilities	8 786 ..	192.3	230.4	279.7	396.9	308.5	374.6	339.3	328.3
Monetary authorities	8 787 ..	....	....	....	....	....	....	....	....
of which: Short-term	8 789 ..	....	....	....	....	....	....	....	....
General government	8 790 ..	....	....	....	....	....	....	....	....
of which: Short-term	8 792 ..	....	....	....	....	....	....	....	....
Banks	8 793 ..	....	....	....	....	....	....	....	....
of which: Short-term	8 795 ..	....	....	....	....	....	....	....	....
Other sectors	8 796 ..	192.3	230.4	279.7	396.9	308.5	374.6	339.3	328.3
of which: Short-term	8 798 ..	*192.3*	*171.2*	*279.7*	....	....	....	....	....
NET INTERNATIONAL INVESTMENT POSITION	8 995 ..	4,335.1	5,051.3	5,646.6	6,336.3	6,951.8	7,970.1	10,018.8	12,310.3
Conversion rates: pula per U.S. dollar (end of period)	0 102 ..	5.3619	6.9832	5.4675	4.4425	4.2808	5.5127	6.0314	6.0060

Table 1. ANALYTIC PRESENTATION, 2000–2007

(Millions of U.S. dollars)

	Code	2000	2001	2002	2003	2004	2005	2006	2007
A. Current Account[1]	4 993 Z.	**−24,225**	**−23,215**	**−7,637**	**4,177**	**11,738**	**13,984**	**13,620**	**1,460**
Goods: exports f.o.b.	2 100 ..	55,086	58,223	60,362	73,084	96,475	118,308	137,807	160,649
Goods: imports f.o.b.	3 100 ..	−55,783	−55,572	−47,240	−48,290	−62,809	−73,606	−91,350	−120,621
Balance on Goods	4 100 ..	*−698*	*2,650*	*13,121*	*24,794*	*33,666*	*44,703*	*46,458*	*40,028*
Services: credit	2 200 ..	9,498	9,322	9,551	10,447	12,584	16,047	19,462	23,895
Services: debit	3 200 ..	−16,660	−17,081	−14,509	−15,378	−17,260	−24,356	−29,116	−37,250
Balance on Goods and Services	4 991 ..	*−7,860*	*−5,109*	*8,164*	*19,863*	*28,990*	*36,394*	*36,804*	*26,673*
Income: credit	2 300 ..	3,621	3,280	3,295	3,339	3,199	3,194	6,438	11,493
Income: debit	3 300 ..	−21,507	−23,023	−21,486	−21,891	−23,719	−29,162	−33,927	−40,734
Balance on Goods, Services, and Income	4 992 ..	*−25,746*	*−24,852*	*−10,026*	*1,311*	*8,469*	*10,427*	*9,315*	*−2,569*
Current transfers: credit	2 379 Z.	1,828	1,934	2,627	3,132	3,582	4,050	4,846	4,972
Current transfers: debit	3 379 ..	−307	−296	−237	−265	−314	−493	−541	−943
B. Capital Account[1]	4 994 Z.	**273**	**−36**	**433**	**498**	**339**	**663**	**869**	**756**
Capital account: credit	2 994 Z.	300	328	464	535	764	906	1,084	1,089
Capital account: debit	3 994 ..	−28	−364	−31	−37	−425	−243	−215	−333
Total, Groups A Plus B	4 981 ..	*−23,952*	*−23,251*	*−7,204*	*4,675*	*12,077*	*14,647*	*14,489*	*2,216*
C. Financial Account[1]	4 995 W.	**29,376**	**20,331**	**−3,909**	**−157**	**−3,333**	**13,144**	**15,113**	**88,399**
Direct investment abroad	4 505 ..	−2,282	2,258	−2,482	−249	−9,471	−2,517	−28,202	−7,067
Direct investment in Brazil	4 555 Z.	32,779	22,457	16,590	10,144	18,166	15,066	18,782	34,585
Portfolio investment assets	4 602 ..	−1,696	−795	−321	179	−755	−1,771	523	286
Equity securities	4 610 ..	−1,953	−1,121	−389	−258	−121	−831	−915	−1,413
Debt securities	4 619 ..	258	326	67	437	−633	−940	1,438	1,699
Portfolio investment liabilities	4 652 Z.	8,651	872	−4,797	5,129	−3,996	6,655	9,051	48,104
Equity securities	4 660 ..	3,076	2,481	1,981	2,973	2,081	6,451	7,716	26,217
Debt securities	4 669 Z.	5,575	−1,609	−6,778	2,156	−6,076	204	1,335	21,887
Financial derivatives	4 910 ..	−197	−471	−356	−151	−677	−40	383	−710
Financial derivatives assets	4 900 ..	386	567	933	683	467	508	482	88
Financial derivatives liabilities	4 905 ..	−583	−1,038	−1,289	−834	−1,145	−548	−99	−799
Other investment assets	4 703 ..	−2,989	−6,586	−3,211	−9,483	−2,196	−5,035	−8,914	−18,723
Monetary authorities	4 701 ..	−18	2,430	2	....	....	....	2	....
General government	4 704 ..	193	−1,085	−979	−1,101	−1,227	−229	17	−328
Banks	4 705 ..	1,551	−3,561	4,335	−6,999	1,122	−2,211	−3,323	−11,337
Other sectors	4 728 ..	−4,715	−4,370	−6,569	−1,383	−2,091	−2,595	−5,610	−7,058
Other investment liabilities	4 753 W.	−4,890	2,596	−9,331	−5,724	−4,404	785	23,491	31,923
Monetary authorities	4 753 WA	−201	−171	−156	−162	−163	−164	−250	−209
General government	4 753 ZB	1,540	−26	−493	−1,561	−2,633	−1,637	−384	−618
Banks	4 753 ZC	1,718	−741	−3,835	348	1,385	841	3,426	17,897
Other sectors	4 753 ZD	−7,946	3,534	−4,847	−4,350	−2,993	1,745	20,699	14,852
Total, Groups A Through C	4 983 ..	*5,424*	*−2,919*	*−11,113*	*4,519*	*8,744*	*27,791*	*29,602*	*90,615*
D. Net Errors and Omissions	4 998 ..	**2,557**	**−498**	**−154**	**−933**	**−2,145**	**−225**	**967**	**−3,131**
Total, Groups A Through D	4 984 ..	*7,981*	*−3,418*	*−11,266*	*3,586*	*6,599*	*27,566*	*30,569*	*87,484*
E. Reserves and Related Items	4 802 A.	**−7,981**	**3,418**	**11,266**	**−3,586**	**−6,599**	**−27,566**	**−30,569**	**−87,484**
Reserve assets	4 802 ..	2,260	−3,311	−314	−8,479	−2,238	−4,324	−30,571	−87,484
Use of Fund credit and loans	4 766 ..	−6,795	6,729	11,580	4,893	−4,362	−23,243	....	....
Exceptional financing	4 920 ..	−3,446	....	....	....	....	....	2	....
Conversion rates: reais per U.S. dollar	0 101 ..	**1.82942**	**2.34963**	**2.92036**	**3.07748**	**2.92512**	**2.43439**	**2.17533**	**1.94706**

[1] Excludes components that have been classified in the categories of Group E.

Table 2. STANDARD PRESENTATION, 2000–2007

(Millions of U.S. dollars)

	Code	2000	2001	2002	2003	2004	2005	2006	2007
CURRENT ACCOUNT............................	4 993 ..	**−24,225**	**−23,215**	**−7,637**	**4,177**	**11,738**	**13,985**	**13,621**	**1,460**
A. GOODS............................	4 100 ..	**−698**	**2,650**	**13,121**	**24,794**	**33,666**	**44,703**	**46,458**	**40,028**
Credit............................	2 100 ..	**55,086**	**58,223**	**60,362**	**73,084**	**96,475**	**118,308**	**137,807**	**160,649**
General merchandise: exports f.o.b............	2 110 ..	53,676	56,820	59,178	71,636	96,091	117,850	137,149	157,059
Goods for processing: exports f.o.b...........	2 150 ..	....	....	....	....	....	....	....	....
Repairs on goods........................	2 160 ..	....	....	....	....	....	....	....	....
Goods procured in ports by carriers.........	2 170 ..	1,034	1,073	866	1,121	281	....	....	2,799
Nonmonetary gold.......................	2 180 ..	375	330	318	327	104	459	659	791
Debit............................	3 100 ..	**−55,783**	**−55,572**	**−47,240**	**−48,290**	**−62,809**	**−73,606**	**−91,350**	**−120,621**
General merchandise: imports f.o.b...........	3 110 ..	−55,121	−54,905	−46,616	−47,809	−62,348	−73,140	−91,349	−120,621
Goods for processing: imports f.o.b..........	3 150 ..	−472	−591	−537	−481	−461	−466	....	....
Repairs on goods........................	3 160 ..	....	....	....	....	....	....	....	....
Goods procured in ports by carriers.........	3 170 ..	....	....	....	....	....	....	....	....
Nonmonetary gold.......................	3 180 ..	−190	−76	−88	....	....	....	....	....
B. SERVICES............................	4 200 ..	**−7,162**	**−7,759**	**−4,957**	**−4,931**	**−4,677**	**−8,309**	**−9,654**	**−13,355**
Total credit............................	2 200 ..	*9,498*	*9,322*	*9,551*	*10,447*	*12,584*	*16,047*	*19,462*	*23,895*
Total debit............................	3 200 ..	*−16,660*	*−17,081*	*−14,509*	*−15,378*	*−17,260*	*−24,356*	*−29,116*	*−37,250*
Transportation services, credit............	2 205 ..	**1,409**	**1,422**	**1,536**	**1,822**	**2,467**	**3,139**	**3,439**	**4,059**
Passenger............................	2 850 ..	*159*	*113*	*144*	*194*	*167*	*307*	*261*	*331*
Freight............................	2 851 ..	*585*	*497*	*586*	*659*	*936*	*1,032*	*1,160*	*1,473*
Other............................	2 852 ..	*666*	*811*	*807*	*969*	*1,364*	*1,799*	*2,017*	*2,256*
Sea transport, passenger.................	2 207 ..	....	....	....	....	....	....	....	....
Sea transport, freight...................	2 208 ..	480	328	459	553	792	861	979	1,124
Sea transport, other....................	2 209 ..	622	752	752	889	1,286	1,740	1,918	2,170
Air transport, passenger.................	2 211 ..	159	113	143	193	165	306	260	330
Air transport, freight...................	2 212 ..	79	148	99	61	76	90	77	241
Air transport, other....................	2 213 ..	36	48	37	64	62	47	89	72
Other transport, passenger...............	2 215 ..	....	....	....	1	2	1	1	1
Other transport, freight.................	2 216 ..	26	21	28	44	69	81	104	108
Other transport, other..................	2 217 ..	8	11	18	16	15	12	10	15
Transportation services, debit............	3 205 ..	**−4,305**	**−4,388**	**−3,494**	**−3,412**	**−4,452**	**−5,089**	**−6,565**	**−8,580**
Passenger............................	3 850 ..	*−654*	*−566*	*−533*	*−613*	*−881*	*−1,185*	*−1,737*	*−2,223*
Freight............................	3 851 ..	*−1,473*	*−1,788*	*−1,278*	*−1,247*	*−1,613*	*−1,897*	*−2,296*	*−3,068*
Other............................	3 852 ..	*−2,178*	*−2,034*	*−1,683*	*−1,552*	*−1,957*	*−2,007*	*−2,531*	*−3,289*
Sea transport, passenger.................	3 207 ..	−2	−6	−2	−2	−8	−8	−1	−2
Sea transport, freight...................	3 208 ..	−1,333	−1,635	−1,147	−1,119	−1,438	−1,699	−2,055	−2,755
Sea transport, other....................	3 209 ..	−1,290	−1,262	−871	−939	−1,342	−1,587	−2,127	−2,849
Air transport, passenger.................	3 211 ..	−651	−560	−531	−611	−873	−1,178	−1,736	−2,222
Air transport, freight...................	3 212 ..	−71	−83	−72	−69	−97	−109	−130	−166
Air transport, other....................	3 213 ..	−888	−772	−811	−612	−615	−418	−403	−437
Other transport, passenger...............	3 215 ..	....	....	....	....	....	....	....	....
Other transport, freight.................	3 216 ..	−69	−70	−59	−59	−78	−90	−111	−146
Other transport, other..................	3 217 ..	−1	−1	−1	−1	−1	−1	−1	−3
Travel, credit............................	2 236 ..	**1,810**	**1,731**	**1,998**	**2,479**	**3,222**	**3,861**	**4,316**	**4,953**
Business travel.........................	2 237 ..	30	25	45	46	51	68	63	70
Personal travel.........................	2 240 ..	1,779	1,706	1,953	2,433	3,171	3,794	4,253	4,883
Travel, debit............................	3 236 ..	**−3,894**	**−3,199**	**−2,396**	**−2,261**	**−2,871**	**−4,720**	**−5,764**	**−8,211**
Business travel.........................	3 237 ..	−206	−194	−195	−198	−236	−291	−319	−370
Personal travel.........................	3 240 ..	−3,688	−3,004	−2,200	−2,063	−2,635	−4,429	−5,444	−7,841
Other services, credit......................	2 200 BA	**6,279**	**6,170**	**6,018**	**6,146**	**6,895**	**9,047**	**11,708**	**14,882**
Communications.........................	2 245 ..	36	242	135	449	243	239	205	276
Construction...........................	2 249 ..	228	18	12	10	3	8	23	17
Insurance..............................	2 253 ..	312	180	206	124	105	134	324	543
Financial..............................	2 260 ..	376	317	390	363	423	507	738	1,090
Computer and information................	2 262 ..	34	27	36	29	53	88	102	161
Royalties and licence fees................	2 266 ..	125	112	100	108	114	102	150	319
Other business services..................	2 268 ..	4,568	4,613	4,319	4,133	4,938	6,722	8,568	11,064
Personal, cultural, and recreational.........	2 287 ..	63	58	58	54	47	56	81	73
Government, n.i.e.......................	2 291 ..	537	604	761	877	969	1,192	1,517	1,340
Other services, debit......................	3 200 BA	**−8,461**	**−9,495**	**−8,618**	**−9,705**	**−9,937**	**−14,547**	**−16,788**	**−20,458**
Communications.........................	3 245 ..	−32	−213	−122	−366	−70	−112	−102	−96
Construction...........................	3 249 ..	....	....	....	....	−1	....	−4	−4
Insurance..............................	3 253 ..	−317	−455	−626	−560	−649	−702	−755	−1,308
Financial..............................	3 260 ..	−670	−624	−623	−745	−499	−737	−861	−807
Computer and information................	3 262 ..	−1,145	−1,133	−1,155	−1,063	−1,281	−1,713	−2,005	−2,273
Royalties and licence fees................	3 266 ..	−1,415	−1,244	−1,229	−1,228	−1,197	−1,404	−1,664	−2,259
Other business services..................	3 268 ..	−3,434	−4,203	−3,543	−4,379	−4,682	−7,480	−8,898	−10,586
Personal, cultural, and recreational.........	3 287 ..	−363	−365	−309	−337	−409	−451	−533	−651
Government, n.i.e.......................	3 291 ..	−1,087	−1,256	−1,013	−1,028	−1,149	−1,947	−1,967	−2,473

Table 2 (Continued). STANDARD PRESENTATION, 2000–2007

(Millions of U.S. dollars)

	Code	2000	2001	2002	2003	2004	2005	2006	2007
C. INCOME	4 300	**−17,886**	**−19,743**	**−18,191**	**−18,552**	**−20,520**	**−25,967**	**−27,489**	**−29,242**
Total credit	2 300	*3,621*	*3,280*	*3,295*	*3,339*	*3,199*	*3,194*	*6,438*	*11,493*
Total debit	3 300	*−21,507*	*−23,023*	*−21,486*	*−21,891*	*−23,719*	*−29,162*	*−33,927*	*−40,734*
Compensation of employees, credit	2 310	**237**	**270**	**293**	**269**	**354**	**325**	**397**	**497**
Compensation of employees, debit	3 310	**−158**	**−175**	**−191**	**−160**	**−173**	**−111**	**−220**	**−49**
Investment income, credit	2 320	**3,383**	**3,009**	**3,002**	**3,070**	**2,845**	**2,869**	**6,041**	**10,996**
Direct investment income	2 330	999	367	967	886	1,061	733	1,073	2,202
Dividends and distributed branch profits	2 332	932	264	857	760	916	641	928	1,152
Reinvested earnings and undistributed branch profits	2 333	....	....	....	....	....	....	....	....
Income on debt (interest)	2 334	67	103	109	126	145	92	145	1,050
Portfolio investment income	2 339	859	1,463	1,383	1,323	733	785	3,049	6,955
Income on equity	2 340	5	1	1	3	4	10	21	13
Income on bonds and notes	2 350	819	1,461	1,382	1,320	729	717	3,024	6,656
Income on money market instruments	2 360	35	1	....	....	....	58	4	286
Other investment income	2 370	1,525	1,179	653	861	1,051	1,351	1,919	1,839
Investment income, debit	3 320	**−21,348**	**−22,847**	**−21,295**	**−21,731**	**−23,546**	**−29,050**	**−33,707**	**−40,686**
Direct investment income	3 330	−4,238	−5,005	−5,950	−5,984	−6,860	−11,035	−13,884	−19,692
Dividends and distributed branch profits	3 332	−3,105	−3,702	−4,891	−4,836	−5,853	−9,783	−12,359	−17,898
Reinvested earnings and undistributed branch profits	3 333	....	....	....	....	....	....	....	....
Income on debt (interest)	3 334	−1,133	−1,303	−1,058	−1,148	−1,007	−1,253	−1,525	−1,794
Portfolio investment income	3 339	−9,404	−11,084	−9,767	−10,066	−11,173	−12,563	−14,101	−14,020
Income on equity	3 340	−1,148	−1,524	−1,129	−1,568	−2,404	−3,554	−4,945	−5,702
Income on bonds and notes	3 350	−8,256	−9,559	−8,638	−8,499	−8,768	−9,009	−9,156	−8,318
Income on money market instruments	3 360	....	....	....	....	....	....	....	....
Other investment income	3 370	−7,707	−6,758	−5,578	−5,681	−5,514	−5,452	−5,723	−6,974
D. CURRENT TRANSFERS	4 379	**1,521**	**1,638**	**2,390**	**2,867**	**3,268**	**3,558**	**4,306**	**4,029**
Credit	2 379	**1,828**	**1,934**	**2,627**	**3,132**	**3,582**	**4,051**	**4,847**	**4,972**
General government	2 380	42	73	57	48	54	81	86	139
Other sectors	2 390	1,785	1,860	2,570	3,084	3,529	3,969	4,761	4,833
Workers' remittances	2 391	1,112	1,178	1,711	2,018	2,459	2,480	2,890	2,809
Other current transfers	2 392	673	682	859	1,066	1,070	1,490	1,871	2,024
Debit	3 379	**−307**	**−296**	**−237**	**−265**	**−314**	**−493**	**−541**	**−943**
General government	3 380	−74	−64	−58	−68	−86	−140	−122	−129
Other sectors	3 390	−233	−232	−179	−197	−228	−353	−419	−813
Workers' remittances	3 391	−180	−169	−138	−136	−167	−263	−309	−514
Other current transfers	3 392	−53	−62	−41	−61	−61	−91	−110	−299
CAPITAL AND FINANCIAL ACCOUNT	4 996	**21,667**	**23,713**	**7,790**	**−3,245**	**−9,593**	**−13,760**	**−14,589**	**1,670**
CAPITAL ACCOUNT	4 994	**273**	**−36**	**433**	**498**	**339**	**663**	**869**	**756**
Total credit	2 994	*300*	*328*	*464*	*535*	*764*	*906*	*1,084*	*1,089*
Total debit	3 994	*−28*	*−364*	*−31*	*−37*	*−425*	*−243*	*−215*	*−333*
Capital transfers, credit	2 400	**300**	**326**	**445**	**535**	**763**	**905**	**1,083**	**1,077**
General government	2 401	....	....	....	....	....	....	....	....
Debt forgiveness	2 402	....	....	....	....	....	....	....	....
Other capital transfers	2 410	....	....	....	....	....	....	....	....
Other sectors	2 430	300	326	445	535	763	905	1,082	1,077
Migrants' transfers	2 431	300	326	445	535	763	735	966	1,077
Debt forgiveness	2 432	....	....	....	....	....	....	....	....
Other capital transfers	2 440	....	....	....	....	....	170	117	....
Capital transfers, debit	3 400	**−28**	**−364**	**−31**	**−37**	**−425**	**−243**	**−213**	**−333**
General government	3 401	....	....	....	....	−364	....	....	....
Debt forgiveness	3 402	....	....	....	....	−364	....	....	....
Other capital transfers	3 410	....	....	....	....	....	....	....	....
Other sectors	3 430	−28	−364	−31	−37	−61	−243	−213	−333
Migrants' transfers	3 431	−28	−364	−31	−37	−61	−124	−161	−333
Debt forgiveness	3 432	....	....	....	....	....	−85	....	....
Other capital transfers	3 440	....	....	....	....	....	−34	−52	....
Nonproduced nonfinancial assets, credit	2 480	**....**	**2**	**19**	**1**	**2**	**1**	**1**	**12**
Nonproduced nonfinancial assets, debit	3 480	**....**	**....**	**....**	**....**	**....**	**....**	**−1**	**....**

Table 2 (Continued). STANDARD PRESENTATION, 2000–2007

(Millions of U.S. dollars)

	Code	2000	2001	2002	2003	2004	2005	2006	2007
FINANCIAL ACCOUNT	4 995	21,395	23,749	7,358	−3,743	−9,932	−14,423	−15,458	915
A. DIRECT INVESTMENT	4 500	30,498	24,715	14,108	9,894	8,695	12,550	−9,420	27,518
Direct investment abroad	4 505	−2,282	2,258	−2,482	−249	−9,471	−2,517	−28,202	−7,067
Equity capital	4 510	−1,755	1,752	−2,402	−62	−6,640	−2,695	−23,413	−10,091
Claims on affiliated enterprises	4 515	−1,755	1,752	−2,402	−62	−6,640	−2,695	−23,413	−10,091
Liabilities to affiliated enterprises	4 520	....	....	....	....	....	....	....	....
Reinvested earnings	4 525	....	....	....	....	....	....	....	....
Other capital	4 530	−527	505	−81	−187	−2,831	178	−4,789	3,025
Claims on affiliated enterprises	4 535	−547	−268	−79	−187	−2,834	103	−4,773	−5,823
Liabilities to affiliated enterprises	4 540	20	773	−2	....	3	75	−16	8,848
Direct investment in Brazil	4 555	32,779	22,457	16,590	10,144	18,166	15,066	18,782	34,585
Equity capital	4 560	30,016	18,765	17,118	9,320	18,570	15,045	15,373	26,074
Claims on direct investors	4 565	....	....	....	....	....	....	....	....
Liabilities to direct investors	4 570	30,016	18,765	17,118	9,320	18,570	15,045	15,373	26,074
Reinvested earnings	4 575	....	....	....	....	....	....	....	....
Other capital	4 580	2,763	3,692	−528	823	−405	21	3,409	8,510
Claims on direct investors	4 585	−196	4	2	21	−12	−319	−612	−1,147
Liabilities to direct investors	4 590	2,959	3,688	−529	803	−392	340	4,021	9,657
B. PORTFOLIO INVESTMENT	4 600	6,955	77	−5,119	5,308	−4,750	4,885	9,573	48,390
Assets	4 602	−1,696	−795	−321	179	−755	−1,771	523	286
Equity securities	4 610	−1,953	−1,121	−389	−258	−121	−831	−915	−1,413
Monetary authorities	4 611	....	....	....	....	....	....	....	....
General government	4 612	....	....	....	....	....	....	....	....
Banks	4 613	−2,891	−605	−335	−155	−71	−383	−811	−1,409
Other sectors	4 614	938	−516	−54	−103	−50	−448	−104	−5
Debt securities	4 619	258	326	67	437	−633	−940	1,438	1,699
Bonds and notes	4 620	258	326	67	437	−633	−519	858	1,789
Monetary authorities	4 621	....	....	....	....	....	....	....	140
General government	4 622	245	353	34	359	8	....	846	....
Banks	4 623	27	75	35	−66	−144	−891	−235	998
Other sectors	4 624	−15	−103	−2	143	−496	372	248	652
Money market instruments	4 630	....	....	....	....	....	−421	579	−90
Monetary authorities	4 631	....	....	....	....	....	....	....	....
General government	4 632	....	....	....	....	....	....	....	....
Banks	4 633	....	....	....	....	....	....	....	−90
Other sectors	4 634	....	....	....	....	....	−421	579	....
Liabilities	4 652	8,651	872	−4,797	5,129	−3,996	6,655	9,051	48,104
Equity securities	4 660	3,076	2,481	1,981	2,973	2,081	6,451	7,716	26,217
Banks	4 663	518	1,410	1,874	989	278	1,380	2,085	3,459
Other sectors	4 664	2,558	1,071	107	1,983	1,803	5,071	5,631	22,759
Debt securities	4 669	5,575	−1,609	−6,778	2,156	−6,076	204	1,335	21,887
Bonds and notes	4 670	5,335	−2,205	−5,959	1,721	−6,513	−506	−2,827	11,302
Monetary authorities	4 671	−16	−6	−7	27	16	69	43	....
General government	4 672	3,809	3,398	1,910	1,154	192	2,976	−6,614	5,878
Banks	4 673	−103	−4,472	−3,384	541	−2,913	−101	3,130	4,542
Other sectors	4 674	1,645	−1,124	−4,477	−1	−3,808	−3,450	614	882
Money market instruments	4 680	240	596	−819	435	436	710	4,161	10,585
Monetary authorities	4 681	−10	−4	−5	17	10	44	28	....
General government	4 682	−54	−21	−14	91	54	232	4,043	6,934
Banks	4 683	154	554	−391	−233	−310	577	805	3,765
Other sectors	4 684	150	67	−409	560	682	−142	−714	−114
C. FINANCIAL DERIVATIVES	4 910	−197	−471	−356	−151	−677	−40	383	−710
Monetary authorities	4 911	....	....	....	....	....	....	....	....
General government	4 912	....	....	....	....	....	....	....	....
Banks	4 913	−194	−441	−301	71	58	206	362	−196
Other sectors	4 914	−3	−30	−56	−222	−735	−246	21	−514
Assets	4 900	386	567	933	683	467	508	482	88
Monetary authorities	4 901	....	....	....	....	....	....	....	....
General government	4 902	....	....	....	....	....	....	....	....
Banks	4 903	296	458	752	623	814	411	134	37
Other sectors	4 904	90	108	181	59	−347	97	348	51
Liabilities	4 905	−583	−1,038	−1,289	−834	−1,145	−548	−99	−799
Monetary authorities	4 906	....	....	....	....	....	....	....	....
General government	4 907	....	....	....	....	....	....	....	....
Banks	4 908	−490	−900	−1,052	−552	−757	−205	228	−234
Other sectors	4 909	−93	−138	−237	−282	−388	−343	−327	−565

Table 2 (Concluded). STANDARD PRESENTATION, 2000–2007

(Millions of U.S. dollars)

	Code	2000	2001	2002	2003	2004	2005	2006	2007
D. OTHER INVESTMENT	4 700	−18,121	2,739	−962	−10,314	−10,962	−27,493	14,577	13,201
Assets	4 703	−2,989	−6,586	−3,211	−9,483	−2,196	−5,035	−8,914	−18,723
Trade credits	4 706	....	....	....	....	....	....	....	....
General government	4 707	....	....	....	....	....	....	....	....
of which: Short-term	4 709	....	....	....	....	....	....	....	....
Other sectors	4 710	....	....	....	....	....	....	....	....
of which: Short-term	4 712	....	....	....	....	....	....	....	....
Loans	4 714	−282	−1,050	−1,740	−541	−1,599	−1,840	−5,015	−1,773
Monetary authorities	4 715	....	....	....	....	....	....	....	....
of which: Short-term	4 718	....	....	....	....	....	....	....	....
General government	4 719	365	−1,286	−717	−910	−1,183	....	....	....
of which: Short-term	4 721	12	14	64	43	56	....	....	....
Banks	4 722	238	390	−6	8	−279	−1,014	−1,600	−592
of which: Short-term	4 724	238	390	−6	8	−279	−12	−11	−305
Other sectors	4 725	−885	−154	−1,017	361	−137	−825	−3,414	−1,182
of which: Short-term	4 727	−157	−96	−74	73	−48	44	−25	122
Currency and deposits	4 730	−1,774	−8,001	−1,300	−8,579	−668	−2,930	−3,241	−16,283
Monetary authorities	4 731	....	−10	....	....	....	....	....	....
General government	4 732	−127	201	−159	−115	20	−198	17	−328
Banks	4 733	1,321	−3,857	4,341	−7,009	1,407	−1,187	−1,732	−10,712
Other sectors	4 734	−2,968	−4,335	−5,482	−1,455	−2,096	−1,546	−1,526	−5,243
Other assets	4 736	−933	2,465	−172	−363	72	−265	−658	−666
Monetary authorities	4 737	−18	2,440	2	....	....	....	2	....
of which: Short-term	4 739	....	....	....	....	....	....	....	....
General government	4 740	−45	1	−104	−76	−64	−32	....	....
of which: Short-term	4 742	....	−3	....	−3	....	....	....	....
Banks	4 743	−8	−94	....	1	−6	−10	10	−33
of which: Short-term	4 745	−8	−94	....	1	−6	−10	10	−33
Other sectors	4 746	−862	119	−70	−288	142	−223	−670	−633
of which: Short-term	4 748	−820	138	−49	−284	116	−86	−470	−373
Liabilities	4 753	−15,131	9,325	2,250	−831	−8,766	−22,458	23,491	31,923
Trade credits	4 756	−6,409	4,233	1,741	−34	1,156	3,585	12,314	17,511
General government	4 757	....	....	....	....	....	....	....	....
of which: Short-term	4 759	....	....	....	....	....	....	....	....
Other sectors	4 760	−6,409	4,233	1,741	−34	1,156	3,585	12,314	17,511
of which: Short-term	4 762	−3,422	3,753	3,111	926	2,542	4,526	13,155	17,378
Loans	4 764	−8,693	5,687	1,131	−1,425	−10,440	−26,725	9,753	13,794
Monetary authorities	4 765	−10,352	6,611	11,463	4,768	−4,493	−23,374	−138	−138
of which: Use of Fund credit and loans from the Fund	4 766	−6,795	6,729	11,580	4,893	−4,362	−23,243	....	....
of which: Short-term	4 768	....	....	....	....	....	....	....	....
General government	4 769	1,540	−26	−493	−1,561	−2,633	−1,637	−384	−618
of which: Short-term	4 771	....	....	....	....	....	....	....	....
Banks	4 772	1,658	−201	−3,251	−316	835	127	1,889	17,214
of which: Short-term	4 774	−254	−655	−2,246	−89	−130	−398	153	13,806
Other sectors	4 775	−1,537	−698	−6,588	−4,316	−4,149	−1,840	8,387	−2,664
of which: Short-term	4 777	−823	−1,220	−2,765	−1,354	−1,054	−661	−669	−36
Currency and deposits	4 780	−33	−596	−621	625	517	567	1,419	607
Monetary authorities	4 781	−90	−53	−38	−37	−31	−33	−112	−70
General government	4 782	....	....	....	....	....	....	....	....
Banks	4 783	57	−543	−583	662	549	600	1,532	672
Other sectors	4 784	....	....	....	....	....	....	−1	5
Other liabilities	4 786	4	2	....	3	1	115	5	11
Monetary authorities	4 787	....	....	....	....	....	....	....	....
of which: Short-term	4 789	....	....	....	....	....	....	....	....
General government	4 790	....	....	....	....	....	....	....	....
of which: Short-term	4 792	....	....	....	....	....	....	....	....
Banks	4 793	4	3	....	3	1	115	5	11
of which: Short-term	4 795	....	....	....	....	....	115	5	11
Other sectors	4 796	....	−1	....	....	....	....	....	....
of which: Short-term	4 798	....	−1	....	....	....	....	....	....
E. RESERVE ASSETS	4 802	2,260	−3,311	−314	−8,479	−2,238	−4,324	−30,571	−87,484
Monetary gold	4 812	330	394	53	43	14	51	76	129
Special drawing rights	4 811	6	−11	−256	278	3	−30	21	6
Reserve position in the Fund	4 810	....	....	....	....	....	....	....	....
Foreign exchange	4 803	1,897	−3,721	−120	−8,776	−2,283	−4,308	−30,665	−87,631
Other claims	4 813	28	26	9	−24	28	−37	−3	11
NET ERRORS AND OMISSIONS	4 998	2,557	−498	−154	−933	−2,145	−225	967	−3,131

Table 3. INTERNATIONAL INVESTMENT POSITION (End-period stocks), 2000–2007

(Millions of U.S. dollars)

	Code	2000	2001	2002	2003	2004	2005	2006	2007
ASSETS	8 995 C.	....	107,086	112,914	134,223	148,536	168,182	238,924	369,862
Direct investment abroad	8 505 ..	....	49,689	54,423	54,892	69,196	79,259	113,925	130,986
Equity capital and reinvested earnings	8 506 ..	....	42,584	43,397	44,769	54,027	65,418	97,465	107,556
Claims on affiliated enterprises	8 507 ..	....	42,584	43,397	44,769	54,027	65,418	97,465	107,556
Liabilities to affiliated enterprises	8 508 ..	....	....	....	....	....	....	....	....
Other capital	8 530 ..	....	7,104	11,026	10,123	15,169	13,842	16,460	23,430
Claims on affiliated enterprises	8 535 ..	....	7,104	11,026	10,123	15,169	13,842	16,460	23,430
Liabilities to affiliated enterprises	8 540 ..	....	....	....	....	....	....	....	....
Portfolio investment	8 602 ..	....	6,402	5,845	6,950	9,353	10,834	14,429	15,337
Equity securities	8 610 ..	....	3,001	2,388	2,596	2,352	2,809	3,754	5,167
Monetary authorities	8 611 ..	....	....	....	....	....	....	....	....
General government	8 612 ..	....	....	....	....	....	....	....	....
Banks	8 613 ..	....	625	120	140	170	143	1,100	2,509
Other sectors	8 614 ..	....	2,376	2,268	2,456	2,182	2,666	2,654	2,658
Debt securities	8 619 ..	....	3,401	3,457	4,354	7,001	8,026	10,675	10,170
Bonds and notes	8 620 ..	....	1,816	2,337	2,496	4,028	4,850	6,185	5,590
Monetary authorities	8 621 ..	....	1,239	1,395	1,004	1,129	1,249	....	1,054
General government	8 622 ..	....	....	....	....	....	....	....	....
Banks	8 623 ..	....	84	200	291	772	1,265	4,361	3,364
Other sectors	8 624 ..	....	493	742	1,200	2,127	2,336	1,824	1,172
Money market instruments	8 630 ..	....	1,585	1,120	1,859	2,973	3,176	4,490	4,580
Monetary authorities	8 631 ..	....	....	....	....	....	....	....	....
General government	8 632 ..	....	....	....	....	....	....	....	....
Banks	8 633 ..	....	230	182	340	862	580	1,994	2,084
Other sectors	8 634 ..	....	1,355	938	1,519	2,111	2,596	2,496	2,496
Financial derivatives	8 900 ..	....	42	105	81	109	119	113	25
Monetary authorities	8 901 ..	....	....	....	....	....	....	....	....
General government	8 902 ..	....	....	....	....	....	....	....	....
Banks	8 903 ..	....	....	58	3	30	....	....	−37
Other sectors	8 904 ..	....	42	47	78	79	119	113	62
Other investment	8 703 ..	....	15,087	14,705	23,004	16,943	24,171	24,617	43,180
Trade credits	8 706 ..	....	155	313	186	68	98	70	70
General government	8 707 ..	....	....	....	....	....	....	....	....
of which: Short-term	8 709 ..	....	....	....	....	....	....	....	....
Other sectors	8 710 ..	....	155	313	186	68	98	70	70
of which: Short-term	8 712 ..	....	*99*	*228*	*160*	*51*	*76*	*49*	*49*
Loans	8 714 ..	....	697	540	687	631	727	562	2,336
Monetary authorities	8 715 ..	....	....	....	....	....	....	....	....
of which: Short-term	8 718 ..	....	....	....	....	....	....	....	....
General government	8 719 ..	....	....	....	....	....	....	....	....
of which: Short-term	8 721 ..	....	....	....	....	....	....	....	....
Banks	8 722 ..	....	5	7	20	7	5	3	594
of which: Short-term	8 724 ..	....	....	*5*	*15*	*5*	*2*	*1*	*306*
Other sectors	8 725 ..	....	692	533	667	625	722	560	1,741
of which: Short-term	8 727 ..	....	*213*	*66*	*36*	*65*	*158*	*101*	*−21*
Currency and deposits	8 730 ..	....	9,441	7,890	16,412	10,418	17,077	17,200	33,368
Monetary authorities	8 731 ..	....	....	....	....	....	....	....	57
General government	8 732 ..	....	....	....	....	....	2	2	330
Banks	8 733 ..	....	5,328	3,872	10,740	6,824	12,334	10,477	21,168
Other sectors	8 734 ..	....	4,113	4,018	5,672	3,594	4,741	6,721	11,814
Other assets	8 736 ..	....	4,794	5,962	5,718	5,826	6,269	6,785	7,407
Monetary authorities	8 737 ..	....	1,383	1,357	1,230	1,230	1,363	1,121	1,076
of which: Short-term	8 739 ..	....	....	....	....	....	....	....	....
General government	8 740 ..	....	....	....	....	....	32	....	....
of which: Short-term	8 742 ..	....	....	....	....	....	....	....	....
Banks	8 743 ..	....	188	172	90	1	1	219	252
of which: Short-term	8 745 ..	....	*188*	*33*	*2*	....	....	*5*	*39*
Other sectors	8 746 ..	....	3,223	4,433	4,398	4,596	4,874	5,445	6,078
of which: Short-term	8 748 ..	....	*429*	*238*	*215*	*274*	*979*	*1,523*	*1,896*
Reserve assets	8 802 ..	....	35,866	37,837	49,296	52,935	53,799	85,839	180,334
Monetary gold	8 812 ..	....	127	153	186	195	225	277	366
Special drawing rights	8 811 ..	....	11	275	2	4	29	8	2
Reserve position in the Fund	8 810 ..	....	....	....	....	....	....	....	....
Foreign exchange	8 803 ..	....	35,700	37,375	49,051	52,707	53,479	85,484	179,908
Other claims	8 813 ..	....	29	33	57	29	66	69	58

Table 3 (Concluded). INTERNATIONAL INVESTMENT POSITION (End-period stocks), 2000–2007

(Millions of U.S. dollars)

	Code	2000	2001	2002	2003	2004	2005	2006	2007
LIABILITIES	8 995 D.	....	372,052	343,466	406,778	446,229	499,268	623,300	939,071
Direct investment in Brazil	8 555 ..	....	121,948	100,863	132,818	161,259	195,562	236,186	328,455
Equity capital and reinvested earnings	8 556 ..	....	105,815	83,884	112,334	142,451	177,024	209,403	281,179
Claims on direct investors	8 557 ..	....	....	....	....	....	....	....	....
Liabilities to direct investors	8 558 ..	....	105,815	83,884	112,334	142,451	177,024	209,403	281,179
Other capital	8 580 ..	....	16,133	16,978	20,484	18,808	18,537	26,783	47,276
Claims on direct investors	8 585 ..	....	....	....	....	....	....	....	....
Liabilities to direct investors	8 590 ..	....	16,133	16,978	20,484	18,808	18,537	26,783	47,276
Portfolio investment	8 652 ..	....	151,741	137,355	166,095	184,758	232,627	303,583	509,648
Equity securities	8 660 ..	....	36,910	27,249	53,138	77,261	125,532	191,513	363,999
Banks	8 663 ..	....	....	....	....	....	....	....	....
Other sectors	8 664 ..	....	36,910	27,249	53,138	77,261	125,532	191,513	363,999
Debt securities	8 669 ..	....	114,831	110,106	112,957	107,497	107,096	112,070	145,650
Bonds and notes	8 670 ..	....	113,631	109,106	111,343	107,253	106,195	110,282	139,711
Monetary authorities	8 671 ..	....	....	....	....	....	....	....	....
General government	8 672 ..	....	....	....	....	....	....	....	....
Banks	8 673 ..	....	....	....	....	....	....	....	....
Other sectors	8 674 ..	....	113,631	109,106	111,343	107,253	106,195	110,282	139,711
Money market instruments	8 680 ..	....	1,200	1,000	1,614	244	901	1,788	5,939
Monetary authorities	8 681 ..	....	....	....	....	....	....	....	....
General government	8 682 ..	....	....	....	....	....	....	....	....
Banks	8 683 ..	....	....	....	....	....	....	....	....
Other sectors	8 684 ..	....	1,200	1,000	1,614	244	901	1,788	5,939
Financial derivatives	8 905 ..	....	45	250	125	320	219	445	1,771
Monetary authorities	8 906 ..	....	....	....	....	....	....	....	....
General government	8 907 ..	....	....	....	....	....	....	....	....
Banks	8 908 ..	....	....	....	....	....	....	....	....
Other sectors	8 909 ..	....	45	250	125	320	219	445	1,771
Other investment	8 753 ..	....	98,317	104,999	107,740	99,892	70,859	83,087	99,197
Trade credits	8 756 ..	....	6,025	5,919	5,465	4,728	4,772	5,216	5,197
General government	8 757 ..	....	....	....	....	....	....	....	....
of which: Short-term	8 759 ..	....	....	....	....	....	....	....	....
Other sectors	8 760 ..	....	6,025	5,919	5,465	4,728	4,772	5,216	5,197
of which: Short-term	8 762 ..	....	*628*	*1,023*	*428*	*314*	*349*	*347*	*134*
Loans	8 764 ..	....	90,711	97,213	99,436	92,216	62,729	73,466	89,003
Monetary authorities	8 765 ..	....	9,121	21,492	28,857	25,477	301	157	14
of which: Use of Fund credit and loans from the Fund	8 766 ..	*1,768*	*8,337*	*20,827*	*28,317*	*25,029*	....	....	....
of which: Short-term	8 768 ..	....	....	....	....	....	....	....	....
General government	8 769 ..	....	....	....	....	....	....	....	....
of which: Short-term	8 771 ..	....	....	....	....	....	....	....	....
Banks	8 772 ..	....	6,324	7,102	5,768	7,161	5,012	4,348	7,801
of which: Short-term	8 774 ..	....	*6,324*	*7,102*	*5,768*	*7,161*	*5,012*	*4,348*	*7,801*
Other sectors	8 775 ..	....	75,265	68,619	64,811	59,578	57,416	68,962	81,188
of which: Short-term	8 777 ..	....	*19,506*	*14,271*	*12,384*	*11,025*	*12,514*	*13,840*	*25,026*
Currency and deposits	8 780 ..	....	1,582	1,867	2,839	2,948	3,358	4,405	4,996
Monetary authorities	8 781 ..	....	129	237	108	100	111	83	73
General government	8 782 ..	....	....	....	....	....	....	....	....
Banks	8 783 ..	....	1,453	1,630	2,731	2,848	3,246	4,321	4,923
Other sectors	8 784 ..	....	....	....	....	....	....	....	....
Other liabilities	8 786 ..	....	....	....	....	....	....	....	....
Monetary authorities	8 787 ..	....	....	....	....	....	....	....	....
of which: Short-term	8 789 ..	....	....	....	....	....	....	....	....
General government	8 790 ..	....	....	....	....	....	....	....	....
of which: Short-term	8 792 ..	....	....	....	....	....	....	....	....
Banks	8 793 ..	....	....	....	....	....	....	....	....
of which: Short-term	8 795 ..	....	....	....	....	....	....	....	....
Other sectors	8 796 ..	....	....	....	....	....	....	....	....
of which: Short-term	8 798 ..	....	....	....	....	....	....	....	....
NET INTERNATIONAL INVESTMENT POSITION	8 995 ..	....	−264,965	−230,552	−272,555	−297,693	−331,085	−384,377	−569,209
Conversion rates: reais per U.S. dollar (end of period)	0 102 ..	1.95460	2.31960	3.53250	2.88840	2.65360	2.33990	2.13720	1.77050

Table 1. ANALYTIC PRESENTATION, 2000–2007
(Millions of U.S. dollars)

	Code	2000	2001	2002	2003	2004	2005	2006	2007
A. Current Account¹................................	4 993 Z.	. . . .	**1,775**	**1,531**	**2,279**	**2,896**	**4,038**	**5,232**	. . . .
Goods: exports f.o.b.....................	2 100 ..	. . . .	3,640	3,702	4,422	5,066	6,247	7,627	. . . .
Goods: imports f.o.b.....................	3 100 ..	. . . .	−1,082	−1,475	−1,258	−1,338	−1,413	−1,586	. . . .
Balance on Goods.............................	4 100 ..	. . . .	*2,558*	*2,227*	*3,164*	*3,728*	*4,834*	*6,041*	. . . .
Services: credit............................	2 200 ..	. . . .	482	427	437	544	617	744	. . . .
Services: debit............................	3 200 ..	. . . .	−1,053	−876	−1,032	−1,075	−1,110	−1,213	. . . .
Balance on Goods and Services..........	4 991 ..	. . . .	*1,986*	*1,777*	*2,569*	*3,197*	*4,340*	*5,572*	. . . .
Income: credit............................	2 300 ..	. . . .	244	235	214	236	263	248	. . . .
Income: debit............................	3 300 ..	. . . .	−186	−172	−214	−228	−190	−183	. . . .
Balance on Goods, Services, and Income......	4 992 ..	. . . .	*2,044*	*1,840*	*2,569*	*3,205*	*4,413*	*5,638*	. . . .
Current transfers: credit................	2 379 Z.	. . . .	. . . .	. . . .	. . . .	. . . .	. . . .	. . . .	. . . .
Current transfers: debit................	3 379 ..	. . . .	−269	−310	−290	−309	−376	−405	. . . .
B. Capital Account¹................................	4 994 Z.	. . . .	**−1**	**−1**	**−1**	**−11**	**−11**	**−7**	. . . .
Capital account: credit................	2 994 Z.	. . . .	. . . .	. . . .	. . . .	. . . .	. . . .	. . . .	. . . .
Capital account: debit................	3 994 ..	. . . .	−1	−1	−1	−11	−11	−7	. . . .
Total, Groups A Plus B...................	4 981 ..	. . . .	*1,774*	*1,530*	*2,277*	*2,885*	*4,026*	*5,225*	. . . .
C. Financial Account¹...........................	4 995 W.	. . . .	**234**	**612**	**−627**	**−1,152**	**−85**	**575**	. . . .
Direct investment abroad................	4 505 ..	. . . .	. . . .	. . . .	. . . .	−41	. . . .	−18	. . . .
Direct investment in Brunei Darussalam........	4 555 Z.	. . . .	74	234	114	81	176	88	. . . .
Portfolio investment assets............	4 602 ..	. . . .	−180	8	60	−45	21	−90	. . . .
Equity securities.....................	4 610 ..	. . . .	−161	1	68	−56	12	−90	. . . .
Debt securities......................	4 619 ..	. . . .	−18	7	−8	11	9	. . . .	. . . .
Portfolio investment liabilities........	4 652 Z.	. . . .	. . . .	. . . .	. . . .	. . . .	. . . .	. . . .	. . . .
Equity securities.....................	4 660 ..	. . . .	. . . .	. . . .	. . . .	. . . .	. . . .	. . . .	. . . .
Debt securities......................	4 669 Z.	. . . .	. . . .	. . . .	. . . .	. . . .	. . . .	. . . .	. . . .
Financial derivatives...................	4 910 ..	. . . .	. . . .	. . . .	. . . .	. . . .	. . . .	. . . .	. . . .
Financial derivatives assets............	4 900 ..	. . . .	. . . .	. . . .	. . . .	. . . .	. . . .	. . . .	. . . .
Financial derivatives liabilities........	4 905 ..	. . . .	. . . .	. . . .	. . . .	. . . .	. . . .	. . . .	. . . .
Other investment assets................	4 703 ..	. . . .	349	308	−604	−1,559	−498	334	. . . .
Monetary authorities................	4 701 ..	. . . .	. . . .	. . . .	. . . .	. . . .	. . . .	. . . .	. . . .
General government................	4 704 ..	. . . .	−1	−1	−1	−1	−1	−1	. . . .
Banks................................	4 705 ..	. . . .	385	237	−528	−991	−650	637	. . . .
Other sectors.......................	4 728 ..	. . . .	−35	72	−75	−568	153	−302	. . . .
Other investment liabilities............	4 753 W.	. . . .	−10	62	−198	413	217	261	. . . .
Monetary authorities................	4 753 WA	. . . .	. . . .	. . . .	. . . .	. . . .	. . . .	. . . .	. . . .
General government................	4 753 ZB	. . . .	. . . .	. . . .	. . . .	. . . .	. . . .	. . . .	. . . .
Banks................................	4 753 ZC	. . . .	126	−19	−73	−22	210	210	. . . .
Other sectors.......................	4 753 ZD	. . . .	−136	80	−124	435	6	50	. . . .
Total, Groups A Through C...............	4 983 ..	. . . .	*2,008*	*2,142*	*1,650*	*1,733*	*3,941*	*5,800*	. . . .
D. Net Errors and Omissions...................	4 998 ..	. . . .	**−2,016**	**−2,102**	**−1,628**	**−1,705**	**−3,950**	**−5,770**	. . . .
Total, Groups A Through D...............	4 984 ..	. . . .	*−8*	*40*	*23*	*28*	*−9*	*30*	. . . .
E. Reserves and Related Items...............	4 802 A.	. . . .	**8**	**−40**	**−23**	**−28**	**9**	**−30**	. . . .
Reserve assets.........................	4 802 ..	. . . .	8	−40	−23	−28	9	−30	. . . .
Use of Fund credit and loans............	4 766 ..	. . . .	. . . .	. . . .	. . . .	. . . .	. . . .	. . . .	. . . .
Exceptional financing...................	4 920 ..	. . . .	. . . .	. . . .	. . . .	. . . .	. . . .	. . . .	. . . .
Conversion rates: Brunei Dollars per U.S. dollar...................	0 101 ..	**1.7240**	**1.7917**	**1.7906**	**1.7422**	**1.6902**	**1.6644**	**1.5889**	**1.5071**

¹ Excludes components that have been classified in the categories of Group E.

Table 2. STANDARD PRESENTATION, 2000–2007

(Millions of U.S. dollars)

	Code	2000	2001	2002	2003	2004	2005	2006	2007
CURRENT ACCOUNT	4 993	....	**1,775**	**1,531**	**2,279**	**2,896**	**4,038**	**5,232**	....
A. GOODS	4 100	....	**2,558**	**2,227**	**3,164**	**3,728**	**4,834**	**6,041**	....
Credit	2 100	....	**3,640**	**3,702**	**4,422**	**5,066**	**6,247**	**7,627**	....
General merchandise: exports f.o.b.	2 110	....	3,640	3,702	4,422	5,066	6,247	7,627	....
Goods for processing: exports f.o.b.	2 150	....	....	....	....	....	....	....	....
Repairs on goods	2 160	....	....	....	....	....	....	....	....
Goods procured in ports by carriers	2 170	....	....	....	....	....	....	....	....
Nonmonetary gold	2 180	....	....	....	....	....	....	....	....
Debit	3 100	....	**−1,082**	**−1,475**	**−1,258**	**−1,338**	**−1,413**	**−1,586**	....
General merchandise: imports f.o.b.	3 110	....	−1,082	−1,475	−1,258	−1,338	−1,413	−1,586	....
Goods for processing: imports f.o.b.	3 150	....	....	....	....	....	....	....	....
Repairs on goods	3 160	....	....	....	....	....	....	....	....
Goods procured in ports by carriers	3 170	....	....	....	....	....	....	....	....
Nonmonetary gold	3 180	....	....	....	....	....	....	....	....
B. SERVICES	4 200	....	**−571**	**−450**	**−595**	**−531**	**−494**	**−469**	....
Total credit	2 200	....	*482*	*427*	*437*	*544*	*617*	*744*	....
Total debit	3 200	....	*−1,053*	*−876*	*−1,032*	*−1,075*	*−1,110*	*−1,213*	....
Transportation services, credit	2 205	....	**267**	**256**	**247**	**285**	**313**	**381**	....
Passenger	2 850	....	....	....	....	....	....	....	....
Freight	2 851	....	....	....	....	....	....	....	....
Other	2 852	....	....	....	....	....	....	....	....
Sea transport, passenger	2 207	....	....	....	....	....	....	....	....
Sea transport, freight	2 208	....	....	....	....	....	....	....	....
Sea transport, other	2 209	....	....	....	....	....	....	....	....
Air transport, passenger	2 211	....	....	....	....	....	....	....	....
Air transport, freight	2 212	....	....	....	....	....	....	....	....
Air transport, other	2 213	....	....	....	....	....	....	....	....
Other transport, passenger	2 215	....	....	....	....	....	....	....	....
Other transport, freight	2 216	....	....	....	....	....	....	....	....
Other transport, other	2 217	....	....	....	....	....	....	....	....
Transportation services, debit	3 205	....	**−251**	**−188**	**−229**	**−297**	**−322**	**−369**	....
Passenger	3 850	....	....	....	....	....	....	....	....
Freight	3 851	....	....	....	....	....	....	....	....
Other	3 852	....	....	....	....	....	....	....	....
Sea transport, passenger	3 207	....	....	....	....	....	....	....	....
Sea transport, freight	3 208	....	....	....	....	....	....	....	....
Sea transport, other	3 209	....	....	....	....	....	....	....	....
Air transport, passenger	3 211	....	....	....	....	....	....	....	....
Air transport, freight	3 212	....	....	....	....	....	....	....	....
Air transport, other	3 213	....	....	....	....	....	....	....	....
Other transport, passenger	3 215	....	....	....	....	....	....	....	....
Other transport, freight	3 216	....	....	....	....	....	....	....	....
Other transport, other	3 217	....	....	....	....	....	....	....	....
Travel, credit	2 236	....	**155**	**114**	**124**	**181**	**191**	**224**	....
Business travel	2 237	....	....	....	....	....	....	....	....
Personal travel	2 240	....	....	....	....	....	....	....	....
Travel, debit	3 236	....	**−456**	**−398**	**−468**	**−382**	**−374**	**−408**	....
Business travel	3 237	....	....	....	....	....	....	....	....
Personal travel	3 240	....	....	....	....	....	....	....	....
Other services, credit	2 200 BA	....	**60**	**57**	**66**	**77**	**112**	**140**	....
Communications	2 245	....	3	3	4	7	10	13	....
Construction	2 249	....	....	....	....	....	....	....	....
Insurance	2 253	....	3	3	4	6	7	10	....
Financial	2 260	....	....	....	....	....	....	....	....
Computer and information	2 262	....	....	....	....	....	....	....	....
Royalties and licence fees	2 266	....	....	....	....	....	....	....	....
Other business services	2 268	....	54	50	58	65	95	116	....
Personal, cultural, and recreational	2 287	....	....	....	....	....	....	....	....
Government, n.i.e.	2 291	....	....	....	....	....	....	....	....
Other services, debit	3 200 BA	....	**−347**	**−290**	**−335**	**−397**	**−415**	**−436**	....
Communications	3 245	....	−2	−2	−2	−3	−5	−8	....
Construction	3 249	....	....	....	....	....	....	....	....
Insurance	3 253	....	−9	−7	−8	−9	−10	−11	....
Financial	3 260	....	−1	−1	−1	−2	−3	−5	....
Computer and information	3 262	....	....	....	....	....	....	....	....
Royalties and licence fees	3 266	....	−2	−2	−3	−3	−4	−6	....
Other business services	3 268	....	−212	−164	−173	−225	−223	−228	....
Personal, cultural, and recreational	3 287	....	....	....	....	....	....	....	....
Government, n.i.e.	3 291	....	−121	−114	−147	−154	−170	−179	....

Table 2 (Continued). STANDARD PRESENTATION, 2000–2007

(Millions of U.S. dollars)

	Code	2000	2001	2002	2003	2004	2005	2006	2007
C. INCOME	4 300	....	**58**	**63**	....	**8**	**73**	**65**	....
Total credit	2 300	....	*244*	*235*	*214*	*236*	*263*	*248*	....
Total debit	3 300	....	*−186*	*−172*	*−214*	*−228*	*−190*	*−183*	....
Compensation of employees, credit	2 310	....	....	....	....	....	....	....	....
Compensation of employees, debit	3 310	....	**−2**	**−3**	**−12**	**−14**	....	....	....
Investment income, credit	2 320	....	**244**	**235**	**214**	**236**	**263**	**248**	....
Direct investment income	2 330	....	....	....	....	....	....	....	....
Dividends and distributed branch profits	2 332	....	....	....	....	....	....	....	....
Reinvested earnings and undistributed branch profits	2 333	....	....	....	....	....	....	....	....
Income on debt (interest)	2 334	....	....	....	....	....	....	....	....
Portfolio investment income	2 339	....	....	....	....	....	....	....	....
Income on equity	2 340	....	....	....	....	....	....	....	....
Income on bonds and notes	2 350	....	....	....	....	....	....	....	....
Income on money market instruments	2 360	....	....	....	....	....	....	....	....
Other investment income	2 370	....	244	235	214	236	263	248	....
Investment income, debit	3 320	....	**−184**	**−169**	**−201**	**−214**	**−190**	**−183**	....
Direct investment income	3 330	....	....	....	....	....	....	....	....
Dividends and distributed branch profits	3 332	....	....	....	....	....	....	....	....
Reinvested earnings and undistributed branch profits	3 333	....	....	....	....	....	....	....	....
Income on debt (interest)	3 334	....	....	....	....	....	....	....	....
Portfolio investment income	3 339	....	....	....	....	....	....	....	....
Income on equity	3 340	....	....	....	....	....	....	....	....
Income on bonds and notes	3 350	....	....	....	....	....	....	....	....
Income on money market instruments	3 360	....	....	....	....	....	....	....	....
Other investment income	3 370	....	−184	−169	−201	−214	−190	−183	....
D. CURRENT TRANSFERS	4 379	....	**−269**	**−310**	**−290**	**−309**	**−376**	**−405**	....
Credit	2 379	....	....	....	....	....	....	....	....
General government	2 380	....	....	....	....	....	....	....	....
Other sectors	2 390	....	....	....	....	....	....	....	....
Workers' remittances	2 391	....	....	....	....	....	....	....	....
Other current transfers	2 392	....	....	....	....	....	....	....	....
Debit	3 379	....	**−269**	**−310**	**−290**	**−309**	**−376**	**−405**	....
General government	3 380	....	....	....	....	....	....	....	....
Other sectors	3 390	....	−269	−310	−290	−309	−376	−405	....
Workers' remittances	3 391	....	−269	−310	−290	−309	−376	−405	....
Other current transfers	3 392	....	....	....	....	....	....	....	....
CAPITAL AND FINANCIAL ACCOUNT	4 996	....	**240**	**571**	**−651**	**−1,191**	**−88**	**538**	....
CAPITAL ACCOUNT	4 994	....	**−1**	**−1**	**−1**	**−11**	**−11**	**−7**	....
Total credit	2 994	....	....	....	....	....	....	....	....
Total debit	3 994	....	*−1*	*−1*	*−1*	*−11*	*−11*	*−7*	....
Capital transfers, credit	2 400	....	....	....	....	....	....	....	....
General government	2 401	....	....	....	....	....	....	....	....
Debt forgiveness	2 402	....	....	....	....	....	....	....	....
Other capital transfers	2 410	....	....	....	....	....	....	....	....
Other sectors	2 430	....	....	....	....	....	....	....	....
Migrants' transfers	2 431	....	....	....	....	....	....	....	....
Debt forgiveness	2 432	....	....	....	....	....	....	....	....
Other capital transfers	2 440	....	....	....	....	....	....	....	....
Capital transfers, debit	3 400	....	....	....	....	....	....	....	....
General government	3 401	....	....	....	....	....	....	....	....
Debt forgiveness	3 402	....	....	....	....	....	....	....	....
Other capital transfers	3 410	....	....	....	....	....	....	....	....
Other sectors	3 430	....	....	....	....	....	....	....	....
Migrants' transfers	3 431	....	....	....	....	....	....	....	....
Debt forgiveness	3 432	....	....	....	....	....	....	....	....
Other capital transfers	3 440	....	....	....	....	....	....	....	....
Nonproduced nonfinancial assets, credit	2 480	....	....	....	....	....	....	....	....
Nonproduced nonfinancial assets, debit	3 480	....	....	....	....	....	....	....	....

Table 2 (Continued). STANDARD PRESENTATION, 2000–2007

(Millions of U.S. dollars)

	Code	2000	2001	2002	2003	2004	2005	2006	2007
FINANCIAL ACCOUNT	4 995	....	241	572	−650	−1,180	−76	545	....
A. DIRECT INVESTMENT	4 500	....	74	234	114	40	176	70	....
Direct investment abroad	4 505	....	....	....	....	−41	....	−18	....
Equity capital	4 510	....	....	....	....	....	....	....	....
Claims on affiliated enterprises	4 515	....	....	....	....	....	....	....	....
Liabilities to affiliated enterprises	4 520	....	....	....	....	....	....	....	....
Reinvested earnings	4 525	....	....	....	....	....	....	....	....
Other capital	4 530	....	....	....	....	−41	....	−18	....
Claims on affiliated enterprises	4 535	....	....	....	....	....	....	....	....
Liabilities to affiliated enterprises	4 540	....	....	....	....	....	....	....	....
Direct investment in Brunei Darussalam	4 555	....	74	234	114	81	176	88	....
Equity capital	4 560	....	69	177	105	79	154	85	....
Claims on direct investors	4 565	....	....	....	....	....	....	....	....
Liabilities to direct investors	4 570	....	....	....	....	....	....	....	....
Reinvested earnings	4 575	....	....	....	....	....	....	....	....
Other capital	4 580	....	5	57	9	2	22	3	....
Claims on direct investors	4 585	....	....	....	....	....	....	....	....
Liabilities to direct investors	4 590	....	....	....	....	....	....	....	....
B. PORTFOLIO INVESTMENT	4 600	....	−180	8	60	−45	21	−90	....
Assets	4 602	....	−180	8	60	−45	21	−90	....
Equity securities	4 610	....	−161	1	68	−56	12	−90	....
Monetary authorities	4 611	....	....	....	....	....	....	....	....
General government	4 612	....	....	....	....	....	....	....	....
Banks	4 613	....	....	....	....	....	....	....	....
Other sectors	4 614	....	....	....	....	....	....	....	....
Debt securities	4 619	....	−18	7	−8	11	9		....
Bonds and notes	4 620	....	....	....	....	....	....	....	....
Monetary authorities	4 621	....	....	....	....	....	....	....	....
General government	4 622	....	....	....	....	....	....	....	....
Banks	4 623	....	....	....	....	....	....	....	....
Other sectors	4 624	....	....	....	....	....	....	....	....
Money market instruments	4 630	....	....	....	....	....	....	....	....
Monetary authorities	4 631	....	....	....	....	....	....	....	....
General government	4 632	....	....	....	....	....	....	....	....
Banks	4 633	....	....	....	....	....	....	....	....
Other sectors	4 634	....	....	....	....	....	....	....	....
Liabilities	4 652	....	....	....	....	....	....	....	....
Equity securities	4 660	....	....	....	....	....	....	....	....
Banks	4 663	....	....	....	....	....	....	....	....
Other sectors	4 664	....	....	....	....	....	....	....	....
Debt securities	4 669	....	....	....	....	....	....	....	....
Bonds and notes	4 670	....	....	....	....	....	....	....	....
Monetary authorities	4 671	....	....	....	....	....	....	....	....
General government	4 672	....	....	....	....	....	....	....	....
Banks	4 673	....	....	....	....	....	....	....	....
Other sectors	4 674	....	....	....	....	....	....	....	....
Money market instruments	4 680	....	....	....	....	....	....	....	....
Monetary authorities	4 681	....	....	....	....	....	....	....	....
General government	4 682	....	....	....	....	....	....	....	....
Banks	4 683	....	....	....	....	....	....	....	....
Other sectors	4 684	....	....	....	....	....	....	....	....
C. FINANCIAL DERIVATIVES	4 910	....	....	....	....	....	....	....	....
Monetary authorities	4 911	....	....	....	....	....	....	....	....
General government	4 912	....	....	....	....	....	....	....	....
Banks	4 913	....	....	....	....	....	....	....	....
Other sectors	4 914	....	....	....	....	....	....	....	....
Assets	4 900	....	....	....	....	....	....	....	....
Monetary authorities	4 901	....	....	....	....	....	....	....	....
General government	4 902	....	....	....	....	....	....	....	....
Banks	4 903	....	....	....	....	....	....	....	....
Other sectors	4 904	....	....	....	....	....	....	....	....
Liabilities	4 905	....	....	....	....	....	....	....	....
Monetary authorities	4 906	....	....	....	....	....	....	....	....
General government	4 907	....	....	....	....	....	....	....	....
Banks	4 908	....	....	....	....	....	....	....	....
Other sectors	4 909	....	....	....	....	....	....	....	....

Table 2 (Concluded). STANDARD PRESENTATION, 2000–2007

(Millions of U.S. dollars)

	Code	2000	2001	2002	2003	2004	2005	2006	2007
D. OTHER INVESTMENT	4 700	....	339	370	−801	−1,147	−282	594	....
Assets	4 703	....	349	308	−604	−1,559	−498	334	....
Trade credits	4 706	....	....	....	....	....	....	....	....
General government	4 707	....	....	....	....	....	....	....	....
of which: Short-term	4 709	....	....	....	....	....	....	....	....
Other sectors	4 710	....	....	....	....	....	....	....	....
of which: Short-term	4 712	....	....	....	....	....	....	....	....
Loans	4 714	....	170	54	−162	−757	−461	936	....
Monetary authorities	4 715	....	....	....	....	....	....	....	....
of which: Short-term	4 718	....	....	....	....	....	....	....	....
General government	4 719	....	....	....	....	....	....	....	....
of which: Short-term	4 721	....	....	....	....	....	....	....	....
Banks	4 722	....	170	54	−162	−757	−461	936	....
of which: Short-term	4 724	....	....	....	....	....	....	....	....
Other sectors	4 725	....	....	....	....	....	....	....	....
of which: Short-term	4 727	....	....	....	....	....	....	....	....
Currency and deposits	4 730	....	180	255	−441	−802	−37	−602	....
Monetary authorities	4 731	....	....	....	....	....	....	....	....
General government	4 732	....	....	....	....	....	....	....	....
Banks	4 733	....	215	183	−366	−234	−190	−299	....
Other sectors	4 734	....	−35	72	−75	−568	153	−302	....
Other assets	4 736	....	−1	−1	−1	−1	−1	−1	....
Monetary authorities	4 737	....	....	....	....	....	....	....	....
of which: Short-term	4 739	....	....	....	....	....	....	....	....
General government	4 740	....	−1	−1	−1	−1	−1	−1	....
of which: Short-term	4 742	....	....	....	....	....	....	....	....
Banks	4 743	....	....	....	....	....	....	....	....
of which: Short-term	4 745	....	....	....	....	....	....	....	....
Other sectors	4 746	....	....	....	....	....	....	....	....
of which: Short-term	4 748	....	....	....	....	....	....	....	....
Liabilities	4 753	....	−10	62	−198	413	217	261	....
Trade credits	4 756	....	−29	160	−2	451	68	69	....
General government	4 757	....	....	....	....	....	....	....	....
of which: Short-term	4 759	....	....	....	....	....	....	....	....
Other sectors	4 760	....	−29	160	−2	451	68	69	....
of which: Short-term	4 762	....	....	....	....	....	....	....	....
Loans	4 764	....	−107	−80	−122	−17	−62	−19	....
Monetary authorities	4 765	....	....	....	....	....	....	....	....
of which: Use of Fund credit and loans from the Fund	4 766	....	....	....	....	....	....	....	....
of which: Short-term	4 768	....	....	....	....	....	....	....	....
General government	4 769	....	....	....	....	....	....	....	....
of which: Short-term	4 771	....	....	....	....	....	....	....	....
Banks	4 772	....	....	....	....	....	....	....	....
of which: Short-term	4 774	....	....	....	....	....	....	....	....
Other sectors	4 775	....	−107	−80	−122	−17	−62	−19	....
of which: Short-term	4 777	....	....	....	....	....	....	....	....
Currency and deposits	4 780	....	126	−19	−73	−22	210	210	....
Monetary authorities	4 781	....	....	....	....	....	....	....	....
General government	4 782	....	....	....	....	....	....	....	....
Banks	4 783	....	126	−19	−73	−22	210	210	....
Other sectors	4 784	....	....	....	....	....	....	....	....
Other liabilities	4 786	....	....	....	....	....	....	....	....
Monetary authorities	4 787	....	....	....	....	....	....	....	....
of which: Short-term	4 789	....	....	....	....	....	....	....	....
General government	4 790	....	....	....	....	....	....	....	....
of which: Short-term	4 792	....	....	....	....	....	....	....	....
Banks	4 793	....	....	....	....	....	....	....	....
of which: Short-term	4 795	....	....	....	....	....	....	....	....
Other sectors	4 796	....	....	....	....	....	....	....	....
of which: Short-term	4 798	....	....	....	....	....	....	....	....
E. RESERVE ASSETS	4 802	....	8	−40	−23	−28	9	−30	....
Monetary gold	4 812	....	....	....	....	....	....	....	....
Special drawing rights	4 811	....	−2	−1	−1	−1	−2	−2	....
Reserve position in the Fund	4 810	....	....	−22	−9	....	38	11	....
Foreign exchange	4 803	....	9	−17	−13	−27	−27	−40	....
Other claims	4 813	....	....	....	....	....	....	....	....
NET ERRORS AND OMISSIONS	4 998	....	−2,016	−2,102	−1,628	−1,705	−3,950	−5,770	....

Table 1. ANALYTIC PRESENTATION, 2000–2007

(Millions of U.S. dollars)

	Code	2000	2001	2002	2003	2004	2005	2006	2007
A. Current Account[1]	4 993 Z.	**−703.1**	**−804.6**	**−319.0**	**−1,022.2**	**−1,671.1**	**−3,347.0**	**−5,658.8**	**−8,715.6**
Goods: exports f.o.b.	2 100 ..	4,824.6	5,112.9	5,354.1	7,081.4	9,931.2	11,754.1	15,101.4	18,575.3
Goods: imports f.o.b.	3 100 ..	−6,000.2	−6,693.4	−7,012.6	−9,657.3	−13,619.1	−17,204.4	−22,129.5	−28,646.1
Balance on Goods	4 100 ..	*−1,175.5*	*−1,580.5*	*−1,658.5*	*−2,575.9*	*−3,688.0*	*−5,450.3*	*−7,028.1*	*−10,070.9*
Services: credit	2 200 ..	2,175.2	2,163.0	2,203.3	2,961.4	4,029.4	4,404.1	5,289.4	6,335.9
Services: debit	3 200 ..	−1,669.6	−1,910.5	−1,754.7	−2,447.1	−3,238.4	−3,403.8	−4,100.1	−4,821.1
Balance on Goods and Services	4 991 ..	*−670.0*	*−1,327.9*	*−1,209.9*	*−2,061.6*	*−2,896.9*	*−4,450.0*	*−5,838.9*	*−8,556.1*
Income: credit	2 300 ..	320.8	705.6	924.4	1,297.7	1,539.3	1,515.6	1,607.2	2,103.2
Income: debit	3 300 ..	−644.2	−680.7	−580.9	−953.9	−1,235.9	−1,426.0	−2,271.3	−2,726.8
Balance on Goods, Services, and Income	4 992 ..	*−993.4*	*−1,303.0*	*−866.4*	*−1,717.8*	*−2,593.5*	*−4,360.4*	*−6,503.0*	*−9,179.6*
Current transfers: credit	2 379 Z.	354.7	598.5	653.6	865.5	1,121.0	1,238.0	1,065.7	1,253.0
Current transfers: debit	3 379 ..	−64.3	−100.2	−106.2	−169.8	−198.6	−224.7	−221.5	−789.0
B. Capital Account[1]	4 994 Z.	**24.9**	**−.1**	**−.1**	**−.2**	**204.0**	**289.7**	**228.0**	**505.5**
Capital account: credit	2 994 Z.	25.0	....	....	....	204.1	293.6	228.0	515.4
Capital account: debit	3 994 ..	−.1	−.1	−.1	−.2	−.1	−3.9	....	−9.9
Total, Groups A Plus B	4 981 ..	*−678.1*	*−804.8*	*−319.1*	*−1,022.4*	*−1,467.1*	*−3,057.3*	*−5,430.8*	*−8,210.2*
C. Financial Account[1]	4 995 W.	**781.3**	**662.8**	**3,513.0**	**2,738.0**	**3,428.1**	**6,903.1**	**8,625.0**	**15,008.3**
Direct investment abroad	4 505 ..	−3.3	−9.7	−28.3	−26.5	217.0	−307.6	−174.9	−278.4
Direct investment in Bulgaria	4 555 Z.	1,001.5	812.9	904.7	2,096.8	2,662.2	4,312.4	7,507.4	8,974.1
Portfolio investment assets	4 602 ..	−62.2	−40.3	218.3	−78.6	9.6	29.1	−324.8	−102.7
Equity securities	4 610 ..	−8.2	−33.5	−16.8	−15.7	−7.2	−6.0	−125.3	−134.7
Debt securities	4 619 ..	−54.0	−6.8	235.1	−62.9	16.7	35.1	−199.5	32.0
Portfolio investment liabilities	4 652 Z.	−114.7	105.1	1,460.7	−36.2	57.9	584.5	703.1	−159.0
Equity securities	4 660 ..	4.9	−8.6	−22.9	−23.2	21.5	449.0	94.7	100.6
Debt securities	4 669 Z.	−119.6	113.7	1,483.6	−13.0	36.4	135.5	608.4	−259.6
Financial derivatives	4 910 ..	−1.8	17.5	6.8	−1.1	−85.9	−112.0	−143.0	−84.6
Financial derivatives assets	4 900 ..	....	....	....	....	−85.9	−112.5	−168.0	−139.5
Financial derivatives liabilities	4 905 ..	−1.8	17.5	6.8	−1.1	....	.5	25.1	54.9
Other investment assets	4 703 ..	−332.1	−100.4	283.0	250.9	−1,784.5	15.7	−2,975.5	−662.4
Monetary authorities	4 701 ..	.9	−2.1	2.1	....	....	....	....	....
General government	4 704 ..	−9.1	−20.7	10.1	2.9	−723.5	703.5	−265.9	30.4
Banks	4 705 ..	−495.8	−129.8	263.1	263.2	−763.2	−470.4	−1,774.3	−289.5
Other sectors	4 728 ..	171.9	52.2	7.6	−15.2	−297.8	−217.4	−935.3	−403.3
Other investment liabilities	4 753 W.	293.8	−122.3	667.9	532.7	2,351.9	2,381.0	4,032.6	7,321.2
Monetary authorities	4 753 WA	....	....	....	....	....	....	....	....
General government	4 753 ZB	−223.9	−310.0	−130.6	−99.9	−45.6	−122.2	−366.6	36.9
Banks	4 753 ZC	108.4	154.3	344.4	445.2	1,096.4	1,178.4	1,091.1	3,186.8
Other sectors	4 753 ZD	409.3	33.4	454.2	187.5	1,301.1	1,324.8	3,308.0	4,097.5
Total, Groups A Through C	4 983 ..	*103.2*	*−142.0*	*3,193.9*	*1,715.6*	*1,961.0*	*3,845.8*	*3,194.2*	*6,798.1*
D. Net Errors and Omissions	4 998 ..	**33.9**	**515.4**	**−715.9**	**−889.0**	**370.8**	**−1,219.4**	**−907.4**	**−2,074.1**
Total, Groups A Through D	4 984 ..	*137.0*	*373.4*	*2,478.0*	*826.6*	*2,331.8*	*2,626.4*	*2,286.8*	*4,724.1*
E. Reserves and Related Items	4 802 A.	**−137.0**	**−373.4**	**−2,478.0**	**−826.6**	**−2,331.8**	**−2,626.4**	**−2,286.8**	**−4,724.1**
Reserve assets	4 802 ..	−408.9	−275.4	−586.3	−929.9	−1,846.4	−415.0	−1,924.2	−4,017.0
Use of Fund credit and loans	4 766 ..	136.0	−168.5	−142.3	36.4	−55.2	−436.2	−341.4	−344.2
Exceptional financing	4 920 ..	136.0	70.5	−1,749.4	66.9	−430.1	−1,775.2	−21.2	−362.9
Conversion rates: leva per U.S. dollar	0 101 ..	**2.1233**	**2.1847**	**2.0770**	**1.7327**	**1.5751**	**1.5741**	**1.5593**	**1.4291**

[1] Excludes components that have been classified in the categories of Group E.

Table 2. STANDARD PRESENTATION, 2000–2007

(Millions of U.S. dollars)

	Code	2000	2001	2002	2003	2004	2005	2006	2007
CURRENT ACCOUNT	4 993 ..	−703.1	−804.6	−319.0	−1,022.2	−1,671.1	−3,347.0	−5,658.8	−8,715.6
A. GOODS	4 100 ..	−1,175.5	−1,580.5	−1,658.5	−2,575.9	−3,688.0	−5,450.3	−7,028.1	−10,070.9
Credit	2 100 ..	4,824.6	5,112.9	5,354.1	7,081.4	9,931.2	11,754.1	15,101.4	18,575.3
General merchandise: exports f.o.b.	2 110 ..	4,824.6	5,112.9	5,354.1	7,081.4	9,931.2	11,754.1	15,101.4	18,575.3
Goods for processing: exports f.o.b.	2 150 ..	....	....	....	....	....	....	....	....
Repairs on goods	2 160 ..	....	....	....	....	....	....	....	....
Goods procured in ports by carriers	2 170 ..	....	....	....	....	....	....	....	....
Nonmonetary gold	2 180 ..	....	....	....	....	....	....	....	....
Debit	3 100 ..	−6,000.2	−6,693.4	−7,012.6	−9,657.3	−13,619.1	−17,204.4	−22,129.5	−28,646.1
General merchandise: imports f.o.b.	3 110 ..	−6,000.2	−6,693.4	−7,012.6	−9,657.3	−13,619.1	−17,204.4	−22,129.5	−28,646.1
Goods for processing: imports f.o.b.	3 150 ..	....	....	....	....	....	....	....	....
Repairs on goods	3 160 ..	....	....	....	....	....	....	....	....
Goods procured in ports by carriers	3 170 ..	....	....	....	....	....	....	....	....
Nonmonetary gold	3 180 ..	....	....	....	....	....	....	....	....
B. SERVICES	4 200 ..	505.5	252.5	448.6	514.3	791.0	1,000.3	1,189.2	1,514.8
Total credit	2 200 ..	*2,175.2*	*2,163.0*	*2,203.3*	*2,961.4*	*4,029.4*	*4,404.1*	*5,289.4*	*6,335.9*
Total debit	3 200 ..	*−1,669.6*	*−1,910.5*	*−1,754.7*	*−2,447.1*	*−3,238.4*	*−3,403.8*	*−4,100.1*	*−4,821.1*
Transportation services, credit	2 205 ..	631.9	642.2	617.9	778.0	1,020.8	1,194.1	1,589.9	1,896.9
Passenger	2 850 ..	*290.0*	*268.3*	*296.0*	*429.9*	*594.5*	*650.9*	*705.2*	*845.1*
Freight	2 851 ..	*241.2*	*373.9*	*321.9*	*348.1*	*426.3*	*543.2*	*774.3*	*910.1*
Other	2 852 ..	*100.6*	*....*	*....*	*....*	*....*	*....*	*110.5*	*141.8*
Sea transport, passenger	2 207 ..	....	....	....	....	....	32.5	35.3	42.3
Sea transport, freight	2 208 ..	....	....	....	....	29.3	47.8	63.3	69.0
Sea transport, other	2 209 ..	....	....	....	....	....	....	11.8	16.6
Air transport, passenger	2 211 ..	....	....	....	....	....	130.2	141.0	169.0
Air transport, freight	2 212 ..	....	....	....	....	7.7	23.1	25.8	21.6
Air transport, other	2 213 ..	....	....	....	....	....	....	98.6	119.2
Other transport, passenger	2 215 ..	....	....	....	....	....	488.1	528.9	633.8
Other transport, freight	2 216 ..	....	....	....	....	389.2	472.3	685.1	819.4
Other transport, other	2 217 ..	....	....	....	....	....	....	.1	5.9
Transportation services, debit	3 205 ..	−732.9	−814.7	−528.5	−748.6	−1,082.3	−1,094.9	−1,311.5	−1,630.9
Passenger	3 850 ..	*−225.9*	*−247.3*	*−301.2*	*−433.9*	*−572.3*	*−549.0*	*−619.0*	*−768.2*
Freight	3 851 ..	*−506.9*	*−567.4*	*−227.3*	*−314.7*	*−510.0*	*−545.9*	*−630.3*	*−781.2*
Other	3 852 ..	*....*	*....*	*....*	*....*	*....*	*....*	*−62.2*	*−81.5*
Sea transport, passenger	3 207 ..	....	....	....	....	....	−43.9	−49.5	−61.5
Sea transport, freight	3 208 ..	....	....	....	....	−234.6	−337.2	−410.8	−486.5
Sea transport, other	3 209 ..	....	....	....	....	....	....	−25.7	−38.3
Air transport, passenger	3 211 ..	....	....	....	....	....	−164.7	−185.7	−230.5
Air transport, freight	3 212 ..	....	....	....	....	−38.3	−36.1	−33.0	−39.8
Air transport, other	3 213 ..	....	....	....	....	....	....	−35.1	−42.0
Other transport, passenger	3 215 ..	....	....	....	....	....	−340.4	−383.8	−476.3
Other transport, freight	3 216 ..	....	....	....	....	−237.2	−172.7	−186.6	−255.0
Other transport, other	3 217 ..	....	....	....	....	....	....	−1.4	−1.2
Travel, credit	2 236 ..	1,074.2	993.5	1,096.3	1,620.6	2,201.8	2,411.8	2,611.7	3,130.0
Business travel	2 237 ..	136.4	113.6	115.1	169.8	230.0	273.9	291.4	356.8
Personal travel	2 240 ..	937.8	879.9	981.3	1,450.8	1,971.9	2,137.9	2,320.3	2,773.2
Travel, debit	3 236 ..	−538.0	−588.7	−717.1	−1,033.1	−1,363.3	−1,308.9	−1,473.7	−1,829.1
Business travel	3 237 ..	−230.5	−428.5	−568.4	−784.6	−1,042.6	−943.4	−1,064.2	−1,415.2
Personal travel	3 240 ..	−307.5	−160.2	−148.6	−248.6	−320.6	−365.5	−409.4	−413.9
Other services, credit	2 200 BA	469.1	527.3	489.0	562.8	806.8	798.2	1,087.7	1,309.0
Communications	2 245 ..	45.3	46.9	42.9	44.8	81.8	145.8	150.6	164.4
Construction	2 249 ..	50.2	69.4	60.7	78.2	122.7	102.8	168.5	136.1
Insurance	2 253 ..	17.3	12.2	14.2	18.0	27.4	30.0	37.5	48.3
Financial	2 260 ..	12.9	33.2	13.6	18.0	38.7	18.3	34.5	32.5
Computer and information	2 262 ..	5.1	12.4	7.4	14.8	28.3	32.6	55.9	117.2
Royalties and licence fees	2 266 ..	3.5	2.6	3.9	4.7	7.1	5.0	10.5	10.4
Other business services	2 268 ..	266.2	279.9	273.6	307.0	413.1	409.0	571.4	717.8
Personal, cultural, and recreational	2 287 ..	22.2	28.2	31.4	37.0	42.4	39.3	56.3	79.5
Government, n.i.e.	2 291 ..	46.4	42.6	41.3	40.3	45.3	15.5	2.4	2.9
Other services, debit	3 200 BA	−398.8	−507.1	−509.2	−665.4	−792.8	−1,000.1	−1,314.9	−1,361.1
Communications	3 245 ..	−28.9	−19.7	−29.2	−35.7	−52.5	−47.8	−79.9	−111.8
Construction	3 249 ..	−21.7	−55.2	−33.5	−28.7	−67.7	−77.4	−59.9	−16.5
Insurance	3 253 ..	−42.6	−37.8	−48.7	−77.2	−85.8	−93.6	−116.9	−134.6
Financial	3 260 ..	−46.7	−23.3	−30.9	−18.5	−32.9	−33.1	−66.9	−102.2
Computer and information	3 262 ..	−5.3	−13.7	−13.7	−18.2	−23.2	−39.6	−54.4	−69.9
Royalties and licence fees	3 266 ..	−9.9	−11.5	−23.3	−24.4	−30.5	−80.6	−69.4	−72.5
Other business services	3 268 ..	−230.3	−321.1	−305.0	−422.3	−459.3	−589.3	−839.5	−815.6
Personal, cultural, and recreational	3 287 ..	−4.0	−8.5	−10.2	−17.3	−15.1	−16.5	−19.3	−29.1
Government, n.i.e.	3 291 ..	−9.3	−16.3	−14.6	−22.9	−25.7	−22.3	−8.8	−8.8

Table 2 (Continued). STANDARD PRESENTATION, 2000–2007

(Millions of U.S. dollars)

	Code	2000	2001	2002	2003	2004	2005	2006	2007
C. INCOME	4 300	−323.4	24.9	343.5	343.8	303.4	89.6	−664.1	−623.6
Total credit	2 300	*320.8*	*705.6*	*924.4*	*1,297.7*	*1,539.3*	*1,515.6*	*1,607.2*	*2,103.2*
Total debit	3 300	*−644.2*	*−680.7*	*−580.9*	*−953.9*	*−1,235.9*	*−1,426.0*	*−2,271.3*	*−2,726.8*
Compensation of employees, credit	2 310	58.2	424.1	677.2	1,037.2	1,286.5	1,151.0	1,287.5	1,688.1
Compensation of employees, debit	3 310	−26.0	−27.0	−14.5	−12.6	−11.1	−13.8	−28.6	−54.1
Investment income, credit	2 320	262.6	281.5	247.2	260.5	252.8	364.7	319.7	415.1
Direct investment income	2 330	−2.2	.6	1.1	1.1	−2.3	−1.8	4.1	−5.0
Dividends and distributed branch profits	2 332	.8	.6	1.1	1.1	.4	1.0	2.3	6.9
Reinvested earnings and undistributed branch profits	2 333	−3.3	....	....	....	−1.0	6.6	1.6	−17.5
Income on debt (interest)	2 334	.4	....	....	....	−1.6	−9.5	.1	5.5
Portfolio investment income	2 339	48.9	64.7	25.8	172.7	140.7	245.9	160.6	192.9
Income on equity	2 340	....	....	....	2.3	....	....	.1	.6
Income on bonds and notes	2 350	47.8	63.2	25.0	169.7	140.2	245.3	159.2	190.3
Income on money market instruments	2 360	1.1	1.5	.8	.7	.5	.6	1.4	1.9
Other investment income	2 370	215.9	216.2	220.3	86.7	114.4	120.6	155.0	227.3
Investment income, debit	3 320	−618.3	−653.8	−566.4	−941.3	−1,224.8	−1,412.2	−2,242.7	−2,672.8
Direct investment income	3 330	−107.1	−148.7	−228.3	−550.6	−755.5	−912.1	−1,683.7	−1,863.1
Dividends and distributed branch profits	3 332	−19.9	−115.5	−115.0	−253.8	−140.3	−316.2	−408.3	−712.0
Reinvested earnings and undistributed branch profits	3 333	−58.3	−6.3	−83.7	−249.8	−548.1	−509.0	−1,045.5	−567.9
Income on debt (interest)	3 334	−28.9	−26.9	−29.6	−47.0	−67.0	−86.9	−229.9	−583.2
Portfolio investment income	3 339	−293.9	−301.7	−175.3	−222.7	−232.3	−220.9	−161.9	−165.9
Income on equity	3 340	−3.8	−2.4	....	−.5	....	....	....	....
Income on bonds and notes	3 350	−290.0	−299.2	−174.0	−220.1	−232.2	−220.9	−161.9	−165.9
Income on money market instruments	3 360	−.1	−.1	−1.3	−2.2	....	....	....	....
Other investment income	3 370	−217.3	−203.3	−162.9	−168.0	−237.1	−279.2	−397.0	−643.8
D. CURRENT TRANSFERS	4 379	290.3	498.4	547.4	695.6	922.4	1,013.4	844.2	464.0
Credit	2 379	354.7	598.5	653.6	865.5	1,121.0	1,238.0	1,065.7	1,253.0
General government	2 380	74.4	177.2	140.0	169.8	104.5	109.5	175.0	355.6
Other sectors	2 390	280.3	421.4	513.6	695.7	1,016.5	1,128.5	890.7	897.5
Workers' remittances	2 391	....	402.1	499.8	681.2	436.3	462.0	419.7	397.5
Other current transfers	2 392	280.3	19.3	13.8	14.5	580.2	666.6	471.1	500.0
Debit	3 379	−64.3	−100.2	−106.2	−169.8	−198.6	−224.7	−221.5	−789.0
General government	3 380	−19.4	−40.9	−15.8	−31.6	−32.4	−38.0	−24.4	−484.3
Other sectors	3 390	−44.9	−59.3	−90.4	−138.3	−166.2	−186.7	−197.1	−304.7
Workers' remittances	3 391	....	....	....	....	−18.3	−21.6	−21.0	−31.5
Other current transfers	3 392	−44.9	−59.3	−90.4	−138.3	−147.9	−165.0	−176.1	−273.2
CAPITAL AND FINANCIAL ACCOUNT	4 996	669.2	289.3	1,034.9	1,911.2	1,300.4	4,566.3	6,566.2	10,789.7
CAPITAL ACCOUNT	4 994	24.9	−.1	−.1	−.2	204.0	289.7	228.0	505.5
Total credit	2 994	*25.0*	....	....	....	*204.1*	*293.6*	*228.0*	*515.4*
Total debit	3 994	*−.1*	*−.1*	*−.1*	*−.2*	*−.1*	*−3.9*	....	*−9.9*
Capital transfers, credit	2 400	25.0	....	....	....	204.1	293.6	228.0	515.4
General government	2 401	25.0	....	....	....	179.2	220.3	222.4	504.9
Debt forgiveness	2 402	....	....	....	....	....	....	....	....
Other capital transfers	2 410	25.0	....	....	....	179.2	220.3	222.4	504.9
Other sectors	2 430	....	....	....	....	24.9	73.3	5.6	10.5
Migrants' transfers	2 431	....	....	....	....	....	....	....	....
Debt forgiveness	2 432	....	....	....	....	24.9	73.1	5.4	10.4
Other capital transfers	2 440	....	....	....	....	....	.1	.3	....
Capital transfers, debit	3 400	−.1	−.1	−.1	−.2	−.1	−3.9	....	−9.9
General government	3 401	....	....	....	....	....	....	....	−9.8
Debt forgiveness	3 402	....	....	....	....	....	....	....	....
Other capital transfers	3 410	....	....	....	....	....	....	....	−9.8
Other sectors	3 430	−.1	−.1	−.1	−.2	−.1	−3.9	....	−.1
Migrants' transfers	3 431	....	....	....	....	....	....	....	....
Debt forgiveness	3 432	....	....	....	....	....	−2.4	....	....
Other capital transfers	3 440	−.1	−.1	−.1	−.2	−.1	−1.5	....	....
Nonproduced nonfinancial assets, credit	2 480	....	....	....	....	....	....	....	....
Nonproduced nonfinancial assets, debit	3 480	....	....	....	....	....	....	....	....

Table 2 (Continued). STANDARD PRESENTATION, 2000–2007

(Millions of U.S. dollars)

	Code	2000	2001	2002	2003	2004	2005	2006	2007
FINANCIAL ACCOUNT	4 995	644.3	289.4	1,035.0	1,911.4	1,096.3	4,276.7	6,338.2	10,284.2
A. DIRECT INVESTMENT	4 500	998.2	803.3	876.3	2,070.3	2,879.2	4,004.8	7,332.5	8,695.8
Direct investment abroad	4 505	−3.3	−9.7	−28.3	−26.5	217.0	−307.6	−174.9	−278.4
Equity capital	4 510	1.5	−6.2	−26.2	−24.0	−33.1	−65.8	−97.2	−278.8
Claims on affiliated enterprises	4 515	....	−6.2	−26.2	−24.0	−33.1	−65.8	−97.2	−278.8
Liabilities to affiliated enterprises	4 520	....	....	....	....	....	....	....	....
Reinvested earnings	4 525	3.3	....	....	....	1.0	−6.6	−1.6	17.5
Other capital	4 530	−8.2	−3.4	−2.1	−2.5	249.0	−235.2	−76.0	−17.0
Claims on affiliated enterprises	4 535	−8.2	−3.4	−2.1	−2.5	−7.5	−10.3	−75.2	−40.1
Liabilities to affiliated enterprises	4 540	....	....	....	....	256.6	−224.9	−.8	23.1
Direct investment in Bulgaria	4 555	1,001.5	812.9	904.7	2,096.8	2,662.2	4,312.4	7,507.4	8,974.1
Equity capital	4 560	754.8	566.7	588.2	1,233.7	1,554.5	1,508.3	4,009.9	3,092.4
Claims on direct investors	4 565	....	....	....	....	....	....	....	....
Liabilities to direct investors	4 570	....	566.7	588.2	1,233.7	1,554.5	1,508.3	4,009.9	3,092.4
Reinvested earnings	4 575	58.3	6.3	83.7	249.8	548.1	509.0	1,045.5	567.9
Other capital	4 580	188.5	240.0	232.7	613.3	559.6	2,295.1	2,451.9	5,313.9
Claims on direct investors	4 585	....	....	....	....	−153.8	−10.6	−105.1	−408.4
Liabilities to direct investors	4 590	188.5	240.0	232.7	613.3	713.3	2,305.7	2,557.0	5,722.3
B. PORTFOLIO INVESTMENT	4 600	−176.9	64.8	−83.8	−211.8	−521.0	−1,304.1	347.1	−631.9
Assets	4 602	−62.2	−40.3	218.3	−78.6	9.6	29.1	−324.8	−102.7
Equity securities	4 610	−8.2	−33.5	−16.8	−15.7	−7.2	−6.0	−125.3	−134.7
Monetary authorities	4 611	....	....	....	....	....	....	....	....
General government	4 612	....	....	....	....	....	....	....	....
Banks	4 613	−7.7	−31.2	1.3	−9.2	−.7	−.3	−.2	−1.4
Other sectors	4 614	−.5	−2.4	−18.1	−6.6	−6.5	−5.7	−125.1	−133.3
Debt securities	4 619	−54.0	−6.8	235.1	−62.9	16.7	35.1	−199.5	32.0
Bonds and notes	4 620	−43.5	−50.1	224.1	−87.0	70.3	136.7	−252.8	11.6
Monetary authorities	4 621	....	80.5	....	....	....	....	....	....
General government	4 622	−25.6	−40.1	305.1	−11.7	255.2	....	....	....
Banks	4 623	−2.2	−90.6	−81.4	−74.5	−181.5	153.6	−187.2	242.7
Other sectors	4 624	−15.7	.1	.4	−.8	−3.4	−16.9	−65.6	−231.1
Money market instruments	4 630	−10.5	43.3	11.0	24.1	−53.6	−101.7	53.4	20.4
Monetary authorities	4 631	.1	−3.4	....	....	....	....	....	....
General government	4 632	.1	39.6	15.0	21.9	25.7	....	....	....
Banks	4 633	−10.6	6.7	−3.8	2.2	−80.4	−103.4	53.1	21.9
Other sectors	4 634	....	.3	−.2	....	1.1	1.7	.3	−1.6
Liabilities	4 652	−114.7	105.1	−302.1	−133.2	−530.6	−1,333.2	671.9	−529.2
Equity securities	4 660	4.9	−8.6	−22.9	−23.2	21.5	449.0	94.7	100.6
Banks	4 663	6.9	2.9	−2.7	−4.4	−4.3	4.6	28.8	77.6
Other sectors	4 664	−2.0	−11.5	−20.2	−18.8	25.8	444.4	66.0	23.0
Debt securities	4 669	−119.6	113.7	−279.1	−110.0	−552.1	−1,782.2	577.1	−629.7
Bonds and notes	4 670	−119.4	113.7	−279.5	−110.5	−552.1	−1,782.2	349.2	−382.0
Monetary authorities	4 671	....	....	....	....	....	....	....	....
General government	4 672	−120.7	123.3	−277.6	−113.2	−588.5	−1,917.7	−31.3	−370.1
Banks	4 673	1.0	−9.5	−1.0	3.2	4.9	123.1	41.2	−13.0
Other sectors	4 674	.3	....	−.9	−.4	31.6	12.3	339.3	1.2
Money market instruments	4 680	−.2	....	.4	.5	....	....	227.9	−247.8
Monetary authorities	4 681	....	....	....	....	....	....	....	....
General government	4 682	−.5	....	....	....	....	....	....	....
Banks	4 683	....	....	....	....	....	....	....	....
Other sectors	4 684	.4	....	.4	.5	....	....	227.9	−247.8
C. FINANCIAL DERIVATIVES	4 910	−1.8	17.5	6.8	−1.1	−85.9	−112.0	−143.0	−84.6
Monetary authorities	4 911	....	....	....	....	....	....	....	....
General government	4 912	....	....	....	....	....	....	....	....
Banks	4 913	−1.8	17.5	6.8	−1.1	−2.7	−2.9	−.8	10.8
Other sectors	4 914	....	....	....	....	−83.3	−109.1	−142.2	−95.4
Assets	4 900	....	....	....	....	−85.9	−112.5	−168.0	−139.5
Monetary authorities	4 901	....	....	....	....	....	....	....	....
General government	4 902	....	....	....	....	....	....	....	....
Banks	4 903	....	....	....	....	−2.7	−3.0	−.6	.1
Other sectors	4 904	....	....	....	....	−83.3	−109.5	−167.4	−139.6
Liabilities	4 905	−1.8	17.5	6.8	−1.1	....	.5	25.1	54.9
Monetary authorities	4 906	....	....	....	....	....	....	....	....
General government	4 907	....	....	....	....	....	....	....	....
Banks	4 908	−1.8	17.5	6.8	−1.1	....	....	−.2	10.6
Other sectors	4 909	....	....	....	....	....	.4	25.3	44.3

Table 2 (Concluded). STANDARD PRESENTATION, 2000–2007

(Millions of U.S. dollars)

	Code	2000	2001	2002	2003	2004	2005	2006	2007
D. OTHER INVESTMENT....................................	4 700 ..	**233.6**	**−320.7**	**822.0**	**984.0**	**670.5**	**2,103.0**	**725.8**	**6,321.9**
Assets...	4 703 ..	**−332.1**	**−100.4**	**283.0**	**250.9**	**−1,784.5**	**15.7**	**−2,975.5**	**−662.4**
Trade credits..	4 706 ..	120.8	....	−1.4	....	−185.8	−38.8	−155.7	−174.5
General government....................................	4 707 ..	....	....	....	....	....	....	....	....
of which: Short-term................................	4 709 ..	....	....	....	....	....	....	....	....
Other sectors..	4 710 ..	120.8	....	−1.4	....	−185.8	−38.8	−155.7	−174.5
of which: Short-term................................	4 712 ..	120.8	....	−1.4	....	−185.8	−38.8	−155.7	−174.5
Loans..	4 714 ..	−7.4	16.2	−17.1	−35.1	−57.3	−85.0	−174.4	−254.2
Monetary authorities..................................	4 715 ..	....	....	....	....	....	....	....	....
of which: Short-term................................	4 718 ..	....	....	....	....	....	....	....	....
General government....................................	4 719 ..	....	....	....	....	....	....	....	....
of which: Short-term................................	4 721 ..	....	....	....	....	....	....	....	....
Banks..	4 722 ..	−7.5	.1	−41.1	−36.9	−42.5	−53.2	−16.8	−136.7
of which: Short-term................................	4 724 ..	−3.3	−.8	−25.5	−20.4	−17.1	7.3	−15.6	5.4
Other sectors..	4 725 ..	....	16.2	24.0	1.8	−14.7	−31.8	−157.7	−117.4
of which: Short-term................................	4 727 ..	....	−.4	−11.6	.2	−7.2	−12.3	−56.6	−117.0
Currency and deposits................................	4 730 ..	−435.5	−92.7	284.0	294.3	−790.0	−540.1	−2,654.4	−95.5
Monetary authorities..................................	4 731 ..	....	....	....	....	....	....	....	....
General government....................................	4 732 ..	....	....	....	....	22.5	−1.7	−246.3	64.3
Banks..	4 733 ..	−486.7	−128.7	299.0	311.3	−715.1	−391.6	−1,786.3	−48.6
Other sectors..	4 734 ..	51.1	36.1	−14.9	−17.0	−97.4	−146.9	−621.8	−111.2
Other assets..	4 736 ..	−9.9	−24.0	17.5	−8.4	−751.5	679.6	9.0	−138.2
Monetary authorities..................................	4 737 ..	.9	−2.1	2.1	....	....	....	....	....
of which: Short-term................................	4 739 ..	.9	−2.1	2.1	....	....	....	....	....
General government....................................	4 740 ..	−9.1	−20.7	10.1	2.9	−746.0	705.2	−19.7	−33.9
of which: Short-term................................	4 742 ..	−9.1	−20.7	10.1	2.9	−746.0	705.2	−19.7	−33.9
Banks..	4 743 ..	−1.7	−1.2	5.2	−11.2	−5.6	−25.6	28.8	−104.2
of which: Short-term................................	4 745 ..	−1.7	−1.2	5.2	−11.2	−5.6	−25.6	28.8	−104.2
Other sectors..	4 746 ..	....	....	....	....	.1	....	−.1	−.1
of which: Short-term................................	4 748 ..	....	....	....	....	.1	....	−.1	−.1
Liabilities...	4 753 ..	**565.7**	**−220.2**	**539.0**	**733.1**	**2,455.1**	**2,087.3**	**3,701.3**	**6,984.3**
Trade credits..	4 756 ..	127.9	−128.1	193.2	−103.4	107.8	282.0	405.8	359.2
General government....................................	4 757 ..	....	....	....	....	....	....	....	....
of which: Short-term................................	4 759 ..	....	....	....	....	....	....	....	....
Other sectors..	4 760 ..	127.9	−128.1	193.2	−103.4	107.8	282.0	405.8	359.2
of which: Short-term................................	4 762 ..	127.9	−128.1	193.2	−103.4	107.8	282.0	405.8	359.2
Loans..	4 764 ..	330.3	−276.0	31.3	429.7	1,723.4	1,269.1	2,631.6	3,708.8
Monetary authorities..................................	4 765 ..	136.0	−168.5	−142.3	36.4	−55.2	−436.2	−341.4	−344.2
of which: Use of Fund credit and loans from the Fund..	4 766 ..	136.0	−168.5	−142.3	36.4	−55.2	−436.2	−341.4	−344.2
of which: Short-term................................	4 768 ..	....	....	....	....	....	....	....	....
General government....................................	4 769 ..	−80.3	−237.3	−117.2	64.0	105.4	14.6	−366.6	36.9
of which: Short-term................................	4 771 ..	....	....	....	....	....	....	....	....
Banks..	4 772 ..	37.6	8.6	42.3	62.1	479.8	647.9	437.3	277.7
of which: Short-term................................	4 774 ..	5.6	1.6	−3.2	−2.2	119.0	421.4	261.3	−422.4
Other sectors..	4 775 ..	237.1	121.3	248.5	267.1	1,193.3	1,042.7	2,902.2	3,738.3
of which: Short-term................................	4 777 ..	79.8	−54.8	41.0	140.1	280.9	493.4	1,286.6	2,540.9
Currency and deposits................................	4 780 ..	73.1	44.7	99.2	303.1	650.4	499.9	633.4	2,877.3
Monetary authorities..................................	4 781 ..	....	....	....	....	....	....	....	....
General government....................................	4 782 ..	....	....	....	....	....	....	....	....
Banks..	4 783 ..	73.1	44.7	99.2	303.1	650.4	499.9	633.4	2,877.3
Other sectors..	4 784 ..	....	....	....	....	....	....	....	....
Other liabilities..	4 786 ..	34.4	139.2	215.2	103.8	−26.4	36.2	30.5	39.0
Monetary authorities..................................	4 787 ..	....	....	....	....	....	....	....	....
of which: Short-term................................	4 789 ..	....	....	....	....	....	....	....	....
General government....................................	4 790 ..	−7.7	−2.1	....	....	....	....	....	....
of which: Short-term................................	4 792 ..	−7.7	−2.1	....	....	....	....	....	....
Banks..	4 793 ..	−2.2	101.0	202.8	80.0	−33.8	30.4	20.4	31.7
of which: Short-term................................	4 795 ..	−2.2	101.0	202.8	80.0	−33.8	30.4	20.4	31.7
Other sectors..	4 796 ..	44.3	40.3	12.4	23.8	7.4	5.8	10.1	7.2
of which: Short-term................................	4 798 ..	44.3	40.3	12.4	23.8	7.4	5.8	10.1	7.2
E. RESERVE ASSETS..	4 802 ..	**−408.9**	**−275.4**	**−586.3**	**−929.9**	**−1,846.4**	**−415.0**	**−1,924.2**	**−4,017.0**
Monetary gold..	4 812 ..	....	....	....	....	....	....	....	....
Special drawing rights.................................	4 811 ..	−6.0	81.4	2.9	−60.1	54.1	11.7	.1	.1
Reserve position in the Fund........................	4 810 ..	−.1	....	....	....	−.2	−.2	−.2	−.3
Foreign exchange..	4 803 ..	−402.9	−356.8	−589.2	−869.9	−1,900.3	−426.5	−1,924.2	−4,016.8
Other claims..	4 813 ..	....	....	....	....	....	....	....	....
NET ERRORS AND OMISSIONS...........................	4 998 ..	**33.9**	**515.4**	**−715.9**	**−889.0**	**370.8**	**−1,219.4**	**−907.4**	**−2,074.1**

Table 3. INTERNATIONAL INVESTMENT POSITION (End-period stocks), 2000–2007

(Millions of U.S. dollars)

	Code	2000	2001	2002	2003	2004	2005	2006	2007
ASSETS	8 995 C.	8,826.0	9,145.8	10,028.9	12,016.6	16,472.4	15,657.9	22,768.5	30,194.3
Direct investment abroad	8 505	87.0	96.7	125.0	102.6	−118.1	123.5	288.0	613.5
Equity capital and reinvested earnings	8 506	45.2	51.5	77.7	106.1	142.7	120.8	203.6	488.1
Claims on affiliated enterprises	8 507	45.2	51.5	77.7	106.1	142.7	120.8	203.6	488.1
Liabilities to affiliated enterprises	8 508	....	....	....	....	....	....	....	....
Other capital	8 530	41.8	45.2	47.3	−3.5	−260.8	2.7	84.4	125.4
Claims on affiliated enterprises	8 535	95.6	99.0	101.1	5.6	17.4	30.3	110.7	155.3
Liabilities to affiliated enterprises	8 540	−53.8	−53.8	−53.8	−9.1	−278.1	−27.6	−26.3	−29.8
Portfolio investment	8 602	728.3	798.7	667.5	803.3	883.0	790.5	1,250.1	1,506.6
Equity securities	8 610	28.7	.4	.8	2.7	31.2	23.2	174.7	378.5
Monetary authorities	8 611	....	....	....	....	....	....	....	....
General government	8 612	....	....	....	....	....	....	....	....
Banks	8 613	27.8	.1	.1	1.4	1.3	1.4	1.8	3.4
Other sectors	8 614	.9	.3	.7	1.2	29.8	21.7	173.0	375.1
Debt securities	8 619	699.6	798.3	666.7	800.6	851.8	767.4	1,075.4	1,128.1
Bonds and notes	8 620	517.9	650.1	576.9	765.4	761.0	591.6	928.4	993.1
Monetary authorities	8 621	....	....	....	....	....	....	....	....
General government	8 622	356.9	495.7	237.2	239.9	....	....	....	....
Banks	8 623	135.3	124.3	323.8	519.6	751.2	574.1	841.8	658.3
Other sectors	8 624	25.7	30.1	15.9	5.9	9.8	17.5	86.5	334.8
Money market instruments	8 630	181.7	148.2	89.8	35.2	90.9	175.8	147.0	135.0
Monetary authorities	8 631	79.8	....	....	....	....	....	....	....
General government	8 632	85.5	64.9	50.0	26.6	....	....	....	....
Banks	8 633	11.3	82.7	38.3	7.3	88.7	175.8	147.0	133.3
Other sectors	8 634	5.1	.6	1.5	1.3	2.2	....	....	1.8
Financial derivatives	8 900	....	....	....	....	....	28.6	265.9	151.0
Monetary authorities	8 901	....	....	....	....	....	....	....	....
General government	8 902	....	....	....	....	....	....	....	....
Banks	8 903	....	....	....	....	....	2.7	.6	.1
Other sectors	8 904	....	....	....	....	....	25.9	265.2	150.9
Other investment	8 703	4,550.4	4,669.9	4,489.4	4,284.2	6,371.2	6,020.5	9,208.4	10,385.8
Trade credits	8 706	....	....	....	249.1	464.5	516.9	730.6	930.8
General government	8 707	....	....	....	....	....	....	....	....
of which: Short-term	8 709	....	....	....	....	....	....	....	....
Other sectors	8 710	....	....	....	249.1	464.5	516.9	730.6	930.8
of which: Short-term	8 712	....	....	....	249.1	464.5	516.9	730.6	930.8
Loans	8 714	21.6	18.3	40.9	63.6	140.8	192.7	370.3	670.5
Monetary authorities	8 715	....	....	....	....	....	....	....	....
of which: Short-term	8 718	....	....	....	....	....	....	....	....
General government	8 719	....	....	....	....	....	....	....	....
of which: Short-term	8 721	....	....	....	....	....	....	....	....
Banks	8 722	21.5	18.2	40.2	57.2	115.9	142.7	174.7	329.6
of which: Short-term	8 724	11.3	7.3	34.7	32.6	32.1	14.9	33.0	28.9
Other sectors	8 725	.1	.1	.7	6.3	24.9	50.1	195.6	340.9
of which: Short-term	8 727	....	....	.6	4.6	15.1	23.7	69.3	202.7
Currency and deposits	8 730	2,093.6	2,184.5	1,972.0	1,804.9	2,760.5	3,038.1	5,998.3	6,544.8
Monetary authorities	8 731	....	....	3.2	....	....	....	....	....
General government	8 732	....	....	....	....	....	10.8	282.1	247.1
Banks	8 733	1,766.6	1,810.5	1,577.8	1,350.9	2,183.5	2,383.3	4,408.2	4,734.7
Other sectors	8 734	327.0	374.0	391.0	454.0	577.0	644.0	1,308.0	1,563.0
Other assets	8 736	2,435.2	2,467.1	2,476.5	2,166.7	3,005.4	2,272.7	2,109.2	2,239.6
Monetary authorities	8 737	.4	.4	.4	.5	16.0	13.5	16.0	....
of which: Short-term	8 739	....	....	....	....	....	....	....	....
General government	8 740	2,416.7	2,446.7	2,461.1	2,135.9	1,963.3	2,205.8	2,065.0	2,101.9
of which: Short-term	8 742	2,416.7	2,446.7	2,461.1	2,135.9	1,963.3	2,147.9	2,004.1	2,037.9
Banks	8 743	18.1	20.0	15.0	30.3	1,026.1	53.5	28.2	137.7
of which: Short-term	8 745	18.1	20.0	15.0	30.3	1,026.1	53.5	28.2	137.7
Other sectors	8 746	....	....	....	....	....	....	....	....
of which: Short-term	8 748	....	....	....	....	....	....	....	....
Reserve assets	8 802	3,460.3	3,580.5	4,747.0	6,826.5	9,336.4	8,694.8	11,756.1	17,537.4
Monetary gold	8 812	305.3	289.6	340.0	535.5	560.1	654.2	813.1	1,059.5
Special drawing rights	8 811	84.6	2.3	.7	67.7	13.1	1.0	1.1	1.0
Reserve position in the Fund	8 810	42.7	41.2	44.6	48.7	51.0	47.2	49.9	52.7
Foreign exchange	8 803	2,998.2	3,221.1	4,280.0	6,051.4	8,582.7	7,891.7	10,790.3	16,424.2
Other claims	8 813	29.5	26.3	81.7	123.2	129.4	100.7	101.7	....

Table 3 (Concluded). INTERNATIONAL INVESTMENT POSITION (End-period stocks), 2000–2007

(Millions of U.S. dollars)

	Code	2000	2001	2002	2003	2004	2005	2006	2007
LIABILITIES	8 995 D.	**13,215.7**	**13,019.1**	**14,506.5**	**18,022.4**	**23,443.6**	**27,918.2**	**43,114.3**	**66,116.4**
Direct investment in Bulgaria	8 555	**2,257.3**	**2,757.7**	**3,662.3**	**6,247.0**	**9,219.7**	**13,851.0**	**23,080.4**	**37,312.7**
Equity capital and reinvested earnings	8 556	1,867.8	2,188.3	2,860.2	4,634.0	7,142.6	9,342.7	15,542.8	23,257.5
Claims on direct investors	8 557	....	....	....	....	....	....	....	....
Liabilities to direct investors	8 558	1,867.8	2,188.3	2,860.2	4,634.0	7,142.6	9,342.7	15,542.8	23,257.5
Other capital	8 580	389.5	569.4	802.1	1,613.1	2,077.1	4,508.3	7,537.6	14,055.2
Claims on direct investors	8 585	−39.0	−20.3	−53.6	−78.2	−368.6	−328.5	−452.8	−792.4
Liabilities to direct investors	8 590	428.5	589.7	855.7	1,691.3	2,445.7	4,836.8	7,990.3	14,847.6
Portfolio investment	8 652	**5,193.6**	**5,073.2**	**4,667.0**	**4,559.6**	**3,942.2**	**2,646.7**	**3,620.9**	**3,718.5**
Equity securities	8 660	99.9	95.3	76.4	31.1	39.2	439.7	675.0	1,237.8
Banks	8 663	24.4	31.3	29.6	26.3	32.8	30.6	99.0	561.7
Other sectors	8 664	75.5	64.0	46.8	4.8	6.4	409.1	576.0	676.1
Debt securities	8 669	5,093.7	4,977.9	4,590.6	4,528.5	3,903.1	2,207.0	2,945.9	2,480.6
Bonds and notes	8 670	5,093.7	4,977.9	4,590.6	4,528.5	3,903.1	2,207.0	2,710.2	2,480.6
Monetary authorities	8 671	....	....	....	....	....	....	....	....
General government	8 672	5,093.7	4,977.9	4,590.6	4,524.8	3,891.3	2,037.4	2,113.2	1,832.5
Banks	8 673	....	....	....	....	7.9	125.8	186.5	194.6
Other sectors	8 674	....	....	....	3.7	3.9	43.8	410.5	453.5
Money market instruments	8 680	....	....	....	....	....	....	235.7	....
Monetary authorities	8 681	....	....	....	....	....	....	....	....
General government	8 682	....	....	....	....	....	....	....	....
Banks	8 683	....	....	....	....	....	....	....	....
Other sectors	8 684	....	....	....	....	....	....	235.7	....
Financial derivatives	8 905	**1.8**	**19.2**	....	....	....	**38.6**	**84.2**	**50.0**
Monetary authorities	8 906	....	....	....	....	....	....	....	....
General government	8 907	....	....	....	....	....	23.3	31.6	31.4
Banks	8 908	1.8	19.2	....	....	....	....	....	4.2
Other sectors	8 909	....	....	....	....	....	15.3	52.6	14.4
Other investment	8 753	**5,763.0**	**5,169.0**	**6,177.2**	**7,215.8**	**10,281.6**	**11,381.9**	**16,328.7**	**25,035.2**
Trade credits	8 756	837.4	712.4	1,146.9	826.2	1,088.4	1,262.1	1,892.6	2,293.0
General government	8 757	....	....	....	....	....	....	....	....
of which: Short-term	8 759	....	....	....	....	....	....	....	....
Other sectors	8 760	837.4	712.4	1,146.9	826.2	1,088.4	1,262.1	1,892.6	2,293.0
of which: Short-term	8 762	*803.7*	*654.5*	*1,094.5*	*826.2*	*1,088.4*	*1,262.1*	*1,892.6*	*2,293.0*
Loans	8 764	4,568.1	4,131.0	4,475.5	5,640.2	7,693.8	8,350.0	11,780.7	16,801.5
Monetary authorities	8 765	1,322.0	1,109.7	1,049.2	1,187.5	1,183.3	660.1	340.9	....
of which: Use of Fund credit and loans from the Fund	8 766	*1,322.0*	*1,109.7*	*1,049.2*	*1,187.5*	*1,183.3*	*660.1*	*340.9*	....
of which: Short-term	8 768	....	....	....	....	....	....	....	....
General government	8 769	2,332.6	2,109.7	2,193.7	2,668.3	2,859.2	2,558.3	2,420.7	2,720.3
of which: Short-term	8 771	....	....	....	....	....	....	....	....
Banks	8 772	43.2	49.9	94.3	249.3	798.5	1,439.7	1,957.5	2,371.5
of which: Short-term	8 774	*9.3*	*10.6*	*13.7*	*12.2*	*35.2*	*674.4*	*940.9*	*480.9*
Other sectors	8 775	870.3	861.7	1,138.3	1,535.1	2,852.8	3,691.9	7,061.5	11,709.7
of which: Short-term	8 777	*155.2*	*97.4*	*155.2*	*339.0*	*969.3*	*1,112.0*	*2,652.5*	*5,615.0*
Currency and deposits	8 780	174.5	195.7	309.0	627.4	1,360.6	1,647.6	2,502.4	5,759.1
Monetary authorities	8 781	....	....	....	....	....	....	....	....
General government	8 782	....	....	....	....	....	....	....	....
Banks	8 783	174.5	195.7	309.0	627.4	1,360.6	1,647.6	2,502.4	5,759.1
Other sectors	8 784	....	....	....	....	....	....	....	....
Other liabilities	8 786	183.0	129.9	245.8	121.9	138.9	122.2	153.1	181.6
Monetary authorities	8 787	.9	.3	.1	....	....	....	....	....
of which: Short-term	8 789	*.9*	*.3*	*.1*	....	....	....	....	....
General government	8 790	3.5	1.4	1.4	.8	.5	.5	.5	.2
of which: Short-term	8 792	*3.5*	*1.4*	*1.4*	*.8*	*.5*	*.5*	*.5*	*.2*
Banks	8 793	178.6	128.2	244.3	121.1	138.4	121.8	152.6	181.4
of which: Short-term	8 795	*178.6*	*128.2*	*244.3*	*121.1*	*138.4*	*121.8*	*152.6*	*181.4*
Other sectors	8 796	....	....	....	....	....	....	....	....
of which: Short-term	8 798	....	....	....	....	....	....	....	....
NET INTERNATIONAL INVESTMENT POSITION	8 995	**−4,389.7**	**−3,873.3**	**−4,477.6**	**−6,005.8**	**−6,971.1**	**−12,260.2**	**−20,345.7**	**−35,922.0**
Conversion rates: leva per U.S. dollar (end of period)	0 102	2.1019	2.2193	1.8850	1.5486	1.4359	1.6579	1.4851	1.3312

Table 1. ANALYTIC PRESENTATION, 2000–2007

(Millions of U.S. dollars)

	Code	2000	2001	2002	2003	2004	2005	2006	2007
A. Current Account[1]	4 993 Z.	**−392.0**	**−380.8**	....	....	....	....	....	....
Goods: exports f.o.b.	2 100 ..	205.6	223.5	....	....	....	....	....	....
Goods: imports f.o.b.	3 100 ..	−517.7	−509.3	....	....	....	....	....	....
Balance on Goods	4 100 ..	*−312.1*	*−285.8*	....	....	....	....	....	....
Services: credit	2 200 ..	31.4	36.5	....	....	....	....	....	....
Services: debit	3 200 ..	−139.9	−141.2	....	....	....	....	....	....
Balance on Goods and Services	4 991 ..	*−420.6*	*−390.5*	....	....	....	....	....	....
Income: credit	2 300 ..	13.5	15.2	....	....	....	....	....	....
Income: debit	3 300 ..	−33.6	−39.7	....	....	....	....	....	....
Balance on Goods, Services, and Income	4 992 ..	*−440.7*	*−414.9*	....	....	....	....	....	....
Current transfers: credit	2 379 Z.	87.6	72.0	....	....	....	....	....	....
Current transfers: debit	3 379 ..	−38.9	−37.9	....	....	....	....	....	....
B. Capital Account[1]	4 994 Z.	**175.9**	**165.2**	....	....	....	....	....	....
Capital account: credit	2 994 Z.	175.9	165.2	....	....	....	....	....	....
Capital account: debit	3 994 ..	....	....	....	....	....	....	....	....
Total, Groups A Plus B	4 981 ..	*−216.1*	*−215.6*	....	....	....	....	....	....
C. Financial Account[1]	4 995 W.	**19.2**	**25.2**	....	....	....	....	....	....
Direct investment abroad	4 505 ..	−.2	−.6	....	....	....	....	....	....
Direct investment in Burkina Faso	4 555 Z.	23.2	8.8	....	....	....	....	....	....
Portfolio investment assets	4 602 ..	6.2	10.0	....	....	....	....	....	....
Equity securities	4 610 ..	.4	−2.1	....	....	....	....	....	....
Debt securities	4 619 ..	5.8	12.2	....	....	....	....	....	....
Portfolio investment liabilities	4 652 Z.	−2.6	.7	....	....	....	....	....	....
Equity securities	4 660 ..	−2.6	.7	....	....	....	....	....	....
Debt securities	4 669 Z.	....	....	....	....	....	....	....	....
Financial derivatives	4 910 ..	....	....	....	....	....	....	....	....
Financial derivatives assets	4 900 ..	....	....	....	....	....	....	....	....
Financial derivatives liabilities	4 905 ..	....	....	....	....	....	....	....	....
Other investment assets	4 703 ..	−9.7	5.6	....	....	....	....	....	....
Monetary authorities	4 701 ..	....	....	....	....	....	....	....	....
General government	4 704 ..	−2.1	−.5	....	....	....	....	....	....
Banks	4 705 ..	−3.0	16.4	....	....	....	....	....	....
Other sectors	4 728 ..	−4.6	−10.3	....	....	....	....	....	....
Other investment liabilities	4 753 W.	2.2	.6	....	....	....	....	....	....
Monetary authorities	4 753 WA	5.7	.7	....	....	....	....	....	....
General government	4 753 ZB	....	....	....	....	....	....	....	....
Banks	4 753 ZC	−13.7	−4.2	....	....	....	....	....	....
Other sectors	4 753 ZD	10.2	4.2	....	....	....	....	....	....
Total, Groups A Through C	4 983 ..	*−196.9*	*−190.4*	....	....	....	....	....	....
D. Net Errors and Omissions	4 998 ..	**5.1**	**3.4**	....	....	....	....	....	....
Total, Groups A Through D	4 984 ..	*−191.8*	*−187.0*	....	....	....	....	....	....
E. Reserves and Related Items	4 802 A.	**191.8**	**187.0**	....	....	....	....	....	....
Reserve assets	4 802 ..	30.6	−31.0	....	....	....	....	....	....
Use of Fund credit and loans	4 766 ..	−2.4	8.5	....	....	....	....	....	....
Exceptional financing	4 920 ..	163.6	209.6	....	....	....	....	....	....
Conversion rates: CFA francs per U.S. dollar	0 101 ..	**711.98**	**733.04**	**696.99**	**581.20**	**528.28**	**527.47**	**522.89**	**479.27**

[1] Excludes components that have been classified in the categories of Group E.

Table 2. STANDARD PRESENTATION, 2000–2007

(Millions of U.S. dollars)

	Code	2000	2001	2002	2003	2004	2005	2006	2007
CURRENT ACCOUNT.....................................	4 993 ..	**−318.8**	**−291.0**	....	....	....	....	....	....
A. GOODS...	4 100 ..	**−312.1**	**−285.8**	....	....	....	....	....	....
Credit..	2 100 ..	**205.6**	**223.5**	....	....	....	....	....	....
General merchandise: exports f.o.b.	2 110 ..	196.9	220.5	....	....	....	....	....	....
Goods for processing: exports f.o.b.	2 150 ..	....	....	....	....	....	....	....	....
Repairs on goods	2 160 ..	....	....	....	....	....	....	....	....
Goods procured in ports by carriers	2 170 ..	....	....	....	....	....	....	....	....
Nonmonetary gold	2 180 ..	8.7	3.0	....	....	....	....	....	....
Debit...	3 100 ..	**−517.7**	**−509.3**	....	....	....	....	....	....
General merchandise: imports f.o.b.	3 110 ..	−513.6	−505.3	....	....	....	....	....	....
Goods for processing: imports f.o.b.	3 150 ..	....	....	....	....	....	....	....	....
Repairs on goods	3 160 ..	−1.1	−1.1	....	....	....	....	....	....
Goods procured in ports by carriers	3 170 ..	−2.9	−2.8	....	....	....	....	....	....
Nonmonetary gold	3 180 ..	....	....	....	....	....	....	....	....
B. SERVICES..	4 200 ..	**−108.5**	**−104.7**	....	....	....	....	....	....
Total credit...	2 200 ..	*31.4*	*36.5*	....	....	....	....	....	....
Total debit...	3 200 ..	*−139.9*	*−141.2*	....	....	....	....	....	....
Transportation services, credit................	2 205 ..	**3.7**	**4.7**	....	....	....	....	....	....
Passenger..	2 850 ..	*3.7*	*4.7*	....	....	....	....	....	....
Freight...	2 851 ..	....	....	....	....	....	....	....	....
Other...	2 852 ..	....	....	....	....	....	....	....	....
Sea transport, passenger	2 207 ..	....	....	....	....	....	....	....	....
Sea transport, freight	2 208 ..	....	....	....	....	....	....	....	....
Sea transport, other	2 209 ..	....	....	....	....	....	....	....	....
Air transport, passenger	2 211 ..	3.6	4.5	....	....	....	....	....	....
Air transport, freight	2 212 ..	....	....	....	....	....	....	....	....
Air transport, other	2 213 ..	....	....	....	....	....	....	....	....
Other transport, passenger	2 215 ..	.1	.2	....	....	....	....	....	....
Other transport, freight	2 216 ..	....	....	....	....	....	....	....	....
Other transport, other	2 217 ..	....	....	....	....	....	....	....	....
Transportation services, debit.................	3 205 ..	**−84.8**	**−87.8**	....	....	....	....	....	....
Passenger..	3 850 ..	*−10.3*	*−13.0*	....	....	....	....	....	....
Freight...	3 851 ..	*−73.5*	*−74.0*	....	....	....	....	....	....
Other...	3 852 ..	*−.9*	*−.8*	....	....	....	....	....	....
Sea transport, passenger	3 207 ..	....	....	....	....	....	....	....	....
Sea transport, freight	3 208 ..	−48.2	−53.6	....	....	....	....	....	....
Sea transport, other	3 209 ..	....	....	....	....	....	....	....	....
Air transport, passenger	3 211 ..	−10.3	−13.0	....	....	....	....	....	....
Air transport, freight	3 212 ..	−18.6	−17.7	....	....	....	....	....	....
Air transport, other	3 213 ..	−.9	−.8	....	....	....	....	....	....
Other transport, passenger	3 215 ..	....	....	....	....	....	....	....	....
Other transport, freight	3 216 ..	−6.7	−2.7	....	....	....	....	....	....
Other transport, other	3 217 ..	....	....	....	....	....	....	....	....
Travel, credit.......................................	2 236 ..	**19.1**	**19.9**	....	....	....	....	....	....
Business travel	2 237 ..	10.8	11.2	....	....	....	....	....	....
Personal travel	2 240 ..	8.3	8.7	....	....	....	....	....	....
Travel, debit..	3 236 ..	**−20.0**	**−21.7**	....	....	....	....	....	....
Business travel	3 237 ..	−20.0	−18.2	....	....	....	....	....	....
Personal travel	3 240 ..	....	−3.5	....	....	....	....	....	....
Other services, credit............................	2 200 BA	**8.6**	**11.9**	....	....	....	....	....	....
Communications	2 245 ..	2.3	3.3	....	....	....	....	....	....
Construction	2 249 ..	.5	....	....	....	....	....	....	....
Insurance	2 253 ..	.1	.1	....	....	....	....	....	....
Financial	2 260 ..	....	....	....	....	....	....	....	....
Computer and information	2 262 ..	....	....	....	....	....	....	....	....
Royalties and licence fees	2 266 ..	....	....	....	....	....	....	....	....
Other business services	2 268 ..	2.7	4.3	....	....	....	....	....	....
Personal, cultural, and recreational	2 287 ..	....	....	....	....	....	....	....	....
Government, n.i.e.	2 291 ..	3.0	4.2	....	....	....	....	....	....
Other services, debit.............................	3 200 BA	**−35.1**	**−31.7**	....	....	....	....	....	....
Communications	3 245 ..	−.6	−1.4	....	....	....	....	....	....
Construction	3 249 ..	−.1	....	....	....	....	....	....	....
Insurance	3 253 ..	−23.1	−19.6	....	....	....	....	....	....
Financial	3 260 ..	−.2	−.3	....	....	....	....	....	....
Computer and information	3 262 ..	−.7	−.5	....	....	....	....	....	....
Royalties and licence fees	3 266 ..	....	−.3	....	....	....	....	....	....
Other business services	3 268 ..	−2.1	−3.4	....	....	....	....	....	....
Personal, cultural, and recreational	3 287 ..	....	....	....	....	....	....	....	....
Government, n.i.e.	3 291 ..	−8.2	−6.2	....	....	....	....	....	....

Table 2 (Continued). STANDARD PRESENTATION, 2000–2007

(Millions of U.S. dollars)

	Code	2000	2001	2002	2003	2004	2005	2006	2007
C. INCOME...	4 300 ..	**−20.1**	**−24.4**	....	....	....	....	....	....
Total credit..	2 300 ..	*13.5*	*15.2*	....	....	....	....	....	....
Total debit..	3 300 ..	*−33.6*	*−39.7*	....	....	....	....	....	....
Compensation of employees, credit..................	2 310 ..	**4.9**	**6.3**	....	....	....	....	....	....
Compensation of employees, debit....................	3 310 ..	**−7.3**	**−7.2**	....	....	....	....	....	....
Investment income, credit...............................	2 320 ..	**8.7**	**8.9**	....	....	....	....	....	....
Direct investment income.................................	2 330 ..	....	.2	....	....	....	....	....	....
Dividends and distributed branch profits..........	2 332 ..	....	.2	....	....	....	....	....	....
Reinvested earnings and undistributed branch profits.....	2 333 ..	....	....	....	....	....	....	....	....
Income on debt (interest)................................	2 334 ..	....	....	....	....	....	....	....	....
Portfolio investment income.............................	2 339 ..	2.5	4.9	....	....	....	....	....	....
Income on equity.......................................	2 340 ..	.2	.1	....	....	....	....	....	....
Income on bonds and notes...........................	2 350 ..	2.3	3.4	....	....	....	....	....	....
Income on money market instruments...............	2 360 ..	....	1.5	....	....	....	....	....	....
Other investment income................................	2 370 ..	6.2	3.8	....	....	....	....	....	....
Investment income, debit.................................	3 320 ..	**−26.3**	**−32.5**	....	....	....	....	....	....
Direct investment income.................................	3 330 ..	−3.1	−4.7	....	....	....	....	....	....
Dividends and distributed branch profits..........	3 332 ..	−3.0	−2.0	....	....	....	....	....	....
Reinvested earnings and undistributed branch profits.....	3 333 ..	....	−2.6	....	....	....	....	....	....
Income on debt (interest)................................	3 334 ..	....	....	....	....	....	....	....	....
Portfolio investment income.............................	3 339 ..	−3.5	−3.8	....	....	....	....	....	....
Income on equity.......................................	3 340 ..	−.2	−3.1	....	....	....	....	....	....
Income on bonds and notes...........................	3 350 ..	−3.3	−.7	....	....	....	....	....	....
Income on money market instruments...............	3 360 ..	....	....	....	....	....	....	....	....
Other investment income................................	3 370 ..	−19.7	−24.0	....	....	....	....	....	....
D. CURRENT TRANSFERS...............................	4 379 ..	**121.9**	**123.9**	....	....	....	....	....	....
Credit...	2 379 ..	**160.8**	**161.8**	....	....	....	....	....	....
General government...	2 380 ..	73.2	89.8	....	....	....	....	....	....
Other sectors...	2 390 ..	87.6	72.0	....	....	....	....	....	....
Workers' remittances....................................	2 391 ..	62.5	43.6	....	....	....	....	....	....
Other current transfers.................................	2 392 ..	25.1	28.4	....	....	....	....	....	....
Debit..	3 379 ..	**−38.9**	**−37.9**	....	....	....	....	....	....
General government...	3 380 ..	−1.3	−1.1	....	....	....	....	....	....
Other sectors...	3 390 ..	−37.6	−36.8	....	....	....	....	....	....
Workers' remittances....................................	3 391 ..	−37.2	−36.8	....	....	....	....	....	....
Other current transfers.................................	3 392 ..	−.3	....	....	....	....	....	....	....
CAPITAL AND FINANCIAL ACCOUNT......................	4 996 ..	**313.7**	**287.6**	....	....	....	....	....	....
CAPITAL ACCOUNT...	4 994 ..	**186.2**	**197.2**	....	....	....	....	....	....
Total credit...	2 994 ..	*186.2*	*197.2*	....	....	....	....	....	....
Total debit..	3 994 ..	....	....	....	....	....	....	....	....
Capital transfers, credit...................................	2 400 ..	**186.2**	**197.2**	....	....	....	....	....	....
General government...	2 401 ..	181.3	190.5	....	....	....	....	....	....
Debt forgiveness...	2 402 ..	10.3	32.1	....	....	....	....	....	....
Other capital transfers.................................	2 410 ..	171.0	158.4	....	....	....	....	....	....
Other sectors...	2 430 ..	4.9	6.8	....	....	....	....	....	....
Migrants' transfers......................................	2 431 ..	....	....	....	....	....	....	....	....
Debt forgiveness...	2 432 ..	....	....	....	....	....	....	....	....
Other capital transfers.................................	2 440 ..	4.9	6.8	....	....	....	....	....	....
Capital transfers, debit....................................	3 400 ..	....	....	....	....	....	....	....	....
General government...	3 401 ..	....	....	....	....	....	....	....	....
Debt forgiveness...	3 402 ..	....	....	....	....	....	....	....	....
Other capital transfers.................................	3 410 ..	....	....	....	....	....	....	....	....
Other sectors...	3 430 ..	....	....	....	....	....	....	....	....
Migrants' transfers......................................	3 431 ..	....	....	....	....	....	....	....	....
Debt forgiveness...	3 432 ..	....	....	....	....	....	....	....	....
Other capital transfers.................................	3 440 ..	....	....	....	....	....	....	....	....
Nonproduced nonfinancial assets, credit..............	2 480 ..	....	....	....	....	....	....	....	....
Nonproduced nonfinancial assets, debit..............	3 480 ..	....	....	....	....	....	....	....	....

Table 2 (Continued). STANDARD PRESENTATION, 2000–2007

(Millions of U.S. dollars)

	Code	2000	2001	2002	2003	2004	2005	2006	2007
FINANCIAL ACCOUNT..	4 995 ..	**127.5**	**90.4**	....	....	....	....	....	....
A. DIRECT INVESTMENT..................................	4 500 ..	**22.9**	**8.2**	....	....	....	....	....	....
Direct investment abroad...................................	4 505 ..	**−.2**	**−.6**	....	....	....	....	....	....
Equity capital...	4 510 ..	−.1	−.6	....	....	....	....	....	....
Claims on affiliated enterprises......................	4 515 ..	....	....	....	....	....	....	....	....
Liabilities to affiliated enterprises..................	4 520 ..	−.1	−.6	....	....	....	....	....	....
Reinvested earnings.......................................	4 525 ..	....	....	....	....	....	....	....	....
Other capital...	4 530 ..	−.1	....	....	....	....	....	....	....
Claims on affiliated enterprises......................	4 535 ..	....	....	....	....	....	....	....	....
Liabilities to affiliated enterprises..................	4 540 ..	−.1	....	....	....	....	....	....	....
Direct investment in Burkina Faso..................	4 555 ..	**23.1**	**8.8**	....	....	....	....	....	....
Equity capital...	4 560 ..	22.6	4.9	....	....	....	....	....	....
Claims on direct investors.............................	4 565 ..	22.8	5.2	....	....	....	....	....	....
Liabilities to direct investors.........................	4 570 ..	−.1	−.3	....	....	....	....	....	....
Reinvested earnings.......................................	4 575 ..	....	2.6	....	....	....	....	....	....
Other capital...	4 580 ..	.4	1.3	....	....	....	....	....	....
Claims on direct investors.............................	4 585 ..	....	....	....	....	....	....	....	....
Liabilities to direct investors.........................	4 590 ..	.4	1.3	....	....	....	....	....	....
B. PORTFOLIO INVESTMENT..............................	4 600 ..	**6.4**	**12.1**	....	....	....	....	....	....
Assets..	4 602 ..	**6.2**	**10.0**	....	....	....	....	....	....
Equity securities..	4 610 ..	.4	−2.1	....	....	....	....	....	....
Monetary authorities......................................	4 611 ..	....	....	....	....	....	....	....	....
General government.......................................	4 612 ..	....	....	....	....	....	....	....	....
Banks..	4 613 ..	.5	−.3	....	....	....	....	....	....
Other sectors..	4 614 ..	−.1	−1.8	....	....	....	....	....	....
Debt securities..	4 619 ..	5.8	12.2	....	....	....	....	....	....
Bonds and notes...	4 620 ..	5.1	12.6	....	....	....	....	....	....
Monetary authorities......................................	4 621 ..	....	....	....	....	....	....	....	....
General government.......................................	4 622 ..	....	....	....	....	....	....	....	....
Banks..	4 623 ..	8.5	8.6	....	....	....	....	....	....
Other sectors..	4 624 ..	−3.4	4.0	....	....	....	....	....	....
Money market instruments.............................	4 630 ..	.7	−.4	....	....	....	....	....	....
Monetary authorities......................................	4 631 ..	....	....	....	....	....	....	....	....
General government.......................................	4 632 ..	....	....	....	....	....	....	....	....
Banks..	4 633 ..	.7	....	....	....	....	....	....	....
Other sectors..	4 634 ..	....	−.4	....	....	....	....	....	....
Liabilities...	4 652 ..	**.2**	**2.1**	....	....	....	....	....	....
Equity securities..	4 660 ..	−2.6	.7	....	....	....	....	....	....
Banks..	4 663 ..	−3.2	.3	....	....	....	....	....	....
Other sectors..	4 664 ..	.7	.4	....	....	....	....	....	....
Debt securities..	4 669 ..	2.8	1.4	....	....	....	....	....	....
Bonds and notes...	4 670 ..	2.8	1.4	....	....	....	....	....	....
Monetary authorities......................................	4 671 ..	....	....	....	....	....	....	....	....
General government.......................................	4 672 ..	....	....	....	....	....	....	....	....
Banks..	4 673 ..	....	....	....	....	....	....	....	....
Other sectors..	4 674 ..	2.8	1.4	....	....	....	....	....	....
Money market instruments.............................	4 680 ..	....	....	....	....	....	....	....	....
Monetary authorities......................................	4 681 ..	....	....	....	....	....	....	....	....
General government.......................................	4 682 ..	....	....	....	....	....	....	....	....
Banks..	4 683 ..	....	....	....	....	....	....	....	....
Other sectors..	4 684 ..	....	....	....	....	....	....	....	....
C. FINANCIAL DERIVATIVES..............................	4 910 ..	....	....	....	....	....	....	....	....
Monetary authorities......................................	4 911 ..	....	....	....	....	....	....	....	....
General government.......................................	4 912 ..	....	....	....	....	....	....	....	....
Banks..	4 913 ..	....	....	....	....	....	....	....	....
Other sectors..	4 914 ..	....	....	....	....	....	....	....	....
Assets..	4 900 ..	....	....	....	....	....	....	....	....
Monetary authorities......................................	4 901 ..	....	....	....	....	....	....	....	....
General government.......................................	4 902 ..	....	....	....	....	....	....	....	....
Banks..	4 903 ..	....	....	....	....	....	....	....	....
Other sectors..	4 904 ..	....	....	....	....	....	....	....	....
Liabilities...	4 905 ..	....	....	....	....	....	....	....	....
Monetary authorities......................................	4 906 ..	....	....	....	....	....	....	....	....
General government.......................................	4 907 ..	....	....	....	....	....	....	....	....
Banks..	4 908 ..	....	....	....	....	....	....	....	....
Other sectors..	4 909 ..	....	....	....	....	....	....	....	....

Table 2 (Concluded). STANDARD PRESENTATION, 2000–2007

(Millions of U.S. dollars)

	Code	2000	2001	2002	2003	2004	2005	2006	2007
D. OTHER INVESTMENT	4 700 ..	**67.5**	**101.0**	....	....	....	....	....	....
Assets	4 703 ..	**−9.7**	**5.6**	....	....	....	....	....	....
Trade credits	4 706 ..	−1.2	−2.0	....	....	....	....	....	....
General government	4 707 ..	....	....	....	....	....	....	....	....
of which: Short-term	4 709 ..	....	....	....	....	....	....	....	....
Other sectors	4 710 ..	−1.2	−2.0	....	....	....	....	....	....
of which: Short-term	4 712 ..	....	....	....	....	....	....	....	....
Loans	4 714 ..	−2.4	5.0	....	....	....	....	....	....
Monetary authorities	4 715 ..	....	....	....	....	....	....	....	....
of which: Short-term	4 718 ..	....	....	....	....	....	....	....	....
General government	4 719 ..	....	....	....	....	....	....	....	....
of which: Short-term	4 721 ..	....	....	....	....	....	....	....	....
Banks	4 722 ..	−2.4	5.0	....	....	....	....	....	....
of which: Short-term	4 724 ..	−1.7	−7.1	....	....	....	....	....	....
Other sectors	4 725 ..	....	....	....	....	....	....	....	....
of which: Short-term	4 727 ..	....	....	....	....	....	....	....	....
Currency and deposits	4 730 ..	−5.6	10.5	....	....	....	....	....	....
Monetary authorities	4 731 ..	....	....	....	....	....	....	....	....
General government	4 732 ..	−1.9	1.0	....	....	....	....	....	....
Banks	4 733 ..	−.4	12.3	....	....	....	....	....	....
Other sectors	4 734 ..	−3.3	−2.9	....	....	....	....	....	....
Other assets	4 736 ..	−.4	−7.9	....	....	....	....	....	....
Monetary authorities	4 737 ..	....	....	....	....	....	....	....	....
of which: Short-term	4 739 ..	....	....	....	....	....	....	....	....
General government	4 740 ..	−.2	−1.5	....	....	....	....	....	....
of which: Short-term	4 742 ..	....	....	....	....	....	....	....	....
Banks	4 743 ..	−.2	−.9	....	....	....	....	....	....
of which: Short-term	4 745 ..	−.2	−.9	....	....	....	....	....	....
Other sectors	4 746 ..	−.1	−5.5	....	....	....	....	....	....
of which: Short-term	4 748 ..	....	....	....	....	....	....	....	....
Liabilities	4 753 ..	**77.2**	**95.5**	....	....	....	....	....	....
Trade credits	4 756 ..	10.2	4.2	....	....	....	....	....	....
General government	4 757 ..	....	....	....	....	....	....	....	....
of which: Short-term	4 759 ..	....	....	....	....	....	....	....	....
Other sectors	4 760 ..	10.2	4.2	....	....	....	....	....	....
of which: Short-term	4 762 ..	....	....	....	....	....	....	....	....
Loans	4 764 ..	60.7	95.5	....	....	....	....	....	....
Monetary authorities	4 765 ..	−2.4	8.5	....	....	....	....	....	....
of which: Use of Fund credit and loans from the Fund	4 766 ..	−2.4	8.5	....	....	....	....	....	....
of which: Short-term	4 768 ..	....	....	....	....	....	....	....	....
General government	4 769 ..	45.7	75.0	....	....	....	....	....	....
of which: Short-term	4 771 ..	....	....	....	....	....	....	....	....
Banks	4 772 ..	12.6	−3.8	....	....	....	....	....	....
of which: Short-term	4 774 ..	12.6	−12.2	....	....	....	....	....	....
Other sectors	4 775 ..	4.8	15.8	....	....	....	....	....	....
of which: Short-term	4 777 ..	....	....	....	....	....	....	....	....
Currency and deposits	4 780 ..	−8.0	−3.5	....	....	....	....	....	....
Monetary authorities	4 781 ..	5.7	.7	....	....	....	....	....	....
General government	4 782 ..	....	....	....	....	....	....	....	....
Banks	4 783 ..	−13.7	−4.2	....	....	....	....	....	....
Other sectors	4 784 ..	....	....	....	....	....	....	....	....
Other liabilities	4 786 ..	14.4	−.7	....	....	....	....	....	....
Monetary authorities	4 787 ..	4.4	−4.9	....	....	....	....	....	....
of which: Short-term	4 789 ..	4.4	−4.9	....	....	....	....	....	....
General government	4 790 ..	....	....	....	....	....	....	....	....
of which: Short-term	4 792 ..	....	....	....	....	....	....	....	....
Banks	4 793 ..	....	3.4	....	....	....	....	....	....
of which: Short-term	4 795 ..	....	3.4	....	....	....	....	....	....
Other sectors	4 796 ..	10.0	.8	....	....	....	....	....	....
of which: Short-term	4 798 ..	10.0	.8	....	....	....	....	....	....
E. RESERVE ASSETS	4 802 ..	**30.6**	**−31.0**	....	....	....	....	....	....
Monetary gold	4 812 ..	....	....	....	....	....	....	....	....
Special drawing rights	4 811 ..	.3	−.1	....	....	....	....	....	....
Reserve position in the Fund	4 810 ..	....	....	....	....	....	....	....	....
Foreign exchange	4 803 ..	30.3	−30.9	....	....	....	....	....	....
Other claims	4 813 ..	....	....	....	....	....	....	....	....
NET ERRORS AND OMISSIONS	4 998 ..	**5.1**	**3.4**	....	....	....	....	....	....

Table 3. INTERNATIONAL INVESTMENT POSITION (End-period stocks), 2000–2007

(Millions of U.S. dollars)

	Code	2000	2001	2002	2003	2004	2005	2006	2007
ASSETS	8 995 C.	**457.2**	**428.8**	....	....	....	....	....	....
Direct investment abroad	8 505 ..	.4	.7	....	....	....	....	....	....
Equity capital and reinvested earnings	8 506 ..	.5	.7	....	....	....	....	....	....
Claims on affiliated enterprises	8 507 ..	.5	.7	....	....	....	....	....	....
Liabilities to affiliated enterprises	8 508 ..	....	....	....	....	....	....	....	....
Other capital	8 530 ..	−.1	....	....	....	....	....	....	....
Claims on affiliated enterprises	8 535 ..	....	....	....	....	....	....	....	....
Liabilities to affiliated enterprises	8 540 ..	−.1	....	....	....	....	....	....	....
Portfolio investment	8 602 ..	**84.0**	**51.8**	....	....	....	....	....	....
Equity securities	8 610 ..	1.3	3.1	....	....	....	....	....	....
Monetary authorities	8 611 ..	.9	2.7	....	....	....	....	....	....
General government	8 612 ..	....	....	....	....	....	....	....	....
Banks	8 613 ..	.4	.4	....	....	....	....	....	....
Other sectors	8 614 ..	....	....	....	....	....	....	....	....
Debt securities	8 619 ..	82.7	48.7	....	....	....	....	....	....
Bonds and notes	8 620 ..	82.0	47.3	....	....	....	....	....	....
Monetary authorities	8 621 ..	....	....	....	....	....	....	....	....
General government	8 622 ..	4.6	2.2	....	....	....	....	....	....
Banks	8 623 ..	77.4	45.1	....	....	....	....	....	....
Other sectors	8 624 ..	....	....	....	....	....	....	....	....
Money market instruments	8 630 ..	.7	1.4	....	....	....	....	....	....
Monetary authorities	8 631 ..	....	....	....	....	....	....	....	....
General government	8 632 ..	....	1.1	....	....	....	....	....	....
Banks	8 633 ..	.7	.3	....	....	....	....	....	....
Other sectors	8 634 ..	....	....	....	....	....	....	....	....
Financial derivatives	8 900 ..	....	....	....	....	....	....	....	....
Monetary authorities	8 901 ..	....	....	....	....	....	....	....	....
General government	8 902 ..	....	....	....	....	....	....	....	....
Banks	8 903 ..	....	....	....	....	....	....	....	....
Other sectors	8 904 ..	....	....	....	....	....	....	....	....
Other investment	8 703 ..	**130.1**	**115.8**	....	....	....	....	....	....
Trade credits	8 706 ..	1.6	2.7	....	....	....	....	....	....
General government	8 707 ..	1.6	2.7	....	....	....	....	....	....
of which: Short-term	8 709 ..	....	....	....	....	....	....	....	....
Other sectors	8 710 ..	....	....	....	....	....	....	....	....
of which: Short-term	8 712 ..	....	....	....	....	....	....	....	....
Loans	8 714 ..	24.8	18.6	....	....	....	....	....	....
Monetary authorities	8 715 ..	....	....	....	....	....	....	....	....
of which: Short-term	8 718 ..	....	....	....	....	....	....	....	....
General government	8 719 ..	....	....	....	....	....	....	....	....
of which: Short-term	8 721 ..	....	....	....	....	....	....	....	....
Banks	8 722 ..	24.8	18.6	....	....	....	....	....	....
of which: Short-term	8 724 ..	*5.0*	*11.7*	....	....	....	....	....	....
Other sectors	8 725 ..	....	....	....	....	....	....	....	....
of which: Short-term	8 727 ..	....	....	....	....	....	....	....	....
Currency and deposits	8 730 ..	100.3	81.5	....	....	....	....	....	....
Monetary authorities	8 731 ..	....	....	....	....	....	....	....	....
General government	8 732 ..	1.9	.8	....	....	....	....	....	....
Banks	8 733 ..	97.2	79.9	....	....	....	....	....	....
Other sectors	8 734 ..	1.2	.8	....	....	....	....	....	....
Other assets	8 736 ..	3.3	13.0	....	....	....	....	....	....
Monetary authorities	8 737 ..	....	....	....	....	....	....	....	....
of which: Short-term	8 739 ..	....	....	....	....	....	....	....	....
General government	8 740 ..	.2	3.8	....	....	....	....	....	....
of which: Short-term	8 742 ..	....	*3.8*	....	....	....	....	....	....
Banks	8 743 ..	3.1	3.8	....	....	....	....	....	....
of which: Short-term	8 745 ..	*3.1*	*3.8*	....	....	....	....	....	....
Other sectors	8 746 ..	.1	5.5	....	....	....	....	....	....
of which: Short-term	8 748 ..	*.1*	*5.5*	....	....	....	....	....	....
Reserve assets	8 802 ..	**242.6**	**260.5**	....	....	....	....	....	....
Monetary gold	8 812 ..	....	....	....	....	....	....	....	....
Special drawing rights	8 811 ..	.4	.5	.4	.3	.2	.2	....	.1
Reserve position in the Fund	8 810 ..	9.4	9.1	9.9	10.8	11.3	10.5	11.1	11.7
Foreign exchange	8 803 ..	232.8	250.9	....	....	....	....	....	....
Other claims	8 813 ..	....	....	....	....	....	....	....	....

Table 3 (Concluded). INTERNATIONAL INVESTMENT POSITION (End-period stocks), 2000–2007

(Millions of U.S. dollars)

	Code	2000	2001	2002	2003	2004	2005	2006	2007
LIABILITIES	8 995 D.	**1,815.3**	**1,513.9**	....	....	....	....	....	....
Direct investment in Burkina Faso	8 555 ..	**27.8**	**15.9**	....	....	....	....	....	....
Equity capital and reinvested earnings	8 556 ..	27.4	14.6	....	....	....	....	....	....
Claims on direct investors	8 557 ..	....	....	....	....	....	....	....	....
Liabilities to direct investors	8 558 ..	27.4	14.6	....	....	....	....	....	....
Other capital	8 580 ..	.4	1.3	....	....	....	....	....	....
Claims on direct investors	8 585 ..	....	....	....	....	....	....	....	....
Liabilities to direct investors	8 590 ..	.4	1.3	....	....	....	....	....	....
Portfolio investment	8 652 ..	**4.3**	**2.9**	....	....	....	....	....	....
Equity securities	8 660 ..	1.5	1.6	....	....	....	....	....	....
Banks	8 663 ..	.6	1.1	....	....	....	....	....	....
Other sectors	8 664 ..	.9	.5	....	....	....	....	....	....
Debt securities	8 669 ..	2.8	1.3	....	....	....	....	....	....
Bonds and notes	8 670 ..	2.8	1.3	....	....	....	....	....	....
Monetary authorities	8 671 ..	....	....	....	....	....	....	....	....
General government	8 672 ..	....	....	....	....	....	....	....	....
Banks	8 673 ..	....	....	....	....	....	....	....	....
Other sectors	8 674 ..	2.8	1.3	....	....	....	....	....	....
Money market instruments	8 680 ..	....	....	....	....	....	....	....	....
Monetary authorities	8 681 ..	....	....	....	....	....	....	....	....
General government	8 682 ..	....	....	....	....	....	....	....	....
Banks	8 683 ..	....	....	....	....	....	....	....	....
Other sectors	8 684 ..	....	....	....	....	....	....	....	....
Financial derivatives	8 905 ..	....	....	....	....	....	....	....	....
Monetary authorities	8 906 ..	....	....	....	....	....	....	....	....
General government	8 907 ..	....	....	....	....	....	....	....	....
Banks	8 908 ..	....	....	....	....	....	....	....	....
Other sectors	8 909 ..	....	....	....	....	....	....	....	....
Other investment	8 753 ..	**1,783.2**	**1,495.1**	....	....	....	....	....	....
Trade credits	8 756 ..	10.7	4.2	....	....	....	....	....	....
General government	8 757 ..	10.7	4.2	....	....	....	....	....	....
of which: Short-term	8 759 ..	....	....	....	....	....	....	....	....
Other sectors	8 760 ..	....	....	....	....	....	....	....	....
of which: Short-term	8 762 ..	....	....	....	....	....	....	....	....
Loans	8 764 ..	1,639.4	1,399.2	....	....	....	....	....	....
Monetary authorities	8 765 ..	112.1	116.5	....	....	....	....	....	....
of which: Use of Fund credit and loans from the Fund	8 766 ..	*112.1*	*116.5*	*126.5*	*124.7*	*114.7*	*103.5*	*34.9*	*37.5*
of which: Short-term	8 768 ..	....	....	....	....	....	....	....	....
General government	8 769 ..	1,508.8	1,248.4	....	....	....	....	....	....
of which: Short-term	8 771 ..	....	....	....	....	....	....	....	....
Banks	8 772 ..	12.7	8.3	....	....	....	....	....	....
of which: Short-term	8 774 ..	*12.7*	....	....	....	....	....	....	....
Other sectors	8 775 ..	5.8	26.0	....	....	....	....	....	....
of which: Short-term	8 777 ..	*5.8*	*20.4*	....	....	....	....	....	....
Currency and deposits	8 780 ..	118.4	79.8	....	....	....	....	....	....
Monetary authorities	8 781 ..	32.4	3.0	....	....	....	....	....	....
General government	8 782 ..	....	....	....	....	....	....	....	....
Banks	8 783 ..	86.0	76.8	....	....	....	....	....	....
Other sectors	8 784 ..	....	....	....	....	....	....	....	....
Other liabilities	8 786 ..	14.6	11.8	....	....	....	....	....	....
Monetary authorities	8 787 ..	4.9	−.2	....	....	....	....	....	....
of which: Short-term	8 789 ..	*4.9*	*−.2*	....	....	....	....	....	....
General government	8 790 ..	....	....	....	....	....	....	....	....
of which: Short-term	8 792 ..	....	....	....	....	....	....	....	....
Banks	8 793 ..	....	....	....	....	....	....	....	....
of which: Short-term	8 795 ..	....	....	....	....	....	....	....	....
Other sectors	8 796 ..	9.7	12.0	....	....	....	....	....	....
of which: Short-term	8 798 ..	*9.7*	*12.0*	....	....	....	....	....	....
NET INTERNATIONAL INVESTMENT POSITION	8 995 ..	**−1,358.2**	**−1,085.2**	....	....	....	....	....	....
Conversion rates: CFA francs per U.S. dollar (end of period)	0 102 ..	704.95	744.31	625.50	519.36	481.58	556.04	498.07	445.59

Table 1. ANALYTIC PRESENTATION, 2000–2007

(Millions of U.S. dollars)

	Code	2000	2001	2002	2003	2004	2005	2006	2007
A. Current Account[1]	4 993 Z.	**−103.1**	**−108.6**	**−111.2**	**−131.0**	**−166.1**	**−225.9**	**−324.0**	**−275.7**
Goods: exports f.o.b.	2 100 ..	49.1	39.2	31.0	37.5	47.9	56.9	58.7	52.9
Goods: imports f.o.b.	3 100 ..	−107.9	−108.3	−104.8	−130.0	−145.4	−188.9	−244.7	−257.6
Balance on Goods	4 100 ..	*−58.8*	*−69.1*	*−73.8*	*−92.5*	*−97.6*	*−132.1*	*−186.0*	*−204.7*
Services: credit	2 200 ..	4.0	5.2	7.5	7.3	15.8	34.8	34.5	30.8
Services: debit	3 200 ..	−42.6	−38.2	−42.7	−45.3	−86.6	−134.1	−202.2	−177.1
Balance on Goods and Services	4 991 ..	*−97.5*	*−102.1*	*−109.0*	*−130.5*	*−168.4*	*−231.3*	*−353.8*	*−351.0*
Income: credit	2 300 ..	2.4	1.9	.9	1.3	1.3	3.2	4.6	8.7
Income: debit	3 300 ..	−14.5	−15.8	−12.6	−18.6	−20.5	−20.9	−13.4	−14.6
Balance on Goods, Services, and Income	4 992 ..	*−109.5*	*−116.0*	*−120.7*	*−147.8*	*−187.6*	*−249.1*	*−362.6*	*−356.9*
Current transfers: credit	2 379 Z.	8.3	10.4	12.8	20.3	24.3	26.5	41.3	81.6
Current transfers: debit	3 379 ..	−1.8	−2.9	−3.3	−3.5	−2.8	−3.3	−2.7	−.4
B. Capital Account[1]	4 994 Z.	**. . . .**	**. . . .**	**−.5**	**−.9**	**17.9**	**24.4**	**46.3**	**79.4**
Capital account: credit	2 994 Z.	. . . .	. . . .	. . . .	. . . .	18.9	25.3	47.4	80.7
Capital account: debit	3 994 ..	. . . .	. . . .	−.5	−.9	−.9	−.9	−1.1	−1.3
Total, Groups A Plus B	4 981 ..	*−103.1*	*−108.6*	*−111.6*	*−132.0*	*−148.2*	*−201.5*	*−277.7*	*−196.3*
C. Financial Account[1]	4 995 W.	**−7.5**	**−4.0**	**−40.5**	**−50.3**	**−23.3**	**−10.9**	**−15.5**	**−42.4**
Direct investment abroad	4 505 ..	. . . .	. . . .	. . . .	. . . .	. . . .	. . . .	. . . .	. . . .
Direct investment in Burundi	4 555 Z.	11.7	. . . .	. . . .	. . . .	. . . .	.6	. . . .	.5
Portfolio investment assets	4 602 ..	. . . .	. . . .	. . . .	. . . .	. . . .	. . . .	. . . .	. . . .
Equity securities	4 610 ..	. . . .	. . . .	. . . .	. . . .	. . . .	. . . .	. . . .	. . . .
Debt securities	4 619 ..	. . . .	. . . .	. . . .	. . . .	. . . .	. . . .	. . . .	. . . .
Portfolio investment liabilities	4 652 Z.	. . . .	. . . .	. . . .	. . . .	. . . .	. . . .	. . . .	. . . .
Equity securities	4 660 ..	. . . .	. . . .	. . . .	. . . .	. . . .	. . . .	. . . .	. . . .
Debt securities	4 669 Z.	. . . .	. . . .	. . . .	. . . .	. . . .	. . . .	. . . .	. . . .
Financial derivatives	4 910 ..	. . . .	. . . .	. . . .	. . . .	. . . .	. . . .	. . . .	. . . .
Financial derivatives assets	4 900 ..	. . . .	. . . .	. . . .	. . . .	. . . .	. . . .	. . . .	. . . .
Financial derivatives liabilities	4 905 ..	. . . .	. . . .	. . . .	. . . .	. . . .	. . . .	. . . .	. . . .
Other investment assets	4 703 ..	6.8	24.0	−4.3	−19.9	−22.0	−7.8	−30.2	−34.2
Monetary authorities	4 701 ..	. . . .	. . . .	. . . .	. . . .	. . . .	. . . .	. . . .	. . . .
General government	4 704 ..	. . . .	. . . .	. . . .	. . . .	−.1	. . . .	. . . .	−1.9
Banks	4 705 ..	−8.2	2.4	−7.7	−22.2	−10.2	−4.5	−15.0	−22.0
Other sectors	4 728 ..	15.0	21.6	3.4	2.3	−11.7	−3.4	−15.2	−10.3
Other investment liabilities	4 753 W.	−25.9	−28.0	−36.2	−30.4	−1.4	−3.6	14.7	−8.6
Monetary authorities	4 753 WA	. . . .	. . . .	. . . .	. . . .	. . . .	. . . .	. . . .	. . . .
General government	4 753 ZB	−35.8	−34.6	−42.9	−41.0	−18.0	−14.2	−35.4	−26.1
Banks	4 753 ZC	8.7	6.6	6.8	9.7	15.3	.6	6.0	21.7
Other sectors	4 753 ZD	1.2	.1	−.1	.9	1.3	10.0	44.0	−4.1
Total, Groups A Through C	4 983 ..	*−110.5*	*−112.6*	*−152.1*	*−182.3*	*−171.5*	*−212.4*	*−293.2*	*−238.6*
D. Net Errors and Omissions	4 998 ..	**−34.3**	**−30.9**	**2.2**	**−13.8**	**−18.9**	**−80.3**	**3.8**	**−34.7**
Total, Groups A Through D	4 984 ..	*−144.8*	*−143.5*	*−149.9*	*−196.1*	*−190.3*	*−292.7*	*−289.3*	*−273.4*
E. Reserves and Related Items	4 802 A.	**144.8**	**143.5**	**149.9**	**196.1**	**190.3**	**292.7**	**289.3**	**273.4**
Reserve assets	4 802 ..	1.2	16.1	−46.9	−9.6	−2.0	−33.9	−18.2	−62.5
Use of Fund credit and loans	4 766 ..	−5.0	−4.8	9.9	13.6	10.7	21.3	21.3	10.8
Exceptional financing	4 920 ..	148.7	132.3	187.0	192.2	181.7	305.3	286.3	325.1
Conversion rates: Burundi francs per U.S. dollar	0 101 ..	**720.67**	**830.35**	**930.75**	**1,082.62**	**1,100.90**	**1,081.58**	**1,028.68**	**1,081.87**

[1] Excludes components that have been classified in the categories of Group E.

Table 2. STANDARD PRESENTATION, 2000–2007

(Millions of U.S. dollars)

	Code	2000	2001	2002	2003	2004	2005	2006	2007
CURRENT ACCOUNT	4 993 ..	**−50.2**	**−36.8**	**−3.4**	**−24.0**	**−33.0**	**−9.6**	**−133.5**	**−115.6**
A. GOODS	4 100 ..	**−58.8**	**−69.1**	**−73.8**	**−92.5**	**−97.6**	**−132.1**	**−186.0**	**−204.7**
Credit	2 100 ..	**49.1**	**39.2**	**31.0**	**37.5**	**47.9**	**56.9**	**58.7**	**52.9**
General merchandise: exports f.o.b.	2 110 ..	49.1	39.2	31.0	37.5	47.9	56.9	58.7	52.9
Goods for processing: exports f.o.b.	2 150 ..	....	....	....	....	....	....	....	....
Repairs on goods	2 160 ..	....	....	....	....	....	....	....	....
Goods procured in ports by carriers	2 170 ..	....	....	....	....	....	....	....	....
Nonmonetary gold	2 180 ..	....	....	....	....	....	....	....	....
Debit	3 100 ..	**−107.9**	**−108.3**	**−104.8**	**−130.0**	**−145.4**	**−188.9**	**−244.7**	**−257.6**
General merchandise: imports f.o.b.	3 110 ..	−107.9	−108.3	−104.8	−130.0	−145.4	−188.9	−244.7	−257.6
Goods for processing: imports f.o.b.	3 150 ..	....	....	....	....	....	....	....	....
Repairs on goods	3 160 ..	....	....	....	....	....	....	....	....
Goods procured in ports by carriers	3 170 ..	....	....	....	....	....	....	....	....
Nonmonetary gold	3 180 ..	....	....	....	....	....	....	....	....
B. SERVICES	4 200 ..	**−38.7**	**−33.0**	**−35.2**	**−38.0**	**−70.9**	**−99.3**	**−167.7**	**−146.3**
Total credit	2 200 ..	*4.0*	*5.2*	*7.5*	*7.3*	*15.8*	*34.8*	*34.5*	*30.8*
Total debit	3 200 ..	*−42.6*	*−38.2*	*−42.7*	*−45.3*	*−86.6*	*−134.1*	*−202.2*	*−177.1*
Transportation services, credit	2 205 ..	**.9**	**.8**	**.9**	**.7**	**1.4**	**1.7**	**.8**	**1.4**
Passenger	2 850 ..	*.6*	*.4*	*.5*	*.5*	*.6*	*.4*	*.3*	*1.0*
Freight	2 851 ..	*.2*	*.4*	*.3*	*.2*	....	....	....	....
Other	2 852 ..	....	....	....	....	*.8*	*1.3*	*.5*	*.4*
Sea transport, passenger	2 207 ..	....	....	....	....	....	....	....	....
Sea transport, freight	2 208 ..	.2	.4	.3	.2	....	....	....	....
Sea transport, other	2 209 ..	....	....	....	....	.8	1.3	.5	.4
Air transport, passenger	2 211 ..	.6	.4	.5	.5	.6	.4	.3	1.0
Air transport, freight	2 212 ..	....	....	....	....	....	....	....	....
Air transport, other	2 213 ..	....	....	....	....	....	....	....	....
Other transport, passenger	2 215 ..	....	....	....	....	....	....	....	....
Other transport, freight.	2 216 ..	....	....	....	....	....	....	....	....
Other transport, other...	2 217 ..	....	....	....	....	....	....	....	....
Transportation services, debit	3 205 ..	**−19.0**	**−17.5**	**−18.1**	**−20.9**	**−38.3**	**−43.9**	**−55.4**	**−53.8**
Passenger	3 850 ..	....	....	....	....	*−6.3*	*−2.4*	*−1.2*	*−2.5*
Freight	3 851 ..	*−19.0*	*−17.5*	*−18.1*	*−20.9*	*−31.9*	*−41.5*	*−54.1*	*−50.7*
Other	3 852 ..	....	....	....	....	....	....	*−.1*	*−.6*
Sea transport, passenger	3 207 ..	....	....	....	....	....	....	....	....
Sea transport, freight	3 208 ..	−19.0	−17.5	−18.1	−20.9	−6.4	−8.3	−10.8	−10.3
Sea transport, other	3 209 ..	....	....	....	....	....	....	−.1	−.6
Air transport, passenger	3 211 ..	....	....	....	....	−6.3	−2.4	−1.2	−2.5
Air transport, freight	3 212 ..	....	....	....	....	−4.8	−6.2	−8.1	−7.7
Air transport, other	3 213 ..	....	....	....	....	....	....	....	....
Other transport, passenger	3 215 ..	....	....	....	....	....	....	....	....
Other transport, freight	3 216 ..	....	....	....	....	−20.8	−27.0	−35.2	−32.7
Other transport, other	3 217 ..	....	....	....	....	....	....	....	....
Travel, credit	2 236 ..	**.8**	**.5**	**1.1**	**.7**	**1.2**	**1.5**	**1.3**	**1.3**
Business travel	2 237 ..	....	....	....	....	....	....	....	....
Personal travel	2 240 ..	.8	.5	1.1	.7	1.2	1.5	1.3	1.3
Travel, debit	3 236 ..	**−13.5**	**−11.9**	**−13.8**	**−14.5**	**−23.5**	**−60.3**	**−125.2**	**−103.6**
Business travel	3 237 ..	....	....	....	....	−20.1	−54.3	−120.5	−98.6
Personal travel	3 240 ..	−13.5	−11.9	−13.8	−14.5	−3.3	−6.0	−4.6	−5.0
Other services, credit	2 200 BA	**2.3**	**3.9**	**5.5**	**5.9**	**13.2**	**31.7**	**32.4**	**28.1**
Communications	2 245 ..	....	....	....	....	....	....	....	....
Construction	2 249 ..	....	....	....	....	....	....	....	....
Insurance	2 253 ..	....	.4	1.1	....	....	....	....	....
Financial	2 260 ..	....	....	....	....	....	....	....	....
Computer and information	2 262 ..	....	....	....	....	....	....	....	....
Royalties and licence fees	2 266 ..	....	....	....	....	....	....	....	....
Other business services	2 268 ..	.4	.6	.7	.8	1.4	3.4	3.4	3.8
Personal, cultural, and recreational	2 287 ..	....	....	....	....	....	....	....	....
Government, n.i.e.	2 291 ..	1.9	2.9	3.8	5.1	11.8	28.3	28.9	24.2
Other services, debit	3 200 BA	**−10.1**	**−8.9**	**−10.7**	**−9.9**	**−24.9**	**−29.9**	**−21.6**	**−19.7**
Communications	3 245 ..	−1.1	−.5	−.8	−1.0	....	....	....	....
Construction	3 249 ..	....	....	....	....	....	....	....	....
Insurance	3 253 ..	−1.5	−1.5	−1.2	−1.5	−2.6	−2.0	−2.5	−1.3
Financial	3 260 ..	....	....	....	....	−1.7	−2.4	−2.2	−1.9
Computer and information	3 262 ..	....	....	....	....	....	....	....	....
Royalties and licence fees	3 266 ..	....	....	....	....	....	....	....	....
Other business services	3 268 ..	−.4	−.1	−.4	−.2	−8.9	−16.1	−8.2	−7.2
Personal, cultural, and recreational	3 287 ..	....	....	....	....	....	....	....	....
Government, n.i.e.	3 291 ..	−7.1	−6.8	−8.3	−7.1	−11.7	−9.4	−8.7	−9.3

Table 2 (Continued). STANDARD PRESENTATION, 2000–2007

(Millions of U.S. dollars)

	Code	2000	2001	2002	2003	2004	2005	2006	2007
C. INCOME	4 300	**−12.1**	**−13.9**	**−11.7**	**−17.3**	**−19.2**	**−17.8**	**−8.8**	**−5.9**
Total credit	2 300	*2.4*	*1.9*	*.9*	*1.3*	*1.3*	*3.2*	*4.6*	*8.7*
Total debit	3 300	*−14.5*	*−15.8*	*−12.6*	*−18.6*	*−20.5*	*−20.9*	*−13.4*	*−14.6*
Compensation of employees, credit	2 310	....	....	....	....	....	....	....	....
Compensation of employees, debit	3 310	**−2.5**	**−2.4**	**−2.8**	**−3.3**	....	....	....	....
Investment income, credit	2 320	**2.4**	**1.9**	**.9**	**1.3**	**1.3**	**3.2**	**4.6**	**8.7**
Direct investment income	2 330	....	....	....	....	....	....	....	....
Dividends and distributed branch profits	2 332	....	....	....	....	....	....	....	....
Reinvested earnings and undistributed branch profits	2 333	....	....	....	....	....	....	....	....
Income on debt (interest)	2 334	....	....	....	....	....	....	....	....
Portfolio investment income	2 339	2.4	1.9	.9	1.3	1.3	3.2	4.6	8.7
Income on equity	2 340	....	....	....	....	1.3	3.2	4.6	8.7
Income on bonds and notes	2 350	2.4	1.9	.9	1.3				
Income on money market instruments	2 360	....	....	....	....	....	....	....	....
Other investment income	2 370	....	....	....	....	....	....	....	....
Investment income, debit	3 320	**−12.0**	**−13.4**	**−9.7**	**−15.3**	**−20.5**	**−20.9**	**−13.4**	**−14.6**
Direct investment income	3 330	−.4	−1.5		−4.7	−6.0	−2.1	−3.4	−4.8
Dividends and distributed branch profits	3 332	−.4	−1.5	....	−4.7	−6.0	−2.1	−3.4	−4.8
Reinvested earnings and undistributed branch profits	3 333	....	....	....	....	....	....	....	....
Income on debt (interest)	3 334	....	....	....	....	....	....	....	....
Portfolio investment income	3 339	−11.6	−11.9	−9.7	−10.6	....	....	....	....
Income on equity	3 340	....	....	....	....	....	....	....	....
Income on bonds and notes	3 350	−11.6	−11.9	−9.7	−10.6	....	....	....	....
Income on money market instruments	3 360	....	....	....	....	....	....	....	....
Other investment income	3 370	....	−.1	−.1	−.1	−14.5	−18.8	−10.1	−9.8
D. CURRENT TRANSFERS	4 379	**59.4**	**79.2**	**117.3**	**123.8**	**154.6**	**239.5**	**229.0**	**241.2**
Credit	2 379	**61.1**	**82.1**	**120.6**	**127.3**	**157.4**	**242.8**	**231.8**	**241.7**
General government	2 380	55.8	74.3	112.9	118.9	144.2	223.2	200.2	160.0
Other sectors	2 390	5.4	7.9	7.7	8.4	13.2	19.5	31.6	81.6
Workers' remittances	2 391	....	....	....	....	....	.1	....	.2
Other current transfers	2 392	5.4	7.9	7.7	8.4	13.2	19.5	31.6	81.5
Debit	3 379	**−1.8**	**−2.9**	**−3.3**	**−3.5**	**−2.8**	**−3.3**	**−2.7**	**−.4**
General government	3 380	−1.0	−1.6	−1.5	−2.0	−1.1	−1.6	−.2	−.2
Other sectors	3 390	−.7	−1.3	−1.8	−1.4	−1.7	−1.7	−2.5	−.2
Workers' remittances	3 391	....	....	....	....	−.3	−.2	−.2	−.2
Other current transfers	3 392	−.7	−1.3	−1.8	−1.4	−1.4	−1.5	−2.3	....
CAPITAL AND FINANCIAL ACCOUNT	4 996	**84.5**	**67.7**	**1.2**	**37.8**	**51.9**	**90.0**	**129.7**	**150.4**
CAPITAL ACCOUNT	4 994	....	**17.4**	**−.5**	**−.9**	**17.9**	**31.8**	**62.0**	**128.0**
Total credit	2 994	....	*17.4*	....	....	*18.9*	*32.7*	*63.1*	*129.3*
Total debit	3 994	....	....	*−.5*	*−.9*	*−.9*	*−.9*	*−1.1*	*−1.3*
Capital transfers, credit	2 400	....	**17.4**	....	....	**18.9**	**32.7**	**63.1**	**129.3**
General government	2 401	....	17.4	....	....	18.9	32.7	63.1	129.3
Debt forgiveness	2 402	....	17.4	....	....	....	7.4	15.7	48.6
Other capital transfers	2 410	....	....	....	....	18.9	25.3	47.4	80.7
Other sectors	2 430	....	....	....	....	....	....	....	....
Migrants' transfers	2 431	....	....	....	....	....	....	....	....
Debt forgiveness	2 432	....	....	....	....	....	....	....	....
Other capital transfers	2 440	....	....	....	....	....	....	....	....
Capital transfers, debit	3 400	....	....	**−.5**	**−.9**	**−.9**	**−.9**	**−1.1**	**−1.3**
General government	3 401	....	....	....	....	−.3	−.7	−1.1	−1.3
Debt forgiveness	3 402	....	....	....	....	....	....	....	....
Other capital transfers	3 410	....	....	....	....	−.3	−.7	−1.1	−1.3
Other sectors	3 430	....	....	−.5	−.9	−.6	−.1	....	....
Migrants' transfers	3 431	....	....	−.5	−.9	−.6	−.1	....	....
Debt forgiveness	3 432	....	....	....	....	....	....	....	....
Other capital transfers	3 440	....	....	....	....	....	....	....	....
Nonproduced nonfinancial assets, credit	2 480	....	....	....	....	....	....	....	....
Nonproduced nonfinancial assets, debit	3 480	....	....	....	....	....	....	....	....

Table 2 (Continued). STANDARD PRESENTATION, 2000–2007

(Millions of U.S. dollars)

	Code	2000	2001	2002	2003	2004	2005	2006	2007
FINANCIAL ACCOUNT...	4 995 ..	**84.5**	**50.3**	**1.6**	**38.8**	**33.9**	**58.2**	**67.7**	**22.3**
A. DIRECT INVESTMENT.....................................	4 500 ..	**11.7**	....	....	....	....	**.6**	....	**.5**
Direct investment abroad.................................	4 505 ..	....	....	....	....	....	....	....	....
Equity capital...	4 510 ..	....	....	....	....	....	....	....	....
Claims on affiliated enterprises.....................	4 515 ..	....	....	....	....	....	....	....	....
Liabilities to affiliated enterprises................	4 520 ..	....	....	....	....	....	....	....	....
Reinvested earnings......................................	4 525 ..	....	....	....	....	....	....	....	....
Other capital...	4 530 ..	....	....	....	....	....	....	....	....
Claims on affiliated enterprises.....................	4 535 ..	....	....	....	....	....	....	....	....
Liabilities to affiliated enterprises................	4 540 ..	....	....	....	....	....	....	....	....
Direct investment in Burundi...........................	4 555 ..	**11.7**	....	....	....	....	**.6**	....	**.5**
Equity capital...	4 560 ..	11.7	....	....	....	....	.6	....	.5
Claims on direct investors............................	4 565 ..	11.7	....	....	....	....	....	....	....
Liabilities to direct investors........................	4 570 ..	....	....	....	....	....	.6	....	.5
Reinvested earnings......................................	4 575 ..	....	....	....	....	....	....	....	....
Other capital...	4 580 ..	....	....	....	....	....	....	....	....
Claims on direct investors............................	4 585 ..	....	....	....	....	....	....	....	....
Liabilities to direct investors........................	4 590 ..	....	....	....	....	....	....	....	....
B. PORTFOLIO INVESTMENT...............................	4 600 ..	....	....	....	....	....	....	....	....
Assets...	4 602 ..	....	....	....	....	....	....	....	....
Equity securities..	4 610 ..	....	....	....	....	....	....	....	....
Monetary authorities.....................................	4 611 ..	....	....	....	....	....	....	....	....
General government......................................	4 612 ..	....	....	....	....	....	....	....	....
Banks..	4 613 ..	....	....	....	....	....	....	....	....
Other sectors...	4 614 ..	....	....	....	....	....	....	....	....
Debt securities..	4 619 ..	....	....	....	....	....	....	....	....
Bonds and notes...	4 620 ..	....	....	....	....	....	....	....	....
Monetary authorities...................................	4 621 ..	....	....	....	....	....	....	....	....
General government....................................	4 622 ..	....	....	....	....	....	....	....	....
Banks..	4 623 ..	....	....	....	....	....	....	....	....
Other sectors...	4 624 ..	....	....	....	....	....	....	....	....
Money market instruments............................	4 630 ..	....	....	....	....	....	....	....	....
Monetary authorities...................................	4 631 ..	....	....	....	....	....	....	....	....
General government....................................	4 632 ..	....	....	....	....	....	....	....	....
Banks..	4 633 ..	....	....	....	....	....	....	....	....
Other sectors...	4 634 ..	....	....	....	....	....	....	....	....
Liabilities..	4 652 ..	....	....	....	....	....	....	....	....
Equity securities..	4 660 ..	....	....	....	....	....	....	....	....
Banks..	4 663 ..	....	....	....	....	....	....	....	....
Other sectors...	4 664 ..	....	....	....	....	....	....	....	....
Debt securities..	4 669 ..	....	....	....	....	....	....	....	....
Bonds and notes...	4 670 ..	....	....	....	....	....	....	....	....
Monetary authorities...................................	4 671 ..	....	....	....	....	....	....	....	....
General government....................................	4 672 ..	....	....	....	....	....	....	....	....
Banks..	4 673 ..	....	....	....	....	....	....	....	....
Other sectors...	4 674 ..	....	....	....	....	....	....	....	....
Money market instruments............................	4 680 ..	....	....	....	....	....	....	....	....
Monetary authorities...................................	4 681 ..	....	....	....	....	....	....	....	....
General government....................................	4 682 ..	....	....	....	....	....	....	....	....
Banks..	4 683 ..	....	....	....	....	....	....	....	....
Other sectors...	4 684 ..	....	....	....	....	....	....	....	....
C. FINANCIAL DERIVATIVES...............................	4 910 ..	....	....	....	....	....	....	....	....
Monetary authorities.....................................	4 911 ..	....	....	....	....	....	....	....	....
General government......................................	4 912 ..	....	....	....	....	....	....	....	....
Banks..	4 913 ..	....	....	....	....	....	....	....	....
Other sectors...	4 914 ..	....	....	....	....	....	....	....	....
Assets...	4 900 ..	....	....	....	....	....	....	....	....
Monetary authorities.....................................	4 901 ..	....	....	....	....	....	....	....	....
General government......................................	4 902 ..	....	....	....	....	....	....	....	....
Banks..	4 903 ..	....	....	....	....	....	....	....	....
Other sectors...	4 904 ..	....	....	....	....	....	....	....	....
Liabilities..	4 905 ..	....	....	....	....	....	....	....	....
Monetary authorities.....................................	4 906 ..	....	....	....	....	....	....	....	....
General government......................................	4 907 ..	....	....	....	....	....	....	....	....
Banks..	4 908 ..	....	....	....	....	....	....	....	....
Other sectors...	4 909 ..	....	....	....	....	....	....	....	....

Table 2 (Concluded). STANDARD PRESENTATION, 2000–2007

(Millions of U.S. dollars)

	Code	2000	2001	2002	2003	2004	2005	2006	2007
D. OTHER INVESTMENT	4 700 ..	**71.6**	**34.3**	**48.6**	**48.4**	**35.9**	**91.5**	**85.8**	**84.4**
Assets	4 703 ..	**6.8**	**24.0**	**−4.3**	**−19.9**	**−22.0**	**−7.8**	**−30.2**	**−34.2**
Trade credits	4 706 ..	....	....	....	....	−11.7	−3.4	−15.2	−10.3
General government	4 707 ..	....	....	....	....	....	....	....	....
of which: Short-term	4 709 ..	....	....	....	....	....	....	....	....
Other sectors	4 710 ..	....	....	....	....	−11.7	−3.4	−15.2	−10.3
of which: Short-term	4 712 ..	....	....	....	....	−11.7	−3.4	−15.2	−10.3
Loans	4 714 ..	15.3	22.1	3.4	3.1	....	....	....	....
Monetary authorities	4 715 ..	....	....	....	....	....	....	....	....
of which: Short-term	4 718 ..	....	....	....	....	....	....	....	....
General government	4 719 ..	....	....	....	....	....	....	....	....
of which: Short-term	4 721 ..	....	....	....	....	....	....	....	....
Banks	4 722 ..	....	....	....	....	....	....	....	....
of which: Short-term	4 724 ..	....	....	....	....	....	....	....	....
Other sectors	4 725 ..	15.3	22.1	3.4	3.1	....	....	....	....
of which: Short-term	4 727 ..	15.3	22.1	3.4	3.1	....	....	....	....
Currency and deposits	4 730 ..	−8.6	1.9	−7.7	−23.0	−10.2	−4.5	−15.0	−22.0
Monetary authorities	4 731 ..	....	....	....	....	....	....	....	....
General government	4 732 ..	....	....	....	....	....	....	....	....
Banks	4 733 ..	−8.2	2.4	−7.7	−22.2	−10.2	−4.5	−15.0	−22.0
Other sectors	4 734 ..	−.4	−.6	....	−.8	....	....	....	....
Other assets	4 736 ..	....	....	....	....	−.1	....	....	−1.9
Monetary authorities	4 737 ..	....	....	....	....	....	....	....	....
of which: Short-term	4 739 ..	....	....	....	....	....	....	....	....
General government	4 740 ..	....	....	....	....	−.1	....	....	−1.9
of which: Short-term	4 742 ..	....	....	....	....	....	....	....	....
Banks	4 743 ..	....	....	....	....	....	....	....	....
of which: Short-term	4 745 ..	....	....	....	....	....	....	....	....
Other sectors	4 746 ..	....	....	....	....	....	....	....	....
of which: Short-term	4 748 ..	....	....	....	....	....	....	....	....
Liabilities	4 753 ..	**64.9**	**10.3**	**52.8**	**68.3**	**57.9**	**99.3**	**116.1**	**118.6**
Trade credits	4 756 ..	....	....	....	....	.9	10.0	44.5	−4.3
General government	4 757 ..	....	....	....	....	....	....	....	....
of which: Short-term	4 759 ..	....	....	....	....	....	....	....	....
Other sectors	4 760 ..	....	....	....	....	.9	10.0	44.5	−4.3
of which: Short-term	4 762 ..	....	....	....	....	1.6	11.4	46.5	−2.2
Loans	4 764 ..	27.2	−19.4	20.0	30.4	41.7	88.8	65.6	101.2
Monetary authorities	4 765 ..	−5.0	−4.8	9.9	13.6	10.7	21.3	21.3	10.8
of which: Use of Fund credit and loans from the Fund..	4 766 ..	−5.0	−4.8	9.9	13.6	10.7	21.3	21.3	10.8
of which: Short-term	4 768 ..	....	....	....	....	....	....	....	....
General government	4 769 ..	32.2	−14.5	10.1	16.8	30.6	67.4	44.7	90.3
of which: Short-term	4 771 ..	....	....	....	....	17.5	6.4	1.4	3.1
Banks	4 772 ..	....	....	....	....	....	....	....	....
of which: Short-term	4 774 ..	....	....	....	....	....	....	....	....
Other sectors	4 775 ..	....	....	....	....	.4	.1	−.4	.2
of which: Short-term	4 777 ..	....	....	....	....	.4	.1	−.4	.2
Currency and deposits	4 780 ..	8.7	6.6	6.8	9.7	15.3	.6	6.0	21.7
Monetary authorities	4 781 ..	....	....	....	....	....	....	....	....
General government	4 782 ..	....	....	....	....	....	....	....	....
Banks	4 783 ..	8.7	6.6	6.8	9.7	15.3	.6	6.0	21.7
Other sectors	4 784 ..	....	....	....	....	....	....	....	....
Other liabilities	4 786 ..	29.0	23.1	26.1	28.2	....	....	....	....
Monetary authorities	4 787 ..	....	....	....	....	....	....	....	....
of which: Short-term	4 789 ..	....	....	....	....	....	....	....	....
General government	4 790 ..	27.8	23.0	26.1	27.3	....	....	....	....
of which: Short-term	4 792 ..	27.8	23.0	26.1	27.3	....	....	....	....
Banks	4 793 ..	....	....	....	....	....	....	....	....
of which: Short-term	4 795 ..	....	....	....	....	....	....	....	....
Other sectors	4 796 ..	1.2	.1	−.1	.9	....	....	....	....
of which: Short-term	4 798 ..	1.2	.1	.1	1.0	....	....	....	....
E. RESERVE ASSETS	4 802 ..	**1.2**	**16.1**	**−46.9**	**−9.6**	**−2.0**	**−33.9**	**−18.2**	**−62.5**
Monetary gold	4 812 ..	−.7	4.2	−.1	−.1	....	....	−.1	−.3
Special drawing rights	4 811 ..	....	....	−.1	....	−.2	.1	....	....
Reserve position in the Fund	4 810 ..	....	6.9	....	....	....	....	....	....
Foreign exchange	4 803 ..	1.9	5.0	−46.7	−9.6	−.7	−35.0	−18.4	−61.4
Other claims	4 813 ..	....	....	....	....	−1.1	1.0	.4	−.8
NET ERRORS AND OMISSIONS	4 998 ..	**−34.3**	**−30.9**	**2.2**	**−13.8**	**−18.9**	**−80.3**	**3.8**	**−34.7**

Table 3. INTERNATIONAL INVESTMENT POSITION (End-period stocks), 2000–2007

(Millions of U.S. dollars)

	Code	2000	2001	2002	2003	2004	2005	2006	2007
ASSETS	8 995 C.	**76.0**	**59.4**	**86.7**	**116.6**	**129.8**	**176.8**	**222.4**	**259.3**
Direct investment abroad	8 505 ..	....	....	.1	.1	.7	....	....	....
Equity capital and reinvested earnings	8 506 ..	....	....	.1	.1	.7	....	....	....
Claims on affiliated enterprises	8 507 ..	....	....	.1	.1	.7	....	....	....
Liabilities to affiliated enterprises	8 508 ..	....	....	....	....	....	....	....	....
Other capital	8 530 ..	....	....	....	....	....	....	....	....
Claims on affiliated enterprises	8 535 ..	....	....	....	....	....	....	....	....
Liabilities to affiliated enterprises	8 540 ..	....	....	....	....	....	....	....	....
Portfolio investment	8 602 ..	....	....	....	....	....	....	....	....
Equity securities	8 610 ..	....	....	....	....	....	....	....	....
Monetary authorities	8 611 ..	....	....	....	....	....	....	....	....
General government	8 612 ..	....	....	....	....	....	....	....	....
Banks	8 613 ..	....	....	....	....	....	....	....	....
Other sectors	8 614 ..	....	....	....	....	....	....	....	....
Debt securities	8 619 ..	....	....	....	....	....	....	....	....
Bonds and notes	8 620 ..	....	....	....	....	....	....	....	....
Monetary authorities	8 621 ..	....	....	....	....	....	....	....	....
General government	8 622 ..	....	....	....	....	....	....	....	....
Banks	8 623 ..	....	....	....	....	....	....	....	....
Other sectors	8 624 ..	....	....	....	....	....	....	....	....
Money market instruments	8 630 ..	....	....	....	....	....	....	....	....
Monetary authorities	8 631 ..	....	....	....	....	....	....	....	....
General government	8 632 ..	....	....	....	....	....	....	....	....
Banks	8 633 ..	....	....	....	....	....	....	....	....
Other sectors	8 634 ..	....	....	....	....	....	....	....	....
Financial derivatives	8 900 ..	....	....	....	....	....	....	....	....
Monetary authorities	8 901 ..	....	....	....	....	....	....	....	....
General government	8 902 ..	....	....	....	....	....	....	....	....
Banks	8 903 ..	....	....	....	....	....	....	....	....
Other sectors	8 904 ..	....	....	....	....	....	....	....	....
Other investment	8 703 ..	**32.6**	**35.5**	**21.1**	**42.7**	**60.6**	**62.8**	**89.9**	**80.5**
Trade credits	8 706 ..	14.2	21.3	2.9	3.3	11.6	3.7	15.6	14.0
General government	8 707 ..	....	....	....	....	....	....	....	....
of which: Short-term	8 709 ..	....	....	....	....	....	....	....	....
Other sectors	8 710 ..	14.2	21.3	2.9	3.3	11.6	3.7	15.6	14.0
of which: Short-term	8 712 ..	*14.2*	*21.3*	*2.9*	*3.3*	*11.6*	*3.7*	*15.6*	*14.0*
Loans	8 714 ..	....	....	....	....	....	....	....	....
Monetary authorities	8 715 ..	....	....	....	....	....	....	....	....
of which: Short-term	8 718 ..	....	....	....	....	....	....	....	....
General government	8 719 ..	....	....	....	....	....	....	....	....
of which: Short-term	8 721 ..	....	....	....	....	....	....	....	....
Banks	8 722 ..	....	....	....	....	....	....	....	....
of which: Short-term	8 724 ..	....	....	....	....	....	....	....	....
Other sectors	8 725 ..	....	....	....	....	....	....	....	....
of which: Short-term	8 727 ..	....	....	....	....	....	....	....	....
Currency and deposits	8 730 ..	18.4	14.3	18.2	39.3	48.9	59.2	74.3	66.5
Monetary authorities	8 731 ..	....	....	....	....	....	....	....	....
General government	8 732 ..	....	....	....	....	....	....	....	....
Banks	8 733 ..	18.4	14.3	18.2	39.3	48.9	59.2	74.3	66.5
Other sectors	8 734 ..	....	....	....	....	....	....	....	....
Other assets	8 736 ..	....	....	....	....	.1	....	....	....
Monetary authorities	8 737 ..	....	....	....	....	....	....	....	....
of which: Short-term	8 739 ..	....	....	....	....	....	....	....	....
General government	8 740 ..	....	....	....	....	.1	....	....	....
of which: Short-term	8 742 ..	....	....	....	....	*.1*	....	....	....
Banks	8 743 ..	....	....	....	....	....	....	....	....
of which: Short-term	8 745 ..	....	....	....	....	....	....	....	....
Other sectors	8 746 ..	....	....	....	....	....	....	....	....
of which: Short-term	8 748 ..	....	....	....	....	....	....	....	....
Reserve assets	8 802 ..	**43.3**	**23.8**	**65.5**	**73.8**	**68.5**	**113.9**	**132.5**	**178.8**
Monetary gold	8 812 ..	4.7	.3	.3	.4	.4	.5	.6	.5
Special drawing rights	8 811 ..	....	.1	.2	.1	.4	.3	.3	.4
Reserve position in the Fund	8 810 ..	7.6	.5	.5	.5	.6	.5	.5	.6
Foreign exchange	8 803 ..	30.9	23.0	64.5	72.7	67.2	112.7	131.0	177.3
Other claims	8 813 ..	....	....	....	....	....	....	....	....

Table 3 (Concluded). INTERNATIONAL INVESTMENT POSITION (End-period stocks), 2000–2007

(Millions of U.S. dollars)

	Code	2000	2001	2002	2003	2004	2005	2006	2007
LIABILITIES	8 995 D.	1,129.5	1,049.8	1,130.7	1,313.1	1,406.9	1,361.7	1,492.7	1,522.7
Direct investment in Burundi	8 555 ..	10.8	....	....	....	....	.6	....	.5
Equity capital and reinvested earnings	8 556 ..	10.8	....	....	....	....	.6	....	.5
Claims on direct investors	8 557 ..	....	....	....	....	....	....	....	....
Liabilities to direct investors	8 558 ..	10.8	....	....	....	....	.6	....	.5
Other capital	8 580 ..	....	....	....	....	....	....	....	....
Claims on direct investors	8 585 ..	....	....	....	....	....	....	....	....
Liabilities to direct investors	8 590 ..	....	....	....	....	....	....	....	....
Portfolio investment	8 652 ..	....	....	....	....	....	....	....	....
Equity securities	8 660 ..	....	....	....	....	....	....	....	....
Banks	8 663 ..	....	....	....	....	....	....	....	....
Other sectors	8 664 ..	....	....	....	....	....	....	....	....
Debt securities	8 669 ..	....	....	....	....	....	....	....	....
Bonds and notes	8 670 ..	....	....	....	....	....	....	....	....
Monetary authorities	8 671 ..	....	....	....	....	....	....	....	....
General government	8 672 ..	....	....	....	....	....	....	....	....
Banks	8 673 ..	....	....	....	....	....	....	....	....
Other sectors	8 674 ..	....	....	....	....	....	....	....	....
Money market instruments	8 680 ..	....	....	....	....	....	....	....	....
Monetary authorities	8 681 ..	....	....	....	....	....	....	....	....
General government	8 682 ..	....	....	....	....	....	....	....	....
Banks	8 683 ..	....	....	....	....	....	....	....	....
Other sectors	8 684 ..	....	....	....	....	....	....	....	....
Financial derivatives	8 905 ..	....	....	....	....	....	....	....	....
Monetary authorities	8 906 ..	....	....	....	....	....	....	....	....
General government	8 907 ..	....	....	....	....	....	....	....	....
Banks	8 908 ..	....	....	....	....	....	....	....	....
Other sectors	8 909 ..	....	....	....	....	....	....	....	....
Other investment	8 753 ..	1,118.7	1,049.8	1,130.7	1,313.1	1,406.8	1,361.0	1,492.7	1,522.2
Trade credits	8 756 ..	....	....	....	....	.9	10.8	45.6	−4.1
General government	8 757 ..	....	....	....	....	....	....	....	....
of which: Short-term	8 759 ..	....	....	....	....	....	....	....	....
Other sectors	8 760 ..	....	....	....	....	.9	10.8	45.6	−4.1
of which: Short-term	8 762 ..	....	....	....	....	.9	10.8	45.6	−4.1
Loans	8 764 ..	1,103.3	1,030.5	1,109.3	1,282.5	1,354.9	1,305.6	1,404.8	1,465.3
Monetary authorities	8 765 ..	7.8	2.7	13.1	28.6	41.0	58.2	82.7	98.2
of which: Use of Fund credit and loans from the Fund	8 766 ..	7.8	2.7	13.1	28.6	41.0	58.2	82.7	98.2
of which: Short-term	8 768 ..	....	....	....	....	....	....	....	....
General government	8 769 ..	1,095.5	1,027.9	1,096.2	1,253.9	1,313.9	1,247.4	1,322.1	1,367.1
of which: Short-term	8 771 ..	....	....	....	....	....	....	....	....
Banks	8 772 ..	....	....	....	....	....	....	....	....
of which: Short-term	8 774 ..	....	....	....	....	....	....	....	....
Other sectors	8 775 ..	....	....	....	....	....	....	....	....
of which: Short-term	8 777 ..	....	....	....	....	....	....	....	....
Currency and deposits	8 780 ..	14.3	19.2	21.4	30.6	33.3	37.6	41.3	57.9
Monetary authorities	8 781 ..	....	....	....	....	....	....	....	....
General government	8 782 ..	....	....	....	....	....	....	....	....
Banks	8 783 ..	14.3	19.2	21.4	30.6	33.3	37.6	41.3	57.9
Other sectors	8 784 ..	....	....	....	....	....	....	....	....
Other liabilities	8 786 ..	1.2	.1	.1	....	17.8	7.0	1.0	3.1
Monetary authorities	8 787 ..	....	....	....	....	....	....	....	....
of which: Short-term	8 789 ..	....	....	....	....	....	....	....	....
General government	8 790 ..	....	....	....	....	....	....	....	....
of which: Short-term	8 792 ..	....	....	....	....	....	....	....	....
Banks	8 793 ..	....	....	....	....	....	....	....	....
of which: Short-term	8 795 ..	....	....	....	....	....	....	....	....
Other sectors	8 796 ..	1.2	.1	.1	....	17.8	7.0	1.0	3.1
of which: Short-term	8 798 ..	1.2	.1	.1	....	17.8	7.0	1.0	3.1
NET INTERNATIONAL INVESTMENT POSITION	8 995 ..	−1,053.6	−990.5	−1,044.0	−1,196.5	−1,277.1	−1,184.9	−1,270.3	−1,263.3
Conversion rates: Burundi francs per U.S. dollar (end of period)	0 102 ..	778.20	864.20	1,071.23	1,093.00	1,109.51	997.78	1,002.47	1,119.54

Table 1. ANALYTIC PRESENTATION, 2000–2007

(Millions of U.S. dollars)

	Code	2000	2001	2002	2003	2004	2005	2006	2007
A. Current Account[1]	4 993 Z.	**−136.1**	**−87.9**	**−107.3**	**−233.4**	**−182.9**	**−360.5**	**−339.1**	**−506.3**
Goods: exports f.o.b.	2 100 ..	1,397.1	1,571.2	1,769.8	2,086.8	2,588.9	2,910.3	3,693.7	4,089.0
Goods: imports f.o.b.	3 100 ..	−1,935.7	−2,094.0	−2,360.5	−2,668.1	−3,269.5	−3,927.8	−4,749.2	−5,423.6
Balance on Goods	4 100 ..	*−538.6*	*−522.8*	*−590.7*	*−581.3*	*−680.6*	*−1,017.6*	*−1,055.6*	*−1,334.6*
Services: credit	2 200 ..	428.4	524.6	604.2	548.0	804.9	1,118.1	1,296.3	1,547.5
Services: debit	3 200 ..	−327.5	−347.3	−375.5	−433.9	−514.4	−647.1	−792.1	−903.2
Balance on Goods and Services	4 991 ..	*−437.7*	*−345.5*	*−362.1*	*−467.2*	*−390.1*	*−546.5*	*−551.3*	*−690.2*
Income: credit	2 300 ..	67.1	57.5	50.6	43.7	48.6	67.7	90.0	112.0
Income: debit	3 300 ..	−190.2	−195.4	−234.4	−223.0	−269.6	−321.8	−380.4	−472.0
Balance on Goods, Services, and Income	4 992 ..	*−560.8*	*−483.4*	*−545.9*	*−646.5*	*−611.1*	*−800.6*	*−841.8*	*−1,050.3*
Current transfers: credit	2 379 Z.	432.0	403.8	447.9	425.3	443.7	460.8	527.2	569.7
Current transfers: debit	3 379 ..	−7.3	−8.3	−9.3	−12.2	−15.5	−20.7	−24.5	−25.8
B. Capital Account[1]	4 994 Z.	**35.6**	**44.9**	**8.1**	**66.2**	**68.1**	**94.9**	**267.6**	**252.8**
Capital account: credit	2 994 Z.	79.8	102.8	71.5	119.5	141.3	150.4	320.8	295.6
Capital account: debit	3 994 ..	−44.2	−58.0	−63.4	−53.3	−73.2	−55.5	−53.2	−42.8
Total, Groups A Plus B	4 981 ..	*−100.5*	*−43.0*	*−99.2*	*−167.3*	*−114.8*	*−265.6*	*−71.5*	*−253.6*
C. Financial Account[1]	4 995 W.	**183.6**	**58.7**	**164.8**	**243.7**	**219.1**	**334.9**	**323.8**	**671.6**
Direct investment abroad	4 505 ..	−6.6	−7.3	−6.0	−9.7	−10.2	−6.3	−8.4	−1.1
Direct investment in Cambodia	4 555 Z.	148.5	149.4	145.1	84.0	131.4	381.2	483.2	867.3
Portfolio investment assets	4 602 ..	−7.2	−7.7	−7.5	−7.7	−8.0	−7.2	−12.1	−12.4
Equity securities	4 610 ..	−7.2	−7.7	−7.5	−7.7	−8.0	−7.2	−12.1	−12.4
Debt securities	4 619 ..	....	....	....	....	....	....	....	....
Portfolio investment liabilities	4 652 Z.	....	....	....	....	....	....	....	....
Equity securities	4 660 ..	....	....	....	....	....	....	....	....
Debt securities	4 669 Z.	....	....	....	....	....	....	....	....
Financial derivatives	4 910 ..	....	....	....	....	....	....	....	....
Financial derivatives assets	4 900 ..	....	....	....	....	....	....	....	....
Financial derivatives liabilities	4 905 ..	....	....	....	....	....	....	....	....
Other investment assets	4 703 ..	−176.3	−216.8	−228.3	−127.0	−91.3	−302.8	−540.1	−699.5
Monetary authorities	4 701 ..	....	−26.2	−98.4	6.3	−66.9	68.6	−70.8	−210.7
General government	4 704 ..	....	....	....	....	....	....	....	....
Banks	4 705 ..	−11.2	−45.4	39.8	−78.5	−34.1	−94.7	−139.6	−353.7
Other sectors	4 728 ..	−165.1	−145.2	−169.8	−54.9	9.7	−276.8	−329.7	−135.1
Other investment liabilities	4 753 W.	225.2	141.1	261.6	304.1	197.2	270.0	401.2	517.3
Monetary authorities	4 753 WA	....	....	....	....	....	....	....	....
General government	4 753 ZB	74.6	78.1	124.2	148.6	154.4	144.0	122.7	119.6
Banks	4 753 ZC	−6.7	.1	−8.6	34.3	−3.2	8.3	23.9	183.8
Other sectors	4 753 ZD	157.3	62.9	146.0	121.2	46.0	117.8	254.6	214.0
Total, Groups A Through C	4 983 ..	*83.1*	*15.7*	*65.6*	*76.5*	*104.3*	*69.3*	*252.3*	*418.1*
D. Net Errors and Omissions	4 998 ..	**8.9**	**26.2**	**1.7**	**−40.0**	**−45.8**	**5.1**	**−44.1**	**−4.0**
Total, Groups A Through D	4 984 ..	*92.0*	*41.9*	*67.3*	*36.5*	*58.5*	*74.5*	*208.2*	*414.1*
E. Reserves and Related Items	4 802 A.	**−92.0**	**−41.9**	**−67.3**	**−36.5**	**−58.5**	**−74.5**	**−208.2**	**−414.1**
Reserve assets	4 802 ..	−108.7	−64.0	−89.4	−47.5	−61.0	−78.4	−138.7	−426.8
Use of Fund credit and loans	4 766 ..	4.0	9.3	9.3	−1.7	−10.3	−8.8	−82.2	....
Exceptional financing	4 920 ..	12.8	12.8	12.8	12.8	12.8	12.8	12.8	12.8
Conversion rates: riels per U.S. dollar	0 101 ..	**3,840.8**	**3,916.3**	**3,912.1**	**3,973.3**	**4,016.3**	**4,092.5**	**4,103.3**	**4,056.2**

[1] Excludes components that have been classified in the categories of Group E.

Table 2. STANDARD PRESENTATION, 2000–2007

(Millions of U.S. dollars)

	Code	2000	2001	2002	2003	2004	2005	2006	2007
CURRENT ACCOUNT	4 993	−136.1	−87.9	−107.3	−233.4	−182.9	−360.5	−339.1	−506.3
A. GOODS	4 100	−538.6	−522.8	−590.7	−581.3	−680.6	−1,017.6	−1,055.6	−1,334.6
Credit	2 100	1,397.1	1,571.2	1,769.8	2,086.8	2,588.9	2,910.3	3,693.7	4,089.0
General merchandise: exports f.o.b.	2 110	1,385.7	1,562.1	1,760.5	2,076.7	2,575.0	2,898.6	3,678.9	4,072.5
Goods for processing: exports f.o.b.	2 150	....	....	....	....	....	....	....	....
Repairs on goods	2 160	....	....	....	....	....	....	....	....
Goods procured in ports by carriers	2 170	7.3	7.6	8.1	8.2	9.6	10.8	14.4	16.4
Nonmonetary gold	2 180	4.2	1.4	1.2	2.0	4.2	.8	.3	.1
Debit	3 100	−1,935.7	−2,094.0	−2,360.5	−2,668.1	−3,269.5	−3,927.8	−4,749.2	−5,423.6
General merchandise: imports f.o.b.	3 110	−1,896.4	−2,077.8	−2,340.3	−2,645.0	−3,232.1	−3,909.2	−4,731.3	−5,404.7
Goods for processing: imports f.o.b.	3 150	....	....	....	....	....	....	....	....
Repairs on goods	3 160	....	....	....	....	....	....	....	....
Goods procured in ports by carriers	3 170	−4.7	−4.7	−9.9	−9.7	−12.3	−13.9	−15.9	−18.1
Nonmonetary gold	3 180	−34.7	−11.6	−10.3	−13.4	−25.0	−4.7	−2.0	−.8
B. SERVICES	4 200	100.9	177.3	228.7	114.1	290.5	471.1	504.2	644.4
Total credit	2 200	*428.4*	*524.6*	*604.2*	*548.0*	*804.9*	*1,118.1*	*1,296.3*	*1,547.5*
Total debit	3 200	*−327.5*	*−347.3*	*−375.5*	*−433.9*	*−514.4*	*−647.1*	*−792.1*	*−903.2*
Transportation services, credit	2 205	71.4	86.9	88.9	84.3	104.8	126.9	166.8	209.7
Passenger	2 850	*41.2*	*48.6*	*55.4*	*52.4*	*69.8*	*88.7*	*116.6*	*149.4*
Freight	2 851	*5.6*	*2.9*	*4.7*	*4.0*	*5.5*	*5.3*	*6.7*	*10.4*
Other	2 852	*24.6*	*35.5*	*28.9*	*28.0*	*29.5*	*32.9*	*43.5*	*49.8*
Sea transport, passenger	2 207	....	....	....	.3	....	....	....	.1
Sea transport, freight	2 208	2.4	.2	.1	.1	.2	.2	.2	.3
Sea transport, other	2 209	13.5	23.7	15.6	14.3	12.5	13.8	17.9	21.1
Air transport, passenger	2 211	41.2	48.6	55.4	52.0	69.6	88.6	116.6	149.3
Air transport, freight	2 212	3.2	2.7	4.5	3.6	5.1	5.0	6.4	7.1
Air transport, other	2 213	11.1	11.8	13.3	12.9	16.4	18.5	21.2	24.2
Other transport, passenger	2 215	....	....	....	....	.2	.1	....	.1
Other transport, freight	2 216	....	....	....	.2	.3	.2	.1	3.0
Other transport, other	2 217	....	....	....	.7	.6	.6	4.5	4.6
Transportation services, debit	3 205	−169.9	−187.1	−217.3	−241.4	−298.4	−360.3	−438.3	−510.2
Passenger	3 850	*−19.0*	*−22.4*	*−25.6*	*−24.1*	*−32.2*	*−40.9*	*−53.8*	*−70.6*
Freight	3 851	*−148.4*	*−162.6*	*−183.2*	*−207.9*	*−253.8*	*−306.5*	*−370.3*	*−423.6*
Other	3 852	*−2.5*	*−2.0*	*−8.6*	*−9.3*	*−12.4*	*−12.9*	*−14.2*	*−16.0*
Sea transport, passenger	3 207	....	....	....	−.1	....	....	....	−1.8
Sea transport, freight	3 208	−144.5	−157.9	−174.9	−201.3	−245.9	−299.2	−361.2	−411.8
Sea transport, other	3 209	−.5	....	....	....	....	....	....	−.1
Air transport, passenger	3 211	−19.0	−22.4	−25.6	−24.0	−32.1	−40.9	−53.8	−68.8
Air transport, freight	3 212	−3.9	−4.7	−8.3	−5.7	−7.1	−6.7	−9.1	−11.2
Air transport, other	3 213	−2.0	−2.0	−8.5	−8.3	−10.6	−11.9	−13.6	−15.5
Other transport, passenger	3 215	....	....	....	....	....	....	....	....
Other transport, freight	3 216	....	....	....	−.9	−.8	−.6	....	−.6
Other transport, other	3 217	....	....	....	−1.0	−1.8	−.9	−.5	−.4
Travel, credit	2 236	303.9	380.4	453.5	389.0	603.5	839.5	963.2	1,134.8
Business travel	2 237	52.6	61.2	56.3	50.4	46.1	64.2	80.8	96.3
Personal travel	2 240	251.3	319.3	397.2	338.6	557.4	775.3	882.4	1,038.5
Travel, debit	3 236	−33.2	−37.0	−38.2	−36.2	−47.6	−96.9	−122.2	−122.7
Business travel	3 237	−29.0	−34.4	−35.0	−33.5	−43.9	−89.2	−114.3	−113.7
Personal travel	3 240	−4.2	−2.6	−3.2	−2.7	−3.8	−7.7	−7.9	−9.0
Other services, credit	2 200 BA	53.1	57.3	61.7	74.6	96.7	151.6	166.3	203.0
Communications	2 245	37.5	39.4	41.3	38.7	40.7	42.7	40.3	45.8
Construction	2 249	....	....	....	1.2	1.9	2.0	2.5	3.4
Insurance	2 253	....	....	....	.3	1.1	.8	.9	3.9
Financial	2 260	....	....	....	1.6	2.7	10.6	13.4	9.1
Computer and information	2 262	....	....	....	....	.2	.1	....	1.6
Royalties and licence fees	2 266	....	....	....	.4	....	.4	.1	.1
Other business services	2 268	9.1	9.8	11.7	24.5	31.7	39.1	54.7	100.4
Personal, cultural, and recreational	2 287	.7	.8	1.0	1.1	1.2	1.4	1.6	1.8
Government, n.i.e.	2 291	5.8	7.3	7.7	6.8	17.2	54.5	52.7	37.1
Other services, debit	3 200 BA	−124.4	−123.2	−120.0	−156.3	−168.4	−189.9	−231.7	−270.2
Communications	3 245	−29.5	−31.0	−32.5	−33.1	−33.9	−32.6	−36.4	−41.0
Construction	3 249	−37.6	−30.3	−20.0	−43.6	−41.9	−42.8	−48.4	−52.5
Insurance	3 253	−14.3	−15.7	−17.2	−20.9	−25.0	−29.0	−32.8	−39.9
Financial	3 260	....	....	....	−.2	−.9	−14.4	−12.1	−7.7
Computer and information	3 262	....	....	....	−.5	−1.3	−.4	−.1	−1.2
Royalties and licence fees	3 266	−4.4	−4.8	−5.2	−6.0	−6.4	−7.3	−7.0	−10.2
Other business services	3 268	−29.6	−31.8	−34.8	−40.1	−42.4	−48.5	−46.5	−68.2
Personal, cultural, and recreational	3 287	−2.2	−2.5	−2.9	−3.2	−4.2	−4.2	−4.7	−5.4
Government, n.i.e.	3 291	−6.9	−7.2	−7.5	−8.6	−12.4	−10.9	−43.6	−44.3

Table 2 (Continued). STANDARD PRESENTATION, 2000–2007

(Millions of U.S. dollars)

	Code	2000	2001	2002	2003	2004	2005	2006	2007
C. INCOME............	4 300 ..	**−123.1**	**−137.9**	**−183.8**	**−179.3**	**−221.0**	**−254.0**	**−290.4**	**−360.0**
Total credit............	2 300 ..	*67.1*	*57.5*	*50.6*	*43.7*	*48.6*	*67.7*	*90.0*	*112.0*
Total debit............	3 300 ..	*−190.2*	*−195.4*	*−234.4*	*−223.0*	*−269.6*	*−321.8*	*−380.4*	*−472.0*
Compensation of employees, credit............	2 310 ..	**2.6**	**2.8**	**3.0**	**3.2**	**3.4**	**3.7**	**3.7**	**4.0**
Compensation of employees, debit............	3 310 ..	**−52.6**	**−44.3**	**−60.7**	**−46.2**	**−44.2**	**−72.0**	**−84.5**	**−90.3**
Investment income, credit............	2 320 ..	**64.5**	**54.7**	**47.6**	**40.5**	**45.2**	**64.0**	**86.3**	**108.0**
Direct investment income............	2 330 ..	4.8	5.3	5.7	7.1	7.5	7.8	8.3	8.5
Dividends and distributed branch profits............	2 332 ..	4.8	5.3	5.7	7.1	7.5	7.8	8.3	8.5
Reinvested earnings and undistributed branch profits.....	2 333 ..	....	....	....	....	....	....	....	....
Income on debt (interest)............	2 334 ..	....	....	....	....	....	....	....	....
Portfolio investment income............	2 339 ..	8.0	8.7	9.5	9.9	10.5	11.2	12.1	12.4
Income on equity............	2 340 ..	8.0	8.7	9.5	9.9	10.5	11.2	12.1	12.4
Income on bonds and notes............	2 350 ..	....	....	....	....	....	....	....	....
Income on money market instruments............	2 360 ..	....	....	....	....	....	....	....	....
Other investment income............	2 370 ..	51.7	40.7	32.4	23.5	27.1	45.0	65.9	87.2
Investment income, debit............	3 320 ..	**−137.6**	**−151.1**	**−173.8**	**−176.8**	**−225.4**	**−249.8**	**−295.9**	**−381.8**
Direct investment income............	3 330 ..	−123.0	−135.7	−158.9	−159.8	−205.4	−227.1	−270.2	−353.0
Dividends and distributed branch profits............	3 332 ..	−101.0	−120.3	−141.9	−158.2	−185.4	−193.6	−225.3	−265.4
Reinvested earnings and undistributed branch profits.....	3 333 ..	−8.9	−2.3	−3.8	11.9	−6.5	−20.0	−31.4	−74.0
Income on debt (interest)............	3 334 ..	−13.1	−13.2	−13.2	−13.5	−13.5	−13.6	−13.6	−13.6
Portfolio investment income............	3 339 ..	....	....	....	....	....	....	....	....
Income on equity............	3 340 ..	....	....	....	....	....	....	....	....
Income on bonds and notes............	3 350 ..	....	....	....	....	....	....	....	....
Income on money market instruments............	3 360 ..	....	....	....	....	....	....	....	....
Other investment income............	3 370 ..	−14.6	−15.3	−14.8	−17.0	−19.9	−22.6	−25.7	−28.8
D. CURRENT TRANSFERS............	4 379 ..	**424.7**	**395.5**	**438.6**	**413.1**	**428.2**	**440.1**	**502.7**	**544.0**
Credit............	2 379 ..	**432.0**	**403.8**	**447.9**	**425.3**	**443.7**	**460.8**	**527.2**	**569.7**
General government............	2 380 ..	255.2	220.3	247.3	216.8	209.5	211.5	248.4	285.7
Other sectors............	2 390 ..	176.9	183.6	200.6	208.5	234.2	249.2	278.8	284.1
Workers' remittances............	2 391 ..	100.0	110.0	120.0	125.0	144.0	160.0	180.0	183.6
Other current transfers............	2 392 ..	76.9	73.6	80.6	83.5	90.2	89.2	98.8	100.5
Debit............	3 379 ..	**−7.3**	**−8.3**	**−9.3**	**−12.2**	**−15.5**	**−20.7**	**−24.5**	**−25.8**
General government............	3 380 ..	−.3	−.3	−.3	−.3	−.3	−.3	−.3	−.3
Other sectors............	3 390 ..	−7.0	−8.0	−9.0	−11.9	−15.2	−20.4	−24.3	−25.5
Workers' remittances............	3 391 ..	−7.0	−8.0	−9.0	−10.0	−12.0	−16.0	−20.0	−24.0
Other current transfers............	3 392 ..	....	....	....	−1.9	−3.2	−4.4	−4.3	−1.5
CAPITAL AND FINANCIAL ACCOUNT............	4 996 ..	**127.2**	**61.6**	**105.6**	**273.4**	**228.7**	**355.3**	**383.2**	**510.3**
CAPITAL ACCOUNT............	4 994 ..	**35.6**	**44.9**	**8.1**	**66.2**	**68.1**	**94.9**	**267.6**	**252.8**
Total credit............	2 994 ..	*79.8*	*102.8*	*71.5*	*119.5*	*141.3*	*150.4*	*320.8*	*295.6*
Total debit............	3 994 ..	*−44.2*	*−58.0*	*−63.4*	*−53.3*	*−73.2*	*−55.5*	*−53.2*	*−42.8*
Capital transfers, credit............	2 400 ..	**79.8**	**102.8**	**71.5**	**119.5**	**141.3**	**150.4**	**320.8**	**295.6**
General government............	2 401 ..	61.9	83.1	54.8	109.4	111.3	114.4	207.0	130.6
Debt forgiveness............	2 402 ..	....	....	....	....	....	....	....	....
Other capital transfers............	2 410 ..	61.9	83.1	54.8	109.4	111.3	114.4	207.0	130.6
Other sectors............	2 430 ..	17.9	19.7	16.7	10.1	30.0	36.0	113.7	165.0
Migrants' transfers............	2 431 ..	17.9	19.7	16.7	10.1	30.0	36.0	113.7	165.0
Debt forgiveness............	2 432 ..	....	....	....	....	....	....	....	....
Other capital transfers............	2 440 ..	....	....	....	....	....	....	....	....
Capital transfers, debit............	3 400 ..	**−44.2**	**−58.0**	**−63.4**	**−53.3**	**−73.2**	**−55.5**	**−53.2**	**−42.8**
General government............	3 401 ..	....	....	....	....	....	....	....	....
Debt forgiveness............	3 402 ..	....	....	....	....	....	....	....	....
Other capital transfers............	3 410 ..	....	....	....	....	....	....	....	....
Other sectors............	3 430 ..	−44.2	−58.0	−63.4	−53.3	−73.2	−55.5	−53.2	−42.8
Migrants' transfers............	3 431 ..	−44.2	−58.0	−63.4	−53.3	−73.2	−55.5	−53.2	−42.8
Debt forgiveness............	3 432 ..	....	....	....	....	....	....	....	....
Other capital transfers............	3 440 ..	....	....	....	....	....	....	....	....
Nonproduced nonfinancial assets, credit............	2 480 ..	....	....	....	....	....	....	....	....
Nonproduced nonfinancial assets, debit............	3 480 ..	....	....	....	....	....	....	....	....

Table 2 (Continued). STANDARD PRESENTATION, 2000–2007

(Millions of U.S. dollars)

	Code	2000	2001	2002	2003	2004	2005	2006	2007
FINANCIAL ACCOUNT	4 995 ..	**91.6**	**16.8**	**97.5**	**207.3**	**160.6**	**260.5**	**115.6**	**257.6**
A. DIRECT INVESTMENT	4 500 ..	**141.9**	**142.1**	**139.1**	**74.3**	**121.2**	**374.9**	**474.8**	**866.2**
Direct investment abroad	4 505 ..	**−6.6**	**−7.3**	**−6.0**	**−9.7**	**−10.2**	**−6.3**	**−8.4**	**−1.1**
Equity capital	4 510 ..	−6.6	−7.3	−6.0	−9.7	−10.2	−6.3	−8.4	−1.1
Claims on affiliated enterprises	4 515 ..	−6.6	−7.3	−6.0	−9.7	−10.2	−6.3	−8.4	−1.1
Liabilities to affiliated enterprises	4 520 ..	....	....	....	....	....	....	....	....
Reinvested earnings	4 525 ..	....	....	....	....	....	....	....	....
Other capital	4 530 ..	....	....	....	....	....	....	....	....
Claims on affiliated enterprises	4 535 ..	....	....	....	....	....	....	....	....
Liabilities to affiliated enterprises	4 540 ..	....	....	....	....	....	....	....	....
Direct investment in Cambodia	4 555 ..	**148.5**	**149.4**	**145.1**	**84.0**	**131.4**	**381.2**	**483.2**	**867.3**
Equity capital	4 560 ..	109.4	144.1	127.1	93.5	124.9	359.2	451.9	793.3
Claims on direct investors	4 565 ..	....	....	....	....	....	....	....	....
Liabilities to direct investors	4 570 ..	109.4	144.1	127.1	93.5	124.9	359.2	451.9	793.3
Reinvested earnings	4 575 ..	8.9	2.3	3.8	−11.9	6.5	20.0	31.4	74.0
Other capital	4 580 ..	30.2	2.9	14.2	2.4	....	2.0	....	....
Claims on direct investors	4 585 ..	30.2	2.9	14.2	2.4	....	2.0	....	....
Liabilities to direct investors	4 590 ..	....	....	....	....	....	....	....	....
B. PORTFOLIO INVESTMENT	4 600 ..	**−7.2**	**−7.7**	**−7.5**	**−7.7**	**−8.0**	**−7.2**	**−12.1**	**−12.4**
Assets	4 602 ..	**−7.2**	**−7.7**	**−7.5**	**−7.7**	**−8.0**	**−7.2**	**−12.1**	**−12.4**
Equity securities	4 610 ..	−7.2	−7.7	−7.5	−7.7	−8.0	−7.2	−12.1	−12.4
Monetary authorities	4 611 ..	....	....	....	....	....	....	....	....
General government	4 612 ..	....	....	....	....	....	....	....	....
Banks	4 613 ..	....	....	....	....	....	....	....	....
Other sectors	4 614 ..	−7.2	−7.7	−7.5	−7.7	−8.0	−7.2	−12.1	−12.4
Debt securities	4 619 ..	....	....	....	....	....	....	....	....
Bonds and notes	4 620 ..	....	....	....	....	....	....	....	....
Monetary authorities	4 621 ..	....	....	....	....	....	....	....	....
General government	4 622 ..	....	....	....	....	....	....	....	....
Banks	4 623 ..	....	....	....	....	....	....	....	....
Other sectors	4 624 ..	....	....	....	....	....	....	....	....
Money market instruments	4 630 ..	....	....	....	....	....	....	....	....
Monetary authorities	4 631 ..	....	....	....	....	....	....	....	....
General government	4 632 ..	....	....	....	....	....	....	....	....
Banks	4 633 ..	....	....	....	....	....	....	....	....
Other sectors	4 634 ..	....	....	....	....	....	....	....	....
Liabilities	4 652 ..	....	....	....	....	....	....	....	....
Equity securities	4 660 ..	....	....	....	....	....	....	....	....
Banks	4 663 ..	....	....	....	....	....	....	....	....
Other sectors	4 664 ..	....	....	....	....	....	....	....	....
Debt securities	4 669 ..	....	....	....	....	....	....	....	....
Bonds and notes	4 670 ..	....	....	....	....	....	....	....	....
Monetary authorities	4 671 ..	....	....	....	....	....	....	....	....
General government	4 672 ..	....	....	....	....	....	....	....	....
Banks	4 673 ..	....	....	....	....	....	....	....	....
Other sectors	4 674 ..	....	....	....	....	....	....	....	....
Money market instruments	4 680 ..	....	....	....	....	....	....	....	....
Monetary authorities	4 681 ..	....	....	....	....	....	....	....	....
General government	4 682 ..	....	....	....	....	....	....	....	....
Banks	4 683 ..	....	....	....	....	....	....	....	....
Other sectors	4 684 ..	....	....	....	....	....	....	....	....
C. FINANCIAL DERIVATIVES	4 910 ..	....	....	....	....	....	....	....	....
Monetary authorities	4 911 ..	....	....	....	....	....	....	....	....
General government	4 912 ..	....	....	....	....	....	....	....	....
Banks	4 913 ..	....	....	....	....	....	....	....	....
Other sectors	4 914 ..	....	....	....	....	....	....	....	....
Assets	4 900 ..	....	....	....	....	....	....	....	....
Monetary authorities	4 901 ..	....	....	....	....	....	....	....	....
General government	4 902 ..	....	....	....	....	....	....	....	....
Banks	4 903 ..	....	....	....	....	....	....	....	....
Other sectors	4 904 ..	....	....	....	....	....	....	....	....
Liabilities	4 905 ..	....	....	....	....	....	....	....	....
Monetary authorities	4 906 ..	....	....	....	....	....	....	....	....
General government	4 907 ..	....	....	....	....	....	....	....	....
Banks	4 908 ..	....	....	....	....	....	....	....	....
Other sectors	4 909 ..	....	....	....	....	....	....	....	....

Table 2 (Concluded). STANDARD PRESENTATION, 2000–2007

(Millions of U.S. dollars)

	Code	2000	2001	2002	2003	2004	2005	2006	2007
D. OTHER INVESTMENT	4 700 ..	**65.7**	**−53.6**	**55.4**	**188.1**	**108.4**	**−28.9**	**−208.4**	**−169.4**
Assets	4 703 ..	**−176.3**	**−216.8**	**−228.3**	**−127.0**	**−91.3**	**−302.8**	**−540.1**	**−699.5**
Trade credits	4 706 ..	−159.4	−24.9	−127.3	−95.1	−47.0	−145.2	−168.9	−90.3
General government	4 707 ..	....	....	....	....	....	....	....	....
of which: Short-term	4 709 ..	....	....	....	....	....	....	....	....
Other sectors	4 710 ..	−159.4	−24.9	−127.3	−95.1	−47.0	−145.2	−168.9	−90.3
of which: Short-term	4 712 ..	−159.4	−24.9	−127.3	−95.1	−47.0	−145.2	−168.9	−90.3
Loans	4 714 ..	....	....	....	....	....	....	....	....
Monetary authorities	4 715 ..	....	....	....	....	....	....	....	....
of which: Short-term	4 718 ..	....	....	....	....	....	....	....	....
General government	4 719 ..	....	....	....	....	....	....	....	....
of which: Short-term	4 721 ..	....	....	....	....	....	....	....	....
Banks	4 722 ..	....	....	....	....	....	....	....	....
of which: Short-term	4 724 ..	....	....	....	....	....	....	....	....
Other sectors	4 725 ..	....	....	....	....	....	....	....	....
of which: Short-term	4 727 ..	....	....	....	....	....	....	....	....
Currency and deposits	4 730 ..	−12.5	−186.8	−98.3	−25.0	−35.6	−153.0	−362.8	−601.4
Monetary authorities	4 731 ..	....	−26.2	−98.4	6.3	−66.9	68.6	−70.8	−210.7
General government	4 732 ..	....	....	....	....	....	....	....	....
Banks	4 733 ..	−11.1	−45.0	38.0	−78.0	−32.1	−96.9	−139.9	−353.7
Other sectors	4 734 ..	−1.4	−115.6	−37.9	46.7	63.3	−124.7	−152.1	−37.0
Other assets	4 736 ..	−4.4	−5.0	−2.7	−6.9	−8.8	−4.6	−8.5	−7.8
Monetary authorities	4 737 ..	....	....	....	....	....	....	....	....
of which: Short-term	4 739 ..	....	....	....	....	....	....	....	....
General government	4 740 ..	....	....	....	....	....	....	....	....
of which: Short-term	4 742 ..	....	....	....	....	....	....	....	....
Banks	4 743 ..	−.1	−.4	1.8	−.4	−2.1	2.2	.3	....
of which: Short-term	4 745 ..	−.1	−.4	1.8	−.4	−2.1	2.2	.3	....
Other sectors	4 746 ..	−4.3	−4.6	−4.5	−6.5	−6.7	−6.9	−8.7	−7.8
of which: Short-term	4 748 ..	−4.3	−4.6	−4.5	−6.5	−6.7	−6.9	−8.7	−7.8
Liabilities	4 753 ..	**241.9**	**163.1**	**283.7**	**315.2**	**199.8**	**274.0**	**331.7**	**530.1**
Trade credits	4 756 ..	157.3	54.9	141.0	117.2	43.0	107.8	211.6	195.3
General government	4 757 ..	....	....	....	....	....	....	....	....
of which: Short-term	4 759 ..	....	....	....	....	....	....	....	....
Other sectors	4 760 ..	157.3	54.9	141.0	117.2	43.0	107.8	211.6	195.3
of which: Short-term	4 762 ..	157.3	54.9	141.0	117.2	43.0	107.8	211.6	195.3
Loans	4 764 ..	81.2	93.0	144.7	163.0	175.7	149.5	89.0	124.0
Monetary authorities	4 765 ..	4.0	9.3	9.3	−1.7	−10.3	−8.8	−82.2	....
of which: Use of Fund credit and loans from the Fund	4 766 ..	4.0	9.3	9.3	−1.7	−10.3	−8.8	−82.2	....
of which: Short-term	4 768 ..	....	....	....	....	....	....	....	....
General government	4 769 ..	74.6	78.1	124.2	148.6	154.4	144.0	122.7	119.6
of which: Short-term	4 771 ..	....	....	....	....	....	....	....	....
Banks	4 772 ..	2.6	−2.4	6.1	12.1	28.6	4.3	5.5	−14.3
of which: Short-term	4 774 ..	....	....	....	....	....	....	....	....
Other sectors	4 775 ..	....	8.0	5.0	4.0	3.0	10.0	43.0	18.7
of which: Short-term	4 777 ..	....	....	....	....	....	....	....	....
Currency and deposits	4 780 ..	−7.3	.1	−12.3	22.2	−31.8	4.0	18.4	198.0
Monetary authorities	4 781 ..	....	....	....	....	....	....	....	....
General government	4 782 ..	....	....	....	....	....	....	....	....
Banks	4 783 ..	−7.3	.1	−12.3	22.2	−31.8	4.0	18.4	198.0
Other sectors	4 784 ..	....	....	....	....	....	....	....	....
Other liabilities	4 786 ..	10.7	15.2	10.4	12.8	12.8	12.8	12.8	12.8
Monetary authorities	4 787 ..	....	....	....	....	....	....	....	....
of which: Short-term	4 789 ..	....	....	....	....	....	....	....	....
General government	4 790 ..	12.8	12.8	12.8	12.8	12.8	12.8	12.8	12.8
of which: Short-term	4 792 ..	12.8	12.8	12.8	12.8	12.8	12.8	12.8	12.8
Banks	4 793 ..	−2.1	2.4	−2.4	....	....	....	....	....
of which: Short-term	4 795 ..	−2.1	2.4	−2.4	....	....	....	....	....
Other sectors	4 796 ..	....	....	....	....	....	....	....	....
of which: Short-term	4 798 ..	....	....	....	....	....	....	....	....
E. RESERVE ASSETS	4 802 ..	**−108.7**	**−64.0**	**−89.4**	**−47.5**	**−61.0**	**−78.4**	**−138.7**	**−426.8**
Monetary gold	4 812 ..	....	....	....	....	....	....	....	....
Special drawing rights	4 811 ..	4.8	−.4	.1	.5	.1	−.2	.1	....
Reserve position in the Fund	4 810 ..	....	....	....	....	....	....	....	....
Foreign exchange	4 803 ..	−113.5	−63.6	−89.5	−48.0	−61.1	−78.2	−138.8	−426.8
Other claims	4 813 ..	....	....	....	....	....	....	....	....
NET ERRORS AND OMISSIONS	4 998 ..	**8.9**	**26.2**	**1.7**	**−40.0**	**−45.8**	**5.1**	**−44.1**	**−4.0**

Table 3. INTERNATIONAL INVESTMENT POSITION (End-period stocks), 2000–2007

(Millions of U.S. dollars)

	Code	2000	2001	2002	2003	2004	2005	2006	2007
ASSETS	8 995 C.	**2,333.2**	**2,684.7**	**3,098.6**	**3,348.0**	**3,558.4**	**4,009.0**	**4,809.6**	**6,062.7**
Direct investment abroad	8 505 ..	**193.2**	**211.0**	**228.5**	**241.5**	**255.6**	**267.0**	**279.0**	**283.8**
Equity capital and reinvested earnings	8 506 ..	193.2	211.0	228.5	241.5	255.6	267.0	279.0	283.8
Claims on affiliated enterprises	8 507 ..	193.2	211.0	228.5	241.5	255.6	267.0	279.0	283.8
Liabilities to affiliated enterprises	8 508 ..	....	....	....	....	....	....	....	....
Other capital	8 530 ..	....	....	....	....	....	....	....	....
Claims on affiliated enterprises	8 535 ..	....	....	....	....	....	....	....	....
Liabilities to affiliated enterprises	8 540 ..	....	....	....	....	....	....	....	....
Portfolio investment	8 602 ..	**198.8**	**217.4**	**236.8**	**253.8**	**270.3**	**286.4**	**312.8**	**332.3**
Equity securities	8 610 ..	178.9	195.6	213.1	228.5	243.3	257.8	281.6	299.1
Monetary authorities	8 611 ..	....	....	....	....	....	....	....	....
General government	8 612 ..	....	....	....	....	....	....	....	....
Banks	8 613 ..	....	....	....	....	....	....	....	....
Other sectors	8 614 ..	178.9	195.6	213.1	228.5	243.3	257.8	281.6	299.1
Debt securities	8 619 ..	19.9	21.7	23.7	25.4	27.0	28.6	31.3	33.2
Bonds and notes	8 620 ..	19.9	21.7	23.7	25.4	27.0	28.6	31.3	33.2
Monetary authorities	8 621 ..	....	....	....	....	....	....	....	....
General government	8 622 ..	....	....	....	....	....	....	....	....
Banks	8 623 ..	....	....	....	....	....	....	....	....
Other sectors	8 624 ..	19.9	21.7	23.7	25.4	27.0	28.6	31.3	33.2
Money market instruments	8 630 ..	....	....	....	....	....	....	....	....
Monetary authorities	8 631 ..	....	....	....	....	....	....	....	....
General government	8 632 ..	....	....	....	....	....	....	....	....
Banks	8 633 ..	....	....	....	....	....	....	....	....
Other sectors	8 634 ..	....	....	....	....	....	....	....	....
Financial derivatives	8 900 ..	....	....	....	....	....	....	....	....
Monetary authorities	8 901 ..	....	....	....	....	....	....	....	....
General government	8 902 ..	....	....	....	....	....	....	....	....
Banks	8 903 ..	....	....	....	....	....	....	....	....
Other sectors	8 904 ..	....	....	....	....	....	....	....	....
Other investment	8 703 ..	**1,330.5**	**1,579.9**	**1,843.7**	**1,989.4**	**2,096.8**	**2,413.8**	**2,989.5**	**3,708.6**
Trade credits	8 706 ..	375.8	400.7	528.1	623.1	670.1	815.3	984.2	1,074.5
General government	8 707 ..	....	....	....	....	....	....	....	....
of which: Short-term	8 709 ..	....	....	....	....	....	....	....	....
Other sectors	8 710 ..	375.8	400.7	528.1	623.1	670.1	815.3	984.2	1,074.5
of which: Short-term	8 712 ..	*375.8*	*400.7*	*528.1*	*623.1*	*670.1*	*815.3*	*984.2*	*1,074.5*
Loans	8 714 ..	....	....	....	....	....	....	....	....
Monetary authorities	8 715 ..	....	....	....	....	....	....	....	....
of which: Short-term	8 718 ..	....	....	....	....	....	....	....	....
General government	8 719 ..	....	....	....	....	....	....	....	....
of which: Short-term	8 721 ..	....	....	....	....	....	....	....	....
Banks	8 722 ..	....	....	....	....	....	....	....	....
of which: Short-term	8 724 ..	....	....	....	....	....	....	....	....
Other sectors	8 725 ..	....	....	....	....	....	....	....	....
of which: Short-term	8 727 ..	....	....	....	....	....	....	....	....
Currency and deposits	8 730 ..	834.0	1,046.9	1,173.6	1,213.5	1,262.0	1,426.4	1,817.6	2,434.7
Monetary authorities	8 731 ..	....	....	....	....	....	....	....	....
General government	8 732 ..	....	....	....	....	....	....	....	....
Banks	8 733 ..	....	....	....	....	....	....	....	....
Other sectors	8 734 ..	834.0	1,046.9	1,173.6	1,213.5	1,262.0	1,426.4	1,817.6	2,434.7
Other assets	8 736 ..	120.7	132.2	142.1	152.7	164.7	172.1	187.7	199.4
Monetary authorities	8 737 ..	....	....	....	....	....	....	....	....
of which: Short-term	8 739 ..	....	....	....	....	....	....	....	....
General government	8 740 ..	....	....	....	....	....	....	....	....
of which: Short-term	8 742 ..	....	....	....	....	....	....	....	....
Banks	8 743 ..	1.4	1.8	....	.4	2.5	.3	....	....
of which: Short-term	8 745 ..	*1.4*	*1.8*	....	*.4*	*2.5*	*.3*	....	....
Other sectors	8 746 ..	119.3	130.4	142.1	152.3	162.2	171.9	187.7	199.4
of which: Short-term	8 748 ..	*119.3*	*130.4*	*142.1*	*152.3*	*162.2*	*171.9*	*187.7*	*199.4*
Reserve assets	8 802 ..	**610.7**	**676.4**	**789.6**	**863.2**	**935.7**	**1,041.7**	**1,228.3**	**1,738.0**
Monetary gold	8 812 ..	109.0	110.8	137.5	166.4	177.9	205.6	253.4	336.3
Special drawing rights	8 811 ..	.2	.5	.5	.2	.1	.2	.2	.2
Reserve position in the Fund	8 810 ..	....	....	....	....	....	....	....	....
Foreign exchange	8 803 ..	501.5	565.1	651.6	696.6	757.7	835.9	974.7	1,401.5
Other claims	8 813 ..	....	....	....	....	....	....	....	....

Table 3 (Concluded). INTERNATIONAL INVESTMENT POSITION (End-period stocks), 2000–2007

(Millions of U.S. dollars)

	Code	2000	2001	2002	2003	2004	2005	2006	2007
LIABILITIES	8 995 D.	2,968.7	3,278.4	3,714.3	4,122.6	4,457.8	5,105.6	5,921.5	7,318.9
Direct investment in Cambodia	8 555 ..	1,579.9	1,729.3	1,874.4	1,958.4	2,089.8	2,471.0	2,954.2	3,821.5
Equity capital and reinvested earnings	8 556 ..	923.7	1,070.1	1,201.1	1,282.7	1,414.1	1,793.3	2,276.5	3,143.8
Claims on direct investors	8 557 ..	....	....	....	....	....	....	....	....
Liabilities to direct investors	8 558 ..	923.7	1,070.1	1,201.1	1,282.7	1,414.1	1,793.3	2,276.5	3,143.8
Other capital	8 580 ..	656.3	659.2	673.3	675.7	675.7	677.7	677.7	677.7
Claims on direct investors	8 585 ..	....	....	....	....	....	....	....	....
Liabilities to direct investors	8 590 ..	656.3	659.2	673.3	675.7	675.7	677.7	677.7	677.7
Portfolio investment	8 652 ..	....	....	....	....	....	....	....	....
Equity securities	8 660 ..	....	....	....	....	....	....	....	....
Banks	8 663 ..	....	....	....	....	....	....	....	....
Other sectors	8 664 ..	....	....	....	....	....	....	....	....
Debt securities	8 669 ..	....	....	....	....	....	....	....	....
Bonds and notes	8 670 ..	....	....	....	....	....	....	....	....
Monetary authorities	8 671 ..	....	....	....	....	....	....	....	....
General government	8 672 ..	....	....	....	....	....	....	....	....
Banks	8 673 ..	....	....	....	....	....	....	....	....
Other sectors	8 674 ..	....	....	....	....	....	....	....	....
Money market instruments	8 680 ..	....	....	....	....	....	....	....	....
Monetary authorities	8 681 ..	....	....	....	....	....	....	....	....
General government	8 682 ..	....	....	....	....	....	....	....	....
Banks	8 683 ..	....	....	....	....	....	....	....	....
Other sectors	8 684 ..	....	....	....	....	....	....	....	....
Financial derivatives	8 905 ..	....	....	....	....	....	....	....	....
Monetary authorities	8 906 ..	....	....	....	....	....	....	....	....
General government	8 907 ..	....	....	....	....	....	....	....	....
Banks	8 908 ..	....	....	....	....	....	....	....	....
Other sectors	8 909 ..	....	....	....	....	....	....	....	....
Other investment	8 753 ..	1,388.8	1,549.1	1,839.9	2,164.2	2,368.0	2,634.6	2,967.3	3,497.4
Trade credits	8 756 ..	496.5	551.4	692.4	809.6	852.7	960.4	1,172.0	1,367.3
General government	8 757 ..	....	....	....	....	....	....	....	....
of which: Short-term	8 759 ..	....	....	....	....	....	....	....	....
Other sectors	8 760 ..	496.5	551.4	692.4	809.6	852.7	960.4	1,172.0	1,367.3
of which: Short-term	8 762 ..	*496.5*	*551.4*	*692.4*	*809.6*	*852.7*	*960.4*	*1,172.0*	*1,367.3*
Loans	8 764 ..	614.9	705.2	857.0	1,029.0	1,208.8	1,350.9	1,440.8	1,564.8
Monetary authorities	8 765 ..	73.3	79.8	96.2	103.6	97.4	81.2	....	....
of which: Use of Fund credit and loans from the Fund	8 766 ..	*73.3*	*79.8*	*96.2*	*103.6*	*97.4*	*81.2*	....	....
of which: Short-term	8 768 ..	....	....	....	....	....	....	....	....
General government	8 769 ..	535.0	613.1	737.3	885.9	1,040.3	1,184.3	1,306.9	1,426.6
of which: Short-term	8 771 ..	....	....	....	....	....	....	....	....
Banks	8 772 ..	2.7	.3	6.4	18.5	47.1	51.4	56.9	42.6
of which: Short-term	8 774 ..	....	....	....	....	....	....	....	....
Other sectors	8 775 ..	4.0	12.0	17.0	21.0	24.0	34.0	77.0	95.7
of which: Short-term	8 777 ..	....	....	....	....	....	....	....	....
Currency and deposits	8 780 ..	47.5	47.5	35.2	57.4	25.6	29.6	48.0	246.1
Monetary authorities	8 781 ..	....	....	....	....	....	....	....	....
General government	8 782 ..	....	....	....	....	....	....	....	....
Banks	8 783 ..	47.5	47.5	35.2	57.4	25.6	29.6	48.0	246.1
Other sectors	8 784 ..	....	....	....	....	....	....	....	....
Other liabilities	8 786 ..	229.9	245.0	255.4	268.1	280.9	293.7	306.4	319.2
Monetary authorities	8 787 ..	....	....	....	....	....	....	....	....
of which: Short-term	8 789 ..	....	....	....	....	....	....	....	....
General government	8 790 ..	229.9	242.6	255.4	268.1	280.9	293.7	306.4	319.2
of which: Short-term	8 792 ..	*229.9*	*242.6*	*255.4*	*268.1*	*280.9*	*293.7*	*306.4*	*319.2*
Banks	8 793 ..	....	2.4	....	....	....	....	....	....
of which: Short-term	8 795 ..	....	*2.4*	....	....	....	....	....	....
Other sectors	8 796 ..	....	....	....	....	....	....	....	....
of which: Short-term	8 798 ..	....	....	....	....	....	....	....	....
NET INTERNATIONAL INVESTMENT POSITION	8 995 ..	−635.5	−593.7	−615.7	−774.6	−899.4	−1,096.6	−1,111.9	−1,256.2
Conversion rates: riels per U.S. dollar (end of period)	0 102 ..	3,905.0	3,895.0	3,930.0	3,984.0	4,027.0	4,112.0	4,057.0	3,999.0

Table 1. ANALYTIC PRESENTATION, 2000–2007

(Millions of U.S. dollars)

	Code	2000	2001	2002	2003	2004	2005	2006	2007
A. Current Account[1]................................	4 993 Z.	**−249.1**	**−376.1**	**−444.8**	**−627.6**	**−626.3**	**−777.2**	**−150.9**	**−547.1**
Goods: exports f.o.b................................	2 100 ..	1,985.8	1,891.5	1,964.3	2,483.4	2,904.2	3,265.2	3,848.6	4,345.0
Goods: imports f.o.b................................	3 100 ..	−1,483.9	−1,797.4	−1,811.6	−2,214.1	−2,695.3	−2,889.8	−3,178.5	−4,049.6
Balance on Goods................................	4 100 ..	*501.9*	*94.1*	*152.7*	*269.4*	*208.9*	*375.4*	*670.1*	*295.3*
Services: credit................................	2 200 ..	590.3	858.0	938.6	644.6	940.2	686.7	672.3	607.0
Services: debit................................	3 200 ..	−957.1	−1,082.5	−1,211.6	−1,222.5	−1,484.8	−1,455.3	−1,474.9	−1,481.0
Balance on Goods and Services.................	4 991 ..	*135.1*	*−130.4*	*−120.3*	*−308.5*	*−335.8*	*−393.3*	*−132.5*	*−578.6*
Income: credit................................	2 300 ..	26.2	47.4	42.6	108.5	97.6	44.9	46.3	58.2
Income: debit................................	3 300 ..	−519.3	−379.8	−419.5	−549.4	−545.0	−665.3	−377.5	−442.9
Balance on Goods, Services, and Income........	4 992 ..	*−358.0*	*−462.7*	*−497.2*	*−749.4*	*−783.1*	*−1,013.7*	*−463.7*	*−963.4*
Current transfers: credit................................	2 379 Z.	173.2	147.3	127.0	205.0	206.2	331.7	526.8	592.9
Current transfers: debit................................	3 379 ..	−64.2	−60.6	−74.7	−83.2	−49.4	−95.3	−214.0	−176.6
B. Capital Account[1]................................	4 994 Z.	**17.5**	**55.6**	**61.0**	**111.8**	**−104.7**	**203.8**	**1,585.5**	**356.3**
Capital account: credit................................	2 994 Z.	17.5	56.4	62.1	123.0	5.1	204.1	1,586.0	356.8
Capital account: debit................................	3 994 ..	−.1	−.8	−1.1	−11.1	−109.8	−.3	−.5	−.5
Total, Groups A Plus B................................	4 981 ..	*−231.6*	*−320.5*	*−383.9*	*−515.8*	*−731.0*	*−573.4*	*1,434.6*	*−190.8*
C. Financial Account[1]................................	4 995 W.	**−145.3**	**325.8**	**593.2**	**−603.1**	**209.7**	**67.0**	**69.4**	**936.4**
Direct investment abroad................................	4 505 ..	−9.7	−35.2	33.1	−8.5	−2.1	23.2	48.0	156.1
Direct investment in Cameroon................................	4 555 Z.	158.8	73.3	601.7	351.8	85.6	244.4	16.4	433.1
Portfolio investment assets................................	4 602 ..	−1.6	4.7	4.6	−2.4	38.9	−9.8	−.8	−8.1
Equity securities................................	4 610 ..	−.4	−4.5	4.9	−1.6	....	−10.2	−.8	−6.3
Debt securities................................	4 619 ..	−1.2	9.2	−.3	−.8	38.9	.4	....	−1.9
Portfolio investment liabilities................................	4 652 Z.	.1	89.7	.7	.1	−8.2	−3.1	−3.8	−13.3
Equity securities................................	4 660 ..	....	2.2	1.0	.2	−8.2	−4.2	−5.6	−13.3
Debt securities................................	4 669 Z.	.1	87.6	−.4	−.1	.1	1.1	1.8	....
Financial derivatives................................	4 910 ..	....	....	....	....	....	....	....	....
Financial derivatives assets................................	4 900 ..	....	....	....	....	....	....	....	....
Financial derivatives liabilities................................	4 905 ..	....	....	....	....	....	....	....	....
Other investment assets................................	4 703 ..	63.6	−162.9	−271.6	79.9	148.8	67.0	139.5	−105.5
Monetary authorities................................	4 701 ..	....	....	....	....	....	....	....	....
General government................................	4 704 ..	....	....	....	....	....	1.3	−9.5	−4.1
Banks................................	4 705 ..	−13.2	7.3	−64.7	−15.7	−44.9	−76.1	−81.9	−136.2
Other sectors................................	4 728 ..	76.8	−170.2	−206.9	95.6	193.6	141.8	230.8	34.8
Other investment liabilities................................	4 753 W.	−356.5	356.2	224.6	−1,024.1	−53.3	−254.6	−130.0	474.2
Monetary authorities................................	4 753 WA	−111.1	−1.8	−4.0	−4.1	−2.4	3.7	−3.3	−10.9
General government................................	4 753 ZB	−198.7	3.4	19.4	−746.1	−446.4	−465.4	−483.3	−70.2
Banks................................	4 753 ZC	−16.3	−12.3	11.2	−4.8	26.2	78.5	−31.0	−30.1
Other sectors................................	4 753 ZD	−30.4	366.9	198.0	−269.1	369.5	128.6	387.6	585.4
Total, Groups A Through C................................	4 983 ..	*−376.9*	*5.3*	*209.3*	*−1,118.9*	*−521.3*	*−506.4*	*1,504.0*	*745.7*
D. Net Errors and Omissions................................	4 998 ..	**111.7**	**−123.8**	**−129.9**	**92.7**	**113.0**	**−31.9**	**112.6**	**93.1**
Total, Groups A Through D................................	4 984 ..	*−265.2*	*−118.5*	*79.5*	*−1,026.2*	*−408.3*	*−538.3*	*1,616.6*	*838.8*
E. Reserves and Related Items................................	4 802 A.	**265.2**	**118.5**	**−79.5**	**1,026.2**	**408.3**	**538.3**	**−1,616.6**	**−838.8**
Reserve assets................................	4 802 ..	−205.7	−132.8	−210.9	105.9	−127.2	−243.4	−627.0	−919.3
Use of Fund credit and loans................................	4 766 ..	49.2	16.7	40.9	12.0	−27.9	−36.2	−268.3	8.0
Exceptional financing................................	4 920 ..	421.7	234.5	90.6	908.3	563.3	818.0	−721.2	72.6
Conversion rates: CFA francs per U.S. dollar..........	0 101 ..	**712.0**	**733.0**	**697.0**	**581.2**	**528.3**	**527.5**	**522.9**	**479.3**

[1] Excludes components that have been classified in the categories of Group E.

Table 2. STANDARD PRESENTATION, 2000–2007

(Millions of U.S. dollars)

	Code	2000	2001	2002	2003	2004	2005	2006	2007
CURRENT ACCOUNT	4 993	−249.1	−376.1	−444.8	−627.6	−626.3	−777.2	−150.9	−547.1
A. GOODS	4 100	**501.9**	**94.1**	**152.7**	**269.4**	**208.9**	**375.4**	**670.1**	**295.3**
Credit	2 100	1,985.8	1,891.5	1,964.3	2,483.4	2,904.2	3,265.2	3,848.6	4,345.0
General merchandise: exports f.o.b.	2 110	1,967.1	1,868.3	1,954.8	2,473.0	2,886.4	3,222.4	3,807.4	4,280.6
Goods for processing: exports f.o.b.	2 150	1.0	....	2.1	....	....	....	....	....
Repairs on goods	2 160	10.7	16.4	....	....	.2	....	....	....
Goods procured in ports by carriers	2 170	7.1	6.8	7.3	10.4	17.7	42.9	41.3	64.4
Nonmonetary gold	2 180	....	....	....	....	....	....	....	....
Debit	3 100	−1,483.9	−1,797.4	−1,811.6	−2,214.1	−2,695.3	−2,889.8	−3,178.5	−4,049.6
General merchandise: imports f.o.b.	3 110	−1,468.4	−1,779.9	−1,791.9	−2,205.7	−2,681.3	−2,869.1	−3,159.4	−4,043.4
Goods for processing: imports f.o.b.	3 150	−1.0	−1.7	−.7	....	....	....	....	....
Repairs on goods	3 160	−9.7	−10.5	−12.3	....	−1.1	−6.3	−10.3	....
Goods procured in ports by carriers	3 170	−4.8	−5.2	−6.8	−8.4	−12.9	−14.4	−8.8	−6.2
Nonmonetary gold	3 180	....	....	....	....	....	....	....	....
B. SERVICES	4 200	**−366.8**	**−224.5**	**−273.0**	**−577.9**	**−544.7**	**−768.7**	**−802.7**	**−874.0**
Total credit	2 200	*590.3*	*858.0*	*938.6*	*644.6*	*940.2*	*686.7*	*672.3*	*607.0*
Total debit	3 200	*−957.1*	*−1,082.5*	*−1,211.6*	*−1,222.5*	*−1,484.8*	*−1,455.3*	*−1,474.9*	*−1,481.0*
Transportation services, credit	2 205	**136.8**	**185.6**	**127.7**	**235.2**	**145.9**	**140.4**	**158.3**	**184.5**
Passenger	2 850	*74.9*	*108.5*	*61.6*	*84.0*	*53.5*	*53.6*	*50.4*	*44.0*
Freight	2 851	*32.6*	*49.9*	*32.7*	*48.6*	*33.6*	*19.8*	*27.7*	*46.7*
Other	2 852	*29.3*	*27.2*	*33.3*	*102.6*	*58.8*	*67.0*	*80.2*	*93.8*
Sea transport, passenger	2 207	....	....	....	....	....	....	....	....
Sea transport, freight	2 208	18.0	26.4	18.0	12.7	20.4	5.3	11.1	....
Sea transport, other	2 209	11.4	5.5	24.6	43.1	16.6	28.2	19.7	21.5
Air transport, passenger	2 211	74.9	108.5	61.6	84.0	53.5	53.6	50.4	44.0
Air transport, freight	2 212	14.2	17.0	6.2	10.2	6.8	9.6	10.3	14.0
Air transport, other	2 213	17.2	21.0	8.7	30.1	17.8	11.4	36.6	46.0
Other transport, passenger	2 215	....	....	....	....	....	....	....	....
Other transport, freight	2 216	.3	6.5	8.6	25.7	6.4	5.0	6.4	32.7
Other transport, other	2 217	.7	.7	....	29.4	24.4	27.4	23.8	26.3
Transportation services, debit	3 205	**−223.0**	**−282.9**	**−274.1**	**−353.1**	**−383.5**	**−467.4**	**−452.9**	**−703.0**
Passenger	3 850	*−36.2*	*−39.1*	*−33.8*	*−101.4*	*−71.4*	*−124.6*	*−109.2*	*−157.7*
Freight	3 851	*−167.4*	*−229.8*	*−197.6*	*−236.0*	*−297.0*	*−314.4*	*−309.6*	*−517.4*
Other	3 852	*−19.3*	*−14.0*	*−42.7*	*−15.8*	*−15.1*	*−28.4*	*−34.1*	*−27.8*
Sea transport, passenger	3 207	....	....	....	....	....	....	....	....
Sea transport, freight	3 208	−166.8	−224.4	−193.8	−224.6	−284.8	−301.4	−272.8	−462.0
Sea transport, other	3 209	−5.6	−1.2	−15.0	−3.4	−3.3	−3.0	−7.4	−8.1
Air transport, passenger	3 211	−36.2	−39.1	−33.8	−101.4	−71.4	−124.6	−109.2	−157.7
Air transport, freight	3 212	−.6	−5.3	−3.8	−10.7	−10.8	−11.5	−33.2	−55.4
Air transport, other	3 213	−13.7	−12.7	−27.5	−11.4	−11.5	−24.3	−24.5	−13.4
Other transport, passenger	3 215	....	....	....	....	....	....	....	....
Other transport, freight	3 216	....	....	....	−.7	−1.4	−1.6	−3.6	....
Other transport, other	3 217	....	....	−.2	−.9	−.3	−1.0	−2.1	−6.4
Travel, credit	2 236	**57.4**	**72.6**	**62.3**	**182.3**	**157.7**	**175.1**	**181.1**	**177.0**
Business travel	2 237	17.2	26.8	19.0	12.4	9.5	16.2	22.9	12.3
Personal travel	2 240	40.2	45.8	43.3	169.9	148.2	158.8	158.2	164.7
Travel, debit	3 236	**−205.1**	**−160.2**	**−170.5**	**−171.2**	**−323.1**	**−355.1**	**−412.5**	**−317.7**
Business travel	3 237	−105.6	−101.8	−104.6	−88.3	−92.7	−152.8	−176.4	−168.6
Personal travel	3 240	−99.5	−58.3	−65.9	−82.8	−230.3	−202.2	−236.1	−149.1
Other services, credit	2 200 BA	**396.1**	**599.7**	**748.6**	**227.1**	**636.6**	**371.2**	**332.8**	**245.6**
Communications	2 245	8.4	4.0	25.3	19.2	52.2	56.0	42.2	79.0
Construction	2 249	7.0	7.0	4.3	1.4	2.5	2.2	1.4	2.0
Insurance	2 253	11.7	51.0	1.8	35.6	43.8	47.6	12.7	21.1
Financial	2 260	5.5	4.6	11.1	1.8	3.4	4.4	2.9	3.1
Computer and information	2 262	.1	....	....	2.4	2.1	.2	.1	.2
Royalties and licence fees	2 266	2.5	....	.1	.2	.1	.3	.2	.3
Other business services	2 268	344.3	517.5	685.6	104.0	404.0	129.3	143.9	9.0
Personal, cultural, and recreational	2 287	1.2	1.2	2.5	10.6	16.8	17.9	12.8	....
Government, n.i.e.	2 291	15.4	14.3	17.9	51.9	111.6	113.2	116.5	130.9
Other services, debit	3 200 BA	**−529.1**	**−639.4**	**−766.9**	**−698.2**	**−778.3**	**−632.9**	**−609.5**	**−460.3**
Communications	3 245	−3.8	−4.0	−19.9	−57.7	−28.8	−46.8	−21.3	−9.3
Construction	3 249	−4.5	−4.6	....	−11.2	−4.1	−16.4	−10.4	−11.3
Insurance	3 253	−29.9	−34.3	−20.1	−81.1	−95.6	−101.3	−78.8	−85.9
Financial	3 260	−9.0	−4.4	−7.7	−11.7	−5.7	−13.7	−8.7	−9.5
Computer and information	3 262	−.5	−.3	−.2	−22.3	−6.7	−2.7	−1.8	−2.0
Royalties and licence fees	3 266	−4.6	−2.0	−.6	−1.7	−1.0	−8.2	−5.2	−5.7
Other business services	3 268	−452.9	−562.6	−703.5	−463.1	−589.7	−414.7	−415.5	−269.2
Personal, cultural, and recreational	3 287	−.7	−.7	−1.2	−4.2	−3.9	−2.4	−8.9	....
Government, n.i.e.	3 291	−23.2	−26.6	−13.8	−45.1	−42.9	−26.7	−58.9	−67.5

Table 2 (Continued). STANDARD PRESENTATION, 2000–2007

(Millions of U.S. dollars)

	Code	2000	2001	2002	2003	2004	2005	2006	2007
C. INCOME	4 300	**−493.1**	**−332.3**	**−376.9**	**−440.9**	**−447.4**	**−620.4**	**−331.2**	**−384.7**
Total credit	2 300	*26.2*	*47.4*	*42.6*	*108.5*	*97.6*	*44.9*	*46.3*	*58.2*
Total debit	3 300	*−519.3*	*−379.8*	*−419.5*	*−549.4*	*−545.0*	*−665.3*	*−377.5*	*−442.9*
Compensation of employees, credit	2 310	**10.3**	**10.0**	**15.3**	**14.9**	**5.0**	**9.9**	**12.3**	**13.4**
Compensation of employees, debit	3 310	**−16.2**	**−23.5**	**−28.3**	**−27.7**	**−19.6**	**−36.0**	**−43.6**	**−47.6**
Investment income, credit	2 320	**16.0**	**37.4**	**27.3**	**93.6**	**92.6**	**35.1**	**34.0**	**44.8**
Direct investment income	2 330	11.5	6.3	5.7	75.7	70.4	10.1	17.6	26.5
Dividends and distributed branch profits	2 332	1.1	2.1	1.7	56.9	70.8	10.5	20.4	25.9
Reinvested earnings and undistributed branch profits	2 333	9.7	2.1	4.1	18.9	−.4	−.4	−2.8	.7
Income on debt (interest)	2 334	.7	2.1	....	....	....	....	....	....
Portfolio investment income	2 339	.5	.8	.5	4.4	3.3	.3	1.0	1.6
Income on equity	2 340	.5	.7	.3	2.6	3.2	.2	....	.3
Income on bonds and notes	2 350	....	....	....	....	....	....	....	....
Income on money market instruments	2 360	....	....	....	....	....	....	....	....
Other investment income	2 370	3.9	30.2	21.1	13.5	18.9	24.7	15.4	16.7
Investment income, debit	3 320	**−503.1**	**−356.2**	**−391.2**	**−521.7**	**−525.4**	**−629.3**	**−333.9**	**−395.4**
Direct investment income	3 330	−40.9	−53.9	−89.5	−123.9	−183.4	−288.6	−9.8	−259.8
Dividends and distributed branch profits	3 332	−14.3	−28.8	−61.8	−62.7	−119.1	−168.8	−92.5	−148.3
Reinvested earnings and undistributed branch profits	3 333	−26.5	−24.9	−27.3	−61.2	−64.3	−119.7	82.6	−111.5
Income on debt (interest)	3 334	−.1	−.2	−.4	....	....	....	....	....
Portfolio investment income	3 339	−4.0	−.3	−1.1	−44.1	−15.1	−.2	−2.7	−1.1
Income on equity	3 340	−2.8	−.1	−.6	−38.1	−14.8	−.1	....	−.3
Income on bonds and notes	3 350	....	....	....	....	....	....	....	....
Income on money market instruments	3 360	....	....	....	....	....	....	....	....
Other investment income	3 370	−458.1	−302.0	−300.7	−353.6	−326.9	−340.5	−321.3	−134.5
D. CURRENT TRANSFERS	4 379	**109.0**	**86.7**	**52.4**	**121.8**	**156.8**	**236.4**	**312.8**	**416.3**
Credit	2 379	**173.2**	**147.3**	**127.0**	**205.0**	**206.2**	**331.7**	**526.8**	**592.9**
General government	2 380	73.5	44.9	27.8	91.5	70.0	50.2	123.6	116.9
Other sectors	2 390	99.7	102.4	99.3	113.5	136.2	281.5	403.1	475.9
Workers' remittances	2 391	11.8	6.8	14.1	60.6	98.4	67.1	117.6	154.0
Other current transfers	2 392	87.9	95.6	85.1	52.9	37.8	214.3	285.5	321.9
Debit	3 379	**−64.2**	**−60.6**	**−74.7**	**−83.2**	**−49.4**	**−95.3**	**−214.0**	**−176.6**
General government	3 380	−2.2	−2.7	−.9	−8.5	−9.7	−7.4	−9.5	−12.8
Other sectors	3 390	−62.1	−57.9	−73.7	−74.8	−39.7	−87.9	−204.5	−163.8
Workers' remittances	3 391	−13.7	−18.2	−27.3	−29.0	−22.5	−20.2	−48.1	−55.1
Other current transfers	3 392	−48.3	−39.7	−46.4	−45.7	−17.1	−67.7	−156.4	−108.8
CAPITAL AND FINANCIAL ACCOUNT	4 996	**137.3**	**499.9**	**574.7**	**534.9**	**513.3**	**809.2**	**38.3**	**454.0**
CAPITAL ACCOUNT	4 994	**17.5**	**55.6**	**61.0**	**111.8**	**−104.7**	**203.8**	**1,585.5**	**356.3**
Total credit	2 994	*17.5*	*56.4*	*62.1*	*123.0*	*5.1*	*204.1*	*1,586.0*	*356.8*
Total debit	3 994	*−.1*	*−.8*	*−1.1*	*−11.1*	*−109.8*	*−.3*	*−.5*	*−.5*
Capital transfers, credit	2 400	**17.5**	**56.3**	**61.8**	**123.0**	**5.1**	**204.1**	**1,586.0**	**356.8**
General government	2 401	9.5	52.8	55.8	96.7	....	174.5	1,537.9	356.8
Debt forgiveness	2 402	9.5	52.8	55.8	96.7	....	101.5	1,249.6	....
Other capital transfers	2 410	....	....	....	....	....	73.0	288.3	356.8
Other sectors	2 430	8.1	3.5	5.9	26.3	5.1	29.6	48.2	....
Migrants' transfers	2 431	8.1	3.5	5.9	.1	....	.3	....	....
Debt forgiveness	2 432	....	....	....	....	....	....	....	....
Other capital transfers	2 440	....	....	....	26.2	5.1	29.3	48.2	....
Capital transfers, debit	3 400	**....**	**....**	**....**	**....**	**−109.3**	**−.3**	**....**	**....**
General government	3 401	....	....	....	....	−109.3	....	....	....
Debt forgiveness	3 402	....	....	....	....	....	....	....	....
Other capital transfers	3 410	....	....	....	....	−109.3	....	....	....
Other sectors	3 430	....	....	....	....	....	−.3	....	....
Migrants' transfers	3 431	....	....	....	....	....	−.2	....	....
Debt forgiveness	3 432	....	....	....	....	....	....	....	....
Other capital transfers	3 440	....	....	....	....	....	−.1	....	....
Nonproduced nonfinancial assets, credit	2 480	**....**	**.1**	**.3**	**....**	**....**	**....**	**....**	**....**
Nonproduced nonfinancial assets, debit	3 480	**−.1**	**−.7**	**−1.1**	**−11.1**	**−.5**	**....**	**−.5**	**−.5**

Table 2 (Continued). STANDARD PRESENTATION, 2000–2007

(Millions of U.S. dollars)

	Code	2000	2001	2002	2003	2004	2005	2006	2007
FINANCIAL ACCOUNT	4 995	**119.9**	**444.3**	**513.7**	**423.0**	**618.0**	**605.4**	**–1,547.2**	**97.6**
A. DIRECT INVESTMENT	4 500	**149.1**	**38.1**	**634.9**	**343.4**	**83.5**	**267.5**	**64.4**	**589.2**
Direct investment abroad	4 505	**–9.7**	**–35.2**	**33.1**	**–8.5**	**–2.1**	**23.2**	**48.0**	**156.1**
Equity capital	4 510	–.3	–1.0	....	3.3	–2.3	–6.5	–3.5	–3.5
Claims on affiliated enterprises	4 515	....	....	....	–1.8	–4.1	–7.1	–3.7	–11.3
Liabilities to affiliated enterprises	4 520	....	....	....	5.1	1.8	.6	.2	7.8
Reinvested earnings	4 525	–9.7	–2.1	–4.1	–18.9	.4	.4	2.8	.7
Other capital	4 530	.3	–32.1	37.2	7.1	–.2	29.3	48.7	158.9
Claims on affiliated enterprises	4 535	–.2	–12.2	38.3	–1.0	–1.6	–.8	25.0	–3.7
Liabilities to affiliated enterprises	4 540	.6	–19.9	–1.1	8.1	1.4	30.1	23.7	162.6
Direct investment in Cameroon	4 555	**158.8**	**73.3**	**601.7**	**351.8**	**85.6**	**244.4**	**16.4**	**433.1**
Equity capital	4 560	.1	36.4	47.5	64.8	57.3	23.4	15.2	99.5
Claims on direct investors	4 565	.1	36.4	47.5	....	....	....	....	–11.9
Liabilities to direct investors	4 570	....	....	....	64.8	57.3	23.4	15.2	111.4
Reinvested earnings	4 575	26.5	24.9	27.3	61.2	64.3	119.7	–82.6	111.5
Other capital	4 580	132.3	12.0	526.9	225.9	–36.0	101.2	83.8	222.1
Claims on direct investors	4 585	....	28.6	50.3	26.1	19.6	21.3	–18.8	2.4
Liabilities to direct investors	4 590	132.3	–16.6	476.7	199.7	–55.6	80.0	102.5	219.7
B. PORTFOLIO INVESTMENT	4 600	**–1.6**	**94.4**	**5.3**	**–2.3**	**30.7**	**–12.9**	**–4.6**	**–21.4**
Assets	4 602	**–1.6**	**4.7**	**4.6**	**–2.4**	**38.9**	**–9.8**	**–.8**	**–8.1**
Equity securities	4 610	–.4	–4.5	4.9	–1.6	....	–10.2	–.8	–6.3
Monetary authorities	4 611	....	....	....	....	....	....	....	....
General government	4 612	....	....	....	....	....	....	....	....
Banks	4 613	1.5	–2.3	1.3	–.2	....	–7.7	–.9	–5.8
Other sectors	4 614	–1.9	–2.2	3.6	–1.4	....	–2.6	.1	–.4
Debt securities	4 619	–1.2	9.2	–.3	–.8	38.9	.4	....	–1.9
Bonds and notes	4 620	–1.2	9.2	–.3	–.8	38.9	.4	....	–1.9
Monetary authorities	4 621	....	....	....	....	....	....	....	....
General government	4 622	....	....	....	....	....	....	....	....
Banks	4 623	....	....	....	....	.3	–.4	....	–1.9
Other sectors	4 624	–1.2	9.2	–.3	–.8	38.7	.8	....	....
Money market instruments	4 630	....	....	....	....	....	....	....	....
Monetary authorities	4 631	....	....	....	....	....	....	....	....
General government	4 632	....	....	....	....	....	....	....	....
Banks	4 633	....	....	....	....	....	....	....	....
Other sectors	4 634	....	....	....	....	....	....	....	....
Liabilities	4 652	**....**	**89.7**	**.7**	**.1**	**–8.2**	**–3.1**	**–3.8**	**–13.3**
Equity securities	4 660	....	2.2	1.0	.2	–8.2	–4.2	–5.6	–13.3
Banks	4 663	....	....	....	.1	....	–.9	....	....
Other sectors	4 664	....	2.2	1.0	.1	–8.2	–3.3	–5.6	–13.3
Debt securities	4 669	....	87.6	–.4	–.1	.1	1.1	1.8	....
Bonds and notes	4 670	....	87.6	–.4	–.1	.1	1.1	1.8	....
Monetary authorities	4 671	....	....	....	....	....	....	....	....
General government	4 672	....	....	....	....	....	....	....	....
Banks	4 673	....	....	....	....	....	....	....	....
Other sectors	4 674	....	87.6	–.4	–.1	.1	1.1	1.8	....
Money market instruments	4 680	....	....	....	....	....	....	....	....
Monetary authorities	4 681	....	....	....	....	....	....	....	....
General government	4 682	....	....	....	....	....	....	....	....
Banks	4 683	....	....	....	....	....	....	....	....
Other sectors	4 684	....	....	....	....	....	....	....	....
C. FINANCIAL DERIVATIVES	4 910	**....**	**....**	**....**	**....**	**....**	**....**	**....**	**....**
Monetary authorities	4 911	....	....	....	....	....	....	....	....
General government	4 912	....	....	....	....	....	....	....	....
Banks	4 913	....	....	....	....	....	....	....	....
Other sectors	4 914	....	....	....	....	....	....	....	....
Assets	4 900	**....**	**....**	**....**	**....**	**....**	**....**	**....**	**....**
Monetary authorities	4 901	....	....	....	....	....	....	....	....
General government	4 902	....	....	....	....	....	....	....	....
Banks	4 903	....	....	....	....	....	....	....	....
Other sectors	4 904	....	....	....	....	....	....	....	....
Liabilities	4 905	**....**	**....**	**....**	**....**	**....**	**....**	**....**	**....**
Monetary authorities	4 906	....	....	....	....	....	....	....	....
General government	4 907	....	....	....	....	....	....	....	....
Banks	4 908	....	....	....	....	....	....	....	....
Other sectors	4 909	....	....	....	....	....	....	....	....

Table 2 (Concluded). STANDARD PRESENTATION, 2000–2007

(Millions of U.S. dollars)

	Code	2000	2001	2002	2003	2004	2005	2006	2007
D. OTHER INVESTMENT	4 700 ..	**178.0**	**444.5**	**84.4**	**−23.8**	**631.0**	**594.2**	**−980.0**	**449.2**
Assets	4 703 ..	**63.6**	**−162.9**	**−271.6**	**79.9**	**148.8**	**67.0**	**139.5**	**−105.5**
Trade credits	4 706 ..	16.2	−130.8	−285.8	1.8	157.2	11.0	−201.5	28.0
General government	4 707 ..	....	....	....	....	....	....	....	....
of which: Short-term	4 709 ..	....	....	....	....	....	....	....	....
Other sectors	4 710 ..	16.2	−130.8	−285.8	1.8	157.2	11.0	−201.5	28.0
of which: Short-term	4 712 ..	*14.0*	*−118.9*	*−292.3*	*1.8*	*80.7*	*11.0*	*−204.8*	*29.9*
Loans	4 714 ..	−5.4	−65.0	45.5	−25.6	−4.6	−15.2	−30.8	−39.5
Monetary authorities	4 715 ..	....	....	....	....	....	....	....	....
of which: Short-term	4 718 ..	....	....	....	....	....	....	....	....
General government	4 719 ..	....	....	....	....	....	....	....	....
of which: Short-term	4 721 ..	....	....	....	....	....	....	....	....
Banks	4 722 ..	−6.3	−6.0	2.1	−26.6	.1	−22.3	−27.6	−30.9
of which: Short-term	4 724 ..	*−.6*	*2.1*	*2.8*	....	....	....	....	....
Other sectors	4 725 ..	.9	−59.0	43.5	1.0	−4.7	7.0	−3.2	−8.5
of which: Short-term	4 727 ..	*.9*	*−29.1*	*43.8*	*.3*	*.6*	*2.1*	*−.4*	*−8.5*
Currency and deposits	4 730 ..	44.7	8.5	−12.0	55.6	−1.7	29.1	13.6	−75.4
Monetary authorities	4 731 ..	....	....	....	....	....	....	....	....
General government	4 732 ..	....	....	....	....	....	1.3	−9.5	−4.1
Banks	4 733 ..	−8.0	12.3	−67.7	10.5	−46.1	−52.5	−52.3	−104.0
Other sectors	4 734 ..	52.7	−3.9	55.7	45.1	44.4	80.3	75.4	32.7
Other assets	4 736 ..	8.1	24.4	−19.3	48.1	−2.1	42.1	358.3	−18.6
Monetary authorities	4 737 ..	....	....	....	....	....	....	....	....
of which: Short-term	4 739 ..	....	....	....	....	....	....	....	....
General government	4 740 ..	....	....	....	....	....	....	....	....
of which: Short-term	4 742 ..	....	....	....	....	....	....	....	....
Banks	4 743 ..	1.1	.9	.9	.4	1.2	−1.3	−1.9	−1.3
of which: Short-term	4 745 ..	*1.1*	*.9*	*.9*	*.4*	*1.2*	*−1.3*	*−1.9*	*−1.3*
Other sectors	4 746 ..	7.0	23.5	−20.2	47.7	−3.3	43.4	360.1	−17.3
of which: Short-term	4 748 ..	*7.0*	*23.5*	*−20.2*	*47.7*	*−3.3*	*43.4*	*360.1*	*−17.3*
Liabilities	4 753 ..	**114.4**	**607.5**	**356.0**	**−103.8**	**482.2**	**527.2**	**−1,119.5**	**554.7**
Trade credits	4 756 ..	−172.2	193.0	38.2	4.4	224.7	49.1	322.5	555.8
General government	4 757 ..	....	....	....	....	....	....	....	....
of which: Short-term	4 759 ..	....	....	....	....	....	....	....	....
Other sectors	4 760 ..	−172.2	193.0	38.2	4.4	224.7	49.1	322.5	555.8
of which: Short-term	4 762 ..	*−171.2*	*218.8*	*51.0*	*−61.7*	*42.8*	*61.2*	*142.4*	*491.4*
Loans	4 764 ..	−304.7	16.5	−188.7	−358.8	−359.0	−272.4	−1,927.2	−140.8
Monetary authorities	4 765 ..	49.2	16.7	40.9	12.0	−27.9	−36.2	−268.3	8.0
of which: Use of Fund credit and loans from the Fund	4 766 ..	*49.2*	*16.7*	*40.9*	*12.0*	*−27.9*	*−36.2*	*−268.3*	*8.0*
of which: Short-term	4 768 ..	....	....	....	....	....	....	....	....
General government	4 769 ..	−325.5	−142.8	−319.6	−337.3	−356.5	−361.0	−1,608.5	−43.3
of which: Short-term	4 771 ..	....	....	....	....	....	....	....	....
Banks	4 772 ..	−19.3	4.9	−4.6	15.9	10.8	−9.9	−11.4	−4.3
of which: Short-term	4 774 ..	*−19.3*	*13.8*	*−3.3*	*−.7*	*12.6*	*−5.6*	*−11.4*	*−6.3*
Other sectors	4 775 ..	−9.1	137.6	94.6	−49.5	14.5	134.7	−38.9	−101.2
of which: Short-term	4 777 ..	*−16.5*	*48.3*	*−5.3*	*−6.8*	*−13.2*	*175.2*	*59.4*	*−.9*
Currency and deposits	4 780 ..	8.3	4.3	11.8	−24.9	12.9	79.3	−38.2	−54.1
Monetary authorities	4 781 ..	4.2	−1.8	−4.0	−4.1	−2.4	3.7	−3.3	−10.9
General government	4 782 ..	....	....	....	....	....	....	....	....
Banks	4 783 ..	3.0	−3.4	15.8	−20.8	15.3	75.5	−34.9	−43.2
Other sectors	4 784 ..	1.1	9.5	....	....	....	....	....	....
Other liabilities	4 786 ..	583.0	393.7	494.7	275.5	603.6	671.3	523.3	193.8
Monetary authorities	4 787 ..	−115.3	....	....	....	....	....	....	....
of which: Short-term	4 789 ..	*−115.3*	....	....	....	....	....	....	....
General government	4 790 ..	546.5	300.9	428.1	499.5	473.3	491.1	344.0	45.1
of which: Short-term	4 792 ..	*360.9*	*230.3*	*353.5*	*404.3*	*395.4*	*415.6*	*344.0*	*−25.7*
Banks	4 793 ..	....	....	....	....	....	12.8	15.3	17.3
of which: Short-term	4 795 ..	....	....	....	....	....	*12.8*	*15.3*	*17.3*
Other sectors	4 796 ..	151.8	92.8	66.6	−224.0	130.3	167.4	164.0	131.4
of which: Short-term	4 798 ..	*151.8*	*92.8*	*66.6*	*−224.0*	*130.3*	*167.4*	*164.0*	*131.4*
E. RESERVE ASSETS	4 802 ..	**−205.7**	**−132.8**	**−210.9**	**105.9**	**−127.2**	**−243.4**	**−627.0**	**−919.3**
Monetary gold	4 812 ..	....	....	....	....	....	....	....	....
Special drawing rights	4 811 ..	−5.1	7.7	−1.1	−.2	.8	−1.5	−2.4	.1
Reserve position in the Fund	4 810 ..	....	....	−.1	−.1	−.1	−.1	....	−.1
Foreign exchange	4 803 ..	−200.2	−138.6	−212.1	106.9	−126.6	−243.3	−623.1	−918.1
Other claims	4 813 ..	−.3	−1.8	2.5	−.8	−1.4	1.5	−1.5	−1.2
NET ERRORS AND OMISSIONS	4 998 ..	**111.7**	**−123.8**	**−129.9**	**92.7**	**113.0**	**−31.9**	**112.6**	**93.1**

Table 1. ANALYTIC PRESENTATION, 2000–2007

(Millions of U.S. dollars)

	Code	2000	2001	2002	2003	2004	2005	2006	2007
A. Current Account[1]	4 993 Z.	**19,622**	**16,281**	**12,604**	**10,696**	**22,946**	**22,179**	**17,859**	**12,639**
Goods: exports f.o.b.	2 100 ..	289,022	271,849	263,908	285,186	330,011	371,899	400,056	432,028
Goods: imports f.o.b.	3 100 ..	−243,975	−226,132	−227,410	−244,904	−279,508	−320,181	−356,514	−387,665
Balance on Goods	4 100 ..	*45,047*	*45,716*	*36,498*	*40,283*	*50,503*	*51,717*	*43,541*	*44,363*
Services: credit	2 200 ..	40,230	38,804	40,481	44,242	50,286	55,444	59,330	62,988
Services: debit	3 200 ..	−44,118	−43,843	−45,069	−52,454	−58,776	−65,434	−72,295	−80,837
Balance on Goods and Services	4 991 ..	*41,159*	*40,678*	*31,910*	*32,070*	*42,013*	*41,727*	*30,576*	*26,515*
Income: credit	2 300 ..	24,746	16,822	19,444	21,050	29,374	39,944	56,912	66,958
Income: debit	3 300 ..	−47,036	−42,238	−38,745	−42,295	−47,926	−58,401	−68,662	−79,946
Balance on Goods, Services, and Income	4 992 ..	*18,868*	*15,262*	*12,609*	*10,825*	*23,461*	*23,271*	*18,825*	*13,527*
Current transfers: credit	2 379 Z.	4,122	4,499	4,387	4,814	5,518	6,754	8,532	8,938
Current transfers: debit	3 379 ..	−3,368	−3,480	−4,391	−4,943	−6,033	−7,845	−9,498	−9,826
B. Capital Account[1]	4 994 Z.	**3,581**	**3,721**	**3,145**	**3,020**	**3,416**	**4,828**	**3,642**	**3,899**
Capital account: credit	2 994 Z.	4,045	4,191	3,589	3,431	3,949	5,446	4,322	4,652
Capital account: debit	3 994 ..	−464	−471	−444	−410	−533	−618	−680	−753
Total, Groups A Plus B	4 981 ..	*23,204*	*20,002*	*15,749*	*13,717*	*26,361*	*27,008*	*21,501*	*16,537*
C. Financial Account[1]	4 995 W.	**−14,500**	**−11,609**	**−14,360**	**−18,070**	**−31,510**	**−25,568**	**−17,986**	**−15,802**
Direct investment abroad	4 505 ..	−44,487	−36,152	−26,818	−23,623	−42,639	−29,690	−39,265	−53,980
Direct investment in Canada	4 555 Z.	66,144	27,711	22,053	7,206	−741	27,184	62,772	111,772
Portfolio investment assets	4 602 ..	−42,975	−24,374	−18,632	−13,829	−18,924	−44,072	−69,225	−42,772
Equity securities	4 610 ..	−40,229	−23,120	−13,500	−5,816	−6,197	−18,167	−24,760	−28,888
Debt securities	4 619 ..	−2,746	−1,254	−5,132	−8,013	−12,727	−25,905	−44,465	−13,885
Portfolio investment liabilities	4 652 Z.	10,259	24,166	11,869	14,127	41,807	7,817	27,879	−32,483
Equity securities	4 660 ..	24,239	2,713	−914	9,947	27,145	7,565	9,501	−42,041
Debt securities	4 669 Z.	−13,980	21,454	12,783	4,180	14,662	252	18,378	9,559
Financial derivatives	4 910 ..	....	....	....	....	....	....	....	....
Financial derivatives assets	4 900 ..	....	....	....	....	....	....	....	....
Financial derivatives liabilities	4 905 ..	....	....	....	....	....	....	....	....
Other investment assets	4 703 ..	−4,195	−10,739	−7,938	−14,209	−7,065	−16,571	−30,974	−55,099
Monetary authorities	4 701 ..	....	....	....	....	....	....	....	....
General government	4 704 ..	−232	−131	−19	339	−210	−395	−281	−477
Banks	4 705 ..	−7,301	−2,183	2,278	−15,172	−983	−16,291	−9,566	−43,690
Other sectors	4 728 ..	3,338	−8,425	−10,197	624	−5,872	115	−21,128	−10,932
Other investment liabilities	4 753 W.	754	7,779	5,106	12,257	−3,948	29,764	30,829	56,760
Monetary authorities	4 753 WA	....	....	....	....	....	....	....	....
General government	4 753 ZB	−350	−237	−116	−527	−754	−138	−109	−133
Banks	4 753 ZC	−626	15,314	8,525	12,557	−1,000	40,912	18,130	45,456
Other sectors	4 753 ZD	1,730	−7,298	−3,303	227	−2,194	−11,010	12,808	11,436
Total, Groups A Through C	4 983 ..	*8,704*	*8,392*	*1,389*	*−4,353*	*−5,149*	*1,440*	*3,515*	*735*
D. Net Errors and Omissions	4 998 ..	**−4,984**	**−6,220**	**−1,574**	**1,098**	**2,313**	**−104**	**−2,689**	**3,171**
Total, Groups A Through D	4 984 ..	*3,720*	*2,172*	*−185*	*−3,255*	*−2,836*	*1,335*	*826*	*3,906*
E. Reserves and Related Items	4 802 A.	**−3,720**	**−2,172**	**185**	**3,255**	**2,836**	**−1,335**	**−826**	**−3,906**
Reserve assets	4 802 ..	−3,720	−2,172	185	3,255	2,836	−1,335	−826	−3,906
Use of Fund credit and loans	4 766 ..	....	....	....	....	....	....	....	....
Exceptional financing	4 920 ..	....	....	....	....	....	....	....	....
Conversion rates: Canadian dollars per U.S. dollar	0 101 ..	**1.4851**	**1.5488**	**1.5693**	**1.4011**	**1.3010**	**1.2118**	**1.1344**	**1.0741**

[1] Excludes components that have been classified in the categories of Group E.

Table 2. STANDARD PRESENTATION, 2000–2007

(Millions of U.S. dollars)

	Code	2000	2001	2002	2003	2004	2005	2006	2007
CURRENT ACCOUNT	4 993	**19,622**	**16,281**	**12,604**	**10,696**	**22,946**	**22,179**	**17,859**	**12,639**
A. GOODS	4 100	**45,047**	**45,716**	**36,498**	**40,283**	**50,503**	**51,717**	**43,541**	**44,363**
Credit	2 100	**289,022**	**271,849**	**263,908**	**285,186**	**330,011**	**371,899**	**400,056**	**432,028**
General merchandise: exports f.o.b.	2 110	287,270	270,440	262,173	283,351	327,427	368,512	395,226	426,341
Goods for processing: exports f.o.b.	2 150	....	....	....	....	....	....	....	....
Repairs on goods	2 160	....	....	....	....	....	....	....	....
Goods procured in ports by carriers	2 170	....	....	....	....	....	....	....	....
Nonmonetary gold	2 180	1,752	1,409	1,735	1,835	2,585	3,387	4,830	5,687
Debit	3 100	**−243,975**	**−226,132**	**−227,410**	**−244,904**	**−279,508**	**−320,181**	**−356,514**	**−387,665**
General merchandise: imports f.o.b.	3 110	−243,332	−225,625	−227,025	−244,533	−278,006	−317,889	−353,141	−383,528
Goods for processing: imports f.o.b.	3 150	....	....	....	....	....	....	....	....
Repairs on goods	3 160	....	....	....	....	....	....	....	....
Goods procured in ports by carriers	3 170	....	....	....	....	....	....	....	....
Nonmonetary gold	3 180	−643	−508	−385	−371	−1,502	−2,292	−3,374	−4,137
B. SERVICES	4 200	**−3,889**	**−5,039**	**−4,588**	**−8,212**	**−8,490**	**−9,990**	**−12,965**	**−17,849**
Total credit	2 200	*40,230*	*38,804*	*40,481*	*44,242*	*50,286*	*55,444*	*59,330*	*62,988*
Total debit	3 200	*−44,118*	*−43,843*	*−45,069*	*−52,454*	*−58,776*	*−65,434*	*−72,295*	*−80,837*
Transportation services, credit	2 205	**7,539**	**6,864**	**7,055**	**7,125**	**8,486**	**9,689**	**10,485**	**11,382**
Passenger	2 850	*2,257*	*2,057*	*2,057*	*1,634*	*2,106*	*2,238*	*2,289*	*2,371*
Freight	2 851	*3,061*	*2,765*	*2,906*	*3,098*	*3,462*	*3,810*	*4,084*	*4,340*
Other	2 852	*2,221*	*2,042*	*2,093*	*2,393*	*2,917*	*3,641*	*4,111*	*4,672*
Sea transport, passenger	2 207	10	15	16	13	14	19	20	29
Sea transport, freight	2 208	594	592	553	664	820	930	1,055	1,236
Sea transport, other	2 209	965	956	973	1,088	1,419	1,839	2,074	2,588
Air transport, passenger	2 211	2,225	2,018	2,021	1,602	2,073	2,200	2,254	2,325
Air transport, freight	2 212	....	....	....	....	....	....	....	....
Air transport, other	2 213	1,256	1,086	1,120	1,306	1,498	1,802	2,037	2,084
Other transport, passenger	2 215	22	23	20	20	19	19	15	17
Other transport, freight	2 216	2,466	2,173	2,353	2,433	2,643	2,880	3,029	3,104
Other transport, other	2 217	....	....	....	....	....	....	....	....
Transportation services, debit	3 205	**−9,373**	**−9,029**	**−9,206**	**−10,390**	**−12,248**	**−14,525**	**−16,493**	**−18,763**
Passenger	3 850	*−2,687*	*−2,673*	*−2,535*	*−2,972*	*−3,743*	*−4,717*	*−5,455*	*−6,483*
Freight	3 851	*−6,366*	*−6,063*	*−6,273*	*−7,012*	*−8,019*	*−9,181*	*−10,457*	*−11,393*
Other	3 852	*−319*	*−292*	*−397*	*−406*	*−486*	*−627*	*−581*	*−887*
Sea transport, passenger	3 207	−65	−75	−81	−90	−111	−107	−133	−181
Sea transport, freight	3 208	−3,114	−3,096	−3,206	−3,862	−4,619	−5,413	−6,367	−7,100
Sea transport, other	3 209	−319	−292	−397	−406	−486	−627	−581	−887
Air transport, passenger	3 211	−2,556	−2,534	−2,398	−2,775	−3,554	−4,506	−5,205	−6,126
Air transport, freight	3 212	−1,467	−1,353	−1,404	−1,475	−1,608	−1,886	−2,111	−2,293
Air transport, other	3 213	....	....	....	....	....	....	....	....
Other transport, passenger	3 215	−67	−64	−56	−107	−78	−104	−117	−176
Other transport, freight	3 216	−1,785	−1,614	−1,663	−1,674	−1,792	−1,882	−1,980	−2,000
Other transport, other	3 217	....	....	....	....	....	....	....	....
Travel, credit	2 236	**10,778**	**10,623**	**10,687**	**10,601**	**13,029**	**13,768**	**14,689**	**15,614**
Business travel	2 237	1,967	1,718	1,747	1,703	2,043	2,301	2,552	2,704
Personal travel	2 240	8,811	8,906	8,941	8,899	10,986	11,467	12,137	12,910
Travel, debit	3 236	**−12,438**	**−11,961**	**−11,722**	**−13,337**	**−15,524**	**−18,017**	**−20,620**	**−24,882**
Business travel	3 237	−2,638	−2,200	−2,178	−2,423	−2,408	−2,941	−3,293	−3,979
Personal travel	3 240	−9,799	−9,761	−9,544	−10,914	−13,115	−15,076	−17,327	−20,903
Other services, credit	2 200 BA	**21,912**	**21,317**	**22,739**	**26,516**	**28,771**	**31,987**	**34,156**	**35,992**
Communications	2 245	1,379	1,510	1,505	1,697	1,881	2,109	2,210	2,545
Construction	2 249	218	178	100	95	128	181	249	152
Insurance	2 253	1,939	2,395	3,244	3,433	3,188	3,212	3,373	3,598
Financial	2 260	879	749	974	1,149	1,132	1,583	1,916	1,997
Computer and information	2 262	2,428	2,331	2,266	2,796	3,014	3,600	4,296	4,426
Royalties and licence fees	2 266	2,259	2,412	2,496	2,810	3,008	2,765	3,173	3,635
Other business services	2 268	10,402	9,451	9,966	12,011	13,354	15,035	15,401	16,043
Personal, cultural, and recreational	2 287	1,451	1,350	1,271	1,414	1,838	2,111	2,012	1,993
Government, n.i.e.	2 291	959	942	915	1,111	1,228	1,390	1,525	1,602
Other services, debit	3 200 BA	**−22,308**	**−22,853**	**−24,142**	**−28,727**	**−31,004**	**−32,892**	**−35,182**	**−37,192**
Communications	3 245	−1,381	−1,390	−1,469	−1,468	−1,651	−1,640	−1,723	−1,830
Construction	3 249	−80	−62	−59	−86	−147	−175	−103	−171
Insurance	3 253	−2,840	−3,527	−4,215	−4,931	−4,715	−5,008	−5,452	−5,579
Financial	3 260	−1,546	−1,652	−1,730	−1,958	−2,158	−2,360	−3,031	−3,406
Computer and information	3 262	−899	−926	−1,304	−1,636	−1,705	−1,802	−2,033	−2,108
Royalties and licence fees	3 266	−3,768	−3,777	−4,487	−5,622	−6,574	−6,903	−6,978	−7,552
Other business services	3 268	−9,626	−9,421	−8,665	−10,624	−11,457	−12,458	−13,036	−13,477
Personal, cultural, and recreational	3 287	−1,647	−1,492	−1,598	−1,720	−1,844	−1,723	−1,907	−2,056
Government, n.i.e.	3 291	−521	−607	−615	−683	−753	−822	−918	−1,013

Table 2 (Continued). STANDARD PRESENTATION, 2000–2007

(Millions of U.S. dollars)

	Code	2000	2001	2002	2003	2004	2005	2006	2007
C. INCOME	4 300	**−22,291**	**−25,416**	**−19,301**	**−21,245**	**−18,552**	**−18,457**	**−11,751**	**−12,988**
Total credit	2 300	*24,746*	*16,822*	*19,444*	*21,050*	*29,374*	*39,944*	*56,912*	*66,958*
Total debit	3 300	*−47,036*	*−42,238*	*−38,745*	*−42,295*	*−47,926*	*−58,401*	*−68,662*	*−79,946*
Compensation of employees, credit	2 310	....	....	....	....	....	....	....	....
Compensation of employees, debit	3 310	....	....	....	....	....	....	....	....
Investment income, credit	2 320	**24,746**	**16,822**	**19,444**	**21,050**	**29,374**	**39,944**	**56,912**	**66,958**
Direct investment income	2 330	10,164	4,154	8,778	9,950	16,331	21,598	30,868	34,841
Dividends and distributed branch profits	2 332	4,543	2,446	3,934	3,533	4,662	7,892	14,060	12,643
Reinvested earnings and undistributed branch profits	2 333	5,227	1,484	4,528	6,179	11,089	12,842	15,506	20,388
Income on debt (interest)	2 334	393	224	316	238	581	864	1,302	1,810
Portfolio investment income	2 339	4,767	5,141	5,647	6,183	7,764	10,238	15,338	20,256
Income on equity	2 340	3,369	3,805	4,326	4,778	5,901	7,214	9,893	12,715
Income on bonds and notes	2 350	1,398	1,336	1,246	1,312	1,708	2,748	4,858	6,894
Income on money market instruments	2 360	....	....	74	93	155	277	587	648
Other investment income	2 370	9,815	7,528	5,019	4,916	5,278	8,108	10,705	11,861
Investment income, debit	3 320	**−47,036**	**−42,238**	**−38,745**	**−42,295**	**−47,926**	**−58,401**	**−68,662**	**−79,946**
Direct investment income	3 330	−16,468	−14,424	−13,723	−16,931	−21,188	−28,443	−30,303	−35,876
Dividends and distributed branch profits	3 332	−6,082	−5,774	−6,398	−8,055	−9,603	−15,306	−16,635	−18,665
Reinvested earnings and undistributed branch profits	3 333	−9,075	−7,166	−5,953	−7,491	−9,987	−11,715	−11,491	−14,889
Income on debt (interest)	3 334	−1,311	−1,485	−1,371	−1,385	−1,597	−1,421	−2,177	−2,322
Portfolio investment income	3 339	−20,100	−19,801	−19,631	−20,590	−21,518	−23,158	−25,812	−28,775
Income on equity	3 340	−1,514	−2,094	−1,946	−2,354	−2,874	−3,926	−6,155	−7,548
Income on bonds and notes	3 350	−17,604	−16,881	−17,312	−17,871	−18,353	−18,780	−18,786	−20,259
Income on money market instruments	3 360	−982	−826	−373	−365	−291	−452	−871	−968
Other investment income	3 370	−10,469	−8,013	−5,391	−4,774	−5,220	−6,800	−12,547	−15,295
D. CURRENT TRANSFERS	4 379	**754**	**1,019**	**−5**	**−129**	**−515**	**−1,091**	**−966**	**−888**
Credit	2 379	**4,122**	**4,499**	**4,387**	**4,814**	**5,518**	**6,754**	**8,532**	**8,938**
General government	2 380	2,531	2,925	2,789	2,969	3,585	4,527	6,155	6,465
Other sectors	2 390	1,591	1,575	1,597	1,846	1,933	2,226	2,378	2,473
Workers' remittances	2 391	....	....	....	....	....	....	....	....
Other current transfers	2 392	1,591	1,575	1,597	1,846	1,933	2,226	2,378	2,473
Debit	3 379	**−3,368**	**−3,480**	**−4,391**	**−4,943**	**−6,033**	**−7,845**	**−9,498**	**−9,826**
General government	3 380	−1,498	−1,582	−1,629	−2,059	−2,351	−3,213	−3,111	−3,504
Other sectors	3 390	−1,870	−1,898	−2,762	−2,883	−3,682	−4,632	−6,387	−6,322
Workers' remittances	3 391	....	....	....	....	....	....	....	....
Other current transfers	3 392	−1,870	−1,898	−2,762	−2,883	−3,682	−4,632	−6,387	−6,322
CAPITAL AND FINANCIAL ACCOUNT	4 996	**−14,639**	**−10,061**	**−11,030**	**−11,795**	**−25,259**	**−22,075**	**−15,170**	**−15,810**
CAPITAL ACCOUNT	4 994	**3,581**	**3,721**	**3,145**	**3,020**	**3,416**	**4,828**	**3,642**	**3,899**
Total credit	2 994	*4,045*	*4,191*	*3,589*	*3,431*	*3,949*	*5,446*	*4,322*	*4,652*
Total debit	3 994	*−464*	*−471*	*−444*	*−410*	*−533*	*−618*	*−680*	*−753*
Capital transfers, credit	2 400	**4,045**	**4,163**	**3,589**	**3,431**	**3,949**	**5,446**	**4,322**	**4,652**
General government	2 401	....	....	....	....	....	....	....	....
Debt forgiveness	2 402	....	....	....	....	....	....	....	....
Other capital transfers	2 410	....	....	....	....	....	....	....	....
Other sectors	2 430	....	....	....	....	....	....	....	....
Migrants' transfers	2 431	....	....	....	....	....	....	....	....
Debt forgiveness	2 432	....	....	....	....	....	....	....	....
Other capital transfers	2 440	....	....	....	....	....	....	....	....
Capital transfers, debit	3 400	**−463**	**−467**	**−442**	**−406**	**−533**	**−618**	**−680**	**−753**
General government	3 401	....	....	....	....	....	....	....	....
Debt forgiveness	3 402	....	....	....	....	....	....	....	....
Other capital transfers	3 410	....	....	....	....	....	....	....	....
Other sectors	3 430	....	....	....	....	....	....	....	....
Migrants' transfers	3 431	....	....	....	....	....	....	....	....
Debt forgiveness	3 432	....	....	....	....	....	....	....	....
Other capital transfers	3 440	....	....	....	....	....	....	....	....
Nonproduced nonfinancial assets, credit	2 480	....	28	....	....	....	....	....	....
Nonproduced nonfinancial assets, debit	3 480	−1	−3	−1	−4	....	....	....	....

Table 2 (Continued). STANDARD PRESENTATION, 2000–2007

(Millions of U.S. dollars)

	Code	2000	2001	2002	2003	2004	2005	2006	2007
FINANCIAL ACCOUNT	4 995	−18,220	−13,782	−14,175	−14,815	−28,675	−26,903	−18,812	−19,709
A. DIRECT INVESTMENT	4 500	21,657	−8,441	−4,765	−16,417	−43,380	−2,506	23,507	57,792
Direct investment abroad	4 505	−44,487	−36,152	−26,818	−23,623	−42,639	−29,690	−39,265	−53,980
Equity capital	4 510	....	....	....	....	....	....	....	....
Claims on affiliated enterprises	4 515	....	....	....	....	....	....	....	....
Liabilities to affiliated enterprises	4 520	....	....	....	....	....	....	....	....
Reinvested earnings	4 525	−5,227	−1,484	−4,528	−6,179	−11,089	−12,842	−15,506	−20,388
Other capital	4 530	−39,259	−34,668	−22,290	−17,444	−31,550	−16,848	−23,759	−33,592
Claims on affiliated enterprises	4 535	−42,453	−36,681	−24,660	−16,575	−32,130	−16,451	−26,615	−34,278
Liabilities to affiliated enterprises	4 540	3,194	2,013	2,370	−869	580	−397	2,856	687
Direct investment in Canada	4 555	66,144	27,711	22,053	7,206	−741	27,184	62,772	111,772
Equity capital	4 560	....	....	....	....	....	....	....	....
Claims on direct investors	4 565	....	....	....	....	....	....	....	....
Liabilities to direct investors	4 570	....	....	....	....	....	....	....	....
Reinvested earnings	4 575	9,075	7,166	5,953	7,491	9,987	11,715	11,491	14,889
Other capital	4 580	57,070	20,545	16,100	−285	−10,729	15,469	51,281	96,883
Claims on direct investors	4 585	1,029	1,331	−74	−675	−1,603	−314	−1,285	1,591
Liabilities to direct investors	4 590	56,041	19,214	16,174	390	−9,126	15,783	52,565	95,292
B. PORTFOLIO INVESTMENT	4 600	−32,717	−208	−6,763	298	22,883	−36,255	−41,347	−75,255
Assets	4 602	−42,975	−24,374	−18,632	−13,829	−18,924	−44,072	−69,225	−42,772
Equity securities	4 610	−40,229	−23,120	−13,500	−5,816	−6,197	−18,167	−24,760	−28,888
Monetary authorities	4 611	....	....	....	....	....	....	....	....
General government	4 612	....	....	....	....	....	....	....	....
Banks	4 613	....	....	....	....	....	....	....	....
Other sectors	4 614	−40,229	−23,120	−13,500	−5,816	−6,197	−18,167	−24,760	−28,888
Debt securities	4 619	−2,746	−1,254	−5,132	−8,013	−12,727	−25,905	−44,465	−13,885
Bonds and notes	4 620	−2,746	−1,254	−3,963	−5,603	−11,956	−24,180	−38,452	−24,948
Monetary authorities	4 621	....	....	....	....	....	....	....	....
General government	4 622	....	....	....	....	....	....	....	....
Banks	4 623	....	....	....	....	....	....	....	....
Other sectors	4 624	−2,746	−1,254	−3,963	−5,603	−11,956	−24,180	−38,452	−24,948
Money market instruments	4 630	....	....	−1,169	−2,410	−771	−1,725	−6,013	11,064
Monetary authorities	4 631	....	....	....	....	....	....	....	....
General government	4 632	....	....	....	....	....	....	....	....
Banks	4 633	....	....	....	....	....	....	....	....
Other sectors	4 634	....	....	−1,169	−2,410	−771	−1,725	−6,013	11,064
Liabilities	4 652	10,259	24,166	11,869	14,127	41,807	7,817	27,879	−32,483
Equity securities	4 660	24,239	2,713	−914	9,947	27,145	7,565	9,501	−42,041
Banks	4 663	....	....	....	....	....	....	....	....
Other sectors	4 664	24,239	2,713	−914	9,947	27,145	7,565	9,501	−42,041
Debt securities	4 669	−13,980	21,454	12,783	4,180	14,662	252	18,378	9,559
Bonds and notes	4 670	−14,515	26,273	11,634	5,285	14,938	−253	15,100	10,639
Monetary authorities	4 671	....	....	....	....	....	....	....	....
General government	4 672	−12,956	−4,268	2,551	−14,260	−2,967	−1,146	211	−9,315
Banks	4 673	−95	−400	−446	−423	−65	−37	−402	−44
Other sectors	4 674	−1,464	30,941	9,529	19,968	17,970	930	15,291	19,997
Money market instruments	4 680	535	−4,820	1,150	−1,105	−277	505	3,278	−1,080
Monetary authorities	4 681	....	....	....	....	....	....	....	....
General government	4 682	91	−3,680	1,003	−219	−2,033	970	2,895	−1,953
Banks	4 683	....	....	....	....	....	....	....	....
Other sectors	4 684	444	−1,140	147	−886	1,756	−465	384	873
C. FINANCIAL DERIVATIVES	4 910	....	....	....	....	....	....	....	....
Monetary authorities	4 911	....	....	....	....	....	....	....	....
General government	4 912	....	....	....	....	....	....	....	....
Banks	4 913	....	....	....	....	....	....	....	....
Other sectors	4 914	....	....	....	....	....	....	....	....
Assets	4 900	....	....	....	....	....	....	....	....
Monetary authorities	4 901	....	....	....	....	....	....	....	....
General government	4 902	....	....	....	....	....	....	....	....
Banks	4 903	....	....	....	....	....	....	....	....
Other sectors	4 904	....	....	....	....	....	....	....	....
Liabilities	4 905	....	....	....	....	....	....	....	....
Monetary authorities	4 906	....	....	....	....	....	....	....	....
General government	4 907	....	....	....	....	....	....	....	....
Banks	4 908	....	....	....	....	....	....	....	....
Other sectors	4 909	....	....	....	....	....	....	....	....

Table 2 (Concluded). STANDARD PRESENTATION, 2000–2007

(Millions of U.S. dollars)

	Code	2000	2001	2002	2003	2004	2005	2006	2007
D. OTHER INVESTMENT	4 700 ..	**−3,441**	**−2,960**	**−2,832**	**−1,951**	**−11,013**	**13,193**	**−146**	**1,661**
Assets	4 703 ..	**−4,195**	**−10,739**	**−7,938**	**−14,209**	**−7,065**	**−16,571**	**−30,974**	**−55,099**
Trade credits	4 706 ..	−1,402	−128	−281	666	−75	287	−1,437	−237
General government	4 707 ..	....	....	....	....	....	....	....	....
of which: Short-term	4 709 ..	....	....	....	....	....	....	....	....
Other sectors	4 710 ..	−1,402	−128	−281	666	−75	287	−1,437	−237
of which: Short-term	4 712 ..	....	....	....	....	....	....	....	....
Loans	4 714 ..	−3,405	−5,097	−5,446	5,909	2,971	6,634	−10,934	−8,898
Monetary authorities	4 715 ..	....	....	....	....	....	....	....	....
of which: Short-term	4 718 ..	....	....	....	....	....	....	....	....
General government	4 719 ..	−80	−109	119	507	−22	−165	9	−193
of which: Short-term	4 721 ..	....	....	....	....	....	....	....	....
Banks	4 722 ..	−863	−1,800	515	3,221	−1,545	−1,987	−5,642	−2,026
of which: Short-term	4 724 ..	....	....	....	....	....	....	....	....
Other sectors	4 725 ..	−2,462	−3,189	−6,079	2,181	4,539	8,786	−5,301	−6,680
of which: Short-term	4 727 ..	....	....	....	....	....	....	....	....
Currency and deposits	4 730 ..	2,606	−1,168	3,759	−13,237	−8,351	−12,645	−8,011	−39,415
Monetary authorities	4 731 ..	....	....	....	....	....	....	....	....
General government	4 732 ..	....	....	....	....	....	....	....	....
Banks	4 733 ..	−5,293	1,250	3,705	−11,699	−1,978	−7,786	7,074	−28,638
Other sectors	4 734 ..	7,900	−2,418	55	−1,537	−6,373	−4,859	−15,084	−10,777
Other assets	4 736 ..	−1,995	−4,347	−5,970	−7,548	−1,610	−10,846	−10,593	−6,549
Monetary authorities	4 737 ..	....	....	....	....	....	....	....	....
of which: Short-term	4 739 ..	....	....	....	....	....	....	....	....
General government	4 740 ..	−152	−22	−138	−168	−188	−230	−290	−284
of which: Short-term	4 742 ..	....	....	....	....	....	....	....	....
Banks	4 743 ..	−1,145	−1,634	−1,941	−6,693	2,540	−6,517	−10,997	−13,026
of which: Short-term	4 745 ..	....	....	....	....	....	....	....	....
Other sectors	4 746 ..	−698	−2,690	−3,891	−686	−3,963	−4,099	694	6,761
of which: Short-term	4 748 ..	....	....	....	....	....	....	....	....
Liabilities	4 753 ..	**754**	**7,779**	**5,106**	**12,257**	**−3,948**	**29,764**	**30,829**	**56,760**
Trade credits	4 756 ..	305	−968	−216	−645	158	492	254	−356
General government	4 757 ..	....	....	....	....	....	....	....	....
of which: Short-term	4 759 ..	....	....	....	....	....	....	....	....
Other sectors	4 760 ..	305	−968	−216	−645	158	492	254	−356
of which: Short-term	4 762 ..	....	....	....	....	....	....	....	....
Loans	4 764 ..	2,327	−3,767	873	1,724	−1,744	4,378	12,991	10,076
Monetary authorities	4 765 ..	....	....	....	....	....	....	....	....
of which: Use of Fund credit and loans from the Fund	4 766 ..	....	....	....	....	....	....	....	....
of which: Short-term	4 768 ..	....	....	....	....	....	....	....	....
General government	4 769 ..	−83	−24	−89	−315	−639	....	....	....
of which: Short-term	4 771 ..	....	....	....	....	....	....	....	....
Banks	4 772 ..	....	....	....	....	....	....	....	....
of which: Short-term	4 774 ..	....	....	....	....	....	....	....	....
Other sectors	4 775 ..	2,411	−3,743	962	2,039	−1,104	4,378	12,991	10,076
of which: Short-term	4 777 ..	....	....	....	....	....	....	....	....
Currency and deposits	4 780 ..	−746	15,319	8,592	12,494	−985	23,971	18,127	43,461
Monetary authorities	4 781 ..	....	....	....	....	....	....	....	....
General government	4 782 ..	....	....	....	....	....	....	....	....
Banks	4 783 ..	−626	15,314	8,525	12,557	−1,000	40,912	18,130	45,456
Other sectors	4 784 ..	−120	4	67	−64	15	−16,942	−2	−1,995
Other liabilities	4 786 ..	−1,132	−2,804	−4,144	−1,316	−1,377	923	−544	3,579
Monetary authorities	4 787 ..	....	....	....	....	....	....	....	....
of which: Short-term	4 789 ..	....	....	....	....	....	....	....	....
General government	4 790 ..	−266	−213	−27	−212	−115	−138	−109	−133
of which: Short-term	4 792 ..	....	....	....	....	....	....	....	....
Banks	4 793 ..	....	....	....	....	....	....	....	....
of which: Short-term	4 795 ..	....	....	....	....	....	....	....	....
Other sectors	4 796 ..	−866	−2,591	−4,117	−1,104	−1,262	1,062	−434	3,712
of which: Short-term	4 798 ..	....	....	....	....	....	....	....	....
E. RESERVE ASSETS	4 802 ..	**−3,720**	**−2,172**	**185**	**3,255**	**2,836**	**−1,335**	**−826**	**−3,906**
Monetary gold	4 812 ..	....	....	....	....	....	....	....	....
Special drawing rights	4 811 ..	−75	−62	−52	−49	−46	−48	−19	−4
Reserve position in the Fund	4 810 ..	514	−457	−467	69	648	1,702	624	204
Foreign exchange	4 803 ..	−4,160	−1,653	704	3,235	2,233	−2,989	−1,431	−4,106
Other claims	4 813 ..	....	....	....	....	....	....	....	....
NET ERRORS AND OMISSIONS	4 998 ..	**−4,984**	**−6,220**	**−1,574**	**1,098**	**2,313**	**−104**	**−2,689**	**3,171**

Table 3. INTERNATIONAL INVESTMENT POSITION (End-period stocks), 2000–2007

(Millions of U.S. dollars)

	Code	2000	2001	2002	2003	2004	2005	2006	2007
ASSETS	8 995 C.	**551,648**	**578,917**	**620,047**	**710,478**	**791,633**	**858,555**	**1,022,836**	**1,198,642**
Direct investment abroad	8 505 ..	**237,639**	**250,692**	**274,350**	**312,167**	**372,671**	**390,907**	**454,792**	**520,737**
Equity capital and reinvested earnings	8 506 ..	214,164	227,020	256,551	288,234	340,948	366,676	427,358	489,326
Claims on affiliated enterprises	8 507 ..	....	....	....	....	....	....	....	....
Liabilities to affiliated enterprises	8 508 ..	....	....	....	....	....	....	....	....
Other capital	8 530 ..	23,476	23,673	17,800	23,933	31,723	24,231	27,433	31,411
Claims on affiliated enterprises	8 535 ..	....	....	....	....	....	....	....	....
Liabilities to affiliated enterprises	8 540 ..	....	....	....	....	....	....	....	....
Portfolio investment	8 602 ..	**139,456**	**150,547**	**169,960**	**194,196**	**220,515**	**251,294**	**319,420**	**358,543**
Equity securities	8 610 ..	115,699	126,141	136,440	150,797	162,656	169,322	195,560	212,594
Monetary authorities	8 611 ..	....	....	....	....	....	....	....	....
General government	8 612 ..	....	....	....	....	....	....	....	....
Banks	8 613 ..	....	....	....	....	....	....	....	....
Other sectors	8 614 ..	115,699	126,141	136,440	150,797	162,656	169,322	195,560	212,594
Debt securities	8 619 ..	23,757	24,407	33,520	43,400	57,859	81,972	123,860	145,949
Bonds and notes	8 620 ..	23,757	24,407	27,775	34,925	48,654	70,761	106,726	138,347
Monetary authorities	8 621 ..	....	....	....	....	....	....	....	....
General government	8 622 ..	....	....	....	....	....	....	....	....
Banks	8 623 ..	....	....	....	....	....	....	....	....
Other sectors	8 624 ..	23,757	24,407	27,775	34,925	48,654	70,761	106,726	138,347
Money market instruments	8 630 ..	....	....	5,746	8,475	9,205	11,211	17,133	7,602
Monetary authorities	8 631 ..	....	....	....	....	....	....	....	....
General government	8 632 ..	....	....	....	....	....	....	....	....
Banks	8 633 ..	....	....	....	....	....	....	....	....
Other sectors	8 634 ..	....	....	5,746	8,475	9,205	11,211	17,133	7,602
Financial derivatives	8 900 ..	....	....	....	....	....	....	....	....
Monetary authorities	8 901 ..	....	....	....	....	....	....	....	....
General government	8 902 ..	....	....	....	....	....	....	....	....
Banks	8 903 ..	....	....	....	....	....	....	....	....
Other sectors	8 904 ..	....	....	....	....	....	....	....	....
Other investment	8 703 ..	**142,687**	**144,189**	**140,113**	**168,777**	**164,936**	**183,694**	**213,476**	**278,284**
Trade credits	8 706 ..	5,592	5,396	5,437	6,151	6,359	6,026	7,208	8,756
General government	8 707 ..	....	....	....	....	....	....	....	....
of which: Short-term	8 709 ..	....	....	....	....	....	....	....	....
Other sectors	8 710 ..	5,592	5,396	5,437	6,151	6,359	6,026	7,208	8,756
of which: Short-term	8 712 ..	....	....	....	....	....	....	....	....
Loans	8 714 ..	40,342	42,950	45,409	45,208	41,100	39,604	62,101	77,039
Monetary authorities	8 715 ..	....	....	....	....	....	....	....	....
of which: Short-term	8 718 ..	....	....	....	....	....	....	....	....
General government	8 719 ..	21,983	22,857	23,396	23,525	17,862	16,826	19,269	20,653
of which: Short-term	8 721 ..	....	....	....	....	....	....	....	....
Banks	8 722 ..	11,704	13,118	12,629	11,118	13,397	15,690	30,480	36,071
of which: Short-term	8 724 ..	....	....	....	....	....	....	....	....
Other sectors	8 725 ..	6,654	6,975	9,385	10,565	9,840	7,087	12,352	20,315
of which: Short-term	8 727 ..	....	....	....	....	....	....	....	....
Currency and deposits	8 730 ..	67,623	68,397	65,019	85,018	90,929	103,746	112,778	158,780
Monetary authorities	8 731 ..	....	....	....	....	....	....	....	....
General government	8 732 ..	....	....	....	....	....	....	....	....
Banks	8 733 ..	46,745	45,283	41,723	55,934	59,401	67,492	61,959	93,839
Other sectors	8 734 ..	20,878	23,114	23,296	29,084	31,528	36,254	50,820	64,941
Other assets	8 736 ..	29,130	27,445	24,248	32,401	26,548	34,317	31,388	33,709
Monetary authorities	8 737 ..	....	....	....	....	....	....	....	....
of which: Short-term	8 739 ..	....	....	....	....	....	....	....	....
General government	8 740 ..	....	....	....	....	....	....	....	....
of which: Short-term	8 742 ..	....	....	....	....	....	....	....	....
Banks	8 743 ..	9,856	8,011	6,798	10,562	274	2,579	....	3,768
of which: Short-term	8 745 ..	....	....	....	....	....	....	....	....
Other sectors	8 746 ..	19,273	19,434	17,451	21,838	26,274	31,739	31,388	29,942
of which: Short-term	8 748 ..	....	....	....	....	....	....	....	....
Reserve assets	8 802 ..	**31,866**	**33,488**	**35,622**	**35,338**	**33,512**	**32,661**	**35,149**	**41,078**
Monetary gold	8 812 ..	54	46	28	6	6	5	6	6
Special drawing rights	8 811 ..	574	614	719	838	924	897	963	1,016
Reserve position in the Fund	8 810 ..	2,509	2,863	3,580	3,847	3,338	1,401	833	661
Foreign exchange	8 803 ..	28,728	29,964	31,295	30,647	29,243	30,358	33,347	39,395
Other claims	8 813 ..	....	....	....	....	....	....	....	....

Table 3 (Concluded). INTERNATIONAL INVESTMENT POSITION (End-period stocks), 2000–2007

(Millions of U.S. dollars)

	Code	2000	2001	2002	2003	2004	2005	2006	2007
LIABILITIES..	8 995 D.	**690,851**	**706,652**	**751,033**	**870,018**	**949,830**	**995,488**	**1,089,173**	**1,325,162**
Direct investment in Canada.....................	8 555 ..	**212,716**	**213,757**	**224,185**	**274,269**	**315,262**	**339,406**	**375,698**	**506,883**
Equity capital and reinvested earnings............	8 556 ..	178,047	173,684	178,633	225,080	261,179	281,255	311,824	434,629
Claims on direct investors.........................	8 557 ..	....	....	....	....	....	....	....	....
Liabilities to direct investors....................	8 558 ..	....	....	....	....	....	....	....	....
Other capital..	8 580 ..	34,669	40,073	45,552	49,189	54,083	58,151	63,874	72,254
Claims on direct investors.........................	8 585 ..	....	....	....	....	....	....	....	....
Liabilities to direct investors....................	8 590 ..	....	....	....	....	....	....	....	....
Portfolio investment...............................	8 652 ..	**324,968**	**330,389**	**351,916**	**394,960**	**433,614**	**428,058**	**454,444**	**492,599**
Equity securities...................................	8 660 ..	58,070	48,654	51,084	64,466	83,119	80,326	83,235	83,653
Banks...	8 663 ..	....	....	....	....	....	....	....	....
Other sectors.......................................	8 664 ..	58,070	48,654	51,084	64,466	83,119	80,326	83,235	83,653
Debt securities.....................................	8 669 ..	266,899	281,735	300,833	330,494	350,496	347,732	371,209	408,946
Bonds and notes....................................	8 670 ..	248,260	268,258	284,886	313,945	334,194	329,884	350,172	386,682
Monetary authorities...............................	8 671 ..	....	....	....	....	....	....	....	....
General government................................	8 672 ..	127,437	118,252	124,528	127,214	130,862	127,808	130,614	133,802
Banks...	8 673 ..	2,599	2,280	1,786	1,536	1,881	1,973	1,746	1,765
Other sectors......................................	8 674 ..	118,224	147,726	158,572	185,195	201,451	200,103	217,811	251,115
Money market instruments.........................	8 680 ..	18,638	13,477	15,946	16,549	16,302	17,847	21,037	22,264
Monetary authorities...............................	8 681 ..	....	....	....	....	....	....	....	....
General government................................	8 682 ..	10,754	6,923	8,145	9,281	7,577	8,917	11,751	11,482
Banks...	8 683 ..	....	....	....	....	....	....	....	....
Other sectors......................................	8 684 ..	7,885	6,554	7,802	7,268	8,725	8,930	9,287	10,783
Financial derivatives..............................	8 905 ..	....	....	....	....	....	....	....	....
Monetary authorities...............................	8 906 ..	....	....	....	....	....	....	....	....
General government................................	8 907 ..	....	....	....	....	....	....	....	....
Banks...	8 908 ..	....	....	....	....	....	....	....	....
Other sectors.......................................	8 909 ..	....	....	....	....	....	....	....	....
Other investment..................................	8 753 ..	**153,167**	**162,506**	**174,932**	**200,789**	**200,953**	**228,024**	**259,032**	**325,680**
Trade credits.......................................	8 756 ..	4,562	4,656	4,511	4,873	5,142	5,712	6,127	6,897
General government................................	8 757 ..	....	....	....	....	....	....	....	....
of which: Short-term.............................	8 759 ..	....	....	....	....	....	....	....	....
Other sectors......................................	8 760 ..	4,562	4,656	4,511	4,873	5,142	5,712	6,127	6,897
of which: Short-term.............................	8 762 ..	....	....	....	....	....	....	....	....
Loans..	8 764 ..	40,445	35,185	37,359	42,173	36,681	36,678	45,139	53,609
Monetary authorities...............................	8 765 ..	....	....	....	....	....	....	....	....
of which: Use of Fund credit and loans from the Fund....	8 766 ..	....	....	....	....	....	....	....	....
of which: Short-term.............................	8 768 ..	....	....	....	....	....	....	....	....
General government................................	8 769 ..	1,306	1,126	1,143	924	292	254	252	269
of which: Short-term.............................	8 771 ..	....	....	....	....	....	....	....	....
Banks...	8 772 ..	....	....	....	....	....	....	....	....
of which: Short-term.............................	8 774 ..	....	....	....	....	....	....	....	....
Other sectors......................................	8 775 ..	39,138	34,059	36,216	41,248	36,388	36,424	44,887	53,340
of which: Short-term.............................	8 777 ..	....	....	....	....	....	....	....	....
Currency and deposits............................	8 780 ..	98,487	113,685	123,472	141,704	146,210	172,627	194,612	246,458
Monetary authorities...............................	8 781 ..	....	....	....	....	....	....	....	....
General government................................	8 782 ..	....	....	....	....	....	....	....	....
Banks...	8 783 ..	98,443	113,639	123,359	141,643	146,127	172,526	194,515	246,302
Other sectors......................................	8 784 ..	44	46	112	62	83	102	97	156
Other liabilities....................................	8 786 ..	9,674	8,980	9,590	12,039	12,920	13,007	13,154	18,715
Monetary authorities...............................	8 787 ..	....	....	....	....	....	....	....	....
of which: Short-term.............................	8 789 ..	....	....	....	....	....	....	....	....
General government................................	8 790 ..	705	484	494	375	316	217	158	111
of which: Short-term.............................	8 792 ..	....	....	....	....	....	....	....	....
Banks...	8 793 ..	....	....	....	....	....	....	....	....
of which: Short-term.............................	8 795 ..	....	....	....	....	....	....	....	....
Other sectors......................................	8 796 ..	8,969	8,496	9,096	11,664	12,604	12,790	12,996	18,604
of which: Short-term.............................	8 798 ..	....	....	....	....	....	....	....	....
NET INTERNATIONAL INVESTMENT POSITION........	8 995 ..	**–139,204**	**–127,735**	**–130,987**	**–159,541**	**–158,197**	**–136,932**	**–66,338**	**–126,519**
Conversion rates: Canadian dollars per U.S. dollar (end of period)...	0 102 ..	**1.5002**	**1.5926**	**1.5796**	**1.2924**	**1.2036**	**1.1645**	**1.1653**	**.9881**

Table 1. ANALYTIC PRESENTATION, 2000–2007

(Millions of U.S. dollars)

	Code	2000	2001	2002	2003	2004	2005	2006	2007
A. Current Account[1]	4 993 Z.	**−58.03**	**−55.73**	**−71.52**	**−90.63**	**−130.01**	**−34.61**	**−39.98**	**−132.57**
Goods: exports f.o.b.	2 100 ..	38.30	37.17	41.76	52.80	57.45	88.85	121.82	76.47
Goods: imports f.o.b.	3 100 ..	−225.66	−231.52	−278.02	−361.37	−435.40	−437.67	−563.33	−743.61
Balance on Goods	4 100 ..	*−187.36*	*−194.35*	*−236.26*	*−308.57*	*−377.95*	*−348.83*	*−441.50*	*−667.14*
Services: credit	2 200 ..	107.58	129.68	152.83	202.46	238.79	277.00	397.45	548.72
Services: debit	3 200 ..	−100.24	−119.01	−142.08	−188.51	−206.67	−208.39	−245.33	−296.61
Balance on Goods and Services	4 991 ..	*−180.01*	*−183.68*	*−225.51*	*−294.61*	*−345.83*	*−280.21*	*−289.38*	*−415.03*
Income: credit	2 300 ..	5.03	7.53	6.41	16.20	17.76	18.80	18.54	24.31
Income: debit	3 300 ..	−17.67	−12.66	−18.26	−29.38	−36.25	−52.18	−63.77	−50.82
Balance on Goods, Services, and Income	4 992 ..	*−192.66*	*−188.81*	*−237.36*	*−307.80*	*−364.31*	*−313.59*	*−334.61*	*−441.54*
Current transfers: credit	2 379 Z.	146.28	155.55	181.57	235.42	277.63	309.97	335.74	415.25
Current transfers: debit	3 379 ..	−11.66	−22.47	−15.73	−18.24	−43.33	−30.98	−41.10	−106.29
B. Capital Account[1]	4 994 Z.	**10.76**	**24.36**	**8.64**	**25.15**	**23.57**	**20.37**	**27.10**	**28.26**
Capital account: credit	2 994 Z.	10.76	24.36	8.64	25.15	23.57	20.73	27.10	28.46
Capital account: debit	3 994 ..	....	....	....	....	....	−.36	....	−.20
Total, Groups A Plus B	4 981 ..	*−47.27*	*−31.37*	*−62.88*	*−65.47*	*−106.44*	*−14.24*	*−12.89*	*−104.31*
C. Financial Account[1]	4 995 W.	**31.53**	**38.53**	**80.67**	**81.55**	**124.48**	**4.02**	**111.46**	**216.96**
Direct investment abroad	4 505 ..	−1.36	−.52	....	−.86	....	....	....	−.35
Direct investment in Cape Verde	4 555 Z.	33.42	9.11	14.81	39.26	67.59	16.70	122.60	130.29
Portfolio investment assets	4 602 ..	−.12	1.45	....	....	....	....	....	−.38
Equity securities	4 610 ..	....	1.56	....	....	....	....	....	−.38
Debt securities	4 619 ..	−.12	−.11	....	....	....	....	....	....
Portfolio investment liabilities	4 652 Z.	....	....	....	....	....	....	.29	7.34
Equity securities	4 660 ..	....	....	....	....	....	....	.29	5.43
Debt securities	4 669 Z.	....	....	....	....	....	....	....	1.91
Financial derivatives	4 910 ..	....	....	....	....	....	....	....	....
Financial derivatives assets	4 900 ..	....	....	....	....	....	....	....	....
Financial derivatives liabilities	4 905 ..	....	....	....	....	....	....	....	....
Other investment assets	4 703 ..	−22.01	−3.30	−2.02	−7.54	−7.54	−55.11	14.78	−23.20
Monetary authorities	4 701 ..	....	−.10	−.07	2.00	4.78	−.37	.30	.30
General government	4 704 ..	−21.33	....	....	−5.22	....	−2.21	....	....
Banks	4 705 ..	−.68	−1.64	−1.95	−4.32	−12.32	−52.56	14.48	−23.50
Other sectors	4 728 ..	....	−1.56	....	....	.01	.03	....	....
Other investment liabilities	4 753 W.	21.60	31.79	67.89	50.70	64.42	42.43	−26.21	103.26
Monetary authorities	4 753 WA	....	.03	2.97	−.66	−.28	−.93	−.07	.25
General government	4 753 ZB	9.68	2.98	9.58	14.30	6.62	24.10	25.48	24.05
Banks	4 753 ZC	18.83	26.93	35.96	33.86	7.79	6.03	−51.80	14.86
Other sectors	4 753 ZD	−6.91	1.85	19.37	3.20	50.30	13.22	.18	64.11
Total, Groups A Through C	4 983 ..	*−15.74*	*7.17*	*17.79*	*16.08*	*18.04*	*−10.22*	*98.57*	*112.65*
D. Net Errors and Omissions	4 998 ..	**−12.03**	**−23.91**	**−7.67**	**−12.40**	**9.74**	**62.57**	**−40.59**	**−25.61**
Total, Groups A Through D	4 984 ..	*−27.77*	*−16.74*	*10.13*	*3.68*	*27.78*	*52.35*	*57.99*	*87.05*
E. Reserves and Related Items	4 802 A.	**27.77**	**16.74**	**−10.13**	**−3.68**	**−27.78**	**−52.35**	**−57.99**	**−87.05**
Reserve assets	4 802 ..	10.27	23.37	.17	1.46	−37.40	−56.06	−57.99	−86.86
Use of Fund credit and loans	4 766 ..	....	....	3.19	3.52	1.80	3.72	....	−.19
Exceptional financing	4 920 ..	17.49	−6.63	−13.49	−8.67	7.83	....	....	....
Conversion rates: Cape Verde escudos per U.S. dollar	0 101 ..	**119.687**	**123.228**	**117.168**	**97.703**	**88.808**	**88.670**	**87.901**	**80.567**

[1] Excludes components that have been classified in the categories of Group E.

Table 2. STANDARD PRESENTATION, 2000–2007

(Millions of U.S. dollars)

	Code	2000	2001	2002	2003	2004	2005	2006	2007
CURRENT ACCOUNT	4 993	−58.03	−55.73	−71.52	−90.63	−130.01	−34.61	−39.98	−132.57
A. GOODS	4 100	−187.36	−194.35	−236.26	−308.57	−377.95	−348.83	−441.50	−667.14
Credit	2 100	38.30	37.17	41.76	52.80	57.45	88.85	121.82	76.47
General merchandise: exports f.o.b.	2 110	2.50	1.96	2.39	3.00	2.65	9.09	12.88	9.71
Goods for processing: exports f.o.b.	2 150	8.93	8.49	8.95	11.09	13.47	9.75	8.85	11.33
Repairs on goods	2 160	1.39	1.41	1.27	1.69	1.66	1.96	.39	.77
Goods procured in ports by carriers	2 170	25.49	25.32	29.14	37.02	39.66	68.05	99.71	54.66
Nonmonetary gold	2 180	....	....	....	....	....	....	....	....
Debit	3 100	−225.66	−231.52	−278.02	−361.37	−435.40	−437.67	−563.33	−743.61
General merchandise: imports f.o.b.	3 110	−210.55	−215.61	−263.43	−339.53	−415.25	−413.82	−528.55	−717.05
Goods for processing: imports f.o.b.	3 150	−8.28	−5.60	−5.94	−7.28	−8.43	−4.49	−5.66	−6.65
Repairs on goods	3 160	−2.13	−5.74	−3.15	−7.27	−5.10	−6.00	−7.99	−9.15
Goods procured in ports by carriers	3 170	−4.70	−4.57	−5.50	−7.28	−6.61	−13.36	−21.12	−10.75
Nonmonetary gold	3 180	....	....	....	....	....	....	....	....
B. SERVICES	4 200	7.35	10.67	10.75	13.95	32.12	68.62	152.12	252.11
Total credit	2 200	*107.58*	*129.68*	*152.83*	*202.46*	*238.79*	*277.00*	*397.45*	*548.72*
Total debit	3 200	*−100.24*	*−119.01*	*−142.08*	*−188.51*	*−206.67*	*−208.39*	*−245.33*	*−296.61*
Transportation services, credit	2 205	44.20	50.62	62.59	83.15	99.05	106.10	128.09	128.92
Passenger	2 850	*22.52*	*23.22*	*34.75*	*47.81*	*53.57*	*55.27*	*70.99*	*79.85*
Freight	2 851	*1.11*	*.70*	*.07*	*.01*	*....*	*.59*	*.53*	*.03*
Other	2 852	*20.57*	*26.70*	*27.78*	*35.34*	*45.48*	*50.24*	*56.57*	*49.04*
Sea transport, passenger	2 207	....	....	....	....	....	....	....	....
Sea transport, freight	2 208	1.08	.38	.07	.01	....	.59	.53	.03
Sea transport, other	2 209	1.83	2.85	1.67	1.96	3.71	6.39	5.31	5.99
Air transport, passenger	2 211	22.52	23.22	34.75	47.81	53.57	55.27	70.99	79.85
Air transport, freight	2 212	.02	.32	....	....	....	....	....	....
Air transport, other	2 213	18.74	23.85	26.11	33.37	41.77	43.86	51.26	43.05
Other transport, passenger	2 215	....	....	....	....	....	....	....	....
Other transport, freight	2 216	....	....	....	....	....	....	....	....
Other transport, other	2 217	....	....	....	....	....	....	....	....
Transportation services, debit	3 205	−44.48	−50.15	−64.78	−90.00	−91.13	−97.79	−125.70	−140.40
Passenger	3 850	*−5.30*	*−7.65*	*−6.60*	*−15.64*	*−14.60*	*−15.43*	*−22.43*	*−25.25*
Freight	3 851	*−22.12*	*−23.11*	*−28.50*	*−31.49*	*−33.23*	*−39.17*	*−51.02*	*−63.21*
Other	3 852	*−17.07*	*−19.38*	*−29.68*	*−42.87*	*−43.30*	*−43.19*	*−52.25*	*−51.94*
Sea transport, passenger	3 207	....	....	....	....	....	....	−50.26	−63.21
Sea transport, freight	3 208	−22.12	−23.11	−27.08	−31.48	−33.18	−39.16	−2.92	−1.69
Sea transport, other	3 209	−2.23	−1.96	−.42	−.22	....	−.01	−22.43	−25.25
Air transport, passenger	3 211	−5.30	−7.65	−6.60	−15.64	−14.60	−15.43	−.77	....
Air transport, freight	3 212	....	....	−1.42	−.01	−.05	−.02	−49.33	−50.26
Air transport, other	3 213	−14.83	−17.42	−29.26	−42.65	−43.29	−43.18		
Other transport, passenger	3 215	....	....	....	....	....	....	....	....
Other transport, freight	3 216	....	....	....	....	....	....	....	....
Other transport, other	3 217	....	....	....	....	....	....	....	....
Travel, credit	2 236	40.69	53.78	65.45	86.80	99.41	121.79	215.11	346.11
Business travel	2 237	.37	.67	1.10	1.52	2.58	4.49	5.37	11.17
Personal travel	2 240	40.31	53.11	64.36	85.28	96.83	117.29	209.74	334.94
Travel, debit	3 236	−36.30	−47.26	−56.36	−72.70	−77.74	−67.23	−82.40	−107.41
Business travel	3 237	−4.41	−4.31	−6.09	−9.39	−7.28	−11.68	....	−29.09
Personal travel	3 240	−31.89	−42.95	−50.27	−63.31	−70.46	−55.55	−82.40	−78.32
Other services, credit	2 200 BA	22.70	25.29	24.79	32.51	40.33	49.11	54.25	73.69
Communications	2 245	10.45	10.81	12.75	14.59	17.05	18.83	22.72	28.90
Construction	2 249	.96	.16	.06	....	....	....	....	....
Insurance	2 253	1.06	2.48	.41	1.17	1.73	1.62	4.17	8.70
Financial	2 260	.01	.04	.04	.15	.06	.64	1.16	.93
Computer and information	2 262	.08	.10	.03	.04	.10	.02	.02	.01
Royalties and licence fees	2 266	....	.13	.56	.07	....	....	....	....
Other business services	2 268	3.10	2.17	2.28	3.52	3.00	2.69	.87	1.58
Personal, cultural, and recreational	2 287	.01	.07	.07	.05	.04	.01	.01	1.93
Government, n.i.e.	2 291	7.02	9.34	8.58	12.92	18.35	25.30	25.29	31.64
Other services, debit	3 200 BA	−19.45	−21.60	−20.94	−25.80	−37.80	−43.36	−37.23	−48.80
Communications	3 245	−4.00	−4.27	−4.52	−3.43	−2.88	−3.34	−3.27	−3.94
Construction	3 249	−.01	....	....	....	....	....	....	....
Insurance	3 253	−3.09	−3.69	−4.63	−5.23	−7.24	−7.51	−9.23	−11.31
Financial	3 260	−.16	−2.77	−.71	−1.91	−2.55	−3.85	−2.55	−1.16
Computer and information	3 262	−3.18	−1.94	−1.81	−2.94	−3.80	−4.69	−3.25	−8.96
Royalties and licence fees	3 266	....	−.14	−.19	−.05	−.26	−.07	....	−1.29
Other business services	3 268	−5.41	−2.72	−3.88	−6.34	−8.28	−15.66	−10.13	−10.74
Personal, cultural, and recreational	3 287	−.20	−.49	−.75	−.31	−.30	−.64	−.72	−1.81
Government, n.i.e.	3 291	−3.41	−5.58	−4.44	−5.60	−12.49	−7.60	−8.07	−9.58

Table 2 (Continued). STANDARD PRESENTATION, 2000–2007

(Millions of U.S. dollars)

	Code	2000	2001	2002	2003	2004	2005	2006	2007
C. INCOME	4 300	**−12.64**	**−5.13**	**−11.85**	**−13.19**	**−18.49**	**−33.38**	**−45.23**	**−26.51**
Total credit	2 300	*5.03*	*7.53*	*6.41*	*16.20*	*17.76*	*18.80*	*18.54*	*24.31*
Total debit	3 300	*−17.67*	*−12.66*	*−18.26*	*−29.38*	*−36.25*	*−52.18*	*−63.77*	*−50.82*
Compensation of employees, credit	2 310	**1.21**	**1.20**	**.39**	**.17**	**.39**	**.15**	**.78**	**.41**
Compensation of employees, debit	3 310	**−.38**	**−.28**	**−.27**	**−.54**	**−.62**	**−1.27**	**−.61**	**−1.47**
Investment income, credit	2 320	**3.81**	**6.33**	**6.03**	**16.03**	**17.37**	**18.65**	**17.76**	**23.89**
Direct investment income	2 330	2.17	3.90	4.00	.96	....	....	.03	....
Dividends and distributed branch profits	2 332	....	.01	....	.11	....	....	.03	....
Reinvested earnings and undistributed branch profits	2 333	1.36	.52	....	.86	....	....	....	....
Income on debt (interest)	2 334	.82	3.37	4.00	....	....	....	....	....
Portfolio investment income	2 339	....	.04	....	5.91	8.58	7.41	4.11	4.69
Income on equity	2 340	....	....	....	4.95	6.97	7.41	4.11	4.69
Income on bonds and notes	2 350	....	....	....	.97	1.61	....	....	....
Income on money market instruments	2 360	....	.04	....	....	....	....	....	....
Other investment income	2 370	1.64	2.39	2.03	9.15	8.79	11.23	13.62	19.20
Investment income, debit	3 320	**−17.29**	**−12.38**	**−17.99**	**−28.84**	**−35.62**	**−50.91**	**−63.16**	**−49.35**
Direct investment income	3 330	−5.05	−1.43	−4.13	−2.78	−3.75	−10.35	−29.47	−21.36
Dividends and distributed branch profits	3 332	−3.70	−.30	−3.05	−1.82	−3.49	−10.00	−29.14	−20.83
Reinvested earnings and undistributed branch profits	3 333	−1.36	−1.03	−1.08	−.96	−.26	−.09	....	....
Income on debt (interest)	3 334	....	−.10	....	....	....	−.26	−.33	−.53
Portfolio investment income	3 339	....	−.06	....	....	....	....	−.03	−.54
Income on equity	3 340	....	....	....	....	....	....	−.03	−.54
Income on bonds and notes	3 350	....	....	....	....	....	....	....	....
Income on money market instruments	3 360	....	−.06	....	....	....	....	....	....
Other investment income	3 370	−12.23	−10.88	−13.86	−26.06	−31.87	−40.56	−33.66	−27.44
D. CURRENT TRANSFERS	4 379	**134.63**	**133.08**	**165.84**	**217.17**	**234.30**	**278.99**	**294.63**	**308.96**
Credit	2 379	**146.28**	**155.55**	**181.57**	**235.42**	**277.63**	**309.97**	**335.74**	**415.25**
General government	2 380	25.55	21.82	34.99	50.21	54.85	48.12	53.25	69.49
Other sectors	2 390	120.73	133.73	146.58	185.21	222.78	261.85	282.49	345.75
Workers' remittances	2 391	85.69	79.75	84.69	108.37	112.97	136.50	135.83	138.44
Other current transfers	2 392	35.04	53.98	61.88	76.84	109.82	125.35	146.66	207.31
Debit	3 379	**−11.66**	**−22.47**	**−15.73**	**−18.24**	**−43.33**	**−30.98**	**−41.10**	**−106.29**
General government	3 380	−3.89	−.68	−.45	−1.06	−1.20	−1.99	−4.04	−5.59
Other sectors	3 390	−7.76	−21.79	−15.28	−17.18	−42.13	−29.00	−37.06	−100.70
Workers' remittances	3 391	−.08	....	−1.25	−6.65	−11.35	−3.90	−5.07	−4.55
Other current transfers	3 392	−7.68	−21.79	−14.03	−10.53	−30.78	−25.09	−32.00	−96.15
CAPITAL AND FINANCIAL ACCOUNT	4 996	**70.06**	**79.64**	**79.19**	**103.02**	**120.27**	**−27.97**	**80.57**	**158.18**
CAPITAL ACCOUNT	4 994	**10.76**	**24.36**	**8.64**	**25.15**	**23.57**	**20.37**	**27.10**	**28.26**
Total credit	2 994	*10.76*	*24.36*	*8.64*	*25.15*	*23.57*	*20.73*	*27.10*	*28.46*
Total debit	3 994	....	....	....	....	....	*−.36*	....	*−.20*
Capital transfers, credit	2 400	**10.76**	**24.36**	**8.64**	**25.15**	**23.57**	**20.73**	**27.10**	**28.46**
General government	2 401	.35	....	2.16	25.15	23.57	20.60	27.10	28.18
Debt forgiveness	2 402	....	....	....	....	....	....	....	....
Other capital transfers	2 410	.35	....	2.16	25.15	23.57	20.60	27.10	28.18
Other sectors	2 430	10.41	24.36	6.48	....	....	.13	....	.28
Migrants' transfers	2 431	....	....	....	....	....	....	....	....
Debt forgiveness	2 432	....	....	....	....	....	....	....	....
Other capital transfers	2 440	10.41	24.36	6.48	....	....	.13	....	.28
Capital transfers, debit	3 400	....	....	....	....	....	**−.36**	....	**−.20**
General government	3 401	....	....	....	....	....	−.12	....	−.20
Debt forgiveness	3 402	....	....	....	....	....	....	....	....
Other capital transfers	3 410	....	....	....	....	....	−.12	....	−.20
Other sectors	3 430	....	....	....	....	....	−.24	....	....
Migrants' transfers	3 431	....	....	....	....	....	....	....	....
Debt forgiveness	3 432	....	....	....	....	....	....	....	....
Other capital transfers	3 440	....	....	....	....	....	−.24	....	....
Nonproduced nonfinancial assets, credit	2 480	....	....	....	....	....	....	....	....
Nonproduced nonfinancial assets, debit	3 480	....	....	....	....	....	....	....	....

Table 2 (Continued). STANDARD PRESENTATION, 2000–2007

(Millions of U.S. dollars)

	Code	2000	2001	2002	2003	2004	2005	2006	2007
FINANCIAL ACCOUNT..	4 995 ..	**59.30**	**55.27**	**70.55**	**77.87**	**96.71**	**−48.33**	**53.47**	**129.92**
A. DIRECT INVESTMENT.......................................	4 500 ..	**32.07**	**8.59**	**14.81**	**38.40**	**67.59**	**16.70**	**122.60**	**129.94**
Direct investment abroad...................................	4 505 ..	−1.36	−.52	....	−.86	....	....	....	−.35
Equity capital..	4 510 ..	....	....	....	....	....	....	....	−.35
Claims on affiliated enterprises....................	4 515 ..	....	....	....	....	....	....	....	....
Liabilities to affiliated enterprises................	4 520 ..	....	....	....	....	....	....	....	....
Reinvested earnings..	4 525 ..	−1.36	−.52	....	−.86	....	....	....	....
Other capital...	4 530 ..	....	....	....	....	....	....	....	....
Claims on affiliated enterprises....................	4 535 ..	....	....	....	....	....	....	....	....
Liabilities to affiliated enterprises................	4 540 ..	....	....	....	....	....	....	....	....
Direct investment in Cape Verde......................	4 555 ..	**33.42**	**9.11**	**14.81**	**39.26**	**67.59**	**16.70**	**122.60**	**130.29**
Equity capital..	4 560 ..	32.40	7.98	13.70	38.29	54.12	....	97.84	132.88
Claims on direct investors..........................	4 565 ..	32.40	7.98	13.70	38.92	54.12	....	....	....
Liabilities to direct investors......................	4 570 ..	....	....	....	−.63	....	....	....	....
Reinvested earnings..	4 575 ..	1.36	1.03	1.08	.96	.26	.09	....	....
Other capital...	4 580 ..	−.34	.10	.03	.01	13.22	16.60	24.76	−2.59
Claims on direct investors..........................	4 585 ..	....	.10	.03	.01	....	−.01	28.90	....
Liabilities to direct investors......................	4 590 ..	−.34	....	....	....	13.22	16.61	−4.14	−2.59
B. PORTFOLIO INVESTMENT.................................	4 600 ..	**−.12**	**1.45**	**....**	**....**	**....**	**....**	**.29**	**6.96**
Assets...	4 602 ..	−.12	1.45	....	....	....	....	....	−.38
Equity securities..	4 610 ..	....	1.56	....	....	....	....	....	−.38
Monetary authorities..................................	4 611 ..	....	....	....	....	....	....	....	....
General government..................................	4 612 ..	....	....	....	....	....	....	....	....
Banks..	4 613 ..	....	....	....	....	....	....	....	....
Other sectors...	4 614 ..	....	1.56	....	....	....	....	....	−.38
Debt securities..	4 619 ..	−.12	−.11	....	....	....	....	....	....
Bonds and notes.......................................	4 620 ..	....	....	....	....	....	....	....	....
Monetary authorities..............................	4 621 ..	....	....	....	....	....	....	....	....
General government..............................	4 622 ..	....	....	....	....	....	....	....	....
Banks..	4 623 ..	....	....	....	....	....	....	....	....
Other sectors.......................................	4 624 ..	....	....	....	....	....	....	....	....
Money market instruments.........................	4 630 ..	−.12	−.11	....	....	....	....	....	....
Monetary authorities..............................	4 631 ..	....	....	....	....	....	....	....	....
General government..............................	4 632 ..	....	....	....	....	....	....	....	....
Banks..	4 633 ..	....	....	....	....	....	....	....	....
Other sectors.......................................	4 634 ..	−.12	−.11	....	....	....	....	....	....
Liabilities..	4 652 ..	....	....	....	....	....	....	.29	7.34
Equity securities..	4 660 ..	....	....	....	....	....	....	.29	5.43
Banks..	4 663 ..	....	....	....	....	....	....	....	....
Other sectors...	4 664 ..	....	....	....	....	....	....	.29	5.43
Debt securities..	4 669 ..	....	....	....	....	....	....	....	1.91
Bonds and notes.......................................	4 670 ..	....	....	....	....	....	....	....	1.91
Monetary authorities..............................	4 671 ..	....	....	....	....	....	....	....	....
General government..............................	4 672 ..	....	....	....	....	....	....	....	....
Banks..	4 673 ..	....	....	....	....	....	....	....	....
Other sectors.......................................	4 674 ..	....	....	....	....	....	....	....	1.91
Money market instruments.........................	4 680 ..	....	....	....	....	....	....	....	....
Monetary authorities..............................	4 681 ..	....	....	....	....	....	....	....	....
General government..............................	4 682 ..	....	....	....	....	....	....	....	....
Banks..	4 683 ..	....	....	....	....	....	....	....	....
Other sectors.......................................	4 684 ..	....	....	....	....	....	....	....	....
C. FINANCIAL DERIVATIVES.................................	4 910 ..	....	....	....	....	....	....	....	....
Monetary authorities...	4 911 ..	....	....	....	....	....	....	....	....
General government..	4 912 ..	....	....	....	....	....	....	....	....
Banks..	4 913 ..	....	....	....	....	....	....	....	....
Other sectors..	4 914 ..	....	....	....	....	....	....	....	....
Assets...	4 900 ..	....	....	....	....	....	....	....	....
Monetary authorities....................................	4 901 ..	....	....	....	....	....	....	....	....
General government....................................	4 902 ..	....	....	....	....	....	....	....	....
Banks..	4 903 ..	....	....	....	....	....	....	....	....
Other sectors...	4 904 ..	....	....	....	....	....	....	....	....
Liabilities..	4 905 ..	....	....	....	....	....	....	....	....
Monetary authorities....................................	4 906 ..	....	....	....	....	....	....	....	....
General government....................................	4 907 ..	....	....	....	....	....	....	....	....
Banks..	4 908 ..	....	....	....	....	....	....	....	....
Other sectors...	4 909 ..	....	....	....	....	....	....	....	....

Table 2 (Concluded). STANDARD PRESENTATION, 2000–2007

(Millions of U.S. dollars)

	Code	2000	2001	2002	2003	2004	2005	2006	2007
D. OTHER INVESTMENT	4 700	**17.08**	**21.86**	**55.57**	**38.01**	**66.52**	**−8.96**	**−11.43**	**79.87**
Assets	4 703	**−22.01**	**−3.30**	**−2.02**	**−7.54**	**−7.54**	**−55.11**	**14.78**	**−23.20**
Trade credits	4 706	....	....	....	....	.01	.03	....	....
General government	4 707	....	....	....	....	....	....	....	....
of which: Short-term	4 709	....	....	....	....	....	....	....	....
Other sectors	4 710	....	....	....	....	.01	.03	....	....
of which: Short-term	4 712	....	....	....	....	.01	.03	....	....
Loans	4 714	−.12	.06	−.10	.61	.66	−.60	−1.88	−6.54
Monetary authorities	4 715	....	....	....	....	....	....	....	....
of which: Short-term	4 718	....	....	....	....	....	....	....	....
General government	4 719	....	....	....	....	....	....	....	....
of which: Short-term	4 721	....	....	....	....	....	....	....	....
Banks	4 722	−.12	.06	−.10	.61	.66	−.60	−1.88	−6.54
of which: Short-term	4 724	−.12	.06	−.10	.53	.84	−.08	−.16	−5.52
Other sectors	4 725	....	....	....	....	....	....	....	....
of which: Short-term	4 727	....	....	....	....	....	....	....	....
Currency and deposits	4 730	....	−1.56	....	....	....	....	....	....
Monetary authorities	4 731	....	....	....	....	....	....	....	....
General government	4 732	....	....	....	....	....	....	....	....
Banks	4 733	....	....	....	....	....	....	....	....
Other sectors	4 734	....	−1.56	....	....	....	....	....	....
Other assets	4 736	−21.90	−1.80	−1.92	−8.15	−8.20	−54.54	16.66	−16.65
Monetary authorities	4 737	....	−.10	−.07	2.00	4.78	−.37	.30	.30
of which: Short-term	4 739	....	....	....	−1.01	3.29	−.23	.19	.19
General government	4 740	−21.33	....	....	−5.22	....	−2.21	....	....
of which: Short-term	4 742	−21.33	....	....	−5.22	....	−2.21	....	....
Banks	4 743	−.56	−1.69	−1.85	−4.93	−12.98	−51.96	16.35	−16.95
of which: Short-term	4 745	−.23	−1.69	−1.85	−4.78	−2.31	2.25	1.49	−27.71
Other sectors	4 746	....	....	....	....	....	....	....	....
of which: Short-term	4 748	....	....	....	....	....	....	....	....
Liabilities	4 753	**39.09**	**25.16**	**57.59**	**45.56**	**74.05**	**46.14**	**−26.21**	**103.07**
Trade credits	4 756	−2.24	5.62	20.45	−1.82	1.66	6.15	3.14	5.01
General government	4 757	....	....	....	....	....	....	....	....
of which: Short-term	4 759	....	....	....	....	....	....	....	....
Other sectors	4 760	−2.24	5.62	20.45	−1.82	1.66	6.15	3.14	5.01
of which: Short-term	4 762	−2.24	5.62	20.45	−1.82	1.66	6.15	3.14	5.01
Loans	4 764	15.10	1.95	17.07	13.84	71.18	40.27	−25.82	78.07
Monetary authorities	4 765	....	....	3.19	2.86	1.52	2.79	....	.06
of which: Use of Fund credit and loans from the Fund	4 766	....	....	3.19	3.52	1.80	3.72	....	−.19
of which: Short-term	4 768	....	....	....	−.11	....	−.93	....	....
General government	4 769	23.06	9.87	9.58	14.41	5.21	24.10	25.48	24.04
of which: Short-term	4 771	13.35	−5.99	−.48	.11	−.17	−1.31	....	....
Banks	4 772	−3.30	−1.68	5.37	−2.91	7.80	6.31	−48.34	−5.13
of which: Short-term	4 774	−3.33	.30	1.44	....	....	....	−50.80	−1.47
Other sectors	4 775	−4.66	−6.23	−1.07	−.53	56.65	7.07	−2.96	59.10
of which: Short-term	4 777	....	.47	....	−5.55	8.00	−11.25	−17.95	−20.78
Currency and deposits	4 780	21.88	26.34	29.15	33.27	....	....	....	19.99
Monetary authorities	4 781	....	....	....	....	....	....	....	....
General government	4 782	....	....	....	....	....	....	....	....
Banks	4 783	21.88	26.34	29.15	33.27	....	....	....	19.99
Other sectors	4 784	....	....	....	....	....	....	....	....
Other liabilities	4 786	4.35	−8.75	−9.07	.27	1.22	−.28	−3.52	.01
Monetary authorities	4 787	....	.03	2.97	....	....	....	−.07	....
of which: Short-term	4 789	....	.03	−.10	....	....	....	....	....
General government	4 790	4.11	−11.06	−13.49	....	1.23	....	....	.01
of which: Short-term	4 792	4.11	−11.06	−13.49	....	....	....	....	....
Banks	4 793	.25	2.28	1.45	.27	−.02	−.28	−3.45	....
of which: Short-term	4 795	.25	2.28	1.82	.27	−.02	−.28	−3.45	....
Other sectors	4 796	....	....	....	....	....	....	....	....
of which: Short-term	4 798	....	....	....	....	....	....	....	....
E. RESERVE ASSETS	4 802	**10.27**	**23.37**	**.17**	**1.46**	**−37.40**	**−56.06**	**−57.99**	**−86.86**
Monetary gold	4 812	....	....	....	....	....	....	....	....
Special drawing rights	4 811	−.03	.03	.02	....	−.03	.01	.02	−.11
Reserve position in the Fund	4 810	....	....	....	....	....	−.02	....	....
Foreign exchange	4 803	10.31	23.34	.16	1.46	−37.37	−56.06	−58.01	−86.75
Other claims	4 813	....	....	....	....	....	....	....	....
NET ERRORS AND OMISSIONS	4 998	**−12.03**	**−23.91**	**−7.67**	**−12.40**	**9.74**	**62.57**	**−40.59**	**−25.61**

Table 1. ANALYTIC PRESENTATION, 2000–2007

(Millions of U.S. dollars)

	Code	2000	2001	2002	2003	2004	2005	2006	2007
A. Current Account[1].....................	4 993 Z.	−898	−1,100	−580	−779	2,074	1,449	6,838	7,200
Goods: exports f.o.b..........................	2 100 ..	19,210	18,272	18,180	21,664	32,520	41,267	58,485	67,644
Goods: imports f.o.b..........................	3 100 ..	−17,091	−16,428	−15,794	−17,941	−22,935	−30,492	−35,899	−43,991
Balance on Goods..........................	4 100 ..	*2,119*	*1,844*	*2,386*	*3,723*	*9,585*	*10,775*	*22,587*	*23,653*
Services: credit................................	2 200 ..	4,083	4,138	4,386	5,070	6,034	7,134	7,824	8,786
Services: debit.................................	3 200 ..	−4,802	−4,983	−5,087	−5,688	−6,780	−7,756	−8,452	−9,947
Balance on Goods and Services............	4 991 ..	*1,400*	*999*	*1,684*	*3,105*	*8,839*	*10,153*	*21,959*	*22,491*
Income: credit.................................	2 300 ..	1,598	1,458	1,114	1,552	1,983	2,452	3,457	5,587
Income: debit..................................	3 300 ..	−4,453	−3,985	−3,960	−6,041	−9,820	−12,939	−21,876	−23,853
Balance on Goods, Services, and Income.........	4 992 ..	*−1,456*	*−1,527*	*−1,163*	*−1,384*	*1,003*	*−334*	*3,541*	*4,226*
Current transfers: credit....................	2 379 Z.	765	713	954	901	1,411	2,199	3,801	3,574
Current transfers: debit....................	3 379 ..	−207	−286	−372	−296	−339	−416	−504	−600
B. Capital Account[1]......................	4 994 Z.	....	....	83	....	5	41	13	16
Capital account: credit....................	2 994 Z.	....	....	83	....	5	41	13	16
Capital account: debit....................	3 994 ..	....	....	....	....	....	....	....	....
Total, Groups A Plus B....................	4 981 ..	*−898*	*−1,100*	*−497*	*−779*	*2,080*	*1,490*	*6,851*	*7,215*
C. Financial Account[1].....................	4 995 W.	787	1,362	1,634	1,145	−2,001	1,550	−5,057	−9,436
Direct investment abroad...................	4 505 ..	−3,987	−1,610	−343	−1,606	−1,563	−2,183	−2,876	−3,830
Direct investment in Chile.................	4 555 Z.	4,860	4,200	2,550	4,307	7,173	6,984	7,358	14,457
Portfolio investment assets................	4 602 ..	766	−1,386	−3,316	−4,699	−4,430	−4,227	−10,851	−15,390
Equity securities............................	4 610 ..	821	−2,094	−3,272	−4,853	−3,205	−4,025	−3,000	−9,597
Debt securities.............................	4 619 ..	−55	708	−44	154	−1,225	−203	−7,851	−5,793
Portfolio investment liabilities............	4 652 Z.	−127	1,525	999	2,054	1,122	1,394	776	−373
Equity securities............................	4 660 ..	−427	−217	−320	318	8	1,571	−194	404
Debt securities.............................	4 669 Z.	300	1,742	1,319	1,736	1,114	−176	970	−777
Financial derivatives........................	4 910 ..	2	−86	−124	118	−84	−63	304	511
Financial derivatives assets................	4 900 ..	....	....	1,788	1,840	639	1,244	1,501	2,650
Financial derivatives liabilities............	4 905 ..	2	−86	−1,912	−1,722	−723	−1,307	−1,197	−2,139
Other investment assets...................	4 703 ..	−2,065	−1,326	1,141	−571	−3,389	−2,384	−3,974	−11,628
Monetary authorities.....................	4 701 ..	....	....	....	−60	....	....	....	....
General government......................	4 704 ..	....	....	....	1	....	....	−591	−5,468
Banks..	4 705 ..	653	145	635	299	−166	−557	−1,042	−1,838
Other sectors..............................	4 728 ..	−2,717	−1,471	505	−811	−3,223	−1,827	−2,341	−4,323
Other investment liabilities...............	4 753 W.	1,338	44	728	1,543	−829	2,028	4,206	6,817
Monetary authorities.....................	4 753 WA	36	−47	−2	−3	6	....	−3	−1
General government......................	4 753 ZB	−128	−132	−294	−117	−115	−443	−53	−12
Banks..	4 753 ZC	−278	771	1,302	1,606	170	1,276	15	2,761
Other sectors..............................	4 753 ZD	1,707	−548	−279	57	−890	1,195	4,247	4,070
Total, Groups A Through C...............	4 983 ..	*−110*	*262*	*1,137*	*367*	*79*	*3,040*	*1,795*	*−2,221*
D. Net Errors and Omissions................	4 998 ..	427	−861	−952	−724	−270	−1,329	204	−993
Total, Groups A Through D...............	4 984 ..	*317*	*−599*	*185*	*−357*	*−191*	*1,711*	*1,998*	*−3,214*
E. Reserves and Related Items.............	4 802 A.	−317	599	−185	357	191	−1,711	−1,998	3,214
Reserve assets................................	4 802 ..	−317	599	−185	357	191	−1,711	−1,998	3,214
Use of Fund credit and loans..............	4 766 ..	....	....	....	....	....	....	....	....
Exceptional financing.......................	4 920 ..	....	....	....	....	....	....	....	....
Conversion rates: Chilean pesos per U.S. dollar	0 101 ..	539.59	634.94	688.94	691.40	609.53	559.77	530.28	522.46

[1] Excludes components that have been classified in the categories of Group E.

Table 2. STANDARD PRESENTATION, 2000–2007

(Millions of U.S. dollars)

	Code	2000	2001	2002	2003	2004	2005	2006	2007
CURRENT ACCOUNT..	4 993 ..	−898	−1,100	−580	−779	2,074	1,449	6,838	7,200
A. GOODS..	4 100 ..	2,119	1,844	2,386	3,723	9,585	10,775	22,587	23,653
Credit..	2 100 ..	19,210	18,272	18,180	21,664	32,520	41,267	58,485	67,644
General merchandise: exports f.o.b..........	2 110 ..	18,679	17,839	17,793	21,128	31,959	40,557	57,532	66,636
Goods for processing: exports f.o.b..........	2 150 ..	....	....	....	....	....	....	....	....
Repairs on goods..	2 160 ..	....	....	2	1	1	1	2	1
Goods procured in ports by carriers..........	2 170 ..	188	168	129	187	243	358	420	434
Nonmonetary gold......................................	2 180 ..	343	264	256	348	318	351	532	574
Debit...	3 100 ..	−17,091	−16,428	−15,794	−17,941	−22,935	−30,492	−35,899	−43,991
General merchandise: imports f.o.b..........	3 110 ..	−16,805	−16,132	−15,526	−17,554	−22,468	−29,809	−35,049	−43,080
Goods for processing: imports f.o.b..........	3 150 ..	....	....	....	....	....	....	....	....
Repairs on goods..	3 160 ..	−63	−72	−52	−56	−66	−63	−37	−58
Goods procured in ports by carriers..........	3 170 ..	−224	−224	−217	−332	−401	−621	−813	−853
Nonmonetary gold......................................	3 180 ..								
B. SERVICES...	4 200 ..	−719	−844	−701	−618	−746	−622	−628	−1,162
Total credit..	2 200 ..	*4,083*	*4,138*	*4,386*	*5,070*	*6,034*	*7,134*	*7,824*	*8,786*
Total debit...	3 200 ..	*−4,802*	*−4,983*	*−5,087*	*−5,688*	*−6,780*	*−7,756*	*−8,452*	*−9,947*
Transportation services, credit..................	2 205 ..	2,188	2,294	2,205	2,771	3,457	4,301	4,675	5,131
Passenger..	2 850 ..	*360*	*385*	*323*	*426*	*476*	*573*	*671*	*753*
Freight...	2 851 ..	*1,316*	*1,294*	*1,229*	*1,537*	*1,964*	*2,498*	*2,589*	*2,824*
Other...	2 852 ..	*512*	*615*	*653*	*807*	*1,017*	*1,230*	*1,414*	*1,554*
Sea transport, passenger............................	2 207 ..	3	5	4	7	9	9	9	15
Sea transport, freight.................................	2 208 ..	863	858	838	1,016	1,300	1,745	1,729	1,928
Sea transport, other...................................	2 209 ..	408	484	495	602	792	998	1,146	1,261
Air transport, passenger............................	2 211 ..	349	373	312	410	458	551	644	716
Air transport, freight.................................	2 212 ..	399	361	320	397	541	605	692	695
Air transport, other...................................	2 213 ..	78	103	126	167	178	181	213	230
Other transport, passenger........................	2 215 ..	8	7	8	9	10	14	19	22
Other transport, freight.............................	2 216 ..	54	75	71	125	123	149	168	201
Other transport, other...............................	2 217 ..	26	28	32	39	47	50	56	63
Transportation services, debit....................	3 205 ..	−2,191	−2,260	−2,300	−2,585	−3,354	−4,135	−4,571	−5,275
Passenger..	3 850 ..	*−284*	*−231*	*−259*	*−259*	*−274*	*−304*	*−334*	*−378*
Freight...	3 851 ..	*−815*	*−861*	*−960*	*−960*	*−1,347*	*−1,571*	*−1,779*	*−2,294*
Other...	3 852 ..	*−1,093*	*−1,167*	*−1,081*	*−1,366*	*−1,733*	*−2,260*	*−2,458*	*−2,603*
Sea transport, passenger............................	3 207 ..	....	....	....	....	....	....	....	....
Sea transport, freight.................................	3 208 ..	−513	−517	−576	−576	−808	−1,021	−1,162	−1,625
Sea transport, other...................................	3 209 ..	−872	−981	−880	−1,027	−1,405	−1,893	−2,040	−2,164
Air transport, passenger............................	3 211 ..	−266	−215	−238	−235	−247	−272	−295	−336
Air transport, freight.................................	3 212 ..	−168	−181	−202	−202	−283	−236	−283	−346
Air transport, other...................................	3 213 ..	−59	−116	−125	−211	−227	−251	−289	−292
Other transport, passenger........................	3 215 ..	−17	−16	−21	−24	−27	−31	−39	−42
Other transport, freight.............................	3 216 ..	−134	−164	−182	−182	−256	−314	−334	−323
Other transport, other...............................	3 217 ..	−162	−70	−77	−128	−101	−116	−130	−147
Travel, credit..	2 236 ..	819	799	898	883	1,095	1,109	1,222	1,419
Business travel..	2 237 ..	79	98	256	678	167	151	173	252
Personal travel...	2 240 ..	741	700	641	206	928	958	1,049	1,168
Travel, debit...	3 236 ..	−620	−708	−673	−850	−977	−1,051	−1,239	−1,762
Business travel..	3 237 ..	−41	−168	−227	−541	−359	−379	−445	−537
Personal travel...	3 240 ..	−579	−540	−446	−309	−618	−671	−794	−1,225
Other services, credit................................	2 200 BA ..	1,076	1,046	1,282	1,415	1,482	1,724	1,927	2,235
Communications...	2 245 ..	207	125	162	158	163	148	143	154
Construction...	2 249 ..	....	....	....	....	....	....	....	....
Insurance..	2 253 ..	76	71	138	124	136	163	189	216
Financial...	2 260 ..	38	34	25	30	31	34	37	40
Computer and information..........................	2 262 ..	33	43	63	81	71	74	78	82
Royalties and licence fees...........................	2 266 ..	10	25	41	45	48	54	55	61
Other business services..............................	2 268 ..	602	652	745	830	890	1,087	1,241	1,487
Personal, cultural, and recreational...........	2 287 ..	22	29	39	68	58	69	78	84
Government, n.i.e..	2 291 ..	88	68	70	79	84	94	104	109
Other services, debit.................................	3 200 BA ..	−1,991	−2,015	−2,114	−2,252	−2,449	−2,570	−2,642	−2,911
Communications...	3 245 ..	−110	−95	−137	−156	−160	−158	−137	−150
Construction...	3 249 ..	....	....	....	....	....	....	....	....
Insurance..	3 253 ..	−192	−211	−353	−435	−451	−463	−431	−479
Financial...	3 260 ..	−222	−203	−230	−214	−283	−256	−319	−368
Computer and information..........................	3 262 ..	−78	−47	−41	−75	−74	−71	−73	−67
Royalties and licence fees...........................	3 266 ..	−297	−269	−251	−257	−307	−348	−384	−434
Other business services..............................	3 268 ..	−909	−1,019	−925	−935	−999	−1,037	−1,031	−1,125
Personal, cultural, and recreational...........	3 287 ..	−44	−36	−44	−47	−48	−53	−55	−59
Government, n.i.e..	3 291 ..	−138	−135	−134	−132	−127	−184	−212	−229

Table 2 (Continued). STANDARD PRESENTATION, 2000–2007

(Millions of U.S. dollars)

	Code	2000	2001	2002	2003	2004	2005	2006	2007
C. INCOME	4 300	**−2,856**	**−2,526**	**−2,847**	**−4,489**	**−7,837**	**−10,487**	**−18,418**	**−18,265**
Total credit	2 300	*1,598*	*1,458*	*1,114*	*1,552*	*1,983*	*2,452*	*3,457*	*5,587*
Total debit	3 300	*−4,453*	*−3,985*	*−3,960*	*−6,041*	*−9,820*	*−12,939*	*−21,876*	*−23,853*
Compensation of employees, credit	2 310	**13**	**12**	**12**	**12**	**12**	**13**	**3**	**3**
Compensation of employees, debit	3 310	**−16**	**−16**	**−16**	**−15**	**−15**	**−16**	**−6**	**−6**
Investment income, credit	2 320	**1,584**	**1,446**	**1,101**	**1,541**	**1,972**	**2,439**	**3,455**	**5,585**
Direct investment income	2 330	568	646	289	652	951	1,063	1,121	2,006
Dividends and distributed branch profits	2 332	166	256	46	103	115	87	118	196
Reinvested earnings anc undistributed branch profits	2 333	385	331	231	547	824	946	956	1,777
Income on debt (interest)	2 334	17	59	12	2	12	30	47	33
Portfolio investment income	2 339	88	25	251	449	591	761	1,258	2,300
Income on equity	2 340	88	25	137	341	351	545	891	1,376
Income on bonds and notes	2 350	....	....	92	101	231	202	201	640
Income on money market instruments	2 360	....	....	21	6	9	13	166	285
Other investment income	2 370	929	776	561	439	429	615	1,076	1,278
Investment income, debit	3 320	**−4,438**	**−3,969**	**−3,944**	**−6,026**	**−9,805**	**−12,923**	**−21,870**	**−23,847**
Direct investment income	3 330	−2,539	−2,250	−2,447	−4,611	−8,231	−11,416	−19,991	−21,754
Dividends and distributed branch profits	3 332	−1,093	−859	−818	−1,154	−2,076	−4,729	−12,716	−11,873
Reinvested earnings and undistributed branch profits	3 333	−1,171	−1,105	−1,367	−3,335	−5,952	−6,539	−7,220	−9,784
Income on debt (interest)	3 334	−276	−287	−262	−123	−203	−148	−54	−97
Portfolio investment income	3 339	−490	−527	−711	−817	−1,137	−928	−950	−1,157
Income on equity	3 340	−154	−143	−230	−193	−424	−224	−240	−317
Income on bonds and notes	3 350	−336	−383	−481	−624	−713	−704	−711	−840
Income on money market instruments	3 360	....	....	....	....	....	....	....	....
Other investment income	3 370	−1,408	−1,192	−787	−598	−437	−579	−929	−936
D. CURRENT TRANSFERS	4 379	**558**	**427**	**583**	**605**	**1,072**	**1,783**	**3,297**	**2,974**
Credit	2 379	**765**	**713**	**954**	**901**	**1,411**	**2,199**	**3,801**	**3,574**
General government	2 380	370	320	454	519	878	1,352	2,951	2,538
Other sectors	2 390	395	393	500	382	533	847	850	1,036
Workers' remittances	2 391	....	....	....	....	....	....	....	....
Other current transfers	2 392	395	393	500	382	533	847	850	1,036
Debit	3 379	**−207**	**−286**	**−372**	**−296**	**−339**	**−416**	**−504**	**−600**
General government	3 380	−45	−40	−42	−52	−37	−35	−38	−50
Other sectors	3 390	−162	−247	−330	−244	−302	−381	−466	−550
Workers' remittances	3 391	....	....	....	....	....	....	....	....
Other current transfers	3 392	−162	−247	−330	−244	−302	−381	−466	−550
CAPITAL AND FINANCIAL ACCOUNT	4 996	**471**	**1,961**	**1,532**	**1,503**	**−1,804**	**−120**	**−7,042**	**−6,207**
CAPITAL ACCOUNT	4 994	....	....	**83**	....	**5**	**41**	**13**	**16**
Total credit	2 994	....	....	*83*	....	*5*	*41*	*13*	*16*
Total debit	3 994	....	....	....	....	....	....	....	....
Capital transfers, credit	2 400	....	....	**83**	....	**5**	**11**	**13**	**16**
General government	2 401	....	....	....	....	....	....	....	....
Debt forgiveness	2 402	....	....	....	....	....	....	....	....
Other capital transfers	2 410	....	....	....	....	....	....	....	....
Other sectors	2 430	....	....	83	....	5	11	13	16
Migrants' transfers	2 431	....	....	....	....	....	....	....	....
Debt forgiveness	2 432	....	....	83	....	5	11	13	16
Other capital transfers	2 440	....	....	....	....	....	....	....	....
Capital transfers, debit	3 400	....	....	....	....	....	....	....	....
General government	3 401	....	....	....	....	....	....	....	....
Debt forgiveness	3 402	....	....	....	....	....	....	....	....
Other capital transfers	3 410	....	....	....	....	....	....	....	....
Other sectors	3 430	....	....	....	....	....	....	....	....
Migrants' transfers	3 431	....	....	....	....	....	....	....	....
Debt forgiveness	3 432	....	....	....	....	....	....	....	....
Other capital transfers	3 440	....	....	....	....	....	....	....	....
Nonproduced nonfinancial assets, credit	2 480	....	....	....	....	....	**30**	....	....
Nonproduced nonfinancial assets, debit	3 480	....	....	....	....	....	....	....	....

Table 2 (Continued). STANDARD PRESENTATION, 2000–2007

(Millions of U.S. dollars)

	Code	2000	2001	2002	2003	2004	2005	2006	2007
FINANCIAL ACCOUNT	4 995	471	1,961	1,449	1,503	−1,809	−161	−7,055	−6,223
A. DIRECT INVESTMENT	4 500	873	2,590	2,207	2,701	5,610	4,801	4,482	10,627
Direct investment abroad	4 505	−3,987	−1,610	−343	−1,606	−1,563	−2,183	−2,876	−3,830
Equity capital	4 510	−3,573	−1,111	310	−588	−507	−763	−1,007	−1,079
Claims on affiliated enterprises	4 515	−3,573	−1,111	310	−588	−507	−763	−1,007	−1,079
Liabilities to affiliated enterprises	4 520	....	....	....	....	....	....	....	....
Reinvested earnings	4 525	−385	−331	−231	−547	−824	−946	−956	−1,777
Other capital	4 530	−28	−168	−421	−472	−232	−475	−912	−974
Claims on affiliated enterprises	4 535	−28	−168	−421	−472	−232	−475	−912	−974
Liabilities to affiliated enterprises	4 540	....	....	....	....	....	....	....	....
Direct investment in Chile	4 555	4,860	4,200	2,550	4,307	7,173	6,984	7,358	14,457
Equity capital	4 560	2,817	3,424	1,309	1,546	1,243	781	1,958	4,693
Claims on direct investors	4 565	....	....	....	....	....	....	....	....
Liabilities to direct investors	4 570	2,817	3,424	1,309	1,546	1,243	781	1,958	4,693
Reinvested earnings	4 575	1,171	1,105	1,367	3,335	5,952	6,539	7,220	9,784
Other capital	4 580	872	−329	−126	−574	−22	−336	−1,820	−20
Claims on direct investors	4 585	....	....	....	....	....	....	....	....
Liabilities to direct investors	4 590	872	−329	−126	−574	−22	−336	−1,820	−20
B. PORTFOLIO INVESTMENT	4 600	639	139	−2,317	−2,645	−3,308	−2,833	−10,074	−15,763
Assets	4 602	766	−1,386	−3,316	−4,699	−4,430	−4,227	−10,851	−15,390
Equity securities	4 610	821	−2,094	−3,272	−4,853	−3,205	−4,025	−3,000	−9,597
Monetary authorities	4 611	....	....	....	....	....	....	....	....
General government	4 612	....	....	....	....	....	....	....	....
Banks	4 613	....	....	....	....	−3	−17	−17	....
Other sectors	4 614	821	−2,094	−3,272	−4,853	−3,202	−4,008	−2,983	−9,597
Debt securities	4 619	−55	708	−44	154	−1,225	−203	−7,851	−5,793
Bonds and notes	4 620	−64	740	−434	−9	−131	−139	−943	−10,737
Monetary authorities	4 621	....	....	....	....	....	....	....	....
General government	4 622	....	....	....	....	....	....	−418	−9,860
Banks	4 623	78	1,209	341	−96	−72	−26	92	−61
Other sectors	4 624	−142	−469	−775	87	−59	−114	−617	−817
Money market instruments	4 630	10	−32	390	163	−1,095	−63	−6,908	4,944
Monetary authorities	4 631	....	....	....	....	....	....	....	....
General government	4 632	....	....	....	....	....	....	−6,756	5,094
Banks	4 633	....	....	22	6	....	−3	3	....
Other sectors	4 634	10	−32	368	157	−1,095	−60	−155	−150
Liabilities	4 652	−127	1,525	999	2,054	1,122	1,394	776	−373
Equity securities	4 660	−427	−217	−320	318	8	1,571	−194	404
Banks	4 663	5	−34	78	74	−58	85	−209	−39
Other sectors	4 664	−432	−183	−399	244	66	1,485	16	443
Debt securities	4 669	300	1,742	1,319	1,736	1,114	−176	970	−777
Bonds and notes	4 670	300	1,742	1,319	1,736	1,114	−176	932	−873
Monetary authorities	4 671	....	....	....	....	....	....	....	....
General government	4 672	....	650	904	999	242	−461	43	−550
Banks	4 673	....	....	−5	−8	700	−207	197	−84
Other sectors	4 674	300	1,092	420	745	172	492	691	−239
Money market instruments	4 680	....	....	....	....	....	....	39	96
Monetary authorities	4 681	....	....	....	....	....	....	3	....
General government	4 682	....	....	....	....	....	....	....	....
Banks	4 683	....	....	....	....	....	....	36	96
Other sectors	4 684	....	....	....	....	....	....	....	....
C. FINANCIAL DERIVATIVES	4 910	2	−86	−124	118	−84	−63	304	511
Monetary authorities	4 911	....	....	....	....	....	....	....	....
General government	4 912	....	....	....	....	....	....	....	....
Banks	4 913	....	....	−4	48	12	239	140	268
Other sectors	4 914	....	....	−120	70	−96	−301	164	243
Assets	4 900	....	....	1,788	1,840	639	1,244	1,501	2,650
Monetary authorities	4 901	....	....	....	....	....	....	....	....
General government	4 902	....	....	....	....	....	....	....	....
Banks	4 903	....	....	1,569	1,614	257	733	1,082	2,075
Other sectors	4 904	....	....	220	227	382	512	419	575
Liabilities	4 905	2	−86	−1,912	−1,722	−723	−1,307	−1,197	−2,139
Monetary authorities	4 906	....	....	....	....	....	....	....	....
General government	4 907	....	....	....	....	....	....	....	....
Banks	4 908	....	....	−1,573	−1,566	−246	−494	−942	−1,807
Other sectors	4 909	....	....	−339	−156	−477	−813	−255	−333

Table 2 (Concluded). STANDARD PRESENTATION, 2000–2007

(Millions of U.S. dollars)

	Code	2000	2001	2002	2003	2004	2005	2006	2007
D. OTHER INVESTMENT	4 700	**−727**	**−1,282**	**1,869**	**972**	**−4,218**	**−356**	**232**	**−4,811**
Assets	4 703	**−2,065**	**−1,326**	**1,141**	**−571**	**−3,389**	**−2,384**	**−3,974**	**−11,628**
Trade credits	4 706	−1,135	−397	685	−996	−1,601	−1,584	−1,379	−2,501
General government	4 707	....	....	....	....	....	....	....	....
of which: Short-term	4 709	....	....	....	....	....	....	....	....
Other sectors	4 710	−1,135	−397	685	−996	−1,601	−1,584	−1,379	−2,501
of which: Short-term	4 712	−1,135	−397	685	−996	−1,601	−1,584	−1,379	−2,501
Loans	4 714	−82	−193	427	44	....	−5	−243	−728
Monetary authorities	4 715	....	....	....	....	....	....	....	....
of which: Short-term	4 718	....	....	....	....	....	....	....	....
General government	4 719	....	....	....	....	....	....	....	....
of which: Short-term	4 721	....	....	....	....	....	....	....	....
Banks	4 722	−82	−193	427	44	....	−3	−223	−725
of which: Short-term	4 724	61	−105	360	112	−111	37	−147	−503
Other sectors	4 725	....	....	....	....	....	−2	−20	−2
of which: Short-term	4 727	....	....	....	....	....	−2	−20	−2
Currency and deposits	4 730	1,503	648	28	441	−1,788	−795	−2,352	−8,400
Monetary authorities	4 731	....	....	....	....	....	....	....	....
General government	4 732	....	....	....	1	....	....	−591	−5,468
Banks	4 733	735	338	208	255	−166	−554	−819	−1,113
Other sectors	4 734	768	310	−180	185	−1,622	−241	−941	−1,819
Other assets	4 736	−2,351	−1,384	....	−60	....	....	....	....
Monetary authorities	4 737	....	....	....	−60	....	....	....	....
of which: Short-term	4 739	....	....	....	....	....	....	....	....
General government	4 740	....	....	....	....	....	....	....	....
of which: Short-term	4 742	....	....	....	....	....	....	....	....
Banks	4 743	....	....	....	....	....	....	....	....
of which: Short-term	4 745	....	....	....	....	....	....	....	....
Other sectors	4 746	−2,351	−1,384	....	....	....	....	....	....
of which: Short-term	4 748	−2,351	−1,384	....	....	....	....	....	....
Liabilities	4 753	**1,338**	**44**	**728**	**1,543**	**−829**	**2,028**	**4,206**	**6,817**
Trade credits	4 756	271	−262	−60	−35	831	437	1,713	1,484
General government	4 757	....	....	....	....	....	−229	−101	−23
of which: Short-term	4 759	....	....	....	....	....	....	....	....
Other sectors	4 760	271	−262	−60	−35	831	665	1,814	1,507
of which: Short-term	4 762	323	−228	78	102	929	795	1,420	1,947
Loans	4 764	1,029	318	777	1,459	−1,576	1,617	2,469	5,341
Monetary authorities	4 765	....	....	....	....	....	....	....	....
of which: Use of Fund credit and loans from the Fund	4 766	....	....	....	....	....	....	....	....
of which: Short-term	4 768	....	....	....	....	....	....	....	....
General government	4 769	−128	−132	−294	−117	−115	−215	48	11
of which: Short-term	4 771	....	....	....	....	....	....	....	....
Banks	4 772	−279	736	1,290	1,485	260	1,302	−12	2,768
of which: Short-term	4 774	168	614	191	1,016	−15	−1,133	647	−987
Other sectors	4 775	1,436	−286	−219	92	−1,721	530	2,433	2,562
of which: Short-term	4 777	1,267	−403	819	765	−290	−214	74	771
Currency and deposits	4 780	1	35	12	121	−91	−26	27	−8
Monetary authorities	4 781	....	....	....	....	....	....	....	....
General government	4 782	....	....	....	....	....	....	....	....
Banks	4 783	1	35	12	121	−91	−26	27	−8
Other sectors	4 784	....	....	....	....	....	....	....	....
Other liabilities	4 786	36	−47	−2	−2	7	1	−3	−1
Monetary authorities	4 787	36	−47	−2	−2	7	1	−3	−1
of which: Short-term	4 789	36	−47	−2	−2	7	1	−3	−1
General government	4 790	....	....	....	....	....	....	....	....
of which: Short-term	4 792	....	....	....	....	....	....	....	....
Banks	4 793	....	....	....	....	....	....	....	....
of which: Short-term	4 795	....	....	....	....	....	....	....	....
Other sectors	4 796	....	....	....	....	....	....	....	....
of which: Short-term	4 798	....	....	....	....	....	....	....	....
E. RESERVE ASSETS	4 802	**−317**	**599**	**−185**	**357**	**191**	**−1,711**	**−1,998**	**3,214**
Monetary gold	4 812	328	....	17	....	....	....	....	....
Special drawing rights	4 811	−7	−5	−5	−5	−5	−4	1	4
Reserve position in the Fund	4 810	67	4	−148	−40	156	228	82	29
Foreign exchange	4 803	−663	550	−53	404	50	−1,924	−2,079	3,217
Other claims	4 813	−41	50	4	−1	−10	−10	−2	−36
NET ERRORS AND OMISSIONS	4 998	**427**	**−861**	**−952**	**−724**	**−270**	**−1,329**	**204**	**−993**

Table 3. INTERNATIONAL INVESTMENT POSITION (End-period stocks), 2000–2007

(Millions of U.S. dollars)

	Code	2000	2001	2002	2003	2004	2005	2006	2007
ASSETS	8 995 C.	**47,007**	**47,245**	**49,839**	**60,998**	**75,975**	**91,898**	**122,566**	**166,378**
Direct investment abroad	8 505	**11,154**	**11,720**	**12,239**	**13,681**	**17,413**	**21,359**	**26,762**	**32,469**
Equity capital and reinvested earnings	8 506	10,139	10,723	10,820	11,790	15,290	18,761	23,252	27,986
Claims on affiliated enterprises	8 507	10,139	10,723	10,820	11,790	15,290	18,761	23,252	27,986
Liabilities to affiliated enterprises	8 508	....	....	....	....	....	....	....	....
Other capital	8 530	1,015	998	1,419	1,891	2,123	2,597	3,510	4,483
Claims on affiliated enterprises	8 535	1,015	998	1,419	1,891	2,123	2,597	3,510	4,483
Liabilities to affiliated enterprises	8 540	....	....	....	....	....	....	....	....
Portfolio investment	8 602	**9,876**	**10,562**	**13,019**	**21,374**	**28,551**	**37,041**	**56,307**	**84,350**
Equity securities	8 610	6,911	7,870	10,682	18,753	24,321	32,741	43,969	65,057
Monetary authorities	8 611	....	....	....	....	....	....	....	....
General government	8 612	....	....	....	....	....	....	....	....
Banks	8 613	....	....	....	....	3	18	36	62
Other sectors	8 614	6,911	7,870	10,682	18,753	24,319	32,724	43,933	64,995
Debt securities	8 619	2,965	2,692	2,337	2,621	4,229	4,300	12,338	19,293
Bonds and notes	8 620	2,894	2,027	2,180	2,559	3,006	3,039	3,813	15,322
Monetary authorities	8 621	....	....	....	....	....	....	....	....
General government	8 622	....	....	....	....	....	....	418	10,889
Banks	8 623	1,990	452	111	206	279	305	237	366
Other sectors	8 624	904	1,575	2,069	2,353	2,727	2,734	3,158	4,068
Money market instruments	8 630	71	666	157	62	1,223	1,261	8,525	3,971
Monetary authorities	8 631	....	....	....	....	....	....	....	....
General government	8 632	....	....	....	....	....	....	6,756	1,967
Banks	8 633	....	29	7	....	....	3	....	....
Other sectors	8 634	71	637	151	61	1,222	1,258	1,769	2,004
Financial derivatives	8 900	**....**	**406**	**268**	**535**	**995**	**1,023**	**779**	**1,419**
Monetary authorities	8 901	....	....	....	....	....	....	....	....
General government	8 902	....	....	....	....	....	....	....	....
Banks	8 903	....	....	183	309	579	782	652	1,274
Other sectors	8 904	....	....	85	225	416	241	128	145
Other investment	8 703	**10,863**	**10,148**	**8,961**	**9,557**	**13,001**	**15,513**	**19,289**	**31,230**
Trade credits	8 706	3,239	3,161	2,475	3,471	5,072	6,656	8,035	10,536
General government	8 707	....	....	....	....	....	....	....	....
of which: Short-term	8 709	....	....	....	....	....	....	....	....
Other sectors	8 710	3,239	3,161	2,475	3,471	5,072	6,656	8,035	10,536
of which: Short-term	8 712	*3,239*	*3,161*	*2,475*	*3,471*	*5,072*	*6,656*	*8,035*	*10,536*
Loans	8 714	954	1,147	720	679	676	681	1,005	1,731
Monetary authorities	8 715	....	....	....	....	....	....	....	....
of which: Short-term	8 718	....	....	....	....	....	....	....	....
General government	8 719	....	....	....	....	....	....	....	....
of which: Short-term	8 721	....	....	....	....	....	....	....	....
Banks	8 722	954	1,147	720	679	676	679	983	1,706
of which: Short-term	8 724	*757*	*861*	*502*	*392*	*501*	*464*	*684*	*1,187*
Other sectors	8 725	....	....	....	....	....	2	22	24
of which: Short-term	8 727	....	....	....	....	....	*2*	*22*	*24*
Currency and deposits	8 730	6,670	5,840	5,766	5,345	7,188	7,824	9,893	18,606
Monetary authorities	8 731	....	....	....	....	....	....	....	....
General government	8 732	....	....	....	....	....	....	591	6,288
Banks	8 733	1,532	1,194	986	725	897	1,451	2,031	3,182
Other sectors	8 734	5,138	4,646	4,780	4,620	6,291	6,373	7,271	9,136
Other assets	8 736	....	....	....	62	65	352	355	358
Monetary authorities	8 737	....	....	....	62	65	244	248	251
of which: Short-term	8 739	....	....	....	....	....	....	....	....
General government	8 740	....	....	....	....	....	108	108	108
of which: Short-term	8 742	....	....	....	....	....	....	....	....
Banks	8 743	....	....	....	....	....	....	....	....
of which: Short-term	8 745	....	....	....	....	....	....	....	....
Other sectors	8 746	....	....	....	....	....	....	....	....
of which: Short-term	8 748	....	....	....	....	....	....	....	....
Reserve assets	8 802	**15,114**	**14,410**	**15,352**	**15,852**	**16,016**	**16,962**	**19,428**	**16,910**
Monetary gold	8 812	18	19	2	3	3	3	4	5
Special drawing rights	8 811	25	29	37	46	53	52	54	53
Reserve position in the Fund	8 810	324	309	491	583	446	188	113	88
Foreign exchange	8 803	14,686	14,041	14,814	15,211	15,495	16,689	19,225	16,695
Other claims	8 813	61	12	8	10	19	30	32	68

Table 3 (Concluded). INTERNATIONAL INVESTMENT POSITION (End-period stocks), 2000–2007

(Millions of U.S. dollars)

	Code	2000	2001	2002	2003	2004	2005	2006	2007
LIABILITIES	8 995 D.	**82,219**	**81,218**	**80,906**	**98,494**	**106,169**	**124,564**	**136,956**	**169,491**
Direct investment in Chile	8 555 ..	**45,753**	**43,482**	**42,311**	**54,082**	**60,540**	**74,196**	**80,501**	**105,558**
Equity capital and reinvested earnings	8 556 ..	40,456	38,534	37,489	49,841	56,319	69,932	78,114	102,391
Claims on direct investors	8 557 ..	....	....	....	....	....	....	....	....
Liabilities to direct investors	8 558 ..	40,456	38,534	37,489	49,841	56,319	69,932	78,114	102,391
Other capital	8 580 ..	5,297	4,948	4,822	4,240	4,221	4,264	2,388	3,168
Claims on direct investors	8 585 ..	....	....	....	....	....	....	....	....
Liabilities to direct investors	8 590 ..	5,297	4,948	4,822	4,240	4,221	4,264	2,388	3,168
Portfolio investment	8 652 ..	**9,187**	**10,121**	**10,527**	**14,632**	**16,192**	**17,985**	**19,943**	**20,218**
Equity securities	8 660 ..	4,701	3,590	2,304	3,974	4,622	6,832	8,172	9,317
Banks	8 663 ..	537	605	548	815	1,057	1,420	1,329	1,326
Other sectors	8 664 ..	4,164	2,985	1,756	3,158	3,565	5,412	6,843	7,991
Debt securities	8 669 ..	4,486	6,532	8,223	10,658	11,571	11,153	11,771	10,901
Bonds and notes	8 670 ..	4,486	6,532	8,223	10,658	11,571	11,153	11,733	10,766
Monetary authorities	8 671 ..	....	....	....	....	....	....	....	....
General government	8 672 ..	481	1,167	2,275	3,520	3,667	3,206	3,078	2,519
Banks	8 673 ..	593	620	605	650	1,335	1,108	1,315	1,232
Other sectors	8 674 ..	3,413	4,745	5,343	6,489	6,569	6,840	7,339	7,015
Money market instruments	8 680 ..	....	....	....	....	....	....	39	134
Monetary authorities	8 681 ..	....	....	....	....	....	....	3	3
General government	8 682 ..	....	....	....	....	....	....	....	....
Banks	8 683 ..	....	....	....	....	....	....	36	132
Other sectors	8 684 ..	....	....	....	....	....	....	....	....
Financial derivatives	8 905 ..	**....**	**363**	**102**	**222**	**695**	**954**	**938**	**1,755**
Monetary authorities	8 906 ..	....	....	....	....	....	....	....	....
General government	8 907 ..	....	....	....	....	....	....	....	....
Banks	8 908 ..	....	....	....	....	....	....	....	....
Other sectors	8 909 ..	....	....	....	....	....	....	....	....
Other investment	8 753 ..	**27,278**	**27,252**	**27,966**	**29,558**	**28,741**	**31,429**	**35,574**	**41,960**
Trade credits	8 756 ..	5,629	5,360	5,305	5,275	6,108	6,774	8,589	10,096
General government	8 757 ..	....	....	....	....	....	....	....	....
of which: Short-term	8 759 ..	....	....	....	....	....	....	....	....
Other sectors	8 760 ..	5,629	5,360	5,305	5,275	6,108	6,774	8,589	10,096
of which: Short-term	8 762 ..	*3,411*	*3,184*	*3,262*	*3,364*	*4,293*	*5,088*	*6,508*	*8,454*
Loans	8 764 ..	21,582	21,836	22,595	24,100	22,533	24,415	26,733	31,619
Monetary authorities	8 765 ..	2	2	1	1	1	....	....	....
of which: Use of Fund credit and loans from the Fund	8 766 ..	....	....	....	....	....	....	....	....
of which: Short-term	8 768 ..	....	....	....	....	....	....	....	....
General government	8 769 ..	1,920	1,742	1,467	1,392	1,287	1,068	1,127	1,152
of which: Short-term	8 771 ..	....	....	....	....	....	....	....	....
Banks	8 772 ..	1,151	1,885	3,175	4,660	4,915	6,230	6,220	9,069
of which: Short-term	8 774 ..	*428*	*1,043*	*1,234*	*2,250*	*2,236*	*1,104*	*1,752*	*765*
Other sectors	8 775 ..	18,510	18,208	17,951	18,047	16,330	17,117	19,385	21,398
of which: Short-term	8 777 ..	*1,866*	*876*	*668*	*1,219*	*823*	*612*	*682*	*1,452*
Currency and deposits	8 780 ..	7	42	55	175	85	223	239	232
Monetary authorities	8 781 ..	....	....	....	....	....	165	154	155
General government	8 782 ..	....	....	....	....	....	....	....	....
Banks	8 783 ..	7	42	55	175	85	58	85	77
Other sectors	8 784 ..	....	....	....	....	....	....	....	....
Other liabilities	8 786 ..	60	13	11	9	16	16	14	13
Monetary authorities	8 787 ..	60	13	11	9	16	16	14	13
of which: Short-term	8 789 ..	*60*	*13*	*11*	*9*	*16*	*16*	*14*	*13*
General government	8 790 ..	....	....	....	....	....	....	....	....
of which: Short-term	8 792 ..	....	....	....	....	....	....	....	....
Banks	8 793 ..	....	....	....	....	....	....	....	....
of which: Short-term	8 795 ..	....	....	....	....	....	....	....	....
Other sectors	8 796 ..	....	....	....	....	....	....	....	....
of which: Short-term	8 798 ..	....	....	....	....	....	....	....	....
NET INTERNATIONAL INVESTMENT POSITION	8 995 ..	**−35,212**	**−33,973**	**−31,067**	**−37,496**	**−30,194**	**−32,665**	**−14,391**	**−3,113**
Conversion rates: Chilean pesos per U.S. dollar (end of period)	0 102 ..	572.68	656.20	712.38	599.42	559.83	514.21	534.43	495.82

Table 1. ANALYTIC PRESENTATION, 2000–2007

(Millions of U.S. dollars)

	Code	2000	2001	2002	2003	2004	2005	2006	2007
A. Current Account[1]............................	4 993 Z.	**20,518**	**17,401**	**35,422**	**45,875**	**68,659**	**160,818**	**253,268**	**371,833**
Goods: exports f.o.b............................	2 100 ..	249,131	266,075	325,651	438,270	593,393	762,484	969,682	1,220,000
Goods: imports f.o.b............................	3 100 ..	−214,657	−232,058	−281,484	−393,618	−534,410	−628,295	−751,936	−904,618
Balance on Goods............................	4 100 ..	*34,474*	*34,017*	*44,167*	*44,652*	*58,982*	*134,189*	*217,746*	*315,381*
Services: credit............................	2 200 ..	30,430	33,334	39,745	46,734	62,434	74,404	91,999	122,206
Services: debit............................	3 200 ..	−36,031	−39,267	−46,528	−55,306	−72,133	−83,795	−100,833	−130,111
Balance on Goods and Services............................	4 991 ..	*28,874*	*28,084*	*37,383*	*36,079*	*49,284*	*124,798*	*208,912*	*307,477*
Income: credit............................	2 300 ..	12,550	9,388	8,344	16,095	20,544	38,959	54,642	83,030
Income: debit............................	3 300 ..	−27,216	−28,563	−23,289	−23,933	−24,067	−28,324	−39,485	−57,342
Balance on Goods, Services, and Income............................	4 992 ..	*14,207*	*8,909*	*22,438*	*28,241*	*45,761*	*135,433*	*224,069*	*333,165*
Current transfers: credit............................	2 379 Z.	6,861	9,125	13,795	18,482	24,326	27,735	31,578	42,646
Current transfers: debit............................	3 379 ..	−550	−633	−811	−848	−1,428	−2,349	−2,378	−3,978
B. Capital Account[1]............................	4 994 Z.	**−35**	**−54**	**−50**	**−48**	**−69**	**4,102**	**4,020**	**3,099**
Capital account: credit............................	2 994 Z.	. . . .	. . . .	. . . .	. . . .	. . . .	4,155	4,102	3,315
Capital account: debit............................	3 994 ..	−35	−54	−50	−48	−69	−53	−82	−216
Total, Groups A Plus B............................	4 981 ..	*20,483*	*17,347*	*35,372*	*45,827*	*68,590*	*164,920*	*257,288*	*374,932*
C. Financial Account[1]............................	4 995 W.	**1,958**	**34,832**	**32,341**	**52,774**	**110,729**	**58,862**	**2,642**	**70,410**
Direct investment abroad............................	4 505 ..	−916	−6,884	−2,518	152	−1,805	−11,306	−21,160	−16,995
Direct investment in China, P.R.: Mainland............................	4 555 Z.	38,399	44,241	49,308	47,077	54,936	79,127	78,095	138,413
Portfolio investment assets............................	4 602 ..	−11,307	−20,654	−12,095	2,983	6,486	−26,157	−110,419	−2,324
Equity securities............................	4 610 ..	. . . .	32	. . . .	. . . .	. . . .	. . . .	−1,454	−15,189
Debt securities............................	4 619 ..	−11,307	−20,686	−12,095	2,983	6,486	−26,157	−108,965	12,865
Portfolio investment liabilities............................	4 652 Z.	7,317	1,249	1,752	8,444	13,203	21,224	42,861	20,996
Equity securities............................	4 660 ..	6,912	849	2,249	7,729	10,923	20,346	42,861	18,510
Debt securities............................	4 669 Z.	405	400	−497	715	2,280	878	. . . .	2,486
Financial derivatives............................	4 910 ..	. . . .	. . . .	. . . .	. . . .	. . . .	. . . .	. . . .	. . . .
Financial derivatives assets............................	4 900 ..	. . . .	. . . .	. . . .	. . . .	. . . .	. . . .	. . . .	. . . .
Financial derivatives liabilities............................	4 905 ..	. . . .	. . . .	. . . .	. . . .	. . . .	. . . .	. . . .	. . . .
Other investment assets............................	4 703 ..	−43,864	20,813	−3,077	−17,922	1,980	−48,947	−31,853	−151,486
Monetary authorities............................	4 701 ..	−7,261	−5,387	. . . .	. . . .	. . . .	−4,354	−3,572	−113,980
General government............................	4 704 ..	. . . .	. . . .	. . . .	. . . .	. . . .	. . . .	. . . .	. . . .
Banks............................	4 705 ..	−21,430	16,800	−10,258	−15,733	2,959	−23,656	3,049	−23,360
Other sectors............................	4 728 ..	−15,173	9,400	7,181	−2,189	−979	−20,938	−31,331	−14,146
Other investment liabilities............................	4 753 W.	12,329	−3,933	−1,029	12,040	35,928	44,921	45,118	81,806
Monetary authorities............................	4 753 WA	. . . .	. . . .	. . . .	. . . .	. . . .	1,778	4,101	1,795
General government............................	4 753 ZB	3,153	1,124	40	−2,758	999	−360	483	−550
Banks............................	4 753 ZC	−8,281	−1,305	−1,725	10,269	13,375	9,186	25,279	6,853
Other sectors............................	4 753 ZD	17,457	−3,752	655	4,529	21,554	34,318	15,255	73,709
Total, Groups A Through C............................	4 983 ..	*22,441*	*52,179*	*67,713*	*98,601*	*179,319*	*223,782*	*259,930*	*445,342*
D. Net Errors and Omissions............................	4 998 ..	**−11,748**	**−4,732**	**7,504**	**17,985**	**26,834**	**−16,441**	**−13,075**	**16,349**
Total, Groups A Through D............................	4 984 ..	*10,693*	*47,447*	*75,217*	*116,586*	*206,153*	*207,342*	*246,855*	*461,691*
E. Reserves and Related Items............................	4 802 A.	**−10,693**	**−47,447**	**−75,217**	**−116,586**	**−206,153**	**−207,342**	**−246,855**	**−461,691**
Reserve assets............................	4 802 ..	−10,693	−47,447	−75,217	−116,586	−206,153	−207,342	−246,855	−461,691
Use of Fund credit and loans............................	4 766 ..	. . . .	. . . .	. . . .	. . . .	. . . .	. . . .	. . . .	. . . .
Exceptional financing............................	4 920 ..	. . . .	. . . .	. . . .	. . . .	. . . .	. . . .	. . . .	. . . .
Conversion rates: yuan per U.S. dollar............................	0 101 ..	**8.2785**	**8.2771**	**8.2770**	**8.2770**	**8.2768**	**8.1943**	**7.9734**	**7.6075**

[1] Excludes components that have been classified in the categories of Group E.

Table 2. STANDARD PRESENTATION, 2000–2007

(Millions of U.S. dollars)

	Code	2000	2001	2002	2003	2004	2005	2006	2007
CURRENT ACCOUNT	4 993	**20,518**	**17,401**	**35,422**	**45,875**	**68,659**	**160,818**	**253,268**	**371,833**
A. GOODS	4 100	**34,474**	**34,017**	**44,167**	**44,652**	**58,982**	**134,189**	**217,746**	**315,381**
Credit	2 100	**249,131**	**266,075**	**325,651**	**438,270**	**593,393**	**762,484**	**969,682**	**1,220,000**
General merchandise: exports f.o.b.	2 110	111,178	118,210	145,202	195,810	264,314	344,229	456,878	597,127
Goods for processing: exports f.o.b.	2 150	137,674	147,477	179,959	241,869	328,015	416,509	510,399	617,700
Repairs on goods	2 160	125	135	232	271	432	584	788	2,943
Goods procured in ports by carriers	2 170	154	253	258	318	632	1,162	1,618	2,229
Nonmonetary gold	2 180	....	....	....	....	....	....	....	....
Debit	3 100	**−214,657**	**−232,058**	**−281,484**	**−393,618**	**−534,410**	**−628,295**	**−751,936**	**−904,618**
General merchandise: imports f.o.b.	3 110	−124,075	−140,329	−162,610	−235,619	−319,651	−363,093	−441,216	−549,026
Goods for processing: imports f.o.b.	3 150	−89,522	−90,837	−117,769	−156,673	−213,149	−263,078	−308,129	−352,009
Repairs on goods	3 160	−238	−190	−235	−240	−160	−216	−203	−171
Goods procured in ports by carriers	3 170	−822	−702	−871	−1,085	−1,450	−1,908	−2,388	−3,412
Nonmonetary gold	3 180	....	....	....	....	....	....	....	....
B. SERVICES	4 200	**−5,600**	**−5,933**	**−6,783**	**−8,573**	**−9,699**	**−9,391**	**−8,834**	**−7,905**
Total credit	2 200	*30,430*	*33,334*	*39,745*	*46,734*	*62,434*	*74,404*	*91,999*	*122,206*
Total debit	3 200	*−36,031*	*−39,267*	*−46,528*	*−55,306*	*−72,133*	*−83,795*	*−100,833*	*−130,111*
Transportation services, credit	2 205	**3,671**	**4,635**	**5,720**	**7,906**	**12,067**	**15,427**	**21,015**	**31,324**
Passenger	2 850	*1,087*	*1,214*	*1,357*	*1,301*	*2,016*	*2,546*	*3,183*	*3,893*
Freight	2 851	*1,826*	*2,358*	*3,093*	*4,952*	*8,118*	*10,680*	*15,098*	*24,085*
Other	2 852	*757*	*1,063*	*1,271*	*1,653*	*1,933*	*2,200*	*2,734*	*3,346*
Sea transport, passenger	2 207	111	68	40	47	39	41	24	26
Sea transport, freight	2 208	1,440	1,944	2,476	3,973	6,582	8,819	12,502	19,836
Sea transport, other	2 209	....	....	....	....	....	....	....	....
Air transport, passenger	2 211	775	969	1,114	1,078	1,760	2,230	2,796	3,449
Air transport, freight	2 212	268	299	539	871	1,322	1,651	2,321	3,832
Air transport, other	2 213	....	....	....	....	....	....	....	....
Other transport, passenger	2 215	201	177	203	177	218	274	363	417
Other transport, freight	2 216	119	115	78	108	213	210	276	417
Other transport, other	2 217	757	1,063	1,271	1,653	1,933	2,200	2,734	3,346
Transportation services, debit	3 205	**−10,396**	**−11,325**	**−13,612**	**−18,233**	**−24,544**	**−28,448**	**−34,369**	**−43,271**
Passenger	3 850	*−1,055*	*−1,083*	*−1,361*	*−1,529*	*−2,211*	*−2,956*	*−3,920*	*−3,478*
Freight	3 851	*−8,705*	*−9,378*	*−11,472*	*−15,938*	*−21,270*	*−24,436*	*−29,382*	*−38,202*
Other	3 852	*−636*	*−864*	*−779*	*−765*	*−1,063*	*−1,056*	*−1,066*	*−1,591*
Sea transport, passenger	3 207	−149	−51	−14	−11	−13	−8	−11	−9
Sea transport, freight	3 208	−5,969	−6,844	−8,412	−13,121	−18,561	−21,745	−25,853	−35,132
Sea transport, other	3 209	....	....	....	....	....	....	....	....
Air transport, passenger	3 211	−836	−969	−1,308	−1,490	−2,165	−2,909	−3,877	−3,421
Air transport, freight	3 212	−750	−1,397	−2,190	−2,167	−2,100	−1,865	−2,250	−2,403
Air transport, other	3 213	....	....	....	....	....	....	....	....
Other transport, passenger	3 215	−70	−63	−39	−28	−34	−39	−32	−48
Other transport, freight	3 216	−1,986	−1,137	−870	−651	−609	−826	−1,279	−667
Other transport, other	3 217	−636	−864	−779	−765	−1,063	−1,056	−1,066	−1,591
Travel, credit	2 236	**16,231**	**17,792**	**20,385**	**17,406**	**25,739**	**29,296**	**33,949**	**37,233**
Business travel	2 237	....	....	....	....	....	....	....	....
Personal travel	2 240	....	....	....	....	....	....	....	....
Travel, debit	3 236	**−13,114**	**−13,909**	**−15,398**	**−15,187**	**−19,149**	**−21,759**	**−24,322**	**−29,786**
Business travel	3 237	....	....	....	....	....	....	....	....
Personal travel	3 240	....	....	....	....	....	....	....	....
Other services, credit	2 200 BA	**10,529**	**10,907**	**13,639**	**21,421**	**24,628**	**29,682**	**37,035**	**53,650**
Communications	2 245	1,345	271	550	638	440	485	738	1,175
Construction	2 249	602	830	1,246	1,290	1,467	2,593	2,753	5,377
Insurance	2 253	108	227	209	313	381	549	548	904
Financial	2 260	78	99	51	152	94	145	145	230
Computer and information	2 262	356	461	638	1,102	1,637	1,840	2,958	4,345
Royalties and licence fees	2 266	80	110	133	107	236	157	205	343
Other business services	2 268	7,663	8,448	10,419	17,427	19,952	23,283	28,973	40,408
Personal, cultural, and recreational	2 287	11	28	30	33	41	134	137	316
Government, n.i.e.	2 291	285	433	363	359	378	495	579	552
Other services, debit	3 200 BA	**−12,521**	**−14,033**	**−17,518**	**−21,886**	**−28,440**	**−33,589**	**−42,142**	**−57,054**
Communications	3 245	−242	−326	−470	−427	−472	−603	−764	−1,082
Construction	3 249	−994	−847	−964	−1,183	−1,339	−1,619	−2,050	−2,910
Insurance	3 253	−2,471	−2,711	−3,246	−4,564	−6,124	−7,200	−8,831	−10,664
Financial	3 260	−97	−77	−90	−233	−138	−159	−891	−557
Computer and information	3 262	−265	−345	−1,133	−1,036	−1,253	−1,623	−1,739	−2,208
Royalties and licence fees	3 266	−1,281	−1,938	−3,114	−3,548	−4,497	−5,321	−6,634	−8,192
Other business services	3 268	−6,959	−7,504	−7,957	−10,371	−13,911	−16,286	−20,605	−30,431
Personal, cultural, and recreational	3 287	−37	−50	−96	−70	−176	−154	−121	−154
Government, n.i.e.	3 291	−173	−235	−448	−454	−531	−623	−506	−857

Table 2 (Continued). STANDARD PRESENTATION, 2000–2007

(Millions of U.S. dollars)

	Code	2000	2001	2002	2003	2004	2005	2006	2007
C. INCOME	4 300	−14,666	−19,175	−14,946	−7,838	−3,523	10,635	15,156	25,688
Total credit	2 300	*12,550*	*9,388*	*8,344*	*16,095*	*20,544*	*38,959*	*54,642*	*83,030*
Total debit	3 300	*−27,216*	*−28,563*	*−23,289*	*−23,933*	*−24,067*	*−28,324*	*−39,485*	*−57,342*
Compensation of employees, credit	2 310	202	297	674	1,283	2,014	3,337	4,319	6,833
Compensation of employees, debit	3 310	−679	−852	−950	−1,120	−1,382	−1,817	−2,330	−2,493
Investment income, credit	2 320	12,348	9,091	7,670	14,812	18,530	35,622	50,322	76,197
Direct investment income	2 330	62	146	126	100	218	3,385	7,831	9,663
Dividends and distributed branch profits	2 332	62	146	126	100	218	462	1,181	3,591
Reinvested earnings and undistributed branch profits	2 333	....	....	....	....	....	2,924	6,650	6,072
Income on debt (interest)	2 334	....	....	....	....	....	....	....	....
Portfolio investment income	2 339	173	173	131	369	831	2,758	2,849	4,457
Income on equity	2 340	169	168	117	349	749	1,341	1,763	903
Income on bonds and notes	2 350	....	....	....	....	....	....	....	....
Income on money market instruments	2 360	....	....	....	....	....	....	....	....
Other investment income	2 370	12,113	8,772	7,413	14,342	17,480	29,479	39,642	62,077
Investment income, debit	3 320	−26,537	−27,711	−22,339	−22,813	−22,685	−26,507	−37,155	−54,849
Direct investment income	3 330	−20,198	−21,489	−17,823	−17,353	−17,415	−21,040	−29,236	−43,711
Dividends and distributed branch profits	3 332	−4,176	−6,808	−8,418	−10,158	−14,031	−18,928	−24,411	−39,514
Reinvested earnings and undistributed branch profits	3 333	−16,022	−14,681	−9,405	−7,195	−3,000	−1,609	−4,191	−3,300
Income on debt (interest)	3 334	....	....	....	....	−383	−503	−634	−897
Portfolio investment income	3 339	−712	−714	−457	....	−225	−424	−162	−528
Income on equity	3 340	−365	....	....	....	....	....	....	....
Income on bonds and notes	3 350	....	....	....	....	....	....	....	....
Income on money market instruments	3 360	....	....	....	....	....	....	....	....
Other investment income	3 370	−5,626	−5,508	−4,059	−5,460	−5,045	−5,042	−7,757	−10,610
D. CURRENT TRANSFERS	4 379	6,311	8,492	12,984	17,634	22,898	25,385	29,199	38,668
Credit	2 379	6,861	9,125	13,795	18,482	24,326	27,735	31,578	42,646
General government	2 380	147	138	86	114	98	49	65	35
Other sectors	2 390	6,713	8,987	13,709	18,369	24,229	27,686	31,513	42,611
Workers' remittances	2 391	556	912	1,679	3,343	4,627	5,495	6,830	10,679
Other current transfers	2 392	6,157	8,075	12,030	15,026	19,602	22,191	24,682	31,931
Debit	3 379	−550	−633	−811	−848	−1,428	−2,349	−2,378	−3,978
General government	3 380	−94	−205	−160	−106	−187	−225	−211	−201
Other sectors	3 390	−456	−428	−651	−743	−1,242	−2,124	−2,167	−3,777
Workers' remittances	3 391	−75	−84	−223	−477	−616	−732	−695	−1,879
Other current transfers	3 392	−381	−344	−428	−266	−626	−1,392	−1,472	−1,898
CAPITAL AND FINANCIAL ACCOUNT	4 996	−8,770	−12,669	−42,926	−63,860	−95,493	−144,378	−240,193	−388,182
CAPITAL ACCOUNT	4 994	−35	−54	−50	−48	−69	4,102	4,020	3,099
Total credit	2 994	....	....	....	....	....	*4,155*	*4,102*	*3,315*
Total debit	3 994	*−35*	*−54*	*−50*	*−48*	*−69*	*−53*	*−82*	*−216*
Capital transfers, credit	2 400	....	....	....	....	....	4,155	4,102	3,315
General government	2 401	....	....	....	....	....	....	....	....
Debt forgiveness	2 402	....	....	....	....	....	....	....	....
Other capital transfers	2 410	....	....	....	....	....	....	....	....
Other sectors	2 430	....	....	....	....	....	4,155	4,102	3,315
Migrants' transfers	2 431	....	....	....	....	....	....	....	....
Debt forgiveness	2 432	....	....	....	....	....	....	....	....
Other capital transfers	2 440	....	....	....	....	....	....	....	....
Capital transfers, debit	3 400	−35	−54	−50	−48	−69	−53	−82	−216
General government	3 401	....	....	....	....	....	....	....	....
Debt forgiveness	3 402	....	....	....	....	....	....	....	....
Other capital transfers	3 410	....	....	....	....	....	....	....	....
Other sectors	3 430	−35	−54	−50	−48	−69	−53	−82	−216
Migrants' transfers	3 431	−35	−54	−50	−48	−69	−53	....	....
Debt forgiveness	3 432	....	....	....	....	....	....	....	....
Other capital transfers	3 440	....	....	....	....	....	....	....	....
Nonproduced nonfinancial assets, credit	2 480	....	....	....	....	....	....	....	....
Nonproduced nonfinancial assets, debit	3 480	....	....	....	....	....	....	....	....

Table 2 (Continued). STANDARD PRESENTATION, 2000–2007

(Millions of U.S. dollars)

	Code	2000	2001	2002	2003	2004	2005	2006	2007
FINANCIAL ACCOUNT	4 995	−8,735	−12,615	−42,876	−63,812	−95,424	−148,480	−244,213	−391,281
A. DIRECT INVESTMENT	4 500	37,483	37,357	46,790	47,229	53,131	67,821	56,935	121,418
Direct investment abroad	4 505	−916	−6,884	−2,518	152	−1,805	−11,306	−21,160	−16,995
Equity capital	4 510	−587	−6,868	−896	−817	−1,540	−4,238	−5,170	−6,748
Claims on affiliated enterprises	4 515	−640	−6,973	−1,044	−924	−1,659	−4,553	−5,424	−7,652
Liabilities to affiliated enterprises	4 520	53	105	148	106	119	315	254	904
Reinvested earnings	4 525	....	....	....	....	....	−2,924	−6,650	−6,072
Other capital	4 530	−329	−16	−1,622	970	−265	−4,144	−9,340	−4,174
Claims on affiliated enterprises	4 535	−1,599	−118	−1,805	−926	−422	−4,394	−9,803	−5,200
Liabilities to affiliated enterprises	4 540	1,270	102	182	1,896	157	250	463	1,026
Direct investment in China, P.R.: Mainland	4 555	38,399	44,241	49,308	47,077	54,936	79,127	78,095	138,413
Equity capital	4 560	20,841	27,361	36,051	37,397	51,764	67,572	62,242	75,063
Claims on direct investors	4 565	−872	−1,180	−1,226	−3,055	−2,267	−2,831	−3,035	−4,248
Liabilities to direct investors	4 570	21,713	28,541	37,277	40,452	54,032	70,403	65,277	79,311
Reinvested earnings	4 575	16,022	14,681	9,405	7,195	3,000	1,609	4,191	3,300
Other capital	4 580	1,536	2,199	3,852	2,485	172	9,946	11,662	60,050
Claims on direct investors	4 585	−1,501	−1,425	−2,210	−3,373	−3,426	−3,548	−5,437	−6,963
Liabilities to direct investors	4 590	3,037	3,624	6,061	5,858	3,598	13,494	17,099	67,013
B. PORTFOLIO INVESTMENT	4 600	−3,991	−19,405	−10,342	11,427	19,690	−4,933	−67,558	18,672
Assets	4 602	−11,307	−20,654	−12,095	2,983	6,486	−26,157	−110,419	−2,324
Equity securities	4 610	....	32	....	....	....	....	−1,454	−15,189
Monetary authorities	4 611	....	....	....	....	....	....	....	....
General government	4 612	....	....	....	....	....	....	....	....
Banks	4 613	....	32	....	....	....	....	....	....
Other sectors	4 614	....	....	....	....	....	....	−1,454	−15,189
Debt securities	4 619	−11,307	−20,686	−12,095	2,983	6,486	−26,157	−108,965	12,865
Bonds and notes	4 620	−11,307	−5,588	−3,273	2,983	6,486	−25,482	−106,737	10,591
Monetary authorities	4 621	....	....	....	....	....	....	....	....
General government	4 622	....	....	....	....	....	....	....	....
Banks	4 623	−11,360	−5,584	−3,263	2,973	6,528	−25,032	−53,234	21,543
Other sectors	4 624	53	−4	−11	10	−41	−450	−53,503	−10,952
Money market instruments	4 630	....	−15,098	−8,821	....	....	−675	−2,228	2,274
Monetary authorities	4 631	....	....	....	....	....	....	....	....
General government	4 632	....	....	....	....	....	....	....	....
Banks	4 633	....	−15,098	−8,821	....	....	....	−2,228	2,274
Other sectors	4 634	....	....	....	....	....	....	....	....
Liabilities	4 652	7,317	1,249	1,752	8,444	13,203	21,224	42,861	20,996
Equity securities	4 660	6,912	849	2,249	7,729	10,923	20,346	42,861	18,510
Banks	4 663	....	....	51	141	558	....	....	....
Other sectors	4 664	6,912	849	2,198	7,588	10,365	20,346	....	....
Debt securities	4 669	405	400	−497	715	2,280	878	....	2,486
Bonds and notes	4 670	405	400	−505	717	2,283	567	....	2,486
Monetary authorities	4 671	....	....	....	....	....	....	....	....
General government	4 672	276	786	....	1,450	1,732	....	....	....
Banks	4 673	129	−226	−281	−506	519	548	....	989
Other sectors	4 674	....	−160	−224	−227	33	19	....	1,497
Money market instruments	4 680	....	....	8	−2	−3	311	....	....
Monetary authorities	4 681	....	....	....	....	....	....	....	....
General government	4 682	....	....	....	....	....	....	....	....
Banks	4 683	....	....	....	....	....	−3	....	....
Other sectors	4 684	....	....	8	−2	−3	314	....	....
C. FINANCIAL DERIVATIVES	4 910	....	....	....	....	....	....	....	....
Monetary authorities	4 911	....	....	....	....	....	....	....	....
General government	4 912	....	....	....	....	....	....	....	....
Banks	4 913	....	....	....	....	....	....	....	....
Other sectors	4 914	....	....	....	....	....	....	....	....
Assets	4 900	....	....	....	....	....	....	....	....
Monetary authorities	4 901	....	....	....	....	....	....	....	....
General government	4 902	....	....	....	....	....	....	....	....
Banks	4 903	....	....	....	....	....	....	....	....
Other sectors	4 904	....	....	....	....	....	....	....	....
Liabilities	4 905	....	....	....	....	....	....	....	....
Monetary authorities	4 906	....	....	....	....	....	....	....	....
General government	4 907	....	....	....	....	....	....	....	....
Banks	4 908	....	....	....	....	....	....	....	....
Other sectors	4 909	....	....	....	....	....	....	....	....

Table 2 (Concluded). STANDARD PRESENTATION, 2000–2007

(Millions of U.S. dollars)

	Code	2000	2001	2002	2003	2004	2005	2006	2007
D. OTHER INVESTMENT	4 700	−31,535	16,880	−4,106	−5,882	37,908	−4,026	13,265	−69,680
Assets	4 703	−43,864	20,813	−3,077	−17,922	1,980	−48,947	−31,853	−151,486
Trade credits	4 706	−12,960	702	1,098	−1,465	−15,897	−22,905	−26,148	−23,800
General government	4 707	....	....	....	....	....	....	....	....
of which: Short-term	4 709	....	....	....	....	....	....	....	....
Other sectors	4 710	−12,960	702	1,098	−1,465	−15,897	−22,905	−26,148	−23,800
of which: Short-term	4 712	−12,960	702	1,098	−1,465	−14,561	−21,989	−24,318	−22,134
Loans	4 714	−18,430	15,314	−5,391	13,927	−9,658	−12,993	4,928	−20,806
Monetary authorities	4 715	....	....	....	....	....	....	....	....
of which: Short-term	4 718	....	....	....	....	....	....	....	....
General government	4 719	....	....	....	....	....	....	....	....
of which: Short-term	4 721	....	....	....	....	....	....	....	....
Banks	4 722	−18,293	15,535	−5,524	20,822	−9,070	−13,464	5,148	−20,412
of which: Short-term	4 724	−18,293	15,712	−5,495	21,515	−8,013	−11,959	8,095	−16,293
Other sectors	4 725	−137	−221	133	−6,895	−588	471	−220	−394
of which: Short-term	4 727	−137	−221	133	−6,895	−588	471	−220	−394
Currency and deposits	4 730	−6,049	−3,214	−2,486	−6,552	20,207	−10,317	−9,904	−2,382
Monetary authorities	4 731	....	....	....	....	....	....	....	....
General government	4 732	....	....	....	....	....	....	....	....
Banks	4 733	−5,870	−2,395	−2,580	−6,125	20,182	−10,192	−2,099	−2,948
Other sectors	4 734	−179	−819	94	−427	25	−126	−7,806	566
Other assets	4 736	−6,425	8,011	3,703	−23,832	7,328	−2,732	−728	−104,499
Monetary authorities	4 737	−7,261	−5,387	....	....	....	−4,354	−3,572	−113,980
of which: Short-term	4 739	....	....	....	....	....	....	....	−113,980
General government	4 740	....	....	....	....	....	....	....	....
of which: Short-term	4 742	....	....	....	....	....	....	....	....
Banks	4 743	2,733	3,660	−2,154	−30,430	−8,153	....	....	....
of which: Short-term	4 745	2,733	3,660	−2,154	14,570	−8,153	....	....	....
Other sectors	4 746	−1,897	9,738	5,857	6,598	15,481	1,622	2,844	9,481
of which: Short-term	4 748	−1,897	9,738	5,857	6,598	15,481	1,622	2,844	9,481
Liabilities	4 753	12,329	−3,933	−1,029	12,040	35,928	44,921	45,118	81,806
Trade credits	4 756	18,232	−2,442	2,849	4,720	18,595	25,412	13,227	29,100
General government	4 757	....	....	....	....	....	....	....	....
of which: Short-term	4 759	....	....	....	....	....	....	....	....
Other sectors	4 760	18,232	−2,442	2,849	4,720	18,595	25,412	13,227	29,100
of which: Short-term	4 762	18,232	−2,442	2,849	4,720	15,733	24,243	12,301	27,063
Loans	4 764	−2,391	−1,489	−4,140	6,614	13,753	2,924	11,038	17,296
Monetary authorities	4 765	....	....	....	....	....	....	....	....
of which: Use of Fund credit and loans from the Fund	4 766	....	....	....	....	....	....	....	....
of which: Short-term	4 768	....	....	....	....	....	....	....	....
General government	4 769	3,153	1,124	40	−2,758	986	−360	483	−550
of which: Short-term	4 771	....	....	98	10	....	....	....	17
Banks	4 772	−3,712	−1,543	−1,894	9,684	9,828	2,353	8,429	14,975
of which: Short-term	4 774	−363	−314	−785	11,965	6,862	809	5,954	8,927
Other sectors	4 775	−1,832	−1,070	−2,286	−312	2,939	931	2,126	2,871
of which: Short-term	4 777	−172	23	1,079	−5	2,076	670	990	1,364
Currency and deposits	4 780	−54	492	287	742	1,561	13,366	10,710	34,317
Monetary authorities	4 781	....	....	....	....	....	1,371	188	689
General government	4 782	....	....	....	....	12	....	....	....
Banks	4 783	−54	490	284	738	1,547	3,999	10,522	−8,137
Other sectors	4 784	....	2	3	4	1	7,995	....	41,765
Other liabilities	4 786	−3,459	−494	−26	−37	2,019	3,220	10,143	1,093
Monetary authorities	4 787	....	....	....	....	....	407	3,913	1,105
of which: Short-term	4 789	....	....	....	....	....	....	....	....
General government	4 790	....	....	....	....	....	....	....	....
of which: Short-term	4 792	....	....	....	....	....	....	....	....
Banks	4 793	−4,516	−252	−114	−153	2,000	2,834	6,328	15
of which: Short-term	4 795	−4,366	−4	−100	−148	2,018	2,745	6,260	−8
Other sectors	4 796	1,057	−242	88	116	19	−20	−98	−27
of which: Short-term	4 798	431	616	67	1,127	−32	14	20	−32
E. RESERVE ASSETS	4 802	−10,693	−47,447	−75,217	−116,586	−206,153	−207,342	−246,855	−461,691
Monetary gold	4 812	....	....	....	....	....	....	....	....
Special drawing rights	4 811	−96	−82	−74	−11	−92	−107	245	−68
Reserve position in the Fund	4 810	301	−774	−901	269	619	1,705	371	282
Foreign exchange	4 803	−10,898	−46,591	−74,242	−116,844	−206,681	−208,940	−247,472	−461,905
Other claims	4 813	....	....	....	....	....	....	....	....
NET ERRORS AND OMISSIONS	4 998	−11,748	−4,732	7,504	17,985	26,834	−16,441	−13,075	16,349

Table 3. INTERNATIONAL INVESTMENT POSITION (End-period stocks), 2000–2007

(Millions of U.S. dollars)

	Code	2000	2001	2002	2003	2004	2005	2006	2007
ASSETS	8 995 C.	....	....	....	....	929,896	1,222,638	1,644,204	2,288,079
Direct investment abroad	8 505 ..	....	....	....	....	52,704	64,493	90,630	107,625
Equity capital and reinvested earnings	8 506 ..	....	....	....	....	....	....	....	....
Claims on affiliated enterprises	8 507 ..	....	....	....	....	....	....	....	....
Liabilities to affiliated enterprises	8 508 ..	....	....	....	....	....	....	....	....
Other capital	8 530 ..	....	....	....	....	....	....	....	....
Claims on affiliated enterprises	8 535 ..	....	....	....	....	....	....	....	....
Liabilities to affiliated enterprises	8 540 ..	....	....	....	....	....	....	....	....
Portfolio investment	8 602 ..	....	....	....	....	92,028	116,739	229,244	239,460
Equity securities	8 610 ..	....	....	....	....	....	....	1,454	18,886
Monetary authorities	8 611 ..	....	....	....	....	....	....	....	....
General government	8 612 ..	....	....	....	....	....	....	....	....
Banks	8 613 ..	....	....	....	....	....	....	....	....
Other sectors	8 614 ..	....	....	....	....	....	....	....	....
Debt securities	8 619 ..	....	....	....	....	92,028	116,739	227,790	220,574
Bonds and notes	8 620 ..	....	....	....	....	....	....	....	....
Monetary authorities	8 621 ..	....	....	....	....	....	....	....	....
General government	8 622 ..	....	....	....	....	....	....	....	....
Banks	8 623 ..	....	....	....	....	....	....	....	....
Other sectors	8 624 ..	....	....	....	....	....	....	....	....
Money market instruments	8 630 ..	....	....	....	....	....	....	....	....
Monetary authorities	8 631 ..	....	....	....	....	....	....	....	....
General government	8 632 ..	....	....	....	....	....	....	....	....
Banks	8 633 ..	....	....	....	....	....	....	....	....
Other sectors	8 634 ..	....	....	....	....	....	....	....	....
Financial derivatives	8 900 ..	....	....	....	....	....	....	....	....
Monetary authorities	8 901 ..	....	....	....	....	....	....	....	....
General government	8 902 ..	....	....	....	....	....	....	....	....
Banks	8 903 ..	....	....	....	....	....	....	....	....
Other sectors	8 904 ..	....	....	....	....	....	....	....	....
Other investment	8 703 ..	....	....	....	....	166,589	215,713	251,519	406,096
Trade credits	8 706 ..	....	....	....	....	67,046	89,952	116,064	141,452
General government	8 707 ..	....	....	....	....	....	....	....	....
of which: Short-term	8 709 ..	....	....	....	....	....	....	....	....
Other sectors	8 710 ..	....	....	....	....	....	....	....	....
of which: Short-term	8 712 ..	....	....	....	....	....	....	....	....
Loans	8 714 ..	....	....	....	....	58,960	71,935	67,019	88,755
Monetary authorities	8 715 ..	....	....	....	....	....	....	....	....
of which: Short-term	8 718 ..	....	....	....	....	....	....	....	....
General government	8 719 ..	....	....	....	....	....	....	....	....
of which: Short-term	8 721 ..	....	....	....	....	....	....	....	....
Banks	8 722 ..	....	....	....	....	....	....	....	....
of which: Short-term	8 724 ..	....	....	....	....	....	....	....	....
Other sectors	8 725 ..	....	....	....	....	....	....	....	....
of which: Short-term	8 727 ..	....	....	....	....	....	....	....	....
Currency and deposits	8 730 ..	....	....	....	....	32,285	42,942	47,386	50,341
Monetary authorities	8 731 ..	....	....	....	....	....	....	....	....
General government	8 732 ..	....	....	....	....	....	....	....	....
Banks	8 733 ..	....	....	....	....	....	....	....	....
Other sectors	8 734 ..	....	....	....	....	....	....	....	....
Other assets	8 736 ..	....	....	....	....	8,298	10,884	21,050	125,548
Monetary authorities	8 737 ..	....	....	....	....	....	....	....	....
of which: Short-term	8 739 ..	....	....	....	....	....	....	....	....
General government	8 740 ..	....	....	....	....	....	....	....	....
of which: Short-term	8 742 ..	....	....	....	....	....	....	....	....
Banks	8 743 ..	....	....	....	....	....	....	....	....
of which: Short-term	8 745 ..	....	....	....	....	....	....	....	....
Other sectors	8 746 ..	....	....	....	....	....	....	....	....
of which: Short-term	8 748 ..	....	....	....	....	....	....	....	....
Reserve assets	8 802 ..	....	....	....	....	618,574	825,693	1,072,812	1,534,898
Monetary gold	8 812 ..	....	....	....	....	4,075	4,179	4,319	4,617
Special drawing rights	8 811 ..	798	851	998	1,102	1,247	1,251	1,068	1,192
Reserve position in the Fund	8 810 ..	1,905	2,590	3,723	3,798	3,320	1,391	1,081	840
Foreign exchange	8 803 ..	....	....	....	....	609,932	818,872	1,066,344	1,528,249
Other claims	8 813 ..	....	....	....	....	....	....	....	....

Table 3 (Concluded). INTERNATIONAL INVESTMENT POSITION (End-period stocks), 2000–2007

(Millions of U.S. dollars)

	Code	2000	2001	2002	2003	2004	2005	2006	2007
LIABILITIES	8 995 D.	....	....	....	....	637,121	800,077	1,032,835	1,266,056
Direct investment in China, P.R.: Mainland	8 555	....	....	....	....	368,970	471,549	612,508	742,388
Equity capital and reinvested earnings	8 556	....	....	....	....	....	....	....	....
Claims on direct investors	8 557	....	....	....	....	....	....	....	....
Liabilities to direct investors	8 558	....	....	....	....	....	....	....	....
Other capital	8 580	....	....	....	....	....	....	....	....
Claims on direct investors	8 585	....	....	....	....	....	....	....	....
Liabilities to direct investors	8 590	....	....	....	....	....	....	....	....
Portfolio investment	8 652	....	....	....	....	56,623	76,617	120,715	142,642
Equity securities	8 660	....	....	....	....	43,290	63,636	106,497	125,007
Banks	8 663	....	....	....	....	....	....	....	....
Other sectors	8 664	....	....	....	....	....	....	....	....
Debt securities	8 669	....	....	....	....	13,332	12,981	14,217	17,635
Bonds and notes	8 670	....	....	....	....	....	....	....	....
Monetary authorities	8 671	....	....	....	....	....	....	....	....
General government	8 672	....	....	....	....	....	....	....	....
Banks	8 673	....	....	....	....	....	....	....	....
Other sectors	8 674	....	....	....	....	....	....	....	....
Money market instruments	8 680	....	....	....	....	....	....	....	....
Monetary authorities	8 681	....	....	....	....	....	....	....	....
General government	8 682	....	....	....	....	....	....	....	....
Banks	8 683	....	....	....	....	....	....	....	....
Other sectors	8 684	....	....	....	....	....	....	....	....
Financial derivatives	8 905	....	....	....	....	....	....	....	....
Monetary authorities	8 906	....	....	....	....	....	....	....	....
General government	8 907	....	....	....	....	....	....	....	....
Banks	8 908	....	....	....	....	....	....	....	....
Other sectors	8 909	....	....	....	....	....	....	....	....
Other investment	8 753	....	....	....	....	211,529	251,911	299,612	381,026
Trade credits	8 756	....	....	....	....	65,361	90,773	104,000	132,264
General government	8 757	....	....	....	....	....	....	....	....
of which: Short-term	8 759	....	....	....	....	....	....	....	....
Other sectors	8 760	....	....	....	....	....	....	....	....
of which: Short-term	8 762	....	....	....	....	....	....	....	....
Loans	8 764	....	....	....	....	88,048	86,988	98,480	103,349
Monetary authorities	8 765	....	....	....	....	....	....	....	....
of which: Use of Fund credit and loans from the Fund	8 766	....	....	....	....	....	....	....	....
of which: Short-term	8 768	....	....	....	....	....	....	....	....
General government	8 769	....	....	....	....	....	....	....	....
of which: Short-term	8 771	....	....	....	....	....	....	....	....
Banks	8 772	....	....	....	....	....	....	....	....
of which: Short-term	8 774	....	....	....	....	....	....	....	....
Other sectors	8 775	....	....	....	....	....	....	....	....
of which: Short-term	8 777	....	....	....	....	....	....	....	....
Currency and deposits	8 780	....	....	....	....	37,891	48,186	58,914	98,098
Monetary authorities	8 781	....	....	....	....	....	....	....	....
General government	8 782	....	....	....	....	....	....	....	....
Banks	8 783	....	....	....	....	....	....	....	....
Other sectors	8 784	....	....	....	....	....	....	....	....
Other liabilities	8 786	....	....	....	....	20,228	25,964	38,218	47,316
Monetary authorities	8 787	....	....	....	....	....	....	....	....
of which: Short-term	8 789	....	....	....	....	....	....	....	....
General government	8 790	....	....	....	....	....	....	....	....
of which: Short-term	8 792	....	....	....	....	....	....	....	....
Banks	8 793	....	....	....	....	....	....	....	....
of which: Short-term	8 795	....	....	....	....	....	....	....	....
Other sectors	8 796	....	....	....	....	....	....	....	....
of which: Short-term	8 798	....	....	....	....	....	....	....	....
NET INTERNATIONAL INVESTMENT POSITION	8 995	....	....	....	....	292,774	422,560	611,369	1,022,022
Conversion rates: yuan per U.S. dollar (end of period)	0 102	8.2774	8.2768	8.2773	8.2767	8.2765	8.0702	7.8087	7.3046

Table 1. ANALYTIC PRESENTATION, 2000–2007

(Millions of U.S. dollars)

	Code	2000	2001	2002	2003	2004	2005	2006	2007
A. Current Account[1]	4 993 Z.	**6,993**	**9,786**	**12,412**	**16,470**	**15,731**	**20,181**	**22,928**	**28,046**
Goods: exports f.o.b.	2 100 ..	202,698	190,926	200,300	224,656	260,263	289,579	317,600	345,979
Goods: imports f.o.b.	3 100 ..	−210,891	−199,257	−205,353	−230,435	−269,575	−297,206	−331,634	−365,679
Balance on Goods	4 100 ..	*−8,193*	*−8,331*	*−5,053*	*−5,779*	*−9,312*	*−7,627*	*−14,033*	*−19,701*
Services: credit	2 200 ..	40,430	41,135	44,600	46,555	55,160	63,709	72,735	83,563
Services: debit	3 200 ..	−24,698	−24,899	−25,964	−26,126	−31,138	−33,979	−37,060	−41,234
Balance on Goods and Services	4 991 ..	*7,538*	*7,905*	*13,583*	*14,651*	*14,710*	*22,104*	*21,642*	*22,629*
Income: credit	2 300 ..	54,483	48,058	41,511	43,181	52,003	64,806	83,865	111,168
Income: debit	3 300 ..	−53,359	−44,398	−40,787	−39,525	−48,997	−64,604	−80,346	−103,184
Balance on Goods, Services, and Income	4 992 ..	*8,663*	*11,565*	*14,308*	*18,307*	*17,716*	*22,305*	*25,161*	*30,613*
Current transfers: credit	2 379 Z.	538	605	777	529	626	943	960	943
Current transfers: debit	3 379 ..	−2,208	−2,385	−2,673	−2,366	−2,611	−3,067	−3,194	−3,509
B. Capital Account[1]	4 994 Z.	**−1,546**	**−1,174**	**−2,011**	**−1,065**	**−329**	**−634**	**−373**	**1,365**
Capital account: credit	2 994 Z.	57	41	31	132	1,152	1,001	1,415	3,476
Capital account: debit	3 994 ..	−1,602	−1,215	−2,042	−1,197	−1,480	−1,636	−1,788	−2,111
Total, Groups A Plus B	4 981 ..	*5,447*	*8,611*	*10,400*	*15,405*	*15,402*	*19,546*	*22,555*	*29,411*
C. Financial Account[1]	4 995 W.	**4,165**	**−6,626**	**−19,751**	**−20,953**	**−20,094**	**−21,448**	**−20,621**	**−18,775**
Direct investment abroad	4 505 ..	−59,352	−11,345	−17,463	−5,492	−45,715	−27,201	−44,978	−53,188
Direct investment in China, P.R.: Hong Kong	4 555 Z.	61,924	23,776	9,682	13,624	34,032	33,618	45,054	59,899
Portfolio investment assets	4 602 ..	−22,022	−40,133	−37,702	−35,386	−43,214	−40,723	−41,751	−64,798
Equity securities	4 610 ..	−17,606	−22,682	−15,756	−9,951	−30,486	−27,954	−15,601	−57,205
Debt securities	4 619 ..	−4,416	−17,452	−21,946	−25,435	−12,728	−12,768	−26,149	−7,593
Portfolio investment liabilities	4 652 Z.	46,508	−1,161	−1,084	1,386	3,882	9,256	15,038	69,518
Equity securities	4 660 ..	46,976	−855	1,391	5,771	1,979	9,961	14,480	39,373
Debt securities	4 669 Z.	−468	−305	−2,475	−4,385	1,902	−705	558	30,145
Financial derivatives	4 910 ..	205	5,083	6,612	10,047	5,693	3,920	3,338	7,499
Financial derivatives assets	4 900 ..	8,445	17,971	20,035	30,005	20,605	20,797	19,437	31,463
Financial derivatives liabilities	4 905 ..	−8,240	−12,888	−13,424	−19,958	−14,912	−16,877	−16,099	−23,964
Other investment assets	4 703 ..	18,279	59,137	46,617	−28,671	−32,609	−18,750	−58,465	−161,007
Monetary authorities	4 701 ..	....	....	....	....	....	....	....	....
General government	4 704 ..	....	....	....	....	....	....	....	....
Banks	4 705 ..	23,857	61,452	46,037	−18,154	−37,563	−4,062	−57,693	−145,520
Other sectors	4 728 ..	−5,578	−2,315	580	−10,517	4,954	−14,688	−772	−15,486
Other investment liabilities	4 753 W.	−41,375	−41,985	−26,412	23,539	57,838	18,432	61,143	123,301
Monetary authorities	4 753 WA	....	....	....	....	....	....	....	....
General government	4 753 ZB	....	....	....	....	....	....	....	....
Banks	4 753 ZC	−44,259	−42,888	−20,937	20,199	56,992	5,623	52,411	119,736
Other sectors	4 753 ZD	2,884	903	−5,475	3,340	845	12,809	8,732	3,565
Total, Groups A Through C	4 983 ..	*9,613*	*1,985*	*−9,350*	*−5,548*	*−4,691*	*−1,901*	*1,934*	*10,636*
D. Net Errors and Omissions	4 998 ..	**431**	**2,699**	**6,973**	**6,542**	**7,977**	**3,279**	**4,082**	**4,068**
Total, Groups A Through D	4 984 ..	*10,044*	*4,684*	*−2,377*	*994*	*3,286*	*1,378*	*6,016*	*14,704*
E. Reserves and Related Items	4 802 A.	**−10,044**	**−4,684**	**2,377**	**−994**	**−3,286**	**−1,378**	**−6,016**	**−14,704**
Reserve assets	4 802 ..	−10,044	−4,684	2,377	−994	−3,286	−1,378	−6,016	−14,704
Use of Fund credit and loans	4 766 ..	....	....	....	....	....	....	....	....
Exceptional financing	4 920 ..	....	....	....	....	....	....	....	....
Conversion rates: Hong Kong dollars per U.S. dollar	0 101 ..	**7.7912**	**7.7988**	**7.7989**	**7.7868**	**7.7880**	**7.7773**	**7.7678**	**7.8014**

[1] Excludes components that have been classified in the categories of Group E.

Table 2. STANDARD PRESENTATION, 2000–2007

(Millions of U.S. dollars)

	Code	2000	2001	2002	2003	2004	2005	2006	2007
CURRENT ACCOUNT	4 993	6,993	9,786	12,412	16,470	15,731	20,181	22,928	28,046
A. GOODS	4 100	−8,193	−8,331	−5,053	−5,779	−9,312	−7,627	−14,033	−19,701
Credit	2 100	202,698	190,926	200,300	224,656	260,263	289,579	317,600	345,979
General merchandise: exports f.o.b.	2 110	....	....	....	....	....	....	....	....
Goods for processing: exports f.o.b.	2 150	....	....	....	....	....	....	....	....
Repairs on goods	2 160	....	....	....	....	....	....	....	....
Goods procured in ports by carriers	2 170	....	....	....	....	....	....	....	....
Nonmonetary gold	2 180	....	....	....	....	....	....	....	....
Debit	3 100	−210,891	−199,257	−205,353	−230,435	−269,575	−297,206	−331,634	−365,679
General merchandise: imports f.o.b.	3 110	....	....	....	....	....	....	....	....
Goods for processing: imports f.o.b.	3 150	....	....	....	....	....	....	....	....
Repairs on goods	3 160	....	....	....	....	....	....	....	....
Goods procured in ports by carriers	3 170	....	....	....	....	....	....	....	....
Nonmonetary gold	3 180	....	....	....	....	....	....	....	....
B. SERVICES	4 200	15,732	16,236	18,636	20,430	24,022	29,730	35,675	42,329
Total credit	2 200	*40,430*	*41,135*	*44,600*	*46,555*	*55,160*	*63,709*	*72,735*	*83,563*
Total debit	3 200	*−24,698*	*−24,899*	*−25,964*	*−26,126*	*−31,138*	*−33,979*	*−37,060*	*−41,234*
Transportation services, credit	2 205	12,772	12,012	13,303	13,832	17,358	20,318	22,423	....
Passenger	2 850	....	....	....	....	....	....	....	....
Freight	2 851	....	....	....	....	....	....	....	....
Other	2 852	....	....	....	....	....	....	....	....
Sea transport, passenger	2 207	....	....	....	....	....	....	....	....
Sea transport, freight	2 208	....	....	....	....	....	....	....	....
Sea transport, other	2 209	....	....	....	....	....	....	....	....
Air transport, passenger	2 211	....	....	....	....	....	....	....	....
Air transport, freight	2 212	....	....	....	....	....	....	....	....
Air transport, other	2 213	....	....	....	....	....	....	....	....
Other transport, passenger	2 215	....	....	....	....	....	....	....	....
Other transport, freight	2 216	....	....	....	....	....	....	....	....
Other transport, other	2 217	....	....	....	....	....	....	....	....
Transportation services, debit	3 205	−6,241	−6,529	−6,221	−6,719	−8,687	−10,462	−11,616	....
Passenger	3 850	....	....	....	....	....	....	....	....
Freight	3 851	....	....	....	....	....	....	....	....
Other	3 852	....	....	....	....	....	....	....	....
Sea transport, passenger	3 207	....	....	....	....	....	....	....	....
Sea transport, freight	3 208	....	....	....	....	....	....	....	....
Sea transport, other	3 209	....	....	....	....	....	....	....	....
Air transport, passenger	3 211	....	....	....	....	....	....	....	....
Air transport, freight	3 212	....	....	....	....	....	....	....	....
Air transport, other	3 213	....	....	....	....	....	....	....	....
Other transport, passenger	3 215	....	....	....	....	....	....	....	....
Other transport, freight	3 216	....	....	....	....	....	....	....	....
Other transport, other	3 217	....	....	....	....	....	....	....	....
Travel, credit	2 236	5,906	5,945	7,454	7,141	8,999	10,296	11,637	....
Business travel	2 237	....	....	....	....	....	....	....	....
Personal travel	2 240	....	....	....	....	....	....	....	....
Travel, debit	3 236	−12,502	−12,317	−12,418	−11,448	−13,269	−13,305	−14,043	....
Business travel	3 237	....	....	....	....	....	....	....	....
Personal travel	3 240	....	....	....	....	....	....	....	....
Other services, credit	2 200 BA	21,751	23,178	23,843	25,582	28,803	33,095	38,676	....
Communications	2 245	362	505	706	756	852	942	834	....
Construction	2 249	338	411	343	510	378	313	268	....
Insurance	2 253	443	456	439	394	411	414	417	....
Financial	2 260	4,372	4,484	4,194	3,763	4,556	6,270	9,268	....
Computer and information	2 262	60	154	208	245	245	265	358	....
Royalties and licence fees	2 266	107	196	229	341	218	245	259	....
Other business services	2 268	15,952	16,795	17,558	19,382	21,798	24,318	26,930	....
Personal, cultural, and recreational	2 287	51	99	112	137	290	270	280	....
Government, n.i.e.	2 291	67	79	55	55	56	58	61	....
Other services, debit	3 200 BA	−5,955	−6,053	−7,325	−7,959	−9,181	−10,211	−11,402	....
Communications	3 245	−698	−586	−830	−941	−1,124	−1,141	−1,072	....
Construction	3 249	−415	−406	−350	−399	−346	−273	−241	....
Insurance	3 253	−528	−516	−592	−622	−611	−606	−613	....
Financial	3 260	−824	−894	−987	−878	−1,165	−1,406	−2,017	....
Computer and information	3 262	−128	−145	−225	−282	−395	−427	−371	....
Royalties and licence fees	3 266	−461	−491	−696	−864	−1,111	−1,289	−1,357	....
Other business services	3 268	−2,726	−2,843	−3,446	−3,772	−4,223	−4,878	−5,519	....
Personal, cultural, and recreational	3 287	−65	−70	−68	−68	−52	−52	−56	....
Government, n.i.e.	3 291	−110	−102	−131	−132	−154	−141	−155	....

Table 2 (Continued). STANDARD PRESENTATION, 2000–2007

(Millions of U.S. dollars)

	Code	2000	2001	2002	2003	2004	2005	2006	2007
C. INCOME	4 300	**1,125**	**3,660**	**724**	**3,656**	**3,006**	**201**	**3,520**	**7,984**
Total credit	2 300	*54,483*	*48,058*	*41,511*	*43,181*	*52,003*	*64,806*	*83,865*	*111,168*
Total debit	3 300	*−53,359*	*−44,398*	*−40,787*	*−39,525*	*−48,997*	*−64,604*	*−80,346*	*−103,184*
Compensation of employees, credit	2 310	**136**	**153**	**121**	**120**	**240**	**297**	**294**	**348**
Compensation of employees, debit	3 310	**−225**	**−309**	**−299**	**−317**	**−321**	**−348**	**−377**	**−380**
Investment income, credit	2 320	**54,348**	**47,905**	**41,391**	**43,061**	**51,763**	**64,509**	**83,571**	**110,820**
Direct investment income	2 330	19,748	21,606	22,953	25,143	29,543	35,046	44,593	60,359
Dividends and distributed branch profits	2 332	8,402	7,894	16,787	15,764	19,781	14,472	17,446	21,405
Reinvested earnings and undistributed branch profits	2 333	10,450	13,231	5,873	8,931	9,084	19,975	26,246	37,987
Income on debt (interest)	2 334	896	481	293	448	678	599	901	967
Portfolio investment income	2 339	12,204	12,353	11,823	13,586	16,041	18,077	22,022	27,147
Income on equity	2 340	2,822	2,517	2,747	4,690	6,435	6,764	7,674	10,621
Income on bonds and notes	2 350	8,388	9,063	8,485	8,329	8,958	10,510	13,018	14,754
Income on money market instruments	2 360	994	773	591	566	648	803	1,330	1,772
Other investment income	2 370	22,396	13,946	6,615	4,332	6,179	11,386	16,957	23,314
Investment income, debit	3 320	**−53,133**	**−44,089**	**−40,488**	**−39,208**	**−48,677**	**−64,256**	**−79,969**	**−102,804**
Direct investment income	3 330	−34,183	−31,395	−32,662	−32,700	−40,269	−50,800	−60,643	−77,704
Dividends and distributed branch profits	3 332	−13,933	−18,180	−14,058	−15,981	−17,219	−24,668	−24,254	−26,274
Reinvested earnings and undistributed branch profits	3 333	−19,289	−12,355	−17,968	−16,027	−22,443	−25,508	−35,736	−50,804
Income on debt (interest)	3 334	−961	−859	−636	−691	−607	−624	−653	−627
Portfolio investment income	3 339	−3,452	−3,441	−3,460	−3,597	−4,032	−4,927	−6,663	−8,426
Income on equity	3 340	−2,645	−2,647	−2,853	−3,172	−3,685	−4,523	−6,254	−7,818
Income on bonds and notes	3 350	−597	−641	−524	−404	−339	−393	−367	−523
Income on money market instruments	3 360	−210	−153	−82	−21	−7	−11	−42	−85
Other investment income	3 370	−15,498	−9,254	−4,366	−2,911	−4,376	−8,530	−12,663	−16,673
D. CURRENT TRANSFERS	4 379	**−1,670**	**−1,780**	**−1,896**	**−1,837**	**−1,985**	**−2,124**	**−2,234**	**−2,566**
Credit	2 379	**538**	**605**	**777**	**529**	**626**	**943**	**960**	**943**
General government	2 380	....	....	....	....	....	....	....	....
Other sectors	2 390	538	605	777	529	626	943	960	943
Workers' remittances	2 391	....	....	....	....	....	....	....	....
Other current transfers	2 392	....	....	....	....	....	....	....	....
Debit	3 379	**−2,208**	**−2,385**	**−2,673**	**−2,366**	**−2,611**	**−3,067**	**−3,194**	**−3,509**
General government	3 380	−166	−167	−172	−171	−171	−181	−196	−225
Other sectors	3 390	−2,042	−2,218	−2,501	−2,194	−2,440	−2,886	−2,998	−3,285
Workers' remittances	3 391	....	....	....	....	....	....	....	....
Other current transfers	3 392	....	....	....	....	....	....	....	....
CAPITAL AND FINANCIAL ACCOUNT	4 996	**−7,424**	**−12,484**	**−19,385**	**−23,011**	**−23,708**	**−23,460**	**−27,010**	**−32,115**
CAPITAL ACCOUNT	4 994	**−1,546**	**−1,174**	**−2,011**	**−1,065**	**−329**	**−634**	**−373**	**1,365**
Total credit	2 994	*57*	*41*	*31*	*132*	*1,152*	*1,001*	*1,415*	*3,476*
Total debit	3 994	*−1,602*	*−1,215*	*−2,042*	*−1,197*	*−1,480*	*−1,636*	*−1,788*	*−2,111*
Capital transfers, credit	2 400	**57**	**41**	**31**	**132**	**1,152**	**1,001**	**1,415**	**3,476**
General government	2 401	....	....	....	....	....	....	....	....
Debt forgiveness	2 402	....	....	....	....	....	....	....	....
Other capital transfers	2 410	....	....	....	....	....	....	....	....
Other sectors	2 430	57	41	31	132	1,152	1,001	1,415	3,476
Migrants' transfers	2 431	....	....	....	....	....	....	....	....
Debt forgiveness	2 432	....	....	....	....	....	....	....	....
Other capital transfers	2 440	....	....	....	....	....	....	....	....
Capital transfers, debit	3 400	**−1,602**	**−1,215**	**−2,042**	**−1,197**	**−1,480**	**−1,636**	**−1,788**	**−2,111**
General government	3 401	....	....	....	....	....	....	....	....
Debt forgiveness	3 402	....	....	....	....	....	....	....	....
Other capital transfers	3 410	....	....	....	....	....	....	....	....
Other sectors	3 430	−1,602	−1,215	−2,042	−1,197	−1,480	−1,636	−1,788	−2,111
Migrants' transfers	3 431	....	....	....	....	....	....	....	....
Debt forgiveness	3 432	....	....	....	....	....	....	....	....
Other capital transfers	3 440	....	....	....	....	....	....	....	....
Nonproduced nonfinancial assets, credit	2 480	....	....	....	....	....	....	....	....
Nonproduced nonfinancial assets, debit	3 480	....	....	....	....	....	....	....	....

Table 2 (Continued). STANDARD PRESENTATION, 2000–2007

(Millions of U.S. dollars)

	Code	2000	2001	2002	2003	2004	2005	2006	2007
FINANCIAL ACCOUNT	4 995	−5,878	−11,310	−17,373	−21,946	−23,380	−22,825	−26,637	−33,479
A. DIRECT INVESTMENT	4 500	2,572	12,431	−7,781	8,132	−11,683	6,417	75	6,712
Direct investment abroad	4 505	−59,352	−11,345	−17,463	−5,492	−45,715	−27,201	−44,978	−53,188
Equity capital	4 510	−49,153	−622	−8,825	−3,097	−11,401	−8,207	−5,917	−11,046
Claims on affiliated enterprises	4 515	−49,153	−622	−8,825	−3,097	−11,401	−8,207	−5,917	−11,046
Liabilities to affiliated enterprises	4 520	....	....	....	....	....	....	....	....
Reinvested earnings	4 525	−10,450	−13,231	−5,873	−8,931	−9,084	−19,975	−26,246	−37,987
Other capital	4 530	251	2,508	−2,764	6,536	−25,230	981	−12,815	−4,154
Claims on affiliated enterprises	4 535	−8,270	−3,834	−1,295	4,307	−13,337	−3,247	−12,905	−7,583
Liabilities to affiliated enterprises	4 540	8,521	6,341	−1,470	2,229	−11,892	4,228	89	3,429
Direct investment in China, P.R.: Hong Kong	4 555	61,924	23,776	9,682	13,624	34,032	33,618	45,054	59,899
Equity capital	4 560	32,940	7,716	1,379	590	3,793	3,665	1,999	3,814
Claims on direct investors	4 565	....	....	....	....	....	....	....	....
Liabilities to direct investors	4 570	32,940	7,716	1,379	590	3,793	3,665	1,999	3,814
Reinvested earnings	4 575	19,289	12,355	17,968	16,027	22,443	25,508	35,736	50,804
Other capital	4 580	9,695	3,705	−9,664	−2,993	7,796	4,445	7,318	5,282
Claims on direct investors	4 585	−231	−1,318	−251	−3,061	−563	−915	604	−1,312
Liabilities to direct investors	4 590	9,925	5,023	−9,414	68	8,360	5,359	6,714	6,594
B. PORTFOLIO INVESTMENT	4 600	24,485	−41,294	−38,786	−34,000	−39,332	−31,467	−26,712	4,720
Assets	4 602	−22,022	−40,133	−37,702	−35,386	−43,214	−40,723	−41,751	−64,798
Equity securities	4 610	−17,606	−22,682	−15,756	−9,951	−30,486	−27,954	−15,601	−57,205
Monetary authorities	4 611	....	....	....	....	....	....	....	....
General government	4 612	....	....	....	....	....	....	....	....
Banks	4 613	−24	9	−26	−139	−765	−1,548	−96	611
Other sectors	4 614	−17,582	−22,691	−15,730	−9,811	−29,721	−26,406	−15,505	−57,816
Debt securities	4 619	−4,416	−17,452	−21,946	−25,435	−12,728	−12,768	−26,149	−7,593
Bonds and notes	4 620	−4,487	−15,549	−22,311	−23,791	−9,083	−11,045	−7,579	1,125
Monetary authorities	4 621	....	....	....	....	....	....	....	....
General government	4 622	....	....	....	....	....	....	....	....
Banks	4 623	−15,022	−15,366	−20,538	−10,340	−1,381	−8,320	−7,722	−919
Other sectors	4 624	10,535	−183	−1,772	−13,450	−7,701	−2,725	143	2,044
Money market instruments	4 630	71	−1,903	365	−1,644	−3,646	−1,723	−18,571	−8,719
Monetary authorities	4 631	....	....	....	....	....	....	....	....
General government	4 632	....	....	....	....	....	....	....	....
Banks	4 633	344	−352	175	−991	−3,524	300	−18,132	−9,574
Other sectors	4 634	−273	−1,551	190	−653	−122	−2,024	−439	855
Liabilities	4 652	46,508	−1,161	−1,084	1,386	3,882	9,256	15,038	69,518
Equity securities	4 660	46,976	−855	1,391	5,771	1,979	9,961	14,480	39,373
Banks	4 663	1,658	−15	459	349	−397	−718	1,076	2,073
Other sectors	4 664	45,318	−841	933	5,422	2,377	10,678	13,404	37,300
Debt securities	4 669	−468	−305	−2,475	−4,385	1,902	−705	558	30,145
Bonds and notes	4 670	−5	−968	−41	−3,825	1,774	−856	517	10,055
Monetary authorities	4 671	....	....	....	....	....	....	....	....
General government	4 672	....	....	....	....	....	....	....	....
Banks	4 673	−378	−344	370	−2,056	973	888	−335	1,117
Other sectors	4 674	373	−624	−411	−1,769	801	−1,744	852	8,939
Money market instruments	4 680	−463	662	−2,434	−560	129	151	42	20,089
Monetary authorities	4 681	....	....	....	....	....	....	....	....
General government	4 682	....	....	....	....	....	....	....	....
Banks	4 683	−59	551	10	−265	181	135	−42	19,844
Other sectors	4 684	−404	111	−2,444	−295	−52	16	84	246
C. FINANCIAL DERIVATIVES	4 910	205	5,083	6,612	10,047	5,693	3,920	3,338	7,499
Monetary authorities	4 911	....	....	....	....	....	....	....	....
General government	4 912	....	....	....	....	....	....	....	....
Banks	4 913	−741	4,338	6,068	9,505	5,787	2,788	1,993	6,537
Other sectors	4 914	947	745	544	542	−94	1,132	1,345	962
Assets	4 900	8,445	17,971	20,035	30,005	20,605	20,797	19,437	31,463
Monetary authorities	4 901	....	....	....	....	....	....	....	....
General government	4 902	....	....	....	....	....	....	....	....
Banks	4 903	7,146	16,811	18,528	27,666	19,041	18,086	16,262	26,419
Other sectors	4 904	1,298	1,160	1,508	2,339	1,564	2,711	3,175	5,044
Liabilities	4 905	−8,240	−12,888	−13,424	−19,958	−14,912	−16,877	−16,099	−23,964
Monetary authorities	4 906	....	....	....	....	....	....	....	....
General government	4 907	....	....	....	....	....	....	....	....
Banks	4 908	−7,888	−12,473	−12,460	−18,162	−13,254	−15,298	−14,269	−19,882
Other sectors	4 909	−352	−415	−964	−1,796	−1,658	−1,579	−1,831	−4,082

Table 2 (Concluded). STANDARD PRESENTATION, 2000–2007

(Millions of U.S. dollars)

	Code	2000	2001	2002	2003	2004	2005	2006	2007
D. OTHER INVESTMENT	4 700 ..	**−23,097**	**17,153**	**20,204**	**−5,132**	**25,229**	**−318**	**2,678**	**−37,705**
Assets	4 703 ..	**18,279**	**59,137**	**46,617**	**−28,671**	**−32,609**	**−18,750**	**−58,465**	**−161,007**
Trade credits	4 706 ..	−712	449	−3,389	−7,049	−9,251	−3,617	373	−1,117
General government	4 707 ..	....	....	....	....	....	....	....	....
of which: Short-term	4 709 ..	....	....	....	....	....	....	....	....
Other sectors	4 710 ..	−712	449	−3,389	−7,049	−9,251	−3,617	373	−1,117
of which: Short-term	4 712 ..	....	....	....	....	....	....	....	....
Loans	4 714 ..	42,591	27,146	6,255	3,957	−5,776	−128	−2,830	−33,761
Monetary authorities	4 715 ..	....	....	....	....	....	....	....	....
of which: Short-term	4 718 ..	....	....	....	....	....	....	....	....
General government	4 719 ..	....	....	....	....	....	....	....	....
of which: Short-term	4 721 ..	....	....	....	....	....	....	....	....
Banks	4 722 ..	42,141	28,280	1,799	3,667	−4,163	−700	−3,172	−27,221
of which: Short-term	4 724 ..	....	....	....	....	....	....	....	....
Other sectors	4 725 ..	450	−1,134	4,456	290	−1,613	572	343	−6,539
of which: Short-term	4 727 ..	....	....	....	....	....	....	....	....
Currency and deposits	4 730 ..	−22,504	29,898	41,708	−25,276	−17,990	−14,663	−53,667	−124,979
Monetary authorities	4 731 ..	....	....	....	....	....	....	....	....
General government	4 732 ..	....	....	....	....	....	....	....	....
Banks	4 733 ..	−18,208	32,927	44,263	−21,908	−33,672	−2,774	−52,415	−118,292
Other sectors	4 734 ..	−4,296	−3,029	−2,555	−3,368	15,682	−11,888	−1,252	−6,687
Other assets	4 736 ..	−1,096	1,644	2,042	−303	409	−343	−2,340	−1,150
Monetary authorities	4 737 ..	....	....	....	....	....	....	....	....
of which: Short-term	4 739 ..	....	....	....	....	....	....	....	....
General government	4 740 ..	....	....	....	....	....	....	....	....
of which: Short-term	4 742 ..	....	....	....	....	....	....	....	....
Banks	4 743 ..	−76	246	−26	87	273	−588	−2,105	−7
of which: Short-term	4 745 ..	....	....	....	....	....	....	....	....
Other sectors	4 746 ..	−1,020	1,398	2,068	−390	136	246	−235	−1,143
of which: Short-term	4 748 ..	....	....	....	....	....	....	....	....
Liabilities	4 753 ..	**−41,375**	**−41,985**	**−26,412**	**23,539**	**57,838**	**18,432**	**61,143**	**123,301**
Trade credits	4 756 ..	602	−623	609	1,847	1,453	647	−1,936	−195
General government	4 757 ..	....	....	....	....	....	....	....	....
of which: Short-term	4 759 ..	....	....	....	....	....	....	....	....
Other sectors	4 760 ..	602	−623	609	1,847	1,453	647	−1,936	−195
of which: Short-term	4 762 ..	....	....	....	....	....	....	....	....
Loans	4 764 ..	654	−4,008	−12,720	784	128	8,881	10,298	2,292
Monetary authorities	4 765 ..	....	....	....	....	....	....	....	....
of which: Use of Fund credit and loans from the Fund	4 766 ..	....	....	....	....	....	....	....	....
of which: Short-term	4 768 ..	....	....	....	....	....	....	....	....
General government	4 769 ..	....	....	....	....	....	....	....	....
of which: Short-term	4 771 ..	....	....	....	....	....	....	....	....
Banks	4 772 ..	−1,272	−5,763	−5,867	−931	1,477	−673	−897	1,109
of which: Short-term	4 774 ..	....	....	....	....	....	....	....	....
Other sectors	4 775 ..	1,926	1,755	−6,852	1,715	−1,349	9,554	11,195	1,183
of which: Short-term	4 777 ..	....	....	....	....	....	....	....	....
Currency and deposits	4 780 ..	−43,004	−37,095	−15,255	20,914	56,562	6,069	52,612	118,988
Monetary authorities	4 781 ..	....	....	....	....	....	....	....	....
General government	4 782 ..	....	....	....	....	....	....	....	....
Banks	4 783 ..	−43,015	−37,092	−15,250	20,932	56,484	5,964	52,242	118,794
Other sectors	4 784 ..	12	−3	−6	−18	79	105	370	194
Other liabilities	4 786 ..	372	−259	953	−6	−305	2,834	169	2,216
Monetary authorities	4 787 ..	....	....	....	....	....	....	....	....
of which: Short-term	4 789 ..	....	....	....	....	....	....	....	....
General government	4 790 ..	....	....	....	....	....	....	....	....
of which: Short-term	4 792 ..	....	....	....	....	....	....	....	....
Banks	4 793 ..	28	−32	180	199	−968	331	1,066	−167
of which: Short-term	4 795 ..	....	....	....	....	....	....	....	....
Other sectors	4 796 ..	344	−226	774	−204	663	2,504	−897	2,383
of which: Short-term	4 798 ..	....	....	....	....	....	....	....	....
E. RESERVE ASSETS	4 802 ..	**−10,044**	**−4,684**	**2,377**	**−994**	**−3,286**	**−1,378**	**−6,016**	**−14,704**
Monetary gold	4 812 ..	....	....	....	....	....	....	....	....
Special drawing rights	4 811 ..	....	....	....	....	....	....	....	....
Reserve position in the Fund	4 810 ..	....	....	....	....	....	....	....	....
Foreign exchange	4 803 ..	−10,044	−4,684	2,377	−994	−3,286	−1,378	−6,016	−14,704
Other claims	4 813 ..	....	....	....	....	....	....	....	....
NET ERRORS AND OMISSIONS	4 998 ..	**431**	**2,699**	**6,973**	**6,542**	**7,977**	**3,279**	**4,082**	**4,068**

Table 3. INTERNATIONAL INVESTMENT POSITION (End-period stocks), 2000–2007

(Billions of U.S. dollars)

	Code	2000	2001	2002	2003	2004	2005	2006	2007
ASSETS	8 995 C.	**1,141.52**	**1,071.00**	**1,030.10**	**1,185.41**	**1,376.31**	**1,494.78**	**1,929.22**	**2,730.10**
Direct investment abroad	8 505	**388.38**	**352.60**	**309.43**	**339.65**	**403.12**	**471.32**	**677.15**	**1,026.65**
Equity capital and reinvested earnings	8 506	317.11	282.77	244.01	276.42	310.18	375.76	561.29	896.96
Claims on affiliated enterprises	8 507	317.11	282.77	244.01	276.42	310.18	375.76	561.29	896.96
Liabilities to affiliated enterprises	8 508	....	....	....	....	....	....	....	....
Other capital	8 530	71.27	69.83	65.42	63.23	92.94	95.56	115.87	129.69
Claims on affiliated enterprises	8 535	94.38	99.58	96.41	95.41	113.88	121.92	139.42	158.11
Liabilities to affiliated enterprises	8 540	−23.11	−29.75	−30.99	−32.18	−20.93	−26.36	−23.56	−28.42
Portfolio investment	8 602	**178.85**	**205.60**	**244.07**	**334.91**	**400.89**	**436.60**	**580.55**	**782.27**
Equity securities	8 610	88.32	94.62	95.72	152.83	199.68	227.85	338.90	518.75
Monetary authorities	8 611	....	....	....	....	....	....	....	....
General government	8 612	....	....	....	....	....	....	....	....
Banks	8 613	.07	.07	.07	.27	1.16	2.88	3.20	5.14
Other sectors	8 614	88.25	94.55	95.65	152.56	198.52	224.97	335.70	513.61
Debt securities	8 619	90.53	110.98	148.35	182.08	201.20	208.75	241.65	263.52
Bonds and notes	8 620	67.22	85.88	123.53	154.10	169.49	175.11	189.32	205.52
Monetary authorities	8 621	....	....	....	....	....	....	....	....
General government	8 622	....	....	....	....	....	....	....	....
Banks	8 623	41.96	58.90	85.12	98.19	101.44	107.59	118.55	123.56
Other sectors	8 624	25.26	26.98	38.41	55.90	68.05	67.52	70.77	81.96
Money market instruments	8 630	23.31	25.11	24.82	27.98	31.72	33.64	52.34	58.00
Monetary authorities	8 631	....	....	....	....	....	....	....	....
General government	8 632	....	....	....	....	....	....	....	....
Banks	8 633	21.15	21.45	21.37	23.91	27.34	27.18	45.42	53.01
Other sectors	8 634	2.15	3.65	3.45	4.08	4.38	6.45	6.91	4.99
Financial derivatives	8 900	**16.81**	**17.53**	**22.52**	**19.85**	**22.44**	**17.19**	**22.54**	**48.15**
Monetary authorities	8 901	....	....	....	....	....	....	....	....
General government	8 902	....	....	....	....	....	....	....	....
Banks	8 903	15.80	16.48	20.47	16.62	17.60	12.93	16.96	33.84
Other sectors	8 904	1.01	1.05	2.05	3.23	4.84	4.26	5.58	14.30
Other investment	8 703	**449.88**	**384.09**	**342.16**	**372.60**	**426.30**	**445.38**	**515.72**	**720.41**
Trade credits	8 706	4.03	5.87	7.28	8.86	8.84	9.80	11.21	14.95
General government	8 707	....	....	....	....	....	....	....	....
of which: Short-term	8 709	....	....	....	....	....	....	....	....
Other sectors	8 710	4.03	5.87	7.28	8.86	8.84	9.80	11.21	14.95
of which: Short-term	8 712	....	....	....	....	....	....	....	....
Loans	8 714	83.23	57.83	52.05	49.55	54.14	55.17	59.46	107.36
Monetary authorities	8 715	....	....	....	....	....	....	....	....
of which: Short-term	8 718	....	....	....	....	....	....	....	....
General government	8 719	....	....	....	....	....	....	....	....
of which: Short-term	8 721	....	....	....	....	....	....	....	....
Banks	8 722	76.86	45.89	45.68	43.02	46.15	46.62	51.57	86.51
of which: Short-term	8 724	....	....	....	....	....	....	....	....
Other sectors	8 725	6.37	11.93	6.36	6.53	7.99	8.55	7.90	20.85
of which: Short-term	8 727	....	....	....	....	....	....	....	....
Currency and deposits	8 730	356.95	314.48	278.01	308.06	357.14	371.72	434.14	571.30
Monetary authorities	8 731	....	....	....	....	....	....	....	....
General government	8 732	....	....	....	....	....	....	....	....
Banks	8 733	315.01	271.33	229.01	255.50	292.28	301.47	357.95	477.78
Other sectors	8 734	41.94	43.15	49.00	52.56	64.86	70.25	76.20	93.52
Other assets	8 736	5.67	5.91	4.83	6.14	6.17	8.69	10.90	26.81
Monetary authorities	8 737	....	....	....	....	....	....	....	....
of which: Short-term	8 739	....	....	....	....	....	....	....	....
General government	8 740	....	....	....	....	....	....	....	....
of which: Short-term	8 742	....	....	....	....	....	....	....	....
Banks	8 743	1.29	1.18	1.14	1.12	2.16	2.66	4.85	5.55
of which: Short-term	8 745	....	....	....	....	....	....	....	....
Other sectors	8 746	4.37	4.74	3.69	5.02	4.01	6.02	6.05	21.26
of which: Short-term	8 748	....	....	....	....	....	....	....	....
Reserve assets	8 802	**107.60**	**111.19**	**111.93**	**118.40**	**123.56**	**124.30**	**133.26**	**152.62**
Monetary gold	8 812	....	....	....	....	....	....	....	....
Special drawing rights	8 811	....	....	....	....	....	....	....	....
Reserve position in the Fund	8 810	....	....	....	....	....	....	....	....
Foreign exchange	8 803	....	....	....	....	....	....	....	....
Other claims	8 813	....	....	....	....	....	....	....	....

Table 3 (Concluded). INTERNATIONAL INVESTMENT POSITION (End-period stocks), 2000–2007

(Billions of U.S. dollars)

	Code	2000	2001	2002	2003	2004	2005	2006	2007
LIABILITIES	8 995 D.	**919.67**	**805.78**	**686.76**	**791.25**	**951.56**	**1,055.42**	**1,410.89**	**2,208.31**
Direct investment in China: P.R.: Hong Kong	8 555 ..	**455.47**	**419.35**	**336.28**	**381.34**	**453.06**	**523.22**	**742.42**	**1,184.55**
Equity capital and reinvested earnings	8 556 ..	402.08	354.63	278.73	330.62	392.61	457.19	662.30	1,093.56
Claims on direct investors	8 557 ..	....	....	....	....	....	....	....	....
Liabilities to direct investors	8 558 ..	402.08	354.63	278.73	330.62	392.61	457.19	662.30	1,093.56
Other capital	8 580 ..	53.39	64.72	57.55	50.72	60.45	66.03	80.12	90.98
Claims on direct investors	8 585 ..	−13.34	−12.48	−12.20	−15.19	−14.81	−14.69	−12.50	−16.52
Liabilities to direct investors	8 590 ..	66.74	77.20	69.75	65.91	75.26	80.73	92.62	107.50
Portfolio investment	8 652 ..	**153.22**	**117.03**	**93.54**	**125.31**	**155.26**	**178.44**	**259.66**	**478.48**
Equity securities	8 660 ..	138.08	102.83	79.29	115.69	143.41	167.57	247.87	435.52
Banks	8 663 ..	8.10	6.42	5.74	8.33	8.48	6.71	11.08	16.77
Other sectors	8 664 ..	129.98	96.42	73.55	107.36	134.93	160.86	236.79	418.75
Debt securities	8 669 ..	15.14	14.20	14.25	9.62	11.86	10.87	11.79	42.96
Bonds and notes	8 670 ..	9.61	8.08	10.44	6.44	8.50	7.52	7.84	18.71
Monetary authorities	8 671 ..	....	....	....	....	....	....	....	....
General government	8 672 ..	....	....	....	....	....	....	....	....
Banks	8 673 ..	3.56	2.98	4.57	2.60	3.77	4.46	3.59	4.88
Other sectors	8 674 ..	6.06	5.10	5.87	3.84	4.73	3.05	4.24	13.84
Money market instruments	8 680 ..	5.53	6.11	3.82	3.18	3.36	3.35	3.96	24.25
Monetary authorities	8 681 ..	....	....	....	....	....	....	....	....
General government	8 682 ..	....	....	....	....	....	....	....	....
Banks	8 683 ..	2.72	3.20	3.16	2.88	3.12	3.10	3.63	24.03
Other sectors	8 684 ..	2.81	2.92	.66	.30	.24	.25	.33	.22
Financial derivatives	8 905 ..	**12.52**	**12.06**	**21.20**	**19.60**	**21.14**	**17.10**	**20.37**	**32.87**
Monetary authorities	8 906 ..	....	....	....	....	....	....	....	....
General government	8 907 ..	....	....	....	....	....	....	....	....
Banks	8 908 ..	11.92	11.57	20.44	17.01	18.25	14.18	16.47	29.00
Other sectors	8 909 ..	.60	.49	.76	2.59	2.89	2.92	3.90	3.87
Other investment	8 753 ..	**298.47**	**257.34**	**235.74**	**265.00**	**322.10**	**336.67**	**388.45**	**512.41**
Trade credits	8 756 ..	2.12	3.02	3.92	5.82	5.95	6.58	6.02	7.58
General government	8 757 ..	....	....	....	....	....	....	....	....
of which: Short-term	8 759 ..	....	....	....	....	....	....	....	....
Other sectors	8 760 ..	2.12	3.02	3.92	5.82	5.95	6.58	6.02	7.58
of which: Short-term	8 762 ..	....	....	....	....	....	....	....	....
Loans	8 764 ..	34.80	34.51	22.06	21.84	20.78	29.99	38.86	39.02
Monetary authorities	8 765 ..	....	....	....	....	....	....	....	....
of which: Use of Fund credit and loans from the Fund	8 766 ..	....	....	....	....	....	....	....	....
of which: Short-term	8 768 ..	....	....	....	....	....	....	....	....
General government	8 769 ..	....	....	....	....	....	....	....	....
of which: Short-term	8 771 ..	....	....	....	....	....	....	....	....
Banks	8 772 ..	19.53	13.50	6.82	5.61	6.39	4.70	3.80	6.70
of which: Short-term	8 774 ..	....	....	....	....	....	....	....	....
Other sectors	8 775 ..	15.27	21.01	15.24	16.22	14.40	25.29	35.06	32.32
of which: Short-term	8 777 ..	....	....	....	....	....	....	....	....
Currency and deposits	8 780 ..	259.35	217.18	205.78	230.55	288.86	288.85	333.18	450.89
Monetary authorities	8 781 ..	....	....	....	....	....	....	....	....
General government	8 782 ..	....	....	....	....	....	....	....	....
Banks	8 783 ..	259.10	217.14	205.66	230.44	288.70	288.63	332.45	449.85
Other sectors	8 784 ..	.25	.04	.12	.10	.16	.22	.73	1.04
Other liabilities	8 786 ..	2.20	2.63	3.99	6.80	6.50	11.25	10.39	14.92
Monetary authorities	8 787 ..	....	....	....	....	....	....	....	....
of which: Short-term	8 789 ..	....	....	....	....	....	....	....	....
General government	8 790 ..	....	....	....	....	....	....	....	....
of which: Short-term	8 792 ..	....	....	....	....	....	....	....	....
Banks	8 793 ..	.39	.54	.68	.91	1.43	1.76	2.81	4.90
of which: Short-term	8 795 ..	....	....	....	....	....	....	....	....
Other sectors	8 796 ..	1.81	2.10	3.30	5.88	5.07	9.49	7.57	10.02
of which: Short-term	8 798 ..	....	....	....	....	....	....	....	....
NET INTERNATIONAL INVESTMENT POSITION	8 995 ..	**221.85**	**265.23**	**343.34**	**394.16**	**424.75**	**439.36**	**518.33**	**521.79**
Conversion rates: Hong Kong dollars per U.S. dollar (end of period)	0 102 ..	**7.7960**	**7.7970**	**7.7980**	**7.7630**	**7.7735**	**7.7525**	**7.7745**	**7.8015**

Table 1. ANALYTIC PRESENTATION, 2000–2007

(Millions of U.S. dollars)

	Code	2000	2001	2002	2003	2004	2005	2006	2007
A. Current Account[1]	4 993 Z.	....	....	**2,719**	**3,160**	**4,240**	**3,367**	**2,946**	....
Goods: exports f.o.b.	2 100 ..	....	....	2,358	2,585	2,816	2,478	2,559	....
Goods: imports f.o.b.	3 100 ..	....	....	−3,277	−3,678	−4,658	−5,270	−6,496	....
Balance on Goods	4 100 ..	....	....	*−920*	*−1,093*	*−1,842*	*−2,792*	*−3,937*	....
Services: credit	2 200 ..	....	....	4,758	5,605	8,063	8,612	10,538	....
Services: debit	3 200 ..	....	....	−1,071	−1,175	−1,364	−1,576	−1,866	....
Balance on Goods and Services	4 991 ..	....	....	*2,767*	*3,337*	*4,857*	*4,244*	*4,736*	....
Income: credit	2 300 ..	....	....	450	395	387	806	1,426	....
Income: debit	3 300 ..	....	....	−468	−547	−959	−1,582	−2,981	....
Balance on Goods, Services, and Income	4 992 ..	....	....	*2,749*	*3,185*	*4,285*	*3,468*	*3,181*	....
Current transfers: credit	2 379 Z.	....	....	69	83	79	83	108	....
Current transfers: debit	3 379 ..	....	....	−99	−108	−124	−184	−343	....
B. Capital Account[1]	4 994 Z.	....	....	**139**	**88**	**274**	**515**	**438**	....
Capital account: credit	2 994 Z.	....	....	161	113	302	534	456	....
Capital account: debit	3 994 ..	....	....	−23	−25	−28	−20	−18	....
Total, Groups A Plus B	4 981 ..	....	....	*2,857*	*3,248*	*4,514*	*3,882*	*3,385*	....
C. Financial Account[1]	4 995 W.	....	....	**−1,084**	**−1,680**	**−1,558**	**−262**	**−806**	....
Direct investment abroad	4 505 ..	....	....	−69	2	81	−60	−512	....
Direct investment in China, P.R.: Macao	4 555 Z.	....	....	415	517	768	1,767	2,654	....
Portfolio investment assets	4 602 ..	....	....	−903	−1,191	−2,181	−617	−1,436	....
Equity securities	4 610 ..	....	....	−290	−358	−487	−356	−212	....
Debt securities	4 619 ..	....	....	−613	−834	−1,694	−261	−1,224	....
Portfolio investment liabilities	4 652 Z.	....	....	1	....	....	....	....	....
Equity securities	4 660 ..	....	....	1	....	....	....	....	....
Debt securities	4 669 Z.	....	....	....	....	....	....	....	....
Financial derivatives	4 910 ..	....	....	118	−114	−584	−522	−212	....
Financial derivatives assets	4 900 ..	....	....	118	−114	−584	−522	−212	....
Financial derivatives liabilities	4 905 ..	....	....	....	....	....	....	....	....
Other investment assets	4 703 ..	....	....	−878	−816	−179	−4,428	−5,520	....
Monetary authorities	4 701 ..	....	....	....	....	....	....	....	....
General government	4 704 ..	....	....	−15	−12	−107	−173	−26	....
Banks	4 705 ..	....	....	−1,015	−760	−58	−4,158	−4,781	....
Other sectors	4 728 ..	....	....	152	−44	−14	−97	−712	....
Other investment liabilities	4 753 W.	....	....	232	−78	538	3,599	4,220	....
Monetary authorities	4 753 WA	....	....	....	....	....	....	....	....
General government	4 753 ZB	....	....	....	....	....	....	....	....
Banks	4 753 ZC	....	....	265	−119	414	3,441	2,671	....
Other sectors	4 753 ZD	....	....	−32	41	124	159	1,548	....
Total, Groups A Through C	4 983 ..	....	....	*1,774*	*1,568*	*2,956*	*3,620*	*2,578*	....
D. Net Errors and Omissions	4 998 ..	....	....	**−1,572**	**−1,077**	**−1,932**	**−2,494**	**−520**	....
Total, Groups A Through D	4 984 ..	....	....	*202*	*491*	*1,024*	*1,126*	*2,058*	....
E. Reserves and Related Items	4 802 A.	....	....	**−202**	**−491**	**−1,024**	**−1,126**	**−2,058**	....
Reserve assets	4 802 ..	....	....	−202	−491	−1,024	−1,126	−2,058	....
Use of Fund credit and loans	4 766 ..	....	....	....	....	....	....	....	....
Exceptional financing	4 920 ..	....	....	....	....	....	....	....	....
Conversion rates: patacas per U.S. dollar	0 101 ..	8.0259	8.0335	8.0334	8.0212	8.0222	8.0111	8.0014	8.0359

[1] Excludes components that have been classified in the categories of Group E.

Table 2. STANDARD PRESENTATION, 2000–2007

(Millions of U.S. dollars)

	Code	2000	2001	2002	2003	2004	2005	2006	2007
CURRENT ACCOUNT	4 993	....	....	2,719	3,160	4,240	3,367	2,946	....
A. GOODS	4 100	....	....	−920	−1,093	−1,842	−2,792	−3,937	....
Credit	2 100	....	....	2,358	2,585	2,816	2,478	2,559	....
General merchandise: exports f.o.b.	2 110	....	....	2,356	2,581	2,812	2,474	2,557	....
Goods for processing: exports f.o.b.	2 150	....	....	....	....	....	....	....	....
Repairs on goods	2 160	....	....	2	4	3	4	2	....
Goods procured in ports by carriers	2 170	....	....	....	....	....	....	....	....
Nonmonetary gold	2 180	....	....	....	....	....	....	....	....
Debit	3 100	....	....	−3,277	−3,678	−4,658	−5,270	−6,496	....
General merchandise: imports f.o.b.	3 110	....	....	−3,213	−3,610	−4,584	−5,164	−6,378	....
Goods for processing: imports f.o.b.	3 150	....	....	....	....	....	....	....	....
Repairs on goods	3 160	....	....	−43	−42	−34	−44	−46	....
Goods procured in ports by carriers	3 170	....	....	−21	−26	−40	−61	−71	....
Nonmonetary gold	3 180	....	....	....	....	....	−2	....	....
B. SERVICES	4 200	....	....	3,687	4,430	6,700	7,036	8,672	....
Total credit	2 200	....	....	*4,758*	*5,605*	*8,063*	*8,612*	*10,538*	....
Total debit	3 200	....	....	*−1,071*	*−1,175*	*−1,364*	*−1,576*	*−1,866*	....
Transportation services, credit	2 205	....	....	285	241	346	399	458	....
Passenger	2 850	....	....	*212*	*164*	*225*	*257*	*306*	....
Freight	2 851	....	....	*38*	*46*	*83*	*107*	*116*	....
Other	2 852	....	....	*34*	*31*	*37*	*34*	*35*	....
Sea transport, passenger	2 207	....	....	....	....	....	....	....	....
Sea transport, freight	2 208	....	....	....	....	....	....	....	....
Sea transport, other	2 209	....	....	....	....	....	....	....	....
Air transport, passenger	2 211	....	....	....	....	....	....	....	....
Air transport, freight	2 212	....	....	....	....	....	....	....	....
Air transport, other	2 213	....	....	....	....	....	....	....	....
Other transport, passenger	2 215	....	....	....	....	....	....	....	....
Other transport, freight	2 216	....	....	....	....	....	....	....	....
Other transport, other	2 217	....	....	....	....	....	....	....	....
Transportation services, debit	3 205	....	....	−122	−125	−163	−231	−268	....
Passenger	3 850	....	....	*−26*	*−21*	*−25*	*−70*	*−74*	....
Freight	3 851	....	....	*−70*	*−79*	*−104*	*−119*	*−147*	....
Other	3 852	....	....	*−27*	*−25*	*−34*	*−42*	*−47*	....
Sea transport, passenger	3 207	....	....	....	....	....	....	....	....
Sea transport, freight	3 208	....	....	....	....	....	....	....	....
Sea transport, other	3 209	....	....	....	....	....	....	....	....
Air transport, passenger	3 211	....	....	....	....	....	....	....	....
Air transport, freight	3 212	....	....	....	....	....	....	....	....
Air transport, other	3 213	....	....	....	....	....	....	....	....
Other transport, passenger	3 215	....	....	....	....	....	....	....	....
Other transport, freight	3 216	....	....	....	....	....	....	....	....
Other transport, other	3 217	....	....	....	....	....	....	....	....
Travel, credit	2 236	....	....	4,306	5,155	7,479	7,979	9,828	....
Business travel	2 237	....	....	471	616	895	1,271	1,272	....
Personal travel	2 240	....	....	3,835	4,539	6,585	6,707	8,557	....
Travel, debit	3 236	....	....	−318	−291	−332	−358	−378	....
Business travel	3 237	....	....	−5	−4	−9	−7	−12	....
Personal travel	3 240	....	....	−314	−287	−323	−351	−366	....
Other services, credit	2 200 BA	....	....	168	210	238	235	252	....
Communications	2 245	....	....	41	45	48	56	57	....
Construction	2 249	....	....	....	....	....	....	....	....
Insurance	2 253	....	....	16	19	19	15	19	....
Financial	2 260	....	....	18	23	32	32	46	....
Computer and information	2 262	....	....	....	....	....	....	....	....
Royalties and licence fees	2 266	....	....	....	....	....	....	....	....
Other business services	2 268	....	....	92	122	139	132	131	....
Personal, cultural, and recreational	2 287	....	....	....	....	....	....	....	....
Government, n.i.e.	2 291	....	....	....	....	....	....	....	....
Other services, debit	3 200 BA	....	....	−630	−759	−868	−987	−1,220	....
Communications	3 245	....	....	−31	−38	−39	−41	−43	....
Construction	3 249	....	....	....	....	....	....	....	....
Insurance	3 253	....	....	−69	−73	−77	−94	−103	....
Financial	3 260	....	....	−10	−10	−12	−12	−14	....
Computer and information	3 262	....	....	−16	−17	−24	−25	−33	....
Royalties and licence fees	3 266	....	....	−2	−2	−3	−5	−6	....
Other business services	3 268	....	....	−478	−592	−684	−770	−973	....
Personal, cultural, and recreational	3 287	....	....	....	....	....	....	....	....
Government, n.i.e.	3 291	....	....	−25	−28	−30	−39	−47	....

Table 2 (Continued). STANDARD PRESENTATION, 2000–2007

(Millions of U.S. dollars)

	Code	2000	2001	2002	2003	2004	2005	2006	2007
C. INCOME	4 300	....	....	**−19**	**−152**	**−572**	**−776**	**−1,554**	....
Total credit	2 300	....	....	*450*	*395*	*387*	*806*	*1,426*	....
Total debit	3 300	....	....	*−468*	*−547*	*−959*	*−1,582*	*−2,981*	....
Compensation of employees, credit	2 310	....	....	....	....	....	....	....	....
Compensation of employees, debit	3 310	....	....	−10	−11	−26	−54	−151	....
Investment income, credit	2 320	....	....	450	395	387	806	1,426	....
Direct investment income	2 330	....	....	9	−5	−2	35	56	....
Dividends and distributed branch profits	2 332	....	....	15	8	12	4	16	....
Reinvested earnings and undistributed branch profits	2 333	....	....	−5	−13	−15	31	40	....
Income on debt (interest)	2 334	....	....	....	....	....	1	1	....
Portfolio investment income	2 339	....	....	177	194	213	271	334	....
Income on equity	2 340	....	....	24	36	44	51	59	....
Income on bonds and notes	2 350	....	....	142	143	155	200	252	....
Income on money market instruments	2 360	....	....	11	15	14	21	23	....
Other investment income	2 370	....	....	263	206	176	501	1,036	....
Investment income, debit	3 320	....	....	**−458**	**−536**	**−933**	**−1,529**	**−2,830**	....
Direct investment income	3 330	....	....	−400	−494	−899	−1,408	−2,467	....
Dividends and distributed branch profits	3 332	....	....	−222	−226	−609	−707	−800	....
Reinvested earnings and undistributed branch profits	3 333	....	....	−174	−263	−285	−695	−1,662	....
Income on debt (interest)	3 334	....	....	−4	−5	−5	−6	−5	....
Portfolio investment income	3 339	....	....	−6	−6	−7	−8	−12	....
Income on equity	3 340	....	....	−2	−2	−3	−5	−8	....
Income on bonds and notes	3 350	....	....	....	....	....	....	....	....
Income on money market instruments	3 360	....	....	−5	−4	−5	−3	−4	....
Other investment income	3 370	....	....	−51	−36	−27	−113	−351	....
D. CURRENT TRANSFERS	4 379	....	....	**−30**	**−25**	**−45**	**−101**	**−235**	....
Credit	2 379	....	....	**69**	**83**	**79**	**83**	**108**	....
General government	2 380	....	....	....	....	....	....	....	....
Other sectors	2 390	....	....	69	83	79	83	108	....
Workers' remittances	2 391	....	....	47	48	53	53	55	....
Other current transfers	2 392	....	....	22	35	26	30	53	....
Debit	3 379	....	....	**−99**	**−108**	**−124**	**−184**	**−343**	....
General government	3 380	....	....	−1	−2	−2	−11	−3	....
Other sectors	3 390	....	....	−98	−105	−122	−173	−340	....
Workers' remittances	3 391	....	....	−84	−83	−106	−156	−326	....
Other current transfers	3 392	....	....	−14	−22	−16	−17	−14	....
CAPITAL AND FINANCIAL ACCOUNT	4 996	....	....	**−1,147**	**−2,082**	**−2,308**	**−874**	**−2,426**	....
CAPITAL ACCOUNT	4 994	....	....	**139**	**88**	**274**	**515**	**438**	....
Total credit	2 994	....	....	*161*	*113*	*302*	*534*	*456*	....
Total debit	3 994	....	....	*−23*	*−25*	*−28*	*−20*	*−18*	....
Capital transfers, credit	2 400	....	....	**161**	**113**	**302**	**534**	**456**	....
General government	2 401	....	....	....	....	....	....	....	....
Debt forgiveness	2 402	....	....	....	....	....	....	....	....
Other capital transfers	2 410	....	....	....	....	....	....	....	....
Other sectors	2 430	....	....	161	113	302	534	456	....
Migrants' transfers	2 431	....	....	161	113	302	534	456	....
Debt forgiveness	2 432	....	....	....	....	....	....	....	....
Other capital transfers	2 440	....	....	....	....	....	....	....	....
Capital transfers, debit	3 400	....	....	**−20**	**−25**	**−28**	**−20**	**−17**	....
General government	3 401	....	....	....	....	....	....	....	....
Debt forgiveness	3 402	....	....	....	....	....	....	....	....
Other capital transfers	3 410	....	....	....	....	....	....	....	....
Other sectors	3 430	....	....	−20	−25	−28	−20	−17	....
Migrants' transfers	3 431	....	....	−20	−25	−28	−20	−17	....
Debt forgiveness	3 432	....	....	....	....	....	....	....	....
Other capital transfers	3 440	....	....	....	....	....	....	....	....
Nonproduced nonfinancial assets, credit	2 480	....	....	....	....	....	....	....	....
Nonproduced nonfinancial assets, debit	3 480	....	....	**−3**	**−1**	....	....	....	....

Table 2 (Continued). STANDARD PRESENTATION, 2000–2007

(Millions of U.S. dollars)

	Code	2000	2001	2002	2003	2004	2005	2006	2007
FINANCIAL ACCOUNT	4 995	....	....	−1,285	−2,170	−2,582	−1,388	−2,865	....
A. DIRECT INVESTMENT	4 500	....	....	346	519	849	1,706	2,142	....
Direct investment abroad	4 505	....	....	−69	2	81	−60	−512	....
Equity capital	4 510	....	....	−23	3	86	−1	106	....
Claims on affiliated enterprises	4 515	....	....	−23	3	86	−1	106	....
Liabilities to affiliated enterprises	4 520	....	....	....	....	....	....	....	....
Reinvested earnings	4 525	....	....	5	13	15	−31	−40	....
Other capital	4 530	....	....	−51	−14	−20	−29	−579	....
Claims on affiliated enterprises	4 535	....	....	−54	2	−20	−36	−578	....
Liabilities to affiliated enterprises	4 540	....	....	3	−16	....	8	−1	....
Direct investment in China, P.R.: Macao	4 555	....	....	415	517	768	1,767	2,654	....
Equity capital	4 560	....	....	83	76	2	132	173	....
Claims on direct investors	4 565	....	....	....	....	....	....	....	....
Liabilities to direct investors	4 570	....	....	83	76	2	132	173	....
Reinvested earnings	4 575	....	....	174	263	285	695	1,662	....
Other capital	4 580	....	....	158	177	481	940	819	....
Claims on direct investors	4 585	....	....	24	−5	−4	3	−132	....
Liabilities to direct investors	4 590	....	....	134	182	485	938	951	....
B. PORTFOLIO INVESTMENT	4 600	....	....	−903	−1,192	−2,181	−617	−1,436	....
Assets	4 602	....	....	−903	−1,191	−2,181	−617	−1,436	....
Equity securities	4 610	....	....	−290	−358	−487	−356	−212	....
Monetary authorities	4 611	....	....	....	....	....	....	....	....
General government	4 612	....	....	....	−76	−172	2	....	....
Banks	4 613	....	....	−26	6	−2	17	20	....
Other sectors	4 614	....	....	−264	−287	−313	−376	−232	....
Debt securities	4 619	....	....	−613	−834	−1,694	−261	−1,224	....
Bonds and notes	4 620	....	....	−577	−777	−824	−199	−1,317	....
Monetary authorities	4 621	....	....	....	....	....	....	....	....
General government	4 622	....	....	−62	−161	151	−107	−137	....
Banks	4 623	....	....	−383	−504	−671	−13	−629	....
Other sectors	4 624	....	....	−133	−113	−303	−79	−551	....
Money market instruments	4 630	....	....	−36	−56	−870	−62	92	....
Monetary authorities	4 631	....	....	....	....	....	....	....	....
General government	4 632	....	....	....	....	1	−1	....	....
Banks	4 633	....	....	−33	47	−327	−78	−23	....
Other sectors	4 634	....	....	−3	−103	−544	17	115	....
Liabilities	4 652	....	....	1	....	....	....	....	....
Equity securities	4 660	....	....	1	....	....	....	....	....
Banks	4 663	....	....	....	....	....	....	....	....
Other sectors	4 664	....	....	1	....	....	....	....	....
Debt securities	4 669	....	....	....	....	....	....	....	....
Bonds and notes	4 670	....	....	....	....	....	....	....	....
Monetary authorities	4 671	....	....	....	....	....	....	....	....
General government	4 672	....	....	....	....	....	....	....	....
Banks	4 673	....	....	....	....	....	....	....	....
Other sectors	4 674	....	....	....	....	....	....	....	....
Money market instruments	4 680	....	....	....	....	....	....	....	....
Monetary authorities	4 681	....	....	....	....	....	....	....	....
General government	4 682	....	....	....	....	....	....	....	....
Banks	4 683	....	....	....	....	....	....	....	....
Other sectors	4 684	....	....	....	....	....	....	....	....
C. FINANCIAL DERIVATIVES	4 910	....	....	118	−114	−584	−522	−212	....
Monetary authorities	4 911	....	....	....	....	....	....	....	....
General government	4 912	....	....	....	....	....	....	....	....
Banks	4 913	....	....	164	−144	−348	−632	−211	....
Other sectors	4 914	....	....	−46	30	−236	109	−1	....
Assets	4 900	....	....	118	−114	−584	−522	−212	....
Monetary authorities	4 901	....	....	....	....	....	....	....	....
General government	4 902	....	....	....	....	....	....	....	....
Banks	4 903	....	....	164	−144	−348	−632	−211	....
Other sectors	4 904	....	....	−46	30	−236	109	−1	....
Liabilities	4 905	....	....	....	....	....	....	....	....
Monetary authorities	4 906	....	....	....	....	....	....	....	....
General government	4 907	....	....	....	....	....	....	....	....
Banks	4 908	....	....	....	....	....	....	....	....
Other sectors	4 909	....	....	....	....	....	....	....	....

Table 2 (Concluded). STANDARD PRESENTATION, 2000–2007

(Millions of U.S. dollars)

	Code	2000	2001	2002	2003	2004	2005	2006	2007
D. OTHER INVESTMENT	4 700 ..	....	....	−645	−893	359	−829	−1,300	....
Assets	4 703 ..	....	....	−878	−816	−179	−4,428	−5,520	....
Trade credits	4 706 ..	....	....	15	−17	10	−35	−1	....
General government	4 707 ..	....	....	....	....	....	....	....	....
of which: Short-term	4 709 ..	....	....	....	....	....	....	....	....
Other sectors	4 710 ..	....	....	15	−17	10	−35	−1	....
of which: Short-term	4 712 ..	....	....	....	....	....	....	....	....
Loans	4 714 ..	....	....	−159	43	−167	−764	−971	....
Monetary authorities	4 715 ..	....	....	....	....	....	....	....	....
of which: Short-term	4 718 ..	....	....	....	....	....	....	....	....
General government	4 719 ..	....	....	....	....	....	....	....	....
of which: Short-term	4 721 ..	....	....	....	....	....	....	....	....
Banks	4 722 ..	....	....	−163	49	−180	−764	−968	....
of which: Short-term	4 724 ..	....	....	....	....	....	....	....	....
Other sectors	4 725 ..	....	....	4	−6	13	....	−3	....
of which: Short-term	4 727 ..	....	....	....	....	....	....	....	....
Currency and deposits	4 730 ..	....	....	−262	−446	56	127	−1,730	....
Monetary authorities	4 731 ..	....	....	....	....	....	....	....	....
General government	4 732 ..	....	....	−15	−12	−107	−173	−26	....
Banks	4 733 ..	....	....	−330	−416	202	342	−1,012	....
Other sectors	4 734 ..	....	....	83	−18	−39	−42	−692	....
Other assets	4 736 ..	....	....	−472	−396	−78	−3,757	−2,818	....
Monetary authorities	4 737 ..	....	....	....	....	....	....	....	....
of which: Short-term	4 739 ..	....	....	....	....	....	....	....	....
General government	4 740 ..	....	....	....	....	....	....	....	....
of which: Short-term	4 742 ..	....	....	....	....	....	....	....	....
Banks	4 743 ..	....	....	−522	−393	−80	−3,737	−2,801	....
of which: Short-term	4 745 ..	....	....	....	....	....	....	....	....
Other sectors	4 746 ..	....	....	50	−3	1	−20	−17	....
of which: Short-term	4 748 ..	....	....	....	....	....	....	....	....
Liabilities	4 753 ..	....	....	232	−78	538	3,599	4,220	....
Trade credits	4 756 ..	....	....	−16	16	−4	30	125	....
General government	4 757 ..	....	....	....	....	....	....	....	....
of which: Short-term	4 759 ..	....	....	....	....	....	....	....	....
Other sectors	4 760 ..	....	....	−16	16	−4	30	125	....
of which: Short-term	4 762 ..	....	....	....	....	....	....	....	....
Loans	4 764 ..	....	....	−54	27	149	37	1,399	....
Monetary authorities	4 765 ..	....	....	....	....	....	....	....	....
of which: Use of Fund credit and loans from the Fund..	4 766 ..	....	....	....	....	....	....	....	....
of which: Short-term	4 768 ..	....	....	....	....	....	....	....	....
General government	4 769 ..	....	....	....	....	....	....	....	....
of which: Short-term	4 771 ..	....	....	....	....	....	....	....	....
Banks	4 772 ..	....	....	−14	4	22	−56	144	....
of which: Short-term	4 774 ..	....	....	....	....	....	....	....	....
Other sectors	4 775 ..	....	....	−41	22	127	93	1,255	....
of which: Short-term	4 777 ..	....	....	....	....	....	....	....	....
Currency and deposits	4 780 ..	....	....	222	42	390	2,887	1,667	....
Monetary authorities	4 781 ..	....	....	....	....	....	....	....	....
General government	4 782 ..	....	....	....	....	....	....	....	....
Banks	4 783 ..	....	....	222	42	390	2,887	1,667	....
Other sectors	4 784 ..	....	....	....	....	....	....	....	....
Other liabilities	4 786 ..	....	....	81	−163	3	645	1,029	....
Monetary authorities	4 787 ..	....	....	....	....	....	....	....	....
of which: Short-term	4 789 ..	....	....	....	....	....	....	....	....
General government	4 790 ..	....	....	....	....	....	....	....	....
of which: Short-term	4 792 ..	....	....	....	....	....	....	....	....
Banks	4 793 ..	....	....	57	−165	2	609	860	....
of which: Short-term	4 795 ..	....	....	....	....	....	....	....	....
Other sectors	4 796 ..	....	....	24	3	1	36	169	....
of which: Short-term	4 798 ..	....	....	....	....	....	....	....	....
E. RESERVE ASSETS	4 802 ..	....	....	−202	−491	−1,024	−1,126	−2,058	....
Monetary gold	4 812 ..	....	....	....	....	....	....	....	....
Special drawing rights	4 811 ..	....	....	....	....	....	....	....	....
Reserve position in the Fund	4 810 ..	....	....	....	....	....	....	....	....
Foreign exchange	4 803 ..	....	....	−202	−491	−1,024	−1,127	−2,059	....
Other claims	4 813 ..	....	....	....	....	−1	1	1	....
NET ERRORS AND OMISSIONS	4 998 ..	....	....	−1,572	−1,077	−1,932	−2,494	−520	....

Table 1. ANALYTIC PRESENTATION, 2000–2007

(Millions of U.S. dollars)

	Code	2000	2001	2002	2003	2004	2005	2006	2007
A. Current Account[1].....................	4 993 Z.	808	−1,067	−1,290	−973	−908	−1,881	−2,982	−5,859
Goods: exports f.o.b........................	2 100 ..	13,760	12,869	12,384	13,813	17,224	21,729	25,181	30,577
Goods: imports f.o.b........................	3 100 ..	−11,090	−12,269	−12,077	−13,258	−15,878	−20,134	−24,859	−31,173
Balance on Goods.........................	4 100 ..	*2,670*	*600*	*306*	*556*	*1,346*	*1,595*	*322*	*−596*
Services: credit.............................	2 200 ..	2,049	2,190	1,867	1,921	2,256	2,668	3,377	3,636
Services: debit.............................	3 200 ..	−3,307	−3,602	−3,302	−3,360	−3,938	−4,770	−5,496	−6,243
Balance on Goods and Services..........	4 991 ..	*1,411*	*−812*	*−1,129*	*−883*	*−335*	*−507*	*−1,797*	*−3,203*
Income: credit.............................	2 300 ..	1,054	919	717	553	671	1,075	1,525	1,868
Income: debit.............................	3 300 ..	−3,331	−3,528	−3,584	−3,951	−4,967	−6,531	−7,454	−9,755
Balance on Goods, Services, and Income.........	4 992 ..	*−866*	*−3,421*	*−3,995*	*−4,281*	*−4,632*	*−5,963*	*−7,726*	*−11,090*
Current transfers: credit....................	2 379 Z.	1,911	2,656	3,010	3,565	3,994	4,342	5,037	5,642
Current transfers: debit....................	3 379 ..	−238	−302	−304	−256	−270	−260	−293	−410
B. Capital Account[1]....................	4 994 Z.	....	....	....	....	....	....	....	....
Capital account: credit....................	2 994 Z.	....	....	....	....	....	....	....	....
Capital account: debit....................	3 994 ..	....	....	....	....	....	....	....	....
Total, Groups A Plus B...................	4 981 ..	*808*	*−1,067*	*−1,290*	*−973*	*−908*	*−1,881*	*−2,982*	*−5,859*
C. Financial Account[1]....................	4 995 W.	50	2,453	1,301	650	3,135	3,238	2,954	10,337
Direct investment abroad....................	4 505 ..	−325	−16	−857	−938	−142	−4,662	−1,098	−913
Direct investment in Colombia..............	4 555 Z.	2,436	2,542	2,134	1,720	3,016	10,252	6,656	9,040
Portfolio investment assets..................	4 602 ..	−1,173	−3,460	2,030	−1,753	−1,565	−1,689	−3,333	−1,098
Equity securities........................	4 610 ..	....	....	....	....	....	....	....	....
Debt securities.........................	4 619 ..	−1,173	−3,460	2,030	−1,753	−1,565	−1,689	−3,333	−1,098
Portfolio investment liabilities..............	4 652 Z.	1,453	3,449	−933	130	1,306	−53	902	1,719
Equity securities........................	4 660 ..	17	−42	17	−52	130	86	−30	790
Debt securities.........................	4 669 Z.	1,436	3,492	−950	181	1,176	−138	932	929
Financial derivatives.......................	4 910 ..	−125	−133	−111	−101	−190	−62	−9	....
Financial derivatives assets................	4 900 ..	....	....	....	....	....	....	....	....
Financial derivatives liabilities.............	4 905 ..	−125	−133	−111	−101	−190	−62	−9	....
Other investment assets....................	4 703 ..	−551	231	277	1,640	433	−177	−723	−2,220
Monetary authorities....................	4 701 ..	−8	7	....	−4	−71	−3	10	−9
General government.....................	4 704 ..	−40	−35	−30	−30	−51	−48	−47	−20
Banks.................................	4 705 ..	145	102	57	−149	59	−474	223	−971
Other sectors..........................	4 728 ..	−648	157	250	1,822	497	348	−909	−1,220
Other investment liabilities.................	4 753 W.	−1,665	−161	−1,240	−48	278	−371	559	3,809
Monetary authorities....................	4 753 WA	−15	−12	−13	−12	−68	5	−5	50
General government.....................	4 753 ZB	340	226	−203	2,180	598	−1,063	852	130
Banks.................................	4 753 ZC	−1,149	−331	−376	−577	619	690	−542	1,319
Other sectors..........................	4 753 ZD	−841	−43	−648	−1,639	−871	−3	254	2,310
Total, Groups A Through C................	4 983 ..	*858*	*1,386*	*11*	*−323*	*2,228*	*1,356*	*−29*	*4,478*
D. Net Errors and Omissions....................	4 998 ..	4	−161	128	135	242	369	60	243
Total, Groups A Through D................	4 984 ..	*862*	*1,225*	*139*	*−188*	*2,470*	*1,726*	*32*	*4,721*
E. Reserves and Related Items................	4 802 A.	−862	−1,225	−139	188	−2,470	−1,726	−32	−4,721
Reserve assets............................	4 802 ..	−862	−1,225	−139	188	−2,470	−1,726	−32	−4,721
Use of Fund credit and loans...............	4 766 ..	....	....	....	....	....	....	....	....
Exceptional financing......................	4 920 ..	....	....	....	....	....	....	....	....
Conversion rates: Colombian pesos per U.S. dollar...............	0 101 ..	2,087.90	2,299.63	2,504.24	2,877.65	2,628.61	2,320.83	2,361.14	2,078.29

[1] Excludes components that have been classified in the categories of Group E.

Table 2. STANDARD PRESENTATION, 2000–2007

(Millions of U.S. dollars)

	Code	2000	2001	2002	2003	2004	2005	2006	2007
CURRENT ACCOUNT....................................	4 993 ..	**808**	**−1,067**	**−1,290**	**−973**	**−908**	**−1,881**	**−2,982**	**−5,859**
A. GOODS..	4 100 ..	**2,670**	**600**	**306**	**556**	**1,346**	**1,595**	**322**	**−596**
Credit..	2 100 ..	**13,760**	**12,869**	**12,384**	**13,813**	**17,224**	**21,729**	**25,181**	**30,577**
General merchandise: exports f.o.b.........	2 110 ..	13,582	12,728	12,214	13,153	16,550	21,053	24,710	30,048
Goods for processing: exports f.o.b.........	2 150 ..	12	7	9	5	6	9	12	15
Repairs on goods...........................	2 160 ..	....	4	7	10	23	9	3	5
Goods procured in ports by carriers.........	2 170 ..	74	62	49	57	84	141	175	177
Nonmonetary gold...........................	2 180 ..	91	68	105	588	561	517	281	332
Debit..	3 100 ..	**−11,090**	**−12,269**	**−12,077**	**−13,258**	**−15,878**	**−20,134**	**−24,859**	**−31,173**
General merchandise: imports f.o.b.........	3 110 ..	−10,945	−12,155	−11,978	−13,149	−15,750	−19,972	−24,646	−30,941
Goods for processing: imports f.o.b.........	3 150 ..	....	....	....	....	....	....	....	....
Repairs on goods...........................	3 160 ..	−34	−39	−53	−50	−40	−39	−48	−44
Goods procured in ports by carriers.........	3 170 ..	−110	−74	−47	−60	−88	−124	−166	−187
Nonmonetary gold...........................	3 180 ..	....	....	....	....	....	....	....	....
B. SERVICES..	4 200 ..	**−1,259**	**−1,412**	**−1,435**	**−1,439**	**−1,682**	**−2,102**	**−2,119**	**−2,607**
Total credit...........................	2 200 ..	*2,049*	*2,190*	*1,867*	*1,921*	*2,256*	*2,668*	*3,377*	*3,636*
Total debit...........................	3 200 ..	*−3,307*	*−3,602*	*−3,302*	*−3,360*	*−3,938*	*−4,770*	*−5,496*	*−6,243*
Transportation services, credit...........	2 205 ..	**588**	**567**	**539**	**623**	**679**	**780**	**899**	**1,104**
Passenger...........................	2 850 ..	*283*	*266*	*270*	*298*	*308*	*352*	*455*	*593*
Freight...........................	2 851 ..	*143*	*120*	*112*	*152*	*177*	*200*	*215*	*269*
Other...........................	2 852 ..	*162*	*181*	*157*	*172*	*195*	*227*	*229*	*242*
Sea transport, passenger...................	2 207 ..	....	....	....	....	....	....		
Sea transport, freight.....................	2 208 ..	19	11	12	18	36	42	40	64
Sea transport, other......................	2 209 ..	63	78	82	95	101	118	115	142
Air transport, passenger...................	2 211 ..	283	266	270	298	308	352	455	593
Air transport, freight.....................	2 212 ..	88	69	69	105	103	105	108	105
Air transport, other......................	2 213 ..	97	101	75	77	94	109	114	100
Other transport, passenger.................	2 215 ..	....	....	....	....	....	....	....	....
Other transport, freight...................	2 216 ..	37	40	31	30	38	53	67	99
Other transport, other....................	2 217 ..	1	1	....	....	....	....	....	....
Transportation services, debit...........	3 205 ..	**−1,307**	**−1,414**	**−1,202**	**−1,260**	**−1,613**	**−2,107**	**−2,253**	**−2,623**
Passenger...........................	3 850 ..	*−392*	*−392*	*−280*	*−287*	*−358*	*−435*	*−467*	*−556*
Freight...........................	3 851 ..	*−672*	*−795*	*−736*	*−789*	*−1,002*	*−1,366*	*−1,399*	*−1,686*
Other...........................	3 852 ..	*−242*	*−228*	*−185*	*−184*	*−253*	*−306*	*−387*	*−381*
Sea transport, passenger...................	3 207 ..	....	....	....	....	....	....		
Sea transport, freight.....................	3 208 ..	−545	−637	−598	−654	−831	−1,147	−1,157	−1,450
Sea transport, other......................	3 209 ..	−39	−19	−18	−22	−48	−59	−73	−79
Air transport, passenger...................	3 211 ..	−392	−392	−280	−287	−358	−435	−467	−556
Air transport, freight.....................	3 212 ..	−96	−121	−110	−112	−143	−188	−209	−199
Air transport, other......................	3 213 ..	−203	−209	−168	−162	−206	−247	−314	−302
Other transport, passenger.................	3 215 ..	....	....	....	....	....	....	....	....
Other transport, freight...................	3 216 ..	−31	−36	−28	−23	−27	−31	−32	−37
Other transport, other....................	3 217 ..	....	....	....	....	....	....		
Travel, credit..	2 236 ..	**1,030**	**1,217**	**967**	**893**	**1,061**	**1,222**	**1,554**	**1,669**
Business travel...........................	2 237 ..	....	....	....	....	....	....		
Personal travel..........................	2 240 ..	1,030	1,217	967	893	1,061	1,222	1,554	1,669
Travel, debit..	3 236 ..	**−1,060**	**−1,164**	**−1,075**	**−1,062**	**−1,111**	**−1,130**	**−1,332**	**−1,537**
Business travel...........................	3 237 ..	....	....	....	....	....	....		
Personal travel..........................	3 240 ..	−1,060	−1,164	−1,075	−1,062	−1,111	−1,130	−1,332	−1,537
Other services, credit........................	2 200 BA	**430**	**406**	**361**	**405**	**516**	**666**	**924**	**863**
Communications...........................	2 245 ..	182	182	146	133	183	217	252	256
Construction..............................	2 249 ..	....	....	....	....	....	....	....	....
Insurance.................................	2 253 ..	....	....	....	....	....	....		
Financial.................................	2 260 ..	74	53	36	36	31	31	59	68
Computer and information.................	2 262 ..	4	8	6	16	17	21	35	30
Royalties and licence fees.................	2 266 ..	5	3	4	6	6	10	11	17
Other business services...................	2 268 ..	78	68	74	113	171	272	445	376
Personal, cultural, and recreational.........	2 287 ..	23	25	27	31	39	41	46	38
Government, n.i.e.........................	2 291 ..	64	67	68	69	70	74	76	77
Other services, debit........................	3 200 BA	**−941**	**−1,024**	**−1,026**	**−1,039**	**−1,214**	**−1,532**	**−1,911**	**−2,082**
Communications...........................	3 245 ..	−123	−113	−113	−108	−144	−152	−199	−201
Construction..............................	3 249 ..	....	....	....	....	....	....	....	....
Insurance.................................	3 253 ..	−202	−239	−282	−238	−249	−290	−317	−375
Financial.................................	3 260 ..	−115	−135	−113	−101	−95	−145	−162	−125
Computer and information.................	3 262 ..	−46	−40	−29	−72	−66	−119	−143	−72
Royalties and licence fees.................	3 266 ..	−74	−77	−86	−76	−82	−118	−127	−188
Other business services...................	3 268 ..	−289	−324	−307	−354	−481	−600	−837	−994
Personal, cultural, and recreational.........	3 287 ..	−27	−27	−28	−29	−31	−44	−58	−54
Government, n.i.e.........................	3 291 ..	−65	−67	−68	−62	−65	−66	−68	−73

Table 2 (Continued). STANDARD PRESENTATION, 2000–2007

(Millions of U.S. dollars)

	Code	2000	2001	2002	2003	2004	2005	2006	2007
C. INCOME	4 300	**−2,277**	**−2,609**	**−2,866**	**−3,398**	**−4,296**	**−5,456**	**−5,929**	**−7,886**
Total credit	2 300	*1,054*	*919*	*717*	*553*	*671*	*1,075*	*1,525*	*1,868*
Total debit	3 300	*−3,331*	*−3,528*	*−3,584*	*−3,951*	*−4,967*	*−6,531*	*−7,454*	*−9,755*
Compensation of employees, credit	2 310	**32**	**35**	**26**	**16**	**20**	**32**	**38**	**30**
Compensation of employees, debit	3 310	**−12**	**−12**	**−14**	**−12**	**−19**	**−19**	**−19**	**−29**
Investment income, credit	2 320	**1,022**	**884**	**691**	**537**	**651**	**1,043**	**1,486**	**1,838**
Direct investment income	2 330	31	38	88	120	152	166	359	401
Dividends and distributed branch profits	2 332	31	38	88	120	152	166	359	401
Reinvested earnings and undistributed branch profits	2 333	....	....	....	....	....	....	....	....
Income on debt (interest)	2 334	....	....	....	....	....	....	....	....
Portfolio investment income	2 339	745	685	514	326	440	785	1,018	1,260
Income on equity	2 340	135	119	90	66	113	224	304	350
Income on bonds and notes	2 350	....	....	....	....	....	....	....	....
Income on money market instruments	2 360	610	566	424	260	327	560	714	911
Other investment income	2 370	246	161	89	92	59	92	109	177
Investment income, debit	3 320	**−3,319**	**−3,515**	**−3,570**	**−3,938**	**−4,948**	**−6,512**	**−7,435**	**−9,726**
Direct investment income	3 330	−655	−924	−1,058	−1,515	−2,433	−3,565	−4,591	−6,466
Dividends and distributed branch profits	3 332	−1,132	−595	−945	−1,193	−1,838	−2,568	−3,096	−4,633
Reinvested earnings and undistributed branch profits	3 333	476	−328	−112	−322	−595	−996	−1,495	−1,833
Income on debt (interest)	3 334	....	....	....	....	....	....	....	....
Portfolio investment income	3 339	−758	−960	−1,177	−1,219	−1,340	−1,630	−1,381	−1,523
Income on equity	3 340	−18	−14	−12	−10	−20	−20	−24	−69
Income on bonds and notes	3 350	−740	−946	−1,165	−1,209	−1,320	−1,610	−1,356	−1,454
Income on money market instruments	3 360	....	....	....	....	....	....	....	....
Other investment income	3 370	−1,905	−1,632	−1,335	−1,204	−1,175	−1,317	−1,464	−1,737
D. CURRENT TRANSFERS	4 379	**1,673**	**2,354**	**2,706**	**3,309**	**3,724**	**4,082**	**4,743**	**5,231**
Credit	2 379	**1,911**	**2,656**	**3,010**	**3,565**	**3,994**	**4,342**	**5,037**	**5,642**
General government	2 380	250	596	406	340	397	501	531	267
Other sectors	2 390	1,661	2,060	2,604	3,225	3,597	3,841	4,505	5,374
Workers' remittances	2 391	1,578	2,021	2,454	3,060	3,170	3,314	3,890	4,493
Other current transfers	2 392	83	39	151	165	427	527	616	882
Debit	3 379	**−238**	**−302**	**−304**	**−256**	**−270**	**−260**	**−293**	**−410**
General government	3 380	−10	−8	−4	−7	−6	−34	−27	−19
Other sectors	3 390	−228	−293	−300	−249	−264	−227	−266	−391
Workers' remittances	3 391	−207	−192	−144	−52	−31	−37	−47	−66
Other current transfers	3 392	−22	−101	−156	−196	−232	−189	−219	−325
CAPITAL AND FINANCIAL ACCOUNT	4 996	**−812**	**1,228**	**1,162**	**838**	**666**	**1,512**	**2,922**	**5,616**
CAPITAL ACCOUNT	4 994	....	....	....	....	....	....	....	....
Total credit	2 994	....	....	....	....	....	....	....	....
Total debit	3 994	....	....	....	....	....	....	....	....
Capital transfers, credit	2 400	....	....	....	....	....	....	....	....
General government	2 401	....	....	....	....	....	....	....	....
Debt forgiveness	2 402	....	....	....	....	....	....	....	....
Other capital transfers	2 410	....	....	....	....	....	....	....	....
Other sectors	2 430	....	....	....	....	....	....	....	....
Migrants' transfers	2 431	....	....	....	....	....	....	....	....
Debt forgiveness	2 432	....	....	....	....	....	....	....	....
Other capital transfers	2 440	....	....	....	....	....	....	....	....
Capital transfers, debit	3 400	....	....	....	....	....	....	....	....
General government	3 401	....	....	....	....	....	....	....	....
Debt forgiveness	3 402	....	....	....	....	....	....	....	....
Other capital transfers	3 410	....	....	....	....	....	....	....	....
Other sectors	3 430	....	....	....	....	....	....	....	....
Migrants' transfers	3 431	....	....	....	....	....	....	....	....
Debt forgiveness	3 432	....	....	....	....	....	....	....	....
Other capital transfers	3 440	....	....	....	....	....	....	....	....
Nonproduced nonfinancial assets, credit	2 480	....	....	....	....	....	....	....	....
Nonproduced nonfinancial assets, debit	3 480	....	....	....	....	....	....	....	....

Table 2 (Continued). STANDARD PRESENTATION, 2000–2007

(Millions of U.S. dollars)

	Code	2000	2001	2002	2003	2004	2005	2006	2007
FINANCIAL ACCOUNT..	4 995 ..	**−812**	**1,228**	**1,162**	**838**	**666**	**1,512**	**2,922**	**5,616**
A. DIRECT INVESTMENT...................................	4 500 ..	**2,111**	**2,526**	**1,277**	**783**	**2,873**	**5,590**	**5,558**	**8,127**
Direct investment abroad................................	4 505 ..	**−325**	**−16**	**−857**	**−938**	**−142**	**−4,662**	**−1,098**	**−913**
Equity capital..	4 510 ..	−325	−16	−857	−938	−142	−4,662	−1,098	−913
Claims on affiliated enterprises..............	4 515 ..	−325	−16	−857	−938	−142	−4,662	−1,098	−913
Liabilities to affiliated enterprises...........	4 520 ..	....	....	....	....	....	....	....	....
Reinvested earnings...................................	4 525 ..	....	....	....	....	....	....	....	....
Other capital..	4 530 ..	....	....	....	....	....	....	....	....
Claims on affiliated enterprises..............	4 535 ..	....	....	....	....	....	....	....	....
Liabilities to affiliated enterprises...........	4 540 ..	....	....	....	....	....	....	....	....
Direct investment in Colombia........................	4 555 ..	**2,436**	**2,542**	**2,134**	**1,720**	**3,016**	**10,252**	**6,656**	**9,040**
Equity capital..	4 560 ..	2,871	2,197	2,027	1,436	2,489	9,270	5,193	7,603
Claims on direct investors.....................	4 565 ..	....	....	....	....	....	....	....	....
Liabilities to direct investors.................	4 570 ..	2,871	2,197	2,027	1,436	2,489	9,270	5,193	7,603
Reinvested earnings...................................	4 575 ..	−476	328	112	322	595	996	1,495	1,833
Other capital..	4 580 ..	42	17	−6	−37	−68	−15	−31	−396
Claims on direct investors.....................	4 585 ..	....	....	....	....	....	....	....	−438
Liabilities to direct investors.................	4 590 ..	42	17	−6	−37	−68	−15	−31	42
B. PORTFOLIO INVESTMENT................................	4 600 ..	**280**	**−10**	**1,098**	**−1,624**	**−259**	**−1,742**	**−2,431**	**621**
Assets..	4 602 ..	**−1,173**	**−3,460**	**2,030**	**−1,753**	**−1,565**	**−1,689**	**−3,333**	**−1,098**
Equity securities..	4 610 ..	....	....	....	....	....	....	....	....
Monetary authorities...............................	4 611 ..	....	....	....	....	....	....	....	....
General government...............................	4 612 ..	....	....	....	....	....	....	....	....
Banks..	4 613 ..	....	....	....	....	....	....	....	....
Other sectors..	4 614 ..	....	....	....	....	....	....	....	....
Debt securities..	4 619 ..	−1,173	−3,460	2,030	−1,753	−1,565	−1,689	−3,333	−1,098
Bonds and notes....................................	4 620 ..	−945	−1,849	431	−1,135	−391	98	−953	−489
Monetary authorities............................	4 621 ..	....	....	....	....	....	....	....	....
General government............................	4 622 ..	....	....	....	....	....	....	....	....
Banks..	4 623 ..	....	....	....	....	....	....	....	....
Other sectors....................................	4 624 ..	−945	−1,849	431	−1,135	−391	98	−953	−489
Money market instruments.......................	4 630 ..	−229	−1,611	1,599	−618	−1,174	−1,787	−2,379	−609
Monetary authorities............................	4 631 ..	....	....	....	....	....	....	....	....
General government............................	4 632 ..	106	−1,138	1,419	−260	−488	−264	−593	1,505
Banks..	4 633 ..	30	−77	32	−36	−446	−938	−782	53
Other sectors....................................	4 634 ..	−365	−396	148	−322	−240	−585	−1,005	−2,167
Liabilities..	4 652 ..	**1,453**	**3,449**	**−933**	**130**	**1,306**	**−53**	**902**	**1,719**
Equity securities..	4 660 ..	17	−42	17	−52	130	86	−30	790
Banks..	4 663 ..	....	....	....	....	....	....	....	....
Other sectors..	4 664 ..	17	−42	17	−52	130	86	−30	790
Debt securities..	4 669 ..	1,436	3,492	−950	181	1,176	−138	932	929
Bonds and notes....................................	4 670 ..	1,436	3,492	−950	181	1,176	−138	932	929
Monetary authorities............................	4 671 ..	....	....	....	....	....	....	....	....
General government............................	4 672 ..	1,565	3,602	−419	−186	1,080	−61	1,817	300
Banks..	4 673 ..	−124	−184	....	....	....	....	−250	400
Other sectors....................................	4 674 ..	−5	74	−530	367	96	−77	−635	228
Money market instruments.......................	4 680 ..	....	....	....	....	....	....	....	....
Monetary authorities............................	4 681 ..	....	....	....	....	....	....	....	....
General government............................	4 682 ..	....	....	....	....	....	....	....	....
Banks..	4 683 ..	....	....	....	....	....	....	....	....
Other sectors....................................	4 684 ..	....	....	....	....	....	....	....	....
C. FINANCIAL DERIVATIVES...............................	4 910 ..	**−125**	**−133**	**−111**	**−101**	**−190**	**−62**	**−9**	**....**
Monetary authorities..................................	4 911 ..	....	....	....	....	....	....	....	....
General government....................................	4 912 ..	....	....	....	....	....	....	....	....
Banks..	4 913 ..	....	....	....	....	....	....	....	....
Other sectors...	4 914 ..	−125	−133	−111	−101	−190	−62	−9	....
Assets..	4 900 ..	**....**	**....**	**....**	**....**	**....**	**....**	**....**	**....**
Monetary authorities..................................	4 901 ..	....	....	....	....	....	....	....	....
General government....................................	4 902 ..	....	....	....	....	....	....	....	....
Banks..	4 903 ..	....	....	....	....	....	....	....	....
Other sectors...	4 904 ..	....	....	....	....	....	....	....	....
Liabilities..	4 905 ..	**−125**	**−133**	**−111**	**−101**	**−190**	**−62**	**−9**	**....**
Monetary authorities..................................	4 906 ..	....	....	....	....	....	....	....	....
General government....................................	4 907 ..	....	....	....	....	....	....	....	....
Banks..	4 908 ..	....	....	....	....	....	....	....	....
Other sectors...	4 909 ..	−125	−133	−111	−101	−190	−62	−9	....

Table 2 (Concluded). STANDARD PRESENTATION, 2000–2007

(Millions of U.S. dollars)

	Code	2000	2001	2002	2003	2004	2005	2006	2007
D. OTHER INVESTMENT	4 700 ..	**−2,216**	**71**	**−963**	**1,592**	**711**	**−549**	**−164**	**1,588**
Assets	4 703 ..	**−551**	**231**	**277**	**1,640**	**433**	**−177**	**−723**	**−2,220**
Trade credits	4 706 ..	−278	32	426	394	15	−219	−402	−308
General government	4 707 ..	....	....	....	....	....	....	....	....
of which: Short-term	4 709 ..	....	....	....	....	....	....	....	....
Other sectors	4 710 ..	−278	32	426	394	15	−219	−402	−308
of which: Short-term	4 712 ..	*−278*	*32*	*426*	*394*	*15*	*−219*	*−402*	*−308*
Loans	4 714 ..	34	131	−295	227	66	−629	−313	−1,510
Monetary authorities	4 715 ..	....	....	....	....	....	....	....	....
of which: Short-term	4 718 ..	....	....	....	....	....	....	....	....
General government	4 719 ..	....	....	....	....	....	....	....	....
of which: Short-term	4 721 ..	....	....	....	....	....	....	....	....
Banks	4 722 ..	113	94	4	−25	44	−447	228	−872
of which: Short-term	4 724 ..	*113*	*92*	*−2*	*−30*	*39*	*−450*	*228*	*−872*
Other sectors	4 725 ..	−79	38	−299	252	21	−181	−541	−639
of which: Short-term	4 727 ..	*−79*	*38*	*−299*	*252*	*21*	*−181*	*−541*	*−639*
Currency and deposits	4 730 ..	−259	95	175	1,052	473	720	28	−354
Monetary authorities	4 731 ..	....	....	....	....	....	....	....	....
General government	4 732 ..	....	....	....	....	....	....	....	....
Banks	4 733 ..	31	8	53	−124	14	−27	−6	−100
Other sectors	4 734 ..	−290	87	122	1,176	459	747	33	−255
Other assets	4 736 ..	−48	−28	−29	−33	−121	−50	−36	−48
Monetary authorities	4 737 ..	−8	7		−4	−71	−3	10	−9
of which: Short-term	4 739 ..	*−8*	*7*	....	*−4*	*−71*	*−3*	*10*	*−9*
General government	4 740 ..	−40	−35	−30	−30	−51	−48	−47	−20
of which: Short-term	4 742 ..	....	....	....	....	....	....	....	....
Banks	4 743 ..	....	....	....	....	....	....	....	....
of which: Short-term	4 745 ..	....	....	....	....	....	....	....	....
Other sectors	4 746 ..	....	....	1	1	1	1	1	−18
of which: Short-term	4 748 ..	....	....	....	....	....	....	....	*−19*
Liabilities	4 753 ..	**−1,665**	**−161**	**−1,240**	**−48**	**278**	**−371**	**559**	**3,809**
Trade credits	4 756 ..	−182	78	33	319	265	288	−36	302
General government	4 757 ..	−8	5	6	−24	−7	12	−27	−10
of which: Short-term	4 759 ..	....	....	....	....	....	....	....	....
Other sectors	4 760 ..	−173	73	26	342	272	276	−9	312
of which: Short-term	4 762 ..	*−163*	*120*	*53*	*320*	*317*	*238*	*52*	*187*
Loans	4 764 ..	−1,522	−305	−1,276	−390	21	−666	587	3,451
Monetary authorities	4 765 ..	−15	−12	−13	−12	−68	5	−5	50
of which: Use of Fund credit and loans from the Fund	4 766 ..	....	....	....	....	....	....	....	....
of which: Short-term	4 768 ..	....	*1*	*1*	*2*	*−2*	*5*	*−5*	*50*
General government	4 769 ..	348	221	−210	2,204	605	−1,075	878	140
of which: Short-term	4 771 ..	*−56*	....	....	....	*24*	*−24*	....	....
Banks	4 772 ..	−1,149	−331	−376	−577	619	690	−542	1,319
of which: Short-term	4 774 ..	*−260*	*279*	*38*	*−349*	*698*	*358*	*−396*	*735*
Other sectors	4 775 ..	−706	−182	−677	−2,004	−1,134	−286	255	1,942
of which: Short-term	4 777 ..	*103*	*208*	*278*	*−147*	*366*	*55*	*−316*	*−308*
Currency and deposits	4 780 ..	....	....	....	....	....	....	....	....
Monetary authorities	4 781 ..	....	....	....	....	....	....	....	....
General government	4 782 ..	....	....	....	....	....	....	....	....
Banks	4 783 ..	....	....	....	....	....	....	....	....
Other sectors	4 784 ..	....	....	....	....	....	....	....	....
Other liabilities	4 786 ..	39	66	3	23	−8	7	7	56
Monetary authorities	4 787 ..	....	....	....	....	....	....	....	....
of which: Short-term	4 789 ..	....	....	....	....	....	....	....	....
General government	4 790 ..	....	....	....	....	....	....	....	....
of which: Short-term	4 792 ..	....	....	....	....	....	....	....	....
Banks	4 793 ..	....	....	....	....	....	....	....	....
of which: Short-term	4 795 ..	....	....	....	....	....	....	....	....
Other sectors	4 796 ..	39	66	3	23	−8	7	7	56
of which: Short-term	4 798 ..	*39*	*66*	*3*	*23*	*−8*	*7*	*7*	*56*
E. RESERVE ASSETS	4 802 ..	**−862**	**−1,225**	**−139**	**188**	**−2,470**	**−1,726**	**−32**	**−4,721**
Monetary gold	4 812 ..	7	−1	−6	−10	−8	−19	3	−20
Special drawing rights	4 811 ..	−11	−6	−7	−3	−2	−6	−11	−16
Reserve position in the Fund	4 810 ..	....	....	....	....	....	....	....	....
Foreign exchange	4 803 ..	−858	−1,219	−126	201	−2,459	−1,700	−23	−4,684
Other claims	4 813 ..	....	....	....	....	....	....	....	....
NET ERRORS AND OMISSIONS	4 998 ..	**4**	**−161**	**128**	**135**	**242**	**369**	**60**	**243**

Table 3. INTERNATIONAL INVESTMENT POSITION (End-period stocks), 2000–2007

(Millions of U.S. dollars)

	Code	2000	2001	2002	2003	2004	2005	2006	2007
ASSETS	8 995 C.	25,417	29,852	28,752	29,792	33,450	41,296	47,000	56,769
Direct investment abroad	8 505 ..	2,989	2,952	3,553	4,390	4,357	8,915	10,013	10,926
Equity capital and reinvested earnings	8 506 ..	2,989	2,952	3,553	4,390	4,357	8,915	10,013	10,926
Claims on affiliated enterprises	8 507 ..	2,989	2,952	3,553	4,390	4,357	8,915	10,013	10,926
Liabilities to affiliated enterprises	8 508 ..	....	....	....	....	....	....	....	....
Other capital	8 530 ..	....	....	....	....	....	....	....	....
Claims on affiliated enterprises	8 535 ..	....	....	....	....	....	....	....	....
Liabilities to affiliated enterprises	8 540 ..	....	....	....	....	....	....	....	....
Portfolio investment	8 602 ..	5,454	8,914	6,884	8,637	10,201	11,891	15,223	16,321
Equity securities	8 610 ..	....	....	....	....	....	....	....	....
Monetary authorities	8 611 ..	....	....	....	....	....	....	....	....
General government	8 612 ..	....	....	....	....	....	....	....	....
Banks	8 613 ..	....	....	....	....	....	....	....	....
Other sectors	8 614 ..	....	....	....	....	....	....	....	....
Debt securities	8 619 ..	5,454	8,914	6,884	8,637	10,201	11,891	15,223	16,321
Bonds and notes	8 620 ..	2,809	4,659	4,228	5,363	5,754	5,656	6,609	7,098
Monetary authorities	8 621 ..	....	....	....	....	....	....	....	....
General government	8 622 ..	....	....	....	....	....	....	....	....
Banks	8 623 ..	....	....	....	....	....	....	....	....
Other sectors	8 624 ..	2,809	4,659	4,228	5,363	5,754	5,656	6,609	7,098
Money market instruments	8 630 ..	2,644	4,255	2,656	3,274	4,448	6,235	8,615	9,224
Monetary authorities	8 631 ..	....	....	....	....	....	....	....	....
General government	8 632 ..	647	1,784	365	626	1,113	1,377	1,970	465
Banks	8 633 ..	198	274	242	278	725	1,663	2,445	2,392
Other sectors	8 634 ..	1,800	2,196	2,048	2,370	2,610	3,195	4,199	6,367
Financial derivatives	8 900 ..	....	....	....	....	....	....	....	....
Monetary authorities	8 901 ..	....	....	....	....	....	....	....	....
General government	8 902 ..	....	....	....	....	....	....	....	....
Banks	8 903 ..	....	....	....	....	....	....	....	....
Other sectors	8 904 ..	....	....	....	....	....	....	....	....
Other investment	8 703 ..	7,979	7,745	7,472	5,851	5,430	5,616	6,396	8,632
Trade credits	8 706 ..	2,207	2,175	1,748	1,355	1,339	1,558	1,960	2,268
General government	8 707 ..	....	....	....	....	....	....	....	....
of which: Short-term	8 709 ..	....	....	....	....	....	....	....	....
Other sectors	8 710 ..	2,207	2,175	1,748	1,355	1,339	1,558	1,960	2,268
of which: Short-term	8 712 ..	*2,207*	*2,175*	*1,748*	*1,355*	*1,339*	*1,558*	*1,960*	*2,268*
Loans	8 714 ..	1,116	985	1,280	1,053	987	1,616	1,929	3,439
Monetary authorities	8 715 ..	....	....	....	....	....	....	....	....
of which: Short-term	8 718 ..	....	....	....	....	....	....	....	....
General government	8 719 ..	....	....	....	....	....	....	....	....
of which: Short-term	8 721 ..	....	....	....	....	....	....	....	....
Banks	8 722 ..	234	140	137	162	117	565	337	1,208
of which: Short-term	8 724 ..	*214*	*122*	*124*	*154*	*115*	*565*	*337*	*1,208*
Other sectors	8 725 ..	882	844	1,143	891	870	1,051	1,592	2,231
of which: Short-term	8 727 ..	*882*	*844*	*1,142*	*891*	*869*	*1,051*	*1,592*	*2,230*
Currency and deposits	8 730 ..	3,941	3,846	3,671	2,619	2,146	1,426	1,398	1,752
Monetary authorities	8 731 ..	....	....	....	....	....	....	....	....
General government	8 732 ..	....	....	....	....	....	....	....	....
Banks	8 733 ..	172	164	111	234	220	247	252	352
Other sectors	8 734 ..	3,769	3,682	3,561	2,385	1,926	1,179	1,146	1,400
Other assets	8 736 ..	714	739	773	825	958	1,016	1,109	1,172
Monetary authorities	8 737 ..	509	499	503	525	607	617	623	646
of which: Short-term	8 739 ..	*10*	*2*	*2*	*6*	*77*	*80*	*69*	*78*
General government	8 740 ..	205	240	270	300	351	399	446	467
of which: Short-term	8 742 ..	....	....	....	....	....	....	....	....
Banks	8 743 ..	....	....	....	....	....	....	....	....
of which: Short-term	8 745 ..	....	....	....	....	....	....	....	....
Other sectors	8 746 ..	....	....	....	....	....	....	40	60
of which: Short-term	8 748 ..	....	....	....	....	....	....	*40*	*60*
Reserve assets	8 802 ..	8,995	10,242	10,843	10,914	13,461	14,875	15,367	20,890
Monetary gold	8 812 ..	89	91	112	136	143	168	141	185
Special drawing rights	8 811 ..	135	135	154	171	181	173	193	220
Reserve position in the Fund	8 810 ..	372	359	389	425	444	408	430	452
Foreign exchange	8 803 ..	8,113	9,347	9,865	9,848	12,353	13,784	14,252	19,666
Other claims	8 813 ..	286	309	324	333	340	342	351	368

Table 3 (Concluded). INTERNATIONAL INVESTMENT POSITION (End-period stocks), 2000–2007

(Millions of U.S. dollars)

	Code	2000	2001	2002	2003	2004	2005	2006	2007
LIABILITIES	8 995 D.	**47,707**	**54,900**	**55,756**	**59,097**	**65,525**	**76,905**	**87,162**	**104,682**
Direct investment in Colombia	8 555 ..	**11,157**	**15,377**	**18,032**	**20,540**	**24,783**	**36,903**	**45,228**	**56,439**
Equity capital and reinvested earnings	8 556 ..	10,991	15,194	17,855	20,400	24,712	36,846	45,202	56,810
Claims on direct investors	8 557 ..	....	....	....	....	....	....	....	....
Liabilities to direct investors	8 558 ..	10,991	15,194	17,855	20,400	24,712	36,846	45,202	56,810
Other capital	8 580 ..	166	183	177	140	72	57	26	−370
Claims on direct investors	8 585 ..	....	....	....	....	....	....	....	−438
Liabilities to direct investors	8 590 ..	166	183	177	140	72	57	26	68
Portfolio investment	8 652 ..	**9,621**	**13,004**	**12,326**	**12,952**	**14,750**	**14,632**	**15,880**	**18,230**
Equity securities	8 660 ..	397	325	325	405	719	899	874	1,890
Banks	8 663 ..	....	....	....	....	....	....	....	....
Other sectors	8 664 ..	397	325	325	405	719	899	874	1,890
Debt securities	8 669 ..	9,224	12,679	12,001	12,546	14,031	13,733	15,007	16,340
Bonds and notes	8 670 ..	9,224	12,679	12,001	12,546	14,031	13,733	15,007	16,340
Monetary authorities	8 671 ..	....	....	....	....	....	....	....	....
General government	8 672 ..	7,746	11,311	11,163	11,342	12,731	12,510	14,669	15,383
Banks	8 673 ..	434	250	250	250	250	250	....	400
Other sectors	8 674 ..	1,044	1,118	587	955	1,050	973	338	557
Money market instruments	8 680 ..	....	....	....	....	....	....	....	....
Monetary authorities	8 681 ..	....	....	....	....	....	....	....	....
General government	8 682 ..	....	....	....	....	....	....	....	....
Banks	8 683 ..	....	....	....	....	....	....	....	....
Other sectors	8 684 ..	....	....	....	....	....	....	....	....
Financial derivatives	8 905 ..	**253**	**139**	**57**	**12**	....	....	....	....
Monetary authorities	8 906 ..	....	....	....	....	....	....	....	....
General government	8 907 ..	....	....	....	....	....	....	....	....
Banks	8 908 ..	....	....	....	....	....	....	....	....
Other sectors	8 909 ..	253	139	57	12	....	....	....	....
Other investment	8 753 ..	**26,676**	**26,379**	**25,341**	**25,593**	**25,991**	**25,371**	**26,054**	**30,013**
Trade credits	8 756 ..	1,358	1,437	1,449	1,748	2,012	2,291	2,256	2,551
General government	8 757 ..	52	58	79	56	49	60	34	24
of which: Short-term	8 759 ..	....	....	....	....	....	....	....	....
Other sectors	8 760 ..	1,306	1,379	1,370	1,691	1,963	2,232	2,223	2,527
of which: Short-term	8 762 ..	*284*	*403*	*456*	*776*	*1,094*	*1,332*	*1,385*	*1,572*
Loans	8 764 ..	25,131	24,661	23,666	23,597	23,739	22,832	23,513	27,130
Monetary authorities	8 765 ..	98	82	77	73	7	9	4	54
of which: Use of Fund credit and loans from the Fund	8 766 ..	....	....	....	....	....	....	....	....
of which: Short-term	8 768 ..	*2*	*3*	*4*	*6*	*4*	*9*	*4*	*54*
General government	8 769 ..	6,528	6,821	6,797	9,301	9,978	8,747	9,694	9,916
of which: Short-term	8 771 ..	....	....	....	....	*24*	....	....	....
Banks	8 772 ..	2,712	2,332	1,959	1,326	1,944	2,630	2,093	3,421
of which: Short-term	8 774 ..	*916*	*1,195*	*1,232*	*884*	*1,581*	*1,940*	*1,544*	*2,280*
Other sectors	8 775 ..	15,792	15,426	14,834	12,897	11,810	11,446	11,721	13,739
of which: Short-term	8 777 ..	*1,313*	*1,522*	*1,800*	*1,653*	*2,019*	*2,074*	*1,458*	*1,150*
Currency and deposits	8 780 ..	....	....	....	....	....	....	....	....
Monetary authorities	8 781 ..	....	....	....	....	....	....	....	....
General government	8 782 ..	....	....	....	....	....	....	....	....
Banks	8 783 ..	....	....	....	....	....	....	....	....
Other sectors	8 784 ..	....	....	....	....	....	....	....	....
Other liabilities	8 786 ..	187	281	225	248	239	247	286	332
Monetary authorities	8 787 ..	89	116	57	57	56	57	48	38
of which: Short-term	8 789 ..	....	*50*	....	....	....	....	....	....
General government	8 790 ..	....	....	....	....	....	....	....	....
of which: Short-term	8 792 ..	....	....	....	....	....	....	....	....
Banks	8 793 ..	....	....	....	....	....	....	....	....
of which: Short-term	8 795 ..	....	....	....	....	....	....	....	....
Other sectors	8 796 ..	98	165	168	191	183	190	238	294
of which: Short-term	8 798 ..	*98*	*165*	*168*	*191*	*183*	*190*	*238*	*294*
NET INTERNATIONAL INVESTMENT POSITION	8 995 ..	**−22,289**	**−25,048**	**−27,004**	**−29,305**	**−32,075**	**−35,610**	**−40,162**	**−47,913**
Conversion rates: Colombian pesos per U.S. dollar (end of period)	0 102 ..	2,187.02	2,301.33	2,864.79	2,780.82	2,412.10	2,284.22	2,225.44	1,987.81

Table 1. ANALYTIC PRESENTATION, 2000–2007

(Millions of U.S. dollars)

	Code	2000	2001	2002	2003	2004	2005	2006	2007
A. Current Account[1]	4 993 Z.	**648.1**	**−28.4**	**−34.5**	**520.5**	**674.4**	**695.6**	**124.1**	**−2,181.0**
Goods: exports f.o.b.	2 100 ..	2,491.8	2,055.3	2,288.8	2,636.6	3,433.2	4,745.3	6,065.7	5,808.0
Goods: imports f.o.b.	3 100 ..	−455.3	−681.3	−691.1	−831.2	−969.0	−1,305.5	−2,003.5	−2,858.1
Balance on Goods	4 100 ..	*2,036.5*	*1,373.9*	*1,597.7*	*1,805.4*	*2,464.2*	*3,439.8*	*4,062.2*	*2,949.9*
Services: credit	2 200 ..	136.5	143.8	164.8	194.1	196.7	220.5	266.0	319.4
Services: debit	3 200 ..	−738.3	−852.2	−926.9	−875.4	−1,016.3	−1,417.1	−2,425.9	−3,527.7
Balance on Goods and Services	4 991 ..	*1,434.7*	*665.6*	*835.6*	*1,124.1*	*1,644.6*	*2,243.2*	*1,902.3*	*−258.3*
Income: credit	2 300 ..	14.0	15.2	6.2	10.3	13.3	17.6	20.1	23.4
Income: debit	3 300 ..	−819.3	−694.0	−866.4	−596.4	−961.8	−1,595.5	−1,772.6	−1,908.1
Balance on Goods, Services, and Income	4 992 ..	*629.3*	*−13.2*	*−24.7*	*538.0*	*696.0*	*665.3*	*149.7*	*−2,143.1*
Current transfers: credit	2 379 Z.	38.9	18.3	12.9	26.5	34.5	87.2	37.9	43.0
Current transfers: debit	3 379 ..	−20.1	−33.5	−22.7	−44.0	−56.0	−56.9	−63.5	−81.0
B. Capital Account[1]	4 994 Z.	**8.4**	**12.7**	**5.3**	**16.9**	**12.7**	**11.2**	**9.6**	**31.7**
Capital account: credit	2 994 Z.	8.9	13.3	5.3	17.7	15.1	11.2	9.6	31.7
Capital account: debit	3 994 ..	−.6	−.7	....	−.9	−2.5	....	....	....
Total, Groups A Plus B	4 981 ..	*656.5*	*−15.8*	*−29.1*	*537.3*	*687.1*	*706.8*	*133.7*	*−2,149.3*
C. Financial Account[1]	4 995 W.	**−821.8**	**−653.1**	**−464.3**	**−701.5**	**−775.0**	**1,069.6**	**1,828.5**	**4,197.9**
Direct investment abroad	4 505 ..	−3.8	−5.9	−4.2	−1.7	−4.5	....	....	....
Direct investment in the Republic of Congo	4 555 Z.	165.9	77.2	331.2	323.1	−8.5	1,810.0	2,890.3	4,289.5
Portfolio investment assets	4 602 ..	−4.5	−11.5	−7.0	....	....	−1.1	−1.3	−1.5
Equity securities	4 610 ..	−3.9	−10.2	−3.8	....	....	−1.1	−1.3	−1.5
Debt securities	4 619 ..	−.6	−1.3	−3.2	....	....	....	....	....
Portfolio investment liabilities	4 652 Z.	−.1	....	....	−.2	2.1	....	....	....
Equity securities	4 660 ..	−.1	....	....	....	....	....	....	....
Debt securities	4 669 Z.	....	....	....	−.2	2.1	....	....	....
Financial derivatives	4 910 ..	....	....	....	....	....	....	....	....
Financial derivatives assets	4 900 ..	....	....	....	....	....	....	....	....
Financial derivatives liabilities	4 905 ..	....	....	....	....	....	....	....	....
Other investment assets	4 703 ..	−73.8	−41.1	−25.0	−180.3	−440.7	−246.5	−228.9	266.2
Monetary authorities	4 701 ..	....	....	....	....	....	....	....	....
General government	4 704 ..	....	....	....	....	....	....	....	....
Banks	4 705 ..	−20.4	27.1	31.9	125.3	−35.8	....	....	....
Other sectors	4 728 ..	−53.5	−68.2	−56.8	−305.6	−404.9	−246.5	−228.9	266.2
Other investment liabilities	4 753 W.	−905.4	−671.8	−759.3	−842.4	−323.3	−492.7	−831.5	−356.4
Monetary authorities	4 753 WA	1.4	−.4	−47.2	−4.1	.9	....	....	....
General government	4 753 ZB	−365.2	−606.8	−418.8	−283.7	−267.1	−519.8	−562.1	−494.9
Banks	4 753 ZC	−12.5	1.3	14.5	−38.9	12.9	−110.5	−130.6	−49.2
Other sectors	4 753 ZD	−529.2	−65.9	−307.8	−515.6	−70.0	137.6	−138.8	187.8
Total, Groups A Through C	4 983 ..	*−165.3*	*−668.9*	*−493.4*	*−164.1*	*−87.8*	*1,776.4*	*1,962.2*	*2,048.5*
D. Net Errors and Omissions	4 998 ..	**−77.6**	**−11.8**	**−219.7**	**−116.0**	**−92.8**	**−1,265.9**	**−1,260.1**	**−1,852.2**
Total, Groups A Through D	4 984 ..	*−242.8*	*−680.6*	*−713.1*	*−280.1*	*−180.7*	*510.5*	*702.1*	*196.4*
E. Reserves and Related Items	4 802 A.	**242.8**	**680.6**	**713.1**	**280.1**	**180.7**	**−510.5**	**−702.1**	**−196.4**
Reserve assets	4 802 ..	−183.7	143.5	91.1	2.6	−75.4	−659.5	−975.2	−88.1
Use of Fund credit and loans	4 766 ..	13.6	−1.1	−8.2	−7.6	.2	−.4	7.6	....
Exceptional financing	4 920 ..	413.0	538.3	630.3	285.0	255.9	149.4	265.4	−108.3
Conversion rates: CFA francs per U.S. dollar	0 101 ..	**711.98**	**733.04**	**696.99**	**581.20**	**528.28**	**527.47**	**522.89**	**479.27**

[1] Excludes components that have been classified in the categories of Group E.

Table 2. STANDARD PRESENTATION, 2000–2007

(Millions of U.S. dollars)

	Code	2000	2001	2002	2003	2004	2005	2006	2007
CURRENT ACCOUNT	4 993	648.1	−28.4	−34.5	520.5	674.4	695.6	124.1	−2,181.0
A. GOODS	4 100	2,036.5	1,373.9	1,597.7	1,805.4	2,464.2	3,439.8	4,062.2	2,949.9
Credit	2 100	2,491.8	2,055.3	2,288.8	2,636.6	3,433.2	4,745.3	6,065.7	5,808.0
General merchandise: exports f.o.b.	2 110	2,491.8	2,055.3	2,288.8	2,636.6	3,433.2	4,745.3	6,065.7	5,808.0
Goods for processing: exports f.o.b.	2 150	....	....	....	....	....	....	....	....
Repairs on goods	2 160	....	....	....	....	....	....	....	....
Goods procured in ports by carriers	2 170	....	....	....	....	....	....	....	....
Nonmonetary gold	2 180	....	....	....	....	....	....	....	....
Debit	3 100	−455.3	−681.3	−691.1	−831.2	−969.0	−1,305.5	−2,003.5	−2,858.1
General merchandise: imports f.o.b.	3 110	−455.3	−681.3	−691.1	−831.2	−969.0	−1,305.5	−2,003.5	−2,858.1
Goods for processing: imports f.o.b.	3 150	....	....	....	....	....	....	....	....
Repairs on goods	3 160	....	....	....	....	....	....	....	....
Goods procured in ports by carriers	3 170	....	....	....	....	....	....	....	....
Nonmonetary gold	3 180	....	....	....	....	....	....	....	....
B. SERVICES	4 200	−601.8	−708.3	−762.1	−681.3	−819.6	−1,196.7	−2,159.9	−3,208.2
Total credit	2 200	*136.5*	*143.8*	*164.8*	*194.1*	*196.7*	*220.5*	*266.0*	*319.4*
Total debit	3 200	*−738.3*	*−852.2*	*−926.9*	*−875.4*	*−1,016.3*	*−1,417.1*	*−2,425.9*	*−3,527.7*
Transportation services, credit	2 205	33.6	39.8	37.2	31.5	31.6	9.9	12.6	12.1
Passenger	2 850	*.4*	*.6*	*.6*	*1.0*	*1.1*	....	....	....
Freight	2 851	*1.8*	*4.7*	*4.4*	*7.2*	*6.1*	*9.9*	*12.6*	*12.1*
Other	2 852	*31.4*	*34.4*	*32.2*	*23.2*	*24.4*	....	....	....
Sea transport, passenger	2 207	....	....	....	....	....	....	....	....
Sea transport, freight	2 208	1.8	4.7	4.4	....	....	9.9	12.6	12.1
Sea transport, other	2 209	31.4	34.4	32.2	....	....	....	....	....
Air transport, passenger	2 211	.4	.6	.6	....	....	....	....	....
Air transport, freight	2 212	....	....	....	....	....	....	....	....
Air transport, other	2 213	....	....	....	....	....	....	....	....
Other transport, passenger	2 215	....	....	....	....	....	....	....	....
Other transport, freight	2 216	....	....	....	....	....	....	....	....
Other transport, other	2 217	....	....	....	....	....	....	....	....
Transportation services, debit	3 205	−82.2	−118.8	−119.7	−164.0	−220.7	−235.1	−360.7	−529.1
Passenger	3 850	*−9.0*	*−16.9*	*−14.7*	*−40.1*	*−72.7*	....	....	....
Freight	3 851	*−68.1*	*−100.3*	*−103.7*	*−122.5*	*−146.9*	*−235.1*	*−360.7*	*−529.1*
Other	3 852	*−5.1*	*−1.6*	*−1.4*	*−1.4*	*−1.1*	....	....	....
Sea transport, passenger	3 207	....	....	....	....	....	....	....	....
Sea transport, freight	3 208	−57.9	−85.3	−87.9	....	....	−235.1	−360.7	−529.1
Sea transport, other	3 209	−5.1	−1.6	−1.4	....	....	....	....	....
Air transport, passenger	3 211	−9.0	−16.9	−14.7	....	....	....	....	....
Air transport, freight	3 212	−10.2	−15.0	−15.8	....	....	....	....	....
Air transport, other	3 213	....	....	....	....	....	....	....	....
Other transport, passenger	3 215	....	....	....	....	....	....	....	....
Other transport, freight	3 216	....	....	....	....	....	....	....	....
Other transport, other	3 217	....	....	....	....	....	....	....	....
Travel, credit	2 236	12.1	21.8	25.4	28.7	22.1	40.4	45.3	54.5
Business travel	2 237	1.7	4.9	8.5	.7	2.3	....	....	....
Personal travel	2 240	10.5	16.9	16.9	28.0	19.9	40.4	45.3	54.5
Travel, debit	3 236	−49.7	−64.7	−70.3	−77.9	−103.2	−111.9	−132.3	−167.5
Business travel	3 237	−16.1	−30.9	−23.4	−38.9	−49.6	....	....	....
Personal travel	3 240	−33.6	−33.7	−46.8	−39.1	−53.6	−111.9	−132.3	−167.5
Other services, credit	2 200 BA	90.8	82.2	102.2	133.9	142.9	170.2	208.1	252.9
Communications	2 245	.9	2.9	3.7	5.3	9.5	....	....	....
Construction	2 249	....	....	....	....	....	....	....	....
Insurance	2 253	2.1	4.2	3.9	29.4	29.2	58.2	77.5	95.1
Financial	2 260	....	....	....	....	....	....	....	....
Computer and information	2 262	....	....	....	....	....	....	....	....
Royalties and licence fees	2 266	....	....	....	....	....	....	....	....
Other business services	2 268	68.7	51.5	66.1	80.4	80.1	98.0	115.9	141.0
Personal, cultural, and recreational	2 287	12.5	16.7	21.4	9.3	10.8	....	....	....
Government, n.i.e.	2 291	6.6	6.9	7.0	9.5	13.4	14.0	14.7	16.7
Other services, debit	3 200 BA	−606.4	−668.7	−736.9	−633.5	−692.4	−1,070.2	−1,932.9	−2,831.0
Communications	3 245	−8.5	−11.2	−12.4	−13.4	−13.8	....	....	....
Construction	3 249	....	....	....	....	....	....	....	....
Insurance	3 253	−33.8	−36.9	−35.4	−69.0	−63.6	−127.0	−150.3	−182.8
Financial	3 260	....	....	....	....	....	....	....	....
Computer and information	3 262	....	....	....	....	....	....	....	....
Royalties and licence fees	3 266	....	....	....	....	....	....	....	....
Other business services	3 268	−549.2	−605.6	−673.8	−538.4	−607.2	−938.8	−1,778.2	−2,643.2
Personal, cultural, and recreational	3 287	−4.6	−5.0	−5.5	−3.4	−3.6	....	....	....
Government, n.i.e.	3 291	−10.3	−10.0	−9.9	−9.3	−4.2	−4.4	−4.4	−5.0

Table 2 (Continued). STANDARD PRESENTATION, 2000–2007

(Millions of U.S. dollars)

	Code	2000	2001	2002	2003	2004	2005	2006	2007
C. INCOME	4 300	−805.4	−678.8	−860.3	−586.0	−948.5	−1,577.9	−1,752.6	−1,884.8
Total credit	2 300	*14.0*	*15.2*	*6.2*	*10.3*	*13.3*	*17.6*	*20.1*	*23.4*
Total debit	3 300	*−819.3*	*−694.0*	*−866.4*	*−596.4*	*−961.8*	*−1,595.5*	*−1,772.6*	*−1,908.1*
Compensation of employees, credit	2 310	9.0	9.9	....	7.7	9.3	11.4	13.2	14.8
Compensation of employees, debit	3 310	−32.3	−28.8	−30.6	−33.6	−42.6	−58.8	−73.1	−93.3
Investment income, credit	2 320	5.0	5.3	6.2	2.6	4.0	6.3	6.9	8.6
Direct investment income	2 330	....	.1	....	1.2	1.1	....	....	....
Dividends and distributed branch profits	2 332	....	.1	....	1.2	1.1	....	....	....
Reinvested earnings and undistributed branch profits	2 333	....	....	....	....	....	....	....	....
Income on debt (interest)	2 334	....	....	....	....	....	....	....	....
Portfolio investment income	2 339	....	.2	....	.9	1.1	....	....	....
Income on equity	2 340	....	.2	....	.2	.2	....	....	....
Income on bonds and notes	2 350	....	....	....	.7	.9	....	....	....
Income on money market instruments	2 360	....	....	....	....	....	....	....	....
Other investment income	2 370	5.0	5.0	6.2	.5	1.7	6.3	6.9	8.6
Investment income, debit	3 320	−787.1	−665.2	−835.9	−562.8	−919.2	−1,536.8	−1,699.6	−1,814.9
Direct investment income	3 330	−466.1	−369.0	−572.2	−387.8	−647.0	−1,296.4	−1,402.6	−1,651.1
Dividends and distributed branch profits	3 332	−310.2	−396.3	−244.5	−26.8	−341.7	....	....	....
Reinvested earnings and undistributed branch profits	3 333	−155.8	27.3	−327.6	−361.0	−305.3	−1,296.4	−1,402.6	−1,651.1
Income on debt (interest)	3 334	....	....	....	....	....	....	....	....
Portfolio investment income	3 339	....	....	....	−.3	....	....	....	....
Income on equity	3 340	....	....	....	−.3	....	....	....	....
Income on bonds and notes	3 350	....	....	....	....	....	....	....	....
Income on money market instruments	3 360	....	....	....	....	....	....	....	....
Other investment income	3 370	−321.0	−296.2	−263.7	−174.6	−272.2	−240.4	−297.0	−163.8
D. CURRENT TRANSFERS	4 379	18.8	−15.2	−9.8	−17.5	−21.6	30.3	−25.6	−38.0
Credit	2 379	38.9	18.3	12.9	26.5	34.5	87.2	37.9	43.0
General government	2 380	17.9	11.0	8.3	10.3	11.2	63.5	13.2	16.1
Other sectors	2 390	21.0	7.3	4.6	16.2	23.3	23.7	24.7	26.9
Workers' remittances	2 391	1.4	2.2	1.2	4.6	5.7	....	....	....
Other current transfers	2 392	19.6	5.1	3.4	11.5	17.6	23.7	24.7	26.9
Debit	3 379	−20.1	−33.5	−22.7	−44.0	−56.0	−56.9	−63.5	−81.0
General government	3 380	−6.1	−17.7	−2.9	−1.0	−.2	−.2	−.2	−1.3
Other sectors	3 390	−14.0	−15.8	−19.8	−43.0	−55.8	−56.7	−63.3	−79.7
Workers' remittances	3 391	−4.3	−2.7	−4.3	−5.7	−6.8	−7.4	−7.6	−9.0
Other current transfers	3 392	−9.7	−13.1	−15.5	−37.3	−49.0	−49.3	−55.7	−70.7
CAPITAL AND FINANCIAL ACCOUNT	4 996	−570.6	40.2	254.1	−404.5	−581.6	570.3	1,136.0	4,033.2
CAPITAL ACCOUNT	4 994	17.4	19.2	14.4	17.0	201.0	11.2	9.6	31.7
Total credit	2 994	*18.0*	*19.9*	*14.4*	*17.8*	*203.5*	*11.2*	*9.6*	*31.7*
Total debit	3 994	*−.6*	*−.7*	....	*−.9*	*−2.5*	....	....	....
Capital transfers, credit	2 400	18.0	19.9	14.4	17.8	203.5	11.2	9.6	31.7
General government	2 401	16.6	11.6	14.4	17.0	203.3	11.2	9.6	31.7
Debt forgiveness	2 402	9.1	6.5	9.1	.1	188.3	....	....	....
Other capital transfers	2 410	7.6	5.1	5.3	16.9	15.0	....	....	....
Other sectors	2 430	1.4	8.3	....	.9	.2	....	....	....
Migrants' transfers	2 431	....	....	....	....	....	....	....	....
Debt forgiveness	2 432	....	....	....	....	....	....	....	....
Other capital transfers	2 440	1.4	8.3	....	.9	.2	....	....	....
Capital transfers, debit	3 400	....	....	....	....	....	....	....	....
General government	3 401	....	....	....	....	....	....	....	....
Debt forgiveness	3 402	....	....	....	....	....	....	....	....
Other capital transfers	3 410	....	....	....	....	....	....	....	....
Other sectors	3 430	....	....	....	....	....	....	....	....
Migrants' transfers	3 431	....	....	....	....	....	....	....	....
Debt forgiveness	3 432	....	....	....	....	....	....	....	....
Other capital transfers	3 440	....	....	....	....	....	....	....	....
Nonproduced nonfinancial assets, credit	2 480	....	....	....	....	....	....	....	....
Nonproduced nonfinancial assets, debit	3 480	−.6	−.7	....	−.9	−2.5	....	....	....

Table 2 (Continued). STANDARD PRESENTATION, 2000–2007

(Millions of U.S. dollars)

	Code	2000	2001	2002	2003	2004	2005	2006	2007
FINANCIAL ACCOUNT..	4 995 ..	**−588.0**	**21.0**	**239.7**	**−421.5**	**−782.6**	**559.1**	**1,126.4**	**4,001.5**
A. DIRECT INVESTMENT......................................	4 500 ..	**162.1**	**71.3**	**327.0**	**321.4**	**−13.1**	**1,810.0**	**2,890.3**	**4,289.5**
Direct investment abroad..................................	4 505 ..	**−3.8**	**−5.9**	**−4.2**	**−1.7**	**−4.5**	....	....	....
Equity capital..	4 510 ..	....	−.5	....	....	....	....	....	....
Claims on affiliated enterprises........................	4 515 ..	....	....	....	....	....	....	....	....
Liabilities to affiliated enterprises...................	4 520 ..	....	−.5	....	....	....	....	....	....
Reinvested earnings...	4 525 ..	....	....	....	....	....	....	....	....
Other capital...	4 530 ..	−3.8	−5.4	−4.2	−1.7	−4.5	....	....	....
Claims on affiliated enterprises........................	4 535 ..	....	.9	1.5	....	....	....	....	....
Liabilities to affiliated enterprises...................	4 540 ..	−3.8	−6.2	−5.6	−1.7	−4.5	....	....	....
Direct investment in the Republic of Congo......	4 555 ..	**165.9**	**77.2**	**331.2**	**323.1**	**−8.5**	**1,810.0**	**2,890.3**	**4,289.5**
Equity capital..	4 560 ..	.1	10.3	....	.5	4.5	....	....	....
Claims on direct investors...............................	4 565 ..	.1	10.3	....	....	....	....	....	....
Liabilities to direct investors..........................	4 570 ..	....	....	....	.5	4.5	....	....	....
Reinvested earnings...	4 575 ..	155.8	−27.3	327.6	361.0	305.3	1,296.4	1,402.6	1,651.1
Other capital...	4 580 ..	10.0	94.3	3.5	−38.4	−318.4	513.6	1,487.7	2,638.4
Claims on direct investors...............................	4 585 ..	259.9	195.6	126.4	101.9	−101.5	....	....	....
Liabilities to direct investors..........................	4 590 ..	−249.9	−101.3	−122.9	−140.2	−216.9	513.6	1,487.7	2,638.4
B. PORTFOLIO INVESTMENT...............................	4 600 ..	**−4.5**	**−11.5**	**−7.0**	**−.2**	**2.1**	**−1.1**	**−1.3**	**−1.5**
Assets..	4 602 ..	**−4.5**	**−11.5**	**−7.0**	....	....	**−1.1**	**−1.3**	**−1.5**
Equity securities...	4 610 ..	−3.9	−10.2	−3.8	....	....	−1.1	−1.3	−1.5
Monetary authorities......................................	4 611 ..	....	....	....	....	....	....	....	....
General government.......................................	4 612 ..	....	....	....	....	....	....	....	....
Banks...	4 613 ..	....	....	....	....	....	....	....	....
Other sectors...	4 614 ..	−3.9	−10.2	−3.8	....	....	−1.1	−1.3	−1.5
Debt securities..	4 619 ..	−.6	−1.3	−3.2	....	....	....	....	....
Bonds and notes..	4 620 ..	−.6	−1.3	−3.2	....	....	....	....	....
Monetary authorities....................................	4 621 ..	....	....	....	....	....	....	....	....
General government......................................	4 622 ..	....	....	....	....	....	....	....	....
Banks...	4 623 ..	....	....	....	....	....	....	....	....
Other sectors...	4 624 ..	−.6	−1.3	−3.2	....	....	....	....	....
Money market instruments.............................	4 630 ..	....	....	....	....	....	....	....	....
Monetary authorities....................................	4 631 ..	....	....	....	....	....	....	....	....
General government......................................	4 632 ..	....	....	....	....	....	....	....	....
Banks...	4 633 ..	....	....	....	....	....	....	....	....
Other sectors...	4 634 ..	....	....	....	....	....	....	....	....
Liabilities...	4 652 ..	**−.1**	....	....	**−.2**	**2.1**	....	....	....
Equity securities...	4 660 ..	−.1	....	....	....	....	....	....	....
Banks...	4 663 ..	....	....	....	....	....	....	....	....
Other sectors...	4 664 ..	−.1	....	....	....	....	....	....	....
Debt securities..	4 669 ..	....	....	....	−.2	2.1	....	....	....
Bonds and notes..	4 670 ..	....	....	....	−.2	2.1	....	....	....
Monetary authorities....................................	4 671 ..	....	....	....	....	....	....	....	....
General government......................................	4 672 ..	....	....	....	....	....	....	....	....
Banks...	4 673 ..	....	....	....	....	....	....	....	....
Other sectors...	4 674 ..	....	....	....	−.2	2.1	....	....	....
Money market instruments.............................	4 680 ..	....	....	....	....	....	....	....	....
Monetary authorities....................................	4 681 ..	....	....	....	....	....	....	....	....
General government......................................	4 682 ..	....	....	....	....	....	....	....	....
Banks...	4 683 ..	....	....	....	....	....	....	....	....
Other sectors...	4 684 ..	....	....	....	....	....	....	....	....
C. FINANCIAL DERIVATIVES...............................	4 910 ..	....	....	....	....	....	....	....	....
Monetary authorities...	4 911 ..	....	....	....	....	....	....	....	....
General government..	4 912 ..	....	....	....	....	....	....	....	....
Banks..	4 913 ..	....	....	....	....	....	....	....	....
Other sectors..	4 914 ..	....	....	....	....	....	....	....	....
Assets..	4 900 ..	....	....	....	....	....	....	....	....
Monetary authorities...	4 901 ..	....	....	....	....	....	....	....	....
General government..	4 902 ..	....	....	....	....	....	....	....	....
Banks..	4 903 ..	....	....	....	....	....	....	....	....
Other sectors..	4 904 ..	....	....	....	....	....	....	....	....
Liabilities...	4 905 ..	....	....	....	....	....	....	....	....
Monetary authorities...	4 906 ..	....	....	....	....	....	....	....	....
General government..	4 907 ..	....	....	....	....	....	....	....	....
Banks..	4 908 ..	....	....	....	....	....	....	....	....
Other sectors..	4 909 ..	....	....	....	....	....	....	....	....

Table 2 (Concluded). STANDARD PRESENTATION, 2000–2007

(Millions of U.S. dollars)

	Code	2000	2001	2002	2003	2004	2005	2006	2007
D. OTHER INVESTMENT	4 700 ..	**−561.8**	**−182.3**	**−171.3**	**−745.3**	**−696.2**	**−590.2**	**−787.4**	**−198.4**
Assets	4 703 ..	**−73.8**	**−41.1**	**−25.0**	**−180.3**	**−440.7**	**−246.5**	**−228.9**	**266.2**
Trade credits	4 706 ..	−57.4	−77.8	−107.5	−173.6	−279.0	−246.5	−228.9	266.2
General government	4 707 ..	....	....	....	....	....	....	....	....
of which: Short-term	4 709 ..	....	....	....	....	....	....	....	....
Other sectors	4 710 ..	−57.4	−77.8	−107.5	−173.6	−279.0	−246.5	−228.9	266.2
of which: Short-term	4 712 ..	*−57.7*	*−77.8*	*−107.5*	*−173.6*	*−279.0*	*−246.5*	*−228.9*	*266.2*
Loans	4 714 ..	−.5	1.2	....	.3	....	....	....	....
Monetary authorities	4 715 ..	....	....	....	....	....	....	....	....
of which: Short-term	4 718 ..	....	....	....	....	....	....	....	....
General government	4 719 ..	....	....	....	....	....	....	....	....
of which: Short-term	4 721 ..	....	....	....	....	....	....	....	....
Banks	4 722 ..	−1.1	1.2	....	.3	....	....	....	....
of which: Short-term	4 724 ..	....	*1.3*	....	*.3*	....	....	....	....
Other sectors	4 725 ..	.6	....	....	....	....	....	....	....
of which: Short-term	4 727 ..	....	....	....	....	....	....	....	....
Currency and deposits	4 730 ..	−19.4	48.9	62.9	−4.3	−171.9	....	....	....
Monetary authorities	4 731 ..	....	....	....	....	....	....	....	....
General government	4 732 ..	....	....	....	....	....	....	....	....
Banks	4 733 ..	−19.5	25.2	31.1	124.9	−35.8	....	....	....
Other sectors	4 734 ..	.1	23.6	31.8	−129.2	−136.1	....	....	....
Other assets	4 736 ..	3.4	−13.5	19.6	−2.8	10.2	....	....	....
Monetary authorities	4 737 ..	....	....	....	....	....	....	....	....
of which: Short-term	4 739 ..	....	....	....	....	....	....	....	....
General government	4 740 ..	....	....	....	....	....	....	....	....
of which: Short-term	4 742 ..	....	....	....	....	....	....	....	....
Banks	4 743 ..	.3	.7	.8	....	....	....	....	....
of which: Short-term	4 745 ..	*.3*	*.7*	*.8*	....	....	....	....	....
Other sectors	4 746 ..	3.1	−14.1	18.9	−2.8	10.2	....	....	....
of which: Short-term	4 748 ..	*3.1*	*−14.1*	*18.9*	*−2.8*	*10.2*	....	....	....
Liabilities	4 753 ..	**−487.9**	**−141.2**	**−146.3**	**−565.0**	**−255.6**	**−343.8**	**−558.5**	**−464.7**
Trade credits	4 756 ..	−15.9	12.8	−109.2	−193.4	23.7	....	....	....
General government	4 757 ..	....	....	....	....	....	....	....	....
of which: Short-term	4 759 ..	....	....	....	....	....	....	....	....
Other sectors	4 760 ..	−15.9	12.8	−109.2	−193.4	23.7	....	....	....
of which: Short-term	4 762 ..	*−17.0*	*13.0*	*−108.3*	*−193.4*	*23.7*	....	....	....
Loans	4 764 ..	−844.0	−394.1	−305.5	−615.3	−242.7	−493.2	−823.9	−356.4
Monetary authorities	4 765 ..	13.6	−1.1	−8.2	−9.3	138.0	−.4	7.6	....
of which: Use of Fund credit and loans from the Fund	4 766 ..	*13.6*	*−1.1*	*−8.2*	*−7.6*	*.2*	*−.4*	*7.6*	....
of which: Short-term	4 768 ..	....	....	....	*−4.1*	*.9*	....	....	....
General government	4 769 ..	−344.9	−309.4	−99.2	−283.7	−267.1	−519.8	−562.1	−494.9
of which: Short-term	4 771 ..	....	....	....	....	....	....	....	....
Banks	4 772 ..	5.6	....	13.1	....	....	−110.5	−130.6	−49.2
of which: Short-term	4 774 ..	....	....	*13.1*	....	....	*−110.5*	*−130.6*	*−49.2*
Other sectors	4 775 ..	−518.3	−83.5	−211.2	−322.3	−113.6	137.6	−138.8	187.8
of which: Short-term	4 777 ..	*−328.7*	*−8.6*	....	....	....	....	....	....
Currency and deposits	4 780 ..	−8.8	12.8	−33.1	−38.9	13.3	....	....	....
Monetary authorities	4 781 ..	1.4	−.4	−47.2	....	....	....	....	....
General government	4 782 ..	....	....	....	....	....	....	....	....
Banks	4 783 ..	−18.1	.8	1.5	−38.9	12.9	....	....	....
Other sectors	4 784 ..	7.9	12.4	12.6	....	.4	....	....	....
Other liabilities	4 786 ..	380.8	227.3	301.6	282.5	−49.8	149.4	265.4	−108.3
Monetary authorities	4 787 ..	....	....	....	282.5	−69.3	149.4	265.4	−108.3
of which: Short-term	4 789 ..	....	....	....	*282.5*	*−69.3*	*149.4*	*265.4*	*−108.3*
General government	4 790 ..	383.7	234.3	301.6	....	....	....	....	....
of which: Short-term	4 792 ..	*383.7*	*234.3*	*301.6*	....	....	....	....	....
Banks	4 793 ..	....	.6	....	....	....	....	....	....
of which: Short-term	4 795 ..	....	*.6*	....	....	....	....	....	....
Other sectors	4 796 ..	−2.9	−7.7	....	....	19.5	....	....	....
of which: Short-term	4 798 ..	*−2.9*	*−7.7*	....	....	*19.5*	....	....	....
E. RESERVE ASSETS	4 802 ..	**−183.7**	**143.5**	**91.1**	**2.6**	**−75.4**	**−659.5**	**−975.2**	**−88.1**
Monetary gold	4 812 ..	....	....	....	....	....	....	....	....
Special drawing rights	4 811 ..	.1	−.2	−3.0	2.7	−6.5	4.5	2.3	....
Reserve position in the Fund	4 810 ..	....	....	....	....	....	....	....	−.1
Foreign exchange	4 803 ..	−183.8	143.7	94.0	....	−68.9	−663.9	−977.5	−88.1
Other claims	4 813 ..	....	....	....	....	....	....	....	....
NET ERRORS AND OMISSIONS	4 998 ..	**−77.6**	**−11.8**	**−219.7**	**−116.0**	**−92.8**	**−1,265.9**	**−1,260.1**	**−1,852.2**

Table 1. ANALYTIC PRESENTATION, 2000–2007

(Millions of U.S. dollars)

	Code	2000	2001	2002	2003	2004	2005	2006	2007
A. Current Account[1]	4 993 Z.	**−706.8**	**−602.9**	**−856.9**	**−880.1**	**−795.8**	**−981.0**	**−1,052.7**	**−1,577.8**
Goods: exports f.o.b.	2 100 ..	5,813.4	4,923.2	5,269.9	6,163.0	6,369.7	7,099.4	8,068.4	9,265.6
Goods: imports f.o.b.	3 100 ..	−6,023.8	−5,743.3	−6,547.7	−7,252.3	−7,791.0	−9,258.3	−10,838.3	−12,289.6
Balance on Goods	4 100 ..	*−210.5*	*−820.1*	*−1,277.7*	*−1,089.4*	*−1,421.3*	*−2,158.9*	*−2,769.9*	*−3,024.0*
Services: credit	2 200 ..	1,936.3	1,925.5	1,868.2	2,021.0	2,241.8	2,621.6	2,979.4	3,629.7
Services: debit	3 200 ..	−1,273.5	−1,179.9	−1,183.0	−1,244.6	−1,384.5	−1,505.6	−1,615.6	−1,802.7
Balance on Goods and Services	4 991 ..	*452.3*	*−74.5*	*−592.6*	*−313.0*	*−563.9*	*−1,042.9*	*−1,406.1*	*−1,197.0*
Income: credit	2 300 ..	242.8	192.9	158.4	146.5	144.5	806.9	1,135.1	722.1
Income: debit	3 300 ..	−1,495.2	−872.3	−598.2	−922.3	−588.8	−1,015.4	−1,130.8	−1,572.4
Balance on Goods, Services, and Income	4 992 ..	*−800.1*	*−753.8*	*−1,032.4*	*−1,088.8*	*−1,008.2*	*−1,251.4*	*−1,401.9*	*−2,047.4*
Current transfers: credit	2 379 Z.	203.8	266.4	296.9	368.8	371.2	470.6	586.1	734.4
Current transfers: debit	3 379 ..	−110.5	−115.5	−121.5	−160.0	−158.7	−200.1	−237.0	−264.8
B. Capital Account[1]	4 994 Z.	**8.9**	**18.1**	**12.4**	**23.7**	**11.5**	**15.9**	**1.1**	**21.2**
Capital account: credit	2 994 Z.	8.9	19.5	13.3	23.8	11.5	15.9	1.1	21.2
Capital account: debit	3 994 ..	....	−1.5	−.9	−.1	....	....	....	....
Total, Groups A Plus B	4 981 ..	*−697.8*	*−584.8*	*−844.6*	*−856.4*	*−784.3*	*−965.1*	*−1,051.6*	*−1,556.6*
C. Financial Account[1]	4 995 W.	**−34.6**	**270.5**	**857.2**	**595.2**	**471.8**	**877.9**	**1,884.5**	**2,389.3**
Direct investment abroad	4 505 ..	−5.0	−9.5	−34.0	−26.9	−60.6	43.0	−98.1	−262.4
Direct investment in Costa Rica	4 555 Z.	408.6	460.4	659.4	575.1	793.8	861.0	1,469.1	1,896.1
Portfolio investment assets	4 602 ..	−18.5	−81.2	28.4	−91.6	53.1	−680.7	−509.3	−170.4
Equity securities	4 610 ..	−4.0	−21.9	4.6	−1.5	−6.6	−6.1	3.9	−42.2
Debt securities	4 619 ..	−14.4	−59.2	23.8	−90.1	59.8	−674.6	−513.2	−128.2
Portfolio investment liabilities	4 652 Z.	−67.5	−57.9	−125.8	−304.5	−239.5	....	....	....
Equity securities	4 660 ..	....	....	....	....	....	....	....	....
Debt securities	4 669 Z.	−67.5	−57.9	−125.8	−304.5	−239.5	....	....	....
Financial derivatives	4 910 ..	....	....	....	....	....	....	....	....
Financial derivatives assets	4 900 ..	....	....	....	....	....	....	....	....
Financial derivatives liabilities	4 905 ..	....	....	....	....	....	....	....	....
Other investment assets	4 703 ..	−344.3	65.5	233.5	162.4	−308.7	154.5	654.6	−129.8
Monetary authorities	4 701 ..	−.2	−.2	−.2	−27.6	−4.1	−4.0	−3.7	−2.9
General government	4 704 ..	....	....	....	....	....	....	....	....
Banks	4 705 ..	−76.3	13.6	17.3	−35.2	−318.4	−163.3	81.9	119.8
Other sectors	4 728 ..	−267.8	52.0	216.4	225.2	13.9	321.8	576.3	−246.7
Other investment liabilities	4 753 W.	−7.8	−106.7	95.8	280.8	233.5	500.2	368.3	1,055.7
Monetary authorities	4 753 WA	−175.3	−135.2	−76.7	−47.4	−77.0	−66.6	−85.8	−5.9
General government	4 753 ZB	−74.6	−65.3	−57.7	−86.5	−69.9	−2.0	−52.9	−55.3
Banks	4 753 ZC	142.9	127.1	58.1	173.2	106.8	32.4	124.0	608.8
Other sectors	4 753 ZD	99.1	−33.4	172.1	241.5	273.7	536.4	382.9	508.2
Total, Groups A Through C	4 983 ..	*−732.4*	*−314.3*	*12.6*	*−261.2*	*−312.6*	*−87.2*	*832.9*	*832.7*
D. Net Errors and Omissions	4 998 ..	**391.0**	**168.4**	**−51.0**	**35.1**	**63.7**	**144.5**	**181.7**	**145.0**
Total, Groups A Through D	4 984 ..	*−341.4*	*−146.0*	*−38.4*	*−226.1*	*−248.8*	*57.2*	*1,014.7*	*977.7*
E. Reserves and Related Items	4 802 A.	**341.4**	**146.0**	**38.4**	**226.1**	**248.8**	**−57.2**	**−1,014.7**	**−977.7**
Reserve assets	4 802 ..	152.9	−13.0	−163.0	−338.9	−80.3	−393.5	−1,030.8	−1,147.7
Use of Fund credit and loans	4 766 ..	....	....	....	....	....	....	....	....
Exceptional financing	4 920 ..	188.4	159.0	201.4	564.9	329.1	336.2	16.2	170.0
Conversion rates: Costa Rican colones per U.S. dollar	0 101 ..	**308.19**	**328.87**	**359.82**	**398.66**	**437.94**	**477.79**	**511.30**	**516.62**

[1] Excludes components that have been classified in the categories of Group E.

Table 2. STANDARD PRESENTATION, 2000–2007

(Millions of U.S. dollars)

	Code	2000	2001	2002	2003	2004	2005	2006	2007
CURRENT ACCOUNT	4 993	−706.8	−602.9	−856.9	−880.1	−795.8	−981.0	−1,052.7	−1,577.8
A. GOODS	4 100	−210.5	−820.1	−1,277.7	−1,089.4	−1,421.3	−2,158.9	−2,769.9	−3,024.0
Credit	2 100	5,813.4	4,923.2	5,269.9	6,163.0	6,369.7	7,099.4	8,068.4	9,265.6
General merchandise: exports f.o.b.	2 110	2,440.4	2,191.9	2,268.0	2,467.6	2,671.3	2,906.9	3,227.6	3,623.3
Goods for processing: exports f.o.b.	2 150	3,355.2	2,713.8	2,984.7	3,635.0	3,621.1	4,072.3	4,732.0	5,497.9
Repairs on goods	2 160	1.0	....	....	....	....	.3	6.5	5.1
Goods procured in ports by carriers	2 170	16.8	17.5	17.3	60.4	77.3	119.9	102.3	139.4
Nonmonetary gold	2 180	....	....	....	....	....	....	....	....
Debit	3 100	−6,023.8	−5,743.3	−6,547.7	−7,252.3	−7,791.0	−9,258.3	−10,838.3	−12,289.6
General merchandise: imports f.o.b.	3 110	−4,099.5	−3,672.5	−4,292.4	−5,014.8	−5,350.3	−6,303.8	−7,303.4	−8,986.2
Goods for processing: imports f.o.b.	3 150	−1,886.9	−2,037.1	−2,220.1	−2,206.5	−2,393.4	−2,920.7	−3,503.4	−3,265.7
Repairs on goods	3 160	−11.9	−13.8	−14.4	−9.4	−18.0	....	....	−.1
Goods procured in ports by carriers	3 170	−25.5	−19.9	−20.8	−21.6	−29.2	−33.8	−31.5	−37.6
Nonmonetary gold	3 180	....	....	....	....	....	....	....	....
B. SERVICES	4 200	662.8	745.7	685.2	776.4	857.4	1,116.0	1,363.8	1,827.0
Total credit	2 200	*1,936.3*	*1,925.5*	*1,868.2*	*2,021.0*	*2,241.8*	*2,621.6*	*2,979.4*	*3,629.7*
Total debit	3 200	*−1,273.5*	*−1,179.9*	*−1,183.0*	*−1,244.6*	*−1,384.5*	*−1,505.6*	*−1,615.6*	*−1,802.7*
Transportation services, credit	2 205	257.5	267.8	244.2	240.4	245.7	282.4	290.9	341.7
Passenger	2 850	*174.9*	*166.4*	*131.4*	*131.2*	*126.6*	*138.5*	*157.6*	*195.2*
Freight	2 851	*18.6*	*15.2*	*13.4*	*15.1*	*17.6*	*17.5*	*22.8*	*35.4*
Other	2 852	*64.0*	*86.2*	*99.4*	*94.1*	*101.5*	*126.3*	*110.4*	*111.0*
Sea transport, passenger	2 207	....	....	....	....	....	....	....	....
Sea transport, freight	2 208	....	....	....	....	....	....	....	....
Sea transport, other	2 209	16.0	43.3	44.5	43.4	40.3	52.6	46.7	37.9
Air transport, passenger	2 211	174.3	165.7	129.0	128.9	123.9	135.6	155.3	192.6
Air transport, freight	2 212	7.1	2.8	.6	.5	.4	.1	.1	.1
Air transport, other	2 213	47.9	42.9	54.9	50.6	61.1	73.6	63.8	73.1
Other transport, passenger	2 215	.7	.7	2.4	2.3	2.7	2.9	2.3	2.7
Other transport, freight	2 216	11.5	12.4	12.8	14.7	17.2	17.4	22.7	35.3
Other transport, other	2 217	....	....	....	....	....	.1	....	....
Transportation services, debit	3 205	−417.2	−424.9	−447.2	−508.3	−581.8	−632.5	−624.9	−626.1
Passenger	3 850	*−65.8*	*−70.4*	*−85.0*	*−81.0*	*−74.5*	*−86.3*	*−91.7*	*−102.5*
Freight	3 851	*−302.8*	*−306.4*	*−329.2*	*−395.5*	*−473.5*	*−516.7*	*−503.7*	*−487.0*
Other	3 852	*−48.6*	*−48.1*	*−33.0*	*−31.7*	*−33.8*	*−29.5*	*−29.5*	*−36.6*
Sea transport, passenger	3 207	....	....	....	....	....	....	....	....
Sea transport, freight	3 208	−302.8	−306.4	−329.2	−395.5	−473.5	−516.7	−503.7	−487.0
Sea transport, other	3 209	....	....	....	....	....	....	....	....
Air transport, passenger	3 211	−65.8	−70.4	−85.0	−81.0	−74.5	−86.3	−91.7	−102.5
Air transport, freight	3 212	....	....	....	....	....	....	....	....
Air transport, other	3 213	−47.5	−47.2	−31.1	−29.6	−31.6	−27.1	−27.1	−33.7
Other transport, passenger	3 215	....	....	....	....	....	....	....	....
Other transport, freight	3 216	....	....	....	....	....	....	....	....
Other transport, other	3 217	−1.0	−.9	−1.9	−2.2	−2.2	−2.4	−2.4	−2.8
Travel, credit	2 236	1,302.4	1,173.3	1,160.7	1,293.1	1,458.5	1,670.8	1,731.5	2,029.1
Business travel	2 237	3.0	3.2	1.7	1.4	1.1	2.1	1.5	1.6
Personal travel	2 240	1,299.4	1,170.1	1,159.0	1,291.7	1,457.4	1,668.7	1,730.0	2,027.5
Travel, debit	3 236	−485.4	−364.4	−344.9	−353.2	−405.7	−469.5	−485.3	−628.2
Business travel	3 237	−3.0	−3.1	−1.1	−1.0	−1.3	−1.1	−1.2	−1.2
Personal travel	3 240	−482.4	−361.3	−343.8	−352.2	−404.4	−468.5	−484.0	−627.0
Other services, credit	2 200 BA	376.3	484.4	463.3	487.5	537.6	668.4	957.0	1,258.8
Communications	2 245	93.2	86.7	32.1	23.5	25.6	34.9	37.8	40.0
Construction	2 249	....	....	....	....	....	....	....	....
Insurance	2 253	....	....	....	....	....	....	....	....
Financial	2 260	3.8	4.8	5.1	4.7	9.7	9.0	11.7	12.1
Computer and information	2 262	59.7	124.6	153.4	166.8	200.3	254.8	370.9	555.7
Royalties and licence fees	2 266	.2	.9	1.7	.5	.5	.1	....	....
Other business services	2 268	194.1	241.1	243.4	260.6	266.7	332.4	497.4	619.4
Personal, cultural, and recreational	2 287	....	.1	.1	.1	.1	.1	.1	.1
Government, n.i.e.	2 291	25.3	26.2	27.5	31.4	34.6	37.0	38.9	31.5
Other services, debit	3 200 BA	−370.9	−390.6	−390.8	−383.2	−397.0	−403.6	−505.4	−548.3
Communications	3 245	−51.7	−38.2	−45.7	−51.4	−55.1	−60.8	−94.3	−98.0
Construction	3 249	....	....	....	....	....	....	....	....
Insurance	3 253	−45.4	−49.4	−68.9	−64.1	−85.2	−90.0	−86.5	−116.8
Financial	3 260	−2.7	−2.0	−1.6	−1.9	−3.8	−6.4	−14.0	−14.2
Computer and information	3 262	−9.3	−14.3	−14.8	−10.2	−16.4	−11.0	−13.6	−15.0
Royalties and licence fees	3 266	−49.8	−49.0	−51.2	−63.9	−51.4	−56.9	−87.5	−52.6
Other business services	3 268	−200.0	−224.5	−195.1	−178.2	−171.0	−174.6	−205.5	−247.6
Personal, cultural, and recreational	3 287	....	−.1	−.1	−.1	−.1	−.1	−.1	−.1
Government, n.i.e.	3 291	−12.0	−13.0	−13.5	−13.4	−14.1	−3.8	−3.9	−4.0

Table 2 (Continued). STANDARD PRESENTATION, 2000–2007

(Millions of U.S. dollars)

	Code	2000	2001	2002	2003	2004	2005	2006	2007
C. INCOME	4 300	−1,252.4	−679.3	−439.8	−775.9	−444.3	−208.5	4.3	−850.4
Total credit	2 300	*242.8*	*192.9*	*158.4*	*146.5*	*144.5*	*806.9*	*1,135.1*	*722.1*
Total debit	3 300	*−1,495.2*	*−872.3*	*−598.2*	*−922.3*	*−588.8*	*−1,015.4*	*−1,130.8*	*−1,572.4*
Compensation of employees, credit	2 310	15.6	14.5	16.4	14.9	17.3	20.6	23.3	39.7
Compensation of employees, debit	3 310	−34.3	−33.7	−35.4	−36.3	−36.6	−13.1	−13.5	−13.9
Investment income, credit	2 320	227.2	178.5	142.0	131.6	127.1	786.3	1,111.8	682.4
Direct investment income	2 330	11.0	19.9	19.9	18.2	5.0	594.6	739.9	133.3
Dividends and distributed branch profits	2 332	6.0	11.3	23.9	24.0	....	578.2	728.5	105.9
Reinvested earnings and undistributed branch profits	2 333	5.0	8.5	−4.0	−6.0	1.3	9.3	3.7	19.6
Income on debt (interest)	2 334	....	....	.1	.1	3.7	7.0	7.7	7.7
Portfolio investment income	2 339	1.1	5.0	5.5	3.1	8.6	72.1	106.4	144.4
Income on equity	2 340	....	....	....	....	....	....	....	....
Income on bonds and notes	2 350	1.1	5.0	5.5	3.1	8.6	72.1	106.4	144.4
Income on money market instruments	2 360	....	....	....	....	....	....	....	....
Other investment income	2 370	215.0	153.6	116.6	110.3	113.6	119.6	265.6	404.7
Investment income, debit	3 320	−1,460.9	−838.6	−562.8	−886.1	−552.1	−1,002.3	−1,117.3	−1,558.5
Direct investment income	3 330	−1,140.8	−565.8	−348.2	−643.5	−329.6	−742.8	−852.8	−1,131.1
Dividends and distributed branch profits	3 332	−946.8	−241.2	−5.4	−252.6	30.2	−647.2	−440.2	−599.4
Reinvested earnings and undistributed branch profits	3 333	−194.0	−324.6	−341.6	−389.9	−356.9	−91.5	−410.2	−521.0
Income on debt (interest)	3 334	....	....	−1.2	−1.0	−2.9	−4.2	−2.4	−10.8
Portfolio investment income	3 339	−96.9	−41.2	−49.3	−65.2	−61.9	−49.2	−74.5	−79.8
Income on equity	3 340	....	....	....	....	....	....	....	....
Income on bonds and notes	3 350	−96.9	−41.2	−49.3	−65.2	−61.9	−49.2	−74.5	−79.8
Income on money market instruments	3 360	....	....	....	....	....	....	....	....
Other investment income	3 370	−223.2	−231.6	−165.3	−177.3	−160.6	−210.3	−190.0	−347.6
D. CURRENT TRANSFERS	4 379	93.4	150.9	175.5	208.8	212.4	270.4	349.2	469.6
Credit	2 379	203.8	266.4	296.9	368.8	371.2	470.6	586.1	734.4
General government	2 380	51.0	22.3	12.1	7.6	9.8	8.2	25.1	28.9
Other sectors	2 390	152.9	244.1	284.8	361.2	361.3	462.3	561.0	705.5
Workers' remittances	2 391	120.4	184.0	234.3	306.0	302.2	399.8	489.8	595.6
Other current transfers	2 392	32.5	60.1	50.5	55.2	59.1	62.6	71.2	109.9
Debit	3 379	−110.5	−115.5	−121.5	−160.0	−158.7	−200.1	−237.0	−264.8
General government	3 380	−2.0	−7.5	−8.8	−4.0	−3.6	−3.9	−3.8	−7.1
Other sectors	3 390	−108.5	−108.0	−112.6	−156.0	−155.2	−196.2	−233.1	−257.8
Workers' remittances	3 391	−108.1	−106.8	−112.4	−155.7	−154.9	−195.9	−232.9	−257.5
Other current transfers	3 392	−.4	−1.2	−.3	−.2	−.2	−.2	−.3	−.3
CAPITAL AND FINANCIAL ACCOUNT	4 996	315.7	434.6	908.0	844.9	732.1	836.5	871.0	1,432.7
CAPITAL ACCOUNT	4 994	18.1	19.3	13.0	25.3	12.7	15.9	1.1	21.2
Total credit	2 994	*18.1*	*20.8*	*13.9*	*25.4*	*12.7*	*15.9*	*1.1*	*21.2*
Total debit	3 994	....	*−1.5*	*−.9*	*−.1*	....	....	....	....
Capital transfers, credit	2 400	18.1	20.8	13.9	25.4	12.7	15.9	1.1	21.2
General government	2 401	18.1	20.8	13.9	4.7	3.3	....	.4	21.2
Debt forgiveness	2 402	9.2	1.2	.6	1.6	1.2	....	.4	1.2
Other capital transfers	2 410	8.9	19.5	13.3	3.0	2.1	....	....	20.0
Other sectors	2 430	....	....	....	20.8	9.4	15.9	.7	....
Migrants' transfers	2 431	....	....	....	....	....	....	....	....
Debt forgiveness	2 432	....	....	....	....	8.6	....	....	....
Other capital transfers	2 440	....	....	....	20.8	.8	15.9	.7	....
Capital transfers, debit	3 400	....	−1.5	−.9	−.1	....	....	....	....
General government	3 401	....	−1.5	−.9	−.1	....	....	....	....
Debt forgiveness	3 402	....	....	....	....	....	....	....	....
Other capital transfers	3 410	....	−1.5	−.9	−.1	....	....	....	....
Other sectors	3 430	....	....	....	....	....	....	....	....
Migrants' transfers	3 431	....	....	....	....	....	....	....	....
Debt forgiveness	3 432	....	....	....	....	....	....	....	....
Other capital transfers	3 440	....	....	....	....	....	....	....	....
Nonproduced nonfinancial assets, credit	2 480	....	....	....	....	....	....	....	....
Nonproduced nonfinancial assets, debit	3 480	....	....	....	....	....	....	....	....

Table 2 (Continued). STANDARD PRESENTATION, 2000–2007

(Millions of U.S. dollars)

	Code	2000	2001	2002	2003	2004	2005	2006	2007
FINANCIAL ACCOUNT	4 995	297.6	415.3	895.0	819.6	719.4	820.7	869.9	1,411.6
A. DIRECT INVESTMENT	4 500	403.6	450.8	625.3	548.1	733.3	904.0	1,371.0	1,633.7
Direct investment abroad	4 505	−5.0	−9.5	−34.0	−26.9	−60.6	43.0	−98.1	−262.4
Equity capital	4 510	....	−1.0	−24.7	−35.3	−63.3	51.6	−109.8	−236.5
Claims on affiliated enterprises	4 515	....	−1.0	−24.7	−35.3	−63.3	51.6	−109.8	−236.5
Liabilities to affiliated enterprises	4 520	....	....	....	....	....	....	....	....
Reinvested earnings	4 525	−5.0	−8.5	4.0	6.0	−1.3	−9.3	−3.7	−19.6
Other capital	4 530	....	....	−13.4	2.4	4.0	.7	15.4	−6.3
Claims on affiliated enterprises	4 535	....	....	−13.4	2.4	4.0	.7	15.4	−6.3
Liabilities to affiliated enterprises	4 540	....	....	....	....	....	....	....	....
Direct investment in Costa Rica	4 555	408.6	460.4	659.4	575.1	793.8	861.0	1,469.1	1,896.1
Equity capital	4 560	159.3	236.4	375.8	255.9	312.8	483.1	1,034.2	1,377.3
Claims on direct investors	4 565	....	....	....	....	....	....	....	....
Liabilities to direct investors	4 570	159.3	236.4	375.8	255.9	312.8	483.1	1,034.2	1,377.3
Reinvested earnings	4 575	194.0	324.6	341.6	389.9	356.9	91.5	410.2	521.0
Other capital	4 580	55.2	−100.6	−58.0	−70.8	124.1	286.4	24.7	−2.2
Claims on direct investors	4 585	....	....	....	....	....	....	....	....
Liabilities to direct investors	4 590	55.2	−100.6	−58.0	−70.8	124.1	286.4	24.7	−2.2
B. PORTFOLIO INVESTMENT	4 600	−68.8	18.6	103.4	11.2	141.6	−344.5	−493.1	−.4
Assets	4 602	−18.5	−81.2	28.4	−91.6	53.1	−680.7	−509.3	−170.4
Equity securities	4 610	−4.0	−21.9	4.6	−1.5	−6.6	−6.1	3.9	−42.2
Monetary authorities	4 611	....	....	....	....	....	....	....	....
General government	4 612	....	....	....	....	....	....	....	....
Banks	4 613	....	....	....	....	....	....	....	....
Other sectors	4 614	−4.0	−21.9	4.6	−1.5	−6.6	−6.1	3.9	−42.2
Debt securities	4 619	−14.4	−59.2	23.8	−90.1	59.8	−674.6	−513.2	−128.2
Bonds and notes	4 620	−14.4	−59.2	23.8	−90.1	59.8	−674.6	−513.2	−128.2
Monetary authorities	4 621	....	....	....	....	....	....	....	....
General government	4 622	....	....	....	....	....	....	....	....
Banks	4 623	....	....	....	....	....	....	....	....
Other sectors	4 624	−14.4	−59.2	23.8	−90.1	59.8	−674.6	−513.2	−128.2
Money market instruments	4 630	....	....	....	....	....	....	....	....
Monetary authorities	4 631	....	....	....	....	....	....	....	....
General government	4 632	....	....	....	....	....	....	....	....
Banks	4 633	....	....	....	....	....	....	....	....
Other sectors	4 634	....	....	....	....	....	....	....	....
Liabilities	4 652	−50.3	99.8	74.9	102.8	88.4	336.2	16.2	170.0
Equity securities	4 660	....	....	....	....	....	....	....	....
Banks	4 663	....	....	....	....	....	....	....	....
Other sectors	4 664	....	....	....	....	....	....	....	....
Debt securities	4 669	−50.3	99.8	74.9	102.8	88.4	336.2	16.2	170.0
Bonds and notes	4 670	−50.3	99.8	74.9	102.8	88.4	336.2	16.2	170.0
Monetary authorities	4 671	−55.6	63.1	−62.8	−46.1	−184.4	....	....	....
General government	4 672	12.4	33.9	143.9	29.5	242.1	332.6	23.5	136.9
Banks	4 673	....	10.0	1.0	6.6	....	....	....	....
Other sectors	4 674	−7.1	−7.1	−7.1	112.8	30.7	3.6	−7.4	33.1
Money market instruments	4 680	....	....	....	....	....	....	....	....
Monetary authorities	4 681	....	....	....	....	....	....	....	....
General government	4 682	....	....	....	....	....	....	....	....
Banks	4 683	....	....	....	....	....	....	....	....
Other sectors	4 684	....	....	....	....	....	....	....	....
C. FINANCIAL DERIVATIVES	4 910	....	....	....	....	....	....	....	....
Monetary authorities	4 911	....	....	....	....	....	....	....	....
General government	4 912	....	....	....	....	....	....	....	....
Banks	4 913	....	....	....	....	....	....	....	....
Other sectors	4 914	....	....	....	....	....	....	....	....
Assets	4 900	....	....	....	....	....	....	....	....
Monetary authorities	4 901	....	....	....	....	....	....	....	....
General government	4 902	....	....	....	....	....	....	....	....
Banks	4 903	....	....	....	....	....	....	....	....
Other sectors	4 904	....	....	....	....	....	....	....	....
Liabilities	4 905	....	....	....	....	....	....	....	....
Monetary authorities	4 906	....	....	....	....	....	....	....	....
General government	4 907	....	....	....	....	....	....	....	....
Banks	4 908	....	....	....	....	....	....	....	....
Other sectors	4 909	....	....	....	....	....	....	....	....

Table 2 (Concluded). STANDARD PRESENTATION, 2000–2007

(Millions of U.S. dollars)

	Code	2000	2001	2002	2003	2004	2005	2006	2007
D. OTHER INVESTMENT	4 700 ..	**−190.1**	**−41.2**	**329.3**	**599.2**	**−75.2**	**654.6**	**1,022.8**	**926.0**
Assets	4 703 ..	**−344.3**	**65.5**	**233.5**	**162.4**	**−308.7**	**154.5**	**654.6**	**−129.8**
Trade credits	4 706 ..	−44.5	5.0	−118.2	−18.8	−28.8	−52.6	−58.2	−52.3
General government	4 707 ..	....	....	....	....	....	....	....	....
of which: Short-term	4 709 ..	....	....	....	....	....	....	....	....
Other sectors	4 710 ..	−44.5	5.0	−118.2	−18.8	−28.8	−52.6	−58.2	−52.3
of which: Short-term	4 712 ..	*−44.5*	*5.0*	*−104.4*	*−25.1*	*−9.2*	*−46.3*	*−64.7*	*−28.1*
Loans	4 714 ..	−30.5	−46.4	8.1	1.7	4.1	10.6	−28.6	−15.3
Monetary authorities	4 715 ..	....	....	....	....	....	....	....	....
of which: Short-term	4 718 ..	....	....	....	....	....	....	....	....
General government	4 719 ..	....	....	....	....	....	....	....	....
of which: Short-term	4 721 ..	....	....	....	....	....	....	....	....
Banks	4 722 ..	....	....	....	....	.8	−8.7	−2.9	−3.4
of which: Short-term	4 724 ..	....	....	....	....	*.1*	*.2*	....	....
Other sectors	4 725 ..	−30.5	−46.4	8.1	1.7	3.3	19.3	−25.8	−11.9
of which: Short-term	4 727 ..	*−3.7*	*−19.9*	*−2.5*	*1.9*	*2.0*	*9.7*	*−3.0*	*3.5*
Currency and deposits	4 730 ..	−282.9	105.9	342.8	207.2	−278.9	208.7	744.9	−50.5
Monetary authorities	4 731 ..	....	....	....	....	....	....	....	....
General government	4 732 ..	....	....	....	....	....	....	....	....
Banks	4 733 ..	−76.3	13.6	17.3	−35.2	−316.8	−149.0	90.1	126.5
Other sectors	4 734 ..	−206.5	92.3	325.5	242.4	37.9	357.7	654.8	−177.0
Other assets	4 736 ..	13.5	1.0	.8	−27.7	−5.0	−12.1	−3.5	−11.5
Monetary authorities	4 737 ..	−.2	−.2	−.2	−27.6	−4.1	−4.0	−3.7	−2.9
of which: Short-term	4 739 ..	....	....	....	....	....	....	....	....
General government	4 740 ..	....	....	....	....	....	....	....	....
of which: Short-term	4 742 ..	....	....	....	....	....	....	....	....
Banks	4 743 ..	....	....	....	....	−2.5	−5.6	−5.3	−3.2
of which: Short-term	4 745 ..	....	....	....	....	*−2.5*	*−5.6*	*−5.3*	*−3.2*
Other sectors	4 746 ..	13.7	1.1	.9	−.1	1.5	−2.6	5.4	−5.4
of which: Short-term	4 748 ..	*14.2*	*6.4*	*.9*	*−1.1*	*2.7*	*−.8*	*2.5*	*−4.5*
Liabilities	4 753 ..	**154.2**	**−106.7**	**95.8**	**436.8**	**233.5**	**500.2**	**368.3**	**1,055.7**
Trade credits	4 756 ..	71.9	−37.1	113.1	21.8	236.0	443.7	107.7	77.8
General government	4 757 ..	....	....	....	....	....	....	....	....
of which: Short-term	4 759 ..	....	....	....	....	....	....	....	....
Other sectors	4 760 ..	71.9	−37.1	113.1	21.8	236.0	443.7	107.7	77.8
of which: Short-term	4 762 ..	*71.9*	*−37.1*	*92.5*	*28.5*	*208.8*	*298.4*	*59.2*	*39.8*
Loans	4 764 ..	72.4	−80.5	−31.0	427.7	15.2	52.7	262.2	977.9
Monetary authorities	4 765 ..	−68.9	−133.8	−75.4	104.3	−75.1	−64.5	−85.3	−7.2
of which: Use of Fund credit and loans from the Fund	4 766 ..	....	....	....	....	....	....	....	....
of which: Short-term	4 768 ..	....	....	....	....	....	....	....	....
General government	4 769 ..	−17.5	−65.3	−57.7	−86.5	−69.9	−2.0	−52.9	−55.3
of which: Short-term	4 771 ..	....	....	....	....	....	....	....	....
Banks	4 772 ..	142.3	122.8	42.6	197.1	127.4	28.7	119.1	613.8
of which: Short-term	4 774 ..	*128.6*	*102.4*	*−30.3*	*207.2*	*82.4*	*−124.5*	*94.9*	*643.4*
Other sectors	4 775 ..	16.5	−4.3	59.4	212.8	32.9	90.5	281.3	426.6
of which: Short-term	4 777 ..	*1.5*	*18.0*	*91.3*	*41.8*	*−24.9*	*83.0*	*131.3*	*64.8*
Currency and deposits	4 780 ..	.6	4.3	15.5	−23.9	−18.4	3.2	.2	−2.7
Monetary authorities	4 781 ..	....	....	....	....	....	....	....	....
General government	4 782 ..	....	....	....	....	....	....	....	....
Banks	4 783 ..	.6	4.3	15.5	−23.9	−18.4	3.2	.2	−2.7
Other sectors	4 784 ..	....	....	....	....	....	....	....	....
Other liabilities	4 786 ..	9.3	6.6	−1.8	11.2	.6	.6	−1.9	2.8
Monetary authorities	4 787 ..	−1.4	−1.4	−1.4	4.3	−1.9	−2.1	−.5	1.3
of which: Short-term	4 789 ..	....	....	....	....	....	....	....	....
General government	4 790 ..	....	....	....	....	....	....	....	....
of which: Short-term	4 792 ..	....	....	....	....	....	....	....	....
Banks	4 793 ..	....	....	....	....	−2.3	.5	4.6	−2.2
of which: Short-term	4 795 ..	....	....	....	....	*.3*	*.5*	*4.6*	*−2.2*
Other sectors	4 796 ..	10.7	8.0	−.4	6.9	4.7	2.2	−6.1	3.7
of which: Short-term	4 798 ..	*12.6*	*7.9*	*.9*	*5.2*	*3.9*	*1.4*	*−4.6*	*3.8*
E. RESERVE ASSETS	4 802 ..	**152.9**	**−13.0**	**−163.0**	**−338.9**	**−80.3**	**−393.5**	**−1,030.8**	**−1,147.7**
Monetary gold	4 812 ..	....	....	....	....	....	....	....	....
Special drawing rights	4 811 ..	.3	.3	....	....	−.1	.1	....	−.1
Reserve position in the Fund	4 810 ..	....	....	....	....	....	....	....	....
Foreign exchange	4 803 ..	190.1	−1.4	−60.6	−352.9	−77.0	−387.9	−1,015.5	−1,125.1
Other claims	4 813 ..	−37.5	−11.9	−102.4	14.0	−3.2	−5.7	−15.3	−22.6
NET ERRORS AND OMISSIONS	4 998 ..	**391.0**	**168.4**	**−51.0**	**35.1**	**63.7**	**144.5**	**181.7**	**145.0**

Table 3. INTERNATIONAL INVESTMENT POSITION (End-period stocks), 2000–2007

(Millions of U.S. dollars)

	Code	2000	2001	2002	2003	2004	2005	2006	2007
ASSETS	8 995 C.	**4,295.5**	**4,244.6**	**4,150.3**	**4,430.7**	**6,792.0**	**7,847.0**	**9,779.9**	**11,673.9**
Direct investment abroad	8 505 ..	**86.1**	**95.8**	**127.4**	**152.4**	**196.9**	**153.6**	**262.9**	**525.9**
Equity capital and reinvested earnings	8 506 ..	86.1	95.8	114.0	141.4	189.9	147.3	260.6	517.4
Claims on affiliated enterprises	8 507 ..	102.3	112.1	130.3	157.6	206.1	163.5	276.9	533.7
Liabilities to affiliated enterprises	8 508 ..	−16.3	−16.3	−16.3	−16.3	−16.3	−16.3	−16.3	−16.3
Other capital	8 530 ..	....	....	13.4	11.0	7.0	6.3	2.2	8.5
Claims on affiliated enterprises	8 535 ..	....	....	13.4	11.0	7.0	6.3	2.2	8.5
Liabilities to affiliated enterprises	8 540 ..	....	....	....	....	....	....	....	....
Portfolio investment	8 602 ..	**108.5**	**142.5**	**131.1**	**222.7**	**169.5**	**807.1**	**1,317.9**	**1,488.2**
Equity securities	8 610 ..	44.0	7.4	2.7	4.3	10.9	17.0	13.1	55.3
Monetary authorities	8 611 ..	....	....	....	....	....	....	....	....
General government	8 612 ..	....	....	....	....	....	....	....	....
Banks	8 613 ..	....	....	....	....	....	....	....	....
Other sectors	8 614 ..	44.0	7.4	2.7	4.3	10.9	17.0	13.1	55.3
Debt securities	8 619 ..	64.5	135.1	128.3	218.4	158.6	790.0	1,304.7	1,432.9
Bonds and notes	8 620 ..	64.5	135.1	128.3	218.4	158.6	790.0	1,304.7	1,432.9
Monetary authorities	8 621 ..	....	....	....	....	....	....	....	....
General government	8 622 ..	....	....	....	....	....	....	....	....
Banks	8 623 ..	....	....	....	....	....	....	....	....
Other sectors	8 624 ..	64.5	135.1	128.3	218.4	158.6	790.0	1,304.7	1,432.9
Money market instruments	8 630 ..	....	....	....	....	....	....	....	....
Monetary authorities	8 631 ..	....	....	....	....	....	....	....	....
General government	8 632 ..	....	....	....	....	....	....	....	....
Banks	8 633 ..	....	....	....	....	....	....	....	....
Other sectors	8 634 ..	....	....	....	....	....	....	....	....
Financial derivatives	8 900 ..	....	....	....	....	....	....	....	....
Monetary authorities	8 901 ..	....	....	....	....	....	....	....	....
General government	8 902 ..	....	....	....	....	....	....	....	....
Banks	8 903 ..	....	....	....	....	....	....	....	....
Other sectors	8 904 ..	....	....	....	....	....	....	....	....
Other investment	8 703 ..	**2,699.8**	**2,593.1**	**2,313.5**	**2,136.0**	**4,503.8**	**4,573.7**	**5,084.6**	**5,546.1**
Trade credits	8 706 ..	556.5	510.7	595.1	601.6	566.5	593.3	637.4	705.4
General government	8 707 ..	....	....	....	....	....	....	....	....
of which: Short-term	8 709 ..	....	....	....	....	....	....	....	....
Other sectors	8 710 ..	556.5	510.7	595.1	601.6	566.5	593.3	637.4	705.4
of which: Short-term	8 712 ..	*556.5*	*510.7*	*584.9*	*560.7*	*519.1*	*545.1*	*599.0*	*638.0*
Loans	8 714 ..	77.7	119.1	102.6	96.0	81.7	68.4	94.7	119.2
Monetary authorities	8 715 ..	....	....	....	....	....	....	....	....
of which: Short-term	8 718 ..	....	....	....	....	....	....	....	....
General government	8 719 ..	....	....	....	....	....	....	....	....
of which: Short-term	8 721 ..	....	....	....	....	....	....	....	....
Banks	8 722 ..	....	....	....	....	.1	9.5	12.4	15.8
of which: Short-term	8 724 ..	....	....	....	....	....	....	....	....
Other sectors	8 725 ..	77.7	119.1	102.6	96.0	81.6	58.9	82.3	103.4
of which: Short-term	8 727 ..	*19.2*	*39.4*	*38.9*	*38.7*	*32.2*	*21.1*	*23.3*	*24.0*
Currency and deposits	8 730 ..	1,923.2	1,822.8	1,476.5	1,269.3	3,683.2	3,734.3	3,563.4	3,759.8
Monetary authorities	8 731 ..	35.7	35.7	35.7	35.7	35.7	35.7	35.7	35.7
General government	8 732 ..	....	....	....	....	....	....	....	....
Banks	8 733 ..	239.8	231.7	209.0	244.2	561.0	746.8	656.7	523.1
Other sectors	8 734 ..	1,647.7	1,555.4	1,231.9	989.4	3,086.5	2,951.8	2,871.0	3,201.0
Other assets	8 736 ..	142.4	140.5	139.3	169.1	172.5	177.7	789.1	961.6
Monetary authorities	8 737 ..	97.3	97.5	97.6	125.2	129.3	127.2	739.5	902.1
of which: Short-term	8 739 ..	....	....	....	....	....	....	....	....
General government	8 740 ..	....	....	....	....	....	....	....	....
of which: Short-term	8 742 ..	....	....	....	....	....	....	....	....
Banks	8 743 ..	....	....	....	....	2.5	8.0	13.3	16.5
of which: Short-term	8 745 ..	....	....	....	....	*2.5*	*8.0*	*13.3*	*16.5*
Other sectors	8 746 ..	45.1	43.0	41.6	43.9	40.7	42.5	36.3	43.0
of which: Short-term	8 748 ..	*25.8*	*19.8*	*18.4*	*21.7*	*17.3*	*17.3*	*14.0*	*19.8*
Reserve assets	8 802 ..	**1,401.1**	**1,413.2**	**1,578.3**	**1,919.6**	**1,921.8**	**2,312.6**	**3,114.6**	**4,113.6**
Monetary gold	8 812 ..	....	....	....	....	....	....	....	....
Special drawing rights	8 811 ..	.4	.1	.1	.1	.1	....	....	.1
Reserve position in the Fund	8 810 ..	26.1	25.1	27.2	29.7	31.1	28.6	30.1	31.6
Foreign exchange	8 803 ..	1,325.4	1,326.8	1,387.3	1,740.2	1,733.8	2,121.5	2,906.6	4,041.2
Other claims	8 813 ..	49.2	61.2	163.6	149.7	156.8	162.5	177.8	40.6

Table 3 (Concluded). INTERNATIONAL INVESTMENT POSITION (End-period stocks), 2000–2007

(Millions of U.S. dollars)

	Code	2000	2001	2002	2003	2004	2005	2006	2007
LIABILITIES	8 995 D.	**7,561.5**	**8,062.7**	**8,722.5**	**9,553.2**	**9,854.2**	**11,241.3**	**13,059.0**	**16,467.9**
Direct investment in Costa Rica	8 555	**2,709.1**	**3,184.7**	**3,742.1**	**4,261.9**	**4,632.1**	**5,416.9**	**6,780.4**	**8,802.8**
Equity capital and reinvested earnings	8 556	2,252.1	2,787.6	3,395.7	3,952.8	4,193.9	4,684.2	5,975.0	8,020.7
Claims on direct investors	8 557	....	....	....	....	....	....	....	....
Liabilities to direct investors	8 558	2,252.1	2,787.6	3,395.7	3,952.8	4,193.9	4,684.2	5,975.0	8,020.7
Other capital	8 580	457.1	397.0	346.4	309.2	438.2	732.7	805.5	782.0
Claims on direct investors	8 585	....	....	....	....	....	....	....	....
Liabilities to direct investors	8 590	457.1	397.0	346.4	309.2	438.2	732.7	805.5	782.0
Portfolio investment	8 652	**744.6**	**844.4**	**921.8**	**863.6**	**632.7**	**961.2**	**1,004.3**	**1,157.2**
Equity securities	8 660	....	....	....	....	....	....	....	....
Banks	8 663	....	....	....	....	....	....	....	....
Other sectors	8 664	....	....	....	....	....	....	....	....
Debt securities	8 669	744.6	844.4	921.8	863.6	632.7	961.2	1,004.3	1,157.2
Bonds and notes	8 670	744.6	844.4	921.8	863.6	632.7	961.2	1,004.3	1,157.2
Monetary authorities	8 671	341.8	405.0	344.7	181.9	....	....	....	....
General government	8 672	375.9	409.8	553.6	538.8	481.7	955.6	1,001.0	1,122.1
Banks	8 673	....	10.0	11.0	17.6	17.6	....	....	....
Other sectors	8 674	26.8	19.6	12.5	125.3	133.3	5.6	3.3	35.1
Money market instruments	8 680	....	....	....	....	....	....	....	....
Monetary authorities	8 681	....	....	....	....	....	....	....	....
General government	8 682	....	....	....	....	....	....	....	....
Banks	8 683	....	....	....	....	....	....	....	....
Other sectors	8 684	....	....	....	....	....	....	....	....
Financial derivatives	8 905	....	....	....	....	....	....	....	....
Monetary authorities	8 906	....	....	....	....	....	....	....	....
General government	8 907	....	....	....	....	....	....	....	....
Banks	8 908	....	....	....	....	....	....	....	....
Other sectors	8 909	....	....	....	....	....	....	....	....
Other investment	8 753	**4,107.8**	**4,033.6**	**4,058.6**	**4,427.6**	**4,589.5**	**4,863.2**	**5,274.3**	**6,507.9**
Trade credits	8 756	974.8	873.2	950.4	990.2	1,151.0	1,517.2	1,549.4	1,650.8
General government	8 757	....	....	....	....	....	....	....	....
of which: Short-term	8 759	....	....	....	....	....	....	....	....
Other sectors	8 760	974.8	873.2	950.4	990.2	1,151.0	1,517.2	1,549.4	1,650.8
of which: Short-term	8 762	*974.8*	*873.2*	*936.5*	*824.0*	*974.1*	*1,211.1*	*1,255.4*	*1,315.5*
Loans	8 764	3,048.6	3,075.7	3,014.0	3,361.5	3,375.2	3,287.5	3,668.9	4,800.7
Monetary authorities	8 765	394.2	294.7	240.1	308.8	234.3	168.5	84.1	77.7
of which: Use of Fund credit and loans from the Fund	8 766	....	....	....	....	....	....	....	....
of which: Short-term	8 768	....	....	....	....	....	....	....	....
General government	8 769	819.4	807.1	757.1	703.1	651.2	617.4	570.6	528.3
of which: Short-term	8 771	....	....	....	....	....	....	....	....
Banks	8 772	532.3	658.6	701.3	877.3	1,004.6	1,031.1	1,145.5	1,762.9
of which: Short-term	8 774	*324.4*	*432.8*	*402.6*	*588.6*	*671.0*	*551.5*	*641.7*	*1,289.1*
Other sectors	8 775	1,302.7	1,315.4	1,315.4	1,472.2	1,485.0	1,470.5	1,868.7	2,431.8
of which: Short-term	8 777	*152.0*	*148.1*	*223.3*	*252.5*	*221.4*	*289.7*	*413.7*	*486.0*
Currency and deposits	8 780	5.3	9.6	25.1	1.2	....	7.4	7.6	4.9
Monetary authorities	8 781	....	....	....	....	....	....	....	....
General government	8 782	....	....	....	....	....	....	....	....
Banks	8 783	5.3	9.6	25.1	1.2	....	7.4	7.6	4.9
Other sectors	8 784	....	....	....	....	....	....	....	....
Other liabilities	8 786	79.1	75.1	69.0	74.7	63.2	51.1	48.4	51.5
Monetary authorities	8 787	25.3	23.9	22.6	26.8	24.9	10.4	9.9	11.2
of which: Short-term	8 789	....	....	....	....	....	....	....	....
General government	8 790	....	....	....	....	....	....	....	....
of which: Short-term	8 792	....	....	....	....	....	....	....	....
Banks	8 793	....	....	....	....	.3	2.3	6.9	4.7
of which: Short-term	8 795	....	....	....	....	*.3*	*2.3*	*6.9*	*4.7*
Other sectors	8 796	53.8	51.2	46.4	47.8	38.0	38.5	31.6	35.6
of which: Short-term	8 798	*44.7*	*45.3*	*42.5*	*38.2*	*33.7*	*33.5*	*28.0*	*32.8*
NET INTERNATIONAL INVESTMENT POSITION	8 995	**–3,266.0**	**–3,818.1**	**–4,572.2**	**–5,122.5**	**–3,062.2**	**–3,394.3**	**–3,279.1**	**–4,794.0**
Conversion rates: Costa Rican colones per U.S. dollar (end of period)	0 102	318.02	341.67	378.72	418.53	458.61	496.68	517.90	498.10

Table 1. ANALYTIC PRESENTATION, 2000–2007

(Millions of U.S. dollars)

	Code	2000	2001	2002	2003	2004	2005	2006	2007
A. Current Account[1]............	4 993 Z.	**−241.3**	**−61.3**	**768.2**	**294.2**	**240.9**	**39.7**	**479.0**	**−146.0**
Goods: exports f.o.b.	2 100 ..	3,888.0	3,945.9	5,274.8	5,787.7	6,919.3	7,697.4	8,477.3	8,475.9
Goods: imports f.o.b.	3 100 ..	−2,401.8	−2,417.7	−2,455.6	−3,230.9	−4,291.4	−5,251.0	−5,368.3	−5,931.6
Balance on Goods............	4 100 ..	*1,486.2*	*1,528.2*	*2,819.3*	*2,556.8*	*2,627.9*	*2,446.3*	*3,109.0*	*2,544.2*
Services: credit	2 200 ..	482.4	577.8	585.3	664.0	762.7	832.4	844.6	943.1
Services: debit	3 200 ..	−1,226.9	−1,271.3	−1,544.7	−1,780.2	−2,032.6	−2,123.5	−2,233.1	−2,444.0
Balance on Goods and Services............	4 991 ..	*741.7*	*834.8*	*1,859.9*	*1,440.6*	*1,358.0*	*1,155.3*	*1,720.5*	*1,043.3*
Income: credit	2 300 ..	141.6	137.3	141.2	170.6	189.7	193.9	196.2	214.9
Income: debit	3 300 ..	−794.5	−723.1	−770.9	−830.1	−841.3	−847.1	−906.4	−1,025.1
Balance on Goods, Services, and Income............	4 992 ..	*88.8*	*249.0*	*1,230.2*	*781.1*	*706.3*	*502.1*	*1,010.3*	*233.1*
Current transfers: credit	2 379 Z.	79.4	88.5	131.9	196.4	187.4	194.8	217.7	459.0
Current transfers: debit	3 379 ..	−409.4	−398.7	−593.8	−683.3	−652.8	−657.2	−749.0	−838.2
B. Capital Account[1]............	4 994 Z.	**8.4**	**10.0**	**8.3**	**13.7**	**145.9**	**185.2**	**33.0**	**89.9**
Capital account: credit	2 994 Z.	9.9	11.5	9.1	14.1	146.4	185.8	33.6	91.0
Capital account: debit	3 994 ..	−1.4	−1.4	−.8	−.4	−.5	−.6	−.6	−1.0
Total, Groups A Plus B............	4 981 ..	*−232.8*	*−51.2*	*776.5*	*307.9*	*386.7*	*224.9*	*511.9*	*−56.1*
C. Financial Account[1]............	4 995 W.	**−362.6**	**−66.1**	**−1,028.6**	**−1,035.3**	**−263.4**	**−482.5**	**−278.5**	**331.8**
Direct investment abroad	4 505 ..	....	....	....	....	....	....	....	....
Direct investment in Côte d'Ivoire	4 555 Z.	234.7	272.7	212.6	165.3	283.0	311.9	318.9	426.9
Portfolio investment assets	4 602 ..	−12.5	−12.0	−21.1	−33.8	−37.5	−49.9	−24.2	−53.8
Equity securities	4 610 ..	−1.3	−1.3	−2.0	−14.1	−6.6	26.9	−6.0	−53.8
Debt securities	4 619 ..	−11.2	−10.7	−19.1	−19.7	−30.9	−76.8	−18.2	....
Portfolio investment liabilities	4 652 Z.	4.5	4.0	51.7	67.0	8.9	48.1	45.3	147.5
Equity securities	4 660 ..	1.2	2.4	3.6	15.8	−4.9	13.9	1.6	147.5
Debt securities	4 669 Z.	3.4	1.6	48.1	51.3	13.8	34.2	43.7	....
Financial derivatives	4 910 ..	−2.6	−3.8	−4.1	−5.3	4.3	−4.3	−6.3	....
Financial derivatives assets	4 900 ..	−2.6	−3.8	−6.0	−7.9	−6.0	−5.2	−6.3	....
Financial derivatives liabilities	4 905 ..	....	....	1.9	2.6	10.2	.9	....	....
Other investment assets	4 703 ..	−182.4	−129.1	−439.0	−341.7	−402.5	−497.9	−501.1	−390.5
Monetary authorities	4 701 ..	....	....	....	....	....	....	....	....
General government	4 704 ..	−4.5	−5.1	−7.8	−4.0	−6.6	−3.2	−5.4	.2
Banks	4 705 ..	2.8	37.7	−89.8	62.6	−32.9	−66.8	26.0	−17.0
Other sectors	4 728 ..	−180.7	−161.8	−341.5	−400.3	−363.0	−427.9	−521.8	−373.7
Other investment liabilities	4 753 W.	−404.3	−197.8	−828.6	−886.9	−119.6	−290.3	−111.1	201.7
Monetary authorities	4 753 WA	−.7	−14.4	10.5	−8.4	−5.6	−38.7	55.1	.2
General government	4 753 ZB	−523.3	−487.3	−737.2	−678.8	....	....	....	....
Banks	4 753 ZC	23.1	46.1	−136.4	−9.6	39.4	−42.8	47.9	24.2
Other sectors	4 753 ZD	96.6	257.8	34.5	−190.1	−153.5	−208.8	−214.2	177.4
Total, Groups A Through C............	4 983 ..	*−595.4*	*−117.3*	*−252.1*	*−727.3*	*123.3*	*−257.5*	*233.4*	*275.7*
D. Net Errors and Omissions............	4 998 ..	**−12.9**	**31.2**	**−26.3**	**−887.9**	**26.6**	**−57.5**	**−10.1**	**44.9**
Total, Groups A Through D............	4 984 ..	*−608.3*	*−86.1*	*−278.4*	*−1,615.3*	*149.9*	*−315.1*	*223.3*	*320.7*
E. Reserves and Related Items............	4 802 A.	**608.3**	**86.1**	**278.4**	**1,615.3**	**−149.9**	**315.1**	**−223.3**	**−320.7**
Reserve assets	4 802 ..	−89.0	−386.6	−584.1	840.1	−249.7	148.4	−314.8	−473.9
Use of Fund credit and loans	4 766 ..	−38.8	−66.4	−13.5	−106.4	−127.1	−90.6	−57.7	15.1
Exceptional financing	4 920 ..	736.1	539.1	876.1	881.6	226.9	257.3	149.2	138.1
Conversion rates: CFA francs per U.S. dollar............	0 101 ..	**711.98**	**733.04**	**696.99**	**581.20**	**528.28**	**527.47**	**522.89**	**479.27**

[1] Excludes components that have been classified in the categories of Group E.

Table 2. STANDARD PRESENTATION, 2000–2007

(Millions of U.S. dollars)

	Code	2000	2001	2002	2003	2004	2005	2006	2007
CURRENT ACCOUNT.................................	4 993 ..	**−241.3**	**−61.3**	**768.2**	**294.2**	**240.9**	**39.7**	**479.0**	**−146.0**
A. GOODS..	4 100 ..	**1,486.2**	**1,528.2**	**2,819.3**	**2,556.8**	**2,627.9**	**2,446.3**	**3,109.0**	**2,544.2**
Credit..	2 100 ..	**3,888.0**	**3,945.9**	**5,274.8**	**5,787.7**	**6,919.3**	**7,697.4**	**8,477.3**	**8,475.9**
General merchandise: exports f.o.b.............	2 110 ..	3,728.9	3,779.5	5,109.6	5,616.3	6,700.7	7,469.0	8,237.3	8,475.9
Goods for processing: exports f.o.b.............	2 150 ..	72.5	75.4	64.6	72.1	85.3	94.5	96.7	....
Repairs on goods...	2 160 ..	5.9	5.7	15.6	17.4	17.1	14.0	18.4	....
Goods procured in ports by carriers.............	2 170 ..	67.4	69.1	69.2	81.9	100.7	100.2	99.3	....
Nonmonetary gold......................................	2 180 ..	13.4	16.3	15.9	....	15.5	19.8	25.7	....
Debit..	3 100 ..	**−2,401.8**	**−2,417.7**	**−2,455.6**	**−3,230.9**	**−4,291.4**	**−5,251.0**	**−5,368.3**	**−5,931.6**
General merchandise: imports f.o.b.............	3 110 ..	−2,293.6	−2,306.4	−2,342.1	−3,076.2	−4,126.2	−5,079.9	−5,190.3	−5,931.6
Goods for processing: imports f.o.b.............	3 150 ..	−100.3	−103.2	−105.5	−142.6	−149.2	−153.9	−158.9	....
Repairs on goods...	3 160 ..	....	....	....	....	−.1	−.4	....	....
Goods procured in ports by carriers.............	3 170 ..	−7.9	−8.1	−8.0	−12.0	−16.0	−16.8	−19.1	....
Nonmonetary gold......................................	3 180 ..	....	....	....	....	....	....	....	....
B. SERVICES..	4 200 ..	**−744.6**	**−693.4**	**−959.3**	**−1,116.2**	**−1,269.9**	**−1,291.1**	**−1,388.5**	**−1,500.9**
Total credit..	2 200 ..	*482.4*	*577.8*	*585.3*	*664.0*	*762.7*	*832.4*	*844.6*	*943.1*
Total debit...	3 200 ..	*−1,226.9*	*−1,271.3*	*−1,544.7*	*−1,780.2*	*−2,032.6*	*−2,123.5*	*−2,233.1*	*−2,444.0*
Transportation services, credit............	2 205 ..	**84.4**	**91.4**	**102.9**	**114.1**	**138.3**	**188.6**	**202.3**	**225.6**
Passenger...	2 850 ..	*3.9*	*4.7*	*5.3*	*7.4*	*8.9*	*9.6*	*10.7*	....
Freight...	2 851 ..	*22.4*	*21.7*	*28.4*	*31.3*	*40.5*	*50.9*	*42.0*	*48.2*
Other..	2 852 ..	*58.1*	*65.0*	*69.2*	*75.4*	*88.9*	*128.1*	*149.5*	*177.4*
Sea transport, passenger........................	2 207 ..	....	....	....	....	....	....	....	....
Sea transport, freight...........................	2 208 ..	....	....	....	....	....	....	....	48.2
Sea transport, other.............................	2 209 ..	42.6	49.9	53.5	62.1	74.1	82.0	92.3	....
Air transport, passenger........................	2 211 ..	1.0	1.9	2.2	3.6	4.2	4.4	4.7	....
Air transport, freight...........................	2 212 ..	....	....	....	....	....	....	....	....
Air transport, other.............................	2 213 ..	15.5	15.1	15.6	13.2	14.8	46.1	57.2	....
Other transport, passenger.....................	2 215 ..	3.0	2.8	3.2	3.8	4.7	5.2	6.0	....
Other transport, freight.........................	2 216 ..	22.4	21.7	28.4	31.3	40.5	50.9	42.0	....
Other transport, other..........................	2 217 ..								177.4
Transportation services, debit............	3 205 ..	**−516.5**	**−501.2**	**−546.9**	**−702.7**	**−914.7**	**−1,092.4**	**−1,141.4**	**−1,274.2**
Passenger...	3 850 ..	*−101.9*	*−101.8*	*−132.3*	*−164.0*	*−190.1*	*−194.6*	*−210.2*	....
Freight...	3 851 ..	*−367.7*	*−352.9*	*−364.6*	*−477.3*	*−647.5*	*−845.4*	*−877.6*	*−982.5*
Other..	3 852 ..	*−46.8*	*−46.6*	*−50.1*	*−61.4*	*−77.1*	*−52.4*	*−53.6*	*−291.7*
Sea transport, passenger........................	3 207 ..	....	....	....	....	....	....	....	....
Sea transport, freight...........................	3 208 ..	−336.9	−323.2	−333.9	−437.2	−588.0	−771.2	−803.8	−982.5
Sea transport, other.............................	3 209 ..	−29.4	−29.2	−31.4	−38.5	−51.3	−26.2	−27.0	....
Air transport, passenger........................	3 211 ..	−101.9	−101.8	−132.3	−164.0	−190.1	−194.6	−210.2	....
Air transport, freight...........................	3 212 ..	−16.9	−16.2	−16.8	−22.0	−32.6	−40.6	−40.4	....
Air transport, other.............................	3 213 ..	−17.2	−17.1	−18.4	−22.5	−25.3	−25.9	−26.7	....
Other transport, passenger.....................	3 215 ..	....	....	....	....	....	....	....	....
Other transport, freight.........................	3 216 ..	−14.0	−13.4	−13.9	−18.1	−26.9	−33.6	−33.4	....
Other transport, other..........................	3 217 ..	−.2	−.2	−.3	−.3	−.4	−.4	....	−291.7
Travel, credit................................	2 236 ..	**49.2**	**53.0**	**51.3**	**69.0**	**81.6**	**83.3**	**93.1**	**104.1**
Business travel..................................	2 237 ..	20.9	24.3	30.7	42.3	53.5	56.2	65.2	....
Personal travel..................................	2 240 ..	28.3	28.7	20.6	26.7	28.1	27.1	27.8	104.1
Travel, debit.................................	3 236 ..	**−189.1**	**−186.7**	**−357.6**	**−387.3**	**−381.5**	**−353.9**	**−372.7**	**−396.3**
Business travel..................................	3 237 ..	−3.6	−11.7	−14.8	−17.7	−20.1	−21.1	−25.6	....
Personal travel..................................	3 240 ..	−185.5	−175.0	−342.8	−369.6	−361.4	−332.8	−347.1	−396.3
Other services, credit.....................	2 200 BA	**348.8**	**433.3**	**431.2**	**480.9**	**542.8**	**560.5**	**549.2**	**613.4**
Communications.................................	2 245 ..	39.3	42.6	56.2	70.9	81.8	86.0	87.8	....
Construction....................................	2 249 ..	10.4	16.9	17.8	10.7	17.6	16.8	21.7	....
Insurance.......................................	2 253 ..	24.6	23.9	24.7	38.2	42.3	33.5	35.4	....
Financial..	2 260 ..	28.2	46.8	38.7	47.5	53.0	54.0	55.2	....
Computer and information.......................	2 262 ..	.2	.2	3.3	1.6	4.4	4.9	4.9	....
Royalties and licence fees......................	2 266 ..	.1	12.8	....	....	.2	....	....	....
Other business services........................	2 268 ..	178.0	221.8	218.0	207.9	221.5	230.1	206.0	457.4
Personal, cultural, and recreational...........	2 287 ..	.1	.1	....	....	....	....	....	....
Government, n.i.e...............................	2 291 ..	67.8	68.3	72.5	104.1	122.1	135.2	138.3	156.1
Other services, debit......................	3 200 BA	**−521.3**	**−583.3**	**−640.2**	**−690.2**	**−736.5**	**−677.2**	**−719.0**	**−773.5**
Communications.................................	3 245 ..	−33.8	−36.5	−44.6	−66.8	−61.0	−65.4	−66.7	....
Construction....................................	3 249 ..	−4.0	−9.2	−1.7	−1.6	−4.1	−2.4	−4.1	....
Insurance.......................................	3 253 ..	−37.3	−30.8	−34.0	−45.6	−64.4	−63.6	−65.5	....
Financial..	3 260 ..	−87.7	−84.0	−90.2	−110.5	−124.5	−119.6	−129.1	....
Computer and information.......................	3 262 ..	−7.3	−7.1	−7.3	−11.0	−8.3	−6.1	−6.2	....
Royalties and licence fees......................	3 266 ..	−8.5	−23.3	−6.3	−10.7	−21.9	−10.3	−9.6	....
Other business services........................	3 268 ..	−257.6	−308.4	−357.8	−320.0	−314.7	−267.2	−290.6	−552.9
Personal, cultural, and recreational...........	3 287 ..	−.6	−.5	−.6	−.7	−.8	−.8	−.8	....
Government, n.i.e...............................	3 291 ..	−84.6	−83.6	−97.6	−123.4	−136.9	−141.8	−146.4	−220.5

Table 2 (Continued). STANDARD PRESENTATION, 2000–2007

(Millions of U.S. dollars)

	Code	2000	2001	2002	2003	2004	2005	2006	2007
C. INCOME..	4 300 ..	**−652.9**	**−585.8**	**−629.7**	**−659.5**	**−651.7**	**−653.2**	**−710.3**	**−810.2**
Total credit..	2 300 ..	*141.6*	*137.3*	*141.2*	*170.6*	*189.7*	*193.9*	*196.2*	*214.9*
Total debit...	3 300 ..	*−794.5*	*−723.1*	*−770.9*	*−830.1*	*−841.3*	*−847.1*	*−906.4*	*−1,025.1*
Compensation of employees, credit..................	2 310 ..	**119.3**	**116.0**	**120.1**	**141.6**	**158.2**	**161.3**	**164.6**	**179.4**
Compensation of employees, debit....................	3 310 ..	**−11.1**	**−11.1**	**−11.9**	**−14.6**	**−16.4**	**−16.8**	**−17.3**	**−19.0**
Investment income, credit..................................	2 320 ..	**22.3**	**21.3**	**21.1**	**29.0**	**31.5**	**32.6**	**31.5**	**35.5**
Direct investment income......................................	2 330 ..	2.5	1.8	2.0	3.0	3.2	4.6	4.7	....
Dividends and distributed branch profits.............	2 332 ..	1.7	1.7	1.9	2.2	2.6	2.7	2.9	....
Reinvested earnings and undistributed branch profits.....	2 333 ..	....	....	....	....	....	....	....	....
Income on debt (interest)......................................	2 334 ..	.8	.1	.1	.8	.6	1.8	1.9	....
Portfolio investment income.................................	2 339 ..	3.1	3.0	3.4	4.4	4.4	5.3	4.6	....
Income on equity..	2 340 ..	.1	....	.1	.3	....	.2	....	....
Income on bonds and notes.................................	2 350 ..	1.5	1.4	1.6	2.0	2.1	2.7	2.2	....
Income on money market instruments..................	2 360 ..	1.6	1.6	1.7	2.1	2.3	2.3	2.4	....
Other investment income......................................	2 370 ..	16.6	16.5	15.8	21.6	23.9	22.8	22.2	35.5
Investment income, debit..................................	3 320 ..	**−783.4**	**−712.1**	**−759.0**	**−815.4**	**−824.9**	**−830.3**	**−889.2**	**−1,006.1**
Direct investment income......................................	3 330 ..	−284.0	−269.5	−283.6	−334.7	−363.7	−370.1	−477.9	....
Dividends and distributed branch profits.............	3 332 ..	−145.1	−137.7	−144.9	−171.0	−185.0	−188.3	−243.1	....
Reinvested earnings and undistributed branch profits.....	3 333 ..	−84.3	−79.9	−84.2	−99.3	−105.4	−107.2	−138.4	....
Income on debt (interest)......................................	3 334 ..	−54.6	−51.8	−54.5	−64.4	−73.4	−74.7	−96.4	....
Portfolio investment income.................................	3 339 ..	−33.2	−31.5	−33.2	−40.1	−42.3	−48.2	−57.2	....
Income on equity..	3 340 ..	−28.6	−27.2	−28.5	−33.7	−36.5	−37.3	−45.8	....
Income on bonds and notes.................................	3 350 ..	−4.6	−4.3	−4.6	−6.4	−5.8	−10.9	−11.4	....
Income on money market instruments..................	3 360 ..	....	....	−.1	−.1	....	....	....	....
Other investment income......................................	3 370 ..	−466.2	−411.1	−442.2	−440.6	−418.9	−412.0	−354.1	−1,006.1
D. CURRENT TRANSFERS....................................	4 379 ..	**−330.0**	**−310.2**	**−462.0**	**−486.9**	**−465.5**	**−462.4**	**−531.3**	**−379.1**
Credit...	2 379 ..	**79.4**	**88.5**	**131.9**	**196.4**	**187.4**	**194.8**	**217.7**	**459.0**
General government..	2 380 ..	37.2	46.6	34.3	55.4	4.0	....	....	219.1
Other sectors...	2 390 ..	42.2	41.9	97.6	141.0	183.4	194.8	217.7	239.9
Workers' remittances..	2 391 ..	....	....	....	....	1.0	1.9	2.1	....
Other current transfers...	2 392 ..	42.2	41.9	97.6	141.0	182.4	192.9	215.6	239.9
Debit..	3 379 ..	**−409.4**	**−398.7**	**−593.8**	**−683.3**	**−652.8**	**−657.2**	**−749.0**	**−838.2**
General government..	3 380 ..	−14.6	−14.5	−15.6	−19.1	−21.4	−21.8	−36.2	−55.7
Other sectors...	3 390 ..	−394.8	−384.2	−578.2	−664.2	−631.5	−635.4	−712.8	−782.4
Workers' remittances..	3 391 ..	−378.6	−368.5	−562.0	−613.2	−575.0	−580.2	−643.2	....
Other current transfers...	3 392 ..	−16.2	−15.7	−16.2	−50.9	−56.5	−55.2	−69.6	−782.4
CAPITAL AND FINANCIAL ACCOUNT.......................	4 996 ..	**254.2**	**30.1**	**−741.9**	**593.7**	**−267.4**	**17.8**	**−468.9**	**101.1**
CAPITAL ACCOUNT...	4 994 ..	**8.4**	**10.0**	**8.3**	**13.7**	**145.9**	**185.2**	**33.0**	**89.9**
Total credit..	2 994 ..	*9.9*	*11.5*	*9.1*	*14.1*	*146.4*	*185.8*	*33.6*	*91.0*
Total debit...	3 994 ..	*−1.4*	*−1.4*	*−.8*	*−.4*	*−.5*	*−.6*	*−.6*	*−1.0*
Capital transfers, credit.....................................	2 400 ..	**9.9**	**11.5**	**9.1**	**14.1**	**143.7**	**181.2**	**28.9**	**91.0**
General government..	2 401 ..	9.9	11.5	9.0	14.1	143.7	179.3	28.9	91.0
Debt forgiveness...	2 402 ..	....	....	....	....	....	....	....	....
Other capital transfers..	2 410 ..	9.9	11.5	9.0	14.1	143.7	179.3	28.9	91.0
Other sectors...	2 430 ..	....	....	....	....	....	1.9	....	....
Migrants' transfers...	2 431 ..	....	....	....	....	....	....	....	....
Debt forgiveness...	2 432 ..	....	....	....	....	....	....	....	....
Other capital transfers..	2 440 ..	....	....	....	....	....	1.9	....	....
Capital transfers, debit......................................	3 400 ..	....	....	....	....	....	....	....	....
General government..	3 401 ..	....	....	....	....	....	....	....	....
Debt forgiveness...	3 402 ..	....	....	....	....	....	....	....	....
Other capital transfers..	3 410 ..	....	....	....	....	....	....	....	....
Other sectors...	3 430 ..	....	....	....	....	....	....	....	....
Migrants' transfers...	3 431 ..	....	....	....	....	....	....	....	....
Debt forgiveness...	3 432 ..	....	....	....	....	....	....	....	....
Other capital transfers..	3 440 ..	....	....	....	....	....	....	....	....
Nonproduced nonfinancial assets, credit.............	2 480 ..	....	....	....	....	2.7	4.6	4.7	....
Nonproduced nonfinancial assets, debit..............	3 480 ..	−1.4	−1.4	−.8	−.4	−.5	−.6	−.6	−1.0

Table 2 (Continued). STANDARD PRESENTATION, 2000–2007

(Millions of U.S. dollars)

	Code	2000	2001	2002	2003	2004	2005	2006	2007
FINANCIAL ACCOUNT	4 995 ..	**245.7**	**20.1**	**−750.2**	**580.0**	**−413.3**	**−167.4**	**−501.8**	**11.1**
A. DIRECT INVESTMENT	4 500 ..	**234.7**	**272.7**	**212.6**	**165.3**	**283.0**	**311.9**	**318.9**	**426.9**
Direct investment abroad	4 505 ..	....	....	....	....	....	....	....	....
Equity capital	4 510 ..	....	....	....	....	....	....	....	....
Claims on affiliated enterprises	4 515 ..	....	....	....	....	....	....	....	....
Liabilities to affiliated enterprises	4 520 ..	....	....	....	....	....	....	....	....
Reinvested earnings	4 525 ..	....	....	....	....	....	....	....	....
Other capital	4 530 ..	....	....	....	....	....	....	....	....
Claims on affiliated enterprises	4 535 ..	....	....	....	....	....	....	....	....
Liabilities to affiliated enterprises	4 540 ..	....	....	....	....	....	....	....	....
Direct investment in Côte d'Ivoire	4 555 ..	**234.7**	**272.7**	**212.6**	**165.3**	**283.0**	**311.9**	**318.9**	**426.9**
Equity capital	4 560 ..	135.1	144.4	106.3	119.7	221.4	195.1	165.2	....
Claims on direct investors	4 565 ..	....	....	....	....	....	....	....	....
Liabilities to direct investors	4 570 ..	135.1	144.4	106.3	119.7	221.4	195.1	165.2	....
Reinvested earnings	4 575 ..	84.3	79.9	84.2	99.3	105.4	107.2	138.4	....
Other capital	4 580 ..	15.3	48.3	22.1	−53.6	−43.8	9.6	15.2	426.9
Claims on direct investors	4 585 ..	−20.3	−20.7	−32.7	−45.1	−47.1	−37.0	−31.8	−44.0
Liabilities to direct investors	4 590 ..	35.6	69.1	54.8	−8.5	3.3	46.6	47.0	470.9
B. PORTFOLIO INVESTMENT	4 600 ..	**−8.0**	**−8.0**	**30.6**	**33.2**	**−28.6**	**−1.8**	**21.1**	**93.7**
Assets	4 602 ..	**−12.5**	**−12.0**	**−21.1**	**−33.8**	**−37.5**	**−49.9**	**−24.2**	**−53.8**
Equity securities	4 610 ..	−1.3	−1.3	−2.0	−14.1	−6.6	26.9	−6.0	−53.8
Monetary authorities	4 611 ..	....	....	....	....	....	....	....	....
General government	4 612 ..	....	....	....	....	....	....	....	....
Banks	4 613 ..	....	....	....	....	....	15.6	....	....
Other sectors	4 614 ..	−1.3	−1.3	−2.0	−14.1	−6.6	11.3	−6.0	−53.8
Debt securities	4 619 ..	−11.2	−10.7	−19.1	−19.7	−30.9	−76.8	−18.2	....
Bonds and notes	4 620 ..	−7.5	−7.2	−12.9	−11.5	−19.6	−29.5	−20.3	....
Monetary authorities	4 621 ..	....	....	....	....	....	....	....	....
General government	4 622 ..	....	....	....	....	....	....	....	....
Banks	4 623 ..	....	....	....	....	....	−9.5	....	....
Other sectors	4 624 ..	−7.5	−7.2	−12.9	−11.5	−19.6	−20.0	−20.3	....
Money market instruments	4 630 ..	−3.7	−3.5	−6.2	−8.2	−11.2	−47.3	2.1	....
Monetary authorities	4 631 ..	....	....	....	....	....	....	....	....
General government	4 632 ..	....	....	....	....	....	....	....	....
Banks	4 633 ..	....	....	....	....	....	−26.5	....	....
Other sectors	4 634 ..	−3.7	−3.5	−6.2	−8.2	−11.2	−20.8	2.1	....
Liabilities	4 652 ..	**4.5**	**4.0**	**51.7**	**67.0**	**8.9**	**48.1**	**45.3**	**147.5**
Equity securities	4 660 ..	1.2	2.4	3.6	15.8	−4.9	13.9	1.6	147.5
Banks	4 663 ..	....	3.9	....	....	−4.3	12.1	....	....
Other sectors	4 664 ..	1.2	−1.5	3.6	15.8	−.6	1.8	1.6	147.5
Debt securities	4 669 ..	3.4	1.6	48.1	51.3	13.8	34.2	43.7	....
Bonds and notes	4 670 ..	3.4	1.6	48.1	51.3	12.3	29.5	42.4	....
Monetary authorities	4 671 ..	....	....	....	....	....	....	....	....
General government	4 672 ..	....	....	48.1	51.1	2.3	28.2	43.2	....
Banks	4 673 ..	....	....	....	....	....	....	....	....
Other sectors	4 674 ..	3.4	1.6	....	.1	10.0	1.2	−.8	....
Money market instruments	4 680 ..	....	....	....	....	1.5	4.7	1.3	....
Monetary authorities	4 681 ..	....	....	....	....	....	....	....	....
General government	4 682 ..	....	....	....	....	....	4.7	1.3	....
Banks	4 683 ..	....	....	....	....	....	....	....	....
Other sectors	4 684 ..	....	....	....	....	1.5	....	....	....
C. FINANCIAL DERIVATIVES	4 910 ..	**−2.6**	**−3.8**	**−4.1**	**−5.3**	**4.3**	**−4.3**	**−6.3**	**....**
Monetary authorities	4 911 ..	....	....	....	....	....	....	....	....
General government	4 912 ..	....	....	....	....	....	....	....	....
Banks	4 913 ..	....	....	....	....	....	....	....	....
Other sectors	4 914 ..	−2.6	−3.8	−4.1	−5.3	4.3	−4.3	−6.3	....
Assets	4 900 ..	**−2.6**	**−3.8**	**−6.0**	**−7.9**	**−6.0**	**−5.2**	**−6.3**	**....**
Monetary authorities	4 901 ..	....	....	....	....	....	....	....	....
General government	4 902 ..	....	....	....	....	....	....	....	....
Banks	4 903 ..	....	....	....	....	....	....	....	....
Other sectors	4 904 ..	−2.6	−3.8	−6.0	−7.9	−6.0	−5.2	−6.3	....
Liabilities	4 905 ..	**....**	**....**	**1.9**	**2.6**	**10.2**	**.9**	**....**	**....**
Monetary authorities	4 906 ..	....	....	....	....	....	....	....	....
General government	4 907 ..	....	....	....	....	....	....	....	....
Banks	4 908 ..	....	....	....	....	....	....	....	....
Other sectors	4 909 ..	....	....	1.9	2.6	10.2	.9	....	....

Table 2 (Concluded). STANDARD PRESENTATION, 2000–2007

(Millions of U.S. dollars)

	Code	2000	2001	2002	2003	2004	2005	2006	2007
D. OTHER INVESTMENT	4 700 ..	**110.6**	**145.8**	**−405.1**	**−453.3**	**−422.3**	**−621.6**	**−520.7**	**−35.6**
Assets	4 703 ..	−182.4	−129.1	−439.0	−341.7	−402.5	−497.9	−501.1	−390.5
Trade credits	4 706 ..	−11.3	−15.1	−64.9	−74.1	−116.5	−118.9	−134.7	....
General government	4 707 ..	....	....	....	....	....	....	....	....
of which: Short-term	4 709 ..	....	....	....	....	....	....	....	....
Other sectors	4 710 ..	−11.3	−15.1	−64.9	−74.1	−116.5	−118.9	−134.7	....
of which: Short-term	4 712 ..	*−11.3*	*−15.1*	*−64.9*	*−74.1*	*−116.5*	*−118.9*	*−134.7*	....
Loans	4 714 ..	−18.4	2.1	−23.0	38.7	−74.1	−.3	−3.7	....
Monetary authorities	4 715 ..	....	....	....	....	....	....	....	....
of which: Short-term	4 718 ..	....	....	....	....	....	....	....	....
General government	4 719 ..	....	....	....	....	....	....	....	....
of which: Short-term	4 721 ..	....	....	....	....	....	....	....	....
Banks	4 722 ..	−12.3	7.8	−15.9	48.5	−63.3	8.4	7.9	....
of which: Short-term	4 724 ..	*−11.9*	*−24.8*	*14.8*	*44.7*	*−57.8*	*5.7*	*12.4*	....
Other sectors	4 725 ..	−6.1	−5.6	−7.0	−9.8	−10.8	−8.7	−11.6	....
of which: Short-term	4 727 ..	....	....	....	....	....	....	....	....
Currency and deposits	4 730 ..	−75.6	−87.2	−348.4	−236.9	−141.4	−315.5	−263.2	....
Monetary authorities	4 731 ..	....	....	....	....	....	....	....	....
General government	4 732 ..	....	....	....	....	....	....	....	....
Banks	4 733 ..	51.7	42.8	−137.6	11.0	32.1	−78.0	18.1	....
Other sectors	4 734 ..	−127.3	−130.0	−210.8	−247.9	−173.5	−237.5	−281.3	....
Other assets	4 736 ..	−77.1	−29.0	−2.9	−69.4	−70.4	−63.2	−99.6	−390.5
Monetary authorities	4 737 ..	....	....	....	....	....	....	....	....
of which: Short-term	4 739 ..	....	....	....	....	....	....	....	....
General government	4 740 ..	−4.5	−5.1	−7.8	−4.0	−6.6	−3.2	−5.4	.2
of which: Short-term	4 742 ..	*.1*	*.1*	*.1*	*.2*	*.2*	*−3.2*	*−5.4*	*.2*
Banks	4 743 ..	−36.5	−12.8	63.7	3.1	−1.6	2.8	....	−17.0
of which: Short-term	4 745 ..	*−36.5*	*−12.8*	*63.7*	*3.1*	*−1.6*	*2.8*	....	*−17.0*
Other sectors	4 746 ..	−36.0	−11.1	−58.8	−68.5	−62.1	−62.8	−94.2	−373.7
of which: Short-term	4 748 ..	*−36.0*	*−11.1*	*−58.8*	*−68.5*	*−62.1*	*−62.8*	*−94.2*	*−373.7*
Liabilities	4 753 ..	**293.0**	**274.9**	**33.9**	**−111.7**	**−19.8**	**−123.7**	**−19.6**	**354.9**
Trade credits	4 756 ..	63.2	146.6	35.4	−186.6	−168.3	−211.4	−217.4	....
General government	4 757 ..	....	....	....	....	....	....	....	....
of which: Short-term	4 759 ..	....	....	....	....	....	....	....	....
Other sectors	4 760 ..	63.2	146.6	35.4	−186.6	−168.3	−211.4	−217.4	....
of which: Short-term	4 762 ..	*63.2*	*146.6*	*35.4*	*−186.6*	*−168.3*	*−211.4*	*−217.4*	....
Loans	4 764 ..	−137.2	7.3	504.4	−588.1	−714.9	−642.5	−592.9	−403.1
Monetary authorities	4 765 ..	−38.8	−66.4	−13.5	−106.4	−127.1	−90.6	−57.7	15.1
of which: Use of Fund credit and loans from the Fund..	4 766 ..	*−38.8*	*−66.4*	*−13.5*	*−106.4*	*−127.1*	*−90.6*	*−57.7*	*15.1*
of which: Short-term	4 768 ..	....	....	....	....	....	....	....	....
General government	4 769 ..	−53.8	−162.5	713.6	−454.9	−584.5	−534.4	−511.2	−418.1
of which: Short-term	4 771 ..	....	....	....	....	....	....	....	....
Banks	4 772 ..	−43.6	175.4	−160.2	−18.8	23.4	−11.0	−18.2	....
of which: Short-term	4 774 ..	*−18.2*	*−.1*	....	....	....	*−14.8*	*−19.5*	....
Other sectors	4 775 ..	−1.0	60.7	−35.5	−7.9	−26.7	−6.4	−5.8	....
of which: Short-term	4 777 ..	*−8.9*	*−8.6*	*19.7*	*23.5*	*12.7*	*5.0*	*5.8*	....
Currency and deposits	4 780 ..	11.6	−103.5	44.5	9.4	19.1	−33.6	76.5	.2
Monetary authorities	4 781 ..	−7.0	−.3	1.6	−1.2	2.5	−1.8	10.9	.2
General government	4 782 ..	....	....	....	....	....	....	....	....
Banks	4 783 ..	18.6	−103.2	42.9	10.6	16.6	−31.7	65.6	....
Other sectors	4 784 ..	....	....	....	....	....	....	....	....
Other liabilities	4 786 ..	355.4	224.5	−550.4	653.7	844.4	763.8	714.1	757.8
Monetary authorities	4 787 ..	6.2	−14.2	8.9	−7.2	−8.1	−36.9	44.2	....
of which: Short-term	4 789 ..	....	....	....	....	....	....	....	....
General government	4 790 ..	266.6	214.3	−574.8	657.8	811.4	791.7	660.4	556.3
of which: Short-term	4 792 ..	*266.6*	*214.3*	*−574.8*	*657.8*	*811.4*	*791.7*	*660.4*	*556.3*
Banks	4 793 ..	48.2	−26.1	−19.1	−1.4	−.5	−.1	.6	24.2
of which: Short-term	4 795 ..	*48.2*	*−26.1*	*−19.1*	*−1.4*	*−.5*	*−.1*	*.6*	*24.2*
Other sectors	4 796 ..	34.4	50.5	34.6	4.5	41.6	9.1	9.0	177.4
of which: Short-term	4 798 ..	*34.4*	*50.5*	*34.6*	*4.5*	*41.6*	*9.1*	*9.0*	*177.4*
E. RESERVE ASSETS	4 802 ..	**−89.0**	**−386.6**	**−584.1**	**840.1**	**−249.7**	**148.4**	**−314.8**	**−473.9**
Monetary gold	4 812 ..	....	....	....	....	....	....	....	....
Special drawing rights	4 811 ..	2.0	.5	−.4	1.0	.1	−.5	−.3	.5
Reserve position in the Fund	4 810 ..	−.1	....	−.2	−.2	....	−.1	−.1	−.1
Foreign exchange	4 803 ..	−91.0	−387.0	−583.5	839.3	−249.7	148.9	−314.4	−474.3
Other claims	4 813 ..	....	....	....	....	....	....	....	....
NET ERRORS AND OMISSIONS	4 998 ..	**−12.9**	**31.2**	**−26.3**	**−887.9**	**26.6**	**−57.5**	**−10.1**	**44.9**

Table 3. INTERNATIONAL INVESTMENT POSITION (End-period stocks), 2000–2007

(Millions of U.S. dollars)

	Code	2000	2001	2002	2003	2004	2005	2006	2007
ASSETS	8 995 C.	**2,729.6**	**3,114.5**	**4,876.2**	**5,361.5**	**6,545.2**	**6,052.7**	**7,645.5**	**9,533.4**
Direct investment abroad	8 505 ..	....	....	....	....	....	....	....	....
Equity capital and reinvested earnings	8 506 ..	....	....	....	....	....	....	....	....
Claims on affiliated enterprises	8 507 ..	....	....	....	....	....	....	....	....
Liabilities to affiliated enterprises	8 508 ..	....	....	....	....	....	....	....	....
Other capital	8 530 ..	....	....	....	....	....	....	....	....
Claims on affiliated enterprises	8 535 ..	....	....	....	....	....	....	....	....
Liabilities to affiliated enterprises	8 540 ..	....	....	....	....	....	....	....	....
Portfolio investment	8 602 ..	**169.9**	**176.4**	**240.2**	**335.9**	**409.9**	**407.3**	**486.8**	**602.0**
Equity securities	8 610 ..	11.1	11.8	16.3	35.4	45.5	13.8	21.7	82.2
Monetary authorities	8 611 ..	....	....	....	....	....	....	....	....
General government	8 612 ..	....	....	....	....	....	....	....	....
Banks	8 613 ..	....	....	....	....	....	....	....	....
Other sectors	8 614 ..	11.1	11.8	16.3	35.4	45.5	13.8	21.7	82.2
Debt securities	8 619 ..	158.7	164.6	223.9	300.5	364.5	393.5	465.0	519.8
Bonds and notes	8 620 ..	....	....	....	....	....	....	....	....
Monetary authorities	8 621 ..	....	....	....	....	....	....	....	....
General government	8 622 ..	....	....	....	....	....	....	....	....
Banks	8 623 ..	....	....	....	....	....	....	....	....
Other sectors	8 624 ..	....	....	....	....	....	....	....	....
Money market instruments	8 630 ..	158.7	164.6	223.9	300.5	364.5	393.5	465.0	519.8
Monetary authorities	8 631 ..	....	....	....	....	....	....	....	....
General government	8 632 ..	....	....	....	....	....	....	....	....
Banks	8 633 ..	....	....	....	....	....	....	....	....
Other sectors	8 634 ..	158.7	164.6	223.9	300.5	364.5	393.5	465.0	519.8
Financial derivatives	8 900 ..	....	....	....	....	....	....	....	....
Monetary authorities	8 901 ..	....	....	....	....	....	....	....	....
General government	8 902 ..	....	....	....	....	....	....	....	....
Banks	8 903 ..	....	....	....	....	....	....	....	....
Other sectors	8 904 ..	....	....	....	....	....	....	....	....
Other investment	8 703 ..	**1,891.9**	**1,919.0**	**2,772.8**	**3,721.7**	**4,455.3**	**4,331.0**	**5,361.1**	**6,412.5**
Trade credits	8 706 ..	628.1	609.8	797.9	1,043.9	1,253.6	1,198.6	1,479.5	1,653.7
General government	8 707 ..	....	....	....	....	....	....	....	....
of which: Short-term	8 709 ..	....	....	....	....	....	....	....	....
Other sectors	8 710 ..	628.1	609.8	797.9	1,043.9	1,253.6	1,198.6	1,479.5	1,653.7
of which: Short-term	8 712 ..	....	....	....	....	....	....	....	....
Loans	8 714 ..	67.9	62.2	99.6	76.7	163.9	142.3	162.6	181.8
Monetary authorities	8 715 ..	....	....	....	....	....	....	....	....
of which: Short-term	8 718 ..	....	....	....	....	....	....	....	....
General government	8 719 ..	....	....	....	....	....	....	....	....
of which: Short-term	8 721 ..	....	....	....	....	....	....	....	....
Banks	8 722 ..	....	....	....	....	....	....	....	....
of which: Short-term	8 724 ..	....	....	....	....	....	....	....	....
Other sectors	8 725 ..	67.9	62.2	99.6	76.7	163.9	142.3	162.6	181.8
of which: Short-term	8 727 ..	....	....	....	....	....	....	....	....
Currency and deposits	8 730 ..	1,000.8	1,033.8	1,618.3	2,214.1	2,543.0	2,501.7	3,069.1	3,430.5
Monetary authorities	8 731 ..	....	....	....	....	....	....	....	....
General government	8 732 ..	....	....	....	....	....	....	....	....
Banks	8 733 ..	....	....	....	....	....	....	....	....
Other sectors	8 734 ..	1,000.8	1,033.8	1,618.3	2,214.1	2,543.0	2,501.7	3,069.1	3,430.5
Other assets	8 736 ..	195.1	213.3	257.0	387.1	494.7	488.5	649.9	1,146.5
Monetary authorities	8 737 ..	....	....	....	....	....	....	....	....
of which: Short-term	8 739 ..	....	....	....	....	....	....	....	....
General government	8 740 ..	....	....	....	....	....	....	....	....
of which: Short-term	8 742 ..	....	....	....	....	....	....	....	....
Banks	8 743 ..	....	....	....	....	....	....	....	....
of which: Short-term	8 745 ..	....	....	....	....	....	....	....	....
Other sectors	8 746 ..	195.1	213.3	257.0	387.1	494.7	488.5	649.9	1,146.5
of which: Short-term	8 748 ..	....	....	....	....	....	....	....	....
Reserve assets	8 802 ..	**667.8**	**1,019.0**	**1,863.3**	**1,303.8**	**1,680.0**	**1,314.4**	**1,797.7**	**2,519.0**
Monetary gold	8 812 ..	....	....	....	....	....	....	....	....
Special drawing rights	8 811 ..	1.3	.7	1.2	.3	.2	.6	1.0	.6
Reserve position in the Fund	8 810 ..	.4	.4	.6	.8	.9	.9	1.0	1.1
Foreign exchange	8 803 ..	666.2	1,017.9	1,861.5	1,302.7	1,678.9	1,312.8	1,795.7	2,517.3
Other claims	8 813 ..	....	....	....	....	....	....	....	....

Table 3 (Concluded). INTERNATIONAL INVESTMENT POSITION (End-period stocks), 2000–2007

(Millions of U.S. dollars)

	Code	2000	2001	2002	2003	2004	2005	2006	2007
LIABILITIES	8 995 D.	**15,907.8**	**12,696.6**	**15,390.7**	**17,844.4**	**18,863.8**	**16,838.2**	**19,265.3**	**22,787.8**
Direct investment in Côte d'Ivoire	8 555 ..	**2,001.6**	**2,164.4**	**2,812.4**	**3,572.1**	**4,162.8**	**3,901.3**	**4,690.1**	**5,701.6**
Equity capital and reinvested earnings	8 556 ..	....	....	....	....	....	....	....	....
Claims on direct investors	8 557 ..	....	....	....	....	....	....	....	....
Liabilities to direct investors	8 558 ..	....	....	....	....	....	....	....	....
Other capital	8 580 ..	2,001.6	2,164.4	2,812.4	3,572.1	4,162.8	3,901.3	4,690.1	5,701.6
Claims on direct investors	8 585 ..	....	....	....	....	....	....	....	....
Liabilities to direct investors	8 590 ..	....	....	....	....	....	....	....	....
Portfolio investment	8 652 ..	**211.2**	**205.8**	**299.3**	**435.2**	**490.4**	**471.2**	**573.6**	**799.8**
Equity securities	8 660 ..	....	....	....	....	....	....	....	....
Banks	8 663 ..	....	....	....	....	....	....	....	....
Other sectors	8 664 ..	....	....	....	....	....	....	....	....
Debt securities	8 669 ..	211.2	205.8	299.3	435.2	490.4	471.2	573.6	799.8
Bonds and notes	8 670 ..	....	....	....	....	....	....	....	....
Monetary authorities	8 671 ..	....	....	....	....	....	....	....	....
General government	8 672 ..	....	....	....	....	....	....	....	....
Banks	8 673 ..	....	....	....	....	....	....	....	....
Other sectors	8 674 ..	....	....	....	....	....	....	....	....
Money market instruments	8 680 ..	211.2	205.8	299.3	435.2	490.4	471.2	573.6	799.8
Monetary authorities	8 681 ..	....	....	....	....	....	....	....	....
General government	8 682 ..	....	....	....	....	....	....	....	....
Banks	8 683 ..	....	....	....	....	....	....	....	....
Other sectors	8 684 ..	211.2	205.8	299.3	435.2	490.4	471.2	573.6	799.8
Financial derivatives	8 905 ..	....	....	....	....	....	....	....	....
Monetary authorities	8 906 ..	....	....	....	....	....	....	....	....
General government	8 907 ..	....	....	....	....	....	....	....	....
Banks	8 908 ..	....	....	....	....	....	....	....	....
Other sectors	8 909 ..	....	....	....	....	....	....	....	....
Other investment	8 753 ..	**13,695.0**	**10,326.5**	**12,279.0**	**13,837.0**	**14,210.6**	**12,465.7**	**14,001.7**	**16,286.4**
Trade credits	8 756 ..	653.8	763.6	948.0	932.9	821.5	511.0	342.2	382.5
General government	8 757 ..	....	....	....	....	....	....	....	....
of which: Short-term	8 759 ..	....	....	....	....	....	....	....	....
Other sectors	8 760 ..	653.8	763.6	948.0	932.9	821.5	511.0	342.2	382.5
of which: Short-term	8 762 ..	....	....	....	....	....	....	....	....
Loans	8 764 ..	12,672.1	9,305.1	10,947.6	12,436.4	12,827.7	11,526.9	13,044.9	14,401.9
Monetary authorities	8 765 ..	549.3	464.0	490.9	425.0	311.4	198.4	150.1	173.5
of which: Use of Fund credit and loans from the Fund	8 766 ..	*549.3*	*464.0*	*490.9*	*425.0*	*311.4*	*198.4*	*150.1*	*173.5*
of which: Short-term	8 768 ..	....	....	....	....	....	....	....	....
General government	8 769 ..	12,027.6	8,518.3	10,291.1	11,841.9	12,337.1	11,189.9	12,765.4	14,083.7
of which: Short-term	8 771 ..	*5,389.9*	*915.9*	*449.4*	*1,233.8*	*2,263.5*	*2,795.9*	*3,774.0*	*4,883.9*
Banks	8 772 ..	85.7	254.0	123.7	127.9	163.6	131.3	127.4	142.4
of which: Short-term	8 774 ..	*85.7*	*254.0*	*123.7*	*127.9*	*163.6*	*131.3*	*127.4*	*142.4*
Other sectors	8 775 ..	9.4	68.7	41.9	41.6	15.6	7.4	2.1	2.4
of which: Short-term	8 777 ..	....	....	....	....	....	....	....	....
Currency and deposits	8 780 ..	199.5	87.1	153.1	194.9	231.1	168.3	268.3	299.9
Monetary authorities	8 781 ..	....	....	....	....	....	....	....	....
General government	8 782 ..	....	....	....	....	....	....	....	....
Banks	8 783 ..	199.5	87.1	153.1	194.9	231.1	168.3	268.3	299.9
Other sectors	8 784 ..	....	....	....	....	....	....	....	....
Other liabilities	8 786 ..	169.6	170.7	230.3	272.7	330.3	259.6	346.2	1,202.1
Monetary authorities	8 787 ..	....	....	....	....	....	....	....	....
of which: Short-term	8 789 ..	....	....	....	....	....	....	....	....
General government	8 790 ..	....	....	....	....	....	....	....	....
of which: Short-term	8 792 ..	....	....	....	....	....	....	....	....
Banks	8 793 ..	169.6	170.7	230.3	272.7	330.3	259.6	346.2	1,202.1
of which: Short-term	8 795 ..	*169.6*	*170.7*	*230.3*	*272.7*	*330.3*	*259.6*	*346.2*	*1,202.1*
Other sectors	8 796 ..	....	....	....	....	....	....	....	....
of which: Short-term	8 798 ..	....	....	....	....	....	....	....	....
NET INTERNATIONAL INVESTMENT POSITION	8 995 ..	**−13,178.3**	**−9,582.1**	**−10,514.5**	**−12,482.9**	**−12,318.5**	**−10,785.5**	**−11,619.8**	**−13,254.3**
Conversion rates: CFA francs per U.S. dollar (end of period)	0 102 ..	704.95	744.31	625.50	519.36	481.58	556.04	498.07	445.59

Croatia 960

Table 1. ANALYTIC PRESENTATION, 2000–2007

(Millions of U.S. dollars)

	Code	2000	2001	2002	2003	2004	2005	2006	2007
A. Current Account[1]	4 993 Z.	**−532.8**	**−729.2**	**−1,925.5**	**−2,162.3**	**−1,874.7**	**−2,555.0**	**−3,287.1**	**−4,443.0**
Goods: exports f.o.b.	2 100 ..	4,573.7	4,767.0	5,006.2	6,311.4	8,214.5	8,959.8	10,644.4	12,622.7
Goods: imports f.o.b.	3 100 ..	−7,770.2	−8,860.0	−10,652.2	−14,216.0	−16,560.3	−18,301.3	−21,130.9	−25,556.1
Balance on Goods	4 100 ..	*−3,196.5*	*−4,093.0*	*−5,646.0*	*−7,904.6*	*−8,345.8*	*−9,341.5*	*−10,486.5*	*−12,933.4*
Services: credit	2 200 ..	4,070.9	4,883.9	5,582.4	8,568.8	9,373.2	9,921.0	10,809.1	12,529.0
Services: debit	3 200 ..	−1,821.7	−1,949.2	−2,414.4	−2,981.8	−3,565.4	−3,400.3	−3,547.6	−3,924.6
Balance on Goods and Services	4 991 ..	*−947.3*	*−1,158.3*	*−2,478.0*	*−2,317.6*	*−2,538.1*	*−2,820.8*	*−3,224.9*	*−4,329.1*
Income: credit	2 300 ..	346.1	433.8	437.0	508.1	878.8	889.3	1,125.7	1,760.2
Income: debit	3 300 ..	−812.0	−988.0	−975.0	−1,759.9	−1,701.1	−2,098.8	−2,578.0	−3,304.7
Balance on Goods, Services, and Income	4 992 ..	*−1,413.3*	*−1,712.5*	*−3,015.9*	*−3,569.4*	*−3,360.4*	*−4,030.3*	*−4,677.3*	*−5,873.5*
Current transfers: credit	2 379 Z.	1,098.2	1,192.7	1,375.0	1,741.4	1,974.0	2,027.2	2,060.5	2,164.4
Current transfers: debit	3 379 ..	−217.8	−209.3	−284.6	−334.4	−488.2	−551.9	−670.4	−733.9
B. Capital Account[1]	4 994 Z.	**11.0**	**137.3**	**463.3**	**118.5**	**39.4**	**64.2**	**−157.1**	**47.2**
Capital account: credit	2 994 Z.	26.6	142.0	470.3	132.6	48.8	70.5	51.6	62.8
Capital account: debit	3 994 ..	−15.6	−4.6	−7.0	−14.1	−9.4	−6.2	−208.7	−15.6
Total, Groups A Plus B	4 981 ..	*−521.9*	*−591.8*	*−1,462.2*	*−2,043.8*	*−1,835.3*	*−2,490.7*	*−3,444.3*	*−4,395.8*
C. Financial Account[1]	4 995 W.	**1,953.3**	**2,430.9**	**2,724.9**	**4,362.9**	**3,127.7**	**4,826.2**	**6,482.5**	**6,566.2**
Direct investment abroad	4 505 ..	−5.1	−184.6	−547.5	−121.5	−346.3	−237.1	−220.4	−240.5
Direct investment in Croatia	4 555 Z.	1,109.9	1,582.4	1,100.0	2,048.8	1,078.6	1,788.1	3,432.3	4,915.8
Portfolio investment assets	4 602 ..	−22.7	−129.3	−626.5	144.2	−924.8	−701.1	−559.6	−492.2
Equity securities	4 610 ..	−.2	.3	−69.3	−65.7	−47.6	−238.7	−363.0	−1,077.8
Debt securities	4 619 ..	−22.5	−129.6	−557.2	210.0	−877.2	−462.4	−196.6	585.6
Portfolio investment liabilities	4 652 Z.	749.5	746.0	193.7	828.0	1,235.2	−798.4	−44.0	549.0
Equity securities	4 660 ..	−.2	14.0	34.7	15.7	177.6	112.9	417.0	434.8
Debt securities	4 669 Z.	749.7	731.9	159.0	812.3	1,057.6	−911.3	−461.0	114.2
Financial derivatives	4 910 ..	....	....	....	....	....	....	....	....
Financial derivatives assets	4 900 ..	....	....	....	....	....	....	....	....
Financial derivatives liabilities	4 905 ..	....	....	....	....	....	....	....	....
Other investment assets	4 703 ..	−888.2	362.6	365.1	−2,603.7	−619.6	1,317.8	−966.1	−2,332.5
Monetary authorities	4 701 ..	....	−.7	....	....	....	....	....	....
General government	4 704 ..	−24.7	−19.2	−30.5	26.5	94.0	−58.1	32.0	−75.4
Banks	4 705 ..	−878.3	−1,607.9	1,323.9	−2,304.4	−553.2	1,685.6	−781.1	−1,923.1
Other sectors	4 728 ..	14.7	1,990.4	−928.2	−325.8	−160.4	−309.7	−217.0	−334.0
Other investment liabilities	4 753 W.	1,009.9	53.7	2,240.1	4,067.1	2,704.7	3,456.9	4,840.3	4,166.6
Monetary authorities	4 753 WA	−8.2	−4.7	−181.7	378.8	−440.4	.1	.1	−.1
General government	4 753 ZB	289.7	−197.3	386.7	582.7	522.4	310.4	160.5	262.8
Banks	4 753 ZC	34.9	299.0	1,243.0	2,188.8	1,489.5	1,476.6	1,668.4	−1,705.3
Other sectors	4 753 ZD	693.5	−43.3	792.1	916.7	1,133.2	1,669.8	3,011.3	5,609.3
Total, Groups A Through C	4 983 ..	*1,431.4*	*1,839.1*	*1,262.7*	*2,319.1*	*1,292.4*	*2,335.5*	*3,038.2*	*2,170.4*
D. Net Errors and Omissions	4 998 ..	**−775.8**	**−441.5**	**−448.1**	**−918.3**	**−1,224.2**	**−1,313.2**	**−1,311.0**	**−1,188.5**
Total, Groups A Through D	4 984 ..	*655.6*	*1,397.6*	*814.6*	*1,400.8*	*68.2*	*1,022.3*	*1,727.2*	*981.9*
E. Reserves and Related Items	4 802 A.	**−655.6**	**−1,397.6**	**−814.6**	**−1,400.8**	**−68.2**	**−1,022.3**	**−1,727.2**	**−981.9**
Reserve assets	4 802 ..	−627.0	−1,366.7	−685.7	−1,400.8	−68.2	−1,022.3	−1,727.2	−981.9
Use of Fund credit and loans	4 766 ..	−28.6	−30.8	−128.9	....	....	....	....	....
Exceptional financing	4 920 ..	....	....	....	....	....	....	....	....
Conversion rates: kunas per U.S. dollar	0 101 ..	**8.2777**	**8.3415**	**7.8717**	**6.7050**	**6.0343**	**5.9492**	**5.8378**	**5.3645**

[1] Excludes components that have been classified in the categories of Group E.

Table 2. STANDARD PRESENTATION, 2000–2007

(Millions of U.S. dollars)

	Code	2000	2001	2002	2003	2004	2005	2006	2007
CURRENT ACCOUNT	4 993 ..	**−532.8**	**−729.2**	**−1,925.5**	**−2,162.3**	**−1,874.7**	**−2,555.0**	**−3,287.1**	**−4,443.0**
A. GOODS	4 100 ..	**−3,196.5**	**−4,093.0**	**−5,646.0**	**−7,904.6**	**−8,345.8**	**−9,341.5**	**−10,486.5**	**−12,933.4**
Credit	2 100 ..	**4,573.7**	**4,767.0**	**5,006.2**	**6,311.4**	**8,214.5**	**8,959.8**	**10,644.4**	**12,622.7**
General merchandise: exports f.o.b.	2 110 ..	4,497.6	4,695.8	4,949.5	6,241.4	8,130.1	8,868.6	10,507.4	12,457.8
Goods for processing: exports f.o.b.	2 150 ..	....	....	....	....	....	....	....	....
Repairs on goods	2 160 ..	69.5	63.4	54.4	66.6	79.8	86.6	99.5	115.3
Goods procured in ports by carriers	2 170 ..	6.6	7.7	2.3	3.4	4.6	4.6	37.5	49.6
Nonmonetary gold	2 180 ..	....	....	....	....	....	....	....	....
Debit	3 100 ..	**−7,770.2**	**−8,860.0**	**−10,652.2**	**−14,216.0**	**−16,560.3**	**−18,301.3**	**−21,130.9**	**−25,556.1**
General merchandise: imports f.o.b.	3 110 ..	−7,745.6	−8,837.2	−10,622.8	−14,149.7	−16,482.2	−18,191.7	−21,016.9	−25,403.0
Goods for processing: imports f.o.b.	3 150 ..	....	....	....	....	....	....	....	....
Repairs on goods	3 160 ..	−15.3	−14.9	−18.3	−34.2	−39.0	−47.4	−50.7	−71.8
Goods procured in ports by carriers	3 170 ..	−9.2	−8.0	−11.1	−32.1	−39.1	−62.2	−63.2	−81.4
Nonmonetary gold	3 180 ..	....	....	....	....	....	....	....	....
B. SERVICES	4 200 ..	**2,249.2**	**2,934.7**	**3,168.0**	**5,587.0**	**5,807.8**	**6,520.7**	**7,261.5**	**8,604.4**
Total credit	2 200 ..	*4,070.9*	*4,883.9*	*5,582.4*	*8,568.8*	*9,373.2*	*9,921.0*	*10,809.1*	*12,529.0*
Total debit	3 200 ..	*−1,821.7*	*−1,949.2*	*−2,414.4*	*−2,981.8*	*−3,565.4*	*−3,400.3*	*−3,547.6*	*−3,924.6*
Transportation services, credit	2 205 ..	**555.7**	**589.2**	**590.6**	**788.4**	**982.4**	**1,093.2**	**1,243.9**	**1,508.1**
Passenger	2 850 ..	*112.8*	*127.7*	*141.4*	*203.5*	*217.6*	*255.1*	*306.0*	*364.6*
Freight	2 851 ..	*338.9*	*348.5*	*324.8*	*429.8*	*564.2*	*582.4*	*631.2*	*772.4*
Other	2 852 ..	*104.0*	*113.0*	*124.4*	*155.1*	*200.6*	*255.7*	*306.7*	*371.1*
Sea transport, passenger	2 207 ..	8.4	9.3	10.6	14.0	16.0	15.7	19.9	22.2
Sea transport, freight	2 208 ..	258.9	248.1	201.4	268.8	363.2	368.0	385.5	466.7
Sea transport, other	2 209 ..	27.2	28.5	26.6	31.8	40.8	67.5	73.9	90.0
Air transport, passenger	2 211 ..	93.2	106.4	116.1	171.5	181.4	219.9	269.0	323.7
Air transport, freight	2 212 ..	1.2	1.9	1.5	1.2	1.6	1.7	1.8	3.0
Air transport, other	2 213 ..	50.2	53.0	59.0	74.7	93.2	103.2	114.1	138.3
Other transport, passenger	2 215 ..	11.2	12.0	14.7	18.0	20.1	19.5	17.1	18.8
Other transport, freight	2 216 ..	78.8	98.6	121.9	159.9	199.4	212.7	243.9	302.7
Other transport, other	2 217 ..	26.6	31.4	38.8	48.6	66.6	85.0	118.7	142.8
Transportation services, debit	3 205 ..	**−378.0**	**−421.9**	**−426.9**	**−503.5**	**−610.6**	**−625.6**	**−709.0**	**−871.0**
Passenger	3 850 ..	*−66.5*	*−70.7*	*−71.4*	*−37.0*	*−33.0*	*−32.0*	*−33.4*	*−39.7*
Freight	3 851 ..	*−178.3*	*−206.7*	*−221.6*	*−290.0*	*−376.0*	*−381.0*	*−441.4*	*−560.2*
Other	3 852 ..	*−133.2*	*−144.5*	*−133.8*	*−176.4*	*−201.6*	*−212.5*	*−234.3*	*−271.2*
Sea transport, passenger	3 207 ..	−.2	−.1	−.2	−.2	−.3	−.3	−.2	−.8
Sea transport, freight	3 208 ..	−16.5	−19.3	−19.5	−25.8	−63.3	−36.7	−41.2	−49.2
Sea transport, other	3 209 ..	−79.1	−84.6	−66.4	−83.7	−86.0	−94.3	−92.3	−105.6
Air transport, passenger	3 211 ..	−59.0	−65.0	−63.9	−27.9	−23.2	−21.3	−22.3	−27.9
Air transport, freight	3 212 ..	−15.4	−18.2	−18.3	−24.3	−28.3	−32.3	−36.6	−45.4
Air transport, other	3 213 ..	−38.7	−42.7	−45.2	−63.2	−81.9	−81.0	−98.9	−131.2
Other transport, passenger	3 215 ..	−7.2	−5.5	−7.3	−8.9	−9.6	−10.5	−10.9	−11.0
Other transport, freight	3 216 ..	−146.4	−169.2	−183.8	−240.0	−284.3	−312.1	−363.5	−465.6
Other transport, other	3 217 ..	−15.4	−17.2	−22.2	−29.5	−33.6	−37.2	−43.0	−34.4
Travel, credit	2 236 ..	**2,758.0**	**3,335.0**	**3,811.4**	**6,310.5**	**6,726.7**	**7,370.1**	**7,990.1**	**9,233.2**
Business travel	2 237 ..	263.6	273.9	323.0	297.1	403.0	623.3	489.1	533.5
Personal travel	2 240 ..	2,494.4	3,061.1	3,488.5	6,013.3	6,323.7	6,746.8	7,501.0	8,699.7
Travel, debit	3 236 ..	**−568.1**	**−606.4**	**−781.3**	**−672.4**	**−847.9**	**−753.9**	**−736.6**	**−985.2**
Business travel	3 237 ..	−260.5	−289.1	−460.0	−330.1	−370.1	−333.7	−288.8	−369.1
Personal travel	3 240 ..	−307.6	−317.3	−321.3	−342.3	−477.9	−420.2	−447.7	−616.1
Other services, credit	2 200 BA	**757.2**	**959.7**	**1,180.4**	**1,469.9**	**1,664.2**	**1,457.7**	**1,575.2**	**1,787.7**
Communications	2 245 ..	102.9	153.8	156.2	212.8	190.2	238.3	327.4	438.5
Construction	2 249 ..	199.2	232.3	327.2	444.3	467.4	42.9	78.3	85.1
Insurance	2 253 ..	33.9	39.4	16.9	19.7	19.3	21.8	25.5	31.2
Financial	2 260 ..	10.6	21.2	90.7	48.2	33.8	34.2	47.5	50.7
Computer and information	2 262 ..	33.5	43.8	45.7	62.2	65.0	84.7	84.4	116.3
Royalties and licence fees	2 266 ..	66.0	106.4	84.8	34.6	40.5	73.1	47.2	39.6
Other business services	2 268 ..	265.5	334.6	428.5	614.5	817.7	933.2	915.2	959.9
Personal, cultural, and recreational	2 287 ..	30.1	27.0	28.2	33.3	29.6	28.7	49.0	65.8
Government, n.i.e.	2 291 ..	15.4	1.4	1.8	.3	.8	.8	.7	.7
Other services, debit	3 200 BA	**−875.7**	**−920.9**	**−1,206.2**	**−1,805.9**	**−2,106.9**	**−2,020.8**	**−2,102.0**	**−2,068.4**
Communications	3 245 ..	−25.1	−77.5	−76.3	−73.5	−104.1	−124.8	−118.3	−158.6
Construction	3 249 ..	−63.1	−70.9	−75.0	−279.0	−335.4	−4.9	−4.0	−11.7
Insurance	3 253 ..	−36.3	−44.9	−38.0	−45.3	−42.6	−47.4	−59.3	−70.6
Financial	3 260 ..	−48.8	−36.4	−94.3	−142.2	−84.8	−88.3	−126.3	−83.7
Computer and information	3 262 ..	−57.0	−70.3	−92.1	−108.2	−124.6	−148.1	−178.5	−216.2
Royalties and licence fees	3 266 ..	−60.8	−62.5	−77.1	−131.1	−146.0	−192.5	−174.8	−213.6
Other business services	3 268 ..	−515.3	−495.8	−685.1	−953.2	−1,173.3	−1,307.8	−1,312.6	−1,154.2
Personal, cultural, and recreational	3 287 ..	−30.1	−31.7	−31.6	−41.5	−53.1	−56.2	−71.2	−93.5
Government, n.i.e.	3 291 ..	−39.3	−30.8	−36.7	−31.9	−42.8	−51.0	−56.9	−66.2

Table 2 (Continued). STANDARD PRESENTATION, 2000–2007

(Millions of U.S. dollars)

	Code	2000	2001	2002	2003	2004	2005	2006	2007
C. INCOME....................	4 300 ..	**−465.9**	**−554.2**	**−537.9**	**−1,251.8**	**−822.3**	**−1,209.5**	**−1,452.3**	**−1,544.5**
Total credit....................	2 300 ..	*346.1*	*433.8*	*437.0*	*508.1*	*878.8*	*889.3*	*1,125.7*	*1,760.2*
Total debit....................	3 300 ..	*−812.0*	*−988.0*	*−975.0*	*−1,759.9*	*−1,701.1*	*−2,098.8*	*−2,578.0*	*−3,304.7*
Compensation of employees, credit....................	2 310 ..	**82.7**	**140.7**	**177.1**	**246.8**	**333.5**	**359.2**	**510.5**	**724.4**
Compensation of employees, debit....................	3 310 ..	**−13.1**	**−12.8**	**−18.5**	**−38.4**	**−42.6**	**−36.3**	**−39.0**	**−46.1**
Investment income, credit....................	2 320 ..	**263.4**	**293.0**	**259.9**	**261.3**	**545.3**	**530.1**	**615.2**	**1,035.8**
Direct investment income....................	2 330 ..	10.3	30.4	24.8	39.2	215.2	138.3	101.3	240.4
Dividends and distributed branch profits....................	2 332 ..	1.2	11.4	14.8	2.2	8.4	53.0	12.6	60.2
Reinvested earnings and undistributed branch profits.....	2 333 ..	7.5	17.6	8.6	35.3	203.2	78.4	82.0	168.2
Income on debt (interest)....................	2 334 ..	1.6	1.3	1.4	1.7	3.6	7.0	6.8	12.1
Portfolio investment income....................	2 339 ..	....	....	....	....	40.4	57.3	72.2	102.4
Income on equity....................	2 340 ..	....	....	....	....	....	....	....	....
Income on bonds and notes....................	2 350 ..	....	....	....	....	36.4	52.3	60.2	80.3
Income on money market instruments....................	2 360 ..	....	....	....	....	4.0	4.9	12.1	22.2
Other investment income....................	2 370 ..	253.1	262.6	235.1	222.1	289.7	334.5	441.7	692.9
Investment income, debit....................	3 320 ..	**−798.9**	**−975.2**	**−956.4**	**−1,721.5**	**−1,658.5**	**−2,062.5**	**−2,539.0**	**−3,258.5**
Direct investment income....................	3 330 ..	−160.6	−327.1	−350.4	−1,018.5	−753.1	−1,072.9	−1,328.3	−1,497.5
Dividends and distributed branch profits....................	3 332 ..	−56.5	−136.1	−173.4	−296.4	−338.9	−275.5	−352.0	−672.7
Reinvested earnings and undistributed branch profits.....	3 333 ..	−80.2	−162.1	−146.1	−673.9	−351.3	−720.4	−877.6	−661.8
Income on debt (interest)....................	3 334 ..	−23.9	−28.9	−30.9	−48.2	−62.8	−77.0	−98.7	−163.0
Portfolio investment income....................	3 339 ..	−210.0	−234.9	−206.9	−270.1	−351.2	−329.1	−292.8	−324.7
Income on equity....................	3 340 ..	−11.6	−18.3	−3.9	−5.8	−4.8	−2.7	−5.1	−9.4
Income on bonds and notes....................	3 350 ..	−196.3	−215.0	−202.6	−264.0	−345.7	−326.5	−287.7	−315.3
Income on money market instruments....................	3 360 ..	−2.2	−1.6	−.4	−.3	−.7	....	....	....
Other investment income....................	3 370 ..	−428.3	−413.2	−399.2	−433.0	−554.2	−660.5	−918.0	−1,436.3
D. CURRENT TRANSFERS....................	4 379 ..	**880.5**	**983.4**	**1,090.4**	**1,407.0**	**1,485.7**	**1,475.3**	**1,390.1**	**1,430.5**
Credit....................	2 379 ..	**1,098.2**	**1,192.7**	**1,375.0**	**1,741.4**	**1,974.0**	**2,027.2**	**2,060.5**	**2,164.4**
General government....................	2 380 ..	118.0	127.4	136.0	240.3	223.3	276.0	322.8	358.7
Other sectors....................	2 390 ..	980.2	1,065.3	1,239.0	1,501.2	1,750.7	1,751.3	1,737.8	1,805.8
Workers' remittances....................	2 391 ..	534.4	582.9	677.0	797.2	851.4	844.8	689.4	610.5
Other current transfers....................	2 392 ..	445.8	482.4	562.0	704.0	899.3	906.5	1,048.3	1,195.2
Debit....................	3 379 ..	**−217.8**	**−209.3**	**−284.6**	**−334.4**	**−488.2**	**−551.9**	**−670.4**	**−733.9**
General government....................	3 380 ..	−96.3	−69.3	−105.1	−161.7	−220.0	−260.2	−332.4	−379.9
Other sectors....................	3 390 ..	−121.4	−140.0	−179.5	−172.7	−268.2	−291.7	−338.0	−354.0
Workers' remittances....................	3 391 ..	−27.3	−29.1	−26.0	−17.2	−17.2	−20.9	−27.2	−31.0
Other current transfers....................	3 392 ..	−94.1	−110.9	−153.6	−155.5	−251.0	−270.7	−310.8	−323.0
CAPITAL AND FINANCIAL ACCOUNT....................	4 996 ..	**1,308.6**	**1,170.6**	**2,373.6**	**3,080.7**	**3,098.9**	**3,868.2**	**4,598.1**	**5,631.4**
CAPITAL ACCOUNT....................	4 994 ..	**11.0**	**137.3**	**463.3**	**118.5**	**39.4**	**64.2**	**−157.1**	**47.2**
Total credit....................	2 994 ..	*26.6*	*142.0*	*470.3*	*132.6*	*48.8*	*70.5*	*51.6*	*62.8*
Total debit....................	3 994 ..	*−15.6*	*−4.6*	*−7.0*	*−14.1*	*−9.4*	*−6.2*	*−208.7*	*−15.6*
Capital transfers, credit....................	2 400 ..	**26.6**	**142.0**	**50.8**	**77.9**	**48.8**	**70.5**	**51.6**	**62.8**
General government....................	2 401 ..	2.4	118.7	20.0	37.0	11.4	52.0	17.5	3.9
Debt forgiveness....................	2 402 ..	2.4	3.8	20.0	37.0	11.4	5.1	17.5	3.9
Other capital transfers....................	2 410 ..	....	114.9	....	....	....	46.9	....	....
Other sectors....................	2 430 ..	24.2	23.3	30.8	40.9	37.3	18.4	34.1	58.9
Migrants' transfers....................	2 431 ..	24.2	23.3	30.8	40.9	37.3	18.4	34.1	58.9
Debt forgiveness....................	2 432 ..	....	....	....	....	....	....	....	....
Other capital transfers....................	2 440 ..	....	....	....	....	....	....	....	....
Capital transfers, debit....................	3 400 ..	**−15.6**	**−4.6**	**−7.0**	**−14.1**	**−9.4**	**−6.2**	**−208.7**	**−15.6**
General government....................	3 401 ..	−12.0	....	−.2	−2.4	−.5	−1.7	−.4	−7.2
Debt forgiveness....................	3 402 ..	−12.0	....	−.2	−2.4	−.5	−1.7	−.4	−7.2
Other capital transfers....................	3 410 ..	....	....	....	....	....	....	....	....
Other sectors....................	3 430 ..	−3.6	−4.6	−6.8	−11.7	−8.9	−4.6	−208.3	−8.4
Migrants' transfers....................	3 431 ..	−3.6	−4.6	−6.8	−11.7	−8.9	−4.6	−208.3	−8.4
Debt forgiveness....................	3 432 ..	....	....	....	....	....	....	....	....
Other capital transfers....................	3 440 ..	....	....	....	....	....	....	....	....
Nonproduced nonfinancial assets, credit....................	2 480 ..	....	....	419.4	54.7	....	....	....	....
Nonproduced nonfinancial assets, debit....................	3 480 ..	....	....	....	....	....	....	....	....

Table 2 (Continued). STANDARD PRESENTATION, 2000–2007

(Millions of U.S. dollars)

	Code	2000	2001	2002	2003	2004	2005	2006	2007
FINANCIAL ACCOUNT	4 995	**1,297.6**	**1,033.3**	**1,910.3**	**2,962.1**	**3,059.5**	**3,803.9**	**4,755.3**	**5,584.3**
A. DIRECT INVESTMENT	4 500	**1,104.8**	**1,397.8**	**552.5**	**1,927.3**	**732.3**	**1,551.0**	**3,211.9**	**4,675.2**
Direct investment abroad	4 505	**−5.1**	**−184.6**	**−547.5**	**−121.5**	**−346.3**	**−237.1**	**−220.4**	**−240.5**
Equity capital	4 510	−33.3	−109.7	−532.7	−80.2	−117.9	−70.1	−142.7	−150.0
Claims on affiliated enterprises	4 515	−33.3	−109.7	−532.7	−80.2	−118.4	−70.4	−142.7	−150.1
Liabilities to affiliated enterprises	4 520	....	....	....	....	.4	.3	....	.1
Reinvested earnings	4 525	−7.5	−17.6	−8.6	−35.3	−203.2	−78.4	−82.0	−168.2
Other capital	4 530	35.6	−57.2	−6.1	−6.1	−25.2	−88.7	4.3	77.7
Claims on affiliated enterprises	4 535	−4.5	9.2	−7.4	−18.1	−30.8	−74.2	−17.3	29.7
Liabilities to affiliated enterprises	4 540	40.1	−66.4	1.3	12.0	5.6	−14.4	21.6	48.0
Direct investment in Croatia	4 555	**1,109.9**	**1,582.4**	**1,100.0**	**2,048.8**	**1,078.6**	**1,788.1**	**3,432.3**	**4,915.8**
Equity capital	4 560	724.2	820.7	677.3	894.2	381.1	1,001.8	2,180.9	2,928.4
Claims on direct investors	4 565	....	....	....	....	−.3	....	−.1	....
Liabilities to direct investors	4 570	724.2	820.7	677.3	894.2	381.4	1,001.9	2,181.0	2,928.5
Reinvested earnings	4 575	80.2	162.1	146.1	673.9	351.3	720.4	877.6	661.8
Other capital	4 580	305.6	599.6	276.6	480.7	346.1	65.8	373.9	1,325.5
Claims on direct investors	4 585	.6	.1	−.3	−1.8	−21.5	−3.2	21.0	−3.4
Liabilities to direct investors	4 590	304.9	599.5	276.9	482.6	367.6	69.0	352.8	1,329.0
B. PORTFOLIO INVESTMENT	4 600	**726.9**	**616.6**	**−432.8**	**972.2**	**310.4**	**−1,499.5**	**−603.6**	**56.8**
Assets	4 602	**−22.7**	**−129.3**	**−626.5**	**144.2**	**−924.8**	**−701.1**	**−559.6**	**−492.2**
Equity securities	4 610	−.2	.3	−69.3	−65.7	−47.6	−238.7	−363.0	−1,077.8
Monetary authorities	4 611	....	....	....	....	....	....	....	....
General government	4 612	....	....	....	....	....	....	....	....
Banks	4 613	....	....	−2.5	.4	....	....	3.3	−.9
Other sectors	4 614	−.2	.3	−66.9	−66.1	−47.6	−238.7	−366.2	−1,076.9
Debt securities	4 619	−22.5	−129.6	−557.2	210.0	−877.2	−462.4	−196.6	585.6
Bonds and notes	4 620	−17.7	−116.2	−569.8	194.8	−715.0	−485.3	121.6	438.4
Monetary authorities	4 621	....	....	....	....	....	....	....	....
General government	4 622	....	....	....	....	....	....	....	....
Banks	4 623	−17.7	−116.2	−549.8	211.8	−724.7	−440.9	178.3	355.1
Other sectors	4 624	....	....	−20.0	−16.9	9.7	−44.4	−56.6	83.3
Money market instruments	4 630	−4.8	−13.4	12.6	15.1	−162.2	22.9	−318.3	147.2
Monetary authorities	4 631	....	....	....	....	....	....	....	....
General government	4 632	....	....	....	....	....	....	....	....
Banks	4 633	−4.8	−13.4	18.5	7.8	−162.2	22.9	−318.3	147.2
Other sectors	4 634	....	....	....	−5.9	7.3	....	....	....
Liabilities	4 652	**749.5**	**746.0**	**193.7**	**828.0**	**1,235.2**	**−798.4**	**−44.0**	**549.0**
Equity securities	4 660	−.2	14.0	34.7	15.7	177.6	112.9	417.0	434.8
Banks	4 663	−.1	−5.3	1.5	−2.8	.9	−16.9	53.6	12.4
Other sectors	4 664	−.1	19.3	33.2	18.5	176.8	129.7	363.4	422.3
Debt securities	4 669	749.7	731.9	159.0	812.3	1,057.6	−911.3	−461.0	114.2
Bonds and notes	4 670	755.8	713.4	187.8	773.2	1,097.6	−911.3	−461.0	114.2
Monetary authorities	4 671	....	....	....	....	....	....	....	....
General government	4 672	755.7	713.4	62.5	588.9	504.6	−905.9	−369.7	−1.0
Banks	4 673	....	....	....	....	556.1	5.1	1.2	1.3
Other sectors	4 674	....	....	125.3	184.2	36.9	−10.5	−92.5	113.9
Money market instruments	4 680	−6.1	18.5	−28.8	39.1	−39.9	....	....	....
Monetary authorities	4 681	....	....	....	....	....	....	....	....
General government	4 682	....	....	....	....	....	....	....	....
Banks	4 683	....	....	....	....	....	....	....	....
Other sectors	4 684	−6.1	18.5	−28.8	39.1	−39.9	....	....	....
C. FINANCIAL DERIVATIVES	4 910	....	....	....	....	....	....	....	....
Monetary authorities	4 911	....	....	....	....	....	....	....	....
General government	4 912	....	....	....	....	....	....	....	....
Banks	4 913	....	....	....	....	....	....	....	....
Other sectors	4 914	....	....	....	....	....	....	....	....
Assets	4 900	....	....	....	....	....	....	....	....
Monetary authorities	4 901	....	....	....	....	....	....	....	....
General government	4 902	....	....	....	....	....	....	....	....
Banks	4 903	....	....	....	....	....	....	....	....
Other sectors	4 904	....	....	....	....	....	....	....	....
Liabilities	4 905	....	....	....	....	....	....	....	....
Monetary authorities	4 906	....	....	....	....	....	....	....	....
General government	4 907	....	....	....	....	....	....	....	....
Banks	4 908	....	....	....	....	....	....	....	....
Other sectors	4 909	....	....	....	....	....	....	....	....

Table 2 (Concluded). STANDARD PRESENTATION, 2000–2007

(Millions of U.S. dollars)

	Code	2000	2001	2002	2003	2004	2005	2006	2007
D. OTHER INVESTMENT	4 700 ..	**93.0**	**385.5**	**2,476.4**	**1,463.4**	**2,085.0**	**4,774.7**	**3,874.2**	**1,834.2**
Assets	4 703 ..	**−888.2**	**362.6**	**365.1**	**−2,603.7**	**−619.6**	**1,317.8**	**−966.1**	**−2,332.5**
Trade credits	4 706 ..	105.8	56.8	−83.6	−188.4	−234.5	−160.8	−38.0	−129.9
General government	4 707 ..	....	....	....	....	....	−.3	.2	.2
of which: Short-term	4 709 ..	....	....	....	....	....	....	....	....
Other sectors	4 710 ..	105.8	56.8	−83.6	−188.4	−234.5	−160.5	−38.2	−130.1
of which: Short-term	4 712 ..	*96.3*	*57.2*	*−77.5*	*−160.1*	*−256.5*	*−175.0*	*−32.2*	*−41.0*
Loans	4 714 ..	−23.5	36.9	−56.7	−102.1	53.7	−140.8	−189.9	−1.5
Monetary authorities	4 715 ..	....	−.7	....	....	....	....	....	....
of which: Short-term	4 718 ..	....	....	....	....	....	....	....	....
General government	4 719 ..	1.1	−3.1	.6	−1.1	−2.4	−1.8	−1.7	−13.3
of which: Short-term	4 721 ..	....	....	....	....	....	....	....	....
Banks	4 722 ..	23.5	−5.9	−20.1	4.3	4.1	−34.9	−98.4	−45.4
of which: Short-term	4 724 ..	*9.6*	*3.3*	*−.6*	*−1.3*	*5.1*	*−10.0*	*−24.3*	*−11.4*
Other sectors	4 725 ..	−48.1	46.6	−37.2	−105.4	52.0	−104.2	−89.8	57.1
of which: Short-term	4 727 ..	....	....	*−.1*	*.1*	*−1.7*	*1.2*	*.3*	*.6*
Currency and deposits	4 730 ..	−970.5	269.0	505.4	−2,313.2	−438.8	1,619.4	−738.2	−2,201.1
Monetary authorities	4 731 ..	....	....	....	....	....	....	....	....
General government	4 732 ..	−25.8	−16.1	−31.1	27.6	96.4	−56.0	33.5	−62.3
Banks	4 733 ..	−901.8	−1,602.0	1,343.9	−2,308.8	−557.3	1,720.4	−682.7	−1,877.8
Other sectors	4 734 ..	−43.0	1,887.0	−807.4	−32.0	22.0	−45.0	−89.0	−261.0
Other assets	4 736 ..	....	....	....	....	....	....	....	....
Monetary authorities	4 737 ..	....	....	....	....	....	....	....	....
of which: Short-term	4 739 ..	....	....	....	....	....	....	....	....
General government	4 740 ..	....	....	....	....	....	....	....	....
of which: Short-term	4 742 ..	....	....	....	....	....	....	....	....
Banks	4 743 ..	....	....	....	....	....	....	....	....
of which: Short-term	4 745 ..	....	....	....	....	....	....	....	....
Other sectors	4 746 ..	....	....	....	....	....	....	....	....
of which: Short-term	4 748 ..	....	....	....	....	....	....	....	....
Liabilities	4 753 ..	**981.3**	**22.9**	**2,111.2**	**4,067.1**	**2,704.7**	**3,456.9**	**4,840.3**	**4,166.6**
Trade credits	4 756 ..	271.0	62.4	478.8	−249.1	−70.5	25.1	−.9	407.8
General government	4 757 ..	−3.3	1.1	−.1	1.8	−.4	.6	−.9	−.9
of which: Short-term	4 759 ..	*−2.8*	....	....	....	....	....	....	....
Other sectors	4 760 ..	274.3	61.3	478.9	−250.9	−70.1	24.5	....	408.7
of which: Short-term	4 762 ..	*288.7*	*82.2*	*480.5*	*−198.1*	*−49.3*	*−9.4*	*5.3*	*180.7*
Loans	4 764 ..	778.3	−257.8	473.6	3,282.3	2,109.6	2,994.2	3,835.5	4,077.9
Monetary authorities	4 765 ..	−37.1	−35.7	−310.7	378.7	−440.4	....	....	....
of which: Use of Fund credit and loans from the Fund	4 766 ..	*−28.6*	*−30.8*	*−128.9*	....	....	....	....	....
of which: Short-term	4 768 ..	*19.9*	*26.7*	*−52.9*	*379.1*	*−440.4*	....	....	....
General government	4 769 ..	293.0	−198.3	386.8	581.0	522.8	309.0	161.4	265.0
of which: Short-term	4 771 ..	*284.1*	*−361.8*	....	....	....	....	....	....
Banks	4 772 ..	103.1	80.8	83.4	1,154.1	827.7	1,043.4	666.0	−1,384.0
of which: Short-term	4 774 ..	*−6.7*	*−4.8*	*−2.1*	*86.5*	*−101.8*	*699.4*	*168.1*	*−563.6*
Other sectors	4 775 ..	419.2	−104.6	314.1	1,168.4	1,199.5	1,641.9	3,008.0	5,196.9
of which: Short-term	4 777 ..	*−104.4*	*.3*	*−22.1*	*53.2*	*43.0*	*69.1*	*106.2*	*825.0*
Currency and deposits	4 780 ..	−68.0	218.4	1,159.7	1,034.8	661.8	434.2	1,002.4	−322.8
Monetary authorities	4 781 ..	.2	.2	.1	.1	....	.1	.1	−.1
General government	4 782 ..	....	....	....	....	....	.9	−.1	−1.4
Banks	4 783 ..	−68.2	218.2	1,159.6	1,034.7	661.8	433.2	1,002.4	−321.3
Other sectors	4 784 ..	....	....	....	....	....	....	....	....
Other liabilities	4 786 ..	....	−.1	−.9	−.8	3.8	3.5	3.3	3.7
Monetary authorities	4 787 ..	....	....	....	....	....	....	....	....
of which: Short-term	4 789 ..	....	....	....	....	....	....	....	....
General government	4 790 ..	....	....	....	....	....	....	....	....
of which: Short-term	4 792 ..	....	....	....	....	....	....	....	....
Banks	4 793 ..	....	....	....	....	....	....	....	....
of which: Short-term	4 795 ..	....	−.1	−.9	−.8	3.8	3.5	3.3	3.7
Other sectors	4 796 ..	....	....	....	....	....	....	....	....
of which: Short-term	4 798 ..	....	....	....	....	....	....	....	....
E. RESERVE ASSETS	4 802 ..	**−627.0**	**−1,366.7**	**−685.7**	**−1,400.8**	**−68.2**	**−1,022.3**	**−1,727.2**	**−981.9**
Monetary gold	4 812 ..	....	....	....	....	....	....	....	....
Special drawing rights	4 811 ..	32.9	35.1	111.6	1.5	....	−.2	.1	−.1
Reserve position in the Fund	4 810 ..	....	....	....	....	....	....	....	....
Foreign exchange	4 803 ..	−659.9	−1,401.8	−797.3	−1,402.3	−68.2	−1,022.1	−1,727.4	−981.8
Other claims	4 813 ..	....	....	....	....	....	....	....	....
NET ERRORS AND OMISSIONS	4 998 ..	**−775.8**	**−441.5**	**−448.1**	**−918.3**	**−1,224.2**	**−1,313.2**	**−1,311.0**	**−1,188.5**

Table 3. INTERNATIONAL INVESTMENT POSITION (End-period stocks), 2000–2007

(Millions of U.S. dollars)

	Code	2000	2001	2002	2003	2004	2005	2006	2007
ASSETS	8 995 C.	**8,334.3**	**11,218.6**	**13,009.5**	**17,930.9**	**20,572.8**	**18,980.9**	**24,019.7**	**31,150.7**
Direct investment abroad	8 505 ..	**825.4**	**889.1**	**1,673.5**	**2,033.0**	**2,127.6**	**2,046.7**	**2,413.7**	**3,479.6**
Equity capital and reinvested earnings	8 506 ..	824.1	859.9	1,634.3	1,983.4	2,044.4	1,905.5	2,271.2	3,317.3
Claims on affiliated enterprises	8 507 ..	824.1	859.9	1,634.3	1,983.4	2,044.4	1,905.5	2,271.2	3,317.3
Liabilities to affiliated enterprises	8 508 ..	....	....	....	....	....	....	....	....
Other capital	8 530 ..	1.3	29.1	39.3	49.6	83.2	141.2	142.4	162.3
Claims on affiliated enterprises	8 535 ..	....	....	....	....	....	....	....	....
Liabilities to affiliated enterprises	8 540 ..	....	....	....	....	....	....	....	....
Portfolio investment	8 602 ..	**87.0**	**221.5**	**912.9**	**921.6**	**2,049.5**	**2,528.3**	**3,391.7**	**4,440.2**
Equity securities	8 610 ..	14.3	20.8	82.4	176.6	240.7	494.6	948.6	2,353.2
Monetary authorities	8 611 ..	....	....	....	....	....	....	....	....
General government	8 612 ..	....	....	2.2	2.9	....	....	....	....
Banks	8 613 ..	7.2	6.6	7.7	5.9	6.9	7.0	8.8	12.2
Other sectors	8 614 ..	7.1	14.2	72.5	167.8	233.8	487.6	939.8	2,341.1
Debt securities	8 619 ..	72.7	200.7	830.5	745.1	1,808.8	2,033.7	2,443.1	2,087.0
Bonds and notes	8 620 ..	58.8	173.3	820.1	742.0	1,590.5	1,859.6	1,927.7	1,675.0
Monetary authorities	8 621 ..	....	....	....	....	....	....	....	....
General government	8 622 ..	....	....	....	....	....	....	....	1.1
Banks	8 623 ..	58.8	173.3	792.5	699.9	1,555.0	1,784.8	1,786.0	1,605.9
Other sectors	8 624 ..	....	....	27.6	42.1	35.5	74.8	141.7	68.0
Money market instruments	8 630 ..	13.9	27.4	10.3	3.0	218.3	174.1	515.4	412.0
Monetary authorities	8 631 ..	....	....	....	....	....	....	....	....
General government	8 632 ..	....	....	....	....	....	....	....	....
Banks	8 633 ..	13.9	27.4	10.3	3.0	218.3	174.1	515.4	412.0
Other sectors	8 634 ..	....	....	....	....	....	....	....	....
Financial derivatives	8 900 ..	....	....	....	....	....	....	....	....
Monetary authorities	8 901 ..	....	....	....	....	....	....	....	....
General government	8 902 ..	....	....	....	....	....	....	....	....
Banks	8 903 ..	....	....	....	....	....	....	....	....
Other sectors	8 904 ..	....	....	....	....	....	....	....	....
Other investment	8 703 ..	**3,900.2**	**5,404.8**	**4,538.3**	**6,785.7**	**7,637.5**	**5,605.7**	**6,726.5**	**9,556.4**
Trade credits	8 706 ..	222.6	219.9	231.8	316.7	301.6	311.2	303.6	366.5
General government	8 707 ..	....	....	....	....	....	.3	.2	....
of which: Short-term	8 709 ..	....	....	....	....	....	....	....	....
Other sectors	8 710 ..	222.6	219.9	231.7	316.7	301.6	310.9	303.4	366.5
of which: Short-term	8 712 ..	*6.0*	*5.3*	*6.5*	*52.3*	*54.7*	*85.3*	*69.8*	*30.4*
Loans	8 714 ..	76.3	84.3	113.4	127.6	139.1	172.9	315.3	434.4
Monetary authorities	8 715 ..	....	.7	.7	.8	.8	.7	.8	.8
of which: Short-term	8 718 ..	....	....	....	....	....	....	....	....
General government	8 719 ..	2.3	5.4	5.0	6.6	9.5	10.3	12.5	26.1
of which: Short-term	8 721 ..	....	....	....	....	....	....	....	....
Banks	8 722 ..	69.5	73.6	101.5	108.8	111.1	133.9	248.2	315.6
of which: Short-term	8 724 ..	*25.9*	*22.2*	*25.6*	*29.9*	*25.9*	*33.0*	*63.8*	*80.5*
Other sectors	8 725 ..	4.5	4.8	6.1	11.3	17.7	27.9	53.8	91.9
of which: Short-term	8 727 ..	....	....	*.1*	....	*1.8*	*.4*	*.3*	*.1*
Currency and deposits	8 730 ..	3,601.2	5,100.5	4,193.1	6,341.5	7,196.8	5,121.5	6,107.2	8,755.4
Monetary authorities	8 731 ..	....	....	....	....	....	....	....	....
General government	8 732 ..	69.0	83.5	120.5	102.3	12.1	64.1	34.8	102.5
Banks	8 733 ..	2,389.2	3,915.0	2,868.6	4,895.2	5,878.7	3,682.4	4,608.4	6,927.9
Other sectors	8 734 ..	1,143.0	1,102.0	1,204.0	1,344.0	1,306.0	1,375.0	1,464.0	1,725.0
Other assets	8 736 ..	....	....	....	....	....	....	.5	....
Monetary authorities	8 737 ..	....	....	....	....	....	....	....	....
of which: Short-term	8 739 ..	....	....	....	....	....	....	....	....
General government	8 740 ..	....	....	....	....	....	....	....	....
of which: Short-term	8 742 ..	....	....	....	....	....	....	....	....
Banks	8 743 ..	....	....	....	....	....	....	.5	....
of which: Short-term	8 745 ..	....	....	....	....	....	....	*.5*	....
Other sectors	8 746 ..	....	....	....	....	....	....	....	....
of which: Short-term	8 748 ..	....	....	....	....	....	....	....	....
Reserve assets	8 802 ..	**3,521.8**	**4,703.3**	**5,884.9**	**8,190.5**	**8,758.2**	**8,800.3**	**11,487.8**	**13,674.5**
Monetary gold	8 812 ..	....	....	....	....	....	....	....	....
Special drawing rights	8 811 ..	147.2	107.4	1.5	....	.1	.3	.2	.3
Reserve position in the Fund	8 810 ..	.2	.2	.2	.2	.2	.2	.2	.3
Foreign exchange	8 803 ..	3,374.4	4,595.6	5,883.2	8,190.2	8,757.9	8,799.8	11,487.4	13,674.0
Other claims	8 813 ..	....	....	....	....	....	....	....	....

Table 3 (Concluded). INTERNATIONAL INVESTMENT POSITION (End-period stocks), 2000–2007

(Millions of U.S. dollars)

	Code	2000	2001	2002	2003	2004	2005	2006	2007
LIABILITIES	8 995 D.	13,648.8	15,060.4	20,587.5	31,325.4	41,492.7	42,916.6	63,484.7	89,325.7
Direct investment in Croatia	8 555 ..	2,787.5	3,893.2	6,031.1	8,509.4	12,403.5	14,591.7	27,363.7	44,640.0
Equity capital and reinvested earnings	8 556 ..	2,173.8	2,945.3	4,583.2	6,214.8	9,684.6	11,738.1	23,649.6	39,415.5
Claims on direct investors	8 557 ..	....	....	....	....	....	....	....	....
Liabilities to direct investors	8 558 ..	2,173.8	2,945.3	4,583.2	6,214.8	9,684.6	11,738.1	23,649.6	39,415.5
Other capital	8 580 ..	613.7	947.9	1,447.9	2,294.5	2,718.8	2,853.7	3,714.1	5,224.4
Claims on direct investors	8 585 ..	....	....	....	....	....	....	....	....
Liabilities to direct investors	8 590 ..	....	....	....	....	....	....	....	....
Portfolio investment	8 652 ..	3,394.5	3,978.5	4,541.9	6,147.1	8,140.3	6,543.6	7,165.9	8,581.8
Equity securities	8 660 ..	108.8	127.1	248.6	291.7	664.2	765.0	1,366.1	2,081.3
Banks	8 663 ..	36.5	35.9	46.3	57.9	88.0	99.3	206.3	246.9
Other sectors	8 664 ..	72.3	91.2	202.3	233.8	576.2	665.7	1,159.8	1,834.5
Debt securities	8 669 ..	3,285.7	3,851.4	4,293.3	5,855.4	7,476.1	5,778.6	5,799.8	6,500.4
Bonds and notes	8 670 ..	3,276.1	3,822.9	4,293.3	5,813.3	7,476.1	5,778.6	5,799.8	6,500.4
Monetary authorities	8 671 ..	....	....	....	....	....	....	....	....
General government	8 672 ..	3,247.0	3,795.4	4,114.3	5,382.4	6,345.0	4,794.4	4,793.5	5,235.9
Banks	8 673 ..	....	....	....	....	616.8	540.2	602.9	674.3
Other sectors	8 674 ..	29.1	27.5	179.0	431.0	514.3	444.0	403.5	590.1
Money market instruments	8 680 ..	9.5	28.5	....	42.1	....	....	....	....
Monetary authorities	8 681 ..	....	....	....	....	....	....	....	....
General government	8 682 ..	....	....	....	....	....	....	....	....
Banks	8 683 ..	....	....	....	....	....	....	....	....
Other sectors	8 684 ..	9.5	28.5	....	42.1	....	....	....	....
Financial derivatives	8 905 ..	....	....	....	....	....	....	....	....
Monetary authorities	8 906 ..	....	....	....	....	....	....	....	....
General government	8 907 ..	....	....	....	....	....	....	....	....
Banks	8 908 ..	....	....	....	....	....	....	....	....
Other sectors	8 909 ..	....	....	....	....	....	....	....	....
Other investment	8 753 ..	7,466.8	7,188.7	10,014.5	16,669.0	20,948.9	21,781.2	28,955.1	36,103.9
Trade credits	8 756 ..	274.6	238.3	270.8	224.4	211.0	229.8	241.3	473.3
General government	8 757 ..	.1	1.2	1.1	2.9	2.8	3.1	2.5	1.7
of which: Short-term	8 759 ..	....	....	....	....	....	....	....	....
Other sectors	8 760 ..	274.5	237.1	269.7	221.5	208.2	226.7	238.8	471.5
of which: Short-term	8 762 ..	*42.0*	*36.1*	*49.5*	*27.7*	*31.6*	*32.8*	*47.3*	*45.7*
Loans	8 764 ..	6,434.3	6,024.7	7,347.7	12,532.8	15,757.4	16,606.8	22,247.7	28,404.6
Monetary authorities	8 765 ..	198.8	188.6	22.4	454.1	....	....	....	....
of which: Use of Fund credit and loans from the Fund	8 766 ..	*158.2*	*122.2*	....	....	....	....	....	....
of which: Short-term	8 768 ..	*40.6*	*66.4*	*22.4*	*454.1*	....	....	....	....
General government	8 769 ..	1,715.9	1,478.9	2,012.3	2,825.2	3,525.0	3,538.5	3,981.8	4,544.5
of which: Short-term	8 771 ..	*362.0*	....	....	....	....	....	....	....
Banks	8 772 ..	1,629.8	1,627.8	1,979.8	4,253.1	5,494.3	5,782.9	7,067.7	6,282.5
of which: Short-term	8 774 ..	*7.3*	*2.3*	*.4*	*755.6*	*707.6*	*1,259.9*	*1,514.8*	*1,044.3*
Other sectors	8 775 ..	2,889.8	2,729.4	3,333.2	5,000.5	6,738.2	7,285.4	11,198.2	17,577.7
of which: Short-term	8 777 ..	*43.3*	*47.6*	*26.5*	*85.1*	*134.1*	*165.9*	*204.0*	*1,000.6*
Currency and deposits	8 780 ..	434.0	635.0	1,977.4	3,422.9	4,413.0	4,301.6	5,791.3	6,090.2
Monetary authorities	8 781 ..	1.2	1.5	1.8	3.2	3.2	3.1	3.4	3.5
General government	8 782 ..	....	....	....	....	....	....	....	....
Banks	8 783 ..	432.8	633.5	1,975.7	3,419.7	4,409.7	4,298.5	5,787.9	6,086.8
Other sectors	8 784 ..	....	....	....	....	....	....	....	....
Other liabilities	8 786 ..	324.0	290.7	418.5	488.9	567.5	643.1	674.8	1,135.8
Monetary authorities	8 787 ..	....	....	....	....	....	....	....	....
of which: Short-term	8 789 ..	....	....	....	....	....	....	....	....
General government	8 790 ..	1.5	.5	1.3	1.6	3.6	2.3	1.6	7.8
of which: Short-term	8 792 ..	*1.5*	*.5*	*1.3*	*1.6*	*3.6*	*2.3*	*1.6*	*7.8*
Banks	8 793 ..	2.6	1.5	.9	1.1	1.2	2.0	1.6	2.4
of which: Short-term	8 795 ..	*2.6*	*1.5*	*.9*	*1.1*	*1.2*	*2.0*	*1.6*	*2.4*
Other sectors	8 796 ..	319.9	288.7	416.3	486.2	562.7	638.7	671.5	1,125.5
of which: Short-term	8 798 ..	*319.9*	*288.7*	*416.3*	*486.2*	*562.7*	*638.7*	*671.5*	*1,125.5*
NET INTERNATIONAL INVESTMENT POSITION	8 995 ..	−5,314.5	−3,841.8	−7,577.9	−13,394.5	−20,919.9	−23,935.6	−39,465.1	−58,175.0
Conversion rates: kunas per U.S. dollar (end of period)	0 102 ..	8.1553	8.3560	7.1457	6.1185	5.6369	6.2336	5.5784	4.9855

Table 1. ANALYTIC PRESENTATION, 2000–2007

(Millions of U.S. dollars)

	Code	2000	2001	2002	2003	2004	2005	2006	2007
A. Current Account[1]	4 993 Z.	**−488.1**	**−322.2**	**−379.2**	**−292.1**	**−826.8**	**−970.9**	**−1,279.4**	**−2,594.9**
Goods: exports f.o.b.	2 100 ..	950.9	975.2	851.8	925.0	1,173.5	1,544.7	1,393.0	1,482.9
Goods: imports f.o.b.	3 100 ..	−3,556.6	−3,552.5	−3,735.4	−4,107.8	−5,222.1	−5,791.8	−6,334.9	−7,957.3
Balance on Goods	4 100 ..	*−2,605.7*	*−2,577.3*	*−2,883.7*	*−3,182.8*	*−4,048.7*	*−4,247.1*	*−4,941.9*	*−6,474.4*
Services: credit	2 200 ..	4,068.1	4,340.0	4,530.5	5,371.8	6,235.0	6,502.0	7,159.6	8,801.7
Services: debit	3 200 ..	−1,585.3	−1,614.6	−1,741.8	−2,236.7	−2,644.1	−2,706.0	−2,938.7	−3,763.6
Balance on Goods and Services	4 991 ..	*−122.9*	*148.1*	*−94.9*	*−47.7*	*−457.8*	*−451.2*	*−720.9*	*−1,436.3*
Income: credit	2 300 ..	572.4	558.9	756.9	905.5	1,160.1	1,634.8	2,139.1	3,348.7
Income: debit	3 300 ..	−1,114.8	−1,083.3	−1,158.0	−1,294.5	−1,697.3	−2,246.6	−2,903.6	−4,493.9
Balance on Goods, Services, and Income	4 992 ..	*−665.3*	*−376.2*	*−496.0*	*−436.8*	*−995.0*	*−1,063.0*	*−1,485.4*	*−2,581.6*
Current transfers: credit	2 379 Z.	236.8	147.3	269.9	386.3	585.1	631.2	822.3	822.2
Current transfers: debit	3 379 ..	−59.6	−93.3	−153.1	−241.6	−416.9	−539.1	−616.2	−835.5
B. Capital Account[1]	4 994 Z.	**4.8**	**5.7**	**19.6**	**37.9**	**133.9**	**86.9**	**33.2**	**8.1**
Capital account: credit	2 994 Z.	19.3	27.1	46.0	59.0	191.7	131.1	97.8	87.8
Capital account: debit	3 994 ..	−14.5	−21.5	−26.3	−21.0	−57.8	−44.2	−64.6	−79.6
Total, Groups A Plus B	4 981 ..	*−483.2*	*−316.6*	*−359.5*	*−254.1*	*−692.9*	*−884.0*	*−1,246.1*	*−2,586.8*
C. Financial Account[1]	4 995 W.	**530.3**	**965.1**	**825.9**	**46.0**	**912.2**	**1,421.5**	**1,909.3**	**2,681.8**
Direct investment abroad	4 505 ..	−172.1	−249.1	−548.1	−589.7	−711.7	−547.6	−896.3	−1,221.7
Direct investment in Cyprus	4 555 Z.	854.9	944.7	1,103.4	908.1	1,118.8	1,162.0	1,870.9	2,239.5
Portfolio investment assets	4 602 ..	−453.4	−249.2	−1,129.2	−521.2	−1,812.6	−1,620.3	−3,158.4	593.8
Equity securities	4 610 ..	−94.5	−52.0	−578.4	161.9	−74.4	−18.4	31.9	−93.6
Debt securities	4 619 ..	−358.9	−197.3	−550.8	−683.1	−1,738.1	−1,601.9	−3,190.2	687.4
Portfolio investment liabilities	4 652 Z.	169.7	517.7	552.6	802.5	2,979.0	1,566.5	2,658.8	−883.5
Equity securities	4 660 ..	29.1	88.9	−3.8	−.1	−13.9	13.2	45.9	1.5
Debt securities	4 669 Z.	140.5	428.8	556.5	802.6	2,992.9	1,553.3	2,612.8	−885.0
Financial derivatives	4 910 ..	3.2	....	−50.3	16.6	−44.7	−15.2	−160.4	127.5
Financial derivatives assets	4 900 ..	....	....	−50.3	16.6	−23.6	−16.5	−151.9	125.0
Financial derivatives liabilities	4 905 ..	3.2	....	....	....	−21.1	1.3	−8.5	2.5
Other investment assets	4 703 ..	−1,285.3	−1,478.4	1,385.6	−2,357.0	−3,133.5	−7,154.0	−3,569.3	−13,802.5
Monetary authorities	4 701 ..	....	....	....	....	35.9	....	....	....
General government	4 704 ..	....	....	13.1	−20.8	−17.6	11.2	18.6	−38.1
Banks	4 705 ..	....	....	1,379.4	−2,482.3	−3,078.9	−7,807.0	−3,866.7	−13,480.9
Other sectors	4 728 ..	−1,285.3	−1,478.4	−6.9	146.1	−72.8	641.7	278.8	−283.5
Other investment liabilities	4 753 W.	1,413.4	1,479.4	−488.2	1,786.6	2,516.8	8,030.1	5,163.9	15,628.7
Monetary authorities	4 753 WA	....	....	−.8	−2.5	−1.8	1.1	6.6	170.6
General government	4 753 ZB	....	....	−38.1	244.6	162.9	135.2	28.9	172.3
Banks	4 753 ZC	....	....	−558.2	1,590.5	2,425.2	7,613.5	5,237.1	15,264.1
Other sectors	4 753 ZD	1,413.4	1,479.4	108.8	−46.0	−69.5	280.4	−108.7	21.7
Total, Groups A Through C	4 983 ..	*47.1*	*648.5*	*466.3*	*−208.2*	*219.3*	*537.5*	*663.1*	*95.0*
D. Net Errors and Omissions	4 998 ..	**−55.2**	**−37.9**	**−77.4**	**20.6**	**152.1**	**165.2**	**347.6**	**−344.9**
Total, Groups A Through D	4 984 ..	*−8.2*	*610.6*	*389.0*	*−187.6*	*371.4*	*702.7*	*1,010.7*	*−249.8*
E. Reserves and Related Items	4 802 A.	**8.2**	**−610.6**	**−389.0**	**187.6**	**−371.4**	**−702.7**	**−1,010.7**	**249.8**
Reserve assets	4 802 ..	8.2	−610.6	−389.0	187.6	−371.4	−702.7	−1,012.2	249.8
Use of Fund credit and loans	4 766 ..	....	....	....	....	....	....	....	....
Exceptional financing	4 920 ..	....	....	....	....	....	....	1.6	....
Conversion rates: Cyprus pounds per U.S. dollar	0 101 ..	**.6224**	**.6431**	**.6107**	**.5174**	**.4686**	**.4641**	**.4589**	**.4261**
Conversion rates: euros per U.S. dollar	0 103 ..	**1.0854**	**1.1175**	**1.0626**	**.8860**	**.8054**	**.8041**	**.7971**	**.7306**

---

[1] Excludes components that have been classified in the categories of Group E.

Table 2. STANDARD PRESENTATION, 2000–2007

(Millions of U.S. dollars)

	Code	2000	2001	2002	2003	2004	2005	2006	2007
CURRENT ACCOUNT	4 993	−488.1	−322.2	−379.2	−292.1	−826.8	−970.9	−1,279.4	−2,594.9
A. GOODS	4 100	−2,605.7	−2,577.3	−2,883.7	−3,182.8	−4,048.7	−4,247.1	−4,941.9	−6,474.4
Credit	2 100	950.9	975.2	851.8	925.0	1,173.5	1,544.7	1,393.0	1,482.9
General merchandise: exports f.o.b.	2 110	841.1	886.7	779.6	834.5	1,082.8	1,302.8	1,133.4	1,248.7
Goods for processing: exports f.o.b.	2 150	....	....	....	....	....	....	....	....
Repairs on goods	2 160	....	....	2.1	.7	.4	.2	....	.8
Goods procured in ports by carriers	2 170	109.8	88.5	70.1	89.6	90.1	241.5	259.7	233.3
Nonmonetary gold	2 180	....	....	....	.1	.1	.2	....	.1
Debit	3 100	−3,556.6	−3,552.5	−3,735.4	−4,107.8	−5,222.1	−5,791.8	−6,334.9	−7,957.3
General merchandise: imports f.o.b.	3 110	−3,556.6	−3,552.5	−3,676.7	−3,981.4	−5,154.4	−5,698.1	−6,207.1	−7,853.3
Goods for processing: imports f.o.b.	3 150	....	....	....	....	....	....	....	....
Repairs on goods	3 160	....	....	−25.9	−44.2	−6.0	−5.9	−38.3	−9.6
Goods procured in ports by carriers	3 170	....	....	−32.9	−81.3	−59.3	−86.8	−88.2	−91.9
Nonmonetary gold	3 180	....	....	....	−1.0	−2.4	−1.0	−1.3	−2.5
B. SERVICES	4 200	2,482.8	2,725.4	2,788.7	3,135.1	3,590.9	3,796.0	4,221.0	5,038.1
Total credit	2 200	*4,068.1*	*4,340.0*	*4,530.5*	*5,371.8*	*6,235.0*	*6,502.0*	*7,159.6*	*8,801.7*
Total debit	3 200	*−1,585.3*	*−1,614.6*	*−1,741.8*	*−2,236.7*	*−2,644.1*	*−2,706.0*	*−2,938.7*	*−3,763.6*
Transportation services, credit	2 205	706.3	748.4	904.4	1,239.6	1,436.2	1,543.4	1,657.4	2,119.0
Passenger	2 850	*195.9*	*209.6*	*219.4*	*227.8*	*311.4*	*325.6*	*309.7*	*422.4*
Freight	2 851	*27.3*	*30.2*	*140.9*	*264.6*	*309.0*	*317.7*	*443.4*	*644.3*
Other	2 852	*483.1*	*508.7*	*544.1*	*747.2*	*815.8*	*900.1*	*904.3*	*1,052.4*
Sea transport, passenger	2 207	22.5	25.5	2.7	1.8	75.8	75.9	81.5	85.7
Sea transport, freight	2 208	10.1	11.4	112.8	246.9	285.1	295.3	309.6	418.7
Sea transport, other	2 209	353.5	370.6	357.6	537.3	697.0	744.7	755.8	893.2
Air transport, passenger	2 211	173.4	184.0	216.7	226.0	235.6	249.7	228.2	336.7
Air transport, freight	2 212	17.2	18.7	28.1	17.4	23.1	21.9	116.0	190.2
Air transport, other	2 213	129.7	138.1	186.5	205.0	100.8	106.9	136.9	155.1
Other transport, passenger	2 215	....	....	....	....	....	....	....	....
Other transport, freight	2 216	....	....	....	.4	.8	.5	17.8	35.3
Other transport, other	2 217	....	....	....	4.9	18.0	48.4	11.5	4.1
Transportation services, debit	3 205	−873.5	−877.6	−828.6	−1,077.3	−1,116.4	−1,079.7	−1,075.3	−1,208.1
Passenger	3 850	*−129.7*	*−140.2*	*−70.5*	*−89.4*	*−96.0*	*−69.0*	*−64.2*	*−75.2*
Freight	3 851	*−355.7*	*−352.4*	*−408.5*	*−449.3*	*−574.1*	*−511.4*	*−555.8*	*−701.8*
Other	3 852	*−388.2*	*−385.0*	*−349.7*	*−538.6*	*−446.3*	*−499.2*	*−455.3*	*−431.1*
Sea transport, passenger	3 207	....	....	−1.9	−8.2	−2.5	−2.8	−1.4	−3.2
Sea transport, freight	3 208	−270.6	−352.4	−272.3	−297.2	−380.7	−339.4	−369.2	−465.3
Sea transport, other	3 209	−305.3	−309.6	−290.3	−396.8	−273.8	−335.7	−368.3	−294.1
Air transport, passenger	3 211	−129.7	−140.2	−68.6	−81.2	−93.5	−66.2	−62.7	−72.0
Air transport, freight	3 212	−85.2	....	−136.2	−148.6	−190.4	−169.7	−184.6	−232.7
Air transport, other	3 213	−82.9	−75.5	−59.4	−117.2	−154.7	−159.0	−79.6	−133.0
Other transport, passenger	3 215	....	....	....	....	....	....	....	....
Other transport, freight	3 216	....	....	....	−3.5	−3.0	−2.3	−2.0	−3.8
Other transport, other	3 217	....	....	....	−24.5	−17.9	−4.5	−7.4	−4.0
Travel, credit	2 236	1,940.8	1,993.3	1,959.1	2,097.1	2,241.3	2,317.8	2,380.9	2,686.8
Business travel	2 237	....	....	97.3	104.6	119.5	120.1	134.2	198.7
Personal travel	2 240	1,940.8	1,993.3	1,861.8	1,992.5	2,121.7	2,197.7	2,246.7	2,488.1
Travel, debit	3 236	−413.4	−427.6	−512.4	−611.2	−811.1	−931.8	−966.5	−1,479.3
Business travel	3 237	−20.4	−19.9	−19.9	−15.4	−28.4	−17.5	−21.9	−31.5
Personal travel	3 240	−393.0	−407.7	−492.5	−595.8	−782.7	−914.3	−944.6	−1,447.7
Other services, credit	2 200 BA	1,420.9	1,598.3	1,667.0	2,035.1	2,557.6	2,640.8	3,121.4	3,995.8
Communications	2 245	27.2	30.3	22.9	50.7	35.2	35.6	92.4	117.4
Construction	2 249	61.1	70.7	95.9	153.2	145.6	165.7	199.2	202.3
Insurance	2 253	27.3	28.3	35.0	34.3	44.7	56.4	113.8	116.8
Financial	2 260	192.8	156.0	138.6	147.2	220.2	264.4	313.8	734.3
Computer and information	2 262	57.8	86.8	104.0	91.9	250.3	229.2	202.1	274.6
Royalties and licence fees	2 266	16.1	26.2	42.7	15.0	17.7	15.1	16.0	21.1
Other business services	2 268	763.2	916.4	919.2	1,169.9	1,461.4	1,508.5	1,743.4	1,953.9
Personal, cultural, and recreational	2 287	5.6	10.4	14.6	9.7	24.8	41.1	52.9	77.0
Government, n.i.e.	2 291	269.9	273.3	294.1	363.3	357.7	324.8	387.8	498.4
Other services, debit	3 200 BA	−298.4	−309.4	−400.8	−548.2	−716.6	−694.6	−896.9	−1,076.2
Communications	3 245	−16.4	−19.9	−46.9	−66.1	−78.3	−94.5	−125.9	−142.0
Construction	3 249	−7.2	−8.4	−8.3	−14.4	−15.1	−10.9	−23.3	−28.5
Insurance	3 253	−66.0	−61.4	−31.1	−46.4	−71.2	−65.1	−75.6	−84.8
Financial	3 260	−48.2	−49.6	−60.0	−45.5	−100.1	−92.8	−131.8	−161.6
Computer and information	3 262	−20.9	−15.6	−10.2	−36.8	−32.8	−34.8	−34.0	−38.2
Royalties and licence fees	3 266	−20.7	−20.2	−15.0	−38.6	−53.4	−44.7	−60.5	−55.6
Other business services	3 268	−83.5	−102.1	−109.1	−130.4	−225.3	−203.4	−291.8	−355.3
Personal, cultural, and recreational	3 287	−13.0	−9.7	−13.2	−22.3	−48.6	−56.0	−64.9	−81.3
Government, n.i.e.	3 291	−22.3	−22.7	−106.9	−147.6	−91.9	−92.3	−89.0	−129.1

Table 2 (Continued). STANDARD PRESENTATION, 2000–2007

(Millions of U.S. dollars)

	Code	2000	2001	2002	2003	2004	2005	2006	2007
C. INCOME	4 300	**−542.4**	**−524.4**	**−401.0**	**−389.0**	**−537.2**	**−611.8**	**−764.5**	**−1,145.2**
Total credit	2 300	*572.4*	*558.9*	*756.9*	*905.5*	*1,160.1*	*1,634.8*	*2,139.1*	*3,348.7*
Total debit	3 300	*−1,114.8*	*−1,083.3*	*−1,158.0*	*−1,294.5*	*−1,697.3*	*−2,246.6*	*−2,903.6*	*−4,493.9*
Compensation of employees, credit	2 310	**45.0**	**77.9**	**15.5**	**25.4**	**33.1**	**53.9**	**34.5**	**43.5**
Compensation of employees, debit	3 310	**−48.2**	**−79.3**	**−81.1**	**−137.2**	**−159.2**	**−185.3**	**−184.3**	**−223.4**
Investment income, credit	2 320	**527.4**	**481.1**	**741.5**	**880.1**	**1,127.0**	**1,580.8**	**2,104.6**	**3,305.2**
Direct investment income	2 330	39.0	41.6	147.7	306.8	390.3	518.8	607.3	847.6
Dividends and distributed branch profits	2 332	29.3	39.2	11.0	10.8	14.2	120.6	113.1	174.4
Reinvested earnings and undistributed branch profits	2 333	9.7	2.4	80.7	246.8	290.2	238.9	317.3	422.9
Income on debt (interest)	2 334	....	....	56.1	49.2	85.9	159.4	176.9	250.3
Portfolio investment income	2 339	156.6	151.5	125.5	126.3	190.1	228.0	488.9	866.2
Income on equity	2 340	40.6	112.7	31.9	28.9	36.9	37.8	76.8	144.5
Income on bonds and notes	2 350	97.6	22.2	73.8	81.1	142.2	182.5	408.6	646.1
Income on money market instruments	2 360	18.4	16.6	19.9	16.4	11.1	7.6	3.4	75.6
Other investment income	2 370	331.8	288.0	468.2	447.0	546.6	834.1	1,008.4	1,591.4
Investment income, debit	3 320	**−1,066.6**	**−1,004.0**	**−1,076.9**	**−1,157.3**	**−1,538.1**	**−2,061.3**	**−2,719.3**	**−4,270.5**
Direct investment income	3 330	−846.3	−708.8	−618.2	−727.4	−961.7	−1,222.9	−1,646.0	−2,354.1
Dividends and distributed branch profits	3 332	−254.0	−244.0	−248.9	−329.1	−409.3	−535.1	−602.3	−1,102.5
Reinvested earnings and undistributed branch profits	3 333	−592.3	−464.8	−298.7	−262.0	−482.4	−538.1	−823.6	−927.9
Income on debt (interest)	3 334	....	....	−70.5	−136.3	−70.1	−149.8	−220.1	−323.6
Portfolio investment income	3 339	−49.0	−94.5	−72.4	−105.1	−228.0	−249.4	−387.2	−880.3
Income on equity	3 340	−6.4	−5.6	−4.7	−10.2	−44.6	−12.3	−60.3	−351.1
Income on bonds and notes	3 350	−37.0	−81.7	−62.4	−93.4	−142.8	−187.5	−280.7	−443.3
Income on money market instruments	3 360	−5.6	−7.3	−5.3	−1.5	−40.6	−49.6	−46.2	−85.9
Other investment income	3 370	−171.3	−200.7	−386.3	−324.8	−348.3	−589.0	−686.1	−1,036.1
D. CURRENT TRANSFERS	4 379	**177.2**	**54.0**	**116.8**	**144.7**	**168.2**	**92.1**	**206.0**	**−13.3**
Credit	2 379	**236.8**	**147.3**	**269.9**	**386.3**	**585.1**	**631.2**	**822.3**	**822.2**
General government	2 380	128.4	22.9	26.7	48.9	173.7	234.5	308.3	241.4
Other sectors	2 390	108.4	124.4	243.2	337.3	411.4	396.7	514.0	580.8
Workers' remittances	2 391	....	....	5.2	6.4	44.3	50.9	69.9	98.7
Other current transfers	2 392	108.4	....	238.0	330.9	367.1	345.8	444.1	482.2
Debit	3 379	**−59.6**	**−93.3**	**−153.1**	**−241.6**	**−416.9**	**−539.1**	**−616.2**	**−835.5**
General government	3 380	....	....	−1.8	−2.7	−132.3	−210.9	−203.6	−272.9
Other sectors	3 390	−59.6	−93.3	−151.4	−238.9	−284.5	−328.2	−412.7	−562.7
Workers' remittances	3 391	....	....	−25.9	−46.7	−54.2	−55.4	−55.2	−81.3
Other current transfers	3 392	−59.6	....	−125.4	−192.2	−230.3	−272.8	−357.5	−481.4
CAPITAL AND FINANCIAL ACCOUNT	4 996	**543.3**	**360.1**	**456.5**	**271.5**	**674.7**	**805.7**	**931.8**	**2,939.8**
CAPITAL ACCOUNT	4 994	**4.8**	**5.7**	**19.6**	**37.9**	**133.9**	**86.9**	**33.2**	**8.1**
Total credit	2 994	*19.3*	*27.1*	*46.0*	*59.0*	*191.7*	*131.1*	*97.8*	*87.8*
Total debit	3 994	*−14.5*	*−21.5*	*−26.3*	*−21.0*	*−57.8*	*−44.2*	*−64.6*	*−79.6*
Capital transfers, credit	2 400	**19.3**	**27.1**	**46.0**	**59.0**	**191.7**	**131.1**	**97.8**	**87.8**
General government	2 401	....	....	5.0	6.5	24.1	46.5	33.2	57.8
Debt forgiveness	2 402	....	....	....	....	....	....	....	....
Other capital transfers	2 410	....	....	5.0	6.5	24.1	46.5	33.2	57.8
Other sectors	2 430	19.3	27.1	41.0	52.5	167.5	84.7	64.7	29.9
Migrants' transfers	2 431	19.3	27.1	41.0	52.5	167.5	84.7	64.7	29.9
Debt forgiveness	2 432	....	....	....	....	....	....	....	....
Other capital transfers	2 440	....	....	....	....	....	....	....	....
Capital transfers, debit	3 400	**−14.5**	**−21.5**	**−16.5**	**−21.0**	**−57.8**	**−44.2**	**−64.6**	**−79.6**
General government	3 401	....	....	−6.9	−2.8	−15.8	−11.6	−25.3	−14.0
Debt forgiveness	3 402	....	....	....	....	....	....	....	....
Other capital transfers	3 410	....	....	−6.9	−2.8	−15.8	−11.6	−25.3	−14.0
Other sectors	3 430	−14.5	−21.5	−9.5	−18.2	−41.9	−32.6	−39.3	−65.6
Migrants' transfers	3 431	−14.5	−21.5	−9.5	−18.2	−41.9	−32.6	−39.3	−65.6
Debt forgiveness	3 432	....	....	....	....	....	....	....	....
Other capital transfers	3 440	....	....	....	....	....	....	....	....
Nonproduced nonfinancial assets, credit	2 480	....	....	....	....	....	....	....	....
Nonproduced nonfinancial assets, debit	3 480	....	....	**−9.9**	....	....	....	....	....

Table 2 (Continued). STANDARD PRESENTATION, 2000–2007

(Millions of U.S. dollars)

	Code	2000	2001	2002	2003	2004	2005	2006	2007
FINANCIAL ACCOUNT	4 995	**538.5**	**354.5**	**436.9**	**233.6**	**540.8**	**718.8**	**898.6**	**2,931.6**
A. DIRECT INVESTMENT	4 500	**682.8**	**695.6**	**555.4**	**318.5**	**407.1**	**614.4**	**974.6**	**1,017.8**
Direct investment abroad	4 505	−172.1	−249.1	−548.1	−589.7	−711.7	−547.6	−896.3	−1,221.7
Equity capital	4 510	−132.2	−176.8	−387.9	−137.6	−253.8	−122.3	−2,386.9	−741.7
Claims on affiliated enterprises	4 515	−132.2	−176.8	−387.9	−137.6	−253.8	−122.3	−2,386.9	−741.7
Liabilities to affiliated enterprises	4 520	....	....	....	....	....	....	....	....
Reinvested earnings	4 525	−9.7	−2.4	−80.7	−246.8	−290.2	−238.9	−317.3	−422.9
Other capital	4 530	−30.1	−69.9	−79.5	−205.3	−167.7	−186.5	1,807.9	−57.2
Claims on affiliated enterprises	4 535	−30.1	−69.9	−79.5	−205.3	−167.7	−186.5	1,807.9	−57.2
Liabilities to affiliated enterprises	4 540	....	....	....	....	....	....	....	....
Direct investment in Cyprus	4 555	854.9	944.7	1,103.4	908.1	1,118.8	1,162.0	1,870.9	2,239.5
Equity capital	4 560	75.8	186.1	535.9	254.3	386.1	503.8	629.2	952.7
Claims on direct investors	4 565	....	....	....	....	....	....	....	....
Liabilities to direct investors	4 570	75.8	186.1	535.9	254.3	386.1	503.8	629.2	952.7
Reinvested earnings	4 575	592.3	464.8	298.7	262.0	482.4	538.1	823.6	927.9
Other capital	4 580	186.7	293.8	268.8	391.8	250.3	120.1	418.1	358.8
Claims on direct investors	4 585	....	....	....	....	....	....	−1.5	....
Liabilities to direct investors	4 590	186.7	293.8	268.8	391.8	250.3	120.1	419.6	358.8
B. PORTFOLIO INVESTMENT	4 600	**−283.7**	**268.5**	**−576.6**	**281.3**	**1,166.5**	**−53.7**	**−498.0**	**−289.7**
Assets	4 602	**−453.4**	**−249.2**	**−1,129.2**	**−521.2**	**−1,812.6**	**−1,620.3**	**−3,158.4**	**593.8**
Equity securities	4 610	−94.5	−52.0	−578.4	161.9	−74.4	−18.4	31.9	−93.6
Monetary authorities	4 611	....	....	....	....	....	....	....	....
General government	4 612	....	....	....	....	....	....	....	....
Banks	4 613	−46.0	−25.3	−563.8	158.5	−58.5	−31.3	−181.8	175.2
Other sectors	4 614	−48.6	−26.7	−14.7	3.4	−16.0	12.9	213.6	−268.8
Debt securities	4 619	−358.9	−197.3	−550.8	−683.1	−1,738.1	−1,601.9	−3,190.2	687.4
Bonds and notes	4 620	−311.7	−171.4	−541.3	−644.5	−1,724.3	−1,783.0	−3,317.6	858.2
Monetary authorities	4 621	....	....	....	....	....	....	....	....
General government	4 622	....	....	....	....	....	....	....	....
Banks	4 623	−284.4	−156.4	−541.3	−644.5	−1,730.9	−1,782.4	−3,316.8	803.3
Other sectors	4 624	−27.3	−15.0	....	....	6.6	−.5	−.7	54.9
Money market instruments	4 630	−47.1	−25.9	−9.6	−38.6	−13.8	181.1	127.4	−170.8
Monetary authorities	4 631	....	....	....	....	....	....	....	....
General government	4 632	....	....	....	....	....	....	....	....
Banks	4 633	−9.8	−5.4	−9.6	−38.6	−13.8	181.1	127.6	−170.8
Other sectors	4 634	−37.3	−20.5	....	....	....	....	−.2	....
Liabilities	4 652	**169.7**	**517.7**	**552.6**	**802.5**	**2,979.0**	**1,566.5**	**2,660.3**	**−883.5**
Equity securities	4 660	29.1	88.9	−3.8	−.1	−13.9	13.2	45.9	1.5
Banks	4 663	27.2	82.8	−1.9	−3.5	−21.4	−3.4	−21.9	10.4
Other sectors	4 664	2.0	6.1	−1.9	3.5	7.5	16.6	67.8	−8.9
Debt securities	4 669	140.5	428.8	556.5	802.6	2,992.9	1,553.3	2,614.4	−885.0
Bonds and notes	4 670	137.9	420.7	443.5	618.8	1,409.0	1,215.2	163.6	1,752.2
Monetary authorities	4 671	....	....	....	....	....	....	....	....
General government	4 672	93.8	286.2	476.0	....	608.5	....	−351.3	....
Banks	4 673	44.1	134.5	−32.5	618.8	800.5	1,215.2	860.3	1,752.2
Other sectors	4 674	....	....	....	....	....	....	−345.5	....
Money market instruments	4 680	2.7	8.1	113.0	183.8	1,583.9	338.1	2,450.8	−2,637.2
Monetary authorities	4 681	....	....	....	....	....	....	....	....
General government	4 682	2.7	8.1	20.7	183.1	10.8	−244.6	....	....
Banks	4 683	....	....	92.3	.6	1,573.1	582.7	2,450.8	−2,637.2
Other sectors	4 684	....	....	....	....	....	....	....	....
C. FINANCIAL DERIVATIVES	4 910	**3.2**	**....**	**−50.3**	**16.6**	**−44.7**	**−15.2**	**−160.4**	**127.5**
Monetary authorities	4 911	....	....	....	....	....	....	....	....
General government	4 912	....	....	....	....	....	....	....	....
Banks	4 913	....	....	−49.8	16.4	−40.3	−13.9	−164.7	142.2
Other sectors	4 914	3.2	....	−.5	.2	−4.4	−1.3	4.3	−14.7
Assets	4 900	**....**	**....**	**−50.3**	**16.6**	**−23.6**	**−16.5**	**−151.9**	**125.0**
Monetary authorities	4 901	....	....	....	....	....	....	....	....
General government	4 902	....	....	....	....	....	....	....	....
Banks	4 903	....	....	−49.8	16.4	−19.2	−13.9	−151.9	134.3
Other sectors	4 904	....	....	−.5	.2	−4.4	−2.6	....	−9.3
Liabilities	4 905	**3.2**	**....**	**....**	**....**	**−21.1**	**1.3**	**−8.5**	**2.5**
Monetary authorities	4 906	....	....	....	....	....	....	....	....
General government	4 907	....	....	....	....	....	....	....	....
Banks	4 908	....	....	....	....	−21.1	....	−12.8	7.9
Other sectors	4 909	3.2	....	....	....	....	1.3	4.3	−5.4

Table 2 (Concluded). STANDARD PRESENTATION, 2000–2007

(Millions of U.S. dollars)

	Code	2000	2001	2002	2003	2004	2005	2006	2007
D. OTHER INVESTMENT	4 700	**128.1**	**1.0**	**897.3**	**−570.4**	**−616.7**	**876.1**	**1,594.6**	**1,826.2**
Assets	4 703	**−1,285.3**	**−1,478.4**	**1,385.6**	**−2,357.0**	**−3,133.5**	**−7,154.0**	**−3,569.3**	**−13,802.5**
Trade credits	4 706	....	....	15.9	−17.7	−15.9	13.8	21.2	−33.2
General government	4 707	....	....	15.9	−17.7	−15.9	13.8	21.2	−36.0
of which: Short-term	4 709	....	....	....	....	....	....	....	*−22.3*
Other sectors	4 710	....	....	....	....	....	....	....	2.8
of which: Short-term	4 712	....	....	....	....	....	....	....	*2.8*
Loans	4 714	....	....	−343.6	−651.8	−2,417.4	−1,122.2	−782.6	−6,018.1
Monetary authorities	4 715	....	....	....	....	....	....	....	....
of which: Short-term	4 718	....	....	....	....	....	....	....	....
General government	4 719	....	....	....	....	....	....	....	....
of which: Short-term	4 721	....	....	....	....	....	....	....	....
Banks	4 722	....	....	−343.6	−651.8	−2,417.4	−1,122.2	−782.6	−6,018.1
of which: Short-term	4 724	....	....	*.7*	*−1.2*	*3.0*	*.8*	*−52.5*	*−416.4*
Other sectors	4 725	....	....	....	....	....	....	....	....
of which: Short-term	4 727	....	....	....	....	....	....	....	....
Currency and deposits	4 730	....	....	1,741.4	−1,700.9	−694.1	−6,049.4	−2,795.6	−7,749.7
Monetary authorities	4 731	....	....	....	....	35.9	....	....	....
General government	4 732	....	....	....	....	....	....	....	....
Banks	4 733	....	....	1,748.3	−1,847.0	−657.1	−6,691.1	−3,074.4	−7,463.5
Other sectors	4 734	....	....	−6.9	146.1	−72.8	641.7	278.8	−286.2
Other assets	4 736	−1,285.3	−1,478.4	−28.1	13.4	−6.2	3.7	−12.2	−1.4
Monetary authorities	4 737	....	....	....	....	....	....	....	....
of which: Short-term	4 739	....	....	....	....	....	....	....	....
General government	4 740	....	....	−2.8	−3.1	−1.7	−2.6	−2.6	−2.1
of which: Short-term	4 742	....	....	....	....	....	....	....	....
Banks	4 743	....	....	−25.3	16.5	−4.5	6.3	−9.7	.7
of which: Short-term	4 745	....	....	....	....	....	....	*−1.4*	*.9*
Other sectors	4 746	−1,285.3	−1,478.4	....	....	....	....	....	....
of which: Short-term	4 748	....	....	....	....	....	....	....	....
Liabilities	4 753	**1,413.4**	**1,479.4**	**−488.2**	**1,786.6**	**2,516.8**	**8,030.1**	**5,163.9**	**15,628.7**
Trade credits	4 756	....	....	34.6	11.7	68.7	91.8	−32.6	212.5
General government	4 757	....	....	....	....	....	....	....	66.1
of which: Short-term	4 759	....	....	....	....	....	....	....	*66.1*
Other sectors	4 760	....	....	34.6	11.7	68.7	91.8	−32.6	146.4
of which: Short-term	4 762	....	....	*36.2*	*13.2*	*71.3*	*94.4*	*−31.9*	*147.8*
Loans	4 764	....	....	340.0	636.5	905.1	1,099.4	1,008.8	3,330.1
Monetary authorities	4 765	....	....	....	....	....	....	....	....
of which: Use of Fund credit and loans from the Fund	4 766	....	....	....	....	....	....	....	....
of which: Short-term	4 768	....	....	....	....	....	....	....	....
General government	4 769	....	....	−38.1	244.6	162.9	135.2	28.9	101.0
of which: Short-term	4 771	....	....	....	....	....	....	....	....
Banks	4 772	....	....	299.3	449.6	880.5	775.7	1,056.1	3,353.7
of which: Short-term	4 774	....	....	....	....	....	....	*252.3*	*1,116.7*
Other sectors	4 775	....	....	78.8	−57.7	−138.2	188.6	−76.2	−124.6
of which: Short-term	4 777	....	....	*13.5*	*11.2*	*−.6*	*233.9*	*12.7*	*−108.5*
Currency and deposits	4 780	....	....	−862.8	1,138.4	1,543.0	6,838.9	4,187.7	12,086.1
Monetary authorities	4 781	....	....	−.8	−2.5	−1.8	1.1	6.6	170.6
General government	4 782	....	....	....	....	....	....	....	5.2
Banks	4 783	....	....	−857.5	1,140.9	1,544.7	6,837.8	4,181.1	11,910.3
Other sectors	4 784	....	....	−4.6	....	....	....	....	....
Other liabilities	4 786	1,413.4	1,479.4	....	....	....	....	....	....
Monetary authorities	4 787	....	....	....	....	....	....	....	....
of which: Short-term	4 789	....	....	....	....	....	....	....	....
General government	4 790	....	....	....	....	....	....	....	....
of which: Short-term	4 792	....	....	....	....	....	....	....	....
Banks	4 793	....	....	....	....	....	....	....	....
of which: Short-term	4 795	....	....	....	....	....	....	....	....
Other sectors	4 796	1,413.4	1,479.4	....	....	....	....	....	....
of which: Short-term	4 798	*1,413.4*	*1,479.4*	....	....	....	....	....	....
E. RESERVE ASSETS	4 802	**8.2**	**−610.6**	**−389.0**	**187.6**	**−371.4**	**−702.7**	**−1,012.2**	**249.8**
Monetary gold	4 812	....	....	....	....	....	....	....	....
Special drawing rights	4 811	−.5	−.5	−.5	−.6	−.8	−.6	.3	.8
Reserve position in the Fund	4 810	....	....	−17.4	−25.3	29.0	37.3	11.1	6.9
Foreign exchange	4 803	8.7	−610.2	−371.0	213.5	−399.7	−739.4	−1,023.7	242.2
Other claims	4 813	....	....	....	....	....	....	....	....
NET ERRORS AND OMISSIONS	4 998	**−55.2**	**−37.9**	**−77.4**	**20.6**	**152.1**	**165.2**	**347.6**	**−344.9**

Table 3. INTERNATIONAL INVESTMENT POSITION (End-period stocks), 2000–2007

(Millions of U.S. dollars)

	Code	2000	2001	2002	2003	2004	2005	2006	2007
ASSETS	8 995 C.	....	....	**23,535.6**	**29,276.2**	**40,613.7**	**47,756.8**	**71,366.8**	**91,976.0**
Direct investment abroad	8 505 ..	....	....	**1,279.0**	**2,058.3**	**3,155.4**	**3,587.2**	**6,833.9**	**8,930.8**
Equity capital and reinvested earnings	8 506 ..	....	....	1,038.4	1,553.6	2,431.3	2,778.0	5,882.2	7,807.3
Claims on affiliated enterprises	8 507 ..	....	....	1,038.4	1,553.6	2,431.3	2,778.0	5,882.2	7,807.3
Liabilities to affiliated enterprises	8 508 ..	....	....	....	....	....	....	....	....
Other capital	8 530 ..	....	....	240.7	504.7	724.1	809.2	951.7	1,123.5
Claims on affiliated enterprises	8 535 ..	....	....	244.4	515.2	734.5	809.2	951.7	1,123.5
Liabilities to affiliated enterprises	8 540 ..	....	....	–3.7	–10.5	–10.4	....	....	....
Portfolio investment	8 602 ..	**1,088.3**	**1,590.3**	**5,383.4**	**6,581.0**	**10,378.8**	**13,378.5**	**26,437.3**	**26,033.1**
Equity securities	8 610 ..	.3	129.3	1,122.5	1,211.0	1,909.1	2,373.4	4,432.4	5,012.2
Monetary authorities	8 611 ..	....	....	....	....	....	....	....	....
General government	8 612 ..	....	....	....	....	....	....	....	....
Banks	8 613 ..	.3	.3	545.7	202.4	147.3	125.6	237.5	49.3
Other sectors	8 614 ..	....	129.0	576.8	1,008.5	1,761.8	2,247.8	4,195.0	4,962.9
Debt securities	8 619 ..	1,088.0	1,460.9	4,260.9	5,370.0	8,469.7	11,005.1	22,004.8	21,020.9
Bonds and notes	8 620 ..	972.8	1,304.8	3,701.5	4,662.7	7,773.1	10,682.4	21,403.6	20,417.8
Monetary authorities	8 621 ..	....	....	....	....	....	....	....	....
General government	8 622 ..	....	....	....	....	....	....	....	....
Banks	8 623 ..	972.8	1,279.6	3,377.3	4,155.0	7,382.1	10,034.0	20,377.3	19,328.4
Other sectors	8 624 ..	....	25.2	324.1	507.7	391.0	648.4	1,026.2	1,089.4
Money market instruments	8 630 ..	115.1	156.1	559.4	707.3	696.7	322.6	601.3	603.1
Monetary authorities	8 631 ..	....	....	....	....	....	....	....	....
General government	8 632 ..	....	....	....	....	....	....	....	....
Banks	8 633 ..	115.1	156.0	116.6	368.0	600.4	176.8	287.8	252.7
Other sectors	8 634 ..	....	.2	442.8	339.4	96.2	145.8	313.4	350.4
Financial derivatives	8 900 ..	....	....	**2.7**	**5.0**	**42.6**	**51.8**	**506.8**	**331.9**
Monetary authorities	8 901 ..	....	....	....	....	....	....	....	....
General government	8 902 ..	....	....	....	....	....	....	....	....
Banks	8 903 ..	....	....	....	2.8	37.7	45.2	498.0	317.9
Other sectors	8 904 ..	....	....	2.7	2.2	4.9	6.7	8.8	14.0
Other investment	8 703 ..	**3,951.0**	**4,269.6**	**13,686.1**	**17,142.5**	**22,962.2**	**26,410.7**	**31,724.4**	**50,168.5**
Trade credits	8 706 ..	....	....	114.8	122.6	179.2	209.8	170.3	214.3
General government	8 707 ..	....	....	43.2	45.3	58.2	63.5	51.8	75.2
of which: Short-term	8 709 ..	....	....	....	....	....	....	....	....
Other sectors	8 710 ..	....	....	71.7	77.3	121.0	146.3	118.6	139.1
of which: Short-term	8 712 ..	....	....	*71.7*	*77.3*	*121.0*	*146.3*	*118.6*	*139.1*
Loans	8 714 ..	399.4	394.5	3,493.6	3,718.0	6,592.8	6,026.4	11,933.6	19,181.7
Monetary authorities	8 715 ..	....	....	....	....	....	....	....	....
of which: Short-term	8 718 ..	....	....	....	....	....	....	....	....
General government	8 719 ..	....	....	....	....	....	....	....	....
of which: Short-term	8 721 ..	....	....	....	....	....	....	....	....
Banks	8 722 ..	399.4	394.5	3,474.4	3,690.6	6,567.7	6,001.2	11,911.1	19,181.7
of which: Short-term	8 724 ..	....	....	*6.1*	*6.9*	*4.7*	*3.2*	*7,749.1*	*10,664.3*
Other sectors	8 725 ..	....	....	19.2	27.4	25.1	25.2	22.5	....
of which: Short-term	8 727 ..	....	....	....	....	....	....	....	....
Currency and deposits	8 730 ..	3,539.7	3,866.5	10,071.2	13,265.2	16,162.5	20,154.6	19,611.4	30,759.5
Monetary authorities	8 731 ..	....	....	....	....	....	....	....	....
General government	8 732 ..	....	....	....	....	....	....	....	....
Banks	8 733 ..	3,539.7	3,865.8	5,568.0	8,171.3	9,701.8	14,761.5	13,648.3	23,598.9
Other sectors	8 734 ..	....	....	4,503.1	5,093.9	6,460.8	5,393.0	5,963.1	7,160.6
Other assets	8 736 ..	12.0	8.6	6.5	36.7	27.6	20.0	9.0	13.1
Monetary authorities	8 737 ..	....	....	....	....	....	....	....	....
of which: Short-term	8 739 ..	....	....	....	....	....	....	....	....
General government	8 740 ..	....	....	....	3.5	1.9	4.0	9.0	13.1
of which: Short-term	8 742 ..	....	....	....	....	....	....	....	....
Banks	8 743 ..	12.0	8.6	6.5	33.3	25.8	15.9	....	....
of which: Short-term	8 745 ..	....	....	....	....	....	....	....	....
Other sectors	8 746 ..	....	....	....	....	....	....	....	....
of which: Short-term	8 748 ..	....	....	....	....	....	....	....	....
Reserve assets	8 802 ..	**1,869.9**	**2,396.4**	**3,184.5**	**3,489.4**	**4,074.7**	**4,328.7**	**5,864.6**	**6,511.7**
Monetary gold	8 812 ..	127.6	127.5	149.2	197.0	201.9	232.4	292.2	388.7
Special drawing rights	8 811 ..	1.0	1.4	2.1	3.0	3.9	4.2	4.1	3.5
Reserve position in the Fund	8 810 ..	46.1	44.4	66.8	99.3	73.4	31.1	21.2	15.0
Foreign exchange	8 803 ..	1,694.0	2,221.9	2,965.1	3,188.6	3,793.8	4,059.6	5,545.5	6,102.7
Other claims	8 813 ..	1.1	1.1	1.3	1.5	1.6	1.4	1.6	1.8

Table 3 (Concluded). INTERNATIONAL INVESTMENT POSITION (End-period stocks), 2000–2007

(Millions of U.S. dollars)

	Code	2000	2001	2002	2003	2004	2005	2006	2007
LIABILITIES	8 995 D.	....	....	**22,299.7**	**28,648.7**	**38,200.5**	**44,546.2**	**64,088.1**	**88,942.4**
Direct investment in Cyprus	8 555	....	....	**4,912.3**	**6,754.8**	**8,500.0**	**8,482.8**	**13,754.0**	**17,711.4**
Equity capital and reinvested earnings	8 556	....	....	3,422.9	4,591.7	5,879.3	6,092.1	10,654.9	13,881.8
Claims on direct investors	8 557	....	....	−.5	−.6	−.6	....	....	....
Liabilities to direct investors	8 558	....	....	3,423.4	4,592.2	5,879.9	6,092.1	10,654.9	13,881.8
Other capital	8 580	....	....	1,489.4	2,163.2	2,620.8	2,390.8	3,099.0	3,829.5
Claims on direct investors	8 585	....	....	−37.4	....	....	....	....	....
Liabilities to direct investors	8 590	....	....	1,526.8	2,163.2	2,620.8	2,390.8	3,099.0	3,829.5
Portfolio investment	8 652	**979.3**	**1,445.1**	**2,086.0**	**3,158.0**	**7,272.5**	**8,692.9**	**13,444.3**	**14,355.3**
Equity securities	8 660	....	....	235.5	151.1	176.4	313.2	1,077.8	1,003.9
Banks	8 663	....	....	209.4	107.9	121.5	203.0	807.7	830.7
Other sectors	8 664	....	....	26.1	43.2	54.9	110.3	270.0	173.3
Debt securities	8 669	979.3	1,445.1	1,850.5	3,006.9	7,096.1	8,379.7	12,366.6	13,351.4
Bonds and notes	8 670	886.1	1,344.1	1,815.6	2,765.9	5,047.9	5,682.8	6,245.1	8,694.7
Monetary authorities	8 671	....	....	....	....	....	....	....	....
General government	8 672	886.1	855.1	1,235.3	1,491.6	2,264.2	1,942.1	1,821.1	2,035.6
Banks	8 673	....	488.9	580.3	1,273.8	2,783.7	3,740.7	4,423.9	6,659.1
Other sectors	8 674	....	....	....	.4	....	....	....	....
Money market instruments	8 680	93.2	101.0	34.9	241.0	2,048.2	2,696.9	6,121.5	4,656.7
Monetary authorities	8 681	....	....	....	....	....	....	....	....
General government	8 682	93.2	101.0	34.9	241.0	266.0	....	....	....
Banks	8 683	....	....	....	....	1,782.2	2,696.9	6,121.5	4,656.7
Other sectors	8 684	....	....	....	....	....	....	....	....
Financial derivatives	8 905	....	....	**3.0**	**23.3**	**27.9**	**23.0**	**421.5**	**481.5**
Monetary authorities	8 906	....	....	....	....	....	....	....	....
General government	8 907	....	....	....	....	....	....	....	....
Banks	8 908	....	....	2.9	22.5	27.9	21.8	409.5	474.1
Other sectors	8 909	....	....	.1	.9	....	1.2	11.9	7.3
Other investment	8 753	**8,691.0**	**9,367.7**	**15,298.4**	**18,712.6**	**22,400.0**	**27,347.4**	**36,468.3**	**56,394.2**
Trade credits	8 756	497.8	489.1	532.2	596.0	698.4	659.2	761.8	903.3
General government	8 757	....	....	....	....	....	....	....	....
of which: Short-term	8 759	....	....	....	....	....	....	....	....
Other sectors	8 760	497.8	489.1	532.2	596.0	698.4	659.2	761.8	903.3
of which: Short-term	8 762	*437.8*	*430.6*	*475.5*	*528.5*	*634.0*	*598.4*	*696.4*	*820.3*
Loans	8 764	1,469.6	1,310.4	3,196.2	4,068.5	5,049.1	5,601.4	11,215.8	14,215.5
Monetary authorities	8 765	....	....	26.3	29.1	30.1	27.2	28.9	39.7
of which: Use of Fund credit and loans from the Fund	8 766	....	....	....	....	....	....	....	....
of which: Short-term	8 768	....	....	....	....	....	....	....	....
General government	8 769	403.9	279.9	280.0	591.7	753.6	754.3	864.5	961.6
of which: Short-term	8 771	....	....	....	....	....	....	....	....
Banks	8 772	....	....	1,767.0	2,100.6	3,017.1	3,601.4	8,999.6	11,760.0
of which: Short-term	8 774	....	....	....	....	....	....	*5,989.4*	*7,466.2*
Other sectors	8 775	1,065.7	1,030.5	1,122.8	1,347.0	1,248.4	1,218.5	1,322.8	1,454.2
of which: Short-term	8 777	*38.9*	*30.8*	*45.7*	*63.2*	*22.6*	*63.5*	*81.5*	*96.2*
Currency and deposits	8 780	6,723.5	7,568.0	11,568.0	14,047.9	16,652.2	21,086.6	24,490.7	41,275.5
Monetary authorities	8 781	....	....	15.4	15.9	15.3	14.3	22.4	....
General government	8 782	....	....	....	....	....	....	....	....
Banks	8 783	6,723.5	7,568.0	11,552.7	14,032.0	16,637.0	21,072.3	24,468.3	41,275.5
Other sectors	8 784	....	....	....	....	....	....	....	....
Other liabilities	8 786	.2	.2	2.0	.2	.2	.2	....	....
Monetary authorities	8 787	.2	.2	2.0	.2	.2	.2	....	....
of which: Short-term	8 789	....	....	*1.8*	....	....	....	....	....
General government	8 790	....	....	....	....	....	....	....	....
of which: Short-term	8 792	....	....	....	....	....	....	....	....
Banks	8 793	....	....	....	....	....	....	....	....
of which: Short-term	8 795	....	....	....	....	....	....	....	....
Other sectors	8 796	....	....	....	....	....	....	....	....
of which: Short-term	8 798	....	....	....	....	....	....	....	....
NET INTERNATIONAL INVESTMENT POSITION	8 995	....	....	**1,236**	**627**	**2,413**	**3,211**	**7,279**	**3,034**
Conversion rates: Cyprus pounds per U.S. dollar (end of period)	0 102	.6168	.6502	.5468	.4652	.4250	.4844	.4391	.3978
Conversion rates: euros per U.S. dollar (end of period)	0 104	1.0747	1.1347	.9536	.7918	.7342	.8477	.7593	.6793

Table 1. ANALYTIC PRESENTATION, 2000–2007

(Millions of U.S. dollars)

	Code	2000	2001	2002	2003	2004	2005	2006	2007
A. Current Account[1]	4 993 Z.	**−2,690**	**−3,273**	**−4,265**	**−5,785**	**−5,749**	**−1,577**	**−3,783**	**−3,232**
Goods: exports f.o.b.	2 100 ..	29,019	33,404	38,480	48,705	67,220	77,951	95,151	122,791
Goods: imports f.o.b.	3 100 ..	−32,114	−36,482	−40,720	−51,224	−67,748	−75,430	−92,308	−116,878
Balance on Goods	4 100 ..	*−3,095*	*−3,078*	*−2,240*	*−2,519*	*−529*	*2,522*	*2,843*	*5,913*
Services: credit	2 200 ..	6,839	7,092	7,083	7,789	9,643	11,765	13,941	17,180
Services: debit	3 200 ..	−5,436	−5,567	−6,439	−7,320	−9,008	−10,217	−11,883	−14,397
Balance on Goods and Services	4 991 ..	*−1,692*	*−1,554*	*−1,597*	*−2,049*	*107*	*4,070*	*4,901*	*8,696*
Income: credit	2 300 ..	1,952	2,233	2,052	2,681	3,405	4,390	5,674	6,977
Income: debit	3 300 ..	−3,323	−4,422	−5,632	−6,966	−9,497	−10,364	−13,778	−18,017
Balance on Goods, Services, and Income	4 992 ..	*−3,063*	*−3,743*	*−5,177*	*−6,334*	*−5,985*	*−1,904*	*−3,204*	*−2,345*
Current transfers: credit	2 379 Z.	948	959	1,465	1,663	2,081	3,219	2,482	3,466
Current transfers: debit	3 379 ..	−575	−489	−553	−1,114	−1,845	−2,892	−3,061	−4,353
B. Capital Account[1]	4 994 Z.	**−5**	**−9**	**−4**	**−3**	**−602**	**196**	**380**	**1,026**
Capital account: credit	2 994 Z.	6	2	7	7	218	230	636	1,109
Capital account: debit	3 994 ..	−11	−11	−11	−10	−820	−35	−257	−83
Total, Groups A Plus B	4 981 ..	*−2,695*	*−3,281*	*−4,269*	*−5,788*	*−6,351*	*−1,382*	*−3,403*	*−2,205*
C. Financial Account[1]	4 995 W.	**3,835**	**4,569**	**10,621**	**5,620**	**7,036**	**6,379**	**4,205**	**4,921**
Direct investment abroad	4 505 ..	−43	−165	−211	−208	−1,037	27	−1,479	−1,356
Direct investment in Czech Republic	4 555 Z.	4,987	5,641	8,497	2,021	4,978	11,602	5,522	9,294
Portfolio investment assets	4 602 ..	−2,236	125	−2,373	−2,934	−2,806	−3,467	−3,004	−4,662
Equity securities	4 610 ..	−1,167	247	−231	188	−1,448	−1,472	−1,938	−3,026
Debt securities	4 619 ..	−1,069	−121	−2,142	−3,122	−1,359	−1,994	−1,066	−1,635
Portfolio investment liabilities	4 652 Z.	482	798	814	1,753	4,795	79	1,877	2,161
Equity securities	4 660 ..	619	616	−265	1,104	738	−1,540	268	−268
Debt securities	4 669 Z.	−137	181	1,079	649	4,057	1,619	1,608	2,430
Financial derivatives	4 910 ..	−40	−87	−130	143	−146	−112	−282	54
Financial derivatives assets	4 900 ..	−129	−254	−476	257	−660	−130	−504	−783
Financial derivatives liabilities	4 905 ..	89	168	347	−114	514	18	222	837
Other investment assets	4 703 ..	984	−1,199	4,015	2,279	−1,072	−4,728	−1,480	−7,876
Monetary authorities	4 701 ..	....	....	....	....	−7	−7	....	....
General government	4 704 ..	76	180	651	278	941	583	217	−33
Banks	4 705 ..	1,011	−1,299	3,844	1,469	−1,252	−4,599	527	−6,693
Other sectors	4 728 ..	−102	−80	−480	533	−754	−705	−2,224	−1,151
Other investment liabilities	4 753 W.	−300	−544	9	2,565	2,325	2,978	3,052	7,305
Monetary authorities	4 753 WA	....	1	−1	−2	27	204	−172	−28
General government	4 753 ZB	−49	−129	−45	372	411	862	442	144
Banks	4 753 ZC	−974	−1,152	−282	1,214	−477	536	792	5,827
Other sectors	4 753 ZD	723	735	338	981	2,365	1,376	1,989	1,362
Total, Groups A Through C	4 983 ..	*1,140*	*1,288*	*6,352*	*−168*	*685*	*4,997*	*802*	*2,715*
D. Net Errors and Omissions	4 998 ..	**−296**	**499**	**266**	**611**	**−422**	**−1,118**	**−710**	**−1,844**
Total, Groups A Through D	4 984 ..	*844*	*1,787*	*6,618*	*442*	*263*	*3,879*	*92*	*872*
E. Reserves and Related Items	4 802 A.	**−844**	**−1,787**	**−6,618**	**−442**	**−263**	**−3,879**	**−92**	**−872**
Reserve assets	4 802 ..	−844	−1,787	−6,618	−442	−263	−3,879	−92	−872
Use of Fund credit and loans	4 766 ..	....	....	....	....	....	....	....	....
Exceptional financing	4 920 ..	....	....	....	....	....	....	....	....
Conversion rates: Czech koruny per U.S. dollar	0 101 ..	**38.598**	**38.035**	**32.739**	**28.209**	**25.700**	**23.957**	**22.596**	**20.294**

[1] Excludes components that have been classified in the categories of Group E.

Czech Republic   935

Table 2. STANDARD PRESENTATION, 2000–2007

(Millions of U.S. dollars)

	Code	2000	2001	2002	2003	2004	2005	2006	2007
CURRENT ACCOUNT	4 993	−2,690	−3,273	−4,265	−5,785	−5,749	−1,577	−3,783	−3,232
A. GOODS	4 100	−3,095	−3,078	−2,240	−2,519	−529	2,522	2,843	5,913
Credit	2 100	29,019	33,404	38,480	48,705	67,220	77,951	95,151	122,791
General merchandise: exports f.o.b.	2 110	19,660	22,885	26,987	35,277	55,902	70,737	87,978	115,146
Goods for processing: exports f.o.b.	2 150	9,335	10,142	11,072	13,172	10,958	7,203	7,159	7,624
Repairs on goods	2 160	....	345	366	196	333	....	....	....
Goods procured in ports by carriers	2 170	....	....	....	....	....	....	....	....
Nonmonetary gold	2 180	24	32	54	60	26	12	14	21
Debit	3 100	−32,114	−36,482	−40,720	−51,224	−67,748	−75,430	−92,308	−116,878
General merchandise: imports f.o.b.	3 110	−25,535	−28,781	−32,337	−41,278	−59,148	−69,270	−86,164	−110,288
Goods for processing: imports f.o.b.	3 150	−6,570	−7,542	−8,269	−9,716	−8,252	−5,963	−5,960	−6,381
Repairs on goods	3 160	....	−151	−108	−219	−254	....	....	....
Goods procured in ports by carriers	3 170	....	....	....	....	−89	−189	−160	−176
Nonmonetary gold	3 180	−9	−7	−7	−11	−6	−8	−24	−33
B. SERVICES	4 200	1,403	1,524	643	470	636	1,548	2,058	2,783
Total credit	2 200	*6,839*	*7,092*	*7,083*	*7,789*	*9,643*	*11,765*	*13,941*	*17,180*
Total debit	3 200	*−5,436*	*−5,567*	*−6,439*	*−7,320*	*−9,008*	*−10,217*	*−11,883*	*−14,397*
Transportation services, credit	2 205	1,390	1,512	1,732	2,154	2,724	3,197	3,800	5,040
Passenger	2 850	....	....	*412*	*503*	*744*	*959*	*818*	*859*
Freight	2 851	....	....	*1,176*	*1,463*	*1,785*	*1,974*	*2,603*	*3,446*
Other	2 852	....	....	*144*	*187*	*195*	*263*	*378*	*735*
Sea transport, passenger	2 207	....	....	1	3	3	....	....	....
Sea transport, freight	2 208	....	....	22	16	27	25	53	47
Sea transport, other	2 209	....	....	....	24	12	10	15	7
Air transport, passenger	2 211	....	....	390	494	731	952	802	834
Air transport, freight	2 212	....	....	16	26	46	74	55	223
Air transport, other	2 213	....	....	....	49	80	111	157	202
Other transport, passenger	2 215	....	....	22	7	10	7	16	25
Other transport, freight	2 216	....	....	1,137	1,421	1,711	1,875	2,495	3,176
Other transport, other	2 217	....	....	144	114	103	143	207	525
Transportation services, debit	3 205	−715	−805	−895	−1,200	−1,862	−2,342	−2,754	−3,624
Passenger	3 850	....	....	*−200*	*−243*	*−402*	*−198*	*−109*	*−124*
Freight	3 851	....	....	*−493*	*−660*	*−1,225*	*−1,634*	*−2,130*	*−2,774*
Other	3 852	....	....	*−202*	*−297*	*−235*	*−510*	*−515*	*−727*
Sea transport, passenger	3 207	....	....	−3	−3	−4	....	....	....
Sea transport, freight	3 208	....	....	−79	−23	−44	−68	−79	−133
Sea transport, other	3 209	....	....	....	−123	−96	−41	−80	−50
Air transport, passenger	3 211	....	....	−188	−232	−387	−195	−95	−105
Air transport, freight	3 212	....	....	−8	−55	−105	−126	−147	−246
Air transport, other	3 213	....	....	....	−50	−53	−358	−299	−450
Other transport, passenger	3 215	....	....	−9	−9	−11	−3	−13	−18
Other transport, freight	3 216	....	....	−406	−582	−1,075	−1,440	−1,905	−2,395
Other transport, other	3 217	....	....	−202	−124	−86	−110	−136	−227
Travel, credit	2 236	2,973	3,104	2,964	3,566	4,187	4,676	5,541	6,637
Business travel	2 237	....	....	635	831	967	1,088	1,179	1,582
Personal travel	2 240	....	....	2,329	2,735	3,220	3,588	4,362	5,055
Travel, debit	3 236	−1,276	−1,386	−1,597	−1,934	−2,280	−2,405	−2,765	−3,647
Business travel	3 237	....	....	−265	−333	−441	−465	−490	−589
Personal travel	3 240	....	....	−1,333	−1,602	−1,840	−1,939	−2,276	−3,057
Other services, credit	2 200 BA	2,476	2,477	2,387	2,070	2,732	3,893	4,600	5,502
Communications	2 245	122	211	169	104	219	381	433	573
Construction	2 249	167	157	122	112	117	230	215	312
Insurance	2 253	3	7	9	1	8	10	9	12
Financial	2 260	376	196	185	174	421	424	391	299
Computer and information	2 262	95	123	144	77	141	587	885	803
Royalties and licence fees	2 266	44	36	45	50	38	39	31	35
Other business services	2 268	1,393	1,526	1,489	1,406	1,553	2,097	2,486	3,243
Personal, cultural, and recreational	2 287	189	161	165	111	199	90	116	190
Government, n.i.e.	2 291	88	58	59	35	36	35	35	36
Other services, debit	3 200 BA	−3,445	−3,376	−3,947	−4,185	−4,865	−5,470	−6,363	−7,126
Communications	3 245	−46	−69	−271	−302	−493	−372	−439	−523
Construction	3 249	−146	−168	−161	−275	−203	−184	−175	−184
Insurance	3 253	−66	−78	−179	−147	−195	−269	−241	−247
Financial	3 260	−408	−263	−609	−555	−948	−906	−1,090	−744
Computer and information	3 262	−83	−107	−122	−150	−220	−457	−538	−759
Royalties and licence fees	3 266	−82	−93	−119	−176	−174	−484	−528	−653
Other business services	3 268	−2,415	−2,382	−2,244	−2,347	−2,439	−2,601	−3,149	−3,768
Personal, cultural, and recreational	3 287	−127	−136	−175	−155	−118	−89	−129	−160
Government, n.i.e.	3 291	−72	−81	−67	−80	−75	−108	−75	−88

2008, International Monetary Fund: *Balance of Payments Statistics Yearbook*

Table 2 (Continued). STANDARD PRESENTATION, 2000–2007

(Millions of U.S. dollars)

	Code	2000	2001	2002	2003	2004	2005	2006	2007
C. INCOME	4 300	−1,371	−2,189	−3,580	−4,285	−6,092	−5,973	−8,104	−11,041
Total credit	2 300	*1,952*	*2,233*	*2,052*	*2,681*	*3,405*	*4,390*	*5,674*	*6,977*
Total debit	3 300	*−3,323*	*−4,422*	*−5,632*	*−6,966*	*−9,497*	*−10,364*	*−13,778*	*−18,017*
Compensation of employees, credit	2 310	294	256	333	494	805	917	1,054	1,174
Compensation of employees, debit	3 310	−603	−711	−893	−1,100	−1,426	−1,384	−1,634	−2,153
Investment income, credit	2 320	1,658	1,977	1,719	2,188	2,599	3,474	4,620	5,803
Direct investment income	2 330	−11	70	−70	129	387	489	685	701
Dividends and distributed branch profits	2 332	4	4	6	2	48	634	167	172
Reinvested earnings and undistributed branch profits	2 333	−19	62	−78	123	337	−155	511	517
Income on debt (interest)	2 334	4	4	2	5	2	10	6	12
Portfolio investment income	2 339	39	214	232	456	565	748	1,032	1,362
Income on equity	2 340	8	15	8	22	66	133	242	423
Income on bonds and notes	2 350	31	183	218	424	492	602	788	937
Income on money market instruments	2 360	....	16	6	10	7	13	2	1
Other investment income	2 370	1,630	1,692	1,556	1,602	1,648	2,236	2,903	3,740
Investment income, debit	3 320	−2,720	−3,711	−4,739	−5,866	−8,070	−8,979	−12,144	−15,864
Direct investment income	3 330	−1,379	−2,129	−3,207	−4,222	−6,089	−6,641	−9,219	−12,288
Dividends and distributed branch profits	3 332	−279	−429	−1,041	−1,874	−2,851	−3,009	−4,997	−5,426
Reinvested earnings and undistributed branch profits	3 333	−957	−1,519	−1,974	−2,161	−2,952	−3,265	−3,863	−6,458
Income on debt (interest)	3 334	−144	−181	−192	−187	−286	−367	−359	−403
Portfolio investment income	3 339	−234	−446	−384	−417	−454	−483	−847	−926
Income on equity	3 340	−12	−76	−65	−148	−237	−178	−442	−246
Income on bonds and notes	3 350	−221	−370	−319	−269	−217	−304	−405	−680
Income on money market instruments	3 360	−1	....	....	....	....	−2	....	−1
Other investment income	3 370	−1,107	−1,136	−1,148	−1,227	−1,527	−1,856	−2,078	−2,651
D. CURRENT TRANSFERS	4 379	373	470	912	548	236	327	−579	−887
Credit	2 379	948	959	1,465	1,663	2,081	3,219	2,482	3,466
General government	2 380	331	373	454	851	1,524	1,681	1,773	2,318
Other sectors	2 390	617	586	1,010	812	557	1,538	708	1,148
Workers' remittances	2 391	....	....	....	....	....	100	128	150
Other current transfers	2 392	617	586	1,010	812	557	1,437	581	999
Debit	3 379	−575	−489	−553	−1,114	−1,845	−2,892	−3,061	−4,353
General government	3 380	−92	−131	−136	−582	−958	−1,846	−1,775	−2,133
Other sectors	3 390	−483	−357	−417	−532	−888	−1,046	−1,286	−2,220
Workers' remittances	3 391	....	....	....	....	....	−291	−393	−469
Other current transfers	3 392	−483	−357	−417	−532	−888	−755	−892	−1,751
CAPITAL AND FINANCIAL ACCOUNT	4 996	2,986	2,773	3,999	5,175	6,172	2,696	4,493	5,075
CAPITAL ACCOUNT	4 994	−5	−9	−4	−3	−602	196	380	1,026
Total credit	2 994	*6*	*2*	*7*	*7*	*218*	*230*	*636*	*1,109*
Total debit	3 994	*−11*	*−11*	*−11*	*−10*	*−820*	*−35*	*−257*	*−83*
Capital transfers, credit	2 400	3	....	2	5	211	225	545	1,032
General government	2 401	....	....	....	....	201	216	537	1,023
Debt forgiveness	2 402	....	....	....	....	....	....	....	....
Other capital transfers	2 410	....	....	....	....	201	216	537	1,023
Other sectors	2 430	3	....	2	5	9	9	8	9
Migrants' transfers	2 431	3	....	2	5	9	9	8	9
Debt forgiveness	2 432	....	....	....	....	....	....	....	....
Other capital transfers	2 440	....	....	....	....	....	....	....	....
Capital transfers, debit	3 400	−2	−7	−5	−3	−801	−20	−209	−20
General government	3 401	....	....	....	....	−795	−18	−206	−18
Debt forgiveness	3 402	....	....	....	....	−789	−11	−196	−10
Other capital transfers	3 410	....	....	....	....	−7	−7	−10	−8
Other sectors	3 430	−2	−7	−5	−3	−5	−2	−3	−2
Migrants' transfers	3 431	−2	−7	−5	−3	−5	−2	−3	−2
Debt forgiveness	3 432	....	....	....	....	....	....	....	....
Other capital transfers	3 440	....	....	....	....	....	....	....	....
Nonproduced nonfinancial assets, credit	2 480	3	2	5	2	7	5	91	77
Nonproduced nonfinancial assets, debit	3 480	−9	−4	−6	−7	−19	−15	−47	−62

Table 2 (Continued). STANDARD PRESENTATION, 2000–2007

(Millions of U.S. dollars)

	Code	2000	2001	2002	2003	2004	2005	2006	2007
FINANCIAL ACCOUNT	4 995	**2,991**	**2,782**	**4,003**	**5,178**	**6,773**	**2,500**	**4,113**	**4,049**
A. DIRECT INVESTMENT	4 500	**4,944**	**5,476**	**8,285**	**1,813**	**3,940**	**11,629**	**4,043**	**7,938**
Direct investment abroad	4 505	**−43**	**−165**	**−211**	**−208**	**−1,037**	**27**	**−1,479**	**−1,356**
Equity capital	4 510	−51	−91	−245	12	−476	−321	−1,003	−268
Claims on affiliated enterprises	4 515	−51	−91	−245	12	−476	−321	−1,003	−268
Liabilities to affiliated enterprises	4 520	....	....	....	....	....	....	....	....
Reinvested earnings	4 525	19	−62	78	−123	−337	155	−511	−517
Other capital	4 530	−11	−12	−44	−97	−225	193	35	−571
Claims on affiliated enterprises	4 535	−11	−12	−44	−97	−225	193	35	−571
Liabilities to affiliated enterprises	4 540	....	....	....	....	....	....	....	....
Direct investment in Czech Republic	4 555	**4,987**	**5,641**	**8,497**	**2,021**	**4,978**	**11,602**	**5,522**	**9,294**
Equity capital	4 560	3,497	3,374	6,287	−130	1,777	7,629	1,941	2,849
Claims on direct investors	4 565	....	....	....	....	....	....	....	....
Liabilities to direct investors	4 570	3,497	3,374	6,287	−130	1,777	7,629	1,941	2,849
Reinvested earnings	4 575	957	1,519	1,974	2,161	2,952	3,265	3,863	6,458
Other capital	4 580	533	747	236	−9	249	708	−282	−13
Claims on direct investors	4 585	....	....	....	....	....	....	....	....
Liabilities to direct investors	4 590	533	747	236	−9	249	708	−282	−13
B. PORTFOLIO INVESTMENT	4 600	**−1,754**	**923**	**−1,559**	**−1,181**	**1,988**	**−3,388**	**−1,127**	**−2,500**
Assets	4 602	**−2,236**	**125**	**−2,373**	**−2,934**	**−2,806**	**−3,467**	**−3,004**	**−4,662**
Equity securities	4 610	−1,167	247	−231	188	−1,448	−1,472	−1,938	−3,026
Monetary authorities	4 611	....	....	....	....	....	....	....	....
General government	4 612	−1	....	1	565	−125	−5	1	−4
Banks	4 613	−512	41	−15	−138	−58	−10	−174	−90
Other sectors	4 614	−654	206	−217	−239	−1,264	−1,458	−1,764	−2,932
Debt securities	4 619	−1,069	−121	−2,142	−3,122	−1,359	−1,994	−1,066	−1,635
Bonds and notes	4 620	−987	−147	−2,209	−3,002	−1,717	−1,992	−960	−1,823
Monetary authorities	4 621	....	....	....	....	....	....	....	....
General government	4 622	....	....	−9	−42	−241	−122	140	37
Banks	4 623	−873	167	−1,606	−1,640	−861	−882	−742	−691
Other sectors	4 624	−114	−314	−594	−1,320	−614	−988	−358	−1,170
Money market instruments	4 630	−82	26	67	−120	358	−2	−107	188
Monetary authorities	4 631	....	....	....	....	....	....	....	....
General government	4 632	6	50	−19	−34	247	−2	18	−3
Banks	4 633	−3	107	−31	−3	36	4	−15	26
Other sectors	4 634	−86	−132	117	−82	75	−4	−110	165
Liabilities	4 652	**482**	**798**	**814**	**1,753**	**4,795**	**79**	**1,877**	**2,161**
Equity securities	4 660	619	616	−265	1,104	738	−1,540	268	−268
Banks	4 663	226	69	−397	97	−14	54	−102	245
Other sectors	4 664	393	548	132	1,008	751	−1,595	371	−513
Debt securities	4 669	−137	181	1,079	649	4,057	1,619	1,608	2,430
Bonds and notes	4 670	−218	132	1,039	644	3,759	1,920	1,619	2,196
Monetary authorities	4 671	−319	....	....	....	....	....	....	....
General government	4 672	13	232	690	97	2,709	2,267	409	790
Banks	4 673	28	79	231	221	196	−3	236	391
Other sectors	4 674	61	−179	117	326	854	−344	974	1,015
Money market instruments	4 680	81	49	40	5	298	−301	−10	234
Monetary authorities	4 681	....	....	....	....	....	....	....	....
General government	4 682	76	−29	56	−2	106	−167	−33	285
Banks	4 683	5	78	−16	7	85	−92	64	−72
Other sectors	4 684	....	....	....	....	107	−42	−42	22
C. FINANCIAL DERIVATIVES	4 910	**−40**	**−87**	**−130**	**143**	**−146**	**−112**	**−282**	**54**
Monetary authorities	4 911	....	....	....	....	....	....	....	....
General government	4 912	....	....	....	....	....	....	....	....
Banks	4 913	−40	−87	−130	143	−146	−112	−282	54
Other sectors	4 914	....	....	....	....	....	....	....	....
Assets	4 900	**−129**	**−254**	**−476**	**257**	**−660**	**−130**	**−504**	**−783**
Monetary authorities	4 901	....	....	....	....	....	....	....	....
General government	4 902	....	....	....	....	....	....	....	....
Banks	4 903	−129	−254	−476	257	−660	−130	−504	−783
Other sectors	4 904	....	....	....	....	....	....	....	....
Liabilities	4 905	**89**	**168**	**347**	**−114**	**514**	**18**	**222**	**837**
Monetary authorities	4 906	....	....	....	....	....	....	....	....
General government	4 907	....	....	....	....	....	....	....	....
Banks	4 908	89	168	347	−114	514	18	222	837
Other sectors	4 909	....	....	....	....	....	....	....	....

Table 2 (Concluded). STANDARD PRESENTATION, 2000–2007

(Millions of U.S. dollars)

	Code	2000	2001	2002	2003	2004	2005	2006	2007
D. OTHER INVESTMENT..................................	4 700 ..	**684**	**−1,743**	**4,024**	**4,845**	**1,253**	**−1,750**	**1,572**	**−571**
Assets...	4 703 ..	**984**	**−1,199**	**4,015**	**2,279**	**−1,072**	**−4,728**	**−1,480**	**−7,876**
Trade credits..	4 706 ..	−61	77	−475	809	−659	−614	−429	−1,687
General government.............................	4 707 ..	....	....	....	....	....	....	....	....
of which: Short-term............................	4 709 ..	....	....	....	....	....	....	....	....
Other sectors.......................................	4 710 ..	−61	77	−475	809	−659	−614	−429	−1,687
of which: Short-term............................	4 712 ..	*−166*	*2*	*−480*	*816*	*−655*	*−618*	*−413*	*−1,634*
Loans...	4 714 ..	315	397	661	−1,365	1,086	−1,335	−553	−2,480
Monetary authorities............................	4 715 ..	....	....	....	....	....	....	....	....
of which: Short-term............................	4 718 ..	....	....	....	....	....	....	....	....
General government.............................	4 719 ..	....	−9	−1	9	3	....	....	....
of which: Short-term..	4 721 ..	....	....	....	*−3*	*3*	....	....	....
Banks..	4 722 ..	332	406	652	−1,375	1,083	−1,335	−555	−2,424
of which: Short-term..	4 724 ..	*−218*	*235*	*603*	*−819*	*950*	*−260*	*−44*	*−623*
Other sectors.......................................	4 725 ..	−18	....	10	....	....	....	2	−56
of which: Short-term..	4 727 ..	*−18*	....	*10*	....	....	....	*2*	*−56*
Currency and deposits.............................	4 730 ..	500	−1,762	3,166	2,736	−2,329	−3,119	−691	−3,648
Monetary authorities............................	4 731 ..	....	....	....	....	....	....	....	....
General government.............................	4 732 ..	....	−2	−68	78	....	....	....	....
Banks..	4 733 ..	524	−1,717	3,188	2,815	−2,332	−3,267	1,105	−4,241
Other sectors.......................................	4 734 ..	−24	−43	47	−156	3	148	−1,796	592
Other assets...	4 736 ..	230	89	663	99	830	341	193	−60
Monetary authorities............................	4 737 ..	....	....	....	....	−7	−7	....	....
of which: Short-term............................	4 739 ..	....	....	....	....	....	....	....	....
General government.............................	4 740 ..	76	191	721	191	938	583	217	−33
of which: Short-term............................	4 742 ..	....	....	....	....	....	....	....	....
Banks..	4 743 ..	155	12	4	28	−4	4	−23	−28
of which: Short-term............................	4 745 ..	*154*	*11*	*8*	*35*	*3*	*1*	*−12*	*−22*
Other sectors.......................................	4 746 ..	....	−114	−62	−120	−98	−238	−1	....
of which: Short-term............................	4 748 ..	....	....	....	....	....	....	....	....
Liabilities..	4 753 ..	**−300**	**−544**	**9**	**2,565**	**2,325**	**2,978**	**3,052**	**7,305**
Trade credits..	4 756 ..	171	−268	170	−500	846	1,034	−37	826
General government.............................	4 757 ..	....	....	....	....	....	397	−3	−41
of which: Short-term............................	4 759 ..	....	....	....	....	....	....	....	....
Other sectors.......................................	4 760 ..	171	−268	170	−500	846	637	−34	866
of which: Short-term............................	4 762 ..	*385*	*−239*	*270*	*−482*	*891*	*417*	*−64*	*659*
Loans...	4 764 ..	−400	304	38	1,707	2,128	1,332	3,230	2,103
Monetary authorities............................	4 765 ..	−1	−1	−1	−1	−1	−1	−1	−1
of which: Use of Fund credit and loans from the Fund..	4 766 ..	....	....	....	....	....	....	....	....
of which: Short-term............................	4 768 ..	....	....	....	....	....	....	....	....
General government.............................	4 769 ..	−49	−13	−45	372	411	465	446	185
of which: Short-term............................	4 771 ..	....	....	....	....	....	....	....	....
Banks..	4 772 ..	−902	−685	−84	−146	199	129	763	1,425
of which: Short-term............................	4 774 ..	*−356*	*−388*	*−148*	*−27*	*231*	*212*	*271*	*640*
Other sectors.......................................	4 775 ..	551	1,003	168	1,482	1,519	739	2,022	495
of which: Short-term............................	4 777 ..	*140*	*761*	*−313*	*697*	*408*	*−193*	*13*	*314*
Currency and deposits.............................	4 780 ..	40	−452	−125	1,385	−738	492	−165	4,355
Monetary authorities............................	4 781 ..	1	2	−1	−1	28	205	−171	−27
General government.............................	4 782 ..	....	....	....	....	....	....	....	....
Banks..	4 783 ..	39	−453	−124	1,386	−766	287	5	4,383
Other sectors.......................................	4 784 ..	....	....	....	....	....	....	....	....
Other liabilities......................................	4 786 ..	−111	−129	−73	−26	90	120	24	20
Monetary authorities............................	4 787 ..	....	....	....	....	....	....	....	....
of which: Short-term............................	4 789 ..	....	....	....	....	....	....	....	....
General government.............................	4 790 ..	....	−116	....	....	....	....	....	....
of which: Short-term............................	4 792 ..	....	....	....	....	....	....	....	....
Banks..	4 793 ..	−111	−13	−73	−26	90	120	24	20
of which: Short-term............................	4 795 ..	*−111*	*−19*	*−67*	*−34*	*90*	*118*	*26*	*16*
Other sectors.......................................	4 796 ..	....	....	....	....	....	....	....	....
of which: Short-term............................	4 798 ..	....	....	....	....	....	....	....	....
E. RESERVE ASSETS...................................	4 802 ..	**−844**	**−1,787**	**−6,618**	**−442**	**−263**	**−3,879**	**−92**	**−872**
Monetary gold..	4 812 ..	....	....	−1	....	4	....	−4	....
Special drawing rights.............................	4 811 ..	....	−1	−3	−4	4	−7	−4	−3
Reserve position in the Fund....................	4 810 ..	−3	−150	−71	−200	75	201	76	31
Foreign exchange....................................	4 803 ..	−840	−1,640	−6,154	−918	−315	−4,064	−160	−631
Other claims..	4 813 ..	....	3	−391	679	−28	−8	−5	−270
NET ERRORS AND OMISSIONS...........................	4 998 ..	**−296**	**499**	**266**	**611**	**−422**	**−1,118**	**−710**	**−1,844**

Table 3. INTERNATIONAL INVESTMENT POSITION (End-period stocks), 2000–2007

(Millions of U.S. dollars)

	Code	2000	2001	2002	2003	2004	2005	2006	2007
ASSETS..	8 995 C.	**38,304**	**42,609**	**52,419**	**59,926**	**69,276**	**76,273**	**90,451**	**115,554**
Direct investment abroad........................	8 505 ..	**738**	**1,136**	**1,473**	**2,284**	**3,760**	**3,610**	**5,017**	**6,971**
Equity capital and reinvested earnings...........	8 506 ..	656	1,038	1,310	1,987	3,160	3,256	4,634	5,967
Claims on affiliated enterprises................	8 507 ..	656	1,038	1,310	1,987	3,160	3,256	4,634	5,967
Liabilities to affiliated enterprises............	8 508 ..	....	....	....	....	....	....	....	....
Other capital...	8 530 ..	82	98	163	297	600	354	383	1,004
Claims on affiliated enterprises................	8 535 ..	82	98	163	297	600	354	383	1,004
Liabilities to affiliated enterprises............	8 540 ..	....	....	....	....	....	....	....	....
Portfolio investment.............................	8 602 ..	**4,772**	**5,106**	**9,102**	**13,408**	**16,644**	**19,026**	**25,492**	**33,544**
Equity securities.......................................	8 610 ..	2,439	1,894	2,869	1,845	3,404	5,977	9,692	14,204
Monetary authorities.............................	8 611 ..	....	....	....	....	....	....	....	....
General government..............................	8 612 ..	....	....	....	31	179	160	194	196
Banks..	8 613 ..	1,191	1,245	1,522	258	379	300	582	1,053
Other sectors..	8 614 ..	1,248	649	1,346	1,557	2,846	5,517	8,916	12,955
Debt securities...	8 619 ..	2,333	3,212	6,233	11,563	13,240	13,049	15,800	19,340
Bonds and notes.....................................	8 620 ..	2,200	2,981	5,973	11,183	13,098	12,980	15,601	19,293
Monetary authorities...........................	8 621 ..	....	....	....	....	....	....	....	....
General government............................	8 622 ..	....	....	3	211	145	215	118	215
Banks..	8 623 ..	1,603	1,693	3,831	6,348	8,055	7,744	9,280	10,445
Other sectors......................................	8 624 ..	596	1,287	2,139	4,623	4,898	5,022	6,203	8,633
Money market instruments.......................	8 630 ..	133	231	260	380	142	69	199	47
Monetary authorities...........................	8 631 ..	....	....	....	....	....	....	....	....
General government............................	8 632 ..	123	111	170	254	....	35	....	1
Banks..	8 633 ..	10	120	89	39	98	11	26	....
Other sectors......................................	8 634 ..	....	....	....	87	44	23	173	46
Financial derivatives............................	8 900 ..	**168**	**435**	**1,036**	**941**	**1,775**	**1,731**	**2,558**	**3,733**
Monetary authorities................................	8 901 ..	....	....	....	....	....	....	....	....
General government.................................	8 902 ..	....	....	....	....	....	....	....	....
Banks..	8 903 ..	168	435	1,036	941	1,775	1,731	2,558	3,733
Other sectors...	8 904 ..	....	....	....	....	....	....	....	....
Other investment.................................	8 703 ..	**19,488**	**21,469**	**17,098**	**16,336**	**18,648**	**22,351**	**25,929**	**36,401**
Trade credits..	8 706 ..	3,335	3,387	4,324	4,271	5,492	6,050	8,891	10,485
General government..............................	8 707 ..	....	....	....	....	....	....	....	....
of which: Short-term.........................	8 709 ..	....	....	....	....	....	....	....	....
Other sectors..	8 710 ..	3,335	3,387	4,324	4,271	5,492	6,050	8,891	10,485
of which: Short-term.........................	8 712 ..	*2,833*	*2,993*	*3,955*	*3,903*	*5,096*	*5,665*	*8,574*	*10,153*
Loans..	8 714 ..	2,916	2,630	2,229	4,048	3,044	4,098	5,070	8,110
Monetary authorities.............................	8 715 ..	7	7	8	8	9	8	9	9
of which: Short-term.........................	8 718 ..	....	....	....	....	....	....	....	....
General government..............................	8 719 ..	....	9	12	3	....	....	....	....
of which: Short-term.........................	8 721 ..	....	....	....	*3*	....	....	....	....
Banks..	8 722 ..	2,909	2,614	2,210	4,036	3,035	4,089	5,061	8,101
of which: Short-term.........................	8 724 ..	*1,420*	*1,244*	*752*	*1,841*	*988*	*1,139*	*1,305*	*2,093*
Other sectors..	8 725 ..	....	....	....	....	....	....	....	....
of which: Short-term.........................	8 727 ..	....	....	....	....	....	....	....	....
Currency and deposits..............................	8 730 ..	7,285	9,389	7,092	4,715	7,700	10,331	10,204	15,915
Monetary authorities.............................	8 731 ..	....	....	....	....	....	....	....	....
General government..............................	8 732 ..	....	2	77	1	....	....	....	....
Banks..	8 733 ..	7,285	9,387	7,015	4,714	7,699	10,331	10,204	15,915
Other sectors..	8 734 ..	....	....	....	....	....	....	....	....
Other assets..	8 736 ..	5,952	6,064	3,454	3,303	2,413	1,872	1,765	1,891
Monetary authorities.............................	8 737 ..	3	3	14	14	21	124	141	154
of which: Short-term.........................	8 739 ..	*1*	*1*	*12*	*4*	*3*	*3*	*6*	*6*
General government..............................	8 740 ..	5,839	5,802	3,212	3,098	2,171	1,562	1,432	1,513
of which: Short-term.........................	8 742 ..	....	....	....	....	....	....	....	....
Banks..	8 743 ..	110	115	124	109	119	103	136	176
of which: Short-term.........................	8 745 ..	*65*	*69*	*68*	*40*	*40*	*33*	*50*	*77*
Other sectors..	8 746 ..	....	143	103	82	101	82	56	47
of which: Short-term.........................	8 748 ..	....	....	....	....	....	....	....	....
Reserve assets.....................................	8 802 ..	**13,139**	**14,464**	**23,710**	**26,957**	**28,449**	**29,555**	**31,454**	**34,905**
Monetary gold..	8 812 ..	123	123	154	186	190	225	273	356
Special drawing rights..............................	8 811 ..	....	1	5	9	5	12	17	20
Reserve position in the Fund....................	8 810 ..	3	151	236	468	410	181	111	84
Foreign exchange......................................	8 803 ..	12,985	14,181	22,777	26,290	27,838	29,133	31,050	34,188
Other claims...	8 813 ..	28	8	538	4	6	5	4	257

Table 3 (Concluded). INTERNATIONAL INVESTMENT POSITION (End-period stocks), 2000–2007

(Millions of U.S. dollars)

	Code	2000	2001	2002	2003	2004	2005	2006	2007
LIABILITIES	8 995 D.	**43,378**	**49,340**	**65,598**	**80,485**	**106,163**	**110,243**	**142,232**	**184,161**
Direct investment in Czech Republic	8 555 ..	**21,644**	**27,092**	**38,669**	**45,287**	**57,259**	**60,662**	**79,841**	**101,074**
Equity capital and reinvested earnings	8 556 ..	18,571	23,099	33,612	39,346	50,161	53,526	71,731	92,132
Claims on direct investors	8 557 ..	....	....	....	....	....	....	....	....
Liabilities to direct investors	8 558 ..	18,571	23,099	33,612	39,346	50,161	53,526	71,731	92,132
Other capital	8 580 ..	3,073	3,993	5,057	5,940	7,098	7,136	8,110	8,942
Claims on direct investors	8 585 ..	....	....	....	....	....	....	....	....
Liabilities to direct investors	8 590 ..	3,073	3,993	5,057	5,940	7,098	7,136	8,110	8,942
Portfolio investment	8 652 ..	**4,353**	**4,974**	**6,673**	**8,717**	**17,036**	**17,806**	**23,376**	**30,775**
Equity securities	8 660 ..	3,059	3,551	4,250	5,488	9,339	8,968	11,573	14,521
Banks	8 663 ..	1,279	1,435	1,868	1,168	2,598	2,507	2,407	3,153
Other sectors	8 664 ..	1,780	2,115	2,382	4,320	6,741	6,461	9,166	11,369
Debt securities	8 669 ..	1,294	1,423	2,423	3,229	7,697	8,838	11,803	16,253
Bonds and notes	8 670 ..	1,233	1,357	2,355	3,143	7,309	8,702	11,656	15,708
Monetary authorities	8 671 ..	....	....	....	....	....	....	....	....
General government	8 672 ..	503	589	1,268	1,815	5,172	6,860	8,878	11,218
Banks	8 673 ..	294	406	548	593	551	560	678	1,129
Other sectors	8 674 ..	436	362	539	735	1,586	1,281	2,100	3,362
Money market instruments	8 680 ..	61	67	68	85	388	136	147	545
Monetary authorities	8 681 ..	....	....	....	....	....	....	....	....
General government	8 682 ..	56	13	25	28	149	45	17	317
Banks	8 683 ..	2	54	42	58	155	53	130	111
Other sectors	8 684 ..	3	....	....	....	84	38	....	117
Financial derivatives	8 905 ..	**140**	**317**	**752**	**758**	**1,422**	**1,296**	**1,748**	**2,897**
Monetary authorities	8 906 ..	....	....	....	....	....	....	....	....
General government	8 907 ..	....	....	....	....	....	....	....	....
Banks	8 908 ..	140	317	752	758	1,422	1,296	1,748	2,897
Other sectors	8 909 ..	....	....	....	....	....	....	....	....
Other investment	8 753 ..	**17,242**	**16,957**	**19,504**	**25,724**	**30,445**	**30,479**	**37,267**	**49,416**
Trade credits	8 756 ..	2,390	2,135	2,610	2,435	3,718	4,352	4,721	6,037
General government	8 757 ..	....	....	....	....	....	392	458	480
of which: Short-term	8 759 ..	....	....	....	....	....	....	....	....
Other sectors	8 760 ..	2,390	2,135	2,610	2,435	3,718	3,960	4,263	5,556
of which: Short-term	8 762 ..	*1,723*	*1,527*	*2,036*	*1,881*	*3,142*	*3,201*	*3,535*	*4,660*
Loans	8 764 ..	8,836	9,254	10,883	14,634	18,279	17,645	23,301	28,404
Monetary authorities	8 765 ..	4	4	4	4	3	2	1	....
of which: Use of Fund credit and loans from the Fund	8 766 ..	....	....	....	....	....	....	....	....
of which: Short-term	8 768 ..	....	....	....	....	....	....	....	....
General government	8 769 ..	284	261	314	875	1,434	1,736	2,497	3,071
of which: Short-term	8 771 ..	....	....	....	....	....	....	....	....
Banks	8 772 ..	2,440	1,719	1,944	2,125	2,454	2,323	3,432	5,402
of which: Short-term	8 774 ..	*668*	*295*	*194*	*202*	*474*	*629*	*989*	*1,792*
Other sectors	8 775 ..	6,107	7,269	8,620	11,630	14,388	13,584	17,370	19,931
of which: Short-term	8 777 ..	*220*	*1,002*	*794*	*1,670*	*2,294*	*1,864*	*2,133*	*2,741*
Currency and deposits	8 780 ..	5,429	5,215	5,697	7,927	7,721	7,674	8,286	13,870
Monetary authorities	8 781 ..	....	2	1	1	39	241	85	68
General government	8 782 ..	....	....	....	....	....	....	....	....
Banks	8 783 ..	5,429	5,213	5,696	7,926	7,683	7,433	8,201	13,802
Other sectors	8 784 ..	....	....	....	....	....	....	....	....
Other liabilities	8 786 ..	587	354	314	729	726	809	959	1,105
Monetary authorities	8 787 ..	....	....	....	....	....	....	....	....
of which: Short-term	8 789 ..	....	....	....	....	....	....	....	....
General government	8 790 ..	237	....	....	....	....	....	....	....
of which: Short-term	8 792 ..	....	....	....	....	....	....	....	....
Banks	8 793 ..	350	354	314	341	462	532	634	720
of which: Short-term	8 795 ..	*350*	*347*	*314*	*325*	*444*	*513*	*614*	*694*
Other sectors	8 796 ..	....	....	....	387	264	276	326	385
of which: Short-term	8 798 ..	....	....	....	....	....	....	....	....
NET INTERNATIONAL INVESTMENT POSITION	8 995 ..	**−5,074**	**−6,731**	**−13,179**	**−20,560**	**−36,886**	**−33,970**	**−51,781**	**−68,607**
Conversion rates: Czech koruny per U.S. dollar (end of period)	0 102 ..	37.813	36.259	30.141	25.654	22.365	24.588	20.876	18.078

Table 1. ANALYTIC PRESENTATION, 2000–2007

(Millions of U.S. dollars)

	Code	2000	2001	2002	2003	2004	2005	2006	2007
A. Current Account[1]	4 993 Z.	**2,262**	**4,848**	**3,460**	**6,963**	**5,941**	**11,349**	**8,089**	**3,404**
Goods: exports f.o.b.	2 100 ..	50,084	50,466	55,473	64,537	75,050	82,610	90,570	100,820
Goods: imports f.o.b.	3 100 ..	–43,443	–43,048	–47,810	–54,840	–65,524	–75,070	–87,671	–101,831
Balance on Goods	4 100 ..	*6,641*	*7,418*	*7,662*	*9,697*	*9,527*	*7,540*	*2,899*	*–1,011*
Services: credit	2 200 ..	23,721	25,134	26,667	31,672	36,304	43,395	52,494	61,734
Services: debit	3 200 ..	–21,063	–22,121	–24,305	–28,254	–33,401	–36,986	–45,405	–54,233
Balance on Goods and Services	4 991 ..	*9,300*	*10,431*	*10,024*	*13,116*	*12,430*	*13,949*	*9,988*	*6,491*
Income: credit	2 300 ..	11,883	10,737	9,265	11,180	12,784	24,928	27,643	35,163
Income: debit	3 300 ..	–15,907	–13,748	–12,805	–13,796	–15,114	–23,333	–24,952	–33,154
Balance on Goods, Services, and Income	4 992 ..	*5,276*	*7,420*	*6,484*	*10,499*	*10,100*	*15,545*	*12,679*	*8,499*
Current transfers: credit	2 379 Z.	3,395	3,719	3,466	4,615	5,120	3,562	3,537	4,061
Current transfers: debit	3 379 ..	–6,410	–6,291	–6,489	–8,151	–9,279	–7,758	–8,127	–9,157
B. Capital Account[1]	4 994 Z.	**–11**	**14**	**152**	**–7**	**13**	**518**	**4**	**54**
Capital account: credit	2 994 Z.	320	300	411	344	511	1,032	458	447
Capital account: debit	3 994 ..	–332	–286	–258	–351	–498	–514	–453	–393
Total, Groups A Plus B	4 981 ..	*2,250*	*4,863*	*3,613*	*6,957*	*5,954*	*11,867*	*8,093*	*3,458*
C. Financial Account[1]	4 995 W.	**–3,311**	**–5,712**	**3,819**	**–5,129**	**–19,023**	**–10,223**	**–9,225**	**–5,732**
Direct investment abroad	4 505 ..	–28,381	–13,154	–2,650	–856	9,930	–16,207	–8,202	–16,513
Direct investment in Denmark	4 555 Z.	36,013	9,286	4,431	1,185	–8,804	12,853	3,343	11,313
Portfolio investment assets	4 602 ..	–23,582	–14,772	–4,356	–21,930	–24,768	–32,808	–26,033	–28,993
Equity securities	4 610 ..	–13,944	–4,318	199	–3,467	–7,299	–14,118	–21,922	–8,989
Debt securities	4 619 ..	–9,638	–10,454	–4,555	–18,463	–17,469	–18,690	–4,111	–20,003
Portfolio investment liabilities	4 652 Z.	5,783	10,510	4,843	6,010	10,055	21,038	7,890	17,944
Equity securities	4 660 ..	2,341	861	591	1,389	1,562	–3,050	–5,488	2,409
Debt securities	4 669 Z.	3,442	9,649	4,253	4,621	8,493	24,087	13,378	15,535
Financial derivatives	4 910 ..	326	694	390	–12	3,206	2,161	2,902	442
Financial derivatives assets	4 900 ..	....	....	....	....	....	....	....	....
Financial derivatives liabilities	4 905 ..	326	694	390	–12	3,206	2,161	2,902	442
Other investment assets	4 703 ..	–2,025	9,054	–6,839	–9,314	–9,021	–19,820	–24,367	–47,890
Monetary authorities	4 701 ..	15	–13	–41	56	–13	....	....	....
General government	4 704 ..	25	41	18	365	31	473	–147	195
Banks	4 705 ..	–1,713	7,232	–6,062	–12,623	–14,576	–20,658	–23,405	–45,265
Other sectors	4 728 ..	–352	1,794	–755	2,888	5,537	365	–815	–2,820
Other investment liabilities	4 753 W.	8,554	–7,331	8,000	19,789	378	22,561	35,240	57,965
Monetary authorities	4 753 WA	113	61	–30	–27	–230	116	280	246
General government	4 753 ZB	–329	–191	–158	–158	–177	7	–14	2
Banks	4 753 ZC	10,466	–1,720	10,806	24,714	9,567	14,496	25,764	57,370
Other sectors	4 753 ZD	–1,696	–5,481	–2,619	–4,461	–8,782	7,942	9,211	347
Total, Groups A Through C	4 983 ..	*–1,061*	*–850*	*7,432*	*1,828*	*–13,069*	*1,644*	*–1,133*	*–2,275*
D. Net Errors and Omissions	4 998 ..	**–4,460**	**4,167**	**–1,887**	**2,846**	**11,644**	**–3,150**	**–4,855**	**2,064**
Total, Groups A Through D	4 984 ..	*–5,521*	*3,317*	*5,546*	*4,674*	*–1,426*	*–1,506*	*–5,988*	*–211*
E. Reserves and Related Items	4 802 A.	**5,521**	**–3,317**	**–5,546**	**–4,674**	**1,426**	**1,506**	**5,988**	**211**
Reserve assets	4 802 ..	5,521	–3,317	–5,546	–4,674	1,426	1,506	5,988	211
Use of Fund credit and loans	4 766 ..	....	....	....	....	....	....	....	....
Exceptional financing	4 920 ..	....	....	....	....	....	....	....	....
Conversion rates: Danish kroner per U.S. dollar	0 101 ..	**8.0831**	**8.3228**	**7.8947**	**6.5877**	**5.9911**	**5.9969**	**5.9468**	**5.4437**

[1] Excludes components that have been classified in the categories of Group E.

Table 2. STANDARD PRESENTATION, 2000–2007

(Millions of U.S. dollars)

	Code	2000	2001	2002	2003	2004	2005	2006	2007
CURRENT ACCOUNT....................................	4 993 ..	2,262	4,848	3,460	6,963	5,941	11,349	8,089	3,404
A. GOODS...	4 100 ..	6,641	7,418	7,662	9,697	9,527	7,540	2,899	−1,011
Credit..	2 100 ..	50,084	50,466	55,473	64,537	75,050	82,610	90,570	100,820
General merchandise: exports f.o.b...............	2 110 ..	50,084	50,466	55,473	64,537	75,050	82,610	90,570	100,820
Goods for processing: exports f.o.b...............	2 150 ..	....	....	....	....	....	....	....	....
Repairs on goods....................................	2 160 ..	....	....	....	....	....	....	....	....
Goods procured in ports by carriers...............	2 170 ..	....	....	....	....	....	....	....	....
Nonmonetary gold..................................	2 180 ..	....	....	....	....	....	....	....	....
Debit..	3 100 ..	−43,443	−43,048	−47,810	−54,840	−65,524	−75,070	−87,671	−101,831
General merchandise: imports f.o.b...............	3 110 ..	−43,443	−43,048	−47,810	−54,840	−65,524	−75,070	−87,671	−101,831
Goods for processing: imports f.o.b...............	3 150 ..	....	....	....	....	....	....	....	....
Repairs on goods....................................	3 160 ..	....	....	....	....	....	....	....	....
Goods procured in ports by carriers...............	3 170 ..	....	....	....	....	....	....	....	....
Nonmonetary gold..................................	3 180 ..	....	....	....	....	....	....	....	....
B. SERVICES...	4 200 ..	2,659	3,013	2,361	3,418	2,903	6,409	7,089	7,502
Total credit	2 200 ..	*23,721*	*25,134*	*26,667*	*31,672*	*36,304*	*43,395*	*52,494*	*61,734*
Total debit	3 200 ..	*−21,063*	*−22,121*	*−24,305*	*−28,254*	*−33,401*	*−36,986*	*−45,405*	*−54,233*
Transportation services, credit..................	2 205 ..	10,790	11,288	10,988	14,023	17,089	....	....	....
Passenger	2 850 ..	....	....	....	....	....	....	....	....
Freight....................................	2 851 ..	....	....	....	....	....	....	....	....
Other	2 852 ..	*10,790*	*11,288*	*10,988*	*14,023*	*17,089*	....	....	....
Sea transport, passenger..........................	2 207 ..	....	....	....	....	....	....	....	....
Sea transport, freight..............................	2 208 ..	....	....	....	....	....	....	....	....
Sea transport, other...............................	2 209 ..	10,790	11,288	10,988	14,023	17,089	....	....	....
Air transport, passenger...........................	2 211 ..	....	....	....	....	....	....	....	....
Air transport, freight..............................	2 212 ..	....	....	....	....	....	....	....	....
Air transport, other...............................	2 213 ..	....	....	....	....	....	....	....	....
Other transport, passenger........................	2 215 ..	....	....	....	....	....	....	....	....
Other transport, freight...........................	2 216 ..	....	....	....	....	....	....	....	....
Other transport, other............................	2 217 ..	....	....	....	....	....	....	....	....
Transportation services, debit..................	3 205 ..	−9,344	−10,036	−9,720	−12,027	−14,484	....	....	....
Passenger	3 850 ..	....	....	....	....	....	....	....	....
Freight....................................	3 851 ..	....	....	....	....	....	....	....	....
Other....................................	3 852 ..	*−9,344*	*−10,036*	*−9,720*	*−12,027*	*−14,484*	....	....	....
Sea transport, passenger..........................	3 207 ..	....	....	....	....	....	....	....	....
Sea transport, freight..............................	3 208 ..	....	....	....	....	....	....	....	....
Sea transport, other...............................	3 209 ..	−9,344	−10,036	−9,720	−12,027	−14,484	....	....	....
Air transport, passenger...........................	3 211 ..	....	....	....	....	....	....	....	....
Air transport, freight..............................	3 212 ..	....	....	....	....	....	....	....	....
Air transport, other...............................	3 213 ..	....	....	....	....	....	....	....	....
Other transport, passenger........................	3 215 ..	....	....	....	....	....	....	....	....
Other transport, freight...........................	3 216 ..	....	....	....	....	....	....	....	....
Other transport, other............................	3 217 ..	....	....	....	....	....	....	....	....
Travel, credit......................................	2 236 ..	3,671	4,003	4,791	5,271	5,652	....	....	....
Business travel.....................................	2 237 ..	....	....	....	....	....	....	....	....
Personal travel.....................................	2 240 ..	3,671	4,003	4,791	5,271	5,652	....	....	....
Travel, debit.......................................	3 236 ..	−4,669	−4,861	−5,838	−6,659	−7,279	....	....	....
Business travel.....................................	3 237 ..	....	....	....	....	....	....	....	....
Personal travel.....................................	3 240 ..	−4,669	−4,861	−5,838	−6,659	−7,279	....	....	....
Other services, credit............................	2 200 BA	9,260	9,843	10,887	12,378	13,563	....	....	....
Communications....................................	2 245 ..	....	....	....	....	....	....	....	....
Construction..	2 249 ..	....	....	....	....	....	....	....	....
Insurance...	2 253 ..	....	....	....	....	....	....	....	....
Financial...	2 260 ..	....	....	....	....	....	....	....	....
Computer and information........................	2 262 ..	....	....	....	....	....	....	....	....
Royalties and licence fees........................	2 266 ..	....	....	....	....	....	....	....	....
Other business services.	2 268 ..	9,260	9,843	10,887	12,378	13,563	....	....	....
Personal, cultural, and recreational..............	2 287 ..	....	....	....	....	....	....	....	....
Government, n.i.e..................................	2 291 ..	....	....	....	....	....	....	....	....
Other services, debit.............................	3 200 BA	−7,049	−7,224	−8,748	−9,568	−11,638	....	....	....
Communications....................................	3 245 ..	....	....	....	....	....	....	....	....
Construction..	3 249 ..	....	....	....	....	....	....	....	....
Insurance...	3 253 ..	....	....	....	....	....	....	....	....
Financial...	3 260 ..	....	....	....	....	....	....	....	....
Computer and information........................	3 262 ..	....	....	....	....	....	....	....	....
Royalties and licence fees........................	3 266 ..	....	....	....	....	....	....	....	....
Other business services............................	3 268 ..	−7,049	−7,224	−8,748	−9,568	−11,638	....	....	....
Personal, cultural, and recreational..............	3 287 ..	....	....	....	....	....	....	....	....
Government, n.i.e..................................	3 291 ..	....	....	....	....	....	....	....	....

Table 2 (Continued). STANDARD PRESENTATION, 2000–2007

(Millions of U.S. dollars)

	Code	2000	2001	2002	2003	2004	2005	2006	2007
C. INCOME	4 300	**−4,023**	**−3,011**	**−3,540**	**−2,616**	**−2,330**	**1,596**	**2,691**	**2,009**
Total credit	2 300	*11,883*	*10,737*	*9,265*	*11,180*	*12,784*	*24,928*	*27,643*	*35,163*
Total debit	3 300	*−15,907*	*−13,748*	*−12,805*	*−13,796*	*−15,114*	*−23,333*	*−24,952*	*−33,154*
Compensation of employees, credit	2 310	**667**	**699**	**785**	**941**	**1,075**	**866**	**985**	**989**
Compensation of employees, debit	3 310	**−662**	**−745**	**−860**	**−1,029**	**−1,226**	**−1,489**	**−1,766**	**−2,958**
Investment income, credit	2 320	**11,217**	**10,038**	**8,480**	**10,239**	**11,709**	**24,062**	**26,657**	**34,173**
Direct investment income	2 330	5,108	4,115	2,474	4,534	4,163	13,592	12,489	15,247
Dividends and distributed branch profits	2 332	1,757	3,864	5,272	4,195	2,730	6,872	7,875	6,189
Reinvested earnings and undistributed branch profits	2 333	2,929	−279	−3,264	−296	931	5,038	2,592	6,740
Income on debt (interest)	2 334	421	531	465	635	501	1,682	2,022	2,318
Portfolio investment income	2 339	2,371	2,402	2,820	3,206	5,152	6,654	9,008	10,475
Income on equity	2 340	705	772	749	628	1,226	1,729	4,093	5,068
Income on bonds and notes	2 350	1,311	1,576	2,039	2,567	3,839	4,531	4,522	4,974
Income on money market instruments	2 360	354	53	32	11	87	394	393	432
Other investment income	2 370	3,738	3,521	3,186	2,499	2,394	3,817	5,159	8,452
Investment income, debit	3 320	**−15,245**	**−13,004**	**−11,945**	**−12,767**	**−13,888**	**−21,844**	**−23,186**	**−30,196**
Direct investment income	3 330	−6,539	−4,252	−3,979	−4,413	−4,715	−10,918	−8,809	−11,927
Dividends and distributed branch profits	3 332	−3,028	−5,139	−5,193	−5,240	−2,893	−7,799	−6,917	−5,199
Reinvested earnings and undistributed branch profits	3 333	−2,755	1,920	2,204	1,516	−1,174	−1,777	−30	−4,393
Income on debt (interest)	3 334	−756	−1,033	−990	−689	−648	−1,341	−1,862	−2,335
Portfolio investment income	3 339	−4,030	−4,100	−3,844	−4,486	−4,928	−6,907	−7,905	−8,452
Income on equity	3 340	−391	−351	−378	−482	−633	−1,201	−1,656	−1,187
Income on bonds and notes	3 350	−3,432	−3,651	−3,411	−3,985	−4,272	−5,592	−6,124	−7,120
Income on money market instruments	3 360	−206	−98	−55	−19	−23	−114	−125	−145
Other investment income	3 370	−4,676	−4,652	−4,122	−3,867	−4,245	−4,019	−6,472	−9,818
D. CURRENT TRANSFERS	4 379	**−3,014**	**−2,572**	**−3,023**	**−3,536**	**−4,159**	**−4,196**	**−4,590**	**−5,096**
Credit	2 379	**3,395**	**3,719**	**3,466**	**4,615**	**5,120**	**3,562**	**3,537**	**4,061**
General government	2 380	441	483	451	600	666	....	....	....
Other sectors	2 390	2,954	3,235	3,016	4,015	4,454	....	....	....
Workers' remittances	2 391	....	....	....	....	....	....	....	....
Other current transfers	2 392	....	....	....	....	....	....	....	....
Debit	3 379	**−6,410**	**−6,291**	**−6,489**	**−8,151**	**−9,279**	**−7,758**	**−8,127**	**−9,157**
General government	3 380	−3,846	−3,775	−3,894	−4,890	−5,567	....	....	....
Other sectors	3 390	−2,564	−2,516	−2,596	−3,260	−3,712	....	....	....
Workers' remittances	3 391	....	....	....	....	....	....	....	....
Other current transfers	3 392	....	....	....	....	....	....	....	....
CAPITAL AND FINANCIAL ACCOUNT	4 996	**2,199**	**−9,015**	**−1,574**	**−9,809**	**−17,585**	**−8,200**	**−3,233**	**−5,468**
CAPITAL ACCOUNT	4 994	**−11**	**14**	**152**	**−7**	**13**	**518**	**4**	**54**
Total credit	2 994	*320*	*300*	*411*	*344*	*511*	*1,032*	*458*	*447*
Total debit	3 994	*−332*	*−286*	*−258*	*−351*	*−498*	*−514*	*−453*	*−393*
Capital transfers, credit	2 400	**320**	**300**	**411**	**344**	**511**	**....**	**....**	**....**
General government	2 401	....	....	....	....	....	....	....	....
Debt forgiveness	2 402	....	....	....	....	....	....	....	....
Other capital transfers	2 410	....	....	....	....	....	....	....	....
Other sectors	2 430	....	....	....	....	....	....	....	....
Migrants' transfers	2 431	....	....	....	....	....	....	....	....
Debt forgiveness	2 432	....	....	....	....	....	....	....	....
Other capital transfers	2 440	....	....	....	....	....	....	....	....
Capital transfers, debit	3 400	**−332**	**−286**	**−258**	**−351**	**−498**	**....**	**....**	**....**
General government	3 401	....	....	....	....	....	....	....	....
Debt forgiveness	3 402	....	....	....	....	....	....	....	....
Other capital transfers	3 410	....	....	....	....	....	....	....	....
Other sectors	3 430	....	....	....	....	....	....	....	....
Migrants' transfers	3 431	....	....	....	....	....	....	....	....
Debt forgiveness	3 432	....	....	....	....	....	....	....	....
Other capital transfers	3 440	....	....	....	....	....	....	....	....
Nonproduced nonfinancial assets, credit	2 480	**....**	**....**	**....**	**....**	**....**	**....**	**....**	**....**
Nonproduced nonfinancial assets, debit	3 480	**....**	**....**	**....**	**....**	**....**	**....**	**....**	**....**

Table 2 (Continued). STANDARD PRESENTATION, 2000–2007

(Millions of U.S. dollars)

	Code	2000	2001	2002	2003	2004	2005	2006	2007
FINANCIAL ACCOUNT	4 995	**2,210**	**−9,029**	**−1,726**	**−9,803**	**−17,598**	**−8,717**	**−3,237**	**−5,522**
A. DIRECT INVESTMENT	4 500	**7,632**	**−3,867**	**1,781**	**329**	**1,126**	**−3,355**	**−4,858**	**−5,200**
Direct investment abroad	4 505	**−28,381**	**−13,154**	**−2,650**	**−856**	**9,930**	**−16,207**	**−8,202**	**−16,513**
Equity capital	4 510	−20,766	−11,774	−3,657	6,995	−1,882	−6,716	−5,476	−4,869
Claims on affiliated enterprises	4 515	....	....	....	....	....	....	....	....
Liabilities to affiliated enterprises	4 520	....	....	....	....	....	....	....	....
Reinvested earnings	4 525	−2,929	279	3,264	296	−931	−5,038	−2,592	−6,740
Other capital	4 530	−4,686	−1,659	−2,257	−8,148	12,743	−4,453	−134	−4,904
Claims on affiliated enterprises	4 535	....	....	....	....	....	....	....	....
Liabilities to affiliated enterprises	4 540	....	....	....	....	....	....	....	....
Direct investment in Denmark	4 555	**36,013**	**9,286**	**4,431**	**1,185**	**−8,804**	**12,853**	**3,343**	**11,313**
Equity capital	4 560	23,638	5,675	4,711	2,413	−8,324	8,682	−3,338	6,075
Claims on direct investors	4 565	....	....	....	....	....	....	....	....
Liabilities to direct investors	4 570	....	....	....	....	....	....	....	....
Reinvested earnings	4 575	2,755	−1,920	−2,204	−1,516	1,174	1,777	30	4,393
Other capital	4 580	9,620	5,532	1,923	287	−1,655	2,393	6,651	845
Claims on direct investors	4 585	....	....	....	....	....	....	....	....
Liabilities to direct investors	4 590	....	....	....	....	....	....	....	....
B. PORTFOLIO INVESTMENT	4 600	**−17,799**	**−4,262**	**488**	**−15,920**	**−14,713**	**−11,770**	**−18,143**	**−11,049**
Assets	4 602	**−23,582**	**−14,772**	**−4,356**	**−21,930**	**−24,768**	**−32,808**	**−26,033**	**−28,993**
Equity securities	4 610	−13,944	−4,318	199	−3,467	−7,299	−14,118	−21,922	−8,989
Monetary authorities	4 611	....	....	....	....	....	5	....	....
General government	4 612	−767	−1,565	813	322	34	−8	....	−9
Banks	4 613	−210	−218	−946	−298	−432	−2,595	−2,014	1,002
Other sectors	4 614	−12,967	−2,534	332	−3,491	−6,900	−11,521	−19,909	−9,982
Debt securities	4 619	−9,638	−10,454	−4,555	−18,463	−17,469	−18,690	−4,111	−20,003
Bonds and notes	4 620	−9,762	−10,315	−4,207	−16,603	−17,542	−18,454	−1,529	−7,162
Monetary authorities	4 621	....	....	....	....	....	....	....	....
General government	4 622	−2,312	−1,632	−3,691	−5,331	−1,525	−43	16	−33
Banks	4 623	−3,259	−480	4,233	−4,729	−1,730	919	−6,423	−5,041
Other sectors	4 624	−4,191	−8,204	−4,749	−6,543	−14,286	−19,330	4,878	−2,088
Money market instruments	4 630	123	−139	−348	−1,859	73	−236	−2,582	−12,841
Monetary authorities	4 631	....	....	....	....	....	....	....	....
General government	4 632	....	....	....	....	....	−5	2	....
Banks	4 633	367	−195	310	−1,346	894	−110	330	−1,864
Other sectors	4 634	−244	56	−658	−514	−821	−121	−2,914	−10,977
Liabilities	4 652	**5,783**	**10,510**	**4,843**	**6,010**	**10,055**	**21,038**	**7,890**	**17,944**
Equity securities	4 660	2,341	861	591	1,389	1,562	−3,050	−5,488	2,409
Banks	4 663	−1,393	830	255	−616	−674	−211	1,323	−1,702
Other sectors	4 664	3,734	31	336	2,005	2,235	−2,839	−6,810	4,111
Debt securities	4 669	3,442	9,649	4,253	4,621	8,493	24,087	13,378	15,535
Bonds and notes	4 670	658	4,927	1,746	2,951	3,864	20,417	14,039	16,428
Monetary authorities	4 671	....	....	....	....	....	....	....	....
General government	4 672	−2,998	−5,514	−38	−6,802	−6,080	−2,320	−4,129	2,370
Banks	4 673	3,154	9,368	553	6,448	7,962	21,662	17,997	17,563
Other sectors	4 674	502	1,072	1,231	3,305	1,983	1,075	171	−3,505
Money market instruments	4 680	2,784	4,723	2,506	1,671	4,629	3,671	−661	−894
Monetary authorities	4 681	....	....	....	....	....	....	....	....
General government	4 682	259	216	196	−1,070	991	−75	−1,614	−1,470
Banks	4 683	2,136	3,759	3,447	2,710	3,587	3,632	1,028	373
Other sectors	4 684	390	747	−1,137	31	51	114	−75	203
C. FINANCIAL DERIVATIVES	4 910	**326**	**694**	**390**	**−12**	**3,206**	**2,161**	**2,902**	**442**
Monetary authorities	4 911	....	....	....	....	....	....	....	....
General government	4 912	....	....	....	....	....	278	−147	160
Banks	4 913	75	207	19	37	−32	−367	−75	836
Other sectors	4 914	251	487	371	−50	3,239	2,251	3,124	−554
Assets	4 900	....	....	....	....	....	....	....	....
Monetary authorities	4 901	....	....	....	....	....	....	....	....
General government	4 902	....	....	....	....	....	....	....	....
Banks	4 903	....	....	....	....	....	....	....	....
Other sectors	4 904	....	....	....	....	....	....	....	....
Liabilities	4 905	**326**	**694**	**390**	**−12**	**3,206**	**2,161**	**2,902**	**442**
Monetary authorities	4 906	....	....	....	....	....	....	....	....
General government	4 907	....	....	....	....	....	278	−147	160
Banks	4 908	75	207	19	37	−32	−367	−75	836
Other sectors	4 909	251	487	371	−50	3,239	2,251	3,124	−554

Table 2 (Concluded). STANDARD PRESENTATION, 2000–2007

(Millions of U.S. dollars)

	Code	2000	2001	2002	2003	2004	2005	2006	2007
D. OTHER INVESTMENT	4 700	**6,529**	**1,723**	**1,161**	**10,475**	**−8,642**	**2,741**	**10,873**	**10,074**
Assets	4 703	**−2,025**	**9,054**	**−6,839**	**−9,314**	**−9,021**	**−19,820**	**−24,367**	**−47,890**
Trade credits	4 706	579	1,971	−390	2,663	5,716	−318	−740	−1,606
General government	4 707	....	....	....	....	....	−11	11	1
of which: Short-term	4 709	....	....	....	....	....	....	....	....
Other sectors	4 710	579	1,971	−390	2,663	5,716	−306	−752	−1,607
of which: Short-term	4 712	....	....	....	....	....	....	....	....
Loans	4 714	....	....	....	....	....	....	....	....
Monetary authorities	4 715	....	....	....	....	....	....	....	....
of which: Short-term	4 718	....	....	....	....	....	....	....	....
General government	4 719	....	....	....	....	....	....	....	....
of which: Short-term	4 721	....	....	....	....	....	....	....	....
Banks	4 722	....	....	....	....	....	....	....	....
of which: Short-term	4 724	....	....	....	....	....	....	....	....
Other sectors	4 725	....	....	....	....	....	....	....	....
of which: Short-term	4 727	....	....	....	....	....	....	....	....
Currency and deposits	4 730	−2,799	7,078	−6,458	−11,959	−14,742	−19,668	−21,784	−45,866
Monetary authorities	4 731	15	−13	−41	56	−13	....	....	....
General government	4 732	25	41	18	365	31	280	−8	171
Banks	4 733	−1,898	7,232	−6,062	−12,623	−14,576	−20,573	−21,693	−44,896
Other sectors	4 734	−941	−182	−373	243	−183	625	−82	−1,141
Other assets	4 736	195	5	9	−19	5	166	−1,843	−419
Monetary authorities	4 737	....	....	....	....	....	....	....	....
of which: Short-term	4 739	....	....	....	....	....	....	....	....
General government	4 740	....	....	....	....	....	205	−150	22
of which: Short-term	4 742	....	....	....	....	....	....	....	....
Banks	4 743	185	....	....	....	....	−85	−1,712	−369
of which: Short-term	4 745	....	....	....	....	....	....	....	....
Other sectors	4 746	10	5	9	−19	5	46	19	−72
of which: Short-term	4 748	....	....	....	....	....	....	....	....
Liabilities	4 753	**8,554**	**−7,331**	**8,000**	**19,789**	**378**	**22,561**	**35,240**	**57,965**
Trade credits	4 756	−1,223	−879	−385	−3,838	−7,134	1,011	920	1,091
General government	4 757	....	....	....	....	....	7	49	−26
of which: Short-term	4 759	....	....	....	....	....	....	....	....
Other sectors	4 760	−1,223	−879	−385	−3,838	−7,134	1,004	872	1,117
of which: Short-term	4 762	....	....	....	....	....	....	....	....
Loans	4 764	9,898	−6,434	8,402	23,652	7,536	7,129	7,869	−839
Monetary authorities	4 765	113	61	−30	−27	−230	....	....	....
of which: Use of Fund credit and loans from the Fund	4 766	....	....	....	....	....	....	....	....
of which: Short-term	4 768	....	....	....	....	....	....	....	....
General government	4 769	−329	−191	−158	−438	−177	....	−63	28
of which: Short-term	4 771	....	....	....	....	....	....	....	....
Banks	4 772	10,563	−1,720	10,806	24,714	9,567	....	....	....
of which: Short-term	4 774	....	....	....	....	....	....	....	....
Other sectors	4 775	−449	−4,584	−2,217	−598	−1,624	7,130	7,931	−866
of which: Short-term	4 777	....	....	....	....	....	....	....	....
Currency and deposits	4 780	....	....	....	....	....	14,450	24,764	56,874
Monetary authorities	4 781	....	....	....	....	....	116	280	246
General government	4 782	....	....	....	....	....	....	....	....
Banks	4 783	....	....	....	....	....	14,333	24,484	56,628
Other sectors	4 784	....	....	....	....	....	....	....	....
Other liabilities	4 786	−121	−18	−17	−25	−24	−29	1,687	839
Monetary authorities	4 787	....	....	....	....	....	....	....	....
of which: Short-term	4 789	....	....	....	....	....	....	....	....
General government	4 790	....	....	....	....	....	....	....	....
of which: Short-term	4 792	....	....	....	....	....	....	....	....
Banks	4 793	−97	....	....	....	....	162	1,279	742
of which: Short-term	4 795	....	....	....	....	....	....	....	....
Other sectors	4 796	−24	−18	−17	−25	−24	−192	408	96
of which: Short-term	4 798	....	....	....	....	....	....	....	....
E. RESERVE ASSETS	4 802	**5,521**	**−3,317**	**−5,546**	**−4,674**	**1,426**	**1,506**	**5,988**	**211**
Monetary gold	4 812	....	....	....	....	−1	....	....	....
Special drawing rights	4 811	262	−221	183	31	38	−71	−225	23
Reserve position in the Fund	4 810	187	−160	−203	49	214	474	98	60
Foreign exchange	4 803	5,072	−2,909	−5,474	−4,713	1,175	1,107	6,169	205
Other claims	4 813	....	−27	−51	−42	....	−4	−54	−77
NET ERRORS AND OMISSIONS	4 998	**−4,460**	**4,167**	**−1,887**	**2,846**	**11,644**	**−3,150**	**−4,855**	**2,064**

Table 3. INTERNATIONAL INVESTMENT POSITION (End-period stocks), 2000–2007

(Millions of U.S. dollars)

	Code	2000	2001	2002	2003	2004	2005	2006	2007
ASSETS	8 995 C.	**249,021**	**253,228**	**307,886**	**393,205**	**474,364**	**473,109**	**573,458**	**712,983**
Direct investment abroad	8 505 ..	**65,890**	**78,252**	**86,679**	**102,596**	**111,678**	**111,288**	**126,654**	**153,944**
Equity capital and reinvested earnings	8 506 ..	54,003	61,831	65,718	69,342	75,444	89,580	104,126	123,632
Claims on affiliated enterprises	8 507 ..	....	....	....	....	....	....	....	....
Liabilities to affiliated enterprises	8 508 ..	....	....	....	....	....	....	....	....
Other capital	8 530 ..	11,887	16,421	20,961	33,254	36,234	21,707	22,529	30,312
Claims on affiliated enterprises	8 535 ..	15,243	12,316	16,702	27,935	30,438	....	....	46,217
Liabilities to affiliated enterprises	8 540 ..	−3,356	4,105	4,259	5,319	5,796	....	....	−15,905
Portfolio investment	8 602 ..	**84,973**	**85,731**	**86,424**	**127,033**	**160,851**	**196,204**	**248,954**	**300,700**
Equity securities	8 610 ..	56,480	47,978	35,796	52,118	65,428	88,108	130,725	156,106
Monetary authorities	8 611 ..	....	109	114	171	258	209	239	268
General government	8 612 ..	5,212	6,021	3,175	3,457	4,448	208	186	66
Banks	8 613 ..	2,711	2,325	2,277	3,338	4,363	6,104	9,090	9,789
Other sectors	8 614 ..	48,557	39,523	30,230	45,152	56,359	81,588	121,209	145,984
Debt securities	8 619 ..	28,493	37,753	50,628	74,915	95,423	108,096	118,229	144,593
Bonds and notes	8 620 ..	27,638	36,876	48,757	73,561	94,233	106,314	116,970	138,201
Monetary authorities	8 621 ..	....	....	....	....	....	....	....	....
General government	8 622 ..	3,171	4,881	8,777	14,946	17,930	101	85	110
Banks	8 623 ..	11,322	11,135	8,895	15,811	18,887	15,387	23,988	30,310
Other sectors	8 624 ..	13,145	20,861	31,084	42,803	57,416	90,826	92,897	107,781
Money market instruments	8 630 ..	855	877	1,871	1,354	1,190	1,781	1,259	6,392
Monetary authorities	8 631 ..	....	....	....	....	....	....	....	....
General government	8 632 ..	....	....	1,416	246	....	5	3	....
Banks	8 633 ..	232	420	−54	674	487	418	171	2,133
Other sectors	8 634 ..	624	457	509	435	703	1,358	1,086	4,258
Financial derivatives	8 900 ..	**14,093**	**11,203**	**30,577**	**23,566**	**36,560**	**8,858**	**8,320**	**1,411**
Monetary authorities	8 901 ..	469	52	239	249	218	....	....	....
General government	8 902 ..	99	4	1,811	1,446	1,579	697	585	96
Banks	8 903 ..	11,541	10,002	24,966	17,893	30,428	275	2,278	1,993
Other sectors	8 904 ..	1,984	1,145	3,561	3,978	4,334	7,887	5,457	−678
Other investment	8 703 ..	**69,009**	**59,937**	**76,433**	**101,816**	**125,174**	**122,702**	**158,311**	**222,536**
Trade credits	8 706 ..	6,412	6,803	8,007	9,538	10,393	5,906	7,224	9,581
General government	8 707 ..	877	856	1,067	1,222	1,331	16	5	5
of which: Short-term	8 709 ..	....	....	....	....	....	....	....	....
Other sectors	8 710 ..	5,535	5,946	6,940	8,316	9,062	5,890	7,219	9,575
of which: Short-term	8 712 ..	....	....	....	....	....	....	....	....
Loans	8 714 ..	20,137	18,616	23,035	26,960	33,100	....	....	....
Monetary authorities	8 715 ..	....	....	....	....	....	....	....	....
of which: Short-term	8 718 ..	....	....	....	....	....	....	....	....
General government	8 719 ..	64	....	....	....	....	....	....	....
of which: Short-term	8 721 ..	....	....	....	....	....	....	....	....
Banks	8 722 ..	13,129	15,798	20,790	24,864	30,816	....	....	....
of which: Short-term	8 724 ..	....	....	....	....	....	....	....	....
Other sectors	8 725 ..	6,944	2,817	2,245	2,096	2,284	....	....	....
of which: Short-term	8 727 ..	....	....	....	....	....	....	....	....
Currency and deposits	8 730 ..	38,730	30,917	40,634	60,060	75,804	....	....	....
Monetary authorities	8 731 ..	....	....	....	....	....	....	....	....
General government	8 732 ..	....	....	1	1	2	....	....	....
Banks	8 733 ..	38,657	29,268	38,718	57,038	72,417	....	....	....
Other sectors	8 734 ..	73	1,649	1,915	3,021	3,385	....	....	....
Other assets	8 736 ..	3,730	3,601	4,757	5,257	5,876	....	....	....
Monetary authorities	8 737 ..	....	....	....	....	....	....	....	....
of which: Short-term	8 739 ..	....	....	....	....	....	....	....	....
General government	8 740 ..	2,455	2,506	3,128	3,745	4,081	2,270	2,700	2,992
of which: Short-term	8 742 ..	....	....	....	....	....	....	....	....
Banks	8 743 ..	....	....	....	318	496	442	2,303	2,959
of which: Short-term	8 745 ..	....	....	....	....	....	....	....	....
Other sectors	8 746 ..	1,275	1,095	1,630	1,193	1,300	244	256	3,271
of which: Short-term	8 748 ..	....	....	....	....	....	....	....	....
Reserve assets	8 802 ..	**15,056**	**18,106**	**27,773**	**38,194**	**40,102**	**34,057**	**31,218**	**34,392**
Monetary gold	8 812 ..	584	592	734	889	931	1,098	1,360	1,790
Special drawing rights	8 811 ..	66	281	103	81	45	112	342	335
Reserve position in the Fund	8 810 ..	573	712	982	1,020	843	309	222	171
Foreign exchange	8 803 ..	13,833	16,521	25,955	36,204	38,283	26,334	23,811	27,647
Other claims	8 813 ..	....	....	....	....	....	6,205	5,483	4,450

Table 3 (Concluded). INTERNATIONAL INVESTMENT POSITION (End-period stocks), 2000–2007

(Millions of U.S. dollars)

	Code	2000	2001	2002	2003	2004	2005	2006	2007
LIABILITIES	8 995 D.	**272,052**	**279,551**	**339,698**	**421,714**	**503,500**	**469,065**	**576,448**	**725,597**
Direct investment in Denmark	8 555	**66,459**	**75,438**	**82,809**	**100,191**	**109,170**	**97,658**	**112,843**	**128,069**
Equity capital and reinvested earnings	8 556	48,073	46,685	55,459	72,924	79,459	79,492	87,669	101,792
Claims on direct investors	8 557	....	....	....	....	....	....	....	....
Liabilities to direct investors	8 558	....	....	....	....	....	....	....	....
Other capital	8 580	18,387	28,753	27,350	27,268	29,711	18,166	25,174	26,276
Claims on direct investors	8 585	−3,624	3,924	4,765	6,984	7,610	....	....	−10,225
Liabilities to direct investors	8 590	22,011	24,829	22,585	20,283	22,101	....	....	36,501
Portfolio investment	8 652	**104,119**	**112,507**	**127,484**	**159,180**	**197,683**	**210,333**	**250,214**	**303,868**
Equity securities	8 660	26,023	23,842	20,672	31,258	44,459	49,212	63,176	84,425
Banks	8 663	3,646	4,545	5,041	6,557	7,874	8,574	12,690	9,788
Other sectors	8 664	22,377	19,297	15,631	24,700	36,585	40,638	50,486	74,637
Debt securities	8 669	78,095	88,665	106,812	127,923	153,225	161,121	187,038	219,443
Bonds and notes	8 670	71,883	75,296	91,722	109,645	127,090	134,601	160,614	193,617
Monetary authorities	8 671	....	....	....	....	....	....	....	....
General government	8 672	37,822	30,883	36,987	36,198	37,772	30,954	28,956	34,282
Banks	8 673	6,418	37,068	43,738	58,212	69,817	84,062	110,310	139,803
Other sectors	8 674	27,643	7,345	10,997	15,234	19,501	19,585	21,348	19,533
Money market instruments	8 680	6,212	13,369	15,090	18,278	26,134	26,520	26,424	25,825
Monetary authorities	8 681	82	73	88	93	131	....	....	....
General government	8 682	1,133	2,820	2,296	2,218	5,705	4,035	2,802	1,487
Banks	8 683	4,219	9,111	12,348	15,498	19,651	21,619	22,793	23,243
Other sectors	8 684	778	1,366	358	469	647	866	829	1,095
Financial derivatives	8 905	**13,363**	**10,828**	**28,301**	**20,442**	**32,582**	....	....	....
Monetary authorities	8 906	7	50	....	....	2	....	....	....
General government	8 907	44	282	155	199	217	....	....	....
Banks	8 908	11,748	10,032	25,868	17,978	29,895	....	....	....
Other sectors	8 909	1,564	465	2,277	2,265	2,467	....	....	....
Other investment	8 753	**88,111**	**80,778**	**101,105**	**141,900**	**164,064**	**161,074**	**213,391**	**293,660**
Trade credits	8 756	3,047	3,605	4,204	4,707	5,129	4,261	5,611	7,102
General government	8 758	....	....	....	....	....	....	....	....
of which: Short-term	8 759	....	....	....	....	....	....	....	....
Other sectors	8 760	2,986	3,470	4,141	4,650	5,066	4,249	5,548	7,063
of which: Short-term	8 762	....	....	....	....	....	....	....	....
Loans	8 764	74,287	65,996	81,925	120,410	134,348	....	....	....
Monetary authorities	8 765	420	....	....	....	....	....	....	....
of which: Use of Fund credit and loans from the Fund	8 766	....	....	....	....	....	....	....	....
of which: Short-term	8 768	....	....	....	....	....	....	....	....
General government	8 769	407	512	488	32	21	284	132	82
of which: Short-term	8 771	....	....	....	....	....	....	....	....
Banks	8 772	51,473	49,701	63,252	96,514	107,647	....	....	....
of which: Short-term	8 774	....	....	....	....	....	....	....	....
Other sectors	8 775	21,986	15,784	18,185	23,863	26,680	24,419	34,980	39,869
of which: Short-term	8 777	....	....	....	....	....	....	....	....
Currency and deposits	8 780	9,082	9,447	13,099	14,633	22,219	....	....	....
Monetary authorities	8 781	....	463	522	519	321	....	....	....
General government	8 782	....	....	....	....	....	....	....	....
Banks	8 783	9,074	8,984	12,577	14,114	21,898	....	....	....
Other sectors	8 784	8	....	....	....	....	....	....	....
Other liabilities	8 786	1,695	1,729	1,877	2,151	2,369	....	....	....
Monetary authorities	8 787	....	....	....	....	....	....	....	....
of which: Short-term	8 789	....	....	....	....	....	....	....	....
General government	8 790	....	....	....	....	....	....	....	....
of which: Short-term	8 792	....	....	....	....	....	....	....	....
Banks	8 793	....	....	....	275	324	447	1,869	2,897
of which: Short-term	8 795	....	....	....	....	....	....	....	....
Other sectors	8 796	1,695	1,729	1,877	1,877	2,045	2,973	4,182	4,267
of which: Short-term	8 798	....	....	....	....	....	....	....	....
NET INTERNATIONAL INVESTMENT POSITION	8 995	**−23,031**	**−26,323**	**−31,812**	**−28,509**	**−29,136**	**4,045**	**−2,990**	**−12,614**
Conversion rates: Danish kroner per U.S. dollar (end of period)	0 102	**8.0205**	**8.4095**	**7.0822**	**5.9576**	**5.4676**	**6.3241**	**5.6614**	**5.0753**

Table 1. ANALYTIC PRESENTATION, 2000–2007

(Millions of U.S. dollars)

	Code	2000	2001	2002	2003	2004	2005	2006	2007
A. Current Account[1]..............................	4 993 Z.	**−71.2**	**−37.8**	**−16.8**	**−34.2**	**−68.0**	**−55.2**	**−99.1**	....
Goods: exports f.o.b............................	2 100 ..	31.6	31.6	35.6	37.2	38.0	39.5	55.2	....
Goods: imports f.o.b............................	3 100 ..	−206.5	−195.6	−197.1	−238.2	−261.4	−277.3	−335.7	....
Balance on Goods................................	4 100 ..	*−174.9*	*−164.0*	*−161.4*	*−201.0*	*−223.4*	*−237.8*	*−280.5*	....
Services: credit....................................	2 200 ..	161.6	181.9	192.4	215.7	212.7	248.4	257.1	....
Services: debit.....................................	3 200 ..	−71.2	−66.4	−61.6	−67.0	−77.2	−83.8	−95.6	....
Balance on Goods and Services...........	4 991 ..	*−84.5*	*−48.5*	*−30.6*	*−52.2*	*−87.9*	*−73.2*	*−119.0*	....
Income: credit.....................................	2 300 ..	25.2	21.5	24.5	31.2	33.3	32.0	34.9	....
Income: debit......................................	3 300 ..	−9.4	−9.1	−9.2	−10.3	−10.7	−11.2	−11.8	....
Balance on Goods, Services, and Income........	4 992 ..	*−68.7*	*−36.1*	*−15.3*	*−31.3*	*−65.3*	*−52.4*	*−96.0*	....
Current transfers: credit......................	2 379 Z.	.7	.7	.8	2.9	3.0	3.0	3.7	....
Current transfers: debit.......................	3 379 ..	−3.2	−2.5	−2.3	−5.8	−5.6	−5.8	−6.8	....
B. Capital Account[1]..............................	4 994 Z.	**9.2**	**5.0**	**10.1**	**−7.2**	**19.7**	**26.8**	**16.8**	....
Capital account: credit.........................	2 994 Z.	9.2	5.0	10.1	4.8	19.7	26.8	16.8	....
Capital account: debit..........................	3 994 ..	....	....	....	−12.0	....	....	....	....
Total, Groups A Plus B.......................	4 981 ..	*−62.0*	*−32.9*	*−6.7*	*−41.5*	*−48.3*	*−28.4*	*−82.3*	....
C. Financial Account[1]...........................	4 995 W.	**29.6**	**−64.6**	**−58.4**	**−37.1**	**−35.7**	**−32.8**	**65.1**	....
Direct investment abroad......................	4 505 ..	....	....	....	....	....	....	....	....
Direct investment in Djibouti................	4 555 Z.	3.3	3.4	3.4	14.2	38.5	22.2	108.3	....
Portfolio investment assets...................	4 602 ..	....	....	....	....	....	....	....	....
Equity securities..............................	4 610 ..	....	....	....	....	....	....	....	....
Debt securities................................	4 619 ..	....	....	....	....	....	....	....	....
Portfolio investment liabilities...............	4 652 Z.	....	....	....	....	....	....	....	....
Equity securities..............................	4 660 ..	....	....	....	....	....	....	....	....
Debt securities................................	4 669 Z.	....	....	....	....	....	....	....	....
Financial derivatives............................	4 910 ..	....	....	....	....	....	....	....	....
Financial derivatives assets..................	4 900 ..	....	....	....	....	....	....	....	....
Financial derivatives liabilities..............	4 905 ..	....	....	....	....	....	....	....	....
Other investment assets......................	4 703 ..	.5	−46.8	−58.5	−53.9	−84.0	−65.1	−62.0	....
Monetary authorities.........................	4 701 ..	....	....	....	....	....	....	....	....
General government.........................	4 704 ..	....	....	....	....	....	....	....	....
Banks..	4 705 ..	12.2	−35.8	−49.6	−44.8	−76.7	−57.8	−54.8	....
Other sectors...................................	4 728 ..	−11.8	−11.0	−8.9	−9.2	−7.3	−7.3	−7.2	....
Other investment liabilities...................	4 753 W.	25.9	−21.2	−3.3	2.6	9.8	10.2	18.8	....
Monetary authorities.........................	4 753 WA	....	−.2	....	....	....	....	....	....
General government.........................	4 753 ZB	−3.8	−2.8	−2.5	−3.6	−4.1	−5.7	−6.6	....
Banks..	4 753 ZC	4.8	−11.4	4.3	−6.7	5.5	4.1	15.2	....
Other sectors...................................	4 753 ZD	24.8	−6.8	−5.2	12.9	8.3	11.8	10.2	....
Total, Groups A Through C..................	4 983 ..	*−32.4*	*−97.5*	*−65.1*	*−78.6*	*−84.0*	*−61.2*	*−17.2*	....
D. Net Errors and Omissions...................	4 998 ..	**−30.6**	**33.9**	**8.9**	**1.5**	**−15.7**	**−45.4**	**−57.8**	....
Total, Groups A Through D..................	4 984 ..	*−63.0*	*−63.6*	*−56.2*	*−77.1*	*−99.7*	*−106.6*	*−75.0*	....
E. Reserves and Related Items...............	4 802 A.	**63.0**	**63.6**	**56.2**	**77.1**	**99.7**	**106.6**	**75.0**	....
Reserve assets.....................................	4 802 ..	2.5	−2.5	−5.1	−25.5	5.9	7.4	−32.9	....
Use of Fund credit and loans...............	4 766 ..	1.3	2.5	3.8	−1.8	−.2	−.8	−1.6	....
Exceptional financing...........................	4 920 ..	59.2	63.5	57.5	104.4	93.9	100.0	109.5	....
Conversion rates: Djibouti francs per U.S. dollar.................	0 101 ..	**177.72**	**177.72**	**177.72**	**177.72**	**177.72**	**177.72**	**177.72**	**177.72**

[1] Excludes components that have been classified in the categories of Group E.

Table 2. STANDARD PRESENTATION, 2000–2007

(Millions of U.S. dollars)

	Code	2000	2001	2002	2003	2004	2005	2006	2007
CURRENT ACCOUNT..................................	4 993 ..	**−19.0**	**15.5**	**26.5**	**38.1**	**3.2**	**20.1**	**−17.2**	....
A. GOODS..	4 100 ..	**−174.9**	**−164.0**	**−161.4**	**−201.0**	**−223.4**	**−237.8**	**−280.5**	....
Credit..	2 100 ..	**31.6**	**31.6**	**35.6**	**37.2**	**38.0**	**39.5**	**55.2**	....
General merchandise: exports f.o.b................	2 110 ..	31.6	31.6	35.6	37.2	38.0	39.5	55.2	....
Goods for processing: exports f.o.b................	2 150 ..	....	....	....	....	....	....	....	....
Repairs on goods..............................	2 160 ..	....	....	....	....	....	....	....	....
Goods procured in ports by carriers..............	2 170 ..	....	....	....	....	....	....	....	....
Nonmonetary gold..............................	2 180 ..	....	....	....	....	....	....	....	....
Debit...	3 100 ..	**−206.5**	**−195.6**	**−197.1**	**−238.2**	**−261.4**	**−277.3**	**−335.7**	....
General merchandise: imports f.o.b................	3 110 ..	−206.5	−195.6	−197.1	−238.2	−261.4	−277.3	−335.7	....
Goods for processing: imports f.o.b................	3 150 ..	....	....	....	....	....	....	....	....
Repairs on goods..............................	3 160 ..	....	....	....	....	....	....	....	....
Goods procured in ports by carriers..............	3 170 ..	....	....	....	....	....	....	....	....
Nonmonetary gold..............................	3 180 ..	....	....	....	....	....	....	....	....
B. SERVICES.......................................	4 200 ..	**90.4**	**115.5**	**130.8**	**148.7**	**135.5**	**164.6**	**161.5**	....
Total credit.....................................	2 200 ..	*161.6*	*181.9*	*192.4*	*215.7*	*212.7*	*248.4*	*257.1*	....
Total debit......................................	3 200 ..	*−71.2*	*−66.4*	*−61.6*	*−67.0*	*−77.2*	*−83.8*	*−95.6*	....
Transportation services, credit................	2 205 ..	**52.6**	**56.2**	**59.6**	**68.2**	**67.8**	**74.9**	**79.9**	....
Passenger...................................	2 850 ..	....	....	....	....	....	....	....	....
Freight......................................	2 851 ..	....	....	....	....	....	....	....	....
Other.......................................	2 852 ..	*52.6*	*56.2*	*59.6*	*68.2*	*67.8*	*74.9*	*79.9*	....
Sea transport, passenger......................	2 207 ..	....	....	....	....	....	....	....	....
Sea transport, freight.........................	2 208 ..	....	....	....	....	....	....	....	....
Sea transport, other..........................	2 209 ..	27.5	30.5	31.7	38.6	38.2	42.8	48.1	....
Air transport, passenger......................	2 211 ..	....	....	....	....	....	....	....	....
Air transport, freight.........................	2 212 ..	....	....	....	....	....	....	....	....
Air transport, other..........................	2 213 ..	8.3	9.0	9.7	10.0	10.0	10.1	10.3	....
Other transport, passenger....................	2 215 ..	....	....	....	....	....	....	....	....
Other transport, freight.......................	2 216 ..	....	....	....	....	....	....	....	....
Other transport, other........................	2 217 ..	16.8	16.7	18.2	19.6	19.7	22.0	21.6	....
Transportation services, debit.................	3 205 ..	**−40.5**	**−38.6**	**−34.7**	**−39.2**	**−47.7**	**−53.0**	**−63.1**	....
Passenger...................................	3 850 ..	*−8.9*	*−8.9*	*−4.9*	*−7.1*	*−11.2*	*−11.5*	*−11.5*	....
Freight......................................	3 851 ..	*−31.5*	*−29.7*	*−29.9*	*−32.2*	*−36.5*	*−41.6*	*−51.7*	....
Other.......................................	3 852 ..	....	....	....	....	....	....	....	....
Sea transport, passenger......................	3 207 ..	....	....	....	....	....	....	....	....
Sea transport, freight.........................	3 208 ..	−31.5	−29.7	−29.9	−32.2	−36.5	−41.6	−51.7	....
Sea transport, other..........................	3 209 ..	....	....	....	....	....	....	....	....
Air transport, passenger......................	3 211 ..	−8.9	−8.9	−4.9	−7.1	−11.2	−11.5	−11.5	....
Air transport, freight.........................	3 212 ..	....	....	....	....	....	....	....	....
Air transport, other..........................	3 213 ..	....	....	....	....	....	....	....	....
Other transport, passenger....................	3 215 ..	....	....	....	....	....	....	....	....
Other transport, freight.......................	3 216 ..	....	....	....	....	....	....	....	....
Other transport, other........................	3 217 ..	....	....	....	....	....	....	....	....
Travel, credit.................................	2 236 ..	**8.1**	**8.6**	**8.9**	**6.9**	**6.8**	**7.1**	**9.2**	....
Business travel...............................	2 237 ..	8.1	8.6	8.9	6.9	6.8	7.1	9.2	....
Personal travel...............................	2 240 ..	....	....	....	....	....	....	....	....
Travel, debit..................................	3 236 ..	**−5.9**	**−4.0**	**−2.8**	**−2.8**	**−2.8**	**−2.8**	**−3.4**	....
Business travel...............................	3 237 ..	....	....	....	....	....	....	....	....
Personal travel...............................	3 240 ..	−5.9	−4.0	−2.8	−2.8	−2.8	−2.8	−3.4	....
Other services, credit.........................	2 200 BA	**100.9**	**117.1**	**123.8**	**140.6**	**138.1**	**166.3**	**168.1**	....
Communications..............................	2 245 ..	3.3	3.3	4.0	5.6	5.6	5.8	6.1	....
Construction.................................	2 249 ..	....	....	....	....	....	....	....	....
Insurance....................................	2 253 ..	....	....	....	....	....	....	....	....
Financial....................................	2 260 ..	....	....	....	....	....	....	....	....
Computer and information.....................	2 262 ..	....	....	....	....	....	....	....	....
Royalties and licence fees.....................	2 266 ..	....	....	....	....	....	....	....	....
Other business services.......................	2 268 ..	5.0	5.5	6.3	6.5	6.7	6.9	7.3	....
Personal, cultural, and recreational.............	2 287 ..	....	....	....	....	....	....	....	....
Government, n.i.e.............................	2 291 ..	92.6	108.2	113.5	128.5	125.8	153.6	154.6	....
Other services, debit..........................	3 200 BA	**−24.8**	**−23.8**	**−24.0**	**−25.0**	**−26.7**	**−27.9**	**−29.0**	....
Communications..............................	3 245 ..	....	....	....	....	....	....	....	....
Construction.................................	3 249 ..	....	....	....	....	....	....	....	....
Insurance....................................	3 253 ..	−8.0	−7.3	−7.3	−7.4	−8.6	−8.6	−8.5	....
Financial....................................	3 260 ..	....	....	....	....	....	....	....	....
Computer and information.....................	3 262 ..	....	....	....	....	....	....	....	....
Royalties and licence fees.....................	3 266 ..	....	....	....	....	....	....	....	....
Other business services.......................	3 268 ..	−10.6	−10.6	−10.6	−10.9	−11.2	−11.6	−11.9	....
Personal, cultural, and recreational.............	3 287 ..	....	....	....	....	....	....	....	....
Government, n.i.e.............................	3 291 ..	−6.2	−5.9	−6.1	−6.7	−6.9	−7.7	−8.6	....

Table 2 (Continued). STANDARD PRESENTATION, 2000–2007

(Millions of U.S. dollars)

	Code	2000	2001	2002	2003	2004	2005	2006	2007
C. INCOME	4 300	**15.8**	**12.4**	**15.3**	**20.9**	**22.5**	**20.8**	**23.0**	....
Total credit	2 300	*25.2*	*21.5*	*24.5*	*31.2*	*33.3*	*32.0*	*34.9*	....
Total debit	3 300	*–9.4*	*–9.1*	*–9.2*	*–10.3*	*–10.7*	*–11.2*	*–11.8*	....
Compensation of employees, credit	2 310	**11.6**	**11.2**	**14.2**	**21.8**	**21.8**	**22.9**	**24.8**	....
Compensation of employees, debit	3 310	....	....	....	....	....	....	....	....
Investment income, credit	2 320	**13.6**	**10.2**	**10.3**	**9.5**	**11.5**	**9.1**	**10.0**	....
Direct investment income	2 330	....	....	....	....	....	....	....	....
Dividends and distributed branch profits	2 332	....	....	....	....	....	....	....	....
Reinvested earnings and undistributed branch profits	2 333	....	....	....	....	....	....	....	....
Income on debt (interest)	2 334	....	....	....	....	....	....	....	....
Portfolio investment income	2 339	....	....	....	....	....	....	....	....
Income on equity	2 340	....	....	....	....	....	....	....	....
Income on bonds and notes	2 350	....	....	....	....	....	....	....	....
Income on money market instruments	2 360	....	....	....	....	....	....	....	....
Other investment income	2 370	13.6	10.2	10.3	9.5	11.5	9.1	10.0	....
Investment income, debit	3 320	**–9.4**	**–9.1**	**–9.2**	**–10.3**	**–10.7**	**–11.2**	**–11.8**	....
Direct investment income	3 330	–4.2	–4.3	–4.4	–6.0	–6.0	–5.9	–5.9	....
Dividends and distributed branch profits	3 332	–.9	–.9	–.9	–2.4	–2.4	–2.3	–2.3	....
Reinvested earnings and undistributed branch profits	3 333	–3.3	–3.4	–3.4	–3.5	–3.5	–3.6	–3.6	....
Income on debt (interest)	3 334	....	....	....	....	....	....	....	....
Portfolio investment income	3 339	....	....	....	....	....	....	....	....
Income on equity	3 340	....	....	....	....	....	....	....	....
Income on bonds and notes	3 350	....	....	....	....	....	....	....	....
Income on money market instruments	3 360	....	....	....	....	....	....	....	....
Other investment income	3 370	–5.2	–4.8	–4.8	–4.3	–4.8	–5.3	–6.0	....
D. CURRENT TRANSFERS	4 379	**49.7**	**51.6**	**41.9**	**69.4**	**68.5**	**72.6**	**78.8**	....
Credit	2 379	**53.0**	**54.1**	**44.2**	**75.3**	**74.1**	**78.3**	**85.5**	....
General government	2 380	52.3	53.3	43.4	72.3	71.2	75.3	81.9	....
Other sectors	2 390	.7	.7	.8	2.9	3.0	3.0	3.7	....
Workers' remittances	2 391	.7	.7	.8	2.9	3.0	3.0	3.7	....
Other current transfers	2 392	....	....	....	....	....	....	....	....
Debit	3 379	**–3.2**	**–2.5**	**–2.3**	**–5.8**	**–5.6**	**–5.8**	**–6.8**	....
General government	3 380	–1.5	–.7	–.6	–1.0	–1.0	–1.1	–2.0	....
Other sectors	3 390	–1.8	–1.8	–1.7	–4.8	–4.7	–4.7	–4.7	....
Workers' remittances	3 391	–1.8	–1.8	–1.7	–4.8	–4.7	–4.7	–4.7	....
Other current transfers	3 392	....	....	....	....	....	....	....	....
CAPITAL AND FINANCIAL ACCOUNT	4 996	**49.6**	**–49.4**	**–35.4**	**–39.6**	**12.5**	**25.3**	**75.0**	....
CAPITAL ACCOUNT	4 994	**9.2**	**5.0**	**10.1**	**–7.2**	**19.7**	**26.8**	**16.8**	....
Total credit	2 994	*9.2*	*5.0*	*10.1*	*4.8*	*19.7*	*26.8*	*16.8*	....
Total debit	3 994	....	....	....	*–12.0*	....	....	....	....
Capital transfers, credit	2 400	**9.2**	**5.0**	**10.1**	**4.8**	**19.7**	**26.8**	**16.8**	....
General government	2 401	9.2	5.0	10.1	4.8	19.7	26.8	16.8	....
Debt forgiveness	2 402	....	....	....	....	....	....	....	....
Other capital transfers	2 410	9.2	5.0	10.1	4.8	19.7	26.8	16.8	....
Other sectors	2 430	....	....	....	....	....	....	....	....
Migrants' transfers	2 431	....	....	....	....	....	....	....	....
Debt forgiveness	2 432	....	....	....	....	....	....	....	....
Other capital transfers	2 440	....	....	....	....	....	....	....	....
Capital transfers, debit	3 400	....	....	....	**–12.0**	....	....	....	....
General government	3 401	....	....	....	....	....	....	....	....
Debt forgiveness	3 402	....	....	....	....	....	....	....	....
Other capital transfers	3 410	....	....	....	....	....	....	....	....
Other sectors	3 430	....	....	....	–12.0	....	....	....	....
Migrants' transfers	3 431	....	....	....	....	....	....	....	....
Debt forgiveness	3 432	....	....	....	....	....	....	....	....
Other capital transfers	3 440	....	....	....	–12.0	....	....	....	....
Nonproduced nonfinancial assets, credit	2 480	....	....	....	....	....	....	....	....
Nonproduced nonfinancial assets, debit	3 480	....	....	....	....	....	....	....	....

Table 2 (Continued). STANDARD PRESENTATION, 2000–2007

(Millions of U.S. dollars)

	Code	2000	2001	2002	2003	2004	2005	2006	2007
FINANCIAL ACCOUNT..	4 995 ..	**40.4**	**−54.4**	**−45.5**	**−32.4**	**−7.2**	**−1.5**	**58.2**	....
A. DIRECT INVESTMENT.......................................	4 500 ..	**3.3**	**3.4**	**3.4**	**14.2**	**38.5**	**22.2**	**108.3**	....
Direct investment abroad...................................	4 505 ..	....	....	....	....	....	....	....	....
Equity capital..	4 510 ..	....	....	....	....	....	....	....	....
Claims on affiliated enterprises................................	4 515 ..	....	....	....	....	....	....	....	....
Liabilities to affiliated enterprises.............................	4 520 ..	....	....	....	....	....	....	....	....
Reinvested earnings..	4 525 ..	....	....	....	....	....	....	....	....
Other capital..	4 530 ..	....	....	....	....	....	....	....	....
Claims on affiliated enterprises................................	4 535 ..	....	....	....	....	....	....	....	....
Liabilities to affiliated enterprises.............................	4 540 ..	....	....	....	....	....	....	....	....
Direct investment in Djibouti...........................	4 555 ..	**3.3**	**3.4**	**3.4**	**14.2**	**38.5**	**22.2**	**108.3**	....
Equity capital..	4 560 ..	....	....	....	10.7	35.0	18.7	104.7	....
Claims on direct investors.......................................	4 565 ..	....	....	....	....	....	....	....	....
Liabilities to direct investors...................................	4 570 ..	....	....	....	10.7	35.0	18.7	104.7	....
Reinvested earnings..	4 575 ..	3.3	3.4	3.4	3.5	3.5	3.6	3.6	....
Other capital..	4 580 ..	....	....	....	....	....	....	....	....
Claims on direct investors.......................................	4 585 ..	....	....	....	....	....	....	....	....
Liabilities to direct investors...................................	4 590 ..	....	....	....	....	....	....	....	....
B. PORTFOLIO INVESTMENT................................	4 600 ..	....	....	....	....	....	....	....	....
Assets..	4 602 ..	....	....	....	....	....	....	....	....
Equity securities..	4 610 ..	....	....	....	....	....	....	....	....
Monetary authorities..	4 611 ..	....	....	....	....	....	....	....	....
General government...	4 612 ..	....	....	....	....	....	....	....	....
Banks..	4 613 ..	....	....	....	....	....	....	....	....
Other sectors..	4 614 ..	....	....	....	....	....	....	....	....
Debt securities..	4 619 ..	....	....	....	....	....	....	....	....
Bonds and notes..	4 620 ..	....	....	....	....	....	....	....	....
Monetary authorities..	4 621 ..	....	....	....	....	....	....	....	....
General government...	4 622 ..	....	....	....	....	....	....	....	....
Banks..	4 623 ..	....	....	....	....	....	....	....	....
Other sectors..	4 624 ..	....	....	....	....	....	....	....	....
Money market instruments.....................................	4 630 ..	....	....	....	....	....	....	....	....
Monetary authorities..	4 631 ..	....	....	....	....	....	....	....	....
General government...	4 632 ..	....	....	....	....	....	....	....	....
Banks..	4 633 ..	....	....	....	....	....	....	....	....
Other sectors..	4 634 ..	....	....	....	....	....	....	....	....
Liabilities..	4 652 ..	....	....	....	....	....	....	....	....
Equity securities..	4 660 ..	....	....	....	....	....	....	....	....
Banks..	4 663 ..	....	....	....	....	....	....	....	....
Other sectors..	4 664 ..	....	....	....	....	....	....	....	....
Debt securities..	4 669 ..	....	....	....	....	....	....	....	....
Bonds and notes..	4 670 ..	....	....	....	....	....	....	....	....
Monetary authorities..	4 671 ..	....	....	....	....	....	....	....	....
General government...	4 672 ..	....	....	....	....	....	....	....	....
Banks..	4 673 ..	....	....	....	....	....	....	....	....
Other sectors..	4 674 ..	....	....	....	....	....	....	....	....
Money market instruments.....................................	4 680 ..	....	....	....	....	....	....	....	....
Monetary authorities..	4 681 ..	....	....	....	....	....	....	....	....
General government...	4 682 ..	....	....	....	....	....	....	....	....
Banks..	4 683 ..	....	....	....	....	....	....	....	....
Other sectors..	4 684 ..	....	....	....	....	....	....	....	....
C. FINANCIAL DERIVATIVES.................................	4 910 ..	....	....	....	....	....	....	....	....
Monetary authorities..	4 911 ..	....	....	....	....	....	....	....	....
General government...	4 912 ..	....	....	....	....	....	....	....	....
Banks..	4 913 ..	....	....	....	....	....	....	....	....
Other sectors..	4 914 ..	....	....	....	....	....	....	....	....
Assets..	4 900 ..	....	....	....	....	....	....	....	....
Monetary authorities..	4 901 ..	....	....	....	....	....	....	....	....
General government...	4 902 ..	....	....	....	....	....	....	....	....
Banks..	4 903 ..	....	....	....	....	....	....	....	....
Other sectors..	4 904 ..	....	....	....	....	....	....	....	....
Liabilities..	4 905 ..	....	....	....	....	....	....	....	....
Monetary authorities..	4 906 ..	....	....	....	....	....	....	....	....
General government...	4 907 ..	....	....	....	....	....	....	....	....
Banks..	4 908 ..	....	....	....	....	....	....	....	....
Other sectors..	4 909 ..	....	....	....	....	....	....	....	....

Table 2 (Concluded). STANDARD PRESENTATION, 2000–2007

(Millions of U.S. dollars)

	Code	2000	2001	2002	2003	2004	2005	2006	2007
D. OTHER INVESTMENT	4 700 ..	**34.6**	**−55.3**	**−43.9**	**−21.1**	**−51.6**	**−31.1**	**−17.1**	....
Assets	4 703 ..	**.5**	**−46.8**	**−58.5**	**−53.9**	**−84.0**	**−65.1**	**−62.0**	....
Trade credits	4 706 ..	....	....	....	....	....	....	....	....
General government	4 707 ..	....	....	....	....	....	....	....	....
of which: Short-term	4 709 ..	....	....	....	....	....	....	....	....
Other sectors	4 710 ..	....	....	....	....	....	....	....	....
of which: Short-term	4 712 ..	....	....	....	....	....	....	....	....
Loans	4 714 ..	....	....	....	....	....	....	....	....
Monetary authorities	4 715 ..	....	....	....	....	....	....	....	....
of which: Short-term	4 718 ..	....	....	....	....	....	....	....	....
General government	4 719 ..	....	....	....	....	....	....	....	....
of which: Short-term	4 721 ..	....	....	....	....	....	....	....	....
Banks	4 722 ..	....	....	....	....	....	....	....	....
of which: Short-term	4 724 ..	....	....	....	....	....	....	....	....
Other sectors	4 725 ..	....	....	....	....	....	....	....	....
of which: Short-term	4 727 ..	....	....	....	....	....	....	....	....
Currency and deposits	4 730 ..	.5	−46.8	−58.5	−53.9	−84.0	−65.1	−62.0	....
Monetary authorities	4 731 ..	....	....	....	....	....	....	....	....
General government	4 732 ..	....	....	....	....	....	....	....	....
Banks	4 733 ..	12.2	−35.8	−49.6	−44.8	−76.7	−57.8	−54.8	....
Other sectors	4 734 ..	−11.8	−11.0	−8.9	−9.2	−7.3	−7.3	−7.2	....
Other assets	4 736 ..	....	....	....	....	....	....	....	....
Monetary authorities	4 737 ..	....	....	....	....	....	....	....	....
of which: Short-term	4 739 ..	....	....	....	....	....	....	....	....
General government	4 740 ..	....	....	....	....	....	....	....	....
of which: Short-term	4 742 ..	....	....	....	....	....	....	....	....
Banks	4 743 ..	....	....	....	....	....	....	....	....
of which: Short-term	4 745 ..	....	....	....	....	....	....	....	....
Other sectors	4 746 ..	....	....	....	....	....	....	....	....
of which: Short-term	4 748 ..	....	....	....	....	....	....	....	....
Liabilities	4 753 ..	**34.1**	**−8.4**	**14.6**	**32.8**	**32.4**	**34.0**	**44.9**	....
Trade credits	4 756 ..	....	....	....	....	....	....	....	....
General government	4 757 ..	....	....	....	....	....	....	....	....
of which: Short-term	4 759 ..	....	....	....	....	....	....	....	....
Other sectors	4 760 ..	....	....	....	....	....	....	....	....
of which: Short-term	4 762 ..	....	....	....	....	....	....	....	....
Loans	4 764 ..	29.3	2.9	10.3	39.5	26.8	30.0	29.7	....
Monetary authorities	4 765 ..	2.1	2.4	4.4	−1.8	.8	−.8	−1.6	....
of which: Use of Fund credit and loans from the Fund..	4 766 ..	1.3	2.5	3.8	−1.8	−.2	−.8	−1.6	....
of which: Short-term	4 768 ..	....	....	....	....	1.0	....	....	....
General government	4 769 ..	2.4	7.4	11.1	28.4	17.7	19.0	21.0	....
of which: Short-term	4 771 ..	....	....	....	....	....	....	....	....
Banks	4 772 ..	....	....	....	....	....	....	....	....
of which: Short-term	4 774 ..	....	....	....	....	....	....	....	....
Other sectors	4 775 ..	24.8	−6.8	−5.2	12.9	8.3	11.8	10.2	....
of which: Short-term	4 777 ..	....	....	....	....	....	....	....	....
Currency and deposits	4 780 ..	4.8	−11.4	4.3	−6.7	5.5	4.1	15.2	....
Monetary authorities	4 781 ..	....	....	....	....	....	....	....	....
General government	4 782 ..	....	....	....	....	....	....	....	....
Banks	4 783 ..	4.8	−11.4	4.3	−6.7	5.5	4.1	15.2	....
Other sectors	4 784 ..	....	....	....	....	....	....	....	....
Other liabilities	4 786 ..	....	....	....	....	....	....	....	....
Monetary authorities	4 787 ..	....	....	....	....	....	....	....	....
of which: Short-term	4 789 ..	....	....	....	....	....	....	....	....
General government	4 790 ..	....	....	....	....	....	....	....	....
of which: Short-term	4 792 ..	....	....	....	....	....	....	....	....
Banks	4 793 ..	....	....	....	....	....	....	....	....
of which: Short-term	4 795 ..	....	....	....	....	....	....	....	....
Other sectors	4 796 ..	....	....	....	....	....	....	....	....
of which: Short-term	4 798 ..	....	....	....	....	....	....	....	....
E. RESERVE ASSETS	4 802 ..	**2.5**	**−2.5**	**−5.1**	**−25.5**	**5.9**	**7.4**	**−32.9**	....
Monetary gold	4 812 ..	....	....	....	....	....	....	....	....
Special drawing rights	4 811 ..	−.3	.2	−.9	.9	−.8	.9	−.8	....
Reserve position in the Fund	4 810 ..	....	....	....	....	....	....	....	....
Foreign exchange	4 803 ..	2.8	−2.7	−4.2	−26.4	6.8	6.5	−32.1	....
Other claims	4 813 ..	....	....	....	....	....	....	....	....
NET ERRORS AND OMISSIONS	4 998 ..	**−30.6**	**33.9**	**8.9**	**1.5**	**−15.7**	**−45.4**	**−57.8**	....

Table 3. INTERNATIONAL INVESTMENT POSITION (End-period stocks), 2000–2007

(Millions of U.S. dollars)

	Code	2000	2001	2002	2003	2004	2005	2006	2007
ASSETS	8 995 C.	....	....	....	560.8	....	....	....	....
Direct investment abroad	8 505 ..	....	....	....	....	....	....	....	....
Equity capital and reinvested earnings	8 506 ..	....	....	....	....	....	....	....	....
Claims on affiliated enterprises	8 507 ..	....	....	....	....	....	....	....	....
Liabilities to affiliated enterprises	8 508 ..	....	....	....	....	....	....	....	....
Other capital	8 530 ..	....	....	....	....	....	....	....	....
Claims on affiliated enterprises	8 535 ..	....	....	....	....	....	....	....	....
Liabilities to affiliated enterprises	8 540 ..	....	....	....	....	....	....	....	....
Portfolio investment	8 602 ..	....	....	....	....	....	....	....	....
Equity securities	8 610 ..	....	....	....	....	....	....	....	....
Monetary authorities	8 611 ..	....	....	....	....	....	....	....	....
General government	8 612 ..	....	....	....	....	....	....	....	....
Banks	8 613 ..	....	....	....	....	....	....	....	....
Other sectors	8 614 ..	....	....	....	....	....	....	....	....
Debt securities	8 619 ..	....	....	....	....	....	....	....	....
Bonds and notes	8 620 ..	....	....	....	....	....	....	....	....
Monetary authorities	8 621 ..	....	....	....	....	....	....	....	....
General government	8 622 ..	....	....	....	....	....	....	....	....
Banks	8 623 ..	....	....	....	....	....	....	....	....
Other sectors	8 624 ..	....	....	....	....	....	....	....	....
Money market instruments	8 630 ..	....	....	....	....	....	....	....	....
Monetary authorities	8 631 ..	....	....	....	....	....	....	....	....
General government	8 632 ..	....	....	....	....	....	....	....	....
Banks	8 633 ..	....	....	....	....	....	....	....	....
Other sectors	8 634 ..	....	....	....	....	....	....	....	....
Financial derivatives	8 900 ..	....	....	....	....	....	....	....	....
Monetary authorities	8 901 ..	....	....	....	....	....	....	....	....
General government	8 902 ..	....	....	....	....	....	....	....	....
Banks	8 903 ..	....	....	....	....	....	....	....	....
Other sectors	8 904 ..	....	....	....	....	....	....	....	....
Other investment	8 703 ..	....	....	....	459.7	....	....	....	....
Trade credits	8 706 ..	....	....	....	....	....	....	....	....
General government	8 707 ..	....	....	....	....	....	....	....	....
of which: Short-term	8 709 ..	....	....	....	....	....	....	....	....
Other sectors	8 710 ..	....	....	....	....	....	....	....	....
of which: Short-term	8 712 ..	....	....	....	....	....	....	....	....
Loans	8 714 ..	....	....	....	281.4	....	....	....	....
Monetary authorities	8 715 ..	....	....	....	....	....	....	....	....
of which: Short-term	8 718 ..	....	....	....	....	....	....	....	....
General government	8 719 ..	....	....	....	....	....	....	....	....
of which: Short-term	8 721 ..	....	....	....	....	....	....	....	....
Banks	8 722 ..	....	....	....	281.4	....	....	....	....
of which: Short-term	8 724 ..	....	....	....	*281.4*	....	....	....	....
Other sectors	8 725 ..	....	....	....	....	....	....	....	....
of which: Short-term	8 727 ..	....	....	....	....	....	....	....	....
Currency and deposits	8 730 ..	....	....	....	178.4	....	....	....	....
Monetary authorities	8 731 ..	....	....	....	....	....	....	....	....
General government	8 732 ..	....	....	....	....	....	....	....	....
Banks	8 733 ..	....	....	....	10.4	....	....	....	....
Other sectors	8 734 ..	....	....	....	168.0	....	....	....	....
Other assets	8 736 ..	....	....	....	....	....	....	....	....
Monetary authorities	8 737 ..	....	....	....	....	....	....	....	....
of which: Short-term	8 739 ..	....	....	....	....	....	....	....	....
General government	8 740 ..	....	....	....	....	....	....	....	....
of which: Short-term	8 742 ..	....	....	....	....	....	....	....	....
Banks	8 743 ..	....	....	....	....	....	....	....	....
of which: Short-term	8 745 ..	....	....	....	....	....	....	....	....
Other sectors	8 746 ..	....	....	....	....	....	....	....	....
of which: Short-term	8 748 ..	....	....	....	....	....	....	....	....
Reserve assets	8 802 ..	....	....	....	101.1	....	....	....	....
Monetary gold	8 812 ..	....	....	....	....	....	....	....	....
Special drawing rights	8 811 ..	.4	.1	1.0	.1	1.0	....	.8	.1
Reserve position in the Fund	8 810 ..	1.4	1.4	1.5	1.6	1.7	1.6	1.7	1.7
Foreign exchange	8 803 ..	....	....	....	99.4	....	....	....	....
Other claims	8 813 ..	....	....	....	....	....	....	....	....

Table 3 (Concluded). INTERNATIONAL INVESTMENT POSITION (End-period stocks), 2000–2007

(Millions of U.S. dollars)

	Code	2000	2001	2002	2003	2004	2005	2006	2007
LIABILITIES...	8 995 D.	....	....	....	**463.5**	....	....	....	....
Direct investment in Djibouti.............................	8 555 ..	....	....	....	**61.2**	....	....	....	....
Equity capital and reinvested earnings...........................	8 556 ..	....	....	....	61.2	....	....	....	....
Claims on direct investors..	8 557 ..	....	....	....	61.2	....	....	....	....
Liabilities to direct investors..................................	8 558 ..	....	....	....	....	....	....	....	....
Other capital..	8 580 ..	....	....	....	....	....	....	....	....
Claims on direct investors..	8 585 ..	....	....	....	....	....	....	....	....
Liabilities to direct investors..................................	8 590 ..	....	....	....	....	....	....	....	....
Portfolio investment.....................................	8 652 ..	....	....	....	....	....	....	....	....
Equity securities..	8 660 ..	....	....	....	....	....	....	....	....
Banks...	8 663 ..	....	....	....	....	....	....	....	....
Other sectors..	8 664 ..	....	....	....	....	....	....	....	....
Debt securities..	8 669 ..	....	....	....	....	....	....	....	....
Bonds and notes..	8 670 ..	....	....	....	....	....	....	....	....
Monetary authorities..	8 671 ..	....	....	....	....	....	....	....	....
General government...	8 672 ..	....	....	....	....	....	....	....	....
Banks..	8 673 ..	....	....	....	....	....	....	....	....
Other sectors..	8 674 ..	....	....	....	....	....	....	....	....
Money market instruments.....................................	8 680 ..	....	....	....	....	....	....	....	....
Monetary authorities..	8 681 ..	....	....	....	....	....	....	....	....
General government...	8 682 ..	....	....	....	....	....	....	....	....
Banks..	8 683 ..	....	....	....	....	....	....	....	....
Other sectors..	8 684 ..	....	....	....	....	....	....	....	....
Financial derivatives....................................	8 905 ..	....	....	....	....	....	....	....	....
Monetary authorities..	8 906 ..	....	....	....	....	....	....	....	....
General government...	8 907 ..	....	....	....	....	....	....	....	....
Banks...	8 908 ..	....	....	....	....	....	....	....	....
Other sectors..	8 909 ..	....	....	....	....	....	....	....	....
Other investment...	8 753 ..	....	....	....	**402.3**	....	....	....	....
Trade credits..	8 756 ..	....	....	....	....	....	....	....	....
General government...	8 757 ..	....	....	....	....	....	....	....	....
of which: Short-term..	8 759 ..	....	....	....	....	....	....	....	....
Other sectors..	8 760 ..	....	....	....	....	....	....	....	....
of which: Short-term..	8 762 ..	....	....	....	....	....	....	....	....
Loans..	8 764 ..	....	....	....	387.4	....	....	....	....
Monetary authorities..	8 765 ..	....	....	....	20.4	....	....	....	....
of which: Use of Fund credit and loans from the Fund....	8 766 ..	*13.4*	*15.5*	*20.5*	*20.4*	*21.2*	*18.7*	*18.0*	*16.1*
of which: Short-term..	8 768 ..	....	....	....	....	....	....	....	....
General government...	8 769 ..	....	....	....	233.6	....	....	....	....
of which: Short-term..	8 771 ..	....	....	....	....	....	....	....	....
Banks..	8 772 ..	....	....	....	3.6	....	....	....	....
of which: Short-term..	8 774 ..	....	....	....	*3.6*	....	....	....	....
Other sectors..	8 775 ..	....	....	....	129.7	....	....	....	....
of which: Short-term..	8 777 ..	....	....	....	....	....	....	....	....
Currency and deposits..	8 780 ..	....	....	....	14.9	....	....	....	....
Monetary authorities..	8 781 ..	....	....	....	1.0	....	....	....	....
General government...	8 782 ..	....	....	....	....	....	....	....	....
Banks..	8 783 ..	....	....	....	13.9	....	....	....	....
Other sectors..	8 784 ..	....	....	....	....	....	....	....	....
Other liabilities..	8 786 ..	....	....	....	....	....	....	....	....
Monetary authorities..	8 787 ..	....	....	....	....	....	....	....	....
of which: Short-term..	8 789 ..	....	....	....	....	....	....	....	....
General government...	8 790 ..	....	....	....	....	....	....	....	....
of which: Short-term..	8 792 ..	....	....	....	....	....	....	....	....
Banks..	8 793 ..	....	....	....	....	....	....	....	....
of which: Short-term..	8 795 ..	....	....	....	....	....	....	....	....
Other sectors..	8 796 ..	....	....	....	....	....	....	....	....
of which: Short-term..	8 798 ..	....	....	....	....	....	....	....	....
NET INTERNATIONAL INVESTMENT POSITION........	8 995 ..	....	....	....	**97.4**	....	....	....	....
Conversion rates: Djibouti francs per U.S. dollar (end of period)...	0 102 ..	**177.72**	**177.72**	**177.72**	**177.72**	**177.72**	**177.72**	**177.72**	**177.72**

Table 1. ANALYTIC PRESENTATION, 2000–2007

(Millions of U.S. dollars)

	Code	2000	2001	2002	2003	2004	2005	2006	2007
A. Current Account[1]	4 993 Z.	−70.22	−60.86	−51.20	−56.37	−61.69	−80.73	−54.39	−92.56
Goods: exports f.o.b.	2 100 ..	54.75	44.39	43.61	41.01	42.92	42.91	44.26	39.78
Goods: imports f.o.b.	3 100 ..	−130.39	−115.71	−102.36	−112.59	−127.76	−145.93	−146.87	−173.98
Balance on Goods	4 100 ..	*−75.64*	*−71.32*	*−58.74*	*−71.58*	*−84.84*	*−103.02*	*−102.61*	*−134.20*
Services: credit	2 200 ..	89.76	76.86	79.55	77.40	87.56	86.45	100.17	100.01
Services: debit	3 200 ..	−52.69	−50.04	−53.88	−44.75	−46.35	−50.19	−51.98	−59.05
Balance on Goods and Services	4 991 ..	*−38.57*	*−44.50*	*−33.07*	*−38.93*	*−43.63*	*−66.77*	*−54.42*	*−93.23*
Income: credit	2 300 ..	4.67	3.57	2.74	2.23	3.81	5.93	6.17	6.20
Income: debit	3 300 ..	−43.99	−28.68	−30.67	−29.24	−37.14	−34.91	−22.95	−22.80
Balance on Goods, Services, and Income	4 992 ..	*−77.89*	*−69.61*	*−61.00*	*−65.94*	*−76.97*	*−95.75*	*−71.21*	*−109.83*
Current transfers: credit	2 379 Z.	14.69	16.05	16.53	17.43	21.61	23.76	22.77	23.34
Current transfers: debit	3 379 ..	−7.02	−7.30	−6.73	−7.85	−6.33	−8.74	−5.95	−6.06
B. Capital Account[1]	4 994 Z.	**10.89**	**17.98**	**20.50**	**18.78**	**26.83**	**18.28**	**27.96**	**31.14**
Capital account: credit	2 994 Z.	12.41	18.10	20.62	18.91	26.96	18.43	28.11	31.29
Capital account: debit	3 994 ..	−1.52	−.13	−.12	−.13	−.13	−.14	−.15	−.16
Total, Groups A Plus B	4 981 ..	*−59.33*	*−42.89*	*−30.71*	*−37.58*	*−34.87*	*−62.44*	*−26.44*	*−61.42*
C. Financial Account[1]	4 995 W.	**55.41**	**30.31**	**18.08**	**17.63**	**11.05**	**56.19**	**27.26**	**47.68**
Direct investment abroad	4 505 ..	....	....	....	....	....	....	....	....
Direct investment in Dominica	4 555 Z.	17.60	17.12	20.11	31.47	26.17	19.24	26.78	46.42
Portfolio investment assets	4 602 ..	−.40	.01	.01	−.17	−2.30	−.46	−.73	1.85
Equity securities	4 610 ..	....	....	....	....	....	....	....	....
Debt securities	4 619 ..	....	....	....	....	....	....	....	....
Portfolio investment liabilities	4 652 Z.	14.03	−.24	12.10	3.64	−.17	4.24	.62	.62
Equity securities	4 660 ..	....	....	....	....	....	....	....	....
Debt securities	4 669 Z.	....	....	....	....	....	....	....	....
Financial derivatives	4 910 ..	....	....	....	....	....	....	....	....
Financial derivatives assets	4 900 ..	....	....	....	....	....	....	....	....
Financial derivatives liabilities	4 905 ..	....	....	....	....	....	....	....	....
Other investment assets	4 703 ..	39.44	33.19	21.43	32.81	29.80	49.43	40.02	46.89
Monetary authorities	4 701 ..	....	....	....	....	....	....	....	....
General government	4 704 ..	....	....	....	....	....	....	....	....
Banks	4 705 ..	....	....	....	....	....	....	....	....
Other sectors	4 728 ..	....	....	....	....	....	....	....	....
Other investment liabilities	4 753 W.	−15.26	−19.77	−35.57	−50.12	−42.45	−16.26	−39.44	−48.10
Monetary authorities	4 753 WA	....	....	....	....	....	....	....	....
General government	4 753 ZB	....	....	....	....	....	....	....	....
Banks	4 753 ZC	....	....	....	....	....	....	....	....
Other sectors	4 753 ZD	−15.26	−19.77	−32.86	−45.35	−41.55	−13.09	−37.59	−50.56
Total, Groups A Through C	4 983 ..	*−3.92*	*−12.58*	*−12.62*	*−19.95*	*−23.81*	*−6.25*	*.82*	*−13.74*
D. Net Errors and Omissions	4 998 ..	**−6.00**	**7.32**	**18.61**	**14.71**	**15.61**	**12.53**	**7.98**	**12.15**
Total, Groups A Through D	4 984 ..	*−9.93*	*−5.26*	*5.98*	*−5.24*	*−8.20*	*6.27*	*8.80*	*−1.59*
E. Reserves and Related Items	4 802 A.	**9.92**	**5.26**	**−5.98**	**5.24**	**8.20**	**−6.27**	**−8.80**	**1.59**
Reserve assets	4 802 ..	−.48	−3.46	−12.54	−2.72	5.82	−14.40	−13.42	1.16
Use of Fund credit and loans	4 766 ..	....	....	2.71	4.77	.90	3.17	1.85	−2.46
Exceptional financing	4 920 ..	10.40	8.72	3.85	3.19	1.48	4.96	2.76	2.89
Conversion rates: Eastern Caribbean dollars per U.S. dollar	0 101 ..	**2.7000**	**2.7000**	**2.7000**	**2.7000**	**2.7000**	**2.7000**	**2.7000**	**2.7000**

[1] Excludes components that have been classified in the categories of Group E.

Table 2. STANDARD PRESENTATION, 2000–2007

(Millions of U.S. dollars)

	Code	2000	2001	2002	2003	2004	2005	2006	2007
CURRENT ACCOUNT	4 993	−59.82	−52.14	−47.35	−53.18	−60.22	−76.08	−51.64	−89.67
A. GOODS	4 100	−75.64	−71.32	−58.74	−71.58	−84.84	−103.02	−102.61	−134.20
Credit	2 100	54.75	44.39	43.61	41.01	42.92	42.91	44.26	39.78
General merchandise: exports f.o.b.	2 110	53.58	43.41	42.66	40.00	41.39	41.43	41.47	37.28
Goods for processing: exports f.o.b.	2 150	....	....	....	....	....	....	....	....
Repairs on goods	2 160	.01	.01	.01	....	....	....	....	....
Goods procured in ports by carriers	2 170	1.16	.97	.94	1.01	1.53	1.48	2.79	2.50
Nonmonetary gold	2 180	....	....	....	....	....	....	....	....
Debit	3 100	−130.39	−115.71	−102.36	−112.59	−127.76	−145.93	−146.87	−173.98
General merchandise: imports f.o.b.	3 110	−130.39	−115.71	−102.36	−112.59	−127.76	−145.93	−146.87	−173.98
Goods for processing: imports f.o.b.	3 150	....	....	....	....	....	....	....	....
Repairs on goods	3 160	....	....	....	....	....	....	....	....
Goods procured in ports by carriers	3 170	....	....	....	....	....	....	....	....
Nonmonetary gold	3 180	....	....	....	....	....	....	....	....
B. SERVICES	4 200	37.07	26.82	25.68	32.66	41.21	36.25	48.19	40.96
Total credit	2 200	*89.76*	*76.86*	*79.55*	*77.40*	*87.56*	*86.45*	*100.17*	*100.01*
Total debit	3 200	*−52.69*	*−50.04*	*−53.88*	*−44.75*	*−46.35*	*−50.19*	*−51.98*	*−59.05*
Transportation services, credit	2 205	7.06	6.14	5.41	4.94	6.08	4.02	3.70	3.79
Passenger	2 850	....	....	....	....	....	....	....	....
Freight	2 851	....	....	....	....	....	....	....	....
Other	2 852	....	....	....	....	....	....	....	....
Sea transport, passenger	2 207	....	....	....	....	....	....	....	....
Sea transport, freight	2 208	....	....	....	....	....	....	....	....
Sea transport, other	2 209	....	....	....	....	....	....	....	....
Air transport, passenger	2 211	....	....	....	....	....	....	....	....
Air transport, freight	2 212	....	....	....	....	....	....	....	....
Air transport, other	2 213	....	....	....	....	....	....	....	....
Other transport, passenger	2 215	....	....	....	....	....	....	....	....
Other transport, freight	2 216	....	....	....	....	....	....	....	....
Other transport, other	2 217	....	....	....	....	....	....	....	....
Transportation services, debit	3 205	−21.77	−20.02	−18.46	−19.85	−21.94	−26.90	−24.88	−28.34
Passenger	3 850	....	....	....	....	....	....	....	....
Freight	3 851	....	....	....	....	....	....	....	....
Other	3 852	....	....	....	....	....	....	....	....
Sea transport, passenger	3 207	....	....	....	....	....	....	....	....
Sea transport, freight	3 208	....	....	....	....	....	....	....	....
Sea transport, other	3 209	....	....	....	....	....	....	....	....
Air transport, passenger	3 211	....	....	....	....	....	....	....	....
Air transport, freight	3 212	....	....	....	....	....	....	....	....
Air transport, other	3 213	....	....	....	....	....	....	....	....
Other transport, passenger	3 215	....	....	....	....	....	....	....	....
Other transport, freight	3 216	....	....	....	....	....	....	....	....
Other transport, other	3 217	....	....	....	....	....	....	....	....
Travel, credit	2 236	48.19	46.42	45.53	52.35	60.63	57.03	71.69	70.52
Business travel	2 237	....	....	....	....	....	....	....	....
Personal travel	2 240	....	....	....	....	....	....	....	....
Travel, debit	3 236	−8.93	−9.19	−9.11	−8.92	−9.17	−9.74	−9.79	−10.25
Business travel	3 237	....	....	....	....	....	....	....	....
Personal travel	3 240	....	....	....	....	....	....	....	....
Other services, credit	2 200 BA	34.51	24.29	28.62	20.11	20.84	25.40	24.79	25.70
Communications	2 245	18.84	9.49	14.90	7.15	8.25	8.12	9.14	9.37
Construction	2 249	....	....	....	....	....	....	....	....
Insurance	2 253	3.41	2.37	2.08	1.99	1.30	1.76	2.23	2.33
Financial	2 260	....	....	....	....	....	....	....	....
Computer and information	2 262	....	....	....	....	....	....	....	....
Royalties and licence fees	2 266	.03	....	....	....	....	....	....	....
Other business services	2 268	9.83	10.71	9.84	10.00	9.96	14.31	11.84	12.39
Personal, cultural, and recreational	2 287	....	....	....	....	....	....	....	....
Government, n.i.e.	2 291	2.40	1.72	1.80	.97	1.34	1.22	1.57	1.61
Other services, debit	3 200 BA	−21.99	−20.83	−26.31	−15.97	−15.23	−13.56	−17.32	−20.46
Communications	3 245	−5.89	−5.63	−12.18	−1.83	−1.61	−1.31	−3.11	−3.26
Construction	3 249	−.51	−1.70	−.90	−.86	−.33	−.48	−.42	−2.34
Insurance	3 253	−4.71	−4.43	−5.02	−4.43	−5.17	−5.74	−6.96	−7.75
Financial	3 260	....	....	....	....	....	....	....	....
Computer and information	3 262	....	....	....	....	....	−.02	−.02	−.02
Royalties and licence fees	3 266	−.12	−.11	−.12	−.06	−.08	−.11	−.24	−.24
Other business services	3 268	−5.70	−5.70	−4.06	−4.90	−6.47	−3.80	−4.92	−5.16
Personal, cultural, and recreational	3 287	....	....	....	....	....	....	....	....
Government, n.i.e.	3 291	−5.07	−3.26	−4.02	−3.88	−1.57	−2.10	−1.65	−1.70

Table 2 (Continued). STANDARD PRESENTATION, 2000–2007

(Millions of U.S. dollars)

	Code	2000	2001	2002	2003	2004	2005	2006	2007
C. INCOME	4 300	−39.32	−25.11	−27.93	−27.02	−33.33	−28.98	−16.79	−16.60
Total credit	2 300	*4.67*	*3.57*	*2.74*	*2.23*	*3.81*	*5.93*	*6.17*	*6.20*
Total debit	3 300	*−43.99*	*−28.68*	*−30.67*	*−29.24*	*−37.14*	*−34.91*	*−22.95*	*−22.80*
Compensation of employees, credit	2 310	.65	1.39	.57	.62	1.57	1.38	1.09	1.09
Compensation of employees, debit	3 310	....	....	....	....	....	....	....	....
Investment income, credit	2 320	4.03	2.18	2.17	1.61	2.24	4.55	5.08	5.11
Direct investment income	2 330	.41	.07	....	.04	....	....	....	....
Dividends and distributed branch profits	2 332	.41	.07	....	....	....	....	....	....
Reinvested earnings and undistributed branch profits	2 333	....	....	....	....	....	....	....	....
Income on debt (interest)	2 334	....	....	....	.04	....	....	....	....
Portfolio investment income	2 339	.55	.35	.48	.43	.06	.08	.70	.54
Income on equity	2 340	.55	.35	.48	.43	.06	.08	.70	.54
Income on bonds and notes	2 350	....	....	....	....	....	....	....	....
Income on money market instruments	2 360	....	....	....	....	....	....	....	....
Other investment income	2 370	3.06	1.76	1.69	1.14	2.17	4.46	4.38	4.58
Investment income, debit	3 320	−43.99	−28.68	−30.67	−29.24	−37.14	−34.91	−22.95	−22.80
Direct investment income	3 330	−33.04	−18.85	−18.22	−15.82	−21.79	−22.68	−9.16	−9.58
Dividends and distributed branch profits	3 332	−17.96	−6.92	−5.08	−2.85	−4.96	−6.04	−2.22	−2.32
Reinvested earnings and undistributed branch profits	3 333	−14.53	−11.65	−12.59	−12.63	−16.60	−16.40	−6.77	−7.09
Income on debt (interest)	3 334	−.55	−.28	−.55	−.34	−.22	−.24	−.17	−.17
Portfolio investment income	3 339	−3.73	−4.53	−4.53	−4.74	−4.60	−3.20	−3.27	−.37
Income on equity	3 340	−3.73	−4.53	−4.53	−4.74	−4.60	−3.20	−3.27	−.37
Income on bonds and notes	3 350	....	....	....	....	....	....	....	....
Income on money market instruments	3 360	....	....	....	....	....	....	....	....
Other investment income	3 370	−7.22	−5.30	−7.92	−8.68	−10.75	−9.02	−10.52	−12.85
D. CURRENT TRANSFERS	4 379	18.07	17.47	13.64	12.77	16.75	19.67	19.57	20.16
Credit	2 379	25.09	24.77	20.38	20.61	23.08	28.40	25.52	26.22
General government	2 380	10.40	8.72	3.85	3.19	1.48	4.64	2.76	2.89
Other sectors	2 390	14.69	16.05	16.53	17.43	21.61	23.76	22.77	23.34
Workers' remittances	2 391	12.87	12.95	13.89	14.18	18.46	20.39	20.98	21.51
Other current transfers	2 392	1.81	3.10	2.63	3.24	3.15	3.37	1.78	1.83
Debit	3 379	−7.02	−7.30	−6.73	−7.85	−6.33	−8.74	−5.95	−6.06
General government	3 380	−2.96	−2.80	−2.81	−2.81	−3.09	−4.38	−2.47	−2.59
Other sectors	3 390	−4.07	−4.51	−3.92	−5.04	−3.24	−4.36	−3.47	−3.47
Workers' remittances	3 391	−.01	−.01	−.01	−.01	−.01	−.01	−.01	−.01
Other current transfers	3 392	−4.06	−4.50	−3.92	−5.03	−3.24	−4.35	−3.47	−3.47
CAPITAL AND FINANCIAL ACCOUNT	4 996	65.82	44.82	28.75	38.47	44.60	63.55	43.66	77.52
CAPITAL ACCOUNT	4 994	10.89	17.98	20.50	18.78	26.83	18.28	27.96	31.14
Total credit	2 994	*12.41*	*18.10*	*20.62*	*18.91*	*26.96*	*18.43*	*28.11*	*31.29*
Total debit	3 994	*−1.52*	*−.13*	*−.12*	*−.13*	*−.13*	*−.14*	*−.15*	*−.16*
Capital transfers, credit	2 400	12.41	18.10	20.62	18.91	26.96	18.43	28.10	31.29
General government	2 401	9.62	15.30	17.67	15.90	23.84	15.23	24.80	27.91
Debt forgiveness	2 402	....	....	....	....	....	....	....	....
Other capital transfers	2 410	9.62	15.30	17.67	15.90	23.84	15.23	24.80	27.91
Other sectors	2 430	2.79	2.80	2.95	3.01	3.12	3.20	3.30	3.38
Migrants' transfers	2 431	2.79	2.80	2.95	3.01	3.12	3.20	3.30	3.38
Debt forgiveness	2 432	....	....	....	....	....	....	....	....
Other capital transfers	2 440	....	....	....	....	....	....	....	....
Capital transfers, debit	3 400	−.13	−.13	−.12	−.13	−.13	−.14	−.15	−.16
General government	3 401	....	....	....	....	....	....	....	....
Debt forgiveness	3 402	....	....	....	....	....	....	....	....
Other capital transfers	3 410	....	....	....	....	....	....	....	....
Other sectors	3 430	−.13	−.13	−.12	−.13	−.13	−.14	−.15	−.16
Migrants' transfers	3 431	−.13	−.13	−.12	−.13	−.13	−.14	−.15	−.16
Debt forgiveness	3 432	....	....	....	....	....	....	....	....
Other capital transfers	3 440	....	....	....	....	....	....	....	....
Nonproduced nonfinancial assets, credit	2 480	....	....	....	....	....	....	.01	....
Nonproduced nonfinancial assets, debit	3 480	−1.39	....	....	....	....	....	....	....

Table 2 (Continued). STANDARD PRESENTATION, 2000–2007

(Millions of U.S. dollars)

	Code	2000	2001	2002	2003	2004	2005	2006	2007
FINANCIAL ACCOUNT	4 995 ..	**54.93**	**26.85**	**8.25**	**19.69**	**17.77**	**45.27**	**15.70**	**46.39**
A. DIRECT INVESTMENT	4 500 ..	**17.60**	**17.12**	**20.11**	**31.47**	**26.17**	**19.24**	**26.78**	**46.42**
Direct investment abroad	4 505 ..	....	....	....	....	....	....	....	....
Equity capital	4 510 ..	....	....	....	....	....	....	....	....
Claims on affiliated enterprises	4 515 ..	....	....	....	....	....	....	....	....
Liabilities to affiliated enterprises	4 520 ..	....	....	....	....	....	....	....	....
Reinvested earnings	4 525 ..	....	....	....	....	....	....	....	....
Other capital	4 530 ..	....	....	....	....	....	....	....	....
Claims on affiliated enterprises	4 535 ..	....	....	....	....	....	....	....	....
Liabilities to affiliated enterprises	4 540 ..	....	....	....	....	....	....	....	....
Direct investment in Dominica	4 555 ..	**17.60**	**17.12**	**20.11**	**31.47**	**26.17**	**19.24**	**26.78**	**46.42**
Equity capital	4 560 ..	5.09	8.65	7.54	11.72	3.33	5.28	4.78	23.40
Claims on direct investors	4 565 ..	....	....	....	....	....	....	....	....
Liabilities to direct investors	4 570 ..	5.09	8.65	7.54	11.72	3.33	5.28	4.78	23.40
Reinvested earnings	4 575 ..	14.53	11.65	12.59	12.63	16.60	16.40	6.77	7.09
Other capital	4 580 ..	−2.02	−3.18	−.02	7.12	6.24	−2.45	15.23	15.94
Claims on direct investors	4 585 ..	....	....	....	....	....	....	....	....
Liabilities to direct investors	4 590 ..	−2.02	−3.18	−.02	7.12	6.24	−2.45	15.23	15.94
B. PORTFOLIO INVESTMENT	4 600 ..	**13.63**	**−.23**	**12.11**	**3.47**	**−2.47**	**3.78**	**−.10**	**2.48**
Assets	4 602 ..	**−.40**	**.01**	**.01**	**−.17**	**−2.30**	**−.46**	**−.73**	**1.85**
Equity securities	4 610 ..	....	....	....	....	....	....	....	....
Monetary authorities	4 611 ..	....	....	....	....	....	....	....	....
General government	4 612 ..	....	....	....	....	....	....	....	....
Banks	4 613 ..	....	....	....	....	....	....	....	....
Other sectors	4 614 ..	....	....	....	....	....	....	....	....
Debt securities	4 619 ..	....	....	....	....	....	....	....	....
Bonds and notes	4 620 ..	....	....	....	....	....	....	....	....
Monetary authorities	4 621 ..	....	....	....	....	....	....	....	....
General government	4 622 ..	....	....	....	....	....	....	....	....
Banks	4 623 ..	....	....	....	....	....	....	....	....
Other sectors	4 624 ..	....	....	....	....	....	....	....	....
Money market instruments	4 630 ..	....	....	....	....	....	....	....	....
Monetary authorities	4 631 ..	....	....	....	....	....	....	....	....
General government	4 632 ..	....	....	....	....	....	....	....	....
Banks	4 633 ..	....	....	....	....	....	....	....	....
Other sectors	4 634 ..	....	....	....	....	....	....	....	....
Liabilities	4 652 ..	**14.03**	**−.24**	**12.10**	**3.64**	**−.17**	**4.24**	**.62**	**.62**
Equity securities	4 660 ..	....	....	....	....	....	....	....	....
Banks	4 663 ..	....	....	....	....	....	....	....	....
Other sectors	4 664 ..	....	....	....	....	....	....	....	....
Debt securities	4 669 ..	....	....	....	....	....	....	....	....
Bonds and notes	4 670 ..	....	....	....	....	....	....	....	....
Monetary authorities	4 671 ..	....	....	....	....	....	....	....	....
General government	4 672 ..	....	....	....	....	....	....	....	....
Banks	4 673 ..	....	....	....	....	....	....	....	....
Other sectors	4 674 ..	....	....	....	....	....	....	....	....
Money market instruments	4 680 ..	....	....	....	....	....	....	....	....
Monetary authorities	4 681 ..	....	....	....	....	....	....	....	....
General government	4 682 ..	....	....	....	....	....	....	....	....
Banks	4 683 ..	....	....	....	....	....	....	....	....
Other sectors	4 684 ..	....	....	....	....	....	....	....	....
C. FINANCIAL DERIVATIVES	4 910 ..	....	....	....	....	....	....	....	....
Monetary authorities	4 911 ..	....	....	....	....	....	....	....	....
General government	4 912 ..	....	....	....	....	....	....	....	....
Banks	4 913 ..	....	....	....	....	....	....	....	....
Other sectors	4 914 ..	....	....	....	....	....	....	....	....
Assets	4 900 ..	....	....	....	....	....	....	....	....
Monetary authorities	4 901 ..	....	....	....	....	....	....	....	....
General government	4 902 ..	....	....	....	....	....	....	....	....
Banks	4 903 ..	....	....	....	....	....	....	....	....
Other sectors	4 904 ..	....	....	....	....	....	....	....	....
Liabilities	4 905 ..	....	....	....	....	....	....	....	....
Monetary authorities	4 906 ..	....	....	....	....	....	....	....	....
General government	4 907 ..	....	....	....	....	....	....	....	....
Banks	4 908 ..	....	....	....	....	....	....	....	....
Other sectors	4 909 ..	....	....	....	....	....	....	....	....

Table 2 (Concluded). STANDARD PRESENTATION, 2000–2007

(Millions of U.S. dollars)

	Code	2000	2001	2002	2003	2004	2005	2006	2007
D. OTHER INVESTMENT	4 700 ..	24.18	13.42	−11.43	−12.54	−11.75	36.65	2.44	−3.67
Assets	4 703 ..	39.44	33.19	21.43	32.81	29.80	49.43	40.02	46.89
Trade credits	4 706 ..	....	....	....	....	....	....	....	....
General government	4 707 ..	....	....	....	....	....	....	....	....
of which: Short-term	4 709 ..	....	....	....	....	....	....	....	....
Other sectors	4 710 ..	....	....	....	....	....	....	....	....
of which: Short-term	4 712 ..	....	....	....	....	....	....	....	....
Loans	4 714 ..	....	....	....	....	....	....	....	....
Monetary authorities	4 715 ..	....	....	....	....	....	....	....	....
of which: Short-term	4 718 ..	....	....	....	....	....	....	....	....
General government	4 719 ..	....	....	....	....	....	....	....	....
of which: Short-term	4 721 ..	....	....	....	....	....	....	....	....
Banks	4 722 ..	....	....	....	....	....	....	....	....
of which: Short-term	4 724 ..	....	....	....	....	....	....	....	....
Other sectors	4 725 ..	....	....	....	....	....	....	....	....
of which: Short-term	4 727 ..	....	....	....	....	....	....	....	....
Currency and deposits	4 730 ..	....	....	....	....	....	....	....	....
Monetary authorities	4 731 ..	....	....	....	....	....	....	....	....
General government	4 732 ..	....	....	....	....	....	....	....	....
Banks	4 733 ..	....	....	....	....	....	....	....	....
Other sectors	4 734 ..	....	....	....	....	....	....	....	....
Other assets	4 736 ..	....	....	....	....	....	....	....	....
Monetary authorities	4 737 ..	....	....	....	....	....	....	....	....
of which: Short-term	4 739 ..	....	....	....	....	....	....	....	....
General government	4 740 ..	....	....	....	....	....	....	....	....
of which: Short-term	4 742 ..	....	....	....	....	....	....	....	....
Banks	4 743 ..	....	....	....	....	....	....	....	....
of which: Short-term	4 745 ..	....	....	....	....	....	....	....	....
Other sectors	4 746 ..	....	....	....	....	....	....	....	....
of which: Short-term	4 748 ..	....	....	....	....	....	....	....	....
Liabilities	4 753 ..	−15.26	−19.77	−32.86	−45.35	−41.55	−12.78	−37.58	−50.56
Trade credits	4 756 ..	....	....	....	....	....	....	....	....
General government	4 757 ..	....	....	....	....	....	....	....	....
of which: Short-term	4 759 ..	....	....	....	....	....	....	....	....
Other sectors	4 760 ..	....	....	....	....	....	....	....	....
of which: Short-term	4 762 ..	....	....	....	....	....	....	....	....
Loans	4 764 ..	....	....	2.71	4.77	.90	3.17	1.85	−2.46
Monetary authorities	4 765 ..	....	....	2.71	4.77	.90	3.17	1.85	−2.46
of which: Use of Fund credit and loans from the Fund	4 766 ..	....	....	*2.71*	*4.77*	*.90*	*3.17*	*1.85*	*−2.46*
of which: Short-term	4 768 ..	....	....	....	....	....	....	....	....
General government	4 769 ..	....	....	....	....	....	....	....	....
of which: Short-term	4 771 ..	....	....	....	....	....	....	....	....
Banks	4 772 ..	....	....	....	....	....	....	....	....
of which: Short-term	4 774 ..	....	....	....	....	....	....	....	....
Other sectors	4 775 ..	....	....	....	....	....	....	....	....
of which: Short-term	4 777 ..	....	....	....	....	....	....	....	....
Currency and deposits	4 780 ..	....	....	....	....	....	....	....	....
Monetary authorities	4 781 ..	....	....	....	....	....	....	....	....
General government	4 782 ..	....	....	....	....	....	....	....	....
Banks	4 783 ..	....	....	....	....	....	....	....	....
Other sectors	4 784 ..	....	....	....	....	....	....	....	....
Other liabilities	4 786 ..	−15.26	−19.77	−32.86	−45.35	−41.55	−12.78	−37.58	−50.56
Monetary authorities	4 787 ..	....	....	....	....	....	....	....	....
of which: Short-term	4 789 ..	....	....	....	....	....	....	....	....
General government	4 790 ..	....	....	....	....	....	....	....	....
of which: Short-term	4 792 ..	....	....	....	....	....	....	....	....
Banks	4 793 ..	....	....	....	....	....	....	....	....
of which: Short-term	4 795 ..	....	....	....	....	....	....	....	....
Other sectors	4 796 ..	−15.26	−19.77	−32.86	−45.35	−41.55	−12.78	−37.58	−50.56
of which: Short-term	4 798 ..	*−15.26*	*−19.77*	*−32.86*	*−45.35*	*−41.55*	*−12.78*	*−37.58*	*−50.56*
E. RESERVE ASSETS	4 802 ..	**−.48**	**−3.46**	**−12.54**	**−2.72**	**5.82**	**−14.40**	**−13.42**	**1.16**
Monetary gold	4 812 ..	....	....	....	....	....	....	....	....
Special drawing rights	4 811 ..	.01	....	....	....	−.05	.04	....	−.03
Reserve position in the Fund	4 810 ..	....	....	....	....	....	....	....	....
Foreign exchange	4 803 ..	2.19	−1.85	−14.27	−2.24	5.46	−6.89	−13.87	2.57
Other claims	4 813 ..	−2.67	−1.61	1.73	−.48	.40	−7.54	.46	−1.38
NET ERRORS AND OMISSIONS	4 998 ..	**−6.00**	**7.32**	**18.61**	**14.71**	**15.61**	**12.53**	**7.98**	**12.15**

Table 1. ANALYTIC PRESENTATION, 2000–2007

(Millions of U.S. dollars)

	Code	2000	2001	2002	2003	2004	2005	2006	2007
A. Current Account¹	4 993 Z.	**−1,026.5**	**−740.8**	**−797.9**	**1,036.2**	**1,041.5**	**−473.0**	**−1,261.8**	**−2,230.8**
Goods: exports f.o.b.	2 100 ..	5,736.7	5,276.3	5,165.0	5,470.8	5,935.9	6,144.7	6,610.2	7,237.2
Goods: imports f.o.b.	3 100 ..	−9,478.5	−8,779.3	−8,837.7	−7,626.8	−7,888.0	−9,869.4	−12,173.9	−13,817.1
Balance on Goods	4 100 ..	*−3,741.8*	*−3,503.0*	*−3,672.7*	*−2,156.0*	*−1,952.1*	*−3,724.7*	*−5,563.7*	*−6,579.9*
Services: credit	2 200 ..	3,227.6	3,110.3	3,070.8	3,468.8	3,503.9	3,935.0	4,567.2	4,717.4
Services: debit	3 200 ..	−1,373.3	−1,283.9	−1,313.5	−1,219.4	−1,213.2	−1,478.2	−1,582.2	−1,749.8
Balance on Goods and Services	4 991 ..	*−1,887.5*	*−1,676.6*	*−1,915.4*	*93.4*	*338.6*	*−1,267.9*	*−2,578.7*	*−3,612.3*
Income: credit	2 300 ..	299.7	271.2	300.4	340.7	321.8	418.1	699.7	798.4
Income: debit	3 300 ..	−1,341.0	−1,362.9	−1,452.2	−1,733.8	−2,146.4	−2,320.4	−2,526.9	−2,826.5
Balance on Goods, Services, and Income	4 992 ..	*−2,928.8*	*−2,768.3*	*−3,067.2*	*−1,299.7*	*−1,486.0*	*−3,170.1*	*−4,405.9*	*−5,640.4*
Current transfers: credit	2 379 Z.	2,095.6	2,232.0	2,451.9	2,512.2	2,701.4	2,907.7	3,365.6	3,662.6
Current transfers: debit	3 379 ..	−193.3	−204.5	−182.6	−176.3	−173.9	−210.6	−221.5	−253.0
B. Capital Account¹	4 994 Z.	....	....	....	....	....	....	**254.2**	**201.9**
Capital account: credit	2 994 Z.	....	....	....	....	....	....	254.2	201.9
Capital account: debit	3 994 ..	....	....	....	....	....	....	....	....
Total, Groups A Plus B	4 981 ..	*−1,026.5*	*−740.8*	*−797.9*	*1,036.2*	*1,041.5*	*−473.0*	*−1,007.6*	*−2,028.9*
C. Financial Account¹	4 995 W.	**1,596.6**	**1,707.4**	**383.0**	**−15.9**	**117.6**	**1,635.9**	**1,536.3**	**2,352.6**
Direct investment abroad	4 505 ..	....	....	....	....	....	....	....	....
Direct investment in Dominican Republic	4 555 Z.	952.9	1,079.1	916.8	613.0	909.0	1,122.7	1,459.4	1,698.0
Portfolio investment assets	4 602 ..	268.4	123.5	−14.0	−19.7	−7.6	−82.2	−328.6	173.7
Equity securities	4 610 ..	270.6	128.2	−2.5	−6.5	−2.2	.9	17.8	....
Debt securities	4 619 ..	−2.2	−4.7	−11.5	−13.2	−5.4	−83.1	−346.4	173.7
Portfolio investment liabilities	4 652 Z.	−3.9	480.2	−11.7	563.5	−16.7	326.4	1,104.3	817.6
Equity securities	4 660 ..	....	....	....	....	....	....	....	....
Debt securities	4 669 Z.	−3.9	480.2	−11.7	563.5	−16.7	326.4	1,104.3	817.6
Financial derivatives	4 910 ..	....	....	....	....	....	....	....	....
Financial derivatives assets	4 900 ..	....	....	....	....	....	....	....	....
Financial derivatives liabilities	4 905 ..	....	....	....	....	....	....	....	....
Other investment assets	4 703 ..	−165.0	−155.5	−1,402.2	−1,159.1	−428.7	62.4	−1,465.0	−513.3
Monetary authorities	4 701 ..	−1.2	−.8	−3.9	1.8	−1.9	−44.5	−11.5	−5.4
General government	4 704 ..	....	....	....	....	....	....	....	....
Banks	4 705 ..	−64.4	−94.9	11.0	−136.6	−377.7	21.7	117.2	−345.0
Other sectors	4 728 ..	−99.4	−59.8	−1,409.3	−1,024.3	−49.1	85.2	−1,570.7	−162.9
Other investment liabilities	4 753 W.	544.2	180.1	894.1	−13.6	−338.4	206.7	766.3	176.6
Monetary authorities	4 753 WA	72.0	−22.3	91.0	−223.3	−38.6	−38.0	−30.2	−24.2
General government	4 753 ZB	119.1	119.3	252.6	445.8	305.8	94.4	366.6	291.2
Banks	4 753 ZC	234.2	−37.0	115.6	−100.5	−254.5	−72.1	23.3	4.5
Other sectors	4 753 ZD	118.9	120.1	434.9	−135.6	−351.1	222.4	406.6	−94.9
Total, Groups A Through C	4 983 ..	*570.1*	*966.6*	*−414.9*	*1,020.3*	*1,159.1*	*1,162.9*	*528.7*	*323.7*
D. Net Errors and Omissions	4 998 ..	**−618.5**	**−451.9**	**−139.3**	**−1,568.2**	**−981.2**	**−456.3**	**−338.5**	**329.7**
Total, Groups A Through D	4 984 ..	*−48.4*	*514.7*	*−554.2*	*−548.0*	*177.9*	*706.6*	*190.2*	*653.4*
E. Reserves and Related Items	4 802 A.	**48.4**	**−514.7**	**554.2**	**548.0**	**−177.9**	**−706.6**	**−190.2**	**−653.4**
Reserve assets	4 802 ..	69.9	−518.2	526.0	357.8	−540.2	−1,110.3	−314.7	−687.9
Use of Fund credit and loans	4 766 ..	....	....	−25.7	94.5	65.5	219.0	37.8	62.9
Exceptional financing	4 920 ..	−21.5	3.5	53.9	95.7	296.9	184.7	86.7	−28.3
Conversion rates: Dominican pesos per U.S. dollar	0 101 ..	**16.415**	**16.952**	**18.610**	**30.831**	**42.120**	**30.409**	**33.365**	**33.263**

¹ Excludes components that have been classified in the categories of Group E.

Table 2. STANDARD PRESENTATION, 2000–2007

(Millions of U.S. dollars)

	Code	2000	2001	2002	2003	2004	2005	2006	2007
CURRENT ACCOUNT	4 993	−1,026.5	−740.8	−797.9	1,036.2	1,041.5	−473.0	−1,261.8	−2,230.8
A. GOODS	4 100	−3,741.8	−3,503.0	−3,672.7	−2,156.0	−1,952.1	−3,724.7	−5,563.7	−6,579.9
Credit	2 100	5,736.7	5,276.3	5,165.0	5,470.8	5,935.9	6,144.7	6,610.2	7,237.2
General merchandise: exports f.o.b.	2 110	783.0	652.4	734.9	912.2	1,016.8	1,058.3	1,556.3	2,259.5
Goods for processing: exports f.o.b.	2 150	4,770.6	4,481.6	4,317.3	4,406.8	4,685.2	4,749.6	4,678.8	4,562.9
Repairs on goods	2 160	....	....	....	....	....	....	....	....
Goods procured in ports by carriers	2 170	183.1	142.3	112.8	151.8	233.9	336.8	375.1	414.8
Nonmonetary gold	2 180	....	....	....	....	....	....	....	....
Debit	3 100	−9,478.5	−8,779.3	−8,837.7	−7,626.8	−7,888.0	−9,869.4	−12,173.9	−13,817.1
General merchandise: imports f.o.b.	3 110	−6,416.0	−5,952.9	−6,237.3	−5,095.9	−5,368.1	−7,366.3	−9,558.8	−11,288.9
Goods for processing: imports f.o.b.	3 150	−3,062.5	−2,826.4	−2,600.4	−2,530.9	−2,519.9	−2,503.1	−2,615.1	−2,528.2
Repairs on goods	3 160	....	....	....	....	....	....	....	....
Goods procured in ports by carriers	3 170	....	....	....	....	....	....	....	....
Nonmonetary gold	3 180	....	....	....	....	....	....	....	....
B. SERVICES	4 200	1,854.3	1,826.4	1,757.3	2,249.4	2,290.7	2,456.8	2,985.0	2,967.6
Total credit	2 200	*3,227.6*	*3,110.3*	*3,070.8*	*3,468.8*	*3,503.9*	*3,935.0*	*4,567.2*	*4,717.4*
Total debit	3 200	*−1,373.3*	*−1,283.9*	*−1,313.5*	*−1,219.4*	*−1,213.2*	*−1,478.2*	*−1,582.2*	*−1,749.8*
Transportation services, credit	2 205	71.3	67.1	92.1	98.1	100.3	128.4	297.5	326.0
Passenger	2 850	....	....	....	....	....	....	....	....
Freight	2 851	*5.2*	*4.7*	*58.7*	*63.3*	*63.0*	*89.6*	*98.9*	*114.1*
Other	2 852	*66.1*	*62.4*	*33.4*	*34.8*	*37.3*	*38.8*	*198.6*	*211.9*
Sea transport, passenger	2 207	....	....	....	....	....	....	....	....
Sea transport, freight	2 208	....	....	54.6	59.8	59.7	85.1	94.0	108.8
Sea transport, other	2 209	51.1	50.6	....	....	....	....	....	....
Air transport, passenger	2 211	....	....	....	....	....	....	....	....
Air transport, freight	2 212	5.2	4.7	4.1	3.5	3.3	4.5	4.9	5.3
Air transport, other	2 213	4.0	3.8	3.5	3.6	3.8	3.9	4.1	4.3
Other transport, passenger	2 215	....	....	....	....	....	....	....	....
Other transport, freight	2 216	....	....	....	....	....	....	....	....
Other transport, other	2 217	11.0	8.0	29.9	31.2	33.5	34.9	194.5	207.6
Transportation services, debit	3 205	−828.0	−763.5	−764.2	−689.1	−650.3	−865.8	−938.6	−1,080.4
Passenger	3 850	*−130.8*	*−133.5*	*−134.1*	*−136.2*	*−137.5*	*−159.1*	*−161.7*	*−190.8*
Freight	3 851	*−694.6*	*−627.4*	*−627.6*	*−550.2*	*−509.8*	*−706.7*	*−776.9*	*−889.6*
Other	3 852	*−2.6*	*−2.6*	*−2.5*	*−2.7*	*−3.0*	....	....	....
Sea transport, passenger	3 207	....	....	....	....	....	....	....	....
Sea transport, freight	3 208	−647.2	−585.4	−586.1	−515.2	−476.3	−661.9	−726.8	−832.0
Sea transport, other	3 209	....	....	....	....	....	....	....	....
Air transport, passenger	3 211	−130.8	−133.5	−134.1	−136.2	−137.5	−159.1	−161.7	−190.8
Air transport, freight	3 212	−47.4	−42.0	−41.5	−35.0	−33.5	−44.8	−50.1	−57.6
Air transport, other	3 213	−2.6	−2.6	−2.5	−2.7	−3.0	....	....	....
Other transport, passenger	3 215	....	....	....	....	....	....	....	....
Other transport, freight	3 216	....	....	....	....	....	....	....	....
Other transport, other	3 217	....	....	....	....	....	....	....	....
Travel, credit	2 236	2,860.2	2,798.3	2,730.4	3,127.8	3,151.6	3,518.3	3,916.8	4,025.5
Business travel	2 237	17.4	19.5	20.2	20.6	18.0	21.3	22.4	23.4
Personal travel	2 240	2,842.8	2,778.8	2,710.2	3,107.2	3,133.6	3,497.0	3,894.4	4,002.1
Travel, debit	3 236	−309.0	−290.8	−295.3	−271.6	−309.8	−352.2	−333.0	−325.9
Business travel	3 237	....	....	....	....	....	....	....	....
Personal travel	3 240	−309.0	−290.8	−295.3	−271.6	−309.8	−352.2	−333.0	−325.9
Other services, credit	2 200 BA	296.1	244.9	248.3	242.9	252.0	288.3	352.9	365.9
Communications	2 245	139.2	98.7	102.5	113.5	118.2	117.9	157.3	162.9
Construction	2 249	....	....	....	....	....	....	....	....
Insurance	2 253	....	....	....	....	....	21.8	24.7	27.4
Financial	2 260	....	....	....	3.0	3.2	18.4	29.0	26.6
Computer and information	2 262	....	....	17.8	17.6	18.2	15.4	12.8	13.2
Royalties and licence fees	2 266	....	....	....	....	....	....	....	....
Other business services	2 268	71.8	59.4	39.5	41.1	43.1	44.7	58.2	64.0
Personal, cultural, and recreational	2 287	....	....	....	....	....	....	....	....
Government, n.i.e.	2 291	85.1	86.8	88.5	67.7	69.3	70.1	70.9	71.8
Other services, debit	3 200 BA	−236.3	−229.6	−254.0	−258.7	−253.1	−260.2	−310.6	−343.5
Communications	3 245	−50.2	−37.9	−30.6	−20.1	−23.7	−20.6	−28.6	−41.4
Construction	3 249	....	....	....	....	....	....	....	....
Insurance	3 253	−86.9	−93.9	−100.0	−89.7	−87.0	−101.9	−98.9	−108.4
Financial	3 260	−8.8	−13.1	−16.9	−38.2	−25.7	−18.1	−31.8	−25.6
Computer and information	3 262	....	....	−7.0	−6.5	−6.7	−7.6	−10.7	−11.6
Royalties and licence fees	3 266	−29.7	−22.0	−29.6	−30.1	−30.1	−30.8	−31.5	−31.9
Other business services	3 268	−27.1	−27.3	−27.2	−33.5	−34.3	−33.8	−37.4	−40.9
Personal, cultural, and recreational	3 287	....	....	....	....	....	....	....	....
Government, n.i.e.	3 291	−33.6	−35.4	−42.7	−40.6	−45.6	−47.4	−71.7	−83.7

Table 2 (Continued). STANDARD PRESENTATION, 2000–2007

(Millions of U.S. dollars)

	Code	2000	2001	2002	2003	2004	2005	2006	2007
C. INCOME	4 300 ..	**−1,041.3**	**−1,091.7**	**−1,151.8**	**−1,393.1**	**−1,824.6**	**−1,902.2**	**−1,827.2**	**−2,028.1**
Total credit	2 300 ..	*299.7*	*271.2*	*300.4*	*340.7*	*321.8*	*418.1*	*699.7*	*798.4*
Total debit	3 300 ..	*−1,341.0*	*−1,362.9*	*−1,452.2*	*−1,733.8*	*−2,146.4*	*−2,320.4*	*−2,526.9*	*−2,826.5*
Compensation of employees, credit	2 310 ..	**149.8**	**173.9**	**234.7**	**264.9**	**271.0**	**289.4**	**316.0**	**351.3**
Compensation of employees, debit	3 310 ..	**−19.3**	**−21.7**	**−22.5**	**−22.9**	**−23.9**	**−24.7**	**−26.6**	**−28.2**
Investment income, credit	2 320 ..	**149.9**	**97.3**	**65.7**	**75.8**	**50.8**	**128.7**	**383.7**	**447.1**
Direct investment income	2 330 ..	....	....	....	....	....	....	....	....
Dividends and distributed branch profits	2 332 ..	....	....	....	....	....	....	....	....
Reinvested earnings and undistributed branch profits	2 333 ..	....	....	....	....	....	....	....	....
Income on debt (interest)	2 334 ..	....	....	....	....	....	....	....	....
Portfolio investment income	2 339 ..	20.4	17.0	9.3	7.6	11.2	10.6	66.3	34.0
Income on equity	2 340 ..	....	....	....	....	....	....	....	....
Income on bonds and notes	2 350 ..	20.4	17.0	9.3	7.6	11.2	10.6	66.3	34.0
Income on money market instruments	2 360 ..	....	....	....	....	....	....	....	....
Other investment income	2 370 ..	129.5	80.3	56.4	68.2	39.6	118.1	317.4	413.1
Investment income, debit	3 320 ..	**−1,321.7**	**−1,341.2**	**−1,429.7**	**−1,710.9**	**−2,122.5**	**−2,295.7**	**−2,500.3**	**−2,798.3**
Direct investment income	3 330 ..	−1,068.3	−1,090.3	−1,153.4	−1,390.5	−1,651.8	−1,765.0	−1,938.5	−2,079.0
Dividends and distributed branch profits	3 332 ..	−793.6	−786.0	−775.6	−1,401.8	−1,118.7	−1,269.7	−1,217.4	−1,613.1
Reinvested earnings and undistributed branch profits	3 333 ..	−210.7	−221.0	−267.8	118.8	−506.0	−483.8	−698.3	−461.3
Income on debt (interest)	3 334 ..	−64.0	−83.3	−110.0	−107.5	−27.1	−11.5	−22.8	−4.6
Portfolio investment income	3 339 ..	−47.6	−33.5	−73.9	−85.2	−137.1	−154.6	−223.5	−358.6
Income on equity	3 340 ..	−10.0	−.8	−10.9	....	−5.0	−3.9	−1.1	−2.5
Income on bonds and notes	3 350 ..	−37.6	−32.7	−63.0	−85.2	−111.6	−118.0	−157.7	−222.7
Income on money market instruments	3 360 ..	....	....	....	....	−20.5	−32.7	−64.7	−133.4
Other investment income	3 370 ..	−205.8	−217.4	−202.4	−235.2	−333.6	−376.1	−338.3	−360.7
D. CURRENT TRANSFERS	4 379 ..	**1,902.3**	**2,027.5**	**2,269.3**	**2,335.9**	**2,527.5**	**2,697.1**	**3,144.1**	**3,409.6**
Credit	2 379 ..	**2,095.6**	**2,232.0**	**2,451.9**	**2,512.2**	**2,701.4**	**2,907.7**	**3,365.6**	**3,662.6**
General government	2 380 ..	115.5	116.2	147.9	125.5	140.6	176.5	232.5	284.5
Other sectors	2 390 ..	1,980.1	2,115.8	2,304.0	2,386.7	2,560.8	2,731.2	3,133.1	3,378.1
Workers' remittances	2 391 ..	1,689.0	1,807.9	1,959.6	2,060.5	2,230.2	2,429.8	2,737.8	3,032.7
Other current transfers	2 392 ..	291.1	307.9	344.4	326.2	330.6	301.4	395.3	345.4
Debit	3 379 ..	**−193.3**	**−204.5**	**−182.6**	**−176.3**	**−173.9**	**−210.6**	**−221.5**	**−253.0**
General government	3 380 ..	−2.8	−2.5	−2.7	−2.4	−2.5	−2.7	−2.5	−2.5
Other sectors	3 390 ..	−190.5	−202.0	−179.9	−173.9	−171.4	−207.9	−219.0	−250.5
Workers' remittances	3 391 ..	....	....	....	....	....	....	....	....
Other current transfers	3 392 ..	−190.5	−202.0	−179.9	−173.9	−171.4	−207.9	−219.0	−250.5
CAPITAL AND FINANCIAL ACCOUNT	4 996 ..	**1,645.0**	**1,192.7**	**937.2**	**532.1**	**−60.2**	**929.3**	**1,600.3**	**1,901.1**
CAPITAL ACCOUNT	4 994 ..	**1.7**	**4.2**	**7.3**	**6.0**	**4.3**	**....**	**290.1**	**212.8**
Total credit	2 994 ..	*1.7*	*4.2*	*7.3*	*6.0*	*4.3*	*....*	*290.1*	*212.8*
Total debit	3 994 ..	....	....	....	....	....	....	....	....
Capital transfers, credit	2 400 ..	**1.7**	**4.2**	**7.3**	**6.0**	**4.3**	**....**	**290.1**	**212.8**
General government	2 401 ..	1.7	4.2	7.3	6.0	4.3	....	42.3	11.6
Debt forgiveness	2 402 ..	1.7	4.2	7.3	6.0	4.3	....	35.9	10.9
Other capital transfers	2 410 ..	....	....	....	....	....	....	6.4	.7
Other sectors	2 430 ..	....	....	....	....	....	....	247.8	201.2
Migrants' transfers	2 431 ..	....	....	....	....	....	....	30.5	29.9
Debt forgiveness	2 432 ..	....	....	....	....	....	....	....	....
Other capital transfers	2 440 ..	....	....	....	....	....	....	217.3	171.3
Capital transfers, debit	3 400 ..	**....**	**....**	**....**	**....**	**....**	**....**	**....**	**....**
General government	3 401 ..	....	....	....	....	....	....	....	....
Debt forgiveness	3 402 ..	....	....	....	....	....	....	....	....
Other capital transfers	3 410 ..	....	....	....	....	....	....	....	....
Other sectors	3 430 ..	....	....	....	....	....	....	....	....
Migrants' transfers	3 431 ..	....	....	....	....	....	....	....	....
Debt forgiveness	3 432 ..	....	....	....	....	....	....	....	....
Other capital transfers	3 440 ..	....	....	....	....	....	....	....	....
Nonproduced nonfinancial assets, credit	2 480 ..	**....**	**....**	**....**	**....**	**....**	**....**	**....**	**....**
Nonproduced nonfinancial assets, debit	3 480 ..	**....**	**....**	**....**	**....**	**....**	**....**	**....**	**....**

Table 2 (Continued). STANDARD PRESENTATION, 2000–2007

(Millions of U.S. dollars)

	Code	2000	2001	2002	2003	2004	2005	2006	2007
FINANCIAL ACCOUNT..............................	4 995 ..	**1,643.3**	**1,188.5**	**929.9**	**526.1**	**−64.6**	**929.3**	**1,310.2**	**1,688.3**
A. DIRECT INVESTMENT..............................	4 500 ..	**952.9**	**1,079.1**	**916.8**	**613.0**	**909.0**	**1,122.7**	**1,459.4**	**1,698.0**
Direct investment abroad..............................	4 505 ..	....	....	....	....	....	....	....	....
Equity capital..............................	4 510 ..	....	....	....	....	....	....	....	....
Claims on affiliated enterprises..............................	4 515 ..	....	....	....	....	....	....	....	....
Liabilities to affiliated enterprises..............................	4 520 ..	....	....	....	....	....	....	....	....
Reinvested earnings..............................	4 525 ..	....	....	....	....	....	....	....	....
Other capital..............................	4 530 ..	....	....	....	....	....	....	....	....
Claims on affiliated enterprises..............................	4 535 ..	....	....	....	....	....	....	....	....
Liabilities to affiliated enterprises..............................	4 540 ..	....	....	....	....	....	....	....	....
Direct investment in Dominican Republic..........	4 555 ..	**952.9**	**1,079.1**	**916.8**	**613.0**	**909.0**	**1,122.7**	**1,459.4**	**1,698.0**
Equity capital..............................	4 560 ..	632.9	648.7	669.5	583.1	482.2	687.8	755.3	1,112.7
Claims on direct investors..............................	4 565 ..	−25.5	....	....	....	....	....	....	....
Liabilities to direct investors..............................	4 570 ..	658.4	648.7	669.5	583.1	482.2	687.8	755.3	1,112.7
Reinvested earnings..............................	4 575 ..	210.7	221.0	267.8	−118.8	506.0	483.8	698.3	461.3
Other capital..............................	4 580 ..	109.3	209.4	−20.5	148.7	−79.2	−48.9	5.8	124.0
Claims on direct investors..............................	4 585 ..	−10.6	−8.8	−9.2	−3.5	−25.4	4.3	.1	−2.6
Liabilities to direct investors..............................	4 590 ..	119.9	218.2	−11.3	152.2	−53.7	−53.2	5.7	126.6
B. PORTFOLIO INVESTMENT..............................	4 600 ..	**264.5**	**603.7**	**−25.7**	**543.8**	**−24.3**	**244.2**	**775.7**	**991.3**
Assets..............................	4 602 ..	**268.4**	**123.5**	**−14.0**	**−19.7**	**−7.6**	**−82.2**	**−328.6**	**173.7**
Equity securities..............................	4 610 ..	270.6	128.2	−2.5	−6.5	−2.2	.9	17.8	....
Monetary authorities..............................	4 611 ..	....	....	....	....	....	....	....	....
General government..............................	4 612 ..	....	....	....	....	....	....	....	....
Banks..............................	4 613 ..	7.3	−2.7	−2.5	−6.5	−2.2	.9	17.8	....
Other sectors..............................	4 614 ..	263.3	130.9						
Debt securities..............................	4 619 ..	−2.2	−4.7	−11.5	−13.2	−5.4	−83.1	−346.4	173.7
Bonds and notes..............................	4 620 ..	−2.2	−4.7	−11.5	−5.7	−6.1	−6.5	−7.1	−11.8
Monetary authorities..............................	4 621 ..	−2.2	−4.7	−5.1	−5.7	−6.1	−6.5	−7.1	−11.8
General government..............................	4 622 ..	....	....	....	....	....	....	....	....
Banks..............................	4 623 ..	....	....	....	−6.4	....	....	....	....
Other sectors..............................	4 624 ..	....	....	....	....	....	....	....	....
Money market instruments..............................	4 630 ..	....	....	....	−7.5	.7	−76.6	−339.3	185.5
Monetary authorities..............................	4 631 ..	....	....	....	....	....	....	....	....
General government..............................	4 632 ..	....	....	....	....	....	....	....	....
Banks..............................	4 633 ..	....	....	....	−7.5	.7	−76.6	−339.3	185.5
Other sectors..............................	4 634 ..	....	....	....	....	....	....	....	....
Liabilities..............................	4 652 ..	**−3.9**	**480.2**	**−11.7**	**563.5**	**−16.7**	**326.4**	**1,104.3**	**817.6**
Equity securities..............................	4 660 ..	....	....	....	....	....	....	....	....
Banks..............................	4 663 ..	....	....	....	....	....	....	....	....
Other sectors..............................	4 664 ..	....	....	....	....	....	....	....	....
Debt securities..............................	4 669 ..	−3.9	480.2	−11.7	563.5	−16.7	326.4	1,104.3	817.6
Bonds and notes..............................	4 670 ..	−3.9	480.2	−19.8	579.8	−19.8	29.6	737.8	328.6
Monetary authorities..............................	4 671 ..	−3.7	−19.0	−19.0	−19.0	−19.0	−19.0	−19.0	−19.0
General government..............................	4 672 ..	....	500.0	....	599.6	....	49.3	333.8	−105.4
Banks..............................	4 673 ..	−.1	−.1	−.1	−.1	−.1	−.1	−.1	
Other sectors..............................	4 674 ..	−.1	−.7	−.7	−.7	−.7	−.7	423.0	453.0
Money market instruments..............................	4 680 ..	....	....	8.1	−16.3	3.1	296.8	366.5	489.0
Monetary authorities..............................	4 681 ..	....	....	....	11.3	3.1	281.0	381.8	488.5
General government..............................	4 682 ..	....	....	....	....	....	....	....	....
Banks..............................	4 683 ..	....	....	8.1	−27.6	....	15.8	−15.3	.5
Other sectors..............................	4 684 ..	....	....	....	....	....	....	....	....
C. FINANCIAL DERIVATIVES..............................	4 910 ..	....	....	....	....	....	....	....	....
Monetary authorities..............................	4 911 ..	....	....	....	....	....	....	....	....
General government..............................	4 912 ..	....	....	....	....	....	....	....	....
Banks..............................	4 913 ..	....	....	....	....	....	....	....	....
Other sectors..............................	4 914 ..	....	....	....	....	....	....	....	....
Assets..............................	4 900 ..	....	....	....	....	....	....	....	....
Monetary authorities..............................	4 901 ..	....	....	....	....	....	....	....	....
General government..............................	4 902 ..	....	....	....	....	....	....	....	....
Banks..............................	4 903 ..	....	....	....	....	....	....	....	....
Other sectors..............................	4 904 ..	....	....	....	....	....	....	....	....
Liabilities..............................	4 905 ..	....	....	....	....	....	....	....	....
Monetary authorities..............................	4 906 ..	....	....	....	....	....	....	....	....
General government..............................	4 907 ..	....	....	....	....	....	....	....	....
Banks..............................	4 908 ..	....	....	....	....	....	....	....	....
Other sectors..............................	4 909 ..	....	....	....	....	....	....	....	....

Table 2 (Concluded). STANDARD PRESENTATION, 2000–2007

(Millions of U.S. dollars)

	Code	2000	2001	2002	2003	2004	2005	2006	2007
D. OTHER INVESTMENT	4 700	**356.0**	**23.9**	**−487.2**	**−988.5**	**−409.1**	**672.7**	**−610.1**	**−313.0**
Assets	4 703	**−165.0**	**−155.5**	**−1,402.2**	**−1,159.1**	**−428.7**	**62.4**	**−1,465.0**	**−513.3**
Trade credits	4 706	−10.7	−17.4	−5.7	23.8	....	....	....	....
General government	4 707	....	....	....	....	....	....	....	....
of which: Short-term	4 709	....	....	....	....	....	....	....	....
Other sectors	4 710	−10.7	−17.4	−5.7	23.8	....	....	....	....
of which: Short-term	4 712	−10.7	−17.4	−5.7	23.8				
Loans	4 714	....	....	....	....	30.3	2.9	3.0	....
Monetary authorities	4 715	....	....	....	....	....	....	....	....
of which: Short-term	4 718	....	....	....	....	....	....	....	....
General government	4 719	....	....	....	....	....	....	....	....
of which: Short-term	4 721	....	....	....	....	....	....	....	....
Banks	4 722	....	....	....	....	30.3	2.9	3.0	....
of which: Short-term	4 724	....	....	....	....	30.3	2.9	3.0	....
Other sectors	4 725	....	....	....	....	....	....	....	....
of which: Short-term	4 727	....	....	....	....	....	....	....	....
Currency and deposits	4 730	−154.6	−136.6	−1,390.5	−1,102.5	−562.6	242.5	−687.7	−217.8
Monetary authorities	4 731	....	....	....	−.2	−.3	−.7	−1.2	−1.2
General government	4 732	....	....	....	....	....	....	....	....
Banks	4 733	−65.9	−94.2	13.1	−61.8	−453.5	21.1	270.6	−222.5
Other sectors	4 734	−88.7	−42.4	−1,403.6	−1,040.5	−108.8	222.1	−957.1	5.9
Other assets	4 736	.3	−1.5	−6.0	−80.4	103.6	−183.0	−780.3	−295.5
Monetary authorities	4 737	−1.2	−.8	−3.9	2.0	−1.6	−43.8	−10.3	−4.2
of which: Short-term	4 739	....	....	....	2.4	−1.1	−43.2	−9.4	1.0
General government	4 740	....	....	....	....	....	....	....	....
of which: Short-term	4 742	....	....	....	....	....	....	....	....
Banks	4 743	1.5	−.7	−2.1	−74.8	45.5	−2.3	−156.4	−122.5
of which: Short-term	4 745	1.5	−.7	−2.1	−74.8	45.5	−2.3	−156.4	−122.5
Other sectors	4 746	....	....	....	−7.6	59.7	−136.9	−613.6	−168.8
of which: Short-term	4 748	....	....	....	−7.6	59.7	−136.9	−613.6	−168.8
Liabilities	4 753	**521.0**	**179.4**	**915.0**	**170.6**	**19.6**	**610.4**	**854.9**	**200.3**
Trade credits	4 756	26.6	−92.3	267.4	−141.0	27.3	190.1	130.2	185.3
General government	4 757	....	....	....	....	....	....	....	....
of which: Short-term	4 759	....	....	....	....	....	....	....	....
Other sectors	4 760	26.6	−92.3	267.4	−141.0	27.3	190.1	130.2	185.3
of which: Short-term	4 762	26.6	−92.3	267.4	−130.2	27.3	190.1	130.2	185.3
Loans	4 764	465.4	272.6	534.7	317.6	−304.7	681.6	714.1	81.0
Monetary authorities	4 765	33.7	−25.7	23.3	−61.5	33.2	191.3	15.4	38.1
of which: Use of Fund credit and loans from the Fund	4 766	....	....	−25.7	94.5	65.5	219.0	37.8	62.9
of which: Short-term	4 768	54.3	−3.8	42.2	−129.4	−4.9	−3.2	−.1	....
General government	4 769	119.1	119.3	252.6	445.8	305.8	510.6	444.3	323.2
of which: Short-term	4 771	....	1.1	....	9.6	4.7	−14.2	....	....
Banks	4 772	220.3	−33.4	91.3	−55.6	−250.4	−72.0	−6.4	13.1
of which: Short-term	4 774	191.3	−46.8	43.8	−58.8	−180.9	−21.6	−4.8	18.4
Other sectors	4 775	92.3	212.4	167.5	−11.1	−393.3	51.7	260.8	−293.4
of which: Short-term	4 777	35.6	−4.2	61.2	−107.9	−46.4	−10.2	271.6	−144.4
Currency and deposits	4 780	49.2	.5	63.2	−109.3	−7.0	−9.7	23.1	−9.2
Monetary authorities	4 781	38.3	3.4	42.0	−67.3	−6.3	−10.3	−5.4	.6
General government	4 782	....	....	....	....	....	....	....	....
Banks	4 783	10.9	−2.9	21.2	−42.0	−.7	.6	28.5	−9.8
Other sectors	4 784	....	....	....	....	....	....	....	....
Other liabilities	4 786	−20.2	−1.4	49.7	103.3	304.0	−251.6	−12.5	−56.8
Monetary authorities	4 787	−1.6	....	....	.1	1.1	1.3	−2.5	....
of which: Short-term	4 789	−1.6	....	....	.1	1.1	1.3	−2.5	....
General government	4 790	−17.3	−.5	44.8	59.7	58.7	−259.5	−25.5	−70.3
of which: Short-term	4 792	−17.3	−.5	44.8	59.7	58.7	−259.5	−25.5	−70.3
Banks	4 793	3.1	−.7	3.4	−3.0	−3.4	−.7	1.3	1.2
of which: Short-term	4 795	3.1	−.7	3.4	−3.0	−3.4	−.7	1.3	1.2
Other sectors	4 796	−4.4	−.2	1.5	46.5	247.6	7.3	14.2	12.3
of which: Short-term	4 798	−4.4	−.2	1.5	46.5	247.6	7.3	14.2	12.3
E. RESERVE ASSETS	4 802	**69.9**	**−518.2**	**526.0**	**357.8**	**−540.2**	**−1,110.3**	**−314.7**	**−687.9**
Monetary gold	4 812	.2	−.1	....	....	....	....	....	....
Special drawing rights	4 811	−.1	−.1	.2	.2	−1.3	.9	−23.7	−70.4
Reserve position in the Fund	4 810	....	....	....	....	....	....	....	....
Foreign exchange	4 803	69.8	−518.0	525.8	357.6	−538.9	−1,111.2	−291.0	−617.5
Other claims	4 813	....	....	....	....	....	....	....	....
NET ERRORS AND OMISSIONS	4 998	**−618.5**	**−451.9**	**−139.3**	**−1,568.2**	**−981.2**	**−456.3**	**−338.5**	**329.7**

Table 3. INTERNATIONAL INVESTMENT POSITION (End-period stocks), 2000–2007

(Millions of U.S. dollars)

	Code	2000	2001	2002	2003	2004	2005	2006	2007
ASSETS	8 995 C.	. . . .	. . . .	2,119.3	3,069.4	3,964.8	5,148.1	9,521.7	. . . .
Direct investment abroad	8 505 ..	. . . .	. . . .	. . . .	. . . .	. . . .	. . . .	. . . .	. . . .
Equity capital and reinvested earnings	8 506 ..	. . . .	. . . .	. . . .	. . . .	. . . .	. . . .	. . . .	. . . .
Claims on affiliated enterprises	8 507 ..	. . . .	. . . .	. . . .	. . . .	. . . .	. . . .	. . . .	. . . .
Liabilities to affiliated enterprises	8 508 ..	. . . .	. . . .	. . . .	. . . .	. . . .	. . . .	. . . .	. . . .
Other capital	8 530 ..	. . . .	. . . .	. . . .	. . . .	. . . .	. . . .	. . . .	. . . .
Claims on affiliated enterprises	8 535 ..	. . . .	. . . .	. . . .	. . . .	. . . .	. . . .	. . . .	. . . .
Liabilities to affiliated enterprises	8 540 ..	. . . .	. . . .	. . . .	. . . .	. . . .	. . . .	. . . .	. . . .
Portfolio investment	8 602 ..	. . . .	. . . .	95.2	114.7	122.3	204.6	533.2	. . . .
Equity securities	8 610 ..	. . . .	. . . .	11.6	18.0	20.2	19.3	1.5	. . . .
Monetary authorities	8 611 ..	. . . .	. . . .	. . . .	. . . .	. . . .	. . . .	. . . .	. . . .
General government	8 612 ..	. . . .	. . . .	. . . .	. . . .	. . . .	. . . .	. . . .	. . . .
Banks	8 613 ..	. . . .	. . . .	11.6	18.0	20.2	19.3	1.5	. . . .
Other sectors	8 614 ..	. . . .	. . . .	. . . .	. . . .	. . . .	. . . .	. . . .	. . . .
Debt securities	8 619 ..	. . . .	. . . .	83.6	96.7	102.1	185.3	531.7	. . . .
Bonds and notes	8 620 ..	. . . .	. . . .	83.6	78.3	84.4	91.0	98.1	. . . .
Monetary authorities	8 621 ..	. . . .	. . . .	72.7	78.3	84.4	91.0	98.1	. . . .
General government	8 622 ..	. . . .	. . . .	. . . .	. . . .	. . . .	. . . .	. . . .	. . . .
Banks	8 623 ..	. . . .	. . . .	10.9	. . . .	. . . .	. . . .	. . . .	. . . .
Other sectors	8 624 ..	. . . .	. . . .	. . . .	. . . .	. . . .	. . . .	. . . .	. . . .
Money market instruments	8 630 ..	. . . .	. . . .	. . . .	18.4	17.7	94.3	433.6	. . . .
Monetary authorities	8 631 ..	. . . .	. . . .	. . . .	. . . .	. . . .	. . . .	. . . .	. . . .
General government	8 632 ..	. . . .	. . . .	. . . .	. . . .	. . . .	. . . .	. . . .	. . . .
Banks	8 633 ..	. . . .	. . . .	. . . .	18.4	17.7	94.3	433.6	. . . .
Other sectors	8 634 ..	. . . .	. . . .	. . . .	. . . .	. . . .	. . . .	. . . .	. . . .
Financial derivatives	8 900 ..	. . . .	. . . .	. . . .	. . . .	. . . .	. . . .	. . . .	. . . .
Monetary authorities	8 901 ..	. . . .	. . . .	. . . .	. . . .	. . . .	. . . .	. . . .	. . . .
General government	8 902 ..	. . . .	. . . .	. . . .	. . . .	. . . .	. . . .	. . . .	. . . .
Banks	8 903 C.	. . . .	. . . .	. . . .	. . . .	. . . .	. . . .	. . . .	. . . .
Other sectors	8 904 ..	. . . .	. . . .	. . . .	. . . .	. . . .	. . . .	. . . .	. . . .
Other investment	8 703 ..	. . . .	. . . .	1,394.5	2,675.4	3,019.3	3,014.3	6,737.6	. . . .
Trade credits	8 706 ..	. . . .	. . . .	64.8	. . . .	. . . .	. . . .	. . . .	. . . .
General government	8 707 ..	. . . .	. . . .	. . . .	. . . .	. . . .	. . . .	. . . .	. . . .
of which: Short-term	8 709 ..	. . . .	. . . .	. . . .	. . . .	. . . .	. . . .	. . . .	. . . .
Other sectors	8 710 ..	. . . .	. . . .	64.8	. . . .	. . . .	. . . .	. . . .	. . . .
of which: Short-term	8 712 ..	. . . .	. . . .	64.8	. . . .	. . . .	. . . .	. . . .	. . . .
Loans	8 714 ..	. . . .	. . . .	. . . .	41.0	10.7	7.8	4.8	. . . .
Monetary authorities	8 715 ..	. . . .	. . . .	. . . .	. . . .	. . . .	. . . .	. . . .	. . . .
of which: Short-term	8 718 ..	. . . .	. . . .	. . . .	. . . .	. . . .	. . . .	. . . .	. . . .
General government	8 719 ..	. . . .	. . . .	. . . .	. . . .	. . . .	. . . .	. . . .	. . . .
of which: Short-term	8 721 ..	. . . .	. . . .	. . . .	. . . .	. . . .	. . . .	. . . .	. . . .
Banks	8 722 ..	. . . .	. . . .	. . . .	41.0	10.7	7.8	4.8	. . . .
of which: Short-term	8 724 ..	. . . .	. . . .	. . . .	41.0	10.7	7.8	4.8	. . . .
Other sectors	8 725 ..	. . . .	. . . .	. . . .	. . . .	. . . .	. . . .	. . . .	. . . .
of which: Short-term	8 727 ..	. . . .	. . . .	. . . .	. . . .	. . . .	. . . .	. . . .	. . . .
Currency and deposits	8 730 ..	. . . .	. . . .	1,174.3	2,352.6	2,850.7	2,592.7	5,560.0	. . . .
Monetary authorities	8 731 ..	. . . .	. . . .	22.0	22.2	22.5	23.2	24.4	. . . .
General government	8 732 ..	. . . .	. . . .	. . . .	. . . .	. . . .	. . . .	. . . .	. . . .
Banks	8 733 ..	. . . .	. . . .	443.8	505.6	959.1	938.0	667.4	. . . .
Other sectors	8 734 ..	. . . .	. . . .	708.5	1,824.8	1,869.1	1,631.5	4,868.2	. . . .
Other assets	8 736 ..	. . . .	. . . .	155.4	281.8	157.9	413.7	1,172.8	. . . .
Monetary authorities	8 737 ..	. . . .	. . . .	34.6	32.5	34.1	77.9	91.8	. . . .
of which: Short-term	8 739 ..	. . . .	. . . .	2.7	.6	1.7	44.9	58.0	. . . .
General government	8 740 ..	. . . .	. . . .	. . . .	. . . .	. . . .	. . . .	. . . .	. . . .
of which: Short-term	8 742 ..	. . . .	. . . .	. . . .	. . . .	. . . .	. . . .	. . . .	. . . .
Banks	8 743 ..	. . . .	. . . .	4.2	79.0	33.5	35.8	192.2	. . . .
of which: Short-term	8 745 ..	. . . .	. . . .	4.2	79.0	33.5	35.8	192.2	. . . .
Other sectors	8 746 ..	. . . .	. . . .	116.6	170.3	90.3	300.0	888.8	. . . .
of which: Short-term	8 748 ..	. . . .	. . . .	116.6	170.3	90.3	300.0	888.8	. . . .
Reserve assets	8 802 ..	. . . .	. . . .	629.6	279.3	823.2	1,929.3	2,250.9	. . . .
Monetary gold	8 812 ..	. . . .	. . . .	6.1	7.6	8.0	9.4	11.6	. . . .
Special drawing rights	8 811 ..	.4	.4	.3	.1	1.6	.6	24.5	. . . .
Reserve position in the Fund	8 810 ..	. . . .	. . . .	. . . .	. . . .	. . . .	. . . .	. . . .	98.6
Foreign exchange	8 803 ..	. . . .	. . . .	623.2	271.6	813.6	1,919.3	2,214.8	. . . .
Other claims	8 813 ..	. . . .	. . . .	. . . .	. . . .	. . . .	. . . .	. . . .	. . . .

Table 3 (Concluded). INTERNATIONAL INVESTMENT POSITION (End-period stocks), 2000–2007

(Millions of U.S. dollars)

	Code	2000	2001	2002	2003	2004	2005	2006	2007
LIABILITIES	8 995 D.	....	....	**10,917.2**	**11,612.1**	**12,348.9**	**14,562.0**	**17,919.6**	....
Direct investment in Dominican Republic	8 555 ..	....	....	**3,668.7**	**3,598.4**	**3,955.7**	**5,275.9**	**6,570.7**	....
Equity capital and reinvested earnings	8 556 ..	....	....	3,139.1	3,127.9	3,597.3	4,923.0	6,192.9	....
Claims on direct investors	8 557 ..	....	....	....	....	....	....	....	....
Liabilities to direct investors	8 558 ..	....	....	3,139.1	3,127.9	3,597.3	4,923.0	6,192.9	....
Other capital	8 580 ..	....	....	529.6	470.5	358.5	352.9	377.8	....
Claims on direct investors	8 585 ..	....	....	−106.4	−155.1	−119.2	−43.7	−14.8	....
Liabilities to direct investors	8 590 ..	....	....	636.0	625.6	477.7	396.7	392.7	....
Portfolio investment	8 652 ..	....	....	**1,031.2**	**1,401.9**	**1,564.4**	**1,980.5**	**3,154.7**	....
Equity securities	8 660 ..	....	....	....	....	....	....	....	....
Banks	8 663 ..	....	....	....	....	....	....	....	....
Other sectors	8 664 ..	....	....	....	....	....	....	....	....
Debt securities	8 669 ..	....	....	1,031.2	1,401.9	1,564.4	1,980.5	3,154.7	....
Bonds and notes	8 670 ..	....	....	1,003.4	1,319.6	1,392.2	1,562.6	2,364.8	....
Monetary authorities	8 671 ..	....	....	450.6	431.1	412.5	394.4	375.6	....
General government	8 672 ..	....	....	534.5	871.0	963.0	1,152.2	1,550.3	....
Banks	8 673 ..	....	....	1.2	1.1	1.1	1.0	1.0	....
Other sectors	8 674 ..	....	....	17.1	16.4	15.7	15.0	438.0	....
Money market instruments	8 680 ..	....	....	27.8	82.3	172.2	417.9	789.9	....
Monetary authorities	8 681 ..	....	....	....	82.1	172.2	402.1	789.4	....
General government	8 682 ..	....	....	....	....	....	....	....	....
Banks	8 683 ..	....	....	27.8	.2	....	15.8	.5	....
Other sectors	8 684 ..	....	....	....	....	....	....	....	....
Financial derivatives	8 905 ..	....	....	....	....	....	....	....	....
Monetary authorities	8 906 ..	....	....	....	....	....	....	....	....
General government	8 907 ..	....	....	....	....	....	....	....	....
Banks	8 908 ..	....	....	....	....	....	....	....	....
Other sectors	8 909 ..	....	....	....	....	....	....	....	....
Other investment	8 753 ..	....	....	**6,217.3**	**6,611.8**	**6,828.7**	**7,305.6**	**8,194.1**	....
Trade credits	8 756 ..	....	....	519.3	199.9	227.3	417.3	547.5	....
General government	8 757 ..	....	....	....	....	....	....	....	....
of which: Short-term	8 759 ..	....	....	....	....	....	....	....	....
Other sectors	8 760 ..	....	....	519.3	199.9	227.3	417.3	547.5	....
of which: Short-term	8 762 ..	....	....	*462.5*	*199.9*	*227.3*	*417.3*	*547.5*	....
Loans	8 764 ..	....	....	5,409.4	6,083.7	5,959.6	6,514.4	7,262.7	....
Monetary authorities	8 765 ..	....	....	372.1	329.2	374.8	536.8	570.2	....
of which: Use of Fund credit and loans from the Fund	8 766 ..	*51.7*	*49.9*	*27.0*	*130.1*	*204.0*	*400.5*	*459.4*	*547.6*
of which: Short-term	8 768 ..	....	....	*139.4*	*10.0*	*4.6*	*1.5*	*1.5*	....
General government	8 769 ..	....	....	3,064.3	3,624.7	3,935.1	4,353.5	4,829.7	....
of which: Short-term	8 771 ..	....	....	....	*9.6*	*15.4*	*6.8*	*6.8*	....
Banks	8 772 ..	....	....	474.3	481.9	231.8	162.6	156.2	....
of which: Short-term	8 774 ..	....	....	*191.4*	*289.4*	*111.7*	*90.9*	*86.1*	....
Other sectors	8 775 ..	....	....	1,498.7	1,647.9	1,417.9	1,461.5	1,706.6	....
of which: Short-term	8 777 ..	....	....	*222.7*	*81.3*	*20.7*	*10.5*	*282.1*	....
Currency and deposits	8 780 ..	....	....	136.1	26.8	19.8	10.1	33.2	....
Monetary authorities	8 781 ..	....	....	92.9	25.6	19.3	9.0	3.6	....
General government	8 782 ..	....	....	....	....	....	....	....	....
Banks	8 783 ..	....	....	43.2	1.2	.5	1.1	29.6	....
Other sectors	8 784 ..	....	....	....	....	....	....	....	....
Other liabilities	8 786 ..	....	....	152.5	301.4	622.1	363.8	350.7	....
Monetary authorities	8 787 ..	....	....	.3	.4	1.2	2.4	−.1	....
of which: Short-term	8 789 ..	....	....	*.3*	*.4*	*1.2*	*2.4*	*−.1*	....
General government	8 790 ..	....	....	113.6	173.5	234.0	−25.5	−51.0	....
of which: Short-term	8 792 ..	....	....	*113.6*	*173.5*	*234.0*	*−25.5*	*−51.0*	....
Banks	8 793 ..	....	....	11.2	8.2	4.8	4.1	4.1	....
of which: Short-term	8 795 ..	....	....	*5.2*	*2.9*	*1.9*	*1.8*	*1.5*	....
Other sectors	8 796 ..	....	....	27.4	119.3	382.1	382.8	397.7	....
of which: Short-term	8 798 ..	....	....	*27.4*	*119.3*	*382.1*	*382.8*	*397.7*	....
NET INTERNATIONAL INVESTMENT POSITION	8 995 ..	....	....	**−8,797.9**	**−8,542.7**	**−8,384.1**	**−9,413.8**	**−8,397.9**	....
Conversion rates: Dominican pesos per U.S. dollar (end of period)	0 102 ..	**16.674**	**17.149**	**21.194**	**37.250**	**31.109**	**34.879**	**33.797**	**34.342**

Table 1. ANALYTIC PRESENTATION, 2000–2007

(Millions of U.S. dollars)

	Code	2000	2001	2002	2003	2004	2005	2006	2007
A. Current Account[1]............................	4 993 Z.	**−468.31**	**−510.43**	**−574.02**	**−686.95**	**−523.87**	**−814.96**	**−1,246.36**	**−1,579.36**
Goods: exports f.o.b..........................	2 100 ..	351.70	309.19	298.60	307.05	342.77	370.03	359.87	394.96
Goods: imports f.o.b...........................	3 100 ..	−1,425.52	−1,306.26	−1,278.05	−1,492.62	−1,575.60	−1,851.47	−2,192.00	−2,507.08
Balance on Goods..............................	4 100 ..	*−1,073.82*	*−997.07*	*−979.45*	*−1,185.57*	*−1,232.83*	*−1,481.44*	*−1,832.13*	*−2,112.12*
Services: credit...................................	2 200 ..	1,288.36	1,200.78	1,161.66	1,272.93	1,461.94	1,510.06	1,524.67	1,586.99
Services: debit....................................	3 200 ..	−627.12	−626.84	−635.81	−661.88	−699.63	−799.63	−886.32	−999.72
Balance on Goods and Services............	4 991 ..	*−412.58*	*−423.14*	*−453.60*	*−574.52*	*−470.52*	*−771.02*	*−1,193.78*	*−1,524.85*
Income: credit....................................	2 300 ..	43.07	38.38	29.73	31.50	48.27	75.64	100.42	104.30
Income: debit.....................................	3 300 ..	−266.42	−235.93	−248.16	−273.08	−321.71	−307.68	−316.86	−317.36
Balance on Goods, Services, and Income..........	4 992 ..	*−635.93*	*−620.68*	*−672.02*	*−816.09*	*−743.96*	*−1,003.05*	*−1,410.21*	*−1,737.91*
Current transfers: credit......................	2 379 Z.	230.95	188.44	185.67	218.80	302.86	273.81	263.65	268.76
Current transfers: debit.......................	3 379 ..	−63.32	−78.18	−87.67	−89.66	−82.78	−85.71	−99.80	−110.21
B. Capital Account[1]............................	4 994 Z.	**122.31**	**134.07**	**131.94**	**131.18**	**135.76**	**337.66**	**181.06**	**276.70**
Capital account: credit........................	2 994 Z.	133.93	141.70	140.08	139.45	144.26	346.41	190.13	286.70
Capital account: debit.........................	3 994 ..	−11.62	−7.62	−8.14	−8.27	−8.50	−8.74	−9.06	−10.00
Total, Groups A Plus B.......................	4 981 ..	*−346.00*	*−376.36*	*−442.09*	*−555.77*	*−388.12*	*−477.29*	*−1,065.29*	*−1,302.66*
C. Financial Account[1].........................	4 995 W.	**414.75**	**403.37**	**471.00**	**480.61**	**606.64**	**393.10**	**983.84**	**1,319.33**
Direct investment abroad....................	4 505 ..	....	−.13	....	....	....	....	....	....
Direct investment in Eastern Caribbean Currency Union......	4 555 Z.	327.83	372.54	340.10	555.64	448.97	632.38	1,105.95	1,291.40
Portfolio investment assets.................	4 602 ..	−1.67	−5.68	−26.53	−1.20	−12.05	−3.17	−5.03	−10.45
Equity securities..............................	4 610 ..	....	....	....	....	....	....	....	....
Debt securities................................	4 619 ..	....	....	....	....	....	....	....	....
Portfolio investment liabilities.............	4 652 Z.	72.47	61.14	192.18	152.15	84.55	34.82	26.91	.84
Equity securities..............................	4 660 Z.	....	....	....	....	....	....	....	....
Debt securities................................	4 669 Z.	....	....	....	....	....	....	....	....
Financial derivatives...........................	4 910 ..	....	....	....	....	....	....	....	....
Financial derivatives assets..............	4 900 ..	....	....	....	....	....	....	....	....
Financial derivatives liabilities..........	4 905 ..	....	....	....	....	....	....	....	....
Other investment assets.....................	4 703 ..	213.66	225.01	224.73	296.29	319.94	477.15	229.51	448.02
Monetary authorities.......................	4 701 ..	....	....	....	....	....	....	....	....
General government........................	4 704 ..	....	....	....	....	....	....	....	....
Banks..	4 705 ..	....	....	....	....	....	....	....	....
Other sectors..................................	4 728 ..	....	....	....	....	....	....	....	....
Other investment liabilities................	4 753 W.	−197.54	−249.52	−259.47	−522.26	−234.77	−748.08	−373.50	−410.48
Monetary authorities.......................	4 753 WA	....	....	....	....	....	....	....	....
General government........................	4 753 ZB	....	....	....	....	....	....	....	....
Banks..	4 753 ZC	....	....	....	....	....	....	....	....
Other sectors..................................	4 753 ZD	....	....	....	....	....	....	....	....
Total, Groups A Through C.................	4 983 ..	*68.75*	*27.01*	*28.92*	*−75.16*	*218.52*	*−84.20*	*−81.45*	*16.67*
D. Net Errors and Omissions................	4 998 ..	**−47.95**	**39.62**	**30.09**	**113.39**	**−114.22**	**59.62**	**170.91**	**34.43**
Total, Groups A Through D.................	4 984 ..	*20.80*	*66.64*	*59.01*	*38.24*	*104.31*	*−24.57*	*89.45*	*51.10*
E. Reserves and Related Items............	4 802 A.	**−20.80**	**−66.63**	**−59.01**	**−38.24**	**−104.31**	**24.57**	**−89.45**	**−51.10**
Reserve assets....................................	4 802 ..	−20.80	−66.63	−60.67	−45.82	−109.63	21.39	−91.95	−46.40
Use of Fund credit and loans...............	4 766 ..	....	....	1.66	7.58	5.33	3.17	2.50	−4.70
Exceptional financing..........................	4 920 ..	....	....	....	....	....	....	....	....
Conversion rates: Eastern Caribbean dollars per U.S. dollar...................	0 101 ..	**2.7000**	**2.7000**	**2.7000**	**2.7000**	**2.7000**	**2.7000**	**2.7000**	**2.7000**

[1] Excludes components that have been classified in the categories of Group E.

Table 2. STANDARD PRESENTATION, 2000–2007

(Millions of U.S. dollars)

	Code	2000	2001	2002	2003	2004	2005	2006	2007
CURRENT ACCOUNT	4 993 ..	**−468.31**	**−510.43**	**−574.02**	**−686.95**	**−523.87**	**−814.96**	**−1,246.36**	**−1,579.36**
A. GOODS	4 100 ..	**−1,073.82**	**−997.07**	**−979.45**	**−1,185.57**	**−1,232.83**	**−1,481.44**	**−1,832.13**	**−2,112.12**
Credit	2 100 ..	**351.70**	**309.19**	**298.60**	**307.05**	**342.77**	**370.03**	**359.87**	**394.96**
General merchandise: exports f.o.b.	2 110 ..	304.25	266.14	261.97	261.10	275.86	282.68	266.37	290.66
Goods for processing: exports f.o.b.	2 150 ..	....	....	....	....	....	....	....	....
Repairs on goods	2 160 ..	..	.04	.07	.05	.03	.14	.15	.14	.13
Goods procured in ports by carriers	2 170 ..	47.40	42.98	36.57	45.91	66.77	87.20	93.36	104.18
Nonmonetary gold	2 180 ..	....	....	....	....	....	....	....	....
Debit	3 100 ..	**−1,425.52**	**−1,306.26**	**−1,278.05**	**−1,492.62**	**−1,575.60**	**−1,851.47**	**−2,192.00**	**−2,507.08**
General merchandise: imports f.o.b.	3 110 ..	−1,420.39	−1,297.82	−1,270.04	−1,484.03	−1,566.12	−1,839.71	−2,179.37	−2,492.97
Goods for processing: imports f.o.b.	3 150 ..	....	....	....	....	....	....	....	....
Repairs on goods	3 160 ..	....	....	....	....	....	....	....	....
Goods procured in ports by carriers	3 170 ..	−5.13	−8.44	−8.01	−8.59	−9.48	−11.76	−12.63	−14.11
Nonmonetary gold	3 180 ..	....	....	....	....	....	....	....	....
B. SERVICES	4 200 ..	**661.24**	**573.94**	**525.85**	**611.05**	**762.31**	**710.42**	**638.36**	**587.27**
Total credit	2 200 ..	*1,288.36*	*1,200.78*	*1,161.66*	*1,272.93*	*1,461.94*	*1,510.06*	*1,524.67*	*1,586.99*
Total debit	3 200 ..	*−627.12*	*−626.84*	*−635.81*	*−661.88*	*−699.63*	*−799.63*	*−886.32*	*−999.72*
Transportation services, credit	2 205 ..	**115.80**	**124.88**	**125.56**	**123.01**	**134.25**	**146.55**	**150.28**	**156.50**
Passenger	2 850 ..	....	....	....	....	....	....	....	....
Freight	2 851 ..	....	....	....	....	....	....	....	....
Other	2 852 ..	....	....	....	....	....	....	....	....
Sea transport, passenger	2 207 ..	....	....	....	....	....	....	....	....
Sea transport, freight	2 208 ..	....	....	....	....	....	....	....	....
Sea transport, other	2 209 ..	....	....	....	....	....	....	....	....
Air transport, passenger	2 211 ..	....	....	....	....	....	....	....	....
Air transport, freight	2 212 ..	....	....	....	....	....	....	....	....
Air transport, other	2 213 ..	....	....	....	....	....	....	....	....
Other transport, passenger	2 215 ..	....	....	....	....	....	....	....	....
Other transport, freight	2 216 ..	....	....	....	....	....	....	....	....
Other transport, other	2 217 ..	....	....	....	....	....	....	....	....
Transportation services, debit	3 205 ..	**−240.17**	**−234.33**	**−226.95**	**−261.63**	**−275.15**	**−320.07**	**−354.19**	**−400.47**
Passenger	3 850 ..	....	....	....	....	....	....	....	....
Freight	3 851 ..	....	....	....	....	....	....	....	....
Other	3 852 ..	....	....	....	....	....	....	....	....
Sea transport, passenger	3 207 ..	....	....	....	....	....	....	....	....
Sea transport, freight	3 208 ..	....	....	....	....	....	....	....	....
Sea transport, other	3 209 ..	....	....	....	....	....	....	....	....
Air transport, passenger	3 211 ..	....	....	....	....	....	....	....	....
Air transport, freight	3 212 ..	....	....	....	....	....	....	....	....
Air transport, other	3 213 ..	....	....	....	....	....	....	....	....
Other transport, passenger	3 215 ..	....	....	....	....	....	....	....	....
Other transport, freight	3 216 ..	....	....	....	....	....	....	....	....
Other transport, other	3 217 ..	....	....	....	....	....	....	....	....
Travel, credit	2 236 ..	**917.78**	**855.97**	**834.50**	**976.28**	**1,083.72**	**1,113.94**	**1,127.04**	**1,166.17**
Business travel	2 237 ..	....	....	....	....	....	....	....	....
Personal travel	2 240 ..	....	....	....	....	....	....	....	....
Travel, debit	3 236 ..	**−109.83**	**−110.26**	**−111.67**	**−119.45**	**−127.13**	**−137.02**	**−154.64**	**−162.52**
Business travel	3 237 ..	....	....	....	....	....	....	....	....
Personal travel	3 240 ..	....	....	....	....	....	....	....	....
Other services, credit	2 200 BA ..	**254.78**	**219.93**	**201.60**	**173.64**	**243.98**	**249.57**	**247.35**	**264.32**
Communications	2 245 ..	99.01	75.80	71.31	50.45	54.21	58.00	54.39	57.33
Construction	2 249 ..	1.56	1.62	1.85	.06	.25	.38	.19	.20
Insurance	2 253 ..	31.99	27.35	25.16	21.07	69.53	43.16	30.42	33.05
Financial	2 260 ..	....	....	....	....	....	....	....	....
Computer and information	2 262 ..	5.00	3.50	2.43	2.43	2.43	3.33	....	....
Royalties and licence fees	2 266 ..	.03	....	....	.11	....	....	....	....
Other business services	2 268 ..	90.73	88.93	81.85	82.93	99.35	123.53	135.95	146.73
Personal, cultural, and recreational	2 287 ..	....	....	....	....	....	....	....	....
Government, n.i.e.	2 291 ..	26.48	22.73	19.00	16.59	18.21	21.16	26.40	27.00
Other services, debit	3 200 BA ..	**−277.12**	**−282.25**	**−297.19**	**−280.81**	**−297.35**	**−342.54**	**−377.49**	**−436.72**
Communications	3 245 ..	−57.06	−39.06	−43.19	−21.52	−24.13	−31.36	−24.12	−25.19
Construction	3 249 ..	−9.88	−11.36	−14.19	−18.72	−15.36	−32.65	−60.70	−90.14
Insurance	3 253 ..	−54.13	−65.28	−70.82	−74.67	−76.55	−91.03	−106.67	−119.33
Financial	3 260 ..	....	....	....	....	....	....	....	....
Computer and information	3 262 ..	....	−.36	−.41	−.75	−.53	−.13	−.26	−.07
Royalties and licence fees	3 266 ..	−3.98	−4.10	−4.72	−5.41	−6.28	−6.86	−8.32	−8.69
Other business services	3 268 ..	−105.29	−118.33	−125.16	−120.48	−130.99	−138.36	−142.78	−157.14
Personal, cultural, and recreational	3 287 ..	....	....	....	....	....	....	....	....
Government, n.i.e.	3 291 ..	−46.79	−43.74	−38.70	−39.26	−43.51	−42.15	−34.65	−36.16

Table 2 (Continued). STANDARD PRESENTATION, 2000–2007

(Millions of U.S. dollars)

	Code	2000	2001	2002	2003	2004	2005	2006	2007
C. INCOME	4 300	**−223.35**	**−197.55**	**−218.43**	**−241.57**	**−273.43**	**−232.04**	**−216.43**	**−213.06**
Total credit	2 300	*43.07*	*38.38*	*29.73*	*31.50*	*48.27*	*75.64*	*100.42*	*104.30*
Total debit	3 300	*−266.42*	*−235.93*	*−248.16*	*−273.08*	*−321.71*	*−307.68*	*−316.86*	*−317.36*
Compensation of employees, credit	2 310	**8.44**	**15.53**	**5.40**	**7.34**	**12.63**	**12.48**	**16.87**	**17.29**
Compensation of employees, debit	3 310	**−3.09**	**−3.64**	**−3.20**	**−3.81**	**−3.96**	**−3.96**	**−1.59**	**−2.41**
Investment income, credit	2 320	**34.63**	**22.85**	**24.34**	**24.16**	**35.64**	**63.16**	**83.55**	**87.02**
Direct investment income	2 330	.63	.33	.26	.22	.15	.10	.15	.15
Dividends and distributed branch profits	2 332	.41	.07	.13	.16	.15	.09	.10	.11
Reinvested earnings and undistributed branch profits	2 333	....	....	....	....	....	....	....	....
Income on debt (interest)	2 334	.21	.26	.12	.06	....	....	.04	.04
Portfolio investment income	2 339	6.70	6.35	6.48	7.43	7.56	8.36	18.13	13.72
Income on equity	2 340	6.70	6.35	6.48	7.43	7.56	8.36	18.13	13.72
Income on bonds and notes	2 350	....	....	....	....	....	....	....	....
Income on money market instruments	2 360	....	....	....	....	....	....	....	....
Other investment income	2 370	27.31	16.17	17.60	16.51	27.93	54.70	65.27	73.14
Investment income, debit	3 320	**−263.33**	**−232.29**	**−244.96**	**−269.27**	**−317.75**	**−303.71**	**−315.27**	**−314.95**
Direct investment income	3 330	−163.72	−153.24	−144.76	−149.15	−171.56	−176.50	−156.41	−168.29
Dividends and distributed branch profits	3 332	−81.11	−62.57	−61.14	−63.39	−73.02	−80.58	−84.98	−92.24
Reinvested earnings and undistributed branch profits	3 333	−73.43	−75.39	−67.77	−71.35	−85.70	−82.27	−58.23	−62.11
Income on debt (interest)	3 334	−9.18	−15.28	−15.85	−14.41	−12.84	−13.65	−13.19	−13.94
Portfolio investment income	3 339	−7.80	−14.27	−23.87	−35.89	−43.09	−26.04	−29.22	−22.54
Income on equity	3 340	−7.80	−14.27	−23.87	−35.89	−43.09	−26.04	−29.22	−22.54
Income on bonds and notes	3 350	....	....	....	....	....	....	....	....
Income on money market instruments	3 360	....	....	....	....	....	....	....	....
Other investment income	3 370	−91.81	−64.78	−76.34	−84.23	−103.10	−101.17	−129.64	−124.11
D. CURRENT TRANSFERS	4 379	**167.62**	**110.26**	**98.00**	**129.14**	**220.08**	**188.10**	**163.85**	**158.55**
Credit	2 379	**230.95**	**188.44**	**185.67**	**218.80**	**302.86**	**273.81**	**263.65**	**268.76**
General government	2 380	55.07	53.36	46.15	68.87	93.57	87.86	81.77	82.15
Other sectors	2 390	175.88	135.07	139.51	149.94	209.29	185.95	181.88	186.61
Workers' remittances	2 391	120.22	121.35	125.01	128.72	159.87	144.06	150.02	153.95
Other current transfers	2 392	55.66	13.72	14.51	21.22	49.42	41.90	31.87	32.66
Debit	3 379	**−63.32**	**−78.18**	**−87.67**	**−89.66**	**−82.78**	**−85.71**	**−99.80**	**−110.21**
General government	3 380	−17.46	−24.54	−25.52	−23.31	−24.27	−25.94	−23.86	−27.07
Other sectors	3 390	−45.86	−53.64	−62.15	−66.35	−58.50	−59.77	−75.94	−83.14
Workers' remittances	3 391	−22.82	−23.65	−21.86	−21.02	−22.64	−24.04	−27.87	−31.19
Other current transfers	3 392	−23.04	−29.99	−40.28	−45.33	−35.86	−35.73	−48.07	−51.95
CAPITAL AND FINANCIAL ACCOUNT	4 996	**516.26**	**470.80**	**543.93**	**573.56**	**638.09**	**755.33**	**1,075.45**	**1,544.93**
CAPITAL ACCOUNT	4 994	**122.31**	**134.07**	**131.94**	**131.18**	**135.76**	**337.66**	**181.06**	**276.70**
Total credit	2 994	*133.93*	*141.70*	*140.08*	*139.45*	*144.26*	*346.41*	*190.13*	*286.70*
Total debit	3 994	*−11.62*	*−7.62*	*−8.14*	*−8.27*	*−8.50*	*−8.74*	*−9.06*	*−10.00*
Capital transfers, credit	2 400	**132.97**	**141.45**	**139.89**	**139.27**	**144.26**	**346.41**	**190.04**	**286.62**
General government	2 401	88.25	95.50	94.40	92.88	95.50	291.88	133.08	228.19
Debt forgiveness	2 402	32.37	10.00	3.83	....	15.65	202.69	....	150.00
Other capital transfers	2 410	55.88	85.50	90.58	92.88	79.86	89.20	133.08	78.19
Other sectors	2 430	44.72	45.95	45.49	46.38	48.76	54.52	56.96	58.42
Migrants' transfers	2 431	44.72	45.95	45.49	46.38	48.76	54.52	56.96	58.42
Debt forgiveness	2 432	....	....	....	....	....	....	....	....
Other capital transfers	2 440	....	....	....	....	....	....	....	....
Capital transfers, debit	3 400	**−8.64**	**−7.62**	**−8.14**	**−8.27**	**−8.50**	**−8.74**	**−9.06**	**−10.00**
General government	3 401	....	....	....	....	....	....	....	....
Debt forgiveness	3 402	....	....	....	....	....	....	....	....
Other capital transfers	3 410	....	....	....	....	....	....	....	....
Other sectors	3 430	−8.64	−7.62	−8.14	−8.27	−8.50	−8.74	−9.06	−10.00
Migrants' transfers	3 431	−8.64	−7.62	−8.14	−8.27	−8.50	−8.74	−9.06	−10.00
Debt forgiveness	3 432	....	....	....	....	....	....	....	....
Other capital transfers	3 440	....	....	....	....	....	....	....	....
Nonproduced nonfinancial assets, credit	2 480	**.96**	**.25**	**.19**	**.19**	**....**	**....**	**.09**	**.09**
Nonproduced nonfinancial assets, debit	3 480	**−2.99**	**....**	**....**	**....**	**....**	**....**	**....**	**....**

Table 2 (Continued). STANDARD PRESENTATION, 2000–2007

(Millions of U.S. dollars)

	Code	2000	2001	2002	2003	2004	2005	2006	2007
FINANCIAL ACCOUNT	4 995 ..	393.95	336.73	411.99	442.37	502.33	417.67	894.39	1,268.23
A. DIRECT INVESTMENT	4 500 ..	327.83	372.42	340.10	555.64	448.97	632.38	1,105.95	1,291.40
Direct investment abroad	4 505 ..	....	–.13	....	....	....	....	....	....
Equity capital	4 510 ..	....	....	....	....	....	....	....	....
Claims on affiliated enterprises	4 515 ..	....	....	....	....	....	....	....	....
Liabilities to affiliated enterprises	4 520 ..	....	....	....	....	....	....	....	....
Reinvested earnings	4 525 ..	....	....	....	....	....	....	....	....
Other capital	4 530 ..	....	....	....	....	....	....	....	....
Claims on affiliated enterprises	4 535 ..	....	....	....	....	....	....	....	....
Liabilities to affiliated enterprises	4 540 ..	....	....	....	....	....	....	....	....
Direct investment in ECCU	4 555 ..	327.83	372.54	340.10	555.64	448.97	632.38	1,105.95	1,291.40
Equity capital	4 560 ..	163.28	199.13	214.17	284.75	343.44	554.87	1,003.07	1,180.72
Claims on direct investors	4 565 ..	....	....	....	....	....	....	....	....
Liabilities to direct investors	4 570 ..	163.28	199.13	214.17	284.75	343.44	554.87	1,003.07	1,180.72
Reinvested earnings	4 575 ..	73.43	75.39	67.77	71.35	85.70	82.27	58.23	62.11
Other capital	4 580 ..	91.13	98.02	58.15	199.54	19.83	–4.76	44.64	48.57
Claims on direct investors	4 585 ..	....	....	....	....	....	....	....	....
Liabilities to direct investors	4 590 ..	91.13	98.02	58.15	199.54	19.83	–4.76	44.64	48.57
B. PORTFOLIO INVESTMENT	4 600 ..	70.79	55.46	165.64	150.95	72.50	31.11	21.88	–9.61
Assets	4 602 ..	–1.67	–5.68	–26.53	–1.20	–12.05	–3.17	–5.03	–10.45
Equity securities	4 610 ..	....	....	....	....	....	....	....	....
Monetary authorities	4 611 ..	....	....	....	....	....	....	....	....
General government	4 612 ..	....	....	....	....	....	....	....	....
Banks	4 613 ..	....	....	....	....	....	....	....	....
Other sectors	4 614 ..	....	....	....	....	....	....	....	....
Debt securities	4 619 ..	....	....	....	....	....	....	....	....
Bonds and notes	4 620 ..	....	....	....	....	....	....	....	....
Monetary authorities	4 621 ..	....	....	....	....	....	....	....	....
General government	4 622 ..	....	....	....	....	....	....	....	....
Banks	4 623 ..	....	....	....	....	....	....	....	....
Other sectors	4 624 ..	....	....	....	....	....	....	....	....
Money market instruments	4 630 ..	....	....	....	....	....	....	....	....
Monetary authorities	4 631 ..	....	....	....	....	....	....	....	....
General government	4 632 ..	....	....	....	....	....	....	....	....
Banks	4 633 ..	....	....	....	....	....	....	....	....
Other sectors	4 634 ..	....	....	....	....	....	....	....	....
Liabilities	4 652 ..	72.47	61.14	192.18	152.15	84.55	34.28	26.91	.84
Equity securities	4 660 ..	....	....	....	....	....	....	....	....
Banks	4 663 ..	....	....	....	....	....	....	....	....
Other sectors	4 664 ..	....	....	....	....	....	....	....	....
Debt securities	4 669 ..	....	....	....	....	....	....	....	....
Bonds and notes	4 670 ..	....	....	....	....	....	....	....	....
Monetary authorities	4 671 ..	....	....	....	....	....	....	....	....
General government	4 672 ..	....	....	....	....	....	....	....	....
Banks	4 673 ..	....	....	....	....	....	....	....	....
Other sectors	4 674 ..	....	....	....	....	....	....	....	....
Money market instruments	4 680 ..	....	....	....	....	....	....	....	....
Monetary authorities	4 681 ..	....	....	....	....	....	....	....	....
General government	4 682 ..	....	....	....	....	....	....	....	....
Banks	4 683 ..	....	....	....	....	....	....	....	....
Other sectors	4 684 ..	....	....	....	....	....	....	....	....
C. FINANCIAL DERIVATIVES	4 910 ..	....	....	....	....	....	....	....	....
Monetary authorities	4 911 ..	....	....	....	....	....	....	....	....
General government	4 912 ..	....	....	....	....	....	....	....	....
Banks	4 913 ..	....	....	....	....	....	....	....	....
Other sectors	4 914 ..	....	....	....	....	....	....	....	....
Assets	4 900 ..	....	....	....	....	....	....	....	....
Monetary authorities	4 901 ..	....	....	....	....	....	....	....	....
General government	4 902 ..	....	....	....	....	....	....	....	....
Banks	4 903 ..	....	....	....	....	....	....	....	....
Other sectors	4 904 ..	....	....	....	....	....	....	....	....
Liabilities	4 905 ..	....	....	....	....	....	....	....	....
Monetary authorities	4 906 ..	....	....	....	....	....	....	....	....
General government	4 907 ..	....	....	....	....	....	....	....	....
Banks	4 908 ..	....	....	....	....	....	....	....	....
Other sectors	4 909 ..	....	....	....	....	....	....	....	....

Table 2 (Concluded). STANDARD PRESENTATION, 2000–2007

(Millions of U.S. dollars)

	Code	2000	2001	2002	2003	2004	2005	2006	2007
D. OTHER INVESTMENT	4 700	**16.13**	**−24.51**	**−33.08**	**−218.39**	**90.50**	**−267.21**	**−141.49**	**32.84**
Assets	4 703	**213.66**	**225.01**	**224.73**	**296.29**	**319.94**	**477.15**	**229.51**	**448.02**
Trade credits	4 706	....	....	....	....	....	....	....	....
General government	4 707	....	....	....	....	....	....	....	....
of which: Short-term	4 709	....	....	....	....	....	....	....	....
Other sectors	4 710	....	....	....	....	....	....	....	....
of which: Short-term	4 712	....	....	....	....	....	....	....	....
Loans	4 714	....	....	....	....	....	....	....	....
Monetary authorities	4 715	....	....	....	....	....	....	....	....
of which: Short-term	4 718	....	....	....	....	....	....	....	....
General government	4 719	....	....	....	....	....	....	....	....
of which: Short-term	4 721	....	....	....	....	....	....	....	....
Banks	4 722	....	....	....	....	....	....	....	....
of which: Short-term	4 724	....	....	....	....	....	....	....	....
Other sectors	4 725	....	....	....	....	....	....	....	....
of which: Short-term	4 727	....	....	....	....	....	....	....	....
Currency and deposits	4 730	....	....	....	....	....	....	....	....
Monetary authorities	4 731	....	....	....	....	....	....	....	....
General government	4 732	....	....	....	....	....	....	....	....
Banks	4 733	....	....	....	....	....	....	....	....
Other sectors	4 734	....	....	....	....	....	....	....	....
Other assets	4 736	....	....	....	....	....	....	....	....
Monetary authorities	4 737	....	....	....	....	....	....	....	....
of which: Short-term	4 739	....	....	....	....	....	....	....	....
General government	4 740	....	....	....	....	....	....	....	....
of which: Short-term	4 742	....	....	....	....	....	....	....	....
Banks	4 743	....	....	....	....	....	....	....	....
of which: Short-term	4 745	....	....	....	....	....	....	....	....
Other sectors	4 746	....	....	....	....	....	....	....	....
of which: Short-term	4 748	....	....	....	....	....	....	....	....
Liabilities	4 753	**−197.53**	**−249.52**	**−257.81**	**−514.68**	**−229.44**	**−744.36**	**−371.00**	**−415.18**
Trade credits	4 756	....	....	....	....	....	....	....	....
General government	4 757	....	....	....	....	....	....	....	....
of which: Short-term	4 759	....	....	....	....	....	....	....	....
Other sectors	4 760	....	....	....	....	....	....	....	....
of which: Short-term	4 762	....	....	....	....	....	....	....	....
Loans	4 764	....	....	1.66	7.58	5.33	3.17	2.50	−4.70
Monetary authorities	4 765	....	....	1.66	7.58	5.33	3.17	2.50	−4.70
of which: Use of Fund credit and loans from the Fund	4 766	....	....	*1.66*	*7.58*	*5.33*	*3.17*	*2.50*	*−4.70*
of which: Short-term	4 768	....	....	....	....	....	....	....	....
General government	4 769	....	....	....	....	....	....	....	....
of which: Short-term	4 771	....	....	....	....	....	....	....	....
Banks	4 772	....	....	....	....	....	....	....	....
of which: Short-term	4 774	....	....	....	....	....	....	....	....
Other sectors	4 775	....	....	....	....	....	....	....	....
of which: Short-term	4 777	....	....	....	....	....	....	....	....
Currency and deposits	4 780	....	....	....	....	....	....	....	....
Monetary authorities	4 781	....	....	....	....	....	....	....	....
General government	4 782	....	....	....	....	....	....	....	....
Banks	4 783	....	....	....	....	....	....	....	....
Other sectors	4 784	....	....	....	....	....	....	....	....
Other liabilities	4 786	....	....	....	....	....	....	....	....
Monetary authorities	4 787	....	....	....	....	....	....	....	....
of which: Short-term	4 789	....	....	....	....	....	....	....	....
General government	4 790	....	....	....	....	....	....	....	....
of which: Short-term	4 792	....	....	....	....	....	....	....	....
Banks	4 793	....	....	....	....	....	....	....	....
of which: Short-term	4 795	....	....	....	....	....	....	....	....
Other sectors	4 796	....	....	....	....	....	....	....	....
of which: Short-term	4 798	....	....	....	....	....	....	....	....
E. RESERVE ASSETS	4 802	**−20.80**	**−66.63**	**−60.67**	**−45.82**	**−109.63**	**21.39**	**−91.95**	**−46.40**
Monetary gold	4 812	....	....	....	....	....	....	....	....
Special drawing rights	4 811	....	....	....	....	....	....	....	....
Reserve position in the Fund	4 810	−.01	....	....	−.01	....	....	....	....
Foreign exchange	4 803	−7.91	−60.44	−53.62	−46.26	−97.20	28.36	−93.87	−56.01
Other claims	4 813	−12.88	−6.20	−7.05	.46	−12.43	−6.96	1.92	9.61
NET ERRORS AND OMISSIONS	4 998	**−47.95**	**39.62**	**30.09**	**113.39**	**−114.22**	**59.62**	**170.91**	**34.43**

Table 1. ANALYTIC PRESENTATION, 2000–2007

(Millions of U.S. dollars)

	Code	2000	2001	2002	2003	2004	2005	2006	2007
A. Current Account[1]	4 993 Z.	**926**	**−654**	**−1,272**	**−422**	**−542**	**347**	**1,615**	**1,598**
Goods: exports f.o.b.	2 100 ..	5,057	4,821	5,258	6,446	7,968	10,468	13,188	14,863
Goods: imports f.o.b.	3 100 ..	−3,657	−5,178	−6,160	−6,366	−7,684	−9,709	−11,423	−13,067
Balance on Goods	4 100 ..	*1,399*	*−356*	*−902*	*80*	*284*	*758*	*1,765*	*1,797*
Services: credit	2 200 ..	849	862	884	881	1,014	1,012	1,037	1,175
Services: debit	3 200 ..	−1,269	−1,434	−1,600	−1,624	−1,968	−2,142	−2,341	−2,572
Balance on Goods and Services	4 991 ..	*979*	*−928*	*−1,618*	*−664*	*−670*	*−371*	*460*	*400*
Income: credit	2 300 ..	70	48	30	27	37	86	165	259
Income: debit	3 300 ..	−1,476	−1,412	−1,335	−1,555	−1,940	−2,029	−2,114	−2,306
Balance on Goods, Services, and Income	4 992 ..	*−426*	*−2,293*	*−2,923*	*−2,192*	*−2,572*	*−2,314*	*−1,489*	*−1,648*
Current transfers: credit	2 379 Z.	1,437	1,686	1,709	1,791	2,049	2,781	3,234	3,395
Current transfers: debit	3 379 ..	−85	−47	−58	−22	−18	−120	−130	−149
B. Capital Account[1]	4 994 Z.	**−1**	**15**	**16**	**8**	**8**	**13**	**19**	**22**
Capital account: credit	2 994 Z.	8	21	24	17	18	23	29	32
Capital account: debit	3 994 ..	−10	−7	−8	−9	−10	−10	−10	−10
Total, Groups A Plus B	4 981 ..	*924*	*−639*	*−1,256*	*−415*	*−534*	*360*	*1,634*	*1,620*
C. Financial Account[1]	4 995 W.	**−6,360**	**626**	**1,193**	**322**	**244**	**−515**	**−2,050**	**−257**
Direct investment abroad	4 505 ..	. . . .	. . . .	. . . .	. . . .	. . . .	. . . .	. . . .	. . . .
Direct investment in Ecuador	4 555 Z.	−23	539	783	872	837	493	271	183
Portfolio investment assets	4 602 ..	. . . .	. . . .	. . . .	−312	−191	−228	−641	−116
Equity securities	4 610 ..	. . . .	. . . .	. . . .	1	−24	−22	−61	−40
Debt securities	4 619 ..	. . . .	. . . .	. . . .	−313	−167	−206	−580	−76
Portfolio investment liabilities	4 652 Z.	−5,583	−16	. . . .	8	. . . .	−2	−743	−3
Equity securities	4 660 ..	. . . .	1	1	9	1	2	. . . .	. . . .
Debt securities	4 669 Z.	−5,583	−17	−1	−1	−1	−3	−743	−3
Financial derivatives	4 910 ..	. . . .	. . . .	. . . .	. . . .	. . . .	. . . .	. . . .	. . . .
Financial derivatives assets	4 900 ..	. . . .	. . . .	. . . .	. . . .	. . . .	. . . .	. . . .	. . . .
Financial derivatives liabilities	4 905 ..	. . . .	. . . .	. . . .	. . . .	. . . .	. . . .	. . . .	. . . .
Other investment assets	4 703 ..	−473	−280	−676	−286	−999	−845	−2,083	−1,467
Monetary authorities	4 701 ..	345	621	309	298	227	403	−780	−141
General government	4 704 ..	. . . .	. . . .	. . . .	. . . .	. . . .	. . . .	. . . .	−163
Banks	4 705 ..	. . . .	. . . .	. . . .	311	158	238	579	90
Other sectors	4 728 ..	−818	−901	−985	−895	−1,383	−1,486	−1,882	−1,253
Other investment liabilities	4 753 W.	−280	384	1,085	40	596	67	1,146	1,146
Monetary authorities	4 753 WA	−135	−144	−138	28	24	−50	17	23
General government	4 753 ZB	202	190	−23	−5	−377	−419	62	257
Banks	4 753 ZC	−33	−108	−19	−20	13	−34	49	19
Other sectors	4 753 ZD	−314	446	1,265	37	935	570	1,018	847
Total, Groups A Through C	4 983 ..	*−5,435*	*−12*	*−63*	*−93*	*−290*	*−155*	*−416*	*1,362*
D. Net Errors and Omissions	4 998 ..	**−262**	**−301**	**−157**	**163**	**681**	**424**	**342**	**45**
Total, Groups A Through D	4 984 ..	*−5,697*	*−313*	*−221*	*70*	*391*	*269*	*−74*	*1,407*
E. Reserves and Related Items	4 802 A.	**5,697**	**313**	**221**	**−70**	**−391**	**−269**	**74**	**−1,407**
Reserve assets	4 802 ..	−307	105	68	−150	−275	−714	125	−1,495
Use of Fund credit and loans	4 766 ..	151	48	95	48	−112	−196	−58	−23
Exceptional financing	4 920 ..	5,853	160	58	32	−4	640	7	111

[1] Excludes components that have been classified in the categories of Group E.

Table 2. STANDARD PRESENTATION, 2000–2007

(Millions of U.S. dollars)

	Code	2000	2001	2002	2003	2004	2005	2006	2007
CURRENT ACCOUNT................................	4 993 ..	926	−654	−1,272	−422	−542	347	1,615	1,598
A. GOODS..	4 100 ..	1,399	−356	−902	80	284	758	1,765	1,797
Credit..	2 100 ..	5,057	4,821	5,258	6,446	7,968	10,468	13,188	14,863
General merchandise: exports f.o.b.............	2 110 ..	4,941	4,730	5,116	6,306	7,832	10,247	12,916	14,549
Goods for processing: exports f.o.b............	2 150 ..	....	....	....	....	....	....	....	....
Repairs on goods..................................	2 160 ..	5	8	7	5	6	6	6	6
Goods procured in ports by carriers............	2 170 ..	111	84	136	135	130	214	266	308
Nonmonetary gold................................	2 180 ..	....	....	....	....	....	....	....	....
Debit..	3 100 ..	−3,657	−5,178	−6,160	−6,366	−7,684	−9,709	−11,423	−13,067
General merchandise: imports f.o.b.............	3 110 ..	−3,637	−5,148	−6,135	−6,344	−7,657	−9,687	−11,400	−13,044
Goods for processing: imports f.o.b............	3 150 ..	....	....	....	....	....	....	....	....
Repairs on goods..................................	3 160 ..	−4	−8	−6	−5	−10	−6	−6	−6
Goods procured in ports by carriers............	3 170 ..	−16	−22	−19	−17	−17	−17	−17	−17
Nonmonetary gold................................	3 180 ..	....	....	....	....	....	....	....	....
B. SERVICES......................................	4 200 ..	−420	−572	−716	−743	−954	−1,130	−1,305	−1,397
Total credit....................................	2 200 ..	*849*	*862*	*884*	*881*	*1,014*	*1,012*	*1,037*	*1,175*
Total debit.....................................	3 200 ..	*−1,269*	*−1,434*	*−1,600*	*−1,624*	*−1,968*	*−2,142*	*−2,341*	*−2,572*
Transportation services, credit............	2 205 ..	290	248	243	269	340	335	352	347
Passenger......................................	2 850 ..	*49*	*8*	*2*	*2*	*2*	*2*	*2*	*3*
Freight...	2 851 ..	*218*	*215*	*210*	*236*	*302*	*292*	*300*	*293*
Other...	2 852 ..	*23*	*26*	*31*	*30*	*36*	*41*	*50*	*51*
Sea transport, passenger....................	2 207 ..	....	....	....	....	....	....	....	....
Sea transport, freight.......................	2 208 ..	204	202	208	220	275	271	276	269
Sea transport, other.........................	2 209 ..	18	12	19	17	24	31	40	43
Air transport, passenger.....................	2 211 ..	49	8	2	2	2	2	2	3
Air transport, freight........................	2 212 ..	14	13	2	17	28	21	25	23
Air transport, other.........................	2 213 ..	5	14	12	13	12	10	9	8
Other transport, passenger..................	2 215 ..	....	....	....	....	....	....	....	....
Other transport, freight....................	2 216 ..	....	....	....	....	....	....	....	....
Other transport, other......................	2 217 ..	....	....	....	....	....	....	....	....
Transportation services, debit............	3 205 ..	−439	−557	−675	−668	−911	−1,043	−1,171	−1,327
Passenger......................................	3 850 ..	*−117*	*−125*	*−143*	*−146*	*−186*	*−215*	*−240*	*−229*
Freight...	3 851 ..	*−270*	*−373*	*−462*	*−460*	*−654*	*−722*	*−830*	*−981*
Other...	3 852 ..	*−52*	*−59*	*−70*	*−62*	*−71*	*−105*	*−101*	*−118*
Sea transport, passenger....................	3 207 ..	....	....	....	....	....	....	....	....
Sea transport, freight.......................	3 208 ..	−239	−308	−365	−358	−530	−573	−677	−829
Sea transport, other.........................	3 209 ..	−44	−46	−24	−25	−32	−38	−47	−58
Air transport, passenger.....................	3 211 ..	−117	−125	−143	−146	−186	−215	−240	−229
Air transport, freight........................	3 212 ..	−15	−50	−55	−62	−80	−98	−100	−94
Air transport, other.........................	3 213 ..	−8	−13	−45	−37	−39	−67	−54	−59
Other transport, passenger..................	3 215 ..	....	....	....	....	....	....	....	....
Other transport, freight....................	3 216 ..	−16	−16	−42	−39	−44	−51	−53	−58
Other transport, other......................	3 217 ..	....	....	....	....	....	....	....	....
Travel, credit................................	2 236 ..	402	430	447	406	462	486	490	623
Business travel................................	2 237 ..	98	101	98	96	112	123	126	161
Personal travel................................	2 240 ..	304	329	349	311	351	363	364	462
Travel, debit.................................	3 236 ..	−299	−340	−364	−354	−391	−429	−466	−504
Business travel................................	3 237 ..	−82	−99	−108	−96	−106	−116	−127	−137
Personal travel................................	3 240 ..	−217	−241	−256	−258	−285	−312	−340	−367
Other services, credit.....................	2 200 BA	157	184	193	206	211	191	194	204
Communications................................	2 245 ..	61	96	98	103	100	80	76	72
Construction....................................	2 249 ..	....	....	....	....	....	....	....	....
Insurance.......................................	2 253 ..	1	1	....	1	....	1	....	....
Financial.......................................	2 260 ..	....	....	....	....	....	....	....	....
Computer and information....................	2 262 ..	....	....	....	....	....	....	....	....
Royalties and licence fees...................	2 266 ..	....	....	....	....	....	....	....	....
Other business services......................	2 268 ..	....	....	....	....	....	....	....	....
Personal, cultural, and recreational.........	2 287 ..	39	24	32	34	36	39	41	44
Government, n.i.e.............................	2 291 ..	56	63	63	69	74	72	78	88
Other services, debit......................	3 200 BA	−532	−537	−561	−602	−666	−671	−704	−741
Communications................................	3 245 ..	−38	−19	−11	−5	−6	−6	−7	−7
Construction....................................	3 249 ..	....	....	....	....	....	....	....	....
Insurance.......................................	3 253 ..	−33	−65	−99	−117	−137	−140	−139	−140
Financial.......................................	3 260 ..	−8	−12	−7	−6	−4	−5	−5	−5
Computer and information....................	3 262 ..	....	....	....	....	....	....	....	....
Royalties and licence fees...................	3 266 ..	−62	−52	−44	−43	−43	−43	−44	−45
Other business services......................	3 268 ..	−294	−277	−272	−289	−298	−308	−318	−327
Personal, cultural, and recreational.........	3 287 ..	−52	−71	−86	−92	−98	−106	−116	−126
Government, n.i.e.............................	3 291 ..	−44	−39	−41	−50	−79	−63	−77	−91

Table 2 (Continued). STANDARD PRESENTATION, 2000–2007

(Millions of U.S. dollars)

	Code	2000	2001	2002	2003	2004	2005	2006	2007
C. INCOME	4 300	**−1,405**	**−1,364**	**−1,306**	**−1,528**	**−1,903**	**−1,942**	**−1,949**	**−2,048**
Total credit	2 300	*70*	*48*	*30*	*27*	*37*	*86*	*165*	*259*
Total debit	3 300	*−1,476*	*−1,412*	*−1,335*	*−1,555*	*−1,940*	*−2,029*	*−2,114*	*−2,306*
Compensation of employees, credit	2 310	**6**	**6**	**6**	**6**	**6**	**7**	**6**	**6**
Compensation of employees, debit	3 310	**−6**	**−7**	**−7**	**−7**	**−7**	**−6**	**−5**	**−5**
Investment income, credit	2 320	**65**	**41**	**24**	**21**	**31**	**80**	**159**	**253**
Direct investment income	2 330	....	....	....	....	....	....	....	....
Dividends and distributed branch profits	2 332	....	....	....	....	....	....	....	....
Reinvested earnings and undistributed branch profits	2 333	....	....	....	....	....	....	....	....
Income on debt (interest)	2 334	....	....	....	....	....	....	....	....
Portfolio investment income	2 339	....	....	....	....	....	....	....	....
Income on equity	2 340	....	....	....	....	....	....	....	....
Income on bonds and notes	2 350	....	....	....	....	....	....	....	....
Income on money market instruments	2 360	....	....	....	....	....	....	....	....
Other investment income	2 370	65	41	24	21	31	80	159	253
Investment income, debit	3 320	**−1,470**	**−1,405**	**−1,328**	**−1,548**	**−1,934**	**−2,023**	**−2,109**	**−2,301**
Direct investment income	3 330	−329	−382	−406	−595	−964	−1,004	−977	−1,160
Dividends and distributed branch profits	3 332	−239	−286	−264	−289	−278	−369	−389	−508
Reinvested earnings and undistributed branch profits	3 333	−41	−47	−38	−141	−422	−400	−395	−411
Income on debt (interest)	3 334	−50	−49	−104	−165	−264	−235	−193	−241
Portfolio investment income	3 339	−464	−301	−292	−317	−344	−372	−416	−399
Income on equity	3 340	....	....	....	....	....	....	....	....
Income on bonds and notes	3 350	−464	−301	−292	−317	−344	−372	−416	−399
Income on money market instruments	3 360	....	....	....	....	....	....	....	....
Other investment income	3 370	−677	−723	−631	−636	−626	−647	−715	−742
D. CURRENT TRANSFERS	4 379	**1,352**	**1,639**	**1,652**	**1,769**	**2,030**	**2,661**	**3,104**	**3,246**
Credit	2 379	**1,437**	**1,686**	**1,709**	**1,791**	**2,049**	**2,781**	**3,234**	**3,395**
General government	2 380	73	200	186	130	135	194	221	244
Other sectors	2 390	1,364	1,485	1,523	1,662	1,914	2,587	3,013	3,151
Workers' remittances	2 391	1,317	1,415	1,432	1,627	1,832	2,454	2,928	3,088
Other current transfers	2 392	47	71	91	34	82	133	85	63
Debit	3 379	**−85**	**−47**	**−58**	**−22**	**−18**	**−120**	**−130**	**−149**
General government	3 380	−15	−4	−3	−21	−18	−32	−22	−13
Other sectors	3 390	−70	−43	−55	−1	−1	−88	−108	−136
Workers' remittances	3 391	....	....	....	....	....	−48	−57	−78
Other current transfers	3 392	−70	−43	−55	−1	−1	−40	−51	−58
CAPITAL AND FINANCIAL ACCOUNT	4 996	**−664**	**954**	**1,429**	**259**	**−139**	**−771**	**−1,958**	**−1,643**
CAPITAL ACCOUNT	4 994	**1,977**	**18**	**27**	**61**	**14**	**70**	**26**	**65**
Total credit	2 994	*1,987*	*25*	*35*	*70*	*24*	*80*	*37*	*75*
Total debit	3 994	*−10*	*−7*	*−8*	*−9*	*−10*	*−10*	*−10*	*−10*
Capital transfers, credit	2 400	**1,987**	**25**	**35**	**70**	**24**	**80**	**37**	**75**
General government	2 401	1,987	21	30	66	20	74	31	68
Debt forgiveness	2 402	1,978	3	11	53	6	57	8	43
Other capital transfers	2 410	8	18	19	13	14	17	23	26
Other sectors	2 430	....	3	4	3	4	6	6	7
Migrants' transfers	2 431	....	....	....	....	....	....	....	....
Debt forgiveness	2 432	....	....	....	....	....	....	....	....
Other capital transfers	2 440	....	3	4	3	4	6	6	7
Capital transfers, debit	3 400	....	....	....	....	....	....	....	....
General government	3 401	....	....	....	....	....	....	....	....
Debt forgiveness	3 402	....	....	....	....	....	....	....	....
Other capital transfers	3 410	....	....	....	....	....	....	....	....
Other sectors	3 430	....	....	....	....	....	....	....	....
Migrants' transfers	3 431	....	....	....	....	....	....	....	....
Debt forgiveness	3 432	....	....	....	....	....	....	....	....
Other capital transfers	3 440	....	....	....	....	....	....	....	....
Nonproduced nonfinancial assets, credit	2 480	....	....	....	....	....	....	....	....
Nonproduced nonfinancial assets, debit	3 480	**−10**	**−7**	**−8**	**−9**	**−10**	**−10**	**−10**	**−10**

Table 2 (Continued). STANDARD PRESENTATION, 2000–2007

(Millions of U.S. dollars)

	Code	2000	2001	2002	2003	2004	2005	2006	2007
FINANCIAL ACCOUNT	4 995	−2,641	936	1,403	199	−153	−841	−1,984	−1,707
A. DIRECT INVESTMENT	4 500	−23	539	783	872	837	493	271	183
Direct investment abroad	4 505	....	....	....	....	....	....	....	....
Equity capital	4 510	....	....	....	....	....	....	....	....
Claims on affiliated enterprises	4 515	....	....	....	....	....	....	....	....
Liabilities to affiliated enterprises	4 520	....	....	....	....	....	....	....	....
Reinvested earnings	4 525	....	....	....	....	....	....	....	....
Other capital	4 530	....	....	....	....	....	....	....	....
Claims on affiliated enterprises	4 535	....	....	....	....	....	....	....	....
Liabilities to affiliated enterprises	4 540	....	....	....	....	....	....	....	....
Direct investment in Ecuador	4 555	−23	539	783	872	837	493	271	183
Equity capital	4 560	34	196	179	207	145	119	136	151
Claims on direct investors	4 565	....	....	....	....	....	....	−719	....
Liabilities to direct investors	4 570	34	196	179	207	145	119	855	151
Reinvested earnings	4 575	41	47	38	141	422	400	395	411
Other capital	4 580	−98	296	565	524	269	−26	−261	−380
Claims on direct investors	4 585	....	....	....	....	....	....	....	....
Liabilities to direct investors	4 590	−98	296	565	524	269	−26	−261	−380
B. PORTFOLIO INVESTMENT	4 600	−1,725	40	....	−304	−190	366	−1,384	−118
Assets	4 602	....	....	....	−312	−191	−228	−641	−116
Equity securities	4 610	....	....	....	1	−24	−22	−61	−40
Monetary authorities	4 611	....	....	....	....	....	....	....	....
General government	4 612	....	....	....	....	....	....	....	....
Banks	4 613	....	....	....	....	....	....	....	....
Other sectors	4 614	....	....	....	1	−24	−22	−61	−40
Debt securities	4 619	....	....	....	−313	−167	−206	−580	−76
Bonds and notes	4 620	....	....	....	−313	−167	−206	−580	−76
Monetary authorities	4 621	....	....	....	....	....	....	....	....
General government	4 622	....	....	....	....	....	....	....	....
Banks	4 623	....	....	....	−313	−167	−206	−580	−76
Other sectors	4 624	....	....	....	....	....	....	....	....
Money market instruments	4 630	....	....	....	....	....	....	....	....
Monetary authorities	4 631	....	....	....	....	....	....	....	....
General government	4 632	....	....	....	....	....	....	....	....
Banks	4 633	....	....	....	....	....	....	....	....
Other sectors	4 634	....	....	....	....	....	....	....	....
Liabilities	4 652	−1,725	40	....	8	....	594	−743	−3
Equity securities	4 660	....	1	1	9	1	2	....	....
Banks	4 663	....	....	....	....	....	....	....	....
Other sectors	4 664	....	1	1	9	1	2	....	....
Debt securities	4 669	−1,725	39	−1	−1	−1	593	−743	−3
Bonds and notes	4 670	−1,725	39	−1	−1	−1	593	−743	−3
Monetary authorities	4 671	....	....	....	....	....	....	....	....
General government	4 672	−1,725	39	−1	−1	−1	593	−743	−3
Banks	4 673	....	....	....	....	....	....	....	....
Other sectors	4 674	....	....	....	....	....	....	....	....
Money market instruments	4 680	....	....	....	....	....	....	....	....
Monetary authorities	4 681	....	....	....	....	....	....	....	....
General government	4 682	....	....	....	....	....	....	....	....
Banks	4 683	....	....	....	....	....	....	....	....
Other sectors	4 684	....	....	....	....	....	....	....	....
C. FINANCIAL DERIVATIVES	4 910	....	....	....	....	....	....	....	....
Monetary authorities	4 911	....	....	....	....	....	....	....	....
General government	4 912	....	....	....	....	....	....	....	....
Banks	4 913	....	....	....	....	....	....	....	....
Other sectors	4 914	....	....	....	....	....	....	....	....
Assets	4 900	....	....	....	....	....	....	....	....
Monetary authorities	4 901	....	....	....	....	....	....	....	....
General government	4 902	....	....	....	....	....	....	....	....
Banks	4 903	....	....	....	....	....	....	....	....
Other sectors	4 904	....	....	....	....	....	....	....	....
Liabilities	4 905	....	....	....	....	....	....	....	....
Monetary authorities	4 906	....	....	....	....	....	....	....	....
General government	4 907	....	....	....	....	....	....	....	....
Banks	4 908	....	....	....	....	....	....	....	....
Other sectors	4 909	....	....	....	....	....	....	....	....

Table 2 (Concluded). STANDARD PRESENTATION, 2000–2007

(Millions of U.S. dollars)

	Code	2000	2001	2002	2003	2004	2005	2006	2007
D. OTHER INVESTMENT	4 700 ..	**−586**	**253**	**551**	**−219**	**−524**	**−987**	**−996**	**−277**
Assets	4 703 ..	**−473**	**−280**	**−676**	**−286**	**−999**	**−845**	**−2,083**	**−1,467**
Trade credits	4 706 ..	−187	−226	−271	−277	−312	−309	−391	−548
General government	4 707 ..	....	....	....	....	....	....	....	−163
of which: Short-term	4 709 ..	....	....	....	....	....	....	....	−163
Other sectors	4 710 ..	−187	−226	−271	−277	−312	−309	−391	−385
of which: Short-term	4 712 ..	−187	−226	−271	−277	−312	−309	−391	−385
Loans	4 714 ..	....	....	....	....	....	....	....	....
Monetary authorities	4 715 ..	....	....	....	....	....	....	....	....
of which: Short-term	4 718 ..	....	....	....	....	....	....	....	....
General government	4 719 ..	....	....	....	....	....	....	....	....
of which: Short-term	4 721 ..	....	....	....	....	....	....	....	....
Banks	4 722 ..	....	....	....	....	....	....	....	....
of which: Short-term	4 724 ..	....	....	....	....	....	....	....	....
Other sectors	4 725 ..	....	....	....	....	....	....	....	....
of which: Short-term	4 727 ..	....	....	....	....	....	....	....	....
Currency and deposits	4 730 ..	−287	−54	−405	282	−313	−377	−515	6
Monetary authorities	4 731 ..	345	621	309	438	284	513	164	−726
General government	4 732 ..	....	....	....	....	29	−109	409	770
Banks	4 733 ..	....	....	....	462	446	396	403	830
Other sectors	4 734 ..	−631	−675	−714	−617	−1,071	−1,177	−1,491	−868
Other assets	4 736 ..	....	....	....	−291	−374	−160	−1,177	−926
Monetary authorities	4 737 ..	....	....	....	−140	−57	−111	−945	585
of which: Short-term	4 739 ..	....	....	....	−140	−57	−111	−945	585
General government	4 740 ..	....	....	....	....	−29	109	−409	−770
of which: Short-term	4 742 ..	....	....	....	....	−29	109	−409	−770
Banks	4 743 ..	....	....	....	−151	−289	−158	176	−740
of which: Short-term	4 745 ..	....	....	....	−151	−289	−158	176	−740
Other sectors	4 746 ..	....	....	....	....	....	....	....	....
of which: Short-term	4 748 ..	....	....	....	....	....	....	....	....
Liabilities	4 753 ..	**−113**	**533**	**1,227**	**67**	**475**	**−141**	**1,087**	**1,191**
Trade credits	4 756 ..	−8	−183	−22	106	342	312	362	514
General government	4 757 ..	98	−113	−2	1	1	−10	−8	−9
of which: Short-term	4 759 ..	....	....	....	....	....	....	....	....
Other sectors	4 760 ..	−106	−69	−21	106	342	322	369	524
of which: Short-term	4 762 ..	....	....	....	....	....	....	....	....
Loans	4 764 ..	−117	1,480	1,202	14	86	−382	647	559
Monetary authorities	4 765 ..	16	−96	−43	31	−112	−196	−59	−23
of which: Use of Fund credit and loans from the Fund..	4 766 ..	151	48	95	48	−112	−196	−58	−23
of which: Short-term	4 768 ..	....	....	....	....	....	....	....	....
General government	4 769 ..	108	1,170	−21	73	−376	−408	70	266
of which: Short-term	4 771 ..	....	....	....	....	....	....	....	....
Banks	4 772 ..	−33	−108	−19	−21	−20	−25	−13	−7
of which: Short-term	4 774 ..	....	....	....	....	....	....	....	....
Other sectors	4 775 ..	−208	515	1,285	−69	594	248	649	323
of which: Short-term	4 777 ..	....	....	....	....	....	....	....	....
Currency and deposits	4 780 ..	....	....	....	46	58	−58	79	49
Monetary authorities	4 781 ..	....	....	....	45	25	−49	17	24
General government	4 782 ..	....	....	....	....	....	....	....	....
Banks	4 783 ..	....	....	....	1	33	−9	62	25
Other sectors	4 784 ..	....	....	....	....	....	....	....	....
Other liabilities	4 786 ..	12	−764	47	−99	−11	−13	−1	68
Monetary authorities	4 787 ..	....	....	−4	....	....	....	....	....
of which: Short-term	4 789 ..	....	....	−4	....	....	....	....	....
General government	4 790 ..	39	−773	69	−89	−9	−12	−1	69
of which: Short-term	4 792 ..	39	−773	69	−89	−9	−12	−1	69
Banks	4 793 ..	−22	9	−18	−11	−2	−1	....	−1
of which: Short-term	4 795 ..	−22	9	−18	−11	−2	−1	....	−1
Other sectors	4 796 ..	−5	....	....	....	....	....	....	....
of which: Short-term	4 798 ..	−5	....	....	....	....	....	....	....
E. RESERVE ASSETS	4 802 ..	**−307**	**105**	**68**	**−150**	**−275**	**−714**	**125**	**−1,495**
Monetary gold	4 812 ..	13	−1	−59	−55	−20	−65	−101	−170
Special drawing rights	4 811 ..	2	−2	1	1	−55	32	15	−16
Reserve position in the Fund	4 810 ..	....	....	....	....	....	....	....	....
Foreign exchange	4 803 ..	−331	123	126	−94	−196	−684	212	−1,307
Other claims	4 813 ..	10	−15	....	−3	−5	3	−1	−2
NET ERRORS AND OMISSIONS	4 998 ..	**−262**	**−301**	**−157**	**163**	**681**	**424**	**342**	**45**

Table 3. INTERNATIONAL INVESTMENT POSITION (End-period stocks), 2000–2007

(Millions of U.S. dollars)

	Code	2000	2001	2002	2003	2004	2005	2006	2007
ASSETS	8 995 C.	**1,904**	**2,451**	**3,136**	**4,439**	**5,446**	**6,930**	**8,911**	**10,865**
Direct investment abroad	8 505 ..	....	....	....	....	....	....	....	....
Equity capital and reinvested earnings	8 506 ..	....	....	....	....	....	....	....	....
Claims on affiliated enterprises	8 507 ..	....	....	....	....	....	....	....	....
Liabilities to affiliated enterprises	8 508 ..	....	....	....	....	....	....	....	....
Other capital	8 530 ..	....	....	....	....	....	....	....	....
Claims on affiliated enterprises	8 535 ..	....	....	....	....	....	....	....	....
Liabilities to affiliated enterprises	8 540 ..	....	....	....	....	....	....	....	....
Portfolio investment	8 602 ..	....	....	428	740	931	1,159	1,800	1,916
Equity securities	8 610 ..	....	....	137	135	159	182	242	282
Monetary authorities	8 611 .	....	....	....	....	....	....	....	....
General government	8 612 ..	....	....	....	....	....	....	....	....
Banks	8 613 ..	....	....	137	135	159	182	242	282
Other sectors	8 614 ..	....	....	....	....	....	....	....	....
Debt securities	8 619 ..	....	....	292	605	771	977	1,558	1,633
Bonds and notes	8 620 ..	....	....	292	605	771	977	1,558	1,633
Monetary authorities	8 621 ..	....	....	....	....	....	....	....	....
General government	8 622 ..	....	....	....	....	....	....	....	....
Banks	8 623 ..	....	....	292	605	771	977	1,558	1,633
Other sectors	8 624 ..	....	....	....	....	....	....	....	....
Money market instruments	8 630 ..	....	....	....	....	....	....	....	....
Monetary authorities	8 631 ..	....	....	....	....	....	....	....	....
General government	8 632 ..	....	....	....	....	....	....	....	....
Banks	8 633 ..	....	....	....	....	....	....	....	....
Other sectors	8 634 ..	....	....	....	....	....	....	....	....
Financial derivatives	8 900 ..	....	....	....	....	....	....	....	....
Monetary authorities	8 901 ..	....	....	....	....	....	....	....	....
General government	8 902 ..	....	....	....	....	....	....	....	....
Banks	8 903 ..	....	....	....	....	....	....	....	....
Other sectors	8 904 ..	....	....	....	....	....	....	....	....
Other investment	8 703 ..	**724**	**1,377**	**1,700**	**2,538**	**3,078**	**3,624**	**5,087**	**5,429**
Trade credits	8 706 ..	....	....	....	....	....	....	....	....
General government	8 707 ..	....	....	....	....	....	....	....	....
of which: Short-term	8 709 ..	....	....	....	....	....	....	....	....
Other sectors	8 710 ..	....	....	....	....	....	....	....	....
of which: Short-term	8 712 ..	....	....	....	....	....	....	....	....
Loans	8 714 ..	....	....	....	....	....	....	....	....
Monetary authorities	8 715 ..	....	....	....	....	....	....	....	....
of which: Short-term	8 718 ..	....	....	....	....	....	....	....	....
General government	8 719 ..	....	....	....	....	....	....	....	....
of which: Short-term	8 721 ..	....	....	....	....	....	....	....	....
Banks	8 722 ..	....	....	....	....	....	....	....	....
of which: Short-term	8 724 ..	....	....	....	....	....	....	....	....
Other sectors	8 725 ..	....	....	....	....	....	....	....	....
of which: Short-term	8 727 ..	....	....	....	....	....	....	....	....
Currency and deposits	8 730 ..	724	1,377	1,700	2,538	3,078	3,624	5,087	5,429
Monetary authorities	8 731 ..	....	....	....	....	....	....	....	....
General government	8 732 ..	....	....	....	....	....	....	....	....
Banks	8 733 ..	724	1,377	1,700	2,538	3,078	3,624	5,087	5,429
Other sectors	8 734 ..	....	....	....	....	....	....	....	....
Other assets	8 736 ..	....	....	....	....	....	....	....	....
Monetary authorities	8 737 ..	....	....	....	....	....	....	....	....
of which: Short-term	8 739 ..	....	....	....	....	....	....	....	....
General government	8 740 ..	....	....	....	....	....	....	....	....
of which: Short-term	8 742 ..	....	....	....	....	....	....	....	....
Banks	8 743 ..	....	....	....	....	....	....	....	....
of which: Short-term	8 745 ..	....	....	....	....	....	....	....	....
Other sectors	8 746 ..	....	....	....	....	....	....	....	....
of which: Short-term	8 748 ..	....	....	....	....	....	....	....	....
Reserve assets	8 802 ..	**1,180**	**1,074**	**1,008**	**1,161**	**1,438**	**2,147**	**2,023**	**3,521**
Monetary gold	8 812 ..	233	234	293	348	368	433	534	704
Special drawing rights	8 811 ..	....	2	2	1	56	22	8	24
Reserve position in the Fund	8 810 ..	22	22	23	25	27	25	26	27
Foreign exchange	8 803 ..	944	821	695	789	984	1,668	1,456	2,763
Other claims	8 813 ..	−20	−5	−5	−3	2	−1	....	2

Table 3 (Concluded). INTERNATIONAL INVESTMENT POSITION (End-period stocks), 2000–2007

(Millions of U.S. dollars)

	Code	2000	2001	2002	2003	2004	2005	2006	2007
LIABILITIES	8 995 D.	21,331	24,059	26,941	28,452	30,044	30,736	30,865	31,801
Direct investment in Ecuador	8 555	7,081	8,410	9,686	10,557	11,394	11,888	12,158	12,341
Equity capital and reinvested earnings	8 556	1,577	1,820	2,037	2,327	2,567	2,759	3,011	3,283
Claims on direct investors	8 557	....	....	....	....	....	....	....	....
Liabilities to direct investors	8 558	1,577	1,820	2,037	2,327	2,567	2,759	3,011	3,283
Other capital	8 580	5,504	6,591	7,648	8,231	8,827	9,129	9,148	9,058
Claims on direct investors	8 585	....	....	....	....	....	....	....	....
Liabilities to direct investors	8 590	5,504	6,591	7,648	8,231	8,827	9,129	9,148	9,058
Portfolio investment	8 652	4,017	4,134	4,134	4,142	4,143	4,791	4,048	4,045
Equity securities	8 660	54	55	56	66	67	69	69	69
Banks	8 663	....	....	....	....	....	....	....	....
Other sectors	8 664	54	55	56	66	67	69	69	69
Debt securities	8 669	3,963	4,079	4,078	4,077	4,076	4,723	3,979	3,976
Bonds and notes	8 670	3,963	4,079	4,078	4,077	4,076	4,723	3,979	3,976
Monetary authorities	8 671	....	....	....	....	....	....	....	....
General government	8 672	3,963	4,079	4,078	4,077	4,076	4,723	3,979	3,976
Banks	8 673	....	....	....	....	....	....	....	....
Other sectors	8 674	....	....	....	....	....	....	....	....
Money market instruments	8 680	....	....	....	....	....	....	....	....
Monetary authorities	8 681	....	....	....	....	....	....	....	....
General government	8 682	....	....	....	....	....	....	....	....
Banks	8 683	....	....	....	....	....	....	....	....
Other sectors	8 684	....	....	....	....	....	....	....	....
Financial derivatives	8 905	....	....	....	....	....	....	....	....
Monetary authorities	8 906	....	....	....	....	....	....	....	....
General government	8 907	....	....	....	....	....	....	....	....
Banks	8 908	....	....	....	....	....	....	....	....
Other sectors	8 909	....	....	....	....	....	....	....	....
Other investment	8 753	10,234	11,515	13,121	13,753	14,507	14,057	14,659	15,415
Trade credits	8 756	246	118	95	202	544	856	848	840
General government	8 757	153	39	37	38	39	28	21	12
of which: Short-term	8 759	....	....	....	....	....	....	....	....
Other sectors	8 760	94	79	58	164	505	828	828	828
of which: Short-term	8 762	....	....	....	....	....	....	....	....
Loans	8 764	8,490	10,125	12,117	12,918	13,316	12,540	12,959	13,547
Monetary authorities	8 765	458	356	334	398	298	85	30	6
of which: Use of Fund credit and loans from the Fund	8 766	*148*	*190*	*308*	*390*	*290*	*78*	*23*	....
of which: Short-term	8 768	....	....	....	....	....	....	....	....
General government	8 769	4,999	6,043	6,507	6,904	6,579	5,828	5,892	6,255
of which: Short-term	8 771	....	....	....	....	....	....	....	....
Banks	8 772	550	435	120	98	77	53	42	35
of which: Short-term	8 774	....	....	....	....	....	....	....	....
Other sectors	8 775	2,483	3,291	5,156	5,518	6,362	6,574	6,996	7,250
of which: Short-term	8 777	*2,229*	*3,038*	*4,899*	*5,272*	*6,128*	*6,363*	*6,782*	*7,051*
Currency and deposits	8 780	632	1,183	772	607	632	660	850	959
Monetary authorities	8 781	....	....	....	....	....	....	....	....
General government	8 782	....	....	....	....	....	....	....	....
Banks	8 783	632	1,183	772	607	632	660	850	959
Other sectors	8 784	....	....	....	....	....	....	....	....
Other liabilities	8 786	866	89	137	26	15	1	1	69
Monetary authorities	8 787	....	....	....	....	....	....	....	....
of which: Short-term	8 789	....	....	....	....	....	....	....	....
General government	8 790	863	80	131	26	15	1	1	69
of which: Short-term	8 792	*863*	*80*	*131*	*26*	*15*	*1*	*1*	*69*
Banks	8 793	2	9	5	....	....	....	....	....
of which: Short-term	8 795	*2*	*9*	*5*	....	....	....	....	....
Other sectors	8 796	....	....	....	....	....	....	....	....
of which: Short-term	8 798	....	....	....	....	....	....	....	....
NET INTERNATIONAL INVESTMENT POSITION	8 995	−19,427	−21,609	−23,805	−24,014	−24,598	−23,806	−21,954	−20,937

Table 1. ANALYTIC PRESENTATION, 2000–2007

(Millions of U.S. dollars)

	Code	2000	2001	2002	2003	2004	2005	2006	2007
A. Current Account[1]..................................	4 993 Z.	**−971**	**−388**	**622**	**3,743**	**3,922**	**2,103**	**2,635**	**412**
Goods: exports f.o.b........................	2 100 ..	7,061	7,025	7,118	8,987	12,320	16,073	20,546	24,455
Goods: imports f.o.b........................	3 100 ..	−15,382	−13,960	−12,879	−13,189	−18,895	−23,818	−28,984	−39,354
Balance on Goods.........................	4 100 ..	*−8,321*	*−6,935*	*−5,762*	*−4,201*	*−6,576*	*−7,745*	*−8,438*	*−14,900*
Services: credit............................	2 200 ..	9,803	9,042	9,320	11,073	14,197	14,643	16,135	19,943
Services: debit.............................	3 200 ..	−7,513	−7,037	−6,629	−6,474	−8,020	−10,508	−11,569	−14,342
Balance on Goods and Services.........	4 991 ..	*−6,031*	*−4,929*	*−3,071*	*398*	*−399*	*−3,611*	*−3,873*	*−9,299*
Income: credit.............................	2 300 ..	1,871	1,468	698	578	572	1,425	2,560	3,309
Income: debit..............................	3 300 ..	−983	−885	−965	−832	−818	−1,460	−1,822	−1,921
Balance on Goods, Services, and Income.........	4 992 ..	*−5,143*	*−4,346*	*−3,338*	*145*	*−645*	*−3,645*	*−3,134*	*−7,911*
Current transfers: credit..................	2 379 Z.	4,224	4,056	4,002	3,708	4,615	5,831	5,933	8,562
Current transfers: debit..................	3 379 ..	−52	−98	−42	−109	−48	−82	−163	−240
B. Capital Account[1]..................................	4 994 Z.	....	....	....	....	....	**−40**	**−36**	**2**
Capital account: credit...................	2 994 Z.	....	....	....	....	....	....	5	5
Capital account: debit....................	3 994 ..	....	....	....	....	....	−40	−41	−3
Total, Groups A Plus B....................	4 981 ..	*−971*	*−388*	*622*	*3,743*	*3,922*	*2,063*	*2,600*	*414*
C. Financial Account[1]..................	4 995 W.	**−1,646**	**190**	**−3,333**	**−5,725**	**−4,461**	**5,591**	**−297**	**3,023**
Direct investment abroad................	4 505 ..	−51	−12	−28	−21	−159	−92	−148	−665
Direct investment in Egypt...............	4 555 Z.	1,235	510	647	237	1,253	5,376	10,043	11,578
Portfolio investment assets..............	4 602 ..	−3	−2	−6	−25	324	−60	−703	−846
Equity securities.......................	4 610 ..	−3	−2	−6	−25	324	−60	−703	−846
Debt securities.........................	4 619 ..	....	....	....	....	....	....	....	....
Portfolio investment liabilities..........	4 652 Z.	269	1,463	−672	−18	−85	3,528	3	−2,728
Equity securities.......................	4 660 ..	269	39	−217	37	26	729	502	−3,199
Debt securities.........................	4 669 Z.	....	1,424	−455	−55	−111	2,799	−499	471
Financial derivatives.....................	4 910 ..	....	....	....	....	....	....	....	....
Financial derivatives assets..............	4 900 ..	....	....	....	....	....	....	....	....
Financial derivatives liabilities..........	4 905 ..	....	....	....	....	....	....	....	....
Other investment assets.................	4 703 ..	−2,991	−1,261	−2,943	−4,651	−5,888	−3,246	−9,743	−5,498
Monetary authorities...................	4 701 ..	−21	−73	29	−38	−4	....	−100	−101
General government....................	4 704 ..	....	....	....	....	....	....	....	....
Banks.................................	4 705 ..	257	1,369	−331	−1,682	−3,215	−2,765	−8,573	−4,585
Other sectors..........................	4 728 ..	−3,227	−2,556	−2,641	−2,931	−2,669	−481	−1,070	−812
Other investment liabilities..............	4 753 W.	−105	−509	−331	−1,248	94	85	252	1,182
Monetary authorities...................	4 753 WA	−5	104	5	6	−16	−2	3	16
General government....................	4 753 ZB	−1,109	−1,157	−1,358	−1,673	−1,740	−1,901	−1,697	−1,792
Banks.................................	4 753 ZC	−129	−56	−9	−601	−326	128	−300	930
Other sectors..........................	4 753 ZD	1,138	601	1,031	1,020	2,175	1,860	2,246	2,028
Total, Groups A Through C..............	4 983 ..	*−2,617*	*−199*	*−2,710*	*−1,982*	*−539*	*7,653*	*2,303*	*3,436*
D. Net Errors and Omissions.............	4 998 ..	**587**	**−1,146**	**1,906**	**1,575**	**−45**	**−2,427**	**634**	**251**
Total, Groups A Through D..............	4 984 ..	*−2,030*	*−1,345*	*−804*	*−407*	*−584*	*5,226*	*2,937*	*3,687*
E. Reserves and Related Items.............	4 802 A.	**2,030**	**1,345**	**804**	**407**	**584**	**−5,226**	**−2,937**	**−3,687**
Reserve assets............................	4 802 ..	1,306	507	−57	−395	−684	−6,319	−3,608	−5,475
Use of Fund credit and loans............	4 766 ..	....	....	....	....	....	....	....	....
Exceptional financing....................	4 920 ..	724	838	861	801	1,269	1,093	671	1,788
Conversion rates: Egyptian pounds per U.S. dollar............................	0 101 ..	**3.4721**	**3.9730**	**4.4997**	**5.8509**	**6.1962**	**5.7788**	**5.7332**	**5.5038**

[1] Excludes components that have been classified in the categories of Group E.

Table 2. STANDARD PRESENTATION, 2000–2007

(Millions of U.S. dollars)

	Code	2000	2001	2002	2003	2004	2005	2006	2007
CURRENT ACCOUNT	4 993 ..	**−971**	**−388**	**622**	**3,743**	**3,922**	**2,103**	**2,635**	**412**
A. GOODS	4 100 ..	**−8,321**	**−6,935**	**−5,762**	**−4,201**	**−6,576**	**−7,745**	**−8,438**	**−14,900**
Credit	2 100 ..	**7,061**	**7,025**	**7,118**	**8,987**	**12,320**	**16,073**	**20,546**	**24,455**
General merchandise: exports f.o.b.	2 110 ..	6,465	6,468	6,668	8,368	11,478	15,238	19,590	23,363
Goods for processing: exports f.o.b.	2 150 ..	....	....	....	....	....	....	....	....
Repairs on goods	2 160 ..	....	....	....	....	....	....	....	....
Goods procured in ports by carriers	2 170 ..	596	557	450	620	842	836	956	1,092
Nonmonetary gold	2 180 ..	....	....	....	....	....	....	....	....
Debit	3 100 ..	**−15,382**	**−13,960**	**−12,879**	**−13,189**	**−18,895**	**−23,818**	**−28,984**	**−39,354**
General merchandise: imports f.o.b.	3 110 ..	−15,346	−13,884	−12,810	−13,105	−18,834	−23,676	−28,843	−39,160
Goods for processing: imports f.o.b.	3 150 ..	....	....	....	....	....	....	....	....
Repairs on goods	3 160 ..	....	....	....	....	....	....	....	....
Goods procured in ports by carriers	3 170 ..	−36	−76	−70	−84	−61	−143	−140	−195
Nonmonetary gold	3 180 ..	....	....	....	....	....	....	....	....
B. SERVICES	4 200 ..	**2,290**	**2,006**	**2,691**	**4,599**	**6,177**	**4,135**	**4,565**	**5,601**
Total credit	2 200 ..	*9,803*	*9,042*	*9,320*	*11,073*	*14,197*	*14,643*	*16,135*	*19,943*
Total debit	3 200 ..	*−7,513*	*−7,037*	*−6,629*	*−6,474*	*−8,020*	*−10,508*	*−11,569*	*−14,342*
Transportation services, credit	2 205 ..	**2,645**	**2,738**	**2,797**	**3,299**	**4,016**	**4,746**	**5,489**	**6,949**
Passenger	2 850 ..	*312*	*319*	*369*	*120*	*203*	*355*	*542*	*1,024*
Freight	2 851 ..	*321*	*347*	*301*	*350*	*398*	*522*	*674*	*610*
Other	2 852 ..	*2,012*	*2,072*	*2,127*	*2,829*	*3,415*	*3,869*	*4,273*	*5,315*
Sea transport, passenger	2 207 ..	....	....	1	1	2	4	21	22
Sea transport, freight	2 208 ..	320	339	297	347	393	486	651	578
Sea transport, other	2 209 ..	....	....	....	....	....	....	....	....
Air transport, passenger	2 211 ..	312	319	368	119	201	351	522	1,002
Air transport, freight	2 212 ..	1	8	4	3	5	36	22	32
Air transport, other	2 213 ..	....	....	....	....	....	....	....	....
Other transport, passenger	2 215 ..	....	....	....	....	....	....	....	....
Other transport, freight	2 216 ..	....	....	....	....	....	....	....	....
Other transport, other	2 217 ..	2,012	2,072	2,127	2,829	3,415	3,869	4,273	5,315
Transportation services, debit	3 205 ..	**−2,212**	**−2,037**	**−1,782**	**−2,013**	**−2,986**	**−3,731**	**−4,525**	**−6,017**
Passenger	3 850 ..	*−134*	*−116*	*−43*	*−144*	*−286*	*−303*	*−372*	*−440*
Freight	3 851 ..	*−2,013*	*−1,857*	*−1,697*	*−1,783*	*−2,632*	*−3,222*	*−3,865*	*−5,129*
Other	3 852 ..	*−65*	*−64*	*−42*	*−86*	*−69*	*−207*	*−288*	*−448*
Sea transport, passenger	3 207 ..	....	−11	−1	−2	−2	−2	−1	−3
Sea transport, freight	3 208 ..	−2,002	−1,849	−1,686	−1,774	−2,619	−3,212	−3,843	−5,094
Sea transport, other	3 209 ..	....	−11	−3	−2	−2	−1	−2	−2
Air transport, passenger	3 211 ..	−134	−105	−42	−143	−284	−301	−371	−437
Air transport, freight	3 212 ..	−2	−1	−5	−3	−3	−1	−8	−22
Air transport, other	3 213 ..	−65	−53	−40	−84	−29	−140	−72	−253
Other transport, passenger	3 215 ..	....	....	....	....	....	....	....	....
Other transport, freight	3 216 ..	−9	−7	−6	−6	−9	−9	−14	−13
Other transport, other	3 217 ..	....	....	....	....	−39	−66	−214	−194
Travel, credit	2 236 ..	**4,345**	**3,800**	**3,764**	**4,584**	**6,125**	**6,851**	**7,591**	**9,303**
Business travel	2 237 ..	....	....	....	....	....	....	....	....
Personal travel	2 240 ..	....	....	....	....	....	....	....	....
Travel, debit	3 236 ..	**−1,072**	**−1,132**	**−1,266**	**−1,321**	**−1,257**	**−1,629**	**−1,784**	**−2,446**
Business travel	3 237 ..	−88	−94	−101	−89	−83	−80	−79	−102
Personal travel	3 240 ..	−984	−1,038	−1,165	−1,232	−1,175	−1,549	−1,705	−2,344
Other services, credit	2 200 BA	**2,813**	**2,504**	**2,759**	**3,190**	**4,055**	**3,046**	**3,055**	**3,691**
Communications	2 245 ..	306	232	221	309	405	362	496	757
Construction	2 249 ..	93	141	172	222	406	503	430	984
Insurance	2 253 ..	30	9	22	37	38	58	36	82
Financial	2 260 ..	52	70	85	80	74	137	149	86
Computer and information	2 262 ..	23	22	27	23	33	25	52	88
Royalties and licence fees	2 266 ..	59	46	38	121	100	136	138	122
Other business services	2 268 ..	2,119	1,737	1,948	2,092	2,780	1,549	1,337	1,197
Personal, cultural, and recreational	2 287 ..	15	19	54	72	69	83	116	92
Government, n.i.e.	2 291 ..	116	227	193	236	150	194	301	284
Other services, debit	3 200 BA	**−4,229**	**−3,868**	**−3,580**	**−3,140**	**−3,776**	**−5,148**	**−5,260**	**−5,879**
Communications	3 245 ..	−102	−128	−125	−148	−224	−406	−309	−471
Construction	3 249 ..	....	....	−124	−108	−171	−231	−166	−257
Insurance	3 253 ..	−450	−411	−398	−423	−588	−781	−978	−1,282
Financial	3 260 ..	−21	−27	−28	−26	−27	−198	−67	−85
Computer and information	3 262 ..	−20	−13	−14	−27	−24	−27	−30	−36
Royalties and licence fees	3 266 ..	−401	−361	−171	−165	−108	−182	−159	−241
Other business services	3 268 ..	−2,862	−2,225	−2,090	−1,793	−2,069	−2,301	−2,232	−2,224
Personal, cultural, and recreational	3 287 ..	−21	−22	−14	−15	−15	−22	−39	−29
Government, n.i.e.	3 291 ..	−352	−680	−616	−436	−550	−1,001	−1,281	−1,255

Table 2 (Continued). STANDARD PRESENTATION, 2000–2007

(Millions of U.S. dollars)

	Code	2000	2001	2002	2003	2004	2005	2006	2007
C. INCOME	4 300	**888**	**583**	**−267**	**−253**	**−246**	**−35**	**738**	**1,388**
Total credit	2 300	*1,871*	*1,468*	*698*	*578*	*572*	*1,425*	*2,560*	*3,309*
Total debit	3 300	*−983*	*−885*	*−965*	*−832*	*−818*	*−1,460*	*−1,822*	*−1,921*
Compensation of employees, credit	2 310	....	....	....	....	....	....	....	....
Compensation of employees, debit	3 310	....	....	....	....	....	....	....	....
Investment income, credit	2 320	**1,871**	**1,468**	**698**	**578**	**572**	**1,425**	**2,560**	**3,309**
Direct investment income	2 330	71	85	56	76	16	92	110	46
Dividends and distributed branch profits	2 332	71	85	56	76	16	92	110	46
Reinvested earnings and undistributed branch profits	2 333	....	....	....	....	....	....	....	....
Income on debt (interest)	2 334	....	....	....	....	....	....	....	....
Portfolio investment income	2 339	176	151	87	91	92	132	152	679
Income on equity	2 340	....	....	....	....	....	....	....	....
Income on bonds and notes	2 350	176	151	87	91	92	132	152	679
Income on money market instruments	2 360	....	....	....	....	....	....	....	....
Other investment income	2 370	1,624	1,232	556	412	465	1,201	2,298	2,585
Investment income, debit	3 320	**−983**	**−885**	**−965**	**−832**	**−818**	**−1,460**	**−1,822**	**−1,921**
Direct investment income	3 330	−92	−28	−89	−47	−56	−647	−915	−1,015
Dividends and distributed branch profits	3 332	−92	−28	−89	−47	−56	−647	−843	−914
Reinvested earnings and undistributed branch profits	3 333	....	....	....	....	....	....	−72	−101
Income on debt (interest)	3 334	....	....	....	....	....	....	....	....
Portfolio investment income	3 339	....	....	−128	−65	−61	−153	−209	−180
Income on equity	3 340	....	....	....	....	....	....	....	....
Income on bonds and notes	3 350	....	....	−128	−65	−61	−153	−209	−180
Income on money market instruments	3 360	....	....	....	....	....	....	....	....
Other investment income	3 370	−891	−857	−748	−720	−702	−661	−699	−726
D. CURRENT TRANSFERS	4 379	**4,172**	**3,957**	**3,960**	**3,599**	**4,567**	**5,748**	**5,770**	**8,322**
Credit	2 379	**4,224**	**4,056**	**4,002**	**3,708**	**4,615**	**5,831**	**5,933**	**8,562**
General government	2 380	857	849	1,056	696	1,218	766	541	824
Other sectors	2 390	3,367	3,207	2,946	3,012	3,397	5,064	5,392	7,738
Workers' remittances	2 391	2,852	2,911	2,893	2,961	3,341	5,017	5,330	7,656
Other current transfers	2 392	515	295	53	51	56	47	63	82
Debit	3 379	**−52**	**−98**	**−42**	**−109**	**−48**	**−82**	**−163**	**−240**
General government	3 380	−17	−64	−27	−29	−32	−25	−28	−60
Other sectors	3 390	−35	−35	−15	−80	−16	−57	−135	−180
Workers' remittances	3 391	−32	−35	−14	−79	−13	−57	−135	−180
Other current transfers	3 392	−3	....	−1	−1	−3	....	....	....
CAPITAL AND FINANCIAL ACCOUNT	4 996	**384**	**1,534**	**−2,529**	**−5,318**	**−3,876**	**324**	**−3,269**	**−662**
CAPITAL ACCOUNT	4 994	....	....	....	....	....	**−40**	**−36**	**2**
Total credit	2 994	....	....	....	....	....	....	*5*	*5*
Total debit	3 994	....	....	....	....	....	*−40*	*−41*	*−3*
Capital transfers, credit	2 400	....	....	....	....	....	....	**5**	**5**
General government	2 401	....	....	....	....	....	....	....	....
Debt forgiveness	2 402	....	....	....	....	....	....	....	....
Other capital transfers	2 410	....	....	....	....	....	....	....	....
Other sectors	2 430	....	....	....	....	....	....	5	5
Migrants' transfers	2 431	....	....	....	....	....	....	....	....
Debt forgiveness	2 432	....	....	....	....	....	....	....	....
Other capital transfers	2 440	....	....	....	....	....	....	5	5
Capital transfers, debit	3 400	....	....	....	....	....	**−40**	**−41**	**−3**
General government	3 401	....	....	....	....	....	−40	−40	....
Debt forgiveness	3 402	....	....	....	....	....	....	....	....
Other capital transfers	3 410	....	....	....	....	....	−40	−40	....
Other sectors	3 430	....	....	....	....	....	....	−1	−3
Migrants' transfers	3 431	....	....	....	....	....	....	....	....
Debt forgiveness	3 432	....	....	....	....	....	....	....	....
Other capital transfers	3 440	....	....	....	....	....	....	−1	−3
Nonproduced nonfinancial assets, credit	2 480	....	....	....	....	....	....	....	....
Nonproduced nonfinancial assets, debit	3 480	....	....	....	....	....	....	....	....

Table 2 (Continued). STANDARD PRESENTATION, 2000–2007

(Millions of U.S. dollars)

	Code	2000	2001	2002	2003	2004	2005	2006	2007
FINANCIAL ACCOUNT	4 995	384	1,534	−2,529	−5,318	−3,876	364	−3,234	−664
A. DIRECT INVESTMENT	4 500	1,184	498	619	217	1,094	5,284	9,894	10,913
Direct investment abroad	4 505	−51	−12	−28	−21	−159	−92	−148	−665
Equity capital	4 510	....	....	....	....	....	....	....	....
Claims on affiliated enterprises	4 515	....	....	....	....	....	....	....	....
Liabilities to affiliated enterprises	4 520	....	....	....	....	....	....	....	....
Reinvested earnings	4 525	....	....	....	....	....	....	....	....
Other capital	4 530	−51	−12	−28	−21	−159	−92	−148	−665
Claims on affiliated enterprises	4 535	−51	−12	−28	−21	−159	−92	−148	−665
Liabilities to affiliated enterprises	4 540	....	....	....	....	....	....	....	....
Direct investment in Egypt	4 555	1,235	510	647	237	1,253	5,376	10,043	11,578
Equity capital	4 560	....	....	....	....	....	....	....	....
Claims on direct investors	4 565	....	....	....	....	....	....	....	....
Liabilities to direct investors	4 570	....	....	....	....	....	....	....	....
Reinvested earnings	4 575	....	....	....	....	....	....	72	101
Other capital	4 580	1,235	510	647	237	1,253	5,376	9,971	11,478
Claims on direct investors	4 585	....	....	....	....	....	....	....	....
Liabilities to direct investors	4 590	1,235	510	647	237	1,253	5,376	9,971	11,478
B. PORTFOLIO INVESTMENT	4 600	266	1,461	−678	−43	239	3,468	−700	−3,574
Assets	4 602	−3	−2	−6	−25	324	−60	−703	−846
Equity securities	4 610	−3	−2	−6	−25	324	−60	−703	−846
Monetary authorities	4 611	....	....	....	....	....	....	....	....
General government	4 612	....	....	....	....	....	....	....	....
Banks	4 613	....	....	....	....	....	....	....	....
Other sectors	4 614	−3	−2	−6	−25	324	−60	−703	−846
Debt securities	4 619	....	....	....	....	....	....	....	....
Bonds and notes	4 620	....	....	....	....	....	....	....	....
Monetary authorities	4 621	....	....	....	....	....	....	....	....
General government	4 622	....	....	....	....	....	....	....	....
Banks	4 623	....	....	....	....	....	....	....	....
Other sectors	4 624	....	....	....	....	....	....	....	....
Money market instruments	4 630	....	....	....	....	....	....	....	....
Monetary authorities	4 631	....	....	....	....	....	....	....	....
General government	4 632	....	....	....	....	....	....	....	....
Banks	4 633	....	....	....	....	....	....	....	....
Other sectors	4 634	....	....	....	....	....	....	....	....
Liabilities	4 652	269	1,463	−672	−18	−85	3,528	3	−2,728
Equity securities	4 660	269	39	−217	37	26	729	502	−3,199
Banks	4 663	....	....	....	....	....	....	....	....
Other sectors	4 664	269	39	−217	37	26	729	502	−3,199
Debt securities	4 669	....	1,424	−455	−55	−111	2,799	−499	471
Bonds and notes	4 670	....	1,424	−455	−55	−111	2,799	−499	789
Monetary authorities	4 671	....	....	....	....	....	....	....	....
General government	4 672	....	1,424	−455	−55	−111	2,799	−499	789
Banks	4 673	....	....	....	....	....	....	....	....
Other sectors	4 674	....	....	....	....	....	....	....	....
Money market instruments	4 680	....	....	....	....	....	....	....	−317
Monetary authorities	4 681	....	....	....	....	....	....	....	−660
General government	4 682	....	....	....	....	....	....	....	343
Banks	4 683	....	....	....	....	....	....	....	....
Other sectors	4 684	....	....	....	....	....	....	....	....
C. FINANCIAL DERIVATIVES	4 910	....	....	....	....	....	....	....	....
Monetary authorities	4 911	....	....	....	....	....	....	....	....
General government	4 912	....	....	....	....	....	....	....	....
Banks	4 913	....	....	....	....	....	....	....	....
Other sectors	4 914	....	....	....	....	....	....	....	....
Assets	4 900	....	....	....	....	....	....	....	....
Monetary authorities	4 901	....	....	....	....	....	....	....	....
General government	4 902	....	....	....	....	....	....	....	....
Banks	4 903	....	....	....	....	....	....	....	....
Other sectors	4 904	....	....	....	....	....	....	....	....
Liabilities	4 905	....	....	....	....	....	....	....	....
Monetary authorities	4 906	....	....	....	....	....	....	....	....
General government	4 907	....	....	....	....	....	....	....	....
Banks	4 908	....	....	....	....	....	....	....	....
Other sectors	4 909	....	....	....	....	....	....	....	....

Table 2 (Concluded). STANDARD PRESENTATION, 2000–2007

(Millions of U.S. dollars)

	Code	2000	2001	2002	2003	2004	2005	2006	2007
D. OTHER INVESTMENT	4 700	**−2,372**	**−932**	**−2,413**	**−5,098**	**−4,525**	**−2,068**	**−8,820**	**−2,529**
Assets	4 703	**−2,991**	**−1,261**	**−2,943**	**−4,651**	**−5,888**	**−3,246**	**−9,743**	**−5,498**
Trade credits	4 706	....	....	....	....	....	....	....	....
General government	4 707	....	....	....	....	....	....	....	....
of which: Short-term	4 709	....	....	....	....	....	....	....	....
Other sectors	4 710	....	....	....	....	....	....	....	....
of which: Short-term	4 712	....	....	....	....	....	....	....	....
Loans	4 714	....	....	....	....	....	....	....	....
Monetary authorities	4 715	....	....	....	....	....	....	....	....
of which: Short-term	4 718	....	....	....	....	....	....	....	....
General government	4 719	....	....	....	....	....	....	....	....
of which: Short-term	4 721	....	....	....	....	....	....	....	....
Banks	4 722	....	....	....	....	....	....	....	....
of which: Short-term	4 724	....	....	....	....	....	....	....	....
Other sectors	4 725	....	....	....	....	....	....	....	....
of which: Short-term	4 727	....	....	....	....	....	....	....	....
Currency and deposits	4 730	257	1,369	−331	−1,682	−3,215	−2,765	−8,573	−4,585
Monetary authorities	4 731	....	....	....	....	....	....	....	....
General government	4 732	....	....	....	....	....	....	....	....
Banks	4 733	257	1,369	−331	−1,682	−3,215	−2,765	−8,573	−4,585
Other sectors	4 734	....	....	....	....	....	....	....	....
Other assets	4 736	−3,248	−2,629	−2,612	−2,969	−2,673	−481	−1,170	−913
Monetary authorities	4 737	−21	−73	29	−38	−4	....	−100	−101
of which: Short-term	4 739	....	....	....	....	....	....	....	....
General government	4 740	....	....	....	....	....	....	....	....
of which: Short-term	4 742	....	....	....	....	....	....	....	....
Banks	4 743	....	....	....	....	....	....	....	....
of which: Short-term	4 745	....	....	....	....	....	....	....	....
Other sectors	4 746	−3,227	−2,556	−2,641	−2,931	−2,669	−481	−1,070	−812
of which: Short-term	4 748	*−3,227*	*−2,556*	*−2,641*	*−2,931*	*−2,669*	*−481*	*−1,070*	*−812*
Liabilities	4 753	**619**	**329**	**530**	**−446**	**1,363**	**1,178**	**923**	**2,970**
Trade credits	4 756	1,138	601	1,031	1,020	2,175	1,860	2,246	2,028
General government	4 757	....	....	....	....	....	....	....	....
of which: Short-term	4 759	....	....	....	....	....	....	....	....
Other sectors	4 760	1,138	601	1,031	1,020	2,175	1,860	2,246	2,028
of which: Short-term	4 762	*1,275*	*569*	*1,317*	*1,280*	*2,270*	*2,033*	*2,743*	*2,199*
Loans	4 764	−385	−320	−497	−871	−471	−808	−1,026	−4
Monetary authorities	4 765	....	....	....	....	....	....	....	....
of which: Use of Fund credit and loans from the Fund	4 766	....	....	....	....	....	....	....	....
of which: Short-term	4 768	....	....	....	....	....	....	....	....
General government	4 769	−385	−320	−497	−871	−471	−808	−1,026	−4
of which: Short-term	4 771	....	....	....	....	....	....	....	....
Banks	4 772	....	....	....	....	....	....	....	....
of which: Short-term	4 774	....	....	....	....	....	....	....	....
Other sectors	4 775	....	....	....	....	....	....	....	....
of which: Short-term	4 777	....	....	....	....	....	....	....	....
Currency and deposits	4 780	−129	−56	−9	−601	−326	128	−300	930
Monetary authorities	4 781	....	....	....	....	....	....	....	....
General government	4 782	....	....	....	....	....	....	....	....
Banks	4 783	−129	−56	−9	−601	−326	128	−300	930
Other sectors	4 784	....	....	....	....	....	....	....	....
Other liabilities	4 786	−5	104	5	6	−16	−2	3	16
Monetary authorities	4 787	−5	104	5	6	−16	−2	3	16
of which: Short-term	4 789	*−7*	*94*	*−1*	*−1*	*1*	....	*−1*	*−3*
General government	4 790	....	....	....	....	....	....	....	....
of which: Short-term	4 792	....	....	....	....	....	....	....	....
Banks	4 793	....	....	....	....	....	....	....	....
of which: Short-term	4 795	....	....	....	....	....	....	....	....
Other sectors	4 796	....	....	....	....	....	....	....	....
of which: Short-term	4 798	....	....	....	....	....	....	....	....
E. RESERVE ASSETS	4 802	**1,306**	**507**	**−57**	**−395**	**−684**	**−6,319**	**−3,608**	**−5,475**
Monetary gold	4 812	....	....	....	....	....	....	....	....
Special drawing rights	4 811	−9	13	−53	−90	29	55	−14	−7
Reserve position in the Fund	4 810	....	152	....	....	....	....	....	....
Foreign exchange	4 803	1,315	342	−4	−304	−713	−6,374	−3,594	−5,469
Other claims	4 813	....	....	....	....	....	....	....	....
NET ERRORS AND OMISSIONS	4 998	**587**	**−1,146**	**1,906**	**1,575**	**−45**	**−2,427**	**634**	**251**

Table 3. INTERNATIONAL INVESTMENT POSITION (End-period stocks), 2000–2007

(Millions of U.S. dollars)

	Code	2000	2001	2002	2003	2004	2005	2006	2007
ASSETS	8 995 C.	....	....	....	....	36,003	46,723	61,559	76,365
Direct investment abroad	8 505 ..	....	....	....	....	875	967	1,116	1,781
Equity capital and reinvested earnings	8 506 ..	....	....	....	....	....	....	....	....
Claims on affiliated enterprises	8 507 ..	....	....	....	....	....	....	....	....
Liabilities to affiliated enterprises	8 508 ..	....	....	....	....	....	....	....	....
Other capital	8 530 ..	....	....	....	....	....	....	....	....
Claims on affiliated enterprises	8 535 ..	....	....	....	....	....	....	....	....
Liabilities to affiliated enterprises	8 540 ..	....	....	....	....	....	....	....	....
Portfolio investment	8 602 ..	....	....	....	....	1,790	2,150	2,434	2,779
Equity securities	8 610 ..	....	....	....	....	782	898	886	1,098
Monetary authorities	8 611 ..	....	....	....	....	....	....	....	....
General government	8 612 ..	....	....	....	....	....	....	....	....
Banks	8 613 ..	....	....	....	....	762	879	865	1,079
Other sectors	8 614 ..	....	....	....	....	20	20	21	19
Debt securities	8 619 ..	....	....	....	....	1,008	1,252	1,548	1,681
Bonds and notes	8 620 ..	....	....	....	....	986	1,202	1,498	1,545
Monetary authorities	8 621 ..	....	....	....	....	....	....	....	....
General government	8 622 ..	....	....	....	....	....	....	....	....
Banks	8 623 ..	....	....	....	....	986	1,202	1,498	1,545
Other sectors	8 624 ..	....	....	....	....	....	....	....	....
Money market instruments	8 630 ..	....	....	....	....	22	50	50	136
Monetary authorities	8 631 ..	....	....	....	....	....	....	....	....
General government	8 632 ..	....	....	....	....	....	....	....	....
Banks	8 633 ..	....	....	....	....	22	50	50	136
Other sectors	8 634 ..	....	....	....	....	....	....	....	....
Financial derivatives	8 900 ..	....	....	....	....	....	....	....	....
Monetary authorities	8 901 ..	....	....	....	....	....	....	....	....
General government	8 902 ..	....	....	....	....	....	....	....	....
Banks	8 903 ..	....	....	....	....	....	....	....	....
Other sectors	8 904 ..	....	....	....	....	....	....	....	....
Other investment	8 703 ..	....	....	....	....	18,861	22,374	32,854	40,628
Trade credits	8 706 ..	....	....	....	....	....	....	....	....
General government	8 707 ..	....	....	....	....	....	....	....	....
of which: Short-term	8 709 ..	....	....	....	....	....	....	....	....
Other sectors	8 710 ..	....	....	....	....	....	....	....	....
of which: Short-term	8 712 ..	....	....	....	....	....	....	....	....
Loans	8 714 ..	....	....	....	....	271	428	476	1,486
Monetary authorities	8 715 ..	....	....	....	....	....	....	....	....
of which: Short-term	8 718 ..	....	....	....	....	....	....	....	....
General government	8 719 ..	....	....	....	....	....	....	....	....
of which: Short-term	8 721 ..	....	....	....	....	....	....	....	....
Banks	8 722 ..	....	....	....	....	271	428	476	1,486
of which: Short-term	8 724 ..	....	....	....	....	*203*	*299*	*324*	*997*
Other sectors	8 725 ..	....	....	....	....	....	....	....	....
of which: Short-term	8 727 ..	....	....	....	....	....	....	....	....
Currency and deposits	8 730 ..	....	....	....	....	17,525	21,355	31,495	36,355
Monetary authorities	8 731 ..	....	....	....	....	....	....	....	....
General government	8 732 ..	....	....	....	....	....	....	....	....
Banks	8 733 ..	....	....	....	....	8,730	11,165	19,231	22,061
Other sectors	8 734 ..	....	....	....	....	8,795	10,190	12,264	14,294
Other assets	8 736 ..	....	....	....	....	1,065	591	884	2,787
Monetary authorities	8 737 ..	....	....	....	....	1,065	591	884	2,787
of which: Short-term	8 739 ..	....	....	....	....	*1,065*	*591*	*884*	*2,787*
General government	8 740 ..	....	....	....	....	....	....	....	....
of which: Short-term	8 742 ..	....	....	....	....	....	....	....	....
Banks	8 743 ..	....	....	....	....	....	....	....	....
of which: Short-term	8 745 ..	....	....	....	....	....	....	....	....
Other sectors	8 746 ..	....	....	....	....	....	....	....	....
of which: Short-term	8 748 ..	....	....	....	....	....	....	....	....
Reserve assets	8 802 ..	....	....	....	....	14,477	21,231	25,155	31,178
Monetary gold	8 812 ..	....	....	....	....	717	1,259	1,526	2,042
Special drawing rights	8 811 ..	48	35	91	189	165	101	121	134
Reserve position in the Fund	8 810 ..	156	....	....	....	....	....	....	....
Foreign exchange	8 803 ..	....	....	....	....	13,595	19,872	23,509	29,002
Other claims	8 813 ..	....	....	....	....	....	....	....	....

Table 3 (Concluded). INTERNATIONAL INVESTMENT POSITION (End-period stocks), 2000–2007

(Millions of U.S. dollars)

	Code	2000	2001	2002	2003	2004	2005	2006	2007
LIABILITIES...	8 995 D.	....	....	....	....	56,552	62,803	72,369	84,729
Direct investment in Egypt...............................	8 555 ..	....	....	....	....	23,506	28,882	38,925	50,503
Equity capital and reinvested earnings.............................	8 556 ..	....	....	....	....	....	....	....	....
Claims on direct investors..............................	8 557 ..	....	....	....	....	....	....	....	....
Liabilities to direct investors...........................	8 558 ..	....	....	....	....	....	....	....	....
Other capital...	8 580 ..	....	....	....	....	....	....	....	....
Claims on direct investors..............................	8 585 ..	....	....	....	....	....	....	....	....
Liabilities to direct investors...........................	8 590 ..	....	....	....	....	....	....	....	....
Portfolio investment...............................	8 652 ..	....	....	....	....	2,530	6,058	6,063	4,032
Equity securities.......................................	8 660 ..	....	....	....	....	1,946	2,676	3,178	....
Banks...	8 663 ..	....	....	....	....	....	....	....	....
Other sectors..	8 664 ..	....	....	....	....	1,946	2,676	3,178	....
Debt securities...	8 669 ..	....	....	....	....	584	3,382	2,885	4,032
Bonds and notes.....................................	8 670 ..	....	....	....	....	584	3,382	2,885	3,689
Monetary authorities..............................	8 671 ..	....	....	....	....	....	....	....	....
General government...............................	8 672 ..	....	....	....	....	584	3,382	2,885	3,689
Banks...	8 673 ..	....	....	....	....	....	....	....	....
Other sectors.....................................	8 674 ..	....	....	....	....	....	....	....	....
Money market instruments...........................	8 680 ..	....	....	....	....	....	....	....	343
Monetary authorities..............................	8 681 ..	....	....	....	....	....	....	....	....
General government...............................	8 682 ..	....	....	....	....	....	....	....	343
Banks...	8 683 ..	....	....	....	....	....	....	....	....
Other sectors.....................................	8 684 ..	....	....	....	....	....	....	....	....
Financial derivatives.................................	8 905 ..	....	....	....	....	....	....	....	....
Monetary authorities...................................	8 906 ..	....	....	....	....	....	....	....	....
General government.....................................	8 907 ..	....	....	....	....	....	....	....	....
Banks..	8 908 ..	....	....	....	....	....	....	....	....
Other sectors...	8 909 ..	....	....	....	....	....	....	....	....
Other investment....................................	8 753 ..	....	....	....	....	30,516	27,863	27,382	30,194
Trade credits...	8 756 ..	....	....	....	....	694	814	973	1,005
General government..................................	8 757 ..	....	....	....	....	....	....	....	....
of which: Short-term...............................	8 759 ..	....	....	....	....	....	....	....	....
Other sectors..	8 760 ..	....	....	....	....	694	814	973	1,005
of which: Short-term...............................	8 762 ..	....	....	....	....	*694*	*814*	*973*	*1,005*
Loans...	8 764 ..	....	....	....	....	28,349	25,839	25,672	27,989
Monetary authorities.................................	8 765 ..	....	....	....	....	336	381	343	311
of which: Use of Fund credit and loans from the Fund....	8 766 ..	....	....	....	....	....	....	....	....
of which: Short-term.............................	8 768 ..	....	....	....	....	....	....	....	....
General government.................................	8 769 ..	....	....	....	....	19,163	16,917	17,051	18,605
of which: Short-term.............................	8 771 ..	....	....	....	....	....	....	....	....
Banks...	8 772 ..	....	....	....	....	1,096	1,602	1,277	1,388
of which: Short-term.............................	8 774 ..	....	....	....	....	*51*	*30*	*9*	*30*
Other sectors.......................................	8 775 ..	....	....	....	....	7,755	6,940	7,002	7,685
of which: Short-term.............................	8 777 ..	....	....	....	....	....	....	....	....
Currency and deposits..................................	8 780 ..	....	....	....	....	1,208	1,090	610	1,009
Monetary authorities.................................	8 781 ..	....	....	....	....	650	550	....	....
General government.................................	8 782 ..	....	....	....	....	....	....	....	....
Banks...	8 783 ..	....	....	....	....	558	540	610	1,009
Other sectors.......................................	8 784 ..	....	....	....	....	....	....	....	....
Other liabilities..	8 786 ..	....	....	....	....	264	120	127	191
Monetary authorities.................................	8 787 ..	....	....	....	....	....	....	....	....
of which: Short-term.............................	8 789 ..	....	....	....	....	....	....	....	....
General government.................................	8 790 ..	....	....	....	....	....	....	....	....
of which: Short-term.............................	8 792 ..	....	....	....	....	....	....	....	....
Banks...	8 793 ..	....	....	....	....	264	120	127	191
of which: Short-term.............................	8 795 ..	....	....	....	....	*264*	*120*	*127*	*191*
Other sectors.......................................	8 796 ..	....	....	....	....	....	....	....	....
of which: Short-term.............................	8 798 ..	....	....	....	....	....	....	....	....
NET INTERNATIONAL INVESTMENT POSITION........	8 995 ..	....	....	....	....	−20,549	−16,080	−10,810	−8,364
Conversion rates: Egyptian pounds per U.S. dollar (end of period)..	0 102 ..	3.6900	4.4900	4.5000	6.1532	6.1314	5.7322	5.7036	5.5038

Table 1. ANALYTIC PRESENTATION, 2000–2007

(Millions of U.S. dollars)

	Code	2000	2001	2002	2003	2004	2005	2006	2007
A. Current Account[1]	4 993 Z.	**−430.5**	**−150.3**	**−405.2**	**−702.2**	**−627.7**	**−568.5**	**−676.9**	**−1,118.8**
Goods: exports f.o.b.	2 100 ..	2,963.2	2,891.6	3,019.7	3,152.6	3,339.2	3,446.5	3,757.6	4,034.9
Goods: imports f.o.b.	3 100 ..	−4,702.8	−4,824.1	−4,884.7	−5,439.2	−5,999.6	−6,384.8	−7,299.6	−8,108.2
Balance on Goods	4 100 ..	*−1,739.6*	*−1,932.5*	*−1,865.0*	*−2,286.6*	*−2,660.3*	*−2,938.3*	*−3,542.0*	*−4,073.3*
Services: credit	2 200 ..	698.4	703.6	783.3	949.0	1,089.6	1,128.2	1,426.4	1,491.9
Services: debit	3 200 ..	−933.3	−954.0	−1,023.0	−1,055.8	−1,154.1	−1,214.4	−1,505.4	−1,733.6
Balance on Goods and Services	4 991 ..	*−1,974.5*	*−2,182.9*	*−2,104.7*	*−2,393.4*	*−2,724.8*	*−3,024.6*	*−3,621.0*	*−4,315.0*
Income: credit	2 300 ..	141.3	168.9	159.1	140.4	143.7	174.7	234.1	285.5
Income: debit	3 300 ..	−394.4	−434.6	−482.5	−563.4	−601.6	−753.5	−761.8	−864.9
Balance on Goods, Services, and Income	4 992 ..	*−2,227.6*	*−2,448.6*	*−2,428.1*	*−2,816.5*	*−3,182.7*	*−3,603.4*	*−4,148.7*	*−4,894.4*
Current transfers: credit	2 379 Z.	1,830.3	2,373.5	2,111.1	2,200.2	2,615.1	3,106.3	3,548.7	3,835.3
Current transfers: debit	3 379 ..	−33.2	−75.2	−88.2	−85.9	−60.1	−71.4	−76.9	−59.7
B. Capital Account[1]	4 994 Z.	**109.0**	**198.9**	**208.9**	**112.9**	**100.3**	**93.6**	**106.3**	**150.2**
Capital account: credit	2 994 Z.	109.4	199.3	209.4	113.4	100.8	94.0	106.8	151.2
Capital account: debit	3 994 ..	−.4	−.4	−.5	−.5	−.5	−.4	−.5	−1.0
Total, Groups A Plus B	4 981 ..	*−321.5*	*48.6*	*−196.3*	*−589.3*	*−527.4*	*−474.9*	*−570.6*	*−968.6*
C. Financial Account[1]	4 995 W.	**287.5**	**230.4**	**688.2**	**1,049.7**	**123.0**	**776.5**	**1,031.6**	**600.1**
Direct investment abroad	4 505 ..	5.0	9.7	25.7	−18.6	2.8	−112.9	26.3	−99.8
Direct investment in El Salvador	4 555 Z.	173.4	279.0	470.2	141.7	363.3	511.1	218.9	1,525.6
Portfolio investment assets	4 602 ..	−8.9	−126.5	−289.2	−263.7	−124.8	18.1	62.3	−92.5
Equity securities	4 610 ..	....	....	....	....	....	....	−.4	−21.9
Debt securities	4 619 ..	−8.9	−126.5	−289.2	−263.7	−124.8	18.1	62.7	−70.6
Portfolio investment liabilities	4 652 Z.	−16.8	155.5	554.8	453.2	181.9	86.4	715.1	−103.9
Equity securities	4 660 ..	....	2.4	−2.4	....	....	....	....	....
Debt securities	4 669 Z.	−16.8	153.1	557.2	453.2	181.9	86.4	715.1	−103.9
Financial derivatives	4 910 ..	....	....	....	....	....	....	....	....
Financial derivatives assets	4 900 ..	....	....	....	....	....	....	....	....
Financial derivatives liabilities	4 905 ..	....	....	....	....	....	....	....	....
Other investment assets	4 703 ..	−245.2	−629.1	−223.7	19.6	−159.8	−256.8	−62.1	−148.9
Monetary authorities	4 701 ..	....	....	....	....	....	....	....	....
General government	4 704 ..	....	....	....	....	....	....	....	....
Banks	4 705 ..	−146.4	−391.3	−83.1	133.7	−19.7	−181.9	50.3	−205.5
Other sectors	4 728 ..	−98.8	−237.8	−140.6	−114.1	−140.2	−74.8	−112.4	56.6
Other investment liabilities	4 753 W.	380.0	541.8	150.4	717.5	−140.4	530.6	71.1	−480.4
Monetary authorities	4 753 WA	−19.5	−30.8	−27.7	76.7	−31.0	25.6	−78.1	−35.2
General government	4 753 ZB	83.3	201.0	217.6	33.2	−76.6	41.4	−42.3	−99.3
Banks	4 753 ZC	120.0	278.3	139.2	491.6	214.0	11.4	−250.0	−360.5
Other sectors	4 753 ZD	196.2	93.3	−178.7	116.0	−246.8	452.2	441.5	14.5
Total, Groups A Through C	4 983 ..	*−34.0*	*279.0*	*492.0*	*460.4*	*−404.5*	*301.6*	*461.0*	*−368.6*
D. Net Errors and Omissions	4 998 ..	**−11.5**	**−456.7**	**−615.4**	**−144.2**	**352.0**	**−360.5**	**−389.4**	**648.8**
Total, Groups A Through D	4 984 ..	*−45.5*	*−177.7*	*−123.5*	*316.2*	*−52.5*	*−58.9*	*71.6*	*280.2*
E. Reserves and Related Items	4 802 A.	**45.5**	**177.7**	**123.5**	**−316.2**	**52.5**	**58.9**	**−71.6**	**−280.2**
Reserve assets	4 802 ..	45.5	177.7	123.5	−316.2	52.5	58.9	−71.6	−280.2
Use of Fund credit and loans	4 766 ..	....	....	....	....	....	....	....	....
Exceptional financing	4 920 ..	....	....	....	....	....	....	....	....

[1] Excludes components that have been classified in the categories of Group E.

Table 2. STANDARD PRESENTATION, 2000–2007

(Millions of U.S. dollars)

	Code	2000	2001	2002	2003	2004	2005	2006	2007
CURRENT ACCOUNT	4 993 ..	−430.5	−150.3	−405.2	−702.2	−627.7	−568.5	−676.9	−1,118.8
A. GOODS	4 100 ..	−1,739.6	−1,932.5	−1,865.0	−2,286.6	−2,660.3	−2,938.3	−3,542.0	−4,073.3
Credit	2 100 ..	2,963.2	2,891.6	3,019.7	3,152.6	3,339.2	3,446.5	3,757.6	4,034.9
General merchandise: exports f.o.b.	2 110 ..	1,319.9	1,202.5	1,233.0	1,250.4	1,375.6	1,583.8	1,914.3	2,159.7
Goods for processing: exports f.o.b.	2 150 ..	1,609.0	1,650.3	1,757.3	1,873.0	1,923.2	1,821.3	1,777.4	1,801.1
Repairs on goods	2 160 ..	19.3	24.5	21.8	21.8	31.5	25.0	49.2	51.2
Goods procured in ports by carriers	2 170 ..	14.9	13.9	7.6	7.4	8.6	16.1	16.7	22.9
Nonmonetary gold	2 180 ..	.1	.4	....	....	.4	.3	....	....
Debit	3 100 ..	−4,702.8	−4,824.1	−4,884.7	−5,439.2	−5,999.6	−6,384.8	−7,299.6	−8,108.2
General merchandise: imports f.o.b.	3 110 ..	−3,459.3	−3,569.9	−3,535.8	−3,992.0	−4,469.1	−5,082.0	−6,027.6	−6,761.9
Goods for processing: imports f.o.b.	3 150 ..	−1,152.7	−1,160.6	−1,282.5	−1,379.3	−1,458.2	−1,204.9	−1,156.9	−1,237.1
Repairs on goods	3 160 ..	−35.6	−39.6	−24.3	−35.7	−31.3	−40.2	−52.9	−46.2
Goods procured in ports by carriers	3 170 ..	−54.9	−53.6	−41.7	−31.8	−40.9	−57.7	−62.2	−63.1
Nonmonetary gold	3 180 ..	−.3	−.4	−.4	−.4	−.1	....	....	....
B. SERVICES	4 200 ..	−234.9	−250.4	−239.7	−106.8	−64.5	−86.2	−79.0	−241.7
Total credit	2 200 ..	*698.4*	*703.6*	*783.3*	*949.0*	*1,089.6*	*1,128.2*	*1,426.4*	*1,491.9*
Total debit	3 200 ..	*−933.3*	*−954.0*	*−1,023.0*	*−1,055.8*	*−1,154.1*	*−1,214.4*	*−1,505.4*	*−1,733.6*
Transportation services, credit	2 205 ..	248.6	289.4	311.4	330.8	342.6	345.1	352.3	366.8
Passenger	2 850 ..	*219.6*	*250.8*	*275.5*	*282.1*	*295.5*	*295.1*	*304.2*	*311.1*
Freight	2 851 ..	*11.4*	*19.8*	*5.9*	*6.6*	*7.7*	*7.2*	*6.8*	*6.6*
Other	2 852 ..	*17.6*	*18.8*	*30.0*	*42.1*	*39.5*	*42.9*	*41.3*	*49.2*
Sea transport, passenger	2 207 ..	....	....	....	....	....	....	....	....
Sea transport, freight	2 208 ..	....	....	....	....	....	....	....	....
Sea transport, other	2 209 ..	1.1	7.1	14.9	28.1	28.3	27.9	30.6	31.6
Air transport, passenger	2 211 ..	218.6	249.7	274.8	280.5	293.6	292.5	302.1	309.2
Air transport, freight	2 212 ..	10.8	19.8	5.9	6.6	7.7	7.2	6.8	6.6
Air transport, other	2 213 ..	11.6	11.1	14.3	13.3	11.2	14.5	10.6	10.3
Other transport, passenger	2 215 ..	1.0	1.1	.7	1.6	1.9	2.6	2.1	1.9
Other transport, freight	2 216 ..	.6	....	....	....	....	....	....	....
Other transport, other	2 217 ..	4.9	.6	.8	.7	....	.5	.1	7.3
Transportation services, debit	3 205 ..	−405.0	−365.4	−447.7	−477.8	−504.6	−520.3	−589.4	−726.9
Passenger	3 850 ..	*−53.6*	*−51.9*	*−75.1*	*−81.9*	*−80.9*	*−82.5*	*−83.1*	*−84.8*
Freight	3 851 ..	*−300.5*	*−258.3*	*−320.9*	*−340.5*	*−357.1*	*−359.9*	*−426.7*	*−551.3*
Other	3 852 ..	*−50.9*	*−55.2*	*−51.7*	*−55.4*	*−66.6*	*−77.9*	*−79.7*	*−90.8*
Sea transport, passenger	3 207 ..	....	....	....	....	....	....	....	....
Sea transport, freight	3 208 ..	−104.4	−99.4	−120.5	−148.4	−151.7	−146.9	−202.8	−255.5
Sea transport, other	3 209 ..	....	−.1	....	....	....	−.2	−.2	....
Air transport, passenger	3 211 ..	−53.2	−51.8	−74.8	−80.8	−80.3	−81.8	−82.5	−84.4
Air transport, freight	3 212 ..	−2.3	−3.3	−11.5	−24.3	−24.8	−33.9	−36.0	−51.7
Air transport, other	3 213 ..	−50.6	−55.1	−51.7	−54.7	−66.6	−77.5	−79.4	−90.8
Other transport, passenger	3 215 ..	−.4	−.1	−.3	−1.1	−.6	−.7	−.6	−.4
Other transport, freight	3 216 ..	−193.8	−155.6	−188.9	−167.8	−180.6	−179.1	−187.8	−244.1
Other transport, other	3 217 ..	−.3	....	....	−.7	....	−.2	−.1	....
Travel, credit	2 236 ..	216.9	201.1	245.3	383.1	452.5	542.9	792.9	846.5
Business travel	2 237 ..	83.3	63.1	75.8	119.6	41.7	44.9	145.7	183.5
Personal travel	2 240 ..	133.6	138.0	169.5	263.5	410.8	498.0	647.2	663.1
Travel, debit	3 236 ..	−165.2	−195.3	−191.2	−229.6	−292.0	−346.7	−523.2	−604.8
Business travel	3 237 ..	−33.1	−27.5	−24.2	−29.1	−68.5	−70.9	−131.7	−148.7
Personal travel	3 240 ..	−132.1	−167.8	−167.0	−200.6	−223.5	−275.9	−391.5	−456.1
Other services, credit	2 200 BA	232.9	213.1	226.6	235.1	294.5	240.2	281.2	278.6
Communications	2 245 ..	86.3	108.8	93.4	122.9	139.3	122.7	135.7	162.2
Construction	2 249 ..	14.0	15.6	22.0	10.0	18.6	24.1	45.4	22.9
Insurance	2 253 ..	63.1	26.8	31.6	31.2	34.8	32.3	34.7	35.5
Financial	2 260 ..	6.7	1.8	2.0	2.8	9.7	7.1	3.4	4.2
Computer and information	2 262 ..	3.9	.2	.1	.4	.4	....	.7	....
Royalties and licence fees	2 266 ..	2.4	1.2	1.5	.2	.1	2.4	.5	....
Other business services	2 268 ..	30.6	34.8	42.6	25.3	40.4	21.3	22.0	15.8
Personal, cultural, and recreational	2 287 ..	.6	.4	.2	....	.2	....	....	....
Government, n.i.e.	2 291 ..	25.3	23.5	33.2	42.3	51.0	30.3	38.8	38.0
Other services, debit	3 200 BA	−363.1	−393.3	−384.1	−348.4	−357.5	−347.4	−392.8	−401.9
Communications	3 245 ..	−27.2	−40.4	−25.0	−36.9	−34.0	−25.2	−25.5	−30.8
Construction	3 249 ..	−8.2	−8.6	−15.5	−6.3	−6.5	−12.7	−8.5	−8.0
Insurance	3 253 ..	−113.2	−91.7	−105.6	−106.2	−108.4	−101.6	−128.3	−139.1
Financial	3 260 ..	−38.1	−19.5	−25.2	−19.7	−28.5	−13.0	−9.3	−9.8
Computer and information	3 262 ..	−14.1	−9.6	−8.9	−3.1	−6.1	−2.9	−3.9	−7.4
Royalties and licence fees	3 266 ..	−20.5	−22.1	−20.4	−22.2	−17.8	−30.4	−27.3	−24.1
Other business services	3 268 ..	−119.2	−184.3	−165.3	−137.2	−130.8	−138.2	−162.4	−152.8
Personal, cultural, and recreational	3 287 ..	−1.0	−1.3	−1.9	−1.2	−1.5	−1.6	−1.3	−1.9
Government, n.i.e.	3 291 ..	−21.6	−15.8	−16.3	−15.6	−24.0	−21.8	−26.4	−28.0

2008, International Monetary Fund: *Balance of Payments Statistics Yearbook*

Table 2 (Continued). STANDARD PRESENTATION, 2000–2007

(Millions of U.S. dollars)

	Code	2000	2001	2002	2003	2004	2005	2006	2007
C. INCOME	4 300	**−253.1**	**−265.7**	**−323.4**	**−423.0**	**−457.9**	**−578.8**	**−527.7**	**−579.4**
Total credit	2 300	*141.3*	*168.9*	*159.1*	*140.4*	*143.7*	*174.7*	*234.1*	*285.5*
Total debit	3 300	*−394.4*	*−434.6*	*−482.5*	*−563.4*	*−601.6*	*−753.5*	*−761.8*	*−864.9*
Compensation of employees, credit	2 310	**13.5**	**13.8**	**17.4**	**16.0**	**15.4**	**11.3**	**11.9**	**13.8**
Compensation of employees, debit	3 310	**−19.2**	**−25.7**	**−21.6**	**−24.3**	**−32.3**	**−24.0**	**−28.0**	**−27.5**
Investment income, credit	2 320	**127.8**	**155.1**	**141.7**	**124.4**	**128.3**	**163.4**	**222.2**	**271.7**
Direct investment income	2 330	....	3.4	2.1	7.5	5.3	14.4	19.5	34.1
Dividends and distributed branch profits	2 332	....	3.4	2.1	....	1.1	1.4	2.1	2.0
Reinvested earnings and undistributed branch profits	2 333	....	....	....	....	....	....	....	....
Income on debt (interest)	2 334	....	....	....	7.5	4.2	13.0	17.4	32.1
Portfolio investment income	2 339	....	.3	7.7	13.9	39.9	36.9	40.2	47.0
Income on equity	2 340	....	....	7.7	....	....	....	....	....
Income on bonds and notes	2 350	....	....	....	....	....	....	....	....
Income on money market instruments	2 360	....	.3	....	13.9	39.9	36.9	40.2	47.0
Other investment income	2 370	127.8	151.4	131.9	103.0	83.1	112.1	162.5	190.6
Investment income, debit	3 320	**−375.2**	**−408.9**	**−460.9**	**−539.1**	**−569.3**	**−729.5**	**−733.8**	**−837.4**
Direct investment income	3 330	−59.5	−73.4	−89.3	−84.9	−80.4	−181.0	−89.8	−172.0
Dividends and distributed branch profits	3 332	−41.4	−39.8	−34.2	−41.0	−33.8	−87.7	−41.9	−119.3
Reinvested earnings and undistributed branch profits	3 333	−18.1	−33.6	−6.5	−3.3	−9.3	−56.1	−3.3	−2.0
Income on debt (interest)	3 334	....	....	−48.6	−40.6	−37.4	−37.2	−44.6	−50.8
Portfolio investment income	3 339	−21.2	−10.4	−86.5	−163.3	−184.5	−222.9	−268.8	−260.4
Income on equity	3 340	....	....	....	....	....	....	....	....
Income on bonds and notes	3 350	....	....	....	....	....	....	....	....
Income on money market instruments	3 360	−21.2	−10.4	−86.5	−163.3	−184.5	−222.9	−268.8	−260.4
Other investment income	3 370	−294.5	−325.1	−285.1	−290.9	−304.4	−325.6	−375.2	−405.0
D. CURRENT TRANSFERS	4 379	**1,797.1**	**2,298.3**	**2,022.9**	**2,114.3**	**2,555.0**	**3,034.9**	**3,471.8**	**3,775.6**
Credit	2 379	**1,830.3**	**2,373.5**	**2,111.1**	**2,200.2**	**2,615.1**	**3,106.3**	**3,548.7**	**3,835.3**
General government	2 380	29.4	39.4	25.3	13.6	13.6	19.2	14.8	30.7
Other sectors	2 390	1,800.9	2,334.1	2,085.8	2,186.6	2,601.5	3,087.1	3,533.9	3,804.6
Workers' remittances	2 391	1,750.7	1,910.5	1,935.2	2,105.3	2,547.6	3,017.3	3,470.8	3,695.3
Other current transfers	2 392	50.2	423.6	150.6	81.3	53.9	69.8	63.1	109.3
Debit	3 379	**−33.2**	**−75.2**	**−88.2**	**−85.9**	**−60.1**	**−71.4**	**−76.9**	**−59.7**
General government	3 380	−1.3	....	....	....	....	....	....	....
Other sectors	3 390	−31.9	−75.2	−88.2	−85.9	−60.1	−71.4	−76.9	−59.7
Workers' remittances	3 391	....	....	....	....	....	....	....	....
Other current transfers	3 392	−31.9	−75.2	−88.2	−85.9	−60.1	−71.4	−76.9	−59.7
CAPITAL AND FINANCIAL ACCOUNT	4 996	**442.0**	**607.0**	**1,020.6**	**846.4**	**275.8**	**929.0**	**1,066.3**	**470.0**
CAPITAL ACCOUNT	4 994	**109.0**	**198.9**	**208.9**	**112.9**	**100.3**	**93.6**	**106.3**	**150.2**
Total credit	2 994	*109.4*	*199.3*	*209.4*	*113.4*	*100.8*	*94.0*	*106.8*	*151.2*
Total debit	3 994	*−.4*	*−.4*	*−.5*	*−.5*	*−.5*	*−.4*	*−.5*	*−1.0*
Capital transfers, credit	2 400	**109.4**	**199.3**	**209.4**	**113.4**	**100.8**	**94.0**	**106.8**	**151.2**
General government	2 401	22.7	59.4	2.2	1.8	2.0	42.4	53.4	94.0
Debt forgiveness	2 402	....	....	....	....	....	....	....	....
Other capital transfers	2 410	22.7	59.4	2.2	1.8	2.0	42.4	53.4	....
Other sectors	2 430	86.7	139.9	207.2	111.6	98.8	51.6	53.4	57.2
Migrants' transfers	2 431	1.2	1.7	1.1	1.1	1.1	1.1	1.8	2.2
Debt forgiveness	2 432	....	....	....	....	....	....	....	....
Other capital transfers	2 440	85.5	138.2	206.1	110.5	97.7	50.5	51.6	55.0
Capital transfers, debit	3 400	**−.4**	**−.4**	**−.5**	**−.5**	**−.5**	**−.4**	**−.5**	**−1.0**
General government	3 401	....	....	....	....	....	....	....	....
Debt forgiveness	3 402	....	....	....	....	....	....	....	....
Other capital transfers	3 410	....	....	....	....	....	....	....	....
Other sectors	3 430	−.4	−.4	−.5	−.5	−.5	−.4	−.5	−1.0
Migrants' transfers	3 431	−.4	−.4	−.5	−.5	−.5	−.4	−.5	−1.0
Debt forgiveness	3 432	....	....	....	....	....	....	....	....
Other capital transfers	3 440	....	....	....	....	....	....	....	....
Nonproduced nonfinancial assets, credit	2 480	....	....	....	....	....	....	....	....
Nonproduced nonfinancial assets, debit	3 480	....	....	....	....	....	....	....	....

Table 2 (Continued). STANDARD PRESENTATION, 2000–2007

(Millions of U.S. dollars)

	Code	2000	2001	2002	2003	2004	2005	2006	2007
FINANCIAL ACCOUNT..	4 995 ..	**333.0**	**408.1**	**811.7**	**733.5**	**175.5**	**835.4**	**960.0**	**319.9**
A. DIRECT INVESTMENT...............................	4 500 ..	**178.4**	**288.7**	**495.9**	**123.1**	**366.0**	**398.2**	**245.2**	**1,425.8**
Direct investment abroad............................	4 505 ..	**5.0**	**9.7**	**25.7**	**−18.6**	**2.8**	**−112.9**	**26.3**	**−99.8**
Equity capital.......................................	4 510 ..	5.0	9.7	25.7	−18.6	3.6	−14.3	1.1	3.4
Claims on affiliated enterprises...........	4 515 ..	5.0	9.7	25.7	−18.6	3.6	−14.3	1.1	3.4
Liabilities to affiliated enterprises........	4 520 ..	....	....	....	....	....	....	....	....
Reinvested earnings.............................	4 525 ..	....	....	....	....	....	....	....	....
Other capital.......................................	4 530 ..	....	....	....	....	−.8	−98.6	25.2	−103.2
Claims on affiliated enterprises...........	4 535 ..	....	....	....	....	−.8	−98.6	25.2	−103.2
Liabilities to affiliated enterprises........	4 540 ..	....	....	....	....	....	....	....	....
Direct investment in El Salvador....................	4 555 ..	**173.4**	**279.0**	**470.2**	**141.7**	**363.3**	**511.1**	**218.9**	**1,525.6**
Equity capital.......................................	4 560 ..	155.3	245.3	201.2	125.4	397.6	456.0	223.6	1,445.5
Claims on direct investors..................	4 565 ..	....	....	....	....	....	....	....	....
Liabilities to direct investors...............	4 570 ..	155.3	245.3	201.2	125.4	397.6	456.0	223.6	1,445.5
Reinvested earnings.............................	4 575 ..	18.1	33.7	6.7	3.8	9.3	56.1	3.3	2.0
Other capital.......................................	4 580 ..	....	....	262.3	12.5	−43.7	−1.0	−8.0	78.2
Claims on direct investors..................	4 585 ..	....	....	....	....	....	....	....	....
Liabilities to direct investors...............	4 590 ..	....	....	262.3	12.5	−43.7	−1.0	−8.0	78.2
B. PORTFOLIO INVESTMENT............................	4 600 ..	**−25.7**	**29.0**	**265.6**	**189.5**	**57.1**	**104.5**	**777.4**	**−196.4**
Assets...	4 602 ..	**−8.9**	**−126.5**	**−289.2**	**−263.7**	**−124.8**	**18.1**	**62.3**	**−92.5**
Equity securities.................................	4 610 ..	....	....	....	....	....	....	−.4	−21.9
Monetary authorities.........................	4 611 ..	....	....	....	....	....	....	....	....
General government..........................	4 612 ..	....	....	....	....	....	....	....	....
Banks...	4 613 ..	....	....	....	....	....	....	....	....
Other sectors....................................	4 614 ..	....	....	....	....	....	....	−.4	−21.9
Debt securities...................................	4 619 ..	−8.9	−126.5	−289.2	−263.7	−124.8	18.1	62.7	−70.6
Bonds and notes...............................	4 620 ..	....	....	....	....	....	−9.9	....	....
Monetary authorities.....................	4 621 ..	....	....	....	....	....	....	....	....
General government......................	4 622 ..	....	....	....	....	....	....	....	....
Banks...	4 623 ..	....	....	....	....	....	....	....	....
Other sectors................................	4 624 ..	....	....	....	....	....	−9.9	....	....
Money market instruments.................	4 630 ..	−8.9	−126.5	−289.2	−263.7	−124.8	28.0	62.7	−70.6
Monetary authorities.....................	4 631 ..	....	....	....	....	....	....	....	....
General government......................	4 632 ..	....	....	....	....	....	....	....	....
Banks...	4 633 ..	−8.1	−122.1	9.8	−242.5	−106.6	23.2	69.3	98.7
Other sectors................................	4 634 ..	−.8	−4.4	−299.0	−21.2	−18.2	4.8	−6.6	−169.3
Liabilities...	4 652 ..	**−16.8**	**155.5**	**554.8**	**453.2**	**181.9**	**86.4**	**715.1**	**−103.9**
Equity securities.................................	4 660 ..	....	2.4	−2.4	....	....	....	....	....
Banks...	4 663 ..	....	....	....	....	....	....	....	....
Other sectors....................................	4 664 ..	....	2.4	−2.4	....	....	....	....	....
Debt securities...................................	4 669 ..	−16.8	153.1	557.2	453.2	181.9	86.4	715.1	−103.9
Bonds and notes...............................	4 670 ..	−95.2	101.1	780.2	394.6	133.7	179.5	711.6	−96.8
Monetary authorities.....................	4 671 ..	....	....	....	92.0	−34.8	−30.5	−21.7	....
General government......................	4 672 ..	−95.2	101.1	780.3	302.2	168.5	210.0	733.3	−96.8
Banks...	4 673 ..	....	....	....	....	....	....	....	....
Other sectors................................	4 674 ..	....	....	−.1	.4	....	....	....	....
Money market instruments.................	4 680 ..	78.4	52.0	−223.0	58.6	48.2	−93.1	3.5	−7.1
Monetary authorities.....................	4 681 ..	8.7	−9.7	....	....	....	....	....	....
General government......................	4 682 ..	68.5	65.8	−223.3	58.3	48.2	−93.1	3.5	−7.1
Banks...	4 683 ..	....	....	....	....	....	....	....	....
Other sectors................................	4 684 ..	1.2	−4.1	.3	.3	....	....	....	....
C. FINANCIAL DERIVATIVES............................	4 910 ..	....	....	....	....	....	....	....	....
Monetary authorities.............................	4 911 ..	....	....	....	....	....	....	....	....
General government..............................	4 912 ..	....	....	....	....	....	....	....	....
Banks...	4 913 ..	....	....	....	....	....	....	....	....
Other sectors..	4 914 ..	....	....	....	....	....	....	....	....
Assets...	4 900 ..	....	....	....	....	....	....	....	....
Monetary authorities.........................	4 901 ..	....	....	....	....	....	....	....	....
General government..........................	4 902 ..	....	....	....	....	....	....	....	....
Banks...	4 903 ..	....	....	....	....	....	....	....	....
Other sectors....................................	4 904 ..	....	....	....	....	....	....	....	....
Liabilities...	4 905 ..	....	....	....	....	....	....	....	....
Monetary authorities.........................	4 906 ..	....	....	....	....	....	....	....	....
General government..........................	4 907 ..	....	....	....	....	....	....	....	....
Banks...	4 908 ..	....	....	....	....	....	....	....	....
Other sectors....................................	4 909 ..	....	....	....	....	....	....	....	....

Table 2 (Concluded). STANDARD PRESENTATION, 2000–2007

(Millions of U.S. dollars)

	Code	2000	2001	2002	2003	2004	2005	2006	2007
D. OTHER INVESTMENT	4 700 ..	**134.8**	**−87.3**	**−73.3**	**737.1**	**−300.2**	**273.8**	**9.0**	**−629.4**
Assets	4 703 ..	−245.2	−629.1	−223.7	19.6	−159.8	−256.8	−62.1	−148.9
Trade credits	4 706 ..	−92.7	2.3	24.8	−17.3	−72.5	−99.2	−74.1	−11.2
General government	4 707 ..	....	....	....	....	....	....	....	....
of which: Short-term.	4 709 ..	....	....	....	....	....	....	....	....
Other sectors	4 710 ..	−92.7	2.3	24.8	−17.3	−72.5	−99.2	−74.1	−11.2
of which: Short-term.	4 712 ..	*−92.7*	*2.3*	*24.8*	*−17.3*	*−72.5*	*−99.2*	*−74.1*	*−11.2*
Loans	4 714 ..	−72.7	−186.7	−119.4	61.6	−7.0	−117.6	9.4	−49.2
Monetary authorities	4 715 ..	....	....	....	....	....	....	....	....
of which: Short-term.	4 718 ..	....	....	....	....	....	....	....	....
General government	4 719 ..	....	....	....	....	....	....	....	....
of which: Short-term.	4 721 ..	....	....	....	....	....	....	....	....
Banks	4 722 ..	−65.9	−182.9	−124.0	59.4	3.7	−119.6	9.1	−68.1
of which: Short-term.	4 724 ..	*−65.9*	*−182.9*	*−124.0*	*59.4*	*3.7*	*−119.6*	*9.1*	*−68.1*
Other sectors	4 725 ..	−6.8	−3.8	4.6	2.2	−10.8	2.0	.3	18.9
of which: Short-term.	4 727 ..	....	....	....	....	....	....	....	....
Currency and deposits	4 730 ..	−75.3	−448.8	−129.3	−12.3	−90.6	−46.1	.8	−94.2
Monetary authorities	4 731 ..	....	....	....	....	....	....	....	....
General government	4 732 ..	....	....	....	....	....	....	....	....
Banks	4 733 ..	−77.8	−208.1	41.4	73.5	−23.4	−62.3	41.4	−137.3
Other sectors	4 734 ..	2.5	−240.7	−170.7	−85.8	−67.2	16.2	−40.6	43.1
Other assets	4 736 ..	−4.5	4.1	.2	−12.4	10.3	6.2	1.8	5.6
Monetary authorities..	4 737 ..	....	....	....	....	....	....	....	....
of which: Short-term.	4 739 ..	....	....	....	....	....	....	....	....
General government	4 740 ..	....	....	....	....	....	....	....	....
of which: Short-term.	4 742 ..	....	....	....	....	....	....	....	....
Banks	4 743 ..	−2.7	−.3	−.5	.8	....	....	−.2	−.2
of which: Short-term.	4 745 ..	*−2.7*	*−.3*	*−.5*	*.8*	....	....	....	*−.2*
Other sectors	4 746 ..	−1.8	4.4	.7	−13.2	10.3	6.2	2.0	5.8
of which: Short-term.	4 748 ..	*−1.8*	*4.4*	*.7*	*−13.2*	*10.3*	*6.2*	*2.0*	*5.8*
Liabilities	4 753 ..	**380.0**	**541.8**	**150.4**	**717.5**	**−140.4**	**530.6**	**71.1**	**−480.4**
Trade credits	4 756 ..	62.9	−87.4	117.3	59.7	41.1	184.3	−155.6	8.6
General government	4 757 ..	....	....	....	....	....	....	....	....
of which: Short-term.	4 759 ..	....	....	....	....	....	....	....	....
Other sectors	4 760 ..	62.9	−87.4	117.3	59.7	41.1	184.3	−155.6	8.6
of which: Short-term.	4 762 ..	*62.9*	*−87.4*	*117.3*	*59.7*	*41.1*	*184.3*	*−155.6*	*8.6*
Loans	4 764 ..	317.4	633.9	77.0	692.8	−169.8	356.8	228.4	−487.9
Monetary authorities	4 765 ..	−15.0	−24.3	−24.6	75.4	−29.6	27.9	−75.7	−35.2
of which: Use of Fund credit and loans from the Fund..	4 766 ..	....	....	....	....	....	....	....	....
of which: Short-term.	4 768 ..	....	....	....	....	....	....	....	....
General government	4 769 ..	83.3	201.0	217.6	33.2	−76.6	41.4	−42.3	−99.3
of which: Short-term.	4 771 ..	....	....	....	....	....	....	....	....
Banks	4 772 ..	120.0	278.3	139.2	491.6	214.0	11.4	−250.0	−360.5
of which: Short-term.	4 774 ..	*77.4*	*338.2*	*−60.0*	*284.0*	*30.1*	*−19.8*	*−420.3*	*−136.8*
Other sectors	4 775 ..	129.1	178.9	−255.2	92.6	−277.6	276.1	596.4	7.1
of which: Short-term.	4 777 ..	*−320.9*	*297.4*	*−75.7*	*−29.0*	*−112.9*	*−6.8*	*48.6*	*99.0*
Currency and deposits.	4 780 ..	−.3	−3.9	−9.2	−1.2	−1.7	−1.4	.8	.1
Monetary authorities.	4 781 ..	−4.5	−5.7	−2.7	−1.2	−1.7	−1.4	.8	.1
General government	4 782 ..	....	....	....	....	....	....	....	....
Banks	4 783 ..	....	....	....	....	....	....	....	....
Other sectors	4 784 ..	4.2	1.8	−6.5	....	....	....	....	....
Other liabilities	4 786 ..	....	−.8	−34.7	−33.8	−10.0	−9.1	−2.5	−1.3
Monetary authorities	4 787 ..	....	−.8	−.4	2.5	.3	−.9	−3.2	−.1
of which: Short-term.	4 789 ..	....	....	....	....	....	....	....	....
General government	4 790 ..	....	....	....	....	....	....	....	....
of which: Short-term.	4 792 ..	....	....	....	....	....	....	....	....
Banks	4 793 ..	....	....	....	....	....	....	....	....
of which: Short-term.	4 795 ..	....	....	....	....	....	....	....	....
Other sectors	4 796 ..	....	....	−34.3	−36.3	−10.3	−8.2	.7	−1.2
of which: Short-term.	4 798 ..	....	....	....	*−36.3*	*−10.3*	*−8.2*	*.7*	*−1.2*
E. RESERVE ASSETS	4 802 ..	**45.5**	**177.7**	**123.5**	**−316.2**	**52.5**	**58.9**	**−71.6**	**−280.2**
Monetary gold	4 812 ..	....	....	....	....	....	....	....	....
Special drawing rights	4 811 ..	....	....	....	....	....	....	....	....
Reserve position in the Fund	4 810 ..	....	....	....	....	....	....	....	....
Foreign exchange	4 803 ..	45.5	177.7	123.5	−316.2	52.5	58.9	−71.6	−280.2
Other claims	4 813 ..	....	....	....	....	....	....	....	....
NET ERRORS AND OMISSIONS	4 998 ..	**−11.5**	**−456.7**	**−615.4**	**−144.2**	**352.0**	**−360.5**	**−389.4**	**648.8**

Table 3. INTERNATIONAL INVESTMENT POSITION (End-period stocks), 2000–2007

(Millions of U.S. dollars)

	Code	2000	2001	2002	2003	2004	2005	2006	2007
ASSETS	8 995 C.	**3,004.0**	**3,353.3**	**3,879.3**	**4,473.4**	**4,750.8**	**4,997.4**	**5,047.2**	**5,684.5**
Direct investment abroad	8 505 ..	**103.9**	**64.3**	**127.6**	**146.3**	**93.0**	**310.1**	**284.0**	**383.5**
Equity capital and reinvested earnings	8 506 ..	103.9	64.3	34.0	23.7	19.0	33.6	32.7	29.0
Claims on affiliated enterprises	8 507 ..	103.9	64.3	34.0	23.7	19.0	33.6	32.7	29.0
Liabilities to affiliated enterprises	8 508 ..	....	....	....	....	....	....	....	....
Other capital	8 530 ..	....	....	93.6	122.6	73.9	276.6	251.3	354.5
Claims on affiliated enterprises	8 535 ..	....	....	93.6	122.6	73.9	276.6	251.3	354.5
Liabilities to affiliated enterprises	8 540 ..	....	....	....	....	....	....	....	....
Portfolio investment	8 602 ..	**11.0**	**152.5**	**595.8**	**859.6**	**1,069.2**	**680.8**	**618.5**	**711.0**
Equity securities	8 610 ..	....	17.8	260.1	260.4	257.9	3.1	3.6	25.5
Monetary authorities	8 611 ..	....	....	....	....	....	....	....	....
General government	8 612 ..	....	....	....	....	....	....	....	....
Banks	8 613 ..	....	....	....	....	....	....	....	....
Other sectors	8 614 ..	....	17.8	260.1	260.4	257.9	3.1	3.6	25.5
Debt securities	8 619 ..	11.0	134.7	335.7	599.2	811.3	677.7	614.9	685.4
Bonds and notes	8 620 ..	....	134.7	335.7	599.2	811.3	677.7	614.9	685.4
Monetary authorities	8 621 ..	....	....	....	....	....	....	....	....
General government	8 622 ..	....	....	....	....	....	....	....	....
Banks	8 623 ..	....	134.7	124.8	367.4	473.9	450.7	381.3	282.6
Other sectors	8 624 ..	....	....	210.9	231.8	337.4	226.9	233.6	402.8
Money market instruments	8 630 ..	11.0	....	....	....	....	....	....	....
Monetary authorities	8 631 ..	....	....	....	....	....	....	....	....
General government	8 632 ..	....	....	....	....	....	....	....	....
Banks	8 633 ..	8.1	....	....	....	....	....	....	....
Other sectors	8 634 ..	2.9	....	....	....	....	....	....	....
Financial derivatives	8 900 ..	....	....	....	....	....	....	....	....
Monetary authorities	8 901 ..	....	....	....	....	....	....	....	....
General government	8 902 ..	....	....	....	....	....	....	....	....
Banks	8 903 C.	....	....	....	....	....	....	....	....
Other sectors	8 904 ..	....	....	....	....	....	....	....	....
Other investment	8 703 ..	**995.8**	**1,424.9**	**1,565.2**	**1,557.4**	**1,695.7**	**2,173.5**	**2,236.4**	**2,391.3**
Trade credits	8 706 ..	400.6	405.3	300.7	328.2	386.9	414.3	488.4	499.6
General government	8 707 ..	....	....	....	....	....	....	....	....
of which: Short-term	8 709 ..	....	....	....	....	....	....	....	....
Other sectors	8 710 ..	400.6	405.3	300.7	328.2	386.9	414.3	488.4	499.6
of which: Short-term	8 712 ..	*400.6*	*405.3*	*300.7*	*328.2*	*386.9*	*414.3*	*488.4*	*499.6*
Loans	8 714 ..	74.2	274.0	400.4	338.7	349.1	455.8	446.4	495.6
Monetary authorities	8 715 ..	....	....	....	....	....	....	....	....
of which: Short-term	8 718 ..	....	....	....	....	....	....	....	....
General government	8 719 ..	....	....	....	....	....	....	....	....
of which: Short-term	8 721 ..	....	....	....	....	....	....	....	....
Banks	8 722 ..	63.9	248.8	372.8	313.4	309.7	429.3	420.2	488.4
of which: Short-term	8 724 ..	*63.9*	*248.8*	*372.8*	*313.4*	*309.7*	*429.3*	*420.2*	*488.4*
Other sectors	8 725 ..	10.3	25.2	27.6	25.3	39.4	26.5	26.2	7.2
of which: Short-term	8 727 ..	*10.3*	*25.2*	*27.6*	*25.3*	*39.4*	*26.5*	*26.2*	*7.2*
Currency and deposits	8 730 ..	534.1	702.4	838.2	852.1	938.3	1,290.2	1,290.2	1,384.5
Monetary authorities	8 731 ..	....	....	....	....	....	....	....	....
General government	8 732 ..	22.0	....	....	....	....	....	....	....
Banks	8 733 ..	225.8	409.9	368.5	295.0	318.4	525.7	529.9	666.1
Other sectors	8 734 ..	286.3	292.5	469.7	557.1	619.9	764.5	760.4	718.4
Other assets	8 736 ..	−13.1	43.3	25.9	38.4	21.4	13.3	11.3	11.5
Monetary authorities	8 737 ..	....	....	....	....	....	....	....	....
of which: Short-term	8 739 ..	....	....	....	....	....	....	....	....
General government	8 740 ..	....	....	....	....	....	....	....	....
of which: Short-term	8 742 ..	....	....	....	....	....	....	....	....
Banks	8 743 ..	−16.6	.4	.9	.1	.1	.1	.2	.4
of which: Short-term	8 745 ..	*−16.6*	*.4*	*.9*	*.1*	*.1*	*.1*	*.2*	*.4*
Other sectors	8 746 ..	3.5	42.8	25.0	38.4	21.3	13.2	11.1	11.1
of which: Short-term	8 748 ..	*3.5*	....	....	....	....	....	....	....
Reserve assets	8 802 ..	**1,893.2**	**1,711.6**	**1,590.7**	**1,910.1**	**1,892.9**	**1,833.0**	**1,908.3**	**2,198.7**
Monetary gold	8 812 ..	120.7	117.8	117.8	117.8	138.9	110.2	84.0	88.8
Special drawing rights	8 811 ..	32.6	31.4	34.0	37.1	38.8	35.7	37.6	39.5
Reserve position in the Fund	8 810 ..	....	....	....	....	....	....	....	....
Foreign exchange	8 803 ..	1,706.7	1,535.3	1,422.3	1,754.4	1,714.1	1,684.9	1,782.3	2,069.5
Other claims	8 813 ..	33.3	27.1	16.6	.8	1.1	2.2	4.4	.9

Table 3 (Concluded). INTERNATIONAL INVESTMENT POSITION (End-period stocks), 2000–2007

(Millions of U.S. dollars)

	Code	2000	2001	2002	2003	2004	2005	2006	2007
LIABILITIES...	8 995 D.	**7,358.3**	**8,351.7**	**9,743.9**	**11,192.1**	**11,866.1**	**12,927.9**	**13,969.7**	**14,970.7**
Direct investment in El Salvador.........................	8 555 ..	**2,000.6**	**2,252.1**	**3,133.7**	**3,275.4**	**3,655.5**	**4,166.5**	**4,385.4**	**5,911.0**
Equity capital and reinvested earnings............................	8 556 ..	2,000.6	2,252.1	2,460.0	2,589.2	2,996.1	3,508.1	3,735.0	5,182.5
Claims on direct investors.............................	8 557 ..	....	....						
Liabilities to direct investors..........................	8 558 ..	2,000.6	2,252.1	2,460.0	2,589.2	2,996.1	3,508.1	3,735.0	5,182.5
Other capital...	8 580 ..	....	....	673.6	686.2	659.4	658.4	650.4	728.5
Claims on direct investors.............................	8 585 ..	....	....	....	....	....	....	....	....
Liabilities to direct investors..........................	8 590 ..	....	....	673.6	686.2	659.4	658.4	650.4	728.5
Portfolio investment..	8 652 ..	**202.8**	**352.7**	**948.7**	**1,402.5**	**1,569.6**	**1,651.7**	**2,357.6**	**2,244.3**
Equity securities.......................................	8 660 ..	....	2.4	....	....	....	....	....	....
Banks..	8 663 ..	....	....	....	....	....	....	....	....
Other sectors...	8 664 ..	....	2.4	....	....	....	....	....	....
Debt securities...	8 669 ..	202.8	350.3	948.7	1,402.5	1,569.6	1,651.7	2,357.6	2,244.3
Bonds and notes.....................................	8 670 ..	34.0	126.3	948.4	1,250.5	1,410.4	1,616.0	2,340.6	2,234.3
Monetary authorities...............................	8 671 ..	....	....	....	....	....	....	....	....
General government................................	8 672 ..	34.0	126.3	948.3	1,250.5	1,410.4	1,616.0	2,340.6	2,234.3
Banks...	8 673 ..	....	....	....	....	....	....	....	....
Other sectors.......................................	8 674 ..	....	....	.1	....	....	....	....	....
Money market instruments..........................	8 680 ..	168.8	224.0	.3	152.0	159.2	35.7	17.0	10.0
Monetary authorities...............................	8 681 ..	9.7	....	....	92.0	52.2	21.7	....	....
General government................................	8 682 ..	157.9	223.3	....	60.0	107.0	14.0	17.0	10.0
Banks...	8 683 ..	....	....	....	....	....	....	....	....
Other sectors.......................................	8 684 ..	1.2	.7	.3	....	....	....	....	....
Financial derivatives..	8 905 ..	....	....	....	....	....	....	....	....
Monetary authorities..................................	8 906 ..	....	....	....	....	....	....	....	....
General government...................................	8 907 ..	....	....	....	....	....	....	....	....
Banks..	8 908 ..	....	....	....	....	....	....	....	....
Other sectors...	8 909 ..	....	....	....	....	....	....	....	....
Other investment...	8 753 ..	**5,154.9**	**5,746.9**	**5,661.6**	**6,514.3**	**6,641.0**	**7,109.7**	**7,226.7**	**6,815.4**
Trade credits...	8 756 ..	400.8	397.0	248.7	308.3	408.1	592.4	436.9	445.4
General government...................................	8 757 ..	....	....	....	....	....	....	....	....
of which: Short-term.............................	8 759 ..	....	....	....	....	....	....	....	....
Other sectors...	8 760 ..	400.8	397.0	248.7	308.3	408.1	592.4	436.9	445.4
of which: Short-term.............................	8 762 ..	*400.8*	*397.0*	*248.7*	*308.3*	*408.1*	*592.4*	*436.9*	*445.4*
Loans..	8 764 ..	4,712.6	5,309.8	5,322.2	6,149.6	6,186.8	6,482.2	6,757.4	6,338.7
Monetary authorities.................................	8 765 ..	144.6	120.2	95.4	170.5	145.7	173.6	96.2	61.0
of which: Use of Fund credit and loans from the Fund....	8 766 ..	....	....	....	....	....	....	....	....
of which: Short-term.............................	8 768 ..	....	....	....	....	....	....	....	....
General government................................	8 769 ..	2,448.3	2,678.0	2,510.7	2,629.0	2,626.4	2,637.7	2,646.6	2,626.4
of which: Short-term.............................	8 771 ..	....	....	....	....	....	....	....	....
Banks...	8 772 ..	673.8	950.0	1,100.3	1,592.1	1,806.2	1,817.5	1,568.0	1,207.7
of which: Short-term.............................	8 774 ..	*360.8*	*676.8*	*616.7*	*900.7*	*930.8*	*910.9*	*490.7*	*354.0*
Other sectors.......................................	8 775 ..	1,445.9	1,561.6	1,615.9	1,758.0	1,608.5	1,853.4	2,446.7	2,443.6
of which: Short-term.............................	8 777 ..	*720.4*	*603.1*	*388.0*	*359.0*	*292.3*	*285.4*	*334.0*	*433.0*
Currency and deposits..............................	8 780 ..	41.5	38.1	28.9	27.6	26.0	24.7	23.6	23.7
Monetary authorities.................................	8 781 ..	37.3	31.6	28.9	27.6	26.0	24.7	23.6	23.7
General government................................	8 782 ..	....	....	....	....	....	....	....	....
Banks...	8 783 ..	....	....	....	....	....	....	....	....
Other sectors.......................................	8 784 ..	4.2	6.5	....	....	....	....	....	....
Other liabilities.......................................	8 786 ..	....	2.0	61.8	28.7	20.1	10.4	8.8	7.7
Monetary authorities.................................	8 787 ..	....	2.0	1.7	4.2	4.5	3.6	1.0	.9
of which: Short-term.............................	8 789 ..	....	*2.0*	*1.7*	*4.2*	*4.5*	*3.6*	*1.0*	*.9*
General government................................	8 790 ..	....	....	....	....	....	....	....	....
of which: Short-term.............................	8 792 ..	....	....	....	....	....	....	....	....
Banks...	8 793 ..	....	....	3.7	4.3	4.5	3.8	4.1	4.3
of which: Short-term.............................	8 795 ..	....	....	*3.7*	*4.3*	*4.5*	*3.8*	*4.1*	*4.3*
Other sectors.......................................	8 796 ..	....	....	56.4	20.2	11.1	3.0	3.7	2.5
of which: Short-term.............................	8 798 ..	....	....	....	....	....	....	....	....
NET INTERNATIONAL INVESTMENT POSITION........	8 995 ..	**–4,354.4**	**–4,998.3**	**–5,864.6**	**–6,718.7**	**–7,115.3**	**–7,930.5**	**–8,922.5**	**–9,286.2**

Table 1. ANALYTIC PRESENTATION, 2000–2007

(Millions of U.S. dollars)

	Code	2000	2001	2002	2003	2004	2005	2006	2007
A. Current Account[1].....................	4 993 Z.	**−299.0**	**−324.6**	**−779.3**	**−1,115.4**	**−1,412.7**	**−1,381.6**	**−2,758.7**	**−3,771.8**
Goods: exports f.o.b....................	2 100 ..	3,298.0	3,367.4	3,507.9	4,597.0	5,887.0	7,792.4	9,754.8	11,077.7
Goods: imports f.o.b....................	3 100 ..	−4,079.5	−4,142.1	−4,625.9	−6,164.0	−7,876.6	−9,703.6	−12,777.2	−14,755.7
Balance on Goods....................	4 100 ..	*−781.5*	*−774.7*	*−1,118.0*	*−1,567.0*	*−1,989.7*	*−1,911.2*	*−3,022.4*	*−3,678.0*
Services: credit....................	2 200 ..	1,485.6	1,607.4	1,705.8	2,223.7	2,847.9	3,187.2	3,512.0	4,393.6
Services: debit....................	3 200 ..	−885.9	−962.6	−1,106.3	−1,393.0	−1,746.8	−2,149.6	−2,440.3	−3,072.2
Balance on Goods and Services....................	4 991 ..	*−181.8*	*−129.9*	*−518.5*	*−736.3*	*−888.6*	*−873.6*	*−1,950.7*	*−2,356.6*
Income: credit....................	2 300 ..	119.0	172.9	205.0	249.3	436.2	730.7	1,091.0	1,518.1
Income: debit....................	3 300 ..	−321.7	−453.5	−530.2	−785.3	−1,074.2	−1,300.3	−1,956.4	−3,092.3
Balance on Goods, Services, and Income....................	4 992 ..	*−384.5*	*−410.6*	*−843.7*	*−1,272.3*	*−1,526.6*	*−1,443.2*	*−2,816.0*	*−3,930.9*
Current transfers: credit....................	2 379 Z.	114.6	115.3	125.7	266.5	416.7	465.7	523.5	707.3
Current transfers: debit....................	3 379 ..	−29.1	−29.4	−61.3	−109.5	−302.7	−404.1	−466.2	−548.2
B. Capital Account[1]....................	4 994 Z.	**25.9**	**14.5**	**38.2**	**49.6**	**86.4**	**103.0**	**352.1**	**240.0**
Capital account: credit....................	2 994 Z.	26.2	14.9	39.2	57.8	93.2	109.5	372.5	273.2
Capital account: debit....................	3 994 ..	−.2	−.4	−1.0	−8.2	−6.8	−6.5	−20.4	−33.2
Total, Groups A Plus B....................	4 981 ..	*−273.1*	*−310.2*	*−741.2*	*−1,065.8*	*−1,326.2*	*−1,278.7*	*−2,406.6*	*−3,531.8*
C. Financial Account[1]....................	4 995 W.	**392.9**	**269.4**	**751.5**	**1,274.6**	**−32.4**	**−2,783.2**	**1,593.8**	**−141.8**
Direct investment abroad....................	4 505 ..	−63.4	−200.1	−131.9	−156.1	−268.2	−687.5	−1,114.3	−1,570.9
Direct investment in Estonia....................	4 555 Z.	387.3	542.5	284.5	919.0	597.8	641.4	1,610.3	2,314.7
Portfolio investment assets....................	4 602 ..	15.5	−118.8	−192.0	−394.3	−380.6	−871.6	−1,211.2	−722.4
Equity securities....................	4 610 ..	3.5	14.3	.3	−75.5	−232.4	−387.7	−366.8	−654.1
Debt securities....................	4 619 ..	12.1	−133.2	−192.3	−318.8	−148.2	−483.9	−844.4	−68.3
Portfolio investment liabilities....................	4 652 Z.	75.6	84.7	344.9	561.2	176.1	−1,362.8	308.5	260.1
Equity securities....................	4 660 ..	−28.5	31.9	53.3	110.6	176.1	−1,362.8	308.5	260.1
Debt securities....................	4 669 Z.	104.1	52.8	291.6	450.5	....	....	....	....
Financial derivatives....................	4 910 ..	.7	−2.2	−4.0	−1.8	−.3	−7.5	5.8	−71.5
Financial derivatives assets....................	4 900 ..	−4.7	−.1	−2.6	−9.9	−2.9	1.3	−15.4	−77.2
Financial derivatives liabilities....................	4 905 ..	5.4	−2.1	−1.4	8.1	2.6	−8.8	21.2	5.7
Other investment assets....................	4 703 ..	−166.7	−220.3	50.5	−154.4	−901.2	−866.9	40.0	−1,997.2
Monetary authorities....................	4 701 ..	−9.6	−11.3	−2.8	.1	−.8	−.1	....	....
General government....................	4 704 ..	43.1	35.9	−23.4	39.8	−12.6	−6.0	28.9	−5.1
Banks....................	4 705 ..	−77.0	−219.3	−28.3	−87.0	−674.6	−1,004.2	597.7	−1,581.1
Other sectors....................	4 728 ..	−123.3	−25.6	105.1	−107.3	−213.2	143.4	−586.6	−411.0
Other investment liabilities....................	4 753 W.	143.8	183.6	399.4	501.1	744.0	371.7	1,954.8	1,645.4
Monetary authorities....................	4 753 WA	1.7	−5.4	32.5	43.5	....	....	....	....
General government....................	4 753 ZB	−17.2	−7.3	−53.1	29.2	....	....	....	....
Banks....................	4 753 ZC	76.8	59.4	344.1	336.3	697.8	235.7	1,690.9	1,663.3
Other sectors....................	4 753 ZD	82.5	136.9	75.9	92.0	46.2	136.1	263.9	−17.9
Total, Groups A Through C....................	4 983 ..	*119.8*	*−40.7*	*10.4*	*208.8*	*−1,358.6*	*−4,061.9*	*−812.8*	*−3,673.6*
D. Net Errors and Omissions....................	4 998 ..	**7.8**	**−1.2**	**58.9**	**−39.4**	**1,629.9**	**4,447.4**	**1,433.2**	**3,782.4**
Total, Groups A Through D....................	4 984 ..	*127.6*	*−41.9*	*69.3*	*169.4*	*271.2*	*385.5*	*620.4*	*108.9*
E. Reserves and Related Items....................	4 802 A.	**−127.6**	**41.9**	**−69.3**	**−169.4**	**−271.2**	**−385.5**	**−620.4**	**−108.9**
Reserve assets....................	4 802 ..	−122.4	46.9	−55.2	−169.4	−271.2	−385.5	−620.4	−108.9
Use of Fund credit and loans....................	4 766 ..	−5.2	−4.9	−14.0	....	....	....	....	....
Exceptional financing....................	4 920 ..	....	....	....	....	....	....	....	....
Conversion rates: krooni per U.S. dollar....................	0 101 ..	**16.969**	**17.478**	**16.612**	**13.856**	**12.596**	**12.584**	**12.465**	**11.434**

[1] Excludes components that have been classified in the categories of Group E.

2008, International Monetary Fund: *Balance of Payments Statistics Yearbook*

Table 2. STANDARD PRESENTATION, 2000–2007

(Millions of U.S. dollars)

	Code	2000	2001	2002	2003	2004	2005	2006	2007
CURRENT ACCOUNT....................................	4 993 ..	**−299.0**	**−324.6**	**−779.3**	**−1,115.4**	**−1,412.7**	**−1,381.6**	**−2,758.7**	**−3,771.8**
A. GOODS	4 100 ..	**−781.5**	**−774.7**	**−1,118.0**	**−1,567.0**	**−1,989.7**	**−1,911.2**	**−3,022.4**	**−3,678.0**
Credit	2 100 ..	**3,298.0**	**3,367.4**	**3,507.9**	**4,597.0**	**5,887.0**	**7,792.4**	**9,754.8**	**11,077.7**
General merchandise: exports f.o.b.	2 110 ..	1,883.5	2,064.5	2,389.3	3,203.5	4,853.4	6,934.8	8,113.4	9,678.1
Goods for processing: exports f.o.b.	2 150 ..	1,396.3	1,276.7	1,087.1	1,365.3	1,000.7	805.4	1,606.6	1,348.3
Repairs on goods	2 160 ..	9.3	12.6	19.3	19.1	31.1	45.8	32.9	48.1
Goods procured in ports by carriers	2 170 ..	9.0	13.6	12.2	9.1	1.7	6.2	1.9	3.1
Nonmonetary gold	2 180 ..	....	....	....	....	....	.1	....	....
Debit	3 100 ..	**−4,079.5**	**−4,142.1**	**−4,625.9**	**−6,164.0**	**−7,876.6**	**−9,703.6**	**−12,777.2**	**−14,755.7**
General merchandise: imports f.o.b.	3 110 ..	−2,780.5	−3,074.2	−3,674.0	−5,037.5	−6,984.4	−8,899.4	−11,193.1	−13,279.4
Goods for processing: imports f.o.b.	3 150 ..	−1,260.9	−1,026.4	−915.5	−1,090.4	−837.3	−729.1	−1,470.8	−1,322.0
Repairs on goods	3 160 ..	−2.7	−5.9	−5.1	−6.2	−10.4	−21.0	−22.0	−22.5
Goods procured in ports by carriers	3 170 ..	−34.7	−34.9	−30.8	−29.1	−43.7	−52.5	−84.6	−117.3
Nonmonetary gold	3 180 ..	−.8	−.7	−.5	−.5	−.8	−1.1	−6.8	−14.6
B. SERVICES	4 200 ..	**599.7**	**644.8**	**599.4**	**830.6**	**1,101.1**	**1,037.6**	**1,071.7**	**1,321.3**
Total credit	2 200 ..	*1,485.6*	*1,607.4*	*1,705.8*	*2,223.7*	*2,847.9*	*3,187.2*	*3,512.0*	*4,393.6*
Total debit	3 200 ..	*−885.9*	*−962.6*	*−1,106.3*	*−1,393.0*	*−1,746.8*	*−2,149.6*	*−2,440.3*	*−3,072.2*
Transportation services, credit	2 205 ..	**710.8**	**751.5**	**795.6**	**972.0**	**1,216.0**	**1,245.6**	**1,432.4**	**1,794.5**
Passenger	2 850 ..	*148.5*	*153.9*	*181.5*	*212.0*	*224.4*	*258.1*	*337.6*	*378.9*
Freight	2 851 ..	*299.3*	*348.6*	*365.0*	*506.8*	*695.4*	*665.2*	*760.5*	*940.1*
Other	2 852 ..	*263.1*	*248.9*	*249.0*	*253.3*	*296.2*	*322.2*	*334.4*	*475.5*
Sea transport, passenger	2 207 ..	109.6	113.0	131.2	152.6	124.8	140.4	184.8	243.3
Sea transport, freight	2 208 ..	118.9	120.2	150.5	165.8	234.5	228.8	279.5	409.7
Sea transport, other	2 209 ..	144.7	155.8	157.9	139.6	132.3	162.0	184.8	205.1
Air transport, passenger	2 211 ..	35.3	35.9	45.8	54.0	93.0	110.1	143.1	126.7
Air transport, freight	2 212 ..	2.9	3.5	2.9	13.9	16.1	39.2	30.6	40.2
Air transport, other	2 213 ..	11.2	10.4	13.4	16.1	25.8	28.7	22.5	30.2
Other transport, passenger	2 215 ..	3.6	5.1	4.6	5.4	6.7	7.6	9.6	8.9
Other transport, freight	2 216 ..	177.4	225.0	211.5	327.1	444.7	397.3	450.4	490.2
Other transport, other	2 217 ..	107.2	82.7	77.8	97.5	138.1	131.5	127.1	240.3
Transportation services, debit	3 205 ..	**−419.7**	**−456.0**	**−491.2**	**−515.7**	**−724.3**	**−950.1**	**−1,058.7**	**−1,267.9**
Passenger	3 850 ..	*−48.7*	*−61.3*	*−73.8*	*−85.0*	*−86.7*	*−90.9*	*−120.0*	*−134.0*
Freight	3 851 ..	*−301.5*	*−330.7*	*−336.4*	*−316.2*	*−462.8*	*−631.8*	*−706.6*	*−828.0*
Other	3 852 ..	*−69.5*	*−64.0*	*−81.0*	*−114.5*	*−174.7*	*−227.4*	*−232.1*	*−305.9*
Sea transport, passenger	3 207 ..	−37.8	−48.1	−55.1	−26.3	−26.7	−27.5	−34.2	−32.9
Sea transport, freight	3 208 ..	−112.7	−98.0	−136.3	−132.3	−174.2	−255.9	−293.8	−355.2
Sea transport, other	3 209 ..	−38.2	−40.2	−55.2	−48.7	−71.9	−96.7	−92.2	−144.4
Air transport, passenger	3 211 ..	−8.7	−9.2	−16.2	−49.7	−51.1	−54.2	−74.8	−88.3
Air transport, freight	3 212 ..	−3.4	−4.3	−4.3	−47.7	−72.2	−103.9	−114.9	−127.9
Air transport, other	3 213 ..	−11.3	−11.5	−12.3	−13.8	−33.0	−50.5	−41.9	−28.5
Other transport, passenger	3 215 ..	−2.2	−4.0	−2.6	−9.0	−8.9	−9.2	−11.0	−12.7
Other transport, freight	3 216 ..	−185.4	−228.4	−195.8	−136.2	−216.4	−272.0	−297.9	−344.9
Other transport, other	3 217 ..	−19.9	−12.3	−13.4	−52.0	−69.8	−80.2	−98.0	−132.9
Travel, credit	2 236 ..	**508.2**	**507.2**	**554.8**	**671.0**	**886.6**	**970.7**	**1,023.8**	**1,035.5**
Business travel	2 237 ..	146.1	129.2	152.1	180.4	229.5	229.7	228.2	249.5
Personal travel	2 240 ..	362.1	377.9	402.8	490.5	657.1	741.0	795.6	786.0
Travel, debit	3 236 ..	**−203.7**	**−191.6**	**−230.9**	**−319.0**	**−398.8**	**−437.4**	**−585.9**	**−670.0**
Business travel	3 237 ..	−73.7	−64.3	−71.2	−105.6	−146.6	−173.4	−223.4	−245.7
Personal travel	3 240 ..	−130.0	−127.4	−159.7	−213.4	−252.2	−264.0	−362.5	−424.4
Other services, credit	2 200 BA ..	**266.5**	**348.7**	**355.4**	**580.7**	**745.2**	**971.0**	**1,055.8**	**1,563.6**
Communications	2 245 ..	20.8	18.6	22.4	38.7	63.6	78.0	80.1	125.5
Construction	2 249 ..	38.0	78.7	79.5	85.6	88.6	187.3	87.3	199.3
Insurance	2 253 ..	6.1	4.1	10.3	15.1	14.5	10.4	11.4	14.2
Financial	2 260 ..	10.4	16.7	9.0	16.0	22.9	45.8	71.4	128.8
Computer and information	2 262 ..	21.2	23.3	24.3	31.1	38.8	43.8	92.4	140.9
Royalties and licence fees	2 266 ..	1.6	2.1	4.9	5.2	4.0	5.4	6.3	10.3
Other business services	2 268 ..	140.4	171.0	170.2	352.1	467.2	546.9	654.1	875.9
Personal, cultural, and recreational	2 287 ..	.9	2.5	1.1	1.8	3.5	5.2	7.0	11.1
Government, n.i.e.	2 291 ..	27.3	31.8	33.7	35.1	42.2	48.2	45.7	57.7
Other services, debit	3 200 BA ..	**−262.6**	**−315.0**	**−384.2**	**−558.3**	**−623.7**	**−762.1**	**−795.7**	**−1,134.4**
Communications	3 245 ..	−19.0	−21.4	−23.5	−45.5	−72.4	−90.9	−90.7	−116.1
Construction	3 249 ..	−17.6	−31.3	−85.0	−92.9	−91.7	−184.5	−135.8	−95.3
Insurance	3 253 ..	−2.5	−1.1	−1.6	−1.9	−1.3	−1.2	−1.7	−1.1
Financial	3 260 ..	−8.2	−13.5	−13.2	−20.4	−23.5	−39.0	−52.0	−86.3
Computer and information	3 262 ..	−11.6	−13.2	−15.1	−21.5	−28.6	−32.7	−47.1	−70.9
Royalties and licence fees	3 266 ..	−7.9	−11.2	−14.1	−14.2	−18.0	−24.9	−29.4	−40.3
Other business services	3 268 ..	−178.4	−205.8	−205.2	−336.8	−355.1	−359.7	−399.2	−664.7
Personal, cultural, and recreational	3 287 ..	−1.6	−3.4	−1.0	−1.7	−2.5	−4.6	−6.8	−9.0
Government, n.i.e.	3 291 ..	−15.8	−14.1	−25.4	−23.4	−30.7	−24.4	−33.0	−50.5

Table 2 (Continued). STANDARD PRESENTATION, 2000–2007

(Millions of U.S. dollars)

	Code	2000	2001	2002	2003	2004	2005	2006	2007
C. INCOME	4 300	−202.7	−280.7	−325.2	−536.0	−638.0	−569.6	−865.4	−1,574.3
Total credit	2 300	*119.0*	*172.9*	*205.0*	*249.3*	*436.2*	*730.7*	*1,091.0*	*1,518.1*
Total debit	3 300	*−321.7*	*−453.5*	*−530.2*	*−785.3*	*−1,074.2*	*−1,300.3*	*−1,956.4*	*−3,092.3*
Compensation of employees, credit	2 310	3.7	7.8	13.7	42.0	155.0	254.5	392.2	396.3
Compensation of employees, debit	3 310	−1.6	−.9	−1.6	−16.4	−25.2	−49.2	−73.9	−93.8
Investment income, credit	2 320	115.3	165.1	191.3	207.2	281.2	476.2	698.8	1,121.8
Direct investment income	2 330	13.0	26.1	51.9	91.9	152.4	314.7	456.1	647.6
Dividends and distributed branch profits	2 332	1.6	2.5	4.1	30.6	64.1	83.2	37.3	291.6
Reinvested earnings and undistributed branch profits	2 333	3.6	17.5	41.2	53.2	74.6	212.0	390.6	290.6
Income on debt (interest)	2 334	7.8	6.1	6.6	8.2	13.7	19.5	28.2	65.4
Portfolio investment income	2 339	60.3	92.6	90.1	58.1	69.0	82.6	154.9	262.9
Income on equity	2 340	.5	4.0	.3	6.5	9.8	10.8	15.8	28.8
Income on bonds and notes	2 350	59.8	88.6	89.8	33.3	44.4	58.7	93.5	155.2
Income on money market instruments	2 360	....	....	....	18.3	14.8	13.1	45.5	78.9
Other investment income	2 370	42.0	46.3	49.3	57.2	59.8	78.9	87.8	211.3
Investment income, debit	3 320	−320.2	−452.6	−528.5	−768.9	−1,049.0	−1,251.1	−1,882.5	−2,998.5
Direct investment income	3 330	−204.6	−310.8	−396.7	−628.5	−861.1	−1,006.8	−1,550.9	−2,294.2
Dividends and distributed branch profits	3 332	−83.2	−68.5	−170.3	−133.2	−177.1	−250.4	−213.1	−280.0
Reinvested earnings and undistributed branch profits	3 333	−105.9	−223.9	−205.4	−465.6	−643.0	−704.7	−1,258.9	−1,853.3
Income on debt (interest)	3 334	−15.5	−18.3	−20.9	−29.7	−41.0	−51.7	−78.8	−160.9
Portfolio investment income	3 339	−41.8	−66.1	−57.5	−57.9	−84.5	−112.9	−88.3	−218.0
Income on equity	3 340	−6.9	−19.1	−11.8	−15.6	−26.7	−35.1	−21.9	−127.7
Income on bonds and notes	3 350	−34.9	−47.0	−45.7	−38.8	−49.0	−66.3	−64.8	−88.5
Income on money market instruments	3 360	....	....	....	−3.6	−8.8	−11.5	−1.7	−1.8
Other investment income	3 370	−73.8	−75.7	−74.3	−82.5	−103.5	−131.3	−243.3	−486.4
D. CURRENT TRANSFERS	4 379	**85.5**	**85.9**	**64.4**	**157.0**	**113.9**	**61.5**	**57.3**	**159.1**
Credit	2 379	**114.6**	**115.3**	**125.7**	**266.5**	**416.7**	**465.7**	**523.5**	**707.3**
General government	2 380	61.9	59.6	53.5	147.4	186.8	225.7	240.6	252.1
Other sectors	2 390	52.8	55.7	72.2	119.0	229.8	240.0	283.0	455.2
Workers' remittances	2 391	.3	3.2	5.4	9.2	11.9	9.5	9.6	29.7
Other current transfers	2 392	52.5	52.5	66.8	109.8	217.9	230.4	273.3	425.5
Debit	3 379	**−29.1**	**−29.4**	**−61.3**	**−109.5**	**−302.7**	**−404.1**	**−466.2**	**−548.2**
General government	3 380	−4.2	−2.7	−9.2	−17.7	−153.0	−258.6	−258.5	−321.3
Other sectors	3 390	−25.0	−26.7	−52.1	−91.8	−149.7	−145.6	−207.7	−226.9
Workers' remittances	3 391	−1.5	−1.3	−3.1	−2.2	−1.3	−1.2	−1.5	−1.9
Other current transfers	3 392	−23.5	−25.4	−49.0	−89.6	−148.4	−144.4	−206.2	−225.0
CAPITAL AND FINANCIAL ACCOUNT	4 996	**291.2**	**325.9**	**720.4**	**1,154.8**	**−217.2**	**−3,065.8**	**1,325.5**	**−10.6**
CAPITAL ACCOUNT	4 994	**25.9**	**14.5**	**38.2**	**49.6**	**86.4**	**103.0**	**352.1**	**240.0**
Total credit	2 994	*26.2*	*14.9*	*39.2*	*57.8*	*93.2*	*109.5*	*372.5*	*273.2*
Total debit	3 994	*−.2*	*−.4*	*−1.0*	*−8.2*	*−6.8*	*−6.5*	*−20.4*	*−33.2*
Capital transfers, credit	2 400	**26.2**	**14.9**	**39.2**	**55.6**	**90.8**	**94.2**	**183.9**	**258.7**
General government	2 401	23.6	10.5	34.4	40.9	40.9	35.6	127.3	161.9
Debt forgiveness	2 402	....	....	....	....	....	....	....	....
Other capital transfers	2 410	....	....	....	40.9	40.9	35.6	127.3	161.9
Other sectors	2 430	2.6	4.4	4.8	14.7	50.0	58.6	56.6	96.8
Migrants' transfers	2 431	....	....	....	....	....	....	....	....
Debt forgiveness	2 432	....	....	....	14.3	1.7	3.3	10.9	5.3
Other capital transfers	2 440	....	....	....	.3	48.3	55.3	45.7	91.5
Capital transfers, debit	3 400	**−.2**	**−.4**	**−1.0**	**−2.1**	**−2.1**	**−3.8**	**−13.5**	**−26.2**
General government	3 401	−.2	−.3	−.3	....	....	....	−.1	−.1
Debt forgiveness	3 402	....	....	....	....	....	....	....	....
Other capital transfers	3 410	....	....	....	....	....	....	−.1	−.1
Other sectors	3 430	....	−.1	−.8	−2.1	−2.1	−3.8	−13.5	−26.1
Migrants' transfers	3 431	....	....	....	....	....	....	....	....
Debt forgiveness	3 432	....	....	....	−1.8	−2.1	−3.8	−11.9	−23.6
Other capital transfers	3 440	....	....	....	−.4	....	....	−1.6	−2.5
Nonproduced nonfinancial assets, credit	2 480	....	....	....	2.2	2.4	15.2	188.6	14.5
Nonproduced nonfinancial assets, debit	3 480	....	....	....	−6.0	−4.7	−2.6	−6.8	−7.0

Table 2 (Continued). STANDARD PRESENTATION, 2000–2007

(Millions of U.S. dollars)

	Code	2000	2001	2002	2003	2004	2005	2006	2007
FINANCIAL ACCOUNT	4 995 ..	**265.3**	**311.4**	**682.3**	**1,105.2**	**−303.6**	**−3,168.8**	**973.4**	**−250.7**
A. DIRECT INVESTMENT	4 500 ..	**323.9**	**342.4**	**152.6**	**762.9**	**329.6**	**−46.2**	**496.0**	**743.8**
Direct investment abroad	4 505 ..	**−63.4**	**−200.1**	**−131.9**	**−156.1**	**−268.2**	**−687.5**	**−1,114.3**	**−1,570.9**
Equity capital	4 510 ..	−36.0	−107.0	−55.6	−79.2	−169.0	−407.6	−476.7	−897.6
Claims on affiliated enterprises	4 515 ..	−36.0	−107.0	−55.6	−79.2	−169.0	−407.6	−476.7	−897.6
Liabilities to affiliated enterprises	4 520 ..	....	....	....	....	....	....	....	....
Reinvested earnings	4 525 ..	−3.6	−17.5	−41.2	−53.2	−74.6	−212.0	−390.6	−290.6
Other capital	4 530 ..	−23.8	−75.6	−35.2	−23.8	−24.6	−67.8	−246.9	−382.8
Claims on affiliated enterprises	4 535 ..	−28.7	−70.8	−41.9	−45.6	−34.7	−90.6	−308.5	−514.2
Liabilities to affiliated enterprises	4 540 ..	4.9	−4.8	6.7	21.8	10.1	22.8	61.7	131.4
Direct investment in Estonia	4 555 ..	**387.3**	**542.5**	**284.5**	**919.0**	**597.8**	**641.4**	**1,610.3**	**2,314.7**
Equity capital	4 560 ..	227.4	210.6	46.0	378.4	....	....	....	....
Claims on direct investors	4 565 ..	....	....	....	....	....	....	....	....
Liabilities to direct investors	4 570 ..	227.4	210.6	46.0	378.4	....	....	....	....
Reinvested earnings	4 575 ..	105.9	223.9	205.4	465.6	643.0	704.7	1,258.9	1,853.3
Other capital	4 580 ..	53.9	108.0	33.1	75.0	−45.2	−63.4	351.3	461.4
Claims on direct investors	4 585 ..	−24.0	−55.2	−47.0	−96.9	−110.5	−163.2	−363.1	−567.0
Liabilities to direct investors	4 590 ..	77.9	163.2	80.0	171.9	65.4	99.9	714.5	1,028.4
B. PORTFOLIO INVESTMENT	4 600 ..	**91.2**	**−34.2**	**153.0**	**166.8**	**−204.5**	**−2,234.4**	**−902.8**	**−462.3**
Assets	4 602 ..	**15.5**	**−118.8**	**−192.0**	**−394.3**	**−380.6**	**−871.6**	**−1,211.2**	**−722.4**
Equity securities	4 610 ..	3.5	14.3	.3	−75.5	−232.4	−387.7	−366.8	−654.1
Monetary authorities	4 611 ..	....	....	....	....	....	−.3	....	....
General government	4 612 ..	....	....	....	−4.1	−3.3	−.7	−13.6	−9.9
Banks	4 613 ..	−3.9	23.5	.8	−.4	−1.9	−10.1	−.6	5.5
Other sectors	4 614 ..	7.4	−9.2	−.5	−71.0	−227.2	−376.7	−352.6	−649.7
Debt securities	4 619 ..	12.1	−133.2	−192.3	−318.8	−148.2	−483.9	−844.4	−68.3
Bonds and notes	4 620 ..	−38.5	−159.8	−103.5	−84.4	−290.5	−217.3	−906.3	210.1
Monetary authorities	4 621 ..	....	4.6	....	....	....	....	....	−42.6
General government	4 622 ..	−24.3	−140.0	−127.8	38.3	−106.1	51.2	−713.4	−42.6
Banks	4 623 ..	3.5	−2.1	12.5	.1	−117.5	−13.7	−23.8	56.1
Other sectors	4 624 ..	−17.7	−22.2	11.8	−122.8	−67.0	−254.8	−169.1	196.5
Money market instruments	4 630 ..	50.6	26.6	−88.7	−234.4	142.3	−266.6	61.9	−278.3
Monetary authorities	4 631 ..	....	....	....	....	....	....	....	....
General government	4 632 ..	....	−.5	−76.2	−343.3	57.9	−166.5	265.2	−270.6
Banks	4 633 ..	31.2	26.8	−12.2	77.1	79.8	−46.0	−189.1	129.4
Other sectors	4 634 ..	19.3	.3	−.4	31.9	4.7	−54.1	−14.2	−137.2
Liabilities	4 652 ..	**75.6**	**84.7**	**344.9**	**561.2**	**176.1**	**−1,362.8**	**308.5**	**260.1**
Equity securities	4 660 ..	−28.5	31.9	53.3	110.6	176.1	−1,362.8	308.5	260.1
Banks	4 663 ..	−36.2	24.0	7.1	16.8	11.5	−1,807.9	2.1	1.9
Other sectors	4 664 ..	7.7	7.8	46.3	93.8	164.7	445.1	306.4	258.2
Debt securities	4 669 ..	104.1	52.8	291.6	450.5	....	....	....	....
Bonds and notes	4 670 ..	107.0	65.4	294.2	99.5	....	....	....	....
Monetary authorities	4 671 ..	....	....	....	....	....	....	....	....
General government	4 672 ..	−4.0	−6.5	84.7	−6.6	....	....	....	....
Banks	4 673 ..	99.5	48.5	19.7	125.9	....	....	....	....
Other sectors	4 674 ..	11.5	23.5	189.8	−19.7	....	....	....	....
Money market instruments	4 680 ..	−2.9	−12.6	−2.6	351.0	....	....	....	....
Monetary authorities	4 681 ..	....	....	....	....	....	....	....	....
General government	4 682 ..	....	....	....	....	....	....	....	....
Banks	4 683 ..	−2.9	−12.6	−2.6	353.0	....	....	....	....
Other sectors	4 684 ..	....	....	....	−2.0	....	....	....	....
C. FINANCIAL DERIVATIVES	4 910 ..	**.7**	**−2.2**	**−4.0**	**−1.8**	**−.3**	**−7.5**	**5.8**	**−71.5**
Monetary authorities	4 911 ..	....	....	....	....	....	....	....	....
General government	4 912 ..	....	....	....	....	....	−.2	.8	1.6
Banks	4 913 ..	1.2	−2.1	−4.0	−1.8	−.3	−5.5	15.3	−72.4
Other sectors	4 914 ..	−.5	....	....	....	....	−1.8	−10.2	−.7
Assets	4 900 ..	**−4.7**	**−.1**	**−2.6**	**−9.9**	**−2.9**	**1.3**	**−15.4**	**−77.2**
Monetary authorities	4 901 ..	....	....	....	....	....	....	....	....
General government	4 902 ..	....	....	....	....	....	.1	1.5	3.0
Banks	4 903 ..	−4.1	−.1	−2.5	−9.9	−2.9	3.0	−5.6	−72.1
Other sectors	4 904 ..	−.6	....	−.2	....	....	−1.8	−11.3	−8.0
Liabilities	4 905 ..	**5.4**	**−2.1**	**−1.4**	**8.1**	**2.6**	**−8.8**	**21.2**	**5.7**
Monetary authorities	4 906 ..	....	....	....	....	....	....	....	....
General government	4 907 ..	....	....	....	....	....	−.3	−.7	−1.4
Banks	4 908 ..	5.3	−2.1	−1.5	8.1	2.6	−8.5	20.8	−.3
Other sectors	4 909 ..	.1	....	.2	....	....	.1	1.1	7.4

Table 2 (Concluded). STANDARD PRESENTATION, 2000–2007

(Millions of U.S. dollars)

	Code	2000	2001	2002	2003	2004	2005	2006	2007
D. OTHER INVESTMENT	4 700 ..	**−28.0**	**−41.6**	**435.9**	**346.7**	**−157.2**	**−495.1**	**1,994.7**	**−351.8**
Assets	4 703 ..	**−166.7**	**−220.3**	**50.5**	**−154.4**	**−901.2**	**−866.9**	**40.0**	**−1,997.2**
Trade credits	4 706 ..	−5.7	−33.0	68.8	−68.8	−81.2	−161.6	−284.6	−67.1
General government	4 707 ..	....	....	−6.1	−2.8	5.9	.1	−1.5	5.2
of which: Short-term	4 709 ..	....	....	*−6.1*	*−2.8*	*5.9*	*.1*	*−1.5*	*5.2*
Other sectors	4 710 ..	−5.7	−33.0	74.9	−65.9	−87.2	−161.7	−283.1	−72.3
of which: Short-term	4 712 ..	*−5.7*	*−33.0*	*74.9*	*−65.9*	*−87.2*	*−161.7*	*−283.1*	*−72.3*
Loans	4 714 ..	−165.6	−132.5	−83.9	−236.7	−676.9	280.5	−195.9	−898.0
Monetary authorities	4 715 ..	....	....	....	....	....	....	....	....
of which: Short-term	4 718 ..	....	....	....	....	....	....	....	....
General government	4 719 ..	....	....	....	....	....	....	....	....
of which: Short-term	4 721 ..	....	....	....	....	....	....	....	....
Banks	4 722 ..	−58.6	−161.6	3.5	−171.3	−509.0	−104.1	−74.9	−807.4
of which: Short-term	4 724 ..	*−45.5*	*−153.8*	*14.1*	*−150.0*	*−106.7*	*−316.9*	*113.0*	*−694.9*
Other sectors	4 725 ..	−107.0	29.1	−87.4	−65.3	−167.8	384.6	−121.1	−90.6
of which: Short-term	4 727 ..	*−54.6*	*40.2*	*−27.0*	*−43.2*	*−86.5*	*188.5*	*−69.7*	*9.7*
Currency and deposits	4 730 ..	−17.3	−48.0	48.4	140.9	−135.8	−945.6	516.7	−982.4
Monetary authorities	4 731 ..	....	....	....	....	....	....	....	....
General government	4 732 ..	43.1	35.9	−17.3	43.2	−15.1	−1.3	34.8	−1.9
Banks	4 733 ..	−47.2	−60.8	−55.1	66.9	−164.3	−866.1	665.2	−744.7
Other sectors	4 734 ..	−13.2	−23.1	120.9	30.9	43.6	−78.2	−183.3	−235.9
Other assets	4 736 ..	22.0	−6.7	17.2	10.1	−7.3	−40.2	3.8	−49.7
Monetary authorities	4 737 ..	−9.6	−11.3	−2.8	.1	−.8	−.1	....	....
of which: Short-term	4 739 ..	*−9.6*	*−11.4*	*−3.1*	....	....	....	....	....
General government	4 740 ..	....	....	....	−.5	−3.4	−4.9	−4.4	−8.5
of which: Short-term	4 742 ..	....	....	....	*−.2*	*.1*	....	*.1*	....
Banks	4 743 ..	28.9	3.1	23.4	17.5	−1.2	−34.0	7.3	−29.0
of which: Short-term	4 745 ..	*28.9*	*3.1*	*23.4*	*17.5*	*−1.2*	*−34.0*	*7.3*	*−29.0*
Other sectors	4 746 ..	2.6	1.5	−3.3	−6.9	−1.8	−1.3	.9	−12.2
of which: Short-term	4 748 ..	*3.1*	*1.6*	*−3.3*	*−6.9*	*−1.8*	*−1.3*	*.9*	*−12.3*
Liabilities	4 753 ..	**138.7**	**178.7**	**385.4**	**501.1**	**744.0**	**371.7**	**1,954.8**	**1,645.4**
Trade credits	4 756 ..	62.3	4.0	42.9	−8.0	46.2	135.4	260.4	−25.9
General government	4 757 ..	....	....	....	....	....	....	....	....
of which: Short-term	4 759 ..	....	....	....	....	....	....	....	....
Other sectors	4 760 ..	62.3	4.0	42.9	−8.0	46.2	135.4	260.4	−25.9
of which: Short-term	4 762 ..	*62.3*	*4.0*	*42.9*	*−8.0*	*46.2*	*135.4*	*260.4*	*−25.9*
Loans	4 764 ..	−59.2	142.4	104.9	234.5	....	....	....	....
Monetary authorities	4 765 ..	−2.9	−9.1	−3.2	43.5	....	....	....	....
of which: Use of Fund credit and loans from the Fund	4 766 ..	*−5.2*	*−4.9*	*−14.0*	....	....	....	....	....
of which: Short-term	4 768 ..	*2.5*	*−4.0*	*10.8*	*43.5*	....	....	....	....
General government	4 769 ..	−17.2	−7.3	−53.1	29.2	....	....	....	....
of which: Short-term	4 771 ..	....	....	....	....	....	....	....	....
Banks	4 772 ..	−59.3	24.1	128.8	57.5	....	....	....	....
of which: Short-term	4 774 ..	*−14.2*	*34.4*	*27.6*	*−150.8*	....	....	....	....
Other sectors	4 775 ..	20.3	134.7	32.4	104.2	....	....	....	....
of which: Short-term	4 777 ..	*−7.0*	*33.5*	*−30.6*	*31.1*	....	....	....	....
Currency and deposits	4 780 ..	116.8	2.8	226.8	341.7	697.8	235.7	1,690.9	1,663.3
Monetary authorities	4 781 ..	−.5	.1	.1	....	....	....	....	....
General government	4 782 ..	....	....	....	....	....	....	....	....
Banks	4 783 ..	117.3	2.7	226.7	341.6	697.8	235.7	1,690.9	1,663.3
Other sectors	4 784 ..	....	....	....	....	....	....	....	....
Other liabilities	4 786 ..	18.7	29.5	10.8	−67.1	....	.7	3.5	8.0
Monetary authorities	4 787 ..	....	−1.3	21.6	....	....	....	....	....
of which: Short-term	4 789 ..	....	*−1.3*	*21.6*	....	....	....	....	....
General government	4 790 ..	....	....	....	....	....	....	....	....
of which: Short-term	4 792 ..	....	....	....	....	....	....	....	....
Banks	4 793 ..	18.8	32.6	−11.4	−62.8	....	....	....	....
of which: Short-term	4 795 ..	*21.0*	*12.1*	*−11.3*	*−62.8*	....	....	....	....
Other sectors	4 796 ..	....	−1.8	.6	−4.2	....	.7	3.5	8.0
of which: Short-term	4 798 ..	....	*−1.8*	*.6*	*−4.2*	....	....	....	....
E. RESERVE ASSETS	4 802 ..	**−122.4**	**46.9**	**−55.2**	**−169.4**	**−271.2**	**−385.5**	**−620.4**	**−108.9**
Monetary gold	4 812 ..	....	....	....	....	....	....	....	....
Special drawing rights	4 811 ..	1.3	....	....	....	....	....	....	....
Reserve position in the Fund	4 810 ..	....	....	....	....	....	....	....	....
Foreign exchange	4 803 ..	−123.8	46.9	−63.9	−167.5	−269.0	−383.5	−620.5	−99.1
Other claims	4 813 ..	....	....	8.7	−1.8	−2.2	−2.0	....	−9.7
NET ERRORS AND OMISSIONS	4 998 ..	**7.8**	**−1.2**	**58.9**	**−39.4**	**1,629.9**	**4,447.4**	**1,433.2**	**3,782.4**

Table 3. INTERNATIONAL INVESTMENT POSITION (End-period stocks), 2000–2007

(Millions of U.S. dollars)

	Code	2000	2001	2002	2003	2004	2005	2006	2007
ASSETS	8 995 C.	2,614.0	2,920.5	4,078.2	6,137.7	8,783.7	10,705.6	15,518.0	22,790.7
Direct investment abroad	8 505	259.1	441.8	676.0	1,028.3	1,418.8	1,939.5	3,637.8	5,986.1
Equity capital and reinvested earnings	8 506	173.5	285.9	444.3	721.6	1,057.3	1,524.2	2,876.1	4,727.5
Claims on affiliated enterprises	8 507	173.5	285.9	444.3	721.6	1,057.3	1,524.2	2,876.1	4,727.5
Liabilities to affiliated enterprises	8 508	....	....	....	....	....	....	....	....
Other capital	8 530	85.6	155.8	231.8	306.7	361.5	415.3	761.7	1,258.6
Claims on affiliated enterprises	8 535	103.0	167.8	253.3	364.1	443.0	531.4	946.8	1,611.4
Liabilities to affiliated enterprises	8 540	−17.4	−12.0	−21.5	−57.4	−81.5	−116.1	−185.1	−352.8
Portfolio investment	8 602	271.8	262.1	824.1	1,560.5	2,244.0	2,962.9	4,823.7	6,466.0
Equity securities	8 610	26.4	22.5	36.8	210.3	534.9	1,014.8	1,788.6	2,937.9
Monetary authorities	8 611	....	....	....	....	....	.3	.3	.3
General government	8 612	....	....	....	4.7	9.5	9.3	24.2	39.4
Banks	8 613	15.1	2.5	2.0	2.6	4.9	14.7	21.3	17.3
Other sectors	8 614	11.3	19.9	34.8	203.0	520.5	990.6	1,742.8	2,880.9
Debt securities	8 619	245.4	239.6	787.3	1,350.2	1,709.1	1,948.1	3,035.0	3,528.2
Bonds and notes	8 620	75.8	91.4	522.6	690.0	1,078.9	1,139.3	2,180.2	2,209.3
Monetary authorities	8 621	....	....	....	....	....	....	....	....
General government	8 622	....	....	300.5	345.7	490.2	370.5	1,144.6	1,328.4
Banks	8 623	15.6	13.5	3.1	3.7	130.0	124.6	159.6	116.0
Other sectors	8 624	60.1	77.8	219.0	340.7	458.7	644.2	875.9	765.0
Money market instruments	8 630	169.6	148.3	264.7	660.2	630.1	808.8	854.9	1,318.9
Monetary authorities	8 631	....	....	....	....	....	....	....	....
General government	8 632	....	....	77.1	485.5	464.5	556.1	355.0	676.7
Banks	8 633	151.0	124.5	158.6	98.7	19.8	62.1	271.2	184.6
Other sectors	8 634	18.6	23.8	29.0	76.0	145.8	190.5	228.7	457.6
Financial derivatives	8 900	9.1	8.7	13.0	26.9	32.1	27.2	46.0	137.9
Monetary authorities	8 901	....	....	....	....	....	....	....	....
General government	8 902	....	....	....	....	....	....	1.6	2.3
Banks	8 903	9.1	8.7	13.0	26.9	32.1	25.2	29.3	109.6
Other sectors	8 904	....	....	....	....	....	2.1	15.1	26.0
Other investment	8 703	1,151.0	1,385.3	1,561.8	2,137.4	3,292.6	3,826.5	4,220.2	6,908.4
Trade credits	8 706	229.5	282.1	281.2	459.1	609.1	678.9	1,080.5	1,394.2
General government	8 707	....	....	....	11.6	5.9	5.4	7.6	2.8
of which: Short-term	8 709	....	....	....	*11.6*	*5.9*	*5.4*	*7.6*	*2.8*
Other sectors	8 710	229.5	282.1	281.2	447.5	603.1	673.5	1,072.8	1,391.3
of which: Short-term	8 712	*229.5*	*282.1*	*281.2*	*447.5*	*603.1*	*673.5*	*1,072.8*	*1,391.3*
Loans	8 714	416.2	523.1	712.8	1,146.2	1,949.2	1,552.5	1,859.8	2,973.5
Monetary authorities	8 715	....	....	....	....	....	....	....	....
of which: Short-term	8 718	....	....	....	....	....	....	....	....
General government	8 719	....	....	....	....	....	....	....	....
of which: Short-term	8 721	....	....	....	....	....	....	....	....
Banks	8 722	155.6	305.7	355.9	642.5	1,251.0	1,156.9	1,323.1	2,302.7
of which: Short-term	8 724	*100.8*	*246.3*	*275.1*	*521.0*	*682.4*	*899.4*	*869.8*	*1,701.6*
Other sectors	8 725	260.7	217.4	356.8	503.8	698.2	395.5	536.8	670.7
of which: Short-term	8 727	*100.3*	*53.3*	*98.0*	*172.2*	*272.3*	*211.3*	*327.3*	*357.8*
Currency and deposits	8 730	474.2	551.7	527.0	479.4	668.2	1,521.8	1,183.0	2,375.6
Monetary authorities	8 731	....	....	....	....	....	....	....	....
General government	8 732	87.5	98.0	52.7	18.2	36.8	36.2	2.3	4.7
Banks	8 733	235.3	278.9	395.9	376.3	574.9	1,353.2	822.4	1,696.6
Other sectors	8 734	151.4	174.8	78.4	84.9	56.5	132.4	358.2	674.3
Other assets	8 736	31.1	28.4	40.9	52.7	66.2	73.3	96.9	165.1
Monetary authorities	8 737	1.0	6.9	.9	.9	1.9	1.7	1.8	2.0
of which: Short-term	8 739	*1.0*	*5.9*	*.1*	....	....	....	....	....
General government	8 740	....	....	....	7.5	11.7	14.7	21.7	32.7
of which: Short-term	8 742	....	....	....	*.3*	....	....	*.6*	....
Banks	8 743	20.9	16.6	30.8	24.6	31.9	45.4	45.2	75.7
of which: Short-term	8 745	*20.9*	*16.6*	*30.8*	*24.6*	*31.9*	*45.4*	*45.2*	*75.7*
Other sectors	8 746	9.2	4.9	9.2	19.7	20.7	11.5	28.2	54.7
of which: Short-term	8 748	*6.7*	*4.9*	*9.1*	*19.6*	*20.6*	*11.4*	*28.1*	*54.6*
Reserve assets	8 802	922.9	822.5	1,003.2	1,384.7	1,796.2	1,949.5	2,790.4	3,292.4
Monetary gold	8 812	2.3	2.3	2.8	3.4	3.6	4.2	5.2	6.9
Special drawing rights	8 811	....	....	.1	.1	.1	.1	.1	.1
Reserve position in the Fund	8 810	....	....	....	....	....	....	....	....
Foreign exchange	8 803	920.6	820.2	1,009.4	1,373.3	1,788.1	1,943.1	2,783.3	3,270.3
Other claims	8 813	....	....	−9.1	7.9	4.4	2.0	1.8	15.1

Table 3 (Concluded). INTERNATIONAL INVESTMENT POSITION (End-period stocks), 2000–2007

(Millions of U.S. dollars)

	Code	2000	2001	2002	2003	2004	2005	2006	2007
LIABILITIES	8 995 D.	**5,389.5**	**6,017.7**	**8,488.0**	**13,378.7**	**20,094.2**	**21,915.0**	**28,425.4**	**39,669.4**
Direct investment in Estonia	8 555 ..	**2,644.7**	**3,159.9**	**4,226.4**	**7,001.8**	**10,058.6**	**11,289.6**	**12,721.0**	**16,667.4**
Equity capital and reinvested earnings	8 556 ..	2,064.6	2,486.5	3,408.8	5,808.5	8,766.1	10,187.8	10,964.4	14,161.9
Claims on direct investors	8 557 ..	....	....	....	....	....	....	....	....
Liabilities to direct investors	8 558 ..	2,064.6	2,486.5	3,408.8	5,808.5	8,766.1	10,187.8	10,964.4	14,161.9
Other capital	8 580 ..	580.2	673.4	817.6	1,193.3	1,292.5	1,101.8	1,756.6	2,505.5
Claims on direct investors	8 585 ..	−106.6	−158.2	−243.9	−403.6	−564.4	−668.7	−1,133.6	−1,864.8
Liabilities to direct investors	8 590 ..	686.7	831.6	1,061.5	1,596.9	1,856.9	1,770.5	2,890.2	4,370.3
Portfolio investment	8 652 ..	**761.4**	**764.3**	**1,378.9**	**2,383.4**	**4,504.7**	**3,380.6**	**3,893.0**	**4,588.1**
Equity securities	8 660 ..	431.6	403.0	634.9	949.6	1,942.0	1,195.7	1,887.6	2,430.7
Banks	8 663 ..	187.5	230.7	426.6	712.0	1,403.7	.6	3.6	6.1
Other sectors	8 664 ..	244.1	172.2	208.3	237.6	538.3	1,195.1	1,884.0	2,424.6
Debt securities	8 669 ..	329.8	361.3	744.0	1,433.9	2,562.7	2,184.9	2,005.4	2,157.4
Bonds and notes	8 670 ..	312.8	358.1	743.0	1,055.3	2,321.0	2,147.8	1,994.9	2,151.4
Monetary authorities	8 671 ..	....	....	....	....	....	....	....	....
General government	8 672 ..	20.8	13.2	112.7	138.6	179.9	161.8	248.9	181.1
Banks	8 673 ..	266.0	298.5	373.3	640.7	1,809.4	1,505.1	1,243.1	1,358.4
Other sectors	8 674 ..	26.0	46.3	257.0	276.1	331.7	480.9	502.9	611.8
Money market instruments	8 680 ..	17.1	3.2	1.1	378.6	241.8	37.2	10.5	6.1
Monetary authorities	8 681 ..	....	....	....	....	....	....	....	....
General government	8 682 ..	....	....	....	....	....	....	....	....
Banks	8 683 ..	17.1	3.2	1.1	375.9	241.1	36.0	9.1	3.5
Other sectors	8 684 ..	....	....	....	2.7	.6	1.1	1.3	2.6
Financial derivatives	8 905 ..	**10.2**	**6.3**	**5.9**	**16.8**	**20.7**	**10.0**	**33.2**	**47.3**
Monetary authorities	8 906 ..	....	....	....	....	....	....	....	....
General government	8 907 ..	....	....	....	....	....	....	.4	.1
Banks	8 908 ..	10.1	6.3	5.9	16.8	20.5	9.7	31.3	36.8
Other sectors	8 909 ..	.1	....	....	....	.2	.4	1.5	10.3
Other investment	8 753 ..	**1,973.1**	**2,087.2**	**2,876.7**	**3,976.6**	**5,510.1**	**7,234.8**	**11,778.2**	**18,366.6**
Trade credits	8 756 ..	366.9	346.6	452.8	583.8	721.2	802.4	1,159.2	1,272.9
General government	8 757 ..	....	....	....	....	....	....	....	....
of which: Short-term	8 759 ..	....	....	....	....	....	....	....	....
Other sectors	8 760 ..	366.9	346.6	452.8	583.8	721.2	802.4	1,159.2	1,272.9
of which: Short-term	8 762 ..	*366.9*	*346.6*	*452.8*	*583.8*	*721.2*	*802.4*	*1,159.2*	*1,272.9*
Loans	8 764 ..	1,009.2	1,135.6	1,453.8	1,965.0	2,498.7	4,101.1	6,163.8	10,425.7
Monetary authorities	8 765 ..	22.0	13.4	11.8	38.7	43.9	3.4	37.2	122.3
of which: Use of Fund credit and loans from the Fund	8 766 ..	*18.9*	*13.4*						
of which: Short-term	8 768 ..	*2.9*	....	*11.8*	*38.7*	*43.9*	*3.4*	*37.2*	*122.3*
General government	8 769 ..	153.6	155.6	113.9	174.2	171.5	135.3	147.8	143.3
of which: Short-term	8 771 ..	....	....	....	....	....	....	....	....
Banks	8 772 ..	216.9	230.3	410.9	560.7	892.2	2,369.0	2,933.2	6,394.7
of which: Short-term	8 774 ..	*69.8*	*100.7*	*147.4*	*6.8*	*77.3*	*826.3*	*461.2*	*810.9*
Other sectors	8 775 ..	616.7	736.4	917.3	1,191.3	1,391.1	1,593.4	3,045.6	3,765.4
of which: Short-term	8 777 ..	*108.7*	*144.6*	*119.2*	*198.0*	*189.8*	*145.0*	*713.0*	*1,042.9*
Currency and deposits	8 780 ..	476.7	457.8	794.3	1,325.4	2,201.4	2,133.5	4,148.1	6,425.7
Monetary authorities	8 781 ..	.1	.1	.3	.3	.4	.3	.3	.4
General government	8 782 ..	....	....	....	....	....	....	....	....
Banks	8 783 ..	476.7	457.7	794.0	1,325.0	2,201.0	2,133.2	4,147.7	6,425.4
Other sectors	8 784 ..	....	....	....	....	....	....	....	....
Other liabilities	8 786 ..	120.4	147.2	175.8	102.5	88.9	197.9	307.2	242.3
Monetary authorities	8 787 ..	....	.9	5.0	....	....	....	1.1	1.2
of which: Short-term	8 789 ..	....	*.9*	*5.0*	....	....	....	*1.1*	*1.2*
General government	8 790 ..	....	....	....	....	....	57.1	58.0	....
of which: Short-term	8 792 ..	....	....	....	....	....	*57.1*	*58.0*	....
Banks	8 793 ..	115.4	139.8	157.6	85.4	81.0	120.0	211.1	197.5
of which: Short-term	8 795 ..	*61.0*	*69.2*	*74.4*	*85.4*	*81.0*	*120.0*	*211.1*	*197.5*
Other sectors	8 796 ..	5.0	6.5	13.2	17.1	7.9	20.9	37.0	43.6
of which: Short-term	8 798 ..	*4.9*	*6.5*	*13.2*	*17.1*	*7.9*	*20.2*	*32.6*	*30.3*
NET INTERNATIONAL INVESTMENT POSITION	8 995 ..	**−2,775.5**	**−3,097.3**	**−4,409.8**	**−7,240.9**	**−11,310.5**	**−11,209.4**	**−12,907.3**	**−16,878.7**
Conversion rates: krooni per U.S. dollar (end of period)	0 102 ..	**16.820**	**17.692**	**14.936**	**12.410**	**11.471**	**13.221**	**11.882**	**10.638**

Table 1. ANALYTIC PRESENTATION, 2000–2007

(Millions of U.S. dollars)

	Code	2000	2001	2002	2003	2004	2005	2006	2007
A. Current Account[1]	4 993 Z.	**13.5**	**−373.4**	**−136.6**	**−136.4**	**−667.8**	**−1,567.8**	**−1,785.9**	**−826.8**
Goods: exports f.o.b.	2 100 ..	486.1	455.6	480.2	496.4	678.3	917.3	1,024.7	1,287.9
Goods: imports f.o.b.	3 100 ..	−1,131.4	−1,625.8	−1,455.0	−1,895.0	−2,768.5	−3,700.9	−4,105.6	−5,164.7
Balance on Goods	*4 100 ..*	*−645.3*	*−1,170.3*	*−974.8*	*−1,398.6*	*−2,090.2*	*−2,783.5*	*−3,080.9*	*−3,876.8*
Services: credit	2 200 ..	506.2	523.1	585.4	761.7	1,005.5	1,012.1	1,174.0	1,370.5
Services: debit	3 200 ..	−489.6	−524.5	−580.4	−708.7	−958.3	−1,193.8	−1,170.7	−1,755.2
Balance on Goods and Services	*4 991 ..*	*−628.7*	*−1,171.6*	*−969.8*	*−1,345.6*	*−2,043.0*	*−2,965.2*	*−3,077.6*	*−4,261.4*
Income: credit	2 300 ..	16.2	16.3	14.3	18.9	31.7	43.4	55.8	76.6
Income: debit	3 300 ..	−52.0	−48.3	−36.9	−43.1	−60.3	−48.0	−37.8	−37.0
Balance on Goods, Services, and Income	*4 992 ..*	*−664.5*	*−1,203.7*	*−992.3*	*−1,369.8*	*−2,071.6*	*−2,969.8*	*−3,059.7*	*−4,221.8*
Current transfers: credit	2 379 Z.	697.9	854.3	876.4	1,266.5	1,420.6	1,426.0	1,297.2	3,422.5
Current transfers: debit	3 379 ..	−19.9	−24.0	−20.7	−33.1	−16.8	−23.9	−23.4	−27.6
B. Capital Account[1]	4 994 Z.	....	....	....	....	....	....	....	....
Capital account: credit	2 994 Z.	....	....	....	....	....	....	....	....
Capital account: debit	3 994 ..	....	....	....	....	....	....	....	....
Total, Groups A Plus B	*4 981 ..*	*13.5*	*−373.4*	*−136.6*	*−136.4*	*−667.8*	*−1,567.8*	*−1,785.9*	*−826.8*
C. Financial Account[1]	4 995 W.	**28.4**	**−178.4**	**−82.7**	**246.9**	**73.2**	**758.6**	**976.3**	**449.1**
Direct investment abroad	4 505 ..	....	....	....	....	....	....	....	....
Direct investment in Ethiopia	4 555 Z.	....	....	....	....	....	265.1	545.3	222.6
Portfolio investment assets	4 602 ..	....	....	....	....	....	....	....	....
Equity securities	4 610 ..	....	....	....	....	....	....	....	....
Debt securities	4 619 ..	....	....	....	....	....	....	....	....
Portfolio investment liabilities	4 652 Z.	....	....	....	....	....	....	....	....
Equity securities	4 660 ..	....	....	....	....	....	....	....	....
Debt securities	4 669 Z.	....	....	....	....	....	....	....	....
Financial derivatives	4 910 ..	....	....	....	....	....	....	....	....
Financial derivatives assets	4 900 ..	....	....	....	....	....	....	....	....
Financial derivatives liabilities	4 905 ..	....	....	....	....	....	....	....	....
Other investment assets	4 703 ..	116.1	22.9	−4.1	68.8	−261.8	302.2	73.3	−107.5
Monetary authorities	4 701 ..	....	....	....	....	....	....	....	....
General government	4 704 ..	....	....	....	....	....	....	....	....
Banks	4 705 ..	23.2	29.7	75.2	95.0	−251.0	245.8	60.0	−171.4
Other sectors	4 728 ..	92.8	−6.8	−79.4	−26.2	−10.7	56.5	13.3	63.9
Other investment liabilities	4 753 W.	−87.7	−201.3	−78.6	178.1	335.0	191.2	357.7	334.0
Monetary authorities	4 753 WA	47.0	−54.6	5.7	11.0	9.2	−17.0	−4.4	1.8
General government	4 753 ZB	−171.9	−107.9	−78.8	147.7	386.2	224.9	332.8	303.0
Banks	4 753 ZC	4.1	−70.5	6.7	24.0	−18.6	1.0	13.6	49.0
Other sectors	4 753 ZD	33.0	31.7	−12.2	−4.5	−41.7	−17.6	15.8	−19.8
Total, Groups A Through C	*4 983 ..*	*41.8*	*−551.8*	*−219.3*	*110.5*	*−594.7*	*−809.2*	*−809.6*	*−377.8*
D. Net Errors and Omissions	4 998 ..	**−231.3**	**−229.0**	**−915.1**	**−390.1**	**−354.1**	**486.3**	**1,161.3**	**−161.7**
Total, Groups A Through D	*4 984 ..*	*−189.5*	*−780.8*	*−1,134.5*	*−279.6*	*−948.8*	*−322.9*	*351.7*	*−539.5*
E. Reserves and Related Items	4 802 A.	**189.5**	**780.8**	**1,134.5**	**279.6**	**948.8**	**322.9**	**−351.7**	**539.5**
Reserve assets	4 802 ..	−108.6	126.7	471.4	76.9	544.3	330.3	−189.6	539.5
Use of Fund credit and loans	4 766 ..	−13.0	31.8	27.1	.6	17.8	−8.7	−162.2	....
Exceptional financing	4 920 ..	311.0	622.2	635.9	202.1	386.8	1.2	....	....
Conversion rates: birr per U.S. dollar	0 101 ..	**8.217**	**8.457**	**8.568**	**8.600**	**8.636**	**8.666**	**8.699**	**8.950**

[1] Excludes components that have been classified in the categories of Group E.

Table 2. STANDARD PRESENTATION, 2000–2007

(Millions of U.S. dollars)

	Code	2000	2001	2002	2003	2004	2005	2006	2007
CURRENT ACCOUNT..	4 993 ..	13.5	−373.4	−136.6	−136.4	−667.8	−1,567.8	−1,785.9	−826.8
A. GOODS..	4 100 ..	−645.3	−1,170.3	−974.8	−1,398.6	−2,090.2	−2,783.5	−3,080.9	−3,876.8
Credit..	2 100 ..	486.1	455.6	480.2	496.4	678.3	917.3	1,024.7	1,287.9
General merchandise: exports f.o.b..........................	2 110 ..	486.1	455.6	480.2	496.4	678.3	917.3	1,024.7	1,287.9
Goods for processing: exports f.o.b..........................	2 150 ..	....	....	....	....	....	....	....	....
Repairs on goods..	2 160 ..	....	....	....	....	....	....	....	....
Goods procured in ports by carriers.........................	2 170 ..	....	....	....	....	....	....	....	....
Nonmonetary gold..	2 180 ..	....	....	....	....	....	....	....	....
Debit...	3 100 ..	−1,131.4	−1,625.8	−1,455.0	−1,895.0	−2,768.5	−3,700.9	−4,105.6	−5,164.7
General merchandise: imports f.o.b...........................	3 110 ..	−1,131.4	−1,625.8	−1,455.0	−1,895.0	−2,768.5	−3,700.9	−4,105.6	−5,164.7
Goods for processing: imports f.o.b..........................	3 150 ..	....	....	....	....	....	....	....	....
Repairs on goods..	3 160 ..	....	....	....	....	....	....	....	....
Goods procured in ports by carriers.........................	3 170 ..	....	....	....	....	....	....	....	....
Nonmonetary gold..	3 180 ..	....	....	....	....	....	....	....	....
B. SERVICES...	4 200 ..	16.6	−1.4	5.0	53.1	47.2	−181.7	3.3	−384.7
Total credit...	2 200 ..	*506.2*	*523.1*	*585.4*	*761.7*	*1,005.5*	*1,012.1*	*1,174.0*	*1,370.5*
Total debit..	3 200 ..	*−489.6*	*−524.5*	*−580.4*	*−708.7*	*−958.3*	*−1,193.8*	*−1,170.7*	*−1,755.2*
Transportation services, credit........................	2 205 ..	215.4	234.4	250.6	298.5	369.7	465.6	584.0	733.6
Passenger...	2 850 ..	*148.4*	*166.7*	*189.3*	*221.7*	*284.4*	*365.3*	*477.2*	*615.4*
Freight...	2 851 ..	*37.8*	*35.4*	*33.2*	*43.6*	*54.7*	*63.3*	*81.9*	*88.1*
Other...	2 852 ..	*29.2*	*32.2*	*28.1*	*33.2*	*30.5*	*37.0*	*24.9*	*30.0*
Sea transport, passenger...	2 207 ..	....	....	....	....	....	....	....	....
Sea transport, freight..	2 208 ..	11.8	8.0	8.0	9.9	14.0	18.3	12.4	19.6
Sea transport, other..	2 209 ..	....	....	....	....	....	....	....	....
Air transport, passenger..	2 211 ..	148.4	166.7	189.3	221.7	284.4	365.3	477.2	615.4
Air transport, freight...	2 212 ..	26.0	27.4	25.2	33.6	40.7	45.0	69.5	68.5
Air transport, other...	2 213 ..	22.7	27.5	22.1	19.3	24.6	30.8	16.9	19.9
Other transport, passenger......................................	2 215 ..	....	....	....	....	....	....	....	....
Other transport, freight...	2 216 ..	....	....	....	....	....	....	....	....
Other transport, other...	2 217 ..	6.4	4.7	6.0	13.9	5.9	6.2	7.9	10.1
Transportation services, debit.........................	3 205 ..	−285.9	−326.8	−319.1	−410.5	−580.5	−764.5	−634.1	−1,124.8
Passenger...	3 850 ..	*−5.8*	*−6.0*	*−10.5*	*−13.1*	*−1.1*	....	....	....
Freight...	3 851 ..	*−112.9*	*−162.3*	*−145.2*	*−189.1*	*−276.3*	*−369.4*	*−97.1*	*−515.5*
Other...	3 852 ..	*−167.2*	*−158.6*	*−163.4*	*−208.3*	*−303.0*	*−395.1*	*−537.0*	*−609.3*
Sea transport, passenger...	3 207 ..	....	....	....	....	....	....	....	....
Sea transport, freight..	3 208 ..	....	....	....	....	....	....	....	....
Sea transport, other..	3 209 ..	−18.7	−13.2	−12.1	−30.1	−80.7	−127.7	−160.2	−169.3
Air transport, passenger..	3 211 ..	−5.8	−6.0	−10.5	−13.1	−1.1	....	....	....
Air transport, freight...	3 212 ..	....	....	....	....	....	....	....	....
Air transport, other...	3 213 ..	−144.8	−140.1	−146.6	−172.1	−213.3	−255.2	−366.7	−423.1
Other transport, passenger......................................	3 215 ..	....	....	....	....	....	....	....	....
Other transport, freight...	3 216 ..	....	....	....	....	....	....	....	....
Other transport, other...	3 217 ..	−3.7	−5.3	−4.7	−6.1	−9.0	−12.1	−10.2	−16.8
Travel, credit..	2 236 ..	56.7	50.8	71.9	114.3	173.6	168.3	162.0	176.7
Business travel..	2 237 ..	1.0	.9	1.4	1.6	6.3	35.1	29.6	9.2
Personal travel..	2 240 ..	55.7	49.8	70.5	112.6	167.2	133.1	132.4	167.5
Travel, debit...	3 236 ..	−73.8	−43.8	−45.4	−49.6	−58.3	−76.7	−96.8	−107.1
Business travel..	3 237 ..	−27.6	−27.5	−32.7	−33.8	−39.5	−48.9	−65.1	−74.7
Personal travel..	3 240 ..	−46.2	−16.3	−12.7	−15.8	−18.8	−27.8	−31.7	−32.4
Other services, credit.....................................	2 200 BA	234.1	238.0	262.9	349.0	462.2	378.2	428.0	460.3
Communications..	2 245 ..	17.7	15.7	24.4	21.4	41.6	41.2	55.7	85.6
Construction...	2 249 ..	10.4	1.5	....	....	....	12.6	11.1	18.4
Insurance..	2 253 ..	1.1	1.9	2.9	.8	1.1	5.5	9.3	4.2
Financial...	2 260 ..	3.6	4.1	4.1	5.0	2.9	25.7	10.9	54.3
Computer and information.......................................	2 262 ..	.4	2.0	.6	.3	....	.1	.5	.6
Royalties and licence fees.......................................	2 266 ..	....	....	....	....	....	....	....	.1
Other business services...	2 268 ..	80.1	79.2	92.5	147.5	211.4	70.0	56.0	111.3
Personal, cultural, and recreational.........................	2 287 ..	1.5	1.4	3.4	.6	....	....	.5	.4
Government, n.i.e..	2 291 ..	119.3	132.1	135.0	173.4	205.2	223.0	284.0	185.5
Other services, debit.......................................	3 200 BA	−129.9	−153.8	−215.9	−248.5	−319.5	−352.6	−439.8	−523.3
Communications..	3 245 ..	−6.0	−6.1	−9.5	−10.1	−14.2	−17.9	−32.0	−16.8
Construction...	3 249 ..	−10.3	−29.6	−80.8	−67.3	−77.6	−120.9	−178.7	−262.2
Insurance..	3 253 ..	−16.3	−29.4	−29.0	−37.8	−45.9	−56.3	−64.6	−69.7
Financial...	3 260 ..	−.8	−.3	−1.0	−5.0	−.7	−3.3	−1.3	−1.9
Computer and information.......................................	3 262 ..	−1.6	−1.2	−1.3	−1.6	−3.2	−4.3	−3.5	−5.1
Royalties and licence fees.......................................	3 266 ..	−.3	−.1	−.4	−.1	−.5	−.6	−.8	−2.1
Other business services...	3 268 ..	−83.6	−77.5	−69.3	−106.6	−150.8	−133.7	−142.5	−150.1
Personal, cultural, and recreational.........................	3 287 ..	−.2	−.6	....	−.1	−.2	....	....	....
Government, n.i.e..	3 291 ..	−10.7	−9.0	−24.6	−19.9	−26.5	−15.8	−16.3	−15.4

Table 2 (Continued). STANDARD PRESENTATION, 2000–2007

(Millions of U.S. dollars)

	Code	2000	2001	2002	2003	2004	2005	2006	2007
C. INCOME..	4 300 ..	**−35.8**	**−32.0**	**−22.6**	**−24.2**	**−28.6**	**−4.6**	**17.9**	**39.6**
Total credit..	2 300 ..	*16.2*	*16.3*	*14.3*	*18.9*	*31.7*	*43.4*	*55.8*	*76.6*
Total debit...	3 300 ..	*−52.0*	*−48.3*	*−36.9*	*−43.1*	*−60.3*	*−48.0*	*−37.8*	*−37.0*
Compensation of employees, credit...............	2 310 ..	....	....	....	....	....	....	3.0	1.9
Compensation of employees, debit.................	3 310 ..	....	....	....	−.7	....	....	....	....
Investment income, credit.............................	2 320 ..	**16.2**	**16.3**	**14.3**	**18.9**	**31.7**	**43.4**	**52.8**	**74.7**
Direct investment income.........................	2 330 ..	....	....	.1	....	.6	.1	.1	.4
Dividends and distributed branch profits.........	2 332 ..	....	....	.1	....	.6	.1	.1	.4
Reinvested earnings and undistributed branch profits.....	2 333 ..	....	....	....	....	....	....	....	....
Income on debt (interest)........................	2 334 ..	....	....	....	....	....	....	....	....
Portfolio investment income...........................	2 339 ..	....	....	....	....	....	....	....	....
Income on equity...................................	2 340 ..	....	....	....	....	....	....	....	....
Income on bonds and notes..........................	2 350 ..	....	....	....	....	....	....	....	....
Income on money market instruments...............	2 360 ..	....	....	....	....	....	....	....	....
Other investment income...........................	2 370 ..	16.2	16.2	14.3	18.9	31.1	43.3	52.7	74.3
Investment income, debit..............................	3 320 ..	**−52.0**	**−48.3**	**−36.9**	**−42.3**	**−60.3**	**−48.0**	**−37.8**	**−37.0**
Direct investment income.........................	3 330 ..	−9.3	−11.7	−11.1	−16.9	−27.9	−21.5	−23.7	−18.1
Dividends and distributed branch profits.........	3 332 ..	−9.3	−11.7	−11.1	−16.9	−27.9	−21.5	−23.7	−18.1
Reinvested earnings and undistributed branch profits.....	3 333 ..	....	....	....	....	....	....	....	....
Income on debt (interest)........................	3 334 ..	....	....	....	....	....	....	....	....
Portfolio investment income...........................	3 339 ..	....	....	....	....	....	....	....	....
Income on equity...................................	3 340 ..	....	....	....	....	....	....	....	....
Income on bonds and notes..........................	3 350 ..	....	....	....	....	....	....	....	....
Income on money market instruments...............	3 360 ..	....	....	....	....	....	....	....	....
Other investment income...........................	3 370 ..	−42.7	−36.6	−25.7	−25.4	−32.4	−26.6	−14.2	−18.9
D. CURRENT TRANSFERS..........................	4 379 ..	**678.0**	**830.3**	**855.7**	**1,233.4**	**1,403.8**	**1,402.1**	**1,273.8**	**3,395.0**
Credit...	2 379 ..	**697.9**	**854.3**	**876.4**	**1,266.5**	**1,420.6**	**1,426.0**	**1,297.2**	**3,422.5**
General government..................................	2 380 ..	257.8	494.6	464.6	660.5	664.9	562.8	381.1	1,342.8
Other sectors...	2 390 ..	440.1	359.7	411.8	606.0	755.7	863.2	916.1	2,079.8
Workers' remittances................................	2 391 ..	53.2	18.3	33.0	46.5	133.7	173.5	169.2	356.6
Other current transfers.............................	2 392 ..	387.0	341.4	378.8	559.6	621.9	689.7	746.9	1,723.2
Debit...	3 379 ..	**−19.9**	**−24.0**	**−20.7**	**−33.1**	**−16.8**	**−23.9**	**−23.4**	**−27.6**
General government..................................	3 380 ..	−3.5	−8.6	−2.9	−4.9	−6.2	−5.9	−8.6	−11.5
Other sectors...	3 390 ..	−16.4	−15.4	−17.7	−28.2	−10.6	−18.0	−14.8	−16.0
Workers' remittances................................	3 391 ..	−12.6	−14.0	−16.6	−16.5	−9.2	−16.4	−14.1	−14.6
Other current transfers.............................	3 392 ..	−3.8	−1.4	−1.1	−11.7	−1.4	−1.6	−.7	−1.4
CAPITAL AND FINANCIAL ACCOUNT............	4 996 ..	**217.9**	**602.4**	**1,051.7**	**526.5**	**1,022.0**	**1,081.4**	**624.6**	**988.6**
CAPITAL ACCOUNT..................................	4 994 ..	....	....	....	**13.8**	....	....	....	....
Total credit..	2 994 ..	....	....	....	*13.8*	....	....	....	....
Total debit...	3 994 ..	....	....	....	....	....	....	....	....
Capital transfers, credit...............................	2 400 ..	....	....	....	**13.8**	....	....	....	....
General government..................................	2 401 ..	....	....	....	13.8	....	....	....	....
Debt forgiveness.....................................	2 402 ..	....	....	....	13.8	....	....	....	....
Other capital transfers..............................	2 410 ..	....	....	....	....	....	....	....	....
Other sectors...	2 430 ..	....	....	....	....	....	....	....	....
Migrants' transfers..................................	2 431 ..	....	....	....	....	....	....	....	....
Debt forgiveness.....................................	2 432 ..	....	....	....	....	....	....	....	....
Other capital transfers..............................	2 440 ..	....	....	....	....	....	....	....	....
Capital transfers, debit................................	3 400 ..	....	....	....	....	....	....	....	....
General government..................................	3 401 ..	....	....	....	....	....	....	....	....
Debt forgiveness.....................................	3 402 ..	....	....	....	....	....	....	....	....
Other capital transfers..............................	3 410 ..	....	....	....	....	....	....	....	....
Other sectors...	3 430 ..	....	....	....	....	....	....	....	....
Migrants' transfers..................................	3 431 ..	....	....	....	....	....	....	....	....
Debt forgiveness.....................................	3 432 ..	....	....	....	....	....	....	....	....
Other capital transfers..............................	3 440 ..	....	....	....	....	....	....	....	....
Nonproduced nonfinancial assets, credit............	2 480 ..	....	....	....	....	....	....	....	....
Nonproduced nonfinancial assets, debit.............	3 480 ..	....	....	....	....	....	....	....	....

Table 2 (Continued). STANDARD PRESENTATION, 2000–2007

(Millions of U.S. dollars)

	Code	2000	2001	2002	2003	2004	2005	2006	2007
FINANCIAL ACCOUNT	4 995 ..	**217.9**	**602.4**	**1,051.7**	**512.7**	**1,022.0**	**1,081.4**	**624.6**	**988.6**
A. DIRECT INVESTMENT	4 500 ..	....	....	....	....	....	**265.1**	**545.3**	**222.6**
Direct investment abroad	4 505 ..	....	....	....	....	....	....	....	....
Equity capital	4 510 ..	....	....	....	....	....	....	....	....
Claims on affiliated enterprises	4 515 ..	....	....	....	....	....	....	....	....
Liabilities to affiliated enterprises	4 520 ..	....	....	....	....	....	....	....	....
Reinvested earnings	4 525 ..	....	....	....	....	....	....	....	....
Other capital	4 530 ..	....	....	....	....	....	....	....	....
Claims on affiliated enterprises	4 535 ..	....	....	....	....	....	....	....	....
Liabilities to affiliated enterprises	4 540 ..	....	....	....	....	....	....	....	....
Direct investment in Ethiopia	4 555 ..	....	....	....	....	....	**265.1**	**545.3**	**222.6**
Equity capital	4 560 ..	....	....	....	....	....	....	....	....
Claims on direct investors	4 565 ..	....	....	....	....	....	....	....	....
Liabilities to direct investors	4 570 ..	....	....	....	....	....	....	....	....
Reinvested earnings	4 575 ..	....	....	....	....	....	....	....	....
Other capital	4 580 ..	....	....	....	....	....	265.1	545.3	222.6
Claims on direct investors	4 585 ..	....	....	....	....	....	265.1	545.3	222.6
Liabilities to direct investors	4 590 ..	....	....	....	....	....	....	....	....
B. PORTFOLIO INVESTMENT	4 600 ..	....	....	....	....	....	....	....	....
Assets	4 602 ..	....	....	....	....	....	....	....	....
Equity securities	4 610 ..	....	....	....	....	....	....	....	....
Monetary authorities	4 611 ..	....	....	....	....	....	....	....	....
General government	4 612 ..	....	....	....	....	....	....	....	....
Banks	4 613 ..	....	....	....	....	....	....	....	....
Other sectors	4 614 ..	....	....	....	....	....	....	....	....
Debt securities	4 619 ..	....	....	....	....	....	....	....	....
Bonds and notes	4 620 ..	....	....	....	....	....	....	....	....
Monetary authorities	4 621 ..	....	....	....	....	....	....	....	....
General government	4 622 ..	....	....	....	....	....	....	....	....
Banks	4 623 ..	....	....	....	....	....	....	....	....
Other sectors	4 624 ..	....	....	....	....	....	....	....	....
Money market instruments	4 630 ..	....	....	....	....	....	....	....	....
Monetary authorities	4 631 ..	....	....	....	....	....	....	....	....
General government	4 632 ..	....	....	....	....	....	....	....	....
Banks	4 633 ..	....	....	....	....	....	....	....	....
Other sectors	4 634 ..	....	....	....	....	....	....	....	....
Liabilities	4 652 ..	....	....	....	....	....	....	....	....
Equity securities	4 660 ..	....	....	....	....	....	....	....	....
Banks	4 663 ..	....	....	....	....	....	....	....	....
Other sectors	4 664 ..	....	....	....	....	....	....	....	....
Debt securities	4 669 ..	....	....	....	....	....	....	....	....
Bonds and notes	4 670 ..	....	....	....	....	....	....	....	....
Monetary authorities	4 671 ..	....	....	....	....	....	....	....	....
General government	4 672 ..	....	....	....	....	....	....	....	....
Banks	4 673 ..	....	....	....	....	....	....	....	....
Other sectors	4 674 ..	....	....	....	....	....	....	....	....
Money market instruments	4 680 ..	....	....	....	....	....	....	....	....
Monetary authorities	4 681 ..	....	....	....	....	....	....	....	....
General government	4 682 ..	....	....	....	....	....	....	....	....
Banks	4 683 ..	....	....	....	....	....	....	....	....
Other sectors	4 684 ..	....	....	....	....	....	....	....	....
C. FINANCIAL DERIVATIVES	4 910 ..	....	....	....	....	....	....	....	....
Monetary authorities	4 911 ..	....	....	....	....	....	....	....	....
General government	4 912 ..	....	....	....	....	....	....	....	....
Banks	4 913 ..	....	....	....	....	....	....	....	....
Other sectors	4 914 ..	....	....	....	....	....	....	....	....
Assets	4 900 ..	....	....	....	....	....	....	....	....
Monetary authorities	4 901 ..	....	....	....	....	....	....	....	....
General government	4 902 ..	....	....	....	....	....	....	....	....
Banks	4 903 ..	....	....	....	....	....	....	....	....
Other sectors	4 904 ..	....	....	....	....	....	....	....	....
Liabilities	4 905 ..	....	....	....	....	....	....	....	....
Monetary authorities	4 906 ..	....	....	....	....	....	....	....	....
General government	4 907 ..	....	....	....	....	....	....	....	....
Banks	4 908 ..	....	....	....	....	....	....	....	....
Other sectors	4 909 ..	....	....	....	....	....	....	....	....

Table 2 (Concluded). STANDARD PRESENTATION, 2000–2007

(Millions of U.S. dollars)

	Code	2000	2001	2002	2003	2004	2005	2006	2007
D. OTHER INVESTMENT	4 700 ..	**326.5**	**475.6**	**580.3**	**435.8**	**477.7**	**486.0**	**268.9**	**226.5**
Assets	4 703 ..	**116.1**	**22.9**	**–4.1**	**68.8**	**–261.8**	**302.2**	**73.3**	**–107.5**
Trade credits	4 706 ..	90.6	2.3	–51.5	21.9	–24.7	....	....	....
General government	4 707 ..	....	....	....	....	....	....	....	....
of which: Short-term	4 709 ..	....	....	....	....	....	....	....	....
Other sectors	4 710 ..	90.6	2.3	–51.5	21.9	–24.7	....	....	....
of which: Short-term	4 712 ..	*90.6*	*2.3*	*–51.5*	*21.9*	*–24.7*	....	....	....
Loans	4 714 ..	....	....	....	....	....	....	....	....
Monetary authorities	4 715 ..	....	....	....	....	....	....	....	....
of which: Short-term	4 718 ..	....	....	....	....	....	....	....	....
General government	4 719 ..	....	....	....	....	....	....	....	....
of which: Short-term	4 721 ..	....	....	....	....	....	....	....	....
Banks	4 722 ..	....	....	....	....	....	....	....	....
of which: Short-term	4 724 ..	....	....	....	....	....	....	....	....
Other sectors	4 725 ..	....	....	....	....	....	....	....	....
of which: Short-term	4 727 ..	....	....	....	....	....	....	....	....
Currency and deposits	4 730 ..	25.4	20.6	47.3	46.9	–237.1	302.2	73.3	–107.5
Monetary authorities	4 731 ..	....	....	....	....	....	....	....	....
General government	4 732 ..	....	....	....	....	....	....	....	....
Banks	4 733 ..	23.2	29.7	75.2	95.0	–251.0	245.8	60.0	–171.4
Other sectors	4 734 ..	2.2	–9.2	–27.9	–48.1	14.0	56.5	13.3	63.9
Other assets	4 736 ..	....	....	....	....	....	....	....	....
Monetary authorities	4 737 ..	....	....	....	....	....	....	....	....
of which: Short-term	4 739 ..	....	....	....	....	....	....	....	....
General government	4 740 ..	....	....	....	....	....	....	....	....
of which: Short-term	4 742 ..	....	....	....	....	....	....	....	....
Banks	4 743 ..	....	....	....	....	....	....	....	....
of which: Short-term	4 745 ..	....	....	....	....	....	....	....	....
Other sectors	4 746 ..	....	....	....	....	....	....	....	....
of which: Short-term	4 748 ..	....	....	....	....	....	....	....	....
Liabilities	4 753 ..	**210.4**	**452.7**	**584.5**	**367.0**	**739.5**	**183.7**	**195.6**	**334.0**
Trade credits	4 756 ..	29.4	6.3	–11.8	7.7	–10.0	....	....	....
General government	4 757 ..	....	....	....	....	....	....	....	....
of which: Short-term	4 759 ..	....	....	....	....	....	....	....	....
Other sectors	4 760 ..	29.4	6.3	–11.8	7.7	–10.0	....	....	....
of which: Short-term	4 762 ..	*29.4*	*6.3*	*–11.8*	*7.7*	*–10.0*	....	....	....
Loans	4 764 ..	–2.3	489.5	523.5	242.3	704.3	199.8	186.3	283.2
Monetary authorities	4 765 ..	–13.0	31.8	27.1	.6	17.8	–8.7	–162.2	....
of which: Use of Fund credit and loans from the Fund..	4 766 ..	*–13.0*	*31.8*	*27.1*	*.6*	*17.8*	*–8.7*	*–162.2*	....
of which: Short-term	4 768 ..	....	....	....	....	....	....	....	....
General government	4 769 ..	6.9	410.6	483.0	147.7	386.2	224.9	332.8	303.0
of which: Short-term	4 771 ..	....	....	....	....	....	....	....	....
Banks	4 772 ..	....	....	....	....	....	....	....	....
of which: Short-term	4 774 ..	....	....	....	....	....	....	....	....
Other sectors	4 775 ..	3.7	47.0	13.4	94.0	300.4	–16.4	15.8	–19.8
of which: Short-term	4 777 ..	*15.9*	*35.0*	*12.8*	*6.4*	*–1.3*	*6.7*	*15.8*	*–10.3*
Currency and deposits	4 780 ..	51.1	–125.1	12.5	35.0	–9.5	–16.0	9.2	50.8
Monetary authorities	4 781 ..	47.0	–54.6	5.7	11.0	9.2	–17.0	–4.4	1.8
General government	4 782 ..	....	....	....	....	....	....	....	....
Banks	4 783 ..	4.1	–70.5	6.7	24.0	–18.6	1.0	13.6	49.0
Other sectors	4 784 ..	....	....	....	....	....	....	....	....
Other liabilities	4 786 ..	132.2	82.0	60.4	82.1	54.6	....	....	....
Monetary authorities	4 787 ..	....	....	....	....	....	....	....	....
of which: Short-term	4 789 ..	....	....	....	....	....	....	....	....
General government	4 790 ..	123.1	76.1	60.3	82.1	54.6	....	....	....
of which: Short-term	4 792 ..	*123.1*	*76.1*	*60.3*	*82.1*	*54.6*	....	....	....
Banks	4 793 ..	....	....	....	....	....	....	....	....
of which: Short-term	4 795 ..	....	....	....	....	....	....	....	....
Other sectors	4 796 ..	9.1	5.9	.1	....	....	....	....	....
of which: Short-term	4 798 ..	*9.1*	*5.9*	*.1*	....	....	....	....	....
E. RESERVE ASSETS	4 802 ..	**–108.6**	**126.7**	**471.4**	**76.9**	**544.3**	**330.3**	**–189.6**	**539.5**
Monetary gold	4 812 ..	....	....	....	....	....	–11.2	8.6	26.5
Special drawing rights	4 811 ..	.1	–.2	.1	.1	–.4	.3	.1	....
Reserve position in the Fund	4 810 ..	....	....	–.1	....	....	....	–.2	–.1
Foreign exchange	4 803 ..	–108.6	127.0	471.4	76.9	544.6	341.2	–198.1	513.1
Other claims	4 813 ..	....	....	....	....	....	....	....	....
NET ERRORS AND OMISSIONS	4 998 ..	**–231.3**	**–229.0**	**–915.1**	**–390.1**	**–354.1**	**486.3**	**1,161.3**	**–161.7**

Table 1. ANALYTIC PRESENTATION, 2000–2007

(Billions of U.S. dollars)

	Code	2000	2001	2002	2003	2004	2005	2006	2007
A. Current Account[1]	4 993 Z.	**−81.84**	**−19.74**	**54.78**	**38.78**	**79.76**	**22.53**	**1.55**	**38.56**
Goods: exports f.o.b.	2 100 ..	907.88	920.86	998.20	1,172.75	1,406.25	1,527.09	1,759.89	2,073.03
Goods: imports f.o.b.	3 100 ..	−879.08	−855.64	−876.73	−1,053.44	−1,276.97	−1,460.10	−1,726.95	−1,989.90
Balance on Goods	4 100 ..	*28.80*	*65.22*	*121.47*	*119.30*	*129.28*	*66.99*	*32.93*	*83.14*
Services: credit	2 200 ..	258.84	287.12	316.49	378.51	452.27	500.04	545.19	670.47
Services: debit	3 200 ..	−278.42	−290.55	−299.88	−353.27	−416.90	−460.03	−497.78	−606.54
Balance on Goods and Services	4 991 ..	*9.22*	*61.79*	*138.08*	*144.55*	*164.66*	*106.99*	*80.35*	*147.07*
Income: credit	2 300 ..	258.08	244.24	232.38	275.92	362.74	470.11	607.85	763.69
Income: debit	3 300 ..	−299.57	−279.96	−269.60	−317.87	−373.61	−463.32	−589.07	−757.14
Balance on Goods, Services, and Income	4 992 ..	*−32.28*	*26.07*	*100.86*	*102.60*	*153.79*	*113.78*	*99.13*	*153.61*
Current transfers: credit	2 379 Z.	62.63	71.19	81.08	93.24	101.78	104.84	108.63	120.36
Current transfers: debit	3 379 ..	−112.19	−117.00	−127.16	−157.06	−175.80	−196.08	−206.20	−235.42
B. Capital Account[1]	4 994 Z.	**8.41**	**5.62**	**9.70**	**14.31**	**20.56**	**13.86**	**11.71**	**19.08**
Capital account: credit	2 994 Z.	16.16	15.50	18.13	27.24	30.39	29.75	29.66	35.13
Capital account: debit	3 994 ..	−7.75	−9.88	−8.43	−12.92	−9.83	−15.89	−17.94	−16.06
Total, Groups A Plus B	4 981 ..	*−73.43*	*−14.12*	*64.48*	*53.09*	*100.32*	*36.40*	*13.26*	*57.63*
C. Financial Account[1]	4 995 W.	**50.73**	**−41.17**	**−17.05**	**−48.88**	**−39.07**	**−14.33**	**130.53**	**123.28**
Direct investment abroad	4 505 ..	−413.73	−297.98	−163.84	−165.44	−205.06	−459.75	−447.98	−552.00
Direct investment in the Euro Area	4 555 Z.	416.35	199.81	184.95	153.20	121.37	189.20	258.70	391.00
Portfolio investment assets	4 602 ..	−385.31	−255.02	−163.19	−318.33	−428.12	−512.44	−667.80	−585.06
Equity securities	4 610 ..	−267.63	−90.84	−34.01	−90.34	−132.52	−165.97	−188.87	−74.77
Debt securities	4 619 ..	−117.67	−164.17	−129.19	−227.99	−295.60	−346.47	−478.93	−510.30
Portfolio investment liabilities	4 652 Z.	268.06	318.31	298.36	383.29	519.98	682.43	1,008.76	891.69
Equity securities	4 660 ..	37.96	207.33	78.44	127.39	165.37	313.20	377.91	249.26
Debt securities	4 669 Z.	230.10	110.98	219.92	255.90	354.61	369.23	630.84	642.43
Financial derivatives	4 910 ..	−9.00	−.84	−12.40	−15.58	−10.42	−22.68	3.45	−125.25
Financial derivatives assets	4 900 ..	. . . .	. . . .	. . . .	. . . .	. . . .	. . . .	. . . .	. . . .
Financial derivatives liabilities	4 905 ..	−9.00	−.84	−12.40	−15.58	−10.42	−22.68	3.45	−125.25
Other investment assets	4 703 ..	−165.90	−243.59	−220.82	−283.99	−392.61	−689.75	−906.43	−1,152.94
Monetary authorities	4 701 ..	−1.11	.21	−.90	−.81	−.25	−.62	−3.26	−13.50
General government	4 704 ..	−2.42	2.91	−.94	−.35	−1.81	6.11	2.16	9.35
Banks	4 705 ..	−118.43	−209.01	−164.43	−173.60	−329.62	−498.58	−662.48	−742.35
Other sectors	4 728 ..	−43.94	−37.70	−54.56	−109.24	−60.93	−196.66	−242.86	−406.44
Other investment liabilities	4 753 W.	340.26	238.13	59.90	197.97	355.79	798.65	881.84	1,255.85
Monetary authorities	4 753 WA	.55	3.82	18.34	12.04	9.74	8.41	23.12	74.35
General government	4 753 ZB	.01	−.67	−7.29	−3.63	−5.06	−2.55	2.65	3.83
Banks	4 753 ZC	273.42	216.66	23.59	151.81	307.47	606.09	615.90	842.53
Other sectors	4 753 ZD	66.28	18.33	25.26	37.76	43.65	186.70	240.17	335.15
Total, Groups A Through C	4 983 ..	*−22.70*	*−55.29*	*47.43*	*4.21*	*61.25*	*22.07*	*143.79*	*180.91*
D. Net Errors and Omissions	4 998 ..	**6.55**	**38.85**	**−44.45**	**−37.01**	**−76.81**	**−44.98**	**−141.23**	**−174.95**
Total, Groups A Through D	4 984 ..	*−16.15*	*−16.45*	*2.98*	*−32.80*	*−15.56*	*−22.91*	*2.56*	*5.96*
E. Reserves and Related Items	4 802 A.	**16.15**	**16.45**	**−2.98**	**32.80**	**15.56**	**22.91**	**−2.56**	**−5.96**
Reserve assets	4 802 ..	16.15	16.45	−2.98	32.80	15.56	22.91	−2.56	−5.96
Use of Fund credit and loans	4 766 ..	. . . .	. . . .	. . . .	. . . .	. . . .	. . . .	. . . .	. . . .
Exceptional financing	4 920 ..	. . . .	. . . .	. . . .	. . . .	. . . .	. . . .	. . . .	. . . .
Conversion rates: euros per U.S. dollar	0 103 ..	**1.0854**	**1.1175**	**1.0626**	**.8860**	**.8054**	**.8041**	**.7971**	**.7306**

[1] Excludes components that have been classified in the categories of Group E.

Table 2. STANDARD PRESENTATION, 2000–2007

(Billions of U.S. dollars)

	Code	2000	2001	2002	2003	2004	2005	2006	2007
CURRENT ACCOUNT	4 993 ..	−81.84	−19.74	54.78	38.78	79.76	22.53	1.55	38.56
A. GOODS	4 100 ..	28.80	65.22	121.47	119.30	129.28	66.99	32.93	83.14
Credit	2 100 ..	907.88	920.86	998.20	1,172.75	1,406.25	1,527.09	1,759.89	2,073.03
General merchandise: exports f.o.b.	2 110 ..	....	....	....	....	....	....	....	....
Goods for processing: exports f.o.b.	2 150 ..	....	....	....	....	....	....	....	....
Repairs on goods	2 160 ..	....	....	....	....	....	....	....	....
Goods procured in ports by carriers	2 170 ..	....	....	....	....	....	....	....	....
Nonmonetary gold	2 180 ..	....	....	....	....	....	....	....	....
Debit	3 100 ..	−879.08	−855.64	−876.73	−1,053.44	−1,276.97	−1,460.10	−1,726.95	−1,989.90
General merchandise: imports f.o.b.	3 110 ..	....	....	....	....	....	....	....	....
Goods for processing: imports f.o.b.	3 150 ..	....	....	....	....	....	....	....	....
Repairs on goods	3 160 ..	....	....	....	....	....	....	....	....
Goods procured in ports by carriers	3 170 ..	....	....	....	....	....	....	....	....
Nonmonetary gold	3 180 ..	....	....	....	....	....	....	....	....
B. SERVICES	4 200 ..	−19.58	−3.43	16.61	25.25	35.37	40.01	47.41	63.93
Total credit	2 200 ..	*258.84*	*287.12*	*316.49*	*378.51*	*452.27*	*500.04*	*545.19*	*670.47*
Total debit	3 200 ..	*−278.42*	*−290.55*	*−299.88*	*−353.27*	*−416.90*	*−460.03*	*−497.78*	*−606.54*
Transportation services, credit	2 205 ..	....	....	....	....	....	....	....	....
Passenger	2 850 ..	....	....	....	....	....	....	....	....
Freight	2 851 ..	....	....	....	....	....	....	....	....
Other	2 852 ..	....	....	....	....	....	....	....	....
Sea transport, passenger	2 207 ..	....	....	....	....	....	....	....	....
Sea transport, freight	2 208 ..	....	....	....	....	....	....	....	....
Sea transport, other	2 209 ..	....	....	....	....	....	....	....	....
Air transport, passenger	2 211 ..	....	....	....	....	....	....	....	....
Air transport, freight	2 212 ..	....	....	....	....	....	....	....	....
Air transport, other	2 213 ..	....	....	....	....	....	....	....	....
Other transport, passenger	2 215 ..	....	....	....	....	....	....	....	....
Other transport, freight	2 216 ..	....	....	....	....	....	....	....	....
Other transport, other	2 217 ..	....	....	....	....	....	....	....	....
Transportation services, debit	3 205 ..	....	....	....	....	....	....	....	....
Passenger	3 850 ..	....	....	....	....	....	....	....	....
Freight	3 851 ..	....	....	....	....	....	....	....	....
Other	3 852 ..	....	....	....	....	....	....	....	....
Sea transport, passenger	3 207 ..	....	....	....	....	....	....	....	....
Sea transport, freight	3 208 ..	....	....	....	....	....	....	....	....
Sea transport, other	3 209 ..	....	....	....	....	....	....	....	....
Air transport, passenger	3 211 ..	....	....	....	....	....	....	....	....
Air transport, freight	3 212 ..	....	....	....	....	....	....	....	....
Air transport, other	3 213 ..	....	....	....	....	....	....	....	....
Other transport, passenger	3 215 ..	....	....	....	....	....	....	....	....
Other transport, freight	3 216 ..	....	....	....	....	....	....	....	....
Other transport, other	3 217 ..	....	....	....	....	....	....	....	....
Travel, credit	2 236 ..	....	....	....	....	....	....	....	....
Business travel	2 237 ..	....	....	....	....	....	....	....	....
Personal travel	2 240 ..	....	....	....	....	....	....	....	....
Travel, debit	3 236 ..	....	....	....	....	....	....	....	....
Business travel	3 237 ..	....	....	....	....	....	....	....	....
Personal travel	3 240 ..	....	....	....	....	....	....	....	....
Other services, credit	2 200 BA	....	....	....	....	....	....	....	....
Communications	2 245 ..	....	....	....	....	....	....	....	....
Construction	2 249 ..	....	....	....	....	....	....	....	....
Insurance	2 253 ..	....	....	....	....	....	....	....	....
Financial	2 260 ..	....	....	....	....	....	....	....	....
Computer and information	2 262 ..	....	....	....	....	....	....	....	....
Royalties and licence fees	2 266 ..	....	....	....	....	....	....	....	....
Other business services	2 268 ..	....	....	....	....	....	....	....	....
Personal, cultural, and recreational	2 287 ..	....	....	....	....	....	....	....	....
Government, n.i.e.	2 291 ..	....	....	....	....	....	....	....	....
Other services, debit	3 200 BA	....	....	....	....	....	....	....	....
Communications	3 245 ..	....	....	....	....	....	....	....	....
Construction	3 249 ..	....	....	....	....	....	....	....	....
Insurance	3 253 ..	....	....	....	....	....	....	....	....
Financial	3 260 ..	....	....	....	....	....	....	....	....
Computer and information	3 262 ..	....	....	....	....	....	....	....	....
Royalties and licence fees	3 266 ..	....	....	....	....	....	....	....	....
Other business services	3 268 ..	....	....	....	....	....	....	....	....
Personal, cultural, and recreational	3 287 ..	....	....	....	....	....	....	....	....
Government, n.i.e.	3 291 ..	....	....	....	....	....	....	....	....

Table 2 (Continued). STANDARD PRESENTATION, 2000–2007

(Billions of U.S. dollars)

	Code	2000	2001	2002	2003	2004	2005	2006	2007
C. INCOME	4 300	−41.49	−35.72	−37.22	−41.95	−10.87	6.79	18.78	6.54
Total credit	2 300	*258.08*	*244.24*	*232.38*	*275.92*	*362.74*	*470.11*	*607.85*	*763.69*
Total debit	3 300	*−299.57*	*−279.96*	*−269.60*	*−317.87*	*−373.61*	*−463.32*	*−589.07*	*−757.14*
Compensation of employees, credit	2 310	12.34	13.40	14.50	17.05	19.05	19.48	20.75	23.64
Compensation of employees, debit	3 310	−5.70	−6.52	−7.24	−8.40	−9.43	−11.35	−12.42	−14.40
Investment income, credit	2 320	245.73	230.84	217.88	258.87	343.69	450.63	587.10	740.05
Direct investment income	2 330	62.75	51.29	59.41	85.63	140.29	193.60	240.64	271.96
Dividends and distributed branch profits	2 332	45.34	59.81	45.02	57.59	78.06	125.50	168.98	162.94
Reinvested earnings and undistributed branch profits	2 333	6.98	−16.97	7.35	16.36	46.22	49.14	46.99	75.28
Income on debt (interest)	2 334	10.44	8.46	7.03	11.69	16.02	18.96	24.68	33.74
Portfolio investment income	2 339	70.54	75.78	79.46	95.46	119.69	140.84	176.89	225.17
Income on equity	2 340	13.02	16.03	18.69	21.24	29.47	39.14	48.99	61.59
Income on bonds and notes	2 350	....	....	....	....	....	....	....	....
Income on money market instruments	2 360	....	....	....	....	....	....	....	....
Other investment income	2 370	112.44	103.77	79.01	77.79	83.71	116.18	169.56	242.92
Investment income, debit	3 320	−293.87	−273.44	−262.36	−309.48	−364.19	−451.97	−576.65	−742.74
Direct investment income	3 330	−79.56	−55.09	−60.24	−77.81	−113.11	−138.88	−154.94	−170.61
Dividends and distributed branch profits	3 332	−32.41	−33.45	−33.30	−45.18	−57.95	−137.16	−84.16	−107.58
Reinvested earnings and undistributed branch profits	3 333	−39.31	−13.25	−19.93	−20.42	−39.45	16.12	−49.00	−34.61
Income on debt (interest)	3 334	−7.84	−8.40	−7.01	−12.22	−15.71	−17.84	−21.79	−28.43
Portfolio investment income	3 339	−101.64	−104.43	−117.31	−149.19	−160.79	−187.81	−232.90	−306.42
Income on equity	3 340	−28.10	−39.99	−48.43	−59.87	−66.75	−86.42	−124.67	−157.50
Income on bonds and notes	3 350	....	....	....	....	....	....	....	....
Income on money market instruments	3 360	....	....	....	....	....	....	....	....
Other investment income	3 370	−112.67	−113.92	−84.80	−82.48	−90.28	−125.28	−188.80	−265.71
D. CURRENT TRANSFERS	4 379	−49.56	−45.82	−46.08	−63.82	−74.02	−91.25	−97.58	−115.06
Credit	2 379	62.63	71.19	81.08	93.24	101.78	104.84	108.63	120.36
General government	2 380	....	....	....	....	....	....	....	....
Other sectors	2 390	....	....	....	....	....	....	....	....
Workers' remittances	2 391	....	....	....	....	....	....	....	....
Other current transfers	2 392	....	....	....	....	....	....	....	....
Debit	3 379	−112.19	−117.00	−127.16	−157.06	−175.80	−196.08	−206.20	−235.42
General government	3 380	....	....	....	....	....	....	....	....
Other sectors	3 390	....	....	....	....	....	....	....	....
Workers' remittances	3 391	....	....	....	....	....	....	....	....
Other current transfers	3 392	....	....	....	....	....	....	....	....
CAPITAL AND FINANCIAL ACCOUNT	4 996	75.29	−19.10	−10.33	−1.77	−2.95	22.44	139.68	136.40
CAPITAL ACCOUNT	4 994	8.41	5.62	9.70	14.31	20.56	13.86	11.71	19.08
Total credit	2 994	*16.16*	*15.50*	*18.13*	*27.24*	*30.39*	*29.75*	*29.66*	*35.13*
Total debit	3 994	*−7.75*	*−9.88*	*−8.43*	*−12.92*	*−9.83*	*−15.89*	*−17.94*	*−16.06*
Capital transfers, credit	2 400	....	....	....	....	....	....	....	....
General government	2 401	....	....	....	....	....	....	....	....
Debt forgiveness	2 402	....	....	....	....	....	....	....	....
Other capital transfers	2 410	....	....	....	....	....	....	....	....
Other sectors	2 430	....	....	....	....	....	....	....	....
Migrants' transfers	2 431	....	....	....	....	....	....	....	....
Debt forgiveness	2 432	....	....	....	....	....	....	....	....
Other capital transfers	2 440	....	....	....	....	....	....	....	....
Capital transfers, debit	3 400	....	....	....	....	....	....	....	....
General government	3 401	....	....	....	....	....	....	....	....
Debt forgiveness	3 402	....	....	....	....	....	....	....	....
Other capital transfers	3 410	....	....	....	....	....	....	....	....
Other sectors	3 430	....	....	....	....	....	....	....	....
Migrants' transfers	3 431	....	....	....	....	....	....	....	....
Debt forgiveness	3 432	....	....	....	....	....	....	....	....
Other capital transfers	3 440	....	....	....	....	....	....	....	....
Nonproduced nonfinancial assets, credit	2 480	....	....	....	....	....	....	....	....
Nonproduced nonfinancial assets, debit	3 480	....	....	....	....	....	....	....	....

Table 2 (Continued). STANDARD PRESENTATION, 2000–2007

(Billions of U.S. dollars)

	Code	2000	2001	2002	2003	2004	2005	2006	2007
FINANCIAL ACCOUNT	4 995 ..	**66.88**	**–24.72**	**–20.03**	**–16.08**	**–23.51**	**8.58**	**127.97**	**117.32**
A. DIRECT INVESTMENT	4 500 ..	**2.62**	**–98.17**	**21.12**	**–12.24**	**–83.70**	**–270.55**	**–189.28**	**–161.00**
Direct investment abroad	4 505 ..	–413.73	–297.98	–163.84	–165.44	–205.06	–459.75	–447.98	–552.00
Equity capital	4 510 ..	–318.14	–229.70	–161.90	–131.41	–168.74	–337.17	–308.72	–351.53
Claims on affiliated enterprises	4 515 ..	....	....	....	....	....	....	....	....
Liabilities to affiliated enterprises	4 520 ..	....	....	....	....	....	....	....	....
Reinvested earnings	4 525 ..	–6.98	16.97	–7.35	–16.36	–46.22	–49.14	–46.99	–75.28
Other capital	4 530 ..	–88.61	–85.26	5.41	–17.68	9.89	–73.44	–92.26	–125.19
Claims on affiliated enterprises	4 535 ..	....	....	....	....	....	....	....	....
Liabilities to affiliated enterprises	4 540 ..	....	....	....	....	....	....	....	....
Direct investment in the Euro Area	4 555 ..	**416.35**	**199.81**	**184.95**	**153.20**	**121.37**	**189.20**	**258.70**	**391.00**
Equity capital	4 560 ..	260.82	118.45	116.81	123.67	82.88	168.55	171.74	217.54
Claims on direct investors	4 565 ..	....	....	....	....	....	....	....	....
Liabilities to direct investors	4 570 ..	....	....	....	....	....	....	....	....
Reinvested earnings	4 575 ..	39.31	13.25	19.93	20.42	39.45	–16.12	49.00	34.61
Other capital	4 580 ..	116.22	68.11	48.21	9.11	–.97	36.77	37.96	138.85
Claims on direct investors	4 585 ..	....	....	....	....	....	....	....	....
Liabilities to direct investors	4 590 ..	....	....	....	....	....	....	....	....
B. PORTFOLIO INVESTMENT	4 600 ..	**–117.25**	**63.29**	**135.16**	**64.96**	**91.87**	**169.99**	**340.95**	**306.62**
Assets	4 602 ..	**–385.31**	**–255.02**	**–163.19**	**–318.33**	**–428.12**	**–512.44**	**–667.80**	**–585.06**
Equity securities	4 610 ..	–267.63	–90.84	–34.01	–90.34	–132.52	–165.97	–188.87	–74.77
Monetary authorities	4 611 ..	–.05	–.32	–.37	–.39	–.02	–.17	–.03	.12
General government	4 612 ..	–2.45	–1.83	–4.13	–2.95	–4.51	–4.29	–7.72	–7.41
Banks	4 613 ..	–3.55	3.19	–6.59	–15.69	–27.32	–18.85	–22.92	–47.75
Other sectors	4 614 ..	–261.59	–91.87	–22.92	–71.31	–100.67	–142.65	–158.20	–19.73
Debt securities	4 619 ..	–117.67	–164.17	–129.19	–227.99	–295.60	–346.47	–478.93	–510.30
Bonds and notes	4 620 ..	–106.82	–140.63	–83.45	–200.23	–223.85	–324.87	–391.29	–436.25
Monetary authorities	4 621 ..	–.33	.20	–.56	–2.66	1.23	–.90	–3.50	–3.06
General government	4 622 ..	–1.39	–.99	–.84	–.23	–2.63	–1.00	–1.43	–3.32
Banks	4 623 ..	–44.28	–60.14	–16.12	–51.44	–102.14	–145.86	–211.03	–215.97
Other sectors	4 624 ..	–60.81	–79.70	–65.93	–145.89	–120.32	–177.12	–175.33	–213.90
Money market instruments	4 630 ..	–10.86	–23.54	–45.73	–27.77	–71.75	–21.60	–87.65	–74.05
Monetary authorities	4 631 ..	2.05	–2.13	1.93	.24	–.06	.13	–10.02	–8.87
General government	4 632 ..	–.91	.09	–.89	.80	.49	–.56	.52	.77
Banks	4 633 ..	–14.30	–36.70	–29.96	–51.05	–53.89	–17.37	–62.38	–63.06
Other sectors	4 634 ..	2.30	15.19	–16.81	22.24	–18.29	–3.80	–15.77	–2.88
Liabilities	4 652 ..	**268.06**	**318.31**	**298.36**	**383.29**	**519.98**	**682.43**	**1,008.76**	**891.69**
Equity securities	4 660 ..	37.96	207.33	78.44	127.39	165.37	313.20	377.91	249.26
Banks	4 663 ..	....	....	....	....	....	....	....	....
Other sectors	4 664 ..	....	....	....	....	....	....	....	....
Debt securities	4 669 ..	230.10	110.98	219.92	255.90	354.61	369.23	630.84	642.43
Bonds and notes	4 670 ..	216.45	101.17	165.17	221.90	334.72	299.85	631.62	572.51
Monetary authorities	4 671 ..	....	....	....	....	....	....	....	....
General government	4 672 ..	....	....	....	....	....	....	....	....
Banks	4 673 ..	....	....	....	....	....	....	....	....
Other sectors	4 674 ..	....	....	....	....	....	....	....	....
Money market instruments	4 680 ..	13.65	9.81	54.75	34.01	19.90	69.38	–.77	69.92
Monetary authorities	4 681 ..	....	....	....	....	....	....		....
General government	4 682 ..	....	....	....	....	....	....	–26.33	....
Banks	4 683 ..	....	....	....	....	....	....	33.34	....
Other sectors	4 684 ..	....	....	....	....	....	....	–7.78	....
C. FINANCIAL DERIVATIVES	4 910 ..	**–9.00**	**–.84**	**–12.40**	**–15.58**	**–10.42**	**–22.68**	**3.45**	**–125.25**
Monetary authorities	4 911 ..	....	....	....	....	....	....	....	....
General government	4 912 ..	....	....	....	....	....	....	....	....
Banks	4 913 ..	....	....	....	....	....	....	....	....
Other sectors	4 914 ..	....	....	....	....	....	....	....	....
Assets	4 900 ..	....	....	....	....	....	....	....	....
Monetary authorities	4 901 ..	....	....	....	....	....	....	....	....
General government	4 902 ..	....	....	....	....	....	....	....	....
Banks	4 903 ..	....	....	....	....	....	....	....	....
Other sectors	4 904 ..	....	....	....	....	....	....	....	....
Liabilities	4 905 ..	**–9.00**	**–.84**	**–12.40**	**–15.58**	**–10.42**	**–22.68**	**3.45**	**–125.25**
Monetary authorities	4 906 ..	....	....	....	....	....	....	....	....
General government	4 907 ..	....	....	....	....	....	....	....	....
Banks	4 908 ..	....	....	....	....	....	....	....	....
Other sectors	4 909 ..	....	....	....	....	....	....	....	....

Table 2 (Concluded).　STANDARD PRESENTATION, 2000–2007

(Billions of U.S. dollars)

	Code	2000	2001	2002	2003	2004	2005	2006	2007
D. OTHER INVESTMENT	4 700 ..	**174.36**	**−5.46**	**−160.93**	**−86.03**	**−36.82**	**108.90**	**−24.60**	**102.91**
Assets	4 703 ..	**−165.90**	**−243.59**	**−220.82**	**−283.99**	**−392.61**	**−689.75**	**−906.43**	**−1,152.94**
Trade credits	4 706 ..	−13.20	−3.11	−.46	−1.22	−7.40	−11.31	−6.21	−13.15
General government	4 707 ..	.05	−.09	1.33	−.07	−.01	−.05	....	.77
of which: Short-term	4 709 ..	....	....	....	....	....	....	....	....
Other sectors	4 710 ..	−13.25	−3.02	−1.79	−1.15	−7.39	−11.25	−6.21	−13.92
of which: Short-term	4 712 ..	....	....	....	....	....	....	....	....
Loans	4 714 ..	−137.20	−169.31	−181.61	−185.94	−360.30	−641.11	−844.33	−1,087.58
Monetary authorities	4 715 ..	−1.11	.21	−.90	−.81	.09	−.49	−3.25	−13.50
of which: Short-term	4 718 ..	....	....	....	....	....	....	....	....
General government	4 719 ..	.60	.72	−.55	−.52	1.86	10.63	7.13	6.78
of which: Short-term	4 721 ..	....	....	....	....	....	....	....	....
Banks	4 722 ..	−114.67	−196.39	−160.28	−173.07	−324.83	−494.44	−657.42	−727.15
of which: Short-term	4 724 ..	....	....	....	....	....	....	....	....
Other sectors	4 725 ..	−22.02	26.14	−19.88	−11.55	−37.41	−156.81	−190.78	−353.71
of which: Short-term	4 727 ..	....	....	....	....	....	....	....	....
Currency and deposits	4 730 ..	−5.88	−49.08	−30.25	−92.55	−13.10	−10.10	−33.55	−17.33
Monetary authorities	4 731 ..	....	....	....	....	....	....	....	....
General government	4 732 ..	−2.23	3.48	−.68	1.28	−2.12	−3.02	−4.06	2.85
Banks	4 733 ..	....	....	....	....	....	....	....	....
Other sectors	4 734 ..	−3.66	−52.57	−29.57	−93.83	−10.97	−7.09	−29.49	−20.18
Other assets	4 736 ..	−9.61	−22.09	−8.51	−4.29	−11.82	−27.23	−22.35	−34.88
Monetary authorities	4 737 ..	....	....	....	....	−.34	−.13	....	....
of which: Short-term	4 739 ..	....	....	....	....	....	....	....	....
General government	4 740 ..	−.83	−1.21	−1.04	−1.04	−1.54	−1.45	−.91	−1.05
of which: Short-term	4 742 ..	....	....	....	....	....	....	....	....
Banks	4 743 ..	−3.76	−12.62	−4.16	−.53	−4.79	−4.14	−5.05	−15.20
of which: Short-term	4 745 ..	....	....	....	....	....	....	....	....
Other sectors	4 746 ..	−5.02	−8.26	−3.32	−2.71	−5.15	−21.51	−16.38	−18.63
of which: Short-term	4 748 ..	....	....	....	....	....	....	....	....
Liabilities	4 753 ..	**340.26**	**238.13**	**59.90**	**197.97**	**355.79**	**798.65**	**881.84**	**1,255.85**
Trade credits	4 756 ..	9.85	1.17	−3.22	4.80	11.72	16.56	14.52	15.07
General government	4 757 ..	.01	.01	−.01	....	....	....	....	.02
of which: Short-term	4 759 ..	....	....	....	....	....	....	....	....
Other sectors	4 760 ..	9.84	1.17	−3.22	4.80	11.72	16.56	14.52	15.05
of which: Short-term	4 762 ..	....	....	....	....	....	....	....	....
Loans	4 764 ..	330.81	223.19	59.82	192.68	338.70	771.53	848.69	1,245.49
Monetary authorities	4 765 ..	.55	3.82	18.32	12.08	9.69	8.40	23.10	74.37
of which: Use of Fund credit and loans from the Fund..	4 766 ..	....	....	....	....	....	....	....	....
of which: Short-term	4 768 ..	....	....	....	....	....	....	....	....
General government	4 769 ..	−.03	−.74	−7.02	−3.95	−4.86	−2.22	2.77	4.04
of which: Short-term	4 771 ..	....	....	....	....	....	....	....	....
Banks	4 772 ..	268.72	207.53	26.33	151.98	303.91	603.74	611.86	835.84
of which: Short-term	4 774 ..	....	....	....	....	....	....	....	....
Other sectors	4 775 ..	61.58	12.57	22.19	32.57	29.97	161.61	210.96	331.23
of which: Short-term	4 777 ..	....	....	....	....	....	....	....	....
Currency and deposits	4 780 ..	....	....	....	....	....	....	....	....
Monetary authorities	4 781 ..	....	....	....	....	....	....	....	....
General government	4 782 ..	....	....	....	....	....	....	....	....
Banks	4 783 ..	....	....	....	....	....	....	....	....
Other sectors	4 784 ..	....	....	....	....	....	....	....	....
Other liabilities	4 786 ..	−.40	13.77	3.30	.49	5.37	10.56	18.63	−4.71
Monetary authorities	4 787 ..	.01	−.01	.02	−.04	.06	.01	.02	−.02
of which: Short-term	4 789 ..	....	....	....	....	....	....	....	....
General government	4 790 ..	.04	.06	−.27	.32	−.21	−.33	−.12	−.23
of which: Short-term	4 792 ..	....	....	....	....	....	....	....	....
Banks	4 793 ..	4.70	9.12	−2.74	−.17	3.56	2.35	4.04	6.68
of which: Short-term	4 795 ..	....	....	....	....	....	....	....	....
Other sectors	4 796 ..	−5.14	4.60	6.28	.39	1.96	8.53	14.69	−11.14
of which: Short-term	4 798 ..	....	....	....	....	....	....	....	....
E. RESERVE ASSETS	4 802 ..	**16.15**	**16.45**	**−2.98**	**32.80**	**15.56**	**22.91**	**−2.56**	**−5.96**
Monetary gold	4 812 ..	.92	.50	.66	1.95	1.46	4.81	5.28	4.08
Special drawing rights	4 811 ..	.30	−.94	.16	−.03	.46	−.21	−.70	−.47
Reserve position in the Fund	4 810 ..	3.45	−3.39	−2.13	−.51	5.07	11.24	6.02	1.92
Foreign exchange	4 803 ..	11.44	20.29	−1.67	31.40	8.58	7.07	−13.17	−11.49
Other claims	4 813 ..	.04	....	....	....	....	....	....	....
NET ERRORS AND OMISSIONS	4 998 ..	**6.55**	**38.85**	**−44.45**	**−37.01**	**−76.81**	**−44.98**	**−141.23**	**−174.95**

Table 3. INTERNATIONAL INVESTMENT POSITION (End-period stocks), 2000–2007

(Billions of U.S. dollars)

	Code	2000	2001	2002	2003	2004	2005	2006	2007
ASSETS	8 995 C.	**6,427.07**	**6,830.53**	**7,780.97**	**10,098.34**	**11,994.97**	**12,983.25**	**16,470.71**	**20,793.72**
Direct investment abroad	8 505 ..	1,623.08	1,837.55	2,103.57	2,742.06	3,163.72	3,316.76	4,047.14	5,152.94
Equity capital and reinvested earnings	8 506 ..	1,193.20	1,371.56	1,619.81	2,183.31	2,580.92	2,704.74	3,303.57	4,189.22
Claims on affiliated enterprises	8 507 ..	....	....	....	....	....	....	....	....
Liabilities to affiliated enterprises	8 508 ..	....	....	....	....	....	....	....	....
Other capital	8 530 ..	429.88	465.99	483.77	558.75	582.81	612.02	743.57	963.72
Claims on affiliated enterprises	8 535 ..	....	....	....	....	....	....	....	....
Liabilities to affiliated enterprises	8 540 ..	....	....	....	....	....	....	....	....
Portfolio investment	8 602 ..	**2,206.10**	**2,211.62**	**2,403.50**	**3,354.80**	**4,136.17**	**4,572.04**	**5,844.46**	**6,922.38**
Equity securities	8 610 ..	1,104.40	982.19	893.20	1,377.83	1,702.63	2,034.38	2,648.10	3,012.19
Monetary authorities	8 611 ..	.48	.56	.71	2.19	2.85	3.49	3.70	4.06
General government	8 612 ..	5.30	5.88	8.71	14.46	22.24	32.02	48.68	61.35
Banks	8 613 ..	40.42	33.89	45.69	67.69	100.75	117.40	157.14	209.68
Other sectors	8 614 ..	1,058.20	941.86	838.10	1,293.48	1,576.78	1,881.48	2,438.58	2,737.10
Debt securities	8 619 ..	1,101.70	1,229.43	1,510.30	1,976.98	2,433.53	2,537.66	3,196.36	3,910.18
Bonds and notes	8 620 ..	936.48	1,042.28	1,259.73	1,672.16	2,042.54	2,164.74	2,698.84	3,315.83
Monetary authorities	8 621 ..	4.68	2.44	7.50	10.43	8.80	8.08	12.17	16.46
General government	8 622 ..	3.89	5.74	6.64	10.12	13.16	13.71	17.62	22.39
Banks	8 623 ..	276.82	343.57	422.69	582.37	739.12	817.78	1,077.72	1,338.85
Other sectors	8 624 ..	651.08	690.53	822.89	1,069.23	1,281.45	1,325.17	1,591.33	1,938.14
Money market instruments	8 630 ..	165.23	187.15	250.57	304.82	391.00	372.92	497.52	594.35
Monetary authorities	8 631 ..	3.06	2.51	1.32	1.39	1.24	.89	11.50	12.01
General government	8 632 ..	.11	.17	1.19	.70	.53	.44	.35	.64
Banks	8 633 ..	117.87	154.65	198.63	241.88	315.26	309.31	397.49	464.15
Other sectors	8 634 ..	44.18	29.83	49.43	60.86	73.96	62.28	88.18	117.55
Financial derivatives	8 900 ..	**98.45**	**114.50**	**139.61**	**192.14**	**215.05**	**262.91**	**373.19**	**600.46**
Monetary authorities	8 901 ..	....	....	....	....	....	....	....	....
General government	8 902 ..	....	....	....	1.93	1.58	1.71	1.95	6.07
Banks	8 903 ..	....	....	....	74.28	96.87	96.70	124.57	183.72
Other sectors	8 904 ..	....	....	....	38.85	30.50	32.88	44.37	94.76
Other investment	8 703 ..	**2,147.46**	**2,320.81**	**2,750.36**	**3,421.99**	**4,097.23**	**4,454.00**	**5,776.74**	**7,606.57**
Trade credits	8 706 ..	164.09	158.20	184.31	238.09	263.15	245.74	263.32	310.09
General government	8 707 ..	2.64	2.69	1.43	30.25	31.99	23.20	18.61	19.65
of which: Short-term	8 709 ..	....	....	....	....	....	....	....	....
Other sectors	8 710 ..	161.44	155.51	182.89	207.84	231.16	222.54	244.71	290.44
of which: Short-term	8 712 ..	....	....	....	....	....	....	....	....
Loans	8 714 ..	1,805.81	1,980.79	2,348.54	2,553.82	3,127.88	3,512.15	4,663.65	6,271.26
Monetary authorities	8 715 ..	8.95	2.85	5.10	5.59	6.12	5.71	10.80	30.32
of which: Short-term	8 718 ..	....	....	....	....	....	....	....	....
General government	8 719 ..	73.68	63.51	65.14	70.39	77.05	58.35	55.81	70.37
of which: Short-term	8 721 ..	....	....	....	....	....	....	....	....
Banks	8 722 ..	1,323.22	1,467.83	1,767.20	2,197.39	2,666.85	2,911.13	3,789.61	4,819.74
of which: Short-term	8 724 ..	....	....	....	....	....	....	....	....
Other sectors	8 725 ..	399.97	446.60	511.11	280.45	377.86	536.97	807.43	1,350.83
of which: Short-term	8 727 ..	....	....	....	....	....	....	....	....
Currency and deposits	8 730 ..	....	....	....	421.49	460.04	420.95	513.44	659.25
Monetary authorities	8 731 ..	....	....	....	....	....	....	....	....
General government	8 732 ..	....	....	....	7.31	11.25	13.92	20.30	19.84
Banks	8 733 ..	....	....	....	....	....	....	....	....
Other sectors	8 734 ..	....	....	....	414.18	448.80	407.03	493.14	639.41
Other assets	8 736 ..	177.56	181.82	217.50	208.58	246.16	275.16	336.33	365.97
Monetary authorities	8 737 ..	2.43	.88	.34	.73	.13	.20	.22	.40
of which: Short-term	8 739 ..	....	....	....	....	....	....	....	....
General government	8 740 ..	49.78	49.98	58.06	52.50	56.87	54.58	59.23	67.60
of which: Short-term	8 742 ..	....	....	....	....	....	....	....	....
Banks	8 743 ..	32.07	43.29	63.94	48.47	61.58	66.28	77.69	105.98
of which: Short-term	8 745 ..	....	....	....	....	....	....	....	....
Other sectors	8 746 ..	93.28	87.68	95.17	106.89	127.58	154.10	199.19	191.99
of which: Short-term	8 748 ..	....	....	....	....	....	....	....	....
Reserve assets	8 802 ..	**351.98**	**346.05**	**383.93**	**387.35**	**382.79**	**377.55**	**429.18**	**511.38**
Monetary gold	8 812 ..	109.65	111.12	136.77	164.21	170.82	192.82	232.17	295.86
Special drawing rights	8 811 ..	4.03	4.82	5.04	5.54	5.32	5.11	6.08	6.87
Reserve position in the Fund	8 810 ..	19.66	22.29	26.32	29.43	25.45	12.46	6.89	5.24
Foreign exchange	8 803 ..	218.63	207.82	215.81	188.18	181.20	167.17	184.04	203.41
Other claims	8 813 ..	....	....	....	....	....	....	....	....

Table 3 (Concluded). INTERNATIONAL INVESTMENT POSITION (End-period stocks), 2000–2007

(Billions of U.S. dollars)

	Code	2000	2001	2002	2003	2004	2005	2006	2007
LIABILITIES	8 995 D.	6,901.90	7,179.69	8,530.66	11,092.32	13,198.40	13,964.66	17,831.17	22,674.86
Direct investment in the Euro Area	8 555	1,294.32	1,465.83	1,915.30	2,630.29	3,053.06	2,885.55	3,499.12	4,410.64
Equity capital and reinvested earnings	8 556	924.30	1,027.62	1,358.65	1,905.29	2,272.16	2,170.09	2,684.06	3,330.95
Claims on direct investors	8 557	....	....	....	....	....	....	....	....
Liabilities to direct investors	8 558	....	....	....	....	....	....	....	....
Other capital	8 580	370.03	438.21	556.65	725.00	780.90	715.46	815.06	1,079.69
Claims on direct investors	8 585	....	....	....	....	....	....	....	....
Liabilities to direct investors	8 590	....	....	....	....	....	....	....	....
Portfolio investment	8 652	2,980.09	2,949.11	3,390.18	4,534.13	5,565.52	6,034.51	7,859.80	9,900.63
Equity securities	8 660	1,544.19	1,448.81	1,430.81	1,985.03	2,406.38	2,872.43	3,862.49	4,805.88
Banks	8 663	....	....	....	....	....	....	....	1,093.64
Other sectors	8 664	....	....	....	....	....	....	....	3,712.24
Debt securities	8 669	1,435.90	1,500.30	1,959.37	2,549.09	3,159.14	3,162.08	3,997.31	5,094.75
Bonds and notes	8 670	1,278.36	1,335.96	1,740.99	2,245.94	2,851.19	2,802.24	3,609.95	4,594.43
Monetary authorities	8 671	....	....	....	....	....	....	....	−3.71
General government	8 672	....	....	....	....	....	....	....	1,923.02
Banks	8 673	....	....	....	....	....	....	....	1,556.00
Other sectors	8 674	....	....	....	....	....	....	....	1,119.12
Money market instruments	8 680	157.54	164.33	218.38	303.16	307.95	359.84	387.36	500.33
Monetary authorities	8 681	....	....	....	....	....	....	....	−.95
General government	8 682	....	....	....	....	....	....	....	210.69
Banks	8 683	....	....	....	....	....	....	....	260.74
Other sectors	8 684	....	....	....	....	....	....	....	29.84
Financial derivatives	8 905	96.55	112.28	152.78	217.10	265.81	317.36	430.48	531.95
Monetary authorities	8 906	....	....	....	....	....	....	....	....
General government	8 907	....	....	....	1.50	1.73	1.31	2.48	....
Banks	8 908	....	....	....	89.53	116.90	102.45	149.90	186.70
Other sectors	8 909	....	....	....	27.91	27.98	39.77	45.12	75.81
Other investment	8 753	2,530.94	2,652.48	3,072.40	3,710.80	4,314.01	4,727.24	6,041.77	7,831.65
Trade credits	8 756	101.26	96.70	109.73	139.76	156.80	156.38	188.71	230.55
General government	8 757	.15	.14	.13	.04	.01	.01	.01	.02
of which: Short-term	8 759	....	....	....	....	....	....	....	....
Other sectors	8 760	101.11	96.56	109.60	139.72	156.79	156.37	188.70	230.53
of which: Short-term	8 762	....	....	....	....	....	....	....	....
Loans	8 764	2,346.75	2,465.48	2,847.12	3,468.77	4,027.06	4,421.87	5,661.47	7,329.61
Monetary authorities	8 765	38.12	35.41	60.01	83.35	101.40	96.93	131.59	202.69
of which: Use of Fund credit and loans from the Fund	8 766	....	....	....	....	....	....	....	....
of which: Short-term	8 768	....	....	....	....	....	....	....	....
General government	8 769	39.83	40.11	44.71	53.14	57.21	47.50	57.54	67.14
of which: Short-term	8 771	....	....	....	....	....	....	....	....
Banks	8 772	1,976.79	2,081.16	2,360.39	2,832.93	3,301.40	3,593.68	4,493.50	5,665.54
of which: Short-term	8 774	....	....	....	....	....	....	....	....
Other sectors	8 775	292.01	308.80	382.01	499.34	567.05	683.77	978.84	1,394.24
of which: Short-term	8 777	....	....	....	....	....	....	....	....
Currency and deposits	8 780	....	....	....	....	....	....	....	....
Monetary authorities	8 781	....	....	....	....	....	....	....	....
General government	8 782	....	....	....	....	....	....	....	....
Banks	8 783	....	....	....	....	....	....	....	....
Other sectors	8 784	....	....	....	....	....	....	....	....
Other liabilities	8 786	82.93	90.30	115.55	102.28	130.16	148.99	191.59	271.49
Monetary authorities	8 787	.27	.10	.13	.20	.30	.27	.32	.36
of which: Short-term	8 789	....	....	....	....	....	....	....	....
General government	8 790	11.29	10.86	14.50	4.84	4.85	4.49	5.07	8.28
of which: Short-term	8 792	....	....	....	....	....	....	....	....
Banks	8 793	34.52	43.46	50.79	39.51	57.26	61.57	70.76	101.01
of which: Short-term	8 795	....	....	....	....	....	....	....	....
Other sectors	8 796	36.86	35.87	50.12	57.72	67.75	82.66	115.44	161.83
of which: Short-term	8 798	....	....	....	....	....	....	....	....
NET INTERNATIONAL INVESTMENT POSITION	8 995	−474.83	−349.17	−749.68	−993.98	−1,203.43	−981.40	−1,360.46	−1,881.14
Conversion rates: euros per U.S. dollar (end of period)	0 104	1.0747	1.1347	.9536	.7918	.7342	.8477	.7593	.6793

Table 1. ANALYTIC PRESENTATION, 2000–2007

(Millions of U.S. dollars)

	Code	2000	2001	2002	2003	2004	2005	2006	2007
A. Current Account[1].....................	4 993 Z.	**99.2**	**146.2**	**125.7**	**–6.6**	....	....	....	....
Goods: exports f.o.b...................	2 100 ..	476.8	516.2	537.4	593.7	....	....	....	....
Goods: imports f.o.b...................	3 100 ..	–514.6	–478.8	–471.6	–683.5	....	....	....	....
Balance on Goods.................	4 100 ..	*–37.8*	*37.3*	*65.8*	*–89.8*	....	....	....	....
Services: credit........................	2 200 ..	54.0	56.8	71.3	77.5	....	....	....	....
Services: debit.........................	3 200 ..	–97.2	–105.3	–132.1	–146.9	....	....	....	....
Balance on Goods and Services............	4 991 ..	*–81.0*	*–11.1*	*5.0*	*–159.2*	....	....	....	....
Income: credit.........................	2 300 ..	101.5	90.6	92.0	106.3	....	....	....	....
Income: debit..........................	3 300 ..	–67.2	–76.0	–73.3	–76.3	....	....	....	....
Balance on Goods, Services, and Income.........	4 992 ..	*–46.7*	*3.6*	*23.7*	*–129.2*	....	....	....	....
Current transfers: credit............	2 379 Z.	148.3	146.9	109.2	128.2	....	....	....	....
Current transfers: debit.............	3 379 ..	–2.3	–4.2	–7.1	–5.6	....	....	....	....
B. Capital Account[1]	4 994 Z.	....	....	....	....	....	....	....	....
Capital account: credit...............	2 994 Z.	....	....	....	....	....	....	....	....
Capital account: debit...............	3 994 ..	....	....	....	....	....	....	....	....
Total, Groups A Plus B................	4 981 ..	*99.2*	*146.2*	*125.7*	*–6.6*	....	....	....	....
C. Financial Account[1]	4 995 W.	....	....	....	....	....	....	....	....
Direct investment abroad..........	4 505 ..	....	....	....	....	....	....	....	....
Direct investment in Faroe Islands..........	4 555 Z.	....	....	....	....	....	....	....	....
Portfolio investment assets..........	4 602 ..	....	....	....	....	....	....	....	....
Equity securities..................	4 610 ..	....	....	....	....	....	....	....	....
Debt securities....................	4 619 ..	....	....	....	....	....	....	....	....
Portfolio investment liabilities........	4 652 Z.	....	....	....	....	....	....	....	....
Equity securities..................	4 660 ..	....	....	....	....	....	....	....	....
Debt securities....................	4 669 Z.	....	....	....	....	....	....	....	....
Financial derivatives................	4 910 ..	....	....	....	....	....	....	....	....
Financial derivatives assets........	4 900 ..	....	....	....	....	....	....	....	....
Financial derivatives liabilities.....	4 905 ..	....	....	....	....	....	....	....	....
Other investment assets............	4 703 ..	....	....	....	....	....	....	....	....
Monetary authorities..............	4 701 ..	....	....	....	....	....	....	....	....
General government...............	4 704 ..	....	....	....	....	....	....	....	....
Banks.............................	4 705 ..	....	....	....	....	....	....	....	....
Other sectors.....................	4 728 ..	....	....	....	....	....	....	....	....
Other investment liabilities.........	4 753 W.	....	....	....	....	....	....	....	....
Monetary authorities..............	4 753 WA	....	....	....	....	....	....	....	....
General government...............	4 753 ZB	....	....	....	....	....	....	....	....
Banks.............................	4 753 ZC	....	....	....	....	....	....	....	....
Other sectors.....................	4 753 ZD	....	....	....	....	....	....	....	....
Total, Groups A Through C...........	4 983 ..	*99.2*	*146.2*	*125.7*	*–6.6*	....	....	....	....
D. Net Errors and Omissions...................	4 998 ..	....	....	....	....	....	....	....	....
Total, Groups A Through D...........	4 984 ..	....	....	....	....	....	....	....	....
E. Reserves and Related Items...............	4 802 A.	....	....	....	....	....	....	....	....
Reserve assets.......................	4 802 ..	....	....	....	....	....	....	....	....
Use of Fund credit and loans........	4 766 ..	....	....	....	....	....	....	....	....
Exceptional financing................	4 920 ..	....	....	....	....	....	....	....	....
Conversion rates: Danish kroner per U.S. dollar....	0 101 ..	**8.0831**	**8.3228**	**7.8947**	**6.5877**	**5.9911**	**5.9969**	**5.9468**	**5.4437**

[1] Excludes components that have been classified in the categories of Group E.

Table 2. STANDARD PRESENTATION, 2000–2007

(Millions of U.S. dollars)

	Code	2000	2001	2002	2003	2004	2005	2006	2007
CURRENT ACCOUNT...	4 993 ..	**99.2**	**146.2**	**125.7**	**−6.6**	....	....	....	....
A. GOODS..	4 100 ..	**−37.8**	**37.3**	**65.8**	**−89.8**	....	....	....	....
Credit..	2 100 ..	**476.8**	**516.2**	**537.4**	**593.7**	....	....	....	....
General merchandise: exports f.o.b............	2 110 ..	....	....	....	....	....	....	....	....
Goods for processing: exports f.o.b...........	2 150 ..	....	....	....	....	....	....	....	....
Repairs on goods..	2 160 ..	....	....	....	....	....	....	....	....
Goods procured in ports by carriers............	2 170 ..	....	....	....	....	....	....	....	....
Nonmonetary gold.......................................	2 180 ..	....	....	....	....	....	....	....	....
Debit...	3 100 ..	**−514.6**	**−478.8**	**−471.6**	**−683.5**	....	....	....	....
General merchandise: imports f.o.b............	3 110 ..	....	....	....	....	....	....	....	....
Goods for processing: imports f.o.b............	3 150 ..	....	....	....	....	....	....	....	....
Repairs on goods..	3 160 ..	....	....	....	....	....	....	....	....
Goods procured in ports by carriers............	3 170 ..	....	....	....	....	....	....	....	....
Nonmonetary gold.......................................	3 180 ..	....	....	....	....	....	....	....	....
B. SERVICES..	4 200 ..	**−43.2**	**−48.4**	**−60.8**	**−69.4**	....	....	....	....
Total credit	2 200 ..	*54.0*	*56.8*	*71.3*	*77.5*	....	....	....	....
Total debit	3 200 ..	*−97.2*	*−105.3*	*−132.1*	*−146.9*	....	....	....	....
Transportation services, credit............	2 205 ..	**18.5**	**22.3**	**25.7**	**34.3**	....	....	....	....
Passenger	2 850 ..	....	....	....	....	....	....	....	....
Freight	2 851 ..	....	....	....	....	....	....	....	....
Other	2 852 ..	....	....	....	....	....	....	....	....
Sea transport, passenger.............................	2 207 ..	....	....	....	....	....	....	....	....
Sea transport, freight...................................	2 208 ..	....	....	....	....	....	....	....	....
Sea transport, other.....................................	2 209 ..	....	....	....	....	....	....	....	....
Air transport, passenger...............................	2 211 ..	....	....	....	....	....	....	....	....
Air transport, freight....................................	2 212 ..	....	....	....	....	....	....	....	....
Air transport, other......................................	2 213 ..	....	....	....	....	....	....	....	....
Other transport, passenger..........................	2 215 ..	....	....	....	....	....	....	....	....
Other transport, freight................................	2 216 ..	....	....	....	....	....	....	....	....
Other transport, other..................................	2 217 ..	....	....	....	....	....	....	....	....
Transportation services, debit.............	3 205 ..	**−28.5**	**−34.7**	**−36.5**	**−39.2**	....	....	....	....
Passenger	3 850 ..	....	....	....	....	....	....	....	....
Freight	3 851 ..	....	....	....	....	....	....	....	....
Other	3 852 ..	....	....	....	....	....	....	....	....
Sea transport, passenger.............................	3 207 ..	....	....	....	....	....	....	....	....
Sea transport, freight...................................	3 208 ..	....	....	....	....	....	....	....	....
Sea transport, other.....................................	3 209 ..	....	....	....	....	....	....	....	....
Air transport, passenger...............................	3 211 ..	....	....	....	....	....	....	....	....
Air transport, freight....................................	3 212 ..	....	....	....	....	....	....	....	....
Air transport, other......................................	3 213 ..	....	....	....	....	....	....	....	....
Other transport, passenger..........................	3 215 ..	....	....	....	....	....	....	....	....
Other transport, freight................................	3 216 ..	....	....	....	....	....	....	....	....
Other transport, other..................................	3 217 ..	....	....	....	....	....	....	....	....
Travel, credit.......................................	2 236 ..	**21.1**	**21.8**	**23.9**	**31.0**	....	....	....	....
Business travel..	2 237 ..	14.5	15.1	17.3	21.8	....	....	....	....
Personal travel..	2 240 ..	6.6	6.7	6.6	9.2	....	....	....	....
Travel, debit..	3 236 ..	**−32.6**	**−34.8**	**−40.7**	**−56.9**	....	....	....	....
Business travel..	3 237 ..	−21.6	−23.6	−27.4	−39.1	....	....	....	....
Personal travel..	3 240 ..	−11.0	−11.2	−13.3	−17.8	....	....	....	....
Other services, credit...........................	2 200 BA	**14.5**	**12.8**	**21.6**	**12.3**	....	....	....	....
Communications...	2 245 ..	.8	1.6	1.9	1.9	....	....	....	....
Construction..	2 249 ..	4.3	3.8	6.1	4.6	....	....	....	....
Insurance...	2 253 ..	7.6	4.3	8.4	2.6	....	....	....	....
Financial..	2 260 ..	.3	.2	2.2	.5	....	....	....	....
Computer and information............................	2 262 ..	.2	.2	.3	.2	....	....	....	....
Royalties and licence fees............................	2 266 ..	....	....	....	....	....	....	....	....
Other business services................................	2 268 ..	.8	2.2	1.9	1.4	....	....	....	....
Personal, cultural, and recreational.............	2 287 ..	.6	.4	.8	.9	....	....	....	....
Government, n.i.e...	2 291 ..	....	....	....	.1	....	....	....	....
Other services, debit............................	3 200 BA	**−36.0**	**−35.8**	**−54.8**	**−50.8**	....	....	....	....
Communications...	3 245 ..	−3.5	−3.6	−4.8	−3.3	....	....	....	....
Construction..	3 249 ..	−12.8	−9.5	−22.3	−19.0	....	....	....	....
Insurance...	3 253 ..	−7.4	−10.3	−10.8	−7.2	....	....	....	....
Financial..	3 260 ..	−.9	−.3	−1.1	−.3	....	....	....	....
Computer and information............................	3 262 ..	−2.5	−2.7	−3.5	−4.6	....	....	....	....
Royalties and licence fees............................	3 266 ..	−2.6	−3.1	−3.0	−3.2	....	....	....	....
Other business services................................	3 268 ..	−4.7	−5.2	−7.4	−10.2	....	....	....	....
Personal, cultural, and recreational.............	3 287 ..	−1.0	−.7	−1.3	−1.5	....	....	....	....
Government, n.i.e...	3 291 ..	−.6	−.6	−.7	−1.4	....	....	....	....

Table 2 (Continued). STANDARD PRESENTATION, 2000–2007

(Millions of U.S. dollars)

	Code	2000	2001	2002	2003	2004	2005	2006	2007
C. INCOME	4 300	**34.3**	**14.6**	**18.7**	**30.0**	....	....	....	....
Total credit	2 300	*101.5*	*90.6*	*92.0*	*106.3*	....	....	....	....
Total debit	3 300	*−67.2*	*−76.0*	*−73.3*	*−76.3*	....	....	....	....
Compensation of employees, credit	2 310	**43.0**	**39.0**	**39.8**	**44.4**	....	....	....	....
Compensation of employees, debit	3 310	**−5.7**	**−13.4**	**−9.6**	**−5.1**	....	....	....	....
Investment income, credit	2 320	**58.5**	**51.6**	**52.2**	**61.9**	....	....	....	....
Direct investment income	2 330	1.1	1.2	1.4	1.6	....	....	....	....
Dividends and distributed branch profits	2 332	....	....	....	....	....	....	....	....
Reinvested earnings and undistributed branch profits	2 333	....	....	....	....	....	....	....	....
Income on debt (interest)	2 334	....	....	....	....	....	....	....	....
Portfolio investment income	2 339	2.1	2.3	2.5	2.3	....	....	....	....
Income on equity	2 340	....	....	....	....	....	....	....	....
Income on bonds and notes	2 350	....	....	....	....	....	....	....	....
Income on money market instruments	2 360	....	....	....	....	....	....	....	....
Other investment income	2 370	55.4	48.1	48.3	58.1	....	....	....	....
Investment income, debit	3 320	**−61.5**	**−62.6**	**−63.7**	**−71.2**	....	....	....	....
Direct investment income	3 330	−4.5	−8.7	−8.6	−6.2	....	....	....	....
Dividends and distributed branch profits	3 332	....	....	....	....	....	....	....	....
Reinvested earnings and undistributed branch profits	3 333	....	....	....	....	....	....	....	....
Income on debt (interest)	3 334	....	....	....	....	....	....	....	....
Portfolio investment income	3 339	−1.6	−1.7	−2.0	−2.0	....	....	....	....
Income on equity	3 340	....	....	....	....	....	....	....	....
Income on bonds and notes	3 350	....	....	....	....	....	....	....	....
Income on money market instruments	3 360	....	....	....	....	....	....	....	....
Other investment income	3 370	−55.5	−52.2	−53.1	−63.0	....	....	....	....
D. CURRENT TRANSFERS	4 379	**145.9**	**142.7**	**102.1**	**122.6**	....	....	....	....
Credit	2 379	**148.3**	**146.9**	**109.2**	**128.2**	....	....	....	....
General government	2 380	133.2	132.6	94.5	111.7	....	....	....	....
Other sectors	2 390	15.1	14.3	14.7	16.5	....	....	....	....
Workers' remittances	2 391	....	....	....	....	....	....	....	....
Other current transfers	2 392	....	....	....	....	....	....	....	....
Debit	3 379	**−2.3**	**−4.2**	**−7.1**	**−5.6**	....	....	....	....
General government	3 380	−.3	−.5	−2.4	−.8	....	....	....	....
Other sectors	3 390	−2.0	−3.7	−4.7	−4.8	....	....	....	....
Workers' remittances	3 391	....	....	....	....	....	....	....	....
Other current transfers	3 392	....	....	....	....	....	....	....	....
CAPITAL AND FINANCIAL ACCOUNT	4 996	....	....	....	....	....	....	....	....
CAPITAL ACCOUNT	4 994	....	....	....	....	....	....	....	....
Total credit	2 994	....	....	....	....	....	....	....	....
Total debit	3 994	....	....	....	....	....	....	....	....
Capital transfers, credit	2 400	....	....	....	....	....	....	....	....
General government	2 401	....	....	....	....	....	....	....	....
Debt forgiveness	2 402	....	....	....	....	....	....	....	....
Other capital transfers	2 410	....	....	....	....	....	....	....	....
Other sectors	2 430	....	....	....	....	....	....	....	....
Migrants' transfers	2 431	....	....	....	....	....	....	....	....
Debt forgiveness	2 432	....	....	....	....	....	....	....	....
Other capital transfers	2 440	....	....	....	....	....	....	....	....
Capital transfers, debit	3 400	....	....	....	....	....	....	....	....
General government	3 401	....	....	....	....	....	....	....	....
Debt forgiveness	3 402	....	....	....	....	....	....	....	....
Other capital transfers	3 410	....	....	....	....	....	....	....	....
Other sectors	3 430	....	....	....	....	....	....	....	....
Migrants' transfers	3 431	....	....	....	....	....	....	....	....
Debt forgiveness	3 432	....	....	....	....	....	....	....	....
Other capital transfers	3 440	....	....	....	....	....	....	....	....
Nonproduced nonfinancial assets, credit	2 480	....	....	....	....	....	....	....	....
Nonproduced nonfinancial assets, debit	3 480	....	....	....	....	....	....	....	....

Table 2 (Continued). STANDARD PRESENTATION, 2000–2007

(Millions of U.S. dollars)

	Code	2000	2001	2002	2003	2004	2005	2006	2007
FINANCIAL ACCOUNT	4 995 ..	....	....	....	....	....	....	....	....
A. DIRECT INVESTMENT	4 500 ..	....	....	....	....	....	....	....	....
Direct investment abroad	4 505 ..	....	....	....	....	....	....	....	....
Equity capital	4 510 ..	....	....	....	....	....	....	....	....
Claims on affiliated enterprises	4 515 ..	....	....	....	....	....	....	....	....
Liabilities to affiliated enterprises	4 520 ..	....	....	....	....	....	....	....	....
Reinvested earnings	4 525 ..	....	....	....	....	....	....	....	....
Other capital	4 530 ..	....	....	....	....	....	....	....	....
Claims on affiliated enterprises	4 535 ..	....	....	....	....	....	....	....	....
Liabilities to affiliated enterprises	4 540 ..	....	....	....	....	....	....	....	....
Direct investment in Faroe Islands	4 555 ..	....	....	....	....	....	....	....	....
Equity capital	4 560 ..	....	....	....	....	....	....	....	....
Claims on direct investors	4 565 ..	....	....	....	....	....	....	....	....
Liabilities to direct investors	4 570 ..	....	....	....	....	....	....	....	....
Reinvested earnings	4 575 ..	....	....	....	....	....	....	....	....
Other capital	4 580 ..	....	....	....	....	....	....	....	....
Claims on direct investors	4 585 ..	....	....	....	....	....	....	....	....
Liabilities to direct investors	4 590 ..	....	....	....	....	....	....	....	....
B. PORTFOLIO INVESTMENT	4 600 ..	....	....	....	....	....	....	....	....
Assets	4 602 ..	....	....	....	....	....	....	....	....
Equity securities	4 610 ..	....	....	....	....	....	....	....	....
Monetary authorities	4 611 ..	....	....	....	....	....	....	....	....
General government	4 612 ..	....	....	....	....	....	....	....	....
Banks	4 613 ..	....	....	....	....	....	....	....	....
Other sectors	4 614 ..	....	....	....	....	....	....	....	....
Debt securities	4 619 ..	....	....	....	....	....	....	....	....
Bonds and notes	4 620 ..	....	....	....	....	....	....	....	....
Monetary authorities	4 621 ..	....	....	....	....	....	....	....	....
General government	4 622 ..	....	....	....	....	....	....	....	....
Banks	4 623 ..	....	....	....	....	....	....	....	....
Other sectors	4 624 ..	....	....	....	....	....	....	....	....
Money market instruments	4 630 ..	....	....	....	....	....	....	....	....
Monetary authorities	4 631 ..	....	....	....	....	....	....	....	....
General government	4 632 ..	....	....	....	....	....	....	....	....
Banks	4 633 ..	....	....	....	....	....	....	....	....
Other sectors	4 634 ..	....	....	....	....	....	....	....	....
Liabilities	4 652 ..	....	....	....	....	....	....	....	....
Equity securities	4 660 ..	....	....	....	....	....	....	....	....
Banks	4 663 ..	....	....	....	....	....	....	....	....
Other sectors	4 664 ..	....	....	....	....	....	....	....	....
Debt securities	4 669 ..	....	....	....	....	....	....	....	....
Bonds and notes	4 670 ..	....	....	....	....	....	....	....	....
Monetary authorities	4 671 ..	....	....	....	....	....	....	....	....
General government	4 672 ..	....	....	....	....	....	....	....	....
Banks	4 673 ..	....	....	....	....	....	....	....	....
Other sectors	4 674 ..	....	....	....	....	....	....	....	....
Money market instruments	4 680 ..	....	....	....	....	....	....	....	....
Monetary authorities	4 681 ..	....	....	....	....	....	....	....	....
General government	4 682 ..	....	....	....	....	....	....	....	....
Banks	4 683 ..	....	....	....	....	....	....	....	....
Other sectors	4 684 ..	....	....	....	....	....	....	....	....
C. FINANCIAL DERIVATIVES	4 910 ..	....	....	....	....	....	....	....	....
Monetary authorities	4 911 ..	....	....	....	....	....	....	....	....
General government	4 912 ..	....	....	....	....	....	....	....	....
Banks	4 913 ..	....	....	....	....	....	....	....	....
Other sectors	4 914 ..	....	....	....	....	....	....	....	....
Assets	4 900 ..	....	....	....	....	....	....	....	....
Monetary authorities	4 901 ..	....	....	....	....	....	....	....	....
General government	4 902 ..	....	....	....	....	....	....	....	....
Banks	4 903 ..	....	....	....	....	....	....	....	....
Other sectors	4 904 ..	....	....	....	....	....	....	....	....
Liabilities	4 905 ..	....	....	....	....	....	....	....	....
Monetary authorities	4 906 ..	....	....	....	....	....	....	....	....
General government	4 907 ..	....	....	....	....	....	....	....	....
Banks	4 908 ..	....	....	....	....	....	....	....	....
Other sectors	4 909 ..	....	....	....	....	....	....	....	....

Table 2 (Concluded). STANDARD PRESENTATION, 2000–2007

(Millions of U.S. dollars)

	Code	2000	2001	2002	2003	2004	2005	2006	2007
D. OTHER INVESTMENT..	4 700 ..	....	....	....	....	....	....	....	....
Assets..	4 703 ..	....	....	....	....	....	....	....	....
Trade credits...	4 706 ..	....	....	....	....	....	....	....	....
General government............................	4 707 ..	....	....	....	....	....	....	....	....
of which: Short-term............................	4 709 ..	....	....	....	....	....	....	....	....
Other sectors......................................	4 710 ..	....	....	....	....	....	....	....	....
of which: Short-term............................	4 712 ..	....	....	....	....	....	....	....	....
Loans..	4 714 ..	....	....	....	....	....	....	....	....
Monetary authorities...........................	4 715 ..	....	....	....	....	....	....	....	....
of which: Short-term............................	4 718 ..	....	....	....	....	....	....	....	....
General government............................	4 719 ..	....	....	....	....	....	....	....	....
of which: Short-term............................	4 721 ..	....	....	....	....	....	....	....	....
Banks..	4 722 ..	....	....	....	....	....	....	....	....
of which: Short-term............................	4 724 ..	....	....	....	....	....	....	....	....
Other sectors......................................	4 725 ..	....	....	....	....	....	....	....	....
of which: Short-term............................	4 727 ..	....	....	....	....	....	....	....	....
Currency and deposits..............................	4 730 ..	....	....	....	....	....	....	....	....
Monetary authorities...........................	4 731 ..	....	....	....	....	....	....	....	....
General government............................	4 732 ..	....	....	....	....	....	....	....	....
Banks..	4 733 ..	....	....	....	....	....	....	....	....
Other sectors......................................	4 734 ..	....	....	....	....	....	....	....	....
Other assets...	4 736 ..	....	....	....	....	....	....	....	....
Monetary authorities...........................	4 737 ..	....	....	....	....	....	....	....	....
of which: Short-term.............................	4 739 ..	....	....	....	....	....	....	....	....
General government............................	4 740 ..	....	....	....	....	....	....	....	....
of which: Short-term.............................	4 742 ..	....	....	....	....	....	....	....	....
Banks..	4 743 ..	....	....	....	....	....	....	....	....
of which: Short-term.............................	4 745 ..	....	....	....	....	....	....	....	....
Other sectors......................................	4 746 ..	....	....	....	....	....	....	....	....
of which: Short-term.............................	4 748 ..	....	....	....	....	....	....	....	....
Liabilities..	4 753 ..	....	....	....	....	....	....	....	....
Trade credits...	4 756 ..	....	....	....	....	....	....	....	....
General government............................	4 757 ..	....	....	....	....	....	....	....	....
of which: Short-term............................	4 759 ..	....	....	....	....	....	....	....	....
Other sectors......................................	4 760 ..	....	....	....	....	....	....	....	....
of which: Short-term............................	4 762 ..	....	....	....	....	....	....	....	....
Loans..	4 764 ..	....	....	....	....	....	....	....	....
Monetary authorities...........................	4 765 ..	....	....	....	....	....	....	....	....
of which: Use of Fund credit and loans from the Fund..	4 766 ..	....	....	....	....	....	....	....	....
of which: Short-term............................	4 768 ..	....	....	....	....	....	....	....	....
General government............................	4 769 ..	....	....	....	....	....	....	....	....
of which: Short-term............................	4 771 ..	....	....	....	....	....	....	....	....
Banks..	4 772 ..	....	....	....	....	....	....	....	....
of which: Short-term............................	4 774 ..	....	....	....	....	....	....	....	....
Other sectors......................................	4 775 ..	....	....	....	....	....	....	....	....
of which: Short-term............................	4 777 ..	....	....	....	....	....	....	....	....
Currency and deposits..............................	4 780 ..	....	....	....	....	....	....	....	....
Monetary authorities...........................	4 781 ..	....	....	....	....	....	....	....	....
General government............................	4 782 ..	....	....	....	....	....	....	....	....
Banks..	4 783 ..	....	....	....	....	....	....	....	....
Other sectors......................................	4 784 ..	....	....	....	....	....	....	....	....
Other liabilities..	4 786 ..	....	....	....	....	....	....	....	....
Monetary authorities..	4 787 ..	....	....	....	....	....	....	....	....
of which: Short-term............................	4 789 ..	....	....	....	....	....	....	....	....
General government............................	4 790 ..	....	....	....	....	....	....	....	....
of which: Short-term............................	4 792 ..	....	....	....	....	....	....	....	....
Banks..	4 793 ..	....	....	....	....	....	....	....	....
of which: Short-term............................	4 795 ..	....	....	....	....	....	....	....	....
Other sectors......................................	4 796 ..	....	....	....	....	....	....	....	....
of which: Short-term............................	4 798 ..	....	....	....	....	....	....	....	....
E. RESERVE ASSETS..	4 802 ..	....	....	....	....	....	....	....	....
Monetary gold......................................	4 812 ..	....	....	....	....	....	....	....	....
Special drawing rights...........................	4 811 ..	....	....	....	....	....	....	....	....
Reserve position in the Fund.................	4 810 ..	....	....	....	....	....	....	....	....
Foreign exchange..................................	4 803 ..	....	....	....	....	....	....	....	....
Other claims...	4 813 ..	....	....	....	....	....	....	....	....
NET ERRORS AND OMISSIONS...........................	4 998 ..	....	....	....	....	....	....	....	....

Table 1. ANALYTIC PRESENTATION, 2000–2007

(Millions of U.S. dollars)

	Code	2000	2001	2002	2003	2004	2005	2006	2007
A. Current Account[1].........	4 993 Z.	**−67.7**	**−113.2**	**−20.7**	**−95.6**	**−372.3**	**−399.0**	**−718.9**	....
Goods: exports f.o.b.........	2 100 ..	547.0	507.0	484.2	679.4	653.2	697.8	711.3	....
Goods: imports f.o.b.........	3 100 ..	−774.1	−777.1	−799.9	−1,064.2	−1,285.9	−1,461.7	−1,640.1	....
Balance on Goods.........	4 100 ..	*−227.1*	*−270.1*	*−315.7*	*−384.9*	*−632.8*	*−763.9*	*−928.7*	....
Services: credit.........	2 200 ..	423.3	404.1	502.4	613.9	687.8	809.6	773.7	....
Services: debit.........	3 200 ..	−333.1	−296.9	−289.7	−396.7	−485.5	−525.1	−542.5	....
Balance on Goods and Services.........	4 991 ..	*−136.8*	*−163.0*	*−103.0*	*−167.6*	*−430.5*	*−479.4*	*−697.5*	....
Income: credit.........	2 300 ..	52.8	66.5	71.6	91.7	145.4	80.3	64.6	....
Income: debit.........	3 300 ..	−35.7	−84.0	−67.5	−103.0	−156.4	−126.5	−185.5	....
Balance on Goods, Services, and Income.........	4 992 ..	*−119.7*	*−180.4*	*−99.0*	*−178.9*	*−441.5*	*−525.6*	*−818.4*	....
Current transfers: credit.........	2 379 Z.	111.0	122.0	133.4	164.3	165.0	228.9	210.9	....
Current transfers: debit.........	3 379 ..	−59.0	−54.8	−55.1	−81.0	−95.8	−102.2	−111.4	....
B. Capital Account[1].........	4 994 Z.	**−28.6**	**−10.0**	**−9.9**	**−5.7**	**−11.6**	**−17.8**	**−17.2**	....
Capital account: credit.........	2 994 Z.	7.0	15.3	13.9	28.4	27.9	33.2	21.7	....
Capital account: debit.........	3 994 ..	−35.6	−25.3	−23.8	−34.1	−39.5	−51.0	−38.9	....
Total, Groups A Plus B.........	4 981 ..	*−96.3*	*−123.2*	*−30.6*	*−101.3*	*−383.9*	*−416.8*	*−736.1*	....
C. Financial Account[1].........	4 995 W.	**17.8**	**44.5**	**97.7**	**35.7**	**235.6**	**107.4**	**417.2**	....
Direct investment abroad.........	4 505 ..	−2.3	−2.6	−1.7	−3.8	−3.2	−10.3	−.6	....
Direct investment in Fiji.........	4 555 Z.	3.4	46.4	36.5	45.1	187.1	160.0	373.7	....
Portfolio investment assets.........	4 602 ..	....	....	....	....	....	....	−.1	....
Equity securities.........	4 610 ..	....	....	....	....	....	....	−.1	....
Debt securities.........	4 619 ..	....	....	....	....	....	....	....	....
Portfolio investment liabilities.........	4 652 Z.	....	....	....	....	1.0	.9	−1.6	....
Equity securities.........	4 660 ..	....	....	....	....	1.0	.9	−1.6	....
Debt securities.........	4 669 Z.	....	....	....	....	....	....	....	....
Financial derivatives.........	4 910 ..	....	....	....	....	....	....	....	....
Financial derivatives assets.........	4 900 ..	....	....	....	....	....	....	....	....
Financial derivatives liabilities.........	4 905 ..	....	....	....	....	....	....	....	....
Other investment assets.........	4 703 ..	48.0	−24.7	29.6	−55.3	70.6	−49.7	12.9	....
Monetary authorities.........	4 701 ..	....	....	....	....	....	....	....	....
General government.........	4 704 ..	−1.0	−1.2	−2.2	−2.0	−.9	−2.0	−1.8	....
Banks.........	4 705 ..	28.2	−9.8	−4.6	−30.0	107.2	−22.4	47.0	....
Other sectors.........	4 728 ..	20.9	−13.7	36.4	−23.4	−35.6	−25.4	−32.2	....
Other investment liabilities.........	4 753 W.	−31.4	25.4	33.3	49.7	−19.9	6.7	32.9	....
Monetary authorities.........	4 753 WA	1.5	−1.4	.6	−.3	−.2	....	−1.0	....
General government.........	4 753 ZB	....	....	....	....	....	....	....	....
Banks.........	4 753 ZC	−43.5	23.6	13.4	−8.6	−43.3	35.9	−29.3	....
Other sectors.........	4 753 ZD	10.7	3.2	19.3	58.6	23.5	−29.2	63.2	....
Total, Groups A Through C.........	4 983 ..	*−78.5*	*−78.8*	*67.1*	*−65.7*	*−148.4*	*−309.3*	*−319.0*	....
D. Net Errors and Omissions.........	4 998 ..	**107.1**	**94.1**	**−96.3**	**1.6**	**230.4**	**159.0**	**171.4**	....
Total, Groups A Through D.........	4 984 ..	*28.7*	*15.4*	*−29.2*	*−64.0*	*82.1*	*−150.4*	*−147.6*	....
E. Reserves and Related Items.........	4 802 A.	**−28.7**	**−15.4**	**29.2**	**64.0**	**−82.1**	**150.4**	**147.6**	....
Reserve assets.........	4 802 ..	−14.7	20.7	41.4	−24.6	−59.0	131.2	−33.1	....
Use of Fund credit and loans.........	4 766 ..	....	....	....	....	....	....	....	....
Exceptional financing.........	4 920 ..	−14.0	−36.1	−12.2	88.7	−23.1	19.2	180.6	....
Conversion rates: Fiji dollars per U.S. dollar.........	0 101 ..	**2.1286**	**2.2766**	**2.1869**	**1.8958**	**1.7330**	**1.6911**	**1.7313**	**1.6104**

[1] Excludes components that have been classified in the categories of Group E.

Table 2. STANDARD PRESENTATION, 2000–2007

(Millions of U.S. dollars)

	Code	2000	2001	2002	2003	2004	2005	2006	2007
CURRENT ACCOUNT	4 993 ..	**−67.2**	**−113.0**	**−20.5**	**−94.6**	**−370.4**	**−396.4**	**−715.2**	....
A. GOODS	4 100 ..	**−227.1**	**−270.1**	**−315.7**	**−384.9**	**−632.8**	**−763.9**	**−928.7**	....
Credit	2 100 ..	**547.0**	**507.0**	**484.2**	**679.4**	**653.2**	**697.8**	**711.3**	....
General merchandise: exports f.o.b.	2 110 ..	479.2	443.5	421.3	589.3	557.3	591.9	613.1	....
Goods for processing: exports f.o.b.	2 150 ..	13.8	7.6	16.5	22.0	13.0	36.8	37.8	....
Repairs on goods	2 160 ..	4.0	3.5	3.7	8.3	6.5	4.6	4.4	....
Goods procured in ports by carriers	2 170 ..	17.2	14.9	11.8	19.4	25.3	29.3	31.0	....
Nonmonetary gold	2 180 ..	32.7	37.5	31.0	40.3	51.0	35.1	24.9	....
Debit	3 100 ..	**−774.1**	**−777.1**	**−799.9**	**−1,064.2**	**−1,285.9**	**−1,461.7**	**−1,640.1**	....
General merchandise: imports f.o.b.	3 110 ..	−740.1	−743.8	−765.3	−1,021.9	−1,233.4	−1,379.7	−1,552.5	....
Goods for processing: imports f.o.b.	3 150 ..	−9.1	−5.0	−6.7	−13.7	−9.8	−22.8	−32.9	....
Repairs on goods	3 160 ..	−2.1	−2.3	−2.4	−2.9	−3.6	−3.6	−2.5	....
Goods procured in ports by carriers	3 170 ..	−22.5	−25.7	−25.5	−25.5	−39.1	−55.5	−52.1	....
Nonmonetary gold	3 180 ..	−.2	−.3	....	−.2	−.2	−.1	−.1	....
B. SERVICES	4 200 ..	**90.2**	**107.1**	**212.7**	**217.2**	**202.3**	**284.5**	**231.2**	....
Total credit	2 200 ..	*423.3*	*404.1*	*502.4*	*613.9*	*687.8*	*809.6*	*773.7*	....
Total debit	3 200 ..	*−333.1*	*−296.9*	*−289.7*	*−396.7*	*−485.5*	*−525.1*	*−542.5*	....
Transportation services, credit	2 205 ..	**127.3**	**138.3**	**151.2**	**183.6**	**194.2**	**290.8**	**249.0**	....
Passenger	2 850 ..	*101.1*	*111.3*	*124.1*	*150.2*	*164.6*	*236.9*	*203.4*	....
Freight	2 851 ..	*12.5*	*10.9*	*11.8*	*12.1*	*12.1*	*26.1*	*21.7*	....
Other	2 852 ..	*13.7*	*16.0*	*15.2*	*21.2*	*17.5*	*27.9*	*23.9*	....
Sea transport, passenger	2 207 ..	....	....	....	....	....	....	....	....
Sea transport, freight	2 208 ..	2.3	.9	2.4	2.9	2.5	4.7	6.9	....
Sea transport, other	2 209 ..	3.7	5.6	4.8	8.3	9.2	8.8	10.3	....
Air transport, passenger	2 211 ..	101.1	111.3	124.1	150.2	164.6	236.9	203.4	....
Air transport, freight	2 212 ..	10.2	10.1	9.4	9.2	9.5	21.3	14.8	....
Air transport, other	2 213 ..	10.1	10.4	10.4	12.9	8.3	19.0	13.6	....
Other transport, passenger	2 215 ..	....	....	....	....	....	....	....	....
Other transport, freight	2 216 ..	....	....	....	....	....	....	....	....
Other transport, other	2 217 ..	....	....	....	....	....	....	....	....
Transportation services, debit	3 205 ..	**−154.4**	**−158.2**	**−158.6**	**−232.1**	**−278.7**	**−287.8**	**−297.1**	....
Passenger	3 850 ..	*−13.2*	*−19.4*	*−24.1*	*−18.4*	*−24.5*	*−26.2*	*−22.4*	....
Freight	3 851 ..	*−84.0*	*−87.5*	*−89.8*	*−121.3*	*−142.5*	*−155.9*	*−184.4*	....
Other	3 852 ..	*−57.2*	*−51.3*	*−44.8*	*−92.4*	*−111.8*	*−105.6*	*−90.3*	....
Sea transport, passenger	3 207 ..	....	....	....	....	....	....	....	....
Sea transport, freight	3 208 ..	−79.1	−81.9	−83.2	−111.4	−133.3	−148.8	−166.5	....
Sea transport, other	3 209 ..	....	....	....	....	....	....	....	....
Air transport, passenger	3 211 ..	−13.2	−19.4	−24.1	−18.4	−24.5	−26.2	−22.4	....
Air transport, freight	3 212 ..	−4.9	−5.6	−6.5	−9.9	−9.1	−7.2	−17.8	....
Air transport, other	3 213 ..	−57.2	−51.3	−44.8	−92.4	−111.8	−105.6	−90.3	....
Other transport, passenger	3 215 ..	....	....	....	....	....	....	....	....
Other transport, freight	3 216 ..	....	....	....	....	....	....	....	....
Other transport, other	3 217 ..	....	....	....	....	....	....	....	....
Travel, credit	2 236 ..	**183.5**	**197.9**	**255.5**	**340.5**	**419.7**	**438.7**	**433.3**	....
Business travel	2 237 ..	12.4	12.7	18.4	23.9	24.7	28.6	28.4	....
Personal travel	2 240 ..	171.1	185.2	237.1	316.6	395.0	410.0	405.0	....
Travel, debit	3 236 ..	**−82.5**	**−64.6**	**−54.7**	**−69.4**	**−93.6**	**−106.0**	**−101.4**	....
Business travel	3 237 ..	−4.4	−3.5	−1.4	−1.8	−5.5	−6.3	−6.5	....
Personal travel	3 240 ..	−78.2	−61.1	−53.4	−67.6	−88.1	−99.8	−95.0	....
Other services, credit	2 200 BA	**112.5**	**67.8**	**95.8**	**89.9**	**74.0**	**80.1**	**91.4**	....
Communications	2 245 ..	24.1	21.4	26.4	26.2	29.1	28.7	21.7	....
Construction	2 249 ..	....	....	....	.2	....	....	.6	....
Insurance	2 253 ..	.6	.3	....	.8	.5	.5	1.5	....
Financial	2 260 ..	.8	1.3	1.3	1.1	1.4	1.5	1.5	....
Computer and information	2 262 ..	.2	.5	.3	.4	2.5	2.5	2.4	....
Royalties and licence fees	2 266 ..	2.8	1.3	3.8	1.1	.1	.1	.2	....
Other business services	2 268 ..	57.5	26.3	39.4	31.3	20.0	27.0	30.4	....
Personal, cultural, and recreational	2 287 ..	.5	....	....	.1	.3	.7	.8	....
Government, n.i.e.	2 291 ..	25.9	16.8	24.5	28.8	20.1	19.2	33.8	....
Other services, debit	3 200 BA	**−96.1**	**−74.1**	**−76.3**	**−95.3**	**−113.2**	**−131.3**	**−144.0**	....
Communications	3 245 ..	−18.7	−12.4	−12.3	−12.8	−16.0	−19.1	−16.0	....
Construction	3 249 ..	....	....	−.2	−1.9	....	−.1	−.3	....
Insurance	3 253 ..	−17.7	−15.7	−18.0	−23.5	−25.6	−29.7	−29.8	....
Financial	3 260 ..	−.8	−.9	−.7	−1.1	−1.2	−.9	−.9	....
Computer and information	3 262 ..	−3.6	−2.9	−3.6	−4.9	−10.8	−12.4	−7.9	....
Royalties and licence fees	3 266 ..	−.7	−.5	−1.5	−1.0	−.8	−1.2	−1.0	....
Other business services	3 268 ..	−40.5	−28.0	−21.1	−33.2	−33.6	−43.7	−55.0	....
Personal, cultural, and recreational	3 287 ..	−2.2	−2.1	−1.7	−2.4	−2.4	−2.4	−4.4	....
Government, n.i.e.	3 291 ..	−12.0	−11.6	−17.2	−14.5	−22.8	−21.8	−28.8	....

Table 2 (Continued). STANDARD PRESENTATION, 2000–2007

(Millions of U.S. dollars)

	Code	2000	2001	2002	2003	2004	2005	2006	2007
C. INCOME	4 300 ..	**17.1**	**−17.4**	**4.0**	**−11.3**	**−11.0**	**−46.2**	**−120.9**	....
Total credit	2 300 ..	*52.8*	*66.5*	*71.6*	*91.7*	*145.4*	*80.3*	*64.6*	....
Total debit	3 300 ..	*−35.7*	*−84.0*	*−67.5*	*−103.0*	*−156.4*	*−126.5*	*−185.5*	....
Compensation of employees, credit	2 310 ..	**17.4**	**40.1**	**51.0**	**68.9**	**116.2**	**47.4**	**37.5**	....
Compensation of employees, debit	3 310 ..	**−.5**	**−1.9**	**−2.3**	**−1.7**	**−1.8**	**−2.5**	**−4.4**	....
Investment income, credit	2 320 ..	**35.4**	**26.4**	**20.6**	**22.8**	**29.3**	**32.9**	**27.1**	....
Direct investment income	2 330 ..	3.7	2.7	1.8	3.9	3.7	5.9	2.2	....
Dividends and distributed branch profits	2 332 ..	.2	.1	.1	.1	.6	....	.5	....
Reinvested earnings and undistributed branch profits	2 333 ..	2.3	2.6	1.7	3.8	3.0	5.9	.6	....
Income on debt (interest)	2 334 ..	1.2	....	....	....	.1	....	1.2	....
Portfolio investment income	2 339 ..	5.4	4.1	4.3	5.1	8.2	9.8	15.0	....
Income on equity	2 340 ..	4.6	3.7	3.8	4.3	6.2	8.2	10.8	....
Income on bonds and notes	2 350 ..	....	....	....	....	....	....	2.4	....
Income on money market instruments	2 360 ..	.8	.4	.5	.7	2.0	1.6	1.8	....
Other investment income	2 370 ..	26.3	19.6	14.4	13.9	17.4	17.3	10.0	....
Investment income, debit	3 320 ..	**−35.2**	**−82.1**	**−65.2**	**−101.3**	**−154.6**	**−124.0**	**−181.1**	....
Direct investment income	3 330 ..	−9.8	−57.7	−53.4	−84.0	−140.7	−114.4	−162.2	....
Dividends and distributed branch profits	3 332 ..	−9.5	−15.5	−24.8	−38.1	−45.5	−24.7	−30.8	....
Reinvested earnings and undistributed branch profits	3 333 ..	6.1	−35.0	−23.5	−41.6	−89.5	−78.2	−127.4	....
Income on debt (interest)	3 334 ..	−6.3	−7.2	−5.0	−4.3	−5.7	−11.5	−4.0	....
Portfolio investment income	3 339 ..	−7.3	−7.2	−1.8	−7.5	−4.9	−3.0	−12.5	....
Income on equity	3 340 ..	−7.3	−7.2	−1.8	−7.5	−4.9	−3.0	−12.5	....
Income on bonds and notes	3 350 ..	....	....	....	....	....	....	....	....
Income on money market instruments	3 360 ..	....	....	....	....	....	....	....	....
Other investment income	3 370 ..	−18.1	−17.2	−10.0	−9.8	−9.1	−6.6	−6.4	....
D. CURRENT TRANSFERS	4 379 ..	**52.5**	**67.4**	**78.5**	**84.3**	**71.1**	**129.2**	**103.2**	....
Credit	2 379 ..	**111.5**	**122.2**	**133.6**	**165.4**	**166.9**	**231.5**	**214.6**	....
General government	2 380 ..	.5	.2	.1	1.1	2.0	2.6	3.7	....
Other sectors	2 390 ..	111.0	122.0	133.4	164.3	165.0	228.9	210.9	....
Workers' remittances	2 391 ..	25.7	36.7	46.1	53.5	55.2	134.6	126.6	....
Other current transfers	2 392 ..	85.2	85.3	87.3	110.8	109.8	94.3	84.3	....
Debit	3 379 ..	**−59.0**	**−54.8**	**−55.1**	**−81.0**	**−95.8**	**−102.2**	**−111.4**	....
General government	3 380 ..	....	....	....	....	....	....	....	....
Other sectors	3 390 ..	−59.0	−54.8	−55.1	−81.0	−95.8	−102.2	−111.4	....
Workers' remittances	3 391 ..	−1.7	−1.9	−1.5	−2.1	−13.4	−4.6	−4.6	....
Other current transfers	3 392 ..	−57.2	−52.9	−53.6	−79.0	−82.4	−97.6	−106.8	....
CAPITAL AND FINANCIAL ACCOUNT	4 996 ..	**−39.9**	**18.9**	**116.8**	**92.9**	**140.0**	**237.4**	**543.8**	....
CAPITAL ACCOUNT	4 994 ..	**−28.6**	**−10.0**	**−9.9**	**−5.7**	**−11.6**	**−17.8**	**−17.2**	....
Total credit	2 994 ..	*7.0*	*15.3*	*13.9*	*28.4*	*27.9*	*33.2*	*21.7*	....
Total debit	3 994 ..	*−35.6*	*−25.3*	*−23.8*	*−34.1*	*−39.5*	*−51.0*	*−38.9*	....
Capital transfers, credit	2 400 ..	**7.0**	**15.3**	**13.9**	**28.4**	**27.9**	**33.2**	**21.7**	....
General government	2 401 ..	5.9	9.5	13.8	23.2	24.5	27.3	17.4	....
Debt forgiveness	2 402 ..	5.9	9.5	13.8	23.2	24.5	27.3	17.4	....
Other capital transfers	2 410 ..	....	....	....	....	....	....	....	....
Other sectors	2 430 ..	1.2	5.8	.1	5.2	3.3	6.0	4.2	....
Migrants' transfers	2 431 ..	.7	5.7	....	.5	.6	2.2	1.4	....
Debt forgiveness	2 432 ..	....	....	....	....	....	....	....	....
Other capital transfers	2 440 ..	.5	....	....	4.6	2.8	3.8	2.8	....
Capital transfers, debit	3 400 ..	**−35.6**	**−25.3**	**−23.8**	**−34.1**	**−39.5**	**−51.0**	**−38.9**	....
General government	3 401 ..	....	....	....	....	....	....	....	....
Debt forgiveness	3 402 ..	....	....	....	....	....	....	....	....
Other capital transfers	3 410 ..	....	....	....	....	....	....	....	....
Other sectors	3 430 ..	−35.6	−25.3	−23.8	−34.1	−39.5	−51.0	−38.9	....
Migrants' transfers	3 431 ..	−23.4	−19.8	−15.9	−22.4	−25.8	−26.4	−22.5	....
Debt forgiveness	3 432 ..	....	....	....	....	....	....	....	....
Other capital transfers	3 440 ..	−12.2	−5.4	−7.9	−11.7	−13.7	−24.7	−16.3	....
Nonproduced nonfinancial assets, credit	2 480 ..	....	....	....	....	....	....	....	....
Nonproduced nonfinancial assets, debit	3 480 ..	....	....	....	....	....	....	....	....

2008, International Monetary Fund: *Balance of Payments Statistics Yearbook*

Table 2 (Continued). STANDARD PRESENTATION, 2000–2007

(Millions of U.S. dollars)

	Code	2000	2001	2002	2003	2004	2005	2006	2007
FINANCIAL ACCOUNT	4 995 ..	**−11.4**	**28.8**	**126.7**	**98.6**	**151.6**	**255.2**	**561.0**	**.…**
A. DIRECT INVESTMENT	4 500 ..	**1.2**	**43.7**	**34.8**	**41.3**	**183.9**	**149.6**	**373.1**	**.…**
Direct investment abroad	4 505 ..	**−2.3**	**−2.6**	**−1.7**	**−3.8**	**−3.2**	**−10.3**	**−.6**	**.…**
Equity capital	4 510 ..	.…	.…	.…	.…	−.2	−4.5	.…	.…
Claims on affiliated enterprises	4 515 ..	.…	.…	.…	.…	−.2	−4.5	.…	.…
Liabilities to affiliated enterprises	4 520 ..	.…	.…	.…	.…	.…	.…	.…	.…
Reinvested earnings	4 525 ..	−2.3	−2.6	−1.7	−3.8	−3.0	−5.9	−.6	.…
Other capital	4 530 ..	.…	.…	.…	.…	.…	.…	.…	.…
Claims on affiliated enterprises	4 535 ..	.…	.…	.…	.…	.…	.…	.…	.…
Liabilities to affiliated enterprises	4 540 ..	.…	.…	.…	.…	.…	.…	.…	.…
Direct investment in Fiji	4 555 ..	**3.4**	**46.4**	**36.5**	**45.1**	**187.1**	**160.0**	**373.7**	**.…**
Equity capital	4 560 ..	5.3	5.0	8.5	.9	99.0	72.5	241.2	.…
Claims on direct investors	4 565 ..	.…	.…	.…	.…	.…	.…	.…	.…
Liabilities to direct investors	4 570 ..	5.3	5.0	8.5	.9	99.0	72.5	241.2	.…
Reinvested earnings	4 575 ..	−6.1	35.0	23.5	41.6	89.5	78.2	127.4	.…
Other capital	4 580 ..	4.3	6.4	4.5	2.6	−1.4	9.2	5.1	.…
Claims on direct investors	4 585 ..	.…	.…	.…	.…	.…	.…	.…	.…
Liabilities to direct investors	4 590 ..	4.3	6.4	4.5	2.6	−1.4	9.2	5.1	.…
B. PORTFOLIO INVESTMENT	4 600 ..	.…	.…	.…	.…	**1.0**	**.9**	**145.6**	**.…**
Assets	4 602 ..	.…	.…	.…	.…	.…	.…	**−.1**	**.…**
Equity securities	4 610 ..	.…	.…	.…	.…	.…	.…	−.1	.…
Monetary authorities	4 611 ..	.…	.…	.…	.…	.…	.…	.…	.…
General government	4 612 ..	.…	.…	.…	.…	.…	.…	.…	.…
Banks	4 613 ..	.…	.…	.…	.…	.…	.…	−.1	.…
Other sectors	4 614 ..	.…	.…	.…	.…	.…	.…	.…	.…
Debt securities	4 619 ..	.…	.…	.…	.…	.…	.…	.…	.…
Bonds and notes	4 620 ..	.…	.…	.…	.…	.…	.…	.…	.…
Monetary authorities	4 621 ..	.…	.…	.…	.…	.…	.…	.…	.…
General government	4 622 ..	.…	.…	.…	.…	.…	.…	.…	.…
Banks	4 623 ..	.…	.…	.…	.…	.…	.…	.…	.…
Other sectors	4 624 ..	.…	.…	.…	.…	.…	.…	.…	.…
Money market instruments	4 630 ..	.…	.…	.…	.…	.…	.…	.…	.…
Monetary authorities	4 631 ..	.…	.…	.…	.…	.…	.…	.…	.…
General government	4 632 ..	.…	.…	.…	.…	.…	.…	.…	.…
Banks	4 633 ..	.…	.…	.…	.…	.…	.…	.…	.…
Other sectors	4 634 ..	.…	.…	.…	.…	.…	.…	.…	.…
Liabilities	4 652 ..	.…	.…	.…	.…	**1.0**	**.9**	**145.7**	**.…**
Equity securities	4 660 ..	.…	.…	.…	.…	1.0	.9	−1.6	.…
Banks	4 663 ..	.…	.…	.…	.…	1.0	.9	−1.6	.…
Other sectors	4 664 ..	.…	.…	.…	.…	.…	.…	.…	.…
Debt securities	4 669 ..	.…	.…	.…	.…	.…	.…	147.3	.…
Bonds and notes	4 670 ..	.…	.…	.…	.…	.…	.…	147.3	.…
Monetary authorities	4 671 ..	.…	.…	.…	.…	.…	.…	147.3	.…
General government	4 672 ..	.…	.…	.…	.…	.…	.…	.…	.…
Banks	4 673 ..	.…	.…	.…	.…	.…	.…	.…	.…
Other sectors	4 674 ..	.…	.…	.…	.…	.…	.…	.…	.…
Money market instruments	4 680 ..	.…	.…	.…	.…	.…	.…	.…	.…
Monetary authorities	4 681 ..	.…	.…	.…	.…	.…	.…	.…	.…
General government	4 682 ..	.…	.…	.…	.…	.…	.…	.…	.…
Banks	4 683 ..	.…	.…	.…	.…	.…	.…	.…	.…
Other sectors	4 684 ..	.…	.…	.…	.…	.…	.…	.…	.…
C. FINANCIAL DERIVATIVES	4 910 ..	.…	.…	.…	.…	.…	.…	.…	.…
Monetary authorities	4 911 ..	.…	.…	.…	.…	.…	.…	.…	.…
General government	4 912 ..	.…	.…	.…	.…	.…	.…	.…	.…
Banks	4 913 ..	.…	.…	.…	.…	.…	.…	.…	.…
Other sectors	4 914 ..	.…	.…	.…	.…	.…	.…	.…	.…
Assets	4 900 ..	.…	.…	.…	.…	.…	.…	.…	.…
Monetary authorities	4 901 ..	.…	.…	.…	.…	.…	.…	.…	.…
General government	4 902 ..	.…	.…	.…	.…	.…	.…	.…	.…
Banks	4 903 ..	.…	.…	.…	.…	.…	.…	.…	.…
Other sectors	4 904 ..	.…	.…	.…	.…	.…	.…	.…	.…
Liabilities	4 905 ..	.…	.…	.…	.…	.…	.…	.…	.…
Monetary authorities	4 906 ..	.…	.…	.…	.…	.…	.…	.…	.…
General government	4 907 ..	.…	.…	.…	.…	.…	.…	.…	.…
Banks	4 908 ..	.…	.…	.…	.…	.…	.…	.…	.…
Other sectors	4 909 ..	.…	.…	.…	.…	.…	.…	.…	.…

Table 2 (Concluded). STANDARD PRESENTATION, 2000–2007

(Millions of U.S. dollars)

	Code	2000	2001	2002	2003	2004	2005	2006	2007
D. OTHER INVESTMENT	4 700	2.2	−35.6	50.5	82.0	25.7	−26.5	75.4	....
Assets	4 703	48.0	−24.7	29.6	−55.3	70.6	−49.7	12.9	....
Trade credits	4 706	−8.9	−19.9	34.1	−70.4	−29.4	−27.3	−25.5	....
General government	4 707	....	....	....	....	....	....	....	....
of which: Short-term	4 709	....	....	....	....	....	....	....	....
Other sectors	4 710	−8.9	−19.9	34.1	−70.4	−29.4	−27.3	−25.5	....
of which: Short-term	4 712	−8.9	−19.9	34.1	−70.4	−29.4	−27.3	−25.5	....
Loans	4 714	25.7	3.4	−1.6	36.2	64.1	−8.3	12.4	....
Monetary authorities	4 715	....	....	....	....	....	....	....	....
of which: Short-term	4 718	....	....	....	....	....	....	....	....
General government	4 719	....	....	....	....	....	....	....	....
of which: Short-term	4 721	....	....	....	....	....	....	....	....
Banks	4 722	−4.1	−2.7	−4.0	−10.8	70.3	−10.2	19.2	....
of which: Short-term	4 724	....	....	....	....	....	....	....	....
Other sectors	4 725	29.8	6.1	2.3	47.0	−6.2	1.9	−6.8	....
of which: Short-term	4 727	....	....	....	....	....	....	....	....
Currency and deposits	4 730	−.3	.6	−1.0	−.8	1.3	−1.1	1.1	....
Monetary authorities	4 731	....	....	....	....	....	....	....	....
General government	4 732	....	−.1	−.9	....	.6	−.4	−.2	....
Banks	4 733	−.4	.7	−.1	−.8	.7	−.8	1.3	....
Other sectors	4 734	....	....	....	....	....	....	....	....
Other assets	4 736	31.6	−8.9	−1.8	−20.4	34.7	−13.0	24.9	....
Monetary authorities	4 737	....	....	....	....	....	....	....	....
of which: Short-term	4 739	....	....	....	....	....	....	....	....
General government	4 740	−1.1	−1.1	−1.3	−2.0	−1.5	−1.7	−1.6	....
of which: Short-term	4 742	−1.1	−1.1	−1.3	−2.0	−1.5	−1.7	−1.6	....
Banks	4 743	32.7	−7.9	−.5	−18.4	36.2	−11.4	26.5	....
of which: Short-term	4 745	28.3	−11.2	−15.0	−13.6	52.7	−12.8	50.2	....
Other sectors	4 746	....	....	....	....	....	....	....	....
of which: Short-term	4 748	....	....	....	....	....	....	....	....
Liabilities	4 753	−45.9	−10.9	20.9	137.3	−44.9	23.2	62.5	....
Trade credits	4 756	10.7	3.2	19.3	58.6	23.5	−29.2	63.2	....
General government	4 757	....	....	....	....	....	....	....	....
of which: Short-term	4 759	....	....	....	....	....	....	....	....
Other sectors	4 760	10.7	3.2	19.3	58.6	23.5	−29.2	63.2	....
of which: Short-term	4 762	10.7	3.2	19.3	58.6	23.5	−29.2	63.2	....
Loans	4 764	−14.5	−36.3	−12.3	87.6	−25.0	16.6	29.6	....
Monetary authorities	4 765	....	....	....	....	....	....	....	....
of which: Use of Fund credit and loans from the Fund	4 766	....	....	....	....	....	....	....	....
of which: Short-term	4 768	....	....	....	....	....	....	....	....
General government	4 769	−8.1	−4.4	2.1	7.2	.6	−2.4	1.4	....
of which: Short-term	4 771	....	....	....	....	....	....	....	....
Banks	4 772	....	....	....	....	....	....	....	....
of which: Short-term	4 774	....	....	....	....	....	....	....	....
Other sectors	4 775	−6.4	−31.9	−14.4	80.4	−25.6	19.0	28.2	....
of which: Short-term	4 777	....	....	....	....	....	....	....	....
Currency and deposits	4 780	−29.1	14.4	10.9	.6	−48.6	25.7	−56.5	....
Monetary authorities	4 781	....	....	....	....	....	....	....	....
General government	4 782	....	....	....	....	....	....	....	....
Banks	4 783	−29.1	14.4	10.9	.6	−48.6	25.7	−56.5	....
Other sectors	4 784	....	....	....	....	....	....	....	....
Other liabilities	4 786	−13.0	7.9	3.1	−9.4	5.1	10.2	26.2	....
Monetary authorities	4 787	1.5	−1.4	.6	−.3	−.2	....	−1.0	....
of which: Short-term	4 789	1.5	−1.4	.6	−.3	−.2	....	−1.0	....
General government	4 790	....	....	....	....	....	....	....	....
of which: Short-term	4 792	....	....	....	....	....	....	....	....
Banks	4 793	−14.4	9.2	2.5	−9.2	5.3	10.2	27.2	....
of which: Short-term	4 795	−1.0	−1.6	1.6	3.2	−3.4	9.9	4.4	....
Other sectors	4 796	....	....	....	....	....	....	....	....
of which: Short-term	4 798	....	....	....	....	....	....	....	....
E. RESERVE ASSETS	4 802	−14.7	20.7	41.4	−24.6	−59.0	131.2	−33.1	....
Monetary gold	4 812	....	....	....	....	....	−.1	−.1	....
Special drawing rights	4 811	−.5	−.4	−.3	−.2	−.2	−.4	−.5	....
Reserve position in the Fund	4 810	−.1	....	−.1	−.2	−.1	−.1	−.3	....
Foreign exchange	4 803	−32.1	24.5	47.6	4.0	−32.8	140.0	20.4	....
Other claims	4 813	17.9	−3.3	−5.8	−28.2	−25.9	−8.3	−52.6	....
NET ERRORS AND OMISSIONS	4 998	107.1	94.1	−96.3	1.6	230.4	159.0	171.4	....

Table 1. ANALYTIC PRESENTATION, 2000–2007

(Millions of U.S. dollars)

	Code	2000	2001	2002	2003	2004	2005	2006	2007
A. Current Account[1]	4 993 Z.	**10,526**	**12,077**	**12,078**	**8,534**	**12,542**	**6,951**	**9,562**	**10,048**
Goods: exports f.o.b.	2 100 ..	45,703	42,980	44,863	52,740	61,139	65,451	77,552	90,126
Goods: imports f.o.b.	3 100 ..	−32,019	−30,321	−32,022	−39,790	−48,368	−55,887	−66,046	−78,190
Balance on Goods	4 100 ..	*13,684*	*12,659*	*12,841*	*12,950*	*12,770*	*9,564*	*11,505*	*11,936*
Services: credit	2 200 ..	7,728	9,205	10,441	11,470	15,168	17,010	17,520	20,212
Services: debit	3 200 ..	−8,440	−8,105	−9,870	−12,149	−14,563	−17,732	−18,641	−21,763
Balance on Goods and Services	4 991 ..	*12,973*	*13,760*	*13,412*	*12,271*	*13,375*	*8,841*	*10,385*	*10,384*
Income: credit	2 300 ..	7,265	8,568	8,607	9,349	13,129	14,406	18,317	22,354
Income: debit	3 300 ..	−8,989	−9,573	−9,210	−11,980	−12,884	−14,753	−17,457	−20,793
Balance on Goods, Services, and Income	4 992 ..	*11,249*	*12,754*	*12,809*	*9,639*	*13,620*	*8,495*	*11,245*	*11,945*
Current transfers: credit	2 379 Z.	1,611	1,562	1,621	1,911	2,040	1,904	1,946	2,129
Current transfers: debit	3 379 ..	−2,334	−2,239	−2,353	−3,016	−3,118	−3,448	−3,628	−4,026
B. Capital Account[1]	4 994 Z.	**103**	**83**	**125**	**149**	**188**	**336**	**223**	**237**
Capital account: credit	2 994 Z.	111	93	126	154	189	337	225	237
Capital account: debit	3 994 ..	−7	−10	−2	−5	−1	−1	−1	....
Total, Groups A Plus B	4 981 ..	*10,630*	*12,161*	*12,202*	*8,683*	*12,730*	*7,287*	*9,786*	*10,285*
C. Financial Account[1]	4 995 W.	**−8,841**	**−10,942**	**−7,312**	**−11,978**	**−9,476**	**−3,634**	**−15,656**	**−10,241**
Direct investment abroad	4 505 ..	−23,898	−8,458	−7,522	2,272	1,146	−4,415	−3,196	−8,625
Direct investment in Finland	4 555 Z.	9,125	3,739	8,276	3,472	2,871	4,806	5,509	8,680
Portfolio investment assets	4 602 ..	−18,920	−11,594	−13,441	−9,801	−24,504	−17,942	−33,329	−15,803
Equity securities	4 610 ..	−7,164	−5,153	−5,390	−5,532	−10,218	−9,410	−14,790	−13,725
Debt securities	4 619 ..	−11,756	−6,441	−8,051	−4,270	−14,286	−8,532	−18,539	−2,078
Portfolio investment liabilities	4 652 Z.	17,116	5,985	9,002	7,901	13,110	10,456	19,149	5,599
Equity securities	4 660 ..	10,114	3,960	2,527	−597	103	4,989	5,366	5,279
Debt securities	4 669 Z.	7,002	2,025	6,475	8,498	13,007	5,467	13,783	320
Financial derivatives	4 910 ..	−630	38	−325	1,715	522	2,168	146	−907
Financial derivatives assets	4 900 ..	....	....	....	....	....	....	....	....
Financial derivatives liabilities	4 905 ..	−630	38	−325	1,715	522	2,168	146	−907
Other investment assets	4 703 ..	−5,636	−10,117	−50	−15,407	−11,851	−1,775	−15,897	−11,523
Monetary authorities	4 701 ..	−129	77	−51	−54	157	9	−287	144
General government	4 704 ..	−171	−966	−143	−3,049	−968	1,415	−2,809	−793
Banks	4 705 ..	−4,107	−8,197	1,205	−10,282	−11,185	−2,272	−11,203	−9,312
Other sectors	4 728 ..	−1,229	−1,032	−1,060	−2,022	146	−927	−1,598	−1,561
Other investment liabilities	4 753 W.	14,001	9,465	−3,253	−2,129	9,230	3,069	11,962	12,338
Monetary authorities	4 753 WA	1,433	282	1,234	696	−2,132	−3,393	193	−2,706
General government	4 753 ZB	−1,272	467	343	2,396	122	−864	−1,853	214
Banks	4 753 ZC	4,098	8,762	−4,663	−3,459	13,197	6,084	12,780	11,149
Other sectors	4 753 ZD	9,742	−47	−166	−1,762	−1,958	1,242	842	3,681
Total, Groups A Through C	4 983 ..	*1,789*	*1,218*	*4,890*	*−3,294*	*3,254*	*3,653*	*−5,870*	*44*
D. Net Errors and Omissions	4 998 ..	**−1,437**	**−808**	**−5,005**	**2,786**	**−2,440**	**−3,833**	**1,550**	**276**
Total, Groups A Through D	4 984 ..	*351*	*410*	*−115*	*−508*	*814*	*−180*	*−4,321*	*320*
E. Reserves and Related Items	4 802 A.	**−351**	**−410**	**115**	**508**	**−814**	**180**	**4,321**	**−320**
Reserve assets	4 802 ..	−351	−410	115	508	−814	180	4,321	−320
Use of Fund credit and loans	4 766 ..	....	....	....	....	....	....	....	....
Exceptional financing	4 920 ..	....	....	....	....	....	....	....	....
Conversion rates: euros per U.S. dollar	0 103 ..	**1.0854**	**1.1175**	**1.0626**	**.8860**	**.8054**	**.8041**	**.7971**	**.7306**

[1] Excludes components that have been classified in the categories of Group E.

Table 2. STANDARD PRESENTATION, 2000–2007

(Millions of U.S. dollars)

	Code	2000	2001	2002	2003	2004	2005	2006	2007
CURRENT ACCOUNT	4 993	**10,526**	**12,077**	**12,078**	**8,534**	**12,542**	**6,951**	**9,562**	**10,048**
A. GOODS	4 100	**13,684**	**12,659**	**12,841**	**12,950**	**12,770**	**9,564**	**11,505**	**11,936**
Credit	2 100	**45,703**	**42,980**	**44,863**	**52,740**	**61,139**	**65,451**	**77,552**	**90,126**
General merchandise: exports f.o.b.	2 110	44,957	42,253	44,097	51,812	60,124	64,452	75,816	88,484
Goods for processing: exports f.o.b.	2 150	650	630	666	798	877	879	1,587	1,506
Repairs on goods	2 160	....	....	....	....	....	....	....	....
Goods procured in ports by carriers	2 170	52	50	53	64	70	70	71	77
Nonmonetary gold	2 180	45	46	47	67	68	50	78	59
Debit	3 100	**−32,019**	**−30,321**	**−32,022**	**−39,790**	**−48,368**	**−55,887**	**−66,046**	**−78,190**
General merchandise: imports f.o.b.	3 110	−31,161	−29,519	−31,166	−38,552	−47,093	−54,480	−63,639	−75,741
Goods for processing: imports f.o.b.	3 150	−687	−666	−705	−844	−928	−930	−1,862	−1,819
Repairs on goods	3 160	....	....	....	....	....	....	....	....
Goods procured in ports by carriers	3 170	−160	−123	−141	−381	−333	−464	−527	−604
Nonmonetary gold	3 180	−10	−13	−10	−13	−15	−13	−18	−26
B. SERVICES	4 200	**−712**	**1,101**	**571**	**−679**	**605**	**−723**	**−1,121**	**−1,552**
Total credit	2 200	*7,728*	*9,205*	*10,441*	*11,470*	*15,168*	*17,010*	*17,520*	*20,212*
Total debit	3 200	*−8,440*	*−8,105*	*−9,870*	*−12,149*	*−14,563*	*−17,732*	*−18,641*	*−21,763*
Transportation services, credit	2 205	**1,677**	**1,565**	**1,649**	**2,000**	**2,400**	**2,440**	**2,757**	**2,771**
Passenger	2 850	*629*	*628*	*658*	*807*	*908*	*890*	*1,129*	*1,068*
Freight	2 851	*657*	*582*	*646*	*830*	*1,073*	*1,112*	*1,185*	*1,260*
Other	2 852	*391*	*355*	*345*	*363*	*419*	*438*	*444*	*443*
Sea transport, passenger	2 207	270	273	276	316	330	326	431	494
Sea transport, freight	2 208	479	392	453	589	782	799	846	943
Sea transport, other	2 209	258	254	219	261	286	285	289	316
Air transport, passenger	2 211	359	355	382	492	578	564	698	574
Air transport, freight	2 212	67	64	67	90	125	146	170	179
Air transport, other	2 213	129	97	125	102	132	152	154	126
Other transport, passenger	2 215	....	....	....	....	....	....	....	....
Other transport, freight	2 216	111	125	126	151	166	167	168	138
Other transport, other	2 217	4	4	....	....	1	1	....	....
Transportation services, debit	3 205	**−2,566**	**−2,573**	**−2,320**	**−2,897**	**−3,606**	**−4,248**	**−4,822**	**−5,254**
Passenger	3 850	*−441*	*−590*	*−432*	*−521*	*−562*	*−565*	*−670*	*−646*
Freight	3 851	*−1,818*	*−1,717*	*−1,587*	*−1,982*	*−2,571*	*−3,125*	*−3,768*	*−4,268*
Other	3 852	*−307*	*−266*	*−302*	*−394*	*−472*	*−559*	*−383*	*−340*
Sea transport, passenger	3 207	−185	−178	−187	−215	−209	−211	−314	−360
Sea transport, freight	3 208	−1,688	−1,588	−1,373	−1,678	−2,050	−2,431	−2,902	−3,428
Sea transport, other	3 209	−228	−189	−230	−311	−377	−462	−282	−259
Air transport, passenger	3 211	−256	−412	−245	−306	−353	−354	−356	−286
Air transport, freight	3 212	−70	−71	−74	−92	−112	−128	−134	−108
Air transport, other	3 213	−79	−70	−71	−80	−92	−94	−98	−78
Other transport, passenger	3 215	....	....	....	....	....	....	....	....
Other transport, freight	3 216	−60	−59	−139	−212	−409	−565	−733	−732
Other transport, other	3 217	....	−7	−1	−3	−4	−4	−3	−3
Travel, credit	2 236	**1,406**	**1,437**	**1,577**	**1,869**	**2,067**	**2,180**	**2,380**	**2,822**
Business travel	2 237	619	632	625	740	904	882	1,029	1,075
Personal travel	2 240	787	805	953	1,129	1,162	1,299	1,351	1,747
Travel, debit	3 236	**−1,852**	**−1,852**	**−2,006**	**−2,433**	**−2,821**	**−3,057**	**−3,424**	**−3,986**
Business travel	3 237	−704	−704	−658	−732	−842	−1,009	−1,204	−1,165
Personal travel	3 240	−1,148	−1,148	−1,348	−1,701	−1,979	−2,047	−2,220	−2,821
Other services, credit	2 200 BA	**4,646**	**6,203**	**7,214**	**7,600**	**10,701**	**12,389**	**12,383**	**14,618**
Communications	2 245	211	229	238	229	312	393	387	403
Construction	2 249	439	397	260	410	746	573	351	273
Insurance	2 253	−33	−39	−3	47	62	62	67	36
Financial	2 260	....	....	....	....	124	81	74	278
Computer and information	2 262	203	304	503	566	755	1,511	1,450	1,303
Royalties and licence fees	2 266	886	584	560	501	839	1,206	1,070	1,216
Other business services	2 268	2,877	4,660	5,553	5,732	7,744	8,439	8,854	11,035
Personal, cultural, and recreational	2 287	4	11	12	30	16	13	24	16
Government, n.i.e.	2 291	59	57	90	86	103	112	106	58
Other services, debit	3 200 BA	**−4,022**	**−3,680**	**−5,544**	**−6,820**	**−8,136**	**−10,427**	**−10,396**	**−12,523**
Communications	3 245	−299	−347	−277	−281	−283	−590	−538	−492
Construction	3 249	−52	−115	−210	−295	−617	−483	−329	−320
Insurance	3 253	−37	−61	−98	−70	−145	−145	−192	−252
Financial	3 260	....	....	....	....	−65	−95	−173	−225
Computer and information	3 262	−307	−340	−372	−482	−735	−1,157	−1,126	−1,155
Royalties and licence fees	3 266	−565	−534	−605	−616	−800	−1,123	−1,299	−1,326
Other business services	3 268	−2,587	−2,137	−3,813	−4,923	−5,321	−6,669	−6,689	−8,711
Personal, cultural, and recreational	3 287	−59	−36	−61	−25	−29	−23	−27	−23
Government, n.i.e.	3 291	−116	−111	−107	−128	−141	−141	−23	−18

2008, International Monetary Fund: *Balance of Payments Statistics Yearbook*

Table 2 (Continued). STANDARD PRESENTATION, 2000–2007

(Millions of U.S. dollars)

	Code	2000	2001	2002	2003	2004	2005	2006	2007
C. INCOME	4 300	**−1,724**	**−1,005**	**−603**	**−2,631**	**245**	**−347**	**860**	**1,560**
Total credit	2 300	*7,265*	*8,568*	*8,607*	*9,349*	*13,129*	*14,406*	*18,317*	*22,354*
Total debit	3 300	*−8,989*	*−9,573*	*−9,210*	*−11,980*	*−12,884*	*−14,753*	*−17,457*	*−20,793*
Compensation of employees, credit	2 310	**473**	**491**	**477**	**526**	**666**	**693**	**698**	**762**
Compensation of employees, debit	3 310	**−100**	**−97**	**−113**	**−149**	**−225**	**−249**	**−309**	**−367**
Investment income, credit	2 320	**6,793**	**8,077**	**8,130**	**8,823**	**12,462**	**13,714**	**17,619**	**21,591**
Direct investment income	2 330	3,825	4,665	4,487	4,581	6,471	7,030	9,260	10,219
Dividends and distributed branch profits	2 332	1,956	6,416	3,109	3,645	2,693	4,552	9,833	6,562
Reinvested earnings and undistributed branch profits	2 333	1,288	−2,420	742	515	3,189	1,906	−1,118	2,934
Income on debt (interest)	2 334	581	670	636	420	589	572	545	723
Portfolio investment income	2 339	1,376	1,759	2,197	2,927	4,272	4,708	5,744	7,597
Income on equity	2 340	203	214	283	420	885	1,151	1,588	2,336
Income on bonds and notes	2 350	1,151	1,489	1,863	2,425	3,308	3,472	4,041	5,050
Income on money market instruments	2 360	23	56	50	82	79	85	114	211
Other investment income	2 370	1,592	1,653	1,447	1,315	1,719	1,976	2,615	3,776
Investment income, debit	3 320	**−8,889**	**−9,476**	**−9,096**	**−11,831**	**−12,659**	**−14,504**	**−17,148**	**−20,426**
Direct investment income	3 330	−2,837	−2,760	−2,761	−4,314	−4,918	−4,829	−6,220	−6,410
Dividends and distributed branch profits	3 332	−1,213	−1,946	−1,997	−2,022	−3,194	−3,296	−2,757	−7,540
Reinvested earnings and undistributed branch profits	3 333	−1,381	−539	−463	−1,822	−1,257	−1,234	−3,052	1,243
Income on debt (interest)	3 334	−243	−275	−302	−470	−467	−299	−411	−113
Portfolio investment income	3 339	−4,047	−4,161	−4,309	−5,924	−6,318	−7,733	−8,596	−10,771
Income on equity	3 340	−1,467	−1,662	−1,652	−2,046	−2,524	−3,572	−3,843	−4,969
Income on bonds and notes	3 350	−2,530	−2,386	−2,586	−3,818	−3,582	−3,667	−3,799	−5,001
Income on money market instruments	3 360	−50	−113	−70	−60	−212	−494	−954	−802
Other investment income	3 370	−2,006	−2,555	−2,026	−1,593	−1,424	−1,942	−2,332	−3,244
D. CURRENT TRANSFERS	4 379	**−723**	**−677**	**−731**	**−1,105**	**−1,078**	**−1,544**	**−1,682**	**−1,897**
Credit	2 379	**1,611**	**1,562**	**1,621**	**1,911**	**2,040**	**1,904**	**1,946**	**2,129**
General government	2 380	199	207	255	315	339	357	376	410
Other sectors	2 390	1,412	1,355	1,367	1,596	1,701	1,547	1,569	1,719
Workers' remittances	2 391	....	....	....	....	....	....	....	10
Other current transfers	2 392	1,412	1,355	1,367	1,596	1,701	1,547	1,569	1,709
Debit	3 379	**−2,334**	**−2,239**	**−2,353**	**−3,016**	**−3,118**	**−3,448**	**−3,628**	**−4,026**
General government	3 380	−1,713	−1,673	−1,785	−2,401	−2,629	−2,960	−3,132	−3,481
Other sectors	3 390	−620	−566	−567	−615	−489	−488	−496	−545
Workers' remittances	3 391	....	....	....	....	....	....	....	−24
Other current transfers	3 392	−620	−566	−567	−615	−489	−488	−496	−521
CAPITAL AND FINANCIAL ACCOUNT	4 996	**−9,089**	**−11,269**	**−7,072**	**−11,321**	**−10,103**	**−3,118**	**−11,112**	**−10,324**
CAPITAL ACCOUNT	4 994	**103**	**83**	**125**	**149**	**188**	**336**	**223**	**237**
Total credit	2 994	*111*	*93*	*126*	*154*	*189*	*337*	*225*	*237*
Total debit	3 994	*−7*	*−10*	*−2*	*−5*	*−1*	*−1*	*−1*	....
Capital transfers, credit	2 400	**111**	**93**	**126**	**154**	**189**	**181**	**211**	**222**
General government	2 401	52	39	115	128	152	148	166	180
Debt forgiveness	2 402	....	....	....	....	....	....	....	....
Other capital transfers	2 410	52	39	115	128	152	148	166	180
Other sectors	2 430	59	54	11	26	37	32	45	42
Migrants' transfers	2 431	....	....	....	....	....	....	....	....
Debt forgiveness	2 432	....	....	....	....	....	....	....	....
Other capital transfers	2 440	59	54	11	26	37	32	45	42
Capital transfers, debit	3 400	**−7**	**−10**	**−2**	**−5**	**−1**	**−1**	**−1**	....
General government	3 401	−7	−10	−2	−5	−1	−1	−1	....
Debt forgiveness	3 402	....	−3	....	....	....	....	....	....
Other capital transfers	3 410	−7	−7	−2	−5	−1	−1	−1	....
Other sectors	3 430	....	....	....	....	....	....	....	....
Migrants' transfers	3 431	....	....	....	....	....	....	....	....
Debt forgiveness	3 432	....	....	....	....	....	....	....	....
Other capital transfers	3 440	....	....	....	....	....	....	....	....
Nonproduced nonfinancial assets, credit	2 480	....	....	....	....	....	157	14	15
Nonproduced nonfinancial assets, debit	3 480	....	....	....	....	....	....	....	....

Table 2 (Continued). STANDARD PRESENTATION, 2000–2007

(Millions of U.S. dollars)

	Code	2000	2001	2002	2003	2004	2005	2006	2007
FINANCIAL ACCOUNT	4 995	−9,192	−11,352	−7,197	−11,470	−10,290	−3,455	−11,335	−10,561
A. DIRECT INVESTMENT	4 500	−14,773	−4,719	753	5,744	4,017	390	2,313	55
Direct investment abroad	4 505	−23,898	−8,458	−7,522	2,272	1,146	−4,415	−3,196	−8,625
Equity capital	4 510	−15,725	−5,607	−6,866	7,963	−1,780	−2,307	−8,595	−7,201
Claims on affiliated enterprises	4 515	−15,725	−5,606	−6,866	7,899	−1,712	−2,307	−8,595	−7,201
Liabilities to affiliated enterprises	4 520	....	....	−1	64	−68	....	....	....
Reinvested earnings	4 525	−1,288	2,420	−742	−515	−3,189	−1,906	1,118	−2,934
Other capital	4 530	−6,885	−5,271	85	−5,176	6,115	−202	4,281	1,510
Claims on affiliated enterprises	4 535	−11,215	−4,424	966	−6,337	2,253	−6,419	9,847	−3,940
Liabilities to affiliated enterprises	4 540	4,329	−848	−880	1,161	3,862	6,217	−5,566	5,450
Direct investment in Finland	4 555	9,125	3,739	8,276	3,472	2,871	4,806	5,509	8,680
Equity capital	4 560	4,871	3,324	5,662	1,080	739	1,233	1,723	9,533
Claims on direct investors	4 565	....	....	....	....	....	....	....	....
Liabilities to direct investors	4 570	4,871	3,324	5,662	1,080	739	1,233	1,723	9,533
Reinvested earnings	4 575	1,381	539	463	1,822	1,257	1,234	3,052	−1,243
Other capital	4 580	2,874	−124	2,151	570	876	2,339	734	389
Claims on direct investors	4 585	−45	−331	−685	−1,266	−107	147	−2,471	−2,005
Liabilities to direct investors	4 590	2,918	208	2,837	1,836	982	2,192	3,205	2,395
B. PORTFOLIO INVESTMENT	4 600	−1,804	−5,609	−4,439	−1,900	−11,394	−7,486	−14,180	−10,204
Assets	4 602	−18,920	−11,594	−13,441	−9,801	−24,504	−17,942	−33,329	−15,803
Equity securities	4 610	−7,164	−5,153	−5,390	−5,532	−10,218	−9,410	−14,790	−13,725
Monetary authorities	4 611	....	....	−257	−65	−20	−54	−44	−15
General government	4 612	−2,743	−3,436	−2,720	−3,427	−6,238	−3,876	−8,320	−8,723
Banks	4 613	−21	−22	84	−23	−104	−146	−359	175
Other sectors	4 614	−4,400	−1,695	−2,496	−2,016	−3,857	−5,333	−6,067	−5,162
Debt securities	4 619	−11,756	−6,441	−8,051	−4,270	−14,286	−8,532	−18,539	−2,078
Bonds and notes	4 620	−11,948	−6,678	−6,230	−3,631	−13,630	−9,850	−16,509	−1,196
Monetary authorities	4 621	−130	−59	116	−27	−88	−46	−5,800	−3,144
General government	4 622	−9,239	−4,611	−4,003	−1,048	−6,259	−4,111	−2,528	4,298
Banks	4 623	−513	927	−1,864	−410	−2,385	−1,354	−5,456	−2,672
Other sectors	4 624	−2,067	−2,935	−479	−2,146	−4,898	−4,338	−2,725	322
Money market instruments	4 630	192	237	−1,821	−639	−657	1,317	−2,030	−882
Monetary authorities	4 631	102	69	....	....	−27	−56	−617	640
General government	4 632	106	−49	107	−264	−8	29	176	−178
Banks	4 633	−131	−134	−934	−321	−274	410	−417	−365
Other sectors	4 634	115	351	−995	−53	−348	934	−1,172	−979
Liabilities	4 652	17,116	5,985	9,002	7,901	13,110	10,456	19,149	5,599
Equity securities	4 660	10,114	3,960	2,527	−597	103	4,989	5,366	5,279
Banks	4 663	−1,884	38	137	295	261	927	1,093	616
Other sectors	4 664	11,998	3,922	2,390	−892	−158	4,061	4,273	4,663
Debt securities	4 669	7,002	2,025	6,475	8,498	13,007	5,467	13,783	320
Bonds and notes	4 670	2,437	444	4,426	8,354	5,356	6,367	12,098	3,548
Monetary authorities	4 671	....	....	....	....	−1	....	....	....
General government	4 672	−72	−816	2,973	6,442	1,274	2,646	1,610	−186
Banks	4 673	303	−1,190	523	1,257	3,860	4,756	9,421	3,876
Other sectors	4 674	2,206	2,449	930	655	222	−1,035	1,068	−143
Money market instruments	4 680	4,565	1,581	2,049	144	7,652	−899	1,685	−3,227
Monetary authorities	4 681	....	....	....	....	....	....	....	....
General government	4 682	3,102	461	1,482	−1,383	3,111	−4,651	3,798	−149
Banks	4 683	1,782	1,743	858	1,248	5,327	3,373	−681	−430
Other sectors	4 684	−319	−623	−291	279	−786	379	−1,431	−2,649
C. FINANCIAL DERIVATIVES	4 910	−630	38	−325	1,715	522	2,168	146	−907
Monetary authorities	4 911	....	....	....	....	....	....	....	....
General government	4 912	91	−7	10	575	−184	330	−7	−1,387
Banks	4 913	−164	−16	−532	234	−156	966	−301	−130
Other sectors	4 914	−557	62	198	905	862	872	453	609
Assets	4 900	....	....	....	....	....	....	....	....
Monetary authorities	4 901	....	....	....	....	....	....	....	....
General government	4 902	....	....	....	....	....	....	....	....
Banks	4 903	....	....	....	....	....	....	....	....
Other sectors	4 904	....	....	....	....	....	....	....	....
Liabilities	4 905	−630	38	−325	1,715	522	2,168	146	−907
Monetary authorities	4 906	....	....	....	....	....	....	....	....
General government	4 907	91	−7	10	575	−184	330	−7	−1,387
Banks	4 908	−164	−16	−532	234	−156	966	−7	−1,387
Other sectors	4 909	−557	62	198	905	862	872	453	609

Table 2 (Concluded). STANDARD PRESENTATION, 2000–2007

(Millions of U.S. dollars)

	Code	2000	2001	2002	2003	2004	2005	2006	2007
D. OTHER INVESTMENT	4 700	**8,366**	**−652**	**−3,302**	**−17,536**	**−2,621**	**1,294**	**−3,935**	**815**
Assets	4 703	−5,636	−10,117	−50	−15,407	−11,851	−1,775	−15,897	−11,523
Trade credits	4 706	−897	−332	−392	370	450	125	−251	−831
General government	4 707	−156	−190	615	−121	−11	−35	123	33
of which: Short-term	4 709	*−1*	*1*	....	....	....	....	....	....
Other sectors	4 710	−741	−142	−1,007	491	461	160	−374	−864
of which: Short-term	4 712	*−767*	*−75*	*−888*	*290*	*465*	*167*	*−660*	*−859*
Loans	4 714	−1,189	809	855	1,465	−860	−1,987	−2,968	−1,945
Monetary authorities	4 715	....	....	....	....	....	....	5	−244
of which: Short-term	4 718	....	....	....	....	....	....	*5*	*−244*
General government	4 719	2	4	....	....	....	....	....	....
of which: Short-term	4 721	....	....	....	....	....	....	....	....
Banks	4 722	−1,096	2,002	1,114	711	−1,022	−2,166	−2,583	−1,456
of which: Short-term	4 724	*−953*	*1,288*	*274*	*320*	*−1,042*	*−1,190*	*−906*	*−1,819*
Other sectors	4 725	−94	−1,196	−259	754	163	179	−391	−245
of which: Short-term	4 727	*−115*	*−16*	*−162*	*234*	*−3*	....	*9*	*−2*
Currency and deposits	4 730	−85	−1,138	−527	−17,334	−10,082	183	−12,959	−8,276
Monetary authorities	4 731	−129	77	−51	−54	161	9	−291	389
General government	4 732	−23	−786	−766	−2,970	−1,132	1,233	−3,234	−838
Banks	4 733	71	−76	37	−11,151	−8,894	−123	−9,074	−7,214
Other sectors	4 734	−4	−353	254	−3,159	−217	−936	−359	−613
Other assets	4 736	−3,465	−9,457	14	93	−1,359	−96	281	−470
Monetary authorities	4 737	....	....	....	....	−5	....	−1	....
of which: Short-term	4 739	....	....	....	....	....	....	*−1*	*−1*
General government	4 740	5	7	7	43	175	217	302	11
of which: Short-term	4 742	*51*	....	....	....	*−1*	*1*	....	....
Banks	4 743	−3,081	−10,122	54	157	−1,270	17	454	−642
of which: Short-term	4 745	*−3,727*	*−10,136*	*107*	*141*	*−1,270*	*18*	*454*	*−543*
Other sectors	4 746	−390	658	−48	−108	−261	−330	−474	160
of which: Short-term	4 748	*−408*	*661*	*−60*	*−94*	*−274*	*−346*	*−474*	*177*
Liabilities	4 753	**14,001**	**9,465**	**−3,253**	**−2,129**	**9,230**	**3,069**	**11,962**	**12,338**
Trade credits	4 756	622	−108	552	171	243	650	−16	454
General government	4 757	....	....	....	....	....	....	....	....
of which: Short-term	4 759	....	....	....	....	....	....	....	....
Other sectors	4 760	622	−108	552	171	243	650	−16	454
of which: Short-term	4 762	*663*	*−196*	*553*	*413*	*164*	*616*	*−6*	*487*
Loans	4 764	4,065	−1,825	−920	513	−1,113	−23	−1,534	2,921
Monetary authorities	4 765	49	−185	....	....	831	−685	−515	118
of which: Use of Fund credit and loans from the Fund	4 766	....	....	....	....	....	....	....	....
of which: Short-term	4 768	*49*	*−185*	....	....	*831*	*−685*	*−515*	*118*
General government	4 769	−1,189	483	358	2,404	104	−829	−1,846	219
of which: Short-term	4 771	*−244*	*54*	*141*	*2,036*	*311*	*−710*	*−1,872*	*431*
Banks	4 772	−91	−1,935	−357	63	373	569	315	610
of which: Short-term	4 774	*756*	*−1,057*	*−225*	*−15*	*89*	*461*	*64*	*334*
Other sectors	4 775	5,294	−187	−921	−1,954	−2,421	923	512	1,974
of which: Short-term	4 777	*2,655*	*−2,168*	*319*	*−241*	*−392*	*119*	*41*	*−95*
Currency and deposits	4 780	1,910	1,041	959	−2,873	8,569	2,646	11,986	8,187
Monetary authorities	4 781	1,383	467	1,234	696	−2,963	−2,708	708	−2,824
General government	4 782	....	....	....	....	....	....	....	....
Banks	4 783	19	574	−275	−3,569	11,532	5,354	11,278	11,011
Other sectors	4 784	508	....	....	....	....	....	....	....
Other liabilities	4 786	7,405	10,357	−3,844	60	1,531	−204	1,526	777
Monetary authorities	4 787	....	....	....	....	....	1	....	....
of which: Short-term	4 789	....	....	....	....	....	*1*	....	....
General government	4 790	−83	−15	−15	−8	19	−34	−7	−5
of which: Short-term	4 792	*−79*	....	....	....	*28*	*−25*	....	....
Banks	4 793	4,170	10,124	−4,032	47	1,292	161	1,188	−472
of which: Short-term	4 795	*5,087*	*9,296*	*−3,964*	*28*	*1,218*	*251*	*1,182*	*−483*
Other sectors	4 796	3,318	248	202	21	220	−331	345	1,253
of which: Short-term	4 798	*2,826*	*98*	*−28*	*136*	*214*	*216*	*271*	*981*
E. RESERVE ASSETS	4 802	**−351**	**−410**	**115**	**508**	**−814**	**180**	**4,321**	**−320**
Monetary gold	4 812	....	....	....	....	....	....	....	....
Special drawing rights	4 811	137	−101	49	24	39	−8	−23	−38
Reserve position in the Fund	4 810	109	−71	−50	−61	173	301	128	42
Foreign exchange	4 803	−597	−239	116	545	−1,026	−113	4,216	−323
Other claims	4 813	....	....	....	....	....	....	....	....
NET ERRORS AND OMISSIONS	4 998	**−1,437**	**−808**	**−5,005**	**2,786**	**−2,440**	**−3,833**	**1,550**	**276**

Table 3. INTERNATIONAL INVESTMENT POSITION (End-period stocks), 2000–2007

(Millions of U.S. dollars)

	Code	2000	2001	2002	2003	2004	2005	2006	2007
ASSETS	8 995 C.	**148,094**	**161,069**	**200,871**	**290,033**	**369,413**	**360,878**	**455,077**	**552,225**
Direct investment abroad	8 505 ..	**52,109**	**52,226**	**63,933**	**76,050**	**85,022**	**81,663**	**94,586**	**113,046**
Equity capital and reinvested earnings	8 506 ..	36,445	32,368	40,514	43,706	57,195	56,877	72,440	90,607
Claims on affiliated enterprises	8 507 ..	36,474	32,387	40,536	43,801	57,311	56,877	72,441	90,607
Liabilities to affiliated enterprises	8 508 ..	−29	−19	−22	−95	−116	. . . .	. . . .	. . . .
Other capital	8 530 ..	15,664	19,857	23,419	32,344	27,828	24,786	22,146	22,439
Claims on affiliated enterprises	8 535 ..	25,701	28,395	32,655	44,691	44,801	45,467	39,703	47,553
Liabilities to affiliated enterprises	8 540 ..	−10,037	−8,538	−9,236	−12,347	−16,973	−20,681	−17,557	−25,114
Portfolio investment	8 602 ..	**51,125**	**55,905**	**76,043**	**107,008**	**146,401**	**154,399**	**214,063**	**253,527**
Equity securities	8 610 ..	20,263	20,157	22,943	36,089	53,290	64,518	96,259	121,587
Monetary authorities	8 611 ..	. . . .	. . . .	271	401	463	465	540	616
General government	8 612 ..	7,057	8,471	9,718	16,722	27,219	32,834	49,628	65,205
Banks	8 613 ..	87	100	25	64	186	328	755	693
Other sectors	8 614 ..	13,119	11,586	12,930	18,903	25,422	30,891	45,336	55,072
Debt securities	8 619 ..	30,862	35,748	53,100	70,919	93,111	89,881	117,804	131,940
Bonds and notes	8 620 ..	29,817	34,897	49,988	66,279	87,380	86,087	111,304	123,921
Monetary authorities	8 621 ..	543	568	547	690	798	769	6,906	10,986
General government	8 622 ..	16,376	20,264	29,546	37,520	47,521	45,133	50,659	50,013
Banks	8 623 ..	4,679	4,394	7,421	9,547	13,083	12,708	19,739	25,552
Other sectors	8 624 ..	8,219	9,671	12,474	18,521	25,977	27,477	34,000	37,371
Money market instruments	8 630 ..	1,045	851	3,112	4,641	5,732	3,794	6,500	8,019
Monetary authorities	8 631 ..	70	. . . .	. . . .	. . . .	30	74	767	163
General government	8 632 ..	118	160	112	405	458	354	299	534
Banks	8 633 ..	220	419	1,634	2,489	2,966	2,257	2,957	3,384
Other sectors	8 634 ..	637	272	1,366	1,746	2,278	1,109	2,477	3,937
Financial derivatives	8 900 ..	**2,816**	**2,110**	**4,068**	**26,131**	**38,806**	**34,927**	**36,687**	**53,394**
Monetary authorities	8 901 ..	. . . .	. . . .	. . . .	47	. . . .	. . . .	. . . .	6
General government	8 902 ..	477	430	1,127	1,588	2,100	1,869	3,755	5,678
Banks	8 903 ..	1,462	1,354	1,693	23,214	35,643	32,216	32,064	46,650
Other sectors	8 904 ..	877	326	1,249	1,283	1,062	842	868	1,061
Other investment	8 703 ..	**33,637**	**42,407**	**47,000**	**69,671**	**86,271**	**78,559**	**102,243**	**123,874**
Trade credits	8 706 ..	4,557	4,448	5,174	6,444	8,903	7,076	7,730	10,788
General government	8 707 ..	1,341	1,499	1,042	1,380	1,434	1,149	1,136	1,253
of which: Short-term	8 709 ..	*1*	. . . .	. . . .	. . . .	. . . .	. . . .	. . . .	*8*
Other sectors	8 710 ..	3,216	2,949	4,132	5,064	7,468	5,926	6,593	9,535
of which: Short-term	8 712 ..	*3,085*	*2,432*	*3,666*	*4,737*	*7,433*	*5,885*	*6,499*	*9,404*
Loans	8 714 ..	6,313	5,324	5,096	3,823	4,624	5,996	9,686	12,383
Monetary authorities	8 715 ..	. . . .	. . . .	. . . .	. . . .	. . . .	. . . .	. . . .	293
of which: Short-term	8 718 ..	. . . .	. . . .	. . . .	. . . .	. . . .	. . . .	. . . .	*293*
General government	8 719 ..	41	35	. . . .	. . . .	69	60	66	74
of which: Short-term	8 721 ..	. . . .	. . . .	. . . .	. . . .	. . . .	. . . .	. . . .	. . . .
Banks	8 722 ..	2,843	3,378	2,614	2,231	3,551	5,229	8,441	10,714
of which: Short-term	8 724 ..	*1,974*	*1,056*	*954*	*800*	*1,901*	*2,839*	*4,074*	*6,340*
Other sectors	8 725 ..	3,429	1,911	2,481	1,592	1,004	707	1,178	1,302
of which: Short-term	8 727 ..	*606*	*184*	*383*	*194*	*10*	*8*	*1*	*8*
Currency and deposits	8 730 ..	2,104	2,993	4,174	56,388	68,036	61,205	80,522	96,140
Monetary authorities	8 731 ..	822	705	924	1,173	1,094	929	1,347	1,091
General government	8 732 ..	315	1,097	2,220	5,775	7,544	5,708	9,639	11,220
Banks	8 733 ..	112	182	176	44,960	57,424	51,759	65,933	79,245
Other sectors	8 734 ..	856	1,009	854	4,481	1,974	2,809	3,603	4,583
Other assets	8 736 ..	20,664	29,643	32,557	3,016	4,709	4,282	4,306	4,563
Monetary authorities	8 737 ..	65	62	73	88	100	87	117	139
of which: Short-term	8 739 ..	. . . .	. . . .	. . . .	. . . .	. . . .	. . . .	*20*	*30*
General government	8 740 ..	1,763	1,720	1,937	2,042	2,094	1,759	1,613	1,687
of which: Short-term	8 742 ..	. . . .	. . . .	. . . .	. . . .	*1*	. . . .	*1*	. . . .
Banks	8 743 ..	18,002	27,743	30,355	603	2,089	1,783	1,476	2,299
of which: Short-term	8 745 ..	*17,092*	*26,859*	*29,335*	*603*	*2,069*	*1,775*	*1,476*	*2,210*
Other sectors	8 746 ..	833	117	191	283	425	653	1,099	438
of which: Short-term	8 748 ..	*786*	*71*	*146*	*219*	*399*	*648*	*1,094*	*435*
Reserve assets	8 802 ..	**8,408**	**8,420**	**9,825**	**11,174**	**12,912**	**11,330**	**7,498**	**8,383**
Monetary gold	8 812 ..	430	438	541	658	691	809	1,002	1,319
Special drawing rights	8 811 ..	139	234	200	195	166	162	193	243
Reserve position in the Fund	8 810 ..	498	552	648	776	631	283	166	131
Foreign exchange	8 803 ..	7,342	7,197	8,437	9,545	11,425	10,076	6,136	6,691
Other claims	8 813 ..	. . . .	. . . .	. . . .	. . . .	. . . .	. . . .	. . . .	. . . .

Table 3 (Concluded). INTERNATIONAL INVESTMENT POSITION (End-period stocks), 2000–2007

(Millions of U.S. dollars)

	Code	2000	2001	2002	2003	2004	2005	2006	2007
LIABILITIES	8 995 D.	**329,900**	**261,959**	**256,067**	**335,466**	**390,092**	**389,588**	**483,224**	**621,272**
Direct investment in Finland	8 555	**24,272**	**24,071**	**33,987**	**50,257**	**57,379**	**54,587**	**67,991**	**85,237**
Equity capital and reinvested earnings	8 556	17,636	18,727	25,392	37,404	43,708	41,011	53,326	68,616
Claims on direct investors	8 557	....	....	–6	–4	–20	–6	–6	–7
Liabilities to direct investors	8 558	17,636	18,727	25,398	37,408	43,729	41,016	53,333	68,623
Other capital	8 580	6,636	5,344	8,595	12,853	13,671	13,576	14,665	16,621
Claims on direct investors	8 585	–1,807	–1,945	–2,502	–4,635	–4,680	–3,436	–6,271	–9,044
Liabilities to direct investors	8 590	8,443	7,289	11,097	17,489	18,351	17,012	20,935	25,665
Portfolio investment	8 652	**253,376**	**178,121**	**159,555**	**198,870**	**221,820**	**230,331**	**289,620**	**378,932**
Equity securities	8 660	204,361	128,039	89,173	103,315	102,974	119,952	154,943	229,461
Banks	8 663	291	391	667	1,703	2,563	3,022	3,815	4,168
Other sectors	8 664	204,070	127,647	88,506	101,612	100,411	116,930	151,128	225,293
Debt securities	8 669	49,015	50,083	70,382	95,555	118,846	110,379	134,677	149,471
Bonds and notes	8 670	42,956	42,469	59,490	81,155	96,197	90,451	110,033	122,845
Monetary authorities	8 671	....	....	....	....	....	....	....	....
General government	8 672	30,016	30,019	41,909	55,207	63,845	56,237	58,764	62,781
Banks	8 673	2,718	5,691	7,289	11,012	15,249	19,340	31,754	38,713
Other sectors	8 674	10,222	6,759	10,293	14,936	17,103	14,874	19,515	21,350
Money market instruments	8 680	6,059	7,614	10,892	14,400	22,648	19,928	24,645	26,627
Monetary authorities	8 681	....	....	....	....	....	....	....	....
General government	8 682	3,308	3,665	5,658	5,082	9,604	4,476	8,926	9,832
Banks	8 683	2,122	3,712	5,080	8,693	12,635	14,742	15,332	16,033
Other sectors	8 684	630	236	154	624	409	710	386	761
Financial derivatives	8 905	**1,925**	**1,678**	**3,102**	**26,021**	**37,544**	**34,019**	**35,644**	**51,096**
Monetary authorities	8 906	....	....	....	45	....	1	....	4
General government	8 907	239	288	643	1,878	2,058	1,365	2,862	3,564
Banks	8 908	1,037	1,153	1,835	23,179	34,649	32,048	31,747	46,429
Other sectors	8 909	649	237	625	919	838	605	1,034	1,099
Other investment	8 753	**50,327**	**58,089**	**59,423**	**60,318**	**73,349**	**70,651**	**89,969**	**106,007**
Trade credits	8 756	2,908	2,644	3,682	4,384	5,246	5,758	6,117	7,719
General government	8 757	....	....	....	....	....	....	....	....
of which: Short-term	8 759	....	....	....	....	....	....	....	....
Other sectors	8 760	2,908	2,644	3,682	4,384	5,246	5,758	6,117	7,719
of which: Short-term	8 762	*2,723*	*2,387*	*3,356*	*4,230*	*5,034*	*5,520*	*5,881*	*7,508*
Loans	8 764	24,452	23,386	24,458	24,690	24,871	22,182	24,827	27,016
Monetary authorities	8 765	278	93	....	314	1,266	503	....	129
of which: Use of Fund credit and loans from the Fund	8 766	....	....	....	....	....	....	....	....
of which: Short-term	8 768	*278*	*93*	....	*314*	*1,266*	*503*	....	*129*
General government	8 769	3,980	4,230	5,188	6,744	7,788	6,277	4,983	5,369
of which: Short-term	8 771	....	*56*	*217*	*2,451*	*2,922*	*2,000*	*211*	*700*
Banks	8 772	1,613	2,401	2,384	1,798	2,214	2,609	3,082	3,894
of which: Short-term	8 774	*1,089*	*206*	*86*	*97*	*130*	*572*	*665*	*1,039*
Other sectors	8 775	18,580	16,662	16,887	15,834	13,604	12,793	16,762	17,623
of which: Short-term	8 777	*4,585*	*2,193*	*2,405*	*2,446*	*380*	*444*	*472*	*419*
Currency and deposits	8 780	1,634	2,089	3,418	29,033	39,115	38,984	53,288	64,548
Monetary authorities	8 781	336	794	2,274	3,502	711	–1,981	–1,521	–4,341
General government	8 782	....	....	....	....	....	....	....	....
Banks	8 783	769	1,295	1,144	25,531	38,404	40,964	54,809	68,889
Other sectors	8 784	529	....	....	....	....	....	....	....
Other liabilities	8 786	21,334	29,970	27,865	2,211	4,116	3,727	5,738	6,723
Monetary authorities	8 787	....	....	....	....	....	....	....	....
of which: Short-term	8 789	....	....	....	....	....	....	....	....
General government	8 790	60	42	33	31	54	14	4	4
of which: Short-term	8 792	....	....	....	....	*31*	*4*	....	*4*
Banks	8 793	15,443	28,090	26,245	633	2,149	2,135	3,517	3,264
of which: Short-term	8 795	*13,874*	*25,756*	*23,922*	*613*	*2,040*	*2,134*	*3,517*	*3,133*
Other sectors	8 796	5,831	1,838	1,587	1,546	1,913	1,578	2,217	3,455
of which: Short-term	8 798	*3,162*	*147*	*143*	*295*	*492*	*591*	*1,158*	*1,106*
NET INTERNATIONAL INVESTMENT POSITION	8 995	**–181,806**	**–100,891**	**–55,196**	**–45,432**	**–20,680**	**–28,710**	**–28,147**	**–69,047**
Conversion rates: euros per U.S. dollar (end of period)	0 104	**1.0747**	**1.1347**	**.9536**	**.7918**	**.7342**	**.8477**	**.7593**	**.6793**

Table 1. ANALYTIC PRESENTATION, 2000–2007

(Billions of U.S. dollars)

	Code	2000	2001	2002	2003	2004	2005	2006	2007
A. Current Account¹...	4 993 Z.	**22.31**	**26.19**	**19.70**	**14.76**	**12.36**	**−13.56**	**−15.45**	**−31.25**
Goods: exports f.o.b.........................	2 100 ..	297.56	294.18	307.20	361.93	421.11	439.45	484.77	546.04
Goods: imports f.o.b.........................	3 100 ..	−300.73	−290.67	−299.58	−358.50	−425.95	−467.29	−521.70	−600.92
Balance on Goods.............................	4 100 ..	*−3.17*	*3.51*	*7.62*	*3.43*	*−4.85*	*−27.84*	*−36.93*	*−54.88*
Services: credit...............................	2 200 ..	80.49	80.12	86.16	98.81	114.63	122.21	126.29	145.74
Services: debit................................	3 200 ..	−60.69	−62.37	−68.96	−82.90	−98.37	−105.69	−113.73	−130.75
Balance on Goods and Services...........	4 991 ..	*16.63*	*21.27*	*24.82*	*19.35*	*11.41*	*−11.32*	*−24.38*	*−39.90*
Income: credit...............................	2 300 ..	73.99	75.93	66.87	89.36	119.72	149.02	195.42	252.73
Income: debit................................	3 300 ..	−54.54	−56.36	−57.51	−74.49	−97.08	−124.18	−159.14	−213.42
Balance on Goods, Services, and Income........................	4 992 ..	*36.08*	*40.84*	*34.19*	*34.22*	*34.05*	*13.52*	*11.90*	*−.59*
Current transfers: credit..................	2 379 Z.	17.34	17.18	19.77	24.05	25.44	25.41	26.89	28.08
Current transfers: debit...................	3 379 ..	−31.11	−31.83	−34.26	−43.51	−47.14	−52.49	−54.25	−58.73
B. Capital Account¹..............................	4 994 Z.	**1.35**	**−.33**	**−.21**	**−8.26**	**1.81**	**.66**	**−.27**	**2.47**
Capital account: credit....................	2 994 Z.	1.92	1.10	.90	1.94	3.35	2.57	1.90	3.42
Capital account: debit.....................	3 994 ..	−.57	−1.43	−1.12	−10.20	−1.54	−1.91	−2.17	−.95
Total, Groups A Plus B.....................	4 981 ..	*23.66*	*25.86*	*19.49*	*6.50*	*14.17*	*−12.90*	*−15.72*	*−28.78*
C. Financial Account¹...........................	4 995 W.	**−31.96**	**−33.09**	**−20.29**	**13.53**	**−6.27**	**−9.44**	**96.37**	**27.41**
Direct investment abroad................	4 505 ..	−174.31	−86.97	−50.61	−53.38	−56.93	−113.83	−122.26	−227.09
Direct investment in France.............	4 555 Z.	42.38	50.34	49.57	43.06	32.83	85.00	78.24	159.46
Portfolio investment assets..............	4 602 ..	−97.43	−85.46	−84.64	−192.71	−232.48	−243.64	−338.89	−219.61
Equity securities........................	4 610 ..	−32.54	−19.14	−16.34	−48.09	−60.85	−53.98	−60.81	−76.30
Debt securities.........................	4 619 ..	−64.90	−66.32	−68.30	−144.62	−171.63	−189.67	−278.08	−143.31
Portfolio investment liabilities..........	4 652 Z.	132.32	106.90	76.77	198.84	166.34	225.25	265.59	36.98
Equity securities........................	4 660 ..	49.97	13.65	−4.37	20.71	31.77	64.15	74.14	−68.58
Debt securities.........................	4 669 Z.	82.35	93.25	81.14	178.13	134.57	161.10	191.46	105.56
Financial derivatives......................	4 910 ..	4.78	2.29	5.30	−7.05	6.21	6.36	4.17	59.12
Financial derivatives assets.............	4 900 ..	. . . .	. . . .	. . . .	. . . .	. . . .	. . . .	. . . .	. . . .
Financial derivatives liabilities.........	4 905 ..	4.78	2.29	5.30	−7.05	6.21	6.36	4.17	59.12
Other investment assets.................	4 703 ..	1.27	−59.07	−44.15	−14.83	−116.16	−276.81	−154.20	−266.77
Monetary authorities..................	4 701 ..	−5.99	−12.51	−4.62	.01	11.42	4.34	14.48	−20.14
General government...................	4 704 ..	.43	.13	.53	−.76	3.74	4.56	2.01	10.27
Banks..	4 705 ..	7.17	−46.89	−35.09	−3.91	−121.43	−287.81	−161.97	−249.82
Other sectors............................	4 728 ..	−.33	.19	−4.97	−10.17	−9.88	2.09	−8.72	−7.08
Other investment liabilities.............	4 753 W.	59.02	38.87	27.47	39.60	193.91	308.24	363.73	485.32
Monetary authorities..................	4 753 WA	−23.38	1.16	−1.29	2.11	1.82	−3.40	10.41	96.24
General government...................	4 753 ZB	2.69	1.32	.25	−.45	2.41	−6.20	3.74	.89
Banks..	4 753 ZC	55.57	42.85	29.23	39.26	169.34	285.22	328.50	378.21
Other sectors............................	4 753 ZD	24.13	−6.46	−.72	−1.32	20.35	32.61	21.08	9.98
Total, Groups A Through C...............	4 983 ..	*−8.31*	*−7.23*	*−.81*	*20.03*	*7.90*	*−22.35*	*80.65*	*−1.37*
D. Net Errors and Omissions...............	4 998 ..	**5.87**	**1.66**	**−3.16**	**−18.74**	**−3.79**	**13.30**	**−68.86**	**1.05**
Total, Groups A Through D...............	4 984 ..	*−2.44*	*−5.57*	*−3.97*	*1.29*	*4.11*	*−9.05*	*11.78*	*−.33*
E. Reserves and Related Items............	4 802 A.	**2.44**	**5.57**	**3.97**	**−1.29**	**−4.11**	**9.05**	**−11.78**	**.33**
Reserve assets..............................	4 802 ..	2.44	5.57	3.97	−1.29	−4.11	9.05	−11.78	.33
Use of Fund credit and loans...........	4 766 ..	. . . .	. . . .	. . . .	. . . .	. . . .	. . . .	. . . .	. . . .
Exceptional financing.....................	4 920 ..	. . . .	. . . .	. . . .	. . . .	. . . .	. . . .	. . . .	. . . .
Conversion rates: euros per U.S. dollar.............	0 103 ..	**1.0854**	**1.1175**	**1.0626**	**.8860**	**.8054**	**.8041**	**.7971**	**.7306**

¹ Excludes components that have been classified in the categories of Group E.

Table 2. STANDARD PRESENTATION, 2000–2007

(Billions of U.S. dollars)

	Code	2000	2001	2002	2003	2004	2005	2006	2007
CURRENT ACCOUNT.........................	4 993 ..	**22.31**	**26.19**	**19.70**	**14.76**	**12.36**	**−13.56**	**−15.45**	**−31.25**
A. GOODS..........................	4 100 ..	**−3.17**	**3.51**	**7.62**	**3.43**	**−4.85**	**−27.84**	**−36.93**	**−54.88**
Credit..........................	2 100 ..	297.56	294.18	307.20	361.93	421.11	439.45	484.77	546.04
General merchandise: exports f.o.b...............	2 110 ..	287.94	284.54	298.26	351.87	409.29	428.04	472.42	530.35
Goods for processing: exports f.o.b...............	2 150 ..	8.44	8.91	8.27	9.25	10.60	9.90	10.46	13.51
Repairs on goods...........................	2 160 ..	....	....	....	....	....	....	....	....
Goods procured in ports by carriers...............	2 170 ..	1.18	.74	.67	.81	1.22	1.51	1.89	2.18
Nonmonetary gold...........................	2 180 ..	....	....	....	....	....	....	....	....
Debit..........................	3 100 ..	**−300.73**	**−290.67**	**−299.58**	**−358.50**	**−425.95**	**−467.29**	**−521.70**	**−600.92**
General merchandise: imports f.o.b...............	3 110 ..	−291.45	−281.26	−290.68	−347.74	−413.49	−453.78	−506.59	−582.16
Goods for processing: imports f.o.b...............	3 150 ..	−8.06	−8.29	−7.76	−9.07	−10.65	−10.79	−11.32	−14.78
Repairs on goods...........................	3 160 ..	....	....	....	....	....	....	....	....
Goods procured in ports by carriers...............	3 170 ..	−1.22	−1.12	−1.14	−1.69	−1.81	−2.73	−3.79	−3.98
Nonmonetary gold...........................	3 180 ..	....	....	....	....	....	....	....	....
B. SERVICES..........................	4 200 ..	**19.80**	**17.75**	**17.20**	**15.92**	**16.26**	**16.52**	**12.55**	**14.99**
Total credit	2 200 ..	*80.49*	*80.12*	*86.16*	*98.81*	*114.63*	*122.21*	*126.29*	*145.74*
Total debit	3 200 ..	*−60.69*	*−62.37*	*−68.96*	*−82.90*	*−98.37*	*−105.69*	*−113.73*	*−130.75*
Transportation services, credit...............	2 205 ..	**18.46**	**18.00**	**18.72**	**21.60**	**26.41**	**28.20**	**29.34**	**33.44**
Passenger	2 850 ..	....	....	....	....	....	....	....	....
Freight	2 851 ..	....	....	....	....	....	....	....	....
Other	2 852 ..	....	....	....	....	....	....	....	....
Sea transport, passenger........................	2 207 ..	....	....	....	....	....	....	....	....
Sea transport, freight..........................	2 208 ..	....	....	....	....	....	....	....	....
Sea transport, other...........................	2 209 ..	....	....	....	....	....	....	....	....
Air transport, passenger........................	2 211 ..	....	....	....	....	....	....	....	....
Air transport, freight..........................	2 212 ..	....	....	....	....	....	....	....	....
Air transport, other...........................	2 213 ..	....	....	....	....	....	....	....	....
Other transport, passenger......................	2 215 ..	....	....	....	....	....	....	....	....
Other transport, freight........................	2 216 ..	....	....	....	....	....	....	....	....
Other transport, other.........................	2 217 ..	....	....	....	....	....	....	....	....
Transportation services, debit...............	3 205 ..	**−17.86**	**−17.19**	**−17.85**	**−21.28**	**−30.12**	**−32.46**	**−34.35**	**−37.67**
Passenger	3 850 ..	....	....	....	....	....	....	....	....
Freight	3 851 ..	....	....	....	....	....	....	....	....
Other	3 852 ..	....	....	....	....	....	....	....	....
Sea transport, passenger........................	3 207 ..	....	....	....	....	....	....	....	....
Sea transport, freight..........................	3 208 ..	....	....	....	....	....	....	....	....
Sea transport, other...........................	3 209 ..	....	....	....	....	....	....	....	....
Air transport, passenger........................	3 211 ..	....	....	....	....	....	....	....	....
Air transport, freight..........................	3 212 ..	....	....	....	....	....	....	....	....
Air transport, other...........................	3 213 ..	....	....	....	....	....	....	....	....
Other transport, passenger......................	3 215 ..	....	....	....	....	....	....	....	....
Other transport, freight........................	3 216 ..	....	....	....	....	....	....	....	....
Other transport, other.........................	3 217 ..	....	....	....	....	....	....	....	....
Travel, credit..........................	2 236 ..	**30.64**	**30.08**	**32.44**	**36.62**	**44.90**	**43.94**	**46.51**	**54.17**
Business travel.............................	2 237 ..	....	....	....	....	....	....	....	....
Personal travel.............................	2 240 ..	....	....	....	....	....	....	....	....
Travel, debit..........................	3 236 ..	**−17.71**	**−17.93**	**−19.52**	**−23.39**	**−28.70**	**−30.46**	**−31.26**	**−36.74**
Business travel.............................	3 237 ..	....	....	....	....	....	....	....	....
Personal travel.............................	3 240 ..	....	....	....	....	....	....	....	....
Other services, credit......................	2 200 BA	**31.39**	**32.05**	**35.00**	**40.59**	**43.32**	**50.07**	**50.43**	**58.13**
Communications.............................	2 245 ..	1.33	1.57	2.16	2.51	3.06	3.53	3.78	4.20
Construction.............................	2 249 ..	2.87	2.80	3.10	2.80	3.19	3.63	4.15	5.30
Insurance.............................	2 253 ..	1.33	.89	1.08	2.07	.87	1.13	.82	1.04
Financial.............................	2 260 ..	1.27	1.09	1.13	1.08	1.46	1.43	1.36	2.03
Computer and information......................	2 262 ..	.80	1.12	1.19	1.26	1.49	1.71	1.96	1.81
Royalties and licence fees......................	2 266 ..	2.32	2.60	3.34	4.07	5.17	6.22	6.23	8.83
Other business services........................	2 268 ..	19.30	20.01	20.65	24.13	24.93	29.41	29.50	31.90
Personal, cultural, and recreational................	2 287 ..	1.59	1.43	1.52	1.86	2.30	2.16	1.74	1.96
Government, n.i.e.............................	2 291 ..	.59	.53	.83	.79	.86	.86	.89	1.06
Other services, debit......................	3 200 BA	**−25.12**	**−27.24**	**−31.59**	**−38.23**	**−39.55**	**−42.78**	**−48.12**	**−56.33**
Communications.............................	3 245 ..	−1.15	−1.52	−1.71	−1.98	−1.94	−2.17	−2.14	−2.69
Construction.............................	3 249 ..	−1.53	−1.60	−1.61	−1.36	−1.75	−1.62	−1.77	−2.11
Insurance.............................	3 253 ..	.33	−.63	−1.55	−2.39	−1.41	−2.27	−2.33	−2.10
Financial.............................	3 260 ..	−1.45	−1.47	−1.55	−1.93	−2.50	−2.38	−3.74	−3.89
Computer and information......................	3 262 ..	−.74	−.98	−1.20	−1.24	−1.44	−1.79	−1.99	−2.18
Royalties and licence fees......................	3 266 ..	−2.04	−1.88	−1.90	−2.43	−3.06	−3.09	−3.31	−4.60
Other business services........................	3 268 ..	−15.46	−16.17	−19.21	−23.47	−23.70	−25.65	−29.11	−34.27
Personal, cultural, and recreational................	3 287 ..	−1.96	−2.07	−2.08	−2.34	−2.62	−2.82	−2.69	−3.20
Government, n.i.e.............................	3 291 ..	−1.11	−.93	−.78	−1.09	−1.13	−.98	−1.05	−1.28

Table 2 (Continued). STANDARD PRESENTATION, 2000–2007

(Billions of U.S. dollars)

	Code	2000	2001	2002	2003	2004	2005	2006	2007
C. INCOME..	4 300 ..	**19.45**	**19.57**	**9.37**	**14.87**	**22.64**	**24.84**	**36.28**	**39.30**
Total credit..	2 300 ..	*73.99*	*75.93*	*66.87*	*89.36*	*119.72*	*149.02*	*195.42*	*252.73*
Total debit..	3 300 ..	*−54.54*	*−56.36*	*−57.51*	*−74.49*	*−97.08*	*−124.18*	*−159.14*	*−213.42*
Compensation of employees, credit..................	2 310 ..	**7.93**	**8.44**	**9.60**	**10.86**	**11.82**	**11.43**	**11.86**	**13.29**
Compensation of employees, debit..................	3 310 ..	**−1.09**	**−1.11**	**−1.28**	**−1.54**	**−1.17**	**−1.07**	**−1.10**	**−1.22**
Investment income, credit..........................	2 320 ..	**66.06**	**67.48**	**57.28**	**78.50**	**107.90**	**137.59**	**183.55**	**239.44**
Direct investment income............................	2 330 ..	14.75	14.20	4.65	16.33	32.52	46.20	59.34	66.74
Dividends and distributed branch profits..........	2 332 ..	7.54	13.80	13.67	14.34	19.45	19.20	28.51	29.52
Reinvested earnings and undistributed branch profits.....	2 333 ..	7.20	.39	−9.02	1.99	13.07	27.00	30.83	37.22
Income on debt (interest)..........................	2 334 ..	....	....	....	....	....	....	....	....
Portfolio investment income........................	2 339 ..	27.50	29.39	32.22	39.73	54.75	62.63	79.31	102.82
Income on equity................................	2 340 ..	2.43	2.55	2.30	1.95	4.66	7.01	9.11	12.25
Income on bonds and notes......................	2 350 ..	....	....	....	....	....	....	....	....
Income on money market instruments............	2 360 ..	....	....	....	....	....	....	....	....
Other investment income..........................	2 370 ..	23.82	23.89	20.41	22.44	20.64	28.76	44.91	69.87
Investment income, debit..........................	3 320 ..	**−53.45**	**−55.25**	**−56.23**	**−72.95**	**−95.91**	**−123.11**	**−158.04**	**−212.21**
Direct investment income............................	3 330 ..	−5.39	−1.54	.27	−4.80	−13.11	−24.62	−26.34	−33.82
Dividends and distributed branch profits..........	3 332 ..	−2.96	−4.09	−4.26	−6.97	−7.10	−6.93	−14.29	−9.70
Reinvested earnings and undistributed branch profits.....	3 333 ..	−2.44	2.54	4.53	2.17	−6.01	−17.68	−12.05	−24.12
Income on debt (interest)..........................	3 334 ..	....	....	....	....	....	....	....	....
Portfolio investment income........................	3 339 ..	−23.65	−28.32	−34.25	−45.23	−59.25	−65.30	−80.46	−98.41
Income on equity................................	3 340 ..	−3.82	−4.93	−5.70	−6.29	−8.21	−9.67	−13.27	−16.36
Income on bonds and notes......................	3 350 ..	....	....	....	....	....	....	....	....
Income on money market instruments............	3 360 ..	....	....	....	....	....	....	....	....
Other investment income..........................	3 370 ..	−24.41	−25.38	−22.24	−22.93	−23.55	−33.19	−51.24	−79.98
D. CURRENT TRANSFERS..........................	4 379 ..	**−13.77**	**−14.65**	**−14.49**	**−19.46**	**−21.69**	**−27.08**	**−27.35**	**−30.66**
Credit..	2 379 ..	**17.34**	**17.18**	**19.77**	**24.05**	**25.44**	**25.41**	**26.89**	**28.08**
General government................................	2 380 ..	11.36	10.79	11.56	14.69	16.48	16.96	17.95	18.54
Other sectors......................................	2 390 ..	5.98	6.39	8.21	9.36	8.96	8.45	8.94	9.54
Workers' remittances............................	2 391 ..	.68	.75	.77	.45	.46	.51	.44	.45
Other current transfers..........................	2 392 ..	5.30	5.63	7.44	8.91	8.50	7.93	8.50	9.09
Debit..	3 379 ..	**−31.11**	**−31.83**	**−34.26**	**−43.51**	**−47.14**	**−52.49**	**−54.25**	**−58.73**
General government................................	3 380 ..	−19.55	−19.40	−20.97	−27.54	−30.12	−35.26	−35.37	−37.79
Other sectors......................................	3 390 ..	−11.56	−12.43	−13.28	−15.97	−17.01	−17.23	−18.88	−20.94
Workers' remittances............................	3 391 ..	−2.68	−2.84	−2.53	−2.85	−3.09	−3.11	−3.11	−3.16
Other current transfers..........................	3 392 ..	−8.88	−9.59	−10.75	−13.12	−13.92	−14.12	−15.76	−17.78
CAPITAL AND FINANCIAL ACCOUNT......................	4 996 ..	**−28.18**	**−27.85**	**−16.54**	**3.98**	**−8.57**	**.27**	**84.32**	**30.20**
CAPITAL ACCOUNT....................................	4 994 ..	**1.35**	**−.33**	**−.21**	**−8.26**	**1.81**	**.66**	**−.27**	**2.47**
Total credit..	2 994 ..	*1.92*	*1.10*	*.90*	*1.94*	*3.35*	*2.57*	*1.90*	*3.42*
Total debit..	3 994 ..	*−.57*	*−1.43*	*−1.12*	*−10.20*	*−1.54*	*−1.91*	*−2.17*	*−.95*
Capital transfers, credit............................	2 400 ..	**1.89**	**1.08**	**.87**	**1.91**	**2.30**	**2.37**	**1.71**	**2.03**
General government................................	2 401 ..	1.65	.82	.60	1.58	1.87	1.83	1.33	1.72
Debt forgiveness..................................	2 402 ..	....	....	....	....	....	....	....	....
Other capital transfers............................	2 410 ..	1.65	.82	.60	1.58	1.87	1.83	1.33	1.72
Other sectors......................................	2 430 ..	.24	.26	.27	.34	.43	.54	.38	.32
Migrants' transfers..............................	2 431 ..	....	....	....	....	....	....	....	....
Debt forgiveness................................	2 432 ..	.01	....	....	....	.09	.10	....	.01
Other capital transfers..........................	2 440 ..	.23	.26	.27	.34	.35	.45	.38	.30
Capital transfers, debit............................	3 400 ..	**−.46**	**−1.27**	**−.98**	**−10.12**	**−1.44**	**−1.79**	**−1.52**	**−.79**
General government................................	3 401 ..	−.23	−.30	−.57	−1.73	−1.06	−1.12	−1.20	−.42
Debt forgiveness..................................	3 402 ..	−.05	−.13	−.39	−1.50	−.75	−.87	−.95	−.14
Other capital transfers............................	3 410 ..	−.18	−.18	−.19	−.23	−.31	−.25	−.25	−.27
Other sectors......................................	3 430 ..	−.23	−.97	−.41	−8.39	−.38	−.67	−.32	−.37
Migrants' transfers..............................	3 431 ..	....	....	....	....	....	....	....	....
Debt forgiveness................................	3 432 ..	−.04	−.81	−.24	−8.18	−.20	−.45	−.10	−.11
Other capital transfers..........................	3 440 ..	−.18	−.16	−.17	−.20	−.19	−.22	−.21	−.26
Nonproduced nonfinancial assets, credit.............	2 480 ..	**.03**	**.02**	**.03**	**.02**	**1.05**	**.20**	**.19**	**1.39**
Nonproduced nonfinancial assets, debit.............	3 480 ..	**−.11**	**−.16**	**−.13**	**−.08**	**−.10**	**−.11**	**−.65**	**−.16**

2008, International Monetary Fund: *Balance of Payments Statistics Yearbook*

Table 2 (Continued). STANDARD PRESENTATION, 2000–2007

(Billions of U.S. dollars)

	Code	2000	2001	2002	2003	2004	2005	2006	2007
FINANCIAL ACCOUNT	4 995 ..	**−29.53**	**−27.52**	**−16.32**	**12.24**	**−10.38**	**−.40**	**84.59**	**27.73**
A. DIRECT INVESTMENT	4 500 ..	**−131.93**	**−36.62**	**−1.04**	**−10.32**	**−24.10**	**−28.83**	**−44.03**	**−67.63**
Direct investment abroad	4 505 ..	**−174.31**	**−86.97**	**−50.61**	**−53.38**	**−56.93**	**−113.83**	**−122.26**	**−227.09**
Equity capital	4 510 ..	−136.10	−54.61	−39.46	−13.82	−32.00	−33.78	−73.29	−78.22
Claims on affiliated enterprises	4 515 ..	−136.10	−54.61	−39.46	−13.82	−32.00	−33.78	−73.29	−78.22
Liabilities to affiliated enterprises	4 520 ..	....	....	....	....	....	....	....	....
Reinvested earnings	4 525 ..	−7.20	−.39	9.02	−1.99	−13.07	−27.00	−30.83	−37.22
Other capital	4 530 ..	−31.00	−31.96	−20.18	−37.57	−11.85	−53.04	−18.15	−111.64
Claims on affiliated enterprises	4 535 ..	−30.64	−33.34	−21.82	−35.73	−14.49	−57.08	−34.17	−108.09
Liabilities to affiliated enterprises	4 540 ..	−.36	1.38	1.64	−1.84	2.63	4.04	16.02	−3.55
Direct investment in France	4 555 ..	**42.38**	**50.34**	**49.57**	**43.06**	**32.83**	**85.00**	**78.24**	**159.46**
Equity capital	4 560 ..	27.04	20.66	34.15	17.61	5.23	22.94	27.38	30.02
Claims on direct investors	4 565 ..	....	....	....	....	....	....	....	....
Liabilities to direct investors	4 570 ..	27.04	20.66	34.15	17.61	5.23	22.94	27.38	30.02
Reinvested earnings	4 575 ..	2.44	−2.54	−4.53	−2.17	6.01	17.68	12.05	24.12
Other capital	4 580 ..	12.90	32.23	19.95	27.62	21.59	44.37	38.81	105.32
Claims on direct investors	4 585 ..	−.01	−.13	−.95	−1.57	−1.26	.25	−.85	−4.06
Liabilities to direct investors	4 590 ..	12.91	32.36	20.90	29.19	22.85	44.12	39.66	109.38
B. PORTFOLIO INVESTMENT	4 600 ..	**34.89**	**21.45**	**−7.87**	**6.13**	**−66.14**	**−18.40**	**−73.30**	**−182.63**
Assets	4 602 ..	**−97.43**	**−85.46**	**−84.64**	**−192.71**	**−232.48**	**−243.64**	**−338.89**	**−219.61**
Equity securities	4 610 ..	−32.54	−19.14	−16.34	−48.09	−60.85	−53.98	−60.81	−76.30
Monetary authorities	4 611 ..	....	....	....	....	....	....	....	.49
General government	4 612 ..	....	....	....	....	....	....	....	....
Banks	4 613 ..	−2.43	1.95	−5.37	−16.27	−24.60	9.66	−9.17	−48.84
Other sectors	4 614 ..	−30.11	−21.08	−10.97	−31.81	−36.25	−63.63	−51.64	−27.95
Debt securities	4 619 ..	−64.90	−66.32	−68.30	−144.62	−171.63	−189.67	−278.08	−143.31
Bonds and notes	4 620 ..	−56.59	−56.27	−54.97	−115.14	−156.05	−176.21	−282.40	−137.69
Monetary authorities	4 621 ..	....	....	....	....	−6.72	−7.72	−6.70	−18.45
General government	4 622 ..	....	....	....	....	....	....	....	....
Banks	4 623 ..	−41.00	−14.77	−17.67	−35.75	−74.56	−95.30	−123.39	−104.99
Other sectors	4 624 ..	−15.59	−41.50	−37.30	−79.38	−74.78	−73.19	−152.30	−14.24
Money market instruments	4 630 ..	−8.30	−10.05	−13.33	−29.49	−15.58	−13.45	4.31	−5.62
Monetary authorities	4 631 ..	....	....	....	....	−.25	−.55	−12.80	−30.54
General government	4 632 ..	....	....	....	....	....	....	....	....
Banks	4 633 ..	8.35	−1.73	−15.47	−28.24	−5.24	−7.84	26.20	14.77
Other sectors	4 634 ..	−16.65	−8.33	2.14	−1.25	−10.09	−5.07	−9.08	10.15
Liabilities	4 652 ..	**132.32**	**106.90**	**76.77**	**198.84**	**166.34**	**225.25**	**265.59**	**36.98**
Equity securities	4 660 ..	49.97	13.65	−4.37	20.71	31.77	64.15	74.14	−68.58
Banks	4 663 ..	−2.18	3.94	−.08	−2.53	−3.02	8.09	13.55	−15.89
Other sectors	4 664 ..	52.16	9.71	−4.29	23.24	34.79	56.06	60.58	−52.70
Debt securities	4 669 ..	82.35	93.25	81.14	178.13	134.57	161.10	191.46	105.56
Bonds and notes	4 670 ..	70.24	85.93	80.40	161.87	118.27	136.60	208.76	107.04
Monetary authorities	4 671 ..	....	....	....	....	....	....	....	....
General government	4 672 ..	36.54	29.64	32.46	66.84	95.73	90.42	66.30	16.54
Banks	4 673 ..	15.30	18.92	35.44	53.05	43.35	48.56	104.54	73.06
Other sectors	4 674 ..	18.40	37.37	12.50	41.98	−20.80	−2.39	37.92	17.44
Money market instruments	4 680 ..	12.11	7.33	.74	16.27	16.29	24.50	−17.31	−1.48
Monetary authorities	4 681 ..	....	....	....	....	....	....	....	....
General government	4 682 ..	3.35	2.88	10.67	17.99	14.07	2.00	−34.80	3.65
Banks	4 683 ..	3.62	12.66	−11.60	−5.31	3.18	18.94	15.18	5.28
Other sectors	4 684 ..	5.14	−8.21	1.67	3.59	−.95	3.57	2.31	−10.41
C. FINANCIAL DERIVATIVES	4 910 ..	**4.78**	**2.29**	**5.30**	**−7.05**	**6.21**	**6.36**	**4.17**	**59.12**
Monetary authorities	4 911 ..	....	....	....	....	....	....	....	....
General government	4 912 ..	....	....	....	....	....	....	....	....
Banks	4 913 ..	4.78	2.29	5.30	−7.05	6.21	6.36	4.17	59.12
Other sectors	4 914 ..	....	....	....	....	....	....	....	....
Assets	4 900 ..	**....**	**....**	**....**	**....**	**....**	**....**	**....**	**....**
Monetary authorities	4 901 ..	....	....	....	....	....	....	....	....
General government	4 902 ..	....	....	....	....	....	....	....	....
Banks	4 903 ..	....	....	....	....	....	....	....	....
Other sectors	4 904 ..	....	....	....	....	....	....	....	....
Liabilities	4 905 ..	**4.78**	**2.29**	**5.30**	**−7.05**	**6.21**	**6.36**	**4.17**	**59.12**
Monetary authorities	4 906 ..	....	....	....	....	....	....	....	....
General government	4 907 ..	....	....	....	....	....	....	....	....
Banks	4 908 ..	4.78	2.29	5.30	−7.05	6.21	6.36	4.17	59.12
Other sectors	4 909 ..	....	....	....	....	....	....	....	....

Table 2 (Concluded). STANDARD PRESENTATION, 2000–2007

(Billions of U.S. dollars)

	Code	2000	2001	2002	2003	2004	2005	2006	2007
D. OTHER INVESTMENT	4 700	**60.29**	**−20.20**	**−16.68**	**24.77**	**77.76**	**31.43**	**209.53**	**218.55**
Assets	4 703	**1.27**	**−59.07**	**−44.15**	**−14.83**	**−116.16**	**−276.81**	**−154.20**	**−266.77**
Trade credits	4 706	1.20	.60	−1.01	.87	−3.10	5.70	4.10	2.31
General government	4 707	....	....	....	1.67	1.73	3.45	6.66	2.11
of which: Short-term	4 709	....	....	....	....	....	....	....	....
Other sectors	4 710	1.20	.60	−1.01	−.80	−4.84	2.25	−2.55	.19
of which: Short-term	4 712	....	....	....	....	....	....	....	....
Loans	4 714	.17	−59.65	−47.88	−7.13	−109.76	−283.79	−156.65	−261.15
Monetary authorities	4 715	−5.99	−12.51	−4.62	.01	11.42	4.34	14.48	−20.14
of which: Short-term	4 718	....	....	....	....	....	....	....	....
General government	4 719	.53	.16	.56	−2.40	2.05	1.14	−4.67	8.16
of which: Short-term	4 721	....	....	....	....	.89	.89	−5.16	7.14
Banks	4 722	7.17	−46.89	−35.09	−3.91	−121.43	−287.81	−161.97	−249.82
of which: Short-term	4 724	18.34	−38.59	−23.26	24.58	−103.24	−244.89	−93.00	−180.43
Other sectors	4 725	−1.53	−.41	−8.74	−.82	−1.79	−1.47	−4.49	.66
of which: Short-term	4 727	....	....	....	....	−1.26	−1.19	−4.06	.74
Currency and deposits	4 730	....	....	4.77	−8.55	−3.27	1.30	−1.66	−7.93
Monetary authorities	4 731	....	....	....	....	....	....	....	....
General government	4 732	....	....	−.01	.01	−.02	−.01	.03	....
Banks	4 733	....	....	....	....	....	....	....	....
Other sectors	4 734	....	....	4.78	−8.55	−3.25	1.31	−1.68	−7.93
Other assets	4 736	−.10	−.03	−.02	−.03	−.02	−.03	....	....
Monetary authorities	4 737	....	....	....	....	....	....	....	....
of which: Short-term	4 739	....	....	....	....	....	....	....	....
General government	4 740	−.10	−.03	−.02	−.03	−.02	−.03	....	....
of which: Short-term	4 742	....	....	....	....	....	....	....	....
Banks	4 743	....	....	....	....	....	....	....	....
of which: Short-term	4 745	....	....	....	....	....	....	....	....
Other sectors	4 746	....	....	....	....	....	....	....	....
of which: Short-term	4 748	....	....	....	....	....	....	....	....
Liabilities	4 753	**59.02**	**38.87**	**27.47**	**39.60**	**193.91**	**308.24**	**363.73**	**485.32**
Trade credits	4 756	3.07	−.61	−1.84	−3.32	9.16	5.46	2.50	−4.18
General government	4 757	....	....	....	....	....	....	....	....
of which: Short-term	4 759	....	....	....	....	....	....	....	....
Other sectors	4 760	3.07	−.61	−1.84	−3.32	9.16	5.46	2.50	−4.18
of which: Short-term	4 762	3.07	−.61	−1.84	−3.32	9.16	5.46	2.50	−4.18
Loans	4 764	55.95	39.48	29.31	42.92	184.76	302.78	361.23	489.50
Monetary authorities	4 765	−23.38	1.16	−1.29	2.11	1.82	−3.40	10.41	96.24
of which: Use of Fund credit and loans from the Fund	4 766	....	....	....	....	....	....	....	....
of which: Short-term	4 768	−23.38	1.16	−1.29	2.11	1.82	−3.40	10.41	96.24
General government	4 769	2.69	1.32	.25	−.45	2.41	−6.20	3.74	.89
of which: Short-term	4 771	....	....	....	....	2.88	−5.22	3.71	.68
Banks	4 772	55.57	42.85	29.23	39.26	169.34	285.22	328.50	378.21
of which: Short-term	4 774	53.57	41.20	6.19	−3.05	144.46	199.47	238.20	238.68
Other sectors	4 775	21.06	−5.85	1.12	1.99	11.19	27.15	18.58	14.16
of which: Short-term	4 777	....	....	....	....	11.66	18.16	6.84	6.54
Currency and deposits	4 780	....	....	....	....	....	....	....	....
Monetary authorities	4 781	....	....	....	....	....	....	....	....
General government	4 782	....	....	....	....	....	....	....	....
Banks	4 783	....	....	....	....	....	....	....	....
Other sectors	4 784	....	....	....	....	....	....	....	....
Other liabilities	4 786	....	....	....	....	....	....	....	....
Monetary authorities	4 787	....	....	....	....	....	....	....	....
of which: Short-term	4 789	....	....	....	....	....	....	....	....
General government	4 790	....	....	....	....	....	....	....	....
of which: Short-term	4 792	....	....	....	....	....	....	....	....
Banks	4 793	....	....	....	....	....	....	....	....
of which: Short-term	4 795	....	....	....	....	....	....	....	....
Other sectors	4 796	....	....	....	....	....	....	....	....
of which: Short-term	4 798	....	....	....	....	....	....	....	....
E. RESERVE ASSETS	4 802	**2.44**	**5.57**	**3.97**	**−1.29**	**−4.11**	**9.05**	**−11.78**	**.33**
Monetary gold	4 812	....	....	....	....	.56	2.35	2.09	2.32
Special drawing rights	4 811	−.07	−.11	−.09	−.08	−.08	−.08	−.02	....
Reserve position in the Fund	4 810	.65	−.54	−.47	.04	1.17	2.11	1.55	.35
Foreign exchange	4 803	1.86	6.22	4.53	−1.25	−5.76	4.67	−15.41	−2.34
Other claims	4 813	....	....	....	....	....	....	....	....
NET ERRORS AND OMISSIONS	4 998	**5.87**	**1.66**	**−3.16**	**−18.74**	**−3.79**	**13.30**	**−68.86**	**1.05**

Table 3. INTERNATIONAL INVESTMENT POSITION (End-period stocks), 2000–2007

(Billions of U.S. dollars)

	Code	2000	2001	2002	2003	2004	2005	2006	2007
ASSETS	8 995 C	**2,369.05**	**2,443.06**	**2,786.45**	**3,681.85**	**4,541.36**	**4,869.97**	**6,276.57**	**7,757.95**
Direct investment abroad	8 505	**942.50**	**900.69**	**896.32**	**1,212.80**	**1,459.16**	**1,522.90**	**1,981.62**	**2,449.24**
Equity capital and reinvested earnings	8 506	826.00	752.81	719.20	968.41	1,183.20	1,234.06	1,647.78	1,966.80
Claims on affiliated enterprises	8 507	....	....	....	....	....	....	....	....
Liabilities to affiliated enterprises	8 508	....	....	....	....	....	....	....	....
Other capital	8 530	116.50	147.88	177.13	244.39	275.96	288.84	333.85	482.44
Claims on affiliated enterprises	8 535	....	....	....	....	....	....	....	....
Liabilities to affiliated enterprises	8 540	....	....	....	....	....	....	....	....
Portfolio investment	8 602	**663.73**	**728.48**	**931.87**	**1,369.56**	**1,750.72**	**1,873.26**	**2,454.10**	**3,013.30**
Equity securities	8 610	210.01	201.73	200.09	340.24	442.66	524.88	709.18	857.90
Monetary authorities	8 611	....	.09	....	.01	.53	.63	.71	.22
General government	8 612	.19	1.15	.31	.54	3.42	11.90	18.10	24.51
Banks	8 613	30.06	25.03	40.40	75.86	106.60	107.25	142.38	179.49
Other sectors	8 614	179.77	175.47	159.38	263.83	332.11	405.11	547.99	653.67
Debt securities	8 619	453.71	526.75	731.78	1,029.32	1,308.07	1,348.37	1,744.92	2,155.40
Bonds and notes	8 620	409.51	480.31	660.48	909.76	1,163.83	1,199.73	1,585.63	1,969.92
Monetary authorities	8 621	....	.44	.60	.80	8.20	14.26	21.56	43.49
General government	8 622	.47	1.67	.78	1.16	.93	3.16	9.46	19.24
Banks	8 623	188.71	200.41	306.09	424.97	531.78	547.72	735.24	850.56
Other sectors	8 624	220.34	277.79	353.01	482.83	622.93	634.58	819.37	1,056.63
Money market instruments	8 630	44.20	46.44	71.30	119.56	144.23	148.64	159.29	185.48
Monetary authorities	8 631	....	....	....	....	.27	1.50	16.05	50.27
General government	8 632	....	....	....	....	....	.05	.30	.38
Banks	8 633	36.66	40.63	62.98	105.74	127.64	130.64	116.21	102.22
Other sectors	8 634	7.54	5.82	8.32	13.82	16.32	16.46	26.72	32.61
Financial derivatives	8 900	**95.00**	**109.81**	**108.11**	**117.55**	**159.19**	**146.87**	**209.69**	**233.33**
Monetary authorities	8 901	....	....	....	....	....	....	....	....
General government	8 902	....	....	....	....	....	....	....	....
Banks	8 903	....	....	....	....	....	....	....	....
Other sectors	8 904	95.00	109.81	108.11	117.55	159.19	146.87	209.69	233.33
Other investment	8 703	**604.27**	**645.38**	**788.37**	**911.20**	**1,094.93**	**1,252.58**	**1,532.90**	**1,946.37**
Trade credits	8 706	78.16	69.80	100.30	111.89	124.32	104.91	110.33	120.46
General government	8 707	....	....	26.19	30.44	32.31	23.56	18.96	18.83
of which: Short-term	8 709	....	....	....	....	....	....	....	....
Other sectors	8 710	78.16	69.80	74.11	81.45	92.01	81.35	91.36	101.63
of which: Short-term	8 712	....	....	....	....	....	....	....	....
Loans	8 714	513.26	562.80	674.06	782.44	953.05	1,129.32	1,403.30	1,805.78
Monetary authorities	8 715	15.35	27.23	36.49	42.64	33.58	26.05	31.73	57.12
of which: Short-term	8 718	*15.35*	*27.23*	*36.49*	*42.64*	*33.58*	*26.05*	*31.73*	*57.12*
General government	8 719	15.07	14.19	15.52	20.07	20.62	16.82	24.48	18.71
of which: Short-term	8 721	*2.05*	*2.20*	*1.92*	*3.07*	*3.58*	*2.29*	*8.77*	*2.30*
Banks	8 722	429.70	453.08	541.55	621.45	788.51	991.77	1,245.33	1,611.49
of which: Short-term	8 724	*321.86*	*340.01*	*406.37*	*439.08*	*574.93*	*757.18*	*920.77*	*1,185.72*
Other sectors	8 725	53.13	68.30	80.50	98.29	110.35	94.67	101.76	118.46
of which: Short-term	8 727	*52.11*	*67.33*	*80.14*	*97.28*	*108.35*	*94.67*	*101.76*	*118.46*
Currency and deposits	8 730	....	....	....	....	....	....	....	....
Monetary authorities	8 731	....	....	....	....	....	....	....	....
General government	8 732	....	....	....	....	....	....	....	....
Banks	8 733	....	....	....	....	....	....	....	....
Other sectors	8 734	....	....	....	....	....	....	....	....
Other assets	8 736	12.84	12.78	14.01	16.87	17.56	18.36	19.27	20.12
Monetary authorities	8 737	.74	.71	.84	1.06	1.13	.98	1.09	1.22
of which: Short-term	8 739	....	....	....	....	....	....	....	....
General government	8 740	12.10	12.07	13.17	15.81	16.43	17.38	18.17	18.90
of which: Short-term	8 742	....	....	....	....	....	....	....	....
Banks	8 743	....	....	....	....	....	....	....	....
of which: Short-term	8 745	....	....	....	....	....	....	....	....
Other sectors	8 746	....	....	....	....	....	....	....	....
of which: Short-term	8 748	....	....	....	....	....	....	....	....
Reserve assets	8 802	**63.55**	**58.70**	**61.77**	**70.75**	**77.36**	**74.36**	**98.26**	**115.72**
Monetary gold	8 812	26.52	26.97	33.35	40.58	42.03	46.61	55.59	70.01
Special drawing rights	8 811	.40	.49	.62	.76	.87	.88	.95	.99
Reserve position in the Fund	8 810	4.52	4.89	5.78	6.30	5.36	2.88	1.42	1.13
Foreign exchange	8 803	32.10	26.35	22.02	23.10	29.09	24.00	40.30	43.59
Other claims	8 813	....	....	....	....	....	....	....	....

Table 3 (Concluded). INTERNATIONAL INVESTMENT POSITION (End-period stocks), 2000–2007

(Billions of U.S. dollars)

	Code	2000	2001	2002	2003	2004	2005	2006	2007
LIABILITIES	8 995 D.	**2,250.41**	**2,245.20**	**2,607.31**	**3,525.66**	**4,349.16**	**4,667.45**	**6,123.18**	**7,383.21**
Direct investment in France	8 555	**536.81**	**463.39**	**564.77**	**776.03**	**957.42**	**999.82**	**1,294.64**	**1,616.53**
Equity capital and reinvested earnings	8 556	458.74	355.08	423.09	586.13	717.68	755.21	983.14	1,163.00
Claims on direct investors	8 557	....	....	....	....	....	....	....	....
Liabilities to direct investors	8 558	....	....	....	....	....	....	....	....
Other capital	8 580	78.07	108.31	141.68	189.89	239.74	244.61	311.50	453.52
Claims on direct investors	8 585	....	....	....	....	....	....	....	....
Liabilities to direct investors	8 590	....	....	....	....	....	....	....	....
Portfolio investment	8 652	**949.20**	**985.38**	**1,105.85**	**1,626.50**	**1,988.41**	**2,081.90**	**2,657.21**	**2,847.50**
Equity securities	8 660	502.10	415.97	345.13	490.90	593.86	690.45	973.00	1,002.35
Banks	8 663	38.43	43.62	43.00	69.33	76.75	90.57	131.91	129.82
Other sectors	8 664	463.67	372.35	302.13	421.58	517.11	599.89	841.09	872.53
Debt securities	8 669	447.11	569.41	760.73	1,135.60	1,394.55	1,391.44	1,684.21	1,845.14
Bonds and notes	8 670	389.69	508.77	684.59	1,025.27	1,257.38	1,246.64	1,543.77	1,684.86
Monetary authorities	8 671	....	....	....	....	....	....	....	....
General government	8 672	194.94	227.55	313.46	464.24	626.92	635.59	751.18	825.10
Banks	8 673	112.96	147.79	188.77	267.78	336.36	353.30	479.35	559.06
Other sectors	8 674	81.79	133.43	182.37	293.24	294.10	257.75	313.25	300.71
Money market instruments	8 680	57.41	60.63	76.14	110.34	137.16	144.81	140.43	160.28
Monetary authorities	8 681	....	....	....	....	....	....	....	....
General government	8 682	26.98	28.38	48.55	77.78	101.00	91.21	64.81	79.76
Banks	8 683	18.80	29.52	22.97	26.18	30.27	45.11	63.57	76.71
Other sectors	8 684	11.63	2.73	4.61	6.38	5.90	8.48	12.05	3.81
Financial derivatives	8 905	**98.26**	**104.79**	**112.35**	**147.80**	**186.04**	**173.89**	**248.85**	**338.89**
Monetary authorities	8 906	....	....	....	....	....	....	....	....
General government	8 907	....	....	....	....	....	....	....	....
Banks	8 908	....	....	....	....	....	....	....	....
Other sectors	8 909	98.26	104.79	112.35	147.80	186.04	173.89	248.85	338.89
Other investment	8 753	**666.14**	**691.64**	**824.34**	**975.34**	**1,217.29**	**1,411.84**	**1,922.49**	**2,580.30**
Trade credits	8 756	66.16	63.19	71.59	81.78	89.01	87.81	96.63	107.29
General government	8 757	....	....	....	....	....	....	....	....
of which: Short-term	8 759	....	....	....	....	....	....	....	....
Other sectors	8 760	66.16	63.19	71.59	81.78	89.01	87.81	96.63	107.29
of which: Short-term	8 762	....	....	....	....	....	....	....	....
Loans	8 764	599.99	628.46	752.75	893.56	1,128.28	1,324.04	1,825.86	2,473.01
Monetary authorities	8 765	2.33	3.35	2.21	4.40	6.17	2.87	31.52	130.65
of which: Use of Fund credit and loans from the Fund	8 766	....	....	....	....	....	....	....	....
of which: Short-term	8 768	*2.33*	*3.35*	*2.21*	*4.40*	*6.17*	*2.87*	*31.52*	*130.65*
General government	8 769	15.82	17.01	20.40	23.74	28.25	19.00	24.97	28.68
of which: Short-term	8 771	*8.84*	*9.17*	*11.20*	*13.29*	*17.61*	*10.64*	*15.63*	*18.02*
Banks	8 772	530.29	548.26	662.88	788.33	1,008.49	1,198.74	1,639.65	2,157.55
of which: Short-term	8 774	*476.70*	*492.21*	*554.47*	*619.07*	*786.95*	*909.84*	*1,222.91*	*1,559.28*
Other sectors	8 775	51.55	59.84	67.25	77.09	85.38	103.42	129.72	156.13
of which: Short-term	8 777	*40.29*	*48.30*	*52.26*	*64.70*	*73.48*	*92.41*	*104.77*	*120.37*
Currency and deposits	8 780	....	....	....	....	....	....	....	....
Monetary authorities	8 781	....	....	....	....	....	....	....	....
General government	8 782	....	....	....	....	....	....	....	....
Banks	8 783	....	....	....	....	....	....	....	....
Other sectors	8 784	....	....	....	....	....	....	....	....
Other liabilities	8 786	....	....	....	....	....	....	....	....
Monetary authorities	8 787	....	....	....	....	....	....	....	....
of which: Short-term	8 789	....	....	....	....	....	....	....	....
General government	8 790	....	....	....	....	....	....	....	....
of which: Short-term	8 792	....	....	....	....	....	....	....	....
Banks	8 793	....	....	....	....	....	....	....	....
of which: Short-term	8 795	....	....	....	....	....	....	....	....
Other sectors	8 796	....	....	....	....	....	....	....	....
of which: Short-term	8 798	....	....	....	....	....	....	....	....
NET INTERNATIONAL INVESTMENT POSITION	8 995	**118.63**	**197.86**	**179.14**	**156.19**	**192.20**	**202.52**	**153.39**	**374.74**
Conversion rates: euros per U.S. dollar (end of period)	0 104	1.0747	1.1347	.9536	.7918	.7342	.8477	.7593	.6793

Table 1. ANALYTIC PRESENTATION, 2000–2007

(Millions of U.S. dollars)

	Code	2000	2001	2002	2003	2004	2005	2006	2007
A. Current Account[1]	4 993 Z.	....	....	6	−119	186	9	−98	131
Goods: exports f.o.b.	2 100 ..	....	....	165	149	179	212	197	193
Goods: imports f.o.b.	3 100 ..	....	....	−1,128	−1,530	−1,440	−1,593	−1,612	−1,829
Balance on Goods	4 100 ..	....	....	*−962*	*−1,381*	*−1,260*	*−1,381*	*−1,415*	*−1,636*
Services: credit	2 200 ..	....	....	765	954	1,028	1,081	1,098	1,247
Services: debit	3 200 ..	....	....	−531	−599	−666	−737	−849	−811
Balance on Goods and Services	4 991 ..	....	....	*−728*	*−1,025*	*−899*	*−1,037*	*−1,166*	*−1,200*
Income: credit	2 300 ..	....	....	523	567	658	588	647	708
Income: debit	3 300 ..	....	....	−119	−102	−98	−67	−74	−107
Balance on Goods, Services, and Income	4 992 ..	....	....	*−324*	*−560*	*−339*	*−515*	*−593*	*−599*
Current transfers: credit	2 379 Z.	....	....	487	638	754	751	786	1,079
Current transfers: debit	3 379 ..	....	....	−157	−197	−229	−227	−290	−349
B. Capital Account[1]	4 994 Z.	....	....	−1	−1	−1	−1	....	....
Capital account: credit	2 994 Z.	....	....	....	....	....	....	....	....
Capital account: debit	3 994 ..	....	....	−1	−1	−1	−1	....	....
Total, Groups A Plus B	4 981 ..	....	....	*5*	*−120*	*185*	*8*	*−98*	*131*
C. Financial Account[1]	4 995 W.	....	....	66	104	−125	−32	−11	−330
Direct investment abroad	4 505 ..	....	....	−14	−6	−9	−16	−10	−14
Direct investment in French Polynesia	4 555 Z.	....	....	11	58	6	8	31	58
Portfolio investment assets	4 602 ..	....	....	39	−75	−20	−66	4	−9
Equity securities	4 610 ..	....	....	....	....	....	....	....	....
Debt securities	4 619 ..	....	....	39	−75	−20	−66	4	−9
Portfolio investment liabilities	4 652 Z.	....	....	....	....	....	....	....	....
Equity securities	4 660 ..	....	....	....	....	....	....	....	....
Debt securities	4 669 Z.	....	....	....	....	....	....	....	....
Financial derivatives	4 910 ..	....	....	....	....	....	....	....	....
Financial derivatives assets	4 900 ..	....	....	....	....	....	....	....	....
Financial derivatives liabilities	4 905 ..	....	....	....	....	....	....	....	....
Other investment assets	4 703 ..	....	....	−48	64	−227	−235	90	518
Monetary authorities	4 701 ..	....	....	60	15	54	76	338	733
General government	4 704 ..	....	....	....	....	....	....	....	....
Banks	4 705 ..	....	....	−2	141	−55	−212	−175	−74
Other sectors	4 728 ..	....	....	−107	−93	−227	−99	−73	−140
Other investment liabilities	4 753 W.	....	....	78	63	125	276	−125	−883
Monetary authorities	4 753 WA	....	....	....	....	....	....	....	....
General government	4 753 ZB	....	....	5	−4	−42	67	−387	−783
Banks	4 753 ZC	....	....	10	−19	180	224	235	−91
Other sectors	4 753 ZD	....	....	64	85	−14	−14	26	−9
Total, Groups A Through C	4 983 ..	....	....	*72*	*−16*	*60*	*−25*	*−108*	*−199*
D. Net Errors and Omissions	4 998 ..	....	....	−72	16	−60	25	108	199
Total, Groups A Through D	4 984 ..	....	....	....	....	....	....	....	....
E. Reserves and Related Items	4 802 A.	....	....	....	....	....	....	....	....
Reserve assets	4 802 ..	....	....	....	....	....	....	....	....
Use of Fund credit and loans	4 766 ..	....	....	....	....	....	....	....	....
Exceptional financing	4 920 ..	....	....	....	....	....	....	....	....
Conversion rates: CFP francs per U.S. dollar	0 101 ..	**129.5227**	**133.3544**	**126.7961**	**105.7320**	**96.1056**	**95.9570**	**95.1242**	**87.1882**

[1] Excludes components that have been classified in the categories of Group E.

Table 2. STANDARD PRESENTATION, 2000–2007

(Millions of U.S. dollars)

	Code	2000	2001	2002	2003	2004	2005	2006	2007
CURRENT ACCOUNT..................................	4 993 ..	....	....	6	−119	186	9	−98	131
A. GOODS..................................	4 100 ..	....	....	−962	−1,381	−1,260	−1,381	−1,415	−1,636
Credit..................................	2 100 ..	....	....	165	149	179	212	197	193
General merchandise: exports f.o.b.	2 110 ..	....	....	165	148	179	211	196	191
Goods for processing: exports f.o.b.	2 150 ..	....	....	....	....	....	....	....	....
Repairs on goods.	2 160 ..	....	....	....	....	....	....	....	....
Goods procured in ports by carriers.	2 170 ..	....	....	1	1	1	1	1	1
Nonmonetary gold.	2 180 ..	....	....	....	....	....	....	....	....
Debit..................................	3 100 ..	....	....	−1,128	−1,530	−1,440	−1,593	−1,612	−1,829
General merchandise: imports f.o.b.	3 110 ..	....	....	−1,126	−1,513	−1,423	−1,555	−1,549	−1,746
Goods for processing: imports f.o.b.	3 150 ..	....	....	....	....	....	....	....	....
Repairs on goods.	3 160 ..	....	....	−1	−2	....	....	....	....
Goods procured in ports by carriers.	3 170 ..	....	....	−1	−15	−17	−38	−63	−83
Nonmonetary gold.	3 180 ..	....	....	....	....	....	....	....	....
B. SERVICES..................................	4 200 ..	....	....	234	355	362	344	249	436
Total credit	2 200 ..	....	....	*765*	*954*	*1,028*	*1,081*	*1,098*	*1,247*
Total debit	3 200 ..	....	....	*−531*	*−599*	*−666*	*−737*	*−849*	*−811*
Transportation services, credit.	2 205 ..	....	....	115	186	226	246	233	291
Passenger	2 850 ..	....	....	*99*	*171*	*214*	*229*	*217*	*267*
Freight	2 851 ..	....	....	*17*	*16*	*12*	*17*	*16*	*24*
Other	2 852 ..	....	....	....	....	....	....	....	....
Sea transport, passenger.	2 207 ..	....	....	....	....	....	....	....	....
Sea transport, freight.	2 208 ..	....	....	17	16	12	17	16	24
Sea transport, other.	2 209 ..	....	....	....	....	....	....	....	....
Air transport, passenger.	2 211 ..	....	....	99	171	214	229	217	267
Air transport, freight.	2 212 ..	....	....	....	....	....	....	....	....
Air transport, other.	2 213 ..	....	....	....	....	....	....	....	....
Other transport, passenger.	2 215 ..	....	....	....	....	....	....	....	....
Other transport, freight.	2 216 ..	....	....	....	....	....	....	....	....
Other transport, other.	2 217 ..	....	....	....	....	....	....	....	....
Transportation services, debit.	3 205 ..	....	....	−163	−180	−198	−203	−334	−346
Passenger	3 850 ..	....	....	*−84*	*−99*	*−114*	*−118*	*−246*	*−257*
Freight	3 851 ..	....	....	*−79*	*−81*	*−84*	*−86*	*−88*	*−89*
Other	3 852 ..	....	....	....	....	....	....	....	....
Sea transport, passenger.	3 207 ..	....	....	....	....	....	....	....	....
Sea transport, freight.	3 208 ..	....	....	−79	−81	−84	−86	−88	−89
Sea transport, other.	3 209 ..	....	....	....	....	....	....	....	....
Air transport, passenger.	3 211 ..	....	....	−84	−99	−114	−118	−246	−257
Air transport, freight.	3 212 ..	....	....	....	....	....	....	....	....
Air transport, other.	3 213 ..	....	....	....	....	....	....	....	....
Other transport, passenger.	3 215 ..	....	....	....	....	....	....	....	....
Other transport, freight.	3 216 ..	....	....	....	....	....	....	....	....
Other transport, other.	3 217 ..	....	....	....	....	....	....	....	....
Travel, credit..................................	2 236 ..	....	....	372	480	523	530	564	609
Business travel.	2 237 ..	....	....	....	....	....	....	....	....
Personal travel.	2 240 ..	....	....	372	480	523	530	564	609
Travel, debit..................................	3 236 ..	....	....	−180	−236	−311	−312	−314	−343
Business travel.	3 237 ..	....	....	....	....	....	....	....	....
Personal travel.	3 240 ..	....	....	−180	−236	−311	−312	−314	−343
Other services, credit.	2 200 BA	....	....	278	288	279	304	301	347
Communications.	2 245 ..	....	....	3	4	16	19	19	11
Construction.	2 249 ..	....	....	13	2	4	3	....	....
Insurance.	2 253 ..	....	....	2	2	4	4	9	12
Financial.	2 260 ..	....	....	1	1	6	15	4	6
Computer and information.	2 262 ..	....	....	....	....	....	....	....	....
Royalties and licence fees.	2 266 ..	....	....	....	1	1	1	....	....
Other business services.	2 268 ..	....	....	134	125	104	134	137	167
Personal, cultural, and recreational.	2 287 ..	....	....	16	8	5	4	4	9
Government, n.i.e.	2 291 ..	....	....	109	146	139	124	128	142
Other services, debit.	3 200 BA	....	....	−188	−184	−158	−222	−201	−121
Communications.	3 245 ..	....	....	−11	−4	−7	−9	−8	−6
Construction.	3 249 ..	....	....	−15	−10	−8	−6	....	−3
Insurance.	3 253 ..	....	....	−15	−20	−17	−22	−21	−10
Financial.	3 260 ..	....	....	−1	−1	−6	−5	−5	−4
Computer and information.	3 262 ..	....	....	....	....	−2	−1	....	....
Royalties and licence fees.	3 266 ..	....	....	−2	−2	−2	−1	−2	−1
Other business services.	3 268 ..	....	....	−135	−138	−106	−166	−154	−91
Personal, cultural, and recreational.	3 287 ..	....	....	−8	−7	−10	−10	−9	−6
Government, n.i.e.	3 291 ..	....	....	−1	−1	−1	−1	−1	−1

Table 2 (Continued). STANDARD PRESENTATION, 2000–2007

(Millions of U.S. dollars)

	Code	2000	2001	2002	2003	2004	2005	2006	2007
C. INCOME	4 300	....	....	**404**	**465**	**560**	**521**	**573**	**601**
Total credit	2 300	....	....	*523*	*567*	*658*	*588*	*647*	*708*
Total debit	3 300	....	....	*−119*	*−102*	*−98*	*−67*	*−74*	*−107*
Compensation of employees, credit	2 310	....	....	**398**	**496**	**583**	**546**	**586**	**652**
Compensation of employees, debit	3 310	....	....	**−38**	**−25**	**−14**	**−14**	**−15**	**−16**
Investment income, credit	2 320	....	....	**125**	**71**	**74**	**42**	**60**	**56**
Direct investment income	2 330	....	....	1	....	....	1	....	2
Dividends and distributed branch profits	2 332	....	....	1	....	....	1	....	2
Reinvested earnings anc undistributed branch profits	2 333	....	....	....	....	....	....	....	....
Income on debt (interest)	2 334	....	....	....	....	....	....	....	....
Portfolio investment income	2 339	....	....	74	37	44	23	22	15
Income on equity	2 340	....	....	....	....	....	....	....	....
Income on bonds and notes	2 350	....	....	74	37	44	23	22	15
Income on money market instruments	2 360	....	....	....	....	....	....	....	....
Other investment income	2 370	....	....	50	34	30	19	38	39
Investment income, debit	3 320	....	....	**−81**	**−78**	**−84**	**−52**	**−59**	**−91**
Direct investment income	3 330	....	....	−2	−2	−2	−2	−5	−8
Dividends and distributed branch profits	3 332	....	....	−2	−2	−2	−2	−5	−8
Reinvested earnings and undistributed branch profits	3 333	....	....	....	....	....	....	....	....
Income on debt (interest)	3 334	....	....	....	....	....	....	....	....
Portfolio investment income	3 339	....	....	−5	−3	−21	−2	−1	−26
Income on equity	3 340	....	....	....	....	....	....	....	....
Income on bonds and notes	3 350	....	....	−5	−3	−21	−2	−1	−26
Income on money market instruments	3 360	....	....	....	....	....	....	....	....
Other investment income	3 370	....	....	−74	−73	−61	−49	−53	−58
D. CURRENT TRANSFERS	4 379	....	....	**330**	**441**	**524**	**524**	**496**	**730**
Credit	2 379	....	....	**487**	**638**	**754**	**751**	**786**	**1,079**
General government	2 380	....	....	449	586	670	669	712	879
Other sectors	2 390	....	....	39	52	84	83	73	200
Workers' remittances	2 391	....	....	10	12	15	11	14	14
Other current transfers	2 392	....	....	28	40	69	71	59	186
Debit	3 379	....	....	**−157**	**−197**	**−229**	**−227**	**−290**	**−349**
General government	3 380	....	....	−38	−40	−50	−64	−136	−158
Other sectors	3 390	....	....	−119	−156	−179	−163	−154	−191
Workers' remittances	3 391	....	....	−24	−27	−32	−33	−36	−40
Other current transfers	3 392	....	....	−95	−130	−147	−130	−118	−152
CAPITAL AND FINANCIAL ACCOUNT	4 996	....	....	**66**	**103**	**−126**	**−33**	**−11**	**−330**
CAPITAL ACCOUNT	4 994	....	....	**−1**	**−1**	**−1**	**−1**	....	....
Total credit	2 994	....	....	....	....	....	....	....	....
Total debit	3 994	....	....	*−1*	*−1*	*−1*	*−1*	....	....
Capital transfers, credit	2 400	....	....	....	....	....	....	....	....
General government	2 401	....	....	....	....	....	....	....	....
Debt forgiveness	2 402	....	....	....	....	....	....	....	....
Other capital transfers	2 410	....	....	....	....	....	....	....	....
Other sectors	2 430	....	....	....	....	....	....	....	....
Migrants' transfers	2 431	....	....	....	....	....	....	....	....
Debt forgiveness	2 432	....	....	....	....	....	....	....	....
Other capital transfers	2 440	....	....	....	....	....	....	....	....
Capital transfers, debit	3 400	....	....	**−1**	**−1**	**−1**	**−1**	....	....
General government	3 401	....	....	....	....	....	....	....	....
Debt forgiveness	3 402	....	....	....	....	....	....	....	....
Other capital transfers	3 410	....	....	....	....	....	....	....	....
Other sectors	3 430	....	....	−1	−1	−1	−1	....	....
Migrants' transfers	3 431	....	....	....	....	....	....	....	....
Debt forgiveness	3 432	....	....	....	....	....	....	....	....
Other capital transfers	3 440	....	....	−1	−1	−1	−1	....	....
Nonproduced nonfinancial assets, credit	2 480	....	....	....	....	....	....	....	....
Nonproduced nonfinancial assets, debit	3 480	....	....	....	....	....	....	....	....

Table 2 (Continued). STANDARD PRESENTATION, 2000–2007

(Millions of U.S. dollars)

	Code	2000	2001	2002	2003	2004	2005	2006	2007
FINANCIAL ACCOUNT	4 995	....	....	66	104	−125	−32	−11	−330
A. DIRECT INVESTMENT	4 500	....	....	−3	53	−3	−8	20	45
Direct investment abroad	4 505	....	....	−14	−6	−9	−16	−10	−14
Equity capital	4 510	....	....	−14	−7	−13	−16	−10	−14
Claims on affiliated enterprises	4 515	....	....	−14	−7	−13	−16	−10	−14
Liabilities to affiliated enterprises	4 520	....	....	....	....	....	....	....	....
Reinvested earnings	4 525	....	....	....	....	....	....	....	....
Other capital	4 530	....	....	....	2	3	....	....	1
Claims on affiliated enterprises	4 535	....	....	....	2	3	....	....	1
Liabilities to affiliated enterprises	4 540	....	....	....	....	....	....	....	....
Direct investment in French Polynesia	4 555	....	....	11	58	6	8	31	58
Equity capital	4 560	....	....	11	58	8	9	31	55
Claims on direct investors	4 565	....	....	....	....	....	....	....	....
Liabilities to direct investors	4 570	....	....	11	58	8	9	31	55
Reinvested earnings	4 575	....	....	....	....	....	....	....	....
Other capital	4 580	....	....	....	....	−2	−1	....	3
Claims on direct investors	4 585	....	....	....	....	....	....	....	....
Liabilities to direct investors	4 590	....	....	....	....	−2	−1	....	3
B. PORTFOLIO INVESTMENT	4 600	....	....	39	−75	−20	−66	4	−9
Assets	4 602	....	....	39	−75	−20	−66	4	−9
Equity securities	4 610	....	....	....	....	....	....	....	....
Monetary authorities	4 611	....	....	....	....	....	....	....	....
General government	4 612	....	....	....	....	....	....	....	....
Banks	4 613	....	....	....	....	....	....	....	....
Other sectors	4 614	....	....	....	....	....	....	....	....
Debt securities	4 619	....	....	39	−75	−20	−66	4	−9
Bonds and notes	4 620	....	....	39	−75	−20	−66	4	−9
Monetary authorities	4 621	....	....	....	....	....	....	....	....
General government	4 622	....	....	....	....	....	....	....	....
Banks	4 623	....	....	....	....	....	....	....	....
Other sectors	4 624	....	....	39	−75	−20	−66	4	−9
Money market instruments	4 630	....	....	....	....	....	....	....	....
Monetary authorities	4 631	....	....	....	....	....	....	....	....
General government	4 632	....	....	....	....	....	....	....	....
Banks	4 633	....	....	....	....	....	....	....	....
Other sectors	4 634	....	....	....	....	....	....	....	....
Liabilities	4 652	....	....	....	....	....	....	....	....
Equity securities	4 660	....	....	....	....	....	....	....	....
Banks	4 663	....	....	....	....	....	....	....	....
Other sectors	4 664	....	....	....	....	....	....	....	....
Debt securities	4 669	....	....	....	....	....	....	....	....
Bonds and notes	4 670	....	....	....	....	....	....	....	....
Monetary authorities	4 671	....	....	....	....	....	....	....	....
General government	4 672	....	....	....	....	....	....	....	....
Banks	4 673	....	....	....	....	....	....	....	....
Other sectors	4 674	....	....	....	....	....	....	....	....
Money market instruments	4 680	....	....	....	....	....	....	....	....
Monetary authorities	4 681	....	....	....	....	....	....	....	....
General government	4 682	....	....	....	....	....	....	....	....
Banks	4 683	....	....	....	....	....	....	....	....
Other sectors	4 684	....	....	....	....	....	....	....	....
C. FINANCIAL DERIVATIVES	4 910	....	....	....	....	....	....	....	....
Monetary authorities	4 911	....	....	....	....	....	....	....	....
General government	4 912	....	....	....	....	....	....	....	....
Banks	4 913	....	....	....	....	....	....	....	....
Other sectors	4 914	....	....	....	....	....	....	....	....
Assets	4 900	....	....	....	....	....	....	....	....
Monetary authorities	4 901	....	....	....	....	....	....	....	....
General government	4 902	....	....	....	....	....	....	....	....
Banks	4 903	....	....	....	....	....	....	....	....
Other sectors	4 904	....	....	....	....	....	....	....	....
Liabilities	4 905	....	....	....	....	....	....	....	....
Monetary authorities	4 906	....	....	....	....	....	....	....	....
General government	4 907	....	....	....	....	....	....	....	....
Banks	4 908	....	....	....	....	....	....	....	....
Other sectors	4 909	....	....	....	....	....	....	....	....

Table 2 (Concluded). STANDARD PRESENTATION, 2000–2007

(Millions of U.S. dollars)

	Code	2000	2001	2002	2003	2004	2005	2006	2007
D. OTHER INVESTMENT	4 700 ..	....	....	**30**	**127**	**−103**	**41**	**−35**	**−365**
Assets	4 703 ..	....	....	**−48**	**64**	**−227**	**−235**	**90**	**518**
Trade credits	4 706 ..	....	....	....	....	....	....	....	....
General government	4 707 ..	....	....	....	....	....	....	....	....
of which: Short-term	4 709 ..	....	....	....	....	....	....	....	....
Other sectors	4 710 ..	....	....	....	....	....	....	....	....
of which: Short-term	4 712 ..	....	....	....	....	....	....	....	....
Loans	4 714 ..	....	....	−48	64	−227	−235	90	518
Monetary authorities	4 715 ..	....	....	60	15	54	76	338	733
of which: Short-term	4 718 ..	....	....	*60*	*15*	*54*	*76*	*338*	*733*
General government	4 719 ..	....	....	....	....	....	....	....	....
of which: Short-term	4 721 ..	....	....	....	....	....	....	....	....
Banks	4 722 ..	....	....	−2	141	−55	−212	−175	−74
of which: Short-term	4 724 ..	....	....	*−2*	*141*	*−55*	*−212*	*−175*	*−74*
Other sectors	4 725 ..	....	....	−107	−93	−227	−99	−73	−140
of which: Short-term	4 727 ..	....	....	*−107*	*−93*	*−227*	*−99*	*−73*	*−140*
Currency and deposits	4 730 ..	....	....	....	....	....	....	....	....
Monetary authorities	4 731 ..	....	....	....	....	....	....	....	....
General government	4 732 ..	....	....	....	....	....	....	....	....
Banks	4 733 ..	....	....	....	....	....	....	....	....
Other sectors	4 734 ..	....	....	....	....	....	....	....	....
Other assets	4 736 ..	....	....	....	....	....	....	....	....
Monetary authorities	4 737 ..	....	....	....	....	....	....	....	....
of which: Short-term	4 739 ..	....	....	....	....	....	....	....	....
General government	4 740 ..	....	....	....	....	....	....	....	....
of which: Short-term	4 742 ..	....	....	....	....	....	....	....	....
Banks	4 743 ..	....	....	....	....	....	....	....	....
of which: Short-term	4 745 ..	....	....	....	....	....	....	....	....
Other sectors	4 746 ..	....	....	....	....	....	....	....	....
of which: Short-term	4 748 ..	....	....	....	....	....	....	....	....
Liabilities	4 753 ..	....	....	**78**	**63**	**125**	**276**	**−125**	**−883**
Trade credits	4 756 ..	....	....	....	....	....	....	....	....
General government	4 757 ..	....	....	....	....	....	....	....	....
of which: Short-term	4 759 ..	....	....	....	....	....	....	....	....
Other sectors	4 760 ..	....	....	....	....	....	....	....	....
of which: Short-term	4 762 ..	....	....	....	....	....	....	....	....
Loans	4 764 ..	....	....	78	63	125	276	−125	−883
Monetary authorities	4 765 ..	....	....	....	....	....	....	....	....
of which: Use of Fund credit and loans from the Fund	4 766 ..	....	....	....	....	....	....	....	....
of which: Short-term	4 768 ..	....	....	....	....	....	....	....	....
General government	4 769 ..	....	....	5	−4	−42	67	−387	−783
of which: Short-term	4 771 ..	....	....	*5*	*−4*	*−42*	*67*	*−387*	*−783*
Banks	4 772 ..	....	....	10	−19	180	224	235	−91
of which: Short-term	4 774 ..	....	....	*10*	*−19*	*180*	*224*	*235*	*−91*
Other sectors	4 775 ..	....	....	64	85	−14	−14	26	−9
of which: Short-term	4 777 ..	....	....	*64*	*85*	*−14*	*−14*	*26*	*−9*
Currency and deposits	4 780 ..	....	....	....	....	....	....	....	....
Monetary authorities	4 781 ..	....	....	....	....	....	....	....	....
General government	4 782 ..	....	....	....	....	....	....	....	....
Banks	4 783 ..	....	....	....	....	....	....	....	....
Other sectors	4 784 ..	....	....	....	....	....	....	....	....
Other liabilities	4 786 ..	....	....	....	....	....	....	....	....
Monetary authorities	4 787 ..	....	....	....	....	....	....	....	....
of which: Short-term	4 789 ..	....	....	....	....	....	....	....	....
General government	4 790 ..	....	....	....	....	....	....	....	....
of which: Short-term	4 792 ..	....	....	....	....	....	....	....	....
Banks	4 793 ..	....	....	....	....	....	....	....	....
of which: Short-term	4 795 ..	....	....	....	....	....	....	....	....
Other sectors	4 796 ..	....	....	....	....	....	....	....	....
of which: Short-term	4 798 ..	....	....	....	....	....	....	....	....
E. RESERVE ASSETS	4 802 ..	....	....	....	....	....	....	....	....
Monetary gold	4 812 ..	....	....	....	....	....	....	....	....
Special drawing rights	4 811 ..	....	....	....	....	....	....	....	....
Reserve position in the Fund	4 810 ..	....	....	....	....	....	....	....	....
Foreign exchange	4 803 ..	....	....	....	....	....	....	....	....
Other claims	4 813 ..	....	....	....	....	....	....	....	....
NET ERRORS AND OMISSIONS	4 998 ..	....	....	**−72**	**16**	**−60**	**25**	**108**	**199**

Table 1. ANALYTIC PRESENTATION, 2000–2007

(Millions of U.S. dollars)

	Code	2000	2001	2002	2003	2004	2005	2006	2007
A. Current Account[1]	4 993 Z.	....	....	−107	−37	257	−112	−533	−445
Goods: exports f.o.b.	2 100 ..	....	....	461	783	1,009	1,090	1,194	1,925
Goods: imports f.o.b.	3 100 ..	....	....	−1,070	−1,408	−1,473	−1,641	−1,933	−2,593
Balance on Goods	4 100 ..	....	....	*−609*	*−625*	*−464*	*−551*	*−739*	*−667*
Services: credit	2 200 ..	....	....	349	429	487	380	473	543
Services: debit	3 200 ..	....	....	−418	−538	−599	−841	−1,118	−1,311
Balance on Goods and Services	4 991 ..	....	....	*−677*	*−735*	*−576*	*−1,012*	*−1,383*	*−1,435*
Income: credit	2 300 ..	....	....	360	478	529	596	599	695
Income: debit	3 300 ..	....	....	−90	−140	−116	−114	−178	−198
Balance on Goods, Services, and Income	4 992 ..	....	....	*−407*	*−396*	*−163*	*−530*	*−962*	*−938*
Current transfers: credit	2 379 Z.	....	....	414	543	609	626	648	763
Current transfers: debit	3 379 ..	....	....	−114	−183	−189	−209	−220	−270
B. Capital Account[1]	4 994 Z.	....	....	−2	1	6	9	4	4
Capital account: credit	2 994 Z.	....	....	4	7	9	11	11	14
Capital account: debit	3 994 ..	....	....	−7	−5	−3	−2	−7	−10
Total, Groups A Plus B	4 981 ..	....	....	*−109*	*−36*	*262*	*−103*	*−530*	*−441*
C. Financial Account[1]	4 995 W.	....	....	175	124	−196	19	469	299
Direct investment abroad	4 505 ..	....	....	−4	−14	−11	−31	−31	−7
Direct investment in New Caledonia	4 555 Z.	....	....	59	116	27	−7	749	659
Portfolio investment assets	4 602 ..	....	....	46	8	135	241	−44	−143
Equity securities	4 610 ..	....	....	....	....	....	....	....	....
Debt securities	4 619 ..	....	....	46	8	135	241	−44	−143
Portfolio investment liabilities	4 652 Z.	....	....	....	....	....	....	....	....
Equity securities	4 660 ..	....	....	....	....	....	....	....	....
Debt securities	4 669 Z.	....	....	....	....	....	....	....	....
Financial derivatives	4 910 ..	....	....	....	....	....	....	....	....
Financial derivatives assets	4 900 ..	....	....	....	....	....	....	....	....
Financial derivatives liabilities	4 905 ..	....	....	....	....	....	....	....	....
Other investment assets	4 703 ..	....	....	−65	8	−549	−379	−204	−182
Monetary authorities	4 701 ..	....	....	44	....	−42	−41	−70	−74
General government	4 704 ..	....	....	....	....	....	....	....	....
Banks	4 705 ..	....	....	−6	−15	−328	−230	1	−26
Other sectors	4 728 ..	....	....	−103	22	−179	−109	−135	−82
Other investment liabilities	4 753 W.	....	....	138	6	201	194	−1	−28
Monetary authorities	4 753 WA	....	....	....	....	....	....	....	....
General government	4 753 ZB	....	....	52	6	−49	−33	−32	−43
Banks	4 753 ZC	....	....	80	−27	186	213	28	211
Other sectors	4 753 ZD	....	....	7	27	64	14	3	−197
Total, Groups A Through C	4 983 ..	....	....	*66*	*89*	*67*	*−85*	*−61*	*−141*
D. Net Errors and Omissions	4 998 ..	....	....	−66	−89	−67	85	61	141
Total, Groups A Through D	4 984 ..	....	....	....	....	....	....	....	....
E. Reserves and Related Items	4 802 A.	....	....	....	....	....	....	....	....
Reserve assets	4 802 ..	....	....	....	....	....	....	....	....
Use of Fund credit and loans	4 766 ..	....	....	....	....	....	....	....	....
Exceptional financing	4 920 ..	....	....	....	....	....	....	....	....
Conversion rates: CFP francs per U.S.dollar	0 101 ..	129.5227	133.3544	126.7961	105.7320	96.1056	95.9570	95.1242	87.1882

[1] Excludes components that have been classified in the categories of Group E.

Table 2. STANDARD PRESENTATION, 2000–2007

(Millions of U.S. dollars)

	Code	2000	2001	2002	2003	2004	2005	2006	2007
CURRENT ACCOUNT	4 993	....	....	−107	−37	257	−112	−533	−445
A. GOODS	4 100	....	....	−609	−625	−464	−551	−739	−667
Credit	2 100	....	....	461	783	1,009	1,090	1,194	1,925
General merchandise: exports f.o.b.	2 110	....	....	458	780	1,008	1,088	1,191	1,915
Goods for processing: exports f.o.b.	2 150	....	....	....	....	....	....	....	....
Repairs on goods	2 160	....	....	....	....	....	....	....	....
Goods procured in ports by carriers	2 170	....	....	3	2	1	1	2	10
Nonmonetary gold	2 180	....	....	....	....	....	....	....	....
Debit	3 100	....	....	−1,070	−1,408	−1,473	−1,641	−1,933	−2,593
General merchandise: imports f.o.b.	3 110	....	....	−1,066	−1,401	−1,465	−1,625	−1,910	−2,568
Goods for processing: imports f.o.b.	3 150	....	....	....	....	....	....	....	....
Repairs on goods	3 160	....	....	−2	....	....	−2	....	....
Goods procured in ports by carriers	3 170	....	....	−2	−6	−8	−14	−22	−25
Nonmonetary gold	3 180	....	....	....	....	....	....	....	....
B. SERVICES	4 200	....	....	−69	−110	−112	−461	−644	−767
Total credit	2 200	....	....	*349*	*429*	*487*	*380*	*473*	*543*
Total debit	3 200	....	....	*−418*	*−538*	*−599*	*−841*	*−1,118*	*−1,311*
Transportation services, credit	2 205	....	....	38	66	65	66	78	99
Passenger	2 850	....	....	....	....	....	....	....	....
Freight	2 851	....	....	*38*	*66*	*65*	*66*	*78*	*99*
Other	2 852	....	....	....	....	....	....	....	....
Sea transport, passenger	2 207	....	....	....	....	....	....	....	....
Sea transport, freight	2 208	....	....	15	21	28	17	27	42
Sea transport, other	2 209	....	....	....	....	....	....	....	....
Air transport, passenger	2 211	....	....	....	....	....	....	....	....
Air transport, freight	2 212	....	....	23	45	37	49	51	58
Air transport, other	2 213	....	....	....	....	....	....	....	....
Other transport, passenger	2 215	....	....	....	....	....	....	....	....
Other transport, freight	2 216	....	....	....	....	....	....	....	....
Other transport, other	2 217	....	....	....	....	....	....	....	....
Transportation services, debit	3 205	....	....	−118	−151	−167	−212	−257	−326
Passenger	3 850	....	....	....	....	....	....	....	....
Freight	3 851	....	....	*−118*	*−151*	*−167*	*−212*	*−257*	*−326*
Other	3 852	....	....	....	....	....	....	....	....
Sea transport, passenger	3 207	....	....	....	....	....	....	....	....
Sea transport, freight	3 208	....	....	−51	−62	−72	−106	−141	−184
Sea transport, other	3 209	....	....	....	....	....	....	....	....
Air transport, passenger	3 211	....	....	....	....	....	....	....	....
Air transport, freight	3 212	....	....	−67	−89	−94	−105	−116	−142
Air transport, other	3 213	....	....	....	....	....	....	....	....
Other transport, passenger	3 215	....	....	....	....	....	....	....	....
Other transport, freight	3 216	....	....	....	....	....	....	....	....
Other transport, other	3 217	....	....	....	....	....	....	....	....
Travel, credit	2 236	....	....	156	196	241	149	169	197
Business travel	2 237	....	....	....	....	....	....	....	....
Personal travel	2 240	....	....	156	196	241	149	169	197
Travel, debit	3 236	....	....	−104	−128	−167	−122	−129	−149
Business travel	3 237	....	....	....	....	....	....	....	....
Personal travel	3 240	....	....	−104	−128	−167	−122	−129	−149
Other services, credit	2 200 BA	....	....	156	166	181	166	226	247
Communications	2 245	....	....	4	5	6	1	5	2
Construction	2 249	....	....	24	27	29	5	25	16
Insurance	2 253	....	....	1	1	2	1	1	6
Financial	2 260	....	....	....	....	2	1	....	4
Computer and information	2 262	....	....	1	....	....	....	....	....
Royalties and licence fees	2 266	....	....	....	....	....	....	1	....
Other business services	2 268	....	....	38	35	40	40	66	69
Personal, cultural, and recreational	2 287	....	....	1	2	2	1	5	15
Government, n.i.e.	2 291	....	....	87	95	100	117	121	135
Other services, debit	3 200 BA	....	....	−196	−259	−265	−507	−732	−835
Communications	3 245	....	....	−3	−8	−9	−12	−22	−9
Construction	3 249	....	....	−43	−33	−11	−93	−118	−322
Insurance	3 253	....	....	−14	−22	−26	−20	−18	−23
Financial	3 260	....	....	−2	−2	−3	−1	....	−2
Computer and information	3 262	....	....	−7	−6	−5	−4	−4	−7
Royalties and licence fees	3 266	....	....	−2	−3	−3	−2	−2	−3
Other business services	3 268	....	....	−119	−177	−198	−336	−526	−413
Personal, cultural, and recreational	3 287	....	....	−6	−8	−11	−38	−41	−56
Government, n.i.e.	3 291	....	....	....	....	−1	−1	−1	−1

Table 2 (Continued). STANDARD PRESENTATION, 2000–2007

(Millions of U.S. dollars)

	Code	2000	2001	2002	2003	2004	2005	2006	2007
C. INCOME	4 300	....	....	**270**	**338**	**413**	**482**	**422**	**497**
Total credit	2 300	....	....	*360*	*478*	*529*	*596*	*599*	*695*
Total debit	3 300	....	....	*–90*	*–140*	*–116*	*–114*	*–178*	*–198*
Compensation of employees, credit	2 310	....	....	**331**	**444**	**485**	**507**	**532**	**582**
Compensation of employees, debit	3 310	....	....	**–13**	**–15**	**–15**	**–17**	**–32**	**–37**
Investment income, credit	2 320	....	....	**29**	**34**	**44**	**89**	**67**	**113**
Direct investment income	2 330	....	....	2	....	1	3	6	32
Dividends and distributed branch profits	2 332	....	....	2	....	1	3	6	32
Reinvested earnings and undistributed branch profits	2 333	....	....	....	....	....	....	....	....
Income on debt (interest)	2 334	....	....	....	....	....	....	....	....
Portfolio investment income	2 339	....	....	11	17	24	61	33	43
Income on equity	2 340	....	....	....	....	....	....	....	....
Income on bonds and notes	2 350	....	....	11	17	24	61	33	43
Income on money market instruments	2 360	....	....	....	....	....	....	....	....
Other investment income	2 370	....	....	17	18	19	25	27	38
Investment income, debit	3 320	....	....	**–78**	**–125**	**–102**	**–96**	**–146**	**–161**
Direct investment income	3 330	....	....	–20	–7	–3	–42	–85	–66
Dividends and distributed branch profits	3 332	....	....	–20	–7	–3	–42	–85	–66
Reinvested earnings and undistributed branch profits	3 333	....	....	....	....	....	....	....	....
Income on debt (interest)	3 334	....	....	....	....	....	....	....	....
Portfolio investment income	3 339	....	....	–13	–34	–43	–3	–2	–8
Income on equity	3 340	....	....	....	....	....	....	....	....
Income on bonds and notes	3 350	....	....	–13	–34	–43	–3	–2	–8
Income on money market instruments	3 360	....	....	....	....	....	....	....	....
Other investment income	3 370	....	....	–45	–85	–56	–52	–59	–87
D. CURRENT TRANSFERS	4 379	....	....	**300**	**359**	**420**	**417**	**428**	**493**
Credit	2 379	....	....	**414**	**543**	**609**	**626**	**648**	**763**
General government	2 380	....	....	363	483	570	585	596	703
Other sectors	2 390	....	....	51	60	39	41	52	61
Workers' remittances	2 391	....	....	2	5	8	5	4	3
Other current transfers	2 392	....	....	50	55	31	36	48	57
Debit	3 379	....	....	**–114**	**–183**	**–189**	**–209**	**–220**	**–270**
General government	3 380	....	....	–84	–130	–152	–155	–150	–195
Other sectors	3 390	....	....	–30	–54	–37	–55	–70	–76
Workers' remittances	3 391	....	....	–7	–6	–7	–10	–18	–18
Other current transfers	3 392	....	....	–24	–48	–30	–44	–51	–57
CAPITAL AND FINANCIAL ACCOUNT	4 996	....	....	**173**	**126**	**–190**	**28**	**472**	**303**
CAPITAL ACCOUNT	4 994	....	....	**–2**	**1**	**6**	**9**	**4**	**4**
Total credit	2 994	....	....	*4*	*7*	*9*	*11*	*11*	*14*
Total debit	3 994	....	....	*–7*	*–5*	*–3*	*–2*	*–7*	*–10*
Capital transfers, credit	2 400	....	....	**4**	**7**	**9**	**11**	**11**	**14**
General government	2 401	....	....	....	....	....	....	....	....
Debt forgiveness	2 402	....	....	....	....	....	....	....	....
Other capital transfers	2 410	....	....	....	....	....	....	....	....
Other sectors	2 430	....	....	4	7	9	11	11	14
Migrants' transfers	2 431	....	....	....	....	....	....	....	....
Debt forgiveness	2 432	....	....	....	....	....	....	....	....
Other capital transfers	2 440	....	....	4	7	9	11	11	14
Capital transfers, debit	3 400	....	....	**–7**	**–5**	**–3**	**–2**	**–7**	**–10**
General government	3 401	....	....	....	....	....	....	....	....
Debt forgiveness	3 402	....	....	....	....	....	....	....	....
Other capital transfers	3 410	....	....	....	....	....	....	....	....
Other sectors	3 430	....	....	–7	–5	–3	–2	–7	–10
Migrants' transfers	3 431	....	....	....	....	....	....	....	....
Debt forgiveness	3 432	....	....	....	....	....	....	....	....
Other capital transfers	3 440	....	....	–7	–5	–3	–2	–7	–10
Nonproduced nonfinancial assets, credit	2 480	....	....	....	....	....	....	....	....
Nonproduced nonfinancial assets, debit	3 480	....	....	....	....	....	....	....	....

Table 2 (Continued). STANDARD PRESENTATION, 2000–2007

(Millions of U.S. dollars)

	Code	2000	2001	2002	2003	2004	2005	2006	2007
FINANCIAL ACCOUNT	4 995	....	....	175	124	−196	19	469	299
A. DIRECT INVESTMENT	4 500	....	....	55	102	16	−37	719	653
Direct investment abroad	4 505	....	....	−4	−14	−11	−31	−31	−7
Equity capital	4 510	....	....	−3	−1	−11	−29	−33	−3
Claims on affiliated enterprises	4 515	....	....	−3	−1	−11	−29	−33	−3
Liabilities to affiliated enterprises	4 520	....	....	....	....	....	....	....	....
Reinvested earnings	4 525	....	....	....	....	....	....	....	....
Other capital	4 530	....	....	−1	−13	....	−1	3	−4
Claims on affiliated enterprises	4 535	....	....	−1	−13	....	−1	3	−4
Liabilities to affiliated enterprises	4 540	....	....	....	....	....	....	....	....
Direct investment in New Caledonia	4 555	....	....	59	116	27	−7	749	659
Equity capital	4 560	....	....	39	1	36	14	80	−2
Claims on direct investors	4 565	....	....	....	....	....	....	....	....
Liabilities to direct investors	4 570	....	....	39	1	36	14	80	−2
Reinvested earnings	4 575	....	....	....	....	....	....	....	....
Other capital	4 580	....	....	20	115	−8	−20	669	661
Claims on direct investors	4 585	....	....	....	....	....	....	....	....
Liabilities to direct investors	4 590	....	....	20	115	−8	−20	669	661
B. PORTFOLIO INVESTMENT	4 600	....	....	46	8	135	241	−44	−143
Assets	4 602	....	....	46	8	135	241	−44	−143
Equity securities	4 610	....	....	....	....	....	....	....	....
Monetary authorities	4 611	....	....	....	....	....	....	....	....
General government	4 612	....	....	....	....	....	....	....	....
Banks	4 613	....	....	....	....	....	....	....	....
Other sectors	4 614	....	....	....	....	....	....	....	....
Debt securities	4 619	....	....	46	8	135	241	−44	−143
Bonds and notes	4 620	....	....	46	8	135	241	−44	−143
Monetary authorities	4 621	....	....	....	....	....	....	....	....
General government	4 622	....	....	....	....	....	....	....	....
Banks	4 623	....	....	....	....	....	....	....	....
Other sectors	4 624	....	....	46	8	135	241	−44	−143
Money market instruments	4 630	....	....	....	....	....	....	....	....
Monetary authorities	4 631	....	....	....	....	....	....	....	....
General government	4 632	....	....	....	....	....	....	....	....
Banks	4 633	....	....	....	....	....	....	....	....
Other sectors	4 634	....	....	....	....	....	....	....	....
Liabilities	4 652	....	....	....	....	....	....	....	....
Equity securities	4 660	....	....	....	....	....	....	....	....
Banks	4 663	....	....	....	....	....	....	....	....
Other sectors	4 664	....	....	....	....	....	....	....	....
Debt securities	4 669	....	....	....	....	....	....	....	....
Bonds and notes	4 670	....	....	....	....	....	....	....	....
Monetary authorities	4 671	....	....	....	....	....	....	....	....
General government	4 672	....	....	....	....	....	....	....	....
Banks	4 673	....	....	....	....	....	....	....	....
Other sectors	4 674	....	....	....	....	....	....	....	....
Money market instruments	4 680	....	....	....	....	....	....	....	....
Monetary authorities	4 681	....	....	....	....	....	....	....	....
General government	4 682	....	....	....	....	....	....	....	....
Banks	4 683	....	....	....	....	....	....	....	....
Other sectors	4 684	....	....	....	....	....	....	....	....
C. FINANCIAL DERIVATIVES	4 910	....	....	....	....	....	....	....	....
Monetary authorities	4 911	....	....	....	....	....	....	....	....
General government	4 912	....	....	....	....	....	....	....	....
Banks	4 913	....	....	....	....	....	....	....	....
Other sectors	4 914	....	....	....	....	....	....	....	....
Assets	4 900	....	....	....	....	....	....	....	....
Monetary authorities	4 901	....	....	....	....	....	....	....	....
General government	4 902	....	....	....	....	....	....	....	....
Banks	4 903	....	....	....	....	....	....	....	....
Other sectors	4 904	....	....	....	....	....	....	....	....
Liabilities	4 905	....	....	....	....	....	....	....	....
Monetary authorities	4 906	....	....	....	....	....	....	....	....
General government	4 907	....	....	....	....	....	....	....	....
Banks	4 908	....	....	....	....	....	....	....	....
Other sectors	4 909	....	....	....	....	....	....	....	....

Table 2 (Concluded). STANDARD PRESENTATION, 2000–2007

(Millions of U.S. dollars)

	Code	2000	2001	2002	2003	2004	2005	2006	2007
D. OTHER INVESTMENT	4 700	....	....	**74**	**14**	**−347**	**−185**	**−206**	**−210**
Assets	4 703	....	....	**−65**	**8**	**−549**	**−379**	**−204**	**−182**
Trade credits	4 706	....	....	....	....	....	....	....	....
General government	4 707	....	....	....	....	....	....	....	....
of which: Short-term	4 709	....	....	....	....	....	....	....	....
Other sectors	4 710	....	....	....	....	....	....	....	....
of which: Short-term	4 712	....	....	....	....	....	....	....	....
Loans	4 714	....	....	−65	8	−549	−379	−204	−182
Monetary authorities	4 715	....	....	44	....	−42	−41	−70	−74
of which: Short-term	4 718	....	....	*44*	....	*−42*	*−41*	*−70*	*−74*
General government	4 719	....	....	....	....	....	....	....	....
of which: Short-term	4 721	....	....	....	....	....	....	....	....
Banks	4 722	....	....	−6	−15	−328	−230	1	−26
of which: Short-term	4 724	....	....	*−6*	*−15*	*−328*	*−230*	*1*	*−26*
Other sectors	4 725	....	....	−103	22	−179	−109	−135	−82
of which: Short-term	4 727	....	....	*−103*	*22*	*−179*	*−109*	*−135*	*−82*
Currency and deposits	4 730	....	....	....	....	....	....	....	....
Monetary authorities	4 731	....	....	....	....	....	....	....	....
General government	4 732	....	....	....	....	....	....	....	....
Banks	4 733	....	....	....	....	....	....	....	....
Other sectors	4 734	....	....	....	....	....	....	....	....
Other assets	4 736	....	....	....	....	....	....	....	....
Monetary authorities	4 737	....	....	....	....	....	....	....	....
of which: Short-term	4 739	....	....	....	....	....	....	....	....
General government	4 740	....	....	....	....	....	....	....	....
of which: Short-term	4 742	....	....	....	....	....	....	....	....
Banks	4 743	....	....	....	....	....	....	....	....
of which: Short-term	4 745	....	....	....	....	....	....	....	....
Other sectors	4 746	....	....	....	....	....	....	....	....
of which: Short-term	4 748	....	....	....	....	....	....	....	....
Liabilities	4 753	....	....	**138**	**6**	**201**	**194**	**−1**	**−28**
Trade credits	4 756	....	....	....	....	....	....	....	....
General government	4 757	....	....	....	....	....	....	....	....
of which: Short-term	4 759	....	....	....	....	....	....	....	....
Other sectors	4 760	....	....	....	....	....	....	....	....
of which: Short-term	4 762	....	....	....	....	....	....	....	....
Loans	4 764	....	....	138	6	201	194	−1	−28
Monetary authorities	4 765	....	....	....	....	....	....	....	....
of which: Use of Fund credit and loans from the Fund	4 766	....	....	....	....	....	....	....	....
of which: Short-term	4 768	....	....	....	....	....	....	....	....
General government	4 769	....	....	52	6	−49	−33	−32	−43
of which: Short-term	4 771	....	....	*52*	*6*	*−49*	*−33*	*−32*	*−43*
Banks	4 772	....	....	80	−27	186	213	28	211
of which: Short-term	4 774	....	....	*80*	*−27*	*186*	*213*	*28*	*211*
Other sectors	4 775	....	....	7	27	64	14	3	−197
of which: Short-term	4 777	....	....	*7*	*27*	*64*	*14*	*3*	*−197*
Currency and deposits	4 780	....	....	....	....	....	....	....	....
Monetary authorities	4 781	....	....	....	....	....	....	....	....
General government	4 782	....	....	....	....	....	....	....	....
Banks	4 783	....	....	....	....	....	....	....	....
Other sectors	4 784	....	....	....	....	....	....	....	....
Other liabilities	4 786	....	....	....	....	....	....	....	....
Monetary authorities	4 787	....	....	....	....	....	....	....	....
of which: Short-term	4 789	....	....	....	....	....	....	....	....
General government	4 790	....	....	....	....	....	....	....	....
of which: Short-term	4 792	....	....	....	....	....	....	....	....
Banks	4 793	....	....	....	....	....	....	....	....
of which: Short-term	4 795	....	....	....	....	....	....	....	....
Other sectors	4 796	....	....	....	....	....	....	....	....
of which: Short-term	4 798	....	....	....	....	....	....	....	....
E. RESERVE ASSETS	4 802	....	....	....	....	....	....	....	....
Monetary gold	4 812	....	....	....	....	....	....	....	....
Special drawing rights	4 811	....	....	....	....	....	....	....	....
Reserve position in the Fund	4 810	....	....	....	....	....	....	....	....
Foreign exchange	4 803	....	....	....	....	....	....	....	....
Other claims	4 813	....	....	....	....	....	....	....	....
NET ERRORS AND OMISSIONS	4 998	....	....	**−66**	**−89**	**−67**	**85**	**61**	**141**

Table 1. ANALYTIC PRESENTATION, 2000–2007

(Millions of U.S. dollars)

	Code	2000	2001	2002	2003	2004	2005	2006	2007
A. Current Account[1]	4 993 Z.	**1,001.0**	**517.4**	**338.0**	**765.9**	**924.5**	**1,983.0**	....	....
Goods: exports f.o.b.	2 100 ..	3,320.6	2,613.8	2,555.5	3,178.5	4,071.6	5,463.9	....	....
Goods: imports f.o.b.	3 100 ..	−798.1	−847.5	−935.0	−1,042.9	−1,215.6	−1,358.8	....	....
Balance on Goods	4 100 ..	*2,522.6*	*1,766.3*	*1,620.5*	*2,135.6*	*2,855.9*	*4,105.0*	....	....
Services: credit	2 200 ..	177.8	168.3	86.0	172.5	156.3	146.2	....	....
Services: debit	3 200 ..	−857.6	−709.8	−758.6	−839.6	−939.1	−1,041.6	....	....
Balance on Goods and Services	4 991 ..	*1,842.8*	*1,224.9*	*947.9*	*1,468.5*	*2,073.1*	*3,209.6*	....	....
Income: credit	2 300 ..	48.4	29.8	17.7	48.3	13.3	36.5	....	....
Income: debit	3 300 ..	−827.1	−659.0	−496.5	−569.9	−978.1	−994.1	....	....
Balance on Goods, Services, and Income	4 992 ..	*1,064.1*	*595.7*	*469.2*	*946.9*	*1,108.3*	*2,252.0*	....	....
Current transfers: credit	2 379 Z.	16.0	34.3	4.7	7.2	9.9	17.7	....	....
Current transfers: debit	3 379 ..	−79.1	−112.6	−135.9	−188.2	−193.7	−286.7	....	....
B. Capital Account[1]	4 994 Z.	**−.3**	**2.9**	**2.6**	**43.1**	....	....	....	....
Capital account: credit	2 994 Z.	....	2.9	2.6	43.1	....	....	....	....
Capital account: debit	3 994 ..	−.3	−.1	....	....	....	....	....	....
Total, Groups A Plus B	4 981 ..	*1,000.7*	*520.2*	*340.6*	*809.0*	*924.5*	*1,983.0*	....	....
C. Financial Account[1]	4 995 W.	**−567.8**	**−674.0**	**−437.3**	**−650.1**	**−499.2**	**−1,342.0**	....	....
Direct investment abroad	4 505 ..	−25.3	−3.8	23.0	20.9	24.8	−75.4	....	....
Direct investment in Gabon	4 555 Z.	−42.6	−89.1	39.0	158.0	319.5	242.3	....	....
Portfolio investment assets	4 602 ..	−9.2	−.8	.6	2.5	−9.4	7.6	....	....
Equity securities	4 610 ..	−9.6	−.9	....	−.1	−7.6	8.3	....	....
Debt securities	4 619 ..	.4	.1	.5	2.6	−1.9	−.7	....	....
Portfolio investment liabilities	4 652 Z.	−1.6	1.2	−2.1	3.7	−1.4	.7	....	....
Equity securities	4 660 ..	....	....	....	....	....	....	....	....
Debt securities	4 669 Z.	−1.6	1.2	−2.1	3.7	−1.4	.7	....	....
Financial derivatives	4 910 ..	....	....	....	....	....	....	....	....
Financial derivatives assets	4 900 ..	....	....	....	....	....	....	....	....
Financial derivatives liabilities	4 905 ..	....	....	....	....	....	....	....	....
Other investment assets	4 703 ..	−729.2	−296.3	−150.5	−355.7	−511.8	−1,079.1	....	....
Monetary authorities	4 701 ..	....	....	....	....	....	....	....	....
General government	4 704 ..	....	....	....	....	....	....	....	....
Banks	4 705 ..	−168.6	96.1	37.3	−24.2	−196.6	−141.5	....	....
Other sectors	4 728 ..	−560.6	−392.5	−187.8	−331.4	−315.2	−937.6	....	....
Other investment liabilities	4 753 W.	240.2	−285.2	−347.3	−479.5	−320.9	−438.1	....	....
Monetary authorities	4 753 WA	10.4	−10.5	−17.0	−10.5	24.7	−18.2	....	....
General government	4 753 ZB	76.7	−355.4	−331.3	−340.1	−273.6	−262.1	....	....
Banks	4 753 ZC	18.0	−5.5	18.3	−18.1	−7.4	−19.8	....	....
Other sectors	4 753 ZD	135.0	86.2	−17.1	−110.8	−64.6	−138.0	....	....
Total, Groups A Through C	4 983 ..	*432.9*	*−153.7*	*−96.7*	*158.9*	*425.2*	*641.0*	....	....
D. Net Errors and Omissions	4 998 ..	**−152.4**	**−104.0**	**−125.4**	**−259.8**	**−357.0**	**−415.1**	....	....
Total, Groups A Through D	4 984 ..	*280.5*	*−257.8*	*−222.1*	*−100.9*	*68.2*	*225.9*	....	....
E. Reserves and Related Items	4 802 A.	**−280.5**	**257.8**	**222.1**	**100.9**	**−68.2**	**−225.9**	....	....
Reserve assets	4 802 ..	−171.8	173.0	−115.0	−25.4	−210.9	−299.5	....	....
Use of Fund credit and loans	4 766 ..	7.2	−11.0	−13.3	−14.6	37.2	−24.5	....	....
Exceptional financing	4 920 ..	−115.9	95.8	350.4	140.8	105.5	98.1	....	....
Conversion rates: CFA francs per U.S. dollar	0 101 ..	**711.98**	**733.04**	**696.99**	**581.20**	**528.28**	**527.47**	**522.89**	**479.27**

[1] Excludes components that have been classified in the categories of Group E.

Table 2. STANDARD PRESENTATION, 2000–2007

(Millions of U.S. dollars)

	Code	2000	2001	2002	2003	2004	2005	2006	2007
CURRENT ACCOUNT	4 993 ..	**1,001.0**	**517.4**	**338.0**	**765.9**	**924.5**	**1,983.0**	....	....
A. GOODS	4 100 ..	**2,522.6**	**1,766.3**	**1,620.5**	**2,135.6**	**2,855.9**	**4,105.0**	....	....
Credit	2 100 ..	**3,320.6**	**2,613.8**	**2,555.5**	**3,178.5**	**4,071.6**	**5,463.9**	....	....
General merchandise: exports f.o.b.	2 110 ..	3,312.8	2,611.1	2,552.7	3,176.4	4,070.8	5,458.2	....	....
Goods for processing: exports f.o.b.	2 150 ..	....	....	....	....	....	....		
Repairs on goods	2 160 ..	....	....	....	....	....	....		
Goods procured in ports by carriers	2 170 ..	7.9	2.7	2.8	2.1	.7	5.7		
Nonmonetary gold	2 180 ..	....	....	....	....	....	....		
Debit	3 100 ..	**−798.1**	**−847.5**	**−935.0**	**−1,042.9**	**−1,215.6**	**−1,358.8**	....	....
General merchandise: imports f.o.b.	3 110 ..	−792.5	−842.5	−934.2	−1,040.9	−1,207.0	−1,358.7		
Goods for processing: imports f.o.b.	3 150 ..	....	....	....	....	....	....		
Repairs on goods	3 160 ..	....	....	....	....	....	....		
Goods procured in ports by carriers	3 170 ..	−5.6	−4.9	−.8	−2.0	−8.7	−.2		
Nonmonetary gold	3 180 ..	....	....	....	....	....	....		
B. SERVICES	4 200 ..	**−679.8**	**−541.5**	**−672.6**	**−667.1**	**−782.8**	**−895.4**	....	....
Total credit	2 200 ..	*177.8*	*168.3*	*86.0*	*172.5*	*156.3*	*146.2*		
Total debit	3 200 ..	*−857.6*	*−709.8*	*−758.6*	*−839.6*	*−939.1*	*−1,041.6*		
Transportation services, credit	2 205 ..	**94.9**	**70.0**	**16.7**	**84.6**	**81.3**	**26.4**	....	....
Passenger	2 850 ..	*79.4*	*30.5*	*1.5*	*69.4*	*63.7*	*3.9*		
Freight	2 851 ..	*6.4*	*37.6*	*14.2*	*15.1*	*17.3*	*19.9*		
Other	2 852 ..	*9.1*	*1.9*	*1.0*	*.1*	*.2*	*2.6*		
Sea transport, passenger	2 207 ..	....	....	....	....	....	....		
Sea transport, freight	2 208 ..	6.4	37.6	14.2	15.1	17.3	19.9		
Sea transport, other	2 209 ..	....	....	....	....	....	....		
Air transport, passenger	2 211 ..	79.4	30.5	1.5	69.4	63.7	3.9		
Air transport, freight	2 212 ..	....	....	....	....	....	....		
Air transport, other	2 213 ..	9.1	1.9	1.0	.1	.2	2.6		
Other transport, passenger	2 215 ..	....	....	....	....	....	....		
Other transport, freight	2 216 ..	....	....	....	....	....	....		
Other transport, other	2 217 ..	....	....	....	....	....	....		
Transportation services, debit	3 205 ..	**−268.2**	**−207.6**	**−216.9**	**−265.0**	**−308.8**	**−320.2**	....	....
Passenger	3 850 ..	*−98.6*	*−30.5*	*−39.6*	*−45.0*	*−60.8*	*−71.9*		
Freight	3 851 ..	*−143.3*	*−162.9*	*−175.4*	*−186.6*	*−222.1*	*−247.1*		
Other	3 852 ..	*−26.3*	*−14.2*	*−2.0*	*−33.4*	*−26.0*	*−1.2*		
Sea transport, passenger	3 207 ..	....	....	....	....	....	....		
Sea transport, freight	3 208 ..	−95.6	−108.6	−116.9	−124.4	−148.1	−164.7		
Sea transport, other	3 209 ..	....	....	....	....	....	....		
Air transport, passenger	3 211 ..	−98.6	−30.5	−39.6	−45.0	−60.8	−71.9		
Air transport, freight	3 212 ..	−47.8	−54.3	−58.5	−62.2	−74.0	−82.4		
Air transport, other	3 213 ..	−26.3	−14.2	−2.0	−33.4	−26.0	−1.2		
Other transport, passenger	3 215 ..	....	....	....	....	....	....		
Other transport, freight	3 216 ..	....	....	....	....	....	....		
Other transport, other	3 217 ..	....	....	....	....	....	....		
Travel, credit	2 236 ..	**20.2**	**15.0**	**18.1**	**14.5**	**9.8**	**9.3**	....	....
Business travel	2 237 ..	1.6	8.7	4.0	2.2	2.0	1.8		
Personal travel	2 240 ..	18.7	6.4	14.1	12.3	7.8	7.4		
Travel, debit	3 236 ..	**−83.9**	**−224.9**	**−194.0**	**−193.9**	**−213.9**	**−274.3**	....	....
Business travel	3 237 ..	−48.9	−146.8	−95.1	−122.9	−108.4	−97.3		
Personal travel	3 240 ..	−34.9	−78.1	−98.9	−70.9	−105.5	−177.0		
Other services, credit	2 200 BA ..	**62.6**	**83.3**	**51.2**	**73.4**	**65.3**	**110.5**	....	....
Communications	2 245 ..	....	....	....	....	....	....		
Construction	2 249 ..	....	....	....	....	....	....		
Insurance	2 253 ..	.8	23.5	21.1	51.3	23.2	29.0		
Financial	2 260 ..	....	....	....	....	....	....		
Computer and information	2 262 ..	1.7	.8	.6	2.1	1.5	6.1		
Royalties and licence fees	2 266 ..	....	....	....	....	....	....		
Other business services	2 268 ..	53.0	33.9	17.1	14.3	20.1	49.5		
Personal, cultural, and recreational	2 287 ..	....	....	....	....	....	....		
Government, n.i.e.	2 291 ..	7.2	25.0	12.4	5.7	20.5	26.0		
Other services, debit	3 200 BA ..	**−505.5**	**−277.3**	**−347.7**	**−380.7**	**−416.4**	**−447.1**	....	....
Communications	3 245 ..	....	....	....	....	....	....		
Construction	3 249 ..	....	....	....	....	....	....		
Insurance	3 253 ..	−69.9	−48.0	−47.9	−46.9	−53.2	−66.3		
Financial	3 260 ..	....	....	....	....	....	....		
Computer and information	3 262 ..	−20.5	−1.9	−6.4	−11.1	−8.5	−10.6		
Royalties and licence fees	3 266 ..	....	....	....	....	....	....		
Other business services	3 268 ..	−403.7	−212.2	−276.1	−304.5	−336.4	−348.9		
Personal, cultural, and recreational	3 287 ..	....	....	....	....	....	....		
Government, n.i.e.	3 291 ..	−11.3	−15.2	−17.4	−18.2	−18.3	−21.3	....	....

Table 2 (Continued). STANDARD PRESENTATION, 2000–2007

(Millions of U.S. dollars)

	Code	2000	2001	2002	2003	2004	2005	2006	2007
C. INCOME	4 300	**−778.7**	**−629.2**	**−478.8**	**−521.6**	**−964.8**	**−957.6**	....	....
Total credit	2 300	*48.4*	*29.8*	*17.7*	*48.3*	*13.3*	*36.5*	....	....
Total debit	3 300	*−827.1*	*−659.0*	*−496.5*	*−569.9*	*−978.1*	*−994.1*	....	....
Compensation of employees, credit	2 310	**3.8**	**4.1**	**1.7**	**2.2**	**5.4**	**9.5**	....	....
Compensation of employees, debit	3 310	**−35.6**	**−14.3**	**−17.2**	**−5.7**	**−19.1**	**−22.2**	....	....
Investment income, credit	2 320	**44.6**	**25.7**	**16.1**	**46.1**	**7.9**	**26.9**	....	....
Direct investment income	2 330	12.3	11.4	11.7	41.3	1.9	13.7	....	....
Dividends and distributed branch profits	2 332	12.3	10.5	3.8	4.6	1.4	3.0	....	....
Reinvested earnings and undistributed branch profits	2 333	....	.9	7.9	36.6	.5	10.7	....	....
Income on debt (interest)	2 334	....	....	....	....	....	....	....	....
Portfolio investment income	2 339	.1	.6	.6	.6	.6	.5	....	....
Income on equity	2 340	....	.5	.6	.1	.4	....	....	....
Income on bonds and notes	2 350	....	.1	.1	.5	.2	.5	....	....
Income on money market instruments	2 360	....	....	....	....	....	....	....	....
Other investment income	2 370	32.2	13.6	3.7	4.3	5.3	12.7	....	....
Investment income, debit	3 320	**−791.5**	**−644.7**	**−479.3**	**−564.2**	**−959.0**	**−971.9**	....	....
Direct investment income	3 330	−472.6	−192.8	−300.5	−358.7	−722.5	−764.7	....	....
Dividends and distributed branch profits	3 332	−304.7	−329.4	−267.1	−246.4	−376.9	−435.1	....	....
Reinvested earnings anc undistributed branch profits	3 333	−167.9	136.6	−33.5	−112.2	−345.6	−329.6	....	....
Income on debt (interest)	3 334	....	....	....	....	....	....	....	....
Portfolio investment income	3 339	−23.4	−1.0	−.7	−.7	−.6	−1.6	....	....
Income on equity	3 340	−4.4	−.8	−.7	....	−.5	−1.3	....	....
Income on bonds and notes	3 350	−19.1	−.2	....	−.7	....	−.3	....	....
Income on money market instruments	3 360	....	....	....	....	....	....	....	....
Other investment income	3 370	−295.5	−451.0	−178.0	−204.9	−236.0	−205.6	....	....
D. CURRENT TRANSFERS	4 379	**−63.1**	**−78.3**	**−131.1**	**−181.0**	**−183.9**	**−269.0**	....	....
Credit	2 379	**16.0**	**34.3**	**4.7**	**7.2**	**9.9**	**17.7**	....	....
General government	2 380	2.7	26.0	.6	.8	2.1	3.0	....	....
Other sectors	2 390	13.3	8.3	4.2	6.4	7.8	14.7	....	....
Workers' remittances	2 391	2.3	1.2	1.2	3.8	1.4	1.5	....	....
Other current transfers	2 392	11.0	7.1	3.0	2.6	6.4	13.2	....	....
Debit	3 379	**−79.1**	**−112.6**	**−135.9**	**−188.2**	**−193.7**	**−286.7**	....	....
General government	3 380	−16.2	−17.1	−32.4	−46.3	−65.0	−56.0	....	....
Other sectors	3 390	−62.8	−95.5	−103.5	−142.0	−128.8	−230.7	....	....
Workers' remittances	3 391	−42.0	−81.6	−79.2	−109.5	−91.2	−163.4	....	....
Other current transfers	3 392	−20.8	−13.8	−24.3	−32.5	−37.5	−67.3	....	....
CAPITAL AND FINANCIAL ACCOUNT	4 996	**−848.6**	**−413.4**	**−212.7**	**−506.1**	**−567.5**	**−1,567.9**	....	....
CAPITAL ACCOUNT	4 994	**−.3**	**2.9**	**2.6**	**43.1**	....	....	....	....
Total credit	2 994	....	*2.9*	*2.6*	*43.1*	....	....	....	....
Total debit	3 994	*−.3*	*−.1*	....	....	....	....	....	....
Capital transfers, credit	2 400	....	**2.6**	**2.6**	**43.1**	....	....	....	....
General government	2 401	....	2.3	2.6	43.1	....	....	....	....
Debt forgiveness	2 402	....	....	....	42.6	....	....	....	....
Other capital transfers	2 410	....	2.3	2.6	.6	....	....	....	....
Other sectors	2 430	....	.3	....	....	....	....	....	....
Migrants' transfers	2 431	....	....	....	....	....	....	....	....
Debt forgiveness	2 432	....	....	....	....	....	....	....	....
Other capital transfers	2 440	....	.3	....	....	....	....	....	....
Capital transfers, debit	3 400	....	....	....	....	....	....	....	....
General government	3 401	....	....	....	....	....	....	....	....
Debt forgiveness	3 402	....	....	....	....	....	....	....	....
Other capital transfers	3 410	....	....	....	....	....	....	....	....
Other sectors	3 430	....	....	....	....	....	....	....	....
Migrants' transfers	3 431	....	....	....	....	....	....	....	....
Debt forgiveness	3 432	....	....	....	....	....	....	....	....
Other capital transfers	3 440	....	....	....	....	....	....	....	....
Nonproduced nonfinancial assets, credit	2 480	....	**.3**	....	....	....	....	....	....
Nonproduced nonfinancial assets, debit	3 480	**−.3**	....	....	....	....	....	....	....

Table 2 (Continued). STANDARD PRESENTATION, 2000–2007

(Millions of U.S. dollars)

	Code	2000	2001	2002	2003	2004	2005	2006	2007
FINANCIAL ACCOUNT	4 995 ..	−848.3	−416.2	−215.3	−549.2	−567.5	−1,567.9	....	....
A. DIRECT INVESTMENT	4 500 ..	−68.0	−92.8	62.0	178.9	344.3	166.9	....	....
Direct investment abroad	4 505 ..	−25.3	−3.8	23.0	20.9	24.8	−75.4	....	....
Equity capital	4 510 ..	−13.7	12.0	17.3	2.0	1.3	−9.0		
Claims on affiliated enterprises	4 515 ..	....	14.1	19.0	3.6	3.1	....		
Liabilities to affiliated enterprises	4 520 ..	−13.7	−2.0	−1.7	−1.7	−1.9	−9.0		
Reinvested earnings	4 525 ..	....	−.9	−7.9	−36.6	−.5	−10.7		
Other capital	4 530 ..	−11.7	−14.9	13.6	55.5	24.0	−55.7		
Claims on affiliated enterprises	4 535 ..	−11.7	−4.7	11.5	52.1	30.6	−53.1		
Liabilities to affiliated enterprises	4 540 ..	....	−10.2	2.1	3.4	−6.6	−2.7		
Direct investment in Gabon	4 555 ..	−42.6	−89.1	39.0	158.0	319.5	242.3	....	....
Equity capital	4 560 ..	29.6	−8.5	7.6	6.1	−25.2	26.3		
Claims on direct investors	4 565 ..	29.6	....	7.6	6.1	.3	26.3		
Liabilities to direct investors	4 570 ..	....	−8.5	....	....	−25.5	....		
Reinvested earnings	4 575 ..	167.9	−136.6	33.5	112.2	345.6	329.6		
Other capital	4 580 ..	−240.0	56.0	−2.1	39.7	−.8	−113.5		
Claims on direct investors	4 585 ..	−363.9	−.7	30.6	54.0	−3.2	−121.8		
Liabilities to direct investors	4 590 ..	123.9	56.7	−32.7	−14.4	2.4	8.2		
B. PORTFOLIO INVESTMENT	4 600 ..	−10.8	.4	−1.5	6.2	−10.8	8.7	....	....
Assets	4 602 ..	−9.2	−.8	.6	2.5	−9.4	7.6	....	....
Equity securities	4 610 ..	−9.6	−.9	....	−.1	−7.6	8.3		
Monetary authorities	4 611 ..	....	....			....	....		
General government	4 612 ..	....	....			....	....		
Banks	4 613 ..	....	....		....	−7.5	7.2		
Other sectors	4 614 ..	−9.6	−.9	....	−.1	−.1	1.0		
Debt securities	4 619 ..	.4	.1	.5	2.6	−1.9	−.7		
Bonds and notes	4 620 ..	.4	.1	.5	2.6	−1.9	−.7		
Monetary authorities	4 621 ..	....	....	....	....	....	....		
General government	4 622 ..	....	....	....	....	....	....		
Banks	4 623 ..	....	....	....	....	....	....		
Other sectors	4 624 ..	.4	.1	.5	2.6	−1.9	−.7		
Money market instruments	4 630 ..	....	....	....	....	....	....		
Monetary authorities	4 631 ..	....	....	....	....	....	....		
General government	4 632 ..	....	....	....	....	....	....		
Banks	4 633 ..	....	....	....	....	....	....		
Other sectors	4 634 ..	....	....	....	....	....	....		
Liabilities	4 652 ..	−1.6	1.2	−2.1	3.7	−1.4	1.1	....	....
Equity securities	4 660 ..	....	....	....	....	....	....		
Banks	4 663 ..	....	....	....	....	....	....		
Other sectors	4 664 ..	....	....	....	....	....	....		
Debt securities	4 669 ..	−1.6	1.2	−2.1	3.7	−1.4	1.1		
Bonds and notes	4 670 ..	....	2.4	−2.1	−.1	....	1.1		
Monetary authorities	4 671 ..	....	....	....	....	....	....		
General government	4 672 ..	....	....	....	....	....	....		
Banks	4 673 ..	....	4.0	−1.9	....	....	....		
Other sectors	4 674 ..	....	−1.5	−.2	−.1	....	1.1		
Money market instruments	4 680 ..	−1.6	−1.2	....	3.8	−1.4	....		
Monetary authorities	4 681 ..	....	....	....	....	....	....		
General government	4 682 ..	....	....	....	....	....	....		
Banks	4 683 ..	....	....	....	....	−.2	....		
Other sectors	4 684 ..	−1.6	−1.2	....	3.8	−1.2	....		
C. FINANCIAL DERIVATIVES	4 910 ..	....	....	....	....	....	....	....	....
Monetary authorities	4 911 ..	....	....	....	....	....	....	....	....
General government	4 912 ..	....	....	....	....	....	....	....	....
Banks	4 913 ..	....	....	....	....	....	....	....	....
Other sectors	4 914 ..	....	....	....	....	....	....	....	....
Assets	4 900 ..	....	....	....	....	....	....	....	....
Monetary authorities	4 901 ..	....	....	....	....	....	....	....	....
General government	4 902 ..	....	....	....	....	....	....	....	....
Banks	4 903 ..	....	....	....	....	....	....	....	....
Other sectors	4 904 ..	....	....	....	....	....	....	....	....
Liabilities	4 905 ..	....	....	....	....	....	....	....	....
Monetary authorities	4 906 ..	....	....	....	....	....	....	....	....
General government	4 907 ..	....	....	....	....	....	....	....	....
Banks	4 908 ..	....	....	....	....	....	....	....	....
Other sectors	4 909 ..	....	....	....	....	....	....	....	....

Table 2 (Concluded). STANDARD PRESENTATION, 2000–2007

(Millions of U.S. dollars)

	Code	2000	2001	2002	2003	2004	2005	2006	2007
D. OTHER INVESTMENT	4 700 ..	−597.8	−496.8	−160.7	−708.9	−690.0	−1,444.0	....	....
Assets	4 703 ..	−729.2	−296.3	−150.5	−355.7	−511.8	−1,079.1	....	....
Trade credits	4 706 ..	9.6	35.3	80.9	80.3	−171.9	−350.8	....	....
General government	4 707 ..	....	....	....	....	....	....	....	....
of which: Short-term	4 709 ..	....	....	....	....	....	....	....	....
Other sectors	4 710 ..	9.6	35.3	80.9	80.3	−171.9	−350.8	....	....
of which: Short-term	4 712 ..	....	....	....	....	....	....	....	....
Loans	4 714 ..	−3.4	13.1	−13.2	1.5	−17.5	19.3	....	....
Monetary authorities	4 715 ..	....	....	....	....	....	....	....	....
of which: Short-term	4 718 ..	....	....	....	....	....	....	....	....
General government	4 719 ..	....	....	....	....	....	....	....	....
of which: Short-term	4 721 ..	....	....	....	....	....	....	....	....
Banks	4 722 ..	−2.6	6.5	2.2	−5.6	−22.3	27.0	....	....
of which: Short-term	4 724 ..	2.6	−.9	2.8	....	....	....	....	....
Other sectors	4 725 ..	−.8	6.5	−15.3	7.0	4.8	−7.8	....	....
of which: Short-term	4 727 ..	−2.9	−.2	....	....	....	....	....	....
Currency and deposits	4 730 ..	−730.3	−339.5	−218.2	−436.9	−303.7	−740.6	....	....
Monetary authorities	4 731 ..	....	....	....	....	....	....	....	....
General government	4 732 ..	....	....	....	....	....	....	....	....
Banks	4 733 ..	−166.0	91.2	34.8	−19.8	−159.7	−183.8	....	....
Other sectors	4 734 ..	−564.3	−430.7	−253.0	−417.1	−144.0	−556.8	....	....
Other assets	4 736 ..	−5.1	−5.2	−.1	−.5	−18.6	−7.0	....	....
Monetary authorities	4 737 ..	....	....	....	....	....	....	....	....
of which: Short-term	4 739 ..	....	....	....	....	....	....	....	....
General government	4 740 ..	....	....	....	....	....	....	....	....
of which: Short-term	4 742 ..	....	....	....	....	....	....	....	....
Banks	4 743 ..	....	−1.6	.3	1.1	−14.6	15.2	....	....
of which: Short-term	4 745 ..	....	−1.6	.3	1.1	−14.6	15.2	....	....
Other sectors	4 746 ..	−5.1	−3.6	−.4	−1.6	−4.0	−22.2	....	....
of which: Short-term	4 748 ..	−5.1	−3.6	−.4	−1.6	−4.0	−22.2	....	....
Liabilities	4 753 ..	131.4	−200.4	−10.2	−353.2	−178.2	−364.9	....	....
Trade credits	4 756 ..	67.9	8.8	9.6	−81.4	−55.6	11.1	....	....
General government	4 757 ..	....	....	....	....	....	....	....	....
of which: Short-term	4 759 ..	....	....	....	....	....	....	....	....
Other sectors	4 760 ..	67.9	8.8	9.6	−81.4	−55.6	11.1	....	....
of which: Short-term	4 762 ..	30.4	9.2	9.9	−77.1	−55.6	11.1	....	....
Loans	4 764 ..	−220.2	−302.6	−329.8	−359.4	−393.3	−321.1	....	....
Monetary authorities	4 765 ..	7.2	−11.0	−13.3	−14.6	37.2	−24.5	....	....
of which: Use of Fund credit and loans from the Fund..	4 766 ..	7.2	−11.0	−13.3	−14.6	37.2	−24.5	....	....
of which: Short-term	4 768 ..	....	....	....	....	....	....	....	....
General government	4 769 ..	−304.8	−365.9	−324.9	−327.5	−411.1	−295.1	....	....
of which: Short-term	4 771 ..	....	....	....	....	....	....	....	....
Banks	4 772 ..	1.4	−.8	13.1	−7.6	−.1	3.3	....	....
of which: Short-term	4 774 ..	1.4	−.8	13.1	−7.6	−1.8	1.9	....	....
Other sectors	4 775 ..	76.0	75.1	−4.7	−9.7	−19.3	−4.8	....	....
of which: Short-term	4 777 ..	7.2	−1.7	−9.0	−4.0	−22.5	−10.2	....	....
Currency and deposits	4 780 ..	31.3	15.5	26.3	.2	−2.0	−13.4	....	....
Monetary authorities	4 781 ..	....	....	....	....	....	....	....	....
General government	4 782 ..	....	....	....	....	....	....	....	....
Banks	4 783 ..	18.0	−4.7	18.3	−10.7	−7.2	−21.1	....	....
Other sectors	4 784 ..	13.2	20.2	8.0	10.9	5.2	7.7	....	....
Other liabilities	4 786 ..	252.5	78.0	283.8	87.3	272.7	−41.5	....	....
Monetary authorities	4 787 ..	10.4	−10.5	−17.0	−10.5	24.7	−18.2	....	....
of which: Short-term	4 789 ..	10.4	−10.5	−17.0	−10.5	24.7	−18.2	....	....
General government	4 790 ..	256.5	106.3	330.8	128.3	243.1	128.7	....	....
of which: Short-term	4 792 ..	−156.8	83.1	311.9	114.4	−8.7	−8.4	....	....
Banks	4 793 ..	....	....	....	.2	−.1	....	....	....
of which: Short-term	4 795 ..	....	....	....	.2	−.1	....	....	....
Other sectors	4 796 ..	−14.4	−17.8	−30.0	−30.6	5.1	−152.0	....	....
of which: Short-term	4 798 ..	−14.4	−17.8	−30.0	−30.6	5.1	−152.0	....	....
E. RESERVE ASSETS	4 802 ..	−171.8	173.0	−115.0	−25.4	−210.9	−299.5	....	....
Monetary gold	4 812 ..	....	....	....	....	....	....	....	....
Special drawing rights	4 811 ..	−.1	....	.1	....	−5.7	6.0	....	....
Reserve position in the Fund	4 810 ..	−.1	....	....	....	....	−.1	....	....
Foreign exchange	4 803 ..	−171.6	173.0	−115.0	−25.4	−205.3	−305.4	....	....
Other claims	4 813 ..	....	....	....	....	....	....	....	....
NET ERRORS AND OMISSIONS	4 998 ..	−152.4	−104.0	−125.4	−259.8	−357.0	−415.1	....	....

Table 1. ANALYTIC PRESENTATION, FISCAL YEARS 2000–2007 ENDING JUNE 30

(Millions of U.S. dollars)

	Code	2000	2001	2002	2003	2004	2005	2006	2007
A. Current Account[1]	4 993 Z.	....	....	....	**−2.39**	**−44.46**	**−50.44**	**−72.30**	**−58.65**
Goods: exports f.o.b.	2 100 ..	....	....	....	77.63	109.16	100.98	108.68	118.37
Goods: imports f.o.b.	3 100 ..	....	....	....	−156.37	−207.24	−215.47	−221.84	−245.07
Balance on Goods	4 100 ..	....	....	....	*−78.74*	*−98.08*	*−114.49*	*−113.16*	*−126.70*
Services: credit	2 200 ..	....	....	....	83.84	73.14	79.58	91.92	114.37
Services: debit	3 200 ..	....	....	....	−36.26	−45.72	−45.38	−93.92	−76.75
Balance on Goods and Services	4 991 ..	....	....	....	*−31.17*	*−70.66*	*−80.30*	*−115.15*	*−89.09*
Income: credit	2 300 ..	....	....	....	4.70	1.78	3.13	4.48	7.61
Income: debit	3 300 ..	....	....	....	−31.94	−29.57	−35.37	−42.35	−47.59
Balance on Goods, Services, and Income	4 992 ..	....	....	....	*−58.40*	*−98.45*	*−112.54*	*−153.02*	*−129.07*
Current transfers: credit	2 379 Z.	....	....	....	88.92	78.23	88.01	107.42	89.84
Current transfers: debit	3 379 ..	....	....	....	−32.91	−24.24	−25.90	−26.70	−19.43
B. Capital Account[1]	4 994 Z.	....	....	....	**4.80**	**5.15**	**.58**	....	**.36**
Capital account: credit	2 994 Z.	....	....	....	4.80	5.15	.58	....	.36
Capital account: debit	3 994 ..	....	....	....	....	....	....	....	....
Total, Groups A Plus B	4 981 ..	....	....	....	*2.41*	*−39.30*	*−49.86*	*−72.30*	*−58.29*
C. Financial Account[1]	4 995 W.	....	....	....	**−9.84**	**46.94**	**68.45**	**78.44**	**78.31**
Direct investment abroad	4 505 ..	....	....	....	....	....	....	....	....
Direct investment in The Gambia	4 555 Z.	....	....	....	21.90	56.75	51.93	82.07	68.45
Portfolio investment assets	4 602 ..	....	....	....	....	....	....	....	....
Equity securities	4 610 ..	....	....	....	....	....	....	....	....
Debt securities	4 619 ..	....	....	....	....	....	....	....	....
Portfolio investment liabilities	4 652 Z.	....	....	....	....	....	....	....	....
Equity securities	4 660 ..	....	....	....	....	....	....	....	....
Debt securities	4 669 Z.	....	....	....	....	....	....	....	....
Financial derivatives	4 910 ..	....	....	....	....	....	....	....	....
Financial derivatives assets	4 900 ..	....	....	....	....	....	....	....	....
Financial derivatives liabilities	4 905 ..	....	....	....	....	....	....	....	....
Other investment assets	4 703 ..	....	....	....	−19.64	−15.37	13.60	−14.08	25.95
Monetary authorities	4 701 ..	....	....	....	....	....	....	....	....
General government	4 704 ..	....	....	....	....	....	....	....	....
Banks	4 705 ..	....	....	....	−19.64	−15.37	13.60	−14.08	14.09
Other sectors	4 728 ..	....	....	....	....	....	....	....	11.86
Other investment liabilities	4 753 W.	....	....	....	−12.10	5.56	2.93	10.44	−16.10
Monetary authorities	4 753 WA	....	....	....	....	....	....	....	....
General government	4 753 ZB	....	....	....	....	....	....	....	....
Banks	4 753 ZC	....	....	....	−16.13	1.32	−1.46	.67	15.46
Other sectors	4 753 ZD	....	....	....	4.03	4.24	4.38	9.77	−31.55
Total, Groups A Through C	4 983 ..	....	....	....	*−7.43*	*7.64*	*18.60*	*6.14*	*20.02*
D. Net Errors and Omissions	4 998 ..	....	....	....	**2.52**	**−8.89**	**−54.32**	**−6.23**	**−28.74**
Total, Groups A Through D	4 984 ..	....	....	....	*−4.91*	*−1.25*	*−35.73*	*−.09*	*−8.72*
E. Reserves and Related Items	4 802 A.	....	....	....	**4.91**	**1.25**	**35.73**	**.09**	**8.72**
Reserve assets	4 802 ..	....	....	....	−11.03	−31.34	−9.41	−20.40	5.56
Use of Fund credit and loans	4 766 ..	....	....	....	3.83	−5.52	−6.66	−3.00	−1.11
Exceptional financing	4 920 ..	....	....	....	12.10	38.11	51.79	23.48	4.28
Conversion rates: dalasis per U.S. dollar	0 101 ..	**11.858**	**14.316**	**17.168**	**23.802**	**29.383**	**29.522**	**28.113**	**27.785**

[1] Excludes components that have been classified in the categories of Group E.

Table 2. STANDARD PRESENTATION, FISCAL YEARS 2000–2007 ENDING JUNE 30

(Millions of U.S. dollars)

	Code	2000	2001	2002	2003	2004	2005	2006	2007
CURRENT ACCOUNT	4 993	....	....	....	3.16	−30.99	−43.56	−65.56	−52.66
A. GOODS	4 100	....	....	....	−78.74	−98.08	−114.49	−113.16	−126.70
Credit	2 100	....	....	....	77.63	109.16	100.98	108.68	118.37
General merchandise: exports f.o.b.	2 110	....	....	....	69.50	103.07	93.00	102.04	109.67
Goods for processing: exports f.o.b.	2 150	....	....	....	....	....	....	....	....
Repairs on goods	2 160	....	....	....	....	....	....	....	....
Goods procured in ports by carriers	2 170	....	....	....	8.12	6.08	7.98	6.64	8.69
Nonmonetary gold	2 180	....	....	....	....	....	....	....	....
Debit	3 100	....	....	....	−156.37	−207.24	−215.47	−221.84	−245.07
General merchandise: imports f.o.b.	3 110	....	....	....	−156.37	−207.24	−215.47	−221.84	−245.07
Goods for processing: imports f.o.b.	3 150	....	....	....	....	....	....	....	....
Repairs on goods	3 160	....	....	....	....	....	....	....	....
Goods procured in ports by carriers	3 170	....	....	....	....	....	....	....	....
Nonmonetary gold	3 180	....	....	....	....	....	....	....	....
B. SERVICES	4 200	....	....	....	47.58	27.42	34.20	−1.99	37.62
Total credit	2 200	....	....	....	*83.84*	*73.14*	*79.58*	*91.92*	*114.37*
Total debit	3 200	....	....	....	*−36.26*	*−45.72*	*−45.38*	*−93.92*	*−76.75*
Transportation services, credit	2 205	....	....	....	22.33	18.34	15.40	16.06	19.88
Passenger	2 850	....	....	....	*2.37*	*3.51*	*.64*	*3.41*	*2.21*
Freight	2 851	....	....	....	*16.79*	*12.70*	*12.80*	*10.86*	*8.67*
Other	2 852	....	....	....	*3.17*	*2.13*	*1.96*	*1.80*	*9.01*
Sea transport, passenger	2 207	....	....	....	....	....	....	....	....
Sea transport, freight	2 208	....	....	....	16.76	12.70	12.80	10.84	8.58
Sea transport, other	2 209	....	....	....	....	....	....	....	....
Air transport, passenger	2 211	....	....	....	2.37	3.51	.64	3.41	2.21
Air transport, freight	2 212	....	....	....	.03	....	....	.02	.08
Air transport, other	2 213	....	....	....	3.17	2.13	1.96	1.80	9.01
Other transport, passenger	2 215	....	....	....	....	....	....	....	....
Other transport, freight	2 216	....	....	....	....	....	....	....	....
Other transport, other	2 217	....	....	....	....	....	....	....	....
Transportation services, debit	3 205	....	....	....	−28.40	−36.46	−34.20	−33.89	−36.24
Passenger	3 850	....	....	....	*−4.08*	*−1.81*	*−1.86*	*−1.55*	*....*
Freight	3 851	....	....	....	*−22.63*	*−29.99*	*−31.18*	*−32.10*	*−35.46*
Other	3 852	....	....	....	*−1.70*	*−4.66*	*−1.16*	*−.24*	*−.78*
Sea transport, passenger	3 207	....	....	....	....	....	....	....	....
Sea transport, freight	3 208	....	....	....	−22.63	−29.99	−31.18	−32.10	−35.46
Sea transport, other	3 209	....	....	....	....	....	....	....	....
Air transport, passenger	3 211	....	....	....	−4.08	−1.81	−1.86	−1.55	....
Air transport, freight	3 212	....	....	....	....	....	....	....	....
Air transport, other	3 213	....	....	....	−1.70	−4.66	−1.16	−.24	−.78
Other transport, passenger	3 215	....	....	....	....	....	....	....	....
Other transport, freight	3 216	....	....	....	....	....	....	....	....
Other transport, other	3 217	....	....	....	....	....	....	....	....
Travel, credit	2 236	....	....	....	56.20	47.33	56.32	66.06	74.66
Business travel	2 237	....	....	....	....	....	....	....	....
Personal travel	2 240	....	....	....	56.20	47.33	56.32	66.06	74.66
Travel, debit	3 236	....	....	....	−4.01	−4.07	−5.29	−6.39	−7.40
Business travel	3 237	....	....	....	−2.71	−2.78	−3.54	−3.54	−5.11
Personal travel	3 240	....	....	....	−1.29	−1.29	−1.75	−2.85	−2.29
Other services, credit	2 200 BA	....	....	....	5.30	7.46	7.85	9.80	19.83
Communications	2 245	....	....	....	4.79	7.00	7.49	9.44	10.97
Construction	2 249	....	....	....	....	....	....	....	8.53
Insurance	2 253	....	....	....	.51	.46	.36	.36	.33
Financial	2 260	....	....	....	....	....	....	....	....
Computer and information	2 262	....	....	....	....	....	....	....	....
Royalties and licence fees	2 266	....	....	....	....	....	....	....	....
Other business services	2 268	....	....	....	....	....	....	....	....
Personal, cultural, and recreational	2 287	....	....	....	....	....	....	....	....
Government, n.i.e.	2 291	....	....	....	....	....	....	....	....
Other services, debit	3 200 BA	....	....	....	−3.85	−5.19	−5.89	−53.64	−33.12
Communications	3 245	....	....	....	−.07	−.26	−.34	−2.97	−7.26
Construction	3 249	....	....	....	....	....	....	....	−.47
Insurance	3 253	....	....	....	−3.58	−4.73	−4.88	−5.04	−6.21
Financial	3 260	....	....	....	....	....	....	....	....
Computer and information	3 262	....	....	....	−.19	−.20	−.66	−.79	−1.19
Royalties and licence fees	3 266	....	....	....	....	....	....	....	....
Other business services	3 268	....	....	....	....	....	....	−44.83	−18.00
Personal, cultural, and recreational	3 287	....	....	....	....	....	....	....	....
Government, n.i.e.	3 291	....	....	....	....	....	....	....	....

Table 2 (Continued). STANDARD PRESENTATION, FISCAL YEARS 2000–2007 ENDING JUNE 30

(Millions of U.S. dollars)

	Code	2000	2001	2002	2003	2004	2005	2006	2007
C. INCOME	4 300	....	....	....	−27.23	−27.79	−32.24	−37.87	−39.98
Total credit	2 300	....	....	....	*4.70*	*1.78*	*3.13*	*4.48*	*7.61*
Total debit	3 300	....	....	....	*−31.94*	*−29.57*	*−35.37*	*−42.35*	*−47.59*
Compensation of employees, credit	2 310	....	....	....	.72	.62	.71	.80	1.68
Compensation of employees, debit	3 310	....	....	....	−.63	−.53	−.72	−.95	−1.02
Investment income, credit	2 320	....	....	....	3.99	1.16	2.42	3.68	5.93
Direct investment income	2 330	....	....	....	....	....	....	....	....
Dividends and distributed branch profits	2 332	....	....	....	....	....	....	....	....
Reinvested earnings and undistributed branch profits	2 333	....	....	....	....	....	....	....	....
Income on debt (interest)	2 334	....	....	....	....	....	....	....	....
Portfolio investment income	2 339	....	....	....	.75	.72	2.28	3.68	5.89
Income on equity	2 340	....	....	....	....	....	....	....	....
Income on bonds and notes	2 350	....	....	....	.75	.72	2.28	3.68	5.89
Income on money market instruments	2 360	....	....	....	....	....	....	....	....
Other investment income	2 370	....	....	....	3.23	.44	.14	....	.04
Investment income, debit	3 320	....	....	....	−31.30	−29.04	−34.65	−41.41	−46.57
Direct investment income	3 330	....	....	....	−24.19	−21.91	−26.01	−32.81	−33.94
Dividends and distributed branch profits	3 332	....	....	....	−19.37	−15.35	−17.34	−21.84	−18.34
Reinvested earnings and undistributed branch profits	3 333	....	....	....	−4.81	−6.56	−8.67	−10.97	−15.60
Income on debt (interest)	3 334	....	....	....	....	....	....	....	....
Portfolio investment income	3 339	....	....	....	−7.12	−7.12	−8.64	−8.56	−12.63
Income on equity	3 340	....	....	....	....	....	....	....	....
Income on bonds and notes	3 350	....	....	....	−7.12	−7.12	−8.64	−.30	−4.54
Income on money market instruments	3 360	....	....	....	....	....	....	−8.26	−8.10
Other investment income	3 370	....	....	....	....	....	....	−.04	....
D. CURRENT TRANSFERS	4 379	....	....	....	61.56	67.46	68.98	87.46	76.40
Credit	2 379	....	....	....	94.46	91.70	94.88	114.16	95.83
General government	2 380	....	....	....	5.55	13.47	6.88	6.73	5.99
Other sectors	2 390	....	....	....	88.92	78.23	88.01	107.42	89.84
Workers' remittances	2 391	....	....	....	64.09	61.46	56.69	62.87	45.65
Other current transfers	2 392	....	....	....	24.82	16.77	31.31	44.56	44.19
Debit	3 379	....	....	....	−32.91	−24.24	−25.90	−26.70	−19.43
General government	3 380	....	....	....	−1.27	−1.52	−1.71	−.73	−1.30
Other sectors	3 390	....	....	....	−31.64	−22.72	−24.19	−25.97	−18.13
Workers' remittances	3 391	....	....	....	....	....	....	....	−10.93
Other current transfers	3 392	....	....	....	−31.64	−22.72	−24.19	−25.97	−7.21
CAPITAL AND FINANCIAL ACCOUNT	4 996	....	....	....	−5.68	39.88	97.88	71.79	81.40
CAPITAL ACCOUNT	4 994	....	....	....	4.80	5.15	.58	....	1.55
Total credit	2 994	....	....	....	*4.80*	*5.15*	*.58*	....	*1.55*
Total debit	3 994	....	....	....	....	....	....	....	....
Capital transfers, credit	2 400	....	....	....	4.80	5.15	.58	....	1.55
General government	2 401	....	....	....	4.80	5.15	.58	....	1.55
Debt forgiveness	2 402	....	....	....	4.80	5.15	.58	....	1.55
Other capital transfers	2 410	....	....	....	....	....	....	....	....
Other sectors	2 430	....	....	....	....	....	....	....	....
Migrants' transfers	2 431	....	....	....	....	....	....	....	....
Debt forgiveness	2 432	....	....	....	....	....	....	....	....
Other capital transfers	2 440	....	....	....	....	....	....	....	....
Capital transfers, debit	3 400	....	....	....	....	....	....	....	....
General government	3 401	....	....	....	....	....	....	....	....
Debt forgiveness	3 402	....	....	....	....	....	....	....	....
Other capital transfers	3 410	....	....	....	....	....	....	....	....
Other sectors	3 430	....	....	....	....	....	....	....	....
Migrants' transfers	3 431	....	....	....	....	....	....	....	....
Debt forgiveness	3 432	....	....	....	....	....	....	....	....
Other capital transfers	3 440	....	....	....	....	....	....	....	....
Nonproduced nonfinancial assets, credit	2 480	....	....	....	....	....	....	....	....
Nonproduced nonfinancial assets, debit	3 480	....	....	....	....	....	....	....	....

Table 2 (Continued). STANDARD PRESENTATION, FISCAL YEARS 2000–2007 ENDING JUNE 30

(Millions of U.S. dollars)

	Code	2000	2001	2002	2003	2004	2005	2006	2007
FINANCIAL ACCOUNT	4 995 ..	....	....	....	−10.48	34.73	97.30	71.79	79.86
A. DIRECT INVESTMENT	4 500 ..	....	....	....	21.90	56.75	51.93	82.07	68.45
Direct investment abroad	4 505 ..	....	....	....	....	....	....	....	....
Equity capital	4 510 ..	....	....	....	....	....	....	....	....
Claims on affiliated enterprises	4 515 ..	....	....	....	....	....	....	....	....
Liabilities to affiliated enterprises	4 520 ..	....	....	....	....	....	....	....	....
Reinvested earnings	4 525 ..	....	....	....	....	....	....	....	....
Other capital	4 530 ..	....	....	....	....	....	....	....	....
Claims on affiliated enterprises	4 535 ..	....	....	....	....	....	....	....	....
Liabilities to affiliated enterprises	4 540 ..	....	....	....	....	....	....	....	....
Direct investment in The Gambia	4 555 ..	....	....	....	21.90	56.75	51.93	82.07	68.45
Equity capital	4 560 ..	....	....	....	17.09	50.19	43.26	71.10	52.85
Claims on direct investors	4 565 ..	....	....	....	....	....	....	....	....
Liabilities to direct investors	4 570 ..	....	....	....	17.09	50.19	43.26	71.10	52.85
Reinvested earnings	4 575 ..	....	....	....	4.81	6.56	8.67	10.97	15.60
Other capital	4 580 ..	....	....	....	....	....	....	....	....
Claims on direct investors	4 585 ..	....	....	....	....	....	....	....	....
Liabilities to direct investors	4 590 ..	....	....	....	....	....	....	....	....
B. PORTFOLIO INVESTMENT	4 600 ..	....	....	....	....	....	....	....	....
Assets	4 602 ..	....	....	....	....	....	....	....	....
Equity securities	4 610 ..	....	....	....	....	....	....	....	....
Monetary authorities	4 611 ..	....	....	....	....	....	....	....	....
General government	4 612 ..	....	....	....	....	....	....	....	....
Banks	4 613 ..	....	....	....	....	....	....	....	....
Other sectors	4 614 ..	....	....	....	....	....	....	....	....
Debt securities	4 619 ..	....	....	....	....	....	....	....	....
Bonds and notes	4 620 ..	....	....	....	....	....	....	....	....
Monetary authorities	4 621 ..	....	....	....	....	....	....	....	....
General government	4 622 ..	....	....	....	....	....	....	....	....
Banks	4 623 ..	....	....	....	....	....	....	....	....
Other sectors	4 624 ..	....	....	....	....	....	....	....	....
Money market instruments	4 630 ..	....	....	....	....	....	....	....	....
Monetary authorities	4 631 ..	....	....	....	....	....	....	....	....
General government	4 632 ..	....	....	....	....	....	....	....	....
Banks	4 633 ..	....	....	....	....	....	....	....	....
Other sectors	4 634 ..	....	....	....	....	....	....	....	....
Liabilities	4 652 ..	....	....	....	....	....	....	....	....
Equity securities	4 660 ..	....	....	....	....	....	....	....	....
Banks	4 663 ..	....	....	....	....	....	....	....	....
Other sectors	4 664 ..	....	....	....	....	....	....	....	....
Debt securities	4 669 ..	....	....	....	....	....	....	....	....
Bonds and notes	4 670 ..	....	....	....	....	....	....	....	....
Monetary authorities	4 671 ..	....	....	....	....	....	....	....	....
General government	4 672 ..	....	....	....	....	....	....	....	....
Banks	4 673 ..	....	....	....	....	....	....	....	....
Other sectors	4 674 ..	....	....	....	....	....	....	....	....
Money market instruments	4 680 ..	....	....	....	....	....	....	....	....
Monetary authorities	4 681 ..	....	....	....	....	....	....	....	....
General government	4 682 ..	....	....	....	....	....	....	....	....
Banks	4 683 ..	....	....	....	....	....	....	....	....
Other sectors	4 684 ..	....	....	....	....	....	....	....	....
C. FINANCIAL DERIVATIVES	4 910 ..	....	....	....	....	....	....	....	....
Monetary authorities	4 911 ..	....	....	....	....	....	....	....	....
General government	4 912 ..	....	....	....	....	....	....	....	....
Banks	4 913 ..	....	....	....	....	....	....	....	....
Other sectors	4 914 ..	....	....	....	....	....	....	....	....
Assets	4 900 ..	....	....	....	....	....	....	....	....
Monetary authorities	4 901 ..	....	....	....	....	....	....	....	....
General government	4 902 ..	....	....	....	....	....	....	....	....
Banks	4 903 ..	....	....	....	....	....	....	....	....
Other sectors	4 904 ..	....	....	....	....	....	....	....	....
Liabilities	4 905 ..	....	....	....	....	....	....	....	....
Monetary authorities	4 906 ..	....	....	....	....	....	....	....	....
General government	4 907 ..	....	....	....	....	....	....	....	....
Banks	4 908 ..	....	....	....	....	....	....	....	....
Other sectors	4 909 ..	....	....	....	....	....	....	....	....

Table 2 (Concluded). STANDARD PRESENTATION, FISCAL YEARS 2000–2007 ENDING JUNE 30

(Millions of U.S. dollars)

	Code	2000	2001	2002	2003	2004	2005	2006	2007
D. OTHER INVESTMENT	4 700	....	....	....	−21.35	9.32	54.78	10.12	5.85
Assets	4 703	....	....	....	−19.64	−15.37	13.60	−14.08	25.95
Trade credits	4 706	....	....	....	....	....	....	....	....
General government	4 707	....	....	....	....	....	....	....	....
of which: Short-term	4 709	....	....	....	....	....	....	....	....
Other sectors	4 710	....	....	....	....	....	....	....	....
of which: Short-term	4 712	....	....	....	....	....	....	....	....
Loans	4 714	....	....	....	....	....	....	....	11.86
Monetary authorities	4 715	....	....	....	....	....	....	....	....
of which: Short-term	4 718	....	....	....	....	....	....	....	....
General government	4 719	....	....	....	....	....	....	....	....
of which: Short-term	4 721	....	....	....	....	....	....	....	....
Banks	4 722	....	....	....	....	....	....	....	....
of which: Short-term	4 724	....	....	....	....	....	....	....	....
Other sectors	4 725	....	....	....	....	....	....	....	11.86
of which: Short-term	4 727				....	....	....	....	*11.86*
Currency and deposits	4 730	....	....	....	−19.64	−15.37	13.60	−14.08	14.09
Monetary authorities	4 731	....	....	....	....	....	....	....	....
General government	4 732	....	....	....	....	....	....	....	....
Banks	4 733	....	....	....	−19.64	−15.37	13.60	−14.08	14.09
Other sectors	4 734	....	....	....	....	....	....	....	....
Other assets	4 736	....	....	....	....	....	....	....	....
Monetary authorities	4 737	....	....	....	....	....	....	....	....
of which: Short-term	4 739	....	....	....	....	....	....	....	....
General government	4 740	....	....	....	....	....	....	....	....
of which: Short-term	4 742	....	....	....	....	....	....	....	....
Banks	4 743	....	....	....	....	....	....	....	....
of which: Short-term	4 745	....	....	....	....	....	....	....	....
Other sectors	4 746	....	....	....	....	....	....	....	....
of which: Short-term	4 748	....	....	....	....	....	....	....	....
Liabilities	4 753	....	....	....	−1.71	24.69	41.18	24.20	−20.11
Trade credits	4 756	....	....	....	4.03	4.24	4.38	9.77	−31.55
General government	4 757	....	....	....	....	....	....	....	....
of which: Short-term	4 759	....	....	....	....	....	....	....	....
Other sectors	4 760	....	....	....	4.03	4.24	4.38	9.77	−31.55
of which: Short-term	4 762	....	....	....	*4.03*	*4.24*	*4.38*	*9.77*	*−31.55*
Loans	4 764	....	....	....	10.39	19.12	38.26	13.75	−4.01
Monetary authorities	4 765	....	....	....	3.83	−5.52	−6.66	−3.00	−1.11
of which: Use of Fund credit and loans from the Fund	4 766	....	....	....	*3.83*	*−5.52*	*−6.66*	*−3.00*	*−1.11*
of which: Short-term	4 768	....	....	....	....	....	....	....	....
General government	4 769	....	....	....	6.56	24.65	44.91	16.75	−2.90
of which: Short-term	4 771	....	....	....	....	....	....	....	....
Banks	4 772	....	....	....	....	....	....	....	....
of which: Short-term	4 774	....	....	....	....	....	....	....	....
Other sectors	4 775	....	....	....	....	....	....	....	....
of which: Short-term	4 777	....	....	....	....	....	....	....	....
Currency and deposits	4 780	....	....	....	−16.13	1.32	−1.46	.67	15.46
Monetary authorities	4 781	....	....	....	....	....	....	....	....
General government	4 782	....	....	....	....	....	....	....	....
Banks	4 783	....	....	....	−16.13	1.32	−1.46	.67	15.46
Other sectors	4 784	....	....	....	....	....	....	....	....
Other liabilities	4 786	....	....	....	....	....	....	....	....
Monetary authorities	4 787	....	....	....	....	....	....	....	....
of which: Short-term	4 789	....	....	....	....	....	....	....	....
General government	4 790	....	....	....	....	....	....	....	....
of which: Short-term	4 792	....	....	....	....	....	....	....	....
Banks	4 793	....	....	....	....	....	....	....	....
of which: Short-term	4 795	....	....	....	....	....	....	....	....
Other sectors	4 796	....	....	....	....	....	....	....	....
of which: Short-term	4 798	....	....	....	....	....	....	....	....
E. RESERVE ASSETS	4 802	....	....	....	−11.03	−31.34	−9.41	−20.40	5.56
Monetary gold	4 812	....	....	....	....	....	....	....	....
Special drawing rights	4 811	....	....	....	.01	−1.10	.93	−1.14	.20
Reserve position in the Fund	4 810	....	....	....	....	....	....	....	....
Foreign exchange	4 803	....	....	....	−8.23	−24.88	−10.45	−19.26	5.35
Other claims	4 813	....	....	....	−2.81	−5.36	.11	....	....
NET ERRORS AND OMISSIONS	4 998	....	....	....	2.52	−8.89	−54.32	−6.23	−28.74

Table 1. ANALYTIC PRESENTATION, 2000–2007

(Millions of U.S. dollars)

	Code	2000	2001	2002	2003	2004	2005	2006	2007
A. Current Account[1]	4 993 Z.	**−269.0**	**−211.7**	**−239.5**	**−391.4**	**−429.5**	**−771.7**	**−1,255.1**	**−2,118.5**
Goods: exports f.o.b.	2 100 ..	459.0	496.1	603.3	830.6	1,092.1	1,472.4	1,666.5	2,088.3
Goods: imports f.o.b.	3 100 ..	−970.5	−1,045.6	−1,092.3	−1,468.6	−2,007.7	−2,686.6	−3,685.9	−4,984.0
Balance on Goods	4 100 ..	*−511.5*	*−549.5*	*−489.0*	*−638.0*	*−915.5*	*−1,214.2*	*−2,019.4*	*−2,895.8*
Services: credit	2 200 ..	206.4	314.1	408.4	458.0	554.8	715.0	885.0	1,094.1
Services: debit	3 200 ..	−216.3	−236.9	−363.4	−396.7	−484.8	−631.5	−727.0	−932.6
Balance on Goods and Services	4 991 ..	*−521.4*	*−472.3*	*−444.1*	*−576.8*	*−845.6*	*−1,130.7*	*−1,861.3*	*−2,734.2*
Income: credit	2 300 ..	178.6	97.7	160.6	177.4	251.7	263.3	341.1	481.8
Income: debit	3 300 ..	−61.1	−65.4	−149.0	−163.9	−173.3	−201.2	−177.5	−442.4
Balance on Goods, Services, and Income	4 992 ..	*−403.9*	*−440.0*	*−432.5*	*−563.3*	*−767.1*	*−1,068.5*	*−1,697.7*	*−2,694.8*
Current transfers: credit	2 379 Z.	163.2	246.4	222.0	208.3	389.1	351.2	505.6	656.4
Current transfers: debit	3 379 ..	−28.3	−18.1	−29.0	−36.3	−51.5	−54.4	−63.0	−80.0
B. Capital Account[1]	4 994 Z.	**−4.8**	**−5.2**	**18.4**	**19.9**	**40.8**	**58.6**	**169.0**	**127.6**
Capital account: credit	2 994 Z.	. . . .	. . . .	27.1	27.9	44.2	61.6	170.0	127.9
Capital account: debit	3 994 ..	−4.8	−5.2	−8.6	−8.0	−3.4	−2.9	−1.0	−.3
Total, Groups A Plus B	4 981 ..	*−273.8*	*−216.9*	*−221.0*	*−371.5*	*−388.7*	*−713.0*	*−1,086.2*	*−1,990.9*
C. Financial Account[1]	4 995 W.	**92.8**	**209.7**	**14.0**	**313.5**	**446.2**	**666.0**	**1,348.3**	**2,196.8**
Direct investment abroad	4 505 ..	.5	.1	−4.1	−3.8	−9.6	89.5	15.8	−74.5
Direct investment in Georgia	4 555 Z.	131.1	109.8	160.2	334.6	492.3	452.8	1,061.0	1,728.3
Portfolio investment assets	4 602 ..	2.7	−.1	. . . .	. . . .	−13.1	13.1	−2.2	−11.0
Equity securities	4 610 ..	2.7	. . . .	. . . .	. . . .	−13.1	13.1	−2.2	−3.4
Debt securities	4 619 ..	. . . .	. . . .	. . . .	. . . .	. . . .	. . . .	. . . .	−7.6
Portfolio investment liabilities	4 652 Z.	. . . .	. . . .	. . . .	. . . .	. . . .	2.5	142.5	33.5
Equity securities	4 660 ..	. . . .	. . . .	. . . .	. . . .	. . . .	2.5	142.5	33.5
Debt securities	4 669 Z.	. . . .	. . . .	. . . .	. . . .	. . . .	. . . .	. . . .	. . . .
Financial derivatives	4 910 ..	. . . .	. . . .	. . . .	. . . .	. . . .	. . . .	. . . .	1.0
Financial derivatives assets	4 900 ..	. . . .	. . . .	. . . .	. . . .	. . . .	. . . .	. . . .	1.2
Financial derivatives liabilities	4 905 ..	. . . .	. . . .	. . . .	. . . .	. . . .	. . . .	. . . .	−.2
Other investment assets	4 703 ..	−7.7	−24.6	−75.2	−15.2	−27.4	−15.5	−45.9	−191.6
Monetary authorities	4 701 ..	. . . .	. . . .	. . . .	. . . .	. . . .	. . . .	−1.9	−44.8
General government	4 704 ..	. . . .	. . . .	−5.1	−5.0	−4.6	−6.9	7.5	5.9
Banks	4 705 ..	−7.7	−24.6	−61.5	.5	−21.4	−3.2	−34.2	−191.1
Other sectors	4 728 ..	. . . .	. . . .	−8.5	−10.7	−1.3	−5.4	−17.3	38.4
Other investment liabilities	4 753 W.	−33.8	124.5	−66.9	−2.2	3.9	123.7	177.0	711.1
Monetary authorities	4 753 WA	. . . .	. . . .	−.6	−.5	−.1	−.1	−.2	−56.6
General government	4 753 ZB	−41.1	99.1	−126.0	−57.2	−72.9	−73.5	−123.4	11.8
Banks	4 753 ZC	7.3	25.4	14.7	4.1	27.6	164.1	223.0	746.6
Other sectors	4 753 ZD	. . . .	. . . .	45.0	51.4	49.3	33.3	77.6	9.3
Total, Groups A Through C	4 983 ..	*−181.0*	*−7.2*	*−207.0*	*−58.1*	*57.4*	*−47.0*	*262.1*	*205.9*
D. Net Errors and Omissions	4 998 ..	**187.4**	**34.9**	**15.6**	**−6.0**	**10.6**	**27.6**	**68.2**	**−10.7**
Total, Groups A Through D	4 984 ..	*6.4*	*27.7*	*−191.5*	*−64.1*	*68.0*	*−19.4*	*330.3*	*195.2*
E. Reserves and Related Items	4 802 A.	**−6.4**	**−27.7**	**191.5**	**64.1**	**−68.0**	**19.4**	**−330.3**	**−195.2**
Reserve assets	4 802 ..	19.8	−47.0	−31.7	18.5	−177.9	−110.6	−438.6	−377.1
Use of Fund credit and loans	4 766 ..	−26.2	19.4	−.1	−47.4	−34.2	−12.5	−7.9	3.2
Exceptional financing	4 920 ..	. . . .	. . . .	223.3	93.0	144.1	142.5	116.2	178.7
Conversion rates: lari per U.S. dollar	0 101 ..	**1.9762**	**2.0730**	**2.1957**	**2.1457**	**1.9167**	**1.8127**	**1.7804**	**1.6705**

[1] Excludes components that have been classified in the categories of Group E.

Table 2. STANDARD PRESENTATION, 2000–2007

(Millions of U.S. dollars)

	Code	2000	2001	2002	2003	2004	2005	2006	2007
CURRENT ACCOUNT...	4 993 ..	**−269.0**	**−211.7**	**−215.7**	**−383.3**	**−353.2**	**−709.7**	**−1,173.8**	**−2,005.6**
A. GOODS..	4 100 ..	**−511.5**	**−549.5**	**−489.0**	**−638.0**	**−915.5**	**−1,214.2**	**−2,019.4**	**−2,895.8**
Credit..	2 100 ..	**459.0**	**496.1**	**603.3**	**830.6**	**1,092.1**	**1,472.4**	**1,666.5**	**2,088.3**
General merchandise: exports f.o.b.	2 110 ..	459.0	496.1	540.8	743.3	1,024.7	1,361.3	1,517.4	1,963.1
Goods for processing: exports f.o.b.	2 150 ..	....	....	20.0	39.9	23.6	50.2	76.2	31.8
Repairs on goods................................	2 160 ..	....	....	6.2	20.6	12.4	7.9	3.5	.7
Goods procured in ports by carriers..........	2 170 ..	....	....	7.7	8.2	12.6	18.3	20.1	23.2
Nonmonetary gold...............................	2 180 ..	....	....	28.7	18.6	18.8	34.7	49.4	69.4
Debit..	3 100 ..	**−970.5**	**−1,045.6**	**−1,092.3**	**−1,468.6**	**−2,007.7**	**−2,686.6**	**−3,685.9**	**−4,984.0**
General merchandise: imports f.o.b.	3 110 ..	−970.5	−1,045.6	−1,066.6	−1,420.0	−1,976.4	−2,618.1	−3,630.2	−4,941.5
Goods for processing: imports f.o.b.	3 150 ..	....	....	−18.4	−39.0	−20.4	−49.9	−35.6	−27.3
Repairs on goods................................	3 160 ..	....	....	....	....	−.1	−4.1	−5.8	−1.4
Goods procured in ports by carriers..........	3 170 ..	....	....	−7.3	−9.5	−10.8	−14.4	−14.1	−13.8
Nonmonetary gold...............................	3 180 ..	....	....	....	....	....	....	−.1	−.1
B. SERVICES...	4 200 ..	**−9.9**	**77.2**	**44.9**	**61.2**	**69.9**	**83.5**	**158.0**	**161.5**
Total credit..	2 200 ..	*206.4*	*314.1*	*408.4*	*458.0*	*554.8*	*715.0*	*885.0*	*1,094.1*
Total debit...	3 200 ..	*−216.3*	*−236.9*	*−363.4*	*−396.7*	*−484.8*	*−631.5*	*−727.0*	*−932.6*
Transportation services, credit........................	2 205 ..	**102.5**	**169.6**	**200.7**	**213.4**	**266.0**	**331.8**	**410.8**	**511.5**
Passenger...	2 850 ..	*9.5*	*19.1*	*17.7*	*24.7*	*32.1*	*45.5*	*48.0*	*56.1*
Freight...	2 851 ..	*76.6*	*134.9*	*138.5*	*139.9*	*150.0*	*174.1*	*227.0*	*307.5*
Other...	2 852 ..	*16.4*	*15.6*	*44.5*	*48.8*	*83.9*	*112.1*	*135.8*	*147.9*
Sea transport, passenger......................	2 207 ..	....	....	.6	.6	.8	1.3	1.9	1.8
Sea transport, freight...........................	2 208 ..	14.8	19.1	.7	1.1	2.1	3.9	5.3	5.5
Sea transport, other............................	2 209 ..	12.9	7.5	36.7	39.8	58.4	70.0	87.6	102.4
Air transport, passenger.......................	2 211 ..	9.5	16.2	14.5	21.6	28.8	40.0	39.6	43.7
Air transport, freight............................	2 212 ..	4.1	3.2	....	....	....	.6	.9	1.7
Air transport, other.............................	2 213 ..	3.5	3.7	5.8	6.6	22.2	35.9	43.0	38.0
Other transport, passenger....................	2 215 ..	....	2.9	2.6	2.5	2.5	4.2	6.4	10.5
Other transport, freight........................	2 216 ..	57.7	112.6	137.8	138.8	148.0	169.7	220.8	300.4
Other transport, other..........................	2 217 ..	....	4.4	2.0	2.3	3.3	6.1	5.3	7.4
Transportation services, debit........................	3 205 ..	**−89.2**	**−98.3**	**−108.5**	**−137.2**	**−205.5**	**−288.0**	**−387.8**	**−507.5**
Passenger...	3 850 ..	*−19.0*	*−29.1*	*−39.6*	*−40.3*	*−48.9*	*−68.5*	*−90.2*	*−101.3*
Freight...	3 851 ..	*−44.7*	*−52.4*	*−57.5*	*−83.5*	*−139.7*	*−192.0*	*−272.1*	*−381.3*
Other...	3 852 ..	*−25.5*	*−16.8*	*−11.5*	*−13.3*	*−16.9*	*−27.6*	*−25.4*	*−24.9*
Sea transport, passenger......................	3 207 ..	−9.3	−7.0	−.8	−.8	−.7	−.8	−.9	−.5
Sea transport, freight...........................	3 208 ..	−16.4	−18.5	−21.0	−34.2	−62.1	−75.9	−97.6	−140.6
Sea transport, other............................	3 209 ..	−11.2	−6.8	−2.6	−2.5	−3.1	−4.5	−6.2	−5.5
Air transport, passenger.......................	3 211 ..	−9.7	−14.5	−31.8	−31.4	−38.1	−51.5	−60.0	−65.6
Air transport, freight............................	3 212 ..	−6.8	−7.4	−8.8	−10.2	−15.0	−22.7	−30.1	−52.4
Air transport, other.............................	3 213 ..	−14.3	−10.0	−7.2	−8.9	−11.1	−18.0	−14.9	−13.2
Other transport, passenger....................	3 215 ..	....	−7.6	−7.0	−8.2	−10.2	−16.1	−29.3	−35.3
Other transport, freight........................	3 216 ..	−21.5	−26.5	−27.6	−39.2	−62.6	−93.4	−144.5	−188.2
Other transport, other..........................	3 217 ..	....	....	−1.7	−2.0	−2.6	−5.1	−4.4	−6.3
Travel, credit..	2 236 ..	**96.7**	**117.4**	**125.7**	**147.1**	**176.6**	**241.4**	**312.6**	**383.7**
Business travel...................................	2 237 ..	67.7	71.6	73.9	87.3	105.4	143.3	167.7	210.2
Personal travel...................................	2 240 ..	29.0	45.8	51.8	59.8	71.2	98.1	144.9	173.5
Travel, debit..	3 236 ..	**−110.3**	**−107.0**	**−148.9**	**−130.2**	**−147.4**	**−168.8**	**−166.6**	**−175.8**
Business travel...................................	3 237 ..	−77.3	−62.1	−79.3	−69.7	−101.7	−111.0	−112.6	−115.9
Personal travel...................................	3 240 ..	−33.0	−44.9	−69.6	−60.5	−45.6	−57.8	−54.1	−59.9
Other services, credit..................................	2 200 BA	**7.2**	**27.1**	**82.0**	**97.4**	**112.2**	**141.8**	**161.7**	**198.9**
Communications..................................	2 245 ..	7.2	12.4	17.5	24.2	17.7	19.8	17.5	14.5
Construction......................................	2 249 ..	....	....	....	....	....	....	....	2.8
Insurance..	2 253 ..	....	....	9.3	9.5	10.0	11.0	13.4	13.0
Financial...	2 260 ..	....	....	8.0	10.3	17.4	20.3	18.9	9.1
Computer and information......................	2 262 ..	....	....	....	....	....	.1	.5	1.9
Royalties and licence fees......................	2 266 ..	....	....	5.5	6.3	7.7	9.3	12.9	10.6
Other business services.........................	2 268 ..	....	....	3.7	7.4	10.6	10.8	8.8	20.3
Personal, cultural, and recreational..........	2 287 ..	....	....	.1	.2	2.1	3.2	5.5	8.7
Government, n.i.e................................	2 291 ..	....	14.7	37.9	39.5	46.6	67.4	84.1	118.0
Other services, debit..................................	3 200 BA	**−16.8**	**−31.6**	**−106.0**	**−129.4**	**−132.0**	**−174.6**	**−172.6**	**−249.3**
Communications..................................	3 245 ..	−4.1	−9.7	−10.5	−15.8	−13.3	−17.3	−14.4	−11.4
Construction......................................	3 249 ..	....	....	−14.5	−14.9	−7.1	−16.0	−4.3	−6.2
Insurance..	3 253 ..	−12.7	−13.1	−18.0	−27.9	−42.3	−58.9	−80.4	−110.5
Financial...	3 260 ..	....	....	−2.8	−2.0	−2.6	−2.2	−4.2	−12.1
Computer and information......................	3 262 ..	....	....	−.5	−.7	−.7	−1.1	−.8	−2.3
Royalties and licence fees......................	3 266 ..	....	....	−10.7	−10.6	−5.7	−5.3	−5.0	−4.9
Other business services.........................	3 268 ..	....	−3.0	−9.0	−15.8	−15.1	−26.1	−23.7	−34.8
Personal, cultural, and recreational..........	3 287 ..	....	....	....	....	....	....	....	−6.7
Government, n.i.e................................	3 291 ..	....	−5.8	−39.9	−41.8	−45.1	−47.6	−39.9	−60.6

Table 2 (Continued). STANDARD PRESENTATION, 2000–2007

(Millions of U.S. dollars)

	Code	2000	2001	2002	2003	2004	2005	2006	2007
C. INCOME	4 300	**117.5**	**32.3**	**11.6**	**13.5**	**78.5**	**62.1**	**163.6**	**39.4**
Total credit	2 300	*178.6*	*97.7*	*160.6*	*177.4*	*251.7*	*263.3*	*341.1*	*481.8*
Total debit	3 300	*−61.1*	*−65.4*	*−149.0*	*−163.9*	*−173.3*	*−201.2*	*−177.5*	*−442.4*
Compensation of employees, credit	2 310	**178.6**	**94.2**	**151.6**	**168.0**	**236.3**	**247.2**	**315.3**	**405.8**
Compensation of employees, debit	3 310	**−14.6**	**−7.2**	**−15.4**	**−15.6**	**−15.0**	**−18.0**	**−20.2**	**−26.4**
Investment income, credit	2 320	....	**3.5**	**9.0**	**9.4**	**15.4**	**16.1**	**25.9**	**76.0**
Direct investment income	2 330	....	....	4.2	3.8	9.6	3.5	....	....
Dividends and distributed branch profits	2 332	....	....	....	....	....	....	....	....
Reinvested earnings and undistributed branch profits	2 333	....	....	4.2	3.8	9.6	3.5		
Income on debt (interest)	2 334	....	....	....	....	....	....	....	....
Portfolio investment income	2 339	....	....	2.2	2.3	2.0	5.4	9.0	23.3
Income on equity	2 340	....	....	....	....	....	....	....	....
Income on bonds and notes	2 350	....	....	2.1	2.3	2.0	5.4	9.0	23.3
Income on money market instruments	2 360	....	....	....	....	....	....	....	....
Other investment income	2 370	....	3.5	2.6	3.3	3.8	7.2	16.9	52.7
Investment income, debit	3 320	**−46.5**	**−58.2**	**−133.6**	**−148.3**	**−158.3**	**−183.2**	**−157.3**	**−416.0**
Direct investment income	3 330	−.3	−11.0	−76.0	−88.7	−100.2	−116.2	−94.4	−297.6
Dividends and distributed branch profits	3 332	....	....	−31.8	−32.0	−50.3	−60.6	−27.5	−173.3
Reinvested earnings and undistributed branch profits	3 333	....	....	−43.4	−52.0	−45.7	−48.5	−64.5	−49.0
Income on debt (interest)	3 334	....	....	−.8	−4.7	−4.2	−7.2	−2.4	−75.3
Portfolio investment income	3 339	....	−1.8	−.1	−.1	....	−.1	−.5	−1.2
Income on equity	3 340	....	....	−.1	−.1	....	....	−.5	−1.2
Income on bonds and notes	3 350	....	....	....	....	....	....	....	....
Income on money market instruments	3 360	....	....	....	....	....	....	....	....
Other investment income	3 370	−46.2	−45.4	−57.5	−59.5	−58.0	−66.9	−62.4	−117.2
D. CURRENT TRANSFERS	4 379	**134.9**	**228.3**	**216.8**	**180.0**	**413.9**	**358.8**	**523.9**	**689.3**
Credit	2 379	**163.2**	**246.4**	**245.8**	**216.3**	**465.4**	**413.2**	**587.0**	**769.3**
General government	2 380	7.1	103.3	69.8	50.0	231.7	141.2	191.4	207.6
Other sectors	2 390	156.1	143.1	176.0	166.3	233.7	272.0	395.5	561.7
Workers' remittances	2 391	94.9	87.1	74.7	64.5	64.0	93.8	153.0	245.0
Other current transfers	2 392	61.2	56.0	101.3	101.9	169.7	178.2	242.6	316.7
Debit	3 379	**−28.3**	**−18.1**	**−29.0**	**−36.3**	**−51.5**	**−54.4**	**−63.0**	**−80.0**
General government	3 380	−8.9	−4.8	−24.1	−26.8	−39.6	−41.1	−51.6	−68.6
Other sectors	3 390	−19.4	−13.3	−4.9	−9.5	−11.9	−13.3	−11.4	−11.5
Workers' remittances	3 391	−19.4	−13.3	−2.1	−5.7	−7.4	−7.6	−3.8	−1.7
Other current transfers	3 392	....	....	−2.8	−3.8	−4.5	−5.7	−7.6	−9.8
CAPITAL AND FINANCIAL ACCOUNT	4 996	**81.6**	**176.8**	**200.1**	**389.3**	**342.6**	**682.1**	**1,105.6**	**2,016.3**
CAPITAL ACCOUNT	4 994	**−4.8**	**−5.2**	**18.4**	**19.9**	**40.8**	**58.6**	**171.2**	**127.6**
Total credit	2 994	....	....	*27.1*	*27.9*	*44.2*	*61.6*	*172.2*	*127.9*
Total debit	3 994	*−4.8*	*−5.2*	*−8.6*	*−8.0*	*−3.4*	*−2.9*	*−1.0*	*−.3*
Capital transfers, credit	2 400	....	....	**27.1**	**27.9**	**44.2**	**61.6**	**172.2**	**127.9**
General government	2 401	....	....	17.9	21.1	35.1	48.3	145.4	67.9
Debt forgiveness	2 402	....	....	....	....	....	....	54.4	....
Other capital transfers	2 410	....	....	17.9	21.1	35.1	48.3	91.0	67.9
Other sectors	2 430	....	....	9.2	6.8	9.1	13.3	26.8	60.0
Migrants' transfers	2 431	....	....	4.1	3.5	2.9	5.1	17.1	44.9
Debt forgiveness	2 432	....	....	....	....	....	....	....	....
Other capital transfers	2 440	....	....	5.1	3.3	6.2	8.2	9.7	15.1
Capital transfers, debit	3 400	**−4.8**	**−5.2**	**−8.6**	**−8.0**	**−3.4**	**−2.9**	**−1.0**	**−.3**
General government	3 401	....	....	....	....	....	....	....	....
Debt forgiveness	3 402	....	....	....	....	....	....	....	....
Other capital transfers	3 410	....	....	....	....	....	....	....	....
Other sectors	3 430	−4.8	−5.2	−8.6	−8.0	−3.4	−2.9	−1.0	−.3
Migrants' transfers	3 431	−4.8	−5.2	−8.6	−8.0	−3.4	−2.9	−1.0	−.3
Debt forgiveness	3 432	....	....	....	....	....	....	....	....
Other capital transfers	3 440	....	....	....	....	....	....	....	....
Nonproduced nonfinancial assets, credit	2 480	....	....	....	....	....	....	....	....
Nonproduced nonfinancial assets, debit	3 480	....	....	....	....	....	....	....	....

Table 2 (Continued). STANDARD PRESENTATION, 2000–2007

(Millions of U.S. dollars)

	Code	2000	2001	2002	2003	2004	2005	2006	2007
FINANCIAL ACCOUNT	4 995	**86.4**	**182.0**	**181.7**	**369.5**	**301.8**	**623.5**	**934.4**	**1,888.8**
A. DIRECT INVESTMENT	4 500	**131.6**	**109.9**	**156.1**	**330.9**	**482.8**	**542.2**	**1,076.8**	**1,653.8**
Direct investment abroad	4 505	**.5**	**.1**	**−4.1**	**−3.8**	**−9.6**	**89.5**	**15.8**	**−74.5**
Equity capital	4 510	.5	....	.1	....	....	93.0	18.0	−74.5
Claims on affiliated enterprises	4 515	....	....	.1	....	....	93.0	18.0	−74.5
Liabilities to affiliated enterprises	4 520	....	....	....	....	....	....	....	....
Reinvested earnings	4 525	....	....	−4.2	−3.8	−9.6	−3.5	....	....
Other capital	4 530	....	....	....	....	....	....	−2.2	....
Claims on affiliated enterprises	4 535	....	....	....	....	....	....	−2.2	....
Liabilities to affiliated enterprises	4 540	....	....	....	....	....	....	....	....
Direct investment in Georgia	4 555	**131.1**	**109.8**	**160.2**	**334.6**	**492.3**	**452.8**	**1,061.0**	**1,728.3**
Equity capital	4 560	131.1	....	89.5	255.6	394.6	334.9	909.3	839.0
Claims on direct investors	4 565	....	....	....	....	....	....	....	....
Liabilities to direct investors	4 570	....	....	89.5	255.6	394.6	334.9	909.3	839.0
Reinvested earnings	4 575	....	....	43.4	52.0	45.7	48.5	64.5	49.0
Other capital	4 580	....	....	27.4	27.1	52.0	69.4	87.2	840.4
Claims on direct investors	4 585	....	....	....	....	....	....	....	2.6
Liabilities to direct investors	4 590	....	....	27.4	27.1	52.0	69.4	87.2	837.8
B. PORTFOLIO INVESTMENT	4 600	**2.7**	**−.1**	**....**	**....**	**−13.0**	**15.5**	**140.3**	**22.5**
Assets	4 602	**2.7**	**−.1**	**....**	**....**	**−13.1**	**13.1**	**−2.2**	**−11.0**
Equity securities	4 610	2.7	....	....	....	−13.1	13.1	−2.2	−3.4
Monetary authorities	4 611	....	....	....	....	....	....	....	....
General government	4 612	....	....	....	....	....	....	....	....
Banks	4 613	....	....	....	....	−13.1	13.1	−2.2	−3.4
Other sectors	4 614	....	....	....	....	....	....	....	....
Debt securities	4 619	....	....	....	....	....	....	....	−7.6
Bonds and notes	4 620	....	....	....	....	....	....	....	−5.2
Monetary authorities	4 621	....	....	....	....	....	....	....	....
General government	4 622	....	....	....	....	....	....	....	....
Banks	4 623	....	....	....	....	....	....	....	−5.1
Other sectors	4 624	....	....	....	....	....	....	....	−.1
Money market instruments	4 630	....	....	....	....	....	....	....	−2.4
Monetary authorities	4 631	....	....	....	....	....	....	....	....
General government	4 632	....	....	....	....	....	....	....	....
Banks	4 633	....	....	....	....	....	....	....	−2.4
Other sectors	4 634	....	....	....	....	....	....	....	....
Liabilities	4 652	**....**	**....**	**....**	**....**	**.1**	**2.4**	**142.5**	**33.5**
Equity securities	4 660	....	....	....	....	....	2.5	142.5	33.5
Banks	4 663	....	....	....	....	....	2.5	142.5	33.5
Other sectors	4 664	....	....	....	....	....	....	....	....
Debt securities	4 669	....	....	....	....	.1	−.1	....	....
Bonds and notes	4 670	....	....	....	....	....	....	....	....
Monetary authorities	4 671	....	....	....	....	....	....	....	....
General government	4 672	....	....	....	....	....	....	....	....
Banks	4 673	....	....	....	....	....	....	....	....
Other sectors	4 674	....	....	....	....	....	....	....	....
Money market instruments	4 680	....	....	....	....	.1	−.1	....	....
Monetary authorities	4 681	....	....	....	....	....	....	....	....
General government	4 682	....	....	....	....	.1	−.1	....	....
Banks	4 683	....	....	....	....	....	....	....	....
Other sectors	4 684	....	....	....	....	....	....	....	....
C. FINANCIAL DERIVATIVES	4 910	**....**	**....**	**....**	**....**	**....**	**....**	**....**	**1.0**
Monetary authorities	4 911	....	....	....	....	....	....	....	....
General government	4 912	....	....	....	....	....	....	....	....
Banks	4 913	....	....	....	....	....	....	....	....
Other sectors	4 914	....	....	....	....	....	....	....	1.0
Assets	4 900	**....**	**....**	**....**	**....**	**....**	**....**	**....**	**1.2**
Monetary authorities	4 901	....	....	....	....	....	....	....	....
General government	4 902	....	....	....	....	....	....	....	....
Banks	4 903	....	....	....	....	....	....	....	....
Other sectors	4 904	....	....	....	....	....	....	....	1.2
Liabilities	4 905	**....**	**....**	**....**	**....**	**....**	**....**	**....**	**−.2**
Monetary authorities	4 906	....	....	....	....	....	....	....	....
General government	4 907	....	....	....	....	....	....	....	....
Banks	4 908	....	....	....	....	....	....	....	....
Other sectors	4 909	....	....	....	....	....	....	....	−.2

Table 2 (Concluded). STANDARD PRESENTATION, 2000–2007

(Millions of U.S. dollars)

	Code	2000	2001	2002	2003	2004	2005	2006	2007
D. OTHER INVESTMENT	4 700	−67.7	119.3	57.3	20.1	9.9	176.3	155.9	588.6
Assets	4 703	−7.7	−24.6	−75.2	−15.2	−27.4	−15.5	−45.9	−191.6
Trade credits	4 706	....	....	−13.5	−15.7	−4.6	−10.5	−1.6	−5.8
General government	4 707	....	....	−5.0	−5.0	−4.7	−3.7	−2.3	−.8
of which: Short-term	4 709	....	....	....	....	....	....	....	....
Other sectors	4 710	....	....	−8.5	−10.7	.1	−6.8	.7	−5.1
of which: Short-term	4 712	....	....	−8.5	−10.7	.1	−6.8	.7	−5.1
Loans	4 714	−2.7	−1.4	−8.4	5.5	4.2	−.8	−24.7	−101.3
Monetary authorities	4 715	....	....	....	....	....	....	−2.3	−44.8
of which: Short-term	4 718	....	....	....	....	....	....	−2.3	−44.8
General government	4 719	....	....	....	....	....	....	....	....
of which: Short-term	4 721	....	....	....	....	....	....	....	....
Banks	4 722	−2.7	−1.4	−8.4	5.5	4.2	−.8	3.6	−44.8
of which: Short-term	4 724	−1.2	−2.3	−6.3	7.0	2.2	−2.3	2.7	−31.8
Other sectors	4 725	....	....	....	....	....	....	−26.0	−11.8
of which: Short-term	4 727	....	....	....	....	....	....	−26.0	30.3
Currency and deposits	4 730	−2.7	−21.1	−24.5	−1.5	−29.2	−3.7	−19.8	−85.7
Monetary authorities	4 731	....	....	....	....	....	....	.5	....
General government	4 732	....	....	....	....	....	−1.2	9.9	4.9
Banks	4 733	−2.7	−21.1	−24.5	−1.5	−29.2	−2.5	−38.6	−145.8
Other sectors	4 734	....	....	....	....	....	....	8.5	55.2
Other assets	4 736	−2.3	−2.1	−28.8	−3.5	2.2	−.6	.2	1.2
Monetary authorities	4 737	....	....	....	....	....	....	....	....
of which: Short-term	4 739	....	....	....	....	....	....	....	....
General government	4 740	....	....	−.1	....	....	−2.0	−.1	1.8
of which: Short-term	4 742	....	....	−.1	....	....	−2.0	−.1	1.8
Banks	4 743	−2.3	−2.1	−28.7	−3.5	3.6	....	.8	−.6
of which: Short-term	4 745	....	....	−28.7	−3.5	3.6	....	.8	−.6
Other sectors	4 746	....	....	....	....	−1.4	1.4	−.5	....
of which: Short-term	4 748	....	....	....	....	−1.4	1.4	−.5	....
Liabilities	4 753	−60.0	143.9	132.5	35.3	37.3	191.9	201.7	780.2
Trade credits	4 756	....	....	9.1	3.0	14.9	26.0	34.3	−53.1
General government	4 757	....	....	....	....	....	....	....	....
of which: Short-term	4 759	....	....	....	....	....	....	....	....
Other sectors	4 760	....	....	9.1	3.0	14.9	26.0	34.3	−53.1
of which: Short-term	4 762	....	....	9.1	3.0	14.9	26.0	34.3	−53.1
Loans	4 764	−127.7	30.5	34.8	26.0	136.7	99.8	234.3	767.6
Monetary authorities	4 765	−26.2	19.4	.1	−48.0	−33.8	−12.7	−8.1	−53.4
of which: Use of Fund credit and loans from the Fund.	4 766	−26.2	19.4	−.1	−47.4	−34.2	−12.5	−7.9	3.2
of which: Short-term	4 768	....	....	−.1	....	....	....	....	....
General government	4 769	−108.2	−13.0	−3.5	14.6	111.2	48.8	−21.4	111.3
of which: Short-term	4 771	....	....	....	−.1	.6	.4	.5	.2
Banks	4 772	6.7	24.1	−5.1	11.0	24.9	56.4	220.5	646.1
of which: Short-term	4 774	2.3	5.4	−10.3	2.5	3.7	9.8	33.7	80.4
Other sectors	4 775	....	....	43.3	48.4	34.4	7.3	43.3	63.5
of which: Short-term	4 777	....	....	.3	.4	.5	.4	8.3	−15.5
Currency and deposits	4 780	.5	1.8	14.5	−4.3	−1.4	94.7	−5.3	92.0
Monetary authorities	4 781	....	....	....	....	....	....	....	....
General government	4 782	....	....	....	....	....	....	....	....
Banks	4 783	.5	1.8	14.5	−4.3	−1.4	94.7	−5.3	92.0
Other sectors	4 784	....	....	....	....	....	....	....	....
Other liabilities	4 786	67.2	111.6	74.1	10.6	−112.9	−28.6	−61.6	−26.3
Monetary authorities	4 787	....	....	....	.5	−.6	....	....	....
of which: Short-term	4 789	....	....	....	.5	−.6	....	....	....
General government	4 790	67.1	112.1	68.5	10.1	−119.0	−36.0	−86.6	−34.9
of which: Short-term	4 792	67.1	112.1	68.5	10.1	−119.0	−36.0	−86.6	−34.9
Banks	4 793	.1	−.5	4.3	−3.4	2.7	12.0	7.5	2.6
of which: Short-term	4 795	....	....	−1.0	−.8	−1.4	−.8	−.3	2.6
Other sectors	4 796	....	....	1.3	3.4	4.0	−4.7	17.6	6.0
of which: Short-term	4 798	....	....	1.3	3.4	4.0	−4.7	17.6	6.0
E. RESERVE ASSETS	4 802	19.8	−47.0	−31.7	18.5	−177.9	−110.6	−438.6	−377.1
Monetary gold	4 812	....	....	....	....	....	....	....	....
Special drawing rights	4 811	5.0	−.7	1.2	−2.0	−6.1	9.5	.2	−13.7
Reserve position in the Fund	4 810	....	....	....	....	....	....	....	....
Foreign exchange	4 803	14.8	−46.3	−32.9	20.5	−171.8	−120.1	−438.8	−363.4
Other claims	4 813	....	....	....	....	....	....	....	....
NET ERRORS AND OMISSIONS	4 998	187.4	34.9	15.6	−6.0	10.6	27.6	68.2	−10.7

Table 3. INTERNATIONAL INVESTMENT POSITION (End-period stocks), 2000–2007

(Millions of U.S. dollars)

	Code	2000	2001	2002	2003	2004	2005	2006	2007
ASSETS	8 995 C.	....	....	....	....	....	885.2	1,399.7	2,136.2
Direct investment abroad	8 505 ..	....	....	....	....	....	21.2	5.4	79.9
Equity capital and reinvested earnings	8 506 ..	....	....	....	....	....	21.2	3.2	79.9
Claims on affiliated enterprises	8 507 ..	....	....	....	....	....	21.2	3.2	79.9
Liabilities to affiliated enterprises	8 508 ..	....	....	....	....	....	....	....	....
Other capital	8 530 ..	....	....	....	....	....	....	2.3	....
Claims on affiliated enterprises	8 535 ..	....	....	....	....	....	....	2.3	....
Liabilities to affiliated enterprises	8 540 ..	....	....	....	....	....	....	....	....
Portfolio investment	8 602 ..	....	....	....	....	....	....	2.2	7.6
Equity securities	8 610 ..	....						2.2	....
Monetary authorities	8 611 ..	....						....	....
General government	8 612 ..	....						....	....
Banks	8 613 ..	....						2.2	....
Other sectors	8 614 ..	....						....	....
Debt securities	8 619 ..	....						....	7.6
Bonds and notes	8 620 ..	....						....	5.2
Monetary authorities	8 621 ..	....						....	
General government	8 622 ..	....						....	
Banks	8 623 ..	....						....	5.1
Other sectors	8 624 ..	....						....	.1
Money market instruments	8 630 ..	....						....	2.4
Monetary authorities	8 631 ..	....						....	....
General government	8 632 ..	....						....	....
Banks	8 633 ..	....						....	2.4
Other sectors	8 634 ..	....						....	....
Financial derivatives	8 900 ..	....	....	....	....	....	....	....	.1
Monetary authorities	8 901 ..	....						....	....
General government	8 902 ..	....						....	....
Banks	8 903 ..	....						....	.1
Other sectors	8 904 ..	....						....	....
Other investment	8 703 ..	....	....	....	....	....	385.5	461.2	687.4
Trade credits	8 706 ..	....					121.7	129.3	141.3
General government	8 707 ..	....					29.3	31.6	32.4
of which: Short-term	8 709 ..	....					....	....	....
Other sectors	8 710 ..	....					92.4	97.7	108.9
of which: Short-term	8 712 ..	....					*92.4*	*97.7*	*108.9*
Loans	8 714 ..	....					14.3	43.7	156.3
Monetary authorities	8 715 ..	....					.6	2.8	51.5
of which: Short-term	8 718 ..	....					*.6*	*2.8*	*51.5*
General government	8 719 ..	....					....	....	....
of which: Short-term	8 721 ..	....					....	....	....
Banks	8 722 ..	....					13.7	10.1	62.3
of which: Short-term	8 724 ..	....					*11.8*	*8.0*	*47.4*
Other sectors	8 725 ..	....					....	30.8	42.5
of which: Short-term	8 727 ..	....					....	*30.8*	*.5*
Currency and deposits	8 730 ..	....					245.7	282.5	384.2
Monetary authorities	8 731 ..	....					....	....	....
General government	8 732 ..	....					15.0	6.9	3.4
Banks	8 733 ..	....					168.8	211.3	371.5
Other sectors	8 734 ..	....					61.8	64.2	9.3
Other assets	8 736 ..	....					3.9	5.7	5.6
Monetary authorities	8 737 ..	....					....	....	....
of which: Short-term	8 739 ..	....					....	....	....
General government	8 740 ..	....					2.5	2.6	.8
of which: Short-term	8 742 ..	....					*2.5*	*2.6*	*.8*
Banks	8 743 ..	....					1.4	2.6	4.3
of which: Short-term	8 745 ..	....					*1.4*	*2.6*	*4.3*
Other sectors	8 746 ..	....					....	.5	.5
of which: Short-term	8 748 ..	....					....	*.5*	*.5*
Reserve assets	8 802 ..	....	....	....	....	....	478.5	930.8	1,361.2
Monetary gold	8 812 ..	....					....	....	....
Special drawing rights	8 811 ..	3.3	4.0	2.9	4.9	11.2	1.0	.9	14.8
Reserve position in the Fund	8 810 ..	....					....	....	....
Foreign exchange	8 803 ..	....					477.4	929.9	1,346.3
Other claims	8 813 ..	....					....	....	....

Table 3 (Concluded). INTERNATIONAL INVESTMENT POSITION (End-period stocks), 2000–2007

(Millions of U.S. dollars)

	Code	2000	2001	2002	2003	2004	2005	2006	2007
LIABILITIES	8 995 D.	....	....	....	....	....	**4,807.7**	**6,451.3**	**9,283.7**
Direct investment in Georgia	8 555 ..	....	....	....	....	....	**2,379.9**	**3,559.2**	**5,388.7**
Equity capital and reinvested earnings	8 556 ..	....	....	....	....	....	1,822.4	2,738.8	3,706.7
Claims on direct investors	8 557 ..	....	....	....	....	....	....	....	....
Liabilities to direct investors	8 558 ..	....	....	....	....	....	1,822.4	2,738.8	3,706.7
Other capital	8 580 ..	....	....	....	....	....	557.6	820.4	1,682.0
Claims on direct investors	8 585 ..	....	....	....	....	....	....	−6.4	−3.7
Liabilities to direct investors	8 590 ..	....	....	....	....	....	557.6	826.7	1,685.7
Portfolio investment	8 652 ..	....	....	....	....	....	**14.9**	**181.1**	**262.0**
Equity securities	8 660 ..	....	....	....	....	....	14.9	181.1	262.0
Banks	8 663 ..	....	....	....	....	....	14.9	181.1	261.9
Other sectors	8 664 ..	....	....	....	....	....	.1	.1	.1
Debt securities	8 669 ..	....	....	....	....	....	....	....	....
Bonds and notes	8 670 ..	....	....	....	....	....	....	....	....
Monetary authorities	8 671 ..	....	....	....	....	....	....	....	....
General government	8 672 ..	....	....	....	....	....	....	....	....
Banks	8 673 ..	....	....	....	....	....	....	....	....
Other sectors	8 674 ..	....	....	....	....	....	....	....	....
Money market instruments	8 680 ..	....	....	....	....	....	....	....	....
Monetary authorities	8 681 ..	....	....	....	....	....	....	....	....
General government	8 682 ..	....	....	....	....	....	....	....	....
Banks	8 683 ..	....	....	....	....	....	....	....	....
Other sectors	8 684 ..	....	....	....	....	....	....	....	....
Financial derivatives	8 905 ..	....	....	....	....	....	....	**.6**	**1.1**
Monetary authorities	8 906 ..	....	....	....	....	....	....	....	....
General government	8 907 ..	....	....	....	....	....	....	....	....
Banks	8 908 ..	....	....	....	....	....	....	.6	1.1
Other sectors	8 909 ..	....	....	....	....	....	....	....	....
Other investment	8 753 ..	....	....	....	....	....	**2,412.9**	**2,710.3**	**3,631.9**
Trade credits	8 756 ..	....	....	....	....	....	128.3	164.6	146.2
General government	8 757 ..	....	....	....	....	....	....	....	....
of which: Short-term	8 759 ..	....	....	....	....	....	....	....	....
Other sectors	8 760 ..	....	....	....	....	....	128.3	164.6	146.2
of which: Short-term	8 762 ..	....	....	....	....	....	*128.3*	*164.6*	*146.2*
Loans	8 764 ..	....	....	....	....	....	1,970.4	2,288.6	3,160.4
Monetary authorities	8 765 ..	....	....	....	....	....	284.9	294.7	254.2
of which: Use of Fund credit and loans from the Fund	8 766 ..	*278.4*	*287.4*	*310.0*	*288.7*	*266.0*	*232.3*	*236.3*	*251.5*
of which: Short-term	8 768 ..	....	....	....	....	....	....	....	....
General government	8 769 ..	....	....	....	....	....	1,291.8	1,330.5	1,509.3
of which: Short-term	8 771 ..	....	....	....	....	....	*2.8*	*3.3*	*3.6*
Banks	8 772 ..	....	....	....	....	....	187.4	409.9	1,059.1
of which: Short-term	8 774 ..	....	....	....	....	....	*48.4*	*82.6*	*164.1*
Other sectors	8 775 ..	....	....	....	....	....	206.2	253.5	337.8
of which: Short-term	8 777 ..	....	....	....	....	....	*13.0*	*23.0*	*16.9*
Currency and deposits	8 780 ..	....	....	....	....	....	120.2	138.5	232.9
Monetary authorities	8 781 ..	....	....	....	....	....	....	....	....
General government	8 782 ..	....	....	....	....	....	....	....	....
Banks	8 783 ..	....	....	....	....	....	120.1	138.5	232.9
Other sectors	8 784 ..	....	....	....	....	....	....	....	....
Other liabilities	8 786 ..	....	....	....	....	....	194.0	118.6	92.4
Monetary authorities	8 787 ..	....	....	....	....	....	....	....	....
of which: Short-term	8 789 ..	....	....	....	....	....	....	....	....
General government	8 790 ..	....	....	....	....	....	193.2	108.8	73.9
of which: Short-term	8 792 ..	....	....	....	....	....	*193.2*	*108.8*	*73.9*
Banks	8 793 ..	....	....	....	....	....	.7	.2	2.8
of which: Short-term	8 795 ..	....	....	....	....	....	*.1*	*.2*	*2.8*
Other sectors	8 796 ..	....	....	....	....	....	....	9.6	15.6
of which: Short-term	8 798 ..	....	....	....	....	....	....	*9.6*	*15.6*
NET INTERNATIONAL INVESTMENT POSITION	8 995 ..	....	....	....	....	....	**−3,922.5**	**−5,051.5**	**−7,147.6**
Conversion rates: lari per U.S. dollar (end of period)	0 102 ..	**1.9750**	**2.0600**	**2.0900**	**2.0750**	**1.8250**	**1.7925**	**1.7135**	**1.5916**

Table 1. ANALYTIC PRESENTATION, 2000–2007

(Billions of U.S. dollars)

	Code	2000	2001	2002	2003	2004	2005	2006	2007
A. Current Account[1]	4 993 Z.	**−29.04**	**3.00**	**42.97**	**52.78**	**130.45**	**148.00**	**181.20**	**255.53**
Goods: exports f.o.b.	2 100 ..	544.73	565.87	611.84	747.37	907.79	983.07	1,135.73	1,354.12
Goods: imports f.o.b.	3 100 ..	−489.26	−478.45	−486.09	−602.62	−721.73	−788.73	−934.86	−1,075.43
Balance on Goods	4 100 ..	*55.47*	*87.42*	*125.76*	*144.74*	*186.07*	*194.34*	*200.86*	*278.69*
Services: credit	2 200 ..	82.24	87.77	102.22	122.56	144.67	161.68	185.57	214.96
Services: debit	3 200 ..	−133.43	−138.46	−141.97	−169.16	−191.51	−203.71	−219.08	−254.23
Balance on Goods and Services	4 991 ..	*4.27*	*36.73*	*86.00*	*98.14*	*139.23*	*152.32*	*167.36*	*239.41*
Income: credit	2 300 ..	106.64	91.21	97.98	118.53	170.23	199.65	245.55	318.01
Income: debit	3 300 ..	−114.30	−100.96	−115.00	−135.52	−144.63	−167.88	−198.21	−260.12
Balance on Goods, Services, and Income	4 992 ..	*−3.39*	*26.98*	*68.98*	*81.16*	*164.83*	*184.09*	*214.70*	*297.31*
Current transfers: credit	2 379 Z.	14.29	14.31	14.70	20.76	19.04	20.61	24.47	25.43
Current transfers: debit	3 379 ..	−39.95	−38.29	−40.71	−49.14	−53.42	−56.70	−57.97	−67.21
B. Capital Account[1]	4 994 Z.	**6.19**	**−.33**	**−.23**	**.35**	**.52**	**−1.67**	**−.24**	**.24**
Capital account: credit	2 994 Z.	9.41	1.87	2.09	3.23	3.30	4.31	3.97	4.75
Capital account: debit	3 994 ..	−3.22	−2.20	−2.32	−2.87	−2.78	−5.98	−4.21	−4.51
Total, Groups A Plus B	4 981 ..	*−22.86*	*2.67*	*42.74*	*53.13*	*130.97*	*146.33*	*180.96*	*255.77*
C. Financial Account[1]	4 995 W.	**28.98**	**−16.12**	**−40.75**	**−71.60**	**−152.99**	**−165.90**	**−192.58**	**−301.46**
Direct investment abroad	4 505 ..	−59.74	−39.25	−19.63	−5.15	−19.96	−70.10	−94.46	−169.37
Direct investment in Germany	4 555 Z.	210.09	26.17	53.61	30.93	−9.80	41.06	55.94	50.94
Portfolio investment assets	4 602 ..	−191.55	−111.68	−57.85	−52.51	−128.60	−256.45	−201.33	−178.42
Equity securities	4 610 ..	−127.50	−27.65	−10.41	3.89	−4.83	−78.41	−19.94	−25.87
Debt securities	4 619 ..	−64.04	−84.03	−47.44	−56.40	−123.77	−178.04	−181.40	−152.54
Portfolio investment liabilities	4 652 Z.	40.88	138.36	121.37	113.10	147.85	219.40	188.96	370.43
Equity securities	4 660 ..	−27.96	76.89	13.82	25.23	−7.88	22.07	36.95	14.31
Debt securities	4 669 Z.	68.84	61.47	107.55	87.87	155.73	197.33	152.01	356.11
Financial derivatives	4 910 ..	−11.44	6.06	−1.14	−2.38	−9.38	−11.70	−8.07	−99.16
Financial derivatives assets	4 900 ..	....	....	....	....	....	....	....	....
Financial derivatives liabilities	4 905 ..	−11.44	6.06	−1.14	−2.38	−9.38	−11.70	−8.07	−99.16
Other investment assets	4 703 ..	−80.18	−102.46	−164.86	−170.90	−179.47	−161.99	−262.27	−440.27
Monetary authorities	4 701 ..	39.37	20.70	−33.41	−.21	−4.03	−26.05	29.12	−91.18
General government	4 704 ..	−18.62	14.30	6.16	.83	2.67	4.83	1.15	11.16
Banks	4 705 ..	−92.58	−118.51	−127.05	−135.18	−152.35	−113.11	−256.47	−304.32
Other sectors	4 728 ..	−8.34	−18.96	−10.56	−36.35	−25.76	−27.66	−36.08	−55.93
Other investment liabilities	4 753 W.	120.92	66.67	27.76	15.31	46.37	73.87	128.66	164.39
Monetary authorities	4 753 WA	.37	2.35	.53	2.13	−2.98	−2.72	−1.64	16.15
General government	4 753 ZB	.29	.68	−1.37	4.03	−5.65	4.85	−.15	3.64
Banks	4 753 ZC	110.00	52.84	25.88	8.59	42.05	33.67	72.66	94.09
Other sectors	4 753 ZD	10.26	10.80	2.72	.55	12.96	38.07	57.79	50.50
Total, Groups A Through C	4 983 ..	*6.13*	*−13.45*	*1.99*	*−18.47*	*−22.02*	*−19.57*	*−11.62*	*−45.69*
D. Net Errors and Omissions	4 998 ..	**−11.35**	**7.98**	**−3.97**	**17.79**	**20.21**	**16.97**	**7.97**	**46.93**
Total, Groups A Through D	4 984 ..	*−5.22*	*−5.47*	*−1.98*	*−.68*	*−1.81*	*−2.60*	*−3.65*	*1.23*
E. Reserves and Related Items	4 802 A.	**5.22**	**5.47**	**1.98**	**.68**	**1.81**	**2.60**	**3.65**	**−1.23**
Reserve assets	4 802 ..	5.22	5.47	1.98	.68	1.81	2.60	3.65	−1.23
Use of Fund credit and loans	4 766 ..	....	....	....	....	....	....	....	....
Exceptional financing	4 920 ..	....	....	....	....	....	....	....	....
Conversion rates: euros per U.S. dollar	0 103 ..	**1.0854**	**1.1175**	**1.0626**	**.8860**	**.8054**	**.8041**	**.7971**	**.7306**

[1] Excludes components that have been classified in the categories of Group E.

Table 2. STANDARD PRESENTATION, 2000–2007

(Billions of U.S. dollars)

	Code	2000	2001	2002	2003	2004	2005	2006	2007
CURRENT ACCOUNT	4 993 ..	−29.04	3.00	42.97	52.78	130.45	148.00	181.20	255.53
A. GOODS	4 100 ..	55.47	87.42	125.76	144.74	186.07	194.34	200.86	278.69
Credit	2 100 ..	544.73	565.87	611.84	747.37	907.79	983.07	1,135.73	1,354.12
General merchandise: exports f.o.b.	2 110 ..	512.74	534.87	575.54	702.35	852.97	924.01	1,068.49	1,284.98
Goods for processing: exports f.o.b.	2 150 ..	29.99	29.08	33.89	42.30	52.08	55.76	62.87	63.83
Repairs on goods	2 160 ..	1.01	.97	1.36	1.64	1.77	2.26	2.62	2.76
Goods procured in ports by carriers	2 170 ..	.40	.41	.43	.48	.48	.48	.58	.76
Nonmonetary gold	2 180 ..	.59	.54	.62	.60	.51	.56	1.17	1.79
Debit	3 100 ..	−489.26	−478.45	−486.09	−602.62	−721.73	−788.73	−934.86	−1,075.43
General merchandise: imports f.o.b.	3 110 ..	−458.36	−447.38	−451.29	−560.48	−672.71	−736.68	−874.94	−1,012.69
Goods for processing: imports f.o.b.	3 150 ..	−28.47	−28.67	−31.93	−38.56	−44.44	−45.93	−52.13	−53.17
Repairs on goods	3 160 ..	−.15	−.13	−.10	−.06	−.07	−.10	−.11	−.15
Goods procured in ports by carriers	3 170 ..	−1.59	−1.50	−2.16	−2.86	−3.77	−4.95	−6.17	−7.53
Nonmonetary gold	3 180 ..	−.70	−.77	−.62	−.66	−.73	−1.07	−1.51	−1.90
B. SERVICES	4 200 ..	−51.19	−50.69	−39.76	−46.60	−46.83	−42.02	−33.50	−39.27
Total credit	2 200 ..	*82.24*	*87.77*	*102.22*	*122.56*	*144.67*	*161.68*	*185.57*	*214.96*
Total debit	3 200 ..	*−133.43*	*−138.46*	*−141.97*	*−169.16*	*−191.51*	*−203.71*	*−219.08*	*−254.23*
Transportation services, credit	2 205 ..	19.95	20.68	23.77	27.07	33.62	38.47	42.24	51.50
Passenger	2 850 ..	*6.33*	*6.14*	*7.41*	*6.98*	*7.96*	*9.10*	*10.03*	*10.77*
Freight	2 851 ..	*10.44*	*11.41*	*11.98*	*14.70*	*19.85*	*22.71*	*25.04*	*33.23*
Other	2 852 ..	*3.18*	*3.12*	*4.38*	*5.39*	*5.82*	*6.67*	*7.16*	*7.51*
Sea transport, passenger	2 207 ..	.19	.21	.21	.16	.24	.27	.29	.27
Sea transport, freight	2 208 ..	6.77	7.63	7.55	9.57	13.87	16.07	17.86	24.91
Sea transport, other	2 209 ..	.90	.91	.96	1.21	1.08	1.21	1.36	1.68
Air transport, passenger	2 211 ..	5.78	5.58	6.87	6.55	7.45	8.43	9.28	10.01
Air transport, freight	2 212 ..	1.02	1.00	1.49	1.68	1.94	2.13	2.11	2.37
Air transport, other	2 213 ..	1.54	1.49	2.44	3.00	3.43	3.84	4.03	4.48
Other transport, passenger	2 215 ..	.37	.35	.33	.27	.27	.40	.46	.49
Other transport, freight	2 216 ..	2.65	2.78	2.94	3.45	4.05	4.50	5.08	5.95
Other transport, other	2 217 ..	.75	.72	.98	1.18	1.30	1.61	1.77	1.35
Transportation services, debit	3 205 ..	−25.13	−24.84	−29.07	−34.58	−40.55	−43.39	−51.60	−60.84
Passenger	3 850 ..	*−4.78*	*−4.61*	*−6.49*	*−7.54*	*−8.25*	*−8.04*	*−8.94*	*−10.62*
Freight	3 851 ..	*−12.57*	*−12.47*	*−12.99*	*−15.84*	*−19.24*	*−20.66*	*−24.69*	*−28.56*
Other	3 852 ..	*−7.78*	*−7.75*	*−9.60*	*−11.19*	*−13.05*	*−14.69*	*−17.96*	*−21.66*
Sea transport, passenger	3 207 ..	....	....	....	....	....	....	....	....
Sea transport, freight	3 208 ..	−5.05	−4.79	−4.93	−5.98	−7.39	−8.16	−10.05	−11.42
Sea transport, other	3 209 ..	−3.42	−3.46	−3.67	−4.01	−4.97	−5.92	−8.07	−10.67
Air transport, passenger	3 211 ..	−4.52	−4.36	−6.24	−7.29	−8.06	−7.82	−8.68	−10.20
Air transport, freight	3 212 ..	−.45	−.42	−.44	−.45	−.48	−.41	−.40	−.39
Air transport, other	3 213 ..	−1.71	−1.75	−2.65	−2.76	−2.72	−2.80	−3.46	−3.49
Other transport, passenger	3 215 ..	−.25	−.25	−.25	−.25	−.20	−.22	−.27	−.43
Other transport, freight	3 216 ..	−7.07	−7.27	−7.62	−9.40	−11.37	−12.09	−14.25	−16.75
Other transport, other	3 217 ..	−2.65	−2.54	−3.27	−4.43	−5.36	−5.97	−6.43	−7.50
Travel, credit	2 236 ..	18.61	18.03	19.28	23.12	27.61	29.12	32.89	36.09
Business travel	2 237 ..	....	....	....	....	....	....	....	....
Personal travel	2 240 ..	....	....	....	....	....	....	....	....
Travel, debit	3 236 ..	−52.82	−51.92	−53.01	−65.23	−71.19	−74.19	−74.12	−82.97
Business travel	3 237 ..	....	−9.42	−8.20	−9.20	−10.67	−11.69	−11.18	....
Personal travel	3 240 ..	....	−42.49	−44.81	−56.03	−60.52	−62.50	−62.94	....
Other services, credit	2 200 BA	43.67	49.07	59.17	72.36	83.44	94.09	110.45	127.36
Communications	2 245 ..	1.45	1.77	2.03	2.68	3.26	3.44	4.50	4.75
Construction	2 249 ..	4.24	4.28	5.07	7.11	7.10	10.38	12.00	12.34
Insurance	2 253 ..	.55	1.75	7.62	6.76	3.63	2.13	3.77	5.77
Financial	2 260 ..	3.54	3.23	3.48	4.01	5.28	6.58	8.55	11.76
Computer and information	2 262 ..	3.80	4.80	5.53	6.70	8.09	8.36	9.68	12.20
Royalties and licence fees	2 266 ..	2.91	3.32	3.87	4.51	5.51	7.01	5.89	7.25
Other business services	2 268 ..	23.29	24.94	24.67	32.14	41.56	48.65	58.78	65.90
Personal, cultural, and recreational	2 287 ..	.39	.52	.53	1.01	.98	1.17	.92	1.08
Government, n.i.e.	2 291 ..	3.49	4.44	6.36	7.44	8.04	6.37	6.35	6.31
Other services, debit	3 200 BA	−55.48	−61.71	−59.90	−69.35	−79.77	−86.13	−93.35	−110.43
Communications	3 245 ..	−3.15	−3.35	−3.84	−4.07	−4.66	−5.02	−6.29	−6.83
Construction	3 249 ..	−4.93	−4.82	−4.55	−5.45	−5.86	−6.58	−7.31	−9.10
Insurance	3 253 ..	−1.01	−1.16	−1.30	−3.44	−5.30	−4.70	−2.47	−3.21
Financial	3 260 ..	−2.00	−2.27	−2.13	−2.41	−3.63	−4.50	−5.74	−7.66
Computer and information	3 262 ..	−4.97	−6.06	−6.18	−7.27	−8.14	−8.59	−9.25	−11.69
Royalties and licence fees	3 266 ..	−5.67	−5.51	−5.31	−5.33	−5.85	−7.44	−7.84	−9.70
Other business services	3 268 ..	−28.75	−33.18	−32.93	−36.73	−41.74	−44.05	−47.98	−57.55
Personal, cultural, and recreational	3 287 ..	−3.56	−4.03	−2.27	−2.95	−3.19	−3.49	−4.73	−2.78
Government, n.i.e.	3 291 ..	−1.44	−1.32	−1.39	−1.69	−1.40	−1.77	−1.73	−1.92

Table 2 (Continued). STANDARD PRESENTATION, 2000–2007

(Billions of U.S. dollars)

	Code	2000	2001	2002	2003	2004	2005	2006	2007
C. INCOME..	4 300 ..	**−7.66**	**−9.75**	**−17.02**	**−16.99**	**25.60**	**31.77**	**47.34**	**57.89**
Total credit..	2 300 ..	*106.64*	*91.21*	*97.98*	*118.53*	*170.23*	*199.65*	*245.55*	*318.01*
Total debit..	3 300 ..	*−114.30*	*−100.96*	*−115.00*	*−135.52*	*−144.63*	*−167.88*	*−198.21*	*−260.12*
Compensation of employees, credit..................	2 310 ..	**3.60**	**3.88**	**4.65**	**5.74**	**6.51**	**6.64**	**7.12**	**8.45**
Compensation of employees, debit..................	3 310 ..	**−5.16**	**−5.50**	**−6.01**	**−7.10**	**−7.71**	**−8.30**	**−8.36**	**−9.30**
Investment income, credit..............................	2 320 ..	**103.03**	**87.33**	**93.33**	**112.79**	**163.72**	**193.02**	**238.43**	**309.57**
Direct investment income................................	2 330 ..	16.85	4.04	8.44	17.48	51.57	59.02	68.54	81.54
Dividends and distributed branch profits................	2 332 ..	16.84	18.39	18.89	20.21	25.39	31.74	33.53	32.78
Reinvested earnings and undistributed branch profits.....	2 333 ..	−4.77	−17.80	−12.66	−4.59	23.41	23.79	30.47	41.55
Income on debt (interest)............................	2 334 ..	4.78	3.46	2.21	1.86	2.76	3.49	4.55	7.21
Portfolio investment income............................	2 339 ..	36.91	41.04	44.07	50.18	58.63	63.45	71.91	96.61
Income on equity................................	2 340 ..	13.28	13.95	13.87	13.85	18.20	19.03	21.50	27.54
Income on bonds and notes........................	2 350 ..	22.65	26.54	29.77	36.00	40.03	43.92	49.53	66.58
Income on money market instruments..................	2 360 ..	.97	.54	.43	.34	.40	.51	.88	2.49
Other investment income................................	2 370 ..	49.28	42.25	40.83	45.12	53.53	70.54	97.98	131.41
Investment income, debit..............................	3 320 ..	**−109.13**	**−95.46**	**−109.00**	**−128.42**	**−136.91**	**−159.58**	**−189.85**	**−250.81**
Direct investment income................................	3 330 ..	−12.89	−4.40	−19.42	−25.75	−26.64	−36.88	−43.49	−55.20
Dividends and distributed branch profits................	3 332 ..	−9.36	−10.50	−12.26	−13.77	−16.91	−19.72	−21.57	−26.26
Reinvested earnings and undistributed branch profits.....	3 333 ..	6.37	18.97	6.67	3.84	5.08	−2.28	−4.79	−8.54
Income on debt (interest)............................	3 334 ..	−9.90	−12.87	−13.84	−15.82	−14.81	−14.89	−17.14	−20.40
Portfolio investment income............................	3 339 ..	−47.00	−48.46	−52.01	−63.46	−67.75	−70.84	−80.54	−105.47
Income on equity................................	3 340 ..	−7.14	−7.32	−6.79	−9.26	−10.39	−11.88	−17.53	−27.67
Income on bonds and notes........................	3 350 ..	−36.76	−38.74	−42.54	−50.64	−54.48	−56.98	−59.59	−70.74
Income on money market instruments..................	3 360 ..	−3.10	−2.40	−2.68	−3.56	−2.88	−1.97	−3.43	−7.06
Other investment income................................	3 370 ..	−49.24	−42.59	−37.56	−39.21	−42.52	−51.87	−65.82	−90.14
D. CURRENT TRANSFERS......................................	4 379 ..	**−25.65**	**−23.98**	**−26.01**	**−28.38**	**−34.38**	**−36.09**	**−33.50**	**−41.77**
Credit..	2 379 ..	**14.29**	**14.31**	**14.70**	**20.76**	**19.04**	**20.61**	**24.47**	**25.43**
General government................................	2 380 ..	10.98	10.95	11.22	16.54	15.52	16.20	20.68	20.73
Other sectors................................	2 390 ..	3.31	3.36	3.47	4.22	3.51	4.41	3.79	4.70
Workers' remittances................................	2 391 ..	....	....	....	....	....	....	....	....
Other current transfers............................	2 392 ..	3.31	3.36	3.47	4.22	3.51	4.41	3.79	4.70
Debit..	3 379 ..	**−39.95**	**−38.29**	**−40.71**	**−49.14**	**−53.42**	**−56.70**	**−57.97**	**−67.21**
General government................................	3 380 ..	−28.08	−25.55	−26.13	−33.60	−36.07	−38.60	−38.53	−42.62
Other sectors................................	3 390 ..	−11.86	−12.74	−14.58	−15.54	−17.35	−18.10	−19.43	−24.59
Workers' remittances................................	3 391 ..	−3.19	−3.15	−3.28	−3.77	−3.95	−3.65	−3.68	−4.12
Other current transfers............................	3 392 ..	−8.67	−9.59	−11.30	−11.77	−13.40	−14.45	−15.76	−20.47
CAPITAL AND FINANCIAL ACCOUNT......................	4 996 ..	**40.39**	**−10.98**	**−39.00**	**−70.57**	**−150.66**	**−164.97**	**−189.17**	**−302.46**
CAPITAL ACCOUNT..	4 994 ..	**6.19**	**−.33**	**−.23**	**.35**	**.52**	**−1.67**	**−.24**	**.24**
Total credit..	2 994 ..	*9.41*	*1.87*	*2.09*	*3.23*	*3.30*	*4.31*	*3.97*	*4.75*
Total debit..	3 994 ..	*−3.22*	*−2.20*	*−2.32*	*−2.87*	*−2.78*	*−5.98*	*−4.21*	*−4.51*
Capital transfers, credit............................	2 400 ..	**1.79**	**1.87**	**2.09**	**3.23**	**3.30**	**4.31**	**3.97**	**4.75**
General government................................	2 401 ..	....	....	....	....	....	....	....	....
Debt forgiveness................................	2 402 ..	....	....	....	....	....	....	....	....
Other capital transfers............................	2 410 ..	....	....	....	....	....	....	....	....
Other sectors................................	2 430 ..	1.79	1.87	2.09	3.23	3.30	4.31	3.97	4.75
Migrants' transfers................................	2 431 ..	.04	.05	.04	.04	.07	.07	.09	.12
Debt forgiveness................................	2 432 ..	....	....	....	....	....	....	....	....
Other capital transfers............................	2 440 ..	1.75	1.82	2.06	3.19	3.23	4.25	3.89	4.62
Capital transfers, debit............................	3 400 ..	**−3.22**	**−2.20**	**−2.32**	**−2.87**	**−2.78**	**−5.98**	**−4.21**	**−4.51**
General government................................	3 401 ..	−1.09	−1.22	−1.36	−1.41	−1.37	−4.35	−2.43	−2.86
Debt forgiveness................................	3 402 ..	−.06	....	−.20	−.32	−.06	−2.88	−.87	−1.01
Other capital transfers............................	3 410 ..	−1.03	−1.22	−1.16	−1.09	−1.30	−1.47	−1.55	−1.84
Other sectors................................	3 430 ..	−2.13	−.98	−.96	−1.46	−1.41	−1.62	−1.78	−1.65
Migrants' transfers................................	3 431 ..	−.38	−.26	−.28	−.33	−.40	−.44	−.38	−.44
Debt forgiveness................................	3 432 ..	−1.07	−.03	−.01	−.48	−.29	−.42	−.40	−.19
Other capital transfers............................	3 440 ..	−.68	−.68	−.67	−.65	−.72	−.77	−1.00	−1.02
Nonproduced nonfinancial assets, credit.............	2 480 ..	**7.62**	**....**	**....**	**....**	**....**	**....**	**....**	**....**
Nonproduced nonfinancial assets, debit..............	3 480 ..	**....**	**....**	**....**	**....**	**....**	**....**	**....**	**....**

Table 2 (Continued). STANDARD PRESENTATION, 2000–2007

(Billions of U.S. dollars)

	Code	2000	2001	2002	2003	2004	2005	2006	2007
FINANCIAL ACCOUNT	4 995	**34.20**	**−10.66**	**−38.77**	**−70.92**	**−151.18**	**−163.30**	**−188.93**	**−302.70**
A. DIRECT INVESTMENT	4 500	**150.34**	**−13.08**	**33.98**	**25.78**	**−29.76**	**−29.04**	**−38.52**	**−118.43**
Direct investment abroad	4 505	**−59.74**	**−39.25**	**−19.63**	**−5.15**	**−19.96**	**−70.10**	**−94.46**	**−169.37**
Equity capital	4 510	−65.48	−71.06	−51.47	−37.83	19.96	−30.65	−71.73	−65.90
Claims on affiliated enterprises	4 515	−65.48	−71.06	−51.47	−37.83	19.96	−30.65	−71.73	−65.90
Liabilities to affiliated enterprises	4 520	....	....	....	....	....	....	....	....
Reinvested earnings	4 525	4.77	17.80	12.66	4.59	−23.41	−23.79	−30.47	−41.55
Other capital	4 530	.96	14.01	19.18	28.08	−16.51	−15.66	7.74	−61.92
Claims on affiliated enterprises	4 535	−35.35	−10.41	−2.51	−2.95	−8.46	−23.30	−15.79	−30.23
Liabilities to affiliated enterprises	4 540	36.31	24.42	21.69	31.03	−8.05	7.64	23.53	−31.69
Direct investment in Germany	4 555	**210.09**	**26.17**	**53.61**	**30.93**	**−9.80**	**41.06**	**55.94**	**50.94**
Equity capital	4 560	122.26	31.46	35.46	53.08	43.98	32.70	32.28	31.78
Claims on direct investors	4 565	....	....	....	....	....	....	....	....
Liabilities to direct investors	4 570	122.26	31.46	35.46	53.08	43.98	32.70	32.28	31.78
Reinvested earnings	4 575	−6.37	−18.97	−6.67	−3.84	−5.08	2.28	4.79	8.54
Other capital	4 580	94.19	13.68	24.82	−18.31	−48.70	6.09	18.87	10.61
Claims on direct investors	4 585	95.78	20.03	.75	−14.94	−51.30	11.85	23.23	12.53
Liabilities to direct investors	4 590	−1.59	−6.35	24.07	−3.37	2.59	−5.76	−4.36	−1.91
B. PORTFOLIO INVESTMENT	4 600	**−150.66**	**26.69**	**63.52**	**60.60**	**19.25**	**−37.05**	**−12.38**	**192.01**
Assets	4 602	**−191.55**	**−111.68**	**−57.85**	**−52.51**	**−128.60**	**−256.45**	**−201.33**	**−178.42**
Equity securities	4 610	−127.50	−27.65	−10.41	3.89	−4.83	−78.41	−19.94	−25.87
Monetary authorities	4 611	....	....	....	....	....	....	....	....
General government	4 612	....	....	....	....	....	....	....	....
Banks	4 613	−7.32	−4.82	5.12	−6.02	−3.57	−20.11	−15.09	−20.34
Other sectors	4 614	−120.19	−22.82	−15.53	9.92	−1.26	−58.30	−4.85	−5.53
Debt securities	4 619	−64.04	−84.03	−47.44	−56.40	−123.77	−178.04	−181.40	−152.54
Bonds and notes	4 620	−65.90	−85.39	−44.13	−61.17	−109.42	−172.21	−171.82	−126.93
Monetary authorities	4 621	....	....	....	....	−.09	−.29	−.09	−2.28
General government	4 622	....	....	....	....	....	....	....	....
Banks	4 623	−39.07	−35.65	−12.10	−36.15	−80.88	−110.05	−126.12	−128.37
Other sectors	4 624	−26.83	−49.74	−32.03	−25.02	−28.45	−61.87	−45.61	3.72
Money market instruments	4 630	1.86	1.36	−3.31	4.77	−14.35	−5.84	−9.57	−25.62
Monetary authorities	4 631	....	....	....	....	....	....	....	....
General government	4 632	....	....	....	....	....	....	....	....
Banks	4 633	.50	1.78	−4.48	.78	−7.60	−1.48	−7.49	−40.44
Other sectors	4 634	1.36	−.41	1.17	3.99	−6.76	−4.35	−2.09	14.83
Liabilities	4 652	**40.88**	**138.36**	**121.37**	**113.10**	**147.85**	**219.40**	**188.96**	**370.43**
Equity securities	4 660	−27.96	76.89	13.82	25.23	−7.88	22.07	36.95	14.31
Banks	4 663	18.30	7.36	−.25	1.56	−1.61	−10.29	−2.77	−2.73
Other sectors	4 664	−46.26	69.53	14.07	23.68	−6.27	32.37	39.72	17.05
Debt securities	4 669	68.84	61.47	107.55	87.87	155.73	197.33	152.01	356.11
Bonds and notes	4 670	68.45	71.84	81.79	73.88	173.84	200.23	156.33	286.73
Monetary authorities	4 671	....	....	....	....	....	....	....	....
General government	4 672	20.72	6.64	40.85	20.28	58.20	89.88	65.82	90.02
Banks	4 673	47.73	65.20	40.95	53.60	115.64	110.34	90.51	196.71
Other sectors	4 674	....	....	....	....	....	....	....	....
Money market instruments	4 680	.40	−10.37	25.76	13.99	−18.11	−2.90	−4.32	69.38
Monetary authorities	4 681	....	....	....	....	....	....	....	....
General government	4 682	.12	5.93	6.88	5.85	−1.80	3.62	−2.31	−1.63
Banks	4 683	−1.88	−16.83	21.34	5.36	−15.86	−3.67	−4.65	43.11
Other sectors	4 684	2.16	.53	−2.46	2.78	−.45	−2.84	2.64	27.90
C. FINANCIAL DERIVATIVES	4 910	**−11.44**	**6.06**	**−1.14**	**−2.38**	**−9.38**	**−11.70**	**−8.07**	**−99.16**
Monetary authorities	4 911	....	....	....	....	....	....	....	....
General government	4 912	....	....	....	....	....	....	....	....
Banks	4 913	....	....	....	....	....	....	....	....
Other sectors	4 914	....	....	....	....	....	....	....	....
Assets	4 900	....	....	....	....	....	....	....	....
Monetary authorities	4 901	....	....	....	....	....	....	....	....
General government	4 902	....	....	....	....	....	....	....	....
Banks	4 903	....	....	....	....	....	....	....	....
Other sectors	4 904	....	....	....	....	....	....	....	....
Liabilities	4 905	**−11.44**	**6.06**	**−1.14**	**−2.38**	**−9.38**	**−11.70**	**−8.07**	**−99.16**
Monetary authorities	4 906	....	....	....	....	....	....	....	....
General government	4 907	....	....	....	....	....	....	....	....
Banks	4 908	....	....	....	....	....	....	....	....
Other sectors	4 909	....	....	....	....	....	....	....	....

Table 2 (Concluded). STANDARD PRESENTATION, 2000–2007

(Billions of U.S. dollars)

	Code	2000	2001	2002	2003	2004	2005	2006	2007
D. OTHER INVESTMENT	4 700	**40.75**	**−35.79**	**−137.11**	**−155.60**	**−133.09**	**−88.12**	**−133.62**	**−275.89**
Assets	4 703	−80.18	−102.46	−164.86	−170.90	−179.47	−161.99	−262.27	−440.27
Trade credits	4 706	−7.98	1.62	−.27	2.65	−1.96	−8.63	−6.39	−6.42
General government	4 707	....	....	....	....	....	....	....	....
of which: Short-term	4 709	....	....	....	....	....	....	....	....
Other sectors	4 710	−7.98	1.62	−.27	2.65	−1.96	−8.63	−6.39	−6.42
of which: Short-term	4 712	−7.98	1.62	−.27	2.65	−1.96	−8.63	−6.39	−6.42
Loans	4 714	−101.57	−116.06	−130.91	−139.43	−152.99	−106.53	−250.53	−290.69
Monetary authorities	4 715	−.30	....	....	....	....	....	....	....
of which: Short-term	4 718	....	....	....	....	....	....	....	....
General government	4 719	−1.02	.23	.19	.77	1.01	10.52	10.24	.84
of which: Short-term	4 721	−.03	....	....	....	.02	....	.01	−.35
Banks	4 722	−92.60	−118.43	−126.97	−135.13	−151.86	−112.95	−256.18	−304.06
of which: Short-term	4 724	−56.00	−75.91	−95.41	−98.72	−159.42	−26.38	−166.12	−170.95
Other sectors	4 725	−7.65	2.14	−4.13	−5.07	−2.14	−4.09	−4.59	12.53
of which: Short-term	4 727	−7.60	4.42	−2.52	−2.37	−1.06	1.32	−2.42	12.63
Currency and deposits	4 730	30.96	13.00	−32.39	−30.86	−20.66	−41.59	1.28	−136.45
Monetary authorities	4 731	39.66	20.70	−33.41	−.21	−4.08	−26.00	29.12	−91.17
General government	4 732	−17.42	14.39	6.22	.33	2.20	−5.07	−8.40	11.14
Banks	4 733	....	−.04	−.01	.02	.06	−.03	−.17	....
Other sectors	4 734	8.72	−22.05	−5.19	−31.01	−18.84	−10.49	−19.28	−56.43
Other assets	4 736	−1.59	−1.02	−1.29	−3.26	−3.86	−5.24	−6.63	−6.71
Monetary authorities	4 737	....	....	....	....	.05	−.05	....	−.02
of which: Short-term	4 739	....	....	....	....	....	....	....	....
General government	4 740	−.18	−.32	−.25	−.27	−.53	−.63	−.69	−.82
of which: Short-term	4 742	....	....	....	....	....	....	....	....
Banks	4 743	.02	−.04	−.07	−.07	−.55	−.12	−.13	−.26
of which: Short-term	4 745	....	....	....	....	....	....	....	....
Other sectors	4 746	−1.43	−.66	−.97	−2.92	−2.83	−4.44	−5.82	−5.62
of which: Short-term	4 748	....	....	....	....	....	....	....	....
Liabilities	4 753	**120.92**	**66.67**	**27.76**	**15.31**	**46.37**	**73.87**	**128.66**	**164.39**
Trade credits	4 756	5.85	3.37	.25	1.82	4.89	6.92	10.42	15.55
General government	4 757	....	....	....	....	....	....	....	....
of which: Short-term	4 759	....	....	....	....	....	....	....	....
Other sectors	4 760	5.85	3.37	.25	1.82	4.89	6.92	10.42	15.55
of which: Short-term	4 762	5.85	3.37	.25	1.82	4.89	6.92	10.42	15.55
Loans	4 764	105.10	32.09	31.55	−9.95	8.10	47.62	99.60	118.36
Monetary authorities	4 765	....	....	....	....	....	....	....	....
of which: Use of Fund credit and loans from the Fund	4 766	....	....	....	....	....	....	....	....
of which: Short-term	4 768	....	....	....	....	....	....	....	....
General government	4 769	.29	.68	−1.37	4.03	−5.65	4.85	−.15	3.64
of which: Short-term	4 771	.66	.87	−1.30	−1.30	−1.67	1.35	−1.22	5.72
Banks	4 772	100.65	24.03	30.53	−12.72	6.60	12.37	52.49	79.79
of which: Short-term	4 774	85.60	20.45	13.21	−6.45	19.57	24.05	67.87	100.00
Other sectors	4 775	4.16	7.38	2.40	−1.26	7.15	30.40	47.26	34.93
of which: Short-term	4 777	.38	−3.27	−2.57	−1.20	−.85	8.57	12.47	10.86
Currency and deposits	4 780	9.67	31.17	−4.12	23.43	32.41	18.57	18.20	30.31
Monetary authorities	4 781	.37	2.35	.53	2.13	−2.98	−2.72	−1.64	16.15
General government	4 782	....	....	....	....	....	....	....	....
Banks	4 783	9.30	28.82	−4.65	21.30	35.39	21.29	19.84	14.15
Other sectors	4 784	....	....	....	....	....	....	....	....
Other liabilities	4 786	.31	.04	.08	.01	.97	.76	.44	.17
Monetary authorities	4 787	....	....	....	....	....	....	....	....
of which: Short-term	4 789	....	....	....	....	....	....	....	....
General government	4 790	....	....	....	....	....	....	....	....
of which: Short-term	4 792	....	....	....	....	....	....	....	....
Banks	4 793	.06	−.01	....	.01	.06	.01	.33	.15
of which: Short-term	4 795	....	....	....	....	....	....	....	....
Other sectors	4 796	.25	.05	.08	....	.91	.76	.11	.03
of which: Short-term	4 798	....	....	....	....	....	....	....	....
E. RESERVE ASSETS	4 802	**5.22**	**5.47**	**1.98**	**.68**	**1.81**	**2.60**	**3.65**	**−1.23**
Monetary gold	4 812	....	....	....	....	....	....	....	....
Special drawing rights	4 811	.10	−.09	−.04	.21	−.03	....	−.02	−.05
Reserve position in the Fund	4 810	.66	−.65	−.30	−.28	1.08	2.91	1.65	.63
Foreign exchange	4 803	4.46	6.21	2.32	.76	.75	−.31	2.02	−1.82
Other claims	4 813	....	....	....	....	....	....	....	....
NET ERRORS AND OMISSIONS	4 998	**−11.35**	**7.98**	**−3.97**	**17.79**	**20.21**	**16.97**	**7.97**	**46.93**

Table 3. INTERNATIONAL INVESTMENT POSITION (End-period stocks), 2000–2007

(Billions of U.S. dollars)

	Code	2000	2001	2002	2003	2004	2005	2006	2007
ASSETS	8 995 C.	**2,643.28**	**2,747.78**	**3,204.48**	**4,061.54**	**4,768.76**	**4,843.24**	**5,951.44**	**7,230.10**
Direct investment abroad	8 505	**486.75**	**551.09**	**602.80**	**720.52**	**814.79**	**843.94**	**1,025.17**	**1,217.67**
Equity capital and reinvested earnings	8 506	437.56	505.49	580.23	722.33	809.87	824.20	1,018.76	1,175.81
Claims on affiliated enterprises	8 507	....	....	....	....	....	....	....	....
Liabilities to affiliated enterprises	8 508	....	....	....	....	....	....	....	....
Other capital	8 530	49.19	45.60	22.57	−1.80	4.92	19.74	6.41	41.85
Claims on affiliated enterprises	8 535	99.06	109.04	131.16	131.15	144.18	139.39	166.12	207.00
Liabilities to affiliated enterprises	8 540	−49.87	−63.44	−108.59	−132.96	−139.26	−119.65	−159.71	−165.14
Portfolio investment	8 602	**995.95**	**975.78**	**1,079.63**	**1,381.82**	**1,675.94**	**1,818.57**	**2,247.84**	**2,583.87**
Equity securities	8 610	573.06	490.74	437.83	576.24	668.23	768.63	964.73	1,085.78
Monetary authorities	8 611	....	....	....	....	....	....	....	....
General government	8 612	....	....	....	....	....	....	....	....
Banks	8 613	22.64	26.37	23.56	31.35	36.07	52.18	71.11	86.32
Other sectors	8 614	550.42	464.37	414.27	544.89	632.16	716.45	893.62	999.46
Debt securities	8 619	422.89	485.04	641.80	805.58	1,007.72	1,049.94	1,283.11	1,498.08
Bonds and notes	8 620	413.35	477.19	625.94	786.89	977.51	1,022.46	1,246.52	1,415.36
Monetary authorities	8 621	....	....	.17	.57	.91	1.06	1.22	3.72
General government	8 622	....	....	....	....	....	....	....	....
Banks	8 623	214.16	240.35	296.79	401.68	527.32	564.20	743.82	899.75
Other sectors	8 624	199.19	236.85	328.98	384.64	449.28	457.20	501.47	511.89
Money market instruments	8 630	9.54	7.85	15.85	18.69	30.21	27.48	36.60	82.72
Monetary authorities	8 631	....	....	....	....	....	....	....	....
General government	8 632	....	....	....	....	....	....	....	....
Banks	8 633	8.17	6.79	12.28	13.29	22.46	21.67	31.89	67.43
Other sectors	8 634	1.37	1.06	3.57	5.40	7.75	5.81	4.71	15.29
Financial derivatives	8 900	....	....	....	....	....	....	....	....
Monetary authorities	8 901	....	....	....	....	....	....	....	....
General government	8 902	....	....	....	....	....	....	....	....
Banks	8 903	....	....	....	....	....	....	....	....
Other sectors	8 904	....	....	....	....	....	....	....	....
Other investment	8 703	**1,073.28**	**1,138.75**	**1,432.92**	**1,862.36**	**2,180.85**	**2,079.06**	**2,566.79**	**3,292.34**
Trade credits	8 706	84.05	80.50	89.66	110.08	122.19	116.81	141.01	166.74
General government	8 707	....	....	....	....	....	....	....	....
of which: Short-term	8 709	....	....	....	....	....	....	....	....
Other sectors	8 710	84.05	80.50	89.66	110.08	122.19	116.81	141.01	166.74
of which: Short-term	8 712	*84.05*	*80.50*	*89.66*	*110.08*	*122.19*	*116.81*	*141.01*	*166.74*
Loans	8 714	824.15	890.14	1,146.87	1,478.64	1,732.54	1,620.97	2,041.59	2,541.07
Monetary authorities	8 715	5.31	−16.13	18.40	21.50	16.43	14.23	15.89	17.84
of which: Short-term	8 718	....	....	....	....	....	....	....	....
General government	8 719	21.97	20.82	24.33	28.29	36.05	21.16	12.51	13.02
of which: Short-term	8 721	*.35*	*.33*	*.36*	*.46*	*.48*	*.41*	*.46*	*.86*
Banks	8 722	678.49	767.58	995.73	1,289.93	1,530.83	1,472.83	1,875.58	2,353.65
of which: Short-term	8 724	*369.95*	*427.93*	*589.75*	*792.40*	*1,013.88*	*922.48*	*1,186.18*	*1,473.69*
Other sectors	8 725	118.38	117.87	108.42	138.91	149.23	112.75	137.61	156.57
of which: Short-term	8 727	*78.14*	*77.38*	*65.01*	*87.75*	*97.35*	*80.93*	*98.34*	*106.67*
Currency and deposits	8 730	125.65	128.99	149.52	214.85	259.00	277.79	308.04	493.92
Monetary authorities	8 731	....	....	....	....	10.70	35.26	7.11	104.60
General government	8 732	....	....	....	....	....	....	....	....
Banks	8 733	24.00	8.88	4.10	4.56	2.49	17.84	28.39	19.37
Other sectors	8 734	101.64	120.10	145.43	210.28	245.88	224.70	272.54	369.95
Other assets	8 736	39.43	39.12	46.85	58.80	67.06	63.49	76.14	90.60
Monetary authorities	8 737	1.15	1.09	1.30	1.56	1.63	1.45	1.62	1.83
of which: Short-term	8 739	....	....	....	....	....	....	....	....
General government	8 740	15.11	15.09	17.35	20.19	21.96	20.48	22.72	25.23
of which: Short-term	8 742	....	....	....	....	....	....	....	....
Banks	8 743	1.38	1.35	1.68	2.12	2.90	2.63	3.11	3.76
of which: Short-term	8 745	....	....	....	....	....	....	....	....
Other sectors	8 746	21.78	21.59	26.52	34.92	40.57	38.92	48.69	59.77
of which: Short-term	8 748	*.02*	*.34*	*.17*	*.08*	*.32*	*.39*	*.47*	*.43*
Reserve assets	8 802	**87.30**	**82.16**	**89.14**	**96.84**	**97.17**	**101.67**	**111.64**	**136.23**
Monetary gold	8 812	30.41	30.85	37.97	46.14	48.35	56.54	69.95	91.91
Special drawing rights	8 811	1.76	1.79	1.98	1.94	2.06	1.89	2.01	2.16
Reserve position in the Fund	8 810	5.46	5.90	6.70	7.66	6.86	3.48	1.96	1.40
Foreign exchange	8 803	49.67	43.61	42.50	41.10	39.90	39.76	37.72	40.77
Other claims	8 813	....	....	....	....	....	....	....	....

Table 3 (Concluded). INTERNATIONAL INVESTMENT POSITION (End-period stocks), 2000–2007

(Billions of U.S. dollars)

	Code	2000	2001	2002	2003	2004	2005	2006	2007
LIABILITIES	8 995 D.	**2,580.96**	**2,586.18**	**3,090.82**	**3,882.34**	**4,438.77**	**4,267.15**	**5,113.44**	**6,278.22**
Direct investment in Germany	8 555 ..	**462.57**	**416.83**	**529.34**	**666.19**	**719.26**	**631.17**	**750.19**	**856.62**
Equity capital and reinvested earnings	8 556 ..	245.29	186.48	250.62	352.49	423.50	395.59	483.71	537.50
Claims on direct investors	8 557 ..	....	....	....	....	....	....	....	....
Liabilities to direct investors	8 558 ..	....	....	....	....	....	....	....	....
Other capital	8 580 ..	217.28	230.35	278.73	313.70	295.76	235.59	266.48	319.12
Claims on direct investors	8 585 ..	−13.06	−11.82	−13.74	−26.38	−28.56	−24.75	−31.78	−31.84
Liabilities to direct investors	8 590 ..	230.34	242.17	292.46	340.08	324.33	260.34	298.26	350.97
Portfolio investment	8 652 ..	**1,043.22**	**1,063.75**	**1,301.15**	**1,732.88**	**2,079.34**	**2,115.50**	**2,543.00**	**3,252.64**
Equity securities	8 660 ..	300.75	294.69	212.68	362.45	396.04	448.10	641.59	858.36
Banks	8 663 ..	50.73	33.02	19.15	36.04	40.49	45.98	57.88	73.14
Other sectors	8 664 ..	250.02	261.67	193.53	326.41	355.55	402.11	583.70	785.22
Debt securities	8 669 ..	742.47	769.06	1,088.48	1,370.43	1,683.30	1,667.40	1,901.41	2,394.29
Bonds and notes	8 670 ..	680.25	720.15	1,002.98	1,250.19	1,573.21	1,575.63	1,800.64	2,207.82
Monetary authorities	8 671 ..	....	....	....	....	....	....	....	....
General government	8 672 ..	383.50	368.46	508.33	620.77	762.28	758.63	866.14	1,022.91
Banks	8 673 ..	287.60	335.77	473.36	599.84	774.12	782.00	896.07	1,144.57
Other sectors	8 674 ..	9.14	15.92	21.29	29.58	36.81	35.00	38.43	40.34
Money market instruments	8 680 ..	62.22	48.91	85.49	120.24	110.09	91.77	100.77	186.47
Monetary authorities	8 681 ..	....	....	....	....	....	....	....	....
General government	8 682 ..	7.03	12.57	22.00	32.88	33.49	32.34	33.71	35.84
Banks	8 683 ..	49.15	29.99	58.70	77.49	66.45	53.62	57.33	109.70
Other sectors	8 684 ..	6.05	6.35	4.80	9.86	10.15	5.81	9.73	40.93
Financial derivatives	8 905 ..	....	....	....	....	....	....	....	....
Monetary authorities	8 906 ..	....	....	....	....	....	....	....	....
General government	8 907 ..	....	....	....	....	....	....	....	....
Banks	8 908 ..	....	....	....	....	....	....	....	....
Other sectors	8 909 ..	....	....	....	....	....	....	....	....
Other investment	8 753 ..	**1,075.18**	**1,105.60**	**1,260.33**	**1,483.27**	**1,640.17**	**1,520.48**	**1,820.25**	**2,168.96**
Trade credits	8 756 ..	52.92	55.12	61.52	74.99	88.19	85.76	109.37	141.81
General government	8 757 ..	....	....	....	....	....	....	....	....
of which: Short-term	8 759 ..	....	....	....	....	....	....	....	....
Other sectors	8 760 ..	52.92	55.12	61.52	74.99	88.19	85.76	109.37	141.81
of which: Short-term	8 762 ..	*52.92*	*55.12*	*61.52*	*74.99*	*88.19*	*85.76*	*109.37*	*141.81*
Loans	8 764 ..	1,019.50	1,047.80	1,195.65	1,404.38	1,535.34	1,421.46	1,696.97	1,994.50
Monetary authorities	8 765 ..	6.13	7.71	9.44	13.19	10.81	....	....	....
of which: Use of Fund credit and loans from the Fund	8 766 ..	....	....	....	....	....	....	....	....
of which: Short-term	8 768 ..	....	....	....	....	....	....	....	....
General government	8 769 ..	12.21	12.37	14.95	21.07	25.52	26.10	29.12	29.61
of which: Short-term	8 771 ..	*4.86*	*5.68*	*5.98*	*6.06*	*5.26*	*8.10*	*7.72*	*8.14*
Banks	8 772 ..	839.92	859.51	980.56	1,136.43	1,248.06	1,144.41	1,323.06	1,542.10
of which: Short-term	8 774 ..	*556.69*	*583.02*	*666.47*	*782.81*	*888.73*	*833.78*	*1,002.46*	*1,217.15*
Other sectors	8 775 ..	161.23	168.20	190.70	233.68	250.95	250.95	344.79	422.78
of which: Short-term	8 777 ..	*102.01*	*92.69*	*93.76*	*112.96*	*122.76*	*120.82*	*167.18*	*191.93*
Currency and deposits	8 780 ..	....	....	....	....	10.81	7.41	6.35	23.56
Monetary authorities	8 781 ..	....	....	....	....	10.81	7.41	6.35	23.56
General government	8 782 ..	....	....	....	....	....	....	....	....
Banks	8 783 ..	....	....	....	....	....	....	....	....
Other sectors	8 784 ..	....	....	....	....	....	....	....	....
Other liabilities	8 786 ..	2.75	2.67	3.16	3.91	5.83	5.85	7.57	9.09
Monetary authorities	8 787 ..	....	....	....	....	....	....	....	....
of which: Short-term	8 789 ..	....	....	....	....	....	....	....	....
General government	8 790 ..	.46	.46	.44	.57	.83	.73	1.30	1.82
of which: Short-term	8 792 ..	....	....	....	....	....	....	....	....
Banks	8 793 ..	.75	.71	.85	1.03	1.16	1.01	1.46	1.79
of which: Short-term	8 795 ..	....	....	....	....	....	....	....	....
Other sectors	8 796 ..	1.54	1.50	1.87	2.32	3.83	4.11	4.81	5.48
of which: Short-term	8 798 ..	....	....	....	....	....	....	....	....
NET INTERNATIONAL INVESTMENT POSITION	8 995 ..	**62.32**	**161.60**	**113.66**	**179.20**	**329.98**	**576.09**	**838.00**	**951.88**
Conversion rates: euros per U.S. dollar (end of period)	0 104 ..	**1.0747**	**1.1347**	**.9536**	**.7918**	**.7342**	**.8477**	**.7593**	**.6793**

Table 1. ANALYTIC PRESENTATION, 2000–2007

(Millions of U.S. dollars)

	Code	2000	2001	2002	2003	2004	2005	2006	2007
A. Current Account[1]	4 993 Z.	**−386.5**	**−324.6**	**−31.9**	**278.0**	**−566.9**	**−1,104.6**	**−1,042.6**	**−2,151.5**
Goods: exports f.o.b.	2 100 ..	1,936.3	1,867.1	2,015.2	2,562.4	2,704.5	2,802.2	3,726.7	4,172.1
Goods: imports f.o.b.	3 100 ..	−2,766.6	−2,968.5	−2,707.0	−3,232.8	−4,297.3	−5,347.3	−6,753.7	−8,066.1
Balance on Goods	4 100 ..	*−830.3*	*−1,101.4*	*−691.8*	*−670.4*	*−1,592.8*	*−2,545.1*	*−3,027.0*	*−3,894.0*
Services: credit	2 200 ..	504.2	531.7	554.9	630.0	702.3	1,106.5	1,396.3	1,831.9
Services: debit	3 200 ..	−583.7	−606.1	−620.9	−899.8	−1,058.5	−1,273.1	−1,532.8	−1,993.9
Balance on Goods and Services	4 991 ..	*−909.8*	*−1,175.8*	*−757.8*	*−940.2*	*−1,949.0*	*−2,711.7*	*−3,163.5*	*−4,056.0*
Income: credit	2 300 ..	15.6	16.3	14.7	21.4	44.5	43.3	73.3	84.0
Income: debit	3 300 ..	−123.2	−124.1	−189.0	−202.4	−242.4	−230.4	−200.6	−222.6
Balance on Goods, Services, and Income	4 992 ..	*−1,017.4*	*−1,283.6*	*−932.1*	*−1,121.2*	*−2,146.8*	*−2,898.8*	*−3,290.9*	*−4,194.7*
Current transfers: credit	2 379 Z.	649.3	978.4	912.4	1,408.4	1,579.9	1,794.2	2,248.3	2,043.2
Current transfers: debit	3 379 ..	−18.4	−19.4	−12.2	−9.2	....	....	....	....
B. Capital Account[1]	4 994 Z.	....	....	....	....	**251.0**	**331.2**	**229.9**	**188.1**
Capital account: credit	2 994 Z.	....	....	....	....	251.0	331.2	229.9	188.1
Capital account: debit	3 994 ..	....	....	....	....	....	....	....	....
Total, Groups A Plus B	4 981 ..	*−386.5*	*−324.6*	*−31.9*	*278.0*	*−315.8*	*−773.4*	*−812.7*	*−1,963.3*
C. Financial Account[1]	4 995 W.	**369.3**	**392.2**	**−21.0**	**340.4**	**201.6**	**834.5**	**1,255.0**	**2,429.8**
Direct investment abroad	4 505 ..	....	....	....	....	....	....	....	....
Direct investment in Ghana	4 555 Z.	165.9	89.3	58.9	136.8	139.3	145.0	636.0	970.4
Portfolio investment assets	4 602 ..	....	....	....	....	....	....	....	98.4
Equity securities	4 610 ..	....	....	....	....	....	....	....	....
Debt securities	4 619 ..	....	....	....	....	....	....	....	98.4
Portfolio investment liabilities	4 652 Z.	....	....	....	....	....	....	....	666.1
Equity securities	4 660 ..	....	....	....	....	....	....	....	....
Debt securities	4 669 Z.	....	....	....	....	....	....	....	666.1
Financial derivatives	4 910 ..	....	....	....	....	....	....	....	....
Financial derivatives assets	4 900 ..	....	....	....	....	....	....	....	....
Financial derivatives liabilities	4 905 ..	....	....	....	....	....	....	....	....
Other investment assets	4 703 ..	....	....	....	....	....	....	....	....
Monetary authorities	4 701 ..	....	....	....	....	....	....	....	....
General government	4 704 ..	....	....	....	....	....	....	....	....
Banks	4 705 ..	....	....	....	....	....	....	....	....
Other sectors	4 728 ..	....	....	....	....	....	....	....	....
Other investment liabilities	4 753 W.	203.4	302.9	−79.9	203.6	62.3	689.5	618.9	695.0
Monetary authorities	4 753 WA	....	....	....	....	....	....	....	....
General government	4 753 ZB	139.7	84.6	−115.2	85.8	52.5	141.1	212.6	445.1
Banks	4 753 ZC	40.8	144.3	−123.8	9.7	−94.6	27.4	−28.7	252.9
Other sectors	4 753 ZD	22.9	74.0	159.1	108.1	104.5	521.0	435.0	−3.0
Total, Groups A Through C	4 983 ..	*−17.2*	*67.6*	*−52.9*	*618.4*	*−114.3*	*61.1*	*442.3*	*466.4*
D. Net Errors and Omissions	4 998 ..	**−352.1**	**−189.1**	**39.3**	**−114.8**	**115.2**	**64.7**	**77.6**	**−52.2**
Total, Groups A Through D	4 984 ..	*−369.3*	*−121.5*	*−13.6*	*503.6*	*1.0*	*125.8*	*519.9*	*414.2*
E. Reserves and Related Items	4 802 A.	**369.3**	**121.5**	**13.6**	**−503.6**	**−1.0**	**−125.8**	**−519.9**	**−414.2**
Reserve assets	4 802 ..	344.5	−80.3	−155.8	−657.6	−191.7	−335.7	−374.3	−414.2
Use of Fund credit and loans	4 766 ..	−2.3	.8	51.4	54.6	−5.3	−15.1	−267.2	....
Exceptional financing	4 920 ..	27.0	201.0	118.0	99.4	196.0	225.0	121.6	....
Conversion rates: cedis per U.S. dollar	0 101 ..	**.5**	**.7**	**.8**	**.9**	**.9**	**.9**	**.9**	**.9**

[1] Excludes components that have been classified in the categories of Group E.

Table 2. STANDARD PRESENTATION, 2000–2007

(Millions of U.S. dollars)

	Code	2000	2001	2002	2003	2004	2005	2006	2007
CURRENT ACCOUNT...	4 993 ..	**−386.5**	**−324.6**	**−31.9**	**278.0**	**−566.9**	**−1,104.6**	**−1,042.6**	**−2,151.5**
A. GOODS...	4 100 ..	**−830.3**	**−1,101.4**	**−691.8**	**−670.4**	**−1,592.8**	**−2,545.1**	**−3,027.0**	**−3,894.0**
Credit...	2 100 ..	**1,936.3**	**1,867.1**	**2,015.2**	**2,562.4**	**2,704.5**	**2,802.2**	**3,726.7**	**4,172.1**
General merchandise: exports f.o.b............	2 110 ..	1,234.3	1,249.3	1,326.1	1,732.3	1,864.3	1,856.4	2,449.4	2,438.4
Goods for processing: exports f.o.b............	2 150 ..	....	....	....	....	....	....	....	....
Repairs on goods...	2 160 ..	....	....	....	....	....	....	....	....
Goods procured in ports by carriers............	2 170 ..	....	....	....	....	....	....	....	....
Nonmonetary gold...	2 180 ..	702.0	617.8	689.1	830.1	840.2	945.8	1,277.3	1,733.8
Debit...	3 100 ..	**−2,766.6**	**−2,968.5**	**−2,707.0**	**−3,232.8**	**−4,297.3**	**−5,347.3**	**−6,753.7**	**−8,066.1**
General merchandise: imports f.o.b............	3 110 ..	−2,766.6	−2,968.5	−2,707.0	−3,232.8	−4,297.3	−5,347.3	−6,753.7	−8,066.1
Goods for processing: imports f.o.b............	3 150 ..	....	....	....	....	....	....	....	....
Repairs on goods...	3 160 ..	....	....	....	....	....	....	....	....
Goods procured in ports by carriers............	3 170 ..	....	....	....	....	....	....	....	....
Nonmonetary gold...	3 180 ..	....	....	....	....	....	....	....	....
B. SERVICES...	4 200 ..	**−79.5**	**−74.4**	**−66.0**	**−269.8**	**−356.2**	**−166.6**	**−136.5**	**−162.1**
Total credit	2 200 ..	*504.2*	*531.7*	*554.9*	*630.0*	*702.3*	*1,106.5*	*1,396.3*	*1,831.9*
Total debit	3 200 ..	*−583.7*	*−606.1*	*−620.9*	*−899.8*	*−1,058.5*	*−1,273.1*	*−1,532.8*	*−1,993.9*
Transportation services, credit............	2 205 ..	**98.4**	**103.6**	**114.6**	**124.3**	**136.8**	**145.9**	**203.4**	**313.2**
Passenger...	2 850 ..	*22.2*	*23.2*	*25.3*	*26.9*	*29.1*	*31.4*	*49.2*	*82.5*
Freight...	2 851 ..	*41.6*	*44.0*	*49.8*	*55.4*	*62.3*	*65.3*	*77.2*	*101.8*
Other...	2 852 ..	*34.6*	*36.4*	*39.5*	*42.0*	*45.4*	*49.2*	*77.0*	*129.0*
Sea transport, passenger............................	2 207 ..	....	....	....	....	....	....	....	....
Sea transport, freight............................	2 208 ..	41.6	44.0	49.8	55.4	62.3	65.3	77.2	101.8
Sea transport, other............................	2 209 ..	34.6	36.4	39.5	42.0	45.4	49.2	77.0	129.0
Air transport, passenger............................	2 211 ..	22.2	23.2	25.3	26.9	29.1	31.4	49.2	82.5
Air transport, freight............................	2 212 ..	....	....	....	....	....	....	....	....
Air transport, other............................	2 213 ..	....	....	....	....	....	....	....	....
Other transport, passenger............................	2 215 ..	....	....	....	....	....	....	....	....
Other transport, freight............................	2 216 ..	....	....	....	....	....	....	....	....
Other transport, other............................	2 217 ..	....	....	....	....	....	....	....	....
Transportation services, debit............	3 205 ..	**−271.2**	**−281.8**	**−268.5**	**−323.1**	**−401.9**	**−580.9**	**−739.6**	**−855.2**
Passenger...	3 850 ..	*−62.1*	*−59.9*	*−65.0*	*−77.6*	*−83.8*	*−169.1*	*−229.6*	*−257.8*
Freight...	3 851 ..	*−187.3*	*−200.9*	*−180.6*	*−218.3*	*−288.6*	*−352.4*	*−429.3*	*−506.8*
Other...	3 852 ..	*−21.8*	*−21.0*	*−22.9*	*−27.2*	*−29.5*	*−59.4*	*−80.7*	*−90.6*
Sea transport, passenger............................	3 207 ..	....	....	....	....	....	....	....	....
Sea transport, freight............................	3 208 ..	−187.3	−200.9	−180.6	−218.3	−288.6	−352.4	−429.3	−506.8
Sea transport, other............................	3 209 ..	−21.8	−21.0	−22.9	−27.2	−29.5	−59.4	−80.7	−90.6
Air transport, passenger............................	3 211 ..	−62.1	−59.9	−65.0	−77.6	−83.8	−169.1	−229.6	−257.8
Air transport, freight............................	3 212 ..	....	....	....	....	....	....	....	....
Air transport, other............................	3 213 ..	....	....	....	....	....	....	....	....
Other transport, passenger............................	3 215 ..	....	....	....	....	....	....	....	....
Other transport, freight............................	3 216 ..	....	....	....	....	....	....	....	....
Other transport, other............................	3 217 ..	....	....	....	....	....	....	....	....
Travel, credit...	2 236 ..	**334.5**	**351.3**	**358.2**	**414.4**	**466.0**	**836.1**	**861.3**	**908.2**
Business travel...	2 237 ..	234.2	245.9	250.7	290.1	326.2	585.3	602.9	635.8
Personal travel...	2 240 ..	100.4	105.4	107.5	124.3	139.8	250.8	258.4	272.5
Travel, debit...	3 236 ..	**−100.4**	**−105.4**	**−119.4**	**−138.1**	**−186.4**	**−302.8**	**−344.5**	**−558.0**
Business travel...	3 237 ..	−70.3	−73.8	−83.6	−96.7	−130.5	−212.0	−241.2	−390.6
Personal travel...	3 240 ..	−30.1	−31.6	−35.8	−41.4	−55.9	−90.8	−103.4	−167.4
Other services, credit............................	2 200 BA	**71.3**	**76.8**	**82.1**	**91.3**	**99.5**	**124.5**	**331.6**	**610.4**
Communications...	2 245 ..	....	....	....	....	....	....	....	....
Construction...	2 249 ..	....	....	....	....	....	....	....	....
Insurance...	2 253 ..	5.1	5.4	6.2	6.8	7.7	8.1	9.5	12.6
Financial...	2 260 ..	....	....	....	....	....	....	....	....
Computer and information............................	2 262 ..	....	....	....	....	....	....	....	....
Royalties and licence fees............................	2 266 ..	....	....	....	....	....	....	....	....
Other business services............................	2 268 ..	51.7	55.1	59.8	66.8	73.2	92.8	182.1	380.4
Personal, cultural, and recreational............	2 287 ..	....	....	....	....	....	....	....	....
Government, n.i.e...	2 291 ..	14.5	16.3	16.1	17.7	18.6	23.6	140.0	217.5
Other services, debit............................	3 200 BA	**−212.1**	**−218.9**	**−233.0**	**−438.6**	**−470.2**	**−389.4**	**−448.7**	**−580.8**
Communications...	3 245 ..	....	....	....	....	....	....	....	....
Construction...	3 249 ..	....	....	....	....	....	....	....	....
Insurance...	3 253 ..	−30.5	−32.7	−29.4	−35.5	−47.0	−57.4	−69.9	−82.5
Financial...	3 260 ..	....	....	....	....	....	....	....	....
Computer and information............................	3 262 ..	....	....	....	....	....	....	....	....
Royalties and licence fees............................	3 266 ..	....	....	....	....	....	....	....	....
Other business services............................	3 268 ..	−111.6	−118.1	−130.4	−233.7	−245.4	−199.0	−287.8	−312.0
Personal, cultural, and recreational............	3 287 ..	....	....	....	....	....	....	....	....
Government, n.i.e...	3 291 ..	−70.0	−68.1	−73.2	−169.4	−177.8	−133.0	−91.0	−186.3

2008, International Monetary Fund: *Balance of Payments Statistics Yearbook*

Table 2 (Continued). STANDARD PRESENTATION, 2000–2007

(Millions of U.S. dollars)

	Code	2000	2001	2002	2003	2004	2005	2006	2007
C. INCOME	4 300	−107.6	−107.8	−174.3	−181.0	−197.9	−187.1	−127.4	−138.6
Total credit	2 300	*15.6*	*16.3*	*14.7*	*21.4*	*44.5*	*43.3*	*73.3*	*84.0*
Total debit	3 300	*−123.2*	*−124.1*	*−189.0*	*−202.4*	*−242.4*	*−230.4*	*−200.6*	*−222.6*
Compensation of employees, credit	2 310	....	....	....	....	....	....	....	....
Compensation of employees, debit	3 310	....	....	....	....	....	....	....	....
Investment income, credit	2 320	15.6	16.3	14.7	21.4	44.5	43.3	73.3	84.0
Direct investment income	2 330	....	....	....	....	....	....	....	....
Dividends and distributed branch profits	2 332	....	....	....	....	....	....	....	....
Reinvested earnings and undistributed branch profits	2 333	....	....	....	....	....	....	....	....
Income on debt (interest)	2 334	....	....	....	....	....	....	....	....
Portfolio investment income	2 339	....	....	....	....	....	....	....	....
Income on equity	2 340	....	....	....	....	....	....	....	....
Income on bonds and notes	2 350	....	....	....	....	....	....	....	....
Income on money market instruments	2 360	....	....	....	....	....	....	....	....
Other investment income	2 370	15.6	16.3	14.7	21.4	44.5	43.3	73.3	84.0
Investment income, debit	3 320	−123.2	−124.1	−189.0	−202.4	−242.4	−230.4	−200.6	−222.6
Direct investment income	3 330	−17.0	−18.0	−65.9	−85.2	−96.5	−94.3	−91.5	−135.4
Dividends and distributed branch profits	3 332	−16.2	−18.0	−65.0	−84.3	−74.5	−71.1	−91.5	−135.4
Reinvested earnings and undistributed branch profits	3 333	....	....	....	....	....	....	....	....
Income on debt (interest)	3 334	−.8	....	−.9	−.9	−22.0	−23.2	....	....
Portfolio investment income	3 339	....	....	....	....	....	....	....	−28.9
Income on equity	3 340	....	....	....	....	....	....	....	....
Income on bonds and notes	3 350	....	....	....	....	....	....	....	−28.9
Income on money market instruments	3 360	....	....	....	....	....	....	....	....
Other investment income	3 370	−106.2	−106.1	−123.1	−117.2	−145.8	−136.1	−109.1	−58.3
D. CURRENT TRANSFERS	4 379	630.9	959.0	900.2	1,399.2	1,579.9	1,794.2	2,248.3	2,043.2
Credit	2 379	649.3	978.4	912.4	1,408.4	1,579.9	1,794.2	2,248.3	2,043.2
General government	2 380	143.1	261.1	232.4	391.2	292.9	244.5	603.7	209.4
Other sectors	2 390	506.2	717.3	680.0	1,017.2	1,287.1	1,549.8	1,644.6	1,833.8
Workers' remittances	2 391	32.4	45.9	43.5	65.1	82.4	99.2	105.3	117.4
Other current transfers	2 392	473.8	671.4	636.5	952.1	1,204.7	1,450.6	1,539.3	1,716.4
Debit	3 379	−18.4	−19.4	−12.2	−9.2	....	....	....	....
General government	3 380	−11.2	−11.8	−12.2	−9.2	....	....	....	....
Other sectors	3 390	−7.2	−7.6	....	....	....	....	....	....
Workers' remittances	3 391	−6.1	−6.4	....	....	....	....	....	....
Other current transfers	3 392	−1.1	−1.2	....	....	....	....	....	....
CAPITAL AND FINANCIAL ACCOUNT	4 996	738.6	513.7	−7.4	−163.3	451.6	1,039.9	965.0	2,203.7
CAPITAL ACCOUNT	4 994	....	....	....	....	251.0	331.2	229.9	188.1
Total credit	2 994	....	....	....	....	*251.0*	*331.2*	*229.9*	*188.1*
Total debit	3 994	....	....	....	....	....	....	....	....
Capital transfers, credit	2 400	....	....	....	....	251.0	331.2	229.9	188.1
General government	2 401	....	....	....	....	251.0	331.2	229.9	188.1
Debt forgiveness	2 402	....	....	....	....	....	....	....	....
Other capital transfers	2 410	....	....	....	....	251.0	331.2	229.9	188.1
Other sectors	2 430	....	....	....	....	....	....	....	....
Migrants' transfers	2 431	....	....	....	....	....	....	....	....
Debt forgiveness	2 432	....	....	....	....	....	....	....	....
Other capital transfers	2 440	....	....	....	....	....	....	....	....
Capital transfers, debit	3 400	....	....	....	....	....	....	....	....
General government	3 401	....	....	....	....	....	....	....	....
Debt forgiveness	3 402	....	....	....	....	....	....	....	....
Other capital transfers	3 410	....	....	....	....	....	....	....	....
Other sectors	3 430	....	....	....	....	....	....	....	....
Migrants' transfers	3 431	....	....	....	....	....	....	....	....
Debt forgiveness	3 432	....	....	....	....	....	....	....	....
Other capital transfers	3 440	....	....	....	....	....	....	....	....
Nonproduced nonfinancial assets, credit	2 480	....	....	....	....	....	....	....	....
Nonproduced nonfinancial assets, debit	3 480	....	....	....	....	....	....	....	....

Table 2 (Continued). STANDARD PRESENTATION, 2000–2007

(Millions of U.S. dollars)

	Code	2000	2001	2002	2003	2004	2005	2006	2007
FINANCIAL ACCOUNT	4 995 ..	**738.6**	**513.7**	**−7.4**	**−163.3**	**200.6**	**708.7**	**735.0**	**2,015.5**
A. DIRECT INVESTMENT	4 500 ..	**165.9**	**89.3**	**58.9**	**136.8**	**139.3**	**145.0**	**636.0**	**970.4**
Direct investment abroad	4 505 ..	....	....	....	....	....	....	....	....
Equity capital	4 510 ..	....	....	....	....	....	....	....	....
Claims on affiliated enterprises	4 515 ..	....	....	....	....	....	....	....	....
Liabilities to affiliated enterprises	4 520 ..	....	....	....	....	....	....	....	....
Reinvested earnings	4 525 ..	....	....	....	....	....	....	....	....
Other capital	4 530 ..	....	....	....	....	....	....	....	....
Claims on affiliated enterprises	4 535 ..	....	....	....	....	....	....	....	....
Liabilities to affiliated enterprises	4 540 ..	....	....	....	....	....	....	....	....
Direct investment in Ghana	4 555 ..	**165.9**	**89.3**	**58.9**	**136.8**	**139.3**	**145.0**	**636.0**	**970.4**
Equity capital	4 560 ..	165.9	89.3	58.9	136.8	139.3	145.0	636.0	970.4
Claims on direct investors	4 565 ..	....	....	....	....	....	....	....	....
Liabilities to direct investors	4 570 ..	165.9	89.3	58.9	136.8	139.3	145.0	636.0	970.4
Reinvested earnings	4 575 ..	....	....	....	....	....	....	....	....
Other capital	4 580 ..	....	....	....	....	....	....	....	....
Claims on direct investors	4 585 ..	....	....	....	....	....	....	....	....
Liabilities to direct investors	4 590 ..	....	....	....	....	....	....	....	....
B. PORTFOLIO INVESTMENT	4 600 ..	....	....	....	....	....	....	....	**764.4**
Assets	4 602 ..	....	....	....	....	....	....	....	**98.4**
Equity securities	4 610 ..	....	....	....	....	....	....	....	....
Monetary authorities	4 611 ..	....	....	....	....	....	....	....	....
General government	4 612 ..	....	....	....	....	....	....	....	....
Banks	4 613 ..	....	....	....	....	....	....	....	....
Other sectors	4 614 ..	....	....	....	....	....	....	....	....
Debt securities	4 619 ..	....	....	....	....	....	....	....	98.4
Bonds and notes	4 620 ..	....	....	....	....	....	....	....	....
Monetary authorities	4 621 ..	....	....	....	....	....	....	....	....
General government	4 622 ..	....	....	....	....	....	....	....	....
Banks	4 623 ..	....	....	....	....	....	....	....	....
Other sectors	4 624 ..	....	....	....	....	....	....	....	....
Money market instruments	4 630 ..	....	....	....	....	....	....	....	98.4
Monetary authorities	4 631 ..	....	....	....	....	....	....	....	....
General government	4 632 ..	....	....	....	....	....	....	....	....
Banks	4 633 ..	....	....	....	....	....	....	....	....
Other sectors	4 634 ..	....	....	....	....	....	....	....	98.4
Liabilities	4 652 ..	....	....	....	....	....	....	....	**666.1**
Equity securities	4 660 ..	....	....	....	....	....	....	....	....
Banks	4 663 ..	....	....	....	....	....	....	....	....
Other sectors	4 664 ..	....	....	....	....	....	....	....	....
Debt securities	4 669 ..	....	....	....	....	....	....	....	666.1
Bonds and notes	4 670 ..	....	....	....	....	....	....	....	750.0
Monetary authorities	4 671 ..	....	....	....	....	....	....	....	....
General government	4 672 ..	....	....	....	....	....	....	....	750.0
Banks	4 673 ..	....	....	....	....	....	....	....	....
Other sectors	4 674 ..	....	....	....	....	....	....	....	....
Money market instruments	4 680 ..	....	....	....	....	....	....	....	−83.9
Monetary authorities	4 681 ..	....	....	....	....	....	....	....	....
General government	4 682 ..	....	....	....	....	....	....	....	....
Banks	4 683 ..	....	....	....	....	....	....	....	....
Other sectors	4 684 ..	....	....	....	....	....	....	....	−83.9
C. FINANCIAL DERIVATIVES	4 910 ..	....	....	....	....	....	....	....	....
Monetary authorities	4 911 ..	....	....	....	....	....	....	....	....
General government	4 912 ..	....	....	....	....	....	....	....	....
Banks	4 913 ..	....	....	....	....	....	....	....	....
Other sectors	4 914 ..	....	....	....	....	....	....	....	....
Assets	4 900 ..	....	....	....	....	....	....	....	....
Monetary authorities	4 901 ..	....	....	....	....	....	....	....	....
General government	4 902 ..	....	....	....	....	....	....	....	....
Banks	4 903 ..	....	....	....	....	....	....	....	....
Other sectors	4 904 ..	....	....	....	....	....	....	....	....
Liabilities	4 905 ..	....	....	....	....	....	....	....	....
Monetary authorities	4 906 ..	....	....	....	....	....	....	....	....
General government	4 907 ..	....	....	....	....	....	....	....	....
Banks	4 908 ..	....	....	....	....	....	....	....	....
Other sectors	4 909 ..	....	....	....	....	....	....	....	....

Table 2 (Concluded). STANDARD PRESENTATION, 2000–2007

(Millions of U.S. dollars)

	Code	2000	2001	2002	2003	2004	2005	2006	2007
D. OTHER INVESTMENT	4 700	**228.1**	**504.7**	**89.5**	**357.6**	**253.0**	**899.4**	**473.3**	**695.0**
Assets	4 703	....	....	....	....	....	....	....	....
Trade credits	4 706	....	....	....	....	....	....	....	....
General government	4 707	....	....	....	....	....	....	....	....
of which: Short-term	4 709	....	....	....	....	....	....	....	....
Other sectors	4 710	....	....	....	....	....	....	....	....
of which: Short-term	4 712	....	....	....	....	....	....	....	....
Loans	4 714	....	....	....	....	....	....	....	....
Monetary authorities	4 715	....	....	....	....	....	....	....	....
of which: Short-term	4 718	....	....	....	....	....	....	....	....
General government	4 719	....	....	....	....	....	....	....	....
of which: Short-term	4 721	....	....	....	....	....	....	....	....
Banks	4 722	....	....	....	....	....	....	....	....
of which: Short-term	4 724	....	....	....	....	....	....	....	....
Other sectors	4 725	....	....	....	....	....	....	....	....
of which: Short-term	4 727	....	....	....	....	....	....	....	....
Currency and deposits	4 730	....	....	....	....	....	....	....	....
Monetary authorities	4 731	....	....	....	....	....	....	....	....
General government	4 732	....	....	....	....	....	....	....	....
Banks	4 733	....	....	....	....	....	....	....	....
Other sectors	4 734	....	....	....	....	....	....	....	....
Other assets	4 736	....	....	....	....	....	....	....	....
Monetary authorities	4 737	....	....	....	....	....	....	....	....
of which: Short-term	4 739	....	....	....	....	....	....	....	....
General government	4 740	....	....	....	....	....	....	....	....
of which: Short-term	4 742	....	....	....	....	....	....	....	....
Banks	4 743	....	....	....	....	....	....	....	....
of which: Short-term	4 745	....	....	....	....	....	....	....	....
Other sectors	4 746	....	....	....	....	....	....	....	....
of which: Short-term	4 748	....	....	....	....	....	....	....	....
Liabilities	4 753	**228.1**	**504.7**	**89.5**	**357.6**	**253.0**	**899.4**	**473.3**	**695.0**
Trade credits	4 756	12.0	26.0	112.4	45.0	−88.3	106.7	51.6	−94.1
General government	4 757	....	....	....	....	....	....	....	....
of which: Short-term	4 759	....	....	....	....	....	....	....	....
Other sectors	4 760	12.0	26.0	112.4	45.0	−88.3	106.7	51.6	−94.1
of which: Short-term	4 762	*12.0*	*26.0*	*112.4*	*45.0*	*−88.3*	*106.7*	*51.6*	*−94.1*
Loans	4 764	137.4	85.4	−63.8	140.3	47.1	126.1	−54.6	445.1
Monetary authorities	4 765	−2.3	.8	51.4	54.6	−5.3	−15.1	−267.2	....
of which: Use of Fund credit and loans from the Fund	4 766	*−2.3*	*.8*	*51.4*	*54.6*	*−5.3*	*−15.1*	*−267.2*	....
of which: Short-term	4 768	....	....	....	....	....	....	....	....
General government	4 769	139.7	84.6	−115.2	85.8	52.5	141.1	212.6	445.1
of which: Short-term	4 771	....	....	....	....	....	....	....	....
Banks	4 772	....	....	....	....	....	....	....	....
of which: Short-term	4 774	....	....	....	....	....	....	....	....
Other sectors	4 775	....	....	....	....	....	....	....	....
of which: Short-term	4 777	....	....	....	....	....	....	....	....
Currency and deposits	4 780	40.8	144.3	−123.8	9.7	−94.6	27.4	−28.7	252.9
Monetary authorities	4 781	....	....	....	....	....	....	....	....
General government	4 782	....	....	....	....	....	....	....	....
Banks	4 783	40.8	144.3	−123.8	9.7	−94.6	27.4	−28.7	252.9
Other sectors	4 784	....	....	....	....	....	....	....	....
Other liabilities	4 786	37.9	249.0	164.7	162.6	388.8	639.3	505.0	91.1
Monetary authorities	4 787	....	....	....	....	....	....	....	....
of which: Short-term	4 789	....	....	....	....	....	....	....	....
General government	4 790	27.0	201.0	118.0	99.4	196.0	225.0	121.6	....
of which: Short-term	4 792	*27.0*	*201.0*	*118.0*	*99.4*	*196.0*	*225.0*	*121.6*	....
Banks	4 793	....	....	....	....	....	....	....	....
of which: Short-term	4 795	....	....	....	....	....	....	....	....
Other sectors	4 796	10.9	48.0	46.7	63.2	192.7	414.3	383.3	91.1
of which: Short-term	4 798	....	....	....	....	....	....	....	....
E. RESERVE ASSETS	4 802	**344.5**	**−80.3**	**−155.8**	**−657.6**	**−191.7**	**−335.7**	**−374.3**	**−414.2**
Monetary gold	4 812	−.3	−.4	−17.7	−20.6	−5.8	−21.6	−33.7	....
Special drawing rights	4 811	16.4	−3.6	1.4	−41.9	27.0	18.5	....	.6
Reserve position in the Fund	4 810	54.7	....	....	....	....	....	....	....
Foreign exchange	4 803	273.8	−76.4	−139.6	−595.1	−212.9	−332.7	−340.6	−414.9
Other claims	4 813	....	....	....	....	....	....	....	....
NET ERRORS AND OMISSIONS	4 998	**−352.1**	**−189.1**	**39.3**	**−114.8**	**115.2**	**64.7**	**77.6**	**−52.2**

Table 1. ANALYTIC PRESENTATION, 2000–2007

(Millions of U.S. dollars)

	Code	2000	2001	2002	2003	2004	2005	2006	2007
A. Current Account[1]	4 993 Z.	**−9,820**	**−9,400**	**−9,582**	**−12,804**	**−13,476**	**−18,233**	**−29,565**	**−44,587**
Goods: exports f.o.b.	2 100 ..	10,202	10,615	9,865	12,578	15,739	17,631	20,300	23,991
Goods: imports f.o.b.	3 100 ..	−30,440	−29,702	−31,321	−38,184	−47,360	−51,900	−64,585	−81,041
Balance on Goods	4 100 ..	*−20,239*	*−19,087*	*−21,455*	*−25,606*	*−31,621*	*−34,268*	*−44,285*	*−57,050*
Services: credit	2 200 ..	19,239	19,456	20,142	24,283	33,085	33,914	35,762	43,080
Services: debit	3 200 ..	−11,286	−11,589	−9,819	−11,250	−14,020	−14,742	−16,367	−20,270
Balance on Goods and Services	4 991 ..	*−12,286*	*−11,220*	*−11,132*	*−12,573*	*−12,556*	*−15,096*	*−24,889*	*−34,240*
Income: credit	2 300 ..	2,807	1,885	1,532	2,911	3,495	4,072	4,566	6,345
Income: debit	3 300 ..	−3,692	−3,652	−3,488	−7,413	−8,920	−11,102	−13,524	−18,814
Balance on Goods, Services, and Income	4 992 ..	*−13,171*	*−12,987*	*−13,088*	*−17,075*	*−17,980*	*−22,126*	*−33,847*	*−46,709*
Current transfers: credit	2 379 Z.	4,116	4,592	5,536	7,202	7,901	8,615	8,587	9,053
Current transfers: debit	3 379 ..	−764	−1,005	−2,029	−2,930	−3,396	−4,722	−4,305	−6,931
B. Capital Account[1]	4 994 Z.	**2,112**	**2,153**	**1,530**	**1,411**	**2,990**	**2,563**	**3,822**	**5,957**
Capital account: credit	2 994 Z.	2,244	2,320	1,707	1,585	3,278	2,905	4,173	6,426
Capital account: debit	3 994 ..	−131	−167	−177	−173	−288	−342	−351	−469
Total, Groups A Plus B	4 981 ..	*−7,707*	*−7,247*	*−8,052*	*−11,392*	*−10,486*	*−15,670*	*−25,743*	*−38,630*
C. Financial Account[1]	4 995 W.	**10,830**	**537**	**11,578**	**6,417**	**6,836**	**15,633**	**25,661**	**38,027**
Direct investment abroad	4 505 ..	−2,099	−611	−668	−375	−1,028	−1,476	−4,226	−5,262
Direct investment in Greece	4 555 Z.	1,083	1,585	53	1,332	2,105	658	5,401	1,959
Portfolio investment assets	4 602 ..	−1,184	−474	−1,917	−9,805	−13,835	−23,194	−9,374	−21,636
Equity securities	4 610 ..	−846	−1,020	−316	−505	−830	−2,189	−2,923	−593
Debt securities	4 619 ..	−338	546	−1,600	−9,300	−13,005	−21,004	−6,452	−21,043
Portfolio investment liabilities	4 652 Z.	9,262	9,012	12,340	23,456	31,301	32,308	18,738	45,545
Equity securities	4 660 ..	1,637	1,829	1,400	2,568	4,290	6,293	7,529	10,865
Debt securities	4 669 Z.	7,625	7,183	10,939	20,887	27,010	26,015	11,208	34,680
Financial derivatives	4 910 ..	348	74	−175	111	−429	13	920	−623
Financial derivatives assets	4 900 ..	348	74	−175	111	−429	13	920	−623
Financial derivatives liabilities	4 905 ..	. . . .	. . . .	. . . .	. . . .	. . . .	. . . .	. . . .	. . . .
Other investment assets	4 703 ..	6,970	−1,539	−6,952	−4,413	−7,463	−8,740	−7,336	−22,118
Monetary authorities	4 701 ..	. . . .	. . . .	3,622	−1,043	−1,078	−295	11	1,100
General government	4 704 ..	6,970	−1,539	. . . .	. . . .	. . . .	. . . .	. . . .	. . . .
Banks	4 705 ..	. . . .	. . . .	−1,589	−2,602	−5,068	−7,358	−7,514	−22,653
Other sectors	4 728 ..	. . . .	. . . .	−8,984	−768	−1,317	−1,087	166	−565
Other investment liabilities	4 753 W.	−3,551	−7,511	8,897	−3,888	−3,813	16,064	21,539	40,161
Monetary authorities	4 753 WA	. . . .	. . . .	9,176	−2,311	−11,799	1,434	1,058	3,716
General government	4 753 ZB	. . . .	. . . .	−4,326	−2,888	−1,271	−516	728	−3,132
Banks	4 753 ZC	−3,425	−6,989	8,249	2,773	10,661	17,833	20,019	40,386
Other sectors	4 753 ZD	−126	−522	−4,202	−1,462	−1,403	−2,686	−267	−809
Total, Groups A Through C	4 983 ..	*3,123*	*−6,710*	*3,527*	*−4,975*	*−3,650*	*−37*	*−83*	*−603*
D. Net Errors and Omissions	4 998 ..	**−550**	**1,011**	**−1,663**	**253**	**373**	**−67**	**361**	**1,060**
Total, Groups A Through D	4 984 ..	*2,573*	*−5,699*	*1,863*	*−4,722*	*−3,277*	*−104*	*279*	*457*
E. Reserves and Related Items	4 802 A.	**−2,573**	**5,699**	**−1,863**	**4,722**	**3,277**	**104**	**−279**	**−457**
Reserve assets	4 802 ..	−2,573	5,699	−1,863	4,722	3,277	104	−279	−457
Use of Fund credit and loans	4 766 ..	. . . .	. . . .	. . . .	. . . .	. . . .	. . . .	. . . .	. . . .
Exceptional financing	4 920 ..	. . . .	. . . .	. . . .	. . . .	. . . .	. . . .	. . . .	. . . .
Conversion rates: drachmas per U.S. dollar	0 101 ..	**365.40**	. . . .	. . . .	. . . .	. . . .	. . . .	. . . .	. . . .
Conversion rates: euros per U.S. dollar	0 103 ..	**1.0854**	**1.1175**	**1.0626**	**.8860**	**.8054**	**.8041**	**.7971**	**.7306**

[1] Excludes components that have been classified in the categories of Group E.

Table 2. STANDARD PRESENTATION, 2000–2007

(Millions of U.S. dollars)

	Code	2000	2001	2002	2003	2004	2005	2006	2007
CURRENT ACCOUNT	4 993	**−9,820**	**−9,400**	**−9,582**	**−12,804**	**−13,476**	**−18,233**	**−29,565**	**−44,587**
A. GOODS	4 100	**−20,239**	**−19,087**	**−21,455**	**−25,606**	**−31,621**	**−34,268**	**−44,285**	**−57,050**
Credit	2 100	**10,202**	**10,615**	**9,865**	**12,578**	**15,739**	**17,631**	**20,300**	**23,991**
General merchandise: exports f.o.b.	2 110	9,460	9,549	9,158	11,942	14,904	16,701	19,209	22,797
Goods for processing: exports f.o.b.	2 150	37	76	40	29	23	43	44	55
Repairs on goods	2 160	55	54	83	71	91	105	102	170
Goods procured in ports by carriers	2 170	651	936	584	535	721	782	945	969
Nonmonetary gold	2 180	....	....	....	....	....	....	....	....
Debit	3 100	**−30,440**	**−29,702**	**−31,321**	**−38,184**	**−47,360**	**−51,900**	**−64,585**	**−81,041**
General merchandise: imports f.o.b.	3 110	−29,713	−29,218	−31,044	−37,861	−46,912	−51,350	−63,339	−79,668
Goods for processing: imports f.o.b.	3 150	−23	−26	−22	−34	−52	−49	−56	−65
Repairs on goods	3 160	−96	−64	−68	−97	−104	−146	−366	−299
Goods procured in ports by carriers	3 170	−609	−394	−185	−191	−292	−354	−825	−1,010
Nonmonetary gold	3 180	....	....	....	....	....	....	....	....
B. SERVICES	4 200	**7,953**	**7,867**	**10,323**	**13,033**	**19,065**	**19,172**	**19,396**	**22,810**
Total credit	2 200	*19,239*	*19,456*	*20,142*	*24,283*	*33,085*	*33,914*	*35,762*	*43,080*
Total debit	3 200	*−11,286*	*−11,589*	*−9,819*	*−11,250*	*−14,020*	*−14,742*	*−16,367*	*−20,270*
Transportation services, credit	2 205	**7,923**	**8,167**	**8,044**	**10,840**	**16,538**	**17,284**	**17,989**	**23,300**
Passenger	2 850	*43*	*61*	*96*	*76*	*94*	*119*	*93*	*137*
Freight	2 851	*92*	*107*	*49*	*63*	*104*	*62*	*81*	*114*
Other	2 852	*7,788*	*7,999*	*7,899*	*10,701*	*16,340*	*17,103*	*17,815*	*23,049*
Sea transport, passenger	2 207	43	61	96	76	94	119	93	137
Sea transport, freight	2 208	91	106	49	50	64	43	48	90
Sea transport, other	2 209	7,376	7,407	7,396	10,023	15,258	15,983	16,530	21,334
Air transport, passenger	2 211	....	....	....	....	....	....	....	....
Air transport, freight	2 212	....	....	....	....	....	....	....	....
Air transport, other	2 213	....	404	299	386	746	769	863	1,169
Other transport, passenger	2 215	....	....	....	....	....	....	....	....
Other transport, freight	2 216	1	1	1	13	40	20	33	24
Other transport, other	2 217	412	188	203	292	336	351	422	547
Transportation services, debit	3 205	**−4,088**	**−4,794**	**−4,746**	**−5,578**	**−7,122**	**−7,751**	**−8,781**	**−10,681**
Passenger	3 850	*−6*	*−12*	*−17*	*−8*	*−8*	*−6*	*−7*	*−7*
Freight	3 851	*−186*	*−247*	*−174*	*−177*	*−234*	*−242*	*−228*	*−284*
Other	3 852	*−3,896*	*−4,535*	*−4,555*	*−5,394*	*−6,880*	*−7,503*	*−8,547*	*−10,390*
Sea transport, passenger	3 207	−6	−12	−17	−8	−8	−6	−7	−7
Sea transport, freight	3 208	−185	−246	−173	−174	−233	−240	−226	−281
Sea transport, other	3 209	−3,100	−3,622	−3,568	−4,145	−5,335	−5,527	−6,077	−7,168
Air transport, passenger	3 211	....	....	....	....	....	....	....	....
Air transport, freight	3 212	....	....	....	....	....	....	....	....
Air transport, other	3 213	....	−371	−360	−372	−495	−454	−483	−620
Other transport, passenger	3 215	....	....	....	....	....	....	....	....
Other transport, freight	3 216	−1	−1	....	−3	−1	−2	−2	−3
Other transport, other	3 217	−796	−542	−627	−876	−1,050	−1,522	−1,987	−2,602
Travel, credit	2 236	**9,219**	**9,155**	**9,909**	**10,766**	**12,715**	**13,333**	**14,402**	**15,549**
Business travel	2 237	2,820	2,611	1,069	1,034	1,405	1,176	1,156	1,346
Personal travel	2 240	6,399	6,544	8,841	9,732	11,309	12,157	13,246	14,204
Travel, debit	3 236	**−4,558**	**−4,177**	**−2,436**	**−2,431**	**−2,872**	**−3,039**	**−2,997**	**−3,423**
Business travel	3 237	−1,176	−991	−934	−947	−1,167	−1,260	−1,354	−1,459
Personal travel	3 240	−3,382	−3,186	−1,502	−1,484	−1,705	−1,779	−1,643	−1,964
Other services, credit	2 200 BA	**2,097**	**2,134**	**2,189**	**2,678**	**3,832**	**3,297**	**3,372**	**4,231**
Communications	2 245	257	228	209	322	393	395	386	461
Construction	2 249	233	211	183	195	216	286	305	361
Insurance	2 253	169	120	154	199	222	264	266	388
Financial	2 260	112	71	71	85	126	107	105	168
Computer and information	2 262	89	82	80	135	199	173	203	236
Royalties and licence fees	2 266	5	14	13	18	32	60	67	52
Other business services	2 268	927	1,147	1,188	1,310	1,577	1,737	1,795	2,251
Personal, cultural, and recreational	2 287	246	189	194	332	966	166	154	219
Government, n.i.e.	2 291	58	72	98	81	100	108	91	95
Other services, debit	3 200 BA	**−2,641**	**−2,618**	**−2,637**	**−3,241**	**−4,026**	**−3,952**	**−4,588**	**−6,165**
Communications	3 245	−288	−383	−263	−336	−364	−324	−360	−562
Construction	3 249	−417	−145	−83	−108	−138	−99	−143	−138
Insurance	3 253	−210	−240	−370	−501	−598	−732	−935	−1,213
Financial	3 260	−85	−54	−62	−82	−75	−76	−141	−472
Computer and information	3 262	−157	−125	−185	−188	−224	−222	−254	−383
Royalties and licence fees	3 266	−203	−225	−287	−335	−466	−442	−406	−600
Other business services	3 268	−754	−850	−833	−988	−1,344	−1,424	−1,655	−1,958
Personal, cultural, and recreational	3 287	−160	−196	−182	−184	−357	−185	−227	−354
Government, n.i.e.	3 291	−368	−400	−372	−520	−460	−450	−467	−486

Table 2 (Continued). STANDARD PRESENTATION, 2000–2007

(Millions of U.S. dollars)

	Code	2000	2001	2002	2003	2004	2005	2006	2007
C. INCOME	4 300	**−885**	**−1,767**	**−1,956**	**−4,503**	**−5,425**	**−7,030**	**−8,958**	**−12,469**
Total credit	2 300	*2,807*	*1,885*	*1,532*	*2,911*	*3,495*	*4,072*	*4,566*	*6,345*
Total debit	3 300	*−3,692*	*−3,652*	*−3,488*	*−7,413*	*−8,920*	*−11,102*	*−13,524*	*−18,814*
Compensation of employees, credit	2 310	**581**	**543**	**478**	**381**	**348**	**357**	**400**	**504**
Compensation of employees, debit	3 310	**−251**	**−251**	**−226**	**−193**	**−235**	**−273**	**−353**	**−457**
Investment income, credit	2 320	**2,227**	**1,342**	**1,054**	**2,530**	**3,148**	**3,715**	**4,166**	**5,841**
Direct investment income	2 330	48	44	67	481	578	657	681	841
Dividends and distributed branch profits	2 332	42	42	65	113	156	151	176	290
Reinvested earnings and undistributed branch profits	2 333	....	....	....	366	422	498	502	548
Income on debt (interest)	2 334	6	2	2	2	1	8	3	4
Portfolio investment income	2 339	356	170	210	1,197	1,586	1,719	1,839	2,657
Income on equity	2 340	10	14	30	26	33	53	51	81
Income on bonds and notes	2 350	325	155	178	1,169	1,551	1,664	1,783	2,549
Income on money market instruments	2 360	21	1	1	2	2	2	4	27
Other investment income	2 370	1,823	1,128	777	852	983	1,340	1,646	2,343
Investment income, debit	3 320	**−3,442**	**−3,401**	**−3,262**	**−7,221**	**−8,685**	**−10,829**	**−13,171**	**−18,357**
Direct investment income	3 330	−319	−241	−368	−1,219	−1,307	−1,697	−1,569	−1,973
Dividends and distributed branch profits	3 332	−294	−207	−325	−545	−521	−726	−632	−922
Reinvested earnings and undistributed branch profits	3 333	....	....	....	−615	−750	−871	−878	−959
Income on debt (interest)	3 334	−25	−34	−44	−59	−36	−100	−60	−92
Portfolio investment income	3 339	−212	−183	−384	−3,855	−5,112	−6,766	−8,203	−10,943
Income on equity	3 340	−96	−67	−63	−185	−337	−728	−998	−1,618
Income on bonds and notes	3 350	−104	−115	−320	−3,667	−4,773	−6,032	−7,191	−9,190
Income on money market instruments	3 360	−12	−1	−1	−2	−2	−6	−13	−134
Other investment income	3 370	−2,911	−2,977	−2,510	−2,148	−2,266	−2,366	−3,399	−5,442
D. CURRENT TRANSFERS	4 379	**3,352**	**3,587**	**3,507**	**4,272**	**4,504**	**3,893**	**4,282**	**2,122**
Credit	2 379	**4,116**	**4,592**	**5,536**	**7,202**	**7,901**	**8,615**	**8,587**	**9,053**
General government	2 380	1,710	2,315	3,493	4,628	5,077	5,811	5,591	5,966
Other sectors	2 390	2,406	2,277	2,042	2,574	2,824	2,804	2,996	3,087
Workers' remittances	2 391	1,613	1,471	1,181	1,183	894	863	1,143	1,980
Other current transfers	2 392	793	806	861	1,391	1,929	1,941	1,853	1,107
Debit	3 379	**−764**	**−1,005**	**−2,029**	**−2,930**	**−3,396**	**−4,722**	**−4,305**	**−6,931**
General government	3 380	−194	−451	−1,563	−2,453	−2,761	−3,660	−3,087	−5,296
Other sectors	3 390	−570	−554	−466	−478	−635	−1,063	−1,218	−1,636
Workers' remittances	3 391	−295	−285	−186	−187	−262	−630	−629	−1,003
Other current transfers	3 392	−275	−269	−280	−291	−374	−433	−589	−633
CAPITAL AND FINANCIAL ACCOUNT	4 996	**10,369**	**8,389**	**11,245**	**12,551**	**13,103**	**18,300**	**29,204**	**43,528**
CAPITAL ACCOUNT	4 994	**2,112**	**2,153**	**1,530**	**1,411**	**2,990**	**2,563**	**3,822**	**5,957**
Total credit	2 994	*2,244*	*2,320*	*1,707*	*1,585*	*3,278*	*2,905*	*4,173*	*6,426*
Total debit	3 994	*−131*	*−167*	*−177*	*−173*	*−288*	*−342*	*−351*	*−469*
Capital transfers, credit	2 400	**2,239**	**2,093**	**1,702**	**1,560**	**3,251**	**2,879**	**4,124**	**6,375**
General government	2 401	2,116	1,940	1,528	1,397	3,086	2,672	3,917	6,050
Debt forgiveness	2 402	9	18	16	8	7	10	9	12
Other capital transfers	2 410	2,107	1,922	1,512	1,390	3,079	2,663	3,908	6,038
Other sectors	2 430	123	153	174	163	165	207	207	325
Migrants' transfers	2 431	....	....	....	....	....	....	....	....
Debt forgiveness	2 432	9	6	3	4	4	7	4	13
Other capital transfers	2 440	114	147	171	159	161	200	203	312
Capital transfers, debit	3 400	**−129**	**−145**	**−165**	**−165**	**−276**	**−262**	**−302**	**−450**
General government	3 401	−49	−32	−29	−18	−86	−28	−40	−37
Debt forgiveness	3 402	−5	−3	−3	−4	−5	−9	−13	−9
Other capital transfers	3 410	−45	−29	−26	−13	−81	−19	−27	−28
Other sectors	3 430	−80	−113	−136	−147	−190	−233	−262	−413
Migrants' transfers	3 431	....	....	....	....	....	....	....	....
Debt forgiveness	3 432	−7	−8	−3	−7	−20	−19	−12	−23
Other capital transfers	3 440	−72	−105	−133	−140	−170	−214	−249	−390
Nonproduced nonfinancial assets, credit	2 480	**4**	**227**	**5**	**24**	**27**	**26**	**48**	**51**
Nonproduced nonfinancial assets, debit	3 480	**−3**	**−22**	**−12**	**−9**	**−12**	**−80**	**−49**	**−19**

2008, International Monetary Fund: *Balance of Payments Statistics Yearbook*

Greece 174

Table 2 (Continued). STANDARD PRESENTATION, 2000–2007

(Millions of U.S. dollars)

	Code	2000	2001	2002	2003	2004	2005	2006	2007
FINANCIAL ACCOUNT	4 995	**8,257**	**6,236**	**9,715**	**11,140**	**10,113**	**15,737**	**25,382**	**37,571**
A. DIRECT INVESTMENT	4 500	**−1,015**	**974**	**−615**	**957**	**1,077**	**−818**	**1,175**	**−3,303**
Direct investment abroad	4 505	−2,099	−611	−668	−375	−1,028	−1,476	−4,226	−5,262
Equity capital	4 510	−2,071	−546	−612	51	−521	−947	−3,754	−4,611
Claims on affiliated enterprises	4 515	−2,092	−544	−665	25	−536	−953	−3,756	−4,612
Liabilities to affiliated enterprises	4 520	21	−2	53	26	15	6	1	....
Reinvested earnings	4 525	....	....	....	−366	−422	−498	−502	−546
Other capital	4 530	−27	−65	−55	−60	−85	−31	30	−104
Claims on affiliated enterprises	4 535	−19	−71	−51	−79	−96	−50	29	−94
Liabilities to affiliated enterprises	4 540	−8	6	−4	19	11	19	1	−10
Direct investment in Greece	4 555	1,083	1,585	53	1,332	2,105	658	5,401	1,959
Equity capital	4 560	953	1,504	211	1,244	1,729	131	4,780	2,440
Claims on direct investors	4 565	958	1,501	211	−7	−10	−3	−6	−3
Liabilities to direct investors	4 570	−5	3	....	1,251	1,739	134	4,786	2,443
Reinvested earnings	4 575	....	....	....	615	750	872	878	959
Other capital	4 580	130	81	−158	−527	−374	−345	−257	−1,440
Claims on direct investors	4 585	146	86	−144	−23	−7	−4	....	−5
Liabilities to direct investors	4 590	−16	−5	−14	−504	−367	−341	−257	−1,435
B. PORTFOLIO INVESTMENT	4 600	**8,078**	**8,538**	**10,423**	**13,651**	**17,465**	**9,114**	**9,363**	**23,910**
Assets	4 602	−1,184	−474	−1,917	−9,805	−13,835	−23,194	−9,374	−21,636
Equity securities	4 610	−846	−1,020	−316	−505	−830	−2,189	−2,923	−593
Monetary authorities	4 611	....	....	....	....	....	....	....	....
General government	4 612	....	....	....	....	....	....	....	....
Banks	4 613	−79	−151	−34	−223	−267	−768	−1,111	−2,110
Other sectors	4 614	−767	−869	−282	−282	−563	−1,422	−1,812	1,517
Debt securities	4 619	−338	546	−1,600	−9,300	−13,005	−21,004	−6,452	−21,043
Bonds and notes	4 620	−308	546	−1,627	−9,233	−12,734	−18,669	−5,648	−13,532
Monetary authorities	4 621	....	−148	....	1,529	−3,853	−1,290	−114	−3,075
General government	4 622	....	....	....	....	....	....	....	....
Banks	4 623	−133	304	−949	−8,137	−1,948	−2,679	−4,859	−8,774
Other sectors	4 624	−175	390	−678	−2,624	−6,933	−14,699	−674	−1,683
Money market instruments	4 630	−30	....	27	−67	−272	−2,335	−804	−7,511
Monetary authorities	4 631	....	....	....	....	....	....	....	−3,047
General government	4 632	....	....	....	....	....	....	....	....
Banks	4 633	−35	....	1	60	−63	−65	....	....
Other sectors	4 634	5	....	26	−127	−209	−2,270	−804	−4,464
Liabilities	4 652	9,262	9,012	12,340	23,456	31,301	32,308	18,738	45,545
Equity securities	4 660	1,637	1,829	1,400	2,568	4,290	6,293	7,529	10,865
Banks	4 663	469	587	358	668	1,116	1,923	4,010	5,243
Other sectors	4 664	1,168	1,242	1,042	1,901	3,174	4,369	3,519	5,622
Debt securities	4 669	7,625	7,183	10,939	20,887	27,010	26,015	11,208	34,680
Bonds and notes	4 670	7,734	7,298	11,095	20,820	26,738	25,989	11,458	33,558
Monetary authorities	4 671	....	....	....	....	....	....	....	....
General government	4 672	7,734	7,298	11,095	20,820	26,738	25,464	10,368	32,677
Banks	4 673	....	....	....	....	....	....	....	....
Other sectors	4 674	....	....	....	....	....	526	1,090	881
Money market instruments	4 680	−109	−115	−156	68	272	26	−250	1,122
Monetary authorities	4 681	....	....	....	....	....	....	....	....
General government	4 682	−243	−115	−156	68	272	26	−250	1,122
Banks	4 683	135	....	....	....	....	....	....	....
Other sectors	4 684	....	....	....	....	....	....	....	....
C. FINANCIAL DERIVATIVES	4 910	**348**	**74**	**−175**	**111**	**−429**	**13**	**920**	**−623**
Monetary authorities	4 911	....	....	....	....	....	....	....	....
General government	4 912	....	....	....	....	....	....	....	....
Banks	4 913	348	74	−175	111	−429	13	920	−623
Other sectors	4 914	....	....	....	....	....	....	....	....
Assets	4 900	348	74	−175	111	−429	13	920	−623
Monetary authorities	4 901	....	....	....	....	....	....	....	....
General government	4 902	....	....	....	....	....	....	....	....
Banks	4 903	348	74	−175	111	−429	13	920	−623
Other sectors	4 904	....	....	....	....	....	....	....	....
Liabilities	4 905	....	....	....	....	....	....	....	....
Monetary authorities	4 906	....	....	....	....	....	....	....	....
General government	4 907	....	....	....	....	....	....	....	....
Banks	4 908	....	....	....	....	....	....	....	....
Other sectors	4 909	....	....	....	....	....	....	....	....

Table 2 (Concluded). STANDARD PRESENTATION, 2000–2007

(Millions of U.S. dollars)

	Code	2000	2001	2002	2003	2004	2005	2006	2007
D. OTHER INVESTMENT	4 700 ..	**3,419**	**−9,049**	**1,946**	**−8,301**	**−11,277**	**7,324**	**14,202**	**18,043**
Assets	4 703 ..	**6,970**	**−1,539**	**−6,952**	**−4,413**	**−7,463**	**−8,740**	**−7,336**	**−22,118**
Trade credits	4 706 ..	....	....	....	....	....	....	....	....
General government	4 707 ..	....	....	....	....	....	....	....	....
of which: Short-term	4 709 ..	....	....	....	....	....	....	....	....
Other sectors	4 710 ..	....	....	....	....	....	....	....	....
of which: Short-term	4 712 ..	....	....	....	....	....	....	....	....
Loans	4 714 ..	323	−311	−56	−20	8	35	−418	−607
Monetary authorities	4 715 ..	....	....	....	....	....	....	....	....
of which: Short-term	4 718 ..	....	....	....	....	....	....	....	....
General government	4 719 ..	323	−311	....	....	....	....	....	....
of which: Short-term	4 721 ..	....	....	....	....	....	....	....	....
Banks	4 722 ..	....	....	−56	−20	8	35	−418	−607
of which: Short-term	4 724 ..	....	....	....	....	....	....	....	....
Other sectors	4 725 ..	....	....	....	....	....	....	....	....
of which: Short-term	4 727 ..	....	....	....	....	....	....	....	....
Currency and deposits	4 730 ..	6,520	−23	−6,883	−4,448	−7,530	−8,775	−6,918	−21,511
Monetary authorities	4 731 ..	....	....	3,622	−1,043	−1,078	−295	11	1,100
General government	4 732 ..	6,520	−23	....	....	....	....	....	....
Banks	4 733 ..	....	....	−1,533	−2,582	−5,076	−7,393	−7,096	−22,046
Other sectors	4 734 ..	....	....	−8,972	−823	−1,375	−1,087	166	−565
Other assets	4 736 ..	127	−1,205	−12	54	58	....	....	....
Monetary authorities	4 737 ..	....	....	....	....	....	....	....	....
of which: Short-term	4 739 ..	....	....	....	....	....	....	....	....
General government	4 740 ..	127	−1,205	....	....	....	....	....	....
of which: Short-term	4 742 ..	....	....	....	....	....	....	....	....
Banks	4 743 ..	....	....	....	....	....	....	....	....
of which: Short-term	4 745 ..	....	....	....	....	....	....	....	....
Other sectors	4 746 ..	....	....	−12	54	58	....	....	....
of which: Short-term	4 748 ..	....	....	....	....	....	....	....	....
Liabilities	4 753 ..	**−3,551**	**−7,511**	**8,897**	**−3,888**	**−3,813**	**16,064**	**21,539**	**40,161**
Trade credits	4 756 ..	....	....	....	....	....	....	....	....
General government	4 757 ..	....	....	....	....	....	....	....	....
of which: Short-term	4 759 ..	....	....	....	....	....	....	....	....
Other sectors	4 760 ..	....	....	....	....	....	....	....	....
of which: Short-term	4 762 ..	....	....	....	....	....	....	....	....
Loans	4 764 ..	−440	−2,277	−5,268	−4,329	−2,742	−2,433	598	−3,598
Monetary authorities	4 765 ..	....	....	....	....	....	....	....	....
of which: Use of Fund credit and loans from the Fund..	4 766 ..	....	....	....	....	....	....	....	....
of which: Short-term	4 768 ..	....	....	....	....	....	....	....	....
General government	4 769 ..	....	....	−4,326	−2,888	−1,271	−516	728	−3,132
of which: Short-term	4 771 ..	....	....	....	....	....	....	....	....
Banks	4 772 ..	....	....	−452	−393	−687	−343	15	282
of which: Short-term	4 774 ..	....	....	....	....	....	....	....	....
Other sectors	4 775 ..	−440	−2,277	−490	−1,048	−784	−1,574	−145	−748
of which: Short-term	4 777 ..	....	....	....	....	....	....	....	....
Currency and deposits	4 780 ..	−3,425	−6,989	14,183	392	−1,116	18,497	20,941	43,759
Monetary authorities	4 781 ..	....	....	9,176	−2,311	−11,799	1,434	1,058	3,716
General government	4 782 ..	....	....	....	....	....	....	....	....
Banks	4 783 ..	−3,425	−6,989	8,701	3,166	11,347	18,176	20,004	40,104
Other sectors	4 784 ..	....	....	−3,694	−464	−665	−1,112	−121	−60
Other liabilities	4 786 ..	314	1,756	−18	49	46	....	....	....
Monetary authorities	4 787 ..	....	....	....	....	....	....	....	....
of which: Short-term	4 789 ..	....	....	....	....	....	....	....	....
General government	4 790 ..	....	....	....	....	....	....	....	....
of which: Short-term	4 792 ..	....	....	....	....	....	....	....	....
Banks	4 793 ..	....	....	....	....	....	....	....	....
of which: Short-term	4 795 ..	....	....	....	....	....	....	....	....
Other sectors	4 796 ..	314	1,756	−18	49	46	....	....	....
of which: Short-term	4 798 ..	....	....	....	....	....	....	....	....
E. RESERVE ASSETS	4 802 ..	**−2,573**	**5,699**	**−1,863**	**4,722**	**3,277**	**104**	**−279**	**−457**
Monetary gold	4 812 ..	−24	180	−119	161	31	−484	−277	−454
Special drawing rights	4 811 ..	−7	2	−4	−5	−4	−4	1	3
Reserve position in the Fund	4 810 ..	75	−72	−51	−12	94	222	47	47
Foreign exchange	4 803 ..	−2,616	5,589	−1,688	4,578	3,156	370	−50	−53
Other claims	4 813 ..	....	....	....	....	....	....	....	....
NET ERRORS AND OMISSIONS	4 998 ..	**−550**	**1,011**	**−1,663**	**253**	**373**	**−67**	**361**	**1,060**

Table 3. INTERNATIONAL INVESTMENT POSITION (End-period stocks), 2000–2007

(Millions of U.S. dollars)

	Code	2000	2001	2002	2003	2004	2005	2006	2007
ASSETS	8 995 C.	57,194	59,753	83,972	113,718	139,964	153,464	196,273	279,777
Direct investment abroad	8 505	5,852	7,020	9,001	12,337	13,791	13,602	22,418	31,650
Equity capital and reinvested earnings	8 506	5,625	6,753	8,584	11,178	12,969	13,056	21,898	30,578
Claims on affiliated enterprises	8 507	5,625	6,753	8,584	11,178	12,969	13,056	21,898	30,578
Liabilities to affiliated enterprises	8 508	....	....	....	....	....	....	....	....
Other capital	8 530	227	268	417	1,159	823	546	520	1,072
Claims on affiliated enterprises	8 535	227	268	417	1,159	823	546	520	1,072
Liabilities to affiliated enterprises	8 540	....	....	....	....	....	....	....	....
Portfolio investment	8 602	3,848	9,376	17,974	34,966	52,666	69,979	88,496	127,849
Equity securities	8 610	1,346	2,559	3,020	4,893	6,200	8,326	13,356	20,602
Monetary authorities	8 611	....	356	424	506	550	488	545	605
General government	8 612	....	....	....	....	....	....	....	....
Banks	8 613	106	811	1,006	1,786	2,109	2,612	4,687	10,495
Other sectors	8 614	1,239	1,392	1,591	2,601	3,541	5,226	8,123	9,502
Debt securities	8 619	2,502	6,817	14,953	30,073	46,465	61,652	75,140	107,247
Bonds and notes	8 620	2,479	6,708	14,757	29,471	45,820	59,834	72,305	96,130
Monetary authorities	8 621	1,028	1,028	2,080	5,973	11,150	10,479	11,911	16,748
General government	8 622	....	....	....	....	....	....	....	....
Banks	8 623	913	3,005	7,437	13,942	15,847	15,269	21,551	33,537
Other sectors	8 624	538	2,674	5,240	9,556	18,823	34,086	38,842	45,844
Money market instruments	8 630	23	109	196	602	646	1,818	2,836	11,117
Monetary authorities	8 631	....	....	....	....	....	....	....	3,094
General government	8 632	....	....	....	....	....	....	....	....
Banks	8 633	8	12	170	109	78	61	46	184
Other sectors	8 634	15	97	26	494	568	1,757	2,789	7,839
Financial derivatives	8 900	12	88	315	326	821	659	13	740
Monetary authorities	8 901	....	....	....	....	....	....	....	....
General government	8 902	....	....	....	....	....	....	....	....
Banks	8 903	....	88	315	326	821	659	13	740
Other sectors	8 904	12	....	....	....	....	....	....	....
Other investment	8 703	35,227	37,099	47,250	60,288	69,978	66,937	82,497	115,880
Trade credits	8 706	246	749	733	719	613	714	884	844
General government	8 707	....	....	....	....	....	....	....	....
of which: Short-term	8 709	....	....	....	....	....	....	....	....
Other sectors	8 710	246	749	733	719	613	714	884	844
of which: Short-term	8 712	....	....	....	....	....	....	....	....
Loans	8 714	21,320	23,468	28,783	39,490	45,316	44,555	58,753	90,067
Monetary authorities	8 715	411	3,958	2,343	2,708	3,328	3,217	3,569	2,779
of which: Short-term	8 718	....	....	....	....	....	....	....	....
General government	8 719	....	....	....	....	....	....	....	....
of which: Short-term	8 721	....	....	....	....	....	....	....	....
Banks	8 722	20,908	19,510	26,440	36,782	41,988	41,338	55,184	87,288
of which: Short-term	8 724	....	....	....	....	....	....	....	....
Other sectors	8 725	....	....	....	....	....	....	....	....
of which: Short-term	8 727	....	....	....	....	....	....	....	....
Currency and deposits	8 730	13,596	12,882	17,735	20,079	24,049	21,669	22,860	24,969
Monetary authorities	8 731	....	....	....	....	....	....	....	....
General government	8 732	....	....	....	....	....	....	....	....
Banks	8 733	....	....	....	....	....	....	....	....
Other sectors	8 734	13,596	12,882	17,735	20,079	24,049	21,669	22,860	24,969
Other assets	8 736	66	....	....	....	....	....	....	....
Monetary authorities	8 737	66	....	....	....	....	....	....	....
of which: Short-term	8 739	....	....	....	....	....	....	....	....
General government	8 740	....	....	....	....	....	....	....	....
of which: Short-term	8 742	....	....	....	....	....	....	....	....
Banks	8 743	....	....	....	....	....	....	....	....
of which: Short-term	8 745	....	....	....	....	....	....	....	....
Other sectors	8 746	....	....	....	....	....	....	....	....
of which: Short-term	8 748	....	....	....	....	....	....	....	....
Reserve assets	8 802	12,255	6,169	9,432	5,801	2,708	2,287	2,850	3,658
Monetary gold	8 812	1,250	1,015	1,350	1,440	1,517	1,780	2,284	3,027
Special drawing rights	8 811	12	10	15	21	27	29	29	28
Reserve position in the Fund	8 810	297	357	438	497	420	168	128	85
Foreign exchange	8 803	10,697	4,787	7,629	3,843	744	309	408	518
Other claims	8 813	....	....	....	....	....	....	....	....

Table 3 (Concluded). INTERNATIONAL INVESTMENT POSITION (End-period stocks), 2000–2007

(Millions of U.S. dollars)

	Code	2000	2001	2002	2003	2004	2005	2006	2007
LIABILITIES	8 995 D.	106,690	119,763	170,892	242,000	309,039	329,468	430,922	595,504
Direct investment in Greece	8 555	12,480	13,941	15,561	22,454	28,482	29,189	41,288	53,221
Equity capital and reinvested earnings	8 556	11,551	13,117	14,604	21,620	27,420	26,967	38,592	49,655
Claims on direct investors	8 557	....	....	....	....	....	....	....	....
Liabilities to direct investors	8 558	11,551	13,117	14,604	21,620	27,420	26,967	38,592	49,655
Other capital	8 580	929	824	956	834	1,061	2,223	2,696	3,565
Claims on direct investors	8 585	....	....	....	....	....	....	....	....
Liabilities to direct investors	8 590	929	824	956	834	1,061	2,223	2,696	3,565
Portfolio investment	8 652	57,294	62,816	85,388	133,865	188,456	202,113	255,983	348,059
Equity securities	8 660	9,584	7,711	8,425	16,140	28,386	37,963	60,247	93,548
Banks	8 663	3,700	2,150	2,108	5,302	10,837	14,104	25,290	40,830
Other sectors	8 664	5,884	5,561	6,317	10,838	17,549	23,858	34,957	52,717
Debt securities	8 669	47,710	55,105	76,963	117,725	160,070	164,151	195,735	254,512
Bonds and notes	8 670	47,362	54,953	76,952	117,709	159,999	164,061	195,503	252,736
Monetary authorities	8 671	....	....	....	....	....	....	....	....
General government	8 672	43,699	51,620	73,142	112,829	154,093	158,198	188,025	243,208
Banks	8 673	....	....	27	39	41	32	1	1
Other sectors	8 674	3,663	3,334	3,783	4,841	5,865	5,831	7,477	9,527
Money market instruments	8 680	347	152	12	16	71	90	232	1,775
Monetary authorities	8 681	....	....	....	....	....	....	....	....
General government	8 682	347	152	8	6	71	90	232	1,775
Banks	8 683	....	....	3	10	....	....	....	....
Other sectors	8 684	....	....	....	....	....	....	....	....
Financial derivatives	8 905	....	....	....	....	....	....	....	....
Monetary authorities	8 906	....	....	....	....	....	....	....	....
General government	8 907	....	....	....	....	....	....	....	....
Banks	8 908	....	....	....	....	....	....	....	....
Other sectors	8 909	....	....	....	....	....	....	....	....
Other investment	8 753	36,917	43,006	69,943	85,681	92,101	98,165	133,652	194,224
Trade credits	8 756	1,071	1,505	1,895	1,748	1,712	1,236	1,733	1,993
General government	8 757	160	159	157	51	10	6	7	7
of which: Short-term	8 759	....	....	....	....	....	....	....	....
Other sectors	8 760	911	1,347	1,738	1,697	1,703	1,230	1,727	1,986
of which: Short-term	8 762	....	....	....	....	....	....	....	....
Loans	8 764	35,846	41,500	68,048	83,933	90,389	96,929	131,919	192,231
Monetary authorities	8 765	....	7,132	18,259	19,391	8,916	8,514	10,777	15,894
of which: Use of Fund credit and loans from the Fund	8 766	....	....	....	....	....	....	....	....
of which: Short-term	8 768	....	*7,132*	*18,259*	*19,391*	*8,916*	*8,514*	*10,777*	*15,894*
General government	8 769	8,677	9,942	11,764	14,100	15,659	13,035	15,423	15,726
of which: Short-term	8 771	....	....	....	....	....	....	....	....
Banks	8 772	18,846	14,879	26,452	35,378	51,054	61,901	90,376	143,416
of which: Short-term	8 774	....	....	....	....	....	....	....	....
Other sectors	8 775	8,322	9,547	11,572	15,064	14,760	13,479	15,342	17,194
of which: Short-term	8 777	....	....	....	....	....	....	....	....
Currency and deposits	8 780	....	....	....	....	....	....	....	....
Monetary authorities	8 781	....	....	....	....	....	....	....	....
General government	8 782	....	....	....	....	....	....	....	....
Banks	8 783	....	....	....	....	....	....	....	....
Other sectors	8 784	....	....	....	....	....	....	....	....
Other liabilities	8 786	....	....	....	....	....	....	....	....
Monetary authorities	8 787	....	....	....	....	....	....	....	....
of which: Short-term	8 789	....	....	....	....	....	....	....	....
General government	8 790	....	....	....	....	....	....	....	....
of which: Short-term	8 792	....	....	....	....	....	....	....	....
Banks	8 793	....	....	....	....	....	....	....	....
of which: Short-term	8 795	....	....	....	....	....	....	....	....
Other sectors	8 796	....	....	....	....	....	....	....	....
of which: Short-term	8 798	....	....	....	....	....	....	....	....
NET INTERNATIONAL INVESTMENT POSITION	8 995	−49,496	−60,010	−86,920	−128,281	−169,074	−176,004	−234,649	−315,727
Conversion rates: drachmas per U.S. dollar (end of period)	0 102	365.62	....	....	....	....	....	....	....
Conversion rates: euros per U.S. dollar (end of period)	0 104	1.0747	1.1347	.9536	.7918	.7342	.8477	.7593	.6793

Table 1. ANALYTIC PRESENTATION, 2000–2007

(Millions of U.S. dollars)

	Code	2000	2001	2002	2003	2004	2005	2006	2007
A. Current Account[1]	4 993 Z.	**−88.10**	**−102.87**	**−125.55**	**−145.94**	**−54.72**	**−186.43**	**−192.80**	**−222.38**
Goods: exports f.o.b.	2 100 ..	82.96	63.60	41.41	45.54	37.52	32.87	31.42	48.11
Goods: imports f.o.b.	3 100 ..	−220.94	−196.83	−181.42	−228.47	−222.20	−293.95	−263.04	−316.00
Balance on Goods	4 100 ..	*−137.98*	*−133.23*	*−140.00*	*−182.93*	*−184.68*	*−261.08*	*−231.62*	*−267.89*
Services: credit	2 200 ..	152.76	133.53	131.21	133.99	157.26	116.01	130.01	147.47
Services: debit	3 200 ..	−89.20	−83.38	−90.69	−82.99	−91.75	−95.38	−98.61	−108.28
Balance on Goods and Services	4 991 ..	*−74.41*	*−83.07*	*−99.49*	*−131.93*	*−119.18*	*−240.45*	*−200.23*	*−228.70*
Income: credit	2 300 ..	5.08	3.73	4.10	3.73	5.69	11.43	13.26	13.30
Income: debit	3 300 ..	−38.83	−45.18	−51.69	−54.23	−62.11	−39.72	−41.95	−43.88
Balance on Goods, Services, and Income	4 992 ..	*−108.16*	*−124.52*	*−147.08*	*−182.42*	*−175.59*	*−268.74*	*−228.92*	*−259.27*
Current transfers: credit	2 379 Z.	30.31	31.00	31.82	48.24	125.91	87.59	48.79	50.01
Current transfers: debit	3 379 ..	−10.25	−9.36	−10.29	−11.76	−5.03	−5.29	−12.68	−13.12
B. Capital Account[1]	4 994 Z.	**32.13**	**42.53**	**31.83**	**43.19**	**39.83**	**47.00**	**61.76**	**31.50**
Capital account: credit	2 994 Z.	34.21	44.56	33.87	45.23	41.87	49.04	63.80	33.54
Capital account: debit	3 994 ..	−2.08	−2.04	−2.04	−2.04	−2.04	−2.04	−2.04	−2.04
Total, Groups A Plus B	4 981 ..	*−55.96*	*−60.35*	*−93.72*	*−102.75*	*−14.89*	*−139.43*	*−131.04*	*−190.88*
C. Financial Account[1]	4 995 W.	**63.75**	**47.29**	**100.46**	**96.38**	**26.93**	**132.15**	**132.07**	**194.15**
Direct investment abroad	4 505 ..	. . . .	. . . .	. . . .	. . . .	. . . .	. . . .	. . . .	. . . .
Direct investment in Grenada	4 555 Z.	37.41	58.75	54.49	89.17	65.01	70.16	85.17	139.50
Portfolio investment assets	4 602 ..	−.07	−.42	−1.69	−2.59	−7.44	.59	−5.32	.59
Equity securities	4 610 ..	. . . .	. . . .	. . . .	. . . .	. . . .	. . . .	. . . .	. . . .
Debt securities	4 619 ..	. . . .	. . . .	. . . .	. . . .	. . . .	. . . .	. . . .	. . . .
Portfolio investment liabilities	4 652 Z.	19.52	.17	109.36	31.68	37.48	17.21	4.57	.06
Equity securities	4 660 ..	. . . .	. . . .	. . . .	. . . .	. . . .	. . . .	. . . .	. . . .
Debt securities	4 669 Z.	. . . .	. . . .	. . . .	. . . .	. . . .	. . . .	. . . .	. . . .
Financial derivatives	4 910 ..	. . . .	. . . .	. . . .	. . . .	. . . .	. . . .	. . . .	. . . .
Financial derivatives assets	4 900 ..	. . . .	. . . .	. . . .	. . . .	. . . .	. . . .	. . . .	. . . .
Financial derivatives liabilities	4 905 ..	. . . .	. . . .	. . . .	. . . .	. . . .	. . . .	. . . .	. . . .
Other investment assets	4 703 ..	25.32	28.00	25.17	42.95	65.27	287.42	79.94	84.17
Monetary authorities	4 701 ..	. . . .	. . . .	. . . .	. . . .	. . . .	. . . .	. . . .	. . . .
General government	4 704 ..	. . . .	. . . .	. . . .	. . . .	. . . .	. . . .	. . . .	. . . .
Banks	4 705 ..	. . . .	. . . .	. . . .	. . . .	. . . .	. . . .	. . . .	. . . .
Other sectors	4 728 ..	. . . .	. . . .	. . . .	. . . .	. . . .	. . . .	. . . .	. . . .
Other investment liabilities	4 753 W.	−18.43	−39.20	−86.87	−64.83	−133.40	−243.23	−32.29	−30.18
Monetary authorities	4 753 WA	. . . .	. . . .	. . . .	. . . .	. . . .	. . . .	. . . .	. . . .
General government	4 753 ZB	. . . .	. . . .	. . . .	. . . .	. . . .	. . . .	. . . .	. . . .
Banks	4 753 ZC	. . . .	. . . .	. . . .	. . . .	. . . .	. . . .	. . . .	. . . .
Other sectors	4 753 ZD	. . . .	. . . .	. . . .	. . . .	. . . .	248.14	. . . .	. . . .
Total, Groups A Through C	4 983 ..	*7.78*	*−13.05*	*6.74*	*−6.37*	*12.04*	*−7.28*	*1.03*	*3.27*
D. Net Errors and Omissions	4 998 ..	**−1.18**	**18.89**	**24.47**	**−10.44**	**29.87**	**−20.12**	**4.07**	**9.57**
Total, Groups A Through D	4 984 ..	*6.60*	*5.84*	*31.22*	*−16.82*	*41.91*	*−27.40*	*5.10*	*12.84*
E. Reserves and Related Items	4 802 A.	**−6.60**	**−5.84**	**−31.22**	**16.82**	**−41.91**	**27.40**	**−5.10**	**−12.84**
Reserve assets	4 802 ..	−6.60	−5.84	−31.22	12.81	−46.34	32.31	−5.75	−10.60
Use of Fund credit and loans	4 766 ..	. . . .	. . . .	. . . .	4.00	4.43	. . . .	.65	−2.23
Exceptional financing	4 920 ..	. . . .	. . . .	. . . .	. . . .	. . . .	−4.91	. . . .	. . . .
Conversion rates: Eastern Caribbean dollars per U.S. dollar	0 101 ..	2.7000	2.7000	2.7000	2.7000	2.7000	2.7000	2.7000	2.7000

[1] Excludes components that have been classified in the categories of Group E.

Table 2. STANDARD PRESENTATION, 2000–2007

(Millions of U.S. dollars)

	Code	2000	2001	2002	2003	2004	2005	2006	2007
CURRENT ACCOUNT	4 993 ..	−88.10	−102.87	−125.55	−145.94	−54.72	−186.43	−192.80	−222.38
A. GOODS	4 100 ..	−137.98	−133.23	−140.00	−182.93	−184.68	−261.08	−231.62	−267.89
Credit	2 100 ..	82.96	63.60	41.41	45.54	37.52	32.87	31.42	48.11
General merchandise: exports f.o.b.	2 110 ..	78.14	59.53	39.06	41.82	32.04	27.64	24.49	37.51
Goods for processing: exports f.o.b.	2 150 ..	....	....	....	....	....	....	....	....
Repairs on goods	2 160 ..	....	....	....	....	.01	....	.01	....
Goods procured in ports by carriers	2 170 ..	4.82	4.08	2.35	3.72	5.47	5.22	6.91	10.59
Nonmonetary gold	2 180 ..	....	....	....	....	....	....	....	....
Debit	3 100 ..	−220.94	−196.83	−181.42	−228.47	−222.20	−293.95	−263.04	−316.00
General merchandise: imports f.o.b.	3 110 ..	−220.89	−196.83	−181.42	−228.47	−222.20	−293.95	−263.04	−316.00
Goods for processing: imports f.o.b.	3 150 ..	....	....	....	....	....	....	....	....
Repairs on goods	3 160 ..	....	....	....	....	....	....	....	....
Goods procured in ports by carriers	3 170 ..	−.06	....	....	....	....	....	....	....
Nonmonetary gold	3 180 ..	....	....	....	....	....	....	....	....
B. SERVICES	4 200 ..	63.57	50.15	40.52	51.00	65.51	20.63	31.40	39.19
Total credit	2 200 ..	*152.76*	*133.53*	*131.21*	*133.99*	*157.26*	*116.01*	*130.01*	*147.47*
Total debit	3 200 ..	*−89.20*	*−83.38*	*−90.69*	*−82.99*	*−91.75*	*−95.38*	*−98.61*	*−108.28*
Transportation services, credit	2 205 ..	5.80	8.14	10.01	8.96	9.29	11.28	11.59	11.88
Passenger	2 850 ..	....	....	....	....	....	....	....	....
Freight	2 851 ..	....	....	....	....	....	....	....	....
Other	2 852 ..	....	....	....	....	....	....	....	....
Sea transport, passenger	2 207 ..	....	....	....	....	....	....	....	....
Sea transport, freight	2 208 ..	....	....	....	....	....	....	....	....
Sea transport, other	2 209 ..	....	....	....	....	....	....	....	....
Air transport, passenger	2 211 ..	....	....	....	....	....	....	....	....
Air transport, freight	2 212 ..	....	....	....	....	....	....	....	....
Air transport, other	2 213 ..	....	....	....	....	....	....	....	....
Other transport, passenger	2 215 ..	....	....	....	....	....	....	....	....
Other transport, freight	2 216 ..	....	....	....	....	....	....	....	....
Other transport, other	2 217 ..	....	....	....	....	....	....	....	....
Transportation services, debit	3 205 ..	−34.27	−30.77	−29.27	−39.17	−39.82	−48.10	−44.33	−52.30
Passenger	3 850 ..	....	....	....	....	....	....	....	....
Freight	3 851 ..	....	....	....	....	....	....	....	....
Other	3 852 ..	....	....	....	....	....	....	....	....
Sea transport, passenger	3 207 ..	....	....	....	....	....	....	....	....
Sea transport, freight	3 208 ..	....	....	....	....	....	....	....	....
Sea transport, other	3 209 ..	....	....	....	....	....	....	....	....
Air transport, passenger	3 211 ..	....	....	....	....	....	....	....	....
Air transport, freight	3 212 ..	....	....	....	....	....	....	....	....
Air transport, other	3 213 ..	....	....	....	....	....	....	....	....
Other transport, passenger	3 215 ..	....	....	....	....	....	....	....	....
Other transport, freight	3 216 ..	....	....	....	....	....	....	....	....
Other transport, other	3 217 ..	....	....	....	....	....	....	....	....
Travel, credit	2 236 ..	92.50	83.45	91.49	103.74	83.50	71.42	93.47	109.88
Business travel	2 237 ..	....	....	....	....	....	....	....	....
Personal travel	2 240 ..	....	....	....	....	....	....	....	....
Travel, debit	3 236 ..	−7.67	−7.60	−7.76	−8.40	−8.51	−10.04	−15.52	−10.39
Business travel	3 237 ..	....	....	....	....	....	....	....	....
Personal travel	3 240 ..	....	....	....	....	....	....	....	....
Other services, credit	2 200 BA	54.46	41.94	29.71	21.29	64.47	33.31	24.95	25.71
Communications	2 245 ..	29.57	20.11	14.85	7.69	9.14	9.30	10.59	10.86
Construction	2 249 ..	....	....	....	....	....	....	....	....
Insurance	2 253 ..	3.20	3.38	4.90	3.46	45.00	13.64	3.60	3.75
Financial	2 260 ..	....	....	....	....	....	....	....	....
Computer and information	2 262 ..	....	....	....	....	....	....	....	....
Royalties and licence fees	2 266 ..	....	....	....	....	....	....	....	....
Other business services	2 268 ..	15.24	14.05	7.02	8.45	8.69	9.07	9.36	9.68
Personal, cultural, and recreational	2 287 ..	....	....	....	....	....	....	....	....
Government, n.i.e.	2 291 ..	6.45	4.39	2.94	1.70	1.64	1.30	1.40	1.42
Other services, debit	3 200 BA	−47.26	−45.00	−53.67	−35.42	−43.43	−37.24	−38.77	−45.58
Communications	3 245 ..	−16.56	−9.41	−8.79	−4.19	−3.64	−1.88	−2.73	−2.83
Construction	3 249 ..	−1.83	−3.22	−3.43	−4.91	−3.03	−4.08	−5.04	−9.52
Insurance	3 253 ..	−8.22	−7.97	−8.14	−8.95	−9.23	−12.54	−13.44	−15.19
Financial	3 260 ..	....	....	....	....	....	....	....	....
Computer and information	3 262 ..	....	....	....	....	....	....	−.10	....
Royalties and licence fees	3 266 ..	−.61	−.67	−.44	−.57	−.79	−.89	−2.12	−2.19
Other business services	3 268 ..	−16.02	−19.36	−28.59	−11.00	−13.97	−10.07	−11.10	−11.49
Personal, cultural, and recreational	3 287 ..	....	....	....	....	....	....	....	....
Government, n.i.e.	3 291 ..	−4.01	−4.37	−4.27	−5.80	−12.77	−7.80	−4.23	−4.36

Table 2 (Continued). STANDARD PRESENTATION, 2000–2007

(Millions of U.S. dollars)

	Code	2000	2001	2002	2003	2004	2005	2006	2007
C. INCOME	4 300	**−33.75**	**−41.44**	**−47.60**	**−50.49**	**−56.42**	**−28.28**	**−28.70**	**−30.57**
Total credit	2 300	*5.08*	*3.73*	*4.10*	*3.73*	*5.69*	*11.43*	*13.26*	*13.30*
Total debit	3 300	*−38.83*	*−45.18*	*−51.69*	*−54.23*	*−62.11*	*−39.72*	*−41.95*	*−43.88*
Compensation of employees, credit	2 310	**.01**	**.03**	**.04**	**.04**	**.04**	**.03**	**.81**	**.83**
Compensation of employees, debit	3 310	....	....	....	....	....	....	....	....
Investment income, credit	2 320	**5.07**	**3.70**	**4.06**	**3.69**	**5.65**	**11.40**	**12.44**	**12.47**
Direct investment income	2 330	.19	.26	.12	.02	....	....	.04	.04
Dividends and distributed branch profits	2 332	....	....	....	....	....	....	....	....
Reinvested earnings and undistributed branch profits	2 333	....	....	....	....	....	....	....	....
Income on debt (interest)	2 334	.19	.26	.12	.02	....	....	.04	.04
Portfolio investment income	2 339	1.02	.77	.59	.53	.19	1.62	3.09	2.85
Income on equity	2 340	1.02	.77	.59	.53	.19	1.62	3.09	2.85
Income on bonds and notes	2 350	....	....	....	....	....	....	....	....
Income on money market instruments	2 360	....	....	....	....	....	....	....	....
Other investment income	2 370	3.86	2.68	3.34	3.15	5.46	9.77	9.31	9.58
Investment income, debit	3 320	**−38.83**	**−45.18**	**−51.69**	**−54.23**	**−62.11**	**−39.72**	**−41.95**	**−43.88**
Direct investment income	3 330	−27.79	−33.61	−32.15	−26.14	−24.92	−22.74	−21.88	−22.64
Dividends and distributed branch profits	3 332	−12.85	−12.01	−13.64	−16.22	−11.46	−11.11	−7.85	−8.12
Reinvested earnings and undistributed branch profits	3 333	−14.53	−21.06	−16.91	−9.30	−12.61	−10.80	−12.30	−12.73
Income on debt (interest)	3 334	−.41	−.54	−1.59	−.62	−.85	−.84	−1.73	−1.79
Portfolio investment income	3 339	....	−2.05	−6.62	−11.57	−16.39	−.47	−.13	−.13
Income on equity	3 340	....	−2.05	−6.62	−11.57	−16.39	−.47	−.13	−.13
Income on bonds and notes	3 350	....	....	....	....	....	....	....	....
Income on money market instruments	3 360	....	....	....	....	....	....	....	....
Other investment income	3 370	−11.04	−9.52	−12.92	−16.51	−20.79	−16.50	−19.95	−21.11
D. CURRENT TRANSFERS	4 379	**20.06**	**21.64**	**21.53**	**36.48**	**120.87**	**82.31**	**36.12**	**36.90**
Credit	2 379	**30.31**	**31.00**	**31.82**	**48.24**	**125.91**	**87.59**	**48.79**	**50.01**
General government	2 380	5.90	6.24	6.31	21.17	43.42	35.14	15.52	15.90
Other sectors	2 390	24.41	24.76	25.52	27.07	82.49	52.45	33.28	34.11
Workers' remittances	2 391	24.22	24.28	24.72	25.24	48.07	26.80	27.63	28.32
Other current transfers	2 392	.20	.47	.80	1.83	34.41	25.65	5.65	5.79
Debit	3 379	**−10.25**	**−9.36**	**−10.29**	**−11.76**	**−5.03**	**−5.29**	**−12.68**	**−13.12**
General government	3 380	−3.65	−3.65	−4.14	−3.37	−3.82	−3.86	−4.48	−4.64
Other sectors	3 390	−6.60	−5.70	−6.15	−8.39	−1.21	−1.42	−8.19	−8.48
Workers' remittances	3 391	−1.21	−1.21	−1.21	−1.21	−1.21	−1.42	−1.48	−1.53
Other current transfers	3 392	−5.38	−4.49	−4.94	−7.17	....	....	−6.71	−6.95
CAPITAL AND FINANCIAL ACCOUNT	4 996	**89.28**	**83.98**	**101.07**	**156.38**	**24.85**	**206.55**	**188.73**	**212.81**
CAPITAL ACCOUNT	4 994	**32.13**	**42.53**	**31.83**	**43.19**	**39.83**	**47.00**	**61.76**	**31.50**
Total credit	2 994	*34.21*	*44.56*	*33.87*	*45.23*	*41.87*	*49.04*	*63.80*	*33.54*
Total debit	3 994	*−2.08*	*−2.04*	*−2.04*	*−2.04*	*−2.04*	*−2.04*	*−2.04*	*−2.04*
Capital transfers, credit	2 400	**34.21**	**44.31**	**33.87**	**45.23**	**41.87**	**49.04**	**63.80**	**33.54**
General government	2 401	12.07	21.91	11.06	21.94	17.79	24.31	38.30	7.27
Debt forgiveness	2 402	....	5.00	....	....	....	....	....	....
Other capital transfers	2 410	12.07	16.91	11.06	21.94	17.79	24.31	38.30	7.27
Other sectors	2 430	22.14	22.40	22.81	23.29	24.08	24.73	25.50	26.26
Migrants' transfers	2 431	22.14	22.40	22.81	23.29	24.08	24.73	25.50	26.26
Debt forgiveness	2 432	....	....	....	....	....	....	....	....
Other capital transfers	2 440	....	....	....	....	....	....	....	....
Capital transfers, debit	3 400	**−2.08**	**−2.04**	**−2.04**	**−2.04**	**−2.04**	**−2.04**	**−2.04**	**−2.04**
General government	3 401	....	....	....	....	....	....	....	....
Debt forgiveness	3 402	....	....	....	....	....	....	....	....
Other capital transfers	3 410	....	....	....	....	....	....	....	....
Other sectors	3 430	−2.08	−2.04	−2.04	−2.04	−2.04	−2.04	−2.04	−2.04
Migrants' transfers	3 431	−2.08	−2.04	−2.04	−2.04	−2.04	−2.04	−2.04	−2.04
Debt forgiveness	3 432	....	....	....	....	....	....	....	....
Other capital transfers	3 440	....	....	....	....	....	....	....	....
Nonproduced nonfinancial assets, credit	2 480	....	.25	....	....	....	....	....	....
Nonproduced nonfinancial assets, debit	3 480	....	....	....	....	....	....	....	....

Table 2 (Continued). STANDARD PRESENTATION, 2000–2007

(Millions of U.S. dollars)

	Code	2000	2001	2002	2003	2004	2005	2006	2007
FINANCIAL ACCOUNT	4 995	**57.15**	**41.46**	**69.24**	**113.19**	**−14.98**	**159.55**	**126.97**	**181.31**
A. DIRECT INVESTMENT	4 500	**37.41**	**58.75**	**54.49**	**89.17**	**65.01**	**70.16**	**85.17**	**139.50**
Direct investment abroad	4 505	....	....	....	....	....	....	....	....
Equity capital	4 510	....	....	....	....	....	....	....	....
Claims on affiliated enterprises	4 515	....	....	....	....	....	....	....	....
Liabilities to affiliated enterprises	4 520	....	....	....	....	....	....	....	....
Reinvested earnings	4 525	....	....	....	....	....	....	....	....
Other capital	4 530	....	....	....	....	....	....	....	....
Claims on affiliated enterprises	4 535	....	....	....	....	....	....	....	....
Liabilities to affiliated enterprises	4 540	....	....	....	....	....	....	....	....
Direct investment in Grenada	4 555	**37.41**	**58.75**	**54.49**	**89.17**	**65.01**	**70.16**	**85.17**	**139.50**
Equity capital	4 560	....	14.18	29.97	57.14	33.87	38.82	50.41	95.18
Claims on direct investors	4 565	....	....	....	....	....	....	....	....
Liabilities to direct investors	4 570	....	14.18	29.97	57.14	33.87	38.82	50.41	95.18
Reinvested earnings	4 575	14.53	21.06	16.91	9.30	12.61	10.80	12.30	12.73
Other capital	4 580	22.88	23.51	7.60	22.73	18.53	20.54	22.46	31.59
Claims on direct investors	4 585	....	....	....	....	....	....	....	....
Liabilities to direct investors	4 590	22.88	23.51	7.60	22.73	18.53	20.54	22.46	31.59
B. PORTFOLIO INVESTMENT	4 600	**19.45**	**−.25**	**107.67**	**29.09**	**30.04**	**17.80**	**−.75**	**.65**
Assets	4 602	**−.07**	**−.42**	**−1.69**	**−2.59**	**−7.44**	**.59**	**−5.32**	**.59**
Equity securities	4 610	....	....	....	....	....	....	....	....
Monetary authorities	4 611	....	....	....	....	....	....	....	....
General government	4 612	....	....	....	....	....	....	....	....
Banks	4 613	....	....	....	....	....	....	....	....
Other sectors	4 614	....	....	....	....	....	....	....	....
Debt securities	4 619	....	....	....	....	....	....	....	....
Bonds and notes	4 620	....	....	....	....	....	....	....	....
Monetary authorities	4 621	....	....	....	....	....	....	....	....
General government	4 622	....	....	....	....	....	....	....	....
Banks	4 623	....	....	....	....	....	....	....	....
Other sectors	4 624	....	....	....	....	....	....	....	....
Money market instruments	4 630	....	....	....	....	....	....	....	....
Monetary authorities	4 631	....	....	....	....	....	....	....	....
General government	4 632	....	....	....	....	....	....	....	....
Banks	4 633	....	....	....	....	....	....	....	....
Other sectors	4 634	....	....	....	....	....	....	....	....
Liabilities	4 652	**19.52**	**.17**	**109.36**	**31.68**	**37.48**	**17.21**	**4.57**	**.06**
Equity securities	4 660	....	....	....	....	....	....	....	....
Banks	4 663	....	....	....	....	....	....	....	....
Other sectors	4 664	....	....	....	....	....	....	....	....
Debt securities	4 669	....	....	....	....	....	....	....	....
Bonds and notes	4 670	....	....	....	....	....	....	....	....
Monetary authorities	4 671	....	....	....	....	....	....	....	....
General government	4 672	....	....	....	....	....	....	....	....
Banks	4 673	....	....	....	....	....	....	....	....
Other sectors	4 674	....	....	....	....	....	....	....	....
Money market instruments	4 680	....	....	....	....	....	....	....	....
Monetary authorities	4 681	....	....	....	....	....	....	....	....
General government	4 682	....	....	....	....	....	....	....	....
Banks	4 683	....	....	....	....	....	....	....	....
Other sectors	4 684	....	....	....	....	....	....	....	....
C. FINANCIAL DERIVATIVES	4 910	....	....	....	....	....	....	....	....
Monetary authorities	4 911	....	....	....	....	....	....	....	....
General government	4 912	....	....	....	....	....	....	....	....
Banks	4 913	....	....	....	....	....	....	....	....
Other sectors	4 914	....	....	....	....	....	....	....	....
Assets	4 900	....	....	....	....	....	....	....	....
Monetary authorities	4 901	....	....	....	....	....	....	....	....
General government	4 902	....	....	....	....	....	....	....	....
Banks	4 903	....	....	....	....	....	....	....	....
Other sectors	4 904	....	....	....	....	....	....	....	....
Liabilities	4 905	....	....	....	....	....	....	....	....
Monetary authorities	4 906	....	....	....	....	....	....	....	....
General government	4 907	....	....	....	....	....	....	....	....
Banks	4 908	....	....	....	....	....	....	....	....
Other sectors	4 909	....	....	....	....	....	....	....	....

Table 2 (Concluded). STANDARD PRESENTATION, 2000–2007

(Millions of U.S. dollars)

	Code	2000	2001	2002	2003	2004	2005	2006	2007
D. OTHER INVESTMENT	4 700	**6.89**	**−11.20**	**−61.70**	**−17.88**	**−63.70**	**39.28**	**48.30**	**51.76**
Assets	4 703	**25.32**	**28.00**	**25.17**	**42.95**	**65.27**	**287.42**	**79.94**	**84.17**
Trade credits	4 706	....	....	....	....	....	....	....	....
General government	4 707	....	....	....	....	....	....	....	....
of which: Short-term	4 709	....	....	....	....	....	....	....	....
Other sectors	4 710	....	....	....	....	....	....	....	....
of which: Short-term	4 712	....	....	....	....	....	....	....	....
Loans	4 714	....	....	....	....	....	....	....	....
Monetary authorities	4 715	....	....	....	....	....	....	....	....
of which: Short-term	4 718	....	....	....	....	....	....	....	....
General government	4 719	....	....	....	....	....	....	....	....
of which: Short-term	4 721	....	....	....	....	....	....	....	....
Banks	4 722	....	....	....	....	....	....	....	....
of which: Short-term	4 724	....	....	....	....	....	....	....	....
Other sectors	4 725	....	....	....	....	....	....	....	....
of which: Short-term	4 727	....	....	....	....	....	....	....	....
Currency and deposits	4 730	....	....	....	....	....	....	....	....
Monetary authorities	4 731	....	....	....	....	....	....	....	....
General government	4 732	....	....	....	....	....	....	....	....
Banks	4 733	....	....	....	....	....	....	....	....
Other sectors	4 734	....	....	....	....	....	....	....	....
Other assets	4 736	....	....	....	....	....	....	....	....
Monetary authorities	4 737	....	....	....	....	....	....	....	....
of which: Short-term	4 739	....	....	....	....	....	....	....	....
General government	4 740	....	....	....	....	....	....	....	....
of which: Short-term	4 742	....	....	....	....	....	....	....	....
Banks	4 743	....	....	....	....	....	....	....	....
of which: Short-term	4 745	....	....	....	....	....	....	....	....
Other sectors	4 746	....	....	....	....	....	....	....	....
of which: Short-term	4 748	....	....	....	....	....	....	....	....
Liabilities	4 753	**−18.43**	**−39.20**	**−86.87**	**−60.83**	**−128.97**	**−248.14**	**−31.64**	**−32.41**
Trade credits	4 756	....	....	....	....	....	....	....	....
General government	4 757	....	....	....	....	....	....	....	....
of which: Short-term.	4 759	....	....	....	....	....	....	....	....
Other sectors	4 760	....	....	....	....	....	....	....	....
of which: Short-term	4 762	....	....	....	....	....	....	....	....
Loans	4 764	....	....	....	4.00	4.43	....	.65	−2.23
Monetary authorities	4 765	....	....	....	4.00	4.43	....	.65	−2.23
of which: Use of Fund credit and loans from the Fund	4 766	....	....	....	*4.00*	*4.43*	....	*.65*	*−2.23*
of which: Short-term	4 768	....	....	....	....	....	....	....	....
General government	4 769	....	....	....	....	....	....	....	....
of which: Short-term	4 771	....	....	....	....	....	....	....	....
Banks	4 772	....	....	....	....	....	....	....	....
of which: Short-term	4 774	....	....	....	....	....	....	....	....
Other sectors	4 775	....	....	....	....	....	....	....	....
of which: Short-term	4 777	....	....	....	....	....	....	....	....
Currency and deposits	4 780	....	....	....	....	....	....	....	....
Monetary authorities	4 781	....	....	....	....	....	....	....	....
General government	4 782	....	....	....	....	....	....	....	....
Banks	4 783	....	....	....	....	....	....	....	....
Other sectors	4 784	....	....	....	....	....	....	....	....
Other liabilities	4 786	....	....	....	....	....	....	....	....
Monetary authorities.	4 787	....	....	....	....	....	....	....	....
of which: Short-term	4 789	....	....	....	....	....	....	....	....
General government	4 790	....	....	....	....	....	....	....	....
of which: Short-term	4 792	....	....	....	....	....	....	....	....
Banks	4 793	....	....	....	....	....	....	....	....
of which: Short-term	4 795	....	....	....	....	....	....	....	....
Other sectors	4 796	....	....	....	....	....	....	....	....
of which: Short-term	4 798	....	....	....	....	....	*−248.14*	....	....
E. RESERVE ASSETS	4 802	**−6.60**	**−5.84**	**−31.22**	**12.81**	**−46.34**	**32.31**	**−5.75**	**−10.60**
Monetary gold	4 812	....	....	....	....	....	....	....	....
Special drawing rights	4 811	....	....	....	....	−.01	−.01	−.11	.06
Reserve position in the Fund	4 810	....	....	....	....	....	....	....	....
Foreign exchange	4 803	−6.82	−6.28	−23.90	4.62	−38.49	32.39	−5.56	−10.66
Other claims	4 813	.22	.44	−7.32	8.20	−7.84	−.08	−.08	....
NET ERRORS AND OMISSIONS	4 998	**−1.18**	**18.89**	**24.47**	**−10.44**	**29.87**	**−20.12**	**4.07**	**9.57**

Table 1. ANALYTIC PRESENTATION, 2000–2007

(Millions of U.S. dollars)

	Code	2000	2001	2002	2003	2004	2005	2006	2007
A. Current Account[1]	4 993 Z.	−1,049.6	−1,252.9	−1,234.9	−1,039.2	−1,235.8	−1,300.3	−1,573.5	−1,754.2
Goods: exports f.o.b.	2 100 ..	3,085.1	2,859.8	2,818.9	3,059.9	5,105.1	5,459.5	6,082.1	7,011.9
Goods: imports f.o.b.	3 100 ..	−4,742.0	−5,142.0	−5,791.0	−6,175.7	−8,737.0	−9,650.1	−10,934.4	−12,482.1
Balance on Goods	4 100 ..	*−1,656.9*	*−2,282.2*	*−2,972.1*	*−3,115.9*	*−3,632.0*	*−4,190.6*	*−4,852.3*	*−5,470.1*
Services: credit	2 200 ..	777.0	1,044.8	1,145.4	1,058.8	1,100.5	1,307.9	1,518.8	1,709.4
Services: debit	3 200 ..	−825.4	−927.9	−1,066.1	−1,126.1	−1,344.4	−1,449.7	−1,784.7	−2,029.3
Balance on Goods and Services	4 991 ..	*−1,705.3*	*−2,165.3*	*−2,892.8*	*−3,183.2*	*−3,875.9*	*−4,332.4*	*−5,118.2*	*−5,790.0*
Income: credit	2 300 ..	214.4	317.5	161.1	179.1	219.9	301.7	452.8	551.0
Income: debit	3 300 ..	−424.0	−401.9	−479.5	−497.0	−630.0	−786.5	−1,115.0	−1,320.5
Balance on Goods, Services, and Income	4 992 ..	*−1,914.9*	*−2,249.7*	*−3,211.1*	*−3,501.0*	*−4,286.1*	*−4,817.2*	*−5,780.4*	*−6,559.6*
Current transfers: credit	2 379 Z.	908.2	1,024.3	2,077.7	2,558.9	3,085.6	3,555.3	4,244.4	4,816.7
Current transfers: debit	3 379 ..	−42.9	−27.5	−101.5	−97.0	−35.4	−38.5	−37.4	−11.2
B. Capital Account[1]	4 994 Z.	**85.5**	**93.4**	**124.2**	**133.8**	....	....	**142.2**	....
Capital account: credit	2 994 Z.	85.5	93.4	124.2	133.8	....	....	142.2	....
Capital account: debit	3 994 ..	....	....	....	....	....	....	....	....
Total, Groups A Plus B	4 981 ..	*−964.1*	*−1,159.5*	*−1,110.7*	*−905.4*	*−1,235.8*	*−1,300.3*	*−1,431.3*	*−1,754.2*
C. Financial Account[1]	4 995 W.	**1,520.7**	**1,546.7**	**1,196.5**	**1,516.3**	**877.8**	**747.9**	**1,190.1**	**1,628.7**
Direct investment abroad	4 505 ..	....	....	....	....	−41.2	−38.3	−60.4	−65.4
Direct investment in Guatemala	4 555 Z.	229.9	455.5	110.6	131.0	296.0	508.3	591.6	723.5
Portfolio investment assets	4 602 ..	−36.3	−45.0	−38.3	18.1	11.7	−39.7	−55.6	35.7
Equity securities	4 610 ..	....	....	....	....	....	−.4	....	....
Debt securities	4 619 ..	−36.3	−45.0	−38.3	18.1	11.7	−39.3	−55.6	35.7
Portfolio investment liabilities	4 652 Z.	78.9	175.3	−107.8	−11.0	387.2	−37.1	−23.7	−201.6
Equity securities	4 660 ..	....	....	....	....	....	....	....	....
Debt securities	4 669 Z.	78.9	175.3	−107.8	−11.0	387.2	−37.1	−23.7	−201.6
Financial derivatives	4 910 ..	....	....	....	....	....	....	....	....
Financial derivatives assets	4 900 ..	....	....	....	....	....	....	....	....
Financial derivatives liabilities	4 905 ..	....	....	....	....	....	....	....	....
Other investment assets	4 703 ..	213.2	156.7	196.4	173.5	−276.2	−151.8	−236.6	−387.4
Monetary authorities	4 701 ..	....	....	....	....	....	....	....	....
General government	4 704 ..	....	....	....	....	....	....	....	....
Banks	4 705 ..	....	....	....	....	−93.4	−1.0	−250.6	−186.3
Other sectors	4 728 ..	213.2	156.7	196.4	173.5	−182.8	−150.8	13.9	−201.0
Other investment liabilities	4 753 W.	1,035.0	804.0	1,035.6	1,204.7	500.2	506.6	974.9	1,523.9
Monetary authorities	4 753 WA	−24.0	−11.2	−11.3	−11.7	−69.7	−.5	−.3	....
General government	4 753 ZB	92.7	42.6	172.7	307.9	90.3	−43.5	356.3	392.9
Banks	4 753 ZC	−17.4	21.8	....	....	99.0	191.1	293.5	521.3
Other sectors	4 753 ZD	983.7	750.9	874.3	908.5	380.7	359.6	325.5	609.7
Total, Groups A Through C	4 983 ..	*556.6*	*387.1*	*85.8*	*610.9*	*−358.1*	*−552.4*	*−241.1*	*−125.4*
D. Net Errors and Omissions	4 998 ..	**86.1**	**87.2**	**−64.7**	**−60.8**	**890.6**	**730.7**	**430.9**	**282.9**
Total, Groups A Through D	4 984 ..	*642.7*	*474.4*	*21.1*	*550.1*	*532.6*	*178.3*	*189.8*	*157.4*
E. Reserves and Related Items	4 802 A.	**−642.7**	**−474.4**	**−21.1**	**−550.1**	**−532.6**	**−178.3**	**−189.8**	**−157.4**
Reserve assets	4 802 ..	−642.7	−474.4	−21.2	−550.1	−603.8	−237.9	−251.0	−214.6
Use of Fund credit and loans	4 766 ..	....	....	....	....	....	....	....	....
Exceptional financing	4 920 ..	....	....	....	....	71.3	59.6	61.3	57.2
Conversion rates: quetzales per U.S. dollar	0 101 ..	**7.7632**	**7.8586**	**7.8216**	**7.9408**	**7.9465**	**7.6339**	**7.6026**	**7.6733**

[1] Excludes components that have been classified in the categories of Group E.

Table 2. STANDARD PRESENTATION, 2000–2007

(Millions of U.S. dollars)

	Code	2000	2001	2002	2003	2004	2005	2006	2007
CURRENT ACCOUNT	4 993	**−1,049.6**	**−1,252.9**	**−1,234.9**	**−1,039.2**	**−1,164.5**	**−1,240.7**	**−1,512.2**	**−1,697.0**
A. GOODS	4 100	**−1,656.9**	**−2,282.2**	**−2,972.1**	**−3,115.9**	**−3,632.0**	**−4,190.6**	**−4,852.3**	**−5,470.1**
Credit	2 100	**3,085.1**	**2,859.8**	**2,818.9**	**3,059.9**	**5,105.1**	**5,459.5**	**6,082.1**	**7,011.9**
General merchandise: exports f.o.b.	2 110	2,711.2	2,463.6	2,473.2	2,631.7	3,403.9	3,895.2	4,418.3	5,461.0
Goods for processing: exports f.o.b.	2 150	373.9	396.2	345.8	428.1	1,653.6	1,508.4	1,603.5	1,474.5
Repairs on goods	2 160	....	....	....	....	....	....	....	....
Goods procured in ports by carriers	2 170	....	....	....	....	47.5	55.9	60.3	76.4
Nonmonetary gold	2 180	....	....	....	....	....	....	....	....
Debit	3 100	**−4,742.0**	**−5,142.0**	**−5,791.0**	**−6,175.7**	**−8,737.0**	**−9,650.1**	**−10,934.4**	**−12,482.1**
General merchandise: imports f.o.b.	3 110	−4,742.0	−5,142.0	−5,791.0	−6,175.7	−7,522.2	−8,581.8	−9,863.3	−11,524.4
Goods for processing: imports f.o.b.	3 150	....	....	....	....	−1,213.7	−1,067.0	−1,068.8	−954.5
Repairs on goods	3 160	....	....	....	....	....	....	....	....
Goods procured in ports by carriers	3 170	....	....	....	....	−1.1	−1.3	−2.3	−3.2
Nonmonetary gold	3 180	....	....	....	....	....	....	....	....
B. SERVICES	4 200	**−48.4**	**116.9**	**79.3**	**−67.3**	**−243.9**	**−141.8**	**−265.9**	**−319.9**
Total credit	2 200	*777.0*	*1,044.8*	*1,145.4*	*1,058.8*	*1,100.5*	*1,307.9*	*1,518.8*	*1,709.4*
Total debit	3 200	*−825.4*	*−927.9*	*−1,066.1*	*−1,126.1*	*−1,344.4*	*−1,449.7*	*−1,784.7*	*−2,029.3*
Transportation services, credit	2 205	**82.4**	**99.7**	**91.1**	**84.2**	**150.4**	**152.3**	**166.9**	**185.4**
Passenger	2 850	*16.4*	*25.5*	*27.1*	*24.7*	....	....	....	....
Freight	2 851	*23.2*	*21.3*	*9.7*	*3.6*	*53.7*	*57.7*	*63.5*	*79.6*
Other	2 852	*42.8*	*52.8*	*54.2*	*55.9*	*96.7*	*94.5*	*103.3*	*105.8*
Sea transport, passenger	2 207	....	2.9	.4	1.1	....	....	....	....
Sea transport, freight	2 208	14.6	10.6	4.6	.3	....	....	....	....
Sea transport, other	2 209	1.5	4.7	4.1	6.6	87.4	86.5	96.2	100.5
Air transport, passenger	2 211	13.5	9.1	8.5	4.4	....	....	....	....
Air transport, freight	2 212	1.2	.8	1.8	....	....	....	....	....
Air transport, other	2 213	40.0	43.5	43.9	47.3	9.3	8.0	7.1	5.3
Other transport, passenger	2 215	2.9	13.5	18.2	19.3	....	....	....	....
Other transport, freight	2 216	7.4	9.9	3.4	3.3	53.7	57.7	63.5	79.6
Other transport, other	2 217	1.3	4.6	6.2	2.1	....	....	....	....
Transportation services, debit	3 205	**−421.6**	**−465.8**	**−522.9**	**−560.4**	**−684.2**	**−787.3**	**−911.8**	**−1,046.0**
Passenger	3 850	*−34.3*	*−40.5*	*−52.7*	*−61.4*	*−102.9*	*−110.6*	*−125.6*	*−139.5*
Freight	3 851	*−386.8*	*−423.9*	*−464.7*	*−495.0*	*−578.9*	*−674.0*	*−783.4*	*−903.5*
Other	3 852	*−.5*	*−1.5*	*−5.5*	*−4.0*	*−2.3*	*−2.8*	*−2.8*	*−3.0*
Sea transport, passenger	3 207	....	....	−.2	−.2	....	....	....	....
Sea transport, freight	3 208	−244.4	−294.7	−331.0	−331.6	−409.6	−476.5	−554.1	−638.5
Sea transport, other	3 209	....	−.2	−1.5	−.9	....	....	....	....
Air transport, passenger	3 211	−33.2	−35.7	−39.0	−47.6	−102.9	−110.6	−125.6	−139.5
Air transport, freight	3 212	−18.6	−36.2	−43.0	−43.0	−58.5	−68.1	−79.2	−91.2
Air transport, other	3 213	....	....	−2.0	−1.4	....	....	....	....
Other transport, passenger	3 215	−1.1	−4.8	−13.6	−13.6	....	....	....	....
Other transport, freight	3 216	−123.8	−92.9	−90.7	−120.4	−110.8	−129.4	−150.2	−173.8
Other transport, other	3 217	−.5	−1.2	−2.0	−1.8	−2.3	−2.8	−2.8	−3.0
Travel, credit	2 236	**482.2**	**561.5**	**619.6**	**620.7**	**629.9**	**791.1**	**918.6**	**1,054.6**
Business travel	2 237	3.3	76.8	139.8	132.4	107.1	134.5	156.2	179.3
Personal travel	2 240	478.9	484.7	479.8	488.3	522.8	656.6	762.5	875.3
Travel, debit	3 236	**−181.7**	**−225.5**	**−275.6**	**−312.0**	**−385.2**	**−420.4**	**−528.3**	**−597.0**
Business travel	3 237	−2.2	−43.1	−87.6	−122.3	−108.3	−117.7	−147.0	−165.8
Personal travel	3 240	−179.5	−182.4	−188.0	−189.7	−276.9	−302.8	−381.4	−431.2
Other services, credit	2 200 BA	**212.4**	**383.6**	**434.7**	**353.9**	**320.1**	**364.6**	**433.3**	**469.4**
Communications	2 245	.3	25.6	43.2	9.0	167.1	174.0	209.0	238.0
Construction	2 249	....	2.8	23.3	18.2	....	....	5.3	2.7
Insurance	2 253	18.8	30.2	49.4	59.4	12.9	14.0	18.3	20.6
Financial	2 260	5.1	8.6	6.2	4.7	5.2	5.1	8.8	9.8
Computer and information	2 262	3.7	4.8	7.2	1.9	2.5	9.5	13.3	14.6
Royalties and licence fees	2 266	....	....	....	....	2.2	4.5	8.0	9.2
Other business services	2 268	109.2	214.2	212.2	155.5	24.2	44.0	42.0	42.5
Personal, cultural, and recreational	2 287	....	.4	.4	.7	20.8	27.3	19.9	21.9
Government, n.i.e.	2 291	75.3	97.0	92.8	104.6	85.3	86.2	108.7	110.1
Other services, debit	3 200 BA	**−222.1**	**−236.6**	**−267.6**	**−253.7**	**−275.1**	**−241.9**	**−344.6**	**−386.4**
Communications	3 245	−.8	−10.9	−67.1	−5.7	−14.8	−17.2	−29.9	−33.8
Construction	3 249	−4.9	−1.0	−4.5	−3.2	....	−.1	−1.1	−.5
Insurance	3 253	−59.9	−77.6	−104.6	−128.3	−172.5	−124.6	−181.8	−202.6
Financial	3 260	−4.5	−13.0	−11.7	−13.7	−3.5	−6.1	−9.9	−10.2
Computer and information	3 262	−4.3	−1.7	−4.2	−1.1	−3.5	−1.8	−11.3	−12.1
Royalties and licence fees	3 266	....	....	....	....	−40.0	−49.4	−66.5	−78.8
Other business services	3 268	−107.9	−95.1	−22.7	−60.5	−19.1	−21.7	−16.4	−17.6
Personal, cultural, and recreational	3 287	....	−.3	−5.0	−.4	−2.0	−.1	−5.6	−6.5
Government, n.i.e.	3 291	−39.8	−36.9	−47.8	−40.7	−19.8	−20.8	−22.1	−24.1

Table 2 (Continued). STANDARD PRESENTATION, 2000–2007

(Millions of U.S. dollars)

	Code	2000	2001	2002	2003	2004	2005	2006	2007
C. INCOME	4 300	**−209.6**	**−84.4**	**−318.4**	**−317.9**	**−410.1**	**−484.8**	**−662.2**	**−769.6**
Total credit	2 300	*214.4*	*317.5*	*161.1*	*179.1*	*219.9*	*301.7*	*452.8*	*551.0*
Total debit	3 300	*−424.0*	*−401.9*	*−479.5*	*−497.0*	*−630.0*	*−786.5*	*−1,115.0*	*−1,320.5*
Compensation of employees, credit	2 310	**32.8**	**41.4**	**20.8**	**40.5**	**11.4**	**22.1**	**20.4**	**25.5**
Compensation of employees, debit	3 310	**−16.5**	**−11.5**	**−6.3**	**−5.9**	**−1.2**	**−8.7**	**−11.0**	**−11.5**
Investment income, credit	2 320	**181.6**	**276.0**	**140.3**	**138.6**	**208.4**	**279.6**	**432.3**	**525.5**
Direct investment income	2 330	77.7	80.3	88.7	100.4	41.2	38.3	61.3	66.3
Dividends and distributed branch profits	2 332	49.8	53.6	57.8	80.9	....	....	.9	.9
Reinvested earnings and undistributed branch profits	2 333	....	....	....	....	41.2	38.3	60.4	65.4
Income on debt (interest)	2 334	27.9	26.7	30.8	19.5	....	....	....	....
Portfolio investment income	2 339	....	....	....	....	3.7	7.6	11.3	11.1
Income on equity	2 340	....	....	....	....	2.1	2.5	3.0	....
Income on bonds and notes	2 350	....	....	....	....	1.6	5.1	8.3	11.1
Income on money market instruments	2 360	....	....	....	....	....	....	....	....
Other investment income	2 370	103.9	195.8	51.6	38.2	163.5	233.7	359.8	448.0
Investment income, debit	3 320	**−407.5**	**−390.4**	**−473.2**	**−491.0**	**−628.8**	**−777.8**	**−1,104.0**	**−1,309.0**
Direct investment income	3 330	−248.4	−205.3	−286.5	−318.8	−270.2	−369.8	−607.3	−739.8
Dividends and distributed branch profits	3 332	−175.2	−118.2	−170.9	−213.6	−34.9	3.4	−77.5	−118.3
Reinvested earnings and undistributed branch profits	3 333	−48.9	−54.6	−56.2	−57.6	−234.6	−371.7	−525.6	−615.5
Income on debt (interest)	3 334	−24.3	−32.5	−59.4	−47.6	−.7	−1.5	−4.3	−6.0
Portfolio investment income	3 339	−36.9	−48.5	−25.3	−22.4	−87.0	−109.2	−107.5	−104.5
Income on equity	3 340	....	....	....	....	....	....	....	....
Income on bonds and notes	3 350	−36.9	−48.5	−25.3	−22.4	−87.0	−109.2	−107.5	−104.5
Income on money market instruments	3 360	....	....	....	....	....	....	....	....
Other investment income	3 370	−122.2	−136.6	−161.4	−149.8	−271.6	−298.7	−389.2	−464.7
D. CURRENT TRANSFERS	4 379	**865.3**	**996.8**	**1,976.3**	**2,461.9**	**3,121.5**	**3,576.5**	**4,268.2**	**4,862.6**
Credit	2 379	**908.2**	**1,024.3**	**2,077.7**	**2,558.9**	**3,156.9**	**3,614.9**	**4,305.6**	**4,873.8**
General government	2 380	....	8.7	....	....	84.9	76.0	61.3	57.2
Other sectors	2 390	908.2	1,015.6	2,077.7	2,558.9	3,072.0	3,538.9	4,244.4	4,816.7
Workers' remittances	2 391	563.4	592.3	1,579.4	2,106.5	2,616.0	3,044.6	3,679.7	4,228.4
Other current transfers	2 392	344.8	423.2	498.3	452.3	456.0	494.3	564.6	588.2
Debit	3 379	**−42.9**	**−27.5**	**−101.5**	**−97.0**	**−35.4**	**−38.5**	**−37.4**	**−11.2**
General government	3 380	....	.1	....	....	−2.9	−5.2	−2.9	−4.4
Other sectors	3 390	−42.9	−27.6	−101.5	−97.0	−32.5	−33.3	−34.5	−6.8
Workers' remittances	3 391	−39.1	−21.0	−75.7	−80.2	−32.5	−33.3	−34.5	−6.8
Other current transfers	3 392	−3.8	−6.5	−25.8	−16.8	....	....	....	....
CAPITAL AND FINANCIAL ACCOUNT	4 996	**963.5**	**1,165.7**	**1,299.5**	**1,099.9**	**273.9**	**510.0**	**1,081.3**	**1,414.1**
CAPITAL ACCOUNT	4 994	**85.5**	**93.4**	**124.2**	**133.8**	**....**	**....**	**142.2**	**....**
Total credit	2 994	*85.5*	*93.4*	*124.2*	*133.8*	*....*	*....*	*142.2*	*....*
Total debit	3 994	*....*	*....*	*....*	*....*	*....*	*....*	*....*	*....*
Capital transfers, credit	2 400	**85.5**	**93.4**	**124.2**	**133.8**	**....**	**....**	**142.2**	**....**
General government	2 401	85.5	93.4	124.2	133.8	....	....	21.7	....
Debt forgiveness	2 402	....	....	....	....	....	....	21.7	....
Other capital transfers	2 410	85.5	93.4	124.2	133.8	....	....	21.7	....
Other sectors	2 430	....	....	....	....	....	....	120.5	....
Migrants' transfers	2 431	....	....	....	....	....	....	....	....
Debt forgiveness	2 432	....	....	....	....	....	....	120.5	....
Other capital transfers	2 440	....	....	....	....	....	....	....	....
Capital transfers, debit	3 400	**....**	**....**	**....**	**....**	**....**	**....**	**....**	**....**
General government	3 401	....	....	....	....	....	....	....	....
Debt forgiveness	3 402	....	....	....	....	....	....	....	....
Other capital transfers	3 410	....	....	....	....	....	....	....	....
Other sectors	3 430	....	....	....	....	....	....	....	....
Migrants' transfers	3 431	....	....	....	....	....	....	....	....
Debt forgiveness	3 432	....	....	....	....	....	....	....	....
Other capital transfers	3 440	....	....	....	....	....	....	....	....
Nonproduced nonfinancial assets, credit	2 480	**....**	**....**	**....**	**....**	**....**	**....**	**....**	**....**
Nonproduced nonfinancial assets, debit	3 480	**....**	**....**	**....**	**....**	**....**	**....**	**....**	**....**

Table 2 (Continued). STANDARD PRESENTATION, 2000–2007

(Millions of U.S. dollars)

	Code	2000	2001	2002	2003	2004	2005	2006	2007
FINANCIAL ACCOUNT	4 995 ..	**878.0**	**1,072.3**	**1,175.4**	**966.2**	**273.9**	**510.0**	**939.1**	**1,414.1**
A. DIRECT INVESTMENT	4 500 ..	**229.9**	**455.5**	**110.6**	**131.0**	**254.8**	**470.0**	**531.2**	**658.1**
Direct investment abroad	4 505 ..	....	....	....	....	−41.2	−38.3	−60.4	−65.4
Equity capital	4 510 ..	....	....	....	....	....	....	....	....
Claims on affiliated enterprises	4 515 ..	....	....	....	....	....	....	....	....
Liabilities to affiliated enterprises	4 520 ..	....	....	....	....	....	....	....	....
Reinvested earnings	4 525 ..	....	....	....	....	−41.2	−38.3	−60.4	−65.4
Other capital	4 530 ..	....	....	....	....	....	....	....	....
Claims on affiliated enterprises	4 535 ..	....	....	....	....	....	....	....	....
Liabilities to affiliated enterprises	4 540 ..	....	....	....	....	....	....	....	....
Direct investment in Guatemala	4 555 ..	**229.9**	**455.5**	**110.6**	**131.0**	**296.0**	**508.3**	**591.6**	**723.5**
Equity capital	4 560 ..	170.6	389.5	41.5	59.7	22.9	18.1	86.8	130.3
Claims on direct investors	4 565 ..	1,018.5	1,392.0	1,127.6	111.5	2.9	−1.9	....	....
Liabilities to direct investors	4 570 ..	−847.9	−1,002.5	−1,086.1	−51.8	20.0	20.0	86.8	130.3
Reinvested earnings	4 575 ..	48.9	54.6	56.2	57.6	234.6	371.7	525.6	615.5
Other capital	4 580 ..	10.4	11.4	12.9	13.7	38.5	118.4	−20.8	−22.3
Claims on direct investors	4 585 ..	....	....	....	....	−28.2	−29.5	−43.6	−46.8
Liabilities to direct investors	4 590 ..	10.4	11.4	12.9	13.7	66.7	147.9	22.8	24.5
B. PORTFOLIO INVESTMENT	4 600 ..	**42.6**	**130.4**	**−146.1**	**7.1**	**399.0**	**−76.9**	**−79.3**	**−165.9**
Assets	4 602 ..	**−36.3**	**−45.0**	**−38.3**	**18.1**	**11.7**	**−39.7**	**−55.6**	**35.7**
Equity securities	4 610 ..	....	....	....	....	....	−.4	....	....
Monetary authorities	4 611 ..	....	....	....	....	....	....	....	....
General government	4 612 ..	....	....	....	....	....	....	....	....
Banks	4 613 ..	....	....	....	....	....	....	....	....
Other sectors	4 614 ..	....	....	....	....	....	−.4	....	....
Debt securities	4 619 ..	−36.3	−45.0	−38.3	18.1	11.7	−39.3	−55.6	35.7
Bonds and notes	4 620 ..	−36.3	−45.0	−38.3	18.1	11.7	−39.3	−55.6	35.7
Monetary authorities	4 621 ..	....	....	....	....	....	....	....	....
General government	4 622 ..	....	....	....	....	....	....	....	....
Banks	4 623 ..	....	....	....	....	11.7	−42.0	−55.6	35.7
Other sectors	4 624 ..	−36.3	−45.0	−38.3	18.1	....	2.7	....	....
Money market instruments	4 630 ..	....	....	....	....	....	....	....	....
Monetary authorities	4 631 ..	....	....	....	....	....	....	....	....
General government	4 632 ..	....	....	....	....	....	....	....	....
Banks	4 633 ..	....	....	....	....	....	....	....	....
Other sectors	4 634 ..	....	....	....	....	....	....	....	....
Liabilities	4 652 ..	**78.9**	**175.3**	**−107.8**	**−11.0**	**387.2**	**−37.1**	**−23.7**	**−201.6**
Equity securities	4 660 ..	....	....	....	....	....	....	....	....
Banks	4 663 ..	....	....	....	....	....	....	....	....
Other sectors	4 664 ..	....	....	....	....	....	....	....	....
Debt securities	4 669 ..	78.9	175.3	−107.8	−11.0	387.2	−37.1	−23.7	−201.6
Bonds and notes	4 670 ..	78.9	175.3	−107.8	−11.0	387.2	−37.1	−23.7	−201.6
Monetary authorities	4 671 ..	....	....	....	....	....	....	....	....
General government	4 672 ..	78.9	175.3	−107.8	−11.0	238.0	−42.2	−30.1	−160.4
Banks	4 673 ..	....	....	....	....	39.5	−2.6	30.3	−41.2
Other sectors	4 674 ..	....	....	....	....	109.7	7.7	−23.9	....
Money market instruments	4 680 ..	....	....	....	....	....	....	....	....
Monetary authorities	4 681 ..	....	....	....	....	....	....	....	....
General government	4 682 ..	....	....	....	....	....	....	....	....
Banks	4 683 ..	....	....	....	....	....	....	....	....
Other sectors	4 684 ..	....	....	....	....	....	....	....	....
C. FINANCIAL DERIVATIVES	4 910 ..	....	....	....	....	....	....	....	....
Monetary authorities	4 911 ..	....	....	....	....	....	....	....	....
General government	4 912 ..	....	....	....	....	....	....	....	....
Banks	4 913 ..	....	....	....	....	....	....	....	....
Other sectors	4 914 ..	....	....	....	....	....	....	....	....
Assets	4 900 ..	....	....	....	....	....	....	....	....
Monetary authorities	4 901 ..	....	....	....	....	....	....	....	....
General government	4 902 ..	....	....	....	....	....	....	....	....
Banks	4 903 ..	....	....	....	....	....	....	....	....
Other sectors	4 904 ..	....	....	....	....	....	....	....	....
Liabilities	4 905 ..	....	....	....	....	....	....	....	....
Monetary authorities	4 906 ..	....	....	....	....	....	....	....	....
General government	4 907 ..	....	....	....	....	....	....	....	....
Banks	4 908 ..	....	....	....	....	....	....	....	....
Other sectors	4 909 ..	....	....	....	....	....	....	....	....

Table 2 (Concluded). STANDARD PRESENTATION, 2000–2007

(Millions of U.S. dollars)

	Code	2000	2001	2002	2003	2004	2005	2006	2007
D. OTHER INVESTMENT	4 700	**1,248.2**	**960.8**	**1,232.1**	**1,378.3**	**224.0**	**354.8**	**738.3**	**1,136.5**
Assets	4 703	**213.2**	**156.7**	**196.4**	**173.5**	**−276.2**	**−151.8**	**−236.6**	**−387.4**
Trade credits	4 706	....	....	....	....	−72.7	−74.9	−99.7	−191.8
General government	4 707	....	....	....	....	....	....	....	....
of which: Short-term	4 709	....	....	....	....	....	....	....	....
Other sectors	4 710	....	....	....	....	−72.7	−74.9	−99.7	−191.8
of which: Short-term	4 712	....	....	....	....	....	....	....	....
Loans	4 714	....	....	....	....	−62.8	−61.6	−229.4	−99.1
Monetary authorities	4 715	....	....	....	....	....	....	....	....
of which: Short-term	4 718	....	....	....	....	....	....	....	....
General government	4 719	....	....	....	....	....	....	....	....
of which: Short-term	4 721	....	....	....	....	....	....	....	....
Banks	4 722	....	....	....	....	−62.8	−61.6	−229.4	−99.1
of which: Short-term	4 724	....	....	....	....	....	....	....	....
Other sectors	4 725	....	....	....	....	....	....	....	....
of which: Short-term	4 727	....	....	....	....	....	....	....	....
Currency and deposits	4 730	....	....	....	....	−140.7	−15.3	93.7	−96.5
Monetary authorities	4 731	....	....	....	....	....	....	....	....
General government	4 732	....	....	....	....	....	....	....	....
Banks	4 733	....	....	....	....	−30.6	60.6	−21.2	−87.3
Other sectors	4 734	....	....	....	....	−110.1	−76.0	114.9	−9.3
Other assets	4 736	213.2	156.7	196.4	173.5	....	....	−1.2	....
Monetary authorities	4 737	....	....	....	....	....	....	....	....
of which: Short-term	4 739	....	....	....	....	....	....	....	....
General government	4 740	....	....	....	....	....	....	....	....
of which: Short-term	4 742	....	....	....	....	....	....	....	....
Banks	4 743	....	....	....	....	....	....	....	....
of which: Short-term	4 745	....	....	....	....	....	....	....	....
Other sectors	4 746	213.2	156.7	196.4	173.5	....	....	−1.2	....
of which: Short-term	4 748	....	....	....	....	....	....	−1.2	....
Liabilities	4 753	**1,035.0**	**804.0**	**1,035.7**	**1,204.7**	**500.2**	**506.6**	**974.9**	**1,523.9**
Trade credits	4 756	1,233.8	1,277.6	1,580.4	1,058.3	359.6	235.8	305.3	538.9
General government	4 757	....	....	....	....	....	....	....	....
of which: Short-term	4 759	....	....	....	....	....	....	....	....
Other sectors	4 760	1,233.8	1,277.6	1,580.4	1,058.3	359.6	235.8	305.3	538.9
of which: Short-term	4 762	*1,233.8*	*1,277.6*	*1,580.4*	*1,058.3*	*359.6*	*235.8*	*305.3*	*538.9*
Loans	4 764	566.8	733.5	456.6	647.4	154.3	288.8	689.1	931.6
Monetary authorities	4 765	−24.3	−11.2	−11.1	−11.4	−68.1	−.5	−.3	....
of which: Use of Fund credit and loans from the Fund.	4 766	....	....	....	....	....	....	....	....
of which: Short-term	4 768	....	....	....	....	....	....	....	....
General government	4 769	92.7	42.6	172.7	307.9	90.3	−43.5	356.3	392.9
of which: Short-term	4 771	....	....	....	....	....	....	....	....
Banks	4 772	....	....	....	....	111.0	209.1	312.9	467.9
of which: Short-term	4 774	....	....	....	....	....	....	....	....
Other sectors	4 775	498.4	702.1	295.0	351.0	21.1	123.8	20.1	70.8
of which: Short-term	4 777	*−1.8*	*215.2*	*−122.8*	*−25.3*	....	....	....	....
Currency and deposits	4 780	....	....	....	....	−13.6	−18.0	−19.5	53.4
Monetary authorities	4 781	....	....	....	....	−1.6	....	....	....
General government	4 782	....	....	....	....	....	....	....	....
Banks	4 783	....	....	....	....	−12.0	−18.0	−19.5	53.4
Other sectors	4 784	....	....	....	....	....	....	....	....
Other liabilities	4 786	−765.6	−1,207.0	−1,001.3	−501.0	....	....	....	....
Monetary authorities	4 787	.3	....	−.2	−.2	....	....	....	....
of which: Short-term	4 789	*.3*	....	*−.2*	*−.2*	....	....	....	....
General government	4 790	....	....	....	....	....	....	....	....
of which: Short-term	4 792	....	....	....	....	....	....	....	....
Banks	4 793	−17.4	21.8	....	....	....	....	....	....
of which: Short-term	4 795	*−17.4*	*21.8*	....	....	....	....	....	....
Other sectors	4 796	−748.5	−1,228.8	−1,001.1	−500.8	....	....	....	....
of which: Short-term	4 798	*−748.5*	*−1,228.8*	*−1,001.1*	*−500.8*	....	....	....	....
E. RESERVE ASSETS	4 802	**−642.7**	**−474.4**	**−21.2**	**−550.1**	**−603.8**	**−237.9**	**−251.0**	**−214.6**
Monetary gold	4 812	−50.2	−.8	−15.1	−16.4	....	....	....	....
Special drawing rights	4 811	1.1	1.0	.9	.7	.6	.8	1.2	1.5
Reserve position in the Fund	4 810	....	....	....	....	....	....	....	....
Foreign exchange	4 803	−593.6	−474.6	−7.0	−534.5	−593.1	−238.2	−252.4	−216.4
Other claims	4 813	....	....	....	....	−11.4	−.5	.2	.3
NET ERRORS AND OMISSIONS	4 998	**86.1**	**87.2**	**−64.7**	**−60.8**	**890.6**	**730.7**	**430.9**	**282.9**

Table 1. ANALYTIC PRESENTATION, 2000–2007

(Millions of U.S. dollars)

	Code	2000	2001	2002	2003	2004	2005	2006	2007
A. Current Account[1]	4 993 Z.	−155.2	−102.2	−199.8	−187.5	−174.8	. . . .	. . . .	−463.4
Goods: exports f.o.b.	2 100 ..	666.3	731.1	708.6	609.3	725.6	. . . .	. . . .	1,203.2
Goods: imports f.o.b.	3 100 ..	−587.1	−561.9	−668.5	−644.3	−688.4	. . . .	. . . .	−1,217.6
Balance on Goods	4 100 ..	*79.3*	*169.2*	*40.1*	*−35.0*	*37.2*	. . . .	. . . .	*−14.4*
Services: credit	2 200 ..	68.0	102.8	90.5	133.7	85.4	. . . .	. . . .	48.6
Services: debit	3 200 ..	−284.9	−319.0	−330.6	−307.3	−275.2	. . . .	. . . .	−296.0
Balance on Goods and Services	4 991 ..	*−137.7*	*−47.0*	*−200.1*	*−208.6*	*−152.7*	. . . .	. . . .	*−261.8*
Income: credit	2 300 ..	23.5	11.3	6.1	12.6	9.8	. . . .	. . . .	61.0
Income: debit	3 300 ..	−101.1	−113.6	−51.6	−124.3	−37.1	. . . .	. . . .	−124.1
Balance on Goods, Services, and Income	4 992 ..	*−215.3*	*−149.3*	*−245.6*	*−320.3*	*−180.0*	. . . .	. . . .	*−325.0*
Current transfers: credit	2 379 Z.	88.6	91.6	70.5	194.6	55.1	. . . .	. . . .	35.3
Current transfers: debit	3 379 ..	−28.5	−44.5	−24.8	−61.7	−49.9	. . . .	. . . .	−173.7
B. Capital Account[1]	4 994 Z.	. . . .	. . . .	91.9	57.6	−30.2	. . . .	. . . .	90.3
Capital account: credit	2 994 Z.	. . . .	. . . .	91.9	57.6	. . . .	. . . .	. . . .	171.3
Capital account: debit	3 994 ..	. . . .	. . . .	. . . .	. . . .	−30.2	. . . .	. . . .	−81.0
Total, Groups A Plus B	4 981 ..	*−155.2*	*−102.2*	*−107.9*	*−129.9*	*−205.0*	. . . .	. . . .	*−373.1*
C. Financial Account[1]	4 995 W.	8.4	−12.1	−115.1	58.6	77.7	. . . .	. . . .	443.8
Direct investment abroad	4 505 ..	. . . .	. . . .	. . . .	. . . .	. . . .	. . . .	. . . .	. . . .
Direct investment in Guinea	4 555 Z.	9.9	1.7	30.0	79.0	. . . .	. . . .	. . . .	385.9
Portfolio investment assets	4 602 ..	8.7	4.6	5.1	−4.6	14.8	. . . .	. . . .	8.3
Equity securities	4 610 ..	. . . .	. . . .	. . . .	. . . .	. . . .	. . . .	. . . .	. . . .
Debt securities	4 619 ..	8.7	4.6	5.1	−4.6	14.8	. . . .	. . . .	8.3
Portfolio investment liabilities	4 652 Z.	. . . .	. . . .	. . . .	. . . .	. . . .	. . . .	. . . .	. . . .
Equity securities	4 660 ..	. . . .	. . . .	. . . .	. . . .	. . . .	. . . .	. . . .	. . . .
Debt securities	4 669 Z.	. . . .	. . . .	. . . .	. . . .	. . . .	. . . .	. . . .	. . . .
Financial derivatives	4 910 ..	. . . .	. . . .	. . . .	. . . .	. . . .	. . . .	. . . .	. . . .
Financial derivatives assets	4 900 ..	. . . .	. . . .	. . . .	. . . .	. . . .	. . . .	. . . .	. . . .
Financial derivatives liabilities	4 905 ..	. . . .	. . . .	. . . .	. . . .	. . . .	. . . .	. . . .	. . . .
Other investment assets	4 703 ..	−17.0	11.7	−71.0	−4.4	49.5	. . . .	. . . .	33.2
Monetary authorities	4 701 ..	−13.7	1.5	. . . .	1.8	7.0	. . . .	. . . .	−6.6
General government	4 704 ..	. . . .	. . . .	. . . .	. . . .	. . . .	. . . .	. . . .	. . . .
Banks	4 705 ..	−1.3	9.5	−69.1	−6.1	42.5	. . . .	. . . .	39.8
Other sectors	4 728 ..	−2.0	.6	−2.0	. . . .	. . . .	. . . .	. . . .	. . . .
Other investment liabilities	4 753 W.	6.8	−30.1	−79.2	−11.4	13.4	. . . .	. . . .	16.4
Monetary authorities	4 753 WA	−.8	13.4	1.6	2.0	2.9	. . . .	. . . .	−83.2
General government	4 753 ZB	61.6	26.5	−36.3	−8.9	7.2	. . . .	. . . .	79.2
Banks	4 753 ZC	−23.1	−12.4	. . . .	−4.2	3.3	. . . .	. . . .	.4
Other sectors	4 753 ZD	−30.8	−57.5	−44.5	−.4	. . . .	. . . .	. . . .	20.0
Total, Groups A Through C	4 983 ..	*−146.8*	*−114.3*	*−223.0*	*−71.4*	*−127.3*	. . . .	. . . .	*70.7*
D. Net Errors and Omissions	4 998 ..	83.9	−2.2	143.1	−157.1	68.6	. . . .	. . . .	117.4
Total, Groups A Through D	4 984 ..	*−62.9*	*−116.5*	*−79.8*	*−228.5*	*−58.6*	. . . .	. . . .	*188.1*
E. Reserves and Related Items	4 802 A.	62.9	116.5	79.8	228.5	58.6	. . . .	. . . .	−188.1
Reserve assets	4 802 ..	50.5	−3.9	75.7	131.5	11.8	. . . .	. . . .	8.7
Use of Fund credit and loans	4 766 ..	−7.9	14.8	5.7	−14.8	−19.5	. . . .	. . . .	−10.4
Exceptional financing	4 920 ..	20.4	105.7	−1.6	111.8	66.3	. . . .	. . . .	−186.4
Conversion rates: Guinean francs per U.S. dollar	0 101 ..	**1,746.9**	**1,950.6**	**1,975.8**	**1,984.9**	**2,225.0**	**3,644.3**	. . . .	. . . .

[1] Excludes components that have been classified in the categories of Group E.

Table 2. STANDARD PRESENTATION, 2000–2007

(Millions of U.S. dollars)

	Code	2000	2001	2002	2003	2004	2005	2006	2007
CURRENT ACCOUNT	4 993	**−140.1**	**−59.5**	**−199.6**	**−185.3**	**−162.4**	....	....	**−455.6**
A. GOODS	4 100	**79.3**	**169.2**	**40.1**	**−35.0**	**37.2**	....	....	**−14.4**
Credit	2 100	**666.3**	**731.1**	**708.6**	**609.3**	**725.6**	....	....	**1,203.2**
General merchandise: exports f.o.b.	2 110	547.5	534.0	531.2	366.6	514.8	....	....	1,070.1
Goods for processing: exports f.o.b.	2 150	....	1.0	1.6	....	....	....	....	....
Repairs on goods	2 160	....	3.4	....	....	....	....	....	....
Goods procured in ports by carriers	2 170	8.2	27.5	....	....	....	....	....	.3
Nonmonetary gold	2 180	110.7	165.1	175.8	242.7	210.7	....	....	132.8
Debit	3 100	**−587.1**	**−561.9**	**−668.5**	**−644.3**	**−688.4**	....	....	**−1,217.6**
General merchandise: imports f.o.b.	3 110	−582.9	−531.9	−645.6	−617.0	−680.7	....	....	−1,206.4
Goods for processing: imports f.o.b.	3 150	....	−22.5	−22.9	−27.1	−7.7	....	....	−11.2
Repairs on goods	3 160	−1.2	−.9	....	−.1	−.1	....	....	....
Goods procured in ports by carriers	3 170	−3.0	−6.6	....	−.1	....	....	....	....
Nonmonetary gold	3 180	....	....	....	....	....	....	....	....
B. SERVICES	4 200	**−216.9**	**−216.1**	**−240.2**	**−173.6**	**−189.9**	....	....	**−247.4**
Total credit	2 200	*68.0*	*102.8*	*90.5*	*133.7*	*85.4*	....	....	*48.6*
Total debit	3 200	*−284.9*	*−319.0*	*−330.6*	*−307.3*	*−275.2*	....	....	*−296.0*
Transportation services, credit	2 205	**15.6**	**31.7**	**8.9**	**6.7**	**6.7**	....	....	**6.0**
Passenger	2 850	*5.8*	*8.1*	....	*.6*	....	....	....	*.9*
Freight	2 851	*4.8*	*16.2*	*6.2*	*4.9*	*5.7*	....	....	*2.0*
Other	2 852	*5.0*	*7.4*	*2.7*	*1.3*	*1.0*	....	....	*3.1*
Sea transport, passenger	2 207	....	....	....	....	....	....	....	....
Sea transport, freight	2 208	4.8	16.2	6.2	4.4	5.6	....	....	1.0
Sea transport, other	2 209	3.3	5.7	2.2	1.0	.1	....	....	1.2
Air transport, passenger	2 211	5.8	8.1	....	.6	....	....	....	.9
Air transport, freight	2 212	....	....	....	.5	.1	....	....	1.0
Air transport, other	2 213	1.7	1.7	.5	.3	.9	....	....	1.8
Other transport, passenger	2 215	....	....	....	....	....	....	....	....
Other transport, freight	2 216	....	....	....	....	....	....	....	....
Other transport, other	2 217	....	....	....	....	....	....	....	....
Transportation services, debit	3 205	**−111.3**	**−112.5**	**−47.0**	**−54.3**	**−92.5**	....	....	**−96.5**
Passenger	3 850	*−3.8*	*−7.8*	*−7.4*	*−10.2*	*−4.3*	....	....	*−66.5*
Freight	3 851	*−104.2*	*−100.3*	*−38.0*	*−37.5*	*−84.3*	....	....	*−26.5*
Other	3 852	*−3.4*	*−4.4*	*−1.6*	*−6.6*	*−3.9*	....	....	*−3.4*
Sea transport, passenger	3 207	....	....	....	....	....	....	....	−50.7
Sea transport, freight	3 208	−99.0	−95.3	−23.7	−34.6	−75.7	....	....	−7.4
Sea transport, other	3 209	−1.0	−3.7	−1.4	−5.8	−3.3	....	....	−2.4
Air transport, passenger	3 211	−3.8	−7.8	−7.4	−10.2	−4.3	....	....	−15.9
Air transport, freight	3 212	−5.2	−5.0	−14.3	−2.9	−8.6	....	....	−19.2
Air transport, other	3 213	−2.4	−.7	−.2	−.8	−.6	....	....	−1.0
Other transport, passenger	3 215	....	....	....	....	....	....	....	....
Other transport, freight	3 216	....	....	....	....	....	....	....	....
Other transport, other	3 217	....	....	....	....	....	....	....	....
Travel, credit	2 236	**2.0**	**.1**	....	....	....	....	....	**.2**
Business travel	2 237	....	.1	....	....	....	....	....	.1
Personal travel	2 240	2.0	....	....	....	....	....	....	.1
Travel, debit	3 236	**−9.3**	**−17.8**	**−30.6**	**−26.0**	**−25.1**	....	....	**−29.0**
Business travel	3 237	−1.0	−2.9	−1.9	−1.0	−.7	....	....	−.8
Personal travel	3 240	−8.3	−14.9	−28.8	−25.0	−24.3	....	....	−28.2
Other services, credit	2 200 BA	**50.4**	**71.0**	**81.6**	**127.0**	**78.7**	....	....	**42.4**
Communications	2 245	1.1	2.2	.4	.1	.3	....	....	10.7
Construction	2 249	4.1	12.9	28.8	42.0	18.2	....	....	13.6
Insurance	2 253	....	3.7	.5	.3	.1	....	....	.3
Financial	2 260	.1	.3	.2	....	....	....	....	....
Computer and information	2 262	....	.1	....	....	....	....	....	....
Royalties and licence fees	2 266	....	....	....	.3	....	....	....	.1
Other business services	2 268	3.8	21.1	4.3	6.0	5.4	....	....	12.1
Personal, cultural, and recreational	2 287	....	....	.2	....	....	....	....	1.1
Government, n.i.e.	2 291	41.2	30.6	47.1	78.3	54.7	....	....	4.6
Other services, debit	3 200 BA	**−164.3**	**−188.7**	**−253.1**	**−227.0**	**−157.7**	....	....	**−170.6**
Communications	3 245	−9.9	−5.5	−2.2	−5.0	−2.7	....	....	−23.8
Construction	3 249	−5.5	−2.1	−9.8	−27.6	−6.9	....	....	−46.4
Insurance	3 253	−7.0	−6.7	−8.9	−18.8	−24.8	....	....	−15.5
Financial	3 260	−.1	−.3	−.2	....	....	....	....	....
Computer and information	3 262	−3.2	−1.3	−.8	−.4	−.3	....	....	−.4
Royalties and licence fees	3 266	....	−1.0	−.8	−.9	−.2	....	....	....
Other business services	3 268	−37.0	−72.8	−55.5	−54.8	−42.6	....	....	−35.8
Personal, cultural, and recreational	3 287	−.1	−.2	−.2	−.2	−.5	....	....	−.9
Government, n.i.e.	3 291	−101.5	−98.7	−174.7	−119.3	−79.8	....	....	−47.8

Table 2 (Continued). STANDARD PRESENTATION, 2000–2007

(Millions of U.S. dollars)

	Code	2000	2001	2002	2003	2004	2005	2006	2007
C. INCOME	4 300	**−77.7**	**−102.3**	**−45.5**	**−111.7**	**−27.3**	....	....	**−63.2**
Total credit	2 300	*23.5*	*11.3*	*6.1*	*12.6*	*9.8*	....	....	*61.0*
Total debit	3 300	*−101.1*	*−113.6*	*−51.6*	*−124.3*	*−37.1*	....	....	*−124.1*
Compensation of employees, credit	2 310	....	....	....	....	....	....	....	....
Compensation of employees, debit	3 310	**−1.4**	**−3.6**	**−2.8**	**−4.1**	**−1.7**	....	....	**−4.6**
Investment income, credit	2 320	**23.5**	**11.3**	**6.1**	**12.6**	**9.8**	....	....	**61.0**
Direct investment income	2 330	....	.1	.1	....	....	....	....	.1
Dividends and distributed branch profits	2 332	....	....	....	....	....	....	....	....
Reinvested earnings anc undistributed branch profits	2 333	....	....	....	....	....	....	....	....
Income on debt (interest)	2 334	....	.1	.1	....	....	....	....	.1
Portfolio investment income	2 339	....	....	....	....	....	....	....	....
Income on equity	2 340	....	....	....	....	....	....	....	....
Income on bonds and notes	2 350	....	....	....	....	....	....	....	....
Income on money market instruments	2 360	....	....	....	....	....	....	....	....
Other investment income	2 370	23.5	11.2	6.0	12.6	9.8	....	....	60.9
Investment income, debit	3 320	**−99.8**	**−110.0**	**−48.8**	**−120.2**	**−35.4**	....	....	**−119.6**
Direct investment income	3 330	−8.4	−45.6	−1.2	−79.0	....	....	....	−54.0
Dividends and distributed branch profits	3 332	−8.3	−45.5	−1.2	....	....	....	....	....
Reinvested earnings and undistributed branch profits	3 333	....	−.1	....	−79.0	....	....	....	−54.0
Income on debt (interest)	3 334	−.1	....	−.1	....	....	....	....	....
Portfolio investment income	3 339	....	....	....	....	....	....	....	....
Income on equity	3 340	....	....	....	....	....	....	....	....
Income on bonds and notes	3 350	....	....	....	....	....	....	....	....
Income on money market instruments	3 360	....	....	....	....	....	....	....	....
Other investment income	3 370	−91.3	−64.3	−47.5	−41.3	−35.4	....	....	−65.6
D. CURRENT TRANSFERS	4 379	**75.2**	**89.8**	**45.9**	**135.1**	**17.7**	....	....	**−130.6**
Credit	2 379	**103.8**	**134.3**	**70.7**	**196.8**	**67.6**	....	....	**43.1**
General government	2 380	84.1	124.6	55.5	85.8	25.9	....	....	7.8
Other sectors	2 390	19.7	9.7	15.2	111.0	41.6	....	....	35.3
Workers' remittances	2 391	1.2	8.7	15.2	111.0	41.6	....	....	15.1
Other current transfers	2 392	18.5	1.0	....	....	....	....	....	20.3
Debit	3 379	**−28.5**	**−44.5**	**−24.8**	**−61.7**	**−49.9**	....	....	**−173.7**
General government	3 380	−.1	−6.7	−9.1	−8.1	−2.6	....	....	−.4
Other sectors	3 390	−28.4	−37.8	−15.7	−53.7	−47.3	....	....	−173.3
Workers' remittances	3 391	−25.5	−33.2	−15.0	−42.3	−46.3	....	....	−34.4
Other current transfers	3 392	−2.9	−4.6	−.7	−11.4	−1.0	....	....	−138.9
CAPITAL AND FINANCIAL ACCOUNT	4 996	**56.2**	**61.7**	**56.5**	**342.4**	**93.7**	....	....	**338.2**
CAPITAL ACCOUNT	4 994	....	....	**91.9**	**57.6**	**−30.2**	....	....	**106.5**
Total credit	2 994	....	....	*91.9*	*57.6*	....	....	....	*187.5*
Total debit	3 994	....	....	....	....	*−30.2*	....	....	*−81.0*
Capital transfers, credit	2 400	....	....	**91.9**	**57.6**	....	....	....	**187.5**
General government	2 401	....	....	73.7	57.6	....	....	....	51.8
Debt forgiveness	2 402	....	....	....	4.1	....	....	....	16.2
Other capital transfers	2 410	....	....	73.7	53.5	....	....	....	35.7
Other sectors	2 430	....	....	18.3	....	....	....	....	135.7
Migrants' transfers	2 431	....	....	....	....	....	....	....	135.7
Debt forgiveness	2 432	....	....	18.3	....	....	....	....	....
Other capital transfers	2 440	....	....	....	....	....	....	....	....
Capital transfers, debit	3 400	....	....	....	....	**−30.2**	....	....	**−81.0**
General government	3 401	....	....	....	....	....	....	....	....
Debt forgiveness	3 402	....	....	....	....	....	....	....	....
Other capital transfers	3 410	....	....	....	....	....	....	....	....
Other sectors	3 430	....	....	....	....	−30.2	....	....	−81.0
Migrants' transfers	3 431	....	....	....	....	....	....	....	−80.5
Debt forgiveness	3 432	....	....	....	....	....	....	....	....
Other capital transfers	3 440	....	....	....	....	−30.2	....	....	−.5
Nonproduced nonfinancial assets, credit	2 480	....	....	....	....	....	....	....	....
Nonproduced nonfinancial assets, debit	3 480	....	....	....	....	....	....	....	....

Table 2 (Continued). STANDARD PRESENTATION, 2000–2007

(Millions of U.S. dollars)

	Code	2000	2001	2002	2003	2004	2005	2006	2007
FINANCIAL ACCOUNT	4 995 ..	56.2	61.7	−35.4	284.8	123.9	....	....	231.7
A. DIRECT INVESTMENT	4 500 ..	9.9	1.7	30.0	79.0	....	....	....	385.9
Direct investment abroad	4 505 ..	....	....	....	....	....	....	....	....
Equity capital	4 510 ..	....	....	....	....	....	....	....	....
Claims on affiliated enterprises	4 515 ..	....	....	....	....	....	....	....	....
Liabilities to affiliated enterprises	4 520 ..	....	....	....	....	....	....	....	....
Reinvested earnings	4 525 ..	....	....	....	....	....	....	....	....
Other capital	4 530 ..	....	....	....	....	....	....	....	....
Claims on affiliated enterprises	4 535 ..	....	....	....	....	....	....	....	....
Liabilities to affiliated enterprises	4 540 ..	....	....	....	....	....	....	....	....
Direct investment in Guinea	4 555 ..	9.9	1.7	30.0	79.0	....	....	....	385.9
Equity capital	4 560 ..	9.9	1.5	30.0	....	....	....	....	385.9
Claims on direct investors	4 565 ..	....	....	30.0	....	....	....	....	385.9
Liabilities to direct investors	4 570 ..	9.9	1.5	....	....	....	....	....	....
Reinvested earnings	4 575 ..	....	.1	....	79.0	....	....	....	54.0
Other capital	4 580 ..	....	....	....	....	....	....	....	−54.0
Claims on direct investors	4 585 ..	....	....	....	....	....	....	....	....
Liabilities to direct investors	4 590 ..	....	....	....	....	....	....	....	....
B. PORTFOLIO INVESTMENT	4 600 ..	8.7	4.6	5.1	−4.6	14.8	....	....	−129.8
Assets	4 602 ..	8.7	4.6	5.1	−4.6	14.8	....	....	8.3
Equity securities	4 610 ..	....	....	....	....	....	....	....	....
Monetary authorities	4 611 ..	....	....	....	....	....	....	....	....
General government	4 612 ..	....	....	....	....	....	....	....	....
Banks	4 613 ..	....	....	....	....	....	....	....	....
Other sectors	4 614 ..	....	....	....	....	....	....	....	....
Debt securities	4 619 ..	8.7	4.6	5.1	−4.6	14.8	....	....	8.3
Bonds and notes	4 620 ..	8.7	4.6	5.1	−4.6	14.8	....	....	8.3
Monetary authorities	4 621 ..	8.7	4.6	5.1	−4.6	14.8	....	....	8.3
General government	4 622 ..	....	....	....	....	....	....	....	....
Banks	4 623 ..	....	....	....	....	....	....	....	....
Other sectors	4 624 ..	....	....	....	....	....	....	....	....
Money market instruments	4 630 ..	....	....	....	....	....	....	....	....
Monetary authorities	4 631 ..	....	....	....	....	....	....	....	....
General government	4 632 ..	....	....	....	....	....	....	....	....
Banks	4 633 ..	....	....	....	....	....	....	....	....
Other sectors	4 634 ..	....	....	....	....	....	....	....	....
Liabilities	4 652 ..	....	....	....	....	....	....	....	−138.1
Equity securities	4 660 ..	....	....	....	....	....	....	....	....
Banks	4 663 ..	....	....	....	....	....	....	....	....
Other sectors	4 664 ..	....	....	....	....	....	....	....	....
Debt securities	4 669 ..	....	....	....	....	....	....	....	−138.1
Bonds and notes	4 670 ..	....	....	....	....	....	....	....	−138.1
Monetary authorities	4 671 ..	....	....	....	....	....	....	....	....
General government	4 672 ..	....	....	....	....	....	....	....	−138.1
Banks	4 673 ..	....	....	....	....	....	....	....	....
Other sectors	4 674 ..	....	....	....	....	....	....	....	....
Money market instruments	4 680 ..	....	....	....	....	....	....	....	....
Monetary authorities	4 681 ..	....	....	....	....	....	....	....	....
General government	4 682 ..	....	....	....	....	....	....	....	....
Banks	4 683 ..	....	....	....	....	....	....	....	....
Other sectors	4 684 ..	....	....	....	....	....	....	....	....
C. FINANCIAL DERIVATIVES	4 910 ..	....	....	....	....	....	....	....	....
Monetary authorities	4 911 ..	....	....	....	....	....	....	....	....
General government	4 912 ..	....	....	....	....	....	....	....	....
Banks	4 913 ..	....	....	....	....	....	....	....	....
Other sectors	4 914 ..	....	....	....	....	....	....	....	....
Assets	4 900 ..	....	....	....	....	....	....	....	....
Monetary authorities	4 901 ..	....	....	....	....	....	....	....	....
General government	4 902 ..	....	....	....	....	....	....	....	....
Banks	4 903 ..	....	....	....	....	....	....	....	....
Other sectors	4 904 ..	....	....	....	....	....	....	....	....
Liabilities	4 905 ..	....	....	....	....	....	....	....	....
Monetary authorities	4 906 ..	....	....	....	....	....	....	....	....
General government	4 907 ..	....	....	....	....	....	....	....	....
Banks	4 908 ..	....	....	....	....	....	....	....	....
Other sectors	4 909 ..	....	....	....	....	....	....	....	....

Table 2 (Concluded). STANDARD PRESENTATION, 2000–2007

(Millions of U.S. dollars)

	Code	2000	2001	2002	2003	2004	2005	2006	2007
D. OTHER INVESTMENT	4 700	−12.8	59.3	−146.2	78.9	97.2	....	....	−33.2
Assets	4 703	−17.0	11.7	−71.0	−4.4	49.5	....	....	33.2
Trade credits	4 706	....	....	....	....	....	....	....	....
General government	4 707	....	....	....	....	....	....	....	....
of which: Short-term	4 709	....	....	....	....	....	....	....	....
Other sectors	4 710	....	....	....	....	....	....	....	....
of which: Short-term	4 712	....	....	....	....	....	....	....	....
Loans	4 714	....	....	....	....	....	....	....	....
Monetary authorities	4 715	....	....	....	....	....	....	....	....
of which: Short-term	4 718	....	....	....	....	....	....	....	....
General government	4 719	....	....	....	....	....	....	....	....
of which: Short-term	4 721	....	....	....	....	....	....	....	....
Banks	4 722	....	....	....	....	....	....	....	....
of which: Short-term	4 724	....	....	....	....	....	....	....	....
Other sectors	4 725	....	....	....	....	....	....	....	....
of which: Short-term	4 727	....	....	....	....	....	....	....	....
Currency and deposits	4 730	−3.3	10.2	−71.0	−6.1	42.5	....	....	39.8
Monetary authorities	4 731	....	....	....	....	....	....	....	....
General government	4 732	....	....	....	....	....	....	....	....
Banks	4 733	−1.3	9.5	−69.1	−6.1	42.5	....	....	39.8
Other sectors	4 734	−2.0	.6	−2.0	....	....	....	....	....
Other assets	4 736	−13.7	1.5	....	1.8	7.0	....	....	−6.6
Monetary authorities	4 737	−13.7	1.5	....	1.8	7.0	....	....	−6.6
of which: Short-term	4 739	−13.7	1.5	....	1.8	7.0	....	....	−6.6
General government	4 740	....	....	....	....	....	....	....	....
of which: Short-term	4 742	....	....	....	....	....	....	....	....
Banks	4 743	....	....	....	....	....	....	....	....
of which: Short-term	4 745	....	....	....	....	....	....	....	....
Other sectors	4 746	....	....	....	....	....	....	....	....
of which: Short-term	4 748	....	....	....	....	....	....	....	....
Liabilities	4 753	4.1	47.6	−75.2	83.3	47.7	....	....	−66.3
Trade credits	4 756	....	....	58.9	....	....	....	....	....
General government	4 757	....	....	58.9	....	....	....	....	....
of which: Short-term	4 759	....	....	....	....	....	....	....	....
Other sectors	4 760	....	....	....	....	....	....	....	....
of which: Short-term	4 762	....	....	....	....	....	....	....	....
Loans	4 764	24.1	45.3	−135.5	122.0	38.8	....	....	75.0
Monetary authorities	4 765	−7.9	14.8	5.7	−14.8	−19.5	....	....	−10.4
of which: Use of Fund credit and loans from the Fund..	4 766	−7.9	14.8	5.7	−14.8	−19.5	....	....	−10.4
of which: Short-term	4 768	....	....	....	....	....	....	....	....
General government	4 769	63.3	88.0	−96.7	137.2	58.3	....	....	74.4
of which: Short-term	4 771	....	....	....	....	....	....	....	....
Banks	4 772	−.5	....	....	....	....	....	....	....
of which: Short-term	4 774	....	....	....	....	....	....	....	....
Other sectors	4 775	−30.8	−57.5	−44.5	−.4	....	....	....	11.0
of which: Short-term	4 777	10.9	4.9	....	26.5	....	....	....	20.0
Currency and deposits	4 780	−21.3	−13.0	1.6	−4.2	3.2	....	....	−.2
Monetary authorities	4 781	1.4	−.6	1.6	....	−.1	....	....	−.6
General government	4 782	....	....	....	....	....	....	....	....
Banks	4 783	−22.6	−12.4	....	−4.2	3.3	....	....	.4
Other sectors	4 784	....	....	....	....	....	....	....	....
Other liabilities	4 786	1.3	15.4	−.2	−34.6	5.7	....	....	−141.1
Monetary authorities	4 787	−2.2	14.0	....	2.0	3.0	....	....	−82.5
of which: Short-term	4 789	−2.2	14.0	....	2.0	3.0	....	....	−82.5
General government	4 790	3.5	1.4	−.2	−36.6	2.7	....	....	−58.5
of which: Short-term	4 792	3.5	1.4	−.2	−32.5	2.7	....	....	−58.5
Banks	4 793	....	....	....	....	....	....	....	....
of which: Short-term	4 795	....	....	....	....	....	....	....	....
Other sectors	4 796	....	....	....	....	....	....	....	....
of which: Short-term	4 798	....	....	....	....	....	....	....	....
E. RESERVE ASSETS	4 802	50.5	−3.9	75.7	131.5	11.8	....	....	8.7
Monetary gold	4 812	−1.6	3.8	84.6	90.7	−1.1	....	....	−1.8
Special drawing rights	4 811	.9	−.5	−.7	1.5	.2	....	....	−12.0
Reserve position in the Fund	4 810	....	....	....	....	....	....	....	....
Foreign exchange	4 803	51.1	−7.2	−8.2	39.4	12.7	....	....	22.5
Other claims	4 813	....	....	....	....	....	....	....	....
NET ERRORS AND OMISSIONS	4 998	83.9	−2.2	143.1	−157.1	68.6	....	....	117.4

Table 3. INTERNATIONAL INVESTMENT POSITION (End-period stocks), 2000–2007

(Millions of U.S. dollars)

	Code	2000	2001	2002	2003	2004	2005	2006	2007
ASSETS	8 995 C.	....	....	....	....	....	....	....	**74.6**
Direct investment abroad	8 505 ..	....	....	....	....	....	....	....	....
Equity capital and reinvested earnings	8 506 ..	....	....	....	....	....	....	....	....
Claims on affiliated enterprises	8 507 ..	....	....	....	....	....	....	....	....
Liabilities to affiliated enterprises	8 508 ..	....	....	....	....	....	....	....	....
Other capital	8 530 ..	....	....	....	....	....	....	....	....
Claims on affiliated enterprises	8 535 ..	....	....	....	....	....	....	....	....
Liabilities to affiliated enterprises	8 540 ..	....	....	....	....	....	....	....	....
Portfolio investment	8 602 ..	....	....	....	....	....	....	....	**8.3**
Equity securities	8 610 ..	....	....	....	....	....	....	....	....
Monetary authorities	8 611 ..	....	....	....	....	....	....	....	....
General government	8 612 ..	....	....	....	....	....	....	....	....
Banks	8 613 ..	....	....	....	....	....	....	....	....
Other sectors	8 614 ..	....	....	....	....	....	....	....	....
Debt securities	8 619 ..	....	....	....	....	....	....	....	8.3
Bonds and notes	8 620 ..	....	....	....	....	....	....	....	8.3
Monetary authorities	8 621 ..	....	....	....	....	....	....	....	8.3
General government	8 622 ..	....	....	....	....	....	....	....	....
Banks	8 623 ..	....	....	....	....	....	....	....	....
Other sectors	8 624 ..	....	....	....	....	....	....	....	....
Money market instruments	8 630 ..	....	....	....	....	....	....	....	....
Monetary authorities	8 631 ..	....	....	....	....	....	....	....	....
General government	8 632 ..	....	....	....	....	....	....	....	....
Banks	8 633 ..	....	....	....	....	....	....	....	....
Other sectors	8 634 ..	....	....	....	....	....	....	....	....
Financial derivatives	8 900 ..	....	....	....	....	....	....	....	....
Monetary authorities	8 901 ..	....	....	....	....	....	....	....	....
General government	8 902 ..	....	....	....	....	....	....	....	....
Banks	8 903 ..	....	....	....	....	....	....	....	....
Other sectors	8 904 ..	....	....	....	....	....	....	....	....
Other investment	8 703 ..	....	....	....	....	....	....	....	**33.2**
Trade credits	8 706 ..	....	....	....	....	....	....	....	....
General government	8 707 ..	....	....	....	....	....	....	....	....
of which: Short-term	8 709 ..	....	....	....	....	....	....	....	....
Other sectors	8 710 ..	....	....	....	....	....	....	....	....
of which: Short-term	8 712 ..	....	....	....	....	....	....	....	....
Loans	8 714 ..	....	....	....	....	....	....	....	....
Monetary authorities	8 715 ..	....	....	....	....	....	....	....	....
of which: Short-term	8 718 ..	....	....	....	....	....	....	....	....
General government	8 719 ..	....	....	....	....	....	....	....	....
of which: Short-term	8 721 ..	....	....	....	....	....	....	....	....
Banks	8 722 ..	....	....	....	....	....	....	....	....
of which: Short-term	8 724 ..	....	....	....	....	....	....	....	....
Other sectors	8 725 ..	....	....	....	....	....	....	....	....
of which: Short-term	8 727 ..	....	....	....	....	....	....	....	....
Currency and deposits	8 730 ..	....	....	....	....	....	....	....	39.8
Monetary authorities	8 731 ..	....	....	....	....	....	....	....	....
General government	8 732 ..	....	....	....	....	....	....	....	....
Banks	8 733 ..	....	....	....	....	....	....	....	39.8
Other sectors	8 734 ..	....	....	....	....	....	....	....	....
Other assets	8 736 ..	....	....	....	....	....	....	....	−6.6
Monetary authorities	8 737 ..	....	....	....	....	....	....	....	−6.6
of which: Short-term	8 739 ..	....	....	....	....	....	....	....	*−6.6*
General government	8 740 ..	....	....	....	....	....	....	....	....
of which: Short-term	8 742 ..	....	....	....	....	....	....	....	....
Banks	8 743 ..	....	....	....	....	....	....	....	....
of which: Short-term	8 745 ..	....	....	....	....	....	....	....	....
Other sectors	8 746 ..	....	....	....	....	....	....	....	....
of which: Short-term	8 748 ..	....	....	....	....	....	....	....	....
Reserve assets	8 802 ..	....	....	....	....	....	....	....	**33.1**
Monetary gold	8 812 ..	....	....	....	....	....	....	....	−1.8
Special drawing rights	8 811 ..	.2	.8	1.7	.2	....	....	....	12.2
Reserve position in the Fund	8 810 ..	.1	.1	.1	.1	.1	.1	.1	.1
Foreign exchange	8 803 ..	....	....	....	....	....	....	....	22.5
Other claims	8 813 ..	....	....	....	....	....	....	....	....

Table 3 (Concluded). INTERNATIONAL INVESTMENT POSITION (End-period stocks), 2000–2007

(Millions of U.S. dollars)

	Code	2000	2001	2002	2003	2004	2005	2006	2007
LIABILITIES	8 995 D.	....	....	....	....	....	....	....	**284.6**
Direct investment in Guinea	8 555 ..	....	....	....	....	....	....	....	**385.9**
Equity capital and reinvested earnings	8 556 ..	....	....	....	....	....	....	....	385.9
Claims on direct investors	8 557 ..	....	....	....	....	....	....	....	385.9
Liabilities to direct investors	8 558 ..	....	....	....	....	....	....	....	....
Other capital	8 580 ..	....	....	....	....	....	....	....	....
Claims on direct investors	8 585 ..	....	....	....	....	....	....	....	....
Liabilities to direct investors	8 590 ..	....	....	....	....	....	....	....	....
Portfolio investment	8 652 ..	....	....	....	....	....	....	....	**−138.1**
Equity securities	8 660 ..	....	....	....	....	....	....	....	....
Banks	8 663 ..	....	....	....	....	....	....	....	....
Other sectors	8 664 ..	....	....	....	....	....	....	....	....
Debt securities	8 669 ..	....	....	....	....	....	....	....	−138.1
Bonds and notes	8 670 ..	....	....	....	....	....	....	....	−138.1
Monetary authorities	8 671 ..	....	....	....	....	....	....	....	....
General government	8 672 ..	....	....	....	....	....	....	....	−138.1
Banks	8 673 ..	....	....	....	....	....	....	....	....
Other sectors	8 674 ..	....	....	....	....	....	....	....	....
Money market instruments	8 680 ..	....	....	....	....	....	....	....	....
Monetary authorities	8 681 ..	....	....	....	....	....	....	....	....
General government	8 682 ..	....	....	....	....	....	....	....	....
Banks	8 683 ..	....	....	....	....	....	....	....	....
Other sectors	8 684 ..	....	....	....	....	....	....	....	....
Financial derivatives	8 905 ..	....	....	....	....	....	....	....	....
Monetary authorities	8 906 ..	....	....	....	....	....	....	....	....
General government	8 907 ..	....	....	....	....	....	....	....	....
Banks	8 908 ..	....	....	....	....	....	....	....	....
Other sectors	8 909 ..	....	....	....	....	....	....	....	....
Other investment	8 753 ..	....	....	....	....	....	....	....	**36.8**
Trade credits	8 756 ..	....	....	....	....	....	....	....	....
General government	8 757 ..	....	....	....	....	....	....	....	....
of which: Short-term	8 759 ..	....	....	....	....	....	....	....	....
Other sectors	8 760 ..	....	....	....	....	....	....	....	....
of which: Short-term	8 762 ..	....	....	....	....	....	....	....	....
Loans	8 764 ..	....	....	....	....	....	....	....	150.0
Monetary authorities	8 765 ..	....	....	....	....	....	....	....	64.7
of which: Use of Fund credit and loans from the Fund	8 766 ..	*112.9*	*123.3*	*139.0*	*136.3*	*121.9*	*87.3*	*72.1*	*64.7*
of which: Short-term	8 768 ..	....	....	....	....	....	....	....	....
General government	8 769 ..	....	....	....	....	....	....	....	74.4
of which: Short-term	8 771 ..	....	....	....	....	....	....	....	....
Banks	8 772 ..	....	....	....	....	....	....	....	....
of which: Short-term	8 774 ..	....	....	....	....	....	....	....	....
Other sectors	8 775 ..	....	....	....	....	....	....	....	11.0
of which: Short-term	8 777 ..	....	....	....	....	....	....	....	*20.0*
Currency and deposits	8 780 ..	....	....	....	....	....	....	....	−.2
Monetary authorities	8 781 ..	....	....	....	....	....	....	....	−.6
General government	8 782 ..	....	....	....	....	....	....	....	....
Banks	8 783 ..	....	....	....	....	....	....	....	.4
Other sectors	8 784 ..	....	....	....	....	....	....	....	....
Other liabilities	8 786 ..	....	....	....	....	....	....	....	−113.0
Monetary authorities	8 787 ..	....	....	....	....	....	....	....	−68.5
of which: Short-term	8 789 ..	....	....	....	....	....	....	....	*−68.5*
General government	8 790 ..	....	....	....	....	....	....	....	−44.5
of which: Short-term	8 792 ..	....	....	....	....	....	....	....	*−44.5*
Banks	8 793 ..	....	....	....	....	....	....	....	....
of which: Short-term	8 795 ..	....	....	....	....	....	....	....	....
Other sectors	8 796 ..	....	....	....	....	....	....	....	....
of which: Short-term	8 798 ..	....	....	....	....	....	....	....	....
NET INTERNATIONAL INVESTMENT POSITION	8 995 ..	....	....	....	....	....	....	....	**−210.0**
Conversion rates: Guinean francs per U.S. dollar (end of period)	0 102 ..	1,882.3	1,988.3	1,976.0	2,000.0	2,550.0	4,500.0	....	....

Table 1. ANALYTIC PRESENTATION, 2000–2007

(Millions of U.S. dollars)

	Code	2000	2001	2002	2003	2004	2005	2006	2007
A. Current Account[1]	4 993 Z.	....	−26.89	−8.69	−6.51	−13.22	....	....	....
Goods: exports f.o.b.	2 100 ..	....	62.89	54.38	65.01	75.77	....	....	....
Goods: imports f.o.b.	3 100 ..	....	−61.72	−58.50	−65.30	−82.87	....	....	....
Balance on Goods	4 100 ..	....	*1.17*	*−4.12*	*−.29*	*−7.11*	....	....	....
Services: credit	2 200 ..	....	4.46	6.50	6.00	7.70	....	....	....
Services: debit	3 200 ..	....	−30.27	−27.48	−36.25	−44.32	....	....	....
Balance on Goods and Services	4 991 ..	....	*−24.63*	*−25.10*	*−30.54*	*−43.73*	....	....	....
Income: credit	2 300 ..	....	.57	1.29	2.08	1.30	....	....	....
Income: debit	3 300 ..	....	−12.58	−10.05	−10.91	−10.94	....	....	....
Balance on Goods, Services, and Income	4 992 ..	....	*−36.64*	*−33.86*	*−39.38*	*−53.36*	....	....	....
Current transfers: credit	2 379 Z.	....	9.76	30.22	39.69	47.36	....	....	....
Current transfers: debit	3 379 ..	....	−.01	−5.05	−6.83	−7.21	....	....	....
B. Capital Account[1]	4 994 Z.	....	25.33	38.86	42.82	27.40	....	....	....
Capital account: credit	2 994 Z.	....	25.05	40.36	42.82	27.44	....	....	....
Capital account: debit	3 994 ..	....	.28	−1.50	....	−.05	....	....	....
Total, Groups A Plus B	4 981 ..	....	*−1.57*	*30.16*	*36.31*	*14.18*	....	....	....
C. Financial Account[1]	4 995 W.	....	−17.34	−21.40	−13.06	1.18	....	....	....
Direct investment abroad	4 505 ..	....	.40	−1.02	−.52	7.50	....	....	....
Direct investment in Guinea-Bissau	4 555 Z.	....	.40	3.56	4.01	1.73	....	....	....
Portfolio investment assets	4 602 ..	....	....	1.15	.60	.95	....	....	....
Equity securities	4 610 ..	....	....	1.15	....	.91	....	....	....
Debt securities	4 619 ..	....	....	....	.60	.04	....	....	....
Portfolio investment liabilities	4 652 Z.	....	....	.65	.34	....	....	....	....
Equity securities	4 660 ..	....	....	.65	.34	....	....	....	....
Debt securities	4 669 Z.	....	....	....	....	....	....	....	....
Financial derivatives	4 910 ..	....	....	....	....	....	....	....	....
Financial derivatives assets	4 900 ..	....	....	....	....	....	....	....	....
Financial derivatives liabilities	4 905 ..	....	....	....	....	....	....	....	....
Other investment assets	4 703 ..	....	4.21	−6.85	−18.99	−7.65	....	....	....
Monetary authorities	4 701 ..	....	....	....	....	....	....	....	....
General government	4 704 ..	....	....	....	....	....	....	....	....
Banks	4 705 ..	....	4.21	−3.73	−16.33	−2.68	....	....	....
Other sectors	4 728 ..	....	....	−3.12	−2.66	−4.98	....	....	....
Other investment liabilities	4 753 W.	....	−22.34	−18.89	1.50	−1.35	....	....	....
Monetary authorities	4 753 WA	....	1.08	−1.27	−.45	1.28	....	....	....
General government	4 753 ZB	....	−20.08	−29.27	7.63	.51	....	....	....
Banks	4 753 ZC	....	−4.12	−.15	.46	.26	....	....	....
Other sectors	4 753 ZD	....	.78	11.80	−6.14	−3.40	....	....	....
Total, Groups A Through C	4 983 ..	....	*−18.91*	*8.76*	*23.24*	*15.35*	....	....	....
D. Net Errors and Omissions	4 998 ..	....	5.86	−2.90	6.19	−4.16	....	....	....
Total, Groups A Through D	4 984 ..	....	*−13.04*	*5.86*	*29.44*	*11.19*	....	....	....
E. Reserves and Related Items	4 802 A.	....	13.04	−5.86	−29.44	−11.19	....	....	....
Reserve assets	4 802 ..	....	−6.34	−18.00	−38.22	−32.94	....	....	....
Use of Fund credit and loans	4 766 ..	....	−.67	−1.60	−4.85	−5.33	....	....	....
Exceptional financing	4 920 ..	....	20.05	13.73	13.64	27.08	....	....	....
Conversion rates: CFA francs per U.S. dollar	0 101 ..	711.98	733.04	696.99	581.20	528.28	527.47	522.89	479.27

[1] Excludes components that have been classified in the categories of Group E.

Table 2. STANDARD PRESENTATION, 2000–2007

(Millions of U.S. dollars)

	Code	2000	2001	2002	2003	2004	2005	2006	2007
CURRENT ACCOUNT..............................	4 993 ..	....	−11.13	−1.27	−.33	13.86	....	....	....
A. GOODS..............................	4 100 ..	....	1.17	−4.12	−.29	−7.11	....	....	....
Credit..............................	2 100 ..	....	62.89	54.38	65.01	75.77	....	....	....
General merchandise: exports f.o.b..............................	2 110 ..	....	62.89	54.36	64.97	75.71	....	....	....
Goods for processing: exports f.o.b..............................	2 150 ..	....	....	....	....	....	....	....	....
Repairs on goods..............................	2 160 ..	....	....	....	....	....	....	....	....
Goods procured in ports by carriers..............................	2 170 ..	....	....	.02	.04	.05	....	....	....
Nonmonetary gold..............................	2 180 ..	....	....	....	....	....	....	....	....
Debit..............................	3 100 ..	....	−61.72	−58.50	−65.30	−82.87	....	....	....
General merchandise: imports f.o.b..............................	3 110 ..	....	−61.72	−58.50	−65.30	−82.87	....	....	....
Goods for processing: imports f.o.b..............................	3 150 ..	....	....	....	....	....	....	....	....
Repairs on goods..............................	3 160 ..	....	....	....	....	....	....	....	....
Goods procured in ports by carriers..............................	3 170 ..	....	....	....	....	....	....	....	....
Nonmonetary gold..............................	3 180 ..	....	....	....	....	....	....	....	....
B. SERVICES..............................	4 200 ..	....	−25.80	−20.98	−30.25	−36.62	....	....	....
Total credit	2 200 ..	....	*4.46*	*6.50*	*6.00*	*7.70*	....	....	....
Total debit	3 200 ..	....	*−30.27*	*−27.48*	*−36.25*	*−44.32*	....	....	....
Transportation services, credit..............................	2 205 ..	....	....	.12	.77	1.33	....	....	....
Passenger	2 850 ..	....	....	....	*.64*	*1.18*	....	....	....
Freight	2 851 ..	....	....	....	....	....	....	....	....
Other	2 852 ..	....	....	*.12*	*.13*	*.15*	....	....	....
Sea transport, passenger	2 207 ..	....					....	....	....
Sea transport, freight..............................	2 208 ..	....					....	....	....
Sea transport, other..............................	2 209 ..	....					....	....	....
Air transport, passenger.	2 211 ..	....					....	....	....
Air transport, freight.	2 212 ..	....					....	....	....
Air transport, other.	2 213 ..	....		.12	.13	.15	....	....	....
Other transport, passenger..............................	2 215 ..	....			.64	1.18	....	....	....
Other transport, freight..	2 216 ..	....					....	....	....
Other transport, other.....	2 217 ..	....					....	....	....
Transportation services, debit..............................	3 205 ..	....	−27.15	−15.40	−21.29	−22.71	....	....	....
Passenger	3 850 ..	....	*−2.73*	*−5.11*	*−8.02*	*−9.21*	....	....	....
Freight	3 851 ..	....	*−24.42*	*−10.30*	*−13.26*	*−13.49*	....	....	....
Other	3 852 ..	....	....	....	....	....	....	....	....
Sea transport, passenger..............................	3 207 ..	....	....	....	....	....	....	....	....
Sea transport, freight..............................	3 208 ..	....	−21.14	−7.52	−10.99	−8.35	....	....	....
Sea transport, other..............................	3 209 ..	....	....	....	....	....	....	....	....
Air transport, passenger..............................	3 211 ..	....	−2.73	−5.11	−6.73	−7.93	....	....	....
Air transport, freight..............................	3 212 ..	....	....	....	....	....	....	....	....
Air transport, other..............................	3 213 ..	....	....	....	....	....	....	....	....
Other transport, passenger..............................	3 215 ..	....	....	....	−1.29	−1.29	....	....	....
Other transport, freight..............................	3 216 ..	....	−3.27	−2.77	−2.28	−5.14	....	....	....
Other transport, other..............................	3 217 ..	....	....	....	....	....	....	....	....
Travel, credit..............................	2 236 ..	....	2.73	2.25	1.84	.96	....	....	....
Business travel..............................	2 237 ..	....	....	.82	.80	.77	....	....	....
Personal travel..............................	2 240 ..	....	2.73	1.43	1.03	.19	....	....	....
Travel, debit..............................	3 236 ..	....	−2.78	−5.10	−13.28	−13.13	....	....	....
Business travel..............................	3 237 ..	....	....	−1.31	−5.39	−2.81	....	....	....
Personal travel..............................	3 240 ..	....	−2.78	−3.78	−7.90	−10.32	....	....	....
Other services, credit..............................	2 200 BA ..	....	1.73	4.13	3.39	5.41	....	....	....
Communications..............................	2 245 ..	....	....	2.28	.07	.08	....	....	....
Construction..............................	2 249 ..	....	....	....	....	....	....	....	....
Insurance..............................	2 253 ..	....	.08	.63	.01	.02	....	....	....
Financial..............................	2 260 ..	....	....	.02	.73	1.11	....	....	....
Computer and information..............................	2 262 ..	....	....	....	....	....	....	....	....
Royalties and licence fees..............................	2 266 ..	....	....	....	....	....	....	....	....
Other business services..............................	2 268 ..	....	.76	1.00	1.54	2.30	....	....	....
Personal, cultural, and recreational..............................	2 287 ..	....	....	....	....	....	....	....	....
Government, n.i.e..............................	2 291 ..	....	.90	.21	1.03	1.89	....	....	....
Other services, debit..............................	3 200 BA ..	....	−.34	−6.98	−1.68	−8.49	....	....	....
Communications..............................	3 245 ..	....	−.15	−5.03	−.34	−3.97	....	....	....
Construction..............................	3 249 ..	....	−.03	−.06	....	−.01	....	....	....
Insurance..............................	3 253 ..	....	−.02	−.28	−.22	−.12	....	....	....
Financial..............................	3 260 ..	....	−.03	−.03	−.15	−.05	....	....	....
Computer and informat on..............................	3 262 ..	....	−.06	−.69	−.04	−.06	....	....	....
Royalties and licence fees..............................	3 266 ..	....	....	−.07	....	....	....	....	....
Other business services..............................	3 268 ..	....	−.05	−.16	−.58	−2.38	....	....	....
Personal, cultural, and recreational..............................	3 287 ..	....	....	....	....	....	....	....	....
Government, n.i.e..............................	3 291 ..	....	....	−.66	−.35	−1.89	....	....	....

Table 2 (Continued). STANDARD PRESENTATION, 2000–2007

(Millions of U.S. dollars)

	Code	2000	2001	2002	2003	2004	2005	2006	2007
C. INCOME	4 300	....	−12.01	−8.76	−8.83	−9.63	....	....	....
Total credit	2 300	....	*.57*	*1.29*	*2.08*	*1.30*	....	....	....
Total debit	3 300	....	*−12.58*	*−10.05*	*−10.91*	*−10.94*	....	....	....
Compensation of employees, credit	2 310	....	.48	.23	1.83	.79	....	....	....
Compensation of employees, debit	3 310	....	....	−.37	−.17	−.02	....	....	....
Investment income, credit	2 320	....	.09	1.06	.25	.51	....	....	....
Direct investment income	2 330	....	....	.02	....	....	....	....	....
Dividends and distributed branch profits	2 332	....	....	....	....	....	....	....	....
Reinvested earnings and undistributed branch profits	2 333	....	....	.02	....	....	....	....	....
Income on debt (interest)	2 334	....	....	....	....	....	....	....	....
Portfolio investment income	2 339	....	.08	....	....	....	....	....	....
Income on equity	2 340	....	....	....	....	....	....	....	....
Income on bonds and notes	2 350	....	.08	....	....	....	....	....	....
Income on money market instruments	2 360	....	....	....	....	....	....	....	....
Other investment income	2 370	....	.01	1.04	.25	.51	....	....	....
Investment income, debit	3 320	....	−12.58	−9.68	−10.74	−10.92	....	....	....
Direct investment income	3 330	....	....	−.68	−.16	−.05	....	....	....
Dividends and distributed branch profits	3 332	....	....	....	....	....	....	....	....
Reinvested earnings and undistributed branch profits	3 333	....	....	−.68	−.16	−.05	....	....	....
Income on debt (interest)	3 334	....	....	....	....	....	....	....	....
Portfolio investment income	3 339	....	−12.58	....	−.60	....	....	....	....
Income on equity	3 340	....	−1.23	....	−.60	....	....	....	....
Income on bonds and notes	3 350	....	−11.35	....	....	....	....	....	....
Income on money market instruments	3 360	....	....	....	....	....	....	....	....
Other investment income	3 370	....	....	−9.00	−9.98	−10.87	....	....	....
D. CURRENT TRANSFERS	4 379	....	25.51	32.59	39.05	67.23	....	....	....
Credit	2 379	....	25.52	37.64	45.87	74.44	....	....	....
General government	2 380	....	15.76	19.44	18.82	43.57	....	....	....
Other sectors	2 390	....	9.76	18.20	27.06	30.87	....	....	....
Workers' remittances	2 391	....	9.55	17.40	21.30	26.91	....	....	....
Other current transfers	2 392	....	.21	.80	5.76	3.96	....	....	....
Debit	3 379	....	−.01	−5.05	−6.83	−7.21	....	....	....
General government	3 380	....	....	....	....	....	....	....	....
Other sectors	3 390	....	−.01	−5.05	−6.83	−7.21	....	....	....
Workers' remittances	3 391	....	....	−5.05	−6.32	−5.36	....	....	....
Other current transfers	3 392	....	−.01	−.01	−.51	−1.85	....	....	....
CAPITAL AND FINANCIAL ACCOUNT	4 996	....	5.27	4.17	−5.86	−9.70	....	....	....
CAPITAL ACCOUNT	4 994	....	25.33	38.86	42.82	27.40	....	....	....
Total credit	2 994	....	*25.05*	*40.36*	*42.82*	*27.44*	....	....	....
Total debit	3 994	....	*.28*	*−1.50*	....	*−.05*	....	....	....
Capital transfers, credit	2 400	....	25.05	40.36	42.82	27.44	....	....	....
General government	2 401	....	24.83	36.81	36.01	23.15	....	....	....
Debt forgiveness	2 402	....	....	....	....	....	....	....	....
Other capital transfers	2 410	....	24.83	36.81	36.01	23.15	....	....	....
Other sectors	2 430	....	.22	3.55	6.81	4.29	....	....	....
Migrants' transfers	2 431	....	....	....	....	....	....	....	....
Debt forgiveness	2 432	....	....	....	....	....	....	....	....
Other capital transfers	2 440	....	.22	3.55	6.81	4.29	....	....	....
Capital transfers, debit	3 400	....	.28	−1.50	....	....	....	....	....
General government	3 401	....	.28	....	....	....	....	....	....
Debt forgiveness	3 402	....	....	....	....	....	....	....	....
Other capital transfers	3 410	....	.28	....	....	....	....	....	....
Other sectors	3 430	....	....	−1.50	....	....	....	....	....
Migrants' transfers	3 431	....	....	....	....	....	....	....	....
Debt forgiveness	3 432	....	....	....	....	....	....	....	....
Other capital transfers	3 440	....	....	−1.50	....	....	....	....	....
Nonproduced nonfinancial assets, credit	2 480	....	....	....	....	....	....	....	....
Nonproduced nonfinancial assets, debit	3 480	....	....	....	....	−.05	....	....	....

Table 2 (Continued). STANDARD PRESENTATION, 2000–2007

(Millions of U.S. dollars)

	Code	2000	2001	2002	2003	2004	2005	2006	2007
FINANCIAL ACCOUNT	4 995 ..	....	−20.06	−34.69	−48.68	−37.10	....	....	....
A. DIRECT INVESTMENT	4 500 ..	....	.79	2.53	3.49	9.23	....	....	....
Direct investment abroad	4 505 ..	....	.40	−1.02	−.52	7.50	....	....	....
Equity capital	4 510 ..	....	.40	−1.00	−.52	7.76	....	....	....
Claims on affiliated enterprises	4 515 ..	....	.40	−1.00	−.52	8.04	....	....	....
Liabilities to affiliated enterprises	4 520 ..	....	....	....	....	−.28	....	....	....
Reinvested earnings	4 525 ..	....	....	−.02	....	....	....	....	....
Other capital	4 530 ..	....	....	....	....	−.26	....	....	....
Claims on affiliated enterprises	4 535 ..	....	....	....	....	−.26	....	....	....
Liabilities to affiliated enterprises	4 540 ..	....	....	....	....	....	....	....	....
Direct investment in Guinea-Bissau	4 555 ..	....	.40	3.55	4.01	1.73	....	....	....
Equity capital	4 560 ..	....	.40	.73	1.24	2.08	....	....	....
Claims on direct investors	4 565 ..	....	.40	.74	1.24	2.08	....	....	....
Liabilities to direct investors	4 570 ..	....	....	−.02	....	....	....	....	....
Reinvested earnings	4 575 ..	....	....	.68	.16	.05	....	....	....
Other capital	4 580 ..	....	....	2.14	2.61	−.40	....	....	....
Claims on direct investors	4 585 ..	....	....	....	....	−.47	....	....	....
Liabilities to direct investors	4 590 ..	....	....	2.14	2.61	.08	....	....	....
B. PORTFOLIO INVESTMENT	4 600 ..	....	....	1.80	.94	.95	....	....	....
Assets	4 602 ..	....	....	1.15	.60	.95	....	....	....
Equity securities	4 610 ..	....	....	1.15	....	.91	....	....	....
Monetary authorities	4 611 ..	....	....	....	....	....	....	....	....
General government	4 612 ..	....	....	....	....	....	....	....	....
Banks	4 613 ..	....	....	....	....	.91	....	....	....
Other sectors	4 614 ..	....	....	1.15	....	....	....	....	....
Debt securities	4 619 ..	....	....	....	.60	.04	....	....	....
Bonds and notes	4 620 ..	....	....	....	.60	.04	....	....	....
Monetary authorities	4 621 ..	....	....	....	....	....	....	....	....
General government	4 622 ..	....	....	....	....	....	....	....	....
Banks	4 623 ..	....	....	....	.04	.04	....	....	....
Other sectors	4 624 ..	....	....	....	.56	....	....	....	....
Money market instruments	4 630 ..	....	....	....	....	....	....	....	....
Monetary authorities	4 631 ..	....	....	....	....	....	....	....	....
General government	4 632 ..	....	....	....	....	....	....	....	....
Banks	4 633 ..	....	....	....	....	....	....	....	....
Other sectors	4 634 ..	....	....	....	....	....	....	....	....
Liabilities	4 652 ..	....	....	.65	.34	....	....	....	....
Equity securities	4 660 ..	....	....	.65	.34	....	....	....	....
Banks	4 663 ..	....	....	.65	.34	....	....	....	....
Other sectors	4 664 ..	....	....	....	....	....	....	....	....
Debt securities	4 669 ..	....	....	....	....	....	....	....	....
Bonds and notes	4 670 ..	....	....	....	....	....	....	....	....
Monetary authorities	4 671 ..	....	....	....	....	....	....	....	....
General government	4 672 ..	....	....	....	....	....	....	....	....
Banks	4 673 ..	....	....	....	....	....	....	....	....
Other sectors	4 674 ..	....	....	....	....	....	....	....	....
Money market instruments	4 680 ..	....	....	....	....	....	....	....	....
Monetary authorities	4 681 ..	....	....	....	....	....	....	....	....
General government	4 682 ..	....	....	....	....	....	....	....	....
Banks	4 683 ..	....	....	....	....	....	....	....	....
Other sectors	4 684 ..	....	....	....	....	....	....	....	....
C. FINANCIAL DERIVATIVES	4 910 ..	....	....	....	....	....	....	....	....
Monetary authorities	4 911 ..	....	....	....	....	....	....	....	....
General government	4 912 ..	....	....	....	....	....	....	....	....
Banks	4 913 ..	....	....	....	....	....	....	....	....
Other sectors	4 914 ..	....	....	....	....	....	....	....	....
Assets	4 900 ..	....	....	....	....	....	....	....	....
Monetary authorities	4 901 ..	....	....	....	....	....	....	....	....
General government	4 902 ..	....	....	....	....	....	....	....	....
Banks	4 903 ..	....	....	....	....	....	....	....	....
Other sectors	4 904 ..	....	....	....	....	....	....	....	....
Liabilities	4 905 ..	....	....	....	....	....	....	....	....
Monetary authorities	4 906 ..	....	....	....	....	....	....	....	....
General government	4 907 ..	....	....	....	....	....	....	....	....
Banks	4 908 ..	....	....	....	....	....	....	....	....
Other sectors	4 909 ..	....	....	....	....	....	....	....	....

Table 2 (Concluded). STANDARD PRESENTATION, 2000–2007

(Millions of U.S. dollars)

	Code	2000	2001	2002	2003	2004	2005	2006	2007
D. OTHER INVESTMENT	4 700	....	**−14.51**	**−21.01**	**−14.89**	**−14.33**	....	....	....
Assets	4 703	....	**4.21**	**−6.85**	**−18.99**	**−7.65**	....	....	....
Trade credits	4 706	....	....	−.41	−.42	−.05	....	....	....
General government	4 707	....	....	....	....	....	....	....	....
of which: Short-term	4 709	....	....	....	....	....	....	....	....
Other sectors	4 710	....	....	−.41	−.42	−.05	....	....	....
of which: Short-term	4 712	....	....	−.41	−.42	−.05	....	....	....
Loans	4 714	....	4.39	−4.25	....	....	....	....	....
Monetary authorities	4 715	....	....	....	....	....	....	....	....
of which: Short-term	4 718	....	....	....	....	....	....	....	....
General government	4 719	....	....	....	....	....	....	....	....
of which: Short-term	4 721	....	....	....	....	....	....	....	....
Banks	4 722	....	4.39	−4.25	....	....	....	....	....
of which: Short-term	4 724	....	4.39	−4.25	....	....	....	....	....
Other sectors	4 725	....	....	....	....	....	....	....	....
of which: Short-term	4 727	....	....	....	....	....	....	....	....
Currency and deposits	4 730	....	−.61	−2.19	−18.57	−7.53	....	....	....
Monetary authorities	4 731	....	....	....	....	....	....	....	....
General government	4 732	....	....	....	....	....	....	....	....
Banks	4 733	....	−.61	.52	−16.33	−2.61	....	....	....
Other sectors	4 734	....	....	−2.71	−2.24	−4.92	....	....	....
Other assets	4 736	....	.43	....	....	−.08	....	....	....
Monetary authorities	4 737	....	....	....	....	....	....	....	....
of which: Short-term	4 739	....	....	....	....	....	....	....	....
General government	4 740	....	....	....	....	....	....	....	....
of which: Short-term	4 742	....	....	....	....	....	....	....	....
Banks	4 743	....	.43	....	....	−.06	....	....	....
of which: Short-term	4 745	....	....	....	....	−.06	....	....	....
Other sectors	4 746	....	....	....	....	−.01	....	....	....
of which: Short-term	4 748	....	....	....	....	−.01	....	....	....
Liabilities	4 753	....	**−18.72**	**−14.16**	**4.10**	**−6.68**	....	....	....
Trade credits	4 756	....	....	11.79	−7.78	.33	....	....	....
General government	4 757	....	....	....	....	....	....	....	....
of which: Short-term	4 759	....	....	....	....	....	....	....	....
Other sectors	4 760	....	....	11.79	−7.78	.33	....	....	....
of which: Short-term	4 762	....	....	11.79	−7.78	.33	....	....	....
Loans	4 764	....	−20.58	−24.69	10.19	−8.76	....	....	....
Monetary authorities	4 765	....	−.67	−1.60	−4.85	−5.33	....	....	....
of which: Use of Fund credit and loans from the Fund	4 766	....	−.67	−1.60	−4.85	−5.33	....	....	....
of which: Short-term	4 768	....	....	....	....	....	....	....	....
General government	4 769	....	−16.53	−22.94	15.08	.47	....	....	....
of which: Short-term	4 771	....	....	....	37.06	....	....	....	....
Banks	4 772	....	−3.38	−.15	−.03	....	....	....	....
of which: Short-term	4 774	....	−5.07	−.15	−.03	....	....	....	....
Other sectors	4 775	....	....	....	....	−3.90	....	....	....
of which: Short-term	4 777	....	....	....	....	−3.90	....	....	....
Currency and deposits	4 780	....	1.86	−1.33	1.58	−.89	....	....	....
Monetary authorities	4 781	....	1.86	−1.33	1.08	−.94	....	....	....
General government	4 782	....	....	....	....	.05	....	....	....
Banks	4 783	....	....	....	.50	....	....	....	....
Other sectors	4 784	....	....	....	....	....	....	....	....
Other liabilities	4 786	....	....	.07	.10	2.65	....	....	....
Monetary authorities	4 787	....	−.78	.06	−1.53	2.21	....	....	....
of which: Short-term	4 789	....	−.78	.06	−1.53	2.21	....	....	....
General government	4 790	....	....	....	....	....	....	....	....
of which: Short-term	4 792	....	....	....	....	....	....	....	....
Banks	4 793	....	....	....	....	.26	....	....	....
of which: Short-term	4 795	....	....	....	....	.26	....	....	....
Other sectors	4 796	....	.78	.01	1.63	.17	....	....	....
of which: Short-term	4 798	....	.78	.01	1.63	.17	....	....	....
E. RESERVE ASSETS	4 802	....	**−6.34**	**−18.00**	**−38.22**	**−32.94**	....	....	....
Monetary gold	4 812	....	....	....	....	....	....	....	....
Special drawing rights	4 811	....	−.17	−.16	−.74	.53	....	....	....
Reserve position in the Fund	4 810	....	....	....	....	....	....	....	....
Foreign exchange	4 803	....	−6.17	−17.83	−37.48	−33.48	....	....	....
Other claims	4 813	....	....	....	....	....	....	....	....
NET ERRORS AND OMISSIONS	4 998	....	**5.86**	**−2.90**	**6.19**	**−4.16**	....	....	....

Table 3. INTERNATIONAL INVESTMENT POSITION (End-period stocks), 2000–2007

(Millions of U.S. dollars)

	Code	2000	2001	2002	2003	2004	2005	2006	2007
ASSETS	8 995 C.	....	73.33	113.28	180.14	88.54	....	....	....
Direct investment abroad	8 505 ..	....	....	1.12	.58	.60	....	....	....
Equity capital and reinvested earnings	8 506 ..	....	....	1.12	.58	.31	....	....	....
Claims on affiliated enterprises	8 507 ..	....	....	1.12	.58	.31	....	....	....
Liabilities to affiliated enterprises	8 508 ..	....	....	....	....	....	....	....	....
Other capital	8 530 ..	....	....	....	....	.28	....	....	....
Claims on affiliated enterprises	8 535 ..	....	....	....	....	.28	....	....	....
Liabilities to affiliated enterprises	8 540 ..	....	....	....	....	....	....	....	....
Portfolio investment	8 602 ..	....	....	....	....	....	....	....	....
Equity securities	8 610 ..	....	....	....	....	....	....	....	....
Monetary authorities	8 611 ..	....	....	....	....	....	....	....	....
General government	8 612 ..	....	....	....	....	....	....	....	....
Banks	8 613 ..	....	....	....	....	....	....	....	....
Other sectors	8 614 ..	....	....	....	....	....	....	....	....
Debt securities	8 619 ..	....	....	....	....	....	....	....	....
Bonds and notes	8 620 ..	....	....	....	....	....	....	....	....
Monetary authorities	8 621 ..	....	....	....	....	....	....	....	....
General government	8 622 ..	....	....	....	....	....	....	....	....
Banks	8 623 ..	....	....	....	....	....	....	....	....
Other sectors	8 624 ..	....	....	....	....	....	....	....	....
Money market instruments	8 630 ..	....	....	....	....	....	....	....	....
Monetary authorities	8 631 ..	....	....	....	....	....	....	....	....
General government	8 632 ..	....	....	....	....	....	....	....	....
Banks	8 633 ..	....	....	....	....	....	....	....	....
Other sectors	8 634 ..	....	....	....	....	....	....	....	....
Financial derivatives	8 900 ..	....	....	....	....	....	....	....	....
Monetary authorities	8 901 ..	....	....	....	....	....	....	....	....
General government	8 902 ..	....	....	....	....	....	....	....	....
Banks	8 903 ..	....	....	....	....	....	....	....	....
Other sectors	8 904 ..	....	....	....	....	....	....	....	....
Other investment	8 703 ..	....	3.85	9.45	13.21	16.34	....	....	....
Trade credits	8 706 ..	....	....	.46	.47	.05	....	....	....
General government	8 707 ..	....	....	....	....	.05	....	....	....
of which: Short-term	8 709 ..	....	....	....	....	*.05*	....	....	....
Other sectors	8 710 ..	....	....	.46	.47	....	....	....	....
of which: Short-term	8 712 ..	....	....	*.46*	*.47*	....	....	....	....
Loans	8 714 ..	....	3.05	8.38	....	....	....	....	....
Monetary authorities	8 715 ..	....	....	....	....	....	....	....	....
of which: Short-term	8 718 ..	....	....	....	....	....	....	....	....
General government	8 719 ..	....	....	....	....	....	....	....	....
of which: Short-term	8 721 ..	....	....	....	....	....	....	....	....
Banks	8 722 ..	....	3.05	8.37	....	....	....	....	....
of which: Short-term	8 724 ..	....	*3.05*	*8.37*	....	....	....	....	....
Other sectors	8 725 ..	....	....	.02	....	....	....	....	....
of which: Short-term	8 727 ..	....	....	*.02*	....	....	....	....	....
Currency and deposits	8 730 ..	....	.81	.61	12.74	16.20	....	....	....
Monetary authorities	8 731 ..	....	....	....	....	....	....	....	....
General government	8 732 ..	....	....	....	....	....	....	....	....
Banks	8 733 ..	....	.81	.38	11.61	15.39	....	....	....
Other sectors	8 734 ..	....	....	.23	1.13	.81	....	....	....
Other assets	8 736 ..	....	....	....	....	.09	....	....	....
Monetary authorities	8 737 ..	....	....	....	....	....	....	....	....
of which: Short-term	8 739 ..	....	....	....	....	....	....	....	....
General government	8 740 ..	....	....	....	....	....	....	....	....
of which: Short-term	8 742 ..	....	....	....	....	....	....	....	....
Banks	8 743 ..	....	....	....	....	.07	....	....	....
of which: Short-term	8 745 ..	....	....	....	....	*.07*	....	....	....
Other sectors	8 746 ..	....	....	....	....	.01	....	....	....
of which: Short-term	8 748 ..	....	....	....	....	*.01*	....	....	....
Reserve assets	8 802 ..	....	69.48	102.71	166.35	71.61	....	....	....
Monetary gold	8 812 ..	....	....	....	....	....	....	....	....
Special drawing rights	8 811 ..	.04	.20	.40	1.18	.68	.57	.50	.05
Reserve position in the Fund	8 810 ..	....	....	....	....	....	....	....	....
Foreign exchange	8 803 ..	....	69.28	102.31	165.16	70.93	....	....	....
Other claims	8 813 ..	....	....	....	....	....	....	....	....

Table 3 (Concluded). INTERNATIONAL INVESTMENT POSITION (End-period stocks), 2000–2007

(Millions of U.S. dollars)

	Code	2000	2001	2002	2003	2004	2005	2006	2007
LIABILITIES	8 995 D.	....	814.98	1,256.22	1,194.97	1,512.08	....	....	....
Direct investment in Guinea-Bissau	8 555 ..	....	.39	3.02	1.55	.85	....	....	....
Equity capital and reinvested earnings	8 556 ..	....	.39	.64	1.45	1.17	....	....	....
Claims on direct investors	8 557 ..	....	....	....	....	....	....	....	....
Liabilities to direct investors	8 558 ..	....	.39	.64	1.45	1.17	....	....	....
Other capital	8 580 ..	....	....	2.38	.10	−.33	....	....	....
Claims on direct investors	8 585 ..	....	....	....	....	−.33	....	....	....
Liabilities to direct investors	8 590 ..	....	....	2.38	.10	....	....	....	....
Portfolio investment	8 652 ..	....	....	.72	1.26	1.36	....	....	....
Equity securities	8 660 ..	....	....	.72	1.26	1.36	....	....	....
Banks	8 663 ..	....	....	.72	1.26	1.36	....	....	....
Other sectors	8 664 ..	....	....	....	....	....	....	....	....
Debt securities	8 669 ..	....	....	....	....	....	....	....	....
Bonds and notes	8 670 ..	....	....	....	....	....	....	....	....
Monetary authorities	8 671 ..	....	....	....	....	....	....	....	....
General government	8 672 ..	....	....	....	....	....	....	....	....
Banks	8 673 ..	....	....	....	....	....	....	....	....
Other sectors	8 674 ..	....	....	....	....	....	....	....	....
Money market instruments	8 680 ..	....	....	....	....	....	....	....	....
Monetary authorities	8 681 ..	....	....	....	....	....	....	....	....
General government	8 682 ..	....	....	....	....	....	....	....	....
Banks	8 683 ..	....	....	....	....	....	....	....	....
Other sectors	8 684 ..	....	....	....	....	....	....	....	....
Financial derivatives	8 905 ..	....	....	....	....	....	....	....	....
Monetary authorities	8 906 ..	....	....	....	....	....	....	....	....
General government	8 907 ..	....	....	....	....	....	....	....	....
Banks	8 908 ..	....	....	....	....	....	....	....	....
Other sectors	8 909 ..	....	....	....	....	....	....	....	....
Other investment	8 753 ..	....	814.59	1,252.48	1,192.16	1,509.88	....	....	....
Trade credits	8 756 ..	....	....	13.22	....	.36	....	....	....
General government	8 757 ..	....	....	13.22	....	....	....	....	....
of which: Short-term	8 759 ..	....	....	*13.22*	....	....	....	....	....
Other sectors	8 760 ..	....	....	....	....	.36	....	....	....
of which: Short-term	8 762 ..	....	....	....	....	*.36*	....	....	....
Loans	8 764 ..	....	812.70	1,239.12	1,190.00	1,507.46	....	....	....
Monetary authorities	8 765 ..	....	23.18	23.43	20.47	15.79	....	....	....
of which: Use of Fund credit and loans from the Fund	8 766 ..	*24.72*	*23.18*	*23.43*	*20.47*	*15.79*	*11.50*	*8.21*	*5.19*
of which: Short-term	8 768 ..	....	....	....	....	....	....	....	....
General government	8 769 ..	....	778.04	1,202.20	1,169.47	1,491.61	....	....	....
of which: Short-term	8 771 ..	....	....	*230.95*	*263.02*	*303.26*	....	....	....
Banks	8 772 ..	....	11.48	13.49	.06	.07	....	....	....
of which: Short-term	8 774 ..	....	*.73*	*.70*	*.03*	*.03*	....	....	....
Other sectors	8 775 ..	....	....	....	....	....	....	....	....
of which: Short-term	8 777 ..	....	....	....	....	....	....	....	....
Currency and deposits	8 780 ..	....	1.89	.94	3.05	2.43	....	....	....
Monetary authorities	8 781 ..	....	1.83	.70	2.05	1.19	....	....	....
General government	8 782 ..	....	....	....	....	....	....	....	....
Banks	8 783 ..	....	.05	.25	1.00	1.24	....	....	....
Other sectors	8 784 ..	....	....	....	....	....	....	....	....
Other liabilities	8 786 ..	....	....	−.82	−.90	−.38	....	....	....
Monetary authorities	8 787 ..	....	−.77	−.84	−2.73	−.55	....	....	....
of which: Short-term	8 789 ..	....	*−.77*	*−.84*	*−2.73*	*−.55*	....	....	....
General government	8 790 ..	....	....	....	....	....	....	....	....
of which: Short-term	8 792 ..	....	....	....	....	....	....	....	....
Banks	8 793 ..	....	....	....	....	....	....	....	....
of which: Short-term	8 795 ..	....	....	....	....	....	....	....	....
Other sectors	8 796 ..	....	.77	.03	1.83	.18	....	....	....
of which: Short-term	8 798 ..	....	*.77*	*.03*	*1.83*	*.18*	....	....	....
NET INTERNATIONAL INVESTMENT POSITION	8 995 ..	....	−741.65	−1,142.94	−1,014.83	−1,423.53	....	....	....
Conversion rates: CFA francs per U.S. dollar (end of period)	0 102 ..	704.95	744.31	625.50	519.36	481.58	556.04	498.07	445.59

Table 1. ANALYTIC PRESENTATION, 2000–2007

(Millions of U.S. dollars)

	Code	2000	2001	2002	2003	2004	2005	2006	2007
A. Current Account[1]	4 993 Z.	**−82.2**	**−90.9**	**−62.3**	**−44.6**	**−19.9**	**−96.3**	**−180.6**	**−165.7**
Goods: exports f.o.b.	2 100 ..	502.9	485.4	490.1	508.0	584.0	545.6	579.6	674.9
Goods: imports f.o.b.	3 100 ..	−550.1	−541.0	−513.9	−525.3	−591.8	−717.1	−809.8	−982.9
Balance on Goods	4 100 ..	*−47.2*	*−55.6*	*−23.8*	*−17.3*	*−7.8*	*−171.4*	*−230.2*	*−308.0*
Services: credit	2 200 ..	169.3	172.0	172.3	156.8	160.9	147.9	147.6	172.9
Services: debit	3 200 ..	−193.2	−192.4	−195.8	−172.1	−207.6	−200.9	−245.4	−272.5
Balance on Goods and Services	4 991 ..	*−71.1*	*−76.0*	*−47.3*	*−32.6*	*−54.5*	*−224.5*	*−327.9*	*−407.6*
Income: credit	2 300 ..	11.7	10.1	7.8	4.7	4.0	3.3	2.8	2.9
Income: debit	3 300 ..	−69.8	−69.0	−62.8	−59.9	−43.4	−42.3	−71.8	−47.7
Balance on Goods, Services, and Income	4 992 ..	*−129.2*	*−134.9*	*−102.3*	*−87.8*	*−93.9*	*−263.5*	*−396.9*	*−452.5*
Current transfers: credit	2 379 Z.	100.8	98.1	128.7	127.4	193.9	261.9	310.9	423.8
Current transfers: debit	3 379 ..	−53.8	−54.1	−88.7	−84.2	−119.9	−94.6	−94.6	−137.0
B. Capital Account[1]	4 994 Z.	**16.3**	**31.9**	**31.1**	**43.8**	**45.9**	**52.1**	**350.5**	**426.6**
Capital account: credit	2 994 Z.	16.3	31.9	31.1	43.8	45.9	52.1	350.5	426.6
Capital account: debit	3 994 ..	....	....	....	....	....	....	....	....
Total, Groups A Plus B	4 981 ..	*−65.9*	*−59.0*	*−31.2*	*−.8*	*26.0*	*−44.2*	*169.9*	*260.9*
C. Financial Account[1]	4 995 W.	**110.5**	**84.4**	**54.3**	**35.0**	**38.5**	**126.7**	**−52.4**	**−226.6**
Direct investment abroad	4 505 ..	....	....	....	....	....	....	....	....
Direct investment in Guyana	4 555 Z.	67.1	56.0	43.6	26.1	30.0	76.8	102.4	152.4
Portfolio investment assets	4 602 ..	3.0	−8.0	−17.0	−26.8	−16.2	−34.1	−5.5	−95.3
Equity securities	4 610 ..	....	....	....	....	....	....	....	....
Debt securities	4 619 ..	3.0	−8.0	−17.0	−26.8	−16.2	−34.1	−5.5	−95.3
Portfolio investment liabilities	4 652 Z.	−12.0	−3.0	8.0	−.5	10.6	17.3	1.4	.2
Equity securities	4 660 ..	....	....	....	....	....	....	....	....
Debt securities	4 669 Z.	−12.0	−3.0	8.0	−.5	10.6	17.3	1.4	.2
Financial derivatives	4 910 ..	....	....	....	....	....	....	....	....
Financial derivatives assets	4 900 ..	....	....	....	....	....	....	....	....
Financial derivatives liabilities	4 905 ..	....	....	....	....	....	....	....	....
Other investment assets	4 703 ..	66.1	....	....	....	....	....	....	....
Monetary authorities	4 701 ..	....	....	....	....	....	....	....	....
General government	4 704 ..	66.1	....	....	....	....	....	....	....
Banks	4 705 ..	....	....	....	....	....	....	....	....
Other sectors	4 728 ..	....	....	....	....	....	....	....	....
Other investment liabilities	4 753 W.	−13.7	39.4	19.7	36.2	14.1	66.7	−150.7	−283.9
Monetary authorities	4 753 WA	....	....	....	....	....	....	....	....
General government	4 753 ZB	−23.7	39.4	19.7	36.2	14.1	66.7	−150.7	−283.9
Banks	4 753 ZC	....	....	....	....	....	....	....	....
Other sectors	4 753 ZD	10.0	....	....	....	....	....	....	....
Total, Groups A Through C	4 983 ..	*44.6*	*25.4*	*23.1*	*34.2*	*64.5*	*82.5*	*117.4*	*34.3*
D. Net Errors and Omissions	4 998 ..	**−4.4**	**−44.8**	**−1.3**	**−19.9**	**−43.4**	**−68.2**	**−84.1**	**−37.4**
Total, Groups A Through D	4 984 ..	*40.2*	*−19.4*	*21.8*	*14.3*	*21.1*	*14.3*	*33.3*	*−3.1*
E. Reserves and Related Items	4 802 A.	**−40.2**	**19.4**	**−21.8**	**−14.3**	**−21.1**	**−14.3**	**−33.3**	**3.1**
Reserve assets	4 802 ..	−24.0	35.2	−13.0	−5.0	−9.8	−24.9	−25.3	−35.6
Use of Fund credit and loans	4 766 ..	−16.2	−15.8	−8.9	−9.3	−11.2	10.5	−38.2	....
Exceptional financing	4 920 ..	....	....	....	....	....	....	30.2	38.7
Conversion rates: Guyana dollars per U.S. dollar	0 101 ..	**182.43**	**187.32**	**190.67**	**193.88**	**198.31**	**199.88**	**200.19**	**202.35**

[1] Excludes components that have been classified in the categories of Group E.

Table 2. STANDARD PRESENTATION, 2000–2007

(Millions of U.S. dollars)

	Code	2000	2001	2002	2003	2004	2005	2006	2007
CURRENT ACCOUNT	4 993	**−82.2**	**−90.9**	**−62.3**	**−44.6**	**−19.9**	**−96.3**	**−180.6**	**−165.7**
A. GOODS	4 100	**−47.2**	**−55.6**	**−23.8**	**−17.3**	**−7.8**	**−171.4**	**−230.2**	**−308.0**
Credit	2 100	**502.9**	**485.4**	**490.1**	**508.0**	**584.0**	**545.6**	**579.6**	**674.9**
General merchandise: exports f.o.b.	2 110	502.9	485.4	490.1	508.0	584.0	545.6	579.6	674.9
Goods for processing: exports f.o.b.	2 150	....	....	....	....	....	....	....	....
Repairs on goods	2 160	....	....	....	....	....	....	....	....
Goods procured in ports by carriers	2 170	....	....	....	....	....	....	....	....
Nonmonetary gold	2 180	....	....	....	....	....	....	....	....
Debit	3 100	**−550.1**	**−541.0**	**−513.9**	**−525.3**	**−591.8**	**−717.1**	**−809.8**	**−982.9**
General merchandise: imports f.o.b.	3 110	−550.1	−541.0	−513.9	−525.3	−591.8	−717.1	−809.8	−982.9
Goods for processing: imports f.o.b.	3 150	....	....	....	....	....	....	....	....
Repairs on goods	3 160	....	....	....	....	....	....	....	....
Goods procured in ports by carriers	3 170	....	....	....	....	....	....	....	....
Nonmonetary gold	3 180	....	....	....	....	....	....	....	....
B. SERVICES	4 200	**−23.9**	**−20.4**	**−23.5**	**−15.3**	**−46.7**	**−53.0**	**−97.8**	**−99.6**
Total credit	2 200	*169.3*	*172.0*	*172.3*	*156.8*	*160.9*	*147.9*	*147.6*	*172.9*
Total debit	3 200	*−193.2*	*−192.4*	*−195.8*	*−172.1*	*−207.6*	*−200.9*	*−245.4*	*−272.5*
Transportation services, credit	2 205	**7.2**	**9.2**	**9.3**	**6.7**	**7.2**	**7.6**	**8.1**	**8.7**
Passenger	2 850	*4.7*	*4.3*	*3.9*	*2.0*	....	....	....	....
Freight	2 851	*2.5*	*4.9*	*5.4*	*4.7*	*7.2*	*7.6*	*8.1*	*8.7*
Other	2 852	....	....	....	....	....	....	....	....
Sea transport, passenger	2 207	....	....	....	....	....	....	....	....
Sea transport, freight	2 208	2.5	4.9	5.4	4.7	7.2	7.6	8.1	8.7
Sea transport, other	2 209	....	....	....	....	....	....	....	....
Air transport, passenger	2 211	4.7	4.3	3.9	2.0	....	....	....	....
Air transport, freight	2 212	....	....	....	....	....	....	....	....
Air transport, other	2 213	....	....	....	....	....	....	....	....
Other transport, passenger	2 215	....	....	....	....	....	....	....	....
Other transport, freight	2 216	....	....	....	....	....	....	....	....
Other transport, other	2 217	....	....	....	....	....	....	....	....
Transportation services, debit	3 205	**−43.3**	**−50.0**	**−55.3**	**−50.7**	**−59.6**	**−71.6**	**−80.6**	**−85.5**
Passenger	3 850	*−8.0*	*−6.9*	*−6.1*	*−4.3*	....	....	....	....
Freight	3 851	*−35.3*	*−43.1*	*−49.2*	*−46.4*	*−59.6*	*−71.6*	*−80.6*	*−85.5*
Other	3 852	....	....	....	....	....	....	....	....
Sea transport, passenger	3 207	....	....	....	....	....	....	....	....
Sea transport, freight	3 208	−35.3	−43.1	−49.2	−46.4	−59.6	−71.6	−80.6	−85.5
Sea transport, other	3 209	....	....	....	....	....	....	....	....
Air transport, passenger	3 211	−8.0	−6.9	−6.1	−4.3	....	....	....	....
Air transport, freight	3 212	....	....	....	....	....	....	....	....
Air transport, other	3 213	....	....	....	....	....	....	....	....
Other transport, passenger	3 215	....	....	....	....	....	....	....	....
Other transport, freight	3 216	....	....	....	....	....	....	....	....
Other transport, other	3 217	....	....	....	....	....	....	....	....
Travel, credit	2 236	**75.1**	**60.5**	**49.3**	**25.8**	**27.1**	**35.1**	**37.1**	**50.5**
Business travel	2 237	....	....	....	....	....	....	....	....
Personal travel	2 240	75.1	60.5	49.3	25.8	27.1	35.1	37.1	50.5
Travel, debit	3 236	**−68.9**	**−55.1**	**−38.4**	**−26.3**	**−30.4**	**−39.6**	**−49.0**	**−57.5**
Business travel	3 237	....	....	....	....	....	....	....	....
Personal travel	3 240	−68.9	−55.1	−38.4	−26.3	−30.4	−39.6	−49.0	−57.5
Other services, credit	2 200 BA	**87.0**	**102.3**	**113.7**	**124.3**	**126.6**	**105.2**	**102.5**	**113.7**
Communications	2 245	37.7	39.3	25.8	26.4	27.7	29.1	30.6	32.1
Construction	2 249	....	....	....	....	....	....	....	....
Insurance	2 253	8.2	8.5	5.1	6.4	6.7	7.0	7.4	7.8
Financial	2 260	7.0	6.7	6.6	7.8	....	....	....	....
Computer and information	2 262	.5	1.8	4.3	4.1	4.4	4.6	4.8	5.1
Royalties and licence fees	2 266	14.8	23.1	34.4	32.1	33.7	35.4	37.2	40.5
Other business services	2 268	18.8	22.9	37.5	47.5	54.0	29.0	22.5	28.2
Personal, cultural, and recreational	2 287	....	....	....	....	....	....	....	....
Government, n.i.e.	2 291	....	....	....	....	....	....	....	....
Other services, debit	3 200 BA	**−81.0**	**−87.3**	**−102.1**	**−95.1**	**−117.6**	**−89.7**	**−115.8**	**−129.5**
Communications	3 245	−30.7	−32.9	−15.1	−17.6	−18.5	−19.4	−20.4	−21.4
Construction	3 249	....	....	....	....	....	....	....	....
Insurance	3 253	−14.1	−14.5	−17.4	−18.8	−19.7	−20.7	−21.8	−22.8
Financial	3 260	−3.9	−6.0	−6.1	−7.7	....	....	....	....
Computer and information	3 262	−1.5	−1.8	−3.4	−3.2	−3.5	−3.8	−4.1	−4.4
Royalties and licence fees	3 266	−10.8	−5.4	−21.6	−17.6	−18.5	−19.4	−20.4	−21.4
Other business services	3 268	−20.0	−26.7	−38.5	−30.2	−57.4	−26.4	−49.1	−59.4
Personal, cultural, and recreational	3 287	....	....	....	....	....	....	....	....
Government, n.i.e.	3 291	....	....	....	....	....	....	....	....

Table 2 (Continued). STANDARD PRESENTATION, 2000–2007

(Millions of U.S. dollars)

	Code	2000	2001	2002	2003	2004	2005	2006	2007
C. INCOME	4 300	**−58.1**	**−58.9**	**−55.0**	**−55.2**	**−39.4**	**−39.0**	**−69.0**	**−44.9**
Total credit	2 300	*11.7*	*10.1*	*7.8*	*4.7*	*4.0*	*3.3*	*2.8*	*2.9*
Total debit	3 300	*−69.8*	*−69.0*	*−62.8*	*−59.9*	*−43.4*	*−42.3*	*−71.8*	*−47.7*
Compensation of employees, credit	2 310	....	....	....	....	....	....	....	....
Compensation of employees, debit	3 310	**−4.0**	**−5.5**	**−5.5**	**−5.5**	**−5.8**	**−5.9**	**−6.0**	**−7.0**
Investment income, credit	2 320	**11.7**	**10.1**	**7.8**	**4.7**	**4.0**	**3.3**	**2.8**	**2.9**
Direct investment income	2 330	....	....	....	....	....	....	....	....
Dividends and distributed branch profits	2 332	....	....	....	....	....	....	....	....
Reinvested earnings and undistributed branch profits	2 333	....	....	....	....	....	....	....	....
Income on debt (interest)	2 334	....	....	....	....	....	....	....	....
Portfolio investment income	2 339	11.7	10.1	7.8	4.7	....	....	....	....
Income on equity	2 340	1.0	....	....	....	....	....	....	....
Income on bonds and notes	2 350	3.2	10.1	7.8	4.7	....	....	....	....
Income on money market instruments	2 360	7.5	....	....	....	....	....	....	....
Other investment income	2 370	....	....	....	....	4.0	3.3	2.8	2.9
Investment income, debit	3 320	**−65.8**	**−63.5**	**−57.3**	**−54.4**	**−37.6**	**−36.4**	**−65.8**	**−40.7**
Direct investment income	3 330	−6.0	−5.0	−3.9	−2.3	−2.7	−6.9	−9.2	−10.1
Dividends and distributed branch profits	3 332	....	....	....	....	....	....	....	....
Reinvested earnings and undistributed branch profits	3 333	−6.0	−5.0	−3.9	−2.3	−2.7	−6.9	−9.2	−10.1
Income on debt (interest)	3 334	....	....	....	....	....	....	....	....
Portfolio investment income	3 339	−6.0	....	....	....	....	....	....	....
Income on equity	3 340	....	....	....	....	....	....	....	....
Income on bonds and notes	3 350	....	....	....	....	....	....	....	....
Income on money market instruments	3 360	−6.0	....	....	....	....	....	....	....
Other investment income	3 370	−53.8	−58.5	−53.4	−52.1	−34.9	−29.5	−56.6	−30.6
D. CURRENT TRANSFERS	4 379	**47.0**	**44.0**	**40.0**	**43.2**	**74.0**	**167.2**	**216.3**	**286.8**
Credit	2 379	**100.8**	**98.1**	**128.7**	**127.4**	**193.9**	**261.9**	**310.9**	**423.8**
General government	2 380	....	....	....	....	....	....	....	....
Other sectors	2 390	100.8	98.1	128.7	127.4	193.9	261.9	310.9	423.8
Workers' remittances	2 391	27.3	22.3	51.0	99.3	153.0	201.3	218.1	278.5
Other current transfers	2 392	73.5	75.8	77.7	28.1	40.8	60.6	92.8	145.3
Debit	3 379	**−53.8**	**−54.1**	**−88.7**	**−84.2**	**−119.9**	**−94.6**	**−94.6**	**−137.0**
General government	3 380	....	....	....	....	....	....	....	....
Other sectors	3 390	−53.8	−54.1	−88.7	−84.2	−119.9	−94.6	−94.6	−137.0
Workers' remittances	3 391	−23.4	−18.6	−47.6	−44.9	−74.8	−48.9	−42.4	−54.1
Other current transfers	3 392	−30.4	−35.5	−41.1	−39.3	−45.1	−45.7	−52.2	−82.9
CAPITAL AND FINANCIAL ACCOUNT	4 996	**86.6**	**135.7**	**63.6**	**64.5**	**63.4**	**164.5**	**264.8**	**203.1**
CAPITAL ACCOUNT	4 994	**16.3**	**31.9**	**31.1**	**43.8**	**45.9**	**52.1**	**380.7**	**465.3**
Total credit	2 994	*16.3*	*31.9*	*31.1*	*43.8*	*45.9*	*52.1*	*380.7*	*465.3*
Total debit	3 994	....	....	....	....	....	....	....	....
Capital transfers, credit	2 400	**16.3**	**31.9**	**31.1**	**43.8**	**45.9**	**52.1**	**380.7**	**465.3**
General government	2 401	16.3	31.9	31.1	43.8	....	....	251.0	356.5
Debt forgiveness	2 402	....	....	....	....	....	....	251.0	356.5
Other capital transfers	2 410	16.3	31.9	31.1	43.8	....	....	....	....
Other sectors	2 430	....	....	....	....	45.9	52.1	129.7	108.8
Migrants' transfers	2 431	....	....	....	....	....	....	....	....
Debt forgiveness	2 432	....	....	....	....	....	....	....	....
Other capital transfers	2 440	....	....	....	....	....	....	129.7	108.8
Capital transfers, debit	3 400	....	....	....	....	....	....	....	....
General government	3 401	....	....	....	....	....	....	....	....
Debt forgiveness	3 402	....	....	....	....	....	....	....	....
Other capital transfers	3 410	....	....	....	....	....	....	....	....
Other sectors	3 430	....	....	....	....	....	....	....	....
Migrants' transfers	3 431	....	....	....	....	....	....	....	....
Debt forgiveness	3 432	....	....	....	....	....	....	....	....
Other capital transfers	3 440	....	....	....	....	....	....	....	....
Nonproduced nonfinancial assets, credit	2 480	....	....	....	....	....	....	....	....
Nonproduced nonfinancial assets, debit	3 480	....	....	....	....	....	....	....	....

Table 2 (Continued). STANDARD PRESENTATION, 2000–2007

(Millions of U.S. dollars)

	Code	2000	2001	2002	2003	2004	2005	2006	2007
FINANCIAL ACCOUNT	4 995	70.3	103.8	32.5	20.7	17.5	112.4	−115.9	−262.2
A. DIRECT INVESTMENT	4 500	67.1	56.0	43.6	26.1	30.0	76.8	102.4	152.4
Direct investment abroad	4 505	....	....	....	....	....	....	....	....
Equity capital	4 510	....	....	....	....	....	....	....	....
Claims on affiliated enterprises	4 515	....	....	....	....	....	....	....	....
Liabilities to affiliated enterprises	4 520	....	....	....	....	....	....	....	....
Reinvested earnings	4 525	....	....	....	....	....	....	....	....
Other capital	4 530	....	....	....	....	....	....	....	....
Claims on affiliated enterprises	4 535	....	....	....	....	....	....	....	....
Liabilities to affiliated enterprises	4 540	....	....	....	....	....	....	....	....
Direct investment in Guyana	4 555	67.1	56.0	43.6	26.1	30.0	76.8	102.4	152.4
Equity capital	4 560	9.6	8.0	6.2	3.7	4.3	11.0	14.6	15.3
Claims on direct investors	4 565	....	....	....	....	....	....	....	....
Liabilities to direct investors	4 570	9.6	8.0	6.2	3.7	4.3	11.0	14.6	15.3
Reinvested earnings	4 575	6.0	5.0	3.9	2.3	2.7	6.9	9.2	10.1
Other capital	4 580	51.5	43.0	33.5	20.1	23.0	58.9	78.6	127.0
Claims on direct investors	4 585	....	....	....	....	....	....	....	....
Liabilities to direct investors	4 590	51.5	43.0	33.5	20.1	23.0	58.9	78.6	127.0
B. PORTFOLIO INVESTMENT	4 600	−9.0	−11.0	−9.0	−27.3	−5.6	−16.8	−4.1	−95.1
Assets	4 602	3.0	−8.0	−17.0	−26.8	−16.2	−34.1	−5.5	−95.3
Equity securities	4 610	....	....	....	....	....	....	....	....
Monetary authorities	4 611	....	....	....	....	....	....	....	....
General government	4 612	....	....	....	....	....	....	....	....
Banks	4 613	....	....	....	....	....	....	....	....
Other sectors	4 614	....	....	....	....	....	....	....	....
Debt securities	4 619	3.0	−8.0	−17.0	−26.8	−16.2	−34.1	−5.5	−95.3
Bonds and notes	4 620	3.0	−8.0	−17.0	−26.8	−16.2	−34.1	−5.5	−95.3
Monetary authorities	4 621	....	....	....	....	....	....	....	....
General government	4 622	....	....	....	....	....	....	....	....
Banks	4 623	....	....	....	....	−16.2	−34.1	−5.5	−95.3
Other sectors	4 624	3.0	−8.0	−17.0	−26.8	....	....	....	....
Money market instruments	4 630	....	....	....	....	....	....	....	....
Monetary authorities	4 631	....	....	....	....	....	....	....	....
General government	4 632	....	....	....	....	....	....	....	....
Banks	4 633	....	....	....	....	....	....	....	....
Other sectors	4 634	....	....	....	....	....	....	....	....
Liabilities	4 652	−12.0	−3.0	8.0	−.5	10.6	17.3	1.4	.2
Equity securities	4 660	....	....	....	....	....	....	....	....
Banks	4 663	....	....	....	....	....	....	....	....
Other sectors	4 664	....	....	....	....	....	....	....	....
Debt securities	4 669	−12.0	−3.0	8.0	−.5	10.6	17.3	1.4	.2
Bonds and notes	4 670	....	....	....	....	....	....	....	....
Monetary authorities	4 671	....	....	....	....	....	....	....	....
General government	4 672	....	....	....	....	....	....	....	....
Banks	4 673	....	....	....	....	....	....	....	....
Other sectors	4 674	....	....	....	....	....	....	....	....
Money market instruments	4 680	−12.0	−3.0	8.0	−.5	10.6	17.3	1.4	.2
Monetary authorities	4 681	....	....	....	....	....	....	....	....
General government	4 682	....	....	....	....	....	....	....	....
Banks	4 683	....	....	....	....	10.6	17.3	1.4	.2
Other sectors	4 684	−12.0	−3.0	8.0	−.5	....	....	....	....
C. FINANCIAL DERIVATIVES	4 910	....	....	....	....	....	....	....	....
Monetary authorities	4 911	....	....	....	....	....	....	....	....
General government	4 912	....	....	....	....	....	....	....	....
Banks	4 913	....	....	....	....	....	....	....	....
Other sectors	4 914	....	....	....	....	....	....	....	....
Assets	4 900	....	....	....	....	....	....	....	....
Monetary authorities	4 901	....	....	....	....	....	....	....	....
General government	4 902	....	....	....	....	....	....	....	....
Banks	4 903	....	....	....	....	....	....	....	....
Other sectors	4 904	....	....	....	....	....	....	....	....
Liabilities	4 905	....	....	....	....	....	....	....	....
Monetary authorities	4 906	....	....	....	....	....	....	....	....
General government	4 907	....	....	....	....	....	....	....	....
Banks	4 908	....	....	....	....	....	....	....	....
Other sectors	4 909	....	....	....	....	....	....	....	....

Table 2 (Concluded). STANDARD PRESENTATION, 2000–2007

(Millions of U.S. dollars)

	Code	2000	2001	2002	2003	2004	2005	2006	2007
D. OTHER INVESTMENT	4 700	**36.2**	**23.6**	**10.8**	**26.9**	**2.9**	**77.2**	**−188.9**	**−283.9**
Assets	4 703	**66.1**	....	....	....	....	....	....	....
Trade credits	4 706	....	....	....	....	....	....	....	....
General government	4 707	....	....	....	....	....	....	....	....
of which: Short-term	4 709	....	....	....	....	....	....	....	....
Other sectors	4 710	....	....	....	....	....	....	....	....
of which: Short-term	4 712	....	....	....	....	....	....	....	....
Loans	4 714	66.1	....	....	....	....	....	....	....
Monetary authorities	4 715	....	....	....	....	....	....	....	....
of which: Short-term	4 718	....	....	....	....	....	....	....	....
General government	4 719	66.1	....	....	....	....	....	....	....
of which: Short-term	4 721	....	....	....	....	....	....	....	....
Banks	4 722	....	....	....	....	....	....	....	....
of which: Short-term	4 724	....	....	....	....	....	....	....	....
Other sectors	4 725	....	....	....	....	....	....	....	....
of which: Short-term	4 727	....	....	....	....	....	....	....	....
Currency and deposits	4 730	....	....	....	....	....	....	....	....
Monetary authorities	4 731	....	....	....	....	....	....	....	....
General government	4 732	....	....	....	....	....	....	....	....
Banks	4 733	....	....	....	....	....	....	....	....
Other sectors	4 734	....	....	....	....	....	....	....	....
Other assets	4 736	....	....	....	....	....	....	....	....
Monetary authorities	4 737	....	....	....	....	....	....	....	....
of which: Short-term	4 739	....	....	....	....	....	....	....	....
General government	4 740	....	....	....	....	....	....	....	....
of which: Short-term	4 742	....	....	....	....	....	....	....	....
Banks	4 743	....	....	....	....	....	....	....	....
of which: Short-term	4 745	....	....	....	....	....	....	....	....
Other sectors	4 746	....	....	....	....	....	....	....	....
of which: Short-term	4 748	....	....	....	....	....	....	....	....
Liabilities	4 753	**−29.9**	**23.6**	**10.8**	**26.9**	**2.9**	**77.2**	**−188.9**	**−283.9**
Trade credits	4 756	....	....	....	....	....	....	....	....
General government	4 757	....	....	....	....	....	....	....	....
of which: Short-term	4 759	....	....	....	....	....	....	....	....
Other sectors	4 760	....	....	....	....	....	....	....	....
of which: Short-term	4 762	....	....	....	....	....	....	....	....
Loans	4 764	−16.2	23.6	10.8	26.9	50.2	113.0	−153.7	−242.5
Monetary authorities	4 765	−16.2	−15.8	−8.9	−9.3	−11.2	10.5	−38.2	....
of which: Use of Fund credit and loans from the Fund	4 766	−16.2	−15.8	−8.9	−9.3	−11.2	10.5	−38.2	....
of which: Short-term	4 768	....	....	....	....	....	....	....	....
General government	4 769	....	39.4	19.7	36.2	61.4	102.5	−115.5	−242.5
of which: Short-term	4 771	....	....	....	....	....	....	....	....
Banks	4 772	....	....	....	....	....	....	....	....
of which: Short-term	4 774	....	....	....	....	....	....	....	....
Other sectors	4 775	....	....	....	....	....	....	....	....
of which: Short-term	4 777	....	....	....	....	....	....	....	....
Currency and deposits	4 780	....	....	....	....	....	....	....	....
Monetary authorities	4 781	....	....	....	....	....	....	....	....
General government	4 782	....	....	....	....	....	....	....	....
Banks	4 783	....	....	....	....	....	....	....	....
Other sectors	4 784	....	....	....	....	....	....	....	....
Other liabilities	4 786	−13.7	....	....	....	−47.3	−35.8	−35.2	−41.4
Monetary authorities	4 787	....	....	....	....	....	....	....	....
of which: Short-term	4 789	....	....	....	....	....	....	....	....
General government	4 790	−23.7	....	....	....	−47.3	−35.8	−35.2	−41.4
of which: Short-term	4 792	....	....	....	....	....	....	....	....
Banks	4 793	....	....	....	....	....	....	....	....
of which: Short-term	4 795	....	....	....	....	....	....	....	....
Other sectors	4 796	10.0	....	....	....	....	....	....	....
of which: Short-term	4 798	....	....	....	....	....	....	....	....
E. RESERVE ASSETS	4 802	**−24.0**	**35.2**	**−13.0**	**−5.0**	**−9.8**	**−24.9**	**−25.3**	**−35.6**
Monetary gold	4 812	....	....	....	....	....	....	....	....
Special drawing rights	4 811	−7.9	6.4	−2.0	.3	−1.8	6.2	−.6	1.2
Reserve position in the Fund	4 810	....	....	....	....	....	....	....	....
Foreign exchange	4 803	....	28.8	−11.0	−5.3	−8.0	−31.0	−24.8	−36.8
Other claims	4 813	−16.1	....	....	....	....	....	....	....
NET ERRORS AND OMISSIONS	4 998	**−4.4**	**−44.8**	**−1.3**	**−19.9**	**−43.4**	**−68.2**	**−84.1**	**−37.4**

Table 1. ANALYTIC PRESENTATION, FISCAL YEARS 2000–2007 ENDING SEPTEMBER 30

(Millions of U.S. dollars)

	Code	2000	2001	2002	2003	2004	2005	2006	2007
A. Current Account[1]...............................	4 993 Z.	**−114.2**	**−131.9**	**−189.0**	**−181.8**	**−155.6**	**−358.2**	**−446.6**	**−459.6**
Goods: exports f.o.b................................	2 100 ..	331.7	305.2	274.4	333.8	377.5	455.5	491.9	522.1
Goods: imports f.o.b................................	3 100 ..	−1,086.7	−1,055.4	−980.4	−1,116.0	−1,210.5	−1,308.5	−1,548.2	−1,618.1
Balance on Goods.....................	4 100 ..	*−755.0*	*−750.2*	*−706.0*	*−782.2*	*−833.0*	*−853.1*	*−1,056.3*	*−1,096.0*
Services: credit....................................	2 200 ..	172.0	139.0	146.7	136.0	141.6	145.5	203.3	206.7
Services: debit.....................................	3 200 ..	−282.0	−260.5	−269.6	−301.0	−345.3	−542.1	−587.6	−703.2
Balance on Goods and Services........................	4 991 ..	*−865.0*	*−871.7*	*−828.9*	*−947.2*	*−1,036.7*	*−1,249.7*	*−1,440.6*	*−1,592.5*
Income: credit.....................................	2 300 ..	....	....	....	....	....	2.1	18.7	24.8
Income: debit......................................	3 300 ..	−9.2	−9.5	−13.7	−14.3	−11.9	−37.1	−12.1	−17.6
Balance on Goods, Services, and Income..........	4 992 ..	*−874.2*	*−881.1*	*−842.6*	*−961.4*	*−1,048.6*	*−1,284.7*	*−1,434.0*	*−1,585.3*
Current transfers: credit.........................	2 379 Z.	771.0	768.6	675.7	811.0	931.5	986.2	1,062.9	1,222.1
Current transfers: debit..........................	3 379 ..	−11.0	−19.3	−22.0	−31.4	−38.6	−59.7	−75.5	−96.4
B. Capital Account[1]...............................	4 994 Z.	**....**	**....**	**....**	**....**	**....**	**....**	**....**	**....**
Capital account: credit...........................	2 994 Z.	....	....	....	....	....	....	....	....
Capital account: debit...........................	3 994 ..	....	....	....	....	....	....	....	....
Total, Groups A Plus B.........................	4 981 ..	*−114.2*	*−131.9*	*−189.0*	*−181.8*	*−155.6*	*−358.2*	*−446.6*	*−459.6*
C. Financial Account[1]...........................	4 995 W.	**−16.0**	**82.5**	**−33.1**	**−60.1**	**21.9**	**−21.9**	**140.4**	**112.0**
Direct investment abroad........................	4 505 ..	....	....	....	....	....	....	....	....
Direct investment in Haiti.......................	4 555 Z.	13.3	4.4	5.7	13.8	5.9	26.0	160.6	74.5
Portfolio investment assets......................	4 602 ..	....	....	....	....	....	....	....	....
Equity securities...............................	4 610 ..	....	....	....	....	....	....	....	....
Debt securities.................................	4 619 ..	....	....	....	....	....	....	....	....
Portfolio investment liabilities.................	4 652 Z.	....	....	....	....	....	....	....	....
Equity securities...............................	4 660 ..	....	....	....	....	....	....	....	....
Debt securities.................................	4 669 Z.	....	....	....	....	....	....	....	....
Financial derivatives............................	4 910 ..	....	....	....	....	....	....	....	....
Financial derivatives assets....................	4 900 ..	....	....	....	....	....	....	....	....
Financial derivatives liabilities................	4 905 ..	....	....	....	....	....	....	....	....
Other investment assets.........................	4 703 ..	−43.3	−3.0	−22.6	−87.8	−4.4	−64.5	−55.1	−.1
Monetary authorities...........................	4 701 ..	....	....	....	.3	−.1	−.9	.1	−.1
General government............................	4 704 ..	−5.4	2.8	....	....	....	....	....	....
Banks..	4 705 ..	−63.9	17.2	.4	−48.1	.6	−57.6	−75.1	4.1
Other sectors..................................	4 728 ..	26.0	−23.0	−23.0	−40.0	−5.0	−6.0	19.8	−4.0
Other investment liabilities.....................	4 753 W.	14.0	81.1	−16.1	13.8	20.4	16.6	34.9	37.6
Monetary authorities...........................	4 753 WA	....	....	.1	1.4	4.0	−1.3	.9	.5
General government............................	4 753 ZB	22.4	−3.0	−7.0	11.3	−7.2	31.0	42.4	40.8
Banks..	4 753 ZC	8.8	−.9	1.7	1.1	23.6	−13.2	−8.4	10.3
Other sectors..................................	4 753 ZD	−17.2	85.0	−11.0	....	....	....	....	−14.0
Total, Groups A Through C.....................	4 983 ..	*−130.3*	*−49.4*	*−222.0*	*−241.9*	*−133.8*	*−380.1*	*−306.3*	*−347.6*
D. Net Errors and Omissions.....................	4 998 ..	**73.3**	**44.2**	**40.7**	**101.5**	**73.5**	**48.7**	**25.8**	**181.6**
Total, Groups A Through D.....................	4 984 ..	*−56.9*	*−5.2*	*−181.3*	*−140.4*	*−60.3*	*−331.4*	*−280.5*	*−166.0*
E. Reserves and Related Items.....................	4 802 A.	**56.9**	**5.2**	**181.3**	**140.4**	**60.3**	**331.4**	**280.5**	**166.0**
Reserve assets....................................	4 802 ..	57.3	−5.3	49.4	20.7	−50.0	−21.0	−108.1	−208.4
Use of Fund credit and loans....................	4 766 ..	−5.8	....	−9.2	−14.5	−7.1	11.0	10.3	20.8
Exceptional financing............................	4 920 ..	5.5	10.5	141.2	134.2	117.4	341.4	378.3	353.6
Conversion rates: gourdes per U.S. dollar..............	0 101 ..	**19.621**	**23.829**	**27.080**	**40.455**	**39.683**	**38.984**	**41.449**	**37.400**

[1] Excludes components that have been classified in the categories of Group E.

Table 2. STANDARD PRESENTATION, FISCAL YEARS 2000–2007 ENDING SEPTEMBER 30

(Millions of U.S. dollars)

	Code	2000	2001	2002	2003	2004	2005	2006	2007
CURRENT ACCOUNT	4 993	**−114.2**	**−131.9**	**−89.0**	**−44.8**	**−55.6**	**5.2**	**−73.2**	**−80.3**
A. GOODS	4 100	**−755.0**	**−750.2**	**−706.0**	**−782.2**	**−833.0**	**−853.1**	**−1,056.3**	**−1,096.0**
Credit	2 100	**331.7**	**305.2**	**274.4**	**333.8**	**377.5**	**455.5**	**491.9**	**522.1**
General merchandise: exports f.o.b.	2 110	331.7	305.2	274.4	333.8	377.5	455.5	491.9	522.1
Goods for processing: exports f.o.b.	2 150	....	....	....	....	....	....	....	....
Repairs on goods	2 160	....	....	....	....	....	....	....	....
Goods procured in ports by carriers	2 170	....	....	....	....	....	....	....	....
Nonmonetary gold	2 180	....	....	....	....	....	....	....	....
Debit	3 100	**−1,086.7**	**−1,055.4**	**−980.4**	**−1,116.0**	**−1,210.5**	**−1,308.5**	**−1,548.2**	**−1,618.1**
General merchandise: imports f.o.b.	3 110	−1,086.7	−1,055.4	−980.4	−1,116.0	−1,210.5	−1,308.5	−1,548.2	−1,618.1
Goods for processing: imports f.o.b.	3 150	....	....	....	....	....	....	....	....
Repairs on goods	3 160	....	....	....	....	....	....	....	....
Goods procured in ports by carriers	3 170	....	....	....	....	....	....	....	....
Nonmonetary gold	3 180	....	....	....	....	....	....	....	....
B. SERVICES	4 200	**−110.0**	**−121.5**	**−123.0**	**−165.0**	**−203.7**	**−396.6**	**−384.3**	**−496.6**
Total credit	2 200	*172.0*	*139.0*	*146.7*	*136.0*	*141.6*	*145.5*	*203.3*	*206.7*
Total debit	3 200	*−282.0*	*−260.5*	*−269.6*	*−301.0*	*−345.3*	*−542.1*	*−587.6*	*−703.2*
Transportation services, credit	2 205	....	....	....	....	....	....		....
Passenger	2 850	....	....	....	....	....	....	....	....
Freight	2 851	....	....	....	....	....	....	....	....
Other	2 852	....	....	....	....	....	....	....	....
Sea transport, passenger	2 207	....	....	....	....	....	....	....	....
Sea transport, freight	2 208	....	....	....	....	....	....	....	....
Sea transport, other	2 209	....	....	....	....	....	....	....	....
Air transport, passenger	2 211	....	....	....	....	....	....	....	....
Air transport, freight	2 212	....	....	....	....	....	....	....	....
Air transport, other	2 213	....	....	....	....	....	....	....	....
Other transport, passenger	2 215	....	....	....	....	....	....	....	....
Other transport, freight	2 216	....	....	....	....	....	....	....	....
Other transport, other	2 217	....	....	....	....	....	....	....	....
Transportation services, debit	3 205	**−245.0**	**−229.0**	**−246.2**	**−243.5**	**−222.7**	**−215.1**	**−293.9**	**−399.1**
Passenger	3 850	*−155.0*	*−150.0*	*−154.1*	*−159.5*	*−133.8*	*−116.6*	*−176.7*	*−277.3*
Freight	3 851	*−90.0*	*−79.0*	*−74.1*	*−84.0*	*−88.9*	*−98.5*	*−117.1*	*−121.8*
Other	3 852	....	....	*−18.0*	....	....	....	....	....
Sea transport, passenger	3 207	....	....	....	....	....	....	....	....
Sea transport, freight	3 208	−90.0	−79.0	−74.1	−84.0	−88.9	−98.5	−117.1	−121.8
Sea transport, other	3 209	....	....	....	....	....	....	....	....
Air transport, passenger	3 211	−155.0	−150.0	−154.1	−159.5	−133.8	−116.6	−176.7	−277.3
Air transport, freight	3 212	....	....	....	....	....	....	....	....
Air transport, other	3 213	....	....	−18.0	....	....	....	....	....
Other transport, passenger	3 215	....	....	....	....	....	....	....	....
Other transport, freight	3 216	....	....	....	....	....	....	....	....
Other transport, other	3 217	....	....	....	....	....	....	....	....
Travel, credit	2 236	**128.0**	**105.0**	**108.0**	**95.6**	**86.8**	**79.5**	**135.3**	**139.8**
Business travel	2 237	....	....	....	....	....	....	....	....
Personal travel	2 240	128.0	105.0	108.0	95.6	86.8	79.5	135.3	139.8
Travel, debit	3 236	**−18.0**	**−18.0**	....	....	**−71.9**	**−55.4**	**−55.6**	**−55.5**
Business travel	3 237	....	....	....	....	....	....	....	....
Personal travel	3 240	−18.0	−18.0	....	....	−71.9	−55.4	−55.6	−55.5
Other services, credit	2 200 BA	**44.0**	**34.0**	**38.7**	**40.4**	**54.8**	**65.9**	**68.0**	**66.9**
Communications	2 245	30.0	18.0	10.3	12.6	17.1	9.3	9.9	9.1
Construction	2 249	....	....	....	....	....	....	....	....
Insurance	2 253	....	....	....	....	....	....	....	....
Financial	2 260	....	....	....	....	....	....	....	....
Computer and information	2 262	....	....	....	....	....	....	....	....
Royalties and licence fees	2 266	....	....	6.5	5.8	5.9	4.5	3.7	3.4
Other business services	2 268	....	....	....	....	....	....	....	....
Personal, cultural, and recreational	2 287	....	....	....	....	....	....	....	....
Government, n.i.e.	2 291	14.0	16.0	21.9	22.0	31.8	52.2	54.4	54.4
Other services, debit	3 200 BA	**−19.0**	**−13.5**	**−23.5**	**−57.5**	**−50.7**	**−271.7**	**−238.1**	**−248.6**
Communications	3 245	−7.0	−5.0	−3.8	−3.4	−12.4	−19.6	−9.0	−13.9
Construction	3 249	....	....	....	....	....	....	....	....
Insurance	3 253	....	....	....	....	....	....	....	....
Financial	3 260	....	....	....	....	....	−5.8	−6.3	−7.0
Computer and information	3 262	....	....	....	....	....	....	....	....
Royalties and licence fees	3 266	....	....	....	−.9	−.4	−.4	−.4	−.5	−.4
Other business services	3 268	....	....	....	....	....	....	....	....
Personal, cultural, and recreational	3 287	....	....	....	....	....	....	....	....
Government, n.i.e.	3 291	−12.0	−8.5	−18.8	−53.7	−37.9	−245.9	−222.3	−227.3

Table 2 (Continued). STANDARD PRESENTATION, FISCAL YEARS 2000–2007 ENDING SEPTEMBER 30

(Millions of U.S. dollars)

	Code	2000	2001	2002	2003	2004	2005	2006	2007
C. INCOME	4 300	**−9.2**	**−9.5**	**−13.7**	**−14.3**	**−11.9**	**−35.0**	**6.6**	**7.2**
Total credit	2 300	....	....	....	....	....	*2.1*	*18.7*	*24.8*
Total debit	3 300	*−9.2*	*−9.5*	*−13.7*	*−14.3*	*−11.9*	*−37.1*	*−12.1*	*−17.6*
Compensation of employees, credit	2 310	....	....	....	....	....	....	....	....
Compensation of employees, debit	3 310	....	....	....	....	....	....	....	....
Investment income, credit	2 320	....	....	....	....	....	**2.1**	**18.7**	**24.8**
Direct investment income	2 330	....	....	....	....	....	....	....	....
Dividends and distributed branch profits	2 332	....	....	....	....	....	....	....	....
Reinvested earnings and undistributed branch profits	2 333	....	....	....	....	....	....	....	....
Income on debt (interest)	2 334	....	....	....	....	....	....	....	....
Portfolio investment income	2 339	....	....	....	....	....	....	....	....
Income on equity	2 340	....	....	....	....	....	....	....	....
Income on bonds and notes	2 350	....	....	....	....	....	....	....	....
Income on money market instruments	2 360	....	....	....	....	....	....	....	....
Other investment income	2 370	....	....	....	....	....	2.1	18.7	24.8
Investment income, debit	3 320	**−9.2**	**−9.5**	**−13.7**	**−14.3**	**−11.9**	**−37.1**	**−12.1**	**−17.6**
Direct investment income	3 330	....	....	....	....	....	....	....	....
Dividends and distributed branch profits	3 332	....	....	....	....	....	....	....	....
Reinvested earnings and undistributed branch profits	3 333	....	....	....	....	....	....	....	....
Income on debt (interest)	3 334	....	....	....	....	....	....	....	....
Portfolio investment income	3 339	....	....	....	....	....	....	....	....
Income on equity	3 340	....	....	....	....	....	....	....	....
Income on bonds and notes	3 350	....	....	....	....	....	....	....	....
Income on money market instruments	3 360	....	....	....	....	....	....	....	....
Other investment income	3 370	−9.2	−9.5	−13.7	−14.3	−11.9	−37.1	−12.1	−17.6
D. CURRENT TRANSFERS	4 379	**760.0**	**749.2**	**753.7**	**916.7**	**993.0**	**1,289.9**	**1,360.8**	**1,505.0**
Credit	2 379	**771.0**	**768.6**	**775.7**	**948.0**	**1,031.5**	**1,349.6**	**1,436.3**	**1,601.4**
General government	2 380	193.0	145.0	100.0	137.0	100.0	363.4	373.5	379.3
Other sectors	2 390	578.0	623.6	675.7	811.0	931.5	986.2	1,062.9	1,222.1
Workers' remittances	2 391	578.0	623.6	675.7	811.0	931.5	986.2	1,062.9	1,222.1
Other current transfers	2 392	....	....	....	....	....	....	....	....
Debit	3 379	**−11.0**	**−19.3**	**−22.0**	**−31.4**	**−38.6**	**−59.7**	**−75.5**	**−96.4**
General government	3 380	....	....	....	....	....	....	....	....
Other sectors	3 390	−11.0	−19.3	−22.0	−31.4	−38.6	−59.7	−75.5	−96.4
Workers' remittances	3 391	−11.0	−19.3	−22.0	−31.4	−38.6	−59.7	−75.5	−96.4
Other current transfers	3 392	....	....	....	....	....	....	....	....
CAPITAL AND FINANCIAL ACCOUNT	4 996	**40.9**	**87.7**	**48.2**	**−56.7**	**−17.8**	**−53.9**	**47.4**	**−101.3**
CAPITAL ACCOUNT	4 994	....	....	....	....	....	....	....	**30.3**
Total credit	2 994	....	....	....	....	....	....	....	*30.3*
Total debit	3 994	....	....	....	....	....	....	....	....
Capital transfers, credit	2 400	....	....	....	....	....	....	....	**30.3**
General government	2 401	....	....	....	....	....	....	....	30.3
Debt forgiveness	2 402	....	....	....	....	....	....	....	30.3
Other capital transfers	2 410	....	....	....	....	....	....	....	....
Other sectors	2 430	....	....	....	....	....	....	....	....
Migrants' transfers	2 431	....	....	....	....	....	....	....	....
Debt forgiveness	2 432	....	....	....	....	....	....	....	....
Other capital transfers	2 440	....	....	....	....	....	....	....	....
Capital transfers, debit	3 400	....	....	....	....	....	....	....	....
General government	3 401	....	....	....	....	....	....	....	....
Debt forgiveness	3 402	....	....	....	....	....	....	....	....
Other capital transfers	3 410	....	....	....	....	....	....	....	....
Other sectors	3 430	....	....	....	....	....	....	....	....
Migrants' transfers	3 431	....	....	....	....	....	....	....	....
Debt forgiveness	3 432	....	....	....	....	....	....	....	....
Other capital transfers	3 440	....	....	....	....	....	....	....	....
Nonproduced nonfinancial assets, credit	2 480	....	....	....	....	....	....	....	....
Nonproduced nonfinancial assets, debit	3 480	....	....	....	....	....	....	....	....

Table 2 (Continued). STANDARD PRESENTATION, FISCAL YEARS 2000–2007 ENDING SEPTEMBER 30

(Millions of U.S. dollars)

	Code	2000	2001	2002	2003	2004	2005	2006	2007
FINANCIAL ACCOUNT	4 995	**40.9**	**87.7**	**48.2**	**−56.7**	**−17.8**	**−53.9**	**47.4**	**−131.6**
A. DIRECT INVESTMENT	4 500	**13.3**	**4.4**	**5.7**	**13.8**	**5.9**	**26.0**	**160.6**	**74.5**
Direct investment abroad	4 505	....	....	....	....	....	....	....	....
Equity capital	4 510	....	....	....	....	....	....	....	....
Claims on affiliated enterprises	4 515	....	....	....	....	....	....	....	....
Liabilities to affiliated enterprises	4 520	....	....	....	....	....	....	....	....
Reinvested earnings	4 525	....	....	....	....	....	....	....	....
Other capital	4 530	....	....	....	....	....	....	....	....
Claims on affiliated enterprises	4 535	....	....	....	....	....	....	....	....
Liabilities to affiliated enterprises	4 540	....	....	....	....	....	....	....	....
Direct investment in Haiti	4 555	**13.3**	**4.4**	**5.7**	**13.8**	**5.9**	**26.0**	**160.6**	**74.5**
Equity capital	4 560	....	....	5.7	13.8	5.9	26.0	160.6	74.5
Claims on direct investors	4 565	....	....						
Liabilities to direct investors	4 570	....	....	5.7	13.8	5.9	26.0	160.6	74.5
Reinvested earnings	4 575	....	....						
Other capital	4 580	13.3	4.4	....	....	....	....	....	....
Claims on direct investors	4 585	....	....						
Liabilities to direct investors	4 590	13.3	4.4	....	....	....	....	....	....
B. PORTFOLIO INVESTMENT	4 600	....	....	....	....	....	....	....	....
Assets	4 602	....	....	....	....	....	....	....	....
Equity securities	4 610	....	....	....	....	....	....	....	....
Monetary authorities	4 611	....	....	....	....	....	....	....	....
General government	4 612	....	....	....	....	....	....	....	....
Banks	4 613	....	....	....	....	....	....	....	....
Other sectors	4 614	....	....	....	....	....	....	....	....
Debt securities	4 619	....	....	....	....	....	....	....	....
Bonds and notes	4 620	....	....	....	....	....	....	....	....
Monetary authorities	4 621	....	....	....	....	....	....	....	....
General government	4 622	....	....	....	....	....	....	....	....
Banks	4 623	....	....	....	....	....	....	....	....
Other sectors	4 624	....	....	....	....	....	....	....	....
Money market instruments	4 630	....	....	....	....	....	....	....	....
Monetary authorities	4 631	....	....	....	....	....	....	....	....
General government	4 632	....	....	....	....	....	....	....	....
Banks	4 633	....	....	....	....	....	....	....	....
Other sectors	4 634	....	....	....	....	....	....	....	....
Liabilities	4 652	....	....	....	....	....	....	....	....
Equity securities	4 660	....	....	....	....	....	....	....	....
Banks	4 663	....	....	....	....	....	....	....	....
Other sectors	4 664	....	....	....	....	....	....	....	....
Debt securities	4 669	....	....	....	....	....	....	....	....
Bonds and notes	4 670	....	....	....	....	....	....	....	....
Monetary authorities	4 671	....	....	....	....	....	....	....	....
General government	4 672	....	....	....	....	....	....	....	....
Banks	4 673	....	....	....	....	....	....	....	....
Other sectors	4 674	....	....	....	....	....	....	....	....
Money market instruments	4 680	....	....	....	....	....	....	....	....
Monetary authorities	4 681	....	....	....	....	....	....	....	....
General government	4 682	....	....	....	....	....	....	....	....
Banks	4 683	....	....	....	....	....	....	....	....
Other sectors	4 684	....	....	....	....	....	....	....	....
C. FINANCIAL DERIVATIVES	4 910	....	....	....	....	....	....	....	....
Monetary authorities	4 911	....	....	....	....	....	....	....	....
General government	4 912	....	....	....	....	....	....	....	....
Banks	4 913	....	....	....	....	....	....	....	....
Other sectors	4 914	....	....	....	....	....	....	....	....
Assets	4 900	....	....	....	....	....	....	....	....
Monetary authorities	4 901	....	....	....	....	....	....	....	....
General government	4 902	....	....	....	....	....	....	....	....
Banks	4 903	....	....	....	....	....	....	....	....
Other sectors	4 904	....	....	....	....	....	....	....	....
Liabilities	4 905	....	....	....	....	....	....	....	....
Monetary authorities	4 906	....	....	....	....	....	....	....	....
General government	4 907	....	....	....	....	....	....	....	....
Banks	4 908	....	....	....	....	....	....	....	....
Other sectors	4 909	....	....	....	....	....	....	....	....

Table 2 (Concluded). STANDARD PRESENTATION, FISCAL YEARS 2000–2007 ENDING SEPTEMBER 30

(Millions of U.S. dollars)

	Code	2000	2001	2002	2003	2004	2005	2006	2007
D. OTHER INVESTMENT	4 700 ..	−29.6	88.5	−6.8	−91.3	26.2	−58.9	−5.1	2.2
Assets	4 703 ..	−43.3	−3.0	−22.6	−87.8	−4.4	−64.5	−55.1	−.1
Trade credits	4 706 ..	−5.4	2.8	....	....	....	....	....	....
General government	4 707 ..	−5.4	2.8	....	....	....	....	....	....
of which: Short-term	4 709 ..	−5.4	2.8	....	....	....	....	....	....
Other sectors	4 710 ..	....	....	....	....	....	....	....	....
of which: Short-term	4 712 ..	....	....	....	....	....	....	....	....
Loans	4 714 ..	....	....	....	....	....	....	....	....
Monetary authorities	4 715 ..	....	....	....	....	....	....	....	....
of which: Short-term	4 718 ..	....	....	....	....	....	....	....	....
General government	4 719 ..	....	....	....	....	....	....	....	....
of which: Short-term	4 721 ..	....	....	....	....	....	....	....	....
Banks	4 722 ..	....	....	....	....	....	....	....	....
of which: Short-term	4 724 ..	....	....	....	....	....	....	....	....
Other sectors	4 725 ..	....	....	....	....	....	....	....	....
of which: Short-term	4 727 ..	....	....	....	....	....	....	....	....
Currency and deposits	4 730 ..	−37.9	−5.8	−22.4	−26.3	1.0	−30.3	9.3	−20.4
Monetary authorities	4 731 ..	....	....	....	....	....	....	....	....
General government	4 732 ..	....	....	....	....	....	....	....	....
Banks	4 733 ..	−63.9	17.2	.6	13.7	6.0	−24.3	−10.5	−16.4
Other sectors	4 734 ..	26.0	−23.0	−23.0	−40.0	−5.0	−6.0	19.8	−4.0
Other assets	4 736 ..	....	....	−.3	−61.5	−5.4	−34.2	−64.5	20.3
Monetary authorities	4 737 ..	....	....	....	.3	−.1	−.9	.1	−.1
of which: Short-term	4 739 ..	....	....	....	.3	−.1	−.9	.1	−.1
General government	4 740 ..	....	....	....	....	....	....	....	....
of which: Short-term	4 742 ..	....	....	....	....	....	....	....	....
Banks	4 743 ..	....	....	−.3	−61.8	−5.4	−33.3	−64.6	20.5
of which: Short-term	4 745 ..	....	....	−.3	−61.8	−5.4	−33.3	−64.6	20.5
Other sectors	4 746 ..	....	....	....	....	....	....	....	....
of which: Short-term	4 748 ..	....	....	....	....	....	....	....	....
Liabilities	4 753 ..	13.6	91.5	15.8	−3.5	30.7	5.5	50.1	2.3
Trade credits	4 756 ..	.8	1.0	....	....	....	....	....	....
General government	4 757 ..	....	....	....	....	....	....	....	....
of which: Short-term	4 759 ..	....	....	....	....	....	....	....	....
Other sectors	4 760 ..	.8	1.0	....	....	....	....	....	....
of which: Short-term	4 762 ..	.8	1.0	....	....	....	....	....	....
Loans	4 764 ..	20.5	3.9	−3.2	−5.6	.4	45.7	49.0	107.6
Monetary authorities	4 765 ..	−5.8	....	−9.2	−14.5	−7.1	11.0	10.3	20.8
of which: Use of Fund credit and loans from the Fund..	4 766 ..	−5.8	....	−9.2	−14.5	−7.1	11.0	10.3	20.8
of which: Short-term	4 768 ..	....	....	....	....	....	....	....	....
General government	4 769 ..	26.3	3.9	6.1	11.3	7.5	31.0	42.4	76.8
of which: Short-term	4 771 ..	....	....	....	....	....	....	....	−32.4
Banks	4 772 ..	....	....	....	−2.4	....	3.6	−3.6	10.1
of which: Short-term	4 774 ..	....	....	....	....	....	....	....	....
Other sectors	4 775 ..	....	....	....	....	....	....	....	....
of which: Short-term	4 777 ..	....	....	....	....	....	....	....	....
Currency and deposits	4 780 ..	−9.2	83.1	−10.3	4.1	21.5	−13.6	−3.7	−16.5
Monetary authorities	4 781 ..	....	....	....	....	....	....	....	....
General government	4 782 ..	....	....	....	....	....	....	....	....
Banks	4 783 ..	8.8	−.9	.7	4.1	21.5	−13.6	−3.7	−2.5
Other sectors	4 784 ..	−18.0	84.0	−11.0	....	....	....	....	−14.0
Other liabilities	4 786 ..	1.5	3.6	29.2	−1.9	8.8	−26.5	4.7	−88.8
Monetary authorities	4 787 ..	....	....	28.3	1.4	4.0	−1.3	.9	.5
of which: Short-term	4 789 ..	....	....	28.2	1.4	1.2	1.6	.8	.5
General government	4 790 ..	1.5	3.6	....	−2.8	2.7	−22.1	4.9	−92.0
of which: Short-term	4 792 ..	5.5	10.5	....	−2.8	17.4	−22.1	4.9	−92.0
Banks	4 793 ..	....	....	.9	−.6	2.1	−3.2	−1.1	2.7
of which: Short-term	4 795 ..	....	....	....	....	....	....	....	....
Other sectors	4 796 ..	....	....	....	....	....	....	....	....
of which: Short-term	4 798 ..	....	....	....	....	....	....	....	....
E. RESERVE ASSETS	4 802 ..	57.3	−5.3	49.4	20.7	−50.0	−21.0	−108.1	−208.4
Monetary gold	4 812 ..	....	....	....	....	−.2	−.1	−.2	−.2
Special drawing rights	4 811 ..	.5	....	−.5	.4	−.4	.7	−9.7	2.9
Reserve position in the Fund	4 810 ..	....	....	....	....	....	....	....	....
Foreign exchange	4 803 ..	56.8	−5.2	50.0	20.4	−49.3	−21.6	−98.3	−211.1
Other claims	4 813 ..	....	....	−.2	....	....	....	....	....
NET ERRORS AND OMISSIONS	4 998 ..	73.3	44.2	40.7	101.5	73.5	48.7	25.8	181.6

Table 3. INTERNATIONAL INVESTMENT POSITION (End-period stocks), 2000–2007

(Millions of U.S. dollars)

	Code	2000	2001	2002	2003	2004	2005	2006	2007
ASSETS	8 995 C.	**531.1**	**539.3**	**460.2**	**534.1**	**537.5**	**649.9**	**1,038.4**	**1,246.8**
Direct investment abroad	8 505 ..	....	....	....	....	....	....	....	....
Equity capital and reinvested earnings	8 506 ..	....	....	....	....	....	....	....	....
Claims on affiliated enterprises	8 507 ..	....	....	....	....	....	....	....	....
Liabilities to affiliated enterprises	8 508 ..	....	....	....	....	....	....	....	....
Other capital	8 530 ..	....	....	....	....	....	....	....	....
Claims on affiliated enterprises	8 535 ..	....	....	....	....	....	....	....	....
Liabilities to affiliated enterprises	8 540 ..	....	....	....	....	....	....	....	....
Portfolio investment	8 602 ..	....	....	....	....	....	....	....	....
Equity securities	8 610 ..	....	....	....	....	....	....	....	....
Monetary authorities	8 611 ..	....	....	....	....	....	....	....	....
General government	8 612 ..	....	....	....	....	....	....	....	....
Banks	8 613 ..	....	....	....	....	....	....	....	....
Other sectors	8 614 ..	....	....	....	....	....	....	....	....
Debt securities	8 619 ..	....	....	....	....	....	....	....	....
Bonds and notes	8 620 ..	....	....	....	....	....	....	....	....
Monetary authorities	8 621 ..	....	....	....	....	....	....	....	....
General government	8 622 ..	....	....	....	....	....	....	....	....
Banks	8 623 ..	....	....	....	....	....	....	....	....
Other sectors	8 624 ..	....	....	....	....	....	....	....	....
Money market instruments	8 630 ..	....	....	....	....	....	....	....	....
Monetary authorities	8 631 ..	....	....	....	....	....	....	....	....
General government	8 632 ..	....	....	....	....	....	....	....	....
Banks	8 633 ..	....	....	....	....	....	....	....	....
Other sectors	8 634 ..	....	....	....	....	....	....	....	....
Financial derivatives	8 900 ..	....	....	....	....	....	....	....	....
Monetary authorities	8 901 ..	....	....	....	....	....	....	....	....
General government	8 902 ..	....	....	....	....	....	....	....	....
Banks	8 903 ..	....	....	....	....	....	....	....	....
Other sectors	8 904 ..	....	....	....	....	....	....	....	....
Other investment	8 703 ..	**259.2**	**262.2**	**232.5**	**327.4**	**280.8**	**371.4**	**651.5**	**651.0**
Trade credits	8 706 ..	....	....	....	....	....	....	....	....
General government	8 707 ..	....	....	....	....	....	....	....	....
of which: Short-term	8 709 ..	....	....	....	....	....	....	....	....
Other sectors	8 710 ..	....	....	....	....	....	....	....	....
of which: Short-term	8 712 ..	....	....	....	....	....	....	....	....
Loans	8 714 ..	....	....	....	....	....	....	....	....
Monetary authorities	8 715 ..	....	....	....	....	....	....	....	....
of which: Short-term	8 718 ..	....	....	....	....	....	....	....	....
General government	8 719 ..	....	....	....	....	....	....	....	....
of which: Short-term	8 721 ..	....	....	....	....	....	....	....	....
Banks	8 722 ..	....	....	....	....	....	....	....	....
of which: Short-term	8 724 ..	....	....	....	....	....	....	....	....
Other sectors	8 725 ..	....	....	....	....	....	....	....	....
of which: Short-term	8 727 ..	....	....	....	....	....	....	....	....
Currency and deposits	8 730 ..	253.8	259.6	160.3	193.1	141.1	198.4	413.9	433.9
Monetary authorities	8 731 ..	....	....	....	....	....	....	....	....
General government	8 732 ..	....	....	....	....	....	....	....	....
Banks	8 733 ..	188.8	171.6	100.3	86.1	80.1	104.4	114.9	130.9
Other sectors	8 734 ..	65.0	88.0	60.0	107.0	61.0	94.0	299.0	303.0
Other assets	8 736 ..	5.4	2.6	72.1	134.3	139.7	173.0	237.6	217.1
Monetary authorities	8 737 ..	....	....	....	....	....	....	....	....
of which: Short-term	8 739 ..	....	....	....	....	....	....	....	....
General government	8 740 ..	....	....	....	....	....	....	....	....
of which: Short-term	8 742 ..	....	....	....	....	....	....	....	....
Banks	8 743 ..	....	....	72.1	134.3	139.7	173.0	237.6	217.1
of which: Short-term	8 745 ..	....	....	....	....	....	....	....	....
Other sectors	8 746 ..	5.4	2.6	....	....	....	....	....	....
of which: Short-term	8 748 ..	*5.4*	*2.6*	....	....	....	....	....	....
Reserve assets	8 802 ..	**271.9**	**277.0**	**227.7**	**206.7**	**256.6**	**278.5**	**386.9**	**595.8**
Monetary gold	8 812 ..	.4	.3	.3	.3	.5	.6	.8	1.0
Special drawing rights	8 811 ..	.1	.1	.6	.3	.8	.1	10.1	7.6
Reserve position in the Fund	8 810 ..	.1	.1	.1	.1	.1	.1	.1	.1
Foreign exchange	8 803 ..	271.3	276.4	177.0	156.6	205.9	227.6	325.9	536.9
Other claims	8 813 ..	.1	.2	49.7	49.4	49.3	50.2	50.1	50.2

Table 3 (Concluded). INTERNATIONAL INVESTMENT POSITION (End-period stocks), 2000–2007

(Millions of U.S. dollars)

	Code	2000	2001	2002	2003	2004	2005	2006	2007
LIABILITIES..	8 995 D.	**1,437.9**	**1,536.8**	**1,554.4**	**1,640.4**	**1,670.1**	**1,723.5**	**1,967.4**	**2,195.8**
Direct investment in Haiti....................	8 555 ..	**94.7**	**99.1**	**104.8**	**118.6**	**124.5**	**150.5**	**310.5**	**385.0**
Equity capital and reinvested earnings.............................	8 556 ..	94.7	99.1	104.8	118.6	124.5	150.5	310.5	385.0
Claims on direct investors...............................	8 557 ..	....	....	....	....	....	....	....	....
Liabilities to direct investors........................	8 558 ..	94.7	99.1	104.8	118.6	124.5	150.5	310.5	385.0
Other capital..	8 580 ..	....	....	....	....	....	....	....	....
Claims on direct investors...............................	8 585 ..	....	....	....	....	....	....	....	....
Liabilities to direct investors........................	8 590 ..	....	....	....	....	....	....	....	....
Portfolio investment...............................	8 652 ..	....	....	....	....	....	....		....
Equity securities..	8 660 ..	....	....	....	....	....	....		
Banks..	8 663 ..	....	....	....	....	....	....		
Other sectors.....................................	8 664 ..	....	....	....	....	....	....		
Debt securities...	8 669 ..	....	....	....	....	....	....		
Bonds and notes.................................	8 670 ..	....	....	....	....	....	....		
Monetary authorities.......................	8 671 ..	....	....	....	....	....	....		
General government........................	8 672 ..	....	....	....	....	....	....		
Banks...	8 673 ..	....	....	....	....	....	....		
Other sectors..................................	8 674 ..	....	....	....	....	....	....		
Money market instruments.................	8 680 ..	....	....	....	....	....	....		
Monetary authorities.......................	8 681 ..	....	....	....	....	....	....		
General government........................	8 682 ..	....	....	....	....	....	....		
Banks...	8 683 ..	....	....	....	....	....	....		
Other sectors..................................	8 684 ..	....	....	....	....	....	....		
Financial derivatives.............................	8 905 ..	....	....	....	....	....	....		
Monetary authorities..................................	8 906 ..	....	....	....	....	....	....		
General government....................................	8 907 ..	....	....	....	....	....	....		
Banks...	8 908 ..	....	....	....	....	....	....		
Other sectors...	8 909 ..	....	....	....	....	....	....		
Other investment...................................	8 753 ..	**1,343.3**	**1,437.8**	**1,449.6**	**1,521.8**	**1,545.6**	**1,573.0**	**1,657.0**	**1,810.8**
Trade credits..	8 756 ..	....	....	....	....	....	....	....	....
General government....................................	8 757 ..	....	....	....	....	....	....	....	....
of which: Short-term................................	8 759 ..	....	....	....	....	....	....	....	....
Other sectors...	8 760 ..	....	....	....	....	....	....	....	....
of which: Short-term................................	8 762 ..	....	....	....	....	....	....	....	....
Loans..	8 764 ..	1,342.4	1,435.9	1,246.8	1,307.2	1,329.3	1,364.8	1,453.6	1,598.5
Monetary authorities..................................	8 765 ..	99.8	100.9	30.6	17.9	11.1	21.4	32.5	55.6
of which: Use of Fund credit and loans from the Fund....	8 766 ..	*39.4*	*39.1*	*30.6*	*17.9*	*11.1*	*21.4*	*32.5*	*55.6*
of which: Short-term................................	8 768 ..	*.4*	*.6*	....	....	....	....	....	....
General government....................................	8 769 ..	1,179.6	1,188.9	1,211.9	1,287.4	1,316.3	1,337.8	1,419.3	1,541.0
of which: Short-term................................	8 771 ..	....	....	....	....	....	....	....	....
Banks...	8 772 ..	21.0	20.0	4.3	1.9	1.9	5.5	1.9	1.9
of which: Short-term................................	8 774 ..	*21.0*	*20.0*	....	....	....	....	....	....
Other sectors...	8 775 ..	42.0	126.0	....	....	....	....	....	....
of which: Short-term................................	8 777 ..	*42.0*	*126.0*	....	....	....	....	....	....
Currency and deposits.................................	8 780 ..	....	....	129.5	135.5	138.0	134.4	129.7	138.2
Monetary authorities..................................	8 781 ..	....	....	....	....	....	....	....	....
General government....................................	8 782 ..	....	....	....	....	....	....	....	....
Banks...	8 783 ..	....	....	10.5	14.5	36.0	22.4	18.7	16.2
Other sectors...	8 784 ..	....	....	119.0	121.0	102.0	112.0	111.0	122.0
Other liabilities..	8 786 ..	.9	1.9	73.4	79.1	78.3	73.8	73.6	74.1
Monetary authorities..................................	8 787 ..	....	....	61.9	63.4	67.3	66.0	66.9	67.4
of which: Short-term................................	8 789 ..	....	....	....	....	....	....	....	....
General government....................................	8 790 ..	....	....	....	....	....	....	....	....
of which: Short-term................................	8 792 ..	....	....	....	....	....	....	....	....
Banks...	8 793 ..	....	....	9.3	15.0	11.0	7.8	6.7	6.7
of which: Short-term................................	8 795 ..	....	....	....	....	....	....	....	....
Other sectors...	8 796 ..	.9	1.9	2.1	.7	....	....	....	....
of which: Short-term................................	8 798 ..	*.9*	*1.9*	*2.1*	*.7*	*.3*	....	....	....
NET INTERNATIONAL INVESTMENT POSITION........	8 995 ..	**−906.8**	**−997.6**	**−1,094.2**	**−1,106.2**	**−1,132.6**	**−1,073.5**	**−929.1**	**−949.0**
Conversion rates: gourdes per U.S. dollar (end of period)........................	0 102 ..	28.334	25.493	29.698	42.025	36.823	43.043	39.129	36.381

Table 1. ANALYTIC PRESENTATION, 2000–2007

(Millions of U.S. dollars)

	Code	2000	2001	2002	2003	2004	2005	2006	2007
A. Current Account[1]	4 993 Z.	**−508.3**	**−478.7**	**−281.6**	**−552.8**	**−683.4**	**−304.3**	**−510.4**	**−1,225.4**
Goods: exports f.o.b.	2 100 ..	3,343.4	3,422.7	3,744.9	3,754.0	4,533.9	5,048.0	5,195.0	5,594.2
Goods: imports f.o.b.	3 100 ..	−3,987.8	−4,151.9	−4,381.6	−4,774.1	−5,827.2	−6,544.6	−7,317.1	−8,556.3
Balance on Goods	4 100 ..	*−644.4*	*−729.3*	*−636.7*	*−1,020.1*	*−1,293.3*	*−1,496.6*	*−2,122.1*	*−2,962.1*
Services: credit	2 200 ..	507.1	504.8	542.0	591.1	644.7	699.6	685.8	750.1
Services: debit	3 200 ..	−693.6	−711.4	−731.9	−753.2	−848.9	−928.8	−983.9	−1,037.3
Balance on Goods and Services	4 991 ..	*−830.9*	*−935.9*	*−826.7*	*−1,182.2*	*−1,497.5*	*−1,725.8*	*−2,420.2*	*−3,249.4*
Income: credit	2 300 ..	151.0	123.3	84.9	67.9	87.5	145.0	198.2	224.5
Income: debit	3 300 ..	−365.9	−381.1	−386.1	−429.8	−538.7	−618.7	−738.6	−822.4
Balance on Goods, Services, and Income	4 992 ..	*−1,045.9*	*−1,193.6*	*−1,127.8*	*−1,544.0*	*−1,948.7*	*−2,199.5*	*−2,960.6*	*−3,847.3*
Current transfers: credit	2 379 Z.	654.2	840.4	983.4	1,091.9	1,374.0	2,042.4	2,588.7	2,774.0
Current transfers: debit	3 379 ..	−116.6	−125.5	−137.1	−100.7	−108.6	−147.3	−138.4	−152.1
B. Capital Account[1]	4 994 Z.	**164.1**	**160.4**	**85.2**	**49.2**	**50.8**	**593.5**	**1,484.8**	**1,158.1**
Capital account: credit	2 994 Z.	164.1	160.4	85.2	49.2	50.8	593.5	1,484.8	1,158.1
Capital account: debit	3 994 ..	....	....	....	....	....	....	....	....
Total, Groups A Plus B	4 981 ..	*−344.2*	*−318.2*	*−196.3*	*−503.6*	*−632.6*	*289.2*	*974.4*	*−67.3*
C. Financial Account[1]	4 995 W.	**223.7**	**288.1**	**169.8**	**304.3**	**991.1**	**54.8**	**−408.4**	**−4.1**
Direct investment abroad	4 505 ..	−6.5	−2.8	−6.5	−12.2	6.2	−1.0	−.6	−1.0
Direct investment in Honduras	4 555 Z.	381.7	304.2	275.2	402.8	546.9	599.8	674.2	815.9
Portfolio investment assets	4 602 ..	−59.0	−12.9	−6.2	−7.3	−11.8	−23.1	−20.9	−13.1
Equity securities	4 610 ..	1.9	−.3	−2.7	−5.7	−1.2	−11.7	1.8	−1.2
Debt securities	4 619 ..	−60.9	−12.6	−3.5	−1.6	−10.6	−11.4	−22.7	−11.9
Portfolio investment liabilities	4 652 Z.	....	....	....	.2	.2	....	....	....
Equity securities	4 660 ..	....	....	....	.2	.2	....	....	....
Debt securities	4 669 Z.	....	....	....	....	....	....	....	....
Financial derivatives	4 910 ..	....	....	....	....	....	....	....	....
Financial derivatives assets	4 900 ..	....	....	....	....	....	....	....	....
Financial derivatives liabilities	4 905 ..	....	....	....	....	....	....	....	....
Other investment assets	4 703 ..	−139.7	−28.1	−92.6	−62.5	−59.3	12.3	94.8	48.4
Monetary authorities	4 701 ..	....	....	....	1.0	2.6	−.5	....	....
General government	4 704 ..	−7.9	−16.2	−2.3	−.9	−1.0	2.1	−.1	−3.0
Banks	4 705 ..	−67.6	−38.9	−76.4	17.0	−96.1	6.0	34.1	−16.9
Other sectors	4 728 ..	−64.2	27.0	−13.9	−79.6	35.2	4.8	60.8	68.4
Other investment liabilities	4 753 W.	47.2	27.6	−.1	−16.7	508.9	−533.1	−1,155.8	−854.3
Monetary authorities	4 753 WA	−36.7	−18.4	−25.8	−13.1	−7.8	−13.4	−4.9	−4.6
General government	4 753 ZB	−24.5	113.1	−6.2	34.8	247.2	−567.2	−1,257.1	−981.2
Banks	4 753 ZC	−43.1	−45.7	7.7	−19.6	107.1	107.7	123.0	99.5
Other sectors	4 753 ZD	151.5	−21.3	24.2	−18.8	162.4	−60.2	−16.9	31.9
Total, Groups A Through C	4 983 ..	*−120.5*	*−30.1*	*−26.5*	*−199.3*	*358.5*	*344.0*	*566.1*	*−71.4*
D. Net Errors and Omissions	4 998 ..	**−39.9**	**−42.7**	**21.5**	**5.1**	**46.5**	**−188.5**	**−185.9**	**−52.6**
Total, Groups A Through D	4 984 ..	*−160.4*	*−72.8*	*−5.0*	*−194.2*	*405.0*	*155.5*	*380.2*	*−124.0*
E. Reserves and Related Items	4 802 A.	**160.4**	**72.8**	**5.0**	**194.2**	**−405.0**	**−155.5**	**−380.2**	**124.0**
Reserve assets	4 802 ..	−54.6	−101.1	−105.7	96.5	−510.4	−346.4	−309.9	108.6
Use of Fund credit and loans	4 766 ..	16.4	12.0	−39.7	−41.1	15.1	−11.5	−140.8	....
Exceptional financing	4 920 ..	198.6	162.0	150.5	138.8	90.3	202.3	70.5	15.5
Conversion rates: lempiras per U.S. dollar	0 101 ..	**14.8392**	**15.4737**	**16.4334**	**17.3453**	**18.2062**	**18.8323**	**18.8952**	**18.8951**

[1] Excludes components that have been classified in the categories of Group E.

Table 2. STANDARD PRESENTATION, 2000–2007

(Millions of U.S. dollars)

	Code	2000	2001	2002	2003	2004	2005	2006	2007
CURRENT ACCOUNT	4 993	−508.3	−478.7	−281.6	−552.8	−683.4	−304.3	−510.4	−1,225.4
A. GOODS	4 100	−644.4	−729.3	−636.7	−1,020.1	−1,293.3	−1,496.6	−2,122.1	−2,962.1
Credit	2 100	3,343.4	3,422.7	3,744.9	3,754.0	4,533.9	5,048.0	5,195.0	5,594.2
General merchandise: exports f.o.b.	2 110	1,291.2	1,200.1	1,159.3	1,288.3	1,566.8	1,829.2	1,974.0	2,192.3
Goods for processing: exports f.o.b.	2 150	2,037.8	2,147.7	2,494.5	2,389.9	2,888.1	3,149.8	3,128.4	3,313.5
Repairs on goods	2 160	.4	.4	.8	.9	.5	.2	.2	.2
Goods procured in ports by carriers	2 170	7.8	10.7	9.8	4.7	4.8	5.7	12.5	12.8
Nonmonetary gold	2 180	6.2	63.8	80.5	70.1	73.6	63.2	79.9	75.4
Debit	3 100	−3,987.8	−4,151.9	−4,381.6	−4,774.1	−5,827.2	−6,544.6	−7,317.1	−8,556.3
General merchandise: imports f.o.b.	3 110	−2,679.9	−2,761.2	−2,772.9	−3,178.2	−3,883.6	−4,467.4	−5,275.0	−6,468.9
Goods for processing: imports f.o.b.	3 150	−1,307.6	−1,389.6	−1,608.3	−1,592.3	−1,940.8	−2,075.7	−2,041.3	−2,086.4
Repairs on goods	3 160	−.3	−1.2	−.4	−2.6	−.7	−.6	−.2	−.3
Goods procured in ports by carriers	3 170	....	....	....	−.9	−2.1	−.8	−.6	−.7
Nonmonetary gold	3 180	....	....	....	....	....	....	....	....
B. SERVICES	4 200	−186.5	−206.6	−190.0	−162.1	−204.2	−229.3	−298.1	−287.2
Total credit	2 200	*507.1*	*504.8*	*542.0*	*591.1*	*644.7*	*699.6*	*685.8*	*750.1*
Total debit	3 200	*−693.6*	*−711.4*	*−731.9*	*−753.2*	*−848.9*	*−928.8*	*−983.9*	*−1,037.3*
Transportation services, credit	2 205	56.6	62.3	61.6	45.0	37.1	38.7	39.5	41.2
Passenger	2 850	*3.0*	*3.5*	*3.8*	*7.9*	*6.2*	*2.3*	*1.8*	*1.7*
Freight	2 851	*17.2*	*16.5*	*16.4*	*....*	*....*	*....*	*....*	*....*
Other	2 852	*36.4*	*42.3*	*41.4*	*37.2*	*30.9*	*36.4*	*37.7*	*39.5*
Sea transport, passenger	2 207	....	....	....	....	....	....	....	....
Sea transport, freight	2 208	....	....	....	....	....	....	....	....
Sea transport, other	2 209	29.9	36.6	36.4	27.6	29.3	34.9	33.6	34.8
Air transport, passenger	2 211	3.0	3.5	3.8	7.6	5.9	1.7	1.2	1.1
Air transport, freight	2 212	....	....	....	....	....	....	....	....
Air transport, other	2 213	6.5	5.7	5.0	9.6	1.6	1.5	4.1	4.7
Other transport, passenger	2 215	....	....	....	.2	.3	.5	.6	.6
Other transport, freight	2 216	17.2	16.5	16.4	....	....	....	....	....
Other transport, other	2 217	....	....	....	....	....	....	....	....
Transportation services, debit	3 205	−414.5	−425.3	−438.1	−373.8	−439.5	−499.9	−530.5	−625.3
Passenger	3 850	*−78.1*	*−77.3*	*−72.0*	*−56.7*	*−56.1*	*−59.0*	*−71.9*	*−78.8*
Freight	3 851	*−327.0*	*−340.0*	*−359.1*	*−311.4*	*−378.9*	*−437.2*	*−458.6*	*−546.4*
Other	3 852	*−9.4*	*−8.0*	*−7.0*	*−5.6*	*−4.4*	*−3.7*	*−.1*	*−.1*
Sea transport, passenger	3 207	....	....	....	....	....	....	....	....
Sea transport, freight	3 208	−283.7	−295.5	−314.5	−226.2	−280.6	−308.1	−319.9	−380.7
Sea transport, other	3 209	−9.4	−8.0	−7.0	−5.4	−4.0	−3.5		
Air transport, passenger	3 211	−77.4	−76.4	−70.9	−55.5	−55.0	−57.7	−70.4	−77.5
Air transport, freight	3 212	−10.8	−11.1	−11.1	−16.3	−18.2	−24.1	−26.7	−33.9
Air transport, other	3 213	....	....	....	−.2	−.4	−.2	−.1	−.1
Other transport, passenger	3 215	−.7	−.9	−1.1	−1.3	−1.2	−1.3	−1.4	−1.3
Other transport, freight	3 216	−32.4	−33.4	−33.4	−69.0	−80.1	−105.1	−112.0	−131.8
Other transport, other	3 217	....	....	....	....	....	....	....	....
Travel, credit	2 236	259.8	256.3	301.0	364.4	413.5	463.5	488.3	556.7
Business travel	2 237	39.0	102.5	89.2	145.7	165.4	185.4	195.3	211.0
Personal travel	2 240	220.8	153.8	211.8	218.6	248.1	278.1	293.0	345.7
Travel, debit	3 236	−119.6	−127.6	−149.2	−217.5	−244.2	−262.1	−283.2	−305.9
Business travel	3 237	−45.4	−48.5	−56.7	−87.0	−97.7	−104.9	−113.3	−127.0
Personal travel	3 240	−74.2	−79.1	−92.5	−130.5	−146.5	−157.3	−169.9	−178.9
Other services, credit	2 200 BA	190.7	186.2	179.4	181.7	194.0	197.4	157.9	152.2
Communications	2 245	122.5	117.1	109.2	126.4	151.2	143.5	107.8	85.9
Construction	2 249	....	....	....	1.2	1.3	.1	....	....
Insurance	2 253	15.5	17.8	18.2	17.6	17.4	18.2	20.8	23.0
Financial	2 260	.4	.4	.4	2.1	2.5	5.7	....	....
Computer and information	2 262	....	....	....	.3	.2	.1	.1	.2
Royalties and licence fees	2 266	.3	.6	1.5	.8	....	....	....	....
Other business services	2 268	31.7	33.8	32.8	15.6	11.9	13.5	14.1	25.0
Personal, cultural, and recreational	2 287	....	....	....	....	....	.3	....	....
Government, n.i.e.	2 291	20.3	16.5	17.3	17.7	9.5	15.9	15.0	18.0
Other services, debit	3 200 BA	−159.6	−158.5	−144.6	−162.0	−165.2	−166.8	−170.2	−106.1
Communications	3 245	−25.7	−19.4	−16.8	−20.4	−18.1	−19.3	−22.2	−20.1
Construction	3 249	−40.0	−35.0	−35.0	−32.0	−36.0	−38.0	−50.1	−5.0
Insurance	3 253	−2.9	−3.3	−3.7	−7.2	−7.7	−8.8	−9.5	−9.1
Financial	3 260	−8.6	−8.2	−9.0	−22.6	−16.6	−12.5	−14.2	−6.6
Computer and information	3 262	−8.3	−5.1	−1.9	−1.7	−2.8	−4.7	−4.3	−3.2
Royalties and licence fees	3 266	−13.8	−15.7	−15.4	−19.1	−19.4	−20.9	−23.9	−25.0
Other business services	3 268	−46.2	−57.0	−48.1	−48.3	−50.7	−50.9	−28.7	−19.6
Personal, cultural, and recreational	3 287	−8.0	−8.2	−8.5	−3.6	−5.0	−6.1	−5.5	−7.3
Government, n.i.e.	3 291	−6.1	−6.6	−6.2	−7.1	−8.9	−5.6	−11.6	−10.2

Table 2 (Continued). STANDARD PRESENTATION, 2000–2007

(Millions of U.S. dollars)

	Code	2000	2001	2002	2003	2004	2005	2006	2007
C. INCOME	4 300	−214.9	−257.8	−301.2	−361.8	−451.2	−473.6	−540.4	−597.9
Total credit	2 300	*151.0*	*123.3*	*84.9*	*67.9*	*87.5*	*145.0*	*198.2*	*224.5*
Total debit	3 300	*−365.9*	*−381.1*	*−386.1*	*−429.8*	*−538.7*	*−618.7*	*−738.6*	*−822.4*
Compensation of employees, credit	2 310	33.4	35.7	35.4	23.1	31.1	29.4	29.9	32.9
Compensation of employees, debit	3 310	−8.9	−10.8	−10.2	−12.0	−16.6	−.5	−2.1	−2.5
Investment income, credit	2 320	117.6	87.6	49.5	44.9	56.4	115.6	168.3	191.6
Direct investment income	2 330	....	....	....	....	....	....	.7	....
Dividends and distributed branch profits	2 332	....	....	....	....	....	....	....	....
Reinvested earnings anc undistributed branch profits	2 333	....	....	....	....	....	....	....	....
Income on debt (interest)	2 334	....	....	....	....	....	....	.7	....
Portfolio investment income	2 339	1.7	3.6	3.8	5.0	5.6	6.3	4.8	9.1
Income on equity	2 340	....	....	....	.9	1.2	.6	....	....
Income on bonds and notes	2 350	1.7	3.6	3.8	4.1	4.4	5.6	4.8	9.1
Income on money market instruments	2 360	....	....	....	....	....	....	....	....
Other investment income	2 370	115.9	84.0	45.7	39.9	50.8	109.4	162.8	182.5
Investment income, debit	3 320	−357.0	−370.3	−375.9	−417.8	−522.1	−618.2	−736.5	−819.9
Direct investment income	3 330	−160.5	−212.4	−234.5	−291.6	−390.4	−479.5	−624.3	−737.3
Dividends and distributed branch profits	3 332	−95.0	−55.5	−47.4	−66.4	−108.8	−103.9	−195.9	−225.7
Reinvested earnings and undistributed branch profits	3 333	−65.5	−156.9	−187.2	−225.2	−280.4	−367.6	−423.1	−507.8
Income on debt (interest)	3 334	....	....	....	−.1	−1.2	−8.0	−5.4	−3.9
Portfolio investment income	3 339	....	....	....	....	....	....	....	....
Income on equity	3 340	....	....	....	....	....	....	....	....
Income on bonds and notes	3 350	....	....	....	....	....	....	....	....
Income on money market instruments	3 360	....	....	....	....	....	....	....	....
Other investment income	3 370	−196.6	−157.9	−141.4	−126.1	−131.7	−138.7	−112.2	−82.6
D. CURRENT TRANSFERS	4 379	537.6	715.0	846.3	991.2	1,265.3	1,895.1	2,450.3	2,621.9
Credit	2 379	654.2	840.4	983.4	1,091.9	1,374.0	2,042.4	2,588.7	2,774.0
General government	2 380	111.8	119.0	73.4	201.0	185.5	181.4	195.4	132.5
Other sectors	2 390	542.4	721.4	910.0	890.9	1,188.4	1,861.1	2,393.3	2,641.5
Workers' remittances	2 391	441.1	574.7	766.0	842.3	1,138.0	1,775.8	2,328.6	2,561.4
Other current transfers	2 392	101.3	146.7	144.0	48.6	50.4	85.3	64.7	80.0
Debit	3 379	−116.6	−125.5	−137.1	−100.7	−108.6	−147.3	−138.4	−152.1
General government	3 380	−.6	−.8	−.8	−7.0	−4.5	−23.0	−4.5	−2.0
Other sectors	3 390	−116.0	−124.7	−136.3	−93.7	−104.1	−124.3	−134.0	−150.1
Workers' remittances	3 391	−.5	−.7	−.7	....	....	....	....	....
Other current transfers	3 392	−115.5	−124.0	−135.6	−93.7	−104.1	−124.3	−134.0	−150.1
CAPITAL AND FINANCIAL ACCOUNT	4 996	548.1	521.4	260.0	547.7	636.9	492.8	696.2	1,278.0
CAPITAL ACCOUNT	4 994	261.9	269.0	141.8	55.7	142.1	860.1	1,639.5	1,218.2
Total credit	2 994	*261.9*	*269.0*	*141.8*	*55.7*	*142.1*	*860.1*	*1,639.5*	*1,218.2*
Total debit	3 994	....	....	....	....	....	....	....	....
Capital transfers, credit	2 400	261.9	269.0	141.8	55.7	142.1	860.1	1,639.5	1,218.2
General government	2 401	218.7	242.8	112.2	35.9	136.1	844.4	1,607.1	1,186.7
Debt forgiveness	2 402	97.8	108.6	56.6	6.5	91.3	266.6	154.7	60.1
Other capital transfers	2 410	120.9	134.2	55.6	29.4	44.8	577.8	1,452.4	1,126.6
Other sectors	2 430	43.2	26.2	29.6	19.8	6.0	15.7	32.4	31.5
Migrants' transfers	2 431	9.5	12.3	16.4	18.1	6.0	15.7	32.4	30.4
Debt forgiveness	2 432	....	....	....	....	....	....	....	.1
Other capital transfers	2 440	33.7	13.9	13.2	1.8	....	....	....	1.1
Capital transfers, debit	3 400	....	....	....	....	....	....	....	....
General government	3 401	....	....	....	....	....	....	....	....
Debt forgiveness	3 402	....	....	....	....	....	....	....	....
Other capital transfers	3 410	....	....	....	....	....	....	....	....
Other sectors	3 430	....	....	....	....	....	....	....	....
Migrants' transfers	3 431	....	....	....	....	....	....	....	....
Debt forgiveness	3 432	....	....	....	....	....	....	....	....
Other capital transfers	3 440	....	....	....	....	....	....	....	....
Nonproduced nonfinancial assets, credit	2 480	....	....	....	....	....	....	....	....
Nonproduced nonfinancial assets, debit	3 480	....	....	....	....	....	....	....	....

Table 2 (Continued). STANDARD PRESENTATION, 2000–2007

(Millions of U.S. dollars)

	Code	2000	2001	2002	2003	2004	2005	2006	2007
FINANCIAL ACCOUNT	4 995 ..	286.3	252.4	118.2	492.0	494.8	−367.3	−943.2	59.8
A. DIRECT INVESTMENT	4 500 ..	375.2	301.4	268.7	390.6	553.1	598.8	673.6	814.9
Direct investment abroad	4 505 ..	−6.5	−2.8	−6.5	−12.2	6.2	−1.0	−.6	−1.0
Equity capital	4 510 ..	−6.5	−2.8	−6.5	−1.3	....	....	....	....
Claims on affiliated enterprises	4 515 ..	....	....	....	....	....	....	....	....
Liabilities to affiliated enterprises	4 520 ..	−6.5	−2.8	−6.5	−1.3	....	....	....	....
Reinvested earnings	4 525 ..	....	....	....	....	....	....	....	....
Other capital	4 530 ..	....	....	....	−10.9	6.2	−1.0	−.6	−1.0
Claims on affiliated enterprises	4 535 ..	....	....	....	....	6.2	−1.0	−.6	−1.0
Liabilities to affiliated enterprises	4 540 ..	....	....	....	−10.9	....	....	....	....
Direct investment in Honduras	4 555 ..	381.7	304.2	275.2	402.8	546.9	599.8	674.2	815.9
Equity capital	4 560 ..	160.3	94.8	106.0	139.6	182.6	169.0	205.5	263.0
Claims on direct investors	4 565 ..	....	....	....	....	....	....	....	....
Liabilities to direct investors	4 570 ..	160.3	94.8	106.0	139.6	182.6	169.0	205.5	263.0
Reinvested earnings	4 575 ..	65.4	156.9	187.2	225.2	280.4	367.6	423.1	507.8
Other capital	4 580 ..	155.9	52.5	−18.0	38.1	83.9	63.2	45.6	45.2
Claims on direct investors	4 585 ..	25.2	−8.4	−18.6	.4	−45.5	−1.3	−48.5	−56.2
Liabilities to direct investors	4 590 ..	130.7	60.9	.7	37.6	129.4	64.5	94.1	101.4
B. PORTFOLIO INVESTMENT	4 600 ..	−59.0	−12.9	−6.2	−7.1	−11.6	−23.1	−20.9	−13.1
Assets	4 602 ..	−59.0	−12.9	−6.2	−7.3	−11.8	−23.1	−20.9	−13.1
Equity securities	4 610 ..	1.9	−.3	−2.7	−5.7	−1.2	−11.7	1.8	−1.2
Monetary authorities	4 611 ..	....	....	....	....	....	....	....	....
General government	4 612 ..	....	....	....	....	....	....	....	....
Banks	4 613 ..	....	....	....	....	....	−.4	1.8	−.2
Other sectors	4 614 ..	1.9	−.3	−2.7	−5.7	−1.2	−11.3	....	−1.0
Debt securities	4 619 ..	−60.9	−12.6	−3.5	−1.6	−10.6	−11.4	−22.7	−11.9
Bonds and notes	4 620 ..	−60.9	−12.6	−3.5	−1.6	−10.6	−11.4	−22.7	−11.9
Monetary authorities	4 621 ..	−1.5	−1.7	−1.7	−1.9	−2.0	−2.2	−2.3	−2.4
General government	4 622 ..	−59.4	−3.6	−3.8	−4.1	−4.3	−4.6	−4.8	−5.1
Banks	4 623 ..	....	....	....	....	−4.5	−4.7	−14.5	−4.4
Other sectors	4 624 ..	....	−7.3	2.0	4.4	.2	....	−1.0	....
Money market instruments	4 630 ..	....	....	....	....	....	....	....	....
Monetary authorities	4 631 ..	....	....	....	....	....	....	....	....
General government	4 632 ..	....	....	....	....	....	....	....	....
Banks	4 633 ..	....	....	....	....	....	....	....	....
Other sectors	4 634 ..	....	....	....	....	....	....	....	....
Liabilities	4 652 ..	....	....	....	.2	.2	....	....	....
Equity securities	4 660 ..	....	....	....	.2	.2	....	....	....
Banks	4 663 ..	....	....	....	....	....	....	....	....
Other sectors	4 664 ..	....	....	....	.2	.2	....	....	....
Debt securities	4 669 ..	....	....	....	....	....	....	....	....
Bonds and notes	4 670 ..	....	....	....	....	....	....	....	....
Monetary authorities	4 671 ..	....	....	....	....	....	....	....	....
General government	4 672 ..	....	....	....	....	....	....	....	....
Banks	4 673 ..	....	....	....	....	....	....	....	....
Other sectors	4 674 ..	....	....	....	....	....	....	....	....
Money market instruments	4 680 ..	....	....	....	....	....	....	....	....
Monetary authorities	4 681 ..	....	....	....	....	....	....	....	....
General government	4 682 ..	....	....	....	....	....	....	....	....
Banks	4 683 ..	....	....	....	....	....	....	....	....
Other sectors	4 684 ..	....	....	....	....	....	....	....	....
C. FINANCIAL DERIVATIVES	4 910 ..	....	....	....	....	....	....	....	....
Monetary authorities	4 911 ..	....	....	....	....	....	....	....	....
General government	4 912 ..	....	....	....	....	....	....	....	....
Banks	4 913 ..	....	....	....	....	....	....	....	....
Other sectors	4 914 ..	....	....	....	....	....	....	....	....
Assets	4 900 ..	....	....	....	....	....	....	....	....
Monetary authorities	4 901 ..	....	....	....	....	....	....	....	....
General government	4 902 ..	....	....	....	....	....	....	....	....
Banks	4 903 ..	....	....	....	....	....	....	....	....
Other sectors	4 904 ..	....	....	....	....	....	....	....	....
Liabilities	4 905 ..	....	....	....	....	....	....	....	....
Monetary authorities	4 906 ..	....	....	....	....	....	....	....	....
General government	4 907 ..	....	....	....	....	....	....	....	....
Banks	4 908 ..	....	....	....	....	....	....	....	....
Other sectors	4 909 ..	....	....	....	....	....	....	....	....

Table 2 (Concluded). STANDARD PRESENTATION, 2000–2007

(Millions of U.S. dollars)

	Code	2000	2001	2002	2003	2004	2005	2006	2007
D. OTHER INVESTMENT	4 700	24.7	65.0	−38.5	11.9	463.6	−596.6	−1,286.0	−850.6
Assets	4 703	−139.7	−28.1	−92.6	−62.5	−59.3	12.3	94.8	48.4
Trade credits	4 706	−71.4	46.1	−15.7	−66.3	33.8	12.6	37.9	31.8
General government	4 707	....	....	....	....	....	....	....	....
of which: Short-term	4 709	....	....	....	....	....	....	....	....
Other sectors	4 710	−71.4	46.1	−15.7	−66.3	33.8	12.6	37.9	31.8
of which: Short-term	4 712	*−71.4*	*46.1*	*−15.7*	*−66.3*	*33.8*	*12.6*	*37.9*	*31.8*
Loans	4 714	9.5	−5.9	12.9	−2.6	−17.3	5.9	13.2	5.3
Monetary authorities	4 715	....	....	....	....	....	....	....	....
of which: Short-term	4 718	....	....	....	....	....	....	....	....
General government	4 719	....	....	....	....	....	....	....	....
of which: Short-term	4 721	....	....	....	....	....	....	....	....
Banks	4 722	....	....	....	.2	−1.6	11.2	11.6	3.1
of which: Short-term	4 724	....	....	....	*.2*	*−1.6*	*11.2*	*11.6*	*3.1*
Other sectors	4 725	9.5	−5.9	12.9	−2.8	−15.7	−5.3	1.6	2.3
of which: Short-term	4 727	*9.5*	*9.9*	*10.5*	....	*−15.9*	*−5.3*	*1.6*	*2.3*
Currency and deposits	4 730	−69.6	−37.9	−82.5	10.9	−69.3	−4.2	55.4	16.9
Monetary authorities	4 731	....	....	....	....	....	....	....	....
General government	4 732	−7.9	−16.2	−2.3	−.9	−1.0	2.1	−.1	−3.0
Banks	4 733	−67.6	−38.9	−76.4	16.8	−94.4	−5.3	22.5	−20.0
Other sectors	4 734	5.9	17.2	−3.8	−5.0	26.1	−1.0	33.0	39.9
Other assets	4 736	−8.2	−30.4	−7.2	−4.5	−6.5	−1.9	−11.7	−5.6
Monetary authorities	4 737	....	....	....	1.0	2.6	−.5	....	....
of which: Short-term	4 739	....	....	....	*1.0*	*2.6*	*−.5*	....	....
General government	4 740	....	....	....	....	....	....	....	....
of which: Short-term	4 742	....	....	....	....	....	....	....	....
Banks	4 743	....	....	....	....	−.1	....	....	....
of which: Short-term	4 745	....	....	....	....	*−.1*	....	....	....
Other sectors	4 746	−8.2	−30.4	−7.2	−5.5	−9.0	−1.5	−11.7	−5.6
of which: Short-term	4 748	*−3.8*	*−26.0*	*.2*	....	*−3.3*	*5.7*	*−.5*	*.4*
Liabilities	4 753	164.4	93.1	54.1	74.4	522.9	−608.9	−1,380.8	−899.0
Trade credits	4 756	−42.3	−8.4	36.8	.1	23.6	−1.0	−1.0	8.3
General government	4 757	....	....	....	....	....	....	....	....
of which: Short-term	4 759	....	....	....	....	....	....	....	....
Other sectors	4 760	−42.3	−8.4	36.8	.1	23.6	−1.0	−1.0	8.3
of which: Short-term	4 762	*−6.6*	*−9.0*	*36.6*	*10.9*	*19.6*	*−1.0*	*−1.0*	*8.3*
Loans	4 764	358.3	121.2	−51.4	−60.4	413.8	−692.5	−1,388.9	−940.2
Monetary authorities	4 765	−10.0	−8.9	−62.1	−56.9	−6.3	−44.5	−175.9	−7.7
of which: Use of Fund credit and loans from the Fund.	4 766	*16.4*	*12.0*	*−39.7*	*−41.1*	*15.1*	*−11.5*	*−140.8*	....
of which: Short-term	4 768	....	....	....	....	....	*−9.3*	....	....
General government	4 769	215.3	192.3	12.2	34.8	201.1	−670.1	−1,320.3	−1,027.9
of which: Short-term	4 771	*−31.9*	*−14.0*	....	....	*−53.2*	*−141.3*	*−44.9*	*−11.2*
Banks	4 772	−40.8	−49.4	11.0	−23.4	93.4	84.1	113.4	79.1
of which: Short-term	4 774	*−1.3*	*−5.8*	*20.6*	*7.4*	*18.3*	*36.2*	*30.6*	*3.5*
Other sectors	4 775	193.7	−12.9	−12.5	−14.9	125.6	−62.1	−6.0	16.2
of which: Short-term	4 777	*14.4*	*21.4*	*9.0*	*20.8*	*−65.8*	*−28.7*	*−40.1*	*−1.6*
Currency and deposits	4 780	−1.7	1.3	−2.3	4.6	12.0	25.6	11.6	22.1
Monetary authorities	4 781	....	....	....	3.5	4.8	2.0	2.0	3.1
General government	4 782	....	....	....	....	....	....	....	....
Banks	4 783	−1.7	1.3	−2.3	1.1	7.2	23.6	9.6	18.9
Other sectors	4 784	....	....	....	....	....	....	....	....
Other liabilities	4 786	−149.9	−21.0	71.0	130.1	73.4	59.0	−2.5	10.9
Monetary authorities	4 787	.4	−1.9	−.6	3.2	3.9	3.0	2.2	....
of which: Short-term	4 789	*.4*	*−1.9*	*−.6*	*3.2*	*3.9*	*3.0*	*2.2*	....
General government	4 790	−149.7	−21.4	72.7	128.3	49.7	53.2	5.2	2.0
of which: Short-term	4 792	*−149.7*	*−21.4*	*72.7*	*128.3*	*49.7*	*53.2*	*5.2*	*2.0*
Banks	4 793	−.6	2.3	−1.1	2.6	6.5	....	....	1.5
of which: Short-term	4 795	*−.6*	*2.3*	*−1.1*	*2.6*	*6.5*	....	....	*1.5*
Other sectors	4 796	....	....	....	−4.0	13.3	2.8	−9.9	7.4
of which: Short-term	4 798	....	....	....	*−4.0*	*13.3*	*2.8*	*−9.9*	*7.4*
E. RESERVE ASSETS	4 802	−54.6	−101.1	−105.7	96.5	−510.4	−346.4	−309.9	108.6
Monetary gold	4 812	.3	−.1	−.1	....	....	....	....	−.7
Special drawing rights	4 811	.8	−.2	−.1	.4	....	−.2	.3	−.1
Reserve position in the Fund	4 810	....	....	....	....	....	....	....	....
Foreign exchange	4 803	−55.7	−100.8	−105.5	96.2	−510.4	−346.2	−310.2	109.3
Other claims	4 813	....	....	....	....	....	....	....	....
NET ERRORS AND OMISSIONS	4 998	−39.9	−42.7	21.5	5.1	46.5	−188.5	−185.9	−52.6

Table 3. INTERNATIONAL INVESTMENT POSITION (End-period stocks), 2000–2007

(Millions of U.S. dollars)

	Code	2000	2001	2002	2003	2004	2005	2006	2007
ASSETS	8 995 C.	....	....	....	....	**3,297.0**	**3,692.1**	**4,724.9**	**4,874.1**
Direct investment abroad	8 505 ..	....	....	....	....	**24.5**	**23.5**	**24.6**	**26.1**
Equity capital and reinvested earnings	8 506 ..	....	....	....	....	....	....	....	....
Claims on affiliated enterprises	8 507 ..	....	....	....	....	....	....	....	....
Liabilities to affiliated enterprises	8 508 ..	....	....	....	....	....	....	....	....
Other capital	8 530 ..	....	....	....	....	24.5	23.5	24.6	26.1
Claims on affiliated enterprises	8 535 ..	....	....	....	....	24.5	23.5	24.6	26.1
Liabilities to affiliated enterprises	8 540 ..	....	....	....	....	....	....	....	....
Portfolio investment	8 602 ..	....	....	....	....	**187.2**	**210.3**	**237.4**	**262.9**
Equity securities	8 610 ..	....	....	....	....	13.2	24.9	23.1	22.5
Monetary authorities	8 611 ..	....	....	....	....	....	....	....	....
General government	8 612 ..	....	....	....	....	....	....	....	....
Banks	8 613 ..	....	....	....	....	3.4	3.8	2.0	1.6
Other sectors	8 614 ..	....	....	....	....	9.8	21.1	21.1	20.9
Debt securities	8 619 ..	....	....	....	....	174.0	185.4	214.3	240.4
Bonds and notes	8 620 ..	....	....	....	....	174.0	185.4	214.3	240.4
Monetary authorities	8 621 ..	....	....	....	....	30.4	32.6	34.9	37.3
General government	8 622 ..	....	....	....	....	130.5	135.0	139.9	150.3
Banks	8 623 ..	....	....	....	....	10.1	14.8	35.5	48.8
Other sectors	8 624 ..	....	....	....	....	3.0	3.0	4.0	4.0
Money market instruments	8 630 ..	....	....	....	....	....	....	....	....
Monetary authorities	8 631 ..	....	....	....	....	....	....	....	....
General government	8 632 ..	....	....	....	....	....	....	....	....
Banks	8 633 ..	....	....	....	....	....	....	....	....
Other sectors	8 634 ..	....	....	....	....	....	....	....	....
Financial derivatives	8 900 ..	....	....	....	....	....	....	....	....
Monetary authorities	8 901 ..	....	....	....	....	....	....	....	....
General government	8 902 ..	....	....	....	....	....	....	....	....
Banks	8 903 ..	....	....	....	....	....	....	....	....
Other sectors	8 904 ..	....	....	....	....	....	....	....	....
Other investment	8 703 ..	....	....	....	....	**1,135.5**	**1,152.7**	**1,855.4**	**2,077.4**
Trade credits	8 706 ..	....	....	....	....	50.4	37.8	33.8	17.6
General government	8 707 ..	....	....	....	....	....	....	....	....
of which: Short-term	8 709 ..	....	....	....	....	....	....	....	....
Other sectors	8 710 ..	....	....	....	....	50.4	37.8	33.8	17.6
of which: Short-term	8 712 ..	....	....	....	....	*50.4*	*37.8*	*33.8*	*17.6*
Loans	8 714 ..	....	....	....	....	183.5	172.0	164.3	189.4
Monetary authorities	8 715 ..	....	....	....	....	105.5	105.5	105.5	105.5
of which: Short-term	8 718 ..	....	....	....	....	....	....	....	....
General government	8 719 ..	....	....	....	....	....	.1	.1	.1
of which: Short-term	8 721 ..	....	....	....	....	....	....	....	....
Banks	8 722 ..	....	....	....	....	76.0	59.1	53.0	81.3
of which: Short-term	8 724 ..	....	....	....	....	....	....	....	....
Other sectors	8 725 ..	....	....	....	....	2.0	7.3	5.7	2.4
of which: Short-term	8 727 ..	....	....	....	....	*2.0*	*7.3*	*5.7*	*2.4*
Currency and deposits	8 730 ..	....	....	....	....	783.8	823.2	1,525.9	1,725.4
Monetary authorities	8 731 ..	....	....	....	....	....	....	....	....
General government	8 732 ..	....	....	....	....	....	.1	.3	.4
Banks	8 733 ..	....	....	....	....	646.8	652.1	629.6	657.9
Other sectors	8 734 ..	....	....	....	....	137.0	170.9	896.0	1,067.0
Other assets	8 736 ..	....	....	....	....	117.8	119.8	131.4	145.0
Monetary authorities	8 737 ..	....	....	....	....	111.2	111.6	111.6	111.5
of which: Short-term	8 739 ..	....	....	....	....	....	....	....	....
General government	8 740 ..	....	....	....	....	....	....	....	....
of which: Short-term	8 742 ..	....	....	....	....	....	....	....	....
Banks	8 743 ..	....	....	....	....	.1	.1	.1	....
of which: Short-term	8 745 ..	....	....	....	....	*.1*	*.1*	*.1*	....
Other sectors	8 746 ..	....	....	....	....	6.6	8.0	19.7	33.5
of which: Short-term	8 748 ..	....	....	....	....	*6.6*	*8.0*	*19.7*	*33.5*
Reserve assets	8 802 ..	....	....	....	....	**1,949.8**	**2,305.6**	**2,607.5**	**2,507.6**
Monetary gold	8 812 ..	....	....	....	....	9.9	11.3	13.9	18.2
Special drawing rights	8 811 ..	.1	.3	.5	.1	.1	.3	....	.1
Reserve position in the Fund	8 810 ..	11.2	10.8	11.7	12.8	13.4	12.3	13.0	13.6
Foreign exchange	8 803 ..	....	....	....	....	1,926.4	2,281.7	2,580.6	2,475.7
Other claims	8 813 ..	....	....	....	....	....	....	....	....

Table 3 (Concluded). INTERNATIONAL INVESTMENT POSITION (End-period stocks), 2000–2007

(Millions of U.S. dollars)

	Code	2000	2001	2002	2003	2004	2005	2006	2007
LIABILITIES	8 995 D.	....	....	....	....	**8,442.2**	**8,084.4**	**7,437.7**	**7,477.2**
Direct investment in Honduras	8 555 ..	....	....	....	....	**2,012.6**	**2,578.2**	**3,155.4**	**4,005.9**
Equity capital and reinvested earnings	8 556 ..	....	....	....	....	1,794.6	2,271.6	2,803.1	3,448.8
Claims on direct investors	8 557 ..	....	....	....	....	....	....	....	....
Liabilities to direct investors	8 558 ..	....	....	....	....	1,794.6	2,271.6	2,803.1	3,448.8
Other capital	8 580 ..	....	....	....	....	218.0	306.6	352.3	557.1
Claims on direct investors	8 585 ..	....	....	....	....	−128.7	−130.0	−178.5	−217.9
Liabilities to direct investors	8 590 ..	....	....	....	....	346.7	436.6	530.8	775.0
Portfolio investment	8 652 ..	....	....	....	....	....	....	....	....
Equity securities	8 660 ..	....	....	....	....	....	....	....	....
Banks	8 663 ..	....	....	....	....	....	....	....	....
Other sectors	8 664 ..	....	....	....	....	....	....	....	....
Debt securities	8 669 ..	....	....	....	....	....	....	....	....
Bonds and notes	8 670 ..	....	....	....	....	....	....	....	....
Monetary authorities	8 671 ..	....	....	....	....	....	....	....	....
General government	8 672 ..	....	....	....	....	....	....	....	....
Banks	8 673 ..	....	....	....	....	....	....	....	....
Other sectors	8 674 ..	....	....	....	....	....	....	....	....
Money market instruments	8 680 ..	....	....	....	....	....	....	....	....
Monetary authorities	8 681 ..	....	....	....	....	....	....	....	....
General government	8 682 ..	....	....	....	....	....	....	....	....
Banks	8 683 ..	....	....	....	....	....	....	....	....
Other sectors	8 684 ..	....	....	....	....	....	....	....	....
Financial derivatives	8 905 ..	....	....	....	....	....	....	....	....
Monetary authorities	8 906 ..	....	....	....	....	....	....	....	....
General government	8 907 ..	....	....	....	....	....	....	....	....
Banks	8 908 ..	....	....	....	....	....	....	....	....
Other sectors	8 909 ..	....	....	....	....	....	....	....	....
Other investment	8 753 ..	....	....	....	....	**6,429.6**	**5,506.2**	**4,282.3**	**3,471.3**
Trade credits	8 756 ..	....	....	....	....	177.2	152.2	151.3	158.0
General government	8 757 ..	....	....	....	....	....	....	....	....
of which: Short-term	8 759 ..	....	....	....	....	....	....	....	....
Other sectors	8 760 ..	....	....	....	....	177.2	152.2	151.3	158.0
of which: Short-term	8 762 ..	....	....	....	....	*135.1*	*136.7*	*135.8*	*142.5*
Loans	8 764 ..	....	....	....	....	6,180.8	5,256.5	4,029.8	3,195.7
Monetary authorities	8 765 ..	....	....	....	....	368.5	323.8	178.6	172.4
of which: Use of Fund credit and loans from the Fund	8 766 ..	*216.0*	*220.1*	*196.6*	*171.5*	*195.2*	*168.1*	*30.6*	*32.1*
of which: Short-term	8 768 ..	....	....	....	....	....	....	....	....
General government	8 769 ..	....	....	....	....	4,909.1	4,024.0	2,815.8	1,801.2
of which: Short-term	8 771 ..	....	....	....	....	....	....	....	....
Banks	8 772 ..	....	....	....	....	351.8	438.9	563.3	709.5
of which: Short-term	8 774 ..	....	....	....	....	*101.3*	*155.3*	*185.9*	*215.7*
Other sectors	8 775 ..	....	....	....	....	551.4	469.8	472.1	512.6
of which: Short-term	8 777 ..	....	....	....	....	*206.2*	*183.2*	*176.1*	*181.9*
Currency and deposits	8 780 ..	....	....	....	....	48.8	72.0	85.6	102.4
Monetary authorities	8 781 ..	....	....	....	....	19.0	21.0	23.0	25.6
General government	8 782 ..	....	....	....	....	....	....	....	....
Banks	8 783 ..	....	....	....	....	29.8	51.0	62.6	76.9
Other sectors	8 784 ..	....	....	....	....	....	....	....	....
Other liabilities	8 786 ..	....	....	....	....	22.8	25.5	15.7	15.2
Monetary authorities	8 787 ..	....	....	....	....	.5	.4	.5	.5
of which: Short-term	8 789 ..	....	....	....	....	*.5*	*.4*	*.5*	*.5*
General government	8 790 ..	....	....	....	....	....	....	....	....
of which: Short-term	8 792 ..	....	....	....	....	....	....	....	....
Banks	8 793 ..	....	....	....	....	....	....	....	....
of which: Short-term	8 795 ..	....	....	....	....	....	....	....	....
Other sectors	8 796 ..	....	....	....	....	22.4	25.1	15.2	14.7
of which: Short-term	8 798 ..	....	....	....	....	*22.4*	*25.1*	*15.2*	*14.7*
NET INTERNATIONAL INVESTMENT POSITION	8 995 ..	....	....	....	....	**−5,145.2**	**−4,392.3**	**−2,712.8**	**−2,603.1**
Conversion rates: lempiras per U.S. dollar (end of period)	0 102 ..	**15.1407**	**15.9197**	**16.9233**	**17.7482**	**18.6328**	**18.8952**	**18.8952**	**18.8951**

Table 1. ANALYTIC PRESENTATION, 2000–2007

(Millions of U.S. dollars)

	Code	2000	2001	2002	2003	2004	2005	2006	2007
A. Current Account[1]	4 993 Z.	**−4,004**	**−3,205**	**−4,693**	**−6,721**	**−8,561**	**−7,463**	**−6,824**	**−6,743**
Goods: exports f.o.b.	2 100 ..	28,762	31,080	34,792	42,943	55,689	62,245	74,348	94,247
Goods: imports f.o.b.	3 100 ..	−31,675	−33,318	−36,911	−46,221	−58,695	−64,077	−75,494	−92,277
Balance on Goods	4 100 ..	*−2,913*	*−2,237*	*−2,119*	*−3,279*	*−3,006*	*−1,832*	*−1,146*	*1,969*
Services: credit	2 200 ..	5,901	7,029	7,417	9,211	10,890	12,777	13,295	16,758
Services: debit	3 200 ..	−4,775	−5,550	−6,849	−9,150	−10,604	−11,466	−11,674	−15,221
Balance on Goods and Services	4 991 ..	*−1,787*	*−759*	*−1,551*	*−3,217*	*−2,720*	*−520*	*475*	*3,506*
Income: credit	2 300 ..	1,165	1,302	1,236	1,371	1,877	1,931	6,182	7,366
Income: debit	3 300 ..	−3,740	−4,152	−4,870	−5,541	−8,013	−9,089	−13,930	−18,067
Balance on Goods, Services, and Income	4 992 ..	*−4,361*	*−3,609*	*−5,184*	*−7,388*	*−8,856*	*−7,678*	*−7,273*	*−7,196*
Current transfers: credit	2 379 Z.	674	781	1,070	1,283	1,633	2,592	3,117	4,145
Current transfers: debit	3 379 ..	−316	−377	−579	−616	−1,338	−2,377	−2,668	−3,693
B. Capital Account[1]	4 994 Z.	**270**	**317**	**191**	**−27**	**328**	**885**	**732**	**1,447**
Capital account: credit	2 994 Z.	458	417	238	240	518	1,003	1,142	1,891
Capital account: debit	3 994 ..	−188	−101	−48	−267	−190	−118	−410	−444
Total, Groups A Plus B	4 981 ..	*−3,734*	*−2,888*	*−4,503*	*−6,748*	*−8,234*	*−6,578*	*−6,092*	*−5,297*
C. Financial Account[1]	4 995 W.	**4,960**	**2,775**	**2,565**	**6,858**	**11,988**	**14,529**	**11,506**	**9,240**
Direct investment abroad	4 505 ..	−589	−364	−282	−1,661	−1,116	−2,256	−18,862	−35,763
Direct investment in Hungary	4 555 Z.	2,770	3,944	3,013	2,177	4,521	7,626	19,697	37,231
Portfolio investment assets	4 602 ..	−309	−149	−43	15	−441	−1,121	−2,236	−2,632
Equity securities	4 610 ..	−151	−55	−50	−42	−439	−584	−1,717	−2,340
Debt securities	4 619 ..	−158	−95	7	57	−3	−536	−519	−292
Portfolio investment liabilities	4 652 Z.	−141	1,523	1,844	2,902	7,353	5,784	8,751	516
Equity securities	4 660 ..	−369	134	−137	269	1,491	−16	912	−5,014
Debt securities	4 669 Z.	229	1,389	1,982	2,633	5,862	5,801	7,839	5,530
Financial derivatives	4 910 ..	56	111	149	251	412	−151	187	1,127
Financial derivatives assets	4 900 ..	754	582	1,796	2,320	4,214	3,621	4,570	6,335
Financial derivatives liabilities	4 905 ..	−698	−471	−1,647	−2,069	−3,802	−3,771	−4,383	−5,208
Other investment assets	4 703 ..	939	−2,754	−1,599	−2,827	−1,940	−2,122	−2,521	−4,645
Monetary authorities	4 701 ..	−8	4	36	−1,049	1,100	−11	....	....
General government	4 704 ..	38	−9	14	198	−66	−117	226	−418
Banks	4 705 ..	755	−1,463	528	−951	−349	−165	−2,984	−3,895
Other sectors	4 728 ..	154	−1,287	−2,176	−1,026	−2,624	−1,829	237	−332
Other investment liabilities	4 753 W.	2,232	465	−517	6,000	3,199	6,769	6,491	13,405
Monetary authorities	4 753 WA	613	−644	−625	569	−916	−36	56	−112
General government	4 753 ZB	−225	−47	766	319	161	523	721	1,853
Banks	4 753 ZC	401	294	647	3,986	2,662	4,575	4,368	6,458
Other sectors	4 753 ZD	1,442	862	−1,306	1,126	1,293	1,707	1,346	5,206
Total, Groups A Through C	4 983 ..	*1,226*	*−113*	*−1,938*	*110*	*3,754*	*7,951*	*5,414*	*3,943*
D. Net Errors and Omissions	4 998 ..	**−174**	**29**	**145**	**226**	**−1,773**	**−3,047**	**−4,311**	**−3,789**
Total, Groups A Through D	4 984 ..	*1,052*	*−84*	*−1,792*	*336*	*1,981*	*4,904*	*1,102*	*154*
E. Reserves and Related Items	4 802 A.	**−1,052**	**84**	**1,792**	**−336**	**−1,981**	**−4,904**	**−1,102**	**−154**
Reserve assets	4 802 ..	−1,052	84	1,792	−336	−1,981	−4,904	−1,102	−154
Use of Fund credit and loans	4 766 ..	....	....	....	....	....	....	....	....
Exceptional financing	4 920 ..	....	....	....	....	....	....	....	....
Conversion rates: forint per U.S. dollar	0 101 ..	282.18	286.49	257.89	224.31	202.75	199.58	210.39	183.63

[1] Excludes components that have been classified in the categories of Group E.

Table 2. STANDARD PRESENTATION, 2000–2007

(Millions of U.S. dollars)

	Code	2000	2001	2002	2003	2004	2005	2006	2007
CURRENT ACCOUNT	4 993	−4,004	−3,205	−4,693	−6,721	−8,561	−7,463	−6,824	−6,743
A. GOODS	4 100	−2,913	−2,237	−2,119	−3,279	−3,006	−1,832	−1,146	1,969
Credit	2 100	28,762	31,080	34,792	42,943	55,689	62,245	74,348	94,247
General merchandise: exports f.o.b.	2 110	27,326	29,617	33,439	41,321	54,168	60,926	73,011	92,769
Goods for processing: exports f.o.b.	2 150	1,428	1,444	1,316	1,575	1,434	1,108	1,133	1,198
Repairs on goods	2 160	8	19	37	47	86	211	203	279
Goods procured in ports by carriers	2 170	....	....	....	....	....	....	....	....
Nonmonetary gold	2 180	....	....	....	....	....	....	....	....
Debit	3 100	−31,675	−33,318	−36,911	−46,221	−58,695	−64,077	−75,494	−92,277
General merchandise: imports f.o.b.	3 110	−31,616	−33,244	−36,804	−46,060	−58,472	−63,865	−75,199	−91,774
Goods for processing: imports f.o.b.	3 150	−40	−54	−73	−110	−191	−172	−237	−420
Repairs on goods	3 160	−18	−19	−34	−51	−32	−39	−58	−83
Goods procured in ports by carriers	3 170	....	....	....	....	....	....	....	....
Nonmonetary gold	3 180	....	....	....	....	....	....	....	....
B. SERVICES	4 200	1,126	1,478	568	61	286	1,312	1,621	1,537
Total credit	2 200	*5,901*	*7,029*	*7,417*	*9,211*	*10,890*	*12,777*	*13,295*	*16,758*
Total debit	3 200	*−4,775*	*−5,550*	*−6,849*	*−9,150*	*−10,604*	*−11,466*	*−11,674*	*−15,221*
Transportation services, credit	2 205	521	585	697	1,020	1,330	2,049	2,390	3,237
Passenger	2 850	*76*	*37*	*46*	*58*	*95*	*597*	*689*	*954*
Freight	2 851	*326*	*442*	*474*	*615*	*849*	*725*	*853*	*1,110*
Other	2 852	*119*	*106*	*177*	*346*	*386*	*728*	*847*	*1,172*
Sea transport, passenger	2 207	....	....	....	....	....			
Sea transport, freight	2 208	....	....	....	....	....	17	11	7
Sea transport, other	2 209	....	....	....	....	....	12	11	15
Air transport, passenger	2 211	....	....	....	....	....	566	655	915
Air transport, freight	2 212	....	....	....	....	....	22	22	31
Air transport, other	2 213	....	....	....	....	....	225	241	403
Other transport, passenger	2 215	....	....	....	....	....	31	34	39
Other transport, freight	2 216	....	....	....	....	....	686	820	1,072
Other transport, other	2 217	....	....	....	....	....	491	595	754
Transportation services, debit	3 205	−710	−749	−1,057	−1,397	−1,567	−2,195	−2,415	−3,049
Passenger	3 850	*−71*	*−79*	*−78*	*−106*	*−61*	*−444*	*−442*	*−519*
Freight	3 851	*−516*	*−521*	*−599*	*−795*	*−992*	*−984*	*−1,048*	*−1,294*
Other	3 852	*−124*	*−149*	*−381*	*−496*	*−514*	*−766*	*−924*	*−1,236*
Sea transport, passenger	3 207	....	....	....	....	....			
Sea transport, freight	3 208	....	....	....	....	....	−32	−34	−39
Sea transport, other	3 209	....	....	....	....	....	−61	−52	−72
Air transport, passenger	3 211	....	....	....	....	....	−428	−427	−499
Air transport, freight	3 212	....	....	....	....	....	−54	−49	−50
Air transport, other	3 213	....	....	....	....	....	−291	−385	−534
Other transport, passenger	3 215	....	....	....	....	....	−16	−15	−21
Other transport, freight	3 216	....	....	....	....	....	−898	−965	−1,206
Other transport, other	3 217	....	....	....	....	....	−415	−487	−630
Travel, credit	2 236	3,733	4,154	3,728	4,061	4,034	4,120	4,254	4,739
Business travel	2 237	174	179	244	376	598	763	788	903
Personal travel	2 240	3,559	3,975	3,485	3,685	3,437	3,357	3,466	3,836
Travel, debit	3 236	−1,651	−1,808	−2,133	−2,594	−2,848	−2,382	−2,126	−2,949
Business travel	3 237	−255	−265	−319	−341	−280	−353	−512	−760
Personal travel	3 240	−1,396	−1,543	−1,814	−2,254	−2,568	−2,029	−1,614	−2,190
Other services, credit	2 200 BA	1,647	2,290	2,991	4,130	5,526	6,608	6,651	8,783
Communications	2 245	69	95	125	208	292	341	389	475
Construction	2 249	96	97	180	198	167	173	256	377
Insurance	2 253	16	16	14	33	38	7	15	20
Financial	2 260	147	164	146	191	250	147	161	256
Computer and information	2 262	121	176	200	244	338	382	487	661
Royalties and licence fees	2 266	112	96	349	313	540	837	627	841
Other business services	2 268	815	967	1,369	2,018	2,670	3,325	3,546	4,635
Personal, cultural, and recreational	2 287	207	600	527	845	1,167	1,272	1,067	1,400
Government, n.i.e.	2 291	65	80	81	80	65	125	104	117
Other services, debit	3 200 BA	−2,413	−2,994	−3,658	−5,158	−6,189	−6,889	−7,134	−9,223
Communications	3 245	−75	−78	−119	−181	−311	−355	−411	−565
Construction	3 249	−57	−86	−243	−203	−62	−101	−139	−250
Insurance	3 253	−84	−114	−153	−211	−215	−202	−212	−204
Financial	3 260	−225	−216	−150	−277	−376	−224	−246	−337
Computer and information	3 262	−127	−160	−171	−267	−392	−494	−544	−623
Royalties and licence fees	3 266	−259	−269	−417	−464	−1,054	−1,108	−1,056	−1,596
Other business services	3 268	−1,368	−1,427	−1,814	−2,582	−2,597	−3,088	−3,491	−4,546
Personal, cultural, and recreational	3 287	−151	−563	−491	−845	−1,048	−1,144	−846	−913
Government, n.i.e.	3 291	−67	−81	−100	−128	−134	−173	−189	−188

Table 2 (Continued). STANDARD PRESENTATION, 2000–2007

(Millions of U.S. dollars)

	Code	2000	2001	2002	2003	2004	2005	2006	2007
C. INCOME	4 300	**−2,575**	**−2,850**	**−3,634**	**−4,170**	**−6,135**	**−7,157**	**−7,748**	**−10,702**
Total credit	2 300	*1,165*	*1,302*	*1,236*	*1,371*	*1,877*	*1,931*	*6,182*	*7,366*
Total debit	3 300	*−3,740*	*−4,152*	*−4,870*	*−5,541*	*−8,013*	*−9,089*	*−13,930*	*−18,067*
Compensation of employees, credit	2 310	221	242	232	249	265	262	317	379
Compensation of employees, debit	3 310	−70	−84	−90	−91	−108	−136	−170	−218
Investment income, credit	2 320	**945**	**1,060**	**1,005**	**1,122**	**1,612**	**1,669**	**5,865**	**6,987**
Direct investment income	2 330	73	39	73	150	697	649	4,429	4,919
Dividends and distributed branch profits	2 332	11	58	23	39	145	460	2,280	2,797
Reinvested earnings and undistributed branch profits	2 333	59	−44	27	88	497	114	1,324	1,157
Income on debt (interest)	2 334	4	24	23	23	56	75	825	965
Portfolio investment income	2 339	511	603	560	606	434	567	773	994
Income on equity	2 340	10	15	14	18	23	53	64	95
Income on bonds and notes	2 350	405	461	494	525	344	426	553	665
Income on money market instruments	2 360	96	128	52	63	67	89	157	235
Other investment income	2 370	360	417	372	366	482	453	663	1,073
Investment income, debit	3 320	**−3,670**	**−4,068**	**−4,780**	**−5,450**	**−7,905**	**−8,953**	**−13,760**	**−17,849**
Direct investment income	3 330	−2,023	−2,338	−3,178	−3,597	−5,495	−5,900	−10,227	−12,665
Dividends and distributed branch profits	3 332	−954	−960	−1,186	−1,426	−2,213	−3,028	−6,320	−7,951
Reinvested earnings and undistributed branch profits	3 333	−1,022	−1,326	−1,858	−2,057	−2,829	−2,308	−2,900	−3,530
Income on debt (interest)	3 334	−47	−52	−135	−113	−452	−564	−1,006	−1,184
Portfolio investment income	3 339	−997	−998	−1,020	−1,225	−1,671	−2,196	−2,406	−3,279
Income on equity	3 340	−65	−56	−61	−52	−194	−373	−415	−749
Income on bonds and notes	3 350	−923	−938	−958	−1,172	−1,477	−1,822	−1,989	−2,526
Income on money market instruments	3 360	−9	−4	−1	−1	....	−1	−1	−3
Other investment income	3 370	−650	−732	−581	−628	−739	−857	−1,128	−1,906
D. CURRENT TRANSFERS	4 379	**357**	**404**	**491**	**667**	**295**	**215**	**449**	**452**
Credit	2 379	**674**	**781**	**1,070**	**1,283**	**1,633**	**2,592**	**3,117**	**4,145**
General government	2 380	128	146	223	290	415	753	901	1,285
Other sectors	2 390	546	635	847	993	1,218	1,838	2,216	2,860
Workers' remittances	2 391	53	51	39	39	26	18	40	32
Other current transfers	2 392	493	584	808	954	1,192	1,820	2,176	2,828
Debit	3 379	**−316**	**−377**	**−579**	**−616**	**−1,338**	**−2,377**	**−2,668**	**−3,693**
General government	3 380	−99	−114	−157	−162	−696	−1,700	−1,613	−2,214
Other sectors	3 390	−217	−263	−421	−454	−642	−677	−1,056	−1,479
Workers' remittances	3 391	−14	−16	−15	−20	−17	−3	−15	−10
Other current transfers	3 392	−203	−247	−406	−434	−626	−674	−1,040	−1,469
CAPITAL AND FINANCIAL ACCOUNT	4 996	**4,178**	**3,176**	**4,548**	**6,495**	**10,334**	**10,510**	**11,136**	**10,533**
CAPITAL ACCOUNT	4 994	**270**	**317**	**191**	**−27**	**328**	**885**	**732**	**1,447**
Total credit	2 994	*458*	*417*	*238*	*240*	*518*	*1,003*	*1,142*	*1,891*
Total debit	3 994	*−188*	*−101*	*−48*	*−267*	*−190*	*−118*	*−410*	*−444*
Capital transfers, credit	2 400	**317**	**395**	**208**	**215**	**500**	**952**	**1,041**	**1,821**
General government	2 401	82	96	50	96	381	669	900	1,781
Debt forgiveness	2 402	....	....	....	....	....	....	....	....
Other capital transfers	2 410	82	96	50	96	381	669	900	1,781
Other sectors	2 430	235	299	158	119	119	283	141	40
Migrants' transfers	2 431	7	3	8	7	16	....	6	2
Debt forgiveness	2 432	....	....	....	....	....	....	....	....
Other capital transfers	2 440	229	296	150	112	102	283	135	37
Capital transfers, debit	3 400	**−50**	**−94**	**−37**	**−164**	**−59**	**−84**	**−330**	**−122**
General government	3 401	−2	−20	−2	−132	−20	−23	−144	−34
Debt forgiveness	3 402	....	....	....	....	....	....	....	....
Other capital transfers	3 410	−2	−20	−2	−132	−20	−23	−144	−34
Other sectors	3 430	−47	−74	−35	−32	−39	−61	−187	−88
Migrants' transfers	3 431	−3	−1	−1	−3	−3	....	−5	−7
Debt forgiveness	3 432	....	....	....	....	....	....	....	....
Other capital transfers	3 440	−45	−73	−34	−28	−37	−61	−182	−82
Nonproduced nonfinancial assets, credit	2 480	**141**	**23**	**31**	**25**	**18**	**51**	**100**	**70**
Nonproduced nonfinancial assets, debit	3 480	**−139**	**−6**	**−11**	**−104**	**−131**	**−34**	**−80**	**−322**

Table 2 (Continued). STANDARD PRESENTATION, 2000–2007

(Millions of U.S. dollars)

	Code	2000	2001	2002	2003	2004	2005	2006	2007
FINANCIAL ACCOUNT	4 995	3,908	2,859	4,357	6,522	10,007	9,625	10,404	9,086
A. DIRECT INVESTMENT	4 500	2,182	3,580	2,731	516	3,405	5,370	835	1,468
Direct investment abroad	4 505	−589	−364	−282	−1,661	−1,116	−2,256	−18,862	−35,763
Equity capital	4 510	−589	−373	−184	−1,462	−533	−2,324	−16,121	−32,505
Claims on affiliated enterprises	4 515	−589	−373	−184	−1,462	−533	−2,324	−16,121	−32,505
Liabilities to affiliated enterprises	4 520	....	....	....	....	....	....	....	....
Reinvested earnings	4 525	−59	44	−27	−88	−497	−114	−1,324	−1,157
Other capital	4 530	59	−35	−71	−111	−86	182	−1,417	−2,101
Claims on affiliated enterprises	4 535	40	−54	−44	−170	−63	−139	−1,444	−2,092
Liabilities to affiliated enterprises	4 540	19	20	−27	59	−23	321	27	−9
Direct investment in Hungary	4 555	2,770	3,944	3,013	2,177	4,521	7,626	19,697	37,231
Equity capital	4 560	1,395	998	1,097	−862	1,322	4,833	9,817	28,472
Claims on direct investors	4 565	....	....	....	....	....	....	....	....
Liabilities to direct investors	4 570	1,395	998	1,097	−862	1,322	4,833	9,817	28,472
Reinvested earnings	4 575	1,022	1,326	1,858	2,057	2,829	2,308	2,900	3,530
Other capital	4 580	353	1,620	58	982	370	485	6,979	5,229
Claims on direct investors	4 585	−5	−95	−658	−1,921	−279	−558	1,220	−3,466
Liabilities to direct investors	4 590	358	1,715	716	2,903	649	1,043	5,760	8,694
B. PORTFOLIO INVESTMENT	4 600	−450	1,374	1,802	2,917	6,911	4,663	6,515	−2,115
Assets	4 602	−309	−149	−43	15	−441	−1,121	−2,236	−2,632
Equity securities	4 610	−151	−55	−50	−42	−439	−584	−1,717	−2,340
Monetary authorities	4 611	....	....	....	....	....	....	....	....
General government	4 612	....	....	....	....	....	....	....	....
Banks	4 613	....	−20	24	−22	−35	70	13	9
Other sectors	4 614	−151	−34	−74	−20	−404	−654	−1,729	−2,348
Debt securities	4 619	−158	−95	7	57	−3	−536	−519	−292
Bonds and notes	4 620	−162	−102	123	73	16	−503	−531	−283
Monetary authorities	4 621	....	....	....	....	....	....	....	....
General government	4 622	....	....	....	....	....	....	....	....
Banks	4 623	−46	−127	−63	−59	38	−51	−248	279
Other sectors	4 624	−117	25	186	132	−22	−451	−284	−562
Money market instruments	4 630	4	7	−115	−16	−19	−34	12	−9
Monetary authorities	4 631	....	....	....	....	....	....	....	....
General government	4 632	....	....	....	....	....	....	....	....
Banks	4 633	....	4	1	9	....	−22	14	−4
Other sectors	4 634	4	2	−117	−25	−19	−11	−2	−6
Liabilities	4 652	−141	1,523	1,844	2,902	7,353	5,784	8,751	516
Equity securities	4 660	−369	134	−137	269	1,491	−16	912	−5,014
Banks	4 663	65	142	43	40	172	−277	799	−146
Other sectors	4 664	−435	−7	−181	229	1,319	261	113	−4,868
Debt securities	4 669	229	1,389	1,982	2,633	5,862	5,801	7,839	5,530
Bonds and notes	4 670	229	1,117	1,940	2,712	5,633	6,107	7,601	5,437
Monetary authorities	4 671	−1,313	−937	−993	−1,739	−1,274	−868	−21	−382
General government	4 672	1,564	1,736	2,816	4,039	5,325	4,622	4,204	3,360
Banks	4 673	−1	322	116	413	1,483	1,328	3,231	2,546
Other sectors	4 674	−21	−4	1	−1	99	1,025	187	−87
Money market instruments	4 680	−1	272	42	−78	229	−306	238	94
Monetary authorities	4 681	....	−3	....	....	....	....	....	−12
General government	4 682	....	275	41	−85	230	−306	239	86
Banks	4 683	....	....	1	7	....	....	....	22
Other sectors	4 684	−1	....	....	....	−1	....	....	−2
C. FINANCIAL DERIVATIVES	4 910	56	111	149	251	412	−151	187	1,127
Monetary authorities	4 911	23	−45	46	139	35	−320	31	−103
General government	4 912	....	....	....	....	24	52	48	10
Banks	4 913	69	156	189	267	714	125	−15	1,360
Other sectors	4 914	−36	−1	−86	−155	−361	−8	124	−141
Assets	4 900	754	582	1,796	2,320	4,214	3,621	4,570	6,335
Monetary authorities	4 901	366	185	234	324	277	153	284	249
General government	4 902	....	....	....	....	....	67	86	60
Banks	4 903	383	363	1,499	2,049	3,414	2,974	3,930	5,844
Other sectors	4 904	5	33	64	−53	523	425	270	183
Liabilities	4 905	−698	−471	−1,647	−2,069	−3,802	−3,771	−4,383	−5,208
Monetary authorities	4 906	−343	−230	−188	−185	−243	−473	−253	−351
General government	4 907	....	....	....	....	24	−15	−38	−50
Banks	4 908	−314	−207	−1,309	−1,782	−2,700	−2,850	−3,946	−4,483
Other sectors	4 909	−40	−34	−150	−102	−884	−433	−146	−323

Table 2 (Concluded). STANDARD PRESENTATION, 2000–2007

(Millions of U.S. dollars)

	Code	2000	2001	2002	2003	2004	2005	2006	2007
D. OTHER INVESTMENT	4 700	**3,172**	**−2,289**	**−2,116**	**3,173**	**1,259**	**4,646**	**3,970**	**8,760**
Assets	4 703	**939**	**−2,754**	**−1,599**	**−2,827**	**−1,940**	**−2,122**	**−2,521**	**−4,645**
Trade credits	4 706	901	293	−1,082	−300	−1,371	−1,078	−514	−350
General government	4 707	65	−10	19	199	−23	−13	362	14
of which: Short-term	4 709	....	....	....	....	....	....	....	....
Other sectors	4 710	836	303	−1,101	−498	−1,348	−1,065	−876	−364
of which: Short-term	4 712	*968*	*182*	*−1,218*	*−584*	*−1,334*	*−871*	*−1,064*	*−311*
Loans	4 714	409	−2,197	−575	−2,687	−930	−913	−1,898	−4,131
Monetary authorities	4 715	−8	4	36	−1,049	1,100	−11	....	....
of which: Short-term	4 718	*−8*	*4*	*32*	*−1,049*	*1,106*		....	....
General government	4 719	−27	2	−6	....	−43	−104	−137	−432
of which: Short-term	4 721	*−1*	*9*	....	*−9*	*−6*	*−67*	*−110*	*−351*
Banks	4 722	613	−1,302	181	−1,101	−830	−88	−3,536	−3,523
of which: Short-term	4 724	*712*	*−1,079*	*330*	*−727*	*−1,110*	*669*	*−2,142*	*249*
Other sectors	4 725	−169	−901	−785	−537	−1,156	−709	1,774	−177
of which: Short-term	4 727	*3*	*−391*	*−608*	*−629*	*−990*	*−593*	*2,049*	*−263*
Currency and deposits	4 730	−370	−851	57	159	361	−131	−109	−164
Monetary authorities	4 731	....	....	....	....	....	....	....	....
General government	4 732	....	....	....	....	....	....	....	....
Banks	4 733	142	−161	347	150	481	−77	552	−372
Other sectors	4 734	−512	−690	−290	9	−120	−54	−661	209
Other assets	4 736	....	....	....	....	....	....	....	....
Monetary authorities	4 737	....	....	....	....	....	....	....	....
of which: Short-term	4 739	....	....	....	....	....	....	....	....
General government	4 740	....	....	....	....	....	....	....	....
of which: Short-term	4 742	....	....	....	....	....	....	....	....
Banks	4 743	....	....	....	....	....	....	....	....
of which: Short-term	4 745	....	....	....	....	....	....	....	....
Other sectors	4 746	....	....	....	....	....	....	....	....
of which: Short-term	4 748	....	....	....	....	....	....	....	....
Liabilities	4 753	**2,232**	**465**	**−517**	**6,000**	**3,199**	**6,769**	**6,491**	**13,405**
Trade credits	4 756	−141	2	−139	20	34	....	67	129
General government	4 757	−114	−71	....	....	....	....	....	....
of which: Short-term	4 759	....	....	....	....	....	....	....	....
Other sectors	4 760	−28	73	−139	20	34	....	67	129
of which: Short-term	4 762	*−12*	*81*	*−139*	*20*	*34*	....	*67*	*129*
Loans	4 764	1,959	65	−485	6,096	2,835	5,968	5,649	13,123
Monetary authorities	4 765	616	−645	−625	569	−933	−20	24	−89
of which: Use of Fund credit and loans from the Fund	4 766	....	....	....	....	....	....	....	....
of which: Short-term	4 768	*647*	*−209*	*−429*	*625*	*−933*	*−14*	*24*	*−89*
General government	4 769	−111	24	766	319	161	523	721	1,853
of which: Short-term	4 771	....	....	....	....	*4*	*108*	*−79*	*464*
Banks	4 772	301	229	507	4,158	2,440	4,119	4,146	6,568
of which: Short-term	4 774	*−269*	*−206*	*−156*	*2,287*	*485*	*2,091*	*874*	*4,458*
Other sectors	4 775	1,153	457	−1,134	1,051	1,168	1,346	757	4,790
of which: Short-term	4 777	*116*	*278*	*−216*	*237*	*809*	*290*	*−2*	*1,007*
Currency and deposits	4 780	414	398	107	−116	330	801	775	153
Monetary authorities	4 781	−3	1	....	1	17	−16	32	−23
General government	4 782	....	....	....	....	....	....	....	....
Banks	4 783	101	64	140	−171	222	455	222	−111
Other sectors	4 784	317	332	−33	55	91	361	521	287
Other liabilities	4 786	....	....	....	....	....	....	....	....
Monetary authorities	4 787	....	....	....	....	....	....	....	....
of which: Short-term	4 789	....	....	....	....	....	....	....	....
General government	4 790	....	....	....	....	....	....	....	....
of which: Short-term	4 792	....	....	....	....	....	....	....	....
Banks	4 793	....	....	....	....	....	....	....	....
of which: Short-term	4 795	....	....	....	....	....	....	....	....
Other sectors	4 796	....	....	....	....	....	....	....	....
of which: Short-term	4 798	....	....	....	....	....	....	....	....
E. RESERVE ASSETS	4 802	**−1,052**	**84**	**1,792**	**−336**	**−1,981**	**−4,904**	**−1,102**	**−154**
Monetary gold	4 812	....	....	....	....	1	....	....	....
Special drawing rights	4 811	−8	−9	−10	−10	−9	−10	−7	−6
Reserve position in the Fund	4 810	−32	−152	−154	−23	161	309	64	29
Foreign exchange	4 803	−2,011	467	1,702	92	−2,143	−4,898	−1,580	−186
Other claims	4 813	999	−222	254	−395	10	−304	420	9
NET ERRORS AND OMISSIONS	4 998	**−174**	**29**	**145**	**226**	**−1,773**	**−3,047**	**−4,311**	**−3,789**

Table 3. INTERNATIONAL INVESTMENT POSITION (End-period stocks), 2000–2007

(Millions of U.S. dollars)

	Code	2000	2001	2002	2003	2004	2005	2006	2007
ASSETS	8 995 C.	**19,641**	**22,754**	**24,301**	**32,540**	**42,846**	**47,802**	**108,183**	**163,839**
Direct investment abroad	8 505	**1,280**	**1,556**	**2,166**	**3,509**	**6,018**	**7,836**	**54,776**	**96,882**
Equity capital and reinvested earnings	8 506	1,234	1,479	1,999	3,205	5,603	7,636	52,664	91,947
Claims on affiliated enterprises	8 507	1,234	1,479	1,999	3,205	5,603	7,636	52,664	91,947
Liabilities to affiliated enterprises	8 508	....	....	....	....	....	....	....	....
Other capital	8 530	46	77	167	304	415	200	2,112	4,935
Claims on affiliated enterprises	8 535	66	117	180	382	473	571	2,564	5,444
Liabilities to affiliated enterprises	8 540	−20	−40	−13	−78	−58	−371	−452	−509
Portfolio investment	8 602	**667**	**814**	**931**	**1,045**	**1,599**	**2,569**	**5,102**	**8,701**
Equity securities	8 610	221	271	355	425	924	1,432	3,363	6,492
Monetary authorities	8 611	....	....	....	....	....	....	....	....
General government	8 612	....	....	....	....	....	....	....	....
Banks	8 613	....	21	....	22	64	7	4	3
Other sectors	8 614	221	251	355	403	860	1,426	3,359	6,489
Debt securities	8 619	447	543	576	620	675	1,137	1,739	2,209
Bonds and notes	8 620	391	495	481	515	541	989	1,623	2,063
Monetary authorities	8 621	....	....	....	....	....	....	....	....
General government	8 622	....	....	....	....	....	....	....	....
Banks	8 623	151	274	290	323	308	330	625	378
Other sectors	8 624	240	221	191	192	233	659	998	1,685
Money market instruments	8 630	55	48	95	104	135	148	116	145
Monetary authorities	8 631	....	....	....	....	....	....	....	....
General government	8 632	....	....	....	....	....	....	....	....
Banks	8 633	7	3	4	1	2	17	3	6
Other sectors	8 634	48	45	91	103	133	130	114	139
Financial derivatives	8 900	**859**	**1,165**	**909**	**1,604**	**2,481**	**1,447**	**2,025**	**2,438**
Monetary authorities	8 901	831	1,127	540	249	195	138	83	72
General government	8 902	....	....	....	....	34	191	98	111
Banks	8 903	28	38	369	1,356	2,251	1,118	1,845	2,255
Other sectors	8 904	....	....	....	....	....	....	....	....
Other investment	8 703	**5,606**	**8,452**	**9,898**	**13,588**	**16,782**	**17,347**	**24,690**	**31,767**
Trade credits	8 706	1,253	941	2,218	2,756	4,284	4,675	6,029	6,966
General government	8 707	354	367	358	231	282	270	149	147
of which: Short-term	8 709	....	....	....	....	....	....	....	....
Other sectors	8 710	900	575	1,861	2,526	4,002	4,405	5,879	6,818
of which: Short-term	8 712	*299*	*108*	*1,507*	*2,268*	*3,948*	*4,169*	*5,829*	*6,799*
Loans	8 714	2,836	4,957	7,126	10,354	11,843	11,765	16,505	22,159
Monetary authorities	8 715	75	63	30	1,107	23	31	33	35
of which: Short-term	8 718	*68*	*52*	*20*	*1,095*	....	....	....	....
General government	8 719	115	112	173	131	178	229	405	987
of which: Short-term	8 721	*20*	*11*	*12*	*21*	*17*	*49*	*180*	*653*
Banks	8 722	2,330	3,567	3,615	4,991	6,073	5,654	9,686	14,098
of which: Short-term	8 724	*1,373*	*2,424*	*2,253*	*3,141*	*4,345*	*3,306*	*5,707*	*5,844*
Other sectors	8 725	317	1,215	3,307	4,124	5,570	5,851	6,382	7,039
of which: Short-term	8 727	*16*	*406*	*2,232*	*3,035*	*4,205*	*4,485*	*4,686*	*5,344*
Currency and deposits	8 730	1,516	2,554	554	478	655	907	2,156	2,643
Monetary authorities	8 731	....	....	....	....	....	....	....	....
General government	8 732	....	....	....	....	....	....	....	....
Banks	8 733	230	473	247	322	372	565	568	884
Other sectors	8 734	1,286	2,081	307	156	283	342	1,589	1,759
Other assets	8 736	....	....	....	....	....	....	....	....
Monetary authorities	8 737	....	....	....	....	....	....	....	....
of which: Short-term	8 739	....	....	....	....	....	....	....	....
General government	8 740	....	....	....	....	....	....	....	....
of which: Short-term	8 742	....	....	....	....	....	....	....	....
Banks	8 743	....	....	....	....	....	....	....	....
of which: Short-term	8 745	....	....	....	....	....	....	....	....
Other sectors	8 746	....	....	....	....	....	....	....	....
of which: Short-term	8 748	....	....	....	....	....	....	....	....
Reserve assets	8 802	**11,229**	**10,767**	**10,396**	**12,793**	**15,965**	**18,603**	**21,589**	**24,052**
Monetary gold	8 812	28	28	35	42	43	51	63	82
Special drawing rights	8 811	12	21	33	46	58	64	74	83
Reserve position in the Fund	8 810	263	405	595	676	538	192	137	113
Foreign exchange	8 803	10,807	9,979	9,601	11,426	14,723	17,466	20,857	23,197
Other claims	8 813	120	335	132	603	602	831	459	576

Table 3 (Concluded). INTERNATIONAL INVESTMENT POSITION (End-period stocks), 2000–2007

(Millions of U.S. dollars)

	Code	2000	2001	2002	2003	2004	2005	2006	2007
LIABILITIES	8 995 D.	**53,010**	**58,653**	**73,854**	**102,881**	**138,744**	**143,112**	**228,995**	**306,554**
Direct investment in Hungary	8 555	**22,870**	**27,407**	**36,224**	**48,340**	**62,585**	**61,970**	**120,350**	**171,584**
Equity capital and reinvested earnings	8 556	19,585	22,550	31,177	41,921	55,144	55,225	146,865	193,743
Claims on direct investors	8 557	....	....	....	....	....	....	....	....
Liabilities to direct investors	8 558	19,585	22,550	31,177	41,921	55,144	55,225	146,865	193,743
Other capital	8 580	3,284	4,857	5,047	6,419	7,441	6,745	−26,515	−22,159
Claims on direct investors	8 585	−124	−251	−2,118	−4,634	−5,536	−5,368	−62,393	−69,693
Liabilities to direct investors	8 590	3,409	5,108	7,164	11,053	12,977	12,113	35,878	47,534
Portfolio investment	8 652	**14,812**	**15,691**	**20,910**	**27,793**	**43,153**	**46,068**	**63,019**	**70,386**
Equity securities	8 660	2,986	2,906	3,784	5,604	11,359	13,157	18,376	15,263
Banks	8 663	354	477	695	947	1,957	1,998	3,373	2,420
Other sectors	8 664	2,633	2,428	3,089	4,657	9,402	11,159	15,004	12,843
Debt securities	8 669	11,825	12,786	17,126	22,189	31,794	32,911	44,643	55,123
Bonds and notes	8 670	11,763	12,442	16,663	21,763	31,025	32,566	43,983	54,275
Monetary authorities	8 671	6,404	4,973	4,457	3,130	2,035	964	935	579
General government	8 672	5,130	6,904	11,411	17,248	25,678	26,450	33,653	40,541
Banks	8 673	211	544	767	1,349	3,162	3,978	7,884	11,560
Other sectors	8 674	17	22	29	36	149	1,174	1,512	1,595
Money market instruments	8 680	63	344	463	426	770	346	659	848
Monetary authorities	8 681	....	....	....	....	....	....	....	....
General government	8 682	....	279	382	331	660	253	555	711
Banks	8 683	1	1	2	9	10	9	10	33
Other sectors	8 684	62	64	79	86	100	84	94	104
Financial derivatives	8 905	**276**	**483**	**624**	**2,000**	**2,605**	**1,652**	**2,365**	**3,192**
Monetary authorities	8 906	236	448	283	538	611	284	336	232
General government	8 907	....	....	....	....	134	255	563	970
Banks	8 908	40	35	342	1,463	1,861	1,113	1,466	1,990
Other sectors	8 909	....	....	....	....	....	....	....	....
Other investment	8 753	**15,053**	**15,072**	**16,096**	**24,748**	**30,400**	**33,422**	**43,262**	**61,392**
Trade credits	8 756	382	374	28	36	....	115	527	304
General government	8 757	193	116	....	....	....	....	....	....
of which: Short-term	8 759	....	....	....	....	....	....	....	....
Other sectors	8 760	188	258	28	36	....	115	527	304
of which: Short-term	8 762	*86*	*164*	*27*	*35*	....	....	*152*	*304*
Loans	8 764	13,277	12,917	14,941	23,646	28,895	31,123	39,442	57,447
Monetary authorities	8 765	1,856	1,157	589	1,234	318	277	333	299
of which: Use of Fund credit and loans from the Fund	8 766	....	....	....	....	....	....	....	....
of which: Short-term	8 768	*1,168*	*941*	*527*	*1,229*	*311*	*277*	*333*	*299*
General government	8 769	1,053	1,051	2,118	2,806	3,215	3,326	4,452	6,867
of which: Short-term	8 771	....	....	....	....	*3*	*103*	*34*	*537*
Banks	8 772	4,666	4,720	5,695	11,014	14,762	16,911	22,772	31,757
of which: Short-term	8 774	*1,786*	*1,420*	*1,426*	*4,084*	*4,970*	*6,409*	*7,513*	*12,676*
Other sectors	8 775	5,701	5,989	6,539	8,592	10,600	10,609	11,886	18,524
of which: Short-term	8 777	*192*	*476*	*1,188*	*1,548*	*2,477*	*2,614*	*2,129*	*3,361*
Currency and deposits	8 780	1,395	1,781	1,127	1,066	1,504	2,183	3,293	3,641
Monetary authorities	8 781	7	8	10	11	39	16	59	44
General government	8 782	....	....	....	....	....	....	....	....
Banks	8 783	810	862	1,089	979	1,287	1,624	1,962	2,074
Other sectors	8 784	578	912	29	75	178	542	1,273	1,523
Other liabilities	8 786	....	....	....	....	....	....	....	....
Monetary authorities	8 787	....	....	....	....	....	....	....	....
of which: Short-term	8 789	....	....	....	....	....	....	....	....
General government	8 790	....	....	....	....	....	....	....	....
of which: Short-term	8 792	....	....	....	....	....	....	....	....
Banks	8 793	....	....	....	....	....	....	....	....
of which: Short-term	8 795	....	....	....	....	....	....	....	....
Other sectors	8 796	....	....	....	....	....	....	....	....
of which: Short-term	8 798	....	....	....	....	....	....	....	....
NET INTERNATIONAL INVESTMENT POSITION	8 995	−33,369	−35,898	−49,553	−70,342	−95,898	−95,310	−120,811	−142,714
Conversion rates: forint per U.S. dollar (end of period)	0 102	284.73	279.03	225.16	207.92	180.29	213.58	191.62	172.61

Table 1. ANALYTIC PRESENTATION, 2000–2007

(Millions of U.S. dollars)

	Code	2000	2001	2002	2003	2004	2005	2006	2007
A. Current Account[1]	4 993 Z.	**−847**	**−336**	**145**	**−534**	**−1,317**	**−2,645**	**−4,234**	**−3,179**
Goods: exports f.o.b.	2 100 ..	1,902	2,016	2,240	2,386	2,896	3,107	3,477	4,792
Goods: imports f.o.b.	3 100 ..	−2,376	−2,091	−2,090	−2,596	−3,415	−4,590	−5,716	−6,181
Balance on Goods	4 100 ..	*−474*	*−75*	*150*	*−210*	*−519*	*−1,482*	*−2,239*	*−1,388*
Services: credit	2 200 ..	1,044	1,086	1,118	1,378	1,623	2,041	1,834	2,251
Services: debit	3 200 ..	−1,164	−1,074	−1,123	−1,503	−1,838	−2,560	−2,553	−2,949
Balance on Goods and Services	4 991 ..	*−595*	*−63*	*144*	*−335*	*−735*	*−2,001*	*−2,959*	*−2,086*
Income: credit	2 300 ..	147	171	305	376	470	1,456	2,587	5,006
Income: debit	3 300 ..	−390	−435	−318	−559	−1,035	−2,072	−3,827	−6,050
Balance on Goods, Services, and Income	4 992 ..	*−837*	*−326*	*131*	*−519*	*−1,300*	*−2,617*	*−4,199*	*−3,130*
Current transfers: credit	2 379 Z.	6	8	36	12	10	11	8	16
Current transfers: debit	3 379 ..	−16	−17	−22	−28	−27	−38	−42	−66
B. Capital Account[1]	4 994 Z.	**−3**	**4**	**−1**	**−5**	**−3**	**−27**	**−26**	**−30**
Capital account: credit	2 994 Z.	17	15	14	15	32	14	15	16
Capital account: debit	3 994 ..	−21	−12	−15	−20	−35	−41	−41	−46
Total, Groups A Plus B	4 981 ..	*−850*	*−332*	*144*	*−539*	*−1,320*	*−2,672*	*−4,259*	*−3,209*
C. Financial Account[1]	4 995 W.	**846**	**172**	**−64**	**444**	**1,925**	**2,354**	**7,417**	**3,087**
Direct investment abroad	4 505 ..	−375	−332	−342	−384	−2,587	−7,114	−5,354	−12,115
Direct investment in Iceland	4 555 Z.	155	166	93	336	757	3,124	4,049	3,038
Portfolio investment assets.	4 602 ..	−667	−64	−324	−593	−1,675	−4,707	−3,092	−7,230
Equity securities	4 610 ..	−651	−67	−265	−531	−1,612	−3,279	−1,106	−2,565
Debt securities	4 619 ..	−16	3	−59	−62	−63	−1,428	−1,986	−4,665
Portfolio investment liabilities	4 652 Z.	1,142	665	467	3,603	8,401	16,935	14,396	828
Equity securities	4 660 ..	−44	43	55	−46	302	83	1,166	211
Debt securities	4 669 Z.	1,186	622	413	3,650	8,099	16,851	13,230	616
Financial derivatives	4 910 ..	−1	....	....	....	....	....	....	....
Financial derivatives assets	4 900 ..	15	....	....	....	....	....	....	....
Financial derivatives liabilities	4 905 ..	−16	....	....	....	....	....	....	....
Other investment assets	4 703 ..	−79	−475	−336	−2,081	−3,460	−10,922	−11,371	−16,718
Monetary authorities	4 701 ..	....	....	....	....	....	....	....	....
General government	4 704 ..	....	....	....	....	....	....	....	....
Banks	4 705 ..	−71	−216	−380	−2,157	−3,187	−10,466	−11,085	−17,644
Other sectors	4 728 ..	−8	−259	43	76	−274	−456	−286	926
Other investment liabilities	4 753 W.	671	213	379	−437	491	5,038	8,790	35,285
Monetary authorities	4 753 WA	142	−33	48	−206	....	1	−20	−4
General government	4 753 ZB	27	79	41	−76	−51	−137	−75	−6
Banks	4 753 ZC	332	−104	296	−37	668	3,487	7,114	31,872
Other sectors	4 753 ZD	170	271	−5	−118	−126	1,687	1,771	3,423
Total, Groups A Through C	4 983 ..	*−4*	*−160*	*80*	*−95*	*606*	*−318*	*3,157*	*−122*
D. Net Errors and Omissions	4 998 ..	**−70**	**111**	**−19**	**401**	**−404**	**389**	**−1,906**	**230**
Total, Groups A Through D	4 984 ..	*−74*	*−48*	*61*	*307*	*202*	*71*	*1,252*	*108*
E. Reserves and Related Items	4 802 A.	**74**	**48**	**−61**	**−307**	**−202**	**−71**	**−1,252**	**−108**
Reserve assets	4 802 ..	74	48	−61	−307	−202	−71	−1,252	−108
Use of Fund credit and loans	4 766 ..	....	....	....	....	....	....	....	....
Exceptional financing	4 920 ..	....	....	....	....	....	....	....	....
Conversion rates: krónur per U.S. dollar	0 101 ..	**78.616**	**97.425**	**91.662**	**76.709**	**70.192**	**62.982**	**70.180**	**64.055**

[1] Excludes components that have been classified in the categories of Group E.

Table 2. STANDARD PRESENTATION, 2000–2007

(Millions of U.S. dollars)

	Code	2000	2001	2002	2003	2004	2005	2006	2007
CURRENT ACCOUNT	4 993	−847	−336	145	−534	−1,317	−2,645	−4,234	−3,179
A. GOODS	4 100	−474	−75	150	−210	−519	−1,482	−2,239	−1,388
Credit	2 100	1,902	2,016	2,240	2,386	2,896	3,107	3,477	4,792
General merchandise: exports f.o.b.	2 110	1,902	2,016	2,240	2,386	2,896	3,107	3,477	4,792
Goods for processing: exports f.o.b.	2 150	....	....	....	....	....	....	....	....
Repairs on goods	2 160	....	....	....	....	....	....	....	....
Goods procured in ports by carriers	2 170	....	....	....	....	....	....	....	....
Nonmonetary gold	2 180	....	....	....	....	....	....	....	....
Debit	3 100	−2,376	−2,091	−2,090	−2,596	−3,415	−4,590	−5,716	−6,181
General merchandise: imports f.o.b.	3 110	−2,376	−2,091	−2,090	−2,596	−3,415	−4,590	−5,716	−6,181
Goods for processing: imports f.o.b.	3 150	....	....	....	....	....	....	....	....
Repairs on goods	3 160	....	....	....	....	....	....	....	....
Goods procured in ports by carriers	3 170	....	....	....	....	....	....	....	....
Nonmonetary gold	3 180	....	....	....	....	....	....	....	....
B. SERVICES	4 200	−121	12	−5	−125	−215	−519	−719	−698
Total credit	2 200	*1,044*	*1,086*	*1,118*	*1,378*	*1,623*	*2,041*	*1,834*	*2,251*
Total debit	3 200	*−1,164*	*−1,074*	*−1,123*	*−1,503*	*−1,838*	*−2,560*	*−2,553*	*−2,949*
Transportation services, credit	2 205	518	521	534	656	902	1,087	831	930
Passenger	2 850	*159*	*151*	*159*	*167*	*188*	*222*	*224*	*247*
Freight	2 851	*126*	*108*	*124*	*153*	*219*	*182*	*133*	*165*
Other	2 852	*233*	*262*	*251*	*336*	*495*	*683*	*475*	*519*
Sea transport, passenger	2 207	....	....	....	....	....	....	....	....
Sea transport, freight	2 208	90	86	91	107	121	132	116	140
Sea transport, other	2 209	45	48	16	11	9	54	14	54
Air transport, passenger	2 211	159	151	159	167	188	222	224	247
Air transport, freight	2 212	36	23	32	46	99	50	17	25
Air transport, other	2 213	188	214	235	325	486	628	461	465
Other transport, passenger	2 215	....	....	....	....	....	....	....	....
Other transport, freight	2 216	....	....	....	....	....	....	....	....
Other transport, other	2 217	....	....	....	....	....	....	....	....
Transportation services, debit	3 205	−413	−381	−425	−518	−698	−885	−766	−858
Passenger	3 850	....	....	*−2*	*−1*	*−2*	*−11*	*−8*	*−10*
Freight	3 851	*−19*	*−18*	*−16*	*−14*	*−21*	*−28*	*−25*	*−32*
Other	3 852	*−394*	*−363*	*−407*	*−503*	*−675*	*−846*	*−733*	*−816*
Sea transport, passenger	3 207	....	....	....	....	....	....	....	....
Sea transport, freight	3 208	−16	−15	−15	−14	−21	−28	−25	−32
Sea transport, other	3 209	−128	−86	−111	−120	−140	−245	−221	−315
Air transport, passenger	3 211	....	....	−2	−1	−2	−11	−8	−10
Air transport, freight	3 212	−3	−3	−2	....	....	....	....	....
Air transport, other	3 213	−266	−277	−296	−383	−534	−601	−511	−500
Other transport, passenger	3 215	....	....	....	....	....	....	....	....
Other transport, freight	3 216	....	....	....	....	....	....	....	....
Other transport, other	3 217	....	....	....	....	....	....	....	....
Travel, credit	2 236	227	232	256	319	370	408	439	640
Business travel	2 237	....	....	....	....	....	....	....	....
Personal travel	2 240	227	232	256	319	370	408	439	640
Travel, debit	3 236	−471	−372	−371	−523	−697	−980	−1,076	−1,341
Business travel	3 237	....	....	....	....	....	....	....	....
Personal travel	3 240	−471	−372	−371	−523	−697	−980	−1,076	−1,341
Other services, credit	2 200 BA	299	333	328	403	351	546	563	681
Communications	2 245	10	24	8	8	10	9	12	14
Construction	2 249	2	....	1	14	2	....	....	....
Insurance	2 253	6	6	7	7	9	8	10	13
Financial	2 260	....	3	....	1	1	....	1	2
Computer and information	2 262	29	27	35	44	56	69	89	74
Royalties and licence fees	2 266	....	....	....	....	2	....	....	....
Other business services	2 268	138	182	188	227	167	358	380	557
Personal, cultural, and recreational	2 287	7	8	5	4	9	16	12	9
Government, n.i.e.	2 291	107	83	84	97	96	86	59	13
Other services, debit	3 200 BA	−280	−321	−327	−462	−444	−695	−712	−751
Communications	3 245	−2	−27	−38	−45	−21	−43	−46	−45
Construction	3 249	−19	−17	−7	−24	−9	−7	−18	−25
Insurance	3 253	−6	−8	−19	−24	−19	−41	−42	−28
Financial	3 260	−11	−5	−5	−11	−38	−24	−19	−21
Computer and information	3 262	−2	−5	−3	−14	−8	−12	−17	−23
Royalties and licence fees	3 266	−1	−1	−1	−2	−2	−4	−4	−5
Other business services	3 268	−211	−229	−224	−309	−314	−529	−531	−560
Personal, cultural, and recreational	3 287	−15	−13	−12	−11	−12	−13	−14	−17
Government, n.i.e.	3 291	−15	−16	−18	−22	−21	−22	−20	−25

Table 2 (Continued). STANDARD PRESENTATION, 2000–2007

(Millions of U.S. dollars)

	Code	2000	2001	2002	2003	2004	2005	2006	2007
C. INCOME	4 300	**−243**	**−264**	**−13**	**−183**	**−565**	**−616**	**−1,240**	**−1,044**
Total credit	2 300	*147*	*171*	*305*	*376*	*470*	*1,456*	*2,587*	*5,006*
Total debit	3 300	*−390*	*−435*	*−318*	*−559*	*−1,035*	*−2,072*	*−3,827*	*−6,050*
Compensation of employees, credit	2 310	**70**	**59**	**60**	**81**	**80**	**74**	**72**	**25**
Compensation of employees, debit	3 310	**−10**	**−5**	**−8**	**−6**	**−12**	**−24**	**−39**	**−54**
Investment income, credit	2 320	**77**	**112**	**245**	**295**	**390**	**1,382**	**2,515**	**4,982**
Direct investment income	2 330	13	50	168	209	212	966	1,323	2,557
Dividends and distributed branch profits	2 332	2	1	12	18	50	70	29	208
Reinvested earnings and undistributed branch profits	2 333	5	44	143	182	137	870	1,180	2,222
Income on debt (interest)	2 334	6	5	12	9	25	26	113	126
Portfolio investment income	2 339	30	31	32	36	67	94	247	596
Income on equity	2 340	20	28	25	29	52	73	150	241
Income on bonds and notes	2 350	8	2	6	7	15	21	97	354
Income on money market instruments	2 360	3	1	1	....	....	....	....	....
Other investment income	2 370	34	32	46	49	110	321	945	1,829
Investment income, debit	3 320	**−380**	**−430**	**−310**	**−553**	**−1,023**	**−2,048**	**−3,788**	**−5,996**
Direct investment income	3 330	−16	−5	16	−160	−499	−1,044	−1,365	−1,285
Dividends and distributed branch profits	3 332	−27	−15	−19	−81	−23	−30	−92	−307
Reinvested earnings and undistributed branch profits	3 333	19	15	38	−76	−458	−1,007	−1,230	−895
Income on debt (interest)	3 334	−8	−5	−3	−2	−18	−7	−42	−83
Portfolio investment income	3 339	−182	−211	−178	−247	−376	−785	−1,797	−3,009
Income on equity	3 340	−2	....	−6	−8	−16	−25	−49	−106
Income on bonds and notes	3 350	−162	−188	−158	−214	−319	−711	−1,639	−2,749
Income on money market instruments	3 360	−19	−23	−14	−24	−40	−49	−109	−153
Other investment income	3 370	−182	−214	−149	−146	−149	−219	−626	−1,702
D. CURRENT TRANSFERS	4 379	**−10**	**−9**	**14**	**−15**	**−17**	**−27**	**−35**	**−50**
Credit	2 379	**6**	**8**	**36**	**12**	**10**	**11**	**8**	**16**
General government	2 380	....	....	6	11	....	1	....	....
Other sectors	2 390	6	8	30	2	10	10	8	16
Workers' remittances	2 391	....	....	....	....	....	....	....	....
Other current transfers	2 392	6	8	30	2	10	10	8	16
Debit	3 379	**−16**	**−17**	**−22**	**−28**	**−27**	**−38**	**−42**	**−66**
General government	3 380	−10	−12	−15	−19	−19	−26	−29	−45
Other sectors	3 390	−5	−5	−7	−9	−8	−12	−14	−20
Workers' remittances	3 391	....	....	....	....	....	....	....	....
Other current transfers	3 392	−5	−5	−7	−9	−8	−12	−14	−20
CAPITAL AND FINANCIAL ACCOUNT	4 996	**917**	**224**	**−126**	**133**	**1,720**	**2,256**	**6,139**	**2,949**
CAPITAL ACCOUNT	4 994	**−3**	**4**	**−1**	**−5**	**−3**	**−27**	**−26**	**−30**
Total credit	2 994	*17*	*15*	*14*	*15*	*32*	*14*	*15*	*16*
Total debit	3 994	*−21*	*−12*	*−15*	*−20*	*−35*	*−41*	*−41*	*−46*
Capital transfers, credit	2 400	**17**	**15**	**14**	**15**	**32**	**14**	**15**	**16**
General government	2 401	....	....	....	....	....	....	....	....
Debt forgiveness	2 402	....	....	....	....	....	....	....	....
Other capital transfers	2 410	....	....	....	....	....	....	....	....
Other sectors	2 430	17	15	14	15	32	14	15	16
Migrants' transfers	2 431	17	15	14	15	32	14	15	16
Debt forgiveness	2 432	....	....	....	....	....	....	....	....
Other capital transfers	2 440	....	....	....	....	....	....	....	....
Capital transfers, debit	3 400	**−21**	**−12**	**−15**	**−20**	**−35**	**−41**	**−41**	**−46**
General government	3 401	....	....	....	....	....	....	....	....
Debt forgiveness	3 402	....	....	....	....	....	....	....	....
Other capital transfers	3 410	....	....	....	....	....	....	....	....
Other sectors	3 430	−21	−12	−15	−20	−35	−41	−41	−46
Migrants' transfers	3 431	−21	−12	−15	−20	−35	−41	−41	−46
Debt forgiveness	3 432	....	....	....	....	....	....	....	....
Other capital transfers	3 440	....	....	....	....	....	....	....	....
Nonproduced nonfinancial assets, credit	2 480	....	....	....	....	....	....	....	....
Nonproduced nonfinancial assets, debit	3 480	....	....	....	....	....	....	....	....

Table 2 (Continued). STANDARD PRESENTATION, 2000–2007

(Millions of U.S. dollars)

	Code	2000	2001	2002	2003	2004	2005	2006	2007
FINANCIAL ACCOUNT	4 995	**920**	**221**	**−125**	**138**	**1,723**	**2,283**	**6,165**	**2,979**
A. DIRECT INVESTMENT	4 500	**−219**	**−166**	**−250**	**−48**	**−1,830**	**−3,990**	**−1,306**	**−9,077**
Direct investment abroad	4 505	**−375**	**−332**	**−342**	**−384**	**−2,587**	**−7,114**	**−5,354**	**−12,115**
Equity capital	4 510	−391	−267	−258	−274	−2,052	−5,158	−3,243	−8,665
Claims on affiliated enterprises	4 515	....	....	....	....	....	....	....	....
Liabilities to affiliated enterprises	4 520	....	....	....	....	....	....	....	....
Reinvested earnings	4 525	−5	−44	−143	−182	−137	−870	−1,180	−2,222
Other capital	4 530	21	−22	59	72	−399	−1,086	−932	−1,228
Claims on affiliated enterprises	4 535	−52		61	....	....	....	....	....
Liabilities to affiliated enterprises	4 540	74	....	−2	....	....	....	....	....
Direct investment in Iceland	4 555	**155**	**166**	**93**	**336**	**757**	**3,124**	**4,049**	**3,038**
Equity capital	4 560	199	201	116	78	100	1,661	2,106	2,036
Claims on direct investors	4 565	....	....	....	....	....	....	....	....
Liabilities to direct investors	4 570	....	....	....	....	....	....	....	....
Reinvested earnings	4 575	−19	−15	−38	76	458	1,007	1,230	895
Other capital	4 580	−24	−20	15	182	199	456	713	106
Claims on direct investors	4 585	4	....	....	....	....	....	....	....
Liabilities to direct investors	4 590	−28	....	....	....	....	....	....	....
B. PORTFOLIO INVESTMENT	4 600	**475**	**601**	**143**	**3,010**	**6,725**	**12,228**	**11,304**	**−6,403**
Assets	4 602	**−667**	**−64**	**−324**	**−593**	**−1,675**	**−4,707**	**−3,092**	**−7,230**
Equity securities	4 610	−651	−67	−265	−531	−1,612	−3,279	−1,106	−2,565
Monetary authorities	4 611	....	....	....	−1	....	−1	....	....
General government	4 612	....	....	....	....	....	....	....	....
Banks	4 613	−54	....	−54	−47	−366	−1,553	−10	−1,032
Other sectors	4 614	−597	−67	−211	−483	−1,247	−1,724	−1,096	−1,534
Debt securities	4 619	−16	3	−59	−62	−63	−1,428	−1,986	−4,665
Bonds and notes	4 620	−1	−21	−59	−66	−67	−1,430	−1,981	−4,662
Monetary authorities	4 621	....	....	....	1	....	....	....	....
General government	4 622	....	....	....	....	....	....	....	....
Banks	4 623	45	−4	8	−7	−22	−1,092	−1,828	−2,586
Other sectors	4 624	−46	−17	−67	−60	−46	−338	−153	−2,076
Money market instruments	4 630	−15	24	....	4	4	2	−5	−3
Monetary authorities	4 631	....	....	....	....	....	....	....	....
General government	4 632	....	....	....	....	....	....	....	....
Banks	4 633	−15	24	....	4	4	2	....	....
Other sectors	4 634	....	....	....	....	....	....	−5	−3
Liabilities	4 652	**1,142**	**665**	**467**	**3,603**	**8,401**	**16,935**	**14,396**	**828**
Equity securities	4 660	−44	43	55	−46	302	83	1,166	211
Banks	4 663	13	....	89	−12	54	379	629	1,139
Other sectors	4 664	−57	43	−34	−35	248	−295	537	−928
Debt securities	4 669	1,186	622	413	3,650	8,099	16,851	13,230	616
Bonds and notes	4 670	1,133	343	431	2,885	7,789	16,733	13,978	−110
Monetary authorities	4 671	....	....	....	....	....	....	....	....
General government	4 672	37	322	119	137	178	−217	969	138
Banks	4 673	761	−20	210	2,554	7,427	16,949	12,456	−692
Other sectors	4 674	334	40	102	193	184	1	553	444
Money market instruments	4 680	52	279	−18	765	310	118	−748	726
Monetary authorities	4 681	....	....	....	....	....	....	....	....
General government	4 682	134	14	−62	−203	12	−199	17	−5
Banks	4 683	−129	264	43	968	298	317	−894	686
Other sectors	4 684	48	....	....	....	....	....	129	45
C. FINANCIAL DERIVATIVES	4 910	**−1**	....	....	....	....	....	....	....
Monetary authorities	4 911	−1	....	....	....	....	....	....	....
General government	4 912	....	....	....	....	....	....	....	....
Banks	4 913	....	....	....	....	....	....	....	....
Other sectors	4 914	....	....	....	....	....	....	....	....
Assets	4 900	**15**	....	....	....	....	....	....	....
Monetary authorities	4 901	15	....	....	....	....	....	....	....
General government	4 902	....	....	....	....	....	....	....	....
Banks	4 903	....	....	....	....	....	....	....	....
Other sectors	4 904	....	....	....	....	....	....	....	....
Liabilities	4 905	**−16**	....	....	....	....	....	....	....
Monetary authorities	4 906	−16	....	....	....	....	....	....	....
General government	4 907	....	....	....	....	....	....	....	....
Banks	4 908	....	....	....	....	....	....	....	....
Other sectors	4 909	....	....	....	....	....	....	....	....

Table 2 (Concluded). STANDARD PRESENTATION, 2000–2007

(Millions of U.S. dollars)

	Code	2000	2001	2002	2003	2004	2005	2006	2007
D. OTHER INVESTMENT	4 700	**592**	**−262**	**43**	**−2,518**	**−2,969**	**−5,884**	**−2,581**	**18,567**
Assets	4 703	−79	−475	−336	−2,081	−3,460	−10,922	−11,371	−16,718
Trade credits	4 706	−19	−8	25	30	−69	14	−105	58
General government	4 707	....	....	....	....	....	....	....	....
of which: Short-term	4 709	....	....	....	....	....	....	....	....
Other sectors	4 710	−19	−8	25	30	−69	14	−105	58
of which: Short-term	4 712	....	....	....	....	....	....	....	....
Loans	4 714	−31	−313	−431	−1,180	−2,460	−9,287	−9,322	−8,316
Monetary authorities	4 715	....	....	....	....	....	....	....	....
of which: Short-term	4 718	....	....	....	....	....	....	....	....
General government	4 719	....	....	....	....	....	....	....	....
of which: Short-term	4 721	....	....	....	....	....	....	....	....
Banks	4 722	−30	−183	−431	−1,173	−2,257	−8,806	−9,438	−8,860
of which: Short-term	4 724	....	....	....	....	....	....	....	....
Other sectors	4 725	−1	−129	....	−7	−203	−481	116	544
of which: Short-term	4 727	....	....	....	....	....	....	....	....
Currency and deposits	4 730	−29	−154	74	−932	−932	−1,652	−1,917	−8,488
Monetary authorities	4 731	....	....	....	....	....	....	....	....
General government	4 732	....	....	....	....	....	....	....	....
Banks	4 733	−41	−33	51	−985	−930	−1,660	−1,647	−8,784
Other sectors	4 734	11	−122	23	52	−2	7	−270	296
Other assets	4 736	....	....	−5	....	....	3	−28	29
Monetary authorities	4 737	....	....	....	....	....	....	....	....
of which: Short-term	4 739	....	....	....	....	....	....	....	....
General government	4 740	....	....	....	....	....	....	....	....
of which: Short-term	4 742	....	....	....	....	....	....	....	....
Banks	4 743	....	....	....	....	....	....	....	....
of which: Short-term	4 745	....	....	....	....	....	....	....	....
Other sectors	4 746	....	....	−5	....	....	3	−28	29
of which: Short-term	4 748	....	....	....	....	....	....	....	....
Liabilities	4 753	**671**	**213**	**379**	**−437**	**491**	**5,038**	**8,790**	**35,285**
Trade credits	4 756	1	−33	−4	34	34	69	8	46
General government	4 757	....	....	....	....	....	....	....	....
of which: Short-term	4 759	....	....	....	....	....	....	....	....
Other sectors	4 760	1	−33	−4	34	34	69	8	46
of which: Short-term	4 762	*1*	....	....	....	....	....	....	....
Loans	4 764	673	260	303	−537	190	4,583	4,689	20,007
Monetary authorities	4 765	140	−32	49	−206	....	....	−1	....
of which: Use of Fund credit and loans from the Fund	4 766	....	....	....	....	....	....	....	....
of which: Short-term	4 768	*140*	*−32*	*49*	*−206*	....	....	....	....
General government	4 769	27	79	41	−76	−51	−137	−75	−6
of which: Short-term	4 771	....	....	....	....	....	....	....	....
Banks	4 772	347	−112	214	−103	398	3,105	3,015	16,637
of which: Short-term	4 774	*160*	*−96*	*492*	*145*	*524*	*1,981*	*1,134*	*12,117*
Other sectors	4 775	158	325	....	−152	−157	1,614	1,750	3,376
of which: Short-term	4 777	*35*	*78*	....	*−5*	*1*	*1*	*239*	*−263*
Currency and deposits	4 780	−13	7	81	65	270	383	4,079	15,232
Monetary authorities	4 781	2	−1	....	....	....	1	−19	−4
General government	4 782	....	....	....	....	....	....	....	....
Banks	4 783	−15	8	81	66	270	382	4,098	15,236
Other sectors	4 784	....	....	....	....	....	....	....	....
Other liabilities	4 786	10	−21	−1	....	−4	4	13	....
Monetary authorities	4 787	....	....	....	....	....	....	....	....
of which: Short-term	4 789	....	....	....	....	....	....	....	....
General government	4 790	....	....	....	....	....	....	....	....
of which: Short-term	4 792	....	....	....	....	....	....	....	....
Banks	4 793	....	....	....	....	....	....	....	....
of which: Short-term	4 795	....	....	....	....	....	....	....	....
Other sectors	4 796	10	−21	−1	....	−4	4	13	....
of which: Short-term	4 798	....	....	....	....	....	....	....	....
E. RESERVE ASSETS	4 802	**74**	**48**	**−61**	**−307**	**−202**	**−71**	**−1,252**	**−108**
Monetary gold	4 812	1	....	....	....	....	....	....	−11
Special drawing rights	4 811	....	....	....	....	....	....	....	....
Reserve position in the Fund	4 810	....	....	....	....	....	....	....	....
Foreign exchange	4 803	74	48	−61	−306	−202	−71	−1,251	−97
Other claims	4 813	....	....	....	....	....	....	....	....
NET ERRORS AND OMISSIONS	4 998	**−70**	**111**	**−19**	**401**	**−404**	**389**	**−1,906**	**230**

Table 3. INTERNATIONAL INVESTMENT POSITION (End-period stocks), 2000–2007

(Millions of U.S. dollars)

	Code	2000	2001	2002	2003	2004	2005	2006	2007
ASSETS	8 995 C.	**3,738**	**4,040**	**5,081**	**9,983**	**18,920**	**39,405**	**63,118**	**104,499**
Direct investment abroad	8 505 ..	**665**	**843**	**1,257**	**1,733**	**4,040**	**10,004**	**13,768**	**25,346**
Equity capital and reinvested earnings	8 506 ..	485	649	1,023	1,559	3,463	8,470	11,583	21,861
Claims on affiliated enterprises	8 507 ..	....	....	....	....	....	....	....	....
Liabilities to affiliated enterprises	8 508 ..	....	....	....	....	....	....	....	....
Other capital	8 530 ..	180	194	235	175	576	1,534	2,185	3,484
Claims on affiliated enterprises	8 535 ..	266	298	255	386	851	1,940	2,771	4,318
Liabilities to affiliated enterprises	8 540 ..	−86	−104	−21	−211	−275	−407	−586	−833
Portfolio investment	8 602 ..	**2,205**	**1,916**	**1,982**	**3,695**	**6,130**	**10,950**	**16,325**	**26,960**
Equity securities	8 610 ..	2,128	1,795	1,853	3,369	5,838	9,282	12,491	17,345
Monetary authorities	8 611 ..	1	1	1	2	2	3	3	8
General government	8 612 ..	....	4	4	5	5	20	23	27
Banks	8 613 ..	73	96	136	235	695	2,387	2,953	4,578
Other sectors	8 614 ..	2,054	1,695	1,711	3,127	5,137	6,871	9,513	12,733
Debt securities	8 619 ..	78	121	129	326	292	1,668	3,833	9,615
Bonds and notes	8 620 ..	42	94	119	320	290	1,668	3,828	9,606
Monetary authorities	8 621 ..	1	1	1	1	1	1	1	....
General government	8 622 ..	....	....	....	....	....	....	....	....
Banks	8 623 ..	1	10	25	40	73	1,120	3,124	6,670
Other sectors	8 624 ..	40	83	93	279	216	547	703	2,936
Money market instruments	8 630 ..	35	27	10	6	2	....	5	9
Monetary authorities	8 631 ..	....	....	....	....	....	....	....	....
General government	8 632 ..	....	....	....	....	....	....	....	....
Banks	8 633 ..	35	8	9	6	2	....	....	....
Other sectors	8 634 ..	....	19	1	....	....	....	5	9
Financial derivatives	8 900 ..	....	....	....	....	....	....	....	....
Monetary authorities	8 901 ..	....	....	....	....	....	....	....	....
General government	8 902 ..	....	....	....	....	....	....	....	....
Banks	8 903 ..	....	....	....	....	....	....	....	....
Other sectors	8 904 ..	....	....	....	....	....	....	....	....
Other investment	8 703 ..	**463**	**925**	**1,380**	**3,736**	**7,676**	**17,392**	**30,688**	**49,568**
Trade credits	8 706 ..	160	159	151	130	194	163	279	241
General government	8 707 ..	....	....	....	....	....	....	....	4
of which: Short-term	8 709 ..	....	....	....	....	....	....	....	....
Other sectors	8 710 ..	160	159	151	130	194	163	279	237
of which: Short-term	8 712 ..	....	....	....	....	....	....	....	....
Loans	8 714 ..	105	426	925	2,280	5,047	13,461	24,218	33,937
Monetary authorities	8 715 ..	....	....	....	....	....	....	....	....
of which: Short-term	8 718 ..	....	....	....	....	....	....	....	....
General government	8 719 ..	....	....	....	....	....	....	....	....
of which: Short-term	8 721 ..	....	....	....	....	....	....	....	....
Banks	8 722 ..	57	247	925	2,273	4,829	12,799	23,635	33,836
of which: Short-term	8 724 ..	....	....	....	....	....	....	....	....
Other sectors	8 725 ..	48	179	....	7	218	662	583	101
of which: Short-term	8 727 ..	....	....	....	....	....	....	....	....
Currency and deposits	8 730 ..	197	341	298	1,320	2,429	3,765	6,160	15,387
Monetary authorities	8 731 ..	....	....	....	....	....	....	....	....
General government	8 732 ..	....	....	....	....	....	....	....	....
Banks	8 733 ..	172	195	176	1,238	2,335	3,708	5,824	15,336
Other sectors	8 734 ..	25	145	123	83	93	57	336	51
Other assets	8 736 ..	....	....	5	6	6	2	31	3
Monetary authorities	8 737 ..	....	....	....	....	....	....	....	....
of which: Short-term	8 739 ..	....	....	....	....	....	....	....	....
General government	8 740 ..	....	....	....	....	....	....	....	....
of which: Short-term	8 742 ..	....	....	....	....	....	....	....	....
Banks	8 743 ..	....	....	....	....	....	....	....	....
of which: Short-term	8 745 ..	....	....	....	....	....	....	....	....
Other sectors	8 746 ..	....	....	5	6	6	2	31	3
of which: Short-term	8 748 ..	....	....	....	....	....	....	....	....
Reserve assets	8 802 ..	**405**	**355**	**462**	**819**	**1,074**	**1,060**	**2,337**	**2,626**
Monetary gold	8 812 ..	16	17	21	26	28	33	41	53
Special drawing rights	8 811 ..	....	....	....	....	....	....	....	....
Reserve position in the Fund	8 810 ..	24	23	25	28	29	27	28	29
Foreign exchange	8 803 ..	365	315	415	765	1,017	1,000	2,268	2,543
Other claims	8 813 ..	....	....	....	....	....	....	....	....

Table 3 (Concluded). INTERNATIONAL INVESTMENT POSITION (End-period stocks), 2000–2007

(Millions of U.S. dollars)

	Code	2000	2001	2002	2003	2004	2005	2006	2007
LIABILITIES	8 995 D.	**9,050**	**9,833**	**12,055**	**17,402**	**29,186**	**53,030**	**82,489**	**130,048**
Direct investment in Iceland	8 555 ..	**492**	**688**	**798**	**1,193**	**2,088**	**4,668**	**7,625**	**12,239**
Equity capital and reinvested earnings	8 556 ..	391	616	696	869	1,542	3,728	5,877	10,302
Claims on direct investors	8 557 ..	....	....	....	....	....	....	....	....
Liabilities to direct investors	8 558 ..	....	....	....	....	....	....	....	....
Other capital	8 580 ..	101	72	101	325	545	940	1,748	1,938
Claims on direct investors	8 585 ..	135	−41	−64	−98	−113	−145	−248	−357
Liabilities to direct investors	8 590 ..	−35	113	166	422	658	1,085	1,996	2,295
Portfolio investment	8 652 ..	**4,105**	**4,578**	**5,876**	**10,626**	**20,697**	**37,587**	**54,531**	**59,701**
Equity securities	8 660 ..	15	118	236	293	781	3,690	4,953	5,799
Banks	8 663 ..	10	31	149	213	379	1,621	2,206	3,442
Other sectors	8 664 ..	5	86	87	80	402	2,069	2,747	2,357
Debt securities	8 669 ..	4,090	4,460	5,640	10,333	19,916	33,897	49,578	53,902
Bonds and notes	8 670 ..	3,542	3,693	4,836	8,609	17,737	31,613	48,291	52,165
Monetary authorities	8 671 ..	....	....	....	....	....	....	....	....
General government	8 672 ..	1,103	1,376	1,786	2,202	2,574	2,187	3,217	3,782
Banks	8 673 ..	1,770	1,660	2,187	5,316	13,782	28,282	43,314	45,998
Other sectors	8 674 ..	670	658	863	1,091	1,381	1,145	1,760	2,385
Money market instruments	8 680 ..	548	767	803	1,725	2,179	2,284	1,287	1,738
Monetary authorities	8 681 ..	....	....	....	....	....	....	....	....
General government	8 682 ..	423	434	403	196	221	7	21	24
Banks	8 683 ..	124	333	399	1,528	1,958	2,277	1,142	1,523
Other sectors	8 684 ..	....	....	1	....	....	....	124	191
Financial derivatives	8 905 ..	....	....	....	....	....	....	....	....
Monetary authorities	8 906 ..	....	....	....	....	....	....	....	....
General government	8 907 ..	....	....	....	....	....	....	....	....
Banks	8 908 ..	....	....	....	....	....	....	....	....
Other sectors	8 909 ..	....	....	....	....	....	....	....	....
Other investment	8 753 ..	**4,454**	**4,567**	**5,382**	**5,582**	**6,401**	**10,776**	**20,333**	**58,107**
Trade credits	8 756 ..	146	108	113	160	202	250	274	338
General government	8 757 ..	....	....	....	....	....	....	....	4
of which: Short-term	8 759 ..	....	....	....	....	....	....	....	....
Other sectors	8 760 ..	146	108	113	160	202	250	274	334
of which: Short-term	8 762 ..	....	....	....	....	....	....	....	....
Loans	8 764 ..	4,246	4,406	5,130	5,197	5,683	9,682	14,949	36,936
Monetary authorities	8 765 ..	184	144	203	....	....	....	....	....
of which: Use of Fund credit and loans from the Fund	8 766 ..	....	....	....	....	....	....	....	....
of which: Short-term	8 768 ..	*184*	*144*	*203*	....	....	....	....	....
General government	8 769 ..	456	520	631	713	684	237	166	122
of which: Short-term	8 771 ..	....	....	....	....	....	....	....	....
Banks	8 772 ..	2,258	2,067	2,922	3,147	3,756	6,475	9,817	28,421
of which: Short-term	8 774 ..	*475*	*360*	*1,239*	*1,539*	*2,180*	*3,919*	*5,244*	*18,092*
Other sectors	8 775 ..	1,349	1,676	1,374	1,337	1,243	2,970	4,966	8,393
of which: Short-term	8 777 ..	*166*	*241*	*12*	*8*	*9*	*60*	*277*	*99*
Currency and deposits	8 780 ..	19	32	118	203	496	822	5,074	20,796
Monetary authorities	8 781 ..	3	2	2	2	2	2	1	2
General government	8 782 ..	....	....	....	....	....	....	....	....
Banks	8 783 ..	16	31	116	202	493	820	5,073	20,794
Other sectors	8 784 ..	....	....	....	....	....	....	....	....
Other liabilities	8 786 ..	43	20	20	23	20	21	36	38
Monetary authorities	8 787 ..	....	....	....	....	....	....	....	....
of which: Short-term	8 789 ..	....	....	....	....	....	....	....	....
General government	8 790 ..	....	....	....	....	....	....	....	....
of which: Short-term	8 792 ..	....	....	....	....	....	....	....	....
Banks	8 793 ..	....	....	....	....	....	....	....	....
of which: Short-term	8 795 ..	....	....	....	....	....	....	....	....
Other sectors	8 796 ..	43	20	20	23	20	21	36	38
of which: Short-term	8 798 ..	....	....	....	....	....	....	....	....
NET INTERNATIONAL INVESTMENT POSITION	8 995 ..	**−5,312**	**−5,794**	**−6,975**	**−7,419**	**−10,265**	**−13,625**	**−19,371**	**−25,548**
Conversion rates: krónur per U.S. dollar (end of period)	0 102 ..	84.700	102.950	80.580	70.990	61.040	62.980	71.660	61.850

Table 1. ANALYTIC PRESENTATION, 2000–2007

(Millions of U.S. dollars)

	Code	2000	2001	2002	2003	2004	2005	2006	2007
A. Current Account[1]	4 993 Z.	**−4,601**	**1,410**	**7,059**	**8,773**	**780**	**−7,835**	**−9,415**	....
Goods: exports f.o.b.	2 100 ..	43,247	44,793	51,141	60,893	77,939	102,176	123,617	....
Goods: imports f.o.b.	3 100 ..	−53,887	−51,212	−54,702	−68,081	−95,539	−134,702	−166,695	....
Balance on Goods	4 100 ..	*−10,640*	*−6,419*	*−3,561*	*−7,188*	*−17,600*	*−32,526*	*−43,078*	....
Services: credit	2 200 ..	16,684	17,337	19,478	23,902	38,281	55,831	75,354	....
Services: debit	3 200 ..	−19,187	−20,099	−21,039	−24,878	−35,641	−47,989	−63,537	....
Balance on Goods and Services	4 991 ..	*−13,143*	*−9,181*	*−5,122*	*−8,164*	*−14,960*	*−24,684*	*−31,261*	....
Income: credit	2 300 ..	2,521	3,524	3,188	3,491	4,690	5,082	7,795	....
Income: debit	3 300 ..	−7,414	−7,666	−7,097	−8,386	−8,742	−11,475	−12,059	....
Balance on Goods, Services, and Income	4 992 ..	*−18,036*	*−13,323*	*−9,031*	*−13,059*	*−19,012*	*−31,078*	*−35,525*	....
Current transfers: credit	2 379 Z.	13,548	15,140	16,788	22,401	20,615	24,120	27,449	....
Current transfers: debit	3 379 ..	−114	−407	−698	−570	−822	−877	−1,340	....
B. Capital Account[1]	4 994 Z.	**716**	....	....	....	....	....	....	....
Capital account: credit	2 994 Z.	2,758	....	....	....	....	....	....	
Capital account: debit	3 994 ..	−2,042	....	....	....	....	....	....	
Total, Groups A Plus B	4 981 ..	*−3,885*	*1,410*	*7,059*	*8,773*	*780*	*−7,835*	*−9,415*	....
C. Financial Account[1]	4 995 W.	**9,623**	**7,995**	**11,984**	**16,421**	**22,229**	**21,622**	**37,776**	....
Direct investment abroad	4 505 ..	−510	−1,398	−1,678	−1,879	−2,179	−2,495	−9,670	....
Direct investment in India	4 555 Z.	3,584	5,472	5,626	4,323	5,771	6,677	17,453	....
Portfolio investment assets	4 602 ..	....	....	....	....	....	....	....	....
Equity securities	4 610 ..	....	....	....	....	....	....	....	....
Debt securities	4 619 ..	....	....	....	....	....	....	....	....
Portfolio investment liabilities	4 652 Z.	2,345	2,853	1,022	8,216	9,037	12,144	9,549	....
Equity securities	4 660 ..	2,345	2,853	1,022	8,216	9,037	12,144	9,549	....
Debt securities	4 669 Z.	....	....	....	....	....	....	....	....
Financial derivatives	4 910 ..	....	....	....	....	....	....	....	....
Financial derivatives assets	4 900 ..	....	....	....	....	....	....	....	....
Financial derivatives liabilities	4 905 ..	....	....	....	....	....	....	....	....
Other investment assets	4 703 ..	1,712	−381	4,850	4,018	2,899	−5,580	−44	....
Monetary authorities	4 701 ..	9,069	....	....	....	....	....	....	....
General government	4 704 ..	−104	−80	−38	−79	−88	−89	−36	....
Banks	4 705 ..	−369	−1,047	4,777	1,696	−14	−1,100	−4,489	....
Other sectors	4 728 ..	−6,884	746	111	2,402	3,001	−4,391	4,481	....
Other investment liabilities	4 753 W.	2,492	1,449	2,164	1,742	6,701	10,876	20,488	....
Monetary authorities	4 753 WA	−127	211	320	−427	−45	598	453	....
General government	4 753 ZB	1,467	181	−50	−4,754	−578	1,882	1,433	....
Banks	4 753 ZC	562	3,494	3,381	7,589	1,860	4,562	3,431	....
Other sectors	4 753 ZD	590	−2,436	−1,487	−666	5,464	3,834	15,171	....
Total, Groups A Through C	4 983 ..	*5,738*	*9,405*	*19,044*	*25,193*	*23,009*	*13,786*	*28,360*	....
D. Net Errors and Omissions	4 998 ..	**331**	**−715**	**−190**	**471**	**637**	**769**	**−4,623**	....
Total, Groups A Through D	4 984 ..	*6,069*	*8,690*	*18,854*	*25,665*	*23,646*	*14,555*	*23,737*	
E. Reserves and Related Items	4 802 A.	**−6,069**	**−8,690**	**−18,854**	**−25,665**	**−23,646**	**−14,555**	**−23,737**	....
Reserve assets	4 802 ..	−6,017	−8,690	−18,854	−25,665	−23,646	−14,555	−23,737	....
Use of Fund credit and loans	4 766 ..	−52	....	....	....	....	....	....	....
Exceptional financing	4 920 ..	....	....	....	....	....	....	....	....
Conversion rates: Indian rupees per U.S. dollar	0 101 ..	**44.942**	**47.186**	**48.610**	**46.583**	**45.316**	**44.100**	**45.307**	**41.349**

[1] Excludes components that have been classified in the categories of Group E.

Table 2. STANDARD PRESENTATION, 2000–2007

(Millions of U.S. dollars)

	Code	2000	2001	2002	2003	2004	2005	2006	2007
CURRENT ACCOUNT	4 993	−4,601	1,410	7,059	8,773	780	−7,835	−9,415	....
A. GOODS	4 100	−10,640	−6,419	−3,561	−7,188	−17,600	−32,526	−43,078	....
Credit	2 100	43,247	44,793	51,141	60,893	77,939	102,176	123,617	....
General merchandise: exports f.o.b.	2 110	43,247	44,793	51,141	60,893	77,939	102,176	123,617	....
Goods for processing: exports f.o.b.	2 150	....	....	....	....	....	....	....	....
Repairs on goods	2 160	....	....	....	....	....	....	....	....
Goods procured in ports by carriers	2 170	....	....	....	....	....	....	....	....
Nonmonetary gold	2 180	....	....	....	....	....	....	....	....
Debit	3 100	−53,887	−51,212	−54,702	−68,081	−95,539	−134,702	−166,695	....
General merchandise: imports f.o.b.	3 110	−53,887	−51,212	−54,702	−68,081	−95,539	−134,702	−166,695	....
Goods for processing: imports f.o.b.	3 150	....	....	....	....	....	....	....	....
Repairs on goods	3 160	....	....	....	....	....	....	....	....
Goods procured in ports by carriers	3 170	....	....	....	....	....	....	....	....
Nonmonetary gold	3 180	....	....	....	....	....	....	....	....
B. SERVICES	4 200	−2,503	−2,762	−1,561	−976	2,640	7,842	11,817	....
Total credit	2 200	*16,684*	*17,337*	*19,478*	*23,902*	*38,281*	*55,831*	*75,354*	....
Total debit	3 200	*−19,187*	*−20,099*	*−21,039*	*−24,878*	*−35,641*	*−47,989*	*−63,537*	....
Transportation services, credit	2 205	1,979	2,050	2,473	3,022	4,373	5,720	7,629	....
Passenger	2 850	*258*	*144*	*198*	*97*	*137*	*159*	*293*	....
Freight	2 851	*1,534*	*1,435*	*1,716*	*2,284*	*3,317*	*4,245*	*5,251*	....
Other	2 852	*187*	*471*	*559*	*640*	*918*	*1,316*	*2,085*	....
Sea transport, passenger	2 207	238	....	....	....	....	....	....	....
Sea transport, freight	2 208	1,534	1,435	1,716	2,284	3,317	4,245	5,251	....
Sea transport, other	2 209	187	232	285	410	725	949	1,435	....
Air transport, passenger	2 211	20	144	198	97	137	159	293	....
Air transport, freight	2 212	....	....	....	....	....	....	....	....
Air transport, other	2 213	....	25	14	18	123	97	121	....
Other transport, passenger	2 215	....	....	....	....	....	....	....	....
Other transport, freight	2 216	....	....	....	....	....	....	....	....
Other transport, other	2 217	....	214	261	212	70	270	529	....
Transportation services, debit	3 205	−8,704	−8,497	−8,523	−9,312	−13,233	−20,140	−25,198	....
Passenger	3 850	*−1,588*	*−1,361*	*−1,362*	*−800*	*−967*	*−1,785*	*−1,944*	....
Freight	3 851	*−6,286*	*−5,879*	*−5,905*	*−7,492*	*−10,728*	*−15,294*	*−18,223*	....
Other	3 852	*−830*	*−1,257*	*−1,256*	*−1,020*	*−1,538*	*−3,060*	*−5,031*	....
Sea transport, passenger	3 207	−1,456	....	....	....	....	....	....	....
Sea transport, freight	3 208	−6,286	−5,879	−5,905	−7,492	−8,674	−14,182	−16,441	....
Sea transport, other	3 209	−830	−948	−945	−741	−1,153	−2,208	−2,793	....
Air transport, passenger	3 211	−132	−1,361	−1,362	−800	−967	−1,785	−1,944	....
Air transport, freight	3 212	....	....	....	....	−2,054	−1,113	−1,782	....
Air transport, other	3 213	....	−199	−197	−187	−227	−385	−485	....
Other transport, passenger	3 215	....	....	....	....	....	....	....	....
Other transport, freight	3 216	....	....	....	....	....	....	....	....
Other transport, other	3 217	....	−110	−114	−93	−158	−467	−1,754	....
Travel, credit	2 236	3,460	3,198	3,102	4,463	6,170	7,493	8,934	....
Business travel	2 237	3,460	....	....	....	....	....	....	....
Personal travel	2 240	....	3,198	3,102	4,463	6,170	7,493	8,934	....
Travel, debit	3 236	−2,690	−3,006	−2,988	−3,585	−4,816	−6,013	−7,352	....
Business travel	3 237	....	−1,462	−1,840	−2,402	−3,068	−2,694	−1,673	....
Personal travel	3 240	....	−1,544	−1,148	−1,183	−1,747	−3,319	−5,679	....
Other services, credit	2 200 BA	11,245	12,089	13,903	16,417	27,738	42,618	58,791	....
Communications	2 245	599	1,104	779	969	1,094	1,973	2,191	....
Construction	2 249	502	65	231	276	516	1,009	403	....
Insurance	2 253	257	282	332	408	842	929	1,116	....
Financial	2 260	276	306	598	367	341	1,469	2,071	....
Computer and information	2 262	4,727	7,407	8,889	11,876	16,344	22,005	29,186	....
Royalties and licence fees	2 266	83	37	20	24	53	131	112	....
Other business services	2 268	4,148	2,349	2,699	2,229	8,153	14,634	23,198	....
Personal, cultural, and recreational	2 287	....	....	....	....	46	146	218	....
Government, n.i.e.	2 291	654	538	353	269	350	323	297	....
Other services, debit	3 200 BA	−7,793	−8,596	−9,528	−11,981	−17,592	−21,836	−30,987	....
Communications	3 245	−105	−267	−1,003	−611	−579	−667	−899	....
Construction	3 249	−127	−470	−601	−1,209	−829	−665	−906	....
Insurance	3 253	−813	−811	−892	−1,164	−1,748	−2,237	−2,664	....
Financial	3 260	−1,277	−1,780	−1,434	−488	−791	−1,144	−1,316	....
Computer and information	3 262	−577	−911	−905	−686	−932	−1,566	−2,199	....
Royalties and licence fees	3 266	−282	−317	−345	−550	−611	−767	−949	....
Other business services	3 268	−4,321	−3,733	−4,084	−7,075	−11,693	−14,231	−21,453	....
Personal, cultural, and recreational	3 287	....	....	....	....	−61	−115	−118	....
Government, n.i.e.	3 291	−290	−307	−263	−199	−348	−444	−484	....

Table 2 (Continued). STANDARD PRESENTATION, 2000–2007

(Millions of U.S. dollars)

	Code	2000	2001	2002	2003	2004	2005	2006	2007
C. INCOME	4 300 ..	**−4,893**	**−4,142**	**−3,909**	**−4,895**	**−4,052**	**−6,393**	**−4,264**	....
Total credit	2 300 ..	*2,521*	*3,524*	*3,188*	*3,491*	*4,690*	*5,082*	*7,795*	....
Total debit	3 300 ..	*−7,414*	*−7,666*	*−7,097*	*−8,386*	*−8,742*	*−11,475*	*−12,059*	....
Compensation of employees, credit	2 310 ..	**145**	**129**	**107**	**115**	**353**	**263**	**317**	....
Compensation of employees, debit	3 310 ..	**−384**	**−462**	**−549**	**−778**	**−1,200**	**−980**	**−867**	....
Investment income, credit	2 320 ..	**2,376**	**3,395**	**3,081**	**3,376**	**4,337**	**4,819**	**7,478**	....
Direct investment income	2 330 ..	....	670	1,015	704	378	500	1,039	....
Dividends and distributed branch profits	2 332 ..	....	60	12	14	54	165	396	....
Reinvested earnings and undistributed branch profits	2 333 ..	....	610	1,003	690	324	335	643	....
Income on debt (interest)	2 334 ..	....	....	....	....	....	....	....	....
Portfolio investment income	2 339 ..	....	27	9	29	129	139	45	....
Income on equity	2 340 ..	....	....	....	....	....	....	....	....
Income on bonds and notes	2 350 ..	....	27	9	29	129	139	45	....
Income on money market instruments	2 360 ..	....	....	....	....	....	....	....	....
Other investment income	2 370 ..	....	2,698	2,057	2,643	3,830	4,180	6,395	....
Investment income, debit	3 320 ..	**−7,030**	**−7,204**	**−6,549**	**−7,608**	**−7,542**	**−10,495**	**−11,192**	....
Direct investment income	3 330 ..	....	−2,143	−2,323	−2,413	−3,479	−4,431	−5,278	....
Dividends and distributed branch profits	3 332 ..	....	−572	−539	−860	−1,686	−2,698	−2,669	....
Reinvested earnings and undistributed branch profits	3 333 ..	....	−1,571	−1,785	−1,553	−1,793	−1,733	−2,609	....
Income on debt (interest)	3 334 ..	....	....	....	....	....	....	....	....
Portfolio investment income	3 339 ..	....	−40	−43	−31	−146	−216	−55	....
Income on equity	3 340 ..	....	....	....	....	....	....	....	....
Income on bonds and notes	3 350 ..	....	−40	−43	−31	−146	−216	−55	....
Income on money market instruments	3 360 ..	....	....	....	....	....	....	....	....
Other investment income	3 370 ..	....	−5,020	−4,182	−5,164	−3,917	−5,848	−5,859	....
D. CURRENT TRANSFERS	4 379 ..	**13,434**	**14,733**	**16,091**	**21,831**	**19,793**	**23,242**	**26,109**	....
Credit	2 379 ..	**13,548**	**15,140**	**16,788**	**22,401**	**20,615**	**24,120**	**27,449**	....
General government	2 380 ..	286	324	507	517	603	602	770	....
Other sectors	2 390 ..	13,262	14,816	16,282	21,884	20,012	23,518	26,679	....
Workers' remittances	2 391 ..	12,745	14,144	15,629	20,884	18,397	21,030	25,109	....
Other current transfers	2 392 ..	517	672	653	1,000	1,615	2,488	1,570	....
Debit	3 379 ..	**−114**	**−407**	**−698**	**−570**	**−822**	**−877**	**−1,340**	....
General government	3 380 ..	....	....	....	....	−266	−402	−473	....
Other sectors	3 390 ..	−113	−407	−698	−570	−556	−476	−867	....
Workers' remittances	3 391 ..	−102	−289	−638	−487	−453	−361	−713	....
Other current transfers	3 392 ..	−12	−118	−60	−82	−103	−115	−154	....
CAPITAL AND FINANCIAL ACCOUNT	4 996 ..	**4,270**	**−695**	**−6,869**	**−9,244**	**−1,417**	**7,067**	**14,039**	....
CAPITAL ACCOUNT	4 994 ..	**716**	....	....	....	....	....	....	....
Total credit	2 994 ..	*2,758*	....	....	....	....	....	....	....
Total debit	3 994 ..	*−2,042*	....	....	....	....	....	....	....
Capital transfers, credit	2 400 ..	**2,758**	....	....	....	....	....	....	....
General government	2 401 ..	....	....	....	....	....	....	....	....
Debt forgiveness	2 402 ..	....	....	....	....	....	....	....	....
Other capital transfers	2 410 ..	....	....	....	....	....	....	....	....
Other sectors	2 430 ..	2,758	....	....	....	....	....	....	....
Migrants' transfers	2 431 ..	....	....	....	....	....	....	....	....
Debt forgiveness	2 432 ..	....	....	....	....	....	....	....	....
Other capital transfers	2 440 ..	2,758	....	....	....	....	....	....	....
Capital transfers, debit	3 400 ..	**−2,042**	....	....	....	....	....	....	....
General government	3 401 ..	....	....	....	....	....	....	....	....
Debt forgiveness	3 402 ..	....	....	....	....	....	....	....	....
Other capital transfers	3 410 ..	....	....	....	....	....	....	....	....
Other sectors	3 430 ..	−2,042	....	....	....	....	....	....	....
Migrants' transfers	3 431 ..	....	....	....	....	....	....	....	....
Debt forgiveness	3 432 ..	....	....	....	....	....	....	....	....
Other capital transfers	3 440 ..	−2,042	....	....	....	....	....	....	....
Nonproduced nonfinancial assets, credit	2 480 ..	....	....	....	....	....	....	....	....
Nonproduced nonfinancial assets, debit	3 480 ..	....	....	....	....	....	....	....	....

2008, International Monetary Fund: *Balance of Payments Statistics Yearbook*

Table 2 (Continued). STANDARD PRESENTATION, 2000–2007

(Millions of U.S. dollars)

	Code	2000	2001	2002	2003	2004	2005	2006	2007
FINANCIAL ACCOUNT	4 995	**3,555**	**−695**	**−6,869**	**−9,244**	**−1,417**	**7,067**	**14,039**	....
A. DIRECT INVESTMENT	4 500	**3,075**	**4,074**	**3,948**	**2,444**	**3,592**	**4,182**	**7,783**	....
Direct investment abroad	4 505	**−510**	**−1,398**	**−1,678**	**−1,879**	**−2,179**	**−2,495**	**−9,670**	....
Equity capital	4 510	....	−660	−585	−968	−1,601	−1,531	−7,981	....
Claims on affiliated enterprises	4 515	....	−760	−683	−1,058	−1,691	−1,737	−8,458	....
Liabilities to affiliated enterprises	4 520	....	100	98	90	90	206	477	....
Reinvested earnings	4 525	....	−610	−1,003	−690	−324	−335	−643	....
Other capital	4 530	....	−128	−91	−221	−254	−629	−1,046	....
Claims on affiliated enterprises	4 535	....	−128	−91	−221	−254	−629	−1,046	....
Liabilities to affiliated enterprises	4 540	....	....	....	....	....	....	....	....
Direct investment in India	4 555	**3,584**	**5,472**	**5,626**	**4,323**	**5,771**	**6,677**	**17,453**	....
Equity capital	4 560	....	3,557	3,424	2,129	3,636	4,606	14,617	....
Claims on direct investors	4 565	....	−4	−14	−46	−26	−92	−25	....
Liabilities to direct investors	4 570	....	3,561	3,438	2,175	3,662	4,698	14,642	....
Reinvested earnings	4 575	....	1,571	1,785	1,553	1,793	1,733	2,609	....
Other capital	4 580	....	344	417	641	342	337	227	....
Claims on direct investors	4 585	....	....	....	....	....	....	....	....
Liabilities to direct investors	4 590	....	344	417	641	342	337	227	....
B. PORTFOLIO INVESTMENT	4 600	**2,345**	**2,853**	**1,022**	**8,216**	**9,037**	**12,144**	**9,549**	....
Assets	4 602	....	....	....	....	....	....	....	....
Equity securities	4 610	....	....	....	....	....	....	....	....
Monetary authorities	4 611	....	....	....	....	....	....	....	....
General government	4 612	....	....	....	....	....	....	....	....
Banks	4 613	....	....	....	....	....	....	....	....
Other sectors	4 614	....	....	....	....	....	....	....	....
Debt securities	4 619	....	....	....	....	....	....	....	....
Bonds and notes	4 620	....	....	....	....	....	....	....	....
Monetary authorities	4 621	....	....	....	....	....	....	....	....
General government	4 622	....	....	....	....	....	....	....	....
Banks	4 623	....	....	....	....	....	....	....	....
Other sectors	4 624	....	....	....	....	....	....	....	....
Money market instruments	4 630	....	....	....	....	....	....	....	....
Monetary authorities	4 631	....	....	....	....	....	....	....	....
General government	4 632	....	....	....	....	....	....	....	....
Banks	4 633	....	....	....	....	....	....	....	....
Other sectors	4 634	....	....	....	....	....	....	....	....
Liabilities	4 652	**2,345**	**2,853**	**1,022**	**8,216**	**9,037**	**12,144**	**9,549**	....
Equity securities	4 660	2,345	2,853	1,022	8,216	9,037	12,144	9,549	....
Banks	4 663	....	....	....	....	....	....	....	....
Other sectors	4 664	2,345	2,853	1,022	8,216	9,037	12,144	9,549	....
Debt securities	4 669	....	....	....	....	....	....	....	....
Bonds and notes	4 670	....	....	....	....	....	....	....	....
Monetary authorities	4 671	....	....	....	....	....	....	....	....
General government	4 672	....	....	....	....	....	....	....	....
Banks	4 673	....	....	....	....	....	....	....	....
Other sectors	4 674	....	....	....	....	....	....	....	....
Money market instruments	4 680	....	....	....	....	....	....	....	....
Monetary authorities	4 681	....	....	....	....	....	....	....	....
General government	4 682	....	....	....	....	....	....	....	....
Banks	4 683	....	....	....	....	....	....	....	....
Other sectors	4 684	....	....	....	....	....	....	....	....
C. FINANCIAL DERIVATIVES	4 910	....	....	....	....	....	....	....	....
Monetary authorities	4 911	....	....	....	....	....	....	....	....
General government	4 912	....	....	....	....	....	....	....	....
Banks	4 913	....	....	....	....	....	....	....	....
Other sectors	4 914	....	....	....	....	....	....	....	....
Assets	4 900	....	....	....	....	....	....	....	....
Monetary authorities	4 901	....	....	....	....	....	....	....	....
General government	4 902	....	....	....	....	....	....	....	....
Banks	4 903	....	....	....	....	....	....	....	....
Other sectors	4 904	....	....	....	....	....	....	....	....
Liabilities	4 905	....	....	....	....	....	....	....	....
Monetary authorities	4 906	....	....	....	....	....	....	....	....
General government	4 907	....	....	....	....	....	....	....	....
Banks	4 908	....	....	....	....	....	....	....	....
Other sectors	4 909	....	....	....	....	....	....	....	....

Table 2 (Concluded). STANDARD PRESENTATION, 2000–2007

(Millions of U.S. dollars)

	Code	2000	2001	2002	2003	2004	2005	2006	2007
D. OTHER INVESTMENT	4 700 ..	**4,152**	**1,068**	**7,014**	**5,761**	**9,600**	**5,296**	**20,444**	....
Assets	4 703 ..	**1,712**	**–381**	**4,850**	**4,018**	**2,899**	**–5,580**	**–44**	....
Trade credits	4 706 ..	....	....	....	....	....	....	....	
General government	4 707 ..	....	....	....	....	....	....	....	
of which: Short-term	4 709 ..	....	....	....	....	....	....	....	
Other sectors	4 710 ..	....	....	....	....	....	....	....	
of which: Short-term	4 712 ..	....	....	....	....	....	....	....	
Loans	4 714 ..	5,285	–77	–29	–76	–236	–320	–230	....
Monetary authorities	4 715 ..	9,111	....	....	....	....	....	....	
of which: Short-term	4 718 ..	*9,111*	....	....	....	....	....	....	
General government	4 719 ..	–107	–80	–38	–79	–88	–89	–36	
of which: Short-term	4 721 ..	*–1,929*	....	....	....	....	....	....	
Banks	4 722 ..	4,445	....	....	....	....	....	....	
of which: Short-term	4 724 ..	*–3,990*	....	....	....	....	....	....	
Other sectors	4 725 ..	–8,164	3	9	3	–148	–231	–194	
of which: Short-term	4 727 ..	*–8,164*	....	....	....	....	....	....	
Currency and deposits	4 730 ..	–4,773	–1,047	4,777	1,696	–14	–1,100	–4,489	
Monetary authorities	4 731 ..	38	....	....	....	....	....	....	
General government	4 732 ..	3	....	....	....	....	....	....	
Banks	4 733 ..	–4,814	–1,047	4,777	1,696	–14	–1,100	–4,489	
Other sectors	4 734 ..	....	....	....	....	....	....	....	
Other assets	4 736 ..	1,199	743	102	2,399	3,149	–4,160	4,675	
Monetary authorities	4 737 ..	–80	....	....	....	....	....	....	
of which: Short-term	4 739 ..	....	....	....	....	....	....	....	
General government	4 740 ..	....	....	....	....	....	....	....	
of which: Short-term	4 742 ..	....	....	....	....	....	....	....	
Banks	4 743 ..	....	....	....	....	....	....	....	
of which: Short-term	4 745 ..	....	....	....	....	....	....	....	
Other sectors	4 746 ..	1,279	743	102	2,399	3,149	–4,160	4,675	....
of which: Short-term	4 748 ..	....	*743*	*102*	*2,399*	*3,149*	*–4,160*	*4,675*	
Liabilities	4 753 ..	**2,440**	**1,449**	**2,164**	**1,742**	**6,701**	**10,876**	**20,488**	....
Trade credits	4 756 ..	1,646	–1,132	396	2,883	2,016	2,560	1,632	....
General government	4 757 ..	1,646	....	....	....	....	....	....	
of which: Short-term	4 759 ..	....	....	....	....	....	....	....	
Other sectors	4 760 ..	....	–1,132	396	2,883	2,016	2,560	1,632	
of which: Short-term	4 762 ..	....	*–1,132*	*396*	*2,883*	*2,016*	*2,560*	*1,632*	
Loans	4 764 ..	279	–522	–1,422	–5,059	6,136	6,257	13,464	....
Monetary authorities	4 765 ..	–52	....	....	....	....	....	....	
of which: Use of Fund credit and loans from the Fund..	4 766 ..	*–52*	....	....	....	....	....	....	
of which: Short-term	4 768 ..	....	....	....	....	....	....	....	
General government	4 769 ..	–179	181	–50	–4,754	–578	1,882	1,433	
of which: Short-term	4 771 ..	....	....	....	....	....	....	....	
Banks	4 772 ..	....	601	511	3,244	3,266	3,102	–1,508	
of which: Short-term	4 774 ..	....	....	....	....	....	....	....	
Other sectors	4 775 ..	509	–1,304	–1,883	–3,549	3,448	1,274	13,539	
of which: Short-term	4 777 ..	*129*	....	....	....	....	....	....	
Currency and deposits	4 780 ..	562	3,104	3,191	3,918	–1,451	2,058	5,392	
Monetary authorities	4 781 ..	....	211	320	–427	–45	598	453	
General government	4 782 ..	....	....	....	....	....	....	....	
Banks	4 783 ..	562	2,893	2,870	4,345	–1,406	1,460	4,939	
Other sectors	4 784 ..	....	....	....	....	....	....	....	
Other liabilities	4 786 ..	–47	....	....	....	....	....	....	
Monetary authorities	4 787 ..	–127	....	....	....	....	....	....	
of which: Short-term	4 789 ..	*–127*	....	....	....	....	....	....	
General government	4 790 ..	....	....	....	....	....	....	....	
of which: Short-term	4 792 ..	....	....	....	....	....	....	....	
Banks	4 793 ..	....	....	....	....	....	....	....	
of which: Short-term	4 795 ..	....	....	....	....	....	....	....	
Other sectors	4 796 ..	80	....	....	....	....	....	....	
of which: Short-term	4 798 ..	....	....	....	....	....	....	....	
E. RESERVE ASSETS	4 802 ..	**–6,017**	**–8,690**	**–18,854**	**–25,665**	**–23,646**	**–14,555**	**–23,737**	....
Monetary gold	4 812 ..	....	....	....	....	....	....	....	
Special drawing rights	4 811 ..	2	–4	–1	4	–2	....	4	....
Reserve position in the Fund	4 810 ..	....	....	....	–563	–46	405	388	....
Foreign exchange	4 803 ..	–6,019	–8,686	–18,853	–25,107	–23,598	–14,960	–24,129	....
Other claims	4 813 ..	....	....	....	....	....	....	....	....
NET ERRORS AND OMISSIONS	4 998 ..	**331**	**–715**	**–190**	**471**	**637**	**769**	**–4,623**	....

2008, International Monetary Fund: *Balance of Payments Statistics Yearbook*

Table 3. INTERNATIONAL INVESTMENT POSITION (End-March following year stocks), 2000–2007

(Millions of U.S. dollars)

	Code	2000	2001	2002	2003	2004	2005	2006	2007
ASSETS	8 995 C.	**62,348**	**74,555**	**94,556**	**129,520**	**167,482**	**181,093**	**230,663**	**331,426**
Direct investment abroad	8 505 ..	**2,609**	**4,058**	**5,767**	**7,392**	**10,072**	**12,832**	**25,520**	**38,824**
Equity capital and reinvested earnings	8 506 ..	2,536	3,861	5,471	6,859	9,121	11,176	22,791	34,701
Claims on affiliated enterprises	8 507 ..	2,536	3,861	5,471	6,859	9,121	11,176	22,791	34,701
Liabilities to affiliated enterprises	8 508 ..	....	....	....	....	....	....	....	....
Other capital	8 530 ..	73	197	296	532	951	1,657	2,730	4,123
Claims on affiliated enterprises	8 535 ..	73	197	296	532	951	1,657	2,730	4,123
Liabilities to affiliated enterprises	8 540 ..	....	....	....	....	....	....	....	....
Portfolio investment	8 602 ..	**504**	**662**	**774**	**359**	**471**	**962**	**1,115**	**725**
Equity securities	8 610 ..	269	343	370	169	244	491	656	567
Monetary authorities	8 611 ..	....	....	....	....	....	....	....	....
General government	8 612 ..	....	....	....	....	....	....	....	....
Banks	8 613 ..	80	98	90	143	212	438	334	361
Other sectors	8 614 ..	190	246	280	27	32	53	322	206
Debt securities	8 619 ..	234	318	404	190	227	471	459	158
Bonds and notes	8 620 ..	178	238	323	113	186	455	441	144
Monetary authorities	8 621 ..	....	....	....	....	....	....	....	....
General government	8 622 ..	....	....	....	....	....	....	....	....
Banks	8 623 ..	73	118	133	111	183	445	433	141
Other sectors	8 624 ..	105	121	190	2	2	10	8	4
Money market instruments	8 630 ..	57	80	81	77	41	16	18	14
Monetary authorities	8 631 ..	....	....	....	....	....	....	....	....
General government	8 632 ..	....	....	....	....	....	....	....	....
Banks	8 633 ..	57	80	81	77	41	16	18	14
Other sectors	8 634 ..	....	....	....	....	....	....	....	....
Financial derivatives	8 900 ..	....	....	....	....	....	....	....	....
Monetary authorities	8 901 ..	....	....	....	....	....	....	....	....
General government	8 902 ..	....	....	....	....	....	....	....	....
Banks	8 903 ..	....	....	....	....	....	....	....	....
Other sectors	8 904 ..	....	....	....	....	....	....	....	....
Other investment	8 703 ..	**16,417**	**14,424**	**12,753**	**14,224**	**14,909**	**17,053**	**26,833**	**16,596**
Trade credits	8 706 ..	920	762	1,086	544	1,111	−281	2,721	1,086
General government	8 707 ..	....	....	....	....	....	....	....	....
of which: Short-term	8 709 ..	....	....	....	....	....	....	....	....
Other sectors	8 710 ..	920	762	1,086	544	1,111	−281	2,721	1,086
of which: Short-term	8 712 ..	*920*	*762*	*1,086*	*544*	*1,111*	*−281*	*2,721*	*1,086*
Loans	8 714 ..	1,990	2,231	1,397	1,682	1,869	2,554	3,710	3,362
Monetary authorities	8 715 ..	....	....	....	....	....	....	....	....
of which: Short-term	8 718 ..	....	....	....	....	....	....	....	....
General government	8 719 ..	334	373	522	659	791	826	842	956
of which: Short-term	8 721 ..	....	....	....	....	....	....	....	....
Banks	8 722 ..	1,421	1,623	655	762	794	1,405	2,519	1,909
of which: Short-term	8 724 ..	....	....	....	....	....	....	....	....
Other sectors	8 725 ..	235	235	220	261	284	322	349	497
of which: Short-term	8 727 ..	....	....	....	....	....	....	....	....
Currency and deposits	8 730 ..	10,847	8,865	7,442	9,079	8,484	11,499	16,584	7,498
Monetary authorities	8 731 ..	....	....	....	....	....	....	....	....
General government	8 732 ..	10	6	4	5	4	3	2	1
Banks	8 733 ..	9,865	8,158	6,753	8,377	7,582	10,303	15,586	5,872
Other sectors	8 734 ..	973	701	685	696	899	1,193	996	1,625
Other assets	8 736 ..	2,660	2,567	2,828	2,919	3,446	3,281	3,818	4,650
Monetary authorities	8 737 ..	....	....	....	....	....	....	....	....
of which: Short-term	8 739 ..	....	....	....	....	....	....	....	....
General government	8 740 ..	685	696	688	683	729	701	715	726
of which: Short-term	8 742 ..	....	....	....	....	....	....	....	....
Banks	8 743 ..	1,333	1,144	1,359	1,429	1,680	1,785	2,171	2,870
of which: Short-term	8 745 ..	....	....	....	....	....	....	....	....
Other sectors	8 746 ..	641	727	782	808	1,037	795	932	1,054
of which: Short-term	8 748 ..	....	....	....	....	....	....	....	....
Reserve assets	8 802 ..	**42,818**	**55,412**	**75,263**	**107,544**	**142,030**	**150,246**	**177,195**	**275,281**
Monetary gold	8 812 ..	2,719	3,086	3,495	3,994	4,517	5,697	6,515	8,327
Special drawing rights	8 811 ..	2	5	7	3	5	4	1	3
Reserve position in the Fund	8 810 ..	637	614	665	1,318	1,424	902	550	432
Foreign exchange	8 803 ..	39,461	51,706	71,096	102,229	136,084	143,643	170,130	266,519
Other claims	8 813 ..	....	....	....	....	....	....	....	....

Table 3 (Concluded). INTERNATIONAL INVESTMENT POSITION (End-March following year stocks), 2000–2007

(Millions of U.S. dollars)

	Code	2000	2001	2002	2003	2004	2005	2006	2007
LIABILITIES..	8 995 D.	138,301	144,574	154,425	175,761	210,728	228,529	290,028	409,660
Direct investment in India....................	8 555 ..	20,278	25,746	30,906	36,374	44,669	50,614	70,189	103,089
Equity capital and reinvested earnings.............................	8 556 ..	18,935	24,057	28,772	34,012	41,392	47,349	66,657	98,860
Claims on direct investors.....................	8 557 ..	....	....	....	....	....	....	....	....
Liabilities to direct investors.................	8 558 ..	18,935	24,057	28,772	34,012	41,392	47,349	66,657	98,860
Other capital......................	8 580 ..	1,343	1,688	2,134	2,362	3,276	3,265	3,532	4,229
Claims on direct investors.....................	8 585 ..	....	....	....	....	....	....	....	....
Liabilities to direct investors.................	8 590 ..	1,343	1,688	2,134	2,362	3,276	3,265	3,532	4,229
Portfolio investment...........................	8 652 ..	31,222	31,945	32,039	41,614	55,907	63,970	74,183	124,578
Equity securities......................	8 660 ..	17,373	18,853	19,885	32,322	43,323	54,184	60,512	103,502
Banks............................	8 663 ..	....	....	....	....	....	....	....	....
Other sectors............................	8 664 ..	17,373	18,853	19,885	32,322	43,323	54,184	60,512	103,502
Debt securities............................	8 669 ..	13,849	13,092	12,154	9,291	12,583	9,786	13,670	21,076
Bonds and notes............................	8 670 ..	13,849	13,092	12,154	9,291	12,583	9,719	13,182	20,131
Monetary authorities............................	8 671 ..	....	....	....	....	....	....	....	....
General government............................	8 672 ..	188	171	184	177	159	109	109	81
Banks............................	8 673 ..	10,403	10,084	9,558	5,265	5,855	528	532	551
Other sectors............................	8 674 ..	3,258	2,837	2,412	3,850	6,569	9,082	12,541	19,499
Money market instruments............................	8 680 ..	....	....	....	....	....	67	488	945
Monetary authorities............................	8 681 ..	....	....	....	....	....	....	....	....
General government............................	8 682 ..	....	....	....	....	....	67	488	945
Banks............................	8 683 ..	....	....	....	....	....	....	....	....
Other sectors............................	8 684 ..	....	....	....	....	....	....	....	....
Financial derivatives...........................	8 905 ..	....	....	....	....	....	....	....	....
Monetary authorities............................	8 906 ..	....	....	....	....	....	....	....	....
General government............................	8 907 ..	....	....	....	....	....	....	....	....
Banks............................	8 908 ..	....	....	....	....	....	....	....	....
Other sectors............................	8 909 ..	....	....	....	....	....	....	....	....
Other investment..........................	8 753 ..	86,800	86,883	91,480	97,773	110,153	113,945	145,657	181,993
Trade credits............................	8 756 ..	4,866	3,883	4,828	6,013	9,595	10,401	27,007	39,149
General government............................	8 757 ..	13	1,001	1,081	1,101	1,141	1,051	1,061	1,125
of which: Short-term............................	8 759 ..	....	....	....	....	....	....	....	....
Other sectors............................	8 760 ..	4,853	2,883	3,747	4,912	8,454	9,350	25,945	38,023
of which: Short-term............................	8 762 ..	*2,665*	*1,800*	*2,677*	*3,932*	*7,554*	*8,607*	*25,228*	*37,360*
Loans............................	8 764 ..	63,844	63,525	60,450	60,170	65,589	67,164	76,152	97,141
Monetary authorities............................	8 765 ..	....	....	....	....	....	....	....	....
of which: Use of Fund credit and loans from the Fund....	8 766 ..	....	....	....	....	....	....	....	....
of which: Short-term............................	8 768 ..	....	....	....	....	....	....	....	....
General government............................	8 769 ..	43,216	43,424	42,343	41,673	44,811	43,816	46,139	49,793
of which: Short-term............................	8 771 ..	....	....	....	....	....	....	....	....
Banks............................	8 772 ..	2,043	2,087	2,001	2,004	1,710	1,482	1,521	1,606
of which: Short-term............................	8 774 ..	....	....	....	....	....	....	....	....
Other sectors............................	8 775 ..	18,585	18,015	16,106	16,493	19,068	21,866	28,492	45,741
of which: Short-term............................	8 777 ..	....	....	....	....	....	....	....	....
Currency and deposits............................	8 780 ..	17,765	18,747	25,289	30,657	33,772	35,791	41,203	44,129
Monetary authorities............................	8 781 ..	281	391	442	630	901	1,015	996	1,094
General government............................	8 782 ..	....	....	....	....	....	....	....	....
Banks............................	8 783 ..	17,484	18,355	24,847	30,027	32,871	34,775	40,207	43,034
Other sectors............................	8 784 ..	....	....	....	....	....	....	....	....
Other liabilities............................	8 786 ..	325	728	913	934	1,196	590	1,295	1,575
Monetary authorities............................	8 787 ..	....	....	....	....	....	....	....	....
of which: Short-term............................	8 789 ..	....	....	....	....	....	....	....	....
General government............................	8 790 ..	....	....	....	....	....	....	....	....
of which: Short-term............................	8 792 ..	....	....	....	....	....	....	....	....
Banks............................	8 793 ..	22	15	22	15	165	69	345	413
of which: Short-term............................	8 795 ..	*22*	*15*	*22*	*15*	*165*	*69*	*345*	*413*
Other sectors............................	8 796 ..	303	712	890	919	1,032	521	950	1,162
of which: Short-term............................	8 798 ..	*303*	*712*	*890*	*919*	*1,032*	*521*	*950*	*1,162*
NET INTERNATIONAL INVESTMENT POSITION........	8 995 ..	−75,953	−70,018	−59,869	−46,242	−43,246	−47,436	−59,366	−78,234
Conversion rates: Indian rupees per U.S. dollar									
(end of period).................................	0 102 ..	46.750	48.180	48.030	45.605	43.585	45.065	44.245	39.415

Table 1. ANALYTIC PRESENTATION, 2000–2007

(Millions of U.S. dollars)

	Code	2000	2001	2002	2003	2004	2005	2006	2007
A. Current Account[1]	4 993 Z.	**7,992**	**6,901**	**7,824**	**8,107**	**1,563**	**278**	**10,836**	**10,365**
Goods: exports f.o.b.	2 100 ..	65,407	57,365	59,165	64,109	70,767	86,995	103,528	118,014
Goods: imports f.o.b.	3 100 ..	−40,365	−34,668	−35,652	−39,546	−50,615	−69,462	−73,868	−85,296
Balance on Goods	4 100 ..	*25,042*	*22,696*	*23,513*	*24,563*	*20,152*	*17,534*	*29,660*	*32,718*
Services: credit	2 200 ..	5,214	5,500	6,663	5,293	12,045	12,926	11,518	12,478
Services: debit	3 200 ..	−15,637	−15,880	−17,045	−17,400	−20,856	−22,049	−21,406	−24,276
Balance on Goods and Services	4 991 ..	*14,619*	*12,316*	*13,131*	*12,456*	*11,341*	*8,411*	*19,772*	*20,921*
Income: credit	2 300 ..	2,458	2,004	1,318	1,054	1,995	2,338	2,577	3,469
Income: debit	3 300 ..	−10,901	−8,940	−8,365	−7,272	−12,912	−15,264	−16,377	−18,993
Balance on Goods, Services, and Income	4 992 ..	*6,176*	*5,381*	*6,083*	*6,238*	*424*	*−4,515*	*5,973*	*5,397*
Current transfers: credit	2 379 Z.	1,816	1,520	2,210	2,053	2,433	5,993	6,079	6,664
Current transfers: debit	3 379 ..	....	....	−470	−184	−1,294	−1,200	−1,216	−1,697
B. Capital Account[1]	4 994 Z.	**....**	**....**	**....**	**....**	**....**	**334**	**350**	**546**
Capital account: credit	2 994 Z.	....	....	....	....	....	334	350	546
Capital account: debit	3 994 ..	....	....	....	....	....	....	....	....
Total, Groups A Plus B	4 981 ..	*7,992*	*6,901*	*7,824*	*8,107*	*1,563*	*611*	*11,186*	*10,911*
C. Financial Account[1]	4 995 W.	**−7,896**	**−7,617**	**−1,103**	**−949**	**−667**	**−2,587**	**2,594**	**2,776**
Direct investment abroad	4 505 ..	....	....	....	....	−3,408	−3,065	−2,703	−4,790
Direct investment in Indonesia	4 555 Z.	−4,550	−2,977	145	−597	1,896	8,336	4,914	6,928
Portfolio investment assets	4 602 ..	....	....	....	....	353	−1,080	−1,933	−4,459
Equity securities	4 610 ..	....	....	....	....	−106	38	−89	−195
Debt securities	4 619 ..	....	....	....	....	459	−1,118	−1,844	−4,264
Portfolio investment liabilities	4 652 Z.	−1,911	−244	1,222	2,251	4,056	5,270	6,107	9,981
Equity securities	4 660 ..	−1,021	442	877	1,130	2,043	−165	1,898	3,559
Debt securities	4 669 Z.	−890	−686	345	1,121	2,014	5,435	4,210	6,422
Financial derivatives	4 91C ..	....	....	....	....	....	....	....	....
Financial derivatives assets	4 90C ..	....	....	....	....	....	....	....	....
Financial derivatives liabilities	4 905 ..	....	....	....	....	....	....	....	....
Other investment assets	4 703 ..	−150	−125	−500	−5	985	−8,646	−1,588	−4,596
Monetary authorities	4 701 ..	....	....	....	....	....	....	....	....
General government	4 704 ..	....	....	....	....	....	....	....	....
Banks	4 705 ..	....	....	....	....	1,701	−4,662	1,719	2,334
Other sectors	4 728 ..	−150	−125	−500	−5	1,347	−507	−1,002	−2,316
Other investment liabilities	4 753 W.	−1,285	−4,271	−1,970	−2,599	−4,549	−3,401	−2,204	−289
Monetary authorities	4 753 WA	....	....	....	....	−12	....	....	....
General government	4 753 ZB	2,094	635	457	−398	−5,201	−3,446	−2,496	−2,363
Banks	4 753 ZC	−1,420	−1,867	−1,217	−69	441	−1,299	413	71
Other sectors	4 753 ZD	−1,959	−3,039	−1,210	−2,132	222	1,343	−122	2,003
Total, Groups A Through C	4 983 ..	*96*	*−716*	*6,720*	*7,157*	*896*	*−1,975*	*13,780*	*13,687*
D. Net Errors and Omissions	4 998 ..	**3,829**	**701**	**−1,763**	**−3,510**	**−3,094**	**−136**	**1,178**	**−981**
Total, Groups A Through D	4 984 ..	*3,926*	*−15*	*4,958*	*3,647*	*−2,198*	*−2,111*	*14,958*	*12,706*
E. Reserves and Related Items	4 802 A.	**−3,926**	**15**	**−4,958**	**−3,647**	**2,198**	**2,111**	**−14,958**	**−12,706**
Reserve assets	4 802 ..	−5,051	1,371	−4,010	−4,236	686	657	−6,903	−12,706
Use of Fund credit and loans	4 766 ..	1,125	−1,356	−948	588	−1,007	−1,144	−8,055	....
Exceptional financing	4 920 ..	....	....	....	....	2,519	2,598	....	....
Conversion rates: rupiah per U.S. dollar	0 101 ..	**8,421.8**	**10,260.9**	**9,311.2**	**8,577.1**	**8,938.9**	**9,704.7**	**9,159.3**	**9,141.0**

[1] Excludes components that have been classified in the categories of Group E.

Table 2. STANDARD PRESENTATION, 2000–2007

(Millions of U.S. dollars)

	Code	2000	2001	2002	2003	2004	2005	2006	2007
CURRENT ACCOUNT..	4 993 ..	**7,992**	**6,901**	**7,824**	**8,107**	**1,563**	**278**	**10,836**	**10,365**
A. GOODS..	4 100 ..	**25,042**	**22,696**	**23,513**	**24,563**	**20,152**	**17,534**	**29,660**	**32,718**
Credit...	2 100 ..	**65,407**	**57,365**	**59,165**	**64,109**	**70,767**	**86,995**	**103,528**	**118,014**
General merchandise: exports f.o.b...............	2 110 ..	65,407	57,365	58,865	64,109	65,855	80,948	97,490	110,384
Goods for processing: exports f.o.b...............	2 150 ..	....	....	....	....	4,683	5,269	5,213	6,637
Repairs on goods.......................................	2 160 ..	....	....	....	....	....	44	64	74
Goods procured in ports by carriers...............	2 170 ..	....	....	....	....	....	498	223	217
Nonmonetary gold.....................................	2 180 ..	....	....	300	....	229	236	538	701
Debit..	3 100 ..	**–40,365**	**–34,668**	**–35,652**	**–39,546**	**–50,615**	**–69,462**	**–73,868**	**–85,296**
General merchandise: imports f.o.b...............	3 110 ..	–40,365	–34,668	–35,652	–39,546	–46,616	–63,523	–65,609	–76,395
Goods for processing: imports f.o.b...............	3 150 ..	....	....	....	....	–3,999	–5,242	–7,648	–8,234
Repairs on goods.......................................	3 160 ..	....	....	....	....	....	–148	–167	–286
Goods procured in ports by carriers...............	3 170 ..	....	....	....	....	....	–548	–444	–380
Nonmonetary gold.....................................	3 180 ..	....	....	....	....	....	....	....	....
B. SERVICES..	4 200 ..	**–10,423**	**–10,380**	**–10,382**	**–12,108**	**–8,811**	**–9,122**	**–9,888**	**–11,797**
Total credit..	2 200 ..	*5,214*	*5,500*	*6,663*	*5,293*	*12,045*	*12,926*	*11,518*	*12,478*
Total debit...	3 200 ..	*–15,637*	*–15,880*	*–17,045*	*–17,400*	*–20,856*	*–22,049*	*–21,406*	*–24,276*
Transportation services, credit..................	2 205 ..	....	....	**1,058**	**856**	**2,279**	**2,842**	**2,102**	**2,206**
Passenger..	2 850 ..	....	....	*512*	*424*	*428*	*572*	*442*	*485*
Freight...	2 851 ..	....	....	....	....	*1,288*	*1,733*	*1,331*	*1,365*
Other...	2 852 ..	....	....	*546*	*431*	*563*	*538*	*329*	*356*
Sea transport, passenger............................	2 207 ..	....	....	....	....	....	....	....	....
Sea transport, freight................................	2 208 ..	....	....	....	....	....	....	....	....
Sea transport, other..................................	2 209 ..	....	....	....	....	....	....	....	....
Air transport, passenger............................	2 211 ..	....	....	....	....	....	....	....	....
Air transport, freight................................	2 212 ..	....	....	....	....	....	....	....	....
Air transport, other..................................	2 213 ..	....	....	....	....	....	....	....	....
Other transport, passenger.........................	2 215 ..	....	....	....	....	....	....	....	....
Other transport, freight.............................	2 216 ..	....	....	....	....	....	....	....	....
Other transport, other...............................	2 217 ..	....	....	....	....	....	....	....	....
Transportation services, debit...................	3 205 ..	**–4,016**	**–3,877**	**–5,150**	**–4,824**	**–5,474**	**–7,451**	**–8,179**	**–9,501**
Passenger..	3 850 ..	....	....	*–1,753*	*–1,345*	*–1,062*	*–1,156*	*–1,428*	*–1,674*
Freight...	3 851 ..	*–2,907*	*–2,577*	*–2,657*	*–2,697*	*–4,213*	*–6,063*	*–6,478*	*–7,483*
Other...	3 852 ..	*–1,110*	*–1,300*	*–740*	*–781*	*–199*	*–231*	*–273*	*–344*
Sea transport, passenger............................	3 207 ..	....	....	....	....	....	....	....	....
Sea transport, freight................................	3 208 ..	....	....	....	....	....	....	....	....
Sea transport, other..................................	3 209 ..	....	....	....	....	....	....	....	....
Air transport, passenger............................	3 211 ..	....	....	....	....	....	....	....	....
Air transport, freight................................	3 212 ..	....	....	....	....	....	....	....	....
Air transport, other..................................	3 213 ..	....	....	....	....	....	....	....	....
Other transport, passenger.........................	3 215 ..	....	....	....	....	....	....	....	....
Other transport, freight.............................	3 216 ..	....	....	....	....	....	....	....	....
Other transport, other...............................	3 217 ..	....	....	....	....	....	....	....	....
Travel, credit.......................................	2 236 ..	**4,975**	**5,276**	**5,285**	**4,037**	**4,798**	**4,522**	**4,448**	**5,346**
Business travel..	2 237 ..	1,293	1,372	1,374	1,211	1,439	1,357	1,334	1,604
Personal travel..	2 240 ..	3,681	3,905	3,911	2,826	3,358	3,165	3,114	3,742
Travel, debit..	3 236 ..	**–3,197**	**–3,406**	**–3,289**	**–3,082**	**–3,507**	**–3,584**	**–4,030**	**–4,904**
Business travel..	3 237 ..	....	....	–1,283	–1,053	–1,069	–1,076	–1,247	–1,536
Personal travel..	3 240 ..	–3,197	–3,406	–2,006	–2,029	–2,438	–2,509	–2,783	–3,368
Other services, credit.............................	2 200 BA	**239**	**224**	**320**	**400**	**4,969**	**5,563**	**4,968**	**4,926**
Communications.......................................	2 245 ..	86	85	174	248	835	998	1,102	1,343
Construction...	2 249 ..	....	....	....	....	463	484	456	459
Insurance...	2 253 ..	....	....	2	3	8	15	32	19
Financial..	2 260 ..	....	....	....	....	297	367	181	280
Computer and information..........................	2 262 ..	....	....	....	....	138	147	118	141
Royalties and licence fees..........................	2 266 ..	....	....	....	....	221	263	14	31
Other business services.............................	2 268 ..	....	....	....	....	2,669	2,876	2,564	2,185
Personal, cultural, and recreational...............	2 287 ..	....	....	....	....	47	57	74	55
Government, n.i.e.....................................	2 291 ..	153	139	144	150	291	355	427	414
Other services, debit..............................	3 200 BA	**–8,424**	**–8,597**	**–8,606**	**–9,494**	**–11,876**	**–11,014**	**–9,196**	**–9,870**
Communications.......................................	3 245 ..	–49	–51	–171	–131	–359	–495	–571	–641
Construction...	3 249 ..	....	....	....	....	–708	–726	–984	–720
Insurance...	3 253 ..	–323	–286	–313	–300	–353	–338	–384	–664
Financial..	3 260 ..	....	....	....	....	–594	–539	–363	–373
Computer and information..........................	3 262 ..	....	....	....	....	–468	–561	–596	–679
Royalties and licence fees..........................	3 266 ..	....	....	....	....	–990	–961	–870	–1,052
Other business services.............................	3 268 ..	–7,796	–7,976	–7,846	–8,834	–7,984	–7,017	–5,086	–5,380
Personal, cultural, and recreational...............	3 287 ..	....	....	....	....	–184	–166	–124	–107
Government, n.i.e.....................................	3 291 ..	–256	–285	–275	–230	–236	–212	–219	–254

Table 2 (Continued). STANDARD PRESENTATION, 2000–2007

(Millions of U.S. dollars)

	Code	2000	2001	2002	2003	2004	2005	2006	2007
C. INCOME	4 300	**−8,443**	**−6,936**	**−7,048**	**−6,217**	**−10,917**	**−12,927**	**−13,800**	**−15,524**
Total credit	2 300	*2,458*	*2,004*	*1,318*	*1,054*	*1,995*	*2,338*	*2,577*	*3,469*
Total debit	3 300	*−10,901*	*−8,940*	*−8,365*	*−7,272*	*−12,912*	*−15,264*	*−16,377*	*−18,993*
Compensation of employees, credit	2 310	....	....	....	....	166	123	162	171
Compensation of employees, debit	3 310	....	....	....	....	−138	−344	−299	−483
Investment income, credit	2 320	**2,458**	**2,004**	**1,318**	**1,054**	**1,829**	**2,214**	**2,415**	**3,299**
Direct investment income	2 330	....	....	....	....	103	209	116	298
Dividends and distributed branch profits	2 332	....	....	....	....	....	....	....	....
Reinvested earnings and undistributed branch profits	2 333	....	....	....	....	....	....	....	....
Income on debt (interest)	2 334	....	....	....	....	3	6	9	60
Portfolio investment income	2 339	....	....	817	671	1,085	1,258	1,382	1,827
Income on equity	2 340	....	....	....	....	210	272	160	312
Income on bonds and notes	2 350	....	....	....	....	....	....	....	....
Income on money market instruments	2 360	....	....	....	....	....	....	....	....
Other investment income	2 370	2,458	2,004	500	384	641	747	917	1,173
Investment income, debit	3 320	**−10,901**	**−8,940**	**−8,365**	**−7,272**	**−12,774**	**−14,920**	**−16,078**	**−18,509**
Direct investment income	3 330	−3,574	−3,158	−3,215	−2,754	−8,323	−9,525	−9,637	−10,813
Dividends and distributed branch profits	3 332	−1,475	−1,676	−1,970	−1,445	−7,237	....	....	....
Reinvested earnings and undistributed branch profits	3 333	....	....	....	....	....	....	....	....
Income on debt (interest)	3 334	−2,099	−1,482	−1,245	−1,309	−1,087	−146	−129	−215
Portfolio investment income	3 339	....	....	−47	−9	−23	−1,715	−2,898	−3,778
Income on equity	3 340	....	....	....	....	....	−1,495	−1,244	−1,773
Income on bonds and notes	3 350	....	....	....	....	....	....	....	....
Income on money market instruments	3 360	....	....	....	....	....	....	....	....
Other investment income	3 370	−7,327	−5,782	−5,103	−4,508	−4,428	−3,680	−3,542	−3,919
D. CURRENT TRANSFERS	4 379	**1,816**	**1,520**	**1,740**	**1,869**	**1,139**	**4,793**	**4,863**	**4,968**
Credit	2 379	**1,816**	**1,520**	**2,210**	**2,053**	**2,433**	**5,993**	**6,079**	**6,664**
General government	2 380	626	474	573	139	296	44	22	44
Other sectors	2 390	1,190	1,046	1,637	1,914	2,136	5,949	6,057	6,621
Workers' remittances	2 391	1,190	1,046	1,259	1,489	1,700	5,296	5,560	6,004
Other current transfers	2 392	....	....	379	425	436	653	497	617
Debit	3 379	....	....	**−470**	**−184**	**−1,294**	**−1,200**	**−1,216**	**−1,697**
General government	3 380	....	....	....	....	....	....	....	....
Other sectors	3 390	....	....	−470	−184	−1,294	−1,200	−1,216	−1,697
Workers' remittances	3 391	....	....	....	....	−775	−834	−1,060	−1,171
Other current transfers	3 392	....	....	−470	−184	−519	−365	−156	−525
CAPITAL AND FINANCIAL ACCOUNT	4 996	**−11,821**	**−7,602**	**−6,061**	**−4,597**	**1,531**	**−141**	**−12,013**	**−9,384**
CAPITAL ACCOUNT	4 994	....	....	....	....	....	**334**	**350**	**546**
Total credit	2 994	....	....	....	....	....	*334*	*350*	*546*
Total debit	3 994	....	....	....	....	....	....	....	....
Capital transfers, credit	2 400	....	....	....	....	....	**334**	**350**	**546**
General government	2 401	....	....	....	....	....	27	89	81
Debt forgiveness	2 402	....	....	....	....	....	....	....	....
Other capital transfers	2 410	....	....	....	....	....	27	89	81
Other sectors	2 430	....	....	....	....	....	307	261	465
Migrants' transfers	2 431	....	....	....	....	....	....	....	....
Debt forgiveness	2 432	....	....	....	....	....	....	....	....
Other capital transfers	2 440	....	....	....	....	....	307	261	465
Capital transfers, debit	3 400	....	....	....	....	....	....	....	....
General government	3 401	....	....	....	....	....	....	....	....
Debt forgiveness	3 402	....	....	....	....	....	....	....	....
Other capital transfers	3 410	....	....	....	....	....	....	....	....
Other sectors	3 430	....	....	....	....	....	....	....	....
Migrants' transfers	3 431	....	....	....	....	....	....	....	....
Debt forgiveness	3 432	....	....	....	....	....	....	....	....
Other capital transfers	3 440	....	....	....	....	....	....	....	....
Nonproduced nonfinancial assets, credit	2 480	....	....	....	....	....	....	....	....
Nonproduced nonfinancial assets, debit	3 480	....	....	....	....	....	....	....	....

Table 2 (Continued). STANDARD PRESENTATION, 2000–2007

(Millions of U.S. dollars)

	Code	2000	2001	2002	2003	2004	2005	2006	2007
FINANCIAL ACCOUNT	4 995	−11,821	−7,602	−6,061	−4,597	1,531	−475	−12,364	−9,930
A. DIRECT INVESTMENT	4 500	−4,550	−2,977	145	−597	−1,512	5,271	2,211	2,139
Direct investment abroad	4 505	....	....	....	....	−3,408	−3,065	−2,703	−4,790
Equity capital	4 510	....	....	....	....	−470	−331	−723	−998
Claims on affiliated enterprises	4 515	....	....	....	....	....	....	....	....
Liabilities to affiliated enterprises	4 520	....	....	....	....	....	....	....	....
Reinvested earnings	4 525	....	....	....	....	....	....	....	....
Other capital	4 530	....	....	....	....	−2,938	−2,734	−1,980	−3,792
Claims on affiliated enterprises	4 535	....	....	....	....	....	....	....	....
Liabilities to affiliated enterprises	4 540	....	....	....	....	....	....	....	....
Direct investment in Indonesia	4 555	−4,550	−2,977	145	−597	1,896	8,336	4,914	6,928
Equity capital	4 560	892	988	2,560	1,483	2,138	7,812	4,616	7,549
Claims on direct investors	4 565	....	....	....	....	....	....	....	....
Liabilities to direct investors	4 570	892	988	2,560	1,483	2,138	7,812	4,616	7,549
Reinvested earnings	4 575	....	....	....	....	....	....	....	....
Other capital	4 580	−5,442	−3,966	−2,415	−2,080	−242	524	298	−621
Claims on direct investors	4 585	....	....	....	....	....	....	....	....
Liabilities to direct investors	4 590	−5,442	−3,966	−2,415	−2,080	−242	524	298	−621
B. PORTFOLIO INVESTMENT	4 600	−1,911	−244	1,222	2,251	4,409	4,190	4,174	5,523
Assets	4 602	....	....	....	....	353	−1,080	−1,933	−4,459
Equity securities	4 610	....	....	....	....	−106	38	−89	−195
Monetary authorities	4 611	....	....	....	....	....	....	....	....
General government	4 612	....	....	....	....	....	....	....	....
Banks	4 613	....	....	....	....	....	....	....	....
Other sectors	4 614	....	....	....	....	−106	38	−89	−195
Debt securities	4 619	....	....	....	....	459	−1,118	−1,844	−4,264
Bonds and notes	4 620	....	....	....	....	459	−1,118	−1,844	−4,264
Monetary authorities	4 621	....	....	....	....	....	....	....	....
General government	4 622	....	....	....	....	....	....	....	....
Banks	4 623	....	....	....	....	....	....	....	....
Other sectors	4 624	....	....	....	....	459	−1,118	−1,844	−4,264
Money market instruments	4 630	....	....	....	....	....	....	....	....
Monetary authorities	4 631	....	....	....	....	....	....	....	....
General government	4 632	....	....	....	....	....	....	....	....
Banks	4 633	....	....	....	....	....	....	....	....
Other sectors	4 634	....	....	....	....	....	....	....	....
Liabilities	4 652	−1,911	−244	1,222	2,251	4,056	5,270	6,107	9,981
Equity securities	4 660	−1,021	442	877	1,130	2,043	−165	1,898	3,559
Banks	4 663	....	....	....	....	....	....	....	....
Other sectors	4 664	−1,021	442	877	1,130	2,043	−165	1,898	3,559
Debt securities	4 669	−890	−686	345	1,121	2,014	5,435	4,210	6,422
Bonds and notes	4 670	−890	−686	345	1,121	1,241	4,758	3,834	5,190
Monetary authorities	4 671	....	....	345	1,121	....	....	....	....
General government	4 672	−890	−686	....	....	1,479	4,149	4,139	4,037
Banks	4 673	....	....	....	....	....	....	....	....
Other sectors	4 674	....	....	....	....	−238	609	−305	1,152
Money market instruments	4 680	....	....	....	....	773	677	375	1,233
Monetary authorities	4 681	....	....	....	....	773	677	375	1,233
General government	4 682	....	....	....	....	....	....	....	....
Banks	4 683	....	....	....	....	....	....	....	....
Other sectors	4 684	....	....	....	....	....	....	....	....
C. FINANCIAL DERIVATIVES	4 910	....	....	....	....	....	....	....	....
Monetary authorities	4 911	....	....	....	....	....	....	....	....
General government	4 912	....	....	....	....	....	....	....	....
Banks	4 913	....	....	....	....	....	....	....	....
Other sectors	4 914	....	....	....	....	....	....	....	....
Assets	4 900	....	....	....	....	....	....	....	....
Monetary authorities	4 901	....	....	....	....	....	....	....	....
General government	4 902	....	....	....	....	....	....	....	....
Banks	4 903	....	....	....	....	....	....	....	....
Other sectors	4 904	....	....	....	....	....	....	....	....
Liabilities	4 905	....	....	....	....	....	....	....	....
Monetary authorities	4 906	....	....	....	....	....	....	....	....
General government	4 907	....	....	....	....	....	....	....	....
Banks	4 908	....	....	....	....	....	....	....	....
Other sectors	4 909	....	....	....	....	....	....	....	....

2008, International Monetary Fund: *Balance of Payments Statistics Yearbook*

Table 2 (Concluded). STANDARD PRESENTATION, 2000–2007

(Millions of U.S. dollars)

	Code	2000	2001	2002	2003	2004	2005	2006	2007
D. OTHER INVESTMENT	4 700 ..	**−310**	**−5,751**	**−3,418**	**−2,016**	**−2,052**	**−10,593**	**−11,846**	**−4,885**
Assets	4 703 ..	**−150**	**−125**	**−500**	**−5**	**985**	**−8,646**	**−1,588**	**−4,596**
Trade credits	4 706 ..	....	....	....	....	−2,069	−3,664	−2,232	−4,853
General government	4 707 ..	....	....	....	....	....	....	....	....
of which: Short-term	4 709 ..	....	....	....	....	....	....	....	....
Other sectors	4 710 ..	....	....	....	....	....	....	....	....
of which: Short-term	4 712 ..	....	....	....	....	....	....	....	....
Loans	4 714 ..	....	....	....	....	6	187	−73	238
Monetary authorities	4 715 ..	....	....	....	....	....	....	....	....
of which: Short-term	4 718 ..	....	....	....	....	....	....	....	....
General government	4 719 ..	....	....	....	....	....	....	....	....
of which: Short-term	4 721 ..	....	....	....	....	....	....	....	....
Banks	4 722 ..	....	....	....	....	....	....	....	....
of which: Short-term	4 724 ..	....	....	....	....	....	....	....	....
Other sectors	4 725 ..	....	....	....	....	....	....	....	....
of which: Short-term	4 727 ..	....	....	....	....	....	....	....	....
Currency and deposits	4 730 ..	....	....	....	....	2,856	−5,512	690	278
Monetary authorities	4 731 ..	....	....	....	....	....	....	....	....
General government	4 732 ..	....	....	....	....	....	....	....	....
Banks	4 733 ..	....	....	....	....	1,701	−4,662	1,719	2,334
Other sectors	4 734 ..	....	....	....	....	1,155	−850	−1,029	−2,057
Other assets	4 736 ..	−150	−125	−500	−5	192	343	26	−259
Monetary authorities	4 737 ..	....	....	....	....	....	....	....	....
of which: Short-term	4 739 ..	....	....	....	....	....	....	....	....
General government	4 740 ..	....	....	....	....	....	....	....	....
of which: Short-term	4 742 ..	....	....	....	....	....	....	....	....
Banks	4 743 ..	....	....	....	....	....	....	....	....
of which: Short-term	4 745 ..	....	....	....	....	....	....	....	....
Other sectors	4 746 ..	−150	−125	−500	−5	192	343	26	−259
of which: Short-term	4 748 ..	....	....	....	....	....	....	....	....
Liabilities	4 753 ..	**−160**	**−5,626**	**−2,918**	**−2,011**	**−3,037**	**−1,948**	**−10,258**	**−289**
Trade credits	4 756 ..	....	....	....	....	−127	170	168	147
General government	4 757 ..	....	....	....	....	....	....	....	....
of which: Short-term	4 759 ..	....	....	....	....	....	....	....	....
Other sectors	4 760 ..	....	....	....	....	−127	170	168	147
of which: Short-term	4 762 ..	....	....	....	....	....	....	....	....
Loans	4 764 ..	−160	−5,626	−2,918	−2,011	−3,147	−2,267	−10,937	−1,161
Monetary authorities	4 765 ..	1,125	−1,356	−948	588	−1,019	−1,144	−8,055	....
of which: Use of Fund credit and loans from the Fund..	4 766 ..	*1,125*	*−1,356*	*−948*	*588*	*−1,007*	*−1,144*	*−8,055*	....
of which: Short-term	4 768 ..	....	....	....	....	....	....	....	....
General government	4 769 ..	2,094	635	457	−398	−2,682	−848	−2,496	−2,363
of which: Short-term	4 771 ..	....	....	....	....	....	....	....	....
Banks	4 772 ..	−1,420	−1,867	−1,217	−69	441	−1,299	413	71
of which: Short-term	4 774 ..	*−401*	*−555*	*−325*	*115*	....	....	....	....
Other sectors	4 775 ..	−1,959	−3,039	−1,210	−2,132	112	1,024	−800	1,131
of which: Short-term	4 777 ..	*−2,605*	*−2,317*	*−1,676*	*−717*	....	....	....	....
Currency and deposits	4 780 ..	....	....	....	....	237	149	511	725
Monetary authorities	4 781 ..	....	....	....	....	....	....	....	....
General government	4 782 ..	....	....	....	....	....	....	....	....
Banks	4 783 ..	....	....	....	....	....	....	....	....
Other sectors	4 784 ..	....	....	....	....	237	149	511	725
Other liabilities	4 786 ..	....	....	....	....	....	....	....	....
Monetary authorities	4 787 ..	....	....	....	....	....	....	....	....
of which: Short-term	4 789 ..	....	....	....	....	....	....	....	....
General government	4 790 ..	....	....	....	....	....	....	....	....
of which: Short-term	4 792 ..	....	....	....	....	....	....	....	....
Banks	4 793 ..	....	....	....	....	....	....	....	....
of which: Short-term	4 795 ..	....	....	....	....	....	....	....	....
Other sectors	4 796 ..	....	....	....	....	....	....	....	....
of which: Short-term	4 798 ..	....	....	....	....	....	....	....	....
E. RESERVE ASSETS	4 802 ..	**−5,051**	**1,371**	**−4,010**	**−4,236**	**686**	**657**	**−6,903**	**−12,706**
Monetary gold	4 812 ..	52	−7	−303	−213	−147	143	307	....
Special drawing rights	4 811 ..	−40	14	−1	16	3	−7	−8	10
Reserve position in the Fund	4 810 ..	....	....	....	....	....	....	....	....
Foreign exchange	4 803 ..	−5,063	1,363	−3,705	−3,988	830	621	−7,202	−12,715
Other claims	4 813 ..	....	....	....	−50	....	−99	....	....
NET ERRORS AND OMISSIONS	4 998 ..	**3,829**	**701**	**−1,763**	**−3,510**	**−3,094**	**−136**	**1,178**	**−981**

Table 3. INTERNATIONAL INVESTMENT POSITION (End-period stocks), 2000–2007

(Millions of U.S. dollars)

	Code	2000	2001	2002	2003	2004	2005	2006	2007
ASSETS	8 995 C.	....	**41,871**	**49,408**	**56,383**	**56,514**	**60,614**	**69,408**	....
Direct investment abroad	8 505 ..	....	**−1,413**	**−328**	**−208**	**−102**	**−1,762**	**−3,958**	....
Equity capital and reinvested earnings	8 506 ..	....	211	13	6	167	200	174	....
Claims on affiliated enterprises	8 507 ..	....	212	97	95	167	234	208	....
Liabilities to affiliated enterprises	8 508 ..	....	....	−85	−89	....	−34	−34	....
Other capital	8 530 ..	....	−1,625	−341	−214	−269	−1,961	−4,131	....
Claims on affiliated enterprises	8 535 ..	....	53	71	96	59	190	203	....
Liabilities to affiliated enterprises	8 540 ..	....	−1,678	−412	−310	−327	−2,151	−4,335	....
Portfolio investment	8 602 ..	....	**1,921**	**2,379**	**2,888**	**2,802**	**2,510**	**3,666**	....
Equity securities	8 610 ..	....	17	23	31	51	94	354	....
Monetary authorities	8 611 ..	....	....	....	....	....	....	....	....
General government	8 612 ..	....	11	11	....	....	....	....	....
Banks	8 613 ..	....	....	8	3	3	....	....	....
Other sectors	8 614 ..	....	6	4	28	48	93	354	....
Debt securities	8 619 ..	....	1,905	2,357	2,857	2,751	2,416	3,311	....
Bonds and notes	8 620 ..	....	967	1,461	1,814	1,358	1,049	1,676	....
Monetary authorities	8 621 ..	....	....	....	....	....	....	....	....
General government	8 622 ..	....	13	7	....	....	....	....	....
Banks	8 623 ..	....	686	1,186	1,168	854	937	1,256	....
Other sectors	8 624 ..	....	268	268	646	503	112	420	....
Money market instruments	8 630 ..	....	938	895	1,043	1,394	1,367	1,635	....
Monetary authorities	8 631 ..	....	....	....	....	....	....	....	....
General government	8 632 ..	....	....	....	....	....	....	....	....
Banks	8 633 ..	....	921	891	961	1,351	1,366	1,597	....
Other sectors	8 634 ..	....	17	5	82	43	1	39	....
Financial derivatives	8 900 ..	....	....	....	**33**	**40**	**27**	**19**	....
Monetary authorities	8 901 ..	....	....	....	....	....	....	....	....
General government	8 902 ..	....	....	....	....	....	....	....	....
Banks	8 903 ..	....	....	....	33	40	27	19	....
Other sectors	8 904 ..	....	....	....	....	....	....	....	....
Other investment	8 703 ..	....	**13,349**	**15,315**	**17,372**	**17,452**	**25,115**	**27,095**	....
Trade credits	8 706 ..	....	....	1,472	2,545	2,041	3,184	3,072	....
General government	8 707 ..	....	....	....	....	....	....	....	....
of which: Short-term	8 709 ..	....	....	....	....	....	....	....	....
Other sectors	8 710 ..	....	....	1,472	2,545	2,041	3,184	3,072	....
of which: Short-term	8 712 ..	....	....	*1,472*	*2,545*	*2,041*	*3,184*	*3,072*	....
Loans	8 714 ..	....	381	233	524	201	124	231	....
Monetary authorities	8 715 ..	....	....	....	....	....	....	....	....
of which: Short-term	8 718 ..	....	....	....	....	....	....	....	....
General government	8 719 ..	....	....	....	....	....	....	....	....
of which: Short-term	8 721 ..	....	....	....	....	....	....	....	....
Banks	8 722 ..	....	311	176	208	43	74	136	....
of which: Short-term	8 724 ..	....	*171*	*27*	*128*	*25*	*43*	*72*	....
Other sectors	8 725 ..	....	69	57	316	158	49	95	....
of which: Short-term	8 727 ..	....	*69*	....	*225*	*79*	....	....	....
Currency and deposits	8 730 ..	....	11,986	11,384	9,969	8,780	14,007	12,101	....
Monetary authorities	8 731 ..	....	509	335	251	229	156	115	....
General government	8 732 ..	....	....	41	41	670	665	641	....
Banks	8 733 ..	....	8,152	7,062	5,497	3,796	8,458	6,739	....
Other sectors	8 734 ..	....	3,324	3,946	4,180	4,086	4,728	4,606	....
Other assets	8 736 ..	....	982	2,226	4,335	6,430	7,800	11,690	....
Monetary authorities	8 737 ..	....	418	930	1,658	2,101	3,999	8,500	....
of which: Short-term	8 739 ..	....	*294*	*805*	*1,471*	*1,912*	*3,820*	*8,319*	....
General government	8 740 ..	....	....	3	1	180	180	....	....
of which: Short-term	8 742 ..	....	....	*3*	*1*	*180*	*180*	....	....
Banks	8 743 ..	....	563	1,161	1,320	1,247	1,243	707	....
of which: Short-term	8 745 ..	....	*563*	*1,159*	*1,317*	*1,245*	*1,240*	*695*	....
Other sectors	8 746 ..	....	1	132	1,357	2,903	2,379	2,483	....
of which: Short-term	8 748 ..	....	*1*	*132*	*1,357*	*2,903*	*2,379*	*2,483*	....
Reserve assets	8 802 ..	....	**28,014**	**32,042**	**36,297**	**36,321**	**34,724**	**42,587**	....
Monetary gold	8 812 ..	....	768	1,071	1,284	1,316	1,583	1,483	....
Special drawing rights	8 811 ..	32	16	19	4	2	7	18	9
Reserve position in the Fund	8 810 ..	190	183	198	216	226	208	219	230
Foreign exchange	8 803 ..	....	27,048	30,754	34,742	34,724	32,774	40,697	....
Other claims	8 813 ..	....	....	....	50	52	151	169	....

Table 3 (Concluded). INTERNATIONAL INVESTMENT POSITION (End-period stocks), 2000–2007

(Millions of U.S. dollars)

	Code	2000	2001	2002	2003	2004	2005	2006	2007
LIABILITIES..	8 995 D.	. . . .	**155,863**	**148,029**	**162,345**	**173,272**	**185,101**	**209,404**	. . . .
Direct investment in Indonesia...........................	8 555 ..	. . . .	**15,203**	**7,103**	**10,328**	**15,858**	**41,187**	**44,522**	. . . .
Equity capital and reinvested earnings................	8 556 ..	. . . .	7,487	3,133	6,531	9,747	37,654	41,454	. . . .
Claims on direct investors.............................	8 557 ..	. . . .	. . . .	−20	−16	−48	−75	−88	. . . .
Liabilities to direct investors.........................	8 558 ..	. . . .	7,487	3,153	6,547	9,795	37,728	41,543	. . . .
Other capital..	8 580 ..	. . . .	7,716	3,971	3,797	6,111	3,533	3,068	. . . .
Claims on direct investors.............................	8 585 ..	. . . .	−85	−355	−353	−562	−1,416	−1,608	. . . .
Liabilities to direct investors.........................	8 590 ..	. . . .	7,801	4,325	4,150	6,672	4,949	4,676	. . . .
Portfolio investment...................................	8 652 ..	. . . .	**13,315**	**14,332**	**23,297**	**25,732**	**34,592**	**56,571**	. . . .
Equity securities...	8 660 ..	. . . .	4,475	6,452	14,808	15,594	15,854	31,519	. . . .
Banks...	8 663 ..	. . . .	380	511	3,759	5,110	6,021	10,635	. . . .
Other sectors..	8 664 ..	. . . .	4,094	5,941	11,049	10,484	9,833	20,883	. . . .
Debt securities..	8 669 ..	. . . .	8,840	7,881	8,489	10,138	18,738	25,053	. . . .
Bonds and notes..	8 670 ..	. . . .	6,377	7,353	7,805	8,438	15,256	21,059	. . . .
Monetary authorities..................................	8 671 ..	. . . .	. . . .	. . . .	. . . .	. . . .	. . . .	. . . .	. . . .
General government...................................	8 672 ..	. . . .	404	468	1,060	2,469	6,683	11,030	. . . .
Banks..	8 673 ..	. . . .	2,076	927	1,048	729	1,237	1,665	. . . .
Other sectors...	8 674 ..	. . . .	3,897	5,958	5,697	5,240	7,336	8,364	. . . .
Money market instruments...........................	8 680 ..	. . . .	2,462	527	684	1,699	3,482	3,993	. . . .
Monetary authorities..................................	8 681 ..	. . . .	42	95	97	843	1,503	2,002	. . . .
General government...................................	8 682 ..	. . . .	. . . .	. . . .	. . . .	. . . .	. . . .	. . . .	. . . .
Banks..	8 683 ..	. . . .	198	268	388	592	1,487	1,200	. . . .
Other sectors...	8 684 ..	. . . .	2,223	164	200	265	492	791	. . . .
Financial derivatives.................................	8 905 ..	. . . .	. . . .	. . . .	**32**	**40**	**43**	**21**	. . . .
Monetary authorities......................................	8 906 ..	. . . .	. . . .	. . . .	. . . .	. . . .	. . . .	. . . .	
General government.......................................	8 907 ..	. . . .	. . . .	. . . .	. . . .	. . . .	. . . .	. . . .	
Banks...	8 908 ..	. . . .	. . . .	. . . .	32	40	43	21	
Other sectors..	8 909 ..	. . . .	. . . .	. . . .	. . . .	. . . .	. . . .	. . . .	
Other investment.....................................	8 753 ..	. . . .	**127,346**	**126,593**	**128,687**	**131,642**	**109,279**	**108,290**	. . . .
Trade credits..	8 756 ..	. . . .	. . . .	218	268	428	356	757	. . . .
General government......................................	8 757 ..	. . . .	. . . .	. . . .	. . . .	. . . .	. . . .	. . . .	
of which: Short-term..............................	8 759 ..	. . . .	. . . .	. . . .	. . . .	. . . .	. . . .	. . . .	
Other sectors...	8 760 ..	. . . .	. . . .	218	268	428	356	757	
of which. Short-term..............................	8 762 ..	. . . .	. . . .	*138*	*107*	*155*	*232*	*654*	
Loans...	8 764 ..	. . . .	122,326	121,382	125,156	125,388	104,268	102,798	. . . .
Monetary authorities..................................	8 765 ..	. . . .	10,951	10,707	12,130	11,529	9,092	756	
of which: Use of Fund credit and loans from the Fund....	8 766 ..	*10,838*	*9,113*	*8,861*	*10,276*	*9,686*	*7,807*	. . . .	
of which: Short-term..............................	8 768 ..	. . . .	. . . .	. . . .	. . . .	. . . .	. . . .	. . . .	
General government...................................	8 769 ..	. . . .	58,060	63,423	68,417	67,917	62,795	62,021	. . . .
of which: Short-term..............................	8 771 ..	. . . .	. . . .	. . . .	. . . .	. . . .	. . . .	. . . .	
Banks..	8 772 ..	. . . .	4,375	1,780	1,355	1,486	1,321	1,708	
of which: Short-term..............................	8 774 ..	. . . .	. . . .	*71*	*113*	*97*	*92*	*165*	
Other sectors...	8 775 ..	. . . .	48,940	45,473	43,254	44,457	31,060	38,313	. . . .
of which: Short-term..............................	8 777 ..	. . . .	*5,401*	*770*	*1,420*	*2,133*	*2,878*	*3,501*	
Currency and deposits...................................	8 780 ..	. . . .	4,150	2,219	1,338	1,574	1,725	2,235	
Monetary authorities..................................	8 781 ..	. . . .	1,360	6	3	2	4	3	
General government...................................	8 782 ..	. . . .	1,347	. . . .	. . . .	. . . .	. . . .	. . . .	
Banks..	8 783 ..	. . . .	1,443	2,213	1,335	1,572	1,721	2,232	
Other sectors...	8 784 ..	. . . .	. . . .	. . . .	. . . .	. . . .	. . . .	. . . .	
Other liabilities..	8 786 ..	. . . .	870	2,775	1,927	4,252	2,930	2,500	
Monetary authorities..................................	8 787 ..	. . . .	78	56	58	70	80	4	
of which: Short-term..............................	8 789 ..	. . . .	*3*	*56*	*58*	*70*	*80*	*4*	
General government...................................	8 790 ..	. . . .	3	7	3	11	11	. . . .	
of which: Short-term..............................	8 792 ..	. . . .	*3*	*7*	*3*	*11*	*11*	. . . .	
Banks..	8 793 ..	. . . .	783	2,388	1,069	2,106	2,020	1,655	
of which: Short-term..............................	8 795 ..	. . . .	*783*	*2,388*	*1,069*	*2,106*	*2,014*	*1,655*	
Other sectors...	8 796 ..	. . . .	6	324	796	2,065	820	842	
of which: Short-term..............................	8 798 ..	. . . .	. . . .	*324*	*796*	*2,065*	. . . .	. . . .	
NET INTERNATIONAL INVESTMENT POSITION........	8 995 ..	. . . .	**−113,993**	**−98,621**	**−105,962**	**−116,758**	**−124,487**	**−139,996**	. . . .
Conversion rates: rupiah per U.S. dollar (end of period)..	0 102 ..	9,595.0	10,400.0	8,940.0	8,465.0	9,290.0	9,830.0	9,020.0	9,419.0

Table 1. ANALYTIC PRESENTATION, 2000–2007

(Millions of U.S. dollars)

	Code	2000	2001	2002	2003	2004	2005	2006	2007
A. Current Account[1]	4 993 Z.	. . . .	. . . .	. . . .	. . . .	. . . .	−7,513	1,252	. . . .
Goods: exports f.o.b.	2 100 ..	. . . .	. . . .	. . . .	. . . .	. . . .	23,697	30,529	. . . .
Goods: imports f.o.b.	3 100 ..	. . . .	. . . .	. . . .	. . . .	. . . .	−20,002	−18,708	. . . .
Balance on Goods	4 100 ..	. . . .	. . . .	. . . .	. . . .	. . . .	*3,695*	*11,822*	. . . .
Services: credit	2 200 ..	. . . .	. . . .	. . . .	. . . .	. . . .	355	357	. . . .
Services: debit	3 200 ..	. . . .	. . . .	. . . .	. . . .	. . . .	−6,095	−5,490	. . . .
Balance on Goods and Services	4 991 ..	. . . .	. . . .	. . . .	. . . .	. . . .	*−2,044*	*6,689*	. . . .
Income: credit	2 300 ..	. . . .	. . . .	. . . .	. . . .	. . . .	680	1,206	. . . .
Income: debit	3 300 ..	. . . .	. . . .	. . . .	. . . .	. . . .	−5,207	−4,751	. . . .
Balance on Goods, Services, and Income	4 992 ..	. . . .	. . . .	. . . .	. . . .	. . . .	*−6,571*	*3,144*	. . . .
Current transfers: credit	2 379 Z.	. . . .	. . . .	. . . .	. . . .	. . . .	552	261	. . . .
Current transfers: debit	3 379 ..	. . . .	. . . .	. . . .	. . . .	. . . .	−1,493	−2,153	. . . .
B. Capital Account[1]	4 994 Z.	. . . .	. . . .	. . . .	. . . .	. . . .	3,889	2,769	. . . .
Capital account: credit	2 994 Z.	. . . .	. . . .	. . . .	. . . .	. . . .	3,889	2,769	. . . .
Capital account: debit	3 994 ..	. . . .	. . . .	. . . .	. . . .	. . . .	. . . .	. . . .	. . . .
C. Financial Account[1]	4 995 W.	. . . .	. . . .	. . . .	. . . .	. . . .	−1,350	−2,600	. . . .
Direct investment abroad	4 505 ..	. . . .	. . . .	. . . .	. . . .	. . . .	−89	−305	. . . .
Direct investment in Iraq	4 555 Z.	. . . .	. . . .	. . . .	. . . .	. . . .	515	383	. . . .
Portfolio investment assets	4 602 ..	. . . .	. . . .	. . . .	. . . .	. . . .	−1,968	−3,669	. . . .
Equity securities	4 610 ..	. . . .	. . . .	. . . .	. . . .	. . . .	. . . .	. . . .	. . . .
Debt securities	4 619 ..	. . . .	. . . .	. . . .	. . . .	. . . .	−1,968	−3,669	. . . .
Portfolio investment liabilities	4 652 Z.	. . . .	. . . .	. . . .	. . . .	. . . .	. . . .	. . . .	. . . .
Equity securities	4 660 ..	. . . .	. . . .	. . . .	. . . .	. . . .	. . . .	. . . .	. . . .
Debt securities	4 669 Z.	. . . .	. . . .	. . . .	. . . .	. . . .	. . . .	. . . .	. . . .
Financial derivatives	4 910 ..	. . . .	. . . .	. . . .	. . . .	. . . .	. . . .	. . . .	. . . .
Financial derivatives assets	4 900 ..	. . . .	. . . .	. . . .	. . . .	. . . .	. . . .	. . . .	. . . .
Financial derivatives liabilities	4 905 ..	. . . .	. . . .	. . . .	. . . .	. . . .	. . . .	. . . .	. . . .
Other investment assets	4 703 ..	. . . .	. . . .	. . . .	. . . .	. . . .	−283	1,459	. . . .
Monetary authorities	4 701 ..	. . . .	. . . .	. . . .	. . . .	. . . .	. . . .	41	. . . .
General government	4 704 ..	. . . .	. . . .	. . . .	. . . .	. . . .	224	2,363	. . . .
Banks	4 705 ..	. . . .	. . . .	. . . .	. . . .	. . . .	−506	−945	. . . .
Other sectors	4 728 ..	. . . .	. . . .	. . . .	. . . .	. . . .	. . . .	. . . .	. . . .
Other investment liabilities	4 753 W.	. . . .	. . . .	. . . .	. . . .	. . . .	474	−467	. . . .
Monetary authorities	4 753 WA	. . . .	. . . .	. . . .	. . . .	. . . .	203	−929	. . . .
General government	4 753 ZB	. . . .	. . . .	. . . .	. . . .	. . . .	−115	−281	. . . .
Banks	4 753 ZC	. . . .	. . . .	. . . .	. . . .	. . . .	386	743	. . . .
Other sectors	4 753 ZD	. . . .	. . . .	. . . .	. . . .	. . . .	. . . .	. . . .	. . . .
D. Net Errors and Omissions	4 998 ..	. . . .	. . . .	. . . .	. . . .	. . . .	451	112	. . . .
Total, Groups A Through D	4 984 ..	. . . .	. . . .	. . . .	. . . .	. . . .	*−4,523*	*1,533*	. . . .
E. Reserves and Related Items	4 802 A.	. . . .	. . . .	. . . .	. . . .	. . . .	4,523	−1,533	. . . .
Reserve assets	4 802 ..	. . . .	. . . .	. . . .	. . . .	. . . .	−4,338	−7,363	. . . .
Use of Fund credit and loans	4 766 ..	. . . .	. . . .	. . . .	. . . .	. . . .	. . . .	. . . .	. . . .
Exceptional financing	4 920 ..	. . . .	. . . .	. . . .	. . . .	. . . .	8,861	5,830	. . . .
Conversion rates: New Iraqi dinars per U.S. dollar	0 101 ..	.31	.31	.31	. . . .	1,453.42	1,472.00	1,467.42	1,254.57

[1] Excludes components that have been classified in the categories of Group E.

Table 2. STANDARD PRESENTATION, 2000–2007

(Millions of U.S. dollars)

	Code	2000	2001	2002	2003	2004	2005	2006	2007
CURRENT ACCOUNT................................	4 993	....	....	....	....	....	**−3,335**	**2,681**	....
A. GOODS................................	4 100	....	....	....	....	....	**3,695**	**11,822**	....
Credit................................	2 100	....	....	....	....	....	**23,697**	**30,529**	....
General merchandise: exports f.o.b.......	2 110	....	....	....	....	....	23,697	30,529	....
Goods for processing: exports f.o.b.......	2 150	....	....	....	....	....	....	....	....
Repairs on goods................................	2 160	....	....	....	....	....	....	....	....
Goods procured in ports by carriers.......	2 170	....	....	....	....	....	....	....	....
Nonmonetary gold................................	2 180	....	....	....	....	....	....	....	....
Debit................................	3 100	....	....	....	....	....	**−20,002**	**−18,708**	....
General merchandise: imports f.o.b.......	3 110	....	....	....	....	....	−20,002	−18,708	....
Goods for processing: imports f.o.b.......	3 150	....	....	....	....	....	....	....	....
Repairs on goods................................	3 160	....	....	....	....	....	....	....	....
Goods procured in ports by carriers.......	3 170	....	....	....	....	....	....	....	....
Nonmonetary gold................................	3 180	....	....	....	....	....	....	....	....
B. SERVICES................................	4 200	....	....	....	....	....	**−5,739**	**−5,133**	....
Total credit	2 200	....	....	....	....	....	*355*	*357*	....
Total debit	3 200	....	....	....	....	....	*−6,095*	*−5,490*	....
Transportation services, credit........	2 205	....	....	....	....	....	**170**	**204**	....
Passenger	2 850	....	....	....	....	....	*18*	*26*	....
Freight	2 851	....	....	....	....	....	*153*	*172*	....
Other	2 852	....	....	....	....	....	*....*	*6*	....
Sea transport, passenger................	2 207	....	....	....	....	....	....	....	....
Sea transport, freight................	2 208	....	....	....	....	....	4	160	....
Sea transport, other................	2 209	....	....	....	....	....	....	....	....
Air transport, passenger................	2 211	....	....	....	....	....	5	....	....
Air transport, freight................	2 212	....	....	....	....	....	3	....	....
Air transport, other................	2 213	....	....	....	....	....	....	....	....
Other transport, passenger................	2 215	....	....	....	....	....	13	26	....
Other transport, freight................	2 216	....	....	....	....	....	146	12	....
Other transport, other................	2 217	....	....	....	....	....	....	6	....
Transportation services, debit........	3 205	....	....	....	....	....	**−2,811**	**−2,581**	....
Passenger	3 850	....	....	....	....	....	*−188*	*−131*	....
Freight	3 851	....	....	....	....	....	*−2,612*	*−2,444*	....
Other	3 852	....	....	....	....	....	*−11*	*−6*	....
Sea transport, passenger................	3 207	....	....	....	....	....	....	....	....
Sea transport, freight................	3 208	....	....	....	....	....	−522	−8	....
Sea transport, other................	3 209	....	....	....	....	....	....	....	....
Air transport, passenger................	3 211	....	....	....	....	....	−155	−131	....
Air transport, freight................	3 212	....	....	....	....	....	−10	....	....
Air transport, other................	3 213	....	....	....	....	....	−11	−6	....
Other transport, passenger................	3 215	....	....	....	....	....	−33	....	....
Other transport, freight................	3 216	....	....	....	....	....	−2,080	−2,436	....
Other transport, other................	3 217	....	....	....	....	....	....	....	....
Travel, credit................................	2 236	....	....	....	....	....	**168**	**144**	....
Business travel................................	2 237	....	....	....	....	....	....	....	....
Personal travel................................	2 240	....	....	....	....	....	168	144	....
Travel, debit................................	3 236	....	....	....	....	....	**−439**	**−395**	....
Business travel................................	3 237	....	....	....	....	....	−338	−218	....
Personal travel................................	3 240	....	....	....	....	....	−101	−177	....
Other services, credit................	2 200 BA	....	....	....	....	....	**17**	**9**	....
Communications................................	2 245	....	....	....	....	....	6	4	....
Construction................................	2 249	....	....	....	....	....	....	....	....
Insurance................................	2 253	....	....	....	....	....	....	....	....
Financial................................	2 260	....	....	....	....	....	3	1	....
Computer and information................	2 262	....	....	....	....	....	1	....	....
Royalties and licence fees................	2 266	....	....	....	....	....	....	....	....
Other business services................	2 268	....	....	....	....	....	....	....	....
Personal, cultural, and recreational........	2 287	....	....	....	....	....	....	....	....
Government, n.i.e................................	2 291	....	....	....	....	....	8	4	....
Other services, debit................	3 200 BA	....	....	....	....	....	**−2,845**	**−2,514**	....
Communications................................	3 245	....	....	....	....	....	−236	−126	....
Construction................................	3 249	....	....	....	....	....	−394	−330	....
Insurance................................	3 253	....	....	....	....	....	−941	−885	....
Financial................................	3 260	....	....	....	....	....	−40	−93	....
Computer and information................	3 262	....	....	....	....	....	−205	−177	....
Royalties and licence fees................	3 266	....	....	....	....	....	−29	....	....
Other business services................	3 268	....	....	....	....	....	−180	−327	....
Personal, cultural, and recreational........	3 287	....	....	....	....	....	−151	−118	....
Government, n.i.e................................	3 291	....	....	....	....	....	−668	−460	....

Table 2 (Continued). STANDARD PRESENTATION, 2000–2007

(Millions of U.S. dollars)

	Code	2000	2001	2002	2003	2004	2005	2006	2007
C. INCOME	4 300	....	....	....	....	....	**−4,527**	**−3,546**	....
Total credit	2 300	....	....	....	....	....	*680*	*1,206*	....
Total debit	3 300	....	....	....	....	....	*−5,207*	*−4,751*	....
Compensation of employees, credit	2 310	....	....	....	....	....	**258**	**128**	....
Compensation of employees, debit	3 310	....	....	....	....	....	**−83**	**−153**	....
Investment income, credit	2 320	....	....	....	....	....	**423**	**1,078**	....
Direct investment income	2 330	....	....	....	....	....	6	27	....
Dividends and distributed branch profits	2 332	....	....	....	....	....	6	27	....
Reinvested earnings and undistributed branch profits	2 333	....	....	....	....	....	....	....	....
Income on debt (interest)	2 334	....	....	....	....	....	....	....	....
Portfolio investment income	2 339	....	....	....	....	....	185	592	....
Income on equity	2 340	....	....	....	....	....	6	....	....
Income on bonds and notes	2 350	....	....	....	....	....	179	592	....
Income on money market instruments	2 360	....	....	....	....	....	....	....	....
Other investment income	2 370	....	....	....	....	....	233	459	....
Investment income, debit	3 320	....	....	....	....	....	**−5,125**	**−4,598**	....
Direct investment income	3 330	....	....	....	....	....	−36	−67	....
Dividends and distributed branch profits	3 332	....	....	....	....	....	−36	−67	....
Reinvested earnings and undistributed branch profits	3 333	....	....	....	....	....	....	....	....
Income on debt (interest)	3 334	....	....	....	....	....	....	....	....
Portfolio investment income	3 339	....	....	....	....	....	....	....	....
Income on equity	3 340	....	....	....	....	....	....	....	....
Income on bonds and notes	3 350	....	....	....	....	....	....	....	....
Income on money market instruments	3 360	....	....	....	....	....	....	....	....
Other investment income	3 370	....	....	....	....	....	−5,089	−4,531	....
D. CURRENT TRANSFERS	4 379	....	....	....	....	....	**3,236**	**−462**	....
Credit	2 379	....	....	....	....	....	**4,729**	**1,691**	....
General government	2 380	....	....	....	....	....	4,178	1,429	....
Other sectors	2 390	....	....	....	....	....	552	261	....
Workers' remittances	2 391	....	....	....	....	....	454	261	....
Other current transfers	2 392	....	....	....	....	....	98	....	....
Debit	3 379	....	....	....	....	....	**−1,493**	**−2,153**	....
General government	3 380	....	....	....	....	....	−1,153	−1,520	....
Other sectors	3 390	....	....	....	....	....	−340	−632	....
Workers' remittances	3 391	....	....	....	....	....	....	−629	....
Other current transfers	3 392	....	....	....	....	....	−340	−4	....
CAPITAL AND FINANCIAL ACCOUNT	4 996	....	....	....	....	....	**2,884**	**−2,793**	....
CAPITAL ACCOUNT	4 994	....	....	....	....	....	**20,489**	**17,984**	....
Total credit	2 994	....	....	....	....	....	*20,489*	*17,984*	....
Total debit	3 994	....	....	....	....	....	....	....	....
Capital transfers, credit	2 400	....	....	....	....	....	**20,489**	**17,984**	....
General government	2 401	....	....	....	....	....	20,489	17,984	....
Debt forgiveness	2 402	....	....	....	....	....	16,952	15,215	....
Other capital transfers	2 410	....	....	....	....	....	3,537	2,769	....
Other sectors	2 430	....	....	....	....	....	....	....	....
Migrants' transfers	2 431	....	....	....	....	....	....	....	....
Debt forgiveness	2 432	....	....	....	....	....	....	....	....
Other capital transfers	2 440	....	....	....	....	....	....	....	....
Capital transfers, debit	3 400	....	....	....	....	....	....	....	....
General government	3 401	....	....	....	....	....	....	....	....
Debt forgiveness	3 402	....	....	....	....	....	....	....	....
Other capital transfers	3 410	....	....	....	....	....	....	....	....
Other sectors	3 430	....	....	....	....	....	....	....	....
Migrants' transfers	3 431	....	....	....	....	....	....	....	....
Debt forgiveness	3 432	....	....	....	....	....	....	....	....
Other capital transfers	3 440	....	....	....	....	....	....	....	....
Nonproduced nonfinancial assets, credit	2 480	....	....	....	....	....	....	....	....
Nonproduced nonfinancial assets, debit	3 480	....	....	....	....	....	....	....	....

Table 2 (Continued). STANDARD PRESENTATION, 2000–2007

(Millions of U.S. dollars)

	Code	2000	2001	2002	2003	2004	2005	2006	2007
FINANCIAL ACCOUNT	4 995 ..	....	....	....	....	....	**−17,604**	**−20,777**	....
A. DIRECT INVESTMENT	4 500 ..	....	....	....	....	....	427	78	....
Direct investment abroad	4 505 ..	....	....	....	....	....	−89	−305	....
Equity capital	4 510 ..	....	....	....	....	....	−89	−305	....
Claims on affiliated enterprises	4 515 ..	....	....	....	....	....	−89	−305	....
Liabilities to affiliated enterprises	4 520 ..	....	....	....	....	....	....	....	....
Reinvested earnings	4 525 ..	....	....	....	....	....	....	....	....
Other capital	4 530 ..	....	....	....	....	....	....	....	....
Claims on affiliated enterprises	4 535 ..	....	....	....	....	....	....	....	....
Liabilities to affiliated enterprises	4 540 ..	....	....	....	....	....	....	....	....
Direct investment in Iraq	4 555 ..	....	....	....	....	....	515	383	....
Equity capital	4 560 ..						515	383	
Claims on direct investors	4 565 ..						....	....	
Liabilities to direct investors	4 570 ..						515	383	
Reinvested earnings	4 575 ..						....	....	
Other capital	4 580 ..						....	....	
Claims on direct investors	4 585 ..						....	....	
Liabilities to direct investors	4 590 ..						....	....	
B. PORTFOLIO INVESTMENT	4 600 ..	....	....	....	....	....	**−1,968**	**−3,669**	....
Assets	4 602 ..	....	....	....	....	....	**−1,968**	**−3,669**	....
Equity securities	4 610 ..	....	....	....	....	....	....	....	....
Monetary authorities	4 611 ..	....	....	....	....	....	....	....	....
General government	4 612 ..	....	....	....	....	....	....	....	....
Banks	4 613 ..	....	....	....	....	....	....	....	....
Other sectors	4 614 ..	....	....	....	....	....	....	....	....
Debt securities	4 619 ..	....	....	....	....	....	−1,968	−3,669	....
Bonds and notes	4 620 ..	....	....	....	....	....	−1,968	−3,617	....
Monetary authorities	4 621 ..	....	....	....	....	....	....	....	....
General government	4 622 ..	....	....	....	....	....	−1,968	−3,617	....
Banks	4 623 ..	....	....	....	....	....	....	....	....
Other sectors	4 624 ..	....	....	....	....	....	....	....	....
Money market instruments	4 630 ..	....	....	....	....	....	....	−53	....
Monetary authorities	4 631 ..	....	....	....	....	....	....	....	....
General government	4 632 ..	....	....	....	....	....	....	....	....
Banks	4 633 ..	....	....	....	....	....	....	−53	....
Other sectors	4 634 ..	....	....	....	....	....	....	....	....
Liabilities	4 652 ..	....	....	....	....	....	....	....	....
Equity securities	4 660 ..	....	....	....	....	....	....	....	....
Banks	4 663 ..	....	....	....	....	....	....	....	....
Other sectors	4 664 ..	....	....	....	....	....	....	....	....
Debt securities	4 669 ..	....	....	....	....	....	....	....	....
Bonds and notes	4 670 ..	....	....	....	....	....	....	....	....
Monetary authorities	4 671 ..	....	....	....	....	....	....	....	....
General government	4 672 ..	....	....	....	....	....	....	....	....
Banks	4 673 ..	....	....	....	....	....	....	....	....
Other sectors	4 674 ..	....	....	....	....	....	....	....	....
Money market instruments	4 680 ..	....	....	....	....	....	....	....	....
Monetary authorities	4 681 ..	....	....	....	....	....	....	....	....
General government	4 682 ..	....	....	....	....	....	....	....	....
Banks	4 683 ..	....	....	....	....	....	....	....	....
Other sectors	4 684 ..	....	....	....	....	....	....	....	....
C. FINANCIAL DERIVATIVES	4 910 ..	....	....	....	....	....	....	....	....
Monetary authorities	4 911 ..	....	....	....	....	....	....	....	....
General government	4 912 ..	....	....	....	....	....	....	....	....
Banks	4 913 ..	....	....	....	....	....	....	....	....
Other sectors	4 914 ..	....	....	....	....	....	....	....	....
Assets	4 900 ..	....	....	....	....	....	....	....	....
Monetary authorities	4 901 ..	....	....	....	....	....	....	....	....
General government	4 902 ..	....	....	....	....	....	....	....	....
Banks	4 903 ..	....	....	....	....	....	....	....	....
Other sectors	4 904 ..	....	....	....	....	....	....	....	....
Liabilities	4 905 ..	....	....	....	....	....	....	....	....
Monetary authorities	4 906 ..	....	....	....	....	....	....	....	....
General government	4 907 ..	....	....	....	....	....	....	....	....
Banks	4 908 ..	....	....	....	....	....	....	....	....
Other sectors	4 909 ..	....	....	....	....	....	....	....	....

Table 2 (Concluded). STANDARD PRESENTATION, 2000–2007

(Millions of U.S. dollars)

	Code	2000	2001	2002	2003	2004	2005	2006	2007
D. OTHER INVESTMENT	4 700 ..	....	....	....	....	....	−11,726	−9,823	....
Assets	4 703 ..	....	....	....	....	....	−283	1,459	....
Trade credits	4 706 ..	....	....	....	....	....	−71	−55	....
General government	4 707 ..	....	....	....	....	....	−71	−55	....
of which: Short-term	4 709 ..	....	....	....	....	....	....	....	....
Other sectors	4 710 ..	....	....	....	....	....	....	....	....
of which: Short-term	4 712 ..	....	....	....	....	....	....	....	....
Loans	4 714 ..	....	....	....	....	....	....	....	....
Monetary authorities	4 715 ..	....	....	....	....	....	....	....	....
of which: Short-term	4 718 ..	....	....	....	....	....	....	....	....
General government	4 719 ..	....	....	....	....	....	....	....	....
of which: Short-term	4 721 ..	....	....	....	....	....	....	....	....
Banks	4 722 ..	....	....	....	....	....	....	....	....
of which: Short-term	4 724 ..	....	....	....	....	....	....	....	....
Other sectors	4 725 ..	....	....	....	....	....	....	....	....
of which: Short-term	4 727 ..	....	....	....	....	....	....	....	....
Currency and deposits	4 730 ..	....	....	....	....	....	−2,453	1,615	....
Monetary authorities	4 731 ..	....	....	....	....	....	....	....	....
General government	4 732 ..	....	....	....	....	....	−1,947	2,561	....
Banks	4 733 ..	....	....	....	....	....	−506	−945	....
Other sectors	4 734 ..	....	....	....	....	....	....	....	....
Other assets	4 736 ..	....	....	....	....	....	2,242	−102	....
Monetary authorities	4 737 ..	....	....	....	....	....	....	41	....
of which: Short-term	4 739 ..	....	....	....	....	....	....	....	....
General government	4 740 ..	....	....	....	....	....	2,242	−143	....
of which: Short-term	4 742 ..	....	....	....	....	....	*2,291*	*263*	....
Banks	4 743 ..	....	....	....	....	....	....	....	....
of which: Short-term	4 745 ..	....	....	....	....	....	....	....	....
Other sectors	4 746 ..	....	....	....	....	....	....	....	....
of which: Short-term	4 748 ..	....	....	....	....	....	....	....	....
Liabilities	4 753 ..	....	....	....	....	....	−11,443	−11,282	....
Trade credits	4 756 ..	....	....	....	....	....	....	....	....
General government	4 757 ..	....	....	....	....	....	....	....	....
of which: Short-term	4 759 ..	....	....	....	....	....	....	....	....
Other sectors	4 760 ..	....	....	....	....	....	....	....	....
of which: Short-term	4 762 ..	....	....	....	....	....	....	....	....
Loans	4 764 ..	....	....	....	....	....	5,591	3,859	....
Monetary authorities	4 765 ..	....	....	....	....	....	203	−929	....
of which: Use of Fund credit and loans from the Fund	4 766 ..	....	....	....	....	....	....	....	....
of which: Short-term	4 768 ..	....	....	....	....	....	....	....	....
General government	4 769 ..	....	....	....	....	....	4,920	4,120	....
of which: Short-term	4 771 ..	....	....	....	....	....	....	....	....
Banks	4 772 ..	....	....	....	....	....	468	669	....
of which: Short-term	4 774 ..	....	....	....	....	....	....	....	....
Other sectors	4 775 ..	....	....	....	....	....	....	....	....
of which: Short-term	4 777 ..	....	....	....	....	....	....	....	....
Currency and deposits	4 780 ..	....	....	....	....	....	−82	51	....
Monetary authorities	4 781 ..	....	....	....	....	....	....	....	....
General government	4 782 ..	....	....	....	....	....	....	....	....
Banks	4 783 ..	....	....	....	....	....	−82	51	....
Other sectors	4 784 ..	....	....	....	....	....	....	....	....
Other liabilities	4 786 ..	....	....	....	....	....	−16,952	−15,192	....
Monetary authorities	4 787 ..	....	....	....	....	....	....	....	....
of which: Short-term	4 789 ..	....	....	....	....	....	....	....	....
General government	4 790 ..	....	....	....	....	....	−16,952	−15,215	....
of which: Short-term	4 792 ..	....	....	....	....	....	*−16,952*	*−15,215*	....
Banks	4 793 ..	....	....	....	....	....	....	23	....
of which: Short-term	4 795 ..	....	....	....	....	....	....	*12*	....
Other sectors	4 796 ..	....	....	....	....	....	....	....	....
of which: Short-term	4 798 ..	....	....	....	....	....	....	....	....
E. RESERVE ASSETS	4 802 ..	....	....	....	....	....	−4,338	−7,363	....
Monetary gold	4 812 ..	....	....	....	....	....	....	....	....
Special drawing rights	4 811 ..	....	....	....	....	....	4	3	....
Reserve position in the Fund	4 810 ..	....	....	....	....	....	....	....	....
Foreign exchange	4 803 ..	....	....	....	....	....	−4,342	−7,366	....
Other claims	4 813 ..	....	....	....	....	....	....	....	....
NET ERRORS AND OMISSIONS	4 998 ..	....	....	....	....	....	451	112	....

Table 1. ANALYTIC PRESENTATION, 2000–2007

(Millions of U.S. dollars)

	Code	2000	2001	2002	2003	2004	2005	2006	2007
A. Current Account[1]	4 993 Z.	**−516**	**−690**	**−1,101**	**89**	**−1,081**	**−7,150**	**−9,095**	**−12,695**
Goods: exports f.o.b.	2 100 ..	73,530	77,623	84,216	88,590	100,116	102,825	104,667	115,517
Goods: imports f.o.b.	3 100 ..	−48,520	−50,360	−50,769	−51,709	−61,102	−67,730	−72,779	−84,226
Balance on Goods	4 100 ..	*25,010*	*27,263*	*33,447*	*36,882*	*39,014*	*35,096*	*31,888*	*31,292*
Services: credit	2 200 ..	18,538	23,465	29,900	42,061	52,718	59,920	69,191	88,994
Services: debit	3 200 ..	−31,272	−35,339	−42,829	−54,596	−65,384	−71,437	−78,528	−94,472
Balance on Goods and Services	4 991 ..	*12,276*	*15,389*	*20,519*	*24,346*	*26,348*	*23,579*	*22,550*	*25,814*
Income: credit	2 300 ..	27,613	28,850	27,200	34,095	43,457	53,862	75,321	103,989
Income: debit	3 300 ..	−41,160	−45,202	−49,515	−58,879	−71,388	−84,876	−106,422	−140,840
Balance on Goods, Services, and Income	4 992 ..	*−1,271*	*−962*	*−1,796*	*−438*	*−1,583*	*−7,434*	*−8,551*	*−11,037*
Current transfers: credit	2 379 Z.	4,143	7,400	7,538	7,027	6,626	6,963	6,648	6,459
Current transfers: debit	3 379 ..	−3,388	−7,128	−6,842	−6,500	−6,123	−6,679	−7,192	−8,117
B. Capital Account[1]	4 994 Z.	**1,074**	**635**	**512**	**126**	**368**	**323**	**283**	**54**
Capital account: credit	2 994 Z.	1,167	719	656	617	797	534	392	174
Capital account: debit	3 994 ..	−93	−84	−144	−491	−428	−211	−109	−121
Total, Groups A Plus B	4 981 ..	*558*	*−55*	*−589*	*215*	*−712*	*−6,827*	*−8,812*	*−12,641*
C. Financial Account[1]	4 995 W.	**7,912**	**16**	**468**	**−3,481**	**3,301**	**−2,501**	**10,732**	**14,115**
Direct investment abroad	4 505 ..	−4,641	−4,103	−11,065	−5,594	−18,107	−14,491	−14,708	−22,004
Direct investment in Ireland	4 555 Z.	25,501	9,573	29,477	22,411	−10,994	−30,334	−882	26,085
Portfolio investment assets	4 602 ..	−83,075	−111,347	−105,469	−163,841	−168,940	−151,139	−269,093	−228,644
Equity securities	4 610 ..	−28,849	−23,808	−27,200	−29,545	−46,087	−59,602	−73,832	−19,123
Debt securities	4 619 ..	−54,226	−87,539	−78,270	−134,296	−122,853	−91,537	−195,261	−209,521
Portfolio investment liabilities	4 652 Z.	77,906	89,085	69,368	119,397	186,471	215,056	251,426	196,392
Equity securities	4 660 ..	69,606	79,352	69,104	76,776	81,709	93,590	160,765	137,155
Debt securities	4 669 Z.	8,300	9,733	265	42,621	104,761	121,466	90,661	59,236
Financial derivatives	4 910 ..	374	381	1,580	−525	1,042	−8,041	2,049	−16,628
Financial derivatives assets	4 900 ..	416	−576	1,606	−406	−1,903	−5,347	4,239	−18,175
Financial derivatives liabilities	4 905 ..	−42	957	−26	−120	2,945	−2,694	−2,190	1,547
Other investment assets	4 703 ..	−37,036	−21,431	−33,183	−65,871	−57,406	−133,298	−126,184	−170,670
Monetary authorities	4 701 ..	−16	−121	−583	−1,576	308	−296	−1,093	3,402
General government	4 704 ..	−2,057	725	3,327	31	−381	−226	407	1,253
Banks	4 705 ..	−12,563	−5,348	−20,722	−35,458	−40,525	−85,843	−82,992	−109,750
Other sectors	4 728 ..	−22,400	−16,687	−15,205	−28,867	−16,809	−46,934	−42,506	−65,575
Other investment liabilities	4 753 W.	28,882	37,859	49,759	90,542	71,236	119,746	168,124	229,584
Monetary authorities	4 753 WA	3,493	922	−1,583	7,461	−4,349	−9	−2,577	....
General government	4 753 ZB	−160	−2	−34	−286	−9	−149	−5	....
Banks	4 753 ZC	19,637	18,656	32,823	62,487	63,865	50,354	117,764	....
Other sectors	4 753 ZD	5,913	18,283	18,554	20,881	11,729	27,555	52,942	....
Total, Groups A Through C	4 983 ..	*8,471*	*−39*	*−121*	*−3,266*	*2,588*	*−9,328*	*1,920*	*1,473*
D. Net Errors and Omissions	4 998 ..	**−8,509**	**434**	**−171**	**1,375**	**−4,023**	**7,552**	**−2,032**	**−1,457**
Total, Groups A Through D	4 984 ..	*−39*	*395*	*−292*	*−1,890*	*−1,435*	*−1,776*	*−112*	*16*
E. Reserves and Related Items	4 802 A.	**39**	**−395**	**292**	**1,890**	**1,435**	**1,776**	**112**	**−16**
Reserve assets	4 802 ..	−121	−395	292	1,890	1,435	1,776	112	−16
Use of Fund credit and loans	4 766 ..	....	....	....	....	....	....	....	....
Exceptional financing	4 920 ..	160	....	....	....	....	....	....	....
Conversion rates: euros per U.S. dollar	0 103 ..	**1.0854**	**1.1175**	**1.0626**	**.8860**	**.8054**	**.8041**	**.7971**	**.7306**

[1] Excludes components that have been classified in the categories of Group E.

Table 2. STANDARD PRESENTATION, 2000–2007

(Millions of U.S. dollars)

	Code	2000	2001	2002	2003	2004	2005	2006	2007
CURRENT ACCOUNT	4 993	−356	−690	−1,101	89	−1,081	−7,150	−9,095	−12,695
A. GOODS	4 100	25,010	27,263	33,447	36,882	39,014	35,096	31,888	31,292
Credit	2 100	73,530	77,623	84,216	88,590	100,116	102,825	104,667	115,517
General merchandise: exports f.o.b.	2 110	73,530	77,623	84,216	88,590	100,062	102,775	104,652	115,456
Goods for processing: exports f.o.b.	2 150	....	....	....	....	....	....	....	....
Repairs on goods	2 160	....	....	....	....	55	50	15	62
Goods procured in ports by carriers	2 170	....	....	....	....	....	....	....	....
Nonmonetary gold	2 180	....	....	....	....	....	....	....	....
Debit	3 100	−48,520	−50,360	−50,769	−51,709	−61,102	−67,730	−72,779	−84,226
General merchandise: imports f.o.b.	3 110	−48,520	−50,360	−50,769	−51,709	−61,102	−67,730	−72,779	−84,226
Goods for processing: imports f.o.b.	3 150	....	....	....	....	....	....	....	....
Repairs on goods	3 160	....	....	....	....	....	....	....	....
Goods procured in ports by carriers	3 170	....	....	....	....	....	....	....	....
Nonmonetary gold	3 180	....	....	....	....	....	....	....	....
B. SERVICES	4 200	−12,734	−11,874	−12,928	−12,535	−12,666	−11,516	−9,338	−5,478
Total credit	2 200	*18,538*	*23,465*	*29,900*	*42,061*	*52,718*	*59,920*	*69,191*	*88,994*
Total debit	3 200	*−31,272*	*−35,339*	*−42,829*	*−54,596*	*−65,384*	*−71,437*	*−78,528*	*−94,472*
Transportation services, credit	2 205	1,380	1,480	1,622	1,932	2,346	2,646	2,938	3,499
Passenger	2 850	*902*	*998*	*1,131*	*1,344*	*1,700*	*1,998*	*2,295*	*2,723*
Freight	2 851	*127*	*142*	*132*	*158*	*174*	*174*	*166*	*255*
Other	2 852	*351*	*341*	*359*	*429*	*472*	*473*	*477*	*521*
Sea transport, passenger	2 207	65	61	75	82	85	81	74	87
Sea transport, freight	2 208	98	113	102	122	134	134	126	211
Sea transport, other	2 209	37	36	38	45	50	50	50	55
Air transport, passenger	2 211	837	937	1,056	1,262	1,615	1,918	2,221	2,636
Air transport, freight	2 212	30	29	30	36	40	40	40	44
Air transport, other	2 213	314	305	321	384	422	423	427	466
Other transport, passenger	2 215	....	....	....	....	....	....	....	....
Other transport, freight	2 216	....	....	....	....	....	....	....	....
Other transport, other	2 217	....	....	....	....	....	....	....	....
Transportation services, debit	3 205	−2,627	−1,791	−1,794	−1,950	−2,224	−2,467	−2,542	−2,799
Passenger	3 850	*−101*	*−98*	*−80*	*−96*	*−114*	*−112*	*−116*	*−129*
Freight	3 851	*−2,204*	*−1,380*	*−1,385*	*−1,461*	*−1,678*	*−1,921*	*−1,990*	*−2,193*
Other	3 852	*−321*	*−312*	*−328*	*−393*	*−432*	*−433*	*−437*	*−477*
Sea transport, passenger	3 207	−30	−29	−10	−12	−22	−20	−23	−27
Sea transport, freight	3 208	−1,543	−966	−970	−1,022	−1,175	−1,344	−1,392	−1,534
Sea transport, other	3 209	−96	−93	−98	−118	−129	−130	−131	−143
Air transport, passenger	3 211	−72	−70	−70	−84	−92	−92	−93	−101
Air transport, freight	3 212	−441	−276	−277	−293	−336	−384	−399	−440
Air transport, other	3 213	−225	−219	−230	−276	−303	−304	−306	−334
Other transport, passenger	3 215	....	....	....	....	....	....	....	....
Other transport, freight	3 216	−220	−138	−138	−146	−167	−193	−198	−219
Other transport, other	3 217	....	....	....	....	....	....	....	....
Travel, credit	2 236	2,615	2,791	3,097	3,862	4,375	4,782	5,369	6,140
Business travel	2 237	....	....	....	....	....	59	103	155
Personal travel	2 240	....	2,791	3,097	3,862	4,375	4,723	5,266	5,985
Travel, debit	3 236	−2,525	−2,858	−3,755	−4,736	−5,177	−6,074	−6,862	−8,682
Business travel	3 237	....	....	....	....	....	−82	−89	−93
Personal travel	3 240	....	−2,858	−3,755	−4,736	−5,177	−5,992	−6,773	−8,589
Other services, credit	2 200 BA	14,543	19,193	25,181	36,267	45,996	52,492	60,884	79,356
Communications	2 245	941	1,006	984	705	427	538	524	652
Construction	2 249	....	18	21	27	....	....	....	....
Insurance	2 253	1,122	2,325	4,932	8,731	9,726	8,611	11,029	12,245
Financial	2 260	2,069	1,863	2,751	3,817	5,303	6,029	7,778	9,947
Computer and information	2 262	7,490	8,926	10,447	14,238	18,774	19,586	21,039	26,118
Royalties and licence fees	2 266	638	185	282	211	352	773	1,028	1,110
Other business services	2 268	1,908	4,386	5,209	7,862	10,498	16,232	18,724	24,753
Personal, cultural, and recreational	2 287	163	286	320	400	....	413	....	....
Government, n.i.e.	2 291	212	199	235	276	505	518	531	....
Other services, debit	3 200 BA	−26,121	−30,690	−37,280	−47,910	−57,983	−62,896	−69,124	−82,991
Communications	3 245	−794	−500	−599	−860	−773	−882	−961	−1,127
Construction	3 249	−18	−36	−37	−47	....	....	....	....
Insurance	3 253	−1,354	−2,167	−3,963	−6,301	−7,498	−7,434	−9,006	−9,990
Financial	3 260	−1,448	−1,290	−1,609	−2,052	−2,776	−3,303	−4,714	−6,300
Computer and information	3 262	−277	−554	−553	−371	−380	−437	−667	−848
Royalties and licence fees	3 266	−8,329	−9,468	−11,001	−16,077	−18,847	−19,223	−20,815	−24,669
Other business services	3 268	−13,814	−16,597	−19,381	−22,038	−27,539	−31,421	−32,743	−33,483
Personal, cultural, and recreational	3 287	−26	−21	−74	−87	....	−105	....	....
Government, n.i.e.	3 291	−60	−57	−64	−77	−56	−51	−68	....

Table 2 (Continued). STANDARD PRESENTATION, 2000–2007

(Millions of U.S. dollars)

	Code	2000	2001	2002	2003	2004	2005	2006	2007
C. INCOME	4 300	**−13,547**	**−16,351**	**−22,315**	**−24,784**	**−27,931**	**−31,014**	**−31,101**	**−36,851**
Total credit	2 300	*27,613*	*28,850*	*27,200*	*34,095*	*43,457*	*53,862*	*75,321*	*103,989*
Total debit	3 300	*−41,160*	*−45,202*	*−49,515*	*−58,879*	*−71,388*	*−84,876*	*−106,422*	*−140,840*
Compensation of employees, credit	2 310	**197**	**190**	**274**	**304**	**389**	**488**	**513**	**563**
Compensation of employees, debit	3 310	**−107**	**−202**	**−419**	**−548**	**−734**	**−1,063**	**−1,277**	**−1,548**
Investment income, credit	2 320	**27,417**	**28,660**	**26,926**	**33,791**	**43,068**	**53,374**	**74,808**	**100,920**
Direct investment income	2 330	3,061	3,645	3,578	5,003	7,489	8,017	10,560	10,267
Dividends and distributed branch profits	2 332	466	341	....	278	....	202	584	77
Reinvested earnings and undistributed branch profits	2 333	1,293	2,016	....	3,023	....	4,544	4,742	3,647
Income on debt (interest)	2 334	1,303	1,288	1,062	1,702	2,838	3,271	5,234	6,542
Portfolio investment income	2 339	6,666	12,475	14,088	18,435	23,014	27,708	40,214	55,424
Income on equity	2 340	1,075	2,171	2,081	2,386	3,406	4,411	6,316	7,902
Income on bonds and notes	2 350	3,537	8,061	10,692	13,061	15,959	18,062	25,236	33,405
Income on money market instruments	2 360	2,054	2,243	1,315	2,989	3,649	5,236	8,662	14,117
Other investment income	2 370	17,689	12,540	9,259	10,352	12,565	17,649	24,034	35,229
Investment income, debit	3 320	**−41,053**	**−45,000**	**−49,096**	**−58,331**	**−70,655**	**−83,813**	**−105,145**	**−139,291**
Direct investment income	3 330	−21,707	−23,947	−29,100	−34,602	−39,681	−40,889	−39,461	−48,737
Dividends and distributed branch profits	3 332	−10,797	−13,456	−14,043	−15,023	−25,925	−32,446	−24,513	−22,417
Reinvested earnings anc undistributed branch profits	3 333	−9,698	−9,267	−13,831	−17,886	−11,590	−5,680	−12,478	−23,742
Income on debt (interest)	3 334	−1,212	−1,225	−1,225	−1,693	−2,166	−2,763	−2,471	−2,578
Portfolio investment income	3 339	−9,433	−10,519	−10,776	−13,856	−18,434	−23,545	−36,405	−51,038
Income on equity	3 340	−4,065	−6,547	−7,621	−9,029	−10,829	−13,472	−21,077	−27,957
Income on bonds and notes	3 350	−3,056	−2,909	−1,959	−3,877	−6,501	−8,189	−12,127	−19,139
Income on money market instruments	3 360	−2,313	−1,063	−1,196	−950	−1,104	−1,884	−3,201	−3,942
Other investment income	3 370	−9,912	−10,533	−9,220	−9,873	−12,540	−19,379	−29,278	−39,516
D. CURRENT TRANSFERS	4 379	**915**	**272**	**696**	**527**	**503**	**284**	**−544**	**−1,658**
Credit	2 379	**4,303**	**7,400**	**7,538**	**7,027**	**6,626**	**6,963**	**6,648**	**6,459**
General government	2 380	294	135	135	167	303	271	236	224
Other sectors	2 390	4,009	7,265	7,403	6,860	6,323	6,693	6,412	6,235
Workers' remittances	2 391	55	54	42	33	25	25	19	16
Other current transfers	2 392	3,954	7,211	7,361	6,826	6,298	6,668	6,393	6,219
Debit	3 379	**−3,388**	**−7,128**	**−6,842**	**−6,500**	**−6,123**	**−6,679**	**−7,192**	**−8,117**
General government	3 380	−582	−808	−1,000	−1,356	−1,663	−1,975	−2,206	−2,735
Other sectors	3 390	−2,806	−6,320	−5,842	−5,144	−4,460	−4,704	−4,985	−5,382
Workers' remittances	3 391	−4	−4	−97	−154	−169	−378	−575	−902
Other current transfers	3 392	−2,802	−6,316	−5,745	−4,991	−4,291	−4,327	−4,411	−4,481
CAPITAL AND FINANCIAL ACCOUNT	4 996	**8,865**	**256**	**1,271**	**−1,464**	**5,104**	**−402**	**11,127**	**14,153**
CAPITAL ACCOUNT	4 994	**1,074**	**635**	**512**	**126**	**368**	**323**	**283**	**54**
Total credit	2 994	*1,167*	*719*	*656*	*617*	*797*	*534*	*392*	*174*
Total debit	3 994	*−93*	*−84*	*−144*	*−491*	*−428*	*−211*	*−109*	*−121*
Capital transfers, credit	2 400	**654**	**611**	**651**	**588**	**670**	**381**	**357**	**136**
General government	2 401	651	607	647	584	665	376	355	136
Debt forgiveness	2 402	....	....	....	....	....	....	....	....
Other capital transfers	2 410	651	607	647	584	665	376	355	136
Other sectors	2 430	4	4	4	5	5	5	2	....
Migrants' transfers	2 431	....	....	....	....	....	....	....	....
Debt forgiveness	2 432	....	....	....	....	....	....	....	....
Other capital transfers	2 440	4	4	4	5	5	5	2	....
Capital transfers, debit	3 400	**−93**	**−68**	**−72**	**−86**	**−94**	**−95**	**−95**	**−104**
General government	3 401	....	....	....	....	....	....	....	....
Debt forgiveness	3 402	....	....	....	....	....	....	....	....
Other capital transfers	3 410	....	....	....	....	....	....	....	....
Other sectors	3 430	−93	−68	−72	−86	−94	−95	−95	−104
Migrants' transfers	3 431	−70	−68	−72	−86	−94	−95	−95	−104
Debt forgiveness	3 432	....	....	....	....	....	....	....	....
Other capital transfers	3 440	−23	....	....	....	....	....	....	....
Nonproduced nonfinancial assets, credit	2 480	**513**	**108**	**5**	**29**	**127**	**153**	**35**	**38**
Nonproduced nonfinancial assets, debit	3 480	....	**−16**	**−73**	**−405**	**−334**	**−116**	**−14**	**−16**

Table 2 (Continued). STANDARD PRESENTATION, 2000–2007

(Millions of U.S. dollars)

	Code	2000	2001	2002	2003	2004	2005	2006	2007
FINANCIAL ACCOUNT	4 995	7,791	−379	760	−1,591	4,735	−724	10,844	14,099
A. DIRECT INVESTMENT	4 500	20,860	5,470	18,412	16,817	−29,102	−44,824	−15,590	4,081
Direct investment abroad	4 505	−4,641	−4,103	−11,065	−5,594	−18,107	−14,491	−14,708	−22,004
Equity capital	4 510	−3,501	−1,427	....	−2,696	....	−4,426	−14,521	....
Claims on affiliated enterprises	4 515	−3,552	−1,284	....	....	....	....	−14,516	....
Liabilities to affiliated enterprises	4 520	50	−144	....	....	....	....	−5	....
Reinvested earnings	4 525	−1,293	−2,016	....	−3,023	....	−4,544	−4,742	−3,647
Other capital	4 530	154	−660	....	126	....	−5,520	4,555	....
Claims on affiliated enterprises	4 535	117	−862	....	−299	....	....	1,757	....
Liabilities to affiliated enterprises	4 540	37	203	....	425	....	....	2,798	....
Direct investment in Ireland	4 555	25,501	9,573	29,477	22,411	−10,994	−30,334	−882	26,085
Equity capital	4 560	−12,728	8,879	13,666	4,153	−5,952	4,703	−7,252	−3,992
Claims on direct investors	4 565	−7,854	−4	....	....	....	....	....	....
Liabilities to direct investors	4 570	−4,874	8,883	....	....	−5,952	....	−7,252	−3,992
Reinvested earnings	4 575	9,698	9,267	13,831	17,886	11,590	5,680	12,478	23,742
Other capital	4 580	28,530	−8,573	1,980	372	−16,632	−40,717	−6,107	6,335
Claims on direct investors	4 585	−1,350	−2,302	−10,541	−32,576	−46,650	−78,014	−28,156	−29,094
Liabilities to direct investors	4 590	29,880	−6,270	12,521	32,948	30,018	37,297	22,049	35,430
B. PORTFOLIO INVESTMENT	4 600	−5,169	−22,262	−36,101	−44,444	17,530	63,917	−17,667	−32,252
Assets	4 602	−83,075	−111,347	−105,469	−163,841	−168,940	−151,139	−269,093	−228,644
Equity securities	4 610	−28,849	−23,808	−27,200	−29,545	−46,087	−59,602	−73,832	−19,123
Monetary authorities	4 611	....	....	....	....	....	....	....	....
General government	4 612	....	....	....	....	....	−1,411	....	....
Banks	4 613	−23	73	....	....	....	−610	....	....
Other sectors	4 614	−28,826	−23,881	....	....	....	−57,580	....	−19,123
Debt securities	4 619	−54,226	−87,539	−78,270	−134,296	−122,853	−91,537	−195,261	−209,521
Bonds and notes	4 620	−30,292	−45,122	−35,983	−93,015	−79,453	−92,303	−111,797	−122,382
Monetary authorities	4 621	−119	−191	−445	−220	−1,350	−2,808	33	−5,863
General government	4 622	....	....	−853	−68	−69	−251	−953	−1,467
Banks	4 623	−15,747	−16,591	−13,928	−62,099	−64,807	−68,879	−80,435	−58,433
Other sectors	4 624	−14,425	−28,339	−20,757	−30,627	−13,227	−20,366	−30,442	−56,619
Money market instruments	4 630	−23,934	−42,417	−42,287	−41,281	−43,400	766	−83,464	−87,139
Monetary authorities	4 631	−18	−26	....	−1,052	−732	99	−540	2,473
General government	4 632	....	....	....	....	....	....	....	....
Banks	4 633	−20,880	−2,114	1,961	−21,761	−32,890	−21,473	−78,864	−76,214
Other sectors	4 634	−3,036	−40,277	−44,247	−18,469	−9,778	22,139	−4,060	−13,398
Liabilities	4 652	77,906	89,085	69,368	119,397	186,471	215,056	251,426	196,392
Equity securities	4 660	69,606	79,352	69,104	76,776	81,709	93,590	160,765	137,155
Banks	4 663	21,985	−30	....	....	37,954	32,051	87,902	91,868
Other sectors	4 664	47,621	79,381	....	....	43,755	61,539	72,863	45,287
Debt securities	4 669	8,300	9,733	265	42,621	104,761	121,466	90,661	59,236
Bonds and notes	4 670	1,616	−1,280	330	....	80,422	76,548	81,811	51,918
Monetary authorities	4 671	....	....	....	....	....	....	....	....
General government	4 672	1,959	−1,348	1,980	....	4,693	2,074	401	2,944
Banks	4 673	756	−272	1,851	....	45,545	40,602	46,085	2,947
Other sectors	4 674	−1,100	340	−3,501	....	30,184	33,872	35,325	46,027
Money market instruments	4 680	6,684	11,014	−65	....	24,340	44,917	8,850	7,319
Monetary authorities	4 681	....	....	....	....	....	....	....	....
General government	4 682	−345	4,558	−1,108	....	−2,263	−282	....	252
Banks	4 683	7,058	8,646	734	....	18,328	32,424	15,297	20,300
Other sectors	4 684	−30	−2,190	309	....	8,275	12,776	−6,448	−13,234
C. FINANCIAL DERIVATIVES	4 910	374	381	1,580	−525	1,042	−8,041	2,049	−16,628
Monetary authorities	4 911	....	....	....	....	....	....	....	....
General government	4 912	−91	44	8	−31	−18	−19	−4	....
Banks	4 913	294	1,151	2,523	544	−1,056	−5,489	3,167	−10,161
Other sectors	4 914	171	−814	−925	−919	−1,710	−2,533	−1,114	−6,474
Assets	4 900	416	−576	1,606	−406	−1,903	−5,347	4,239	−18,175
Monetary authorities	4 901	....	....	....	....	....	....	....	....
General government	4 902	−91	44	8	−31	....	....	....	....
Banks	4 903	294	131	2,523	544	....	....	....	....
Other sectors	4 904	213	−750	−925	−919	....	....	....	....
Liabilities	4 905	−42	957	−26	−120	2,945	−2,694	−2,190	1,547
Monetary authorities	4 906	....	....	....	....	....	....	....	....
General government	4 907	....	....	....	....	....	....	....	....
Banks	4 908	....	1,021	....	....	....	....	....	....
Other sectors	4 909	−42	−64	....	....	....	....	....	....

Table 2 (Concluded). STANDARD PRESENTATION, 2000–2007

(Millions of U.S. dollars)

	Code	2000	2001	2002	2003	2004	2005	2006	2007
D. OTHER INVESTMENT	4 700	**−8,154**	**16,427**	**16,576**	**24,672**	**13,830**	**−13,552**	**41,939**	**58,914**
Assets	4 703	−37,036	−21,431	−33,183	−65,871	−57,406	−133,298	−126,184	−170,670
Trade credits	4 706	−3,680	−6,137	−980	−126	990	−2,445	−2,198	2,278
General government	4 707	170	....	....	....	....	....	....	....
of which: Short-term	4 709	*170*	....	....	....	....	....	....	....
Other sectors	4 710	−3,850	−6,137	−980	−126	990	−2,445	−2,198	2,278
of which: Short-term	4 712	*−3,020*	*−6,137*	*−980*	*−126*	*990*	*−2,445*	*−2,198*	*2,278*
Loans	4 714	−28,678	−8,462	−11,431	−34,071	−42,180	−62,594	−107,064	−77,522
Monetary authorities	4 715	....	....	....	−1,006	146	127	85	784
of which: Short-term	4 718	....	....	....	*−1,006*	*146*	*127*	*85*	*784*
General government	4 719	−2,250	....	....	....	....	....	....	....
of which: Short-term	4 721	*−2,250*	....	....	....	....	....	....	....
Banks	4 722	−10,839	−3,778	−8,163	−14,223	−31,735	−34,561	−75,390	−20,437
of which: Short-term	4 724	....	*2,848*	*5,730*	*−980*	*−6,341*	*−17,864*	*−26,246*	*1,883*
Other sectors	4 725	−15,590	−4,684	−3,268	−18,842	−10,591	−28,160	−31,759	−57,869
of which: Short-term	4 727	*−852*	*−409*	*−1,315*	*−4,368*	*4,658*	*−5,759*	*−11,034*	*−19,309*
Currency and deposits	4 730	−1,500	−2,435	−13,926	−30,102	−14,486	−47,321	−8,614	−94,603
Monetary authorities	4 731	−19	−121	−583	−570	291	−423	−1,193	2,608
General government	4 732	22	725	3,327	31	−381	−226	407	1,253
Banks	4 733	6	−1,152	−10,036	−22,859	−9,840	−47,415	−7,264	−90,168
Other sectors	4 734	−1,510	−1,887	−6,634	−6,704	−4,556	743	−564	−8,296
Other assets	4 736	−3,178	−4,398	−6,845	−1,572	−1,730	−20,939	−8,308	−823
Monetary authorities	4 737	3	....	....	....	−129	....	15	10
of which: Short-term	4 739	*3*	....	....	....	*−129*	....	*15*	*10*
General government	4 740	....	....	....	....	....	....	....	....
of which: Short-term	4 742	....	....	....	....	....	....	....	....
Banks	4 743	−1,731	−418	−2,523	1,624	1,050	−3,866	−338	855
of which: Short-term	4 745	*−904*	*−305*	....	....	....	....	....	....
Other sectors	4 746	−1,450	−3,980	−4,323	−3,196	−2,652	−17,073	−7,985	−1,688
of which: Short-term	4 748	*−1,441*	*−629*	*−3,705*	*−2,124*	*−1,751*	....	*−5,582*	....
Liabilities	4 753	**28,882**	**37,859**	**49,759**	**90,542**	**71,236**	**119,746**	**168,124**	**229,584**
Trade credits	4 756	2,331	2,505	1,328	2,450	1,442	3,368	6,323	1,055
General government	4 757	−8	....	....	....	....	....	....	....
of which: Short-term	4 759	*−8*	....	....	....	....	....	....	....
Other sectors	4 760	2,339	2,505	1,328	2,450	1,442	3,368	6,323	....
of which: Short-term	4 762	*985*	*2,505*	*1,328*	*2,450*	*1,442*	*3,368*	*6,323*	....
Loans	4 764	25,243	11,562	29,029	64,412	19,841	67,627	117,629	70,934
Monetary authorities	4 765	....	....	....	....	....	....	....	....
of which: Use of Fund credit and loans from the Fund	4 766	....	....	....	....	....	....	....	....
of which: Short-term	4 768	....	....	....	....	....	....	....	....
General government	4 769	−152	−2	−34	−286	−9	−149	−5	....
of which: Short-term	4 771	*−18*	*90*	*117*	*−198*	*67*	*−144*	*−5*	....
Banks	4 772	20,018	5,668	22,473	51,240	16,183	50,740	92,062	....
of which: Short-term	4 774	....	*5,492*	*6,116*	*42,015*	*23,679*	*32,667*	....	....
Other sectors	4 775	5,377	5,896	6,590	13,458	3,668	17,036	25,571	....
of which: Short-term	4 777	*−1,621*	*3,798*	*5,013*	*10,013*	*−226*	*5,106*	*5,056*	....
Currency and deposits	4 780	3,202	13,650	7,542	20,560	43,905	41,994	16,438	138,970
Monetary authorities	4 781	3,327	928	−1,582	7,494	−4,345	....	−2,574	....
General government	4 782	....	....	....	....	....	....	....	....
Banks	4 783	....	13,161	8,836	13,411	48,102	....	19,035	....
Other sectors	4 784	−125	−439	288	−345	148	....	−23	....
Other liabilities	4 786	−1,893	10,141	11,861	3,121	6,048	6,757	27,735	18,625
Monetary authorities	4 787	165	−6	−1	−33	−4	−9	−3	....
of which: Short-term	4 789	*165*	*−6*	*−1*	*−33*	*−4*	*−9*	*−3*	....
General government	4 790	....	....	....	....	....	....	....	....
of which: Short-term	4 792	....	....	....	....	....	....	....	....
Banks	4 793	−381	−173	1,514	−2,164	−420	−385	6,667	....
of which: Short-term	4 795	*−171*	*−192*	*1,514*	*−2,164*	*−420*	*−385*	....	....
Other sectors	4 796	−1,678	10,320	10,349	5,318	6,472	7,151	21,071	....
of which: Short-term	4 798	*−1,678*	*9,899*	*10,128*	*5,186*	....	....	....	....
E. RESERVE ASSETS	4 802	**−121**	**−395**	**292**	**1,890**	**1,435**	**1,776**	**112**	**−16**
Monetary gold	4 812	−1	....	....	−1	8	18	....	5
Special drawing rights	4 811	−10	−8	−7	−6	−6	−6	−2	−1
Reserve position in the Fund	4 810	67	−20	−100	−59	175	212	52	48
Foreign exchange	4 803	−215	−367	398	1,956	1,258	1,552	63	−69
Other claims	4 813	37	....	....	....	....	....	....	....
NET ERRORS AND OMISSIONS	4 998	**−8,509**	**434**	**−171**	**1,375**	**−4,023**	**7,552**	**−2,032**	**−1,457**

Table 3. INTERNATIONAL INVESTMENT POSITION (End-period stocks), 2000–2007

(Millions of U.S. dollars)

	Code	2000	2001	2002	2003	2004	2005	2006	2007
ASSETS	8 995 C.	....	749,233	972,186	1,364,407	1,757,495	1,983,595	2,637,748	3,337,954
Direct investment abroad	8 505 ..	....	40,819	58,881	73,321	106,692	104,152	123,296	145,863
Equity capital and reinvested earnings	8 506 ..	....	35,698	53,071	67,539	91,766	87,684	109,365	127,513
Claims on affiliated enterprises	8 507 ..	....	36,504	53,371	68,076	91,849	87,692	109,405	....
Liabilities to affiliated enterprises	8 508 ..	....	−806	−301	−537	−83	−8	−40	....
Other capital	8 530 ..	....	5,121	5,811	5,782	14,926	16,469	13,931	18,350
Claims on affiliated enterprises	8 535 ..	....	....	14,248	14,605	26,318	24,880	26,796	33,337
Liabilities to affiliated enterprises	8 540 ..	....	....	−8,437	−8,823	−11,393	−8,411	−12,864	−14,987
Portfolio investment	8 602 ..	....	432,843	573,968	834,518	1,072,312	1,182,212	1,593,699	1,969,782
Equity securities	8 610 ..	....	133,758	152,856	222,503	304,943	383,155	543,534	649,321
Monetary authorities	8 611 ..	....	....	....	....	....	....	....	....
General government	8 612 ..	....	....	4,386	8,528	11,955	14,382	19,823	24,119
Banks	8 613 ..	....	316	3,543	201	1,146	1,811	3,959	2,584
Other sectors	8 614 ..	....	133,443	144,928	213,774	291,842	366,962	519,751	622,619
Debt securities	8 619 ..	....	299,084	421,112	612,016	767,369	799,057	1,050,165	1,320,460
Bonds and notes	8 620 ..	....	183,871	249,198	379,235	474,982	535,258	683,104	846,362
Monetary authorities	8 621 ..	....	2,056	2,905	3,740	5,447	7,354	8,065	15,491
General government	8 622 ..	....	190	1,351	1,694	2,023	2,079	3,182	4,982
Banks	8 623 ..	....	79,580	100,267	174,539	253,082	300,204	401,883	482,133
Other sectors	8 624 ..	....	102,045	144,676	199,262	214,430	225,621	269,974	343,756
Money market instruments	8 630 ..	....	115,213	171,913	232,781	292,387	263,799	367,061	474,099
Monetary authorities	8 631 ..	....	....	....	1,163	2,091	1,765	2,576	218
General government	8 632 ..	....	....	....	....	....	....	....	....
Banks	8 633 ..	....	108,169	154,666	200,516	246,678	244,652	339,454	436,531
Other sectors	8 634 ..	....	7,044	17,247	31,101	43,619	17,382	25,031	37,350
Financial derivatives	8 900 ..	....	7,874	4,293	7,317	9,138	11,048	11,405	35,775
Monetary authorities	8 901 ..	....	....	....	....	....	....	....	....
General government	8 902 ..	....	344	191	162	−3	26	−36	−59
Banks	8 903 ..	....	5,387	3,738	3,793	3,578	3,643	3,672	25,403
Other sectors	8 904 ..	....	2,143	365	3,362	5,563	7,379	7,769	10,431
Other investment	8 703 ..	....	262,055	329,562	445,091	566,439	685,304	908,505	1,185,594
Trade credits	8 706 ..	....	32,894	31,555	28,873	29,037	32,878	36,894	48,251
General government	8 707 ..	....	....	....	....	....	....	....	....
of which: Short-term	8 709 ..	....	....	....	....	....	....	....	....
Other sectors	8 710 ..	....	32,894	31,555	28,873	29,037	32,878	36,894	48,251
of which: Short-term	8 712 ..	....	*32,894*	*31,555*	*28,873*	*29,037*	*32,878*	*36,894*	*48,251*
Loans	8 714 ..	....	164,990	190,604	274,548	376,121	438,171	581,212	714,270
Monetary authorities	8 715 ..	....	....	....	1,080	1,000	790	763	....
of which: Short-term	8 718 ..	....	....	....	*1,080*	*1,000*	*790*	*763*	....
General government	8 719 ..	....	....	....	....	....	....	....	....
of which: Short-term	8 721 ..	....	....	....	....	....	....	....	....
Banks	8 722 ..	....	84,866	82,890	104,227	142,709	160,956	214,866	248,960
of which: Short-term	8 724 ..	....	*29,450*	*20,986*	*22,252*	*36,564*	*51,693*	*77,212*	*49,683*
Other sectors	8 725 ..	....	80,124	107,714	169,242	232,412	276,425	365,583	465,310
of which: Short-term	8 727 ..	....	*25,200*	*33,736*	*38,385*	*34,738*	*39,731*	*48,614*	*72,667*
Currency and deposits	8 730 ..	....	43,977	82,200	114,391	134,611	164,245	223,536	347,972
Monetary authorities	8 731 ..	....	257	999	1,920	1,801	1,948	3,435	1,038
General government	8 732 ..	....	3,954	744	928	1,429	1,430	1,192	183
Banks	8 733 ..	....	24,325	56,619	85,491	100,142	132,714	189,011	308,642
Other sectors	8 734 ..	....	15,440	23,838	26,052	31,240	28,154	29,899	38,110
Other assets	8 736 ..	....	20,195	25,202	27,278	26,670	50,010	66,863	75,101
Monetary authorities	8 737 ..	....	412	490	590	776	672	735	811
of which: Short-term	8 739 ..	....	*412*	*490*	*590*	*776*	*672*	*735*	*811*
General government	8 740 ..	....	....	....	....	....	....	....	....
of which: Short-term	8 742 ..	....	....	....	....	....	....	....	....
Banks	8 743 ..	....	8,183	10,074	8,650	3,757	8,352	10,161	13,470
of which: Short-term	8 745 ..	....	*8,018*	*9,755*	....	....	....	....	....
Other sectors	8 746 ..	....	11,601	14,639	18,038	22,137	40,985	55,967	60,820
of which: Short-term	8 748 ..	....	*4,310*	*6,814*	*7,483*	*8,228*	*8,850*	*19,528*	*17,366*
Reserve assets	8 802 ..	....	5,641	5,481	4,159	2,914	879	843	940
Monetary gold	8 812 ..	....	54	66	81	84	99	122	162
Special drawing rights	8 811 ..	48	55	66	79	89	88	95	101
Reserve position in the Fund	8 810 ..	329	336	469	575	418	176	131	87
Foreign exchange	8 803 ..	....	5,196	4,880	3,425	2,322	516	494	590
Other claims	8 813 ..	....	....	....	....	....	....	....	....

Table 3 (Concluded). INTERNATIONAL INVESTMENT POSITION (End-period stocks), 2000–2007

(Millions of U.S. dollars)

	Code	2000	2001	2002	2003	2004	2005	2006	2007
LIABILITIES	8 995 D.	....	764,959	996,758	1,399,964	1,794,149	2,030,767	2,652,430	3,384,243
Direct investment in Ireland	8 555	....	134,052	182,899	222,837	207,648	163,530	156,591	193,452
Equity capital and reinvested earnings	8 556	....	129,339	176,270	224,902	228,371	217,604	225,347	264,603
Claims on direct investors	8 557	....	....	....	....	....	....	....	....
Liabilities to direct investors	8 558	....	....	....	224,902	228,371	217,604	225,347	264,603
Other capital	8 580	....	4,713	6,629	−2,065	−20,723	−54,074	−68,755	−71,151
Claims on direct investors	8 585	....	−46,409	−65,462	−109,438	−157,125	−229,837	−272,840	−319,275
Liabilities to direct investors	8 590	....	51,122	72,091	107,373	136,402	175,764	204,085	248,124
Portfolio investment	8 652	....	363,168	468,835	684,799	982,009	1,210,257	1,612,174	1,955,218
Equity securities	8 660	....	279,225	343,771	481,712	613,830	712,330	951,735	1,147,707
Banks	8 663	....	102,403	169,822	201,419	257,536	277,517	377,673	470,033
Other sectors	8 664	....	176,822	173,949	280,293	356,294	434,813	574,062	677,674
Debt securities	8 669	....	83,943	125,064	203,087	368,178	497,927	660,439	807,512
Bonds and notes	8 670	....	44,414	77,389	149,495	286,034	376,389	526,084	651,292
Monetary authorities	8 671	....	....	....	....	....	....	....	....
General government	8 672	....	16,283	18,219	27,043	34,279	31,677	35,716	42,984
Banks	8 673	....	15,119	20,302	42,132	93,311	125,108	180,267	199,919
Other sectors	8 674	....	13,012	38,868	80,319	158,445	219,604	310,101	408,390
Money market instruments	8 680	....	39,529	47,675	53,592	82,144	121,537	134,355	156,219
Monetary authorities	8 681	....	....	....	....	....	....	....	....
General government	8 682	....	5,057	4,454	2,516	278	....	....	867
Banks	8 683	....	30,058	32,852	34,678	56,328	86,303	102,676	128,030
Other sectors	8 684	....	4,414	10,370	16,398	25,538	35,234	31,679	27,322
Financial derivatives	8 905	....	2,944	....	....	....	2,895	....	42,897
Monetary authorities	8 906	....	....	....	....	....	....	....	....
General government	8 907	....	....	....	....	....	....	....	....
Banks	8 908	....	....	....	....	....	....	....	39,932
Other sectors	8 909	....	....	....	....	....	....	....	2,965
Other investment	8 753	....	264,795	345,024	....	....	654,086	....	1,192,676
Trade credits	8 756	....	10,059	12,607	17,856	18,233	20,002	28,641	33,315
General government	8 757	....	....	....	....	....	....	....	....
of which: Short-term	8 759	....	....	....	....	....	....	....	....
Other sectors	8 760	....	10,059	12,607	17,856	18,233	20,002	28,641	33,315
of which: Short-term	8 762	....	*10,059*	*12,607*	*17,856*	*18,233*	*20,002*	*28,641*	*33,315*
Loans	8 764	....	164,618	207,196	284,347	318,628	357,843	504,568	485,780
Monetary authorities	8 765	....	....	....	....	....	....	....	....
of which: Use of Fund credit and loans from the Fund	8 766	....	....	....	....	....	....	....	....
of which: Short-term	8 768	....	....	....	....	....	....	....	....
General government	8 769	....	501	541	318	385	158	209	542
of which: Short-term	8 771	....	*88*	*215*	*63*	*196*	....	....	*368*
Banks	8 772	....	93,886	128,395	188,539	214,671	243,911	357,523	272,840
of which: Short-term	8 774	....	*75,974*	*100,044*	*139,214*	*186,172*	*201,949*	*264,002*	*215,508*
Other sectors	8 775	....	70,232	78,259	95,489	103,571	113,774	146,835	212,398
of which: Short-term	8 777	....	*29,473*	*41,971*	*50,184*	*49,590*	*51,016*	*58,514*	*99,384*
Currency and deposits	8 780	....	65,554	83,263	128,160	187,605	204,706	242,212	539,744
Monetary authorities	8 781	....	4,506	3,766	13,059	9,100	5,319	3,352	876
General government	8 782	....	....	....	....	....	....	....	....
Banks	8 783	....	57,047	76,159	112,814	174,076	196,724	236,064	536,937
Other sectors	8 784	....	4,001	3,338	2,287	4,428	2,663	2,796	1,931
Other liabilities	8 786	....	24,564	....	....	....	71,535	....	133,837
Monetary authorities	8 787	....	129	139	141	157	137	144	135
of which: Short-term	8 789	....	....	*139*	*141*	*157*	*137*	*144*	*135*
General government	8 790	....	....	....	....	....	....	....	....
of which: Short-term	8 792	....	....	....	....	....	....	....	....
Banks	8 793	....	2,494	....	....	....	....	....	13,038
of which: Short-term	8 795	....	....	....	....	....	....	....	*13,038*
Other sectors	8 796	....	21,942	35,486	50,774	63,079	....	93,674	120,664
of which: Short-term	8 798	....	*21,942*	*35,486*	*50,774*	*63,079*	....	*93,674*	*120,664*
NET INTERNATIONAL INVESTMENT POSITION	8 995	....	−15,726	−24,571	−35,557	−36,654	−47,173	−14,682	−46,289
Conversion rates: euros per U.S. dollar (end of period)	0 104	1.0747	1.1347	.9536	.7918	.7342	.8477	.7593	.6793

Table 1. ANALYTIC PRESENTATION, 2000–2007

(Millions of U.S. dollars)

	Code	2000	2001	2002	2003	2004	2005	2006	2007
A. Current Account[1]	4 993 Z.	**−996**	**−1,287**	**−928**	**1,323**	**2,659**	**3,980**	**8,078**	**4,523**
Goods: exports f.o.b.	2 100 ..	30,864	27,663	27,244	29,918	36,329	39,722	43,278	49,779
Goods: imports f.o.b.	3 100 ..	−34,728	−31,713	−31,971	−33,294	−39,488	−43,868	−47,125	−55,789
Balance on Goods	4 100 ..	*−3,864*	*−4,050*	*−4,727*	*−3,376*	*−3,159*	*−4,147*	*−3,847*	*−6,010*
Services: credit	2 200 ..	15,402	12,852	12,186	13,661	16,035	17,447	19,248	21,122
Services: debit	3 200 ..	−11,901	−11,846	−10,902	−11,201	−12,822	−13,715	−14,866	−17,842
Balance on Goods and Services	4 991 ..	*−363*	*−3,043*	*−3,443*	*−916*	*54*	*−415*	*536*	*−2,730*
Income: credit	2 300 ..	3,630	2,730	2,458	2,814	3,004	5,600	8,419	10,486
Income: debit	3 300 ..	−10,732	−7,632	−6,727	−6,986	−6,675	−7,177	−8,334	−10,511
Balance on Goods, Services, and Income	4 992 ..	*−7,465*	*−7,945*	*−7,713*	*−5,088*	*−3,618*	*−1,992*	*621*	*−2,755*
Current transfers: credit	2 379 Z.	7,466	7,790	8,165	7,556	7,358	7,010	8,575	8,549
Current transfers: debit	3 379 ..	−996	−1,132	−1,380	−1,145	−1,081	−1,038	−1,117	−1,270
B. Capital Account[1]	4 994 Z.	**465**	**720**	**207**	**534**	**667**	**727**	**786**	**782**
Capital account: credit	2 994 Z.	465	720	207	534	667	727	786	782
Capital account: debit	3 994 ..	....	....	....	....	....	....	....	....
Total, Groups A Plus B	4 981 ..	*−530*	*−567*	*−721*	*1,857*	*3,326*	*4,706*	*8,865*	*5,306*
C. Financial Account[1]	4 995 W.	**528**	**391**	**−139**	**−3,758**	**−7,399**	**−6,856**	**−12,825**	**−1,928**
Direct investment abroad	4 505 ..	−3,317	−677	−960	−2,124	−4,547	−2,967	−15,078	−7,047
Direct investment in Israel	4 555 Z.	5,269	3,562	1,611	3,342	2,354	4,301	14,305	9,664
Portfolio investment assets	4 602 ..	−3,312	−1,246	−2,645	−3,247	−2,856	−7,969	−8,054	−4,028
Equity securities	4 610 ..	−1,972	−38	−50	−1,054	−1,152	−3,374	−3,873	−2,199
Debt securities	4 619 ..	−1,340	−1,208	−2,595	−2,193	−1,704	−4,595	−4,180	−1,829
Portfolio investment liabilities	4 652 Z.	3,967	812	1,506	−80	3,549	3,771	4,551	4,282
Equity securities	4 660 ..	3,960	819	1,481	−250	3,661	3,713	4,480	4,306
Debt securities	4 669 Z.	7	−7	25	170	−113	58	71	−24
Financial derivatives	4 910 ..	....	8	−10	14	50	35	−66	20
Financial derivatives assets	4 900 ..	....	....	....	....	....	....	....	....
Financial derivatives liabilities	4 905 ..	....	8	−10	14	50	35	−66	20
Other investment assets	4 703 ..	−4,131	−2,795	−1,217	−1,603	−6,283	−4,924	−10,648	−7,396
Monetary authorities	4 701 ..	....	....	....	....	....	....	....	....
General government	4 704 ..	−1	−561	110	−13	13	1,305	206	−180
Banks	4 705 ..	−1,189	−392	340	−1,255	−3,658	−4,718	−7,153	837
Other sectors	4 728 ..	−2,941	−1,843	−1,667	−335	−2,639	−1,512	−3,700	−8,053
Other investment liabilities	4 753 W.	2,052	728	1,577	−60	335	899	2,166	2,577
Monetary authorities	4 753 WA	....	....	....	....	....	....	....	....
General government	4 753 ZB	40	197	100	30	−120	−432	−497	−371
Banks	4 753 ZC	1,644	1,317	117	−558	−1,120	−132	1,216	993
Other sectors	4 753 ZD	368	−786	1,360	469	1,575	1,464	1,446	1,954
Total, Groups A Through C	4 983 ..	*−2*	*−176*	*−859*	*−1,901*	*−4,073*	*−2,150*	*−3,960*	*3,377*
D. Net Errors and Omissions	4 998 ..	**302**	**385**	**−166**	**1,858**	**1,111**	**3,769**	**−172**	**−2,942**
Total, Groups A Through D	4 984 ..	*300*	*209*	*−1,026*	*−43*	*−2,962*	*1,619*	*−4,132*	*436*
E. Reserves and Related Items	4 802 A.	**−300**	**−209**	**1,026**	**43**	**2,962**	**−1,619**	**4,132**	**−436**
Reserve assets	4 802 ..	−945	104	801	−1,085	−282	−2,041	−425	1,686
Use of Fund credit and loans	4 766 ..	....	....	....	....	....	....	....	....
Exceptional financing	4 920 ..	645	−313	224	1,128	3,244	422	4,557	−2,122
Conversion rates: new sheqalim per U.S. dollar	0 101 ..	**4.0773**	**4.2057**	**4.7378**	**4.5541**	**4.4820**	**4.4877**	**4.4558**	**4.1081**

[1] Excludes components that have been classified in the categories of Group E.

Table 2. STANDARD PRESENTATION, 2000–2007

(Millions of U.S. dollars)

	Code	2000	2001	2002	2003	2004	2005	2006	2007
CURRENT ACCOUNT............................	4 993 ..	**−996**	**−1,287**	**−928**	**1,323**	**2,659**	**3,980**	**8,078**	**4,523**
A. GOODS............................	4 100 ..	**−3,864**	**−4,050**	**−4,727**	**−3,376**	**−3,159**	**−4,147**	**−3,847**	**−6,010**
Credit............................	2 100 ..	**30,864**	**27,663**	**27,244**	**29,918**	**36,329**	**39,722**	**43,278**	**49,779**
General merchandise: exports f.o.b.	2 110 ..	30,643	27,587	27,146	29,792	36,222	39,605	43,200	49,559
Goods for processing: exports f.o.b.	2 150 ..	....	....	....	....	....	....	....	....
Repairs on goods............................	2 160 ..	....	....	....	....	....	....	....	....
Goods procured in ports by carriers............	2 170 ..	221	77	98	126	107	116	78	220
Nonmonetary gold............................	2 180 ..	....	....	....	....	....	....	....	....
Debit............................	3 100 ..	**−34,728**	**−31,713**	**−31,971**	**−33,294**	**−39,488**	**−43,868**	**−47,125**	**−55,789**
General merchandise: imports f.o.b.	3 110 ..	−34,444	−31,461	−31,731	−32,979	−39,088	−43,305	−46,402	−54,922
Goods for processing: imports f.o.b.	3 150 ..	....	....	....	....	....	....	....	....
Repairs on goods............................	3 160 ..	....	....	....	....	....	....	....	....
Goods procured in ports by carriers............	3 170 ..	−284	−252	−240	−315	−400	−563	−723	−867
Nonmonetary gold............................	3 180 ..	....	....	....	....	....	....	....	....
B. SERVICES............................	4 200 ..	**3,501**	**1,006**	**1,284**	**2,460**	**3,213**	**3,732**	**4,382**	**3,280**
Total credit............................	2 200 ..	*15,402*	*12,852*	*12,186*	*13,661*	*16,035*	*17,447*	*19,248*	*21,122*
Total debit............................	3 200 ..	*−11,901*	*−11,846*	*−10,902*	*−11,201*	*−12,822*	*−13,715*	*−14,866*	*−17,842*
Transportation services, credit............	2 205 ..	**2,479**	**2,121**	**2,120**	**2,597**	**3,199**	**3,685**	**3,701**	**4,489**
Passenger............................	2 850 ..	*497*	*294*	*281*	*341*	*432*	*561*	*540*	*653*
Freight............................	2 851 ..	*1,632*	*1,518*	*1,520*	*1,899*	*2,374*	*2,680*	*2,685*	*3,335*
Other............................	2 852 ..	*350*	*309*	*319*	*358*	*393*	*444*	*476*	*501*
Sea transport, passenger............	2 207 ..	....	....	....	....	....	....	....	....
Sea transport, freight............	2 208 ..	1,477	1,398	1,394	1,752	2,172	2,477	2,467	3,120
Sea transport, other............	2 209 ..	200	172	184	217	249	289	319	325
Air transport, passenger............	2 211 ..	497	294	281	341	432	561	540	653
Air transport, freight............	2 212 ..	155	120	126	147	202	203	218	215
Air transport, other............	2 213 ..	116	113	114	114	117	125	129	134
Other transport, passenger............	2 215 ..	....	....	....	....	....	....	....	....
Other transport, freight............	2 216 ..	....	....	....	....	....	....	....	....
Other transport, other............	2 217 ..	34	24	21	27	27	31	28	42
Transportation services, debit............	3 205 ..	**−4,218**	**−3,738**	**−3,458**	**−3,730**	**−4,347**	**−4,711**	**−4,785**	**−5,815**
Passenger............................	3 850 ..	*−929*	*−942*	*−779*	*−791*	*−867*	*−885*	*−887*	*−990*
Freight............................	3 851 ..	*−1,365*	*−1,179*	*−1,043*	*−1,038*	*−1,205*	*−1,293*	*−1,401*	*−1,682*
Other............................	3 852 ..	*−1,924*	*−1,616*	*−1,635*	*−1,901*	*−2,276*	*−2,533*	*−2,497*	*−3,143*
Sea transport, passenger............	3 207 ..	−7	−7	−7	−7	−8	−8	−8	−9
Sea transport, freight............	3 208 ..	−1,220	−1,038	−900	−896	−1,056	−1,121	−1,200	−1,430
Sea transport, other............	3 209 ..	−1,488	−1,262	−1,285	−1,544	−1,845	−2,055	−2,114	−2,743
Air transport, passenger............	3 211 ..	−922	−935	−773	−785	−859	−877	−879	−982
Air transport, freight............	3 212 ..	−145	−141	−143	−142	−149	−173	−201	−252
Air transport, other............	3 213 ..	−422	−346	−345	−352	−423	−461	−367	−380
Other transport, passenger............	3 215 ..	....	....	....	....	....	....	....	....
Other transport, freight............	3 216 ..	....	....	....	....	....	....	....	....
Other transport, other............	3 217 ..	−14	−9	−5	−5	−8	−16	−17	−20
Travel, credit............................	2 236 ..	**4,114**	**2,560**	**2,145**	**2,132**	**2,430**	**2,797**	**2,776**	**3,059**
Business travel............................	2 237 ..	....	....	....	....	....	....	....	....
Personal travel............................	2 240 ..	....	....	....	....	....	....	....	....
Travel, debit............................	3 236 ..	**−2,804**	**−2,945**	**−2,543**	**−2,550**	**−2,796**	**−2,895**	**−2,983**	**−3,260**
Business travel............................	3 237 ..	....	....	....	....	....	....	....	....
Personal travel............................	3 240 ..	....	....	....	....	....	....	....	....
Other services, credit............................	2 200 BA	**8,809**	**8,171**	**7,921**	**8,932**	**10,407**	**10,966**	**12,771**	**13,574**
Communications............................	2 245 ..	176	139	138	171	147	161	221	221
Construction............................	2 249 ..	182	224	216	249	325	348	509	665
Insurance............................	2 253 ..	17	13	15	16	15	16	20	24
Financial............................	2 260 ..	....	....	....	....	....	....	....	....
Computer and information............	2 262 ..	4,246	3,471	4,180	3,409	4,407	4,529	5,289	5,809
Royalties and licence fees............	2 266 ..	496	425	420	425	505	574	593	784
Other business services............	2 268 ..	3,610	3,857	2,926	4,623	4,979	5,296	6,100	6,040
Personal, cultural, and recreational............	2 287 ..	....	....	....	....	....	....	....	....
Government, n.i.e.	2 291 ..	83	41	27	39	31	42	38	31
Other services, debit............................	3 200 BA	**−4,880**	**−5,163**	**−4,902**	**−4,921**	**−5,679**	**−6,110**	**−7,098**	**−8,767**
Communications............................	3 245 ..	−232	−214	−261	−204	−242	−211	−318	−346
Construction............................	3 249 ..	....	....	....	....	....	....	....	....
Insurance............................	3 253 ..	−330	−313	−380	−435	−435	−412	−413	−393
Financial............................	3 260 ..	....	....	....	....	....	....	....	....
Computer and information............	3 262 ..	....	....	....	....	....	....	....	....
Royalties and licence fees............	3 266 ..	−361	−460	−462	−433	−491	−542	−681	−946
Other business services............	3 268 ..	−3,760	−3,975	−3,598	−3,625	−4,301	−4,727	−5,457	−6,828
Personal, cultural, and recreational............	3 287 ..	....	....	....	....	....	....	....	....
Government, n.i.e.	3 291 ..	−198	−202	−201	−224	−211	−218	−230	−255

Table 2 (Continued). STANDARD PRESENTATION, 2000–2007

(Millions of U.S. dollars)

	Code	2000	2001	2002	2003	2004	2005	2006	2007
C. INCOME	4 300	−7,102	−4,902	−4,270	−4,172	−3,672	−1,578	85	−25
Total credit	2 300	*3,630*	*2,730*	*2,458*	*2,814*	*3,004*	*5,600*	*8,419*	*10,486*
Total debit	3 300	*−10,732*	*−7,632*	*−6,727*	*−6,986*	*−6,675*	*−7,177*	*−8,334*	*−10,511*
Compensation of employees, credit	2 310	182	196	167	171	298	377	463	546
Compensation of employees, debit	3 310	−3,255	−3,039	−2,781	−2,502	−2,218	−2,206	−2,334	−2,770
Investment income, credit	2 320	3,447	2,534	2,291	2,643	2,706	5,223	7,956	9,940
Direct investment income	2 330	597	−80	327	1,158	1,119	2,335	3,310	4,076
Dividends and distributed branch profits	2 332	348	314	410	732	495	760	1,349	1,395
Reinvested earnings and undistributed branch profits	2 333	16	−599	−226	314	476	1,311	1,513	2,041
Income on debt (interest)	2 334	234	205	142	112	148	264	449	641
Portfolio investment income	2 339	364	302	322	401	443	887	1,522	1,796
Income on equity	2 340	114	107	138	255	186	310	566	662
Income on bonds and notes	2 350	250	196	184	146	257	577	955	1,134
Income on money market instruments	2 360	....	....	....	....	....	....	....	....
Other investment income	2 370	2,486	2,312	1,642	1,084	1,144	2,000	3,124	4,068
Investment income, debit	3 320	−7,477	−4,593	−3,947	−4,484	−4,457	−4,972	−6,000	−7,741
Direct investment income	3 330	−2,478	−904	−776	−1,355	−1,300	−770	−1,736	−2,888
Dividends and distributed branch profits	3 332	−645	−180	−351	−522	−461	−858	−552	−726
Reinvested earnings and undistributed branch profits	3 333	−1,678	−601	−350	−773	−757	239	−960	−1,895
Income on debt (interest)	3 334	−155	−124	−75	−60	−82	−151	−224	−267
Portfolio investment income	3 339	−2,539	−1,521	−1,540	−1,746	−1,875	−2,595	−2,156	−2,596
Income on equity	3 340	−1,198	−197	−245	−434	−380	−1,026	−476	−845
Income on bonds and notes	3 350	−1,341	−1,324	−1,295	−1,312	−1,495	−1,569	−1,680	−1,751
Income on money market instruments	3 360	....	....	....	....	....	....	....	....
Other investment income	3 370	−2,459	−2,168	−1,631	−1,384	−1,282	−1,607	−2,108	−2,257
D. CURRENT TRANSFERS	4 379	6,470	6,658	6,785	6,411	6,277	5,972	7,458	7,278
Credit	2 379	7,466	7,790	8,165	7,556	7,358	7,010	8,575	8,549
General government	2 380	4,410	4,359	4,506	4,200	3,590	3,325	4,535	3,989
Other sectors	2 390	3,056	3,431	3,659	3,356	3,768	3,685	4,040	4,560
Workers' remittances	2 391	....	....	....	....	....	....	....	....
Other current transfers	2 392	3,056	3,431	3,659	3,356	3,768	3,685	4,040	4,560
Debit	3 379	−996	−1,132	−1,380	−1,145	−1,081	−1,038	−1,117	−1,270
General government	3 380	−68	−76	−86	−85	−71	−104	−107	−111
Other sectors	3 390	−928	−1,057	−1,293	−1,060	−1,009	−934	−1,010	−1,160
Workers' remittances	3 391	....	....	....	....	....	....	....	....
Other current transfers	3 392	−928	−1,057	−1,293	−1,060	−1,009	−934	−1,010	−1,160
CAPITAL AND FINANCIAL ACCOUNT	4 996	694	902	1,094	−3,180	−3,770	−7,748	−7,906	−1,582
CAPITAL ACCOUNT	4 994	465	720	207	534	667	727	786	782
Total credit	2 994	*465*	*720*	*207*	*534*	*667*	*727*	*786*	*782*
Total debit	3 994	....	....	....	....	....	....	....	....
Capital transfers, credit	2 400	465	720	207	534	667	727	786	782
General government	2 401	160	162	−120	191	173	163	203	182
Debt forgiveness	2 402	....	....	....	....	....	....	....	....
Other capital transfers	2 410	160	162	−120	191	173	163	203	182
Other sectors	2 430	305	558	327	344	494	564	584	601
Migrants' transfers	2 431	218	303	243	252	417	473	481	495
Debt forgiveness	2 432	....	....	....	....	....	....	....	....
Other capital transfers	2 440	87	255	84	92	77	91	102	106
Capital transfers, debit	3 400	....	....	....	....	....	....	....	....
General government	3 401	....	....	....	....	....	....	....	....
Debt forgiveness	3 402	....	....	....	....	....	....	....	....
Other capital transfers	3 410	....	....	....	....	....	....	....	....
Other sectors	3 430	....	....	....	....	....	....	....	....
Migrants' transfers	3 431	....	....	....	....	....	....	....	....
Debt forgiveness	3 432	....	....	....	....	....	....	....	....
Other capital transfers	3 440	....	....	....	....	....	....	....	....
Nonproduced nonfinancial assets, credit	2 480	....	....	....	....	....	....	....	....
Nonproduced nonfinancial assets, debit	3 480	....	....	....	....	....	....	....	....

Table 2 (Continued). STANDARD PRESENTATION, 2000–2007

(Millions of U.S. dollars)

	Code	2000	2001	2002	2003	2004	2005	2006	2007
FINANCIAL ACCOUNT	4 995	228	182	887	−3,715	−4,437	−8,475	−8,693	−2,364
A. DIRECT INVESTMENT	4 500	1,952	2,885	651	1,218	−2,193	1,333	−774	2,618
Direct investment abroad	4 505	−3,317	−677	−960	−2,124	−4,547	−2,967	−15,078	−7,047
Equity capital	4 510	−2,538	−598	−277	−848	−3,687	−1,457	−11,019	−3,266
Claims on affiliated enterprises	4 515	....	....	....	....	....	....	....	....
Liabilities to affiliated enterprises	4 520	....	....	....	....	....	....	....	....
Reinvested earnings	4 525	−16	599	226	−314	−476	−1,311	−1,513	−2,041
Other capital	4 530	−763	−678	−909	−962	−384	−200	−2,546	−1,741
Claims on affiliated enterprises	4 535	....	....	....	....	....	....	....	....
Liabilities to affiliated enterprises	4 540	....	....	....	....	....	....	....	....
Direct investment in Israel	4 555	5,269	3,562	1,611	3,342	2,354	4,301	14,305	9,664
Equity capital	4 560	2,879	2,915	1,364	2,413	1,104	4,434	12,695	7,490
Claims on direct investors	4 565	....	....	....	....	....	....	....	....
Liabilities to direct investors	4 570	....	....	....	....	....	....	....	....
Reinvested earnings	4 575	1,678	601	350	773	757	−239	960	1,895
Other capital	4 580	712	47	−103	157	492	105	650	279
Claims on direct investors	4 585	....	....	....	....	....	....	....	....
Liabilities to direct investors	4 590	712	47	−103	157	492	105	650	279
B. PORTFOLIO INVESTMENT	4 600	1,300	−747	−915	−2,199	3,937	−3,776	1,054	−1,868
Assets	4 602	−3,312	−1,246	−2,645	−3,247	−2,856	−7,969	−8,054	−4,028
Equity securities	4 610	−1,972	−38	−50	−1,054	−1,152	−3,374	−3,873	−2,199
Monetary authorities	4 611	....	....	....	....	....	....	....	....
General government	4 612	....	....	....	....	....	....	....	....
Banks	4 613	....	....	....	....	....	....	....	....
Other sectors	4 614	−1,972	−38	−50	−1,054	−1,152	−3,374	−3,873	−2,199
Debt securities	4 619	−1,340	−1,208	−2,595	−2,193	−1,704	−4,595	−4,180	−1,829
Bonds and notes	4 620	−1,340	−1,208	−2,595	−2,193	−1,704	−4,595	−4,180	−1,829
Monetary authorities	4 621	....	....	....	....	....	....	....	....
General government	4 622	19	17	15	13	11	10	8	8
Banks	4 623	−402	357	247	−518	167	−1,555	−1,342	−1,156
Other sectors	4 624	−957	−1,581	−2,856	−1,687	−1,883	−3,050	−2,847	−681
Money market instruments	4 630	....	....	....	....	....	....	....	....
Monetary authorities	4 631	....	....	....	....	....	....	....	....
General government	4 632	....	....	....	....	....	....	....	....
Banks	4 633	....	....	....	....	....	....	....	....
Other sectors	4 634	....	....	....	....	....	....	....	....
Liabilities	4 652	4,612	499	1,730	1,048	6,793	4,193	9,108	2,160
Equity securities	4 660	3,960	819	1,481	−250	3,661	3,713	4,480	4,306
Banks	4 663	....	....	....	....	....	....	....	....
Other sectors	4 664	3,960	819	1,481	−250	3,661	3,713	4,480	4,306
Debt securities	4 669	652	−320	249	1,298	3,132	480	4,628	−2,146
Bonds and notes	4 670	652	−320	249	1,298	3,132	480	4,628	−2,146
Monetary authorities	4 671	7	−7	25	170	−113	58	71	−24
General government	4 672	−110	−555	87	1,863	1,569	714	2,299	−1,523
Banks	4 673	....	....	....	....	....	....	....	....
Other sectors	4 674	755	243	137	−735	1,676	−292	2,258	−599
Money market instruments	4 680	....	....	....	....	....	....	....	....
Monetary authorities	4 681	....	....	....	....	....	....	....	....
General government	4 682	....	....	....	....	....	....	....	....
Banks	4 683	....	....	....	....	....	....	....	....
Other sectors	4 684	....	....	....	....	....	....	....	....
C. FINANCIAL DERIVATIVES	4 910	....	8	−10	14	50	35	−66	20
Monetary authorities	4 911	....	....	....	....	....	....	....	....
General government	4 912	....	....	....	....	....	....	....	....
Banks	4 913	....	....	....	....	....	....	....	....
Other sectors	4 914	....	8	−10	14	50	35	−66	20
Assets	4 900	....	....	....	....	....	....	....	....
Monetary authorities	4 901	....	....	....	....	....	....	....	....
General government	4 902	....	....	....	....	....	....	....	....
Banks	4 903	....	....	....	....	....	....	....	....
Other sectors	4 904	....	....	....	....	....	....	....	....
Liabilities	4 905	....	8	−10	14	50	35	−66	20
Monetary authorities	4 906	....	....	....	....	....	....	....	....
General government	4 907	....	....	....	....	....	....	....	....
Banks	4 908	....	....	....	....	....	....	....	....
Other sectors	4 909	....	8	−10	14	50	35	−66	20

Table 2 (Concluded). STANDARD PRESENTATION, 2000–2007

(Millions of U.S. dollars)

	Code	2000	2001	2002	2003	2004	2005	2006	2007
D. OTHER INVESTMENT	4 700 ..	**−2,079**	**−2,068**	**360**	**−1,662**	**−5,948**	**−4,025**	**−8,482**	**−4,819**
Assets	4 703 ..	**−4,131**	**−2,795**	**−1,217**	**−1,603**	**−6,283**	**−4,924**	**−10,648**	**−7,396**
Trade credits	4 706 ..	−1,532	1,027	116	−594	−1,461	665	−1,364	−2,615
General government	4 707 ..	....	....	....	−153	−71	11	11	11
of which: Short-term	4 709 ..	....	....	....	....	....	....	....	....
Other sectors	4 710 ..	−1,532	1,027	116	−441	−1,390	654	−1,375	−2,626
of which: Short-term	4 712 ..	*−1,532*	*1,027*	*116*	*−441*	*−1,390*	*654*	*−1,375*	*−2,626*
Loans	4 714 ..	−788	−1,266	517	507	610	−686	−888	−98
Monetary authorities	4 715 ..	....	....	....	....	....	....	....	....
of which: Short-term	4 718 ..	....	....	....	....	....	....	....	....
General government	4 719 ..	....	....	....	....	....	....	....	....
of which: Short-term	4 721 ..	....	....	....	....	....	....	....	....
Banks	4 722 ..	−788	−1,266	517	507	610	−686	−888	−98
of which: Short-term	4 724 ..	*−788*	*−1,266*	*517*	*507*	*610*	*−686*	*−888*	*−98*
Other sectors	4 725 ..	....	....	....	....	....	....	....	....
of which: Short-term	4 727 ..	....	....	....	....	....	....	....	....
Currency and deposits	4 730 ..	−1,855	−1,937	−1,892	−1,590	−5,551	−6,004	−7,747	−3,260
Monetary authorities	4 731 ..	....	....	....	....	....	....	....	....
General government	4 732 ..	....	....	....	....	....	....	....	....
Banks	4 733 ..	−401	874	−177	−1,762	−4,267	−4,032	−6,265	936
Other sectors	4 734 ..	−1,454	−2,811	−1,715	172	−1,284	−1,972	−1,482	−4,196
Other assets	4 736 ..	44	−621	42	75	120	1,101	−649	−1,422
Monetary authorities	4 737 ..	....	....	....	....	....	....	....	....
of which: Short-term	4 739 ..	....	....	....	....	....	....	....	....
General government	4 740 ..	−1	−561	110	140	84	1,295	195	−191
of which: Short-term	4 742 ..	*−1*	*−561*	*110*	*140*	*84*	*1,295*	*195*	*−191*
Banks	4 743 ..	....	....	....	....	....	....	....	....
of which: Short-term	4 745 ..	....	....	....	....	....	....	....	....
Other sectors	4 746 ..	46	−60	−69	−65	35	−194	−844	−1,231
of which: Short-term	4 748 ..	*46*	*−60*	*−38*	*−28*	*80*	*73*	*67*	*142*
Liabilities	4 753 ..	**2,052**	**728**	**1,577**	**−60**	**335**	**899**	**2,166**	**2,577**
Trade credits	4 756 ..	474	−822	−183	433	880	958	650	1,732
General government	4 757 ..	....	....	....	....	....	....	....	....
of which: Short-term	4 759 ..	....	....	....	....	....	....	....	....
Other sectors	4 760 ..	474	−822	−183	433	880	958	650	1,732
of which: Short-term	4 762 ..	*474*	*−822*	*−183*	*433*	*880*	*958*	*650*	*1,732*
Loans	4 764 ..	−66	232	1,643	65	575	73	300	−149
Monetary authorities	4 765 ..	....	....	....	....	....	....	....	....
of which: Use of Fund credit and loans from the Fund	4 766 ..	....	....	....	....	....	....	....	....
of which: Short-term	4 768 ..	....	....	....	....	....	....	....	....
General government	4 769 ..	40	197	100	30	−120	−432	−497	−371
of which: Short-term	4 771 ..	....	....	25	....	−25	....	....	....
Banks	4 772 ..	....	....	....	....	....	....	....	....
of which: Short-term	4 774 ..	....	....	....	....	....	....	....	....
Other sectors	4 775 ..	−106	35	1,543	36	695	506	797	222
of which: Short-term	4 777 ..	*41*	*−37*	*103*	*−171*	*−114*	*220*	*226*	*−400*
Currency and deposits	4 780 ..	1,644	1,317	117	−558	−1,120	−132	1,216	993
Monetary authorities	4 781 ..	....	....	....	....	....	....	....	....
General government	4 782 ..	....	....	....	....	....	....	....	....
Banks	4 783 ..	1,644	1,317	117	−558	−1,120	−132	1,216	993
Other sectors	4 784 ..	....	....	....	....	....	....	....	....
Other liabilities	4 786 ..	....	....	....	....	....	....	....	....
Monetary authorities	4 787 ..	....	....	....	....	....	....	....	....
of which: Short-term	4 789 ..	....	....	....	....	....	....	....	....
General government	4 790 ..	....	....	....	....	....	....	....	....
of which: Short-term	4 792 ..	....	....	....	....	....	....	....	....
Banks	4 793 ..	....	....	....	....	....	....	....	....
of which: Short-term	4 795 ..	....	....	....	....	....	....	....	....
Other sectors	4 796 ..	....	....	....	....	....	....	....	....
of which: Short-term	4 798 ..	....	....	....	....	....	....	....	....
E. RESERVE ASSETS	4 802 ..	**−945**	**104**	**801**	**−1,085**	**−282**	**−2,041**	**−425**	**1,686**
Monetary gold	4 812 ..	....	....	....	....	....	....	....	....
Special drawing rights	4 811 ..	−1	−1	−3	−4	−5	−5	....	3
Reserve position in the Fund	4 810 ..	−32	−85	−187	−69	84	229	86	32
Foreign exchange	4 803 ..	−910	192	993	−949	−359	−2,194	−512	1,650
Other claims	4 813 ..	−2	−2	−2	−62	−2	−71	....	....
NET ERRORS AND OMISSIONS	4 998 ..	**302**	**385**	**−166**	**1,858**	**1,111**	**3,769**	**−172**	**−2,942**

Table 3. INTERNATIONAL INVESTMENT POSITION (End-period stocks), 2000–2007

(Millions of U.S. dollars)

	Code	2000	2001	2002	2003	2004	2005	2006	2007
ASSETS	8 995 C.	68,157	72,059	78,057	89,462	105,975	122,877	163,593	188,165
Direct investment abroad	8 505 ..	9,091	9,249	10,319	13,097	18,493	23,010	39,799	47,456
Equity capital and reinvested earnings	8 506 ..	5,522	5,273	6,043	8,560	13,527	17,570	31,427	38,030
Claims on affiliated enterprises	8 507 ..	5,522	5,273	6,043	8,560	13,527	17,570	31,427	38,030
Liabilities to affiliated enterprises	8 508 ..	....	....	....	....	....	....	....	....
Other capital	8 530 ..	3,569	3,976	4,276	4,537	4,966	5,440	8,372	9,426
Claims on affiliated enterprises	8 535 ..	3,569	3,976	4,276	4,537	4,966	5,440	8,372	9,426
Liabilities to affiliated enterprises	8 540 ..	....	....	....	....	....	....	....	....
Portfolio investment	8 602 ..	7,420	8,059	10,839	14,980	18,576	26,583	37,135	45,005
Equity securities	8 610 ..	2,517	1,972	1,893	3,513	5,003	8,663	14,123	17,868
Monetary authorities	8 611 ..	....	....	....	....	....	....	....	....
General government	8 612 ..	....	....	....	....	....	....	....	....
Banks	8 613 ..	....	....	....	....	....	....	....	....
Other sectors	8 614 ..	2,517	1,972	1,893	3,513	5,003	8,663	14,123	17,868
Debt securities	8 619 ..	4,903	6,087	8,947	11,467	13,574	17,920	23,012	27,137
Bonds and notes	8 620 ..	4,903	6,087	8,947	11,467	13,574	17,920	23,012	27,137
Monetary authorities	8 621 ..	....	....	....	....	....	....	....	....
General government	8 622 ..	99	82	67	54	43	33	24	17
Banks	8 623 ..	3,062	2,686	2,465	3,054	2,961	4,339	5,962	7,523
Other sectors	8 624 ..	1,743	3,319	6,415	8,359	10,570	13,548	17,026	19,598
Money market instruments	8 630 ..	....	....	....	....	....	....	....	....
Monetary authorities	8 631 ..	....	....	....	....	....	....	....	....
General government	8 632 ..	....	....	....	....	....	....	....	....
Banks	8 633 ..	....	....	....	....	....	....	....	....
Other sectors	8 634 ..	....	....	....	....	....	....	....	....
Financial derivatives	8 900 ..	....	....	....	....	....	....	....	....
Monetary authorities	8 901 ..	....	....	....	....	....	....	....	....
General government	8 902 ..	....	....	....	....	....	....	....	....
Banks	8 903 ..	....	....	....	....	....	....	....	....
Other sectors	8 904 ..	....	....	....	....	....	....	....	....
Other investment	8 703 ..	28,219	31,223	32,663	34,792	41,527	44,798	57,054	66,720
Trade credits	8 706 ..	6,250	5,190	5,186	5,913	7,456	6,627	8,135	10,916
General government	8 707 ..	....	....	....	153	224	213	202	191
of which: Short-term	8 709 ..	....	....	....	....	....	....	....	....
Other sectors	8 710 ..	6,250	5,190	5,186	5,760	7,232	6,414	7,933	10,725
of which: Short-term	8 712 ..	....	....	....	....	....	....	....	....
Loans	8 714 ..	5,012	6,566	6,262	6,052	5,687	5,945	7,239	7,842
Monetary authorities	8 715 ..	....	....	....	....	....	....	....	....
of which: Short-term	8 718 ..	....	....	....	....	....	....	....	....
General government	8 719 ..	....	....	....	....	....	....	....	....
of which: Short-term	8 721 ..	....	....	....	....	....	....	....	....
Banks	8 722 ..	4,472	5,694	5,221	4,833	4,293	3,866	4,869	5,157
of which: Short-term	8 724 ..	....	....	....	....	....	....	....	....
Other sectors	8 725 ..	540	873	1,040	1,219	1,394	2,079	2,370	2,685
of which: Short-term	8 727 ..	....	....	....	....	....	....	....	....
Currency and deposits	8 730 ..	15,423	17,371	19,199	20,912	26,549	31,684	41,334	44,536
Monetary authorities	8 731 ..	....	....	....	....	....	....	....	....
General government	8 732 ..	....	....	....	....	....	....	....	....
Banks	8 733 ..	8,142	7,194	7,679	9,877	14,424	17,801	24,526	23,979
Other sectors	8 734 ..	7,281	10,177	11,520	11,035	12,125	13,883	16,808	20,557
Other assets	8 736 ..	1,535	2,096	2,016	1,916	1,836	541	346	3,426
Monetary authorities	8 737 ..	....	....	....	....	....	....	....	....
of which: Short-term	8 739 ..	....	....	....	....	....	....	....	....
General government	8 740 ..	1,535	2,096	1,986	1,846	1,761	467	272	343
of which: Short-term	8 742 ..	*1,535*	*2,096*	*1,986*	*1,846*	*1,761*	*467*	*272*	*343*
Banks	8 743 ..	....	....	....	....	....	....	....	....
of which: Short-term	8 745 ..	....	....	....	....	....	....	....	....
Other sectors	8 746 ..	....	....	31	70	75	75	75	3,083
of which: Short-term	8 748 ..	....	....	....	....	....	....	....	....
Reserve assets	8 802 ..	23,426	23,528	24,236	26,593	27,378	28,486	29,605	28,984
Monetary gold	8 812 ..	....	....	....	....	....	....	....	....
Special drawing rights	8 811 ..	1	2	5	9	15	19	19	17
Reserve position in the Fund	8 810 ..	117	198	413	527	463	202	123	96
Foreign exchange	8 803 ..	23,227	23,245	23,734	25,910	26,751	28,046	29,243	28,652
Other claims	8 813 ..	81	83	85	147	149	220	220	220

Table 3 (Concluded). INTERNATIONAL INVESTMENT POSITION (End-period stocks), 2000–2007

(Millions of U.S. dollars)

	Code	2000	2001	2002	2003	2004	2005	2006	2007
LIABILITIES	8 995 D.	**118,655**	**107,560**	**104,191**	**121,834**	**136,011**	**151,670**	**172,618**	**203,394**
Direct investment in Israel	8 555	**22,816**	**23,196**	**22,714**	**28,438**	**31,548**	**35,625**	**49,304**	**58,193**
Equity capital and reinvested earnings	8 556	20,542	20,878	20,489	26,040	28,640	32,630	45,637	54,213
Claims on direct investors	8 557	20,542	20,878	20,489	26,040	28,640	32,630	45,637	54,213
Liabilities to direct investors	8 558	....	....	....	....	....	....	....	....
Other capital	8 580	2,274	2,318	2,225	2,398	2,908	2,995	3,667	3,980
Claims on direct investors	8 585	....	....	....	....	....	....	....	....
Liabilities to direct investors	8 590	2,274	2,318	2,225	2,398	2,908	2,995	3,667	3,980
Portfolio investment	8 652	**50,760**	**38,866**	**33,465**	**44,181**	**54,368**	**66,287**	**70,424**	**88,761**
Equity securities	8 660	32,021	20,626	14,831	23,907	30,807	42,733	41,987	61,491
Banks	8 663	....	....	....	....	....	....	....	....
Other sectors	8 664	32,021	20,626	14,831	23,907	30,807	42,733	41,987	61,491
Debt securities	8 669	18,739	18,240	18,634	20,274	23,561	23,554	28,437	27,270
Bonds and notes	8 670	18,718	18,227	18,596	20,054	23,454	23,393	28,191	27,076
Monetary authorities	8 671	....	....	....	....	....	....	....	....
General government	8 672	14,746	14,100	14,331	16,421	18,112	18,457	20,951	20,334
Banks	8 673	....	....	....	....	....	....	....	....
Other sectors	8 674	3,972	4,128	4,265	3,633	5,342	4,936	7,240	6,743
Money market instruments	8 680	21	12	38	220	107	160	246	194
Monetary authorities	8 681	21	12	38	220	107	160	246	194
General government	8 682	....	....	....	....	....	....	....	....
Banks	8 683	....	....	....	....	....	....	....	....
Other sectors	8 684	....	....	....	....	....	....	....	....
Financial derivatives	8 905	....	....	....	....	....	....	....	....
Monetary authorities	8 906	....	....	....	....	....	....	....	....
General government	8 907	....	....	....	....	....	....	....	....
Banks	8 908	....	....	....	....	....	....	....	....
Other sectors	8 909	....	....	....	....	....	....	....	....
Other investment	8 753	**45,079**	**45,499**	**48,013**	**49,215**	**50,096**	**49,759**	**52,891**	**56,440**
Trade credits	8 756	5,101	4,227	4,225	4,856	5,837	6,610	7,391	9,297
General government	8 757	....	....	....	....	....	....	....	....
of which: Short-term	8 759	....	....	....	....	....	....	....	....
Other sectors	8 760	5,101	4,227	4,225	4,856	5,837	6,610	7,391	9,297
of which: Short-term	8 762	*5,101*	*4,227*	*4,225*	*4,856*	*5,837*	*6,610*	*7,391*	*9,297*
Loans	8 764	17,309	17,482	19,283	19,615	20,271	19,960	20,512	20,598
Monetary authorities	8 765	17	16	16	16	15	14	13	13
of which: Use of Fund credit and loans from the Fund	8 766	....	....	....	....	....	....	....	....
of which: Short-term	8 768	....	....	....	....	....	....	....	....
General government	8 769	12,604	12,781	12,922	13,054	12,899	12,265	11,878	11,588
of which: Short-term	8 771	....	....	*25*	*25*	....	....	....	....
Banks	8 772	....	....	....	....	....	....	....	....
of which: Short-term	8 774	....	....	....	....	....	....	....	....
Other sectors	8 775	4,688	4,685	6,345	6,545	7,357	7,681	8,620	8,997
of which: Short-term	8 777	*537*	*492*	*485*	*377*	*257*	*381*	*645*	*227*
Currency and deposits	8 780	22,668	23,790	24,505	24,745	23,989	23,189	24,988	26,545
Monetary authorities	8 781	....	....	....	....	....	....	....	....
General government	8 782	....	....	....	....	....	....	....	....
Banks	8 783	22,668	23,790	24,505	24,745	23,989	23,189	24,988	26,545
Other sectors	8 784	....	....	....	....	....	....	....	....
Other liabilities	8 786	....	....	....	....	....	....	....	....
Monetary authorities	8 787	....	....	....	....	....	....	....	....
of which: Short-term	8 789	....	....	....	....	....	....	....	....
General government	8 790	....	....	....	....	....	....	....	....
of which: Short-term	8 792	....	....	....	....	....	....	....	....
Banks	8 793	....	....	....	....	....	....	....	....
of which: Short-term	8 795	....	....	....	....	....	....	....	....
Other sectors	8 796	....	....	....	....	....	....	....	....
of which: Short-term	8 798	....	....	....	....	....	....	....	....
NET INTERNATIONAL INVESTMENT POSITION	8 995	**−50,498**	**−35,501**	**−26,134**	**−32,372**	**−30,036**	**−28,793**	**−9,025**	**−15,229**
Conversion rates: new sheqalim per U.S. dollar (end of period)	0 102	4.0410	4.4160	4.7370	4.3790	4.3080	4.6030	4.2250	3.8460

Table 1. ANALYTIC PRESENTATION, 2000–2007

(Billions of U.S. dollars)

	Code	2000	2001	2002	2003	2004	2005	2006	2007
A. Current Account[1]	4 993 Z.	**−5.78**	**−.65**	**−9.37**	**−19.41**	**−16.46**	**−29.71**	**−48.05**	**−51.03**
Goods: exports f.o.b.	2 100 ..	240.47	244.93	252.62	298.12	352.17	372.38	418.07	502.38
Goods: imports f.o.b.	3 100 ..	−230.92	−229.39	−239.21	−286.64	−341.28	−371.81	−430.58	−498.14
Balance on Goods	4 100 ..	*9.55*	*15.54*	*13.41*	*11.48*	*10.89*	*.56*	*−12.51*	*4.24*
Services: credit	2 200 ..	56.56	57.68	60.44	71.77	84.52	89.22	98.98	112.00
Services: debit	3 200 ..	−55.60	−57.75	−63.17	−74.33	−83.25	−90.08	−100.51	−121.45
Balance on Goods and Services	4 991 ..	*10.50*	*15.46*	*10.68*	*8.91*	*12.17*	*−.30*	*−14.04*	*−5.21*
Income: credit	2 300 ..	38.67	38.57	43.30	48.78	53.12	61.32	72.35	88.08
Income: debit	3 300 ..	−50.68	−48.91	−57.85	−69.00	−71.46	−78.43	−89.43	−114.99
Balance on Goods, Services, and Income	4 992 ..	*−1.51*	*5.13*	*−3.87*	*−11.31*	*−6.17*	*−17.41*	*−31.11*	*−32.13*
Current transfers: credit	2 379 Z.	15.80	16.14	20.87	20.65	21.83	23.57	22.01	27.46
Current transfers: debit	3 379 ..	−20.07	−21.92	−26.37	−28.74	−32.12	−35.88	−38.94	−46.36
B. Capital Account[1]	4 994 Z.	**2.88**	**.85**	**−.08**	**2.67**	**2.17**	**1.24**	**2.39**	**3.68**
Capital account: credit	2 994 Z.	4.17	2.10	2.06	4.95	4.11	4.73	5.51	5.70
Capital account: debit	3 994 ..	−1.29	−1.25	−2.14	−2.28	−1.94	−3.49	−3.12	−2.02
Total, Groups A Plus B	4 981 ..	*−2.90*	*.19*	*−9.45*	*−16.74*	*−14.28*	*−28.47*	*−45.65*	*−47.35*
C. Financial Account[1]	4 995 W.	**7.50**	**−3.57**	**11.22**	**20.44**	**8.43**	**25.28**	**30.93**	**37.61**
Direct investment abroad	4 505 ..	−12.08	−21.76	−17.25	−8.99	−19.14	−40.79	−42.48	−92.12
Direct investment in Italy	4 555 Z.	13.18	14.87	14.70	16.54	16.77	19.64	39.01	40.04
Portfolio investment assets	4 602 ..	−80.26	−36.17	−15.26	−57.41	−26.39	−108.09	−61.73	1.58
Equity securities	4 610 ..	−77.04	−9.99	−5.20	−16.00	−16.18	−24.88	−23.04	17.02
Debt securities	4 619 ..	−3.23	−26.18	−10.07	−41.41	−10.22	−83.21	−38.69	−15.44
Portfolio investment liabilities	4 652 Z.	57.02	29.33	32.92	60.15	58.55	164.40	115.29	24.06
Equity securities	4 660 ..	−2.43	−.24	−6.27	−2.01	17.18	2.63	13.56	−14.87
Debt securities	4 669 Z.	59.45	29.57	39.19	62.16	41.37	161.77	101.73	38.93
Financial derivatives	4 910 ..	2.33	−.44	−2.71	−5.47	2.29	3.12	−.59	.74
Financial derivatives assets	4 900 ..	.74	−2.28	−6.14	−10.28	....	....	....	....
Financial derivatives liabilities	4 905 ..	1.59	1.84	3.43	4.81	2.29	3.12	−.59	.74
Other investment assets	4 703 ..	.24	2.03	6.23	−20.58	−47.94	−100.28	−142.42	−82.58
Monetary authorities	4 701 ..	3.03	−27.63	13.54	−.07	−8.70	−4.35	−18.73	−18.29
General government	4 704 ..	−.65	−.35	1.37	1.41	−.56	−1.23	−.36	.02
Banks	4 705 ..	2.39	12.09	−34.00	.43	−27.29	−24.83	−58.87	−39.39
Other sectors	4 728 ..	−4.53	17.92	25.32	−22.35	−11.38	−69.87	−64.45	−24.92
Other investment liabilities	4 753 W.	27.07	8.56	−7.41	36.20	24.29	87.28	123.86	145.90
Monetary authorities	4 753 WA	−.69	1.93	.87	−2.55	.39	1.10	−.94	−1.14
General government	4 753 ZB	−3.55	−.76	−.54	−1.01	−.65	1.30	−.39	−1.29
Banks	4 753 ZC	24.87	12.78	−6.12	43.75	14.72	59.50	113.40	152.67
Other sectors	4 753 ZD	6.44	−5.39	−1.62	−3.98	9.83	25.37	11.79	−4.34
Total, Groups A Through C	4 983 ..	*4.60*	*−3.38*	*1.77*	*3.70*	*−5.86*	*−3.19*	*−14.72*	*−9.74*
D. Net Errors and Omissions	4 998 ..	**−1.36**	**2.79**	**1.39**	**−2.58**	**3.01**	**2.16**	**14.16**	**11.63**
Total, Groups A Through D	4 984 ..	*3.25*	*−.59*	*3.17*	*1.11*	*−2.84*	*−1.03*	*−.57*	*1.89*
E. Reserves and Related Items	4 802 A.	**−3.25**	**.59**	**−3.17**	**−1.11**	**2.84**	**1.03**	**.57**	**−1.89**
Reserve assets	4 802 ..	−3.25	.59	−3.17	−1.11	2.84	1.03	.57	−1.89
Use of Fund credit and loans	4 766 ..	....	....	....	....	....	....	....	....
Exceptional financing	4 920 ..	....	....	....	....	....	....	....	....
Conversion rates: euros per U.S. dollar	0 103 ..	**1.0854**	**1.1175**	**1.0626**	**.8860**	**.8054**	**.8041**	**.7971**	**.7306**

[1] Excludes components that have been classified in the categories of Group E.

Table 2. STANDARD PRESENTATION, 2000–2007

(Billions of U.S. dollars)

	Code	2000	2001	2002	2003	2004	2005	2006	2007
CURRENT ACCOUNT	4 993 ..	**−5.78**	**−.65**	**−9.37**	**−19.41**	**−16.46**	**−29.71**	**−48.05**	**−51.03**
A. GOODS	4 100 ..	**9.55**	**15.54**	**13.41**	**11.48**	**10.89**	**.56**	**−12.51**	**4.24**
Credit	2 100 ..	240.47	244.93	252.62	298.12	352.17	372.38	418.07	502.38
General merchandise: exports f.o.b.	2 110 ..	238.28	242.90	240.58	286.56	338.41	357.51	400.43	480.90
Goods for processing: exports f.o.b.	2 150 ..	.68	.77	11.42	10.98	12.80	13.79	16.42	19.80
Repairs on goods	2 160 ..	.75	.67	.08	.08	.16	.18	.16	.17
Goods procured in ports by carriers	2 170 ..	.55	.33	.22	.28	.49	.55	.54	.88
Nonmonetary gold	2 180 ..	.22	.26	.32	.22	.31	.35	.52	.63
Debit	3 100 ..	−230.92	−229.39	−239.21	−286.64	−341.28	−371.81	−430.58	−498.14
General merchandise: imports f.o.b.	3 110 ..	−226.17	−224.40	−224.18	−272.46	−324.37	−353.85	−409.57	−472.72
Goods for processing: imports f.o.b.	3 150 ..	−1.07	−1.40	−11.40	−10.82	−13.12	−13.61	−15.83	−19.77
Repairs on goods	3 160 ..	−.46	−.35	−.05	−.07	−.09	−.16	−.24	−.26
Goods procured in ports by carriers	3 170 ..	−.63	−.78	−.68	−.69	−.89	−1.33	−1.65	−1.72
Nonmonetary gold	3 180 ..	−2.59	−2.46	−2.90	−2.59	−2.81	−2.87	−3.29	−3.68
B. SERVICES	4 200 ..	**.96**	**−.08**	**−2.73**	**−2.57**	**1.28**	**−.87**	**−1.53**	**−9.45**
Total credit	2 200 ..	*56.56*	*57.68*	*60.44*	*71.77*	*84.52*	*89.22*	*98.98*	*112.00*
Total debit	3 200 ..	*−55.60*	*−57.75*	*−63.17*	*−74.33*	*−83.25*	*−90.08*	*−100.51*	*−121.45*
Transportation services, credit	2 205 ..	**9.29**	**8.30**	**9.31**	**10.58**	**14.89**	**14.76**	**16.20**	**17.84**
Passenger	2 850 ..	*1.21*	*1.09*	*1.32*	*1.34*	*2.49*	*3.05*	*3.39*	*3.48*
Freight	2 851 ..	*3.03*	*2.61*	*2.90*	*3.49*	*4.52*	*4.99*	*5.57*	*6.34*
Other	2 852 ..	*5.04*	*4.59*	*5.09*	*5.74*	*7.88*	*6.72*	*7.25*	*8.01*
Sea transport, passenger	2 207 ..	.02	.01	.02	.02	.02	.05	.05	.05
Sea transport, freight	2 208 ..	2.04	1.77	1.75	2.19	2.68	2.97	3.23	3.77
Sea transport, other	2 209 ..	2.21	2.06	2.44	2.87	3.74	2.84	2.95	3.12
Air transport, passenger	2 211 ..	1.03	.90	1.01	1.04	2.16	2.76	3.11	3.19
Air transport, freight	2 212 ..	.14	.11	.14	.12	.17	.22	.23	.31
Air transport, other	2 213 ..	1.75	1.58	1.79	1.86	2.81	2.70	2.97	3.36
Other transport, passenger	2 215 ..	.16	.19	.28	.28	.31	.24	.23	.24
Other transport, freight	2 216 ..	.86	.73	1.00	1.19	1.67	1.80	2.11	2.27
Other transport, other	2 217 ..	1.09	.95	.86	1.01	1.33	1.17	1.33	1.53
Transportation services, debit	3 205 ..	**−13.14**	**−11.75**	**−13.27**	**−16.20**	**−21.03**	**−21.33**	**−22.69**	**−27.48**
Passenger	3 850 ..	*−2.48*	*−2.20*	*−2.71*	*−3.14*	*−3.60*	*−4.40*	*−4.28*	*−5.43*
Freight	3 851 ..	*−5.33*	*−4.84*	*−5.30*	*−6.71*	*−9.15*	*−10.11*	*−11.01*	*−13.65*
Other	3 852 ..	*−5.32*	*−4.71*	*−5.25*	*−6.35*	*−8.28*	*−6.82*	*−7.40*	*−8.41*
Sea transport, passenger	3 207 ..	−.05	−.06	−.08	−.11	−.13	−.14	−.09	−.12
Sea transport, freight	3 208 ..	−3.16	−2.73	−2.98	−3.78	−5.16	−5.62	−6.05	−7.54
Sea transport, other	3 209 ..	−2.44	−2.22	−2.60	−3.23	−4.18	−3.05	−3.37	−3.63
Air transport, passenger	3 211 ..	−2.27	−1.99	−2.49	−2.89	−3.35	−4.18	−4.11	−5.23
Air transport, freight	3 212 ..	−.42	−.34	−.23	−.35	−.51	−.55	−.58	−.69
Air transport, other	3 213 ..	−1.65	−1.41	−1.71	−2.01	−2.50	−2.33	−2.45	−2.96
Other transport, passenger	3 215 ..	−.16	−.15	−.14	−.15	−.13	−.09	−.08	−.07
Other transport, freight	3 216 ..	−1.75	−1.77	−2.09	−2.58	−3.48	−3.94	−4.39	−5.42
Other transport, other	3 217 ..	−1.23	−1.07	−.94	−1.12	−1.59	−1.44	−1.58	−1.82
Travel, credit	2 236 ..	**27.49**	**25.82**	**26.87**	**31.25**	**35.38**	**35.32**	**38.26**	**42.66**
Business travel	2 237 ..	7.07	6.30	6.27	6.80	7.34	7.15	8.20	9.36
Personal travel	2 240 ..	20.43	19.52	20.60	24.45	28.04	28.17	30.06	33.30
Travel, debit	3 236 ..	**−15.69**	**−14.79**	**−16.92**	**−20.59**	**−20.46**	**−22.37**	**−23.15**	**−27.33**
Business travel	3 237 ..	−6.50	−5.96	−7.17	−8.23	−7.40	−7.89	−8.15	−9.88
Personal travel	3 240 ..	−9.19	−8.84	−9.76	−12.35	−13.06	−14.48	−15.00	−17.45
Other services, credit	2 200 BA	**19.77**	**23.55**	**24.26**	**29.94**	**34.25**	**39.14**	**44.52**	**51.50**
Communications	2 245 ..	1.27	1.43	.99	1.89	2.00	2.19	3.20	3.05
Construction	2 249 ..	1.35	1.64	1.72	2.09	2.05	2.21	2.43	3.17
Insurance	2 253 ..	.82	1.13	1.33	1.16	1.60	1.62	1.70	1.53
Financial	2 260 ..	.43	.41	.64	.89	.94	1.25	2.00	3.89
Computer and information	2 262 ..	.45	.35	.39	.50	.59	.64	.93	.91
Royalties and licence fees	2 266 ..	.56	.44	.54	.52	.77	1.13	1.12	1.05
Other business services	2 268 ..	13.79	17.02	17.04	21.00	24.35	28.22	30.77	35.20
Personal, cultural, and recreational	2 287 ..	.54	.54	.72	.72	.75	.76	.95	1.17
Government, n.i.e.	2 291 ..	.56	.58	.88	1.16	1.22	1.12	1.43	1.53
Other services, debit	3 200 BA	**−26.78**	**−31.21**	**−32.98**	**−37.55**	**−41.75**	**−46.38**	**−54.66**	**−66.64**
Communications	3 245 ..	−1.94	−2.61	−2.59	−3.23	−2.77	−3.11	−4.64	−4.42
Construction	3 249 ..	−1.14	−1.63	−2.27	−2.46	−2.69	−2.19	−2.57	−3.47
Insurance	3 253 ..	−1.10	−1.43	−1.79	−1.79	−2.29	−2.14	−2.89	−3.27
Financial	3 260 ..	−.54	−.56	−.63	−.81	−1.29	−1.22	−1.04	−1.43
Computer and information	3 262 ..	−.93	−.94	−1.06	−1.05	−1.23	−1.53	−1.72	−1.79
Royalties and licence fees	3 266 ..	−1.20	−1.31	−1.27	−1.70	−1.75	−1.94	−1.84	−1.68
Other business services	3 268 ..	−17.80	−19.96	−20.37	−24.25	−26.65	−30.89	−35.92	−45.30
Personal, cultural, and recreational	3 287 ..	−1.16	−1.09	−.93	−1.03	−1.51	−1.64	−1.64	−2.10
Government, n.i.e.	3 291 ..	−.97	−1.67	−2.06	−1.23	−1.57	−1.72	−2.40	−3.19

Table 2 (Continued). STANDARD PRESENTATION, 2000–2007

(Billions of U.S. dollars)

	Code	2000	2001	2002	2003	2004	2005	2006	2007
C. INCOME	4 300	**−12.01**	**−10.34**	**−14.55**	**−20.22**	**−18.34**	**−17.11**	**−17.08**	**−26.92**
Total credit	2 300	*38.67*	*38.57*	*43.30*	*48.78*	*53.12*	*61.32*	*72.35*	*88.08*
Total debit	3 300	*−50.68*	*−48.91*	*−57.85*	*−69.00*	*−71.46*	*−78.43*	*−89.43*	*−114.99*
Compensation of employees, credit	2 310	**1.51**	**1.85**	**1.88**	**1.73**	**1.81**	**2.03**	**2.24**	**2.72**
Compensation of employees, debit	3 310	**−1.96**	**−1.90**	**−2.76**	**−2.98**	**−2.07**	**−2.72**	**−2.65**	**−2.86**
Investment income, credit	2 320	**37.16**	**36.73**	**41.42**	**47.05**	**51.31**	**59.30**	**70.10**	**85.36**
Direct investment income	2 330	1.94	3.00	5.20	5.51	5.01	4.98	7.65	10.71
Dividends and distributed branch profits	2 332	1.69	4.08	2.66	1.90	2.18	2.27	3.37	4.48
Reinvested earnings and undistributed branch profits	2 333	.24	−1.08	2.54	3.61	2.83	2.70	4.29	6.23
Income on debt (interest)	2 334	....	....	....	....	....	....	....	....
Portfolio investment income	2 339	24.16	20.59	24.35	30.10	35.79	40.25	47.92	52.67
Income on equity	2 340	4.01	4.55	5.53	5.03	8.22	10.33	11.23	17.45
Income on bonds and notes	2 350	19.63	15.96	18.44	24.67	27.12	29.81	36.59	35.02
Income on money market instruments	2 360	.52	.08	.38	.40	.45	.10	.11	.19
Other investment income	2 370	11.06	13.13	11.86	11.44	10.52	14.07	14.53	21.98
Investment income, debit	3 320	**−48.72**	**−47.01**	**−55.10**	**−66.02**	**−69.39**	**−75.72**	**−86.78**	**−112.13**
Direct investment income	3 330	−3.54	−4.08	−4.96	−5.39	−5.50	−5.82	−6.80	−7.11
Dividends and distributed branch profits	3 332	−.63	−.37	1.53	−.60	−.59	−.63	−.62	−.59
Reinvested earnings and undistributed branch profits	3 333	−2.91	−3.72	−6.49	−4.79	−4.91	−5.19	−6.18	−6.52
Income on debt (interest)	3 334	....	....	....	....	....	....	....	....
Portfolio investment income	3 339	−30.87	−26.20	−35.36	−44.27	−49.05	−51.74	−54.86	−68.32
Income on equity	3 340	−5.77	−6.07	−8.18	−11.59	−12.76	−15.41	−18.56	−19.61
Income on bonds and notes	3 350	−22.06	−18.08	−24.37	−29.50	−32.78	−34.77	−34.92	−47.01
Income on money market instruments	3 360	−3.03	−2.05	−2.81	−3.19	−3.50	−1.56	−1.38	−1.70
Other investment income	3 370	−14.32	−16.73	−14.78	−16.36	−14.84	−18.16	−25.12	−36.71
D. CURRENT TRANSFERS	4 379	**−4.28**	**−5.78**	**−5.50**	**−8.10**	**−10.29**	**−12.30**	**−16.93**	**−18.91**
Credit	2 379	**15.80**	**16.14**	**20.87**	**20.65**	**21.83**	**23.57**	**22.01**	**27.46**
General government	2 380	9.23	9.63	13.11	11.73	12.20	12.36	12.15	16.55
Other sectors	2 390	6.57	6.51	7.76	8.92	9.63	11.22	9.85	10.90
Workers' remittances	2 391	.36	.32	.30	.29	.28	.29	.31	.35
Other current transfers	2 392	6.21	6.18	7.47	8.63	9.35	10.93	9.54	10.56
Debit	3 379	**−20.07**	**−21.92**	**−26.37**	**−28.74**	**−32.12**	**−35.88**	**−38.94**	**−46.36**
General government	3 380	−12.86	−12.93	−14.16	−18.11	−20.63	−22.67	−22.21	−26.13
Other sectors	3 390	−7.21	−8.98	−12.21	−10.64	−11.49	−13.20	−16.73	−20.23
Workers' remittances	3 391	−.54	−.67	−.75	−1.33	−3.37	−4.83	−5.70	−8.32
Other current transfers	3 392	−6.67	−8.31	−11.46	−9.31	−8.12	−8.37	−11.03	−11.91
CAPITAL AND FINANCIAL ACCOUNT	4 996	**7.14**	**−2.14**	**7.97**	**21.99**	**13.44**	**27.55**	**33.89**	**39.40**
CAPITAL ACCOUNT	4 994	**2.88**	**.85**	**−.08**	**2.67**	**2.17**	**1.24**	**2.39**	**3.68**
Total credit	2 994	*4.17*	*2.10*	*2.06*	*4.95*	*4.11*	*4.73*	*5.51*	*5.70*
Total debit	3 994	*−1.29*	*−1.25*	*−2.14*	*−2.28*	*−1.94*	*−3.49*	*−3.12*	*−2.02*
Capital transfers, credit	2 400	**3.91**	**1.95**	**1.89**	**4.68**	**3.86**	**4.39**	**5.30**	**5.47**
General government	2 401	3.27	1.57	1.51	4.21	3.56	4.22	4.82	5.05
Debt forgiveness	2 402	....	....	....	....	....	....	....	....
Other capital transfers	2 410	....	....	....	4.21	3.56	4.22	4.82	5.05
Other sectors	2 430	.64	.38	.38	.47	.29	.17	.47	.42
Migrants' transfers	2 431	.07	.10	.09	.13	.08	.08	.07	.10
Debt forgiveness	2 432	....	....	....	....	....	....	....	....
Other capital transfers	2 440	.57	.28	.29	.34	.21	.09	.40	.32
Capital transfers, debit	3 400	**−.96**	**−.82**	**−1.77**	**−1.92**	**−1.64**	**−3.23**	**−2.79**	**−1.69**
General government	3 401	−.47	−.51	−1.60	−1.70	−1.31	−2.98	−2.24	−1.38
Debt forgiveness	3 402	....	....	....	−.75	−.29	−1.49	−1.28	−.15
Other capital transfers	3 410	....	....	....	−.95	−1.02	−1.49	−.96	−1.23
Other sectors	3 430	−.49	−.32	−.17	−.22	−.33	−.25	−.55	−.31
Migrants' transfers	3 431	−.08	−.14	−.07	−.06	−.07	−.08	−.09	−.10
Debt forgiveness	3 432	....	−.01	−.01	....	....	−.01	....	....
Other capital transfers	3 440	−.41	−.17	−.09	−.16	−.25	−.16	−.46	−.21
Nonproduced nonfinancial assets, credit	2 480	**.26**	**.15**	**.17**	**.27**	**.26**	**.34**	**.22**	**.23**
Nonproduced nonfinancial assets, debit	3 480	**−.33**	**−.43**	**−.37**	**−.36**	**−.30**	**−.26**	**−.34**	**−.33**

Table 2 (Continued). STANDARD PRESENTATION, 2000–2007

(Billions of U.S. dollars)

	Code	2000	2001	2002	2003	2004	2005	2006	2007
FINANCIAL ACCOUNT...	4 995 ..	**4.26**	**−2.98**	**8.05**	**19.32**	**11.27**	**26.31**	**31.50**	**35.72**
A. DIRECT INVESTMENT.....................................	4 500 ..	**1.10**	**−6.88**	**−2.55**	**7.55**	**−2.37**	**−21.15**	**−3.47**	**−52.08**
Direct investment abroad............................	4 505 ..	**−12.08**	**−21.76**	**−17.25**	**−8.99**	**−19.14**	**−40.79**	**−42.48**	**−92.12**
Equity capital..	4 510 ..	−9.35	−13.37	−10.36	−12.82	−.93	−26.54	−28.66	−67.49
Claims on affiliated enterprises...............	4 515 ..	....	....	....	....	....	....	....	....
Liabilities to affiliated enterprises............	4 520 ..	....	....	....	....	....	....	....	....
Reinvested earnings..................................	4 525 ..	−.24	1.08	−2.54	−3.61	−2.83	−2.70	−4.29	−6.23
Other capital..	4 530 ..	−2.49	−9.46	−4.35	7.45	−15.39	−11.55	−9.53	−18.40
Claims on affiliated enterprises...............	4 535 ..	....	....	....	....	....	....	....	....
Liabilities to affiliated enterprises............	4 540 ..	....	....	....	....	....	....	....	....
Direct investment in Italy..........................	4 555 ..	**13.18**	**14.87**	**14.70**	**16.54**	**16.77**	**19.64**	**39.01**	**40.04**
Equity capital..	4 560 ..	7.36	6.87	5.90	2.81	7.45	8.49	21.98	18.44
Claims on direct investors.......................	4 565 ..	....	....	....	....	....	....	....	....
Liabilities to direct investors...................	4 570 ..	....	....	....	....	....	....	....	....
Reinvested earnings..................................	4 575 ..	2.91	3.72	6.49	4.79	4.91	5.19	6.18	6.52
Other capital..	4 580 ..	2.91	4.29	2.31	8.94	4.41	5.96	10.85	15.08
Claims on direct investors.......................	4 585 ..	....	....	....	....	....	....	....	....
Liabilities to direct investors...................	4 590 ..	....	....	....	....	....	....	....	....
B. PORTFOLIO INVESTMENT...............................	4 600 ..	**−23.24**	**−6.84**	**17.66**	**2.74**	**32.16**	**56.31**	**53.56**	**25.64**
Assets..	4 602 ..	**−80.26**	**−36.17**	**−15.26**	**−57.41**	**−26.39**	**−108.09**	**−61.73**	**1.58**
Equity securities..	4 610 ..	−77.04	−9.99	−5.20	−16.00	−16.18	−24.88	−23.04	17.02
Monetary authorities...............................	4 611 ..	....	....	.03	.03	−.05	−.67	−.18	....
General government................................	4 612 ..	−3.13	−2.70	−.21	−.38	.31	−.27	−.11	−.09
Banks...	4 613 ..	−.14	−.91	−1.09	−.25	−1.25	2.23	−1.50	−11.44
Other sectors...	4 614 ..	−73.77	−6.38	−3.93	−15.39	−15.18	−26.17	−21.25	28.55
Debt securities..	4 619 ..	−3.23	−26.18	−10.07	−41.41	−10.22	−83.21	−38.69	−15.44
Bonds and notes.....................................	4 620 ..	−1.58	−24.48	−9.48	−44.59	−11.05	−80.92	−33.05	−9.10
Monetary authorities............................	4 621 ..	−.03	.01	.18	−.34	.08	−.07	−15.24	−7.25
General government.............................	4 622 ..	−.50	.29	−.19	−.17	−.19	−.68	−.57	−.02
Banks..	4 623 ..	1.64	4.99	−.36	−11.30	−9.83	.18	1.30	−6.94
Other sectors..	4 624 ..	−2.70	−29.77	−9.11	−32.78	−1.10	−80.35	−18.54	5.11
Money market instruments.......................	4 630 ..	−1.64	−1.70	−.59	3.18	.83	−2.28	−5.64	−6.34
Monetary authorities............................	4 631 ..	.43	.01	−2.12	.18	−1.43	−.24	.82	2.34
General government.............................	4 632 ..	−.06	−.01	.09	−.07	−.01	.02	.02	.08
Banks..	4 633 ..	−.70	−1.20	−.38	−.19	.91	.59	−.43	.12
Other sectors..	4 634 ..	−1.31	−.51	1.82	3.27	1.36	−2.65	−6.05	−8.87
Liabilities..	4 652 ..	**57.02**	**29.33**	**32.92**	**60.15**	**58.55**	**164.40**	**115.29**	**24.06**
Equity securities..	4 660 ..	−2.43	−.24	−6.27	−2.01	17.18	2.63	13.56	−14.87
Banks...	4 663 ..	1.90	1.04	.21	4.57	3.27	27.53	4.85	−14.40
Other sectors...	4 664 ..	−4.33	−1.29	−6.48	−6.58	13.91	−24.90	8.71	−.47
Debt securities..	4 669 ..	59.45	29.57	39.19	62.16	41.37	161.77	101.73	38.93
Bonds and notes.....................................	4 670 ..	71.58	39.07	52.14	53.11	58.34	129.85	102.85	33.04
Monetary authorities............................	4 671 ..	....	....	....	....	....	....	....	....
General government.............................	4 672 ..	63.07	20.23	37.18	53.17	25.41	88.70	46.48	−12.88
Banks..	4 673 ..	1.72	.60	−1.42	−.89	18.98	35.27	53.47	42.93
Other sectors..	4 674 ..	6.78	18.25	16.37	.83	13.95	5.88	2.89	3.00
Money market instruments.......................	4 680 ..	−12.13	−9.50	−12.95	9.05	−16.97	31.92	−1.12	5.89
Monetary authorities............................	4 681 ..	....	....	....	....	....	....	....	....
General government.............................	4 682 ..	−11.57	−7.54	−12.39	15.27	−14.29	31.93	−1.05	5.42
Banks..	4 683 ..	−.58	−2.43	−.66	−6.23	−2.68	−.02	−.07	.47
Other sectors..	4 684 ..	.02	.47	.10	....	....	....	....	....
C. FINANCIAL DERIVATIVES...............................	4 910 ..	**2.33**	**−.44**	**−2.71**	**−5.47**	**2.29**	**3.12**	**−.59**	**.74**
Monetary authorities.................................	4 911 ..	....	....	....	....	....	....	....	....
General government.................................	4 912 ..	....	.01	−.04	−.04	−.02	−.07	−.02	−.05
Banks...	4 913 ..	2.97	−1.08	.11	−4.42	−3.52	−6.85	−7.01	−5.95
Other sectors..	4 914 ..	−.65	.63	−2.78	−1.00	5.82	10.05	6.43	6.74
Assets..	4 900 ..	**.74**	**−2.28**	**−6.14**	**−10.28**	....	....	....	....
Monetary authorities.................................	4 901 ..	....	....	....	....	....	....	....	....
General government.................................	4 902 ..	....	.01	−.04	−.04	....	....	....	....
Banks...	4 903 ..	1.60	−1.42	−1.53	−6.93	....	....	....	....
Other sectors..	4 904 ..	−.86	−.87	−4.57	−3.31	....	....	....	....
Liabilities..	4 905 ..	**1.59**	**1.84**	**3.43**	**4.81**	**2.29**	**3.12**	**−.59**	**.74**
Monetary authorities.................................	4 906 ..	....	....	....	....	....	....	....	....
General government.................................	4 907 ..	....	.01	....	....	−.02	−.07	−.02	−.05
Banks...	4 908 ..	1.38	.34	1.64	2.51	−3.52	−6.85	−7.01	−5.95
Other sectors..	4 909 ..	.21	1.50	1.79	2.30	5.82	10.05	6.43	6.74

Table 2 (Concluded). STANDARD PRESENTATION, 2000–2007

(Billions of U.S. dollars)

	Code	2000	2001	2002	2003	2004	2005	2006	2007
D. OTHER INVESTMENT	4 700	**27.32**	**10.59**	**−1.18**	**15.61**	**−23.65**	**−13.00**	**−18.57**	**63.31**
Assets	4 703	.24	2.03	6.23	−20.58	−47.94	−100.28	−142.42	−82.58
Trade credits	4 706	−6.63	.49	2.35	.34	−2.95	−.38	.79	.63
General government	4 707	....	....	.01	−.01	−.01	.01	....	−.01
of which: Short-term	4 709	....	....	....	....	....	....	....	....
Other sectors	4 710	−6.63	.49	2.35	.35	−2.94	−.39	.79	.64
of which: Short-term	4 712	....	....	....	....	....	....	....	....
Loans	4 714	−19.23	−4.59	−8.64	16.31	−14.64	−47.08	−66.58	−62.33
Monetary authorities	4 715	.05	....	....	....	.23	....	....	.06
of which: Short-term	4 718	....	....	....	....	....	....	....	....
General government	4 719	.07	.04	1.44	.57	.44	−.38	−.06	−.15
of which: Short-term	4 721	....	....	....	....	....	....	....	....
Banks	4 722	−17.18	−4.79	−20.63	−.07	−13.95	2.83	−22.16	−19.65
of which: Short-term	4 724	....	....	....	....	*−10.03*	*11.88*	*−14.80*	*−.37*
Other sectors	4 725	−2.15	.16	10.55	15.82	−1.36	−49.53	−44.36	−42.58
of which: Short-term	4 727	....	....	....	....	....	....	....	....
Currency and deposits	4 730	32.25	9.15	17.82	−31.17	−17.88	−39.13	−58.34	−4.93
Monetary authorities	4 731	2.99	−27.62	13.54	−.06	−8.96	−4.34	−18.73	−18.29
General government	4 732	−.40	−.06	.12	1.02	−.64	−.45	−.28	.19
Banks	4 733	20.09	17.02	−11.27	4.01	−6.83	−19.95	−24.48	−12.39
Other sectors	4 734	9.57	19.81	15.43	−36.14	−1.45	−14.39	−14.85	25.56
Other assets	4 736	−6.14	−3.00	−5.30	−6.07	−12.47	−13.69	−18.30	−15.95
Monetary authorities	4 737	....	....	....	....	.02	....	....	−.06
of which: Short-term	4 739	....	....	....	....	....	....	....	....
General government	4 740	−.31	−.34	−.19	−.17	−.35	−.42	−.03	....
of which: Short-term	4 742	....	....	....	....	....	....	....	....
Banks	4 743	−.52	−.13	−2.10	−3.51	−6.51	−7.71	−12.23	−7.35
of which: Short-term	4 745	....	....	....	....	*−5.20*	*−8.65*	*−7.46*	*−11.78*
Other sectors	4 746	−5.31	−2.53	−3.01	−2.39	−5.63	−5.56	−6.03	−8.54
of which: Short-term	4 748	....	....	....	....	....	....	....	....
Liabilities	4 753	**27.07**	**8.56**	**−7.41**	**36.20**	**24.29**	**87.28**	**123.86**	**145.90**
Trade credits	4 756	2.81	−1.72	−2.92	−.49	1.05	3.25	1.60	−.95
General government	4 757	.01	.01	−.01	−.01	....	−.01	−.01	.01
of which: Short-term	4 759	....	....	....	....	....	....	....	....
Other sectors	4 760	2.80	−1.73	−2.91	−.48	1.04	3.26	1.61	−.97
of which: Short-term	4 762	....	....	....	....	....	....	....	....
Loans	4 764	8.33	6.14	18.29	5.87	26.72	12.42	23.54	18.30
Monetary authorities	4 765	−.68	1.91	.86	−2.64	.40	1.01	−.80	−1.11
of which: Use of Fund credit and loans from the Fund	4 766	....	....	....	....	....	....	....	....
of which: Short-term	4 768	*−.68*	*1.91*	*.86*	*−2.64*	*.40*	*1.01*	*−.80*	*−1.11*
General government	4 769	−2.02	−.82	−.60	−.99	−.60	1.70	−.31	−.87
of which: Short-term	4 771	....	....	....	....	....	....	....	....
Banks	4 772	.81	3.09	10.95	13.97	20.65	5.63	16.40	25.92
of which: Short-term	4 774	....	....	....	....	*12.74*	*.72*	*9.10*	*35.35*
Other sectors	4 775	10.22	1.96	7.08	−4.48	6.27	4.08	8.24	−5.64
of which: Short-term	4 777	....	....	....	....	....	....	....	....
Currency and deposits	4 780	23.09	9.32	−17.48	30.36	−5.57	47.93	91.23	111.01
Monetary authorities	4 781	−.01	.02	....	−.01	.01	.07	−.02	−.01
General government	4 782	−1.56	....	....	....	....	....	....	....
Banks	4 783	23.53	9.20	−17.48	30.38	−5.58	47.86	91.25	111.02
Other sectors	4 784	1.13	.11	....	−.01	....	....	....	....
Other liabilities	4 786	−7.16	−5.19	−5.30	.46	2.10	23.68	7.49	17.54
Monetary authorities	4 787	....	....	.01	.09	−.01	.02	−.12	−.02
of which: Short-term	4 789	....	....	....	....	....	....	....	....
General government	4 790	.02	.05	.07	−.02	−.05	−.39	−.07	−.43
of which: Short-term	4 792	....	....	....	....	....	....	....	....
Banks	4 793	.53	.49	.41	−.61	−.35	6.01	5.74	15.73
of which: Short-term	4 795	....	....	....	....	*−.32*	*3.56*	*7.03*	*−6.87*
Other sectors	4 796	−7.71	−5.72	−5.79	.99	2.52	18.03	1.94	2.26
of which: Short-term	4 798	....	....	....	....	....	....	....	....
E. RESERVE ASSETS	4 802	**−3.25**	**.59**	**−3.17**	**−1.11**	**2.84**	**1.03**	**.57**	**−1.89**
Monetary gold	4 812	....	....	....	....	....	....	....	....
Special drawing rights	4 811	−.08	−.07	.20	−.04	.02	−.10	−.03	−.04
Reserve position in the Fund	4 810	.48	−.42	−.41	.13	.61	1.69	.85	.28
Foreign exchange	4 803	−3.65	1.08	−2.96	−1.21	2.22	−.56	−.25	−2.13
Other claims	4 813	....	....	....	....	....	....	....	....
NET ERRORS AND OMISSIONS	4 998	**−1.36**	**2.79**	**1.39**	**−2.58**	**3.01**	**2.16**	**14.16**	**11.63**

Table 3. INTERNATIONAL INVESTMENT POSITION (End-period stocks), 2000–2007

(Billions of U.S. dollars)

	Code	2000	2001	2002	2003	2004	2005	2006	2007
ASSETS..........	8 995 C.	**1,119.40**	**1,078.29**	**1,201.35**	**1,565.54**	**1,832.05**	**1,921.98**	**2,400.91**	**2,828.52**
Direct investment abroad..........	8 505 ..	**180.28**	**182.38**	**194.50**	**238.89**	**280.48**	**293.48**	**378.93**	**520.08**
Equity capital and reinvested earnings..........	8 506 ..	172.30	166.02	170.09	213.49	235.99	240.66	305.54	417.48
Claims on affiliated enterprises..........	8 507 ..	....	....	....	....	....	....	....	....
Liabilities to affiliated enterprises..........	8 508 ..	....	....	....	....	....	....	....	....
Other capital..........	8 530 ..	7.98	16.36	24.41	25.40	44.49	52.82	73.39	102.60
Claims on affiliated enterprises..........	8 535 ..	....	....	....	....	....	....	....	....
Liabilities to affiliated enterprises..........	8 540 ..	....	....	....	....	....	....	....	....
Portfolio investment..........	8 602 ..	**590.76**	**552.03**	**595.92**	**796.33**	**936.49**	**983.91**	**1,156.30**	**1,243.66**
Equity securities..........	8 610 ..	285.55	239.47	247.46	331.05	399.70	416.47	534.88	576.45
Monetary authorities..........	8 611 ..	.52	.52	.57	.62	.69	1.67	2.07	2.45
General government..........	8 612 ..	.27	1.25	.87	.95	1.15	1.64	2.92	3.38
Banks..........	8 613 ..	7.01	7.42	10.24	15.11	18.07	17.20	22.76	35.99
Other sectors..........	8 614 ..	277.76	230.28	235.77	314.37	379.79	395.96	507.14	534.62
Debt securities..........	8 619 ..	305.20	312.55	348.46	465.28	536.79	567.44	621.43	667.21
Bonds and notes..........	8 620 ..	304.30	307.58	339.20	458.90	524.14	560.36	614.62	651.20
Monetary authorities..........	8 621 ..	.04	.18	.02	.41	.35	.40	16.22	25.91
General government..........	8 622 ..	1.54	2.67	2.57	3.96	4.22	4.84	6.03	6.26
Banks..........	8 623 ..	26.58	24.33	29.84	65.92	83.38	71.93	77.16	87.86
Other sectors..........	8 624 ..	276.14	280.40	306.77	388.60	436.19	483.19	515.20	531.18
Money market instruments..........	8 630 ..	.91	4.97	9.26	6.38	12.65	7.08	6.81	16.01
Monetary authorities..........	8 631 ..	.11	.10	2.21	2.05	3.47	3.64	2.90	.57
General government..........	8 632 ..	....	.05	.05	.06	.03	.02	.01	....
Banks..........	8 633 ..	.19	.46	.73	1.02	1.03	.08	.41	2.22
Other sectors..........	8 634 ..	.61	4.36	6.26	3.26	8.12	3.34	3.50	13.22
Financial derivatives..........	8 900 ..	**3.53**	**4.33**	**11.05**	**22.70**	**28.49**	**30.23**	**31.28**	**34.13**
Monetary authorities..........	8 901 ..	....	....	....	....	....	....	....	....
General government..........	8 902 ..	....	.01	.05	.11	.14	.18	.22	.29
Banks..........	8 903 ..	1.30	1.35	2.48	8.63	13.31	15.38	12.66	16.17
Other sectors..........	8 904 ..	2.24	2.97	8.52	13.97	15.04	14.66	18.40	17.66
Other investment..........	8 703 ..	**297.78**	**293.35**	**344.26**	**444.35**	**524.21**	**548.42**	**758.62**	**936.32**
Trade credits..........	8 706 ..	45.01	42.55	48.24	57.75	65.48	57.08	62.94	69.85
General government..........	8 707 ..	.03	.01	.01	.02	.04	.02	.01	.03
of which: Short-term..........	8 709 ..	....	....	....	....	....	....	....	....
Other sectors..........	8 710 ..	44.98	42.53	48.23	57.73	65.45	57.06	62.93	69.82
of which: Short-term..........	8 712 ..	....	....	....	....	....	....	....	....
Loans..........	8 714 ..	198.50	200.01	221.77	289.23	332.87	359.40	535.01	648.35
Monetary authorities..........	8 715 ..	−7.41	19.97	8.16	11.30	22.72	21.11	44.47	68.00
of which: Short-term..........	8 718 ..	....	....	....	....	....	....	....	....
General government..........	8 719 ..	18.61	18.28	19.51	21.63	23.21	25.09	28.10	31.08
of which: Short-term..........	8 721 ..	....	....	....	....	....	....	....	....
Banks..........	8 722 ..	119.94	103.08	153.22	187.59	220.43	199.10	272.52	318.26
of which: Short-term..........	8 724 ..	....	....	....	....	....	....	....	....
Other sectors..........	8 725 ..	67.35	58.68	40.88	68.71	66.51	114.09	189.92	231.01
of which: Short-term..........	8 727 ..	....	....	....	....	....	....	....	....
Currency and deposits..........	8 730 ..								
Monetary authorities..........	8 731 ..								
General government..........	8 732 ..								
Banks..........	8 733 ..								
Other sectors..........	8 734 ..	....	....	....	....	....	....	....	....
Other assets..........	8 736 ..	54.27	50.79	74.25	97.37	125.86	131.94	160.67	218.13
Monetary authorities..........	8 737 ..	.69	.66	.78	.94	.99	.86	.96	1.13
of which: Short-term..........	8 739 ..	....	....	....	....	....	....	....	....
General government..........	8 740 ..	4.68	4.76	5.89	7.28	8.24	7.54	8.45	9.45
of which: Short-term..........	8 742 ..	....	....	....	....	....	....	....	....
Banks..........	8 743 ..	20.50	15.99	27.96	38.75	56.19	65.88	80.48	119.18
of which: Short-term..........	8 745 ..	....	....	....	....	....	....	....	....
Other sectors..........	8 746 ..	28.39	29.38	39.62	50.39	60.44	57.66	70.78	88.36
of which: Short-term..........	8 748 ..	....	....	....	....	....	....	....	....
Reserve assets..........	8 802 ..	**47.06**	**46.21**	**55.62**	**63.26**	**62.39**	**65.95**	**75.77**	**94.32**
Monetary gold..........	8 812 ..	21.49	21.80	27.02	32.89	34.53	40.44	50.11	65.94
Special drawing rights..........	8 811 ..	.24	.30	.11	.16	.14	.23	.27	.33
Reserve position in the Fund..........	8 810 ..	2.91	3.22	3.91	4.15	3.70	1.76	.98	.73
Foreign exchange..........	8 803 ..	22.42	20.90	24.59	26.06	24.01	23.53	24.41	27.32
Other claims..........	8 813 ..	....	....	....	....	....	....	....	....

Table 3 (Concluded). INTERNATIONAL INVESTMENT POSITION (End-period stocks), 2000–2007

(Billions of U.S. dollars)

	Code	2000	2001	2002	2003	2004	2005	2006	2007
LIABILITIES..	8 995 D.	**1,079.98**	**1,055.44**	**1,273.30**	**1,652.97**	**1,932.71**	**1,982.70**	**2,489.26**	**2,946.31**
Direct investment in Italy..........................	8 555 ..	**121.17**	**113.43**	**130.82**	**180.89**	**220.72**	**224.08**	**294.88**	**364.84**
Equity capital and reinvested earnings..............................	8 556 ..	114.56	103.25	115.81	147.00	178.12	178.70	231.53	277.55
Claims on direct investors..................................	8 557 ..	....	....	....	....	....	....	....	....
Liabilities to direct investors..............................	8 558 ..	....	....	....	....	....	....	....	....
Other capital..	8 580 ..	6.61	10.19	15.01	33.89	42.60	45.38	63.34	87.29
Claims on direct investors..................................	8 585 ..	....	....	....	....	....	....	....	....
Liabilities to direct investors..............................	8 590 ..	....	....	....	....	....	....	....	....
Portfolio investment..............................	8 652 ..	**576.34**	**565.87**	**708.82**	**925.48**	**1,081.35**	**1,106.55**	**1,346.93**	**1,485.73**
Equity securities..	8 660 ..	59.29	40.66	33.90	43.24	74.74	81.20	123.87	110.63
Banks..	8 663 ..	6.11	4.92	4.39	12.15	17.82	49.18	73.99	57.99
Other sectors..	8 664 ..	53.18	35.74	29.51	31.09	56.92	32.01	49.88	52.63
Debt securities..	8 669 ..	517.05	525.22	674.92	882.24	1,006.60	1,025.36	1,223.06	1,375.10
Bonds and notes..	8 670 ..	450.00	470.84	624.61	808.06	942.98	941.65	1,129.85	1,263.71
Monetary authorities..................................	8 671 ..	....	....	....	....	....	....	....	....
General government..................................	8 672 ..	371.88	376.13	493.87	647.81	746.24	736.01	846.00	901.99
Banks..	8 673 ..	12.22	13.60	15.49	20.18	27.56	56.87	119.62	180.68
Other sectors..	8 674 ..	65.90	81.11	115.25	140.07	169.18	148.76	164.23	181.03
Money market instruments..........................	8 680 ..	67.05	54.37	50.31	74.18	63.62	83.71	93.21	111.40
Monetary authorities..................................	8 681 ..	....	....	....	....	....	....	....	....
General government..................................	8 682 ..	67.05	53.68	50.25	74.11	63.55	83.65	93.15	110.96
Banks..	8 683 ..	....	....	....	....	....	....	....	.38
Other sectors..	8 684 ..	....	.69	.06	.07	.07	.06	.07	.06
Financial derivatives..............................	8 905 ..	**2.64**	**4.55**	**8.92**	**15.90**	**26.35**	**37.73**	**47.60**	**58.19**
Monetary authorities......................................	8 906 ..	....	....	....	....	....	....	....	....
General government..	8 907 ..	....	.01	.01	.01	.01	.01	.01	.01
Banks..	8 908 ..	.87	1.39	3.12	6.38	9.95	12.57	10.70	12.46
Other sectors..	8 909 ..	1.77	3.16	5.79	9.51	16.38	25.15	36.89	45.72
Other investment..................................	8 753 ..	**379.83**	**371.58**	**424.74**	**530.70**	**604.30**	**614.34**	**799.85**	**1,037.56**
Trade credits..	8 756 ..	26.18	23.31	24.89	29.83	33.09	31.88	37.46	40.60
General government......................................	8 758 ..	....	....	....	....	....	....	....	....
of which: Short-term................................	8 759 ..	....	....	....	....	....	....	....	....
Other sectors..	8 760 ..	26.14	23.28	24.87	29.81	33.07	31.86	37.45	40.57
of which: Short-term................................	8 762 ..	....	....	....	....	....	....	....	....
Loans..	8 764 ..	337.55	334.51	380.00	471.01	524.92	514.95	684.78	883.95
Monetary authorities..................................	8 765 ..	.22	2.18	3.05	.50	.91	2.01	1.22	.11
of which: Use of Fund credit and loans from the Fund....	8 766 ..	....	....	....	....	....	....	....	....
of which: Short-term..............................	8 768 ..	....	....	....	....	....	....	....	....
General government..................................	8 769 ..	7.17	5.93	6.12	6.27	6.08	6.85	6.16	5.10
of which: Short-term..............................	8 771 ..	....	....	....	....	....	....	....	....
Banks..	8 772 ..	254.41	252.49	279.96	361.80	403.91	402.38	553.24	745.60
of which: Short-term..............................	8 774 ..	....	....	....	....	....	....	....	....
Other sectors..	8 775 ..	75.76	73.90	90.88	102.45	114.02	103.72	124.16	133.14
of which: Short-term..............................	8 777 ..	....	....	....	....	....	....	....	....
Currency and deposits..................................	8 780 ..	....	....	....	....	....	....	....	....
Monetary authorities..................................	8 781 ..	....	....	....	....	....	....	....	....
General government..................................	8 782 ..	....	....	....	....	....	....	....	....
Banks..	8 783 ..	....	....	....	....	....	....	....	....
Other sectors..	8 784 ..	....	....	....	....	....	....	....	....
Other liabilities..	8 786 ..	16.10	13.77	19.85	29.86	46.28	67.51	77.61	113.01
Monetary authorities..................................	8 787 ..	.02	.01	.03	.14	.13	.15	.03	.03
of which: Short-term..............................	8 789 ..	....	....	....	....	....	....	....	....
General government..................................	8 790 ..	.06	.11	.20	.22	.17	.10	.45	.04
of which: Short-term..............................	8 792 ..	....	....	....	....	....	....	....	....
Banks..	8 793 ..	10.63	8.32	16.72	25.18	38.27	43.78	49.27	79.44
of which: Short-term..............................	8 795 ..	....	....	....	....	....	....	....	....
Other sectors..	8 796 ..	5.38	5.33	2.90	4.33	7.71	23.48	27.86	33.51
of which: Short-term..............................	8 798 ..	....	....	....	....	....	....	....	....
NET INTERNATIONAL INVESTMENT POSITION........	8 995 ..	**39.42**	**22.86**	**−71.95**	**−87.43**	**−100.66**	**−60.72**	**−88.35**	**−117.79**
Conversion rates: euros per U.S. dollar (end of period)..	0 104 ..	**1.0747**	**1.1347**	**.9536**	**.7918**	**.7342**	**.8477**	**.7593**	**.6793**

Table 1. ANALYTIC PRESENTATION, 2000–2007

(Millions of U.S. dollars)

	Code	2000	2001	2002	2003	2004	2005	2006	2007
A. Current Account[1]	4 993 Z.	**−367.4**	**−758.8**	**−1,074.0**	**−773.4**	**−509.1**	**−1,071.5**	**−1,182.8**	**−1,743.6**
Goods: exports f.o.b.	2 100 ..	1,562.8	1,454.4	1,309.1	1,385.6	1,601.6	1,664.3	2,133.6	2,226.4
Goods: imports f.o.b.	3 100 ..	−3,004.3	−3,072.6	−3,179.6	−3,328.2	−3,546.1	−4,245.5	−5,077.1	−5,789.1
Balance on Goods	4 100 ..	*−1,441.5*	*−1,618.2*	*−1,870.5*	*−1,942.6*	*−1,944.5*	*−2,581.2*	*−2,943.5*	*−3,562.7*
Services: credit	2 200 ..	2,025.7	1,897.0	1,912.3	2,137.7	2,297.1	2,329.7	2,648.7	2,701.8
Services: debit	3 200 ..	−1,422.5	−1,513.9	−1,597.4	−1,586.1	−1,725.4	−1,722.2	−2,021.0	−2,261.0
Balance on Goods and Services	4 991 ..	*−838.3*	*−1,235.1*	*−1,555.6*	*−1,391.1*	*−1,372.8*	*−1,973.7*	*−2,315.8*	*−3,121.9*
Income: credit	2 300 ..	193.1	218.2	221.0	217.6	269.6	327.9	378.4	520.7
Income: debit	3 300 ..	−543.0	−656.0	−826.3	−789.0	−852.1	−1,004.2	−994.0	−1,182.3
Balance on Goods, Services, and Income	4 992 ..	*−1,188.2*	*−1,672.9*	*−2,160.9*	*−1,962.5*	*−1,955.4*	*−2,649.9*	*−2,931.4*	*−3,783.5*
Current transfers: credit	2 379 Z.	969.4	1,090.7	1,337.9	1,523.5	1,892.1	1,935.5	2,088.5	2,385.7
Current transfers: debit	3 379 ..	−148.6	−176.6	−251.0	−334.4	−445.9	−357.0	−339.9	−345.8
B. Capital Account[1]	4 994 Z.	**2.2**	**−22.3**	**−16.9**	**.1**	**2.2**	**−18.3**	**−27.7**	**−35.5**
Capital account: credit	2 994 Z.	29.6	15.2	18.9	19.3	35.8	22.5	26.8	22.2
Capital account: debit	3 994 ..	−27.4	−37.5	−35.8	−19.2	−33.6	−40.8	−54.5	−57.7
Total, Groups A Plus B	4 981 ..	*−365.2*	*−781.1*	*−1,090.9*	*−773.3*	*−506.9*	*−1,089.8*	*−1,210.5*	*−1,779.1*
C. Financial Account[1]	4 995 W.	**853.9**	**1,660.5**	**910.9**	**314.4**	**1,215.8**	**1,297.3**	**1,312.0**	**1,289.2**
Direct investment abroad	4 505 ..	−74.3	−89.0	−73.9	−116.3	−60.0	−101.0	−85.4	−115.0
Direct investment in Jamaica	4 555 Z.	468.3	613.9	481.1	720.7	601.6	682.5	882.2	866.5
Portfolio investment assets	4 602 ..	−70.0	−39.3	−351.3	−1,105.2	−1,132.8	−1,406.4	−506.4	−1,768.6
Equity securities	4 610 ..	....	....	....	....	....	....	....	....
Debt securities	4 619 ..	−70.0	−39.3	−351.3	−1,105.2	−1,132.8	−1,406.4	−506.4	−1,768.6
Portfolio investment liabilities	4 652 Z.	5.9	69.7	155.8	819.6	1,228.8	1,280.4	377.9	1,128.1
Equity securities	4 660 ..	....	....	....	....	....	....	....	....
Debt securities	4 669 Z.	5.9	69.7	155.8	819.6	1,228.8	1,280.4	377.9	1,128.1
Financial derivatives	4 910 ..	....	....	....	....	....	....	....	....
Financial derivatives assets	4 900 ..	....	....	....	....	....	....	....	....
Financial derivatives liabilities	4 905 ..	....	....	....	....	....	....	....	....
Other investment assets	4 703 ..	−95.5	−215.5	−161.3	−307.6	−127.4	−290.8	−269.0	−238.3
Monetary authorities	4 701 ..	....	....	....	....	....	−61.3	.1	53.5
General government	4 704 ..	....	....	3.6	1.2	−1.0	−1.8	.1	−.8
Banks	4 705 ..	−181.5	−282.9	−227.0	−362.8	−175.5	−274.2	−317.6	−338.2
Other sectors	4 728 ..	86.0	67.4	62.1	54.0	49.1	46.5	48.4	47.2
Other investment liabilities	4 753 W.	619.5	1,320.7	860.5	303.1	705.6	1,132.6	912.7	1,416.5
Monetary authorities	4 753 WA	....	....	....	....	....	....	....	....
General government	4 753 ZB	383.6	653.4	78.0	−362.7	481.2	117.8	72.0	105.8
Banks	4 753 ZC	167.9	250.5	158.0	395.5	235.4	506.9	466.2	389.1
Other sectors	4 753 ZD	68.0	416.8	624.5	270.3	−11.0	507.9	374.5	921.5
Total, Groups A Through C	4 983 ..	*488.7*	*879.4*	*−180.0*	*−458.9*	*708.9*	*207.5*	*101.5*	*−489.9*
D. Net Errors and Omissions	4 998 ..	**29.7**	**−14.4**	**−61.0**	**28.3**	**−14.2**	**22.4**	**128.9**	**50.2**
Total, Groups A Through D	4 984 ..	*518.4*	*865.0*	*−241.0*	*−430.5*	*694.7*	*229.9*	*230.3*	*−439.8*
E. Reserves and Related Items	4 802 A.	**−518.4**	**−865.0**	**241.0**	**430.5**	**−694.7**	**−229.9**	**−230.3**	**439.8**
Reserve assets	4 802 ..	−499.4	−846.6	260.8	447.7	−685.6	−227.9	−230.3	439.8
Use of Fund credit and loans	4 766 ..	−19.0	−18.3	−18.9	−16.1	−8.0	−.9	....	....
Exceptional financing	4 920 ..	....	....	−.9	−1.0	−1.1	−1.1	....	....
Conversion rates: Jamaica dollars per U.S. dollar	0 101 ..	**42.986**	**45.996**	**48.416**	**57.741**	**61.197**	**62.281**	**65.744**	**68.950**

[1] Excludes components that have been classified in the categories of Group E.

Table 2. STANDARD PRESENTATION, 2000–2007

(Millions of U.S. dollars)

	Code	2000	2001	2002	2003	2004	2005	2006	2007
CURRENT ACCOUNT	4 993	−367.4	−758.8	−1,074.0	−773.4	−509.1	−1,071.5	−1,182.8	−1,743.6
A. GOODS	4 100	−1,441.5	−1,618.2	−1,870.5	−1,942.6	−1,944.5	−2,581.2	−2,943.5	−3,562.7
Credit	2 100	1,562.8	1,454.4	1,309.1	1,385.6	1,601.6	1,664.3	2,133.6	2,226.4
General merchandise: exports f.o.b.	2 110	1,524.9	1,419.0	1,280.0	1,337.6	1,531.3	1,588.3	2,037.6	2,123.2
Goods for processing: exports f.o.b.	2 150	....	....	....	....	....	....	....	....
Repairs on goods	2 160	....	....	....	....	....	....	....	....
Goods procured in ports by carriers	2 170	37.9	35.4	29.1	48.0	70.3	76.0	96.0	103.3
Nonmonetary gold	2 180	....	....	....	....	....	....	....	....
Debit	3 100	−3,004.3	−3,072.6	−3,179.6	−3,328.2	−3,546.1	−4,245.5	−5,077.1	−5,789.1
General merchandise: imports f.o.b.	3 110	−2,966.0	−3,033.9	−3,141.4	−3,252.0	−3,433.8	−4,134.3	−4,945.1	−5,652.1
Goods for processing: imports f.o.b.	3 150	....	....	....	....	....	....	....	....
Repairs on goods	3 160	....	....	....	....	....	....	....	....
Goods procured in ports by carriers	3 170	−38.3	−38.7	−38.2	−76.2	−112.3	−111.2	−132.0	−137.0
Nonmonetary gold	3 180	....	....	....	....	....	....	....	....
B. SERVICES	4 200	603.2	383.1	314.9	551.6	571.7	607.5	627.7	440.8
Total credit	2 200	*2,025.7*	*1,897.0*	*1,912.3*	*2,137.7*	*2,297.1*	*2,329.7*	*2,648.7*	*2,701.8*
Total debit	3 200	*−1,422.5*	*−1,513.9*	*−1,597.4*	*−1,586.1*	*−1,725.4*	*−1,722.2*	*−2,021.0*	*−2,261.0*
Transportation services, credit	2 205	328.6	350.5	368.7	474.3	497.3	451.1	459.0	447.2
Passenger	2 850	*243.7*	*261.6*	*272.8*	*266.2*	*295.2*	*237.8*	*224.2*	*231.5*
Freight	2 851	*6.5*	*6.9*	*6.9*	*3.6*	*7.6*	*14.6*	*17.8*	*15.3*
Other	2 852	*78.4*	*82.0*	*89.0*	*204.5*	*194.5*	*198.7*	*217.0*	*200.3*
Sea transport, passenger	2 207	....	....	....	....	....	....	....	....
Sea transport, freight	2 208	....	....	....	....	....	....	....	....
Sea transport, other	2 209	....	....	....	....	....	....	....	....
Air transport, passenger	2 211	....	....	....	....	....	....	....	....
Air transport, freight	2 212	....	....	....	....	....	....	....	....
Air transport, other	2 213	....	....	....	....	....	....	....	....
Other transport, passenger	2 215	....	....	....	....	....	....	....	....
Other transport, freight	2 216	....	....	....	....	....	....	....	....
Other transport, other	2 217	....	....	....	....	....	....	....	....
Transportation services, debit	3 205	−585.2	−606.7	−614.3	−617.9	−647.6	−717.7	−885.4	−972.0
Passenger	3 850	*−28.5*	*−20.9*	*−15.8*	*−17.4*	*−31.7*	*−40.8*	*−41.5*	*−41.7*
Freight	3 851	*−431.4*	*−448.2*	*−473.7*	*−467.1*	*−506.2*	*−572.1*	*−666.4*	*−759.5*
Other	3 852	*−125.3*	*−137.6*	*−124.8*	*−133.4*	*−109.7*	*−104.9*	*−177.5*	*−170.8*
Sea transport, passenger	3 207	....	....	....	....	....	....	....	....
Sea transport, freight	3 208	....	....	....	....	....	....	....	....
Sea transport, other	3 209	....	....	....	....	....	....	....	....
Air transport, passenger	3 211	....	....	....	....	....	....	....	....
Air transport, freight	3 212	....	....	....	....	....	....	....	....
Air transport, other	3 213	....	....	....	....	....	....	....	....
Other transport, passenger	3 215	....	....	....	....	....	....	....	....
Other transport, freight	3 216	....	....	....	....	....	....	....	....
Other transport, other	3 217	....	....	....	....	....	....	....	....
Travel, credit	2 236	1,332.6	1,232.2	1,208.7	1,355.1	1,438.0	1,545.2	1,870.1	1,905.3
Business travel	2 237	....	....	....	....	....	....	....	....
Personal travel	2 240	....	....	....	....	....	....	....	....
Travel, debit	3 236	−208.7	−206.0	−258.4	−252.4	−286.2	−249.5	−273.4	−298.2
Business travel	3 237	....	....	....	....	....	....	....	....
Personal travel	3 240	....	....	....	....	....	....	....	....
Other services, credit	2 200 BA	364.5	314.3	334.9	308.3	361.8	333.4	319.7	349.4
Communications	2 245	209.4	164.7	171.1	144.6	192.8	148.4	147.8	157.2
Construction	2 249	....	....	....	....	....	....	....	....
Insurance	2 253	12.1	11.9	15.4	7.8	9.1	14.2	13.8	12.4
Financial	2 260	12.6	15.8	22.4	26.3	27.7	50.4	40.4	66.9
Computer and information	2 262	40.4	36.6	34.1	36.0	33.1	34.5	28.8	27.3
Royalties and licence fees	2 266	6.4	5.9	6.1	12.0	9.7	12.7	12.0	14.9
Other business services	2 268	36.4	40.7	45.2	26.4	26.3	9.6	10.5	4.7
Personal, cultural, and recreational	2 287	9.6	9.0	9.2	20.4	28.4	29.7	31.2	29.1
Government, n.i.e.	2 291	37.6	29.7	31.3	34.8	34.6	34.1	35.2	37.0
Other services, debit	3 200 BA	−628.6	−701.2	−724.7	−715.8	−791.6	−755.0	−862.2	−990.8
Communications	3 245	−31.8	−50.1	−52.9	−45.9	−48.4	−47.2	−79.6	−72.4
Construction	3 249	−10.2	−10.0	−5.9	−4.8	−4.8	−4.8	−4.8	−4.8
Insurance	3 253	−87.2	−94.1	−118.4	−97.3	−124.4	−133.8	−168.2	−175.8
Financial	3 260	−18.4	−29.7	−17.7	−16.3	−32.0	−34.2	−42.7	−54.9
Computer and information	3 262	−7.1	−13.8	−11.6	−20.4	−75.1	−17.2	−23.7	−25.8
Royalties and licence fees	3 266	−41.0	−38.3	−32.1	−10.8	−9.1	−11.0	−11.2	−60.4
Other business services	3 268	−396.8	−427.2	−436.4	−469.5	−447.1	−458.5	−476.1	−538.5
Personal, cultural, and recreational	3 287	−4.1	−4.0	−4.0	−2.4	−2.5	−2.0	−4.4	−2.2
Government, n.i.e.	3 291	−32.0	−34.0	−45.8	−48.4	−48.2	−46.4	−51.6	−56.1

Table 2 (Continued). STANDARD PRESENTATION, 2000–2007

(Millions of U.S. dollars)

	Code	2000	2001	2002	2003	2004	2005	2006	2007
C. INCOME	4 300	−349.9	−437.8	−605.3	−571.4	−582.5	−676.2	−615.6	−661.6
Total credit	2 300	*193.1*	*218.2*	*221.0*	*217.6*	*269.6*	*327.9*	*378.4*	*520.7*
Total debit	3 300	*−543.0*	*−656.0*	*−826.3*	*−789.0*	*−852.1*	*−1,004.2*	*−994.0*	*−1,182.3*
Compensation of employees, credit	2 310	88.2	106.7	111.0	110.1	135.4	140.4	154.4	157.8
Compensation of employees, debit	3 310	−20.8	−32.1	−28.9	−39.4	−51.0	−51.8	−58.4	−93.0
Investment income, credit	2 320	104.9	111.5	110.0	107.5	134.2	187.5	224.1	363.0
Direct investment income	2 330	8.5	5.7	17.2	8.4	24.9	24.4	−.3	9.6
Dividends and distributed branch profits	2 332	6.3	5.7	17.2	8.4	24.9	24.4	−.3	9.6
Reinvested earnings and undistributed branch profits	2 333	....	....	....	....	....	....	....	....
Income on debt (interest)	2 334	2.2	....	....	....	....	....	....	....
Portfolio investment income	2 339	2.7	5.3	12.4	14.8	35.9	56.3	73.8	176.7
Income on equity	2 340	....	....	....	....	....	....	....	....
Income on bonds and notes	2 350	....	....	....	....	....	....	....	....
Income on money market instruments	2 360	....	....	....	....	....	....	....	....
Other investment income	2 370	93.7	100.5	80.4	84.3	73.3	106.9	150.6	176.7
Investment income, debit	3 320	−522.2	−623.9	−797.4	−749.6	−801.1	−952.4	−935.7	−1,089.3
Direct investment income	3 330	−289.9	−300.8	−434.3	−326.3	−361.6	−453.7	−375.6	−532.6
Dividends and distributed branch profits	3 332	−159.0	−171.6	−247.4	−128.6	−175.8	−241.1	−228.8	−316.6
Reinvested earnings and undistributed branch profits	3 333	−116.0	−115.9	−164.3	−158.1	−178.0	−201.6	−132.1	−177.3
Income on debt (interest)	3 334	−14.9	−13.3	−22.6	−39.6	−7.8	−11.0	−14.7	−38.7
Portfolio investment income	3 339	−7.6	−6.7	−9.0	−25.2	−18.6	−35.2	−42.3	−27.1
Income on equity	3 340	....	....	....	....	....	....	....	....
Income on bonds and notes	3 350	....	....	....	....	....	....	....	....
Income on money market instruments	3 360	....	....	....	....	....	....	....	....
Other investment income	3 370	−224.7	−316.4	−354.1	−398.1	−421.0	−463.5	−517.8	−529.6
D. CURRENT TRANSFERS	4 379	820.8	914.1	1,086.9	1,189.1	1,446.3	1,578.4	1,748.6	2,039.9
Credit	2 379	969.4	1,090.7	1,337.9	1,523.5	1,892.1	1,935.5	2,088.5	2,385.7
General government	2 380	155.1	125.0	115.1	110.0	163.5	141.8	152.1	141.2
Other sectors	2 390	814.3	965.7	1,222.8	1,413.5	1,728.6	1,793.7	1,936.4	2,244.4
Workers' remittances	2 391	789.5	939.9	1,130.6	1,269.5	1,465.8	1,621.2	1,769.4	1,964.3
Other current transfers	2 392	24.8	25.8	92.2	144.0	262.8	172.4	167.0	280.1
Debit	3 379	−148.6	−176.6	−251.0	−334.4	−445.9	−357.0	−339.9	−345.8
General government	3 380	−7.2	−6.6	−7.5	−4.8	−3.6	−4.8	−6.7	−8.3
Other sectors	3 390	−141.4	−170.0	−243.5	−329.6	−442.3	−352.2	−333.2	−337.5
Workers' remittances	3 391	−131.2	−147.3	−213.4	−282.8	−339.9	−317.0	−299.6	−303.2
Other current transfers	3 392	−10.2	−22.7	−30.1	−46.8	−102.3	−35.3	−33.6	−34.3
CAPITAL AND FINANCIAL ACCOUNT	4 996	337.7	773.2	1,135.1	745.0	523.3	1,049.1	1,054.0	1,693.4
CAPITAL ACCOUNT	4 994	2.2	−22.3	−16.9	.1	2.2	−18.3	−27.7	−35.5
Total credit	2 994	*29.6*	*15.2*	*18.9*	*19.3*	*35.8*	*22.5*	*26.8*	*22.2*
Total debit	3 994	*−27.4*	*−37.5*	*−35.8*	*−19.2*	*−33.6*	*−40.8*	*−54.5*	*−57.7*
Capital transfers, credit	2 400	29.6	15.2	18.9	18.9	35.8	22.5	26.8	22.2
General government	2 401	15.6	3.5	.2	.1	13.8	.3	4.1	.7
Debt forgiveness	2 402	....	....	....	....	....	....	....	....
Other capital transfers	2 410	15.6	3.5	.2	.1	13.8	.3	4.1	.7
Other sectors	2 430	14.0	11.7	18.7	18.8	22.0	22.2	22.7	21.5
Migrants' transfers	2 431	14.0	11.7	18.7	18.8	22.0	22.2	22.7	21.5
Debt forgiveness	2 432	....	....	....	....	....	....	....	....
Other capital transfers	2 440	....	....	....	....	....	....	....	....
Capital transfers, debit	3 400	−27.4	−37.5	−35.8	−19.2	−33.6	−40.8	−54.5	−57.7
General government	3 401	....	....	....	....	....	....	....	....
Debt forgiveness	3 402	....	....	....	....	....	....	....	....
Other capital transfers	3 410	....	....	....	....	....	....	....	....
Other sectors	3 430	−27.4	−37.5	−35.8	−19.2	−33.6	−40.8	−54.5	−57.7
Migrants' transfers	3 431	−27.4	−37.5	−35.8	−19.2	−33.6	−40.8	−54.5	−57.7
Debt forgiveness	3 432	....	....	....	....	....	....	....	....
Other capital transfers	3 440	....	....	....	....	....	....	....	....
Nonproduced nonfinancial assets, credit	2 480	....	....	....	.4	....	....	....	....
Nonproduced nonfinancial assets, debit	3 480	....	....	....	....	....	....	....	....

2008, International Monetary Fund: *Balance of Payments Statistics Yearbook*

Table 2 (Continued). STANDARD PRESENTATION, 2000–2007

(Millions of U.S. dollars)

	Code	2000	2001	2002	2003	2004	2005	2006	2007
FINANCIAL ACCOUNT	4 995 ..	**335.5**	**795.5**	**1,152.0**	**744.9**	**521.1**	**1,067.4**	**1,081.7**	**1,729.0**
A. DIRECT INVESTMENT	4 500 ..	**394.0**	**524.9**	**407.2**	**604.4**	**541.6**	**581.5**	**796.8**	**751.5**
Direct investment abroad	4 505 ..	**−74.3**	**−89.0**	**−73.9**	**−116.3**	**−60.0**	**−101.0**	**−85.4**	**−115.0**
Equity capital	4 510 ..	−25.6	−51.6	−36.6	−79.1	−17.7	−56.4	−45.6	−60.4
Claims on affiliated enterprises	4 515 ..	−25.6	−51.6	−36.6	−79.1	−17.7	−56.4	−45.6	−60.4
Liabilities to affiliated enterprises	4 520 ..	. . . .	. . . .	. . . .	. . . .	. . . .	. . . .	. . . .	. . . .
Reinvested earnings	4 525 ..	. . . .	. . . .	. . . .	. . . .	. . . .	. . . .	. . . .	. . . .
Other capital	4 530 ..	−48.7	−37.4	−37.3	−37.2	−42.2	−44.6	−39.8	−54.6
Claims on affiliated enterprises	4 535 ..	. . . .	. . . .	. . . .	. . . .	. . . .	. . . .	. . . .	. . . .
Liabilities to affiliated enterprises	4 540 ..	−48.7	−37.4	−37.3	−37.2	−42.2	−44.6	−39.8	−54.6
Direct investment in Jamaica	4 555 ..	**468.3**	**613.9**	**481.1**	**720.7**	**601.6**	**682.5**	**882.2**	**866.5**
Equity capital	4 560 ..	273.8	427.4	271.1	538.7	336.3	458.3	740.1	540.5
Claims on direct investors	4 565 ..	. . . .	. . . .	. . . .	. . . .	. . . .	. . . .	. . . .	. . . .
Liabilities to direct investors	4 570 ..	273.8	427.4	271.1	538.7	336.3	458.3	740.1	540.5
Reinvested earnings	4 575 ..	116.0	115.9	164.3	158.1	178.0	201.6	132.1	177.3
Other capital	4 580 ..	78.5	70.6	45.7	23.9	87.3	22.7	10.0	148.7
Claims on direct investors	4 585 ..	. . . .	. . . .	. . . .	. . . .	. . . .	. . . .	. . . .	. . . .
Liabilities to direct investors	4 590 ..	78.5	70.6	45.7	23.9	87.3	22.7	10.0	148.7
B. PORTFOLIO INVESTMENT	4 600 ..	**−64.1**	**30.4**	**−195.5**	**−285.6**	**96.0**	**−126.0**	**−128.5**	**−640.4**
Assets	4 602 ..	**−70.0**	**−39.3**	**−351.3**	**−1,105.2**	**−1,132.8**	**−1,406.4**	**−506.4**	**−1,768.6**
Equity securities	4 610 ..	. . . .	. . . .	. . . .	. . . .	. . . .	. . . .	. . . .	. . . .
Monetary authorities	4 611 ..	. . . .	. . . .	. . . .	. . . .	. . . .	. . . .	. . . .	. . . .
General government	4 612 ..	. . . .	. . . .	. . . .	. . . .	. . . .	. . . .	. . . .	. . . .
Banks	4 613 ..	. . . .	. . . .	. . . .	. . . .	. . . .	. . . .	. . . .	. . . .
Other sectors	4 614 ..	. . . .	. . . .	. . . .	. . . .	. . . .	. . . .	. . . .	. . . .
Debt securities	4 619 ..	−70.0	−39.3	−351.3	−1,105.2	−1,132.8	−1,406.4	−506.4	−1,768.6
Bonds and notes	4 620 ..	−70.0	−39.3	−351.3	−1,105.2	−1,132.8	−1,406.4	−506.4	−1,768.6
Monetary authorities	4 621 ..	. . . .	. . . .	. . . .	. . . .	. . . .	. . . .	. . . .	. . . .
General government	4 622 ..	. . . .	. . . .	. . . .	. . . .	. . . .	. . . .	. . . .	. . . .
Banks	4 623 ..	. . . .	. . . .	. . . .	. . . .	. . . .	. . . .	. . . .	. . . .
Other sectors	4 624 ..	−70.0	−39.3	−351.3	−1,105.2	−1,132.8	−1,406.4	−506.4	−1,768.6
Money market instruments	4 630 ..	. . . .	. . . .	. . . .	. . . .	. . . .	. . . .	. . . .	. . . .
Monetary authorities	4 631 ..	. . . .	. . . .	. . . .	. . . .	. . . .	. . . .	. . . .	. . . .
General government	4 632 ..	. . . .	. . . .	. . . .	. . . .	. . . .	. . . .	. . . .	. . . .
Banks	4 633 ..	. . . .	. . . .	. . . .	. . . .	. . . .	. . . .	. . . .	. . . .
Other sectors	4 634 ..	. . . .	. . . .	. . . .	. . . .	. . . .	. . . .	. . . .	. . . .
Liabilities	4 652 ..	**5.9**	**69.7**	**155.8**	**819.6**	**1,228.8**	**1,280.4**	**377.9**	**1,128.1**
Equity securities	4 660 ..	. . . .	. . . .	. . . .	. . . .	. . . .	. . . .	. . . .	. . . .
Banks	4 663 ..	. . . .	. . . .	. . . .	. . . .	. . . .	. . . .	. . . .	. . . .
Other sectors	4 664 ..	. . . .	. . . .	. . . .	. . . .	. . . .	. . . .	. . . .	. . . .
Debt securities	4 669 ..	5.9	69.7	155.8	819.6	1,228.8	1,280.4	377.9	1,128.1
Bonds and notes	4 670 ..	5.9	69.7	155.8	819.6	1,228.8	1,280.4	377.9	1,128.1
Monetary authorities	4 671 ..	. . . .	. . . .	. . . .	. . . .	. . . .	. . . .	. . . .	. . . .
General government	4 672 ..	. . . .	. . . .	. . . .	. . . .	. . . .	. . . .	. . . .	. . . .
Banks	4 673 ..	. . . .	. . . .	. . . .	. . . .	. . . .	. . . .	. . . .	. . . .
Other sectors	4 674 ..	5.9	69.7	155.8	819.6	1,228.8	1,280.4	377.9	1,128.1
Money market instruments	4 680 ..	. . . .	. . . .	. . . .	. . . .	. . . .	. . . .	. . . .	. . . .
Monetary authorities	4 681 ..	. . . .	. . . .	. . . .	. . . .	. . . .	. . . .	. . . .	. . . .
General government	4 682 ..	. . . .	. . . .	. . . .	. . . .	. . . .	. . . .	. . . .	. . . .
Banks	4 683 ..	. . . .	. . . .	. . . .	. . . .	. . . .	. . . .	. . . .	. . . .
Other sectors	4 684 ..	. . . .	. . . .	. . . .	. . . .	. . . .	. . . .	. . . .	. . . .
C. FINANCIAL DERIVATIVES	4 910 ..	. . . .	. . . .	. . . .	. . . .	. . . .	. . . .	. . . .	. . . .
Monetary authorities	4 911 ..	. . . .	. . . .	. . . .	. . . .	. . . .	. . . .	. . . .	. . . .
General government	4 912 ..	. . . .	. . . .	. . . .	. . . .	. . . .	. . . .	. . . .	. . . .
Banks	4 913 ..	. . . .	. . . .	. . . .	. . . .	. . . .	. . . .	. . . .	. . . .
Other sectors	4 914 ..	. . . .	. . . .	. . . .	. . . .	. . . .	. . . .	. . . .	. . . .
Assets	4 900 ..	. . . .	. . . .	. . . .	. . . .	. . . .	. . . .	. . . .	. . . .
Monetary authorities	4 901 ..	. . . .	. . . .	. . . .	. . . .	. . . .	. . . .	. . . .	. . . .
General government	4 902 ..	. . . .	. . . .	. . . .	. . . .	. . . .	. . . .	. . . .	. . . .
Banks	4 903 ..	. . . .	. . . .	. . . .	. . . .	. . . .	. . . .	. . . .	. . . .
Other sectors	4 904 ..	. . . .	. . . .	. . . .	. . . .	. . . .	. . . .	. . . .	. . . .
Liabilities	4 905 ..	. . . .	. . . .	. . . .	. . . .	. . . .	. . . .	. . . .	. . . .
Monetary authorities	4 906 ..	. . . .	. . . .	. . . .	. . . .	. . . .	. . . .	. . . .	. . . .
General government	4 907 ..	. . . .	. . . .	. . . .	. . . .	. . . .	. . . .	. . . .	. . . .
Banks	4 908 ..	. . . .	. . . .	. . . .	. . . .	. . . .	. . . .	. . . .	. . . .
Other sectors	4 909 ..	. . . .	. . . .	. . . .	. . . .	. . . .	. . . .	. . . .	. . . .

Table 2 (Concluded). STANDARD PRESENTATION, 2000–2007

(Millions of U.S. dollars)

	Code	2000	2001	2002	2003	2004	2005	2006	2007
D. OTHER INVESTMENT............................	4 700 ..	**505.0**	**1,086.9**	**679.4**	**−21.6**	**569.1**	**839.8**	**643.7**	**1,178.2**
Assets..	4 703 ..	**−95.5**	**−215.5**	**−161.3**	**−307.6**	**−127.4**	**−290.8**	**−269.0**	**−238.3**
Trade credits..........................	4 706 ..	....	....	....	....	....	....	....	....
General government...............	4 707 ..	....	....	....	....	....	....	....	....
of which: Short-term.........	4 709 ..	....	....	....	....	....	....	....	....
Other sectors.........................	4 710 ..	....	....	....	....	....	....	....	....
of which: Short-term.........	4 712 ..	....	....	....	....	....	....	....	....
Loans....................................	4 714 ..	....	....	....	....	....	....	....	....
Monetary authorities...............	4 715 ..	....	....	....	....	....	....	....	....
of which: Short-term.........	4 718 ..	....	....	....	....	....	....	....	....
General government...............	4 719 ..	....	....	....	....	....	....	....	....
of which: Short-term.........	4 721 ..	....	....	....	....	....	....	....	....
Banks.....................................	4 722 ..	....	....	....	....	....	....	....	....
of which: Short-term.........	4 724 ..	....	....	....	....	....	....	....	....
Other sectors.........................	4 725 ..	....	....	....	....	....	....	....	....
of which: Short-term.........	4 727 ..	....	....	....	....	....	....	....	....
Currency and deposits..............	4 730 ..	−181.5	−282.9	−227.0	−362.8	−175.5	−274.2	−317.6	−338.2
Monetary authorities...............	4 731 ..	....	....	....	....	....	....	....	....
General government...............	4 732 ..	....	....	....	....	....	....	....	....
Banks.....................................	4 733 ..	−181.5	−282.9	−227.0	−362.8	−175.5	−274.2	−317.6	−338.2
Other sectors.........................	4 734 ..	....	....	....	....	....	....	....	....
Other assets............................	4 736 ..	86.0	67.4	65.7	55.2	48.1	−16.6	48.6	99.9
Monetary authorities...............	4 737 ..	....	....	....	....	....	−61.3	.1	53.5
of which: Short-term.........	4 739 ..	....	....	....	....	....	*−61.3*	*.1*	*53.5*
General government...............	4 740 ..	....	....	3.6	1.2	−1.0	−1.8	.1	−.8
of which: Short-term.........	4 742 ..	....	....	....	....	....	....	....	....
Banks.....................................	4 743 ..	....	....	....	....	....	....	....	....
of which: Short-term.........	4 745 ..	....	....	....	....	....	....	....	....
Other sectors.........................	4 746 ..	86.0	67.4	62.1	54.0	49.1	46.5	48.4	47.2
of which: Short-term.........	4 748 ..	*87.6*	*88.5*	*63.2*	*55.2*	*50.8*	*48.3*	*50.8*	*50.8*
Liabilities......................................	4 753 ..	**600.5**	**1,302.4**	**840.7**	**286.0**	**696.5**	**1,130.6**	**912.7**	**1,416.5**
Trade credits..........................	4 756 ..	10.1	−42.9	8.1	10.5	−19.8	16.2	−149.9	65.8
General government...............	4 757 ..	....	....	....	....	....	....	....	....
of which: Short-term.........	4 759 ..	....	....	....	....	....	....	....	....
Other sectors.........................	4 760 ..	10.1	−42.9	8.1	10.5	−19.8	16.2	−149.9	65.8
of which: Short-term.........	4 762 ..	*10.1*	*−42.9*	*8.1*	*10.5*	*−19.8*	*16.2*	*−149.9*	*65.8*
Loans....................................	4 764 ..	446.2	730.2	80.7	−77.4	737.9	627.9	1,003.7	519.5
Monetary authorities...............	4 765 ..	−19.0	−18.3	−19.8	−17.1	−9.1	−2.0	....	....
of which: Use of Fund credit and loans from the Fund..	4 766 ..	*−19.0*	*−18.3*	*−18.9*	*−16.1*	*−8.0*	*−.9*	....	....
of which: Short-term.........	4 768 ..	....	....	....	....	....	....	....	....
General government...............	4 769 ..	383.6	653.4	78.0	−362.7	481.2	117.8	72.0	105.8
of which: Short-term.........	4 771 ..	....	....	....	....	....	....	....	....
Banks.....................................	4 772 ..	....	....	....	....	....	....	....	....
of which: Short-term.........	4 774 ..	....	....	....	....	....	....	....	....
Other sectors.........................	4 775 ..	81.6	95.1	22.5	302.4	265.8	512.0	931.6	413.7
of which: Short-term.........	4 777 ..	....	....	....	....	....	....	....	....
Currency and deposits..............	4 780 ..	143.1	614.0	750.3	350.5	−24.2	484.9	57.2	829.4
Monetary authorities...............	4 781 ..	....	....	....	....	....	....	....	....
General government...............	4 782 ..	....	....	....	....	....	....	....	....
Banks.....................................	4 783 ..	167.9	250.5	158.0	395.5	235.4	506.9	466.2	389.1
Other sectors.........................	4 784 ..	−24.8	363.5	592.3	−45.0	−259.6	−22.0	−409.0	440.2
Other liabilities.......................	4 786 ..	1.1	1.1	1.6	2.4	2.6	1.6	1.8	1.8
Monetary authorities...............	4 787 ..	....	....	....	....	....	....	....	....
of which: Short-term.........	4 789 ..	....	....	....	....	....	....	....	....
General government...............	4 790 ..	....	....	....	....	....	....	....	....
of which: Short-term.........	4 792 ..	....	....	....	....	....	....	....	....
Banks.....................................	4 793 ..	....	....	....	....	....	....	....	....
of which: Short-term.........	4 795 ..	....	....	....	....	....	....	....	....
Other sectors.........................	4 796 ..	1.1	1.1	1.6	2.4	2.6	1.6	1.8	1.8
of which: Short-term.........	4 798 ..	....	....	....	....	....	....	....	....
E. RESERVE ASSETS.................................	4 802 ..	**−499.4**	**−846.6**	**260.8**	**447.7**	**−685.6**	**−227.9**	**−230.3**	**439.8**
Monetary gold..........................	4 812 ..	....	....	....	....	....	....	....	....
Special drawing rights................	4 811 ..	.5	−1.4	.6	.9	....	.1	−.2	....
Reserve position in the Fund........	4 810 ..	....	....	....	....	....	....	....	....
Foreign exchange......................	4 803 ..	−500.6	−845.4	260.2	446.8	−685.6	−228.0	−230.1	439.8
Other claims............................	4 813 ..	.7	.2	....	....	....	....	....	....
NET ERRORS AND OMISSIONS...........................	4 998 ..	**29.7**	**−14.4**	**−61.0**	**28.3**	**−14.2**	**22.4**	**128.9**	**50.2**

Table 3. INTERNATIONAL INVESTMENT POSITION (End-period stocks), 2000–2007

(Millions of U.S. dollars)

	Code	2000	2001	2002	2003	2004	2005	2006	2007
ASSETS..	8 995 C.	....	....	....	....	....	3,616.4	4,463.7	5,075.4
Direct investment abroad.............................	8 505 ..	....	....	....	....	....	48.6	96.0	211.0
Equity capital and reinvested earnings.............................	8 506 ..	....	....	....	....	....	....	....	....
Claims on affiliated enterprises................................	8 507 ..	....	....	....	....	....	....	....	....
Liabilities to affiliated enterprises............................	8 508 ..	....	....	....	....	....	....	....	....
Other capital...	8 530 ..	....	....	....	....	....	....	....	....
Claims on affiliated enterprises................................	8 535 ..	....	....	....	....	....	....	....	....
Liabilities to affiliated enterprises............................	8 540 ..	....	....	....	....	....	....	....	....
Portfolio investment.................................	8 602 ..	....	....	....	....	....	602.6	1,114.8	1,462.5
Equity securities...	8 610 ..	....	....	....	....	....	....	....	....
Monetary authorities......................................	8 611 ..	....	....	....	....	....	....	....	....
General government......................................	8 612 ..	....	....	....	....	....	....	....	....
Banks..	8 613 ..	....	....	....	....	....	....	....	....
Other sectors..	8 614 ..	....	....	....	....	....	....	....	....
Debt securities..	8 619 ..	....	....	....	....	....	....	....	....
Bonds and notes...	8 620 ..	....	....	....	....	....	....	....	....
Monetary authorities....................................	8 621 ..	....	....	....	....	....	....	....	....
General government....................................	8 622 ..	....	....	....	....	....	....	....	....
Banks..	8 623 ..	....	....	....	....	....	....	....	....
Other sectors...	8 624 ..	....	....	....	....	....	....	....	....
Money market instruments................................	8 630 ..	....	....	....	....	....	....	....	....
Monetary authorities....................................	8 631 ..	....	....	....	....	....	....	....	....
General government....................................	8 632 ..	....	....	....	....	....	....	....	....
Banks..	8 633 ..	....	....	....	....	....	....	....	....
Other sectors...	8 634 ..	....	....	....	....	....	....	....	....
Financial derivatives..............................	8 900 ..	....	....	....	....	....	19.4	2.8	17.6
Monetary authorities......................................	8 901 ..	....	....	....	....	....	....	....	....
General government......................................	8 902 ..	....	....	....	....	....	....	....	....
Banks...	8 903 ..	....	....	....	....	....	....	....	....
Other sectors...	8 904 ..	....	....	....	....	....	....	....	....
Other investment.................................	8 703 ..	....	....	....	....	....	858.5	932.3	1,506.2
Trade credits...	8 706 ..	....	....	....	....	....	30.5	37.6	121.8
General government......................................	8 707 ..	....	....	....	....	....	....	....	....
of which: Short-term.................................	8 709 ..	....	....	....	....	....	....	....	....
Other sectors..	8 710 ..	....	....	....	....	....	....	....	....
of which: Short-term.................................	8 712 ..	....	....	....	....	....	....	....	....
Loans..	8 714 ..	....	....	....	....	....	26.9	29.4	60.5
Monetary authorities......................................	8 715 ..	....	....	....	....	....	....	....	....
of which: Short-term.................................	8 718 ..	....	....	....	....	....	....	....	....
General government......................................	8 719 ..	....	....	....	....	....	....	....	....
of which: Short-term.................................	8 721 ..	....	....	....	....	....	....	....	....
Banks..	8 722 ..	....	....	....	....	....	....	....	....
of which: Short-term.................................	8 724 ..	....	....	....	....	....	....	....	....
Other sectors..	8 725 ..	....	....	....	....	....	....	....	....
of which: Short-term.................................	8 727 ..	....	....	....	....	....	....	....	....
Currency and deposits....................................	8 730 ..	....	....	....	....	....	623.2	594.4	914.7
Monetary authorities......................................	8 731 ..	....	....	....	....	....	....	....	....
General government......................................	8 732 ..	....	....	....	....	....	....	....	....
Banks..	8 733 ..	....	....	....	....	....	....	....	....
Other sectors..	8 734 ..	....	....	....	....	....	....	....	....
Other assets..	8 736 ..	....	....	....	....	....	177.9	270.9	409.2
Monetary authorities......................................	8 737 ..	....	....	....	....	....	....	....	....
of which: Short-term.................................	8 739 ..	....	....	....	....	....	....	....	....
General government......................................	8 740 ..	....	....	....	....	....	....	....	....
of which: Short-term.................................	8 742 ..	....	....	....	....	....	....	....	....
Banks..	8 743 ..	....	....	....	....	....	....	....	....
of which: Short-term.................................	8 745 ..	....	....	....	....	....	....	....	....
Other sectors..	8 746 ..	....	....	....	....	....	....	....	....
of which: Short-term.................................	8 748 ..	....	....	....	....	....	....	....	....
Reserve assets.................................	8 802 ..	....	....	....	....	....	2,087.4	2,317.8	1,878.1
Monetary gold..	8 812 ..	....	....	....	....	....	....	....	....
Special drawing rights....................................	8 811 ..	.1	1.5	.9	.1	.1	....	.3	.3
Reserve position in the Fund..............................	8 810 ..	....	....	....	....	....	....	....	....
Foreign exchange...	8 803 ..	....	....	....	....	....	2,087.4	2,317.6	1,877.7
Other claims...	8 813 ..	....	....	....	....	....	....	....	....

Table 3 (Concluded). INTERNATIONAL INVESTMENT POSITION (End-period stocks), 2000–2007

(Millions of U.S. dollars)

	Code	2000	2001	2002	2003	2004	2005	2006	2007
LIABILITIES	8 995 D.	....	....	....	....	....	14,440.9	16,696.3	18,729.8
Direct investment in Jamaica	8 555 ..	....	....	....	....	....	6,918.5	7,800.7	8,667.2
Equity capital and reinvested earnings	8 556 ..	....	....	....	....	....	....	....	....
Claims on direct investors	8 557 ..	....	....	....	....	....	....	....	....
Liabilities to direct investors	8 558 ..	....	....	....	....	....	....	....	....
Other capital	8 580 ..	....	....	....	....	....	....	....	....
Claims on direct investors	8 585 ..	....	....	....	....	....	....	....	....
Liabilities to direct investors	8 590 ..	....	....	....	....	....	....	....	....
Portfolio investment	8 652 ..	....	....	....	....	....	357.5	518.5	578.3
Equity securities	8 660 ..	....	....	....	....	....	....	....	....
Banks	8 663 ..	....	....	....	....	....	....	....	....
Other sectors	8 664 ..	....	....	....	....	....	....	....	....
Debt securities	8 669 ..	....	....	....	....	....	....	....	....
Bonds and notes	8 670 ..	....	....	....	....	....	....	....	....
Monetary authorities	8 671 ..	....	....	....	....	....	....	....	....
General government	8 672 ..	....	....	....	....	....	....	....	....
Banks	8 673 ..	....	....	....	....	....	....	....	....
Other sectors	8 674 ..	....	....	....	....	....	....	....	....
Money market instruments	8 680 ..	....	....	....	....	....	....	....	....
Monetary authorities	8 681 ..	....	....	....	....	....	....	....	....
General government	8 682 ..	....	....	....	....	....	....	....	....
Banks	8 683 ..	....	....	....	....	....	....	....	....
Other sectors	8 684 ..	....	....	....	....	....	....	....	....
Financial derivatives	8 905 ..	....	....	....	....	....	11.3	....	11.5
Monetary authorities	8 906 ..	....	....	....	....	....	....	....	....
General government	8 907 ..	....	....	....	....	....	....	....	....
Banks	8 908 ..	....	....	....	....	....	....	....	....
Other sectors	8 909 ..	....	....	....	....	....	....	....	....
Other investment	8 753 ..	....	....	....	....	....	7,153.5	8,377.1	9,472.7
Trade credits	8 756 ..	....	....	....	....	....	48.4	654.9	1,094.3
General government	8 757 ..	....	....	....	....	....	....	....	....
of which: Short-term	8 759 ..	....	....	....	....	....	....	....	....
Other sectors	8 760 ..	....	....	....	....	....	....	....	....
of which: Short-term	8 762 ..	....	....	....	....	....	....	....	....
Loans	8 764 ..	....	....	....	....	....	6,545.1	6,879.7	7,488.9
Monetary authorities	8 765 ..	....	....	....	....	....	....	....	....
of which: Use of Fund credit and loans from the Fund	8 766 ..	60.4	40.0	23.7	8.9	.9	....	....	....
of which: Short-term	8 768 ..	....	....	....	....	....	....	....	....
General government	8 769 ..	....	....	....	....	....	....	....	....
of which: Short-term	8 771 ..	....	....	....	....	....	....	....	....
Banks	8 772 ..	....	....	....	....	....	....	....	....
of which: Short-term	8 774 ..	....	....	....	....	....	....	....	....
Other sectors	8 775 ..	....	....	....	....	....	....	....	....
of which: Short-term	8 777 ..	....	....	....	....	....	....	....	....
Currency and deposits	8 780 ..	....	....	....	....	....	386.7	777.9	827.4
Monetary authorities	8 781 ..	....	....	....	....	....	....	....	....
General government	8 782 ..	....	....	....	....	....	....	....	....
Banks	8 783 ..	....	....	....	....	....	....	....	....
Other sectors	8 784 ..	....	....	....	....	....	....	....	....
Other liabilities	8 786 ..	....	....	....	....	....	173.3	64.6	62.1
Monetary authorities	8 787 ..	....	....	....	....	....	....	....	....
of which: Short-term	8 789 ..	....	....	....	....	....	....	....	....
General government	8 790 ..	....	....	....	....	....	....	....	....
of which: Short-term	8 792 ..	....	....	....	....	....	....	....	....
Banks	8 793 ..	....	....	....	....	....	....	....	....
of which: Short-term	8 795 ..	....	....	....	....	....	....	....	....
Other sectors	8 796 ..	....	....	....	....	....	....	....	....
of which: Short-term	8 798 ..	....	....	....	....	....	....	....	....
NET INTERNATIONAL INVESTMENT POSITION	8 995 ..	....	....	....	....	....	−10,824.4	−12,232.7	−13,654.4
Conversion rates: Jamaica dollars per U.S. dollar (end of period)	0 102 ..	45.415	47.286	50.762	60.517	61.450	64.381	67.032	70.618

Table 1. ANALYTIC PRESENTATION, 2000–2007

(Billions of U.S. dollars)

	Code	2000	2001	2002	2003	2004	2005	2006	2007
A. Current Account[1]	4 993 Z.	**119.66**	**87.80**	**112.45**	**136.22**	**172.06**	**165.78**	**170.52**	**210.49**
Goods: exports f.o.b.	2 100 ..	459.51	383.59	395.58	449.12	539.00	567.57	615.81	678.09
Goods: imports f.o.b.	3 100 ..	−342.80	−313.38	−301.75	−342.72	−406.87	−473.61	−534.51	−573.34
Balance on Goods	4 100 ..	*116.72*	*70.21*	*93.83*	*106.40*	*132.13*	*93.96*	*81.30*	*104.75*
Services: credit	2 200 ..	69.24	64.52	65.71	77.62	97.61	110.21	117.30	129.12
Services: debit	3 200 ..	−116.86	−108.25	−107.94	−111.53	−135.51	−134.26	−135.56	−150.37
Balance on Goods and Services	4 991 ..	*69.09*	*26.48*	*51.60*	*72.49*	*94.23*	*69.91*	*63.05*	*83.50*
Income: credit	2 300 ..	97.20	103.09	91.48	95.21	113.33	141.06	165.80	199.46
Income: debit	3 300 ..	−36.80	−33.87	−25.71	−23.97	−27.63	−37.62	−47.65	−60.96
Balance on Goods, Services, and Income	4 992 ..	*129.49*	*95.70*	*117.37*	*143.73*	*179.93*	*173.36*	*181.20*	*222.00*
Current transfers: credit	2 379 Z.	7.38	6.15	10.04	6.51	6.91	9.74	6.18	6.77
Current transfers: debit	3 379 ..	−17.21	−14.06	−14.96	−14.02	−14.78	−17.31	−16.87	−18.28
B. Capital Account[1]	4 994 Z.	**−9.26**	**−2.87**	**−3.32**	**−4.00**	**−4.79**	**−4.88**	**−4.76**	**−4.03**
Capital account: credit	2 994 Z.	.78	.99	.91	.39	.44	.83	.75	.69
Capital account: debit	3 994 ..	−10.04	−3.86	−4.24	−4.39	−5.23	−5.71	−5.51	−4.72
Total, Groups A Plus B	4 981 ..	*110.40*	*84.93*	*109.13*	*132.22*	*167.27*	*160.91*	*165.76*	*206.46*
C. Financial Account[1]	4 995 W.	**−78.31**	**−48.16**	**−63.38**	**71.92**	**22.50**	**−122.68**	**−102.34**	**−187.24**
Direct investment abroad	4 505 ..	−31.53	−38.50	−32.02	−28.77	−30.96	−45.44	−50.17	−73.49
Direct investment in Japan	4 555 Z.	8.23	6.19	9.09	6.24	7.80	3.21	−6.78	22.18
Portfolio investment assets	4 602 ..	−83.36	−106.79	−85.93	−176.29	−173.77	−196.40	−71.04	−123.45
Equity securities	4 610 ..	−19.72	−11.28	−37.28	−4.47	−31.47	−22.97	−25.04	−26.09
Debt securities	4 619 ..	−63.64	−95.51	−48.65	−171.82	−142.30	−173.43	−46.00	−97.36
Portfolio investment liabilities	4 652 Z.	47.39	60.50	−20.04	81.18	196.72	183.13	198.56	196.58
Equity securities	4 660 ..	−1.29	39.10	−16.69	87.78	98.28	131.32	71.44	45.45
Debt securities	4 669 Z.	48.67	21.40	−3.35	−6.59	98.44	51.81	127.12	151.13
Financial derivatives	4 910 ..	−4.67	1.39	2.48	5.58	2.41	−6.53	2.46	2.80
Financial derivatives assets	4 900 ..	106.74	102.79	77.25	64.96	56.44	230.59	143.48	188.50
Financial derivatives liabilities	4 905 ..	−111.41	−101.40	−74.77	−59.38	−54.04	−237.12	−141.03	−185.71
Other investment assets	4 703 ..	−4.15	46.59	36.41	149.89	−48.01	−106.60	−86.24	−260.78
Monetary authorities	4 701 ..	....	....	....	....	....	....	....	....
General government	4 704 ..	−1.89	−3.95	.92	4.49	3.87	14.29	3.48	−.36
Banks	4 705 ..	36.51	15.59	1.59	140.78	3.24	−29.80	−7.50	−195.65
Other sectors	4 728 ..	−38.77	34.95	33.90	4.62	−55.12	−91.08	−82.22	−64.78
Other investment liabilities	4 753 W.	−10.21	−17.55	26.63	34.10	68.31	45.94	−89.12	48.92
Monetary authorities	4 753 WA	....	....	....	....	....	....	....	....
General government	4 753 ZB	−.93	7.01	.06	5.14	.99	12.24	−25.44	1.28
Banks	4 753 ZC	28.22	4.99	22.46	−26.22	42.73	−9.38	−48.83	.32
Other sectors	4 753 ZD	−37.49	−29.54	4.11	55.17	24.59	43.07	−14.85	47.31
Total, Groups A Through C	4 983 ..	*32.09*	*36.77*	*45.75*	*204.14*	*189.77*	*38.22*	*63.42*	*19.22*
D. Net Errors and Omissions	4 998 ..	**16.87**	**3.72**	**.39**	**−16.99**	**−28.92**	**−15.90**	**−31.44**	**17.30**
Total, Groups A Through D	4 984 ..	*48.95*	*40.49*	*46.13*	*187.15*	*160.85*	*22.33*	*31.98*	*36.52*
E. Reserves and Related Items	4 802 A.	**−48.95**	**−40.49**	**−46.13**	**−187.15**	**−160.85**	**−22.33**	**−31.98**	**−36.52**
Reserve assets	4 802 ..	−48.95	−40.49	−46.13	−187.15	−160.85	−22.33	−31.98	−36.52
Use of Fund credit and loans	4 766 ..	....	....	....	....	....	....	....	....
Exceptional financing	4 920 ..	....	....	....	....	....	....	....	....
Conversion rates: yen per U.S. dollar	0 101 ..	**107.77**	**121.53**	**125.39**	**115.93**	**108.19**	**110.22**	**116.30**	**117.75**

[1] Excludes components that have been classified in the categories of Group E.

Table 2. STANDARD PRESENTATION, 2000–2007

(Billions of U.S. dollars)

	Code	2000	2001	2002	2003	2004	2005	2006	2007
CURRENT ACCOUNT...	4 993 ..	**119.66**	**87.80**	**112.45**	**136.22**	**172.06**	**165.78**	**170.52**	**210.49**
A. GOODS..	4 100 ..	116.72	70.21	93.83	106.40	132.13	93.96	81.30	104.75
Credit...	2 100 ..	459.51	383.59	395.58	449.12	539.00	567.57	615.81	678.09
General merchandise: exports f.o.b...............	2 110 ..	452.33	377.44	389.42	441.70	530.97	558.70	605.02	664.95
Goods for processing: exports f.o.b...............	2 150 ..	5.07	4.30	4.40	5.03	5.27	4.84	4.55	5.00
Repairs on goods.......................................	2 160 ..	.14	.20	.23	.21	.20	.27	.30	.34
Goods procured in ports by carriers..............	2 170 ..	1.54	1.32	1.16	1.31	1.68	2.36	2.97	4.22
Nonmonetary gold....................................	2 180 ..	.43	.33	.38	.87	.88	1.41	2.98	3.57
Debit..	3 100 ..	−342.80	−313.38	−301.75	−342.72	−406.87	−473.61	−534.51	−573.34
General merchandise: imports f.o.b...............	3 110 ..	−328.86	−300.61	−287.59	−327.21	−389.14	−453.43	−523.19	−545.76
Goods for processing: imports f.o.b...............	3 150 ..	−7.97	−7.80	−8.75	−8.99	−9.73	−9.03	−4.64	−12.78
Repairs on goods.......................................	3 160 ..	−.23	−.34	−.38	−.37	−.46	−.57	−.27	−.54
Goods procured in ports by carriers..............	3 170 ..	−5.17	−4.27	−4.30	−5.62	−6.58	−9.48	−6.20	−13.55
Nonmonetary gold....................................	3 180 ..	−.57	−.36	−.73	−.54	−.94	−1.11	−.21	−.71
B. SERVICES..	4 200 ..	**−47.63**	**−43.73**	**−42.23**	**−33.91**	**−37.90**	**−24.05**	**−18.26**	**−21.25**
Total credit..	2 200 ..	*69.24*	*64.52*	*65.71*	*77.62*	*97.61*	*110.21*	*117.30*	*129.12*
Total debit..	3 200 ..	*−116.86*	*−108.25*	*−107.94*	*−111.53*	*−135.51*	*−134.26*	*−135.56*	*−150.37*
Transportation services, credit.................	2 205 ..	**25.60**	**24.01**	**24.02**	**26.50**	**32.15**	**35.75**	**37.65**	**42.02**
Passenger..	2 850 ..	*2.60*	*2.44*	*2.57*	*2.63*	*3.08*	*3.12*	*3.02*	*3.08*
Freight..	2 851 ..	*16.72*	*15.67*	*15.79*	*18.38*	*22.52*	*25.62*	*28.10*	*32.50*
Other..	2 852 ..	*6.28*	*5.89*	*5.66*	*5.50*	*6.55*	*7.01*	*6.53*	*6.44*
Sea transport, passenger............................	2 207 ..	....	.01	.01	.01	.01	.02	.01	.02
Sea transport, freight...............................	2 208 ..	14.05	13.70	13.49	15.85	19.44	22.61	25.05	29.21
Sea transport, other.................................	2 209 ..	2.75	2.71	2.64	2.48	2.70	2.88	2.59	2.70
Air transport, passenger............................	2 211 ..	2.59	2.43	2.56	2.62	3.07	3.11	3.01	3.06
Air transport, freight...............................	2 212 ..	2.66	1.96	2.29	2.52	3.08	3.00	3.04	3.29
Air transport, other.................................	2 213 ..	3.52	3.18	3.02	3.02	3.85	4.13	3.93	3.74
Other transport, passenger.........................	2 215 ..	....	....	....	....	....	....	....	....
Other transport, freight............................	2 216 ..	.01	.01	.01	.01	....	....	.01	....
Other transport, other..............................	2 217 ..	.02	.01	....	....	....	....	....	....
Transportation services, debit.................	3 205 ..	**−35.10**	**−32.38**	**−31.52**	**−34.20**	**−42.72**	**−40.38**	**−42.84**	**−49.04**
Passenger..	3 850 ..	*−10.76*	*−9.00*	*−8.32*	*−7.55*	*−9.92*	*−10.54*	*−10.78*	*−10.75*
Freight..	3 851 ..	*−18.05*	*−17.31*	*−17.00*	*−20.05*	*−24.87*	*−20.71*	*−22.48*	*−27.94*
Other..	3 852 ..	*−6.29*	*−6.07*	*−6.20*	*−6.59*	*−7.93*	*−9.13*	*−9.57*	*−10.35*
Sea transport, passenger............................	3 207 ..	....	....	−.01	....	....	−.01	−.05	−.05
Sea transport, freight...............................	3 208 ..	−15.86	−15.29	−14.90	−17.76	−22.38	−18.06	−19.80	−25.29
Sea transport, other.................................	3 209 ..	−5.21	−5.12	−5.24	−5.65	−6.87	−8.00	−8.53	−9.33
Air transport, passenger............................	3 211 ..	−10.75	−8.99	−8.31	−7.54	−9.91	−10.52	−10.73	−10.69
Air transport, freight...............................	3 212 ..	−2.15	−1.96	−1.99	−2.18	−2.44	−2.60	−2.60	−2.51
Air transport, other.................................	3 213 ..	−1.05	−.93	−.96	−.94	−1.07	−1.12	−1.04	−1.01
Other transport, passenger.........................	3 215 ..	−.01	−.01	−.01	....	−.01	−.01	....	....
Other transport, freight............................	3 216 ..	−.05	−.07	−.11	−.11	−.05	−.05	−.07	−.13
Other transport, other..............................	3 217 ..	−.03	−.01	....	....	....	−.01	....	−.01
Travel, credit...................................	2 236 ..	**3.37**	**3.31**	**3.50**	**8.85**	**11.26**	**12.43**	**8.47**	**9.35**
Business travel.......................................	2 237 ..	.93	....	....	....	3.84	4.07	2.43	2.51
Personal travel......................................	2 240 ..	2.44	....	....	....	7.43	8.36	6.04	6.84
Travel, debit....................................	3 236 ..	**−31.88**	**−26.53**	**−26.66**	**−28.96**	**−38.25**	**−37.56**	**−26.88**	**−26.51**
Business travel.......................................	3 237 ..	−5.73	....	....	....	−6.74	−7.40	−5.38	−4.94
Personal travel......................................	3 240 ..	−26.16	....	....	....	−31.51	−30.16	−21.49	−21.57
Other services, credit.........................	2 200 BA	**40.27**	**37.20**	**38.19**	**42.27**	**54.20**	**62.03**	**71.18**	**77.75**
Communications.....................................	2 245 ..	.82	.72	.74	.66	.45	.39	.44	.55
Construction...	2 249 ..	5.85	4.79	4.63	4.55	6.87	7.22	8.98	10.32
Insurance...	2 253 ..	.17	−.10	−.38	.37	1.07	.87	1.58	1.34
Financial..	2 260 ..	2.86	2.71	3.13	3.47	4.41	5.04	6.15	6.21
Computer and information..........................	2 262 ..	1.57	1.41	1.14	1.08	1.04	1.13	.97	.97
Royalties and licence fees..........................	2 266 ..	10.23	10.46	10.42	12.27	15.70	17.66	20.10	23.23
Other business services..............................	2 268 ..	17.71	16.24	17.40	18.04	21.91	27.28	30.68	32.92
Personal, cultural, and recreational..............	2 287 ..	.12	.12	.32	.14	.07	.10	.14	.16
Government, n.i.e....................................	2 291 ..	.94	.85	.80	1.69	2.68	2.33	2.16	2.06
Other services, debit..........................	3 200 BA	**−49.88**	**−49.34**	**−49.76**	**−48.37**	**−54.54**	**−56.31**	**−65.84**	**−74.82**
Communications.....................................	3 245 ..	−1.15	−1.07	−.91	−.80	−.62	−.62	−.73	−1.03
Construction...	3 249 ..	−4.00	−3.81	−3.59	−3.38	−4.80	−4.77	−6.20	−7.94
Insurance...	3 253 ..	−2.03	−2.64	−3.23	−3.54	−3.44	−1.89	−4.57	−4.12
Financial..	3 260 ..	−1.88	−1.65	−1.63	−2.18	−2.65	−2.69	−2.99	−3.61
Computer and information..........................	3 262 ..	−3.07	−2.64	−2.15	−2.11	−2.19	−2.43	−3.12	−3.61
Royalties and licence fees..........................	3 266 ..	−11.01	−11.10	−11.02	−11.00	−13.64	−14.65	−15.50	−16.68
Other business services..............................	3 268 ..	−24.30	−23.81	−24.71	−23.15	−24.61	−26.50	−29.77	−34.84
Personal, cultural, and recreational..............	3 287 ..	−1.28	−1.39	−1.19	−.95	−1.08	−1.11	−1.30	−1.32
Government, n.i.e....................................	3 291 ..	−1.18	−1.22	−1.33	−1.27	−1.50	−1.66	−1.66	−1.68

2008, International Monetary Fund: *Balance of Payments Statistics Yearbook*

Table 2 (Continued). STANDARD PRESENTATION, 2000–2007

(Billions of U.S. dollars)

	Code	2000	2001	2002	2003	2004	2005	2006	2007
C. INCOME	4 300	**60.40**	**69.22**	**65.77**	**71.24**	**85.70**	**103.44**	**118.16**	**138.50**
Total credit	2 300	*97.20*	*103.09*	*91.48*	*95.21*	*113.33*	*141.06*	*165.80*	*199.46*
Total debit	3 300	*−36.80*	*−33.87*	*−25.71*	*−23.97*	*−27.63*	*−37.62*	*−47.65*	*−60.96*
Compensation of employees, credit	2 310	.27	.21	.18	.15	.17	.17	.15	.12
Compensation of employees, debit	3 310	−.27	−.25	−.27	−.27	−.29	−.30	−.18	−.18
Investment income, credit	2 320	96.93	102.88	91.30	95.06	113.16	140.89	165.65	199.34
Direct investment income	2 330	8.24	16.81	16.69	13.11	18.96	30.37	35.12	45.09
Dividends and distributed branch profits	2 332	8.89	8.66	7.68	7.89	12.27	16.35	17.84	24.40
Reinvested earnings and undistributed branch profits	2 333	−1.82	6.92	8.15	4.58	5.97	13.23	16.39	19.61
Income on debt (interest)	2 334	1.16	1.23	.86	.64	.72	.80	.90	1.09
Portfolio investment income	2 339	61.35	63.15	60.41	68.79	81.33	95.28	111.28	129.22
Income on equity	2 340	7.39	7.26	8.45	10.26	13.72	18.62	22.72	27.28
Income on bonds and notes	2 350	47.87	50.12	49.47	56.52	65.89	73.72	84.30	98.05
Income on money market instruments	2 360	6.09	5.78	2.48	2.01	1.72	2.94	4.26	3.89
Other investment income	2 370	27.34	22.92	14.20	13.16	12.87	15.24	19.25	25.03
Investment income, debit	3 320	−36.53	−33.62	−25.44	−23.70	−27.34	−37.32	−47.47	−60.78
Direct investment income	3 330	−2.61	−4.12	−5.32	−5.04	−6.34	−9.48	−9.01	−14.89
Dividends and distributed branch profits	3 332	−2.40	−2.27	−3.40	−3.25	−3.99	−7.51	−6.50	−10.69
Reinvested earnings and undistributed branch profits	3 333	.10	−1.55	−1.50	−1.41	−1.95	−1.70	−2.25	−3.84
Income on debt (interest)	3 334	−.32	−.31	−.42	−.38	−.41	−.28	−.26	−.36
Portfolio investment income	3 339	−13.87	−11.79	−9.85	−10.09	−12.63	−16.90	−21.14	−26.49
Income on equity	3 340	−2.79	−2.65	−2.48	−3.41	−6.02	−9.93	−13.88	−17.32
Income on bonds and notes	3 350	−11.08	−9.14	−7.36	−6.67	−6.61	−6.97	−7.26	−9.16
Income on money market instruments	3 360	....	....	....	−.01	....	....	....	....
Other investment income	3 370	−20.04	−17.71	−10.28	−8.57	−8.37	−10.93	−17.32	−19.40
D. CURRENT TRANSFERS	4 379	**−9.83**	**−7.90**	**−4.92**	**−7.51**	**−7.88**	**−7.57**	**−10.68**	**−11.51**
Credit	2 379	**7.38**	**6.15**	**10.04**	**6.51**	**6.91**	**9.74**	**6.18**	**6.77**
General government	2 380	.19	.16	2.93	.19	.18	1.21	.14	.23
Other sectors	2 390	7.19	5.99	7.11	6.32	6.73	8.53	6.05	6.54
Workers' remittances	2 391	.50	1.04	.95	.66	.60	.73	1.03	1.26
Other current transfers	2 392	6.69	4.95	6.16	5.66	6.13	7.80	5.02	5.28
Debit	3 379	**−17.21**	**−14.06**	**−14.96**	**−14.02**	**−14.78**	**−17.31**	**−16.87**	**−18.28**
General government	3 380	−3.09	−2.33	−2.86	−3.88	−5.61	−5.21	−4.82	−5.13
Other sectors	3 390	−14.12	−11.73	−12.10	−10.14	−9.17	−12.10	−12.05	−13.16
Workers' remittances	3 391	−2.26	−2.09	−2.41	−1.23	−.93	−.85	−3.15	−3.46
Other current transfers	3 392	−11.86	−9.64	−9.69	−8.91	−8.25	−11.25	−8.89	−9.70
CAPITAL AND FINANCIAL ACCOUNT	4 996	**−136.53**	**−91.52**	**−112.84**	**−119.23**	**−143.14**	**−149.89**	**−139.08**	**−227.79**
CAPITAL ACCOUNT	4 994	**−9.26**	**−2.87**	**−3.32**	**−4.00**	**−4.79**	**−4.88**	**−4.76**	**−4.03**
Total credit	2 994	*.78*	*.99*	*.91*	*.39*	*.44*	*.83*	*.75*	*.69*
Total debit	3 994	*−10.04*	*−3.86*	*−4.24*	*−4.39*	*−5.23*	*−5.71*	*−5.51*	*−4.72*
Capital transfers, credit	2 400	**.65**	**.76**	**.71**	**.28**	**.17**	**.62**	**.42**	**.20**
General government	2 401	.01	....	....	....	....	....	....	....
Debt forgiveness	2 402	....	....	....	....	....	....	....	....
Other capital transfers	2 410	.01	....	....	....	....	....	....	....
Other sectors	2 430	.64	.75	.71	.28	.16	.61	.42	.20
Migrants' transfers	2 431	.60	.73	.69	.27	.16	.18	.20	.19
Debt forgiveness	2 432	....	....	....	....	....	.43	.21	....
Other capital transfers	2 440	.04	.02	.02	.01	.01	.01	.01	.01
Capital transfers, debit	3 400	**−9.18**	**−3.19**	**−3.35**	**−2.54**	**−4.53**	**−4.57**	**−4.43**	**−3.05**
General government	3 401	−1.65	−1.52	−1.43	−1.55	−3.71	−4.25	−4.13	−2.23
Debt forgiveness	3 402	....	....	....	....	....	−2.81	−3.03	−1.18
Other capital transfers	3 410	−1.65	−1.52	−1.43	−1.55	−3.71	−1.44	−1.10	−1.05
Other sectors	3 430	−7.53	−1.67	−1.92	−.99	−.82	−.31	−.30	−.81
Migrants' transfers	3 431	−.64	−.60	−.67	−.27	−.20	−.13	−.14	−.40
Debt forgiveness	3 432	−1.91	−1.01	−1.21	−.70	−.61	−.17	−.15	−.38
Other capital transfers	3 440	−4.98	−.06	−.04	−.02	−.01	−.01	−.01	−.04
Nonproduced nonfinancial assets, credit	2 480	**.13**	**.24**	**.20**	**.12**	**.28**	**.21**	**.33**	**.49**
Nonproduced nonfinancial assets, debit	3 480	**−.86**	**−.67**	**−.89**	**−1.85**	**−.70**	**−1.14**	**−1.08**	**−1.68**

Table 2 (Continued). STANDARD PRESENTATION, 2000–2007

(Billions of U.S. dollars)

	Code	2000	2001	2002	2003	2004	2005	2006	2007
FINANCIAL ACCOUNT	4 995 ..	**−127.27**	**−88.65**	**−109.51**	**−115.23**	**−138.35**	**−145.01**	**−134.32**	**−223.76**
A. DIRECT INVESTMENT	4 500 ..	−23.31	−32.31	−22.93	−22.53	−23.15	−42.22	−56.95	−51.31
Direct investment abroad	4 505 ..	−31.53	−38.50	−32.02	−28.77	−30.96	−45.44	−50.17	−73.49
Equity capital	4 510 ..	−30.79	−27.50	−23.56	−20.79	−20.95	−28.92	−28.74	−51.80
Claims on affiliated enterprises	4 515 ..	−30.80	−26.28	−23.55	−20.79	−20.95	−28.92	−28.74	−51.80
Liabilities to affiliated enterprises	4 520 ..	.01	−1.22	....	....	....	....	....	....
Reinvested earnings	4 525 ..	1.82	−6.92	−8.15	−4.58	−5.97	−13.23	−16.39	−19.61
Other capital	4 530 ..	−2.56	−4.08	−.31	−3.40	−4.04	−3.29	−5.04	−2.08
Claims on affiliated enterprises	4 535 ..	−2.32	−3.28	−2.02	−3.94	−2.76	−4.42	−6.24	−2.68
Liabilities to affiliated enterprises	4 540 ..	−.24	−.80	1.72	.54	−1.28	1.13	1.20	.61
Direct investment in Japan	4 555 ..	8.23	6.19	9.09	6.24	7.80	3.21	−6.78	22.18
Equity capital	4 560 ..	7.59	4.86	−5.70	7.51	7.02	3.78	−8.93	10.53
Claims on direct investors	4 565 ..	−.07	....	−.05	....	....	....	....	....
Liabilities to direct investors	4 570 ..	7.66	4.86	−5.65	7.51	7.02	3.78	−8.92	10.53
Reinvested earnings	4 575 ..	−.10	1.55	1.50	1.41	1.95	1.70	2.25	3.84
Other capital	4 580 ..	.74	−.22	13.28	−2.69	−1.16	−2.27	−.11	7.81
Claims on direct investors	4 585 ..	−.64	−.92	−.67	−1.55	−1.27	.02	−.96	−.13
Liabilities to direct investors	4 590 ..	1.38	.71	13.95	−1.14	.11	−2.28	.85	7.93
B. PORTFOLIO INVESTMENT	4 600 ..	**−35.98**	**−46.29**	**−105.97**	**−95.11**	**22.95**	**−13.27**	**127.52**	**73.13**
Assets	4 602 ..	**−83.36**	**−106.79**	**−85.93**	**−176.29**	**−173.77**	**−196.40**	**−71.04**	**−123.45**
Equity securities	4 610 ..	−19.72	−11.28	−37.28	−4.47	−31.47	−22.97	−25.04	−26.09
Monetary authorities	4 611 ..	....	....	....	....	....	....	....	....
General government	4 612 ..	....	....	....	....	....	−.02	−.02	....
Banks	4 613 ..	−1.13	.29	1.29	−.37	−1.29	−1.80	−1.38	−1.67
Other sectors	4 614 ..	−18.59	−11.57	−38.58	−4.10	−30.18	−21.15	−23.63	−24.42
Debt securities	4 619 ..	−63.64	−95.51	−48.65	−171.82	−142.30	−173.43	−46.00	−97.36
Bonds and notes	4 620 ..	−47.85	−96.71	−54.32	−177.77	−148.54	−182.88	−55.55	−102.31
Monetary authorities	4 621 ..	....	....	....	....	....	....	....	....
General government	4 622 ..	3.88	12.35	14.55	6.56	3.02	.35	.13	−.64
Banks	4 623 ..	−47.93	−18.31	−9.92	−63.50	−61.15	−56.44	17.10	−16.33
Other sectors	4 624 ..	−3.80	−90.74	−58.94	−120.83	−90.41	−126.78	−72.79	−85.34
Money market instruments	4 630 ..	−15.79	1.20	5.67	5.94	6.24	9.45	9.55	4.95
Monetary authorities	4 631 ..	....	....	....	....	....	....	....	....
General government	4 632 ..	.05	.22	.11	.18	.31	....	....	....
Banks	4 633 ..	−8.66	−13.09	−18.61	−12.85	−10.84	5.21	3.20	−.77
Other sectors	4 634 ..	−7.18	14.08	24.16	18.62	16.76	4.24	6.36	5.72
Liabilities	4 652 ..	**47.39**	**60.50**	**−20.04**	**81.18**	**196.72**	**183.13**	**198.56**	**196.58**
Equity securities	4 660 ..	−1.29	39.10	−16.69	87.78	98.28	131.32	71.44	45.45
Banks	4 663 ..	2.72	−1.18	.71	8.41	16.67	13.00	15.51	.39
Other sectors	4 664 ..	−4.01	40.28	−17.40	79.37	81.61	118.31	55.92	45.07
Debt securities	4 669 ..	48.67	21.40	−3.35	−6.59	98.44	51.81	127.12	151.13
Bonds and notes	4 670 ..	56.53	28.35	−10.78	−18.30	53.47	61.01	78.33	66.62
Monetary authorities	4 671 ..	....	....	....	....	....	....	....	....
General government	4 672 ..	54.19	27.87	−.05	−17.14	43.62	55.80	58.76	68.59
Banks	4 673 ..	7.92	2.35	−.56	4.68	9.31	6.73	4.89	.99
Other sectors	4 674 ..	−5.57	−1.87	−10.18	−5.84	.54	−1.52	14.68	−2.95
Money market instruments	4 680 ..	−7.86	−6.95	7.43	11.71	44.97	−9.20	48.78	84.50
Monetary authorities	4 681 ..	....	....	....	....	....	....	....	....
General government	4 682 ..	−7.93	−7.33	6.68	10.68	43.19	−9.30	48.61	84.53
Banks	4 683 ..	.17	−.02	.07	.17	.11	−.02	....	−.01
Other sectors	4 684 ..	−.10	.41	.67	.85	1.67	.12	.18	−.02
C. FINANCIAL DERIVATIVES	4 910 ..	**−4.67**	**1.39**	**2.48**	**5.58**	**2.41**	**−6.53**	**2.46**	**2.80**
Monetary authorities	4 911 ..	....	....	....	....	....	....	....	....
General government	4 912 ..	....	.06	.06	.04	.11	.09	−.17	−.25
Banks	4 913 ..	−.87	.84	2.21	5.49	4.12	3.47	.48	−.79
Other sectors	4 914 ..	−3.80	.49	.21	.04	−1.82	−10.08	2.14	3.84
Assets	4 900 ..	**106.74**	**102.79**	**77.25**	**64.96**	**56.44**	**230.59**	**143.48**	**188.50**
Monetary authorities	4 901 ..	....	....	....	....	....	....	....	....
General government	4 902 ..	....	.07	.13	.56	.14	.19	.07	.13
Banks	4 903 ..	110.07	105.03	72.15	60.63	56.57	78.34	88.50	121.62
Other sectors	4 904 ..	−3.33	−2.32	4.97	3.76	−.27	152.06	54.90	66.75
Liabilities	4 905 ..	**−111.41**	**−101.40**	**−74.77**	**−59.38**	**−54.04**	**−237.12**	**−141.03**	**−185.71**
Monetary authorities	4 906 ..	....	....	....	....	....	....	....	....
General government	4 907 ..	....	−.01	−.06	−.52	−.03	−.10	−.25	−.38
Banks	4 908 ..	−110.95	−104.19	−69.94	−55.14	−52.45	−74.87	−88.02	−122.41
Other sectors	4 909 ..	−.46	2.80	−4.76	−3.72	−1.55	−162.14	−52.76	−62.91

Table 2 (Concluded). STANDARD PRESENTATION, 2000–2007

(Billions of U.S. dollars)

	Code	2000	2001	2002	2003	2004	2005	2006	2007
D. OTHER INVESTMENT	4 700	**−14.36**	**29.04**	**63.04**	**183.99**	**20.30**	**−60.66**	**−175.36**	**−211.86**
Assets	4 703	**−4.15**	**46.59**	**36.41**	**149.89**	**−48.01**	**−106.60**	**−86.24**	**−260.78**
Trade credits	4 706	−1.78	7.66	−.71	−1.82	−1.80	−2.65	−5.05	−3.40
General government	4 707	.30	.18	.08	.34	.29	.53	−.52	.68
of which: Short-term	4 709	....	....	....	....	....	*.12*	....	*.02*
Other sectors	4 710	−2.08	7.48	−.78	−2.16	−2.10	−3.17	−4.53	−4.08
of which: Short-term	4 712	*−4.86*	*5.89*	*−1.41*	*−3.42*	*−3.40*	*−3.49*	*−5.33*	*−4.52*
Loans	4 714	55.97	−25.32	−58.66	86.80	−38.30	−79.10	−62.29	−144.13
Monetary authorities	4 715	....	....	....	....	....	....	....	....
of which: Short-term	4 718	....	....	....	....	....	....	....	....
General government	4 719	−.82	−3.11	1.73	5.03	3.82	2.29	.13	−1.82
of which: Short-term	4 721	....	....	....	....	....	....	....	....
Banks	4 722	71.54	−31.40	−27.86	87.97	7.59	−30.28	8.79	−105.05
of which: Short-term	4 724	*47.21*	*−44.71*	*−43.82*	*92.48*	*3.97*	*−36.52*	*13.14*	*−96.08*
Other sectors	4 725	−14.76	9.20	−32.52	−6.20	−49.71	−51.11	−71.20	−37.26
of which: Short-term	4 727	*−23.81*	*6.04*	*−40.28*	*−10.77*	*−60.32*	*−38.71*	*−70.23*	*−39.01*
Currency and deposits	4 730	−46.56	61.84	55.72	5.12	−14.08	−5.35	−20.49	−117.14
Monetary authorities	4 731	....	....	....	....	....	....	....	....
General government	4 732	....	....	....	....	....	....	....	....
Banks	4 733	−29.90	43.70	37.11	−7.57	−11.64	9.26	−8.24	−96.65
Other sectors	4 734	−16.66	18.14	18.61	12.69	−2.44	−14.61	−12.25	−20.49
Other assets	4 736	−11.77	2.41	40.05	59.79	6.17	−19.50	1.59	3.89
Monetary authorities	4 737	....	....	....	....	....	....	....	....
of which: Short-term	4 739	....	....	....	....	....	....	....	....
General government	4 740	−1.37	−1.02	−.88	−.88	−.24	11.47	3.87	.78
of which: Short-term	4 742	*−.02*	*−.02*	*−.03*	*−.01*	*.70*	*12.40*	*6.41*	*.91*
Banks	4 743	−5.13	3.29	−7.66	60.38	7.30	−8.78	−8.04	6.06
of which: Short-term	4 745	*−.94*	*4.52*	*2.11*	*62.12*	*−.28*	*2.13*	*2.78*	*−4.89*
Other sectors	4 746	−5.27	.14	48.59	.29	−.89	−22.19	5.77	−2.95
of which: Short-term	4 748	*−.29*	*−14.93*	*13.67*	*.99*	*−.21*	*−21.23*	*6.00*	*−2.88*
Liabilities	4 753	**−10.21**	**−17.55**	**26.63**	**34.10**	**68.31**	**45.94**	**−89.12**	**48.92**
Trade credits	4 756	−.25	−1.11	.65	.80	.68	4.82	3.24	4.24
General government	4 757	....	....	....	....	....	....	....	....
of which: Short-term	4 759	....	....	....	....	....	....	....	....
Other sectors	4 760	−.25	−1.11	.65	.80	.68	4.82	3.24	4.24
of which: Short-term	4 762	*.20*	*−.81*	*1.11*	*1.39*	*1.36*	*4.99*	*3.70*	*4.63*
Loans	4 764	−18.18	−31.78	50.07	22.66	81.81	9.83	−74.73	51.90
Monetary authorities	4 765	....	....	....	....	....	....	....	....
of which: Use of Fund credit and loans from the Fund	4 766	....	....	....	....	....	....	....	....
of which: Short-term	4 768	....	....	....	....	....	....	....	....
General government	4 769	....	....	....	....	14.81	18.66	−21.15	1.63
of which: Short-term	4 771	....	....	....	....	*14.80*	*18.66*	*−21.15*	*1.63*
Banks	4 772	25.74	−4.33	49.86	−36.88	35.24	−5.76	−44.42	−6.54
of which: Short-term	4 774	*34.99*	*−7.29*	*58.21*	*−34.84*	*44.60*	*1.80*	*−56.11*	*−16.35*
Other sectors	4 775	−43.92	−27.45	.20	59.54	31.76	−3.08	−9.16	56.81
of which: Short-term	4 777	*−25.10*	*−13.67*	*12.67*	*68.30*	*22.40*	*9.02*	*−13.57*	*50.16*
Currency and deposits	4 780	6.62	15.83	−22.22	17.00	−4.15	2.98	−9.32	6.55
Monetary authorities	4 781	....	....	....	....	....	....	....	....
General government	4 782	−.16	7.41	3.46	5.83	−13.29	−.92	−3.89	.03
Banks	4 783	6.78	8.42	−25.68	11.17	9.14	3.90	−5.42	6.52
Other sectors	4 784	....	....	....	....	....	....	....	....
Other liabilities	4 786	1.60	−.49	−1.86	−6.36	−10.04	28.31	−8.31	−13.76
Monetary authorities	4 787	....	....	....	....	....	....	....	....
of which: Short-term	4 789	....	....	....	....	....	....	....	....
General government	4 790	−.77	−.40	−3.40	−.68	−.53	−5.50	−.40	−.37
of which: Short-term	4 792	*−.77*	*−.40*	*−3.40*	*−.68*	*−.53*	*−5.50*	*−.40*	*−.37*
Banks	4 793	−4.30	.90	−1.72	−.51	−1.65	−7.52	1.01	.35
of which: Short-term	4 795	*−4.56*	*.65*	*−2.84*	*1.63*	*−1.60*	*−6.22*	*1.01*	*.34*
Other sectors	4 796	6.68	−.99	3.26	−5.17	−7.86	41.33	−8.93	−13.73
of which: Short-term	4 798	*9.13*	*−1.15*	*3.71*	*−4.77*	*−7.69*	*39.62*	*−8.61*	*−8.63*
E. RESERVE ASSETS	4 802	**−48.95**	**−40.49**	**−46.13**	**−187.15**	**−160.85**	**−22.33**	**−31.98**	**−36.52**
Monetary gold	4 812	−.11	−.01	....	....	....	....	....	....
Special drawing rights	4 811	.09	−.03	.04	−.01	.05	.03	−.09	−.08
Reserve position in the Fund	4 810	1.00	....	−1.63	.18	1.24	3.44	1.06	.61
Foreign exchange	4 803	−49.93	−40.45	−44.55	−187.33	−162.14	−25.80	−32.95	−37.06
Other claims	4 813	....	....	....	....	....	....	....	....
NET ERRORS AND OMISSIONS	4 998	**16.87**	**3.72**	**.39**	**−16.99**	**−28.92**	**−15.90**	**−31.44**	**17.30**

Table 3. INTERNATIONAL INVESTMENT POSITION (End-period stocks), 2000–2007

(Billions of U.S. dollars)

	Code	2000	2001	2002	2003	2004	2005	2006	2007
ASSETS	8 995 C.	**2,969.59**	**2,881.51**	**3,052.08**	**3,599.80**	**4,166.99**	**4,290.87**	**4,691.94**	**5,355.23**
Direct investment abroad	8 505 ..	**278.44**	**300.11**	**304.23**	**335.50**	**370.54**	**386.59**	**449.57**	**542.62**
Equity capital and reinvested earnings	8 506 ..	254.52	278.53	284.97	315.03	351.27	368.46	429.18	518.91
Claims on affiliated enterprises	8 507 ..	254.60	278.56	284.99	315.06	351.33	368.51	429.28	518.96
Liabilities to affiliated enterprises	8 508 ..	−.08	−.02	−.02	−.03	−.05	−.05	−.10	−.05
Other capital	8 530 ..	23.93	21.58	19.26	20.47	19.27	18.12	20.39	23.70
Claims on affiliated enterprises	8 535 ..	24.99	22.04	21.55	24.04	21.84	20.67	23.32	26.44
Liabilities to affiliated enterprises	8 540 ..	−1.06	−.46	−2.29	−3.57	−2.57	−2.54	−2.94	−2.73
Portfolio investment	8 602 ..	**1,306.48**	**1,289.75**	**1,394.52**	**1,721.32**	**2,009.67**	**2,114.89**	**2,343.48**	**2,523.57**
Equity securities	8 610 ..	262.25	227.35	210.82	274.46	364.69	408.57	510.42	573.47
Monetary authorities	8 611 ..	. . . .	. . . .	. . . .	. . . .	. . . .	. . . .	. . . .	. . . .
General government	8 612 ..	. . . .	. . . .	. . . .	.03	. . . .	. . . .	. . . .	. . . .
Banks	8 613 ..	6.40	4.82	4.51	5.15	5.85	6.86	10.22	13.54
Other sectors	8 614 ..	255.85	222.53	206.31	269.28	358.84	401.72	500.20	559.93
Debt securities	8 619 ..	1,044.23	1,062.40	1,183.70	1,446.86	1,644.98	1,706.31	1,833.06	1,950.10
Bonds and notes	8 620 ..	975.51	1,004.88	1,135.52	1,407.17	1,610.02	1,681.11	1,811.99	1,924.83
Monetary authorities	8 621 ..	. . . .	. . . .	. . . .	. . . .	. . . .	. . . .	. . . .	. . . .
General government	8 622 ..	67.17	52.72	46.93	17.98	16.07	7.36	6.39	4.96
Banks	8 623 ..	290.90	304.24	341.86	422.95	491.32	565.25	558.60	573.11
Other sectors	8 624 ..	617.43	647.92	746.73	966.24	1,102.63	1,108.50	1,247.00	1,346.76
Money market instruments	8 630 ..	68.72	57.52	48.18	39.69	34.97	25.20	21.08	25.27
Monetary authorities	8 631 ..	. . . .	. . . .	. . . .	. . . .	. . . .	. . . .	. . . .	. . . .
General government	8 632 ..	.03	.06	.11	.12	.07	.02	.03	.06
Banks	8 633 ..	8.89	8.30	15.02	14.96	12.99	10.18	6.39	11.85
Other sectors	8 634 ..	59.80	49.16	33.06	24.61	21.91	15.01	14.66	13.36
Financial derivatives	8 900 ..	**3.31**	**3.00**	**3.37**	**4.90**	**5.75**	**26.31**	**23.03**	**38.96**
Monetary authorities	8 901 ..	. . . .	. . . .	. . . .	. . . .	. . . .	. . . .	. . . .	. . . .
General government	8 902 ..	. . . .	. . . .	. . . .	. . . .	. . . .	. . . .	. . . .	. . . .
Banks	8 903 ..	2.45	1.89	1.92	2.90	3.08	7.62	12.65	16.47
Other sectors	8 904 ..	.86	1.11	1.45	2.00	2.67	18.70	10.38	22.49
Other investment	8 703 ..	**1,020.36**	**888.23**	**882.34**	**865.03**	**938.51**	**920.10**	**981.07**	**1,282.69**
Trade credits	8 706 ..	41.40	32.75	36.13	47.89	50.62	51.80	52.47	56.58
General government	8 707 ..	7.76	6.96	7.56	12.41	12.16	11.65	7.85	7.24
of which: Short-term	8 709 ..	*.44*	*.37*	*.44*	*.51*	*.53*	*.58*	*.22*	*.05*
Other sectors	8 710 ..	33.64	25.79	28.57	35.48	38.46	40.15	44.62	49.34
of which: Short-term	8 712 ..	*18.56*	*17.25*	*21.93*	*28.05*	*32.27*	*33.22*	*38.97*	*44.09*
Loans	8 714 ..	649.09	617.97	678.50	656.94	693.57	671.70	699.16	852.55
Monetary authorities	8 715 ..	. . . .	. . . .	. . . .	. . . .	. . . .	. . . .	. . . .	. . . .
of which: Short-term	8 718 ..	. . . .	. . . .	. . . .	. . . .	. . . .	. . . .	. . . .	. . . .
General government	8 719 ..	163.09	148.83	159.34	157.75	158.25	138.26	138.48	144.92
of which: Short-term	8 721 ..	. . . .	. . . .	. . . .	. . . .	. . . .	. . . .	. . . .	. . . .
Banks	8 722 ..	382.33	375.78	407.17	385.52	375.80	371.83	349.47	457.90
of which: Short-term	8 724 ..	*277.08*	*289.96*	*334.87*	*295.08*	*289.93*	*296.16*	*269.57*	*367.27*
Other sectors	8 725 ..	103.67	93.36	112.00	113.67	159.52	161.61	211.20	249.73
of which: Short-term	8 727 ..	*12.59*	*16.11*	*34.69*	*40.09*	*94.95*	*97.78*	*144.98*	*178.16*
Currency and deposits	8 730 ..	189.13	113.85	65.54	64.07	79.98	79.73	102.81	221.84
Monetary authorities	8 731 ..	. . . .	. . . .	. . . .	. . . .	. . . .	. . . .	. . . .	. . . .
General government	8 732 ..	. . . .	. . . .	. . . .	. . . .	. . . .	. . . .	. . . .	. . . .
Banks	8 733 ..	117.22	67.17	32.57	40.52	52.06	40.61	48.73	147.42
Other sectors	8 734 ..	71.91	46.67	32.97	23.55	27.92	39.12	54.08	74.41
Other assets	8 736 ..	140.74	123.66	102.16	96.13	114.34	116.87	126.63	151.73
Monetary authorities	8 737 ..	. . . .	. . . .	. . . .	. . . .	. . . .	. . . .	. . . .	. . . .
of which: Short-term	8 739 ..	. . . .	. . . .	. . . .	. . . .	. . . .	. . . .	. . . .	. . . .
General government	8 740 ..	39.31	36.14	40.07	58.64	62.69	48.89	50.84	52.35
of which: Short-term	8 742 ..	*.08*	*.09*	*.13*	*15.75*	*15.81*	*5.83*	*5.56*	*5.24*
Banks	8 743 ..	29.69	24.51	46.92	21.31	34.22	50.57	58.46	81.67
of which: Short-term	8 745 ..	*20.98*	*12.76*	*25.59*	*−2.02*	*18.17*	*11.54*	*12.80*	*38.78*
Other sectors	8 746 ..	71.74	63.02	15.17	16.18	17.43	17.40	17.34	17.70
of which: Short-term	8 748 ..	*4.57*	*17.82*	*4.39*	*3.78*	*4.07*	*4.29*	*4.07*	*3.99*
Reserve assets	8 802 ..	**360.99**	**400.41**	**467.62**	**673.06**	**842.52**	**842.98**	**894.79**	**967.39**
Monetary gold	8 812 ..	6.74	6.79	8.50	10.23	10.74	12.57	15.64	20.42
Special drawing rights	8 811 ..	2.44	2.38	2.52	2.77	2.84	2.58	2.81	3.03
Reserve position in the Fund	8 810 ..	5.25	5.05	7.20	7.73	6.79	2.88	1.93	1.39
Foreign exchange	8 803 ..	346.56	386.20	449.39	652.33	822.15	824.95	874.07	942.18
Other claims	8 813 ..	. . . .	. . . .	. . . .	. . . .	. . . .	. . . .	.34	.37

Table 3 (Concluded). INTERNATIONAL INVESTMENT POSITION (End-period stocks), 2000–2007

(Billions of U.S. dollars)

	Code	2000	2001	2002	2003	2004	2005	2006	2007
LIABILITIES	8 995 D.	**1,811.65**	**1,521.42**	**1,589.92**	**1,986.18**	**2,382.51**	**2,759.11**	**2,883.77**	**3,160.27**
Direct investment in Japan	8 555 ..	**50.32**	**50.32**	**78.14**	**89.73**	**96.99**	**100.90**	**107.64**	**132.85**
Equity capital and reinvested earnings	8 556 ..	41.60	43.16	55.46	70.69	76.42	82.49	90.70	107.51
Claims on direct investors	8 557 ..	−.28	−.05	−.36	−.08	−.04	−.21	−.25	−.37
Liabilities to direct investors	8 558 ..	41.88	43.21	55.82	70.77	76.46	82.70	90.95	107.88
Other capital	8 580 ..	8.73	7.16	22.68	19.03	20.57	18.41	16.94	25.35
Claims on direct investors	8 585 ..	−1.31	−1.63	−1.76	−3.00	−2.48	−1.21	−1.98	−1.74
Liabilities to direct investors	8 590 ..	10.03	8.79	24.45	22.04	23.05	19.62	18.92	27.09
Portfolio investment	8 652 ..	**884.32**	**665.79**	**610.42**	**867.17**	**1,153.39**	**1,542.42**	**1,762.89**	**1,942.87**
Equity securities	8 660 ..	550.23	376.05	339.93	561.02	743.30	1,126.07	1,254.95	1,245.89
Banks	8 663 ..	32.30	11.32	8.85	31.45	61.33	101.97	110.08	80.57
Other sectors	8 664 ..	517.93	364.73	331.08	529.57	681.98	1,024.10	1,144.87	1,165.32
Debt securities	8 669 ..	334.09	289.75	270.49	306.14	410.09	416.35	507.94	696.98
Bonds and notes	8 670 ..	287.04	254.52	231.85	253.11	325.07	351.17	416.80	528.10
Monetary authorities	8 671 ..	. . . .	. . . .	. . . .	. . . .	. . . .	. . . .	. . . .	. . . .
General government	8 672 ..	207.76	179.45	159.59	169.56	232.03	261.76	311.68	419.14
Banks	8 673 ..	9.29	11.53	9.49	16.43	19.60	23.34	28.10	29.66
Other sectors	8 674 ..	69.98	63.54	62.77	67.12	73.45	66.08	77.02	79.30
Money market instruments	8 680 ..	47.05	35.23	38.64	53.04	85.02	65.18	91.13	168.88
Monetary authorities	8 681 ..	. . . .	. . . .	. . . .	. . . .	. . . .	. . . .	. . . .	. . . .
General government	8 682 ..	47.05	35.23	38.22	53.04	84.25	64.97	90.59	168.09
Banks	8 683 ..	. . . .	. . . .	. . . .	. . . .	.01	. . . .	. . . .	. . . .
Other sectors	8 684 ..	. . . .	. . . .	.42	. . . .	.76	.21	.55	.79
Financial derivatives	8 905 ..	**3.19**	**3.54**	**3.71**	**6.79**	**10.77**	**33.23**	**30.16**	**43.55**
Monetary authorities	8 906 ..	. . . .	. . . .	. . . .	. . . .	. . . .	. . . .	. . . .	. . . .
General government	8 907 ..	. . . .	. . . .	. . . .	. . . .	. . . .	. . . .	. . . .	. . . .
Banks	8 908 ..	2.23	2.46	2.75	3.75	6.07	10.83	16.45	21.23
Other sectors	8 909 ..	.96	1.08	.96	3.04	4.70	22.41	13.70	22.32
Other investment	8 753 ..	**873.82**	**801.77**	**897.65**	**1,022.50**	**1,121.36**	**1,082.55**	**983.09**	**1,041.00**
Trade credits	8 756 ..	9.49	8.71	11.13	10.37	13.22	16.00	20.36	23.47
General government	8 757 ..	. . . .	. . . .	. . . .	. . . .	. . . .	. . . .	. . . .	. . . .
of which: Short-term	8 759 ..	. . . .	. . . .	. . . .	. . . .	. . . .	. . . .	. . . .	. . . .
Other sectors	8 760 ..	9.49	8.71	11.13	10.37	13.22	16.00	20.36	23.47
of which: Short-term	8 762 ..	*8.43*	*7.78*	*10.10*	*10.35*	*12.01*	*14.69*	*18.21*	*22.37*
Loans	8 764 ..	663.29	603.48	698.56	781.19	871.84	803.64	717.57	744.82
Monetary authorities	8 765 ..	. . . .	. . . .	. . . .	. . . .	. . . .	. . . .	. . . .	. . . .
of which: Use of Fund credit and loans from the Fund	8 766 ..	. . . .	. . . .	. . . .	. . . .	. . . .	. . . .	. . . .	. . . .
of which: Short-term	8 768 ..	. . . .	. . . .	. . . .	. . . .	. . . .	. . . .	. . . .	. . . .
General government	8 769 ..	. . . .	. . . .	. . . .	. . . .	15.22	31.33	10.66	12.94
of which: Short-term	8 771 ..	. . . .	. . . .	. . . .	. . . .	*15.22*	*31.33*	*10.66*	*12.94*
Banks	8 772 ..	441.88	411.98	479.57	465.68	507.54	482.04	438.80	422.96
of which: Short-term	8 774 ..	*353.70*	*329.92*	*399.60*	*380.95*	*430.67*	*418.57*	*363.89*	*336.68*
Other sectors	8 775 ..	221.41	191.50	218.99	315.51	349.08	290.27	268.11	308.91
of which: Short-term	8 777 ..	*143.16*	*133.89*	*166.06*	*262.13*	*283.29*	*246.15*	*219.89*	*251.39*
Currency and deposits	8 780 ..	85.30	95.95	77.49	102.51	100.03	93.76	84.26	92.24
Monetary authorities	8 781 ..	. . . .	. . . .	. . . .	. . . .	. . . .	. . . .	. . . .	. . . .
General government	8 782 ..	. . . .	. . . .	. . . .	. . . .	. . . .	. . . .	. . . .	. . . .
Banks	8 783 ..	85.30	95.95	77.49	102.51	100.03	93.76	84.26	92.24
Other sectors	8 784 ..	. . . .	. . . .	. . . .	. . . .	. . . .	. . . .	. . . .	. . . .
Other liabilities	8 786 ..	115.74	93.62	110.47	128.43	136.26	169.16	160.89	180.47
Monetary authorities	8 787 ..	. . . .	. . . .	. . . .	. . . .	. . . .	. . . .	. . . .	. . . .
of which: Short-term	8 789 ..	. . . .	. . . .	. . . .	. . . .	. . . .	. . . .	. . . .	. . . .
General government	8 790 ..	9.68	8.15	5.26	5.14	4.74	3.97	3.61	3.39
of which: Short-term	8 792 ..	*9.68*	*8.15*	*5.26*	*5.14*	*4.74*	*3.97*	*3.61*	*3.39*
Banks	8 793 ..	76.82	60.47	74.07	92.21	101.74	127.09	120.71	147.28
of which: Short-term	8 795 ..	*75.87*	*58.17*	*70.64*	*90.92*	*100.51*	*111.17*	*107.78*	*134.12*
Other sectors	8 796 ..	29.25	25.00	31.15	31.08	29.78	38.10	36.58	29.80
of which: Short-term	8 798 ..	*28.67*	*24.35*	*30.94*	*31.23*	*25.57*	*32.79*	*31.63*	*29.91*
NET INTERNATIONAL INVESTMENT POSITION	8 995 ..	**1,157.94**	**1,360.09**	**1,462.17**	**1,613.63**	**1,784.49**	**1,531.76**	**1,808.17**	**2,194.96**
Conversion rates: yen per U.S. dollar (end of period)	0 102 ..	**114.90**	**131.80**	**119.90**	**107.10**	**104.12**	**117.97**	**118.95**	**114.00**

Table 1. ANALYTIC PRESENTATION, 2000–2007

(Millions of U.S. dollars)

	Code	2000	2001	2002	2003	2004	2005	2006	2007
A. Current Account[1]................................	4 993 Z.	**59.7**	**4.9**	**543.9**	**1,244.9**	**88.7**	**−2,199.6**	**−1,598.4**	**−2,776.2**
Goods: exports f.o.b.........................	2 100 ..	1,899.3	2,294.4	2,770.0	3,081.7	3,882.9	4,301.4	5,204.4	5,700.0
Goods: imports f.o.b.........................	3 100 ..	−4,073.8	−4,301.5	−4,500.9	−5,077.9	−7,261.1	−9,317.3	−10,260.2	−12,021.6
Balance on Goods.....................	4 100 ..	*−2,174.5*	*−2,007.1*	*−1,730.9*	*−1,996.2*	*−3,378.1*	*−5,015.9*	*−5,055.9*	*−6,321.6*
Services: credit................................	2 200 ..	1,639.7	1,487.5	1,774.2	1,748.2	2,072.8	2,333.6	2,907.5	3,410.4
Services: debit.................................	3 200 ..	−1,722.1	−1,725.9	−1,882.9	−1,889.2	−2,145.8	−2,542.0	−2,970.7	−3,478.7
Balance on Goods and Services....................	4 991 ..	*−2,256.9*	*−2,245.5*	*−1,839.6*	*−2,137.2*	*−3,451.2*	*−5,224.4*	*−5,119.0*	*−6,389.8*
Income: credit.................................	2 300 ..	668.1	652.5	491.7	550.5	649.2	791.1	1,031.9	1,395.1
Income: debit..................................	3 300 ..	−535.4	−460.9	−372.3	−374.3	−325.5	−382.7	−451.3	−560.1
Balance on Goods, Services, and Income..............	4 992 ..	*−2,124.2*	*−2,053.9*	*−1,720.2*	*−1,961.1*	*−3,127.5*	*−4,815.9*	*−4,538.5*	*−5,554.9*
Current transfers: credit.................	2 379 Z.	2,611.3	2,365.8	2,524.3	3,501.0	3,562.5	3,029.9	3,378.8	3,510.9
Current transfers: debit..................	3 379 ..	−427.4	−306.9	−260.1	−295.1	−346.3	−413.5	−438.8	−732.2
B. Capital Account[1]................................	4 994 Z.	**64.9**	**21.6**	**68.8**	**93.5**	**2.1**	**8.5**	**62.8**	**12.8**
Capital account: credit..................	2 994 Z.	64.9	21.6	68.8	93.5	2.1	8.5	62.8	12.8
Capital account: debit...................	3 994 ..	....	....	....	....	....	....	....	....
Total, Groups A Plus B...................	4 981 ..	*124.6*	*26.5*	*612.8*	*1,338.4*	*90.8*	*−2,191.1*	*−1,535.7*	*−2,763.3*
C. Financial Account[1]...........................	4 995 W.	**284.9**	**−191.4**	**337.4**	**−210.6**	**−103.2**	**1,638.2**	**2,994.2**	**2,399.6**
Direct investment abroad....................	4 505 ..	−8.6	−31.6	−13.8	3.7	−18.2	−163.2	138.1	−48.1
Direct investment in Jordan.................	4 555 Z.	814.8	179.8	121.6	443.2	816.4	1,774.0	3,219.3	1,835.4
Portfolio investment assets.................	4 602 ..	−38.4	−201.1	−178.0	−122.6	−199.0	143.6	−180.4	493.9
Equity securities........................	4 610 ..	−38.4	−201.1	−178.0	−122.6	−199.0	143.6	−180.4	493.9
Debt securities.........................	4 619 ..	....	....	....	....	....	....	....	....
Portfolio investment liabilities............	4 652 Z.	−140.9	−83.2	−232.7	−349.1	−89.8	169.1	143.6	346.0
Equity securities........................	4 660 ..	−16.8	−56.7	−232.7	−57.8	−89.8	169.1	143.6	346.0
Debt securities.........................	4 669 Z.	−124.1	−26.5	....	−291.3	....	....	....	....
Financial derivatives.......................	4 910 ..	....	....	....	....	....	....	....	....
Financial derivatives assets................	4 900 ..	....	....	....	....	....	....	....	....
Financial derivatives liabilities............	4 905 ..	....	....	....	....	....	....	....	....
Other investment assets....................	4 703 ..	−942.2	−635.5	−3.0	252.9	−680.8	−615.9	−1,148.0	−939.6
Monetary authorities...................	4 701 ..	146.5	6.3	37.4	−22.6	−23.4	−36.0	−58.7	−58.3
General government....................	4 704 ..	....	....	....	....	....	....	....	....
Banks.....................................	4 705 ..	−1,088.7	−641.9	−40.3	275.5	−657.4	−580.0	−1,089.3	−881.4
Other sectors............................	4 728 ..	....	....	....	....	....	....	....	....
Other investment liabilities................	4 753 W.	600.1	580.3	643.3	−438.6	68.3	330.6	821.6	712.0
Monetary authorities...................	4 753 WA	−69.8	4.7	−15.0	−13.4	−29.3	−9.2	97.7	2.3
General government....................	4 753 ZB	173.5	281.1	168.7	−275.7	−114.2	74.6	−183.9	−87.6
Banks.....................................	4 753 ZC	395.2	309.6	466.0	−99.4	329.3	272.6	804.5	776.3
Other sectors............................	4 753 ZD	101.3	−15.1	23.6	−50.1	−117.5	−7.5	103.2	21.0
Total, Groups A Through C..............	4 983 ..	*409.5*	*−164.9*	*950.2*	*1,127.8*	*−12.4*	*−552.9*	*1,458.5*	*−363.8*
D. Net Errors and Omissions..................	4 998 ..	**287.7**	**−90.0**	**−56.0**	**148.9**	**192.3**	**813.7**	**−16.8**	**1,253.8**
Total, Groups A Through D................	4 984 ..	*697.2*	*−254.9*	*894.2*	*1,276.7*	*179.8*	*260.8*	*1,441.7*	*890.0*
E. Reserves and Related Items................	4 802 A.	**−697.2**	**254.9**	**−894.2**	**−1,276.7**	**−179.8**	**−260.8**	**−1,441.7**	**−890.0**
Reserve assets..............................	4 802 ..	−686.1	267.0	−906.7	−1,176.7	−81.8	−183.5	−1,353.3	−813.6
Use of Fund credit and loans................	4 766 ..	−11.2	−12.1	12.5	−100.0	−98.1	−77.2	−88.4	−76.4
Exceptional financing.......................	4 920 ..	....	....	....	....	....	....	....	....
Conversion rates: Jordanian dinar per U.S. dollar...............	0 101 ..	**.7090**	**.7090**	**.7090**	**.7090**	**.7090**	**.7090**	**.7090**	**.7090**

[1] Excludes components that have been classified in the categories of Group E.

Table 2. STANDARD PRESENTATION, 2000–2007

(Millions of U.S. dollars)

	Code	2000	2001	2002	2003	2004	2005	2006	2007
CURRENT ACCOUNT	4 993	**59.7**	**4.9**	**543.9**	**1,244.9**	**88.7**	**−2,199.6**	**−1,598.4**	**−2,776.2**
A. GOODS	4 100	**−2,174.5**	**−2,007.1**	**−1,730.9**	**−1,996.2**	**−3,378.1**	**−5,015.9**	**−5,055.9**	**−6,321.6**
Credit	2 100	**1,899.3**	**2,294.4**	**2,770.0**	**3,081.7**	**3,882.9**	**4,301.4**	**5,204.4**	**5,700.0**
General merchandise: exports f.o.b.	2 110	1,896.5	2,284.1	2,594.6	2,871.2	3,831.9	4,297.6	4,927.5	5,653.6
Goods for processing: exports f.o.b.	2 150	....	....	....	....	....	....	....	....
Repairs on goods	2 160	....	....	....	....	....	....	....	....
Goods procured in ports by carriers	2 170	....	....	....	....	....	....	....	....
Nonmonetary gold	2 180	2.8	10.3	175.3	210.4	51.1	3.8	276.9	46.4
Debit	3 100	**−4,073.8**	**−4,301.5**	**−4,500.9**	**−5,077.9**	**−7,261.1**	**−9,317.3**	**−10,260.2**	**−12,021.6**
General merchandise: imports f.o.b.	3 110	−4,045.6	−4,262.7	−4,468.6	−5,006.5	−7,159.1	−9,248.7	−10,223.7	−11,927.4
Goods for processing: imports f.o.b.	3 150	....	....	....	....	....	....	....	....
Repairs on goods	3 160	....	....	....	....	....	....	....	....
Goods procured in ports by carriers	3 170	....	....	....	....	....	....	....	....
Nonmonetary gold	3 180	−28.2	−38.8	−32.3	−71.4	−102.0	−68.7	−36.5	−94.2
B. SERVICES	4 200	**−82.4**	**−238.4**	**−108.7**	**−141.0**	**−73.1**	**−208.5**	**−63.2**	**−68.3**
Total credit	2 200	*1,639.7*	*1,487.5*	*1,774.2*	*1,748.2*	*2,072.8*	*2,333.6*	*2,907.5*	*3,410.4*
Total debit	3 200	*−1,722.1*	*−1,725.9*	*−1,882.9*	*−1,889.2*	*−2,145.8*	*−2,542.0*	*−2,970.7*	*−3,478.7*
Transportation services, credit	2 205	**299.6**	**260.2**	**292.2**	**303.2**	**426.0**	**469.8**	**527.6**	**636.7**
Passenger	2 850	*212.0*	*184.1*	*205.6*	*203.5*	*291.4*	*317.8*	*366.0*	*443.3*
Freight	2 851	*17.1*	*15.0*	*18.3*	*32.0*	*37.7*	*46.1*	*39.8*	*45.7*
Other	2 852	*70.5*	*61.2*	*68.3*	*67.7*	*96.9*	*105.9*	*121.9*	*147.7*
Sea transport, passenger	2 207	....	....	....	....	....	....	....	....
Sea transport, freight	2 208	....	....	....	....	....	....	....	....
Sea transport, other	2 209	....	....	....	....	....	....	....	....
Air transport, passenger	2 211	....	....	....	....	....	....	....	....
Air transport, freight	2 212	....	....	....	....	....	....	....	....
Air transport, other	2 213	....	....	....	....	....	....	....	....
Other transport, passenger	2 215	....	....	....	....	....	....	....	....
Other transport, freight	2 216	....	....	....	....	....	....	....	....
Other transport, other	2 217	....	....	....	....	....	....	....	....
Transportation services, debit	3 205	**−693.8**	**−739.2**	**−771.4**	**−825.9**	**−1,106.6**	**−1,341.6**	**−1,536.0**	**−1,795.2**
Passenger	3 850	*−37.2*	*−42.5*	*−51.5*	*−51.3*	*−61.4*	*−68.0*	*−119.2*	*−141.3*
Freight	3 851	*−411.9*	*−435.0*	*−455.2*	*−513.5*	*−734.3*	*−942.2*	*−1,037.5*	*−1,215.7*
Other	3 852	*−244.6*	*−261.8*	*−264.7*	*−261.1*	*−311.0*	*−331.5*	*−379.3*	*−438.2*
Sea transport, passenger	3 207	....	....	....	....	....	....	....	....
Sea transport, freight	3 208	....	....	....	....	....	....	....	....
Sea transport, other	3 209	....	....	....	....	....	....	....	....
Air transport, passenger	3 211	....	....	....	....	....	....	....	....
Air transport, freight	3 212	....	....	....	....	....	....	....	....
Air transport, other	3 213	....	....	....	....	....	....	....	....
Other transport, passenger	3 215	....	....	....	....	....	....	....	....
Other transport, freight	3 216	....	....	....	....	....	....	....	....
Other transport, other	3 217	....	....	....	....	....	....	....	....
Travel, credit	2 236	**722.7**	**699.7**	**1,048.4**	**1,061.5**	**1,329.8**	**1,440.6**	**2,060.4**	**2,311.6**
Business travel	2 237	....	....	....	....	....	....	....	....
Personal travel	2 240	....	....	....	....	....	....	....	....
Travel, debit	3 236	**−349.6**	**−377.6**	**−453.2**	**−451.9**	**−523.8**	**−585.2**	**−837.0**	**−882.7**
Business travel	3 237	....	....	....	....	....	....	....	....
Personal travel	3 240	−349.6	−377.6	−453.2	−451.9	−523.8	−585.2	−837.0	−882.7
Other services, credit	2 200 BA	**617.4**	**527.5**	**433.6**	**383.5**	**317.1**	**423.1**	**319.5**	**462.2**
Communications	2 245	....	....	....	....	....	....	....	....
Construction	2 249	....	....	....	....	....	....	....	....
Insurance	2 253	....	....	....	....	....	....	....	....
Financial	2 260	....	....	....	....	....	....	....	....
Computer and information	2 262	....	....	....	....	....	....	....	....
Royalties and licence fees	2 266	....	....	....	....	....	....	....	....
Other business services	2 268	579.4	436.4	402.1	351.9	295.9	328.6	262.2	349.9
Personal, cultural, and recreational	2 287	....	....	....	....	....	....	....	....
Government, n.i.e.	2 291	38.0	91.1	31.5	31.6	21.2	94.5	57.3	112.3
Other services, debit	3 200 BA	**−678.7**	**−609.1**	**−658.3**	**−611.4**	**−515.4**	**−615.2**	**−597.7**	**−800.8**
Communications	3 245	....	....	....	....	....	....	....	....
Construction	3 249	....	....	....	....	....	....	....	....
Insurance	3 253	−91.5	−96.7	−101.2	−114.1	−163.2	−209.4	−230.6	−270.1
Financial	3 260	....	....	....	....	....	....	....	....
Computer and information	3 262	....	....	....	....	....	....	....	....
Royalties and licence fees	3 266	....	....	....	....	....	....	....	....
Other business services	3 268	−327.9	−306.9	−301.6	−297.7	−178.7	−328.6	−250.5	−369.5
Personal, cultural, and recreational	3 287	....	....	....	....	....	....	....	....
Government, n.i.e.	3 291	−259.2	−205.5	−255.6	−199.6	−173.5	−77.2	−116.6	−161.2

Table 2 (Continued). STANDARD PRESENTATION, 2000–2007

(Millions of U.S. dollars)

	Code	2000	2001	2002	2003	2004	2005	2006	2007
C. INCOME	4 300	**132.7**	**191.5**	**119.4**	**176.2**	**323.7**	**408.5**	**580.5**	**835.0**
Total credit	2 300	*668.1*	*652.5*	*491.7*	*550.5*	*649.2*	*791.1*	*1,031.9*	*1,395.1*
Total debit	3 300	*−535.4*	*−460.9*	*−372.3*	*−374.3*	*−325.5*	*−382.7*	*−451.3*	*−560.1*
Compensation of employees, credit	2 310	**184.6**	**201.3**	**221.6**	**220.2**	**271.7**	**320.9**	**369.0**	**440.5**
Compensation of employees, debit	3 310	**−23.1**	**−22.8**	**−22.8**	**−26.8**	**−32.2**	**−41.2**	**−47.4**	**−56.7**
Investment income, credit	2 320	**483.4**	**451.2**	**270.1**	**330.3**	**377.6**	**470.2**	**662.9**	**954.6**
Direct investment income	2 330	....	....	....	....	....	....	....	....
Dividends and distributed branch profits	2 332	....	....	....	....	....	....	....	....
Reinvested earnings and undistributed branch profits	2 333	....	....	....	....	....	....	....	....
Income on debt (interest)	2 334	....	....	....	....	....	....	....	....
Portfolio investment income	2 339	....	....	....	....	....	....	....	....
Income on equity	2 340	....	....	....	....	....	....	....	....
Income on bonds and notes	2 350	....	....	....	....	....	....	....	....
Income on money market instruments	2 360	....	....	....	....	....	....	....	....
Other investment income	2 370	483.4	451.2	270.1	330.3	377.6	470.2	662.9	954.6
Investment income, debit	3 320	**−512.2**	**−438.1**	**−349.4**	**−347.5**	**−293.4**	**−341.5**	**−403.9**	**−503.4**
Direct investment income	3 330	−1.1	−2.0	−.8	−2.1	−1.0	−1.4	−2.4	−2.9
Dividends and distributed branch profits	3 332	....	....	....	....	....	....	....	....
Reinvested earnings and undistributed branch profits	3 333	....	....	....	....	....	....	....	....
Income on debt (interest)	3 334	....	....	....	....	....	....	....	....
Portfolio investment income	3 339	−8.0	−5.2	−3.9	−1.7	−.6	....	....	....
Income on equity	3 340	....	....	....	....	....	....	....	....
Income on bonds and notes	3 350	−8.0	−5.2	−3.9	−1.7	−.6	....	....	....
Income on money market instruments	3 360	....	....	....	....	....	....	....	....
Other investment income	3 370	−503.1	−430.9	−344.7	−343.7	−291.8	−340.1	−401.6	−500.5
D. CURRENT TRANSFERS	4 379	**2,183.9**	**2,058.9**	**2,264.2**	**3,205.9**	**3,216.2**	**2,616.4**	**2,940.1**	**2,778.7**
Credit	2 379	**2,611.3**	**2,365.8**	**2,524.3**	**3,501.0**	**3,562.5**	**3,029.9**	**3,378.8**	**3,510.9**
General government	2 380	410.8	465.5	511.3	1,406.5	1,334.1	752.0	844.6	378.6
Other sectors	2 390	2,200.4	1,900.3	2,013.0	2,094.5	2,228.3	2,277.9	2,534.3	3,132.3
Workers' remittances	2 391	1,660.5	1,810.1	1,921.4	1,981.0	2,058.7	2,178.8	2,514.4	2,993.7
Other current transfers	2 392	539.9	90.3	91.5	113.5	169.7	99.0	19.9	138.6
Debit	3 379	**−427.4**	**−306.9**	**−260.1**	**−295.1**	**−346.3**	**−413.5**	**−438.8**	**−732.2**
General government	3 380	−6.2	−4.2	−1.4	−2.0	−8.9	−6.6	−34.1	−4.9
Other sectors	3 390	−421.2	−302.7	−258.7	−293.1	−337.4	−406.9	−404.7	−727.2
Workers' remittances	3 391	−174.3	−170.4	−171.1	−200.1	−239.9	−308.0	−354.2	−422.6
Other current transfers	3 392	−246.8	−132.3	−87.6	−92.9	−97.5	−98.9	−50.5	−304.7
CAPITAL AND FINANCIAL ACCOUNT	4 996	**−347.5**	**85.0**	**−488.0**	**−1,393.8**	**−281.0**	**1,385.9**	**1,615.2**	**1,522.4**
CAPITAL ACCOUNT	4 994	**64.9**	**21.6**	**68.8**	**93.5**	**2.1**	**8.5**	**62.8**	**12.8**
Total credit	2 994	*64.9*	*21.6*	*68.8*	*93.5*	*2.1*	*8.5*	*62.8*	*12.8*
Total debit	3 994	....	....	....	....	....	....	....	....
Capital transfers, credit	2 400	**64.9**	**21.6**	**68.8**	**93.5**	**2.1**	**8.5**	**62.8**	**12.8**
General government	2 401	....	....	....	....	....	....	....	....
Debt forgiveness	2 402	....	....	....	....	....	....	....	....
Other capital transfers	2 410	....	....	....	....	....	....	....	....
Other sectors	2 430	64.9	21.6	68.8	93.5	2.1	8.5	62.8	12.8
Migrants' transfers	2 431	....	....	....	....	....	....	....	....
Debt forgiveness	2 432	....	....	....	....	....	....	....	....
Other capital transfers	2 440	64.9	21.6	68.8	93.5	2.1	8.5	62.8	12.8
Capital transfers, debit	3 400	....	....	....	....	....	....	....	....
General government	3 401	....	....	....	....	....	....	....	....
Debt forgiveness	3 402	....	....	....	....	....	....	....	....
Other capital transfers	3 410	....	....	....	....	....	....	....	....
Other sectors	3 430	....	....	....	....	....	....	....	....
Migrants' transfers	3 431	....	....	....	....	....	....	....	....
Debt forgiveness	3 432	....	....	....	....	....	....	....	....
Other capital transfers	3 440	....	....	....	....	....	....	....	....
Nonproduced nonfinancial assets, credit	2 480	....	....	....	....	....	....	....	....
Nonproduced nonfinancial assets, debit	3 480	....	....	....	....	....	....	....	....

Table 2 (Continued). STANDARD PRESENTATION, 2000–2007

(Millions of U.S. dollars)

	Code	2000	2001	2002	2003	2004	2005	2006	2007
FINANCIAL ACCOUNT	4 995 ..	−412.3	63.5	−556.8	−1,487.3	−283.1	1,377.5	1,552.5	1,509.6
A. DIRECT INVESTMENT	4 500 ..	806.2	148.2	107.8	446.8	798.2	1,610.9	3,357.4	1,787.3
Direct investment abroad	4 505 ..	−8.6	−31.6	−13.8	3.7	−18.2	−163.2	138.1	−48.1
Equity capital	4 510 ..	....	....	....	....	....	....	....	....
Claims on affiliated enterprises	4 515 ..	....	....	....	....	....	....	....	....
Liabilities to affiliated enterprises	4 520 ..	....	....	....	....	....	....	....	....
Reinvested earnings	4 525 ..	....	....	....	....	....	....	....	....
Other capital	4 530 ..	....	....	....	....	....	....	....	....
Claims on affiliated enterprises	4 535 ..	....	....	....	....	....	....	....	....
Liabilities to affiliated enterprises	4 540 ..	....	....	....	....	....	....	....	....
Direct investment in Jordan	4 555 ..	814.8	179.8	121.6	443.2	816.4	1,774.0	3,219.3	1,835.4
Equity capital	4 560 ..	....	....	....	....	....	....	....	....
Claims on direct investors	4 565 ..	....	....	....	....	....	....	....	....
Liabilities to direct investors	4 570 ..	....	....	....	....	....	....	....	....
Reinvested earnings	4 575 ..	....	....	....	....	....	....	....	....
Other capital	4 580 ..	....	....	....	....	....	....	....	....
Claims on direct investors	4 585 ..	....	....	....	....	....	....	....	....
Liabilities to direct investors	4 590 ..	....	....	....	....	....	....	....	....
B. PORTFOLIO INVESTMENT	4 600 ..	−179.3	−284.4	−410.7	−471.7	−288.9	312.7	−36.8	839.9
Assets	4 602 ..	−38.4	−201.1	−178.0	−122.6	−199.0	143.6	−180.4	493.9
Equity securities	4 610 ..	−38.4	−201.1	−178.0	−122.6	−199.0	143.6	−180.4	493.9
Monetary authorities	4 611 ..	....	....	....	....	....	....	....	....
General government	4 612 ..	....	....	....	....	....	....	....	....
Banks	4 613 ..	−38.4	−201.1	−178.0	−122.6	−199.0	143.6	−180.4	493.9
Other sectors	4 614 ..	....	....	....	....	....	....	....	....
Debt securities	4 619 ..	....	....	....	....	....	....	....	....
Bonds and notes	4 620 ..	....	....	....	....	....	....	....	....
Monetary authorities	4 621 ..	....	....	....	....	....	....	....	....
General government	4 622 ..	....	....	....	....	....	....	....	....
Banks	4 623 ..	....	....	....	....	....	....	....	....
Other sectors	4 624 ..	....	....	....	....	....	....	....	....
Money market instruments	4 630 ..	....	....	....	....	....	....	....	....
Monetary authorities	4 631 ..	....	....	....	....	....	....	....	....
General government	4 632 ..	....	....	....	....	....	....	....	....
Banks	4 633 ..	....	....	....	....	....	....	....	....
Other sectors	4 634 ..	....	....	....	....	....	....	....	....
Liabilities	4 652 ..	−140.9	−83.2	−232.7	−349.1	−89.8	169.1	143.6	346.0
Equity securities	4 660 ..	−16.8	−56.7	−232.7	−57.8	−89.8	169.1	143.6	346.0
Banks	4 663 ..	....	....	....	....	....	....	....	....
Other sectors	4 664 ..	−16.8	−56.7	−232.7	−57.8	−89.8	169.1	143.6	346.0
Debt securities	4 669 ..	−124.1	−26.5	....	−291.3	....	....	....	....
Bonds and notes	4 670 ..	−124.1	−26.5	....	−291.3	....	....	....	....
Monetary authorities	4 671 ..	....	....	....	....	....	....	....	....
General government	4 672 ..	−124.1	−26.5	....	−291.3	....	....	....	....
Banks	4 673 ..	....	....	....	....	....	....	....	....
Other sectors	4 674 ..	....	....	....	....	....	....	....	....
Money market instruments	4 680 ..	....	....	....	....	....	....	....	....
Monetary authorities	4 681 ..	....	....	....	....	....	....	....	....
General government	4 682 ..	....	....	....	....	....	....	....	....
Banks	4 683 ..	....	....	....	....	....	....	....	....
Other sectors	4 684 ..	....	....	....	....	....	....	....	....
C. FINANCIAL DERIVATIVES	4 910 ..	....	....	....	....	....	....	....	....
Monetary authorities	4 911 ..	....	....	....	....	....	....	....	....
General government	4 912 ..	....	....	....	....	....	....	....	....
Banks	4 913 ..	....	....	....	....	....	....	....	....
Other sectors	4 914 ..	....	....	....	....	....	....	....	....
Assets	4 900 ..	....	....	....	....	....	....	....	....
Monetary authorities	4 901 ..	....	....	....	....	....	....	....	....
General government	4 902 ..	....	....	....	....	....	....	....	....
Banks	4 903 ..	....	....	....	....	....	....	....	....
Other sectors	4 904 ..	....	....	....	....	....	....	....	....
Liabilities	4 905 ..	....	....	....	....	....	....	....	....
Monetary authorities	4 906 ..	....	....	....	....	....	....	....	....
General government	4 907 ..	....	....	....	....	....	....	....	....
Banks	4 908 ..	....	....	....	....	....	....	....	....
Other sectors	4 909 ..	....	....	....	....	....	....	....	....

Table 2 (Concluded). STANDARD PRESENTATION, 2000–2007

(Millions of U.S. dollars)

	Code	2000	2001	2002	2003	2004	2005	2006	2007
D. OTHER INVESTMENT	4 700	−353.2	−67.4	652.8	−285.8	−710.6	−362.6	−414.8	−304.1
Assets	4 703	−942.2	−635.5	−3.0	252.9	−680.8	−615.9	−1,148.0	−939.6
Trade credits	4 706	....	....	....	....	....	....	....	....
General government	4 707	....	....	....	....	....	....	....	....
of which: Short-term	4 709	....	....	....	....	....	....	....	....
Other sectors	4 710	....	....	....	....	....	....	....	....
of which: Short-term	4 712	....	....	....	....	....	....	....	....
Loans	4 714	144.9	10.7	14.0	−26.2	50.5	34.7	−117.6	4.5
Monetary authorities	4 715	148.5	30.6	54.7	11.3	....	....	....	....
of which: Short-term	4 718	....	....	....	....	....	....	....	....
General government	4 719	....	....	....	....	....	....	....	....
of which: Short-term	4 721	....	....	....	....	....	....	....	....
Banks	4 722	−3.7	−19.9	−40.8	−37.5	50.5	34.7	−117.6	4.5
of which: Short-term	4 724	....	....	....	....	....	....	....	....
Other sectors	4 725	....	....	....	....	....	....	....	....
of which: Short-term	4 727	....	....	....	....	....	....	....	....
Currency and deposits	4 730	−942.3	−531.0	−75.5	285.9	−682.5	−583.2	−838.6	−857.5
Monetary authorities	4 731	....	....	....	....	....	....	....	....
General government	4 732	....	....	....	....	....	....	....	....
Banks	4 733	−942.3	−531.0	−75.5	285.9	−682.5	−583.2	−838.6	−857.5
Other sectors	4 734	....	....	....	....	....	....	....	....
Other assets	4 736	−144.7	−115.2	58.5	−6.8	−48.8	−67.4	−191.7	−85.6
Monetary authorities	4 737	−2.0	−24.3	−17.3	−33.9	−23.4	−36.0	−58.7	−53.3
of which: Short-term	4 739	−2.0	−24.3	−17.3	−33.9	−23.4	−36.0	−58.7	−53.3
General government	4 740	....	....	....	....	....	....	....	....
of which: Short-term	4 742	....	....	....	....	....	....	....	....
Banks	4 743	−142.7	−91.0	75.9	27.1	−25.4	−31.5	−133.0	−28.3
of which: Short-term	4 745	....	....	....	....	....	....	....	....
Other sectors	4 746	....	....	....	....	....	....	....	....
of which: Short-term	4 748	....	....	....	....	....	....	....	....
Liabilities	4 753	589.0	568.1	655.8	−538.6	−29.8	253.4	733.2	635.6
Trade credits	4 756	35.8	18.5	75.7	3.7	−37.4	−7.9	47.5	−29.9
General government	4 757	....	....	....	....	....	....	....	....
of which: Short-term	4 759	....	....	....	....	....	....	....	....
Other sectors	4 760	35.8	18.5	75.7	3.7	−37.4	−7.9	47.5	−29.9
of which: Short-term	4 762	35.8	18.5	75.7	3.7	−37.4	−7.9	47.5	−29.9
Loans	4 764	70.9	151.6	87.2	−265.3	−269.2	−40.0	−54.7	−154.7
Monetary authorities	4 765	−27.9	−11.1	−1.5	−109.2	−109.7	−86.5	−88.4	−76.4
of which: Use of Fund credit and loans from the Fund	4 766	−11.2	−12.1	12.5	−100.0	−98.1	−77.2	−88.4	−76.4
of which: Short-term	4 768	....	....	....	....	....	....	....	....
General government	4 769	34.8	196.1	130.3	−101.0	−83.1	6.1	−92.0	−125.5
of which: Short-term	4 771	....	....	....	....	....	....	....	....
Banks	4 772	−1.4	.3	10.6	−1.4	3.7	40.1	70.0	−3.7
of which: Short-term	4 774	....	....	....	....	....	....	....	....
Other sectors	4 775	65.4	−33.6	−52.2	−53.7	−80.1	.4	55.7	50.9
of which: Short-term	4 777	....	....	....	....	....	....	....	....
Currency and deposits	4 780	343.6	313.0	454.4	−102.3	307.9	232.7	832.3	782.2
Monetary authorities	4 781	−53.0	3.7	−1.0	−4.2	−17.8	.1	97.7	2.3
General government	4 782	....	....	....	....	....	....	....	....
Banks	4 783	396.6	309.3	455.4	−98.0	325.7	232.6	734.6	780.0
Other sectors	4 784	....	....	....	....	....	....	....	....
Other liabilities	4 786	138.6	85.1	38.4	−174.8	−31.2	68.5	−92.0	37.9
Monetary authorities	4 787	....	....	....	....	....	....	....	....
of which: Short-term	4 789	....	....	....	....	....	....	....	....
General government	4 790	138.6	85.1	38.4	−174.8	−31.2	68.5	−92.0	37.9
of which: Short-term	4 792	....	....	....	....	....	....	....	....
Banks	4 793	....	....	....	....	....	....	....	....
of which: Short-term	4 795	....	....	....	....	....	....	....	....
Other sectors	4 796	....	....	....	....	....	....	....	....
of which: Short-term	4 798	....	....	....	....	....	....	....	....
E. RESERVE ASSETS	4 802	−686.1	267.0	−906.7	−1,176.7	−81.8	−183.5	−1,353.3	−813.6
Monetary gold	4 812	20.9	−1.1	−1.3	−.4	....	....	1.0	−40.6
Special drawing rights	4 811	−.7	−.6	.4	....	−.5	.9	−.5	−.8
Reserve position in the Fund	4 810	−.1	....	....	....	−.1	−.1	−.1	−.1
Foreign exchange	4 803	−706.2	268.7	−905.8	−1,176.3	−81.2	−184.3	−1,353.7	−772.1
Other claims	4 813	....	....	....	....	....	....	....	....
NET ERRORS AND OMISSIONS	4 998	287.7	−90.0	−56.0	148.9	192.3	813.7	−16.8	1,253.8

Table 3. INTERNATIONAL INVESTMENT POSITION (End-period stocks), 2000–2007

(Millions of U.S. dollars)

	Code	2000	2001	2002	2003	2004	2005	2006	2007
ASSETS	8 995 C.	9,889.1	10,472.3	11,603.8	12,684.4	13,849.4	14,452.6	17,138.0	18,529.9
Direct investment abroad	8 505 ..	44.3	70.1	83.9	80.3	286.6	449.6	311.6	359.7
Equity capital and reinvested earnings	8 506 ..	44.3	70.1	83.9	80.3	286.6	449.6	311.6	359.7
Claims on affiliated enterprises	8 507 ..	44.3	70.1	83.9	80.3	286.6	449.6	311.6	359.7
Liabilities to affiliated enterprises	8 508 ..	....	....	....	....	....	....	....	....
Other capital	8 530 ..	....	....	....	....	....	....	....	....
Claims on affiliated enterprises	8 535 ..	....	....	....	....	....	....	....	....
Liabilities to affiliated enterprises	8 540 ..	....	....	....	....	....	....	....	....
Portfolio investment	8 602 ..	140.3	341.6	519.7	642.3	862.6	719.2	902.0	410.7
Equity securities	8 610 ..	12.4	19.7	23.7	22.7	49.1	92.1	61.2	71.1
Monetary authorities	8 611 ..	....	....	....	....	....	....	....	....
General government	8 612 ..	....	....	....	....	....	....	....	....
Banks	8 613 ..	12.4	19.7	23.7	22.7	24.0	60.8	27.4	40.9
Other sectors	8 614 ..	....	....	....	....	25.1	31.3	33.9	30.2
Debt securities	8 619 ..	127.9	321.9	496.1	619.6	813.5	627.1	840.8	339.6
Bonds and notes	8 620 ..	127.9	321.9	496.1	619.6	813.5	627.1	840.8	339.6
Monetary authorities	8 621 ..	....	....	....	....	....	....	....	....
General government	8 622 ..	....	....	....	....	....	....	....	....
Banks	8 623 ..	127.9	321.9	496.1	619.6	813.5	627.1	840.8	339.6
Other sectors	8 624 ..	....	....	....	....	....	....	....	....
Money market instruments	8 630 ..	....	....	....	....	....	....	....	....
Monetary authorities	8 631 ..	....	....	....	....	....	....	....	....
General government	8 632 ..	....	....	....	....	....	....	....	....
Banks	8 633 ..	....	....	....	....	....	....	....	....
Other sectors	8 634 ..	....	....	....	....	....	....	....	....
Financial derivatives	8 900 ..	....	....	....	....	....	....	....	....
Monetary authorities	8 901 ..	....	....	....	....	....	....	....	....
General government	8 902 ..	....	....	....	....	....	....	....	....
Banks	8 903 ..	....	....	....	....	....	....	....	....
Other sectors	8 904 ..	....	....	....	....	....	....	....	....
Other investment	8 703 ..	6,274.1	6,886.3	6,882.9	6,596.2	7,253.9	7,835.8	8,946.1	9,830.5
Trade credits	8 706 ..	....	....	....	....	....	....	....	....
General government	8 707 ..	....	....	....	....	....	....	....	....
of which: Short-term	8 709 ..	....	....	....	....	....	....	....	....
Other sectors	8 710 ..	....	....	....	....	....	....	....	....
of which: Short-term	8 712 ..	....	....	....	....	....	....	....	....
Loans	8 714 ..	1,489.0	1,478.4	1,464.5	1,490.7	1,440.2	1,405.5	1,523.0	1,518.5
Monetary authorities	8 715 ..	1,178.1	1,147.5	1,092.9	1,081.7	1,081.7	1,081.7	1,081.7	1,081.7
of which: Short-term	8 718 ..	....	....	....	....	....	....	....	....
General government	8 719 ..	....	....	....	....	....	....	....	....
of which: Short-term	8 721 ..	....	....	....	....	....	....	....	....
Banks	8 722 ..	310.9	330.9	371.5	409.0	358.5	323.8	441.3	436.8
of which: Short-term	8 724 ..	*285.9*	*302.8*	*348.7*	*387.2*	*315.4*	*245.3*	*327.1*	*301.3*
Other sectors	8 725 ..	....	....	....	....	....	....	....	....
of which: Short-term	8 727 ..	....	....	....	....	....	....	....	....
Currency and deposits	8 730 ..	4,322.0	4,853.0	4,928.8	4,642.9	5,325.5	5,908.6	6,747.3	7,604.8
Monetary authorities	8 731 ..	....	....	....	....	....	....	....	....
General government	8 732 ..	....	....	....	....	....	....	....	....
Banks	8 733 ..	4,322.0	4,853.0	4,928.8	4,642.9	5,325.5	5,908.6	6,747.3	7,604.8
Other sectors	8 734 ..	....	....	....	....	....	....	....	....
Other assets	8 736 ..	463.0	554.9	489.7	462.6	488.2	521.7	675.9	707.2
Monetary authorities	8 737 ..	45.3	46.1	56.8	56.8	57.0	59.1	80.3	83.2
of which: Short-term	8 739 ..	....	....	....	....	....	....	....	....
General government	8 740 ..	....	....	....	....	....	....	....	....
of which: Short-term	8 742 ..	....	....	....	....	....	....	....	....
Banks	8 743 ..	417.8	508.7	432.9	405.8	431.2	462.6	595.6	624.0
of which: Short-term	8 745 ..	....	....	....	....	....	....	....	....
Other sectors	8 746 ..	....	....	....	....	....	....	....	....
of which: Short-term	8 748 ..	....	....	....	....	....	....	....	....
Reserve assets	8 802 ..	3,430.5	3,174.3	4,117.1	5,365.7	5,446.3	5,447.9	6,978.3	7,929.0
Monetary gold	8 812 ..	99.2	112.1	141.2	171.4	179.5	212.3	257.1	387.0
Special drawing rights	8 811 ..	.6	1.2	.9	1.1	1.7	.6	1.3	2.2
Reserve position in the Fund	8 810 ..	.1	.1	.1	.1	.1	.2	.3	.4
Foreign exchange	8 803 ..	3,330.6	3,060.9	3,975.0	5,193.1	5,264.9	5,234.8	6,719.6	7,539.4
Other claims	8 813 ..	....	....	....	....	....	....	....	....

Table 3 (Concluded). INTERNATIONAL INVESTMENT POSITION (End-period stocks), 2000–2007

(Millions of U.S. dollars)

	Code	2000	2001	2002	2003	2004	2005	2006	2007
LIABILITIES..	8 995 D.	**16,337.8**	**17,397.3**	**18,455.0**	**19,878.7**	**24,602.9**	**34,342.5**	**32,593.0**	**39,769.4**
Direct investment in Jordan................................	8 555 ..	**3,135.1**	**3,428.2**	**3,964.0**	**5,004.2**	**8,315.7**	**13,228.8**	**12,713.1**	**16,058.4**
Equity capital and reinvested earnings...........................	8 556 ..	3,135.1	3,428.2	3,964.0	5,004.2	8,315.7	13,228.8	12,713.1	16,058.4
Claims on direct investors....................................	8 557 ..	....	....	....	....	....	....	....	....
Liabilities to direct investors.................................	8 558 ..	3,135.1	3,428.2	3,964.0	5,004.2	8,315.7	13,228.8	12,713.1	16,058.4
Other capital...	8 580 ..	....	....	....	....	....	....	....	....
Claims on direct investors....................................	8 585 ..	....	....	....	....	....	....	....	....
Liabilities to direct investors.................................	8 590 ..	....	....	....	....	....	....	....	....
Portfolio investment..	8 652 ..	**2,076.2**	**2,493.1**	**1,883.6**	**2,210.3**	**3,260.4**	**8,210.0**	**5,896.5**	**8,765.0**
Equity securities...	8 660 ..	1,725.3	2,172.9	1,563.5	2,210.3	3,260.4	8,210.0	5,896.5	8,765.0
Banks..	8 663 ..	1,309.2	1,686.7	1,102.4	1,808.6	2,804.8	7,382.2	5,063.9	6,951.5
Other sectors...	8 664 ..	416.1	486.2	461.1	401.7	455.6	827.8	832.6	1,813.5
Debt securities..	8 669 ..	350.9	320.2	320.2	....	....	....	....	....
Bonds and notes..	8 670 ..	350.9	320.2	320.2	....	....	....	....	....
Monetary authorities.......................................	8 671 ..	....	....	....	....	....	....	....	....
General government..	8 672 ..	350.9	320.2	320.2	....	....	....	....	....
Banks..	8 673 ..	....	....	....	....	....	....	....	....
Other sectors...	8 674 ..	....	....	....	....	....	....	....	....
Money market instruments...................................	8 680 ..	....	....	....	....	....	....	....	....
Monetary authorities.......................................	8 681 ..	....	....	....	....	....	....	....	....
General government..	8 682 ..	....	....	....	....	....	....	....	....
Banks..	8 683 ..	....	....	....	....	....	....	....	....
Other sectors...	8 684 ..	....	....	....	....	....	....	....	....
Financial derivatives...	8 905 ..	....	....	....	....	....	....	....	....
Monetary authorities...	8 906 ..	....	....	....	....	....	....	....	....
General government..	8 907 ..	....	....	....	....	....	....	....	....
Banks..	8 908 ..	....	....	....	....	....	....	....	....
Other sectors...	8 909 ..	....	....	....	....	....	....	....	....
Other investment..	8 753 ..	**11,126.5**	**11,476.0**	**12,607.3**	**12,664.1**	**13,026.9**	**12,903.7**	**13,983.4**	**14,946.0**
Trade credits..	8 756 ..	297.9	315.9	391.5	395.2	357.8	349.9	397.5	427.4
General government..	8 757 ..	....	....	....	....	....	....	....	....
of which: Short-term......................................	8 759 ..	....	....	....	....	....	....	....	....
Other sectors...	8 760 ..	297.9	315.9	391.5	395.2	357.8	349.9	397.5	427.4
of which: Short-term......................................	8 762 ..	*297.9*	*315.9*	*391.5*	*395.2*	*357.8*	*349.9*	*397.5*	*427.4*
Loans..	8 764 ..	6,832.0	6,765.5	7,328.3	7,723.4	7,631.4	7,214.8	7,506.8	7,619.5
Monetary authorities..	8 765 ..	502.5	473.6	510.6	442.2	347.6	236.3	158.3	87.6
of which: Use of Fund credit and loans from the Fund....	8 766 ..	*461.6*	*432.9*	*482.6*	*421.4*	*337.7*	*236.3*	*158.3*	*87.6*
of which: Short-term......................................	8 768 ..	....	....	....	....	....	....	....	....
General government...	8 769 ..	5,845.7	5,860.7	6,411.7	6,907.6	7,055.2	6,561.2	6,784.4	6,915.4
of which: Short-term......................................	8 771 ..	....	....	....	....	....	....	....	....
Banks..	8 772 ..	....	.3	10.9	9.4	13.1	53.2	123.1	119.5
of which: Short-term......................................	8 774 ..	....	*.3*	*10.9*	*9.4*	*13.1*	*53.2*	*123.1*	*119.5*
Other sectors...	8 775 ..	483.8	431.0	395.2	364.0	215.5	364.2	441.0	497.0
of which: Short-term......................................	8 777 ..	....	....	....	....	....	....	....	....
Currency and deposits..	8 780 ..	3,709.6	4,022.4	4,477.0	4,309.9	4,833.2	5,065.9	5,898.0	6,680.1
Monetary authorities..	8 781 ..	177.6	181.2	180.3	176.0	158.3	158.4	256.0	258.1
General government...	8 782 ..	....	....	....	....	....	....	....	....
Banks..	8 783 ..	3,532.0	3,841.2	4,296.8	4,133.9	4,674.9	4,907.5	5,642.0	6,422.0
Other sectors...	8 784 ..	....	....	....	....	....	....	....	....
Other liabilities...	8 786 ..	287.0	372.1	410.4	235.7	204.5	273.1	181.1	219.0
Monetary authorities..	8 787 ..	....	....	....	....	....	....	....	....
of which: Short-term......................................	8 789 ..	....	....	....	....	....	....	....	....
General government...	8 790 ..	....	....	....	....	....	....	....	....
of which: Short-term......................................	8 792 ..	....	....	....	....	....	....	....	....
Banks..	8 793 ..	287.0	372.1	410.4	235.7	204.5	273.1	181.1	219.0
of which: Short-term......................................	8 795 ..	*287.0*	*372.1*	*410.4*	*235.7*	*204.5*	*273.1*	*181.1*	*219.0*
Other sectors...	8 796 ..	....	....	....	....	....	....	....	....
of which: Short-term......................................	8 798 ..	....	....	....	....	....	....	....	....
NET INTERNATIONAL INVESTMENT POSITION........	8 995 ..	**−6,448.7**	**−6,924.9**	**−6,851.3**	**−7,194.2**	**−10,753.6**	**−19,889.9**	**−15,455.1**	**−21,239.6**
Conversion rates: Jordanian dinar per U.S. dollar (end of period)..	0 102 ..	**.7090**	**.7090**	**.7090**	**.7090**	**.7090**	**.7090**	**.7090**	**.7090**

Table 1. ANALYTIC PRESENTATION, 2000–2007

(Millions of U.S. dollars)

	Code	2000	2001	2002	2003	2004	2005	2006	2007
A. Current Account[1]	4 993 Z.	**366.3**	**−1,389.5**	**−1,024.3**	**−272.6**	**335.4**	**−1,055.8**	**−1,998.6**	**−7,333.4**
Goods: exports f.o.b.	2 100 ..	9,288.1	8,927.8	10,026.9	13,232.6	20,603.1	28,300.6	38,762.1	48,351.1
Goods: imports f.o.b.	3 100 ..	−7,119.7	−7,944.4	−8,039.8	−9,553.6	−13,817.7	−17,978.8	−24,120.4	−33,260.2
Balance on Goods	4 100 ..	*2,168.4*	*983.4*	*1,987.1*	*3,679.0*	*6,785.4*	*10,321.8*	*14,641.7*	*15,091.0*
Services: credit	2 200 ..	1,053.0	1,260.2	1,540.4	1,712.3	2,009.2	2,228.4	2,818.7	3,555.0
Services: debit	3 200 ..	−1,850.0	−2,634.6	−3,538.3	−3,752.7	−5,107.9	−7,495.7	−8,760.4	−11,626.8
Balance on Goods and Services	4 991 ..	*1,371.4*	*−391.0*	*−10.7*	*1,638.6*	*3,686.7*	*5,054.5*	*8,700.1*	*7,019.1*
Income: credit	2 300 ..	138.6	224.8	233.8	255.3	422.5	680.3	1,430.5	3,463.0
Income: debit	3 300 ..	−1,392.7	−1,461.7	−1,361.1	−2,001.9	−3,285.6	−6,377.2	−10,922.0	−15,656.0
Balance on Goods, Services, and Income	4 992 ..	*117.3*	*−1,628.0*	*−1,138.1*	*−108.0*	*823.6*	*−642.4*	*−791.3*	*−5,173.9*
Current transfers: credit	2 379 Z.	352.2	394.4	425.9	278.6	352.9	810.0	904.2	903.8
Current transfers: debit	3 379 ..	−103.2	−156.0	−312.1	−443.3	−841.1	−1,223.5	−2,111.4	−3,063.3
B. Capital Account[1]	4 994 Z.	**−290.5**	**−185.0**	**−119.8**	**−27.8**	**−21.3**	**14.0**	**31.9**	**−37.6**
Capital account: credit	2 994 Z.	66.4	99.2	109.8	123.1	113.1	120.9	106.6	85.2
Capital account: debit	3 994 ..	−356.9	−284.2	−229.7	−150.9	−134.3	−106.9	−74.7	−122.8
Total, Groups A Plus B	4 981 ..	*75.8*	*−1,574.5*	*−1,144.1*	*−300.4*	*314.1*	*−1,041.8*	*−1,966.6*	*−7,371.0*
C. Financial Account[1]	4 995 W.	**1,307.0**	**2,613.7**	**1,359.1**	**2,765.8**	**4,700.7**	**898.0**	**16,168.9**	**7,312.5**
Direct investment abroad	4 505 ..	−4.4	25.6	−426.4	121.3	1,278.9	145.9	384.7	−3,243.6
Direct investment in Kazakhstan	4 555 Z.	1,282.5	2,835.0	2,590.2	2,092.0	4,157.2	1,971.2	6,278.2	10,188.6
Portfolio investment assets	4 602 ..	−85.5	−1,348.9	−1,063.9	−2,073.1	−1,092.1	−5,157.1	−9,176.7	−4,095.3
Equity securities	4 610 ..	.7	−10.4	−374.4	−311.8	−362.8	−423.8	−1,847.4	−1,525.6
Debt securities	4 619 ..	−86.2	−1,338.5	−689.5	−1,761.2	−729.3	−4,733.3	−7,329.3	−2,569.7
Portfolio investment liabilities	4 652 Z.	30.4	31.4	−182.9	182.1	675.0	1,204.4	4,675.4	−468.8
Equity securities	4 660 ..	19.3	55.4	39.3	63.8	−12.8	149.7	2,788.9	841.4
Debt securities	4 669 Z.	11.1	−23.9	−222.1	118.3	687.7	1,054.7	1,886.5	−1,310.2
Financial derivatives	4 910 ..	....	....	....	15.9	−46.4	−112.6	−67.8	−366.6
Financial derivatives assets	4 900 ..	....	....	....	....	−44.6	−119.7	−91.6	−614.0
Financial derivatives liabilities	4 905 ..	....	....	....	15.9	−1.8	7.0	23.8	247.3
Other investment assets	4 703 ..	42.9	464.8	−1,116.8	−977.5	−4,466.0	−4,310.4	−8,032.6	−11,815.8
Monetary authorities	4 701 ..	−.4	.3	−14.8	−128.9	−9.3	−73.5	−110.7	−369.0
General government	4 704 ..	−.4	209.7	321.2	275.0	....	....	−212.8	−189.6
Banks	4 705 ..	154.4	−63.6	−624.7	−314.3	−1,755.1	−3,172.4	−6,081.5	−6,466.9
Other sectors	4 728 ..	−110.7	318.5	−798.6	−809.3	−2,701.6	−1,064.5	−1,627.5	−4,790.4
Other investment liabilities	4 753 W.	41.0	605.7	1,558.8	3,405.0	4,194.2	7,156.7	22,107.7	17,114.0
Monetary authorities	4 753 WA	−2.6	.4	−17.2	85.5	−67.4	−17.2	....	−1.8
General government	4 753 ZB	88.1	51.3	1.7	57.4	−65.7	−827.3	−.5	−57.6
Banks	4 753 ZC	165.0	432.8	937.0	2,147.5	2,997.7	6,574.1	16,884.0	11,591.7
Other sectors	4 753 ZD	−209.5	121.2	619.9	1,114.7	1,329.6	1,427.1	5,224.2	5,581.7
Total, Groups A Through C	4 983 ..	*1,382.8*	*1,039.2*	*214.9*	*2,465.4*	*5,014.9*	*−143.8*	*14,202.3*	*−58.5*
D. Net Errors and Omissions	4 998 ..	**−812.7**	**−654.5**	**320.2**	**−931.9**	**−1,015.9**	**−1,800.0**	**−3,127.7**	**−2,970.2**
Total, Groups A Through D	4 984 ..	*570.1*	*384.7*	*535.1*	*1,533.5*	*3,999.0*	*−1,943.8*	*11,074.6*	*−3,028.7*
E. Reserves and Related Items	4 802 A.	**−570.1**	**−384.7**	**−535.1**	**−1,533.5**	**−3,999.0**	**1,943.8**	**−11,074.6**	**3,028.7**
Reserve assets	4 802 ..	−129.1	−384.7	−535.1	−1,533.5	−3,999.0	1,943.8	−11,074.6	3,028.7
Use of Fund credit and loans	4 766 ..	−441.0	....	....	....	....	....	....	....
Exceptional financing	4 920 ..	....	....	....	....	....	....	....	....
Conversion rates: tenge per U.S. dollar	0 101 ..	**142.13**	**146.74**	**153.28**	**149.58**	**136.04**	**132.88**	**126.09**	**122.55**

[1] Excludes components that have been classified in the categories of Group E.

Table 2. STANDARD PRESENTATION, 2000–2007

(Millions of U.S. dollars)

	Code	2000	2001	2002	2003	2004	2005	2006	2007
CURRENT ACCOUNT	4 993	366.3	−1,389.5	−1,024.3	−272.6	335.4	−1,055.8	−1,998.6	−7,333.4
A. GOODS	4 100	2,168.4	983.4	1,987.1	3,679.0	6,785.4	10,321.8	14,641.7	15,091.0
Credit	2 100	9,288.1	8,927.8	10,026.9	13,232.6	20,603.1	28,300.6	38,762.1	48,351.1
General merchandise: exports f.o.b.	2 110	9,276.7	8,909.1	10,004.5	13,201.4	20,536.9	28,180.8	38,608.7	48,197.0
Goods for processing: exports f.o.b.	2 150	....	....	....	....	....	....	....	....
Repairs on goods	2 160	1.1	5.1	8.7	9.3	7.4	1.4	.7	3.0
Goods procured in ports by carriers	2 170	10.3	13.6	13.7	22.0	58.8	118.4	152.7	151.1
Nonmonetary gold	2 180	....	....	....	....	....	....	....	....
Debit	3 100	−7,119.7	−7,944.4	−8,039.8	−9,553.6	−13,817.7	−17,978.8	−24,120.4	−33,260.2
General merchandise: imports f.o.b.	3 110	−7,048.7	−7,762.5	−7,828.7	−9,439.9	−13,783.4	−17,929.4	−24,038.3	−33,076.9
Goods for processing: imports f.o.b.	3 150	....	....	....	....	....	....	....	....
Repairs on goods	3 160	−59.4	−168.8	−198.9	−92.7	−12.8	−25.6	−50.7	−138.3
Goods procured in ports by carriers	3 170	−11.6	−13.1	−12.1	−21.1	−21.5	−23.8	−31.4	−45.0
Nonmonetary gold	3 180	....	....	....	....	....	....	....	....
B. SERVICES	4 200	−797.0	−1,374.4	−1,997.9	−2,040.4	−3,098.7	−5,267.3	−5,941.6	−8,071.8
Total credit	2 200	*1,053.0*	*1,260.2*	*1,540.4*	*1,712.3*	*2,009.2*	*2,228.4*	*2,818.7*	*3,555.0*
Total debit	3 200	*−1,850.0*	*−2,634.6*	*−3,538.3*	*−3,752.7*	*−5,107.9*	*−7,495.7*	*−8,760.4*	*−11,626.8*
Transportation services, credit	2 205	461.4	556.0	615.7	712.9	837.3	1,021.4	1,457.9	1,735.5
Passenger	2 850	*47.0*	*50.4*	*57.8*	*74.0*	*85.1*	*100.2*	*134.5*	*193.7*
Freight	2 851	*350.5*	*433.8*	*477.9*	*545.7*	*616.1*	*757.2*	*1,113.8*	*1,311.4*
Other	2 852	*63.9*	*71.8*	*79.9*	*93.3*	*136.0*	*163.9*	*209.5*	*224.5*
Sea transport, passenger	2 207	....	....	....	....	....	....	....	....
Sea transport, freight	2 208	....	.1	....	....	....	.1	1.2	.4
Sea transport, other	2 209	5.5	11.5	11.5	15.8	21.3	30.0	37.4	24.0
Air transport, passenger	2 211	29.1	30.3	34.1	45.6	49.2	57.5	76.1	123.0
Air transport, freight	2 212	18.7	15.2	15.6	15.8	22.6	25.4	50.4	63.0
Air transport, other	2 213	55.1	56.1	63.4	69.6	94.2	116.5	146.0	175.6
Other transport, passenger	2 215	17.9	20.1	23.8	28.4	35.9	42.7	58.5	75.7
Other transport, freight	2 216	331.7	418.5	462.3	529.8	593.5	731.8	1,062.2	1,247.9
Other transport, other	2 217	3.3	4.2	5.1	7.9	20.6	17.4	26.1	24.9
Transportation services, debit	3 205	−330.2	−437.3	−495.4	−583.3	−871.1	−1,167.5	−1,513.4	−2,120.4
Passenger	3 850	*−75.1*	*−88.0*	*−106.3*	*−114.3*	*−153.2*	*−186.6*	*−238.9*	*−314.0*
Freight	3 851	*−241.1*	*−323.4*	*−356.5*	*−433.3*	*−672.7*	*−898.5*	*−1,207.7*	*−1,670.6*
Other	3 852	*−14.0*	*−25.9*	*−32.6*	*−35.7*	*−45.3*	*−82.4*	*−66.9*	*−135.8*
Sea transport, passenger	3 207	−.2	−.2	−.2	−.7	−.8	−.7	−.3	−.5
Sea transport, freight	3 208	−10.5	−15.1	−26.2	−22.4	−34.7	−42.6	−55.9	−76.6
Sea transport, other	3 209	....	−2.1	−4.3	....	−9.2	−18.2	−7.9	−3.7
Air transport, passenger	3 211	−63.0	−75.1	−90.1	−96.7	−132.2	−163.9	−207.7	−271.1
Air transport, freight	3 212	−44.5	−60.2	−65.4	−80.9	−125.8	−168.5	−226.2	−313.3
Air transport, other	3 213	−12.1	−22.3	−25.0	−31.8	−30.6	−45.2	−52.5	−52.7
Other transport, passenger	3 215	−11.9	−12.6	−16.0	−17.0	−20.2	−22.1	−30.9	−42.3
Other transport, freight	3 216	−186.1	−248.2	−264.9	−330.0	−512.2	−687.4	−925.6	−1,280.8
Other transport, other	3 217	−1.9	−1.5	−3.3	−3.9	−5.5	−19.0	−6.5	−74.5
Travel, credit	2 236	356.4	451.6	621.9	564.0	717.8	700.9	837.9	1,013.1
Business travel	2 237	124.1	91.4	142.8	103.3	171.7	132.8	153.1	167.2
Personal travel	2 240	232.2	360.2	479.1	460.7	546.1	568.1	684.8	845.9
Travel, debit	3 236	−407.8	−672.7	−757.0	−668.7	−843.6	−753.0	−820.7	−1,040.6
Business travel	3 237	−59.3	−57.8	−73.7	−43.5	−156.2	−160.1	−125.1	−151.4
Personal travel	3 240	−348.4	−614.9	−683.3	−625.3	−687.5	−592.9	−695.6	−889.2
Other services, credit	2 200 BA	235.3	252.5	302.8	435.4	454.1	506.2	523.0	806.4
Communications	2 245	34.4	35.6	45.4	60.8	63.1	73.1	79.6	87.8
Construction	2 249	.2	1.8	1.1	19.3	3.3	2.0	3.5	5.5
Insurance	2 253	3.9	5.2	.5	2.0	3.3	3.8	8.9	35.4
Financial	2 260	10.8	5.2	10.7	14.1	18.9	18.3	22.0	75.6
Computer and information	2 262	1.1	.5	.2	.6	.9	1.0	1.3	2.2
Royalties and licence fees	2 266	....	....	....	....	....	....	....	....
Other business services	2 268	37.1	36.8	67.1	153.8	172.1	178.6	172.5	286.2
Personal, cultural, and recreational	2 287	.2	.2	.2	....	.1	.2	.3	.4
Government, n.i.e.	2 291	147.6	167.2	177.6	184.8	192.4	229.1	235.0	313.3
Other services, debit	3 200 BA	−1,112.1	−1,524.6	−2,285.9	−2,500.6	−3,393.1	−5,575.2	−6,426.3	−8,465.8
Communications	3 245	−30.2	−39.2	−64.1	−60.7	−67.7	−72.4	−94.3	−106.5
Construction	3 249	−538.9	−763.2	−1,075.1	−813.3	−733.5	−1,941.4	−3,237.7	−4,352.1
Insurance	3 253	−39.6	−43.4	−71.6	−88.7	−93.8	−173.4	−253.7	−246.1
Financial	3 260	−12.8	−9.9	−20.3	−21.2	−31.9	−47.5	−182.4	−193.1
Computer and information	3 262	−11.6	−17.1	−14.9	−20.6	−29.4	−52.9	−58.3	−76.8
Royalties and licence fees	3 266	−11.8	−13.6	−19.9	−19.6	−25.7	−30.9	−48.4	−68.0
Other business services	3 268	−447.1	−610.8	−985.2	−1,423.1	−2,354.6	−3,119.8	−2,397.3	−3,149.2
Personal, cultural, and recreational	3 287	−1.6	−2.2	−2.7	−12.4	−6.5	−16.5	−15.2	−17.5
Government, n.i.e.	3 291	−18.6	−25.3	−32.0	−41.0	−50.1	−120.4	−138.9	−256.4

Table 2 (Continued). STANDARD PRESENTATION, 2000–2007

(Millions of U.S. dollars)

	Code	2000	2001	2002	2003	2004	2005	2006	2007
C. INCOME	4 300	−1,254.1	−1,237.0	−1,127.4	−1,746.6	−2,863.1	−5,696.9	−9,491.4	−12,193.0
Total credit	2 300	138.6	224.8	233.8	255.3	422.5	680.3	1,430.5	3,463.0
Total debit	3 300	−1,392.7	−1,461.7	−1,361.1	−2,001.9	−3,285.6	−6,377.2	−10,922.0	−15,656.0
Compensation of employees, credit	2 310	3.6	3.6	3.9	3.9	3.9	6.3	10.6	11.1
Compensation of employees, debit	3 310	−47.2	−59.9	−78.7	−229.8	−413.7	−734.7	−959.0	−1,214.4
Investment income, credit	2 320	135.0	221.2	229.9	251.4	418.7	674.1	1,420.0	3,451.9
Direct investment income	2 330	....	−5.6	−7.6	−16.7	−29.7	−162.4	−193.6	59.3
Dividends and distributed branch profits	2 332	....	.4	....	....	.2	7.7	1.4	226.1
Reinvested earnings and undistributed branch profits	2 333	....	....	....	....	7.6	−7.9	.5	31.1
Income on debt (interest)	2 334	....	−6.0	−7.6	−16.7	−37.6	−162.3	−195.4	−197.9
Portfolio investment income	2 339	73.6	149.4	218.4	225.6	294.1	445.7	883.9	1,459.0
Income on equity	2 340	.8	1.9	5.4	7.3	18.6	25.4	51.8	102.6
Income on bonds and notes	2 350	28.7	93.9	200.6	204.1	255.3	356.3	663.9	1,341.7
Income on money market instruments	2 360	44.2	53.5	12.3	14.2	20.2	63.9	168.1	14.6
Other investment income	2 370	61.5	77.4	19.1	42.5	154.3	390.8	729.6	1,933.7
Investment income, debit	3 320	−1,345.5	−1,401.8	−1,282.5	−1,772.1	−2,871.9	−5,642.6	−9,963.0	−14,441.7
Direct investment income	3 330	−1,045.9	−1,141.6	−1,007.2	−1,431.6	−2,346.6	−4,633.1	−7,693.7	−10,410.8
Dividends and distributed branch profits	3 332	−173.6	−294.9	−160.4	−288.2	−1,369.6	−3,601.0	−5,685.4	−7,611.2
Reinvested earnings and undistributed branch profits	3 333	−474.2	−448.9	−498.3	−769.5	−515.6	−206.4	−783.0	−1,302.6
Income on debt (interest)	3 334	−398.0	−397.8	−348.4	−373.9	−461.4	−825.7	−1,225.3	−1,496.9
Portfolio investment income	3 339	−64.1	−56.4	−52.3	−36.5	−84.8	−154.3	−341.9	−394.5
Income on equity	3 340	−.4	−5.7	−10.5	−5.2	−11.5	−25.1	−116.3	−100.4
Income on bonds and notes	3 350	−63.7	−50.7	−41.7	−31.4	−73.3	−129.2	−225.6	−290.2
Income on money market instruments	3 360	....	....	....	....	....	−.1	....	−3.9
Other investment income	3 370	−235.5	−203.8	−223.0	−304.0	−440.5	−855.2	−1,927.4	−3,636.3
D. CURRENT TRANSFERS	4 379	249.0	238.5	113.7	−164.7	−488.2	−413.5	−1,207.2	−2,159.5
Credit	2 379	352.2	394.4	425.9	278.6	352.9	810.0	904.2	903.8
General government	2 380	287.5	305.0	287.3	211.7	275.8	726.2	810.3	739.7
Other sectors	2 390	64.6	89.4	138.5	66.9	77.1	83.8	93.9	164.1
Workers' remittances	2 391	63.9	81.4	107.4	38.3	53.5	55.8	73.0	131.9
Other current transfers	2 392	.8	8.0	31.2	28.6	23.6	28.0	20.9	32.2
Debit	3 379	−103.2	−156.0	−312.1	−443.3	−841.1	−1,223.5	−2,111.4	−3,063.3
General government	3 380	−5.9	−6.8	−5.3	−8.4	−14.5	−16.2	−23.8	−18.9
Other sectors	3 390	−97.3	−149.2	−306.9	−434.9	−826.6	−1,207.2	−2,087.6	−3,044.4
Workers' remittances	3 391	−74.3	−143.3	−286.2	−421.1	−805.8	−1,158.5	−1,999.5	−2,997.9
Other current transfers	3 392	−23.0	−5.9	−20.7	−13.8	−20.8	−48.8	−88.1	−46.5
CAPITAL AND FINANCIAL ACCOUNT	4 996	446.4	2,044.0	704.2	1,204.5	680.5	2,855.8	5,126.2	10,303.6
CAPITAL ACCOUNT	4 994	−290.5	−185.0	−119.8	−27.8	−21.3	14.0	31.9	−37.6
Total credit	2 994	66.4	99.2	109.8	123.1	113.1	120.9	106.6	85.2
Total debit	3 994	−356.9	−284.2	−229.7	−150.9	−134.3	−106.9	−74.7	−122.8
Capital transfers, credit	2 400	66.4	99.2	109.8	123.1	113.1	120.9	106.6	85.2
General government	2 401	11.9	3.8	12.4	9.7	2.4	1.1	2.0	3.4
Debt forgiveness	2 402	....	....	....	....	....	....	....	....
Other capital transfers	2 410	11.9	3.8	12.4	9.7	2.4	1.1	2.0	3.4
Other sectors	2 430	54.5	95.4	97.5	113.4	110.7	119.9	104.6	81.8
Migrants' transfers	2 431	54.3	86.2	93.7	105.3	108.5	116.4	102.8	80.0
Debt forgiveness	2 432	....	....	....	....	....	....	....	.5
Other capital transfers	2 440	.1	9.2	3.8	8.1	2.2	3.4	1.8	1.3
Capital transfers, debit	3 400	−356.9	−284.2	−229.7	−150.9	−134.3	−106.9	−74.7	−122.8
General government	3 401	−.2	....	....	....	−.1	....	....	....
Debt forgiveness	3 402	....	....	....	....	....	....	....	....
Other capital transfers	3 410	−.2	....	....	....	−.1	....	....	....
Other sectors	3 430	−356.7	−284.1	−229.7	−150.8	−134.2	−106.9	−74.7	−122.8
Migrants' transfers	3 431	−318.5	−284.1	−229.7	−150.8	−134.2	−106.9	−74.7	−91.2
Debt forgiveness	3 432	−38.2	....	....	....	....	....	....	−31.6
Other capital transfers	3 440	....	....	....	....	....	....	....	....
Nonproduced nonfinancial assets, credit	2 480	....	....	....	....	....	....	....	....
Nonproduced nonfinancial assets, debit	3 480	....	....	....	....	....	....	....	....

Table 2 (Continued). STANDARD PRESENTATION, 2000–2007

(Millions of U.S. dollars)

	Code	2000	2001	2002	2003	2004	2005	2006	2007
FINANCIAL ACCOUNT	4 995	**736.9**	**2,228.9**	**824.0**	**1,232.3**	**701.8**	**2,841.8**	**5,094.3**	**10,341.1**
A. DIRECT INVESTMENT	4 500	**1,278.2**	**2,860.6**	**2,163.8**	**2,213.4**	**5,436.2**	**2,117.1**	**6,662.9**	**6,945.1**
Direct investment abroad	4 505	**−4.4**	**25.6**	**−426.4**	**121.3**	**1,278.9**	**145.9**	**384.7**	**−3,243.6**
Equity capital	4 510	−4.3	−12.3	−440.4	−7.9	−69.8	−124.5	−821.8	−2,301.2
Claims on affiliated enterprises	4 515	−4.3	−12.3	−440.4	−7.9	−69.7	−124.5	−821.9	−2,301.0
Liabilities to affiliated enterprises	4 520	....	....	....	....	....	....	.2	−.2
Reinvested earnings	4 525	....	....	....	....	−7.6	7.9	−.5	−31.1
Other capital	4 530	....	37.9	14.0	129.2	1,356.3	262.5	1,207.0	−911.3
Claims on affiliated enterprises	4 535	....	−14.4	13.8	4.3	−164.9	−83.2	−29.0	−91.6
Liabilities to affiliated enterprises	4 540	....	52.3	.1	125.0	1,521.2	345.7	1,235.9	−819.6
Direct investment in Kazakhstan	4 555	**1,282.5**	**2,835.0**	**2,590.2**	**2,092.0**	**4,157.2**	**1,971.2**	**6,278.2**	**10,188.6**
Equity capital	4 560	272.3	547.1	243.1	409.1	374.7	40.1	556.8	5,266.1
Claims on direct investors	4 565	....	....	.2	....	−19.1	9.8	−35.0	3.1
Liabilities to direct investors	4 570	272.3	547.1	242.9	409.1	393.8	30.3	591.8	5,263.1
Reinvested earnings	4 575	474.2	448.9	498.3	769.5	515.6	206.4	783.0	1,302.6
Other capital	4 580	536.0	1,839.0	1,848.8	913.4	3,266.9	1,724.8	4,938.4	3,619.9
Claims on direct investors	4 585	−88.0	70.5	1.7	−266.2	82.3	−239.0	−61.9	−1,682.7
Liabilities to direct investors	4 590	624.1	1,768.5	1,847.1	1,179.6	3,184.6	1,963.7	5,000.3	5,302.6
B. PORTFOLIO INVESTMENT	4 600	**−55.0**	**−1,317.5**	**−1,246.7**	**−1,891.0**	**−417.2**	**−3,952.7**	**−4,501.4**	**−4,564.1**
Assets	4 602	**−85.5**	**−1,348.9**	**−1,063.9**	**−2,073.1**	**−1,092.1**	**−5,157.1**	**−9,176.7**	**−4,095.3**
Equity securities	4 610	.7	−10.4	−374.4	−311.8	−362.8	−423.8	−1,847.4	−1,525.6
Monetary authorities	4 611	....	....	−369.1	−256.3	−391.7	−418.3	−1,781.4	−1,036.2
General government	4 612	....	....	....	....	....	....	....	.1
Banks	4 613	....	....	.1	....	....	....	....	.1
Other sectors	4 614	.7	−10.4	−5.4	−55.6	28.9	−5.6	−65.9	−489.6
Debt securities	4 619	−86.2	−1,338.5	−689.5	−1,761.2	−729.3	−4,733.3	−7,329.3	−2,569.7
Bonds and notes	4 620	−86.2	−397.7	−1,070.2	−1,257.7	−363.1	−3,495.1	−7,392.6	−2,032.3
Monetary authorities	4 621	....	−288.7	−750.5	−963.8	−428.2	−1,338.0	−4,101.8	−4,642.4
General government	4 622	....	....	....	....	....	....	....	....
Banks	4 623	−39.6	−65.7	−155.7	−414.1	−45.7	−1,738.9	−1,910.5	1,875.4
Other sectors	4 624	−46.6	−43.3	−164.0	120.2	110.8	−418.2	−1,380.2	734.7
Money market instruments	4 630	....	−940.8	380.7	−503.5	−366.2	−1,238.2	63.2	−537.4
Monetary authorities	4 631	....	−940.8	380.8	−496.0	−369.2	−1,214.6	35.7	−466.2
General government	4 632	....	....	....	....	....	....	....	....
Banks	4 633	....	....	....	−.6	−3.3	−23.6	27.5	....
Other sectors	4 634	....	....	....	−7.0	6.3	....	.1	−71.2
Liabilities	4 652	**30.4**	**31.4**	**−182.9**	**182.1**	**675.0**	**1,204.4**	**4,675.4**	**−468.8**
Equity securities	4 660	19.3	55.4	39.3	63.8	−12.8	149.7	2,788.9	841.4
Banks	4 663	.6	31.7	22.9	46.8	50.9	167.6	1,762.2	361.9
Other sectors	4 664	18.7	23.6	16.4	17.0	−63.7	−17.9	1,026.7	479.5
Debt securities	4 669	11.1	−23.9	−222.1	118.3	687.7	1,054.7	1,886.5	−1,310.2
Bonds and notes	4 670	11.5	−23.9	−222.9	118.4	687.1	955.2	1,115.6	795.9
Monetary authorities	4 671	....	....	....	....	....	....	....	....
General government	4 672	10.6	−102.7	−237.1	54.3	21.2	−59.8	.5	−6.9
Banks	4 673	−10.3	−31.1	53.8	60.2	624.5	1,026.6	1,186.1	248.3
Other sectors	4 674	11.1	109.9	−39.5	3.9	41.4	−11.5	−71.0	554.5
Money market instruments	4 680	−.3	....	.7	−.1	.6	99.5	770.9	−2,106.0
Monetary authorities	4 681	....	....	....	....	....	99.4	740.3	−2,122.5
General government	4 682	−.3	....	.7	−.1	....	−.1	33.1	18.0
Banks	4 683	....	....	....	....	....	....	....	....
Other sectors	4 684	....	....	....	....	.6	.1	−2.4	−1.5
C. FINANCIAL DERIVATIVES	4 910	**....**	**....**	**....**	**15.9**	**−46.4**	**−112.6**	**−67.8**	**−366.6**
Monetary authorities	4 911	....	....	....	15.9	−7.7	−38.8	−4.6	11.3
General government	4 912	....	....	....	....	....	....	....	....
Banks	4 913	....	....	....	....	1.9	−.2	−41.2	−367.8
Other sectors	4 914	....	....	....	....	−40.7	−73.7	−21.9	−10.1
Assets	4 900	**....**	**....**	**....**	**....**	**−44.6**	**−119.7**	**−91.6**	**−614.0**
Monetary authorities	4 901	....	....	....	....	....	−5.6	−4.6	10.2
General government	4 902	....	....	....	....	....	....	....	....
Banks	4 903	....	....	....	....	.7	−2.6	−73.7	−621.7
Other sectors	4 904	....	....	....	....	−45.3	−111.5	−13.3	−2.5
Liabilities	4 905	**....**	**....**	**....**	**15.9**	**−1.8**	**7.0**	**23.8**	**247.3**
Monetary authorities	4 906	....	....	....	15.9	−7.7	−33.2	....	1.1
General government	4 907	....	....	....	....	....	....	....	....
Banks	4 908	....	....	....	....	1.2	2.4	32.5	253.9
Other sectors	4 909	....	....	....	....	4.7	37.8	−8.7	−7.7

Table 2 (Concluded). STANDARD PRESENTATION, 2000–2007

(Millions of U.S. dollars)

	Code	2000	2001	2002	2003	2004	2005	2006	2007
D. OTHER INVESTMENT.................................	4 700 ..	**−357.1**	**1,070.5**	**442.0**	**2,427.6**	**−271.9**	**2,846.3**	**14,075.2**	**5,298.1**
Assets..	4 703 ..	**42.9**	**464.8**	**−1,116.8**	**−977.5**	**−4,466.0**	**−4,310.4**	**−8,032.6**	**−11,815.8**
Trade credits......................................	4 706 ..	−115.3	83.0	−330.9	−617.0	−1,029.4	−1,034.4	−1,641.4	−2,445.7
General government........................	4 707 ..	....	....	....	....	....	....	....	....
of which: Short-term.....................	4 709 ..	....	....	....	....	....	....	....	....
Other sectors................................	4 710 ..	−115.3	83.0	−330.9	−617.0	−1,029.4	−1,034.4	−1,641.4	−2,445.7
of which: Short-term.....................	4 712 ..	*−48.3*	*50.6*	*−352.2*	*−620.1*	*−899.6*	*−958.4*	*−1,592.7*	*−1,716.9*
Loans...	4 714 ..	42.8	−10.4	−92.9	−415.0	−1,394.8	−1,082.1	−5,147.5	−5,258.0
Monetary authorities.......................	4 715 ..	....	....	....	....	....	....	....	....
of which: Short-term.....................	4 718 ..	....	....	....	....	....	....	....	....
General government........................	4 719 ..	....	....	....	....	....	....	1.2	1.2
of which: Short-term.....................	4 721 ..	....	....	....	....	....	....	....	....
Banks...	4 722 ..	42.9	−10.2	−86.6	−358.4	−1,423.6	−865.3	−4,990.1	−4,348.9
of which: Short-term.....................	4 724 ..	*42.3*	*−10.5*	*−65.8*	*−101.5*	*−183.5*	*−314.9*	*−1,136.8*	*−597.6*
Other sectors................................	4 725 ..	....	−.2	−6.3	−56.6	28.9	−216.9	−158.6	−910.4
of which: Short-term.....................	4 727 ..	....	*.2*	*−5.5*	*−21.0*	*22.4*	*−202.0*	*−46.7*	*−559.4*
Currency and deposits........................	4 730 ..	63.0	196.7	−680.2	−218.0	−1,815.9	−1,893.1	−762.0	−3,858.4
Monetary authorities.......................	4 731 ..	−.4	.3	−14.8	−168.1	−9.3	−26.6	−122.3	−404.3
General government........................	4 732 ..	....	....	321.2	....	....	....	....	....
Banks...	4 733 ..	109.1	−45.6	−509.8	65.0	−263.9	−2,316.4	−928.2	−2,155.3
Other sectors................................	4 734 ..	−45.7	242.0	−476.8	−114.9	−1,542.8	449.9	288.5	−1,298.8
Other assets.......................................	4 736 ..	52.3	195.6	−12.8	272.5	−225.9	−300.7	−481.7	−253.7
Monetary authorities.......................	4 737 ..	....	....	....	39.2	....	−46.8	11.6	35.3
of which: Short-term.....................	4 739 ..	....	....	....	*39.2*	....	*−46.8*	*11.6*	*35.3*
General government........................	4 740 ..	−.4	209.7	....	275.0	....	....	−214.0	−190.8
of which: Short-term.....................	4 742 ..	*−.4*	*−.3*	....	....	....	....	....	....
Banks...	4 743 ..	2.4	−7.8	−28.2	−21.0	−67.6	9.2	−163.2	37.2
of which: Short-term.....................	4 745 ..	*2.4*	*−7.8*	*−28.2*	*−21.0*	*−67.6*	*9.2*	*−163.2*	*37.2*
Other sectors................................	4 746 ..	50.3	−6.2	15.5	−20.7	−158.3	−263.2	−116.0	−135.4
of which: Short-term.....................	4 748 ..	*50.3*	*−6.2*	*15.5*	*−20.7*	*−158.3*	*−263.2*	*−116.0*	*−135.4*
Liabilities...	4 753 ..	**−400.0**	**605.7**	**1,558.8**	**3,405.0**	**4,194.2**	**7,156.7**	**22,107.7**	**17,114.0**
Trade credits......................................	4 756 ..	20.0	−41.7	279.5	224.8	413.6	279.0	1,507.3	1,385.0
General government........................	4 757 ..	....	....	....	....	....	....	....	....
of which: Short-term.....................	4 759 ..	....	....	....	....	....	....	....	....
Other sectors................................	4 760 ..	20.0	−41.7	279.5	224.8	413.6	279.0	1,507.3	1,385.0
of which: Short-term.....................	4 762 ..	*42.5*	*50.4*	*202.6*	*180.7*	*267.3*	*115.3*	*1,370.4*	*983.4*
Loans...	4 764 ..	−502.3	524.8	1,126.0	2,919.4	3,666.5	6,406.0	19,781.4	14,802.5
Monetary authorities.......................	4 765 ..	−443.7	....	....	....	....	....	....	....
of which: Use of Fund credit and loans from the Fund.	4 766 ..	*−441.0*	....	....	....	....	....	....	....
of which: Short-term.....................	4 768 ..	....	....	....	....	....	....	....	....
General government........................	4 769 ..	88.2	54.6	3.4	57.4	−65.7	−827.3	−.5	−57.6
of which: Short-term.....................	4 771 ..	....	....	....	....	....	....	....	....
Banks...	4 772 ..	79.0	291.7	780.7	2,007.1	2,763.8	6,078.2	16,038.2	10,707.1
of which: Short-term.....................	4 774 ..	*52.0*	*212.3*	*369.4*	*675.2*	*401.2*	*3,601.8*	*494.0*	*−1,448.7*
Other sectors................................	4 775 ..	−225.8	178.4	341.8	855.0	968.4	1,155.2	3,743.8	4,153.0
of which: Short-term.....................	4 777 ..	*−144.2*	*−3.8*	*73.4*	*85.6*	*71.5*	*123.0*	*766.5*	*378.1*
Currency and deposits........................	4 780 ..	84.2	139.6	157.9	126.4	93.4	497.6	652.6	757.1
Monetary authorities.......................	4 781 ..	....	.2	−.1	....	.2	.1	−.3	−.8
General government........................	4 782 ..	....	....	....	....	....	....	....	....
Banks...	4 783 ..	84.2	139.4	158.0	126.4	93.2	497.5	652.9	757.9
Other sectors................................	4 784 ..	....	....	....	....	....	....	....	....
Other liabilities..................................	4 786 ..	−1.9	−17.0	−4.7	134.5	20.6	−25.9	166.4	169.4
Monetary authorities.......................	4 787 ..	....	.2	.3	85.5	−67.6	−17.3	.3	−1.0
of which: Short-term.....................	4 789 ..	....	*.2*	*.3*	*85.5*	*−67.6*	*−17.3*	*.3*	*−1.0*
General government........................	4 790 ..	....	....	−3.3	−1.7	....	....	....	....
of which: Short-term.....................	4 792 ..	....	....	....	....	....	....	....	....
Banks...	4 793 ..	1.8	1.7	−1.7	14.1	140.7	−1.5	192.9	126.7
of which: Short-term.....................	4 795 ..	*1.8*	*1.7*	*−1.7*	*14.1*	*140.7*	*−1.5*	*192.9*	*126.7*
Other sectors................................	4 796 ..	−3.7	−15.5	−1.5	34.9	−52.4	−7.1	−26.9	43.6
of which: Short-term.....................	4 798 ..	*−3.7*	*−15.5*	*−1.5*	*34.9*	*−52.4*	*−7.1*	*−26.9*	*43.6*
E. RESERVE ASSETS...............................	4 802 ..	**−129.1**	**−384.7**	**−535.1**	**−1,533.5**	**−3,999.0**	**1,943.8**	**−11,074.6**	**3,028.7**
Monetary gold.....................................	4 812 ..	....	....	....	....	....	....	....	....
Special drawing rights.........................	4 811 ..	217.1	....	−1.0	....	....	....	....	−.1
Reserve position in the Fund................	4 810 ..	....	....	....	....	....	....	....	....
Foreign exchange................................	4 803 ..	−346.1	−377.6	−531.1	−1,538.5	−3,997.2	1,950.3	−11,077.2	3,017.8
Other claims.......................................	4 813 ..	....	−7.2	−3.0	5.0	−1.8	−6.5	2.7	10.9
NET ERRORS AND OMISSIONS...............	4 998 ..	**−812.7**	**−654.5**	**320.2**	**−931.9**	**−1,015.9**	**−1,800.0**	**−3,127.7**	**−2,970.2**

Table 3. INTERNATIONAL INVESTMENT POSITION (End-period stocks), 2000–2007

(Millions of U.S. dollars)

	Code	2000	2001	2002	2003	2004	2005	2006	2007
ASSETS...	8 995 C.	4,612.9	6,117.0	9,321.5	14,283.7	23,070.7	30,174.2	59,425.5	77,387.6
Direct investment abroad..........................	8 505 ..	15.5	−9.7	417.2	300.4	−971.7	−1,141.8	−1,006.7	2,254.2
Equity capital and reinvested earnings.............	8 506 ..	15.4	27.9	468.8	475.8	558.3	673.8	1,999.2	4,320.9
Claims on affiliated enterprises..................	8 507 ..	15.4	27.9	468.8	475.8	558.3	673.8	1,999.4	4,320.9
Liabilities to affiliated enterprises..............	8 508 ..	....	....	....	....	....	....	−.2	....
Other capital....................................	8 530 ..	.1	−37.6	−51.6	−175.4	−1,529.9	−1,815.6	−3,005.9	−2,066.6
Claims on affiliated enterprises..................	8 535 ..	.1	14.7	.9	2.1	171.8	231.4	277.6	398.1
Liabilities to affiliated enterprises..............	8 540 ..	....	−52.3	−52.4	−177.4	−1,701.7	−2,047.0	−3,283.5	−2,464.7
Portfolio investment..............................	8 602 ..	69.7	1,430.8	2,396.1	4,563.6	5,903.3	10,962.2	20,104.8	24,835.9
Equity securities.................................	8 610 ..	3.4	15.2	308.9	641.5	1,075.2	1,512.7	3,271.1	4,895.1
Monetary authorities............................	8 611 ..	....	....	287.7	544.0	1,010.4	1,439.5	3,205.0	4,229.4
General government............................	8 612 ..	....	....	....	....	....	....	....	....
Banks..	8 613 ..	....	....	....	....	....	....	....	....
Other sectors..................................	8 614 ..	3.4	15.2	21.2	97.6	64.8	73.2	66.2	665.7
Debt securities...................................	8 619 ..	66.3	1,415.6	2,087.2	3,922.0	4,828.1	9,449.5	16,833.6	19,940.8
Bonds and notes.................................	8 620 ..	66.3	458.9	1,531.8	2,862.7	3,406.0	6,788.9	14,218.8	16,840.4
Monetary authorities..........................	8 621 ..	....	283.5	1,048.0	2,011.8	2,560.5	3,729.9	7,888.8	12,942.4
General government...........................	8 622 ..	....	....	....	....	....	....	....	....
Banks...	8 623 ..	41.3	110.7	264.9	677.2	785.3	2,557.4	4,493.1	2,671.4
Other sectors..................................	8 624 ..	25.0	64.8	218.9	173.7	60.2	501.6	1,836.9	1,226.7
Money market instruments.......................	8 630 ..	....	956.7	555.4	1,059.3	1,422.2	2,660.6	2,614.8	3,100.4
Monetary authorities..........................	8 631 ..	....	956.7	555.4	1,051.3	1,418.9	2,634.1	2,614.8	3,090.4
General government...........................	8 632 ..	....	....	....	....	....	....	....	....
Banks...	8 633 ..	....	....	....	1.8	3.3	26.5	....	....
Other sectors..................................	8 634 ..	....	....	....	6.2	....	....	....	10.0
Financial derivatives.............................	8 900 ..	....	....	....	....	48.4	164.3	258.1	866.5
Monetary authorities.............................	8 901 ..	....	....	....	....	....	5.6	10.2	....
General government..............................	8 902 ..	....	....	....	....	....	....	....	....
Banks...	8 903 ..	....	....	....	....	3.0	1.9	77.8	696.2
Other sectors....................................	8 904 ..	....	....	....	....	45.3	156.9	170.1	170.4
Other investment.................................	8 703 ..	2,432.1	2,187.8	3,367.4	4,457.6	8,810.1	13,119.8	20,942.2	31,801.6
Trade credits....................................	8 706 ..	828.8	784.3	1,151.8	1,878.5	2,957.4	3,949.9	5,614.1	8,231.7
General government.............................	8 707 ..	....	....	....	....	....	....	....	....
of which: Short-term.........................	8 709 ..	....	....	....	....	....	....	....	....
Other sectors..................................	8 710 ..	828.8	784.3	1,151.8	1,878.5	2,957.4	3,949.9	5,614.1	8,231.7
of which: Short-term.........................	8 712 ..	*699.7*	*687.4*	*1,030.0*	*1,725.0*	*2,694.2*	*3,648.0*	*5,258.6*	*7,036.0*
Loans...	8 714 ..	70.5	75.3	169.7	580.6	1,855.6	3,022.3	8,287.1	13,690.1
Monetary authorities...........................	8 715 ..	....	....	....	....	....	....	....	....
of which: Short-term.........................	8 718 ..	....	....	....	....	....	....	....	....
General government............................	8 719 ..	46.1	39.9	39.9	39.9	39.9	39.9	38.7	37.5
of which: Short-term.........................	8 721 ..	....	....	....	....	....	....	....	....
Banks..	8 722 ..	24.1	34.9	121.4	478.1	1,765.2	2,636.3	7,734.3	12,155.9
of which: Short-term.........................	8 724 ..	*12.8*	*23.7*	*89.6*	*191.9*	*326.0*	*632.8*	*1,886.8*	*2,505.4*
Other sectors..................................	8 725 ..	.3	.6	8.4	62.6	50.5	346.1	514.1	1,496.7
of which: Short-term.........................	8 727 ..	*.2*		*5.5*	*24.0*	*18.3*	*290.2*	*342.4*	*916.9*
Currency and deposits...........................	8 730 ..	952.5	944.4	1,625.4	1,848.4	3,630.4	5,499.3	6,118.8	8,679.1
Monetary authorities...........................	8 731 ..	.7	.3	15.1	183.3	192.6	219.2	341.8	746.5
General government............................	8 732 ..	321.2	321.2	....	....	....	....	....	....
Banks..	8 733 ..	329.7	374.1	884.7	798.3	1,062.8	3,355.0	4,321.5	6,751.1
Other sectors..................................	8 734 ..	301.0	248.8	725.6	866.7	2,375.0	1,925.0	1,455.5	1,181.5
Other assets....................................	8 736 ..	580.2	383.7	420.6	150.1	366.8	648.3	922.1	1,200.7
Monetary authorities...........................	8 737 ..	....	....	39.2	....	....	46.8	35.3	....
of which: Short-term.........................	8 739 ..	....	....	*39.2*	....	....	*46.8*	*35.3*	....
General government............................	8 740 ..	485.0	275.0	275.0	....	....	....	214.0	404.8
of which: Short-term.........................	8 742 ..	....	....	....	....	....	....	....	....
Banks..	8 743 ..	6.1	14.0	42.1	63.5	130.3	102.2	266.3	253.9
of which: Short-term.........................	8 745 ..	*6.1*	*14.0*	*42.1*	*63.5*	*130.3*	*102.2*	*266.3*	*253.9*
Other sectors..................................	8 746 ..	89.2	94.7	64.2	86.5	236.5	499.3	406.6	541.9
of which: Short-term.........................	8 748 ..	*89.2*	*94.7*	*64.2*	*86.5*	*236.5*	*499.3*	*406.6*	*541.9*
Reserve assets...................................	8 802 ..	2,095.7	2,508.2	3,140.8	4,962.1	9,280.5	7,069.7	19,127.1	17,629.3
Monetary gold...................................	8 812 ..	501.5	510.7	585.6	725.9	803.6	985.5	1,376.2	1,852.5
Special drawing rights...........................	8 811 ..	....	....	1.0	1.2	1.2	1.2	1.3	1.4
Reserve position in the Fund.....................	8 810 ..	....	....	....	....	....	....	....	....
Foreign exchange................................	8 803 ..	1,594.1	1,990.3	2,544.5	4,229.4	8,468.7	6,069.5	17,738.6	15,775.4
Other claims....................................	8 813 ..	....	7.2	9.8	5.6	7.1	13.6	10.9	....

Table 3 (Concluded). INTERNATIONAL INVESTMENT POSITION (End-period stocks), 2000–2007

(Millions of U.S. dollars)

	Code	2000	2001	2002	2003	2004	2005	2006	2007
LIABILITIES	8 995 D.	**15,726.9**	**19,192.4**	**23,056.5**	**29,041.5**	**38,772.8**	**50,451.5**	**88,390.9**	**120,924.7**
Direct investment in Kazakhstan	8 555	**10,077.7**	**12,916.6**	**15,464.3**	**17,587.1**	**22,376.5**	**25,607.4**	**32,879.4**	**43,583.3**
Equity capital and reinvested earnings	8 556	3,097.7	4,123.8	4,861.1	6,101.6	7,640.4	8,921.0	11,217.1	18,443.5
Claims on direct investors	8 557	....	....	....	....	−19.1	−9.0	−43.6	−41.5
Liabilities to direct investors	8 558	3,097.7	4,123.8	4,861.1	6,101.6	7,659.5	8,930.1	11,260.6	18,485.0
Other capital	8 580	6,980.0	8,792.8	10,603.2	11,485.5	14,736.1	16,686.4	21,662.3	25,139.9
Claims on direct investors	8 585	−106.9	−34.2	−54.0	−320.1	−237.1	−488.6	−567.2	−2,308.9
Liabilities to direct investors	8 590	7,086.9	8,827.0	10,657.2	11,805.6	14,973.3	17,175.0	22,229.5	27,448.8
Portfolio investment	8 652	**695.9**	**725.0**	**337.8**	**581.0**	**1,310.8**	**2,721.1**	**11,142.1**	**14,326.3**
Equity securities	8 660	101.6	146.9	142.0	221.6	291.5	593.2	6,942.5	10,225.3
Banks	8 663	32.9	64.6	85.8	137.4	189.8	476.9	5,466.0	5,915.0
Other sectors	8 664	68.7	82.3	56.2	84.2	101.7	116.3	1,476.5	4,310.3
Debt securities	8 669	594.3	578.1	195.7	359.4	1,019.3	2,127.9	4,199.6	4,101.1
Bonds and notes	8 670	593.8	578.1	195.7	359.4	1,015.3	2,024.0	3,086.2	3,935.7
Monetary authorities	8 671	....	....	....	....	....	....	....	....
General government	8 672	547.7	445.0	40.0	129.1	113.4	52.3	14.3	....
Banks	8 673	31.3	.2	57.2	120.2	754.1	1,824.8	2,984.1	3,266.2
Other sectors	8 674	14.8	132.9	98.6	110.0	147.8	146.8	87.8	669.5
Money market instruments	8 680	.5	....	....	....	4.0	103.9	1,113.4	165.4
Monetary authorities	8 681	....	....	....	....	....	99.8	1,073.0	104.8
General government	8 682	.5	....	....	....	....	....	38.8	60.3
Banks	8 683	....	....	....	....	....	....	....	....
Other sectors	8 684	....	....	....	....	4.0	4.2	1.6	.3
Financial derivatives	8 905	**....**	**....**	**25.0**	**40.9**	**38.8**	**44.3**	**67.9**	**313.6**
Monetary authorities	8 906	....	....	25.0	40.9	33.2	....	....	1.1
General government	8 907	....	....	....	....	....	....	....	....
Banks	8 908	....	....	....	....	1.0	1.8	34.1	278.7
Other sectors	8 909	....	....	....	....	4.7	42.5	33.8	33.8
Other investment	8 753	**4,953.3**	**5,550.8**	**7,229.4**	**10,832.5**	**15,046.7**	**22,078.7**	**44,301.5**	**62,701.4**
Trade credits	8 756	1,434.4	1,459.0	1,811.6	2,165.1	2,628.1	2,915.5	4,469.0	5,900.7
General government	8 757	....	....	....	....	....	....	....	....
of which: Short-term	8 759	....	....	....	....	....	....	....	....
Other sectors	8 760	1,434.4	1,459.0	1,811.6	2,165.1	2,628.1	2,915.5	4,469.0	5,900.7
of which: Short-term	8 762	*470.5*	*541.0*	*771.7*	*1,006.9*	*1,222.3*	*1,259.4*	*2,684.0*	*3,713.7*
Loans	8 764	3,159.1	3,633.7	4,818.1	7,841.8	11,564.2	17,801.2	37,620.7	53,561.9
Monetary authorities	8 765	....	....	....	....	....	....	....	....
of which: Use of Fund credit and loans from the Fund	8 766	....	....	....	....	....	....	....	....
of which: Short-term	8 768	....	....	....	....	....	....	....	....
General government	8 769	2,272.0	2,247.3	2,294.1	2,423.2	2,382.7	1,426.6	1,442.1	1,431.2
of which: Short-term	8 771	....	....	....	....	....	....	....	....
Banks	8 772	222.5	543.0	1,322.5	3,404.1	6,165.2	12,204.2	28,187.9	39,623.3
of which: Short-term	8 774	*98.2*	*310.4*	*673.1*	*1,359.7*	*1,728.7*	*5,318.2*	*5,801.4*	*3,747.5*
Other sectors	8 775	664.6	843.3	1,201.6	2,014.4	3,016.3	4,170.4	7,990.8	12,507.4
of which: Short-term	8 777	*38.8*	*36.1*	*141.1*	*212.9*	*275.0*	*369.2*	*1,162.7*	*1,448.6*
Currency and deposits	8 780	165.3	310.2	465.6	577.5	587.6	1,113.5	1,785.9	2,565.3
Monetary authorities	8 781	....	.2	.1	.1	.3	1.0	.8	....
General government	8 782	....	....	....	....	....	....	....	....
Banks	8 783	165.3	310.1	465.4	577.4	587.3	1,112.5	1,785.2	2,565.3
Other sectors	8 784	....	....	....	....	....	....	....	....
Other liabilities	8 786	194.6	147.8	134.1	248.1	266.8	248.5	425.9	673.6
Monetary authorities	8 787	1.9	2.1	2.4	87.9	20.4	2.8	3.1	2.1
of which: Short-term	8 789	....	*.2*	*.5*	*86.0*	*18.5*	*.9*	*1.2*	*.2*
General government	8 790	5.0	1.7	....	....	....	....	....	....
of which: Short-term	8 792	....	....	....	....	....	....	....	....
Banks	8 793	4.4	6.2	3.9	17.6	174.9	174.8	366.2	491.4
of which: Short-term	8 795	*4.4*	*6.2*	*3.9*	*17.6*	*174.9*	*174.8*	*366.2*	*491.4*
Other sectors	8 796	183.3	137.8	127.8	142.6	71.5	70.9	56.6	180.1
of which: Short-term	8 798	*183.3*	*137.8*	*127.8*	*142.6*	*71.5*	*70.9*	*56.6*	*180.1*
NET INTERNATIONAL INVESTMENT POSITION	8 995	**−11,114.0**	**−13,075.3**	**−13,734.9**	**−14,757.8**	**−15,702.1**	**−20,277.3**	**−28,965.4**	**−43,537.2**
Conversion rates: tenge per U.S. dollar (end of period)	0 102	144.50	150.20	154.60	144.22	130.00	133.98	127.00	120.30

Table 1. ANALYTIC PRESENTATION, 2000–2007

(Millions of U.S. dollars)

	Code	2000	2001	2002	2003	2004	2005	2006	2007
A. Current Account[1]	4 993 Z.	**−199.4**	**−320.3**	**−117.7**	**132.4**	**−131.8**	**−252.3**	**−478.8**	**−1,101.8**
Goods: exports f.o.b.	2 100 ..	1,782.2	1,891.4	2,161.9	2,412.2	2,726.0	3,462.1	3,516.2	4,122.9
Goods: imports f.o.b.	3 100 ..	−3,043.9	−3,238.2	−3,159.0	−3,568.6	−4,350.6	−5,601.7	−6,769.5	−8,381.0
Balance on Goods	4 100 ..	*−1,261.7*	*−1,346.9*	*−997.0*	*−1,156.4*	*−1,624.7*	*−2,139.5*	*−3,253.2*	*−4,258.0*
Services: credit	2 200 ..	993.4	1,120.1	1,053.7	1,197.6	1,556.5	1,880.1	2,461.1	2,699.0
Services: debit	3 200 ..	−718.7	−810.2	−708.4	−690.6	−939.2	−1,137.1	−1,401.5	−1,459.5
Balance on Goods and Services	4 991 ..	*−987.0*	*−1,037.0*	*−651.7*	*−649.3*	*−1,007.3*	*−1,396.6*	*−2,193.6*	*−3,018.5*
Income: credit	2 300 ..	45.0	46.1	35.4	59.6	45.0	73.3	99.4	112.8
Income: debit	3 300 ..	−178.1	−167.7	−178.6	−148.2	−171.5	−181.7	−169.5	−304.4
Balance on Goods, Services, and Income	4 992 ..	*−1,120.2*	*−1,158.6*	*−794.8*	*−737.9*	*−1,133.8*	*−1,505.0*	*−2,263.7*	*−3,210.1*
Current transfers: credit	2 379 Z.	926.6	854.1	689.3	884.5	1,044.7	1,319.2	1,832.8	2,148.8
Current transfers: debit	3 379 ..	−5.8	−15.8	−12.1	−14.1	−42.6	−66.6	−47.9	−40.4
B. Capital Account[1]	4 994 Z.	**49.6**	**51.5**	**82.1**	**163.0**	**145.2**	**103.3**	**168.4**	**156.8**
Capital account: credit	2 994 Z.	49.6	51.5	82.1	163.0	145.2	103.3	168.4	156.8
Capital account: debit	3 994 ..	....	....	....	....	....	....	....	....
Total, Groups A Plus B	4 981 ..	*−149.8*	*−268.8*	*−35.5*	*295.5*	*13.4*	*−149.0*	*−310.4*	*−944.9*
C. Financial Account[1]	4 995 W.	**269.8**	**148.1**	**−173.9**	**406.3**	**40.2**	**511.3**	**673.6**	**2,070.9**
Direct investment abroad	4 505 ..	....	....	−7.4	−2.1	−4.4	−9.7	−24.0	−36.0
Direct investment in Kenya	4 555 Z.	110.9	5.3	27.6	81.7	46.1	21.2	50.7	727.7
Portfolio investment assets	4 602 ..	−10.9	−6.9	−10.0	−38.6	−71.7	−45.9	−23.6	−24.3
Equity securities	4 610 ..	−.5	−.9	−2.0	−12.2	−25.8	−5.4	−3.9	−2.9
Debt securities	4 619 ..	−10.4	−6.0	−8.1	−26.4	−45.9	−40.5	−19.7	−21.5
Portfolio investment liabilities	4 652 Z.	−3.5	5.5	5.3	.9	5.4	15.4	3.0	.8
Equity securities	4 660 ..	−6.0	2.4	3.0	.6	3.2	3.1	1.8	.5
Debt securities	4 669 Z.	2.5	3.1	2.3	.3	2.1	12.3	1.2	.3
Financial derivatives	4 910 ..	....	....	....	....	....	....	....	....
Financial derivatives assets	4 900 ..	....	....	....	....	....	....	....	....
Financial derivatives liabilities	4 905 ..	....	....	....	....	....	....	....	....
Other investment assets	4 703 ..	−55.7	−86.4	−132.6	−67.4	−307.1	−200.6	−259.6	−346.7
Monetary authorities	4 701 ..	....	....	....	....	....	....	....	....
General government	4 704 ..	....	....	....	....	....	....	....	....
Banks	4 705 ..	−5.3	−6.6	−7.8	−11.0	....	....	....	....
Other sectors	4 728 ..	−50.4	−79.8	−124.9	−56.4	−307.1	−200.6	−259.6	−346.7
Other investment liabilities	4 753 W.	228.9	230.6	−56.7	431.7	372.0	730.8	927.1	1,749.4
Monetary authorities	4 753 WA	....	....	....	....	....	....	....	....
General government	4 753 ZB	243.8	−158.4	−133.7	−81.3	−171.4	−46.1	61.9	134.8
Banks	4 753 ZC	....	....	....	....	....	....	....	....
Other sectors	4 753 ZD	−14.9	389.0	77.0	513.0	543.4	776.9	865.2	1,614.6
Total, Groups A Through C	4 983 ..	*119.9*	*−120.7*	*−209.5*	*701.8*	*53.7*	*362.3*	*363.2*	*1,126.0*
D. Net Errors and Omissions	4 998 ..	**−127.1**	**130.7**	**193.1**	**−276.5**	**−66.8**	**−245.3**	**218.1**	**−314.7**
Total, Groups A Through D	4 984 ..	*−7.2*	*10.0*	*−16.4*	*425.2*	*−13.1*	*117.0*	*581.3*	*811.3*
E. Reserves and Related Items	4 802 A.	**7.2**	**−10.0**	**16.4**	**−425.2**	**13.1**	**−117.0**	**−581.3**	**−811.3**
Reserve assets	4 802 ..	−107.1	−167.8	−1.7	−412.6	−36.6	−281.2	−615.8	−938.2
Use of Fund credit and loans	4 766 ..	1.3	−23.6	−18.4	16.7	−14.1	69.1	−13.5	106.2
Exceptional financing	4 920 ..	113.0	181.4	36.5	−29.3	63.8	95.1	48.1	20.7
Conversion rates: Kenya shillings per U.S. dollar	0 101 ..	**76.176**	**78.563**	**78.749**	**75.936**	**79.174**	**75.554**	**72.101**	**67.318**

[1] Excludes components that have been classified in the categories of Group E.

Table 2. STANDARD PRESENTATION, 2000–2007

(Millions of U.S. dollars)

	Code	2000	2001	2002	2003	2004	2005	2006	2007
CURRENT ACCOUNT.....................................	4 993 ..	**−199.4**	**−320.3**	**−117.7**	**132.4**	**−131.8**	**−252.3**	**−478.8**	**−1,101.8**
A. GOODS..	4 100 ..	**−1,261.7**	**−1,346.9**	**−997.0**	**−1,156.4**	**−1,624.7**	**−2,139.5**	**−3,253.2**	**−4,258.0**
Credit..	2 100 ..	**1,782.2**	**1,891.4**	**2,161.9**	**2,412.2**	**2,726.0**	**3,462.1**	**3,516.2**	**4,122.9**
General merchandise: exports f.o.b...............	2 110 ..	1,735.7	1,840.5	2,104.9	2,334.5	2,617.6	3,347.1	3,355.1	3,990.9
Goods for processing: exports f.o.b..............	2 150 ..	....	....	....	....	....	....	....	....
Repairs on goods..	2 160 ..	3.8	2.9	2.6	2.6	2.5	2.7	7.2	9.0
Goods procured in ports by carriers..............	2 170 ..	35.6	35.6	44.0	61.3	100.6	104.8	147.1	68.7
Nonmonetary gold.......................................	2 180 ..	7.1	12.4	10.5	13.8	5.2	7.6	6.8	54.3
Debit..	3 100 ..	**−3,043.9**	**−3,238.2**	**−3,159.0**	**−3,568.6**	**−4,350.6**	**−5,601.7**	**−6,769.5**	**−8,381.0**
General merchandise: imports f.o.b..............	3 110 ..	−2,985.6	−3,183.8	−3,108.1	−3,514.3	−4,299.3	−5,548.6	−6,712.8	−8,361.5
Goods for processing: imports f.o.b..............	3 150 ..	....	....	....	....	....	....	....	....
Repairs on goods..	3 160 ..	−22.4	−23.0	−17.4	−15.5	−16.1	−15.1	−17.4	−19.5
Goods procured in ports by carriers..............	3 170 ..	−36.0	−31.4	−33.5	−38.8	−35.3	−38.0	−39.3	....
Nonmonetary gold.......................................	3 180 ..	....	....	....	....	....	....	....	.1
B. SERVICES..	4 200 ..	**274.7**	**309.9**	**345.4**	**507.0**	**617.4**	**743.0**	**1,059.6**	**1,239.5**
Total credit..	2 200 ..	*993.4*	*1,120.1*	*1,053.7*	*1,197.6*	*1,556.5*	*1,880.1*	*2,461.1*	*2,699.0*
Total debit..	3 200 ..	*−718.7*	*−810.2*	*−708.4*	*−690.6*	*−939.2*	*−1,137.1*	*−1,401.5*	*−1,459.5*
Transportation services, credit..............	2 205 ..	**411.1**	**460.6**	**458.8**	**487.8**	**598.5**	**736.5**	**1,021.6**	**1,124.7**
Passenger..	2 850 ..	*217.3*	*227.2*	*236.6*	*271.8*	*312.9*	*390.0*	*493.5*	*596.5*
Freight...	2 851 ..	*64.6*	*105.7*	*161.2*	*153.9*	*211.0*	*265.2*	*360.3*	*350.7*
Other...	2 852 ..	*129.3*	*127.6*	*61.0*	*62.2*	*74.7*	*81.3*	*167.7*	*177.4*
Sea transport, passenger	2 207 ..	....	....	....	....	....	....	....	....
Sea transport, freight.................................	2 208 ..	....	....	....	....	....	....	....	....
Sea transport, other...................................	2 209 ..	75.4	78.7	49.1	49.2	59.8	62.7	141.8	133.8
Air transport, passenger.............................	2 211 ..	210.0	226.7	236.6	271.8	312.8	390.0	493.5	596.5
Air transport, freight..................................	2 212 ..	12.7	14.0	16.5	17.2	19.7	24.6	71.8	72.7
Air transport, other....................................	2 213 ..	11.5	12.1	11.9	12.9	14.9	18.6	25.9	43.7
Other transport, passenger.........................	2 215 ..	7.3	.5	....	....	....	....	....	....
Other transport, freight..............................	2 216 ..	51.8	91.7	144.6	136.8	191.2	240.6	288.5	278.0
Other transport, other................................	2 217 ..	42.3	36.8	....	....	....	....	....	....
Transportation services, debit..............	3 205 ..	**−341.5**	**−310.9**	**−272.6**	**−249.7**	**−346.3**	**−426.3**	**−670.4**	**−809.7**
Passenger..	3 850 ..	*−24.4*	*−40.1*	*....*	*....*	*....*	*....*	*....*	*....*
Freight...	3 851 ..	*−279.1*	*−236.1*	*−224.5*	*−223.1*	*−287.2*	*−347.1*	*−573.2*	*−727.2*
Other...	3 852 ..	*−38.0*	*−34.6*	*−48.2*	*−26.6*	*−59.0*	*−79.2*	*−97.2*	*−82.5*
Sea transport, passenger	3 207 ..	....	....	....	....	....	....	....	....
Sea transport, freight.................................	3 208 ..	−252.8	−209.9	−175.4	−192.8	−253.5	−301.7	−507.0	−655.2
Sea transport, other...................................	3 209 ..	−2.5	−.7	−2.2	−6.0	−35.3	−41.4	−14.9	−14.5
Air transport, passenger.............................	3 211 ..	−24.1	−38.3	....	....	....	....	....	....
Air transport, freight..................................	3 212 ..	−20.2	−18.6	....	....	....	....	....	....
Air transport, other....................................	3 213 ..	−16.9	−17.4	−46.0	−20.6	−23.7	−37.8	−82.3	−68.0
Other transport, passenger.........................	3 215 ..	−.3	−1.8	....	....	....	....	....	....
Other transport, freight..............................	3 216 ..	−6.2	−7.6	−49.0	−30.4	−33.7	−45.4	−66.2	−72.0
Other transport, other................................	3 217 ..	−18.6	−16.5	....	....	....	....	....	....
Travel, credit..	2 236 ..	**282.9**	**308.7**	**276.0**	**347.4**	**485.7**	**579.1**	**687.5**	**910.3**
Business travel...	2 237 ..	62.7	72.0	49.6	48.5	56.7	64.3	97.7	107.3
Personal travel...	2 240 ..	220.2	236.8	226.4	298.9	429.0	514.8	589.8	803.0
Travel, debit..	3 236 ..	**−131.5**	**−143.1**	**−125.6**	**−127.1**	**−107.5**	**−123.9**	**−177.8**	**−262.3**
Business travel...	3 237 ..	−45.4	−61.2	−69.7	−81.6	−49.3	−53.9	−66.6	−96.3
Personal travel...	3 240 ..	−86.1	−81.9	−55.9	−45.5	−58.2	−69.9	−111.2	−165.9
Other services, credit...........................	2 200 BA	**299.3**	**350.8**	**318.9**	**362.4**	**472.3**	**564.5**	**752.1**	**664.0**
Communications...	2 245 ..	22.0	45.5	15.5	15.2	113.2	177.7	283.3	109.0
Construction..	2 249 ..	....	....	....	....	....	....	....	....
Insurance..	2 253 ..	3.7	3.6	11.2	13.8	12.4	10.5	7.3	7.5
Financial...	2 260 ..	....	....	....	....	....	....	....	....
Computer and information............................	2 262 ..	.4	.3	.7	....	.4	1.1	.7	.8
Royalties and licence fees...........................	2 266 ..	7.1	5.0	9.9	11.6	16.6	17.5	9.9	23.0
Other business services..	2 268 ..	....	....	....	....	....	....	....	....
Personal, cultural, and recreational...............	2 287 ..	....	.1	.4	.3	.3	.4	.7	2.1
Government, n.i.e.......................................	2 291 ..	266.2	296.3	281.1	321.5	329.5	357.4	450.2	521.6
Other services, debit.............................	3 200 BA	**−245.7**	**−356.3**	**−310.1**	**−313.8**	**−485.4**	**−587.0**	**−553.3**	**−387.5**
Communications...	3 245 ..	−7.1	−31.5	−6.4	−6.2	−108.4	−107.5	−130.4	−152.8
Construction..	3 249 ..	....	....	....	....	....	....	....	....
Insurance..	3 253 ..	−47.7	−63.2	−33.7	−40.9	−39.5	−58.9	−72.7	−25.7
Financial...	3 260 ..	−16.2	−24.3	−27.6	−31.7	−69.4	−71.5	−92.6	109.8
Computer and information............................	3 262 ..	−1.3	−1.1	−1.4	−1.6	−.7	−1.5	−1.8	−2.3
Royalties and licence fees...........................	3 266 ..	−77.3	−62.2	−42.4	−39.2	−50.3	−36.9	−19.7	−23.6
Other business services..............................	3 268 ..	−41.0	−74.9	−73.9	−76.5	−79.6	−127.0	−67.7	−100.7
Personal, cultural, and recreational...............	3 287 ..	−1.6	−1.2	−3.9	−2.5	−1.2	−1.1	−1.6	−.8
Government, n.i.e.......................................	3 291 ..	−53.4	−97.9	−120.8	−115.2	−136.3	−182.5	−166.8	−191.3

Table 2 (Continued). STANDARD PRESENTATION, 2000–2007

(Millions of U.S. dollars)

	Code	2000	2001	2002	2003	2004	2005	2006	2007
C. INCOME	4 300	**−133.1**	**−121.7**	**−143.2**	**−88.6**	**−126.5**	**−108.5**	**−70.1**	**−191.6**
Total credit	2 300	*45.0*	*46.1*	*35.4*	*59.6*	*45.0*	*73.3*	*99.4*	*112.8*
Total debit	3 300	*−178.1*	*−167.7*	*−178.6*	*−148.2*	*−171.5*	*−181.7*	*−169.5*	*−304.4*
Compensation of employees, credit	2 310	....	....	....	....	....	....	....	....
Compensation of employees, debit	3 310	....	....	....	....	....	....	....	....
Investment income, credit	2 320	**45.0**	**46.1**	**35.4**	**59.6**	**45.0**	**73.3**	**99.4**	**112.8**
Direct investment income	2 330	....	....	....	....	....	....	....	....
Dividends and distributed branch profits	2 332	....	....	....	....	....	....	....	....
Reinvested earnings and undistributed branch profits	2 333	....	....	....	....	....	....	....	....
Income on debt (interest)	2 334	....	....	....	....	....	....	....	....
Portfolio investment income	2 339	....	....	....	....	....	....	....	....
Income on equity	2 340	....	....	....	....	....	....	....	....
Income on bonds and notes	2 350	....	....	....	....	....	....	....	....
Income on money market instruments	2 360	....	....	....	....	....	....	....	....
Other investment income	2 370	45.0	46.1	35.4	59.6	45.0	73.3	99.4	112.8
Investment income, debit	3 320	**−178.1**	**−167.7**	**−178.6**	**−148.2**	**−171.5**	**−181.7**	**−169.5**	**−304.4**
Direct investment income	3 330	−28.7	−48.4	−75.5	−32.5	−30.6	−34.9	−38.9	−123.6
Dividends and distributed branch profits	3 332	−21.9	−44.3	−19.7	−31.1	−29.8	−34.1	−38.4	−108.2
Reinvested earnings and undistributed branch profits	3 333	....	....	....	....	....	....	....	....
Income on debt (interest)	3 334	−6.8	−4.1	−55.7	−1.3	−.8	−.8	−.5	−15.4
Portfolio investment income	3 339	−1.4	−2.7	−2.8	−2.2	−6.8	−3.8	−5.4	−5.3
Income on equity	3 340	−1.2	−.6	−.6	−1.6	−5.3	−2.9	−3.3	−4.0
Income on bonds and notes	3 350	−.2	−2.1	−2.2	−.7	−1.6	−.9	−2.1	−1.2
Income on money market instruments	3 360	....	....	....	....	....	....	....	....
Other investment income	3 370	−148.0	−116.6	−100.3	−113.5	−134.1	−143.0	−125.2	−175.5
D. CURRENT TRANSFERS	4 379	**920.8**	**838.3**	**677.2**	**870.3**	**1,002.1**	**1,252.7**	**1,784.9**	**2,108.4**
Credit	2 379	**926.6**	**854.1**	**689.3**	**884.5**	**1,044.7**	**1,319.2**	**1,832.8**	**2,148.8**
General government	2 380	111.2	20.2	33.0	69.5	106.1	100.3	123.8	220.1
Other sectors	2 390	815.3	833.9	656.2	815.0	938.5	1,218.9	1,709.0	1,928.7
Workers' remittances	2 391	....	50.9	57.1	65.8	375.8	425.0	570.5	645.2
Other current transfers	2 392	815.3	783.0	599.1	749.1	562.7	793.9	1,138.5	1,283.5
Debit	3 379	**−5.8**	**−15.8**	**−12.1**	**−14.1**	**−42.6**	**−66.6**	**−47.9**	**−40.4**
General government	3 380	−1.6	−10.7	−6.4	−7.5	−8.6	−10.1	−22.5	−24.1
Other sectors	3 390	−4.2	−5.1	−5.7	−6.6	−34.0	−56.4	−25.4	−16.4
Workers' remittances	3 391	....	−5.1	−5.7	−6.6	−34.0	−56.4	−25.4	−16.4
Other current transfers	3 392	−4.2	....	....	....	....	....	....	....
CAPITAL AND FINANCIAL ACCOUNT	4 996	**326.5**	**189.6**	**−75.4**	**144.1**	**198.6**	**497.6**	**260.7**	**1,416.5**
CAPITAL ACCOUNT	4 994	**49.6**	**51.5**	**82.1**	**163.0**	**145.2**	**103.3**	**168.4**	**156.8**
Total credit	2 994	*49.6*	*51.5*	*82.1*	*163.0*	*145.2*	*103.3*	*168.4*	*156.8*
Total debit	3 994	....	....	....	....	....	....	....	....
Capital transfers, credit	2 400	**49.6**	**51.5**	**82.1**	**163.0**	**145.2**	**103.3**	**168.4**	**156.8**
General government	2 401	49.6	51.5	82.1	163.0	145.2	103.3	168.4	156.8
Debt forgiveness	2 402	....	4.0	....	....	....	....	....	....
Other capital transfers	2 410	49.6	47.5	82.1	163.0	145.2	103.3	168.4	156.8
Other sectors	2 430	....	....	....	....	....	....	....	....
Migrants' transfers	2 431	....	....	....	....	....	....	....	....
Debt forgiveness	2 432	....	....	....	....	....	....	....	....
Other capital transfers	2 440	....	....	....	....	....	....	....	....
Capital transfers, debit	3 400	....	....	....	....	....	....	....	....
General government	3 401	....	....	....	....	....	....	....	....
Debt forgiveness	3 402	....	....	....	....	....	....	....	....
Other capital transfers	3 410	....	....	....	....	....	....	....	....
Other sectors	3 430	....	....	....	....	....	....	....	....
Migrants' transfers	3 431	....	....	....	....	....	....	....	....
Debt forgiveness	3 432	....	....	....	....	....	....	....	....
Other capital transfers	3 440	....	....	....	....	....	....	....	....
Nonproduced nonfinancial assets, credit	2 480	....	....	....	....	....	....	....	....
Nonproduced nonfinancial assets, debit	3 480	....	....	....	....	....	....	....	....

Table 2 (Continued). STANDARD PRESENTATION, 2000–2007

(Millions of U.S. dollars)

	Code	2000	2001	2002	2003	2004	2005	2006	2007
FINANCIAL ACCOUNT	4 995	**277.0**	**138.2**	**−157.5**	**−18.9**	**53.4**	**394.3**	**92.3**	**1,259.6**
A. DIRECT INVESTMENT	4 500	**110.9**	**5.3**	**20.2**	**79.7**	**41.6**	**11.5**	**26.7**	**691.7**
Direct investment abroad	4 505	....	....	−7.4	−2.1	−4.4	−9.7	−24.0	−36.0
Equity capital	4 510	....	....	−7.4	−2.1	−4.4	−9.7	−24.0	−36.0
Claims on affiliated enterprises	4 515	....	....	−7.4	−2.1	−4.4	−9.7	−24.0	−36.0
Liabilities to affiliated enterprises	4 520	....	....	....	....	....	....	....	....
Reinvested earnings	4 525	....	....	....	....	....	....	....	....
Other capital	4 530	....	....	....	....	....	....	....	....
Claims on affiliated enterprises	4 535	....	....	....	....	....	....	....	....
Liabilities to affiliated enterprises	4 540	....	....	....	....	....	....	....	....
Direct investment in Kenya	4 555	110.9	5.3	27.6	81.7	46.1	21.2	50.7	727.7
Equity capital	4 560	83.3	.8	13.1	27.0	29.9	5.6	3.0	14.3
Claims on direct investors	4 565	....	....	....	....	....	....	....	....
Liabilities to direct investors	4 570	83.3	.8	13.1	27.0	29.9	5.6	3.0	14.3
Reinvested earnings	4 575	....	....	....	....	....	....	....	....
Other capital	4 580	27.6	4.5	14.5	54.7	16.2	15.6	47.7	713.4
Claims on direct investors	4 585	....	....	....	....	....	....	....	....
Liabilities to direct investors	4 590	27.6	4.5	14.5	54.7	16.2	15.6	47.7	713.4
B. PORTFOLIO INVESTMENT	4 600	**−14.4**	**−1.4**	**−4.8**	**−37.7**	**−66.3**	**−30.5**	**−20.6**	**−23.5**
Assets	4 602	**−10.9**	**−6.9**	**−10.0**	**−38.6**	**−71.7**	**−45.9**	**−23.6**	**−24.3**
Equity securities	4 610	−.5	−.9	−2.0	−12.2	−25.8	−5.4	−3.9	−2.9
Monetary authorities	4 611	....	....	....	....	....	....	....	....
General government	4 612	....	....	....	....	....	....	....	....
Banks	4 613	....	....	....	....	....	....	....	....
Other sectors	4 614	−.5	−.9	−2.0	−12.2	−25.8	−5.4	−3.9	−2.9
Debt securities	4 619	−10.4	−6.0	−8.1	−26.4	−45.9	−40.5	−19.7	−21.5
Bonds and notes	4 620	−10.4	−6.0	−8.1	−26.4	−45.9	−40.5	−19.7	−21.5
Monetary authorities	4 621	−.4	−1.3	−2.2	−.1	....	....	....	....
General government	4 622	....	....	....	....	....	....	....	....
Banks	4 623	....	....	....	....	....	....	....	....
Other sectors	4 624	−10.0	−4.7	−5.9	−26.3	−45.9	−40.5	−19.7	−21.5
Money market instruments	4 630	....	....	....	....	....	....	....	....
Monetary authorities	4 631	....	....	....	....	....	....	....	....
General government	4 632	....	....	....	....	....	....	....	....
Banks	4 633	....	....	....	....	....	....	....	....
Other sectors	4 634	....	....	....	....	....	....	....	....
Liabilities	4 652	**−3.5**	**5.5**	**5.3**	**.9**	**5.4**	**15.4**	**3.0**	**.8**
Equity securities	4 660	−6.0	2.4	3.0	.6	3.2	3.1	1.8	.5
Banks	4 663	.4	1.0	3.0	.6	3.2	3.1	1.8	.5
Other sectors	4 664	−6.4	1.4	....	....	....	....	....	....
Debt securities	4 669	2.5	3.1	2.3	.3	2.1	12.3	1.2	.3
Bonds and notes	4 670	2.5	3.1	2.3	.3	2.1	12.3	1.2	.3
Monetary authorities	4 671	2.5	3.1	2.3	.3	2.1	12.3	1.2	.3
General government	4 672	....	....	....	....	....	....	....	....
Banks	4 673	....	....	....	....	....	....	....	....
Other sectors	4 674	....	....	....	....	....	....	....	....
Money market instruments	4 680	....	....	....	....	....	....	....	....
Monetary authorities	4 681	....	....	....	....	....	....	....	....
General government	4 682	....	....	....	....	....	....	....	....
Banks	4 683	....	....	....	....	....	....	....	....
Other sectors	4 684	....	....	....	....	....	....	....	....
C. FINANCIAL DERIVATIVES	4 910	....	....	....	....	....	....	....	....
Monetary authorities	4 911	....	....	....	....	....	....	....	....
General government	4 912	....	....	....	....	....	....	....	....
Banks	4 913	....	....	....	....	....	....	....	....
Other sectors	4 914	....	....	....	....	....	....	....	....
Assets	4 900	....	....	....	....	....	....	....	....
Monetary authorities	4 901	....	....	....	....	....	....	....	....
General government	4 902	....	....	....	....	....	....	....	....
Banks	4 903	....	....	....	....	....	....	....	....
Other sectors	4 904	....	....	....	....	....	....	....	....
Liabilities	4 905	....	....	....	....	....	....	....	....
Monetary authorities	4 906	....	....	....	....	....	....	....	....
General government	4 907	....	....	....	....	....	....	....	....
Banks	4 908	....	....	....	....	....	....	....	....
Other sectors	4 909	....	....	....	....	....	....	....	....

Table 2 (Concluded). STANDARD PRESENTATION, 2000–2007

(Millions of U.S. dollars)

	Code	2000	2001	2002	2003	2004	2005	2006	2007
D. OTHER INVESTMENT	4 700 ..	**287.5**	**302.0**	**−171.2**	**351.7**	**114.6**	**694.4**	**702.1**	**1,529.7**
Assets	4 703 ..	**−55.7**	**−86.4**	**−132.6**	**−67.4**	**−307.1**	**−200.6**	**−259.6**	**−346.7**
Trade credits	4 706 ..	....	....	....	....	....	....	....	....
General government	4 707 ..	....	....	....	....	....	....	....	....
of which: Short-term	4 709 ..	....	....	....	....	....	....	....	....
Other sectors	4 710 ..	....	....	....	....	....	....	....	....
of which: Short-term	4 712 ..	....	....	....	....	....	....	....	....
Loans	4 714 ..	....	....	....	....	....	....	....	....
Monetary authorities	4 715 ..	....	....	....	....	....	....	....	....
of which: Short-term	4 718 ..	....	....	....	....	....	....	....	....
General government	4 719 ..	....	....	....	....	....	....	....	....
of which: Short-term	4 721 ..	....	....	....	....	....	....	....	....
Banks	4 722 ..	....	....	....	....	....	....	....	....
of which: Short-term	4 724 ..	....	....	....	....	....	....	....	....
Other sectors	4 725 ..	....	....	....	....	....	....	....	....
of which: Short-term	4 727 ..	....	....	....	....	....	....	....	....
Currency and deposits	4 730 ..	....	....	....	....	−211.3	−117.0	−180.8	−286.1
Monetary authorities	4 731 ..	....	....	....	....	....	....	....	....
General government	4 732 ..	....	....	....	....	....	....	....	....
Banks	4 733 ..	....	....	....	....	....	....	....	....
Other sectors	4 734 ..	....	....	....	....	−211.3	−117.0	−180.8	−286.1
Other assets	4 736 ..	−55.7	−86.4	−132.6	−67.4	−95.8	−83.6	−78.8	−60.5
Monetary authorities	4 737 ..	....	....	....	....	....	....	....	....
of which: Short-term	4 739 ..	....	....	....	....	....	....	....	....
General government	4 740 ..	....	....	....	....	....	....	....	....
of which: Short-term	4 742 ..	....	....	....	....	....	....	....	....
Banks	4 743 ..	−5.3	−6.6	−7.8	−11.0	....	....	....	....
of which: Short-term	4 745 ..	*−5.3*	*−6.6*	*−7.8*	*−11.0*	....	....	....	....
Other sectors	4 746 ..	−50.4	−79.8	−124.9	−56.4	−95.8	−83.6	−78.8	−60.5
of which: Short-term	4 748 ..	*13.0*	*12.1*	*11.6*	*12.5*	*13.4*	*15.8*	*18.5*	*22.2*
Liabilities	4 753 ..	**343.2**	**388.4**	**−38.6**	**419.1**	**421.7**	**895.0**	**961.6**	**1,876.4**
Trade credits	4 756 ..	....	....	....	....	....	....	....	....
General government	4 757 ..	....	....	....	....	....	....	....	....
of which: Short-term	4 759 ..	....	....	....	....	....	....	....	....
Other sectors	4 760 ..	....	....	....	....	....	....	....	....
of which: Short-term	4 762 ..	....	....	....	....	....	....	....	....
Loans	4 764 ..	125.6	−212.0	−216.4	−135.3	−265.2	146.6	58.7	351.2
Monetary authorities	4 765 ..	1.3	−23.6	−18.4	16.7	−14.1	69.1	−13.5	106.2
of which: Use of Fund credit and loans from the Fund..	4 766 ..	*1.3*	*−23.6*	*−18.4*	*16.7*	*−14.1*	*69.1*	*−13.5*	*106.2*
of which: Short-term	4 768 ..	....	....	....	....	....	....	....	....
General government	4 769 ..	243.8	−158.4	−133.7	−81.3	−171.4	−46.1	61.9	134.8
of which: Short-term	4 771 ..	....	....	....	....	....	....	....	....
Banks	4 772 ..	....	....	....	....	....	....	....	....
of which: Short-term	4 774 ..	....	....	....	....	....	....	....	....
Other sectors	4 775 ..	−119.5	−30.0	−64.3	−70.7	−79.7	123.6	10.3	110.2
of which: Short-term	4 777 ..	*20.9*	*17.0*	....	....	....	....	....	....
Currency and deposits	4 780 ..	−232.0	92.0	−169.0	109.5	53.3	−42.7	26.4	325.1
Monetary authorities	4 781 ..	....	....	....	....	....	....	....	....
General government	4 782 ..	....	....	....	....	....	....	....	....
Banks	4 783 ..	....	....	....	....	....	....	....	....
Other sectors	4 784 ..	−232.0	92.0	−169.0	109.5	53.3	−42.7	26.4	325.1
Other liabilities	4 786 ..	449.6	508.4	346.7	444.9	633.6	791.1	876.5	1,200.0
Monetary authorities	4 787 ..	....	....	....	....	....	....	....	....
of which: Short-term	4 789 ..	....	....	....	....	....	....	....	....
General government	4 790 ..	113.0	181.4	36.5	−29.3	63.8	95.1	48.1	20.7
of which: Short-term	4 792 ..	*113.0*	*181.4*	*36.5*	*−29.3*	*63.8*	*95.1*	*48.1*	*20.7*
Banks	4 793 ..	....	....	....	....	....	....	....	....
of which: Short-term	4 795 ..	....	....	....	....	....	....	....	....
Other sectors	4 796 ..	336.6	327.0	310.3	474.2	569.8	696.0	828.5	1,179.3
of which: Short-term	4 798 ..	*336.6*	*327.0*	*310.3*	*474.2*	*569.8*	*696.0*	*828.5*	*1,179.3*
E. RESERVE ASSETS	4 802 ..	**−107.1**	**−167.8**	**−1.7**	**−412.6**	**−36.6**	**−281.2**	**−615.8**	**−938.2**
Monetary gold	4 812 ..	....	....	....	....	....	....	....	....
Special drawing rights	4 811 ..	2.0	−.7	.2	−.8	1.4	.5	−.3	.4
Reserve position in the Fund	4 810 ..	....	−.1	−.1	−.1	....	−.1	−.1	....
Foreign exchange	4 803 ..	−108.8	−167.2	−1.8	−411.3	−38.3	−281.3	−615.4	−938.3
Other claims	4 813 ..	−.2	.2	−.1	−.3	.3	−.3	−.1	−.3
NET ERRORS AND OMISSIONS	4 998 ..	**−127.1**	**130.7**	**193.1**	**−276.5**	**−66.8**	**−245.3**	**218.1**	**−314.7**

Table 1. ANALYTIC PRESENTATION, 2000–2007

(Millions of U.S. dollars)

	Code	2000	2001	2002	2003	2004	2005	2006	2007
A. Current Account[1]	4 993 Z.	**12,251**	**8,033**	**5,394**	**11,950**	**28,174**	**14,981**	**5,385**	**5,954**
Goods: exports f.o.b.	2 100 ..	176,221	151,478	163,414	197,289	257,710	288,971	331,842	378,982
Goods: imports f.o.b.	3 100 ..	−159,267	−137,990	−148,637	−175,337	−220,141	−256,288	−303,937	−349,573
Balance on Goods	4 100 ..	*16,954*	*13,488*	*14,777*	*21,952*	*37,569*	*32,683*	*27,905*	*29,409*
Services: credit	2 200 ..	30,534	29,055	28,388	32,957	41,882	45,129	49,891	63,034
Services: debit	3 200 ..	−33,381	−32,927	−36,585	−40,381	−49,928	−58,788	−68,851	−83,609
Balance on Goods and Services	4 991 ..	*14,106*	*9,616*	*6,580*	*14,528*	*29,523*	*19,025*	*8,945*	*8,835*
Income: credit	2 300 ..	6,375	6,650	6,900	7,176	9,410	10,432	14,547	19,327
Income: debit	3 300 ..	−8,797	−7,848	−6,467	−6,850	−8,328	−11,994	−14,014	−18,558
Balance on Goods, Services, and Income	4 992 ..	*11,685*	*8,418*	*7,012*	*14,854*	*30,606*	*17,462*	*9,478*	*9,603*
Current transfers: credit	2 379 Z.	6,500	6,687	7,314	7,859	9,151	10,004	9,588	10,934
Current transfers: debit	3 379 ..	−5,934	−7,072	−8,932	−10,764	−11,583	−12,486	−13,680	−14,583
B. Capital Account[1]	4 994 Z.	**−615**	**−731**	**−1,087**	**−1,398**	**−1,753**	**−2,340**	**−3,126**	**−2,390**
Capital account: credit	2 994 Z.	98	42	47	59	72	147	290	522
Capital account: debit	3 994 ..	−713	−773	−1,133	−1,457	−1,825	−2,487	−3,416	−2,912
Total, Groups A Plus B	4 981 ..	*11,636*	*7,302*	*4,307*	*10,551*	*26,421*	*12,641*	*2,259*	*3,565*
C. Financial Account[1]	4 995 W.	**12,725**	**3,025**	**7,338**	**15,308**	**9,359**	**7,104**	**21,098**	**8,622**
Direct investment abroad	4 505 ..	−4,999	−2,420	−2,617	−3,426	−4,650	−4,291	−8,127	−15,276
Direct investment in Republic of Korea	4 555 Z.	9,283	3,528	2,392	3,526	9,246	6,309	3,586	1,579
Portfolio investment assets	4 602 ..	−520	−5,521	−5,032	−4,390	−9,918	−14,136	−26,912	−54,602
Equity securities	4 610 ..	−480	−492	−1,460	−1,993	−3,622	−3,686	−15,262	−52,436
Debt securities	4 619 ..	−40	−5,029	−3,571	−2,397	−6,297	−10,450	−11,650	−2,166
Portfolio investment liabilities	4 652 Z.	12,697	12,227	5,378	22,690	18,375	14,114	8,056	29,974
Equity securities	4 660 ..	13,094	10,266	395	14,419	9,469	3,282	−8,391	−28,726
Debt securities	4 669 Z.	−397	1,962	4,983	8,272	8,906	10,831	16,447	58,700
Financial derivatives	4 910 ..	−179	−123	362	−394	163	−1,706	−3,890	5,534
Financial derivatives assets	4 900 ..	532	463	1,288	800	2,523	3,461	4,559	12,188
Financial derivatives liabilities	4 905 ..	−711	−586	−926	−1,194	−2,360	−5,167	−8,449	−6,654
Other investment assets	4 703 ..	−2,289	7,085	1,591	−5,132	−8,138	−2,658	−7,945	−18,424
Monetary authorities	4 701 ..	−44	−38	−40	−48	−55	−8	−1,299	−132
General government	4 704 ..	−155	−509	−311	−27	−1,577	−394	−390	−191
Banks	4 705 ..	−1,219	8,755	3,087	−4,210	−5,666	−1,525	−3,747	−11,222
Other sectors	4 728 ..	−871	−1,124	−1,145	−848	−841	−732	−2,510	−6,878
Other investment liabilities	4 753 W.	−1,268	−11,751	5,263	2,434	4,282	9,473	56,330	59,836
Monetary authorities	4 753 WA	28	63	−52	−35	−10	433	1,596	270
General government	4 753 ZB	110	−397	−1,436	−5,255	−2,549	−2,602	−924	−873
Banks	4 753 ZC	−4,538	−4,147	6,257	669	1,154	5,733	42,195	40,549
Other sectors	4 753 ZD	3,132	−7,271	493	7,055	5,687	5,909	13,462	19,890
Total, Groups A Through C	4 983 ..	*24,361*	*10,326*	*11,645*	*25,859*	*35,780*	*19,745*	*23,357*	*12,187*
D. Net Errors and Omissions	4 998 ..	**−571**	**2,951**	**124**	**−68**	**2,895**	**119**	**−1,267**	**2,922**
Total, Groups A Through D	4 984 ..	*23,790*	*13,278*	*11,769*	*25,791*	*38,675*	*19,864*	*22,090*	*15,109*
E. Reserves and Related Items	4 802 A.	**−23,790**	**−13,278**	**−11,769**	**−25,791**	**−38,675**	**−19,864**	**−22,090**	**−15,109**
Reserve assets	4 802 ..	−23,790	−7,586	−11,769	−25,791	−38,675	−19,864	−22,090	−15,109
Use of Fund credit and loans	4 766 ..	....	−5,692	....	....	....	....	....	....
Exceptional financing	4 920 ..	....	....	....	....	....	....	....	....
Conversion rates: won per U.S. dollar	0 101 ..	**1,131.0**	**1,291.0**	**1,251.1**	**1,191.6**	**1,145.3**	**1,024.1**	**954.8**	**929.3**

[1] Excludes components that have been classified in the categories of Group E.

Table 2. STANDARD PRESENTATION, 2000–2007

(Millions of U.S. dollars)

	Code	2000	2001	2002	2003	2004	2005	2006	2007
CURRENT ACCOUNT	4 993 ..	**12,251**	**8,033**	**5,394**	**11,950**	**28,174**	**14,981**	**5,385**	**5,954**
A. GOODS	4 100 ..	**16,954**	**13,488**	**14,777**	**21,952**	**37,569**	**32,683**	**27,905**	**29,409**
Credit	2 100 ..	**176,221**	**151,478**	**163,414**	**197,289**	**257,710**	**288,971**	**331,842**	**378,982**
General merchandise: exports f.o.b.	2 110 ..	159,409	139,597	151,233	181,792	238,309	265,500	303,173	345,188
Goods for processing: exports f.o.b.	2 150 ..	13,907	9,681	9,988	11,920	14,153	20,596	24,605	29,624
Repairs on goods	2 160 ..	103	37	25	17	99	19	82	77
Goods procured in ports by carriers	2 170 ..	1,278	1,108	1,241	1,613	2,205	2,640	3,205	3,412
Nonmonetary gold	2 180 ..	1,523	1,056	927	1,947	2,945	216	777	682
Debit	3 100 ..	**−159,267**	**−137,990**	**−148,637**	**−175,337**	**−220,141**	**−256,288**	**−303,937**	**−349,573**
General merchandise: imports f.o.b.	3 110 ..	−146,973	−128,964	−139,042	−161,877	−203,353	−238,551	−283,477	−326,495
Goods for processing: imports f.o.b.	3 150 ..	−8,508	−6,088	−6,522	−8,805	−10,739	−13,730	−16,016	−17,805
Repairs on goods	3 160 ..	−24	−31	−7	−6	−85	−36	−18	−37
Goods procured in ports by carriers	3 170 ..	−1,609	−1,349	−1,402	−1,882	−2,603	−3,213	−3,684	−3,956
Nonmonetary gold	3 180 ..	−2,153	−1,558	−1,665	−2,767	−3,361	−757	−742	−1,280
B. SERVICES	4 200 ..	**−2,848**	**−3,872**	**−8,198**	**−7,424**	**−8,046**	**−13,658**	**−18,961**	**−20,575**
Total credit	2 200 ..	*30,534*	*29,055*	*28,388*	*32,957*	*41,882*	*45,129*	*49,891*	*63,034*
Total debit	3 200 ..	*−33,381*	*−32,927*	*−36,585*	*−40,381*	*−49,928*	*−58,788*	*−68,851*	*−83,609*
Transportation services, credit	2 205 ..	**13,687**	**13,180**	**13,216**	**17,180**	**22,529**	**23,877**	**25,807**	**33,767**
Passenger	2 850 ..	*1,693*	*1,535*	*1,685*	*1,647*	*2,157*	*2,484*	*2,720*	*3,150*
Freight	2 851 ..	*9,995*	*9,573*	*9,810*	*13,502*	*17,422*	*18,360*	*20,099*	*27,931*
Other	2 852 ..	*2,000*	*2,073*	*1,721*	*2,031*	*2,951*	*3,033*	*2,989*	*2,686*
Sea transport, passenger	2 207 ..	....	....	....	....	....	....	13	7
Sea transport, freight	2 208 ..	....	....	....	....	....	....	17,420	25,087
Sea transport, other	2 209 ..	....	....	....	....	....	....	2,866	2,583
Air transport, passenger	2 211 ..	....	....	....	....	....	....	2,707	3,143
Air transport, freight	2 212 ..	....	....	....	....	....	....	2,679	2,844
Air transport, other	2 213 ..	....	....	....	....	....	....	123	103
Other transport, passenger	2 215 ..	....	....	....	....	....	....	....	....
Other transport, freight	2 216 ..	....	....	....	....	....	....	....	....
Other transport, other	2 217 ..	....	....	....	....	....	....	....	....
Transportation services, debit	3 205 ..	**−11,048**	**−11,043**	**−11,301**	**−13,613**	**−17,655**	**−20,144**	**−23,133**	**−29,874**
Passenger	3 850 ..	*−813*	*−732*	*−975*	*−960*	*−1,157*	*−1,518*	*−2,138*	*−2,469*
Freight	3 851 ..	*−3,203*	*−3,028*	*−3,698*	*−4,566*	*−6,930*	*−7,997*	*−9,623*	*−13,743*
Other	3 852 ..	*−7,032*	*−7,282*	*−6,628*	*−8,087*	*−9,568*	*−10,629*	*−11,372*	*−13,662*
Sea transport, passenger	3 207 ..	....	....	....	....	....	....	−33	−54
Sea transport, freight	3 208 ..	....	....	....	....	....	....	−9,347	−13,393
Sea transport, other	3 209 ..	....	....	....	....	....	....	−8,917	−10,846
Air transport, passenger	3 211 ..	....	....	....	....	....	....	−2,105	−2,415
Air transport, freight	3 212 ..	....	....	....	....	....	....	−276	−350
Air transport, other	3 213 ..	....	....	....	....	....	....	−2,455	−2,817
Other transport, passenger	3 215 ..	....	....	....	....	....	....	....	....
Other transport, freight	3 216 ..	....	....	....	....	....	....	....	....
Other transport, other	3 217 ..	....	....	....	....	....	....	....	....
Travel, credit	2 236 ..	**6,834**	**6,384**	**5,936**	**5,358**	**6,069**	**5,806**	**5,788**	**5,797**
Business travel	2 237 ..	....	....	....	....	....	....	2,454	2,490
Personal travel	2 240 ..	....	....	....	....	....	....	3,334	3,307
Travel, debit	3 236 ..	**−7,132**	**−7,617**	**−10,465**	**−10,103**	**−12,350**	**−15,406**	**−18,851**	**−20,890**
Business travel	3 237 ..	....	....	....	....	....	....	−3,928	−3,438
Personal travel	3 240 ..	....	....	....	....	....	....	−14,922	−17,452
Other services, credit	2 200 BA	**10,012**	**9,491**	**9,237**	**10,419**	**13,283**	**15,447**	**18,296**	**23,471**
Communications	2 245 ..	387	398	378	341	446	443	642	574
Construction	2 249 ..	29	82	39	37	99	111	133	136
Insurance	2 253 ..	68	60	37	34	139	169	274	319
Financial	2 260 ..	705	533	695	699	1,083	1,651	2,543	4,146
Computer and information	2 262 ..	11	16	20	30	25	57	248	339
Royalties and licence fees	2 266 ..	688	924	835	1,311	1,861	1,908	2,046	1,920
Other business services	2 268 ..	7,200	6,388	6,006	6,687	8,125	9,422	10,532	14,124
Personal, cultural, and recreational	2 287 ..	137	138	185	76	128	268	369	416
Government, n.i.e.	2 291 ..	787	952	1,043	1,203	1,377	1,418	1,509	1,497
Other services, debit	3 200 BA	**−15,201**	**−14,267**	**−14,820**	**−16,665**	**−19,923**	**−23,238**	**−26,868**	**−32,845**
Communications	3 245 ..	−623	−742	−685	−693	−636	−773	−1,012	−930
Construction	3 249 ..	−16	−15	−24	−14	−4	−6	−3	−17
Insurance	3 253 ..	−146	−374	−571	−390	−461	−733	−854	−1,116
Financial	3 260 ..	−191	−83	−70	−101	−127	−235	−547	−711
Computer and information	3 262 ..	−92	−104	−124	−134	−157	−183	−598	−539
Royalties and licence fees	3 266 ..	−3,221	−3,053	−3,002	−3,570	−4,446	−4,561	−4,650	−5,075
Other business services	3 268 ..	−10,328	−9,237	−9,607	−11,049	−13,163	−15,538	−17,705	−22,508
Personal, cultural, and recreational	3 287 ..	−160	−206	−283	−261	−376	−477	−671	−864
Government, n.i.e.	3 291 ..	−425	−454	−454	−453	−554	−733	−828	−1,086

Table 2 (Continued). STANDARD PRESENTATION, 2000–2007

(Millions of U.S. dollars)

	Code	2000	2001	2002	2003	2004	2005	2006	2007
C. INCOME	4 300	**−2,421**	**−1,198**	**432**	**326**	**1,083**	**−1,563**	**534**	**769**
Total credit	2 300	*6,375*	*6,650*	*6,900*	*7,176*	*9,410*	*10,432*	*14,547*	*19,327*
Total debit	3 300	*−8,797*	*−7,848*	*−6,467*	*−6,850*	*−8,328*	*−11,994*	*−14,014*	*−18,558*
Compensation of employees, credit	2 310	**582**	**566**	**590**	**732**	**713**	**745**	**685**	**661**
Compensation of employees, debit	3 310	**−51**	**−69**	**−64**	**−97**	**−126**	**−119**	**−141**	**−185**
Investment income, credit	2 320	**5,794**	**6,084**	**6,309**	**6,444**	**8,697**	**9,687**	**13,862**	**18,666**
Direct investment income	2 330	449	503	475	822	1,559	1,748	2,006	2,151
Dividends and distributed branch profits	2 332	648	629	547	928	1,550	1,732	1,980	2,034
Reinvested earnings and undistributed branch profits	2 333	−248	−167	−104	−164	−8	−7	−2	−1
Income on debt (interest)	2 334	49	41	32	57	16	24	28	118
Portfolio investment income	2 339	3,446	4,492	5,080	5,172	5,786	6,567	9,726	13,552
Income on equity	2 340	22	28	35	114	163	326	779	924
Income on bonds and notes	2 350	....	....	....	....	....	....	....	....
Income on money market instruments	2 360	....	....	....	....	....	....	....	....
Other investment income	2 370	1,899	1,089	754	451	1,352	1,372	2,131	2,963
Investment income, debit	3 320	**−8,746**	**−7,779**	**−6,404**	**−6,752**	**−8,202**	**−11,875**	**−13,873**	**−18,373**
Direct investment income	3 330	−1,194	−1,661	−1,836	−2,240	−2,533	−4,351	−4,176	−5,172
Dividends and distributed branch profits	3 332	−1,157	−1,644	−1,802	−2,223	−2,525	−4,294	−4,115	−5,101
Reinvested earnings and undistributed branch profits	3 333	....	....	....	....	....	....	....	....
Income on debt (interest)	3 334	−37	−17	−34	−17	−8	−57	−61	−71
Portfolio investment income	3 339	−3,126	−2,709	−2,224	−2,468	−3,612	−5,014	−6,012	−7,201
Income on equity	3 340	−687	−600	−640	−1,343	−2,489	−3,025	−3,041	−3,835
Income on bonds and notes	3 350	....	....	....	....	....	....	....	....
Income on money market instruments	3 360	....	....	....	....	....	....	....	....
Other investment income	3 370	−4,427	−3,408	−2,344	−2,044	−2,057	−2,510	−3,685	−6,001
D. CURRENT TRANSFERS	4 379	**566**	**−385**	**−1,618**	**−2,905**	**−2,432**	**−2,482**	**−4,093**	**−3,649**
Credit	2 379	**6,500**	**6,687**	**7,314**	**7,859**	**9,151**	**10,004**	**9,588**	**10,934**
General government	2 380	47	266	125	76	98	188	313	251
Other sectors	2 390	6,453	6,421	7,189	7,784	9,053	9,816	9,275	10,684
Workers' remittances	2 391	63	48	34	42	30	64	138	172
Other current transfers	2 392	6,390	6,373	7,156	7,741	9,022	9,752	9,137	10,512
Debit	3 379	**−5,934**	**−7,072**	**−8,932**	**−10,764**	**−11,583**	**−12,486**	**−13,680**	**−14,583**
General government	3 380	−559	−628	−764	−989	−1,005	−1,252	−1,402	−1,444
Other sectors	3 390	−5,374	−6,444	−8,169	−9,775	−10,578	−11,234	−12,278	−13,139
Workers' remittances	3 391	−227	−239	−297	−359	−559	−839	−982	−1,248
Other current transfers	3 392	−5,147	−6,204	−7,872	−9,416	−10,019	−10,395	−11,296	−11,891
CAPITAL AND FINANCIAL ACCOUNT	4 996	**−11,680**	**−10,984**	**−5,518**	**−11,882**	**−31,069**	**−15,100**	**−4,118**	**−8,877**
CAPITAL ACCOUNT	4 994	**−615**	**−731**	**−1,087**	**−1,398**	**−1,753**	**−2,340**	**−3,126**	**−2,390**
Total credit	2 994	*98*	*42*	*47*	*59*	*72*	*147*	*290*	*522*
Total debit	3 994	*−713*	*−773*	*−1,133*	*−1,457*	*−1,825*	*−2,487*	*−3,416*	*−2,912*
Capital transfers, credit	2 400	**90**	**38**	**38**	**53**	**56**	**38**	**171**	**295**
General government	2 401	....	....	....	....	....	....	....	....
Debt forgiveness	2 402	....	....	....	....	....	....	....	....
Other capital transfers	2 410	....	....	....	....	....	....	....	....
Other sectors	2 430	90	38	38	53	56	38	171	295
Migrants' transfers	2 431	90	38	38	53	56	38	171	295
Debt forgiveness	2 432	....	....	....	....	....	....	....	....
Other capital transfers	2 440	....	....	....	....	....	....	....	....
Capital transfers, debit	3 400	**−694**	**−706**	**−1,113**	**−1,396**	**−1,812**	**−2,378**	**−3,190**	**−2,636**
General government	3 401	....	....	....	....	....	....	....	....
Debt forgiveness	3 402	....	....	....	....	....	....	....	....
Other capital transfers	3 410	....	....	....	....	....	....	....	....
Other sectors	3 430	−694	−706	−1,113	−1,396	−1,812	−2,378	−3,190	−2,636
Migrants' transfers	3 431	−694	−706	−1,113	−1,396	−1,812	−2,378	−3,190	−2,636
Debt forgiveness	3 432	....	....	....	....	....	....	....	....
Other capital transfers	3 440	....	....	....	....	....	....	....	....
Nonproduced nonfinancial assets, credit	2 480	**8**	**4**	**8**	**6**	**16**	**109**	**119**	**228**
Nonproduced nonfinancial assets, debit	3 480	**−19**	**−68**	**−20**	**−61**	**−12**	**−109**	**−226**	**−276**

Table 2 (Continued). STANDARD PRESENTATION, 2000–2007

(Millions of U.S. dollars)

	Code	2000	2001	2002	2003	2004	2005	2006	2007
FINANCIAL ACCOUNT	4 995 ..	**−11,065**	**−10,253**	**−4,431**	**−10,483**	**−29,316**	**−12,760**	**−992**	**−6,487**
A. DIRECT INVESTMENT	4 500 ..	**4,285**	**1,108**	**−224**	**100**	**4,596**	**2,018**	**−4,540**	**−13,697**
Direct investment abroad	4 505 ..	**−4,999**	**−2,420**	**−2,617**	**−3,426**	**−4,650**	**−4,291**	**−8,127**	**−15,276**
Equity capital	4 510 ..	−4,617	−2,192	−2,383	−3,662	−4,213	−3,897	−6,671	−13,278
Claims on affiliated enterprises	4 515 ..	−4,617	−2,192	−2,383	−3,662	−4,213	−3,897	−6,671	−13,278
Liabilities to affiliated enterprises	4 520 ..	....	....	....	....	....	....	....	....
Reinvested earnings	4 525 ..	248	167	104	164	8	7	2	1
Other capital	4 530 ..	−630	−395	−338	73	−445	−401	−1,458	−1,999
Claims on affiliated enterprises	4 535 ..	−630	−395	−338	73	−445	−401	−1,458	−1,999
Liabilities to affiliated enterprises	4 540 ..	....	....	....	....	....	....	....	....
Direct investment in Republic of Korea	4 555 ..	**9,283**	**3,528**	**2,392**	**3,526**	**9,246**	**6,309**	**3,586**	**1,579**
Equity capital	4 560 ..	8,282	3,189	2,033	2,975	7,880	5,775	2,400	561
Claims on direct investors	4 565 ..	....	....	....	....	....	....	....	....
Liabilities to direct investors	4 570 ..	8,282	3,189	2,033	2,975	7,880	5,775	2,400	561
Reinvested earnings	4 575 ..	....	....	....	....	....	....	....	....
Other capital	4 580 ..	1,001	339	360	551	1,366	534	1,186	1,018
Claims on direct investors	4 585 ..	....	....	....	....	....	....	....	....
Liabilities to direct investors	4 590 ..	1,001	339	360	551	1,366	534	1,186	1,018
B. PORTFOLIO INVESTMENT	4 600 ..	**12,177**	**6,706**	**346**	**18,300**	**8,457**	**−23**	**−18,856**	**−24,627**
Assets	4 602 ..	**−520**	**−5,521**	**−5,032**	**−4,390**	**−9,918**	**−14,136**	**−26,912**	**−54,602**
Equity securities	4 610 ..	−480	−492	−1,460	−1,993	−3,622	−3,686	−15,262	−52,436
Monetary authorities	4 611 ..	....	....	....	....	....	....		
General government	4 612 ..	....	....	....	....	....	....	−82	−1,393
Banks	4 613 ..	16	14	−19	−434	−3,303	−3,456	−12,769	−52,047
Other sectors	4 614 ..	−496	−506	−1,441	−1,559	−319	−230	−2,411	1,004
Debt securities	4 619 ..	−40	−5,029	−3,571	−2,397	−6,297	−10,450	−11,650	−2,166
Bonds and notes	4 620 ..	5	−3,819	−4,819	−2,223	−6,080	−10,563	−11,576	−1,807
Monetary authorities	4 621 ..	....	....	....	....				
General government	4 622 ..	....	....	....	....	−3,203	−7,795	−3,557	−100
Banks	4 623 ..	144	−572	−899	258	−325	−841	−3,593	−320
Other sectors	4 624 ..	−140	−3,247	−3,920	−2,481	−2,551	−1,928	−4,426	−1,387
Money market instruments	4 630 ..	−45	−1,210	1,248	−174	−217	113	−75	−359
Monetary authorities	4 631 ..	....	....	....	....	....	....	....	
General government	4 632 ..	....	....	....	....	....	....	....	
Banks	4 633 ..	37	−1,147	1,276	−162	−227	142	−106	−71
Other sectors	4 634 ..	−82	−64	−29	−12	11	−29	31	−288
Liabilities	4 652 ..	**12,697**	**12,227**	**5,378**	**22,690**	**18,375**	**14,114**	**8,056**	**29,974**
Equity securities	4 660 ..	13,094	10,266	395	14,419	9,469	3,282	−8,391	−28,726
Banks	4 663 ..	....	....	....	....	....	....	....	
Other sectors	4 664 ..	....	....	....	....	....	....	....	
Debt securities	4 669 ..	−397	1,962	4,983	8,272	8,906	10,831	16,447	58,700
Bonds and notes	4 670 ..	−1,649	2,926	4,579	8,589	9,038	10,305	16,004	56,587
Monetary authorities	4 671 ..	....	....	....	−15	371	730	928	94
General government	4 672 ..	....	....	309	−11	8	47	62	50
Banks	4 673 ..	199	−1,205	−1,569	4,680	5,442	4,424	6,019	11,898
Other sectors	4 674 ..	−1,848	4,131	5,838	3,934	3,218	5,104	8,995	44,545
Money market instruments	4 680 ..	1,252	−965	404	−317	−132	527	443	2,113
Monetary authorities	4 681 ..	....	....	....	....	....	....	....	
General government	4 682 ..	....	....	....	....	....	....	....	
Banks	4 683 ..	1,200	−1,080	431	−386	−125	632	487	1,695
Other sectors	4 684 ..	52	115	−27	69	−6	−105	−44	417
C. FINANCIAL DERIVATIVES	4 910 ..	**−179**	**−123**	**362**	**−394**	**163**	**−1,706**	**−3,890**	**5,534**
Monetary authorities	4 911 ..	....	....	....	....	....	....	....	
General government	4 912 ..	....	....	....	....	....	....	....	
Banks	4 913 ..	−180	−55	386	−6	646	217	1,425	617
Other sectors	4 914 ..	....	−68	−24	−388	−483	−1,922	−5,314	4,917
Assets	4 900 ..	**532**	**463**	**1,288**	**800**	**2,523**	**3,461**	**4,559**	**12,188**
Monetary authorities	4 901 ..	....	....	....	....	....	....	....	
General government	4 902 ..	....	....	....	....	....	....	....	
Banks	4 903 ..	532	544	1,332	1,216	3,490	6,671	12,184	14,547
Other sectors	4 904 ..	....	−81	−44	−416	−967	−3,210	−7,625	−2,360
Liabilities	4 905 ..	**−711**	**−586**	**−926**	**−1,194**	**−2,360**	**−5,167**	**−8,449**	**−6,654**
Monetary authorities	4 906 ..	....	....	....	....	....	....	....	
General government	4 907 ..	....	....	....	....	....	....	....	
Banks	4 908 ..	−711	−600	−946	−1,221	−2,844	−6,454	−10,759	−13,930
Other sectors	4 909 ..	....	14	20	28	484	1,288	2,311	7,277

Table 2 (Concluded). STANDARD PRESENTATION, 2000–2007

(Millions of U.S. dollars)

	Code	2000	2001	2002	2003	2004	2005	2006	2007
D. OTHER INVESTMENT	4 700	**−3,557**	**−10,358**	**6,854**	**−2,699**	**−3,856**	**6,815**	**48,384**	**41,412**
Assets	4 703	**−2,289**	**7,085**	**1,591**	**−5,132**	**−8,138**	**−2,658**	**−7,945**	**−18,424**
Trade credits	4 706	−634	−875	−515	23	−987	454	−1,591	−2,022
General government	4 707	....	....	....	....	....	....	....	....
of which: Short-term	4 709	....	....	....	....	....	....	....	....
Other sectors	4 710	−634	−875	−515	23	−987	454	−1,591	−2,022
of which: Short-term	4 712	*−885*	*−1,209*	*−689*	*−47*	*−999*	*292*	*−1,613*	*−2,040*
Loans	4 714	−2,239	3,105	4,753	−4,493	−2,386	246	−1,275	−10,325
Monetary authorities	4 715	10	5	8	12	8	10	31	....
of which: Short-term	4 718	....	....	....	....	....	....	....	....
General government	4 719	−81	−117	−153	−99	−1,408	−131	−116	−99
of which: Short-term	4 721	....	....	....	....	....	....	....	....
Banks	4 722	−1,865	2,959	4,962	−4,497	−1,045	786	−751	−9,203
of which: Short-term	4 724	*−2,422*	*2,158*	*4,238*	*−4,705*	*−1,316*	*1,758*	*3,472*	*−916*
Other sectors	4 725	−303	259	−65	91	59	−418	−439	−1,022
of which: Short-term	4 727	*−1,303*	*210*	*31*	*91*	*59*	*−418*	*−301*	*−436*
Currency and deposits	4 730	1,390	2,349	−159	−1,326	−130	−1,247	−1,354	−4,730
Monetary authorities	4 731	....	....	....	....	....	....	....	....
General government	4 732	−74	−392	−158	72	−169	−262	−274	−92
Banks	4 733	−67	2,116	189	−431	−49	−183	−465	−805
Other sectors	4 734	1,530	624	−189	−967	87	−802	−615	−3,833
Other assets	4 736	−807	2,506	−2,488	663	−4,636	−2,111	−3,725	−1,346
Monetary authorities	4 737	−54	−43	−48	−60	−63	−17	−1,331	−132
of which: Short-term	4 739	....	....	....	....	....	....	....	....
General government	4 740	....	....	....	....	....	....	....	....
of which: Short-term	4 742	....	....	....	....	....	....	....	....
Banks	4 743	712	3,680	−2,064	718	−4,573	−2,128	−2,530	−1,214
of which: Short-term	4 745	....	....	....	....	....	....	....	....
Other sectors	4 746	−1,465	−1,131	−376	5	....	35	136	−1
of which: Short-term	4 748	....	....	....	....	....	....	....	....
Liabilities	4 753	**−1,268**	**−17,443**	**5,263**	**2,434**	**4,282**	**9,473**	**56,330**	**59,836**
Trade credits	4 756	4,282	−3,071	3,289	6,301	8,088	7,780	13,091	13,547
General government	4 757	....	....	....	....	....	....	....	....
of which: Short-term	4 759	....	....	....	....	....	....	....	....
Other sectors	4 760	4,282	−3,071	3,289	6,301	8,088	7,780	13,091	13,547
of which: Short-term	4 762	*4,323*	*−2,916*	*2,722*	*1,410*	*3,160*	*5,018*	*7,073*	*989*
Loans	4 764	−4,858	−13,215	1,934	−5,032	−935	1,022	44,180	41,554
Monetary authorities	4 765	....	−5,692	....	....	....	....	....	....
of which: Use of Fund credit and loans from the Fund..	4 766	....	−5,692	....	....	....	....	....	....
of which: Short-term	4 768	....	....	....	....	....	....	....	....
General government	4 769	110	−397	−1,436	−5,255	−2,549	−2,602	−924	−873
of which: Short-term	4 771	....	....	....	....	....	....	....	....
Banks	4 772	−4,992	−2,936	6,004	1,075	2,027	4,410	44,914	39,447
of which: Short-term	4 774	*−1,804*	*−3,193*	*6,162*	*648*	*3,515*	*5,538*	*42,568*	*33,210*
Other sectors	4 775	23	−4,191	−2,634	−852	−414	−787	189	2,980
of which: Short-term	4 777	*844*	*−1,011*	*−1,080*	*−582*	*−220*	*186*	*−128*	*755*
Currency and deposits	4 780	−869	−971	−153	840	−2,650	−717	−2,416	5,496
Monetary authorities	4 781	....	....	....	....	....	....	....	....
General government	4 782	....	....	....	....	....	....	....	....
Banks	4 783	324	−1,212	−49	239	−440	64	−2,598	2,133
Other sectors	4 784	−1,193	241	−104	601	−2,211	−780	183	3,363
Other liabilities	4 786	177	−186	192	325	−220	1,387	1,475	−761
Monetary authorities	4 787	28	63	−52	−35	−10	433	1,596	270
of which: Short-term	4 789	....	....	....	....	....	....	....	....
General government	4 790	....	....	....	....	....	....	....	....
of which: Short-term	4 792	....	....	....	....	....	....	....	....
Banks	4 793	130	1	302	−645	−434	1,259	−121	−1,031
of which: Short-term	4 795	....	....	....	....	....	....	....	....
Other sectors	4 796	19	−250	−59	1,005	224	−305	....	....
of which: Short-term	4 798	....	....	....	....	....	....	....	....
E. RESERVE ASSETS	4 802	**−23,790**	**−7,586**	**−11,769**	**−25,791**	**−38,675**	**−19,864**	**−22,090**	**−15,109**
Monetary gold	4 812	−1	−1	−1	−2	−1	−1	−1	....
Special drawing rights	4 811	−7	....	−8	−8	−10	−14	−8	−11
Reserve position in the Fund	4 810	....	....	−228	−175	....	425	−114	146
Foreign exchange	4 803	−23,783	−7,585	−11,532	−25,607	−38,663	−20,274	−21,968	−15,243
Other claims	4 813	....	....	....	....	....	....	....	....
NET ERRORS AND OMISSIONS	4 998	**−571**	**2,951**	**124**	**−68**	**2,895**	**119**	**−1,267**	**2,922**

Table 3. INTERNATIONAL INVESTMENT POSITION (End-period stocks), 2000–2007

(Millions of U.S. dollars)

	Code	2000	2001	2002	2003	2004	2005	2006	2007
ASSETS	8 995 C.	....	**185,042**	**206,818**	**255,996**	**325,021**	**359,968**	**451,316**	**587,643**
Direct investment abroad	8 505 ..	....	**19,967**	**20,735**	**24,986**	**32,166**	**38,683**	**49,187**	**66,225**
Equity capital and reinvested earnings	8 506 ..	....	18,236	18,742	23,045	30,041	35,741	45,652	60,552
Claims on affiliated enterprises	8 507 ..	....	18,236	18,742	23,045	30,041	35,741	45,652	60,552
Liabilities to affiliated enterprises	8 508 ..	....	....	....	....	....	....	....	....
Other capital	8 530 ..	....	1,731	1,993	1,942	2,124	2,942	3,535	5,673
Claims on affiliated enterprises	8 535 ..	....	1,731	1,993	1,942	2,124	2,942	3,535	5,673
Liabilities to affiliated enterprises	8 540 ..	....	....	....	....	....	....	....	....
Portfolio investment	8 602 ..	....	**7,928**	**11,551**	**17,394**	**28,371**	**43,668**	**83,521**	**158,734**
Equity securities	8 610 ..	....	1,156	1,794	3,416	9,009	13,914	36,819	106,110
Monetary authorities	8 611 ..	....	....	....	....	....	....	....	....
General government	8 612 ..	....	....	....	....	....	....	....	9,865
Banks	8 613 ..	....	271	582	1,347	5,625	9,774	28,119	76,286
Other sectors	8 614 ..	....	885	1,212	2,068	3,384	4,139	8,700	19,959
Debt securities	8 619 ..	....	6,773	9,757	13,978	19,362	29,755	46,702	52,625
Bonds and notes	8 620 ..	....	5,322	9,667	13,878	19,097	29,583	46,491	52,228
Monetary authorities	8 621 ..	....	....	....	....	....	....	....	....
General government	8 622 ..	....	....	....	49	3,057	10,365	13,829	16,636
Banks	8 623 ..	....	2,510	2,771	2,847	3,204	4,211	9,044	8,246
Other sectors	8 624 ..	....	2,812	6,896	10,981	12,835	15,007	23,618	27,345
Money market instruments	8 630 ..	....	1,451	90	101	265	171	211	397
Monetary authorities	8 631 ..	....	....	....	....	....	....	....	....
General government	8 632 ..	....	....	....	....	....	....	....	....
Banks	8 633 ..	....	1,411	39	22	229	123	185	42
Other sectors	8 634 ..	....	40	51	79	37	49	26	355
Financial derivatives	8 900 ..	....	**414**	**917**	**777**	**1,078**	**1,009**	**1,392**	**2,303**
Monetary authorities	8 901 ..	....	....	....	....	....	....	....	....
General government	8 902 ..	....	....	....	....	....	....	....	....
Banks	8 903 ..	....	414	917	777	1,078	1,009	1,392	2,303
Other sectors	8 904 ..	....	....	....	....	....	....	....	....
Other investment	8 703 ..	....	**53,911**	**52,202**	**57,483**	**64,337**	**66,217**	**78,260**	**98,156**
Trade credits	8 706 ..	....	9,942	7,931	9,766	8,787	9,526	12,792	15,936
General government	8 707 ..	....	....	....	....	....	....	....	....
of which: Short-term	8 709 ..	....	....	....	....	....	....	....	....
Other sectors	8 710 ..	....	9,942	7,931	9,766	8,787	9,526	12,792	15,936
of which: Short-term	8 712 ..	....	*9,433*	*7,510*	*9,412*	*8,445*	*9,374*	*12,667*	*15,832*
Loans	8 714 ..	....	20,477	17,539	21,160	23,911	23,213	25,471	35,801
Monetary authorities	8 715 ..	....	69	61	49	41	31	....	....
of which: Short-term	8 718 ..	....	....	....	....	....	....	....	....
General government	8 719 ..	....	555	769	869	2,346	2,470	2,666	2,715
of which: Short-term	8 721 ..	....	....	....	....	....	....	....	....
Banks	8 722 ..	....	18,566	16,303	19,845	21,277	20,580	21,717	31,111
of which: Short-term	8 724 ..	....	*8,651*	*7,493*	*11,163*	*12,453*	*10,549*	*7,127*	*8,614*
Other sectors	8 725 ..	....	1,286	406	398	248	132	1,088	1,976
of which: Short-term	8 727 ..	....	*3*	*4*	....	....	....	....	*370*
Currency and deposits	8 730 ..	....	3,709	3,816	4,556	4,064	4,108	5,599	9,724
Monetary authorities	8 731 ..	....	....	....	....	....	....	....	....
General government	8 732 ..	....	394	316	315	348	381	431	525
Banks	8 733 ..	....	2,756	2,575	3,164	3,237	3,419	4,331	4,524
Other sectors	8 734 ..	....	559	926	1,077	479	307	836	4,675
Other assets	8 736 ..	....	19,784	22,915	22,001	27,575	29,370	34,398	36,695
Monetary authorities	8 737 ..	....	2,377	2,297	2,141	2,493	3,019	4,980	5,236
of which: Short-term	8 739 ..	....	*1,777*	*1,612*	*1,384*	*1,605*	*2,003*	*3,882*	*4,048*
General government	8 740 ..	....	25	27	27	29	29	30	30
of which: Short-term	8 742 ..	....	*15*	*16*	*17*	*18*	*18*	*19*	*20*
Banks	8 743 ..	....	17,087	19,957	18,977	24,207	25,403	28,679	30,835
of which: Short-term	8 745 ..	....	*16,687*	*19,660*	*18,532*	*23,810*	*25,241*	*28,533*	*30,664*
Other sectors	8 746 ..	....	296	635	856	847	919	710	594
of which: Short-term	8 748 ..	....	*271*	*419*	*544*	*293*	*485*	*393*	*555*
Reserve assets	8 802 ..	....	**102,822**	**121,415**	**155,355**	**199,069**	**210,391**	**238,957**	**262,224**
Monetary gold	8 812 ..	....	68	69	71	72	74	74	74
Special drawing rights	8 811 ..	4	3	12	21	33	44	54	69
Reserve position in the Fund	8 810 ..	272	262	522	754	788	306	440	311
Foreign exchange	8 803 ..	....	102,488	120,812	154,509	198,175	209,968	238,388	261,771
Other claims	8 813 ..	....	....	....	....	....	....	....	....

Table 3 (Concluded). INTERNATIONAL INVESTMENT POSITION (End-period stocks), 2000–2007

(Millions of U.S. dollars)

	Code	2000	2001	2002	2003	2004	2005	2006	2007
LIABILITIES	8 995 D.	....	**248,825**	**277,173**	**337,755**	**413,494**	**539,444**	**652,264**	**820,102**
Direct investment in Republic of Korea	8 555 ..	....	**53,208**	**62,658**	**66,070**	**87,766**	**104,879**	**119,143**	**119,631**
Equity capital and reinvested earnings	8 556 ..	....	49,719	59,101	62,704	83,914	100,768	113,393	112,922
Claims on direct investors	8 557 ..	....	....	....	....	....	....	....	....
Liabilities to direct investors	8 558 ..	....	49,719	59,101	62,704	83,914	100,768	113,393	112,922
Other capital	8 580 ..	....	3,489	3,558	3,366	3,852	4,112	5,750	6,709
Claims on direct investors	8 585 ..	....	....	....	....	....	....	....	....
Liabilities to direct investors	8 590 ..	....	3,489	3,558	3,366	3,852	4,112	5,750	6,709
Portfolio investment	8 652 ..	....	**106,387**	**116,201**	**165,029**	**210,313**	**310,456**	**352,393**	**456,506**
Equity securities	8 660 ..	....	70,002	75,666	116,758	156,417	249,475	276,388	320,065
Banks	8 663 ..	....	10,361	11,196	18,092	22,826	38,503	42,622	49,514
Other sectors	8 664 ..	....	59,642	64,470	98,666	133,590	210,972	233,766	270,552
Debt securities	8 669 ..	....	36,385	40,535	48,271	53,897	60,981	76,005	136,441
Bonds and notes	8 670 ..	....	35,960	39,157	47,265	53,306	59,638	73,577	128,832
Monetary authorities	8 671 ..	....	2,608	2,470	2,745	3,512	4,292	5,194	12,704
General government	8 672 ..	....	388	913	1,261	2,237	3,005	5,664	28,131
Banks	8 673 ..	....	14,249	11,999	17,161	22,559	26,001	32,007	46,578
Other sectors	8 674 ..	....	18,716	23,775	26,099	24,999	26,339	30,712	41,419
Money market instruments	8 680 ..	....	425	1,379	1,005	591	1,343	2,428	7,609
Monetary authorities	8 681 ..	....	212	372	669	311	300	150	4,259
General government	8 682 ..	....	1	2	2	....	....	2	1
Banks	8 683 ..	....	121	979	260	171	1,026	2,226	3,231
Other sectors	8 684 ..	....	92	26	73	109	17	50	118
Financial derivatives	8 905 ..	....	**417**	**936**	**899**	**904**	**1,319**	**2,423**	**4,933**
Monetary authorities	8 906 ..	....	....	....	....	....	....	....	....
General government	8 907 ..	....	....	....	....	....	....	....	....
Banks	8 908 ..	....	417	936	899	904	1,319	2,423	4,933
Other sectors	8 909 ..	....	....	....	....	....	....	....	....
Other investment	8 753 ..	....	**88,814**	**97,378**	**105,758**	**114,510**	**122,789**	**178,305**	**239,033**
Trade credits	8 756 ..	....	13,299	13,641	20,225	27,307	33,210	42,351	55,349
General government	8 757 ..	....	....	....	....	....	....	....	....
of which: Short-term	8 759 ..	....	....	....	....	....	....	....	....
Other sectors	8 760 ..	....	13,299	13,641	20,225	27,307	33,210	42,351	55,349
of which: Short-term	8 762 ..	....	*5,919*	*4,889*	*4,442*	*5,625*	*6,680*	*7,386*	*8,188*
Loans	8 764 ..	....	67,297	73,216	73,780	73,968	75,635	119,468	160,214
Monetary authorities	8 765 ..	....	....	....	....	....	....	....	....
of which: Use of Fund credit and loans from the Fund	8 766 ..	5,814	....	....	....	....	....	....	....
of which: Short-term	8 768 ..	....	....	....	....	....	....	....	....
General government	8 769 ..	....	17,883	16,662	10,300	8,143	5,448	4,601	3,787
of which: Short-term	8 771 ..	....	....	....	....	....	....	....	....
Banks	8 772 ..	....	34,193	41,271	46,077	46,993	51,181	96,182	135,398
of which: Short-term	8 774 ..	....	*27,359*	*32,953*	*36,285*	*39,511*	*45,030*	*87,748*	*121,746*
Other sectors	8 775 ..	....	15,221	15,283	17,402	18,832	19,006	18,685	21,029
of which: Short-term	8 777 ..	....	*1,598*	*1,676*	*1,505*	*1,812*	*2,238*	*2,188*	*2,356*
Currency and deposits	8 780 ..	....	4,239	5,712	6,408	7,722	9,027	11,806	17,149
Monetary authorities	8 781 ..	....	1,664	1,608	1,433	1,665	1,923	3,756	3,923
General government	8 782 ..	....	....	....	....	....	....	....	1
Banks	8 783 ..	....	2,294	3,210	3,772	4,026	4,361	4,625	6,503
Other sectors	8 784 ..	....	281	894	1,203	2,031	2,743	3,424	6,722
Other liabilities	8 786 ..	....	3,979	4,808	5,345	5,514	4,917	4,680	6,320
Monetary authorities	8 787 ..	....	409	453	452	496	553	510	511
of which: Short-term	8 789 ..	....	....	....	....	....	....	....	....
General government	8 790 ..	....	9	10	10	9	11	12	12
of which: Short-term	8 792 ..	....	....	....	....	....	....	....	....
Banks	8 793 ..	....	444	1,012	459	743	860	1,493	2,335
of which: Short-term	8 795 ..	....	*444*	*1,012*	*459*	*743*	*860*	*1,493*	*2,335*
Other sectors	8 796 ..	....	3,118	3,334	4,425	4,267	3,493	2,665	3,462
of which: Short-term	8 798 ..	....	*309*	*558*	*702*	*344*	*734*	*698*	*882*
NET INTERNATIONAL INVESTMENT POSITION	8 995 ..	....	**–63,783**	**–70,355**	**–81,759**	**–88,474**	**–179,476**	**–200,948**	**–232,459**
Conversion rates: won per U.S. dollar (end of period)	0 102 ..	**1,264.5**	**1,313.5**	**1,186.2**	**1,192.6**	**1,035.1**	**1,011.6**	**929.8**	**936.1**

Table 1. ANALYTIC PRESENTATION, 2000–2007

(Millions of U.S. dollars)

	Code	2000	2001	2002	2003	2004	2005	2006	2007
A. Current Account[1]	4 993 Z.	**14,672**	**8,324**	**4,265**	**9,424**	**18,162**	**34,308**	**51,571**	**47,471**
Goods: exports f.o.b.	2 100 ..	19,478	16,237	15,367	21,794	30,089	46,971	58,638	63,681
Goods: imports f.o.b.	3 100 ..	−6,451	−7,047	−8,117	−9,880	−11,663	−14,238	−14,331	−20,625
Balance on Goods	4 100 ..	*13,027*	*9,190*	*7,250*	*11,914*	*18,426*	*32,733*	*44,308*	*43,056*
Services: credit	2 200 ..	1,823	1,664	1,648	3,144	3,743	4,723	7,931	9,636
Services: debit	3 200 ..	−4,921	−5,355	−5,838	−6,615	−7,586	−8,604	−10,215	−13,082
Balance on Goods and Services	4 991 ..	*9,929*	*5,499*	*3,059*	*8,443*	*14,583*	*28,852*	*42,023*	*39,610*
Income: credit	2 300 ..	7,315	5,427	3,716	3,733	6,584	9,413	14,667	15,688
Income: debit	3 300 ..	−616	−524	−369	−372	−456	−556	−1,499	−2,751
Balance on Goods, Services, and Income	4 992 ..	*16,628*	*10,403*	*6,406*	*11,804*	*20,712*	*37,709*	*55,191*	*52,547*
Current transfers: credit	2 379 Z.	85	53	50	66	88	86	113	127
Current transfers: debit	3 379 ..	−2,041	−2,132	−2,192	−2,446	−2,638	−3,487	−3,733	−5,203
B. Capital Account[1]	4 994 Z.	**2,217**	**2,931**	**1,672**	**1,431**	**433**	**797**	**882**	**1,573**
Capital account: credit	2 994 Z.	2,236	2,950	1,707	1,463	474	824	916	1,596
Capital account: debit	3 994 ..	−20	−18	−35	−32	−40	−27	−34	−23
Total, Groups A Plus B	4 981 ..	*16,889*	*11,255*	*5,937*	*10,856*	*18,595*	*35,104*	*52,453*	*49,044*
C. Financial Account[1]	4 995 W.	**−13,779**	**−5,478**	**−5,038**	**−12,106**	**−16,836**	**−31,087**	**−47,962**	**−37,285**
Direct investment abroad	4 505 ..	303	1,914	77	4,960	−2,526	−5,142	−8,177	−13,682
Direct investment in Kuwait	4 555 Z.	16	−112	4	−67	24	234	121	119
Portfolio investment assets	4 602 ..	−12,923	−8,641	−3,388	−13,708	−14,223	−10,016	−25,758	−33,575
Equity securities	4 610 ..	....	....	....	....	....	....	....	....
Debt securities	4 619 ..	−12,923	−8,641	−3,388	−13,708	−14,223	−10,016	−25,758	−33,575
Portfolio investment liabilities	4 652 Z.	254	−79	162	334	288	−459	45	675
Equity securities	4 660 ..	....	....	....	....	....	....	....	....
Debt securities	4 669 Z.	254	−79	162	334	288	−459	45	675
Financial derivatives	4 910 ..	....	....	....	....	....	....	....	....
Financial derivatives assets	4 900 ..	....	....	....	....	....	....	....	....
Financial derivatives liabilities	4 905 ..	....	....	....	....	....	....	....	....
Other investment assets	4 703 ..	−1,109	230	−3,751	−3,391	−292	−19,963	−23,947	−10,915
Monetary authorities	4 701 ..	....	....	....	....	....	....	....	....
General government	4 704 ..	−284	920	−3,877	−3,319	2,043	−18,163	−17,867	−3,743
Banks	4 705 ..	−1,004	244	−599	58	−2,148	−1,622	−4,382	−6,337
Other sectors	4 728 ..	179	−934	725	−130	−187	−178	−1,698	−835
Other investment liabilities	4 753 W.	−321	1,209	1,859	−234	−107	4,260	9,754	20,093
Monetary authorities	4 753 WA	2	−2	26	30	34	259	94	47
General government	4 753 ZB	−838	−31	404	−179	−28	836	352	2,848
Banks	4 753 ZC	−297	1,303	1,355	−549	−419	1,988	2,984	11,004
Other sectors	4 753 ZD	812	−61	74	464	306	1,176	6,323	6,194
Total, Groups A Through C	4 983 ..	*3,110*	*5,777*	*899*	*−1,250*	*1,759*	*4,018*	*4,490*	*11,759*
D. Net Errors and Omissions	4 998 ..	**−842**	**−2,869**	**−1,869**	**−574**	**−1,130**	**−3,398**	**−907**	**−8,541**
Total, Groups A Through D	4 984 ..	*2,268*	*2,908*	*−970*	*−1,824*	*629*	*619*	*3,583*	*3,218*
E. Reserves and Related Items	4 802 A.	**−2,268**	**−2,908**	**970**	**1,824**	**−629**	**−619**	**−3,583**	**−3,218**
Reserve assets	4 802 ..	−2,268	−2,908	970	1,824	−629	−619	−3,583	−3,218
Use of Fund credit and loans	4 766 ..	....	....	....	....	....	....	....	....
Exceptional financing	4 920 ..	....	....	....	....	....	....	....	....
Conversion rates: Kuwaiti dinar per U.S. dollar	0 101 ..	**.3068**	**.3067**	**.3039**	**.2980**	**.2947**	**.2920**	**.2902**	**.2842**

[1] Excludes components that have been classified in the categories of Group E.

2008, International Monetary Fund: *Balance of Payments Statistics Yearbook*

Table 2. STANDARD PRESENTATION, 2000–2007

(Millions of U.S. dollars)

	Code	2000	2001	2002	2003	2004	2005	2006	2007
CURRENT ACCOUNT...	4 993 ..	**14,672**	**8,324**	**4,265**	**9,424**	**18,162**	**34,308**	**51,571**	**47,471**
A. GOODS...	4 100 ..	**13,027**	**9,190**	**7,250**	**11,914**	**18,426**	**32,733**	**44,308**	**43,056**
Credit..	2 100 ..	**19,478**	**16,237**	**15,367**	**21,794**	**30,089**	**46,971**	**58,638**	**63,681**
General merchandise: exports f.o.b.............	2 110 ..	19,478	16,237	15,367	21,794	30,089	46,971	58,638	63,681
Goods for processing: exports f.o.b.............	2 150 ..	....	....	....	....	....	....	....	....
Repairs on goods..	2 160 ..	....	....	....	....	....	....	....	....
Goods procured in ports by carriers.............	2 170 ..	....	....	....	....	....	....	....	....
Nonmonetary gold......................................	2 180 ..	....	....	....	....	....	....	....	....
Debit...	3 100 ..	**−6,451**	**−7,047**	**−8,117**	**−9,880**	**−11,663**	**−14,238**	**−14,331**	**−20,625**
General merchandise: imports f.o.b.............	3 110 ..	−6,451	−7,047	−8,117	−9,880	−11,663	−14,238	−14,331	−20,625
Goods for processing: imports f.o.b.............	3 150 ..	....	....	....	....	....	....	....	....
Repairs on goods..	3 160 ..	....	....	....	....	....	....	....	....
Goods procured in ports by carriers.............	3 170 ..	....	....	....	....	....	....	....	....
Nonmonetary gold......................................	3 180 ..	....	....	....	....	....	....	....	....
B. SERVICES...	4 200 ..	**−3,098**	**−3,691**	**−4,190**	**−3,471**	**−3,843**	**−3,881**	**−2,284**	**−3,446**
Total credit	2 200 ..	*1,823*	*1,664*	*1,648*	*3,144*	*3,743*	*4,723*	*7,931*	*9,636*
Total debit	3 200 ..	*−4,921*	*−5,355*	*−5,838*	*−6,615*	*−7,586*	*−8,604*	*−10,215*	*−13,082*
Transportation services, credit.............	2 205 ..	**1,383**	**1,205**	**1,129**	**1,516**	**1,683**	**2,211**	**2,665**	**2,924**
Passenger	2 850 ..	*296*	*180*	*203*	*210*	*234*	*245*	*264*	*289*
Freight	2 851 ..	*1,066*	*1,004*	*905*	*1,200*	*1,343*	*1,858*	*2,293*	*2,555*
Other	2 852 ..	*21*	*21*	*21*	*106*	*107*	*108*	*108*	*80*
Sea transport, passenger...........................	2 207 ..	....	....	....	....	....	....	....	....
Sea transport, freight.................................	2 208 ..	....	....	....	....	....	....	....	....
Sea transport, other..................................	2 209 ..	....	....	....	....	....	....	....	....
Air transport, passenger............................	2 211 ..	....	....	....	....	....	....	....	....
Air transport, freight.................................	2 212 ..	....	....	....	....	....	....	....	....
Air transport, other...................................	2 213 ..	....	....	....	....	....	....	....	....
Other transport, passenger.........................	2 215 ..	....	....	....	....	....	....	....	....
Other transport, freight..............................	2 216 ..	....	....	....	....	....	....	....	....
Other transport, other................................	2 217 ..	....	....	....	....	....	....	....	....
Transportation services, debit...............	3 205 ..	**−1,536**	**−1,574**	**−1,747**	**−2,026**	**−2,297**	**−2,789**	**−2,862**	**−3,974**
Passenger	3 850 ..	*−357*	*−365*	*−391*	*−402*	*−447*	*−464*	*−501*	*−550*
Freight	3 851 ..	*−1,130*	*−1,161*	*−1,306*	*−1,573*	*−1,793*	*−2,271*	*−2,307*	*−3,365*
Other	3 852 ..	*−49*	*−49*	*−50*	*−51*	*−57*	*−55*	*−55*	*−59*
Sea transport, passenger...........................	3 207 ..	....	....	....	....	....	....	....	....
Sea transport, freight.................................	3 208 ..	....	....	....	....	....	....	....	....
Sea transport, other..................................	3 209 ..	....	....	....	....	....	....	....	....
Air transport, passenger............................	3 211 ..	....	....	....	....	....	....	....	....
Air transport, freight.................................	3 212 ..	....	....	....	....	....	....	....	....
Air transport, other...................................	3 213 ..	....	....	....	....	....	....	....	....
Other transport, passenger.........................	3 215 ..	....	....	....	....	....	....	....	....
Other transport, freight..............................	3 216 ..	....	....	....	....	....	....	....	....
Other transport, other................................	3 217 ..	....	....	....	....	....	....	....	....
Travel, credit.....................................	2 236 ..	**98**	**106**	**117**	**118**	**178**	**165**	**205**	**223**
Business travel..	2 237 ..	98	106	117	118	178	165	205	223
Personal travel...	2 240 ..	....	....	....	....	....	....	....	....
Travel, debit......................................	3 236 ..	**−2,495**	**−2,842**	**−3,021**	**−3,348**	**−3,701**	**−4,277**	**−5,253**	**−6,128**
Business travel..	3 237 ..	−2,495	−2,842	−3,021	−3,348	−3,701	−4,277	−5,253	−6,128
Personal travel...	3 240 ..	....	....	....	....	....	....	....	....
Other services, credit...........................	2 200 BA ..	**342**	**353**	**402**	**1,509**	**1,881**	**2,347**	**5,061**	**6,489**
Communications.......................................	2 245 ..	....	....	....	....	506	1,295	3,398	4,667
Construction...	2 249 ..	....	....	....	....	....	....	....	....
Insurance..	2 253 ..	72	70	109	83	79	83	64	68
Financial...	2 260 ..	18	20	17	46	42	35	35	53
Computer and information.........................	2 262 ..	....	....	....	....	....	....	....	....
Royalties and licence fees..........................	2 266 ..	....	....	....	....	....	....	....	....
Other business services.............................	2 268 ..	....	....	....	....	....	....	615	637
Personal, cultural, and recreational.............	2 287 ..	....	....	....	....	....	....	....	....
Government, n.i.e.......................................	2 291 ..	252	263	275	1,380	1,255	934	949	1,064
Other services, debit............................	3 200 BA ..	**−890**	**−938**	**−1,070**	**−1,242**	**−1,587**	**−1,538**	**−2,099**	**−2,981**
Communications.......................................	3 245 ..	....	....	....	....	−122	−96	−93	−89
Construction...	3 249 ..	−26	−40	−41	−42	−42	−42	−43	−45
Insurance..	3 253 ..	−58	−63	−72	−88	−101	−126	−128	−189
Financial...	3 260 ..	....	....	....	−31	−29	−2	−2	−6
Computer and information.........................	3 262 ..	....	....	....	....	....	....	....	....
Royalties and licence fees..........................	3 266 ..	....	....	....	....	....	....	....	....
Other business services.............................	3 268 ..	....	....	....	....	....	....	....	....
Personal, cultural, and recreational.............	3 287 ..	....	....	....	....	....	....	....	....
Government, n.i.e.......................................	3 291 ..	−806	−835	−958	−1,081	−1,293	−1,271	−1,833	−2,652

Table 2 (Continued). STANDARD PRESENTATION, 2000–2007

(Millions of U.S. dollars)

	Code	2000	2001	2002	2003	2004	2005	2006	2007
C. INCOME....................	4 300 ..	**6,699**	**4,903**	**3,347**	**3,361**	**6,129**	**8,857**	**13,167**	**12,937**
Total credit....................	2 300 ..	*7,315*	*5,427*	*3,716*	*3,733*	*6,584*	*9,413*	*14,667*	*15,688*
Total debit....................	3 300 ..	*−616*	*−524*	*−369*	*−372*	*−456*	*−556*	*−1,499*	*−2,751*
Compensation of employees, credit..........	2 310 ..	....	....	....	....	....	....	....	....
Compensation of employees, debit..........	3 310 ..	....	....	....	....	....	....	....	....
Investment income, credit....................	2 320 ..	**7,315**	**5,427**	**3,716**	**3,733**	**6,584**	**9,413**	**14,667**	**15,688**
Direct investment income....................	2 330 ..	....	....	....	....	....	....	....	....
Dividends and distributed branch profits..........	2 332 ..	....	....	....	....	....	....	....	....
Reinvested earnings and undistributed branch profits.....	2 333 ..	....	....	....	....	....	....	....	....
Income on debt (interest)....................	2 334 ..	....	....	....	....	....	....	....	....
Portfolio investment income....................	2 339 ..	....	....	....	....	....	....	....	....
Income on equity....................	2 340 ..	....	....	....	....	....	....	....	....
Income on bonds and notes....................	2 350 ..	....	....	....	....	....	....	....	....
Income on money market instruments..........	2 360 ..	....	....	....	....	....	....	....	....
Other investment income....................	2 370 ..	7,315	5,427	3,716	3,733	6,584	9,413	14,667	15,688
Investment income, debit....................	3 320 ..	**−616**	**−524**	**−369**	**−372**	**−456**	**−556**	**−1,499**	**−2,751**
Direct investment income....................	3 330 ..	....	....	....	....	....	....	....	....
Dividends and distributed branch profits..........	3 332 ..	....	....	....	....	....	....	....	....
Reinvested earnings and undistributed branch profits.....	3 333 ..	....	....	....	....	....	....	....	....
Income on debt (interest)....................	3 334 ..	....	....	....	....	....	....	....	....
Portfolio investment income....................	3 339 ..	....	....	....	....	....	....	....	....
Income on equity....................	3 340 ..	....	....	....	....	....	....	....	....
Income on bonds and notes....................	3 350 ..	....	....	....	....	....	....	....	....
Income on money market instruments..........	3 360 ..	....	....	....	....	....	....	....	....
Other investment income....................	3 370 ..	−616	−524	−369	−372	−456	−556	−1,499	−2,751
D. CURRENT TRANSFERS....................	4 379 ..	**−1,956**	**−2,079**	**−2,142**	**−2,379**	**−2,550**	**−3,401**	**−3,620**	**−5,076**
Credit....................	2 379 ..	**85**	**53**	**50**	**66**	**88**	**86**	**113**	**127**
General government....................	2 380 ..	85	53	50	66	88	86	113	127
Other sectors....................	2 390 ..	....	....	....	....	....	....	....	....
Workers' remittances....................	2 391 ..	....	....	....	....	....	....	....	....
Other current transfers....................	2 392 ..	....	....	....	....	....	....	....	....
Debit....................	3 379 ..	**−2,041**	**−2,132**	**−2,192**	**−2,446**	**−2,638**	**−3,487**	**−3,733**	**−5,203**
General government....................	3 380 ..	−225	−259	−173	−189	−162	−715	−405	−574
Other sectors....................	3 390 ..	−1,816	−1,873	−2,019	−2,257	−2,476	−2,772	−3,328	−4,630
Workers' remittances....................	3 391 ..	−1,734	−1,785	−1,926	−2,144	−2,403	−2,648	−3,183	−3,824
Other current transfers....................	3 392 ..	−81	−88	−93	−113	−74	−124	−145	−806
CAPITAL AND FINANCIAL ACCOUNT..........	4 996 ..	**−13,830**	**−5,455**	**−2,396**	**−8,850**	**−17,032**	**−30,909**	**−50,664**	**−38,930**
CAPITAL ACCOUNT....................	4 994 ..	**2,217**	**2,931**	**1,672**	**1,431**	**433**	**797**	**882**	**1,573**
Total credit....................	2 994 ..	*2,236*	*2,950*	*1,707*	*1,463*	*474*	*824*	*916*	*1,596*
Total debit....................	3 994 ..	*−20*	*−18*	*−35*	*−32*	*−40*	*−27*	*−34*	*−23*
Capital transfers, credit....................	2 400 ..	**2,236**	**2,950**	**1,707**	**1,463**	**474**	**824**	**916**	**1,596**
General government....................	2 401 ..	88	1,227	318	703	3	55	498	1,361
Debt forgiveness....................	2 402 ..	....	....	....	....	....	....	....	....
Other capital transfers....................	2 410 ..	88	1,227	318	703	3	55	498	1,361
Other sectors....................	2 430 ..	2,148	1,723	1,389	761	471	770	418	235
Migrants' transfers....................	2 431 ..	....	....	....	....	....	....	....	....
Debt forgiveness....................	2 432 ..	....	....	....	....	....	....	....	....
Other capital transfers....................	2 440 ..	2,148	1,723	1,389	761	471	770	418	235
Capital transfers, debit....................	3 400 ..	**−20**	**−18**	**−35**	**−32**	**−40**	**−27**	**−34**	**−23**
General government....................	3 401 ..	−20	−18	−35	−32	−40	−27	−34	−23
Debt forgiveness....................	3 402 ..	....	....	....	....	....	....	....	....
Other capital transfers....................	3 410 ..	−20	−18	−35	−32	−40	−27	−34	−23
Other sectors....................	3 430 ..	....	....	....	....	....	....	....	....
Migrants' transfers....................	3 431 ..	....	....	....	....	....	....	....	....
Debt forgiveness....................	3 432 ..	....	....	....	....	....	....	....	....
Other capital transfers....................	3 440 ..	....	....	....	....	....	....	....	....
Nonproduced nonfinancial assets, credit..........	2 480 ..	....	....	....	....	....	....	....	....
Nonproduced nonfinancial assets, debit..........	3 480 ..	....	....	....	....	....	....	....	....

Table 2 (Continued). STANDARD PRESENTATION, 2000–2007

(Millions of U.S. dollars)

	Code	2000	2001	2002	2003	2004	2005	2006	2007
FINANCIAL ACCOUNT...............	4 995 ..	**−16,047**	**−8,386**	**−4,068**	**−10,281**	**−17,465**	**−31,706**	**−51,545**	**−40,503**
A. DIRECT INVESTMENT..................	4 500 ..	**319**	**1,802**	**80**	**4,893**	**−2,502**	**−4,908**	**−8,056**	**−13,563**
Direct investment abroad...............	4 505 ..	**303**	**1,914**	**77**	**4,960**	**−2,526**	**−5,142**	**−8,177**	**−13,682**
Equity capital...............................	4 510 ..	−346	−14	−1,038	−789	−2,556	−5,868	−8,201	−13,693
Claims on affiliated enterprises...........	4 515 ..	−346	−14	−1,038	−789	−2,556	−5,868	−8,201	−13,693
Liabilities to affiliated enterprises........	4 520 ..	....	....	....	....	....	....	....	....
Reinvested earnings..........................	4 525 ..	....	....	....	....	....	....	....	....
Other capital..................................	4 530 ..	649	1,927	1,114	5,749	30	726	24	11
Claims on affiliated enterprises...........	4 535 ..	649	1,927	1,114	5,749	30	726	24	11
Liabilities to affiliated enterprises........	4 540 ..	....	....	....	....	....	....	....	....
Direct investment in Kuwait............	4 555 ..	**16**	**−112**	**4**	**−67**	**24**	**234**	**121**	**119**
Equity capital...............................	4 560 ..	16	−112	4	−67	24	234	121	119
Claims on direct investors.................	4 565 ..	....	....	....	....	....	....	....	....
Liabilities to direct investors..............	4 570 ..	16	−112	4	−67	24	234	121	119
Reinvested earnings..........................	4 575 ..	....	....	....	....	....	....	....	....
Other capital..................................	4 580 ..	....	....	....	....	....	....	....	....
Claims on direct investors.................	4 585 ..	....	....	....	....	....	....	....	....
Liabilities to direct investors..............	4 590 ..	....	....	....	....	....	....	....	....
B. PORTFOLIO INVESTMENT...............	4 600 ..	**−12,668**	**−8,719**	**−3,227**	**−13,374**	**−13,935**	**−10,475**	**−25,714**	**−32,900**
Assets...	4 602 ..	**−12,923**	**−8,641**	**−3,388**	**−13,708**	**−14,223**	**−10,016**	**−25,758**	**−33,575**
Equity securities............................	4 610 ..	....	....	....	....	....	....	....	....
Monetary authorities......................	4 611 ..	....	....	....	....	....	....	....	....
General government.......................	4 612 ..	....	....	....	....	....	....	....	....
Banks.......................................	4 613 ..	....	....	....	....	....	....	....	....
Other sectors..............................	4 614 ..	....	....	....	....	....	....	....	....
Debt securities.............................	4 619 ..	−12,923	−8,641	−3,388	−13,708	−14,223	−10,016	−25,758	−33,575
Bonds and notes...........................	4 620 ..	−12,923	−8,641	−3,388	−13,708	−14,223	−10,016	−25,758	−33,575
Monetary authorities.....................	4 621 ..	....	....	....	....	....	....	....	....
General government......................	4 622 ..	−12,006	−7,876	−1,924	−12,073	−12,501	−5,546	−20,604	−27,061
Banks......................................	4 623 ..	411	−434	−764	−6	−432	−440	−512	−1,770
Other sectors.............................	4 624 ..	−1,327	−331	−700	−1,629	−1,290	−4,031	−4,643	−4,744
Money market instruments................	4 630 ..	....	....	....	....	....	....	....	....
Monetary authorities.....................	4 631 ..	....	....	....	....	....	....	....	....
General government......................	4 632 ..	....	....	....	....	....	....	....	....
Banks......................................	4 633 ..	....	....	....	....	....	....	....	....
Other sectors.............................	4 634 ..	....	....	....	....	....	....	....	....
Liabilities....................................	4 652 ..	**254**	**−79**	**162**	**334**	**288**	**−459**	**45**	**675**
Equity securities............................	4 660 ..	....	....	....	....	....	....	....	....
Banks.......................................	4 663 ..	....	....	....	....	....	....	....	....
Other sectors..............................	4 664 ..	....	....	....	....	....	....	....	....
Debt securities.............................	4 669 ..	254	−79	162	334	288	−459	45	675
Bonds and notes...........................	4 670 ..	254	−79	162	334	288	−459	45	675
Monetary authorities.	4 671 ..	....	....	....	....	....	....	....	....
General government......................	4 672 ..	....	....	....	....	....	....	....	....
Banks......................................	4 673 ..	254	−79	162	191	71	−487	−35	−12
Other sectors.............................	4 674 ..	....	....	....	143	217	28	80	686
Money market instruments................	4 680 ..	....	....	....	....	....	....	....	....
Monetary authorities.	4 681 ..	....	....	....	....	....	....	....	....
General government......................	4 682 ..	....	....	....	....	....	....	....	....
Banks......................................	4 683 ..	....	....	....	....	....	....	....	....
Other sectors.............................	4 684 ..	....	....	....	....	....	....	....	....
C. FINANCIAL DERIVATIVES...............	4 910 ..	....	....	....	....	....	....	....	....
Monetary authorities.........................	4 911 ..	....	....	....	....	....	....	....	....
General government..........................	4 912 ..	....	....	....	....	....	....	....	....
Banks...	4 913 ..	....	....	....	....	....	....	....	....
Other sectors..................................	4 914 ..	....	....	....	....	....	....	....	....
Assets..	4 900 ..	....	....	....	....	....	....	....	....
Monetary authorities.........................	4 901 ..	....	....	....	....	....	....	....	....
General government..........................	4 902 ..	....	....	....	....	....	....	....	....
Banks...	4 903 ..	....	....	....	....	....	....	....	....
Other sectors..................................	4 904 ..	....	....	....	....	....	....	....	....
Liabilities....................................	4 905 ..	....	....	....	....	....	....	....	....
Monetary authorities.........................	4 906 ..	....	....	....	....	....	....	....	....
General government..........................	4 907 ..	....	....	....	....	....	....	....	....
Banks...	4 908 ..	....	....	....	....	....	....	....	....
Other sectors..................................	4 909 ..	....	....	....	....	....	....	....	....

Table 2 (Concluded). STANDARD PRESENTATION, 2000–2007

(Millions of U.S. dollars)

	Code	2000	2001	2002	2003	2004	2005	2006	2007
D. OTHER INVESTMENT	4 700 ..	**−1,430**	**1,439**	**−1,892**	**−3,624**	**−399**	**−15,703**	**−14,192**	**9,178**
Assets	4 703 ..	**−1,109**	**230**	**−3,751**	**−3,391**	**−292**	**−19,963**	**−23,947**	**−10,915**
Trade credits	4 706 ..	−130	471	−404	−846	−1,746	−3,140	−2,926	−2,639
General government	4 707 ..	−130	471	−404	−846	−1,746	−3,140	−2,926	−2,639
of which: Short-term	4 709 ..	*−130*	*471*	*−404*	*−846*	*−1,746*	*−3,140*	*−2,926*	*−2,639*
Other sectors	4 710 ..	....	....	....	....	....	....	....	....
of which: Short-term	4 712 ..	....	....	....	....	....	....	....	....
Loans	4 714 ..	−313	−38	−87	952	90	−939	−356	−1,089
Monetary authorities	4 715 ..	....	....	....	....	....	....	....	....
of which: Short-term	4 718 ..	....	....	....	....	....	....	....	....
General government	4 719 ..	−535	−476	−125	−343	−428	−513	410	226
of which: Short-term	4 721 ..	....	....	....	....	....	....	....	....
Banks	4 722 ..	114	389	−198	1,317	496	−365	−716	−1,203
of which: Short-term	4 724 ..	*114*	*389*	*−198*	*1,317*	*496*	*−365*	*−716*	*−1,203*
Other sectors	4 725 ..	108	48	236	−21	23	−62	−51	−112
of which: Short-term	4 727 ..	*108*	*48*	*236*	*−21*	*23*	*−62*	*−51*	*−112*
Currency and deposits	4 730 ..	−711	732	−2,858	−3,274	1,279	−16,028	−19,590	−5,069
Monetary authorities	4 731 ..	....	....	....	....	....	....	....	....
General government	4 732 ..	329	1,051	−2,732	−1,921	4,279	−14,392	−14,657	−1,104
Banks	4 733 ..	−1,115	−130	−408	−1,198	−2,509	−1,366	−3,640	−4,251
Other sectors	4 734 ..	75	−188	282	−155	−491	−270	−1,293	286
Other assets	4 736 ..	46	−935	−402	−223	84	145	−1,074	−2,118
Monetary authorities	4 737 ..	....	....	....	....	....	....	....	....
of which: Short-term	4 739 ..	....	....	....	....	....	....	....	....
General government	4 740 ..	52	−127	−617	−209	−62	−118	−694	−226
of which: Short-term	4 742 ..	....	....	....	....	....	....	....	....
Banks	4 743 ..	−3	−15	7	−61	−135	109	−27	−882
of which: Short-term	4 745 ..	*−3*	*−15*	*7*	*−61*	*−135*	*109*	*−27*	*−882*
Other sectors	4 746 ..	−3	−794	207	47	281	153	−354	−1,010
of which: Short-term	4 748 ..	*−3*	*−794*	*207*	*47*	*281*	*153*	*−354*	*−1,010*
Liabilities	4 753 ..	**−321**	**1,209**	**1,859**	**−234**	**−107**	**4,260**	**9,754**	**20,093**
Trade credits	4 756 ..	−143	....	....	....	....	....	....	....
General government	4 757 ..	−143	....	....	....	....	....	....	....
of which: Short-term	4 759 ..	*−143*	....	....	....	....	....	....	....
Other sectors	4 760 ..	....	....	....	....	....	....	....	....
of which: Short-term	4 762 ..	....	....	....	....	....	....	....	....
Loans	4 764 ..	−176	14	−53	357	154	976	5,593	5,747
Monetary authorities	4 765 ..	....	....	....	....	....	....	....	....
of which: Use of Fund credit and loans from the Fund	4 766 ..	....	....	....	....	....	....	....	....
of which: Short-term	4 768 ..	....	....	....	....	....	....	....	....
General government	4 769 ..	−851	−31	−45	−36	−37	−41	−38	−24
of which: Short-term	4 771 ..	....	....	....	....	....	....	....	....
Banks	4 772 ..	....	....	....	....	....	....	....	....
of which: Short-term	4 774 ..	....	....	....	....	....	....	....	....
Other sectors	4 775 ..	675	45	−8	393	192	1,016	5,630	5,771
of which: Short-term	4 777 ..	....	....	....	....	....	....	....	....
Currency and deposits	4 780 ..	−329	1,295	1,368	−534	−437	1,925	3,036	10,832
Monetary authorities	4 781 ..	....	....	....	....	....	....	....	....
General government	4 782 ..	....	....	....	....	....	....	....	....
Banks	4 783 ..	−329	1,295	1,368	−534	−469	1,877	3,039	10,843
Other sectors	4 784 ..	....	....	....	....	32	48	−3	−11
Other liabilities	4 786 ..	328	−100	544	−57	176	1,359	1,126	3,514
Monetary authorities	4 787 ..	2	−2	26	30	34	259	94	47
of which: Short-term	4 789 ..	*2*	*−2*	*26*	*30*	*34*	*259*	*94*	*47*
General government	4 790 ..	156	....	449	−143	9	877	390	2,871
of which: Short-term	4 792 ..	*156*	....	*449*	*−143*	*9*	*877*	*390*	*2,871*
Banks	4 793 ..	33	7	−13	−15	51	111	−54	161
of which: Short-term	4 795 ..	*33*	*7*	*−13*	*−15*	*51*	*111*	*−54*	*161*
Other sectors	4 796 ..	137	−106	82	71	82	112	696	434
of which: Short-term	4 798 ..	*137*	*−106*	*82*	*71*	*82*	*112*	*696*	*434*
E. RESERVE ASSETS	4 802 ..	**−2,268**	**−2,908**	**970**	**1,824**	**−629**	**−619**	**−3,583**	**−3,218**
Monetary gold	4 812 ..	....	....	....	....	....	....	....	....
Special drawing rights	4 811 ..	−21	−21	−15	−14	−14	−17	−13	−13
Reserve position in the Fund	4 810 ..	−8	−129	−68	9	94	363	129	45
Foreign exchange	4 803 ..	−2,240	−2,759	1,053	1,829	−709	−965	−3,699	−3,250
Other claims	4 813 ..	....	....	....	....	....	....	....	....
NET ERRORS AND OMISSIONS	4 998 ..	**−842**	**−2,869**	**−1,869**	**−574**	**−1,130**	**−3,398**	**−907**	**−8,541**

Table 3. INTERNATIONAL INVESTMENT POSITION (End-period stocks), 2000–2007

(Millions of U.S. dollars)

	Code	2000	2001	2002	2003	2004	2005	2006	2007
ASSETS	8 995 C.	....	**29,094**	**31,040**	**32,499**	**39,690**	**54,694**	**78,162**	**108,966**
Direct investment abroad	8 505 ..	....	**616**	**728**	**766**	**1,468**	**5,893**	**10,812**	**16,934**
Equity capital and reinvested earnings	8 506 ..	....	616	728	766	1,468	5,893	10,812	16,934
Claims on affiliated enterprises	8 507 ..	....	616	728	766	1,468	5,893	10,812	16,934
Liabilities to affiliated enterprises	8 508 ..	....	....	....	....	....	....	....	....
Other capital	8 530 ..	....	....	....	....	....	....	....	....
Claims on affiliated enterprises	8 535 ..	....	....	....	....	....	....	....	....
Liabilities to affiliated enterprises	8 540 ..	....	....	....	....	....	....	....	....
Portfolio investment	8 602 ..	....	**6,087**	**7,968**	**9,756**	**11,416**	**15,999**	**21,330**	**29,373**
Equity securities	8 610 ..	....	2,715	3,725	4,228	5,887	8,057	10,451	14,687
Monetary authorities	8 611 ..	....	....	....	....	....	....	....	....
General government	8 612 ..	....	....	....	....	....	....	....	....
Banks	8 613 ..	....	1,049	1,682	1,714	2,168	2,559	3,015	4,741
Other sectors	8 614 ..	....	1,666	2,043	2,514	3,719	5,498	7,436	9,946
Debt securities	8 619 ..	....	3,372	4,243	5,528	5,529	7,942	10,879	14,686
Bonds and notes	8 620 ..	....	3,372	4,243	5,528	5,529	7,942	10,879	14,686
Monetary authorities	8 621 ..	....	....	....	....	....	....	....	....
General government	8 622 ..	....	....	....	....	....	....	....	....
Banks	8 623 ..	....	302	481	492	414	487	575	904
Other sectors	8 624 ..	....	3,069	3,762	5,036	5,115	7,455	10,304	13,782
Money market instruments	8 630 ..	....	....	....	....	....	....	....	....
Monetary authorities	8 631 ..	....	....	....	....	....	....	....	....
General government	8 632 ..	....	....	....	....	....	....	....	....
Banks	8 633 ..	....	....	....	....	....	....	....	....
Other sectors	8 634 ..	....	....	....	....	....	....	....	....
Financial derivatives	8 900 ..	....	....	....	....	....	....	....	....
Monetary authorities	8 901 ..	....	....	....	....	....	....	....	....
General government	8 902 ..	....	....	....	....	....	....	....	....
Banks	8 903 ..	....	....	....	....	....	....	....	....
Other sectors	8 904 ..	....	....	....	....	....	....	....	....
Other investment	8 703 ..	....	**12,417**	**13,037**	**14,297**	**18,461**	**23,834**	**33,349**	**45,893**
Trade credits	8 706 ..	....	952	1,389	2,267	4,011	7,188	10,196	13,546
General government	8 707 ..	....	952	1,389	2,267	4,011	7,188	10,196	13,546
of which: Short-term	8 709 ..	....	*952*	*1,389*	*2,267*	*4,011*	*7,188*	*10,196*	*13,546*
Other sectors	8 710 ..	....	....	....	....	....	....	....	....
of which: Short-term	8 712 ..	....	....	....	....	....	....	....	....
Loans	8 714 ..	....	5,449	5,555	6,529	6,073	6,760	7,741	9,694
Monetary authorities	8 715 ..	....	....	....	....	....	....	....	....
of which: Short-term	8 718 ..	....	....	....	....	....	....	....	....
General government	8 719 ..	....	3,987	4,091	4,280	4,342	4,587	4,777	5,186
of which: Short-term	8 721 ..	....	....	....	....	....	....	....	....
Banks	8 722 ..	....	972	1,199	1,958	1,462	1,841	2,577	3,982
of which: Short-term	8 724 ..	....	*972*	*1,199*	*1,958*	*1,462*	*1,841*	*2,577*	*3,982*
Other sectors	8 725 ..	....	491	265	291	269	333	387	526
of which: Short-term	8 727 ..	....	*491*	*265*	*291*	*269*	*333*	*387*	*526*
Currency and deposits	8 730 ..	....	4,706	4,965	4,340	7,362	9,124	14,262	19,466
Monetary authorities	8 731 ..	....	....	....	....	....	....	....	....
General government	8 732 ..	....	....	....	....	....	....	....	....
Banks	8 733 ..	....	4,133	4,662	3,880	6,411	7,851	11,678	17,028
Other sectors	8 734 ..	....	573	303	460	951	1,273	2,583	2,438
Other assets	8 736 ..	....	1,309	1,128	1,161	1,015	761	1,150	3,186
Monetary authorities	8 737 ..	....	....	....	....	....	....	....	....
of which: Short-term	8 739 ..	....	....	....	....	....	....	....	....
General government	8 740 ..	....	....	....	....	....	....	....	....
of which: Short-term	8 742 ..	....	....	....	....	....	....	....	....
Banks	8 743 ..	....	127	123	187	321	215	244	1,177
of which: Short-term	8 745 ..	....	*127*	*123*	*187*	*321*	*215*	*244*	*1,177*
Other sectors	8 746 ..	....	1,182	1,005	974	693	546	906	2,010
of which: Short-term	8 748 ..	....	*1,182*	*1,005*	*974*	*693*	*546*	*906*	*2,010*
Reserve assets	8 802 ..	....	**9,975**	**9,306**	**7,681**	**8,345**	**8,967**	**12,670**	**16,766**
Monetary gold	8 812 ..	....	103	106	108	108	109	110	116
Special drawing rights	8 811 ..	91	108	133	160	182	184	207	231
Reserve position in the Fund	8 810 ..	487	598	718	777	713	298	181	144
Foreign exchange	8 803 ..	....	9,165	8,349	6,637	7,343	8,376	12,172	16,276
Other claims	8 813 ..	....	....	....	....	....	....	....	....

Table 3 (Concluded). INTERNATIONAL INVESTMENT POSITION (End-period stocks), 2000–2007

(Millions of U.S. dollars)

	Code	2000	2001	2002	2003	2004	2005	2006	2007
LIABILITIES	8 995 D.	. . . .	**10,946**	**13,162**	**13,496**	**13,700**	**17,862**	**27,994**	**51,394**
Direct investment in Kuwait	8 555 ..	. . . .	**429**	**444**	**384**	**408**	**645**	**773**	**942**
Equity capital and reinvested earnings	8 556 ..	. . . .	429	444	384	408	645	773	942
Claims on direct investors	8 557 ..	. . . .	. . . .	. . . .	. . . .	. . . .	. . . .	. . . .	. . . .
Liabilities to direct investors	8 558 ..	. . . .	429	444	384	408	645	773	942
Other capital	8 580 ..	. . . .	. . . .	. . . .	. . . .	. . . .	. . . .	. . . .	. . . .
Claims on direct investors	8 585 ..	. . . .	. . . .	. . . .	. . . .	. . . .	. . . .	. . . .	. . . .
Liabilities to direct investors	8 590 ..	. . . .	. . . .	. . . .	. . . .	. . . .	. . . .	. . . .	. . . .
Portfolio investment	8 652 ..	. . . .	**279**	**451**	**882**	**1,171**	**722**	**774**	**1,522**
Equity securities	8 660 ..	. . . .	. . . .	. . . .	. . . .	. . . .	. . . .	. . . .	. . . .
Banks	8 663 ..	. . . .	. . . .	. . . .	. . . .	. . . .	. . . .	. . . .	. . . .
Other sectors	8 664 ..	. . . .	. . . .	. . . .	. . . .	. . . .	. . . .	. . . .	. . . .
Debt securities	8 669 ..	. . . .	279	451	882	1,171	722	774	1,522
Bonds and notes	8 670 ..	. . . .	279	451	882	1,171	722	774	1,522
Monetary authorities	8 671 ..	. . . .	. . . .	. . . .	. . . .	. . . .	. . . .	. . . .	. . . .
General government	8 672 ..	. . . .	. . . .	. . . .	. . . .	. . . .	. . . .	. . . .	. . . .
Banks	8 673 ..	. . . .	279	451	652	723	241	209	209
Other sectors	8 674 ..	. . . .		. . . .	231	448	480	565	1,314
Money market instruments	8 680 ..	. . . .			. . . .	. . . .	. . . .	. . . .	. . . .
Monetary authorities	8 681 ..	. . . .			. . . .	. . . .	. . . .	. . . .	. . . .
General government	8 682 ..	. . . .			. . . .	. . . .	. . . .	. . . .	. . . .
Banks	8 683 ..	. . . .			. . . .	. . . .	. . . .	. . . .	. . . .
Other sectors	8 684 ..	. . . .			. . . .	. . . .	. . . .	. . . .	. . . .
Financial derivatives	8 905 ..	. . . .	. . . .	. . . .	. . . .	. . . .	. . . .	. . . .	. . . .
Monetary authorities	8 906 ..	. . . .	. . . .	. . . .	. . . .	. . . .	. . . .	. . . .	. . . .
General government	8 907 ..	. . . .	. . . .	. . . .	. . . .	. . . .	. . . .	. . . .	. . . .
Banks	8 908 ..	. . . .	. . . .	. . . .	. . . .	. . . .	. . . .	. . . .	. . . .
Other sectors	8 909 ..	. . . .	. . . .	. . . .	. . . .	. . . .	. . . .	. . . .	. . . .
Other investment	8 753 ..	. . . .	**10,238**	**12,266**	**12,230**	**12,122**	**16,495**	**26,447**	**48,929**
Trade credits	8 756 ..	. . . .	. . . .	. . . .	. . . .	. . . .	. . . .	. . . .	. . . .
General government	8 757 ..	. . . .	. . . .	. . . .	. . . .	. . . .	. . . .	. . . .	. . . .
of which: Short-term	8 759 ..	. . . .	. . . .	. . . .	. . . .	. . . .	. . . .	. . . .	. . . .
Other sectors	8 760 ..	. . . .	. . . .	. . . .	. . . .	. . . .	. . . .	. . . .	. . . .
of which: Short-term	8 762 ..	. . . .	. . . .	. . . .	. . . .	. . . .	. . . .	. . . .	. . . .
Loans	8 764 ..	. . . .	4,812	4,745	5,184	5,339	6,365	12,040	18,736
Monetary authorities	8 765 ..	. . . .	. . . .	. . . .	. . . .	. . . .	. . . .	. . . .	. . . .
of which: Use of Fund credit and loans from the Fund	8 766 ..	. . . .	. . . .	. . . .	. . . .	. . . .	. . . .	. . . .	. . . .
of which: Short-term	8 768 ..	. . . .	. . . .	. . . .	. . . .	. . . .	. . . .	. . . .	. . . .
General government	8 769 ..	. . . .	214	175	141	104	64	27	4
of which: Short-term	8 771 ..	. . . .	*214*	*175*	*141*	*104*	*64*	*27*	*4*
Banks	8 772 ..	. . . .	. . . .	. . . .	. . . .	. . . .	. . . .	. . . .	. . . .
of which: Short-term	8 774 ..	. . . .	. . . .	. . . .	. . . .	. . . .	. . . .	. . . .	. . . .
Other sectors	8 775 ..	. . . .	4,598	4,570	5,043	5,235	6,300	12,013	18,732
of which: Short-term	8 777 ..	. . . .	*4,598*	*4,570*	*5,043*	*5,235*	*6,300*	*12,013*	*18,732*
Currency and deposits	8 780 ..	. . . .	4,757	6,277	5,841	5,404	7,379	10,499	22,396
Monetary authorities	8 781 ..	. . . .	. . . .	. . . .	. . . .	. . . .	. . . .	. . . .	. . . .
General government	8 782 ..	. . . .	. . . .	. . . .	. . . .	. . . .	. . . .	. . . .	. . . .
Banks	8 783 ..	. . . .	4,757	6,277	5,841	5,372	7,299	10,421	22,325
Other sectors	8 784 ..	. . . .	. . . .	. . . .	. . . .	32	80	78	71
Other liabilities	8 786 ..	. . . .	670	1,244	1,204	1,380	2,751	3,908	7,797
Monetary authorities	8 787 ..	. . . .	14	45	74	108	367	466	543
of which: Short-term	8 789 ..	. . . .	*14*	*45*	*74*	*108*	*367*	*466*	*543*
General government	8 790 ..	. . . .	194	655	521	530	1,412	1,817	4,914
of which: Short-term	8 792 ..	. . . .	*194*	*655*	*521*	*530*	*1,412*	*1,817*	*4,914*
Banks	8 793 ..	. . . .	65	54	39	90	201	148	325
of which: Short-term	8 795 ..	. . . .	*65*	*54*	*39*	*90*	*201*	*148*	*325*
Other sectors	8 796 ..	. . . .	396	490	570	652	770	1,476	2,015
of which: Short-term	8 798 ..	. . . .	*396*	*490*	*570*	*652*	*770*	*1,476*	*2,015*
NET INTERNATIONAL INVESTMENT POSITION	8 995 ..	. . . .	**18,148**	**17,878**	**19,004**	**25,990**	**36,832**	**50,168**	**57,572**
Conversion rates: Kuwaiti dinar per U.S. dollar (end of period)	0 102 ..	**.3054**	**.3079**	**.2996**	**.2947**	**.2947**	**.2920**	**.2891**	**.2730**

Table 1. ANALYTIC PRESENTATION, 2000–2007

(Millions of U.S. dollars)

	Code	2000	2001	2002	2003	2004	2005	2006	2007
A. Current Account[1]	4 993 Z.	**−122.9**	**−51.6**	**−60.9**	**−60.8**	**3.4**	**−60.0**	**−299.2**	**−262.7**
Goods: exports f.o.b.	2 100 ..	510.9	480.3	498.1	590.3	733.2	686.8	906.0	1,337.0
Goods: imports f.o.b.	3 100 ..	−506.2	−449.2	−571.4	−723.1	−903.8	−1,105.5	−1,792.4	−2,635.5
Balance on Goods	4 100 ..	*4.7*	*31.1*	*−73.3*	*−132.8*	*−170.6*	*−418.7*	*−886.5*	*−1,298.5*
Services: credit	2 200 ..	62.0	82.8	142.0	158.2	209.8	259.4	378.7	684.3
Services: debit	3 200 ..	−148.2	−124.8	−148.0	−159.9	−223.5	−291.3	−460.8	−582.2
Balance on Goods and Services	4 991 ..	*−81.4*	*−10.9*	*−79.2*	*−134.5*	*−184.3*	*−450.5*	*−968.5*	*−1,196.4*
Income: credit	2 300 ..	17.0	12.4	6.3	5.2	7.8	16.5	41.6	42.6
Income: debit	3 300 ..	−99.0	−71.5	−64.1	−67.2	−109.4	−101.7	−84.7	−95.0
Balance on Goods, Services, and Income	4 992 ..	*−163.4*	*−70.0*	*−137.0*	*−196.5*	*−285.9*	*−535.7*	*−1,011.6*	*−1,248.8*
Current transfers: credit	2 379 Z.	42.9	22.8	79.0	142.7	306.9	513.6	762.4	1,065.2
Current transfers: debit	3 379 ..	−2.4	−4.5	−2.9	−7.0	−17.6	−37.9	−50.0	−79.0
B. Capital Account[1]	4 994 Z.	**−11.4**	**−32.0**	**−7.9**	**−.9**	**−19.9**	**−20.5**	**−43.9**	**−74.9**
Capital account: credit	2 994 Z.	22.8	9.2	35.1	36.0	33.7	51.6	37.8	54.3
Capital account: debit	3 994 ..	−34.2	−41.2	−43.0	−36.9	−53.6	−72.2	−81.7	−129.1
Total, Groups A Plus B	4 981 ..	*−134.3*	*−83.6*	*−68.9*	*−61.6*	*−16.5*	*−80.6*	*−343.1*	*−337.5*
C. Financial Account[1]	4 995 W.	**83.4**	**46.3**	**110.5**	**27.7**	**180.1**	**85.4**	**337.3**	**354.4**
Direct investment abroad	4 505 ..	−4.5	−6.1	....	....	−43.9	....	....	.2
Direct investment in Kyrgyz Republic	4 555 Z.	−2.4	5.0	4.7	45.5	175.5	42.6	182.0	207.9
Portfolio investment assets	4 602 ..	−1.6	1.2	−2.5	1.1	−9.5	2.3	−3.0	−19.2
Equity securities	4 610 ..	....	....	....	....	....	....	....	−.2
Debt securities	4 619 ..	−1.6	1.2	−2.5	1.1	−9.5	2.3	−3.0	−19.0
Portfolio investment liabilities	4 652 Z.	.3	....	−9.5	5.0	....	....	....	1.5
Equity securities	4 660 ..	....	....	−9.5	5.0	....	....	....	1.5
Debt securities	4 669 Z.	.3	....	....	....	....	....	....	....
Financial derivatives	4 910 ..	25.8	17.6	−5.1	−20.0	−20.5	....	....	....
Financial derivatives assets	4 900 ..	25.8	17.6	−5.1	−20.0	−20.5	....	....	....
Financial derivatives liabilities	4 905 ..	....	....	....	....	....	....	....	....
Other investment assets	4 703 ..	−29.1	−9.4	28.2	−76.6	−35.8	−47.5	−24.0	19.5
Monetary authorities	4 701 ..	8.6	−5.6	37.0	1.7	9.3	18.7	1.0	20.0
General government	4 704 ..	−.1	−.1	....	−.2	....	....	....	....
Banks	4 705 ..	−1.6	−16.5	−42.8	−50.2	−63.2	−15.1	−17.0	37.7
Other sectors	4 728 ..	−36.1	12.7	34.1	−28.0	18.1	−51.1	−8.0	−38.2
Other investment liabilities	4 753 W.	94.9	38.1	94.8	72.8	114.3	88.1	182.3	144.4
Monetary authorities	4 753 WA	....	....	....	....	....	....	....	....
General government	4 753 ZB	119.7	86.2	66.6	76.7	101.5	88.1	61.0	31.7
Banks	4 753 ZC	−.3	3.9	32.7	36.6	42.2	−11.9	−26.6	66.6
Other sectors	4 753 ZD	−24.4	−52.0	−4.5	−40.5	−29.5	12.0	147.9	46.2
Total, Groups A Through C	4 983 ..	*−50.8*	*−37.3*	*41.6*	*−33.9*	*163.6*	*4.8*	*−5.7*	*16.8*
D. Net Errors and Omissions	4 998 ..	**18.0**	**24.5**	**−21.3**	**80.7**	**−19.0**	**63.6**	**182.4**	**276.3**
Total, Groups A Through D	4 984 ..	*−32.9*	*−12.8*	*20.4*	*46.8*	*144.5*	*68.4*	*176.7*	*293.1*
E. Reserves and Related Items	4 802 A.	**32.9**	**12.8**	**−20.4**	**−46.8**	**−144.5**	**−68.4**	**−176.7**	**−293.1**
Reserve assets	4 802 ..	−21.3	−17.7	−43.0	−64.2	−166.2	−80.5	−170.3	−306.7
Use of Fund credit and loans	4 766 ..	7.4	−2.1	−8.0	−.9	−3.9	−12.5	−23.5	−20.7
Exceptional financing	4 920 ..	46.8	32.7	30.6	18.3	25.6	24.6	17.1	34.3
Conversion rates: soms per U.S. dollar	0 101 ..	**47.704**	**48.378**	**46.937**	**43.648**	**42.650**	**41.012**	**40.153**	**37.316**

[1] Excludes components that have been classified in the categories of Group E.

Table 2. STANDARD PRESENTATION, 2000–2007

(Millions of U.S. dollars)

	Code	2000	2001	2002	2003	2004	2005	2006	2007
CURRENT ACCOUNT	4 993	**−76.1**	**−19.0**	**−30.4**	**−42.5**	**28.9**	**−35.4**	**−282.1**	**−228.3**
A. GOODS	4 100	**4.7**	**31.1**	**−73.3**	**−132.8**	**−170.6**	**−418.7**	**−886.5**	**−1,298.5**
Credit	2 100	**510.9**	**480.3**	**498.1**	**590.3**	**733.2**	**686.8**	**906.0**	**1,337.0**
General merchandise: exports f.o.b.	2 110	315.6	255.7	335.3	330.7	445.8	456.1	700.0	1,112.2
Goods for processing: exports f.o.b.	2 150	....	....	....	....	....	....	....	....
Repairs on goods	2 160	....	....	....	....	....	....	....	....
Goods procured in ports by carriers	2 170	....	....	....	....	....	....	....	....
Nonmonetary gold	2 180	195.3	224.6	162.8	259.6	287.4	230.7	206.0	224.8
Debit	3 100	**−506.2**	**−449.2**	**−571.4**	**−723.1**	**−903.8**	**−1,105.5**	**−1,792.4**	**−2,635.5**
General merchandise: imports f.o.b.	3 110	−504.6	−448.2	−568.5	−720.2	−900.4	−1,102.7	−1,790.0	−2,627.0
Goods for processing: imports f.o.b.	3 150	....	....	....	....	....	....	....	....
Repairs on goods	3 160	....	....	....	....	....	....	....	....
Goods procured in ports by carriers	3 170	−1.6	−.9	−2.9	−2.9	−3.4	−2.8	−2.4	−8.4
Nonmonetary gold	3 180	....	....	....	....	....	....	....	....
B. SERVICES	4 200	**−86.1**	**−42.0**	**−6.0**	**−1.7**	**−13.7**	**−31.8**	**−82.0**	**102.1**
Total credit	2 200	*62.0*	*82.8*	*142.0*	*158.2*	*209.8*	*259.4*	*378.7*	*684.3*
Total debit	3 200	*−148.2*	*−124.8*	*−148.0*	*−159.9*	*−223.5*	*−291.3*	*−460.8*	*−582.2*
Transportation services, credit	2 205	**16.6**	**20.4**	**37.5**	**41.9**	**50.8**	**60.6**	**56.6**	**139.3**
Passenger	2 850	*5.3*	*8.0*	*12.0*	*13.5*	*15.6*	*20.9*	*22.1*	*45.9*
Freight	2 851	*5.6*	*4.7*	*15.2*	*16.5*	*20.5*	*20.8*	*17.6*	*43.7*
Other	2 852	*5.7*	*7.6*	*10.4*	*11.9*	*14.6*	*18.9*	*16.8*	*49.8*
Sea transport, passenger	2 207	....	....	....	....	....	....	....	....
Sea transport, freight	2 208	....	....	....	....	....	....	....	....
Sea transport, other	2 209	....	....	....	....	....	....	....	....
Air transport, passenger	2 211	1.9	3.1	4.8	5.6	7.0	7.8	6.8	19.7
Air transport, freight	2 212	2.5	.9	8.8	10.1	12.6	14.1	12.4	35.6
Air transport, other	2 213	3.3	5.3	9.1	10.5	13.2	14.7	12.9	37.2
Other transport, passenger	2 215	3.4	5.0	7.1	8.0	8.6	13.1	15.3	26.2
Other transport, freight	2 216	3.1	3.8	6.4	6.4	7.9	6.7	5.3	8.1
Other transport, other	2 217	2.4	2.3	1.2	1.4	1.5	4.2	3.9	12.6
Transportation services, debit	3 205	**−49.9**	**−42.3**	**−55.9**	**−64.2**	**−88.7**	**−125.5**	**−178.0**	**−337.1**
Passenger	3 850	*−11.8*	*−8.6*	*−16.2*	*−17.9*	*−23.2*	*−36.1*	*−50.2*	*−103.3*
Freight	3 851	*−18.2*	*−24.6*	*−20.0*	*−25.4*	*−33.7*	*−43.8*	*−62.9*	*−92.5*
Other	3 852	*−20.0*	*−9.1*	*−19.8*	*−20.9*	*−31.8*	*−45.5*	*−64.8*	*−141.4*
Sea transport, passenger	3 207	....	....	....	....	....	....	....	....
Sea transport, freight	3 208	....	....	....	....	....	....	....	....
Sea transport, other	3 209	....	....	....	....	....	....	....	....
Air transport, passenger	3 211	−3.9	−5.2	−5.4	−4.8	−6.1	−10.1	−12.0	−29.0
Air transport, freight	3 212	−1.0	−.8	−1.0	−.9	−1.1	−1.9	−2.2	−5.3
Air transport, other	3 213	−7.1	−4.0	−8.4	−7.6	−9.6	−15.9	−18.8	−45.6
Other transport, passenger	3 215	−7.9	−3.4	−10.8	−13.0	−17.2	−26.0	−38.2	−74.3
Other transport, freight	3 216	−17.1	−23.7	−19.0	−24.5	−32.6	−42.0	−60.7	−87.2
Other transport, other	3 217	−12.9	−5.1	−11.4	−13.4	−22.2	−29.6	−46.0	−95.8
Travel, credit	2 236	**15.3**	**24.4**	**35.7**	**47.8**	**75.6**	**73.0**	**167.0**	**345.5**
Business travel	2 237	4.0	13.1	19.7	25.8	40.7	39.1	86.4	176.2
Personal travel	2 240	11.2	11.3	16.0	21.9	35.0	33.9	80.6	169.3
Travel, debit	3 236	**−15.6**	**−11.9**	**−9.9**	**−16.6**	**−50.3**	**−58.4**	**−91.6**	**−89.7**
Business travel	3 237	−8.5	−8.3	−6.9	−11.6	−35.2	−40.9	−64.2	−62.8
Personal travel	3 240	−7.1	−3.6	−3.0	−5.0	−15.1	−17.5	−27.5	−26.9
Other services, credit	2 200 BA	**30.1**	**38.0**	**68.9**	**68.6**	**83.4**	**125.8**	**155.2**	**199.4**
Communications	2 245	9.3	8.7	8.9	8.7	8.0	6.4	10.1	12.0
Construction	2 249	1.8	4.5	4.9	5.7	8.3	19.0	19.7	16.8
Insurance	2 253	.5	.2	.3	1.3	.2	.2	1.4	5.0
Financial	2 260	1.0	.6	3.6	.6	1.9	3.8	2.0	3.7
Computer and information	2 262	.5	.5	.7	1.5	.7	1.2	1.3	1.1
Royalties and licence fees	2 266	4.8	1.3	.6	.5	1.0	1.7	2.4	2.4
Other business services	2 268	4.7	12.0	26.1	23.6	37.4	61.0	80.8	82.5
Personal, cultural, and recreational	2 287	2.7	3.3	2.0	5.6	8.6	6.7	10.2	45.3
Government, n.i.e.	2 291	4.9	6.9	21.9	21.2	17.3	25.9	27.3	30.7
Other services, debit	3 200 BA	**−82.6**	**−70.6**	**−82.2**	**−79.1**	**−84.5**	**−107.4**	**−191.1**	**−155.3**
Communications	3 245	−7.3	−7.9	−7.0	−8.2	−6.1	−6.0	−5.9	−7.4
Construction	3 249	−6.0	−6.7	−8.5	−2.7	−1.6	−2.1	−3.3	−11.8
Insurance	3 253	−8.9	−8.3	−9.4	−15.0	−13.2	−14.9	−18.3	−9.4
Financial	3 260	−4.2	−3.3	−12.5	−4.4	−12.7	−4.4	−3.6	−9.0
Computer and information	3 262	−.9	−1.0	−1.8	−3.5	−3.3	−2.2	−1.7	−4.4
Royalties and licence fees	3 266	−9.2	−6.9	−3.4	−3.5	−3.0	−6.0	−19.5	−11.7
Other business services	3 268	−39.4	−30.8	−35.7	−36.0	−33.7	−46.5	−104.2	−70.3
Personal, cultural, and recreational	3 287	−3.0	−2.2	−.5	−3.1	−6.3	−21.0	−29.9	−26.2
Government, n.i.e.	3 291	−3.9	−3.4	−3.5	−2.6	−4.8	−4.2	−4.8	−5.2

Table 2 (Continued). STANDARD PRESENTATION, 2000–2007

(Millions of U.S. dollars)

	Code	2000	2001	2002	2003	2004	2005	2006	2007
C. INCOME	4 300	**−82.0**	**−59.1**	**−57.8**	**−62.0**	**−101.6**	**−85.2**	**−43.1**	**−52.4**
Total credit	2 300	*17.0*	*12.4*	*6.3*	*5.2*	*7.8*	*16.5*	*41.6*	*42.6*
Total debit	3 300	*−99.0*	*−71.5*	*−64.1*	*−67.2*	*−109.4*	*−101.7*	*−84.7*	*−95.0*
Compensation of employees, credit	2 310	....	....	....	....	....	....	....	....
Compensation of employees, debit	3 310	**−10.3**	**−10.3**	**−12.2**	**−13.3**	**−13.7**	**−17.4**	**−19.1**	**−20.8**
Investment income, credit	2 320	**17.0**	**12.4**	**6.3**	**5.2**	**7.8**	**16.5**	**41.6**	**42.6**
Direct investment income	2 330	....	....	....	....	....	....	....	....
Dividends and distributed branch profits	2 332	....	....	....	....	....	....	....	....
Reinvested earnings and undistributed branch profits	2 333	....	....	....	....	....	....	....	....
Income on debt (interest)	2 334	....	....	....	....	....	....	....	....
Portfolio investment income	2 339	....	.5	.3	.3	.1	....	.1	.2
Income on equity	2 340	....	....	....	....	....	....	....	....
Income on bonds and notes	2 350	....	.5	.3	.3	.1	....	.1	.2
Income on money market instruments	2 360	....	....	....	....	....	....	....	....
Other investment income	2 370	16.9	11.9	6.0	4.9	7.6	16.5	41.5	42.4
Investment income, debit	3 320	**−88.7**	**−61.2**	**−51.9**	**−54.0**	**−95.7**	**−84.3**	**−65.6**	**−74.2**
Direct investment income	3 330	−37.3	−25.7	−19.6	−26.7	−57.6	−36.0	−39.8	−39.5
Dividends and distributed branch profits	3 332	−1.3	−.5	−.1	−.1	....	−2.3	−14.0	−.2
Reinvested earnings and undistributed branch profits	3 333	−8.0	−13.5	−9.0	−21.8	−48.0	−30.7	−21.0	−33.6
Income on debt (interest)	3 334	−28.0	−11.7	−10.5	−4.9	−9.5	−3.0	−4.8	−5.8
Portfolio investment income	3 339	....	....	....	....	....	....	....	....
Income on equity	3 340	....	....	....	....	....	....	....	....
Income on bonds and notes	3 350	....	....	....	....	....	....	....	....
Income on money market instruments	3 360	....	....	....	....	....	....	....	....
Other investment income	3 370	−51.4	−35.5	−32.3	−27.2	−38.2	−48.3	−25.8	−34.7
D. CURRENT TRANSFERS	4 379	**87.4**	**51.0**	**106.7**	**154.0**	**314.9**	**500.3**	**729.5**	**1,020.5**
Credit	2 379	**89.8**	**55.5**	**109.5**	**161.0**	**332.5**	**538.2**	**779.5**	**1,099.5**
General government	2 380	46.8	32.7	30.6	18.3	25.6	24.6	17.1	34.3
Other sectors	2 390	42.9	22.8	79.0	142.7	306.9	513.6	762.4	1,065.2
Workers' remittances	2 391	2.2	4.5	30.3	70.3	179.1	313.3	473.1	705.4
Other current transfers	2 392	40.7	18.3	48.7	72.4	127.9	200.3	289.3	359.8
Debit	3 379	**−2.4**	**−4.5**	**−2.9**	**−7.0**	**−17.6**	**−37.9**	**−50.0**	**−79.0**
General government	3 380	−1.3	−1.1	−.7	−1.3	−1.9	−1.6	−4.7	−3.4
Other sectors	3 390	−1.1	−3.4	−2.2	−5.7	−15.7	−36.3	−45.3	−75.6
Workers' remittances	3 391	−.9	−3.0	−2.1	−5.2	−15.4	−32.8	−43.9	−69.8
Other current transfers	3 392	−.2	−.3	....	−.6	−.3	−3.4	−1.4	−5.8
CAPITAL AND FINANCIAL ACCOUNT	4 996	**58.1**	**−5.5**	**51.6**	**−38.3**	**−9.9**	**−28.1**	**99.7**	**−47.9**
CAPITAL ACCOUNT	4 994	**−11.4**	**−32.0**	**−7.9**	**−.9**	**−19.9**	**−20.5**	**−43.9**	**−74.9**
Total credit	2 994	*22.8*	*9.2*	*35.1*	*36.0*	*33.7*	*51.6*	*37.8*	*54.3*
Total debit	3 994	*−34.2*	*−41.2*	*−43.0*	*−36.9*	*−53.6*	*−72.2*	*−81.7*	*−129.1*
Capital transfers, credit	2 400	**22.8**	**9.2**	**35.1**	**36.0**	**33.7**	**51.6**	**37.8**	**54.3**
General government	2 401	3.0	1.8	27.7	27.5	22.7	23.1	29.4	36.3
Debt forgiveness	2 402	....	....	....	....	....	....	....	....
Other capital transfers	2 410	3.0	1.8	27.7	27.5	22.7	23.1	29.4	36.3
Other sectors	2 430	19.8	7.4	7.4	8.6	11.0	28.5	8.4	18.0
Migrants' transfers	2 431	6.6	6.6	6.4	7.8	9.6	8.7	8.1	9.4
Debt forgiveness	2 432	6.1	....	....	....	....	19.0	....	....
Other capital transfers	2 440	7.1	.8	1.0	.7	1.4	.8	.3	8.6
Capital transfers, debit	3 400	**−34.2**	**−41.2**	**−43.0**	**−36.9**	**−53.6**	**−72.2**	**−81.7**	**−129.1**
General government	3 401	....	....	....	....	....	....	....	....
Debt forgiveness	3 402	....	....	....	....	....	....	....	....
Other capital transfers	3 410	....	....	....	....	....	....	....	....
Other sectors	3 430	−34.2	−41.2	−43.0	−36.9	−53.6	−72.2	−81.7	−129.1
Migrants' transfers	3 431	−34.2	−41.2	−43.0	−36.8	−53.4	−72.2	−81.7	−129.1
Debt forgiveness	3 432	....	....	....	....	....	....	....	....
Other capital transfers	3 440	....	....	....	−.1	−.2	....	....	....
Nonproduced nonfinancial assets, credit	2 480	....	....	....	....	....	....	....	....
Nonproduced nonfinancial assets, debit	3 480	....	....	....	....	....	....	....	....

Table 2 (Continued). STANDARD PRESENTATION, 2000–2007

(Millions of U.S. dollars)

	Code	2000	2001	2002	2003	2004	2005	2006	2007
FINANCIAL ACCOUNT	4 995	69.5	26.5	59.6	−37.4	10.0	−7.6	143.5	26.9
A. DIRECT INVESTMENT	4 500	−6.9	−1.1	4.7	45.5	131.5	42.6	182.0	208.1
Direct investment abroad	4 505	−4.5	−6.1	....	....	−43.9	....	....	.2
Equity capital	4 510	−4.5	−6.1	....	....	−43.9	....	....	.2
Claims on affiliated enterprises	4 515	−4.5	−6.1	....	....	−43.9	....	....	.2
Liabilities to affiliated enterprises	4 520	....	....	....	....	....	....	....	....
Reinvested earnings	4 525	....	....	....	....	....	....	....	....
Other capital	4 530	....	....	....	....	....	....	....	....
Claims on affiliated enterprises	4 535	....	....	....	....	....	....	....	....
Liabilities to affiliated enterprises	4 540	....	....	....	....	....	....	....	....
Direct investment in Kyrgyz Republic	4 555	−2.4	5.0	4.7	45.5	175.5	42.6	182.0	207.9
Equity capital	4 560	17.6	12.3	4.9	14.9	149.5	16.2	31.5	16.4
Claims on direct investors	4 565	....	....	....	....	....	....	....	....
Liabilities to direct investors	4 570	17.6	12.3	4.9	14.9	149.5	16.2	31.5	16.4
Reinvested earnings	4 575	8.0	13.5	9.0	21.8	48.0	30.7	21.0	33.6
Other capital	4 580	−28.0	−20.8	−9.2	8.8	−22.1	−4.3	129.5	157.9
Claims on direct investors	4 585	....	....	....	....	....	....	....	....
Liabilities to direct investors	4 590	−28.0	−20.8	−9.2	8.8	−22.1	−4.3	129.5	157.9
B. PORTFOLIO INVESTMENT	4 600	−1.3	1.2	−12.0	6.0	−9.5	2.3	−3.0	−17.7
Assets	4 602	−1.6	1.2	−2.5	1.1	−9.5	2.3	−3.0	−19.2
Equity securities	4 610	....	....	....	....	....	....	....	−.2
Monetary authorities	4 611	....	....	....	....	....	....	....	....
General government	4 612	....	....	....	....	....	....	....	....
Banks	4 613	....	....	....	....	....	....	....	....
Other sectors	4 614	....	....	....	....	....	....	....	−.2
Debt securities	4 619	−1.6	1.2	−2.5	1.1	−9.5	2.3	−3.0	−19.0
Bonds and notes	4 620	−1.6	1.2	−2.5	1.1	−9.5	2.3	−3.0	−19.0
Monetary authorities	4 621	....	....	....	....	....	....	....	....
General government	4 622	....	....	....	....	....	....	....	....
Banks	4 623	−1.6	1.2	−2.5	1.1	−9.5	2.3	−3.0	−19.0
Other sectors	4 624	....	....	....	....	....	....	....	....
Money market instruments	4 630	....	....	....	....	....	....	....	....
Monetary authorities	4 631	....	....	....	....	....	....	....	....
General government	4 632	....	....	....	....	....	....	....	....
Banks	4 633	....	....	....	....	....	....	....	....
Other sectors	4 634	....	....	....	....	....	....	....	....
Liabilities	4 652	.3	....	−9.5	5.0	....	....	....	1.5
Equity securities	4 660	....	....	−9.5	5.0	....	....	....	1.5
Banks	4 663	....	....	−6.7	3.5	....	....	....	1.0
Other sectors	4 664	....	....	−2.9	1.5	....	....	....	.4
Debt securities	4 669	.3	....	....	....	....	....	....	....
Bonds and notes	4 670	....	....	....	....	....	....	....	....
Monetary authorities	4 671	....	....	....	....	....	....	....	....
General government	4 672	....	....	....	....	....	....	....	....
Banks	4 673	....	....	....	....	....	....	....	....
Other sectors	4 674	....	....	....	....	....	....	....	....
Money market instruments	4 680	.3	....	....	....	....	....	....	....
Monetary authorities	4 681	.3	....	....	....	....	....	....	....
General government	4 682	....	....	....	....	....	....	....	....
Banks	4 683	....	....	....	....	....	....	....	....
Other sectors	4 684	....	....	....	....	....	....	....	....
C. FINANCIAL DERIVATIVES	4 910	25.8	17.6	−5.1	−20.0	−20.5	....	....	....
Monetary authorities	4 911	....	....	....	....	....	....	....	....
General government	4 912	....	....	....	....	....	....	....	....
Banks	4 913	....	....	....	....	....	....	....	....
Other sectors	4 914	25.8	17.6	−5.1	−20.0	−20.5	....	....	....
Assets	4 900	25.8	17.6	−5.1	−20.0	−20.5	....	....	....
Monetary authorities	4 901	....	....	....	....	....	....	....	....
General government	4 902	....	....	....	....	....	....	....	....
Banks	4 903	....	....	....	....	....	....	....	....
Other sectors	4 904	25.8	17.6	−5.1	−20.0	−20.5	....	....	....
Liabilities	4 905	....	....	....	....	....	....	....	....
Monetary authorities	4 906	....	....	....	....	....	....	....	....
General government	4 907	....	....	....	....	....	....	....	....
Banks	4 908	....	....	....	....	....	....	....	....
Other sectors	4 909	....	....	....	....	....	....	....	....

Table 2 (Concluded). STANDARD PRESENTATION, 2000–2007

(Millions of U.S. dollars)

	Code	2000	2001	2002	2003	2004	2005	2006	2007
D. OTHER INVESTMENT	4 700	**73.2**	**26.5**	**115.0**	**−4.7**	**74.6**	**28.1**	**134.8**	**143.3**
Assets	4 703	**−29.1**	**−9.4**	**28.2**	**−76.6**	**−35.8**	**−47.5**	**−24.0**	**19.5**
Trade credits	4 706	−32.8	−2.8	24.6	−18.2	8.4	−45.1	−13.5	−27.6
General government	4 707	....	....	....	....	....	....	....	....
of which: Short-term	4 709	....	....	....	....	....	....	....	....
Other sectors	4 710	−32.8	−2.8	24.6	−18.2	8.4	−45.1	−13.5	−27.6
of which: Short-term	4 712	*−10.8*	*−.9*	*8.1*	*−6.0*	*2.8*	*−14.9*	*−4.5*	*−9.1*
Loans	4 714	−.2	−.3	−4.4	.1	−8.3	−2.9	.5	−3.3
Monetary authorities	4 715	....	....	....	....	....	....	....	....
of which: Short-term	4 718	....	....	....	....	....	....	....	....
General government	4 719	....	....	....	....	....	....	....	....
of which: Short-term	4 721	....	....	....	....	....	....	....	....
Banks	4 722	−.2	−.3	−4.4	.1	−8.3	−2.9	.5	−3.3
of which: Short-term	4 724	*−.2*	*−.3*	*−4.4*	*.1*	*−8.3*	*−2.9*	*.5*	*−3.3*
Other sectors	4 725	....	....	....	....	....	....	....	....
of which: Short-term	4 727	....	....	....	....	....	....	....	....
Currency and deposits	4 730	−4.6	−.9	−29.2	−60.3	−45.4	−18.5	−12.2	30.1
Monetary authorities	4 731	....	....	....	....	....	....	....	....
General government	4 732	....	....	....	....	....	....	....	....
Banks	4 733	−1.4	−16.1	−38.4	−50.3	−54.9	−12.2	−17.5	40.9
Other sectors	4 734	−3.3	15.2	9.2	−10.0	9.5	−6.3	5.2	−10.8
Other assets	4 736	8.5	−5.4	37.2	1.8	9.6	19.0	1.3	20.3
Monetary authorities	4 737	8.6	−5.6	37.0	1.7	9.3	18.7	1.0	20.0
of which: Short-term	4 739	....	....	....	....	....	....	....	....
General government	4 740	−.1	−.1	....	−.2	....	....	....	....
of which: Short-term	4 742	....	....	....	....	....	....	....	....
Banks	4 743	....	....	....	....	....	....	....	....
of which: Short-term	4 745	....	....	....	....	....	....	....	....
Other sectors	4 746	....	.3	.3	.3	.3	.3	.3	.3
of which: Short-term	4 748	....	*.3*	*.3*	*.3*	*.3*	*.3*	*.3*	*.3*
Liabilities	4 753	**102.3**	**35.9**	**86.8**	**71.9**	**110.4**	**75.6**	**158.8**	**123.7**
Trade credits	4 756	26.0	.7	12.7	9.9	−21.2	19.8	132.7	13.3
General government	4 757	....	....	....	....	....	....	....	....
of which: Short-term	4 759	....	....	....	....	....	....	....	....
Other sectors	4 760	26.0	.7	12.7	9.9	−21.2	19.8	132.7	13.3
of which: Short-term	4 762	*11.7*	*.3*	*5.7*	*4.5*	*−9.5*	*8.9*	*59.7*	*6.0*
Loans	4 764	49.3	19.4	29.0	−19.7	46.9	12.1	52.6	9.2
Monetary authorities	4 765	7.4	−2.1	−8.0	−.9	−3.9	−12.5	−23.5	−20.7
of which: Use of Fund credit and loans from the Fund	4 766	*7.4*	*−2.1*	*−8.0*	*−.9*	*−3.9*	*−12.5*	*−23.5*	*−20.7*
of which: Short-term	4 768	....	....	....	....	....	....	....	....
General government	4 769	92.9	68.2	47.1	34.0	56.3	17.2	54.4	28.1
of which: Short-term	4 771	....	....	....	....	....	....	....	....
Banks	4 772	.6	2.9	6.7	−4.9	1.5	6.2	9.7	−14.5
of which: Short-term	4 774	*.6*	*2.9*	*6.7*	*−4.9*	*1.5*	*6.2*	*9.7*	*−14.5*
Other sectors	4 775	−51.7	−49.6	−16.8	−47.9	−7.0	1.2	12.1	16.4
of which: Short-term	4 777	....	....	....	....	....	....	....	....
Currency and deposits	4 780	−1.0	1.0	26.0	41.5	40.7	−18.2	−36.3	81.1
Monetary authorities	4 781	....	....	....	....	....	....	....	....
General government	4 782	....	....	....	....	....	....	....	....
Banks	4 783	−1.0	1.0	26.0	41.5	40.7	−18.2	−36.3	81.1
Other sectors	4 784	....	....	....	....	....	....	....	....
Other liabilities	4 786	28.0	14.9	19.1	40.1	44.0	61.8	9.7	20.1
Monetary authorities	4 787	....	....	....	....	....	....	....	....
of which: Short-term	4 789	....	....	....	....	....	....	....	....
General government	4 790	26.7	18.0	19.5	42.7	45.2	70.8	6.6	3.6
of which: Short-term	4 792	*26.7*	*18.0*	*19.5*	*42.7*	*45.2*	*70.8*	*6.6*	*3.6*
Banks	4 793	....	....	....	....	....	....	....	....
of which: Short-term	4 795	....	....	....	....	....	....	....	....
Other sectors	4 796	1.3	−3.1	−.4	−2.6	−1.3	−9.0	3.1	16.5
of which: Short-term	4 798	*1.3*	*1.3*	*1.7*	*−.5*	*.5*	*−6.9*	*3.1*	*16.5*
E. RESERVE ASSETS	4 802	**−21.3**	**−17.7**	**−43.0**	**−64.2**	**−166.2**	**−80.5**	**−170.3**	**−306.7**
Monetary gold	4 812	....	....	....	....	....	−18.7	....	....
Special drawing rights	4 811	4.2	−.8	.8	−8.7	−8.6	13.0	−27.2	20.4
Reserve position in the Fund	4 810	....	....	....	....	....	....	....	....
Foreign exchange	4 803	−25.5	−16.9	−43.8	−55.5	−157.6	−74.8	−143.1	−327.1
Other claims	4 813	....	....	....	....	....	....	....	....
NET ERRORS AND OMISSIONS	4 998	**18.0**	**24.5**	**−21.3**	**80.7**	**−19.0**	**63.6**	**182.4**	**276.3**

Table 3. INTERNATIONAL INVESTMENT POSITION (End-period stocks), 2000–2007

(Millions of U.S. dollars)

	Code	2000	2001	2002	2003	2004	2005	2006	2007
ASSETS	8 995 C.	**489.9**	**488.7**	**551.3**	**711.5**	**991.5**	**1,159.3**	**1,270.4**	**1,695.9**
Direct investment abroad	8 505	**33.2**	**39.3**	**39.3**	**39.3**	**83.2**	**147.5**	**3.4**	**17.9**
Equity capital and reinvested earnings	8 506	33.2	39.3	39.3	39.3	83.2	147.5	3.4	17.9
Claims on affiliated enterprises	8 507	33.2	39.3	39.3	39.3	83.2	147.5	3.4	17.9
Liabilities to affiliated enterprises	8 508	....	....	....	....	....	....	....	....
Other capital	8 530	....	....	....	....	....	....	....	....
Claims on affiliated enterprises	8 535	....	....	....	....	....	....	....	....
Liabilities to affiliated enterprises	8 540	....	....	....	....	....	....	....	....
Portfolio investment	8 602	**3.1**	**3.7**	**6.2**	**7.6**	**17.4**	**14.9**	**19.3**	**50.5**
Equity securities	8 610	....	....	....	....	....	....	....	27.7
Monetary authorities	8 611	....	....	....	....	....	....	....	....
General government	8 612	....	....	....	....	....	....	....	....
Banks	8 613	....	....	....	....	....	....	....	....
Other sectors	8 614	....	....	....	....	....	....	....	27.7
Debt securities	8 619	3.1	3.7	6.2	7.6	17.4	14.9	19.3	22.8
Bonds and notes	8 620	3.1	3.7	6.2	7.6	17.4	14.9	19.3	22.8
Monetary authorities	8 621	....	....	....	....	....	....	....	....
General government	8 622	....	....	....	....	....	....	....	....
Banks	8 623	....	....	....	....	....	....	....	....
Other sectors	8 624	3.1	3.7	6.2	7.6	17.4	14.9	19.3	22.8
Money market instruments	8 630	....	....	....	....	....	....	....	....
Monetary authorities	8 631	....	....	....	....	....	....	....	....
General government	8 632	....	....	....	....	....	....	....	....
Banks	8 633	....	....	....	....	....	....	....	....
Other sectors	8 634	....	....	....	....	....	....	....	....
Financial derivatives	8 900	**19.5**	**17.2**	....	....	....	....	....	....
Monetary authorities	8 901	....	....	....	....	....	....	....	....
General government	8 902	....	....	....	....	....	....	....	....
Banks	8 903	....	....	....	....	....	....	....	....
Other sectors	8 904	19.5	17.2	....	....	....	....	....	....
Other investment	8 703	**230.1**	**192.7**	**216.0**	**305.4**	**347.0**	**388.4**	**433.4**	**433.7**
Trade credits	8 706	99.3	105.4	93.6	117.8	110.1	150.0	177.1	221.5
General government	8 707	....	....	....	....	....	....	....	....
of which: Short-term	8 709	....	....	....	....	....	....	....	....
Other sectors	8 710	99.3	105.4	93.6	117.8	110.1	150.0	177.1	221.5
of which: Short-term	8 712	*33.8*	*35.8*	*31.8*	*40.0*	*37.4*	*51.0*	*60.2*	*75.3*
Loans	8 714	2.4	2.8	6.8	6.5	15.0	17.9	17.4	20.6
Monetary authorities	8 715	2.4	2.3	....	....	....	....	....	....
of which: Short-term	8 718	....	....	....	....	....	....	....	....
General government	8 719	....	....	1.4	1.1	.8	.6	.3	....
of which: Short-term	8 721	....	....	....	....	....	....	....	....
Banks	8 722	....	.5	5.4	5.4	14.2	17.3	17.1	20.6
of which: Short-term	8 724	....	*.5*	....	....	....	....	....	....
Other sectors	8 725	....	....	....	....	....	....	....	....
of which: Short-term	8 727	....	....	....	....	....	....	....	....
Currency and deposits	8 730	71.3	35.2	88.7	151.3	200.4	216.7	236.0	208.8
Monetary authorities	8 731	....	....	....	....	....	....	....	....
General government	8 732	....	....	....	....	....	....	....	....
Banks	8 733	71.3	35.2	88.7	151.3	200.4	216.7	236.0	208.8
Other sectors	8 734	....	....	....	....	....	....	....	....
Other assets	8 736	57.1	49.3	27.0	29.8	21.4	3.9	2.9	−17.1
Monetary authorities	8 737	....	....	27.0	29.8	21.4	3.9	2.9	−17.1
of which: Short-term	8 739	....	....	....	....	....	....	....	....
General government	8 740	57.1	49.3	....	....	....	....	....	....
of which: Short-term	8 742	....	....	....	....	....	....	....	....
Banks	8 743	....	....	....	....	....	....	....	....
of which: Short-term	8 745	....	....	....	....	....	....	....	....
Other sectors	8 746	....	....	....	....	....	....	....	....
of which: Short-term	8 748	....	....	....	....	....	....	....	....
Reserve assets	8 802	**204.0**	**235.8**	**289.7**	**359.3**	**543.9**	**608.5**	**814.3**	**1,193.8**
Monetary gold	8 812	6.3	6.4	7.9	9.6	18.9	42.6	52.8	69.5
Special drawing rights	8 811	.7	1.3	.6	10.3	19.9	5.3	33.3	13.8
Reserve position in the Fund	8 810	....	....	....	....	....	....	....	....
Foreign exchange	8 803	197.0	228.1	281.2	339.3	505.1	560.6	728.2	1,110.5
Other claims	8 813	....	....	....	....	....	....	....	....

Table 3 (Concluded). INTERNATIONAL INVESTMENT POSITION (End-period stocks), 2000–2007

(Millions of U.S. dollars)

	Code	2000	2001	2002	2003	2004	2005	2006	2007
LIABILITIES	8 995 D.	**2,353.1**	**2,148.8**	**2,348.1**	**2,603.5**	**2,957.9**	**2,843.1**	**3,075.3**	**3,568.8**
Direct investment in Kyrgyz Republic	8 555 ..	**446.5**	**440.8**	**479.1**	**523.4**	**724.9**	**562.8**	**630.4**	**893.5**
Equity capital and reinvested earnings	8 556 ..	249.7	265.6	226.5	260.7	471.4	288.4	298.3	316.4
Claims on direct investors	8 557 ..	....	....	....	....	....	....	....	....
Liabilities to direct investors	8 558 ..	249.7	265.6	226.5	260.7	471.4	288.4	298.3	316.4
Other capital	8 580 ..	196.8	175.2	252.6	262.7	253.4	274.4	332.1	577.2
Claims on direct investors	8 585 ..	....	....	....	....	6.2	16.4	12.3	15.3
Liabilities to direct investors	8 590 ..	196.8	175.2	252.6	262.7	247.2	258.0	319.8	561.9
Portfolio investment	8 652 ..	**9.6**	**9.7**	**.5**	**5.7**	**6.0**	**6.1**	**6.6**	**8.7**
Equity securities	8 660 ..	....	....	.5	5.7	6.0	6.1	6.6	8.7
Banks	8 663 ..	....	....	.4	4.0	4.2	4.3	4.6	8.7
Other sectors	8 664 ..	....	....	.2	1.7	1.8	1.8	2.0	....
Debt securities	8 669 ..	9.6	9.7	....	....	....	....	....	....
Bonds and notes	8 670 ..	9.6	9.7	....	....	....	....	....	....
Monetary authorities	8 671 ..	....	....	....	....	....	....	....	....
General government	8 672 ..	....	....	....	....	....	....	....	....
Banks	8 673 ..	....	....	....	....	....	....	....	....
Other sectors	8 674 ..	9.6	9.7	....	....	....	....	....	....
Money market instruments	8 680 ..	....	....	....	....	....	....	....	....
Monetary authorities	8 681 ..	....	....	....	....	....	....	....	....
General government	8 682 ..	....	....	....	....	....	....	....	....
Banks	8 683 ..	....	....	....	....	....	....	....	....
Other sectors	8 684 ..	....	....	....	....	....	....	....	....
Financial derivatives	8 905 ..	**....**	**....**	**29.7**	**24.6**	**....**	**....**	**....**	**....**
Monetary authorities	8 906 ..	....	....	....	....	....	....	....	....
General government	8 907 ..	....	....	....	....	....	....	....	....
Banks	8 908 ..	....	....	....	....	....	....	....	....
Other sectors	8 909 ..	....	....	29.7	24.6	....	....	....	....
Other investment	8 753 ..	**1,897.0**	**1,698.3**	**1,838.8**	**2,049.8**	**2,227.0**	**2,274.1**	**2,438.3**	**2,666.5**
Trade credits	8 756 ..	128.5	131.1	116.4	148.0	110.7	218.9	286.4	326.4
General government	8 757 ..	....	....	....	....	....	....	....	....
of which: Short-term	8 759 ..	....	....	....	....	....	....	....	....
Other sectors	8 760 ..	128.5	131.1	116.4	148.0	110.7	218.9	286.4	326.4
of which: Short-term	8 762 ..	*42.4*	*43.3*	*38.4*	*48.8*	*36.5*	*72.2*	*94.5*	*107.7*
Loans	8 764 ..	1,761.9	1,563.9	1,695.2	1,831.7	2,003.9	1,902.5	2,032.4	2,135.7
Monetary authorities	8 765 ..	188.0	179.3	185.2	201.9	206.9	177.9	163.1	149.8
of which: Use of Fund credit and loans from the Fund	8 766 ..	*188.0*	*179.3*	*185.2*	*201.9*	*206.9*	*177.9*	*163.1*	*149.8*
of which: Short-term	8 768 ..	....	....	....	....	....	....	....	....
General government	8 769 ..	1,407.5	1,264.4	1,401.1	1,574.5	1,752.3	1,681.4	1,814.6	1,918.3
of which: Short-term	8 771 ..	....	....	....	....	....	....	....	....
Banks	8 772 ..	1.6	4.5	10.1	5.4	7.2	8.3	18.0	22.1
of which: Short-term	8 774 ..	*.4*	*1.9*	....	....	....	....	....	....
Other sectors	8 775 ..	164.8	115.7	98.8	49.9	37.5	34.9	36.8	45.4
of which: Short-term	8 777 ..	....	....	....	....	....	....	....	....
Currency and deposits	8 780 ..	.1	1.1	27.1	70.1	112.4	152.7	119.6	204.5
Monetary authorities	8 781 ..	....	....	....	....	....	....	....	....
General government	8 782 ..	....	....	....	....	....	....	....	....
Banks	8 783 ..	.1	1.1	27.1	70.1	112.4	152.7	119.6	204.5
Other sectors	8 784 ..	....	....	....	....	....	....	....	....
Other liabilities	8 786 ..	6.5	2.2	.1	....	....	....	....	....
Monetary authorities	8 787 ..	....	....	....	....	....	....	....	....
of which: Short-term	8 789 ..	....	....	....	....	....	....	....	....
General government	8 790 ..	....	....	....	....	....	....	....	....
of which: Short-term	8 792 ..	....	....	....	....	....	....	....	....
Banks	8 793 ..	....	....	....	....	....	....	....	....
of which: Short-term	8 795 ..	....	....	....	....	....	....	....	....
Other sectors	8 796 ..	6.5	2.2	.1	....	....	....	....	....
of which: Short-term	8 798 ..	*6.5*	*2.2*	*.1*	....	....	....	....	....
NET INTERNATIONAL INVESTMENT POSITION	8 995 ..	**−1,863.2**	**−1,660.1**	**−1,796.9**	**−1,892.0**	**−1,966.4**	**−1,683.8**	**−1,804.9**	**−1,872.9**
Conversion rates: soms per U.S. dollar (end of period)	0 102 ..	48.304	47.719	46.095	44.190	41.625	41.301	38.124	35.499

Table 1. ANALYTIC PRESENTATION, 2000–2007

(Millions of U.S. dollars)

	Code	2000	2001	2002	2003	2004	2005	2006	2007
A. Current Account[1]...............................	4 993 Z.	**−8.5**	**−82.4**	**3.2**	**−62.3**	**−189.3**	**−192.5**	**49.6**	**107.3**
Goods: exports f.o.b.............................	2 100 ..	330.3	311.1	300.6	335.4	363.4	553.1	882.0	922.7
Goods: imports f.o.b.............................	3 100 ..	−535.3	−527.9	−446.9	−462.1	−712.7	−882.0	−1,060.3	−1,064.7
Balance on Goods...............................	4 100 ..	*−205.0*	*−216.8*	*−146.3*	*−126.7*	*−349.3*	*−328.9*	*−178.3*	*−142.0*
Services: credit..................................	2 200 ..	175.7	166.1	176.2	127.4	178.8	204.3	223.5	278.1
Services: debit...................................	3 200 ..	−43.1	−31.6	−32.4	−37.1	−41.1	−56.4	−62.2	−76.0
Balance on Goods and Services..............	4 991 ..	*−72.4*	*−82.3*	*−2.5*	*−36.4*	*−211.6*	*−181.0*	*−17.0*	*60.1*
Income: credit...................................	2 300 ..	7.3	5.8	4.6	3.6	3.9	5.1	16.2	43.7
Income: debit....................................	3 300 ..	−59.7	−39.6	−46.9	−50.5	−60.3	−83.8	−76.2	−94.0
Balance on Goods, Services, and Income.......	4 992 ..	*−124.7*	*−116.1*	*−44.8*	*−83.3*	*−268.0*	*−259.7*	*−77.0*	*9.8*
Current transfers: credit.......................	2 379 Z.	116.3	33.7	48.0	21.0	78.7	67.2	126.6	97.5
Current transfers: debit........................	3 379 ..	....	....	....	....	....	....	....	....
B. Capital Account[1]...............................	4 994 Z.	....	....	....	....	....	....	....	....
Capital account: credit.........................	2 994 Z.	....	....	....	....	....	....	....	....
Capital account: debit.........................	3 994 ..	....	....	....	....	....	....	....	....
Total, Groups A Plus B........................	4 981 ..	*−8.5*	*−82.4*	*3.2*	*−62.3*	*−189.3*	*−192.5*	*49.6*	*107.3*
C. Financial Account[1]...........................	4 995 W.	**126.1**	**135.7**	**69.1**	**118.7**	**94.2**	**154.8**	**229.9**	**397.1**
Direct investment abroad........................	4 505 ..	....	....	....	....	....	....	....	....
Direct investment in Lao PDR...................	4 555 Z.	33.9	23.9	4.5	19.4	17.0	27.7	187.4	323.5
Portfolio investment assets.....................	4 602 ..	....	....	....	....	....	....	....	....
Equity securities..............................	4 610 ..	....	....	....	....	....	....	....	....
Debt securities................................	4 619 ..	....	....	....	....	....	....	....	....
Portfolio investment liabilities................	4 652 Z.	....	....	....	....	....	....	....	....
Equity securities..............................	4 660 ..	....	....	....	....	....	....	....	....
Debt securities................................	4 669 Z.	....	....	....	....	....	....	....	....
Financial derivatives...........................	4 910 ..	....	....	....	....	....	....	....	....
Financial derivatives assets....................	4 900 ..	....	....	....	....	....	....	....	....
Financial derivatives liabilities...............	4 905 ..	....	....	....	....	....	....	....	....
Other investment assets........................	4 703 ..	18.8	25.2	−9.8	−47.1	−53.0	−3.4	−111.1	−134.9
Monetary authorities..........................	4 701 ..	....	....	....	....	....	....	....	....
General government...........................	4 704 ..	....	....	....	....	....	....	....	....
Banks...	4 705 ..	18.8	25.2	−9.8	−47.1	−53.0	−3.4	−111.1	−134.9
Other sectors.................................	4 728 ..	....	....	....	....	....	....	....	....
Other investment liabilities....................	4 753 W.	73.3	86.6	74.4	146.4	130.2	130.5	153.6	208.5
Monetary authorities..........................	4 753 WA	....	....	6.9	.2	−6.4	−7.1	−1.9	−2.0
General government...........................	4 753 ZB	67.2	79.0	71.7	117.1	117.6	124.0	130.9	192.8
Banks...	4 753 ZC	6.2	7.6	−4.2	29.1	19.0	13.6	24.6	17.7
Other sectors.................................	4 753 ZD	....	....	....	....	....	....	....	....
Total, Groups A Through C....................	4 983 ..	*117.6*	*53.3*	*72.3*	*56.4*	*−95.1*	*−37.7*	*279.5*	*504.4*
D. Net Errors and Omissions..................	4 998 ..	**−74.2**	**−57.2**	**−13.4**	**−34.7**	**114.6**	**55.7**	**−179.7**	**−306.5**
Total, Groups A Through D....................	4 984 ..	*43.4*	*−3.9*	*58.9*	*21.7*	*19.5*	*18.0*	*99.8*	*197.9*
E. Reserves and Related Items...............	4 802 A.	**−43.4**	**3.9**	**−58.9**	**−21.7**	**−19.5**	**−18.0**	**−99.8**	**−197.9**
Reserve assets..................................	4 802 ..	−35.7	7.4	−61.4	−19.0	−11.6	−11.9	−96.6	−194.9
Use of Fund credit and loans...................	4 766 ..	−7.7	−3.6	2.5	−2.7	−7.9	−6.1	−3.3	−3.0
Exceptional financing...........................	4 920 ..	....	....	....	....	....	....	....	....
Conversion rates: kip per U.S. dollar......	0 101 ..	**7,887.6**	**8,954.6**	**10,056.3**	**10,569.0**	**10,585.4**	**10,655.2**	**10,159.9**	**9,603.2**

[1] Excludes components that have been classified in the categories of Group E.

Table 2. STANDARD PRESENTATION, 2000–2007

(Millions of U.S. dollars)

	Code	2000	2001	2002	2003	2004	2005	2006	2007
CURRENT ACCOUNT	4 993	−8.5	−82.4	3.2	−62.3	−189.3	−192.5	49.6	107.3
A. GOODS	4 100	−205.0	−216.8	−146.3	−126.7	−349.3	−328.9	−178.3	−142.0
Credit	2 100	330.3	311.1	300.6	335.4	363.4	553.1	882.0	922.7
General merchandise: exports f.o.b.	2 110	330.3	311.1	....	....	....	....	....	....
Goods for processing: exports f.o.b.	2 150	....	....	....	....	....	....	....	....
Repairs on goods	2 160	....	....	....	....	....	....	....	....
Goods procured in ports by carriers	2 170	....	....	....	....	....	....	....	....
Nonmonetary gold	2 180	....	....	....	....	....	....	....	....
Debit	3 100	−535.3	−527.9	−446.9	−462.1	−712.7	−882.0	−1,060.3	−1,064.7
General merchandise: imports f.o.b.	3 110	−535.3	−527.9	....	....	....	....	....	....
Goods for processing: imports f.o.b.	3 150	....	....	....	....	....	....	....	....
Repairs on goods	3 160	....	....	....	....	....	....	....	....
Goods procured in ports by carriers	3 170	....	....	....	....	....	....	....	....
Nonmonetary gold	3 180	....	....	....	....	....	....	....	....
B. SERVICES	4 200	132.6	134.5	143.8	90.3	137.7	147.9	161.3	202.1
Total credit	2 200	*175.7*	*166.1*	*176.2*	*127.4*	*178.8*	*204.3*	*223.5*	*278.1*
Total debit	3 200	*−43.1*	*−31.6*	*−32.4*	*−37.1*	*−41.1*	*−56.4*	*−62.2*	*−76.0*
Transportation services, credit	2 205	19.7	22.7	....	....	....	....	....	....
Passenger	2 850	....	....	....	....	....	....	....	....
Freight	2 851	....	....	....	....	....	....	....	....
Other	2 852	....	....	....	....	....	....	....	....
Sea transport, passenger	2 207	....	....	....	....	....	....	....	....
Sea transport, freight	2 208	....	....	....	....	....	....	....	....
Sea transport, other	2 209	....	....	....	....	....	....	....	....
Air transport, passenger	2 211	....	....	....	....	....	....	....	....
Air transport, freight	2 212	....	....	....	....	....	....	....	....
Air transport, other	2 213	....	....	....	....	....	....	....	....
Other transport, passenger	2 215	....	....	....	....	....	....	....	....
Other transport, freight	2 216	....	....	....	....	....	....	....	....
Other transport, other	2 217	....	....	....	....	....	....	....	....
Transportation services, debit	3 205	−4.9	−4.9	....	....	....	....	....	....
Passenger	3 850	....	....	....	....	....	....	....	....
Freight	3 851	....	....	....	....	....	....	....	....
Other	3 852	....	....	....	....	....	....	....	....
Sea transport, passenger	3 207	....	....	....	....	....	....	....	....
Sea transport, freight	3 208	....	....	....	....	....	....	....	....
Sea transport, other	3 209	....	....	....	....	....	....	....	....
Air transport, passenger	3 211	....	....	....	....	....	....	....	....
Air transport, freight	3 212	....	....	....	....	....	....	....	....
Air transport, other	3 213	....	....	....	....	....	....	....	....
Other transport, passenger	3 215	....	....	....	....	....	....	....	....
Other transport, freight	3 216	....	....	....	....	....	....	....	....
Other transport, other	3 217	....	....	....	....	....	....	....	....
Travel, credit	2 236	113.9	103.8	....	....	....	....	....	....
Business travel	2 237	....	....	....	....	....	....	....	....
Personal travel	2 240	....	....	....	....	....	....	....	....
Travel, debit	3 236	−8.1	−.1	....	....	....	....	....	....
Business travel	3 237	....	....	....	....	....	....	....	....
Personal travel	3 240	....	....	....	....	....	....	....	....
Other services, credit	2 200 BA	42.1	39.6	....	....	....	....	....	....
Communications	2 245	....	....	....	....	....	....	....	....
Construction	2 249	....	....	....	....	....	....	....	....
Insurance	2 253	....	....	....	....	....	....	....	....
Financial	2 260	....	....	....	....	....	....	....	....
Computer and information	2 262	....	....	....	....	....	....	....	....
Royalties and licence fees	2 266	....	....	....	....	....	....	....	....
Other business services	2 268	....	....	....	....	....	....	....	....
Personal, cultural, and recreational	2 287	....	....	....	....	....	....	....	....
Government, n.i.e.	2 291	42.1	39.6	....	....	....	....	....	....
Other services, debit	3 200 BA	−30.1	−26.7	....	....	....	....	....	....
Communications	3 245	....	....	....	....	....	....	....	....
Construction	3 249	....	....	....	....	....	....	....	....
Insurance	3 253	....	....	....	....	....	....	....	....
Financial	3 260	....	....	....	....	....	....	....	....
Computer and information	3 262	....	....	....	....	....	....	....	....
Royalties and licence fees	3 266	....	....	....	....	....	....	....	....
Other business services	3 268	....	....	....	....	....	....	....	....
Personal, cultural, and recreational	3 287	....	....	....	....	....	....	....	....
Government, n.i.e.	3 291	−30.1	−26.7	....	....	....	....	....	....

Table 2 (Continued). STANDARD PRESENTATION, 2000–2007

(Millions of U.S. dollars)

	Code	2000	2001	2002	2003	2004	2005	2006	2007
C. INCOME	4 300	−52.4	−33.8	−42.3	−46.9	−56.4	−78.7	−60.0	−50.3
Total credit	2 300	*7.3*	*5.8*	*4.6*	*3.6*	*3.9*	*5.1*	*16.2*	*43.7*
Total debit	3 300	*−59.7*	*−39.6*	*−46.9*	*−50.5*	*−60.3*	*−83.8*	*−76.2*	*−94.0*
Compensation of employees, credit	2 310	.7	.7	....	....	....	....	....	....
Compensation of employees, debit	3 310	−.4	−.5	....	....	....	....	....	....
Investment income, credit	2 320	6.6	5.1	....	....	....	....	....	....
Direct investment income	2 330	....	....	....	....	....	....	....	....
Dividends and distributed branch profits	2 332	....	....	....	....	....	....	....	....
Reinvested earnings and undistributed branch profits	2 333	....	....	....	....	....	....	....	....
Income on debt (interest)	2 334	....	....	....	....	....	....	....	....
Portfolio investment income	2 339	....	....	....	....	....	....	....	....
Income on equity	2 340	....	....	....	....	....	....	....	....
Income on bonds and notes	2 350	....	....	....	....	....	....	....	....
Income on money market instruments	2 360	....	....	....	....	....	....	....	....
Other investment income	2 370	....	....	....	....	....	....	....	....
Investment income, debit	3 320	−59.2	−39.2	....	....	....	....	....	....
Direct investment income	3 330	....	....	....	....	....	....	....	....
Dividends and distributed branch profits	3 332	....	....	....	....	....	....	....	....
Reinvested earnings and undistributed branch profits	3 333	....	....	....	....	....	....	....	....
Income on debt (interest)	3 334	....	....	....	....	....	....	....	....
Portfolio investment income	3 339	....	....	....	....	....	....	....	....
Income on equity	3 340	....	....	....	....	....	....	....	....
Income on bonds and notes	3 350	....	....	....	....	....	....	....	....
Income on money market instruments	3 360	....	....	....	....	....	....	....	....
Other investment income	3 370	....	....	....	....	....	....	....	....
D. CURRENT TRANSFERS	4 379	116.3	33.7	48.0	21.0	78.7	67.2	126.6	97.5
Credit	2 379	116.3	33.7	48.0	21.0	78.7	67.2	126.6	97.5
General government	2 380	115.6	23.0	....	....	....	....	....	....
Other sectors	2 390	.6	10.7	....	....	....	....	....	....
Workers' remittances	2 391	....	....	....	....	....	....	....	....
Other current transfers	2 392	....	....	....	....	....	....	....	....
Debit	3 379	....	....	....	....	....	....	....	....
General government	3 380	....	....	....	....	....	....	....	....
Other sectors	3 390	....	....	....	....	....	....	....	....
Workers' remittances	3 391	....	....	....	....	....	....	....	....
Other current transfers	3 392	....	....	....	....	....	....	....	....
CAPITAL AND FINANCIAL ACCOUNT	4 996	82.7	139.6	10.2	97.0	74.7	136.8	130.1	199.2
CAPITAL ACCOUNT	4 994	....	....	....	....	....	....	....	....
Total credit	2 994	....	....	....	....	....	....	....	....
Total debit	3 994	....	....	....	....	....	....	....	....
Capital transfers, credit	2 400	....	....	....	....	....	....	....	....
General government	2 401	....	....	....	....	....	....	....	....
Debt forgiveness	2 402	....	....	....	....	....	....	....	....
Other capital transfers	2 410	....	....	....	....	....	....	....	....
Other sectors	2 430	....	....	....	....	....	....	....	....
Migrants' transfers	2 431	....	....	....	....	....	....	....	....
Debt forgiveness	2 432	....	....	....	....	....	....	....	....
Other capital transfers	2 440	....	....	....	....	....	....	....	....
Capital transfers, debit	3 400	....	....	....	....	....	....	....	....
General government	3 401	....	....	....	....	....	....	....	....
Debt forgiveness	3 402	....	....	....	....	....	....	....	....
Other capital transfers	3 410	....	....	....	....	....	....	....	....
Other sectors	3 430	....	....	....	....	....	....	....	....
Migrants' transfers	3 431	....	....	....	....	....	....	....	....
Debt forgiveness	3 432	....	....	....	....	....	....	....	....
Other capital transfers	3 440	....	....	....	....	....	....	....	....
Nonproduced nonfinancial assets, credit	2 480	....	....	....	....	....	....	....	....
Nonproduced nonfinancial assets, debit	3 480	....	....	....	....	....	....	....	....

Table 2 (Continued). STANDARD PRESENTATION, 2000–2007

(Millions of U.S. dollars)

	Code	2000	2001	2002	2003	2004	2005	2006	2007
FINANCIAL ACCOUNT............................	4 995 ..	**82.7**	**139.6**	**10.2**	**97.0**	**74.7**	**136.8**	**130.1**	**199.2**
A. DIRECT INVESTMENT..........................	4 500 ..	**33.9**	**23.9**	**4.5**	**19.4**	**17.0**	**27.7**	**187.4**	**323.5**
Direct investment abroad......................	4 505 ..	....	....	....	....	....	....	....	....
Equity capital...................................	4 510 ..	....	....	....	....	....	....	....	....
Claims on affiliated enterprises..................	4 515 ..	....	....	....	....	....	....	....	....
Liabilities to affiliated enterprises.............	4 520 ..	....	....	....	....	....	....	....	....
Reinvested earnings..............................	4 525 ..	....	....	....	....	....	....	....	....
Other capital...................................	4 530 ..	....	....	....	....	....	....	....	....
Claims on affiliated enterprises..................	4 535 ..	....	....	....	....	....	....	....	....
Liabilities to affiliated enterprises.............	4 540 ..	....	....	....	....	....	....	....	....
Direct investment in Lao PDR..........................	4 555 ..	**33.9**	**23.9**	**4.5**	**19.4**	**17.0**	**27.7**	**187.4**	**323.5**
Equity capital...................................	4 560 ..	33.9	23.9	4.5	19.4	17.0	27.7	187.4	323.5
Claims on direct investors........................	4 565 ..	....	....	....	....	....	....	....	....
Liabilities to direct investors...................	4 570 ..	33.9	23.9	4.5	19.4	17.0	27.7	187.4	323.5
Reinvested earnings..............................	4 575 ..	....	....	....	....	....	....	....	....
Other capital...................................	4 580 ..	....	....	....	....	....	....	....	....
Claims on direct investors........................	4 585 ..	....	....	....	....	....	....	....	....
Liabilities to direct investors...................	4 590 ..	....	....	....	....	....	....	....	....
B. PORTFOLIO INVESTMENT............................	4 600 ..	....	....	....	....	....	....	....	....
Assets..	4 602 ..	....	....	....	....	....	....	....	....
Equity securities................................	4 610 ..	....	....	....	....	....	....	....	....
Monetary authorities............................	4 611 ..	....	....	....	....	....	....	....	....
General government.............................	4 612 ..	....	....	....	....	....	....	....	....
Banks...	4 613 ..	....	....	....	....	....	....	....	....
Other sectors...................................	4 614 ..	....	....	....	....	....	....	....	....
Debt securities.................................	4 619 ..	....	....	....	....	....	....	....	....
Bonds and notes................................	4 620 ..	....	....	....	....	....	....	....	....
Monetary authorities...........................	4 621 ..	....	....	....	....	....	....	....	....
General government...........................	4 622 ..	....	....	....	....	....	....	....	....
Banks...	4 623 ..	....	....	....	....	....	....	....	....
Other sectors.................................	4 624 ..	....	....	....	....	....	....	....	....
Money market instruments.......................	4 630 ..	....	....	....	....	....	....	....	....
Monetary authorities...........................	4 631 ..	....	....	....	....	....	....	....	....
General government...........................	4 632 ..	....	....	....	....	....	....	....	....
Banks...	4 633 ..	....	....	....	....	....	....	....	....
Other sectors.................................	4 634 ..	....	....	....	....	....	....	....	....
Liabilities....................................	4 652 ..	....	....	....	....	....	....	....	....
Equity securities................................	4 660 ..	....	....	....	....	....	....	....	....
Banks...	4 663 ..	....	....	....	....	....	....	....	....
Other sectors...................................	4 664 ..	....	....	....	....	....	....	....	....
Debt securities.................................	4 669 ..	....	....	....	....	....	....	....	....
Bonds and notes................................	4 670 ..	....	....	....	....	....	....	....	....
Monetary authorities...........................	4 671 ..	....	....	....	....	....	....	....	....
General government...........................	4 672 ..	....	....	....	....	....	....	....	....
Banks...	4 673 ..	....	....	....	....	....	....	....	....
Other sectors.................................	4 674 ..	....	....	....	....	....	....	....	....
Money market instruments.......................	4 680 ..	....	....	....	....	....	....	....	....
Monetary authorities...........................	4 681 ..	....	....	....	....	....	....	....	....
General government...........................	4 682 ..	....	....	....	....	....	....	....	....
Banks...	4 683 ..	....	....	....	....	....	....	....	....
Other sectors.................................	4 684 ..	....	....	....	....	....	....	....	....
C. FINANCIAL DERIVATIVES............................	4 910 ..	....	....	....	....	....	....	....	....
Monetary authorities............................	4 911 ..	....	....	....	....	....	....	....	....
General government.............................	4 912 ..	....	....	....	....	....	....	....	....
Banks...	4 913 ..	....	....	....	....	....	....	....	....
Other sectors...................................	4 914 ..	....	....	....	....	....	....	....	....
Assets..	4 900 ..	....	....	**4.5**	**19.4**	**17.0**	**27.7**	....	**323.5**
Monetary authorities............................	4 901 ..	....	....	....	....	....	....	....	....
General government.............................	4 902 ..	....	....	....	....	....	....	....	....
Banks...	4 903 ..	....	....	....	....	....	....	....	....
Other sectors...................................	4 904 ..	....	....	....	....	....	....	....	....
Liabilities....................................	4 905 ..	....	....	....	....	....	....	....	....
Monetary authorities............................	4 906 ..	....	....	....	....	....	....	....	....
General government.............................	4 907 ..	....	....	....	....	....	....	....	....
Banks...	4 908 ..	....	....	....	....	....	....	....	....
Other sectors...................................	4 909 ..	....	....	....	....	....	....	....	....

Table 2 (Concluded). STANDARD PRESENTATION, 2000–2007

(Millions of U.S. dollars)

	Code	2000	2001	2002	2003	2004	2005	2006	2007
D. OTHER INVESTMENT	4 700 ..	84.5	108.2	67.1	96.6	69.3	121.0	39.2	70.6
Assets	4 703 ..	18.8	25.2	−9.8	−47.1	−53.0	−3.4	−111.1	−134.9
Trade credits	4 706 ..	....	....	....	....	....	....	....	....
General government	4 707 ..	....	....	....	....	....	....	....	....
of which: Short-term	4 709 ..	....	....	....	....	....	....	....	....
Other sectors	4 710 ..	....	....	....	....	....	....	....	....
of which: Short-term	4 712 ..	....	....	....	....	....	....	....	....
Loans	4 714 ..	18.8	25.2	....	....	....	....	....	....
Monetary authorities	4 715 ..	....	....	....	....	....	....	....	....
of which: Short-term	4 718 ..	....	....	....	....	....	....	....	....
General government	4 719 ..	....	....	....	....	....	....	....	....
of which: Short-term	4 721 ..	....	....	....	....	....	....	....	....
Banks	4 722 ..	18.8	25.2	....	....	....	....	....	....
of which: Short-term	4 724 ..	....	....	....	....	....	....	....	....
Other sectors	4 725 ..	....	....	....	....	....	....	....	....
of which: Short-term	4 727 ..	....	....	....	....	....	....	....	....
Currency and deposits	4 730 ..	....	....	−9.8	−47.1	−53.0	−3.4	−111.1	−134.9
Monetary authorities	4 731 ..	....	....	....	....	....	....	....	....
General government	4 732 ..	....	....	....	....	....	....	....	....
Banks	4 733 ..	....	....	−9.8	−47.1	−53.0	−3.4	−111.1	−134.9
Other sectors	4 734 ..	....	....	....	....	....	....	....	....
Other assets	4 736 ..	....	....	....	....	....	....	....	....
Monetary authorities	4 737 ..	....	....	....	....	....	....	....	....
of which: Short-term	4 739 ..	....	....	....	....	....	....	....	....
General government	4 740 ..	....	....	....	....	....	....	....	....
of which: Short-term	4 742 ..	....	....	....	....	....	....	....	....
Banks	4 743 ..	....	....	....	....	....	....	....	....
of which: Short-term	4 745 ..	....	....	....	....	....	....	....	....
Other sectors	4 746 ..	....	....	....	....	....	....	....	....
of which: Short-term	4 748 ..	....	....	....	....	....	....	....	....
Liabilities	4 753 ..	65.6	83.1	76.9	143.7	122.3	124.4	150.3	205.5
Trade credits	4 756 ..	67.2	79.0	....	....	....	....	....	....
General government	4 757 ..	67.2	79.0	....	....	....	....	....	....
of which: Short-term	4 759 ..	....	....	....	....	....	....	....	....
Other sectors	4 760 ..	....	....	....	....	....	....	....	....
of which: Short-term	4 762 ..	....	....	....	....	....	....	....	....
Loans	4 764 ..	−1.5	4.1	9.4	−2.5	−14.3	−13.2	−5.2	−5.0
Monetary authorities	4 765 ..	−7.7	−3.6	9.4	−2.5	−14.3	−13.2	−5.2	−5.0
of which: Use of Fund credit and loans from the Fund	4 766 ..	−7.7	−3.6	2.5	−2.7	−7.9	−6.1	−3.3	−3.0
of which: Short-term	4 768 ..	....	....	....	....	....	....	....	....
General government	4 769 ..	....	....	....	....	....	....	....	....
of which: Short-term	4 771 ..	....	....	....	....	....	....	....	....
Banks	4 772 ..	6.2	7.6	....	....	....	....	....	....
of which: Short-term	4 774 ..	....	....	....	....	....	....	....	....
Other sectors	4 775 ..	....	....	....	....	....	....	....	....
of which: Short-term	4 777 ..	....	....	....	....	....	....	....	....
Currency and deposits	4 780 ..	....	....	67.5	146.2	136.6	137.6	155.5	210.5
Monetary authorities	4 781 ..	....	....	....	....	....	....	....	....
General government	4 782 ..	....	....	71.7	117.1	117.6	124.0	130.9	192.8
Banks	4 783 ..	....	....	−4.2	29.1	19.0	13.6	24.6	17.7
Other sectors	4 784 ..	....	....	....	....	....	....	....	....
Other liabilities	4 786 ..	....	....	....	....	....	....	....	....
Monetary authorities	4 787 ..	....	....	....	....	....	....	....	....
of which: Short-term	4 789 ..	....	....	....	....	....	....	....	....
General government	4 790 ..	....	....	....	....	....	....	....	....
of which: Short-term	4 792 ..	....	....	....	....	....	....	....	....
Banks	4 793 ..	....	....	....	....	....	....	....	....
of which: Short-term	4 795 ..	....	....	....	....	....	....	....	....
Other sectors	4 796 ..	....	....	....	....	....	....	....	....
of which: Short-term	4 798 ..	....	....	....	....	....	....	....	....
E. RESERVE ASSETS	4 802 ..	−35.7	7.4	−61.4	−19.0	−11.6	−11.9	−96.6	−194.9
Monetary gold	4 812 ..	3.5	−1.8	....	....	....	....	....	....
Special drawing rights	4 811 ..	−.1	−3.4	−2.1	−11.7	4.4	.1	.1	....
Reserve position in the Fund	4 810 ..	....	....	....	....	....	....	....	....
Foreign exchange	4 803 ..	−39.1	12.7	−59.3	−7.3	−16.0	−12.0	−96.7	−194.9
Other claims	4 813 ..	....	....	....	....	....	....	....	....
NET ERRORS AND OMISSIONS	4 998 ..	−74.2	−57.2	−13.4	−34.7	114.6	55.7	−179.7	−306.5

Table 1. ANALYTIC PRESENTATION, 2000–2007

(Millions of U.S. dollars)

	Code	2000	2001	2002	2003	2004	2005	2006	2007
A. Current Account[1]	4 993 Z.	**−371**	**−626**	**−625**	**−921**	**−1,762**	**−1,992**	**−4,522**	**−6,485**
Goods: exports f.o.b.	2 100 ..	2,079	2,243	2,545	3,171	4,221	5,361	6,140	8,227
Goods: imports f.o.b.	3 100 ..	−3,123	−3,578	−4,024	−5,173	−7,002	−8,379	−11,271	−15,125
Balance on Goods	4 100 ..	*−1,044*	*−1,336*	*−1,479*	*−2,003*	*−2,781*	*−3,018*	*−5,131*	*−6,899*
Services: credit	2 200 ..	1,150	1,179	1,238	1,506	1,779	2,163	2,642	3,671
Services: debit	3 200 ..	−690	−671	−701	−929	−1,178	−1,557	−1,980	−2,702
Balance on Goods and Services	4 991 ..	*−583*	*−828*	*−942*	*−1,427*	*−2,180*	*−2,413*	*−4,469*	*−5,930*
Income: credit	2 300 ..	215	278	289	368	500	772	1,078	1,488
Income: debit	3 300 ..	−198	−221	−235	−393	−775	−948	−1,610	−2,425
Balance on Goods, Services, and Income	4 992 ..	*−566*	*−771*	*−888*	*−1,451*	*−2,455*	*−2,589*	*−5,001*	*−6,867*
Current transfers: credit	2 379 Z.	406	373	538	924	1,289	1,373	1,789	2,035
Current transfers: debit	3 379 ..	−211	−229	−275	−394	−595	−776	−1,310	−1,654
B. Capital Account[1]	4 994 Z.	**36**	**41**	**21**	**76**	**144**	**212**	**239**	**578**
Capital account: credit	2 994 Z.	40	50	27	80	151	220	249	588
Capital account: debit	3 994 ..	−5	−9	−6	−4	−7	−8	−10	−10
Total, Groups A Plus B	4 981 ..	*−335*	*−585*	*−604*	*−844*	*−1,618*	*−1,780*	*−4,283*	*−5,907*
C. Financial Account[1]	4 995 W.	**413**	**900**	**687**	**937**	**2,013**	**2,600**	**6,141**	**7,063**
Direct investment abroad	4 505 ..	−12	−18	−3	−50	−110	−128	−173	−335
Direct investment in Latvia	4 555 Z.	413	132	254	304	637	714	1,664	2,247
Portfolio investment assets	4 602 ..	−351	−57	−219	−286	−21	−270	−246	−607
Equity securities	4 610 ..	−34	7	−2	7	−29	−73	−73	−170
Debt securities	4 619 ..	−317	−64	−218	−292	8	−197	−174	−437
Portfolio investment liabilities	4 652 Z.	27	187	20	70	255	131	294	−50
Equity securities	4 660 ..	−7	1	23	39	32	12	22	−13
Debt securities	4 669 Z.	34	186	−3	31	223	119	272	−38
Financial derivatives	4 910 ..	2	1	13	6	−47	−76	60	229
Financial derivatives assets	4 900 ..	2	3	−7	−5	−35	58	130	334
Financial derivatives liabilities	4 905 ..	....	−3	20	11	−13	−134	−70	−105
Other investment assets	4 703 ..	−389	−79	−472	−687	−1,776	−398	−1,953	−6,135
Monetary authorities	4 701 ..	....	....	....	1	−2	−1	−1	−1
General government	4 704 ..	....	−5	6	....	−31	−23	1	−32
Banks	4 705 ..	−370	−106	−469	−635	−1,601	169	−687	−3,896
Other sectors	4 728 ..	−18	32	−8	−53	−143	−542	−1,267	−2,206
Other investment liabilities	4 753 W.	724	734	1,094	1,580	3,076	2,626	6,495	11,714
Monetary authorities	4 753 WA	....	1	−1	....	44	−36	33	−21
General government	4 753 ZB	−8	7	−3	−66	19	−50	56	201
Banks	4 753 ZC	719	529	984	1,480	2,533	2,482	5,131	8,477
Other sectors	4 753 ZD	12	196	115	165	480	230	1,275	3,057
Total, Groups A Through C	4 983 ..	*78*	*315*	*83*	*92*	*395*	*820*	*1,858*	*1,156*
D. Net Errors and Omissions	4 998 ..	**−75**	**....**	**−71**	**−13**	**8**	**−296**	**120**	**−173**
Total, Groups A Through D	4 984 ..	*3*	*314*	*12*	*79*	*403*	*524*	*1,979*	*982*
E. Reserves and Related Items	4 802 A.	**−3**	**−314**	**−12**	**−79**	**−403**	**−524**	**−1,979**	**−982**
Reserve assets	4 802 ..	7	−305	−2	−68	−398	−524	−1,979	−982
Use of Fund credit and loans	4 766 ..	−10	−10	−10	−11	−6	....	....	....
Exceptional financing	4 920 ..	....	....	....	....	....	....	....	....
Conversion rates: lats per U.S. dollar	0 101 ..	**.6065**	**.6279**	**.6182**	**.5715**	**.5402**	**.5647**	**.5604**	**.5138**

[1] Excludes components that have been classified in the categories of Group E.

Table 2. STANDARD PRESENTATION, 2000–2007

(Millions of U.S. dollars)

	Code	2000	2001	2002	2003	2004	2005	2006	2007
CURRENT ACCOUNT..	4 993 ..	−371	−626	−625	−921	−1,762	−1,992	−4,522	−6,485
A. GOODS..	4 100 ..	−1,044	−1,336	−1,479	−2,003	−2,781	−3,018	−5,131	−6,899
Credit..	2 100 ..	2,079	2,243	2,545	3,171	4,221	5,361	6,140	8,227
General merchandise: exports f.o.b.	2 110 ..	1,584	1,736	1,959	2,307	3,393	4,647	5,469	7,534
Goods for processing: exports f.o.b.	2 150 ..	445	433	503	765	708	530	509	520
Repairs on goods.	2 160 ..	35	35	43	49	65	94	71	77
Goods procured in ports by carriers.	2 170 ..	16	39	39	49	56	90	92	96
Nonmonetary gold.	2 180 ..	....	....	....	....	....	....	....	....
Debit..	3 100 ..	−3,123	−3,578	−4,024	−5,173	−7,002	−8,379	−11,271	−15,125
General merchandise: imports f.o.b.	3 110 ..	−2,719	−3,212	−3,599	−4,580	−6,429	−7,860	−10,716	−14,600
Goods for processing: imports f.o.b.	3 150 ..	−342	−296	−338	−485	−456	−383	−376	−296
Repairs on goods.	3 160 ..	−12	−15	−17	−17	−19	−10	−23	−39
Goods procured in ports by carriers.	3 170 ..	−50	−55	−70	−91	−97	−127	−157	−190
Nonmonetary gold.	3 180 ..	....	....	....	....	....	....	....	....
B. SERVICES..	4 200 ..	461	508	537	576	601	606	662	969
Total credit.	2 200 ..	*1,150*	*1,179*	*1,238*	*1,506*	*1,779*	*2,163*	*2,642*	*3,671*
Total debit.	3 200 ..	*−690*	*−671*	*−701*	*−929*	*−1,178*	*−1,557*	*−1,980*	*−2,702*
Transportation services, credit................	2 205 ..	770	768	769	892	991	1,219	1,414	1,846
Passenger.	2 850 ..	*41*	*34*	*40*	*49*	*76*	*105*	*142*	*209*
Freight.	2 851 ..	*327*	*413*	*453*	*560*	*592*	*714*	*845*	*1,068*
Other.	2 852 ..	*402*	*321*	*277*	*284*	*323*	*400*	*426*	*570*
Sea transport, passenger.	2 207 ..	1	1	1	3	3	3	....	6
Sea transport, freight.	2 208 ..	144	179	189	212	199	222	238	271
Sea transport, other.	2 209 ..	320	260	221	209	248	319	321	430
Air transport, passenger.	2 211 ..	36	27	31	36	61	89	125	180
Air transport, freight.	2 212 ..	3	4	5	5	6	6	8	11
Air transport, other.	2 213 ..	22	22	22	25	35	41	54	83
Other transport, passenger.	2 215 ..	5	7	8	10	11	14	17	23
Other transport, freight.	2 216 ..	180	231	260	343	388	485	599	786
Other transport, other.	2 217 ..	60	39	34	49	39	41	52	56
Transportation services, debit.................	3 205 ..	−214	−208	−233	−301	−413	−501	−639	−786
Passenger.	3 850 ..	*−34*	*−32*	*−37*	*−37*	*−51*	*−71*	*−84*	*−94*
Freight.	3 851 ..	*−110*	*−84*	*−100*	*−134*	*−201*	*−245*	*−323*	*−440*
Other.	3 852 ..	*−70*	*−91*	*−95*	*−130*	*−161*	*−185*	*−232*	*−252*
Sea transport, passenger.	3 207 ..	−1	−1	−5	−1	−1	−1	−2	−2
Sea transport, freight.	3 208 ..	−26	−15	−20	−27	−46	−54	−79	−118
Sea transport, other.	3 209 ..	−32	−46	−51	−66	−61	−53	−70	−68
Air transport, passenger.	3 211 ..	−32	−30	−31	−35	−48	−69	−81	−89
Air transport, freight.	3 212 ..	−10	−11	−13	−17	−23	−23	−30	−40
Air transport, other.	3 213 ..	−24	−20	−19	−22	−54	−84	−111	−130
Other transport, passenger.	3 215 ..	−2	−1	−1	−1	−2	−1	−1	−2
Other transport, freight.	3 216 ..	−74	−58	−67	−91	−132	−169	−214	−283
Other transport, other.	3 217 ..	−14	−25	−25	−42	−46	−47	−51	−55
Travel, credit..	2 236 ..	131	119	161	222	267	341	480	672
Business travel.	2 237 ..	79	60	67	93	103	109	142	200
Personal travel.	2 240 ..	52	59	94	130	164	232	337	471
Travel, debit...	3 236 ..	−247	−223	−230	−328	−377	−584	−704	−927
Business travel.	3 237 ..	−55	−42	−50	−77	−114	−160	−141	−155
Personal travel.	3 240 ..	−192	−181	−180	−251	−263	−423	−564	−772
Other services, credit...............................	2 200 BA	249	292	308	391	521	603	749	1,154
Communications.	2 245 ..	20	23	25	36	53	61	82	81
Construction.	2 249 ..	14	13	7	32	47	14	25	48
Insurance.	2 253 ..	8	12	11	10	12	11	10	17
Financial.	2 260 ..	35	43	58	93	115	129	179	264
Computer and information.	2 262 ..	20	22	25	33	43	54	73	99
Royalties and licence fees.	2 266 ..	2	3	3	4	8	10	11	13
Other business services.	2 268 ..	130	156	161	162	214	290	332	585
Personal, cultural, and recreational.	2 287 ..	1	1	1	4	3	5	6	9
Government, n.i.e.	2 291 ..	19	18	17	18	28	29	30	38
Other services, debit.................................	3 200 BA	−229	−241	−239	−301	−387	−472	−637	−989
Communications.	3 245 ..	−10	−10	−14	−22	−47	−58	−81	−106
Construction.	3 249 ..	−29	−17	−10	−17	−18	−12	−42	−157
Insurance.	3 253 ..	−55	−42	−37	−51	−40	−28	−27	−53
Financial.	3 260 ..	−12	−23	−24	−25	−28	−31	−30	−55
Computer and information.	3 262 ..	−15	−16	−17	−23	−28	−51	−63	−88
Royalties and licence fees.	3 266 ..	−12	−7	−7	−10	−14	−14	−20	−40
Other business services.	3 268 ..	−83	−113	−116	−134	−184	−249	−343	−447
Personal, cultural, and recreational.	3 287 ..	−4	−5	−5	−7	−15	−13	−15	−21
Government, n.i.e.	3 291 ..	−9	−9	−10	−12	−14	−16	−18	−24

Table 2 (Continued). STANDARD PRESENTATION, 2000–2007

(Millions of U.S. dollars)

	Code	2000	2001	2002	2003	2004	2005	2006	2007
C. INCOME	4 300	17	58	54	−24	−275	−176	−532	−937
Total credit	2 300	*215*	*278*	*289*	*368*	*500*	*772*	*1,078*	*1,488*
Total debit	3 300	*−198*	*−221*	*−235*	*−393*	*−775*	*−948*	*−1,610*	*−2,425*
Compensation of employees, credit	2 310	70	110	136	172	228	379	481	551
Compensation of employees, debit	3 310	−4	−5	−5	−5	−10	−16	−25	−40
Investment income, credit	2 320	146	168	153	197	272	392	597	937
Direct investment income	2 330	1	3	1	5	6	35	35	68
Dividends and distributed branch profits	2 332	....	....	1	1	2	13	14	18
Reinvested earnings and undistributed branch profits	2 333	....	2	....	4	4	21	20	49
Income on debt (interest)	2 334	1	1	....	....	....	....	....	1
Portfolio investment income	2 339	65	92	88	131	163	186	302	377
Income on equity	2 340	1	....	....	....	1	1	2	2
Income on bonds and notes	2 350	59	87	85	98	109	132	189	295
Income on money market instruments	2 360	6	5	3	33	54	54	112	81
Other investment income	2 370	79	73	64	61	103	171	261	493
Investment income, debit	3 320	−194	−216	−230	−388	−766	−932	−1,585	−2,385
Direct investment income	3 330	−92	−98	−105	−211	−529	−617	−983	−1,267
Dividends and distributed branch profits	3 332	−17	−36	−53	−85	−200	−250	−216	−507
Reinvested earnings and undistributed branch profits	3 333	−59	−36	−28	−95	−304	−335	−735	−691
Income on debt (interest)	3 334	−16	−26	−23	−31	−26	−32	−32	−69
Portfolio investment income	3 339	−15	−16	−29	−73	−110	−110	−190	−150
Income on equity	3 340	....	−1	....	−3	−2	−3	−4	−7
Income on bonds and notes	3 350	−13	−14	−25	−40	−57	−62	−89	−108
Income on money market instruments	3 360	−1	−1	−4	−29	−51	−45	−97	−35
Other investment income	3 370	−87	−101	−97	−104	−127	−205	−413	−968
D. CURRENT TRANSFERS	4 379	195	144	263	530	694	596	479	382
Credit	2 379	406	373	538	924	1,289	1,373	1,789	2,035
General government	2 380	47	39	47	98	218	251	254	363
Other sectors	2 390	359	335	491	826	1,071	1,122	1,535	1,673
Workers' remittances	2 391	3	2	2	2	2	2	2	2
Other current transfers	2 392	356	332	489	825	1,069	1,120	1,534	1,671
Debit	3 379	−211	−229	−275	−394	−595	−776	−1,310	−1,654
General government	3 380	−10	−12	−10	−15	−101	−183	−224	−295
Other sectors	3 390	−201	−217	−265	−380	−494	−594	−1,086	−1,359
Workers' remittances	3 391	−3	−3	−3	−3	−4	−4	−4	−5
Other current transfers	3 392	−198	−214	−262	−376	−491	−590	−1,081	−1,353
CAPITAL AND FINANCIAL ACCOUNT	4 996	446	627	695	934	1,754	2,288	4,401	6,658
CAPITAL ACCOUNT	4 994	36	41	21	76	144	212	239	578
Total credit	2 994	*40*	*50*	*27*	*80*	*151*	*220*	*249*	*588*
Total debit	3 994	*−5*	*−9*	*−6*	*−4*	*−7*	*−8*	*−10*	*−10*
Capital transfers, credit	2 400	40	50	27	80	151	220	242	586
General government	2 401	30	40	22	69	149	218	242	586
Debt forgiveness	2 402	....	....	....	....	....	....	....	....
Other capital transfers	2 410	30	40	22	69	149	218	242	586
Other sectors	2 430	10	10	4	10	2	2	....	1
Migrants' transfers	2 431	....	....	....	....	....	....	....	....
Debt forgiveness	2 432	....	....	....	....	....	....	....	....
Other capital transfers	2 440	10	10	4	10	2	2	....	1
Capital transfers, debit	3 400	−5	−9	−6	−4	−6	−5	−9	−10
General government	3 401	−1	....	....	....	....	....	....	....
Debt forgiveness	3 402	....	....	....	....	....	....	....	....
Other capital transfers	3 410	−1	....	....	....	....	....	....	....
Other sectors	3 430	−4	−9	−5	−3	−6	−5	−9	−10
Migrants' transfers	3 431	....	....	....	....	....	....	....	....
Debt forgiveness	3 432	....	....	....	....	....	....	....	....
Other capital transfers	3 440	−4	−9	−5	−3	−6	−5	−9	−10
Nonproduced nonfinancial assets, credit	2 480	....	....	....	....	....	....	7	1
Nonproduced nonfinancial assets, debit	3 480	....	....	....	....	−1	−2	−1	....

Table 2 (Continued). STANDARD PRESENTATION, 2000–2007

(Millions of U.S. dollars)

	Code	2000	2001	2002	2003	2004	2005	2006	2007
FINANCIAL ACCOUNT	4 995	**410**	**585**	**675**	**857**	**1,610**	**2,076**	**4,162**	**6,081**
A. DIRECT INVESTMENT	4 500	**400**	**114**	**250**	**254**	**527**	**585**	**1,491**	**1,913**
Direct investment abroad	4 505	−12	−18	−3	−50	−110	−128	−173	−335
Equity capital	4 510	−1	−11	−7	−42	−60	−62	−98	−206
Claims on affiliated enterprises	4 515	−1	−11	−7	−42	−60	−62	−98	−206
Liabilities to affiliated enterprises	4 520	....	....	....	....	....	....	....	....
Reinvested earnings	4 525	....	−2	....	−4	−4	−21	−20	−49
Other capital	4 530	−11	−5	3	−4	−46	−45	−55	−80
Claims on affiliated enterprises	4 535	−10	−6	4	−5	−46	−49	−66	−101
Liabilities to affiliated enterprises	4 540	−1	1	....	1	....	4	11	21
Direct investment in Latvia	4 555	413	132	254	304	637	714	1,664	2,247
Equity capital	4 560	213	217	249	177	246	237	532	1,297
Claims on direct investors	4 565	5	−81	72	−22	29	−22	21	−2
Liabilities to direct investors	4 570	208	298	177	199	217	260	511	1,300
Reinvested earnings	4 575	59	36	28	95	304	335	735	691
Other capital	4 580	140	−121	−24	31	88	141	398	259
Claims on direct investors	4 585	−2	−5	−10	−19	−8	−72	−48	−375
Liabilities to direct investors	4 590	142	−116	−13	51	95	213	446	634
B. PORTFOLIO INVESTMENT	4 600	**−324**	**130**	**−199**	**−216**	**234**	**−138**	**48**	**−658**
Assets	4 602	−351	−57	−219	−286	−21	−270	−246	−607
Equity securities	4 610	−34	7	−2	7	−29	−73	−73	−170
Monetary authorities	4 611	....	....	....	....	....	....	....	....
General government	4 612	....	....	....	....	....	....	....	....
Banks	4 613	−29	7	−2	15	−1	−13	−23	1
Other sectors	4 614	−5	....	....	−9	−28	−60	−50	−171
Debt securities	4 619	−317	−64	−218	−292	8	−197	−174	−437
Bonds and notes	4 620	−340	−55	−267	−290	23	−207	−159	−402
Monetary authorities	4 621	....	....	....	....	....	....	....	....
General government	4 622	....	....	....	....	....	....	....	....
Banks	4 623	−341	−56	−266	−276	37	−183	−134	−207
Other sectors	4 624	....	1	−1	−14	−13	−24	−26	−196
Money market instruments	4 630	23	−9	49	−3	−16	10	−14	−35
Monetary authorities	4 631	....	....	....	....	....	....	....	....
General government	4 632	....	....	....	....	....	....	....	....
Banks	4 633	23	−9	50	−1	−16	11	−9	−21
Other sectors	4 634	....	1	−1	−2	....	−2	−5	−14
Liabilities	4 652	**27**	**187**	**20**	**70**	**255**	**131**	**294**	**−50**
Equity securities	4 660	−7	1	23	39	32	12	22	−13
Banks	4 663	−9	−3	3	25	−1	−10	13	20
Other sectors	4 664	2	3	21	15	32	23	9	−33
Debt securities	4 669	34	186	−3	31	223	119	272	−38
Bonds and notes	4 670	40	185	−2	31	221	120	271	−48
Monetary authorities	4 671	....	....	....	....	....	....	....	....
General government	4 672	39	186	−27	30	185	....	13	15
Banks	4 673	....	....	25	1	36	119	258	−61
Other sectors	4 674	....	−1	....	....	....	....	....	−2
Money market instruments	4 680	−6	1	−1	....	2	−1	1	10
Monetary authorities	4 681	....	....	....	....	....	....	....	....
General government	4 682	−3	....	....	....	2	−1	1	−1
Banks	4 683	....	....	....	....	....	....	....	11
Other sectors	4 684	−3	1	−1	....	....	....	....	....
C. FINANCIAL DERIVATIVES	4 910	**2**	**1**	**13**	**6**	**−47**	**−76**	**60**	**229**
Monetary authorities	4 911	....	....	−1	2	−42	−55	55	245
General government	4 912	....	....	....	....	....	....	1	−2
Banks	4 913	....	....	12	3	−5	−6	2	−8
Other sectors	4 914	2	....	2	1	....	−15	2	−6
Assets	4 900	**2**	**3**	**−7**	**−5**	**−35**	**58**	**130**	**334**
Monetary authorities	4 901	....	3	−3	−2	−36	76	136	373
General government	4 902	....	....	....	....	....	....	1	−1
Banks	4 903	....	....	−3	−3	2	−3	−9	−32
Other sectors	4 904	2	....	−1	1	....	−15	2	−6
Liabilities	4 905	....	**−3**	**20**	**11**	**−13**	**−134**	**−70**	**−105**
Monetary authorities	4 906	....	−3	1	4	−6	−131	−81	−128
General government	4 907	....	....	....	....	....	....	1	−1
Banks	4 908	....	....	15	6	−7	−3	11	24
Other sectors	4 909	....	....	3	....	....	....	....	....

Table 2 (Concluded). STANDARD PRESENTATION, 2000–2007

(Millions of U.S. dollars)

	Code	2000	2001	2002	2003	2004	2005	2006	2007
D. OTHER INVESTMENT	4 700 ..	**325**	**645**	**613**	**882**	**1,294**	**2,229**	**4,542**	**5,579**
Assets	4 703 ..	**–389**	**–79**	**–472**	**–687**	**–1,776**	**–398**	**–1,953**	**–6,135**
Trade credits	4 706 ..	–18	–20	–22	–20	–125	–168	–133	–216
General government	4 707 ..	....	....	....	....	....	....	....	....
of which: Short-term	4 709 ..	....	....	....	....	....	....	....	....
Other sectors	4 710 ..	–18	–20	–22	–20	–125	–168	–133	–216
of which: Short-term	4 712 ..	*–18*	*–25*	*–22*	*–20*	*–125*	*–168*	*–133*	*–216*
Loans	4 714 ..	73	–24	–376	–122	–990	35	–632	–2,294
Monetary authorities	4 715 ..	....	....	....	....	....	....	....	....
of which: Short-term	4 718 ..	....	....	....	....	....	....	....	....
General government	4 719 ..	....	....	....	....	....	....	....	....
of which: Short-term	4 721 ..	....	....	....	....	....	....	....	....
Banks	4 722 ..	74	–24	–352	–98	–943	119	–549	–1,635
of which: Short-term	4 724 ..	*61*	*22*	*–287*	*13*	*–523*	*220*	*–53*	*–1,066*
Other sectors	4 725 ..	–1	1	–24	–24	–47	–84	–83	–659
of which: Short-term	4 727 ..	*–5*	*6*	*–22*	*–11*	*–4*	*–46*	*–53*	*–56*
Currency and deposits	4 730 ..	–449	–41	–69	–551	–619	–219	–1,158	–3,600
Monetary authorities	4 731 ..	....	....	....	....	....	....	....	....
General government	4 732 ..	....	–5	6	....	1	....	1	–32
Banks	4 733 ..	–454	–88	–125	–531	–650	55	–112	–2,238
Other sectors	4 734 ..	5	51	50	–21	30	–275	–1,047	–1,330
Other assets	4 736 ..	5	6	–5	6	–41	–45	–31	–25
Monetary authorities	4 737 ..	....	....	....	1	–2	–1	–1	–1
of which: Short-term	4 739 ..	....	....	....	*1*	....	*1*	*–1*	*–1*
General government	4 740 ..	....	....	....	....	–32	–23	....	....
of which: Short-term	4 742 ..	....	....	....	....	....	....	....	....
Banks	4 743 ..	9	6	7	–6	–8	–6	–27	–23
of which: Short-term	4 745 ..	*9*	*6*	*7*	*–6*	*–8*	*–6*	*–27*	*–23*
Other sectors	4 746 ..	–4	–1	–12	11	....	–15	–3	–1
of which: Short-term	4 748 ..	*–4*	*–1*	*–12*	*11*	....	*–15*	*–3*	*4*
Liabilities	4 753 ..	**714**	**724**	**1,084**	**1,569**	**3,070**	**2,626**	**6,495**	**11,714**
Trade credits	4 756 ..	17	20	55	54	192	122	128	306
General government	4 757 ..	....	....	....	....	....	....	....	....
of which: Short-term	4 759 ..	....	....	....	....	....	....	....	....
Other sectors	4 760 ..	17	20	55	54	192	122	128	306
of which: Short-term	4 762 ..	*17*	*14*	*55*	*54*	*192*	*122*	*128*	*306*
Loans	4 764 ..	–18	358	180	579	1,676	2,810	5,732	7,972
Monetary authorities	4 765 ..	–10	–10	–10	–11	–6	....	....	....
of which: Use of Fund credit and loans from the Fund..	4 766 ..	*–10*	*–10*	*–10*	*–11*	*–6*	....	....	....
of which: Short-term	4 768 ..	....	....	....	....	....	....	....	....
General government	4 769 ..	–8	7	–3	–66	–5	–71	62	212
of which: Short-term	4 771 ..	....	....	....	....	....	....	....	*37*
Banks	4 772 ..	10	201	141	543	1,417	2,777	4,542	5,049
of which: Short-term	4 774 ..	....	*141*	*84*	*287*	*349*	*573*	*1,703*	*1,391*
Other sectors	4 775 ..	–10	160	52	113	269	105	1,128	2,711
of which: Short-term	4 777 ..	*–17*	*40*	*–11*	*–20*	*43*	*–19*	*144*	*222*
Currency and deposits	4 780 ..	587	337	846	937	1,112	–300	561	3,337
Monetary authorities	4 781 ..	....	1	....	....	43	–35	33	–21
General government	4 782 ..	....	....	....	....	....	....	....	....
Banks	4 783 ..	588	337	846	937	1,068	–265	528	3,358
Other sectors	4 784 ..	....	....	....	....	....	....	....	....
Other liabilities	4 786 ..	127	9	3	–1	90	–6	73	98
Monetary authorities	4 787 ..	....	1	–2	....	1	–1	....	....
of which: Short-term	4 789 ..	....	*1*	*–2*	....	*1*	*–1*	....	....
General government	4 790 ..	....	....	....	....	23	21	–6	–11
of which: Short-term	4 792 ..	....	....	....	....	....	....	....	....
Banks	4 793 ..	121	–9	–3	....	48	–30	61	70
of which: Short-term	4 795 ..	*121*	*–9*	*–3*	....	*48*	*–30*	*61*	*70*
Other sectors	4 796 ..	6	17	7	–2	18	4	18	39
of which: Short-term	4 798 ..	*6*	*17*	*7*	*–2*	*18*	*4*	*18*	*39*
E. RESERVE ASSETS	4 802 ..	**7**	**–305**	**–2**	**–68**	**–398**	**–524**	**–1,979**	**–982**
Monetary gold	4 812 ..	1	3	1	....	....	....	....	....
Special drawing rights	4 811 ..	3	....	....	....	....	....	....	....
Reserve position in the Fund	4 810 ..	....	....	....	....	....	....	....	....
Foreign exchange	4 803 ..	3	–307	–3	–68	–398	–524	–1,979	–982
Other claims	4 813 ..	....	....	....	....	....	....	....	....
NET ERRORS AND OMISSIONS	4 998 ..	**–75**	....	**–71**	**–13**	**8**	**–296**	**120**	**–173**

Table 3. INTERNATIONAL INVESTMENT POSITION (End-period stocks), 2000–2007

(Millions of U.S. dollars)

	Code	2000	2001	2002	2003	2004	2005	2006	2007
ASSETS	8 995 C.	**3,840**	**4,128**	**5,136**	**6,674**	**9,380**	**10,045**	**15,174**	**24,533**
Direct investment abroad	8 505	**24**	**39**	**59**	**114**	**239**	**282**	**475**	**880**
Equity capital and reinvested earnings	8 506	13	24	36	83	152	169	293	583
Claims on affiliated enterprises	8 507	13	24	36	84	153	169	293	583
Liabilities to affiliated enterprises	8 508	....	....	....	....	....	....	....	....
Other capital	8 530	11	15	23	31	86	114	182	298
Claims on affiliated enterprises	8 535	13	19	27	37	94	124	205	342
Liabilities to affiliated enterprises	8 540	−2	−4	−3	−6	−8	−10	−23	−44
Portfolio investment	8 602	**858**	**671**	**912**	**1,255**	**1,340**	**1,601**	**2,041**	**2,807**
Equity securities	8 610	57	50	53	48	83	168	300	530
Monetary authorities	8 611	....	....	....	....	....	....	....	....
General government	8 612	....	....	....	....	....	....	....	....
Banks	8 613	49	42	44	29	30	51	94	106
Other sectors	8 614	8	8	9	19	52	117	206	424
Debt securities	8 619	801	621	859	1,207	1,258	1,433	1,742	2,277
Bonds and notes	8 620	755	566	850	1,194	1,228	1,417	1,709	2,204
Monetary authorities	8 621	....	....	....	....	....	....	....	....
General government	8 622	....	....	....	....	....	....	....	....
Banks	8 623	748	558	841	1,170	1,173	1,338	1,580	1,862
Other sectors	8 624	7	7	9	24	55	79	129	342
Money market instruments	8 630	46	55	9	13	30	16	33	73
Monetary authorities	8 631	....	....	....	....	....	....	....	....
General government	8 632	....	....	....	....	....	....	....	....
Banks	8 633	40	49	1	2	18	7	16	40
Other sectors	8 634	6	6	9	11	12	10	17	33
Financial derivatives	8 900	**1**	**4**	**12**	**18**	**52**	**21**	**80**	**101**
Monetary authorities	8 901	....	2	6	9	46	6	58	34
General government	8 902	....	....	....	....	....	4	....	1
Banks	8 903	....	....	4	7	6	8	18	52
Other sectors	8 904	1	1	2	3	....	4	5	13
Other investment	8 703	**2,038**	**2,196**	**2,825**	**3,752**	**5,726**	**5,780**	**8,068**	**14,987**
Trade credits	8 706	372	428	506	625	808	874	1,152	1,609
General government	8 707	....	....	....	....	....	....	....	....
of which: Short-term	8 709	....	....	....	....	....	....	....	....
Other sectors	8 710	372	428	506	625	808	874	1,152	1,609
of which: Short-term	8 712	*365*	*418*	*506*	*625*	*808*	*874*	*1,152*	*1,609*
Loans	8 714	276	719	1,124	1,301	2,352	2,199	2,913	5,459
Monetary authorities	8 715	....	....	....	....	....	....	....	....
of which: Short-term	8 718	....	....	....	....	....	....	....	....
General government	8 719	....	....	....	....	....	....	....	....
of which: Short-term	8 721	....	....	....	....	....	....	....	....
Banks	8 722	252	681	1,049	1,184	2,173	1,978	2,567	4,368
of which: Short-term	8 724	*120*	*504*	*799*	*802*	*1,339*	*1,098*	*1,151*	*2,282*
Other sectors	8 725	24	38	75	118	179	221	346	1,091
of which: Short-term	8 727	*19*	*19*	*51*	*74*	*82*	*103*	*155*	*210*
Currency and deposits	8 730	1,335	1,002	1,135	1,755	2,444	2,561	3,826	7,720
Monetary authorities	8 731	1	....	....	....	....	....	....	....
General government	8 732	3	7	1	2	....	....	....	35
Banks	8 733	1,233	916	1,059	1,641	2,346	2,211	2,361	4,659
Other sectors	8 734	98	79	75	113	97	350	1,465	3,026
Other assets	8 736	56	48	61	70	122	146	177	200
Monetary authorities	8 737	2	2	3	2	4	5	6	7
of which: Short-term	8 739	....	*1*	*1*	*1*	*1*	....	*1*	*2*
General government	8 740	16	16	17	18	55	70	77	84
of which: Short-term	8 742	....	....	....	....	....	....	....	....
Banks	8 743	30	19	12	18	26	31	58	82
of which: Short-term	8 745	*30*	*19*	*12*	*18*	*26*	*31*	*58*	*82*
Other sectors	8 746	8	12	29	32	36	41	37	27
of which: Short-term	8 748	*8*	*12*	*29*	*32*	*35*	*40*	*35*	*20*
Reserve assets	8 802	**919**	**1,218**	**1,327**	**1,535**	**2,022**	**2,361**	**4,509**	**5,758**
Monetary gold	8 812	68	70	86	103	110	128	156	205
Special drawing rights	8 811	....	....	....	....	....	....	....	....
Reserve position in the Fund	8 810	....	....	....	....	....	....	....	....
Foreign exchange	8 803	851	1,149	1,241	1,432	1,912	2,232	4,353	5,553
Other claims	8 813	....	....	....	....	....	....	....	....

Table 3 (Concluded). INTERNATIONAL INVESTMENT POSITION (End-period stocks), 2000–2007

(Millions of U.S. dollars)

	Code	2000	2001	2002	2003	2004	2005	2006	2007
LIABILITIES	8 995 D.	**6,164**	**7,167**	**9,105**	**11,836**	**16,900**	**19,096**	**29,693**	**47,204**
Direct investment in Latvia	8 555	**2,084**	**2,328**	**2,751**	**3,277**	**4,529**	**4,929**	**7,476**	**10,637**
Equity capital and reinvested earnings	8 556	1,414	1,634	2,054	2,406	3,433	3,836	5,791	8,537
Claims on direct investors	8 557	−3	−85	−21	−51	−26	−28	−11	−16
Liabilities to direct investors	8 558	1,417	1,719	2,074	2,458	3,460	3,865	5,802	8,553
Other capital	8 580	669	694	698	870	1,095	1,093	1,685	2,101
Claims on direct investors	8 585	−47	−83	−87	−129	−154	−174	−232	−731
Liabilities to direct investors	8 590	717	777	785	999	1,250	1,266	1,917	2,831
Portfolio investment	8 652	**255**	**428**	**511**	**687**	**1,035**	**1,118**	**1,599**	**1,760**
Equity securities	8 660	40	42	70	121	152	233	329	378
Banks	8 663	13	12	17	45	46	55	98	144
Other sectors	8 664	27	30	53	76	106	178	230	234
Debt securities	8 669	215	386	442	566	882	885	1,271	1,381
Bonds and notes	8 670	214	384	441	566	881	885	1,270	1,368
Monetary authorities	8 671	....	....	....	....	....	....	....	....
General government	8 672	213	384	416	537	810	706	794	898
Banks	8 673	....	....	25	28	70	179	463	448
Other sectors	8 674	1	....	....	....	....	....	13	22
Money market instruments	8 680	1	2	1	....	2	....	1	13
Monetary authorities	8 681	....	....	....	....	....	....	....	....
General government	8 682	....	....	....	....	2	....	1	....
Banks	8 683	....	....	....	....	....	....	....	12
Other sectors	8 684	1	2	1	....	....	....	....	1
Financial derivatives	8 905	....	**7**	**29**	**43**	**27**	**31**	**60**	**110**
Monetary authorities	8 906	....	7	9	15	9	17	25	39
General government	8 907	....	....	....	....	....	....	9	18
Banks	8 908	....	....	16	24	18	14	26	53
Other sectors	8 909	....	....	4	4	....	....	....	....
Other investment	8 753	**3,826**	**4,404**	**5,813**	**7,828**	**11,309**	**13,018**	**20,558**	**34,697**
Trade credits	8 756	515	548	652	788	1,044	1,004	1,272	1,795
General government	8 757	....	....	....	....	....	....	....	....
of which: Short-term	8 759	....	....	....	....	....	....	....	....
Other sectors	8 760	515	548	652	788	1,044	1,004	1,272	1,795
of which: Short-term	8 762	*515*	*527*	*652*	*788*	*1,044*	*1,004*	*1,272*	*1,795*
Loans	8 764	1,160	2,166	2,582	3,443	5,373	7,618	14,204	24,081
Monetary authorities	8 765	35	24	16	6	....	....	....	....
of which: Use of Fund credit and loans from the Fund	8 766	*35*	*24*	*16*	*6*	....	....	....	....
of which: Short-term	8 768	....	....	....	....	....	....	....	....
General government	8 769	327	324	337	314	327	264	355	601
of which: Short-term	8 771	....	....	....	....	....	....	....	*36*
Banks	8 772	201	971	1,168	1,841	3,423	5,800	10,950	17,374
of which: Short-term	8 774	....	*646*	*758*	*1,114*	*1,535*	*1,996*	*3,840*	*5,617*
Other sectors	8 775	598	847	1,062	1,282	1,623	1,554	2,899	6,106
of which: Short-term	8 777	*148*	*161*	*179*	*181*	*263*	*129*	*322*	*564*
Currency and deposits	8 780	1,824	1,622	2,500	3,519	4,714	4,263	4,863	8,381
Monetary authorities	8 781	....	1	1	2	47	8	43	24
General government	8 782	....	....	....	....	....	....	....	....
Banks	8 783	1,824	1,621	2,499	3,518	4,667	4,254	4,820	8,358
Other sectors	8 784	....	....	....	....	....	....	....	....
Other liabilities	8 786	327	69	79	79	178	132	218	440
Monetary authorities	8 787	1	2	....	1	1	....	....	1
of which: Short-term	8 789	*1*	*2*	....	*1*	*1*	....	....	*1*
General government	8 790	....	....	....	....	27	43	41	34
of which: Short-term	8 792	....	....	....	....	....	....	....	....
Banks	8 793	303	24	21	21	69	38	100	171
of which: Short-term	8 795	*303*	*24*	*21*	*21*	*69*	*38*	*100*	*171*
Other sectors	8 796	22	44	57	57	81	51	77	236
of which: Short-term	8 798	*22*	*44*	*57*	*57*	*81*	*51*	*77*	*236*
NET INTERNATIONAL INVESTMENT POSITION	8 995	**−2,325**	**−3,039**	**−3,970**	**−5,162**	**−7,520**	**−9,051**	**−14,519**	**−22,671**
Conversion rates: lats per U.S. dollar (end of period)	0 102	.6130	.6380	.5940	.5410	.5160	.5930	.5360	.4840

Table 1. ANALYTIC PRESENTATION, 2000–2007

(Millions of U.S. dollars)

	Code	2000	2001	2002	2003	2004	2005	2006	2007
A. Current Account[1]	4 993 Z.	....	....	**−4,415**	**−4,930**	**−4,080**	**−2,748**	**−1,202**	**−2,046**
Goods: exports f.o.b.	2 100 ..	....	....	1,210	1,733	2,050	2,652	3,207	4,077
Goods: imports f.o.b.	3 100 ..	....	....	−5,910	−6,528	−8,502	−9,239	−9,345	−11,926
Balance on Goods	4 100 ..	....	....	*−4,700*	*−4,794*	*−6,452*	*−6,588*	*−6,138*	*−7,850*
Services: credit	2 200 ..	....	....	4,429	9,462	9,704	10,858	11,565	12,527
Services: debit	3 200 ..	....	....	−3,354	−6,488	−8,230	−7,895	−8,734	−9,986
Balance on Goods and Services	4 991 ..	....	....	*−3,625*	*−1,821*	*−4,978*	*−3,624*	*−3,307*	*−5,309*
Income: credit	2 300 ..	....	....	395	1,399	1,060	1,733	2,440	2,663
Income: debit	3 300 ..	....	....	−1,263	−4,836	−1,878	−1,919	−2,145	−2,286
Balance on Goods, Services, and Income	4 992 ..	....	....	*−4,493*	*−5,258*	*−5,796*	*−3,811*	*−3,013*	*−4,932*
Current transfers: credit	2 379 Z.	....	....	2,591	4,079	5,325	4,399	5,053	5,219
Current transfers: debit	3 379 ..	....	....	−2,513	−3,751	−3,609	−3,337	−3,242	−2,333
B. Capital Account[1]	4 994 Z.	....	....	**13**	**29**	**50**	**27**	**1,940**	**590**
Capital account: credit	2 994 Z.	....	....	13	30	54	27	1,944	591
Capital account: debit	3 994 ..	....	....	....	−1	−3	....	−4	−1
Total, Groups A Plus B	4 981 ..	....	....	*−4,403*	*−4,901*	*−4,030*	*−2,721*	*739*	*−1,456*
C. Financial Account[1]	4 995 W.	....	....	**348**	**9,963**	**6,148**	**6,897**	**2,982**	**7,772**
Direct investment abroad	4 505 ..	....	....	....	−40	−213	−122	−70	233
Direct investment in Lebanon	4 555 Z.	....	....	1,336	2,977	1,993	2,791	2,739	2,845
Portfolio investment assets	4 602 ..	....	....	101	−559	−614	−110	−355	−992
Equity securities	4 610 ..	....	....	158	−40	−349	−151	−203	−83
Debt securities	4 619 ..	....	....	−57	−519	−265	40	−152	−909
Portfolio investment liabilities	4 652 Z.	....	....	749	644	−93	648	1,308	1,695
Equity securities	4 660 ..	....	....	....	207	148	1,436	551	791
Debt securities	4 669 Z.	....	....	749	437	−241	−788	757	904
Financial derivatives	4 910 ..	....	....	....	....	....	....	....	....
Financial derivatives assets	4 900 ..	....	....	....	....	....	....	....	....
Financial derivatives liabilities	4 905 ..	....	....	....	....	....	....	....	....
Other investment assets	4 703 ..	....	....	−1,744	5,015	3,864	3,658	−1,494	1,962
Monetary authorities	4 701 ..	....	....	....	....	....	....	....	....
General government	4 704 ..	....	....	....	136	92	82	47	54
Banks	4 705 ..	....	....	−901	5,201	4,186	4,700	1,617	2,207
Other sectors	4 728 ..	....	....	−843	−322	−414	−1,125	−3,159	−299
Other investment liabilities	4 753 W.	....	....	−94	1,926	1,211	32	854	2,029
Monetary authorities	4 753 WA	....	....	....	....	....	−22	2	244
General government	4 753 ZB	....	....	−16	612	−11	−69	4	50
Banks	4 753 ZC	....	....	1	190	41	−423	591	1,481
Other sectors	4 753 ZD	....	....	−78	1,124	1,182	547	257	254
Total, Groups A Through C	4 983 ..	....	....	*−4,055*	*5,063*	*2,118*	*4,176*	*3,720*	*6,316*
D. Net Errors and Omissions	4 998 ..	....	....	**4,719**	**−25**	**−2,898**	**−3,719**	**−3,575**	**−6,981**
Total, Groups A Through D	4 984 ..	....	....	*664*	*5,037*	*−780*	*458*	*146*	*−665*
E. Reserves and Related Items	4 802 A.	....	....	**−664**	**−5,037**	**780**	**−458**	**−146**	**665**
Reserve assets	4 802 ..	....	....	−664	−5,037	780	−458	−250	588
Use of Fund credit and loans	4 766 ..	....	....	....	....	....	....	....	77
Exceptional financing	4 920 ..	....	....	....	....	....	....	105	....
Conversion rates: Lebanese pounds per U.S. dollar	0 101 ..	**1,507.5**	**1,507.5**	**1,507.5**	**1,507.5**	**1,507.5**	**1,507.5**	**1,507.5**	**1,507.5**

[1] Excludes components that have been classified in the categories of Group E.

Table 2. STANDARD PRESENTATION, 2000–2007

(Millions of U.S. dollars)

	Code	2000	2001	2002	2003	2004	2005	2006	2007
CURRENT ACCOUNT	4 993 ..	....	....	**–4,415**	**–4,930**	**–4,080**	**–2,748**	**–1,097**	**–2,046**
A. GOODS	4 100 ..	....	....	**–4,700**	**–4,794**	**–6,452**	**–6,588**	**–6,138**	**–7,850**
Credit	2 100 ..	....	....	**1,210**	**1,733**	**2,050**	**2,652**	**3,207**	**4,077**
General merchandise: exports f.o.b.	2 110 ..	....	....	1,018	1,273	1,661	2,158	2,278	3,201
Goods for processing: exports f.o.b.	2 150 ..	....	....	63	105	207	291	416	472
Repairs on goods	2 160 ..	....	....	....	....	....	....	....	....
Goods procured in ports by carriers	2 170 ..	....	....	....	....	....	83	68	89
Nonmonetary gold	2 180 ..	....	....	129	355	182	120	445	315
Debit	3 100 ..	....	....	**–5,910**	**–6,528**	**–8,502**	**–9,239**	**–9,345**	**–11,926**
General merchandise: imports f.o.b.	3 110 ..	....	....	–5,739	–6,362	–8,168	–8,625	–8,879	–11,197
Goods for processing: imports f.o.b.	3 150 ..	....	....	....	....	....	–278	–319	–463
Repairs on goods	3 160 ..	....	....	–5	–2	–2	–2	–1	....
Goods procured in ports by carriers	3 170 ..	....	....	....	....	....	....	....	....
Nonmonetary gold	3 180 ..	....	....	–166	–164	–332	–334	–146	–266
B. SERVICES	4 200 ..	....	....	**1,075**	**2,974**	**1,474**	**2,963**	**2,830**	**2,541**
Total credit	2 200 ..	....	....	*4,429*	*9,462*	*9,704*	*10,858*	*11,565*	*12,527*
Total debit	3 200 ..	....	....	*–3,354*	*–6,488*	*–8,230*	*–7,895*	*–8,734*	*–9,986*
Transportation services, credit	2 205 ..	....	....	....	408	520	438	477	580
Passenger	2 850 ..	....	....	....	*408*	*520*	*437*	*476*	*580*
Freight	2 851 ..	....	....	....	....	....	....	....	....
Other	2 852 ..	....	....	....	....	....	....	....	....
Sea transport, passenger	2 207 ..	....	....	....	....	....	....	....	....
Sea transport, freight	2 208 ..	....	....	....	....	....	....	....	....
Sea transport, other	2 209 ..	....	....	....	....	....	....	....	....
Air transport, passenger	2 211 ..	....	....	....	408	520	437	476	580
Air transport, freight	2 212 ..	....	....	....	....	....	....	....	....
Air transport, other	2 213 ..	....	....	....	....	....	....	....	....
Other transport, passenger	2 215 ..	....	....	....	....	....	....	....	....
Other transport, freight	2 216 ..	....	....	....	....	....	....	....	....
Other transport, other	2 217 ..	....	....	....	....	....	....	....	....
Transportation services, debit	3 205 ..	....	....	**–471**	**–902**	**–1,229**	**–1,332**	**–1,500**	**–1,719**
Passenger	3 850 ..	....	....	....	*–376*	*–549*	*–657*	*–777*	*–800*
Freight	3 851 ..	....	....	*–471*	*–525*	*–680*	*–675*	*–723*	*–919*
Other	3 852 ..	....	....	....	....	....	....	....	....
Sea transport, passenger	3 207 ..	....	....	....	....	....	....	....	....
Sea transport, freight	3 208 ..	....	....	–351	–388	–513	–516	–553	–708
Sea transport, other	3 209 ..	....	....	....	....	....	....	....	....
Air transport, passenger	3 211 ..	....	....	....	–376	–549	–657	–777	–800
Air transport, freight	3 212 ..	....	....	–92	–103	–124	–117	–119	–150
Air transport, other	3 213 ..	....	....	....	....	....	....	....	....
Other transport, passenger	3 215 ..	....	....	....	....	....	....	....	....
Other transport, freight	3 216 ..	....	....	–28	–34	–43	–42	–51	–61
Other transport, other	3 217 ..	....	....	....	....	....	....	....	....
Travel, credit	2 236 ..	....	....	**4,284**	**6,374**	**5,411**	**5,532**	**4,965**	**4,993**
Business travel	2 237 ..	....	....	....	1,690	89	529	72	100
Personal travel	2 240 ..	....	....	4,284	4,683	5,322	5,002	4,893	4,893
Travel, debit	3 236 ..	....	....	**–2,683**	**–2,943**	**–3,170**	**–2,908**	**–3,006**	**–3,114**
Business travel	3 237 ..	....	....	....	–76	–111	–179	–82	–94
Personal travel	3 240 ..	....	....	–2,683	–2,867	–3,059	–2,729	–2,924	–3,020
Other services, credit	2 200 BA	....	....	**145**	**2,680**	**3,773**	**4,889**	**6,123**	**6,954**
Communications	2 245 ..	....	....	60	163	229	241	305	250
Construction	2 249 ..	....	....	....	....	....	....	....	....
Insurance	2 253 ..	....	....	65	124	141	209	189	260
Financial	2 260 ..	....	....	....	27	40	58	129	129
Computer and information	2 262 ..	....	....	....	....	....	....	....	....
Royalties and licence fees	2 266 ..	....	....	....	....	....	....	....	....
Other business services	2 268 ..	....	....	3	2,351	3,340	4,362	5,485	6,304
Personal, cultural, and recreational	2 287 ..	....	....	....	....	....	....	....	....
Government, n.i.e.	2 291 ..	....	....	17	16	22	19	16	11
Other services, debit	3 200 BA	....	....	**–200**	**–2,644**	**–3,831**	**–3,655**	**–4,228**	**–5,153**
Communications	3 245 ..	....	....	–4	–97	–203	–138	–217	–210
Construction	3 249 ..	....	....	....	....	....	....	....	....
Insurance	3 253 ..	....	....	–118	–217	–176	–248	–260	–285
Financial	3 260 ..	....	....	–1	–6	–9	–10	–19	–11
Computer and information	3 262 ..	....	....	....	....	....	....	....	–1
Royalties and licence fees	3 266 ..	....	....	....	....	....	....	....	....
Other business services	3 268 ..	....	....	–63	–2,310	–3,426	–3,242	–3,717	–4,630
Personal, cultural, and recreational	3 287 ..	....	....	....	....	....	....	....	....
Government, n.i.e.	3 291 ..	....	....	–14	–14	–16	–16	–15	–16

Table 2 (Continued). STANDARD PRESENTATION, 2000–2007

(Millions of U.S. dollars)

	Code	2000	2001	2002	2003	2004	2005	2006	2007
C. INCOME	4 300	....	....	**−868**	**−3,438**	**−818**	**−186**	**295**	**377**
Total credit	2 300	....	....	*395*	*1,399*	*1,060*	*1,733*	*2,440*	*2,663*
Total debit	3 300	....	....	*−1,263*	*−4,836*	*−1,878*	*−1,919*	*−2,145*	*−2,286*
Compensation of employees, credit	2 310	....	....	....	**779**	**409**	**667**	**579**	**747**
Compensation of employees, debit	3 310	....	....	**−11**	**−387**	**−660**	**−731**	**−661**	**−597**
Investment income, credit	2 320	....	....	**395**	**619**	**651**	**1,066**	**1,860**	**1,916**
Direct investment income	2 330	....	....	....	87	63	122	79	68
Dividends and distributed branch profits	2 332	....	....	....	87	63	122	79	68
Reinvested earnings and undistributed branch profits	2 333	....	....	....	....	....	....	....	....
Income on debt (interest)	2 334	....	....	....	....	....	....	....	....
Portfolio investment income	2 339	....	....	....	213	135	64	70	75
Income on equity	2 340	....	....	....	....	....	....	....	....
Income on bonds and notes	2 350	....	....	....	....	....	....	....	....
Income on money market instruments	2 360	....	....	....	213	135	64	70	75
Other investment income	2 370	....	....	395	319	453	881	1,712	1,773
Investment income, debit	3 320	....	....	**−1,252**	**−4,449**	**−1,218**	**−1,188**	**−1,484**	**−1,689**
Direct investment income	3 330	....	....	....	−69	−91	−95	−96	−64
Dividends and distributed branch profits	3 332	....	....	....	−69	−91	−95	−96	−64
Reinvested earnings and undistributed branch profits	3 333	....	....	....	....	....	....	....	....
Income on debt (interest)	3 334	....	....	....	....	....	....	....	....
Portfolio investment income	3 339	....	....	−710	−3,876	−573	−447	−467	−519
Income on equity	3 340	....	....	....	....	....	....	....	....
Income on bonds and notes	3 350	....	....	−440	−417	−377	−377	−357	−385
Income on money market instruments	3 360	....	....	−270	−3,460	−196	−70	−110	−135
Other investment income	3 370	....	....	−542	−503	−555	−646	−921	−1,106
D. CURRENT TRANSFERS	4 379	....	....	**78**	**328**	**1,716**	**1,063**	**1,916**	**2,886**
Credit	2 379	....	....	**2,591**	**4,079**	**5,325**	**4,399**	**5,157**	**5,219**
General government	2 380	....	....	47	8	11	8	113	13
Other sectors	2 390	....	....	2,544	4,071	5,314	4,392	5,045	5,205
Workers' remittances	2 391	....	....	2,544	3,964	5,183	4,257	4,623	5,022
Other current transfers	2 392	....	....	....	108	132	134	422	183
Debit	3 379	....	....	**−2,513**	**−3,751**	**−3,609**	**−3,337**	**−3,242**	**−2,333**
General government	3 380	....	....	−4	−4	−5	−8	−3	−10
Other sectors	3 390	....	....	−2,510	−3,747	−3,604	−3,329	−3,238	−2,323
Workers' remittances	3 391	....	....	−2,510	−3,694	−3,573	−3,281	−2,837	−2,248
Other current transfers	3 392	....	....	....	−53	−31	−48	−401	−75
CAPITAL AND FINANCIAL ACCOUNT	4 996	....	....	**−304**	**4,955**	**6,978**	**6,467**	**4,672**	**9,027**
CAPITAL ACCOUNT	4 994	....	....	**13**	**29**	**50**	**27**	**1,940**	**590**
Total credit	2 994	....	....	*13*	*30*	*54*	*27*	*1,944*	*591*
Total debit	3 994	....	....	....	*−1*	*−3*	....	*−4*	*−1*
Capital transfers, credit	2 400	....	....	**13**	**30**	**54**	**27**	**1,944**	**591**
General government	2 401	....	....	13	30	54	27	1,944	591
Debt forgiveness	2 402	....	....	....	....	....	....	....	....
Other capital transfers	2 410	....	....	13	30	54	27	1,944	591
Other sectors	2 430	....	....	....	....	....	....	....	....
Migrants' transfers	2 431	....	....	....	....	....	....	....	....
Debt forgiveness	2 432	....	....	....	....	....	....	....	....
Other capital transfers	2 440	....	....	....	....	....	....	....	....
Capital transfers, debit	3 400	....	....	....	**−1**	**−3**	....	**−4**	**−1**
General government	3 401	....	....	....	−1	−3	....	−4	−1
Debt forgiveness	3 402	....	....	....	....	....	....	....	....
Other capital transfers	3 410	....	....	....	−1	−3	....	−4	−1
Other sectors	3 430	....	....	....	....	....	....	....	....
Migrants' transfers	3 431	....	....	....	....	....	....	....	....
Debt forgiveness	3 432	....	....	....	....	....	....	....	....
Other capital transfers	3 440	....	....	....	....	....	....	....	....
Nonproduced nonfinancial assets, credit	2 480	....	....	....	....	....	....	....	....
Nonproduced nonfinancial assets, debit	3 480	....	....	....	....	....	....	....	....

Table 2 (Continued). STANDARD PRESENTATION, 2000–2007

(Millions of U.S. dollars)

	Code	2000	2001	2002	2003	2004	2005	2006	2007
FINANCIAL ACCOUNT	4 995	....	....	−317	4,926	6,928	6,439	2,731	8,437
A. DIRECT INVESTMENT	4 500	....	....	1,336	2,937	1,780	2,669	2,669	3,077
Direct investment abroad	4 505	....	....	....	−40	−213	−122	−70	233
Equity capital	4 510	....	....	....	−40	−213	−122	−70	233
Claims on affiliated enterprises	4 515	....	....	....	−40	−213	−122	−70	233
Liabilities to affiliated enterprises	4 520	....	....	....	....	....	....	....	....
Reinvested earnings	4 525	....	....	....	....	....	....	....	....
Other capital	4 530	....	....	....	....	....	....	....	....
Claims on affiliated enterprises	4 535	....	....	....	....	....	....	....	....
Liabilities to affiliated enterprises	4 540	....	....	....	....	....	....	....	....
Direct investment in Lebanon	4 555	....	....	1,336	2,977	1,993	2,791	2,739	2,845
Equity capital	4 560			1,336	2,977	1,993	2,791	2,739	2,845
Claims on direct investors	4 565	....	....	....	....	....	....	....	....
Liabilities to direct investors	4 570	....	....	1,336	2,977	1,993	2,791	2,739	2,845
Reinvested earnings	4 575	....	....	....	....	....	....	....	....
Other capital	4 580	....	....	....	....	....	....	....	....
Claims on direct investors	4 585	....	....	....	....	....	....	....	....
Liabilities to direct investors	4 590	....	....	....	....	....	....	....	....
B. PORTFOLIO INVESTMENT	4 600	....	....	850	85	−707	537	953	703
Assets	4 602	....	....	101	−559	−614	−110	−355	−992
Equity securities	4 610	....	....	158	−40	−349	−151	−203	−83
Monetary authorities	4 611	....	....	....	....	....	....	....	....
General government	4 612	....	....	....	107	....	1	1	3
Banks	4 613	....	....	132	−89	−294	−115	−201	186
Other sectors	4 614	....	....	26	−58	−55	−36	−3	−272
Debt securities	4 619	....	....	−57	−519	−265	40	−152	−909
Bonds and notes	4 620	....	....	−54	−514	−274	39	−139	−813
Monetary authorities	4 621	....	....	....	....	....	....	....	....
General government	4 622	....	....	....	....	....	....	....	....
Banks	4 623	....	....	34	−452	−218	64	−89	−861
Other sectors	4 624	....	....	−88	−62	−55	−25	−51	48
Money market instruments	4 630	....	....	−3	−5	8	1	−13	−97
Monetary authorities	4 631	....	....	....	....	....	....	....	....
General government	4 632	....	....	....	....	....	....	....	....
Banks	4 633	....	....	−3	−2	4	2	−12	−100
Other sectors	4 634	....	....		−2	5	−1	−1	4
Liabilities	4 652	....	....	749	644	−93	648	1,308	1,695
Equity securities	4 660	....	....	....	207	148	1,436	551	791
Banks	4 663	....	....	....	22	42	153	163	183
Other sectors	4 664	....	....	....	185	106	1,283	388	609
Debt securities	4 669	....	....	749	437	−241	−788	757	904
Bonds and notes	4 670	....	....	891	563	−272	−642	732	890
Monetary authorities	4 671	....	....	22	−50	−253	−313	1,752	....
General government	4 672	....	....	869	−323	−1,285	−600	−1,789	−634
Banks	4 673	....	....	....	93	171	152	143	112
Other sectors	4 674	....	....	....	843	1,095	119	625	1,412
Money market instruments	4 680	....	....	−143	−127	32	−146	25	15
Monetary authorities	4 681	....	....	....	....	....	....	....	....
General government	4 682	....	....	−143	−127	32	−146	25	15
Banks	4 683	....	....	....	....	....	....	....	....
Other sectors	4 684	....	....	....	....	....	....	....	....
C. FINANCIAL DERIVATIVES	4 910	....	....	....	....	....	....	....	....
Monetary authorities	4 911	....	....	....	....	....	....	....	....
General government	4 912	....	....	....	....	....	....	....	....
Banks	4 913	....	....	....	....	....	....	....	....
Other sectors	4 914	....	....	....	....	....	....	....	....
Assets	4 900	....	....	....	....	....	....	....	....
Monetary authorities	4 901	....	....	....	....	....	....	....	....
General government	4 902	....	....	....	....	....	....	....	....
Banks	4 903	....	....	....	....	....	....	....	....
Other sectors	4 904	....	....	....	....	....	....	....	....
Liabilities	4 905	....	....	....	....	....	....	....	....
Monetary authorities	4 906	....	....	....	....	....	....	....	....
General government	4 907	....	....	....	....	....	....	....	....
Banks	4 908	....	....	....	....	....	....	....	....
Other sectors	4 909	....	....	....	....	....	....	....	....

Table 2 (Concluded). STANDARD PRESENTATION, 2000–2007

(Millions of U.S. dollars)

	Code	2000	2001	2002	2003	2004	2005	2006	2007
D. OTHER INVESTMENT	4 700 ..	....	....	−1,838	6,941	5,075	3,690	−641	4,069
Assets	4 703 ..	....	....	−1,744	5,015	3,864	3,658	−1,494	1,962
Trade credits	4 706 ..	....	....	....	....	....	....	....	....
General government	4 707 ..	....	....	....	....	....	....	....	....
of which: Short-term	4 709 ..	....	....	....	....	....	....	....	....
Other sectors	4 710 ..	....	....	....	....	....	....	....	....
of which: Short-term	4 712 ..	....	....	....	....	....	....	....	....
Loans	4 714 ..	....	....	....	3,615	5,232	4,649	5,083	6,619
Monetary authorities	4 715 ..	....	....	....	....	....	....	....	....
of which: Short-term	4 718 ..	....	....	....	....	....	....	....	....
General government	4 719 ..	....	....	....	1	....	....	1	6
of which: Short-term	4 721 ..	....	....	....	....	....	....	....	....
Banks	4 722 ..	....	....	....	3,551	5,135	4,516	4,688	6,543
of which: Short-term	4 724 ..	....	....	....	....	....	....	....	....
Other sectors	4 725 ..	....	....	....	64	97	132	394	70
of which: Short-term	4 727 ..	....	....	....	....	....	....	....	....
Currency and deposits	4 730 ..	....	....	−1,744	1,400	−1,368	−991	−6,578	−4,657
Monetary authorities	4 731 ..	....	....	....	....	....	....	....	....
General government	4 732 ..	....	....	....	135	92	82	45	48
Banks	4 733 ..	....	....	−901	1,651	−949	184	−3,070	−4,336
Other sectors	4 734 ..	....	....	−843	−386	−511	−1,257	−3,553	−369
Other assets	4 736 ..	....	....	....	....	....	....	....	....
Monetary authorities	4 737 ..	....	....	....	....	....	....	....	....
of which: Short-term	4 739 ..	....	....	....	....	....	....	....	....
General government	4 740 ..	....	....	....	....	....	....	....	....
of which: Short-term	4 742 ..	....	....	....	....	....	....	....	....
Banks	4 743 ..	....	....	....	....	....	....	....	....
of which: Short-term	4 745 ..	....	....	....	....	....	....	....	....
Other sectors	4 746 ..	....	....	....	....	....	....	....	....
of which: Short-term	4 748 ..	....	....	....	....	....	....	....	....
Liabilities	4 753 ..	....	....	−94	1,926	1,211	32	854	2,106
Trade credits	4 756 ..	....	....	....	....	....	....	....	....
General government	4 757 ..	....	....	....	....	....	....	....	....
of which: Short-term	4 759 ..	....	....	....	....	....	....	....	....
Other sectors	4 760 ..	....	....	....	....	....	....	....	....
of which: Short-term	4 762 ..	....	....	....	....	....	....	....	....
Loans	4 764 ..	....	....	−16	992	285	960	304	441
Monetary authorities	4 765 ..	....	....	....	....	....	....	....	77
of which: Use of Fund credit and loans from the Fund..	4 766 ..	....	....	....	....	....	....	....	77
of which: Short-term	4 768 ..	....	....	....	....	....	....	....	....
General government	4 769 ..	....	....	−16	581	−12	−70	1	....
of which: Short-term	4 771 ..	....	....	....	....	....	....	....	....
Banks	4 772 ..	....	....	....	190	41	30	68	13
of which: Short-term	4 774 ..	....	....	....	....	....	....	....	....
Other sectors	4 775 ..	....	....	....	221	257	1,000	235	350
of which: Short-term	4 777 ..	....	....	....	....	....	....	....	....
Currency and deposits	4 780 ..	....	....	−77	934	926	−927	549	1,666
Monetary authorities	4 781 ..	....	....	....	....	....	−22	2	244
General government	4 782 ..	....	....	....	31	1	....	3	49
Banks	4 783 ..	....	....	1	....	....	−453	523	1,469
Other sectors	4 784 ..	....	....	−78	903	925	−453	22	−96
Other liabilities	4 786 ..	....	....	....	....	....	....	....	....
Monetary authorities	4 787 ..	....	....	....	....	....	....	....	....
of which: Short-term	4 789 ..	....	....	....	....	....	....	....	....
General government	4 790 ..	....	....	....	....	....	....	....	....
of which: Short-term	4 792 ..	....	....	....	....	....	....	....	....
Banks	4 793 ..	....	....	....	....	....	....	....	....
of which: Short-term	4 795 ..	....	....	....	....	....	....	....	....
Other sectors	4 796 ..	....	....	....	....	....	....	....	....
of which: Short-term	4 798 ..	....	....	....	....	....	....	....	....
E. RESERVE ASSETS	4 802 ..	....	....	−664	−5,037	780	−458	−250	588
Monetary gold	4 812 ..	....	....	....	....	....	....	....	....
Special drawing rights	4 811 ..	....	....	−1	−1	−1	−1	−2	1
Reserve position in the Fund	4 810 ..	....	....	....	....	....	....	....	....
Foreign exchange	4 803 ..	....	....	−663	−5,037	781	−456	−248	587
Other claims	4 813 ..	....	....	....	....	....	....	....	....
NET ERRORS AND OMISSIONS	4 998 ..	....	....	4,719	−25	−2,898	−3,719	−3,575	−6,981

Table 1. ANALYTIC PRESENTATION, 2000–2007

(Millions of U.S. dollars)

	Code	2000	2001	2002	2003	2004	2005	2006	2007
A. Current Account[1]	4 993 Z.	**−151.4**	**−95.1**	**−142.5**	**−134.7**	**−68.0**	**−102.0**	**66.3**	**211.8**
Goods: exports f.o.b.	2 100 ..	211.1	278.6	357.3	475.0	707.3	650.0	693.6	805.0
Goods: imports f.o.b.	3 100 ..	−727.6	−678.6	−762.7	−994.4	−1,302.0	−1,306.3	−1,361.3	−1,604.4
Balance on Goods	4 100 ..	*−516.5*	*−400.0*	*−405.5*	*−519.4*	*−594.7*	*−656.3*	*−667.7*	*−799.4*
Services: credit	2 200 ..	42.7	40.5	34.9	49.9	71.9	52.2	59.1	76.2
Services: debit	3 200 ..	−42.5	−49.0	−55.4	−84.9	−96.1	−103.3	−95.2	−110.2
Balance on Goods and Services	4 991 ..	*−516.4*	*−408.5*	*−426.0*	*−554.4*	*−618.9*	*−707.4*	*−703.8*	*−833.4*
Income: credit	2 300 ..	288.8	235.3	206.8	304.1	379.1	370.0	412.7	517.3
Income: debit	3 300 ..	−62.6	−56.7	−44.9	−54.3	−76.3	−65.2	−32.1	−97.1
Balance on Goods, Services, and Income	4 992 ..	*−290.2*	*−229.9*	*−264.1*	*−304.7*	*−316.1*	*−402.6*	*−323.2*	*−413.2*
Current transfers: credit	2 379 Z.	139.8	137.2	123.3	171.8	250.7	303.8	392.0	628.7
Current transfers: debit	3 379 ..	−1.0	−2.5	−1.7	−1.9	−2.5	−3.2	−2.6	−3.6
B. Capital Account[1]	4 994 Z.	**22.0**	**16.8**	**23.5**	**27.5**	**33.4**	**21.3**	**11.0**	**32.0**
Capital account: credit	2 994 Z.	22.0	16.8	23.5	27.5	33.4	21.3	11.0	32.0
Capital account: debit	3 994 ..	....	....	....	....	....	....	....	....
Total, Groups A Plus B	4 981 ..	*−129.4*	*−78.3*	*−119.0*	*−107.3*	*−34.6*	*−80.7*	*77.3*	*243.9*
C. Financial Account[1]	4 995 W.	**85.2**	**88.6**	**88.8**	**98.2**	**63.3**	**127.0**	**3.6**	**84.6**
Direct investment abroad	4 505 ..	....	....	....	....	−.1	....	....	....
Direct investment in Lesotho	4 555 Z.	117.8	117.0	84.1	115.7	123.5	92.6	113.0	130.3
Portfolio investment assets	4 602 ..	....	....	....	....	....	....	....	....
Equity securities	4 610 ..	....	....	....	....	....	....	....	....
Debt securities	4 619 ..	....	....	....	....	....	....	....	....
Portfolio investment liabilities	4 652 Z.	....	....	....	....	....	....	....	....
Equity securities	4 660 ..	....	....	....	....	....	....	....	....
Debt securities	4 669 Z.	....	....	....	....	....	....	....	....
Financial derivatives	4 910 ..	....	....	....	....	....	....	....	....
Financial derivatives assets	4 900 ..	....	....	....	....	....	....	....	....
Financial derivatives liabilities	4 905 ..	....	....	....	....	....	....	....	....
Other investment assets	4 703 ..	−19.1	−20.2	1.5	−8.8	−48.9	−.1	−87.8	−62.2
Monetary authorities	4 701 ..	....	....	....	....	....	....	....	....
General government	4 704 ..	....	....	....	....	....	....	....	....
Banks	4 705 ..	−19.1	−20.2	1.5	−8.8	−48.9	−.1	−87.8	−62.2
Other sectors	4 728 ..	....	....	....	....	....	....	....	....
Other investment liabilities	4 753 W.	−13.5	−8.2	3.2	−8.7	−11.2	34.5	−21.7	16.4
Monetary authorities	4 753 WA	−3.5	16.0	.8	−17.8	.9	94.2	−1.0	9.3
General government	4 753 ZB	−15.1	−19.0	2.9	−10.0	1.6	−46.1	−16.2	7.4
Banks	4 753 ZC	5.2	−4.8	....	19.2	−13.7	−13.6	−5.2	−.3
Other sectors	4 753 ZD	−.1	−.5	−.5	−.1	....	....	.7	....
Total, Groups A Through C	4 983 ..	*−44.3*	*10.3*	*−30.2*	*−9.0*	*28.7*	*46.3*	*80.9*	*328.5*
D. Net Errors and Omissions	4 998 ..	**62.1**	**155.4**	**−97.9**	**−55.8**	**−25.0**	**−2.7**	**109.9**	**−58.6**
Total, Groups A Through D	4 984 ..	*17.8*	*165.7*	*−128.2*	*−64.8*	*3.8*	*43.7*	*190.8*	*269.9*
E. Reserves and Related Items	4 802 A.	**−17.8**	**−165.7**	**128.2**	**64.8**	**−3.8**	**−43.7**	**−190.8**	**−269.9**
Reserve assets	4 802 ..	−12.6	−170.2	122.9	62.3	−13.6	−43.7	−190.3	−267.2
Use of Fund credit and loans	4 766 ..	−5.2	4.5	5.2	2.5	9.8	....	−.5	−2.7
Exceptional financing	4 920 ..	....	....	....	....	....	....	....	....
Conversion rates: maloti per U.S. dollar	0 101 ..	**6.940**	**8.609**	**10.541**	**7.565**	**6.460**	**6.359**	**6.772**	**7.045**

[1] Excludes components that have been classified in the categories of Group E.

Table 2. STANDARD PRESENTATION, 2000–2007

(Millions of U.S. dollars)

	Code	2000	2001	2002	2003	2004	2005	2006	2007
CURRENT ACCOUNT	4 993 ..	−151.4	−95.1	−142.5	−134.7	−68.0	−102.0	66.3	211.8
A. GOODS	4 100 ..	−516.5	−400.0	−405.5	−519.4	−594.7	−656.3	−667.7	−799.4
Credit	2 100 ..	211.1	278.6	357.3	475.0	707.3	650.0	693.6	805.0
General merchandise: exports f.o.b.	2 110 ..	211.1	278.6	357.3	475.0	707.3	650.0	693.6	805.0
Goods for processing: exports f.o.b.	2 150 ..	....	....	....	....	....	....	....	....
Repairs on goods	2 160 ..	....	....	....	....	....	....	....	....
Goods procured in ports by carriers	2 170 ..	....	....	....	....	....	....	....	....
Nonmonetary gold	2 180 ..	....	....	....	....	....	....	....	....
Debit	3 100 ..	−727.6	−678.6	−762.7	−994.4	−1,302.0	−1,306.3	−1,361.3	−1,604.4
General merchandise: imports f.o.b.	3 110 ..	−727.6	−678.6	−762.7	−994.4	−1,302.0	−1,306.3	−1,361.3	−1,604.4
Goods for processing: imports f.o.b.	3 150 ..	....	....	....	....	....	....	....	....
Repairs on goods	3 160 ..	....	....	....	....	....	....	....	....
Goods procured in ports by carriers	3 170 ..	....	....	....	....	....	....	....	....
Nonmonetary gold	3 180 ..	....	....	....	....	....	....	....	....
B. SERVICES	4 200 ..	.1	−8.5	−20.5	−35.1	−24.2	−51.1	−36.1	−34.0
Total credit	2 200 ..	*42.7*	*40.5*	*34.9*	*49.9*	*71.9*	*52.2*	*59.1*	*76.2*
Total debit	3 200 ..	*−42.5*	*−49.0*	*−55.4*	*−84.9*	*−96.1*	*−103.3*	*−95.2*	*−110.2*
Transportation services, credit	2 205 ..	.5	.4	.4	.5	.6	.8	.7	.7
Passenger	2 850 ..	....	....	....	....	....	....	....	....
Freight	2 851 ..	....	....	....	....	....	....	....	....
Other	2 852 ..	*.5*	*.4*	*.4*	*.5*	*.6*	*.8*	*.7*	*.7*
Sea transport, passenger	2 207 ..	....	....	....	....	....	....	....	....
Sea transport, freight	2 208 ..	....	....	....	....	....	....	....	....
Sea transport, other	2 209 ..	....	....	....	....	....	....	....	....
Air transport, passenger	2 211 ..	....	....	....	....	....	....	....	....
Air transport, freight	2 212 ..	....	....	....	....	....	....	....	....
Air transport, other	2 213 ..	.5	.4	.1	....	.1	.2	.2	.2
Other transport, passenger	2 215 ..	....	....	....	....	....	....	....	....
Other transport, freight	2 216 ..	....	....	....	....	....	....	....	....
Other transport, other	2 217 ..	....	....	.3	.5	.6	.6	.5	.5
Transportation services, debit	3 205 ..	−31.5	−28.6	−30.8	−43.5	−55.5	−59.2	−54.7	−69.4
Passenger	3 850 ..	*−3.2*	*−2.5*	*−2.3*	*−3.9*	*−6.6*	*−8.9*	*−3.0*	*−7.7*
Freight	3 851 ..	*−28.3*	*−26.1*	*−28.5*	*−39.6*	*−48.9*	*−50.2*	*−51.7*	*−61.7*
Other	3 852 ..	....	....	....	....	....	....	....	....
Sea transport, passenger	3 207 ..	....	....	....	....	....	....	....	....
Sea transport, freight	3 208 ..	....	....	....	....	....	....	....	....
Sea transport, other	3 209 ..	....	....	....	....	....	....	....	....
Air transport, passenger	3 211 ..	−3.2	−2.5	−2.3	−3.9	−6.6	−8.9	−3.0	−7.7
Air transport, freight	3 212 ..	....	....	....	....	....	....	....	....
Air transport, other	3 213 ..	....	....	....	....	....	....	....	....
Other transport, passenger	3 215 ..	....	....	....	....	....	....	....	....
Other transport, freight	3 216 ..	−28.3	−26.1	−28.5	−39.6	−48.9	−50.2	−51.7	−61.7
Other transport, other	3 217 ..	....	....	....	....	....	....	....	....
Travel, credit	2 236 ..	24.2	22.8	19.5	27.6	41.5	26.0	26.8	42.6
Business travel	2 237 ..	9.8	8.6	5.9	6.9	8.4	3.5	3.3	8.0
Personal travel	2 240 ..	14.4	14.1	13.7	20.7	33.1	22.5	23.5	34.6
Travel, debit	3 236 ..	−9.4	−9.1	−14.0	−25.9	−30.3	−27.0	−18.8	−16.3
Business travel	3 237 ..	−.6	−.2	−.4	−1.6	−1.9	−1.9	−2.2	−1.8
Personal travel	3 240 ..	−8.8	−8.9	−13.6	−24.3	−28.4	−25.1	−16.6	−14.6
Other services, credit	2 200 BA	18.0	17.3	15.0	21.8	29.7	25.5	31.6	32.9
Communications	2 245 ..	....	....	....	....	....	1.3	4.7	4.1
Construction	2 249 ..	....	....	....	....	....	....	....	....
Insurance	2 253 ..	−.5	....	−.5	....	2.6	−2.3	−.2	−.1
Financial	2 260 ..	....	....	....	....	....	....	....	....
Computer and information	2 262 ..	....	....	....	....	....	....	....	....
Royalties and licence fees	2 266 ..	11.7	11.5	10.5	14.9	17.0	18.1	18.5	20.4
Other business services	2 268 ..	....	....	.1	.1	1.7	....	.1	....
Personal, cultural, and recreational	2 287 ..	....	....	....	....	....	....	....	....
Government, n.i.e.	2 291 ..	6.7	5.8	4.9	6.9	8.3	8.4	8.6	8.5
Other services, debit	3 200 BA	−1.7	−11.2	−10.6	−15.5	−10.3	−17.1	−21.6	−24.5
Communications	3 245 ..	....	....	....	....	....	−2.0	−1.5	−2.7
Construction	3 249 ..	....	....	....	....	....	....	....	....
Insurance	3 253 ..	....	−.5	....	....	....	....	....	....
Financial	3 260 ..	....	....	....	....	....	....	....	....
Computer and information	3 262 ..	....	....	....	....	....	....	....	....
Royalties and licence fees	3 266 ..	....	−.2	....	....	....	....	....	....
Other business services	3 268 ..	....	....	....	....	−.1	....	....	....
Personal, cultural, and recreational	3 287 ..	....	....	....	....	....	....	....	....
Government, n.i.e.	3 291 ..	−1.6	−10.6	−10.6	−15.5	−10.2	−15.1	−20.2	−21.8

Table 2 (Continued). STANDARD PRESENTATION, 2000–2007

(Millions of U.S. dollars)

	Code	2000	2001	2002	2003	2004	2005	2006	2007
C. INCOME..	4 300 ..	**226.1**	**178.6**	**161.9**	**249.8**	**302.8**	**304.8**	**380.7**	**420.2**
Total credit......................................	2 300 ..	*288.8*	*235.3*	*206.8*	*304.1*	*379.1*	*370.0*	*412.7*	*517.3*
Total debit..	3 300 ..	*−62.6*	*−56.7*	*−44.9*	*−54.3*	*−76.3*	*−65.2*	*−32.1*	*−97.1*
Compensation of employees, credit..................	2 310 ..	**252.1**	**208.1**	**184.5**	**276.5**	**340.5**	**319.6**	**357.0**	**430.4**
Compensation of employees, debit....................	3 310 ..	**−27.5**	**−24.7**	**−21.2**	**−27.0**	**−29.4**	**−16.9**	**−10.9**	**−21.0**
Investment income, credit.................................	2 320 ..	**36.7**	**27.1**	**22.3**	**27.7**	**38.6**	**50.4**	**55.8**	**86.8**
Direct investment income...............................	2 330 ..	....	....	....	....	....	....	....	....
Dividends and distributed branch profits........................	2 332 ..	....	....	....	....	....	....	....	....
Reinvested earnings and undistributed branch profits.....	2 333 ..	....	....	....	....	....	....	....	....
Income on debt (interest)............................	2 334 ..	....	....	....	....	....	....	....	....
Portfolio investment income...........................	2 339 ..	....	....	....	....	....	....	....	....
Income on equity..................................	2 340 ..	....	....	....	....	....	....	....	....
Income on bonds and notes........................	2 350 ..	....	....	....	....	....	....	....	....
Income on money market instruments........................	2 360 ..	....	....	....	....	....	....	....	....
Other investment income..............................	2 370 ..	36.7	27.1	22.3	27.7	38.6	50.4	55.8	86.8
Investment income, debit.................................	3 320 ..	**−35.1**	**−31.9**	**−23.7**	**−27.4**	**−46.9**	**−48.3**	**−21.2**	**−76.1**
Direct investment income...............................	3 330 ..	−15.0	−16.0	−11.7	−14.4	−20.6	−10.7	−11.6	−12.9
Dividends and distributed branch profits........................	3 332 ..	−15.0	−16.0	−11.7	−14.4	−20.6	−10.7	−11.6	−12.9
Reinvested earnings and undistributed branch profits.....	3 333 ..	....	....	....	....	....	....	....	....
Income on debt (interest)............................	3 334 ..	....	....	....	....	....	....	....	....
Portfolio investment income...........................	3 339 ..	....	....	....	....	....	....	....	....
Income on equity..................................	3 340 ..	....	....	....	....	....	....	....	....
Income on bonds and notes........................	3 350 ..	....	....	....	....	....	....	....	....
Income on money market instruments........................	3 360 ..	....	....	....	....	....	....	....	....
Other investment income..............................	3 370 ..	−20.1	−15.9	−11.9	−13.0	−26.2	−37.5	−9.5	−63.1
D. CURRENT TRANSFERS..	4 379 ..	**138.8**	**134.7**	**121.6**	**169.9**	**248.1**	**300.6**	**389.5**	**625.0**
Credit..	2 379 ..	**139.8**	**137.2**	**123.3**	**171.8**	**250.7**	**303.8**	**392.0**	**628.7**
General government..	2 380 ..	137.4	133.6	110.0	151.9	217.6	274.0	369.9	614.7
Other sectors..	2 390 ..	2.4	3.6	13.3	19.9	33.0	29.8	22.1	14.0
Workers' remittances..................................	2 391 ..	.1	1.3	9.8	11.5	14.4	6.9	4.5	12.9
Other current transfers...............................	2 392 ..	2.3	2.3	3.6	8.4	18.7	22.9	17.6	1.1
Debit..	3 379 ..	**−1.0**	**−2.5**	**−1.7**	**−1.9**	**−2.5**	**−3.2**	**−2.6**	**−3.6**
General government..	3 380 ..	−1.0	−2.5	−1.6	−1.7	−2.4	−3.0	−2.5	−3.5
Other sectors..	3 390 ..	....	....	−.1	−.2	−.2	−.1	....	−.1
Workers' remittances..................................	3 391 ..	....	....	....	....	....	....	....	....
Other current transfers...............................	3 392 ..	....	....	−.1	−.2	−.2	−.1	....	−.1
CAPITAL AND FINANCIAL ACCOUNT........................	4 996 ..	**89.4**	**−60.2**	**240.4**	**190.5**	**92.9**	**104.7**	**−176.2**	**−153.2**
CAPITAL ACCOUNT...	4 994 ..	**22.0**	**16.8**	**23.5**	**27.5**	**33.4**	**21.3**	**11.0**	**32.0**
Total credit......................................	2 994 ..	*22.0*	*16.8*	*23.5*	*27.5*	*33.4*	*21.3*	*11.0*	*32.0*
Total debit..	3 994 ..	....	....	....	....	....	....	....	....
Capital transfers, credit..................................	2 400 ..	**22.0**	**16.8**	**23.5**	**27.5**	**33.4**	**21.3**	**11.0**	**32.0**
General government..	2 401 ..	22.0	16.8	23.5	27.5	33.4	21.3	11.0	32.0
Debt forgiveness...................................	2 402 ..	....	....	....	....	....	....	....	....
Other capital transfers.............................	2 410 ..	22.0	16.8	23.5	27.5	33.4	21.3	11.0	32.0
Other sectors..	2 430 ..	....	....	....	....	....	....	....	....
Migrants' transfers..................................	2 431 ..	....	....	....	....	....	....	....	....
Debt forgiveness...................................	2 432 ..	....	....	....	....	....	....	....	....
Other capital transfers.............................	2 440 ..	....	....	....	....	....	....	....	....
Capital transfers, debit....................................	3 400 ..	....	....	....	....	....	....	....	....
General government..	3 401 ..	....	....	....	....	....	....	....	....
Debt forgiveness...................................	3 402 ..	....	....	....	....	....	....	....	....
Other capital transfers.............................	3 410 ..	....	....	....	....	....	....	....	....
Other sectors..	3 430 ..	....	....	....	....	....	....	....	....
Migrants' transfers..................................	3 431 ..	....	....	....	....	....	....	....	....
Debt forgiveness...................................	3 432 ..	....	....	....	....	....	....	....	....
Other capital transfers.............................	3 440 ..	....	....	....	....	....	....	....	....
Nonproduced nonfinancial assets, credit.............	2 480 ..	....	....	....	....	....	....	....	....
Nonproduced nonfinancial assets, debit..............	3 480 ..	....	....	....	....	....	....	....	....

Table 2 (Continued). STANDARD PRESENTATION, 2000–2007

(Millions of U.S. dollars)

	Code	2000	2001	2002	2003	2004	2005	2006	2007
FINANCIAL ACCOUNT	4 995 ..	**67.4**	**−77.1**	**216.9**	**163.0**	**59.5**	**83.4**	**−187.2**	**−185.3**
A. DIRECT INVESTMENT	4 500 ..	**117.8**	**117.0**	**84.0**	**115.7**	**123.4**	**92.6**	**113.0**	**130.3**
Direct investment abroad	4 505 ..	....	....	....	....	−.1	....	....	....
Equity capital	4 510 ..	....	....	....	....	....	....	....	....
Claims on affiliated enterprises	4 515 ..	....	....	....	....	....	....	....	....
Liabilities to affiliated enterprises	4 520 ..	....	....	....	....	....	....	....	....
Reinvested earnings	4 525 ..	....	....	....	....	....	....	....	....
Other capital	4 530 ..	....	....	....	....	−.1	....	....	....
Claims on affiliated enterprises	4 535 ..	....	....	....	....	−.1	....	....	....
Liabilities to affiliated enterprises	4 540 ..	....	....	....	....	....	....	....	....
Direct investment in Lesotho	4 555 ..	**117.8**	**117.0**	**84.1**	**115.7**	**123.5**	**92.6**	**113.0**	**130.3**
Equity capital	4 560 ..	31.5	28.5	27.1	42.2	53.5	57.3	92.5	105.8
Claims on direct investors	4 565 ..	....	....	....	....	....	....	....	....
Liabilities to direct investors	4 570 ..	31.5	28.5	27.1	42.2	53.5	57.3	92.5	105.8
Reinvested earnings	4 575 ..	....	....	....	....	....	....	....	....
Other capital	4 580 ..	86.3	88.5	57.0	73.5	70.0	35.3	20.6	24.5
Claims on direct investors	4 585 ..	....	....	....	....	....	....	....	....
Liabilities to direct investors	4 590 ..	86.3	88.5	57.0	73.5	70.0	35.3	20.6	24.5
B. PORTFOLIO INVESTMENT	4 600 ..	....	....	....	....	....	....	....	....
Assets	4 602 ..	....	....	....	....	....	....	....	....
Equity securities	4 610 ..	....	....	....	....	....	....	....	....
Monetary authorities	4 611 ..	....	....	....	....	....	....	....	....
General government	4 612 ..	....	....	....	....	....	....	....	....
Banks	4 613 ..	....	....	....	....	....	....	....	....
Other sectors	4 614 ..	....	....	....	....	....	....	....	....
Debt securities	4 619 ..	....	....	....	....	....	....	....	....
Bonds and notes	4 620 ..	....	....	....	....	....	....	....	....
Monetary authorities	4 621 ..	....	....	....	....	....	....	....	....
General government	4 622 ..	....	....	....	....	....	....	....	....
Banks	4 623 ..	....	....	....	....	....	....	....	....
Other sectors	4 624 ..	....	....	....	....	....	....	....	....
Money market instruments	4 630 ..	....	....	....	....	....	....	....	....
Monetary authorities	4 631 ..	....	....	....	....	....	....	....	....
General government	4 632 ..	....	....	....	....	....	....	....	....
Banks	4 633 ..	....	....	....	....	....	....	....	....
Other sectors	4 634 ..	....	....	....	....	....	....	....	....
Liabilities	4 652 ..	....	....	....	....	....	....	....	....
Equity securities	4 660 ..	....	....	....	....	....	....	....	....
Banks	4 663 ..	....	....	....	....	....	....	....	....
Other sectors	4 664 ..	....	....	....	....	....	....	....	....
Debt securities	4 669 ..	....	....	....	....	....	....	....	....
Bonds and notes	4 670 ..	....	....	....	....	....	....	....	....
Monetary authorities	4 671 ..	....	....	....	....	....	....	....	....
General government	4 672 ..	....	....	....	....	....	....	....	....
Banks	4 673 ..	....	....	....	....	....	....	....	....
Other sectors	4 674 ..	....	....	....	....	....	....	....	....
Money market instruments	4 680 ..	....	....	....	....	....	....	....	....
Monetary authorities	4 681 ..	....	....	....	....	....	....	....	....
General government	4 682 ..	....	....	....	....	....	....	....	....
Banks	4 683 ..	....	....	....	....	....	....	....	....
Other sectors	4 684 ..	....	....	....	....	....	....	....	....
C. FINANCIAL DERIVATIVES	4 910 ..	....	....	....	....	....	....	....	....
Monetary authorities	4 911 ..	....	....	....	....	....	....	....	....
General government	4 912 ..	....	....	....	....	....	....	....	....
Banks	4 913 ..	....	....	....	....	....	....	....	....
Other sectors	4 914 ..	....	....	....	....	....	....	....	....
Assets	4 900 ..	....	....	....	....	....	....	....	....
Monetary authorities	4 901 ..	....	....	....	....	....	....	....	....
General government	4 902 ..	....	....	....	....	....	....	....	....
Banks	4 903 ..	....	....	....	....	....	....	....	....
Other sectors	4 904 ..	....	....	....	....	....	....	....	....
Liabilities	4 905 ..	....	....	....	....	....	....	....	....
Monetary authorities	4 906 ..	....	....	....	....	....	....	....	....
General government	4 907 ..	....	....	....	....	....	....	....	....
Banks	4 908 ..	....	....	....	....	....	....	....	....
Other sectors	4 909 ..	....	....	....	....	....	....	....	....

Table 2 (Concluded). STANDARD PRESENTATION, 2000–2007

(Millions of U.S. dollars)

	Code	2000	2001	2002	2003	2004	2005	2006	2007
D. OTHER INVESTMENT...	4 700 ..	**−37.8**	**−23.9**	**9.9**	**−15.0**	**−50.3**	**34.4**	**−110.0**	**−48.4**
Assets...	4 703 ..	**−19.1**	**−20.2**	**1.5**	**−8.8**	**−48.9**	**−.1**	**−87.8**	**−62.2**
Trade credits..................................	4 706 ..	....	....	....	....	....	....	....	....
General government......................	4 707 ..	....	....	....	....	....	....	....	....
of which: Short-term..................	4 709 ..	....	....	....	....	....	....	....	....
Other sectors..............................	4 710 ..	....	....	....	....	....	....	....	....
of which: Short-term..................	4 712 ..	....	....	....	....	....	....	....	....
Loans..	4 714 ..	....	....	....	....	....	....	....	....
Monetary authorities....................	4 715 ..	....	....	....	....	....	....	....	....
of which: Short-term..................	4 718 ..	....	....	....	....	....	....	....	....
General government......................	4 719 ..	....	....	....	....	....	....	....	....
of which: Short-term..................	4 721 ..	....	....	....	....	....	....	....	....
Banks..	4 722 ..	....	....	....	....	....	....	....	....
of which: Short-term..................	4 724 ..	....	....	....	....	....	....	....	....
Other sectors..............................	4 725 ..	....	....	....	....	....	....	....	....
of which: Short-term..................	4 727 ..	....	....	....	....	....	....	....	....
Currency and deposits.....................	4 730 ..	−19.1	−20.2	1.5	−8.8	−48.9	−.1	−87.8	−62.2
Monetary authorities....................	4 731 ..	....	....	....	....	....	....	....	....
General government......................	4 732 ..	....	....	....	....	....	....	....	....
Banks..	4 733 ..	−19.1	−20.2	1.5	−8.8	−48.9	−.1	−87.8	−62.2
Other sectors..............................	4 734 ..	....	....	....	....	....	....	....	....
Other assets..................................	4 736 ..	....	....	....	....	....	....	....	....
Monetary authorities....................	4 737 ..	....	....	....	....	....	....	....	....
of which: Short-term..................	4 739 ..	....	....	....	....	....	....	....	....
General government......................	4 740 ..	....	....	....	....	....	....	....	....
of which: Short-term..................	4 742 ..	....	....	....	....	....	....	....	....
Banks..	4 743 ..	....	....	....	....	....	....	....	....
of which: Short-term..................	4 745 ..	....	....	....	....	....	....	....	....
Other sectors..............................	4 746 ..	....	....	....	....	....	....	....	....
of which: Short-term..................	4 748 ..	....	....	....	....	....	....	....	....
Liabilities...	4 753 ..	**−18.7**	**−3.7**	**8.4**	**−6.2**	**−1.4**	**34.5**	**−22.2**	**13.8**
Trade credits..................................	4 756 ..	....	....	....	....	....	....	....	....
General government......................	4 757 ..	....	....	....	....	....	....	....	....
of which: Short-term..................	4 759 ..	....	....	....	....	....	....	....	....
Other sectors..............................	4 760 ..	....	....	....	....	....	....	....	....
of which: Short-term..................	4 762 ..	....	....	....	....	....	....	....	....
Loans..	4 764 ..	−20.4	−14.9	7.6	−7.6	11.4	−46.1	−16.7	4.7
Monetary authorities....................	4 765 ..	−5.2	4.5	5.2	2.5	9.8	....	−.5	−2.7
of which: Use of Fund credit and loans from the Fund..	4 766 ..	*−5.2*	*4.5*	*5.2*	*2.5*	*9.8*	....	*−.5*	*−2.7*
of which: Short-term..................	4 768 ..	....	....	....	....	....	....	....	....
General government......................	4 769 ..	−15.1	−19.0	2.9	−10.0	1.6	−46.1	−16.2	7.4
of which: Short-term..................	4 771 ..	....	....	....	....	....	....	....	....
Banks..	4 772 ..	....	....	....	....	....	....	....	....
of which: Short-term..................	4 774 ..	....	....	....	....	....	....	....	....
Other sectors..............................	4 775 ..	−.1	−.5	−.5	−.1	....	....	....	....
of which: Short-term..................	4 777 ..	....	....	....	....	....	....	....	....
Currency and deposits.....................	4 780 ..	....	....	....	....	....	....	....	....
Monetary authorities....................	4 781 ..	....	....	....	....	....	....	....	....
General government......................	4 782 ..	....	....	....	....	....	....	....	....
Banks..	4 783 ..	....	....	....	....	....	....	....	....
Other sectors..............................	4 784 ..	....	....	....	....	....	....	....	....
Other liabilities.............................	4 786 ..	1.7	11.2	.8	1.4	−12.8	80.6	−5.5	9.1
Monetary authorities....................	4 787 ..	−3.5	16.0	.8	−17.8	.9	94.2	−1.0	9.3
of which: Short-term..................	4 789 ..	*−3.5*	*16.0*	*.8*	*−17.8*	*.9*	*94.2*	*−1.0*	*9.3*
General government......................	4 790 ..	....	....	....	....	....	....	....	....
of which: Short-term..................	4 792 ..	....	....	....	....	....	....	....	....
Banks..	4 793 ..	5.2	−4.8	....	19.2	−13.7	−13.6	−5.2	−.3
of which: Short-term..................	4 795 ..	*5.2*	*−4.8*	....	*19.2*	*−13.7*	*−13.6*	*−5.2*	*−.3*
Other sectors..............................	4 796 ..	....	....	....	....	....	....	.7	....
of which: Short-term..................	4 798 ..	....	....	....	....	....	....	*.7*	....
E. RESERVE ASSETS.................................	4 802 ..	**−12.6**	**−170.2**	**122.9**	**62.3**	**−13.6**	**−43.7**	**−190.3**	**−267.2**
Monetary gold................................	4 812 ..	....	....	....	....	....	....	....	....
Special drawing rights.....................	4 811 ..	.5	.1	....	....	....	.1	.2	−6.0
Reserve position in the Fund............	4 810 ..	....	....	....	....	....	−.1	....	....
Foreign exchange............................	4 803 ..	−13.1	−170.2	122.9	63.2	−14.7	−40.4	−190.7	−259.0
Other claims..................................	4 813 ..	....	....	....	−.9	1.1	−3.4	.2	−2.3
NET ERRORS AND OMISSIONS............................	4 998 ..	**62.1**	**155.4**	**−97.9**	**−55.8**	**−25.0**	**−2.7**	**109.9**	**−58.6**

Table 3. INTERNATIONAL INVESTMENT POSITION (End-period stocks), 2000–2007

(Millions of U.S. dollars)

	Code	2000	2001	2002	2003	2004	2005	2006	2007
ASSETS..	8 995 C.	**500.3**	**488.8**	**536.0**	**629.4**	**818.0**	**769.4**	**970.4**	**1,336.6**
Direct investment abroad....................................	8 505 ..	....	....	....	....	....	....	....	....
Equity capital and reinvested earnings..........................	8 506 ..	....	....	....	....	....	....	....	....
Claims on affiliated enterprises..........................	8 507 ..	....	....	....	....	....	....	....	....
Liabilities to affiliated enterprises........................	8 508 ..	....	....	....	....	....	....	....	....
Other capital..	8 530 ..	....	....	....	....	....	....	....	....
Claims on affiliated enterprises..........................	8 535 ..	....	....	....	....	....	....	....	....
Liabilities to affiliated enterprises........................	8 540 ..	....	....	....	....	....	....	....	....
Portfolio investment..	8 602 ..	....	....	....	....	....	....		....
Equity securities...	8 610 ..	....	....	....	....	....	....		....
Monetary authorities......................................	8 611 ..	....	....	....	....	....	....		....
General government.......................................	8 612 ..	....	....	....	....	....	....		....
Banks..	8 613 ..	....	....	....	....	....	....		....
Other sectors..	8 614 ..	....	....	....	....	....	....		....
Debt securities..	8 619 ..	....	....	....	....	....	....		....
Bonds and notes...	8 620 ..	....	....	....	....	....	....		....
Monetary authorities..................................	8 621 ..	....	....	....	....	....	....		....
General government...................................	8 622 ..	....	....	....	....	....	....		....
Banks..	8 623 ..	....	....	....	....	....	....		....
Other sectors...	8 624 ..	....	....	....	....	....	....		....
Money market instruments..............................	8 630 ..	....	....	....	....	....	....		....
Monetary authorities..................................	8 631 ..	....	....	....	....	....	....		....
General government...................................	8 632 ..	....	....	....	....	....	....		....
Banks..	8 633 ..	....	....	....	....	....	....		....
Other sectors...	8 634 ..	....	....	....	....	....	....		....
Financial derivatives.......................................	8 900 ..	....	....	....	....	....	....		....
Monetary authorities..	8 901 ..	....	....	....	....	....	....		....
General government...	8 902 ..	....	....	....	....	....	....		....
Banks..	8 903 ..	....	....	....	....	....	....		....
Other sectors..	8 904 ..	....	....	....	....	....	....		....
Other investment...	8 703 ..	**80.5**	**65.1**	**89.4**	**126.1**	**222.7**	**196.3**	**264.8**	**333.9**
Trade credits...	8 706 ..	....	....	....	....	....	....	....	....
General government.......................................	8 707 ..	....	....	....	....	....	....	....	....
of which: Short-term.....................................	8 709 ..	....	....	....	....	....	....	....	....
Other sectors..	8 710 ..	....	....	....	....	....	....	....	....
of which: Short-term.....................................	8 712 ..	....	....	....	....	....	....	....	....
Loans..	8 714 ..	....	....	....	....	....	....	....	....
Monetary authorities......................................	8 715 ..	....	....	....	....	....	....	....	....
of which: Short-term...................................	8 718 ..	....	....	....	....	....	....	....	....
General government.......................................	8 719 ..	....	....	....	....	....	....	....	....
of which: Short-term...................................	8 721 ..	....	....	....	....	....	....	....	....
Banks..	8 722 ..	....	....	....	....	....	....	....	....
of which: Short-term...................................	8 724 ..	....	....	....	....	....	....	....	....
Other sectors..	8 725 ..	....	....	....	....	....	....	....	....
of which: Short-term...................................	8 727 ..	....	....	....	....	....	....	....	....
Currency and deposits......................................	8 730 ..	80.5	65.1	....	....	....	....	....	....
Monetary authorities......................................	8 731 ..	....	....	....	....	....	....	....	....
General government.......................................	8 732 ..	....	....	....	....	....	....	....	....
Banks..	8 733 ..	80.5	65.1	....	....	....	....	....	....
Other sectors..	8 734 ..	....	....	....	....	....	....	....	....
Other assets...	8 736 ..	....	....	89.4	126.1	222.7	196.3	264.8	333.9
Monetary authorities......................................	8 737 ..	....	....	....	....	....	....	....	....
of which: Short-term...................................	8 739 ..	....	....	....	....	....	....	....	....
General government.......................................	8 740 ..	....	....	....	....	....	....	....	....
of which: Short-term...................................	8 742 ..	....	....	....	....	....	....	....	....
Banks..	8 743 ..	....	....	89.4	126.1	222.7	196.3	264.8	333.9
of which: Short-term...................................	8 745 ..	....	....	*89.4*	*126.1*	*222.7*	*196.3*	*264.8*	*333.9*
Other sectors..	8 746 ..	....	....	....	....	....	....	....	....
of which: Short-term...................................	8 748 ..	....	....	....	....	....	....	....	....
Reserve assets..	8 802 ..	**419.8**	**423.7**	**446.6**	**503.2**	**595.3**	**573.1**	**705.6**	**1,002.8**
Monetary gold...	8 812 ..	....	....	....	....	....	....	....	....
Special drawing rights......................................	8 811 ..	.7	.6	.6	.6	.6	.4	.2	6.3
Reserve position in the Fund..............................	8 810 ..	4.6	4.4	4.8	5.3	5.5	5.1	5.4	5.7
Foreign exchange...	8 803 ..	414.6	418.7	298.6	384.9	431.5	299.0	300.8	411.2
Other claims...	8 813 ..	....	....	142.5	112.4	157.7	268.5	399.2	579.5

Table 3 (Concluded). INTERNATIONAL INVESTMENT POSITION (End-period stocks), 2000–2007

(Millions of U.S. dollars)

	Code	2000	2001	2002	2003	2004	2005	2006	2007
LIABILITIES	8 995 D.	**600.9**	**580.9**	**702.2**	**802.1**	**881.0**	**773.0**	**772.2**	**822.9**
Direct investment in Lesotho	8 555	....	....	....	....	....	....	....	....
Equity capital and reinvested earnings	8 556	....	....	....	....	....	....	....	....
Claims on direct investors	8 557	....	....	....	....	....	....	....	....
Liabilities to direct investors	8 558	....	....	....	....	....	....	....	....
Other capital	8 580	....	....	....	....	....	....	....	....
Claims on direct investors	8 585	....	....	....	....	....	....	....	....
Liabilities to direct investors	8 590	....	....	....	....	....	....	....	....
Portfolio investment	8 652	....	....	....	....	....	....	....	....
Equity securities	8 660	....	....	....	....	....	....	....	....
Banks	8 663	....	....	....	....	....	....	....	....
Other sectors	8 664	....	....	....	....	....	....	....	....
Debt securities	8 669	....	....	....	....	....	....	....	....
Bonds and notes	8 670	....	....	....	....	....	....	....	....
Monetary authorities	8 671	....	....	....	....	....	....	....	....
General government	8 672	....	....	....	....	....	....	....	....
Banks	8 673	....	....	....	....	....	....	....	....
Other sectors	8 674	....	....	....	....	....	....	....	....
Money market instruments	8 680	....	....	....	....	....	....	....	....
Monetary authorities	8 681	....	....	....	....	....	....	....	....
General government	8 682	....	....	....	....	....	....	....	....
Banks	8 683	....	....	....	....	....	....	....	....
Other sectors	8 684	....	....	....	....	....	....	....	....
Financial derivatives	8 905	....	....	....	....	....	....	....	....
Monetary authorities	8 906	....	....	....	....	....	....	....	....
General government	8 907	....	....	....	....	....	....	....	....
Banks	8 908	....	....	....	....	....	....	....	....
Other sectors	8 909	....	....	....	....	....	....	....	....
Other investment	8 753	**600.9**	**580.9**	**702.2**	**802.1**	**881.0**	**773.0**	**772.2**	**822.9**
Trade credits	8 756	....	....	....	....	....	....	....	....
General government	8 757	....	....	....	....	....	....	....	....
of which: Short-term	8 759	....	....	....	....	....	....	....	....
Other sectors	8 760	....	....	....	....	....	....	....	....
of which: Short-term	8 762	....	....	....	....	....	....	....	....
Loans	8 764	11.1	530.4	615.8	694.0	768.6	669.3	684.0	722.7
Monetary authorities	8 765	11.1	15.2	22.0	26.6	38.0	35.0	36.3	35.4
of which: Use of Fund credit and loans from the Fund	8 766	*11.1*	*15.2*	*22.0*	*26.6*	*38.0*	*35.0*	*36.3*	*35.4*
of which: Short-term	8 768	....	....	....	....	....	....	....	....
General government	8 769	....	515.1	593.8	667.5	730.5	634.2	647.7	687.3
of which: Short-term	8 771	....	....	....	....	....	....	....	....
Banks	8 772	....	....	....	....	....	....	....	....
of which: Short-term	8 774	....	....	....	....	....	....	....	....
Other sectors	8 775	....	....	....	....	....	....	....	....
of which: Short-term	8 777	....	....	....	....	....	....	....	....
Currency and deposits	8 780	.6	8.5	11.5	34.6	24.1	16.9	10.5	10.8
Monetary authorities	8 781	.6	....	....	....	....	....	....	....
General government	8 782	....	....	....	....	....	....	....	....
Banks	8 783	....	8.5	11.5	34.6	24.1	16.9	10.5	10.8
Other sectors	8 784	....	....	....	....	....	....	....	....
Other liabilities	8 786	589.2	42.0	74.9	73.5	88.3	86.9	77.7	89.4
Monetary authorities	8 787	....	42.0	74.9	73.5	88.3	86.9	77.7	89.4
of which: Short-term	8 789	....	....	*74.9*	*73.5*	*88.3*	*86.9*	*77.7*	*89.4*
General government	8 790	570.7	....	....	....	....	....	....	....
of which: Short-term	8 792	....	....	....	....	....	....	....	....
Banks	8 793	18.5	....	....	....	....	....	....	....
of which: Short-term	8 795	....	....	....	....	....	....	....	....
Other sectors	8 796	....	....	....	....	....	....	....	....
of which: Short-term	8 798	....	....	....	....	....	....	....	....
NET INTERNATIONAL INVESTMENT POSITION	8 995	**−100.6**	**−92.0**	**−166.2**	**−172.8**	**−63.0**	**−3.6**	**198.2**	**513.7**
Conversion rates: maloti per U.S. dollar (end of period)	0 102	**7.569**	**12.127**	**8.640**	**6.640**	**5.630**	**6.325**	**6.970**	**6.810**

Table 1. ANALYTIC PRESENTATION, 2000–2007

(Millions of U.S. dollars)

	Code	2000	2001	2002	2003	2004	2005	2006	2007
A. Current Account[1]	4 993 Z.	....	....	....	....	**−164.6**	**−198.7**	**−369.2**	**−383.2**
Goods: exports f.o.b.	2 100 ..	....	....	....	....	104.8	132.3	154.6	196.2
Goods: imports f.o.b.	3 100 ..	....	....	....	....	−278.9	−306.4	−441.1	−498.5
Balance on Goods	4 100 ..	....	....	....	....	*−174.1*	*−174.1*	*−286.5*	*−302.3*
Services: credit	2 200 ..	....	....	....	....	210.6	211.3	336.5	346.2
Services: debit	3 200 ..	....	....	....	....	−769.7	−844.3	−1,274.6	−1,244.0
Balance on Goods and Services	4 991 ..	....	....	....	....	*−733.2*	*−807.1*	*−1,224.6*	*−1,200.1*
Income: credit	2 300 ..	....	....	....	....	5.0	9.2	18.3	19.9
Income: debit	3 300 ..	....	....	....	....	−167.6	−155.8	−166.7	−169.8
Balance on Goods, Services, and Income	4 992 ..	....	....	....	....	*−895.8*	*−953.8*	*−1,372.9*	*−1,350.1*
Current transfers: credit	2 379 Z.	....	....	....	....	731.2	755.0	1,003.7	966.8
Current transfers: debit	3 379 ..	....	....	....	....	....	....	....	....
B. Capital Account[1]	4 994 Z.	....	....	....	....	....	....	....	....
Capital account: credit	2 994 Z.	....	....	....	....	....	....	....	....
Capital account: debit	3 994 Z.	....	....	....	....	....	....	....	....
Total, Groups A Plus B	4 981 ..	....	....	....	....	*−164.6*	*−198.7*	*−369.2*	*−383.2*
C. Financial Account[1]	4 995 W.	....	....	....	....	**46.1**	**54.2**	**87.3**	**113.5**
Direct investment abroad	4 505 ..	....	....	....	....	....	....	....	....
Direct investment in Liberia	4 555 Z.	....	....	....	....	69.3	75.8	107.9	131.6
Portfolio investment assets	4 602 ..	....	....	....	....	....	....	....	....
Equity securities	4 610 ..	....	....	....	....	....	....	....	....
Debt securities	4 619 ..	....	....	....	....	....	....	....	....
Portfolio investment liabilities	4 652 Z.	....	....	....	....	....	....	....	....
Equity securities	4 660 ..	....	....	....	....	....	....	....	....
Debt securities	4 669 Z.	....	....	....	....	....	....	....	....
Financial derivatives	4 910 ..	....	....	....	....	....	....	....	....
Financial derivatives assets	4 900 ..	....	....	....	....	....	....	....	....
Financial derivatives liabilities	4 905 ..	....	....	....	....	....	....	....	....
Other investment assets	4 703 ..	....	....	....	....	−3.3	−3.1	−15.5	−13.2
Monetary authorities	4 701 ..	....	....	....	....	−3.3	−3.1	−15.5	−13.2
General government	4 704 ..	....	....	....	....	....	....	....	....
Banks	4 705 ..	....	....	....	....	....	....	....	....
Other sectors	4 728 ..	....	....	....	....	....	....	....	....
Other investment liabilities	4 753 W.	....	....	....	....	−19.9	−18.6	−5.0	−4.9
Monetary authorities	4 753 WA	....	....	....	....	....	....	....	....
General government	4 753 ZB	....	....	....	....	−19.9	−18.6	−5.0	−4.9
Banks	4 753 ZC	....	....	....	....	....	....	....	....
Other sectors	4 753 ZD	....	....	....	....	....	....	....	....
Total, Groups A Through C	4 983 ..	....	....	....	....	*−118.5*	*−144.6*	*−281.9*	*−269.7*
D. Net Errors and Omissions	4 998 ..	....	....	....	....	**−48.8**	**−36.5**	**−20.9**	**−9.5**
Total, Groups A Through D	4 984 ..	....	....	....	....	*−167.3*	*−181.0*	*−302.8*	*−279.2*
E. Reserves and Related Items	4 802 A.	....	....	....	....	**167.3**	**181.0**	**302.8**	**279.2**
Reserve assets	4 802 ..	....	....	....	....	−5.3	−2.3	−38.6	−38.8
Use of Fund credit and loans	4 766 ..	....	....	....	....	....	−.1	−.7	−.7
Exceptional financing	4 920 ..	....	....	....	....	172.6	183.4	342.1	318.7
Conversion rates: Liberian dollar per U.S. dollar	0 101 ..	**40.9525**	**48.5833**	**61.7542**	**59.3788**	**54.9058**	**57.0958**	**58.0133**	**61.2722**

[1] Excludes components that have been classified in the categories of Group E.

Table 2. STANDARD PRESENTATION, 2000–2007

(Millions of U.S. dollars)

	Code	2000	2001	2002	2003	2004	2005	2006	2007
CURRENT ACCOUNT	4 993	....	....	....	....	−151.8	−174.7	−173.2	−211.3
A. GOODS	4 100	....	....	....	....	−174.1	−174.1	−286.5	−302.3
Credit	2 100	....	....	....	....	104.8	132.3	154.6	196.2
General merchandise: exports f.o.b.	2 110	....	....	....	....	103.8	131.3	153.0	189.1
Goods for processing: exports f.o.b.	2 150	....	....	....	....	....	....	....	....
Repairs on goods	2 160	....	....	....	....	....	....	....	....
Goods procured in ports by carriers	2 170	....	....	....	....	.9	1.0	1.5	1.6
Nonmonetary gold	2 180	....	....	....	....	....	....	.2	5.5
Debit	3 100	....	....	....	....	−278.9	−306.4	−441.1	−498.5
General merchandise: imports f.o.b.	3 110	....	....	....	....	−278.9	−306.4	−441.1	−498.5
Goods for processing: imports f.o.b.	3 150	....	....	....	....	....	....	....	....
Repairs on goods	3 160	....	....	....	....	....	....	....	....
Goods procured in ports by carriers	3 170	....	....	....	....	....	....	....	....
Nonmonetary gold	3 180	....	....	....	....	....	....	....	....
B. SERVICES	4 200	....	....	....	....	−559.1	−633.0	−938.1	−897.8
Total credit	2 200	....	....	....	....	*210.6*	*211.3*	*336.5*	*346.2*
Total debit	3 200	....	....	....	....	*−769.7*	*−844.3*	*−1,274.6*	*−1,244.0*
Transportation services, credit	2 205	....	....	....	....	6.0	9.9	15.0	20.2
Passenger	2 850	....	....	....	....	....	....	....	....
Freight	2 851	....	....	....	....	....	....	....	....
Other	2 852	....	....	....	....	*6.0*	*9.9*	*15.0*	*20.2*
Sea transport, passenger	2 207	....	....	....	....	....	....	....	....
Sea transport, freight	2 208	....	....	....	....	....	....	....	....
Sea transport, other	2 209	....	....	....	....	5.2	9.0	13.6	18.4
Air transport, passenger	2 211	....	....	....	....	....	....	....	....
Air transport, freight	2 212	....	....	....	....	....	....	....	....
Air transport, other	2 213	....	....	....	....	.9	1.0	1.5	1.7
Other transport, passenger	2 215	....	....	....	....	....	....	....	....
Other transport, freight	2 216	....	....	....	....	....	....	....	....
Other transport, other	2 217	....	....	....	....	....	....	....	....
Transportation services, debit	3 205	....	....	....	....	−63.9	−70.7	−114.5	−122.7
Passenger	3 850	....	....	....	....	*−13.9*	*−15.9*	*−23.7*	*−27.3*
Freight	3 851	....	....	....	....	*−49.9*	*−54.9*	*−90.8*	*−95.3*
Other	3 852	....	....	....	....	....	....	....	....
Sea transport, passenger	3 207	....	....	....	....	....	....	....	....
Sea transport, freight	3 208	....	....	....	....	−47.4	−52.1	−86.3	−90.6
Sea transport, other	3 209	....	....	....	....	....	....	....	....
Air transport, passenger	3 211	....	....	....	....	−13.9	−15.9	−23.7	−27.3
Air transport, freight	3 212	....	....	....	....	−2.5	−2.7	−4.5	−4.8
Air transport, other	3 213	....	....	....	....	....	....	....	....
Other transport, passenger	3 215	....	....	....	....	....	....	....	....
Other transport, freight	3 216	....	....	....	....	....	....	....	....
Other transport, other	3 217	....	....	....	....	....	....	....	....
Travel, credit	2 236	....	....	....	....	58.6	67.2	124.4	131.1
Business travel	2 237	....	....	....	....	58.6	67.2	124.4	131.1
Personal travel	2 240	....	....	....	....	....	....	....	....
Travel, debit	3 236	....	....	....	....	−13.1	−14.7	−17.3	−20.9
Business travel	3 237	....	....	....	....	−4.5	−5.0	−2.7	−3.3
Personal travel	3 240	....	....	....	....	−8.6	−9.8	−14.6	−17.7
Other services, credit	2 200 BA	....	....	....	....	145.9	134.1	197.1	194.9
Communications	2 245	....	....	....	....	....	....	....	....
Construction	2 249	....	....	....	....	....	....	....	....
Insurance	2 253	....	....	....	....	....	....	....	....
Financial	2 260	....	....	....	....	....	....	....	....
Computer and information	2 262	....	....	....	....	....	....	....	....
Royalties and licence fees	2 266	....	....	....	....	....	....	....	....
Other business services	2 268	....	....	....	....	2.2	2.6	3.8	4.3
Personal, cultural, and recreational	2 287	....	....	....	....	....	....	....	....
Government, n.i.e.	2 291	....	....	....	....	143.7	131.6	193.3	190.6
Other services, debit	3 200 BA	....	....	....	....	−692.8	−758.9	−1,142.8	−1,100.4
Communications	3 245	....	....	....	....	....	....	....	....
Construction	3 249	....	....	....	....	....	....	....	....
Insurance	3 253	....	....	....	....	−2.6	−2.9	−4.8	−5.0
Financial	3 260	....	....	....	....	....	....	....	....
Computer and information	3 262	....	....	....	....	....	....	....	....
Royalties and licence fees	3 266	....	....	....	....	....	....	....	....
Other business services	3 268	....	....	....	....	....	....	−44.8	−42.4
Personal, cultural, and recreational	3 287	....	....	....	....	....	....	−35.5	−23.1
Government, n.i.e.	3 291	....	....	....	....	−690.2	−756.0	−1,057.7	−1,029.9

Table 2 (Continued). STANDARD PRESENTATION, 2000–2007

(Millions of U.S. dollars)

	Code	2000	2001	2002	2003	2004	2005	2006	2007
C. INCOME	4 300	....	....	....	....	−162.6	−146.6	−148.3	−149.9
Total credit	2 300	....	....	....	....	*5.0*	*9.2*	*18.3*	*19.9*
Total debit	3 300	....	....	....	....	*−167.6*	*−155.8*	*−166.7*	*−169.8*
Compensation of employees, credit	2 310	....	....	....	....	5.0	9.2	18.3	19.9
Compensation of employees, debit	3 310	....	....	....	....	−.2	−.2	−.2	−.3
Investment income, credit	2 320	....	....	....	....	....	....	....	....
Direct investment income	2 330	....	....	....	....	....	....	....	....
Dividends and distributed branch profits	2 332	....	....	....	....	....	....	....	....
Reinvested earnings and undistributed branch profits	2 333	....	....	....	....	....	....	....	....
Income on debt (interest)	2 334	....	....	....	....	....	....	....	....
Portfolio investment income	2 339	....	....	....	....	....	....	....	....
Income on equity	2 340	....	....	....	....	....	....	....	....
Income on bonds and notes	2 350	....	....	....	....	....	....	....	....
Income on money market instruments	2 360	....	....	....	....	....	....	....	....
Other investment income	2 370	....	....	....	....	....	....	....	....
Investment income, debit	3 320	....	....	....	....	−167.4	−155.7	−166.4	−169.5
Direct investment income	3 330	....	....	....	....	−5.7	−7.1	−14.0	−14.7
Dividends and distributed branch profits	3 332	....	....	....	....	−2.8	−3.5	−7.0	−7.3
Reinvested earnings and undistributed branch profits	3 333	....	....	....	....	−2.8	−3.5	−7.0	−7.3
Income on debt (interest)	3 334	....	....	....	....	....	....	....	....
Portfolio investment income	3 339	....	....	....	....	....	....	....	....
Income on equity	3 340	....	....	....	....	....	....	....	....
Income on bonds and notes	3 350	....	....	....	....	....	....	....	....
Income on money market instruments	3 360	....	....	....	....	....	....	....	....
Other investment income	3 370	....	....	....	....	−161.8	−148.6	−152.4	−154.9
D. CURRENT TRANSFERS	4 379	....	....	....	....	744.0	779.1	1,199.7	1,138.8
Credit	2 379	....	....	....	....	744.0	779.1	1,199.7	1,138.8
General government	2 380	....	....	....	....	689.3	755.0	1,137.0	1,094.1
Other sectors	2 390	....	....	....	....	54.7	24.0	62.8	44.7
Workers' remittances	2 391	....	....	....	....	....	....	....	....
Other current transfers	2 392	....	....	....	....	54.7	24.0	62.8	44.7
Debit	3 379	....	....	....	....	....	....	....	....
General government	3 380	....	....	....	....	....	....	....	....
Other sectors	3 390	....	....	....	....	....	....	....	....
Workers' remittances	3 391	....	....	....	....	....	....	....	....
Other current transfers	3 392	....	....	....	....	....	....	....	....
CAPITAL AND FINANCIAL ACCOUNT	4 996	....	....	....	....	200.6	211.2	194.0	220.7
CAPITAL ACCOUNT	4 994	....	....	....	....	....	....	....	....
Total credit	2 994	....	....	....	....	....	....	....	....
Total debit	3 994	....	....	....	....	....	....	....	....
Capital transfers, credit	2 400	....	....	....	....	....	....	....	....
General government	2 401	....	....	....	....	....	....	....	....
Debt forgiveness	2 402	....	....	....	....	....	....	....	....
Other capital transfers	2 410	....	....	....	....	....	....	....	....
Other sectors	2 430	....	....	....	....	....	....	....	....
Migrants' transfers	2 431	....	....	....	....	....	....	....	....
Debt forgiveness	2 432	....	....	....	....	....	....	....	....
Other capital transfers	2 440	....	....	....	....	....	....	....	....
Capital transfers, debit	3 400	....	....	....	....	....	....	....	....
General government	3 401	....	....	....	....	....	....	....	....
Debt forgiveness	3 402	....	....	....	....	....	....	....	....
Other capital transfers	3 410	....	....	....	....	....	....	....	....
Other sectors	3 430	....	....	....	....	....	....	....	....
Migrants' transfers	3 431	....	....	....	....	....	....	....	....
Debt forgiveness	3 432	....	....	....	....	....	....	....	....
Other capital transfers	3 440	....	....	....	....	....	....	....	....
Nonproduced nonfinancial assets, credit	2 480	....	....	....	....	....	....	....	....
Nonproduced nonfinancial assets, debit	3 480	....	....	....	....	....	....	....	....

Table 2 (Continued). STANDARD PRESENTATION, 2000–2007

(Millions of U.S. dollars)

	Code	2000	2001	2002	2003	2004	2005	2006	2007
FINANCIAL ACCOUNT	4 995	....	....	....	....	200.6	211.2	194.0	220.7
A. DIRECT INVESTMENT	4 500	....	....	....	....	69.3	75.8	107.9	131.6
Direct investment abroad	4 505	....	....	....	....	....	....	....	....
Equity capital	4 510	....	....	....	....	....	....	....	....
Claims on affiliated enterprises	4 515	....	....	....	....	....	....	....	....
Liabilities to affiliated enterprises	4 520	....	....	....	....	....	....	....	....
Reinvested earnings	4 525	....	....	....	....	....	....	....	....
Other capital	4 530	....	....	....	....	....	....	....	....
Claims on affiliated enterprises	4 535	....	....	....	....	....	....	....	....
Liabilities to affiliated enterprises	4 540	....	....	....	....	....	....	....	....
Direct investment in Liberia	4 555	....	....	....	....	69.3	75.8	107.9	131.6
Equity capital	4 560	....	....	....	....	....	....	....	....
Claims on direct investors	4 565	....	....	....	....	....	....	....	....
Liabilities to direct investors	4 570	....	....	....	....	....	....	....	....
Reinvested earnings	4 575	....	....	....	....	2.8	3.5	7.0	7.3
Other capital	4 580	....	....	....	....	66.4	72.3	100.8	124.3
Claims on direct investors	4 585	....	....	....	....	....	....	....	....
Liabilities to direct investors	4 590	....	....	....	....	66.4	72.3	100.8	124.3
B. PORTFOLIO INVESTMENT	4 600	....	....	....	....	....	....	....	....
Assets	4 602	....	....	....	....	....	....	....	....
Equity securities	4 610	....	....	....	....	....	....	....	....
Monetary authorities	4 611	....	....	....	....	....	....	....	....
General government	4 612	....	....	....	....	....	....	....	....
Banks	4 613	....	....	....	....	....	....	....	....
Other sectors	4 614	....	....	....	....	....	....	....	....
Debt securities	4 619	....	....	....	....	....	....	....	....
Bonds and notes	4 620	....	....	....	....	....	....	....	....
Monetary authorities	4 621	....	....	....	....	....	....	....	....
General government	4 622	....	....	....	....	....	....	....	....
Banks	4 623	....	....	....	....	....	....	....	....
Other sectors	4 624	....	....	....	....	....	....	....	....
Money market instruments	4 630	....	....	....	....	....	....	....	....
Monetary authorities	4 631	....	....	....	....	....	....	....	....
General government	4 632	....	....	....	....	....	....	....	....
Banks	4 633	....	....	....	....	....	....	....	....
Other sectors	4 634	....	....	....	....	....	....	....	....
Liabilities	4 652	....	....	....	....	....	....	....	....
Equity securities	4 660	....	....	....	....	....	....	....	....
Banks	4 663	....	....	....	....	....	....	....	....
Other sectors	4 664	....	....	....	....	....	....	....	....
Debt securities	4 669	....	....	....	....	....	....	....	....
Bonds and notes	4 670	....	....	....	....	....	....	....	....
Monetary authorities	4 671	....	....	....	....	....	....	....	....
General government	4 672	....	....	....	....	....	....	....	....
Banks	4 673	....	....	....	....	....	....	....	....
Other sectors	4 674	....	....	....	....	....	....	....	....
Money market instruments	4 680	....	....	....	....	....	....	....	....
Monetary authorities	4 681	....	....	....	....	....	....	....	....
General government	4 682	....	....	....	....	....	....	....	....
Banks	4 683	....	....	....	....	....	....	....	....
Other sectors	4 684	....	....	....	....	....	....	....	....
C. FINANCIAL DERIVATIVES	4 910	....	....	....	....	....	....	....	....
Monetary authorities	4 911	....	....	....	....	....	....	....	....
General government	4 912	....	....	....	....	....	....	....	....
Banks	4 913	....	....	....	....	....	....	....	....
Other sectors	4 914	....	....	....	....	....	....	....	....
Assets	4 900	....	....	....	....	....	....	....	....
Monetary authorities	4 901	....	....	....	....	....	....	....	....
General government	4 902	....	....	....	....	....	....	....	....
Banks	4 903	....	....	....	....	....	....	....	....
Other sectors	4 904	....	....	....	....	....	....	....	....
Liabilities	4 905	....	....	....	....	....	....	....	....
Monetary authorities	4 906	....	....	....	....	....	....	....	....
General government	4 907	....	....	....	....	....	....	....	....
Banks	4 908	....	....	....	....	....	....	....	....
Other sectors	4 909	....	....	....	....	....	....	....	....

Table 2 (Concluded). STANDARD PRESENTATION, 2000–2007

(Millions of U.S. dollars)

	Code	2000	2001	2002	2003	2004	2005	2006	2007
D. OTHER INVESTMENT	4 700 ..	....	....	....	....	**136.6**	**137.7**	**124.8**	**127.9**
Assets	4 703 ..	....	....	....	....	–3.3	–3.1	–15.5	–13.2
Trade credits	4 706 ..	....	....	....	....	....	....	....	....
General government	4 707 ..	....	....	....	....	....	....	....	....
of which: Short-term	4 709 ..	....	....	....	....	....	....	....	....
Other sectors	4 710 ..	....	....	....	....	....	....	....	....
of which: Short-term	4 712 ..	....	....	....	....	....	....	....	....
Loans	4 714 ..	....	....	....	....	....	....	....	....
Monetary authorities	4 715 ..	....	....	....	....	....	....	....	....
of which: Short-term	4 718 ..	....	....	....	....	....	....	....	....
General government	4 719 ..	....	....	....	....	....	....	....	....
of which: Short-term	4 721 ..	....	....	....	....	....	....	....	....
Banks	4 722 ..	....	....	....	....	....	....	....	....
of which: Short-term	4 724 ..	....	....	....	....	....	....	....	....
Other sectors	4 725 ..	....	....	....	....	....	....	....	....
of which: Short-term	4 727 ..	....	....	....	....	....	....	....	....
Currency and deposits	4 730 ..	....	....	....	....	–3.3	–3.1	–15.5	–13.2
Monetary authorities	4 731 ..	....	....	....	....	–3.3	–3.1	–15.5	–13.2
General government	4 732 ..	....	....	....	....	....	....	....	....
Banks	4 733 ..	....	....	....	....	....	....	....	....
Other sectors	4 734 ..	....	....	....	....	....	....	....	....
Other assets	4 736 ..	....	....	....	....	....	....	....	....
Monetary authorities	4 737 ..	....	....	....	....	....	....	....	....
of which: Short-term	4 739 ..	....	....	....	....	....	....	....	....
General government	4 740 ..	....	....	....	....	....	....	....	....
of which: Short-term	4 742 ..	....	....	....	....	....	....	....	....
Banks	4 743 ..	....	....	....	....	....	....	....	....
of which: Short-term	4 745 ..	....	....	....	....	....	....	....	....
Other sectors	4 746 ..	....	....	....	....	....	....	....	....
of which: Short-term	4 748 ..	....	....	....	....	....	....	....	....
Liabilities	4 753 ..	....	....	....	....	**140.0**	**140.8**	**140.3**	**141.1**
Trade credits	4 756 ..	....	....	....	....	....	....	....	....
General government	4 757 ..	....	....	....	....	....	....	....	....
of which: Short-term	4 759 ..	....	....	....	....	....	....	....	....
Other sectors	4 760 ..	....	....	....	....	....	....	....	....
of which: Short-term	4 762 ..	....	....	....	....	....	....	....	....
Loans	4 764 ..	....	....	....	....	–19.9	–18.7	–5.7	–5.7
Monetary authorities	4 765 ..	....	....	....	....	....	–.1	–.7	–.7
of which: Use of Fund credit and loans from the Fund	4 766 ..	....	....	....	....	....	–.1	–.7	–.7
of which: Short-term	4 768 ..	....	....	....	....	....	....	....	....
General government	4 769 ..	....	....	....	....	–19.9	–18.6	–5.0	–4.9
of which: Short-term	4 771 ..	....	....	....	....	....	....	....	....
Banks	4 772 ..	....	....	....	....	....	....	....	....
of which: Short-term	4 774 ..	....	....	....	....	....	....	....	....
Other sectors	4 775 ..	....	....	....	....	....	....	....	....
of which: Short-term	4 777 ..	....	....	....	....	....	....	....	....
Currency and deposits	4 780 ..	....	....	....	....	....	....	....	....
Monetary authorities	4 781 ..	....	....	....	....	....	....	....	....
General government	4 782 ..	....	....	....	....	....	....	....	....
Banks	4 783 ..	....	....	....	....	....	....	....	....
Other sectors	4 784 ..	....	....	....	....	....	....	....	....
Other liabilities	4 786 ..	....	....	....	....	159.8	159.4	146.0	146.8
Monetary authorities	4 787 ..	....	....	....	....	....	....	....	....
of which: Short-term	4 789 ..	....	....	....	....	....	....	....	....
General government	4 790 ..	....	....	....	....	159.8	159.4	146.0	146.8
of which: Short-term	4 792 ..	....	....	....	....	*159.8*	*159.4*	*146.0*	*146.8*
Banks	4 793 ..	....	....	....	....	....	....	....	....
of which: Short-term	4 795 ..	....	....	....	....	....	....	....	....
Other sectors	4 796 ..	....	....	....	....	....	....	....	....
of which: Short-term	4 798 ..	....	....	....	....	....	....	....	....
E. RESERVE ASSETS	4 802 ..	....	....	....	....	**–5.3**	**–2.3**	**–38.6**	**–38.8**
Monetary gold	4 812 ..	....	....	....	....	....	....	....	....
Special drawing rights	4 811 ..	....	....	....	....	....	....	....	....
Reserve position in the Fund	4 810 ..	....	....	....	....	....	....	....	....
Foreign exchange	4 803 ..	....	....	....	....	–5.3	–2.3	–38.6	–38.8
Other claims	4 813 ..	....	....	....	....	....	....	....	....
NET ERRORS AND OMISSIONS	4 998 ..	....	....	....	....	**–48.8**	**–36.5**	**–20.9**	**–9.5**

Table 1. ANALYTIC PRESENTATION, 2000–2007

(Millions of U.S. dollars)

	Code	2000	2001	2002	2003	2004	2005	2006	2007
A. Current Account[1].....................	4 993 Z.	**6,270**	**3,332**	**694**	**3,402**	**4,616**	**14,945**	**22,170**	....
Goods: exports f.o.b..........	2 100 ..	12,038	10,634	9,851	12,878	17,425	28,849	37,473	....
Goods: imports f.o.b..........	3 100 ..	−4,129	−4,825	−7,408	−7,200	−8,768	−11,174	−13,219	....
Balance on Goods.................	4 100 ..	*7,909*	*5,809*	*2,443*	*5,678*	*8,657*	*17,675*	*24,254*	....
Services: credit..........	2 200 ..	172	184	401	442	437	534	489	....
Services: debit..........	3 200 ..	−895	−1,034	−1,544	−1,597	−1,914	−2,349	−2,564	....
Balance on Goods and Services...........	4 991 ..	*7,186*	*4,959*	*1,300*	*4,523*	*7,180*	*15,860*	*22,179*	....
Income: credit..........	2 300 ..	723	684	1,773	1,689	1,339	1,837	2,180	....
Income: debit..........	3 300 ..	−1,152	−1,583	−1,508	−1,149	−1,394	−2,118	−2,775	....
Balance on Goods, Services, and Income........	4 992 ..	*6,757*	*4,060*	*1,565*	*5,063*	*7,125*	*15,579*	*21,584*	....
Current transfers: credit..........	2 379 Z.	16	20	13	255	254	418	1,646	....
Current transfers: debit..........	3 379 ..	−503	−748	−884	−1,916	−2,763	−1,052	−1,060	....
B. Capital Account[1].................	4 994 Z.	....	....	....	....	....	....	....	....
Capital account: credit..........	2 994 Z.	....	....	....	....	....	....	....	
Capital account: debit..........	3 994 ..	....	....	....	....	....	....	....	
Total, Groups A Plus B............	4 981 ..	*6,270*	*3,332*	*694*	*3,402*	*4,616*	*14,945*	*22,170*	....
C. Financial Account[1].................	4 995 W.	**−149**	**−977**	**89**	**−166**	**−238**	**392**	**−4,731**	....
Direct investment abroad..........	4 505 ..	−98	−175	136	−63	−286	−128	−474	....
Direct investment in Libya..........	4 555 Z.	141	−133	145	143	357	1,038	2,064	....
Portfolio investment assets..........	4 602 ..	−706	−1,359	72	−607	−187	−393	−5,198	....
Equity securities..........	4 610 ..	−13	−985	21	−18	27	−47	−60	....
Debt securities..........	4 619 ..	−693	−374	51	−589	−214	−346	−5,138	....
Portfolio investment liabilities..........	4 652 Z.	....	....	....	....	....	....	....	....
Equity securities..........	4 660 ..	....	....	....	....	....	....	....	....
Debt securities..........	4 669 Z.	....	....	....	....	....	....	....	....
Financial derivatives..........	4 910 ..	....	....	....	....	....	....	....	....
Financial derivatives assets..........	4 900 ..	....	....	....	....	....	....	....	....
Financial derivatives liabilities..........	4 905 ..	....	....	....	....	....	....	....	....
Other investment assets..........	4 703 ..	−333	−97	62	−163	−1,767	−416	−1,194	....
Monetary authorities..........	4 701 ..	....	....	....	....	....	....	....	....
General government..........	4 704 ..	....	....	....	6	....	....	....	....
Banks..........	4 705 ..	−294	−121	102	−152	−2,077	328	291	....
Other sectors..........	4 728 ..	−39	24	−40	−17	310	−744	−1,485	....
Other investment liabilities..........	4 753 W.	847	787	−326	524	1,645	291	71	....
Monetary authorities..........	4 753 WA	....	309	−197	−7	....	....	....	....
General government..........	4 753 ZB	....	....	....	....	....	....	....	....
Banks..........	4 753 ZC	847	488	−149	548	1,855	224	387	....
Other sectors..........	4 753 ZD	....	−10	20	−17	−210	67	−316	....
Total, Groups A Through C............	4 983 ..	*6,121*	*2,355*	*783*	*3,236*	*4,378*	*15,337*	*17,439*	....
D. Net Errors and Omissions.................	4 998 ..	**−764**	**−1,206**	**362**	**1,890**	**1,733**	**−1,497**	**2,008**	....
Total, Groups A Through D............	4 984 ..	*5,357*	*1,149*	*1,145*	*5,126*	*6,111*	*13,840*	*19,447*	....
E. Reserves and Related Items.................	4 802 A.	**−5,357**	**−1,149**	**−1,145**	**−5,126**	**−6,111**	**−13,840**	**−19,447**	....
Reserve assets..........	4 802 ..	−5,357	−1,149	−1,145	−5,126	−6,040	−13,840	−19,447	....
Use of Fund credit and loans..........	4 766 ..	....	....	....	....	....	....	....	....
Exceptional financing..........	4 920 ..	....	....	....	....	−71	....	....	....
Conversion rates: Libyan dinars per U.S. dollar	0 101 ..	.51219	.60506	1.27068	1.29294	1.30497	1.30838	1.31357	1.26264

[1] Excludes components that have been classified in the categories of Group E.

Table 2. STANDARD PRESENTATION, 2000–2007

(Millions of U.S. dollars)

	Code	2000	2001	2002	2003	2004	2005	2006	2007
CURRENT ACCOUNT	4 993	6,270	3,332	694	3,402	4,616	14,945	22,170	....
A. GOODS	4 100	7,909	5,809	2,443	5,678	8,657	17,675	24,254	....
Credit	2 100	12,038	10,634	9,851	12,878	17,425	28,849	37,473	....
General merchandise: exports f.o.b.	2 110	12,038	10,634	9,851	12,878	17,425	28,849	37,473	....
Goods for processing: exports f.o.b.	2 150	....	....	....	....	....	....	....	....
Repairs on goods	2 160	....	....	....	....	....	....	....	....
Goods procured in ports by carriers	2 170	....	....	....	....	....	....	....	....
Nonmonetary gold	2 180	....	....	....	....	....	....	....	....
Debit	3 100	–4,129	–4,825	–7,408	–7,200	–8,768	–11,174	–13,219	....
General merchandise: imports f.o.b.	3 110	–4,129	–4,825	–7,408	–7,200	–8,768	–11,174	–13,219	....
Goods for processing: imports f.o.b.	3 150	....	....	....	....	....	....	....	....
Repairs on goods	3 160	....	....	....	....	....	....	....	....
Goods procured in ports by carriers	3 170	....	....	....	....	....	....	....	....
Nonmonetary gold	3 180	....	....	....	....	....	....	....	....
B. SERVICES	4 200	–723	–850	–1,143	–1,155	–1,477	–1,815	–2,075	....
Total credit	2 200	*172*	*184*	*401*	*442*	*437*	*534*	*489*	....
Total debit	3 200	*–895*	*–1,034*	*–1,544*	*–1,597*	*–1,914*	*–2,349*	*–2,564*	....
Transportation services, credit	2 205	16	18	41	58	63	116	128	....
Passenger	2 850	*9*	*12*	*21*	*38*	*43*	*51*	*54*	....
Freight	2 851	*7*	*6*	*20*	*20*	*20*	*65*	*74*	....
Other	2 852	....	....	....	....	....	....	....	....
Sea transport, passenger	2 207	3	4	3	2	2	2	2	....
Sea transport, freight	2 208	7	6	20	20	20	25	30	....
Sea transport, other	2 209	....	....	....	....	....	....	....	....
Air transport, passenger	2 211	3	4	9	16	16	19	20	....
Air transport, freight	2 212	....	....	....	....	....	....	....	....
Air transport, other	2 213	....	....	....	....	....	....	....	....
Other transport, passenger	2 215	3	4	9	20	25	30	32	....
Other transport, freight	2 216	....	....	....	....	....	40	44	....
Other transport, other	2 217	....	....	....	....	....	....	....	....
Transportation services, debit	3 205	–350	–453	–522	–661	–766	–1,016	–1,182	....
Passenger	3 850	*–98*	*–127*	*–68*	*–132*	*–186*	*–240*	*–247*	....
Freight	3 851	*–252*	*–326*	*–454*	*–529*	*–580*	*–776*	*–935*	....
Other	3 852	....	....	....	....	....	....	....	....
Sea transport, passenger	3 207	....	....	....	....	....	....	....	....
Sea transport, freight	3 208	–191	–266	–380	–481	–522	–691	–840	....
Sea transport, other	3 209	....	....	....	....	....	....	....	....
Air transport, passenger	3 211	–98	–127	–68	–132	–186	–225	–230	....
Air transport, freight	3 212	–61	–60	–74	–48	–58	–60	–65	....
Air transport, other	3 213	....	....	....	....	....	....	....	....
Other transport, passenger	3 215	....	....	....	....	....	–15	–17	....
Other transport, freight	3 216	....	....	....	....	....	–25	–30	....
Other transport, other	3 217	....	....	....	....	....	....	....	....
Travel, credit	2 236	75	78	181	205	218	250	190	....
Business travel	2 237	70	73	175	200	211	241	180	....
Personal travel	2 240	5	5	6	5	7	9	10	....
Travel, debit	3 236	–397	–445	–586	–557	–603	–680	–668	....
Business travel	3 237	–10	–15	–15	–23	–21	–25	–30	....
Personal travel	3 240	–387	–430	–571	–534	–582	–655	–638	....
Other services, credit	2 200 BA	81	88	179	179	156	168	171	....
Communications	2 245	4	3	6	11	10	10	12	....
Construction	2 249	....	....	....	....	....	....	....	....
Insurance	2 253	20	33	37	55	60	43	55	....
Financial	2 260	....	....	....	....	....	....	....	....
Computer and information	2 262	....	....	....	....	....	....	....	....
Royalties and licence fees	2 266	4	2	10	....	....	....	....	....
Other business services	2 268	....	....	....	....	....	....	....	....
Personal, cultural, and recreational	2 287	....	....	....	....	....	....	....	....
Government, n.i.e.	2 291	53	50	126	113	86	115	104	....
Other services, debit	3 200 BA	–148	–136	–436	–379	–545	–653	–714	....
Communications	3 245	–8	–6	–10	–13	–15	–18	–22	....
Construction	3 249	–50	–50	–188	–168	–183	–149	–160	....
Insurance	3 253	–5	–5	–24	–59	–104	–160	–182	....
Financial	3 260	....	....	....	–10	–13	–20	–16	....
Computer and information	3 262	....	....	–2	–12	–15	–25	–30	....
Royalties and licence fees	3 266	....	....	....	....	....	....	....	....
Other business services	3 268	–5	–5	–10	–39	–45	–50	–52	....
Personal, cultural, and recreational	3 287	....	....	–1	–9	–9	–10	–12	....
Government, n.i.e.	3 291	–80	–70	–201	–69	–161	–221	–240	....

Table 2 (Continued). STANDARD PRESENTATION, 2000–2007

(Millions of U.S. dollars)

	Code	2000	2001	2002	2003	2004	2005	2006	2007
C. INCOME	4 300 ..	−429	−899	265	540	−55	−281	−595	....
Total credit	2 300 ..	*723*	*684*	*1,773*	*1,689*	*1,339*	*1,837*	*2,180*	....
Total debit	3 300 ..	*−1,152*	*−1,583*	*−1,508*	*−1,149*	*−1,394*	*−2,118*	*−2,775*	....
Compensation of employees, credit	2 310 ..	3	5	4	5	5	8	10	....
Compensation of employees, debit	3 310 ..	−9	−8	−10	−32	−35	−60	−65	....
Investment income, credit	2 320 ..	720	679	1,769	1,684	1,334	1,829	2,170	....
Direct investment income	2 330 ..	....	....	873	232	156	224	320	....
Dividends and distributed branch profits	2 332 ..	....	....	873	232	156	224	320	....
Reinvested earnings and undistributed branch profits	2 333 ..	....	....	....	....	....	....	....	....
Income on debt (interest)	2 334 ..	....	....	....	....	....	....	....	....
Portfolio investment income	2 339 ..	720	679	896	1,452	1,178	1,605	1,850	....
Income on equity	2 340 ..	720	679	896	1,452	1,178	1,605	1,850	....
Income on bonds and notes	2 350 ..	....	....	....	....	....	....	....	....
Income on money market instruments	2 360 ..	....	....	....	....	....	....	....	....
Other investment income.	2 370 ..	....	....	....	....	....	....	....	....
Investment income, debit	3 320 ..	−1,143	−1,575	−1,498	−1,117	−1,359	−2,058	−2,710	....
Direct investment income	3 330 ..	−1,143	−1,575	−1,458	−1,078	−1,359	−2,058	−2,710	....
Dividends and distributed branch profits	3 332 ..	−1,002	−1,708	−1,313	−935	−1,146	−1,895	−2,460	....
Reinvested earnings and undistributed branch profits	3 333 ..	−141	133	−145	−143	−213	−163	−250	....
Income on debt (interest)	3 334 ..	....	....	....	....	....	....	....	....
Portfolio investment income	3 339 ..	....	....	−40	−39	....	....	....	....
Income on equity	3 340 ..	....	....	−40	−39	....	....	....	....
Income on bonds and notes	3 350 ..	....	....	....	....	....	....	....	....
Income on money market instruments	3 360 ..	....	....	....	....	....	....	....	....
Other investment income.	3 370 ..	....	....	....	....	....	....	....	....
D. CURRENT TRANSFERS	4 379 ..	−487	−728	−871	−1,661	−2,509	−634	586	....
Credit	2 379 ..	16	20	13	255	254	418	1,646	....
General government	2 380 ..	10	15	10	12	15	18	1,300	....
Other sectors	2 390 ..	6	5	3	243	239	400	346	....
Workers' remittances	2 391 ..	6	5	3	3	5	7	6	....
Other current transfers	2 392 ..	....	....	....	240	234	393	340	....
Debit	3 379 ..	−503	−748	−884	−1,916	−2,763	−1,052	−1,060	....
General government	3 380 ..	−49	−73	−108	−1,186	−1,756	−130	−110	....
Other sectors	3 390 ..	−454	−675	−776	−730	−1,007	−922	−950	....
Workers' remittances	3 391 ..	−454	−675	−776	−644	−940	−854	−880	....
Other current transfers	3 392 ..	....	....	....	−86	−67	−68	−70	....
CAPITAL AND FINANCIAL ACCOUNT	4 996 ..	−5,506	−2,126	−1,056	−5,292	−6,349	−13,448	−24,178	....
CAPITAL ACCOUNT	4 994 ..	....	....	....	....	....	....	....	....
Total credit	2 994 ..	....	....	....	....	....	....	....	....
Total debit	3 994 ..	....	....	....	....	....	....	....	....
Capital transfers, credit	2 400 ..	....	....	....	....	....	....	....	....
General government	2 401 ..	....	....	....	....	....	....	....	....
Debt forgiveness	2 402 ..	....	....	....	....	....	....	....	....
Other capital transfers	2 410 ..	....	....	....	....	....	....	....	....
Other sectors	2 430 ..	....	....	....	....	....	....	....	....
Migrants' transfers	2 431 ..	....	....	....	....	....	....	....	....
Debt forgiveness	2 432 ..	....	....	....	....	....	....	....	....
Other capital transfers	2 440 ..	....	....	....	....	....	....	....	....
Capital transfers, debit	3 400 ..	....	....	....	....	....	....	....	....
General government	3 401 ..	....	....	....	....	....	....	....	....
Debt forgiveness	3 402 ..	....	....	....	....	....	....	....	....
Other capital transfers	3 410 ..	....	....	....	....	....	....	....	....
Other sectors	3 430 ..	....	....	....	....	....	....	....	....
Migrants' transfers	3 431 ..	....	....	....	....	....	....	....	....
Debt forgiveness	3 432 ..	....	....	....	....	....	....	....	....
Other capital transfers	3 440 ..	....	....	....	....	....	....	....	....
Nonproduced nonfinancial assets, credit	2 480 ..	....	....	....	....	....	....	....	....
Nonproduced nonfinancial assets, debit	3 480 ..	....	....	....	....	....	....	....	....

Table 2 (Continued). STANDARD PRESENTATION, 2000–2007

(Millions of U.S. dollars)

	Code	2000	2001	2002	2003	2004	2005	2006	2007
FINANCIAL ACCOUNT	4 995	−5,506	−2,126	−1,056	−5,292	−6,349	−13,448	−24,178	....
A. DIRECT INVESTMENT	4 500	43	−308	281	80	71	910	1,590	....
Direct investment abroad	4 505	−98	−175	136	−63	−286	−128	−474	....
Equity capital	4 510	−98	−175	136	−63	−286	−128	−474	....
Claims on affiliated enterprises	4 515	−98	−175	136	−63	−286	−128	−474	....
Liabilities to affiliated enterprises	4 520	....	....	....	....	....	....	....	....
Reinvested earnings	4 525	....	....	....	....	....	....	....	....
Other capital	4 530	....	....	....	....	....	....	....	....
Claims on affiliated enterprises	4 535	....	....	....	....	....	....	....	....
Liabilities to affiliated enterprises	4 540	....	....	....	....	....	....	....	....
Direct investment in Libya	4 555	141	−133	145	143	357	1,038	2,064	....
Equity capital	4 560	....	....	....	....	....	....	....	....
Claims on direct investors	4 565	....	....	....	....	....	....	....	....
Liabilities to direct investors	4 570	....	....	....	....	....	....	....	....
Reinvested earnings	4 575	141	−133	145	143	213	163	250	....
Other capital	4 580	....	....	....	....	144	875	1,814	....
Claims on direct investors	4 585	....	....	....	....	....	....	....	....
Liabilities to direct investors	4 590	....	....	....	....	144	875	1,814	....
B. PORTFOLIO INVESTMENT	4 600	−706	−1,359	72	−607	−187	−393	−5,198	....
Assets	4 602	−706	−1,359	72	−607	−187	−393	−5,198	....
Equity securities	4 610	−13	−985	21	−18	27	−47	−60	....
Monetary authorities	4 611	....	....	....	....	....	....	....	....
General government	4 612	....	....	....	....	....	....	....	....
Banks	4 613	....	....	....	....	....	....	....	....
Other sectors	4 614	−13	−985	21	−18	27	−47	−60	....
Debt securities	4 619	−693	−374	51	−589	−214	−346	−5,138	....
Bonds and notes	4 620	−535	−302	126	−333	61	−333	−5,125	....
Monetary authorities	4 621	....	....	....	....	....	....	....	....
General government	4 622	....	....	....	....	....	....	....	....
Banks	4 623	−535	−302	126	−333	61	−333	−5,125	....
Other sectors	4 624	....	....	....	....	....	....	....	....
Money market instruments	4 630	−158	−72	−75	−256	−275	−13	−13	....
Monetary authorities	4 631	....	....	....	....	....	....	....	....
General government	4 632	....	....	....	....	....	....	....	....
Banks	4 633	....	....	....	....	....	....	....	....
Other sectors	4 634	−158	−72	−75	−256	−275	−13	−13	....
Liabilities	4 652	....	....	....	....	....	....	....	....
Equity securities	4 660	....	....	....	....	....	....	....	....
Banks	4 663	....	....	....	....	....	....	....	....
Other sectors	4 664	....	....	....	....	....	....	....	....
Debt securities	4 669	....	....	....	....	....	....	....	....
Bonds and notes	4 670	....	....	....	....	....	....	....	....
Monetary authorities	4 671	....	....	....	....	....	....	....	....
General government	4 672	....	....	....	....	....	....	....	....
Banks	4 673	....	....	....	....	....	....	....	....
Other sectors	4 674	....	....	....	....	....	....	....	....
Money market instruments	4 680	....	....	....	....	....	....	....	....
Monetary authorities	4 681	....	....	....	....	....	....	....	....
General government	4 682	....	....	....	....	....	....	....	....
Banks	4 683	....	....	....	....	....	....	....	....
Other sectors	4 684	....	....	....	....	....	....	....	....
C. FINANCIAL DERIVATIVES	4 910	....	....	....	....	....	....	....	....
Monetary authorities	4 911	....	....	....	....	....	....	....	....
General government	4 912	....	....	....	....	....	....	....	....
Banks	4 913	....	....	....	....	....	....	....	....
Other sectors	4 914	....	....	....	....	....	....	....	....
Assets	4 900	....	....	....	....	....	....	....	....
Monetary authorities	4 901	....	....	....	....	....	....	....	....
General government	4 902	....	....	....	....	....	....	....	....
Banks	4 903	....	....	....	....	....	....	....	....
Other sectors	4 904	....	....	....	....	....	....	....	....
Liabilities	4 905	....	....	....	....	....	....	....	....
Monetary authorities	4 906	....	....	....	....	....	....	....	....
General government	4 907	....	....	....	....	....	....	....	....
Banks	4 908	....	....	....	....	....	....	....	....
Other sectors	4 909	....	....	....	....	....	....	....	....

Table 2 (Concluded). STANDARD PRESENTATION, 2000–2007

(Millions of U.S. dollars)

	Code	2000	2001	2002	2003	2004	2005	2006	2007
D. OTHER INVESTMENT	4 700 ..	**514**	**690**	**−264**	**361**	**−193**	**−125**	**−1,123**	....
Assets	4 703 ..	**−333**	**−97**	**62**	**−163**	**−1,767**	**−416**	**−1,194**	....
Trade credits	4 706 ..	....	....	....	....	....	....	....	....
General government	4 707 ..	....	....	....	....	....	....	....	....
of which: Short-term	4 709 ..	....	....	....	....	....	....	....	....
Other sectors	4 710 ..	....	....	....	....	....	....	....	....
of which: Short-term	4 712 ..	....	....	....	....	....	....	....	....
Loans	4 714 ..	−314	−90	69	−78	446	156	156	....
Monetary authorities	4 715 ..	....	....	....	....	....	....	....	....
of which: Short-term	4 718 ..	....	....	....	....	....	....	....	....
General government	4 719 ..	....	....	....	4	....	....	....	....
of which: Short-term	4 721 ..	....	....	....	....	....	....	....	....
Banks	4 722 ..	−294	−121	45	−82	446	141	141	....
of which: Short-term	4 724 ..	*−294*	*−121*	*45*	*−82*	*446*	*141*	*141*	....
Other sectors	4 725 ..	−20	31	24	....	....	15	15	....
of which: Short-term	4 727 ..	*−20*	*31*	*24*	....	....	*15*	*15*	....
Currency and deposits	4 730 ..	−19	−7	−7	−85	−2,213	−572	−1,350	....
Monetary authorities	4 731 ..	....	....	....	....	....	....	....	....
General government	4 732 ..	....	....	....	2	....	....	....	....
Banks	4 733 ..	....	....	57	−70	−2,523	187	150	....
Other sectors	4 734 ..	−19	−7	−64	−17	310	−759	−1,500	....
Other assets	4 736 ..	....	....	....	....	....	....	....	....
Monetary authorities	4 737 ..	....	....	....	....	....	....	....	....
of which: Short-term	4 739 ..	....	....	....	....	....	....	....	....
General government	4 740 ..	....	....	....	....	....	....	....	....
of which: Short-term	4 742 ..	....	....	....	....	....	....	....	....
Banks	4 743 ..	....	....	....	....	....	....	....	....
of which: Short-term	4 745 ..	....	....	....	....	....	....	....	....
Other sectors	4 746 ..	....	....	....	....	....	....	....	....
of which: Short-term	4 748 ..	....	....	....	....	....	....	....	....
Liabilities	4 753 ..	**847**	**787**	**−326**	**524**	**1,574**	**291**	**71**	....
Trade credits	4 756 ..	....	....	....	....	....	....	....	....
General government	4 757 ..	....	....	....	....	....	....	....	....
of which: Short-term	4 759 ..	....	....	....	....	....	....	....	....
Other sectors	4 760 ..	....	....	....	....	....	....	....	....
of which: Short-term	4 762 ..	....	....	....	....	....	....	....	....
Loans	4 764 ..	....	....	....	....	−71	....	....	....
Monetary authorities	4 765 ..	....	....	....	....	....	....	....	....
of which: Use of Fund credit and loans from the Fund	4 766 ..	....	....	....	....	....	....	....	....
of which: Short-term	4 768 ..	....	....	....	....	....	....	....	....
General government	4 769 ..	....	....	....	....	....	....	....	....
of which: Short-term	4 771 ..	....	....	....	....	....	....	....	....
Banks	4 772 ..	....	....	....	....	−71	....	....	....
of which: Short-term	4 774 ..	....	....	....	....	....	....	....	....
Other sectors	4 775 ..	....	....	....	....	....	....	....	....
of which: Short-term	4 777 ..	....	....	....	....	....	....	....	....
Currency and deposits	4 780 ..	847	797	−917	221	....	−63	−63	....
Monetary authorities	4 781 ..	....	309	−197	−7	....	....	....	....
General government	4 782 ..	....	....	....	....	....	....	....	....
Banks	4 783 ..	847	488	−720	228	....	−63	−63	....
Other sectors	4 784 ..	....	....	....	....	....	....	....	....
Other liabilities	4 786 ..	....	−10	591	303	1,645	354	134	....
Monetary authorities	4 787 ..	....	....	....	....	....	....	....	....
of which: Short-term	4 789 ..	....	....	....	....	....	....	....	....
General government	4 790 ..	....	....	....	....	....	....	....	....
of which: Short-term	4 792 ..	....	....	....	....	....	....	....	....
Banks	4 793 ..	....	....	571	320	1,855	287	450	....
of which: Short-term	4 795 ..	....	....	....	....	....	....	....	....
Other sectors	4 796 ..	....	−10	20	−17	−210	67	−316	....
of which: Short-term	4 798 ..	....	*−10*	*20*	*−17*	*−210*	*67*	*−316*	....
E. RESERVE ASSETS	4 802 ..	**−5,357**	**−1,149**	**−1,145**	**−5,126**	**−6,040**	**−13,840**	**−19,447**	....
Monetary gold	4 812 ..	....	....	....	....	....	....	....	....
Special drawing rights	4 811 ..	−53	−36	−10	−18	−20	−29	−42	....
Reserve position in the Fund	4 810 ..	....	....	....	....	....	....	....	....
Foreign exchange	4 803 ..	−5,304	−1,113	−1,135	−5,108	−6,018	−13,814	−19,400	....
Other claims	4 813 ..	....	....	....	1	−2	3	−5	....
NET ERRORS AND OMISSIONS	4 998 ..	**−764**	**−1,206**	**362**	**1,890**	**1,733**	**−1,497**	**2,008**	....

Table 1. ANALYTIC PRESENTATION, 2000–2007

(Millions of U.S. dollars)

	Code	2000	2001	2002	2003	2004	2005	2006	2007
A. Current Account[1].....................	4 993 Z.	**−674.9**	**−573.6**	**−720.7**	**−1,278.4**	**−1,724.6**	**−1,831.2**	**−3,218.1**	**−5,260.5**
Goods: exports f.o.b..........................	2 100 ..	4,050.4	4,889.0	6,028.4	7,657.8	9,306.3	11,774.4	14,150.6	17,179.6
Goods: imports f.o.b..........................	3 100 ..	−5,154.1	−5,997.0	−7,343.3	−9,362.0	−11,688.9	−14,690.4	−18,359.8	−22,802.6
Balance on Goods...........................	4 100 ..	*−1,103.8*	*−1,108.0*	*−1,314.9*	*−1,704.2*	*−2,382.6*	*−2,916.0*	*−4,209.3*	*−5,623.1*
Services: credit................................	2 200 ..	1,058.8	1,157.0	1,463.7	1,878.0	2,444.4	3,104.3	3,623.2	4,063.2
Services: debit................................	3 200 ..	−678.7	−700.3	−915.0	−1,263.6	−1,632.1	−2,054.6	−2,540.0	−3,236.3
Balance on Goods and Services..........	4 991 ..	*−723.7*	*−651.4*	*−766.1*	*−1,089.8*	*−1,570.2*	*−1,866.3*	*−3,126.0*	*−4,796.2*
Income: credit................................	2 300 ..	185.5	205.7	191.6	235.2	354.9	448.3	589.9	793.0
Income: debit................................	3 300 ..	−379.3	−385.5	−375.0	−717.4	−967.3	−1,075.4	−1,406.9	−2,415.9
Balance on Goods, Services, and Income.........	4 992 ..	*−917.5*	*−831.1*	*−949.5*	*−1,572.0*	*−2,182.5*	*−2,493.4*	*−3,943.0*	*−6,419.1*
Current transfers: credit....................	2 379 Z.	246.8	262.0	231.7	301.5	612.1	951.3	1,425.1	2,036.2
Current transfers: debit....................	3 379 ..	−4.3	−4.5	−2.9	−7.8	−154.2	−289.1	−700.2	−877.6
B. Capital Account[1].....................	4 994 Z.	**2.1**	**1.4**	**56.5**	**67.5**	**287.2**	**331.1**	**351.4**	**690.1**
Capital account: credit......................	2 994 Z.	2.6	1.5	56.8	68.3	288.1	331.2	351.6	690.1
Capital account: debit......................	3 994 ..	−.4	−.1	−.4	−.8	−1.0	−.1	−.2	....
Total, Groups A Plus B....................	4 981 ..	*−672.8*	*−572.2*	*−664.2*	*−1,210.8*	*−1,437.5*	*−1,500.1*	*−2,866.7*	*−4,570.3*
C. Financial Account[1]..................	4 995 W.	**702.4**	**777.6**	**1,048.4**	**1,642.3**	**1,141.2**	**2,261.8**	**4,662.6**	**6,016.4**
Direct investment abroad..................	4 505 ..	−3.7	−7.1	−17.7	−37.2	−262.6	−343.0	−289.5	−600.4
Direct investment in Lithuania..........	4 555 Z.	378.9	445.8	712.5	179.2	773.2	1,031.8	1,840.2	1,934.1
Portfolio investment assets..............	4 602 ..	−141.4	26.2	−124.5	29.8	−219.9	−778.5	−1,105.8	−847.2
Equity securities........................	4 610 ..	−1.4	1.1	−3.7	−1.8	−18.8	−185.1	−286.4	−366.2
Debt securities........................	4 619 ..	−140.0	25.1	−120.9	31.6	−201.0	−593.4	−819.4	−481.0
Portfolio investment liabilities..........	4 652 Z.	405.9	238.0	148.8	222.3	431.1	541.6	852.1	608.8
Equity securities........................	4 660 ..	121.5	−16.3	5.6	4.2	7.9	130.0	72.0	−166.3
Debt securities........................	4 669 Z.	284.4	254.3	143.2	218.0	423.1	411.6	780.1	775.0
Financial derivatives......................	4 910 ..	....	−1.3	−3.0	−28.0	2.6	12.9	−11.0	−2.4
Financial derivatives assets..............	4 900 ..	....	18.3	19.6	28.1	60.0	27.4	9.5	4.8
Financial derivatives liabilities..........	4 905 ..	....	−19.6	−22.7	−56.2	−57.4	−14.5	−20.5	−7.1
Other investment assets..................	4 703 ..	39.9	−225.0	154.7	−100.9	−683.8	−785.6	−475.7	−1,677.5
Monetary authorities..................	4 701 ..	....	....	....	....	....	....	....	....
General government..................	4 704 ..	....	−2.6	....	....	−7.3	....	....	....
Banks........................	4 705 ..	−142.2	−158.2	212.7	−161.0	−671.1	−394.7	−335.3	−720.5
Other sectors........................	4 728 ..	182.1	−64.2	−58.0	60.1	−5.4	−390.9	−140.4	−957.0
Other investment liabilities..............	4 753 W.	22.8	300.9	177.7	1,377.2	1,100.7	2,582.6	3,852.4	6,600.8
Monetary authorities..................	4 753 WA	−102.0	51.7	−3.6	−8.0	−66.7	5.5	75.3	323.4
General government..................	4 753 ZB	....	−53.7	−70.6	−9.4	−308.2	−191.0	−24.5	−120.1
Banks........................	4 753 ZC	53.1	169.4	111.8	737.6	870.3	2,577.3	2,560.0	4,702.7
Other sectors........................	4 753 ZD	71.7	133.5	140.0	657.0	605.3	190.8	1,241.6	1,694.9
Total, Groups A Through C..............	4 983 ..	*29.6*	*205.4*	*384.2*	*431.5*	*−296.3*	*761.7*	*1,795.9*	*1,446.0*
D. Net Errors and Omissions............	4 998 ..	**128.3**	**153.6**	**78.5**	**181.2**	**191.8**	**−49.4**	**−289.1**	**−230.7**
Total, Groups A Through D..............	4 984 ..	*158.0*	*359.0*	*462.7*	*612.7*	*−104.4*	*712.3*	*1,506.7*	*1,215.3*
E. Reserves and Related Items..........	4 802 A.	**−158.0**	**−359.0**	**−462.7**	**−612.7**	**104.4**	**−712.3**	**−1,506.7**	**−1,215.3**
Reserve assets..............................	4 802 ..	−130.7	−325.0	−422.5	−531.2	124.2	−686.8	−1,506.7	−1,215.3
Use of Fund credit and loans..........	4 766 ..	−27.3	−34.0	−40.2	−81.4	−19.8	−25.5	....	....
Exceptional financing......................	4 920 ..	....	....	....	....	....	....	....	....
Conversion rates: litai per U.S. dollar........	0 101 ..	**4.0000**	**4.0000**	**3.6770**	**3.0609**	**2.7806**	**2.7740**	**2.7522**	**2.5237**

[1] Excludes components that have been classified in the categories of Group E.

Table 2. STANDARD PRESENTATION, 2000–2007

(Millions of U.S. dollars)

	Code	2000	2001	2002	2003	2004	2005	2006	2007
CURRENT ACCOUNT..	4 993 ..	**−674.9**	**−573.6**	**−720.7**	**−1,278.4**	**−1,724.6**	**−1,831.2**	**−3,218.1**	**−5,260.5**
A. GOODS...	4 100 ..	**−1,103.8**	**−1,108.0**	**−1,314.9**	**−1,704.2**	**−2,382.6**	**−2,916.0**	**−4,209.3**	**−5,623.1**
Credit...	2 100 ..	**4,050.4**	**4,889.0**	**6,028.4**	**7,657.8**	**9,306.3**	**11,774.4**	**14,150.6**	**17,179.6**
General merchandise: exports f.o.b.....................	2 110 ..	3,102.6	3,844.8	4,539.6	5,761.4	7,879.4	10,622.4	12,869.8	15,677.2
Goods for processing: exports f.o.b....................	2 150 ..	937.5	1,033.6	1,476.5	1,880.1	1,409.7	1,120.6	1,237.4	1,419.1
Repairs on goods...	2 160 ..	. . . .	. . . .	. . . .	. . . .	. . . .	. . . .	. . . .	. . . .
Goods procured in ports by carriers...................	2 170 ..	2.4	3.0	3.9	4.8	.3	7.5	.3	.9
Nonmonetary gold...	2 180 ..	7.9	7.5	8.5	11.5	17.0	23.9	43.0	82.4
Debit...	3 100 ..	**−5,154.1**	**−5,997.0**	**−7,343.3**	**−9,362.0**	**−11,688.9**	**−14,690.4**	**−18,359.8**	**−22,802.6**
General merchandise: imports f.o.b....................	3 110 ..	−4,440.9	−5,173.0	−6,042.7	−7,864.6	−10,475.2	−13,610.5	−17,048.8	−21,247.4
Goods for processing: imports f.o.b...................	3 150 ..	−652.6	−754.4	−1,196.6	−1,419.7	−1,068.2	−899.0	−999.3	−1,197.4
Repairs on goods...	3 160 ..	. . . .	. . . .	. . . .	. . . .	. . . .	. . . .	. . . .	. . . .
Goods procured in ports by carriers...................	3 170 ..	−50.1	−59.2	−79.8	−62.4	−127.5	−158.6	−274.6	−295.8
Nonmonetary gold...	3 180 ..	−10.5	−10.3	−24.2	−15.3	−18.0	−22.3	−37.0	−62.1
B. SERVICES..	4 200 ..	**380.1**	**456.7**	**548.7**	**614.4**	**812.4**	**1,049.7**	**1,083.3**	**826.9**
Total credit...	2 200 ..	*1,058.8*	*1,157.0*	*1,463.7*	*1,878.0*	*2,444.4*	*3,104.3*	*3,623.2*	*4,063.2*
Total debit..	3 200 ..	*−678.7*	*−700.3*	*−915.0*	*−1,263.6*	*−1,632.1*	*−2,054.6*	*−2,540.0*	*−3,236.3*
Transportation services, credit........................	2 205 ..	**491.6**	**531.9**	**653.7**	**932.6**	**1,353.4**	**1,587.2**	**1,945.2**	**2,342.2**
Passenger...	2 850 ..	*38.5*	*41.6*	*51.0*	*61.9*	*57.9*	*54.3*	*38.5*	*38.9*
Freight..	2 851 ..	*321.9*	*358.1*	*436.2*	*625.6*	*960.9*	*1,181.8*	*1,476.0*	*1,808.5*
Other..	2 852 ..	*131.3*	*132.2*	*166.5*	*245.1*	*334.5*	*351.1*	*430.7*	*494.8*
Sea transport, passenger.....................................	2 207 ..	2.8	4.7	5.7	3.8	6.3	5.5	7.5	8.0
Sea transport, freight..	2 208 ..	65.7	65.9	65.3	105.3	127.8	191.5	184.1	172.8
Sea transport, other..	2 209 ..	111.7	109.7	137.2	114.3	49.0	43.3	36.3	48.6
Air transport, passenger......................................	2 211 ..	26.9	28.0	34.3	37.6	40.4	36.5	18.3	13.8
Air transport, freight...	2 212 ..	3.6	3.8	3.6	4.5	6.9	6.2	5.6	8.6
Air transport, other...	2 213 ..	13.1	14.4	15.5	25.2	35.0	43.9	43.1	52.1
Other transport, passenger..................................	2 215 ..	8.8	9.0	11.0	20.6	11.2	12.4	12.7	17.1
Other transport, freight.......................................	2 216 ..	252.5	288.5	367.3	515.8	826.2	984.1	1,286.2	1,627.1
Other transport, other...	2 217 ..	6.4	8.1	13.7	105.6	250.6	263.9	351.3	394.2
Transportation services, debit.........................	3 205 ..	**−221.1**	**−236.6**	**−297.1**	**−509.6**	**−663.5**	**−896.7**	**−1,111.2**	**−1,409.4**
Passenger...	3 850 ..	*−8.2*	*−8.3*	*−7.5*	*−5.0*	*−6.9*	*−12.7*	*−21.8*	*−24.4*
Freight..	3 851 ..	*−161.4*	*−173.1*	*−233.9*	*−371.3*	*−505.1*	*−659.7*	*−801.1*	*−1,060.3*
Other..	3 852 ..	*−51.5*	*−55.2*	*−55.7*	*−133.2*	*−151.5*	*−224.3*	*−288.3*	*−324.6*
Sea transport, passenger.....................................	3 207 ..	. . . .	. . . .	. . . .	. . . .	−.1	. . . .	−.4	−.2
Sea transport, freight..	3 208 ..	−31.5	−30.4	−60.6	−107.7	−131.9	−203.6	−243.5	−314.8
Sea transport, other..	3 209 ..	−14.7	−10.9	−10.6	−16.2	−6.4	−10.9	−18.9	−22.1
Air transport, passenger......................................	3 211 ..	−4.4	−3.3	−3.2	−.2	−.4	−5.4	−12.7	−13.5
Air transport, freight...	3 212 ..	−5.6	−5.3	−6.6	−10.8	−11.7	−12.6	−16.9	−28.7
Air transport, other...	3 213 ..	−15.9	−20.8	−17.7	−17.7	−19.7	−31.4	−25.4	−31.4
Other transport, passenger..................................	3 215 ..	−3.8	−5.0	−4.3	−4.8	−6.4	−7.3	−8.7	−10.7
Other transport, freight.......................................	3 216 ..	−124.4	−137.4	−166.7	−252.8	−361.5	−443.6	−540.7	−716.8
Other transport, other...	3 217 ..	−20.8	−23.6	−27.4	−99.4	−125.5	−181.9	−244.0	−271.1
Travel, credit..	2 236 ..	**391.3**	**383.0**	**504.9**	**638.0**	**776.4**	**921.1**	**1,038.0**	**1,153.0**
Business travel..	2 237 ..	106.8	82.1	92.4	111.2	135.3	170.6	277.2	358.1
Personal travel..	2 240 ..	284.5	301.0	412.5	526.8	641.1	750.5	760.8	795.0
Travel, debit...	3 236 ..	**−253.1**	**−218.5**	**−326.2**	**−470.6**	**−635.8**	**−744.0**	**−909.1**	**−1,143.5**
Business travel..	3 237 ..	−69.4	−47.0	−94.5	−140.0	−189.2	−207.4	−266.7	−160.5
Personal travel..	3 240 ..	−183.7	−171.6	−231.6	−330.6	−446.6	−536.6	−642.4	−983.0
Other services, credit......................................	2 200 BA	**175.8**	**242.1**	**305.2**	**307.4**	**314.7**	**595.9**	**640.0**	**567.9**
Communications..	2 245 ..	35.4	37.0	39.4	59.5	64.2	76.8	87.4	99.9
Construction...	2 249 ..	13.9	17.5	27.6	24.2	30.2	34.0	31.4	67.7
Insurance..	2 253 ..	2.7	9.3	4.6	.1	.7	−.6	−10.0	−13.0
Financial...	2 260 ..	3.1	9.5	6.2	7.1	11.1	16.5	29.3	37.8
Computer and information...................................	2 262 ..	15.5	24.2	18.8	28.6	31.0	28.4	18.4	24.5
Royalties and licence fees...................................	2 266 ..	. . . .	.5	.2	.5	.8	1.9	.7	.2
Other business services.......................................	2 268 ..	87.3	123.6	175.8	154.9	153.5	398.9	426.6	291.8
Personal, cultural, and recreational.....................	2 287 ..	11.3	10.4	20.0	18.3	9.4	10.3	15.7	14.3
Government, n.i.e..	2 291 ..	6.7	10.2	12.7	14.0	13.8	29.8	40.4	44.6
Other services, debit.......................................	3 200 BA	**−204.5**	**−245.2**	**−291.7**	**−283.4**	**−332.8**	**−413.9**	**−519.6**	**−683.4**
Communications..	3 245 ..	−33.3	−38.2	−48.1	−50.4	−57.1	−66.3	−79.4	−94.0
Construction...	3 249 ..	−9.2	−14.1	−12.6	−8.2	−7.6	−13.4	−19.5	−88.1
Insurance..	3 253 ..	−7.8	−20.5	−30.6	−12.3	−21.5	−27.1	−44.8	−82.0
Financial...	3 260 ..	−5.3	−6.9	−7.1	−3.7	−5.0	−5.9	−17.5	−22.5
Computer and information...................................	3 262 ..	−13.0	−9.7	−11.4	−15.9	−20.1	−22.8	−22.9	−26.9
Royalties and licence fees...................................	3 266 ..	−12.3	−10.2	−11.5	−18.1	−18.0	−20.7	−24.4	−21.6
Other business services.......................................	3 268 ..	−96.0	−108.3	−130.1	−125.7	−147.6	−190.0	−230.7	−235.9
Personal, cultural, and recreational.....................	3 287 ..	−4.2	−5.8	−3.5	−1.0	−1.5	−2.4	−2.4	−2.2
Government, n.i.e..	3 291 ..	−23.5	−31.7	−36.6	−48.2	−54.5	−65.2	−78.0	−110.3

Table 2 (Continued). STANDARD PRESENTATION, 2000–2007

(Millions of U.S. dollars)

	Code	2000	2001	2002	2003	2004	2005	2006	2007
C. INCOME	4 300	**−193.8**	**−179.8**	**−183.3**	**−482.3**	**−612.4**	**−627.1**	**−817.0**	**−1,622.9**
Total credit	2 300	*185.5*	*205.7*	*191.6*	*235.2*	*354.9*	*448.3*	*589.9*	*793.0*
Total debit	3 300	*−379.3*	*−385.5*	*−375.0*	*−717.4*	*−967.3*	*−1,075.4*	*−1,406.9*	*−2,415.9*
Compensation of employees, credit	2 310	**47.7**	**76.1**	**74.0**	**81.6**	**162.7**	**224.5**	**248.1**	**255.7**
Compensation of employees, debit	3 310	**−36.8**	**−28.2**	**−30.1**	**−36.1**	**−25.9**	**−45.2**	**−51.3**	**−85.4**
Investment income, credit	2 320	**137.8**	**129.6**	**117.6**	**153.6**	**192.2**	**223.9**	**341.8**	**537.4**
Direct investment income	2 330	15.4	4.9	6.8	8.0	16.3	10.5	42.6	9.5
Dividends and distributed branch profits	2 332	....	....	....	....	.1	.3	1.8	.3
Reinvested earnings and undistributed branch profits	2 333	.2	−.5	−.4	−1.1	5.1	4.3	2.6	−20.4
Income on debt (interest)	2 334	15.1	5.3	7.2	9.1	11.1	5.9	38.2	29.7
Portfolio investment income	2 339	59.5	60.7	70.7	105.1	127.0	138.0	187.8	336.1
Income on equity	2 340	....	.3	.3	.4	.4	.4	.5	.6
Income on bonds and notes	2 350	59.5	60.4	66.1	93.8	119.4	128.8	172.2	310.7
Income on money market instruments	2 360	....	....	4.3	10.9	7.3	8.8	15.0	24.7
Other investment income	2 370	63.0	64.1	40.1	40.5	48.9	75.4	111.5	191.8
Investment income, debit	3 320	**−342.5**	**−357.3**	**−344.8**	**−681.4**	**−941.4**	**−1,030.2**	**−1,355.6**	**−2,330.6**
Direct investment income	3 330	−123.5	−144.9	−123.7	−401.4	−649.1	−711.2	−877.6	−1,428.0
Dividends and distributed branch profits	3 332	−29.2	−53.4	−43.1	−166.6	−229.7	−396.0	−177.7	−287.4
Reinvested earnings and undistributed branch profits	3 333	−88.4	−85.7	−66.2	−222.1	−409.0	−299.2	−678.1	−1,063.0
Income on debt (interest)	3 334	−5.9	−5.8	−14.4	−12.7	−10.4	−16.0	−21.8	−77.6
Portfolio investment income	3 339	−63.7	−68.6	−75.7	−144.5	−178.4	−170.1	−183.2	−223.2
Income on equity	3 340	−7.1	−10.1	−7.0	−8.5	−6.1	−11.3	−12.6	−21.6
Income on bonds and notes	3 350	−56.7	−58.4	−68.5	−134.2	−170.2	−158.5	−169.6	−191.2
Income on money market instruments	3 360	....	....	−.2	−1.8	−2.2	−.3	−1.0	−10.4
Other investment income	3 370	−155.2	−143.9	−145.4	−135.5	−113.8	−148.9	−294.8	−679.3
D. CURRENT TRANSFERS	4 379	**242.6**	**257.5**	**228.8**	**293.7**	**457.9**	**662.2**	**724.8**	**1,158.6**
Credit	2 379	**246.8**	**262.0**	**231.7**	**301.5**	**612.1**	**951.3**	**1,425.1**	**2,036.2**
General government	2 380	66.1	38.4	84.4	99.4	229.5	405.5	464.0	789.1
Other sectors	2 390	180.8	223.7	147.3	202.1	382.6	545.8	961.1	1,247.1
Workers' remittances	2 391	2.3	3.1	35.2	33.2	161.8	309.8	745.9	1,171.6
Other current transfers	2 392	178.5	220.6	112.1	168.9	220.8	235.9	215.1	75.5
Debit	3 379	**−4.3**	**−4.5**	**−2.9**	**−7.8**	**−154.2**	**−289.1**	**−700.2**	**−877.6**
General government	3 380	−2.9	−3.1	−1.6	−1.6	−151.6	−285.5	−323.2	−394.0
Other sectors	3 390	−1.4	−1.4	−1.4	−6.3	−2.6	−3.6	−377.0	−483.5
Workers' remittances	3 391	−1.3	−1.3	−1.1	−5.9	−1.7	−2.2	−374.5	−480.2
Other current transfers	3 392	−.1	−.2	−.2	−.4	−.9	−1.5	−2.5	−3.3
CAPITAL AND FINANCIAL ACCOUNT	4 996	**546.6**	**420.0**	**642.2**	**1,097.2**	**1,532.8**	**1,880.6**	**3,507.2**	**5,491.2**
CAPITAL ACCOUNT	4 994	**2.1**	**1.4**	**56.5**	**67.5**	**287.2**	**331.1**	**351.4**	**690.1**
Total credit	2 994	*2.6*	*1.5*	*56.8*	*68.3*	*288.1*	*331.2*	*351.6*	*690.1*
Total debit	3 994	*−.4*	*−.1*	*−.4*	*−.8*	*−1.0*	*−.1*	*−.2*	*....*
Capital transfers, credit	2 400	**2.6**	**1.5**	**56.8**	**68.3**	**288.1**	**331.2**	**351.6**	**690.1**
General government	2 401	1.2	....	56.1	68.0	287.8	331.2	351.1	690.1
Debt forgiveness	2 402	....	....	....	....	....	....	....	....
Other capital transfers	2 410	1.2	....	56.1	68.0	287.8	331.2	351.1	690.1
Other sectors	2 430	1.4	1.5	.8	.3	.4	....	.5	....
Migrants' transfers	2 431	....	....	....	....	....	....	....	....
Debt forgiveness	2 432	.8	1.5	.8	.3	.4	....	....	....
Other capital transfers	2 440	.5	....	....	....	....	....	.5	....
Capital transfers, debit	3 400	**−.4**	**−.1**	**−.4**	**−.8**	**−1.0**	**−.1**	**−.2**	**....**
General government	3 401	....	....	....	....	....	....	....	....
Debt forgiveness	3 402	....	....	....	....	....	....	....	....
Other capital transfers	3 410	....	....	....	....	....	....	....	....
Other sectors	3 430	−.4	−.1	−.4	−.8	−1.0	−.1	−.2	....
Migrants' transfers	3 431	....	....	....	....	....	....	....	....
Debt forgiveness	3 432	−.4	−.1	−.4	−.8	−1.0	−.1	....	....
Other capital transfers	3 440	....	....	....	....	....	....	−.2	....
Nonproduced nonfinancial assets, credit	2 480	....	....	....	....	....	....	....	....
Nonproduced nonfinancial assets, debit	3 480	....	....	....	....	....	....	....	....

Table 2 (Continued). STANDARD PRESENTATION, 2000–2007

(Millions of U.S. dollars)

	Code	2000	2001	2002	2003	2004	2005	2006	2007
FINANCIAL ACCOUNT	4 995 ..	544.4	418.6	585.7	1,029.6	1,245.6	1,549.4	3,155.8	4,801.0
A. DIRECT INVESTMENT	4 500 ..	375.2	438.7	694.8	142.0	510.5	688.8	1,550.6	1,333.7
Direct investment abroad	4 505 ..	−3.7	−7.1	−17.7	−37.2	−262.6	−343.0	−289.5	−600.4
Equity capital	4 510 ..	−1.7	−5.4	−13.4	−10.4	−194.6	−204.1	−104.5	−673.8
Claims on affiliated enterprises	4 515 ..	−1.7	−5.4	−13.4	−10.4	−197.1	−201.7	−104.5	−673.8
Liabilities to affiliated enterprises	4 520 ..	....	....	....	....	2.5	−2.4	....	....
Reinvested earnings	4 525 ..	−.2	.5	.4	1.1	−5.1	−4.3	−2.6	20.4
Other capital	4 530 ..	−1.8	−2.2	−4.8	−27.8	−62.9	−134.6	−182.5	53.0
Claims on affiliated enterprises	4 535 ..	−1.8	−3.3	−5.8	−26.3	−63.9	−147.4	−192.5	14.6
Liabilities to affiliated enterprises	4 540 ..	....	1.0	1.1	−1.5	1.0	12.8	10.0	38.4
Direct investment in Lithuania	4 555 ..	378.9	445.8	712.5	179.2	773.2	1,031.8	1,840.2	1,934.1
Equity capital	4 560 ..	181.4	260.7	515.8	192.4	315.6	432.0	1,076.0	328.7
Claims on direct investors	4 565 ..	....	....	....	....	−.1			.4
Liabilities to direct investors	4 570 ..	181.4	260.7	515.8	192.4	315.7	432.0	1,076.0	328.3
Reinvested earnings	4 575 ..	88.4	85.7	66.2	222.1	409.0	299.2	678.1	1,063.0
Other capital	4 580 ..	109.1	99.5	130.4	−235.3	48.5	300.6	86.0	542.4
Claims on direct investors	4 585 ..	−1.4	4.5	52.7	−39.7	−31.3	−146.9	−201.9	−268.4
Liabilities to direct investors	4 590 ..	110.5	95.0	77.6	−195.6	79.8	447.4	287.9	810.8
B. PORTFOLIO INVESTMENT	4 600 ..	264.5	264.3	24.3	252.1	211.2	−236.9	−253.7	−238.4
Assets	4 602 ..	−141.4	26.2	−124.5	29.8	−219.9	−778.5	−1,105.8	−847.2
Equity securities	4 610 ..	−1.4	1.1	−3.7	−1.8	−18.8	−185.1	−286.4	−366.2
Monetary authorities	4 611 ..	....	....	....	....	−2.1	−1.4	....	.1
General government	4 612 ..	....	....	....	....	....	....	....	....
Banks	4 613 ..	−1.4	1.1	....	....	.3	−31.6	−33.8	14.2
Other sectors	4 614 ..	.1	....	−3.6	−1.8	−17.0	−152.1	−252.6	−380.4
Debt securities	4 619 ..	−140.0	25.1	−120.9	31.6	−201.0	−593.4	−819.4	−481.0
Bonds and notes	4 620 ..	−79.9	−18.5	−56.4	3.0	−219.7	−439.2	−543.9	−220.4
Monetary authorities	4 621 ..	....	....	....	....	....	....	....	....
General government	4 622 ..	....	....	....	....	....	....	....	....
Banks	4 623 ..	−79.9	−18.5	−30.3	4.0	−182.1	−319.7	−365.1	57.9
Other sectors	4 624 ..	....	....	−26.0	−.9	−37.6	−119.5	−178.8	−278.3
Money market instruments	4 630 ..	−60.1	43.6	−64.5	28.6	18.6	−154.3	−275.5	−260.6
Monetary authorities	4 631 ..	....	....	....	....	....	....	....	....
General government	4 632 ..	....	....	....	....	....	....	....	....
Banks	4 633 ..	−53.8	43.7	−65.7	29.1	19.4	−154.1	−277.2	−253.6
Other sectors	4 634 ..	−6.4	−.1	1.2	−.5	−.7	−.2	1.7	−7.0
Liabilities	4 652 ..	405.9	238.0	148.8	222.3	431.1	541.6	852.1	608.8
Equity securities	4 660 ..	121.5	−16.3	5.6	4.2	7.9	130.0	72.0	−166.3
Banks	4 663 ..	−17.1	−4.4	4.6	6.3	−12.9	−10.0	34.2	−115.0
Other sectors	4 664 ..	138.7	−11.9	1.0	−2.1	20.8	140.0	37.8	−51.3
Debt securities	4 669 ..	284.4	254.3	143.2	218.0	423.1	411.6	780.1	775.0
Bonds and notes	4 670 ..	309.8	245.5	153.1	191.1	455.8	349.4	881.9	772.6
Monetary authorities	4 671 ..	....	....	....	....	....	....	....	....
General government	4 672 ..	306.4	165.3	168.8	161.7	405.2	313.0	924.2	569.4
Banks	4 673 ..	−.3	2.7	−1.8	57.4	63.6	38.3	−46.9	199.7
Other sectors	4 674 ..	3.7	77.6	−13.9	−27.9	−13.0	−1.8	4.7	3.6
Money market instruments	4 680 ..	−25.4	8.8	−9.9	26.9	−32.6	62.2	−101.9	2.4
Monetary authorities	4 681 ..	....	....	....	....	....	....	....	....
General government	4 682 ..	−22.0	−.6	.2	27.1	−14.0	88.1	−89.1	....
Banks	4 683 ..	−.2	9.4	−10.1	−.2	34.1	−24.4	−12.7	2.4
Other sectors	4 684 ..	−3.2	−.1	....	....	−52.7	−1.6	−.1	....
C. FINANCIAL DERIVATIVES	4 910 ..	....	−1.3	−3.0	−28.0	2.6	12.9	−11.0	−2.4
Monetary authorities	4 911 ..	....	....	....	....	....	....	....	....
General government	4 912 ..	....	....	....	....	....	....	....	....
Banks	4 913 ..	....	−1.3	−12.0	−31.2	2.6	12.9	−11.1	−2.4
Other sectors	4 914 ..	....	....	8.9	3.2	−.1	....	....	....
Assets	4 900 ..	....	18.3	19.6	28.1	60.0	27.4	9.5	4.8
Monetary authorities	4 901 ..	....	....	....	....	....	....	....	....
General government	4 902 ..	....	....	....	....	....	....	....	....
Banks	4 903 ..	....	18.3	19.6	28.1	60.1	27.4	9.4	4.8
Other sectors	4 904 ..	....	....	....	.1	−.1	....	....	....
Liabilities	4 905 ..	....	−19.6	−22.7	−56.2	−57.4	−14.5	−20.5	−7.1
Monetary authorities	4 906 ..	....	....	....	....	....	....	....	....
General government	4 907 ..	....	....	....	....	....	....	....	....
Banks	4 908 ..	....	−19.6	−31.6	−59.3	−57.4	−14.5	−20.5	−7.1
Other sectors	4 909 ..	....	....	8.9	3.2	....	....	....	....

Table 2 (Concluded). STANDARD PRESENTATION, 2000–2007

(Millions of U.S. dollars)

	Code	2000	2001	2002	2003	2004	2005	2006	2007
D. OTHER INVESTMENT...........................	4 700 ..	**35.4**	**41.9**	**292.2**	**1,194.8**	**397.1**	**1,771.5**	**3,376.6**	**4,923.4**
Assets...	4 703 ..	**39.9**	**−225.0**	**154.7**	**−100.9**	**−683.8**	**−785.6**	**−475.7**	**−1,677.5**
Trade credits.................................	4 706 ..	74.5	−79.9	−44.4	61.5	−58.3	−392.9	−52.6	−465.3
General government......................	4 707 ..	....	....	....	....	....	....	....	....
of which: Short-term.................	4 709 ..	....	....	....	....	....	....	....	....
Other sectors..............................	4 710 ..	74.5	−79.9	−44.4	61.5	−58.3	−392.9	−52.6	−465.3
of which: Short-term.................	4 712 ..	*74.5*	*−79.9*	*−44.4*	*61.5*	*−58.3*	*−392.9*	*−52.6*	*−465.3*
Loans..	4 714 ..	22.8	−97.9	196.3	−9.7	−429.5	−271.2	41.1	−991.4
Monetary authorities....................	4 715 ..	....	....	....	....	....	....	....	....
of which: Short-term.................	4 718 ..	....	....	....	....	....	....	....	....
General government......................	4 719 ..	....	....	....	....	....	....	....	....
of which: Short-term.................	4 721 ..	....	....	....	....	....	....	....	....
Banks...	4 722 ..	20.8	−96.0	214.3	16.3	−431.0	−220.6	115.5	−962.8
of which: Short-term.................	4 724 ..	*22.0*	*−100.9*	*250.8*	*31.3*	*−408.2*	*−228.2*	*215.7*	*−733.4*
Other sectors..............................	4 725 ..	2.0	−1.9	−18.0	−26.0	1.4	−50.6	−74.4	−28.6
of which: Short-term.................	4 727 ..	*1.8*	*−.5*	*−10.4*	*−23.7*	*11.3*	*−23.3*	*−43.2*	*−48.3*
Currency and deposits...................	4 730 ..	−51.6	−38.1	1.2	−143.8	−208.0	−106.2	−473.4	−216.3
Monetary authorities....................	4 731 ..	....	....	....	....	....	....	....	....
General government......................	4 732 ..	....	−2.6	....	....	−7.3	....	....	....
Banks...	4 733 ..	−157.9	−57.6	−2.4	−171.3	−243.3	−163.2	−459.7	245.3
Other sectors..............................	4 734 ..	106.3	22.2	3.6	27.5	42.5	57.0	−13.7	−461.6
Other assets.................................	4 736 ..	−5.9	−9.2	1.6	−8.9	12.0	−15.3	9.2	−4.4
Monetary authorities....................	4 737 ..	....	....	....	....	....	....	....	....
of which: Short-term.................	4 739 ..	....	....	....	....	....	....	....	....
General government......................	4 740 ..	....	....	....	....	....	....	....	....
of which: Short-term.................	4 742 ..	....	....	....	....	....	....	....	....
Banks...	4 743 ..	−5.1	−4.5	.9	−6.0	3.1	−10.9	8.9	−3.0
of which: Short-term.................	4 745 ..	*−5.1*	*−4.5*	*.9*	*−6.0*	*3.1*	*−10.9*	*8.9*	*−3.0*
Other sectors..............................	4 746 ..	−.8	−4.7	.7	−2.9	8.9	−4.4	.3	−1.4
of which: Short-term.................	4 748 ..	*−.8*	*−4.7*	*.7*	*−2.9*	*8.9*	*−4.4*	*.3*	*−1.4*
Liabilities.......................................	4 753 ..	**−4.5**	**266.9**	**137.5**	**1,295.7**	**1,081.0**	**2,557.0**	**3,852.4**	**6,600.8**
Trade credits.................................	4 756 ..	−2.5	143.4	190.4	272.7	243.4	530.1	−1.1	210.3
General government......................	4 757 ..	....	....	....	....	....	....	....	....
of which: Short-term.................	4 759 ..	....	....	....	....	....	....	....	....
Other sectors..............................	4 760 ..	−2.5	143.4	190.4	272.7	243.4	530.1	−1.1	210.3
of which: Short-term.................	4 762 ..	*−2.5*	*143.4*	*190.4*	*272.7*	*243.4*	*530.1*	*−1.1*	*210.3*
Loans..	4 764 ..	−85.0	−.5	−65.1	995.2	648.7	1,880.7	3,549.6	6,099.7
Monetary authorities....................	4 765 ..	−129.2	−34.0	−40.2	−81.4	−19.8	−25.5	....	....
of which: Use of Fund credit and loans from the Fund..	4 766 ..	*−27.3*	*−34.0*	*−40.2*	*−81.4*	*−19.8*	*−25.5*	....	....
of which: Short-term.................	4 768 ..	*−25.0*	....	....	....	....	....	....	....
General government......................	4 769 ..	....	−53.7	−70.6	−9.4	−308.2	−191.0	−24.5	−120.1
of which: Short-term.................	4 771 ..	....	....	....	*80.0*	*−85.3*	....	....	....
Banks...	4 772 ..	−6.4	90.7	101.6	683.2	594.4	2,434.4	2,336.3	4,771.7
of which: Short-term.................	4 774 ..	*30.3*	*192.1*	*115.5*	*455.6*	*27.9*	*953.9*	*264.7*	*810.9*
Other sectors..............................	4 775 ..	50.6	−3.5	−56.0	402.9	382.2	−337.1	1,237.9	1,448.1
of which: Short-term.................	4 777 ..	*−14.6*	*13.2*	*9.5*	*1.3*	*65.4*	*−62.4*	*34.3*	*82.1*
Currency and deposits...................	4 780 ..	58.6	30.6	10.0	80.6	286.8	156.2	260.8	−110.7
Monetary authorities....................	4 781 ..	−.1	.1	....	−.2	1.8	5.5	77.9	−27.0
General government......................	4 782 ..	....	....	....	....	....	....	....	....
Banks...	4 783 ..	58.7	30.5	10.0	80.8	285.0	150.6	182.8	−83.7
Other sectors..............................	4 784 ..	....	....	....	....	....	....	....	....
Other liabilities............................	4 786 ..	24.5	93.4	2.2	−52.8	−97.9	−9.9	43.2	401.6
Monetary authorities....................	4 787 ..	....	51.6	−3.6	−7.8	−68.6	....	−2.7	350.4
of which: Short-term.................	4 789 ..	....	*51.6*	*−3.6*	*−7.8*	*−68.6*	....	*−2.7*	*350.4*
General government......................	4 790 ..	....	....	....	....	....	....	....	....
of which: Short-term.................	4 792 ..	....	....	....	....	....	....	....	....
Banks...	4 793 ..	.8	48.2	.1	−26.4	−9.1	−7.7	40.9	14.7
of which: Short-term.................	4 795 ..	*.8*	*48.2*	*.1*	*−26.4*	*−9.1*	*−7.7*	*40.9*	*14.7*
Other sectors..............................	4 796 ..	23.7	−6.4	5.7	−18.6	−20.2	−2.2	4.9	36.5
of which: Short-term.................	4 798 ..	*23.7*	*−6.4*	*5.7*	*−18.6*	*−20.2*	*−2.2*	*4.9*	*36.5*
E. RESERVE ASSETS................................	4 802 ..	**−130.7**	**−325.0**	**−422.5**	**−531.2**	**124.2**	**−686.8**	**−1,506.7**	**−1,215.3**
Monetary gold................................	4 812 ..	....	....	....	....	.1	....	....	....
Special drawing rights.....................	4 811 ..	2.9	−17.3	−30.3	53.6	....	....	....	....
Reserve position in the Fund............	4 810 ..	....	....	....	....	....	....	....	....
Foreign exchange............................	4 803 ..	−133.6	−307.8	−392.2	−584.9	124.1	−686.8	−1,506.7	−1,215.3
Other claims..................................	4 813 ..	....	....	....	....	....	....	....	....
NET ERRORS AND OMISSIONS.............................	4 998 ..	**128.3**	**153.6**	**78.5**	**181.2**	**191.8**	**−49.4**	**−289.1**	**−230.7**

Table 3. INTERNATIONAL INVESTMENT POSITION (End-period stocks), 2000–2007

(Millions of U.S. dollars)

	Code	2000	2001	2002	2003	2004	2005	2006	2007
ASSETS	8 995 C.	**2,677.7**	**3,126.3**	**4,225.5**	**5,717.0**	**7,413.0**	**9,129.0**	**13,457.3**	**19,195.5**
Direct investment abroad	8 505 ..	**29.3**	**47.9**	**59.5**	**119.7**	**422.8**	**721.1**	**1,041.4**	**1,570.5**
Equity capital and reinvested earnings	8 506 ..	17.6	26.4	36.3	62.7	287.2	490.7	558.8	1,074.3
Claims on affiliated enterprises	8 507 ..	17.6	26.4	36.3	62.7	289.9	490.7	558.8	1,074.3
Liabilities to affiliated enterprises	8 508 ..	....	....	....	....	−2.6	....	....	....
Other capital	8 530 ..	11.7	21.4	23.2	57.0	135.6	230.4	482.6	496.1
Claims on affiliated enterprises	8 535 ..	12.0	22.7	24.8	57.2	136.9	243.6	507.3	563.9
Liabilities to affiliated enterprises	8 540 ..	−.3	−1.3	−1.6	−.2	−1.3	−13.1	−24.7	−67.8
Portfolio investment	8 602 ..	**172.3**	**138.2**	**286.3**	**268.8**	**516.7**	**1,255.2**	**2,517.2**	**3,617.0**
Equity securities	8 610 ..	6.0	4.9	10.5	11.8	36.2	220.5	561.4	1,038.6
Monetary authorities	8 611 ..	2.0	2.0	2.4	2.8	5.4	6.0	6.6	7.4
General government	8 612 ..	....	....	....	....	....	....	....	....
Banks	8 613 ..	2.0	.9	1.5	1.6	1.5	5.2	40.9	29.3
Other sectors	8 614 ..	2.1	2.1	6.7	7.3	29.3	209.3	513.9	1,001.9
Debt securities	8 619 ..	166.4	133.2	275.8	257.0	480.5	1,034.8	1,955.8	2,578.4
Bonds and notes	8 620 ..	91.0	109.2	84.9	91.2	345.0	756.9	1,363.7	1,626.4
Monetary authorities	8 621 ..	....	....	....	....	....	....	....	....
General government	8 622 ..	....	....	....	....	....	....	....	....
Banks	8 623 ..	91.0	108.5	55.0	59.4	252.3	547.2	968.5	987.1
Other sectors	8 624 ..	....	.8	29.9	31.9	92.7	209.7	395.2	639.3
Money market instruments	8 630 ..	75.4	24.0	190.9	165.7	135.5	277.8	592.1	952.1
Monetary authorities	8 631 ..	....	....	....	....	....	....	....	....
General government	8 632 ..	....	....	....	....	....	....	....	....
Banks	8 633 ..	65.1	15.2	175.8	147.3	134.3	276.4	587.6	939.6
Other sectors	8 634 ..	10.3	8.8	15.1	18.5	1.2	1.4	4.5	12.5
Financial derivatives	8 900 ..	**....**	**....**	**....**	**.2**	**....**	**9.6**	**69.0**	**222.0**
Monetary authorities	8 901 ..	....	....	....	....	....	....	....	....
General government	8 902 ..	....	....	....	....	....	....	....	....
Banks	8 903 ..	....	....	....	....	....	9.5	69.0	222.0
Other sectors	8 904 ..	....	....	....	.2	....	....	....	....
Other investment	8 703 ..	**1,117.4**	**1,271.1**	**1,459.7**	**1,878.7**	**2,879.5**	**3,327.5**	**4,057.1**	**6,064.9**
Trade credits	8 706 ..	437.7	518.7	688.0	828.7	1,115.5	1,355.1	1,518.3	2,118.5
General government	8 707 ..	....	....	....	....	....	....	....	....
of which: Short-term	8 709 ..	....	....	....	....	....	....	....	....
Other sectors	8 710 ..	437.7	518.7	688.0	828.7	1,115.5	1,355.1	1,518.3	2,118.5
of which: Short-term	8 712 ..	*437.7*	*518.7*	*688.0*	*828.7*	*1,115.5*	*1,355.1*	*1,518.3*	*2,118.5*
Loans	8 714 ..	357.4	447.8	288.8	328.9	786.5	992.9	998.2	2,068.0
Monetary authorities	8 715 ..	....	....	....	....	....	....	....	....
of which: Short-term	8 718 ..	....	....	....	....	....	....	....	....
General government	8 719 ..	....	....	....	....	....	....	....	....
of which: Short-term	8 721 ..	....	....	....	....	....	....	....	....
Banks	8 722 ..	344.9	439.4	259.7	257.5	733.7	867.2	789.0	1,802.7
of which: Short-term	8 724 ..	*331.5*	*430.9*	*209.6*	*172.9*	*613.3*	*774.9*	*589.2*	*1,345.3*
Other sectors	8 725 ..	12.6	8.4	29.1	71.4	52.9	125.7	209.2	265.3
of which: Short-term	8 727 ..	*5.9*	*2.0*	*14.3*	*43.9*	*33.2*	*55.7*	*105.2*	*169.8*
Currency and deposits	8 730 ..	309.3	282.3	457.7	684.6	957.6	944.2	1,511.3	1,815.0
Monetary authorities	8 731 ..	....	....	....	....	....	....	....	....
General government	8 732 ..	....	....	....	....	....	....	....	....
Banks	8 733 ..	188.9	186.6	231.7	463.6	731.6	784.2	1,324.3	1,197.0
Other sectors	8 734 ..	120.4	95.6	225.9	221.0	226.0	160.0	187.0	618.0
Other assets	8 736 ..	12.9	22.3	25.2	36.5	19.9	35.3	29.3	63.5
Monetary authorities	8 737 ..	....	....	....	....	....	....	....	....
of which: Short-term	8 739 ..	....	....	....	....	....	....	....	....
General government	8 740 ..	....	....	....	....	....	....	....	....
of which: Short-term	8 742 ..	....	....	....	....	....	....	....	....
Banks	8 743 ..	6.0	10.5	12.6	15.2	13.8	19.1	11.4	15.4
of which: Short-term	8 745 ..	*6.0*	*10.5*	*12.6*	*15.2*	*13.8*	*19.1*	*11.4*	*15.4*
Other sectors	8 746 ..	7.0	11.8	12.6	21.3	6.0	16.1	17.9	48.0
of which: Short-term	8 748 ..	*7.0*	*11.8*	*12.6*	*21.3*	*6.0*	*16.1*	*17.9*	*48.0*
Reserve assets	8 802 ..	**1,358.7**	**1,669.2**	**2,420.0**	**3,449.7**	**3,594.0**	**3,815.6**	**5,772.6**	**7,721.1**
Monetary gold	8 812 ..	47.1	51.5	63.8	77.7	81.4	95.3	118.1	155.4
Special drawing rights	8 811 ..	1.3	18.4	53.4	.1	.1	.1	.1	.1
Reserve position in the Fund	8 810 ..							.1	.1
Foreign exchange	8 803 ..	1,097.1	1,599.3	2,302.8	3,371.9	3,512.5	3,720.1	5,654.3	7,565.6
Other claims	8 813 ..	213.1	....	....	....	....	....	....	....

Table 3 (Concluded). INTERNATIONAL INVESTMENT POSITION (End-period stocks), 2000–2007

(Millions of U.S. dollars)

	Code	2000	2001	2002	2003	2004	2005	2006	2007
LIABILITIES	8 995 D.	**6,693.3**	**7,331.4**	**9,373.3**	**12,575.8**	**15,956.7**	**19,717.0**	**28,931.5**	**42,683.0**
Direct investment in Lithuania	8 555 ..	**2,334.3**	**2,665.5**	**3,981.3**	**4,959.8**	**6,388.9**	**8,211.0**	**10,996.3**	**15,061.9**
Equity capital and reinvested earnings	8 556 ..	1,809.5	2,069.5	3,106.7	4,193.9	5,475.9	7,129.0	9,663.6	12,714.2
Claims on direct investors	8 557 ..	−.1	−.1	....	....	−.1	−.1	−.5	....
Liabilities to direct investors	8 558 ..	1,809.6	2,069.6	3,106.7	4,193.9	5,476.0	7,129.1	9,664.1	12,714.2
Other capital	8 580 ..	524.8	596.0	874.6	765.9	913.0	1,082.0	1,332.7	2,347.8
Claims on direct investors	8 585 ..	−100.4	−100.7	−52.4	−110.0	−165.0	−282.6	−504.0	−845.2
Liabilities to direct investors	8 590 ..	625.2	696.7	927.0	875.9	1,077.9	1,364.7	1,836.7	3,193.0
Portfolio investment	8 652 ..	**1,140.4**	**1,312.6**	**1,511.2**	**2,077.3**	**2,812.0**	**2,981.6**	**4,572.3**	**5,705.0**
Equity securities	8 660 ..	128.1	95.6	111.0	144.0	172.5	319.5	809.4	743.5
Banks	8 663 ..	31.7	26.8	37.4	51.8	42.8	27.8	205.3	128.3
Other sectors	8 664 ..	96.3	68.8	73.6	92.1	129.7	291.8	604.0	615.3
Debt securities	8 669 ..	1,012.3	1,217.1	1,400.3	1,933.3	2,639.5	2,662.1	3,762.9	4,961.5
Bonds and notes	8 670 ..	1,008.1	1,204.5	1,394.3	1,834.0	2,535.8	2,560.9	3,762.9	4,958.8
Monetary authorities	8 671 ..	....	....	....	....	....	....	....	....
General government	8 672 ..	986.1	1,103.9	1,293.1	1,756.8	2,395.2	2,402.4	3,628.9	4,609.6
Banks	8 673 ..	.4	3.0	1.7	62.3	138.5	158.5	128.6	339.4
Other sectors	8 674 ..	21.6	97.7	99.4	15.0	2.1	....	5.4	9.9
Money market instruments	8 680 ..	4.2	12.6	6.0	99.2	103.7	101.2	....	2.7
Monetary authorities	8 681 ..	....	....	....	....	....	....	....	....
General government	8 682 ..	4.2	2.9	4.7	39.9	62.0	87.8	....	....
Banks	8 683 ..	....	9.6	1.2	1.4	39.9	13.3	....	2.7
Other sectors	8 684 ..	.1	....	....	57.9	1.8	.1	....	....
Financial derivatives	8 905 ..	....	....	**10.1**	**10.2**	**2.9**	**4.0**	**30.1**	**41.0**
Monetary authorities	8 906 ..	....	....	....	....	....	....	....	....
General government	8 907 ..	....	....	....	....	....	....	....	....
Banks	8 908 ..	....	....	....	....	....	3.1	30.1	41.0
Other sectors	8 909 ..	....	....	10.1	10.2	2.9	.9	....	....
Other investment	8 753 ..	**3,218.6**	**3,353.3**	**3,870.5**	**5,528.6**	**6,752.9**	**8,520.4**	**13,332.8**	**21,875.1**
Trade credits	8 756 ..	732.3	862.3	1,163.4	1,437.3	1,644.2	1,945.5	2,169.2	2,719.8
General government	8 757 ..	....	....	....	....	....	....	....	....
of which: Short-term	8 759 ..	....	....	....	....	....	....	....	....
Other sectors	8 760 ..	732.3	862.3	1,163.4	1,437.3	1,644.2	1,945.5	2,169.2	2,719.8
of which: Short-term	8 762 ..	*732.3*	*862.3*	*1,163.4*	*1,437.3*	*1,644.2*	*1,945.5*	*2,169.2*	*2,719.8*
Loans	8 764 ..	2,261.5	2,149.3	2,274.1	3,524.8	4,321.3	5,720.3	9,933.5	17,498.5
Monetary authorities	8 765 ..	191.6	151.2	121.4	44.9	26.1	....	....	....
of which: Use of Fund credit and loans from the Fund	8 766 ..	*191.6*	*151.2*	*121.4*	*44.9*	*26.1*	....	....	....
of which: Short-term	8 768 ..	....	....	....	....	....	....	....	....
General government	8 769 ..	767.0	694.1	669.2	717.7	478.0	254.7	256.2	153.1
of which: Short-term	8 771 ..	....	....	....	*87.5*	....	....	....	....
Banks	8 772 ..	412.3	474.0	652.1	1,470.6	2,097.6	4,274.4	7,124.3	12,900.9
of which: Short-term	8 774 ..	*126.5*	*298.3*	*461.4*	*1,006.3*	*985.4*	*1,805.2*	*2,080.4*	*3,063.9*
Other sectors	8 775 ..	890.7	830.0	831.5	1,291.5	1,719.6	1,191.2	2,553.0	4,444.4
of which: Short-term	8 777 ..	*26.1*	*43.6*	*58.6*	*79.7*	*245.4*	*165.8*	*192.3*	*319.9*
Currency and deposits	8 780 ..	147.9	166.1	219.3	387.8	695.2	785.7	1,101.7	1,053.5
Monetary authorities	8 781 ..	.2	.3	.3	.2	4.0	8.9	89.9	64.3
General government	8 782 ..	....	....	....	....	....	....	....	....
Banks	8 783 ..	147.7	165.8	219.0	387.6	691.1	776.9	1,011.8	989.2
Other sectors	8 784 ..	....	....	....	....	....	....	....	....
Other liabilities	8 786 ..	76.9	175.6	213.7	178.8	92.3	68.9	128.4	603.4
Monetary authorities	8 787 ..	....	51.6	58.3	67.1	....	....	....	391.5
of which: Short-term	8 789 ..	....	*51.6*	*58.3*	*67.1*	....	....	....	*391.5*
General government	8 790 ..	....	....	....	....	....	....	....	....
of which: Short-term	8 792 ..	....	....	....	....	....	....	....	....
Banks	8 793 ..	8.2	51.3	62.3	51.9	50.4	35.6	86.4	123.1
of which: Short-term	8 795 ..	*8.2*	*51.3*	*62.3*	*51.9*	*50.4*	*35.6*	*86.4*	*123.1*
Other sectors	8 796 ..	68.7	72.8	93.0	59.7	41.9	33.3	42.0	88.7
of which: Short-term	8 798 ..	*68.7*	*72.8*	*93.0*	*59.7*	*41.9*	*33.3*	*42.0*	*88.7*
NET INTERNATIONAL INVESTMENT POSITION	8 995 ..	**−4,015.6**	**−4,205.1**	**−5,147.7**	**−6,858.9**	**−8,543.7**	**−10,588.0**	**−15,474.2**	**−23,487.5**
Conversion rates: litai per U.S. dollar (end of period)	0 102 ..	4.0000	4.0000	3.3114	2.7621	2.5345	2.9102	2.6304	2.3572

Table 1. ANALYTIC PRESENTATION, 2000–2007

(Millions of U.S. dollars)

	Code	2000	2001	2002	2003	2004	2005	2006	2007
A. Current Account[1].....	4 993 Z.	**2,562**	**1,674**	**2,306**	**2,409**	**4,088**	**4,148**	**4,435**	**4,928**
Goods: exports f.o.b.....	2 100 ..	8,635	8,996	9,467	10,942	13,526	14,602	16,383	18,256
Goods: imports f.o.b.....	3 100 ..	−11,056	−11,395	−11,612	−13,937	−17,078	−18,802	−20,795	−23,066
Balance on Goods.....	4 100 ..	*−2,420*	*−2,399*	*−2,145*	*−2,995*	*−3,552*	*−4,200*	*−4,411*	*−4,810*
Services: credit.....	2 200 ..	20,301	19,945	20,504	25,499	33,957	40,842	50,906	64,524
Services: debit.....	3 200 ..	−13,581	−13,708	−12,412	−15,531	−20,940	−24,594	−30,218	−37,453
Balance on Goods and Services.....	4 991 ..	*4,300*	*3,838*	*5,946*	*6,973*	*9,465*	*12,047*	*16,276*	*22,261*
Income: credit.....	2 300 ..	50,400	52,302	60,400	69,291	76,855	90,229	117,521	162,971
Income: debit.....	3 300 ..	−51,678	−53,941	−63,759	−73,247	−81,166	−96,950	−128,091	−177,946
Balance on Goods, Services, and Income.....	4 992 ..	*3,022*	*2,199*	*2,587*	*3,017*	*5,154*	*5,327*	*5,705*	*7,286*
Current transfers: credit.....	2 379 Z.	2,750	2,269	3,579	3,889	4,025	4,716	5,612	6,134
Current transfers: debit.....	3 379 ..	−3,211	−2,793	−3,860	−4,497	−5,090	−5,895	−6,882	−8,492
B. Capital Account[1].....	4 994 Z.	....	....	**−89**	**−140**	**−772**	**1,183**	**−299**	**−166**
Capital account: credit.....	2 994 Z.	....	....	92	63	51	1,509	54	77
Capital account: debit.....	3 994 ..	....	....	−181	−204	−823	−326	−354	−243
Total, Groups A Plus B.....	4 981 ..	*2,562*	*1,674*	*2,217*	*2,268*	*3,316*	*5,331*	*4,136*	*4,762*
C. Financial Account[1].....	4 995 W.	....	....	**−2,456**	**−2,084**	**−3,528**	**−5,883**	**−4,631**	**−5,097**
Direct investment abroad.....	4 505 ..	....	....	−128,789	−100,458	−85,310	−122,039	−111,658	−250,036
Direct investment in Luxembourg.....	4 555 Z.	....	....	118,512	89,784	80,098	113,905	126,268	188,119
Portfolio investment assets.....	4 602 ..	....	....	6,253	−78,422	−87,546	−267,098	−176,160	−174,516
Equity securities.....	4 610 ..	....	....	4,301	−35,857	−45,835	−123,620	−102,723	−52,572
Debt securities.....	4 619 ..	....	....	1,952	−42,565	−41,711	−143,477	−73,437	−121,944
Portfolio investment liabilities.....	4 652 Z.	....	....	64,161	99,486	139,610	315,806	248,629	309,874
Equity securities.....	4 660 ..	....	....	36,031	70,443	121,546	275,574	220,275	281,525
Debt securities.....	4 669 Z.	....	....	28,130	29,043	18,064	40,232	28,353	28,349
Financial derivatives.....	4 910 ..	....	....	−1,346	6,158	−2,998	−4,216	10,364	15,754
Financial derivatives assets.....	4 900 ..	....	....	....	....	....	....	....	....
Financial derivatives liabilities.....	4 905 ..	....	....	....	....	....	....	....	....
Other investment assets.....	4 703 ..	....	....	−40,902	−33,924	−117,163	−191,630	−264,794	−250,140
Monetary authorities.....	4 701 ..	....	....	....	−7,641	−7,210	−5,755	3,281	−18,671
General government.....	4 704 ..	....	....	....	−1	....	−1	−9	−317
Banks.....	4 705 ..	....	....	19,337	−3,623	−43,871	−36,573	−57,181	−118,631
Other sectors.....	4 728 ..	....	....	−60,239	−22,658	−66,081	−149,300	−210,885	−112,520
Other investment liabilities.....	4 753 W.	....	....	−20,345	15,292	69,781	149,388	162,721	155,847
Monetary authorities.....	4 753 WA	....	....	−887	−5,824	6,208	322	−343	454
General government.....	4 753 ZB	....	....	3	−1	−16	....	....	−1
Banks.....	4 753 ZC	....	....	−27,719	17,866	31,295	41,383	43,908	75,326
Other sectors.....	4 753 ZD	....	....	8,258	3,251	32,294	107,684	119,155	80,068
Total, Groups A Through C.....	4 983 ..	*2,562*	*1,674*	*−239*	*184*	*−212*	*−552*	*−495*	*−335*
D. Net Errors and Omissions.....	4 998 ..	....	....	**275**	**−76**	**220**	**504**	**467**	**247**
Total, Groups A Through D.....	4 984 ..	....	....	*35*	*108*	*8*	*−48*	*−28*	*−89*
E. Reserves and Related Items.....	4 802 A.	....	....	**−35**	**−108**	**−8**	**48**	**28**	**89**
Reserve assets.....	4 802 ..	....	....	−35	−108	−8	48	28	89
Use of Fund credit and loans.....	4 766 ..	....	....	....	....	....	....	....	....
Exceptional financing.....	4 920 ..	....	....	....	....	....	....	....	....
Conversion rates: euros per U.S. dollar.....	0 103 ..	**1.0854**	**1.1175**	**1.0626**	**.8860**	**.8054**	**.8041**	**.7971**	**.7306**

[1] Excludes components that have been classified in the categories of Group E.

Table 2. STANDARD PRESENTATION, 2000–2007

(Millions of U.S. dollars)

	Code	2000	2001	2002	2003	2004	2005	2006	2007
CURRENT ACCOUNT	4 993 ..	**2,562**	**1,674**	**2,306**	**2,409**	**4,088**	**4,148**	**4,435**	**4,928**
A. GOODS	4 100 ..	**−2,420**	**−2,399**	**−2,145**	**−2,995**	**−3,552**	**−4,200**	**−4,411**	**−4,810**
Credit	2 100 ..	**8,635**	**8,996**	**9,467**	**10,942**	**13,526**	**14,602**	**16,383**	**18,256**
General merchandise: exports f.o.b.	2 110 ..	....	....	8,190	9,487	11,705	12,565	13,753	15,613
Goods for processing: exports f.o.b.	2 150 ..	....	....	187	194	199	191	149	245
Repairs on goods	2 160 ..	....	....	1	1	3	3	4	3
Goods procured in ports by carriers	2 170 ..	....	....	572	799	1,043	1,340	1,445	1,534
Nonmonetary gold	2 180 ..	....	....	518	461	576	503	1,032	861
Debit	3 100 ..	**−11,056**	**−11,395**	**−11,612**	**−13,937**	**−17,078**	**−18,802**	**−20,795**	**−23,066**
General merchandise: imports f.o.b.	3 110 ..	....	....	−10,963	−12,988	−16,140	−17,104	−18,921	−21,464
Goods for processing: imports f.o.b.	3 150 ..	....	....	−160	−191	−202	−182	−156	−219
Repairs on goods	3 160 ..	....	....	−9	−13	−15	−12	−12	−9
Goods procured in ports by carriers	3 170 ..	....	....	−144	−206	−266	−433	−590	−653
Nonmonetary gold	3 180 ..	....	....	−336	−541	−455	−1,071	−1,116	−721
B. SERVICES	4 200 ..	**6,720**	**6,237**	**8,091**	**9,968**	**13,017**	**16,248**	**20,687**	**27,071**
Total credit	2 200 ..	*20,301*	*19,945*	*20,504*	*25,499*	*33,957*	*40,842*	*50,906*	*64,524*
Total debit	3 200 ..	*−13,581*	*−13,708*	*−12,412*	*−15,531*	*−20,940*	*−24,594*	*−30,218*	*−37,453*
Transportation services, credit	2 205 ..	**1,331**	**1,368**	**1,462**	**1,765**	**2,179**	**2,663**	**2,893**	**3,441**
Passenger	2 850 ..	....	....	....	....	....	....	....	....
Freight	2 851 ..	....	....	....	....	....	....	....	....
Other	2 852 ..	....	....	....	....	....	....	....	....
Sea transport, passenger	2 207 ..	....	....	....	....	....	....	....	....
Sea transport, freight	2 208 ..	....	....	....	....	....	....	....	....
Sea transport, other	2 209 ..	....	....	....	....	....	....	....	....
Air transport, passenger	2 211 ..	....	....	....	....	....	....	....	....
Air transport, freight	2 212 ..	....	....	....	....	....	....	....	....
Air transport, other	2 213 ..	....	....	....	....	....	....	....	....
Other transport, passenger	2 215 ..	....	....	....	....	....	....	....	....
Other transport, freight	2 216 ..	....	....	....	....	....	....	....	....
Other transport, other	2 217 ..	....	....	....	....	....	....	....	....
Transportation services, debit	3 205 ..	**−834**	**−917**	**−746**	**−784**	**−1,062**	**−1,264**	**−1,352**	**−1,738**
Passenger	3 850 ..	....	....	....	....	....	....	....	....
Freight	3 851 ..	....	....	....	....	....	....	....	....
Other	3 852 ..	....	....	....	....	....	....	....	....
Sea transport, passenger	3 207 ..	....	....	....	....	....	....	....	....
Sea transport, freight	3 208 ..	....	....	....	....	....	....	....	....
Sea transport, other	3 209 ..	....	....	....	....	....	....	....	....
Air transport, passenger	3 211 ..	....	....	....	....	....	....	....	....
Air transport, freight	3 212 ..	....	....	....	....	....	....	....	....
Air transport, other	3 213 ..	....	....	....	....	....	....	....	....
Other transport, passenger	3 215 ..	....	....	....	....	....	....	....	....
Other transport, freight	3 216 ..	....	....	....	....	....	....	....	....
Other transport, other	3 217 ..	....	....	....	....	....	....	....	....
Travel, credit	2 236 ..	**1,686**	**1,780**	**2,406**	**2,994**	**3,650**	**3,612**	**3,620**	**4,009**
Business travel	2 237 ..	529	587	....	....	....	....	....	....
Personal travel	2 240 ..	1,157	1,194	....	....	....	....	....	....
Travel, debit	3 236 ..	**−1,309**	**−1,464**	**−1,942**	**−2,423**	**−2,911**	**−2,976**	**−3,136**	**−3,552**
Business travel	3 237 ..	−170	−220	....	....	....	....	....	....
Personal travel	3 240 ..	−1,139	−1,244	....	....	....	....	....	....
Other services, credit	2 200 BA ..	**17,283**	**16,797**	**16,636**	**20,739**	**28,127**	**34,567**	**44,392**	**57,073**
Communications	2 245 ..	683	736	685	828	951	1,056	1,349	2,067
Construction	2 249 ..	32	45	121	165	232	282	336	479
Insurance	2 253 ..	955	807	1,038	1,300	1,671	1,955	2,290	2,338
Financial	2 260 ..	13,198	12,628	12,195	14,323	19,449	24,973	33,324	43,006
Computer and information	2 262 ..	172	172	308	1,199	2,283	2,325	2,209	1,306
Royalties and licence fees	2 266 ..	134	202	116	128	200	298	393	388
Other business services	2 268 ..	1,521	1,666	1,799	2,371	2,834	3,108	3,835	6,492
Personal, cultural, and recreational	2 287 ..	376	330	161	162	189	239	328	619
Government, n.i.e.	2 291 ..	212	211	212	262	319	332	327	376
Other services, debit	3 200 BA ..	**−11,438**	**−11,327**	**−9,725**	**−12,324**	**−16,966**	**−20,354**	**−25,731**	**−32,162**
Communications	3 245 ..	−138	−159	−96	−584	−1,083	−1,163	−1,335	−1,045
Construction	3 249 ..	−113	−102	−232	−318	−399	−426	−488	−639
Insurance	3 253 ..	−691	−559	−770	−842	−1,134	−1,232	−1,631	−1,424
Financial	3 260 ..	−7,340	−7,103	−6,426	−7,549	−10,125	−13,075	−17,184	−21,687
Computer and information	3 262 ..	−278	−283	−283	−366	−582	−678	−668	−654
Royalties and licence fees	3 266 ..	−122	−243	−99	−109	−147	−137	−161	−394
Other business services	3 268 ..	−2,238	−2,402	−1,487	−2,118	−2,992	−3,280	−3,805	−5,672
Personal, cultural, and recreational	3 287 ..	−481	−435	−309	−418	−477	−332	−428	−616
Government, n.i.e.	3 291 ..	−37	−40	−24	−20	−27	−30	−30	−33

2008, International Monetary Fund: *Balance of Payments Statistics Yearbook*

Table 2 (Continued). STANDARD PRESENTATION, 2000–2007

(Millions of U.S. dollars)

	Code	2000	2001	2002	2003	2004	2005	2006	2007
C. INCOME	4 300	**−1,278**	**−1,639**	**−3,359**	**−3,956**	**−4,311**	**−6,721**	**−10,571**	**−14,975**
Total credit	2 300	*50,400*	*52,302*	*60,400*	*69,291*	*76,855*	*90,229*	*117,521*	*162,971*
Total debit	3 300	*−51,678*	*−53,941*	*−63,759*	*−73,247*	*−81,166*	*−96,950*	*−128,091*	*−177,946*
Compensation of employees, credit	2 310	**579**	**576**	**785**	**994**	**1,115**	**1,259**	**1,354**	**1,537**
Compensation of employees, debit	3 310	**−2,720**	**−3,138**	**−3,886**	**−4,930**	**−5,928**	**−6,542**	**−7,450**	**−9,176**
Investment income, credit	2 320	**49,821**	**51,725**	**59,615**	**68,297**	**75,740**	**88,970**	**116,167**	**161,434**
Direct investment income	2 330	....	....	12,672	19,976	20,518	25,126	26,845	43,944
Dividends and distributed branch profits	2 332	....	....	7,726	14,862	13,803	18,465	20,651	34,304
Reinvested earnings and undistributed branch profits	2 333	....	....	−36	−534	1,912	2,014	676	740
Income on debt (interest)	2 334	....	....	4,982	5,647	4,803	4,647	5,518	8,900
Portfolio investment income	2 339	....	....	32,615	35,345	41,766	49,081	68,329	86,465
Income on equity	2 340	....	....	7,718	8,355	9,601	14,681	22,027	26,527
Income on bonds and notes	2 350	....	....	22,291	24,740	29,457	30,915	40,912	50,686
Income on money market instruments	2 360	....	....	2,605	2,250	2,708	3,485	5,390	9,252
Other investment income	2 370	....	....	14,328	12,977	13,456	14,764	20,993	31,025
Investment income, debit	3 320	**−48,958**	**−50,803**	**−59,874**	**−68,317**	**−75,238**	**−90,408**	**−120,642**	**−168,770**
Direct investment income	3 330	....	....	−18,495	−26,299	−26,145	−30,212	−33,108	−53,730
Dividends and distributed branch profits	3 332	....	....	−13,808	−21,359	−21,655	−26,318	−30,302	−48,344
Reinvested earnings and undistributed branch profits	3 333	....	....	−2,305	−2,002	−2,491	−1,435	−1	394
Income on debt (interest)	3 334	....	....	−2,382	−2,939	−2,000	−2,460	−2,805	−5,780
Portfolio investment income	3 339	....	....	−29,530	−31,542	−38,223	−46,183	−64,836	−82,559
Income on equity	3 340	....	....	−27,415	−29,706	−36,354	−43,995	−62,813	−80,046
Income on bonds and notes	3 350	....	....	−1,315	−1,347	−1,345	−1,455	−1,240	−1,498
Income on money market instruments	3 360	....	....	−800	−490	−524	−733	−783	−1,015
Other investment income	3 370	....	....	−11,849	−10,475	−10,869	−14,012	−22,698	−32,481
D. CURRENT TRANSFERS	4 379	**−461**	**−525**	**−281**	**−608**	**−1,065**	**−1,179**	**−1,270**	**−2,358**
Credit	2 379	**2,750**	**2,269**	**3,579**	**3,889**	**4,025**	**4,716**	**5,612**	**6,134**
General government	2 380	876	958	1,133	1,626	1,804	2,051	2,497	2,836
Other sectors	2 390	1,874	1,310	2,446	2,263	2,221	2,665	3,115	3,298
Workers' remittances	2 391	....	....	1	1	4	4	6	5
Other current transfers	2 392	....	....	2,445	2,262	2,216	2,660	3,108	3,293
Debit	3 379	**−3,211**	**−2,793**	**−3,860**	**−4,497**	**−5,090**	**−5,895**	**−6,882**	**−8,492**
General government	3 380	−901	−998	−1,204	−1,397	−1,637	−1,894	−1,905	−2,304
Other sectors	3 390	−2,309	−1,796	−2,656	−3,100	−3,453	−4,000	−4,977	−6,188
Workers' remittances	3 391	....	....	−44	−53	−65	−68	−81	−91
Other current transfers	3 392	....	....	−2,612	−3,047	−3,388	−3,932	−4,896	−6,096
CAPITAL AND FINANCIAL ACCOUNT	4 996	....	....	**−2,580**	**−2,332**	**−4,308**	**−4,652**	**−4,902**	**−5,175**
CAPITAL ACCOUNT	4 994	....	....	**−89**	**−140**	**−772**	**1,183**	**−299**	**−166**
Total credit	2 994	....	....	*92*	*63*	*51*	*1,509*	*54*	*77*
Total debit	3 994	....	....	*−181*	*−204*	*−823*	*−326*	*−354*	*−243*
Capital transfers, credit	2 400	....	....	**56**	**48**	**37**	**43**	**48**	**65**
General government	2 401	....	....	33	20	26	37	36	41
Debt forgiveness	2 402	....	....	....	....	....	....	....	....
Other capital transfers	2 410	....	....	33	20	26	37	36	41
Other sectors	2 430	....	....	24	28	11	5	12	23
Migrants' transfers	2 431	....	....	24	28	11	5	12	23
Debt forgiveness	2 432	....	....	....	....	....	....	....	....
Other capital transfers	2 440	....	....	....	....	....	....	....	....
Capital transfers, debit	3 400	....	....	**−106**	**−144**	**−247**	**−189**	**−224**	**−211**
General government	3 401	....	....	−81	−109	−235	−164	−184	−191
Debt forgiveness	3 402	....	....	....	....	....	....	....	....
Other capital transfers	3 410	....	....	−81	−109	−235	−164	−184	−191
Other sectors	3 430	....	....	−25	−35	−13	−25	−41	−20
Migrants' transfers	3 431	....	....	−18	−27	−7	−17	−30	−13
Debt forgiveness	3 432	....	....	....	....	....	....	....	....
Other capital transfers	3 440	....	....	−6	−8	−5	−8	−10	−7
Nonproduced nonfinancial assets, credit	2 480	....	....	**36**	**16**	**14**	**1,467**	**6**	**12**
Nonproduced nonfinancial assets, debit	3 480	....	....	**−75**	**−60**	**−575**	**−137**	**−129**	**−32**

Table 2 (Continued). STANDARD PRESENTATION, 2000–2007

(Millions of U.S. dollars)

	Code	2000	2001	2002	2003	2004	2005	2006	2007
FINANCIAL ACCOUNT	4 995	....	....	−2,491	−2,192	−3,536	−5,835	−4,603	−5,009
A. DIRECT INVESTMENT	4 500	....	....	−10,277	−10,674	−5,212	−8,134	14,609	−61,917
Direct investment abroad	4 505	....	....	−128,789	−100,458	−85,310	−122,039	−111,658	−250,036
Equity capital	4 510	....	....	−119,395	−88,178	−103,908	−108,145	−90,396	−214,664
Claims on affiliated enterprises	4 515	....	....	....	....	....	....	....	....
Liabilities to affiliated enterprises	4 520	....	....	....	....	....	....	....	....
Reinvested earnings	4 525	....	....	36	534	−1,912	−2,014	−676	−740
Other capital	4 530	....	....	−9,430	−12,815	20,510	−11,881	−20,586	−34,631
Claims on affiliated enterprises	4 535	....	....	....	....	....	....	....	....
Liabilities to affiliated enterprises	4 540	....	....	....	....	....	....	....	....
Direct investment in Luxembourg	4 555	....	....	118,512	89,784	80,098	113,905	126,268	188,119
Equity capital	4 560	....	....	115,341	81,288	66,743	95,756	114,855	156,370
Claims on direct investors	4 565	....	....	....	....	....	....	....	....
Liabilities to direct investors	4 570	....	....	....	....	....	....	....	....
Reinvested earnings	4 575	....	....	2,305	2,002	2,491	1,435	1	−394
Other capital	4 580	....	....	866	6,494	10,863	16,715	11,412	32,142
Claims on direct investors	4 585	....	....	....	....	....	....	....	....
Liabilities to direct investors	4 590	....	....	....	....	....	....	....	....
B. PORTFOLIO INVESTMENT	4 600	....	....	70,414	21,064	52,064	48,709	72,469	135,358
Assets	4 602	....	....	6,253	−78,422	−87,546	−267,098	−176,160	−174,516
Equity securities	4 610	....	....	4,301	−35,857	−45,835	−123,620	−102,723	−52,572
Monetary authorities	4 611	....	....	....	....	....	....	....	....
General government	4 612	....	....	....	....	....	....	....	....
Banks	4 613	....	....	−647	1,318	−1,023	192	−4,697	−1,591
Other sectors	4 614	....	....	4,948	−37,175	−44,811	−123,812	−98,025	−50,981
Debt securities	4 619	....	....	1,952	−42,565	−41,711	−143,477	−73,437	−121,944
Bonds and notes	4 620	....	....	−22,253	−64,746	−50,817	−124,442	−53,197	−90,315
Monetary authorities	4 621	....	....	−106	−180	−659	−2,060	−1,338	−254
General government	4 622	....	....	−15	116	124	95	−155	−156
Banks	4 623	....	....	−20,908	−22,630	−4,228	−14,181	−24,774	−23,587
Other sectors	4 624	....	....	−1,224	−42,053	−46,055	−108,297	−26,930	−66,317
Money market instruments	4 630	....	....	24,205	22,182	9,105	−19,035	−20,240	−31,629
Monetary authorities	4 631	....	....	....	....	−499	473	−534	182
General government	4 632	....	....	....	....	....	....	....	....
Banks	4 633	....	....	8,146	−9,936	−1,478	−1,009	−2,636	−22,434
Other sectors	4 634	....	....	16,059	32,118	11,082	−18,499	−17,069	−9,377
Liabilities	4 652	....	....	64,161	99,486	139,610	315,806	248,629	309,874
Equity securities	4 660	....	....	36,031	70,443	121,546	275,574	220,275	281,525
Banks	4 663	....	....	30,170	7,331	2,575	557	13,994	81,906
Other sectors	4 664	....	....	5,861	63,112	118,971	275,017	206,281	199,618
Debt securities	4 669	....	....	28,130	29,043	18,064	40,232	28,353	28,349
Bonds and notes	4 670	....	....	7,962	21,852	20,578	38,041	24,978	22,703
Monetary authorities	4 671	....	....	....	....	....	....	....	....
General government	4 672	....	....	−42	−48	−9	−2	1	−5
Banks	4 673	....	....	4,566	8,644	10,889	8,726	603	6,284
Other sectors	4 674	....	....	3,438	13,257	9,698	29,317	24,374	16,424
Money market instruments	4 680	....	....	20,168	7,191	−2,515	2,191	3,376	5,647
Monetary authorities	4 681	....	....	....	....	....	....	....	....
General government	4 682	....	....	−37	−30	1	....	−320	−112
Banks	4 683	....	....	6,698	−5,429	−7,715	−5,452	3,578	7,794
Other sectors	4 684	....	....	13,507	12,650	5,200	7,642	118	−2,035
C. FINANCIAL DERIVATIVES	4 910	....	....	−1,346	6,158	−2,998	−4,216	10,364	15,754
Monetary authorities	4 911	....	....	....	....	−5	7	13	....
General government	4 912	....	....	....	....	....	....	....	....
Banks	4 913	....	....	3,356	1,733	−1,990	807	3,609	5,443
Other sectors	4 914	....	....	−4,703	4,424	−1,002	−5,030	6,742	10,311
Assets	4 900	....	....	....	....	....	....	....	....
Monetary authorities	4 901	....	....	....	....	....	....	....	....
General government	4 902	....	....	....	....	....	....	....	....
Banks	4 903	....	....	....	....	....	....	....	....
Other sectors	4 904	....	....	....	....	....	....	....	....
Liabilities	4 905	....	....	....	....	....	....	....	....
Monetary authorities	4 906	....	....	....	....	....	....	....	....
General government	4 907	....	....	....	....	....	....	....	....
Banks	4 908	....	....	....	....	....	....	....	....
Other sectors	4 909	....	....	....	....	....	....	....	....

Table 2 (Concluded). STANDARD PRESENTATION, 2000–2007

(Millions of U.S. dollars)

	Code	2000	2001	2002	2003	2004	2005	2006	2007
D. OTHER INVESTMENT	4 700 ..	....	....	**−61,246**	**−18,632**	**−47,382**	**−42,241**	**−102,073**	**−94,292**
Assets	4 703 ..	....	....	**−40,902**	**−33,924**	**−117,163**	**−191,630**	**−264,794**	**−250,140**
Trade credits	4 706 ..	....	....	−189	−363	−626	−155	−551	−558
General government	4 707 ..	....	....	....	....	....	....	....	....
of which: Short-term	4 709 ..	....	....	....	....	....	....	....	....
Other sectors	4 710 ..	....	....	−189	−363	−626	−155	−551	−558
of which: Short-term	4 712 ..	....	....	....	....	....	....	....	....
Loans	4 714 ..	....	....	−5,387	−22,586	−105,652	−179,729	−234,214	−263,610
Monetary authorities	4 715 ..	....	....	....	−7,641	−7,210	−5,755	3,281	−18,671
of which: Short-term	4 718 ..	....	....	....	−7,641	−7,210	−5,755	3,281	−18,671
General government	4 719 ..	....	....	....	....	....	....	....	....
of which: Short-term	4 721 ..	....	....	....	....	....	....	....	....
Banks	4 722 ..	....	....	19,337	−3,623	−43,871	−36,573	−57,181	−118,631
of which: Short-term	4 724 ..	....	....	14,113	4,017	−39,319	−22,173	−41,262	−93,729
Other sectors	4 725 ..	....	....	−24,725	−11,322	−54,571	−137,401	−180,315	−126,308
of which: Short-term	4 727 ..	....	....	−24,606	−6,326	−38,785	−120,601	−154,450	−91,705
Currency and deposits	4 730 ..	....	....	−36,937	−12,701	−9,939	−11,076	−28,231	14,986
Monetary authorities	4 731 ..	....	....	....	....	....	....	....	....
General government	4 732 ..	....	....	....	....	....	....	−1	−9
Banks	4 733 ..	....	....	....	....	....	....	....	....
Other sectors	4 734 ..	....	....	−36,937	−12,701	−9,939	−11,075	−28,230	14,995
Other assets	4 736 ..	....	....	1,612	1,727	−945	−671	−1,797	−957
Monetary authorities	4 737 ..	....	....	....	....	....	....	....	....
of which: Short-term	4 739 ..	....	....	....	....	....	....	....	....
General government	4 740 ..	....	....	....	−1	....	−1	−7	−308
of which: Short-term	4 742 ..	....	....	....	....	....	....	....	....
Banks	4 743 ..	....	....	....	....	....	....	....	....
of which: Short-term	4 745 ..	....	....	....	....	....	....	....	....
Other sectors	4 746 ..	....	....	1,612	1,728	−945	−670	−1,790	−649
of which: Short-term	4 748 ..	....	....	....	....	....	....	....	....
Liabilities	4 753 ..	....	....	**−20,345**	**15,292**	**69,781**	**149,388**	**162,721**	**155,847**
Trade credits	4 756 ..	....	....	−408	121	595	−367	−233	211
General government	4 757 ..	....	....	....	....	....	....	....	....
of which: Short-term	4 759 ..	....	....	....	....	....	....	....	....
Other sectors	4 760 ..	....	....	−408	121	595	−367	−233	211
of which: Short-term	4 762 ..	....	....	....	....	....	....	....	....
Loans	4 764 ..	....	....	−19,135	13,347	63,992	143,266	154,829	149,603
Monetary authorities	4 765 ..	....	....	−887	−5,824	6,208	322	−343	454
of which: Use of Fund credit and loans from the Fund	4 766 ..	....	....	....	....	....	....	....	....
of which: Short-term	4 768 ..	....	....	−887	−5,824	6,208	322	−343	454
General government	4 769 ..	....	....	3	−1	−16	....	....	−1
of which: Short-term	4 771 ..	....	....	....	....	....	....	....	−1
Banks	4 772 ..	....	....	−27,719	17,866	31,295	41,383	43,908	75,326
of which: Short-term	4 774 ..	....	....	−24,683	12,379	7,404	23,807	39,252	68,795
Other sectors	4 775 ..	....	....	9,468	1,306	26,506	101,562	111,263	73,824
of which: Short-term	4 777 ..	....	....	9,525	490	27,266	101,859	112,019	67,400
Currency and deposits	4 780 ..	....	....	....	....	....	....	....	....
Monetary authorities	4 781 ..	....	....	....	....	....	....	....	....
General government	4 782 ..	....	....	....	....	....	....	....	....
Banks	4 783 ..	....	....	....	....	....	....	....	....
Other sectors	4 784 ..	....	....	....	....	....	....	....	....
Other liabilities	4 786 ..	....	....	−802	1,824	5,193	6,490	8,125	6,033
Monetary authorities	4 787 ..	....	....	....	....	....	....	....	....
of which: Short-term	4 789 ..	....	....	....	....	....	....	....	....
General government	4 790 ..	....	....	....	....	....	....	....	....
of which: Short-term	4 792 ..	....	....	....	....	....	....	....	....
Banks	4 793 ..	....	....	....	....	....	....	....	....
of which: Short-term	4 795 ..	....	....	....	....	....	....	....	....
Other sectors	4 796 ..	....	....	−802	1,824	5,193	6,490	8,125	6,033
of which: Short-term	4 798 ..	....	....	....	....	....	....	....	....
E. RESERVE ASSETS	4 802 ..	....	....	**−35**	**−108**	**−8**	**48**	**28**	**89**
Monetary gold	4 812 ..	....	....	....	2	....	....	....	....
Special drawing rights	4 811 ..	....	....	−2	−2	−2	−2	−1	−1
Reserve position in the Fund	4 810 ..	....	....	−33	−21	45	72	17	16
Foreign exchange	4 803 ..	....	....	....	−86	−52	−21	13	74
Other claims	4 813 ..	....	....	....	....	....	....	....	....
NET ERRORS AND OMISSIONS	4 998 ..	....	....	**275**	**−76**	**220**	**504**	**467**	**247**

Table 3. INTERNATIONAL INVESTMENT POSITION (End-period stocks), 2000–2007

(Millions of U.S. dollars)

	Code	2000	2001	2002	2003	2004	2005	2006	2007
ASSETS	8 995 C.	....	....	**2,003,109**	**2,756,955**	**3,356,855**	**3,714,154**	**4,825,422**	**6,089,341**
Direct investment abroad	8 505 ..	....	....	**503,175**	**739,969**	**884,760**	**896,205**	**1,088,947**	**1,460,139**
Equity capital and reinvested earnings	8 506 ..	....	....	408,445	608,768	764,303	779,733	925,660	1,239,415
Claims on affiliated enterprises	8 507 ..	....	....	....	....	....	....	....	....
Liabilities to affiliated enterprises	8 508 ..	....	....	....	....	....	....	....	....
Other capital	8 530 ..	....	....	94,730	131,201	120,457	116,472	163,287	220,724
Claims on affiliated enterprises	8 535 ..	....	....	....	....	....	....	....	....
Liabilities to affiliated enterprises	8 540 ..	....	....	....	....	....	....	....	....
Portfolio investment	8 602 ..	....	....	**923,391**	**1,333,204**	**1,616,314**	**1,840,921**	**2,432,433**	**2,882,607**
Equity securities	8 610 ..	....	....	304,988	488,241	637,837	807,866	1,149,652	1,413,236
Monetary authorities	8 611 ..	....	....						
General government	8 612 ..	....	....	....	....	....	....	....	....
Banks	8 613 ..	....	....	10,542	8,257	12,142	10,540	16,394	19,431
Other sectors	8 614 ..	....	....	294,446	479,983	625,694	797,326	1,133,258	1,393,805
Debt securities	8 619 ..	....	....	618,403	844,964	978,477	1,033,055	1,282,781	1,469,371
Bonds and notes	8 620 ..	....	....	526,432	749,929	868,571	915,332	1,128,293	1,257,695
Monetary authorities	8 621 ..	....	....	1,217	1,892	2,767	4,260	6,105	7,011
General government	8 622 ..	....	....	589	576	481	308	568	717
Banks	8 623 ..	....	....	189,965	302,659	335,108	344,708	402,758	473,123
Other sectors	8 624 ..	....	....	334,661	444,801	530,216	566,056	718,862	776,844
Money market instruments	8 630 ..	....	....	91,971	95,034	109,906	117,723	154,488	211,676
Monetary authorities	8 631 ..	....	....	26	32	578	82	639	564
General government	8 632 ..	....	....	....	....	....	....	....	....
Banks	8 633 ..	....	....	54,753	58,911	64,975	62,518	70,361	101,301
Other sectors	8 634 ..	....	....	37,191	36,092	44,353	55,123	83,488	109,810
Financial derivatives	8 900 ..	....	....	**7,767**	**8,780**	**8,785**	**18,137**	**12,242**	**14,082**
Monetary authorities	8 901 ..	....	....	....	....	....	....	....	....
General government	8 902 ..	....	....	....	....	....	....	....	....
Banks	8 903 ..	....	....	133	3,227	5,528	5,912	8,178	2,639
Other sectors	8 904 ..	....	....	7,634	5,553	3,257	12,224	4,064	11,443
Other investment	8 703 ..	....	....	**568,598**	**674,691**	**846,665**	**958,613**	**1,291,535**	**1,732,307**
Trade credits	8 706 ..	....	....	1,797	2,555	3,448	3,127	4,103	5,168
General government	8 707 ..	....	....	....	....	....	....	....	....
of which: Short-term	8 709 ..	....	....	....	....	....	....	....	....
Other sectors	8 710 ..	....	....	1,797	2,555	3,448	3,127	4,103	5,168
of which: Short-term	8 712 ..	....	....	....	....	....	....	....	....
Loans	8 714 ..	....	....	500,233	574,977	708,743	826,319	1,117,988	1,477,630
Monetary authorities	8 715 ..	....	....	79	3,057	4,755	9,295	7,003	27,112
of which: Short-term	8 718 ..	....	....	....	....	....	....	....	....
General government	8 719 ..	....	....	....	....	....	109	155	174
of which: Short-term	8 721 ..	....	....	....	....	....	....	....	....
Banks	8 722 ..	....	....	425,900	487,900	562,010	538,125	640,400	810,054
of which: Short-term	8 724 ..	....	....	*108,841*	*416,654*	*70,655*	*78,092*	*108,819*	*131,594*
Other sectors	8 725 ..	....	....	74,253	84,019	141,979	278,791	470,429	640,291
of which: Short-term	8 727 ..	....	....	....	....	....	....	....	....
Currency and deposits	8 730 ..	....	....	48,083	79,888	113,172	107,478	142,302	219,821
Monetary authorities	8 731 ..	....	....	....	....	....	....	....	....
General government	8 732 ..	....	....	....	....	....	....	....	....
Banks	8 733 ..	....	....	....	....	....	....	....	....
Other sectors	8 734 ..	....	....	48,083	79,888	113,172	107,478	142,302	219,821
Other assets	8 736 ..	....	....	18,485	17,271	21,302	21,689	27,142	29,688
Monetary authorities	8 737 ..	....	....	8	10	14	11	13	16
of which: Short-term	8 739 ..	....	....	....	....	....	....	....	....
General government	8 740 ..	....	....	28	42	50	47	54	53
of which: Short-term	8 742 ..	....	....	....	....	....	....	....	....
Banks	8 743 ..	....	....	....	....	....	....	....	....
of which: Short-term	8 745 ..	....	....	....	....	....	....	....	....
Other sectors	8 746 ..	....	....	18,449	17,219	21,238	21,631	27,075	29,619
of which: Short-term	8 748 ..	....	....	....	....	....	....	....	....
Reserve assets	8 802 ..	....	....	**178**	**311**	**331**	**278**	**265**	**206**
Monetary gold	8 812 ..	....	....	26	31	33	38	47	62
Special drawing rights	8 811 ..	4	6	9	12	15	16	18	20
Reserve position in the Fund	8 810 ..	72	99	142	179	139	58	44	30
Foreign exchange	8 803 ..			....	89	144	166	156	94
Other claims	8 813 ..	....	....	....	....	....	....	....	....

Table 3 (Concluded). INTERNATIONAL INVESTMENT POSITION (End-period stocks), 2000–2007

(Millions of U.S. dollars)

	Code	2000	2001	2002	2003	2004	2005	2006	2007
LIABILITIES..	8 995 D.	. . . .	. . . .	**1,975,231**	**2,711,497**	**3,314,123**	**3,668,697**	**4,770,943**	**6,033,466**
Direct investment in Luxembourg.......................	8 555 ..	. . . .	. . . .	**514,550**	**768,405**	**950,233**	**912,515**	**1,151,102**	**1,482,046**
Equity capital and reinvested earnings....................	8 556 ..	. . . .	. . . .	449,533	672,053	834,064	797,538	1,009,069	1,294,570
Claims on direct investors............................	8 557 ..	. . . .	. . . .	. . . .	. . . .	. . . .	. . . .	. . . .	. . . .
Liabilities to direct investors.........................	8 558 ..	. . . .	. . . .	. . . .	. . . .	. . . .	. . . .	. . . .	. . . .
Other capital.......................................	8 580 ..	. . . .	. . . .	65,017	96,352	116,169	114,976	142,033	187,476
Claims on direct investors............................	8 585 ..	. . . .	. . . .	. . . .	. . . .	. . . .	. . . .	. . . .	. . . .
Liabilities to direct investors.........................	8 590 ..	. . . .	. . . .	. . . .	. . . .	. . . .	. . . .	. . . .	. . . .
Portfolio investment.................................	8 652 ..	. . . .	. . . .	**982,938**	**1,337,144**	**1,661,113**	**1,944,049**	**2,530,490**	**3,166,601**
Equity securities....................................	8 660 ..	. . . .	. . . .	849,537	1,143,406	1,436,258	1,698,464	2,233,555	2,821,021
Banks..	8 663 ..	. . . .	. . . .	113,377	183,871	196,070	187,957	231,765	355,935
Other sectors...................................	8 664 ..	. . . .	. . . .	736,160	959,535	1,240,188	1,510,508	2,001,791	2,465,086
Debt securities.....................................	8 669 ..	. . . .	. . . .	133,401	193,739	224,856	245,584	296,935	345,579
Bonds and notes.................................	8 670 ..	. . . .	. . . .	100,765	151,267	196,108	218,891	261,740	306,041
Monetary authorities..........................	8 671 ..	. . . .	. . . .	. . . .	. . . .	. . . .	. . . .	. . . .	. . . .
General government...........................	8 672 ..	. . . .	. . . .	. . . .	. . . .	. . . .	. . . .	. . . .	. . . .
Banks......................................	8 673 ..	. . . .	. . . .	33,426	52,873	69,175	75,327	85,759	96,847
Other sectors...............................	8 674 ..	. . . .	. . . .	67,339	98,394	126,933	143,564	175,980	209,194
Money market instruments........................	8 680 ..	. . . .	. . . .	32,636	42,472	28,747	26,693	35,195	39,538
Monetary authorities..........................	8 681 ..	. . . .	. . . .	. . . .	. . . .	. . . .	. . . .	. . . .	. . . .
General government...........................	8 682 ..	. . . .	. . . .	. . . .	. . . .	. . . .	. . . .	. . . .	. . . .
Banks......................................	8 683 ..	. . . .	. . . .	30,494	31,179	25,947	18,792	23,639	31,386
Other sectors...............................	8 684 ..	. . . .	. . . .	2,142	11,293	2,800	7,901	11,557	8,152
Financial derivatives................................	8 905 ..	. . . .	. . . .	**1,166**	**14,353**	**15,478**	**13,423**	**13,671**	**24,443**
Monetary authorities................................	8 906 ..	. . . .	. . . .	. . . .	. . . .	. . . .	. . . .	. . . .	. . . .
General government.................................	8 907 ..	. . . .	. . . .	. . . .	. . . .	. . . .	. . . .	. . . .	. . . .
Banks..	8 908 ..	. . . .	. . . .	127	6,748	7,278	6,303	7,037	10,076
Other sectors.......................................	8 909 ..	. . . .	. . . .	1,039	7,605	8,200	7,120	6,635	14,368
Other investment....................................	8 753 ..	. . . .	. . . .	**476,577**	**591,595**	**687,300**	**798,711**	**1,075,679**	**1,360,376**
Trade credits.......................................	8 756 ..	. . . .	. . . .	923	1,248	1,992	1,422	1,316	1,632
General government.................................	8 757 ..	. . . .	. . . .	. . . .	. . . .	. . . .	. . . .	. . . .	. . . .
of which: Short-term..............................	8 759 ..	. . . .	. . . .	. . . .	. . . .	. . . .	. . . .	. . . .	. . . .
Other sectors......................................	8 760 ..	. . . .	. . . .	923	1,248	1,992	1,422	1,316	1,632
of which: Short-term..............................	8 762 ..	. . . .	. . . .	. . . .	. . . .	. . . .	. . . .	. . . .	. . . .
Loans..	8 764 ..	. . . .	. . . .	458,885	569,826	659,646	767,262	1,035,621	1,313,781
Monetary authorities................................	8 765 ..	. . . .	. . . .	9,824	91	154	427	92	557
of which: Use of Fund credit and loans from the Fund....	8 766 ..	. . . .	. . . .	. . . .	. . . .	. . . .	. . . .	. . . .	. . . .
of which: Short-term..............................	8 768 ..	. . . .	. . . .	*9,824*	*91*	*154*	*427*	*92*	*557*
General government.................................	8 769 ..	. . . .	. . . .	13	15	. . . .	30	60	67
of which: Short-term..............................	8 771 ..	. . . .	. . . .	. . . .	. . . .	. . . .	. . . .	. . . .	. . . .
Banks..	8 772 ..	. . . .	. . . .	379,119	450,011	499,059	486,735	572,958	697,033
of which: Short-term..............................	8 774 ..	. . . .	. . . .	*255,899*	*385,512*	*451,783*	*441,037*	*516,880*	*631,121*
Other sectors......................................	8 775 ..	. . . .	. . . .	69,930	119,709	160,434	280,070	462,511	616,124
of which: Short-term..............................	8 777 ..	. . . .	. . . .	*48,951*	*83,923*	*114,078*	*210,052*	*346,883*	*462,093*
Currency and deposits................................	8 780 ..	. . . .	. . . .	. . . .	. . . .	. . . .	. . . .	. . . .	. . . .
Monetary authorities................................	8 781 ..	. . . .	. . . .	. . . .	. . . .	. . . .	. . . .	. . . .	. . . .
General government.................................	8 782 ..	. . . .	. . . .	. . . .	. . . .	. . . .	. . . .	. . . .	. . . .
Banks..	8 783 ..	. . . .	. . . .	. . . .	. . . .	. . . .	. . . .	. . . .	. . . .
Other sectors......................................	8 784 ..	. . . .	. . . .	. . . .	. . . .	. . . .	. . . .	. . . .	. . . .
Other liabilities.....................................	8 786 ..	. . . .	. . . .	16,769	20,521	25,662	30,028	38,742	44,963
Monetary authorities................................	8 787 ..	. . . .	. . . .	. . . .	. . . .	. . . .	. . . .	. . . .	. . . .
of which: Short-term..............................	8 789 ..	. . . .	. . . .	. . . .	. . . .	. . . .	. . . .	. . . .	. . . .
General government.................................	8 790 ..	. . . .	. . . .	. . . .	. . . .	. . . .	. . . .	. . . .	. . . .
of which: Short-term..............................	8 792 ..	. . . .	. . . .	. . . .	. . . .	. . . .	. . . .	. . . .	. . . .
Banks..	8 793 ..	. . . .	. . . .	. . . .	. . . .	. . . .	. . . .	. . . .	. . . .
of which: Short-term..............................	8 795 ..	. . . .	. . . .	. . . .	. . . .	. . . .	. . . .	. . . .	. . . .
Other sectors......................................	8 796 ..	. . . .	. . . .	16,769	20,521	25,662	30,028	38,742	44,963
of which: Short-term..............................	8 798 ..	. . . .	. . . .	*8,720*	*10,671*	*13,344*	*15,614*	*20,146*	*23,381*
NET INTERNATIONAL INVESTMENT POSITION........	8 995 ..	. . . .	. . . .	**27,878**	**45,458**	**42,731**	**45,457**	**54,479**	**55,875**
Conversion rates: euros per U.S. dollar (end of period)..	0 104 ..	1.0747	1.1347	.9536	.7918	.7342	.8477	.7593	.6793

Table 1. ANALYTIC PRESENTATION, 2000–2007

(Millions of U.S. dollars)

	Code	2000	2001	2002	2003	2004	2005	2006	2007
A. Current Account[1]	4 993 Z.	**−72.4**	**−243.6**	**−357.9**	**−149.0**	**−414.8**	**−81.4**	**−23.7**	....
Goods: exports f.o.b.	2 100 ..	1,320.7	1,155.4	1,112.1	1,362.7	1,672.4	2,039.6	2,396.3	....
Goods: imports f.o.b.	3 100 ..	−2,011.1	−1,681.8	−1,916.5	−2,210.6	−2,784.5	−3,097.1	−3,681.5	....
Balance on Goods	4 100 ..	*−690.4*	*−526.4*	*−804.3*	*−847.9*	*−1,112.1*	*−1,057.5*	*−1,285.2*	....
Services: credit	2 200 ..	316.7	244.6	253.0	326.9	407.9	471.6	601.3	....
Services: debit	3 200 ..	−268.0	−263.8	−275.3	−337.0	−462.3	−505.3	−576.1	....
Balance on Goods and Services	4 991 ..	*−641.7*	*−545.6*	*−826.6*	*−858.1*	*−1,166.4*	*−1,091.2*	*−1,260.0*	....
Income: credit	2 300 ..	41.6	52.6	51.0	60.4	84.6	97.6	134.9	....
Income: debit	3 300 ..	−87.3	−93.3	−80.8	−91.9	−123.8	−152.7	−138.0	....
Balance on Goods, Services, and Income	4 992 ..	*−687.3*	*−586.3*	*−856.4*	*−889.6*	*−1,205.7*	*−1,146.2*	*−1,263.1*	....
Current transfers: credit	2 379 Z.	788.2	725.7	535.7	778.9	836.9	1,109.5	1,282.8	....
Current transfers: debit	3 379 ..	−173.3	−383.0	−37.2	−38.2	−46.0	−44.7	−43.4	....
B. Capital Account[1]	4 994 Z.	**.3**	**1.3**	**8.3**	**−6.7**	**−4.6**	**−2.0**	**−1.1**	....
Capital account: credit	2 994 Z.	.3	3.6	9.9	....	....	....	....	....
Capital account: debit	3 994 ..	....	−2.3	−1.7	−6.7	−4.6	−2.0	−1.1	....
Total, Groups A Plus B	4 981 ..	*−72.1*	*−242.3*	*−349.6*	*−155.6*	*−419.4*	*−83.4*	*−24.8*	....
C. Financial Account[1]	4 995 W.	**290.3**	**325.7**	**257.2**	**237.0**	**439.7**	**506.8**	**400.4**	....
Direct investment abroad	4 505 ..	.6	−.9	−.1	−.3	−1.2	−2.8	−.2	....
Direct investment in Macedonia, FYR	4 555 Z.	174.5	441.5	77.8	96.3	157.0	99.8	350.5	....
Portfolio investment assets	4 602 ..	−.8	3.2	1.2	.3	−.9	.8	−.5	....
Equity securities	4 610 ..	....	....	.3	.1	.2	.1	.1	....
Debt securities	4 619 ..	−.8	3.2	.9	.3	−1.1	.7	−.5	....
Portfolio investment liabilities	4 652 Z.	−.1	.4	.1	3.3	14.7	235.0	83.3	....
Equity securities	4 660 ..	....	....	....	.7	15.3	51.7	76.8	....
Debt securities	4 669 Z.	−.1	.4	....	2.6	−.7	183.3	6.5	....
Financial derivatives	4 910 ..	....	....	....	....	....	....	....	....
Financial derivatives assets	4 900 ..	....	....	....	....	....	....	....	....
Financial derivatives liabilities	4 905 ..	....	....	....	....	....	....	....	....
Other investment assets	4 703 ..	−77.7	−98.1	246.2	−3.8	6.8	−89.2	−150.5	....
Monetary authorities	4 701 ..	14.1	−236.8	223.0	17.8	26.4	.8	−3.3	....
General government	4 704 ..	....	....	....	....	....	....	....	....
Banks	4 705 ..	−62.1	−237.6	159.4	−43.4	−94.8	7.8	−66.4	....
Other sectors	4 728 ..	−29.6	376.2	−136.3	21.8	75.1	−97.8	−80.8	....
Other investment liabilities	4 753 W.	193.7	−20.4	−67.9	141.2	263.4	263.1	117.8	....
Monetary authorities	4 753 WA	14.7	140.1	−154.2	....	....	....	....	....
General government	4 753 ZB	77.3	−65.4	11.0	28.3	38.4	44.3	−157.7	....
Banks	4 753 ZC	−44.0	−38.3	−4.6	−34.2	−23.9	82.5	104.2	....
Other sectors	4 753 ZD	145.7	−56.8	79.9	147.1	248.9	136.3	171.2	....
Total, Groups A Through C	4 983 ..	*218.2*	*83.4*	*−92.4*	*81.3*	*20.4*	*423.4*	*375.6*	....
D. Net Errors and Omissions	4 998 ..	**61.0**	**2.3**	**−29.7**	**−26.0**	**7.7**	**−12.9**	**9.7**	....
Total, Groups A Through D	4 984 ..	*279.2*	*85.6*	*−122.1*	*55.4*	*28.0*	*410.6*	*385.3*	....
E. Reserves and Related Items	4 802 A.	**−279.2**	**−85.6**	**122.1**	**−55.4**	**−28.0**	**−410.6**	**−385.3**	....
Reserve assets	4 802 ..	−263.6	−78.0	130.9	−50.7	−19.4	−415.3	−375.7	....
Use of Fund credit and loans	4 766 ..	−15.6	−7.6	−8.8	−4.7	−8.6	4.7	−9.6	....
Exceptional financing	4 920 ..	....	....	....	....	....	....	....	....
Conversion rates: denars per U.S. dollar	0 101 ..	**65.904**	**68.037**	**64.350**	**54.322**	**49.410**	**49.284**	**48.802**	**44.730**

[1] Excludes components that have been classified in the categories of Group E.

Table 2. STANDARD PRESENTATION, 2000–2007

(Millions of U.S. dollars)

	Code	2000	2001	2002	2003	2004	2005	2006	2007
CURRENT ACCOUNT..	4 993 ..	**−72.4**	**−243.6**	**−357.9**	**−149.0**	**−414.8**	**−81.4**	**−23.7**	....
A. GOODS..	4 100 ..	**−690.4**	**−526.4**	**−804.3**	**−847.9**	**−1,112.1**	**−1,057.5**	**−1,285.2**	....
Credit..	2 100 ..	**1,320.7**	**1,155.4**	**1,112.1**	**1,362.7**	**1,672.4**	**2,039.6**	**2,396.3**	....
General merchandise: exports f.o.b...............	2 110 ..	679.1	600.1	585.1	751.9	1,033.2	1,385.1	1,765.4	....
Goods for processing: exports f.o.b...............	2 150 ..	636.9	552.7	524.1	607.6	633.4	648.6	625.6	....
Repairs on goods...	2 160 ..	1.0	.6	1.2	.9	2.7	2.1	1.2	....
Goods procured in ports by carriers...............	2 170 ..	3.7	2.1	1.8	2.3	3.2	3.9	4.0	....
Nonmonetary gold..	2 180 ..	....	....	....	....	....	....	....	....
Debit..	3 100 ..	**−2,011.1**	**−1,681.8**	**−1,916.5**	**−2,210.6**	**−2,784.5**	**−3,097.1**	**−3,681.5**	....
General merchandise: imports f.o.b...............	3 110 ..	−1,506.4	−1,296.9	−1,534.2	−1,766.4	−2,333.1	−2,639.1	−3,217.7	....
Goods for processing: imports f.o.b...............	3 150 ..	−503.1	−383.2	−380.7	−441.6	−448.7	−454.2	−458.2	....
Repairs on goods...	3 160 ..	−1.6	−1.5	−1.6	−2.5	−2.6	−3.8	−2.4	....
Goods procured in ports by carriers...............	3 170 ..	....	....	....	....	....	....	−3.2	....
Nonmonetary gold..	3 180 ..	−.1	−.2	....	....	....	....	....	....
B. SERVICES..	4 200 ..	**48.7**	**−19.2**	**−22.2**	**−10.1**	**−54.4**	**−33.7**	**25.2**	....
Total credit..	2 200 ..	*316.7*	*244.6*	*253.0*	*326.9*	*407.9*	*471.6*	*601.3*	....
Total debit...	3 200 ..	*−268.0*	*−263.8*	*−275.3*	*−337.0*	*−462.3*	*−505.3*	*−576.1*	....
Transportation services, credit.........................	2 205 ..	**120.5**	**81.8**	**79.9**	**92.7**	**112.4**	**133.7**	**186.2**	....
Passenger...	2 850 ..	*49.6*	*23.2*	*15.9*	*8.0*	*5.4*	*7.8*	*27.4*	....
Freight...	2 851 ..	*47.6*	*37.1*	*40.8*	*56.7*	*72.5*	*87.6*	*115.7*	....
Other..	2 852 ..	*23.3*	*21.4*	*23.3*	*28.0*	*34.5*	*38.3*	*43.1*	....
Sea transport, passenger...............................	2 207 ..	....	....	....	....	....	....	....	....
Sea transport, freight.....................................	2 208 ..	....	....	....	.1	....	.7	.3	....
Sea transport, other.......................................	2 209 ..	....	....	....	....	....	.2	....	....
Air transport, passenger................................	2 211 ..	48.4	22.7	14.7	7.3	4.6	7.2	25.2	....
Air transport, freight......................................	2 212 ..	.6	.3	.1	.2	.2	.3	.5	....
Air transport, other..	2 213 ..	18.7	17.1	14.3	6.0	6.7	9.1	9.9	....
Other transport, passenger............................	2 215 ..	1.2	.6	1.2	.7	.8	.6	2.2	....
Other transport, freight..................................	2 216 ..	47.0	36.8	40.7	56.4	72.3	86.7	114.9	....
Other transport, other...	2 217 ..	4.7	4.3	8.9	22.0	27.8	29.0	33.2	....
Transportation services, debit..........................	3 205 ..	**−129.0**	**−101.9**	**−97.9**	**−132.3**	**−187.0**	**−199.0**	**−232.0**	....
Passenger...	3 850 ..	*−23.6*	*−20.6*	*−16.4*	*−23.2*	*−29.2*	*−34.2*	*−38.6*	....
Freight...	3 851 ..	*−70.1*	*−57.5*	*−61.8*	*−86.3*	*−131.4*	*−135.1*	*−144.1*	....
Other..	3 852 ..	*−35.3*	*−23.8*	*−19.7*	*−22.9*	*−26.4*	*−29.8*	*−49.3*	....
Sea transport, passenger...............................	3 207 ..	....	....	....	−.1	−.2	....	−.2	....
Sea transport, freight.....................................	3 208 ..	−2.0	−2.7	−2.3	−5.9	−13.0	−13.5	−12.8	....
Sea transport, other.......................................	3 209 ..	−4.0	−3.1	−4.0	−2.9	−4.7	−6.1	−8.9	....
Air transport, passenger................................	3 211 ..	−22.9	−19.9	−15.6	−22.2	−28.1	−33.2	−36.3	....
Air transport, freight......................................	3 212 ..	−1.7	−3.5	−2.9	−2.8	−2.9	−2.8	−2.7	....
Air transport, other..	3 213 ..	−14.9	−3.7	−1.6	−1.7	−1.1	−.9	−10.9	....
Other transport, passenger............................	3 215 ..	−.7	−.7	−.8	−.9	−1.0	−1.0	−2.0	....
Other transport, freight..................................	3 216 ..	−66.4	−51.4	−56.6	−77.6	−115.5	−118.7	−128.7	....
Other transport, other....................................	3 217 ..	−16.4	−16.9	−14.2	−18.3	−20.6	−22.9	−29.5	....
Travel, credit...	2 236 ..	**37.9**	**25.9**	**39.0**	**56.7**	**71.8**	**83.9**	**129.2**	....
Business travel...	2 237 ..	....	....	....	....	....	....	....	....
Personal travel...	2 240 ..	37.9	25.9	39.0	56.7	71.8	83.9	129.2	....
Travel, debit..	3 236 ..	**−34.3**	**−38.5**	**−44.5**	**−47.9**	**−54.5**	**−59.6**	**−70.7**	....
Business travel...	3 237 ..	−20.9	−21.3	−18.1	−15.9	−17.8	−20.3	−20.8	....
Personal travel...	3 240 ..	−13.4	−17.2	−26.4	−32.0	−36.7	−39.3	−50.0	....
Other services, credit.......................................	2 200 BA	**158.2**	**136.9**	**134.1**	**177.5**	**223.7**	**254.0**	**285.9**	....
Communications...	2 245 ..	39.3	33.0	38.2	40.5	40.9	37.3	61.0	....
Construction...	2 249 ..	15.4	13.7	7.9	35.3	49.7	55.3	48.5	....
Insurance...	2 253 ..	2.8	2.3	2.7	2.3	4.6	4.9	5.9	....
Financial..	2 260 ..	1.8	1.2	2.1	2.9	3.2	3.4	5.2	....
Computer and information.............................	2 262 ..	1.0	1.6	2.0	4.6	8.9	16.7	23.6	....
Royalties and licence fees..............................	2 266 ..	2.8	3.4	3.2	2.3	3.1	3.1	2.7	....
Other business services.................................	2 268 ..	67.0	33.1	43.0	64.6	82.5	99.9	109.2	....
Personal, cultural, and recreational...............	2 287 ..	1.4	1.7	2.0	4.4	7.0	7.1	10.1	....
Government, n.i.e..	2 291 ..	26.6	46.8	33.0	20.6	23.8	26.3	19.9	....
Other services, debit..	3 200 BA	**−104.7**	**−123.4**	**−132.9**	**−156.7**	**−220.8**	**−246.6**	**−273.4**	....
Communications...	3 245 ..	−6.5	−7.5	−9.5	−8.5	−10.7	−9.5	−27.7	....
Construction...	3 249 ..	−.3	−1.0	−1.9	−4.0	−2.9	−8.9	−2.8	....
Insurance...	3 253 ..	−5.0	−10.4	−6.5	−10.7	−13.6	−16.3	−21.0	....
Financial..	3 260 ..	−2.6	−2.2	−2.5	−2.8	−3.3	−4.3	−3.1	....
Computer and information.............................	3 262 ..	−1.6	−8.2	−9.1	−13.0	−20.9	−24.4	−40.4	....
Royalties and licence fees..............................	3 266 ..	−5.7	−5.5	−10.3	−7.0	−9.4	−10.4	−8.7	....
Other business services.................................	3 268 ..	−72.6	−75.6	−81.8	−88.3	−132.3	−144.5	−134.0	....
Personal, cultural, and recreational...............	3 287 ..	−2.3	−2.5	−3.1	−5.6	−5.3	−6.3	−7.7	....
Government, n.i.e..	3 291 ..	−8.2	−10.4	−8.1	−16.9	−22.4	−22.0	−27.9	....

Table 2 (Continued). STANDARD PRESENTATION, 2000–2007

(Millions of U.S. dollars)

	Code	2000	2001	2002	2003	2004	2005	2006	2007
C. INCOME	4 300	−45.6	−40.7	−29.8	−31.6	−39.2	−55.1	−3.1	....
Total credit	2 300	*41.6*	*52.6*	*51.0*	*60.4*	*84.6*	*97.6*	*134.9*	....
Total debit	3 300	*−87.3*	*−93.3*	*−80.8*	*−91.9*	*−123.8*	*−152.7*	*−138.0*	....
Compensation of employees, credit	2 310	.4	5.4	13.5	27.9	52.0	57.3	68.9	....
Compensation of employees, debit	3 310	....	....	−.7	−.5	−1.3	−1.6	−2.2	....
Investment income, credit	2 320	41.2	47.1	37.5	32.4	32.6	40.4	66.0	....
Direct investment income	2 330	....	....	....	.9	.4	.6	.5	....
Dividends and distributed branch profits	2 332	....	....	....	.9	.4	.6	.5	....
Reinvested earnings and undistributed branch profits	2 333	....	....	....	....	....	....	....	....
Income on debt (interest)	2 334	....	....	....	....	....	....	....	....
Portfolio investment income	2 339	....	....	....	5.5	2.7	1.2	3.0	....
Income on equity	2 340	....	....	....	....	....	....	....	....
Income on bonds and notes	2 350	....	....	....	5.5	2.7	1.2	3.0	....
Income on money market instruments	2 360	....	....	....	....	....	....	....	....
Other investment income	2 370	41.2	47.1	37.4	26.1	29.4	38.6	62.5	....
Investment income, debit	3 320	−87.3	−93.3	−80.1	−91.4	−122.5	−151.1	−135.8	....
Direct investment income	3 330	−6.9	−12.7	−24.0	−34.0	−66.2	−85.8	−38.9	....
Dividends and distributed branch profits	3 332	−6.9	−12.7	−24.0	−34.0	−66.2	−85.8	−38.9	....
Reinvested earnings and undistributed branch profits	3 333	....	....	....	....	....	....	....	....
Income on debt (interest)	3 334	....	....	....	....	....	....	....	....
Portfolio investment income	3 339	....	....	....	−.1	−.6	−.7	−10.0	....
Income on equity	3 340	....	....	....	....	....	....	....	....
Income on bonds and notes	3 350	....	....	....	−.1	−.6	−.7	−10.0	....
Income on money market instruments	3 360	....	....	....	....	....	....	....	....
Other investment income	3 370	−80.3	−80.6	−56.1	−57.3	−55.7	−64.6	−86.8	....
D. CURRENT TRANSFERS	4 379	615.0	342.6	498.4	740.7	790.9	1,064.9	1,239.4	....
Credit	2 379	788.2	725.7	535.7	778.9	836.9	1,109.5	1,282.8	....
General government	2 380	140.0	55.8	103.0	108.0	76.0	73.8	83.2	....
Other sectors	2 390	648.2	669.9	432.6	670.8	760.9	1,035.7	1,199.7	....
Workers' remittances	2 391	80.5	68.0	92.4	145.7	161.1	169.4	197.6	....
Other current transfers	2 392	567.7	601.9	340.3	525.1	599.8	866.4	1,002.0	....
Debit	3 379	−173.3	−383.0	−37.2	−38.2	−46.0	−44.7	−43.4	....
General government	3 380	−7.5	−6.8	−2.5	−4.1	−5.9	−9.4	−9.4	....
Other sectors	3 390	−165.7	−376.2	−34.7	−34.1	−40.1	−35.3	−34.0	....
Workers' remittances	3 391	−14.2	−20.5	−22.5	−15.4	−14.8	−14.0	−15.6	....
Other current transfers	3 392	−151.5	−355.7	−12.2	−18.7	−25.3	−21.3	−18.4	....
CAPITAL AND FINANCIAL ACCOUNT	4 996	11.4	241.4	387.6	174.9	407.1	94.3	14.0	....
CAPITAL ACCOUNT	4 994	.3	1.3	8.3	−6.7	−4.6	−2.0	−1.1	....
Total credit	2 994	*.3*	*3.6*	*9.9*	....	....	....	....	....
Total debit	3 994	....	*−2.3*	*−1.7*	*−6.7*	*−4.6*	*−2.0*	*−1.1*	....
Capital transfers, credit	2 400	.3	3.6	9.9	....	....	....	....	....
General government	2 401	....	3.6	9.9	....	....	....	....	....
Debt forgiveness	2 402	....	....	....	....	....	....	....	....
Other capital transfers	2 410	....	3.6	9.9	....	....	....	....	....
Other sectors	2 430	.3	....	....	....	....	....	....	....
Migrants' transfers	2 431	....	....	....	....	....	....	....	....
Debt forgiveness	2 432	....	....	....	....	....	....	....	....
Other capital transfers	2 440	.3	....	....	....	....	....	....	....
Capital transfers, debit	3 400	....	....	−.1	−6.6	−4.6	−2.0	−1.1	....
General government	3 401	....	....	....	−6.6	....	....	....	....
Debt forgiveness	3 402	....	....	....	....	....	....	....	....
Other capital transfers	3 410	....	....	....	−6.6	....	....	....	....
Other sectors	3 430	....	....	−.1	....	−4.6	−2.0	−1.1	....
Migrants' transfers	3 431	....	....	....	....	....	....	....	....
Debt forgiveness	3 432	....	....	....	....	....	....	....	....
Other capital transfers	3 440	....	....	−.1	....	−4.6	−2.0	−1.1	....
Nonproduced nonfinancial assets, credit	2 480	....	....	....	....	....	....	....	....
Nonproduced nonfinancial assets, debit	3 480	....	−2.3	−1.6	−.1	....	....	....	....

Table 2 (Continued). STANDARD PRESENTATION, 2000–2007

(Millions of U.S. dollars)

	Code	2000	2001	2002	2003	2004	2005	2006	2007
FINANCIAL ACCOUNT	4 995 ..	**11.1**	**240.1**	**379.3**	**181.6**	**411.7**	**96.3**	**15.1**	....
A. DIRECT INVESTMENT	4 500 ..	**175.1**	**440.7**	**77.7**	**96.0**	**155.9**	**97.1**	**350.3**	....
Direct investment abroad	4 505 ..	.6	−.9	−.1	−.3	−1.2	−2.8	−.2	....
Equity capital	4 510 ..	.6	−.9	−.1	−.3	−1.2	−2.8	−.2	....
Claims on affiliated enterprises	4 515 ..	.6	−.9	−.1	−.3	−1.2	−2.8	−.2	....
Liabilities to affiliated enterprises	4 520 ..	....	....	....	....	....	....	....	
Reinvested earnings	4 525 ..	....	....	....	....	....	....	....	
Other capital	4 530 ..	....	....	....	....	....	....	....	
Claims on affiliated enterprises	4 535 ..	....	....	....	....	....	....	....	
Liabilities to affiliated enterprises	4 540 ..	....	....	....	....	....	....	....	
Direct investment in Macedonia, FYR	4 555 ..	**174.5**	**441.5**	**77.8**	**96.3**	**157.0**	**99.8**	**350.5**	....
Equity capital	4 560 ..	174.5	441.5	77.8	96.3	157.0	99.8	350.5	....
Claims on direct investors	4 565 ..	....	....	....	....	....	....	....	
Liabilities to direct investors	4 570 ..	174.5	441.5	77.8	96.3	157.0	99.8	350.5	....
Reinvested earnings	4 575 ..	....	....	....	....	....	....	....	
Other capital	4 580 ..	....	....	....	....	....	....	....	
Claims on direct investors	4 585 ..	....	....	....	....	....	....	....	
Liabilities to direct investors	4 590 ..	....	....	....	....	....	....	....	
B. PORTFOLIO INVESTMENT	4 600 ..	**−.9**	**3.5**	**1.2**	**3.6**	**13.7**	**235.8**	**82.8**	....
Assets	4 602 ..	**−.8**	**3.2**	**1.2**	**.3**	**−.9**	**.8**	**−.5**	....
Equity securities	4 610 ..	....	....	.3	.1	.2	.1	.1	....
Monetary authorities	4 611 ..	....	....	....	....	....	....	....	
General government	4 612 ..	....	....	....	....	....	....	....	
Banks	4 613 ..	....	....	....	....	....	....	....	
Other sectors	4 614 ..	....	....	.3	.1	.2	.1	.1	....
Debt securities	4 619 ..	−.8	3.2	.9	.3	−1.1	.7	−.5	....
Bonds and notes	4 620 ..	−.8	3.2	.9	.2	−1.1	.7	−.5	....
Monetary authorities	4 621 ..	....	....	....	....	....	....	....	
General government	4 622 ..	....	....	....	....	....	....	....	
Banks	4 623 ..	−.8	3.2	.9	.2	−1.1	.7	−.5	....
Other sectors	4 624 ..	....	....	....	....	....	....	....	
Money market instruments	4 630 ..	....	....	....	.1	....	....	....	
Monetary authorities	4 631 ..	....	....	....	....	....	....	....	
General government	4 632 ..	....	....	....	....	....	....	....	
Banks	4 633 ..	....	....	....	....	....	....	....	
Other sectors	4 634 ..	....	....	....	.1	....	....	....	
Liabilities	4 652 ..	**−.1**	**.4**	**.1**	**3.3**	**14.7**	**235.0**	**83.3**	....
Equity securities	4 660 ..	....	....	....	.7	15.3	51.7	76.8	....
Banks	4 663 ..	....	....	....	....	....	....	32.9	....
Other sectors	4 664 ..	....	....	....	.7	15.3	51.7	43.9	....
Debt securities	4 669 ..	−.1	.4	....	2.6	−.7	183.3	6.5	....
Bonds and notes	4 670 ..	−.1	.4	....	2.6	−.7	183.3	6.5	....
Monetary authorities	4 671 ..	....	....	....	....	....	....	....	
General government	4 672 ..	−.1	.4	....	2.6	−.7	183.3	6.5	....
Banks	4 673 ..	....	....	....	....	....	....	....	
Other sectors	4 674 ..	....	....	....	....	....	....	....	
Money market instruments	4 680 ..	....	....	....	....	....	....	....	
Monetary authorities	4 681 ..	....	....	....	....	....	....	....	
General government	4 682 ..	....	....	....	....	....	....	....	
Banks	4 683 ..	....	....	....	....	....	....	....	
Other sectors	4 684 ..	....	....	....	....	....	....	....	
C. FINANCIAL DERIVATIVES	4 910 ..	....	....	....	....	....	....	....	....
Monetary authorities	4 911 ..	....	....	....	....	....	....	....	
General government	4 912 ..	....	....	....	....	....	....	....	
Banks	4 913 ..	....	....	....	....	....	....	....	
Other sectors	4 914 ..	....	....	....	....	....	....	....	
Assets	4 900 ..	....	....	....	....	....	....	....	....
Monetary authorities	4 901 ..	....	....	....	....	....	....	....	
General government	4 902 ..	....	....	....	....	....	....	....	
Banks	4 903 ..	....	....	....	....	....	....	....	
Other sectors	4 904 ..	....	....	....	....	....	....	....	
Liabilities	4 905 ..	....	....	....	....	....	....	....	....
Monetary authorities	4 906 ..	....	....	....	....	....	....	....	
General government	4 907 ..	....	....	....	....	....	....	....	
Banks	4 908 ..	....	....	....	....	....	....	....	
Other sectors	4 909 ..	....	....	....	....	....	....	....	

Table 2 (Concluded). STANDARD PRESENTATION, 2000–2007

(Millions of U.S. dollars)

	Code	2000	2001	2002	2003	2004	2005	2006	2007
D. OTHER INVESTMENT	4 700 ..	100.4	−126.1	169.4	132.7	261.6	178.6	−42.3	....
Assets	4 703 ..	−77.7	−98.1	246.2	−3.8	6.8	−89.2	−150.5	....
Trade credits	4 706 ..	....	....	....	....	....	....	....	....
General government	4 707 ..	....	....	....	....	....	....	....	....
of which: Short-term	4 709 ..	....	....	....	....	....	....	....	....
Other sectors	4 710 ..	....	....	....	....	....	....	....	....
of which: Short-term	4 712 ..	....	....	....	....	....	....	....	....
Loans	4 714 ..	3.1	−10.2	20.0	−15.3	.1	−49.0	6.4	....
Monetary authorities	4 715 ..								
of which: Short-term	4 718 ..	....	....	....	....	....	....	....	....
General government	4 719 ..	....	....	....	....	....	....	....	....
of which: Short-term	4 721 ..	....	....	....	....	....	....	....	....
Banks	4 722 ..	3.1	−10.2	20.0	2.6	....	−3.3	2.3	....
of which: Short-term	4 724 ..	*3.1*	*−13.4*	*19.9*	*1.7*	....	....	*−.5*	....
Other sectors	4 725 ..	....	....	....	−17.9	.1	−45.7	4.1	....
of which: Short-term	4 727 ..	....	....	....	*−17.9*	*.1*	*−45.7*	*4.1*	....
Currency and deposits	4 730 ..	−93.8	−88.9	240.4	13.4	7.2	−43.3	−155.9	....
Monetary authorities	4 731 ..	14.1	−236.8	223.0	17.8	26.4	.8	−3.3	....
General government	4 732 ..	....	....	....	....	....	....	....	....
Banks	4 733 ..	−78.2	−228.3	153.6	−44.1	−94.2	8.0	−67.7	....
Other sectors	4 734 ..	−29.6	376.2	−136.3	39.7	75.0	−52.1	−84.9	....
Other assets	4 736 ..	13.0	1.0	−14.2	−1.9	−.6	3.2	−1.0	....
Monetary authorities	4 737 ..	....	....	....	....	....	....	....	....
of which: Short-term	4 739 ..	....	....	....	....	....	....	....	....
General government	4 740 ..	....	....	....	....	....	....	....	....
of which: Short-term	4 742 ..	....	....	....	....	....	....	....	....
Banks	4 743 ..	13.0	1.0	−14.2	−1.9	−.6	3.2	−1.0	....
of which: Short-term	4 745 ..	*13.0*	*1.0*	*−14.2*	*−1.9*	*−.6*	*3.2*	*−1.0*	....
Other sectors	4 746 ..	....	....	....	....	....	....	....	....
of which: Short-term	4 748 ..	....	....	....	....	....	....	....	....
Liabilities	4 753 ..	178.1	−28.0	−76.7	136.5	254.8	267.9	108.1	....
Trade credits	4 756 ..	147.4	−60.2	83.1	72.9	170.0	24.6	41.2	....
General government	4 757 ..	....	....	....	....	....	....	....	....
of which: Short-term	4 759 ..	....	....	....	....	....	....	....	....
Other sectors	4 760 ..	147.4	−60.2	83.1	72.9	170.0	24.6	41.2	....
of which: Short-term	4 762 ..	*147.4*	*−60.2*	*83.1*	*72.9*	*170.0*	*24.6*	*41.2*	....
Loans	4 764 ..	28.1	−72.0	15.6	56.7	66.7	200.5	−5.2	....
Monetary authorities	4 765 ..	−.9	−21.7	−8.8	−4.7	−8.6	4.7	−9.6	....
of which: Use of Fund credit and loans from the Fund	4 766 ..	*−15.6*	*−7.6*	*−8.8*	*−4.7*	*−8.6*	*4.7*	*−9.6*	....
of which: Short-term	4 768 ..	*14.7*	*−14.1*	....	....	....	....	....	....
General government	4 769 ..	75.3	−64.8	8.7	36.0	38.4	44.3	−157.7	....
of which: Short-term	4 771 ..	....	....	....	....	....	....	....	....
Banks	4 772 ..	−41.5	12.8	17.9	−44.3	−22.5	56.5	50.1	....
of which: Short-term	4 774 ..	*−11.3*	*22.9*	*−21.9*	*−20.7*	*−6.5*	*−6.8*	*−1.5*	....
Other sectors	4 775 ..	−4.9	1.8	−2.3	69.7	59.4	95.0	112.0	....
of which: Short-term	4 777 ..	....	....	....	*2.3*	*24.4*	*63.5*	*9.9*	....
Currency and deposits	4 780 ..	−19.0	93.1	−170.2	9.3	−2.7	24.9	52.9	....
Monetary authorities	4 781 ..	....	154.2	−154.2	....	....	....	....	....
General government	4 782 ..	....	....	....	....	....	....	....	....
Banks	4 783 ..	−19.0	−61.1	−15.9	9.3	−2.7	24.9	52.9	....
Other sectors	4 784 ..	....	....	....	....	....	....	....	....
Other liabilities	4 786 ..	21.7	11.1	−5.2	−2.4	20.8	17.9	19.2	....
Monetary authorities	4 787 ..	....	....	....	....	....	....	....	....
of which: Short-term	4 789 ..	....	....	....	....	....	....	....	....
General government	4 790 ..	2.0	−.6	2.3	−7.6	....	....	....	....
of which: Short-term	4 792 ..	*2.0*	*−.6*	*2.3*	*−7.6*	....	....	....	....
Banks	4 793 ..	16.5	10.1	−6.6	.8	1.3	1.1	1.2	....
of which: Short-term	4 795 ..	*16.5*	*9.8*	*−6.6*	*.8*	*1.3*	*1.1*	*1.2*	....
Other sectors	4 796 ..	3.1	1.6	−1.0	4.5	19.5	16.7	18.0	....
of which: Short-term	4 798 ..	*3.1*	*1.6*	*−1.0*	*4.5*	*19.5*	*16.7*	*18.0*	....
E. RESERVE ASSETS	4 802 ..	−263.6	−78.0	130.9	−50.7	−19.4	−415.3	−375.7	....
Monetary gold	4 812 ..	....	....	....	40.2	−39.5	....	....	....
Special drawing rights	4 811 ..	.4	−1.7	−3.6	6.1	−.4	−.1	−2.1	....
Reserve position in the Fund	4 810 ..	....	....	....	....	....	....	....	....
Foreign exchange	4 803 ..	−263.9	−76.4	134.5	−97.0	20.4	−415.1	−373.6	....
Other claims	4 813 ..	....	....	....	....	....	....	....	....
NET ERRORS AND OMISSIONS	4 998 ..	61.0	2.3	−29.7	−26.0	7.7	−12.9	9.7	....

Table 3. INTERNATIONAL INVESTMENT POSITION (End-period stocks), 2000–2007

(Millions of U.S. dollars)

	Code	2000	2001	2002	2003	2004	2005	2006	2007
ASSETS	8 995 C.	....	....	....	**1,868.4**	**2,162.1**	**2,455.8**	**3,256.5**	....
Direct investment abroad	8 505 ..	....	....	....	42.0	54.2	62.1	39.7	....
Equity capital and reinvested earnings	8 506 ..	....	....	....	35.7	43.9	43.6	37.7	....
Claims on affiliated enterprises	8 507 ..	....	....	....	35.7	43.9	43.6	37.7	....
Liabilities to affiliated enterprises	8 508 ..	....	....	....	....	....	....	....	....
Other capital	8 530 ..	....	....	....	6.3	10.3	18.5	2.0	....
Claims on affiliated enterprises	8 535 ..	....	....	....	10.8	15.3	25.2	19.4	....
Liabilities to affiliated enterprises	8 540 ..	....	....	....	−4.5	−5.0	−6.7	−17.3	....
Portfolio investment	8 602 ..	....	....	**3.5**	**3.8**	**4.1**	**3.6**	**4.2**	....
Equity securities	8 610 ..	....	....	....	3.8	4.1	3.6	4.2	....
Monetary authorities	8 611 ..	....	....	....	....	....	....	....	....
General government	8 612 ..	....	....	....	....	....	....	....	....
Banks	8 613 ..	....	....	....	3.0	3.3	2.9	3.4	....
Other sectors	8 614 ..	....	....	....	.8	.8	.7	.8	....
Debt securities	8 619 ..	....	....	3.5	....	....	....	....	....
Bonds and notes	8 620 ..	....	....	3.5	....	....	....	....	....
Monetary authorities	8 621 ..	....	....	....	....	....	....	....	....
General government	8 622 ..	....	....	....	....	....	....	....	....
Banks	8 623 ..	....	....	3.5	....	....	....	....	....
Other sectors	8 624 ..	....	....	....	....	....	....	....	....
Money market instruments	8 630 ..	....	....	....	....	....	....	....	....
Monetary authorities	8 631 ..	....	....	....	....	....	....	....	....
General government	8 632 ..	....	....	....	....	....	....	....	....
Banks	8 633 ..	....	....	....	....	....	....	....	....
Other sectors	8 634 ..	....	....	....	....	....	....	....	....
Financial derivatives	8 900 ..	....	....	....	....	....	....	....	....
Monetary authorities	8 901 ..	....	....	....	....	....	....	....	....
General government	8 902 ..	....	....	....	....	....	....	....	....
Banks	8 903 C	....	....	....	....	....	....	....	....
Other sectors	8 904 ..	....	....	....	....	....	....	....	....
Other investment	8 703 ..	**458.8**	**895.7**	**601.4**	**929.3**	**1,128.5**	**1,065.4**	**1,346.9**	....
Trade credits	8 706 ..	....	....	....	194.3	267.2	299.0	441.8	....
General government	8 707 ..	....	....	....	....	....	....	....	....
of which: Short-term	8 709 ..	....	....	....	....	....	....	....	....
Other sectors	8 710 ..	....	....	....	194.3	267.2	299.0	441.8	....
of which: Short-term	8 712 ..	....	....	....	*193.9*	*266.8*	*298.2*	*441.0*	....
Loans	8 714 ..	....	....	2.5	25.5	27.4	26.0	2.3	....
Monetary authorities	8 715 ..	....	....	....	....	....	....	....	....
of which: Short-term	8 718 ..	....	....	....	....	....	....	....	....
General government	8 719 ..	....	....	....	....	....	....	....	....
of which: Short-term	8 721 ..	....	....	....	....	....	....	....	....
Banks	8 722 ..	....	....	2.5	24.0	25.7	25.6	2.0	....
of which: Short-term	8 724 ..	....	....	*1.6*	*8.8*	*9.2*	*10.6*	*.5*	....
Other sectors	8 725 ..	....	....	....	1.5	1.7	.4	.3	....
of which: Short-term	8 727 ..	....	....	....	*1.5*	....	*.2*	....	....
Currency and deposits	8 730 ..	458.8	895.7	581.9	706.0	827.7	733.3	868.4	....
Monetary authorities	8 731 ..	21.4	252.7	49.2	41.4	16.2	15.5	23.6	....
General government	8 732 ..	....	....	....	....	....	....	....	....
Banks	8 733 ..	437.4	643.0	532.7	664.6	811.5	717.8	844.8	....
Other sectors	8 734 ..	....	....	....	....	....	....	....	....
Other assets	8 736 ..	....	....	17.0	3.5	6.3	7.1	34.4	....
Monetary authorities	8 737 ..	....	....	....	....	....	....	....	....
of which: Short-term	8 739 ..	....	....	....	....	....	....	....	....
General government	8 740 ..	....	....	....	....	....	....	....	....
of which: Short-term	8 742 ..	....	....	....	....	....	....	....	....
Banks	8 743 ..	....	....	17.0	....	....	....	....	....
of which: Short-term	8 745 ..	....	....	*17.0*	....	....	....	....	....
Other sectors	8 746 ..	....	....	....	3.5	6.3	7.1	34.4	....
of which: Short-term	8 748 ..	....	....	....	*3.5*	*6.3*	*7.1*	*34.4*	....
Reserve assets	8 802 ..	**712.6**	**775.2**	**734.4**	**893.3**	**975.2**	**1,324.7**	**1,865.7**	....
Monetary gold	8 812 ..	30.7	53.7	67.8	37.1	86.5	112.0	138.8	....
Special drawing rights	8 811 ..	.7	2.2	6.1	.3	.8	.8	3.0	1.5
Reserve position in the Fund	8 810 ..	....	....	....	....	....	....	....	....
Foreign exchange	8 803 ..	681.3	719.3	660.5	856.0	888.0	1,212.0	1,724.0	....
Other claims	8 813 ..	....	....	....	....	....	....	....	....

Table 3 (Concluded). INTERNATIONAL INVESTMENT POSITION (End-period stocks), 2000–2007

(Millions of U.S. dollars)

	Code	2000	2001	2002	2003	2004	2005	2006	2007
LIABILITIES	8 995 D.	....	....	....	3,867.5	4,660.7	4,789.7	5,730.4	....
Direct investment in Macedonia, FYR	8 555 ..	....	....	....	1,614.7	2,190.5	2,086.9	2,763.8	....
Equity capital and reinvested earnings	8 556 ..	....	....	....	1,477.0	1,858.5	1,863.5	2,454.0	....
Claims on direct investors	8 557 ..	....	....	....					....
Liabilities to direct investors	8 558 ..	....	....	....	1,477.0	1,858.5	1,863.5	2,454.0	....
Other capital	8 580 ..	....	....	....	137.7	332.1	223.4	309.8	....
Claims on direct investors	8 585 ..	....	....	....	−60.0	−49.9	−87.9	−106.6	....
Liabilities to direct investors	8 590 ..	....	....	....	197.6	382.0	311.3	416.4	....
Portfolio investment	8 652 ..	....	....	....	107.2	71.6	273.9	366.5	....
Equity securities	8 660 ..	....	....	....	80.5	40.0	52.8	114.0	....
Banks	8 663 ..	....	....	....	12.6	19.1	29.5	106.2	....
Other sectors	8 664 ..	....	....	....	67.9	20.9	23.2	7.8	....
Debt securities	8 669 ..	....	....	....	26.8	31.6	221.1	252.5	....
Bonds and notes	8 670 ..	....	....	....	26.8	31.6	221.1	252.5	....
Monetary authorities	8 671 ..	....	....	....	....	....	....	....	....
General government	8 672 ..	....	....	....	26.8	31.6	221.1	252.5	....
Banks	8 673 ..	....	....	....	....	....	....	....	....
Other sectors	8 674 ..	....	....	....	....	....	....	....	....
Money market instruments	8 680 ..	....	....	....	....	....	....	....	....
Monetary authorities	8 681 ..	....	....	....	....	....	....	....	....
General government	8 682 ..	....	....	....	....	....	....	....	....
Banks	8 683 ..	....	....	....	....	....	....	....	....
Other sectors	8 684 ..	....	....	....	....	....	....	....	....
Financial derivatives	8 905 ..	....	....	....	....	....	....	....	....
Monetary authorities	8 906 ..	....	....	....	....	....	....	....	....
General government	8 907 ..	....	....	....	....	....	....	....	....
Banks	8 908 ..	....	....	....	....	....	....	....	....
Other sectors	8 909 ..	....	....	....	....	....	....	....	....
Other investment	8 753 ..	1,603.0	1,654.3	1,642.8	2,145.6	2,398.5	2,428.9	2,600.0	....
Trade credits	8 756 ..	....	....	....	398.2	485.6	456.9	486.2	....
General government	8 757 ..	....	....	....	....	....	....	....	....
of which: Short-term	8 759 ..	....	....	....	....	....	....	....	....
Other sectors	8 760 ..	....	....	....	398.2	485.6	456.9	486.2	....
of which: Short-term	8 762 ..	....	....	....	336.4	438.9	427.6	460.4	....
Loans	8 764 ..	1,600.6	1,493.5	1,590.6	1,657.2	1,814.4	1,852.2	1,853.1	....
Monetary authorities	8 765 ..	95.4	70.8	67.4	68.3	62.5	62.2	55.7	....
of which: Use of Fund credit and loans from the Fund	8 766 ..	81.2	70.8	67.4	68.3	62.5	62.2	55.7	....
of which: Short-term	8 768 ..	14.2	....	....	....	....	....	....	....
General government	8 769 ..	1,216.3	1,147.8	1,131.6	1,256.5	1,351.2	1,292.2	1,152.6	....
of which: Short-term	8 771 ..	....	....	....	....	....	....	....	....
Banks	8 772 ..	215.0	170.7	136.2	90.9	89.1	131.0	192.7	....
of which: Short-term	8 774 ..	172.4	138.5	36.4	10.9	10.7	2.7	....	....
Other sectors	8 775 ..	73.9	104.2	255.4	241.4	311.6	366.9	452.2	....
of which: Short-term	8 777 ..	....	....	....	21.5	18.0	73.4	15.4	....
Currency and deposits	8 780 ..	2.4	160.8	51.9	68.9	70.5	86.9	148.6	....
Monetary authorities	8 781 ..	....	154.2	....	....	....	....	....	....
General government	8 782 ..	....	....	....	....	....	....	....	....
Banks	8 783 ..	2.4	6.6	51.9	68.9	70.5	86.9	148.6	....
Other sectors	8 784 ..	....	....	....	....	....	....	....	....
Other liabilities	8 786 ..	....	....	.3	21.4	27.9	32.8	112.1	....
Monetary authorities	8 787 ..	....	....	....	....	....	....	....	....
of which: Short-term	8 789 ..	....	....	....	....	....	....	....	....
General government	8 790 ..	....	....	....	....	....	....	....	....
of which: Short-term	8 792 ..	....	....	....	....	....	....	....	....
Banks	8 793 ..	....	....	.3	....	....	....	....	....
of which: Short-term	8 795 ..	....	....	....	....	....	....	....	....
Other sectors	8 796 ..	....	....	....	21.4	27.9	32.8	112.1	....
of which: Short-term	8 798 ..	....	....	....	21.4	27.9	32.8	112.1	....
NET INTERNATIONAL INVESTMENT POSITION	8 995 ..	....	....	....	−1,999.1	−2,498.6	−2,333.9	−2,473.8	....
Conversion rates: denars per U.S. dollar (end of period)	0 102 ..	66.328	69.172	58.598	49.050	45.068	51.859	46.450	41.656

Table 1. ANALYTIC PRESENTATION, 2000–2007

(Millions of U.S. dollars)

	Code	2000	2001	2002	2003	2004	2005	2006	2007
A. Current Account[1].....................	4 993 Z.	**−283**	**−170**	**−528**	**−458**	**−541**	**−626**	....	....
Goods: exports f.o.b.................	2 100 ..	824	928	859	854	990	834	....	....
Goods: imports f.o.b.................	3 100 ..	−997	−955	−1,066	−1,111	−1,427	−1,427	....	....
Balance on Goods..................	4 100 ..	*−174*	*−27*	*−207*	*−258*	*−437*	*−592*	....	....
Services: credit......................	2 200 ..	364	351	397	322	425	498	....	....
Services: debit.......................	3 200 ..	−522	−511	−704	−619	−637	−615	....	....
Balance on Goods and Services...................	4 991 ..	*−332*	*−187*	*−515*	*−555*	*−649*	*−710*	....	....
Income: credit........................	2 300 ..	22	24	46	16	15	24	....	....
Income: debit........................	3 300 ..	−64	−106	−178	−94	−89	−104	....	....
Balance on Goods, Services, and Income........................	4 992 ..	*−373*	*−270*	*−647*	*−632*	*−723*	*−790*	....	....
Current transfers: credit...........	2 379 Z.	122	114	156	357	245	208	....	....
Current transfers: debit...........	3 379 ..	−31	−15	−36	−183	−62	−45	....	....
B. Capital Account[1].....................	4 994 Z.	**115**	**113**	**102**	**143**	**182**	**192**	....	....
Capital account: credit.............	2 994 Z.	115	113	102	143	182	192	....	....
Capital account: debit.............	3 994 ..	....	....	....	....	....	....	....	....
Total, Groups A Plus B...........	4 981 ..	*−168*	*−57*	*−425*	*−315*	*−359*	*−435*	....	....
C. Financial Account[1]................	4 995 W.	**−31**	**−139**	**−96**	**−126**	**251**	**−6**	....	....
Direct investment abroad.............	4 505 ..	....	....	....	....	....	....	....	....
Direct investment in Madagascar........	4 555 Z.	83	93	15	13	53	85	....	....
Portfolio investment assets..........	4 602 ..	....	....	....	....	....	....	....	....
Equity securities..................	4 610 ..	....	....	....	....	....	....	....	....
Debt securities....................	4 619 ..	....	....	....	....	....	....	....	....
Portfolio investment liabilit es......	4 652 Z.	....	....	....	....	....	....	....	....
Equity securities..................	4 660 ..	....	....	....	....	....	....	....	....
Debt securities....................	4 669 Z.	....	....	....	....	....	....	....	....
Financial derivatives................	4 910 ..	....	....	....	....	....	....	....	....
Financial derivatives assets.........	4 900 ..	....	....	....	....	....	....	....	....
Financial derivatives liabilities.....	4 905 ..	....	....	....	....	....	....	....	....
Other investment assets.............	4 703 ..	−87	−128	74	−29	295	11	....	....
Monetary authorities.............	4 701 ..	−40	−144	102	4	315	....	....	....
General government..............	4 704 ..	....	....	....	....	....	....	....	....
Banks.............................	4 705 ..	−48	15	−29	−32	−20	11	....	....
Other sectors.....................	4 728 ..	....	....	....	....	....	....	....	....
Other investment liabilities.........	4 753 W.	−26	−103	−184	−110	−97	−102	....	....
Monetary authorities.............	4 753 WA	−1	....	4	−1	−1	....	....	....
General government..............	4 753 ZB	−28	−84	−165	−100	−101	−89	....	....
Banks.............................	4 753 ZC	15	−11	−5	3	6	−14	....	....
Other sectors.....................	4 753 ZD	−12	−8	−18	−13	....	....	....	....
Total, Groups A Through C........	4 983 ..	*−199*	*−196*	*−521*	*−441*	*−108*	*−440*	....	....
D. Net Errors and Omissions...................	4 998 ..	**39**	**−57**	**29**	**67**	**−35**	**91**	....	....
Total, Groups A Through D........	4 984 ..	*−160*	*−253*	*−493*	*−374*	*−143*	*−349*	....	....
E. Reserves and Related Items...........................	4 802 A.	**160**	**253**	**493**	**374**	**143**	**349**	....	....
Reserve assets.......................	4 802 ..	−30	18	14	−25	−384	−10	....	....
Use of Fund credit and loans........	4 766 ..	45	27	12	8	44	5	....	....
Exceptional financing................	4 920 ..	145	208	467	391	483	354	....	....
Conversion rates: Malagasy ariary per U.S. dollar.................	0 101 ..	**1,353.5**	**1,317.7**	**1,366.4**	**1,238.3**	**1,868.9**	**2,003.0**	**2,142.3**	**1,873.9**

[1] Excludes components that have been classified in the categories of Group E.

Table 2. STANDARD PRESENTATION, 2000–2007

(Millions of U.S. dollars)

	Code	2000	2001	2002	2003	2004	2005	2006	2007
CURRENT ACCOUNT..	4 993 ..	**−260**	**−140**	**−477**	**−328**	**−399**	**−554**	....	....
A. GOODS...	4 100 ..	**−174**	**−27**	**−207**	**−258**	**−437**	**−592**	....	....
Credit..	2 100 ..	**824**	**928**	**859**	**854**	**990**	**834**	....	....
General merchandise: exports f.o.b..........................	2 110 ..	414	531	497	449	450	352	....	....
Goods for processing: exports f.o.b.........................	2 150 ..	407	395	358	405	540	482	....	....
Repairs on goods..	2 160 ..	....	....	....	....	....	....	....	....
Goods procured in ports by carriers.......................	2 170 ..	2	2	4	....	....	....	....	....
Nonmonetary gold...	2 180 ..	....	....	....	....	....	....	....	....
Debit..	3 100 ..	**−997**	**−955**	**−1,066**	**−1,111**	**−1,427**	**−1,427**	....	....
General merchandise: imports f.o.b..........................	3 110 ..	−633	−691	−896	−748	−929	−1,024	....	....
Goods for processing: imports f.o.b.........................	3 150 ..	−365	−264	−170	−363	−498	−402	....	....
Repairs on goods..	3 160 ..	....	....	....	....	....	....	....	....
Goods procured in ports by carriers.......................	3 170 ..	....	....	....	....	....	....	....	....
Nonmonetary gold...	3 180 ..	....	....	....	....	....	....	....	....
B. SERVICES..	4 200 ..	**−158**	**−160**	**−308**	**−297**	**−212**	**−117**	....	....
Total credit...	2 200 ..	*364*	*351*	*397*	*322*	*425*	*498*	....	....
Total debit...	3 200 ..	*−522*	*−511*	*−704*	*−619*	*−637*	*−615*	....	....
Transportation services, credit..........................	2 205 ..	**51**	**56**	**75**	**58**	**100**	**118**	....	....
Passenger...	2 850 ..	*31*	*34*	*45*	*43*	*82*	*107*	....	....
Freight...	2 851 ..	*8*	*9*	*6*	*7*	*10*	*9*	....	....
Other..	2 852 ..	*12*	*14*	*23*	*8*	*8*	*3*	....	....
Sea transport, passenger...................................	2 207 ..	....	....	....	....	....	....	....	....
Sea transport, freight.....................................	2 208 ..	8	9	6	7	9	9	....	....
Sea transport, other......................................	2 209 ..	7	8	12	4	6	1	....	....
Air transport, passenger...................................	2 211 ..	31	34	45	43	82	107	....	....
Air transport, freight.....................................	2 212 ..	....	....	....	....	2		....	....
Air transport, other......................................	2 213 ..	5	6	11	4	2	2	....	....
Other transport, passenger................................	2 215 ..	....	....	....	....	....	....	....	....
Other transport, freight...................................	2 216 ..	....	....	....	....	....	....	....	....
Other transport, other....................................	2 217 ..	....	....	....	....	....	....	....	....
Transportation services, debit...........................	3 205 ..	**−191**	**−211**	**−255**	**−230**	**−237**	**−224**	....	....
Passenger...	3 850 ..	*−24*	*−49*	*−32*	*−3*	*−15*	*−6*	....	....
Freight...	3 851 ..	*−148*	*−144*	*−188*	*−167*	*−214*	*−214*	....	....
Other..	3 852 ..	*−19*	*−19*	*−34*	*−61*	*−8*	*−4*	....	....
Sea transport, passenger...................................	3 207 ..	....	....	....	....	....	....	....	....
Sea transport, freight.....................................	3 208 ..	−148	−144	−188	−167	−214	−214	....	....
Sea transport, other......................................	3 209 ..	−3	−3	−5	−1	−4	−1	....	....
Air transport, passenger...................................	3 211 ..	−24	−49	−32	−3	−15	−6	....	....
Air transport, freight.....................................	3 212 ..	....	....	....	....	....	....	....	....
Air transport, other......................................	3 213 ..	−16	−16	−29	−60	−4	−3	....	....
Other transport, passenger................................	3 215 ..	....	....	....	....	....	....	....	....
Other transport, freight...................................	3 216 ..	....	....	....	....	....	....	....	....
Other transport, other....................................	3 217 ..	....	....	....	....	....	....	....	....
Travel, credit...	2 236 ..	**121**	**115**	**64**	**76**	**157**	**183**	....	....
Business travel...	2 237 ..	....	....	....	1	1	....	....	....
Personal travel...	2 240 ..	121	115	64	75	156	183	....	....
Travel, debit..	3 236 ..	**−115**	**−130**	**−160**	**−64**	**−93**	**−74**	....	....
Business travel...	3 237 ..	−9	−10	−7	−7	−8	....	....	....
Personal travel...	3 240 ..	−106	−120	−153	−57	−86	−73	....	....
Other services, credit..................................	2 200 BA	**192**	**180**	**258**	**188**	**168**	**197**	....	....
Communications..	2 245 ..	6	8	....	6	7	2	....	....
Construction...	2 249 ..	20	18	17	74	10	2	....	....
Insurance..	2 253 ..	3	3	1	1	3	....	....	....
Financial..	2 260 ..	1	1	1	4	1	....	....	....
Computer and information................................	2 262 ..	....	....	....	1	1	....	....	....
Royalties and licence fees.................................	2 266 ..	1	1	....	1	....	2	....	....
Other business services...................................	2 268 ..	109	72	120	32	79	111	....	....
Personal, cultural, and recreational........................	2 287 ..	....	....	....	....	....	....	....	....
Government, n.i.e...	2 291 ..	50	77	118	69	66	78	....	....
Other services, debit...................................	3 200 BA	**−216**	**−170**	**−289**	**−325**	**−307**	**−318**	....	....
Communications..	3 245 ..	−2	....	−2	−5	−4	−6	....	....
Construction...	3 249 ..	−37	−47	−72	−39	−5	−2	....	....
Insurance..	3 253 ..	−5	−4	−6	−10	−7	−5	....	....
Financial..	3 260 ..	−1	−2	−3	−5	−5	....	....	....
Computer and information................................	3 262 ..	....	....	....	−2	−3	−1	....	....
Royalties and licence fees.................................	3 266 ..	−11	−8	−23	−7	−23	−9	....	....
Other business services...................................	3 268 ..	−33	−22	−40	−118	−97	−143	....	....
Personal, cultural, and recreational........................	3 287 ..	....	....	....	....	....	....	....	....
Government, n.i.e...	3 291 ..	−127	−87	−143	−139	−164	−153	....	....

Table 2 (Continued). STANDARD PRESENTATION, 2000–2007

(Millions of U.S. dollars)

	Code	2000	2001	2002	2003	2004	2005	2006	2007
C. INCOME	4 300	**−42**	**−82**	**−132**	**−77**	**−74**	**−80**	....	....
Total credit	2 300	*22*	*24*	*46*	*16*	*15*	*24*	....	....
Total debit	3 300	*−64*	*−106*	*−178*	*−94*	*−89*	*−104*	....	....
Compensation of employees, credit	2 310	**11**	**11**	**29**	**8**	**7**	**10**	....	....
Compensation of employees, debit	3 310	**−1**	**−11**	**−5**	**−5**	**−6**	**−13**	....	....
Investment income, credit	2 320	**11**	**13**	**17**	**8**	**8**	**14**	....	....
Direct investment income	2 330	....	....	....	....	....	....	....	....
Dividends and distributed branch profits	2 332	....	....	....	....	....	....	....	....
Reinvested earnings and undistributed branch profits	2 333	....	....	....	....	....	....	....	....
Income on debt (interest)	2 334	....	....	....	....	....	....	....	....
Portfolio investment income	2 339	....	....	....	....	....	....	....	....
Income on equity	2 340	....	....	....	....	....	....	....	....
Income on bonds and notes	2 350	....	....	....	....	....	....	....	....
Income on money market instruments	2 360	....	....	....	....	....	....	....	....
Other investment income	2 370	11	13	17	8	8	14	....	....
Investment income, debit	3 320	**−63**	**−95**	**−173**	**−89**	**−83**	**−90**	....	....
Direct investment income	3 330	−4	−38	−65	−32	−21	−38	....	....
Dividends and distributed branch profits	3 332	−4	−38	−65	−32	−21	−38	....	....
Reinvested earnings and undistributed branch profits	3 333	....	....	....	....	....	....	....	....
Income on debt (interest)	3 334	....	....	....	....	....	....	....	....
Portfolio investment income	3 339	....	....	....	....	....	....	....	....
Income on equity	3 340	....	....	....	....	....	....	....	....
Income on bonds and notes	3 350	....	....	....	....	....	....	....	....
Income on money market instruments	3 360	....	....	....	....	....	....	....	....
Other investment income	3 370	−58	−57	−108	−57	−63	−52	....	....
D. CURRENT TRANSFERS	4 379	**113**	**129**	**170**	**304**	**324**	**236**	....	....
Credit	2 379	**144**	**144**	**206**	**487**	**387**	**281**	....	....
General government	2 380	42	30	51	149	162	72	....	....
Other sectors	2 390	102	114	156	338	224	208	....	....
Workers' remittances	2 391	....	....	....	8	4	1	....	....
Other current transfers	2 392	102	114	156	330	220	207	....	....
Debit	3 379	**−31**	**−15**	**−36**	**−183**	**−62**	**−45**	....	....
General government	3 380	−21	−15	−36	−5	....	−14	....	....
Other sectors	3 390	−10	....	....	−178	−62	−31	....	....
Workers' remittances	3 391	−10	....	....	−13	−3	−8	....	....
Other current transfers	3 392	....	....	....	−165	−59	−23	....	....
CAPITAL AND FINANCIAL ACCOUNT	4 996	**222**	**197**	**448**	**261**	**434**	**463**	....	....
CAPITAL ACCOUNT	4 994	**115**	**113**	**102**	**143**	**182**	**192**	....	....
Total credit	2 994	*115*	*113*	*102*	*143*	*182*	*192*	....	....
Total debit	3 994	....	....	....	....	....	....	....	....
Capital transfers, credit	2 400	**115**	**113**	**102**	**143**	**182**	**192**	....	....
General government	2 401	115	113	102	143	182	192	....	....
Debt forgiveness	2 402	....	....	....	....	....	....	....	....
Other capital transfers	2 410	115	113	102	143	182	192	....	....
Other sectors	2 430	....	....	....	....	....	....	....	....
Migrants' transfers	2 431	....	....	....	....	....	....	....	....
Debt forgiveness	2 432	....	....	....	....	....	....	....	....
Other capital transfers	2 440	....	....	....	....	....	....	....	....
Capital transfers, debit	3 400	....	....	....	....	....	....	....	....
General government	3 401	....	....	....	....	....	....	....	....
Debt forgiveness	3 402	....	....	....	....	....	....	....	....
Other capital transfers	3 410	....	....	....	....	....	....	....	....
Other sectors	3 430	....	....	....	....	....	....	....	....
Migrants' transfers	3 431	....	....	....	....	....	....	....	....
Debt forgiveness	3 432	....	....	....	....	....	....	....	....
Other capital transfers	3 440	....	....	....	....	....	....	....	....
Nonproduced nonfinancial assets, credit	2 480	....	....	....	....	....	....	....	....
Nonproduced nonfinancial assets, debit	3 480	....	....	....	....	....	....	....	....

Table 2 (Continued). STANDARD PRESENTATION, 2000–2007

(Millions of U.S. dollars)

	Code	2000	2001	2002	2003	2004	2005	2006	2007
FINANCIAL ACCOUNT.................................	4 995 ..	107	84	346	118	252	271	....	....
A. DIRECT INVESTMENT..........................	4 500 ..	83	93	15	13	53	85	....	....
Direct investment abroad..................................	4 505 ..	....	....	....	....	....	....	....	....
Equity capital...	4 510 ..	....	....	....	....	....	....	....	....
Claims on affiliated enterprises..................	4 515 ..	....	....	....	....	....	....	....	....
Liabilities to affiliated enterprises..............	4 520 ..	....	....	....	....	....	....	....	....
Reinvested earnings...................................	4 525 ..	....	....	....	....	....	....	....	....
Other capital...	4 530 ..	....	....	....	....	....	....	....	....
Claims on affiliated enterprises..................	4 535 ..	....	....	....	....	....	....	....	....
Liabilities to affiliated enterprises..............	4 540 ..	....	....	....	....	....	....	....	....
Direct investment in Madagascar...................	4 555 ..	83	93	15	13	53	85	....	....
Equity capital...	4 560 ..	83	93	15	13	53	85	....	....
Claims on direct investors.........................	4 565 ..	....	....	....	....	....	....	....	....
Liabilities to direct investors.....................	4 570 ..	83	93	15	13	53	85	....	....
Reinvested earnings...................................	4 575 ..	....	....	....	....	....	....	....	....
Other capital...	4 580 ..	....	....	....	....	....	....	....	....
Claims on direct investors.........................	4 585 ..	....	....	....	....	....	....	....	....
Liabilities to direct investors.....................	4 590 ..	....	....	....	....	....	....	....	....
B. PORTFOLIO INVESTMENT........................	4 600 ..	....	....	....	....	....	....	....	....
Assets...	4 602 ..	....	....	....	....	....	....	....	....
Equity securities..	4 610 ..	....	....	....	....	....	....	....	....
Monetary authorities.................................	4 611 ..	....	....	....	....	....	....	....	....
General government..................................	4 612 ..	....	....	....	....	....	....	....	....
Banks...	4 613 ..	....	....	....	....	....	....	....	....
Other sectors..	4 614 ..	....	....	....	....	....	....	....	....
Debt securities..	4 619 ..	....	....	....	....	....	....	....	....
Bonds and notes.......................................	4 620 ..	....	....	....	....	....	....	....	....
Monetary authorities..............................	4 621 ..	....	....	....	....	....	....	....	....
General government..............................	4 622 ..	....	....	....	....	....	....	....	....
Banks..	4 623 ..	....	....	....	....	....	....	....	....
Other sectors..	4 624 ..	....	....	....	....	....	....	....	....
Money market instruments.........................	4 630 ..	....	....	....	....	....	....	....	....
Monetary authorities..............................	4 631 ..	....	....	....	....	....	....	....	....
General government..............................	4 632 ..	....	....	....	....	....	....	....	....
Banks..	4 633 ..	....	....	....	....	....	....	....	....
Other sectors..	4 634 ..	....	....	....	....	....	....	....	....
Liabilities...	4 652 ..	....	....	....	....	....	....	....	....
Equity securities..	4 660 ..	....	....	....	....	....	....	....	....
Banks...	4 663 ..	....	....	....	....	....	....	....	....
Other sectors..	4 664 ..	....	....	....	....	....	....	....	....
Debt securities..	4 669 ..	....	....	....	....	....	....	....	....
Bonds and notes.......................................	4 670 ..	....	....	....	....	....	....	....	....
Monetary authorities..............................	4 671 ..	....	....	....	....	....	....	....	....
General government..............................	4 672 ..	....	....	....	....	....	....	....	....
Banks..	4 673 ..	....	....	....	....	....	....	....	....
Other sectors..	4 674 ..	....	....	....	....	....	....	....	....
Money market instruments.........................	4 680 ..	....	....	....	....	....	....	....	....
Monetary authorities..............................	4 681 ..	....	....	....	....	....	....	....	....
General government..............................	4 682 ..	....	....	....	....	....	....	....	....
Banks..	4 683 ..	....	....	....	....	....	....	....	....
Other sectors..	4 684 ..	....	....	....	....	....	....	....	....
C. FINANCIAL DERIVATIVES........................	4 910 ..	....	....	....	....	....	....	....	....
Monetary authorities.................................	4 911 ..	....	....	....	....	....	....	....	....
General government..................................	4 912 ..	....	....	....	....	....	....	....	....
Banks...	4 913 ..	....	....	....	....	....	....	....	....
Other sectors..	4 914 ..	....	....	....	....	....	....	....	....
Assets...	4 900 ..	....	....	....	....	....	....	....	....
Monetary authorities.................................	4 901 ..	....	....	....	....	....	....	....	....
General government..................................	4 902 ..	....	....	....	....	....	....	....	....
Banks...	4 903 ..	....	....	....	....	....	....	....	....
Other sectors..	4 904 ..	....	....	....	....	....	....	....	....
Liabilities...	4 905 ..	....	....	....	....	....	....	....	....
Monetary authorities.................................	4 906 ..	....	....	....	....	....	....	....	....
General government..................................	4 907 ..	....	....	....	....	....	....	....	....
Banks...	4 908 ..	....	....	....	....	....	....	....	....
Other sectors..	4 909 ..	....	....	....	....	....	....	....	....

Table 2 (Concluded). STANDARD PRESENTATION, 2000–2007

(Millions of U.S. dollars)

	Code	2000	2001	2002	2003	2004	2005	2006	2007
D. OTHER INVESTMENT	4 700 ..	**54**	**−27**	**317**	**131**	**583**	**196**	....	....
Assets	4 703 ..	**−87**	**−128**	**74**	**−29**	**295**	**11**	....	....
Trade credits	4 706 ..	....	....	....	....	....	....	....	....
General government	4 707 ..	....	....	....	....	....	....	....	....
of which: Short-term	4 709 ..	....	....	....	....	....	....	....	....
Other sectors	4 710 ..	....	....	....	....	....	....	....	....
of which: Short-term	4 712 ..	....	....	....	....	....	....	....	....
Loans	4 714 ..	−52	−2	−22	−23	4	5	....	....
Monetary authorities	4 715 ..	....	....	....	....	....	....	....	....
of which: Short-term	4 718 ..	....	....	....	....	....	....	....	....
General government	4 719 ..	....	....	....	....	....	....	....	....
of which: Short-term	4 721 ..	....	....	....	....	....	....	....	....
Banks	4 722 ..	−52	−2	−22	−23	4	5	....	....
of which: Short-term	4 724 ..	....	....	....	....	....	....	....	....
Other sectors	4 725 ..	....	....	....	....	....	....	....	....
of which: Short-term	4 727 ..	....	....	....	....	....	....	....	....
Currency and deposits	4 730 ..	17	6	−21	−6	−26	9	....	....
Monetary authorities	4 731 ..	....	....	....	....	....	....	....	....
General government	4 732 ..	....	....	....	....	....	....	....	....
Banks	4 733 ..	17	6	−21	−6	−26	9	....	....
Other sectors	4 734 ..	....	....	....	....	....	....	....	....
Other assets	4 736 ..	−53	−133	117	....	317	−4	....	....
Monetary authorities	4 737 ..	−40	−144	102	4	315	....	....	....
of which: Short-term	4 739 ..	*−30*	*21*	*9*	*4*	*−13*	....	....	....
General government	4 740 ..	....	....	....	....	....	....	....	....
of which: Short-term	4 742 ..	....	....	....	....	....	....	....	....
Banks	4 743 ..	−13	11	14	−3	2	−4	....	....
of which: Short-term	4 745 ..	*−13*	*11*	*14*	*−3*	*2*	*−4*	....	....
Other sectors	4 746 ..	....	....	....	....	....	....	....	....
of which: Short-term	4 748 ..	....	....	....	....	....	....	....	....
Liabilities	4 753 ..	**142**	**102**	**244**	**159**	**288**	**184**	....	....
Trade credits	4 756 ..	....	....	....	....	....	....	....	....
General government	4 757 ..	....	....	....	....	....	....	....	....
of which: Short-term	4 759 ..	....	....	....	....	....	....	....	....
Other sectors	4 760 ..	....	....	....	....	....	....	....	....
of which: Short-term	4 762 ..	....	....	....	....	....	....	....	....
Loans	4 764 ..	135	113	241	171	298	206	....	....
Monetary authorities	4 765 ..	45	27	12	8	44	5	....	....
of which: Use of Fund credit and loans from the Fund	4 766 ..	*45*	*27*	*12*	*8*	*44*	*5*	....	....
of which: Short-term	4 768 ..	....	....	....	....	....	....	....	....
General government	4 769 ..	102	94	247	175	268	208	....	....
of which: Short-term	4 771 ..	....	....	....	....	....	....	....	....
Banks	4 772 ..	....	....	....	....	....	....	....	....
of which: Short-term	4 774 ..	....	....	....	....	....	....	....	....
Other sectors	4 775 ..	−12	−8	−18	−13	−14	−7	....	....
of which: Short-term	4 777 ..	....	....	....	....	....	....	....	....
Currency and deposits	4 780 ..	−1	3	3	2	−3	−6	....	....
Monetary authorities	4 781 ..	−1	−1	4	−3	−1	....	....	....
General government	4 782 ..	....	....	....	....	....	....	....	....
Banks	4 783 ..	....	4	−1	4	−2	−6	....	....
Other sectors	4 784 ..	....	....	....	....	....	....	....	....
Other liabilities	4 786 ..	8	−14	....	−13	−7	−15	....	....
Monetary authorities	4 787 ..	....	1	....	1	....	....	....	....
of which: Short-term	4 789 ..	....	*1*	....	*1*	....	....	....	....
General government	4 790 ..	−8	....	3	−13	−14	−7	....	....
of which: Short-term	4 792 ..	*−8*	....	*3*	*−13*	*−14*	*−7*	....	....
Banks	4 793 ..	15	−15	−3	−1	7	−7	....	....
of which: Short-term	4 795 ..	*15*	*−15*	*−3*	*−1*	*7*	*−7*	....	....
Other sectors	4 796 ..	....	....	....	....	....	....	....	....
of which: Short-term	4 798 ..	....	....	....	....	....	....	....	....
E. RESERVE ASSETS	4 802 ..	**−30**	**18**	**14**	**−25**	**−384**	**−10**	....	....
Monetary gold	4 812 ..	....	....	....	....	....	....	....	....
Special drawing rights	4 811 ..	....	....	....	....	....	....	....	....
Reserve position in the Fund	4 810 ..	....	....	....	....	....	....	....	....
Foreign exchange	4 803 ..	−30	18	14	−25	−384	−10	....	....
Other claims	4 813 ..	....	....	....	....	....	....	....	....
NET ERRORS AND OMISSIONS	4 998 ..	**39**	**−57**	**29**	**67**	**−35**	**91**	....	....

Table 1. ANALYTIC PRESENTATION, 2000–2007

(Millions of U.S. dollars)

	Code	2000	2001	2002	2003	2004	2005	2006	2007
A. Current Account[1]	4 993 Z.	**−73.5**	**−60.0**	**−200.7**	....	....	....	....	....
Goods: exports f.o.b.	2 100 ..	403.1	427.9	422.4	....	....	....	....	....
Goods: imports f.o.b.	3 100 ..	−462.0	−472.2	−573.2	....	....	....	....	....
Balance on Goods	4 100 ..	*−58.8*	*−44.3*	*−150.8*	....	....	....	....	....
Services: credit	2 200 ..	34.3	43.6	49.4	....	....	....	....	....
Services: debit	3 200 ..	−167.1	−171.4	−221.9	....	....	....	....	....
Balance on Goods and Services	4 991 ..	*−191.7*	*−172.1*	*−323.3*	....	....	....	....	....
Income: credit	2 300 ..	33.3	12.2	6.0	....	....	....	....	....
Income: debit	3 300 ..	−50.5	−42.6	−44.5	....	....	....	....	....
Balance on Goods, Services, and Income	4 992 ..	*−209.0*	*−202.5*	*−361.8*	....	....	....	....	....
Current transfers: credit	2 379 Z.	143.1	148.8	170.0	....	....	....	....	....
Current transfers: debit	3 379 ..	−7.6	−6.2	−8.9	....	....	....	....	....
B. Capital Account[1]	4 994 Z.	....	....	....	....	....	....	....	....
Capital account: credit	2 994 Z.	....	....	....	....	....	....	....	....
Capital account: debit	3 994 ..	....	....	....	....	....	....	....	....
Total, Groups A Plus B	4 981 ..	*−73.5*	*−60.0*	*−200.7*	....	....	....	....	....
C. Financial Account[1]	4 995 W.	**188.8**	**213.4**	**134.0**	....	....	....	....	....
Direct investment abroad	4 505 ..	....	....	....	....	....	....	....	....
Direct investment in Malawi	4 555 Z.	26.0	19.3	5.9	....	....	....	....	....
Portfolio investment assets	4 602 ..	....	....	....	....	....	....	....	....
Equity securities	4 610 ..	....	....	....	....	....	....	....	....
Debt securities	4 619 ..	....	....	....	....	....	....	....	....
Portfolio investment liabilities	4 652 Z.	....	....	....	....	....	....	....	....
Equity securities	4 660 ..	....	....	....	....	....	....	....	....
Debt securities	4 669 Z.	....	....	....	....	....	....	....	....
Financial derivatives	4 910 ..	....	....	....	....	....	....	....	....
Financial derivatives assets	4 900 ..	....	....	....	....	....	....	....	....
Financial derivatives liabilities	4 905 ..	....	....	....	....	....	....	....	....
Other investment assets	4 703 ..	....	....	....	....	....	....	....	....
Monetary authorities	4 701 ..	....	....	....	....	....	....	....	....
General government	4 704 ..	....	....	....	....	....	....	....	....
Banks	4 705 ..	....	....	....	....	....	....	....	....
Other sectors	4 728 ..	....	....	....	....	....	....	....	....
Other investment liabilities	4 753 W.	162.8	194.1	128.1	....	....	....	....	....
Monetary authorities	4 753 WA	....	....	....	....	....	....	....	....
General government	4 753 ZB	107.9	139.2	73.3	....	....	....	....	....
Banks	4 753 ZC	....	....	....	....	....	....	....	....
Other sectors	4 753 ZD	54.8	54.8	54.8	....	....	....	....	....
Total, Groups A Through C	4 983 ..	*115.3*	*153.4*	*−66.7*	....	....	....	....	....
D. Net Errors and Omissions	4 998 ..	**−23.9**	**−221.5**	**156.7**	....	....	....	....	....
Total, Groups A Through D	4 984 ..	*91.4*	*−68.0*	*90.0*	....	....	....	....	....
E. Reserves and Related Items	4 802 A.	**−91.4**	**68.0**	**−90.0**	....	....	....	....	....
Reserve assets	4 802 ..	−90.6	75.0	−105.5	....	....	....	....	....
Use of Fund credit and loans	4 766 ..	−.8	−7.0	15.5	....	....	....	....	....
Exceptional financing	4 920 ..	....	....	....	....	....	....	....	....
Conversion rates: Malawi kwacha per U.S. dollar	0 101 ..	**59.544**	**72.197**	**76.687**	**97.432**	**108.898**	**118.420**	**136.014**	**139.957**

[1] Excludes components that have been classified in the categories of Group E.

Table 2. STANDARD PRESENTATION, 2000–2007

(Millions of U.S. dollars)

	Code	2000	2001	2002	2003	2004	2005	2006	2007
CURRENT ACCOUNT	4 993 ..	**−73.5**	**−60.0**	**−200.7**	....	....	....	....	....
A. GOODS	4 100 ..	**−58.8**	**−44.3**	**−150.8**	....	....	....	....	....
Credit	2 100 ..	**403.1**	**427.9**	**422.4**	....	....	....	....	....
General merchandise: exports f.o.b.	2 110 ..	401.8	426.6	421.2	....	....	....	....	....
Goods for processing: exports f.o.b.	2 150 ..	....	....	....	....	....	....	....	....
Repairs on goods	2 160 ..	....	....	....	....	....	....	....	....
Goods procured in ports by carriers	2 170 ..	1.3	1.3	1.2	....	....	....	....	....
Nonmonetary gold	2 180 ..	....	....	....	....	....	....	....	....
Debit	3 100 ..	**−462.0**	**−472.2**	**−573.2**	....	....	....	....	....
General merchandise: imports f.o.b.	3 110 ..	−460.4	−471.3	−572.5	....	....	....	....	....
Goods for processing: imports f.o.b.	3 150 ..	....	....	....	....	....	....	....	....
Repairs on goods	3 160 ..	....	....	....	....	....	....	....	....
Goods procured in ports by carriers	3 170 ..	−1.6	−1.0	−.7	....	....	....	....	....
Nonmonetary gold	3 180 ..	....	....	....	....	....	....	....	....
B. SERVICES	4 200 ..	**−132.8**	**−127.8**	**−172.5**	....	....	....	....	....
Total credit	2 200 ..	*34.3*	*43.6*	*49.4*	....	....	....	....	....
Total debit	3 200 ..	*−167.1*	*−171.4*	*−221.9*	....	....	....	....	....
Transportation services, credit	2 205 ..	**8.8**	**19.0**	**16.1**	....	....	....	....	....
Passenger	2 850 ..	*4.2*	*14.7*	*11.6*	....	....	....	....	....
Freight	2 851 ..	*2.1*	*1.3*	*1.5*	....	....	....	....	....
Other	2 852 ..	*2.5*	*3.0*	*3.0*	....	....	....	....	....
Sea transport, passenger	2 207 ..	....	....	....	....	....	....	....	....
Sea transport, freight	2 208 ..	....	....	....	....	....	....	....	....
Sea transport, other	2 209 ..	....	....	....	....	....	....	....	....
Air transport, passenger	2 211 ..	4.2	14.7	11.6	....	....	....	....	....
Air transport, freight	2 212 ..	2.1	1.3	1.5	....	....	....	....	....
Air transport, other	2 213 ..	2.5	3.0	3.0	....	....	....	....	....
Other transport, passenger	2 215 ..	....	....	....	....	....	....	....	....
Other transport, freight	2 216 ..	....	....	....	....	....	....	....	....
Other transport, other	2 217 ..	....	....	....	....	....	....	....	....
Transportation services, debit	3 205 ..	**−88.2**	**−98.4**	**−111.2**	....	....	....	....	....
Passenger	3 850 ..	*−3.4*	*−12.0*	*−7.9*	....	....	....	....	....
Freight	3 851 ..	*−81.2*	*−83.2*	*−101.0*	....	....	....	....	....
Other	3 852 ..	*−3.5*	*−3.2*	*−2.3*	....	....	....	....	....
Sea transport, passenger	3 207 ..	....	....	....	....	....	....	....	....
Sea transport, freight	3 208 ..	....	....	....	....	....	....	....	....
Sea transport, other	3 209 ..	....	....	....	....	....	....	....	....
Air transport, passenger	3 211 ..	−3.4	−12.0	−7.9	....	....	....	....	....
Air transport, freight	3 212 ..	−81.2	−83.2	−101.0	....	....	....	....	....
Air transport, other	3 213 ..	−3.5	−3.2	−2.3	....	....	....	....	....
Other transport, passenger	3 215 ..	....	....	....	....	....	....	....	....
Other transport, freight	3 216 ..	....	....	....	....	....	....	....	....
Other transport, other	3 217 ..	....	....	....	....	....	....	....	....
Travel, credit	2 236 ..	**25.5**	**24.6**	**33.3**	....	....	....	....	....
Business travel	2 237 ..	....	....	....	....	....	....	....	....
Personal travel	2 240 ..	25.5	24.6	33.3	....	....	....	....	....
Travel, debit	3 236 ..	**−49.9**	**−40.5**	**−78.0**	....	....	....	....	....
Business travel	3 237 ..	−46.0	−37.1	−73.6	....	....	....	....	....
Personal travel	3 240 ..	−3.9	−3.3	−4.4	....	....	....	....	....
Other services, credit	2 200 BA	....	....	....	....	....	....	....	....
Communications	2 245 ..	....	....	....	....	....	....	....	....
Construction	2 249 ..	....	....	....	....	....	....	....	....
Insurance	2 253 ..	....	....	....	....	....	....	....	....
Financial	2 260 ..	....	....	....	....	....	....	....	....
Computer and information	2 262 ..	....	....	....	....	....	....	....	....
Royalties and licence fees	2 266 ..	....	....	....	....	....	....	....	....
Other business services	2 268 ..	....	....	....	....	....	....	....	....
Personal, cultural, and recreational	2 287 ..	....	....	....	....	....	....	....	....
Government, n.i.e.	2 291 ..	....	....	....	....	....	....	....	....
Other services, debit	3 200 BA	**−29.1**	**−32.6**	**−32.7**	....	....	....	....	....
Communications	3 245 ..	....	....	....	....	....	....	....	....
Construction	3 249 ..	....	....	....	....	....	....	....	....
Insurance	3 253 ..	−.4	−.1	....	....	....	....	....	....
Financial	3 260 ..	....	....	....	....	....	....	....	....
Computer and information	3 262 ..	....	....	....	....	....	....	....	....
Royalties and licence fees	3 266 ..	−.2	−.5	−.2	....	....	....	....	....
Other business services	3 268 ..	−22.5	−26.6	−23.4	....	....	....	....	....
Personal, cultural, and recreational	3 287 ..	−5.9	−5.4	−9.1	....	....	....	....	....
Government, n.i.e.	3 291 ..	....	....	....	....	....	....	....	....

Table 2 (Continued). STANDARD PRESENTATION, 2000–2007

(Millions of U.S. dollars)

	Code	2000	2001	2002	2003	2004	2005	2006	2007
C. INCOME	4 300	**−17.3**	**−30.4**	**−38.5**	....	....	....	....	....
Total credit	2 300	*33.3*	*12.2*	*6.0*	....	....	....	....	....
Total debit	3 300	*−50.5*	*−42.6*	*−44.5*	....	....	....	....	....
Compensation of employees, credit	2 310	....	....	....	....	....	....	....	....
Compensation of employees, debit	3 310	....	....	....	....	....	....	....	....
Investment income, credit	2 320	**33.3**	**12.2**	**6.0**	....	....	....	....	....
Direct investment income	2 330	....	....	....	....	....	....	....	....
Dividends and distributed branch profits	2 332	....	....	....	....	....	....	....	....
Reinvested earnings and undistributed branch profits	2 333	....	....	....	....	....	....	....	....
Income on debt (interest)	2 334	....	....	....	....	....	....	....	....
Portfolio investment income	2 339	....	....	....	....	....	....	....	....
Income on equity	2 340	....	....	....	....	....	....	....	....
Income on bonds and notes	2 350	....	....	....	....	....	....	....	....
Income on money market instruments	2 360	....	....	....	....	....	....	....	....
Other investment income	2 370	33.3	12.2	6.0	....	....	....	....	....
Investment income, debit	3 320	**−50.5**	**−42.6**	**−44.5**	....	....	....	....	....
Direct investment income	3 330	−15.1	−14.4	−22.5	....	....	....	....	....
Dividends and distributed branch profits	3 332	−15.1	−14.4	−22.5	....	....	....	....	....
Reinvested earnings and undistributed branch profits	3 333	....	....	....	....	....	....	....	....
Income on debt (interest)	3 334	....	....	....	....	....	....	....	....
Portfolio investment income	3 339	....	−.1	−.1	....	....	....	....	....
Income on equity	3 340	....	....	....	....	....	....	....	....
Income on bonds and notes	3 350	....	−.1	−.1	....	....	....	....	....
Income on money market instruments	3 360	....	....	....	....	....	....	....	....
Other investment income	3 370	−35.4	−28.0	−22.0	....	....	....	....	....
D. CURRENT TRANSFERS	4 379	**135.5**	**142.5**	**161.1**	....	....	....	....	....
Credit	2 379	**143.1**	**148.8**	**170.0**	....	....	....	....	....
General government	2 380	121.3	127.0	142.3	....	....	....	....	....
Other sectors	2 390	21.8	21.8	27.7	....	....	....	....	....
Workers' remittances	2 391	.7	.7	.8	....	....	....	....	....
Other current transfers	2 392	21.0	21.0	26.9	....	....	....	....	....
Debit	3 379	**−7.6**	**−6.2**	**−8.9**	....	....	....	....	....
General government	3 380	−.7	−.2	−1.7	....	....	....	....	....
Other sectors	3 390	−6.9	−6.0	−7.2	....	....	....	....	....
Workers' remittances	3 391	−.4	−.6	−.4	....	....	....	....	....
Other current transfers	3 392	−6.5	−5.4	−6.7	....	....	....	....	....
CAPITAL AND FINANCIAL ACCOUNT	4 996	**97.4**	**281.4**	**44.0**	....	....	....	....	....
CAPITAL ACCOUNT	4 994	....	....	....	....	....	....	....	....
Total credit	2 994	....	....	....	....	....	....	....	....
Total debit	3 994	....	....	....	....	....	....	....	....
Capital transfers, credit	2 400	....	....	....	....	....	....	....	....
General government	2 401	....	....	....	....	....	....	....	....
Debt forgiveness	2 402	....	....	....	....	....	....	....	....
Other capital transfers	2 410	....	....	....	....	....	....	....	....
Other sectors	2 430	....	....	....	....	....	....	....	....
Migrants' transfers	2 431	....	....	....	....	....	....	....	....
Debt forgiveness	2 432	....	....	....	....	....	....	....	....
Other capital transfers	2 440	....	....	....	....	....	....	....	....
Capital transfers, debit	3 400	....	....	....	....	....	....	....	....
General government	3 401	....	....	....	....	....	....	....	....
Debt forgiveness	3 402	....	....	....	....	....	....	....	....
Other capital transfers	3 410	....	....	....	....	....	....	....	....
Other sectors	3 430	....	....	....	....	....	....	....	....
Migrants' transfers	3 431	....	....	....	....	....	....	....	....
Debt forgiveness	3 432	....	....	....	....	....	....	....	....
Other capital transfers	3 440	....	....	....	....	....	....	....	....
Nonproduced nonfinancial assets, credit	2 480	....	....	....	....	....	....	....	....
Nonproduced nonfinancial assets, debit	3 480	....	....	....	....	....	....	....	....

Table 2 (Continued). STANDARD PRESENTATION, 2000–2007

(Millions of U.S. dollars)

	Code	2000	2001	2002	2003	2004	2005	2006	2007
FINANCIAL ACCOUNT..............................	4 995 ..	**97.4**	**281.4**	**44.0**	....	....	....	....	....
A. DIRECT INVESTMENT...........................	4 500 ..	**26.0**	**19.3**	**5.9**	....	....	....	....	....
Direct investment abroad....................	4 505 ..	....	....	....	....	....	....	....	....
Equity capital...............................	4 510 ..	....	....	....	....	....	....	....	....
Claims on affiliated enterprises.................	4 515 ..	....	....	....	....	....	....	....	....
Liabilities to affiliated enterprises.............	4 520 ..	....	....	....	....	....	....	....	....
Reinvested earnings........................	4 525 ..	....	....	....	....	....	....	....	....
Other capital..............................	4 530 ..	....	....	....	....	....	....	....	....
Claims on affiliated enterprises.................	4 535 ..	....	....	....	....	....	....	....	....
Liabilities to affiliated enterprises.............	4 540 ..	....	....	....	....	....	....	....	....
Direct investment in Malawi..............	4 555 ..	**26.0**	**19.3**	**5.9**	....	....	....	....	....
Equity capital...............................	4 560 ..	26.0	19.3	5.9	....	....	....	....	....
Claims on direct investors..................	4 565 ..	....	....	....	....	....	....	....	....
Liabilities to direct investors...............	4 570 ..	26.0	19.3	5.9	....	....	....	....	....
Reinvested earnings........................	4 575 ..	....	....	....	....	....	....	....	....
Other capital..............................	4 580 ..	....	....	....	....	....	....	....	....
Claims on direct investors..................	4 585 ..	....	....	....	....	....	....	....	....
Liabilities to direct investors...............	4 590 ..	....	....	....	....	....	....	....	....
B. PORTFOLIO INVESTMENT...................	4 600 ..	....	....	....	....	....	....	....	....
Assets...	4 602 ..	....	....	....	....	....	....	....	....
Equity securities..........................	4 610 ..	....	....	....	....	....	....	....	....
Monetary authorities.......................	4 611 ..	....	....	....	....	....	....	....	....
General government.......................	4 612 ..	....	....	....	....	....	....	....	....
Banks....................................	4 613 ..	....	....	....	....	....	....	....	....
Other sectors.............................	4 614 ..	....	....	....	....	....	....	....	....
Debt securities............................	4 619 ..	....	....	....	....	....	....	....	....
Bonds and notes..........................	4 620 ..	....	....	....	....	....	....	....	....
Monetary authorities.....................	4 621 ..	....	....	....	....	....	....	....	....
General government.....................	4 622 ..	....	....	....	....	....	....	....	....
Banks..................................	4 623 ..	....	....	....	....	....	....	....	....
Other sectors...........................	4 624 ..	....	....	....	....	....	....	....	....
Money market instruments..................	4 630 ..	....	....	....	....	....	....	....	....
Monetary authorities.....................	4 631 ..	....	....	....	....	....	....	....	....
General government.....................	4 632 ..	....	....	....	....	....	....	....	....
Banks..................................	4 633 ..	....	....	....	....	....	....	....	....
Other sectors...........................	4 634 ..	....	....	....	....	....	....	....	....
Liabilities...................................	4 652 ..	....	....	....	....	....	....	....	....
Equity securities..........................	4 660 ..	....	....	....	....	....	....	....	....
Banks....................................	4 663 ..	....	....	....	....	....	....	....	....
Other sectors.............................	4 664 ..	....	....	....	....	....	....	....	....
Debt securities............................	4 669 ..	....	....	....	....	....	....	....	....
Bonds and notes..........................	4 670 ..	....	....	....	....	....	....	....	....
Monetary authorities.....................	4 671 ..	....	....	....	....	....	....	....	....
General government.....................	4 672 ..	....	....	....	....	....	....	....	....
Banks..................................	4 673 ..	....	....	....	....	....	....	....	....
Other sectors...........................	4 674 ..	....	....	....	....	....	....	....	....
Money market instruments..................	4 680 ..	....	....	....	....	....	....	....	....
Monetary authorities.....................	4 681 ..	....	....	....	....	....	....	....	....
General government.....................	4 682 ..	....	....	....	....	....	....	....	....
Banks..................................	4 683 ..	....	....	....	....	....	....	....	....
Other sectors...........................	4 684 ..	....	....	....	....	....	....	....	....
C. FINANCIAL DERIVATIVES...................	4 910 ..	....	....	....	....	....	....	....	....
Monetary authorities.......................	4 911 ..	....	....	....	....	....	....	....	....
General government.......................	4 912 ..	....	....	....	....	....	....	....	....
Banks....................................	4 913 ..	....	....	....	....	....	....	....	....
Other sectors.............................	4 914 ..	....	....	....	....	....	....	....	....
Assets...	4 900 ..	....	....	....	....	....	....	....	....
Monetary authorities.......................	4 901 ..	....	....	....	....	....	....	....	....
General government.......................	4 902 ..	....	....	....	....	....	....	....	....
Banks....................................	4 903 ..	....	....	....	....	....	....	....	....
Other sectors.............................	4 904 ..	....	....	....	....	....	....	....	....
Liabilities...................................	4 905 ..	....	....	....	....	....	....	....	....
Monetary authorities.......................	4 906 ..	....	....	....	....	....	....	....	....
General government.......................	4 907 ..	....	....	....	....	....	....	....	....
Banks....................................	4 908 ..	....	....	....	....	....	....	....	....
Other sectors.............................	4 909 ..	....	....	....	....	....	....	....	....

Table 2 (Concluded). STANDARD PRESENTATION, 2000–2007

(Millions of U.S. dollars)

	Code	2000	2001	2002	2003	2004	2005	2006	2007
D. OTHER INVESTMENT	4 700 ..	**162.0**	**187.1**	**143.6**	....	....	....	....	....
Assets	4 703 ..	....	....	....	....	....	....	....	....
Trade credits	4 706 ..	....	....	....	....	....	....	....	....
General government	4 707 ..	....	....	....	....	....	....	....	....
of which: Short-term	4 709 ..	....	....	....	....	....	....	....	....
Other sectors	4 710 ..	....	....	....	....	....	....	....	....
of which: Short-term	4 712 ..	....	....	....	....	....	....	....	....
Loans	4 714 ..	....	....	....	....	....	....	....	....
Monetary authorities	4 715 ..	....	....	....	....	....	....	....	....
of which: Short-term	4 718 ..	....	....	....	....	....	....	....	....
General government	4 719 ..	....	....	....	....	....	....	....	....
of which: Short-term	4 721 ..	....	....	....	....	....	....	....	....
Banks	4 722 ..	....	....	....	....	....	....	....	....
of which: Short-term	4 724 ..	....	....	....	....	....	....	....	....
Other sectors	4 725 ..	....	....	....	....	....	....	....	....
of which: Short-term	4 727 ..	....	....	....	....	....	....	....	....
Currency and deposits	4 730 ..	....	....	....	....	....	....	....	....
Monetary authorities	4 731 ..	....	....	....	....	....	....	....	....
General government	4 732 ..	....	....	....	....	....	....	....	....
Banks	4 733 ..	....	....	....	....	....	....	....	....
Other sectors	4 734 ..	....	....	....	....	....	....	....	....
Other assets	4 736 ..	....	....	....	....	....	....	....	....
Monetary authorities	4 737 ..	....	....	....	....	....	....	....	....
of which: Short-term	4 739 ..	....	....	....	....	....	....	....	....
General government	4 740 ..	....	....	....	....	....	....	....	....
of which: Short-term	4 742 ..	....	....	....	....	....	....	....	....
Banks	4 743 ..	....	....	....	....	....	....	....	....
of which: Short-term	4 745 ..	....	....	....	....	....	....	....	....
Other sectors	4 746 ..	....	....	....	....	....	....	....	....
of which: Short-term	4 748 ..	....	....	....	....	....	....	....	....
Liabilities	4 753 ..	**162.0**	**187.1**	**143.6**	....	....	....	....	....
Trade credits	4 756 ..	....	....	....	....	....	....	....	....
General government	4 757 ..	....	....	....	....	....	....	....	....
of which: Short-term	4 759 ..	....	....	....	....	....	....	....	....
Other sectors	4 760 ..	....	....	....	....	....	....	....	....
of which: Short-term	4 762 ..	....	....	....	....	....	....	....	....
Loans	4 764 ..	162.0	187.1	143.6	....	....	....	....	....
Monetary authorities	4 765 ..	−.8	−7.0	15.5	....	....	....	....	....
of which: Use of Fund credit and loans from the Fund	4 766 ..	−.8	−7.0	15.5	....	....	....	....	....
of which: Short-term	4 768 ..	....	....	....	....	....	....	....	....
General government	4 769 ..	107.9	139.2	73.3	....	....	....	....	....
of which: Short-term	4 771 ..	....	....	....	....	....	....	....	....
Banks	4 772 ..	....	....	....	....	....	....	....	....
of which: Short-term	4 774 ..	....	....	....	....	....	....	....	....
Other sectors	4 775 ..	54.8	54.8	54.8	....	....	....	....	....
of which: Short-term	4 777 ..	51.2	51.2	51.2	....	....	....	....	....
Currency and deposits	4 780 ..	....	....	....	....	....	....	....	....
Monetary authorities	4 781 ..	....	....	....	....	....	....	....	....
General government	4 782 ..	....	....	....	....	....	....	....	....
Banks	4 783 ..	....	....	....	....	....	....	....	....
Other sectors	4 784 ..	....	....	....	....	....	....	....	....
Other liabilities	4 786 ..	....	....	....	....	....	....	....	....
Monetary authorities	4 787 ..	....	....	....	....	....	....	....	....
of which: Short-term	4 789 ..	....	....	....	....	....	....	....	....
General government	4 790 ..	....	....	....	....	....	....	....	....
of which: Short-term	4 792 ..	....	....	....	....	....	....	....	....
Banks	4 793 ..	....	....	....	....	....	....	....	....
of which: Short-term	4 795 ..	....	....	....	....	....	....	....	....
Other sectors	4 796 ..	....	....	....	....	....	....	....	....
of which: Short-term	4 798 ..	....	....	....	....	....	....	....	....
E. RESERVE ASSETS	4 802 ..	**−90.6**	**75.0**	**−105.5**	....	....	....	....	....
Monetary gold	4 812 ..	....	....	....	....	....	....	....	....
Special drawing rights	4 811 ..	−.2	−.4	.8	....	....	....	....	....
Reserve position in the Fund	4 810 ..	....	....	....	....	....	....	....	....
Foreign exchange	4 803 ..	−90.4	75.4	−106.2	....	....	....	....	....
Other claims	4 813 ..	....	....	....	....	....	....	....	....
NET ERRORS AND OMISSIONS	4 998 ..	**−23.9**	**−221.5**	**156.7**	....	....	....	....	....

Table 1. ANALYTIC PRESENTATION, 2000–2007

(Millions of U.S. dollars)

	Code	2000	2001	2002	2003	2004	2005	2006	2007
A. Current Account[1]...................................	4 993 Z.	**8,488**	**7,287**	**7,190**	**13,381**	**15,079**	**19,980**	**25,488**	**28,931**
Goods: exports f.o.b........................	2 100 ..	98,429	87,981	93,383	104,999	126,817	141,808	160,842	176,403
Goods: imports f.o.b........................	3 100 ..	−77,602	−69,597	−75,248	−79,289	−99,244	−108,653	−124,144	−139,075
Balance on Goods..........................	4 100 ..	*20,827*	*18,383*	*18,135*	*25,711*	*27,572*	*33,156*	*36,698*	*37,328*
Services: credit..............................	2 200 ..	13,941	14,455	14,878	13,577	17,111	19,576	21,831	28,272
Services: debit...............................	3 200 ..	−16,747	−16,657	−16,448	−17,532	−19,269	−21,956	−23,720	−27,986
Balance on Goods and Services..............	4 991 ..	*18,020*	*16,182*	*16,565*	*21,757*	*25,415*	*30,776*	*34,809*	*37,613*
Income: credit..............................	2 300 ..	1,986	1,847	2,139	3,448	4,329	5,373	8,463	11,302
Income: debit...............................	3 300 ..	−9,594	−8,590	−8,734	−9,376	−10,751	−11,691	−13,192	−15,297
Balance on Goods, Services, and Income.........	4 992 ..	*10,412*	*9,439*	*9,970*	*15,829*	*18,993*	*24,457*	*30,080*	*33,618*
Current transfers: credit...................	2 379 Z.	756	537	661	508	422	299	313	342
Current transfers: debit....................	3 379 ..	−2,680	−2,689	−3,442	−2,955	−4,335	−4,776	−4,904	−5,029
B. Capital Account[1]...................................	4 994 Z.	....	....	....	....	....	....	....	**−28**
Capital account: credit....................	2 994 Z.	....	....	....	....	....	....	....	15
Capital account: debit.....................	3 994 ..	....	....	....	....	....	....	....	−42
Total, Groups A Plus B........................	4 981 ..	*8,488*	*7,287*	*7,190*	*13,381*	*15,079*	*19,980*	*25,488*	*28,904*
C. Financial Account[1]................................	4 995 W.	**−6,276**	**−3,892**	**−3,142**	**−3,196**	**5,091**	**−9,806**	**−11,894**	**−10,850**
Direct investment abroad....................	4 505 ..	−2,026	−267	−1,905	−1,369	−2,061	−2,972	−6,043	−11,042
Direct investment in Malaysia..............	4 555 Z.	3,788	554	3,203	2,473	4,624	3,966	6,064	8,456
Portfolio investment assets................	4 602 ..	−387	254	−563	−196	−287	−715	−2,123	−3,940
Equity securities..........................	4 610 ..	....	....	−43	−18	23	7	−1,890	−4,093
Debt securities............................	4 619 ..	....	....	−520	−178	−309	−722	−234	153
Portfolio investment liabilities............	4 652 Z.	−2,145	−666	−836	1,174	8,675	−2,985	5,593	9,320
Equity securities..........................	4 660 ..	....	....	−55	1,339	4,509	−1,200	2,392	−669
Debt securities............................	4 669 Z.	....	....	−781	−165	4,166	−1,786	3,202	9,989
Financial derivatives.......................	4 910 ..	60	−237	−313	119	294	−58	29	−48
Financial derivatives assets................	4 900 ..	279	−234	−174	−24	−1,520	−59	8	198
Financial derivatives liabilities............	4 905 ..	−220	−3	−139	142	1,814	1	21	−246
Other investment assets....................	4 703 ..	−5,565	−2,702	−4,597	−4,502	−10,756	−4,877	−8,531	−17,209
Monetary authorities.......................	4 701 ..	....	....	....	....	....	....	....	....
General government........................	4 704 ..	....	....	−3	5	....	8	−1	−4
Banks.....................................	4 705 ..	....	....	−96	904	−4,698	1,579	−4,291	−12,850
Other sectors..............................	4 728 ..	....	....	−4,497	−5,411	−6,058	−6,464	−4,239	−4,355
Other investment liabilities................	4 753 W.	....	−829	1,868	−895	4,602	−2,164	−6,883	3,614
Monetary authorities.......................	4 753 WA	....	....	....	−62	....	....	....	....
General government........................	4 753 ZB	....	....	1,245	−2,891	633	−841	−2,194	−653
Banks.....................................	4 753 ZC	....	....	862	1,715	1,684	−134	−3,613	6,370
Other sectors..............................	4 753 ZD	....	....	−239	343	2,284	−1,188	−1,076	−2,104
Total, Groups A Through C....................	4 983 ..	*2,212*	*3,394*	*4,047*	*10,185*	*20,170*	*10,174*	*13,595*	*18,054*
D. Net Errors and Omissions...................	4 998 ..	**−3,221**	**−2,394**	**−391**	**−4**	**1,880**	**−6,555**	**−6,731**	**−4,910**
Total, Groups A Through D....................	4 984 ..	*−1,009*	*1,000*	*3,657*	*10,181*	*22,050*	*3,620*	*6,864*	*13,144*
E. Reserves and Related Items...............	4 802 A.	**1,009**	**−1,000**	**−3,657**	**−10,181**	**−22,050**	**−3,620**	**−6,864**	**−13,144**
Reserve assets..............................	4 802 ..	1,009	−1,000	−3,657	−10,181	−22,050	−3,620	−6,864	−13,144
Use of Fund credit and loans...............	4 766 ..	....	....	....	....	....	....	....	....
Exceptional financing......................	4 920 ..	....	....	....	....	....	....	....	....
Conversion rates: ringgit per U.S. dollar...............	0 101 ..	**3.800**	**3.800**	**3.800**	**3.800**	**3.800**	**3.787**	**3.668**	**3.438**

[1] Excludes components that have been classified in the categories of Group E.

Table 2. STANDARD PRESENTATION, 2000–2007

(Millions of U.S. dollars)

	Code	2000	2001	2002	2003	2004	2005	2006	2007
CURRENT ACCOUNT	4 993	8,488	7,287	7,190	13,381	15,079	19,980	25,488	28,931
A. GOODS	4 100	20,827	18,383	18,135	25,711	27,572	33,156	36,698	37,328
Credit	2 100	98,429	87,981	93,383	104,999	126,817	141,808	160,842	176,403
General merchandise: exports f.o.b.	2 110	98,092	87,690	93,072	104,563	126,134	141,068	159,581	175,599
Goods for processing: exports f.o.b.	2 150	93	77	29	14	29	34	38	51
Repairs on goods	2 160	....	....	38	56	199	172	217	193
Goods procured in ports by carriers	2 170	128	128	119	141	207	275	648	308
Nonmonetary gold	2 180	116	86	125	226	248	260	358	252
Debit	3 100	−77,602	−69,597	−75,248	−79,289	−99,244	−108,653	−124,144	−139,075
General merchandise: imports f.o.b.	3 110	−76,222	−68,270	−74,175	−78,175	−97,758	−106,645	−121,926	−136,255
Goods for processing: imports f.o.b.	3 150	−83	−73	−27	−7	−27	−31	−31	−47
Repairs on goods	3 160	....	....	....	....	....	....	....	....
Goods procured in ports by carriers	3 170	−351	−349	−232	−250	−470	−816	−894	−1,010
Nonmonetary gold	3 180	−947	−906	−814	−857	−989	−1,161	−1,294	−1,763
B. SERVICES	4 200	−2,807	−2,202	−1,570	−3,954	−2,158	−2,380	−1,889	285
Total credit	2 200	*13,941*	*14,455*	*14,878*	*13,577*	*17,111*	*19,576*	*21,831*	*28,272*
Total debit	3 200	*−16,747*	*−16,657*	*−16,448*	*−17,532*	*−19,269*	*−21,956*	*−23,720*	*−27,986*
Transportation services, credit	2 205	2,802	2,748	2,855	2,767	3,196	4,056	4,228	7,037
Passenger	2 850	*862*	*764*	*966*	*898*	*980*	*1,543*	*1,928*	*3,893*
Freight	2 851	*1,489*	*1,546*	*1,436*	*1,406*	*1,756*	*2,011*	*1,732*	*2,346*
Other	2 852	*452*	*439*	*452*	*463*	*461*	*501*	*568*	*799*
Sea transport, passenger	2 207	....	....	....	....	....	....	....	1
Sea transport, freight	2 208	1,276	1,391	1,273	1,203	1,455	1,731	1,465	1,750
Sea transport, other	2 209	357	344	384	382	376	404	461	696
Air transport, passenger	2 211	862	764	966	898	980	1,543	1,928	3,889
Air transport, freight	2 212	213	155	163	203	301	280	267	596
Air transport, other	2 213	94	95	69	81	85	97	107	103
Other transport, passenger	2 215	....	....	....	....	....	....	....	3
Other transport, freight	2 216	....	....	....	....	....	....	....	....
Other transport, other	2 217	....	....	....	....	....	....	....	....
Transportation services, debit	3 205	−5,890	−5,736	−5,892	−6,260	−7,814	−8,396	−9,577	−10,975
Passenger	3 850	*−468*	*−777*	*−712*	*−555*	*−644*	*−628*	*−827*	*−993*
Freight	3 851	*−4,957*	*−4,472*	*−4,783*	*−5,029*	*−6,301*	*−6,938*	*−7,935*	*−8,880*
Other	3 852	*−465*	*−486*	*−397*	*−675*	*−868*	*−830*	*−815*	*−1,103*
Sea transport, passenger	3 207	....	....	....	....	....	....	....	....
Sea transport, freight	3 208	−4,957	−4,472	−4,783	−5,029	−6,301	−6,938	−7,935	−8,880
Sea transport, other	3 209	−170	−226	−147	−435	−515	−513	−493	−607
Air transport, passenger	3 211	−468	−777	−712	−555	−644	−628	−827	−993
Air transport, freight	3 212	....	....	....	....	....	....	....	....
Air transport, other	3 213	−295	−261	−249	−241	−353	−316	−321	−496
Other transport, passenger	3 215	....	....	....	....	....	....	....	....
Other transport, freight	3 216	....	....	....	....	....	....	....	....
Other transport, other	3 217	....	....	....	....	....	....	....	....
Travel, credit	2 236	5,011	6,863	7,118	5,901	8,203	8,846	10,427	12,905
Business travel	2 237	....	....	7,050	5,820	8,082	8,738	10,247	12,671
Personal travel	2 240	5,011	6,863	68	80	121	108	180	234
Travel, debit	3 236	−2,075	−2,614	−2,618	−2,846	−3,178	−3,711	−4,020	−5,252
Business travel	3 237	....	....	−1,930	−2,150	−2,323	−2,771	−2,894	−3,897
Personal travel	3 240	−2,075	−2,614	−688	−697	−855	−940	−1,126	−1,355
Other services, credit	2 200 BA	6,127	4,843	4,905	4,910	5,712	6,674	7,177	8,329
Communications	2 245	181	242	235	201	395	615	641	599
Construction	2 249	314	338	427	262	453	811	1,041	1,378
Insurance	2 253	156	265	156	223	280	278	292	370
Financial	2 260	160	110	51	109	97	60	71	90
Computer and information	2 262	82	176	182	216	348	435	572	775
Royalties and licence fees	2 266	18	21	12	20	42	27	26	36
Other business services	2 268	5,055	3,537	2,153	1,924	2,315	2,773	3,559	4,180
Personal, cultural, and recreational	2 287	33	29	1,566	1,835	1,670	1,562	864	812
Government, n.i.e.	2 291	129	124	125	119	112	113	109	87
Other services, debit	3 200 BA	−8,783	−8,307	−7,939	−8,426	−8,277	−9,849	−10,123	−11,759
Communications	3 245	−231	−285	−232	−252	−503	−680	−653	−846
Construction	3 249	−1,091	−757	−476	−410	−518	−1,087	−1,314	−1,699
Insurance	3 253	−289	−340	−434	−480	−494	−518	−612	−681
Financial	3 260	−175	−197	−102	−117	−121	−119	−122	−221
Computer and information	3 262	−201	−215	−172	−197	−325	−379	−518	−650
Royalties and licence fees	3 266	−546	−751	−628	−782	−896	−1,370	−1,052	−1,195
Other business services	3 268	−6,035	−5,539	−2,906	−3,057	−3,219	−3,636	−4,196	−4,735
Personal, cultural, and recreational	3 287	−70	−106	−2,790	−2,922	−1,899	−1,855	−1,428	−1,530
Government, n.i.e.	3 291	−145	−118	−200	−209	−302	−205	−227	−202

Table 2 (Continued). STANDARD PRESENTATION, 2000–2007

(Millions of U.S. dollars)

	Code	2000	2001	2002	2003	2004	2005	2006	2007
C. INCOME	4 300	**−7,608**	**−6,743**	**−6,595**	**−5,928**	**−6,422**	**−6,318**	**−4,729**	**−3,995**
Total credit	2 300	*1,986*	*1,847*	*2,139*	*3,448*	*4,329*	*5,373*	*8,463*	*11,302*
Total debit	3 300	*−9,594*	*−8,590*	*−8,734*	*−9,376*	*−10,751*	*−11,691*	*−13,192*	*−15,297*
Compensation of employees, credit	2 310	**342**	**367**	**435**	**571**	**802**	**1,117**	**1,364**	**1,556**
Compensation of employees, debit	3 310	**−599**	**−634**	**−745**	**−821**	**−1,064**	**−1,244**	**−1,442**	**−1,711**
Investment income, credit	2 320	**1,644**	**1,480**	**1,704**	**2,877**	**3,527**	**4,256**	**7,098**	**9,745**
Direct investment income	2 330	−222	−65	177	517	1,126	1,087	3,247	4,289
Dividends and distributed branch profits	2 332	....	62	....	....	....	....	....	....
Reinvested earnings and undistributed branch profits	2 333	....	−147						
Income on debt (interest)	2 334	....	20	57	128	78	118	303	490
Portfolio investment income	2 339	78	60	42	89	103	100	175	165
Income on equity	2 340	....	29	17	50	76	43	105	100
Income on bonds and notes	2 350	....	4	4	6	9	26	19	32
Income on money market instruments	2 360	....	27	21	33	17	31	51	33
Other investment income	2 370	1,788	1,485	1,486	2,271	2,299	3,068	3,676	5,292
Investment income, debit	3 320	**−8,995**	**−7,956**	**−7,989**	**−8,555**	**−9,687**	**−10,446**	**−11,750**	**−13,586**
Direct investment income	3 330	−7,173	−5,933	−6,121	−6,735	−7,757	−8,330	−8,924	−9,831
Dividends and distributed branch profits	3 332	....	−3,363	....	....	....	....	....	....
Reinvested earnings and undistributed branch profits	3 333	....	−2,491	....	....	....	....	....	....
Income on debt (interest)	3 334	....	−78	−117	−70	−104	−89	−85	−57
Portfolio investment income	3 339	−262	−126	−134	−196	−380	−528	−1,002	−1,847
Income on equity	3 340	....	−88	−103	−183	−322	−396	−635	−1,533
Income on bonds and notes	3 350	....	−37	−25	−11	−58	−132	−367	−314
Income on money market instruments	3 360	....	−2	−5	−1	....	....	....	....
Other investment income	3 370	−1,561	−1,896	−1,735	−1,624	−1,551	−1,589	−1,824	−1,907
D. CURRENT TRANSFERS	4 379	**−1,924**	**−2,152**	**−2,781**	**−2,447**	**−3,914**	**−4,477**	**−4,591**	**−4,687**
Credit	2 379	**756**	**537**	**661**	**508**	**422**	**299**	**313**	**342**
General government	2 380	117	112	137	92	120	134	127	96
Other sectors	2 390	639	425	524	416	302	164	186	247
Workers' remittances	2 391	....	....	....	....	....	....	....	....
Other current transfers	2 392	639	425	524	416	302	164	186	247
Debit	3 379	**−2,680**	**−2,689**	**−3,442**	**−2,955**	**−4,335**	**−4,776**	**−4,904**	**−5,029**
General government	3 380	−39	−42	−50	−46	−63	−152	−101	−89
Other sectors	3 390	−2,642	−2,647	−3,392	−2,909	−4,272	−4,624	−4,803	−4,940
Workers' remittances	3 391	....	....	−3,081	−2,643	−4,001	−4,435	−4,118	−4,644
Other current transfers	3 392	−2,642	−2,647	−311	−267	−271	−189	−685	−296
CAPITAL AND FINANCIAL ACCOUNT	4 996	**−5,267**	**−4,893**	**−6,799**	**−13,377**	**−16,959**	**−13,425**	**−18,758**	**−24,021**
CAPITAL ACCOUNT	4 994	....	....	....	....	....	....	....	**−28**
Total credit	2 994	....	....	....	....	....	....	....	*15*
Total debit	3 994	....	....	....	....	....	....	....	*−42*
Capital transfers, credit	2 400	....	....	....	....	....	....	....	**14**
General government	2 401	....	....	....	....	....	....	....	....
Debt forgiveness	2 402	....	....	....	....	....	....	....	....
Other capital transfers	2 410	....	....	....	....	....	....	....	....
Other sectors	2 430	....	....	....	....	....	....	....	14
Migrants' transfers	2 431	....	....	....	....	....	....	....	7
Debt forgiveness	2 432	....	....	....	....	....	....	....	1
Other capital transfers	2 440	....	....	....	....	....	....	....	5
Capital transfers, debit	3 400	....	....	....	....	....	....	....	**−35**
General government	3 401	....	....	....	....	....	....	....	−1
Debt forgiveness	3 402	....	....	....	....	....	....	....	....
Other capital transfers	3 410	....	....	....	....	....	....	....	−1
Other sectors	3 430	....	....	....	....	....	....	....	−34
Migrants' transfers	3 431	....	....	....	....	....	....	....	−29
Debt forgiveness	3 432	....	....	....	....	....	....	....	....
Other capital transfers	3 440	....	....	....	....	....	....	....	−5
Nonproduced nonfinancial assets, credit	2 480	....	....	....	....	....	....	....	**1**
Nonproduced nonfinancial assets, debit	3 480	....	....	....	....	....	....	....	**−8**

Table 2 (Continued). STANDARD PRESENTATION, 2000–2007

(Millions of U.S. dollars)

	Code	2000	2001	2002	2003	2004	2005	2006	2007
FINANCIAL ACCOUNT	4 995 ..	−5,267	−4,893	−6,799	−13,377	−16,959	−13,425	−18,758	−23,993
A. DIRECT INVESTMENT	4 500 ..	1,762	287	1,299	1,104	2,563	994	20	−2,587
Direct investment abroad	4 505 ..	−2,026	−267	−1,905	−1,369	−2,061	−2,972	−6,043	−11,042
Equity capital	4 510 ..	....	−29	−1,113	−1,089	−957	−1,867	−4,605	−9,165
Claims on affiliated enterprises	4 515 ..	....	....	−1,113	−1,089	−957	−1,867	−4,605	−9,165
Liabilities to affiliated enterprises	4 520 ..	....	....	−1	....	....	....	....	....
Reinvested earnings	4 525 ..	....	147	....	....	....	....	....	....
Other capital	4 530 ..	....	−384	−792	−280	−1,104	−1,105	−1,438	−1,877
Claims on affiliated enterprises	4 535 ..	....	....	−585	−504	−987	−1,021	−1,183	−1,755
Liabilities to affiliated enterprises	4 540 ..	....	....	−207	224	−117	−84	−255	−122
Direct investment in Malaysia	4 555 ..	3,788	554	3,203	2,473	4,624	3,966	6,064	8,456
Equity capital	4 560 ..	....	−854	3,209	3,317	4,438	4,232	7,609	8,612
Claims on direct investors	4 565 ..	....	....	....	....	....	....	....	....
Liabilities to direct investors	4 570 ..	....	....	3,209	3,317	4,438	4,232	7,609	8,612
Reinvested earnings	4 575 ..	....	2,491	....	....	....	....	....	....
Other capital	4 580 ..	....	−1,083	−5	−843	186	−266	−1,545	−156
Claims on direct investors	4 585 ..	....	....	−197	−522	131	−43	−1,869	−634
Liabilities to direct investors	4 590 ..	....	....	191	−322	56	−223	324	478
B. PORTFOLIO INVESTMENT	4 600 ..	−2,532	−412	−1,399	978	8,389	−3,700	3,470	5,380
Assets	4 602 ..	−387	254	−563	−196	−287	−715	−2,123	−3,940
Equity securities	4 610 ..	....	....	−43	−18	23	7	−1,890	−4,093
Monetary authorities	4 611 ..	....	....	....	....	....	....	....	1
General government	4 612 ..	....	....	....	....	....	....	....	....
Banks	4 613 ..	....	....	−1	....	−6	1	1	−33
Other sectors	4 614 ..	....	....	−41	−19	28	7	−1,890	−4,060
Debt securities	4 619 ..	....	....	−520	−178	−309	−722	−234	153
Bonds and notes	4 620 ..	....	....	−429	−191	−111	−398	−602	280
Monetary authorities	4 621 ..	....	....	....	....	....	....	....	1
General government	4 622 ..	....	....	−79	19	91	15	−16	7
Banks	4 623 ..	....	....	−37	−213	−180	−256	−409	409
Other sectors	4 624 ..	....	....	−313	3	−21	−157	−177	−135
Money market instruments	4 630 ..	....	....	−91	13	−198	−325	368	−127
Monetary authorities	4 631 ..	....	....	....	....	....	....	....	1
General government	4 632 ..	....	....	....	....	....	....	....	1
Banks	4 633 ..	....	....	....	8	....	....	....	....
Other sectors	4 634 ..	....	....	−91	5	−198	−325	369	−129
Liabilities	4 652 ..	−2,145	−666	−836	1,174	8,675	−2,985	5,593	9,320
Equity securities	4 660 ..	....	....	−55	1,339	4,509	−1,200	2,392	−669
Banks	4 663 ..	....	....	559	612	466	−928	32	716
Other sectors	4 664 ..	....	....	−614	728	4,043	−272	2,359	−1,385
Debt securities	4 669 ..	....	....	−781	−165	4,166	−1,786	3,202	9,989
Bonds and notes	4 670 ..	....	....	−685	−113	3,666	−630	2,661	3,859
Monetary authorities	4 671 ..	....	....	....	....	....	−894	−188	−76
General government	4 672 ..	....	....	5	41	2,373	595	1,890	3,017
Banks	4 673 ..	....	....	−220	150	478	497	165	−4
Other sectors	4 674 ..	....	....	−470	−304	816	−828	794	922
Money market instruments	4 680 ..	....	....	−96	−52	500	−1,156	541	6,130
Monetary authorities	4 681 ..	....	....	....	....	....	−260	1,000	366
General government	4 682 ..	....	....	....	....	472	−198	47	−495
Banks	4 683 ..	....	....	....	1	−1	−697	−813	95
Other sectors	4 684 ..	....	....	−96	−53	28	−1	307	6,164
C. FINANCIAL DERIVATIVES	4 910 ..	60	−237	−313	119	294	−58	29	−48
Monetary authorities	4 911 ..	....	....	....	....	....	....	....	....
General government	4 912 ..	....	....	....	....	....	....	....	....
Banks	4 913 ..	....	....	−317	116	293	−62	38	19
Other sectors	4 914 ..	....	....	4	3	1	3	−8	−67
Assets	4 900 ..	279	−234	−174	−24	−1,520	−59	8	198
Monetary authorities	4 901 ..	....	....	....	....	....	....	....	....
General government	4 902 ..	....	....	....	....	....	....	....	....
Banks	4 903 ..	....	....	−175	−17	−1,519	−59	13	155
Other sectors	4 904 ..	....	....	2	−6	−1	−1	−5	43
Liabilities	4 905 ..	−220	−3	−139	142	1,814	1	21	−246
Monetary authorities	4 906 ..	....	....	....	....	....	....	....	....
General government	4 907 ..	....	....	....	....	....	....	....	....
Banks	4 908 ..	....	....	−142	133	1,812	−3	25	−136
Other sectors	4 909 ..	....	....	3	9	2	4	−4	−110

Table 2 (Concluded). STANDARD PRESENTATION, 2000–2007

(Millions of U.S. dollars)

	Code	2000	2001	2002	2003	2004	2005	2006	2007
D. OTHER INVESTMENT	4 700	**−5,565**	**−3,531**	**−2,729**	**−5,397**	**−6,154**	**−7,041**	**−15,413**	**−13,595**
Assets	4 703	**−5,565**	**−2,702**	**−4,597**	**−4,502**	**−10,756**	**−4,877**	**−8,531**	**−17,209**
Trade credits	4 706	....	....	−4,147	−2,024	−2,508	−10,166	−1,655	−1,655
General government	4 707	....	....	....	5	1	9	....	−4
of which: Short-term	4 709	....	....	....	*5*	*1*	*9*	....	*−4*
Other sectors	4 710	....	....	−4,147	−2,029	−2,509	−10,175	−1,655	−1,651
of which: Short-term	4 712	....	....	*−4,147*	*−2,029*	*−2,509*	*−10,175*	*−1,655*	*−1,651*
Loans	4 714	....	....	−634	237	−685	−306	−312	−818
Monetary authorities	4 715	....	....	....	....	....	....	....	....
of which: Short-term	4 718	....	....	....	....	....	....	....	....
General government	4 719	....	....	....	....	....	....	....	....
of which: Short-term	4 721	....	....	....	....	....	....	....	....
Banks	4 722	....	....	246	127	−798	−85	−1	−632
of which: Short-term	4 724	....	....	*207*	*209*	*−690*	*−85*	*19*	*−29*
Other sectors	4 725	....	....	−879	111	113	−221	−311	−186
of which: Short-term	4 727	....	....	*−924*	*119*	*−36*	*−65*	*−132*	*−9*
Currency and deposits	4 730	....	....	−566	456	−4,722	2,549	−5,480	−12,417
Monetary authorities	4 731	....	....	....	....	....	....	....	....
General government	4 732	....	....	....	....	....	....	....	....
Banks	4 733	....	....	−421	777	−3,891	1,670	−4,278	−12,320
Other sectors	4 734	....	....	−145	−320	−830	879	−1,202	−97
Other assets	4 736	....	....	749	−3,172	−2,842	3,046	−1,084	−2,319
Monetary authorities	4 737	....	....	....	....	....	....	....	....
of which: Short-term	4 739	....	....	....	....	....	....	....	....
General government	4 740	....	....	−3	....	−2	−1	−1	....
of which: Short-term	4 742	....	....	....	*−1*	*−2*	*−1*	*−1*	....
Banks	4 743	....	....	79	1	−9	−6	−12	102
of which: Short-term	4 745	....	....	*79*	*1*	*−9*	*−6*	*−12*	*192*
Other sectors	4 746	....	....	674	−3,172	−2,831	3,053	−1,071	−2,421
of which: Short-term	4 748	....	....	*647*	*525*	*−2,247*	*2,696*	*−759*	*−2,651*
Liabilities	4 753	....	**−829**	**1,868**	**−895**	**4,602**	**−2,164**	**−6,883**	**3,614**
Trade credits	4 756	....	....	−374	−856	551	−434	−1,010	10
General government	4 757	....	....	....	....	....	....	....	....
of which: Short-term	4 759	....	....	....	....	....	....	....	....
Other sectors	4 760	....	....	−374	−856	551	−434	−1,010	10
of which: Short-term	4 762	....	....	*−374*	*−856*	*551*	*−434*	*−1,010*	*10*
Loans	4 764	....	....	1,098	−3,011	21	−1,116	−2,441	−2,164
Monetary authorities	4 765	....	....	....	−62	....	....	....	....
of which: Use of Fund credit and loans from the Fund	4 766	....	....	....	....	....	....	....	....
of which: Short-term	4 768	....	....	....	....	....	....	....	....
General government	4 769	....	....	1,245	−2,891	633	−840	−2,194	−653
of which: Short-term	4 771	....	....	*969*	*−3,163*	*−754*	*−630*	*−2,360*	*−338*
Banks	4 772	....	....	50	298	−279	−65	−302	−224
of which: Short-term	4 774	....	....	*79*	*305*	*−276*	*−65*	*−252*	*−52*
Other sectors	4 775	....	....	−197	−355	−333	−212	55	−1,287
of which: Short-term	4 777	....	....	*−318*	*−44*	*−152*	*−39*	*20*	*−417*
Currency and deposits	4 780	....	....	921	1,411	1,920	−66	−3,373	6,688
Monetary authorities	4 781	....	....	....	....	....	....	....	....
General government	4 782	....	....	....	....	....	....	....	....
Banks	4 783	....	....	820	1,412	1,920	−66	−3,373	6,679
Other sectors	4 784	....	....	101	−1	....	....	−1	9
Other liabilities	4 786	....	....	222	1,561	2,109	−547	−58	−920
Monetary authorities	4 787	....	....	....	....	....	....	....	....
of which: Short-term	4 789	....	....	....	....	....	....	....	....
General government	4 790	....	....	....	....	....	−2	....	....
of which: Short-term	4 792	....	....	....	....	....	....	....	....
Banks	4 793	....	....	−8	5	43	−3	62	−84
of which: Short-term	4 795	....	....	*−8*	*5*	*43*	*−3*	*62*	*−84*
Other sectors	4 796	....	....	231	1,556	2,066	−543	−120	−836
of which: Short-term	4 798	....	....	*1,299*	*−1,545*	*1,110*	*276*	*262*	*−292*
E. RESERVE ASSETS	4 802	**1,009**	**−1,000**	**−3,657**	**−10,181**	**−22,050**	**−3,620**	**−6,864**	**−13,144**
Monetary gold	4 812	....	....	....	....	....	....	....	....
Special drawing rights	4 811	−26	−24	−15	−12	−12	−13	−7	−5
Reserve position in the Fund	4 810	....	....	36	−5	128	437	103	48
Foreign exchange	4 803	1,035	−976	−3,677	−10,164	−22,166	−4,044	−6,959	−13,187
Other claims	4 813	....	....	....	....	....	....	....	....
NET ERRORS AND OMISSIONS	4 998	**−3,221**	**−2,394**	**−391**	**−4**	**1,880**	**−6,555**	**−6,731**	**−4,910**

Table 3. INTERNATIONAL INVESTMENT POSITION (End-period stocks), 2000–2007

(Millions of U.S. dollars)

	Code	2000	2001	2002	2003	2004	2005	2006	2007
ASSETS	8 995 C.	....	59,558	66,098	77,625	106,132	116,846	157,245	224,587
Direct investment abroad	8 505 ..	....	8,354	10,225	12,019	12,794	22,035	36,073	58,175
Equity capital and reinvested earnings	8 506 ..	....	5,144	5,696	7,033	8,008	13,499	20,212	34,284
Claims on affiliated enterprises	8 507 ..	....	....	....	....	....	....	....	....
Liabilities to affiliated enterprises	8 508 ..	....	....	....	....	....	....	....	....
Other capital	8 530 ..	....	3,210	4,529	4,986	4,787	8,536	15,861	23,891
Claims on affiliated enterprises	8 535 ..	....	....	....	....	....	....	....	....
Liabilities to affiliated enterprises	8 540 ..	....	....	....	....	....	....	....	....
Portfolio investment	8 602 ..	....	1,632	2,207	2,490	2,509	4,183	8,281	15,336
Equity securities	8 610 ..	....	961	1,010	1,083	917	1,715	5,522	12,533
Monetary authorities	8 611 ..	....	....	....	....	....	....	....	....
General government	8 612 ..	....	....	....	....	....	....	....	....
Banks	8 613 ..	....	....	....	....	....	....	....	....
Other sectors	8 614 ..	....	....	....	....	....	....	....	....
Debt securities	8 619 ..	....	671	1,198	1,407	1,592	2,468	2,758	2,803
Bonds and notes	8 620 ..	....	....	....	....	....	....	....	....
Monetary authorities	8 621 ..	....	....	....	....	....	....	....	....
General government	8 622 ..	....	....	....	....	....	....	....	....
Banks	8 623 ..	....	....	....	....	....	....	....	....
Other sectors	8 624 ..	....	....	....	....	....	....	....	....
Money market instruments	8 630 ..	....	....	....	....	....	....	....	....
Monetary authorities	8 631 ..	....	....	....	....	....	....	....	....
General government	8 632 ..	....	....	....	....	....	....	....	....
Banks	8 633 ..	....	....	....	....	....	....	....	....
Other sectors	8 634 ..	....	....	....	....	....	....	....	....
Financial derivatives	8 900 ..	....	11	400	319	166	233	591	546
Monetary authorities	8 901 ..	....	....	....	....	....	....	....	....
General government	8 902 ..	....	....	....	....	....	....	....	....
Banks	8 903 ..	....	....	....	....	....	....	....	....
Other sectors	8 904 ..	....	....	....	....	....	....	....	....
Other investment	8 703 ..	....	19,748	19,619	18,689	24,462	20,256	30,099	49,036
Trade credits	8 706 ..	....	....	....	....	....	....	....	....
General government	8 707 ..	....	....	....	....	....	....	....	....
of which: Short-term	8 709 ..	....	....	....	....	....	....	....	....
Other sectors	8 710 ..	....	....	....	....	....	....	....	....
of which: Short-term	8 712 ..	....	....	....	....	....	....	....	....
Loans	8 714 ..	....	....	....	....	....	....	....	....
Monetary authorities	8 715 ..	....	....	....	....	....	....	....	....
of which: Short-term	8 718 ..	....	....	....	....	....	....	....	....
General government	8 719 ..	....	....	....	....	....	....	....	....
of which: Short-term	8 721 ..	....	....	....	....	....	....	....	....
Banks	8 722 ..	....	....	....	....	....	....	....	....
of which: Short-term	8 724 ..	....	....	....	....	....	....	....	....
Other sectors	8 725 ..	....	....	....	....	....	....	....	....
of which: Short-term	8 727 ..	....	....	....	....	....	....	....	....
Currency and deposits	8 730 ..	....	....	....	....	....	....	....	....
Monetary authorities	8 731 ..	....	....	....	....	....	....	....	....
General government	8 732 ..	....	....	....	....	....	....	....	....
Banks	8 733 ..	....	....	....	....	....	....	....	....
Other sectors	8 734 ..	....	....	....	....	....	....	....	....
Other assets	8 736 ..	....	....	....	....	....	....	....	....
Monetary authorities	8 737 ..	....	....	....	....	....	....	....	....
of which: Short-term	8 739 ..	....	....	....	....	....	....	....	....
General government	8 740 ..	....	....	....	....	....	....	....	....
of which: Short-term	8 742 ..	....	....	....	....	....	....	....	....
Banks	8 743 ..	....	....	....	....	....	....	....	....
of which: Short-term	8 745 ..	....	....	....	....	....	....	....	....
Other sectors	8 746 ..	....	....	....	....	....	....	....	....
of which: Short-term	8 748 ..	....	....	....	....	....	....	....	....
Reserve assets	8 802 ..	....	29,811	33,647	44,109	66,201	70,139	82,201	101,493
Monetary gold	8 812 ..	....	295	295	294	294	294	293	294
Special drawing rights	8 811 ..	105	125	151	178	199	196	214	229
Reserve position in the Fund	8 810 ..	792	764	790	871	776	285	195	155
Foreign exchange	8 803 ..	....	27,492	30,801	40,556	61,744	66,203	78,101	95,062
Other claims	8 813 ..	....	1,135	1,609	2,209	3,187	3,160	3,398	5,753

Table 3 (Concluded). INTERNATIONAL INVESTMENT POSITION (End-period stocks), 2000–2007

(Millions of U.S. dollars)

	Code	2000	2001	2002	2003	2004	2005	2006	2007
LIABILITIES	8 995 D.	....	**95,854**	**102,969**	**115,084**	**139,645**	**136,699**	**163,798**	**230,128**
Direct investment in Malaysia	8 555 ..	....	**33,972**	**37,542**	**41,188**	**43,047**	**44,460**	**53,836**	**76,748**
Equity capital and reinvested earnings	8 556 ..	....	29,769	33,304	37,312	39,754	41,346	51,387	73,424
Claims on direct investors	8 557 ..	....	....	....	....	....	....	....	....
Liabilities to direct investors	8 558 ..	....	....	....	....	....	....	....	....
Other capital	8 580 ..	....	4,203	4,238	3,876	3,293	3,113	2,450	3,323
Claims on direct investors	8 585 ..	....	....	....	....	....	....	....	....
Liabilities to direct investors	8 590 ..	....	....	....	....	....	....	....	....
Portfolio investment	8 652 ..	....	**15,369**	**15,844**	**22,822**	**50,938**	**46,054**	**65,764**	**103,058**
Equity securities	8 660 ..	....	12,631	13,882	20,818	31,285	30,498	45,868	68,013
Banks	8 663 ..	....	....	....	....	....	....	....	....
Other sectors	8 664 ..	....	....	....	....	....	....	....	....
Debt securities	8 669 ..	....	2,739	1,963	2,003	19,653	15,556	19,897	35,045
Bonds and notes	8 670 ..	....	....	....	....	....	....	....	....
Monetary authorities	8 671 ..	....	....	....	....	....	....	....	....
General government	8 672 ..	....	....	....	....	....	....	....	....
Banks	8 673 ..	....	....	....	....	....	....	....	....
Other sectors	8 674 ..	....	....	....	....	....	....	....	....
Money market instruments	8 680 ..	....	....	....	....	....	....	....	....
Monetary authorities	8 681 ..	....	....	....	....	....	....	....	....
General government	8 682 ..	....	....	....	....	....	....	....	....
Banks	8 683 ..	....	....	....	....	....	....	....	....
Other sectors	8 684 ..	....	....	....	....	....	....	....	....
Financial derivatives	8 905 ..	....	**311**	**283**	**208**	**223**	**317**	**527**	**551**
Monetary authorities	8 906 ..	....	....	....	....	....	....	....	....
General government	8 907 ..	....	....	....	....	....	....	....	....
Banks	8 908 ..	....	....	....	....	....	....	....	....
Other sectors	8 909 ..	....	....	....	....	....	....	....	....
Other investment	8 753 ..	....	**46,202**	**49,300**	**50,866**	**45,436**	**45,869**	**43,671**	**49,771**
Trade credits	8 756 ..	....	....	....	....	....	....	....	....
General government	8 757 ..	....	....	....	....	....	....	....	....
of which: Short-term	8 759 ..	....	....	....	....	....	....	....	....
Other sectors	8 760 ..	....	....	....	....	....	....	....	....
of which: Short-term	8 762 ..	....	....	....	....	....	....	....	....
Loans	8 764 ..	....	....	....	....	....	....	....	....
Monetary authorities	8 765 ..	....	....	....	....	....	....	....	....
of which: Use of Fund credit and loans from the Fund	8 766 ..	....	....	....	....	....	....	....	....
of which: Short-term	8 768 ..	....	....	....	....	....	....	....	....
General government	8 769 ..	....	....	....	....	....	....	....	....
of which: Short-term	8 771 ..	....	....	....	....	....	....	....	....
Banks	8 772 ..	....	....	....	....	....	....	....	....
of which: Short-term	8 774 ..	....	....	....	....	....	....	....	....
Other sectors	8 775 ..	....	....	....	....	....	....	....	....
of which: Short-term	8 777 ..	....	....	....	....	....	....	....	....
Currency and deposits	8 780 ..	....	....	....	....	....	....	....	....
Monetary authorities	8 781 ..	....	....	....	....	....	....	....	....
General government	8 782 ..	....	....	....	....	....	....	....	....
Banks	8 783 ..	....	....	....	....	....	....	....	....
Other sectors	8 784 ..	....	....	....	....	....	....	....	....
Other liabilities	8 786 ..	....	....	....	....	....	....	....	....
Monetary authorities	8 787 ..	....	....	....	....	....	....	....	....
of which: Short-term	8 789 ..	....	....	....	....	....	....	....	....
General government	8 790 ..	....	....	....	....	....	....	....	....
of which: Short-term	8 792 ..	....	....	....	....	....	....	....	....
Banks	8 793 ..	....	....	....	....	....	....	....	....
of which: Short-term	8 795 ..	....	....	....	....	....	....	....	....
Other sectors	8 796 ..	....	....	....	....	....	....	....	....
of which: Short-term	8 798 ..	....	....	....	....	....	....	....	....
NET INTERNATIONAL INVESTMENT POSITION	8 995 ..	....	**−36,297**	**−36,871**	**−37,459**	**−33,513**	**−19,853**	**−6,553**	**−5,541**
Conversion rates: ringgit per U.S. dollar (end of period)	0 102 ..	**3.800**	**3.800**	**3.800**	**3.800**	**3.800**	**3.780**	**3.532**	**3.307**

Table 1. ANALYTIC PRESENTATION, 2000–2007

(Millions of U.S. dollars)

	Code	2000	2001	2002	2003	2004	2005	2006	2007
A. Current Account[1]	4 993 Z.	**−56.1**	**−64.6**	**−45.1**	**−31.3**	**−122.4**	**−271.5**	**−300.4**	**−423.0**
Goods: exports f.o.b.	2 100 ..	104.0	104.3	122.9	152.0	181.0	161.6	225.2	228.0
Goods: imports f.o.b.	3 100 ..	−342.0	−346.3	−344.7	−414.3	−564.8	−655.5	−815.3	−964.7
Balance on Goods	4 100 ..	*−238.0*	*−242.0*	*−221.8*	*−262.3*	*−383.8*	*−493.8*	*−590.1*	*−736.8*
Services: credit	2 200 ..	348.5	354.1	362.9	431.9	507.7	322.9	551.9	627.7
Services: debit	3 200 ..	−109.7	−109.8	−111.1	−120.3	−157.5	−211.5	−229.6	−268.5
Balance on Goods and Services	4 991 ..	*.8*	*2.3*	*29.9*	*49.3*	*−33.7*	*−382.5*	*−267.9*	*−377.6*
Income: credit	2 300 ..	10.3	8.2	5.6	6.2	9.8	10.9	15.6	21.7
Income: debit	3 300 ..	−40.3	−45.4	−41.1	−44.6	−44.9	−41.8	−56.3	−63.1
Balance on Goods, Services, and Income	4 992 ..	*−29.2*	*−35.0*	*−5.5*	*10.9*	*−68.9*	*−413.5*	*−308.6*	*−419.0*
Current transfers: credit	2 379 Z.	19.3	19.9	10.6	12.7	7.6	211.5	91.3	98.7
Current transfers: debit	3 379 ..	−46.2	−49.6	−50.2	−54.9	−61.1	−69.5	−83.2	−102.7
B. Capital Account[1]	4 994 Z.	....	....	....	....	....	....	....	....
Capital account: credit	2 994 Z.	....	....	....	....	....	....	....	....
Capital account: debit	3 994 ..	....	....	....	....	....	....	....	....
Total, Groups A Plus B	4 981 ..	*−56.1*	*−64.6*	*−45.1*	*−31.3*	*−122.4*	*−271.5*	*−300.4*	*−423.0*
C. Financial Account[1]	4 995 W.	**40.0**	**33.7**	**73.9**	**50.7**	**153.2**	**263.8**	**294.2**	**445.1**
Direct investment abroad	4 505 ..	....	....	....	....	....	....	....	....
Direct investment in Maldives	4 555 Z.	13.0	11.7	12.4	13.5	14.7	9.5	13.9	15.0
Portfolio investment assets	4 602 ..	....	....	....	....	....	....	....	....
Equity securities	4 610 ..	....	....	....	....	....	....	....	....
Debt securities	4 619 ..	....	....	....	....	....	....	....	....
Portfolio investment liabilities	4 652 Z.	....	....	....	....	....	....	....	....
Equity securities	4 660 ..	....	....	....	....	....	....	....	....
Debt securities	4 669 Z.	....	....	....	....	....	....	....	....
Financial derivatives	4 910 ..	....	....	....	....	....	....	....	....
Financial derivatives assets	4 900 ..	....	....	....	....	....	....	....	....
Financial derivatives liabilities	4 905 ..	....	....	....	....	....	....	....	....
Other investment assets	4 703 ..	22.6	19.6	27.1	26.6	109.9	162.2	113.0	183.4
Monetary authorities	4 701 ..	....	....	....	....	....	....	....	....
General government	4 704 ..	....	....	....	....	....	....	....	....
Banks	4 705 ..	−3.0	−4.8	−6.8	−30.2	−15.5	32.2	−20.9	−14.3
Other sectors	4 728 ..	25.6	24.3	33.9	56.8	125.3	130.0	133.9	197.7
Other investment liabilities	4 753 W.	4.4	2.4	34.4	10.6	28.6	92.1	167.3	246.8
Monetary authorities	4 753 WA	....	−.1	....	....	.1	6.3	....	....
General government	4 753 ZB	−1.9	7.8	26.8	29.9	25.0	18.6	42.2	39.2
Banks	4 753 ZC	6.3	−5.3	7.6	−19.3	3.6	67.2	125.2	207.6
Other sectors	4 753 ZD	....	....	....	....	....	....	....	....
Total, Groups A Through C	4 983 ..	*−16.2*	*−30.9*	*28.8*	*19.4*	*30.8*	*−7.7*	*−6.3*	*22.2*
D. Net Errors and Omissions	4 998 ..	**11.8**	**1.2**	**11.3**	**6.8**	**13.3**	**−15.6**	**51.3**	**53.6**
Total, Groups A Through D	4 984 ..	*−4.3*	*−29.7*	*40.1*	*26.2*	*44.1*	*−23.3*	*45.0*	*75.8*
E. Reserves and Related Items	4 802 A.	**4.3**	**29.7**	**−40.1**	**−26.2**	**−44.1**	**23.3**	**−45.0**	**−75.8**
Reserve assets	4 802 ..	4.3	29.7	−40.1	−26.2	−44.1	17.1	−45.0	−76.8
Use of Fund credit and loans	4 766 ..	....	....	....	....	....	6.3	....	....
Exceptional financing	4 920 ..	....	....	....	....	....	....	....	1.0
Conversion rates: rufiyaa per U.S. dollar	0 101 ..	**11.770**	**12.242**	**12.800**	**12.800**	**12.800**	**12.800**	**12.800**	**12.800**

[1] Excludes components that have been classified in the categories of Group E.

Table 2. STANDARD PRESENTATION, 2000–2007

(Millions of U.S. dollars)

	Code	2000	2001	2002	2003	2004	2005	2006	2007
CURRENT ACCOUNT	4 993	**−56.1**	**−64.6**	**−45.1**	**−31.3**	**−122.4**	**−271.5**	**−300.4**	**−423.0**
A. GOODS	4 100	**−238.0**	**−242.0**	**−221.8**	**−262.3**	**−383.8**	**−493.8**	**−590.1**	**−736.8**
Credit	2 100	**104.0**	**104.3**	**122.9**	**152.0**	**181.0**	**161.6**	**225.2**	**228.0**
General merchandise: exports f.o.b.	2 110	75.9	76.2	90.4	118.1	127.9	112.8	144.5	107.8
Goods for processing: exports f.o.b.	2 150	....	....	....	....	....	....	....	....
Repairs on goods	2 160	....	....	....	....	....	....	....	....
Goods procured in ports by carriers	2 170	28.1	28.1	32.5	33.9	53.1	48.8	80.8	120.2
Nonmonetary gold	2 180	....	....	....	....	....	....	....	....
Debit	3 100	**−342.0**	**−346.3**	**−344.7**	**−414.3**	**−564.8**	**−655.5**	**−815.3**	**−964.7**
General merchandise: imports f.o.b.	3 110	−342.0	−346.3	−344.7	−414.3	−564.8	−655.5	−815.3	−964.7
Goods for processing: imports f.o.b.	3 150	....	....	....	....	....	....	....	....
Repairs on goods	3 160	....	....	....	....	....	....	....	....
Goods procured in ports by carriers	3 170	....	....	....	....	....	....	....	....
Nonmonetary gold	3 180	....	....	....	....	....	....	....	....
B. SERVICES	4 200	**238.8**	**244.2**	**251.7**	**311.6**	**350.1**	**111.3**	**322.2**	**359.1**
Total credit	2 200	*348.5*	*354.1*	*362.9*	*431.9*	*507.7*	*322.9*	*551.9*	*627.7*
Total debit	3 200	*−109.7*	*−109.8*	*−111.1*	*−120.3*	*−157.5*	*−211.5*	*−229.6*	*−268.5*
Transportation services, credit	2 205	**20.2**	**19.6**	**17.3**	**20.1**	**23.3**	**22.0**	**26.0**	**28.6**
Passenger	2 850	....	....	....	....	....	....	....	....
Freight	2 851	*6.9*	*3.6*	*3.6*	*3.6*	*3.6*	*5.0*	*5.9*	*7.3*
Other	2 852	*13.3*	*16.0*	*13.7*	*16.5*	*19.7*	*17.0*	*20.1*	*21.3*
Sea transport, passenger	2 207	....	....	....	....	....	....	....	....
Sea transport, freight	2 208	....	....	....	....	....	....	....	....
Sea transport, other	2 209	....	....	....	....	....	....	....	....
Air transport, passenger	2 211	....	....	....	....	....	....	....	....
Air transport, freight	2 212	....	....	....	....	....	....	....	....
Air transport, other	2 213	13.3	16.0	13.7	16.5	19.7	17.0	20.1	21.3
Other transport, passenger	2 215	....	....	....	....	....	....	....	....
Other transport, freight	2 216	....	....	....	....	....	....	....	....
Other transport, other	2 217	....	....	....	....	....	....	....	....
Transportation services, debit	3 205	**−53.6**	**−52.9**	**−52.0**	**−58.8**	**−80.1**	**−94.5**	**−115.5**	**−137.0**
Passenger	3 850	*−14.1*	*−13.7*	*−13.9*	*−13.8*	*−19.3*	*−24.3*	*−28.2*	*−34.1*
Freight	3 851	*−35.7*	*−36.1*	*−36.0*	*−43.2*	*−58.9*	*−68.4*	*−85.1*	*−100.6*
Other	3 852	*−3.8*	*−3.0*	*−2.1*	*−1.8*	*−1.8*	*−1.8*	*−2.2*	*−2.2*
Sea transport, passenger	3 207	....	....	....	....	....	....	....	....
Sea transport, freight	3 208	....	....	....	....	....	....	....	....
Sea transport, other	3 209	−2.6	−1.3	−1.3	−1.3	−1.3	−1.3	−1.7	−1.7
Air transport, passenger	3 211	−14.1	−13.7	−13.9	−13.8	−19.3	−24.3	−28.2	−34.1
Air transport, freight	3 212	....	....	....	....	....	....	....	....
Air transport, other	3 213	−1.2	−1.7	−.8	−.5	−.5	−.5	−.5	−.5
Other transport, passenger	3 215	....	....	....	....	....	....	....	....
Other transport, freight	3 216	....	....	....	....	....	....	....	....
Other transport, other	3 217	....	....	....	....	....	....	....	....
Travel, credit	2 236	**320.7**	**327.1**	**337.1**	**401.6**	**470.9**	**286.6**	**512.4**	**586.3**
Business travel	2 237	....	....	....	....	....	....	....	....
Personal travel	2 240	320.7	327.1	337.1	401.6	470.9	286.6	512.4	586.3
Travel, debit	3 236	**−46.2**	**−45.1**	**−45.8**	**−46.3**	**−55.6**	**−68.4**	**−76.8**	**−91.7**
Business travel	3 237	−1.5	−1.4	−1.6	−1.5	−1.6	−2.5	−2.5	−2.5
Personal travel	3 240	−44.7	−43.6	−44.2	−44.8	−54.0	−65.9	−74.3	−89.2
Other services, credit	2 200 BA	**7.5**	**7.3**	**8.6**	**10.2**	**13.4**	**14.2**	**13.4**	**12.8**
Communications	2 245	....	....	....	....	....	....	....	....
Construction	2 249	....	....	....	....	....	....	....	....
Insurance	2 253	.8	.4	.4	.4	.4	.6	.7	.8
Financial	2 260	....	....	....	....	....	....	....	....
Computer and information	2 262	....	....	....	....	....	....	....	....
Royalties and licence fees	2 266	3.7	3.8	5.1	6.7	9.9	7.5	10.0	6.5
Other business services	2 268	....	....	....	....	....	....	....	....
Personal, cultural, and recreational	2 287	....	....	....	....	....	....	....	....
Government, n.i.e.	2 291	3.1	3.1	3.1	3.1	3.1	6.1	2.8	5.5
Other services, debit	3 200 BA	**−9.9**	**−11.9**	**−13.4**	**−15.2**	**−21.9**	**−48.6**	**−37.4**	**−39.9**
Communications	3 245	....	....	....	....	....	....	....	....
Construction	3 249	....	....	....	....	....	....	....	....
Insurance	3 253	−4.0	−4.0	−4.0	−4.8	−6.5	−7.6	−9.5	−11.2
Financial	3 260	....	....	....	....	....	....	....	....
Computer and information	3 262	....	....	....	....	....	....	....	....
Royalties and licence fees	3 266	....	....	....	....	....	....	....	....
Other business services	3 268	−4.2	−6.5	−8.1	−8.9	−13.0	−38.1	−23.1	−24.3
Personal, cultural, and recreational	3 287	....	....	....	....	....	....	....	....
Government, n.i.e.	3 291	−1.8	−1.4	−1.3	−1.5	−2.3	−2.9	−4.8	−4.4

Table 2 (Continued). STANDARD PRESENTATION, 2000–2007

(Millions of U.S. dollars)

	Code	2000	2001	2002	2003	2004	2005	2006	2007
C. INCOME	4 300	**−30.0**	**−37.2**	**−35.4**	**−38.4**	**−35.2**	**−31.0**	**−40.8**	**−41.3**
Total credit	2 300	*10.3*	*8.2*	*5.6*	*6.2*	*9.8*	*10.9*	*15.6*	*21.7*
Total debit	3 300	*−40.3*	*−45.4*	*−41.1*	*−44.6*	*−44.9*	*−41.8*	*−56.3*	*−63.1*
Compensation of employees, credit	2 310	**2.2**	**1.8**	**2.0**	**2.0**	**2.9**	**2.3**	**2.8**	**3.0**
Compensation of employees, debit	3 310	**−.1**	**−.4**	**−.4**	**−.4**	**−.4**	**−.4**	**−.4**	**−.4**
Investment income, credit	2 320	**8.1**	**6.4**	**3.6**	**4.2**	**6.9**	**8.6**	**12.8**	**18.8**
Direct investment income	2 330	....	....	....	....	....	....	....	....
Dividends and distributed branch profits	2 332	....	....	....	....	....	....	....	....
Reinvested earnings and undistributed branch profits	2 333	....	....	....	....	....	....	....	....
Income on debt (interest)	2 334	....	....	....	....	....	....	....	....
Portfolio investment income	2 339	....	....	....	....	....	....	....	....
Income on equity	2 340	....	....	....	....	....	....	....	....
Income on bonds and notes	2 350	....	....	....	....	....	....	....	....
Income on money market instruments	2 360	....	....	....	....	....	....	....	....
Other investment income	2 370	8.1	6.4	3.6	4.2	6.9	8.6	12.8	18.8
Investment income, debit	3 320	**−40.2**	**−45.0**	**−40.7**	**−44.2**	**−44.5**	**−41.4**	**−55.9**	**−62.6**
Direct investment income	3 330	−34.4	−39.7	−35.3	−39.0	−36.4	−31.0	−41.0	−44.9
Dividends and distributed branch profits	3 332	−21.4	−28.0	−22.8	−25.5	−21.7	−21.5	−27.2	−29.9
Reinvested earnings and undistributed branch profits	3 333	−13.0	−11.7	−12.5	−13.5	−14.7	−9.5	−13.9	−15.0
Income on debt (interest)	3 334	....	....	....	....	....	....	....	....
Portfolio investment income	3 339	....	....	....	....	....	....	....	....
Income on equity	3 340	....	....	....	....	....	....	....	....
Income on bonds and notes	3 350	....	....	....	....	....	....	....	....
Income on money market instruments	3 360	....	....	....	....	....	....	....	....
Other investment income	3 370	−5.8	−5.3	−5.4	−5.2	−8.1	−10.5	−14.9	−17.7
D. CURRENT TRANSFERS	4 379	**−27.0**	**−29.7**	**−39.6**	**−42.3**	**−53.6**	**142.0**	**8.2**	**−4.0**
Credit	2 379	**19.3**	**19.9**	**10.6**	**12.7**	**7.6**	**211.5**	**91.3**	**98.7**
General government	2 380	19.3	19.9	10.6	12.7	7.6	211.5	91.3	98.7
Other sectors	2 390	....	....	....	....	....	....	....	....
Workers' remittances	2 391	....	....	....	....	....	....	....	....
Other current transfers	2 392	....	....	....	....	....	....	....	....
Debit	3 379	**−46.2**	**−49.6**	**−50.2**	**−54.9**	**−61.1**	**−69.5**	**−83.2**	**−102.7**
General government	3 380	....	....	....	....	....	....	....	....
Other sectors	3 390	−46.2	−49.6	−50.2	−54.9	−61.1	−69.5	−83.2	−102.7
Workers' remittances	3 391	−46.2	−49.6	−50.2	−54.9	−61.1	−69.5	−83.2	−102.7
Other current transfers	3 392	....	....	....	....	....	....	....	....
CAPITAL AND FINANCIAL ACCOUNT	4 996	**44.3**	**63.4**	**33.8**	**24.6**	**109.1**	**287.1**	**249.2**	**369.4**
CAPITAL ACCOUNT	4 994	....	....	....	....	....	....	....	....
Total credit	2 994	....	....	....	....	....	....	....	....
Total debit	3 994	....	....	....	....	....	....	....	....
Capital transfers, credit	2 400	....	....	....	....	....	....	....	....
General government	2 401	....	....	....	....	....	....	....	....
Debt forgiveness	2 402	....	....	....	....	....	....	....	....
Other capital transfers	2 410	....	....	....	....	....	....	....	....
Other sectors	2 430	....	....	....	....	....	....	....	....
Migrants' transfers	2 431	....	....	....	....	....	....	....	....
Debt forgiveness	2 432	....	....	....	....	....	....	....	....
Other capital transfers	2 440	....	....	....	....	....	....	....	....
Capital transfers, debit	3 400	....	....	....	....	....	....	....	....
General government	3 401	....	....	....	....	....	....	....	....
Debt forgiveness	3 402	....	....	....	....	....	....	....	....
Other capital transfers	3 410	....	....	....	....	....	....	....	....
Other sectors	3 430	....	....	....	....	....	....	....	....
Migrants' transfers	3 431	....	....	....	....	....	....	....	....
Debt forgiveness	3 432	....	....	....	....	....	....	....	....
Other capital transfers	3 440	....	....	....	....	....	....	....	....
Nonproduced nonfinancial assets, credit	2 480	....	....	....	....	....	....	....	....
Nonproduced nonfinancial assets, debit	3 480	....	....	....	....	....	....	....	....

Table 2 (Continued). STANDARD PRESENTATION, 2000–2007

(Millions of U.S. dollars)

	Code	2000	2001	2002	2003	2004	2005	2006	2007
FINANCIAL ACCOUNT	4 995 ..	**44.3**	**63.4**	**33.8**	**24.6**	**109.1**	**287.1**	**249.2**	**369.4**
A. DIRECT INVESTMENT	4 500 ..	**13.0**	**11.7**	**12.4**	**13.5**	**14.7**	**9.5**	**13.9**	**15.0**
Direct investment abroad	4 505 ..	....	....	....	....	....	....	....	....
Equity capital	4 510 ..	....	....	....	....	....	....	....	....
Claims on affiliated enterprises	4 515 ..	....	....	....	....	....	....	....	....
Liabilities to affiliated enterprises	4 520 ..	....	....	....	....	....	....	....	....
Reinvested earnings	4 525 ..	....	....	....	....	....	....	....	....
Other capital	4 530 ..	....	....	....	....	....	....	....	....
Claims on affiliated enterprises	4 535 ..	....	....	....	....	....	....	....	....
Liabilities to affiliated enterprises	4 540 ..	....	....	....	....	....	....	....	....
Direct investment in Maldives	4 555 ..	**13.0**	**11.7**	**12.4**	**13.5**	**14.7**	**9.5**	**13.9**	**15.0**
Equity capital	4 560 ..	....	....	....	....	....	....	....	....
Claims on direct investors	4 565 ..	....	....	....	....	....	....	....	....
Liabilities to direct investors	4 570 ..	....	....	....	....	....	....	....	....
Reinvested earnings	4 575 ..	13.0	11.7	12.4	13.5	14.7	9.5	13.9	15.0
Other capital	4 580 ..	....	....	....	....	....	....	....	....
Claims on direct investors	4 585 ..	....	....	....	....	....	....	....	....
Liabilities to direct investors	4 590 ..	....	....	....	....	....	....	....	....
B. PORTFOLIO INVESTMENT	4 600 ..	....	....	....	....	....	....	....	....
Assets	4 602 ..	....	....	....	....	....	....	....	....
Equity securities	4 610 ..	....	....	....	....	....	....	....	....
Monetary authorities	4 611 ..	....	....	....	....	....	....	....	....
General government	4 612 ..	....	....	....	....	....	....	....	....
Banks	4 613 ..	....	....	....	....	....	....	....	....
Other sectors	4 614 ..	....	....	....	....	....	....	....	....
Debt securities	4 619 ..	....	....	....	....	....	....	....	....
Bonds and notes	4 620 ..	....	....	....	....	....	....	....	....
Monetary authorities	4 621 ..	....	....	....	....	....	....	....	....
General government	4 622 ..	....	....	....	....	....	....	....	....
Banks	4 623 ..	....	....	....	....	....	....	....	....
Other sectors	4 624 ..	....	....	....	....	....	....	....	....
Money market instruments	4 630 ..	....	....	....	....	....	....	....	....
Monetary authorities	4 631 ..	....	....	....	....	....	....	....	....
General government	4 632 ..	....	....	....	....	....	....	....	....
Banks	4 633 ..	....	....	....	....	....	....	....	....
Other sectors	4 634 ..	....	....	....	....	....	....	....	....
Liabilities	4 652 ..	....	....	....	....	....	....	....	....
Equity securities	4 660 ..	....	....	....	....	....	....	....	....
Banks	4 663 ..	....	....	....	....	....	....	....	....
Other sectors	4 664 ..	....	....	....	....	....	....	....	....
Debt securities	4 669 ..	....	....	....	....	....	....	....	....
Bonds and notes	4 670 ..	....	....	....	....	....	....	....	....
Monetary authorities	4 671 ..	....	....	....	....	....	....	....	....
General government	4 672 ..	....	....	....	....	....	....	....	....
Banks	4 673 ..	....	....	....	....	....	....	....	....
Other sectors	4 674 ..	....	....	....	....	....	....	....	....
Money market instruments	4 680 ..	....	....	....	....	....	....	....	....
Monetary authorities	4 681 ..	....	....	....	....	....	....	....	....
General government	4 682 ..	....	....	....	....	....	....	....	....
Banks	4 683 ..	....	....	....	....	....	....	....	....
Other sectors	4 684 ..	....	....	....	....	....	....	....	....
C. FINANCIAL DERIVATIVES	4 910 ..	....	....	....	....	....	....	....	....
Monetary authorities	4 911 ..	....	....	....	....	....	....	....	....
General government	4 912 ..	....	....	....	....	....	....	....	....
Banks	4 913 ..	....	....	....	....	....	....	....	....
Other sectors	4 914 ..	....	....	....	....	....	....	....	....
Assets	4 900 ..	....	....	....	....	....	....	....	....
Monetary authorities	4 901 ..	....	....	....	....	....	....	....	....
General government	4 902 ..	....	....	....	....	....	....	....	....
Banks	4 903 ..	....	....	....	....	....	....	....	....
Other sectors	4 904 ..	....	....	....	....	....	....	....	....
Liabilities	4 905 ..	....	....	....	....	....	....	....	....
Monetary authorities	4 906 ..	....	....	....	....	....	....	....	....
General government	4 907 ..	....	....	....	....	....	....	....	....
Banks	4 908 ..	....	....	....	....	....	....	....	....
Other sectors	4 909 ..	....	....	....	....	....	....	....	....

Table 2 (Concluded). STANDARD PRESENTATION, 2000–2007

(Millions of U.S. dollars)

	Code	2000	2001	2002	2003	2004	2005	2006	2007
D. OTHER INVESTMENT	4 700 ..	**26.9**	**22.0**	**61.5**	**37.2**	**138.5**	**260.5**	**280.3**	**431.2**
Assets	4 703 ..	**22.6**	**19.6**	**27.1**	**26.6**	**109.9**	**162.2**	**113.0**	**183.4**
Trade credits	4 706 ..	25.6	24.3	33.9	56.8	125.3	130.0	133.9	197.7
General government	4 707 ..	....	....	....	....	....	....	....	....
of which: Short-term	4 709 ..	....	....	....	....	....	....	....	....
Other sectors	4 710 ..	25.6	24.3	33.9	56.8	125.3	130.0	133.9	197.7
of which: Short-term	4 712 ..	....	....	....	....	....	....	....	....
Loans	4 714 ..	1.2	−2.3	1.2	−4.3	4.7	−1.8	−11.6	6.1
Monetary authorities	4 715 ..	....	....	....	....	....	....	....	....
of which: Short-term	4 718 ..	....	....	....	....	....	....	....	....
General government	4 719 ..	....	....	....	....	....	....	....	....
of which: Short-term	4 721 ..	....	....	....	....	....	....	....	....
Banks	4 722 ..	1.2	−2.3	1.2	−4.3	4.7	−1.8	−11.6	6.1
of which: Short-term	4 724 ..	....	....	....	....	....	....	....	....
Other sectors	4 725 ..	....	....	....	....	....	....	....	....
of which: Short-term	4 727 ..	....	....	....	....	....	....	....	....
Currency and deposits	4 730 ..	−4.2	−2.4	−8.0	−25.9	−20.1	34.0	−9.3	−20.4
Monetary authorities	4 731 ..	....	....	....	....	....	....	....	....
General government	4 732 ..	....	....	....	....	....	....	....	....
Banks	4 733 ..	−4.2	−2.4	−8.0	−25.9	−20.1	34.0	−9.3	−20.4
Other sectors	4 734 ..	....	....	....	....	....	....	....	....
Other assets	4 736 ..	....	....	....	....	....	....	....	....
Monetary authorities	4 737 ..	....	....	....	....	....	....	....	....
of which: Short-term	4 739 ..	....	....	....	....	....	....	....	....
General government	4 740 ..	....	....	....	....	....	....	....	....
of which: Short-term	4 742 ..	....	....	....	....	....	....	....	....
Banks	4 743 ..	....	....	....	....	....	....	....	....
of which: Short-term	4 745 ..	....	....	....	....	....	....	....	....
Other sectors	4 746 ..	....	....	....	....	....	....	....	....
of which: Short-term	4 748 ..	....	....	....	....	....	....	....	....
Liabilities	4 753 ..	**4.4**	**2.4**	**34.4**	**10.6**	**28.6**	**98.3**	**167.3**	**247.8**
Trade credits	4 756 ..	....	....	....	....	....	....	....	....
General government	4 757 ..	....	....	....	....	....	....	....	....
of which: Short-term	4 759 ..	....	....	....	....	....	....	....	....
Other sectors	4 760 ..	....	....	....	....	....	....	....	....
of which: Short-term	4 762 ..	....	....	....	....	....	....	....	....
Loans	4 764 ..	3.6	2.3	34.8	5.8	24.1	90.0	167.6	249.0
Monetary authorities	4 765 ..	....	....	....	....	....	6.3	....	....
of which: Use of Fund credit and loans from the Fund..	4 766 ..	....	....	....	....	....	*6.3*	....	....
of which: Short-term	4 768 ..	....	....	....	....	....	....	....	....
General government	4 769 ..	−1.9	7.8	26.8	29.9	25.0	18.6	42.2	39.2
of which: Short-term	4 771 ..	....	....	....	....	....	....	....	....
Banks	4 772 ..	5.5	−5.6	8.0	−24.1	−.9	65.2	125.4	208.8
of which: Short-term	4 774 ..	....	....	....	....	....	....	....	....
Other sectors	4 775 ..	....	....	....	....	....	....	....	1.0
of which: Short-term	4 777 ..	....	....	....	....	....	....	....	*1.0*
Currency and deposits	4 780 ..	.8	.2	−.4	4.7	4.5	2.0	−.3	−1.2
Monetary authorities	4 781 ..	....	....	....	....	....	....	....	....
General government	4 782 ..	....	....	....	....	....	....	....	....
Banks	4 783 ..	.8	.2	−.4	4.7	4.5	2.0	−.3	−1.2
Other sectors	4 784 ..	....	....	....	....	....	....	....	....
Other liabilities	4 786 ..	....	−.1	....	....	.1	6.3	....	....
Monetary authorities	4 787 ..	....	−.1	....	....	.1	6.3	....	....
of which: Short-term	4 789 ..	....	*−.1*	....	....	*.1*	*6.3*	....	....
General government	4 790 ..	....	....	....	....	....	....	....	....
of which: Short-term	4 792 ..	....	....	....	....	....	....	....	....
Banks	4 793 ..	....	....	....	....	....	....	....	....
of which: Short-term	4 795 ..	....	....	....	....	....	....	....	....
Other sectors	4 796 ..	....	....	....	....	....	....	....	....
of which: Short-term	4 798 ..	....	....	....	....	....	....	....	....
E. RESERVE ASSETS	4 802 ..	**4.3**	**29.7**	**−40.1**	**−26.2**	**−44.1**	**17.1**	**−45.0**	**−76.8**
Monetary gold	4 812 ..	.1	....	−.1	−.1	....	....	....	....
Special drawing rights	4 811 ..	−.1	−.1	....	....	....	....	....	....
Reserve position in the Fund	4 810 ..	....	....	....	....	....	....	....	....
Foreign exchange	4 803 ..	4.3	29.7	−39.8	−26.1	−43.9	17.1	−45.0	−76.8
Other claims	4 813 ..	....	.1	−.1	.1	−.1	....	....	.1
NET ERRORS AND OMISSIONS	4 998 ..	**11.8**	**1.2**	**11.3**	**6.8**	**13.3**	**−15.6**	**51.3**	**53.6**

Maldives   556

Table 3. INTERNATIONAL INVESTMENT POSITION (End-period stocks), 2000–2007

(Millions of U.S. dollars)

	Code	2000	2001	2002	2003	2004	2005	2006	2007
ASSETS	8 995 C.	**146.2**	**121.2**	**168.3**	**224.9**	**284.5**	**234.2**	**300.3**	**391.5**
Direct investment abroad	8 505	....	....	....	....	....	....	....	....
Equity capital and reinvested earnings	8 506	....	....	....	....	....	....	....	....
Claims on affiliated enterprises	8 507	....	....	....	....	....	....	....	....
Liabilities to affiliated enterprises	8 508	....	....	....	....	....	....	....	....
Other capital	8 530	....	....	....	....	....	....	....	....
Claims on affiliated enterprises	8 535	....	....	....	....	....	....	....	....
Liabilities to affiliated enterprises	8 540	....	....	....	....	....	....	....	....
Portfolio investment	8 602	....	....	....	....	....	....	....	....
Equity securities	8 610	....	....	....	....	....	....	....	....
Monetary authorities	8 611	....	....	....	....	....	....	....	....
General government	8 612	....	....	....	....	....	....	....	....
Banks	8 613	....	....	....	....	....	....	....	....
Other sectors	8 614	....	....	....	....	....	....	....	....
Debt securities	8 619	....	....	....	....	....	....	....	....
Bonds and notes	8 620	....	....	....	....	....	....	....	....
Monetary authorities	8 621	....	....	....	....	....	....	....	....
General government	8 622	....	....	....	....	....	....	....	....
Banks	8 623	....	....	....	....	....	....	....	....
Other sectors	8 624	....	....	....	....	....	....	....	....
Money market instruments	8 630	....	....	....	....	....	....	....	....
Monetary authorities	8 631	....	....	....	....	....	....	....	....
General government	8 632	....	....	....	....	....	....	....	....
Banks	8 633	....	....	....	....	....	....	....	....
Other sectors	8 634	....	....	....	....	....	....	....	....
Financial derivatives	8 900	....	....	....	....	....	....	....	....
Monetary authorities	8 901	....	....	....	....	....	....	....	....
General government	8 902	....	....	....	....	....	....	....	....
Banks	8 903	....	....	....	....	....	....	....	....
Other sectors	8 904	....	....	....	....	....	....	....	....
Other investment	8 703	**22.1**	**26.9**	**33.7**	**63.9**	**79.4**	**47.1**	**68.1**	**82.4**
Trade credits	8 706	....	....	....	....	....	....	....	....
General government	8 707	....	....	....	....	....	....	....	....
of which: Short-term	8 709	....	....	....	....	....	....	....	....
Other sectors	8 710	....	....	....	....	....	....	....	....
of which: Short-term	8 712	....	....	....	....	....	....	....	....
Loans	8 714	1.7	4.1	2.9	7.2	2.5	4.3	16.0	9.8
Monetary authorities	8 715	....	....	....	....	....	....	....	....
of which: Short-term	8 718	....	....	....	....	....	....	....	....
General government	8 719	....	....	....	....	....	....	....	....
of which: Short-term	8 721	....	....	....	....	....	....	....	....
Banks	8 722	1.7	4.1	2.9	7.2	2.5	4.3	16.0	9.8
of which: Short-term	8 724	....	....	....	....	....	....	....	....
Other sectors	8 725	....	....	....	....	....	....	....	....
of which: Short-term	8 727	....	....	....	....	....	....	....	....
Currency and deposits	8 730	20.4	22.8	30.8	56.7	76.8	42.8	52.1	72.5
Monetary authorities	8 731	....	....	....	....	....	....	....	....
General government	8 732	....	....	....	....	....	....	....	....
Banks	8 733	20.4	22.8	30.8	56.7	76.8	42.8	52.1	72.5
Other sectors	8 734	....	....	....	....	....	....	....	....
Other assets	8 736	....	....	....	....	....	....	....	....
Monetary authorities	8 737	....	....	....	....	....	....	....	....
of which: Short-term	8 739	....	....	....	....	....	....	....	....
General government	8 740	....	....	....	....	....	....	....	....
of which: Short-term	8 742	....	....	....	....	....	....	....	....
Banks	8 743	....	....	....	....	....	....	....	....
of which: Short-term	8 745	....	....	....	....	....	....	....	....
Other sectors	8 746	....	....	....	....	....	....	....	....
of which: Short-term	8 748	....	....	....	....	....	....	....	....
Reserve assets	8 802	**124.1**	**94.3**	**134.6**	**161.0**	**205.2**	**187.1**	**232.2**	**309.1**
Monetary gold	8 812	.4	.5	.6	.7	.7	....	....	....
Special drawing rights	8 811	.3	.3	.4	.4	.5	.5	.5	.6
Reserve position in the Fund	8 810	2.0	2.0	2.1	2.3	2.4	2.2	2.3	2.5
Foreign exchange	8 803	120.5	90.8	130.6	156.7	200.7	183.6	228.5	305.3
Other claims	8 813	.8	.8	.8	.8	.8	.8	.8	.8

Table 3 (Concluded). INTERNATIONAL INVESTMENT POSITION (End-period stocks), 2000–2007

(Millions of U.S. dollars)

	Code	2000	2001	2002	2003	2004	2005	2006	2007
LIABILITIES...	8 995 D.	**212.4**	**210.6**	**259.8**	**290.3**	**332.5**	**410.0**	**587.6**	**880.6**
Direct investment in Maldives...........................	8 555 ..	....	....	....	....	....	....	....	....
Equity capital and reinvested earnings................	8 556 ..	....	....	....	....	....	....	....	....
Claims on direct investors........................	8 557 ..	....	....	....	....	....	....	....	....
Liabilities to direct investors.....................	8 558 ..	....	....	....	....	....	....	....	....
Other capital..	8 580 ..	....	....	....	....	....	....	....	....
Claims on direct investors........................	8 585 ..	....	....	....	....	....	....	....	....
Liabilities to direct investors.....................	8 590 ..	....	....	....	....	....	....	....	....
Portfolio investment.................................	8 652 ..	....	....	....	....	....	....	....	....
Equity securities...................................	8 660 ..	....	....	....	....	....	....	....	....
Banks...	8 663 ..	....	....	....	....	....	....	....	....
Other sectors...................................	8 664 ..	....	....	....	....	....	....	....	....
Debt securities....................................	8 669 ..	....	....	....	....	....	....	....	....
Bonds and notes...............................	8 670 ..	....	....	....	....	....	....	....	....
Monetary authorities.......................	8 671 ..	....	....	....	....	....	....	....	....
General government........................	8 672 ..	....	....	....	....	....	....	....	....
Banks.......................................	8 673 ..	....	....	....	....	....	....	....	....
Other sectors..............................	8 674 ..	....	....	....	....	....	....	....	....
Money market instruments....................	8 680 ..	....	....	....	....	....	....	....	....
Monetary authorities.......................	8 681 ..	....	....	....	....	....	....	....	....
General government........................	8 682 ..	....	....	....	....	....	....	....	....
Banks.......................................	8 683 ..	....	....	....	....	....	....	....	....
Other sectors..............................	8 684 ..	....	....	....	....	....	....	....	....
Financial derivatives...........................	8 905 ..	....	....	....	....	....	....	....	....
Monetary authorities..............................	8 906 ..	....	....	....	....	....	....	....	....
General government...............................	8 907 ..	....	....	....	....	....	....	....	....
Banks...	8 908 ..	....	....	....	....	....	....	....	....
Other sectors.....................................	8 909 ..	....	....	....	....	....	....	....	....
Other investment..............................	8 753 ..	**212.4**	**210.6**	**259.8**	**290.3**	**332.5**	**410.0**	**587.6**	**880.6**
Trade credits.....................................	8 756 ..	....	....	....	....	....	....	....	....
General government...........................	8 757 ..	....	....	....	....	....	....	....	....
of which: Short-term......................	8 759 ..	....	....	....	....	....	....	....	....
Other sectors.................................	8 760 ..	....	....	....	....	....	....	....	....
of which: Short-term......................	8 762 ..	....	....	....	....	....	....	....	....
Loans..	8 764 ..	210.1	208.1	257.6	283.3	321.1	390.2	568.1	862.4
Monetary authorities.........................	8 765 ..	....	....	....	....	....	5.9	6.2	....
of which: Use of Fund credit and loans from the Fund....	8 766 ..	....	....	....	....	....	*5.9*	*6.2*	*6.5*
of which: Short-term......................	8 768 ..	....	....	....	....	....	....	....	....
General government...........................	8 769 ..	178.0	181.5	223.1	272.9	311.5	309.5	361.8	453.3
of which: Short-term......................	8 771 ..	....	....	....	....	....	....	....	....
Banks..	8 772 ..	32.1	26.6	34.6	10.5	9.6	74.8	200.2	409.0
of which: Short-term......................	8 774 ..	....	....	....	....	....	....	....	....
Other sectors.................................	8 775 ..	....	....	....	....	....	....	....	....
of which: Short-term......................	8 777 ..	....	....	....	....	....	....	....	....
Currency and deposits............................	8 780 ..	1.5	1.8	1.4	6.1	10.6	12.6	12.3	11.2
Monetary authorities.........................	8 781 ..	....	....	....	....	....	....	....	....
General government...........................	8 782 ..	....	....	....	....	....	....	....	....
Banks..	8 783 ..	1.5	1.8	1.4	6.1	10.6	12.6	12.3	11.2
Other sectors.................................	8 784 ..	....	....	....	....	....	....	....	....
Other liabilities..................................	8 786 ..	.9	.8	.8	.8	.9	7.1	7.1	7.1
Monetary authorities.........................	8 787 ..	.9	.8	.8	.8	.9	7.1	7.1	7.1
of which: Short-term......................	8 789 ..	*.9*	*.8*	*.8*	*.8*	*.9*	*7.1*	*7.1*	*7.1*
General government...........................	8 790 ..	....	....	....	....	....	....	....	....
of which: Short-term......................	8 792 ..	....	....	....	....	....	....	....	....
Banks..	8 793 ..	....	....	....	....	....	....	....	....
of which: Short-term......................	8 795 ..	....	....	....	....	....	....	....	....
Other sectors.................................	8 796 ..	....	....	....	....	....	....	....	....
of which: Short-term......................	8 798 ..	....	....	....	....	....	....	....	....
NET INTERNATIONAL INVESTMENT POSITION........	8 995 ..	−66.2	−89.4	−91.5	−65.4	−48.0	−175.7	−287.4	−489.1
Conversion rates: rufiyaa per U.S. dollar (end of period)...	0 102 ..	11.770	12.800	12.800	12.800	12.800	12.800	12.800	12.800

Table 1. ANALYTIC PRESENTATION, 2000–2007

(Millions of U.S. dollars)

	Code	2000	2001	2002	2003	2004	2005	2006	2007
A. Current Account[1]............................	4 993 Z.	**−254.5**	**−310.0**	**−148.8**	**−271.0**	**−409.0**	**−437.6**	**−230.5**	....
Goods: exports f.o.b..............................	2 100 ..	545.1	725.2	875.1	927.8	976.4	1,100.9	1,550.4	....
Goods: imports f.o.b..............................	3 100 ..	−592.1	−734.7	−712.5	−988.3	−1,092.9	−1,245.5	−1,475.4	....
Balance on Goods..............................	4 100 ..	*−46.9*	*−9.6*	*162.7*	*−60.5*	*−116.4*	*−144.6*	*75.0*	....
Services: credit....................................	2 200 ..	99.0	151.2	169.4	224.3	241.1	274.3	313.3	....
Services: debit.....................................	3 200 ..	−334.9	−421.4	−387.0	−482.2	−531.8	−588.0	−674.5	....
Balance on Goods and Services.............	4 991 ..	*−282.8*	*−279.7*	*−54.9*	*−318.5*	*−407.1*	*−458.3*	*−286.2*	....
Income: credit.....................................	2 300 ..	20.6	22.1	36.1	21.3	24.0	32.0	33.2	....
Income: debit......................................	3 300 ..	−118.7	−188.2	−276.3	−181.2	−218.8	−238.9	−302.6	....
Balance on Goods, Services, and Income..........	4 992 ..	*−380.9*	*−445.8*	*−295.1*	*−478.4*	*−601.9*	*−665.2*	*−555.6*	....
Current transfers: credit........................	2 379 Z.	157.2	160.7	182.1	265.5	251.3	286.0	380.9	....
Current transfers: debit.........................	3 379 ..	−30.8	−25.0	−35.7	−58.1	−58.3	−58.5	−55.8	....
B. Capital Account[1]............................	4 994 Z.	**101.6**	**107.4**	**104.2**	**113.7**	**151.4**	**148.9**	**140.6**	....
Capital account: credit..........................	2 994 Z.	101.6	107.5	104.4	113.7	151.5	149.5	141.2	....
Capital account: debit...........................	3 994 ..	....	−.1	−.2	....	....	−.6	−.6	....
Total, Groups A Plus B........................	4 981 ..	*−153.0*	*−202.6*	*−44.6*	*−157.3*	*−257.5*	*−288.7*	*−89.9*	....
C. Financial Account[1]........................	4 995 W.	**220.4**	**146.2**	**188.6**	**288.7**	**99.9**	**333.4**	**−1,910.2**	....
Direct investment abroad......................	4 505 ..	−4.0	−17.3	−1.6	−1.4	−.8	.9	−1.2	....
Direct investment in Mali......................	4 555 Z.	82.4	121.7	243.8	132.3	101.0	223.8	83.4	....
Portfolio investment assets...................	4 602 ..	15.5	−.8	−.5	−27.1	−3.2	−18.0	−6.9	....
Equity securities...............................	4 610 ..	−.1	−.1	−.6	.2	−5.1	....	−.3	....
Debt securities.................................	4 619 ..	15.6	−.7	.1	−27.2	1.9	−18.0	−6.6	....
Portfolio investment liabilities...............	4 652 Z.	1.0	12.4	54.1	27.6	.6	2.9	−4.2	....
Equity securities...............................	4 660 ..	.4	13.5	−2.1	.9	−.7	8.9	2.8	....
Debt securities.................................	4 669 Z.	.6	−1.1	56.2	26.7	1.3	−5.9	−6.9	....
Financial derivatives............................	4 910 ..	....	....	....	....	−.4	−.1	....	....
Financial derivatives assets...................	4 900 ..	....	....	....	....	−.4	−.1	....	....
Financial derivatives liabilities...............	4 905 ..	....	....	....	....	....	....	....	....
Other investment assets.......................	4 703 ..	−87.0	−87.7	−248.4	3.7	−130.9	−109.2	−209.3	....
Monetary authorities.........................	4 701 ..	....	....	....	....	....	....	....	....
General government..........................	4 704 ..	−1.4	....	....	....	−.5	....	−3.7	....
Banks..	4 705 ..	−42.5	−64.2	30.4	15.6	−22.9	.9	−85.9	....
Other sectors..................................	4 728 ..	−43.1	−23.5	−278.7	−11.9	−107.5	−110.0	−119.7	....
Other investment liabilities...................	4 753 W.	212.5	117.8	141.1	153.7	133.5	232.9	−1,771.9	....
Monetary authorities.........................	4 753 WA	−.6	.7	2.6	.3	.3	−.1	1.4	....
General government..........................	4 753 ZB	88.3	111.5	87.5	104.4	86.7	158.1	−1,745.5	....
Banks..	4 753 ZC	−1.9	8.4	25.9	11.1	21.0	81.9	45.0	....
Other sectors..................................	4 753 ZD	126.6	−2.7	25.1	37.9	25.5	−7.0	−72.8	....
Total, Groups A Through C..................	4 983 ..	*67.4*	*−56.4*	*143.9*	*131.4*	*−157.7*	*44.6*	*−2,000.1*	....
D. Net Errors and Omissions..................	4 998 ..	**−4.8**	**9.4**	**−6.1**	**45.2**	**−26.3**	**−29.1**	**−34.9**	....
Total, Groups A Through D..................	4 984 ..	*62.6*	*−47.0*	*137.8*	*176.5*	*−184.0*	*15.5*	*−2,035.0*	....
E. Reserves and Related Items..............	4 802 A.	**−62.6**	**47.0**	**−137.8**	**−176.5**	**184.0**	**−15.5**	**2,035.0**	....
Reserve assets....................................	4 802 ..	−57.9	14.0	−159.0	−216.6	159.9	−122.7	−14.9	....
Use of Fund credit and loans.................	4 766 ..	−8.3	1.5	−18.3	−11.8	−30.1	−24.8	−102.8	....
Exceptional financing...........................	4 920 ..	3.7	31.5	39.5	51.9	54.2	132.0	2,152.7	....
Conversion rates: CFA francs per U.S. dollar..........	0 101 ..	**711.98**	**733.04**	**696.99**	**581.20**	**528.28**	**527.47**	**522.89**	**479.27**

[1] Excludes components that have been classified in the categories of Group E.

Table 2. STANDARD PRESENTATION, 2000–2007

(Millions of U.S. dollars)

	Code	2000	2001	2002	2003	2004	2005	2006	2007
CURRENT ACCOUNT	4 993 ..	**−254.5**	**−310.0**	**−148.8**	**−271.0**	**−409.0**	**−437.6**	**−230.5**	....
A. GOODS	4 100 ..	**−46.9**	**−9.6**	**162.7**	**−60.5**	**−116.4**	**−144.6**	**75.0**	....
Credit	2 100 ..	**545.1**	**725.2**	**875.1**	**927.8**	**976.4**	**1,100.9**	**1,550.4**	....
General merchandise: exports f.o.b.	2 110 ..	278.8	241.8	296.6	361.7	458.4	419.1	422.2	....
Goods for processing: exports f.o.b.	2 150 ..	....	....	....	....	....	....	....	....
Repairs on goods	2 160 ..	....	.1	....	.2	....	....	....	....
Goods procured in ports by carriers	2 170 ..	.3	.7	.9	3.7	5.9	7.8	4.6	....
Nonmonetary gold	2 180 ..	266.0	482.7	577.6	562.3	512.2	674.0	1,123.5	....
Debit	3 100 ..	**−592.1**	**−734.7**	**−712.5**	**−988.3**	**−1,092.9**	**−1,245.5**	**−1,475.4**	....
General merchandise: imports f.o.b.	3 110 ..	−589.9	−732.2	−706.9	−977.0	−1,088.9	−1,243.5	−1,473.2	....
Goods for processing: imports f.o.b.	3 150 ..	....	....	....	....	....	....	....	....
Repairs on goods	3 160 ..	−.9	−1.3	−5.6	−3.1	−2.0	−1.9	−2.2	....
Goods procured in ports by carriers	3 170 ..	−1.3	−1.3	....	−8.3	−2.0	....	....	....
Nonmonetary gold	3 180 ..	....	....	....	....	....	....	....	....
B. SERVICES	4 200 ..	**−235.8**	**−270.2**	**−217.6**	**−258.0**	**−290.7**	**−313.7**	**−361.2**	....
Total credit	2 200 ..	*99.0*	*151.2*	*169.4*	*224.3*	*241.1*	*274.3*	*313.3*	....
Total debit	3 200 ..	*−334.9*	*−421.4*	*−387.0*	*−482.2*	*−531.8*	*−588.0*	*−674.5*	....
Transportation services, credit	2 205 ..	**33.1**	**23.8**	**21.0**	**42.7**	**30.6**	**35.1**	**39.1**	....
Passenger	2 850 ..	*6.6*	*2.7*	*.6*	*7.9*	*2.3*	*1.2*	*.4*	....
Freight	2 851 ..	*17.1*	*18.5*	*19.0*	*30.8*	*25.2*	*25.3*	*32.4*	....
Other	2 852 ..	*9.4*	*2.6*	*1.5*	*3.9*	*3.1*	*8.6*	*6.3*	....
Sea transport, passenger	2 207 ..	....	....	....	....	....	....	....	....
Sea transport, freight	2 208 ..	....	....	....	....	....	....	....	....
Sea transport, other	2 209 ..	....	....	....	....	.1	2.3	.6	....
Air transport, passenger	2 211 ..	6.1	1.8	....	6.4	2.1	....	....	....
Air transport, freight	2 212 ..	2.9	....	....	....	....	....	....	....
Air transport, other	2 213 ..	7.9	2.5	1.4	3.9	3.0	6.3	5.7	....
Other transport, passenger	2 215 ..	.5	.9	.6	1.5	.2	1.2	.4	....
Other transport, freight	2 216 ..	14.2	18.5	19.0	30.8	25.2	25.3	32.4	....
Other transport, other	2 217 ..	1.5	....	....	....	....	....	....	....
Transportation services, debit	3 205 ..	**−238.6**	**−264.7**	**−230.0**	**−312.3**	**−342.8**	**−361.0**	**−405.4**	....
Passenger	3 850 ..	*−25.9*	*−28.5*	*−26.1*	*−46.4*	*−58.6*	*−56.4*	*−75.7*	....
Freight	3 851 ..	*−209.4*	*−234.3*	*−202.0*	*−263.2*	*−277.4*	*−297.2*	*−327.4*	....
Other	3 852 ..	*−3.3*	*−1.8*	*−1.9*	*−2.7*	*−6.8*	*−7.5*	*−2.3*	....
Sea transport, passenger	3 207 ..	....	....	....	....	....	....	....	....
Sea transport, freight	3 208 ..	−76.7	−118.3	−111.0	−144.7	−152.6	−163.5	−180.1	....
Sea transport, other	3 209 ..	....	....	....	....	−2.2	−2.5	....	....
Air transport, passenger	3 211 ..	−25.7	−28.5	−25.8	−46.4	−58.6	−56.4	−75.7	....
Air transport, freight	3 212 ..	−9.1	−17.6	−15.1	−19.7	−20.8	−22.3	−24.6	....
Air transport, other	3 213 ..	−2.3	−1.8	−1.3	−2.7	−1.9	−2.1	−2.3	....
Other transport, passenger	3 215 ..	−.2	....	−.2	....	....	....	....	....
Other transport, freight	3 216 ..	−123.6	−98.4	−75.8	−98.8	−104.0	−111.4	−122.8	....
Other transport, other	3 217 ..	−.9	....	−.6	....	−2.7	−2.8	....	....
Travel, credit	2 236 ..	**40.3**	**88.2**	**104.0**	**127.9**	**140.4**	**148.4**	**175.0**	....
Business travel	2 237 ..	19.7	35.2	41.7	53.6	60.8	67.0	91.6	....
Personal travel	2 240 ..	20.6	53.0	62.3	74.3	79.6	81.4	83.5	....
Travel, debit	3 236 ..	**−40.3**	**−35.7**	**−36.2**	**−47.6**	**−66.5**	**−76.9**	**−120.2**	....
Business travel	3 237 ..	−27.2	−17.4	−20.7	−27.7	−43.9	−53.5	−73.4	....
Personal travel	3 240 ..	−13.1	−18.3	−15.6	−19.9	−22.5	−23.4	−46.7	....
Other services, credit	2 200 BA	**25.6**	**39.2**	**44.4**	**53.7**	**70.1**	**90.8**	**99.2**	....
Communications	2 245 ..	8.7	6.8	10.3	12.2	37.8	44.2	60.8	....
Construction	2 249 ..	1.5	7.9	.1	5.9	2.3	2.0	3.4	....
Insurance	2 253 ..	1.5	2.5	1.7	1.2	1.7	3.2	4.3	....
Financial	2 260 ..	.8	1.5	2.4	2.0	3.6	4.2	2.7	....
Computer and information	2 262 ..	....	....	.1	....	....	....	....	....
Royalties and licence fees	2 266 ..	....	.1	....	....	.2	.2	.2	....
Other business services	2 268 ..	6.2	9.4	10.0	15.7	10.1	15.9	5.6	....
Personal, cultural, and recreational	2 287 ..	....	.1	....	.2	....	.3	.3	....
Government, n.i.e.	2 291 ..	6.8	10.9	19.7	16.5	14.4	20.8	21.9	....
Other services, debit	3 200 BA	**−56.0**	**−121.0**	**−120.8**	**−122.4**	**−122.5**	**−150.1**	**−149.0**	....
Communications	3 245 ..	−4.1	−5.7	−7.1	−9.7	−12.9	−22.9	−24.1	....
Construction	3 249 ..	−1.1	−10.3	−31.8	−22.0	−15.6	−18.8	−16.4	....
Insurance	3 253 ..	−7.1	−12.5	−15.8	−19.1	−32.2	−35.5	−29.5	....
Financial	3 260 ..	−6.1	−1.9	−6.1	−8.1	−2.3	−4.2	−4.2	....
Computer and information	3 262 ..	−1.2	−.8	−.8	−2.1	−6.2	−8.3	−6.1	....
Royalties and licence fees	3 266 ..	−1.3	−1.1	−.6	−.9	−.6	−1.1	−1.1	....
Other business services	3 268 ..	−24.0	−80.9	−51.1	−56.0	−36.2	−39.5	−49.4	....
Personal, cultural, and recreational	3 287 ..	....	−.2	−.1	−.2	−12.9	−14.4	−15.3	....
Government, n.i.e.	3 291 ..	−11.0	−7.5	−7.4	−4.2	−3.6	−5.2	−2.8	....

Table 2 (Continued). STANDARD PRESENTATION, 2000–2007

(Millions of U.S. dollars)

	Code	2000	2001	2002	2003	2004	2005	2006	2007
C. INCOME	4 300	**−98.2**	**−166.0**	**−240.2**	**−159.9**	**−194.8**	**−206.9**	**−269.4**	....
Total credit	2 300	*20.6*	*22.1*	*36.1*	*21.3*	*24.0*	*32.0*	*33.2*	....
Total debit	3 300	*−118.7*	*−188.2*	*−276.3*	*−181.2*	*−218.8*	*−238.9*	*−302.6*	....
Compensation of employees, credit	2 310	**4.0**	**6.1**	**11.2**	**14.9**	**17.4**	**23.9**	**19.1**	....
Compensation of employees, debit	3 310	**−2.4**	**−3.0**	**−6.2**	**−9.7**	**−12.3**	**−18.5**	**−9.9**	....
Investment income, credit	2 320	**16.6**	**16.0**	**25.0**	**6.4**	**6.6**	**8.1**	**14.1**	....
Direct investment income	2 330	.6	.8	.1	.6	.1	.3	.1	....
Dividends and distributed branch profits	2 332	.6	....	....	.6	.1	.3	....	....
Reinvested earnings and undistributed branch profits	2 333	....	.8	....	....	....	....	....	....
Income on debt (interest)	2 334	....	....	.1	....	....	....	.1	....
Portfolio investment income	2 339	2.2	5.6	7.3	2.3	3.2	4.2	7.1	....
Income on equity	2 340	....	....	....	....	.1	.2	.2	....
Income on bonds and notes	2 350	.9	1.9	5.2	2.2	3.1	3.3	4.9	....
Income on money market instruments	2 360	1.3	3.6	2.1	.1	....	.7	1.9	....
Other investment income	2 370	13.7	9.7	17.6	3.4	3.2	3.7	6.9	....
Investment income, debit	3 320	**−116.4**	**−185.1**	**−270.1**	**−171.6**	**−206.5**	**−220.4**	**−292.7**	....
Direct investment income	3 330	−75.9	−140.5	−227.3	−120.0	−152.0	−154.6	−226.9	....
Dividends and distributed branch profits	3 332	−50.9	−23.9	−154.2	−128.7	−60.2	−110.1	−182.7	....
Reinvested earnings and undistributed branch profits	3 333	−24.5	−115.6	−72.2	9.6	−93.9	−38.8	−35.3	....
Income on debt (interest)	3 334	−.5	−1.0	−.8	−1.0	2.1	−5.6	−8.9	....
Portfolio investment income	3 339	−3.4	−24.0	−16.3	−19.6	−21.2	−16.7	−16.9	....
Income on equity	3 340	−.1	−1.2	−3.2	−7.5	−5.7	−5.1	−3.0	....
Income on bonds and notes	3 350	−3.3	−22.5	−12.7	−12.0	−15.5	−11.6	−13.9	....
Income on money market instruments	3 360	....	−.4	−.4	....	....	....	....	....
Other investment income	3 370	−37.1	−20.6	−26.6	−32.0	−33.3	−49.1	−48.8	....
D. CURRENT TRANSFERS	4 379	**126.4**	**135.7**	**146.3**	**207.4**	**193.0**	**227.6**	**325.1**	....
Credit	2 379	**157.2**	**160.7**	**182.1**	**265.5**	**251.3**	**286.0**	**380.9**	....
General government	2 380	70.2	68.8	47.2	119.9	101.6	119.9	169.1	....
Other sectors	2 390	87.0	91.9	134.8	145.6	149.7	166.2	211.8	....
Workers' remittances	2 391	69.2	82.1	126.5	138.9	138.1	153.3	192.7	....
Other current transfers	2 392	17.8	9.9	8.3	6.7	11.6	12.9	19.0	....
Debit	3 379	**−30.8**	**−25.0**	**−35.7**	**−58.1**	**−58.3**	**−58.5**	**−55.8**	....
General government	3 380	−6.0	−2.8	−3.0	−4.0	−4.4	−4.0	−4.4	....
Other sectors	3 390	−24.7	−22.2	−32.8	−54.1	−54.0	−54.4	−51.4	....
Workers' remittances	3 391	−23.9	−20.3	−24.1	−47.9	−51.6	−50.8	−47.2	....
Other current transfers	3 392	−.8	−2.0	−8.6	−6.1	−2.4	−3.6	−4.1	....
CAPITAL AND FINANCIAL ACCOUNT	4 996	**259.4**	**300.7**	**155.0**	**225.8**	**435.3**	**466.7**	**265.4**	....
CAPITAL ACCOUNT	4 994	**105.2**	**139.0**	**143.6**	**165.5**	**205.7**	**205.9**	**2,258.5**	....
Total credit	2 994	*105.3*	*139.0*	*143.8*	*165.6*	*205.7*	*206.5*	*2,259.1*	....
Total debit	3 994	....	*−.1*	*−.2*	....	....	*−.6*	*−.6*	....
Capital transfers, credit	2 400	**105.3**	**139.0**	**143.8**	**165.6**	**205.7**	**206.5**	**2,259.1**	....
General government	2 401	100.6	130.8	138.8	156.3	186.7	194.4	2,247.8	....
Debt forgiveness	2 402	3.7	31.5	39.5	51.9	54.2	57.0	2,117.9	....
Other capital transfers	2 410	96.9	99.3	99.4	104.4	132.5	137.4	129.9	....
Other sectors	2 430	4.7	8.2	5.0	9.3	19.0	12.0	11.3	....
Migrants' transfers	2 431	....	....	....	....	....	....	....	....
Debt forgiveness	2 432	....	....	....	....	....	....	....	....
Other capital transfers	2 440	4.7	8.2	5.0	9.3	19.0	12.0	11.3	....
Capital transfers, debit	3 400	....	....	....	....	....	....	....	....
General government	3 401	....	....	....	....	....	....	....	....
Debt forgiveness	3 402	....	....	....	....	....	....	....	....
Other capital transfers	3 410	....	....	....	....	....	....	....	....
Other sectors	3 430	....	....	....	....	....	....	....	....
Migrants' transfers	3 431	....	....	....	....	....	....	....	....
Debt forgiveness	3 432	....	....	....	....	....	....	....	....
Other capital transfers	3 440	....	....	....	....	....	....	....	....
Nonproduced nonfinancial assets, credit	2 480	....	....	....	....	....	....	....	....
Nonproduced nonfinancial assets, debit	3 480	....	**−.1**	**−.2**	....	....	**−.6**	**−.6**	....

Table 2 (Continued). STANDARD PRESENTATION, 2000–2007

(Millions of U.S. dollars)

	Code	2000	2001	2002	2003	2004	2005	2006	2007
FINANCIAL ACCOUNT	4 995	**154.1**	**161.7**	**11.3**	**60.3**	**229.7**	**260.9**	**−1,993.1**	....
A. DIRECT INVESTMENT	4 500	**78.4**	**104.5**	**242.2**	**130.8**	**100.2**	**224.7**	**82.1**	....
Direct investment abroad	4 505	**−4.0**	**−17.3**	**−1.6**	**−1.4**	**−.8**	**.9**	**−1.2**	....
Equity capital	4 510	−.6	.7	−.3	−.4	−1.7	−1.5	−6.1	....
Claims on affiliated enterprises	4 515	−.6	....	....	....	....	....	1.0	....
Liabilities to affiliated enterprises	4 520	....	.7	−.3	−.4	−1.7	−1.5	−7.1	....
Reinvested earnings	4 525	....	−.8	....	....	....	....	....	....
Other capital	4 530	−3.5	−17.2	−1.2	−1.0	.9	2.4	4.9	....
Claims on affiliated enterprises	4 535	−.7	−17.0	−1.6	−2.6	−1.5	.8	1.1	....
Liabilities to affiliated enterprises	4 540	−2.8	−.2	.3	1.6	2.4	1.6	3.8	....
Direct investment in Mali	4 555	**82.4**	**121.7**	**243.8**	**132.3**	**101.0**	**223.8**	**83.4**	....
Equity capital	4 560	19.5	−80.9	256.3	56.5	−2.1	46.0	49.3	....
Claims on direct investors	4 565	19.5	−80.9	256.3	64.8	24.2	85.8	86.4	....
Liabilities to direct investors	4 570	....	....	....	−8.4	−26.3	−39.8	−37.1	....
Reinvested earnings	4 575	24.5	115.6	72.2	−9.6	93.9	38.8	35.3	....
Other capital	4 580	38.5	87.0	−84.7	85.4	9.2	139.0	−1.3	....
Claims on direct investors	4 585	....	−5.7	−.2	−3.7	−7.3	−1.0	.6	....
Liabilities to direct investors	4 590	38.5	92.7	−84.5	89.1	16.5	140.0	−1.8	....
B. PORTFOLIO INVESTMENT	4 600	**16.5**	**11.7**	**53.6**	**.5**	**−2.6**	**−15.1**	**−11.1**	....
Assets	4 602	**15.5**	**−.8**	**−.5**	**−27.1**	**−3.2**	**−18.0**	**−6.9**	....
Equity securities	4 610	−.1	−.1	−.6	.2	−5.1	....	−.3	....
Monetary authorities	4 611	....	....	....	....	....	....	....	....
General government	4 612	....	....	....	....	....	....	....	....
Banks	4 613	....	....	....	....	....	....	−.3	....
Other sectors	4 614	−.1	−.1	−.6	.2	−5.1	....	....	....
Debt securities	4 619	15.6	−.7	.1	−27.2	1.9	−18.0	−6.6	....
Bonds and notes	4 620	7.2	−1.2	2.1	−27.2	1.9	−17.7	−6.6	....
Monetary authorities	4 621	....	....	....	....	....	....	....	....
General government	4 622	....	....	....	....	....	....	−1.9	....
Banks	4 623	2.2	.4	2.2	−12.5	−7.2	−16.2	−5.7	....
Other sectors	4 624	4.9	−1.7	−.1	−14.7	9.1	−1.5	1.1	....
Money market instruments	4 630	8.4	.5	−2.0	....	....	−.3	....	....
Monetary authorities	4 631	....	....	....	....	....	....	....	....
General government	4 632	....	....	....	....	....	....	....	....
Banks	4 633	8.4	.5	−2.0	.2	....	....	....	....
Other sectors	4 634	....	....	....	−.2	....	−.3	....	....
Liabilities	4 652	**1.0**	**12.4**	**54.1**	**27.6**	**.6**	**2.9**	**−4.2**	....
Equity securities	4 660	.4	13.5	−2.1	.9	−.7	8.9	2.8	....
Banks	4 663	....	.3	.8	−.4	.5	4.7	3.1	....
Other sectors	4 664	.4	13.2	−2.9	1.3	−1.2	4.2	−.4	....
Debt securities	4 669	.6	−1.1	56.2	26.7	1.3	−5.9	−6.9	....
Bonds and notes	4 670	.6	−1.1	56.2	26.7	1.3	−2.5	−6.9	....
Monetary authorities	4 671	....	....	....	....	....	....	....	....
General government	4 672	....	....	....	....	....	....	....	....
Banks	4 673	....	....	....	....	1.2	−4.5	−4.9	....
Other sectors	4 674	.6	−1.1	56.2	26.7	.2	2.0	−2.0	....
Money market instruments	4 680	.1	....	....	....	....	−3.4	....	....
Monetary authorities	4 681	....	....	....	....	....	....	....	....
General government	4 682	....	....	....	....	....	....	....	....
Banks	4 683	....	....	....	....	....	−3.4	....	....
Other sectors	4 684	.1	....	....	....	....	....	....	....
C. FINANCIAL DERIVATIVES	4 910	....	....	....	....	**−.4**	**−.1**	....	....
Monetary authorities	4 911	....	....	....	....	....	....	....	....
General government	4 912	....	....	....	....	....	....	....	....
Banks	4 913	....	....	....	....	−.1	....	....	....
Other sectors	4 914	....	....	....	....	−.3	−.1	....	....
Assets	4 900	**....**	**....**	**....**	**....**	**−.4**	**−.1**	**....**	....
Monetary authorities	4 901	....	....	....	....	....	....	....	....
General government	4 902	....	....	....	....	....	....	....	....
Banks	4 903	....	....	....	....	−.1	....	....	....
Other sectors	4 904	....	....	....	....	−.3	−.1	....	....
Liabilities	4 905	**....**	**....**	**....**	**....**	**....**	**....**	**....**	....
Monetary authorities	4 906	....	....	....	....	....	....	....	....
General government	4 907	....	....	....	....	....	....	....	....
Banks	4 908	....	....	....	....	....	....	....	....
Other sectors	4 909	....	....	....	....	....	....	....	....

Table 2 (Concluded). STANDARD PRESENTATION, 2000–2007

(Millions of U.S. dollars)

	Code	2000	2001	2002	2003	2004	2005	2006	2007
D. OTHER INVESTMENT	4 700	**117.2**	**31.7**	**−125.5**	**145.5**	**−27.4**	**174.0**	**−2,049.3**	....
Assets	4 703	**−87.0**	**−87.7**	**−248.4**	**3.7**	**−130.9**	**−109.2**	**−209.3**	....
Trade credits	4 706	−21.5	−5.0	−85.2	−4.8	−55.3	−4.2	3.3	....
General government	4 707	....	....	....	....	....	....	....	....
of which: Short-term	4 709	....	....	....	....	....	....	....	....
Other sectors	4 710	−21.5	−5.0	−85.2	−4.8	−55.3	−4.2	3.3	....
of which: Short-term	4 712	−21.5	−5.0	−85.2	−4.8	−55.3	−4.2	3.3	....
Loans	4 714	−16.6	−54.4	43.6	−22.9	−4.9	6.0	−19.1	....
Monetary authorities	4 715	....	....	....	....	....	....	....	....
of which: Short-term	4 718	....	....	....	....	....	....	....	....
General government	4 719	....	....	....	....	....	....	....	....
of which: Short-term	4 721	....	....	....	....	....	....	....	....
Banks	4 722	−16.6	−54.4	43.6	−22.9	−4.8	6.1	−19.1	....
of which: Short-term	4 724	−13.9	−55.2	51.0	−13.1	.6	.6	−2.1	....
Other sectors	4 725	....	....	....	....	....	−.1	....	....
of which: Short-term	4 727	....	....	....	....	....	−.1	....	....
Currency and deposits	4 730	−53.3	−29.7	−148.3	34.1	−72.9	−84.0	−148.3	....
Monetary authorities	4 731	....	....	....	....	....	....	....	....
General government	4 732	−1.4	....	....	....	....	....	....	....
Banks	4 733	−28.2	−10.8	−5.6	34.5	−21.6	−2.1	−57.0	....
Other sectors	4 734	−23.8	−18.9	−142.7	−.5	−51.3	−81.9	−91.4	....
Other assets	4 736	4.4	1.3	−58.4	−2.7	2.2	−26.9	−45.2	....
Monetary authorities	4 737	....	....	....	....	....	....	....	....
of which: Short-term	4 739	....	....	....	....	....	....	....	....
General government	4 740	....	....	....	....	−.5	....	−3.7	....
of which: Short-term	4 742	....	....	....	....	−.5	....	−3.7	....
Banks	4 743	2.3	.9	−7.6	3.9	3.6	−3.1	−9.9	....
of which: Short-term	4 745	2.3	.9	−7.6	4.1	3.6	−3.1	−9.9	....
Other sectors	4 746	2.1	.4	−50.8	−6.7	−.8	−23.8	−31.7	....
of which: Short-term	4 748	2.1	.4	−50.8	−6.7	−.8	−23.8	−31.7	....
Liabilities	4 753	**204.2**	**119.4**	**122.8**	**141.8**	**103.4**	**283.1**	**−1,840.0**	....
Trade credits	4 756	76.2	70.9	−26.2	10.6	−1.8	15.4	2.2	....
General government	4 757	....	....	....	....	....	....	....	....
of which: Short-term	4 759	....	....	....	....	....	....	....	....
Other sectors	4 760	76.2	70.9	−26.2	10.6	−1.8	15.4	2.2	....
of which: Short-term	4 762	76.2	70.9	−26.2	10.6	−1.8	15.4	2.2	....
Loans	4 764	108.8	32.8	115.1	113.0	100.5	213.5	−1,832.6	....
Monetary authorities	4 765	−8.3	1.5	−18.3	−11.8	−30.1	−24.8	−102.8	....
of which: Use of Fund credit and loans from the Fund	4 766	−8.3	1.5	−18.3	−11.8	−30.1	−24.8	−102.8	....
of which: Short-term	4 768	....	....	....	....	....	....	....	....
General government	4 769	88.3	111.5	87.5	104.4	86.7	158.1	−1,745.5	....
of which: Short-term	4 771	....	....	....	....	....	....	....	....
Banks	4 772	−6.2	−2.8	9.9	3.2	17.9	9.9	13.2	....
of which: Short-term	4 774	−9.5	3.0	1.0	1.5	8.4	−2.5	2.0	....
Other sectors	4 775	35.0	−77.4	35.9	17.2	26.0	70.3	2.4	....
of which: Short-term	4 777	108.9	....	....	....	....	....	....	....
Currency and deposits	4 780	3.9	12.1	11.2	13.0	−10.1	76.6	32.4	....
Monetary authorities	4 781	−.4	.9	1.7	1.3	−3.7	4.2	−1.2	....
General government	4 782	....	....	....	....	....	....	....	....
Banks	4 783	4.3	11.2	9.5	11.8	−6.4	72.5	33.6	....
Other sectors	4 784	....	....	....	....	....	....	....	....
Other liabilities	4 786	15.2	3.6	22.8	5.3	14.8	−22.5	−42.0	....
Monetary authorities	4 787	−.2	−.2	.9	−1.0	4.0	−4.3	2.6	....
of which: Short-term	4 789	....	....	....	....	4.0	−4.3	2.6	....
General government	4 790	....	....	....	....	....	....	....	....
of which: Short-term	4 792	....	....	....	....	....	....	....	....
Banks	4 793	....	....	6.5	−3.9	9.4	−.5	−1.9	....
of which: Short-term	4 795	....	....	6.5	−3.9	9.4	−.5	−1.9	....
Other sectors	4 796	15.4	3.8	15.3	10.1	1.3	−17.7	−42.7	....
of which: Short-term	4 798	15.4	3.8	15.3	10.1	1.3	−17.7	−42.7	....
E. RESERVE ASSETS	4 802	**−57.9**	**14.0**	**−159.0**	**−216.6**	**159.9**	**−122.7**	**−14.9**	....
Monetary gold	4 812	....	....	....	....	....	....	....	....
Special drawing rights	4 811	.4	−.3	.4	−.8	.3	.3	.2	....
Reserve position in the Fund	4 810	....	−.1	....	−.1	−.1	−.2	−.3	....
Foreign exchange	4 803	−58.1	14.3	−159.3	−215.7	159.7	−122.7	−14.9	....
Other claims	4 813	−.2	....	....	....	....	....	....	....
NET ERRORS AND OMISSIONS	4 998	**−4.8**	**9.4**	**−6.1**	**45.2**	**−26.3**	**−29.1**	**−34.9**	....

Table 3. INTERNATIONAL INVESTMENT POSITION (End-period stocks), 2000–2007

(Millions of U.S. dollars)

	Code	2000	2001	2002	2003	2004	2005	2006	2007
ASSETS	8 995 C.	**596.7**	**671.1**	**1,223.5**	**1,358.3**	**1,409.7**	**1,347.7**	**1,592.3**	....
Direct investment abroad	8 505 ..	**.6**	**15.9**	**2.1**	**6.6**	**10.2**	**7.9**	**3.8**	....
Equity capital and reinvested earnings	8 506 ..	.6	....	.4	5.2	7.5	6.6	7.5	....
Claims on affiliated enterprises	8 507 ..	.6	....	.4	5.2	7.5	6.6	7.5	....
Liabilities to affiliated enterprises	8 508 ..	....	....	....	....	....	....	....	....
Other capital	8 530 ..	.1	15.8	1.7	1.4	2.7	1.3	−3.7	....
Claims on affiliated enterprises	8 535 ..	.1	15.8	1.7	1.4	2.7	1.3		....
Liabilities to affiliated enterprises	8 540 ..	....	....	....	....	....	....	−3.7	....
Portfolio investment	8 602 ..	**28.4**	**35.0**	**41.1**	**98.3**	**96.8**	**65.7**	**120.7**	....
Equity securities	8 610 ..	1.7	.4	1.5	1.1	6.4	6.8	3.3	....
Monetary authorities	8 611 ..	....	....	....	....	....	....	....	....
General government	8 612 ..	....	....	....	....	....	....	....	....
Banks	8 613 ..	1.7	.3	.7	.4	....	6.6	3.2	....
Other sectors	8 614 ..	.1	.1	.8	.7	6.4	.1	.2	....
Debt securities	8 619 ..	26.6	34.6	39.7	97.2	90.4	59.0	117.3	....
Bonds and notes	8 620 ..	25.0	33.1	34.0	95.9	90.1	58.7	104.4	....
Monetary authorities	8 621 ..	....	....	....	....	....	....	....	....
General government	8 622 ..	....	....	....	....	....	....	....	....
Banks	8 623 ..	9.7	17.0	15.7	57.4	58.6	56.3	100.2	....
Other sectors	8 624 ..	15.3	16.1	18.3	38.5	31.5	2.4	4.3	....
Money market instruments	8 630 ..	1.6	1.5	5.7	1.2	.3	.3	12.9	....
Monetary authorities	8 631 ..	....	....	....	....	....	....	....	....
General government	8 632 ..	....	....	....	....	....	....	....	....
Banks	8 633 ..	1.6	1.5	5.7	1.0	.3	....	12.5	....
Other sectors	8 634 ..	....	....	....	.3	....	.3	.3	....
Financial derivatives	8 900 ..	**....**	**.1**	**.1**	**.1**	**.5**	**.4**	**.4**	....
Monetary authorities	8 901 ..	....	....	....	....	....	....	....	....
General government	8 902 ..	....	....	....	....	....	....	....	....
Banks	8 903 C.	....	....	....	....	....	.3	....	....
Other sectors	8 904 ..	....	.1	.1	.1	.5	.2	.4	....
Other investment	8 703 ..	**185.0**	**271.5**	**589.5**	**300.8**	**450.9**	**419.2**	**498.7**	....
Trade credits	8 706 ..	42.9	34.4	137.1	33.3	87.1	52.4	58.0	....
General government	8 707 ..	....	....	....	....	....	....	....	....
of which: Short-term	8 709 ..	....	....	....	....	....	....	....	....
Other sectors	8 710 ..	42.9	34.4	137.1	33.3	87.1	52.4	58.0	....
of which: Short-term	8 712 ..	....	....	....	....	....	....	....	....
Loans	8 714 ..	25.0	70.5	35.3	59.0	68.9	54.0	80.2	....
Monetary authorities	8 715 ..	....	....	....	....	....	....	....	....
of which: Short-term	8 718 ..	....	....	....	....	....	....	....	....
General government	8 719 ..	....	....	....	....	....	....	....	....
of which: Short-term	8 721 ..	....	....	....	....	....	....	....	....
Banks	8 722 ..	24.9	70.5	35.3	58.9	68.9	53.9	80.2	....
of which: Short-term	8 724 ..	*20.1*	*69.8*	*26.2*	*46.1*	*49.1*	*41.9*	*49.1*	....
Other sectors	8 725 ..	....	....	....	....	....	.1	....	....
of which: Short-term	8 727 ..	....	....	....	....	....	....	....	....
Currency and deposits	8 730 ..	98.2	153.3	348.9	183.9	272.4	292.8	301.5	....
Monetary authorities	8 731 ..	....	....	....	....	....	....	....	....
General government	8 732 ..	1.4	....	....	....	....	....	....	....
Banks	8 733 ..	73.2	115.4	149.0	140.8	175.5	146.5	223.4	....
Other sectors	8 734 ..	23.6	38.0	199.9	43.1	96.8	146.3	78.2	....
Other assets	8 736 ..	18.9	13.3	68.2	24.7	22.6	20.0	59.1	....
Monetary authorities	8 737 ..	....	....	....	....	....	....	....	....
of which: Short-term	8 739 ..	....	....	....	....	....	....	....	....
General government	8 740 ..	....	....	....	....	.6	....	3.9	....
of which: Short-term	8 742 ..	....	....	....	....	....	....	....	....
Banks	8 743 ..	2.5	1.5	−1.6	−6.5	−11.0	−6.6	3.0	....
of which: Short-term	8 745 ..	*2.5*	*1.5*	*−1.6*	*−6.6*	*−11.0*	*−6.6*	*3.0*	....
Other sectors	8 746 ..	16.4	11.8	69.8	31.2	33.0	26.6	52.3	....
of which: Short-term	8 748 ..	....	....	....	....	....	....	....	....
Reserve assets	8 802 ..	**382.7**	**348.7**	**590.8**	**952.5**	**851.3**	**854.5**	**968.8**	....
Monetary gold	8 812 ..	....	....	....	....	....	....	....	....
Special drawing rights	8 811 ..	.1	.4	....	.9	.6	.3	.1	.1
Reserve position in the Fund	8 810 ..	11.4	11.1	12.0	13.2	13.9	13.1	14.1	15.1
Foreign exchange	8 803 ..	370.9	337.2	578.8	938.4	836.8	841.2	954.7	....
Other claims	8 813 ..	.2	....	....	....	....	....	....	....

Table 3 (Concluded). INTERNATIONAL INVESTMENT POSITION (End-period stocks), 2000–2007

(Millions of U.S. dollars)

	Code	2000	2001	2002	2003	2004	2005	2006	2007
LIABILITIES	8 995 D.	**3,053.3**	**3,021.8**	**3,766.9**	**4,459.1**	**4,956.7**	**4,440.8**	**2,887.5**	....
Direct investment in Mali	8 555 ..	**132.4**	**210.4**	**524.2**	**682.6**	**756.4**	**871.6**	**965.6**	....
Equity capital and reinvested earnings	8 556 ..	79.2	81.9	461.6	551.4	682.9	654.6	680.5	....
Claims on direct investors	8 557 ..	....	....	....	....	....	....	....	....
Liabilities to direct investors	8 558 ..	....	....	....	....	....	....	....	....
Other capital	8 580 ..	53.2	128.6	62.5	131.2	73.5	217.0	285.1	....
Claims on direct investors	8 585 ..	....	....	....	....	....	....	....	....
Liabilities to direct investors	8 590 ..	....	....	....	....	....	....	....	....
Portfolio investment	8 652 ..	**4.7**	**16.7**	**76.4**	**46.9**	**16.4**	**33.5**	**38.1**	....
Equity securities	8 660 ..	.8	14.0	13.8	17.1	16.2	22.4	28.7	....
Banks	8 663 ..	.4	.7	1.8	1.7	1.7	6.5	10.6	....
Other sectors	8 664 ..	.4	13.3	12.1	15.4	14.5	15.9	18.1	....
Debt securities	8 669 ..	4.0	2.7	62.6	29.8	.2	11.0	9.4	....
Bonds and notes	8 670 ..	4.0	2.7	62.6	29.8	.2	11.0	9.4	....
Monetary authorities	8 671 ..	....	....	....	....	....	....	....	
General government	8 672 ..	....	....	....	....	....	....	....	
Banks	8 673 ..	....	....	....	....	....	9.1	9.4	
Other sectors	8 674 ..	4.0	2.7	62.6	29.8	.2	1.9	....	
Money market instruments	8 680 ..	....	....	....	....	....	....	....	
Monetary authorities	8 681 ..	....	....	....	....	....	....	....	
General government	8 682 ..	....	....	....	....	....	....	....	
Banks	8 683 ..	....	....	....	....	....	....	....	
Other sectors	8 684 ..	....	....	....	....	....	....	....	
Financial derivatives	8 905 ..	....	....	....	....	....	....	....	....
Monetary authorities	8 906 ..	....	....	....	....	....	....	....	
General government	8 907 ..	....	....	....	....	....	....	....	
Banks	8 908 ..	....	....	....	....	....	....	....	
Other sectors	8 909 ..	....	....	....	....	....	....	....	
Other investment	8 753 ..	**2,916.2**	**2,794.6**	**3,166.3**	**3,729.5**	**4,183.9**	**3,535.7**	**1,883.8**	....
Trade credits	8 756 ..	106.6	155.7	155.8	67.5	62.0	58.3	97.9	....
General government	8 757 ..	....	....	....	....	....	....	....	
of which: Short-term	8 759 ..	....	....	....	....	....	....	....	
Other sectors	8 760 ..	106.6	155.7	155.8	67.5	62.0	58.3	97.9	....
of which: Short-term	8 762 ..	....	....	....	....	....	....	....	
Loans	8 764 ..	2,720.3	2,534.4	2,830.8	3,457.6	3,920.5	3,259.7	1,486.6	....
Monetary authorities	8 765 ..	175.5	170.9	165.5	168.8	144.8	109.2	8.0	....
of which: Use of Fund credit and loans from the Fund	8 766 ..	*175.5*	*170.9*	*165.5*	*168.8*	*144.8*	*109.2*	*8.0*	*12.6*
of which: Short-term	8 768 ..	....	....	....	....	....	....	....	
General government	8 769 ..	2,295.1	2,238.5	2,576.0	3,170.3	3,612.8	3,011.5	1,262.9	....
of which: Short-term	8 771 ..	....	....	....	....	....	....	....	
Banks	8 772 ..	20.1	16.3	30.4	40.1	63.0	63.9	85.2	....
of which: Short-term	8 774 ..	*6.1*	*8.7*	*11.5*	*15.5*	*25.9*	*20.0*	*24.5*	....
Other sectors	8 775 ..	229.6	108.7	58.8	78.4	99.9	75.1	130.5	....
of which: Short-term	8 777 ..	....	....	....	....	....	....	....	
Currency and deposits	8 780 ..	61.8	75.9	128.9	174.5	163.4	231.7	276.9	....
Monetary authorities	8 781 ..	2.0	2.6	5.0	7.4	4.0	7.4	8.4	....
General government	8 782 ..	....	....	....	....	....	....	....	
Banks	8 783 ..	59.8	73.3	123.9	167.1	159.5	224.3	268.5	....
Other sectors	8 784 ..	....	....	....	....	....	....	....	
Other liabilities	8 786 ..	27.5	28.7	50.8	29.9	38.0	−14.1	22.4	....
Monetary authorities	8 787 ..	.3	.1	1.1	.3	4.7	....	2.7	....
of which: Short-term	8 789 ..	*.3*	*.1*	*1.1*	*.3*	*4.7*	....	*2.7*	
General government	8 790 ..	....	....	....	....	....	....	....	
of which: Short-term	8 792 ..	....	....	....	....	....	....	....	
Banks	8 793 ..	....	....	....	....	....	....	....	
of which: Short-term	8 795 ..	....	....	....	....	....	....	....	
Other sectors	8 796 ..	27.2	28.6	49.7	29.6	33.3	−14.0	19.6	....
of which: Short-term	8 798 ..	....	....	....	....	....	....	....	
NET INTERNATIONAL INVESTMENT POSITION	8 995 ..	**−2,456.6**	**−2,350.7**	**−2,543.4**	**−3,100.8**	**−3,547.0**	**−3,093.1**	**−1,295.2**	....
Conversion rates: CFA francs per U.S. dollar (end of period)	0 102 ..	704.95	744.31	625.50	519.36	481.58	556.04	498.07	445.59

Table 1. ANALYTIC PRESENTATION, 2000–2007

(Millions of U.S. dollars)

	Code	2000	2001	2002	2003	2004	2005	2006	2007
A. Current Account[1]	4 993 Z.	**−480.4**	**−149.7**	**106.2**	**−156.3**	**−353.0**	**−523.5**	**−584.4**	**−489.2**
Goods: exports f.o.b.	2 100 ..	2,479.0	2,023.1	2,341.9	2,591.8	2,719.9	2,586.9	2,936.5	3,228.4
Goods: imports f.o.b.	3 100 ..	−3,232.6	−2,575.4	−2,681.3	−3,232.0	−3,583.3	−3,709.4	−4,142.9	−4,615.9
Balance on Goods	4 100 ..	*−753.6*	*−552.3*	*−339.4*	*−640.2*	*−863.4*	*−1,122.5*	*−1,206.4*	*−1,387.4*
Services: credit	2 200 ..	1,092.3	1,098.7	1,201.0	1,379.4	1,675.8	2,006.6	2,665.5	3,411.2
Services: debit	3 200 ..	−760.6	−759.3	−797.6	−894.3	−1,051.5	−1,204.0	−1,769.5	−2,247.9
Balance on Goods and Services	4 991 ..	*−421.9*	*−212.9*	*63.9*	*−155.2*	*−239.1*	*−320.0*	*−310.3*	*−224.1*
Income: credit	2 300 ..	917.5	839.1	856.8	905.3	972.9	1,207.8	1,840.7	2,682.4
Income: debit	3 300 ..	−1,008.9	−799.8	−833.1	−934.4	−1,025.6	−1,454.9	−2,103.2	−2,854.3
Balance on Goods, Services, and Income	4 992 ..	*−513.4*	*−173.5*	*87.6*	*−184.3*	*−291.8*	*−567.1*	*−572.8*	*−396.0*
Current transfers: credit	2 379 Z.	93.1	201.4	281.1	276.0	229.5	343.4	529.0	712.8
Current transfers: debit	3 379 ..	−60.2	−177.6	−262.5	−247.9	−290.7	−299.8	−540.5	−806.0
B. Capital Account[1]	4 994 Z.	**18.6**	**1.5**	**6.6**	**17.2**	**83.4**	**193.2**	**193.6**	**71.7**
Capital account: credit	2 994 Z.	24.1	4.4	8.5	18.6	87.3	205.5	200.1	77.8
Capital account: debit	3 994 ..	−5.5	−2.9	−1.9	−1.4	−3.9	−12.3	−6.5	−6.1
Total, Groups A Plus B	4 981 ..	*−461.9*	*−148.2*	*112.9*	*−139.1*	*−269.6*	*−330.3*	*−390.7*	*−417.5*
C. Financial Account[1]	4 995 W.	**231.9**	**142.5**	**230.9**	**259.2**	**−40.0**	**611.0**	**494.9**	**678.5**
Direct investment abroad	4 505 ..	−21.0	−9.5	29.0	−575.2	−8.0	24.3	−30.0	−30.9
Direct investment in Malta	4 555 Z.	601.0	240.1	−429.9	1,007.0	394.4	679.0	1,872.7	931.6
Portfolio investment assets	4 602 ..	−781.7	−282.7	−385.2	−1,571.0	−2,094.6	−2,608.1	−2,454.1	534.0
Equity securities	4 610 ..	2.8	46.7	48.4	−11.6	−51.4	−98.4	−72.0	−117.8
Debt securities	4 619 ..	−784.6	−329.4	−433.6	−1,559.5	−2,043.2	−2,509.7	−2,382.2	651.7
Portfolio investment liabilities	4 652 Z.	70.7	−215.2	2.3	−20.2	4.4	36.1	−18.5	2.2
Equity securities	4 660 ..	67.8	−212.5	13.0	−13.5	7.5	35.5	−9.1	1.7
Debt securities	4 669 Z.	2.9	−2.7	−10.7	−6.7	−3.1	.6	−9.4	.4
Financial derivatives	4 910 ..	....	....	....	25.1	−18.2	−23.9	30.3	167.4
Financial derivatives assets	4 900 ..	....	....	....	−5.0	−17.6	−19.2	51.3	−196.1
Financial derivatives liabilities	4 905 ..	....	....	....	30.0	−.5	−4.7	−21.0	363.5
Other investment assets	4 703 ..	−222.2	1,095.2	−591.9	−68.7	−1,278.9	−2,805.2	−4,114.5	−10,281.5
Monetary authorities	4 701 ..	....	....	....	....	−.1	6.9	....	....
General government	4 704 ..	.4	−1.1	−.5	....	−.4	.3	−.3	1.0
Banks	4 705 ..	−264.6	1,104.8	−635.1	−92.8	−1,168.2	−2,743.2	−3,940.7	−10,235.5
Other sectors	4 728 ..	42.1	−8.5	43.8	24.1	−110.2	−69.2	−173.6	−47.1
Other investment liabilities	4 753 W.	585.1	−685.4	1,606.7	1,462.2	2,960.9	5,308.8	5,209.0	9,355.8
Monetary authorities	4 753 WA	8.0	−8.3	16.6	51.3	−71.1	18.6	9.9	7.7
General government	4 753 ZB	−16.1	5.4	13.4	43.0	−4.7	−26.7	−34.7	−23.0
Banks	4 753 ZC	573.3	−726.8	1,597.3	1,278.0	2,993.2	5,037.1	5,203.0	9,178.0
Other sectors	4 753 ZD	19.9	44.4	−20.6	89.8	43.5	279.9	30.9	193.2
Total, Groups A Through C	4 983 ..	*−230.0*	*−5.7*	*343.8*	*120.1*	*−309.6*	*280.7*	*104.2*	*261.0*
D. Net Errors and Omissions	4 998 ..	**8.1**	**260.7**	**−55.9**	**23.8**	**102.4**	**−63.9**	**7.2**	**234.4**
Total, Groups A Through D	4 984 ..	*−221.9*	*255.0*	*287.9*	*144.0*	*−207.2*	*216.8*	*111.4*	*495.4*
E. Reserves and Related Items	4 802 A.	**221.9**	**−255.0**	**−287.9**	**−144.0**	**207.2**	**−216.8**	**−111.4**	**−495.4**
Reserve assets	4 802 ..	221.9	−255.0	−287.9	−144.0	207.2	−216.8	−111.4	−495.4
Use of Fund credit and loans	4 766 ..	....	....	....	....	....	....	....	....
Exceptional financing	4 920 ..	....	....	....	....	....	....	....	....
Conversion rates: Maltese liri per U.S. dollar	0 101 ..	**.4381**	**.4500**	**.4336**	**.3772**	**.3447**	**.3458**	**.3409**	**.3117**
Conversion rates: euros per U.S. dollar	0 103 ..	**1.0854**	**1.1175**	**1.0626**	**.8860**	**.8054**	**.8041**	**.7971**	**.7306**

[1] Excludes components that have been classified in the categories of Group E.

Table 2. STANDARD PRESENTATION, 2000–2007

(Millions of U.S. dollars)

	Code	2000	2001	2002	2003	2004	2005	2006	2007
CURRENT ACCOUNT	4 993	−480.4	−149.7	106.2	−156.3	−353.0	−523.5	−584.4	−489.2
A. GOODS	4 100	−753.6	−552.3	−339.4	−640.2	−863.4	−1,122.5	−1,206.4	−1,387.4
Credit	2 100	2,479.0	2,023.1	2,341.9	2,591.8	2,719.9	2,586.9	2,936.5	3,228.4
General merchandise: exports f.o.b.	2 110	2,347.8	1,895.8	2,194.3	2,435.7	2,565.8	2,420.2	2,776.6	3,039.9
Goods for processing: exports f.o.b.	2 150	....	....	....	....	....	....	....	....
Repairs on goods	2 160	.1	....	2.2	....	49.0	118.0	110.7	127.4
Goods procured in ports by carriers	2 170	131.1	127.2	145.3	156.1	104.2	48.2	47.0	58.9
Nonmonetary gold	2 180	....	....	....	....	.9	.4	2.2	2.3
Debit	3 100	−3,232.6	−2,575.4	−2,681.3	−3,232.0	−3,583.3	−3,709.4	−4,142.9	−4,615.9
General merchandise: imports f.o.b.	3 110	−3,171.1	−2,511.0	−2,620.0	−3,171.3	−3,526.4	−3,636.4	−4,048.1	−4,488.8
Goods for processing: imports f.o.b.	3 150	....	....	....	....	....	....	....	....
Repairs on goods	3 160	−20.6	−24.8	−25.9	−23.3	−10.7	−12.8	−10.6	−8.3
Goods procured in ports by carriers	3 170	−18.5	−16.6	−13.9	−14.2	−26.1	−38.6	−51.4	−82.2
Nonmonetary gold	3 180	−22.4	−23.1	−21.5	−23.2	−20.0	−21.7	−32.8	−36.5
B. SERVICES	4 200	331.8	339.5	403.4	485.0	624.3	802.5	896.0	1,163.4
Total credit	2 200	*1,092.3*	*1,098.7*	*1,201.0*	*1,379.4*	*1,675.8*	*2,006.6*	*2,665.5*	*3,411.2*
Total debit	3 200	*−760.6*	*−759.3*	*−797.6*	*−894.3*	*−1,051.5*	*−1,204.0*	*−1,769.5*	*−2,247.9*
Transportation services, credit	2 205	300.7	322.3	337.7	329.0	350.3	312.0	391.8	435.1
Passenger	2 850	*144.4*	*142.8*	*143.4*	*146.9*	*182.1*	*168.8*	*198.8*	*229.8*
Freight	2 851	*24.5*	*22.9*	*22.6*	*24.2*	*14.9*	*12.0*	*16.0*	*15.1*
Other	2 852	*131.8*	*156.6*	*171.7*	*157.9*	*153.3*	*131.2*	*177.0*	*190.2*
Sea transport, passenger	2 207	....	....	....	....	....	....	....	....
Sea transport, freight	2 208	....	....	....	....	....	....	....	....
Sea transport, other	2 209	....	....	....	....	....	....	....	....
Air transport, passenger	2 211	144.4	142.8	143.4	146.9	182.1	168.8	198.8	229.8
Air transport, freight	2 212	24.5	22.9	22.6	24.2	14.9	12.0	16.0	15.1
Air transport, other	2 213	131.8	156.6	171.7	157.9	153.3	131.2	177.0	190.2
Other transport, passenger	2 215	....	....	....	....	....	....	....	....
Other transport, freight	2 216	....	....	....	....	....	....	....	....
Other transport, other	2 217	....	....	....	....	....	....	....	....
Transportation services, debit	3 205	−319.5	−312.3	−351.5	−353.7	−272.0	−232.0	−293.4	−298.7
Passenger	3 850	*−23.8*	*−23.5*	*−25.7*	*−23.0*	*−35.7*	*−42.9*	*−42.3*	*−43.5*
Freight	3 851	*−174.5*	*−166.7*	*−179.2*	*−210.1*	*−156.2*	*−144.7*	*−164.7*	*−196.8*
Other	3 852	*−121.2*	*−122.1*	*−146.5*	*−120.7*	*−80.1*	*−44.4*	*−86.3*	*−58.5*
Sea transport, passenger	3 207	....	....	....	....	....	....	....	....
Sea transport, freight	3 208	....	....	....	....	....	....	....	....
Sea transport, other	3 209	....	....	....	....	....	....	....	....
Air transport, passenger	3 211	−23.8	−23.5	−25.7	−23.0	−35.7	−42.9	−42.3	−43.5
Air transport, freight	3 212	−174.5	−166.7	−179.2	−210.1	−156.2	−144.7	−164.7	−196.8
Air transport, other	3 213	−121.2	−122.1	−146.5	−120.7	−80.1	−44.4	−86.3	−58.5
Other transport, passenger	3 215	....	....	....	....	....	....	....	....
Other transport, freight	3 216	....	....	....	....	....	....	....	....
Other transport, other	3 217	....	....	....	....	....	....	....	....
Travel, credit	2 236	586.6	560.8	613.7	722.1	766.6	754.9	767.0	912.8
Business travel	2 237	586.6	560.8	613.7	722.1	766.6	754.9	767.0	912.8
Personal travel	2 240	....	....	....	....	....	....	....	....
Travel, debit	3 236	−200.0	−180.4	−153.5	−215.1	−255.5	−268.0	−319.7	−375.5
Business travel	3 237	−200.0	−180.4	−153.5	−215.1	−255.5	−268.0	−319.7	−375.5
Personal travel	3 240	....	....	....	....	....	....	....	....
Other services, credit	2 200 BA	205.1	215.6	249.5	328.2	558.9	939.6	1,506.7	2,063.3
Communications	2 245	23.8	24.6	28.3	31.8	47.7	61.8	56.4	70.8
Construction	2 249	....	....	....	....	2.6	12.0	5.7	5.8
Insurance	2 253	28.8	29.7	32.9	27.7	42.8	46.0	40.9	41.3
Financial	2 260	....	....	....	....	65.4	65.4	115.8	230.3
Computer and information	2 262	3.4	3.2	3.5	5.1	14.1	45.3	49.2	51.0
Royalties and licence fees	2 266	1.6	....	1.2	1.2	2.9	48.0	143.7	161.0
Other business services	2 268	129.7	138.0	158.0	231.8	208.9	270.2	512.7	809.1
Personal, cultural, and recreational	2 287	....	....	....	....	148.5	361.7	551.8	660.7
Government, n.i.e.	2 291	17.8	20.1	25.6	30.7	26.0	29.2	30.6	33.2
Other services, debit	3 200 BA	−241.0	−266.6	−292.6	−325.5	−524.1	−704.1	−1,156.4	−1,573.6
Communications	3 245	−13.9	−12.0	−10.6	−13.1	−33.1	−33.7	−41.1	−48.2
Construction	3 249	....	....	....	....	−4.0	−.9	−62.3	−65.5
Insurance	3 253	−69.8	−71.8	−72.2	−72.9	−85.6	−97.2	−89.7	−95.1
Financial	3 260	....	....	....	....	−106.0	−75.0	−122.1	−317.8
Computer and information	3 262	−1.8	−2.4	−3.0	−3.6	−15.4	−30.2	−52.4	−73.0
Royalties and licence fees	3 266	−9.8	−10.2	−13.2	−15.2	−16.5	−53.7	−34.4	−42.7
Other business services	3 268	−116.5	−141.7	−158.8	−179.3	−236.3	−387.4	−725.7	−890.5
Personal, cultural, and recreational	3 287	−4.0	−3.7	−5.9	−7.7	−6.4	−7.8	−11.7	−14.8
Government, n.i.e.	3 291	−25.2	−24.7	−28.9	−33.7	−20.7	−18.1	−17.0	−26.1

Table 2 (Continued). STANDARD PRESENTATION, 2000–2007

(Millions of U.S. dollars)

	Code	2000	2001	2002	2003	2004	2005	2006	2007
C. INCOME................	4 300 ..	**−91.5**	**39.3**	**23.7**	**−29.1**	**−52.7**	**−247.1**	**−262.5**	**−171.9**
Total credit................	2 300 ..	*917.5*	*839.1*	*856.8*	*905.3*	*972.9*	*1,207.8*	*1,840.7*	*2,682.4*
Total debit................	3 300 ..	*−1,008.9*	*−799.8*	*−833.1*	*−934.4*	*−1,025.6*	*−1,454.9*	*−2,103.2*	*−2,854.3*
Compensation of employees, credit..........	2 310 ..	**16.2**	**12.4**	**21.0**	**25.2**	**32.6**	**33.3**	**35.3**	**42.8**
Compensation of employees, debit..........	3 310 ..	**−7.3**	**−6.9**	**−8.2**	**−10.2**	**−15.8**	**−21.8**	**−38.8**	**−45.6**
Investment income, credit............	2 320 ..	**901.3**	**826.7**	**835.8**	**880.1**	**940.3**	**1,174.4**	**1,805.4**	**2,639.6**
Direct investment income...........	2 330 ..	901.3	826.7	835.8	880.1	32.9	28.4	15.8	51.9
Dividends and distributed branch profits...........	2 332 ..	6.0	7.9	7.8	1.4	26.4	22.1	12.7	53.2
Reinvested earnings and undistributed branch profits.....	2 333 ..	6.7	7.4	−18.0	.8	3.9	2.8	−.6	−5.8
Income on debt (interest)...........	2 334 ..	888.5	811.4	846.0	877.8	2.6	3.6	3.6	4.5
Portfolio investment income...........	2 339 ..	....	....	....	....	481.7	624.2	986.8	1,243.7
Income on equity...........	2 340 ..	....	....	....	....	6.3	6.6	10.0	11.9
Income on bonds and notes...........	2 350 ..	....	....	....	....	475.4	617.6	976.8	1,231.8
Income on money market instruments...........	2 360 ..	....	....	....	....	....	....	....	....
Other investment income...........	2 370 ..	....	....	....	....	425.7	521.8	802.8	1,344.0
Investment income, debit...............	3 320 ..	**−1,001.7**	**−792.9**	**−825.0**	**−924.2**	**−1,009.8**	**−1,433.1**	**−2,064.4**	**−2,808.7**
Direct investment income...........	3 330 ..	−998.3	−791.9	−824.2	−922.4	−320.5	−556.1	−635.8	−712.7
Dividends and distributed branch profits...........	3 332 ..	−54.9	−59.4	−196.5	−204.4	−235.3	−455.3	−490.6	−436.3
Reinvested earnings and undistributed branch profits.....	3 333 ..	−262.1	−61.9	18.5	−92.9	−82.1	−95.4	−138.6	−266.9
Income on debt (interest)...........	3 334 ..	−681.2	−670.6	−646.2	−625.1	−3.1	−5.4	−6.6	−9.5
Portfolio investment income...........	3 339 ..	....	....	....	....	−22.4	−24.7	−24.0	−20.9
Income on equity...........	3 340 ..	....	....	....	....	−3.9	−6.4	−5.6	−.6
Income on bonds and notes...........	3 350 ..	....	....	....	....	−18.5	−18.3	−18.3	−20.3
Income on money market instruments...........	3 360 ..	....	....	....	....	....	....	....	−.1
Other investment income...........	3 370 ..	−3.4	−1.0	−.8	−1.8	−666.9	−852.3	−1,404.6	−2,075.1
D. CURRENT TRANSFERS............	4 379 ..	**32.9**	**23.9**	**18.6**	**28.1**	**−61.1**	**43.5**	**−11.5**	**−93.2**
Credit............	2 379 ..	**93.1**	**201.4**	**281.1**	**276.0**	**229.5**	**343.4**	**529.0**	**712.8**
General government...........	2 380 ..	25.8	62.6	113.4	54.8	85.4	154.1	402.1	599.2
Other sectors...........	2 390 ..	67.3	138.8	167.7	221.2	144.1	189.3	126.9	113.6
Workers' remittances...........	2 391 ..	1.3	.5	.2	.6	.1	.2	.3	.3
Other current transfers...........	2 392 ..	65.9	138.3	167.5	220.6	144.0	189.1	126.6	113.2
Debit............	3 379 ..	**−60.2**	**−177.6**	**−262.5**	**−247.9**	**−290.7**	**−299.8**	**−540.5**	**−806.0**
General government...........	3 380 ..	−25.1	−54.7	−106.1	−30.9	−71.6	−128.9	−351.2	−601.0
Other sectors...........	3 390 ..	−35.0	−122.9	−156.4	−217.0	−219.0	−171.0	−189.3	−205.0
Workers' remittances...........	3 391 ..	−1.1	−1.5	−1.2	−1.3	−2.5	−6.7	−4.2	−4.1
Other current transfers...........	3 392 ..	−33.9	−121.4	−155.2	−215.7	−216.5	−164.3	−185.1	−200.8
CAPITAL AND FINANCIAL ACCOUNT.........	4 996 ..	**472.3**	**−111.0**	**−50.4**	**132.5**	**250.6**	**587.5**	**577.2**	**254.8**
CAPITAL ACCOUNT............	4 994 ..	**18.6**	**1.5**	**6.6**	**17.2**	**83.4**	**193.2**	**193.6**	**71.7**
Total credit............	2 994 ..	*24.1*	*4.4*	*8.5*	*18.6*	*87.3*	*205.5*	*200.1*	*77.8*
Total debit............	3 994 ..	*−5.5*	*−2.9*	*−1.9*	*−1.4*	*−3.9*	*−12.3*	*−6.5*	*−6.1*
Capital transfers, credit............	2 400 ..	**24.1**	**4.4**	**8.5**	**18.6**	**87.3**	**205.5**	**181.9**	**77.8**
General government...........	2 401 ..	21.6	3.1	6.4	6.7	87.1	192.7	176.9	74.9
Debt forgiveness...........	2 402 ..	....	....	....	....	....	....	....	....
Other capital transfers...........	2 410 ..	21.6	3.1	6.4	6.7	87.1	192.7	176.9	74.9
Other sectors...........	2 430 ..	2.5	1.3	2.2	11.9	.2	12.8	5.1	2.9
Migrants' transfers...........	2 431 ..	2.5	1.3	2.2	1.0	.1	....	.4	.2
Debt forgiveness...........	2 432 ..	....	....	....	10.9	....	12.6	3.0	....
Other capital transfers...........	2 440 ..	....	....	....	....	.1	.1	1.7	2.6
Capital transfers, debit............	3 400 ..	**−5.5**	**−2.9**	**−1.9**	**−1.4**	**−3.4**	**−11.6**	**−5.8**	**−5.9**
General government...........	3 401 ..	....	....	....	....	....	....	−.2	....
Debt forgiveness...........	3 402 ..	....	....	....	....	....	....	....	....
Other capital transfers...........	3 410 ..	....	....	....	....	....	....	−.2	....
Other sectors...........	3 430 ..	−5.5	−2.9	−1.9	−1.4	−3.4	−11.6	−5.6	−5.9
Migrants' transfers...........	3 431 ..	−5.5	−2.9	−1.9	−1.4	−3.3	−4.0	−3.1	−3.8
Debt forgiveness...........	3 432 ..	−.1	....	....	....	−.2	−7.6	−2.5	−2.0
Other capital transfers...........	3 440 ..	....	....	....	....	....	....	....	....
Nonproduced nonfinancial assets, credit.............	2 480 ..	....	....	....	....	....	....	**18.2**	....
Nonproduced nonfinancial assets, debit.............	3 480 ..	....	....	....	....	**−.5**	**−.7**	**−.7**	**−.3**

Table 2 (Continued). STANDARD PRESENTATION, 2000–2007

(Millions of U.S. dollars)

	Code	2000	2001	2002	2003	2004	2005	2006	2007
FINANCIAL ACCOUNT..........................	4 995 ..	453.8	−112.5	−57.0	115.3	167.2	394.3	383.5	183.1
A. DIRECT INVESTMENT........................	4 500 ..	580.1	230.6	−400.9	431.8	386.4	703.3	1,842.7	900.8
Direct investment abroad...................	4 505 ..	−21.0	−9.5	29.0	−575.2	−8.0	24.3	−30.0	−30.9
Equity capital.............	4 510 ..	−17.3	−4.0	7.8	−579.8	−34.3	−26.1	−10.5	14.3
Claims on affiliated enterprises......	4 515 ..	−17.3	−4.0	7.8	−579.8	−34.3	−26.1	−10.5	14.3
Liabilities to affiliated enterprises....	4 520 ..	....	....	....	....	....	....	....	....
Reinvested earnings.............	4 525 ..	−6.7	−7.4	18.0	−.8	−4.1	−2.8	.6	5.8
Other capital.............	4 530 ..	3.0	2.0	3.2	5.5	30.3	53.2	−20.1	−50.9
Claims on affiliated enterprises......	4 535 ..	−1.2	3.0	2.3	1.7	19.3	−27.5	−6.3	−39.2
Liabilities to affiliated enterprises....	4 540 ..	4.2	−1.0	1.0	3.8	10.9	80.8	−13.8	−11.7
Direct investment in Malta................	4 555 ..	601.0	240.1	−429.9	1,007.0	394.4	679.0	1,872.7	931.6
Equity capital.............	4 560 ..	137.7	122.9	100.7	819.7	317.2	391.8	1,149.6	722.9
Claims on direct investors......	4 565 ..	....	....	....	....	....	....	....	....
Liabilities to direct investors......	4 570 ..	137.7	122.9	100.7	819.7	317.2	391.8	1,149.6	722.9
Reinvested earnings.............	4 575 ..	262.1	61.9	−18.5	92.9	81.9	95.4	138.5	266.9
Other capital.............	4 580 ..	201.2	55.3	−512.2	94.4	−4.7	191.8	584.6	−58.1
Claims on direct investors......	4 585 ..	−137.9	−177.8	68.9	99.3	−23.0	66.2	43.8	−196.7
Liabilities to direct investors......	4 590 ..	339.1	233.1	−581.0	−5.0	18.3	125.6	540.8	138.6
B. PORTFOLIO INVESTMENT...................	4 600 ..	−711.1	−498.0	−383.0	−1,591.2	−2,090.2	−2,571.9	−2,472.6	536.1
Assets..........................	4 602 ..	−781.7	−282.7	−385.2	−1,571.0	−2,094.6	−2,608.1	−2,454.1	534.0
Equity securities.............	4 610 ..	2.8	46.7	48.4	−11.6	−51.4	−98.4	−72.0	−117.8
Monetary authorities......	4 611 ..	....	....	....	....	....	....	....	....
General government......	4 612 ..	....	....	....	....	....	3.1	....	−2.0
Banks......	4 613 ..	12.6	−.1	−1.9	−15.6	2.3	−27.0	11.7	7.0
Other sectors......	4 614 ..	−9.8	46.8	50.3	4.0	−53.8	−74.5	−83.6	−122.7
Debt securities.............	4 619 ..	−784.6	−329.4	−433.6	−1,559.5	−2,043.2	−2,509.7	−2,382.2	651.7
Bonds and notes.............	4 620 ..	−836.7	242.4	−1,101.0	−970.7	−2,117.1	−2,504.9	−2,389.2	643.6
Monetary authorities......	4 621 ..	....	....	....	....	....	....	....	....
General government......	4 622 ..	....	....	....	....	....	....	....	....
Banks......	4 623 ..	−798.8	169.0	−1,096.1	−910.0	−2,070.3	−2,476.9	−2,228.5	671.6
Other sectors......	4 624 ..	−37.9	73.3	−5.0	−60.7	−46.8	−28.0	−160.7	−28.0
Money market instruments.............	4 630 ..	52.2	−571.8	667.4	−588.8	73.9	−4.8	7.1	8.2
Monetary authorities......	4 631 ..	....	....	....	....	....	....	....	....
General government......	4 632 ..	....	....	....	....	....	....	....	....
Banks......	4 633 ..	54.1	−609.8	660.3	−539.7	63.8	−14.7	....	....
Other sectors......	4 634 ..	−1.9	38.1	7.1	−49.0	10.2	10.0	7.1	8.2
Liabilities..........................	4 652 ..	70.7	−215.2	2.3	−20.2	4.4	36.1	−18.5	2.2
Equity securities.............	4 660 ..	67.8	−212.5	13.0	−13.5	7.5	35.5	−9.1	1.7
Banks......	4 663 ..	−.4	−2.6	....	−9.8	8.3	34.3	−18.6	1.5
Other sectors......	4 664 ..	68.1	−209.9	13.0	−3.7	−.9	1.2	9.5	.2
Debt securities.............	4 669 ..	2.9	−2.7	−10.7	−6.7	−3.1	.6	−9.4	.4
Bonds and notes.............	4 670 ..	2.7	−12.4	−2.1	1.5	−4.1	3.3	−7.3	.4
Monetary authorities......	4 671 ..	....	....	....	....	....	....	....	....
General government......	4 672 ..	....	....	....	....	.8	.2	−.1	−2.5
Banks......	4 673 ..	−.4	−12.7	−1.9	1.4	−6.1	1.1	−9.6	5.0
Other sectors......	4 674 ..	3.1	.3	−.2	.1	1.2	2.0	2.4	−2.1
Money market instruments.............	4 680 ..	.2	9.7	−8.6	−8.2	1.0	−2.7	−2.1	....
Monetary authorities......	4 681 ..	....	....	....	....	....	....	....	....
General government......	4 682 ..	....	....	....	....	....	....	....	....
Banks......	4 683 ..	.2	9.7	−8.6	−8.2	1.0	−2.7	−2.1	....
Other sectors......	4 684 ..	....	....	....	....	....	....	....	....
C. FINANCIAL DERIVATIVES...................	4 910 ..	....	....	....	25.1	−18.2	−23.9	30.3	167.4
Monetary authorities.............	4 911 ..	....	....	....	....	....	....	....	....
General government.............	4 912 ..	....	....	....	....	....	....	....	....
Banks.............	4 913 ..	....	....	....	25.1	−18.1	−24.0	30.3	167.3
Other sectors.............	4 914 ..	....	....	....	....	−.1	.1	....	.1
Assets..........................	4 900 ..	....	....	....	−5.0	−17.6	−19.2	51.3	−196.1
Monetary authorities.............	4 901 ..	....	....	....	....	....	....	....	....
General government.............	4 902 ..	....	....	....	....	....	....	....	....
Banks.............	4 903 ..	....	....	....	−5.0	−17.6	−19.3	51.3	−196.2
Other sectors.............	4 904 ..	....	....	....	....	−.1	.1	....	.1
Liabilities..........................	4 905 ..	....	....	....	30.0	−.5	−4.7	−21.0	363.5
Monetary authorities.............	4 906 ..	....	....	....	....	....	....	....	....
General government.............	4 907 ..	....	....	....	....	....	....	....	....
Banks.............	4 908 ..	....	....	....	30.0	−.5	−4.7	−21.0	363.5
Other sectors.............	4 909 ..	....	....	....	....	....	....	....	....

Table 2 (Concluded). STANDARD PRESENTATION, 2000–2007

(Millions of U.S. dollars)

	Code	2000	2001	2002	2003	2004	2005	2006	2007
D. OTHER INVESTMENT	4 700 ..	**362.9**	**409.8**	**1,014.7**	**1,393.5**	**1,682.0**	**2,503.6**	**1,094.5**	**−925.8**
Assets	4 703 ..	−222.2	1,095.2	−591.9	−68.7	−1,278.9	−2,805.2	−4,114.5	−10,281.5
Trade credits	4 706 ..	17.8	17.1	−25.4	6.4	−49.8	−123.6	−74.5	−82.9
General government	4 707 ..	.5	.3	−.1	....	....	−.5	.1	.9
of which: Short-term	4 709 ..	.5	.3	−.1	....	....	−.5	.1	.9
Other sectors	4 710 ..	17.3	16.8	−25.3	6.4	−49.8	−123.2	−74.6	−83.8
of which: Short-term	4 712 ..	17.3	16.8	−25.3	6.4	−36.5	−122.2	−58.8	−64.9
Loans	4 714 ..	−289.4	−834.1	−553.7	−357.2	−1,304.6	−2,233.3	−3,605.9	−8,781.1
Monetary authorities	4 715 ..	....	....	....	....	....	....	....	....
of which: Short-term	4 718 ..	....	....	....	....	....	....	....	....
General government	4 719 ..	....	....	....	....	....	....	....	....
of which: Short-term	4 721 ..	....	....	....	....	....	....	....	....
Banks	4 722 ..	−288.2	−826.4	−549.7	−346.8	−1,212.2	−2,224.6	−3,574.3	−8,790.1
of which: Short-term	4 724 ..	....	....	....	−45.8	−4.3	−69.5	−87.3	−520.5
Other sectors	4 725 ..	−1.1	−7.7	−4.0	−10.4	−92.4	−8.7	−31.6	8.9
of which: Short-term	4 727 ..	−1.4	−4.2	2.7	−9.1	−13.6	−11.5	−32.3	7.6
Currency and deposits	4 730 ..	−39.9	1,899.7	−59.1	348.0	116.6	−394.2	−477.0	−1,374.7
Monetary authorities	4 731 ..	....	....	....	....	−.2	6.9	....	....
General government	4 732 ..	−.1	−1.3	−.4	....	−.4	.8	−.4	.2
Banks	4 733 ..	−82.9	1,904.9	−154.3	308.3	74.2	−477.4	−421.8	−1,414.7
Other sectors	4 734 ..	43.1	−3.9	95.6	39.7	43.1	75.6	−54.8	39.9
Other assets	4 736 ..	89.3	12.5	46.3	−65.9	−41.1	−54.1	43.0	−42.8
Monetary authorities	4 737 ..	....	....	....	....	.2	....	....	....
of which: Short-term	4 739 ..	....	....	....	....	....	....	....	....
General government	4 740 ..	....	....	....	....	....	....	....	....
of which: Short-term	4 742 ..	....	....	....	....	....	....	....	....
Banks	4 743 ..	106.5	26.3	68.9	−54.3	−30.2	−41.1	55.5	−30.7
of which: Short-term	4 745 ..	106.5	26.3	68.9	15.1	−29.7	−41.2	20.4	−30.0
Other sectors	4 746 ..	−17.2	−13.7	−22.6	−11.6	−11.1	−12.9	−12.6	−12.1
of which: Short-term	4 748 ..	−9.3	−4.9	−12.7	1.7	2.2	−2.8	−1.3	.7
Liabilities	4 753 ..	**585.1**	**−685.4**	**1,606.7**	**1,462.2**	**2,960.9**	**5,308.8**	**5,209.0**	**9,355.8**
Trade credits	4 756 ..	8.3	22.1	−8.0	20.3	76.5	162.6	7.3	114.7
General government	4 757 ..	−3.2	3.5	.2	....	12.5	−11.5	.9	−3.4
of which: Short-term	4 759 ..	−3.2	3.5	.2	....	12.5	−11.5	.9	−3.4
Other sectors	4 760 ..	11.5	18.6	−8.2	20.3	64.0	174.1	6.3	118.1
of which: Short-term	4 762 ..	11.5	18.6	−8.2	20.3	59.6	174.0	8.7	117.7
Loans	4 764 ..	18.3	443.1	1,103.2	1,692.3	1,086.5	3,651.6	3,980.6	3,684.9
Monetary authorities	4 765 ..	....	....	....	52.5	−55.5	13.7	−.7	....
of which: Use of Fund credit and loans from the Fund	4 766 ..	....	....	....	....	....	....	....	....
of which: Short-term	4 768 ..	....	....	....	52.5	−56.0	13.7	−.7	....
General government	4 769 ..	−12.9	1.8	13.2	43.0	−17.2	−15.2	−35.7	−19.6
of which: Short-term	4 771 ..	....	....	....	....	....	....	....	....
Banks	4 772 ..	35.0	425.6	1,113.6	1,544.7	1,189.9	3,560.2	4,033.4	3,673.5
of which: Short-term	4 774 ..	....	....	....	587.8	−568.0	3,592.3	1,832.9	955.6
Other sectors	4 775 ..	−3.8	15.7	−23.6	52.1	−30.8	92.9	−16.4	30.9
of which: Short-term	4 777 ..	.4	2.6	−4.7	2.7	−19.1	−11.2	−16.3	−2.7
Currency and deposits	4 780 ..	864.2	−1,152.5	470.2	−235.6	1,711.4	1,518.3	1,187.1	4,828.2
Monetary authorities	4 781 ..	8.0	−8.3	16.6	−1.1	−15.6	4.9	10.6	7.7
General government	4 782 ..	....	....	....	....	....	....	....	....
Banks	4 783 ..	856.2	−1,144.2	453.6	−234.5	1,722.5	1,502.0	1,141.2	4,776.4
Other sectors	4 784 ..	....	....	....	....	4.5	11.4	35.3	44.1
Other liabilities	4 786 ..	−305.8	1.9	41.2	−14.8	86.6	−23.6	34.1	728.1
Monetary authorities	4 787 ..	....	....	....	....	....	....	....	....
of which: Short-term	4 789 ..	....	....	....	....	....	....	....	....
General government	4 790 ..	....	....	....	....	....	....	....	....
of which: Short-term	4 792 ..	....	....	....	....	....	....	....	....
Banks	4 793 ..	−317.9	−8.2	30.0	−32.2	80.8	−25.1	28.4	728.1
of which: Short-term	4 795 ..	−317.9	−8.2	30.0	−78.8	16.2	12.7	10.8	537.7
Other sectors	4 796 ..	12.1	10.1	11.2	17.4	5.8	1.5	5.7	....
of which: Short-term	4 798 ..	1.8	−.5	−1.4	4.4	5.8	1.5	5.7	....
E. RESERVE ASSETS	4 802 ..	**221.9**	**−255.0**	**−287.9**	**−144.0**	**207.2**	**−216.8**	**−111.4**	**−495.4**
Monetary gold	4 812 ..	.8	−.3	.5	....	.1	....	−1.1	−8.0
Special drawing rights	4 811 ..	−2.6	−2.4	−3.4	−1.3	−1.4	−2.0	−2.9	−5.8
Reserve position in the Fund	4 810 ..	....	....	....	....	....	....	....	....
Foreign exchange	4 803 ..	227.4	−254.0	−292.3	−135.2	208.8	−214.8	−107.4	−481.4
Other claims	4 813 ..	−3.7	1.8	7.3	−7.5	−.3	....	....	−.2
NET ERRORS AND OMISSIONS	4 998 ..	**8.1**	**260.7**	**−55.9**	**23.8**	**102.4**	**−63.9**	**7.2**	**234.4**

Table 3. INTERNATIONAL INVESTMENT POSITION (End-period stocks), 2000–2007

(Millions of U.S. dollars)

	Code	2000	2001	2002	2003	2004	2005	2006	2007
ASSETS	8 995 C.	**10,224.7**	**9,478.4**	**12,886.6**	**17,980.6**	**22,576.9**	**26,892.0**	**35,376.9**	....
Direct investment abroad	8 505	**203.1**	**258.8**	**271.9**	**923.5**	**1,109.3**	**994.8**	**1,145.0**	....
Equity capital and reinvested earnings	8 506	128.3	191.4	192.7	837.4	911.5	857.3	1,012.4	....
Claims on affiliated enterprises	8 507	128.3	191.4	192.7	837.4	906.3	850.6	1,004.2	....
Liabilities to affiliated enterprises	8 508	....	....	....	....	5.2	6.7	8.2	....
Other capital	8 530	74.8	67.4	79.2	86.1	197.8	137.5	132.5	....
Claims on affiliated enterprises	8 535	83.7	74.9	88.8	101.3	228.9	226.1	227.9	....
Liabilities to affiliated enterprises	8 540	−8.9	−7.5	−9.6	−15.2	−31.2	−88.6	−95.3	....
Portfolio investment	8 602	**2,820.5**	**3,025.6**	**4,352.4**	**7,020.0**	**9,628.5**	**11,899.6**	**14,986.7**	....
Equity securities	8 610	170.9	119.7	297.7	462.0	599.1	777.9	1,060.9	....
Monetary authorities	8 611	....	....	....	....	....	....	....	....
General government	8 612	....	....	....	....	....	....	....	....
Banks	8 613	2.6	2.6	5.3	23.4	9.3	36.7	35.0	....
Other sectors	8 614	168.3	117.1	292.3	438.6	589.8	741.2	1,025.8	....
Debt securities	8 619	2,649.6	2,905.9	4,054.7	6,558.0	9,029.4	11,121.7	13,925.9	....
Bonds and notes	8 620	2,603.2	2,286.6	3,980.2	5,840.7	8,452.7	10,554.8	13,924.9	....
Monetary authorities	8 621	....	....	....	....	....	....	....	....
General government	8 622	....	....	....	....	....	....	....	....
Banks	8 623	2,511.2	2,269.7	3,750.5	5,407.9	7,754.3	9,813.5	13,048.6	....
Other sectors	8 624	92.0	16.9	229.7	432.8	698.4	741.3	876.3	....
Money market instruments	8 630	46.3	619.3	74.5	717.2	576.7	566.9	1.0	....
Monetary authorities	8 631	....	....	....	....	....	....	....	....
General government	8 632	....	....	....	....	....	....	....	....
Banks	8 633	....	604.7	....	577.0	576.3	566.7	....	....
Other sectors	8 634	46.3	14.6	74.5	140.3	.4	.2	1.0	....
Financial derivatives	8 900	....	....	....	**5.2**	**14.4**	**50.1**	**45.4**	....
Monetary authorities	8 901	....	....	....	....	....	....	....	....
General government	8 902	....	....	....	....	....	....	....	....
Banks	8 903	....	....	....	5.2	14.1	49.9	43.2	....
Other sectors	8 904	....	....	....	....	.3	.1	2.2	....
Other investment	8 703	**5,729.7**	**4,511.9**	**6,053.6**	**7,274.1**	**9,090.5**	**11,357.3**	**16,247.5**	....
Trade credits	8 706	200.1	184.3	210.3	219.7	444.2	542.7	682.6	....
General government	8 707	.3	.1	.2	.3	....	.5	.7	....
of which: Short-term	8 709	*.3*	*.1*	*.2*	*.3*	....	*.5*	*.7*	....
Other sectors	8 710	199.8	184.3	210.1	219.4	444.2	542.2	681.9	....
of which: Short-term	8 712	*199.8*	*184.3*	*210.1*	*219.4*	*404.0*	*541.0*	*663.8*	....
Loans	8 714	2,205.6	2,979.2	3,977.1	5,074.8	6,646.1	8,399.4	12,578.7	....
Monetary authorities	8 715	....	....	....	....	....	....	....	....
of which: Short-term	8 718	....	....	....	....	....	....	....	....
General government	8 719	....	....	.1	.1	....	....	....	....
of which: Short-term	8 721	....	....	....	....	....	....	....	....
Banks	8 722	2,187.0	2,960.7	3,943.3	5,024.0	6,544.0	8,286.5	12,417.2	....
of which: Short-term	8 724	....	....	....	*2,132.5*	*211.0*	*151.9*	*567.4*	....
Other sectors	8 725	18.5	18.4	33.7	50.8	102.1	112.9	161.5	....
of which: Short-term	8 727	*18.4*	*14.9*	*20.9*	*34.4*	*25.0*	*35.5*	*77.9*	....
Currency and deposits	8 730	3,104.1	1,153.1	1,672.8	1,676.8	1,903.9	2,315.2	2,934.2	....
Monetary authorities	8 731	....	....	....	....	6.6	....	....	....
General government	8 732	.4	.2	.7	.8	1.1	.4	.4	....
Banks	8 733	3,057.0	1,093.4	1,416.8	1,280.8	1,361.8	1,707.3	2,188.5	....
Other sectors	8 734	46.7	59.6	255.3	395.2	534.5	607.5	745.3	....
Other assets	8 736	219.9	195.3	193.4	302.8	96.3	100.0	51.9	....
Monetary authorities	8 737	....	....	....	....	.3	.2	.2	....
of which: Short-term	8 739	....	....	....	....	....	....	....	....
General government	8 740	2.4	2.7	3.0	3.5	....	....	....	....
of which: Short-term	8 742	....	....	....	....	....	....	....	....
Banks	8 743	202.8	167.3	123.0	207.9	60.0	65.9	42.9	....
of which: Short-term	8 745	*202.8*	*167.3*	*123.0*	*207.9*	*59.4*	*65.5*	*29.0*	....
Other sectors	8 746	14.6	25.4	67.5	91.4	36.1	33.8	8.8	....
of which: Short-term	8 748	*14.6*	*16.7*	*32.0*	*35.4*	*29.3*	*26.0*	....	....
Reserve assets	8 802	**1,471.4**	**1,682.2**	**2,208.7**	**2,757.7**	**2,734.2**	**2,590.3**	**2,952.4**	....
Monetary gold	8 812	1.0	1.4	1.2	1.8	1.9	2.3	4.1	....
Special drawing rights	8 811	31.9	33.2	39.3	44.3	47.8	45.9	51.2	59.8
Reserve position in the Fund	8 810	52.5	50.6	54.7	59.8	62.5	57.5	60.6	63.6
Foreign exchange	8 803	1,386.0	1,597.0	2,113.4	2,651.8	2,622.0	2,484.6	2,836.5	....
Other claims	8 813	....	....	....	....	....	....	....	....

Table 3 (Concluded). INTERNATIONAL INVESTMENT POSITION (End-period stocks), 2000–2007

(Millions of U.S. dollars)

	Code	2000	2001	2002	2003	2004	2005	2006	2007
LIABILITIES..	8 995 D.	**9,991.1**	**8,949.4**	**11,269.9**	**15,745.1**	**20,131.2**	**24,787.0**	**33,405.0**	....
Direct investment in Malta...............................	8 555 ..	**2,385.2**	**2,551.4**	**2,413.4**	**3,281.0**	**4,018.4**	**4,315.0**	**6,498.0**	....
Equity capital and reinvested earnings............................	8 556 ..	1,793.7	1,941.4	2,294.9	3,605.5	4,248.9	4,352.9	6,037.7	....
Claims on direct investors............................	8 557 ..	....	....	....	....	....	....	....	....
Liabilities to direct investors.......................	8 558 ..	1,793.7	1,941.4	2,294.9	3,605.5	4,248.9	4,352.9	6,037.7	....
Other capital...............................	8 580 ..	591.5	610.1	118.5	−324.5	−230.5	−37.9	460.4	....
Claims on direct investors............................	8 585 ..	−475.8	−638.8	−647.4	−655.1	−631.7	−558.1	−609.9	....
Liabilities to direct investors.......................	8 590 ..	1,067.3	1,248.9	765.9	330.5	401.2	520.2	1,070.3	....
Portfolio investment...................................	8 652 ..	**569.4**	**342.4**	**369.3**	**412.7**	**477.9**	**488.9**	**537.5**	....
Equity securities....................................	8 660 ..	262.4	39.3	52.7	47.2	159.1	215.0	245.7	....
Banks....................................	8 663 ..	10.7	7.7	8.7	....	104.7	177.9	180.5	....
Other sectors....................................	8 664 ..	251.7	31.6	44.0	47.2	54.4	37.2	65.2	....
Debt securities....................................	8 669 ..	307.0	303.1	316.6	365.5	318.8	273.8	291.8	....
Bonds and notes....................................	8 670 ..	299.4	286.0	307.0	363.0	314.4	272.9	291.8	....
Monetary authorities....................................	8 671 ..	....	....	....	....	....	....	....	....
General government....................................	8 672 ..	....	....	....	3.7	3.3	2.9	4.7	....
Banks....................................	8 673 ..	37.0	23.3	24.3	30.0	25.3	23.3	14.1	....
Other sectors....................................	8 674 ..	262.4	262.6	282.7	329.3	285.8	246.7	273.0	....
Money market instruments....................................	8 680 ..	7.6	17.1	9.5	2.5	4.4	.9	....	....
Monetary authorities....................................	8 681 ..	....	....	....	....	....	....	....	....
General government....................................	8 682 ..	....	....	....	....	....	....	....	....
Banks....................................	8 683 ..	7.6	17.1	9.5	2.5	4.4	.9	....	....
Other sectors....................................	8 684 ..	....	....	....	....	....	....	....	....
Financial derivatives....................................	8 905 ..	....	....	....	**31.6**	**51.4**	**52.3**	**65.0**	....
Monetary authorities....................................	8 906 ..	....	....	....	....	....	....	....	....
General government....................................	8 907 ..	....	....	....	....	....	....	....	....
Banks....................................	8 908 ..	....	....	....	31.6	51.4	52.3	65.0	....
Other sectors....................................	8 909 ..	....	....	....	....	....	....	....	....
Other investment...................................	8 753 ..	**7,036.5**	**6,055.5**	**8,487.3**	**12,019.8**	**15,583.4**	**19,930.9**	**26,304.4**	....
Trade credits....................................	8 756 ..	167.1	169.2	181.4	234.3	340.3	526.2	558.2	....
General government....................................	8 757 ..	2.3	5.9	5.8	12.7	21.7	8.3	10.0	....
of which: Short-term....................................	8 759 ..	*2.3*	*5.9*	*5.8*	*12.7*	*21.7*	*8.3*	*10.0*	....
Other sectors....................................	8 760 ..	164.9	163.3	175.7	221.6	318.5	518.0	548.2	....
of which: Short-term....................................	8 762 ..	*164.9*	*163.3*	*175.7*	*221.6*	*312.9*	*512.3*	*537.8*	....
Loans....................................	8 764 ..	1,642.5	2,007.6	3,408.6	6,344.6	7,797.3	10,828.6	15,449.9	....
Monetary authorities....................................	8 765 ..	....	....	....	55.2	.6	....	....	....
of which: Use of Fund credit and loans from the Fund....	8 766 ..	....	....	....	....	....	....	....	....
of which: Short-term....................................	8 768 ..	....	....	....	*55.2*	....	....	....	....
General government....................................	8 769 ..	160.2	144.7	174.1	250.1	249.0	202.8	187.5	....
of which: Short-term....................................	8 771 ..	....	....	....	....	....	....	....	....
Banks....................................	8 772 ..	1,240.0	1,602.4	2,994.3	5,702.9	7,170.3	10,150.8	14,794.2	....
of which: Short-term....................................	8 774 ..	....	....	....	*4,562.3*	*4,513.7*	*7,893.7*	*6,657.2*	....
Other sectors....................................	8 775 ..	242.4	260.5	240.2	336.4	377.4	475.0	468.2	....
of which: Short-term....................................	8 777 ..	*26.3*	*27.4*	*24.2*	*31.2*	*39.5*	*33.2*	*27.6*	....
Currency and deposits....................................	8 780 ..	5,041.3	3,708.4	4,671.3	5,207.3	7,223.3	8,409.2	10,146.2	....
Monetary authorities....................................	8 781 ..	8.3	....	17.5	19.8	8.6	20.1	35.2	....
General government....................................	8 782 ..	....	....	....	....	....	....	....	....
Banks....................................	8 783 ..	5,033.0	3,708.4	4,653.8	5,187.5	7,188.9	8,354.0	10,033.7	....
Other sectors....................................	8 784 ..	....	....	....	....	25.9	35.1	77.3	....
Other liabilities....................................	8 786 ..	185.5	170.4	225.9	233.5	222.5	166.8	150.1	....
Monetary authorities....................................	8 787 ..	....	....	....	....	....	....	....	....
of which: Short-term....................................	8 789 ..	....	....	....	....	....	....	....	....
General government....................................	8 790 ..	....	....	....	....	....	....	....	....
of which: Short-term....................................	8 792 ..	....	....	....	....	....	....	....	....
Banks....................................	8 793 ..	173.9	159.5	215.9	217.0	207.7	152.3	150.1	....
of which: Short-term....................................	8 795 ..	*173.9*	*159.5*	*215.9*	*217.0*	*109.2*	*95.7*	*44.8*	....
Other sectors....................................	8 796 ..	11.6	10.8	10.0	16.5	14.8	14.5	....	....
of which: Short-term....................................	8 798 ..	*11.6*	*10.8*	*10.0*	*16.5*	*14.8*	*14.5*	....	....
NET INTERNATIONAL INVESTMENT POSITION........	8 995 ..	**233.6**	**529.0**	**1,616.7**	**2,235.5**	**2,445.7**	**2,105.1**	**1,971.9**	....
Conversion rates: Maltese liris per U.S. dollar (end of period)................	0 102 ..	.4378	.4521	.3988	.3425	.3185	.3627	.3257	.2916
Conversion rates: euros per U.S. dollar (end of period)................	0 104 ..	1.0747	1.1347	.9536	.7918	.7342	.8477	.7593	.6793

Table 1. ANALYTIC PRESENTATION, 2000–2007

(Millions of U.S. dollars)

	Code	2000	2001	2002	2003	2004	2005	2006	2007
A. Current Account[1]	4 993 Z.	**−36.9**	**276.1**	**249.4**	**93.2**	**−111.8**	**−324.0**	**−604.4**	**−408.3**
Goods: exports f.o.b.	2 100 ..	1,552.2	1,628.2	1,801.3	1,898.1	1,993.1	2,138.4	2,328.8	2,230.7
Goods: imports f.o.b.	3 100 ..	−1,944.4	−1,846.0	−2,012.6	−2,201.1	−2,572.6	−2,935.2	−3,408.8	−3,656.4
Balance on Goods	4 100 ..	*−392.1*	*−217.7*	*−211.3*	*−303.0*	*−579.5*	*−796.8*	*−1,080.0*	*−1,425.7*
Services: credit	2 200 ..	1,070.2	1,222.0	1,148.7	1,280.1	1,455.6	1,618.1	1,671.3	2,205.3
Services: debit	3 200 ..	−762.5	−810.1	−792.7	−906.3	−1,023.3	−1,197.7	−1,316.9	−1,545.4
Balance on Goods and Services	4 991 ..	*−84.5*	*194.1*	*144.7*	*70.8*	*−147.2*	*−376.5*	*−725.5*	*−765.8*
Income: credit	2 300 ..	48.7	75.2	79.9	47.0	51.7	142.9	373.9	816.5
Income: debit	3 300 ..	−64.9	−60.9	−66.7	−77.1	−65.7	−151.3	−323.8	−577.6
Balance on Goods, Services, and Income	4 992 ..	*−100.7*	*208.4*	*157.9*	*40.8*	*−161.1*	*−385.0*	*−675.5*	*−526.9*
Current transfers: credit	2 379 Z.	167.6	193.1	195.3	163.0	168.1	162.3	179.3	253.9
Current transfers: debit	3 379 ..	−103.8	−125.4	−103.8	−110.6	−118.7	−101.3	−108.2	−135.3
B. Capital Account[1]	4 994 Z.	**−.6**	**−1.4**	**−1.9**	**−.9**	**−1.6**	**−1.8**	**−2.7**	**−1.6**
Capital account: credit	2 994 Z.	....	.4	....	....	....	....	....	....
Capital account: debit	3 994 ..	−.6	−1.8	−1.9	−.9	−1.6	−1.8	−2.7	−1.6
Total, Groups A Plus B	4 981 ..	*−37.5*	*274.7*	*247.4*	*92.3*	*−113.4*	*−325.7*	*−607.1*	*−410.0*
C. Financial Account[1]	4 995 W.	**258.0**	**−240.2**	**84.2**	**89.7**	**8.1**	**142.1**	**172.8**	**518.9**
Direct investment abroad	4 505 ..	−13.0	−2.9	−8.7	6.0	−31.8	−47.0	−9.6	−59.6
Direct investment in Mauritius	4 555 Z.	265.6	−27.7	32.1	62.6	13.9	41.8	106.8	340.8
Portfolio investment assets	4 602 ..	−18.8	−17.7	−18.3	−27.1	−52.4	−41.6	−110.5	−138.5
Equity securities	4 610 ..	−18.8	−17.7	−18.3	−27.1	−52.4	−41.6	−110.5	−138.5
Debt securities	4 619 ..	....	....	....	....	....	....	....	....
Portfolio investment liabilities	4 652 Z.	−120.4	−1.6	.9	8.9	15.3	25.4	80.6	153.7
Equity securities	4 660 ..	−3.5	−8.7	−.7	8.1	19.3	35.6	35.1	49.7
Debt securities	4 669 Z.	−116.8	7.1	1.6	.8	−3.9	−10.2	45.5	103.9
Financial derivatives	4 910 ..	....	....	....	....	....	....	....	....
Financial derivatives assets	4 900 ..	....	....	....	....	....	....	....	....
Financial derivatives liabilit es	4 905 ..	....	....	....	....	....	....	....	....
Other investment assets	4 703 ..	−307.6	−253.0	−106.7	−22.8	−49.4	−230.9	−371.0	−671.5
Monetary authorities	4 701 ..	....	....	....	....	....	....	....	....
General government	4 704 ..	....	....	....	....	....	....	....	....
Banks	4 705 ..	−51.5	−61.7	−20.4	14.1	−44.2	−195.5	−338.6	−460.0
Other sectors	4 728 ..	−256.1	−191.3	−86.2	−36.9	−5.2	−35.4	−32.4	−211.5
Other investment liabilities	4 753 W.	452.1	62.7	184.9	62.0	112.4	394.3	476.5	894.1
Monetary authorities	4 753 WA	....	....	....	....	....	....	....	....
General government	4 753 ZB	91.6	−118.7	34.5	−8.2	−7.3	10.3	−19.7	46.1
Banks	4 753 ZC	13.7	.4	93.1	6.1	56.7	7.1	−5.0	18.8
Other sectors	4 753 ZD	346.8	181.0	57.3	64.1	63.0	377.0	501.3	829.2
Total, Groups A Through C	4 983 ..	*220.5*	*34.5*	*331.7*	*182.0*	*−105.3*	*−183.6*	*−434.3*	*108.9*
D. Net Errors and Omissions	4 998 ..	**10.1**	**−86.3**	**9.4**	**40.4**	**77.9**	**18.7**	**294.2**	**327.1**
Total, Groups A Through D	4 984 ..	*230.6*	*−51.8*	*341.1*	*222.4*	*−27.5*	*−165.0*	*−140.1*	*436.0*
E. Reserves and Related Items	4 802 A.	**−230.6**	**51.8**	**−341.1**	**−222.4**	**27.5**	**165.0**	**140.1**	**−436.0**
Reserve assets	4 802 ..	−230.6	51.8	−341.1	−222.4	27.5	165.0	140.1	−436.0
Use of Fund credit and loans	4 766 ..	....	....	....	....	....	....	....	....
Exceptional financing	4 920 ..	....	....	....	....	....	....	....	....
Conversion rates: Mauritian rupees per U.S. dollar	0 101 ..	**26.250**	**29.129**	**29.962**	**27.901**	**27.499**	**29.496**	**31.708**	**31.314**

[1] Excludes components that have been classified in the categories of Group E.

Table 2. STANDARD PRESENTATION, 2000–2007

(Millions of U.S. dollars)

	Code	2000	2001	2002	2003	2004	2005	2006	2007
CURRENT ACCOUNT..	4 993 ..	**−36.9**	**276.1**	**249.4**	**93.2**	**−111.8**	**−324.0**	**−604.4**	**−408.3**
A. GOODS...	4 100 ..	**−392.1**	**−217.7**	**−211.3**	**−303.0**	**−579.5**	**−796.8**	**−1,080.0**	**−1,425.7**
Credit...	2 100 ..	**1,552.2**	**1,628.2**	**1,801.3**	**1,898.1**	**1,993.1**	**2,138.4**	**2,328.8**	**2,230.7**
General merchandise: exports f.o.b................	2 110 ..	1,483.8	1,561.5	1,727.3	1,824.8	1,913.2	1,999.2	2,168.9	2,056.0
Goods for processing: exports f.o.b...............	2 150 ..	....	....	....	....	....	....	....	....
Repairs on goods...	2 160 ..	....	....	....	....	....	....	....	....
Goods procured in ports by carriers..............	2 170 ..	68.4	66.8	74.0	73.3	79.9	139.1	159.9	174.7
Nonmonetary gold.......................................	2 180 ..	....	....	....	....	....	....	....	....
Debit..	3 100 ..	**−1,944.4**	**−1,846.0**	**−2,012.6**	**−2,201.1**	**−2,572.6**	**−2,935.2**	**−3,408.8**	**−3,656.4**
General merchandise: imports f.o.b...............	3 110 ..	−1,917.9	−1,817.3	−1,982.6	−2,164.7	−2,517.4	−2,865.2	−3,326.4	−3,564.0
Goods for processing: imports f.o.b..............	3 150 ..	....	....	....	....	....	....	....	....
Repairs on goods...	3 160 ..	....	....	....	....	....	....	....	....
Goods procured in ports by carriers..............	3 170 ..	−26.5	−28.6	−29.9	−36.4	−55.2	−70.0	−82.5	−92.4
Nonmonetary gold.......................................	3 180 ..	....	....	....	....	....	....	....	....
B. SERVICES..	4 200 ..	**307.6**	**411.9**	**356.0**	**373.8**	**432.3**	**420.4**	**354.4**	**659.9**
Total credit..	2 200 ..	*1,070.2*	*1,222.0*	*1,148.7*	*1,280.1*	*1,455.6*	*1,618.1*	*1,671.3*	*2,205.3*
Total debit...	3 200 ..	*−762.5*	*−810.1*	*−792.7*	*−906.3*	*−1,023.3*	*−1,197.7*	*−1,316.9*	*−1,545.4*
Transportation services, credit....................	2 205 ..	**223.2**	**235.1**	**275.1**	**335.1**	**372.9**	**384.1**	**362.5**	**430.8**
Passenger..	2 850 ..	*189.6*	*197.0*	*217.1*	*263.3*	*300.2*	*317.6*	*297.5*	*359.1*
Freight..	2 851 ..	*8.4*	*12.6*	*17.7*	*24.0*	*28.1*	*29.0*	*27.0*	*24.2*
Other..	2 852 ..	*25.1*	*25.5*	*40.3*	*47.8*	*44.5*	*37.5*	*38.1*	*47.4*
Sea transport, passenger.............................	2 207 ..	....	....	....	....	....	....	....	....
Sea transport, freight..................................	2 208 ..	....	....	....	....	....	....	....	....
Sea transport, other....................................	2 209 ..	....	....	....	....	....	....	....	....
Air transport, passenger..............................	2 211 ..	....	....	....	....	....	....	....	....
Air transport, freight...................................	2 212 ..	....	....	....	....	....	....	....	....
Air transport, other.....................................	2 213 ..	....	....	....	....	....	....	....	....
Other transport, passenger.........................	2 215 ..	....	....	....	....	....	....	....	....
Other transport, freight...............................	2 216 ..	....	....	....	....	....	....	....	....
Other transport, other................................	2 217 ..	....	....	....	....	....	....	....	....
Transportation services, debit.....................	3 205 ..	**−261.1**	**−260.8**	**−307.3**	**−400.3**	**−469.0**	**−522.5**	**−534.1**	**−576.0**
Passenger..	3 850 ..	*−20.9*	*−17.9*	*−19.5*	*−19.8*	*−21.9*	*−20.4*	*−20.4*	*−27.3*
Freight..	3 851 ..	*−140.7*	*−140.9*	*−144.5*	*−164.6*	*−212.8*	*−246.8*	*−256.6*	*−258.3*
Other..	3 852 ..	*−99.5*	*−101.9*	*−143.4*	*−215.9*	*−234.3*	*−255.2*	*−257.1*	*−290.4*
Sea transport, passenger.............................	3 207 ..	....	....	....	....	....	....	....	....
Sea transport, freight..................................	3 208 ..	....	....	....	....	....	....	....	....
Sea transport, other....................................	3 209 ..	....	....	....	....	....	....	....	....
Air transport, passenger..............................	3 211 ..	....	....	....	....	....	....	....	....
Air transport, freight...................................	3 212 ..	....	....	....	....	....	....	....	....
Air transport, other.....................................	3 213 ..	....	....	....	....	....	....	....	....
Other transport, passenger.........................	3 215 ..	....	....	....	....	....	....	....	....
Other transport, freight...............................	3 216 ..	....	....	....	....	....	....	....	....
Other transport, other................................	3 217 ..	....	....	....	....	....	....	....	....
Travel, credit...	2 236 ..	**542.0**	**622.9**	**611.8**	**696.7**	**856.1**	**871.0**	**1,005.3**	**1,303.7**
Business travel..	2 237 ..	....	155.7	227.0	244.8	330.7	368.0	367.0	450.2
Personal travel..	2 240 ..	....	467.2	384.8	452.0	525.4	503.0	638.3	853.4
Travel, debit..	3 236 ..	**−181.6**	**−197.6**	**−203.9**	**−216.1**	**−254.8**	**−275.0**	**−326.8**	**−361.1**
Business travel..	3 237 ..	....	−14.9	−33.3	−26.1	−14.0	−24.7	−14.4	−24.5
Personal travel..	3 240 ..	....	−182.7	−170.5	−190.0	−240.8	−250.3	−312.4	−336.6
Other services, credit.................................	2 200 BA	**305.0**	**364.0**	**261.8**	**248.2**	**226.7**	**363.0**	**303.5**	**470.8**
Communications..	2 245 ..	16.0	31.7	30.8	20.5	19.9	19.9	26.1	42.0
Construction...	2 249 ..	9.3	3.4	6.2	3.3	4.6	24.0	17.7	7.5
Insurance..	2 253 ..	41.6	13.6	4.0	8.6	6.5	3.4	6.5	9.4
Financial...	2 260 ..	21.4	68.0	17.6	12.7	17.9	17.1	20.8	32.6
Computer and information............................	2 262 ..	2.8	6.1	6.2	9.2	12.3	16.9	24.3	20.3
Royalties and licence fees............................	2 266 ..	....	....	....	....	.1	....	.2	.5
Other business services...............................	2 268 ..	207.8	234.1	189.4	182.3	155.5	265.2	197.8	343.0
Personal, cultural, and recreational..............	2 287 ..	2.0	2.8	5.0	5.3	3.6	2.4	1.9	4.2
Government, n.i.e...	2 291 ..	4.0	4.2	2.6	6.3	6.3	13.9	8.2	11.3
Other services, debit..................................	3 200 BA	**−319.9**	**−351.7**	**−281.5**	**−289.9**	**−299.5**	**−400.3**	**−455.9**	**−608.3**
Communications..	3 245 ..	−16.2	−12.6	−36.5	−22.5	−20.0	−18.3	−30.3	−25.9
Construction...	3 249 ..	−.4	−5.9	−18.5	−7.1	−3.5	−10.4	−4.3	−10.2
Insurance..	3 253 ..	−28.2	−24.9	−32.5	−39.7	−55.7	−59.6	−58.7	−59.7
Financial...	3 260 ..	−21.5	−57.2	−4.4	−6.3	−5.5	−4.2	−12.2	−24.2
Computer and information............................	3 262 ..	−5.3	−8.8	−8.3	−8.0	−8.4	−6.4	−8.0	−7.4
Royalties and licence fees............................	3 266 ..	−1.2	−1.4	−2.3	−1.7	−4.3	−4.7	−4.4	−6.0
Other business services...............................	3 268 ..	−228.9	−225.2	−152.0	−160.0	−162.6	−261.4	−299.7	−428.3
Personal, cultural, and recreational..............	3 287 ..	−4.1	−4.6	−9.5	−13.8	−21.3	−30.6	−33.5	−39.3
Government, n.i.e...	3 291 ..	−14.1	−11.1	−17.6	−30.8	−18.3	−4.7	−4.7	−7.3

Table 2 (Continued). STANDARD PRESENTATION, 2000–2007

(Millions of U.S. dollars)

	Code	2000	2001	2002	2003	2004	2005	2006	2007
C. INCOME	4 300	−16.2	14.3	13.2	−30.0	−14.0	−8.5	50.1	238.9
Total credit	2 300	*48.7*	*75.2*	*79.9*	*47.0*	*51.7*	*142.9*	*373.9*	*816.5*
Total debit	3 300	*−64.9*	*−60.9*	*−66.7*	*−77.1*	*−65.7*	*−151.3*	*−323.8*	*−577.6*
Compensation of employees, credit	2 310	....	.6	.6	.6	.7	.6	.7	.7
Compensation of employees, debit	3 310	....	−6.3	−8.1	−9.1	−9.3	−9.2	−10.1	−9.9
Investment income, credit	2 320	48.7	74.6	79.2	46.5	51.0	142.2	373.2	815.8
Direct investment income	2 330	.9	2.3	5.2	2.7	3.9	4.5	2.4	4.1
Dividends and distributed branch profits	2 332	.9	2.3	5.2	2.7	3.9	4.5	2.4	4.1
Reinvested earnings and undistributed branch profits	2 333	....	....	....	....	....	....	....	....
Income on debt (interest)	2 334	....	....	....	....	....	....	....	....
Portfolio investment income	2 339	1.4	.7	3.1	3.4	3.5	3.4	3.6	9.9
Income on equity	2 340	1.4	.7	3.1	3.4	3.5	3.4	3.6	9.9
Income on bonds and notes	2 350	....	....	....	....	....	....	....	....
Income on money market instruments	2 360	....	....	....	....	....	....	....	....
Other investment income	2 370	46.3	71.6	70.9	40.4	43.6	134.4	367.2	801.8
Investment income, debit	3 320	−64.9	−54.6	−58.6	−68.0	−56.4	−142.1	−313.8	−567.7
Direct investment income	3 330	−8.1	−5.0	−9.8	−23.6	−13.6	−33.6	−88.1	−75.5
Dividends and distributed branch profits	3 332	−8.1	−5.0	−9.8	−23.6	−13.6	−33.6	−88.1	−75.5
Reinvested earnings and undistributed branch profits	3 333	....	....	....	....	....	....	....	....
Income on debt (interest)	3 334	....	....	....	....	....	....	....	....
Portfolio investment income	3 339	−4.2	−3.2	−11.6	−6.7	−9.0	−17.0	−23.0	−65.3
Income on equity	3 340	−4.2	−3.2	−10.1	−4.5	−8.1	−17.0	−23.0	−65.3
Income on bonds and notes	3 350	....	....	....	....	....	....	....	....
Income on money market instruments	3 360	....	....	−1.5	−2.3	−.8	....	....	....
Other investment income	3 370	−52.5	−46.4	−37.1	−37.6	−33.8	−91.4	−202.7	−426.9
D. CURRENT TRANSFERS	4 379	63.8	67.6	91.5	52.4	49.3	61.0	71.1	118.6
Credit	2 379	167.6	193.1	195.3	163.0	168.1	162.3	179.3	253.9
General government	2 380	8.0	11.1	20.7	15.1	22.0	16.4	17.7	22.8
Other sectors	2 390	159.6	182.0	174.6	147.9	146.0	145.9	161.6	231.1
Workers' remittances	2 391	....	....	....	....	....	....	....	....
Other current transfers	2 392	159.6	182.0	174.6	147.9	146.0	145.9	161.6	231.1
Debit	3 379	−103.8	−125.4	−103.8	−110.6	−118.7	−101.3	−108.2	−135.3
General government	3 380	−.8	−7.5	−6.8	−.5	−4.0	−5.9	−6.1	−5.3
Other sectors	3 390	−103.0	−117.9	−97.0	−110.1	−114.7	−95.4	−102.1	−130.0
Workers' remittances	3 391	....	....	....	....	....	....	....	....
Other current transfers	3 392	−103.0	−117.9	−97.0	−110.1	−114.7	−95.4	−102.1	−130.0
CAPITAL AND FINANCIAL ACCOUNT	4 996	26.8	−189.8	−258.8	−133.5	33.9	305.3	310.2	81.2
CAPITAL ACCOUNT	4 994	−.6	−1.4	−1.9	−.9	−1.6	−1.8	−2.7	−1.6
Total credit	2 994	....	*.4*	....	....	....	....	....	....
Total debit	3 994	*−.6*	*−1.8*	*−1.9*	*−.9*	*−1.6*	*−1.8*	*−2.7*	*−1.6*
Capital transfers, credit	2 400	....	.4	....	....	....	....	....	....
General government	2 401	....	.4	....	....	....	....	....	....
Debt forgiveness	2 402	....	....	....	....	....	....	....	....
Other capital transfers	2 410	....	.4	....	....	....	....	....	....
Other sectors	2 430	....	....	....	....	....	....	....	....
Migrants' transfers	2 431	....	....	....	....	....	....	....	....
Debt forgiveness	2 432	....	....	....	....	....	....	....	....
Other capital transfers	2 440	....	....	....	....	....	....	....	....
Capital transfers, debit	3 400	−.6	−1.8	−1.9	−.9	−1.6	−1.8	−2.7	−1.6
General government	3 401	....	....	....	....	....	....	....	....
Debt forgiveness	3 402	....	....	....	....	....	....	....	....
Other capital transfers	3 410	....	....	....	....	....	....	....	....
Other sectors	3 430	−.6	−1.8	−1.9	−.9	−1.6	−1.8	−2.7	−1.6
Migrants' transfers	3 431	−.6	−1.8	−1.9	−.9	−1.6	−1.8	−2.7	−1.6
Debt forgiveness	3 432	....	....	....	....	....	....	....	....
Other capital transfers	3 440	....	....	....	....	....	....	....	....
Nonproduced nonfinancial assets, credit	2 480	....	....	....	....	....	....	....	....
Nonproduced nonfinancial assets, debit	3 480	....	....	....	....	....	....	....	....

Table 2 (Continued). STANDARD PRESENTATION, 2000–2007

(Millions of U.S. dollars)

	Code	2000	2001	2002	2003	2004	2005	2006	2007
FINANCIAL ACCOUNT................................	4 995 ..	27.5	−188.4	−256.8	−132.7	35.5	307.0	312.9	82.9
A. DIRECT INVESTMENT............................	4 500 ..	252.7	−30.5	23.4	68.6	−17.9	−5.2	97.2	281.2
Direct investment abroad......................	4 505 ..	−13.0	−2.9	−8.7	6.0	−31.8	−47.0	−9.6	−59.6
Equity capital................................	4 510 ..	−13.0	−2.9	−8.7	6.0	−31.8	−47.0	−9.6	−59.6
Claims on affiliated enterprises..........	4 515 ..	....	....	....	....	....	....	....	....
Liabilities to affiliated enterprises......	4 520 ..	....	....	....	....	....	....	....	....
Reinvested earnings........................	4 525 ..	....	....	....	....	....	....	....	....
Other capital................................	4 530 ..	....	....	....	....	....	....	....	....
Claims on affiliated enterprises..........	4 535 ..	....	....	....	....	....	....	....	....
Liabilities to affiliated enterprises......	4 540 ..	....	....	....	....	....	....	....	....
Direct investment in Mauritius..............	4 555 ..	265.6	−27.7	32.1	62.6	13.9	41.8	106.8	340.8
Equity capital................................	4 560 ..	265.6	−27.7	32.1	62.6	13.9	41.8	106.8	340.8
Claims on direct investors................	4 565 ..	....	....	....	....	....	....	....	....
Liabilities to direct investors............	4 570 ..	....	....	....	....	....	....	....	....
Reinvested earnings........................	4 575 ..	....	....	....	....	....	....	....	....
Other capital................................	4 580 ..	....	....	....	....	....	....	....	....
Claims on direct investors................	4 585 ..	....	....	....	....	....	....	....	....
Liabilities to direct investors............	4 590 ..	....	....	....	....	....	....	....	....
B. PORTFOLIO INVESTMENT....................	4 600 ..	−139.2	−19.3	−17.4	−18.1	−37.0	−16.2	−29.9	15.1
Assets..	4 602 ..	−18.8	−17.7	−18.3	−27.1	−52.4	−41.6	−110.5	−138.5
Equity securities............................	4 610 ..	−18.8	−17.7	−18.3	−27.1	−52.4	−41.6	−110.5	−138.5
Monetary authorities......................	4 611 ..	....	....	....	....	....	....	....	....
General government......................	4 612 ..	....	....	....	....	....	....	....	....
Banks....................................	4 613 ..	....	....	....	....	....	....	....	....
Other sectors............................	4 614 ..	−18.8	−17.7	−18.3	−27.1	−52.4	−41.6	−110.5	−138.5
Debt securities............................	4 619 ..	....	....	....	....	....	....	....	....
Bonds and notes..........................	4 620 ..	....	....	....	....	....	....	....	....
Monetary authorities..................	4 621 ..	....	....	....	....	....	....	....	....
General government..................	4 622 ..	....	....	....	....	....	....	....	....
Banks....................................	4 623 ..	....	....	....	....	....	....	....	....
Other sectors............................	4 624 ..	....	....	....	....	....	....	....	....
Money market instruments..............	4 630 ..	....	....	....	....	....	....	....	....
Monetary authorities..................	4 631 ..	....	....	....	....	....	....	....	....
General government..................	4 632 ..	....	....	....	....	....	....	....	....
Banks....................................	4 633 ..	....	....	....	....	....	....	....	....
Other sectors............................	4 634 ..	....	....	....	....	....	....	....	....
Liabilities....................................	4 652 ..	−120.4	−1.6	.9	8.9	15.3	25.4	80.6	153.7
Equity securities............................	4 660 ..	−3.5	−8.7	−.7	8.1	19.3	35.6	35.1	49.7
Banks....................................	4 663 ..	....	....	....	....	....	....	....	....
Other sectors............................	4 664 ..	−3.5	−8.7	−.7	8.1	19.3	35.6	35.1	49.7
Debt securities............................	4 669 ..	−116.8	7.1	1.6	.8	−3.9	−10.2	45.5	103.9
Bonds and notes..........................	4 670 ..	−114.2	....	....	....	....	1.1	46.0	....
Monetary authorities..................	4 671 ..	....	....	....	....	....	....	....	....
General government..................	4 672 ..	−114.2	....	....	....	....	....	....	....
Banks....................................	4 673 ..	....	....	....	....	....	1.1	46.0	....
Other sectors............................	4 674 ..	....	....	....	....	....	....	....	....
Money market instruments..............	4 680 ..	−2.6	7.1	1.6	.8	−3.9	−11.3	−.6	103.9
Monetary authorities..................	4 681 ..	....	....	....	1.5	.7	−2.1	....	1.5
General government..................	4 682 ..	−2.6	7.1	1.6	−.7	−4.7	−9.3	−.6	102.4
Banks....................................	4 683 ..	....	....	....	....	....	....	....	....
Other sectors............................	4 684 ..	....	....	....	....	....	....	....	....
C. FINANCIAL DERIVATIVES....................	4 910 ..	....	....	....	....	....	....	....	....
Monetary authorities......................	4 911 ..	....	....	....	....	....	....	....	....
General government......................	4 912 ..	....	....	....	....	....	....	....	....
Banks....................................	4 913 ..	....	....	....	....	....	....	....	....
Other sectors............................	4 914 ..	....	....	....	....	....	....	....	....
Assets..	4 900 ..	....	....	....	....	....	....	....	....
Monetary authorities......................	4 901 ..	....	....	....	....	....	....	....	....
General government......................	4 902 ..	....	....	....	....	....	....	....	....
Banks....................................	4 903 ..	....	....	....	....	....	....	....	....
Other sectors............................	4 904 ..	....	....	....	....	....	....	....	....
Liabilities....................................	4 905 ..	....	....	....	....	....	....	....	....
Monetary authorities......................	4 906 ..	....	....	....	....	....	....	....	....
General government......................	4 907 ..	....	....	....	....	....	....	....	....
Banks....................................	4 908 ..	....	....	....	....	....	....	....	....
Other sectors............................	4 909 ..	....	....	....	....	....	....	....	....

Table 2 (Concluded). STANDARD PRESENTATION, 2000–2007

(Millions of U.S. dollars)

	Code	2000	2001	2002	2003	2004	2005	2006	2007
D. OTHER INVESTMENT	4 700	**144.5**	**−190.4**	**78.3**	**39.2**	**63.0**	**163.4**	**105.5**	**222.5**
Assets	4 703	−307.6	−253.0	−106.7	−22.8	−49.4	−230.9	−371.0	−671.5
Trade credits	4 706	....	....	....	....	....	....	....	....
General government	4 707	....	....	....	....	....	....	....	....
of which: Short-term	4 709	....	....	....	....	....	....	....	....
Other sectors	4 710	....	....	....	....	....	....	....	....
of which: Short-term	4 712	....	....	....	....	....	....	....	....
Loans	4 714	....	....	....	....	....	−92.6	5.3	−122.8
Monetary authorities	4 715	....	....	....	....	....	....	....	....
of which: Short-term	4 718	....	....	....	....	....	....	....	....
General government	4 719	....	....	....	....	....	....	....	....
of which: Short-term	4 721	....	....	....	....	....	....	....	....
Banks	4 722	....	....	....	....	....	−92.6	5.3	−122.8
of which: Short-term	4 724	....	....	....	....	....	−92.6	5.3	−122.8
Other sectors	4 725	....	....	....	....	....	....	....	....
of which: Short-term	4 727	....	....	....	....	....	....	....	....
Currency and deposits	4 730	−306.9	−252.3	−95.0	−4.3	−63.4	−133.9	−330.3	−583.6
Monetary authorities	4 731	....	....	....	....	....	....	....	....
General government	4 732	....	....	....	....	....	....	....	....
Banks	4 733	−51.5	−61.7	−20.4	14.1	−44.2	−92.6	−306.9	−372.1
Other sectors	4 734	−255.4	−190.6	−74.6	−18.3	−19.2	−41.3	−23.3	−211.5
Other assets	4 736	−.7	−.7	−11.7	−18.5	14.1	−4.4	−46.0	34.9
Monetary authorities	4 737	....	....	....	....	....	....	....	....
of which: Short-term	4 739	....	....	....	....	....	....	....	....
General government	4 740	....	....	....	....	....	....	....	....
of which: Short-term	4 742	....	....	....	....	....	....	....	....
Banks	4 743	....	....	....	....	....	−10.3	−36.9	34.9
of which: Short-term	4 745	....	....	....	....	....	−10.3	−36.9	34.9
Other sectors	4 746	−.7	−.7	−11.7	−18.5	14.1	5.8	−9.1	....
of which: Short-term	4 748	−.7	−.7	−11.7	−18.5	14.1	5.8	−9.1	....
Liabilities	4 753	**452.1**	**62.7**	**184.9**	**62.0**	**112.4**	**394.3**	**476.5**	**894.1**
Trade credits	4 756	....	....	....	....	80.8	210.3	231.2	244.7
General government	4 757	....	....	....	....	....	....	....	....
of which: Short-term	4 759	....	....	....	....	....	....	....	....
Other sectors	4 760	....	....	....	....	80.8	210.3	231.2	244.7
of which: Short-term	4 762	....	....	....	....	80.8	210.3	231.2	244.7
Loans	4 764	112.4	−168.7	−64.6	−90.7	−82.7	49.9	−3.0	98.9
Monetary authorities	4 765	....	....	....	....	....	....	....	....
of which: Use of Fund credit and loans from the Fund	4 766	....	....	....	....	....	....	....	....
of which: Short-term	4 768	....	....	....	....	....	....	....	....
General government	4 769	91.6	−118.7	34.5	−8.2	−7.3	10.3	−19.7	46.1
of which: Short-term	4 771	114.2	−111.3	....	....	....	....	....	....
Banks	4 772	....	....	....	....	....	7.1	−5.0	18.8
of which: Short-term	4 774	....	....	....	....	....	7.1	−5.0	18.8
Other sectors	4 775	20.8	−49.9	−99.1	−82.5	−75.4	32.5	21.8	34.0
of which: Short-term	4 777	....	....	....	....	....	....	....	....
Currency and deposits	4 780	339.7	231.3	249.5	152.7	114.3	134.1	248.3	550.4
Monetary authorities	4 781	....	....	....	....	....	....	....	....
General government	4 782	....	....	....	....	....	....	....	....
Banks	4 783	13.7	.4	93.1	6.1	56.7	....	....	....
Other sectors	4 784	326.0	230.9	156.4	146.6	57.6	134.1	248.3	550.4
Other liabilities	4 786	....	....	....	....	....	....	....	....
Monetary authorities	4 787	....	....	....	....	....	....	....	....
of which: Short-term	4 789	....	....	....	....	....	....	....	....
General government	4 790	....	....	....	....	....	....	....	....
of which: Short-term	4 792	....	....	....	....	....	....	....	....
Banks	4 793	....	....	....	....	....	....	....	....
of which: Short-term	4 795	....	....	....	....	....	....	....	....
Other sectors	4 796	....	....	....	....	....	....	....	....
of which: Short-term	4 798	....	....	....	....	....	....	....	....
E. RESERVE ASSETS	4 802	**−230.6**	**51.8**	**−341.1**	**−222.4**	**27.5**	**165.0**	**140.1**	**−436.0**
Monetary gold	4 812	....	....	....	....	....	....	....	....
Special drawing rights	4 811	−.5	−.5	−.3	−.3	−.4	−.6	−.5	−.3
Reserve position in the Fund	4 810	....	....	....	−10.5	....	6.2	10.2	5.2
Foreign exchange	4 803	−230.1	52.2	−340.8	−211.6	27.9	159.4	130.4	−440.9
Other claims	4 813	....	....	....	....	....	....	....	....
NET ERRORS AND OMISSIONS	4 998	**10.1**	**−86.3**	**9.4**	**40.4**	**77.9**	**18.7**	**294.2**	**327.1**

Table 3. INTERNATIONAL INVESTMENT POSITION (End-period stocks), 2000–2007

(Millions of U.S. dollars)

	Code	2000	2001	2002	2003	2004	2005	2006	2007
ASSETS	8 995 C.	1,329.9	1,293.9	1,736.9	2,159.2	2,184.3	2,139.0	2,484.7	3,561.6
Direct investment abroad	8 505	....	....	....	....	....	....	....	....
Equity capital and reinvested earnings	8 506	....	....	....	....	....	....	....	....
Claims on affiliated enterprises	8 507	....	....	....	....	....	....	....	....
Liabilities to affiliated enterprises	8 508	....	....	....	....	....	....	....	....
Other capital	8 530	....	....	....	....	....	....	....	....
Claims on affiliated enterprises	8 535	....	....	....	....	....	....	....	....
Liabilities to affiliated enterprises	8 540	....	....	....	....	....	....	....	....
Portfolio investment	8 602	....	....	....	....	....	....	....	....
Equity securities	8 610	....	....	....	....	....	....	....	....
Monetary authorities	8 611	....	....	....	....	....	....	....	....
General government	8 612	....	....	....	....	....	....	....	....
Banks	8 613	....	....	....	....	....	....	....	....
Other sectors	8 614	....	....	....	....	....	....	....	....
Debt securities	8 619	....	....	....	....	....	....	....	....
Bonds and notes	8 620	....	....	....	....	....	....	....	....
Monetary authorities	8 621	....	....	....	....	....	....	....	....
General government	8 622	....	....	....	....	....	....	....	....
Banks	8 623	....	....	....	....	....	....	....	....
Other sectors	8 624	....	....	....	....	....	....	....	....
Money market instruments	8 630	....	....	....	....	....	....	....	....
Monetary authorities	8 631	....	....	....	....	....	....	....	....
General government	8 632	....	....	....	....	....	....	....	....
Banks	8 633	....	....	....	....	....	....	....	....
Other sectors	8 634	....	....	....	....	....	....	....	....
Financial derivatives	8 900	....	....	....	....	....	....	....	....
Monetary authorities	8 901	....	....	....	....	....	....	....	....
General government	8 902	....	....	....	....	....	....	....	....
Banks	8 903	....	....	....	....	....	....	....	....
Other sectors	8 904	....	....	....	....	....	....	....	....
Other investment	8 703	420.1	445.9	497.1	560.7	554.4	773.2	1,183.8	1,739.9
Trade credits	8 706	....	....	....	....	....	....	....	....
General government	8 707	....	....	....	....	....	....	....	....
of which: Short-term	8 709	....	....	....	....	....	....	....	....
Other sectors	8 710	....	....	....	....	....	....	....	....
of which: Short-term	8 712	....	....	....	....	....	....	....	....
Loans	8 714	....	....	....	....	....	204.7	195.3	338.3
Monetary authorities	8 715	....	....	....	....	....	....	....	....
of which: Short-term	8 718	....	....	....	....	....	....	....	....
General government	8 719	....	....	....	....	....	....	....	....
of which: Short-term	8 721	....	....	....	....	....	....	....	....
Banks	8 722	....	....	....	....	....	204.7	195.3	338.3
of which: Short-term	8 724	....	....	....	....	....	*204.7*	*195.3*	*338.3*
Other sectors	8 725	....	....	....	....	....	....	....	....
of which: Short-term	8 727	....	....	....	....	....	....	....	....
Currency and deposits	8 730	400.2	427.0	465.5	503.1	512.5	416.1	766.3	1,148.2
Monetary authorities	8 731	....	....	....	....	....	....	....	....
General government	8 732	....	....	....	....	....	....	....	....
Banks	8 733	400.2	427.0	465.5	503.1	512.5	416.1	766.3	1,148.2
Other sectors	8 734	....	....	....	....	....	....	....	....
Other assets	8 736	19.9	19.0	31.6	57.6	41.9	152.5	222.2	253.3
Monetary authorities	8 737	....	....	....	....	....	....	....	....
of which: Short-term	8 739	....	....	....	....	....	....	....	....
General government	8 740	....	....	....	....	....	....	....	....
of which: Short-term	8 742	....	....	....	....	....	....	....	....
Banks	8 743	....	....	....	....	....	109.2	140.1	196.2
of which: Short-term	8 745	....	....	....	....	....	*109.2*	*140.1*	*196.2*
Other sectors	8 746	19.9	19.0	31.6	57.6	41.9	43.3	82.1	57.1
of which: Short-term	8 748	*19.9*	*19.0*	*31.6*	*57.6*	*41.9*	*43.3*	*82.1*	*57.1*
Reserve assets	8 802	909.8	848.0	1,239.8	1,598.4	1,629.9	1,365.8	1,300.9	1,821.8
Monetary gold	8 812	12.3	12.3	12.3	21.1	23.9	25.9	31.3	41.5
Special drawing rights	8 811	21.4	21.1	23.2	25.6	27.2	25.7	27.5	29.3
Reserve position in the Fund	8 810	18.9	18.2	19.7	32.5	34.0	25.0	15.8	11.1
Foreign exchange	8 803	857.2	796.3	1,184.5	1,519.2	1,544.7	1,289.2	1,226.3	1,739.9
Other claims	8 813	....	....	....	....	....	....	....	....

Table 3 (Concluded). INTERNATIONAL INVESTMENT POSITION (End-period stocks), 2000–2007

(Millions of U.S. dollars)

	Code	2000	2001	2002	2003	2004	2005	2006	2007
LIABILITIES	8 995 D.	**1,265.0**	**1,069.9**	**1,197.7**	**1,281.5**	**1,262.8**	**1,233.6**	**1,134.2**	**1,322.8**
Direct investment in Mauritius	8 555	....	....	....	....	....	....	....	....
Equity capital and reinvested earnings	8 556	....	....	....	....	....	....	....	....
Claims on direct investors	8 557	....	....	....	....	....	....	....	....
Liabilities to direct investors	8 558	....	....	....	....	....	....	....	....
Other capital	8 580	....	....	....	....	....	....	....	....
Claims on direct investors	8 585	....	....	....	....	....	....	....	....
Liabilities to direct investors	8 590	....	....	....	....	....	....	....	....
Portfolio investment	8 652	**40.0**	**35.0**	**37.3**	**51.6**	**62.5**	**82.1**	**149.9**	**236.6**
Equity securities	8 660	33.4	22.2	22.5	33.8	49.9	80.3	104.0	180.8
Banks	8 663	....	....	....	....	....	....	....	....
Other sectors	8 664	33.4	22.2	22.5	33.8	49.9	80.3	104.0	180.8
Debt securities	8 669	6.6	12.9	14.9	17.8	12.7	1.8	45.9	55.8
Bonds and notes	8 670	....	....	....	....	....	1.1	45.9	55.8
Monetary authorities	8 671	....	....	....	....	....	....	....	....
General government	8 672	....	....	....	....	....	....	....	....
Banks	8 673	....	....	....	....	....	....	....	....
Other sectors	8 674	....	....	....	....	....	1.1	45.9	55.8
Money market instruments	8 680	6.6	12.9	14.9	17.8	12.7	.6	....	....
Monetary authorities	8 681	....	....	....	1.6	2.1	....	....	2.8
General government	8 682	6.6	12.9	14.9	16.2	10.5	.6	....	117.5
Banks	8 683	....	....	....	....	....	....	....	....
Other sectors	8 684	....	....	....	....	....	....	....	....
Financial derivatives	8 905	....	....	....	....	....	....	....	....
Monetary authorities	8 906	....	....	....	....	....	....	....	....
General government	8 907	....	....	....	....	....	....	....	....
Banks	8 908	....	....	....	....	....	....	....	....
Other sectors	8 909	....	....	....	....	....	....	....	....
Other investment	8 753	**1,225.0**	**1,034.8**	**1,160.4**	**1,229.9**	**1,200.3**	**1,151.5**	**984.3**	**1,086.1**
Trade credits	8 756	....	....	....	....	....	....	....	....
General government	8 757	....	....	....	....	....	....	....	....
of which: Short-term	8 759	....	....	....	....	....	....	....	....
Other sectors	8 760	....	....	....	....	....	....	....	....
of which: Short-term	8 762	....	....	....	....	....	....	....	....
Loans	8 764	1,118.4	936.6	963.7	1,004.6	933.0	1,151.5	984.3	1,086.1
Monetary authorities	8 765	....	....	....	....	....	....	....	....
of which: Use of Fund credit and loans from the Fund	8 766	....	....	....	....	....	....	....	....
of which: Short-term	8 768	....	....	....	....	....	....	....	....
General government	8 769	358.3	230.2	285.6	300.4	294.4	285.9	260.3	343.3
of which: Short-term	8 771	*112.1*	....	....	....	....	....	....	....
Banks	8 772	....	....	....	....	....	251.8	242.0	329.3
of which: Short-term	8 774	....	....	....	....	....	*251.8*	*242.0*	*329.3*
Other sectors	8 775	760.1	706.3	678.2	704.2	638.7	613.8	482.0	413.5
of which: Short-term	8 777	....	....	....	....	....	....	....	....
Currency and deposits	8 780	106.6	98.3	196.7	225.3	267.3	....	....	....
Monetary authorities	8 781	....	....	....	....	....	....	....	....
General government	8 782	....	....	....	....	....	....	....	....
Banks	8 783	106.6	98.3	196.7	225.3	267.3	....	....	....
Other sectors	8 784	....	....	....	....	....	....	....	....
Other liabilities	8 786	....	....	....	....	....	....	....	....
Monetary authorities	8 787	....	....	....	....	....	....	....	....
of which: Short-term	8 789	....	....	....	....	....	....	....	....
General government	8 790	....	....	....	....	....	....	....	....
of which: Short-term	8 792	....	....	....	....	....	....	....	....
Banks	8 793	....	....	....	....	....	....	....	....
of which: Short-term	8 795	....	....	....	....	....	....	....	....
Other sectors	8 796	....	....	....	....	....	....	....	....
of which: Short-term	8 798	....	....	....	....	....	....	....	....
NET INTERNATIONAL INVESTMENT POSITION	8 995	**64.9**	**224.1**	**539.1**	**877.7**	**921.5**	**905.4**	**1,350.6**	**2,238.9**
Conversion rates: Mauritian rupees per U.S. dollar (end of period)	0 102	**27.882**	**30.394**	**29.197**	**26.088**	**28.204**	**30.667**	**34.337**	**28.216**

Table 1. ANALYTIC PRESENTATION, 2000–2007

(Millions of U.S. dollars)

	Code	2000	2001	2002	2003	2004	2005	2006	2007
A. Current Account[1]	4 993 Z.	**−18,708**	**−17,721**	**−14,154**	**−8,588**	**−6,610**	**−5,222**	**−2,244**	**−5,539**
Goods: exports f.o.b.	2 100 ..	166,121	158,780	161,046	164,766	187,999	214,233	249,925	271,875
Goods: imports f.o.b.	3 100 ..	−174,458	−168,397	−168,679	−170,546	−196,810	−221,820	−256,059	−281,949
Balance on Goods	4 100 ..	*−8,337*	*−9,617*	*−7,633*	*−5,780*	*−8,811*	*−7,587*	*−6,133*	*−10,074*
Services: credit	2 200 ..	13,756	12,701	12,740	12,617	14,047	16,137	16,392	17,736
Services: debit	3 200 ..	−17,360	−17,194	−17,660	−18,141	−19,779	−21,440	−22,833	−23,826
Balance on Goods and Services	4 991 ..	*−11,942*	*−14,110*	*−12,553*	*−11,304*	*−14,543*	*−12,890*	*−12,574*	*−16,164*
Income: credit	2 300 ..	5,977	5,326	4,051	3,858	5,617	5,359	6,406	7,876
Income: debit	3 300 ..	−19,713	−18,252	−15,903	−15,239	−14,829	−18,409	−20,186	−21,560
Balance on Goods, Services, and Income	4 992 ..	*−25,678*	*−27,036*	*−24,406*	*−22,685*	*−23,755*	*−25,939*	*−26,353*	*−29,847*
Current transfers: credit	2 379 Z.	6,999	9,336	10,287	14,134	17,226	20,774	24,197	24,409
Current transfers: debit	3 379 ..	−30	−22	−35	−37	−80	−57	−88	−101
B. Capital Account[1]	4 994 Z.	....	....	....	....	....	....	....	....
Capital account: credit	2 994 Z.	....	....	....	....	....	....	....	....
Capital account: debit	3 994 ..	....	....	....	....	....	....	....	....
Total, Groups A Plus B	4 981 ..	*−18,708*	*−17,721*	*−14,154*	*−8,588*	*−6,610*	*−5,222*	*−2,244*	*−5,539*
C. Financial Account[1]	4 995 W.	**24,048**	**27,996**	**30,725**	**23,503**	**12,417**	**13,994**	**−1,980**	**18,307**
Direct investment abroad	4 505 ..	....	−4,404	−891	−1,253	−4,432	−6,474	−5,759	−8,256
Direct investment in Mexico	4 555 Z.	17,977	29,483	23,049	16,594	22,883	20,945	19,291	24,686
Portfolio investment assets	4 602 ..	1,290	3,857	1,134	91	1,718	....	....	....
Equity securities	4 610 ..	....	....	....	....	....	....	....	....
Debt securities	4 619 ..	1,290	3,857	1,134	91	1,718	....	....	....
Portfolio investment liabilities	4 652 Z.	−1,134	3,634	−1,003	3,558	5,238	8,366	1,296	14,773
Equity securities	4 660 ..	447	151	−104	−123	−2,522	3,353	2,805	−482
Debt securities	4 669 Z.	−1,581	3,483	−900	3,681	7,760	5,013	−1,510	15,255
Financial derivatives	4 910 ..	....	....	....	....	....	....	....	....
Financial derivatives assets	4 900 ..	....	....	....	....	....	....	....	....
Financial derivatives liabilities	4 905 ..	....	....	....	....	....	....	....	....
Other investment assets	4 703 ..	5,809	−3,287	11,601	8,627	−9,051	−7,719	−12,156	−21,776
Monetary authorities	4 701 ..	....	....	....	....	....	....	....	....
General government	4 704 ..	....	....	....	....	....	....	....	....
Banks	4 705 ..	45	−5,423	7,401	4,456	−2,724	−5,256	−8,428	−8,476
Other sectors	4 728 ..	5,764	2,136	4,199	4,171	−6,328	−2,463	−3,728	−13,300
Other investment liabilities	4 753 W.	107	−1,287	−3,164	−4,114	−3,939	−1,124	−4,652	8,880
Monetary authorities	4 753 WA	....	....	....	....	....	....	....	....
General government	4 753 ZB	−2,896	−603	316	832	752	1,494	−1,497	1,643
Banks	4 753 ZC	−883	−4,222	−2,861	−1,145	−2,686	−5,401	−7,773	1,766
Other sectors	4 753 ZD	3,886	3,539	−619	−3,800	−2,004	2,784	4,618	5,472
Total, Groups A Through C	4 983 ..	*5,340*	*10,275*	*16,571*	*14,915*	*5,808*	*8,773*	*−4,224*	*12,768*
D. Net Errors and Omissions	4 998 ..	**1,786**	**−2,961**	**−9,212**	**−5,097**	**−1,704**	**−1,808**	**2,921**	**−2,518**
Total, Groups A Through D	4 984 ..	*7,126*	*7,314*	*7,359*	*9,817*	*4,104*	*6,965*	*−1,303*	*10,250*
E. Reserves and Related Items	4 802 A.	**−7,126**	**−7,314**	**−7,359**	**−9,817**	**−4,104**	**−6,965**	**1,303**	**−10,250**
Reserve assets	4 802 ..	−2,862	−7,338	−7,376	−9,833	−4,120	−6,980	1,288	−10,264
Use of Fund credit and loans	4 766 ..	−4,288	....	....	....	....	....	....	....
Exceptional financing	4 920 ..	24	24	16	16	16	15	15	14
Conversion rates: Mexican pesos per U.S. dollar	0 101 ..	**9.4556**	**9.3423**	**9.6560**	**10.7890**	**11.2860**	**10.8979**	**10.8992**	**10.9282**

[1] Excludes components that have been classified in the categories of Group E.

Table 2. STANDARD PRESENTATION, 2000–2007

(Millions of U.S. dollars)

	Code	2000	2001	2002	2003	2004	2005	2006	2007
CURRENT ACCOUNT.....................................	4 993 ..	**−18,684**	**−17,697**	**−14,137**	**−8,573**	**−6,594**	**−5,207**	**−2,229**	**−5,525**
A. GOODS..	4 100 ..	**−8,337**	**−9,617**	**−7,633**	**−5,780**	**−8,811**	**−7,587**	**−6,133**	**−10,074**
Credit...	2 100 ..	**166,121**	**158,780**	**161,046**	**164,766**	**187,999**	**214,233**	**249,925**	**271,875**
General merchandise: exports f.o.b.	2 110 ..	86,653	81,899	82,948	87,299	101,047	116,832	138,101	150,145
Goods for processing: exports f.o.b.	2 150 ..	79,467	76,881	78,098	77,467	86,952	97,401	111,824	121,731
Repairs on goods..........................	2 160 ..	....	....	....	....	....	....	....	....
Goods procured in ports by carriers.	2 170 ..	....	....	....	....	....	....	....	....
Nonmonetary gold........................	2 180 ..	....	....	....	....	....	....	....	....
Debit...	3 100 ..	**−174,458**	**−168,397**	**−168,679**	**−170,546**	**−196,810**	**−221,820**	**−256,059**	**−281,949**
General merchandise: imports f.o.b.	3 110 ..	−112,749	−110,798	−109,383	−111,489	−129,067	−146,141	−168,555	−185,780
Goods for processing: imports f.o.b.	3 150 ..	−61,709	−57,599	−59,296	−59,057	−67,742	−75,679	−87,503	−96,169
Repairs on goods..........................	3 160 ..	....	....	....	....	....	....	....	....
Goods procured in ports by carriers.	3 170 ..	....	....	....	....	....	....	....	....
Nonmonetary gold........................	3 180 ..	....	....	....	....	....	....	....	....
B. SERVICES..	4 200 ..	**−3,604**	**−4,493**	**−4,920**	**−5,524**	**−5,732**	**−5,303**	**−6,441**	**−6,090**
Total credit....................................	2 200 ..	*13,756*	*12,701*	*12,740*	*12,617*	*14,047*	*16,137*	*16,392*	*17,736*
Total debit.....................................	3 200 ..	*−17,360*	*−17,194*	*−17,660*	*−18,141*	*−19,779*	*−21,440*	*−22,833*	*−23,826*
Transportation services, credit...........	2 205 ..	**1,369**	**1,282**	**1,143**	**1,113**	**1,362**	**1,753**	**1,912**	**2,008**
Passenger.....................................	2 850 ..	*839*	*789*	*689*	*696*	*813*	*998*	*1,152*	*1,171*
Freight...	2 851 ..	....	....	....	....	....	....	....	....
Other...	2 852 ..	*530*	*493*	*454*	*417*	*549*	*755*	*760*	*837*
Sea transport, passenger...............	2 207 ..	....	....	....	....	....	....	....	....
Sea transport, freight....................	2 208 ..	....	....	....	....	....	....	....	....
Sea transport, other......................	2 209 ..	106	113	127	105	106	174	138	133
Air transport, passenger................	2 211 ..	839	789	689	696	813	998	1,152	1,171
Air transport, freight.....................	2 212 ..	....	....	....	....	....	....	....	....
Air transport, other.......................	2 213 ..	424	380	327	312	443	581	622	704
Other transport, passenger............	2 215 ..	....	....	....	....	....	....	....	....
Other transport, freight.................	2 216 ..	....	....	....	....	....	....	....	....
Other transport, other...................	2 217 ..	....	....	....	....	....	....	....	....
Transportation services, debit...........	3 205 ..	**−1,983**	**−2,105**	**−1,990**	**−1,930**	**−2,127**	**−2,716**	**−2,684**	**−2,748**
Passenger.....................................	3 850 ..	*−866*	*−983*	*−1,027*	*−999*	*−1,075*	*−1,351*	*−1,279*	*−1,465*
Freight...	3 851 ..	*−273*	*−282*	*−279*	*−284*	*−298*	*−356*	*−327*	*−337*
Other...	3 852 ..	*−844*	*−841*	*−683*	*−647*	*−755*	*−1,009*	*−1,077*	*−946*
Sea transport, passenger...............	3 207 ..	....	....	....	....	....	....	....	....
Sea transport, freight....................	3 208 ..	−10	−10	−10	−6	....	....	....	....
Sea transport, other......................	3 209 ..	−10	−6	−7	−6	....	....	....	....
Air transport, passenger................	3 211 ..	−866	−983	−1,027	−999	−1,075	−1,351	−1,279	−1,465
Air transport, freight.....................	3 212 ..	−263	−272	−270	−278	−298	−356	−327	−337
Air transport, other.......................	3 213 ..	−835	−835	−676	−641	−755	−1,009	−1,077	−946
Other transport, passenger............	3 215 ..	....	....	....	....	....	....	....	....
Other transport, freight.................	3 216 ..	....	....	....	....	....	....	....	....
Other transport, other...................	3 217 ..	....	....	....	....	....	....	....	....
Travel, credit...................................	2 236 ..	**8,294**	**8,401**	**8,858**	**9,362**	**10,796**	**11,803**	**12,177**	**12,901**
Business travel..............................	2 237 ..	383	449	532	439	511	716	732	756
Personal travel..............................	2 240 ..	7,911	7,951	8,326	8,922	10,285	11,087	11,445	12,145
Travel, debit....................................	3 236 ..	**−5,499**	**−5,702**	**−6,060**	**−6,253**	**−6,959**	**−7,600**	**−8,108**	**−8,378**
Business travel..............................	3 237 ..	−328	−443	−590	−614	−702	−827	−806	−971
Personal travel..............................	3 240 ..	−5,171	−5,258	−5,470	−5,640	−6,257	−6,773	−7,303	−7,407
Other services, credit........................	2 200 BA	**4,092**	**3,018**	**2,739**	**2,143**	**1,889**	**2,580**	**2,303**	**2,827**
Communications............................	2 245 ..	1,213	787	557	423	423	548	466	400
Construction.................................	2 249 ..	....	....	....	....	....	....	....	....
Insurance.....................................	2 253 ..	1,799	1,352	1,212	1,163	864	1,550	1,263	1,999
Financial......................................	2 260 ..	....	....	....	....	....	....	....	....
Computer and information..............	2 262 ..	....	....	....	....	....	....	....	....
Royalties and licence fees..............	2 266 ..	43	41	48	84	92	70	171	120
Other business services.................	2 268 ..	520	369	255	41	80	....	....	−11
Personal, cultural, and recreational..	2 287 ..	328	318	400	293	358	373	383	308
Government, n.i.e..........................	2 291 ..	189	151	266	140	74	39	20	11
Other services, debit.........................	3 200 BA	**−9,878**	**−9,387**	**−9,611**	**−9,958**	**−10,693**	**−11,124**	**−12,041**	**−12,701**
Communications............................	3 245 ..	−366	−331	−197	−310	−176	−119	−107	−99
Construction.................................	3 249 ..	....	....	....	....	....	....	....	....
Insurance.....................................	3 253 ..	−6,294	−6,488	−6,520	−6,755	−7,666	−8,714	−9,278	−10,936
Financial......................................	3 260 ..	−918	−557	−200	−400	−412	−550	−374	−270
Computer and information..............	3 262 ..	....	....	....	....	....	....	....	....
Royalties and licence fees..............	3 266 ..	−407	−419	−720	−608	−805	−111	−503	....
Other business services.................	3 268 ..	−1,007	−721	−1,085	−1,094	−880	−830	−950	−300
Personal, cultural, and recreational..	3 287 ..	−245	−198	−260	−221	−225	−275	−326	−259
Government, n.i.e..........................	3 291 ..	−642	−673	−629	−570	−529	−525	−504	−837

Table 2 (Continued). STANDARD PRESENTATION, 2000–2007

(Millions of U.S. dollars)

	Code	2000	2001	2002	2003	2004	2005	2006	2007
C. INCOME	4 300	−13,736	−12,926	−11,853	−11,381	−9,212	−13,049	−13,779	−13,684
Total credit	2 300	*5,977*	*5,326*	*4,051*	*3,858*	*5,617*	*5,359*	*6,406*	*7,876*
Total debit	3 300	*−19,713*	*−18,252*	*−15,903*	*−15,239*	*−14,829*	*−18,409*	*−20,186*	*−21,560*
Compensation of employees, credit	2 310	952	1,251	1,215	1,515	1,530	1,374	1,310	1,068
Compensation of employees, debit	3 310	....	....	....	....	....	....	....	....
Investment income, credit	2 320	5,025	4,075	2,835	2,343	4,087	3,986	5,097	6,808
Direct investment income	2 330	....	....	....	....	1,876	975	....	497
Dividends and distributed branch profits	2 332	....	....	....	....	....	....	....	....
Reinvested earnings and undistributed branch profits	2 333	....	....	....	....	1,876	975	....	497
Income on debt (interest)	2 334	....	....	....	....	....	....	....	....
Portfolio investment income	2 339	....	....	....	....	....	....	....	....
Income on equity	2 340	....	....	....	....	....	....	....	....
Income on bonds and notes	2 350	....	....	....	....	....	....	....	....
Income on money market instruments	2 360	....	....	....	....	....	....	....	....
Other investment income	2 370	5,025	4,075	2,835	2,343	2,211	3,011	5,097	6,312
Investment income, debit	3 320	−19,713	−18,252	−15,903	−15,239	−14,829	−18,409	−20,186	−21,560
Direct investment income	3 330	−6,018	−5,558	−3,937	−3,569	−3,606	−6,149	−6,110	−6,695
Dividends and distributed branch profits	3 332	−2,167	−1,701	−1,470	−1,492	−1,261	−2,662	−1,932	−2,717
Reinvested earnings and undistributed branch profits	3 333	−3,851	−3,857	−2,467	−2,077	−2,345	−3,487	−4,178	−3,978
Income on debt (interest)	3 334	....	....	....	....	....	....	....	....
Portfolio investment income	3 339	−140	−162	−159	−197	−269	−625	−1,201	−1,296
Income on equity	3 340	....	....	....	....	....	....	....	....
Income on bonds and notes	3 350	....	....	....	....	....	....	....	....
Income on money market instruments	3 360	−140	−162	−159	−197	−269	−625	−1,201	−1,296
Other investment income	3 370	−13,555	−12,531	−11,807	−11,473	−10,953	−11,634	−12,875	−13,569
D. CURRENT TRANSFERS	4 379	6,994	9,338	10,269	14,112	17,161	20,733	24,124	24,323
Credit	2 379	7,023	9,360	10,304	14,149	17,241	20,789	24,212	24,424
General government	2 380	62	62	55	54	54	53	53	53
Other sectors	2 390	6,961	9,298	10,249	14,095	17,187	20,736	24,159	24,371
Workers' remittances	2 391	6,573	8,895	9,814	13,650	16,730	20,284	23,742	23,970
Other current transfers	2 392	388	403	435	445	457	453	417	401
Debit	3 379	−30	−22	−35	−37	−80	−57	−88	−101
General government	3 380	....	....	....	....	....	....	....	....
Other sectors	3 390	−30	−22	−35	−37	−80	−57	−88	−101
Workers' remittances	3 391	....	....	....	....	....	....	....	....
Other current transfers	3 392	−30	−22	−35	−37	−80	−57	−88	−101
CAPITAL AND FINANCIAL ACCOUNT	4 996	16,898	20,658	23,349	13,670	8,298	7,015	−692	8,043
CAPITAL ACCOUNT	4 994	....	....	....	....	....	....	....	....
Total credit	2 994	....	....	....	....	....	....	....	....
Total debit	3 994	....	....	....	....	....	....	....	....
Capital transfers, credit	2 400	....	....	....	....	....	....	....	....
General government	2 401	....	....	....	....	....	....	....	....
Debt forgiveness	2 402	....	....	....	....	....	....	....	....
Other capital transfers	2 410	....	....	....	....	....	....	....	....
Other sectors	2 430	....	....	....	....	....	....	....	....
Migrants' transfers	2 431	....	....	....	....	....	....	....	....
Debt forgiveness	2 432	....	....	....	....	....	....	....	....
Other capital transfers	2 440	....	....	....	....	....	....	....	....
Capital transfers, debit	3 400	....	....	....	....	....	....	....	....
General government	3 401	....	....	....	....	....	....	....	....
Debt forgiveness	3 402	....	....	....	....	....	....	....	....
Other capital transfers	3 410	....	....	....	....	....	....	....	....
Other sectors	3 430	....	....	....	....	....	....	....	....
Migrants' transfers	3 431	....	....	....	....	....	....	....	....
Debt forgiveness	3 432	....	....	....	....	....	....	....	....
Other capital transfers	3 440	....	....	....	....	....	....	....	....
Nonproduced nonfinancial assets, credit	2 480	....	....	....	....	....	....	....	....
Nonproduced nonfinancial assets, debit	3 480	....	....	....	....	....	....	....	....

Table 2 (Continued). STANDARD PRESENTATION, 2000–2007

(Millions of U.S. dollars)

	Code	2000	2001	2002	2003	2004	2005	2006	2007
FINANCIAL ACCOUNT	4 995	**16,898**	**20,658**	**23,349**	**13,670**	**8,298**	**7,015**	**−692**	**8,043**
A. DIRECT INVESTMENT	4 500	**17,977**	**25,079**	**22,158**	**15,341**	**18,451**	**14,471**	**13,532**	**16,430**
Direct investment abroad	4 505	....	−4,404	−891	−1,253	−4,432	−6,474	−5,759	−8,256
Equity capital	4 510	....	....	....	....	−1,901	−3,726	−5,452	−4,239
Claims on affiliated enterprises	4 515	....	....	....	....	−1,901	−3,726	−5,452	−4,239
Liabilities to affiliated enterprises	4 520	....	....	....	....			....	
Reinvested earnings	4 525	....	....	....	....	−1,876	−975	....	−497
Other capital	4 530	....	−4,404	−891	−1,253	−655	−1,773	−307	−3,520
Claims on affiliated enterprises	4 535	....	−4,404	−891	−1,253	−655	−1,773	−307	−3,520
Liabilities to affiliated enterprises	4 540	....	....	....	....				
Direct investment in Mexico	4 555	17,977	29,483	23,049	16,594	22,883	20,945	19,291	24,686
Equity capital	4 560	8,387	22,621	15,048	7,247	13,877	10,838	5,638	11,471
Claims on direct investors	4 565	....	....	....	....				
Liabilities to direct investors	4 570	8,387	22,621	15,048	7,247	13,877	10,838	5,638	11,471
Reinvested earnings	4 575	3,851	3,857	2,467	2,077	2,345	3,487	4,178	3,978
Other capital	4 580	5,739	3,005	5,533	7,271	6,661	6,620	9,475	9,237
Claims on direct investors	4 585	....	....	....	....				
Liabilities to direct investors	4 590	5,739	3,005	5,533	7,271	6,661	6,620	9,475	9,237
B. PORTFOLIO INVESTMENT	4 600	**156**	**7,491**	**131**	**3,649**	**6,956**	**8,366**	**1,296**	**14,773**
Assets	4 602	**1,290**	**3,857**	**1,134**	**91**	**1,718**	....	....	....
Equity securities	4 610	....	....	....	....	....	....	....	....
Monetary authorities	4 611	....	....	....	....	....	....	....	....
General government	4 612	....	....	....	....	....	....	....	....
Banks	4 613	....	....	....	....	....	....	....	....
Other sectors	4 614	....	....	....	....	....	....	....	....
Debt securities	4 619	1,290	3,857	1,134	91	1,718	....	....	....
Bonds and notes	4 620	1,290	3,857	1,134	91	1,718	....	....	....
Monetary authorities	4 621	....	....	....	....	....	....	....	....
General government	4 622	1,290	3,857	1,134	91	1,718	....	....	....
Banks	4 623	....	....	....	....	....	....	....	....
Other sectors	4 624	....	....	....	....	....	....	....	....
Money market instruments	4 630	....	....	....	....	....	....	....	....
Monetary authorities	4 631	....	....	....	....	....	....	....	....
General government	4 632	....	....	....	....	....	....	....	....
Banks	4 633	....	....	....	....	....	....	....	....
Other sectors	4 634	....	....	....	....	....	....	....	....
Liabilities	4 652	**−1,134**	**3,634**	**−1,003**	**3,558**	**5,238**	**8,366**	**1,296**	**14,773**
Equity securities	4 660	447	151	−104	−123	−2,522	3,353	2,805	−482
Banks	4 663	....	....	....	....	....	....	....	....
Other sectors	4 664	447	151	−104	−123	−2,522	3,353	2,805	−482
Debt securities	4 669	−1,581	3,483	−900	3,681	7,760	5,013	−1,510	15,255
Bonds and notes	4 670	−1,556	2,543	−1,049	2,779	2,567	1,667	−5,182	6,201
Monetary authorities	4 671	....	....	....	....	....	....	....	....
General government	4 672	−3,086	1,849	−1,425	−258	1,976	−1,550	−9,516	−3,066
Banks	4 673	−1,748	−121	−1,344	−1,025	−900	−347	260	220
Other sectors	4 674	3,278	815	1,720	4,062	1,491	3,563	4,074	9,048
Money market instruments	4 680	−25	941	150	902	5,193	3,346	3,672	9,054
Monetary authorities	4 681	....	....	....	....	....	....	....	....
General government	4 682	−25	941	150	902	5,193	3,346	3,672	9,054
Banks	4 683	....	....	....	....	....	....	....	....
Other sectors	4 684	....	....	....	....	....	....	....	....
C. FINANCIAL DERIVATIVES	4 910	....	....	....	....	....	....	....	....
Monetary authorities	4 911	....	....	....	....	....	....	....	....
General government	4 912	....	....	....	....	....	....	....	....
Banks	4 913	....	....	....	....	....	....	....	....
Other sectors	4 914	....	....	....	....	....	....	....	....
Assets	4 900	....	....	....	....	....	....	....	....
Monetary authorities	4 901	....	....	....	....	....	....	....	....
General government	4 902	....	....	....	....	....	....	....	....
Banks	4 903	....	....	....	....	....	....	....	....
Other sectors	4 904	....	....	....	....	....	....	....	....
Liabilities	4 905	....	....	....	....	....	....	....	....
Monetary authorities	4 906	....	....	....	....	....	....	....	....
General government	4 907	....	....	....	....	....	....	....	....
Banks	4 908	....	....	....	....	....	....	....	....
Other sectors	4 909	....	....	....	....	....	....	....	....

Table 2 (Concluded). STANDARD PRESENTATION, 2000–2007

(Millions of U.S. dollars)

	Code	2000	2001	2002	2003	2004	2005	2006	2007
D. OTHER INVESTMENT	4 700	**1,627**	**−4,574**	**8,437**	**4,513**	**−12,990**	**−8,843**	**−16,808**	**−12,896**
Assets	4 703	**5,809**	**−3,287**	**11,601**	**8,627**	**−9,051**	**−7,719**	**−12,156**	**−21,776**
Trade credits	4 706	413	....	190	46	....	....	....	....
General government	4 707	....	....	....	....	....	....	....	....
of which: Short-term	4 709	....	....	....	....	....	....	....	....
Other sectors	4 710	413	....	190	46	....	....	....	....
of which: Short-term	4 712	*413*	....	*190*	*46*	....	....	....	....
Loans	4 714	....	....	....	....	....	....	....	....
Monetary authorities	4 715	....	....	....	....	....	....	....	....
of which: Short-term	4 718	....	....	....	....	....	....	....	....
General government	4 719	....	....	....	....	....	....	....	....
of which: Short-term	4 721	....	....	....	....	....	....	....	....
Banks	4 722	....	....	....	....	....	....	....	....
of which: Short-term	4 724	....	....	....	....	....	....	....	....
Other sectors	4 725	....	....	....	....	....	....	....	....
of which: Short-term	4 727	....	....	....	....	....	....	....	....
Currency and deposits	4 730	3,550	−1,512	10,773	7,457	−5,579	−4,403	−6,148	−17,046
Monetary authorities	4 731	....	....	....	....	....	....	....	....
General government	4 732	....	....	....	....	....	....	....	....
Banks	4 733	−1,802	−3,647	6,764	3,332	748	−1,940	−2,420	−3,746
Other sectors	4 734	5,352	2,136	4,009	4,125	−6,328	−2,463	−3,728	−13,300
Other assets	4 736	1,847	−1,775	637	1,124	−3,472	−3,316	−6,008	−4,730
Monetary authorities	4 737	....	....	....	....	....	....	....	....
of which: Short-term	4 739	....	....	....	....	....	....	....	....
General government	4 740	....	....	....	....	....	....	....	....
of which: Short-term	4 742	....	....	....	....	....	....	....	....
Banks	4 743	1,847	−1,775	637	1,124	−3,472	−3,316	−6,008	−4,730
of which: Short-term	4 745	*1,847*	*−1,775*	*637*	*1,124*	*−3,472*	*−3,316*	*−6,008*	*−4,730*
Other sectors	4 746	....	....	....	....	....	....	....	....
of which: Short-term	4 748	....	....	....	....	....	....	....	....
Liabilities	4 753	**−4,182**	**−1,287**	**−3,164**	**−4,114**	**−3,939**	**−1,124**	**−4,652**	**8,880**
Trade credits	4 756	−5,006	−4,643	−4,408	−4,493	−5,450	−6,494	−7,418	−8,297
General government	4 757	....	....	....	....	....	....	....	....
of which: Short-term	4 759	....	....	....	....	....	....	....	....
Other sectors	4 760	−5,006	−4,643	−4,408	−4,493	−5,450	−6,494	−7,418	−8,297
of which: Short-term	4 762	....	....	....	....	....	....	....	....
Loans	4 764	825	3,356	1,244	379	1,512	5,370	2,766	17,177
Monetary authorities	4 765	−4,288	....	....	....	....	....	....	....
of which: Use of Fund credit and loans from the Fund	4 766	*−4,288*	....	....	....	....	....	....	....
of which: Short-term	4 768	....	....	....	....	....	....	....	....
General government	4 769	−2,896	−603	316	832	752	1,494	−1,497	1,643
of which: Short-term	4 771	....	....	....	*−1,375*	....	....	....	....
Banks	4 772	−883	−4,222	−2,861	−1,145	−2,686	−5,401	−7,773	1,766
of which: Short-term	4 774	*−423*	*−1,727*	*−741*	*379*	*−693*	*−1,909*	*−120*	*2,824*
Other sectors	4 775	8,892	8,182	3,789	693	3,446	9,278	12,036	13,769
of which: Short-term	4 777	*1,750*	*1,132*	*−1,871*	*−1,680*	*−2,744*	*−3,529*	*−2,734*	*−5,069*
Currency and deposits	4 780	....	....	....	....	....	....	....	....
Monetary authorities	4 781	....	....	....	....	....	....	....	....
General government	4 782	....	....	....	....	....	....	....	....
Banks	4 783	....	....	....	....	....	....	....	....
Other sectors	4 784	....	....	....	....	....	....	....	....
Other liabilities	4 786	....	....	....	....	....	....	....	....
Monetary authorities	4 787	....	....	....	....	....	....	....	....
of which: Short-term	4 789	....	....	....	....	....	....	....	....
General government	4 790	....	....	....	....	....	....	....	....
of which: Short-term	4 792	....	....	....	....	....	....	....	....
Banks	4 793	....	....	....	....	....	....	....	....
of which: Short-term	4 795	....	....	....	....	....	....	....	....
Other sectors	4 796	....	....	....	....	....	....	....	....
of which: Short-term	4 798	....	....	....	....	....	....	....	....
E. RESERVE ASSETS	4 802	**−2,862**	**−7,338**	**−7,376**	**−9,833**	**−4,120**	**−6,980**	**1,288**	**−10,264**
Monetary gold	4 812	−22	5	−13	7	10	5	−3	−40
Special drawing rights	4 811	382	−3	−6	−5	−11	−18	−13	39
Reserve position in the Fund	4 810	....	....	−301	−419	−77	229	275	24
Foreign exchange	4 803	−4,077	−9,346	−5,852	−8,307	−5,140	−9,914	−2,152	−10,785
Other claims	4 813	855	2,006	−1,204	−1,109	1,099	2,718	3,181	498
NET ERRORS AND OMISSIONS	4 998	**1,786**	**−2,961**	**−9,212**	**−5,097**	**−1,704**	**−1,808**	**2,921**	**−2,518**

Table 3. INTERNATIONAL INVESTMENT POSITION (End-period stocks), 2000–2007

(Millions of U.S. dollars)

	Code	2000	2001	2002	2003	2004	2005	2006	2007
ASSETS	8 995 C.	....	**106,690**	**110,193**	**119,161**	**135,788**	**160,430**	**178,185**	**218,505**
Direct investment abroad	8 505	....	**12,078**	**12,869**	**16,587**	**21,673**	**29,641**	**36,447**	**44,703**
Equity capital and reinvested earnings	8 506	....	12,078	12,869	16,587	21,673	29,641	36,447	44,703
Claims on affiliated enterprises	8 507	....	12,078	12,869	16,587	21,673	29,641	36,447	44,703
Liabilities to affiliated enterprises	8 508	....	....	....	....	....	....	....	....
Other capital	8 530	....	....	....	....	....	....	....	....
Claims on affiliated enterprises	8 535	....	....	....	....	....	....	....	....
Liabilities to affiliated enterprises	8 540	....	....	....	....	....	....	....	....
Portfolio investment	8 602	....	**2,828**	**2,023**	**2,472**	**2,204**	**5,880**	**10,291**	**12,490**
Equity securities	8 610	....	....	....	....	....	....	....	....
Monetary authorities	8 611	....	....	....	....	....	....	....	....
General government	8 612	....	....	....	....	....	....	....	....
Banks	8 613	....	....	....	....	....	....	....	....
Other sectors	8 614	....	....	....	....	....	....	....	....
Debt securities	8 619	....	2,828	2,023	2,472	2,204	5,880	10,291	12,490
Bonds and notes	8 620	....	2,828	2,023	2,472	2,204	5,880	10,291	12,490
Monetary authorities	8 621	....	....	....	....	....	....	....	....
General government	8 622	....	3,196	1,809	2,345	627	627	627	....
Banks	8 623	....	2,828	2,023	2,472	2,204	2,966	3,378	1,417
Other sectors	8 624	....	....	....	....	....	2,914	6,913	11,073
Money market instruments	8 630	....	....	....	....	....	....	....	....
Monetary authorities	8 631	....	....	....	....	....	....	....	....
General government	8 632	....	....	....	....	....	....	....	....
Banks	8 633	....	....	....	....	....	....	....	....
Other sectors	8 634	....	....	....	....	....	....	....	....
Financial derivatives	8 900	....	....	....	....	....	....	....	....
Monetary authorities	8 901	....	....	....	....	....	....	....	....
General government	8 902	....	....	....	....	....	....	....	....
Banks	8 903	....	....	....	....	....	....	....	....
Other sectors	8 904	....	....	....	....	....	....	....	....
Other investment	8 703	....	**50,547**	**46,618**	**41,451**	**49,053**	**55,200**	**62,945**	**82,522**
Trade credits	8 706	....	....	....	....	....	....	....	....
General government	8 707	....	....	....	....	....	....	....	....
of which: Short-term	8 709	....	....	....	....	....	....	....	....
Other sectors	8 710	....	....	....	....	....	....	....	....
of which: Short-term	8 712	....	....	....	....	....	....	....	....
Loans	8 714	....	....	....	....	....	....	....	....
Monetary authorities	8 715	....	....	....	....	....	....	....	....
of which: Short-term	8 718	....	....	....	....	....	....	....	....
General government	8 719	....	....	....	....	....	....	....	....
of which: Short-term	8 721	....	....	....	....	....	....	....	....
Banks	8 722	....	....	....	....	....	....	....	....
of which: Short-term	8 724	....	....	....	....	....	....	....	....
Other sectors	8 725	....	....	....	....	....	....	....	....
of which: Short-term	8 727	....	....	....	....	....	....	....	....
Currency and deposits	8 730	....	....	....	....	....	....	....	....
Monetary authorities	8 731	....	....	....	....	....	....	....	....
General government	8 732	....	....	....	....	....	....	....	....
Banks	8 733	....	....	....	....	....	....	....	....
Other sectors	8 734	....	....	....	....	....	....	....	....
Other assets	8 736	....	50,547	46,618	41,451	49,053	55,200	62,945	82,522
Monetary authorities	8 737	....	....	....	....	....	....	....	....
of which: Short-term	8 739	....	....	....	....	....	....	....	....
General government	8 740	....	....	....	....	....	....	....	....
of which: Short-term	8 742	....	....	....	....	....	....	....	....
Banks	8 743	....	15,358	11,118	8,076	12,548	13,536	15,544	19,801
of which: Short-term	8 745	....	....	....	....	....	....	....	....
Other sectors	8 746	....	35,189	35,500	33,375	36,505	41,664	47,401	62,721
of which: Short-term	8 748	....	....	....	....	....	....	....	....
Reserve assets	8 802	....	**41,237**	**48,683**	**58,651**	**62,859**	**69,708**	**68,502**	**78,791**
Monetary gold	8 812	....	64	77	71	61	56	59	99
Special drawing rights	8 811	366	356	392	433	465	445	482	466
Reserve position in the Fund	8 810	....	....	308	782	898	594	340	334
Foreign exchange	8 803	....	40,816	47,907	57,364	61,435	68,613	67,621	77,892
Other claims	8 813	....	....	....	....	....	....	....	....

Table 3 (Concluded). INTERNATIONAL INVESTMENT POSITION (End-period stocks), 2000–2007

(Millions of U.S. dollars)

	Code	2000	2001	2002	2003	2004	2005	2006	2007
LIABILITIES	8 995 D.	....	**355,023**	**365,032**	**395,668**	**441,394**	**497,816**	**559,844**	**611,544**
Direct investment in Mexico	8 555 ..	....	**140,359**	**163,407**	**180,002**	**202,885**	**223,830**	**243,121**	**267,807**
Equity capital and reinvested earnings	8 556 ..	....	140,359	163,407	180,002	202,885	223,830	243,121	267,807
Claims on direct investors	8 557 ..	....	140,359	163,407	180,002	202,885	223,830	243,121	267,807
Liabilities to direct investors	8 558 ..	....	....	....	....	....	....	....	....
Other capital	8 580 ..	....	....	....	....	....	....	....	....
Claims on direct investors	8 585 ..	....	....	....	....	....	....	....	....
Liabilities to direct investors	8 590 ..	....	....	....	....	....	....	....	....
Portfolio investment	8 652 ..	....	**138,322**	**127,294**	**143,862**	**169,708**	**207,358**	**253,836**	**271,781**
Equity securities	8 660 ..	....	54,940	44,564	56,516	73,967	106,555	154,239	154,445
Banks	8 663 ..	....	....	....	....	....	....	....	....
Other sectors	8 664 ..	....	54,940	44,564	56,516	73,967	106,555	154,239	154,445
Debt securities	8 669 ..	....	83,382	82,731	87,346	95,741	100,803	99,597	117,336
Bonds and notes	8 670 ..	....	81,597	81,136	85,238	88,759	90,686	87,155	97,097
Monetary authorities	8 671 ..	....	....	....	....	....	....	....	....
General government	8 672 ..	....	42,741	41,895	42,604	45,511	44,152	36,289	35,429
Banks	8 673 ..	....	6,556	5,213	4,535	3,651	3,255	3,512	3,752
Other sectors	8 674 ..	....	32,300	34,028	38,099	39,596	43,280	47,354	57,916
Money market instruments	8 680 ..	....	1,785	1,595	2,107	6,983	10,117	12,443	20,239
Monetary authorities	8 681 ..	....	....	....	....	....	....	....	....
General government	8 682 ..	....	1,785	1,595	2,107	6,983	10,117	12,443	20,239
Banks	8 683 ..	....	....	....	....	....	....	....	....
Other sectors	8 684 ..	....	....	....	....	....	....	....	....
Financial derivatives	8 905 ..	....	....	....	....	....	....	....	....
Monetary authorities	8 906 ..	....	....	....	....	....	....	....	....
General government	8 907 ..	....	....	....	....	....	....	....	....
Banks	8 908 ..	....	....	....	....	....	....	....	....
Other sectors	8 909 ..	....	....	....	....	....	....	....	....
Other investment	8 753 ..	....	**76,343**	**74,330**	**71,805**	**68,802**	**66,628**	**62,887**	**71,956**
Trade credits	8 756 ..	....	....	....	....	....	....	....	....
General government	8 757 ..	....	....	....	....	....	....	....	....
of which: Short-term	8 759 ..	....	....	....	....	....	....	....	....
Other sectors	8 760 ..	....	....	....	....	....	....	....	....
of which: Short-term	8 762 ..	....	....	....	....	....	....	....	....
Loans	8 764 ..	....	....	....	....	....	....	....	....
Monetary authorities	8 765 ..	....	....	....	....	....	....	....	....
of which: Use of Fund credit and loans from the Fund	8 766 ..	....	....	....	....	....	....	....	....
of which: Short-term	8 768 ..	....	....	....	....	....	....	....	....
General government	8 769 ..	....	....	....	....	....	....	....	....
of which: Short-term	8 771 ..	....	....	....	....	....	....	....	....
Banks	8 772 ..	....	....	....	....	....	....	....	....
of which: Short-term	8 774 ..	....	....	....	....	....	....	....	....
Other sectors	8 775 ..	....	....	....	....	....	....	....	....
of which: Short-term	8 777 ..	....	....	....	....	....	....	....	....
Currency and deposits	8 780 ..	....	....	....	....	....	....	....	....
Monetary authorities	8 781 ..	....	....	....	....	....	....	....	....
General government	8 782 ..	....	....	....	....	....	....	....	....
Banks	8 783 ..	....	....	....	....	....	....	....	....
Other sectors	8 784 ..	....	....	....	....	....	....	....	....
Other liabilities	8 786 ..	....	76,343	74,330	71,805	68,802	66,628	62,887	71,956
Monetary authorities	8 787 ..	....	....	....	....	....	....	....	....
of which: Short-term	8 789 ..	....	....	*2,690*	*1,593*	*2,701*	*5,441*	*8,650*	....
General government	8 790 ..	....	1,329	1,659	2,294	3,051	4,538	3,041	4,685
of which: Short-term	8 792 ..	....	....	....	....	....	....	....	....
Banks	8 793 ..	....	29,676	27,336	26,421	23,853	18,190	10,517	12,418
of which: Short-term	8 795 ..	....	....	....	....	....	....	....	....
Other sectors	8 796 ..	....	45,338	45,335	43,091	41,898	43,900	49,328	54,853
of which: Short-term	8 798 ..	....	....	....	....	....	....	....	....
NET INTERNATIONAL INVESTMENT POSITION	8 995 ..	....	**–248,333**	**–254,839**	**–276,507**	**–305,606**	**–337,387**	**–381,659**	**–393,038**
Conversion rates: Mexican pesos per U.S. dollar (end of period)	0 102 ..	9.5722	9.1423	10.3125	11.2360	11.2648	10.7777	10.8810	10.8662

Table 1. ANALYTIC PRESENTATION, 2000–2007

(Millions of U.S. dollars)

	Code	2000	2001	2002	2003	2004	2005	2006	2007
A. Current Account[1]	4 993 Z.	**−108.4**	**−37.0**	**−25.3**	**−130.3**	**−47.1**	**−247.7**	**−384.5**	**−747.7**
Goods: exports f.o.b.	2 100 ..	476.8	564.6	659.7	805.1	994.1	1,104.6	1,058.7	1,368.4
Goods: imports f.o.b.	3 100 ..	−770.3	−879.7	−1,037.5	−1,428.1	−1,748.2	−2,296.1	−2,644.4	−3,676.4
Balance on Goods	4 100 ..	*−293.6*	*−315.1*	*−377.8*	*−623.0*	*−754.2*	*−1,191.5*	*−1,585.7*	*−2,308.0*
Services: credit	2 200 ..	164.6	170.9	216.7	250.0	332.1	398.9	488.6	649.7
Services: debit	3 200 ..	−201.6	−208.8	−257.0	−294.3	−353.1	−419.7	−484.4	−630.0
Balance on Goods and Services	4 991 ..	*−330.5*	*−352.9*	*−418.1*	*−667.3*	*−775.1*	*−1,212.2*	*−1,581.5*	*−2,288.3*
Income: credit	2 300 ..	139.1	173.9	229.4	340.8	490.0	539.3	605.8	710.0
Income: debit	3 300 ..	−117.5	−78.1	−72.8	−110.0	−133.0	−128.4	−203.8	−295.7
Balance on Goods, Services, and Income	4 992 ..	*−309.0*	*−257.1*	*−261.6*	*−436.5*	*−418.1*	*−801.4*	*−1,179.4*	*−1,874.0*
Current transfers: credit	2 379 Z.	213.6	236.0	255.6	334.0	406.8	596.8	854.9	1,206.6
Current transfers: debit	3 379 ..	−13.1	−15.9	−19.3	−27.8	−35.8	−43.2	−60.0	−80.3
B. Capital Account[1]	4 994 Z.	**−14.3**	**−20.7**	**−19.3**	**−19.0**	**−18.3**	**−16.9**	**−22.8**	**−8.0**
Capital account: credit	2 994 Z.	2.8	1.1	1.2	4.6	7.2	5.2	6.1	7.0
Capital account: debit	3 994 ..	−17.1	−21.8	−20.4	−23.6	−25.5	−22.1	−28.9	−14.9
Total, Groups A Plus B	4 981 ..	*−122.7*	*−57.7*	*−44.6*	*−149.3*	*−65.4*	*−264.6*	*−407.2*	*−755.7*
C. Financial Account[1]	4 995 W.	**126.4**	**19.1**	**20.6**	**84.3**	**113.0**	**200.5**	**359.4**	**989.0**
Direct investment abroad	4 505 ..	−.1	−.1	−.5	−.1	−3.2	.2	.7	−12.0
Direct investment in Moldova	4 555 Z.	127.5	54.5	84.1	73.8	87.7	190.7	251.1	493.4
Portfolio investment assets	4 602 ..	....	−3.2	−1.5	.4	−1.5	−1.2	−.2	−.1
Equity securities	4 610 ..	....	....	....	−.1	−.2	....	−.2	−.1
Debt securities	4 619 ..	....	−3.2	−1.5	.5	−1.3	−1.2	....	....
Portfolio investment liabilities	4 652 Z.	−4.0	−3.9	−25.9	−24.2	−8.3	−5.8	−4.6	−4.4
Equity securities	4 660 ..	2.9	2.8	2.3	.7	−.8	.6	1.8	1.7
Debt securities	4 669 Z.	−6.9	−6.8	−28.2	−24.9	−7.5	−6.4	−6.4	−6.2
Financial derivatives	4 910 ..	....	....	....	.1	.6	−1.6	.2	−.5
Financial derivatives assets	4 900 ..	....	....	....	....	−.5	−1.7	−.1	−.5
Financial derivatives liabilities	4 905 ..	....	....	....	.1	1.0	.1	.3	.1
Other investment assets	4 703 ..	−35.9	−22.2	−40.0	6.5	−31.6	−78.2	−49.4	54.0
Monetary authorities	4 701 ..	.1	....	....	....	−18.8	−14.1	....	....
General government	4 704 ..	....	8.3	.5	−.2	.3	−.2	....	....
Banks	4 705 ..	−16.5	1.2	−15.7	−19.6	5.8	−50.7	−77.6	49.2
Other sectors	4 728 ..	−19.6	−31.7	−24.8	26.4	−18.9	−13.1	28.2	4.8
Other investment liabilities	4 753 W.	38.8	−6.0	4.3	27.8	69.3	96.3	161.6	458.6
Monetary authorities	4 753 WA	−.2	....	....	....	....	....	....	....
General government	4 753 ZB	−11.1	−14.3	−12.6	−25.1	−19.1	−14.8	−29.9	−14.6
Banks	4 753 ZC	4.2	−2.3	11.0	14.1	17.0	13.8	60.5	193.1
Other sectors	4 753 ZD	45.9	10.5	6.0	38.8	71.4	97.3	131.0	280.2
Total, Groups A Through C	4 983 ..	*3.7*	*−38.6*	*−24.0*	*−65.0*	*47.5*	*−64.1*	*−47.8*	*233.3*
D. Net Errors and Omissions	4 998 ..	**−8.6**	**16.0**	**−24.0**	**47.4**	**100.6**	**178.3**	**64.2**	**139.0**
Total, Groups A Through D	4 984 ..	*−4.9*	*−22.6*	*−48.0*	*−17.6*	*148.2*	*114.2*	*16.4*	*372.3*
E. Reserves and Related Items	4 802 A.	**4.9**	**22.6**	**48.0**	**17.6**	**−148.2**	**−114.2**	**−16.4**	**−372.3**
Reserve assets	4 802 ..	−47.4	−9.5	−27.0	−14.1	−148.0	−128.6	−140.7	−528.9
Use of Fund credit and loans	4 766 ..	−12.7	−2.3	−5.6	−22.2	−21.6	−21.7	41.1	11.2
Exceptional financing	4 920 ..	65.0	34.4	80.6	53.9	21.4	36.1	83.2	145.4
Conversion rates: Moldovan lei per U.S. dollar	0 101 ..	**12.434**	**12.865**	**13.570**	**13.945**	**12.330**	**12.600**	**13.131**	**12.140**

[1] Excludes components that have been classified in the categories of Group E.

Table 2. STANDARD PRESENTATION, 2000–2007

(Millions of U.S. dollars)

	Code	2000	2001	2002	2003	2004	2005	2006	2007
CURRENT ACCOUNT................................	4 993 ..	**–98.2**	**–26.8**	**–19.8**	**–130.1**	**–46.1**	**–225.8**	**–379.8**	**–695.5**
A. GOODS..	4 100 ..	**–293.6**	**–315.1**	**–377.8**	**–623.0**	**–754.2**	**–1,191.5**	**–1,585.7**	**–2,308.0**
Credit..	2 100 ..	**476.8**	**564.6**	**659.7**	**805.1**	**994.1**	**1,104.6**	**1,058.7**	**1,368.4**
General merchandise: exports f.o.b.	2 110 ..	375.6	443.5	524.4	655.9	793.9	885.7	779.0	1,013.3
Goods for processing: exports f.o.b.	2 150 ..	100.9	121.0	134.9	149.1	199.2	217.9	273.3	346.8
Repairs on goods	2 160 ..	.1	....	.2	.1	.5	.6	.5	.6
Goods procured in ports by carriers	2 170 ..	.1	.1	.2	....	.5	.4	5.8	7.8
Nonmonetary gold	2 180 ..	....	....	....	....	....	....	....	....
Debit..	3 100 ..	**–770.3**	**–879.7**	**–1,037.5**	**–1,428.1**	**–1,748.2**	**–2,296.1**	**–2,644.4**	**–3,676.4**
General merchandise: imports f.o.b.	3 110 ..	–685.4	–776.4	–912.8	–1,305.9	–1,589.1	–2,113.9	–2,428.9	–3,406.6
Goods for processing: imports f.o.b.	3 150 ..	–81.0	–99.7	–121.1	–117.4	–152.0	–172.0	–208.8	–261.7
Repairs on goods	3 160 ..	–1.3	–1.3	–.6	–1.4	–3.3	–5.3	–.6	–.8
Goods procured in ports by carriers	3 170 ..	–2.4	–2.2	–2.8	–3.3	–3.9	–4.5	–5.6	–6.6
Nonmonetary gold	3 180 ..	–.2	–.1	–.2	–.1	....	–.4	–.5	–.7
B. SERVICES....................................	4 200 ..	**–37.0**	**–37.9**	**–40.3**	**–44.3**	**–21.0**	**–20.7**	**4.2**	**19.7**
Total credit	2 200 ..	*164.6*	*170.9*	*216.7*	*250.0*	*332.1*	*398.9*	*488.6*	*649.7*
Total debit	3 200 ..	*–201.6*	*–208.8*	*–257.0*	*–294.3*	*–353.1*	*–419.7*	*–484.4*	*–630.0*
Transportation services, credit	2 205 ..	**82.9**	**84.6**	**109.2**	**127.1**	**142.6**	**169.6**	**223.8**	**292.1**
Passenger	2 850 ..	*17.8*	*18.7*	*21.5*	*25.2*	*20.6*	*34.7*	*32.8*	*57.5*
Freight	2 851 ..	*63.8*	*63.3*	*84.8*	*97.3*	*116.4*	*127.7*	*183.4*	*221.2*
Other	2 852 ..	*1.3*	*2.5*	*2.9*	*4.7*	*5.7*	*7.1*	*7.6*	*13.4*
Sea transport, passenger	2 207 ..	....	....	....	....	....	....	....	....
Sea transport, freight	2 208 ..	....	....	....	.1	....	.1	.2	.5
Sea transport, other	2 209 ..	....	....	....	....	....	....	....	....
Air transport, passenger	2 211 ..	15.0	15.3	16.1	17.2	13.6	27.9	24.2	45.4
Air transport, freight	2 212 ..	1.5	3.0	4.8	3.2	11.7	7.7	14.9	12.0
Air transport, other	2 213 ..	.3	.8	.5	1.6	2.4	3.1	1.1	4.6
Other transport, passenger	2 215 ..	2.8	3.4	5.5	8.0	7.0	6.9	8.6	12.1
Other transport, freight	2 216 ..	62.3	60.3	79.9	94.0	104.7	119.9	168.3	208.7
Other transport, other	2 217 ..	1.0	1.7	2.4	3.0	3.3	3.3	6.5	8.7
Transportation services, debit	3 205 ..	**–61.5**	**–68.2**	**–76.2**	**–99.9**	**–116.0**	**–147.1**	**–171.6**	**–244.9**
Passenger	3 850 ..	*–12.5*	*–15.1*	*–14.1*	*–19.1*	*–22.2*	*–28.9*	*–33.4*	*–56.8*
Freight	3 851 ..	*–45.3*	*–47.8*	*–52.9*	*–68.2*	*–77.6*	*–99.8*	*–119.3*	*–163.4*
Other	3 852 ..	*–3.6*	*–5.3*	*–9.2*	*–12.6*	*–16.2*	*–18.4*	*–18.9*	*–24.7*
Sea transport, passenger	3 207 ..	....	....	....	....	....	–.1	....	....
Sea transport, freight	3 208 ..	–.8	–.6	–.2	–.1	–.2	....	–2.1	....
Sea transport, other	3 209 ..	....	....	....	....	....	....	....	–.2
Air transport, passenger	3 211 ..	–10.0	–12.8	–10.3	–14.4	–16.9	–25.2	–27.8	–48.4
Air transport, freight	3 212 ..	–3.4	–2.0	–2.3	–2.2	–3.0	–1.7	–5.9	–6.0
Air transport, other	3 213 ..	–2.3	–3.6	–7.0	–9.7	–13.1	–15.1	–14.5	–17.6
Other transport, passenger	3 215 ..	–2.5	–2.3	–3.8	–4.7	–5.3	–3.6	–5.6	–8.4
Other transport, freight	3 216 ..	–41.1	–45.3	–50.5	–66.0	–74.4	–98.0	–111.3	–157.3
Other transport, other	3 217 ..	–1.3	–1.7	–2.1	–2.9	–3.1	–3.3	–4.4	–7.0
Travel, credit	2 236 ..	**39.4**	**38.6**	**50.4**	**54.4**	**91.2**	**103.2**	**111.8**	**164.2**
Business travel	2 237 ..	12.8	11.2	15.2	18.4	20.8	23.9	26.4	38.9
Personal travel	2 240 ..	26.6	27.4	35.1	36.0	70.4	79.3	85.3	125.4
Travel, debit	3 236 ..	**–73.0**	**–75.1**	**–95.4**	**–99.4**	**–113.2**	**–141.2**	**–187.4**	**–213.0**
Business travel	3 237 ..	–31.6	–34.8	–49.6	–54.5	–70.1	–82.7	–100.2	–107.4
Personal travel	3 240 ..	–41.4	–40.3	–45.8	–44.9	–43.0	–58.6	–87.1	–105.6
Other services, credit	2 200 BA ..	**42.3**	**47.7**	**57.1**	**68.5**	**98.2**	**126.2**	**153.1**	**193.4**
Communications	2 245 ..	16.7	17.5	20.0	24.4	45.3	59.4	71.2	85.7
Construction	2 249 ..	.9	.5	.9	.6	4.3	6.1	10.7	15.0
Insurance	2 253 ..	.8	.8	.8	1.0	.8	.6	.9	2.1
Financial	2 260 ..	1.5	2.5	2.1	1.8	1.7	3.2	4.0	4.1
Computer and information	2 262 ..	.6	.4	.9	1.2	2.6	3.6	8.0	14.3
Royalties and licence fees	2 266 ..	.7	1.1	1.3	1.4	2.2	1.6	1.7	6.2
Other business services	2 268 ..	10.9	13.1	20.1	18.3	28.4	36.2	38.3	47.4
Personal, cultural, and recreational	2 287 ..	.3	.8	.7	.5	.8	.8	.6	.3
Government, n.i.e.	2 291 ..	9.9	11.0	10.3	19.3	12.1	14.8	17.8	18.5
Other services, debit	3 200 BA ..	**–67.1**	**–65.5**	**–85.4**	**–94.9**	**–123.8**	**–131.4**	**–125.4**	**–172.1**
Communications	3 245 ..	–7.6	–8.6	–14.0	–19.0	–18.8	–27.3	–29.0	–37.6
Construction	3 249 ..	–11.3	–2.4	–4.6	–2.1	–3.4	–2.5	–4.2	–7.3
Insurance	3 253 ..	–1.2	–1.1	–1.3	–2.4	–2.2	–3.1	–5.6	–5.5
Financial	3 260 ..	–1.9	–2.9	–2.3	–2.9	–2.9	–3.6	–4.9	–6.7
Computer and information	3 262 ..	–2.8	–2.6	–11.8	–2.7	–6.1	–4.4	–5.9	–15.7
Royalties and licence fees	3 266 ..	–1.8	–1.0	–1.2	–3.0	–2.6	–2.3	–4.0	–7.2
Other business services	3 268 ..	–29.1	–33.4	–36.0	–35.8	–65.7	–58.2	–41.4	–54.5
Personal, cultural, and recreational	3 287 ..	....	–.1	–.2	–.6	–.5	–.6	–.7	–.7
Government, n.i.e.	3 291 ..	–11.4	–13.4	–14.0	–26.3	–21.6	–29.5	–29.7	–36.9

Table 2 (Continued). STANDARD PRESENTATION, 2000–2007

(Millions of U.S. dollars)

	Code	2000	2001	2002	2003	2004	2005	2006	2007
C. INCOME	4 300	**21.6**	**95.8**	**156.6**	**230.8**	**357.0**	**410.9**	**402.1**	**414.3**
Total credit	2 300	*139.1*	*173.9*	*229.4*	*340.8*	*490.0*	*539.3*	*605.8*	*710.0*
Total debit	3 300	*−117.5*	*−78.1*	*−72.8*	*−110.0*	*−133.0*	*−128.4*	*−203.8*	*−295.7*
Compensation of employees, credit	2 310	**125.0**	**162.0**	**221.0**	**332.0**	**480.0**	**520.0**	**573.0**	**649.0**
Compensation of employees, debit	3 310	**−29.0**	**−39.0**	**−35.3**	**−43.0**	**−41.1**	**−43.2**	**−50.4**	**−56.1**
Investment income, credit	2 320	**14.1**	**11.9**	**8.4**	**8.8**	**10.0**	**19.3**	**32.8**	**61.0**
Direct investment income	2 330	....	....	....	....	....	....	....	....
Dividends and distributed branch profits	2 332	....	....	....	....	....	....	....	....
Reinvested earnings and undistributed branch profits	2 333	....	....	....	....	....	....	....	....
Income on debt (interest)	2 334	....	....	....	....	....	....	....	....
Portfolio investment income	2 339	5.5	3.2	2.2	2.8	2.4	5.1	10.9	15.0
Income on equity	2 340	....	....	....	....	....	....	....	....
Income on bonds and notes	2 350	5.5	3.2	2.2	2.8	2.4	5.1	10.9	15.0
Income on money market instruments	2 360	....	....	....	....	....	....	....	....
Other investment income	2 370	8.6	8.7	6.2	6.0	7.7	14.2	22.0	46.0
Investment income, debit	3 320	**−88.5**	**−39.1**	**−37.5**	**−67.0**	**−91.9**	**−85.2**	**−153.4**	**−239.6**
Direct investment income	3 330	−2.7	20.7	13.6	−24.7	−49.5	−44.9	−108.5	−183.2
Dividends and distributed branch profits	3 332	−2.3	−4.2	−5.3	−3.3	−3.9	−6.1	−55.1	−52.8
Reinvested earnings and undistributed branch profits	3 333	2.6	36.6	27.4	−15.3	−38.1	−27.4	−41.6	−112.8
Income on debt (interest)	3 334	−3.0	−11.7	−8.6	−6.1	−7.5	−11.4	−11.8	−17.7
Portfolio investment income	3 339	−39.2	−6.4	−3.7	−2.8	−2.3	−2.4	−2.5	−3.2
Income on equity	3 340	−.6	−.5	−.3	−.6	−.2	....	−.2	−1.4
Income on bonds and notes	3 350	−38.7	−5.9	−3.5	−2.2	−2.0	−2.4	−2.3	−1.8
Income on money market instruments	3 360	....	....	....	....	....	....	....	....
Other investment income	3 370	−46.6	−53.4	−47.4	−39.5	−40.2	−37.9	−42.4	−53.2
D. CURRENT TRANSFERS	4 379	**210.8**	**230.3**	**241.8**	**306.4**	**372.0**	**575.5**	**799.7**	**1,178.5**
Credit	2 379	**223.8**	**246.3**	**261.1**	**334.2**	**407.8**	**618.8**	**859.6**	**1,258.8**
General government	2 380	78.8	75.1	64.9	67.4	64.1	81.3	73.9	128.4
Other sectors	2 390	145.0	171.2	196.2	266.8	343.7	537.5	785.7	1,130.4
Workers' remittances	2 391	52.6	80.2	101.6	152.0	221.4	395.1	602.8	842.3
Other current transfers	2 392	92.4	91.0	94.6	114.8	122.3	142.4	182.9	288.1
Debit	3 379	**−13.1**	**−15.9**	**−19.3**	**−27.8**	**−35.8**	**−43.2**	**−60.0**	**−80.3**
General government	3 380	−2.1	−3.1	−3.6	−5.3	−5.4	−5.4	−6.5	−5.1
Other sectors	3 390	−11.0	−12.9	−15.7	−22.6	−30.4	−37.9	−53.4	−75.2
Workers' remittances	3 391	−.2	−.4	−1.0	−.8	−.8	−3.1	−6.5	−15.8
Other current transfers	3 392	−10.8	−12.5	−14.8	−21.7	−29.7	−34.8	−47.0	−59.4
CAPITAL AND FINANCIAL ACCOUNT	4 996	**106.7**	**10.8**	**43.8**	**82.7**	**−54.5**	**47.5**	**315.5**	**556.5**
CAPITAL ACCOUNT	4 994	**−11.9**	**−20.7**	**−19.3**	**−19.0**	**−12.8**	**−3.8**	**−22.8**	**−8.0**
Total credit	2 994	*5.2*	*1.1*	*1.2*	*4.6*	*12.7*	*18.3*	*6.1*	*7.0*
Total debit	3 994	*−17.1*	*−21.8*	*−20.4*	*−23.6*	*−25.5*	*−22.1*	*−28.9*	*−14.9*
Capital transfers, credit	2 400	**5.2**	**1.1**	**1.2**	**4.6**	**12.7**	**18.3**	**6.1**	**7.0**
General government	2 401	2.4	....	....	....	5.5	13.0	....	....
Debt forgiveness	2 402	2.4	....	....	....	5.5	13.0	....	....
Other capital transfers	2 410	....	....	....	....	....	....	....	....
Other sectors	2 430	2.8	1.1	1.2	4.6	7.2	5.2	6.1	7.0
Migrants' transfers	2 431	1.0	1.1	1.2	2.6	3.9	5.2	5.9	7.0
Debt forgiveness	2 432	....	....	....	....	.4	....	....	....
Other capital transfers	2 440	1.7	....	....	2.0	2.9	....	.2	....
Capital transfers, debit	3 400	**−17.1**	**−21.8**	**−20.4**	**−23.6**	**−25.5**	**−22.1**	**−28.9**	**−14.9**
General government	3 401	....	....	....	....	....	....	....	....
Debt forgiveness	3 402	....	....	....	....	....	....	....	....
Other capital transfers	3 410	....	....	....	....	....	....	....	....
Other sectors	3 430	−17.1	−21.8	−20.4	−23.6	−25.5	−22.1	−28.9	−14.9
Migrants' transfers	3 431	−16.8	−19.1	−20.3	−23.6	−25.5	−22.1	−28.8	−14.8
Debt forgiveness	3 432	....	....	....	....	....	....	....	....
Other capital transfers	3 440	−.3	−2.6	−.2	....	−.1	....	....	−.1
Nonproduced nonfinancial assets, credit	2 480	....	....	....	....	....	....	....	....
Nonproduced nonfinancial assets, debit	3 480	....	....	....	....	....	....	....	....

Table 2 (Continued). STANDARD PRESENTATION, 2000–2007

(Millions of U.S. dollars)

	Code	2000	2001	2002	2003	2004	2005	2006	2007
FINANCIAL ACCOUNT	4 995 ..	**118.6**	**31.4**	**63.1**	**101.7**	**−41.7**	**51.3**	**338.3**	**564.5**
A. DIRECT INVESTMENT	4 500 ..	**127.5**	**103.3**	**83.6**	**73.6**	**147.8**	**190.9**	**251.8**	**481.4**
Direct investment abroad	4 505 ..	**−.1**	**−.1**	**−.5**	**−.1**	**−3.2**	**.2**	**.7**	**−12.0**
Equity capital	4 510 ..	−.1	−.1	−.5	−.1	−.2	.2	−.8	−12.6
Claims on affiliated enterprises	4 515 ..	−.1	−.1	−.5	−.1	−.2	.2	−.8	−12.6
Liabilities to affiliated enterprises	4 520 ..	....	....	....	....	....	....	....	....
Reinvested earnings	4 525 ..	....	....	....	....	....	....	....	....
Other capital	4 530 ..	....	....	....	....	−3.0	−.1	1.6	.6
Claims on affiliated enterprises	4 535 ..	....	....	....	....	−3.0	−.1	1.6	.6
Liabilities to affiliated enterprises	4 540 ..	....	....	....	....	....	....	....	....
Direct investment in Moldova	4 555 ..	**127.5**	**103.4**	**84.1**	**73.8**	**151.0**	**190.7**	**251.1**	**493.4**
Equity capital	4 560 ..	83.7	110.9	60.1	39.7	114.1	79.6	119.0	229.3
Claims on direct investors	4 565 ..	....	....	....	....	....	....	....	....
Liabilities to direct investors	4 570 ..	83.7	110.9	60.1	39.7	114.1	79.6	119.0	229.3
Reinvested earnings	4 575 ..	−2.6	−36.6	−27.4	15.3	38.1	27.4	41.6	112.8
Other capital	4 580 ..	46.5	29.2	51.4	18.8	−1.2	83.7	90.4	151.4
Claims on direct investors	4 585 ..	....	....	....	....	....	....	....	....
Liabilities to direct investors	4 590 ..	46.5	29.2	51.4	18.8	−1.2	83.7	90.4	151.4
B. PORTFOLIO INVESTMENT	4 600 ..	**117.2**	**−32.4**	**−27.4**	**−23.8**	**−9.8**	**−7.0**	**−4.8**	**−4.5**
Assets	4 602 ..	....	**−3.2**	**−1.5**	**.4**	**−1.5**	**−1.2**	**−.2**	**−.1**
Equity securities	4 610 ..	....	....	....	−.1	−.2	....	−.2	−.1
Monetary authorities	4 611 ..	....	....	....	....	....	....	....	....
General government	4 612 ..	....	....	....	....	....	....	....	....
Banks	4 613 ..	....	....	....	....	....	....	....	....
Other sectors	4 614 ..	....	....	....	−.1	−.2	....	−.2	....
Debt securities	4 619 ..	....	−3.2	−1.5	.5	−1.3	−1.2	....	....
Bonds and notes	4 620 ..	....	−3.2	−1.5	.5	−1.3	−1.2	....	....
Monetary authorities	4 621 ..	....	....	....	....	....	....	....	....
General government	4 622 ..	....	....	....	....	....	....	....	....
Banks	4 623 ..	....	−3.1	−1.5	.5	−1.3	−1.2	....	....
Other sectors	4 624 ..	....	−.1	....	....	....	....	....	....
Money market instruments	4 630 ..	....	....	....	....	....	....	....	....
Monetary authorities	4 631 ..	....	....	....	....	....	....	....	....
General government	4 632 ..	....	....	....	....	....	....	....	....
Banks	4 633 ..	....	....	....	....	....	....	....	....
Other sectors	4 634 ..	....	....	....	....	....	....	....	....
Liabilities	4 652 ..	**117.2**	**−29.2**	**−25.9**	**−24.2**	**−8.3**	**−5.8**	**−4.6**	**−4.4**
Equity securities	4 660 ..	2.9	2.8	2.3	.7	−.8	.6	1.8	1.7
Banks	4 663 ..	2.9	.1	1.6	−.3	−.6	.6	1.7	1.5
Other sectors	4 664 ..	....	2.8	.8	1.0	−.2	....	.1	.3
Debt securities	4 669 ..	114.3	−32.1	−28.2	−24.9	−7.5	−6.4	−6.4	−6.2
Bonds and notes	4 670 ..	114.3	−32.1	−28.2	−24.9	−7.5	−6.4	−6.4	−6.4
Monetary authorities	4 671 ..	....	....	....	....	....	....	....	....
General government	4 672 ..	114.3	−32.1	−28.2	−24.9	−7.5	−6.4	−6.4	−6.4
Banks	4 673 ..	....	....	....	....	....	....	....	....
Other sectors	4 674 ..	....	....	....	....	....	....	....	....
Money market instruments	4 680 ..	....	....	....	....	....	....	....	.2
Monetary authorities	4 681 ..	....	....	....	....	....	....	....	....
General government	4 682 ..	....	....	....	....	....	....	....	.2
Banks	4 683 ..	....	....	....	....	....	....	....	....
Other sectors	4 684 ..	....	....	....	....	....	....	....	....
C. FINANCIAL DERIVATIVES	4 910 ..	....	....	....	**.1**	**.6**	**−1.6**	**.2**	**−.5**
Monetary authorities	4 911 ..	....	....	....	....	....	....	....	....
General government	4 912 ..	....	....	....	....	....	....	....	....
Banks	4 913 ..	....	....	....	.1	.6	−1.6	.2	−.5
Other sectors	4 914 ..	....	....	....	....	....	....	....	....
Assets	4 900 ..	....	....	....	....	**−.5**	**−1.7**	**−.1**	**−.5**
Monetary authorities	4 901 ..	....	....	....	....	....	....	....	....
General government	4 902 ..	....	....	....	....	....	....	....	....
Banks	4 903 ..	....	....	....	....	−.5	−1.7	−.1	−.5
Other sectors	4 904 ..	....	....	....	....	....	....	....	....
Liabilities	4 905 ..	....	....	....	**.1**	**1.0**	**.1**	**.3**	**.1**
Monetary authorities	4 906 ..	....	....	....	....	....	....	....	....
General government	4 907 ..	....	....	....	....	....	....	....	....
Banks	4 908 ..	....	....	....	.1	1.0	.1	.3	....
Other sectors	4 909 ..	....	....	....	....	....	....	....	.1

Table 2 (Concluded). STANDARD PRESENTATION, 2000–2007

(Millions of U.S. dollars)

	Code	2000	2001	2002	2003	2004	2005	2006	2007
D. OTHER INVESTMENT	4 700 ..	**−78.6**	**−30.0**	**33.9**	**65.8**	**−32.3**	**−2.4**	**231.9**	**616.9**
Assets	4 703 ..	**−35.9**	**−22.2**	**−40.0**	**6.5**	**−31.6**	**−78.2**	**−49.4**	**54.0**
Trade credits	4 706 ..	−12.7	−23.5	−19.5	−17.4	−27.4	−25.7	17.4	−7.6
General government	4 707 ..	....	....	....	....	....	....	....	....
of which: Short-term	4 709 ..	....	....	....	....	....	....	....	....
Other sectors	4 710 ..	−12.7	−23.5	−19.5	−17.4	−27.4	−25.7	17.4	−7.6
of which: Short-term	4 712 ..	*−12.7*	*−23.5*	*−19.5*	*−17.4*	*−27.4*	*−25.7*	*17.4*	*−7.6*
Loans	4 714 ..	....	....	....	....	....	....	....	....
Monetary authorities	4 715 ..	....	....	....	....	....	....	....	....
of which: Short-term	4 718 ..	....	....	....	....	....	....	....	....
General government	4 719 ..	....	....	....	....	....	....	....	....
of which: Short-term	4 721 ..	....	....	....	....	....	....	....	....
Banks	4 722 ..	....	....	....	....	....	....	....	....
of which: Short-term	4 724 ..	....	....	....	....	....	....	....	....
Other sectors	4 725 ..	....	....	....	....	....	....	....	....
of which: Short-term	4 727 ..	....	....	....	....	....	....	....	....
Currency and deposits	4 730 ..	−23.3	1.3	−21.0	24.0	−5.6	−52.5	−66.8	61.6
Monetary authorities	4 731 ..	.1	....	....	....	−18.8	−14.1	....	....
General government	4 732 ..	....	8.3	.5	−.2	.3	−.2	....	....
Banks	4 733 ..	−16.5	1.2	−15.7	−19.6	5.8	−50.7	−77.6	49.2
Other sectors	4 734 ..	−6.9	−8.2	−5.8	43.8	7.1	12.6	10.8	12.4
Other assets	4 736 ..	....	....	.5	....	1.3	....	....	....
Monetary authorities	4 737 ..	....	....	....	....	....	....	....	....
of which: Short-term	4 739 ..	....	....	....	....	....	....	....	....
General government	4 740 ..	....	....	....	....	....	....	....	....
of which: Short-term	4 742 ..	....	....	....	....	....	....	....	....
Banks	4 743 ..	....	....	....	....	....	....	....	....
of which: Short-term	4 745 ..	....	....	....	....	....	....	....	....
Other sectors	4 746 ..	....	....	.5	....	1.3	....	....	....
of which: Short-term	4 748 ..	....	....	*.5*	....	....	....	....	....
Liabilities	4 753 ..	**−42.7**	**−7.8**	**73.8**	**59.3**	**−.7**	**75.8**	**281.2**	**563.0**
Trade credits	4 756 ..	−7.3	−10.0	11.2	27.3	36.6	60.1	44.9	107.1
General government	4 757 ..	....	....	....	....	....	....	....	....
of which: Short-term	4 759 ..	....	....	....	....	....	....	....	....
Other sectors	4 760 ..	−7.3	−10.0	11.2	27.3	36.6	60.1	44.9	107.1
of which: Short-term	4 762 ..	*−7.3*	*−10.0*	*11.2*	*27.3*	*36.6*	*60.1*	*44.9*	*107.1*
Loans	4 764 ..	149.8	13.2	−2.1	−23.8	−4.7	−7.6	191.8	334.1
Monetary authorities	4 765 ..	−12.7	−2.3	−5.6	−22.2	−21.6	−21.7	41.1	11.2
of which: Use of Fund credit and loans from the Fund	4 766 ..	*−12.7*	*−2.3*	*−5.6*	*−22.2*	*−21.6*	*−21.7*	*41.1*	*11.2*
of which: Short-term	4 768 ..	....	....	....	....	....	....	....	....
General government	4 769 ..	128.6	−7.5	.1	−22.6	−19.1	−14.8	57.8	27.6
of which: Short-term	4 771 ..	....	....	....	....	....	....	....	....
Banks	4 772 ..	−6.3	.7	7.1	9.5	2.3	1.2	7.2	122.2
of which: Short-term	4 774 ..	*.1*	*1.8*	*−2.1*	*8.6*	*−6.1*	*−2.0*	....	*18.5*
Other sectors	4 775 ..	40.2	22.3	−3.7	11.5	33.7	27.7	85.6	173.1
of which: Short-term	4 777 ..	*2.3*	*−3.4*	....	*.7*	*−.7*	*1.6*	*7.2*	*2.1*
Currency and deposits	4 780 ..	10.3	−3.0	3.9	4.6	14.7	12.6	53.3	60.6
Monetary authorities	4 781 ..	−.2	....	....	....	....	....	....	....
General government	4 782 ..	....	....	....	....	....	....	....	....
Banks	4 783 ..	10.5	−3.0	3.9	4.6	14.7	12.6	53.3	60.6
Other sectors	4 784 ..	....	....	....	....	....	....	....	....
Other liabilities	4 786 ..	−195.5	−8.0	60.8	51.2	−47.3	10.6	−8.8	61.3
Monetary authorities	4 787 ..	....	....	....	....	....	....	....	....
of which: Short-term	4 789 ..	....	....	....	....	....	....	....	....
General government	4 790 ..	−110.5	4.8	23.2	37.6	−39.9	16.9	−60.9	−.1
of which: Short-term	4 792 ..	*−110.5*	*4.8*	*23.2*	*37.6*	*−39.9*	*16.9*	*−60.9*	*−.1*
Banks	4 793 ..	....	....	....	....	....	....	....	10.3
of which: Short-term	4 795 ..	....	....	....	....	....	....	....	*10.3*
Other sectors	4 796 ..	−84.9	−12.9	37.6	13.6	−7.4	−6.3	52.1	51.1
of which: Short-term	4 798 ..	*−84.9*	*−12.9*	*37.6*	*13.6*	*−7.4*	*−6.3*	*52.1*	*51.1*
E. RESERVE ASSETS	4 802 ..	**−47.4**	**−9.5**	**−27.0**	**−14.1**	**−148.0**	**−128.6**	**−140.7**	**−528.9**
Monetary gold	4 812 ..	....	....	....	....	....	....	....	....
Special drawing rights	4 811 ..	....	−.4	.5	.3	....	....	−.1	....
Reserve position in the Fund	4 810 ..	....	....	....	....	....	....	....	....
Foreign exchange	4 803 ..	−47.4	−9.1	−27.5	−14.3	−148.0	−128.7	−140.6	−528.9
Other claims	4 813 ..	....	....	....	....	....	....	....	....
NET ERRORS AND OMISSIONS	4 998 ..	**−8.6**	**16.0**	**−24.0**	**47.4**	**100.6**	**178.3**	**64.2**	**139.0**

Table 3. INTERNATIONAL INVESTMENT POSITION (End-period stocks), 2000–2007

(Millions of U.S. dollars)

	Code	2000	2001	2002	2003	2004	2005	2006	2007
ASSETS...	8 995 C.	**656.9**	**679.8**	**761.1**	**798.0**	**1,012.0**	**1,185.4**	**1,419.9**	**1,969.9**
Direct investment abroad...........................	8 505 ..	**23.0**	**23.1**	**23.5**	**23.6**	**28.7**	**29.9**	**29.2**	**41.2**
Equity capital and reinvested earnings............	8 506 ..	22.6	22.7	23.2	23.3	23.5	24.6	25.5	38.1
Claims on affiliated enterprises..................	8 507 ..	22.6	22.7	23.2	23.3	23.5	24.6	25.5	38.1
Liabilities to affiliated enterprises...............	8 508 ..	....	....	....	....	....	....	....	....
Other capital..	8 530 ..	.4	.4	.4	.4	5.2	5.3	3.7	3.1
Claims on affiliated enterprises..................	8 535 ..	.4	.4	.4	.4	5.2	5.3	3.7	3.1
Liabilities to affiliated enterprises...............	8 540 ..	....	....	....	....	....	....	....	....
Portfolio investment...............................	8 602 ..	**.4**	**3.6**	**5.1**	**4.7**	**6.1**	**7.3**	**7.5**	**7.6**
Equity securities.......................................	8 610 ..	.4	.4	.4	.5	.7	.7	.9	.9
Monetary authorities..............................	8 611 ..	....	....	....	....	....	....	....	....
General government...............................	8 612 ..	.4	.4	.4	.4	.4	.4	.4	.4
Banks...	8 613 ..	....	....	....	....	....	....	....	....
Other sectors..	8 614 ..	....	....	....	.1	.3	.3	.5	.5
Debt securities...	8 619 ..	....	3.2	4.7	4.2	5.5	6.7	6.7	6.7
Bonds and notes....................................	8 620 ..	....	3.2	4.7	4.2	5.5	6.7	6.7	6.7
Monetary authorities............................	8 621 ..	....	....	....	....	....	....	....	....
General government.............................	8 622 ..	....	....	....	....	....	....	....	....
Banks...	8 623 ..	....	3.1	4.5	4.0	5.3	6.5	6.5	6.5
Other sectors......................................	8 624 ..	....	.1	.1	.1	.1	.1	.1	.1
Money market instruments......................	8 630 ..	....	....	....	....	....	....	....	....
Monetary authorities............................	8 631 ..	....	....	....	....	....	....	....	....
General government.............................	8 632 ..	....	....	....	....	....	....	....	....
Banks...	8 633 ..	....	....	....	....	....	....	....	....
Other sectors......................................	8 634 ..	....	....	....	....	....	....	....	....
Financial derivatives...............................	8 900 ..	**....**	**....**	**....**	**....**	**.4**	**2.1**	**2.2**	**2.8**
Monetary authorities................................	8 901 ..	....	....	....	....	....	....	....	....
General government.................................	8 902 ..	....	....	....	....	....	....	....	....
Banks..	8 903 ..	....	....	....	....	.4	2.1	2.2	2.8
Other sectors..	8 904 ..	....	....	....	....	....	....	....	....
Other investment....................................	8 703 ..	**410.9**	**424.7**	**463.6**	**467.4**	**506.5**	**548.6**	**605.7**	**584.7**
Trade credits...	8 706 ..	228.5	244.2	261.4	283.2	314.4	345.3	330.5	347.9
General government...............................	8 707 ..	.3	....	....	....	....	....	....	....
of which: Short-term............................	8 709 ..	*.3*	....	....	....	....	....	....	....
Other sectors..	8 710 ..	228.2	244.2	261.4	283.2	314.4	345.3	330.5	347.9
of which: Short-term............................	8 712 ..	*228.2*	*244.2*	*261.4*	*283.2*	*314.4*	*345.3*	*330.5*	*347.9*
Loans...	8 714 ..	....	....	....	....	....	....	....	....
Monetary authorities..............................	8 715 ..	....	....	....	....	....	....	....	....
of which: Short-term............................	8 718 ..	....	....	....	....	....	....	....	....
General government...............................	8 719 ..	....	....	....	....	....	....	....	....
of which: Short-term............................	8 721 ..	....	....	....	....	....	....	....	....
Banks...	8 722 ..	....	....	....	....	....	....	....	....
of which: Short-term............................	8 724 ..	....	....	....	....	....	....	....	....
Other sectors..	8 725 ..	....	....	....	....	....	....	....	....
of which: Short-term............................	8 727 ..	....	....	....	....	....	....	....	....
Currency and deposits...............................	8 730 ..	171.6	169.6	191.9	173.9	183.1	194.3	266.2	227.8
Monetary authorities..............................	8 731 ..	....	....	....	....	19.4	....	....	....
General government...............................	8 732 ..	9.6	1.3	.8	1.1	.8	....	....	....
Banks...	8 733 ..	74.4	72.7	89.6	115.2	112.5	156.5	244.2	218.0
Other sectors..	8 734 ..	87.6	95.6	101.4	57.6	50.5	37.8	22.0	9.8
Other assets..	8 736 ..	10.8	10.8	10.4	10.4	9.0	9.0	9.0	9.0
Monetary authorities..............................	8 737 ..	....	....	....	....	....	....	....	....
of which: Short-term............................	8 739 ..	....	....	....	....	....	....	....	....
General government...............................	8 740 ..	....	....	....	....	....	....	....	....
of which: Short-term............................	8 742 ..	....	....	....	....	....	....	....	....
Banks...	8 743 ..	....	....	....	....	....	....	....	....
of which: Short-term............................	8 745 ..	....	....	....	....	....	....	....	....
Other sectors..	8 746 ..	10.8	10.8	10.4	10.4	9.0	9.0	9.0	9.0
of which: Short-term............................	8 748 ..	*.5*	*.5*	....	....	....	....	....	....
Reserve assets..	8 802 ..	**222.6**	**228.5**	**268.9**	**302.3**	**470.3**	**597.4**	**775.3**	**1,333.7**
Monetary gold...	8 812 ..	....	....	....	....	....	....	....	....
Special drawing rights...............................	8 811 ..	.3	.7	.3	....	.1	....	.2	.2
Reserve position in the Fund.......................	8 810 ..	....	....	....	....	....	....	....	....
Foreign exchange......................................	8 803 ..	222.3	227.8	268.6	302.2	470.2	597.4	775.1	1,333.5
Other claims..	8 813 ..	....	....	....	....	....	....	....	....

Table 3 (Concluded). INTERNATIONAL INVESTMENT POSITION (End-period stocks), 2000–2007

(Millions of U.S. dollars)

	Code	2000	2001	2002	2003	2004	2005	2006	2007
LIABILITIES	8 995 D.	**2,106.4**	**2,133.7**	**2,307.2**	**2,478.0**	**2,587.9**	**2,887.4**	**3,506.5**	**4,696.5**
Direct investment in Moldova	8 555 ..	**448.8**	**549.1**	**639.2**	**716.6**	**868.9**	**1,052.4**	**1,306.0**	**1,855.8**
Equity capital and reinvested earnings	8 556 ..	372.5	442.1	473.6	530.5	683.5	788.1	944.8	1,329.4
Claims on direct investors	8 557 ..	....	....	....	....	....	....	....	....
Liabilities to direct investors	8 558 ..	372.5	442.1	473.6	530.5	683.5	788.1	944.8	1,329.4
Other capital	8 580 ..	76.3	107.0	165.6	186.0	185.5	264.3	361.2	526.4
Claims on direct investors	8 585 ..	....	....	....	....	....	....	....	....
Liabilities to direct investors	8 590 ..	76.3	107.0	165.6	186.0	185.5	264.3	361.2	526.4
Portfolio investment	8 652 ..	**201.3**	**161.5**	**133.7**	**110.9**	**51.5**	**46.1**	**51.1**	**53.9**
Equity securities	8 660 ..	11.9	14.1	14.5	16.5	19.7	20.7	32.0	41.0
Banks	8 663 ..	4.2	3.9	4.1	4.7	7.1	8.3	19.6	26.8
Other sectors	8 664 ..	7.7	10.2	10.4	11.9	12.7	12.4	12.4	14.2
Debt securities	8 669 ..	189.5	147.4	119.2	94.3	31.8	25.4	19.0	12.9
Bonds and notes	8 670 ..	189.5	147.4	119.2	94.3	31.8	25.4	19.0	12.7
Monetary authorities	8 671 ..	....	....	....	....	....	....	....	....
General government	8 672 ..	189.5	147.4	119.2	94.3	31.8	25.4	19.0	12.7
Banks	8 673 ..	....	....	....	....	....	....	....	....
Other sectors	8 674 ..	....	....	....	....	....	....	....	....
Money market instruments	8 680 ..	....	....	....	....	....	....	....	.2
Monetary authorities	8 681 ..	....	....	....	....	....	....	....	....
General government	8 682 ..	....	....	....	....	....	....	....	.2
Banks	8 683 ..	....	....	....	....	....	....	....	....
Other sectors	8 684 ..	....	....	....	....	....	....	....	....
Financial derivatives	8 905 ..	....	....	....	....	**1.1**	**1.2**	**1.5**	**1.5**
Monetary authorities	8 906 ..	....	....	....	....	....	....	....	....
General government	8 907 ..	....	....	....	....	....	....	....	....
Banks	8 908 ..	....	....	....	....	1.1	1.2	1.5	1.5
Other sectors	8 909 ..	....	....	....	....	....	....	....	....
Other investment	8 753 ..	**1,456.3**	**1,423.1**	**1,534.2**	**1,650.6**	**1,666.4**	**1,787.7**	**2,148.0**	**2,785.4**
Trade credits	8 756 ..	108.1	98.0	109.4	137.7	175.0	338.6	387.4	502.6
General government	8 757 ..	....	....	....	....	....	....	....	....
of which: Short-term	8 759 ..	....	....	....	....	....	....	....	....
Other sectors	8 760 ..	108.1	98.0	109.4	137.7	175.0	338.6	387.4	502.6
of which: Short-term	8 762 ..	*108.1*	*98.0*	*109.4*	*137.7*	*175.0*	*338.6*	*387.4*	*502.6*
Loans	8 764 ..	970.3	958.0	1,001.2	1,035.6	1,058.9	998.6	1,238.0	1,627.3
Monetary authorities	8 765 ..	154.1	146.1	152.0	142.6	126.4	95.5	141.1	159.5
of which: Use of Fund credit and loans from the Fund	8 766 ..	*154.1*	*146.1*	*152.0*	*142.6*	*126.4*	*95.5*	*141.1*	*159.5*
of which: Short-term	8 768 ..	....	....	....	....	....	....	....	....
General government	8 769 ..	621.0	593.7	623.4	644.2	646.8	596.0	699.1	753.1
of which: Short-term	8 771 ..	....	....	....	....	....	....	....	....
Banks	8 772 ..	15.7	16.3	23.5	33.0	34.8	35.8	44.0	173.6
of which: Short-term	8 774 ..	*.3*	*2.1*		*8.6*	*2.0*	....		*18.5*
Other sectors	8 775 ..	179.4	201.8	202.3	215.8	251.0	271.4	353.9	541.1
of which: Short-term	8 777 ..	*3.6*	*.2*	*.1*	*.8*	*.1*	*1.4*	*8.6*	*10.8*
Currency and deposits	8 780 ..	19.1	15.9	19.7	24.6	39.6	51.0	106.8	178.5
Monetary authorities	8 781 ..	....	....	....	....	....	....	....	....
General government	8 782 ..	....	....	....	....	....	....	....	....
Banks	8 783 ..	19.1	15.9	19.7	24.6	39.6	51.0	106.8	178.5
Other sectors	8 784 ..	....	....	....	....	....	....	....	....
Other liabilities	8 786 ..	358.8	351.3	403.9	452.7	392.9	399.5	415.7	477.0
Monetary authorities	8 787 ..	....	....	....	....	....	....	....	....
of which: Short-term	8 789 ..	....	....	....	....	....	....	....	....
General government	8 790 ..	5.3	9.8	32.7	70.4	20.9	36.3	.1	....
of which: Short-term	8 792 ..	*5.3*	*9.8*	*32.7*	*70.4*	*20.9*	*36.3*	*.1*	....
Banks	8 793 ..	....	....	....	....	....	....	....	10.3
of which: Short-term	8 795 ..	....	....	....	....	....	....	....	*10.3*
Other sectors	8 796 ..	353.5	341.5	371.2	382.3	372.0	363.3	415.6	466.7
of which: Short-term	8 798 ..	*353.5*	*341.5*	*371.2*	*382.3*	*372.0*	*363.3*	*415.6*	*466.7*
NET INTERNATIONAL INVESTMENT POSITION	8 995 ..	**−1,449.5**	**−1,453.9**	**−1,546.1**	**−1,680.0**	**−1,576.0**	**−1,702.0**	**−2,086.6**	**−2,726.6**
Conversion rates: Moldovan lei per U.S. dollar (end of period)	0 102 ..	**12.383**	**13.091**	**13.822**	**13.220**	**12.461**	**12.832**	**12.905**	**11.319**

Table 1. ANALYTIC PRESENTATION, 2000–2007

(Millions of U.S. dollars)

	Code	2000	2001	2002	2003	2004	2005	2006	2007
A. Current Account[1]	4 993 Z.	−156.1	−154.2	−158.0	−148.1	−24.6	−5.1	108.9	....
Goods: exports f.o.b.	2 100 ..	535.8	523.2	524.0	627.3	872.1	1,068.6	1,545.2	....
Goods: imports f.o.b.	3 100 ..	−608.4	−623.8	−680.2	−826.9	−901.0	−1,097.4	−1,356.7	....
Balance on Goods	4 100 ..	*−72.6*	*−100.6*	*−156.2*	*−199.6*	*−28.9*	*−28.8*	*188.5*	....
Services: credit	2 200 ..	77.7	113.5	183.9	207.9	338.4	414.5	485.8	....
Services: debit	3 200 ..	−162.8	−205.4	−265.8	−257.1	−503.7	−476.4	−523.2	....
Balance on Goods and Services	4 991 ..	*−157.7*	*−192.5*	*−238.1*	*−248.8*	*−194.2*	*−90.8*	*151.0*	....
Income: credit	2 300 ..	13.0	14.8	14.1	13.9	16.5	10.7	17.4	....
Income: debit	3 300 ..	−19.5	−16.8	−18.6	−25.4	−27.7	−61.4	−161.9	....
Balance on Goods, Services, and Income	4 992 ..	*−164.2*	*−194.5*	*−242.6*	*−260.3*	*−205.3*	*−141.5*	*6.5*	....
Current transfers: credit	2 379 Z.	25.0	40.3	126.9	167.1	230.9	177.6	179.8	....
Current transfers: debit	3 379 ..	−16.9	....	−42.3	−54.9	−50.2	−41.2	−77.4	....
B. Capital Account[1]	4 994 Z.	....	....	....	....	....	....	....	....
Capital account: credit	2 994 Z.	....	....	....	....	....	....	....	....
Capital account: debit	3 994 ..	....	....	....	....	....	....	....	....
Total, Groups A Plus B	4 981 ..	*−156.1*	*−154.2*	*−158.0*	*−148.1*	*−24.6*	*−5.1*	*108.9*	....
C. Financial Account[1]	4 995 W.	**89.9**	**107.0**	**157.4**	**5.0**	**−23.2**	**45.6**	**181.4**	....
Direct investment abroad	4 505 ..	....	....	....	....	....	....	....	....
Direct investment in Mongolia	4 555 Z.	53.7	43.0	77.8	131.5	92.9	184.6	344.0	....
Portfolio investment assets	4 602 ..	....	....	....	50.0	−2.5	....	....	....
Equity securities	4 610 ..	....	....	....	....	−2.5	....	....	....
Debt securities	4 619 ..	....	....	....	50.0	....	....	....	....
Portfolio investment liabilities	4 652 Z.	....	....	....	....	−50.0	....	....	....
Equity securities	4 660 ..	....	....	....	....	....	....	....	....
Debt securities	4 669 Z.	....	....	....	....	−50.0	....	....	....
Financial derivatives	4 910 ..	....	....	....	....	....	....	....	....
Financial derivatives assets	4 900 ..	....	....	....	....	....	....	....	....
Financial derivatives liabilities	4 905 ..	....	....	....	....	....	....	....	....
Other investment assets	4 703 ..	−44.3	−5.2	−32.1	9.6	−132.2	−124.8	−223.4	....
Monetary authorities	4 701 ..	....	....	....	....	....	....	....	....
General government	4 704 ..	....	....	....	....	....	....	....	....
Banks	4 705 ..	−10.7	1.1	−24.4	46.8	15.0	−1.5	−1.0	....
Other sectors	4 728 ..	−33.6	−6.3	−7.8	−37.2	−147.2	....	....	....
Other investment liabilities	4 753 W.	80.5	69.2	111.7	−186.1	68.6	−14.2	60.8	....
Monetary authorities	4 753 WA	....	....	....	....	....	....	....	....
General government	4 753 ZB	60.5	66.2	72.5	−144.5	112.9	79.6	63.0	....
Banks	4 753 ZC	−2.3	.6	6.9	2.4	27.3	2.5	1.5	....
Other sectors	4 753 ZD	22.3	2.4	32.3	−44.0	−71.6	−96.3	−3.7	....
Total, Groups A Through C	4 983 ..	*−66.2*	*−47.2*	*−.7*	*−143.1*	*−47.7*	*40.5*	*290.4*	....
D. Net Errors and Omissions	4 998 ..	**−19.3**	**−32.2**	**14.1**	**−5.9**	**1.4**	**−74.9**	**−7.8**	....
Total, Groups A Through D	4 984 ..	*−85.5*	*−79.4*	*13.4*	*−149.0*	*−46.3*	*−34.4*	*282.5*	....
E. Reserves and Related Items	4 802 A.	**85.5**	**79.4**	**−13.4**	**149.0**	**46.3**	**34.4**	**−282.5**	....
Reserve assets	4 802 ..	−2.5	−15.8	−58.1	96.8	−34.4	−48.5	−389.2	....
Use of Fund credit and loans	4 766 ..	1.8	−1.6	−7.7	2.8	−7.2	−5.9	−5.9	....
Exceptional financing	4 920 ..	86.2	96.9	52.3	49.4	88.0	88.8	112.6	....
Conversion rates: togrogs per U.S. dollar	0 101 ..	**1,076.7**	**1,097.7**	**1,110.3**	**1,146.5**	**1,185.3**	**1,205.2**	**1,165.4**	**1,171.0**

[1] Excludes components that have been classified in the categories of Group E.

Table 2. STANDARD PRESENTATION, 2000–2007

(Millions of U.S. dollars)

	Code	2000	2001	2002	2003	2004	2005	2006	2007
CURRENT ACCOUNT	4 993 ..	**−69.9**	**−62.1**	**−105.0**	**−98.7**	**63.4**	**83.7**	**221.6**	....
A. GOODS	4 100 ..	**−72.6**	**−100.6**	**−156.2**	**−199.6**	**−28.9**	**−28.8**	**188.5**	....
Credit	2 100 ..	**535.8**	**523.2**	**524.0**	**627.3**	**872.1**	**1,068.6**	**1,545.2**	....
General merchandise: exports f.o.b.	2 110 ..	466.1	448.5	406.4	627.3	872.1	737.2	1,275.1	....
Goods for processing: exports f.o.b.	2 150 ..	....	....	....	....	....	....	....	....
Repairs on goods	2 160 ..	....	....	....	....	....	....	....	....
Goods procured in ports by carriers	2 170 ..	....	....	....	....	....	....	....	....
Nonmonetary gold	2 180 ..	69.7	74.7	117.6	....	....	331.4	270.1	....
Debit	3 100 ..	**−608.4**	**−623.8**	**−680.2**	**−826.9**	**−901.0**	**−1,097.4**	**−1,356.7**	....
General merchandise: imports f.o.b.	3 110 ..	−608.4	−623.8	−680.2	−826.9	−901.0	−1,097.4	−1,356.7	....
Goods for processing: imports f.o.b.	3 150 ..	....	....	....	....	....	....	....	....
Repairs on goods	3 160 ..	....	....	....	....	....	....	....	....
Goods procured in ports by carriers	3 170 ..	....	....	....	....	....	....	....	....
Nonmonetary gold	3 180 ..	....	....	....	....	....	....	....	....
B. SERVICES	4 200 ..	**−85.1**	**−91.9**	**−81.9**	**−49.2**	**−165.3**	**−62.0**	**−37.5**	....
Total credit	2 200 ..	*77.7*	*113.5*	*183.9*	*207.9*	*338.4*	*414.5*	*485.8*	....
Total debit	3 200 ..	*−162.8*	*−205.4*	*−265.8*	*−257.1*	*−503.7*	*−476.4*	*−523.2*	....
Transportation services, credit	2 205 ..	**30.2**	**35.8**	**38.9**	**40.5**	**107.6**	**199.2**	**214.4**	....
Passenger	2 850 ..	*7.3*	*10.1*	*13.1*	*11.0*	*19.6*	*26.4*	*36.2*	....
Freight	2 851 ..	....	....	....	....	*37.0*	*77.9*	*97.6*	....
Other	2 852 ..	*22.9*	*25.7*	*25.8*	*29.5*	*51.1*	*95.0*	*80.6*	....
Sea transport, passenger	2 207 ..	....	....	....	....	....	....	....	....
Sea transport, freight	2 208 ..	....	....	....	....	....	....	....	....
Sea transport, other	2 209 ..	....	....	....	....	....	....	....	....
Air transport, passenger	2 211 ..	5.4	6.4	7.0	6.9	10.4	....	....	....
Air transport, freight	2 212 ..	....	....	....	....	7.4	....	....	....
Air transport, other	2 213 ..	22.3	22.6	23.9	24.1	29.0	....	....	....
Other transport, passenger	2 215 ..	1.9	3.7	6.1	4.1	9.2	....	....	....
Other transport, freight	2 216 ..	....	....	....	....	29.6	....	....	....
Other transport, other	2 217 ..	.6	3.1	1.9	5.4	22.1	....	....	....
Transportation services, debit	3 205 ..	**−85.1**	**−99.7**	**−99.6**	**−44.2**	**−199.4**	**−216.1**	**−254.6**	....
Passenger	3 850 ..	*−3.4*	*−4.4*	*−6.1*	*−5.9*	*−13.6*	*−16.3*	*−24.2*	....
Freight	3 851 ..	*−67.6*	*−69.3*	*−72.5*	....	*−107.2*	*−129.3*	*−151.5*	....
Other	3 852 ..	*−14.1*	*−26.0*	*−20.9*	*−38.3*	*−78.6*	*−70.6*	*−78.9*	....
Sea transport, passenger	3 207 ..	....	....	....	....	....	....	....	....
Sea transport, freight	3 208 ..	....	....	....	....	....	....	....	....
Sea transport, other	3 209 ..	....	....	....	....	....	....	....	....
Air transport, passenger	3 211 ..	−2.3	−3.3	−4.2	−4.4	−7.2	....	....	....
Air transport, freight	3 212 ..	....	....	....	....	−21.4	....	....	....
Air transport, other	3 213 ..	−9.1	−2.4	−2.7	−10.5	−12.9	....	....	....
Other transport, passenger	3 215 ..	−1.1	−1.1	−1.9	−1.5	−6.4	....	....	....
Other transport, freight	3 216 ..	−67.6	−69.3	−72.5	....	−85.8	....	....	....
Other transport, other	3 217 ..	−5.0	−23.6	−18.2	−27.8	−65.7	....	....	....
Travel, credit	2 236 ..	**35.9**	**39.3**	**130.0**	**143.0**	**185.1**	**176.8**	**225.1**	....
Business travel	2 237 ..	....	....	....	....	.4	.7	2.3	....
Personal travel	2 240 ..	....	....	....	143.0	184.7	176.1	222.8	....
Travel, debit	3 236 ..	**−51.3**	**−55.3**	**−119.2**	**−137.5**	**−192.7**	**−156.6**	**−187.9**	....
Business travel	3 237 ..	....	....	....	....	−7.6	−4.7	−5.6	....
Personal travel	3 240 ..	....	....	....	−137.5	−185.1	−151.9	−182.4	....
Other services, credit	2 200 BA ..	**11.6**	**38.4**	**15.0**	**24.4**	**45.7**	**38.5**	**46.3**	....
Communications	2 245 ..	7.7	7.7	6.2	4.8	4.8	14.5	17.9	....
Construction	2 249 ..	....	....	....	....	....	.8	.4	....
Insurance	2 253 ..	.2	.9	1.2	1.2	2.0	2.3	.7	....
Financial	2 260 ..	....	....	.3	.5	2.0	5.0	9.0	....
Computer and information	2 262 ..	....	....	.9	1.8	1.2	.8	.2	....
Royalties and licence fees	2 266 ..	....	....	....	....	....	....	....	....
Other business services	2 268 ..	....	25.5	1.2	10.7	25.4	9.7	15.2	....
Personal, cultural, and recreational	2 287 ..	....	....	....	.2	1.1	.1	....	....
Government, n.i.e.	2 291 ..	3.7	4.3	5.2	5.2	9.2	5.4	2.9	....
Other services, debit	3 200 BA ..	**−26.4**	**−50.4**	**−47.1**	**−75.4**	**−111.6**	**−103.7**	**−80.7**	**....**
Communications	3 245 ..	−4.4	−4.4	−10.5	−7.4	−9.1	−23.4	−9.9	....
Construction	3 249 ..	....	....	....	−.6	−.6	−3.5	−1.5	....
Insurance	3 253 ..	−.8	−1.6	−.4	−1.2	−32.9	−15.2	−16.9	....
Financial	3 260 ..	−.3	....	−6.6	−3.2	−7.9	−7.9	−3.0	....
Computer and information	3 262 ..	....	....	−.4	−.5	−1.3	−2.3	−.5	....
Royalties and licence fees	3 266 ..	....	....	....	....	....	....	....	....
Other business services	3 268 ..	−15.6	−36.7	−23.6	−53.7	−52.6	−43.3	−42.4	....
Personal, cultural, and recreational	3 287 ..	....	....	....	−.2	....	−.2	2.2	....
Government, n.i.e.	3 291 ..	−5.3	−7.7	−5.6	−8.6	−7.2	−8.0	−9.0	....

Table 2 (Continued). STANDARD PRESENTATION, 2000–2007

(Millions of U.S. dollars)

	Code	2000	2001	2002	2003	2004	2005	2006	2007
C. INCOME	4 300	**−6.5**	**−2.0**	**−4.5**	**−11.5**	**−11.1**	**−50.8**	**−144.5**	....
Total credit	2 300	*13.0*	*14.8*	*14.1*	*13.9*	*16.5*	*10.7*	*17.4*	....
Total debit	3 300	*−19.5*	*−16.8*	*−18.6*	*−25.4*	*−27.7*	*−61.4*	*−161.9*	....
Compensation of employees, credit	2 310	....	....	....	....	7.1	2.8	1.6	....
Compensation of employees, debit	3 310	....	....	....	....	....	....	....	....
Investment income, credit	2 320	**13.0**	**14.8**	**14.1**	**13.9**	**9.4**	**7.9**	**15.8**	....
Direct investment income	2 330	....	....	....	....	....	....	....	....
Dividends and distributed branch profits	2 332	....	....	....	....	....	....	....	....
Reinvested earnings and undistributed branch profits	2 333	....	....	....	....	....	....	....	....
Income on debt (interest)	2 334	....	....	....	....	....	....	....	....
Portfolio investment income	2 339	....	....	10.1	7.4	1.0	....	....	....
Income on equity	2 340	....	....	....	....	....	....	....	....
Income on bonds and notes	2 350	....	....	2.6	1.5	1.0	....	....	....
Income on money market instruments	2 360	....	....	7.4	5.9	....	....	....	....
Other investment income	2 370	13.0	14.8	4.0	6.5	8.4	7.9	15.8	....
Investment income, debit	3 320	**−19.5**	**−16.8**	**−18.6**	**−25.4**	**−27.7**	**−61.4**	**−161.9**	....
Direct investment income	3 330	−8.8	−5.9	−5.1	−5.0	−9.5	−41.0	−145.4	....
Dividends and distributed branch profits	3 332	−8.8	−5.9	−5.1	−5.0	−9.5	−41.0	−145.4	....
Reinvested earnings and undistributed branch profits	3 333	....	....	....	....	....	....	....	....
Income on debt (interest)	3 334	....	....	....	....	....	....	....	....
Portfolio investment income	3 339	....	....	....	....	....	....	....	....
Income on equity	3 340	....	....	....	....	....	....	....	....
Income on bonds and notes	3 350	....	....	....	....	....	....	....	....
Income on money market instruments	3 360	....	....	....	....	....	....	....	....
Other investment income	3 370	−10.7	−10.9	−13.5	−20.4	−18.2	−20.4	−16.5	....
D. CURRENT TRANSFERS	4 379	**94.3**	**132.4**	**137.6**	**161.6**	**268.7**	**225.2**	**215.1**	....
Credit	2 379	**111.2**	**132.4**	**179.9**	**216.5**	**318.9**	**266.4**	**292.5**	....
General government	2 380	98.6	107.4	73.2	49.4	88.0	88.8	112.6	....
Other sectors	2 390	12.6	25.0	106.7	167.1	230.9	177.6	179.8	....
Workers' remittances	2 391	12.0	25.0	56.3	128.6	195.4	177.6	179.8	....
Other current transfers	2 392	.6	....	50.4	38.5	35.5	....	....	....
Debit	3 379	**−16.9**	....	**−42.3**	**−54.9**	**−50.2**	**−41.2**	**−77.4**	....
General government	3 380	....	....	....	−.6	−1.1	−.8	−.8	....
Other sectors	3 390	−16.9	....	−42.3	−54.3	−49.1	−40.4	−76.6	....
Workers' remittances	3 391	−3.0	....	−13.7	−54.3	−49.1	−40.4	−76.6	....
Other current transfers	3 392	−13.9	....	−28.6	....	....	....	....	....
CAPITAL AND FINANCIAL ACCOUNT	4 996	**89.2**	**94.3**	**90.9**	**104.6**	**−64.9**	**−8.8**	**−213.7**	....
CAPITAL ACCOUNT	4 994	....	....	....	....	....	....	....	....
Total credit	2 994	....	....	....	....	....	....	....	....
Total debit	3 994	....	....	....	....	....	....	....	....
Capital transfers, credit	2 400	....	....	....	....	....	....	....	....
General government	2 401	....	....	....	....	....	....	....	....
Debt forgiveness	2 402	....	....	....	....	....	....	....	....
Other capital transfers	2 410	....	....	....	....	....	....	....	....
Other sectors	2 430	....	....	....	....	....	....	....	....
Migrants' transfers	2 431	....	....	....	....	....	....	....	....
Debt forgiveness	2 432	....	....	....	....	....	....	....	....
Other capital transfers	2 440	....	....	....	....	....	....	....	....
Capital transfers, debit	3 400	....	....	....	....	....	....	....	....
General government	3 401	....	....	....	....	....	....	....	....
Debt forgiveness	3 402	....	....	....	....	....	....	....	....
Other capital transfers	3 410	....	....	....	....	....	....	....	....
Other sectors	3 430	....	....	....	....	....	....	....	....
Migrants' transfers	3 431	....	....	....	....	....	....	....	....
Debt forgiveness	3 432	....	....	....	....	....	....	....	....
Other capital transfers	3 440	....	....	....	....	....	....	....	....
Nonproduced nonfinancial assets, credit	2 480	....	....	....	....	....	....	....	....
Nonproduced nonfinancial assets, debit	3 480	....	....	....	....	....	....	....	....

Table 2 (Continued). STANDARD PRESENTATION, 2000–2007

(Millions of U.S. dollars)

	Code	2000	2001	2002	2003	2004	2005	2006	2007
FINANCIAL ACCOUNT	4 995	89.2	94.3	90.9	104.6	−64.9	−8.8	−213.7	....
A. DIRECT INVESTMENT	4 500	53.7	43.0	77.8	131.5	92.9	184.6	344.0	....
Direct investment abroad	4 505	....	....	....	....	....	....	....	....
Equity capital	4 510	....	....	....	....	....	....	....	....
Claims on affiliated enterprises	4 515	....	....	....	....	....	....	....	....
Liabilities to affiliated enterprises	4 520	....	....	....	....	....	....	....	....
Reinvested earnings	4 525	....	....	....	....	....	....	....	....
Other capital	4 530	....	....	....	....	....	....	....	....
Claims on affiliated enterprises	4 535	....	....	....	....	....	....	....	....
Liabilities to affiliated enterprises	4 540	....	....	....	....	....	....	....	....
Direct investment in Mongolia	4 555	53.7	43.0	77.8	131.5	92.9	184.6	344.0	....
Equity capital	4 560	53.7	43.0	77.8	131.5	92.9	184.6	344.0	....
Claims on direct investors	4 565	....	....	....	....	....	....	....	....
Liabilities to direct investors	4 570	53.7	43.0	77.8	131.5	92.9	184.6	344.0	....
Reinvested earnings	4 575	....	....	....	....	....	....	....	....
Other capital	4 580	....	....	....	....	....	....	....	....
Claims on direct investors	4 585	....	....	....	....	....	....	....	....
Liabilities to direct investors	4 590	....	....	....	....	....	....	....	....
B. PORTFOLIO INVESTMENT	4 600	....	....	....	50.0	−52.5	....	....	....
Assets	4 602	....	....	....	50.0	−2.5	....	....	....
Equity securities	4 610	....	....	....	....	−2.5	....	....	....
Monetary authorities	4 611	....	....	....	....	....	....	....	....
General government	4 612	....	....	....	....	....	....	....	....
Banks	4 613	....	....	....	....	−2.5	....	....	....
Other sectors	4 614	....	....	....	....	....	....	....	....
Debt securities	4 619	....	....	....	50.0	....	....	....	....
Bonds and notes	4 620	....	....	....	50.0	....	....	....	....
Monetary authorities	4 621	....	....	....	....	....	....	....	....
General government	4 622	....	....	....	50.0	....	....	....	....
Banks	4 623	....	....	....	....	....	....	....	....
Other sectors	4 624	....	....	....	....	....	....	....	....
Money market instruments	4 630	....	....	....	....	....	....	....	....
Monetary authorities	4 631	....	....	....	....	....	....	....	....
General government	4 632	....	....	....	....	....	....	....	....
Banks	4 633	....	....	....	....	....	....	....	....
Other sectors	4 634	....	....	....	....	....	....	....	....
Liabilities	4 652	....	....	....	....	−50.0	....	....	....
Equity securities	4 660	....	....	....	....	....	....	....	....
Banks	4 663	....	....	....	....	....	....	....	....
Other sectors	4 664	....	....	....	....	....	....	....	....
Debt securities	4 669	....	....	....	....	−50.0	....	....	....
Bonds and notes	4 670	....	....	....	....	−50.0	....	....	....
Monetary authorities	4 671	....	....	....	....	....	....	....	....
General government	4 672	....	....	....	....	−50.0	....	....	....
Banks	4 673	....	....	....	....	....	....	....	....
Other sectors	4 674	....	....	....	....	....	....	....	....
Money market instruments	4 680	....	....	....	....	....	....	....	....
Monetary authorities	4 681	....	....	....	....	....	....	....	....
General government	4 682	....	....	....	....	....	....	....	....
Banks	4 683	....	....	....	....	....	....	....	....
Other sectors	4 684	....	....	....	....	....	....	....	....
C. FINANCIAL DERIVATIVES	4 910	....	....	....	....	....	....	....	....
Monetary authorities	4 911	....	....	....	....	....	....	....	....
General government	4 912	....	....	....	....	....	....	....	....
Banks	4 913	....	....	....	....	....	....	....	....
Other sectors	4 914	....	....	....	....	....	....	....	....
Assets	4 900	....	....	....	....	....	....	....	....
Monetary authorities	4 901	....	....	....	....	....	....	....	....
General government	4 902	....	....	....	....	....	....	....	....
Banks	4 903	....	....	....	....	....	....	....	....
Other sectors	4 904	....	....	....	....	....	....	....	....
Liabilities	4 905	....	....	....	....	....	....	....	....
Monetary authorities	4 906	....	....	....	....	....	....	....	....
General government	4 907	....	....	....	....	....	....	....	....
Banks	4 908	....	....	....	....	....	....	....	....
Other sectors	4 909	....	....	....	....	....	....	....	....

Table 2 (Concluded). STANDARD PRESENTATION, 2000–2007

(Millions of U.S. dollars)

	Code	2000	2001	2002	2003	2004	2005	2006	2007
D. OTHER INVESTMENT	4 700 ..	**38.0**	**67.2**	**71.2**	**−173.7**	**−70.8**	**−144.9**	**−168.5**	....
Assets	4 703 ..	**−44.3**	**−5.2**	**−32.1**	**9.6**	**−132.2**	**−124.8**	**−223.4**	....
Trade credits	4 706 ..	−33.6	−6.3	−7.8	−1.0	3.4	16.2	10.6	....
General government	4 707 ..	....	....	....	....	....	....	....	....
of which: Short-term	4 709 ..	....	....	....	....	....	....	....	....
Other sectors	4 710 ..	−33.6	−6.3	−7.8	−1.0	3.4	....	....	....
of which: Short-term	4 712 ..	−33.6	−6.3	−7.8	−1.0	3.4	....	....	....
Loans	4 714 ..	....	....	−8.0	....	3.2	−1.5	−1.0	....
Monetary authorities	4 715 ..	....	....	....	....	....	....	....	....
of which: Short-term	4 718 ..	....	....	....	....	....	....	....	....
General government	4 719 ..	....	....	....	....	....	....	....	....
of which: Short-term	4 721 ..	....	....	....	....	....	....	....	....
Banks	4 722 ..	....	....	−8.0	....	3.2	−1.5	−1.0	....
of which: Short-term	4 724 ..	....	....	....	....	.1	−1.5	−1.0	....
Other sectors	4 725 ..	....	....	....	....	....	....	....	....
of which: Short-term	4 727 ..	....	....	....	....	....	....	....	....
Currency and deposits	4 730 ..	−10.7	1.1	−16.4	10.6	−135.8	−139.6	−233.0	....
Monetary authorities	4 731 ..	....	....	....	....	....	....	....	....
General government	4 732 ..	....	....	....	....	....	....	....	....
Banks	4 733 ..	−10.7	1.1	−16.4	46.8	14.8	....	....	....
Other sectors	4 734 ..	....	....	....	−36.2	−150.6	....	....	....
Other assets	4 736 ..	....	....	....	....	−3.0	....	....	....
Monetary authorities	4 737 ..	....	....	....	....	....	....	....	....
of which: Short-term	4 739 ..	....	....	....	....	....	....	....	....
General government	4 740 ..	....	....	....	....	....	....	....	....
of which: Short-term	4 742 ..	....	....	....	....	....	....	....	....
Banks	4 743 ..	....	....	....	....	−3.0	....	....	....
of which: Short-term	4 745 ..	....	....	....	....	−3.0	....	....	....
Other sectors	4 746 ..	....	....	....	....	....	....	....	....
of which: Short-term	4 748 ..	....	....	....	....	....	....	....	....
Liabilities	4 753 ..	**82.3**	**72.4**	**103.3**	**−183.3**	**61.4**	**−20.1**	**54.9**	....
Trade credits	4 756 ..	....	....	−5.8	−2.5	.8	−9.4	24.7	....
General government	4 757 ..	....	....	....	....	....	....	....	....
of which: Short-term	4 759 ..	....	....	....	....	....	....	....	....
Other sectors	4 760 ..	....	....	−5.8	−2.5	.8	−9.4	24.7	....
of which: Short-term	4 762 ..	....	....	−5.8	−2.5	.8	−9.4	24.7	....
Loans	4 764 ..	84.6	67.0	102.9	−180.1	43.8	−7.9	45.1	....
Monetary authorities	4 765 ..	1.8	−1.6	−7.7	2.8	−7.2	−5.9	−5.9	....
of which: Use of Fund credit and loans from the Fund..	4 766 ..	1.8	−1.6	−7.7	2.8	−7.2	−5.9	−5.9	....
of which: Short-term	4 768 ..	....	....	....	....	....	....	....	....
General government	4 769 ..	60.5	66.2	72.5	−144.5	112.9	79.6	63.0	....
of which: Short-term	4 771 ..	....	....	....	....	....	....	....	....
Banks	4 772 ..	....	....	....	3.1	10.5	5.4	16.3	....
of which: Short-term	4 774 ..	....	....	....	....	....	4.4	....	....
Other sectors	4 775 ..	22.3	2.4	38.1	−41.5	−72.4	−87.0	−28.3	....
of which: Short-term	4 777 ..	....	....	....	−21.0	−26.6	−78.0	−17.3	....
Currency and deposits	4 780 ..	−2.3	.6	6.9	−.7	16.5	−2.9	−14.9	....
Monetary authorities	4 781 ..	....	....	....	....	....	....	....	....
General government	4 782 ..	....	....	....	....	....	....	....	....
Banks	4 783 ..	−2.3	.6	6.9	−.7	16.5	−2.9	−14.9	....
Other sectors	4 784 ..	....	....	....	....	....	....	....	....
Other liabilities	4 786 ..	....	4.8	−.7	....	.3	....	....	....
Monetary authorities	4 787 ..	....	....	....	....	....	....	....	....
of which: Short-term	4 789 ..	....	....	....	....	....	....	....	....
General government	4 790 ..	....	4.8	−.7	....	....	....	....	....
of which: Short-term	4 792 ..	....	4.8	−.7	....	....	....	....	....
Banks	4 793 ..	....	....	....	....	.3	....	....	....
of which: Short-term	4 795 ..	....	....	....	....	.3	....	....	....
Other sectors	4 796 ..	....	....	....	....	....	....	....	....
of which: Short-term	4 798 ..	....	....	....	....	....	....	....	....
E. RESERVE ASSETS	4 802 ..	**−2.5**	**−15.8**	**−58.1**	**96.8**	**−34.4**	**−48.5**	**−389.2**	....
Monetary gold	4 812 ..	....	....	....	43.1	−7.4	14.1	−134.7	....
Special drawing rights	4 811 ..	.1	....	....	....	....	....	....	....
Reserve position in the Fund	4 810 ..	....	....	....	....	....	....	....	....
Foreign exchange	4 803 ..	−2.6	−15.8	−58.0	21.6	3.2	76.8	−33.7	....
Other claims	4 813 ..	....	....	....	32.1	−30.2	−139.4	−220.9	....
NET ERRORS AND OMISSIONS	4 998 ..	**−19.3**	**−32.2**	**14.1**	**−5.9**	**1.4**	**−74.9**	**−7.8**	....

Table 1. ANALYTIC PRESENTATION, 2000–2007

(Millions of U.S. dollars)

	Code	2000	2001	2002	2003	2004	2005	2006	2007
A. Current Account[1]	4 993 Z.	**−7.73**	**−6.27**	**−10.25**	**−8.42**	**−9.00**	**−15.85**	**−8.01**	**−8.99**
Goods: exports f.o.b.	2 100 ..	1.12	.92	1.96	2.32	4.78	1.85	1.72	3.04
Goods: imports f.o.b.	3 100 ..	−19.02	−17.10	−22.40	−25.01	−25.28	−26.19	−26.58	−26.09
Balance on Goods	4 100 ..	*−17.90*	*−16.18*	*−20.44*	*−22.69*	*−20.50*	*−24.34*	*−24.85*	*−23.04*
Services: credit	2 200 ..	16.20	14.69	13.92	11.96	14.87	14.80	14.75	14.57
Services: debit	3 200 ..	−22.64	−21.90	−16.32	−18.53	−23.20	−25.74	−17.31	−18.64
Balance on Goods and Services	4 991 ..	*−24.34*	*−23.40*	*−22.84*	*−29.26*	*−28.83*	*−35.28*	*−27.42*	*−27.11*
Income: credit	2 300 ..	1.48	.87	.78	.84	1.24	2.12	2.51	2.49
Income: debit	3 300 ..	−4.17	−1.52	−3.84	−2.05	−4.63	−4.93	−4.82	−5.86
Balance on Goods, Services, and Income	4 992 ..	*−27.03*	*−24.04*	*−25.90*	*−30.47*	*−32.21*	*−38.09*	*−29.73*	*−30.48*
Current transfers: credit	2 379 Z.	22.44	21.57	20.78	26.93	28.30	28.04	25.44	27.57
Current transfers: debit	3 379 ..	−3.13	−3.81	−5.14	−4.89	−5.09	−5.80	−3.72	−6.07
B. Capital Account[1]	4 994 Z.	**4.43**	**7.70**	**12.74**	**14.37**	**11.84**	**10.94**	**9.21**	**11.63**
Capital account: credit	2 994 Z.	7.32	9.66	14.84	16.52	14.12	13.37	11.77	14.70
Capital account: debit	3 994 ..	−2.89	−1.96	−2.09	−2.16	−2.29	−2.42	−2.56	−3.07
Total, Groups A Plus B	4 981 ..	*−3.30*	*1.43*	*2.49*	*5.95*	*2.83*	*−4.91*	*1.20*	*2.64*
C. Financial Account[1]	4 995 W.	**2.35**	**−3.59**	**−2.52**	**−8.26**	**−1.71**	**6.30**	**2.50**	**−2.39**
Direct investment abroad	4 505 ..	....	....	....	....	....	....	....	....
Direct investment in Montserrat	4 555 Z.	2.29	.53	.64	2.08	2.34	.81	2.19	2.29
Portfolio investment assets	4 602 ..	....	....	....	....	....	....	....	....
Equity securities	4 610 ..	....	....	....	....	....	....	....	....
Debt securities	4 619 ..	....	....	....	....	....	....	....	....
Portfolio investment liabilities	4 652 Z.	.55	−.60	−.21	.08	.05	−.13	.06	.06
Equity securities	4 660 ..	....	....	....	....	....	....	....	....
Debt securities	4 669 Z.	....	....	....	....	....	....	....	....
Financial derivatives	4 910 ..	....	....	....	....	....	....	....	....
Financial derivatives assets	4 900 ..	....	....	....	....	....	....	....	....
Financial derivatives liabilities	4 905 ..	....	....	....	....	....	....	....	....
Other investment assets	4 703 ..	4.27	1.60	.18	.33	1.56	9.48	3.69	.07
Monetary authorities	4 701 ..	....	....	....	....	....	....	....	....
General government	4 704 ..	....	....	....	....	....	....	....	....
Banks	4 705 ..	....	....	....	....	....	....	....	....
Other sectors	4 728 ..	....	....	....	....	....	....	....	....
Other investment liabilities	4 753 W.	−4.76	−5.12	−3.13	−10.75	−5.66	−3.85	−3.44	−4.81
Monetary authorities	4 753 WA	....	....	....	....	....	....	....	....
General government	4 753 ZB	....	....	....	....	....	....	....	....
Banks	4 753 ZC	....	....	....	....	....	....	....	....
Other sectors	4 753 ZD	....	....	....	....	....	....	....	....
Total, Groups A Through C	4 983 ..	*−.95*	*−2.17*	*−.03*	*−2.31*	*1.12*	*1.39*	*3.70*	*.25*
D. Net Errors and Omissions	4 998 ..	**−2.60**	**4.29**	**1.14**	**3.28**	**−.23**	**−.46**	**−3.06**	**−.34**
Total, Groups A Through D	4 984 ..	*−3.55*	*2.12*	*1.12*	*.96*	*.89*	*.93*	*.65*	*−.09*
E. Reserves and Related Items	4 802 A.	**3.55**	**−2.12**	**−1.12**	**−.96**	**−.89**	**−.93**	**−.65**	**.09**
Reserve assets	4 802 ..	3.55	−2.12	−1.12	−.96	−.89	−.93	−.65	.09
Use of Fund credit and loans	4 766 ..	....	....	....	....	....	....	....	....
Exceptional financing	4 920 ..	....	....	....	....	....	....	....	....
Conversion rates: Eastern Caribbean dollars per U.S. dollar	0 101 ..	**2.7000**	**2.7000**	**2.7000**	**2.7000**	**2.7000**	**2.7000**	**2.7000**	**2.7000**

[1] Excludes components that have been classified in the categories of Group E.

Table 2. STANDARD PRESENTATION, 2000–2007

(Millions of U.S. dollars)

	Code	2000	2001	2002	2003	2004	2005	2006	2007
CURRENT ACCOUNT	4 993	**−7.73**	**−6.27**	**−10.25**	**−8.42**	**−9.00**	**−15.85**	**−8.01**	**−8.99**
A. GOODS	4 100	**−17.90**	**−16.18**	**−20.44**	**−22.69**	**−20.50**	**−24.34**	**−24.85**	**−23.04**
Credit	2 100	**1.12**	**.92**	**1.96**	**2.32**	**4.78**	**1.85**	**1.72**	**3.04**
General merchandise: exports f.o.b.	2 110	1.11	.72	1.46	1.77	4.23	1.44	1.31	2.64
Goods for processing: exports f.o.b.	2 150	....	....	....	....	....	....	....	....
Repairs on goods	2 160	....	....	....	....	....	....	....	....
Goods procured in ports by carriers	2 170	....	.19	.49	.55	.56	.41	.41	.40
Nonmonetary gold	2 180	....	....	....	....	....	....	....	....
Debit	3 100	**−19.02**	**−17.10**	**−22.40**	**−25.01**	**−25.28**	**−26.19**	**−26.58**	**−26.09**
General merchandise: imports f.o.b.	3 110	−19.02	−17.10	−22.40	−25.01	−25.28	−26.19	−26.58	−26.09
Goods for processing: imports f.o.b.	3 150	....	....	....	....	....	....	....	....
Repairs on goods	3 160	....	....	....	....	....	....	....	....
Goods procured in ports by carriers	3 170	....	....	....	....	....	....	....	....
Nonmonetary gold	3 180	....	....	....	....	....	....	....	....
B. SERVICES	4 200	**−6.44**	**−7.21**	**−2.40**	**−6.57**	**−8.33**	**−10.94**	**−2.56**	**−4.07**
Total credit	2 200	*16.20*	*14.69*	*13.92*	*11.96*	*14.87*	*14.80*	*14.75*	*14.57*
Total debit	3 200	*−22.64*	*−21.90*	*−16.32*	*−18.53*	*−23.20*	*−25.74*	*−17.31*	*−18.64*
Transportation services, credit	2 205	**1.19**	**1.32**	**1.36**	**1.44**	**1.40**	**1.40**	**1.46**	**1.46**
Passenger	2 850	....	....	....	....	....	....	....	....
Freight	2 851	....	....	....	....	....	....	....	....
Other	2 852	....	....	....	....	....	....	....	....
Sea transport, passenger	2 207	....	....	....	....	....	....	....	....
Sea transport, freight	2 208	....	....	....	....	....	....	....	....
Sea transport, other	2 209	....	....	....	....	....	....	....	....
Air transport, passenger	2 211	....	....	....	....	....	....	....	....
Air transport, freight	2 212	....	....	....	....	....	....	....	....
Air transport, other	2 213	....	....	....	....	....	....	....	....
Other transport, passenger	2 215	....	....	....	....	....	....	....	....
Other transport, freight	2 216	....	....	....	....	....	....	....	....
Other transport, other	2 217	....	....	....	....	....	....	....	....
Transportation services, debit	3 205	**−3.67**	**−3.47**	**−4.18**	**−4.54**	**−4.66**	**−4.79**	**−5.41**	**−6.12**
Passenger	3 850	....	....	....	....	....	....	....	....
Freight	3 851	....	....	....	....	....	....	....	....
Other	3 852	....	....	....	....	....	....	....	....
Sea transport, passenger	3 207	....	....	....	....	....	....	....	....
Sea transport, freight	3 208	....	....	....	....	....	....	....	....
Sea transport, other	3 209	....	....	....	....	....	....	....	....
Air transport, passenger	3 211	....	....	....	....	....	....	....	....
Air transport, freight	3 212	....	....	....	....	....	....	....	....
Air transport, other	3 213	....	....	....	....	....	....	....	....
Other transport, passenger	3 215	....	....	....	....	....	....	....	....
Other transport, freight	3 216	....	....	....	....	....	....	....	....
Other transport, other	3 217	....	....	....	....	....	....	....	....
Travel, credit	2 236	**8.96**	**8.48**	**8.67**	**7.33**	**9.19**	**8.98**	**7.75**	**7.44**
Business travel	2 237	....	....	....	....	....	....	....	....
Personal travel	2 240	....	....	....	....	....	....	....	....
Travel, debit	3 236	**−1.77**	**−1.82**	**−1.86**	**−1.96**	**−2.11**	**−2.61**	**−2.84**	**−2.83**
Business travel	3 237	....	....	....	....	....	....	....	....
Personal travel	3 240	....	....	....	....	....	....	....	....
Other services, credit	2 200 BA	**6.06**	**4.89**	**3.89**	**3.19**	**4.28**	**4.43**	**5.55**	**5.67**
Communications	2 245	5.02	3.82	2.57	1.87	3.00	3.00	3.03	3.09
Construction	2 249	....	....	....	....	....	....	....	....
Insurance	2 253	.23	.24	.29	.30	.41	.56	.46	.46
Financial	2 260	....	....	....	....	....	....	....	....
Computer and information	2 262	....	....	....	....	....	....	....	....
Royalties and licence fees	2 266	....	....	....	....	....	....	....	....
Other business services	2 268	.61	.65	.84	.81	.68	.60	1.74	1.80
Personal, cultural, and recreational	2 287	....	....	....	....	....	....	....	....
Government, n.i.e.	2 291	.19	.17	.20	.20	.18	.27	.31	.32
Other services, debit	3 200 BA	**−17.20**	**−16.61**	**−10.28**	**−12.03**	**−16.43**	**−18.34**	**−9.06**	**−9.70**
Communications	3 245	−3.77	−3.01	−1.22	−1.08	−2.47	−2.47	−2.50	−2.61
Construction	3 249	−.09	−.13	−.03	−1.87	−3.62	−2.93	....	....
Insurance	3 253	−.62	−.50	−.62	−.67	−.84	−.98	−1.01	−1.01
Financial	3 260	....	....	....	....	....	....	....	....
Computer and information	3 262	....	....	−.06	−.06	−.07	−.01	−.01	−.01
Royalties and licence fees	3 266	−.02	−.03	−.05	−.05	−.06	−.06	−.08	−.09
Other business services	3 268	−.70	−2.05	−2.70	−2.67	−2.87	−2.59	−2.86	−3.35
Personal, cultural, and recreational	3 287	....	....	....	....	....	....	....	....
Government, n.i.e.	3 291	−12.01	−10.88	−5.60	−5.62	−6.50	−9.31	−2.61	−2.64

Table 2 (Continued). STANDARD PRESENTATION, 2000–2007

(Millions of U.S. dollars)

	Code	2000	2001	2002	2003	2004	2005	2006	2007
C. INCOME	4 300	**−2.69**	**−.64**	**−3.06**	**−1.21**	**−3.39**	**−2.82**	**−2.32**	**−3.37**
Total credit	2 300	*1.48*	*.87*	*.78*	*.84*	*1.24*	*2.12*	*2.51*	*2.49*
Total debit	3 300	*−4.17*	*−1.52*	*−3.84*	*−2.05*	*−4.63*	*−4.93*	*−4.82*	*−5.86*
Compensation of employees, credit	2 310	....	....	....	....	....	....	....	....
Compensation of employees, debit	3 310	....	....	....	−.21	−.86	−.73	....	−.73
Investment income, credit	2 320	**1.48**	**.87**	**.78**	**.84**	**1.24**	**2.12**	**2.51**	**2.49**
Direct investment income	2 330	....	....	....	....	....	....	....	....
Dividends and distributed branch profits	2 332	....	....	....	....	....	....	....	....
Reinvested earnings and undistributed branch profits	2 333	....	....	....	....	....	....	....	....
Income on debt (interest)	2 334	....	....	....	....	....	....	....	....
Portfolio investment income	2 339	.66	.62	.58	.66	.68	.96	1.00	.99
Income on equity	2 340	.66	.62	.58	.66	.68	.96	1.00	.99
Income on bonds and notes	2 350	....	....	....	....	....	....	....	....
Income on money market instruments	2 360	....	....	....	....	....	....	....	....
Other investment income	2 370	.81	.25	.20	.18	.56	1.16	1.51	1.49
Investment income, debit	3 320	**−4.17**	**−1.52**	**−3.84**	**−1.84**	**−3.77**	**−4.21**	**−4.82**	**−5.13**
Direct investment income	3 330	−3.32	−.86	−3.22	−1.23	−2.31	−2.46	−2.49	−2.87
Dividends and distributed branch profits	3 332	−1.19	−.32	−2.85	−.86	−1.55	−1.65	−1.74	−2.09
Reinvested earnings and undistributed branch profits	3 333	−2.11	−.53	−.37	−.36	−.76	−.80	−.75	−.78
Income on debt (interest)	3 334	−.02	−.01	....	−.01	....	....	....	....
Portfolio investment income	3 339	....	....	....	....	....	....	....	....
Income on equity	3 340	....	....	....	....	....	....	....	....
Income on bonds and notes	3 350	....	....	....	....	....	....	....	....
Income on money market instruments	3 360	....	....	....	....	....	....	....	....
Other investment income	3 370	−.85	−.66	−.62	−.61	−1.46	−1.75	−2.33	−2.27
D. CURRENT TRANSFERS	4 379	**19.30**	**17.77**	**15.65**	**22.05**	**23.21**	**22.24**	**21.72**	**21.50**
Credit	2 379	**22.44**	**21.57**	**20.78**	**26.93**	**28.30**	**28.04**	**25.44**	**27.57**
General government	2 380	21.23	20.82	20.01	25.95	27.47	27.37	24.91	27.02
Other sectors	2 390	1.21	.75	.77	.99	.83	.68	.53	.55
Workers' remittances	2 391	.43	.42	.45	.48	.49	.51	.52	.54
Other current transfers	2 392	.79	.33	.32	.51	.33	.17	.01	.01
Debit	3 379	**−3.13**	**−3.81**	**−5.14**	**−4.89**	**−5.09**	**−5.80**	**−3.72**	**−6.07**
General government	3 380	−1.92	−1.84	−2.14	−1.96	−2.24	−2.63	−.59	−2.31
Other sectors	3 390	−1.21	−1.97	−3.00	−2.92	−2.84	−3.17	−3.13	−3.75
Workers' remittances	3 391	−1.21	−1.21	−1.66	−1.60	−1.70	−1.75	−1.75	−2.09
Other current transfers	3 392	....	−.75	−1.34	−1.32	−1.14	−1.43	−1.38	−1.66
CAPITAL AND FINANCIAL ACCOUNT	4 996	**10.33**	**1.98**	**9.11**	**5.14**	**9.23**	**16.31**	**11.07**	**9.33**
CAPITAL ACCOUNT	4 994	**4.43**	**7.70**	**12.74**	**14.37**	**11.84**	**10.94**	**9.21**	**11.63**
Total credit	2 994	*7.32*	*9.66*	*14.84*	*16.52*	*14.12*	*13.37*	*11.77*	*14.70*
Total debit	3 994	*−2.89*	*−1.96*	*−2.09*	*−2.16*	*−2.29*	*−2.42*	*−2.56*	*−3.07*
Capital transfers, credit	2 400	**7.32**	**9.66**	**14.84**	**16.52**	**14.12**	**13.37**	**11.77**	**14.70**
General government	2 401	6.95	9.11	14.41	15.95	13.53	12.76	11.16	14.07
Debt forgiveness	2 402	....	....	....	....	....	....	....	....
Other capital transfers	2 410	6.95	9.11	14.41	15.95	13.53	12.76	11.16	14.07
Other sectors	2 430	.37	.56	.43	.58	.59	.61	.61	.63
Migrants' transfers	2 431	.37	.56	.43	.58	.59	.61	.61	.63
Debt forgiveness	2 432	....	....	....	....	....	....	....	....
Other capital transfers	2 440	....	....	....	....	....	....	....	....
Capital transfers, debit	3 400	**−2.89**	**−1.96**	**−2.09**	**−2.16**	**−2.29**	**−2.42**	**−2.56**	**−3.07**
General government	3 401	....	....	....	....	....	....	....	....
Debt forgiveness	3 402	....	....	....	....	....	....	....	....
Other capital transfers	3 410	....	....	....	....	....	....	....	....
Other sectors	3 430	−2.89	−1.96	−2.09	−2.16	−2.29	−2.42	−2.56	−3.07
Migrants' transfers	3 431	−2.89	−1.96	−2.09	−2.16	−2.29	−2.42	−2.56	−3.07
Debt forgiveness	3 432	....	....	....	....	....	....	....	....
Other capital transfers	3 440	....	....	....	....	....	....	....	....
Nonproduced nonfinancial assets, credit	2 480	....	....	....	....	....	....	....	....
Nonproduced nonfinancial assets, debit	3 480	....	....	....	....	....	....	....	....

Table 2 (Continued). STANDARD PRESENTATION, 2000–2007

(Millions of U.S. dollars)

	Code	2000	2001	2002	2003	2004	2005	2006	2007
FINANCIAL ACCOUNT	4 995	**5.90**	**−5.71**	**−3.63**	**−9.22**	**−2.60**	**5.37**	**1.86**	**−2.30**
A. DIRECT INVESTMENT	4 500	**2.29**	**.53**	**.64**	**2.08**	**2.34**	**.81**	**2.19**	**2.29**
Direct investment abroad	4 505	....	....	....	....	....	....	....	....
Equity capital	4 510	....	....	....	....	....	....	....	....
Claims on affiliated enterprises	4 515	....	....	....	....	....	....	....	....
Liabilities to affiliated enterprises	4 520	....	....	....	....	....	....	....	....
Reinvested earnings	4 525	....	....	....	....	....	....	....	....
Other capital	4 530	....	....	....	....	....	....	....	....
Claims on affiliated enterprises	4 535	....	....	....	....	....	....	....	....
Liabilities to affiliated enterprises	4 540	....	....	....	....	....	....	....	....
Direct investment in Montserrat	4 555	**2.29**	**.53**	**.64**	**2.08**	**2.34**	**.81**	**2.19**	**2.29**
Equity capital	4 560	....	....	....	1.45	....	....	....	....
Claims on direct investors	4 565	....	....	....	....	....	....	....	....
Liabilities to direct investors	4 570	....	....	....	1.45	....	....	....	....
Reinvested earnings	4 575	2.11	.53	.37	.36	.76	.80	.75	.78
Other capital	4 580	.19	....	.27	.27	1.58	.01	1.44	1.51
Claims on direct investors	4 585	....	....	....	....	....	....	....	....
Liabilities to direct investors	4 590	.19	....	.27	.27	1.58	.01	1.44	1.51
B. PORTFOLIO INVESTMENT	4 600	**.55**	**−.59**	**−.21**	**.08**	**.05**	**−.13**	**.06**	**.06**
Assets	4 602	....	....	....	....	....	....	....	....
Equity securities	4 610	....	....	....	....	....	....	....	....
Monetary authorities	4 611	....	....	....	....	....	....	....	....
General government	4 612	....	....	....	....	....	....	....	....
Banks	4 613	....	....	....	....	....	....	....	....
Other sectors	4 614	....	....	....	....	....	....	....	....
Debt securities	4 619	....	....	....	....	....	....	....	....
Bonds and notes	4 620	....	....	....	....	....	....	....	....
Monetary authorities	4 621	....	....	....	....	....	....	....	....
General government	4 622	....	....	....	....	....	....	....	....
Banks	4 623	....	....	....	....	....	....	....	....
Other sectors	4 624	....	....	....	....	....	....	....	....
Money market instruments	4 630	....	....	....	....	....	....	....	....
Monetary authorities	4 631	....	....	....	....	....	....	....	....
General government	4 632	....	....	....	....	....	....	....	....
Banks	4 633	....	....	....	....	....	....	....	....
Other sectors	4 634	....	....	....	....	....	....	....	....
Liabilities	4 652	**.55**	**−.59**	**−.21**	**.08**	**.05**	**−.13**	**.06**	**.06**
Equity securities	4 660	....	....	....	....	....	....	....	....
Banks	4 663	....	....	....	....	....	....	....	....
Other sectors	4 664	....	....	....	....	....	....	....	....
Debt securities	4 669	....	....	....	....	....	....	....	....
Bonds and notes	4 670	....	....	....	....	....	....	....	....
Monetary authorities	4 671	....	....	....	....	....	....	....	....
General government	4 672	....	....	....	....	....	....	....	....
Banks	4 673	....	....	....	....	....	....	....	....
Other sectors	4 674	....	....	....	....	....	....	....	....
Money market instruments	4 680	....	....	....	....	....	....	....	....
Monetary authorities	4 681	....	....	....	....	....	....	....	....
General government	4 682	....	....	....	....	....	....	....	....
Banks	4 683	....	....	....	....	....	....	....	....
Other sectors	4 684	....	....	....	....	....	....	....	....
C. FINANCIAL DERIVATIVES	4 910	....	....	....	....	....	....	....	....
Monetary authorities	4 911	....	....	....	....	....	....	....	....
General government	4 912	....	....	....	....	....	....	....	....
Banks	4 913	....	....	....	....	....	....	....	....
Other sectors	4 914	....	....	....	....	....	....	....	....
Assets	4 900	....	....	....	....	....	....	....	....
Monetary authorities	4 901	....	....	....	....	....	....	....	....
General government	4 902	....	....	....	....	....	....	....	....
Banks	4 903	....	....	....	....	....	....	....	....
Other sectors	4 904	....	....	....	....	....	....	....	....
Liabilities	4 905	....	....	....	....	....	....	....	....
Monetary authorities	4 906	....	....	....	....	....	....	....	....
General government	4 907	....	....	....	....	....	....	....	....
Banks	4 908	....	....	....	....	....	....	....	....
Other sectors	4 909	....	....	....	....	....	....	....	....

Table 2 (Concluded). STANDARD PRESENTATION, 2000–2007

(Millions of U.S. dollars)

	Code	2000	2001	2002	2003	2004	2005	2006	2007
D. OTHER INVESTMENT	4 700 ..	**−.48**	**−3.53**	**−2.95**	**−10.43**	**−4.10**	**5.62**	**.26**	**−4.74**
Assets	4 703 ..	**4.27**	**1.60**	**.18**	**.33**	**1.56**	**9.48**	**3.69**	**.07**
Trade credits	4 706 ..	....	....	....	....	....	....	....	....
General government	4 707 ..	....	....	....	....	....	....	....	....
of which: Short-term	4 709 ..	....	....	....	....	....	....	....	....
Other sectors	4 710 ..	....	....	....	....	....	....	....	....
of which: Short-term	4 712 ..	....	....	....	....	....	....	....	....
Loans	4 714 ..	....	....	....	....	....	....	....	....
Monetary authorities	4 715 ..	....	....	....	....	....	....	....	....
of which: Short-term	4 718 ..	....	....	....	....	....	....	....	....
General government	4 719 ..	....	....	....	....	....	....	....	....
of which: Short-term	4 721 ..	....	....	....	....	....	....	....	....
Banks	4 722 ..	....	....	....	....	....	....	....	....
of which: Short-term	4 724 ..	....	....	....	....	....	....	....	....
Other sectors	4 725 ..	....	....	....	....	....	....	....	....
of which: Short-term	4 727 ..	....	....	....	....	....	....	....	....
Currency and deposits	4 730 ..	....	....	....	....	....	....	....	....
Monetary authorities	4 731 ..	....	....	....	....	....	....	....	....
General government	4 732 ..	....	....	....	....	....	....	....	....
Banks	4 733 ..	....	....	....	....	....	....	....	....
Other sectors	4 734 ..	....	....	....	....	....	....	....	....
Other assets	4 736 ..	....	....	....	....	....	....	....	....
Monetary authorities	4 737 ..	....	....	....	....	....	....	....	....
of which: Short-term	4 739 ..	....	....	....	....	....	....	....	....
General government	4 740 ..	....	....	....	....	....	....	....	....
of which: Short-term	4 742 ..	....	....	....	....	....	....	....	....
Banks	4 743 ..	....	....	....	....	....	....	....	....
of which: Short-term	4 745 ..	....	....	....	....	....	....	....	....
Other sectors	4 746 ..	....	....	....	....	....	....	....	....
of which: Short-term	4 748 ..	....	....	....	....	....	....	....	....
Liabilities	4 753 ..	**−4.75**	**−5.12**	**−3.13**	**−10.75**	**−5.66**	**−3.85**	**−3.44**	**−4.81**
Trade credits	4 756 ..	....	....	....	....	....	....	....	....
General government	4 757 ..	....	....	....	....	....	....	....	....
of which: Short-term	4 759 ..	....	....	....	....	....	....	....	....
Other sectors	4 760 ..	....	....	....	....	....	....	....	....
of which: Short-term	4 762 ..	....	....	....	....	....	....	....	....
Loans	4 764 ..	....	....	....	....	....	....	....	....
Monetary authorities	4 765 ..	....	....	....	....	....	....	....	....
of which: Use of Fund credit and loans from the Fund	4 766 ..	....	....	....	....	....	....	....	....
of which: Short-term	4 768 ..	....	....	....	....	....	....	....	....
General government	4 769 ..	....	....	....	....	....	....	....	....
of which: Short-term	4 771 ..	....	....	....	....	....	....	....	....
Banks	4 772 ..	....	....	....	....	....	....	....	....
of which: Short-term	4 774 ..	....	....	....	....	....	....	....	....
Other sectors	4 775 ..	....	....	....	....	....	....	....	....
of which: Short-term	4 777 ..	....	....	....	....	....	....	....	....
Currency and deposits	4 780 ..	....	....	....	....	....	....	....	....
Monetary authorities	4 781 ..	....	....	....	....	....	....	....	....
General government	4 782 ..	....	....	....	....	....	....	....	....
Banks	4 783 ..	....	....	....	....	....	....	....	....
Other sectors	4 784 ..	....	....	....	....	....	....	....	....
Other liabilities	4 786 ..	....	....	....	....	....	....	....	....
Monetary authorities	4 787 ..	....	....	....	....	....	....	....	....
of which: Short-term	4 789 ..	....	....	....	....	....	....	....	....
General government	4 790 ..	....	....	....	....	....	....	....	....
of which: Short-term	4 792 ..	....	....	....	....	....	....	....	....
Banks	4 793 ..	....	....	....	....	....	....	....	....
of which: Short-term	4 795 ..	....	....	....	....	....	....	....	....
Other sectors	4 796 ..	....	....	....	....	....	....	....	....
of which: Short-term	4 798 ..	....	....	....	....	....	....	....	....
E. RESERVE ASSETS	4 802 ..	**3.55**	**−2.12**	**−1.12**	**−.96**	**−.89**	**−.93**	**−.65**	**.09**
Monetary gold	4 812 ..	....	....	....	....	....	....	....	....
Special drawing rights	4 811 ..	....	....	....	....	....	....	....	....
Reserve position in the Fund	4 810 ..	....	....	....	....	....	....	....	....
Foreign exchange	4 803 ..	3.62	−2.09	−1.91	−.83	1.13	.15	−.61	.06
Other claims	4 813 ..	−.07	−.03	.79	−.14	−2.01	−1.08	−.04	.03
NET ERRORS AND OMISSIONS	4 998 ..	**−2.60**	**4.29**	**1.14**	**3.28**	**−.23**	**−.46**	**−3.06**	**−.34**

Table 1. ANALYTIC PRESENTATION, 2000–2007

(Millions of U.S. dollars)

	Code	2000	2001	2002	2003	2004	2005	2006	2007
A. Current Account[1]	4 993 Z.	**−501**	**1,606**	**1,472**	**1,552**	**922**	**949**	**1,315**	**−224**
Goods: exports f.o.b.	2 100 ..	7,419	7,142	7,839	8,771	9,922	10,690	11,926	15,146
Goods: imports f.o.b.	3 100 ..	−10,654	−10,164	−10,900	−13,117	−16,408	−18,894	−21,683	−29,316
Balance on Goods	4 100 ..	*−3,235*	*−3,022*	*−3,061*	*−4,345*	*−6,487*	*−8,204*	*−9,756*	*−14,170*
Services: credit	2 200 ..	3,034	4,029	4,360	5,478	6,710	8,098	9,789	12,165
Services: debit	3 200 ..	−1,892	−2,118	−2,413	−2,861	−3,451	−3,845	−4,473	−5,416
Balance on Goods and Services	4 991 ..	*−2,093*	*−1,111*	*−1,115*	*−1,728*	*−3,228*	*−3,951*	*−4,441*	*−7,421*
Income: credit	2 300 ..	276	326	377	370	505	689	750	961
Income: debit	3 300 ..	−1,140	−1,159	−1,115	−1,162	−1,176	−1,072	−1,227	−1,365
Balance on Goods, Services, and Income	4 992 ..	*−2,958*	*−1,944*	*−1,853*	*−2,520*	*−3,898*	*−4,335*	*−4,918*	*−7,825*
Current transfers: credit	2 379 Z.	2,574	3,670	3,441	4,214	4,974	5,441	6,410	7,786
Current transfers: debit	3 379 ..	−118	−120	−115	−141	−154	−158	−177	−185
B. Capital Account[1]	4 994 Z.	**−6**	**−9**	**−6**	**−10**	**−8**	**−5**	**−3**	**−3**
Capital account: credit	2 994 Z.	....	....	....	....	....	....	....	....
Capital account: debit	3 994 ..	−6	−9	−6	−10	−8	−5	−3	−3
Total, Groups A Plus B	4 981 ..	*−507*	*1,597*	*1,466*	*1,542*	*914*	*944*	*1,312*	*−227*
C. Financial Account[1]	4 995 W.	**−774**	**−966**	**−1,336**	**−1,091**	**102**	**−88**	**−185**	**−718**
Direct investment abroad	4 505 ..	−59	−97	−28	−13	−31	−74	−451	−632
Direct investment in Morocco	4 555 Z.	221	144	79	2,313	787	1,620	2,366	2,807
Portfolio investment assets	4 602 ..	....	....	....	....	....	−4	3	−16
Equity securities	4 610 ..	....	....	....	....	....	−4	3	−16
Debt securities	4 619 ..	....	....	....	....	....	....	....	....
Portfolio investment liabilities	4 652 Z.	18	−7	−8	8	597	64	−298	−64
Equity securities	4 660 ..	18	−7	−8	8	597	64	−298	−64
Debt securities	4 669 Z.	....	....	....	....	....	....	....	....
Financial derivatives	4 910 ..	....	....	....	....	....	....	....	....
Financial derivatives assets	4 900 ..	....	....	....	....	....	....	....	....
Financial derivatives liabilities	4 905 ..	....	....	....	....	....	....	....	....
Other investment assets	4 703 ..	....	....	....	−869	−454	−891	−762	−1,617
Monetary authorities	4 701 ..	....	....	....	....	....	....	....	....
General government	4 704 ..	....	....	....	....	....	....	....	....
Banks	4 705 ..	....	....	....	−529	....	−193	....	65
Other sectors	4 728 ..	....	....	....	−340	−454	−699	−762	−1,682
Other investment liabilities	4 753 W.	−953	−1,006	−1,380	−2,529	−797	−803	−1,043	−1,195
Monetary authorities	4 753 WA	....	....	....	....	....	....	....	....
General government	4 753 ZB	−1,208	−1,215	−1,465	−1,830	−1,321	−1,227	−1,108	−1,542
Banks	4 753 ZC	−80	−93	−128	−214	−213	−177	−76	−25
Other sectors	4 753 ZD	335	302	214	−486	737	602	141	372
Total, Groups A Through C	4 983 ..	*−1,280*	*631*	*130*	*451*	*1,015*	*856*	*1,127*	*−945*
D. Net Errors and Omissions	4 998 ..	**114**	**230**	**−182**	**−297**	**−282**	**−407**	**−499**	**105**
Total, Groups A Through D	4 984 ..	*−1,166*	*861*	*−52*	*154*	*733*	*449*	*628*	*−840*
E. Reserves and Related Items	4 802 A.	**1,166**	**−861**	**52**	**−154**	**−733**	**−449**	**−628**	**840**
Reserve assets	4 802 ..	416	−3,842	−644	−1,649	−1,901	−2,352	−2,711	−2,034
Use of Fund credit and loans	4 766 ..	....	....	....	....	....	....	....	....
Exceptional financing	4 920 ..	751	2,982	696	1,495	1,168	1,904	2,083	2,874
Conversion rates: Moroccan dirhams per U.S. dollar	0 101 ..	**10.626**	**11.303**	**11.021**	**9.574**	**8.868**	**8.865**	**8.796**	**8.192**

[1] Excludes components that have been classified in the categories of Group E.

Table 2. STANDARD PRESENTATION, 2000–2007

(Millions of U.S. dollars)

	Code	2000	2001	2002	2003	2004	2005	2006	2007
CURRENT ACCOUNT	4 993	−475	1,611	1,477	1,582	970	1,041	1,411	−122
A. GOODS	4 100	−3,235	−3,022	−3,061	−4,345	−6,487	−8,204	−9,756	−14,170
Credit	2 100	7,419	7,142	7,839	8,771	9,922	10,690	11,926	15,146
General merchandise: exports f.o.b.	2 110	4,843	4,668	5,062	5,481	6,422	7,239	7,904	9,741
Goods for processing: exports f.o.b.	2 150	2,558	2,438	2,741	3,241	3,438	3,362	3,888	5,262
Repairs on goods	2 160	....	....	....	....	....	....	....	....
Goods procured in ports by carriers	2 170	18	36	36	49	62	89	135	144
Nonmonetary gold	2 180	....	....	....	....	....	....	....	....
Debit	3 100	−10,654	−10,164	−10,900	−13,117	−16,408	−18,894	−21,683	−29,316
General merchandise: imports f.o.b.	3 110	−9,043	−8,531	−9,216	−11,194	−14,269	−16,687	−19,372	−25,941
Goods for processing: imports f.o.b.	3 150	−1,602	−1,623	−1,676	−1,916	−2,134	−2,196	−2,300	−3,362
Repairs on goods	3 160	....	....	....	....	....	....	....	....
Goods procured in ports by carriers	3 170	−9	−9	−8	−7	−5	−10	−11	−13
Nonmonetary gold	3 180	....	....	....	....	....	....	....	....
B. SERVICES	4 200	1,142	1,911	1,947	2,617	3,259	4,253	5,316	6,749
Total credit	2 200	*3,034*	*4,029*	*4,360*	*5,478*	*6,710*	*8,098*	*9,789*	*12,165*
Total debit	3 200	*−1,892*	*−2,118*	*−2,413*	*−2,861*	*−3,451*	*−3,845*	*−4,473*	*−5,416*
Transportation services, credit	2 205	485	660	780	910	1,025	1,300	1,489	1,818
Passenger	2 850	*241*	*383*	*511*	*581*	*618*	*816*	*916*	*1,126*
Freight	2 851	*244*	*277*	*270*	*329*	*407*	*485*	*572*	*692*
Other	2 852	....	....	....	....	....	....	....	....
Sea transport, passenger	2 207	6	4	23	22	27	39	35	9
Sea transport, freight	2 208	203	216	203	237	326	386	472	549
Sea transport, other	2 209	....	....	....	....	....	....	....	....
Air transport, passenger	2 211	233	378	486	558	587	773	876	1,114
Air transport, freight	2 212	13	28	30	54	29	19	13	23
Air transport, other	2 213	....	....	....	....	....	....	....	....
Other transport, passenger	2 215	2	1	2	1	3	4	5	3
Other transport, freight	2 216	29	32	36	38	53	79	87	120
Other transport, other	2 217	....	....	....	....	....	....	....	....
Transportation services, debit	3 205	−620	−783	−857	−1,127	−1,375	−1,580	−1,754	−2,211
Passenger	3 850	*−81*	*−200*	*−225*	*−297*	*−338*	*−387*	*−420*	*−538*
Freight	3 851	*−539*	*−582*	*−632*	*−830*	*−1,037*	*−1,193*	*−1,333*	*−1,673*
Other	3 852	....	....	....	....	....	....	....	....
Sea transport, passenger	3 207	−3	−6	−8	−15	−16	−21	−25	−20
Sea transport, freight	3 208	−443	−467	−530	−662	−879	−1,027	−1,173	−1,487
Sea transport, other	3 209	....	....	....	....	....	....	....	....
Air transport, passenger	3 211	−76	−193	−216	−280	−319	−363	−392	−517
Air transport, freight	3 212	−32	−51	−57	−108	−103	−90	−75	−58
Air transport, other	3 213	....	....	....	....	....	....	....	....
Other transport, passenger	3 215	−2	−1	−1	−2	−3	−3	−4	−2
Other transport, freight	3 216	−64	−65	−45	−61	−55	−76	−85	−128
Other transport, other	3 217	....	....	....	....	....	....	....	....
Travel, credit	2 236	2,039	2,583	2,646	3,221	3,922	4,610	5,984	7,181
Business travel	2 237	....	....	....	....	....	....	....	....
Personal travel	2 240	2,039	2,583	2,646	3,221	3,922	4,610	5,984	7,181
Travel, debit	3 236	−425	−389	−444	−548	−574	−612	−693	−880
Business travel	3 237	−86	−75	−81	−88	−96	−97	−99	−150
Personal travel	3 240	−340	−314	−364	−460	−479	−515	−593	−731
Other services, credit	2 200 BA	510	786	933	1,347	1,763	2,188	2,316	3,166
Communications	2 245	114	169	231	250	342	328	387	401
Construction	2 249	....	....	....	....	....	....	....	....
Insurance	2 253	30	29	28	76	95	72	76	72
Financial	2 260	....	....	....	....	....	....	....	....
Computer and information	2 262	....	....	....	....	....	....	....	....
Royalties and licence fees	2 266	22	15	11	26	16	13	3	4
Other business services	2 268	164	331	401	643	904	1,247	1,330	2,014
Personal, cultural, and recreational	2 287	....	....	....	....	....	....	....	....
Government, n.i.e.	2 291	180	242	262	353	406	529	520	675
Other services, debit	3 200 BA	−847	−947	−1,112	−1,186	−1,502	−1,654	−2,027	−2,324
Communications	3 245	−17	−17	−20	−22	−48	−44	−64	−108
Construction	3 249	....	....	....	....	....	....	....	....
Insurance	3 253	−29	−38	−46	−57	−82	−80	−93	−113
Financial	3 260	....	....	....	....	....	....	....	....
Computer and information	3 262	....	....	....	....	....	....	....	....
Royalties and licence fees	3 266	−19	−35	−41	−29	−37	−45	−49	−36
Other business services	3 268	−410	−443	−496	−567	−689	−742	−909	−1,178
Personal, cultural, and recreational	3 287	....	....	....	....	....	....	....	....
Government, n.i.e.	3 291	−372	−414	−511	−512	−646	−742	−911	−889

Table 2 (Continued). STANDARD PRESENTATION, 2000–2007

(Millions of U.S. dollars)

	Code	2000	2001	2002	2003	2004	2005	2006	2007
C. INCOME	4 300	**−864**	**−833**	**−738**	**−792**	**−671**	**−384**	**−477**	**−405**
Total credit	2 300	*276*	*326*	*377*	*370*	*505*	*689*	*750*	*961*
Total debit	3 300	*−1,140*	*−1,159*	*−1,115*	*−1,162*	*−1,176*	*−1,072*	*−1,227*	*−1,365*
Compensation of employees, credit	2 310	....	....	....	....	....	....	....	....
Compensation of employees, debit	3 310	....	....	....	....	....	....	....	....
Investment income, credit	2 320	**276**	**326**	**377**	**370**	**505**	**689**	**750**	**961**
Direct investment income	2 330	13	13	9	13	60	59	72	78
Dividends and distributed branch profits	2 332	8	9	6	11	16	21	25	17
Reinvested earnings and undistributed branch profits	2 333	1	....	....	....	10	....	....	....
Income on debt (interest)	2 334	4	4	2	2	33	38	47	61
Portfolio investment income	2 339	....	....	1	....	....	....	....	....
Income on equity	2 340	....	....	1	....	....	....	....	....
Income on bonds and notes	2 350	....	....	....	....	....	....	....	....
Income on money market instruments	2 360	....	....	....	....	....	....	....	....
Other investment income	2 370	263	312	367	357	445	630	678	883
Investment income, debit	3 320	**−1,140**	**−1,159**	**−1,115**	**−1,162**	**−1,176**	**−1,072**	**−1,227**	**−1,365**
Direct investment income	3 330	−268	−401	−482	−593	−670	−594	−674	−730
Dividends and distributed branch profits	3 332	−154	−278	−396	−504	−572	−435	−533	−544
Reinvested earnings and undistributed branch profits	3 333	−10	−3	....	−8	....	−69	−56	−115
Income on debt (interest)	3 334	−105	−120	−85	−81	−98	−90	−85	−71
Portfolio investment income	3 339	−13	−2	−2	−3	−10	−32	−65	−51
Income on equity	3 340	−13	−2	−2	−3	−10	−32	−65	−51
Income on bonds and notes	3 350	....	....	....	....	....	....	....	....
Income on money market instruments	3 360	....	....	....	....	....	....	....	....
Other investment income	3 370	−859	−756	−632	−566	−496	−447	−488	−585
D. CURRENT TRANSFERS	4 379	**2,483**	**3,555**	**3,330**	**4,102**	**4,868**	**5,375**	**6,329**	**7,703**
Credit	2 379	**2,600**	**3,675**	**3,446**	**4,243**	**5,022**	**5,533**	**6,506**	**7,888**
General government	2 380	142	65	151	142	193	273	328	349
Other sectors	2 390	2,458	3,610	3,294	4,101	4,829	5,260	6,177	7,539
Workers' remittances	2 391	2,161	3,261	2,877	3,614	4,221	4,589	5,451	6,730
Other current transfers	2 392	297	349	417	488	608	671	726	809
Debit	3 379	**−118**	**−120**	**−115**	**−141**	**−154**	**−158**	**−177**	**−185**
General government	3 380	−42	−45	−44	−59	−54	−37	−63	−61
Other sectors	3 390	−76	−75	−71	−82	−101	−120	−114	−124
Workers' remittances	3 391	−23	−27	−30	−34	−34	−35	−38	−49
Other current transfers	3 392	−53	−48	−41	−48	−67	−85	−76	−75
CAPITAL AND FINANCIAL ACCOUNT	4 996	**361**	**−1,841**	**−1,295**	**−1,285**	**−688**	**−633**	**−912**	**17**
CAPITAL ACCOUNT	4 994	**−6**	**−9**	**−6**	**−10**	**−8**	**−5**	**−3**	**−3**
Total credit	2 994	....	....	....	....	....	....	....	....
Total debit	3 994	*−6*	*−9*	*−6*	*−10*	*−8*	*−5*	*−3*	*−3*
Capital transfers, credit	2 400	....	....	....	....	....	....	....	....
General government	2 401	....	....	....	....	....	....	....	....
Debt forgiveness	2 402	....	....	....	....	....	....	....	....
Other capital transfers	2 410	....	....	....	....	....	....	....	....
Other sectors	2 430	....	....	....	....	....	....	....	....
Migrants' transfers	2 431	....	....	....	....	....	....	....	....
Debt forgiveness	2 432	....	....	....	....	....	....	....	....
Other capital transfers	2 440	....	....	....	....	....	....	....	....
Capital transfers, debit	3 400	**−6**	**−9**	**−6**	**−10**	**−8**	**−5**	**−3**	**−3**
General government	3 401	....	....	....	....	....	....	....	....
Debt forgiveness	3 402	....	....	....	....	....	....	....	....
Other capital transfers	3 410	....	....	....	....	....	....	....	....
Other sectors	3 430	−6	−9	−6	−10	−8	−5	−3	−3
Migrants' transfers	3 431	−6	−9	−6	−10	−8	−5	−3	−3
Debt forgiveness	3 432	....	....	....	....	....	....	....	....
Other capital transfers	3 440	....	....	....	....	....	....	....	....
Nonproduced nonfinancial assets, credit	2 480	....	....	....	....	....	....	....	....
Nonproduced nonfinancial assets, debit	3 480	....	....	....	....	....	....	....	....

Table 2 (Continued). STANDARD PRESENTATION, 2000–2007

(Millions of U.S. dollars)

	Code	2000	2001	2002	2003	2004	2005	2006	2007
FINANCIAL ACCOUNT	4 995 ..	**367**	**−1,832**	**−1,289**	**−1,275**	**−680**	**−629**	**−909**	**20**
A. DIRECT INVESTMENT	4 500 ..	**368**	**2,728**	**452**	**2,300**	**862**	**1,596**	**2,010**	**2,194**
Direct investment abroad	4 505 ..	**−59**	**−97**	**−28**	**−13**	**−31**	**−74**	**−451**	**−632**
Equity capital	4 510 ..	−58	−97	−28	−13	−20	−74	−451	−632
Claims on affiliated enterprises	4 515 ..	−58	−97	−28	−13	−20	−74	−451	−632
Liabilities to affiliated enterprises	4 520 ..	....	....	....	....	....	....	....	....
Reinvested earnings	4 525 ..	−1	....	....	....	−10	....	....	....
Other capital	4 530 ..	....	....	....	....	....	....	....	....
Claims on affiliated enterprises	4 535 ..	....	....	....	....	....	....	....	....
Liabilities to affiliated enterprises	4 540 ..	....	....	....	....	....	....	....	....
Direct investment in Morocco	4 555 ..	**427**	**2,825**	**480**	**2,313**	**893**	**1,671**	**2,461**	**2,826**
Equity capital	4 560 ..	206	2,681	401	2,225	764	880	2,629	2,443
Claims on direct investors	4 565 ..	....	....	....	....	....	....	....	....
Liabilities to direct investors	4 570 ..	206	2,681	401	2,225	764	880	2,629	2,443
Reinvested earnings	4 575 ..	10	3	....	8	....	69	56	115
Other capital	4 580 ..	211	141	79	81	130	721	−224	267
Claims on direct investors	4 585 ..	....	....	....	....	....	....	....	....
Liabilities to direct investors	4 590 ..	211	141	79	81	130	721	−224	267
B. PORTFOLIO INVESTMENT	4 600 ..	**18**	**−7**	**−8**	**8**	**597**	**60**	**−295**	**−80**
Assets	4 602 ..	....	....	....	....	....	**−4**	**3**	**−16**
Equity securities	4 610 ..	....	....	....	....	....	−4	3	−16
Monetary authorities	4 611 ..	....	....	....	....	....	....	....	....
General government	4 612 ..	....	....	....	....	....	....	....	....
Banks	4 613 ..	....	....	....	....	....	....	....	....
Other sectors	4 614 ..	....	....	....	....	....	−4	3	−16
Debt securities	4 619 ..	....	....	....	....	....	....	....	....
Bonds and notes	4 620 ..	....	....	....	....	....	....	....	....
Monetary authorities	4 621 ..	....	....	....	....	....	....	....	....
General government	4 622 ..	....	....	....	....	....	....	....	....
Banks	4 623 ..	....	....	....	....	....	....	....	....
Other sectors	4 624 ..	....	....	....	....	....	....	....	....
Money market instruments	4 630 ..	....	....	....	....	....	....	....	....
Monetary authorities	4 631 ..	....	....	....	....	....	....	....	....
General government	4 632 ..	....	....	....	....	....	....	....	....
Banks	4 633 ..	....	....	....	....	....	....	....	....
Other sectors	4 634 ..	....	....	....	....	....	....	....	....
Liabilities	4 652 ..	**18**	**−7**	**−8**	**8**	**597**	**64**	**−298**	**−64**
Equity securities	4 660 ..	18	−7	−8	8	597	64	−298	−64
Banks	4 663 ..	....	....	....	....	....	....	....	....
Other sectors	4 664 ..	18	−7	−8	8	597	64	−298	−64
Debt securities	4 669 ..	....	....	....	....	....	....	....	....
Bonds and notes	4 670 ..	....	....	....	....	....	....	....	....
Monetary authorities	4 671 ..	....	....	....	....	....	....	....	....
General government	4 672 ..	....	....	....	....	....	....	....	....
Banks	4 673 ..	....	....	....	....	....	....	....	....
Other sectors	4 674 ..	....	....	....	....	....	....	....	....
Money market instruments	4 680 ..	....	....	....	....	....	....	....	....
Monetary authorities	4 681 ..	....	....	....	....	....	....	....	....
General government	4 682 ..	....	....	....	....	....	....	....	....
Banks	4 683 ..	....	....	....	....	....	....	....	....
Other sectors	4 684 ..	....	....	....	....	....	....	....	....
C. FINANCIAL DERIVATIVES	4 910 ..	....	....	....	....	....	....	....	....
Monetary authorities	4 911 ..	....	....	....	....	....	....	....	....
General government	4 912 ..	....	....	....	....	....	....	....	....
Banks	4 913 ..	....	....	....	....	....	....	....	....
Other sectors	4 914 ..	....	....	....	....	....	....	....	....
Assets	4 900 ..	....	....	....	....	....	....	....	....
Monetary authorities	4 901 ..	....	....	....	....	....	....	....	....
General government	4 902 ..	....	....	....	....	....	....	....	....
Banks	4 903 ..	....	....	....	....	....	....	....	....
Other sectors	4 904 ..	....	....	....	....	....	....	....	....
Liabilities	4 905 ..	....	....	....	....	....	....	....	....
Monetary authorities	4 906 ..	....	....	....	....	....	....	....	....
General government	4 907 ..	....	....	....	....	....	....	....	....
Banks	4 908 ..	....	....	....	....	....	....	....	....
Other sectors	4 909 ..	....	....	....	....	....	....	....	....

Table 2 (Concluded). STANDARD PRESENTATION, 2000–2007

(Millions of U.S. dollars)

	Code	2000	2001	2002	2003	2004	2005	2006	2007
D. OTHER INVESTMENT	4 700	**−435**	**−710**	**−1,089**	**−1,934**	**−237**	**67**	**87**	**−60**
Assets	4 703	....	....	....	−869	−454	−891	−762	−1,617
Trade credits	4 706	....	....	....	−340	−451	−694	−758	−1,668
General government	4 707	....	....	....	....	....	....	....	....
of which: Short-term	4 709	....	....	....	....	....	....	....	....
Other sectors	4 710	....	....	....	−340	−451	−694	−758	−1,668
of which: Short-term	4 712	....	....	....	*−340*	*−451*	*−694*	*−758*	*−1,668*
Loans	4 714	....	....	....	−529	....	−193	....	65
Monetary authorities	4 715	....	....	....	....	....	....	....	....
of which: Short-term	4 718	....	....	....	....	....	....	....	....
General government	4 719	....	....	....	....	....	....	....	....
of which: Short-term	4 721	....	....	....	....	....	....	....	....
Banks	4 722	....	....	....	−529	....	−193	....	65
of which: Short-term	4 724	....	....	....	....	....	....	....	....
Other sectors	4 725	....	....	....	....	....	....	....	....
of which: Short-term	4 727	....	....	....	....	....	....	....	....
Currency and deposits	4 730	....	....	....	....	−4	−5	−4	−14
Monetary authorities	4 731	....	....	....	....	....	....	....	....
General government	4 732	....	....	....	....	....	....	....	....
Banks	4 733	....	....	....	....	....	....	....	....
Other sectors	4 734	....	....	....	....	−4	−5	−4	−14
Other assets	4 736	....	....	....	....	....	....	....	....
Monetary authorities	4 737	....	....	....	....	....	....	....	....
of which: Short-term	4 739	....	....	....	....	....	....	....	....
General government	4 740	....	....	....	....	....	....	....	....
of which: Short-term	4 742	....	....	....	....	....	....	....	....
Banks	4 743	....	....	....	....	....	....	....	....
of which: Short-term	4 745	....	....	....	....	....	....	....	....
Other sectors	4 746	....	....	....	....	....	....	....	....
of which: Short-term	4 748	....	....	....	....	....	....	....	....
Liabilities	4 753	**−435**	**−710**	**−1,089**	**−1,064**	**217**	**958**	**849**	**1,557**
Trade credits	4 756	416	318	385	392	1,260	1,041	1,154	1,270
General government	4 757	....	....	....	....	....	....	....	....
of which: Short-term	4 759	....	....	....	....	....	....	....	....
Other sectors	4 760	416	318	385	392	1,260	1,041	1,154	1,270
of which: Short-term	4 762	*416*	*318*	*385*	*392*	*1,260*	*1,041*	*1,154*	*1,270*
Loans	4 764	−875	−1,111	−1,459	−1,388	−1,288	−279	−301	312
Monetary authorities	4 765	....	....	....	....	....	....	....	....
of which: Use of Fund credit and loans from the Fund	4 766	....	....	....	....	....	....	....	....
of which: Short-term	4 768	....	....	....	....	....	....	....	....
General government	4 769	−689	−919	−1,174	−991	−936	−393	−376	−16
of which: Short-term	4 771	....	....	....	....	....	....	....	....
Banks	4 772	−80	−93	−128	−211	−213	−174	−76	−25
of which: Short-term	4 774	....	....	....	....	....	....	....	....
Other sectors	4 775	−105	−99	−156	−185	−139	289	151	354
of which: Short-term	4 777	....	....	....	....	....	....	....	....
Currency and deposits	4 780	24	83	−15	−68	245	196	−4	−25
Monetary authorities	4 781	....	....	....	....	....	....	....	....
General government	4 782	....	....	....	....	....	....	....	....
Banks	4 783	....	....	....	....	....	....	....	....
Other sectors	4 784	24	83	−15	−68	245	196	−4	−25
Other liabilities	4 786	....	....	....	....	....	....	....	....
Monetary authorities	4 787	....	....	....	....	....	....	....	....
of which: Short-term	4 789	....	....	....	....	....	....	....	....
General government	4 790	....	....	....	....	....	....	....	....
of which: Short-term	4 792	....	....	....	....	....	....	....	....
Banks	4 793	....	....	....	....	....	....	....	....
of which: Short-term	4 795	....	....	....	....	....	....	....	....
Other sectors	4 796	....	....	....	....	....	....	....	....
of which: Short-term	4 798	....	....	....	....	....	....	....	....
E. RESERVE ASSETS	4 802	**416**	**−3,842**	**−644**	**−1,649**	**−1,901**	**−2,352**	**−2,711**	**−2,034**
Monetary gold	4 812	....	....	....	....	....	....	....	....
Special drawing rights	4 811	−38	−9	10	20	−3	33	29	23
Reserve position in the Fund	4 810	....	....	....	....	....	....	....	....
Foreign exchange	4 803	474	−3,798	−540	−1,789	−1,899	−2,385	−2,740	−2,056
Other claims	4 813	−20	−36	−114	120	....	....	....	....
NET ERRORS AND OMISSIONS	4 998	**114**	**230**	**−182**	**−297**	**−282**	**−407**	**−499**	**105**

Table 3. INTERNATIONAL INVESTMENT POSITION (End-period stocks), 2000–2007

(Millions of U.S. dollars)

	Code	2000	2001	2002	2003	2004	2005	2006	2007
ASSETS	8 995 C.	....	....	12,192	17,022	20,207	20,823	26,710	....
Direct investment abroad	8 505 ..	....	....	453	560	676	666	1,350	....
Equity capital and reinvested earnings	8 506 ..	....	....	427	520	490	535	1,025	....
Claims on affiliated enterprises	8 507 ..	....	....	427	520	490	535	1,025	....
Liabilities to affiliated enterprises	8 508 ..	....	....	....	....	....	....	....	....
Other capital	8 530 ..	....	....	27	41	185	131	325	....
Claims on affiliated enterprises	8 535 ..	....	....	27	41	185	131	325	....
Liabilities to affiliated enterprises	8 540 ..	....	....	....	....	....	....	....	....
Portfolio investment	8 602 ..	....	....	85	116	156	176	178	....
Equity securities	8 610 ..	....	....	82	116	156	176	171	....
Monetary authorities	8 611 ..	....	....	....	....	....	....	....	....
General government	8 612 ..	....	....	....	....	....	....	....	....
Banks	8 613 ..	....	....	49	56	67	60	69	....
Other sectors	8 614 ..	....	....	33	60	89	116	101	....
Debt securities	8 619 ..	....	....	3	....	....	....	8	....
Bonds and notes	8 620 ..	....	....	3	....	....	....	8	....
Monetary authorities	8 621 ..	....	....	....	....	....	....	....	....
General government	8 622 ..	....	....	....	....	....	....	....	....
Banks	8 623 ..	....	....	....	....	....	....	....	....
Other sectors	8 624 ..	....	....	3	....	....	....	8	....
Money market instruments	8 630 ..	....	....	....	....	....	....	....	....
Monetary authorities	8 631 ..	....	....	....	....	....	....	....	....
General government	8 632 ..	....	....	....	....	....	....	....	....
Banks	8 633 ..	....	....	....	....	....	....	....	....
Other sectors	8 634 ..	....	....	....	....	....	....	....	....
Financial derivatives	8 900 ..	....	....	....	....	....	....	....	....
Monetary authorities	8 901 ..	....	....	....	....	....	....	....	....
General government	8 902 ..	....	....	....	....	....	....	....	....
Banks	8 903 ..	....	....	....	....	....	....	....	....
Other sectors	8 904 ..	....	....	....	....	....	....	....	....
Other investment	8 703 ..	....	....	468	1,305	1,221	1,335	1,563	....
Trade credits	8 706 ..	....	....	342	390	450	453	583	....
General government	8 707 ..	....	....	....	....	....	....	....	....
of which: Short-term	8 709 ..	....	....	....	....	....	....	....	....
Other sectors	8 710 ..	....	....	342	390	450	453	583	....
of which: Short-term	8 712 ..	....	....	*342*	*390*	*450*	*453*	*583*	....
Loans	8 714 ..	....	....	3	603	614	720	788	....
Monetary authorities	8 715 ..	....	....	....	....	....	....	....	....
of which: Short-term	8 718 ..	....	....	....	....	....	....	....	....
General government	8 719 ..	....	....	....	....	....	....	....	....
of which: Short-term	8 721 ..	....	....	....	....	....	....	....	....
Banks	8 722 ..	....	....	3	603	614	613	670	....
of which: Short-term	8 724 ..	....	....	*3*	....	....	....	....	....
Other sectors	8 725 ..	....	....	....	....	....	107	118	....
of which: Short-term	8 727 ..	....	....	....	....	....	....	....	....
Currency and deposits	8 730 ..	....	....	59	235	73	85	109	....
Monetary authorities	8 731 ..	....	....	....	....	....	....	....	....
General government	8 732 ..	....	....	....	....	....	....	....	....
Banks	8 733 ..	....	....	23	25	....	....	....	....
Other sectors	8 734 ..	....	....	36	210	73	85	109	....
Other assets	8 736 ..	....	....	64	77	84	77	83	....
Monetary authorities	8 737 ..	....	....	....	....	....	....	....	....
of which: Short-term	8 739 ..	....	....	....	....	....	....	....	....
General government	8 740 ..	....	....	64	77	84	77	83	....
of which: Short-term	8 742 ..	....	....	....	....	....	....	....	....
Banks	8 743 ..	....	....	....	....	....	....	....	....
of which: Short-term	8 745 ..	....	....	....	....	....	....	....	....
Other sectors	8 746 ..	....	....	....	....	....	....	....	....
of which: Short-term	8 748 ..	....	....	....	....	....	....	....	....
Reserve assets	8 802 ..	....	....	11,186	15,040	18,154	18,646	23,620	....
Monetary gold	8 812 ..	....	....	193	224	239	280	450	....
Special drawing rights	8 811 ..	119	123	122	112	120	79	53	32
Reserve position in the Fund	8 810 ..	92	89	96	105	109	101	106	111
Foreign exchange	8 803 ..	....	....	10,775	14,599	17,686	18,187	23,011	....
Other claims	8 813 ..	....	....	....	....	....	....	....	....

Table 3 (Concluded). INTERNATIONAL INVESTMENT POSITION (End-period stocks), 2000–2007

(Millions of U.S. dollars)

	Code	2000	2001	2002	2003	2004	2005	2006	2007
LIABILITIES..	8 995 D.	....	....	**28,641**	**34,727**	**38,675**	**38,119**	**48,520**	....
Direct investment in Morocco...............	8 555 ..	....	....	**12,130**	**17,106**	**19,883**	**20,752**	**29,831**	....
Equity capital and reinvested earnings........	8 556 ..	....	....	11,141	16,037	18,675	19,017	28,167	....
Claims on direct investors................	8 557 ..	....	....	....	....	....	....	....	....
Liabilities to direct investors.............	8 558 ..	....	....	11,141	16,037	18,675	19,017	28,167	....
Other capital..	8 580 ..	....	....	989	1,069	1,208	1,735	1,664	....
Claims on direct investors................	8 585 ..	....	....	....	....	....	....	....	....
Liabilities to direct investors.............	8 590 ..	....	....	989	1,069	1,208	1,735	1,664	....
Portfolio investment...............................	8 652 ..	....	....	**636**	**840**	**1,720**	**2,037**	**2,096**	....
Equity securities...................................	8 660 ..	....	....	613	799	1,679	2,017	2,093	....
Banks...	8 663 ..	....	....	150	156	251	348	433	....
Other sectors................................	8 664 ..	....	....	463	643	1,428	1,669	1,660	....
Debt securities.....................................	8 669 ..	....	....	22	41	41	20	2	....
Bonds and notes............................	8 670 ..	....	....	22	41	41	20	2	....
Monetary authorities..................	8 671 ..	....	....	....	....	....	....	....	....
General government...................	8 672 ..	....	....	15	14	18	2	....	....
Banks..	8 673 ..	....	....	....	....	....	....	....	....
Other sectors............................	8 674 ..	....	....	8	27	23	19	2	....
Money market instruments................	8 680 ..	....	....	....	....	....	....	....	....
Monetary authorities..................	8 681 ..	....	....	....	....	....	....	....	....
General government...................	8 682 ..	....	....	....	....	....	....	....	....
Banks..	8 683 ..	....	....	....	....	....	....	....	....
Other sectors............................	8 684 ..	....	....	....	....	....	....	....	....
Financial derivatives............................	8 905 ..	....	....	....	....	....	....	....	....
Monetary authorities.............................	8 906 ..	....	....	....	....	....	....	....	....
General government..............................	8 907 ..	....	....	....	....	....	....	....	....
Banks..	8 908 ..	....	....	....	....	....	....	....	....
Other sectors.......................................	8 909 ..	....	....	....	....	....	....	....	....
Other investment...................................	8 753 ..	....	....	**15,875**	**16,780**	**17,073**	**15,330**	**16,593**	....
Trade credits..	8 756 ..	....	....	104	362	745	661	818	....
General government...........................	8 757 ..	....	....	....	....	....	....	....	....
of which: Short-term.....................	8 759 ..	....	....	....	....	....	....	....	....
Other sectors..................................	8 760 ..	....	....	104	362	745	661	818	....
of which: Short-term.....................	8 762 ..	....	....	*104*	*362*	*745*	*661*	*818*	....
Loans..	8 764 ..	....	....	15,393	15,834	15,657	13,866	14,707	....
Monetary authorities.........................	8 765 ..	....	....	....	....	....	....	....	....
of which: Use of Fund credit and loans from the Fund....	8 766 ..	....	....	....	....	....	....	....	....
of which: Short-term.....................	8 768 ..	....	....	....	....	....	....	....	....
General government...........................	8 769 ..	....	....	9,104	9,020	8,562	7,464	7,644	....
of which: Short-term.....................	8 771 ..	....	....	....	....	....	....	....	....
Banks..	8 772 ..	....	....	981	853	677	432	341	....
of which: Short-term.....................	8 774 ..	....	....	....	....	....	....	....	....
Other sectors..................................	8 775 ..	....	....	5,308	5,962	6,418	5,970	6,723	....
of which: Short-term.....................	8 777 ..	....	....	....	....	....	....	....	....
Currency and deposits............................	8 780 ..	....	....	378	584	671	803	1,067	....
Monetary authorities.........................	8 781 ..	....	....	80	135	217	261	262	....
General government...........................	8 782 ..	....	....	....	....	....	....	....	....
Banks..	8 783 ..	....	....	299	449	454	542	805	....
Other sectors..................................	8 784 ..	....	....	....	....	....	....	....	....
Other liabilities....................................	8 786 ..	....	....	....	....	....	....	....	....
Monetary authorities.........................	8 787 ..	....	....	....	....	....	....	....	....
of which: Short-term.....................	8 789 ..	....	....	....	....	....	....	....	....
General government...........................	8 790 ..	....	....	....	....	....	....	....	....
of which: Short-term.....................	8 792 ..	....	....	....	....	....	....	....	....
Banks..	8 793 ..	....	....	....	....	....	....	....	....
of which: Short-term.....................	8 795 ..	....	....	....	....	....	....	....	....
Other sectors..................................	8 796 ..	....	....	....	....	....	....	....	....
of which: Short-term.....................	8 798 ..	....	....	....	....	....	....	....	....
NET INTERNATIONAL INVESTMENT POSITION........	8 995 ..	....	....	**−16,449**	**−17,705**	**−18,468**	**−17,297**	**−21,809**	....
Conversion rates: Moroccan dirhams per U.S. dollar (end of period)........................	0 102 ..	10.619	11.560	10.167	8.750	8.218	9.249	8.457	7.713

Table 1. ANALYTIC PRESENTATION, 2000–2007

(Millions of U.S. dollars)

	Code	2000	2001	2002	2003	2004	2005	2006	2007
A. Current Account[1]	4 993 Z.	**−763.6**	**−657.2**	**−869.1**	**−816.5**	**−607.4**	**−760.7**	**−773.2**	**−795.1**
Goods: exports f.o.b.	2 100 ..	364.0	726.0	809.8	1,043.9	1,503.9	1,745.3	2,381.1	2,412.1
Goods: imports f.o.b.	3 100 ..	−1,046.0	−997.3	−1,476.5	−1,648.1	−1,849.7	−2,242.3	−2,648.8	−2,811.1
Balance on Goods	4 100 ..	*−682.0*	*−271.3*	*−666.6*	*−604.2*	*−345.8*	*−497.1*	*−267.7*	*−399.0*
Services: credit	2 200 ..	325.4	249.7	339.4	303.9	255.6	341.9	386.4	458.7
Services: debit	3 200 ..	−445.8	−618.4	−577.0	−573.9	−531.4	−648.6	−758.1	−855.6
Balance on Goods and Services	4 991 ..	*−802.4*	*−640.0*	*−904.2*	*−874.1*	*−621.7*	*−803.8*	*−639.5*	*−795.9*
Income: credit	2 300 ..	79.3	56.0	52.1	55.9	74.5	98.9	159.8	193.6
Income: debit	3 300 ..	−271.4	−290.7	−655.3	−221.4	−374.0	−458.8	−794.3	−785.2
Balance on Goods, Services, and Income	4 992 ..	*−994.5*	*−874.7*	*−1,507.4*	*−1,039.6*	*−921.2*	*−1,163.6*	*−1,273.9*	*−1,387.5*
Current transfers: credit	2 379 Z.	337.3	254.6	827.0	293.2	370.5	479.0	574.5	657.8
Current transfers: debit	3 379 ..	−106.4	−37.1	−188.7	−70.0	−56.7	−76.0	−73.8	−65.4
B. Capital Account[1]	4 994 Z.	**226.8**	**256.7**	**222.0**	**270.7**	**578.1**	**187.9**	**488.5**	**415.1**
Capital account: credit	2 994 Z.	226.8	256.7	222.5	271.2	581.2	191.8	490.8	416.1
Capital account: debit	3 994 ..	....	....	−.4	−.5	−3.1	−3.9	−2.3	−1.0
Total, Groups A Plus B	4 981 ..	*−536.8*	*−400.5*	*−647.1*	*−545.8*	*−29.2*	*−572.8*	*−284.7*	*−379.9*
C. Financial Account[1]	4 995 W.	**83.2**	**−24.8**	**−731.7**	**372.8**	**−46.5**	**95.2**	**−1,501.7**	**352.7**
Direct investment abroad	4 505 ..	....	....	....	....	....	....	−.4	.3
Direct investment in Mozambique	4 555 Z.	139.2	255.4	347.6	336.7	244.7	107.9	153.7	427.4
Portfolio investment assets	4 602 ..	....	....	32.2	5.0	−25.4	−88.8	−124.2	−117.5
Equity securities	4 610 ..	....	....	32.2	5.0	−25.4	−88.8	−.2	−1.5
Debt securities	4 619 ..	....	....	....	....	....	....	−124.0	−116.0
Portfolio investment liabilities	4 652 Z.	....	....	....	....	....	.3	.4	.3
Equity securities	4 660 ..	....	....	....	....	....	.3	.4	.3
Debt securities	4 669 Z.	....	....	....	....	....	....	....	....
Financial derivatives	4 910 ..	....	....	....	....	....	....	....	−16.0
Financial derivatives assets	4 900 ..	....	....	....	....	....	....	....	....
Financial derivatives liabilities	4 905 ..	....	....	....	....	....	....	....	−16.0
Other investment assets	4 703 ..	−145.0	−33.8	−207.7	−77.1	−88.7	−78.5	−13.8	−359.3
Monetary authorities	4 701 ..	....	−.8	−5.6	6.9	−186.4	40.9	17.5	41.6
General government	4 704 ..	....	....	....	....	....	....	....	....
Banks	4 705 ..	−124.0	−23.9	−74.6	13.1	57.8	−76.3	−106.9	−249.6
Other sectors	4 728 ..	−21.0	−9.1	−127.5	−97.1	39.9	−43.1	75.5	−151.3
Other investment liabilities	4 753 W.	89.0	−246.4	−903.8	108.2	−177.1	154.3	−1,517.5	417.5
Monetary authorities	4 753 WA	−40.8	....	10.1	22.3	−48.4	−.3	.3	−.4
General government	4 753 ZB	−171.4	−263.1	−1,302.9	53.0	−47.6	95.8	−1,475.5	216.2
Banks	4 753 ZC	16.6	35.1	−43.0	15.7	9.6	6.4	−35.6	39.6
Other sectors	4 753 ZD	284.6	−18.4	432.0	17.3	−90.8	52.4	−6.6	162.1
Total, Groups A Through C	4 983 ..	*−453.6*	*−425.2*	*−1,378.8*	*−172.9*	*−75.7*	*−477.6*	*−1,786.4*	*−27.2*
D. Net Errors and Omissions	4 998 ..	**37.5**	**−59.6**	**−60.0**	**208.2**	**216.4**	**281.0**	**143.8**	**83.9**
Total, Groups A Through D	4 984 ..	*−416.1*	*−484.9*	*−1,438.8*	*35.3*	*140.7*	*−196.6*	*−1,642.6*	*56.7*
E. Reserves and Related Items	4 802 A.	**416.1**	**484.9**	**1,438.8**	**−35.3**	**−140.7**	**196.6**	**1,642.6**	**−56.7**
Reserve assets	4 802 ..	−76.8	18.8	−97.8	−181.5	−169.1	129.9	−29.3	−204.8
Use of Fund credit and loans	4 766 ..	31.1	−15.8	−11.5	−9.1	−20.4	−25.3	−149.4	4.9
Exceptional financing	4 920 ..	461.8	481.9	1,548.2	155.3	48.8	92.1	1,821.4	143.1
Conversion rates: meticais per U.S. dollar	0 101 ..	**15.2273**	**20.7036**	**23.6780**	**23.7823**	**22.5813**	**23.0610**	**25.4008**	**25.8403**

[1] Excludes components that have been classified in the categories of Group E.

Table 2. STANDARD PRESENTATION, 2000–2007

(Millions of U.S. dollars)

	Code	2000	2001	2002	2003	2004	2005	2006	2007
CURRENT ACCOUNT	4 993	−763.6	−657.2	−869.1	−816.5	−607.4	−760.7	−773.2	−795.1
A. GOODS	4 100	−682.0	−271.3	−666.6	−604.2	−345.8	−497.1	−267.7	−399.0
Credit	2 100	364.0	726.0	809.8	1,043.9	1,503.9	1,745.3	2,381.1	2,412.1
General merchandise: exports f.o.b.	2 110	364.0	726.0	809.8	1,043.9	1,503.9	1,745.3	2,381.1	2,412.1
Goods for processing: exports f.o.b.	2 150	....	....	....	....	....	....	....	....
Repairs on goods	2 160	....	....	....	....	....	....	....	....
Goods procured in ports by carriers	2 170	....	....	....	....	....	....	....	....
Nonmonetary gold	2 180	....	....	....	....	....	....	....	....
Debit	3 100	−1,046.0	−997.3	−1,476.5	−1,648.1	−1,849.7	−2,242.3	−2,648.8	−2,811.1
General merchandise: imports f.o.b.	3 110	−1,046.0	−997.3	−1,476.5	−1,648.1	−1,849.7	−2,242.3	−2,648.8	−2,811.1
Goods for processing: imports f.o.b.	3 150	....	....	....	....	....	....	....	....
Repairs on goods	3 160	....	....	....	....	....	....	....	....
Goods procured in ports by carriers	3 170	....	....	....	....	....	....	....	....
Nonmonetary gold	3 180	....	....	....	....	....	....	....	....
B. SERVICES	4 200	−120.4	−368.7	−237.6	−270.0	−275.8	−306.7	−371.7	−396.8
Total credit	2 200	*325.4*	*249.7*	*339.4*	*303.9*	*255.6*	*341.9*	*386.4*	*458.7*
Total debit	3 200	*−445.8*	*−618.4*	*−577.0*	*−573.9*	*−531.4*	*−648.6*	*−758.1*	*−855.6*
Transportation services, credit	2 205	**97.6**	**55.7**	**101.7**	**90.5**	**80.0**	**89.3**	**105.0**	**128.6**
Passenger	2 850	....	....	*2.1*	*8.0*	*.5*	*7.7*	*5.1*	*19.2*
Freight	2 851	*95.7*	*6.0*	*36.2*	*32.1*	*27.7*	*44.4*	*69.1*	*46.2*
Other	2 852	*1.9*	*49.7*	*63.4*	*50.5*	*51.9*	*37.1*	*30.8*	*63.2*
Sea transport, passenger	2 207	....	....	....	....	....	....	....	....
Sea transport, freight	2 208	....	5.8	10.3	11.5	27.6	33.7	34.8	3.2
Sea transport, other	2 209	....	32.3	35.8	34.3	7.3	13.5	7.6	44.6
Air transport, passenger	2 211	....	....	....	....	.5	7.7	5.1	19.2
Air transport, freight	2 212	.2	.2	....	....	....	.2	2.4	.1
Air transport, other	2 213	1.9	....	4.4	1.5	2.5	5.3	10.7	8.5
Other transport, passenger	2 215	....	....	2.1	8.0	....	.1	....	....
Other transport, freight	2 216	95.5	....	25.9	20.5	....	10.6	31.9	42.9
Other transport, other	2 217	....	17.5	23.3	14.6	42.0	18.3	12.5	10.1
Transportation services, debit	3 205	**−165.3**	**−157.8**	**−179.5**	**−190.4**	**−190.7**	**−229.9**	**−273.1**	**−294.7**
Passenger	3 850	*−14.1*	*−18.0*	*−2.1*	*−.8*	*−6.1*	*−11.3*	*−25.5*	*−29.3*
Freight	3 851	*−114.3*	*−107.7*	*−146.2*	*−163.7*	*−168.6*	*−204.8*	*−242.2*	*−253.2*
Other	3 852	*−36.9*	*−32.2*	*−31.3*	*−25.9*	*−16.0*	*−13.9*	*−5.4*	*−12.2*
Sea transport, passenger	3 207	....	....	....	....	....	....	....	....
Sea transport, freight	3 208	....	−104.2	....	−.1	−2.1	−2.3	−3.5	....
Sea transport, other	3 209	....	−6.4	−.7	−7.4	−.9	−5.2	−1.1	−6.1
Air transport, passenger	3 211	−14.1	−18.0	−.2	....	−6.1	−11.0	−25.5	−29.2
Air transport, freight	3 212	−4.4	−3.5	....	−.6	....	−.7	....	....
Air transport, other	3 213	−.6	−.6	−14.6	−5.0	....	−7.9	−3.6	−3.7
Other transport, passenger	3 215	....	....	−1.9	−.7	....	−.3	....	−.1
Other transport, freight	3 216	−109.9	....	−146.2	−163.1	−166.5	−201.8	−238.7	−253.2
Other transport, other	3 217	−36.3	−25.1	−16.0	−13.6	−15.1	−.8	−.7	−2.5
Travel, credit	2 236	**74.1**	**63.6**	**62.9**	**97.6**	**95.3**	**129.6**	**139.7**	**163.4**
Business travel	2 237	....	....	....	38.0	18.8	5.8	3.7	11.3
Personal travel	2 240	74.1	63.6	62.9	59.6	76.4	123.9	135.9	152.1
Travel, debit	3 236	**−107.6**	**−114.3**	**−113.0**	**−139.8**	**−134.2**	**−176.1**	**−179.5**	**−180.0**
Business travel	3 237	....	....	−40.1	−51.4	−7.6	−5.1	−17.5	−34.9
Personal travel	3 240	−107.6	−114.3	−72.9	−88.4	−126.6	−171.0	−162.0	−145.1
Other services, credit	2 200 BA	**153.7**	**130.4**	**174.8**	**115.8**	**80.2**	**122.9**	**141.7**	**166.8**
Communications	2 245	7.7	10.3	11.0	7.4	8.5	10.6	15.3	19.0
Construction	2 249	.2	1.8	30.6	11.8	11.1	22.1	24.9	18.5
Insurance	2 253	....	....	1.3	.7	.4	....	.1	2.0
Financial	2 260	....	....	8.4	4.0	1.5	1.3	1.7	4.3
Computer and information	2 262	....	....	....	....	1.0	1.6	2.7	3.9
Royalties and licence fees	2 266	....	....	....	15.0	.5	2.2	1.0	....
Other business services	2 268	145.8	117.4	120.2	73.1	48.0	58.4	61.8	64.2
Personal, cultural, and recreational	2 287	....	....	....	.1	.2	.4	2.3	.5
Government, n.i.e.	2 291	....	.9	3.3	3.7	9.1	26.3	31.8	54.4
Other services, debit	3 200 BA	**−172.9**	**−346.2**	**−284.5**	**−243.6**	**−206.5**	**−242.6**	**−305.5**	**−380.8**
Communications	3 245	−1.6	−14.2	−25.3	−10.6	−8.5	−11.2	−16.9	−17.0
Construction	3 249	−28.2	−39.7	−91.2	−60.9	−52.2	−78.6	−93.7	−61.4
Insurance	3 253	−17.6	−17.4	−2.7	−4.5	−.4	−1.6	−1.8	−3.8
Financial	3 260	−9.1	−1.9	−3.3	−3.2	−7.7	−17.6	−12.5	−19.5
Computer and information	3 262	....	....	−.1	−.1	−1.1	−4.2	−6.4	−6.8
Royalties and licence fees	3 266	−.1	....	−.3	−1.4	−3.1	−5.3	−2.3	−2.4
Other business services	3 268	−109.1	−261.5	−143.3	−142.5	−113.3	−101.9	−141.1	−233.2
Personal, cultural, and recreational	3 287	....	....	....	....	−.4	−.9	−1.1	−.7
Government, n.i.e.	3 291	−7.2	−11.5	−18.3	−20.4	−19.9	−21.3	−29.6	−36.1

Table 2 (Continued). STANDARD PRESENTATION, 2000–2007

(Millions of U.S. dollars)

	Code	2000	2001	2002	2003	2004	2005	2006	2007
C. INCOME	4 300	**−192.1**	**−234.7**	**−603.2**	**−165.5**	**−299.5**	**−359.9**	**−634.5**	**−591.6**
Total credit	2 300	*79.3*	*56.0*	*52.1*	*55.9*	*74.5*	*98.9*	*159.8*	*193.6*
Total debit	3 300	*−271.4*	*−290.7*	*−655.3*	*−221.4*	*−374.0*	*−458.8*	*−794.3*	*−785.2*
Compensation of employees, credit	2 310	**36.8**	**.8**	**23.6**	**39.5**	**55.0**	**50.9**	**64.2**	**68.5**
Compensation of employees, debit	3 310	**−53.4**	**−32.0**	**−33.6**	**−9.0**	**−9.0**	**−10.4**	**−13.8**	**−19.3**
Investment income, credit	2 320	**42.5**	**55.2**	**28.5**	**16.4**	**19.5**	**48.0**	**95.6**	**125.1**
Direct investment income	2 330	....	....	....	....	....	....	....	4.1
Dividends and distributed branch profits	2 332	....	....	....	....	....	....	....	4.1
Reinvested earnings and undistributed branch profits	2 333	....	....	....	....	....	....	....	....
Income on debt (interest)	2 334	....	....	....	....	....	....	....	....
Portfolio investment income	2 339	....	....	6.5	6.8	6.6	15.5	28.5	41.8
Income on equity	2 340	....	....	....	6.6	6.1	15.5	.1	.1
Income on bonds and notes	2 350	....	....	....	.2	.5	....	28.4	41.8
Income on money market instruments	2 360	....	....	6.5	....	....	....	....	....
Other investment income	2 370	42.5	55.2	22.1	9.6	12.9	32.5	67.1	79.2
Investment income, debit	3 320	**−218.0**	**−258.7**	**−621.7**	**−212.4**	**−365.0**	**−448.3**	**−780.5**	**−765.9**
Direct investment income	3 330	−.3	−20.3	−27.7	−42.1	−167.6	−284.0	−471.4	−553.6
Dividends and distributed branch profits	3 332	−.3	−20.3	−27.7	−42.1	−162.7	−267.1	−390.4	−523.8
Reinvested earnings and undistributed branch profits	3 333	....	....	....	....	....	....	−77.2	−24.2
Income on debt (interest)	3 334	....	....	....	....	−4.9	−16.9	−3.8	−5.6
Portfolio investment income	3 339	−43.9	....	....	....	−.5	−.7	−.6	−.4
Income on equity	3 340	....	....	....	....	....	−.7	−.6	−.4
Income on bonds and notes	3 350	−43.9	....	....	....	−.5	....	....	....
Income on money market instruments	3 360	....	....	....	....	....	....	....	....
Other investment income	3 370	−173.8	−238.4	−594.0	−170.3	−197.0	−163.6	−308.5	−212.0
D. CURRENT TRANSFERS	4 379	**230.9**	**217.5**	**638.3**	**223.1**	**313.8**	**403.0**	**500.7**	**592.4**
Credit	2 379	**337.3**	**254.6**	**827.0**	**293.2**	**370.5**	**479.0**	**574.5**	**657.8**
General government	2 380	336.9	212.5	628.4	232.4	325.3	373.8	454.9	508.7
Other sectors	2 390	.4	42.1	198.6	60.7	45.2	105.2	119.6	149.2
Workers' remittances	2 391	....	41.0	29.0	29.9	2.5	5.8	15.8	30.9
Other current transfers	2 392	.4	1.1	169.6	30.8	42.7	99.4	103.7	118.3
Debit	3 379	**−106.4**	**−37.1**	**−188.7**	**−70.0**	**−56.7**	**−76.0**	**−73.8**	**−65.4**
General government	3 380	−3.6	−5.0	....	....	−1.6	....	−1.9	−3.6
Other sectors	3 390	−102.8	−32.2	−188.7	−70.0	−55.1	−76.0	−71.8	−61.8
Workers' remittances	3 391	−102.8	−32.2	−16.2	−20.5	−11.3	−10.8	−12.3	−25.9
Other current transfers	3 392	....	....	−172.5	−49.5	−43.8	−65.2	−59.5	−35.8
CAPITAL AND FINANCIAL ACCOUNT	4 996	**726.1**	**716.8**	**929.2**	**608.3**	**391.0**	**479.7**	**629.4**	**711.1**
CAPITAL ACCOUNT	4 994	**305.8**	**256.7**	**1,169.4**	**284.1**	**578.1**	**193.8**	**2,277.9**	**541.9**
Total credit	2 994	*305.8*	*256.7*	*1,169.8*	*284.6*	*581.2*	*197.7*	*2,280.3*	*542.9*
Total debit	3 994	....	....	*−.4*	*−.5*	*−3.1*	*−3.9*	*−2.3*	*−1.0*
Capital transfers, credit	2 400	**305.8**	**256.7**	**1,169.8**	**284.6**	**581.2**	**197.7**	**2,280.3**	**542.8**
General government	2 401	305.8	256.7	1,168.9	272.8	512.9	86.7	1,957.3	386.8
Debt forgiveness	2 402	79.0	....	947.4	13.3	315.1	6.0	1,789.4	126.8
Other capital transfers	2 410	226.8	256.7	221.5	259.5	197.8	80.8	167.9	260.1
Other sectors	2 430	....	....	1.0	11.7	68.3	111.0	322.9	156.0
Migrants' transfers	2 431	....	....	....	....	....	....	....	....
Debt forgiveness	2 432	....	....	....	....	....	....	....	....
Other capital transfers	2 440	....	....	1.0	11.7	68.3	111.0	322.9	156.0
Capital transfers, debit	3 400	....	....	**−.4**	**−.5**	**−3.0**	**−3.9**	**−2.3**	**−.9**
General government	3 401	....	....	....	....	....	....	....	....
Debt forgiveness	3 402	....	....	....	....	....	....	....	....
Other capital transfers	3 410	....	....	....	....	....	....	....	....
Other sectors	3 430	....	....	−.4	−.5	−3.0	−3.9	−2.3	−.9
Migrants' transfers	3 431	....	....	−.1	....	....	....	....	....
Debt forgiveness	3 432	....	....	....	....	....	....	....	....
Other capital transfers	3 440	....	....	−.4	−.5	−3.0	−3.9	−2.3	−.9
Nonproduced nonfinancial assets, credit	2 480	....	....	....	....	....	....	....	....
Nonproduced nonfinancial assets, debit	3 480	....	....	....	....	....	....	....	....

Table 2 (Continued). STANDARD PRESENTATION, 2000–2007

(Millions of U.S. dollars)

	Code	2000	2001	2002	2003	2004	2005	2006	2007
FINANCIAL ACCOUNT....................................	4 995 ..	**420.3**	**460.1**	**−240.3**	**324.2**	**−187.2**	**285.9**	**−1,648.5**	**169.2**
A. DIRECT INVESTMENT....................................	4 500 ..	**139.2**	**255.4**	**347.6**	**336.7**	**244.7**	**107.9**	**153.3**	**427.7**
Direct investment abroad................................	4 505 ..	....	....	....	....	....	....	−.4	.3
Equity capital..	4 510 ..	....	....	....	....	....	....	−.4	....
Claims on affiliated enterprises................	4 515 ..	....	....	....	....	....	....	−.4	....
Liabilities to affiliated enterprises.............	4 520 ..	....	....	....	....	....	....	....	....
Reinvested earnings.................................	4 525 ..	....	....	....	....	....	....	....	....
Other capital..	4 530 ..	....	....	....	....	....	....	....	.3
Claims on affiliated enterprises................	4 535 ..	....	....	....	....	....	....	....	.3
Liabilities to affiliated enterprises.............	4 540 ..	....	....	....	....	....	....	....	....
Direct investment in Mozambique....................	4 555 ..	**139.2**	**255.4**	**347.6**	**336.7**	**244.7**	**107.9**	**153.7**	**427.4**
Equity capital..	4 560 ..	139.2	255.4	347.4	336.7	234.6	59.8	111.8	167.3
Claims on direct investors.....................	4 565 ..	....	....	.2	....	....	....	....	−.8
Liabilities to direct investors.................	4 570 ..	139.2	255.4	347.3	336.7	234.6	59.8	111.8	168.1
Reinvested earnings.................................	4 575 ..	....	....	....	....	....	....	77.2	24.1
Other capital..	4 580 ..	....	....	.2	....	10.1	48.1	−35.2	235.9
Claims on direct investors.....................	4 585 ..	....	....	.2	....	....	−14.6	−31.6	11.5
Liabilities to direct investors.................	4 590 ..	....	....	−.1	....	10.1	62.6	−3.6	224.5
B. PORTFOLIO INVESTMENT..........................	4 600 ..	....	....	**32.2**	**5.0**	**−25.4**	**−88.5**	**−123.8**	**−117.2**
Assets...	4 602 ..	....	....	**32.2**	**5.0**	**−25.4**	**−88.8**	**−124.2**	**−117.5**
Equity securities...................................	4 610 ..	....	....	32.2	5.0	−25.4	−88.8	−.2	−1.5
Monetary authorities............................	4 611 ..	....	....	−.2	−.8	....	−69.9	....	−1.4
General government.............................	4 612 ..	....	....	....	....	....	....	....	....
Banks...	4 613 ..	....	....	32.4	5.8	−25.4	−18.8	....	....
Other sectors....................................	4 614 ..	....	....	....	....	....	−.1	−.2	−.1
Debt securities.....................................	4 619 ..	....	....	....	....	....	....	−124.0	−116.0
Bonds and notes...............................	4 620 ..	....	....	....	....	....	....	−124.0	−116.0
Monetary authorities........................	4 621 ..	....	....	....	....	....	....	−84.1	−77.9
General government.........................	4 622 ..	....	....	....	....	....	....	....	....
Banks..	4 623 ..	....	....	....	....	....	....	−39.9	−38.1
Other sectors.................................	4 624 ..	....	....	....	....	....	....	....	....
Money market instruments....................	4 630 ..	....	....	....	....	....	....	....	....
Monetary authorities........................	4 631 ..	....	....	....	....	....	....	....	....
General government.........................	4 632 ..	....	....	....	....	....	....	....	....
Banks..	4 633 ..	....	....	....	....	....	....	....	....
Other sectors.................................	4 634 ..	....	....	....	....	....	....	....	....
Liabilities.......................................	4 652 ..	....	....	....	....	....	.3	.4	.3
Equity securities...................................	4 660 ..	....	....	....	....	....	.3	.4	.3
Banks...	4 663 ..	....	....	....	....	....	....	....	....
Other sectors....................................	4 664 ..	....	....	....	....	....	.3	.4	.3
Debt securities.....................................	4 669 ..	....	....	....	....	....	....	....	....
Bonds and notes...............................	4 670 ..	....	....	....	....	....	....	....	....
Monetary authorities........................	4 671 ..	....	....	....	....	....	....	....	....
General government.........................	4 672 ..	....	....	....	....	....	....	....	....
Banks..	4 673 ..	....	....	....	....	....	....	....	....
Other sectors.................................	4 674 ..	....	....	....	....	....	....	....	....
Money market instruments....................	4 680 ..	....	....	....	....	....	....	....	....
Monetary authorities........................	4 681 ..	....	....	....	....	....	....	....	....
General government.........................	4 682 ..	....	....	....	....	....	....	....	....
Banks..	4 683 ..	....	....	....	....	....	....	....	....
Other sectors.................................	4 684 ..	....	....	....	....	....	....	....	....
C. FINANCIAL DERIVATIVES...........................	4 910 ..	....	....	....	....	....	....	....	**−16.0**
Monetary authorities...............................	4 911 ..	....	....	....	....	....	....	....	....
General government...............................	4 912 ..	....	....	....	....	....	....	....	....
Banks..	4 913 ..	....	....	....	....	....	....	....	....
Other sectors......................................	4 914 ..	....	....	....	....	....	....	....	−16.0
Assets...	4 900 ..	....	....	....	....	....	....	....	....
Monetary authorities...............................	4 901 ..	....	....	....	....	....	....	....	....
General government...............................	4 902 ..	....	....	....	....	....	....	....	....
Banks..	4 903 ..	....	....	....	....	....	....	....	....
Other sectors......................................	4 904 ..	....	....	....	....	....	....	....	....
Liabilities.......................................	4 905 ..	....	....	....	....	....	....	....	**−16.0**
Monetary authorities...............................	4 906 ..	....	....	....	....	....	....	....	....
General government...............................	4 907 ..	....	....	....	....	....	....	....	....
Banks..	4 908 ..	....	....	....	....	....	....	....	....
Other sectors......................................	4 909 ..	....	....	....	....	....	....	....	−16.0

Table 2 (Concluded). STANDARD PRESENTATION, 2000–2007

(Millions of U.S. dollars)

	Code	2000	2001	2002	2003	2004	2005	2006	2007
D. OTHER INVESTMENT	4 700 ..	**357.9**	**185.9**	**−522.2**	**164.0**	**−237.4**	**136.7**	**−1,648.8**	**79.5**
Assets	4 703 ..	**−145.0**	**−33.8**	**−207.7**	**−77.1**	**−88.7**	**−78.5**	**−13.8**	**−359.3**
Trade credits	4 706 ..	−21.0	−9.1	1.0	−3.3	−2.8	−3.7	−27.8	−65.8
General government	4 707 ..	....	....	....	....	....	....	....	....
of which: Short-term	4 709 ..	....	....	....	....	....	....	....	....
Other sectors	4 710 ..	−21.0	−9.1	1.0	−3.3	−2.8	−3.7	−27.8	−65.8
of which: Short-term	4 712 ..	*−21.0*	*−9.1*	*.8*	*−3.3*	*−2.8*	*−3.7*	*−27.8*	*−65.8*
Loans	4 714 ..	....	....	−.2	....	....	....	6.7	−1.5
Monetary authorities	4 715 ..	....	....	....	....	....	....	....	....
of which: Short-term	4 718 ..	....	....	....	....	....	....	....	....
General government	4 719 ..	....	....	....	....	....	....	....	....
of which: Short-term	4 721 ..	....	....	....	....	....	....	....	....
Banks	4 722 ..	....	....	−.2	....	....	....	....	....
of which: Short-term	4 724 ..	....	....	....	....	....	....	....	....
Other sectors	4 725 ..	....	....	....	....	....	....	6.7	−1.5
of which: Short-term	4 727 ..	....	....	....	....	....	....	*6.7*	*−.9*
Currency and deposits	4 730 ..	−124.0	−23.9	−80.0	20.0	−66.6	−108.8	−30.0	−322.4
Monetary authorities	4 731 ..	....	....	−5.6	6.9	−122.8	....	....	....
General government	4 732 ..	....	....	....	....	....	....	....	....
Banks	4 733 ..	−124.0	−23.9	−74.4	13.1	56.2	−76.6	−105.9	−226.8
Other sectors	4 734 ..	....	....	....	....	....	−32.2	75.8	−95.6
Other assets	4 736 ..	....	−.8	−128.5	−93.8	−19.4	34.0	37.3	30.4
Monetary authorities	4 737 ..	....	−.8	....	....	−63.6	40.9	17.5	41.6
of which: Short-term	4 739 ..	....	*−.8*	....	....	*−63.6*	*40.9*	*17.5*	*41.6*
General government	4 740 ..	....	....	....	....	....	....	....	....
of which: Short-term	4 742 ..	....	....	....	....	....	....	....	....
Banks	4 743 ..	....	....	....	....	1.6	.3	−1.0	−22.8
of which: Short-term	4 745 ..	....	....	....	....	*1.6*	*.3*	*−1.0*	*−22.8*
Other sectors	4 746 ..	....	....	−128.5	−93.8	42.6	−7.3	20.8	11.6
of which: Short-term	4 748 ..	....	....	....	....	*42.6*	*−7.3*	*20.8*	*11.6*
Liabilities	4 753 ..	**502.9**	**219.7**	**−314.6**	**241.1**	**−148.7**	**215.1**	**−1,635.0**	**438.7**
Trade credits	4 756 ..	....	....	9.2	.1	1.3	8.8	−3.8	36.6
General government	4 757 ..	....	....	−.1	....	....	....	....	....
of which: Short-term	4 759 ..	....	....	....	....	....	....	....	....
Other sectors	4 760 ..	....	....	9.4	.1	1.3	8.8	−3.8	36.6
of which: Short-term	4 762 ..	....	....	*−.1*	....	*1.3*	*8.8*	*−3.8*	*36.6*
Loans	4 764 ..	527.1	184.6	−569.5	94.6	−206.2	126.3	−1,866.5	352.4
Monetary authorities	4 765 ..	31.1	−15.8	−1.4	13.2	−68.8	−25.6	−149.1	4.5
of which: Use of Fund credit and loans from the Fund	4 766 ..	*31.1*	*−15.8*	*−11.5*	*−9.1*	*−20.4*	*−25.3*	*−149.4*	*4.9*
of which: Short-term	4 768 ..	....	....	....	....	....	*.1*	....	*−1.2*
General government	4 769 ..	211.4	218.8	−955.6	53.0	−47.6	95.2	−1,475.5	216.2
of which: Short-term	4 771 ..	....	....	....	....	....	*−.6*	....	....
Banks	4 772 ..	....	....	−35.1	11.2	2.3	18.5	−31.7	14.1
of which: Short-term	4 774 ..	....	....	*−35.0*	*12.0*	*−2.8*	*23.7*	*−30.8*	*16.0*
Other sectors	4 775 ..	284.6	−18.4	422.6	17.2	−92.1	38.3	−210.1	117.6
of which: Short-term	4 777 ..	....	....	....	....	....	....	....	*−3.7*
Currency and deposits	4 780 ..	....	35.1	−8.5	.9	7.3	−12.0	−3.9	25.5
Monetary authorities	4 781 ..	....	....	....	....	....	....	....	....
General government	4 782 ..	....	....	....	....	....	....	....	....
Banks	4 783 ..	....	35.1	−8.5	.9	7.3	−12.0	−3.9	25.5
Other sectors	4 784 ..	....	....	....	....	....	....	....	....
Other liabilities	4 786 ..	−24.2	....	254.2	145.5	48.8	92.0	239.2	24.2
Monetary authorities	4 787 ..	−40.8	....	....	....	....	....	....	....
of which: Short-term	4 789 ..	....	....	....	....	....	....	....	....
General government	4 790 ..	....	....	253.7	141.9	48.8	86.7	32.0	16.3
of which: Short-term	4 792 ..	....	....	*253.7*	*141.9*	*48.8*	*86.7*	*32.0*	*16.3*
Banks	4 793 ..	16.6	....	.5	3.5	....	....	....	....
of which: Short-term	4 795 ..	*16.6*	....	*.5*	*3.5*	....	....	....	....
Other sectors	4 796 ..	....	....	....	....	....	5.3	207.2	7.9
of which: Short-term	4 798 ..	....	....	....	....	....	*5.3*	*207.2*	*8.1*
E. RESERVE ASSETS	4 802 ..	**−76.8**	**18.8**	**−97.8**	**−181.5**	**−169.1**	**129.9**	**−29.3**	**−204.8**
Monetary gold	4 812 ..	−5.3	8.8	−8.7	12.3	−18.6	−20.0	−11.5	−18.8
Special drawing rights	4 811 ..	....	....	....	....	....	−.2	....	.1
Reserve position in the Fund	4 810 ..								
Foreign exchange	4 803 ..	−96.3	10.0	−89.1	−193.8	−150.5	150.1	−17.8	−186.1
Other claims	4 813 ..	24.8	....	....	....	....	....	....	....
NET ERRORS AND OMISSIONS	4 998 ..	**37.5**	**−59.6**	**−60.0**	**208.2**	**216.4**	**281.0**	**143.8**	**83.9**

Table 3. INTERNATIONAL INVESTMENT POSITION (End-period stocks), 2000–2007

(Millions of U.S. dollars)

	Code	2000	2001	2002	2003	2004	2005	2006	2007
ASSETS	8 995 C.	....	....	....	....	2,112.2	2,171.7	2,364.6	3,061.8
Direct investment abroad	8 505 ..	....	....	....	....	....	.4	.8	.5
Equity capital and reinvested earnings	8 506 ..	....	....	....	....	....	.2	.6	.3
Claims on affiliated enterprises	8 507 ..	....	....	....	....	....	.2	.6	.3
Liabilities to affiliated enterprises	8 508 ..	....	....	....	....	....	....	....	....
Other capital	8 530 ..	....	....	....	....	....	.2	.2	.2
Claims on affiliated enterprises	8 535 ..	....	....	....	....	....	.2	.2	.2
Liabilities to affiliated enterprises	8 540 ..	....	....	....	....	....	....	....	....
Portfolio investment	8 602 ..	....	....	....	....	68.5	157.3	281.4	398.8
Equity securities	8 610 ..	....	....	....	....	....	.1	.1	1.6
Monetary authorities	8 611 ..	....	....	....	....	....	....	....	1.4
General government	8 612 ..	....	....	....	....	....	....	....	....
Banks	8 613 ..	....	....	....	....	....	....	....	....
Other sectors	8 614 ..	....	....	....	....	....	.1	.1	.2
Debt securities	8 619 ..	....	....	....	....	68.5	157.2	281.3	397.3
Bonds and notes	8 620 ..	....	....	....	....	68.5	157.2	281.3	397.3
Monetary authorities	8 621 ..	....	....	....	....	....	69.9	154.0	232.0
General government	8 622 ..	....	....	....	....	....	....	....	....
Banks	8 623 ..	....	....	....	....	68.5	87.3	127.2	165.3
Other sectors	8 624 ..	....	....	....	....	....	....	....	....
Money market instruments	8 630 ..	....	....	....	....	....	....	....	....
Monetary authorities	8 631 ..	....	....	....	....	....	....	....	....
General government	8 632 ..	....	....	....	....	....	....	....	....
Banks	8 633 ..	....	....	....	....	....	....	....	....
Other sectors	8 634 ..	....	....	....	....	....	....	....	....
Financial derivatives	8 900 ..	....	....	....	....	....	....	....	**16.0**
Monetary authorities	8 901 ..	....	....	....	....	....	....	....	....
General government	8 902 ..	....	....	....	....	....	....	....	....
Banks	8 903 C.	....	....	....	....	....	....	....	....
Other sectors	8 904 ..	....	....	....	....	....	....	....	16.0
Other investment	8 703 ..	....	....	....	....	884.3	984.6	1,023.7	1,383.0
Trade credits	8 706 ..	....	....	....	....	10.8	22.1	46.3	112.1
General government	8 707 ..	....	....	....	....	....	....	....	....
of which: Short-term	8 709 ..	....	....	....	....	....	....	....	....
Other sectors	8 710 ..	....	....	....	....	10.8	22.1	46.3	112.1
of which: Short-term	8 712 ..	....	....	....	....	*10.8*	*22.1*	*46.3*	*112.1*
Loans	8 714 ..	....	....	....	....	....	6.7	....	1.5
Monetary authorities	8 715 ..	....	....	....	....	....	....	....	....
of which: Short-term	8 718 ..	....	....	....	....	....	....	....	....
General government	8 719 ..	....	....	....	....	....	....	....	....
of which: Short-term	8 721 ..	....	....	....	....	....	....	....	....
Banks	8 722 ..	....	....	....	....	....	....	....	....
of which: Short-term	8 724 ..	....	....	....	....	....	....	....	....
Other sectors	8 725 ..	....	....	....	....	....	6.7	....	1.5
of which: Short-term	8 727 ..	....	....	....	....	....	*6.7*	....	*1.5*
Currency and deposits	8 730 ..	....	....	....	....	655.2	735.5	794.9	1,117.3
Monetary authorities	8 731 ..	....	....	....	....	....	....	....	....
General government	8 732 ..	....	....	....	....	....	....	....	....
Banks	8 733 ..	....	....	....	....	261.2	326.8	432.7	659.5
Other sectors	8 734 ..	....	....	....	....	394.0	408.7	362.2	457.8
Other assets	8 736 ..	....	....	....	....	218.3	220.3	182.5	152.1
Monetary authorities	8 737 ..	....	....	....	....	197.5	179.3	161.8	120.1
of which: Short-term	8 739 ..	....	....	....	....	*197.5*	*179.3*	*161.8*	*120.1*
General government	8 740 ..	....	....	....	....	....	....	....	....
of which: Short-term	8 742 ..	....	....	....	....	....	....	....	....
Banks	8 743 ..	....	....	....	....	1.8	1.5	2.5	25.3
of which: Short-term	8 745 ..	....	....	....	....	*1.8*	*1.5*	*2.5*	*25.3*
Other sectors	8 746 ..	....	....	....	....	19.0	39.5	18.2	6.6
of which: Short-term	8 748 ..	....	....	....	....	*19.0*	*39.5*	*18.2*	*6.6*
Reserve assets	8 802 ..	....	....	....	....	1,159.3	1,029.4	1,058.7	1,263.5
Monetary gold	8 812 ..	....	....	....	....	28.9	49.0	60.5	79.3
Special drawing rights	8 811 ..	.1	.1	.1	.1	.1	.2	.2	.2
Reserve position in the Fund	8 810 ..	....	....	....	....	....	....	....	....
Foreign exchange	8 803 ..	....	....	....	....	1,130.2	980.2	998.0	1,184.1
Other claims	8 813 ..	....	....	....	....	....	....	....	....

Table 3 (Concluded). INTERNATIONAL INVESTMENT POSITION (End-period stocks), 2000–2007

(Millions of U.S. dollars)

	Code	2000	2001	2002	2003	2004	2005	2006	2007
LIABILITIES	8 995 D.	....	....	....	....	**11,492.4**	**12,036.8**	**10,722.8**	**9,435.7**
Direct investment in Mozambique	8 555 ..	....	....	....	....	**2,441.5**	**2,630.0**	**2,789.0**	**3,216.3**
Equity capital and reinvested earnings	8 556 ..	....	....	....	....	2,380.9	2,440.7	2,629.6	2,821.1
Claims on direct investors	8 557 ..	....	....	....	....	....	....	....	....
Liabilities to direct investors	8 558 ..	....	....	....	....	2,380.9	2,440.7	2,629.6	2,821.1
Other capital	8 580 ..	....	....	....	....	60.6	189.3	159.3	395.3
Claims on direct investors	8 585 ..	....	....	....	....	−14.2	−28.8	−68.0	−68.0
Liabilities to direct investors	8 590 ..	....	....	....	....	74.8	218.0	227.3	463.2
Portfolio investment	8 652 ..	....	....	....	....	....	**.3**	**.3**	**.6**
Equity securities	8 660 ..	....	....	....	....	....	....	....	....
Banks	8 663 ..	....	....	....	....	....	....	....	....
Other sectors	8 664 ..	....	....	....	....	....	....	....	....
Debt securities	8 669 ..	....	....	....	....	....	.3	.3	.6
Bonds and notes	8 670 ..	....	....	....	....	....	.3	.3	.6
Monetary authorities	8 671 ..	....	....	....	....	....	....	....	....
General government	8 672 ..	....	....	....	....	....	....	....	....
Banks	8 673 ..	....	....	....	....	....	....	....	....
Other sectors	8 674 ..	....	....	....	....	....	.3	.3	.6
Money market instruments	8 680 ..	....	....	....	....	....	....	....	....
Monetary authorities	8 681 ..	....	....	....	....	....	....	....	....
General government	8 682 ..	....	....	....	....	....	....	....	....
Banks	8 683 ..	....	....	....	....	....	....	....	....
Other sectors	8 684 ..	....	....	....	....	....	....	....	....
Financial derivatives	8 905 ..	....	....	....	....	....	....	....	....
Monetary authorities	8 906 ..	....	....	....	....	....	....	....	....
General government	8 907 ..	....	....	....	....	....	....	....	....
Banks	8 908 ..	....	....	....	....	....	....	....	....
Other sectors	8 909 ..	....	....	....	....	....	....	....	....
Other investment	8 753 ..	....	....	....	....	**9,050.9**	**9,406.5**	**7,933.5**	**6,218.8**
Trade credits	8 756 ..	....	....	....	....	6.5	16.3	12.5	49.2
General government	8 757 ..	....	....	....	....	....	....	....	....
of which: Short-term	8 759 ..	....	....	....	....	....	....	....	....
Other sectors	8 760 ..	....	....	....	....	6.5	16.3	12.5	49.2
of which: Short-term	8 762 ..	....	....	....	....	*6.5*	*16.3*	*12.5*	*49.2*
Loans	8 764 ..	....	....	....	....	8,950.4	9,199.3	7,494.7	5,830.7
Monetary authorities	8 765 ..	....	....	....	....	200.3	159.6	12.8	18.0
of which: Use of Fund credit and loans from the Fund	8 766 ..	*219.5*	*195.9*	*200.1*	*209.2*	*197.3*	*156.9*	*9.7*	*15.4*
of which: Short-term	8 768 ..	....	....	....	....	....	*.1*	*.2*	*−1.1*
General government	8 769 ..	....	....	....	....	4,416.1	4,648.9	3,333.0	3,286.9
of which: Short-term	8 771 ..	....	....	....	....	....	....	....	....
Banks	8 772 ..	....	....	....	....	22.2	40.7	8.9	23.0
of which: Short-term	8 774 ..	....	....	....	....	*11.0*	*34.7*	*3.8*	*19.9*
Other sectors	8 775 ..	....	....	....	....	4,311.8	4,350.1	4,140.0	2,502.7
of which: Short-term	8 777 ..	....	....	....	....	....	....	....	....
Currency and deposits	8 780 ..	....	....	....	....	45.2	37.8	33.9	59.4
Monetary authorities	8 781 ..	....	....	....	....	....	....	....	....
General government	8 782 ..	....	....	....	....	....	....	....	....
Banks	8 783 ..	....	....	....	....	45.2	37.8	33.9	59.4
Other sectors	8 784 ..	....	....	....	....	....	....	....	....
Other liabilities	8 786 ..	....	....	....	....	48.8	153.2	392.4	279.6
Monetary authorities	8 787 ..	....	....	....	....	....	....	....	....
of which: Short-term	8 789 ..	....	....	....	....	....	....	....	....
General government	8 790 ..	....	....	....	....	48.8	135.5	167.5	183.8
of which: Short-term	8 792 ..	....	....	....	....	*48.8*	*135.5*	*167.5*	*183.8*
Banks	8 793 ..	....	....	....	....	....	....	....	....
of which: Short-term	8 795 ..	....	....	....	....	....	....	....	....
Other sectors	8 796 ..	....	....	....	....	....	17.7	224.9	95.8
of which: Short-term	8 798 ..	....	....	....	....	....	*17.7*	*224.9*	*96.1*
NET INTERNATIONAL INVESTMENT POSITION	8 995 ..	....	....	....	....	−9,380.2	−9,865.1	−8,358.2	−6,373.9
Conversion rates: meticais per U.S. dollar (end of period)	0 102 ..	**17.1405**	**23.3204**	**23.8543**	**23.8567**	**18.8993**	**24.1830**	**25.9700**	**23.8200**

Table 1. ANALYTIC PRESENTATION, 2000–2007

(Millions of U.S. dollars)

	Code	2000	2001	2002	2003	2004	2005	2006	2007
A. Current Account[1]..............	4 993 Z.	−211.7	−153.5	96.6	−19.3	111.5	582.1	802.0	....
Goods: exports f.o.b..............	2 100 ..	1,661.6	2,521.8	2,421.1	2,709.7	2,926.6	3,752.8	4,554.7	....
Goods: imports f.o.b..............	3 100 ..	−2,165.4	−2,443.7	−2,022.1	−1,911.6	−1,998.7	−1,743.7	−2,343.4	....
Balance on Goods..............	4 100 ..	−503.8	78.1	399.0	798.1	927.9	2,009.1	2,211.3	....
Services: credit..............	2 200 ..	477.9	407.7	426.0	249.1	254.7	256.7	279.5	....
Services: debit..............	3 200 ..	−328.1	−361.2	−309.5	−420.0	−459.6	−497.5	−562.9	....
Balance on Goods and Services..............	4 991 ..	−354.0	124.6	515.5	627.3	723.0	1,768.3	1,928.0	....
Income: credit..............	2 300 ..	35.5	36.6	36.6	29.4	40.4	55.1	97.8	....
Income: debit..............	3 300 ..	−168.8	−549.4	−619.7	−771.0	−785.8	−1,413.7	−1,346.2	....
Balance on Goods, Services, and Income..............	4 992 ..	−487.3	−388.2	−67.6	−114.2	−22.4	409.7	679.6	....
Current transfers: credit..............	2 379 Z.	289.7	248.9	187.6	118.0	160.6	196.0	161.4	....
Current transfers: debit..............	3 379 ..	−14.1	−14.3	−23.4	−23.0	−26.7	−23.6	−39.0	....
B. Capital Account[1]..............	4 994 Z.	....	....	....	....	....	....	....	....
Capital account: credit..............	2 994 Z.	....	....	....	....	....	....	....	....
Capital account: debit..............	3 994 ..	....	....	....	....	....	....	....	....
Total, Groups A Plus B..............	4 981 ..	−211.7	−153.5	96.6	−19.3	111.5	582.1	802.0	....
C. Financial Account[1]..............	4 995 W.	212.8	347.7	−32.0	137.1	125.2	164.7	253.0	....
Direct investment abroad..............	4 505 ..	....	....	....	....	....	....	....	....
Direct investment in Myanmar..............	4 555 Z.	258.3	210.3	152.1	251.5	213.5	235.1	278.6	....
Portfolio investment assets..............	4 602 ..	....	....	....	....	....	....	....	....
Equity securities..............	4 610 ..	....	....	....	....	....	....	....	....
Debt securities..............	4 619 ..	....	....	....	....	....	....	....	....
Portfolio investment liabilities..............	4 652 Z.	....	....	....	....	....	....	....	....
Equity securities..............	4 660 Z.	....	....	....	....	....	....	....	....
Debt securities..............	4 669 Z.	....	....	....	....	....	....	....	....
Financial derivatives..............	4 910 ..	....	....	....	....	....	....	....	....
Financial derivatives assets..............	4 900 ..	....	....	....	....	....	....	....	....
Financial derivatives liabilities..............	4 905 ..	....	....	....	....	....	....	....	....
Other investment assets..............	4 703 ..	....	....	....	....	....	....	....	....
Monetary authorities..............	4 701 ..	....	....	....	....	....	....	....	....
General government..............	4 704 ..	....	....	....	....	....	....	....	....
Banks..............	4 705 ..	....	....	....	....	....	....	....	....
Other sectors..............	4 728 ..	....	....	....	....	....	....	....	....
Other investment liabilities..............	4 753 W.	−45.4	137.4	−184.1	−114.3	−88.3	−70.4	−25.6	....
Monetary authorities..............	4 753 WA	7.2	200.8	−11.6	−21.2	−13.4	10.4	−8.0	....
General government..............	4 753 ZB	−56.8	−62.7	−171.2	−91.2	−85.2	−87.3	−31.8	....
Banks..............	4 753 ZC	4.1	−.8	−1.3	5.3	12.4	9.4	17.8	....
Other sectors..............	4 753 ZD	....	....	....	−7.2	−2.2	−2.9	−3.6	....
Total, Groups A Through C..............	4 983 ..	1.1	194.2	64.6	117.9	236.7	746.8	1,055.0	....
D. Net Errors and Omissions..............	4 998 ..	−24.5	−14.3	−19.1	−78.9	−142.7	−604.6	−632.1	....
Total, Groups A Through D..............	4 984 ..	−23.4	179.8	45.4	38.9	94.0	142.2	422.9	....
E. Reserves and Related Items..............	4 802 A.	23.4	−179.8	−45.4	−38.9	−94.0	−142.2	−422.9	....
Reserve assets..............	4 802 ..	23.4	−179.8	−45.4	−38.9	−94.0	−142.2	−422.9	....
Use of Fund credit and loans..............	4 766 ..	....	....	....	....	....	....	....	....
Exceptional financing..............	4 920 ..	....	....	....	....	....	....	....	....
Conversion rates: kyats per U.S. dollar..............	0 101 ..	6.4257	6.6841	6.5734	6.0764	5.7459	5.8132	5.7838	5.5597

[1] Excludes components that have been classified in the categories of Group E.

Table 2. STANDARD PRESENTATION, 2000–2007

(Millions of U.S. dollars)

	Code	2000	2001	2002	2003	2004	2005	2006	2007
CURRENT ACCOUNT...............................	4 993 ..	**−211.7**	**−153.5**	**96.6**	**−19.3**	**111.5**	**582.1**	**802.0**	....
A. GOODS...	4 100 ..	**−503.8**	**78.1**	**399.0**	**798.1**	**927.9**	**2,009.1**	**2,211.3**	....
Credit...	2 100 ..	**1,661.6**	**2,521.8**	**2,421.1**	**2,709.7**	**2,926.6**	**3,752.8**	**4,554.7**	....
General merchandise: exports f.o.b...........	2 110 ..	1,212.2	2,056.7	2,006.6	2,353.0	2,697.2	3,504.5	4,264.9	....
Goods for processing: exports f.o.b..........	2 150 ..	449.4	465.0	414.5	356.7	229.4	248.3	289.8	....
Repairs on goods.................................	2 160 ..	....	....	....	....	....	....	....	....
Goods procured in ports by carriers..........	2 170 ..	....	....	....	....	....	....	....	....
Nonmonetary gold................................	2 180 ..	....	....	....	....	....	....	....	....
Debit..	3 100 ..	**−2,165.4**	**−2,443.7**	**−2,022.1**	**−1,911.6**	**−1,998.7**	**−1,743.7**	**−2,343.4**	....
General merchandise: imports f.o.b...........	3 110 ..	−2,165.4	−2,009.0	−1,622.7	−1,589.0	−1,768.1	−1,519.6	−2,090.8	....
Goods for processing: imports f.o.b..........	3 150 ..	....	−434.7	−399.4	−322.6	−230.7	−224.1	−252.5	....
Repairs on goods.................................	3 160 ..	....	....	....	....	....	....	....	....
Goods procured in ports by carriers..........	3 170 ..	....	....	....	....	....	....	....	....
Nonmonetary gold................................	3 180 ..	....	....	....	....	....	....	....	....
B. SERVICES..	4 200 ..	**149.8**	**46.5**	**116.5**	**−170.8**	**−204.9**	**−240.8**	**−283.4**	....
Total credit..	2 200 ..	*477.9*	*407.7*	*426.0*	*249.1*	*254.7*	*256.7*	*279.5*	....
Total debit..	3 200 ..	*−328.1*	*−361.2*	*−309.5*	*−420.0*	*−459.6*	*−497.5*	*−562.9*	....
Transportation services, credit...........	2 205 ..	**76.0**	**71.0**	**73.1**	**72.3**	**85.3**	**118.6**	**130.1**	....
Passenger..	2 850 ..	*32.9*	*23.1*	*16.2*	*14.3*	*13.5*	*16.4*	*13.1*	....
Freight...	2 851 ..	*8.2*	*14.6*	*18.2*	*14.1*	*13.0*	*44.8*	*48.3*	....
Other..	2 852 ..	*34.8*	*33.3*	*38.8*	*43.8*	*58.9*	*57.3*	*68.8*	....
Sea transport, passenger.	2 207 ..	....	....	....	....	....	....	....	....
Sea transport, freight..........................	2 208 ..	....	....	....	....	....	....	....	....
Sea transport, other............................	2 209 ..	....	....	....	....	....	....	....	....
Air transport, passenger.......................	2 211 ..	....	....	....	....	....	....	....	....
Air transport, freight...........................	2 212 ..	....	....	....	....	....	....	....	....
Air transport, other............................	2 213 ..	....	....	....	....	....	....	....	....
Other transport, passenger....................	2 215 ..	....	....	....	....	....	....	....	....
Other transport, freight........................	2 216 ..	....	....	....	....	....	....	....	....
Other transport, other.........................	2 217 ..	....	....	....	....	....	....	....	....
Transportation services, debit...........	3 205 ..	**−253.9**	**−285.3**	**−221.9**	**−215.6**	**−227.2**	**−195.3**	**−254.1**	....
Passenger..	3 850 ..	*−5.4*	*−5.0*	*−5.0*	*−3.5*	*−2.8*	*−2.6*	*−2.9*	....
Freight...	3 851 ..	*−248.5*	*−280.3*	*−215.9*	*−211.2*	*−219.9*	*−188.0*	*−249.4*	....
Other..	3 852 ..	....	....	*−1.0*	*−.8*	*−4.5*	*−4.7*	*−1.9*	....
Sea transport, passenger......................	3 207 ..	....	....	....	....	....	....	....	....
Sea transport, freight..........................	3 208 ..	....	....	....	....	....	....	....	....
Sea transport, other............................	3 209 ..	....	....	....	....	....	....	....	....
Air transport, passenger.......................	3 211 ..	....	....	....	....	....	....	....	....
Air transport, freight...........................	3 212 ..	....	....	....	....	....	....	....	....
Air transport, other............................	3 213 ..	....	....	....	....	....	....	....	....
Other transport, passenger....................	3 215 ..	....	....	....	....	....	....	....	....
Other transport, freight........................	3 216 ..	....	....	....	....	....	....	....	....
Other transport, other.........................	3 217 ..	....	....	....	....	....	....	....	....
Travel, credit...............................	2 236 ..	**162.4**	**109.0**	**120.2**	**56.4**	**83.9**	**67.0**	**46.3**	....
Business travel..................................	2 237 ..	....	....	....	....	....	....	....	....
Personal travel..................................	2 240 ..	....	....	....	....	....	....	....	....
Travel, debit.................................	3 236 ..	**−25.2**	**−27.1**	**−28.6**	**−32.0**	**−28.9**	**−30.9**	**−37.0**	....
Business travel..................................	3 237 ..	....	....	....	....	....	....	....	....
Personal travel..................................	3 240 ..	....	....	....	....	....	....	....	....
Other services, credit......................	2 200 BA	**239.5**	**227.7**	**232.6**	**120.5**	**85.5**	**71.2**	**103.0**	....
Communications................................	2 245 ..	.2	.2	....	....	....	....	....	....
Construction.....................................	2 249 ..	....	....	....	....	....	....	....	....
Insurance..	2 253 ..	....	....	....	....	....	....	....	....
Financial...	2 260 ..	....	....	....	....	....	....	....	....
Computer and information....................	2 262 ..	....	....	....	....	....	....	....	....
Royalties and licence fees.....................	2 266 ..	.1	....	....	....	....	....	....	....
Other business services........................	2 268 ..	220.4	207.2	210.0	99.1	62.7	49.7	79.9	....
Personal, cultural, and recreational..........	2 287 ..	....	....	....	....	....	....	....	....
Government, n.i.e...............................	2 291 ..	18.8	20.2	22.6	21.4	22.8	21.5	23.2	....
Other services, debit........................	3 200 BA	**−48.9**	**−48.8**	**−59.0**	**−172.3**	**−203.6**	**−271.4**	**−271.8**	....
Communications................................	3 245 ..	....	....	....	....	....	....	....	....
Construction.....................................	3 249 ..	....	....	....	....	....	....	....	....
Insurance..	3 253 ..	....	....	....	....	....	....	....	....
Financial...	3 260 ..	....	....	....	....	....	....	....	....
Computer and information....................	3 262 ..	....	....	....	....	....	....	....	....
Royalties and licence fees.....................	3 266 ..	....	....	....	....	....	....	....	....
Other business services..	3 268 ..	−30.8	−32.6	−45.7	−149.9	−185.0	−252.9	−249.2	....
Personal, cultural, and recreational..........	3 287 ..	−.2	−.2	−.2	−5.7	−3.1	−2.5	−6.7	....
Government, n.i.e...............................	3 291 ..	−17.9	−16.0	−13.1	−16.7	−15.5	−16.0	−15.9	....

Table 2 (Continued). STANDARD PRESENTATION, 2000–2007

(Millions of U.S. dollars)

	Code	2000	2001	2002	2003	2004	2005	2006	2007
C. INCOME	4 300	**−133.3**	**−512.8**	**−583.1**	**−741.5**	**−745.4**	**−1,358.6**	**−1,248.4**	....
Total credit	2 300	*35.5*	*36.6*	*36.6*	*29.4*	*40.4*	*55.1*	*97.8*	....
Total debit	3 300	*−168.8*	*−549.4*	*−619.7*	*−771.0*	*−785.8*	*−1,413.7*	*−1,346.2*	....
Compensation of employees, credit	2 310	**26.9**	**30.8**	**30.4**	**26.0**	**36.5**	**43.4**	**50.6**	....
Compensation of employees, debit	3 310	....	....	....	....	....	....	....	....
Investment income, credit	2 320	**8.6**	**5.8**	**6.2**	**3.4**	**3.9**	**11.7**	**47.1**	....
Direct investment income	2 330	....	....	....	....	....	....	....	....
Dividends and distributed branch profits	2 332	....	....	....	....	....	....	....	....
Reinvested earnings and undistributed branch profits	2 333	....	....	....	....	....	....	....	....
Income on debt (interest)	2 334	....	....	....	....	....	....	....	....
Portfolio investment income	2 339	....	....	....	....	....	....	....	....
Income on equity	2 340	....	....	....	....	....	....	....	....
Income on bonds and notes	2 350	....	....	....	....	....	....	....	....
Income on money market instruments	2 360	....	....	....	....	....	....	....	....
Other investment income	2 370	8.6	5.8	6.2	3.4	3.9	11.7	47.1	....
Investment income, debit	3 320	**−168.8**	**−549.4**	**−619.7**	**−771.0**	**−785.8**	**−1,413.7**	**−1,346.2**	....
Direct investment income	3 330	−137.2	−527.9	−582.8	−751.6	−761.6	−1,389.1	−1,317.0	....
Dividends and distributed branch profits	3 332	....	....	....	....	....	....	....	....
Reinvested earnings and undistributed branch profits	3 333	....	....	....	....	....	....	....	....
Income on debt (interest)	3 334	....	....	....	....	....	....	....	....
Portfolio investment income	3 339	....	....	....	....	....	....	....	....
Income on equity	3 340	....	....	....	....	....	....	....	....
Income on bonds and notes	3 350	....	....	....	....	....	....	....	....
Income on money market instruments	3 360	....	....	....	....	....	....	....	....
Other investment income	3 370	−31.6	−21.5	−36.9	−19.3	−24.2	−24.6	−29.2	....
D. CURRENT TRANSFERS	4 379	**275.6**	**234.7**	**164.2**	**95.0**	**133.9**	**172.4**	**122.4**	....
Credit	2 379	**289.7**	**248.9**	**187.6**	**118.0**	**160.6**	**196.0**	**161.4**	....
General government	2 380	36.3	41.2	52.4	27.4	26.0	48.2	32.2	....
Other sectors	2 390	253.5	207.7	135.2	90.6	134.6	147.8	129.2	....
Workers' remittances	2 391	76.7	86.5	76.1	59.3	81.3	86.3	65.7	....
Other current transfers	2 392	176.8	121.3	59.1	31.4	53.3	61.5	63.5	....
Debit	3 379	**−14.1**	**−14.3**	**−23.4**	**−23.0**	**−26.7**	**−23.6**	**−39.0**	....
General government	3 380	−.2	−.1	−.2	−.2	−.2	....	....	....
Other sectors	3 390	−14.0	−14.1	−23.3	−22.8	−26.5	−23.6	−39.0	....
Workers' remittances	3 391	−14.0	−14.1	−23.3	−22.8	−24.5	−18.8	−31.7	....
Other current transfers	3 392	....	....	....	....	−2.0	−4.8	−7.4	....
CAPITAL AND FINANCIAL ACCOUNT	4 996	**236.2**	**167.8**	**−77.5**	**98.2**	**31.2**	**22.5**	**−169.9**	....
CAPITAL ACCOUNT	4 994	....	....	....	....	....	....	....	....
Total credit	2 994	....	....	....	....	....	....	....	....
Total debit	3 994	....	....	....	....	....	....	....	....
Capital transfers, credit	2 400	....	....	....	....	....	....	....	....
General government	2 401	....	....	....	....	....	....	....	....
Debt forgiveness	2 402	....	....	....	....	....	....	....	....
Other capital transfers	2 410	....	....	....	....	....	....	....	....
Other sectors	2 430	....	....	....	....	....	....	....	....
Migrants' transfers	2 431	....	....	....	....	....	....	....	....
Debt forgiveness	2 432	....	....	....	....	....	....	....	....
Other capital transfers	2 440	....	....	....	....	....	....	....	....
Capital transfers, debit	3 400	....	....	....	....	....	....	....	....
General government	3 401	....	....	....	....	....	....	....	....
Debt forgiveness	3 402	....	....	....	....	....	....	....	....
Other capital transfers	3 410	....	....	....	....	....	....	....	....
Other sectors	3 430	....	....	....	....	....	....	....	....
Migrants' transfers	3 431	....	....	....	....	....	....	....	....
Debt forgiveness	3 432	....	....	....	....	....	....	....	....
Other capital transfers	3 440	....	....	....	....	....	....	....	....
Nonproduced nonfinancial assets, credit	2 480	....	....	....	....	....	....	....	....
Nonproduced nonfinancial assets, debit	3 480	....	....	....	....	....	....	....	....

Table 2 (Continued). STANDARD PRESENTATION, 2000–2007

(Millions of U.S. dollars)

	Code	2000	2001	2002	2003	2004	2005	2006	2007
FINANCIAL ACCOUNT	4 995 ..	**236.2**	**167.8**	**−77.5**	**98.2**	**31.2**	**22.5**	**−169.9**	....
A. DIRECT INVESTMENT	4 500 ..	**258.3**	**210.3**	**152.1**	**251.5**	**213.5**	**235.1**	**278.6**	....
Direct investment abroad	4 505 ..	....	....	....	....	....	....	....	....
Equity capital	4 510 ..	....	....	....	....	....	....	....	....
Claims on affiliated enterprises	4 515 ..	....	....	....	....	....	....	....	....
Liabilities to affiliated enterprises	4 520 ..	....	....	....	....	....	....	....	....
Reinvested earnings	4 525 ..	....	....	....	....	....	....	....	....
Other capital	4 530 ..	....	....	....	....	....	....	....	....
Claims on affiliated enterprises	4 535 ..	....	....	....	....	....	....	....	....
Liabilities to affiliated enterprises	4 540 ..	....	....	....	....	....	....	....	....
Direct investment in Myanmar	4 555 ..	**258.3**	**210.3**	**152.1**	**251.5**	**213.5**	**235.1**	**278.6**	....
Equity capital	4 560 ..	258.3	210.3	152.1	251.5	213.5	235.1	278.6	....
Claims on direct investors	4 565 ..	....	....	....	....	....	....	....	....
Liabilities to direct investors	4 570 ..	....	....	....	....	....	....	....	....
Reinvested earnings	4 575 ..	....	....	....	....	....	....	....	....
Other capital	4 580 ..	....	....	....	....	....	....	....	....
Claims on direct investors	4 585 ..	....	....	....	....	....	....	....	....
Liabilities to direct investors	4 590 ..	....	....	....	....	....	....	....	....
B. PORTFOLIO INVESTMENT	4 600 ..	....	....	....	....	....	....	....	....
Assets	4 602 ..	....	....	....	....	....	....	....	....
Equity securities	4 610 ..	....	....	....	....	....	....	....	....
Monetary authorities	4 611 ..	....	....	....	....	....	....	....	....
General government	4 612 ..	....	....	....	....	....	....	....	....
Banks	4 613 ..	....	....	....	....	....	....	....	....
Other sectors	4 614 ..	....	....	....	....	....	....	....	....
Debt securities	4 619 ..	....	....	....	....	....	....	....	....
Bonds and notes	4 620 ..	....	....	....	....	....	....	....	....
Monetary authorities	4 621 ..	....	....	....	....	....	....	....	....
General government	4 622 ..	....	....	....	....	....	....	....	....
Banks	4 623 ..	....	....	....	....	....	....	....	....
Other sectors	4 624 ..	....	....	....	....	....	....	....	....
Money market instruments	4 630 ..	....	....	....	....	....	....	....	....
Monetary authorities	4 631 ..	....	....	....	....	....	....	....	....
General government	4 632 ..	....	....	....	....	....	....	....	....
Banks	4 633 ..	....	....	....	....	....	....	....	....
Other sectors	4 634 ..	....	....	....	....	....	....	....	....
Liabilities	4 652 ..	....	....	....	....	....	....	....	....
Equity securities	4 660 ..	....	....	....	....	....	....	....	....
Banks	4 663 ..	....	....	....	....	....	....	....	....
Other sectors	4 664 ..	....	....	....	....	....	....	....	....
Debt securities	4 669 ..	....	....	....	....	....	....	....	....
Bonds and notes	4 670 ..	....	....	....	....	....	....	....	....
Monetary authorities	4 671 ..	....	....	....	....	....	....	....	....
General government	4 672 ..	....	....	....	....	....	....	....	....
Banks	4 673 ..	....	....	....	....	....	....	....	....
Other sectors	4 674 ..	....	....	....	....	....	....	....	....
Money market instruments	4 680 ..	....	....	....	....	....	....	....	....
Monetary authorities	4 681 ..	....	....	....	....	....	....	....	....
General government	4 682 ..	....	....	....	....	....	....	....	....
Banks	4 683 ..	....	....	....	....	....	....	....	....
Other sectors	4 684 ..	....	....	....	....	....	....	....	....
C. FINANCIAL DERIVATIVES	4 910 ..	....	....	....	....	....	....	....	....
Monetary authorities	4 911 ..	....	....	....	....	....	....	....	....
General government	4 912 ..	....	....	....	....	....	....	....	....
Banks	4 913 ..	....	....	....	....	....	....	....	....
Other sectors	4 914 ..	....	....	....	....	....	....	....	....
Assets	4 900 ..	....	....	....	....	....	....	....	....
Monetary authorities	4 901 ..	....	....	....	....	....	....	....	....
General government	4 902 ..	....	....	....	....	....	....	....	....
Banks	4 903 ..	....	....	....	....	....	....	....	....
Other sectors	4 904 ..	....	....	....	....	....	....	....	....
Liabilities	4 905 ..	....	....	....	....	....	....	....	....
Monetary authorities	4 906 ..	....	....	....	....	....	....	....	....
General government	4 907 ..	....	....	....	....	....	....	....	....
Banks	4 908 ..	....	....	....	....	....	....	....	....
Other sectors	4 909 ..	....	....	....	....	....	....	....	....

Table 2 (Concluded). STANDARD PRESENTATION, 2000–2007

(Millions of U.S. dollars)

	Code	2000	2001	2002	2003	2004	2005	2006	2007
D. OTHER INVESTMENT	4 700 ..	−45.4	137.4	−184.1	−114.3	−88.3	−70.4	−25.6	....
Assets	4 703 ..	....	....	....	....	....	....	....	....
Trade credits	4 706 ..	....	....	....	....	....	....	....	....
General government	4 707 ..	....	....	....	....	....	....	....	....
of which: Short-term	4 709 ..	....	....	....	....	....	....	....	....
Other sectors	4 710 ..	....	....	....	....	....	....	....	....
of which: Short-term	4 712 ..	....	....	....	....	....	....	....	....
Loans	4 714 ..	....	....	....	....	....	....	....	....
Monetary authorities	4 715 ..	....	....	....	....	....	....	....	....
of which: Short-term	4 718 ..	....	....	....	....	....	....	....	....
General government	4 719 ..	....	....	....	....	....	....	....	....
of which: Short-term	4 721 ..	....	....	....	....	....	....	....	....
Banks	4 722 ..	....	....	....	....	....	....	....	....
of which: Short-term	4 724 ..	....	....	....	....	....	....	....	....
Other sectors	4 725 ..	....	....	....	....	....	....	....	....
of which: Short-term	4 727 ..	....	....	....	....	....	....	....	....
Currency and deposits	4 730 ..	....	....	....	....	....	....	....	....
Monetary authorities	4 731 ..	....	....	....	....	....	....	....	....
General government	4 732 ..	....	....	....	....	....	....	....	....
Banks	4 733 ..	....	....	....	....	....	....	....	....
Other sectors	4 734 ..	....	....	....	....	....	....	....	....
Other assets	4 736 ..	....	....	....	....	....	....	....	....
Monetary authorities	4 737 ..	....	....	....	....	....	....	....	....
of which: Short-term	4 739 ..	....	....	....	....	....	....	....	....
General government	4 740 ..	....	....	....	....	....	....	....	....
of which: Short-term	4 742 ..	....	....	....	....	....	....	....	....
Banks	4 743 ..	....	....	....	....	....	....	....	....
of which: Short-term	4 745 ..	....	....	....	....	....	....	....	....
Other sectors	4 746 ..	....	....	....	....	....	....	....	....
of which: Short-term	4 748 ..	....	....	....	....	....	....	....	....
Liabilities	4 753 ..	**−45.4**	**137.4**	**−184.1**	**−114.3**	**−88.3**	**−70.4**	**−25.6**	....
Trade credits	4 756 ..	....	....	....	....	....	....	....	....
General government	4 757 ..	....	....	....	....	....	....	....	....
of which: Short-term	4 759 ..	....	....	....	....	....	....	....	....
Other sectors	4 760 ..	....	....	....	....	....	....	....	....
of which: Short-term	4 762 ..	....	....	....	....	....	....	....	....
Loans	4 764 ..	−56.8	−62.7	−171.2	−98.4	−87.4	−90.2	−35.5	....
Monetary authorities	4 765 ..	....	....	....	....	....	....	....	....
of which: Use of Fund credit and loans from the Fund	4 766 ..	....	....	....	....	....	....	....	....
of which: Short-term	4 768 ..	....	....	....	....	....	....	....	....
General government	4 769 ..	−56.8	−62.7	−171.2	−91.2	−85.2	−87.3	−31.8	....
of which: Short-term	4 771 ..	....	....	....	....	....	....	....	....
Banks	4 772 ..	....	....	....	....	....	....	....	....
of which: Short-term	4 774 ..	....	....	....	....	....	....	....	....
Other sectors	4 775 ..	....	....	....	−7.2	−2.2	−2.9	−3.6	....
of which: Short-term	4 777 ..	....	....	....	....	....	....	....	....
Currency and deposits	4 780 ..	1.1	−.1	.4	.9	4.0	2.9	3.6	....
Monetary authorities	4 781 ..	....	....	....	....	....	....	....	....
General government	4 782 ..	....	....	....	....	....	....	....	....
Banks	4 783 ..	1.1	−.1	.4	.9	4.0	2.9	3.6	....
Other sectors	4 784 ..	....	....	....	....	....	....	....	....
Other liabilities	4 786 ..	10.3	200.1	−13.3	−16.8	−5.0	16.9	6.2	....
Monetary authorities	4 787 ..	7.2	200.8	−11.6	−21.2	−13.4	10.4	−8.0	....
of which: Short-term	4 789 ..	....	....	....	....	....	....	....	....
General government	4 790 ..	....	....	....	....	....	....	....	....
of which: Short-term	4 792 ..	....	....	....	....	....	....	....	....
Banks	4 793 ..	3.1	−.7	−1.7	4.4	8.4	6.5	14.2	....
of which: Short-term	4 795 ..	....	....	....	....	....	....	....	....
Other sectors	4 796 ..	....	....	....	....	....	....	....	....
of which: Short-term	4 798 ..	....	....	....	....	....	....	....	....
E. RESERVE ASSETS	4 802 ..	**23.4**	**−179.8**	**−45.4**	**−38.9**	**−94.0**	**−142.2**	**−422.9**	....
Monetary gold	4 812 ..	....	....	....	....	....	....	....	....
Special drawing rights	4 811 ..	....	−.4	.5	....	.1	−.2	.1	....
Reserve position in the Fund	4 810 ..	....	....	....	....	....	....	....	....
Foreign exchange	4 803 ..	.6	−180.6	11.9	15.6	40.1	−142.7	−421.4	....
Other claims	4 813 ..	22.8	1.2	−57.9	−54.6	−134.2	.6	−1.6	....
NET ERRORS AND OMISSIONS	4 998 ..	**−24.5**	**−14.3**	**−19.1**	**−78.9**	**−142.7**	**−604.6**	**−632.1**	....

Table 3. INTERNATIONAL INVESTMENT POSITION (End-period stocks), 2000–2007

(Millions of U.S. dollars)

	Code	2000	2001	2002	2003	2004	2005	2006	2007
ASSETS	8 995 C.	290.4	460.4	560.5	665.5	792.5	890.7	1,390.4	....
Direct investment abroad	8 505 ..	....	....	....	....	....	....	....	....
Equity capital and reinvested earnings	8 506 ..	....	....	....	....	....	....	....	....
Claims on affiliated enterprises	8 507 ..	....	....	....	....	....	....	....	....
Liabilities to affiliated enterprises	8 508 ..	....	....	....	....	....	....	....	....
Other capital	8 530 ..	....	....	....	....	....	....	....	....
Claims on affiliated enterprises	8 535 ..	....	....	....	....	....	....	....	....
Liabilities to affiliated enterprises	8 540 ..	....	....	....	....	....	....	....	....
Portfolio investment	8 602 ..	....	....	....	....	....	....	....	....
Equity securities	8 610 ..	....	....	....	....	....	....	....	....
Monetary authorities	8 611 ..	....	....	....	....	....	....	....	....
General government	8 612 ..	....	....	....	....	....	....	....	....
Banks	8 613 ..	....	....	....	....	....	....	....	....
Other sectors	8 614 ..	....	....	....	....	....	....	....	....
Debt securities	8 619 ..	....	....	....	....	....	....	....	....
Bonds and notes	8 620 ..	....	....	....	....	....	....	....	....
Monetary authorities	8 621 ..	....	....	....	....	....	....	....	....
General government	8 622 ..	....	....	....	....	....	....	....	....
Banks	8 623 ..	....	....	....	....	....	....	....	....
Other sectors	8 624 ..	....	....	....	....	....	....	....	....
Money market instruments	8 630 ..	....	....	....	....	....	....	....	....
Monetary authorities	8 631 ..	....	....	....	....	....	....	....	....
General government	8 632 ..	....	....	....	....	....	....	....	....
Banks	8 633 ..	....	....	....	....	....	....	....	....
Other sectors	8 634 ..	....	....	....	....	....	....	....	....
Financial derivatives	8 900 ..	....	....	....	....	....	....	....	....
Monetary authorities	8 901 ..	....	....	....	....	....	....	....	....
General government	8 902 ..	....	....	....	....	....	....	....	....
Banks	8 903 ..	....	....	....	....	....	....	....	....
Other sectors	8 904 ..	....	....	....	....	....	....	....	....
Other investment	8 703 ..	....	....	....	....	....	....	....	....
Trade credits	8 706 ..	....	....	....	....	....	....	....	....
General government	8 707 ..	....	....	....	....	....	....	....	....
of which: Short-term	8 709 ..	....	....	....	....	....	....	....	....
Other sectors	8 710 ..	....	....	....	....	....	....	....	....
of which: Short-term	8 712 ..	....	....	....	....	....	....	....	....
Loans	8 714 ..	....	....	....	....	....	....	....	....
Monetary authorities	8 715 ..	....	....	....	....	....	....	....	....
of which: Short-term	8 718 ..	....	....	....	....	....	....	....	....
General government	8 719 ..	....	....	....	....	....	....	....	....
of which: Short-term	8 721 ..	....	....	....	....	....	....	....	....
Banks	8 722 ..	....	....	....	....	....	....	....	....
of which: Short-term	8 724 ..	....	....	....	....	....	....	....	....
Other sectors	8 725 ..	....	....	....	....	....	....	....	....
of which: Short-term	8 727 ..	....	....	....	....	....	....	....	....
Currency and deposits	8 730 ..	....	....	....	....	....	....	....	....
Monetary authorities	8 731 ..	....	....	....	....	....	....	....	....
General government	8 732 ..	....	....	....	....	....	....	....	....
Banks	8 733 ..	....	....	....	....	....	....	....	....
Other sectors	8 734 ..	....	....	....	....	....	....	....	....
Other assets	8 736 ..	....	....	....	....	....	....	....	....
Monetary authorities	8 737 ..	....	....	....	....	....	....	....	....
of which: Short-term	8 739 ..	....	....	....	....	....	....	....	....
General government	8 740 ..	....	....	....	....	....	....	....	....
of which: Short-term	8 742 ..	....	....	....	....	....	....	....	....
Banks	8 743 ..	....	....	....	....	....	....	....	....
of which: Short-term	8 745 ..	....	....	....	....	....	....	....	....
Other sectors	8 746 ..	....	....	....	....	....	....	....	....
of which: Short-term	8 748 ..	....	....	....	....	....	....	....	....
Reserve assets	8 802 ..	290.4	460.4	560.5	665.5	792.5	890.7	1,390.4	....
Monetary gold	8 812 ..	64.0	63.5	81.1	99.8	104.0	119.0	146.2	....
Special drawing rights	8 811 ..	.1	.6	.1	.1	....	.2	.2	.4
Reserve position in the Fund	8 810 ..	....	....	....	....	....	....	....	....
Foreign exchange	8 803 ..	24.8	202.6	207.0	210.1	177.9	765.2	1,235.8	....
Other claims	8 813 ..	201.4	193.7	272.3	355.5	510.7	6.3	8.2	....

Table 3 (Concluded). INTERNATIONAL INVESTMENT POSITION (End-period stocks), 2000–2007

(Millions of U.S. dollars)

	Code	2000	2001	2002	2003	2004	2005	2006	2007
LIABILITIES	8 995 D.	**8,321.0**	**8,369.7**	**9,022.6**	**10,101.4**	**10,688.3**	**10,081.1**	**10,868.9**	....
Direct investment in Myanmar	8 555 ..	**3,211.0**	**3,304.8**	**3,735.0**	**4,392.6**	**4,814.6**	**4,714.9**	**5,247.4**	....
Equity capital and reinvested earnings	8 556 ..	3,211.0	3,304.8	3,735.0	4,392.6	4,814.6	4,714.9	5,247.4	....
Claims on direct investors	8 557 ..	....	....	....	....	....	....	5,247.4	....
Liabilities to direct investors	8 558 ..	3,211.0	3,304.8	3,735.0	4,392.6	4,814.6	4,714.9	....	....
Other capital	8 580 ..	....	....	....	....	....	....	....	....
Claims on direct investors	8 585 ..	....	....	....	....	....	....	....	....
Liabilities to direct investors	8 590 ..	....	....	....	....	....	....	....	....
Portfolio investment	8 652 ..	....	....	....	....	....	....	....	....
Equity securities	8 660 ..	....	....	....	....	....	....	....	....
Banks	8 663 ..	....	....	....	....	....	....	....	....
Other sectors	8 664 ..	....	....	....	....	....	....	....	....
Debt securities	8 669 ..	....	....	....	....	....	....	....	....
Bonds and notes	8 670 ..	....	....	....	....	....	....	....	....
Monetary authorities	8 671 ..	....	....	....	....	....	....	....	....
General government	8 672 ..	....	....	....	....	....	....	....	....
Banks	8 673 ..	....	....	....	....	....	....	....	....
Other sectors	8 674 ..	....	....	....	....	....	....	....	....
Money market instruments	8 680 ..	....	....	....	....	....	....	....	....
Monetary authorities	8 681 ..	....	....	....	....	....	....	....	....
General government	8 682 ..	....	....	....	....	....	....	....	....
Banks	8 683 ..	....	....	....	....	....	....	....	....
Other sectors	8 684 ..	....	....	....	....	....	....	....	....
Financial derivatives	8 905 ..	....	....	....	....	....	....	....	....
Monetary authorities	8 906 ..	....	....	....	....	....	....	....	....
General government	8 907 ..	....	....	....	....	....	....	....	....
Banks	8 908 ..	....	....	....	....	....	....	....	....
Other sectors	8 909 ..	....	....	....	....	....	....	....	....
Other investment	8 753 ..	**5,109.9**	**5,064.9**	**5,287.6**	**5,708.7**	**5,873.6**	**5,366.3**	**5,621.5**	....
Trade credits	8 756 ..	....	....	....	....	....	....	....	....
General government	8 757 ..	....	....	....	....	....	....	....	....
of which: Short-term	8 759 ..	....	....	....	....	....	....	....	....
Other sectors	8 760 ..	....	....	....	....	....	....	....	....
of which: Short-term	8 762 ..	....	....	....	....	....	....	....	....
Loans	8 764 ..	5,000.0	4,761.0	4,971.9	5,365.0	5,515.4	5,016.8	5,243.5	....
Monetary authorities	8 765 ..	....	....	....	....	....	....	....	....
of which: Use of Fund credit and loans from the Fund....	8 766 ..	....	....	....	....	....	....	....	....
of which: Short-term	8 768 ..	....	....	....	....	....	....	....	....
General government	8 769 ..	....	....	....	....	....	....	....	....
of which: Short-term	8 771 ..	....	....	....	....	....	....	....	....
Banks	8 772 ..	....	....	....	....	....	....	....	....
of which: Short-term	8 774 ..	....	....	....	....	....	....	....	....
Other sectors	8 775 ..	....	....	....	....	....	....	....	....
of which: Short-term	8 777 ..	....	....	....	....	....	....	....	....
Currency and deposits	8 780 ..	1.1	1.0	1.5	2.5	6.8	9.0	13.3	....
Monetary authorities	8 781 ..	....	....	....	....	....	....	....	....
General government	8 782 ..	....	....	....	....	....	....	....	....
Banks	8 783 ..	1.1	1.0	1.5	2.5	6.8	9.0	13.3	....
Other sectors	8 784 ..	....	....	....	....	....	....	....	....
Other liabilities	8 786 ..	108.8	302.9	314.3	341.2	351.4	340.5	364.7	....
Monetary authorities	8 787 ..	102.1	297.1	309.6	315.9	316.1	301.6	309.3	....
of which: Short-term	8 789 ..	....	....	....	....	....	....	....	....
General government	8 790 ..	....	....	....	....	....	....	....	....
of which: Short-term	8 792 ..	....	....	....	....	....	....	....	....
Banks	8 793 ..	6.8	5.9	4.7	25.3	35.3	38.9	55.4	....
of which: Short-term	8 795 ..	....	....	....	....	....	....	....	....
Other sectors	8 796 ..	....	....	....	....	....	....	....	....
of which: Short-term	8 798 ..	....	....	....	....	....	....	....	....
NET INTERNATIONAL INVESTMENT POSITION	8 995 ..	**−8,030.6**	**−7,909.3**	**−8,462.1**	**−9,435.8**	**−9,895.7**	**−9,190.4**	**−9,478.5**	....
Conversion rates: kyats per U.S. dollar (end of period)	0 102 ..	**6.5303**	**6.7704**	**6.2584**	**5.7259**	**5.4787**	**5.9530**	**5.6558**	**5.3842**

2008, International Monetary Fund: *Balance of Payments Statistics Yearbook*

Table 1. ANALYTIC PRESENTATION, 2000–2007

(Millions of U.S. dollars)

	Code	2000	2001	2002	2003	2004	2005	2006	2007
A. Current Account[1]	4 993 Z.	173.3	−20.4	56.7	204.4	384.5	266.8	1,015.8	693.1
Goods: exports f.o.b.	2 100 ..	1,309.5	1,147.0	1,071.6	1,262.0	1,827.5	2,069.9	2,646.6	2,921.6
Goods: imports f.o.b.	3 100 ..	−1,310.0	−1,349.0	−1,282.5	−1,726.0	−2,110.3	−2,326.2	−2,544.2	−3,101.6
Balance on Goods	4 100 ..	*−.5*	*−202.0*	*−210.9*	*−464.0*	*−282.8*	*−256.3*	*102.4*	*−180.0*
Services: credit	2 200 ..	221.9	293.9	272.5	414.5	475.4	412.6	525.7	599.1
Services: debit	3 200 ..	−332.6	−275.6	−233.7	−276.3	−420.2	−368.8	−429.7	−513.6
Balance on Goods and Services	4 991 ..	*−111.2*	*−183.7*	*−172.1*	*−325.9*	*−227.7*	*−212.4*	*198.4*	*−94.5*
Income: credit	2 300 ..	128.4	120.9	110.2	184.8	217.0	225.4	256.0	273.2
Income: debit	3 300 ..	−226.2	−268.7	−122.1	−53.6	−212.1	−352.6	−318.9	−431.5
Balance on Goods, Services, and Income	4 992 ..	*−209.0*	*−331.5*	*−184.0*	*−194.6*	*−222.8*	*−339.6*	*135.6*	*−252.9*
Current transfers: credit	2 379 Z.	419.2	346.7	270.4	426.2	642.1	651.1	925.6	998.3
Current transfers: debit	3 379 ..	−37.0	−35.6	−29.7	−27.2	−34.9	−44.7	−45.4	−52.3
B. Capital Account[1]	4 994 Z.	112.6	95.8	40.7	68.3	77.2	79.6	83.3	83.4
Capital account: credit	2 994 Z.	112.9	96.0	40.9	68.6	77.6	80.2	83.8	83.9
Capital account: debit	3 994 ..	−.3	−.2	−.2	−.4	−.5	−.5	−.5	−.5
Total, Groups A Plus B	4 981 ..	*285.9*	*75.4*	*97.4*	*272.7*	*461.6*	*346.4*	*1,099.1*	*776.4*
C. Financial Account[1]	4 995 W.	−493.7	−435.3	−365.7	−581.9	−779.0	−874.8	−1,525.3	−1,467.0
Direct investment abroad	4 505 ..	−1.7	12.5	5.0	11.5	22.7	12.3	12.6	−2.7
Direct investment in Namibia	4 555 Z.	118.9	36.1	51.2	33.3	88.2	166.1	−30.9	169.9
Portfolio investment assets	4 602 ..	−470.2	−451.7	−419.1	−612.3	−825.5	−1,052.8	−1,133.0	−1,482.9
Equity securities	4 610 ..	−304.9	−319.2	−262.4	−400.9	−500.4	−754.2	−785.7	−1,210.6
Debt securities	4 619 ..	−165.3	−132.4	−156.7	−211.5	−325.0	−298.7	−347.3	−272.3
Portfolio investment liabilities	4 652 Z.	34.7	25.9	8.2	3.9	4.5	5.1	4.7	4.5
Equity securities	4 660 ..	34.7	25.9	8.2	3.9	4.5	5.1	4.7	4.5
Debt securities	4 669 Z.	....	....	....	....	....	....	....	....
Financial derivatives	4 910 ..	....	....	....	....	....	....	....	....
Financial derivatives assets	4 900 ..	....	....	....	....	....	....	....	....
Financial derivatives liabilities	4 905 ..	....	....	....	....	....	....	....	....
Other investment assets	4 703 ..	−155.6	−42.4	8.6	23.3	44.6	43.2	−353.7	136.2
Monetary authorities	4 701 ..	....	....	....	....	....	....	....	....
General government	4 704 ..	−3.4	−2.8	−2.3	−4.3	−6.2	−6.3	−5.9	−5.6
Banks	4 705 ..	−118.7	34.4	47.7	28.1	59.6	51.1	−356.2	191.4
Other sectors	4 728 ..	−33.5	−73.9	−36.8	−.5	−8.8	−1.6	8.3	−49.6
Other investment liabilities	4 753 W.	−19.8	−15.9	−19.7	−41.5	−113.6	−48.6	−25.0	−292.0
Monetary authorities	4 753 WA	....	....	....	....	....	....	....	....
General government	4 753 ZB	−2.1	−2.0	−2.4	−7.3	−4.5	−16.5	−11.5	−19.2
Banks	4 753 ZC	....	....	....	....	....	.9	51.6	−2.7
Other sectors	4 753 ZD	−17.7	−13.9	−17.3	−34.2	−109.1	−32.9	−65.1	−270.1
Total, Groups A Through C	4 983 ..	*−207.8*	*−360.0*	*−268.3*	*−309.2*	*−317.4*	*−528.4*	*−426.2*	*−690.6*
D. Net Errors and Omissions	4 998 ..	−4.0	−28.2	16.1	−88.8	115.3	127.9	121.6	490.0
Total, Groups A Through D	4 984 ..	*−211.8*	*−388.2*	*−252.2*	*−398.1*	*−202.1*	*−400.5*	*−304.5*	*−200.5*
E. Reserves and Related Items	4 802 A.	211.8	388.2	252.2	398.1	202.1	400.5	304.5	200.5
Reserve assets	4 802 ..	−17.2	−70.2	−8.7	107.2	14.2	−1.1	−163.1	−570.8
Use of Fund credit and loans	4 766 ..	....	....	....	....	....	....	....	....
Exceptional financing	4 920 ..	229.0	458.4	260.8	290.8	187.9	401.6	467.6	771.4
Conversion rates: Namibia dollars per U.S. dollar	0 101 ..	6.940	8.609	10.541	7.565	6.460	6.359	6.772	7.045

[1] Excludes components that have been classified in the categories of Group E.

Table 2. STANDARD PRESENTATION, 2000–2007

(Millions of U.S. dollars)

	Code	2000	2001	2002	2003	2004	2005	2006	2007
CURRENT ACCOUNT	4 993 ..	**227.1**	**20.8**	**90.8**	**265.7**	**446.3**	**333.4**	**1,081.7**	**747.4**
A. GOODS	4 100 ..	**−.5**	**−202.0**	**−210.9**	**−464.0**	**−282.8**	**−256.3**	**102.4**	**−180.0**
Credit	2 100 ..	**1,309.5**	**1,147.0**	**1,071.6**	**1,262.0**	**1,827.5**	**2,069.9**	**2,646.6**	**2,921.6**
General merchandise: exports f.o.b.	2 110 ..	1,309.5	1,147.0	1,071.6	1,262.0	1,827.5	2,069.9	2,646.6	2,921.6
Goods for processing: exports f.o.b.	2 150 ..	....	....	....	....	....	....	....	....
Repairs on goods	2 160 ..	....	....	....	....	....	....	....	....
Goods procured in ports by carriers	2 170 ..	....	....	....	....	....	....	....	....
Nonmonetary gold	2 180 ..	....	....	....	....	....	....	....	....
Debit	3 100 ..	**−1,310.0**	**−1,349.0**	**−1,282.5**	**−1,726.0**	**−2,110.3**	**−2,326.2**	**−2,544.2**	**−3,101.6**
General merchandise: imports f.o.b.	3 110 ..	−1,310.0	−1,349.0	−1,282.5	−1,726.0	−2,110.3	−2,326.2	−2,544.2	−3,101.6
Goods for processing: imports f.o.b.	3 150 ..	....	....	....	....	....	....	....	....
Repairs on goods	3 160 ..	....	....	....	....	....	....	....	....
Goods procured in ports by carriers	3 170 ..	....	....	....	....	....	....	....	....
Nonmonetary gold	3 180 ..	....	....	....	....	....	....	....	....
B. SERVICES	4 200 ..	**−110.7**	**18.3**	**38.8**	**138.2**	**55.2**	**43.8**	**96.0**	**85.5**
Total credit	2 200 ..	*221.9*	*293.9*	*272.5*	*414.5*	*475.4*	*412.6*	*525.7*	*599.1*
Total debit	3 200 ..	*−332.6*	*−275.6*	*−233.7*	*−276.3*	*−420.2*	*−368.8*	*−429.7*	*−513.6*
Transportation services, credit	2 205 ..	**37.5**	**37.0**	**35.9**	**54.1**	**25.5**	**22.5**	**101.5**	**120.2**
Passenger	2 850 ..	*33.0*	*28.3*	*32.8*	*49.6*	*20.8*	*14.1*	*92.4*	*108.4*
Freight	2 851 ..	....	....	....	....	....	....	....	*.4*
Other	2 852 ..	*4.5*	*8.6*	*3.0*	*4.5*	*4.8*	*8.4*	*9.1*	*11.4*
Sea transport, passenger	2 207 ..	....	....	....	....	....	....	....	....
Sea transport, freight	2 208 ..	....	....	....	....	....	....	....	....
Sea transport, other	2 209 ..	....	....	....	....	....	....	....	....
Air transport, passenger	2 211 ..	33.0	28.3	32.8	49.6	20.8	14.1	92.4	108.4
Air transport, freight	2 212 ..	....	....	....	....	....	....	....	....
Air transport, other	2 213 ..	4.5	8.6	3.0	4.5	4.8	8.4	9.1	11.4
Other transport, passenger	2 215 ..	....	....	....	....	....	....	....	....
Other transport, freight	2 216 ..	....	....	....	....	....	....	....	.4
Other transport, other	2 217 ..	....	....	....	....	....	....	....	....
Transportation services, debit	3 205 ..	**−90.8**	**−82.4**	**−73.1**	**−61.1**	**−135.5**	**−130.7**	**−149.8**	**−241.0**
Passenger	3 850 ..	....	....	....	....	....	....	....	....
Freight	3 851 ..	*−90.8*	*−82.4*	*−73.1*	*−61.1*	*−135.5*	*−130.7*	*−149.8*	*−241.0*
Other	3 852 ..	....	....	....	....	....	....	....	....
Sea transport, passenger	3 207 ..	....	....	....	....	....	....	....	....
Sea transport, freight	3 208 ..	−22.7	−20.6	−18.3	−15.3	−33.9	−32.7	−37.4	−60.3
Sea transport, other	3 209 ..	....	....	....	....	....	....	....	....
Air transport, passenger	3 211 ..	....	....	....	....	....	....	....	....
Air transport, freight	3 212 ..	−22.7	−20.6	−18.3	−15.3	−33.9	−32.7	−37.4	−60.3
Air transport, other	3 213 ..	....	....	....	....	....	....	....	....
Other transport, passenger	3 215 ..	....	....	....	....	....	....	....	....
Other transport, freight	3 216 ..	−45.4	−41.2	−36.6	−30.6	−67.8	−65.4	−74.9	−120.5
Other transport, other	3 217 ..	....	....	....	....	....	....	....	....
Travel, credit	2 236 ..	**159.8**	**236.3**	**218.1**	**332.5**	**404.8**	**349.0**	**381.3**	**434.1**
Business travel	2 237 ..	83.9	131.4	99.4	81.5	89.9	89.4	60.7	48.6
Personal travel	2 240 ..	75.9	105.0	118.7	251.0	314.9	259.6	320.6	385.5
Travel, debit	3 236 ..	**−85.6**	**−70.5**	**−64.8**	**−101.0**	**−122.8**	**−108.2**	**−118.3**	**−132.2**
Business travel	3 237 ..	−41.9	−19.7	−14.9	−12.2	−13.5	−13.4	−9.1	−7.3
Personal travel	3 240 ..	−43.7	−50.8	−49.8	−88.8	−109.3	−94.8	−109.2	−124.9
Other services, credit	2 200 BA ..	**24.6**	**20.6**	**18.5**	**27.9**	**45.0**	**41.1**	**42.8**	**44.8**
Communications	2 245 ..	5.6	4.8	4.0	8.5	15.5	16.8	15.7	15.0
Construction	2 249 ..	1.4	1.1	1.5	....	....	....	....	....
Insurance	2 253 ..	−1.8	−.3	.1	....	....	.1	1.7	5.1
Financial	2 260 ..	2.5	1.2	1.3	....	....	....	....	....
Computer and information	2 262 ..	.5	....	....	....	.1	....	1.2	1.2
Royalties and licence fees	2 266 ..	5.5	4.7	3.8	....	....	....	....	....
Other business services	2 268 ..	.5	.4	.4	3.4	9.7	2.4	4.0	4.2
Personal, cultural, and recreational	2 287 ..	....	....	....	....	....	....	....	....
Government, n.i.e.	2 291 ..	10.4	8.8	7.3	16.0	19.8	21.7	20.2	19.3
Other services, debit	3 200 BA ..	**−156.2**	**−122.7**	**−95.8**	**−114.2**	**−161.9**	**−129.9**	**−161.6**	**−140.3**
Communications	3 245 ..	−.3	−.2	−.2	−.2	−.3	−.3	−.3	−.3
Construction	3 249 ..	−27.6	−22.6	−18.4	−2.7	−4.4	−3.9	−24.6	−9.0
Insurance	3 253 ..	−16.6	−13.8	−11.8	−17.5	−17.7	−9.4	−18.8	−27.0
Financial	3 260 ..	−3.4	−2.1	−1.3	−5.4	−3.1	−9.5	−4.4	−4.9
Computer and information	3 262 ..	−14.2	−13.4	−8.8	−12.3	−14.6	−13.1	−21.1	−15.5
Royalties and licence fees	3 266 ..	−8.1	....	−1.7	−3.6	−3.2	−1.7	−3.0	−1.9
Other business services	3 268 ..	−74.0	−60.1	−44.4	−65.1	−109.5	−82.7	−80.6	−73.2
Personal, cultural, and recreational	3 287 ..	....	....	....	....	....	....	....	....
Government, n.i.e.	3 291 ..	−12.1	−10.5	−9.3	−7.5	−9.2	−9.3	−8.8	−8.4

Table 2 (Continued). STANDARD PRESENTATION, 2000–2007

(Millions of U.S. dollars)

	Code	2000	2001	2002	2003	2004	2005	2006	2007
C. INCOME	4 300	**−97.8**	**−147.8**	**−11.9**	**131.3**	**4.9**	**−127.2**	**−62.9**	**−158.4**
Total credit	2 300	*128.4*	*120.9*	*110.2*	*184.8*	*217.0*	*225.4*	*256.0*	*273.2*
Total debit	3 300	*−226.2*	*−268.7*	*−122.1*	*−53.6*	*−212.1*	*−352.6*	*−318.9*	*−431.5*
Compensation of employees, credit	2 310	**4.7**	**4.7**	**4.3**	**7.0**	**8.7**	**10.5**	**9.9**	**9.5**
Compensation of employees, debit	3 310	**−6.1**	**−5.6**	**−5.7**	**−11.1**	**−12.9**	**−14.1**	**−15.7**	**−11.8**
Investment income, credit	2 320	**123.8**	**116.2**	**105.9**	**177.8**	**208.3**	**214.9**	**246.1**	**263.7**
Direct investment income	2 330	−.2	−2.0	−.9	−.5	1.4	7.8	.7	.8
Dividends and distributed branch profits	2 332	.2	.1	.1	.2	.3	.3	.2	.2
Reinvested earnings and undistributed branch profits	2 333	−.4	−2.1	−1.0	−1.8	−2.2	2.1	−1.3	−.5
Income on debt (interest)	2 334	....	....	....	1.1	3.4	5.5	1.7	1.1
Portfolio investment income	2 339	77.4	76.2	66.9	139.4	165.0	163.9	207.6	204.3
Income on equity	2 340	48.7	41.5	35.0	80.8	84.0	88.0	145.0	134.8
Income on bonds and notes	2 350	.6	.6	1.7	2.8	2.8	3.4	3.1	3.0
Income on money market instruments	2 360	28.1	34.1	30.3	55.8	78.2	72.5	59.6	66.6
Other investment income	2 370	46.6	42.0	39.9	38.9	41.9	43.2	37.8	58.6
Investment income, debit	3 320	**−220.2**	**−263.1**	**−116.4**	**−42.5**	**−199.2**	**−338.5**	**−303.2**	**−419.8**
Direct investment income	3 330	−193.7	−242.2	−95.4	2.7	−143.5	−285.2	−257.3	−369.5
Dividends and distributed branch profits	3 332	−84.1	−130.9	−83.5	−64.8	−68.8	−73.6	−96.0	−183.8
Reinvested earnings and undistributed branch profits	3 333	−109.2	−111.0	−11.0	69.8	−70.0	−206.3	−156.2	−185.8
Income on debt (interest)	3 334	−.4	−.3	−.9	−2.4	−4.7	−5.3	−5.1	.1
Portfolio investment income	3 339	−11.1	−9.0	−7.8	−11.0	−23.6	−25.4	−24.9	−24.2
Income on equity	3 340	....	....	....	....	....	....	−.6	−.8
Income on bonds and notes	3 350	−11.1	−9.0	−7.5	−10.0	−21.5	−22.5	−21.7	−20.8
Income on money market instruments	3 360	....	....	−.3	−1.0	−2.1	−2.9	−2.6	−2.5
Other investment income	3 370	−15.4	−12.0	−13.2	−34.2	−32.1	−27.9	−21.1	−26.1
D. CURRENT TRANSFERS	4 379	**436.1**	**352.3**	**274.8**	**460.3**	**669.1**	**673.0**	**946.1**	**1,000.3**
Credit	2 379	**473.0**	**387.9**	**304.4**	**487.5**	**703.9**	**717.7**	**991.5**	**1,052.7**
General government	2 380	452.4	371.2	289.9	462.1	676.8	692.0	964.3	1,029.7
Other sectors	2 390	20.6	16.8	14.6	25.4	27.1	25.8	27.2	22.9
Workers' remittances	2 391	4.5	3.8	3.2	4.8	5.9	7.1	6.5	6.2
Other current transfers	2 392	16.1	13.0	11.3	20.6	21.2	18.7	20.7	16.7
Debit	3 379	**−37.0**	**−35.6**	**−29.7**	**−27.2**	**−34.9**	**−44.7**	**−45.4**	**−52.3**
General government	3 380	−32.8	−32.0	−26.0	−23.0	−30.0	−39.9	−40.8	−47.9
Other sectors	3 390	−4.2	−3.7	−3.7	−4.2	−4.8	−4.8	−4.6	−4.4
Workers' remittances	3 391	−2.6	−2.3	−2.3	−3.6	−4.2	−4.2	−4.0	−3.8
Other current transfers	3 392	−1.6	−1.4	−1.3	−.5	−.6	−.6	−.6	−.6
CAPITAL AND FINANCIAL ACCOUNT	4 996	**−223.1**	**7.4**	**−106.9**	**−176.9**	**−561.6**	**−461.3**	**−1,203.3**	**−1,237.5**
CAPITAL ACCOUNT	4 994	**112.6**	**95.8**	**40.7**	**68.3**	**77.2**	**79.6**	**83.3**	**83.4**
Total credit	2 994	*112.9*	*96.0*	*40.9*	*68.6*	*77.6*	*80.2*	*83.8*	*83.9*
Total debit	3 994	*−.3*	*−.2*	*−.2*	*−.4*	*−.5*	*−.5*	*−.5*	*−.5*
Capital transfers, credit	2 400	**112.9**	**96.0**	**40.9**	**68.6**	**77.6**	**80.2**	**83.8**	**83.9**
General government	2 401	112.1	95.3	40.2	65.1	73.6	76.0	80.0	80.2
Debt forgiveness	2 402	....	....	....	....	....	....	....	....
Other capital transfers	2 410	112.1	95.3	40.2	65.1	73.6	76.0	80.0	80.2
Other sectors	2 430	.8	.7	.7	3.5	4.0	4.1	3.8	3.7
Migrants' transfers	2 431	.3	.4	.4	.4	.6	.5	.5	.5
Debt forgiveness	2 432	....	....	....	....	....	....	....	....
Other capital transfers	2 440	.5	.3	.3	3.0	3.4	3.6	3.4	3.2
Capital transfers, debit	3 400	**−.3**	**−.2**	**−.2**	**−.4**	**−.5**	**−.5**	**−.5**	**−.5**
General government	3 401	....	....	....	....	....	....	....	....
Debt forgiveness	3 402	....	....	....	....	....	....	....	....
Other capital transfers	3 410	....	....	....	....	....	....	....	....
Other sectors	3 430	−.3	−.2	−.2	−.4	−.5	−.5	−.5	−.5
Migrants' transfers	3 431	−.3	−.2	−.2	−.4	−.5	−.5	−.5	−.5
Debt forgiveness	3 432	....	....	....	....	....	....	....	....
Other capital transfers	3 440	....	....	....	....	....	....	....	....
Nonproduced nonfinancial assets, credit	2 480	....	....	....	....	....	....	....	....
Nonproduced nonfinancial assets, debit	3 480	....	....	....	....	....	....	....	....

Table 2 (Continued). STANDARD PRESENTATION, 2000–2007

(Millions of U.S. dollars)

	Code	2000	2001	2002	2003	2004	2005	2006	2007
FINANCIAL ACCOUNT	4 995	**−335.7**	**−88.4**	**−147.6**	**−245.1**	**−638.7**	**−540.9**	**−1,286.6**	**−1,320.8**
A. DIRECT INVESTMENT	4 500	**184.3**	**381.7**	**179.4**	**157.6**	**246.1**	**403.1**	**403.5**	**718.5**
Direct investment abroad	4 505	**−1.7**	**12.5**	**5.0**	**11.5**	**22.7**	**12.3**	**12.6**	**−2.7**
Equity capital	4 510	−1.0	−.1	.9	1.2	1.2	1.5	5.4	−2.8
Claims on affiliated enterprises	4 515	−1.0	−.1	.9	1.2	1.2	1.5	5.4	−2.8
Liabilities to affiliated enterprises	4 520	....	....	....	....	....	....	....	....
Reinvested earnings	4 525	.4	2.1	1.0	1.8	2.2	−2.1	1.3	.5
Other capital	4 530	−1.1	10.5	3.2	8.6	19.2	12.8	5.9	−.5
Claims on affiliated enterprises	4 535	−1.1	10.5	3.2	8.6	19.2	12.8	5.9	−.5
Liabilities to affiliated enterprises	4 540	....	....	....	....	....	....	....	....
Direct investment in Namibia	4 555	**186.0**	**369.1**	**174.4**	**146.1**	**223.4**	**390.8**	**391.0**	**721.3**
Equity capital	4 560	82.5	344.5	132.3	111.3	133.3	222.9	420.1	549.6
Claims on direct investors	4 565	....	....	....	....	....	....	....	....
Liabilities to direct investors	4 570	82.5	344.5	132.3	111.3	133.3	222.9	420.1	549.6
Reinvested earnings	4 575	109.2	111.0	11.0	−69.8	70.0	206.3	156.2	185.8
Other capital	4 580	−5.8	−86.4	31.1	104.7	20.0	−38.3	−185.3	−14.2
Claims on direct investors	4 585	−10.4	−10.2	26.9	81.0	−.2	−1.9	−218.8	51.5
Liabilities to direct investors	4 590	4.6	−76.2	4.2	23.7	20.2	−36.4	33.5	−65.7
B. PORTFOLIO INVESTMENT	4 600	**−455.7**	**−439.7**	**−431.8**	**−635.2**	**−845.4**	**−1,045.6**	**−1,125.8**	**−1,476.6**
Assets	4 602	**−470.2**	**−451.7**	**−419.1**	**−612.3**	**−825.5**	**−1,052.8**	**−1,133.0**	**−1,482.9**
Equity securities	4 610	−304.9	−319.2	−262.4	−400.9	−500.4	−754.2	−785.7	−1,210.6
Monetary authorities	4 611	....	....	....	....	....	....	....	....
General government	4 612	....	....	....	....	....	....	....	....
Banks	4 613	....	....	....	....	....	....	....	....
Other sectors	4 614	−304.9	−319.2	−262.4	−400.9	−500.4	−754.2	−785.7	−1,210.6
Debt securities	4 619	−165.3	−132.4	−156.7	−211.5	−325.0	−298.7	−347.3	−272.3
Bonds and notes	4 620	....	....	....	....	....	....	....	....
Monetary authorities	4 621	....	....	....	....	....	....	....	....
General government	4 622	....	....	....	....	....	....	....	....
Banks	4 623	....	....	....	....	....	....	....	....
Other sectors	4 624	....	....	....	....	....	....	....	....
Money market instruments	4 630	−165.3	−132.4	−156.7	−211.5	−325.0	−298.7	−347.3	−272.3
Monetary authorities	4 631	....	....	....	....	....	....	....	....
General government	4 632	....	....	....	....	....	....	....	....
Banks	4 633	....	....	....	....	....	....	....	....
Other sectors	4 634	−165.3	−132.4	−156.7	−211.5	−325.0	−298.7	−347.3	−272.3
Liabilities	4 652	**14.5**	**11.9**	**−12.7**	**−22.9**	**−19.9**	**7.3**	**7.1**	**6.3**
Equity securities	4 660	34.7	25.9	8.2	3.9	4.5	5.1	4.7	4.5
Banks	4 663	.1	.1	.1	.1	.1	.1	.1	.1
Other sectors	4 664	34.7	25.8	8.1	3.8	4.4	4.9	4.6	4.4
Debt securities	4 669	−20.3	−14.0	−20.8	−26.8	−24.5	2.2	2.4	1.8
Bonds and notes	4 670	−20.3	−14.0	−20.8	−26.8	−24.5	2.2	2.4	1.8
Monetary authorities	4 671	....	....	....	....	....	....	....	....
General government	4 672	−20.3	−14.0	−20.8	−26.8	−24.5	2.2	2.4	1.8
Banks	4 673	....	....	....	....	....	....	....	....
Other sectors	4 674	....	....	....	....	....	....	....	....
Money market instruments	4 680	....	....	....	....	....	....	....	....
Monetary authorities	4 681	....	....	....	....	....	....	....	....
General government	4 682	....	....	....	....	....	....	....	....
Banks	4 683	....	....	....	....	....	....	....	....
Other sectors	4 684	....	....	....	....	....	....	....	....
C. FINANCIAL DERIVATIVES	4 910	....	....	....	....	....	....	....	....
Monetary authorities	4 911	....	....	....	....	....	....	....	....
General government	4 912	....	....	....	....	....	....	....	....
Banks	4 913	....	....	....	....	....	....	....	....
Other sectors	4 914	....	....	....	....	....	....	....	....
Assets	4 900	....	....	....	....	....	....	....	....
Monetary authorities	4 901	....	....	....	....	....	....	....	....
General government	4 902	....	....	....	....	....	....	....	....
Banks	4 903	....	....	....	....	....	....	....	....
Other sectors	4 904	....	....	....	....	....	....	....	....
Liabilities	4 905	....	....	....	....	....	....	....	....
Monetary authorities	4 906	....	....	....	....	....	....	....	....
General government	4 907	....	....	....	....	....	....	....	....
Banks	4 908	....	....	....	....	....	....	....	....
Other sectors	4 909	....	....	....	....	....	....	....	....

Table 2 (Concluded). STANDARD PRESENTATION, 2000–2007

(Millions of U.S. dollars)

	Code	2000	2001	2002	2003	2004	2005	2006	2007
D. OTHER INVESTMENT	4 700 ..	**−47.1**	**39.9**	**113.4**	**125.3**	**−53.6**	**102.6**	**−401.3**	**8.1**
Assets	4 703 ..	−155.6	−42.4	8.6	23.3	44.6	43.2	−353.7	136.2
Trade credits	4 706 ..	....	....	....	....	....	....	....	....
General government	4 707 ..	....	....	....	....	....	....	....	....
of which: Short-term	4 709 ..	....	....	....	....	....	....	....	....
Other sectors	4 710 ..	....	....	....	....	....	....	....	....
of which: Short-term	4 712 ..	....	....	....	....	....	....	....	....
Loans	4 714 ..	−13.5	−54.2	−19.1	4.4	24.5	37.3	−6.1	−11.5
Monetary authorities	4 715 ..	....	....	....	....	....	....	....	....
of which: Short-term	4 718 ..	....	....	....	....	....	....	....	....
General government	4 719 ..	....	....	....	....	....	....	....	....
of which: Short-term	4 721 ..	....	....	....	....	....	....	....	....
Banks	4 722 ..	....	....	....	6.0	6.9	14.5	−1.6	36.5
of which: Short-term	4 724 ..	....	....	....	5.2	−10.9	18.3	−2.7	36.0
Other sectors	4 725 ..	−13.5	−54.2	−19.1	−1.6	17.6	22.8	−4.6	−48.0
of which: Short-term	4 727 ..	−13.5	−54.2	−19.1	−1.6	17.6	22.8	−4.6	−48.0
Currency and deposits	4 730 ..	−119.3	33.9	47.0	21.7	53.3	35.2	−357.1	152.0
Monetary authorities	4 731 ..	....	....	....	....	....	....	....	....
General government	4 732 ..	....	....	....	....	....	....	....	....
Banks	4 733 ..	−118.7	34.4	47.5	22.3	54.0	36.0	−356.4	152.7
Other sectors	4 734 ..	−.6	−.5	−.4	−.6	−.7	−.8	−.7	−.7
Other assets	4 736 ..	−22.8	−22.0	−19.3	−2.9	−33.1	−29.3	9.5	−4.3
Monetary authorities	4 737 ..	....	....	....	....	....	....	....	....
of which: Short-term	4 739 ..	....	....	....	....	....	....	....	....
General government	4 740 ..	−3.4	−2.8	−2.3	−4.3	−6.2	−6.3	−5.9	−5.6
of which: Short-term	4 742 ..	....	....	....	....	....	....	....	....
Banks	4 743 ..	....	....	.2	−.3	−1.2	.6	1.8	2.3
of which: Short-term	4 745 ..	....	....	.2	−.3	−1.2	.6	1.8	2.3
Other sectors	4 746 ..	−19.4	−19.2	−17.2	1.7	−25.7	−23.7	13.6	−.9
of which: Short-term	4 748 ..	....	....	....	....	....	....	....	....
Liabilities	4 753 ..	**108.5**	**82.3**	**104.8**	**102.0**	**−98.2**	**59.4**	**−47.5**	**−128.1**
Trade credits	4 756 ..	....	....	....	....	....	....	....	....
General government	4 757 ..	....	....	....	....	....	....	....	....
of which: Short-term	4 759 ..	....	....	....	....	....	....	....	....
Other sectors	4 760 ..	....	....	....	....	....	....	....	....
of which: Short-term	4 762 ..	....	....	....	....	....	....	....	....
Loans	4 764 ..	108.5	82.3	104.8	102.0	−98.2	59.4	−47.5	−128.1
Monetary authorities	4 765 ..	....	....	....	....	....	....	....	....
of which: Use of Fund credit and loans from the Fund..	4 766 ..	....	....	....	....	....	....	....	....
of which: Short-term	4 768 ..	....	....	....	....	....	....	....	....
General government	4 769 ..	12.3	13.5	84.1	42.2	14.1	14.2	18.5	6.8
of which: Short-term	4 771 ..	....	....	....	....	....	....	....	....
Banks	4 772 ..	79.5	66.6	32.1	36.2	−4.1	61.6	−77.3	−11.7
of which: Short-term	4 774 ..	79.5	66.6	32.1	36.2	−5.0	8.7	−191.6	−9.2
Other sectors	4 775 ..	16.6	2.1	−11.4	23.6	−108.2	−16.3	11.3	−123.2
of which: Short-term	4 777 ..	31.6	9.0	−3.8	7.9	−28.5	−18.3	−33.2	48.4
Currency and deposits	4 780 ..	....	....	....	....	....	....	....	....
Monetary authorities	4 781 ..	....	....	....	....	....	....	....	....
General government	4 782 ..	....	....	....	....	....	....	....	....
Banks	4 783 ..	....	....	....	....	....	....	....	....
Other sectors	4 784 ..	....	....	....	....	....	....	....	....
Other liabilities	4 786 ..	....	....	....	....	....	....	....	....
Monetary authorities	4 787 ..	....	....	....	....	....	....	....	....
of which: Short-term	4 789 ..	....	....	....	....	....	....	....	....
General government	4 790 ..	....	....	....	....	....	....	....	....
of which: Short-term	4 792 ..	....	....	....	....	....	....	....	....
Banks	4 793 ..	....	....	....	....	....	....	....	....
of which: Short-term	4 795 ..	....	....	....	....	....	....	....	....
Other sectors	4 796 ..	....	....	....	....	....	....	....	....
of which: Short-term	4 798 ..	....	....	....	....	....	....	....	....
E. RESERVE ASSETS	4 802 ..	**−17.2**	**−70.2**	**−8.7**	**107.2**	**14.2**	**−1.1**	**−163.1**	**−570.8**
Monetary gold	4 812 ..	....	....	....	....	....	....	....	....
Special drawing rights	4 811 ..	....	....	....	....	....	....	....	....
Reserve position in the Fund	4 810 ..	....	....	....	....	....	....	....	....
Foreign exchange	4 803 ..	−17.2	−70.2	−8.7	107.2	14.2	−1.0	−163.1	−570.8
Other claims	4 813 ..	....	....	....	....	....	....	....	....
NET ERRORS AND OMISSIONS	4 998 ..	**−4.0**	**−28.2**	**16.1**	**−88.8**	**115.3**	**127.9**	**121.6**	**490.0**

Table 3. INTERNATIONAL INVESTMENT POSITION (End-period stocks), 2000–2007

(Millions of U.S. dollars)

	Code	2000	2001	2002	2003	2004	2005	2006	2007
ASSETS	8 995 C.	**1,213.5**	**996.9**	**1,427.3**	**2,937.1**	**2,804.3**	**4,619.5**	**5,849.1**	**8,419.5**
Direct investment abroad	8 505	**44.9**	**10.1**	**19.6**	**33.2**	**53.0**	**25.7**	**7.3**	**15.8**
Equity capital and reinvested earnings	8 506	7.6	4.4	6.7	9.3	28.8	21.6	5.4	12.7
Claims on affiliated enterprises	8 507	....	....	....	....	....	....	....	....
Liabilities to affiliated enterprises	8 508	....	....	....	....	....	....	....	....
Other capital	8 530	37.4	5.7	13.0	23.9	24.2	4.1	1.9	3.1
Claims on affiliated enterprises	8 535	....	....	....	....	....	....	....	....
Liabilities to affiliated enterprises	8 540	....	....	....	....	....	....	....	....
Portfolio investment	8 602	**610.5**	**624.5**	**675.3**	**2,354.4**	**2,206.2**	**4,095.0**	**4,493.4**	**6,022.8**
Equity securities	8 610	603.7	....	....	....	1,706.4	2,977.2	3,304.3	3,643.4
Monetary authorities	8 611	....	....	....	....	....	....	....	....
General government	8 612	....	....	....	....	....	....	....	....
Banks	8 613	....	....	....	....	....	....	....	....
Other sectors	8 614	....	....	....	....	....	....	....	....
Debt securities	8 619	6.8	....	....	....	499.9	1,117.8	1,189.0	2,379.5
Bonds and notes	8 620	5.5	....	....	....	....	....	....	....
Monetary authorities	8 621	....	....	....	....	....	....	....	....
General government	8 622	....	....	....	....	....	....	....	....
Banks	8 623	....	....	....	....	....	....	....	....
Other sectors	8 624	....	....	....	....	....	....	....	....
Money market instruments	8 630	1.3	....	....	....	....	....	....	....
Monetary authorities	8 631	....	....	....	....	....	....	....	....
General government	8 632	....	....	....	....	....	....	....	....
Banks	8 633	....	....	....	....	....	....	....	....
Other sectors	8 634	....	....	....	....	....	....	....	....
Financial derivatives	8 900	....	....	....	....	....	....	....	....
Monetary authorities	8 901	....	....	....	....	....	....	....	....
General government	8 902	....	....	....	....	....	....	....	....
Banks	8 903	....	....	....	....	....	....	....	....
Other sectors	8 904	....	....	....	....	....	....	....	....
Other investment	8 703	**295.1**	**139.3**	**408.2**	**230.5**	**216.9**	**204.5**	**926.6**	**1,440.7**
Trade credits	8 706	5.0	....	....	....	....	....	....	....
General government	8 707	....	....	....	....	....	....	....	....
of which: Short-term	8 709	....	....	....	....	....	....	....	....
Other sectors	8 710	5.0	....	....	....	....	....	....	....
of which: Short-term	8 712	*5.0*	....	....	....	....	....	....	....
Loans	8 714	132.7	111.3	337.3	172.2	174.3	114.9	525.7	250.9
Monetary authorities	8 715	....	....	....	....	....	....	....	....
of which: Short-term	8 718	....	....	....	....	....	....	....	....
General government	8 719	....	....	....	....	....	....	....	....
of which: Short-term	8 721	....	....	....	....	....	....	....	....
Banks	8 722	51.3	62.9	259.1	62.7	69.9	46.1	489.2	144.3
of which: Short-term	8 724	....	....	....	....	*67.0*	*40.3*	*335.7*	*47.3*
Other sectors	8 725	81.4	48.5	78.1	109.5	104.4	68.8	36.5	106.7
of which: Short-term	8 727	*55.9*	*41.5*	*71.6*	*101.9*	*94.7*	*56.9*	*24.4*	*85.2*
Currency and deposits	8 730	.4	.2	.2	.1	7.1	36.4	357.5	1,157.3
Monetary authorities	8 731	....	....	....	....	....	....	....	....
General government	8 732	....	....	....	....	....	....	....	....
Banks	8 733	.4	.2	.2	.1	....	....	....	....
Other sectors	8 734	....	....	....	....	7.1	36.4	357.5	1,157.3
Other assets	8 736	157.0	27.8	70.8	58.2	35.5	53.1	43.3	32.5
Monetary authorities	8 737	....	....	....	....	....	....	....	....
of which: Short-term	8 739	....	....	....	....	....	....	....	....
General government	8 740	....	....	....	....	....	....	....	....
of which: Short-term	8 742	....	....	....	....	....	....	....	....
Banks	8 743	....	....	....	47.8	....	....	....	....
of which: Short-term	8 745	....	....	....	....	....	....	....	....
Other sectors	8 746	157.0	27.8	70.8	10.4	35.5	53.1	43.3	32.5
of which: Short-term	8 748	....	....	....	....	....	....	....	....
Reserve assets	8 802	**262.9**	**222.9**	**324.1**	**319.1**	**328.2**	**294.4**	**421.8**	**940.1**
Monetary gold	8 812	....	....	....	....	....	....	....	....
Special drawing rights	8 811	....	....	....	....	....	....	....	....
Reserve position in the Fund	8 810	....	....	.1	.1	.1	.1	.1	.1
Foreign exchange	8 803	262.8	222.9	324.1	319.0	328.1	294.2	421.7	940.0
Other claims	8 813	....	....	....	....	....	....	....	....

Table 3 (Concluded). INTERNATIONAL INVESTMENT POSITION (End-period stocks), 2000–2007

(Millions of U.S. dollars)

	Code	2000	2001	2002	2003	2004	2005	2006	2007
LIABILITIES	8 995 D.	**1,807.3**	**1,310.8**	**2,556.6**	**4,019.3**	**5,231.7**	**4,123.9**	**4,641.2**	**5,126.5**
Direct investment in Namibia	8 555 ..	**1,276.3**	**715.0**	**1,822.5**	**2,951.9**	**4,120.4**	**2,453.4**	**2,785.7**	**3,854.4**
Equity capital and reinvested earnings	8 556 ..	1,105.7	638.1	1,397.2	2,393.6	3,368.4	2,260.0	2,381.6	2,851.3
Claims on direct investors	8 557 ..	....	....	....	....	....	....	....	....
Liabilities to direct investors	8 558 ..	....	....	....	....	....	....	....	....
Other capital	8 580 ..	170.6	76.9	425.3	558.3	752.1	193.5	404.1	1,003.1
Claims on direct investors	8 585 ..	....	....	....	....	....	....	....	....
Liabilities to direct investors	8 590 ..	....	....	....	....	....	....	....	....
Portfolio investment	8 652 ..	**75.0**	**27.2**	**41.7**	**57.7**	**68.7**	**92.4**	**83.8**	**85.8**
Equity securities	8 660 ..	1.7	4.6	6.8	5.8	6.9	15.6	14.1	14.4
Banks	8 663 ..	....	....	....	....	....	....	....	....
Other sectors	8 664 ..	....	....	....	....	....	....	....	....
Debt securities	8 669 ..	73.3	22.6	34.9	51.8	61.8	76.9	69.7	71.4
Bonds and notes	8 670 ..	....	....	....	....	....	....	....	....
Monetary authorities	8 671 ..	....	....	....	....	....	....	....	....
General government	8 672 ..	....	....	....	....	....	....	....	....
Banks	8 673 ..	....	....	....	....	....	....	....	....
Other sectors	8 674 ..	....	....	....	....	....	....	....	....
Money market instruments	8 680 ..	....	....	....	....	....	....	....	....
Monetary authorities	8 681 ..	....	....	....	....	....	....	....	....
General government	8 682 ..	....	....	....	....	....	....	....	....
Banks	8 683 ..	....	....	....	....	....	....	....	....
Other sectors	8 684 ..	....	....	....	....	....	....	....	....
Financial derivatives	8 905 ..	....	....	....	....	....	....	....	....
Monetary authorities	8 906 ..	....	....	....	....	....	....	....	....
General government	8 907 ..	....	....	....	....	....	....	....	....
Banks	8 908 ..	....	....	....	....	....	....	....	....
Other sectors	8 909 ..	....	....	....	....	....	....	....	....
Other investment	8 753 ..	**455.9**	**568.6**	**692.4**	**1,009.7**	**1,042.6**	**1,578.0**	**1,771.7**	**1,186.3**
Trade credits	8 756 ..	11.3	....	....	....	....	....	....	....
General government	8 757 ..	1.4	....	....	....	....	....	....	....
of which: Short-term	8 759 ..	*1.4*	....	....	....	....	....	....	....
Other sectors	8 760 ..	9.9	....	....	....	....	....	....	....
of which: Short-term	8 762 ..	*9.9*	....	....	....	....	....	....	....
Loans	8 764 ..	372.0	518.5	626.7	873.3	1,042.6	1,395.7	1,607.7	1,032.5
Monetary authorities	8 765 ..	....	....	....	....	....	....	....	....
of which: Use of Fund credit and loans from the Fund	8 766 ..	....	....	....	....	....	....	....	....
of which: Short-term	8 768 ..	....	....	....	....	....	....	....	....
General government	8 769 ..	127.9	155.8	218.0	302.0	391.4	362.1	404.1	464.4
of which: Short-term	8 771 ..	....	*7.1*	*12.2*	*15.9*	*50.9*	*45.9*	*41.1*	*.4*
Banks	8 772 ..	70.1	79.3	187.8	222.4	307.0	115.3	200.7	239.1
of which: Short-term	8 774 ..	*66.6*	*.3*	*187.8*	....	*185.6*	*98.8*	*135.1*	*174.4*
Other sectors	8 775 ..	174.0	283.4	220.9	348.9	344.2	918.3	1,002.9	329.0
of which: Short-term	8 777 ..	*89.8*	*44.0*	*80.7*	*121.7*	*344.2*	*300.0*	*382.6*	*329.0*
Currency and deposits	8 780 ..	....	....	....	....	....	182.3	164.0	153.8
Monetary authorities	8 781 ..	....	....	....	....	....	....	....	....
General government	8 782 ..	....	....	....	....	....	....	....	....
Banks	8 783 ..	....	....	....	....	....	182.3	164.0	153.8
Other sectors	8 784 ..	....	....	....	....	....	....	....	....
Other liabilities	8 786 ..	72.6	50.1	65.7	136.4	....	....	....	....
Monetary authorities	8 787 ..	....	....	....	....	....	....	....	....
of which: Short-term	8 789 ..	....	....	....	....	....	....	....	....
General government	8 790 ..	....	....	....	....	....	....	....	....
of which: Short-term	8 792 ..	....	....	....	....	....	....	....	....
Banks	8 793 ..	....	....	....	136.4	....	....	....	....
of which: Short-term	8 795 ..	....	....	....	....	....	....	....	....
Other sectors	8 796 ..	72.6	50.1	65.7	....	....	....	....	....
of which: Short-term	8 798 ..	*72.6*	....	....	....	....	....	....	....
NET INTERNATIONAL INVESTMENT POSITION	8 995 ..	**−593.8**	**−313.8**	**−1,129.2**	**−1,082.2**	**−2,427.4**	**495.7**	**1,207.9**	**3,293.0**
Conversion rates: Namibia dollars per U.S. dollar (end of period)	0 102 ..	**7.569**	**12.127**	**8.640**	**6.640**	**5.630**	**6.325**	**6.970**	**6.810**

Table 1. ANALYTIC PRESENTATION, 2000–2007

(Millions of U.S. dollars)

	Code	2000	2001	2002	2003	2004	2005	2006	2007
A. Current Account[1]	4 993 Z.	−298.7	−339.3	55.6	119.9	−45.0	1.1	−10.4	−130.0
Goods: exports f.o.b.	2 100 ..	776.1	720.5	632.0	703.2	773.1	902.9	848.8	924.9
Goods: imports f.o.b.	3 100 ..	−1,590.1	−1,485.7	−1,425.4	−1,665.9	−1,908.0	−2,276.5	−2,441.0	−2,932.6
Balance on Goods	4 100 ..	*−814.0*	*−765.2*	*−793.4*	*−962.7*	*−1,134.9*	*−1,373.6*	*−1,592.2*	*−2,007.6*
Services: credit	2 200 ..	505.9	413.3	305.2	372.1	460.9	380.3	385.7	511.3
Services: debit	3 200 ..	−199.9	−214.7	−236.8	−266.2	−385.0	−434.7	−492.8	−722.6
Balance on Goods and Services	4 991 ..	*−508.0*	*−566.6*	*−724.9*	*−856.8*	*−1,059.1*	*−1,428.0*	*−1,699.4*	*−2,218.9*
Income: credit	2 300 ..	72.2	70.3	56.9	48.7	63.0	139.9	158.2	224.3
Income: debit	3 300 ..	−35.2	−58.8	−71.2	−69.0	−78.0	−91.6	−96.1	−87.6
Balance on Goods, Services, and Income	4 992 ..	*−471.0*	*−555.2*	*−739.2*	*−877.1*	*−1,074.1*	*−1,379.7*	*−1,637.3*	*−2,082.2*
Current transfers: credit	2 379 Z.	189.0	240.2	828.1	1,022.5	1,091.8	1,441.3	1,695.7	1,993.7
Current transfers: debit	3 379 ..	−16.7	−24.3	−33.2	−25.4	−62.8	−60.5	−68.9	−41.5
B. Capital Account[1]	4 994 Z.	....	....	102.4	24.8	15.7	40.3	46.3	75.4
Capital account: credit	2 994 Z.	....	....	102.4	24.8	15.7	40.5	46.4	75.5
Capital account: debit	3 994 ..	....	....	....	....	....	−.2	−.1	−.1
Total, Groups A Plus B	4 981 ..	*−298.7*	*−339.3*	*158.0*	*144.8*	*−29.4*	*41.4*	*35.9*	*−54.7*
C. Financial Account[1]	4 995 W.	76.1	−216.9	−404.8	−354.1	−488.5	−276.5	2.8	−132.1
Direct investment abroad	4 505 ..	....	....	....	....	....	....	....	....
Direct investment in Nepal	4 555 Z.	....	....	−6.0	14.8	−.4	2.5	−6.6	5.7
Portfolio investment assets	4 602 ..	....	....	....	....	....	....	....	....
Equity securities	4 610 ..	....	....	....	....	....	....	....	....
Debt securities	4 619 ..	....	....	....	....	....	....	....	....
Portfolio investment liabilities	4 652 Z.	....	....	....	....	....	....	....	....
Equity securities	4 660 ..	....	....	....	....	....	....	....	....
Debt securities	4 669 Z.	....	....	....	....	....	....	....	....
Financial derivatives	4 910 ..	....	....	....	....	....	....	....	....
Financial derivatives assets	4 900 ..	....	....	....	....	....	....	....	....
Financial derivatives liabilities	4 905 ..	....	....	....	....	....	....	....	....
Other investment assets	4 703 ..	128.6	11.2	−470.4	−436.7	−348.0	−242.4	−250.9	−161.0
Monetary authorities	4 701 ..	....	....	....	....	....	....	....	....
General government	4 704 ..	....	....	....	....	....	....	....	....
Banks	4 705 ..	....	....	....	....	....	....	−15.3	−61.8
Other sectors	4 728 ..	128.6	11.2	−470.4	−436.7	−348.0	−242.4	−235.5	−99.2
Other investment liabilities	4 753 W.	−52.6	−228.0	71.5	67.8	−140.0	−36.5	260.3	23.1
Monetary authorities	4 753 WA	4.5	−3.5	1.8	.2	−1.6	−2.3	−.2	.1
General government	4 753 ZB	−61.0	−63.5	−71.3	−67.6	−90.7	−84.3	10.9	24.3
Banks	4 753 ZC	67.4	3.2	33.3	19.2	4.7	22.3	39.1	56.0
Other sectors	4 753 ZD	−63.5	−164.3	107.8	116.0	−52.5	27.8	210.5	−57.2
Total, Groups A Through C	4 983 ..	*−222.7*	*−556.1*	*−246.8*	*−209.3*	*−517.8*	*−235.1*	*38.7*	*−186.7*
D. Net Errors and Omissions	4 998 ..	145.7	256.5	−66.6	309.9	415.9	139.0	108.5	19.1
Total, Groups A Through D	4 984 ..	*−77.0*	*−299.6*	*−313.4*	*100.6*	*−101.9*	*−96.1*	*147.2*	*−167.7*
E. Reserves and Related Items	4 802 A.	77.0	299.6	313.4	−100.6	101.9	96.1	−147.2	167.7
Reserve assets	4 802 ..	−291.0	−5.2	65.5	−218.1	−178.0	−170.9	−329.0	−1.1
Use of Fund credit and loans	4 766 ..	−4.4	−4.3	−4.3	7.1	10.0	....	21.2	33.1
Exceptional financing	4 920 ..	372.4	309.1	252.3	110.4	270.0	267.0	160.5	135.7
Conversion rates: Nepalese rupees per U.S. dollar	0 101 ..	71.094	74.949	77.877	76.141	73.674	71.368	72.756	66.415

[1] Excludes components that have been classified in the categories of Group E.

Table 2. STANDARD PRESENTATION, 2000–2007

(Millions of U.S. dollars)

	Code	2000	2001	2002	2003	2004	2005	2006	2007
CURRENT ACCOUNT	4 993	−130.6	−164.7	215.2	180.3	100.0	153.1	150.1	5.7
A. GOODS	4 100	−814.0	−765.2	−793.4	−962.7	−1,134.9	−1,373.6	−1,592.2	−2,007.6
Credit	2 100	776.1	720.5	632.0	703.2	773.1	902.9	848.8	924.9
General merchandise: exports f.o.b.	2 110	776.1	720.5	632.0	703.2	773.1	902.9	848.8	924.9
Goods for processing: exports f.o.b.	2 150	....	....	....	....	....	....	....	....
Repairs on goods	2 160	....	....	....	....	....	....	....	....
Goods procured in ports by carriers	2 170	....	....	....	....	....	....	....	....
Nonmonetary gold	2 180	....	....	....	....	....	....	....	....
Debit	3 100	−1,590.1	−1,485.7	−1,425.4	−1,665.9	−1,908.0	−2,276.5	−2,441.0	−2,932.6
General merchandise: imports f.o.b.	3 110	−1,590.1	−1,485.7	−1,425.4	−1,665.9	−1,908.0	−2,276.5	−2,441.0	−2,932.6
Goods for processing: imports f.o.b.	3 150	....	....	....	....	....	....	....	....
Repairs on goods	3 160	....	....	....	....	....	....	....	....
Goods procured in ports by carriers	3 170	....	....	....	....	....	....	....	....
Nonmonetary gold	3 180	....	....	....	....	....	....	....	....
B. SERVICES	4 200	306.0	198.6	68.4	105.9	75.9	−54.4	−107.1	−211.3
Total credit	2 200	*505.9*	*413.3*	*305.2*	*372.1*	*460.9*	*380.3*	*385.7*	*511.3*
Total debit	3 200	*−199.9*	*−214.7*	*−236.8*	*−266.2*	*−385.0*	*−434.7*	*−492.8*	*−722.6*
Transportation services, credit	2 205	61.4	47.3	36.2	35.9	32.5	32.6	35.1	37.0
Passenger	2 850	*61.4*	*47.3*	*31.1*	*32.6*	*30.2*	*29.3*	*29.2*	*34.4*
Freight	2 851	....	....	....	....	....	....	....	....
Other	2 852	....	....	*5.1*	*3.3*	*2.3*	*3.3*	*5.9*	*2.7*
Sea transport, passenger	2 207	....	....	....	....	....	....	....	....
Sea transport, freight	2 208	....	....	....	....	....	....	....	....
Sea transport, other	2 209	....	....	....	....	....	....	....	....
Air transport, passenger	2 211	....	....	....	....	....	....	....	....
Air transport, freight	2 212	....	....	....	....	....	....	....	....
Air transport, other	2 213	....	....	....	....	....	....	....	....
Other transport, passenger	2 215	....	....	....	....	....	....	....	....
Other transport, freight	2 216	....	....	....	....	....	....	....	....
Other transport, other	2 217	....	....	....	....	....	....	....	....
Transportation services, debit	3 205	−64.8	−71.6	−110.9	−115.0	−141.5	−160.8	−186.3	−287.3
Passenger	3 850	*−35.9*	*−47.7*	*−38.7*	*−38.1*	*−51.1*	*−57.7*	*−76.4*	*−127.5*
Freight	3 851	*−28.9*	*−24.0*	*−57.7*	*−58.6*	*−69.3*	*−78.0*	*−78.9*	*−85.4*
Other	3 852	....	....	*−14.5*	*−18.3*	*−21.0*	*−25.1*	*−31.1*	*−74.5*
Sea transport, passenger	3 207	....	....	....	....	....	....	....	....
Sea transport, freight	3 208	....	....	....	....	....	....	....	....
Sea transport, other	3 209	....	....	....	....	....	....	....	....
Air transport, passenger	3 211	....	....	....	....	....	....	....	....
Air transport, freight	3 212	....	....	....	....	....	....	....	....
Air transport, other	3 213	....	....	....	....	....	....	....	....
Other transport, passenger	3 215	....	....	....	....	....	....	....	....
Other transport, freight	3 216	....	....	....	....	....	....	....	....
Other transport, other	3 217	....	....	....	....	....	....	....	....
Travel, credit	2 236	157.8	143.8	103.5	199.5	230.2	131.3	127.8	199.9
Business travel	2 237	....	....	....	....	....	....	....	....
Personal travel	2 240	....	....	....	....	....	....	....	....
Travel, debit	3 236	−73.3	−79.7	−69.2	−81.2	−153.8	−163.2	−185.3	−273.6
Business travel	3 237	....	....	....	....	....	....	....	....
Personal travel	3 240	....	....	....	....	....	....	....	....
Other services, credit	2 200 BA	286.7	222.2	165.5	136.7	198.2	216.4	222.7	274.4
Communications	2 245	....	....	8.1	17.2	31.8	39.7	34.7	38.2
Construction	2 249	....	....	....	....	....	....	....	....
Insurance	2 253	....	....	.1	.6	.2	3.9	1.6	3.1
Financial	2 260	....	....	....	....	....	....	....	....
Computer and information	2 262	....	....	....	....	....	....	....	....
Royalties and licence fees	2 266	....	....	....	....	....	....	....	....
Other business services	2 268	190.8	111.6	44.3	49.3	61.1	63.9	52.4	61.3
Personal, cultural, and recreational	2 287	....	....	....	....	....	....	....	....
Government, n.i.e.	2 291	96.0	110.6	113.0	69.7	105.1	109.0	134.0	171.8
Other services, debit	3 200 BA	−61.9	−63.3	−56.7	−70.0	−89.8	−110.7	−121.2	−161.6
Communications	3 245	....	....	−1.6	−5.3	−8.2	−4.1	−4.1	−5.0
Construction	3 249	....	....	....	....	....	....	....	....
Insurance	3 253	....	....	−16.3	−17.2	−18.2	−26.3	−28.7	−30.7
Financial	3 260	....	....	....	....	....	....	....	....
Computer and information	3 262	....	....	....	....	....	....	....	....
Royalties and licence fees	3 266	....	....	....	....	....	....	....	....
Other business services	3 268	−55.2	−54.0	−33.2	−39.0	−54.0	−69.4	−83.8	−119.5
Personal, cultural, and recreational	3 287	....	....	....	....	....	....	....	....
Government, n.i.e.	3 291	−6.7	−9.4	−5.7	−8.5	−9.3	−10.9	−4.6	−6.4

Table 2 (Continued). STANDARD PRESENTATION, 2000–2007

(Millions of U.S. dollars)

	Code	2000	2001	2002	2003	2004	2005	2006	2007
C. INCOME	4 300	**37.0**	**11.5**	**−14.3**	**−20.3**	**−15.0**	**48.3**	**62.1**	**136.7**
Total credit	2 300	*72.2*	*70.3*	*56.9*	*48.7*	*63.0*	*139.9*	*158.2*	*224.3*
Total debit	3 300	*−35.2*	*−58.8*	*−71.2*	*−69.0*	*−78.0*	*−91.6*	*−96.1*	*−87.6*
Compensation of employees, credit	2 310	....	....	23.5	26.7	30.0	85.5	79.9	86.7
Compensation of employees, debit	3 310	....	....	−.9	−.8	−.8	−5.3	−10.3	−4.0
Investment income, credit	2 320	72.2	70.3	33.4	22.0	33.0	54.4	78.2	137.6
Direct investment income	2 330	....	....	....	....	....	....	....	....
Dividends and distributed branch profits	2 332	....	....	....	....	....	....	....	....
Reinvested earnings and undistributed branch profits	2 333	....	....	....	....	....	....	....	....
Income on debt (interest)	2 334	....	....	....	....	....	....	....	....
Portfolio investment income	2 339	....	....	....	....	....	....	....	....
Income on equity	2 340	....	....	....	....	....	....	....	....
Income on bonds and notes	2 350	....	....	....	....	....	....	....	....
Income on money market instruments	2 360	....	....	....	....	....	....	....	....
Other investment income	2 370	72.2	70.3	33.4	22.0	33.0	54.4	78.2	137.6
Investment income, debit	3 320	**−35.2**	**−58.8**	**−70.3**	**−68.2**	**−77.2**	**−86.3**	**−85.8**	**−83.7**
Direct investment income	3 330	....	....	−44.8	−42.1	−44.9	−56.6	−55.7	−54.0
Dividends and distributed branch profits	3 332	....	....	−44.8	−42.1	−44.9	−56.6	−55.7	−54.0
Reinvested earnings and undistributed branch profits	3 333	....	....	....	....	....	....	....	....
Income on debt (interest)	3 334	....	....	....	....	....	....	....	....
Portfolio investment income	3 339	....	....	....	....	....	....	....	....
Income on equity	3 340	....	....	....	....	....	....	....	....
Income on bonds and notes	3 350	....	....	....	....	....	....	....	....
Income on money market instruments	3 360	....	....	....	....	....	....	....	....
Other investment income	3 370	−35.2	−58.8	−25.5	−26.2	−32.3	−29.7	−30.0	−29.7
D. CURRENT TRANSFERS	4 379	**340.3**	**390.5**	**954.4**	**1,057.4**	**1,174.0**	**1,532.8**	**1,787.4**	**2,087.9**
Credit	2 379	**357.1**	**414.8**	**987.6**	**1,082.8**	**1,236.8**	**1,593.3**	**1,856.2**	**2,129.4**
General government	2 380	168.1	174.6	184.0	92.7	190.7	167.1	160.5	182.3
Other sectors	2 390	189.0	240.2	803.6	990.1	1,046.1	1,426.2	1,695.7	1,947.2
Workers' remittances	2 391	111.5	147.0	655.0	744.4	792.6	1,126.3	1,373.3	1,647.1
Other current transfers	2 392	77.5	93.2	148.6	245.7	253.5	299.8	322.4	300.0
Debit	3 379	**−16.7**	**−24.3**	**−33.2**	**−25.4**	**−62.8**	**−60.5**	**−68.9**	**−41.5**
General government	3 380	....	....	....	....	....	....	....	−.1
Other sectors	3 390	−16.7	−24.3	−33.2	−25.4	−62.8	−60.5	−68.9	−41.4
Workers' remittances	3 391	−16.7	−24.3	−33.2	−25.4	−62.8	−60.5	−68.9	....
Other current transfers	3 392	....	....	....	....	....	....	....	....
CAPITAL AND FINANCIAL ACCOUNT	4 996	**−15.1**	**−91.9**	**−148.5**	**−490.2**	**−515.9**	**−292.1**	**−258.6**	**−24.7**
CAPITAL ACCOUNT	4 994	....	....	**102.4**	**24.8**	**15.7**	**40.3**	**46.3**	**75.4**
Total credit	2 994	....	....	*102.4*	*24.8*	*15.7*	*40.5*	*46.4*	*75.5*
Total debit	3 994	....	....	....	....	....	*−.2*	*−.1*	*−.1*
Capital transfers, credit	2 400	....	....	102.4	24.8	15.7	40.5	46.4	75.5
General government	2 401	....	....	57.4	24.8	15.7	40.5	46.4	75.5
Debt forgiveness	2 402	....	....	....	....	....	....	....	....
Other capital transfers	2 410	....	....	57.4	24.8	15.7	40.5	46.4	75.5
Other sectors	2 430	....	....	45.0	....	....	....	....	....
Migrants' transfers	2 431	....	....	....	....	....	....	....	....
Debt forgiveness	2 432	....	....	....	....	....	....	....	....
Other capital transfers	2 440	....	....	45.0	....	....	....	....	....
Capital transfers, debit	3 400	....	....	....	....	....	−.2	−.1	−.1
General government	3 401	....	....	....	....	....	....	....	....
Debt forgiveness	3 402	....	....	....	....	....	....	....	....
Other capital transfers	3 410	....	....	....	....	....	....	....	....
Other sectors	3 430	....	....	....	....	....	−.2	−.1	−.1
Migrants' transfers	3 431	....	....	....	....	....	....	....	....
Debt forgiveness	3 432	....	....	....	....	....	....	....	....
Other capital transfers	3 440	....	....	....	....	....	−.2	−.1	−.1
Nonproduced nonfinancial assets, credit	2 480	....	....	....	....	....	....	....	....
Nonproduced nonfinancial assets, debit	3 480	....	....	....	....	....	....	....	....

Table 2 (Continued). STANDARD PRESENTATION, 2000–2007

(Millions of U.S. dollars)

	Code	2000	2001	2002	2003	2004	2005	2006	2007
FINANCIAL ACCOUNT	4 995	−15.1	−91.9	−251.0	−515.0	−531.5	−332.4	−304.9	−100.1
A. DIRECT INVESTMENT	4 500	−.5	....	−6.0	14.8	−.4	2.5	−6.6	5.7
Direct investment abroad	4 505	....	....	....	....	....	....	....	....
Equity capital	4 510	....	....	....	....	....	....	....	....
Claims on affiliated enterprises	4 515	....	....	....	....	....	....	....	....
Liabilities to affiliated enterprises	4 520	....	....	....	....	....	....	....	....
Reinvested earnings	4 525	....	....	....	....	....	....	....	....
Other capital	4 530	....	....	....	....	....	....	....	....
Claims on affiliated enterprises	4 535	....	....	....	....	....	....	....	....
Liabilities to affiliated enterprises	4 540	....	....	....	....	....	....	....	....
Direct investment in Nepal	4 555	−.5	....	−6.0	14.8	−.4	2.5	−6.6	5.7
Equity capital	4 560	−.5	....	−6.0	14.8	−.4	2.5	−6.6	5.3
Claims on direct investors	4 565	....	....	....	....	....	....	....	....
Liabilities to direct investors	4 570	−.5	....	−6.0	14.8	−.4	2.5	−6.6	5.3
Reinvested earnings	4 575	....	....	....	....	....	....	....	....
Other capital	4 580	....	....	....	....	....	....	....	.5
Claims on direct investors	4 585	....	....	....	....	....	....	....	....
Liabilities to direct investors	4 590	....	....	....	....	....	....	....	....
B. PORTFOLIO INVESTMENT	4 600	....	....	....	....	....	....	....	....
Assets	4 602	....	....	....	....	....	....	....	....
Equity securities	4 610	....	....	....	....	....	....	....	....
Monetary authorities	4 611	....	....	....	....	....	....	....	....
General government	4 612	....	....	....	....	....	....	....	....
Banks	4 613	....	....	....	....	....	....	....	....
Other sectors	4 614	....	....	....	....	....	....	....	....
Debt securities	4 619	....	....	....	....	....	....	....	....
Bonds and notes	4 620	....	....	....	....	....	....	....	....
Monetary authorities	4 621	....	....	....	....	....	....	....	....
General government	4 622	....	....	....	....	....	....	....	....
Banks	4 623	....	....	....	....	....	....	....	....
Other sectors	4 624	....	....	....	....	....	....	....	....
Money market instruments	4 630	....	....	....	....	....	....	....	....
Monetary authorities	4 631	....	....	....	....	....	....	....	....
General government	4 632	....	....	....	....	....	....	....	....
Banks	4 633	....	....	....	....	....	....	....	....
Other sectors	4 634	....	....	....	....	....	....	....	....
Liabilities	4 652	....	....	....	....	....	....	....	....
Equity securities	4 660	....	....	....	....	....	....	....	....
Banks	4 663	....	....	....	....	....	....	....	....
Other sectors	4 664	....	....	....	....	....	....	....	....
Debt securities	4 669	....	....	....	....	....	....	....	....
Bonds and notes	4 670	....	....	....	....	....	....	....	....
Monetary authorities	4 671	....	....	....	....	....	....	....	....
General government	4 672	....	....	....	....	....	....	....	....
Banks	4 673	....	....	....	....	....	....	....	....
Other sectors	4 674	....	....	....	....	....	....	....	....
Money market instruments	4 680	....	....	....	....	....	....	....	....
Monetary authorities	4 681	....	....	....	....	....	....	....	....
General government	4 682	....	....	....	....	....	....	....	....
Banks	4 683	....	....	....	....	....	....	....	....
Other sectors	4 684	....	....	....	....	....	....	....	....
C. FINANCIAL DERIVATIVES	4 910	....	....	....	....	....	....	....	....
Monetary authorities	4 911	....	....	....	....	....	....	....	....
General government	4 912	....	....	....	....	....	....	....	....
Banks	4 913	....	....	....	....	....	....	....	....
Other sectors	4 914	....	....	....	....	....	....	....	....
Assets	4 900	....	....	....	14.8	....	....	....	....
Monetary authorities	4 901	....	....	....	....	....	2.5	....	....
General government	4 902	....	....	....	....	....	....	....	....
Banks	4 903	....	....	....	....	....	....	....	....
Other sectors	4 904	....	....	....	....	....	....	....	....
Liabilities	4 905	....	....	....	....	....	....	....	....
Monetary authorities	4 906	....	....	....	....	....	....	....	....
General government	4 907	....	....	....	....	....	....	....	....
Banks	4 908	....	....	....	....	....	....	....	....
Other sectors	4 909	....	....	....	....	....	....	....	....

Table 2 (Concluded). STANDARD PRESENTATION, 2000–2007

(Millions of U.S. dollars)

	Code	2000	2001	2002	2003	2004	2005	2006	2007
D. OTHER INVESTMENT	4 700 ..	**276.4**	**−86.6**	**−310.5**	**−311.7**	**−353.1**	**−164.0**	**30.7**	**−104.7**
Assets	4 703 ..	**128.6**	**11.2**	**−470.4**	**−436.7**	**−348.0**	**−242.4**	**−250.9**	**−161.0**
Trade credits	4 706 ..	128.6	11.2	5.7	−34.9	17.6	−39.7	−94.9	−44.9
General government	4 707 ..	....	....	....	....	....	....	....	....
of which: Short-term	4 709 ..	....	....	....	....	....	....	....	....
Other sectors	4 710 ..	128.6	11.2	5.7	−34.9	17.6	−39.7	−94.9	−44.9
of which: Short-term	4 712 ..	128.6	11.2	5.7	−34.9	17.6	−39.7	−94.9	−44.9
Loans	4 714 ..	....	....	....	....	....	....	....	....
Monetary authorities	4 715 ..	....	....	....	....	....	....	....	....
of which: Short-term	4 718 ..	....	....	....	....	....	....	....	....
General government	4 719 ..	....	....	....	....	....	....	....	....
of which: Short-term	4 721 ..	....	....	....	....	....	....	....	....
Banks	4 722 ..	....	....	....	....	....	....	....	....
of which: Short-term	4 724 ..	....	....	....	....	....	....	....	....
Other sectors	4 725 ..	....	....	....	....	....	....	....	....
of which: Short-term	4 727 ..	....	....	....	....	....	....	....	....
Currency and deposits	4 730 ..	....	....	....	....	....	....	−15.3	−61.8
Monetary authorities	4 731 ..	....	....	....	....	....	....	....	....
General government	4 732 ..	....	....	....	....	....	....	....	....
Banks	4 733 ..	....	....	....	....	....	....	−15.3	−61.8
Other sectors	4 734 ..	....	....	....	....	....	....	....	....
Other assets	4 736 ..	....	....	−476.0	−401.8	−365.6	−202.7	−140.6	−54.2
Monetary authorities	4 737 ..	....	....	....	....	....	....	....	....
of which: Short-term	4 739 ..	....	....	....	....	....	....	....	....
General government	4 740 ..	....	....	....	....	....	....	....	....
of which: Short-term	4 742 ..	....	....	....	....	....	....	....	....
Banks	4 743 ..	....	....	....	....	....	....	....	....
of which: Short-term	4 745 ..	....	....	....	....	....	....	....	....
Other sectors	4 746 ..	....	....	−476.0	−401.8	−365.6	−202.7	−140.6	−54.2
of which: Short-term	4 748 ..	....	....	−476.0	−401.8	−365.6	−202.7	−140.6	−54.2
Liabilities	4 753 ..	**147.8**	**−97.8**	**159.9**	**125.0**	**−5.1**	**78.5**	**281.6**	**56.3**
Trade credits	4 756 ..	−60.1	−162.6	109.0	119.8	−47.4	37.6	219.1	−54.6
General government	4 757 ..	....	....	....	....	....	....	....	....
of which: Short-term	4 759 ..	....	....	....	....	....	....	....	....
Other sectors	4 760 ..	−60.1	−162.6	109.0	119.8	−47.4	37.6	219.1	−54.6
of which: Short-term	4 762 ..	−60.1	−162.6	109.0	119.8	−47.4	37.6	219.1	−54.6
Loans	4 764 ..	135.3	64.5	15.7	−14.9	39.2	20.8	23.5	54.8
Monetary authorities	4 765 ..	−4.4	−4.3	−4.5	6.4	10.0	....	21.2	33.1
of which: Use of Fund credit and loans from the Fund	4 766 ..	−4.4	−4.3	−4.3	7.1	10.0	....	21.2	33.1
of which: Short-term	4 768 ..	....	....	....	....	....	....	....	....
General government	4 769 ..	132.0	71.1	21.4	−26.4	32.0	28.8	10.9	24.3
of which: Short-term	4 771 ..	....	....	....	....	....	....	....	....
Banks	4 772 ..	....	....	....	....	....	....	....	....
of which: Short-term	4 774 ..	....	....	....	....	....	....	....	....
Other sectors	4 775 ..	7.7	−2.3	−1.1	5.0	−2.8	−8.0	−8.6	−2.6
of which: Short-term	4 777 ..	....	....	....	....	....	....	....	....
Currency and deposits	4 780 ..	67.4	3.2	35.2	20.1	3.1	20.0	39.0	56.1
Monetary authorities	4 781 ..	....	....	1.9	.9	−1.6	−2.3	−.2	.1
General government	4 782 ..	....	....	....	....	....	....	....	....
Banks	4 783 ..	67.4	3.2	33.3	19.2	4.7	22.3	39.1	56.0
Other sectors	4 784 ..	....	....	....	....	....	....	....	....
Other liabilities	4 786 ..	5.2	−2.9	....	....	....	....	....	....
Monetary authorities	4 787 ..	4.5	−3.5	....	....	....	....	....	....
of which: Short-term	4 789 ..	4.5	−3.5	....	....	....	....	....	....
General government	4 790 ..	....	....	....	....	....	....	....	....
of which: Short-term	4 792 ..	....	....	....	....	....	....	....	....
Banks	4 793 ..	....	....	....	....	....	....	....	....
of which: Short-term	4 795 ..	....	....	....	....	....	....	....	....
Other sectors	4 796 ..	.7	.6	....	....	....	....	....	....
of which: Short-term	4 798 ..	.7	.6	....	....	....	....	....	....
E. RESERVE ASSETS	4 802 ..	**−291.0**	**−5.2**	**65.5**	**−218.1**	**−178.0**	**−170.9**	**−329.0**	**−1.1**
Monetary gold	4 812 ..	−.5	−.2	....	....	....	....	....	....
Special drawing rights	4 811 ..	.3	−.1	.1	−.8	−8.4	.1	.2	.4
Reserve position in the Fund	4 810 ..	....	....	....	....	8.5	....	....	....
Foreign exchange	4 803 ..	−290.8	−5.0	65.4	−217.3	−178.1	−171.0	−329.2	−1.5
Other claims	4 813 ..	....	....	....	....	....	....	....	....
NET ERRORS AND OMISSIONS	4 998 ..	**145.7**	**256.5**	**−66.6**	**309.9**	**415.9**	**139.0**	**108.5**	**19.1**

Table 1. ANALYTIC PRESENTATION, 2000–2007

(Millions of U.S. dollars)

	Code	2000	2001	2002	2003	2004	2005	2006	2007
A. Current Account[1]	4 993 Z.	**7,264**	**9,810**	**11,017**	**29,867**	**46,100**	**45,723**	**55,795**	**47,435**
Goods: exports f.o.b.	2 100 ..	205,271	203,201	209,516	264,966	313,429	343,726	386,923	458,042
Goods: imports f.o.b.	3 100 ..	−187,471	−184,015	−190,950	−228,447	−272,590	−298,684	−341,728	−407,374
Balance on Goods	4 100 ..	*17,800*	*19,187*	*18,565*	*36,519*	*40,839*	*45,042*	*45,195*	*50,669*
Services: credit	2 200 ..	49,319	51,248	56,138	63,227	73,772	80,092	82,271	90,594
Services: debit	3 200 ..	−51,339	−53,713	−57,204	−63,897	−69,444	−73,313	−79,539	−87,997
Balance on Goods and Services	4 991 ..	*15,779*	*16,722*	*17,499*	*35,850*	*45,167*	*51,821*	*47,928*	*53,266*
Income: credit	2 300 ..	45,506	43,458	40,304	59,006	80,671	98,837	131,087	152,499
Income: debit	3 300 ..	−47,803	−43,631	−40,245	−57,773	−69,306	−93,529	−110,715	−145,327
Balance on Goods, Services, and Income	4 992 ..	*13,482*	*16,549*	*17,558*	*37,082*	*56,533*	*57,129*	*68,299*	*60,437*
Current transfers: credit	2 379 Z.	4,399	4,475	4,961	8,444	9,764	11,144	12,392	14,864
Current transfers: debit	3 379 ..	−10,618	−11,214	−11,501	−15,659	−20,197	−22,550	−24,897	−27,866
B. Capital Account[1]	4 994 Z.	**−97**	**−3,200**	**−545**	**−3,069**	**−1,614**	**−1,764**	**−2,792**	**−3,534**
Capital account: credit	2 994 Z.	2,216	1,118	857	1,682	1,734	1,929	2,946	3,365
Capital account: debit	3 994 ..	−2,314	−4,317	−1,402	−4,750	−3,349	−3,693	−5,738	−6,899
Total, Groups A Plus B	4 981 ..	*7,166*	*6,611*	*10,472*	*26,798*	*44,485*	*43,959*	*53,003*	*43,901*
C. Financial Account[1]	4 995 W.	**−7,604**	**−3,852**	**−4,527**	**−23,963**	**−46,181**	**−35,746**	**−53,792**	**3,571**
Direct investment abroad	4 505 ..	−74,510	−50,764	−31,758	−44,641	−28,849	−133,929	−46,474	−27,547
Direct investment in the Netherlands	4 555 Z.	63,119	51,980	25,457	20,441	4,379	47,235	7,197	113,627
Portfolio investment assets	4 602 ..	−65,635	−60,994	−64,293	−63,372	−105,084	−81,845	−43,830	−58,055
Equity securities	4 610 ..	−23,448	−29,565	−7,917	−15,394	−34,534	−11,480	−3,044	−34,171
Debt securities	4 619 ..	−42,187	−31,429	−56,375	−47,978	−70,551	−70,365	−40,786	−23,885
Portfolio investment liabilities	4 652 Z.	55,242	74,193	49,777	85,229	74,104	159,993	59,482	−69,174
Equity securities	4 660 ..	16,970	12,947	−149	898	3,379	82,609	18,086	−94,767
Debt securities	4 669 Z.	38,272	61,246	49,926	84,331	70,725	77,384	41,396	25,593
Financial derivatives	4 910 ..	−3,979	−5,836	−6,844	−230	−1,518	−4,181	−6,939	3,870
Financial derivatives assets	4 900 ..	82,999	87,517	70,419	126,911	165,590	150,955	133,924	175,276
Financial derivatives liabilities	4 905 ..	−86,979	−93,354	−77,263	−127,141	−167,108	−155,136	−140,862	−171,406
Other investment assets	4 703 ..	−28,347	−69,657	−28,292	−66,500	−67,053	−52,628	−185,690	−240,426
Monetary authorities	4 701 ..	675	−1,175	360	277	−335	196	−693	1,008
General government	4 704 ..	534	−837	−1,621	−1,660	650	321	1,249	619
Banks	4 705 ..	−18,044	−60,704	−20,587	−56,184	−57,572	−44,049	−177,721	−209,332
Other sectors	4 728 ..	−11,513	−6,940	−6,444	−8,934	−9,795	−9,095	−8,525	−32,720
Other investment liabilities	4 753 W.	46,507	57,227	51,425	45,110	77,840	29,609	162,461	281,276
Monetary authorities	4 753 WA	−3,542	1,977	2,279	−3,544	2,085	−3,182	−8,788	46,126
General government	4 753 ZB	329	2,828	4	−133	−1,845	259	451	815
Banks	4 753 ZC	18,370	57,763	52,158	41,211	77,337	33,290	152,312	211,810
Other sectors	4 753 ZD	31,351	−5,340	−3,016	7,576	263	−759	18,486	22,525
Total, Groups A Through C	4 983 ..	*−438*	*2,759*	*5,945*	*2,835*	*−1,696*	*8,213*	*−789*	*47,472*
D. Net Errors and Omissions	4 998 ..	**657**	**−3,110**	**−6,077**	**−3,272**	**785**	**−10,003**	**1,567**	**−48,373**
Total, Groups A Through D	4 984 ..	*219*	*−351*	*−132*	*−437*	*−911*	*−1,790*	*778*	*−901*
E. Reserves and Related Items	4 802 A.	**−219**	**351**	**132**	**437**	**911**	**1,790**	**−778**	**901**
Reserve assets	4 802 ..	−219	351	132	437	911	1,790	−778	901
Use of Fund credit and loans	4 766 ..	....	....	....	....	....	....	....	....
Exceptional financing	4 920 ..	....	....	....	....	....	....	....	....
Conversion rates: euros per U.S. dollar	0 103 ..	**1.0854**	**1.1175**	**1.0626**	**.8860**	**.8054**	**.8041**	**.7971**	**.7306**

---

[1] Excludes components that have been classified in the categories of Group E.

Table 2. STANDARD PRESENTATION, 2000–2007

(Millions of U.S. dollars)

	Code	2000	2001	2002	2003	2004	2005	2006	2007
CURRENT ACCOUNT..............................	4 993 ..	7,264	9,810	11,017	29,867	46,100	45,723	55,795	47,435
A. GOODS...	4 100 ..	17,800	19,187	18,565	36,519	40,839	45,042	45,195	50,669
Credit..	2 100 ..	205,271	203,201	209,516	264,966	313,429	343,726	386,923	458,042
General merchandise: exports f.o.b............	2 110 ..	195,044	194,689	200,897	254,746	302,795	330,975	373,919	444,260
Goods for processing: exports f.o.b............	2 150 ..	8,621	7,099	7,205	8,683	8,675	10,345	9,961	9,936
Repairs on goods......................................	2 160 ..	257	247	406	....	....	....	....	....
Goods procured in ports by carriers............	2 170 ..	1,319	1,066	921	1,454	1,920	2,281	2,692	3,329
Nonmonetary gold....................................	2 180 ..	29	100	86	83	39	125	351	518
Debit...	3 100 ..	−187,471	−184,015	−190,950	−228,447	−272,590	−298,684	−341,728	−407,374
General merchandise: imports f.o.b............	3 110 ..	−179,035	−176,227	−184,362	−221,000	−263,939	−288,796	−330,980	−393,774
Goods for processing: imports f.o.b............	3 150 ..	−7,144	−6,570	−5,375	−6,258	−7,110	−7,780	−8,311	−10,649
Repairs on goods......................................	3 160 ..	−81	−107	−127	....	....	....	....	....
Goods procured in ports by carriers............	3 170 ..	−1,170	−944	−978	−1,089	−1,435	−1,925	−2,049	−2,412
Nonmonetary gold....................................	3 180 ..	−41	−166	−108	−100	−106	−183	−388	−539
B. SERVICES...	4 200 ..	−2,021	−2,465	−1,066	−670	4,328	6,779	2,733	2,597
Total credit...	2 200 ..	*49,319*	*51,248*	*56,138*	*63,227*	*73,772*	*80,092*	*82,271*	*90,594*
Total debit..	3 200 ..	*−51,339*	*−53,713*	*−57,204*	*−63,897*	*−69,444*	*−73,313*	*−79,539*	*−87,997*
Transportation services, credit..........	2 205 ..	16,787	17,624	17,672	16,271	19,402	21,453	20,578	22,460
Passenger...	2 850 ..	*4,088*	*4,439*	*4,035*	....	....	....	....	....
Freight...	2 851 ..	*9,934*	*10,339*	*10,654*	....	....	....	....	....
Other...	2 852 ..	*2,765*	*2,846*	*2,983*	....	....	....	....	....
Sea transport, passenger...........................	2 207 ..	15	16	11	....	....	....	....	....
Sea transport, freight................................	2 208 ..	5,175	5,286	4,914	....	....	....	....	....
Sea transport, other..................................	2 209 ..	2,186	2,170	2,339	....	....	....	....	....
Air transport, passenger............................	2 211 ..	4,051	4,405	4,001	....	....	....	....	....
Air transport, freight.................................	2 212 ..	885	972	943	....	....	....	....	....
Air transport, other...................................	2 213 ..	364	453	392	....	....	....	....	....
Other transport, passenger........................	2 215 ..	22	18	23	....	....	....	....	....
Other transport, freight.............................	2 216 ..	3,874	4,081	4,797	....	....	....	....	....
Other transport, other...............................	2 217 ..	216	224	252	....	....	....	....	....
Transportation services, debit............	3 205 ..	−12,888	−12,778	−12,860	−12,188	−13,715	−14,956	−17,362	−19,365
Passenger...	3 850 ..	*−1,458*	*−1,067*	*−1,225*	....	....	....	....	....
Freight...	3 851 ..	*−9,748*	*−9,882*	*−9,819*	....	....	....	....	....
Other...	3 852 ..	*−1,682*	*−1,829*	*−1,816*	....	....	....	....	....
Sea transport, passenger...........................	3 207 ..	−101	−99	−108	....	....	....	....	....
Sea transport, freight................................	3 208 ..	−6,954	−6,860	−6,322	....	....	....	....	....
Sea transport, other..................................	3 209 ..	−589	−640	−635	....	....	....	....	....
Air transport, passenger............................	3 211 ..	−1,301	−922	−1,060	....	....	....	....	....
Air transport, freight.................................	3 212 ..	−167	−119	−136	....	....	....	....	....
Air transport, other...................................	3 213 ..	−757	−823	−818	....	....	....	....	....
Other transport, passenger........................	3 215 ..	−56	−46	−57	....	....	....	....	....
Other transport, freight.............................	3 216 ..	−2,627	−2,903	−3,360	....	....	....	....	....
Other transport, other...............................	3 217 ..	−335	−366	−364	....	....	....	....	....
Travel, credit.....................................	2 236 ..	7,197	6,708	7,710	9,163	10,308	10,447	11,380	13,416
Business travel...	2 237 ..	....	....	....	....	3,382	3,464	3,627	4,375
Personal travel...	2 240 ..	....	....	....	....	6,926	6,983	7,754	9,041
Travel, debit......................................	3 236 ..	−12,191	−11,994	−12,976	−15,265	−16,348	−16,140	−17,087	−19,109
Business travel...	3 237 ..	....	....	....	....	−4,058	−3,921	−4,156	−4,682
Personal travel...	3 240 ..	....	....	....	....	−12,289	−12,219	−12,931	−14,427
Other services, credit........................	2 200 BA	25,335	26,916	30,756	37,793	44,062	48,193	50,313	54,718
Communications.......................................	2 245 ..	1,441	1,855	1,486	2,588	3,310	3,762	3,999	4,399
Construction..	2 249 ..	2,581	3,178	2,588	2,145	2,129	2,751	2,295	2,968
Insurance..	2 253 ..	204	231	308	380	414	452	512	597
Financial...	2 260 ..	735	790	809	738	836	910	1,032	1,294
Computer and information..........................	2 262 ..	1,166	864	1,422	2,884	3,702	3,723	3,904	4,220
Royalties and licence fees..........................	2 266 ..	2,171	1,740	1,963	2,930	4,205	3,866	4,126	4,790
Other business services.............................	2 268 ..	15,527	16,598	20,204	23,599	26,704	29,923	31,454	33,131
Personal, cultural, and recreational.............	2 287 ..	552	534	538	618	771	902	901	1,006
Government, n.i.e......................................	2 291 ..	958	1,127	1,438	1,910	1,990	1,904	2,091	2,312
Other services, debit..........................	3 200 BA	−26,261	−28,941	−31,368	−36,444	−39,382	−42,218	−45,090	−49,522
Communications.......................................	3 245 ..	−1,416	−1,770	−1,535	−2,498	−2,868	−3,194	−3,487	−3,568
Construction..	3 249 ..	−977	−1,129	−909	−1,002	−1,071	−1,417	−1,209	−1,593
Insurance..	3 253 ..	−534	−534	−1,089	−1,011	−761	−802	−889	−989
Financial...	3 260 ..	−961	−1,209	−1,255	−887	−888	−1,011	−1,128	−1,506
Computer and information..........................	3 262 ..	−1,187	−1,314	−1,586	−2,352	−3,107	−3,697	−3,745	−4,128
Royalties and licence fees..........................	3 266 ..	−2,505	−2,321	−2,612	−3,360	−3,339	−3,692	−3,865	−4,465
Other business services.............................	3 268 ..	−16,687	−18,537	−21,054	−23,646	−25,590	−26,567	−28,969	−31,521
Personal, cultural, and recreational.............	3 287 ..	−597	−580	−616	−746	−880	−946	−990	−1,047
Government, n.i.e......................................	3 291 ..	−1,398	−1,547	−712	−943	−879	−894	−809	−707

Table 2 (Continued). STANDARD PRESENTATION, 2000–2007

(Millions of U.S. dollars)

	Code	2000	2001	2002	2003	2004	2005	2006	2007
C. INCOME	4 300	**−2,297**	**−172**	**59**	**1,233**	**11,366**	**5,308**	**20,371**	**7,172**
Total credit	2 300	*45,506*	*43,458*	*40,304*	*59,006*	*80,671*	*98,837*	*131,087*	*152,499*
Total debit	3 300	*−47,803*	*−43,631*	*−40,245*	*−57,773*	*−69,306*	*−93,529*	*−110,715*	*−145,327*
Compensation of employees, credit	2 310	**426**	**483**	**484**	**1,120**	**1,251**	**1,233**	**1,121**	**1,304**
Compensation of employees, debit	3 310	**−924**	**−984**	**−1,027**	**−1,812**	**−2,290**	**−2,420**	**−2,972**	**−3,074**
Investment income, credit	2 320	**45,080**	**42,976**	**39,820**	**57,886**	**79,420**	**97,604**	**129,966**	**151,195**
Direct investment income	2 330	20,254	17,089	14,107	25,973	40,787	50,354	68,651	69,811
Dividends and distributed branch profits	2 332	16,666	14,845	9,095	11,889	15,105	46,373	55,442	43,859
Reinvested earnings and undistributed branch profits	2 333	953	−967	2,243	7,923	17,548	−4,510	2,379	15,866
Income on debt (interest)	2 334	2,636	3,210	2,770	6,161	8,134	8,491	10,830	10,085
Portfolio investment income	2 339	10,870	10,232	14,004	20,909	26,743	30,846	35,885	40,789
Income on equity	2 340	1,742	1,413	1,529	4,826	6,491	8,589	9,791	11,887
Income on bonds and notes	2 350	9,128	8,819	12,476	16,043	20,211	22,116	25,952	28,792
Income on money market instruments	2 360	....	....	....	40	41	140	142	109
Other investment income	2 370	13,956	15,655	11,709	11,004	11,890	16,404	25,430	40,596
Investment income, debit	3 320	**−46,879**	**−42,646**	**−39,218**	**−55,960**	**−67,016**	**−91,109**	**−107,744**	**−142,253**
Direct investment income	3 330	−16,144	−9,505	−5,317	−18,099	−23,002	−31,631	−32,096	−40,269
Dividends and distributed branch profits	3 332	−5,266	−5,903	−4,843	−8,749	−8,343	−25,348	−10,426	−26,127
Reinvested earnings and undistributed branch profits	3 333	−9,196	−1,042	1,120	−4,501	−8,698	532	−13,499	−5,512
Income on debt (interest)	3 334	−1,681	−2,560	−1,594	−4,849	−5,960	−6,815	−8,171	−8,631
Portfolio investment income	3 339	−15,123	−16,328	−20,650	−23,953	−27,721	−37,110	−44,070	−53,553
Income on equity	3 340	−5,429	−5,910	−6,016	−6,681	−7,949	−12,810	−16,079	−20,109
Income on bonds and notes	3 350	−9,693	−10,418	−14,633	−16,628	−18,893	−23,464	−26,889	−31,456
Income on money market instruments	3 360	....	....	....	−644	−879	−836	−1,102	−1,988
Other investment income	3 370	−15,612	−16,813	−13,252	−13,908	−16,294	−22,368	−31,577	−48,430
D. CURRENT TRANSFERS	4 379	**−6,219**	**−6,739**	**−6,540**	**−7,216**	**−10,433**	**−11,406**	**−12,504**	**−13,002**
Credit	2 379	**4,399**	**4,475**	**4,961**	**8,444**	**9,764**	**11,144**	**12,392**	**14,864**
General government	2 380	2,911	2,915	3,112	3,090	4,271	5,320	5,973	7,326
Other sectors	2 390	1,488	1,560	1,848	5,354	5,493	5,825	6,420	7,537
Workers' remittances	2 391	....	....	....	....	....	....	....	....
Other current transfers	2 392	1,488	1,560	1,848	5,354	5,493	5,825	6,420	7,537
Debit	3 379	**−10,618**	**−11,214**	**−11,501**	**−15,659**	**−20,197**	**−22,550**	**−24,897**	**−27,866**
General government	3 380	−7,843	−8,331	−8,186	−9,488	−12,374	−13,367	−14,692	−15,027
Other sectors	3 390	−2,774	−2,884	−3,315	−6,171	−7,823	−9,183	−10,205	−12,839
Workers' remittances	3 391	−523	−549	−613	−656	−644	−849	−975	−1,306
Other current transfers	3 392	−2,251	−2,335	−2,702	−5,515	−7,179	−8,334	−9,230	−11,533
CAPITAL AND FINANCIAL ACCOUNT	4 996	**−7,921**	**−6,700**	**−4,940**	**−26,595**	**−46,884**	**−35,720**	**−57,362**	**938**
CAPITAL ACCOUNT	4 994	**−97**	**−3,200**	**−545**	**−3,069**	**−1,614**	**−1,764**	**−2,792**	**−3,534**
Total credit	2 994	*2,216*	*1,118*	*857*	*1,682*	*1,734*	*1,929*	*2,946*	*3,365*
Total debit	3 994	*−2,314*	*−4,317*	*−1,402*	*−4,750*	*−3,349*	*−3,693*	*−5,738*	*−6,899*
Capital transfers, credit	2 400	**1,032**	**1,109**	**854**	**1,675**	**1,593**	**1,911**	**2,346**	**3,356**
General government	2 401	196	145	50	250	256	308	409	17
Debt forgiveness	2 402	....	....	....	....	....	....	....	....
Other capital transfers	2 410	....	....	....	....	....	....	....	....
Other sectors	2 430	835	963	804	1,425	1,338	1,603	1,937	3,339
Migrants' transfers	2 431	731	875	731	904	913	994	1,292	1,701
Debt forgiveness	2 432	....	....	....	....	....	....	....	....
Other capital transfers	2 440	104	89	73	520	425	609	645	1,639
Capital transfers, debit	3 400	**−1,789**	**−1,514**	**−1,401**	**−2,955**	**−3,263**	**−3,693**	**−5,738**	**−6,881**
General government	3 401	−8	−62	−62	−565	−743	−789	−1,650	−2,711
Debt forgiveness	3 402	....	....	....	....	....	....	....	....
Other capital transfers	3 410	....	....	....	....	....	....	....	....
Other sectors	3 430	−1,781	−1,452	−1,340	−2,390	−2,520	−2,904	−4,087	−4,170
Migrants' transfers	3 431	−1,675	−1,316	−1,249	−1,770	−2,098	−2,409	−2,855	−3,270
Debt forgiveness	3 432	....	....	....	....	....	....	....	....
Other capital transfers	3 440	−107	−136	−90	−620	−423	−495	−1,232	−900
Nonproduced nonfinancial assets, credit	2 480	**1,185**	**9**	**3**	**7**	**141**	**18**	**600**	**9**
Nonproduced nonfinancial assets, debit	3 480	**−525**	**−2,804**	**−1**	**−1,796**	**−85**	**....**	**....**	**−17**

Table 2 (Continued). STANDARD PRESENTATION, 2000–2007

(Millions of U.S. dollars)

	Code	2000	2001	2002	2003	2004	2005	2006	2007
FINANCIAL ACCOUNT	4 995 ..	−7,824	−3,501	−4,395	−23,526	−45,270	−33,956	−54,570	4,472
A. DIRECT INVESTMENT	4 500 ..	−11,391	1,215	−6,301	−24,200	−24,471	−86,694	−39,277	86,080
Direct investment abroad	4 505 ..	−74,510	−50,764	−31,758	−44,641	−28,849	−133,929	−46,474	−27,547
Equity capital	4 510 ..	−42,962	−25,657	−20,340	−33,241	−31,276	−113,822	−34,465	−12,295
Claims on affiliated enterprises	4 515 ..	....	....	....	....	−31,276	−113,821	−34,646	−12,389
Liabilities to affiliated enterprises	4 520 ..	....	....	....	....	....	−1	180	94
Reinvested earnings	4 525 ..	−953	967	−2,243	−7,923	−17,548	4,510	−2,379	−15,866
Other capital	4 530 ..	−30,595	−26,075	−9,175	−3,477	19,975	−24,617	−9,630	614
Claims on affiliated enterprises	4 535 ..	....	....	....	....	10,362	−21,962	−18,698	−6,189
Liabilities to affiliated enterprises	4 540 ..	....	....	....	....	9,612	−2,655	9,069	6,803
Direct investment in the Netherlands	4 555 ..	63,119	51,980	25,457	20,441	4,379	47,235	7,197	113,627
Equity capital	4 560 ..	17,052	12,519	4,826	16,637	6,600	4,856	6,024	130,029
Claims on direct investors	4 565 ..	....	....	....	....	553	−27	−58	57
Liabilities to direct investors	4 570 ..	....	....	....	....	6,046	4,883	6,082	129,972
Reinvested earnings	4 575 ..	9,196	1,042	−1,120	4,501	8,698	−532	13,499	5,510
Other capital	4 580 ..	36,871	38,418	21,751	−698	−10,920	42,911	−12,326	−21,912
Claims on direct investors	4 585 ..	....	....	....	....	−1,742	314	−3,631	1,650
Liabilities to direct investors	4 590 ..	....	....	....	....	−9,177	42,597	−8,695	−23,562
B. PORTFOLIO INVESTMENT	4 600 ..	−10,393	13,199	−14,516	21,857	−30,980	78,148	15,652	−127,229
Assets	4 602 ..	−65,635	−60,994	−64,293	−63,372	−105,084	−81,845	−43,830	−58,055
Equity securities	4 610 ..	−23,448	−29,565	−7,917	−15,394	−34,534	−11,480	−3,044	−34,171
Monetary authorities	4 611 ..	....	....	....	....	23	39	....	−4
General government	4 612 ..	....	....	....	....				
Banks	4 613 ..	....	....	....	....	−4,439	−6,322	17,024	−8,986
Other sectors	4 614 ..	....	....	....	....	−30,118	−5,198	−20,068	−25,180
Debt securities	4 619 ..	−42,187	−31,429	−56,375	−47,978	−70,551	−70,365	−40,786	−23,885
Bonds and notes	4 620 ..	−47,387	−33,793	−54,120	−50,239	−61,081	−71,262	−64,356	−32,460
Monetary authorities	4 621 ..	....	....	....	....	121	−1,153	−351	−5,091
General government	4 622 ..	....	....	....	....				
Banks	4 623 ..	....	....	....	....	−6,323	−15,951	−27,553	3,139
Other sectors	4 624 ..	....	....	....	....	−54,879	−54,158	−36,452	−30,507
Money market instruments	4 630 ..	5,200	2,364	−2,256	2,262	−9,470	897	23,571	8,575
Monetary authorities	4 631 ..	....	....	....	....	....	....	23	−802
General government	4 632 ..	....	....	....	....				
Banks	4 633 ..	....	....	....	....	−7,732	−1,257	22,701	8,842
Other sectors	4 634 ..	....	....	....	....	−1,738	2,153	847	535
Liabilities	4 652 ..	55,242	74,193	49,777	85,229	74,104	159,993	59,482	−69,174
Equity securities	4 660 ..	16,970	12,947	−149	898	3,379	82,609	18,086	−94,767
Banks	4 663 ..	....	....	....	....				
Other sectors	4 664 ..	....	....	....	....				
Debt securities	4 669 ..	38,272	61,246	49,926	84,331	70,725	77,384	41,396	25,593
Bonds and notes	4 670 ..	41,647	55,389	39,866	81,011	75,715	83,421	61,234	20,172
Monetary authorities	4 671 ..	....	....	....	....				
General government	4 672 ..	4,991	18,357	9,454	13,113	22,525	13,756	−254	−6,962
Banks	4 673 ..	15,616	20,243	23,370	43,965	48,866	53,227	41,313	23,049
Other sectors	4 674 ..	21,041	16,788	7,042	23,933	4,324	16,438	20,174	4,085
Money market instruments	4 680 ..	−3,375	5,857	10,060	3,320	−4,991	−6,037	−19,838	5,421
Monetary authorities	4 681 ..	−2	−43	....	....				
General government	4 682 ..	122	736	9,142	2,444	−2,455	586	−5,765	2,240
Banks	4 683 ..	−2,456	1,936	−114	−3,702	269	−7,565	−8,868	5,143
Other sectors	4 684 ..	−1,039	3,229	1,032	4,578	−2,804	942	−5,205	−1,962
C. FINANCIAL DERIVATIVES	4 910 ..	−3,979	−5,836	−6,844	−230	−1,518	−4,181	−6,939	3,870
Monetary authorities	4 911 ..	39	....	....	8	....	....	....	....
General government	4 912 ..	−1	....	2	....	....	....	−3	1
Banks	4 913 ..	−3,555	−5,619	−7,216	−362	−1,241	−1,293	−2,759	1,095
Other sectors	4 914 ..	−462	−217	371	123	−278	−2,888	−4,177	2,774
Assets	4 900 ..	82,999	87,517	70,419	126,911	165,590	150,955	133,924	175,276
Monetary authorities	4 901 ..	39	....	....	8	....	....	....	....
General government	4 902 ..	−1	....	2	....	....	....	−3	1
Banks	4 903 ..	82,565	85,507	67,180	96,650	118,004	120,015	111,074	114,531
Other sectors	4 904 ..	396	2,010	3,237	30,252	47,586	30,941	22,852	60,744
Liabilities	4 905 ..	−86,979	−93,354	−77,263	−127,141	−167,108	−155,136	−140,862	−171,406
Monetary authorities	4 906 ..	....	....	....	....	....	....	....	....
General government	4 907 ..	....	....	....	....	....	....	....	....
Banks	4 908 ..	−86,121	−91,126	−74,397	−97,012	−119,245	−121,308	−113,833	−113,436
Other sectors	4 909 ..	−858	−2,228	−2,866	−30,129	−47,864	−33,828	−27,029	−57,970

Table 2 (Concluded). STANDARD PRESENTATION, 2000–2007

(Millions of U.S. dollars)

	Code	2000	2001	2002	2003	2004	2005	2006	2007
D. OTHER INVESTMENT	4 700	**18,160**	**−12,430**	**23,133**	**−21,390**	**10,788**	**−23,019**	**−23,229**	**40,850**
Assets	4 703	−28,347	−69,657	−28,292	−66,500	−67,053	−52,628	−185,690	−240,426
Trade credits	4 706	−3,131	1,233	−205	−1,487	−3,266	−2,978	−2,646	−3,381
General government	4 707	....	....	....	....	....	....	....	....
of which: Short-term	4 709	....	....	....	....	....	....	....	....
Other sectors	4 710	−3,131	1,233	−205	−1,487	−3,266	−2,978	−2,646	−3,381
of which: Short-term	4 712	*−3,131*	*1,233*	*−205*	*−1,787*	*−3,256*	*−2,899*	*−2,829*	*−3,100*
Loans	4 714	−12,273	−7,791	−3,214	−18,306	−4,198	−13,804	−16,344	−76,521
Monetary authorities	4 715	....	....	....	....	....	....	....	....
of which: Short-term	4 718	....	....	....	....	....	....	....	....
General government	4 719	711	−673	−1,483	−1,492	568	−50	455	471
of which: Short-term	4 721	*546*	*−874*	*−1,726*	*−1,625*	....	*−119*	*300*	*188*
Banks	4 722	−10,194	−7,221	−4,833	−13,695	−5,771	−12,834	−14,522	−71,352
of which: Short-term	4 724	....	....	....	....	....	....	....	....
Other sectors	4 725	−2,791	103	3,101	−3,119	1,004	−921	−2,277	−5,639
of which: Short-term	4 727	*−1,353*	*510*	*3,080*	*−2,378*	*1,148*	*−896*	*−2,474*	*−5,294*
Currency and deposits	4 730	−11,519	−59,217	−23,719	−48,139	−58,334	−32,913	−160,886	−143,719
Monetary authorities	4 731	675	−1,175	360	277	−314	220	−693	1,014
General government	4 732	....	....	....	....	....	....	....	....
Banks	4 733	−7,850	−53,483	−15,754	−42,489	−51,801	−31,216	−163,199	−137,980
Other sectors	4 734	−4,343	−4,558	−8,325	−5,928	−6,219	−1,917	3,006	−6,754
Other assets	4 736	−1,425	−3,882	−1,153	1,433	−1,254	−2,932	−5,814	−16,805
Monetary authorities	4 737	....	....	....	....	−21	−24	....	−7
of which: Short-term	4 739	....	....	....	....	....	....	....	....
General government	4 740	−177	−164	−138	−167	82	371	794	148
of which: Short-term	4 742	....	....	....	....	....	....	....	....
Banks	4 743	....	....	....	....	....	....	....	....
of which: Short-term	4 745	....	....	....	....	....	....	....	....
Other sectors	4 746	−1,248	−3,718	−1,015	1,600	−1,315	−3,279	−6,608	−16,947
of which: Short-term	4 748	*−1,543*	*−3,585*	*−1,104*	*1,563*	*−1,316*	*−3,283*	*−6,617*	*−16,946*
Liabilities	4 753	**46,507**	**57,227**	**51,425**	**45,110**	**77,840**	**29,609**	**162,461**	**281,276**
Trade credits	4 756	1,891	−1,193	213	913	2,039	1,860	1,849	1,910
General government	4 757	....	....	....	....	....	....	....	....
of which: Short-term	4 759	....	....	....	....	....	....	....	....
Other sectors	4 760	1,891	−1,193	213	913	2,039	1,860	1,849	1,910
of which: Short-term	4 762	*1,899*	*−1,193*	*213*	*932*	*2,039*	*1,860*	*1,850*	*1,910*
Loans	4 764	21,482	7,048	17,330	19,033	4,145	14,188	14,416	53,357
Monetary authorities	4 765	....	....	....	103	−1,192	292	1,284	−905
of which: Use of Fund credit and loans from the Fund	4 766	....	....	....	....	....	....	....	....
of which: Short-term	4 768	....	....	....	*103*	*−1,192*	*292*	*1,284*	*−905*
General government	4 769	78	2,538	560	−187	−954	6	25	654
of which: Short-term	4 771	*77*	*2,496*	*552*	*−185*	*−944*	*4*	....	*743*
Banks	4 772	−51	−883	10,868	19,604	3,018	22,270	8,957	32,545
of which: Short-term	4 774	....	....	....	....	....	....	....	....
Other sectors	4 775	21,455	5,393	5,902	−487	3,273	−8,381	4,150	21,063
of which: Short-term	4 777	*3,667*	*652*	*2,766*	*413*	*1,132*	*−1,710*	*1,994*	*6,801*
Currency and deposits	4 780	17,293	55,465	43,379	25,404	66,893	16,410	134,849	231,280
Monetary authorities	4 781	−3,542	1,977	2,279	−3,647	3,277	−3,474	−10,072	47,030
General government	4 782	331	303	−531	99	−890	391	228	133
Banks	4 783	18,420	58,645	41,290	20,613	70,716	18,863	141,228	178,801
Other sectors	4 784	2,084	−5,461	341	8,339	−6,210	630	3,465	5,315
Other liabilities	4 786	5,841	−4,093	−9,497	−240	4,763	−2,849	11,348	−5,271
Monetary authorities	4 787	....	....	....	....	....	....	....	....
of which: Short-term	4 789	....	....	....	....	....	....	....	....
General government	4 790	−80	−14	−25	−45	−1	−138	198	28
of which: Short-term	4 792	*−80*	*−14*	*−25*	*−45*	*−1*	*−138*	*198*	*28*
Banks	4 793	....	1	....	995	3,603	−7,843	2,127	464
of which: Short-term	4 795	....	*1*	....	*995*	*3,603*	*−7,843*	*2,127*	*464*
Other sectors	4 796	5,921	−4,081	−9,473	−1,189	1,161	5,132	9,023	−5,763
of which: Short-term	4 798	*321*	*403*	*838*	*−1,823*	*1,172*	*5,141*	*9,038*	*−5,783*
E. RESERVE ASSETS	4 802	**−219**	**351**	**132**	**437**	**911**	**1,790**	**−778**	**901**
Monetary gold	4 812	672	237	337	930	....	1,190	1,000	−27
Special drawing rights	4 811	323	−123	109	−13	34	....	−31	−153
Reserve position in the Fund	4 810	474	−447	−301	69	500	1,295	550	180
Foreign exchange	4 803	−1,689	684	−13	−549	377	−695	−2,297	901
Other claims	4 813	....	....	....	....	....	....	....	....
NET ERRORS AND OMISSIONS	4 998	**657**	**−3,110**	**−6,077**	**−3,272**	**785**	**−10,003**	**1,567**	**−48,373**

Table 3. INTERNATIONAL INVESTMENT POSITION (End-period stocks), 2000–2007

(Billions of U.S. dollars)

	Code	2000	2001	2002	2003	2004	2005	2006	2007
ASSETS..	8 995 C.	**1,135.47**	**1,238.99**	**1,489.74**	**2,000.21**	**2,394.19**	**2,429.20**	**2,956.18**	**3,671.58**
Direct investment abroad....................................	8 505 ..	**305.46**	**332.16**	**396.53**	**521.30**	**587.25**	**613.48**	**718.83**	**845.56**
Equity capital and reinvested earnings............................	8 506 ..	183.75	188.50	226.13	318.97	388.77	403.89	476.04	574.66
Claims on affiliated enterprises..............................	8 507 ..	....	....	....	319.03	389.16	404.21	476.35	575.67
Liabilities to affiliated enterprises...........................	8 508 ..	....	....	....	−.06	−.39	−.32	−.31	−1.01
Other capital...	8 530 ..	121.71	143.65	170.40	202.33	198.48	209.60	242.78	270.90
Claims on affiliated enterprises..............................	8 535 ..	....	....	....	241.31	249.50	251.12	298.84	339.35
Liabilities to affiliated enterprises...........................	8 540 ..	....	....	....	−38.98	−51.02	−41.52	−56.06	−68.45
Portfolio investment...	8 602 ..	**478.30**	**485.70**	**570.00**	**832.42**	**1,058.94**	**1,096.65**	**1,261.23**	**1,474.71**
Equity securities..	8 610 ..	253.59	235.02	217.39	349.82	442.99	475.35	556.58	646.14
Monetary authorities..	8 611 ..	.52	.67	.81	1.40	1.51	1.55	1.59	1.76
General government...	8 612 ..	....	....	....	....	....	....	....	....
Banks..	8 613 ..	2.45	1.94	3.76	6.96	12.75	17.07	−17.67	−7.59
Other sectors..	8 614 ..	250.62	232.41	212.81	341.46	428.74	456.73	572.66	651.97
Debt securities..	8 619 ..	224.71	250.67	352.62	482.60	615.95	621.30	704.65	828.57
Bonds and notes..	8 620 ..	220.21	244.77	343.32	476.17	597.76	605.68	694.32	818.54
Monetary authorities...	8 621 ..	7.29	6.42	9.26	11.67	12.07	10.90	11.89	17.80
General government..	8 622 ..	....	....	....	....	....	....	....	....
Banks...	8 623 ..	67.14	73.00	103.41	143.14	161.49	158.14	182.81	185.13
Other sectors...	8 624 ..	145.79	165.35	230.66	321.36	424.20	436.63	499.61	615.60
Money market instruments...................................	8 630 ..	4.50	5.90	9.29	6.43	18.19	15.62	10.33	10.04
Monetary authorities...	8 631 ..	....	....	....	....	....	....	....	1.00
General government..	8 632 ..	....	....	....	....	....	....	....	....
Banks...	8 633 ..	3.96	1.50	4.30	5.01	14.21	13.32	6.01	2.28
Other sectors...	8 634 ..	.53	4.40	5.00	1.42	3.98	2.31	4.32	6.76
Financial derivatives..	8 900 ..	**29.25**	**44.61**	**71.81**	**86.71**	**85.89**	**70.36**	**81.46**	**116.78**
Monetary authorities...	8 901 ..	....	....	....	....	.01	.23	.03	.04
General government..	8 902 ..	....	....	....	....	....	....	....	....
Banks...	8 903 ..	28.60	43.55	69.65	60.66	68.42	59.15	63.14	96.66
Other sectors..	8 904 ..	.64	1.05	2.16	26.05	17.46	10.97	18.29	20.08
Other investment..	8 703 ..	**304.83**	**359.60**	**432.45**	**538.18**	**640.51**	**628.24**	**870.76**	**1,207.54**
Trade credits..	8 706 ..	21.79	19.46	23.15	28.01	33.64	31.99	38.59	46.77
General government...	8 707 ..	1.49	1.48	1.51	.12	....	....	....	....
of which: Short-term..	8 709 ..	....	....	....	....	....	....	....	....
Other sectors..	8 710 ..	20.30	17.98	21.64	27.89	33.64	31.99	38.59	46.77
of which: Short-term..	8 712 ..	*19.80*	*17.51*	*21.14*	*27.56*	*33.27*	*31.60*	*38.36*	*46.20*
Loans..	8 714 ..	62.61	68.39	76.44	117.60	128.80	127.79	152.02	246.70
Monetary authorities..	8 715 ..	2.33	3.05	3.32	....	....	....	....	....
of which: Short-term..	8 718 ..	....	....	....	....	....	....	....	....
General government...	8 719 ..	5.33	4.95	5.73	2.57	2.17	1.82	1.87	1.78
of which: Short-term..	8 721 ..	....	....	....	....	....	....	....	....
Banks..	8 722 ..	39.84	45.90	54.47	74.42	84.44	92.21	112.58	195.41
of which: Short-term..	8 724 ..	....	....	....	....	....	....	....	....
Other sectors..	8 725 ..	15.11	14.49	12.92	40.61	42.19	33.76	37.58	49.51
of which: Short-term..	8 727 ..	*5.47*	*4.78*	*2.00*	*12.42*	*12.42*	*8.72*	*13.52*	*13.89*
Currency and deposits..	8 730 ..	191.20	240.41	294.08	352.88	433.78	427.70	627.30	842.50
Monetary authorities..	8 731 ..	....	....	....	3.74	4.30	3.62	4.84	4.32
General government...	8 732 ..	....	....	....	3.22	3.64	8.03	2.32	6.55
Banks..	8 733 ..	163.94	209.95	248.18	326.72	398.32	391.87	587.08	769.82
Other sectors..	8 734 ..	27.26	30.46	45.90	19.21	27.51	24.19	33.05	61.81
Other assets..	8 736 ..	29.23	31.35	38.78	39.68	44.29	40.76	52.85	71.57
Monetary authorities..	8 737 ..	.20	.19	.23	.31	.36	.33	.37	.42
of which: Short-term..	8 739 ..	....	....	....	....	....	....	....	....
General government...	8 740 ..	14.09	13.48	16.20	3.54	3.70	2.89	2.38	3.23
of which: Short-term..	8 742 ..	....	....	....	....	....	....	....	.77
Banks..	8 743 ..	....	....	....	2.35	3.94	4.57	6.47	14.42
of which: Short-term..	8 745 ..	....	....	....	*2.35*	*3.94*	*4.57*	*6.47*	*14.42*
Other sectors..	8 746 ..	14.94	17.68	22.35	33.48	36.28	32.97	43.63	53.50
of which: Short-term..	8 748 ..	*15.05*	*17.79*	*22.48*	*27.94*	*30.31*	*27.46*	*37.48*	*46.61*
Reserve assets..	8 802 ..	**17.64**	**16.93**	**18.95**	**21.60**	**21.60**	**20.46**	**23.90**	**26.98**
Monetary gold..	8 812 ..	7.99	7.89	9.38	10.43	10.95	11.46	13.10	16.71
Special drawing rights..	8 811 ..	.65	.75	.70	.78	.78	.72	.78	.98
Reserve position in the Fund.....................................	8 810 ..	1.99	2.35	2.85	3.05	2.67	1.19	.69	.54
Foreign exchange...	8 803 ..	7.00	5.93	6.02	7.34	7.21	7.09	9.33	8.75
Other claims..	8 813 ..	....	....	....	....	....	....	....	....

Table 3 (Concluded). INTERNATIONAL INVESTMENT POSITION (End-period stocks), 2000–2007

(Billions of U.S. dollars)

	Code	2000	2001	2002	2003	2004	2005	2006	2007
LIABILITIES...	8 995 D.	**1,194.73**	**1,291.91**	**1,608.30**	**2,013.86**	**2,369.41**	**2,448.69**	**2,950.59**	**3,722.14**
Direct investment in the Netherlands.................	8 555 ..	**243.73**	**282.88**	**349.97**	**428.05**	**477.22**	**451.08**	**502.23**	**704.56**
Equity capital and reinvested earnings............................	8 556 ..	133.65	140.39	168.19	249.25	295.09	242.82	281.83	466.84
Claims on direct investors................................	8 557 ..	....	....	....	−.04	−.02	−.24	.06	−.08
Liabilities to direct investors............................	8 558 ..	....	....	....	249.29	295.11	243.06	281.77	466.92
Other capital..	8 580 ..	110.09	142.49	181.78	178.79	182.13	208.26	220.39	237.72
Claims on direct investors................................	8 585 ..	....	....	....	−11.01	−12.80	−10.72	−14.63	−15.44
Liabilities to direct investors............................	8 590 ..	....	....	....	189.80	194.93	218.98	235.02	253.16
Portfolio investment................................	8 652 ..	**567.01**	**547.59**	**647.36**	**866.12**	**1,045.45**	**1,199.25**	**1,428.00**	**1,562.69**
Equity securities..	8 660 ..	350.57	283.98	262.25	314.56	368.43	516.08	630.52	662.13
Banks..	8 663 ..	350.57	283.98	262.25	25.60	31.72	36.67	44.78	1.40
Other sectors..	8 664 ..	....	....	....	288.95	336.72	479.41	585.74	660.73
Debt securities..	8 669 ..	216.44	263.61	385.11	551.57	677.02	683.17	797.48	900.56
Bonds and notes..	8 670 ..	208.12	250.71	361.00	504.12	627.93	638.92	763.41	850.27
Monetary authorities.....	8 671 ..	....	....	....	....	....	....	....	....
General government......................	8 672 ..	64.48	79.38	113.45	159.39	198.19	187.58	209.34	220.18
Banks....................................	8 673 ..	96.94	116.51	174.58	230.81	299.14	323.10	395.45	450.25
Other sectors............................	8 674 ..	46.71	54.83	72.96	113.93	130.60	128.24	158.63	179.84
Money market instruments........................	8 680 ..	8.32	12.90	24.11	47.45	49.09	44.24	34.07	50.29
Monetary authorities.....	8 681 ..	....	....	....	....	....	....	....	....
General government......................	8 682 ..	.17	4.20	14.05	23.20	22.67	20.02	17.08	21.82
Banks....................................	8 683 ..	6.08	7.54	7.85	18.64	21.74	17.53	13.66	23.39
Other sectors............................	8 684 ..	2.07	1.16	2.21	5.61	4.68	6.69	3.33	5.08
Financial derivatives.............................	8 905 ..	**24.44**	**49.47**	**86.57**	**94.85**	**98.66**	**86.95**	**86.59**	**121.53**
Monetary authorities...............................	8 906 ..	....	....	....	.01	....	....	.01	.01
General government...............................	8 907 ..	....	....	....	....	....	....	....	....
Banks...	8 908 ..	24.04	48.55	84.40	78.74	92.94	76.03	76.76	102.82
Other sectors.....................................	8 909 ..	.40	.92	2.18	16.10	5.72	10.92	9.82	18.70
Other investment................................	8 753 ..	**359.54**	**411.96**	**524.39**	**624.84**	**748.07**	**711.41**	**933.77**	**1,333.36**
Trade credits..	8 756 ..	13.72	11.80	14.40	18.45	22.10	20.89	25.83	31.05
General government............................	8 757 ..	....	....	....	....	....	....	....	....
of which: Short-term..........................	8 759 ..	....	....	....	....	....	....	....	....
Other sectors................................	8 760 ..	13.72	11.80	14.40	18.45	22.10	20.89	25.83	31.05
of which: Short-term..........................	8 762 ..	*13.30*	*11.40*	*13.96*	*17.92*	*21.54*	*20.41*	*24.83*	*29.94*
Loans..	8 764 ..	85.49	89.19	119.10	150.38	162.32	168.11	203.36	274.48
Monetary authorities............................	8 765 ..	....	....	....	1.34	.13	.39	1.71	.83
of which: Use of Fund credit and loans from the Fund....	8 766 ..	....	....	....	....	....	....	....	....
of which: Short-term..........................	8 768 ..	....	....	....	*1.34*	*.13*	*.39*	*1.71*	*.83*
General government............................	8 769 ..	1.37	3.80	4.91	3.81	2.73	2.54	2.86	3.87
of which: Short-term..........................	8 771 ..	*.79*	*3.21*	*4.20*	*1.06*	*.06*	*.05*	*.05*	*.83*
Banks..	8 772 ..	28.21	26.57	40.85	67.64	74.44	94.71	111.70	154.37
of which: Short-term..........................	8 774 ..	....	....	....	....	....	....	....	....
Other sectors..................................	8 775 ..	55.91	58.82	73.33	77.59	85.02	70.46	87.09	115.41
of which: Short-term..........................	8 777 ..	*10.96*	*11.12*	*15.19*	*17.65*	*19.70*	*16.05*	*22.42*	*33.28*
Currency and deposits..	8 780 ..	244.95	296.04	372.17	433.08	534.73	498.84	670.77	947.11
Monetary authorities............................	8 781 ..	.12	1.67	4.89	1.25	4.97	1.22	−9.22	39.14
General government............................	8 782 ..	1.36	1.35	1.67	1.23	.39	.73	1.01	1.21
Banks..	8 783 ..	240.56	290.26	362.27	428.57	526.58	494.67	675.53	903.93
Other sectors..................................	8 784 ..	2.91	2.76	3.35	2.02	2.79	2.22	3.44	2.82
Other liabilities..	8 786 ..	15.38	14.94	18.72	22.92	28.93	23.57	33.81	80.71
Monetary authorities............................	8 787 ..	....	....	....	....	....	....	....	....
of which: Short-term..........................	8 789 ..	....	....	....	....	....	....	....	....
General government............................	8 790 ..	10.05	9.48	11.26	.58	.63	.42	.66	.78
of which: Short-term..........................	8 792 ..	*10.05*	*9.48*	*11.26*	*.58*	*.63*	*.42*	*.66*	*.78*
Banks..	8 793 ..	.08	.07	.09	12.52	17.27	7.87	5.09	14.55
of which: Short-term..........................	8 795 ..	*.08*	*.07*	*.09*	*12.52*	*17.27*	*7.87*	*5.09*	*14.55*
Other sectors..................................	8 796 ..	5.25	5.38	7.37	9.83	11.04	15.29	28.06	65.39
of which: Short-term..........................	8 798 ..	*3.77*	*3.96*	*5.68*	*3.96*	*4.75*	*9.50*	*21.67*	*58.27*
NET INTERNATIONAL INVESTMENT POSITION........	8 995 ..	**−59.26**	**−52.92**	**−118.55**	**−13.65**	**24.78**	**−19.49**	**5.59**	**−50.56**
Conversion rates: euros per U.S. dollar (end of period)..............	0 104 ..	**1.0747**	**1.1347**	**.9536**	**.7918**	**.7342**	**.8477**	**.7593**	**.6793**

Table 1. ANALYTIC PRESENTATION, 2000–2007

(Millions of U.S. dollars)

	Code	2000	2001	2002	2003	2004	2005	2006	2007
A. Current Account[1]	4 993 Z.	−37.3	−209.8	−59.1	4.5	−113.5	−148.3	−260.1	−589.7
Goods: exports f.o.b.	2 100 ..	674.8	637.0	577.0	654.1	776.3	971.1	694.7	676.5
Goods: imports f.o.b.	3 100 ..	−1,656.2	−1,746.7	−1,597.7	−1,671.6	−1,955.6	−2,285.2	−2,209.3	−2,543.2
Balance on Goods	4 100 ..	*−981.4*	*−1,109.7*	*−1,020.7*	*−1,017.6*	*−1,179.3*	*−1,314.1*	*−1,514.6*	*−1,866.7*
Services: credit	2 200 ..	1,613.7	1,651.4	1,625.8	1,700.7	1,799.3	1,847.3	1,991.1	2,099.7
Services: debit	3 200 ..	−731.6	−789.8	−792.6	−811.8	−801.3	−813.2	−758.3	−802.6
Balance on Goods and Services	4 991 ..	*−99.3*	*−248.2*	*−187.5*	*−128.7*	*−181.4*	*−280.0*	*−281.9*	*−569.6*
Income: credit	2 300 ..	126.1	103.7	91.0	89.9	94.7	103.5	137.0	175.8
Income: debit	3 300 ..	−102.7	−83.8	−90.3	−97.0	−105.0	−107.5	−138.1	−165.6
Balance on Goods, Services, and Income	4 992 ..	*−75.9*	*−228.3*	*−186.8*	*−135.8*	*−191.7*	*−284.1*	*−283.0*	*−559.4*
Current transfers: credit	2 379 Z.	242.7	211.6	361.2	394.7	311.3	401.0	328.8	296.4
Current transfers: debit	3 379 ..	−204.2	−193.1	−233.5	−254.4	−233.1	−265.2	−305.9	−326.8
B. Capital Account[1]	4 994 Z.	**29.8**	**37.2**	**27.7**	**26.2**	**79.4**	**95.6**	**100.3**	**121.6**
Capital account: credit	2 994 Z.	31.2	37.9	29.3	32.8	80.2	96.1	102.6	126.2
Capital account: debit	3 994 ..	−1.4	−.6	−1.6	−6.6	−.8	−.5	−2.3	−4.6
Total, Groups A Plus B	4 981 ..	*−7.5*	*−172.6*	*−31.4*	*30.7*	*−34.1*	*−52.7*	*−159.8*	*−468.1*
C. Financial Account[1]	4 995 W.	**−135.2**	**298.2**	**89.6**	**−36.0**	**−.4**	**21.3**	**139.8**	**514.9**
Direct investment abroad	4 505 ..	1.9	.6	−1.1	.9	−25.1	−72.4	−56.6	3.2
Direct investment in the Netherlands Antilles	4 555 Z.	−12.7	59.6	64.7	1.5	25.7	73.5	−21.9	231.8
Portfolio investment assets	4 602 ..	−37.9	−31.6	−38.4	−.7	−94.1	−25.7	67.3	−67.9
Equity securities	4 610 ..	−33.8	−7.2	−8.5	−42.6	−16.0	−2.2	−12.5	−71.6
Debt securities	4 619 ..	−4.1	−24.4	−29.9	41.9	−78.1	−23.5	79.8	3.7
Portfolio investment liabilities	4 652 Z.	.1	−.2	.9	5.0	93.2	1.6	−8.9	−9.6
Equity securities	4 660 ..	....	....	....	....	....	....	....	....
Debt securities	4 669 Z.	.1	−.2	.9	5.0	93.2	1.6	−8.9	−9.6
Financial derivatives	4 910 ..	....	.1	....	....	....	1.5	−1.6	−4.2
Financial derivatives assets	4 900 ..	....	.1	....	....	....	.9	−1.6	−4.2
Financial derivatives liabilities	4 905 ..	....	....	....	....	....	.6	....	....
Other investment assets	4 703 ..	−40.8	147.6	87.2	−71.2	.9	44.1	193.3	427.7
Monetary authorities	4 701 ..	−.1	−1.2	.4	....	....	....	....	.3
General government	4 704 ..	−.8	−.8	....	−5.7	....	.1	....	−.1
Banks	4 705 ..	13.8	22.2	56.3	1.2	19.5	2.2	6.5	26.7
Other sectors	4 728 ..	−53.7	127.4	30.4	−66.7	−18.6	41.8	186.8	400.9
Other investment liabilities	4 753 W.	−45.7	122.2	−23.7	28.5	−1.0	−1.2	−31.8	−66.2
Monetary authorities	4 753 WA	1.3	....	....	....	....	....	....	....
General government	4 753 ZB	−33.2	−12.9	−20.6	−37.9	−26.8	−34.8	−36.3	−22.8
Banks	4 753 ZC	40.0	−13.4	−44.2	−5.8	−25.1	5.6	−.3	−24.8
Other sectors	4 753 ZD	−53.7	148.5	41.0	72.2	50.9	28.0	4.8	−18.7
Total, Groups A Through C	4 983 ..	*−142.7*	*125.6*	*58.2*	*−5.3*	*−34.5*	*−31.4*	*−20.0*	*46.7*
D. Net Errors and Omissions	4 998 ..	**13.1**	**92.1**	**−6.0**	**32.4**	**42.1**	**80.3**	**35.6**	**82.4**
Total, Groups A Through D	4 984 ..	*−129.6*	*217.7*	*52.2*	*27.1*	*7.6*	*48.9*	*15.6*	*129.2*
E. Reserves and Related Items	4 802 A.	**129.6**	**−217.7**	**−52.2**	**−27.1**	**−7.6**	**−48.9**	**−15.6**	**−129.2**
Reserve assets	4 802 ..	47.8	−231.9	−68.2	−49.8	−36.9	−74.0	−47.1	−155.0
Use of Fund credit and loans	4 766 ..	....	....	....	....	....	....	....	....
Exceptional financing	4 920 ..	81.8	14.2	15.9	22.8	29.3	25.1	31.5	25.8
Conversion rates: Netherlands Antillean guilders per U.S. dollar	0 101 ..	**1.7900**	**1.7900**	**1.7900**	**1.7900**	**1.7900**	**1.7900**	**1.7900**	**1.7900**

[1] Excludes components that have been classified in the categories of Group E.

Table 2. STANDARD PRESENTATION, 2000–2007

(Millions of U.S. dollars)

	Code	2000	2001	2002	2003	2004	2005	2006	2007
CURRENT ACCOUNT	4 993 ..	**−37.3**	**−209.8**	**−59.1**	**4.5**	**−113.5**	**−148.3**	**−260.1**	**−589.7**
A. GOODS	4 100 ..	**−981.4**	**−1,109.7**	**−1,020.7**	**−1,017.6**	**−1,179.3**	**−1,314.1**	**−1,514.6**	**−1,866.7**
Credit	2 100 ..	**674.8**	**637.0**	**577.0**	**654.1**	**776.3**	**971.1**	**694.7**	**676.5**
General merchandise: exports f.o.b.	2 110 ..	406.3	386.4	365.2	339.4	412.0	457.7	484.9	414.1
Goods for processing: exports f.o.b.	2 150 ..	7.0	9.4	20.6	12.9	11.0	10.5	9.5	8.0
Repairs on goods	2 160 ..	53.4	47.8	37.5	35.2	48.5	43.6	55.0	63.1
Goods procured in ports by carriers	2 170 ..	208.1	193.5	153.7	266.5	304.9	459.3	145.3	191.2
Nonmonetary gold	2 180 ..	....	....	....	....	....	....	....	....
Debit	3 100 ..	**−1,656.2**	**−1,746.7**	**−1,597.7**	**−1,671.6**	**−1,955.6**	**−2,285.2**	**−2,209.3**	**−2,543.2**
General merchandise: imports f.o.b.	3 110 ..	−1,609.0	−1,696.6	−1,563.8	−1,643.4	−1,932.3	−2,274.7	−2,203.2	−2,526.6
Goods for processing: imports f.o.b.	3 150 ..	−38.0	−43.0	−25.1	−19.9	−16.9	−9.4	−4.0	−13.6
Repairs on goods	3 160 ..	−1.1	....	−1.4	−.2	−.4	....	−1.0	−.1
Goods procured in ports by carriers	3 170 ..	−8.0	−7.1	−7.4	−8.2	−6.0	−1.0	−1.1	−2.9
Nonmonetary gold	3 180 ..	....	....	....	....	....	....	....	....
B. SERVICES	4 200 ..	**882.1**	**861.5**	**833.2**	**888.9**	**997.9**	**1,034.1**	**1,232.8**	**1,297.1**
Total credit	2 200 ..	*1,613.7*	*1,651.4*	*1,625.8*	*1,700.7*	*1,799.3*	*1,847.3*	*1,991.1*	*2,099.7*
Total debit	3 200 ..	*−731.6*	*−789.8*	*−792.6*	*−811.8*	*−801.3*	*−813.2*	*−758.3*	*−802.6*
Transportation services, credit	2 205 ..	**161.6**	**177.1**	**169.5**	**142.4**	**137.3**	**126.9**	**132.0**	**144.8**
Passenger	2 850 ..	*61.9*	*69.0*	*74.5*	*64.4*	*34.0*	*9.4*	*4.8*	*5.9*
Freight	2 851 ..	*2.1*	*3.5*	*2.5*	*2.4*	*1.5*	*1.1*	*1.0*	*1.8*
Other	2 852 ..	*97.5*	*104.6*	*92.4*	*75.6*	*101.8*	*116.4*	*126.2*	*137.1*
Sea transport, passenger	2 207 ..	.8	2.1	.6	.3	.2	.5	....	.7
Sea transport, freight	2 208 ..	....	....	....	....	....	....	....	....
Sea transport, other	2 209 ..	90.7	99.0	91.7	72.8	94.9	106.9	118.5	127.6
Air transport, passenger	2 211 ..	61.1	66.9	73.9	64.1	33.7	9.0	4.8	5.3
Air transport, freight	2 212 ..	2.1	3.5	2.5	2.4	1.5	1.1	1.0	1.8
Air transport, other	2 213 ..	6.8	5.6	.7	2.8	6.9	9.5	7.7	9.5
Other transport, passenger	2 215 ..	...	....	....	....	....	....	....	....
Other transport, freight	2 216 ..	...	....	....	....	....	....	....	....
Other transport, other	2 217 ..	...	....	....	....	....	....	....	....
Transportation services, debit	3 205 ..	**−105.5**	**−109.5**	**−101.2**	**−78.1**	**−94.0**	**−98.2**	**−83.0**	**−91.9**
Passenger	3 850 ..	*−39.4*	*−47.6*	*−43.7*	*−22.8*	*−31.4*	*−34.7*	*−22.1*	*−20.2*
Freight	3 851 ..	*−41.5*	*−43.7*	*−40.3*	*−42.4*	*−49.8*	*−58.6*	*−56.8*	*−65.1*
Other	3 852 ..	*−24.6*	*−18.2*	*−17.2*	*−12.9*	*−12.8*	*−4.8*	*−4.1*	*−6.6*
Sea transport, passenger	3 207 ..	−2.0	−.1	−.4	−.5	−.4	−.3	−.3	−.6
Sea transport, freight	3 208 ..	−37.3	−39.4	−36.3	−38.1	−44.8	−52.8	−51.1	−58.6
Sea transport, other	3 209 ..	−9.2	−8.2	−5.5	−2.1	−3.5	−2.0	−1.1	−3.2
Air transport, passenger	3 211 ..	−37.4	−47.4	−43.3	−22.3	−30.9	−34.4	−21.8	−19.6
Air transport, freight	3 212 ..	−4.1	−4.4	−4.0	−4.2	−5.0	−5.9	−5.7	−6.5
Air transport, other	3 213 ..	−15.4	−10.0	−11.7	−10.8	−9.3	−2.9	−3.0	−3.4
Other transport, passenger	3 215 ..	...	....	....	....	....	....	....	....
Other transport, freight	3 216 ..	...	....	....	....	....	....	....	....
Other transport, other	3 217 ..	...	....	....	....	....	....	....	....
Travel, credit	2 236 ..	**760.2**	**750.9**	**771.0**	**845.5**	**918.9**	**956.3**	**1,019.3**	**1,098.3**
Business travel	2 237 ..	...	....	....	....	....	....	....	....
Personal travel	2 240 ..	760.2	750.9	771.0	845.5	918.9	956.3	1,019.3	1,098.3
Travel, debit	3 236 ..	**−244.1**	**−267.9**	**−278.6**	**−322.8**	**−285.4**	**−276.5**	**−281.6**	**−311.7**
Business travel	3 237 ..	....	....	....	....	....	....	....	....
Personal travel	3 240 ..	−244.1	−267.9	−278.6	−322.8	−285.4	−276.5	−281.6	−311.7
Other services, credit	2 200 BA	**692.0**	**723.4**	**685.3**	**712.8**	**743.1**	**764.1**	**839.8**	**856.5**
Communications	2 245 ..	17.3	20.1	11.1	9.3	19.4	13.3	11.0	14.9
Construction	2 249 ..	34.1	50.2	47.8	17.7	15.7	23.0	35.5	50.7
Insurance	2 253 ..	3.8	5.4	4.4	5.2	12.2	16.3	.5	.6
Financial	2 260 ..	14.4	8.9	3.2	3.1	2.7	5.7	5.5	2.0
Computer and information	2 262 ..	2.0	1.5	.9	1.3	2.5	1.7	3.5	4.1
Royalties and licence fees	2 266 ..	6.4	2.7	2.0	.5	.2	.3	.2	3.0
Other business services	2 268 ..	591.2	587.7	564.0	622.7	643.6	647.4	727.8	729.8
Personal, cultural, and recreational	2 287 ..	1.6	.6	.9	.6	.5	.2	.7	.2
Government, n.i.e.	2 291 ..	21.2	46.2	51.0	52.3	46.1	56.3	55.1	51.3
Other services, debit	3 200 BA	**−382.1**	**−412.4**	**−412.7**	**−410.9**	**−422.0**	**−438.6**	**−393.8**	**−399.0**
Communications	3 245 ..	−16.7	−18.6	−13.8	−22.8	−23.0	−23.4	−23.2	−20.4
Construction	3 249 ..	−31.7	−55.1	−46.9	−15.6	−8.9	−33.3	−35.3	−51.8
Insurance	3 253 ..	−18.3	−31.9	−31.2	−30.7	−44.7	−49.2	−11.6	−13.3
Financial	3 260 ..	−5.6	−5.9	−4.6	−5.8	−4.9	−5.2	−5.0	−7.5
Computer and information	3 262 ..	−13.7	−5.1	−7.3	−9.2	−8.9	−13.9	−12.9	−15.2
Royalties and licence fees	3 266 ..	−4.1	−4.8	−7.3	−5.3	−5.0	−5.9	−7.0	−12.6
Other business services	3 268 ..	−287.1	−287.1	−295.8	−309.1	−311.3	−299.0	−288.6	−269.3
Personal, cultural, and recreational	3 287 ..	−1.1	−.6	−.7	−2.0	−1.0	−.6	−1.0	−.4
Government, n.i.e.	3 291 ..	−3.8	−3.3	−5.1	−10.4	−14.2	−8.0	−9.3	−8.5

Table 2 (Continued). STANDARD PRESENTATION, 2000–2007

(Millions of U.S. dollars)

	Code	2000	2001	2002	2003	2004	2005	2006	2007
C. INCOME	4 300	**23.4**	**19.9**	**.7**	**−7.1**	**−10.3**	**−4.1**	**−1.1**	**10.3**
Total credit	2 300	*126.1*	*103.7*	*91.0*	*89.9*	*94.7*	*103.5*	*137.0*	*175.8*
Total debit	3 300	*−102.7*	*−83.8*	*−90.3*	*−97.0*	*−105.0*	*−107.5*	*−138.1*	*−165.6*
Compensation of employees, credit	2 310	**6.8**	**8.0**	**5.5**	**5.6**	**3.9**	**7.1**	**17.5**	**28.8**
Compensation of employees, debit	3 310	**−37.3**	**−31.8**	**−32.8**	**−34.3**	**−35.0**	**−42.0**	**−38.0**	**−43.7**
Investment income, credit	2 320	**119.3**	**95.7**	**85.5**	**84.3**	**90.8**	**96.4**	**119.6**	**147.1**
Direct investment income	2 330	1.8	5.7	1.9	2.5	14.0	1.2	31.1	17.6
Dividends and distributed branch profits	2 332	.8	3.7	.1	....	12.0	.1	30.5	17.4
Reinvested earnings and undistributed branch profits	2 333	....	....	....	....	....	....	....	....
Income on debt (interest)	2 334	1.0	2.0	1.8	2.5	2.1	1.1	.6	.2
Portfolio investment income	2 339	61.7	68.0	62.3	67.6	58.2	62.0	44.3	71.9
Income on equity	2 340	14.6	14.3	17.4	22.0	24.4	23.6	7.6	9.9
Income on bonds and notes	2 350	....	....	....	....	....	....	....	....
Income on money market instruments	2 360	47.1	53.7	44.9	45.6	33.8	38.4	36.7	61.9
Other investment income	2 370	55.9	22.0	21.4	14.2	18.6	33.2	44.1	57.6
Investment income, debit	3 320	**−65.4**	**−52.0**	**−57.5**	**−62.7**	**−69.9**	**−65.6**	**−100.2**	**−121.9**
Direct investment income	3 330	−4.0	−3.9	−10.3	−8.3	−9.9	−5.6	−48.9	−60.3
Dividends and distributed branch profits	3 332	−.9	−.5	−7.2	−7.2	−7.1	−2.1	−46.9	−60.6
Reinvested earnings and undistributed branch profits	3 333	−.4	−.5	−.7	.4	−.3	−.9	−.1	2.6
Income on debt (interest)	3 334	−2.7	−2.9	−2.4	−1.5	−2.5	−2.7	−1.9	−2.3
Portfolio investment income	3 339	−25.2	−23.9	−33.6	−39.1	−38.2	−35.7	−21.2	−31.6
Income on equity	3 340	−24.5	−21.8	−31.5	−35.5	−36.1	−32.5	−19.2	−22.5
Income on bonds and notes	3 350	....	....	....	....	....	....	....	....
Income on money market instruments	3 360	−.8	−2.1	−2.1	−3.6	−2.0	−3.2	−2.1	−9.1
Other investment income	3 370	−36.1	−24.2	−13.6	−15.4	−21.9	−24.3	−30.0	−30.0
D. CURRENT TRANSFERS	4 379	**38.5**	**18.5**	**127.7**	**140.3**	**78.2**	**135.8**	**22.9**	**−30.4**
Credit	2 379	**242.7**	**211.6**	**361.2**	**394.7**	**311.3**	**401.0**	**328.8**	**296.4**
General government	2 380	76.3	59.4	69.8	86.7	70.5	176.6	85.4	47.6
Other sectors	2 390	166.4	152.2	291.4	308.0	240.7	224.4	243.4	248.8
Workers' remittances	2 391	5.6	12.2	19.9	.8	1.0	1.0	.4	.5
Other current transfers	2 392	160.8	140.0	271.5	307.2	239.7	223.4	242.9	248.3
Debit	3 379	**−204.2**	**−193.1**	**−233.5**	**−254.4**	**−233.1**	**−265.2**	**−305.9**	**−326.8**
General government	3 380	−9.7	−9.5	−9.1	−11.5	−9.0	−18.9	−12.4	−14.9
Other sectors	3 390	−194.5	−183.6	−224.3	−242.9	−224.1	−246.2	−293.5	−311.9
Workers' remittances	3 391	−9.0	−11.7	−20.2	−18.1	−16.5	−16.5	−21.0	−23.8
Other current transfers	3 392	−185.5	−171.9	−204.1	−224.9	−207.6	−229.7	−272.5	−288.1
CAPITAL AND FINANCIAL ACCOUNT	4 996	**24.2**	**117.7**	**65.1**	**−36.9**	**71.4**	**68.0**	**224.5**	**507.3**
CAPITAL ACCOUNT	4 994	**29.8**	**37.2**	**27.7**	**26.2**	**79.4**	**95.6**	**100.3**	**121.6**
Total credit	2 994	*31.2*	*37.9*	*29.3*	*32.8*	*80.2*	*96.1*	*102.6*	*126.2*
Total debit	3 994	*−1.4*	*−.6*	*−1.6*	*−6.6*	*−.8*	*−.5*	*−2.3*	*−4.6*
Capital transfers, credit	2 400	**31.2**	**37.8**	**29.3**	**32.3**	**80.2**	**96.1**	**102.6**	**126.1**
General government	2 401	31.1	33.7	29.1	30.3	79.7	96.1	101.3	122.3
Debt forgiveness	2 402	....	....	....	....	....	....	....	....
Other capital transfers	2 410	31.1	33.7	29.1	30.3	79.7	96.1	101.3	122.3
Other sectors	2 430	.2	4.1	.2	2.0	.6	....	1.3	3.8
Migrants' transfers	2 431	.1	3.9	.2	1.5	.6	....	1.3	3.1
Debt forgiveness	2 432	....	....	....	....	....	....	....	....
Other capital transfers	2 440	.1	.2	....	.5	....	....	....	.6
Capital transfers, debit	3 400	**−1.4**	**−.6**	**−1.6**	**−6.6**	**−.8**	**−.5**	**−2.3**	**−4.6**
General government	3 401	....	....	....	....	....	....	....	....
Debt forgiveness	3 402	....	....	....	....	....	....	....	....
Other capital transfers	3 410	....	....	....	....	....	....	....	....
Other sectors	3 430	−1.4	−.6	−1.6	−6.6	−.8	−.5	−2.3	−4.6
Migrants' transfers	3 431	−1.2	−.3	−1.6	−6.3	−.8	−.5	−2.2	−4.6
Debt forgiveness	3 432	....	....	....	....	....	....	....	....
Other capital transfers	3 440	−.3	−.3	....	−.3	−.1	....	−.1	....
Nonproduced nonfinancial assets, credit	2 480	**....**	**.1**	**....**	**.4**	**....**	**....**	**....**	**.1**
Nonproduced nonfinancial assets, debit	3 480	**....**	**....**	**....**	**....**	**....**	**....**	**....**	**....**

Table 2 (Continued). STANDARD PRESENTATION, 2000–2007

(Millions of U.S. dollars)

	Code	2000	2001	2002	2003	2004	2005	2006	2007
FINANCIAL ACCOUNT	4 995	−5.6	80.5	37.4	−63.1	−8.0	−27.6	124.2	385.7
A. DIRECT INVESTMENT	4 500	−10.8	60.2	63.6	2.4	.6	1.1	−78.5	235.0
Direct investment abroad	4 505	1.9	.6	−1.1	.9	−25.1	−72.4	−56.6	3.2
Equity capital	4 510	....	....	−.9	.5	−7.1	−71.4	−43.9	−8.8
Claims on affiliated enterprises	4 515	....	....	−.4	.5	−7.1	−71.4	−43.9	−8.8
Liabilities to affiliated enterprises	4 520	....	....	−.5	....	....	....	....	....
Reinvested earnings	4 525	....	....	....	....	....	....	....	....
Other capital	4 530	1.9	.6	−.2	.4	−17.9	−1.0	−12.7	12.1
Claims on affiliated enterprises	4 535	1.9	.6	−.2	.4	−17.9	−1.0	−12.7	12.1
Liabilities to affiliated enterprises	4 540	....	....	....	....	....	....	....	....
Direct investment in the Netherlands Antilles	4 555	−12.7	59.6	64.7	1.5	25.7	73.5	−21.9	231.8
Equity capital	4 560	4.1	32.6	35.9	16.3	52.7	120.8	−8.0	205.5
Claims on direct investors	4 565	....	....	....	....	....	....	....	....
Liabilities to direct investors	4 570	4.1	32.6	35.9	16.3	52.7	120.8	−8.0	205.5
Reinvested earnings	4 575	.4	.5	.7	−.4	.3	.9	.1	−2.6
Other capital	4 580	−17.3	26.4	28.1	−14.4	−27.3	−48.2	−14.0	28.9
Claims on direct investors	4 585	−5.8	13.5	....	1.6	....	−.5	.5	1.0
Liabilities to direct investors	4 590	−11.4	12.9	28.0	−16.0	−27.3	−47.7	−14.5	27.9
B. PORTFOLIO INVESTMENT	4 600	−37.9	−31.8	−37.5	4.3	−.9	−24.1	58.3	−77.4
Assets	4 602	−37.9	−31.6	−38.4	−.7	−94.1	−25.7	67.3	−67.9
Equity securities	4 610	−33.8	−7.2	−8.5	−42.6	−16.0	−2.2	−12.5	−71.6
Monetary authorities	4 611	....	....	....	....	....	....	....	....
General government	4 612	....	−.2	.1	.1	−16.3	−18.3	−3.1	−5.1
Banks	4 613	....	−.1	6.9	−3.1	....	.5	.4	−.9
Other sectors	4 614	−33.8	−6.9	−15.4	−39.5	.2	15.6	−9.8	−65.6
Debt securities	4 619	−4.1	−24.4	−29.9	41.9	−78.1	−23.5	79.8	3.7
Bonds and notes	4 620	6.6	−12.0	−14.3	35.3	−75.2	−32.3	74.9	−7.7
Monetary authorities	4 621	....	....	....	−2.8	....	....	....	....
General government	4 622	....	−.3	−.1	.5	−13.9	−.1	.1	−1.1
Banks	4 623	−.5	....	−.2	1.6	1.3	.1	2.1	2.1
Other sectors	4 624	7.1	−11.7	−14.0	35.9	−62.6	−32.3	72.7	−8.7
Money market instruments	4 630	−10.7	−12.4	−15.6	6.6	−2.9	8.8	4.9	11.4
Monetary authorities	4 631	....	....	....	....	....	.1	....	....
General government	4 632	....	....	....	....	....	−4.3	....	1.9
Banks	4 633	....	−.1	.4	....	....	.5	−2.8	17.7
Other sectors	4 634	−10.7	−12.3	−16.0	6.6	−2.9	12.5	7.7	−8.2
Liabilities	4 652	.1	−.2	.9	5.0	93.2	1.6	−8.9	−9.6
Equity securities	4 660	....	....	....	....	....	....	....	....
Banks	4 663	....	....	....	....	....	....	....	....
Other sectors	4 664	....	....	....	....	....	....	....	....
Debt securities	4 669	.1	−.2	.9	5.0	93.2	1.6	−8.9	−9.6
Bonds and notes	4 670	−1.5	−.4	.9	5.2	4.1	.9	−1.0	29.5
Monetary authorities	4 671	....	....	....	....	....	....	....	....
General government	4 672	−1.5	−.6	.9	.3	4.0	−.1	−.9	22.5
Banks	4 673	....	....	....	5.2	.1	....	....	2.9
Other sectors	4 674	....	.2	....	−.3	−.1	.9	−.1	4.2
Money market instruments	4 680	1.6	.1	....	−.2	89.1	.7	−7.9	−39.1
Monetary authorities	4 681	....	....	....	....	....	....	....	....
General government	4 682	.2	.1	....	....	....	....	....	....
Banks	4 683	....	....	....	−.1	−3.5	....	....	−15.3
Other sectors	4 684	1.4	.1	....	−.2	92.6	.7	−7.9	−23.9
C. FINANCIAL DERIVATIVES	4 910	....	.1	....	....	....	1.5	−1.6	−4.2
Monetary authorities	4 911	....	....	....	....	....	....	....	....
General government	4 912	....	....	....	....	....	....	....	....
Banks	4 913	....	....	....	....	....	....	.3	−4.3
Other sectors	4 914	....	.1	....	....	....	1.5	−1.9	....
Assets	4 900	....	.1	....	....	....	.9	−1.6	−4.2
Monetary authorities	4 901	....	....	....	....	....	....	....	....
General government	4 902	....	....	....	....	....	....	....	....
Banks	4 903	....	....	....	....	....	....	.3	−4.3
Other sectors	4 904	....	.1	....	....	....	.9	−1.9	....
Liabilities	4 905	....	....	....	....	....	.6	....	....
Monetary authorities	4 906	....	....	....	....	....	....	....	....
General government	4 907	....	....	....	....	....	....	....	....
Banks	4 908	....	....	....	....	....	....	....	....
Other sectors	4 909	....	....	....	....	....	.6	....	....

Table 2 (Concluded). STANDARD PRESENTATION, 2000–2007

(Millions of U.S. dollars)

	Code	2000	2001	2002	2003	2004	2005	2006	2007
D. OTHER INVESTMENT	4 700 ..	**−4.6**	**284.0**	**79.4**	**−20.0**	**29.3**	**68.0**	**193.0**	**387.3**
Assets	4 703 ..	**−40.8**	**147.6**	**87.2**	**−71.2**	**.9**	**44.1**	**193.3**	**427.7**
Trade credits	4 706 ..	−42.3	75.6	27.7	−74.4	−42.8	−67.7	−48.8	174.4
General government	4 707 ..	....	....	....	....	....	....	....	....
of which: Short-term	4 709 ..	....	....	....	....	....	....	....	....
Other sectors	4 710 ..	−42.3	75.6	27.7	−74.4	−42.8	−67.7	−48.8	174.4
of which: Short-term	4 712 ..	−43.1	74.1	27.8	−74.8	−42.6	−67.4	−48.7	174.4
Loans	4 714 ..	3.1	8.1	−1.7	−2.4	3.7	.2	8.8	21.8
Monetary authorities	4 715 ..	−.1	....	....	....	....	....	....	....
of which: Short-term	4 718 ..	....	....	....	....	....	....	....	....
General government	4 719 ..	....	....	....	....	....	....	....	....
of which: Short-term	4 721 ..	....	....	....	....	....	....	....	....
Banks	4 722 ..	....	5.9	.7	....	2.5	2.0	6.6	15.7
of which: Short-term	4 724 ..	....	....	....	....	....	....	....	.5
Other sectors	4 725 ..	3.2	2.1	−2.4	−2.4	1.1	−1.8	2.2	6.2
of which: Short-term	4 727 ..	.3	.2	.2	....	....	−.1	−.1	−.3
Currency and deposits	4 730 ..	−3.8	4.3	28.1	−26.7	11.4	92.1	157.8	70.4
Monetary authorities	4 731 ..	....	....	....	....	....	....	....	....
General government	4 732 ..	....	....	....	....	....	....	....	....
Banks	4 733 ..	....	....	....	....	....	....	....	....
Other sectors	4 734 ..	−3.8	4.3	28.1	−26.7	11.4	92.1	157.8	70.4
Other assets	4 736 ..	2.1	59.5	33.0	32.3	28.7	19.5	75.5	161.2
Monetary authorities	4 737 ..	....	−1.2	.4	....	....	....	....	.3
of which: Short-term	4 739 ..	....	−1.2	.4	....	....	....	....	.3
General government	4 740 ..	−.8	−.8	....	−5.7	....	.1	....	−.1
of which: Short-term	4 742 ..	−.8	−.8	....	−5.7	....	.1	....	−.1
Banks	4 743 ..	13.8	16.3	55.6	1.2	17.0	.2	−.1	11.0
of which: Short-term	4 745 ..	15.8	14.8	57.1	6.1	17.2	−.7	....	11.4
Other sectors	4 746 ..	−10.8	45.3	−23.0	36.8	11.7	19.2	75.6	150.0
of which: Short-term	4 748 ..	.6	45.5	−17.3	43.2	29.9	34.3	82.6	168.4
Liabilities	4 753 ..	**36.2**	**136.4**	**−7.8**	**51.2**	**28.3**	**23.9**	**−.3**	**−40.4**
Trade credits	4 756 ..	−14.2	150.2	32.6	123.3	77.1	77.1	16.6	−59.2
General government	4 757 ..	....	....	....	....	....	....	....	....
of which: Short-term	4 759 ..	....	....	....	....	....	....	....	....
Other sectors	4 760 ..	−14.2	150.2	32.6	123.3	77.1	77.1	16.6	−59.2
of which: Short-term	4 762 ..	−13.5	150.1	32.8	123.3	76.4	76.9	16.2	−65.0
Loans	4 764 ..	11.9	−11.7	−28.2	−33.2	−83.2	−51.9	−89.3	−1.5
Monetary authorities	4 765 ..	1.3	....	....	....	....	....	....	....
of which: Use of Fund credit and loans from the Fund..	4 766 ..	....	....	....	....	....	....	....	....
of which: Short-term	4 768 ..	1.3	....	....	....	....	....	....	....
General government	4 769 ..	49.5	−8.4	−16.4	−21.5	−22.6	−23.7	−40.1	−18.8
of which: Short-term	4 771 ..	....	....	....	....	−.8	....	....	....
Banks	4 772 ..	−4.0	−11.7	−2.7	−5.8	−23.8	−.4	−.3	2.8
of which: Short-term	4 774 ..	....	....	....	....	−1.9	−.6	....	....
Other sectors	4 775 ..	−34.8	8.3	−9.1	−5.9	−36.8	−27.8	−48.9	14.5
of which: Short-term	4 777 ..	−3.2	−.5	−.7	−.1	.1	3.1	.1	.3
Currency and deposits	4 780 ..	....	....	....	....	....	....	....	....
Monetary authorities	4 781 ..	....	....	....	....	....	....	....	....
General government	4 782 ..	....	....	....	....	....	....	....	....
Banks	4 783 ..	....	....	....	....	....	....	....	....
Other sectors	4 784 ..	....	....	....	....	....	....	....	....
Other liabilities	4 786 ..	38.4	−2.1	−12.2	−38.9	34.4	−1.3	72.4	20.3
Monetary authorities	4 787 ..	....	....	....	....	....	....	....	....
of which: Short-term	4 789 ..	....	....	....	....	....	....	....	....
General government	4 790 ..	−.8	9.6	11.8	6.4	25.1	14.0	35.3	21.8
of which: Short-term	4 792 ..	18.8	14.2	15.9	22.1	29.3	25.1	35.3	21.8
Banks	4 793 ..	44.0	−1.8	−41.5	....	−1.3	6.0	....	−27.5
of which: Short-term	4 795 ..	43.2	....	−41.5	....	....	....	....	2.3
Other sectors	4 796 ..	−4.8	−10.0	17.5	−45.3	10.6	−21.3	37.1	26.0
of which: Short-term	4 798 ..	1.8	1.7	10.5	−10.3	−24.9	−25.6	10.3	19.6
E. RESERVE ASSETS	4 802 ..	**47.8**	**−231.9**	**−68.2**	**−49.8**	**−36.9**	**−74.0**	**−47.1**	**−155.0**
Monetary gold	4 812 ..	....	....	....	....	....	....	....	....
Special drawing rights	4 811 ..	....	....	....	....	....	....	....	....
Reserve position in the Fund	4 810 ..	....	....	....	....	....	....	....	....
Foreign exchange	4 803 ..	47.8	−231.9	−68.2	−49.8	−36.9	−74.0	−47.1	−155.0
Other claims	4 813 ..	....	....	....	....	....	....	....	....
NET ERRORS AND OMISSIONS	4 998 ..	**13.1**	**92.1**	**−6.0**	**32.4**	**42.1**	**80.3**	**35.6**	**82.4**

Table 1. ANALYTIC PRESENTATION, 2000–2007

(Millions of U.S. dollars)

	Code	2000	2001	2002	2003	2004	2005	2006	2007
A. Current Account[1]................................	4 993 Z.	**−2,678**	**−1,430**	**−2,375**	**−3,469**	**−6,291**	**−9,291**	**−9,087**	**−10,235**
Goods: exports f.o.b..........................	2 100 ..	13,459	13,870	14,495	16,804	20,466	22,005	22,574	27,291
Goods: imports f.o.b..........................	3 100 ..	−12,850	−12,448	−14,351	−17,315	−21,888	−24,583	−24,573	−29,056
Balance on Goods..............................	4 100 ..	*609*	*1,422*	*144*	*−511*	*−1,422*	*−2,578*	*−1,999*	*−1,764*
Services: credit..................................	2 200 ..	4,408	4,441	5,406	6,859	8,146	8,593	8,102	9,299
Services: debit..................................	3 200 ..	−4,490	−4,327	−4,788	−5,760	−7,217	−8,224	−7,795	−9,055
Balance on Goods and Services..............	4 991 ..	*527*	*1,536*	*762*	*589*	*−493*	*−2,209*	*−1,692*	*−1,520*
Income: credit..................................	2 300 ..	694	610	1,133	1,429	1,530	1,444	1,433	2,753
Income: debit..................................	3 300 ..	−4,137	−3,729	−4,343	−5,641	−7,419	−8,856	−9,290	−11,917
Balance on Goods, Services, and Income........	4 992 ..	*−2,916*	*−1,583*	*−2,449*	*−3,623*	*−6,381*	*−9,621*	*−9,549*	*−10,684*
Current transfers: credit....................	2 379 Z.	635	585	642	856	901	1,242	1,291	1,425
Current transfers: debit....................	3 379 ..	−397	−432	−568	−702	−810	−912	−828	−976
B. Capital Account[1]................................	4 994 Z.	**−180**	**480**	**813**	**502**	**156**	**−197**	**−217**	**−564**
Capital account: credit.....................	2 994 Z.	238	844	1,171	1,065	963	740	650	652
Capital account: debit......................	3 994 ..	−418	−364	−357	−563	−807	−937	−867	−1,216
Total, Groups A Plus B......................	4 981 ..	*−2,858*	*−950*	*−1,561*	*−2,967*	*−6,134*	*−9,488*	*−9,304*	*−10,799*
C. Financial Account[1]...........................	4 995 W.	**3,136**	**852**	**2,158**	**3,430**	**8,136**	**11,044**	**13,014**	**13,878**
Direct investment abroad....................	4 505 ..	−739	1,078	−382	−917	508	1,649	−363	−2,807
Direct investment in New Zealand........	4 555 Z.	3,910	−68	1,667	2,475	2,478	1,504	8,013	2,753
Portfolio investment assets................	4 602 ..	−2,188	−1,243	−950	−864	−1,772	−587	−945	−1,199
Equity securities........................	4 610 ..	....	−941	....	−920	−1,556	−1,104	−647	−848
Debt securities..........................	4 619 ..	....	−303	....	56	−216	517	−298	−351
Portfolio investment liabilities............	4 652 Z.	76	2,030	2,637	1,886	8,072	438	−546	12,101
Equity securities........................	4 660 ..	....	24	752	719	99	−141	−378	192
Debt securities..........................	4 669 Z.	....	2,005	1,885	1,167	7,974	578	−168	11,908
Financial derivatives........................	4 910 ..	....	....	....	....	....	....	....	....
Financial derivatives assets................	4 900 ..	....	....	....	....	....	....	....	....
Financial derivatives liabilities............	4 905 ..	....	....	....	....	....	....	....	....
Other investment assets....................	4 703 ..	−394	−3,997	−475	56	482	4,090	−1,569	−2,112
Monetary authorities....................	4 701 ..	....	....	....	....	....	....	....	....
General government....................	4 704 ..	....	....	....	....	....	....	....	....
Banks......................................	4 705 ..	....	....	....	....	....	....	....	....
Other sectors............................	4 728 ..	....	....	....	....	....	....	....	....
Other investment liabilities................	4 753 W.	2,471	3,053	−338	795	−1,631	3,948	8,423	5,142
Monetary authorities....................	4 753 WA	....	....	....	....	....	....	....	....
General government....................	4 753 ZB	....	....	....	....	....	....	....	....
Banks......................................	4 753 ZC	....	....	....	....	....	....	....	....
Other sectors............................	4 753 ZD	....	....	....	....	....	....	....	....
Total, Groups A Through C................	4 983 ..	*278*	*−98*	*597*	*464*	*2,002*	*1,556*	*3,710*	*3,079*
D. Net Errors and Omissions....................	4 998 ..	**−421**	**−89**	**489**	**319**	**−1,372**	**862**	**544**	**9**
Total, Groups A Through D................	4 984 ..	*−143*	*−187*	*1,086*	*783*	*630*	*2,418*	*4,255*	*3,088*
E. Reserves and Related Items..............	4 802 A.	**143**	**187**	**−1,086**	**−783**	**−630**	**−2,418**	**−4,255**	**−3,088**
Reserve assets................................	4 802 ..	143	187	−1,086	−783	−630	−2,418	−4,255	−3,088
Use of Fund credit and loans.............	4 766 ..	....	....	....	....	....	....	....	....
Exceptional financing........................	4 920 ..	....	....	....	....	....	....	....	....
Conversion rates: New Zealand dollars per U.S. dollar................	0 101 ..	**2.2011**	**2.3788**	**2.1622**	**1.7221**	**1.5087**	**1.4203**	**1.5421**	**1.3607**

[1] Excludes components that have been classified in the categories of Group E.

Table 2. STANDARD PRESENTATION, 2000–2007

(Millions of U.S. dollars)

	Code	2000	2001	2002	2003	2004	2005	2006	2007
CURRENT ACCOUNT	4 993	−2,678	−1,430	−2,375	−3,469	−6,291	−9,291	−9,087	−10,235
A. GOODS	4 100	609	1,422	144	−511	−1,422	−2,578	−1,999	−1,764
Credit	2 100	13,459	13,870	14,495	16,804	20,466	22,005	22,574	27,291
General merchandise: exports f.o.b.	2 110	....	....	....	....	....	....	....	....
Goods for processing: exports f.o.b.	2 150	....	....	....	....	....	....	....	....
Repairs on goods	2 160	....	....	....	....	....	....	....	....
Goods procured in ports by carriers	2 170	....	....	....	....	....	....	....	....
Nonmonetary gold	2 180	....	....	....	....	....	....	....	....
Debit	3 100	−12,850	−12,448	−14,351	−17,315	−21,888	−24,583	−24,573	−29,056
General merchandise: imports f.o.b.	3 110	....	....	....	....	....	....	....	....
Goods for processing: imports f.o.b.	3 150	....	....	....	....	....	....	....	....
Repairs on goods	3 160	....	....	....	....	....	....	....	....
Goods procured in ports by carriers	3 170	....	....	....	....	....	....	....	....
Nonmonetary gold	3 180	....	....	....	....	....	....	....	....
B. SERVICES	4 200	−82	114	618	1,100	929	369	307	244
Total credit	2 200	*4,408*	*4,441*	*5,406*	*6,859*	*8,146*	*8,593*	*8,102*	*9,299*
Total debit	3 200	*−4,490*	*−4,327*	*−4,788*	*−5,760*	*−7,217*	*−8,224*	*−7,795*	*−9,055*
Transportation services, credit	2 205	1,220	1,122	1,163	1,353	1,488	1,637	1,669	1,992
Passenger	2 850	....	....	....	....	....	....	....	....
Freight	2 851	....	....	....	....	....	....	....	....
Other	2 852	....	....	....	....	....	....	....	....
Sea transport, passenger	2 207	....	....	....	....	....	....	....	....
Sea transport, freight	2 208	....	....	....	....	....	....	....	....
Sea transport, other	2 209	....	....	....	....	....	....	....	....
Air transport, passenger	2 211	....	....	....	....	....	....	....	....
Air transport, freight	2 212	....	....	....	....	....	....	....	....
Air transport, other	2 213	....	....	....	....	....	....	....	....
Other transport, passenger	2 215	....	....	....	....	....	....	....	....
Other transport, freight	2 216	....	....	....	....	....	....	....	....
Other transport, other	2 217	....	....	....	....	....	....	....	....
Transportation services, debit	3 205	−1,427	−1,451	−1,650	−2,000	−2,531	−2,790	−2,595	−2,955
Passenger	3 850	....	....	....	....	....	....	....	....
Freight	3 851	....	....	....	....	....	....	....	....
Other	3 852	....	....	....	....	....	....	....	....
Sea transport, passenger	3 207	....	....	....	....	....	....	....	....
Sea transport, freight	3 208	....	....	....	....	....	....	....	....
Sea transport, other	3 209	....	....	....	....	....	....	....	....
Air transport, passenger	3 211	....	....	....	....	....	....	....	....
Air transport, freight	3 212	....	....	....	....	....	....	....	....
Air transport, other	3 213	....	....	....	....	....	....	....	....
Other transport, passenger	3 215	....	....	....	....	....	....	....	....
Other transport, freight	3 216	....	....	....	....	....	....	....	....
Other transport, other	3 217	....	....	....	....	....	....	....	....
Travel, credit	2 236	2,272	2,339	3,158	4,201	5,031	5,162	4,777	5,406
Business travel	2 237	250	272	327	435	440	517	462	592
Personal travel	2 240	2,022	2,067	2,832	3,766	4,590	4,645	4,314	4,814
Travel, debit	3 236	−1,450	−1,255	−1,386	−1,649	−2,217	−2,657	−2,526	−3,066
Business travel	3 237	−423	−314	−322	−353	−452	−546	−517	....
Personal travel	3 240	−1,026	−941	−1,064	−1,297	−1,766	−2,110	−2,009	....
Other services, credit	2 200 BA	916	980	1,085	1,306	1,628	1,794	1,657	1,901
Communications	2 245	193	214	216	209	225	274	....	....
Construction	2 249	7	16	17	38	48	54	....	....
Insurance	2 253	13	13	18	25	29	27	27	32
Financial	2 260	27	22	18	33	59	87	80	80
Computer and information	2 262	81	90	118	129	168	192	183	205
Royalties and licence fees	2 266	49	58	79	108	105	93	123	141
Other business services	2 268	357	394	441	540	681	795	820	617
Personal, cultural, and recreational	2 287	135	117	111	152	220	170	153	210
Government, n.i.e.	2 291	53	55	67	72	94	102	97	121
Other services, debit	3 200 BA	−1,613	−1,621	−1,751	−2,109	−2,469	−2,778	−2,667	−3,034
Communications	3 245	−202	−201	−198	−199	−226	−302	−195	−219
Construction	3 249	−3	−5	−6	−6	−14	−29	−50	−76
Insurance	3 253	−99	−98	−134	−183	−223	−245	−217	−248
Financial	3 260	−29	−35	−58	−59	−88	−126	−75	−118
Computer and information	3 262	−98	−107	−122	−134	−197	−248	−270	−305
Royalties and licence fees	3 266	−313	−317	−362	−466	−529	−551	−487	−553
Other business services	3 268	−772	−760	−733	−898	−1,040	−1,130	−1,233	−1,350
Personal, cultural, and recreational	3 287	−36	−37	−65	−72	−57	−43	−41	−51
Government, n.i.e.	3 291	−62	−61	−73	−93	−95	−103	−99	−115

Table 2 (Continued). STANDARD PRESENTATION, 2000–2007

(Millions of U.S. dollars)

	Code	2000	2001	2002	2003	2004	2005	2006	2007
C. INCOME	4 300	−3,443	−3,119	−3,211	−4,212	−5,889	−7,412	−7,857	−9,164
Total credit	2 300	*694*	*610*	*1,133*	*1,429*	*1,530*	*1,444*	*1,433*	*2,753*
Total debit	3 300	*−4,137*	*−3,729*	*−4,343*	*−5,641*	*−7,419*	*−8,856*	*−9,290*	*−11,917*
Compensation of employees, credit	2 310	....	....	....	....	....	....	....	....
Compensation of employees, debit	3 310	....	....	....	....	....	....	....	....
Investment income, credit	2 320	694	610	1,133	1,429	1,530	1,444	1,433	2,753
Direct investment income	2 330	93	−186	268	525	372	160	210	696
Dividends and distributed branch profits	2 332	....	....	....	....	....	....	....	....
Reinvested earnings and undistributed branch profits	2 333	....	....	....	....	....	....	....	....
Income on debt (interest)	2 334	....	....	−41	−72	−96	−112	−48	−97
Portfolio investment income	2 339	366	451	412	443	594	593	833	1,421
Income on equity	2 340	94	98	96	98	187	271	370	547
Income on bonds and notes	2 350	....	....	306	323	379	239	201	266
Income on money market instruments	2 360	....	....	10	22	28	82	262	609
Other investment income	2 370	235	346	453	461	564	691	390	635
Investment income, debit	3 320	−4,137	−3,729	−4,343	−5,641	−7,419	−8,856	−9,290	−11,917
Direct investment income	3 330	−2,055	−1,778	−2,352	−3,345	−4,332	−4,967	−4,679	−6,094
Dividends and distributed branch profits	3 332	....	....	−1,106	−1,884	−1,564	−2,088	−2,431	−3,838
Reinvested earnings and undistributed branch profits	3 333	....	....	−1,086	−1,231	−2,335	−2,412	−1,749	−1,371
Income on debt (interest)	3 334	−360	−266	−160	−231	−434	−468	−499	−885
Portfolio investment income	3 339	−953	−1,071	−1,089	−1,281	−1,756	−2,271	−2,487	−3,232
Income on equity	3 340	−172	−159	−220	−345	−568	−775	−694	−815
Income on bonds and notes	3 350	−583	−702	−739	−785	−998	−1,140	−1,327	−1,550
Income on money market instruments	3 360	−198	−210	−130	−150	−190	−356	−466	−866
Other investment income	3 370	−1,129	−880	−903	−1,016	−1,331	−1,617	−2,125	−2,591
D. CURRENT TRANSFERS	4 379	238	153	74	154	91	330	463	449
Credit	2 379	635	585	642	856	901	1,242	1,291	1,425
General government	2 380	410	369	398	548	558	872	939	1,021
Other sectors	2 390	225	216	244	308	343	370	352	404
Workers' remittances	2 391	....	....	....	....	....	....	....	....
Other current transfers	2 392	....	....	....	....	....	....	....	....
Debit	3 379	−397	−432	−568	−702	−810	−912	−828	−976
General government	3 380	−208	−190	−200	−237	−282	−336	−308	−367
Other sectors	3 390	−189	−242	−368	−465	−528	−575	−520	−609
Workers' remittances	3 391	....	....	....	....	....	....	....	....
Other current transfers	3 392	....	....	....	....	....	....	....	....
CAPITAL AND FINANCIAL ACCOUNT	4 996	3,099	1,521	1,885	3,150	7,662	8,429	8,542	10,226
CAPITAL ACCOUNT	4 994	−180	480	813	502	156	−197	−217	−564
Total credit	2 994	*238*	*844*	*1,171*	*1,065*	*963*	*740*	*650*	*652*
Total debit	3 994	*−418*	*−364*	*−357*	*−563*	*−807*	*−937*	*−867*	*−1,216*
Capital transfers, credit	2 400	236	841	1,148	1,065	958	739	650	650
General government	2 401	....	....	....	....	....	....	....	....
Debt forgiveness	2 402	....	....	....	....	....	....	....	....
Other capital transfers	2 410	....	....	....	....	....	....	....	....
Other sectors	2 430	236	841	1,148	1,065	958	739	650	650
Migrants' transfers	2 431	236	841	1,148	1,065	958	739	650	650
Debt forgiveness	2 432	....	....	....	....	....	....	....	....
Other capital transfers	2 440	....	....	....	....	....	....	....	....
Capital transfers, debit	3 400	−418	....	....	−561	−806	−936	−865	−1,207
General government	3 401	....	....	....	....	....	....	....	....
Debt forgiveness	3 402	....	....	....	....	....	....	....	....
Other capital transfers	3 410	....	....	....	....	....	....	....	....
Other sectors	3 430	−418	....	....	−561	−806	−936	−865	−1,207
Migrants' transfers	3 431	−418	....	....	−561	−806	−936	−865	−1,207
Debt forgiveness	3 432	....	....	....	....	....	....	....	....
Other capital transfers	3 440	....	....	....	....	....	....	....	....
Nonproduced nonfinancial assets, credit	2 480	2	3	23	....	4	1	....	2
Nonproduced nonfinancial assets, debit	3 480	....	....	....	−2	−1	−1	−2	−8

Table 2 (Continued). STANDARD PRESENTATION, 2000–2007

(Millions of U.S. dollars)

	Code	2000	2001	2002	2003	2004	2005	2006	2007
FINANCIAL ACCOUNT	4 995	**3,279**	**1,041**	**1,072**	**2,648**	**7,506**	**8,626**	**8,759**	**10,790**
A. DIRECT INVESTMENT	4 500	**3,171**	**1,012**	**1,285**	**1,558**	**2,985**	**3,154**	**7,651**	**−55**
Direct investment abroad	4 505	**−739**	**1,078**	**−382**	**−917**	**508**	**1,649**	**−363**	**−2,807**
Equity capital	4 510	....	....	....	....	....	....	....	....
Claims on affiliated enterprises	4 515	....	....	....	....	....	....	....	....
Liabilities to affiliated enterprises	4 520	....	....	....	....	....	....	....	....
Reinvested earnings	4 525	....	....	....	....	....	....	....	....
Other capital	4 530	....	....	....	....	....	....	....	....
Claims on affiliated enterprises	4 535	....	....	....	....	....	....	....	....
Liabilities to affiliated enterprises	4 540	....	....	....	....	....	....	....	....
Direct investment in New Zealand	4 555	**3,910**	**−68**	**1,667**	**2,475**	**2,478**	**1,504**	**8,013**	**2,753**
Equity capital	4 560	....	....	18	−1,395	−1,606	−1,889	1,433	1,702
Claims on direct investors	4 565	....	....	....	....	....	....	....	....
Liabilities to direct investors	4 570	....	....	....	....	....	....	....	....
Reinvested earnings	4 575	....	....	1,086	1,231	2,335	2,412	1,749	1,371
Other capital	4 580	....	....	563	2,639	1,749	982	4,831	−320
Claims on direct investors	4 585	....	....	....	....	....	....	....	....
Liabilities to direct investors	4 590	....	....	....	....	....	....	....	....
B. PORTFOLIO INVESTMENT	4 600	**−2,112**	**786**	**1,687**	**1,021**	**6,300**	**−149**	**−1,491**	**10,902**
Assets	4 602	**−2,188**	**−1,243**	**−950**	**−864**	**−1,772**	**−587**	**−945**	**−1,199**
Equity securities	4 610	....	−941	....	−920	−1,556	−1,104	−647	−848
Monetary authorities	4 611	....	....	....	....	....	....	....	....
General government	4 612	....	....	....	....	....	....	....	....
Banks	4 613	....	....	....	....	....	....	....	....
Other sectors	4 614	....	....	....	....	....	....	....	....
Debt securities	4 619	....	−303	....	56	−216	517	−298	−351
Bonds and notes	4 620	....	....	....	....	....	....	....	....
Monetary authorities	4 621	....	....	....	....	....	....	....	....
General government	4 622	....	....	....	....	....	....	....	....
Banks	4 623	....	....	....	....	....	....	....	....
Other sectors	4 624	....	....	....	....	....	....	....	....
Money market instruments	4 630	....	....	....	....	....	....	....	....
Monetary authorities	4 631	....	....	....	....	....	....	....	....
General government	4 632	....	....	....	....	....	....	....	....
Banks	4 633	....	....	....	....	....	....	....	....
Other sectors	4 634	....	....	....	....	....	....	....	....
Liabilities	4 652	**76**	**2,030**	**2,637**	**1,886**	**8,072**	**438**	**−546**	**12,101**
Equity securities	4 660	....	24	752	719	99	−141	−378	192
Banks	4 663	....	....	....	....	....	....	....	....
Other sectors	4 664	....	....	....	....	....	....	....	....
Debt securities	4 669	....	2,005	1,885	1,167	7,974	578	−168	11,908
Bonds and notes	4 670	....	....	....	....	....	....	....	....
Monetary authorities	4 671	....	....	....	....	....	....	....	....
General government	4 672	....	....	....	....	....	....	....	....
Banks	4 673	....	....	....	....	....	....	....	....
Other sectors	4 674	....	....	....	....	....	....	....	....
Money market instruments	4 680	....	....	....	....	....	....	....	....
Monetary authorities	4 681	....	....	....	....	....	....	....	....
General government	4 682	....	....	....	....	....	....	....	....
Banks	4 683	....	....	....	....	....	....	....	....
Other sectors	4 684	....	....	....	....	....	....	....	....
C. FINANCIAL DERIVATIVES	4 910	....	....	....	....	....	....	....	....
Monetary authorities	4 911	....	....	....	....	....	....	....	....
General government	4 912	....	....	....	....	....	....	....	....
Banks	4 913	....	....	....	....	....	....	....	....
Other sectors	4 914	....	....	....	....	....	....	....	....
Assets	4 900	....	....	....	....	....	....	....	....
Monetary authorities	4 901	....	....	....	....	....	....	....	....
General government	4 902	....	....	....	....	....	....	....	....
Banks	4 903	....	....	....	....	....	....	....	....
Other sectors	4 904	....	....	....	....	....	....	....	....
Liabilities	4 905	....	....	....	....	....	....	....	....
Monetary authorities	4 906	....	....	....	....	....	....	....	....
General government	4 907	....	....	....	....	....	....	....	....
Banks	4 908	....	....	....	....	....	....	....	....
Other sectors	4 909	....	....	....	....	....	....	....	....

Table 2 (Concluded). STANDARD PRESENTATION, 2000–2007

(Millions of U.S. dollars)

	Code	2000	2001	2002	2003	2004	2005	2006	2007
D. OTHER INVESTMENT	4 700 ..	**2,077**	**−944**	**−813**	**851**	**−1,149**	**8,039**	**6,855**	**3,030**
Assets	4 703 ..	**−394**	**−3,997**	**−475**	**56**	**482**	**4,090**	**−1,569**	**−2,112**
Trade credits	4 706 ..	....	−232	....	....	....	....	−444	....
General government	4 707 ..	....	....	....	....	....	....	....	....
of which: Short-term	4 709 ..	....	....	....	....	....	....	....	....
Other sectors	4 710 ..	....	....	....	....	....	....	....	....
of which: Short-term	4 712 ..	....	....	....	....	....	....	....	....
Loans	4 714 ..	....	−4,409	−355	−175	747	5,101	186	−2,269
Monetary authorities	4 715 ..	....	....	....	....	....	....	....	....
of which: Short-term	4 718 ..	....	....	....	....	....	....	....	....
General government	4 719 ..	....	....	....	....	....	....	....	....
of which: Short-term	4 721 ..	....	....	....	....	....	....	....	....
Banks	4 722 ..	....	....	....	....	....	....	....	....
of which: Short-term	4 724 ..	....	....	....	....	....	....	....	....
Other sectors	4 725 ..	....	....	....	....	....	....	....	....
of which: Short-term	4 727 ..	....	....	....	....	....	....	....	....
Currency and deposits	4 730 ..	....	351	−203	−117	−16	−579	−1,318	517
Monetary authorities	4 731 ..	....	....	....	....	....	....	....	....
General government	4 732 ..	....	....	....	....	....	....	....	....
Banks	4 733 ..	....	....	....	....	....	....	....	....
Other sectors	4 734 ..	....	....	....	....	....	....	....	....
Other assets	4 736 ..	....	−484	−50	....	....	....	247	....
Monetary authorities	4 737 ..	....	....	....	....	....	....	....	....
of which: Short-term	4 739 ..	....	....	....	....	....	....	....	....
General government	4 740 ..	....	....	....	....	....	....	....	....
of which: Short-term	4 742 ..	....	....	....	....	....	....	....	....
Banks	4 743 ..	....	....	....	....	....	....	....	....
of which: Short-term	4 745 ..	....	....	....	....	....	....	....	....
Other sectors	4 746 ..	....	....	....	....	....	....	....	....
of which: Short-term	4 748 ..	....	....	....	....	....	....	....	....
Liabilities	4 753 ..	**2,471**	**3,053**	**−338**	**795**	**−1,631**	**3,948**	**8,423**	**5,142**
Trade credits	4 756 ..	....	−22	−76	−151	....	42	105	−43
General government	4 757 ..	....	....	....	....	....	....	....	....
of which: Short-term	4 759 ..	....	....	....	....	....	....	....	....
Other sectors	4 760 ..	....	....	....	....	....	....	....	....
of which: Short-term	4 762 ..	....	....	....	....	....	....	....	....
Loans	4 764 ..	....	2,341	−1,492	−83	−2,243	2,544	3,187	4,631
Monetary authorities	4 765 ..	....	....	....	....	....	....	....	....
of which: Use of Fund credit and loans from the Fund..	4 766 ..	....	....	....	....	....	....	....	....
of which: Short-term	4 768 ..	....	....	....	....	....	....	....	....
General government	4 769 ..	....	....	....	....	....	....	....	....
of which: Short-term	4 771 ..	....	....	....	....	....	....	....	....
Banks	4 772 ..	....	....	....	....	....	....	....	....
of which: Short-term	4 774 ..	....	....	....	....	....	....	....	....
Other sectors	4 775 ..	....	....	....	....	....	....	....	....
of which: Short-term	4 777 ..	....	....	....	....	....	....	....	....
Currency and deposits	4 780 ..	....	665	1,164	1,070	599	1,297	4,732	421
Monetary authorities	4 781 ..	....	....	....	....	....	....	....	....
General government	4 782 ..	....	....	....	....	....	....	....	....
Banks	4 783 ..	....	....	....	....	....	....	....	....
Other sectors	4 784 ..	....	....	....	....	....	....	....	....
Other liabilities	4 786 ..	....	221	66	−40	....	66	400	132
Monetary authorities	4 787 ..	....	....	....	....	....	....	....	....
of which: Short-term	4 789 ..	....	....	....	....	....	....	....	....
General government	4 790 ..	....	....	....	....	....	....	....	....
of which: Short-term	4 792 ..	....	....	....	....	....	....	....	....
Banks	4 793 ..	....	....	....	....	....	....	....	....
of which: Short-term	4 795 ..	....	....	....	....	....	....	....	....
Other sectors	4 796 ..	....	....	....	....	....	....	....	....
of which: Short-term	4 798 ..	....	....	....	....	....	....	....	....
E. RESERVE ASSETS	4 802 ..	**143**	**187**	**−1,086**	**−783**	**−630**	**−2,418**	**−4,255**	**−3,088**
Monetary gold	4 812 ..	....	....	....	....	....	....	....	....
Special drawing rights	4 811 ..	−7	−4	−4	−4	−5	−3	3	6
Reserve position in the Fund	4 810 ..	82	−79	−38	−135	189	277	53	29
Foreign exchange	4 803 ..	355	21	−389	244	−625	−2,541	−1,976	−6,546
Other claims	4 813 ..	−288	249	−655	−888	−188	−151	−2,334	3,423
NET ERRORS AND OMISSIONS	4 998 ..	**−421**	**−89**	**489**	**319**	**−1,372**	**862**	**544**	**9**

Table 3. INTERNATIONAL INVESTMENT POSITION (End-March stocks through 1999)

(Millions of U.S. dollars)

	Code	2000	2001	2002	2003	2004	2005	2006	2007
ASSETS	8 995 C.	**32,453**	**33,120**	**42,164**	**55,178**	**63,358**	**58,823**	**73,191**	**91,686**
Direct investment abroad	8 505 ..	**8,491**	**7,175**	**9,425**	**11,883**	**13,957**	**11,584**	**12,825**	**15,065**
Equity capital and reinvested earnings	8 506 ..	7,842	5,580	8,137	10,538	12,045	10,243	11,173	13,150
Claims on affiliated enterprises	8 507 ..	....	....	....	....	....	....	....	....
Liabilities to affiliated enterprises	8 508 ..	....	....	....	....	....	....	....	....
Other capital	8 530 ..	649	1,595	1,289	1,345	1,912	1,341	1,652	1,915
Claims on affiliated enterprises	8 535 ..	....	....	....	....	....	....	....	....
Liabilities to affiliated enterprises	8 540 ..	....	....	....	....	....	....	....	....
Portfolio investment	8 602 ..	**11,264**	**11,788**	**13,468**	**19,271**	**23,751**	**25,309**	**29,598**	**35,602**
Equity securities	8 610 ..	6,721	7,114	7,652	13,432	17,267	19,645	23,380	27,411
Monetary authorities	8 611 ..	....	....	....	....	....	....	....	....
General government	8 612 ..	....	....	....	....	....	....	....	....
Banks	8 613 ..	....	....	....	....	....	....	....	....
Other sectors	8 614 ..	....	....	....	....	....	....	....	....
Debt securities	8 619 ..	4,543	4,673	5,816	5,839	6,484	5,664	6,218	8,190
Bonds and notes	8 620 ..	....	....	....	....	....	....	....	....
Monetary authorities	8 621 ..	....	....	....	....	....	....	....	....
General government	8 622 ..	....	....	....	....	....	....	....	....
Banks	8 623 ..	....	....	....	....	....	....	....	....
Other sectors	8 624 ..	....	....	....	....	....	....	....	....
Money market instruments	8 630 ..	....	....	....	....	....	....	....	....
Monetary authorities	8 631 ..	....	....	....	....	....	....	....	....
General government	8 632 ..	....	....	....	....	....	....	....	....
Banks	8 633 ..	....	....	....	....	....	....	....	....
Other sectors	8 634 ..	....	....	....	....	....	....	....	....
Financial derivatives	8 900 ..	**4,289**	**2,462**	**3,484**	**4,678**	**3,922**	**2,758**	**4,151**	**7,178**
Monetary authorities	8 901 ..	....	....	....	....	....	....	....	....
General government	8 902 ..	....	....	....	....	....	....	....	....
Banks	8 903 ..	....	....	....	....	....	....	....	....
Other sectors	8 904 ..	....	....	....	....	....	....	....	....
Other investment	8 703 ..	**4,456**	**8,130**	**10,824**	**13,298**	**14,782**	**10,276**	**12,549**	**16,595**
Trade credits	8 706 ..	931	946	1,306	1,567	....	1,821	2,302	2,769
General government	8 707 ..	....	....	....	....	....	....	....	....
of which: Short-term	8 709 ..	....	....	....	....	....	....	....	....
Other sectors	8 710 ..	....	....	....	....	....	....	....	....
of which: Short-term	8 712 ..	....	....	....	....	....	....	....	....
Loans	8 714 ..	2,056	6,371	8,178	10,146	10,997	5,481	5,623	8,643
Monetary authorities	8 715 ..	....	....	....	....	....	....	....	....
of which: Short-term	8 718 ..	....	....	....	....	....	....	....	....
General government	8 719 ..	....	....	....	....	....	....	....	....
of which: Short-term	8 721 ..	....	....	....	....	....	....	....	....
Banks	8 722 ..	....	....	....	....	....	....	....	....
of which: Short-term	8 724 ..	....	....	....	....	....	....	....	....
Other sectors	8 725 ..	....	....	....	....	....	....	....	....
of which: Short-term	8 727 ..	....	....	....	....	....	....	....	....
Currency and deposits	8 730 ..	1,166	698	1,062	1,488	1,879	2,114	3,870	4,011
Monetary authorities	8 731 ..	....	....	....	....	....	....	....	....
General government	8 732 ..	....	....	....	....	....	....	....	....
Banks	8 733 ..	....	....	....	....	....	....	....	....
Other sectors	8 734 ..	....	....	....	....	....	....	....	....
Other assets	8 736 ..	304	116	277	97	....	859	753	1,171
Monetary authorities	8 737 ..	....	....	....	....	....	....	....	....
of which: Short-term	8 739 ..	....	....	....	....	....	....	....	....
General government	8 740 ..	....	....	....	....	....	....	....	....
of which: Short-term	8 742 ..	....	....	....	....	....	....	....	....
Banks	8 743 ..	....	....	....	....	....	....	....	....
of which: Short-term	8 745 ..	....	....	....	....	....	....	....	....
Other sectors	8 746 ..	....	....	....	....	....	....	....	....
of which: Short-term	8 748 ..	....	....	....	....	....	....	....	....
Reserve assets	8 802 ..	**3,952**	**3,566**	**4,963**	**6,048**	**6,946**	**8,896**	**14,068**	**17,246**
Monetary gold	8 812 ..	....	....	....	....	....	....	....	....
Special drawing rights	8 811 ..	13	16	22	28	34	34	33	28
Reserve position in the Fund	8 810 ..	320	388	459	644	474	165	119	95
Foreign exchange	8 803 ..	3,025	2,815	3,410	3,367	4,119	6,257	8,935	15,525
Other claims	8 813 ..	594	347	1,072	2,009	2,320	2,439	4,982	1,598

Table 3 (Concluded). INTERNATIONAL INVESTMENT POSITION (End-March stocks through 1999)

(Millions of U.S. dollars)

	Code	2000	2001	2002	2003	2004	2005	2006	2007
LIABILITIES	8 995 D.	**73,187**	**71,057**	**95,018**	**123,473**	**150,648**	**148,149**	**173,535**	**209,754**
Direct investment in New Zealand	8 555	**24,894**	**20,925**	**30,194**	**44,327**	**52,640**	**52,230**	**63,055**	**70,942**
Equity capital and reinvested earnings	8 556	16,851	14,716	20,946	28,142	32,436	31,180	35,611	39,901
Claims on direct investors	8 557	....	....	....	....	....	....	....	....
Liabilities to direct investors	8 558	....	....	....	....	....	....	....	....
Other capital	8 580	8,043	6,210	9,248	16,185	20,204	21,050	27,443	31,040
Claims on direct investors	8 585	....	....	....	....	....	....	....	....
Liabilities to direct investors	8 590	....	....	....	....	....	....	....	....
Portfolio investment	8 652	**24,658**	**25,526**	**33,739**	**43,021**	**58,070**	**54,076**	**55,993**	**70,969**
Equity securities	8 660	4,582	4,170	5,652	8,965	12,078	11,489	11,833	12,612
Banks	8 663	....	....	....	....	....	....	....	....
Other sectors	8 664	....	....	....	....	....	....	....	....
Debt securities	8 669	20,076	21,356	28,087	34,057	45,993	42,587	44,160	58,357
Bonds and notes	8 670	....	....	....	....	....	....	....	....
Monetary authorities	8 671	....	....	....	....	....	....	....	....
General government	8 672	....	....	....	....	....	....	....	....
Banks	8 673	....	....	....	....	....	....	....	....
Other sectors	8 674	....	....	....	....	....	....	....	....
Money market instruments	8 680	....	....	....	....	....	....	....	....
Monetary authorities	8 681	....	....	....	....	....	....	....	....
General government	8 682	....	....	....	....	....	....	....	....
Banks	8 683	....	....	....	....	....	....	....	....
Other sectors	8 684	....	....	....	....	....	....	....	....
Financial derivatives	8 905	**3,256**	**2,640**	**4,138**	**5,466**	**5,206**	**3,543**	**5,195**	**7,196**
Monetary authorities	8 906	....	....	....	....	....	....	....	....
General government	8 907	....	....	....	....	....	....	....	....
Banks	8 908	....	....	....	....	....	....	....	....
Other sectors	8 909	....	....	....	....	....	....	....	....
Other investment	8 753	**20,379**	**21,966**	**26,947**	**30,659**	**34,732**	**38,301**	**49,292**	**60,648**
Trade credits	8 756	971	828	1,236	1,173	1,191	1,242	1,323	1,256
General government	8 758	....	....	....	....	....	....	....	....
of which: Short-term	8 759	....	....	....	....	....	....	....	....
Other sectors	8 760	....	....	....	....	....	....	....	....
of which: Short-term	8 762	....	....	....	....	....	....	....	....
Loans	8 764	15,353	16,688	18,951	20,166	22,683	25,272	30,167	39,740
Monetary authorities	8 765	....	....	....	....	....	....	....	....
of which: Use of Fund credit and loans from the Fund	8 766	....	....	....	....	....	....	....	....
of which: Short-term	8 768	....	....	....	....	....	....	....	....
General government	8 769	....	....	....	....	....	....	....	....
of which: Short-term	8 771	....	....	....	....	....	....	....	....
Banks	8 772	....	....	....	....	....	....	....	....
of which: Short-term	8 774	....	....	....	....	....	....	....	....
Other sectors	8 775	....	....	....	....	....	....	....	....
of which: Short-term	8 777	....	....	....	....	....	....	....	....
Currency and deposits	8 780	3,929	4,293	6,503	9,104	10,549	11,276	16,932	18,574
Monetary authorities	8 781	....	....	....	....	....	....	....	....
General government	8 782	....	....	....	....	....	....	....	....
Banks	8 783	....	....	....	....	....	....	....	....
Other sectors	8 784	....	....	....	....	....	....	....	....
Other liabilities	8 786	125	157	257	216	308	510	869	1,077
Monetary authorities	8 787	....	....	....	....	....	....	....	....
of which: Short-term	8 789	....	....	....	....	....	....	....	....
General government	8 790	....	....	....	....	....	....	....	....
of which: Short-term	8 792	....	....	....	....	....	....	....	....
Banks	8 793	....	....	....	....	....	....	....	....
of which: Short-term	8 795	....	....	....	....	....	....	....	....
Other sectors	8 796	....	....	....	....	....	....	....	....
of which: Short-term	8 798	....	....	....	....	....	....	....	....
NET INTERNATIONAL INVESTMENT POSITION	8 995	**−40,734**	**−37,937**	**−52,854**	**−68,295**	**−87,291**	**−89,327**	**−100,343**	**−118,068**
Conversion rates: New Zealand dollars per U.S. dollar (end of period)	0 102	**2.2717**	**2.4067**	**1.8993**	**1.5385**	**1.3920**	**1.4676**	**1.4166**	**1.2920**

Table 1. ANALYTIC PRESENTATION, 2000–2007

(Millions of U.S. dollars)

	Code	2000	2001	2002	2003	2004	2005	2006	2007
A. Current Account[1].....................................	4 993 Z.	**−841.9**	**−805.0**	**−744.1**	**−663.0**	**−648.7**	**−734.3**	**−678.5**	**−1,047.5**
Goods: exports f.o.b.	2 100 ..	880.6	895.3	914.4	1,056.0	1,369.0	1,654.1	2,033.9	2,313.2
Goods: imports f.o.b.	3 100 ..	−1,801.5	−1,805.1	−1,853.0	−2,027.0	−2,457.4	−2,956.1	−3,450.5	−4,117.0
Balance on Goods.................	4 100 ..	*−920.9*	*−909.8*	*−938.6*	*−971.0*	*−1,088.4*	*−1,302.0*	*−1,416.6*	*−1,803.8*
Services: credit.................	2 200 ..	221.3	223.1	225.5	257.6	285.8	308.5	341.0	372.1
Services: debit.................	3 200 ..	−350.7	−363.7	−355.4	−376.8	−409.0	−448.2	−477.7	−555.8
Balance on Goods and Services.................	4 991 ..	*−1,050.3*	*−1,050.4*	*−1,068.5*	*−1,090.2*	*−1,211.6*	*−1,441.7*	*−1,553.3*	*−1,987.5*
Income: credit.................	2 300 ..	30.7	14.7	9.2	6.8	9.4	22.7	41.4	48.2
Income: debit.................	3 300 ..	−232.5	−255.0	−215.1	−205.0	−201.5	−172.7	−169.9	−182.8
Balance on Goods, Services, and Income.................	4 992 ..	*−1,252.1*	*−1,290.7*	*−1,274.4*	*−1,288.4*	*−1,403.7*	*−1,591.7*	*−1,681.8*	*−2,122.1*
Current transfers: credit.................	2 379 Z.	410.2	485.7	530.3	625.4	755.0	857.4	1,003.3	1,074.6
Current transfers: debit.................	3 379 ..	....	....	....	....	....	....	....	....
B. Capital Account[1]................................	4 994 Z.	**296.4**	**297.6**	**312.0**	**283.9**	**307.4**	**299.8**	**348.0**	**418.1**
Capital account: credit.................	2 994 Z.	296.4	297.6	312.0	283.9	307.4	299.8	348.0	418.1
Capital account: debit.................	3 994 ..	....	....	....	....	....	....	....	....
Total, Groups A Plus B.................	4 981 ..	*−545.5*	*−507.4*	*−432.1*	*−379.1*	*−341.3*	*−434.5*	*−330.5*	*−629.4*
C. Financial Account[1]................................	4 995 W.	**−43.8**	**−171.2**	**359.4**	**36.6**	**360.9**	**183.0**	**515.0**	**489.8**
Direct investment abroad.................	4 505 ..	....	....	....	....	....	....	....	....
Direct investment in Nicaragua.................	4 555 Z.	266.5	150.2	203.9	201.3	250.0	241.1	286.8	381.7
Portfolio investment assets.................	4 602 ..	....	....	....	....	....	....	....	....
Equity securities.................	4 610 ..	....	....	....	....	....	....	....	....
Debt securities.................	4 619 ..	....	....	....	....	....	....	....	....
Portfolio investment liabilities.................	4 652 Z.	34.6	14.2	1.2	.3	−1.0	−7.8	−9.6	−12.2
Equity securities.................	4 660 ..	....	....	....	....	....	....	....	....
Debt securities.................	4 669 Z.	34.6	14.2	1.2	.3	−1.0	−7.8	−9.6	−12.2
Financial derivatives.................	4 910 ..	....	....	....	....	....	....	....	....
Financial derivatives assets.................	4 900 ..	....	....	....	....	....	....	....	....
Financial derivatives liabilities.................	4 905 ..	....	....	....	....	....	....	....	....
Other investment assets.................	4 703 ..	−64.7	−247.8	149.6	−105.5	275.2	−182.3	5.3	−163.8
Monetary authorities.................	4 701 ..	.5	.4	−3.3	3.5	−.2	−53.8	−8.5	−11.2
General government.................	4 704 ..	....	....	....	....	−.3	−1.9	−.8	−21.4
Banks.................	4 705 ..	38.8	−22.2	2.9	−16.0	−8.3	−20.6	9.2	−8.0
Other sectors.................	4 728 ..	−104.0	−226.0	150.0	−93.0	284.0	−106.0	5.4	−123.2
Other investment liabilities.................	4 753 W.	−280.2	−87.8	4.7	−59.5	−163.3	132.0	232.5	284.1
Monetary authorities.................	4 753 WA	−60.8	−13.6	−18.7	2.9	−6.8	−25.4	2.1	−4.4
General government.................	4 753 ZB	−73.6	−81.9	−184.4	−186.0	−155.0	−79.3	−69.1	−77.5
Banks.................	4 753 ZC	−32.6	9.5	5.0	−5.4	3.5	91.9	166.2	36.0
Other sectors.................	4 753 ZD	−113.2	−1.8	202.8	129.0	−5.0	144.8	133.3	330.0
Total, Groups A Through C.................	4 983 ..	*−589.3*	*−678.6*	*−72.7*	*−342.5*	*19.6*	*−251.4*	*184.5*	*−139.6*
D. Net Errors and Omissions................................	4 998 ..	**205.7**	**235.2**	**−318.8**	**−119.4**	**−415.2**	**−57.4**	**−151.5**	**42.9**
Total, Groups A Through D.................	4 984 ..	*−383.6*	*−443.4*	*−391.5*	*−461.9*	*−395.6*	*−308.8*	*33.0*	*−96.7*
E. Reserves and Related Items................................	4 802 A.	**383.6**	**443.4**	**391.5**	**461.9**	**395.6**	**308.8**	**−33.0**	**96.7**
Reserve assets.................	4 802 ..	15.7	109.9	−69.3	−55.0	−159.9	−5.7	−185.8	−172.5
Use of Fund credit and loans.................	4 766 ..	20.9	−5.0	4.0	21.6	23.9	−28.4	−141.5	18.5
Exceptional financing.................	4 920 ..	347.0	338.5	456.7	495.4	531.7	343.0	294.3	250.7
Conversion rates: córdobas per U.S. dollar............	0 101 ..	**12.684**	**13.372**	**14.251**	**15.105**	**15.937**	**16.733**	**17.570**	**18.449**

[1] Excludes components that have been classified in the categories of Group E.

Table 2. STANDARD PRESENTATION, 2000–2007

(Millions of U.S. dollars)

	Code	2000	2001	2002	2003	2004	2005	2006	2007
CURRENT ACCOUNT	4 993	**−841.9**	**−805.0**	**−744.1**	**−663.0**	**−648.7**	**−734.3**	**−678.5**	**−1,047.5**
A. GOODS	4 100	**−920.9**	**−909.8**	**−938.6**	**−971.0**	**−1,088.4**	**−1,302.0**	**−1,416.6**	**−1,803.8**
Credit	2 100	**880.6**	**895.3**	**914.4**	**1,056.0**	**1,369.0**	**1,654.1**	**2,033.9**	**2,313.2**
General merchandise: exports f.o.b.	2 110	613.5	559.5	523.6	575.9	714.6	823.6	994.2	1,140.8
Goods for processing: exports f.o.b.	2 150	230.7	296.3	347.0	433.7	596.7	773.7	966.2	1,088.1
Repairs on goods	2 160	....	....	....	....	....	....	....	....
Goods procured in ports by carriers	2 170	7.1	9.6	8.7	11.4	12.5	14.4	18.2	22.9
Nonmonetary gold	2 180	29.3	29.9	35.1	35.0	45.2	42.4	55.3	61.4
Debit	3 100	**−1,801.5**	**−1,805.1**	**−1,853.0**	**−2,027.0**	**−2,457.4**	**−2,956.1**	**−3,450.5**	**−4,117.0**
General merchandise: imports f.o.b.	3 110	−1,653.2	−1,617.3	−1,617.5	−1,726.1	−2,027.7	−2,404.6	−2,754.7	−3,333.4
Goods for processing: imports f.o.b.	3 150	−148.3	−187.8	−235.5	−300.9	−429.7	−551.5	−695.8	−783.6
Repairs on goods	3 160	....	....	....	....	....	....	....	....
Goods procured in ports by carriers	3 170	....	....	....	....	....	....	....	....
Nonmonetary gold	3 180	....	....	....	....	....	....	....	....
B. SERVICES	4 200	**−129.4**	**−140.6**	**−129.9**	**−119.2**	**−123.2**	**−139.7**	**−136.7**	**−183.7**
Total credit	2 200	*221.3*	*223.1*	*225.5*	*257.6*	*285.8*	*308.5*	*341.0*	*372.1*
Total debit	3 200	*−350.7*	*−363.7*	*−355.4*	*−376.8*	*−409.0*	*−448.2*	*−477.7*	*−555.8*
Transportation services, credit	2 205	**29.6**	**25.0**	**30.6**	**33.0**	**28.1**	**33.8**	**38.4**	**42.6**
Passenger	2 850	....	....	....	....	....	....	....	....
Freight	2 851	*9.6*	*8.8*	*13.0*	*13.9*	*7.9*	*11.3*	*12.5*	*15.2*
Other	2 852	*20.0*	*16.2*	*17.6*	*19.1*	*20.2*	*22.5*	*25.9*	*27.4*
Sea transport, passenger	2 207	....	....	....	....	....	....	....	....
Sea transport, freight	2 208	....	....	....	....	....	....	....	....
Sea transport, other	2 209	6.7	6.3	5.3	5.3	5.3	6.7	9.5	10.7
Air transport, passenger	2 211	....	....	....	....	....	....	....	....
Air transport, freight	2 212	....	....	....	....	....	....	....	....
Air transport, other	2 213	13.3	9.9	12.3	13.8	14.9	15.8	16.4	16.7
Other transport, passenger	2 215	....	....	....	....	....	....	....	....
Other transport, freight	2 216	9.6	8.8	13.0	13.9	7.9	11.3	12.5	15.2
Other transport, other	2 217	....	....	....	....	....	....	....	....
Transportation services, debit	3 205	**−152.3**	**−168.5**	**−171.5**	**−186.0**	**−196.4**	**−233.9**	**−250.1**	**−285.0**
Passenger	3 850	*−48.0*	*−51.8*	*−55.9*	*−63.6*	*−65.4*	*−70.9*	*−74.0*	*−74.0*
Freight	3 851	*−104.3*	*−116.7*	*−115.6*	*−122.4*	*−131.0*	*−163.0*	*−176.1*	*−211.0*
Other	3 852	....	....	....	....	....	....	....	....
Sea transport, passenger	3 207	....	....	....	....	....	....	....	....
Sea transport, freight	3 208	−40.2	−50.6	−39.9	−52.6	−58.6	−75.0	−84.1	−110.2
Sea transport, other	3 209	....	....	....	....	....	....	....	....
Air transport, passenger	3 211	−48.0	−51.8	−55.9	−63.6	−65.4	−70.9	−74.0	−74.0
Air transport, freight	3 212	−10.8	−12.1	−12.3	−13.1	−14.0	−16.0	−17.0	−21.0
Air transport, other	3 213	....	....	....	....	....	....	....	....
Other transport, passenger	3 215	....	....	....	....	....	....	....	....
Other transport, freight	3 216	−53.3	−54.0	−63.4	−56.7	−58.4	−72.0	−75.0	−79.8
Other transport, other	3 217	....	....	....	....	....	....	....	....
Travel, credit	2 236	**128.6**	**135.3**	**134.6**	**160.2**	**192.0**	**206.3**	**230.6**	**255.1**
Business travel	2 237	....	....	....	....	....	....	....	....
Personal travel	2 240	128.6	135.3	134.6	160.2	192.0	206.3	230.6	255.1
Travel, debit	3 236	**−78.4**	**−76.0**	**−69.4**	**−75.0**	**−89.3**	**−90.8**	**−97.0**	**−120.6**
Business travel	3 237	....	....	....	....	....	....	....	....
Personal travel	3 240	−78.4	−76.0	−69.4	−75.0	−89.3	−90.8	−97.0	−120.6
Other services, credit	2 200 BA	**63.1**	**62.8**	**60.3**	**64.4**	**65.7**	**68.4**	**72.0**	**74.4**
Communications	2 245	25.1	24.3	23.3	26.4	27.1	28.3	29.4	30.5
Construction	2 249	....	....	....	....	....	....	....	....
Insurance	2 253	3.2	2.9	2.3	2.3	2.4	2.8	3.5	4.1
Financial	2 260	....	....	....	....	....	....	....	....
Computer and information	2 262	....	....	....	....	....	....	....	....
Royalties and licence fees	2 266	....	....	....	....	....	....	....	....
Other business services	2 268	....	....	....	....	....	....	....	....
Personal, cultural, and recreational	2 287	....	....	....	....	....	....	....	....
Government, n.i.e.	2 291	34.8	35.6	34.7	35.7	36.2	37.3	39.1	39.8
Other services, debit	3 200 BA	**−120.0**	**−119.2**	**−114.5**	**−115.8**	**−123.3**	**−123.5**	**−130.6**	**−150.2**
Communications	3 245	−3.1	−3.6	−3.9	−4.3	−4.7	−5.1	−5.3	−5.6
Construction	3 249	....	....	....	....	....	....	....	....
Insurance	3 253	−25.0	−29.2	−37.1	−28.6	−39.2	−40.8	−43.7	−56.4
Financial	3 260	....	....	....	....	....	....	....	....
Computer and information	3 262	....	....	....	....	....	....	....	....
Royalties and licence fees	3 266	....	....	....	....	....	....	....	....
Other business services	3 268	−75.3	−68.9	−54.2	−59.4	−55.5	−53.0	−55.0	−57.0
Personal, cultural, and recreational	3 287	....	....	....	....	....	....	....	....
Government, n.i.e.	3 291	−16.6	−17.5	−19.3	−23.5	−23.9	−24.6	−26.6	−31.2

Table 2 (Continued). STANDARD PRESENTATION, 2000–2007

(Millions of U.S. dollars)

	Code	2000	2001	2002	2003	2004	2005	2006	2007
C. INCOME	4 300 ..	−201.8	−240.3	−205.9	−198.2	−192.1	−150.0	−128.5	−134.6
Total credit	2 300 ..	*30.7*	*14.7*	*9.2*	*6.8*	*9.4*	*22.7*	*41.4*	*48.2*
Total debit	3 300 ..	*−232.5*	*−255.0*	*−215.1*	*−205.0*	*−201.5*	*−172.7*	*−169.9*	*−182.8*
Compensation of employees, credit	2 310 ..	....	....	....	....	....	....	....	....
Compensation of employees, debit	3 310 ..	....	....	....	....	....	....	....	....
Investment income, credit	2 320 ..	30.7	14.7	9.2	6.8	9.4	22.7	41.4	48.2
Direct investment income	2 330 ..	....	....	....	....	....	....	....	....
Dividends and distributed branch profits	2 332 ..	....	....	....	....	....	....	....	....
Reinvested earnings and undistributed branch profits	2 333 ..	....	....	....	....	....	....	....	....
Income on debt (interest)	2 334 ..	....	....	....	....	....	....	....	....
Portfolio investment income	2 339 ..	....	....	....	....	....	....	....	....
Income on equity	2 340 ..	....	....	....	....	....	....	....	....
Income on bonds and notes	2 350 ..	....	....	....	....	....	....	....	....
Income on money market instruments	2 360 ..	....	....	....	....	....	....	....	....
Other investment income	2 370 ..	30.7	14.7	9.2	6.8	9.4	22.7	41.4	48.2
Investment income, debit	3 320 ..	−232.5	−255.0	−215.1	−205.0	−201.5	−172.7	−169.9	−182.8
Direct investment income	3 330 ..	−69.4	−77.2	−71.4	−76.9	−80.0	−82.4	−84.9	−92.6
Dividends and distributed branch profits	3 332 ..	−69.4	−77.2	−71.4	−76.9	−80.0	−82.4	−84.9	−92.6
Reinvested earnings and undistributed branch profits	3 333 ..	....	....	....	....	....	....	....	....
Income on debt (interest)	3 334 ..	....	....	....	....	....	....	....	....
Portfolio investment income	3 339 ..	....	....	....	....	....	....	....	....
Income on equity	3 340 ..	....	....	....	....	....	....	....	....
Income on bonds and notes	3 350 ..	....	....	....	....	....	....	....	....
Income on money market instruments	3 360 ..	....	....	....	....	....	....	....	....
Other investment income	3 370 ..	−163.1	−177.8	−143.7	−128.1	−121.5	−90.3	−85.0	−90.2
D. CURRENT TRANSFERS	4 379 ..	410.2	485.7	530.3	625.4	755.0	857.4	1,003.3	1,074.6
Credit	2 379 ..	410.2	485.7	530.3	625.4	755.0	857.4	1,003.3	1,074.6
General government	2 380 ..	....	....	....	....	....	....	....	80.0
Other sectors	2 390 ..	410.2	485.7	530.3	625.4	755.0	857.4	1,003.3	994.6
Workers' remittances	2 391 ..	320.0	335.7	376.5	438.8	518.8	615.7	697.5	739.6
Other current transfers	2 392 ..	90.2	150.0	153.8	186.6	236.2	241.7	305.8	255.0
Debit	3 379 ..	....	....	....	....	....	....	....	....
General government	3 380 ..	....	....	....	....	....	....	....	....
Other sectors	3 390 ..	....	....	....	....	....	....	....	....
Workers' remittances	3 391 ..	....	....	....	....	....	....	....	....
Other current transfers	3 392 ..	....	....	....	....	....	....	....	....
CAPITAL AND FINANCIAL ACCOUNT	4 996 ..	636.2	569.8	1,062.9	782.4	1,063.9	791.7	830.0	1,004.6
CAPITAL ACCOUNT	4 994 ..	331.8	834.0	772.0	771.5	1,922.2	481.8	1,578.4	2,938.0
Total credit	2 994 ..	*331.8*	*834.0*	*772.0*	*771.5*	*1,922.2*	*481.8*	*1,578.4*	*2,938.0*
Total debit	3 994 ..	....	....	....	....	....	....	....	....
Capital transfers, credit	2 400 ..	331.8	834.0	772.0	771.5	1,922.2	481.8	1,578.4	2,938.0
General government	2 401 ..	183.0	632.2	559.8	609.3	1,764.1	345.1	1,440.2	2,732.5
Debt forgiveness	2 402 ..	35.4	536.4	460.0	487.6	1,614.8	182.0	1,230.4	2,519.9
Other capital transfers	2 410 ..	147.6	95.8	99.8	121.7	149.3	163.1	209.8	212.6
Other sectors	2 430 ..	148.8	201.8	212.2	162.2	158.1	136.7	138.2	205.5
Migrants' transfers	2 431 ..	....	....	....	....	....	....	....	....
Debt forgiveness	2 432 ..	....	....	....	....	....	....	....	....
Other capital transfers	2 440 ..	148.8	201.8	212.2	162.2	158.1	136.7	138.2	205.5
Capital transfers, debit	3 400 ..	....	....	....	....	....	....	....	....
General government	3 401 ..	....	....	....	....	....	....	....	....
Debt forgiveness	3 402 ..	....	....	....	....	....	....	....	....
Other capital transfers	3 410 ..	....	....	....	....	....	....	....	....
Other sectors	3 430 ..	....	....	....	....	....	....	....	....
Migrants' transfers	3 431 ..	....	....	....	....	....	....	....	....
Debt forgiveness	3 432 ..	....	....	....	....	....	....	....	....
Other capital transfers	3 440 ..	....	....	....	....	....	....	....	....
Nonproduced nonfinancial assets, credit	2 480 ..	....	....	....	....	....	....	....	....
Nonproduced nonfinancial assets, debit	3 480 ..	....	....	....	....	....	....	....	....

2008, International Monetary Fund: *Balance of Payments Statistics Yearbook*

Table 2 (Continued). STANDARD PRESENTATION, 2000–2007

(Millions of U.S. dollars)

	Code	2000	2001	2002	2003	2004	2005	2006	2007
FINANCIAL ACCOUNT	4 995	304.4	−264.2	290.9	10.9	−858.3	309.9	−748.4	−1,933.4
A. DIRECT INVESTMENT	4 500	266.5	150.2	203.9	201.3	250.0	241.1	286.8	381.7
Direct investment abroad	4 505	....	....	....	....	....	....	....	....
Equity capital	4 510	....	....	....	....	....	....	....	....
Claims on affiliated enterprises	4 515	....	....	....	....	....	....	....	....
Liabilities to affiliated enterprises	4 520	....	....	....	....	....	....	....	....
Reinvested earnings	4 525	....	....	....	....	....	....	....	....
Other capital	4 530	....	....	....	....	....	....	....	....
Claims on affiliated enterprises	4 535	....	....	....	....	....	....	....	....
Liabilities to affiliated enterprises	4 540	....	....	....	....	....	....	....	....
Direct investment in Nicaragua	4 555	266.5	150.2	203.9	201.3	250.0	241.1	286.8	381.7
Equity capital	4 560	266.5	150.2	203.9	201.3	250.0	241.1	286.8	381.7
Claims on direct investors	4 565	....	....	....	....	....	....	....	....
Liabilities to direct investors	4 570	266.5	150.2	203.9	201.3	250.0	241.1	286.8	381.7
Reinvested earnings	4 575	....	....	....	....	....	....	....	....
Other capital	4 580	....	....	....	....	....	....	....	....
Claims on direct investors	4 585	....	....	....	....	....	....	....	....
Liabilities to direct investors	4 590	....	....	....	....	....	....	....	....
B. PORTFOLIO INVESTMENT	4 600	34.6	14.2	1.2	.3	−1.0	−7.8	−9.6	−12.2
Assets	4 602	....	....	....	....	....	....	....	....
Equity securities	4 610	....	....	....	....	....	....	....	....
Monetary authorities	4 611	....	....	....	....	....	....	....	....
General government	4 612	....	....	....	....	....	....	....	....
Banks	4 613	....	....	....	....	....	....	....	....
Other sectors	4 614	....	....	....	....	....	....	....	....
Debt securities	4 619	....	....	....	....	....	....	....	....
Bonds and notes	4 620	....	....	....	....	....	....	....	....
Monetary authorities	4 621	....	....	....	....	....	....	....	....
General government	4 622	....	....	....	....	....	....	....	....
Banks	4 623	....	....	....	....	....	....	....	....
Other sectors	4 624	....	....	....	....	....	....	....	....
Money market instruments	4 630	....	....	....	....	....	....	....	....
Monetary authorities	4 631	....	....	....	....	....	....	....	....
General government	4 632	....	....	....	....	....	....	....	....
Banks	4 633	....	....	....	....	....	....	....	....
Other sectors	4 634	....	....	....	....	....	....	....	....
Liabilities	4 652	34.6	14.2	1.2	.3	−1.0	−7.8	−9.6	−12.2
Equity securities	4 660	....	....	....	....	....	....	....	....
Banks	4 663	....	....	....	....	....	....	....	....
Other sectors	4 664	....	....	....	....	....	....	....	....
Debt securities	4 669	34.6	14.2	1.2	.3	−1.0	−7.8	−9.6	−12.2
Bonds and notes	4 670	....	....	....	....	....	....	....	....
Monetary authorities	4 671	....	....	....	....	....	....	....	....
General government	4 672	....	....	....	....	....	....	....	....
Banks	4 673	....	....	....	....	....	....	....	....
Other sectors	4 674	....	....	....	....	....	....	....	....
Money market instruments	4 680	34.6	14.2	1.2	.3	−1.0	−7.8	−9.6	−12.2
Monetary authorities	4 681	34.6	14.2	1.2	.3	−1.0	−7.8	−9.6	−12.2
General government	4 682	....	....	....	....	....	....	....	....
Banks	4 683	....	....	....	....	....	....	....	....
Other sectors	4 684	....	....	....	....	....	....	....	....
C. FINANCIAL DERIVATIVES	4 910	....	....	....	....	....	....	....	....
Monetary authorities	4 911	....	....	....	....	....	....	....	....
General government	4 912	....	....	....	....	....	....	....	....
Banks	4 913	....	....	....	....	....	....	....	....
Other sectors	4 914	....	....	....	....	....	....	....	....
Assets	4 900	....	....	....	....	....	....	....	....
Monetary authorities	4 901	....	....	....	....	....	....	....	....
General government	4 902	....	....	....	....	....	....	....	....
Banks	4 903	....	....	....	....	....	....	....	....
Other sectors	4 904	....	....	....	....	....	....	....	....
Liabilities	4 905	....	....	....	....	....	....	....	....
Monetary authorities	4 906	....	....	....	....	....	....	....	....
General government	4 907	....	....	....	....	....	....	....	....
Banks	4 908	....	....	....	....	....	....	....	....
Other sectors	4 909	....	....	....	....	....	....	....	....

Table 2 (Concluded). STANDARD PRESENTATION, 2000–2007

(Millions of U.S. dollars)

	Code	2000	2001	2002	2003	2004	2005	2006	2007
D. OTHER INVESTMENT	4 700 ..	**−12.4**	**−538.5**	**155.0**	**−135.6**	**−947.3**	**82.3**	**−839.8**	**−2,130.4**
Assets	4 703 ..	**−64.7**	**−247.8**	**149.6**	**−105.5**	**275.2**	**−182.3**	**5.3**	**−163.8**
Trade credits	4 706 ..	....	....	....	....	....	....	....	....
General government	4 707 ..	....	....	....	....	....	....	....	....
of which: Short-term	4 709 ..	....	....	....	....	....	....	....	....
Other sectors	4 710 ..	....	....	....	....	....	....	....	....
of which: Short-term	4 712 ..	....	....	....	....	....	....	....	....
Loans	4 714 ..	....	....	....	....	−.3	−1.9	−.8	−21.4
Monetary authorities	4 715 ..	....	....	....	....	....	....	....	....
of which: Short-term	4 718 ..	....	....	....	....	....	....	....	....
General government	4 719 ..	....	....	....	....	−.3	−1.9	−.8	−21.4
of which: Short-term	4 721 ..	....	....	....	....	....	....	....	....
Banks	4 722 ..	....	....	....	....	....	....	....	....
of which: Short-term	4 724 ..	....	....	....	....	....	....	....	....
Other sectors	4 725 ..	....	....	....	....	....	....	....	....
of which: Short-term	4 727 ..	....	....	....	....	....	....	....	....
Currency and deposits	4 730 ..	−64.7	−248.9	149.9	−104.8	275.2	−127.0	14.2	−133.4
Monetary authorities	4 731 ..	.5	.4	−3.3	3.5	−.2	.2	−.2	−2.3
General government	4 732 ..	....	....	....	....	....	....	....	....
Banks	4 733 ..	38.8	−23.3	3.2	−15.3	−8.6	−21.2	9.0	−7.9
Other sectors	4 734 ..	−104.0	−226.0	150.0	−93.0	284.0	−106.0	5.4	−123.2
Other assets	4 736 ..	....	1.1	−.3	−.7	.3	−53.4	−8.1	−9.0
Monetary authorities	4 737 ..	....	....	....	....	....	−54.0	−8.3	−8.9
of which: Short-term	4 739 ..	....	....	....	....	....	....	....	....
General government	4 740 ..	....	....	....	....	....	....	....	....
of which: Short-term	4 742 ..	....	....	....	....	....	....	....	....
Banks	4 743 ..	....	1.1	−.3	−.7	.3	.6	.2	−.1
of which: Short-term	4 745 ..	....	....	....	....	....	....	....	....
Other sectors	4 746 ..	....	....	....	....	....	....	....	....
of which: Short-term	4 748 ..	....	....	....	....	....	....	....	....
Liabilities	4 753 ..	**52.3**	**−290.7**	**5.4**	**−30.1**	**−1,222.5**	**264.6**	**−845.1**	**−1,966.6**
Trade credits	4 756 ..	−99.8	−14.7	270.2	117.8	−6.8	122.0	102.0	276.3
General government	4 757 ..	....	....	....	....	....	....	....	....
of which: Short-term	4 759 ..	....	....	....	....	....	....	....	....
Other sectors	4 760 ..	−99.8	−14.7	270.2	117.8	−6.8	122.0	102.0	276.3
of which: Short-term	4 762 ..	−99.8	−14.7	270.2	117.8	−6.8	122.0	102.0	276.3
Loans	4 764 ..	152.1	−291.7	−260.8	−172.9	−1,231.8	147.7	−984.5	−2,251.6
Monetary authorities	4 765 ..	−39.5	−417.2	−27.5	5.8	5.8	−38.7	−322.9	−14.5
of which: Use of Fund credit and loans from the Fund..	4 766 ..	20.9	−5.0	4.0	21.6	23.9	−28.4	−141.5	18.5
of which: Short-term	4 768 ..	....	....	....	....	....	....	....	....
General government	4 769 ..	237.6	118.8	−188.1	−178.8	−1,238.6	81.7	−836.1	−2,326.7
of which: Short-term	4 771 ..	....	....	....	....	....	....	....	....
Banks	4 772 ..	−32.6	12.2	4.2	−5.9	1.3	91.0	154.5	41.6
of which: Short-term	4 774 ..	....	....	−26.7	1.7	−6.5	11.8	54.2	−31.0
Other sectors	4 775 ..	−13.4	−5.5	−49.4	6.0	−.3	13.7	20.0	48.0
of which: Short-term	4 777 ..	30.5	36.9	12.7	20.2	10.7	21.7	22.3	51.4
Currency and deposits	4 780 ..	....	−5.8	13.3	18.4	10.4	−13.5	24.0	4.6
Monetary authorities	4 781 ..	....	....	13.1	19.4	10.5	−13.8	11.8	11.2
General government	4 782 ..	....	....	....	....	....	....	....	....
Banks	4 783 ..	....	−5.8	.2	−1.0	−.1	.3	12.2	−6.6
Other sectors	4 784 ..	....	....	....	....	....	....	....	....
Other liabilities	4 786 ..	....	21.5	−17.3	6.6	5.7	8.4	13.4	4.1
Monetary authorities	4 787 ..	....	....	.1	−.1	1.3	−1.3	2.6	−2.6
of which: Short-term	4 789 ..	....	....	.1	−.1	1.3	−1.3	2.6	−2.6
General government	4 790 ..	....	....	....	....	....	....	....	....
of which: Short-term	4 792 ..	....	....	....	....	....	....	....	....
Banks	4 793 ..	....	3.1	.6	1.5	2.3	.6	−.5	1.0
of which: Short-term	4 795 ..	....	3.1	.6	1.5	2.3	.6	−.5	1.0
Other sectors	4 796 ..	....	18.4	−18.0	5.2	2.1	9.1	11.3	5.7
of which: Short-term	4 798 ..	....	18.4	−18.0	5.2	2.1	9.1	11.3	5.7
E. RESERVE ASSETS	4 802 ..	**15.7**	**109.9**	**−69.3**	**−55.0**	**−159.9**	**−5.7**	**−185.8**	**−172.5**
Monetary gold	4 812 ..	−5.3	1.4	−1.1	−1.1	6.2	....	....	....
Special drawing rights	4 811 ..	.1	−.3	.3	....	−.4	.2	−.1	.3
Reserve position in the Fund	4 810 ..	....	....	....	....	....	....	....	....
Foreign exchange	4 803 ..	15.6	108.8	−68.5	−53.9	−165.7	−5.9	−185.7	−172.8
Other claims	4 813 ..	5.3	....	....	....	....	....	....	....
NET ERRORS AND OMISSIONS	4 998 ..	**205.7**	**235.2**	**−318.8**	**−119.4**	**−415.2**	**−57.4**	**−151.5**	**42.9**

Table 3. INTERNATIONAL INVESTMENT POSITION (End-period stocks), 2000–2007

(Millions of U.S. dollars)

	Code	2000	2001	2002	2003	2004	2005	2006	2007
ASSETS	8 995 C.	....	1,196.1	951.7	777.3	990.8	1,116.7	1,375.5	1,618.7
Direct investment abroad	8 505 ..	....	....	....	....	....	....	....	....
Equity capital and reinvested earnings	8 506 ..	....	....	....	....	....	....	....	....
Claims on affiliated enterprises	8 507 ..	....	....	....	....	....	....	....	....
Liabilities to affiliated enterprises	8 508 ..	....	....	....	....	....	....	....	....
Other capital	8 530 ..	....	....	....	....	....	....	....	....
Claims on affiliated enterprises	8 535 ..	....	....	....	....	....	....	....	....
Liabilities to affiliated enterprises	8 540 ..	....	....	....	....	....	....	....	....
Portfolio investment	8 602 ..	....	....	....	....	....	....	....	....
Equity securities	8 610 ..	....	....	....	....	....	....	....	....
Monetary authorities	8 611 ..	....	....	....	....	....	....	....	....
General government	8 612 ..	....	....	....	....	....	....	....	....
Banks	8 613 ..	....	....	....	....	....	....	....	....
Other sectors	8 614 ..	....	....	....	....	....	....	....	....
Debt securities	8 619 ..	....	....	....	....	....	....	....	....
Bonds and notes	8 620 ..	....	....	....	....	....	....	....	....
Monetary authorities	8 621 ..	....	....	....	....	....	....	....	....
General government	8 622 ..	....	....	....	....	....	....	....	....
Banks	8 623 ..	....	....	....	....	....	....	....	....
Other sectors	8 624 ..	....	....	....	....	....	....	....	....
Money market instruments	8 630 ..	....	....	....	....	....	....	....	....
Monetary authorities	8 631 ..	....	....	....	....	....	....	....	....
General government	8 632 ..	....	....	....	....	....	....	....	....
Banks	8 633 ..	....	....	....	....	....	....	....	....
Other sectors	8 634 ..	....	....	....	....	....	....	....	....
Financial derivatives	8 900 ..	....	....	....	....	....	....	....	....
Monetary authorities	8 901 ..	....	....	....	....	....	....	....	....
General government	8 902 ..	....	....	....	....	....	....	....	....
Banks	8 903 ..	....	....	....	....	....	....	....	....
Other sectors	8 904 ..	....	....	....	....	....	....	....	....
Other investment	8 703 ..	....	812.1	498.5	269.0	322.6	442.9	515.9	586.6
Trade credits	8 706 ..	....	....	....	....	....	....	....	....
General government	8 707 ..	....	....	....	....	....	....	....	....
of which: Short-term	8 709 ..	....	....	....	....	....	....	....	....
Other sectors	8 710 ..	....	....	....	....	....	....	....	....
of which: Short-term	8 712 ..	....	....	....	....	....	....	....	....
Loans	8 714 ..	....	....	....	....	....	....	....	....
Monetary authorities	8 715 ..	....	....	....	....	....	....	....	....
of which: Short-term	8 718 ..	....	....	....	....	....	....	....	....
General government	8 719 ..	....	....	....	....	....	....	....	....
of which: Short-term	8 721 ..	....	....	....	....	....	....	....	....
Banks	8 722 ..	....	....	....	....	....	....	....	....
of which: Short-term	8 724 ..	....	....	....	....	....	....	....	....
Other sectors	8 725 ..	....	....	....	....	....	....	....	....
of which: Short-term	8 727 ..	....	....	....	....	....	....	....	....
Currency and deposits	8 730 ..	....	811.9	498.0	267.8	321.7	442.6	515.8	586.4
Monetary authorities	8 731 ..	....	2.3	5.6	2.1	2.3	2.1	2.3	....
General government	8 732 ..	....	....	....	....	....	....	....	....
Banks	8 733 ..	....	87.6	84.4	99.7	108.4	129.5	120.5	128.4
Other sectors	8 734 ..	....	722.0	408.0	166.0	211.0	311.0	393.0	458.0
Other assets	8 736 ..	....	.2	.5	1.2	.9	.3	.1	.2
Monetary authorities	8 737 ..	....	....	....	....	....	....	....	....
of which: Short-term	8 739 ..	....	....	....	....	....	....	....	....
General government	8 740 ..	....	....	....	....	....	....	....	....
of which: Short-term	8 742 ..	....	....	....	....	....	....	....	....
Banks	8 743 ..	....	.2	.5	1.2	.9	.3	.1	.2
of which: Short-term	8 745 ..	....	....	....	....	....	....	....	....
Other sectors	8 746 ..	....	....	....	....	....	....	....	....
of which: Short-term	8 748 ..	....	....	....	....	....	....	....	....
Reserve assets	8 802 ..	....	384.0	453.2	508.3	668.2	673.8	859.6	1,032.1
Monetary gold	8 812 ..	....	4.1	5.1	6.2	....	....	....	....
Special drawing rights	8 811 ..	.1	.3	....	.1	.5	.3	.4	.1
Reserve position in the Fund	8 810 ..	....	....	....	....	....	....	....	....
Foreign exchange	8 803 ..	....	379.6	448.1	502.0	667.7	673.5	859.2	1,032.0
Other claims	8 813 ..	....	....	....	....	....	....	....	....

Table 3 (Concluded). INTERNATIONAL INVESTMENT POSITION (End-period stocks), 2000–2007

(Millions of U.S. dollars)

	Code	2000	2001	2002	2003	2004	2005	2006	2007
LIABILITIES	8 995 D.	....	7,122.9	7,386.5	7,731.6	6,524.1	6,693.9	6,141.2	5,311.6
Direct investment in Nicaragua	8 555 ..	....	....	....	....	....	....	....	....
Equity capital and reinvested earnings	8 556 ..	....	....	....	....	....	....	....	....
Claims on direct investors	8 557 ..	....	....	....	....	....	....	....	....
Liabilities to direct investors	8 558 ..	....	....	....	....	....	....	....	....
Other capital	8 580 ..	....	....	....	....	....	....	....	....
Claims on direct investors	8 585 ..	....	....	....	....	....	....	....	....
Liabilities to direct investors	8 590 ..	....	....	....	....	....	....	....	....
Portfolio investment	8 652 ..	....	....	....	....	....	....	....	....
Equity securities	8 660 ..	....	....	....	....	....	....	....	....
Banks	8 663 ..	....	....	....	....	....	....	....	....
Other sectors	8 664 ..	....	....	....	....	....	....	....	....
Debt securities	8 669 ..	....	....	....	....	....	....	....	....
Bonds and notes	8 670 ..	....	....	....	....	....	....	....	....
Monetary authorities	8 671 ..	....	....	....	....	....	....	....	....
General government	8 672 ..	....	....	....	....	....	....	....	....
Banks	8 673 ..	....	....	....	....	....	....	....	....
Other sectors	8 674 ..	....	....	....	....	....	....	....	....
Money market instruments	8 680 ..	....	....	....	....	....	....	....	....
Monetary authorities	8 681 ..	....	....	....	....	....	....	....	....
General government	8 682 ..	....	....	....	....	....	....	....	....
Banks	8 683 ..	....	....	....	....	....	....	....	....
Other sectors	8 684 ..	....	....	....	....	....	....	....	....
Financial derivatives	8 905 ..	....	....	....	....	....	....	....	....
Monetary authorities	8 906 ..	....	....	....	....	....	....	....	....
General government	8 907 ..	....	....	....	....	....	....	....	....
Banks	8 908 ..	....	....	....	....	....	....	....	....
Other sectors	8 909 ..	....	....	....	....	....	....	....	....
Other investment	8 753 ..	....	7,122.9	7,386.5	7,731.6	6,524.1	6,693.9	6,141.2	5,311.6
Trade credits	8 756 ..	....	646.9	917.1	1,034.9	1,028.1	1,150.0	1,252.0	1,528.3
General government	8 757 ..	....	....	....	....	....	....	....	....
of which: Short-term	8 759 ..	....	....	....	....	....	....	....	....
Other sectors	8 760 ..	....	646.9	917.1	1,034.9	1,028.1	1,150.0	1,252.0	1,528.3
of which: Short-term	8 762 ..	....	*646.9*	*917.1*	*1,034.9*	*1,028.1*	*1,150.0*	*1,252.0*	*1,528.3*
Loans	8 764 ..	....	6,464.7	6,460.3	6,689.9	5,488.0	5,535.3	4,868.9	3,768.6
Monetary authorities	8 765 ..	....	1,900.7	1,931.8	1,987.5	1,927.8	1,921.0	1,835.6	1,886.9
of which: Use of Fund credit and loans from the Fund	8 766 ..	*168.5*	*157.5*	*174.4*	*213.2*	*247.7*	*200.8*	*62.9*	*84.8*
of which: Short-term	8 768 ..	....	*500.2*	*494.0*	*551.5*	*551.0*	*570.6*	*597.4*	*624.8*
General government	8 769 ..	....	4,378.9	4,386.7	4,590.3	3,447.0	3,399.7	2,637.3	1,422.5
of which: Short-term	8 771 ..	....	*.8*	*.8*	*1.2*	*1.0*	*1.0*	*1.1*	*1.3*
Banks	8 772 ..	....	90.1	97.1	94.1	96.6	187.8	342.2	383.8
of which: Short-term	8 774 ..	....	*47.6*	*20.9*	*22.5*	*16.0*	*27.8*	*82.0*	*51.0*
Other sectors	8 775 ..	....	95.0	44.7	18.0	16.6	26.8	53.8	75.4
of which: Short-term	8 777 ..	....	*35.1*	*4.5*	*8.5*	*4.8*	*2.2*	*1.9*	*4.2*
Currency and deposits	8 780 ..	....	.9	1.0	.1	.2	.3	12.5	5.9
Monetary authorities	8 781 ..	....	.1	....	....	.1	....	....	....
General government	8 782 ..	....	....	....	....	....	....	....	....
Banks	8 783 ..	....	.8	1.0	.1	.1	.3	12.5	5.9
Other sectors	8 784 ..	....	....	....	....	....	....	....	....
Other liabilities	8 786 ..	....	10.4	8.1	6.7	7.8	8.3	7.8	8.8
Monetary authorities	8 787 ..	....	....	....	....	....	....	....	....
of which: Short-term	8 789 ..	....	....	....	....	....	....	....	....
General government	8 790 ..	....	....	....	....	....	....	....	....
of which: Short-term	8 792 ..	....	....	....	....	....	....	....	....
Banks	8 793 ..	....	10.4	8.1	6.7	7.8	8.3	7.8	8.8
of which: Short-term	8 795 ..	....	*3.3*	*3.9*	*5.4*	*7.7*	*8.3*	*7.8*	*8.8*
Other sectors	8 796 ..	....	....	....	....	....	....	....	....
of which: Short-term	8 798 ..	....	....	....	....	....	....	....	....
NET INTERNATIONAL INVESTMENT POSITION	8 995 ..	....	−5,926.8	−6,434.8	−6,954.4	−5,533.3	−5,577.2	−4,765.7	−3,692.9
Conversion rates: córdobas per U.S. dollar (end of period)	0 102 ..	13.057	13.841	14.671	15.552	16.329	17.146	18.003	18.903

Table 1. ANALYTIC PRESENTATION, 2000–2007

(Millions of U.S. dollars)

	Code	2000	2001	2002	2003	2004	2005	2006	2007
A. Current Account[1]	4 993 Z.	−104.1	−92.3	−164.8	−218.7	−230.9	−311.5	−313.8	....
Goods: exports f.o.b.	2 100 ..	283.1	272.5	279.4	351.8	436.7	477.6	508.0	....
Goods: imports f.o.b.	3 100 ..	−323.7	−331.3	−371.2	−488.5	−589.7	−769.5	−748.3	....
Balance on Goods	4 100 ..	*−40.6*	*−58.8*	*−91.7*	*−136.7*	*−153.0*	*−291.9*	*−240.3*	*....*
Services: credit	2 200 ..	37.5	56.7	50.6	63.3	93.4	87.5	90.6	....
Services: debit	3 200 ..	−131.9	−147.2	−152.3	−192.5	−262.2	−279.3	−328.6	....
Balance on Goods and Services	4 991 ..	*−134.9*	*−149.2*	*−193.4*	*−265.9*	*−321.8*	*−483.7*	*−478.4*	*....*
Income: credit	2 300 ..	13.1	12.3	13.2	17.3	26.5	37.1	42.0	....
Income: debit	3 300 ..	−29.5	−27.2	−37.4	−43.4	−39.4	−46.6	−40.8	....
Balance on Goods, Services, and Income	4 992 ..	*−151.4*	*−164.1*	*−217.6*	*−292.0*	*−334.7*	*−493.2*	*−477.2*	*....*
Current transfers: credit	2 379 Z.	63.8	87.9	65.1	82.9	128.6	217.1	199.5	....
Current transfers: debit	3 379 ..	−16.5	−16.0	−12.3	−9.5	−24.7	−35.4	−36.1	....
B. Capital Account[1]	4 994 Z.	**55.4**	**40.2**	**91.8**	**92.3**	**249.2**	**49.4**	**219.8**	....
Capital account: credit	2 994 Z.	55.4	40.2	91.9	92.4	384.5	188.3	219.8	....
Capital account: debit	3 994 ..	....	....	−.1	−.1	−135.3	−138.9	....	....
Total, Groups A Plus B	4 981 ..	*−48.8*	*−52.0*	*−73.0*	*−126.4*	*18.4*	*−262.1*	*−94.0*	*....*
C. Financial Account[1]	4 995 W.	**97.5**	**60.5**	**69.1**	**97.1**	**−173.0**	**174.0**	**34.6**	....
Direct investment abroad	4 505 ..	.6	3.6	1.7	....	−13.1	−9.3	1.0	....
Direct investment in Niger	4 555 Z.	8.4	22.9	2.4	14.9	26.3	44.0	50.5	....
Portfolio investment assets	4 602 ..	−.2	−1.9	−.8	−4.4	−.2	−.8	.2	....
Equity securities	4 610 ..	....	−1.9	−.5	−4.3	−.3	−.7	.4	....
Debt securities	4 619 ..	−.2	....	−.3	−.2	.1	−.1	−.2	....
Portfolio investment liabilities	4 652 Z.	8.7	5.7	1.2	6.9	5.0	42.5	−4.1	....
Equity securities	4 660 ..	.5	.5	....	....	3.8	.6	....	....
Debt securities	4 669 Z.	8.3	5.2	1.2	6.9	1.1	41.9	−4.1	....
Financial derivatives	4 910 ..	....	....	....	....	1.1	....	....	....
Financial derivatives assets	4 900 ..	....	....	....	....	....	....	....	....
Financial derivatives liabilities	4 905 ..	....	....	....	....	1.1	....	....	....
Other investment assets	4 703 ..	−14.8	−27.1	15.6	−42.4	−72.8	−19.4	−30.1	....
Monetary authorities	4 701 ..	....	....	....	....	....	....	....	....
General government	4 704 ..	....	....	−.6	.7	....	....	....	....
Banks	4 705 ..	−.1	−19.4	16.4	−5.0	−10.9	−6.4	6.2	....
Other sectors	4 728 ..	−14.7	−7.7	−.2	−38.1	−61.9	−13.0	−36.3	....
Other investment liabilities	4 753 W.	94.8	57.4	49.1	122.1	−119.3	117.0	17.0	....
Monetary authorities	4 753 WA	−.4	−.3	1.5	.4	1.3	1.5	−1.6	....
General government	4 753 ZB	87.8	42.5	48.3	93.7	−148.9	87.2	....	....
Banks	4 753 ZC	4.7	−3.0	−12.0	17.0	−8.5	16.6	7.0	....
Other sectors	4 753 ZD	2.7	18.1	11.2	11.0	36.8	11.7	11.6	....
Total, Groups A Through C	4 983 ..	*48.7*	*8.5*	*−3.9*	*−29.2*	*−154.6*	*−88.1*	*−59.5*	*....*
D. Net Errors and Omissions	4 998 ..	**−13.6**	**13.8**	**−8.6**	**−14.6**	**115.9**	**120.9**	**−23.2**	....
Total, Groups A Through D	4 984 ..	*35.1*	*22.2*	*−12.5*	*−43.8*	*−38.7*	*32.8*	*−82.6*	*....*
E. Reserves and Related Items	4 802 A.	**−35.1**	**−22.2**	**12.5**	**43.8**	**38.7**	**−32.8**	**82.6**	....
Reserve assets	4 802 ..	−44.3	−31.8	−5.4	29.2	40.6	−35.4	−82.2	....
Use of Fund credit and loans	4 766 ..	9.2	9.6	17.9	14.6	−1.9	2.6	−103.5	....
Exceptional financing	4 920 ..	....	....	....	....	....	....	268.4	....
Conversion rates: CFA francs per U.S. dollar	0 101 ..	711.98	733.04	696.99	581.20	528.28	527.47	522.89	479.27

[1] Excludes components that have been classified in the categories of Group E.

Table 2. STANDARD PRESENTATION, 2000–2007

(Millions of U.S. dollars)

	Code	2000	2001	2002	2003	2004	2005	2006	2007
CURRENT ACCOUNT...	4 993 ..	**−104.1**	**−92.3**	**−164.8**	**−218.7**	**−230.9**	**−311.5**	**−313.8**	....
A. GOODS..	4 100 ..	**−40.6**	**−58.8**	**−91.7**	**−136.7**	**−153.0**	**−291.9**	**−240.3**	....
Credit..	2 100 ..	**283.1**	**272.5**	**279.4**	**351.8**	**436.7**	**477.6**	**508.0**	....
General merchandise: exports f.o.b.............	2 110 ..	276.2	266.4	277.0	345.5	409.2	397.0	440.3	....
Goods for processing: exports f.o.b.............	2 150 ..	....	....	....	....	....	....	....	....
Repairs on goods...	2 160 ..	....	....	....	....	....	....	....	....
Goods procured in ports by carriers.............	2 170 ..	6.9	6.0	2.4	6.3	7.1	15.7	21.2	....
Nonmonetary gold..	2 180 ..	....	....	....	....	20.4	64.9	46.4	....
Debit...	3 100 ..	**−323.7**	**−331.3**	**−371.2**	**−488.5**	**−589.7**	**−769.5**	**−748.3**	....
General merchandise: imports f.o.b.............	3 110 ..	−314.8	−320.1	−359.6	−470.9	−573.5	−748.7	−740.4	....
Goods for processing: imports f.o.b.............	3 150 ..	....	....	....	....	....	....	....	....
Repairs on goods...	3 160 ..	−.9	−1.4	−.7	−1.1	−.8	−.9	−.8	....
Goods procured in ports by carriers.............	3 170 ..	−7.7	−9.6	−10.8	−16.3	−15.4	−19.8	−7.1	....
Nonmonetary gold..	3 180 ..	−.2	−.1	−.1	−.1	....	....	....	....
B. SERVICES..	4 200 ..	**−94.4**	**−90.5**	**−101.7**	**−129.2**	**−168.8**	**−191.8**	**−238.1**	....
Total credit...	2 200 ..	*37.5*	*56.7*	*50.6*	*63.3*	*93.4*	*87.5*	*90.6*	....
Total debit..	3 200 ..	*−131.9*	*−147.2*	*−152.3*	*−192.5*	*−262.2*	*−279.3*	*−328.6*	....
Transportation services, credit..................	2 205 ..	**8.3**	**2.6**	**2.4**	**5.0**	**7.5**	**8.5**	**8.8**	....
Passenger...	2 850 ..	*.1*	*.1*	*.2*	*.5*	*1.3*	*.9*	*3.1*	....
Freight...	2 851 ..	*6.5*	*2.2*	*1.9*	*3.8*	*4.4*	*5.8*	*4.2*	....
Other...	2 852 ..	*1.6*	*.2*	*.3*	*.8*	*1.8*	*1.8*	*1.5*	....
Sea transport, passenger.............................	2 207 ..	....	....	....	....	....	....	....	....
Sea transport, freight....................................	2 208 ..	....	....	....	....	....	....	....	....
Sea transport, other......................................	2 209 ..	1.3	.1	....	.1	....	.6	.1	....
Air transport, passenger...............................	2 211 ..	....	....	....	....	....	....	....	....
Air transport, freight.....................................	2 212 ..	....	....	....	....	....	....	....	....
Air transport, other.......................................	2 213 ..	.3	.2	.3	.7	1.8	1.3	1.4	....
Other transport, passenger..........................	2 215 ..	.1	.1	.2	.5	1.3	.9	3.1	....
Other transport, freight.................................	2 216 ..	6.5	2.2	1.9	3.8	4.3	5.8	4.2	....
Other transport, other...................................	2 217 ..	....	....	....	....	....	....	....	....
Transportation services, debit....................	3 205 ..	**−84.1**	**−90.4**	**−103.0**	**−134.7**	**−163.5**	**−213.4**	**−226.7**	....
Passenger...	3 850 ..	*−6.0*	*−7.3*	*−11.9*	*−16.6*	*−19.8*	*−11.7*	*−13.5*	....
Freight...	3 851 ..	*−78.2*	*−83.0*	*−91.1*	*−117.3*	*−142.9*	*−200.5*	*−212.2*	....
Other...	3 852 ..	....	....	....	*−.7*	*−.8*	*−1.1*	*−1.0*	....
Sea transport, passenger.............................	3 207 ..	....	....	....	....	....	....	....	....
Sea transport, freight....................................	3 208 ..	−70.3	−73.1	−82.0	−105.6	−130.2	−27.9	−168.8	....
Sea transport, other......................................	3 209 ..	....	....	....	....	....	....	....	....
Air transport, passenger...............................	3 211 ..	−6.0	−7.3	−11.9	−16.6	−19.8	−11.7	−13.5	....
Air transport, freight.....................................	3 212 ..	−2.3	−2.4	−2.7	−3.5	−4.3	−120.7	−5.6	....
Air transport, other.......................................	3 213 ..	....	....	....	−.7	−.8	−1.1	−1.0	....
Other transport, passenger..........................	3 215 ..	....	....	....	....	....	....	....	....
Other transport, freight.................................	3 216 ..	−5.5	−7.6	−6.4	−8.2	−8.3	−51.9	−37.7	....
Other transport, other...................................	3 217 ..	....	....	....	....	....	....	....	....
Travel, credit...	2 236 ..	**22.6**	**29.6**	**20.2**	**27.5**	**31.2**	**43.2**	**36.1**	....
Business travel..	2 237 ..	22.3	23.6	15.1	19.1	21.3	30.8	23.4	....
Personal travel..	2 240 ..	.3	6.0	5.1	8.4	10.0	12.4	12.7	....
Travel, debit..	3 236 ..	**−26.4**	**−25.8**	**−17.1**	**−22.2**	**−22.4**	**−30.4**	**−27.6**	....
Business travel..	3 237 ..	−21.5	−21.6	−13.0	−15.2	−14.3	−20.6	−18.7	....
Personal travel..	3 240 ..	−5.0	−4.1	−4.1	−7.0	−8.1	−9.8	−8.9	....
Other services, credit.................................	2 200 BA	**6.7**	**24.5**	**28.0**	**30.8**	**54.7**	**35.8**	**45.6**	....
Communications...	2 245 ..	.2	11.3	22.8	16.2	29.2	22.5	29.6	....
Construction...	2 249 ..	....	.1	....	....	11.4	1.6	.8	....
Insurance..	2 253 ..	1.0	.2	.9	.6	1.0	.6	.8	....
Financial...	2 260 ..	.4	.4	.6	.2	.2	.3	2.9	....
Computer and information............................	2 262 ..	....	.1	.1	.2	.1	....	.1	....
Royalties and licence fees............................	2 266 ..	....	....	....	....	....	....	....	....
Other business services................................	2 268 ..	2.6	4.1	1.3	7.0	7.0	7.5	4.6	....
Personal, cultural, and recreational.............	2 287 ..	....	....	....	....	....	....	....	....
Government, n.i.e..	2 291 ..	2.4	8.2	2.3	6.7	5.7	3.2	6.8	....
Other services, debit..................................	3 200 BA	**−21.3**	**−31.0**	**−32.2**	**−35.7**	**−76.3**	**−35.6**	**−74.3**	....
Communications...	3 245 ..	−1.8	−9.1	−6.6	−4.5	−7.9	−12.9	−24.0	....
Construction...	3 249 ..	....	−.3	−.1	....	−27.8	−.6	−.8	....
Insurance..	3 253 ..	−3.0	−2.5	−2.6	−3.2	−5.9	−4.6	−7.0	....
Financial...	3 260 ..	−.5	−.4	−.5	−.4	−1.5	−1.4	−3.2	....
Computer and information............................	3 262 ..	−3.7	−3.9	−4.3	−5.6	−6.9	−7.4	−9.2	....
Royalties and licence fees............................	3 266 ..	−.2	....	−.8	−.2	−.5	−1.1	−.5	....
Other business services................................	3 268 ..	−5.0	−3.4	−4.7	−4.2	−14.0	−5.0	−21.4	....
Personal, cultural, and recreational.............	3 287 ..	....	....	....	−.4	....	....	−6.3	....
Government, n.i.e..	3 291 ..	−7.0	−11.6	−12.6	−17.1	−11.8	−2.6	−2.0	....

Table 2 (Continued). STANDARD PRESENTATION, 2000–2007

(Millions of U.S. dollars)

	Code	2000	2001	2002	2003	2004	2005	2006	2007
C. INCOME	4 300	**−16.5**	**−14.9**	**−24.2**	**−26.1**	**−12.9**	**−9.5**	**1.2**	....
Total credit	2 300	*13.1*	*12.3*	*13.2*	*17.3*	*26.5*	*37.1*	*42.0*	....
Total debit	3 300	*−29.5*	*−27.2*	*−37.4*	*−43.4*	*−39.4*	*−46.6*	*−40.8*	....
Compensation of employees, credit	2 310	**9.9**	**8.2**	**10.2**	**14.0**	**16.8**	**20.9**	**29.0**	....
Compensation of employees, debit	3 310	**−1.3**	**−1.6**	**−1.5**	**−1.9**	**−3.2**	**−2.4**	**−2.0**	....
Investment income, credit	2 320	**3.2**	**4.1**	**3.0**	**3.3**	**9.6**	**16.2**	**12.9**	....
Direct investment income	2 330	−.6	....	.1	.1	6.1	13.7	−.3	....
Dividends and distributed branch profits	2 332	....	....	....	....	.1	....	....	....
Reinvested earnings and undistributed branch profits	2 333	−.6	....	....	....	6.0	13.7	−.3	....
Income on debt (interest)	2 334	....	....	.1	.1	....	....	....	....
Portfolio investment income	2 339	.3	.7	.6	.9	1.2	.8	.7	....
Income on equity	2 340	....	....	....	.1	.1	.1	.2	....
Income on bonds and notes	2 350	.1	.4	.5	.8	.6	.7	.2	....
Income on money market instruments	2 360	.2	.3	....	.1	.5	....	.3	....
Other investment income	2 370	3.4	3.4	2.4	2.3	2.4	1.7	12.6	....
Investment income, debit	3 320	**−28.3**	**−25.6**	**−35.9**	**−41.5**	**−36.1**	**−44.1**	**−38.7**	....
Direct investment income	3 330	−1.9	3.0	−2.7	−9.3	−15.8	−20.9	−12.5	....
Dividends and distributed branch profits	3 332	−.4	−.1	−.3	−1.4	−2.1	−3.3	−5.1	....
Reinvested earnings and undistributed branch profits	3 333	−1.5	3.4	−2.4	−7.6	−13.0	−16.5	−5.2	....
Income on debt (interest)	3 334	....	−.3	....	−.3	−.7	−1.2	−2.3	....
Portfolio investment income	3 339	−1.0	−.9	−1.0	−2.5	−4.1	−5.6	−5.8	....
Income on equity	3 340	−.7	−.3	−.4	−2.0	−2.2	−1.9	−2.5	....
Income on bonds and notes	3 350	−.4	−.6	−.5	−.4	−1.9	−3.0	−3.2	....
Income on money market instruments	3 360	....	....	....	−.1	....	−.7	....	....
Other investment income	3 370	−25.3	−27.7	−32.2	−29.7	−16.2	−17.6	−20.5	....
D. CURRENT TRANSFERS	4 379	**47.3**	**71.9**	**52.8**	**73.3**	**103.9**	**181.7**	**163.4**	....
Credit	2 379	**63.8**	**87.9**	**65.1**	**82.9**	**128.6**	**217.1**	**199.5**	....
General government	2 380	48.5	64.2	47.3	58.2	74.6	113.7	91.9	....
Other sectors	2 390	15.3	23.7	17.8	24.7	54.0	103.4	107.5	....
Workers' remittances	2 391	4.6	13.8	8.7	11.5	42.9	45.5	49.1	....
Other current transfers	2 392	10.7	9.9	9.1	13.1	11.1	57.9	58.5	....
Debit	3 379	**−16.5**	**−16.0**	**−12.3**	**−9.5**	**−24.7**	**−35.4**	**−36.1**	....
General government	3 380	−5.0	−6.7	−6.9	−1.7	−1.4	−3.0	−8.1	....
Other sectors	3 390	−11.5	−9.3	−5.4	−7.9	−23.3	−32.4	−28.0	....
Workers' remittances	3 391	−10.6	−8.8	−4.8	−7.1	−21.6	−26.9	−27.2	....
Other current transfers	3 392	−.9	−.5	−.6	−.8	−1.7	−5.6	−.8	....
CAPITAL AND FINANCIAL ACCOUNT	4 996	**117.8**	**78.5**	**173.4**	**233.3**	**115.0**	**190.6**	**337.0**	....
CAPITAL ACCOUNT	4 994	**55.4**	**40.2**	**91.8**	**92.3**	**249.2**	**49.4**	**1,739.3**	....
Total credit	2 994	*55.4*	*40.2*	*91.9*	*92.4*	*384.5*	*188.3*	*1,739.3*	....
Total debit	3 994	....	....	*−.1*	*−.1*	*−135.3*	*−138.9*	....	....
Capital transfers, credit	2 400	**43.4**	**40.2**	**91.9**	**92.4**	**384.5**	**188.3**	**1,681.1**	....
General government	2 401	41.9	38.1	80.4	87.6	373.6	181.0	1,667.6	....
Debt forgiveness	2 402	....	....	14.8	19.8	285.6	34.5	1,519.8	....
Other capital transfers	2 410	41.9	38.1	65.7	67.8	88.0	146.5	147.8	....
Other sectors	2 430	1.5	2.1	11.4	4.8	10.9	7.3	13.5	....
Migrants' transfers	2 431	....	....	....	....	....	....	....	....
Debt forgiveness	2 432	....	....	....	....	....	....	....	....
Other capital transfers	2 440	1.5	2.1	11.4	4.8	10.9	7.3	13.5	....
Capital transfers, debit	3 400	....	....	....	....	....	....	....	....
General government	3 401	....	....	....	....	....	....	....	....
Debt forgiveness	3 402	....	....	....	....	....	....	....	....
Other capital transfers	3 410	....	....	....	....	....	....	....	....
Other sectors	3 430	....	....	....	....	....	....	....	....
Migrants' transfers	3 431	....	....	....	....	....	....	....	....
Debt forgiveness	3 432	....	....	....	....	....	....	....	....
Other capital transfers	3 440	....	....	....	....	....	....	....	....
Nonproduced nonfinancial assets, credit	2 480	**11.9**	....	....	....	....	....	**58.1**	....
Nonproduced nonfinancial assets, debit	3 480	....	....	**−.1**	**−.1**	**−135.3**	**−138.9**	....	....

Table 2 (Continued). STANDARD PRESENTATION, 2000–2007

(Millions of U.S. dollars)

	Code	2000	2001	2002	2003	2004	2005	2006	2007
FINANCIAL ACCOUNT............	4 995 ..	**62.4**	**38.3**	**81.6**	**141.0**	**−134.3**	**141.2**	**−1,402.3**	....
A. DIRECT INVESTMENT............	4 500 ..	**9.1**	**26.5**	**4.1**	**14.9**	**13.2**	**34.7**	**51.5**	....
Direct investment abroad............	4 505 ..	**.6**	**3.6**	**1.7**	....	**−13.1**	**−9.3**	**1.0**	....
Equity capital............	4 510 ..	−.7	−1.0	−.5	−3.8	−2.3	−.9	−1.1	....
Claims on affiliated enterprises............	4 515 ..	....	....	....	....	....	....		....
Liabilities to affiliated enterprises............	4 520 ..	....	....	....	....	....	....	−1.2	....
Reinvested earnings............	4 525 ..	.6	....	....	....	−6.0	−13.7	.3	....
Other capital............	4 530 ..	.7	4.6	2.2	3.8	−4.8	5.3	1.8	....
Claims on affiliated enterprises............	4 535 ..	−6.5	5.4	−1.4	1.7	−2.1	−.3	−.8	....
Liabilities to affiliated enterprises............	4 540 ..	7.3	−.8	3.6	2.1	−2.8	5.6	2.6	....
Direct investment in Niger............	4 555 ..	**8.4**	**22.9**	**2.4**	**14.9**	**26.3**	**44.0**	**50.5**	....
Equity capital............	4 560 ..	−.8	19.8	−.1	4.9	12.8	6.1	12.4	....
Claims on direct investors............	4 565 ..	....	....	....	....	....	....	12.4	....
Liabilities to direct investors............	4 570 ..	....	....	....	....	....	....		....
Reinvested earnings............	4 575 ..	1.5	−3.4	2.4	7.6	13.0	16.5	5.2	....
Other capital............	4 580 ..	7.7	6.5	.1	2.4	.6	21.3	33.0	....
Claims on direct investors............	4 585 ..	....	−.5	−1.8	−1.4	−.8	−.1	−.7	....
Liabilities to direct investors............	4 590 ..	7.7	7.0	1.9	3.9	1.4	21.4	33.7	....
B. PORTFOLIO INVESTMENT............	4 600 ..	**8.5**	**3.7**	**.4**	**2.5**	**4.8**	**41.7**	**−3.9**	....
Assets............	4 602 ..	**−.2**	**−1.9**	**−.8**	**−4.4**	**−.2**	**−.8**	**.2**	....
Equity securities............	4 610 ..	....	−1.9	−.5	−4.3	−.3	−.7	.4	....
Monetary authorities............	4 611 ..	....	....	....	....	....	....	....	....
General government............	4 612 ..	....	....	....	....	....	....	....	....
Banks............	4 613 ..	....	....	....	....	....	....	....	....
Other sectors............	4 614 ..	....	−1.9	−.5	−4.3	−.3	−.7	.4	....
Debt securities............	4 619 ..	−.2	....	−.3	−.2	.1	−.1	−.2	....
Bonds and notes............	4 620 ..	−.1	....	−.3	−.2	.1	−.1	−.2	....
Monetary authorities............	4 621 ..	....	....	....	....	....	....	....	....
General government............	4 622 ..	....	....	....	....	....	....	....	....
Banks............	4 623 ..	....	....	....	....	....	....	....	....
Other sectors............	4 624 ..	−.1	....	−.3	−.2	.1	−.1	−.2	....
Money market instruments............	4 630 ..	−.2	....	....	....	....	....	....	....
Monetary authorities............	4 631 ..	....	....	....	....	....	....	....	....
General government............	4 632 ..	....	....	....	....	....	....	....	....
Banks............	4 633 ..	....	....	....	....	....	....	....	....
Other sectors............	4 634 ..	−.2	....	....	....	....	....	....	....
Liabilities............	4 652 ..	**8.7**	**5.7**	**1.2**	**6.9**	**5.0**	**42.5**	**−4.1**	....
Equity securities............	4 660 ..	.5	.5	....	....	3.8	.6	....	....
Banks............	4 663 ..	....	....	....	....	....	....	....	....
Other sectors............	4 664 ..	.5	.5	....	....	3.8	.6	....	....
Debt securities............	4 669 ..	8.3	5.2	1.2	6.9	1.1	41.9	−4.1	....
Bonds and notes............	4 670 ..	8.3	5.2	1.2	6.9	....	18.2	−4.1	....
Monetary authorities............	4 671 ..	....	....	....	....	....	....	....	....
General government............	4 672 ..	....	....	....	....	....	−1.9	....	....
Banks............	4 673 ..	....	....	....	....	....	....	....	....
Other sectors............	4 674 ..	8.3	5.2	1.2	6.9	....	20.1	−4.1	....
Money market instruments............	4 680 ..	....	....	....	....	....	23.7	....	....
Monetary authorities............	4 681 ..	....	....	....	....	....	....	....	....
General government............	4 682 ..	....	....	....	....	....	23.7	....	....
Banks............	4 683 ..	....	....	....	....	....	....	....	....
Other sectors............	4 684 ..	....	....	....	....	....	....	....	....
C. FINANCIAL DERIVATIVES............	4 910 ..	....	....	....	....	**1.1**	....	....	....
Monetary authorities............	4 911 ..	....	....	....	....	....	....	....	....
General government............	4 912 ..	....	....	....	....	....	....	....	....
Banks............	4 913 ..	....	....	....	....	....	....	....	....
Other sectors............	4 914 ..	....	....	....	....	1.1	....	....	....
Assets............	4 900 ..	....	....	....	....	....	....	....	....
Monetary authorities............	4 901 ..	....	....	....	....	....	....	....	....
General government............	4 902 ..	....	....	....	....	....	....	....	....
Banks............	4 903 ..	....	....	....	....	....	....	....	....
Other sectors............	4 904 ..	....	....	....	....	....	....	....	....
Liabilities............	4 905 ..	....	....	....	....	**1.1**	....	....	....
Monetary authorities............	4 906 ..	....	....	....	....	....	....	....	....
General government............	4 907 ..	....	....	....	....	....	....	....	....
Banks............	4 908 ..	....	....	....	....	....	....	....	....
Other sectors............	4 909 ..	....	....	....	....	1.1	....	....	....

Table 2 (Concluded). STANDARD PRESENTATION, 2000–2007

(Millions of U.S. dollars)

	Code	2000	2001	2002	2003	2004	2005	2006	2007
D. OTHER INVESTMENT	4 700 ..	**89.1**	**39.8**	**82.5**	**94.4**	**−194.1**	**100.1**	**−1,367.7**	....
Assets	4 703 ..	**−14.8**	**−27.1**	**15.6**	**−42.4**	**−72.8**	**−19.4**	**−30.1**	....
Trade credits	4 706 ..	−11.2	1.5	1.9	−37.6	−29.2	−6.6	−9.2	....
General government	4 707 ..	....	....	....	....	....	....	....	....
of which: Short-term	4 709 ..	....	....	....	....	....	....	....	....
Other sectors	4 710 ..	−11.2	1.5	1.9	−37.6	−29.2	−6.6	−9.2	....
of which: Short-term	4 712 ..	....	....	....	....	....	....	....	....
Loans	4 714 ..	−7.1	−3.5	5.0	−5.0	−3.5	−10.7	6.7	....
Monetary authorities	4 715 ..	....	....	....	....	....	....	....	....
of which: Short-term	4 718 ..	....	....	....	....	....	....	....	....
General government	4 719 ..	....	....	....	....	....	....	....	....
of which: Short-term	4 721 ..	....	....	....	....	....	....	....	....
Banks	4 722 ..	−6.2	−3.5	5.7	−4.9	−1.0	−7.5	6.7	....
of which: Short-term	4 724 ..	−5.2	3.7	−1.1	−.9	−6.7	−6.0	6.4	....
Other sectors	4 725 ..	−.8	....	−.7	....	−2.5	−3.1	....	....
of which: Short-term	4 727 ..	....	....	....	....	....	....	....	....
Currency and deposits	4 730 ..	3.1	−19.2	9.5	−1.4	−26.3	−1.8	−2.6	....
Monetary authorities	4 731 ..	....	....	....	....	....	....	....	....
General government	4 732 ..	....	....	....	....	....	....	....	....
Banks	4 733 ..	5.8	−16.1	10.8	−.6	−10.1	1.3	.3	....
Other sectors	4 734 ..	−2.7	−3.1	−1.3	−.8	−16.2	−3.1	−2.9	....
Other assets	4 736 ..	.5	−5.9	−.9	1.6	−13.9	−.3	−25.1	....
Monetary authorities	4 737 ..	....	....	....	....	....	....	....	....
of which: Short-term	4 739 ..	....	....	....	....	....	....	....	....
General government	4 740 ..	....	....	−.6	.7	....	....	....	....
of which: Short-term	4 742 ..	....	....	....	....	....	....	....	....
Banks	4 743 ..	.4	.2	−.1	.5	.2	−.2	−.9	....
of which: Short-term	4 745 ..	.4	.2	−.1	.5	.5	−.2	.1	....
Other sectors	4 746 ..	....	−6.0	−.1	.4	−14.1	−.1	−24.2	....
of which: Short-term	4 748 ..	....	....	....	....	....	....	....	....
Liabilities	4 753 ..	**103.9**	**66.9**	**66.9**	**136.7**	**−121.2**	**119.5**	**−1,337.6**	....
Trade credits	4 756 ..	.3	11.6	10.3	13.5	15.0	2.4	3.8	....
General government	4 757 ..	....	....	....	....	....	....	....	....
of which: Short-term	4 759 ..	....	....	....	....	....	....	....	....
Other sectors	4 760 ..	.3	11.6	10.3	13.5	15.0	2.4	3.8	....
of which: Short-term	4 762 ..	....	....	....	....	....	....	....	....
Loans	4 764 ..	104.0	41.5	70.5	114.5	−144.3	103.8	−1,354.6	....
Monetary authorities	4 765 ..	9.2	9.6	17.9	14.6	−1.9	2.6	−103.5	....
of which: Use of Fund credit and loans from the Fund..	4 766 ..	9.2	9.6	17.9	14.6	−1.9	2.6	−103.5	....
of which: Short-term	4 768 ..	....	....	....	....	....	....	....	....
General government	4 769 ..	87.8	42.5	48.3	93.7	−148.9	87.2	−1,268.1	....
of which: Short-term	4 771 ..	41.4	−7.1	....	....	....	....	....	....
Banks	4 772 ..	6.2	−10.7	3.4	3.1	−2.3	6.2	12.5	....
of which: Short-term	4 774 ..	6.2	−10.7	3.4	2.6	−6.7	3.4	....	....
Other sectors	4 775 ..	.8	.2	.8	3.1	8.9	7.8	4.5	....
of which: Short-term	4 777 ..	3.6	....	....	....	....	9.4	5.0	....
Currency and deposits	4 780 ..	−.7	7.6	−13.8	11.6	−4.8	10.6	7.0	....
Monetary authorities	4 781 ..	.8	−.2	1.6	−2.4	1.3	.2	....	....
General government	4 782 ..	....	....	....	....	....	....	....	....
Banks	4 783 ..	−1.6	7.8	−15.4	14.0	−6.2	10.4	7.0	....
Other sectors	4 784 ..	....	....	....	....	....	....	....	....
Other liabilities	4 786 ..	.3	6.3	....	−2.8	12.8	2.7	6.2	....
Monetary authorities	4 787 ..	−1.3	....	−.1	2.7	....	1.3	−1.6	....
of which: Short-term	4 789 ..	....	....	....	....	....	....	....	....
General government	4 790 ..	....	....	....	....	....	....	....	....
of which: Short-term	4 792 ..	....	....	....	....	....	....	....	....
Banks	4 793 ..	....	....	....	....	....	....	....	....
of which: Short-term	4 795 ..	....	....	....	....	....	....	....	....
Other sectors	4 796 ..	1.6	6.3	.1	−5.5	12.8	1.4	7.8	....
of which: Short-term	4 798 ..	....	....	....	....	....	....	....	....
E. RESERVE ASSETS	4 802 ..	**−44.3**	**−31.8**	**−5.4**	**29.2**	**40.6**	**−35.4**	**−82.2**	**....**
Monetary gold	4 812 ..	....	....	....	....	....	....	....	....
Special drawing rights	4 811 ..	1.3	−.3	−.3	−1.8	1.8	.6	.2	....
Reserve position in the Fund	4 810 ..	....	....	....	....	....	−.1	....	....
Foreign exchange	4 803 ..	−45.6	−31.5	−5.1	31.0	38.8	−35.9	−87.6	....
Other claims	4 813 ..	....	....	....	....	....	....	5.3	....
NET ERRORS AND OMISSIONS	4 998 ..	**−13.6**	**13.8**	**−8.6**	**−14.6**	**115.9**	**120.9**	**−23.2**	**....**

Table 3. INTERNATIONAL INVESTMENT POSITION (End-period stocks), 2000–2007

(Millions of U.S. dollars)

	Code	2000	2001	2002	2003	2004	2005	2006	2007
ASSETS	8 995 C.	**141.4**	**184.8**	**192.7**	**343.0**	**411.9**	**362.8**	**536.0**	....
Direct investment abroad	8 505 ..	**1.0**	**–1.7**	**–3.9**	**–4.6**	**8.2**	**1.9**	**6.0**	....
Equity capital and reinvested earnings	8 506 ..	3.2	3.7	4.6	9.6	9.5	7.6	9.2	....
Claims on affiliated enterprises	8 507 ..	....	....	....	....	....	....	....	....
Liabilities to affiliated enterprises	8 508 ..	....	....	....	....	....	....	....	....
Other capital	8 530 ..	–2.2	–5.4	–8.5	–14.3	–1.3	–5.7	–3.2	....
Claims on affiliated enterprises	8 535 ..	....	....	....	....	....	....	....	....
Liabilities to affiliated enterprises	8 540 ..	....	....	....	....	....	....	....	....
Portfolio investment	8 602 ..	**6.8**	**8.4**	**10.2**	**5.6**	**3.0**	**15.3**	**31.2**	....
Equity securities	8 610 ..	.5	2.4	1.1	....	2.2	2.4	11.9	....
Monetary authorities	8 611 ..	....	....	....	....	....	....	....	....
General government	8 612 ..	....	....	....	....	....	....	....	....
Banks	8 613 ..	.5	.4	.5	....	1.8	1.6	11.9	....
Other sectors	8 614 ..	....	1.9	.6	....	.4	.7	....	....
Debt securities	8 619 ..	6.3	6.0	9.0	5.6	.8	12.9	19.3	....
Bonds and notes	8 620 ..	2.4	2.5	9.0	....	....	12.8	9.4	....
Monetary authorities	8 621 ..	....	....	....	....	....	....	....	....
General government	8 622 ..	....	....	....	....	....	....	....	....
Banks	8 623 ..	2.0	2.2	8.3	....	....	10.0	8.7	....
Other sectors	8 624 ..	.4	.4	.7	....	....	2.8	.7	....
Money market instruments	8 630 ..	3.9	3.5	....	5.6	.8	.1	10.0	....
Monetary authorities	8 631 ..	....	....	....	....	....	....	10.0	....
General government	8 632 ..	....	....	....	....	....	....	....	....
Banks	8 633 ..	3.5	3.5	....	5.6	.8	....	....	....
Other sectors	8 634 ..	.4	....	....	....	....	.1	....	....
Financial derivatives	8 900 ..	....	....	....	....	....	**1.1**	....	....
Monetary authorities	8 901 ..	....	....	....	....	....	....	....	....
General government	8 902 ..	....	....	....	....	....	....	....	....
Banks	8 903 ..	....	....	....	....	....	1.1	....	....
Other sectors	8 904 ..	....	....	....	....	....	....	....	....
Other investment	8 703 ..	**52.2**	**69.5**	**52.4**	**68.7**	**150.8**	**93.8**	**127.8**	....
Trade credits	8 706 ..	16.5	11.7	6.7	10.5	40.3	19.9	30.5	....
General government	8 707 ..	....	....	....	....	....	....	....	....
of which: Short-term	8 709 ..	....	....	....	....	....	....	....	....
Other sectors	8 710 ..	16.5	11.7	6.7	10.5	40.3	19.9	30.5	....
of which: Short-term	8 712 ..	....	....	....	....	....	....	....	....
Loans	8 714 ..	9.5	12.2	8.9	14.4	19.3	24.5	17.0	....
Monetary authorities	8 715 ..	....	....	....	....	....	....	....	....
of which: Short-term	8 718 ..	....	....	....	....	....	....	....	....
General government	8 719 ..	....	....	....	....	....	....	....	....
of which: Short-term	8 721 ..	....	....	....	....	....	....	....	....
Banks	8 722 ..	8.5	11.5	7.3	14.3	16.6	21.5	16.9	....
of which: Short-term	8 724 ..	*6.5*	*2.5*	*4.2*	*6.1*	*13.9*	*17.7*	*13.0*	....
Other sectors	8 725 ..	1.0	.7	1.6	....	2.7	3.0	....	....
of which: Short-term	8 727 ..	....	....	....	....	....	....	....	....
Currency and deposits	8 730 ..	24.5	38.7	33.9	42.3	74.4	48.2	53.2	....
Monetary authorities	8 731 ..	....	....	....	....	....	....	....	....
General government	8 732 ..	....	....	....	....	....	....	....	....
Banks	8 733 ..	22.9	37.6	32.7	40.0	54.2	45.6	50.6	....
Other sectors	8 734 ..	1.6	1.2	1.2	2.3	20.2	2.6	2.6	....
Other assets	8 736 ..	1.7	6.8	2.9	1.6	16.9	1.1	27.1	....
Monetary authorities	8 737 ..	....	....	....	....	....	....	....	....
of which: Short-term	8 739 ..	....	....	....	....	....	....	....	....
General government	8 740 ..	....	....	.7	....	....	....	....	....
of which: Short-term	8 742 ..	....	....	....	....	....	....	....	....
Banks	8 743 ..	.8	.6	.8	.5	.3	.5	1.5	....
of which: Short-term	8 745 ..	*.8*	*.6*	*.8*	*.5*	....	*.2*	*.2*	....
Other sectors	8 746 ..	.9	6.3	1.4	1.1	16.6	.6	25.7	....
of which: Short-term	8 748 ..	....	....	....	....	....	....	....	....
Reserve assets	8 802 ..	**81.4**	**108.6**	**134.1**	**273.4**	**249.8**	**250.7**	**370.9**	....
Monetary gold	8 812 ..	....	....	....	....	....	....	....	....
Special drawing rights	8 811 ..	....	.3	.7	2.7	.9	.3	.1	.1
Reserve position in the Fund	8 810 ..	11.2	10.8	11.6	12.7	13.3	12.3	13.0	13.6
Foreign exchange	8 803 ..	70.3	97.5	121.7	258.0	235.6	238.1	357.8	....
Other claims	8 813 ..	....	....	....	....	....	....	....	....

Table 3 (Concluded). INTERNATIONAL INVESTMENT POSITION (End-period stocks), 2000–2007

(Millions of U.S. dollars)

	Code	2000	2001	2002	2003	2004	2005	2006	2007
LIABILITIES	8 995 D.	**1,757.0**	**1,585.1**	**2,025.0**	**2,080.3**	**2,227.4**	**2,073.4**	**896.2**	....
Direct investment in Niger	8 555 ..	**45.4**	**61.5**	**70.0**	**78.8**	**115.5**	**100.0**	**161.1**	....
Equity capital and reinvested earnings	8 556 ..	37.2	54.3	60.9	74.6	110.7	76.3	103.8	....
Claims on direct investors	8 557 ..	....	....	....	....	....	....	....	....
Liabilities to direct investors	8 558 ..	....	....	....	....	....	....	....	....
Other capital	8 580 ..	8.2	7.1	9.1	4.3	4.8	23.7	57.3	....
Claims on direct investors	8 585 ..	....	....	....	....	....	....	....	....
Liabilities to direct investors	8 590 ..	....	....	....	....	....	....	....	....
Portfolio investment	8 652 ..	**12.2**	**8.9**	**6.2**	**14.4**	**5.3**	**24.9**	**18.7**	....
Equity securities	8 660 ..	3.9	3.8	4.8	5.2	5.3	5.1	5.1	....
Banks	8 663 ..	.3	.4	.8	.9	.6	.5	.3	....
Other sectors	8 664 ..	3.6	3.5	4.1	4.3	4.6	4.6	4.8	....
Debt securities	8 669 ..	8.3	5.1	1.4	9.2	....	19.8	13.6	....
Bonds and notes	8 670 ..	8.3	5.1	1.4	9.2	....	19.1	8.3	....
Monetary authorities	8 671 ..	....	....	....	....	....	....	....	....
General government	8 672 ..	....	....	....	....	....	....	....	....
Banks	8 673 ..	....	....	....	....	....	....	....	....
Other sectors	8 674 ..	8.3	5.1	1.4	9.2	....	19.1	8.3	....
Money market instruments	8 680 ..	....	....	....	....	....	.7	5.3	....
Monetary authorities	8 681 ..	....	....	....	....	....	....	....	....
General government	8 682 ..	....	....	....	....	....	....	....	....
Banks	8 683 ..	....	....	....	....	....	.7	5.3	....
Other sectors	8 684 ..	....	....	....	....	....	....	....	....
Financial derivatives	8 905 ..	....	....	....	....	....	....	....	....
Monetary authorities	8 906 ..	....	....	....	....	....	....	....	....
General government	8 907 ..	....	....	....	....	....	....	....	....
Banks	8 908 ..	....	....	....	....	....	....	....	....
Other sectors	8 909 ..	....	....	....	....	....	....	....	....
Other investment	8 753 ..	**1,699.4**	**1,514.7**	**1,948.8**	**1,987.1**	**2,106.6**	**1,948.6**	**716.4**	....
Trade credits	8 756 ..	36.4	46.1	46.2	49.8	52.5	35.0	38.5	....
General government	8 757 ..	....	....	....	....	....	....	....	....
of which: Short-term	8 759 ..	....	....	....	....	....	....	....	....
Other sectors	8 760 ..	36.4	46.1	46.2	49.8	52.5	35.0	38.5	....
of which: Short-term	8 762 ..	....	....	....	....	....	....	....	....
Loans	8 764 ..	1,637.1	1,435.9	1,875.4	1,895.3	2,002.3	1,867.3	613.4	....
Monetary authorities	8 765 ..	74.0	80.7	106.4	131.4	135.4	127.6	26.5	....
of which: Use of Fund credit and loans from the Fund	8 766 ..	*74.0*	*80.7*	*106.4*	*131.4*	*135.4*	*127.6*	*26.5*	*40.1*
of which: Short-term	8 768 ..	....	....	....	....	....	....	....	....
General government	8 769 ..	1,549.9	1,353.2	1,762.9	1,753.1	1,843.9	1,704.3	536.7	....
of which: Short-term	8 771 ..	*161.1*	....	....	*7.2*	....	....	....	....
Banks	8 772 ..	13.2	2.0	6.1	10.8	9.2	13.8	28.6	....
of which: Short-term	8 774 ..	*13.2*	*2.0*	*6.1*	*10.3*	*3.8*	*6.5*	*9.8*	....
Other sectors	8 775 ..	....	....	....	....	13.7	21.5	21.6	....
of which: Short-term	8 777 ..	....	....	....	....	....	....	....	....
Currency and deposits	8 780 ..	23.7	30.2	20.8	37.4	35.1	40.6	52.3	....
Monetary authorities	8 781 ..	1.5	1.2	3.2	1.2	2.7	2.2	2.4	....
General government	8 782 ..	....	....	....	....	....	....	....	....
Banks	8 783 ..	22.2	29.0	17.6	36.3	32.4	38.4	49.9	....
Other sectors	8 784 ..	....	....	....	....	....	....	....	....
Other liabilities	8 786 ..	2.2	2.5	6.5	4.6	16.7	5.6	12.1	....
Monetary authorities	8 787 ..	.1	.1	....	3.1	1.9	2.9	1.6	....
of which: Short-term	8 789 ..	....	....	....	....	....	....	....	....
General government	8 790 ..	....	....	....	....	....	....	....	....
of which: Short-term	8 792 ..	....	....	....	....	....	....	....	....
Banks	8 793 ..	....	....	....	....	....	....	....	....
of which: Short-term	8 795 ..	....	....	....	....	....	....	....	....
Other sectors	8 796 ..	2.1	2.4	6.5	1.5	14.7	2.7	10.6	....
of which: Short-term	8 798 ..	....	....	....	....	....	....	....	....
NET INTERNATIONAL INVESTMENT POSITION	8 995 ..	**−1,615.6**	**−1,400.4**	**−1,832.3**	**−1,737.3**	**−1,815.5**	**−1,710.6**	**−360.2**	....
Conversion rates: CFA francs per U.S. dollar (end of period)	0 102 ..	704.95	744.31	625.50	519.36	481.58	556.04	498.07	445.59

Table 1. ANALYTIC PRESENTATION, 2000–2007

(Millions of U.S. dollars)

	Code	2000	2001	2002	2003	2004	2005	2006	2007
A. Current Account[1]	4 993 Z.	**7,427**	**2,478**	**1,083**	**3,391**	**16,840**	**24,202**	....	**21,972**
Goods: exports f.o.b.	2 100 ..	19,132	17,992	15,613	23,976	34,766	48,069	....	65,086
Goods: imports f.o.b.	3 100 ..	−8,717	−11,097	−10,876	−16,152	−15,009	−17,288	....	−31,948
Balance on Goods	4 100 ..	*10,415*	*6,895*	*4,738*	*7,824*	*19,757*	*30,781*	....	*33,138*
Services: credit	2 200 ..	1,833	1,653	2,524	3,473	3,336	4,164	....	1,682
Services: debit	3 200 ..	−3,300	−4,640	−4,922	−5,715	−5,973	−7,321	....	−14,118
Balance on Goods and Services	4 991 ..	*8,948*	*3,909*	*2,340*	*5,582*	*17,120*	*27,624*	....	*20,702*
Income: credit	2 300 ..	218	199	184	82	157	705	....	2,581
Income: debit	3 300 ..	−3,365	−2,997	−2,854	−3,325	−2,689	−7,437	....	−19,327
Balance on Goods, Services, and Income	4 992 ..	*5,800*	*1,111*	*−330*	*2,339*	*14,588*	*20,892*	....	*3,955*
Current transfers: credit	2 379 Z.	1,637	1,373	1,422	1,063	2,273	3,329	....	18,168
Current transfers: debit	3 379 ..	−10	−6	−9	−12	−21	−18	....	−151
B. Capital Account[1]	4 994 Z.	**33**	....	**55**	**20**	**36**	**23**	....	....
Capital account: credit	2 994 Z.	....	....	....	....	....	....	....	....
Capital account: debit	3 994 ..	....	....	....	....	....	....	....	....
Total, Groups A Plus B	4 981 ..	*7,460*	*2,478*	*1,138*	*3,411*	*16,876*	*24,225*	....	*21,972*
C. Financial Account[1]	4 995 W.	**−6,219**	**−3,035**	**−6,609**	**−10,285**	**−13,061**	**−23,586**	....	**5,159**
Direct investment abroad	4 505 ..	....	....	....	....	....	....	....	−468
Direct investment in Nigeria	4 555 Z.	1,140	1,191	1,874	2,005	1,874	2,013	....	6,087
Portfolio investment assets	4 602 ..	502	832	134	183	178	2,869	....	−138
Equity securities	4 610 ..	....	....	....	....	....	....	....	....
Debt securities	4 619 ..	502	832	134	183	178	2,869	....	−138
Portfolio investment liabilities	4 652 Z.	....	....	....	....	....	....	....	5,640
Equity securities	4 660 ..	....	....	....	....	....	....	....	4,648
Debt securities	4 669 Z.	....	....	....	....	....	....	....	992
Financial derivatives	4 910 ..	....	....	....	....	....	....	....	....
Financial derivatives assets	4 900 ..	....	....	....	....	....	....	....	....
Financial derivatives liabilities	4 905 ..	....	....	....	....	....	....	....	....
Other investment assets	4 703 ..	−4,534	−3,071	−5,890	−5,845	−7,301	−15,786	....	−7,400
Monetary authorities	4 701 ..	....	....	....	....	....	....	....	....
General government	4 704 ..	....	....	....	....	....	....	....	....
Banks	4 705 ..	602	738	773	818	1,022	2,210	....	−2,489
Other sectors	4 728 ..	−5,136	−3,809	−6,662	−6,663	−8,323	−17,996	....	−4,911
Other investment liabilities	4 753 W.	−3,327	−1,985	−2,727	−6,628	−7,812	−12,682	....	1,438
Monetary authorities	4 753 WA	....	....	....	....	....	....	....	....
General government	4 753 ZB	−979	−850	582	−4,186	−5,079	−12,682	....	110
Banks	4 753 ZC	....	....	....	....	....	....	....	972
Other sectors	4 753 ZD	−2,348	−1,136	−3,309	−2,442	−2,733	....	....	357
Total, Groups A Through C	4 983 ..	*1,240*	*−557*	*−5,472*	*−6,874*	*3,815*	*639*	....	*27,130*
D. Net Errors and Omissions	4 998 ..	**1,849**	**779**	**782**	**5,614**	**4,676**	**9,758**	....	**−18,095**
Total, Groups A Through D	4 984 ..	*3,089*	*223*	*−4,689*	*−1,260*	*8,491*	*10,397*	....	*9,035*
E. Reserves and Related Items	4 802 A.	**−3,089**	**−223**	**4,689**	**1,260**	**−8,491**	**−10,397**	....	**−9,035**
Reserve assets	4 802 ..	−4,459	−509	2,744	214	−9,531	−11,357	....	−9,035
Use of Fund credit and loans	4 766 ..	....	....	....	....	....	....	....	....
Exceptional financing	4 920 ..	1,369	286	1,945	1,047	1,040	960	....	....
Conversion rates: naira per U.S. dollar	0 101 ..	**101.700**	**111.230**	**120.580**	**129.220**	**132.890**	**131.274**	**128.652**	**125.808**

[1] Excludes components that have been classified in the categories of Group E.

2008, International Monetary Fund: *Balance of Payments Statistics Yearbook*

Table 2. STANDARD PRESENTATION, 2000–2007

(Millions of U.S. dollars)

	Code	2000	2001	2002	2003	2004	2005	2006	2007
CURRENT ACCOUNT	4 993 ..	**7,427**	**2,478**	**1,083**	**3,391**	**16,840**	**24,202**	....	**21,972**
A. GOODS	4 100 ..	**10,415**	**6,895**	**4,738**	**7,824**	**19,757**	**30,781**	....	**33,138**
Credit	2 100 ..	**19,132**	**17,992**	**15,613**	**23,976**	**34,766**	**48,069**	....	**65,086**
General merchandise: exports f.o.b.	2 110 ..	19,132	17,992	15,613	23,976	34,766	48,069	....	65,086
Goods for processing: exports f.o.b.	2 150 ..	....	....	....	....	....	....	....	....
Repairs on goods	2 160 ..	....	....	....	....	....	....	....	....
Goods procured in ports by carriers	2 170 ..	....	....	....	....	....	....	....	....
Nonmonetary gold	2 180 ..	....	....	....	....	....	....	....	....
Debit	3 100 ..	**−8,717**	**−11,097**	**−10,876**	**−16,152**	**−15,009**	**−17,288**	....	**−31,948**
General merchandise: imports f.o.b.	3 110 ..	−8,717	−11,097	−10,876	−16,152	−15,009	−17,288	....	−31,948
Goods for processing: imports f.o.b.	3 150 ..	....	....	....	....	....	....	....	....
Repairs on goods	3 160 ..	....	....	....	....	....	....	....	....
Goods procured in ports by carriers	3 170 ..	....	....	....	....	....	....	....	....
Nonmonetary gold	3 180 ..	....	....	....	....	....	....	....	....
B. SERVICES	4 200 ..	**−1,467**	**−2,986**	**−2,398**	**−2,242**	**−2,637**	**−3,158**	....	**−12,436**
Total credit	2 200 ..	*1,833*	*1,653*	*2,524*	*3,473*	*3,336*	*4,164*	....	*1,682*
Total debit	3 200 ..	*−3,300*	*−4,640*	*−4,922*	*−5,715*	*−5,973*	*−7,321*	....	*−14,118*
Transportation services, credit	2 205 ..	**220**	**199**	**304**	**361**	**673**	**730**	....	**1,104**
Passenger	2 850 ..	*85*	*77*	*117*	*28*	*28*	*28*	....	*125*
Freight	2 851 ..	*49*	*44*	*67*	*83*	*69*	*69*	....	*379*
Other	2 852 ..	*87*	*79*	*120*	*250*	*575*	*633*	....	*600*
Sea transport, passenger	2 207 ..	....	....	....	....	....	....	....	....
Sea transport, freight	2 208 ..	....	....	....	....	....	....	....	....
Sea transport, other	2 209 ..	....	....	....	....	....	....	....	....
Air transport, passenger	2 211 ..	....	....	....	....	....	....	....	....
Air transport, freight	2 212 ..	....	....	....	....	....	....	....	....
Air transport, other	2 213 ..	....	....	....	....	....	....	....	....
Other transport, passenger	2 215 ..	....	....	....	....	....	....	....	....
Other transport, freight	2 216 ..	....	....	....	....	....	....	....	....
Other transport, other	2 217 ..	....	....	....	....	....	....	....	....
Transportation services, debit	3 205 ..	**−624**	**−877**	**−930**	**−1,284**	**−1,463**	**−1,512**	....	**−3,373**
Passenger	3 850 ..	*−19*	*−27*	*−29*	*−281*	*−308*	*−276*	....	*−1,050*
Freight	3 851 ..	*−576*	*−810*	*−859*	*−1,002*	*−1,155*	*−1,236*	....	*−2,322*
Other	3 852 ..	*−28*	*−40*	*−42*	....	....	....	....	*−1*
Sea transport, passenger	3 207 ..	....	....	....	....	....	....	....	....
Sea transport, freight	3 208 ..	....	....	....	....	....	....	....	....
Sea transport, other	3 209 ..	....	....	....	....	....	....	....	....
Air transport, passenger	3 211 ..	....	....	....	....	....	....	....	....
Air transport, freight	3 212 ..	....	....	....	....	....	....	....	....
Air transport, other	3 213 ..	....	....	....	....	....	....	....	....
Other transport, passenger	3 215 ..	....	....	....	....	....	....	....	....
Other transport, freight	3 216 ..	....	....	....	....	....	....	....	....
Other transport, other	3 217 ..	....	....	....	....	....	....	....	....
Travel, credit	2 236 ..	**101**	**91**	**139**	**30**	**21**	**18**	....	**215**
Business travel	2 237 ..	....	....	....	....	....	....	....	....
Personal travel	2 240 ..	....	....	....	....	....	....	....	215
Travel, debit	3 236 ..	**−591**	**−831**	**−881**	**−1,795**	**−1,161**	**−1,109**	....	**−2,444**
Business travel	3 237 ..	....	....	....	....	....	....	....	−271
Personal travel	3 240 ..	....	....	....	....	....	....	....	−2,173
Other services, credit	2 200 BA	**1,512**	**1,363**	**2,081**	**3,082**	**2,642**	**3,415**	....	**363**
Communications	2 245 ..	....	....	....	....	....	....	....	....
Construction	2 249 ..	....	....	....	....	....	....	....	....
Insurance	2 253 ..	16	14	21	4	6	8	....	5
Financial	2 260 ..	....	....	....	....	....	....	....	....
Computer and information	2 262 ..	....	....	....	....	....	....	....	....
Royalties and licence fees	2 266 ..	....	....	....	....	....	....	....	....
Other business services	2 268 ..	1,496	1,349	2,060	3,078	2,637	3,407	....	10
Personal, cultural, and recreational	2 287 ..	....	....	....	....	....	....	....	....
Government, n.i.e.	2 291 ..	....	....	....	....	....	....	....	348
Other services, debit	3 200 BA	**−2,086**	**−2,932**	**−3,110**	**−2,637**	**−64**	**−45**	....	**−8,301**
Communications	3 245 ..	....	....	....	....	....	....	....	....
Construction	3 249 ..	....	....	....	....	....	....	....	....
Insurance	3 253 ..	−88	−124	−132	....	....	....	....	−5
Financial	3 260 ..	....	....	....	....	....	....	....	....
Computer and information	3 262 ..	....	....	....	....	....	....	....	....
Royalties and licence fees	3 266 ..	....	....	....	−50	−64	−45	....	−174
Other business services	3 268 ..	−1,841	−2,588	−2,745	−2,587	....	....	....	−5,841
Personal, cultural, and recreational	3 287 ..	....	....	....	....	....	....	....	....
Government, n.i.e.	3 291 ..	−156	−220	−233	....	....	....	....	−2,281

Table 2 (Continued). STANDARD PRESENTATION, 2000–2007

(Millions of U.S. dollars)

	Code	2000	2001	2002	2003	2004	2005	2006	2007
C. INCOME	4 300	−3,148	−2,798	−2,670	−3,243	−2,532	−6,732	....	−16,746
Total credit	2 300	*218*	*199*	*184*	*82*	*157*	*705*	*....*	*2,581*
Total debit	3 300	*−3,365*	*−2,997*	*−2,854*	*−3,325*	*−2,689*	*−7,437*	*....*	*−19,327*
Compensation of employees, credit	2 310	....	....	....	....	....	....	....	220
Compensation of employees, debit	3 310	....	....	....	....	....	....	....	−76
Investment income, credit	2 320	218	199	184	82	157	705	....	2,361
Direct investment income	2 330	....	....	....	82	157	705	....	17
Dividends and distributed branch profits	2 332	....	....	....	....	....	....	....	14
Reinvested earnings and undistributed branch profits	2 333	....	....	....	....	....	....	....	....
Income on debt (interest)	2 334	....	....	....	82	157	705	....	3
Portfolio investment income	2 339	....	....	....	....	....	....	....	53
Income on equity	2 340	....	....	....	....	....	....	....	....
Income on bonds and notes	2 350	....	....	....	....	....	....	....	53
Income on money market instruments	2 360	....	....	....	....	....	....	....	....
Other investment income	2 370	218	199	184	....	....	....	....	2,291
Investment income, debit	3 320	−3,365	−2,997	−2,854	−3,325	−2,689	−7,437	....	−19,251
Direct investment income	3 330	−2,279	−2,003	−1,937	−3,325	−2,689	−7,437	....	−17,889
Dividends and distributed branch profits	3 332	−2,279	−2,003	−1,937	....	....	....	....	−15,702
Reinvested earnings and undistributed branch profits	3 333	....	....	....	−1,807	−1,616	−1,348	....	−2,112
Income on debt (interest)	3 334	....	....	....	−1,518	−1,074	−6,088	....	−75
Portfolio investment income	3 339	....	....	....	....	....	....	....	−714
Income on equity	3 340	....	....	....	....	....	....	....	....
Income on bonds and notes	3 350	....	....	....	....	....	....	....	−714
Income on money market instruments	3 360	....	....	....	....	....	....	....	....
Other investment income	3 370	−1,087	−994	−916	....	....	....	....	−648
D. CURRENT TRANSFERS	4 379	**1,627**	**1,367**	**1,413**	**1,051**	**2,252**	**3,310**	....	**18,016**
Credit	2 379	**1,637**	**1,373**	**1,422**	**1,063**	**2,273**	**3,329**	....	**18,168**
General government	2 380	246	206	213	....	....	....	....	180
Other sectors	2 390	1,392	1,167	1,209	1,063	2,273	3,329	....	17,988
Workers' remittances	2 391	1,392	1,167	1,209	1,063	2,273	3,329	....	17,946
Other current transfers	2 392	....	....	....	....	....	....	....	42
Debit	3 379	**−10**	**−6**	**−9**	**−12**	**−21**	**−18**	....	**−151**
General government	3 380	−9	−5	−8	....	....	....	....	−84
Other sectors	3 390	−1	−1	−1	−12	−21	−18	....	−68
Workers' remittances	3 391	−1	−1	−1	−12	−21	−18	....	−26
Other current transfers	3 392	....	....	....	....	....	....	....	−41
CAPITAL AND FINANCIAL ACCOUNT	4 996	−9,276	−3,257	−1,865	−9,004	−21,516	−33,960	....	−3,877
CAPITAL ACCOUNT	4 994	33	....	54	20	36	23	....	....
Total credit	2 994	*....*	*....*	*....*	*....*	*....*	*....*	*....*	*....*
Total debit	3 994	*....*	*....*	*....*	*....*	*....*	*....*	*....*	*....*
Capital transfers, credit	2 400	....	....	....	....	....	....	....	....
General government	2 401	....	....	....	....	....	....	....	....
Debt forgiveness	2 402	....	....	....	....	....	....	....	....
Other capital transfers	2 410	....	....	....	....	....	....	....	....
Other sectors	2 430	....	....	....	....	....	....	....	....
Migrants' transfers	2 431	....	....	....	....	....	....	....	....
Debt forgiveness	2 432	....	....	....	....	....	....	....	....
Other capital transfers	2 440	....	....	....	....	....	....	....	....
Capital transfers, debit	3 400	....	....	....	....	....	....	....	....
General government	3 401	....	....	....	....	....	....	....	....
Debt forgiveness	3 402	....	....	....	....	....	....	....	....
Other capital transfers	3 410	....	....	....	....	....	....	....	....
Other sectors	3 430	....	....	....	....	....	....	....	....
Migrants' transfers	3 431	....	....	....	....	....	....	....	....
Debt forgiveness	3 432	....	....	....	....	....	....	....	....
Other capital transfers	3 440	....	....	....	....	....	....	....	....
Nonproduced nonfinancial assets, credit	2 480	....	....	....	....	....	....	....	....
Nonproduced nonfinancial assets, debit	3 480	....	....	....	....	....	....	....	....

2008, International Monetary Fund: *Balance of Payments Statistics Yearbook*

Table 2 (Continued). STANDARD PRESENTATION, 2000–2007

(Millions of U.S. dollars)

	Code	2000	2001	2002	2003	2004	2005	2006	2007
FINANCIAL ACCOUNT	4 995 ..	**−9,309**	**−3,257**	**−1,920**	**−9,025**	**−21,552**	**−33,983**	**. . . .**	**−3,877**
A. DIRECT INVESTMENT	4 500 ..	**1,140**	**1,191**	**1,874**	**2,005**	**1,874**	**2,013**	**. . . .**	**5,619**
Direct investment abroad	4 505 ..	. . . .	. . . .	. . . .	. . . .	. . . .	. . . .	. . . .	**−468**
Equity capital	4 510 ..	. . . .	. . . .	. . . .	. . . .	. . . .	. . . .	. . . .	−468
Claims on affiliated enterprises	4 515 ..	. . . .	. . . .	. . . .	. . . .	. . . .	. . . .	. . . .	. . . .
Liabilities to affiliated enterprises	4 520 ..	. . . .	. . . .	. . . .	. . . .	. . . .	. . . .	. . . .	. . . .
Reinvested earnings	4 525 ..	. . . .	. . . .	. . . .	. . . .	. . . .	. . . .	. . . .	. . . .
Other capital	4 530 ..	. . . .	. . . .	. . . .	. . . .	. . . .	. . . .	. . . .	. . . .
Claims on affiliated enterprises	4 535 ..	. . . .	. . . .	. . . .	. . . .	. . . .	. . . .	. . . .	. . . .
Liabilities to affiliated enterprises	4 540 ..	. . . .	. . . .	. . . .	. . . .	. . . .	. . . .	. . . .	. . . .
Direct investment in Nigeria	4 555 ..	**1,140**	**1,191**	**1,874**	**2,005**	**1,874**	**2,013**	**. . . .**	**6,087**
Equity capital	4 560 ..	. . . .	. . . .	. . . .	. . . .	. . . .	. . . .	. . . .	3,975
Claims on direct investors	4 565 ..	. . . .	. . . .	. . . .	. . . .	. . . .	. . . .	. . . .	. . . .
Liabilities to direct investors	4 570 ..	. . . .	. . . .	. . . .	. . . .	. . . .	. . . .	. . . .	3,975
Reinvested earnings	4 575 ..	. . . .	. . . .	. . . .	1,807	1,616	1,348	. . . .	2,112
Other capital	4 580 ..	1,140	1,191	1,874	198	259	665	. . . .	. . . .
Claims on direct investors	4 585 ..	. . . .	. . . .	. . . .	. . . .	. . . .	. . . .	. . . .	. . . .
Liabilities to direct investors	4 590 ..	. . . .	. . . .	. . . .	. . . .	. . . .	. . . .	. . . .	. . . .
B. PORTFOLIO INVESTMENT	4 600 ..	**502**	**832**	**134**	**183**	**178**	**2,869**	**. . . .**	**5,502**
Assets	4 602 ..	**502**	**832**	**134**	**183**	**178**	**2,869**	**. . . .**	**−138**
Equity securities	4 610 ..	. . . .	. . . .	. . . .	. . . .	. . . .	. . . .	. . . .	. . . .
Monetary authorities	4 611 ..	. . . .	. . . .	. . . .	. . . .	. . . .	. . . .	. . . .	. . . .
General government	4 612 ..	. . . .	. . . .	. . . .	. . . .	. . . .	. . . .	. . . .	. . . .
Banks	4 613 ..	. . . .	. . . .	. . . .	. . . .	. . . .	. . . .	. . . .	. . . .
Other sectors	4 614 ..	. . . .	. . . .	. . . .	. . . .	. . . .	. . . .	. . . .	. . . .
Debt securities	4 619 ..	502	832	134	183	178	2,869	. . . .	−138
Bonds and notes	4 620 ..	. . . .	. . . .	. . . .	. . . .	. . . .	. . . .	. . . .	. . . .
Monetary authorities	4 621 ..	. . . .	. . . .	. . . .	. . . .	. . . .	. . . .	. . . .	. . . .
General government	4 622 ..	. . . .	. . . .	. . . .	. . . .	. . . .	. . . .	. . . .	. . . .
Banks	4 623 ..	. . . .	. . . .	. . . .	. . . .	. . . .	. . . .	. . . .	. . . .
Other sectors	4 624 ..	. . . .	. . . .	. . . .	. . . .	. . . .	. . . .	. . . .	. . . .
Money market instruments	4 630 ..	. . . .	. . . .	. . . .	. . . .	. . . .	. . . .	. . . .	−138
Monetary authorities	4 631 ..	. . . .	. . . .	. . . .	. . . .	. . . .	. . . .	. . . .	. . . .
General government	4 632 ..	. . . .	. . . .	. . . .	. . . .	. . . .	. . . .	. . . .	. . . .
Banks	4 633 ..	. . . .	. . . .	. . . .	. . . .	. . . .	. . . .	. . . .	. . . .
Other sectors	4 634 ..	. . . .	. . . .	. . . .	. . . .	. . . .	. . . .	. . . .	. . . .
Liabilities	4 652 ..	**. . . .**	**. . . .**	**. . . .**	**. . . .**	**. . . .**	**. . . .**	**. . . .**	**5,640**
Equity securities	4 660 ..	. . . .	. . . .	. . . .	. . . .	. . . .	. . . .	. . . .	4,648
Banks	4 663 ..	. . . .	. . . .	. . . .	. . . .	. . . .	. . . .	. . . .	. . . .
Other sectors	4 664 ..	. . . .	. . . .	. . . .	. . . .	. . . .	. . . .	. . . .	4,648
Debt securities	4 669 ..	. . . .	. . . .	. . . .	. . . .	. . . .	. . . .	. . . .	992
Bonds and notes	4 670 ..	. . . .	. . . .	. . . .	. . . .	. . . .	. . . .	. . . .	992
Monetary authorities	4 671 ..	. . . .	. . . .	. . . .	. . . .	. . . .	. . . .	. . . .	. . . .
General government	4 672 ..	. . . .	. . . .	. . . .	. . . .	. . . .	. . . .	. . . .	. . . .
Banks	4 673 ..	. . . .	. . . .	. . . .	. . . .	. . . .	. . . .	. . . .	. . . .
Other sectors	4 674 ..	. . . .	. . . .	. . . .	. . . .	. . . .	. . . .	. . . .	992
Money market instruments	4 680 ..	. . . .	. . . .	. . . .	. . . .	. . . .	. . . .	. . . .	. . . .
Monetary authorities	4 681 ..	. . . .	. . . .	. . . .	. . . .	. . . .	. . . .	. . . .	. . . .
General government	4 682 ..	. . . .	. . . .	. . . .	. . . .	. . . .	. . . .	. . . .	. . . .
Banks	4 683 ..	. . . .	. . . .	. . . .	. . . .	. . . .	. . . .	. . . .	. . . .
Other sectors	4 684 ..	. . . .	. . . .	. . . .	. . . .	. . . .	. . . .	. . . .	. . . .
C. FINANCIAL DERIVATIVES	4 910 ..	. . . .	. . . .	. . . .	. . . .	. . . .	. . . .	. . . .	. . . .
Monetary authorities	4 911 ..	. . . .	. . . .	. . . .	. . . .	. . . .	. . . .	. . . .	. . . .
General government	4 912 ..	. . . .	. . . .	. . . .	. . . .	. . . .	. . . .	. . . .	. . . .
Banks	4 913 ..	. . . .	. . . .	. . . .	. . . .	. . . .	. . . .	. . . .	. . . .
Other sectors	4 914 ..	. . . .	. . . .	. . . .	. . . .	. . . .	. . . .	. . . .	. . . .
Assets	4 900 ..	**. . . .**	**. . . .**	**. . . .**	**. . . .**	**. . . .**	**. . . .**	**. . . .**	**. . . .**
Monetary authorities	4 901 ..	. . . .	. . . .	. . . .	. . . .	. . . .	. . . .	. . . .	. . . .
General government	4 902 ..	. . . .	. . . .	. . . .	. . . .	. . . .	. . . .	. . . .	. . . .
Banks	4 903 ..	. . . .	. . . .	. . . .	. . . .	. . . .	. . . .	. . . .	. . . .
Other sectors	4 904 ..	. . . .	. . . .	. . . .	. . . .	. . . .	. . . .	. . . .	. . . .
Liabilities	4 905 ..	**. . . .**	**. . . .**	**. . . .**	**. . . .**	**. . . .**	**. . . .**	**. . . .**	**. . . .**
Monetary authorities	4 906 ..	. . . .	. . . .	. . . .	. . . .	. . . .	. . . .	. . . .	. . . .
General government	4 907 ..	. . . .	. . . .	. . . .	. . . .	. . . .	. . . .	. . . .	. . . .
Banks	4 908 ..	. . . .	. . . .	. . . .	. . . .	. . . .	. . . .	. . . .	. . . .
Other sectors	4 909 ..	. . . .	. . . .	. . . .	. . . .	. . . .	. . . .	. . . .	. . . .

Table 2 (Concluded). STANDARD PRESENTATION, 2000–2007

(Millions of U.S. dollars)

	Code	2000	2001	2002	2003	2004	2005	2006	2007
D. OTHER INVESTMENT	4 700	**−6,492**	**−4,771**	**−6,672**	**−11,426**	**−14,073**	**−27,507**	. . . .	**−5,962**
Assets	4 703	**−4,534**	**−3,071**	**−5,890**	**−5,845**	**−7,301**	**−15,786**	. . . .	**−7,400**
Trade credits	4 706	. . . .	. . . .	. . . .	. . . .	. . . .	. . . .	. . . .	−1,256
General government	4 707	. . . .	. . . .	. . . .	. . . .	. . . .	. . . .	. . . .	. . . .
of which: Short-term	4 709	. . . .	. . . .	. . . .	. . . .	. . . .	. . . .	. . . .	. . . .
Other sectors	4 710	. . . .	. . . .	. . . .	. . . .	. . . .	. . . .	. . . .	−1,256
of which: Short-term	4 712	. . . .	. . . .	. . . .	. . . .	. . . .	. . . .	. . . .	. . . .
Loans	4 714	. . . .	. . . .	. . . .	. . . .	. . . .	. . . .	. . . .	−117
Monetary authorities	4 715	. . . .	. . . .	. . . .	. . . .	. . . .	. . . .	. . . .	. . . .
of which: Short-term	4 718	. . . .	. . . .	. . . .	. . . .	. . . .	. . . .	. . . .	. . . .
General government	4 719	. . . .	. . . .	. . . .	. . . .	. . . .	. . . .	. . . .	. . . .
of which: Short-term	4 721	. . . .	. . . .	. . . .	. . . .	. . . .	. . . .	. . . .	. . . .
Banks	4 722	. . . .	. . . .	. . . .	. . . .	. . . .	. . . .	. . . .	−117
of which: Short-term	4 724	. . . .	. . . .	. . . .	. . . .	. . . .	. . . .	. . . .	. . . .
Other sectors	4 725	. . . .	. . . .	. . . .	. . . .	. . . .	. . . .	. . . .	. . . .
of which: Short-term	4 727	. . . .	. . . .	. . . .	. . . .	. . . .	. . . .	. . . .	. . . .
Currency and deposits	4 730	−4,534	−3,071	−5,890	−5,845	−7,301	−15,786	. . . .	−4,753
Monetary authorities	4 731	. . . .	. . . .	. . . .	. . . .	. . . .	. . . .	. . . .	. . . .
General government	4 732	. . . .	. . . .	. . . .	. . . .	. . . .	. . . .	. . . .	. . . .
Banks	4 733	602	738	773	818	1,022	2,210	. . . .	−2,372
Other sectors	4 734	−5,136	−3,809	−6,662	−6,663	−8,323	−17,996	. . . .	−2,381
Other assets	4 736	. . . .	. . . .	. . . .	. . . .	. . . .	. . . .	. . . .	−1,274
Monetary authorities	4 737	. . . .	. . . .	. . . .	. . . .	. . . .	. . . .	. . . .	. . . .
of which: Short-term	4 739	. . . .	. . . .	. . . .	. . . .	. . . .	. . . .	. . . .	. . . .
General government	4 740	. . . .	. . . .	. . . .	. . . .	. . . .	. . . .	. . . .	. . . .
of which: Short-term	4 742	. . . .	. . . .	. . . .	. . . .	. . . .	. . . .	. . . .	. . . .
Banks	4 743	. . . .	. . . .	. . . .	. . . .	. . . .	. . . .	. . . .	. . . .
of which: Short-term	4 745	. . . .	. . . .	. . . .	. . . .	. . . .	. . . .	. . . .	. . . .
Other sectors	4 746	. . . .	. . . .	. . . .	. . . .	. . . .	. . . .	. . . .	−1,274
of which: Short-term	4 748	. . . .	. . . .	. . . .	. . . .	. . . .	. . . .	. . . .	. . . .
Liabilities	4 753	**−1,958**	**−1,700**	**−782**	**−5,582**	**−6,772**	**−11,722**	. . . .	**1,438**
Trade credits	4 756	. . . .	. . . .	1,945	−2,791	−3,386	−8,135	. . . .	. . . .
General government	4 757	. . . .	. . . .	1,945	−2,791	−3,386	−8,135	. . . .	. . . .
of which: Short-term	4 759	. . . .	. . . .	. . . .	. . . .	. . . .	. . . .	. . . .	. . . .
Other sectors	4 760	. . . .	. . . .	. . . .	. . . .	. . . .	. . . .	. . . .	. . . .
of which: Short-term	4 762	. . . .	. . . .	. . . .	. . . .	. . . .	. . . .	. . . .	. . . .
Loans	4 764	−979	−850	−1,364	−1,395	−1,693	−4,548	. . . .	588
Monetary authorities	4 765	. . . .	. . . .	. . . .	. . . .	. . . .	. . . .	. . . .	. . . .
of which: Use of Fund credit and loans from the Fund	4 766	. . . .	. . . .	. . . .	. . . .	. . . .	. . . .	. . . .	. . . .
of which: Short-term	4 768	. . . .	. . . .	. . . .	. . . .	. . . .	. . . .	. . . .	. . . .
General government	4 769	−979	−850	−1,364	−1,395	−1,693	−4,548	. . . .	110
of which: Short-term	4 771	. . . .	. . . .	. . . .	. . . .	. . . .	. . . .	. . . .	. . . .
Banks	4 772	. . . .	. . . .	. . . .	. . . .	. . . .	. . . .	. . . .	122
of which: Short-term	4 774	. . . .	. . . .	. . . .	. . . .	. . . .	. . . .	. . . .	. . . .
Other sectors	4 775	. . . .	. . . .	. . . .	. . . .	. . . .	. . . .	. . . .	357
of which: Short-term	4 777	. . . .	. . . .	. . . .	. . . .	. . . .	. . . .	. . . .	. . . .
Currency and deposits	4 780	. . . .	. . . .	. . . .	. . . .	. . . .	. . . .	. . . .	850
Monetary authorities	4 781	. . . .	. . . .	. . . .	. . . .	. . . .	. . . .	. . . .	. . . .
General government	4 782	. . . .	. . . .	. . . .	. . . .	. . . .	. . . .	. . . .	. . . .
Banks	4 783	. . . .	. . . .	. . . .	. . . .	. . . .	. . . .	. . . .	850
Other sectors	4 784	. . . .	. . . .	. . . .	. . . .	. . . .	. . . .	. . . .	. . . .
Other liabilities	4 786	−979	−850	−1,364	−1,395	−1,693	960	. . . .	. . . .
Monetary authorities	4 787	1,369	286	1,945	1,047	1,040	960	. . . .	. . . .
of which: Short-term	4 789	*1,369*	*286*	*1,945*	*1,047*	*1,040*	*960*	. . . .	. . . .
General government	4 790	. . . .	. . . .	. . . .	. . . .	. . . .	. . . .	. . . .	. . . .
of which: Short-term	4 792	. . . .	. . . .	. . . .	. . . .	. . . .	. . . .	. . . .	. . . .
Banks	4 793	. . . .	. . . .	. . . .	. . . .	. . . .	. . . .	. . . .	. . . .
of which: Short-term	4 795	. . . .	. . . .	. . . .	. . . .	. . . .	. . . .	. . . .	. . . .
Other sectors	4 796	−2,348	−1,136	−3,309	−2,442	−2,733	. . . .	. . . .	. . . .
of which: Short-term	4 798	*−2,348*	*−1,136*	*−3,309*	*−2,442*	*−2,733*	. . . .	. . . .	. . . .
E. RESERVE ASSETS	4 802	**−4,459**	**−509**	**2,744**	**214**	**−9,531**	**−11,357**	. . . .	**−9,035**
Monetary gold	4 812	. . . .	. . . .	. . . .	. . . .	. . . .	. . . .	. . . .	. . . .
Special drawing rights	4 811	. . . .	. . . .	1	. . . .	. . . .	. . . .	. . . .	. . . .
Reserve position in the Fund	4 810	. . . .	. . . .	. . . .	. . . .	. . . .	. . . .	. . . .	. . . .
Foreign exchange	4 803	−4,458	−508	2,743	214	−9,531	−11,357	. . . .	−9,035
Other claims	4 813	. . . .	. . . .	. . . .	. . . .	. . . .	. . . .	. . . .	. . . .
NET ERRORS AND OMISSIONS	4 998	**1,849**	**779**	**782**	**5,614**	**4,676**	**9,758**	. . . .	**−18,095**

Table 3. INTERNATIONAL INVESTMENT POSITION (End-period stocks), 2000–2007

(Millions of U.S. dollars)

	Code	2000	2001	2002	2003	2004	2005	2006	2007
ASSETS...	8 995 C.	....	....	....	....	....	**42,955**	**61,880**	**78,865**
Direct investment abroad...................	8 505 ..	....	....	....	....	....	**302**	**700**	**1,168**
Equity capital and reinvested earnings...........................	8 506 ..	....	....	....	....	....	302	700	1,168
Claims on affiliated enterprises............................	8 507 ..	....	....	....	....	....	302	700	1,168
Liabilities to affiliated enterprises........................	8 508 ..	....	....	....	....	....	....	....	....
Other capital..	8 530 ..	....	....	....	....	....	....	....	....
Claims on affiliated enterprises............................	8 535 ..	....	....	....	....	....	....	....	....
Liabilities to affiliated enterprises........................	8 540 ..	....	....	....	....	....	....	....	....
Portfolio investment.............................	8 602 ..	....	....	....	....	....	**1,179**	**1,294**	**1,375**
Equity securities..	8 610 ..	....	....	....	....	....	....	....	....
Monetary authorities..................................	8 611 ..	....	....	....	....	....	....	....	....
General government..................................	8 612 ..	....	....	....	....	....	....	....	....
Banks..	8 613 ..	....	....	....	....	....	....	....	....
Other sectors..	8 614 ..	....	....	....	....	....	....	....	....
Debt securities..	8 619 ..	....	....	....	....	....	1,179	1,294	1,375
Bonds and notes..	8 620 ..	....	....	....	....	....			
Monetary authorities..................................	8 621 ..	....	....	....	....	....			
General government..................................	8 622 ..	....	....	....	....	....			
Banks..	8 623 ..	....	....	....	....	....			
Other sectors..	8 624 ..	....	....	....	....	....			
Money market instruments...........................	8 630 ..	....	....	....	....	....	1,179	1,294	1,375
Monetary authorities..................................	8 631 ..	....	....	....	....	....			
General government..................................	8 632 ..	....	....	....	....	....	....	....	....
Banks..	8 633 ..	....	....	....	....	....			
Other sectors..	8 634 ..	....	....	....	....	....			
Financial derivatives...............................	8 900 ..	....	....	....	....	....	....	....	....
Monetary authorities..................................	8 901 ..	....	....	....	....	....	....	....	....
General government..................................	8 902 ..	....	....	....	....	....	....	....	....
Banks..	8 903 ..	....	....	....	....	....	....	....	....
Other sectors..	8 904 ..	....	....	....	....	....	....	....	....
Other investment................................	8 703 ..	....	....	....	....	....	**13,397**	**17,587**	**24,988**
Trade credits..	8 706 ..	....	....	....	....	....	3,247	5,285	6,541
General government..................................	8 707 ..	....	....	....	....	....	....	....	....
of which: Short-term............................	8 709 ..	....	....	....	....	....	....	....	....
Other sectors..	8 710 ..	....	....	....	....	....	3,247	5,285	6,541
of which: Short-term............................	8 712 ..	....	....	....	....	....	....	....	....
Loans..	8 714 ..	....	....	....	....	....	925	1,051	1,168
Monetary authorities..................................	8 715 ..	....	....	....	....	....	....	....	....
of which: Short-term............................	8 718 ..	....	....	....	....	....	....	....	....
General government..................................	8 719 ..	....	....	....	....	....	....	....	....
of which: Short-term............................	8 721 ..	....	....	....	....	....	....	....	....
Banks..	8 722 ..	....	....	....	....	....	925	1,051	1,168
of which: Short-term............................	8 724 ..	....	....	....	....	....	....	....	....
Other sectors..	8 725 ..	....	....	....	....	....	....	....	....
of which: Short-term............................	8 727 ..	....	....	....	....	....	....	....	....
Currency and deposits................................	8 730 ..	....	....	....	....	....	7,797	9,944	14,697
Monetary authorities..................................	8 731 ..	....	....	....	....	....	....	....	....
General government..................................	8 732 ..	....	....	....	....	....	....	....	....
Banks..	8 733 ..	....	....	....	....	....	3,555	4,975	7,347
Other sectors..	8 734 ..	....	....	....	....	....	4,242	4,969	7,350
Other assets..	8 736 ..	....	....	....	....	....	1,428	1,308	2,582
Monetary authorities..................................	8 737 ..	....	....	....	....	....	....	....	....
of which: Short-term............................	8 739 ..	....	....	....	....	....	....	....	....
General government..................................	8 740 ..	....	....	....	....	....	....	....	....
of which: Short-term............................	8 742 ..	....	....	....	....	....	....	....	....
Banks..	8 743 ..	....	....	....	....	....	....	....	....
of which: Short-term............................	8 745 ..	....	....	....	....	....	....	....	....
Other sectors..	8 746 ..	....	....	....	....	....	1,428	1,308	2,582
of which: Short-term............................	8 748 ..	....	....	....	....	....	....	....	....
Reserve assets...................................	8 802 ..	....	....	....	....	....	**28,077**	**42,299**	**51,334**
Monetary gold..	8 812 ..	....	....	....	....	....	....	....	....
Special drawing rights................................	8 811 ..	....	1	....	....	....	....	....	1
Reserve position in the Fund.......................	8 810 ..	....	....	....	....	....	....	....	....
Foreign exchange....................................	8 803 ..	....	....	....	....	....	28,077	42,298	51,333
Other claims..	8 813 ..	....	....	....	....	....	....	....	....

Table 3 (Concluded). INTERNATIONAL INVESTMENT POSITION (End-period stocks), 2000–2007

(Millions of U.S. dollars)

	Code	2000	2001	2002	2003	2004	2005	2006	2007
LIABILITIES	8 995 D.	....	....	....	....	....	**63,363**	**52,492**	**62,869**
Direct investment in Nigeria	8 555 ..	....	....	....	....	....	**26,345**	**29,313**	**32,613**
Equity capital and reinvested earnings	8 556 ..	....	....	....	....	....	26,345	29,313	32,613
Claims on direct investors	8 557 ..	....	....	....	....	....	....	....	....
Liabilities to direct investors	8 558 ..	....	....	....	....	....	26,345	29,313	32,613
Other capital	8 580 ..	....	....	....	....	....	....	....	....
Claims on direct investors	8 585 ..	....	....	....	....	....	....	....	....
Liabilities to direct investors	8 590 ..	....	....	....	....	....	....	....	....
Portfolio investment	8 652 ..	....	....	....	....	....	**6,613**	**9,028**	**14,635**
Equity securities	8 660 ..	....	....	....	....	....	3,550	4,890	9,538
Banks	8 663 ..	....	....	....	....	....	....	....	....
Other sectors	8 664 ..	....	....	....	....	....	3,550	4,890	9,538
Debt securities	8 669 ..	....	....	....	....	....	3,063	4,138	5,098
Bonds and notes	8 670 ..	....	....	....	....	....	3,063	4,138	5,098
Monetary authorities	8 671 ..	....	....	....	....	....	....	....	....
General government	8 672 ..	....	....	....	....	....	3,063	4,138	5,098
Banks	8 673 ..	....	....	....	....	....	....	....	....
Other sectors	8 674 ..	....	....	....	....	....	....	....	....
Money market instruments	8 680 ..	....	....	....	....	....	....	....	....
Monetary authorities	8 681 ..	....	....	....	....	....	....	....	....
General government	8 682 ..	....	....	....	....	....	....	....	....
Banks	8 683 ..	....	....	....	....	....	....	....	....
Other sectors	8 684 ..	....	....	....	....	....	....	....	....
Financial derivatives	8 905 ..	....	....	....	....	....	....	....	....
Monetary authorities	8 906 ..	....	....	....	....	....	....	....	....
General government	8 907 ..	....	....	....	....	....	....	....	....
Banks	8 908 ..	....	....	....	....	....	....	....	....
Other sectors	8 909 ..	....	....	....	....	....	....	....	....
Other investment	8 753 ..	....	....	....	....	....	**30,405**	**14,151**	**15,621**
Trade credits	8 756 ..	....	....	....	....	....	....	....	....
General government	8 757 ..	....	....	....	....	....	....	....	....
of which: Short-term	8 759 ..	....	....	....	....	....	....	....	....
Other sectors	8 760 ..	....	....	....	....	....	....	....	....
of which: Short-term	8 762 ..	....	....	....	....	....	....	....	....
Loans	8 764 ..	....	....	....	....	....	23,646	7,148	7,615
Monetary authorities	8 765 ..	....	....	....	....	....	....	....	....
of which: Use of Fund credit and loans from the Fund	8 766 ..	....	....	....	....	....	....	....	....
of which: Short-term	8 768 ..	....	....	....	....	....	....	....	....
General government	8 769 ..	....	....	....	....	....	20,476	3,544	3,654
of which: Short-term	8 771 ..	....	....	....	....	....	....	....	....
Banks	8 772 ..	....	....	....	....	....	....	....	....
of which: Short-term	8 774 ..	....	....	....	....	....	....	....	....
Other sectors	8 775 ..	....	....	....	....	....	3,170	3,604	3,961
of which: Short-term	8 777 ..	....	....	....	....	....	....	....	....
Currency and deposits	8 780 ..	....	....	....	....	....	180	284	1,133
Monetary authorities	8 781 ..	....	....	....	....	....	....	....	....
General government	8 782 ..	....	....	....	....	....	....	....	....
Banks	8 783 ..	....	....	....	....	....	180	284	1,133
Other sectors	8 784 ..	....	....	....	....	....	....	....	....
Other liabilities	8 786 ..	....	....	....	....	....	6,579	6,719	6,873
Monetary authorities	8 787 ..	....	....	....	....	....	....	....	....
of which: Short-term	8 789 ..	....	....	....	....	....	....	....	....
General government	8 790 ..	....	....	....	....	....	....	....	....
of which: Short-term	8 792 ..	....	....	....	....	....	....	....	....
Banks	8 793 ..	....	....	....	....	....	....	....	....
of which: Short-term	8 795 ..	....	....	....	....	....	....	....	....
Other sectors	8 796 ..	....	....	....	....	....	6,579	6,719	6,873
of which: Short-term	8 798 ..	....	....	....	....	....	....	....	....
NET INTERNATIONAL INVESTMENT POSITION	8 995 ..	....	....	....	....	....	**−20,408**	**9,388**	**15,995**
Conversion rates: naira per U.S. dollar (end of period)	0 102 ..	109.550	112.950	126.400	136.500	132.350	129.000	128.270	117.968

Table 1. ANALYTIC PRESENTATION, 2000–2007

(Millions of U.S. dollars)

	Code	2000	2001	2002	2003	2004	2005	2006	2007
A. Current Account[1].....................	4 993 Z.	**25,079**	**27,546**	**24,269**	**27,698**	**33,000**	**49,003**	**58,323**	**60,459**
Goods: exports f.o.b.................	2 100 ..	60,393	59,448	59,555	68,666	83,164	104,011	122,789	137,297
Goods: imports f.o.b.................	3 100 ..	−34,485	−33,045	−35,263	−40,504	−49,035	−55,094	−62,933	−77,026
Balance on Goods.................	4 100 ..	*25,908*	*26,402*	*24,291*	*28,162*	*34,129*	*48,917*	*59,856*	*60,271*
Services: credit.................	2 200 ..	17,718	18,355	19,488	21,663	25,263	29,928	33,328	40,592
Services: debit.................	3 200 ..	−14,991	−15,798	−17,972	−20,569	−24,304	−29,182	−31,957	−39,758
Balance on Goods and Services.................	4 991 ..	*28,635*	*28,959*	*25,807*	*29,256*	*35,088*	*49,664*	*61,227*	*61,105*
Income: credit.................	2 300 ..	7,546	9,671	10,351	14,077	17,117	24,557	30,988	39,273
Income: debit.................	3 300 ..	−9,851	−9,502	−9,654	−12,712	−16,570	−22,586	−31,610	−37,272
Balance on Goods, Services, and Income.................	4 992 ..	*26,329*	*29,128*	*26,504*	*30,622*	*35,635*	*51,635*	*60,606*	*63,106*
Current transfers: credit.................	2 379 Z.	1,657	1,815	1,877	2,049	2,553	3,458	3,304	3,554
Current transfers: debit.................	3 379 ..	−2,908	−3,398	−4,112	−4,972	−5,188	−6,090	−5,587	−6,201
B. Capital Account[1].................	4 994 Z.	**−91**	**−90**	**−191**	**678**	**−154**	**−290**	**−146**	**−163**
Capital account: credit.................	2 994 Z.	135	113	44	964	105	....	....	....
Capital account: debit.................	3 994 ..	−225	−203	−235	−286	−260	−290	−146	−163
Total, Groups A Plus B.................	4 981 ..	*24,988*	*27,456*	*24,078*	*28,376*	*32,846*	*48,713*	*58,177*	*60,296*
C. Financial Account[1].................	4 995 W.	**−14,805**	**−28,720**	**−10,534**	**−21,745**	**−22,300**	**−38,694**	**−38,690**	**−30,665**
Direct investment abroad.................	4 505 ..	−9,433	−844	−5,385	−6,052	−5,250	−21,823	−21,170	−12,500
Direct investment in Norway.................	4 555 Z.	6,962	2,104	657	3,550	2,544	5,209	6,617	3,788
Portfolio investment assets.................	4 602 ..	−25,143	−29,669	−22,985	−19,283	−38,031	−38,107	−113,451	−68,808
Equity securities.................	4 610 ..	−11,034	−12,346	−6,831	−8,498	−7,270	−18,286	−19,364	−52,918
Debt securities.................	4 619 ..	−14,109	−17,323	−16,154	−10,785	−30,761	−19,821	−94,087	−15,890
Portfolio investment liabilities.................	4 652 Z.	9,843	2,590	4,675	13,123	9,353	32,321	39,463	44,283
Equity securities.................	4 660 ..	1,630	2,698	352	2,040	4,493	11,661	8,350	6,444
Debt securities.................	4 669 Z.	8,213	−108	4,322	11,083	4,860	20,660	31,112	37,840
Financial derivatives.................	4 910 ..	−460	−1,136	−4,826	−126	144	....	....	....
Financial derivatives assets.................	4 900 ..	−329	−1,228	−4,270	35	−636	....	....	....
Financial derivatives liabilities.................	4 905 ..	−131	92	−556	−161	780	....	....	....
Other investment assets.................	4 703 ..	−15,746	−3,556	−12,392	−25,212	−16,517	−38,085	−29,143	−47,671
Monetary authorities.................	4 701 ..	−514	249	490	−127	243	221	−16	6
General government.................	4 704 ..	−8,552	−3,732	−12,220	−14,642	−17,858	−20,779	−8,729	−22,384
Banks.................	4 705 ..	−1,806	505	674	−4,291	963	−9,850	−17,702	−18,261
Other sectors.................	4 728 ..	−4,874	−578	−1,335	−6,151	135	−7,678	−2,697	−7,033
Other investment liabilities.................	4 753 W.	19,173	1,790	29,723	12,256	25,458	21,791	78,994	50,243
Monetary authorities.................	4 753 WA	3,388	−1,653	3,023	−1,721	382	1,298	5,840	−675
General government.................	4 753 ZB	9,658	79	15,666	9,992	22,306	−437	46,444	12,221
Banks.................	4 753 ZC	1,321	2,320	8,549	377	4,266	19,704	21,518	30,929
Other sectors.................	4 753 ZD	4,805	1,044	2,486	3,608	−1,496	1,227	5,191	7,769
Total, Groups A Through C.................	4 983 ..	*10,184*	*−1,265*	*13,544*	*6,631*	*10,546*	*10,019*	*19,487*	*29,631*
D. Net Errors and Omissions.................	4 998 ..	**−6,498**	**−1,216**	**−6,814**	**−6,303**	**−5,319**	**−5,508**	**−14,012**	**−28,586**
Total, Groups A Through D.................	4 984 ..	*3,686*	*−2,481*	*6,730*	*328*	*5,227*	*4,511*	*5,475*	*1,045*
E. Reserves and Related Items.................	4 802 A.	**−3,686**	**2,481**	**−6,730**	**−328**	**−5,227**	**−4,511**	**−5,475**	**−1,045**
Reserve assets.................	4 802 ..	−3,686	2,481	−6,730	−328	−5,227	−4,511	−5,475	−1,045
Use of Fund credit and loans.................	4 766 ..	....	....	....	....	....	....	....	....
Exceptional financing.................	4 920 ..	....	....	....	....	....	....	....	....
Conversion rates: Norwegian kroner per U.S. dollar.................	0 101 ..	**8.8018**	**8.9917**	**7.9838**	**7.0802**	**6.7408**	**6.4425**	**6.4133**	**5.8617**

[1] Excludes components that have been classified in the categories of Group E.

Table 2. STANDARD PRESENTATION, 2000–2007

(Millions of U.S. dollars)

	Code	2000	2001	2002	2003	2004	2005	2006	2007
CURRENT ACCOUNT	4 993	**25,079**	**27,546**	**24,269**	**27,698**	**33,000**	**49,003**	**58,323**	**60,459**
A. GOODS	4 100	**25,908**	**26,402**	**24,291**	**28,162**	**34,129**	**48,917**	**59,856**	**60,271**
Credit	2 100	**60,393**	**59,448**	**59,555**	**68,666**	**83,164**	**104,011**	**122,789**	**137,297**
General merchandise: exports f.o.b.	2 110	60,102	59,068	59,229	68,250	82,674	103,642	122,187	136,405
Goods for processing: exports f.o.b.	2 150	....	....	....	....	....	....	....	....
Repairs on goods	2 160	143	226	251	298	334	369	602	893
Goods procured in ports by carriers	2 170	147	154	74	117	156	....	....	....
Nonmonetary gold	2 180	....	....	....	....	....	....	....	....
Debit	3 100	**−34,485**	**−33,045**	**−35,263**	**−40,504**	**−49,035**	**−55,094**	**−62,933**	**−77,026**
General merchandise: imports f.o.b.	3 110	−32,790	−31,154	−33,657	−38,848	−47,329	−53,179	−60,940	−75,190
Goods for processing: imports f.o.b.	3 150	....	....	....	....	....	....	....	....
Repairs on goods	3 160	−744	−859	−606	−512	−461	−624	−527	−656
Goods procured in ports by carriers	3 170	−951	−1,033	−1,001	−1,144	−1,245	−1,291	−1,466	−1,180
Nonmonetary gold	3 180	....	....	....	....	....	....	....	....
B. SERVICES	4 200	**2,726**	**2,557**	**1,516**	**1,094**	**959**	**747**	**1,371**	**834**
Total credit	2 200	*17,718*	*18,355*	*19,488*	*21,663*	*25,263*	*29,928*	*33,328*	*40,592*
Total debit	3 200	*−14,991*	*−15,798*	*−17,972*	*−20,569*	*−24,304*	*−29,182*	*−31,957*	*−39,758*
Transportation services, credit	2 205	**9,606**	**10,871**	**11,212**	**12,232**	**13,917**	**16,248**	**16,072**	**19,079**
Passenger	2 850	*471*	*422*	*402*	*489*	*551*	*698*	*638*	*815*
Freight	2 851	*6,406*	*7,280*	*7,770*	*8,000*	*9,162*	*10,398*	*10,889*	*13,140*
Other	2 852	*2,729*	*3,169*	*3,040*	*3,744*	*4,203*	*5,152*	*4,545*	*5,124*
Sea transport, passenger	2 207	206	236	236	240	251	362	265	280
Sea transport, freight	2 208	5,472	6,213	6,449	6,375	7,391	8,328	8,676	10,957
Sea transport, other	2 209	2,086	2,404	2,205	2,771	3,082	3,783	3,250	3,434
Air transport, passenger	2 211	254	177	149	233	281	313	349	496
Air transport, freight	2 212	49	30	25	29	36	40	....	....
Air transport, other	2 213	75	44	52	95	86	204	50	81
Other transport, passenger	2 215	10	9	16	16	19	23	24	39
Other transport, freight	2 216	885	1,037	1,296	1,595	1,735	2,030	2,213	2,184
Other transport, other	2 217	568	721	783	879	1,035	1,165	1,245	1,608
Transportation services, debit	3 205	**−5,138**	**−5,973**	**−6,503**	**−7,156**	**−8,458**	**−9,682**	**−9,900**	**−13,159**
Passenger	3 850	*−292*	*−308*	*−421*	*−373*	*−405*	*−480*	*−486*	*....*
Freight	3 851	*−513*	*−651*	*−614*	*−773*	*−1,062*	*−1,753*	*−2,601*	*−4,516*
Other	3 852	*−4,333*	*−5,015*	*−5,468*	*−6,009*	*−6,991*	*−7,448*	*−6,812*	*−8,642*
Sea transport, passenger	3 207	−15	−36	−33	−37	−38	−48	−48	....
Sea transport, freight	3 208	−322	−407	−383	−452	−711	−799	−1,095	−2,069
Sea transport, other	3 209	−3,851	−4,503	−5,003	−5,467	−6,421	−6,823	−6,162	−7,144
Air transport, passenger	3 211	−269	−263	−375	−315	−355	−413	−419	....
Air transport, freight	3 212	−56	−71	−76	−68	−60	−95	−196	−440
Air transport, other	3 213	−459	−482	−441	−516	−529	−580	−603	−1,433
Other transport, passenger	3 215	−8	−8	−13	−22	−12	−19	−19	....
Other transport, freight	3 216	−135	−174	−156	−254	−290	−860	−1,310	−2,008
Other transport, other	3 217	−23	−29	−23	−25	−41	−45	−47	−65
Travel, credit	2 236	**2,050**	**1,958**	**2,179**	**2,500**	**2,980**	**3,332**	**3,613**	**4,222**
Business travel	2 237	....	....	....	....	....	....	....	....
Personal travel	2 240	2,050	1,958	2,179	2,500	2,980	3,332	3,613	4,222
Travel, debit	3 236	**−4,601**	**−4,410**	**−5,189**	**−6,716**	**−8,489**	**−10,111**	**−11,586**	**−14,043**
Business travel	3 237	−1,474	−1,393	−1,602	−2,080	−2,649	−3,204	−2,524	−2,880
Personal travel	3 240	−3,127	−3,017	−3,588	−4,636	−5,840	−6,907	−9,062	−11,163
Other services, credit	2 200 BA	**6,062**	**5,526**	**6,097**	**6,931**	**8,366**	**10,349**	**13,642**	**17,291**
Communications	2 245	291	322	361	309	321	378	400	595
Construction	2 249	68	87	88	116	116	254	330	342
Insurance	2 253	153	130	294	394	335	367	283	289
Financial	2 260	386	406	462	558	594	707	820	1,021
Computer and information	2 262	660	589	301	373	566	899	1,376	1,126
Royalties and licence fees	2 266	161	159	171	195	242	414	674	700
Other business services	2 268	4,014	3,458	3,986	4,470	5,708	6,670	9,123	12,517
Personal, cultural, and recreational	2 287	139	172	175	210	185	351	422	466
Government, n.i.e.	2 291	190	203	260	306	298	308	214	235
Other services, debit	3 200 BA	**−5,252**	**−5,415**	**−6,280**	**−6,698**	**−7,357**	**−9,389**	**−10,472**	**−12,556**
Communications	3 245	−165	−190	−216	−217	−233	−286	−310	−409
Construction	3 249	−31	−32	−44	−48	−39	−42	−44	−55
Insurance	3 253	−351	−361	−472	−522	−439	−289	−182	−222
Financial	3 260	−585	−651	−818	−1,153	−1,180	−1,137	−879	−1,122
Computer and information	3 262	−243	−374	−601	−507	−573	−1,006	−1,268	−1,678
Royalties and licence fees	3 266	−439	−329	−329	−394	−442	−469	−498	−622
Other business services	3 268	−3,100	−3,146	−3,444	−3,399	−3,634	−5,180	−5,972	−7,063
Personal, cultural, and recreational	3 287	−179	−200	−218	−304	−383	−508	−588	−569
Government, n.i.e.	3 291	−159	−131	−138	−154	−433	−472	−730	−817

Table 2 (Continued). STANDARD PRESENTATION, 2000–2007

(Millions of U.S. dollars)

	Code	2000	2001	2002	2003	2004	2005	2006	2007
C. INCOME	4 300	**−2,305**	**169**	**697**	**1,365**	**547**	**1,971**	**−622**	**2,001**
Total credit	2 300	*7,546*	*9,671*	*10,351*	*14,077*	*17,117*	*24,557*	*30,988*	*39,273*
Total debit	3 300	*−9,851*	*−9,502*	*−9,654*	*−12,712*	*−16,570*	*−22,586*	*−31,610*	*−37,272*
Compensation of employees, credit	2 310	**270**	**279**	**333**	**392**	**465**	**505**	**524**	**613**
Compensation of employees, debit	3 310	**−1,060**	**−1,022**	**−923**	**−1,430**	**−1,749**	**−2,174**	**−2,620**	**−3,642**
Investment income, credit	2 320	**7,275**	**9,392**	**10,018**	**13,686**	**16,652**	**24,052**	**30,463**	**38,660**
Direct investment income	2 330	1,920	2,888	1,695	4,128	4,892	13,914	12,172	14,409
Dividends and distributed branch profits	2 332	634	897	1,202	1,686	2,792	7,418	6,621	8,325
Reinvested earnings and undistributed branch profits	2 333	1,285	1,992	493	2,442	2,100	6,496	5,551	6,085
Income on debt (interest)	2 334	....	....	....	....	....	....	....	....
Portfolio investment income	2 339	884	986	971	879	946	7,891	14,880	19,402
Income on equity	2 340	....	....	....	....	....	....	....	....
Income on bonds and notes	2 350	884	986	971	879	946	7,891	14,880	19,402
Income on money market instruments	2 360	....	....	....	....	....	....	....	....
Other investment income	2 370	4,472	5,517	7,353	8,679	10,814	2,247	3,412	4,849
Investment income, debit	3 320	**−8,792**	**−8,479**	**−8,731**	**−11,282**	**−14,821**	**−20,412**	**−28,990**	**−33,630**
Direct investment income	3 330	−3,499	−2,809	−2,204	−4,050	−6,202	−12,290	−13,431	−13,801
Dividends and distributed branch profits	3 332	−2,816	−3,192	−2,607	−3,030	−4,611	−7,834	−11,192	−11,097
Reinvested earnings and undistributed branch profits	3 333	−683	383	404	−1,021	−1,592	−4,456	−2,239	−2,703
Income on debt (interest)	3 334	....	....	....	....	....	....	....	....
Portfolio investment income	3 339	−433	−449	−513	−502	−735	−3,576	−6,252	−9,775
Income on equity	3 340	....	....	....	....	....	....	....	....
Income on bonds and notes	3 350	−433	−449	−513	−502	−735	−3,576	−6,252	−9,775
Income on money market instruments	3 360	....	....	....	....	....	....	....	....
Other investment income	3 370	−4,859	−5,221	−6,015	−6,729	−7,884	−4,546	−9,306	−10,055
D. CURRENT TRANSFERS	4 379	**−1,250**	**−1,582**	**−2,235**	**−2,924**	**−2,635**	**−2,632**	**−2,283**	**−2,647**
Credit	2 379	**1,657**	**1,815**	**1,877**	**2,049**	**2,553**	**3,458**	**3,304**	**3,554**
General government	2 380	123	112	55	22	25	279	206	377
Other sectors	2 390	1,535	1,703	1,822	2,027	2,528	3,179	3,099	3,177
Workers' remittances	2 391	....	....	....	....	....	....	....	....
Other current transfers	2 392	1,535	1,703	1,822	2,027	2,528	3,179	3,099	3,177
Debit	3 379	**−2,908**	**−3,398**	**−4,112**	**−4,972**	**−5,188**	**−6,090**	**−5,587**	**−6,201**
General government	3 380	−1,086	−1,227	−1,616	−1,892	−2,030	−2,481	−2,749	−3,278
Other sectors	3 390	−1,822	−2,170	−2,495	−3,081	−3,158	−3,608	−2,838	−2,923
Workers' remittances	3 391	....	....	....	....	....	....	....	....
Other current transfers	3 392	−1,822	−2,170	−2,495	−3,081	−3,158	−3,608	−2,838	−2,923
CAPITAL AND FINANCIAL ACCOUNT	4 996	**−18,581**	**−26,330**	**−17,455**	**−21,395**	**−27,681**	**−43,495**	**−44,311**	**−31,873**
CAPITAL ACCOUNT	4 994	**−91**	**−90**	**−191**	**678**	**−154**	**−290**	**−146**	**−163**
Total credit	2 994	*135*	*113*	*44*	*964*	*105*	*....*	*....*	*....*
Total debit	3 994	*−225*	*−203*	*−235*	*−286*	*−260*	*−290*	*−146*	*−163*
Capital transfers, credit	2 400	**34**	**105**	**39**	**963**	**105**	**....**	**....**	**....**
General government	2 401	....	....	....	....	....	....	....	....
Debt forgiveness	2 402	....	....	....	....	....	....	....	....
Other capital transfers	2 410	....	....	....	....	....	....	....	....
Other sectors	2 430	34	105	39	963	105	....	....	....
Migrants' transfers	2 431	....	....	....	....	....	....	....	....
Debt forgiveness	2 432	....	....	....	....	....	....	....	....
Other capital transfers	2 440	34	105	39	963	105	....	....	....
Capital transfers, debit	3 400	**−220**	**−197**	**−233**	**−285**	**−258**	**−290**	**−146**	**−163**
General government	3 401	....	....	....	....	....	−290	−146	−163
Debt forgiveness	3 402	....	....	....	....	....	....	....	....
Other capital transfers	3 410	....	....	....	....	....	−290	−146	−163
Other sectors	3 430	−220	−197	−233	−285	−258	....	....	....
Migrants' transfers	3 431	....	....	....	....	....	....	....	....
Debt forgiveness	3 432	....	....	....	....	....	....	....	....
Other capital transfers	3 440	−220	−197	−233	−285	−258	....	....	....
Nonproduced nonfinancial assets, credit	2 480	**101**	**9**	**5**	**1**	**....**	**....**	**....**	**....**
Nonproduced nonfinancial assets, debit	3 480	**−6**	**−6**	**−2**	**−1**	**−1**	**....**	**....**	**....**

Table 2 (Continued). STANDARD PRESENTATION, 2000–2007

(Millions of U.S. dollars)

	Code	2000	2001	2002	2003	2004	2005	2006	2007
FINANCIAL ACCOUNT	4 995	−18,490	−26,240	−17,264	−22,073	−27,527	−43,205	−44,166	−31,710
A. DIRECT INVESTMENT	4 500	−2,471	1,260	−4,728	−2,503	−2,706	−16,614	−14,552	−8,712
Direct investment abroad	4 505	−9,433	−844	−5,385	−6,052	−5,250	−21,823	−21,170	−12,500
Equity capital	4 510	−8,761	−792	−5,588	−3,576	−3,356	−13,644	−15,656	−18,184
Claims on affiliated enterprises	4 515	....	....	....	....	....	....	....	....
Liabilities to affiliated enterprises	4 520	....	....	....	....	....	....	....	....
Reinvested earnings	4 525	−1,285	−1,992	−493	−2,442	−2,100	−6,496	−5,551	−6,085
Other capital	4 530	613	1,939	696	−35	206	−1,683	37	11,769
Claims on affiliated enterprises	4 535	−317	647	−1,453	−1,018	−2,569	−5,132	415	−942
Liabilities to affiliated enterprises	4 540	930	1,292	2,149	983	2,775	3,449	−378	12,711
Direct investment in Norway	4 555	6,962	2,104	657	3,550	2,544	5,209	6,617	3,788
Equity capital	4 560	7,269	1,369	909	1,232	−2,882	1,800	2,740	−1,137
Claims on direct investors	4 565	....	....	....	....	....	....	....	....
Liabilities to direct investors	4 570	....	....	....	....	....	....	....	....
Reinvested earnings	4 575	683	−383	−404	1,021	1,592	4,456	2,239	2,703
Other capital	4 580	−991	1,118	152	1,297	3,834	−1,047	1,638	2,222
Claims on direct investors	4 585	−440	205	−206	353	400	−2,623	−1,998	−2,274
Liabilities to direct investors	4 590	−550	913	358	944	3,434	1,576	3,637	4,496
B. PORTFOLIO INVESTMENT	4 600	−15,300	−27,079	−18,310	−6,160	−28,678	−5,786	−73,989	−24,525
Assets	4 602	−25,143	−29,669	−22,985	−19,283	−38,031	−38,107	−113,451	−68,808
Equity securities	4 610	−11,034	−12,346	−6,831	−8,498	−7,270	−18,286	−19,364	−52,918
Monetary authorities	4 611	....	....	....	....	....	....	....	....
General government	4 612	−8,164	−12,796	−11,233	−7,821	−7,249	−10,242	−10,708	−45,874
Banks	4 613	−8	73	165	−21	−87	67	−202	−676
Other sectors	4 614	−2,862	377	4,238	−656	66	−8,111	−8,454	−6,368
Debt securities	4 619	−14,109	−17,323	−16,154	−10,785	−30,761	−19,821	−94,087	−15,890
Bonds and notes	4 620	−14,223	−18,197	−15,362	−13,371	−29,665	−18,366	−94,187	−14,301
Monetary authorities	4 621	....	....	....	....	....	....	....	....
General government	4 622	−11,532	−12,721	−10,731	−7,348	−23,035	−7,284	−82,004	−10,910
Banks	4 623	−1,429	−695	438	−1,892	−969	−3,416	−6,070	−318
Other sectors	4 624	−1,263	−4,781	−5,069	−4,131	−5,660	−7,666	−6,112	−3,073
Money market instruments	4 630	114	874	−792	2,585	−1,096	−1,455	100	−1,589
Monetary authorities	4 631	....	....	....	....	....	....	....	....
General government	4 632	17	−340	295	225	1,197	−804	−545	739
Banks	4 633	−42	32	4	4	−36	−77	73	−2
Other sectors	4 634	139	1,183	−1,092	2,356	−2,257	−574	572	−2,326
Liabilities	4 652	9,843	2,590	4,675	13,123	9,353	32,321	39,463	44,283
Equity securities	4 660	1,630	2,698	352	2,040	4,493	11,661	8,350	6,444
Banks	4 663	−658	84	−297	−1	36	219	−8	68
Other sectors	4 664	2,288	2,614	650	2,042	4,457	11,442	8,358	6,375
Debt securities	4 669	8,213	−108	4,322	11,083	4,860	20,660	31,112	37,840
Bonds and notes	4 670	6,306	1,444	5,572	10,875	3,927	17,559	30,621	26,134
Monetary authorities	4 671	....	....	....	....	....	....	....	....
General government	4 672	2,224	−1,614	877	1,361	−752	2,016	4,288	3,438
Banks	4 673	2,561	2,029	−245	6,859	975	7,242	17,678	1,807
Other sectors	4 674	1,521	1,029	4,940	2,655	3,705	8,300	8,655	20,890
Money market instruments	4 680	1,907	−1,552	−1,250	208	932	3,100	491	11,705
Monetary authorities	4 681	....	....	....	....	....	....	....	....
General government	4 682	−196	70	−1,338	−735	−772	31	717	845
Banks	4 683	2,332	−648	−36	1,332	1,532	3,127	−486	5,812
Other sectors	4 684	−229	−974	125	−389	172	−58	261	5,048
C. FINANCIAL DERIVATIVES	4 910	−460	−1,136	−4,826	−126	144	....	....	....
Monetary authorities	4 911	....	....	....	....	....	....	....	....
General government	4 912	−9	−233	−354	82	−5	....	....	....
Banks	4 913	−79	−29	−353	683	−163	....	....	....
Other sectors	4 914	−372	−875	−4,120	−891	312	....	....	....
Assets	4 900	−329	−1,228	−4,270	35	−636	....	....	....
Monetary authorities	4 901	....	....	....	....	....	....	....	....
General government	4 902	−9	−231	−354	58	−45	....	....	....
Banks	4 903	−142	−144	−144	18	−304	....	....	....
Other sectors	4 904	−178	−853	−3,773	−41	−288	....	....	....
Liabilities	4 905	−131	92	−556	−161	780	....	....	....
Monetary authorities	4 906	....	....	....	....	....	....	....	....
General government	4 907	....	−2	....	25	40	....	....	....
Banks	4 908	64	116	−209	665	141	....	....	....
Other sectors	4 909	−195	−22	−347	−851	600	....	....	....

Table 2 (Concluded). STANDARD PRESENTATION, 2000–2007

(Millions of U.S. dollars)

	Code	2000	2001	2002	2003	2004	2005	2006	2007
D. OTHER INVESTMENT	4 700 ..	**3,427**	**−1,765**	**17,331**	**−12,956**	**8,940**	**−16,294**	**49,851**	**2,572**
Assets	4 703 ..	**−15,746**	**−3,556**	**−12,392**	**−25,212**	**−16,517**	**−38,085**	**−29,143**	**−47,671**
Trade credits	4 706 ..	−1,111	1,396	−949	−709	683	−3,418	−1,449	35
General government	4 707 ..	....	....	....	....	....	....	....	....
of which: Short-term	4 709 ..	....	....	....	....	....	....	....	....
Other sectors	4 710 ..	−1,111	1,396	−949	−709	683	−3,418	−1,449	35
of which: Short-term	4 712 ..	−1,112	1,098	−966	−710	671	−3,418	−1,449	35
Loans	4 714 ..	−6,462	−5,600	−13,920	−13,861	−19,590	−27,665	−15,165	−29,102
Monetary authorities	4 715 ..	....	....	....	....	....	....	....	....
of which: Short-term	4 718 ..	....	....	....	....	....	....	....	....
General government	4 719 ..	−6,480	−4,972	−12,509	−12,900	−18,403	−22,745	−10,965	−20,487
of which: Short-term	4 721 ..	....	....	....	....	....	−22,872	−10,984	−20,387
Banks	4 722 ..	484	−255	−464	−467	−402	−3,550	−2,995	−6,188
of which: Short-term	4 724 ..	....	....	....	....	....	−436	−1,034	−4,142
Other sectors	4 725 ..	−466	−373	−947	−494	−784	−1,371	−1,205	−2,427
of which: Short-term	4 727 ..	−441	−462	−584	−418	−631	102	−123	−164
Currency and deposits	4 730 ..	−6,269	1,385	3,751	−6,405	242	−7,712	−11,346	−11,871
Monetary authorities	4 731 ..	....	....	....	....	....	....	....	....
General government	4 732 ..	−2,059	1,389	453	−1,199	1,586	−778	1,069	−1,461
Banks	4 733 ..	−2,289	760	1,137	−3,824	1,365	−5,380	−12,834	−11,113
Other sectors	4 734 ..	−1,920	−764	2,160	−1,382	−2,709	−1,555	419	703
Other assets	4 736 ..	−1,904	−736	−1,274	−4,236	2,148	710	−1,183	−6,733
Monetary authorities	4 737 ..	−514	249	490	−127	243	221	−16	6
of which: Short-term	4 739 ..	....	....	....	....	....	....	....	....
General government	4 740 ..	−13	−148	−165	−543	−1,041	2,744	1,167	−435
of which: Short-term	4 742 ..	....	....	....	....	....	....	....	....
Banks	4 743 ..	....	....	....	....	....	−920	−1,872	−959
of which: Short-term	4 745 ..	....	....	....	....	....	....	....	....
Other sectors	4 746 ..	−1,377	−837	−1,599	−3,566	2,946	−1,334	−462	−5,344
of which: Short-term	4 748 ..	....	....	....	....	....	....	....	....
Liabilities	4 753 ..	**19,173**	**1,790**	**29,723**	**12,256**	**25,458**	**21,791**	**78,994**	**50,243**
Trade credits	4 756 ..	65	−978	−27	−817	−1,350	−407	1,666	620
General government	4 757 ..	....	....	....	....	....	....	....	....
of which: Short-term..	4 759 ..	....	....	....	....	....	....	....	....
Other sectors	4 760 ..	65	−978	−27	−817	−1,350	−407	1,666	620
of which: Short-term	4 762 ..	65	−978	−27	−817	−1,350	−407	1,666	620
Loans	4 764 ..	17,424	1,158	20,480	8,963	23,976	6,315	58,697	14,640
Monetary authorities	4 765 ..	3,385	−1,697	2,613	−1,397	265	1,765	5,886	−1,332
of which: Use of Fund credit and loans from the Fund..	4 766 ..	....	....	....	....	....	....	....	....
of which: Short-term	4 768 ..	....	....	....	....	....	....	....	....
General government	4 769 ..	9,658	−96	15,678	9,893	20,434	3,135	46,596	7,511
of which: Short-term	4 771 ..	9,658	−96	15,678	9,893	20,434	3,135	46,584	7,511
Banks	4 772 ..	330	743	−4	65	−331	1,031	3,534	3,162
of which: Short-term	4 774 ..	....	....	....	....	....	−51	310	1,455
Other sectors	4 775 ..	4,050	2,208	2,193	401	3,609	384	2,681	5,298
of which: Short-term	4 777 ..	....	....	....	....	....	....	....	....
Currency and deposits	4 780 ..	994	1,621	8,963	−12	4,715	16,998	16,860	24,595
Monetary authorities	4 781 ..	3	43	410	−324	117	16	−43	....
General government	4 782 ..	....	....	....	....	....	....	....	....
Banks	4 783 ..	991	1,578	8,553	311	4,597	16,982	16,903	24,595
Other sectors	4 784 ..	....	....	....	....	....	....	....	....
Other liabilities	4 786 ..	690	−11	308	4,122	−1,883	−1,115	1,771	10,388
Monetary authorities	4 787 ..	....	....	....	....	....	−483	−3	656
of which: Short-term	4 789 ..	....	....	....	....	....	....	....	....
General government	4 790 ..	....	175	−12	99	1,872	−3,572	−152	4,709
of which: Short-term	4 792 ..	....	....	....	....	....	....	....	....
Banks	4 793 ..	....	....	....	....	....	1,691	1,081	3,171
of which: Short-term	4 795 ..	....	....	....	....	....	....	....	....
Other sectors	4 796 ..	690	−186	320	4,023	−3,755	1,249	844	1,851
of which: Short-term	4 798 ..	....	....	....	....	....	....	....	....
E. RESERVE ASSETS	4 802 ..	**−3,686**	**2,481**	**−6,730**	**−328**	**−5,227**	**−4,511**	**−5,475**	**−1,045**
Monetary gold	4 812 ..	....	....	....	....	475	....	....	....
Special drawing rights	4 811 ..	85	−57	64	10	−12	28	−130	104
Reserve position in the Fund	4 810 ..	228	−163	−200	86	163	505	105	38
Foreign exchange	4 803 ..	−1,798	6,341	−285	340	−3,912	−2,047	−3,988	−1,732
Other claims	4 813 ..	−2,200	−3,640	−6,309	−763	−1,941	−2,997	−1,463	545
NET ERRORS AND OMISSIONS	4 998 ..	**−6,498**	**−1,216**	**−6,814**	**−6,303**	**−5,319**	**−5,508**	**−14,012**	**−28,586**

Table 3. INTERNATIONAL INVESTMENT POSITION (End-period stocks), 2000–2007

(Millions of U.S. dollars)

	Code	2000	2001	2002	2003	2004	2005	2006	2007
ASSETS	8 995 C.	**193,524**	**210,470**	**282,515**	**369,891**	**499,303**	**568,534**	**794,790**	**1,016,809**
Direct investment abroad	8 505 ..	**22,940**	**29,777**	**37,292**	**45,912**	**88,915**	**95,851**	**118,480**	**158,354**
Equity capital and reinvested earnings	8 506 ..	....	....	....	....	....	....	96,671	135,885
Claims on affiliated enterprises	8 507 ..	....	....	....	....	....	....	....	....
Liabilities to affiliated enterprises	8 508 ..	....	....	....	....	....	....	....	....
Other capital	8 530 ..	....	....	....	....	....	....	21,809	22,470
Claims on affiliated enterprises	8 535 ..	....	....	....	....	....	....	....	....
Liabilities to affiliated enterprises	8 540 ..	....	....	....	....	....	....	....	....
Portfolio investment	8 602 ..	**89,240**	**100,457**	**132,594**	**175,584**	**251,967**	**280,637**	**434,333**	**546,842**
Equity securities	8 610 ..	43,899	41,571	44,996	67,157	99,440	125,959	174,890	249,168
Monetary authorities	8 611 ..	....	....	....	....	....	....	....	....
General government	8 612 ..	....	....	....	....	....	....	....	....
Banks	8 613 ..	....	....	....	....	....	....	....	....
Other sectors	8 614 ..	....	....	....	....	....	....	....	....
Debt securities	8 619 ..	45,341	58,887	87,598	108,426	152,527	154,679	259,443	297,674
Bonds and notes	8 620 ..	....	....	....	....	....	....	....	....
Monetary authorities	8 621 ..	....	....	....	....	....	....	....	....
General government	8 622 ..	....	....	....	....	....	....	....	....
Banks	8 623 ..	....	....	....	....	....	....	....	....
Other sectors	8 624 ..	....	....	....	....	....	....	....	....
Money market instruments	8 630 ..	....	....	....	....	....	....	....	....
Monetary authorities	8 631 ..	....	....	....	....	....	....	....	....
General government	8 632 ..	....	....	....	....	....	....	....	....
Banks	8 633 ..	....	....	....	....	....	....	....	....
Other sectors	8 634 ..	....	....	....	....	....	....	....	....
Financial derivatives	8 900 ..	....	....	....	....	....	....	....	....
Monetary authorities	8 901 ..	....	....	....	....	....	....	....	....
General government	8 902 ..	....	....	....	....	....	....	....	....
Banks	8 903 ..	....	....	....	....	....	....	....	....
Other sectors	8 904 ..	....	....	....	....	....	....	....	....
Other investment	8 703 ..	**53,559**	**56,762**	**80,454**	**110,830**	**113,606**	**144,983**	**185,483**	**250,472**
Trade credits	8 706 ..	....	....	....	....	....	....	15,395	18,716
General government	8 707 ..	....	....	....	....	....	....	....	....
of which: Short-term	8 709 ..	....	....	....	....	....	....	....	....
Other sectors	8 710 ..	....	....	....	....	....	....	....	....
of which: Short-term	8 712 ..	....	....	....	....	....	....	....	....
Loans	8 714 ..	....	....	....	....	....	....	120,093	155,622
Monetary authorities	8 715 ..	....	....	....	....	....	....	....	....
of which: Short-term	8 718 ..	....	....	....	....	....	....	....	....
General government	8 719 ..	....	....	....	....	....	....	....	....
of which: Short-term	8 721 ..	....	....	....	....	....	....	....	....
Banks	8 722 ..	....	....	....	....	....	....	....	....
of which: Short-term	8 724 ..	....	....	....	....	....	....	....	....
Other sectors	8 725 ..	....	....	....	....	....	....	....	....
of which: Short-term	8 727 ..	....	....	....	....	....	....	....	....
Currency and deposits	8 730 C.	....	....	....	....	....	....	32,948	49,643
Monetary authorities	8 731 ..	....	....	....	....	....	....	....	....
General government	8 732 ..	....	....	....	....	....	....	....	....
Banks	8 733 ..	....	....	....	....	....	....	....	....
Other sectors	8 734 ..	....	....	....	....	....	....	....	....
Other assets	8 736 ..	....	....	....	....	....	....	17,047	26,492
Monetary authorities	8 737 ..	....	....	....	....	....	....	....	....
of which: Short-term	8 739 ..	....	....	....	....	....	....	....	....
General government	8 740 ..	....	....	....	....	....	....	....	....
of which: Short-term	8 742 ..	....	....	....	....	....	....	....	....
Banks	8 743 ..	....	....	....	....	....	....	....	....
of which: Short-term	8 745 ..	....	....	....	....	....	....	....	....
Other sectors	8 746 ..	....	....	....	....	....	....	....	....
of which: Short-term	8 748 ..	....	....	....	....	....	....	....	....
Reserve assets	8 802 ..	**27,786**	**23,474**	**32,175**	**37,566**	**44,815**	**47,062**	**56,494**	**61,140**
Monetary gold	8 812 ..	....	....	....	....	....	....	....	....
Special drawing rights	8 811 ..	307	354	316	335	361	307	453	368
Reserve position in the Fund	8 810 ..	584	726	992	995	869	301	207	178
Foreign exchange	8 803 ..	26,895	22,394	30,868	36,236	43,586	46,454	55,834	60,594
Other claims	8 813 ..	....	....	....	....	....	....	....	....

Table 3 (Concluded). INTERNATIONAL INVESTMENT POSITION (End-period stocks), 2000–2007

(Millions of U.S. dollars)

	Code	2000	2001	2002	2003	2004	2005	2006	2007
LIABILITIES	8 995 D.	**159,128**	**160,147**	**217,515**	**269,546**	**373,962**	**402,681**	**591,090**	**784,998**
Direct investment in Norway	8 555 ..	**25,285**	**21,010**	**25,222**	**26,106**	**85,028**	**81,474**	**97,577**	**129,056**
Equity capital and reinvested earnings	8 556 ..	....	....	....	....	....	....	59,061	71,504
Claims on direct investors	8 557 ..	....	....	....	....	....	....	....	....
Liabilities to direct investors	8 558 ..	....	....	....	....	....	....	....	....
Other capital	8 580 ..	....	....	....	....	....	....	38,516	57,552
Claims on direct investors	8 585 ..	....	....	....	....	....	....	....	....
Liabilities to direct investors	8 590 ..	....	....	....	....	....	....	....	....
Portfolio investment	8 652 ..	**63,543**	**65,197**	**76,929**	**103,017**	**131,047**	**158,210**	**238,509**	**324,448**
Equity securities	8 660 ..	9,927	12,808	12,854	21,498	40,549	58,822	100,857	134,695
Banks	8 663 ..	....	....	....	....	....	....	....	....
Other sectors	8 664 ..	....	....	....	....	....	....	....	....
Debt securities	8 669 ..	53,616	52,389	64,075	81,519	90,497	99,388	137,652	189,753
Bonds and notes	8 670 ..	....	....	....	....	....	....	....	....
Monetary authorities	8 671 ..	....	....	....	....	....	....	....	....
General government	8 672 ..	....	....	....	....	....	....	....	....
Banks	8 673 ..	....	....	....	....	....	....	....	....
Other sectors	8 674 ..	....	....	....	....	....	....	....	....
Money market instruments	8 680 ..	....	....	....	....	....	....	....	....
Monetary authorities	8 681 ..	....	....	....	....	....	....	....	....
General government	8 682 ..	....	....	....	....	....	....	....	....
Banks	8 683 ..	....	....	....	....	....	....	....	....
Other sectors	8 684 ..	....	....	....	....	....	....	....	....
Financial derivatives	8 905 ..	....	....	....	....	....	....	....	....
Monetary authorities	8 906 ..	....	....	....	....	....	....	....	....
General government	8 907 ..	....	....	....	....	....	....	....	....
Banks	8 908 ..	....	....	....	....	....	....	....	....
Other sectors	8 909 ..	....	....	....	....	....	....	....	....
Other investment	8 753 ..	**70,300**	**73,940**	**115,364**	**140,424**	**157,887**	**162,997**	**255,003**	**331,494**
Trade credits	8 756 ..	....	....	....	....	....	....	6,440	8,607
General government	8 757 ..	....	....	....	....	....	....	....	....
of which: Short-term	8 759 ..	....	....	....	....	....	....	....	....
Other sectors	8 760 ..	....	....	....	....	....	....	....	....
of which: Short-term	8 762 ..	....	....	....	....	....	....	....	....
Loans	8 764 ..	....	....	....	....	....	....	167,020	194,422
Monetary authorities	8 765 ..	....	....	....	....	....	....	....	....
of which: Use of Fund credit and loans from the Fund	8 766 ..	....	....	....	....	....	....	....	....
of which: Short-term	8 768 ..	....	....	....	....	....	....	....	....
General government	8 769 ..	....	....	....	....	....	....	....	....
of which: Short-term	8 771 ..	....	....	....	....	....	....	....	....
Banks	8 772 ..	....	....	....	....	....	....	....	....
of which: Short-term	8 774 ..	....	....	....	....	....	....	....	....
Other sectors	8 775 ..	....	....	....	....	....	....	....	....
of which: Short-term	8 777 ..	....	....	....	....	....	....	....	....
Currency and deposits	8 780 ..	....	....	....	....	....	....	66,561	99,424
Monetary authorities	8 781 ..	....	....	....	....	....	....	....	....
General government	8 782 ..	....	....	....	....	....	....	....	....
Banks	8 783 ..	....	....	....	....	....	....	....	....
Other sectors	8 784 ..	....	....	....	....	....	....	....	....
Other liabilities	8 786 ..	....	....	....	....	....	....	14,982	29,042
Monetary authorities	8 787 ..	....	....	....	....	....	....	....	....
of which: Short-term	8 789 ..	....	....	....	....	....	....	....	....
General government	8 790 ..	....	....	....	....	....	....	....	....
of which: Short-term	8 792 ..	....	....	....	....	....	....	....	....
Banks	8 793 ..	....	....	....	....	....	....	....	....
of which: Short-term	8 795 ..	....	....	....	....	....	....	....	....
Other sectors	8 796 ..	....	....	....	....	....	....	....	....
of which: Short-term	8 798 ..	....	....	....	....	....	....	....	....
NET INTERNATIONAL INVESTMENT POSITION	8 995 ..	34,396	50,323	65,000	100,345	125,341	165,853	203,700	231,811
Conversion rates: Norwegian kroner per U.S. dollar (end of period)	0 102 ..	8.8485	9.0116	6.9657	6.6800	6.0400	6.7700	6.2600	5.4100

Table 1. ANALYTIC PRESENTATION, 2000–2007

(Millions of U.S. dollars)

	Code	2000	2001	2002	2003	2004	2005	2006	2007
A. Current Account[1]	4 993 Z.	**3,129**	**2,082**	**1,941**	**1,454**	**908**	**4,935**	**5,087**	**1,918**
Goods: exports f.o.b.	2 100 ..	11,318	11,074	11,170	11,670	13,381	18,692	21,586	24,723
Goods: imports f.o.b.	3 100 ..	−4,593	−5,308	−5,633	−6,086	−7,873	−8,029	−9,880	−14,343
Balance on Goods	4 100 ..	*6,725*	*5,766*	*5,537*	*5,584*	*5,508*	*10,663*	*11,706*	*10,380*
Services: credit	2 200 ..	452	606	606	655	739	754	931	1,163
Services: debit	3 200 ..	−1,758	−1,899	−1,880	−2,573	−3,123	−3,255	−3,847	−4,996
Balance on Goods and Services	4 991 ..	*5,418*	*4,473*	*4,263*	*3,666*	*3,124*	*8,163*	*8,790*	*6,546*
Income: credit	2 300 ..	291	307	242	317	761	830	1,549	2,026
Income: debit	3 300 ..	−1,129	−1,165	−962	−857	−1,152	−1,801	−2,464	−2,985
Balance on Goods, Services, and Income	4 992 ..	*4,581*	*3,614*	*3,543*	*3,126*	*2,733*	*7,193*	*7,875*	*5,587*
Current transfers: credit	2 379 Z.	....	....	....	....	....	....	....	....
Current transfers: debit	3 379 ..	−1,451	−1,532	−1,602	−1,672	−1,826	−2,257	−2,788	−3,670
B. Capital Account[1]	4 994 Z.	**8**	**−10**	**5**	**10**	**21**	**−16**	**−96**	**827**
Capital account: credit	2 994 Z.	34	8	5	10	21	....	....	861
Capital account: debit	3 994 ..	−26	−18	....	....	....	−16	−96	−34
Total, Groups A Plus B	4 981 ..	*3,137*	*2,072*	*1,946*	*1,464*	*928*	*4,920*	*4,991*	*2,745*
C. Financial Account[1]	4 995 W.	**−370**	**−502**	**−798**	**−261**	**360**	**−1,437**	**−2,826**	**2,384**
Direct investment abroad	4 505 ..	....	....	−3	−88	−42	−234	−328	−568
Direct investment in Oman	4 555 Z.	82	5	109	25	111	1,688	1,622	2,376
Portfolio investment assets	4 602 ..	....	42	23	−242	−174	−437	−1,495	775
Equity securities	4 610 ..	....	42	23	−242	−174	−437	−1,495	775
Debt securities	4 619 ..	....	....	....	....	....	....	....	....
Portfolio investment liabilities	4 652 Z.	−36	38	−101	12	162	479	806	2,056
Equity securities	4 660 ..	−10	23	−49	51	32	487	806	2,056
Debt securities	4 669 Z.	−26	16	−52	−39	130	−8	....	....
Financial derivatives	4 910 ..	....	....	....	....	....	....	....	....
Financial derivatives assets	4 900 ..	....	....	....	....	....	....	....	....
Financial derivatives liabilities	4 905 ..	....	....	....	....	....	....	....	....
Other investment assets	4 703 ..	−497	91	−296	−136	−977	−3,226	−6,050	−5,135
Monetary authorities	4 701 ..	....	....	....	....	....	....	....	....
General government	4 704 ..	−273	....	....	....	....	....	....	....
Banks	4 705 ..	−224	218	−244	−44	−593	−422	−1,221	−492
Other sectors	4 728 ..	....	....	81	−9	−39	−146	−508	−172
Other investment liabilities	4 753 W.	81	−679	−531	169	1,280	292	2,620	2,880
Monetary authorities	4 753 WA	....	....	....	....	....	....	....	....
General government	4 753 ZB	−114	−447	−598	−421	195	−440	508	8
Banks	4 753 ZC	−21	−112	−133	−226	29	−273	1,028	1,663
Other sectors	4 753 ZD	216	−120	200	760	989	929	997	1,105
Total, Groups A Through C	4 983 ..	*2,767*	*1,570*	*1,149*	*1,204*	*1,289*	*3,482*	*2,165*	*5,128*
D. Net Errors and Omissions	4 998 ..	**−504**	**−555**	**−842**	**−547**	**−427**	**−673**	**41**	**1,159**
Total, Groups A Through D	4 984 ..	*2,263*	*1,015*	*307*	*656*	*861*	*2,809*	*2,206*	*6,287*
E. Reserves and Related Items	4 802 A.	**−2,263**	**−1,015**	**−307**	**−656**	**−861**	**−2,809**	**−2,206**	**−6,287**
Reserve assets	4 802 ..	−2,263	−1,015	−307	−656	−861	−2,809	−2,206	−6,287
Use of Fund credit and loans	4 766 ..	....	....	....	....	....	....	....	....
Exceptional financing	4 920 ..	....	....	....	....	....	....	....	....
Conversion rates: rial Omani per U.S. dollar	0 101 ..	**.3845**	**.3845**	**.3845**	**.3845**	**.3845**	**.3845**	**.3845**	**.3845**

[1] Excludes components that have been classified in the categories of Group E.

Table 2. STANDARD PRESENTATION, 2000–2007

(Millions of U.S. dollars)

	Code	2000	2001	2002	2003	2004	2005	2006	2007
CURRENT ACCOUNT...............	4 993 ..	**3,129**	**2,082**	**1,941**	**1,454**	**908**	**4,935**	**5,087**	**1,918**
A. GOODS...............	4 100 ..	**6,725**	**5,766**	**5,537**	**5,584**	**5,508**	**10,663**	**11,706**	**10,380**
Credit...............	2 100 ..	**11,318**	**11,074**	**11,170**	**11,670**	**13,381**	**18,692**	**21,586**	**24,723**
General merchandise: exports f.o.b............	2 110 ..	11,318	11,074	11,170	11,670	13,381	18,692	21,586	24,723
Goods for processing: exports f.o.b.........	2 150 ..	....	....	....	....	....	....	....	....
Repairs on goods............	2 160 ..	....	....	....	....	....	....	....	....
Goods procured in ports by carriers.........	2 170 ..	....	....	....	....	....	....	....	....
Nonmonetary gold............	2 180 ..	....	....	....	....	....	....	....	....
Debit...............	3 100 ..	**−4,593**	**−5,308**	**−5,633**	**−6,086**	**−7,873**	**−8,029**	**−9,880**	**−14,343**
General merchandise: imports f.o.b............	3 110 ..	−4,593	−5,308	−5,633	−6,086	−7,873	−8,029	−9,880	−14,343
Goods for processing: imports f.o.b.........	3 150 ..	....	....	....	....	....	....	....	....
Repairs on goods............	3 160 ..	....	....	....	....	....	....	....	....
Goods procured in ports by carriers.........	3 170 ..	....	....	....	....	....	....	....	....
Nonmonetary gold............	3 180 ..	....	....	....	....	....	....	....	....
B. SERVICES...............	4 200 ..	**−1,307**	**−1,293**	**−1,274**	**−1,918**	**−2,384**	**−2,500**	**−2,916**	**−3,833**
Total credit...............	2 200 ..	*452*	*606*	*606*	*655*	*739*	*754*	*931*	*1,163*
Total debit...............	3 200 ..	*−1,758*	*−1,899*	*−1,880*	*−2,573*	*−3,123*	*−3,255*	*−3,847*	*−4,996*
Transportation services, credit...............	2 205 ..	**195**	**198**	**190**	**239**	**289**	**299**	**317**	**385**
Passenger...............	2 850 ..	*156*	*153*	*146*	*161*	*190*	*198*	*205*	*257*
Freight...............	2 851 ..	*39*	*44*	*44*	*78*	*99*	*101*	*112*	*127*
Other...............	2 852 ..	....	....	....	....	....	....	....	....
Sea transport, passenger............	2 207 ..	....	....	....	....	....	....	....	....
Sea transport, freight............	2 208 ..	39	44	44	78	99	101	112	127
Sea transport, other............	2 209 ..	....	....	....	....	....	....	....	....
Air transport, passenger............	2 211 ..	156	153	146	161	190	198	205	257
Air transport, freight............	2 212 ..	....	....	....	....	....	....	....	....
Air transport, other............	2 213 ..	....	....	....	....	....	....	....	....
Other transport, passenger............	2 215 ..	....	....	....	....	....	....	....	....
Other transport, freight............	2 216 ..	....	....	....	....	....	....	....	....
Other transport, other............	2 217 ..	....	....	....	....	....	....	....	....
Transportation services, debit...............	3 205 ..	**−647**	**−749**	**−772**	**−820**	**−1,017**	**−1,051**	**−1,260**	**−1,723**
Passenger...............	3 850 ..	*−158*	*−185*	*−172*	*−174*	*−179*	*−195*	*−208*	*−200*
Freight...............	3 851 ..	*−489*	*−565*	*−601*	*−646*	*−837*	*−856*	*−1,053*	*−1,523*
Other...............	3 852 ..	....	....	....	....	....	....	....	....
Sea transport, passenger............	3 207 ..	....	....	....	....	....	....	....	....
Sea transport, freight............	3 208 ..	−489	−565	−601	−646	−837	−856	−1,053	−1,523
Sea transport, other............	3 209 ..	....	....	....	....	....	....	....	....
Air transport, passenger............	3 211 ..	−158	−185	−172	−174	−179	−195	−208	−200
Air transport, freight............	3 212 ..	....	....	....	....	....	....	....	....
Air transport, other............	3 213 ..	....	....	....	....	....	....	....	....
Other transport, passenger............	3 215 ..	....	....	....	....	....	....	....	....
Other transport, freight............	3 216 ..	....	....	....	....	....	....	....	....
Other transport, other............	3 217 ..	....	....	....	....	....	....	....	....
Travel, credit...............	2 236 ..	**221**	**385**	**393**	**385**	**414**	**401**	**538**	**645**
Business travel............	2 237 ..	....	117	120	116	125	121	163	195
Personal travel............	2 240 ..	221	268	273	269	289	280	376	450
Travel, debit...............	3 236 ..	**−471**	**−518**	**−530**	**−630**	**−669**	**−692**	**−711**	**−744**
Business travel............	3 237 ..	....	−68	−67	−83	−92	−102	−107	−120
Personal travel............	3 240 ..	−471	−450	−463	−546	−577	−590	−604	−624
Other services, credit...............	2 200 BA	**36**	**23**	**23**	**31**	**36**	**55**	**75**	**133**
Communications............	2 245 ..	23	21	21	18	21	36	52	75
Construction............	2 249 ..	....	....	....	....	....	....	....	....
Insurance............	2 253 ..	13	3	3	3	3	5	5	8
Financial............	2 260 ..	....	....	....	....	....	....	....	....
Computer and information............	2 262 ..	....	....	....	....	....	....	....	....
Royalties and licence fees............	2 266 ..	....	....	....	....	....	....	....	....
Other business services............	2 268 ..	....	....	....	10	13	13	18	49
Personal, cultural, and recreational............	2 287 ..	....	....	....	....	....	....	....	....
Government, n.i.e............	2 291 ..	....	....	....	....	....	....	....	....
Other services, debit...............	3 200 BA	**−641**	**−632**	**−577**	**−1,124**	**−1,437**	**−1,512**	**−1,876**	**−2,529**
Communications............	3 245 ..	−39	−39	−31	−29	−36	−42	−44	−47
Construction............	3 249 ..	....	....	....	....	....	....	....	....
Insurance............	3 253 ..	−114	−96	−172	−221	−238	−285	−334	−383
Financial............	3 260 ..	....	....	....	....	....	....	....	....
Computer and information............	3 262 ..	....	....	....	....	....	....	....	....
Royalties and licence fees............	3 266 ..	....	....	....	....	....	....	....	....
Other business services............	3 268 ..	−487	−497	−375	−874	−1,163	−1,186	−1,498	−2,099
Personal, cultural, and recreational............	3 287 ..	....	....	....	....	....	....	....	....
Government, n.i.e............	3 291 ..	....	....	....	....	....	....	....	....

Table 2 (Continued). STANDARD PRESENTATION, 2000–2007

(Millions of U.S. dollars)

	Code	2000	2001	2002	2003	2004	2005	2006	2007
C. INCOME	4 300	**−838**	**−859**	**−720**	**−540**	**−391**	**−970**	**−915**	**−959**
Total credit	2 300	*291*	*307*	*242*	*317*	*761*	*830*	*1,549*	*2,026*
Total debit	3 300	*−1,129*	*−1,165*	*−962*	*−857*	*−1,152*	*−1,801*	*−2,464*	*−2,985*
Compensation of employees, credit	2 310	**39**	**39**	**39**	**39**	**39**	**39**	**39**	**39**
Compensation of employees, debit	3 310	....	....	....	....	....	....	....	....
Investment income, credit	2 320	**252**	**268**	**203**	**278**	**722**	**791**	**1,510**	**1,987**
Direct investment income	2 330	....	....	....	39	39	31	94	49
Dividends and distributed branch profits	2 332	....	....	....	....	....	....	....	....
Reinvested earnings and undistributed branch profits	2 333	....	....	....	....	....	....	....	....
Income on debt (interest)	2 334	....	....	....	....	....	....	....	....
Portfolio investment income	2 339	....	....	....	....	....	....	....	....
Income on equity	2 340	....	....	....	....	....	....	....	....
Income on bonds and notes	2 350	....	....	....	....	....	....	....	....
Income on money market instruments	2 360	....	....	....	....	....	....	....	....
Other investment income	2 370	252	268	203	239	683	760	1,416	1,937
Investment income, debit	3 320	**−1,129**	**−1,165**	**−962**	**−857**	**−1,152**	**−1,801**	**−2,464**	**−2,985**
Direct investment income	3 330	−830	−986	−796	−717	−925	−1,486	−1,995	−2,347
Dividends and distributed branch profits	3 332	....	....	....	....	....	....	....	....
Reinvested earnings and undistributed branch profits	3 333	....	....	....	....	....	....	....	....
Income on debt (interest)	3 334	....	....	....	....	....	....	....	....
Portfolio investment income	3 339	....	....	....	....	....	....	....	....
Income on equity	3 340	....	....	....	....	....	....	....	....
Income on bonds and notes	3 350	....	....	....	....	....	....	....	....
Income on money market instruments	3 360	....	....	....	....	....	....	....	....
Other investment income	3 370	−299	−180	−166	−140	−227	−315	−469	−637
D. CURRENT TRANSFERS	4 379	**−1,451**	**−1,532**	**−1,602**	**−1,672**	**−1,826**	**−2,257**	**−2,788**	**−3,670**
Credit	2 379	....	....	....	....	....	....	....	....
General government	2 380	....	....	....	....	....	....	....	....
Other sectors	2 390	....	....	....	....	....	....	....	....
Workers' remittances	2 391	....	....	....	....	....	....	....	....
Other current transfers	2 392	....	....	....	....	....	....	....	....
Debit	3 379	**−1,451**	**−1,532**	**−1,602**	**−1,672**	**−1,826**	**−2,257**	**−2,788**	**−3,670**
General government	3 380	....	....	....	....	....	....	....	....
Other sectors	3 390	−1,451	−1,532	−1,602	−1,672	−1,826	−2,257	−2,788	−3,670
Workers' remittances	3 391	−1,451	−1,532	−1,602	−1,672	−1,826	−2,257	−2,788	−3,670
Other current transfers	3 392	....	....	....	....	....	....	....	....
CAPITAL AND FINANCIAL ACCOUNT	4 996	**−2,626**	**−1,527**	**−1,099**	**−907**	**−480**	**−4,262**	**−5,128**	**−3,076**
CAPITAL ACCOUNT	4 994	**8**	**−10**	**5**	**10**	**21**	**−16**	**−96**	**827**
Total credit	2 994	*34*	*8*	*5*	*10*	*21*	....	....	*861*
Total debit	3 994	*−26*	*−18*	....	....	....	*−16*	*−96*	*−34*
Capital transfers, credit	2 400	**34**	**8**	**5**	**10**	**21**	....	....	**861**
General government	2 401	34	8	5	10	21	....	....	861
Debt forgiveness	2 402	....	....	....	....	....	....	....	....
Other capital transfers	2 410	34	8	5	10	21	....	....	861
Other sectors	2 430	....	....	....	....	....	....	....	....
Migrants' transfers	2 431	....	....	....	....	....	....	....	....
Debt forgiveness	2 432	....	....	....	....	....	....	....	....
Other capital transfers	2 440	....	....	....	....	....	....	....	....
Capital transfers, debit	3 400	**−26**	**−18**	....	....	....	**−16**	**−96**	**−34**
General government	3 401	−26	−18	....	....	....	−16	−96	−34
Debt forgiveness	3 402	....	....	....	....	....	....	....	....
Other capital transfers	3 410	−26	−18	....	....	....	−16	−96	−34
Other sectors	3 430	....	....	....	....	....	....	....	....
Migrants' transfers	3 431	....	....	....	....	....	....	....	....
Debt forgiveness	3 432	....	....	....	....	....	....	....	....
Other capital transfers	3 440	....	....	....	....	....	....	....	....
Nonproduced nonfinancial assets, credit	2 480	....	....	....	....	....	....	....	....
Nonproduced nonfinancial assets, debit	3 480	....	....	....	....	....	....	....	....

Table 2 (Continued). STANDARD PRESENTATION, 2000–2007

(Millions of U.S. dollars)

	Code	2000	2001	2002	2003	2004	2005	2006	2007
FINANCIAL ACCOUNT	4 995	−2,633	−1,517	−1,105	−917	−501	−4,246	−5,032	−3,903
A. DIRECT INVESTMENT	4 500	82	5	107	−63	69	1,455	1,294	1,808
Direct investment abroad	4 505	....	....	−3	−88	−42	−234	−328	−568
Equity capital	4 510	....	....	−3	−88	−42	−234	−328	−568
Claims on affiliated enterprises	4 515	....	....	−3	−88	−42	−234	−328	−568
Liabilities to affiliated enterprises	4 520	....	....	....	....	....	....	....	....
Reinvested earnings	4 525	....	....	....	....	....	....	....	....
Other capital	4 530	....	....	....	....	....	....	....	....
Claims on affiliated enterprises	4 535	....	....	....	....	....	....	....	....
Liabilities to affiliated enterprises	4 540	....	....	....	....	....	....	....	....
Direct investment in Oman	4 555	82	5	109	25	111	1,688	1,622	2,376
Equity capital	4 560	82	5	109	25	111	1,688	1,622	2,376
Claims on direct investors	4 565	....	....	....	....	....	....	....	....
Liabilities to direct investors	4 570	82	5	109	25	111	1,688	1,622	2,376
Reinvested earnings	4 575	....	....	....	....	....	....	....	....
Other capital	4 580	....	....	....	....	....	....	....	....
Claims on direct investors	4 585	....	....	....	....	....	....	....	....
Liabilities to direct investors	4 590	....	....	....	....	....	....	....	....
B. PORTFOLIO INVESTMENT	4 600	−36	80	−77	−229	−12	42	−690	2,830
Assets	4 602	....	42	23	−242	−174	−437	−1,495	775
Equity securities	4 610	....	42	23	−242	−174	−437	−1,495	775
Monetary authorities	4 611	....	....	....	....	....	....	....	....
General government	4 612	....	....	....	....	....	....	....	....
Banks	4 613	....	....	....	....	....	....	....	....
Other sectors	4 614	....	....	....	....	....	....	....	....
Debt securities	4 619	....	....	....	....	....	....	....	....
Bonds and notes	4 620	....	....	....	....	....	....	....	....
Monetary authorities	4 621	....	....	....	....	....	....	....	....
General government	4 622	....	....	....	....	....	....	....	....
Banks	4 623	....	....	....	....	....	....	....	....
Other sectors	4 624	....	....	....	....	....	....	....	....
Money market instruments	4 630	....	....	....	....	....	....	....	....
Monetary authorities	4 631	....	....	....	....	....	....	....	....
General government	4 632	....	....	....	....	....	....	....	....
Banks	4 633	....	....	....	....	....	....	....	....
Other sectors	4 634	....	....	....	....	....	....	....	....
Liabilities	4 652	−36	38	−101	12	162	479	806	2,056
Equity securities	4 660	−10	23	−49	51	32	487	806	2,056
Banks	4 663	8	....	....	....	32	87	50	156
Other sectors	4 664	−18	....	....	51	....	400	756	1,899
Debt securities	4 669	−26	16	−52	−39	130	−8	....	....
Bonds and notes	4 670	−26	16	−52	−39	130	−8	....	....
Monetary authorities	4 671	....	....	....	....	....	....	....	....
General government	4 672	−26	16	−52	−39	130	−8	....	....
Banks	4 673	....	....	....	....	....	....	....	....
Other sectors	4 674	....	....	....	....	....	....	....	....
Money market instruments	4 680	....	....	....	....	....	....	....	....
Monetary authorities	4 681	....	....	....	....	....	....	....	....
General government	4 682	....	....	....	....	....	....	....	....
Banks	4 683	....	....	....	....	....	....	....	....
Other sectors	4 684	....	....	....	....	....	....	....	....
C. FINANCIAL DERIVATIVES	4 910	....	....	....	....	....	....	....	....
Monetary authorities	4 911	....	....	....	....	....	....	....	....
General government	4 912	....	....	....	....	....	....	....	....
Banks	4 913	....	....	....	....	....	....	....	....
Other sectors	4 914	....	....	....	....	....	....	....	....
Assets	4 900	....	....	....	....	....	....	....	....
Monetary authorities	4 901	....	....	....	....	....	....	....	....
General government	4 902	....	....	....	....	....	....	....	....
Banks	4 903	....	....	....	....	....	....	....	....
Other sectors	4 904	....	....	....	....	....	....	....	....
Liabilities	4 905	....	....	....	....	....	....	....	....
Monetary authorities	4 906	....	....	....	....	....	....	....	....
General government	4 907	....	....	....	....	....	....	....	....
Banks	4 908	....	....	....	....	....	....	....	....
Other sectors	4 909	....	....	....	....	....	....	....	....

Table 2 (Concluded). STANDARD PRESENTATION, 2000–2007

(Millions of U.S. dollars)

	Code	2000	2001	2002	2003	2004	2005	2006	2007
D. OTHER INVESTMENT	4 700 ..	−416	−588	−827	32	303	−2,934	−3,430	−2,255
Assets	4 703 ..	−497	91	−296	−136	−977	−3,226	−6,050	−5,135
Trade credits	4 706 ..	16	....	88	−3	1	−48	−68	−119
General government	4 707 ..	16	....	....	....	....	....	....	....
of which: Short-term	4 709 ..	*16*	....	....	....	....	....	....	....
Other sectors	4 710 ..	....	....	88	−3	1	−48	−68	−119
of which: Short-term	4 712 ..	....	....	*88*	*−3*	*1*	*−48*	*−68*	*−119*
Loans	4 714 ..	....	....	....	....	....	....	....	....
Monetary authorities	4 715 ..	....	....	....	....	....	....	....	....
of which: Short-term	4 718 ..	....	....	....	....	....	....	....	....
General government	4 719 ..	....	....	....	....	....	....	....	....
of which: Short-term	4 721 ..	....	....	....	....	....	....	....	....
Banks	4 722 ..	....	....	....	....	....	....	....	....
of which: Short-term	4 724 ..	....	....	....	....	....	....	....	....
Other sectors	4 725 ..	....	....	....	....	....	....	....	....
of which: Short-term	4 727 ..	....	....	....	....	....	....	....	....
Currency and deposits	4 730 ..	−224	218	−252	−51	−633	−520	−1,661	−545
Monetary authorities	4 731 ..	....	....	....	....	....	....	....	....
General government	4 732 ..	....	....	....	....	....	....	....	....
Banks	4 733 ..	−224	218	−244	−44	−593	−422	−1,221	−492
Other sectors	4 734 ..	....	....	−8	−7	−40	−97	−440	−53
Other assets	4 736 ..	−289	−127	−133	−83	−345	−2,658	−4,321	−4,471
Monetary authorities	4 737 ..	....	....	....	....	....	....	....	....
of which: Short-term	4 739 ..	....	....	....	....	....	....	....	....
General government	4 740 ..	−289	....	....	....	....	....	....	....
of which: Short-term	4 742 ..	....	....	....	....	....	....	....	....
Banks	4 743 ..	....	....	....	....	....	....	....	....
of which: Short-term	4 745 ..	....	....	....	....	....	....	....	....
Other sectors	4 746 ..	....	....	....	....	....	....	....	....
of which: Short-term	4 748 ..	....	....	....	....	....	....	....	....
Liabilities	4 753 ..	81	−679	−531	169	1,280	292	2,620	2,880
Trade credits	4 756 ..	....	....	....	56	67	75	86	104
General government	4 757 ..	....	....	....	....	....	....	....	....
of which: Short-term	4 759 ..	....	....	....	....	....	....	....	....
Other sectors	4 760 ..	....	....	....	....	....	....	....	....
of which: Short-term	4 762 ..	....	....	....	....	....	....	....	....
Loans	4 764 ..	102	−567	−398	−135	583	−59	934	489
Monetary authorities	4 765 ..	....	....	....	....	....	....	....	....
of which: Use of Fund credit and loans from the Fund	4 766 ..	....	....	....	....	....	....	....	....
of which: Short-term	4 768 ..	....	....	....	....	....	....	....	....
General government	4 769 ..	−114	−447	−598	−421	195	−440	508	8
of which: Short-term	4 771 ..	....	....	....	....	....	....	....	....
Banks	4 772 ..	....	....	....	....	....	....	....	....
of which: Short-term	4 774 ..	....	....	....	....	....	....	....	....
Other sectors	4 775 ..	216	−120	200	286	388	380	425	481
of which: Short-term	4 777 ..	....	....	....	....	....	....	....	....
Currency and deposits	4 780 ..	−21	−112	−133	−226	29	−273	1,028	1,663
Monetary authorities	4 781 ..	....	....	....	....	....	....	....	....
General government	4 782 ..	....	....	....	....	....	....	....	....
Banks	4 783 ..	−21	−112	−133	−226	29	−273	1,028	1,663
Other sectors	4 784 ..	....	....	....	....	....	....	....	....
Other liabilities	4 786 ..	....	....	....	473	601	549	572	624
Monetary authorities	4 787 ..	....	....	....	....	....	....	....	....
of which: Short-term	4 789 ..	....	....	....	....	....	....	....	....
General government	4 790 ..	....	....	....	....	....	....	....	....
of which: Short-term	4 792 ..	....	....	....	....	....	....	....	....
Banks	4 793 ..	....	....	....	....	....	....	....	....
of which: Short-term	4 795 ..	....	....	....	....	....	....	....	....
Other sectors	4 796 ..	....	....	....	473	601	549	572	624
of which: Short-term	4 798 ..	....	....	....	....	....	....	....	....
E. RESERVE ASSETS	4 802 ..	−2,263	−1,015	−307	−656	−861	−2,809	−2,206	−6,287
Monetary gold	4 812 ..	....	−12	80	....	....	....	....	....
Special drawing rights	4 811 ..	−2	−2	−2	−2	−2	−2	−1	−1
Reserve position in the Fund	4 810 ..	....	−19	−11	−5	20	57	9	8
Foreign exchange	4 803 ..	345	−981	−374	−650	−880	−2,864	−2,213	−6,294
Other claims	4 813 ..	−2,606	....	....	....	....	....	....	....
NET ERRORS AND OMISSIONS	4 998 ..	−504	−555	−842	−547	−427	−673	41	1,159

Table 1. ANALYTIC PRESENTATION, 2000–2007

(Millions of U.S. dollars)

	Code	2000	2001	2002	2003	2004	2005	2006	2007
A. Current Account[1]	4 993 Z.	**−85**	**1,878**	**3,854**	**3,573**	**−817**	**−3,606**	**−6,750**	**−8,253**
Goods: exports f.o.b.	2 100 ..	8,739	9,131	9,832	11,869	13,297	15,432	17,049	18,121
Goods: imports f.o.b.	3 100 ..	−9,896	−9,741	−10,428	−11,978	−16,693	−21,773	−26,696	−28,761
Balance on Goods	4 100 ..	*−1,157*	*−610*	*−596*	*−109*	*−3,396*	*−6,341*	*−9,647*	*−10,640*
Services: credit	2 200 ..	1,380	1,459	2,429	2,968	2,749	3,678	3,506	3,758
Services: debit	3 200 ..	−2,252	−2,330	−2,241	−3,294	−5,333	−7,508	−8,418	−8,764
Balance on Goods and Services	4 991 ..	*−2,029*	*−1,481*	*−408*	*−435*	*−5,980*	*−10,171*	*−14,559*	*−15,646*
Income: credit	2 300 ..	118	113	128	180	221	658	864	1,355
Income: debit	3 300 ..	−2,336	−2,189	−2,414	−2,404	−2,584	−3,172	−3,995	−5,048
Balance on Goods, Services, and Income	4 992 ..	*−4,247*	*−3,557*	*−2,694*	*−2,659*	*−8,343*	*−12,685*	*−17,691*	*−19,339*
Current transfers: credit	2 379 Z.	4,200	5,496	6,593	6,300	7,666	9,169	11,030	11,215
Current transfers: debit	3 379 ..	−38	−61	−45	−68	−140	−90	−89	−129
B. Capital Account[1]	4 994 Z.	....	....	**40**	**1,138**	**591**	**202**	**345**	**175**
Capital account: credit	2 994 Z.	....	....	40	1,140	596	214	351	181
Capital account: debit	3 994 ..	....	....	....	−2	−5	−12	−6	−6
Total, Groups A Plus B	4 981 ..	*−85*	*1,878*	*3,894*	*4,711*	*−226*	*−3,404*	*−6,405*	*−8,078*
C. Financial Account[1]	4 995 W.	**−3,099**	**−389**	**−784**	**−1,751**	**−1,810**	**4,079**	**7,436**	**10,103**
Direct investment abroad	4 505 ..	−11	−31	−28	−19	−56	−44	−109	−98
Direct investment in Pakistan	4 555 Z.	308	383	823	534	1,118	2,201	4,273	5,331
Portfolio investment assets	4 602 ..	....	....	....	−2	9	19	−4	5
Equity securities	4 610 ..	....	....	....	−2	9	19	−4	5
Debt securities	4 619 ..	....	....	....	....	....	....	....	....
Portfolio investment liabilities	4 652 Z.	−451	−192	−567	−119	392	906	1,973	2,083
Equity securities	4 660 ..	35	−130	79	−26	49	451	1,152	1,276
Debt securities	4 669 Z.	−486	−62	−646	−93	343	455	821	807
Financial derivatives	4 910 ..	....	....	....	....	....	....	....	....
Financial derivatives assets	4 900 ..	....	....	....	....	....	....	....	....
Financial derivatives liabilities	4 905 ..	....	....	....	....	....	....	....	....
Other investment assets	4 703 ..	−437	53	−64	−542	−1,339	126	−242	−107
Monetary authorities	4 701 ..	....	....	....	....	....	....	....	....
General government	4 704 ..	−15	44	−5	19	−1	1	−1	6
Banks	4 705 ..	−18	−17	−6	−247	−984	471	−41	−15
Other sectors	4 728 ..	−404	26	−53	−314	−354	−346	−200	−98
Other investment liabilities	4 753 W.	−2,508	−602	−948	−1,603	−1,934	871	1,545	2,889
Monetary authorities	4 753 WA	−168	−13	−254	....	−15	8	2	−10
General government	4 753 ZB	−729	−37	−162	−1,571	−1,335	661	921	1,864
Banks	4 753 ZC	−1,160	−14	−81	29	22	68	−3	186
Other sectors	4 753 ZD	−451	−538	−451	−61	−606	134	625	849
Total, Groups A Through C	4 983 ..	*−3,184*	*1,489*	*3,110*	*2,960*	*−2,036*	*675*	*1,031*	*2,025*
D. Net Errors and Omissions	4 998 ..	**557**	**708**	**974**	**−52**	**685**	**−200**	**520**	**102**
Total, Groups A Through D	4 984 ..	*−2,627*	*2,197*	*4,084*	*2,908*	*−1,351*	*475*	*1,551*	*2,127*
E. Reserves and Related Items	4 802 A.	**2,627**	**−2,197**	**−4,084**	**−2,908**	**1,351**	**−475**	**−1,551**	**−2,127**
Reserve assets	4 802 ..	7	−2,716	−4,525	−3,003	1,728	−176	−1,544	−1,976
Use of Fund credit and loans	4 766 ..	−101	328	68	−112	−323	−244	−106	−151
Exceptional financing	4 920 ..	2,721	192	373	207	−55	−55	100	....
Conversion rates: Pakistan rupees per U.S. dollar	0 101 ..	**53.648**	**61.927**	**59.724**	**57.752**	**58.258**	**59.514**	**60.271**	**60.739**

[1] Excludes components that have been classified in the categories of Group E.

Table 2. STANDARD PRESENTATION, 2000–2007

(Millions of U.S. dollars)

	Code	2000	2001	2002	2003	2004	2005	2006	2007
CURRENT ACCOUNT........................	4 993 ..	−85	1,878	3,854	3,573	−817	−3,606	−6,750	−8,253
A. GOODS........................	4 100 ..	−1,157	−610	−596	−109	−3,396	−6,341	−9,647	−10,640
Credit........................	2 100 ..	8,739	9,131	9,832	11,869	13,297	15,432	17,049	18,121
General merchandise: exports f.o.b........	2 110 ..	8,739	9,131	9,792	11,785	13,237	15,284	16,910	17,943
Goods for processing: exports f.o.b........	2 150 ..	....	....	....	....	....	....	....	....
Repairs on goods........................	2 160 ..	....	....	....	....	6	....	....	....
Goods procured in ports by carriers........	2 170 ..	....	....	40	84	54	148	139	178
Nonmonetary gold........................	2 180 ..	....	....	....	....	....	....	....	....
Debit........................	3 100 ..	−9,896	−9,741	−10,428	−11,978	−16,693	−21,773	−26,696	−28,761
General merchandise: imports f.o.b........	3 110 ..	−9,896	−9,741	−10,428	−11,929	−16,498	−21,456	−26,314	−28,395
Goods for processing: imports f.o.b........	3 150 ..	....	....	....	....	....	....	....	....
Repairs on goods........................	3 160 ..	....	....	....	....	−50	−90	−99	−137
Goods procured in ports by carriers........	3 170 ..	....	....	....	−49	−145	−227	−283	−229
Nonmonetary gold........................	3 180 ..	....	....	....	....	....	....	....	....
B. SERVICES........................	4 200 ..	−872	−871	188	−326	−2,584	−3,830	−4,912	−5,006
Total credit........................	2 200 ..	*1,380*	*1,459*	*2,429*	*2,968*	*2,749*	*3,678*	*3,506*	*3,758*
Total debit........................	3 200 ..	*−2,252*	*−2,330*	*−2,241*	*−3,294*	*−5,333*	*−7,508*	*−8,418*	*−8,764*
Transportation services, credit............	2 205 ..	840	818	792	836	940	1,076	1,112	1,071
Passenger........................	2 850 ..	*470*	*445*	*465*	*498*	*586*	*646*	*664*	*624*
Freight........................	2 851 ..	*77*	*83*	*99*	*122*	*100*	*118*	*135*	*148*
Other........................	2 852 ..	*293*	*290*	*228*	*216*	*254*	*312*	*313*	*299*
Sea transport, passenger..................	2 207 ..	....	....	....	....	....	....	....	....
Sea transport, freight....................	2 208 ..	30	36	49	26	25	27	29	32
Sea transport, other.....................	2 209 ..	94	99	100	113	103	151	145	123
Air transport, passenger..................	2 211 ..	470	445	465	498	586	646	664	624
Air transport, freight....................	2 212 ..	47	47	50	96	75	91	106	116
Air transport, other.....................	2 213 ..	199	191	128	103	151	161	168	176
Other transport, passenger...............	2 215 ..	....	....	....	....	....	....	....	....
Other transport, freight..................	2 216 ..	....	....	....	....	....	....	....	....
Other transport, other...................	2 217 ..	....	....	....	....	....	....	....	....
Transportation services, debit............	3 205 ..	−1,517	−1,553	−1,388	−1,585	−2,076	−2,614	−3,027	−3,253
Passenger........................	3 850 ..	*−324*	*−303*	*−236*	*−238*	*−344*	*−473*	*−484*	*−450*
Freight........................	3 851 ..	*−808*	*−820*	*−855*	*−1,015*	*−1,438*	*−1,837*	*−2,192*	*−2,413*
Other........................	3 852 ..	*−385*	*−430*	*−297*	*−332*	*−294*	*−304*	*−351*	*−390*
Sea transport, passenger..................	3 207 ..	....	....	....	....	....	....	....	....
Sea transport, freight....................	3 208 ..	−808	−820	−855	−955	−1,285	−1,635	−1,935	−2,054
Sea transport, other.....................	3 209 ..	−15	−26	−17	−30	−21	−31	−47	−54
Air transport, passenger..................	3 211 ..	−324	−303	−236	−238	−344	−473	−484	−450
Air transport, freight....................	3 212 ..	....	....	....	−54	−136	−180	−230	−327
Air transport, other.....................	3 213 ..	−370	−404	−280	−302	−275	−275	−304	−336
Other transport, passenger...............	3 215 ..	....	....	....	....	....	....	....	....
Other transport, freight..................	3 216 ..	....	....	....	−6	−17	−22	−27	−32
Other transport, other...................	3 217 ..	....	....	....	....	2	2	....	....
Travel, credit........................	2 236 ..	81	88	97	122	179	182	255	276
Business travel........................	2 237 ..	....	....	....	1	2	8	13	14
Personal travel........................	2 240 ..	81	88	97	121	177	174	242	262
Travel, debit........................	3 236 ..	−250	−252	−255	−925	−1,268	−1,280	−1,545	−1,593
Business travel........................	3 237 ..	−6	−8	−3	−23	−102	−121	−71	−46
Personal travel........................	3 240 ..	−244	−244	−252	−902	−1,166	−1,159	−1,474	−1,547
Other services, credit....................	2 200 BA	459	553	1,540	2,010	1,630	2,420	2,139	2,411
Communications........................	2 245 ..	190	202	332	190	233	284	157	128
Construction........................	2 249 ..	....	....	....	4	24	18	31	66
Insurance........................	2 253 ..	5	18	18	22	19	32	19	36
Financial........................	2 260 ..	10	11	17	12	40	47	65	67
Computer and information................	2 262 ..	22	19	21	34	38	59	87	126
Royalties and licence fees................	2 266 ..	....	2	6	8	10	15	53	37
Other business services..................	2 268 ..	136	144	213	247	236	328	465	413
Personal, cultural, and recreational........	2 287 ..	....	....	....	1	....	2	1	1
Government, n.i.e........................	2 291 ..	96	157	933	1,492	1,030	1,635	1,261	1,537
Other services, debit....................	3 200 BA	−485	−525	−598	−784	−1,989	−3,614	−3,846	−3,918
Communications........................	3 245 ..	−15	−19	−27	−45	−46	−84	−89	−101
Construction........................	3 249 ..	....	....	....	−12	−8	−132	−58	−43
Insurance........................	3 253 ..	−34	−54	−68	−73	−91	−126	−125	−141
Financial........................	3 260 ..	−45	−46	−53	−73	−75	−124	−132	−125
Computer and information................	3 262 ..	....	....	....	−6	−18	−34	−65	−122
Royalties and licence fees................	3 266 ..	−28	−19	−18	−36	−86	−109	−106	−107
Other business services..................	3 268 ..	−220	−273	−286	−347	−1,431	−2,695	−2,944	−2,924
Personal, cultural, and recreational........	3 287 ..	....	....	....	....	−2	−8	−3	....
Government, n.i.e........................	3 291 ..	−143	−114	−146	−192	−232	−302	−324	−355

Table 2 (Continued). STANDARD PRESENTATION, 2000–2007

(Millions of U.S. dollars)

	Code	2000	2001	2002	2003	2004	2005	2006	2007
C. INCOME	4 300	**−2,218**	**−2,076**	**−2,286**	**−2,224**	**−2,363**	**−2,514**	**−3,131**	**−3,693**
Total credit	2 300	*118*	*113*	*128*	*180*	*221*	*658*	*864*	*1,355*
Total debit	3 300	*−2,336*	*−2,189*	*−2,414*	*−2,404*	*−2,584*	*−3,172*	*−3,995*	*−5,048*
Compensation of employees, credit	2 310	....	....	....	1	2	3	8	6
Compensation of employees, debit	3 310	....	....	....	....	−1	−1	−2	....
Investment income, credit	2 320	**118**	**113**	**128**	**179**	**219**	**655**	**856**	**1,349**
Direct investment income	2 330	2	3	2	3	18	18	48	20
Dividends and distributed branch profits	2 332	2	3	2	3	18	18	48	19
Reinvested earnings and undistributed branch profits	2 333	....	....	....	....	....	....	....	....
Income on debt (interest)	2 334	....	....	....	....	....	....	....	1
Portfolio investment income	2 339	....	....	1	5	17	328	357	670
Income on equity	2 340	....	....	1	3	7	1	4	10
Income on bonds and notes	2 350	....	....	....	2	9	27	7	5
Income on money market instruments	2 360	....	....	....	....	1	300	346	655
Other investment income	2 370	116	110	125	171	184	309	451	659
Investment income, debit	3 320	**−2,336**	**−2,189**	**−2,414**	**−2,404**	**−2,583**	**−3,171**	**−3,993**	**−5,048**
Direct investment income	3 330	−429	−470	−576	−893	−1,486	−1,871	−2,580	−2,974
Dividends and distributed branch profits	3 332	−330	−371	−460	−739	−1,238	−1,447	−1,886	−2,003
Reinvested earnings and undistributed branch profits	3 333	−99	−99	−116	−154	−248	−424	−695	−971
Income on debt (interest)	3 334	....	....	....	....	....	....	....	....
Portfolio investment income	3 339	−372	−399	−562	−360	−197	−468	−473	−941
Income on equity	3 340	−149	−206	−421	−257	−104	−137	−155	−271
Income on bonds and notes	3 350	−206	−178	−141	−79	−43	−135	−140	−189
Income on money market instruments	3 360	−17	−15	....	−24	−50	−196	−178	−481
Other investment income	3 370	−1,535	−1,320	−1,276	−1,151	−900	−832	−940	−1,133
D. CURRENT TRANSFERS	4 379	**4,162**	**5,435**	**6,548**	**6,232**	**7,526**	**9,079**	**10,941**	**11,086**
Credit	2 379	**4,200**	**5,496**	**6,593**	**6,300**	**7,666**	**9,169**	**11,030**	**11,215**
General government	2 380	1,005	1,352	1,037	813	163	455	677	424
Other sectors	2 390	3,195	4,144	5,556	5,487	7,503	8,714	10,353	10,791
Workers' remittances	2 391	1,075	1,461	3,554	3,963	3,943	4,277	5,113	5,992
Other current transfers	2 392	2,120	2,683	2,002	1,524	3,560	4,437	5,240	4,799
Debit	3 379	**−38**	**−61**	**−45**	**−68**	**−140**	**−90**	**−89**	**−129**
General government	3 380	−4	−4	−10	−14	−35	−22	−26	−55
Other sectors	3 390	−34	−57	−35	−54	−105	−68	−63	−74
Workers' remittances	3 391	−2	−3	−2	−5	−9	−2	−1	....
Other current transfers	3 392	−32	−54	−33	−49	−96	−66	−62	−74
CAPITAL AND FINANCIAL ACCOUNT	4 996	**−472**	**−2,586**	**−4,828**	**−3,521**	**132**	**3,806**	**6,230**	**8,151**
CAPITAL ACCOUNT	4 994	....	....	**40**	**1,138**	**591**	**202**	**345**	**175**
Total credit	2 994	....	....	*40*	*1,140*	*596*	*214*	*351*	*181*
Total debit	3 994	....	....	....	*−2*	*−5*	*−12*	*−6*	*−6*
Capital transfers, credit	2 400	....	....	**40**	**1,140**	**596**	**202**	**331**	**181**
General government	2 401	....	....	40	1,135	576	161	301	164
Debt forgiveness	2 402	....	....	....	1,000	495	....	....	....
Other capital transfers	2 410	....	....	40	135	81	161	301	164
Other sectors	2 430	....	....	....	5	20	41	30	17
Migrants' transfers	2 431	....	....	....	....	....	....	....	....
Debt forgiveness	2 432	....	....	....	....	....	....	....	....
Other capital transfers	2 440	....	....	....	5	20	41	....	17
Capital transfers, debit	3 400	....	....	....	**−2**	**−5**	**−12**	**−6**	**−3**
General government	3 401	....	....	....	−2	....	−10	−5	....
Debt forgiveness	3 402	....	....	....	....	....	....	....	....
Other capital transfers	3 410	....	....	....	−2	....	−10	−5	....
Other sectors	3 430	....	....	....	....	−5	−2	−1	−3
Migrants' transfers	3 431	....	....	....	....	....	....	....	....
Debt forgiveness	3 432	....	....	....	....	....	....	....	....
Other capital transfers	3 440	....	....	....	....	−5	−2	−1	−3
Nonproduced nonfinancial assets, credit	2 480	....	....	....	....	....	12	20	....
Nonproduced nonfinancial assets, debit	3 480	....	....	....	....	....	....	....	−3

Table 2 (Continued). STANDARD PRESENTATION, 2000–2007

(Millions of U.S. dollars)

	Code	2000	2001	2002	2003	2004	2005	2006	2007
FINANCIAL ACCOUNT	4 995	−472	−2,586	−4,868	−4,659	−459	3,604	5,885	7,976
A. DIRECT INVESTMENT	4 500	297	352	795	515	1,062	2,157	4,164	5,233
Direct investment abroad	4 505	−11	−31	−28	−19	−56	−44	−109	−98
Equity capital	4 510	....	....	....	....	....	....	....	....
Claims on affiliated enterprises	4 515	....	....	....	....	....	....	....	....
Liabilities to affiliated enterprises	4 520	....	....	....	....	....	....	....	....
Reinvested earnings	4 525	....	....	....	....	....	....	....	....
Other capital	4 530	−11	−31	−28	−19	−56	−44	−109	−98
Claims on affiliated enterprises	4 535	−11	−26	−31	−19	−56	−44	−109	−98
Liabilities to affiliated enterprises	4 540	....	−5	3	....	....	....	....	....
Direct investment in Pakistan	4 555	308	383	823	534	1,118	2,201	4,273	5,331
Equity capital	4 560	209	284	707	379	867	1,777	3,518	4,360
Claims on direct investors	4 565	....	....	....	....	....	....	....	....
Liabilities to direct investors	4 570	209	284	707	379	867	1,777	3,518	4,360
Reinvested earnings	4 575	99	99	116	154	248	424	695	971
Other capital	4 580	....	....	....	1	3	....	61	....
Claims on direct investors	4 585	....	....	....	....	....	....	....	....
Liabilities to direct investors	4 590	....	....	....	1	3	....	61	....
B. PORTFOLIO INVESTMENT	4 600	9	−192	−722	−276	246	770	1,969	2,088
Assets	4 602	....	....	....	−2	9	19	−4	5
Equity securities	4 610	....	....	....	−2	9	19	−4	5
Monetary authorities	4 611	....	....	....	....	....	....	....	....
General government	4 612	....	....	....	....	....	....	....	....
Banks	4 613	....	....	....	....	....	....	....	....
Other sectors	4 614	....	....	....	−2	9	19	−4	5
Debt securities	4 619	....	....	....	....	....	....	....	....
Bonds and notes	4 620	....	....	....	....	....	....	....	....
Monetary authorities	4 621	....	....	....	....	....	....	....	....
General government	4 622	....	....	....	....	....	....	....	....
Banks	4 623	....	....	....	....	....	....	....	....
Other sectors	4 624	....	....	....	....	....	....	....	....
Money market instruments	4 630	....	....	....	....	....	....	....	....
Monetary authorities	4 631	....	....	....	....	....	....	....	....
General government	4 632	....	....	....	....	....	....	....	....
Banks	4 633	....	....	....	....	....	....	....	....
Other sectors	4 634	....	....	....	....	....	....	....	....
Liabilities	4 652	9	−192	−722	−274	237	751	1,973	2,083
Equity securities	4 660	35	−130	79	−26	49	451	1,152	1,276
Banks	4 663	....	....	....	....	....	....	150	650
Other sectors	4 664	35	−130	79	−26	49	451	1,002	626
Debt securities	4 669	−26	−62	−801	−248	188	300	821	807
Bonds and notes	4 670	−26	−62	−801	−248	188	300	821	807
Monetary authorities	4 671	....	....	....	....	....	....	....	....
General government	4 672	−26	−62	−801	−248	188	300	623	757
Banks	4 673	....	....	....	....	....	....	....	....
Other sectors	4 674	....	....	....	....	....	....	198	50
Money market instruments	4 680	....	....	....	....	....	....	....	....
Monetary authorities	4 681	....	....	....	....	....	....	....	....
General government	4 682	....	....	....	....	....	....	....	....
Banks	4 683	....	....	....	....	....	....	....	....
Other sectors	4 684	....	....	....	....	....	....	....	....
C. FINANCIAL DERIVATIVES	4 910	....	....	....	....	....	....	....	....
Monetary authorities	4 911	....	....	....	....	....	....	....	....
General government	4 912	....	....	....	....	....	....	....	....
Banks	4 913	....	....	....	....	....	....	....	....
Other sectors	4 914	....	....	....	....	....	....	....	....
Assets	4 900	....	....	....	....	....	....	....	....
Monetary authorities	4 901	....	....	....	....	....	....	....	....
General government	4 902	....	....	....	....	....	....	....	....
Banks	4 903	....	....	....	....	....	....	....	....
Other sectors	4 904	....	....	....	....	....	....	....	....
Liabilities	4 905	....	....	....	....	....	....	....	....
Monetary authorities	4 906	....	....	....	....	....	....	....	....
General government	4 907	....	....	....	....	....	....	....	....
Banks	4 908	....	....	....	....	....	....	....	....
Other sectors	4 909	....	....	....	....	....	....	....	....

Table 2 (Concluded). STANDARD PRESENTATION, 2000–2007

(Millions of U.S. dollars)

	Code	2000	2001	2002	2003	2004	2005	2006	2007
D. OTHER INVESTMENT	4 700	**−785**	**−29**	**−416**	**−1,895**	**−3,496**	**853**	**1,297**	**2,631**
Assets	4 703	**−437**	**53**	**−64**	**−542**	**−1,339**	**126**	**−242**	**−107**
Trade credits	4 706	....	....	....	−198	−265	−301	−282	−268
General government	4 707	....	....	....	....	....	....	....	....
of which: Short-term	4 709	....	....	....	....	....	....	....	....
Other sectors	4 710	....	....	....	−198	−265	−301	−282	−268
of which: Short-term	4 712	....	....	....	−198	−265	−301	−282	−268
Loans	4 714	....	....	....	....	....	....	....	....
Monetary authorities	4 715	....	....	....	....	....	....	....	....
of which: Short-term	4 718	....	....	....	....	....	....	....	....
General government	4 719	....	....	....	....	....	....	....	....
of which: Short-term	4 721	....	....	....	....	....	....	....	....
Banks	4 722	....	....	....	....	....	....	....	....
of which: Short-term	4 724	....	....	....	....	....	....	....	....
Other sectors	4 725	....	....	....	....	....	....	....	....
of which: Short-term	4 727	....	....	....	....	....	....	....	....
Currency and deposits	4 730	....		....	−243	−961	524	125	113
Monetary authorities	4 731	....			....	....	....	....	....
General government	4 732	....			2	−1	....	−2	5
Banks	4 733	....			−171	−871	569	45	−62
Other sectors	4 734	....			−74	−89	−45	82	170
Other assets	4 736	−437	53	−64	−101	−113	−97	−85	48
Monetary authorities	4 737				....	....	....	....	....
of which: Short-term	4 739	....	....	....	....	....	....	....	....
General government	4 740	−15	44	−5	17	....	1	1	1
of which: Short-term	4 742	−15	−1	−51	17	....	....	....	....
Banks	4 743	−18	−17	−6	−76	−113	−98	−86	47
of which: Short-term	4 745	−18	−17	−6	−76	−113	−98	−86	47
Other sectors	4 746	−404	26	−53	−42	....	....	....	....
of which: Short-term	4 748	−404	26	−53	−42	....	....	....	....
Liabilities	4 753	**−348**	**−82**	**−352**	**−1,353**	**−2,157**	**727**	**1,539**	**2,738**
Trade credits	4 756	....	....	....	....	....	....	....	....
General government	4 757	....	....	....	....	....	....	....	....
of which: Short-term	4 759	....	....	....	....	....	....	....	....
Other sectors	4 760	....	....	....	....	....	....	....	....
of which: Short-term	4 762	....	....	....	....	....	....	....	....
Loans	4 764	−112	568	655	−1,488	−1,593	355	1,340	2,147
Monetary authorities	4 765	−101	328	68	−112	−323	−244	−106	−151
of which: Use of Fund credit and loans from the Fund	4 766	−101	328	68	−112	−323	−244	−106	−151
of which: Short-term	4 768	....	....	....	....	....	....	....	....
General government	4 769	348	559	813	−994	−1,211	792	1,044	1,886
of which: Short-term	4 771	−153	−195	−529	−215	−14	230	−132	442
Banks	4 772	....	....	....	....	....	....	....	....
of which: Short-term	4 774	....	....	....	....	....	....	....	....
Other sectors	4 775	−359	−319	−226	−382	−59	−193	402	412
of which: Short-term	4 777	7	20	50	−78	....	....	....	....
Currency and deposits	4 780	....	....	213	328	−421	393	127	462
Monetary authorities	4 781	....	....	−3	....	−15	5	2	....
General government	4 782	....	....	....	....	−2	−10	−1	....
Banks	4 783	....	....	4	18	−8	−3	−1	43
Other sectors	4 784	....	....	212	310	−396	401	127	419
Other liabilities	4 786	−236	−650	−1,220	−193	−143	−21	72	129
Monetary authorities	4 787	82	−13	−251	....	....	3	....	−10
of which: Short-term	4 789	332	−13	−251	....	....	3	....	....
General government	4 790	−10	−21	−18	−24	−22	−21	−22	−22
of which: Short-term	4 792	....	....	1	1	....	1	....	....
Banks	4 793	−326	−340	−327	−180	30	71	−2	143
of which: Short-term	4 795	−322	−338	−327	−150	40	81	−45	105
Other sectors	4 796	18	−276	−624	11	−151	−74	96	18
of which: Short-term	4 798	−3	−286	−153	27	−105	−97	−29	−18
E. RESERVE ASSETS	4 802	**7**	**−2,716**	**−4,525**	**−3,003**	**1,728**	**−176**	**−1,544**	**−1,976**
Monetary gold	4 812	....	....	....	....	....	....	....	....
Special drawing rights	4 811	−13	9	2	−230	13	10	12	11
Reserve position in the Fund	4 810	....	....	....	....	....	....	....	....
Foreign exchange	4 803	43	−2,115	−4,898	−3,134	2,045	−206	−1,402	−2,377
Other claims	4 813	−23	−610	371	361	−330	20	−154	390
NET ERRORS AND OMISSIONS	4 998	**557**	**708**	**974**	**−52**	**685**	**−200**	**520**	**102**

Table 3. INTERNATIONAL INVESTMENT POSITION (End-period stocks), 2000–2007

(Millions of U.S. dollars)

	Code	2000	2001	2002	2003	2004	2005	2006	2007
ASSETS..	8 995 C.	....	....	....	**16,960**	**17,071**	**17,681**	**19,657**	**22,416**
Direct investment abroad..........................	8 505 ..	....	....	....	**604**	**702**	**870**	**1,010**	**1,237**
Equity capital and reinvested earnings..........................	8 506 ..	....	....	....	604	702	870	1,010	1,237
Claims on affiliated enterprises..........................	8 507 ..	....	....	....	604	702	870	1,010	1,237
Liabilities to affiliated enterprises..........................	8 508 ..	....	....	....	....	....	....	....	....
Other capital..........................	8 530 ..	....	....	....	....	....	....	....	....
Claims on affiliated enterprises..........................	8 535 ..	....	....	....	....	....	....	....	....
Liabilities to affiliated enterprises..........................	8 540 ..	....	....	....	....	....	....	....	....
Portfolio investment..........................	8 602 ..	....	....	....	**155**	**158**	**452**	**311**	**329**
Equity securities..........................	8 610 ..	....	....	....	154	155	447	307	315
Monetary authorities..........................	8 611 ..	....	....	....	....	....	....	....	....
General government..........................	8 612 ..	....	....	....	....	....	....	....	....
Banks..........................	8 613 ..	....	....	....	55	98	375	234	254
Other sectors..........................	8 614 ..	....	....	....	99	57	72	73	61
Debt securities..........................	8 619 ..	....	....	....	1	3	5	4	14
Bonds and notes..........................	8 620 ..	....	....	....	1	3	5	4	14
Monetary authorities..........................	8 621 ..	....	....	....	....	....	....	....	....
General government..........................	8 622 ..	....	....	....	....	....	....	....	....
Banks..........................	8 623 ..	....	....	....	1	3	5	3	13
Other sectors..........................	8 624 ..	....	....	....	....	....	....	1	1
Money market instruments..........................	8 630 ..	....	....	....	....	....	....	....	....
Monetary authorities..........................	8 631 ..	....	....	....	....	....	....	....	....
General government..........................	8 632 ..	....	....	....	....	....	....	....	....
Banks..........................	8 633 ..	....	....	....	....	....	....	....	....
Other sectors..........................	8 634 ..	....	....	....	....	....	....	....	....
Financial derivatives..........................	8 900 ..	....	....	....	....	....	....	....	....
Monetary authorities..........................	8 901 ..	....	....	....	....	....	....	....	....
General government..........................	8 902 ..	....	....	....	....	....	....	....	....
Banks..........................	8 903 ..	....	....	....	....	....	....	....	....
Other sectors..........................	8 904 ..	....	....	....	....	....	....	....	....
Other investment..........................	8 703 ..	....	....	....	**3,729**	**5,386**	**5,246**	**5,430**	**5,524**
Trade credits..........................	8 706 ..	....	....	....	1,692	1,957	2,258	2,500	2,765
General government..........................	8 707 ..	....	....	....	....	....	....	....	....
of which: Short-term..........................	8 709 ..	....	....	....	....	....	....	....	....
Other sectors..........................	8 710 ..	....	....	....	1,692	1,957	2,258	2,500	2,765
of which: Short-term..........................	8 712 ..	....	....	....	*1,692*	*1,957*	*2,258*	*2,500*	*2,765*
Loans..........................	8 714 ..	....	....	....	80	83	86	89	92
Monetary authorities..........................	8 715 ..	....	....	....	....	....	....	....	....
of which: Short-term..........................	8 718 ..	....	....	....	....	....	....	....	....
General government..........................	8 719 ..	....	....	....	80	83	86	89	92
of which: Short-term..........................	8 721 ..	....	....	....	....	....	....	....	....
Banks..........................	8 722 ..	....	....	....	....	....	....	....	....
of which: Short-term..........................	8 724 ..	....	....	....	....	....	....	....	....
Other sectors..........................	8 725 ..	....	....	....	....	....	....	....	....
of which: Short-term..........................	8 727 ..	....	....	....	....	....	....	....	....
Currency and deposits..........................	8 730 C.	....	....	....	1,070	2,346	1,804	1,617	1,490
Monetary authorities..........................	8 731 ..	....	....	....	....	....	....	....	....
General government..........................	8 732 ..	....	....	....	4	5	3	5	5
Banks..........................	8 733 ..	....	....	....	1,032	2,216	1,648	1,604	1,663
Other sectors..........................	8 734 ..	....	....	....	34	125	153	8	−178
Other assets..........................	8 736 ..	....	....	....	887	1,000	1,098	1,224	1,177
Monetary authorities..........................	8 737 ..	....	....	....	....	....	....	....	....
of which: Short-term..........................	8 739 ..	....	....	....	....	....	....	....	....
General government..........................	8 740 ..	....	....	....	....	....	....	....	....
of which: Short-term..........................	8 742 ..	....	....	....	....	....	....	....	....
Banks..........................	8 743 ..	....	....	....	887	1,000	1,098	1,224	1,177
of which: Short-term..........................	8 745 ..	....	....	....	*887*	*1,000*	*1,098*	*1,224*	*1,177*
Other sectors..........................	8 746 ..	....	....	....	....	....	....	....	....
of which: Short-term..........................	8 748 ..	....	....	....	....	....	....	....	....
Reserve assets..........................	8 802 ..	....	....	....	**12,472**	**10,825**	**11,113**	**12,906**	**15,326**
Monetary gold..........................	8 812 ..	....	....	....	860	904	1,059	1,313	1,732
Special drawing rights..........................	8 811 ..	14	4	2	248	245	216	216	215
Reserve position in the Fund..........................	8 810 ..	....	....	....	....	....	....	....	....
Foreign exchange..........................	8 803 ..	....	....	....	11,589	9,570	9,748	11,133	13,524
Other claims..........................	8 813 ..	....	....	....	−225	106	90	244	−145

Table 3 (Concluded). INTERNATIONAL INVESTMENT POSITION (End-period stocks), 2000–2007

(Millions of U.S. dollars)

	Code	2000	2001	2002	2003	2004	2005	2006	2007
LIABILITIES	8 995 D.	....	....	....	**44,155**	**45,333**	**47,206**	**55,251**	**66,018**
Direct investment in Pakistan	8 555 ..	....	....	....	**7,195**	**7,606**	**10,209**	**13,682**	**19,015**
Equity capital and reinvested earnings	8 556 ..	....	....	....	6,269	6,628	9,109	12,241	17,572
Claims on direct investors	8 557 ..	....	....	....	....	....	....	....	....
Liabilities to direct investors	8 558 ..	....	....	....	6,269	6,628	9,109	12,241	17,572
Other capital	8 580 ..	....	....	....	926	978	1,100	1,441	1,443
Claims on direct investors	8 585 ..	....	....	....	....	....	....	....	....
Liabilities to direct investors	8 590 ..	....	....	....	926	978	1,100	1,441	1,443
Portfolio investment	8 652 ..	....	....	....	**1,142**	**1,622**	**2,511**	**4,252**	**6,284**
Equity securities	8 660 ..	....	....	....	217	495	1,064	1,960	3,236
Banks	8 663 ..	....	....	....	50	92	283	669	1,319
Other sectors	8 664 ..	....	....	....	167	403	781	1,291	1,917
Debt securities	8 669 ..	....	....	....	925	1,127	1,447	2,292	3,048
Bonds and notes	8 670 ..	....	....	....	925	1,127	1,447	2,292	3,048
Monetary authorities	8 671 ..	....	....	....	....	....	....	....	....
General government	8 672 ..	....	....	....	910	1,115	1,438	2,088	2,795
Banks	8 673 ..	....	....	....	....	....	....	....	....
Other sectors	8 674 ..	....	....	....	15	12	9	204	253
Money market instruments	8 680 ..	....	....	....	....	....	....	....	....
Monetary authorities	8 681 ..	....	....	....	....	....	....	....	....
General government	8 682 ..	....	....	....	....	....	....	....	....
Banks	8 683 ..	....	....	....	....	....	....	....	....
Other sectors	8 684 ..	....	....	....	....	....	....	....	....
Financial derivatives	8 905 ..	....	....	....	....	....	....	....	....
Monetary authorities	8 906 ..	....	....	....	....	....	....	....	....
General government	8 907 ..	....	....	....	....	....	....	....	....
Banks	8 908 ..	....	....	....	....	....	....	....	....
Other sectors	8 909 ..	....	....	....	....	....	....	....	....
Other investment	8 753 ..	....	....	....	**35,818**	**36,105**	**34,486**	**37,317**	**40,719**
Trade credits	8 756 ..	....	....	....	162	140	221	506	506
General government	8 757 ..	....	....	....	....	....	....	....	....
of which: Short-term	8 759 ..	....	....	....	....	....	....	....	....
Other sectors	8 760 ..	....	....	....	162	140	221	506	506
of which: Short-term	8 762 ..	....	....	....	*162*	*140*	*221*	*506*	*506*
Loans	8 764 ..	....	....	....	33,828	34,161	32,414	34,975	38,561
Monetary authorities	8 765 ..	....	....	....	2,117	1,876	1,492	1,462	1,381
of which: Use of Fund credit and loans from the Fund....	8 766 ..	*1,561*	*1,830*	*2,048*	*2,117*	*1,876*	*1,492*	*1,462*	*1,381*
of which: Short-term	8 768 ..	....	....	....	....	....	....	....	....
General government	8 769 ..	....	....	....	29,342	30,510	29,352	31,549	34,846
of which: Short-term	8 771 ..	....	....	....	*95*	*111*	*343*	*26*	*601*
Banks	8 772 ..	....	....	....	....	....	....	....	....
of which: Short-term	8 774 ..	....	....	....	....	....	....	....	....
Other sectors	8 775 ..	....	....	....	2,369	1,775	1,570	1,964	2,334
of which: Short-term	8 777 ..	....	....	....	....	....	....	....	....
Currency and deposits	8 780 ..	....	....	....	1,143	1,152	1,200	1,182	1,159
Monetary authorities	8 781 ..	....	....	....	707	704	701	701	701
General government	8 782 ..	....	....	....	2	3	1	....	1
Banks	8 783 ..	....	....	....	434	445	498	481	457
Other sectors	8 784 ..	....	....	....	....	....	....	....	....
Other liabilities	8 786 ..	....	....	....	685	652	651	654	493
Monetary authorities	8 787 ..	....	....	....	....	....	....	....	....
of which: Short-term	8 789 ..	....	....	....	....	....	....	....	....
General government	8 790 ..	....	....	....	656	631	609	588	466
of which: Short-term	8 792 ..	....	....	....	*500*	*500*	*500*	*500*	*400*
Banks	8 793 ..	....	....	....	....	....	....	....	....
of which: Short-term	8 795 ..	....	....	....	....	....	....	....	....
Other sectors	8 796 ..	....	....	....	29	21	42	66	27
of which: Short-term	8 798 ..	....	....	....	*29*	*21*	*42*	*66*	*27*
NET INTERNATIONAL INVESTMENT POSITION	8 995 ..	....	....	....	**−27,195**	**−28,262**	**−29,525**	**−35,595**	**−43,602**
Conversion rates: Pakistan rupees per U.S. dollar (end of period)	0 102 ..	58.029	60.864	58.534	57.215	59.124	59.830	60.918	61.221

Table 1. ANALYTIC PRESENTATION, 2000–2007

(Millions of U.S. dollars)

	Code	2000	2001	2002	2003	2004	2005	2006	2007
A. Current Account[1]	4 993 Z.	**−672.5**	**−170.3**	**−95.5**	**−536.5**	**−1,003.2**	**−1,021.8**	**−526.8**	**−1,422.4**
Goods: exports f.o.b.	2 100 ..	5,838.5	5,992.4	5,314.7	5,072.4	6,079.9	7,375.2	8,478.1	9,338.4
Goods: imports f.o.b.	3 100 ..	−6,981.4	−6,688.6	−6,349.8	−6,274.4	−7,616.5	−8,933.0	−10,190.0	−12,520.6
Balance on Goods	4 100 ..	*−1,142.9*	*−696.2*	*−1,035.1*	*−1,202.0*	*−1,536.6*	*−1,557.8*	*−1,711.9*	*−3,182.2*
Services: credit	2 200 ..	1,994.4	1,992.8	2,277.9	2,539.6	2,793.7	3,231.3	3,938.0	4,924.4
Services: debit	3 200 ..	−1,140.8	−1,102.9	−1,309.8	−1,299.8	−1,457.0	−1,811.4	−1,727.7	−2,106.7
Balance on Goods and Services	4 991 ..	*−289.3*	*193.7*	*−67.0*	*37.8*	*−199.9*	*−137.9*	*498.4*	*−364.5*
Income: credit	2 300 ..	1,575.3	1,384.0	953.2	805.3	790.9	1,054.8	1,403.0	1,875.7
Income: debit	3 300 ..	−2,135.5	−1,974.1	−1,225.5	−1,614.0	−1,811.3	−2,180.4	−2,680.7	−3,186.8
Balance on Goods, Services, and Income	4 992 ..	*−849.5*	*−396.4*	*−339.3*	*−770.9*	*−1,220.3*	*−1,263.5*	*−779.3*	*−1,675.6*
Current transfers: credit	2 379 Z.	208.7	277.9	298.8	298.6	297.6	338.2	388.4	416.4
Current transfers: debit	3 379 ..	−31.7	−51.8	−55.0	−64.2	−80.5	−96.5	−135.9	−163.2
B. Capital Account[1]	4 994 Z.	**1.7**	**1.6**	**. . . .**	**. . . .**	**. . . .**	**15.8**	**15.2**	**43.7**
Capital account: credit	2 994 Z.	1.7	1.6	. . . .	. . . .	. . . .	15.8	15.2	43.7
Capital account: debit	3 994 ..	. . . .	. . . .	. . . .	. . . .	. . . .	. . . .	. . . .	. . . .
Total, Groups A Plus B	4 981 ..	*−670.8*	*−168.7*	*−95.5*	*−536.5*	*−1,003.2*	*−1,006.0*	*−511.6*	*−1,378.7*
C. Financial Account[1]	4 995 W.	**331.8**	**1,301.0**	**194.3**	**178.0**	**496.7**	**2,040.1**	**375.2**	**2,773.9**
Direct investment abroad	4 505 ..	. . . .	. . . .	. . . .	. . . .	. . . .	. . . .	. . . .	. . . .
Direct investment in Panama	4 555 Z.	623.9	467.1	98.6	817.5	1,019.1	917.6	2,497.9	1,907.2
Portfolio investment assets	4 602 ..	−93.0	−752.7	−11.9	−75.4	−650.9	−1,102.8	−748.0	−1,084.1
Equity securities	4 610 ..	2.0	−1.2	3.0	8.7	6.8	−16.9	−133.1	127.4
Debt securities	4 619 ..	−95.0	−751.5	−14.9	−84.1	−657.7	−1,085.9	−614.9	−1,211.5
Portfolio investment liabilities	4 652 Z.	163.7	727.1	102.2	139.6	775.9	545.7	254.9	450.0
Equity securities	4 660 ..	. . . .	. . . .	. . . .	. . . .	. . . .	. . . .	. . . .	. . . .
Debt securities	4 669 Z.	163.7	727.1	102.2	139.6	775.9	545.7	254.9	450.0
Financial derivatives	4 910 ..	. . . .	. . . .	. . . .	. . . .	. . . .	. . . .	. . . .	. . . .
Financial derivatives assets	4 900 ..	. . . .	. . . .	. . . .	. . . .	. . . .	. . . .	. . . .	. . . .
Financial derivatives liabilities	4 905 ..	. . . .	. . . .	. . . .	. . . .	. . . .	. . . .	. . . .	. . . .
Other investment assets	4 703 ..	489.3	818.4	3,270.4	631.2	−1,542.8	−334.4	−3,781.8	−4,998.4
Monetary authorities	4 701 ..	5.2	. . . .	. . . .	. . . .	. . . .	. . . .	. . . .	. . . .
General government	4 704 ..	−4.0	−2.1	−.9	32.1	−598.5	496.7	−309.1	. . . .
Banks	4 705 ..	185.4	1,016.2	3,294.5	529.2	−710.8	−276.1	−2,848.1	−4,817.5
Other sectors	4 728 ..	302.7	−195.7	−23.2	69.9	−233.5	−555.0	−624.6	−180.9
Other investment liabilities	4 753 W.	−852.1	41.1	−3,265.0	−1,334.9	895.4	2,014.0	2,152.2	6,499.2
Monetary authorities	4 753 WA	−6.4	3.7	−.9	1.6	. . . .	. . . .	2.4	10.1
General government	4 753 ZB	−2.6	3.5	46.1	10.2	−37.0	−54.2	23.7	34.8
Banks	4 753 ZC	−425.5	−3.3	−3,311.7	−1,349.3	820.8	1,866.4	2,100.8	6,111.6
Other sectors	4 753 ZD	−417.6	37.2	1.5	2.6	111.6	201.8	25.4	342.7
Total, Groups A Through C	4 983 ..	*−339.0*	*1,132.3*	*98.8*	*−358.5*	*−506.5*	*1,034.1*	*−136.4*	*1,395.2*
D. Net Errors and Omissions	4 998 ..	**262.5**	**−498.6**	**45.2**	**89.9**	**110.4**	**−357.9**	**308.1**	**−775.3**
Total, Groups A Through D	4 984 ..	*−76.5*	*633.7*	*144.0*	*−268.6*	*−396.1*	*676.2*	*171.7*	*619.9*
E. Reserves and Related Items	4 802 A.	**76.5**	**−633.7**	**−144.0**	**268.6**	**396.1**	**−676.2**	**−171.7**	**−619.9**
Reserve assets	4 802 ..	108.1	−623.3	−135.9	268.2	397.0	−522.8	−161.8	−609.6
Use of Fund credit and loans	4 766 ..	−51.7	−33.3	−8.1	−9.5	−10.0	−9.7	−9.9	−10.3
Exceptional financing	4 920 ..	20.1	22.9	. . . .	10.0	9.1	−143.7	. . . .	. . . .
Conversion rates: balboas per U.S. dollar	0 101 ..	**1.0000**	**1.0000**	**1.0000**	**1.0000**	**1.0000**	**1.0000**	**1.0000**	**1.0000**

[1] Excludes components that have been classified in the categories of Group E.

Table 2. STANDARD PRESENTATION, 2000–2007

(Millions of U.S. dollars)

	Code	2000	2001	2002	2003	2004	2005	2006	2007
CURRENT ACCOUNT	4 993	−672.5	−170.3	−95.5	−536.5	−1,003.2	−1,021.8	−526.8	−1,422.4
A. GOODS	4 100	−1,142.9	−696.2	−1,035.1	−1,202.0	−1,536.6	−1,557.8	−1,711.9	−3,182.2
Credit	2 100	5,838.5	5,992.4	5,314.7	5,072.4	6,079.9	7,375.2	8,478.1	9,338.4
General merchandise: exports f.o.b.	2 110	5,600.3	5,791.8	5,163.6	4,953.5	5,909.0	7,160.2	8,154.3	8,971.8
Goods for processing: exports f.o.b.	2 150	13.4	4.6	3.3	2.6	.7	1.1	.8	.4
Repairs on goods	2 160	.9	1.0	1.9	2.6	3.5	1.5	1.8	3.4
Goods procured in ports by carriers	2 170	223.9	195.0	145.9	113.7	166.7	212.4	321.2	362.8
Nonmonetary gold	2 180	....	....	....	....	....	....	....	....
Debit	3 100	−6,981.4	−6,688.6	−6,349.8	−6,274.4	−7,616.5	−8,933.0	−10,190.0	−12,520.6
General merchandise: imports f.o.b.	3 110	−6,939.3	−6,648.7	−6,310.2	−6,243.8	−7,578.3	−8,869.0	−10,107.9	−12,425.0
Goods for processing: imports f.o.b.	3 150	−4.6	−3.0	−2.7	−1.8	−.8	−.9	−1.1	−.6
Repairs on goods	3 160	−7.1	−7.1	−5.1	....	....	....	....	−1.3
Goods procured in ports by carriers	3 170	−30.4	−29.8	−31.8	−28.8	−37.4	−63.1	−81.0	−93.7
Nonmonetary gold	3 180	....	....	....	....	....	....	....	....
B. SERVICES	4 200	853.6	889.9	968.1	1,239.8	1,336.7	1,419.9	2,210.3	2,817.7
Total credit	2 200	*1,994.4*	*1,992.8*	*2,277.9*	*2,539.6*	*2,793.7*	*3,231.3*	*3,938.0*	*4,924.4*
Total debit	3 200	*−1,140.8*	*−1,102.9*	*−1,309.8*	*−1,299.8*	*−1,457.0*	*−1,811.4*	*−1,727.7*	*−2,106.7*
Transportation services, credit	2 205	1,152.6	1,131.3	1,209.5	1,357.3	1,524.0	1,791.0	2,217.3	2,607.5
Passenger	2 850	*170.4*	*188.2*	*196.6*	*218.5*	*252.0*	*327.7*	*464.6*	*620.9*
Freight	2 851	*9.5*	*9.3*	*10.0*	*8.3*	*10.0*	*11.5*	*13.1*	*21.7*
Other	2 852	*972.7*	*933.8*	*1,002.9*	*1,130.5*	*1,262.0*	*1,451.8*	*1,739.6*	*1,964.9*
Sea transport, passenger	2 207	....	....	....	....	....	....	....	....
Sea transport, freight	2 208	....	....	....	....	....	....	....	....
Sea transport, other	2 209	942.0	908.5	970.2	1,110.3	1,240.2	1,420.6	1,708.6	1,930.2
Air transport, passenger	2 211	170.4	188.2	196.6	218.5	252.0	327.7	464.6	620.9
Air transport, freight	2 212	9.5	9.3	10.0	8.3	10.0	11.5	13.1	21.7
Air transport, other	2 213	30.7	25.3	32.7	20.2	21.8	31.2	31.0	34.7
Other transport, passenger	2 215	....	....	....	....	....	....	....	....
Other transport, freight	2 216	....	....	....	....	....	....	....	....
Other transport, other	2 217	....	....	....	....	....	....	....	....
Transportation services, debit	3 205	−607.5	−597.6	−617.2	−611.9	−746.7	−959.1	−952.8	−1,211.1
Passenger	3 850	*−53.1*	*−53.4*	*−73.0*	*−58.6*	*−54.8*	*−116.7*	*−132.2*	*−149.9*
Freight	3 851	*−535.7*	*−527.4*	*−525.4*	*−497.3*	*−631.5*	*−768.4*	*−725.2*	*−935.1*
Other	3 852	*−18.7*	*−16.8*	*−18.8*	*−56.0*	*−60.4*	*−74.0*	*−95.4*	*−126.1*
Sea transport, passenger	3 207	....	....	....	....	....	....	....	....
Sea transport, freight	3 208	−535.7	−527.4	−525.4	−497.3	−631.5	−768.4	−725.2	−935.1
Sea transport, other	3 209	....	....	....	....	....	....	....	....
Air transport, passenger	3 211	−53.1	−53.4	−73.0	−58.6	−54.8	−116.7	−132.2	−149.9
Air transport, freight	3 212	....	....	....	....	....	....	....	....
Air transport, other	3 213	−18.7	−16.8	−18.8	−56.0	−60.4	−74.0	−95.4	−126.1
Other transport, passenger	3 215	....	....	....	....	....	....	....	....
Other transport, freight	3 216	....	....	....	....	....	....	....	....
Other transport, other	3 217	....	....	....	....	....	....	....	....
Travel, credit	2 236	457.8	477.1	513.0	584.6	651.0	779.8	960.0	1,184.8
Business travel	2 237	89.8	90.6	90.6	99.7	108.4	124.0	151.8	197.1
Personal travel	2 240	368.0	386.5	422.4	484.9	542.6	655.8	808.2	987.7
Travel, debit	3 236	−188.4	−173.5	−178.8	−207.7	−238.9	−271.1	−271.2	−307.0
Business travel	3 237	−22.8	−21.1	−21.6	−25.2	−28.9	−33.1	−33.4	−39.8
Personal travel	3 240	−165.6	−152.4	−157.2	−182.5	−210.0	−238.0	−237.8	−267.2
Other services, credit	2 200 BA	384.0	384.4	555.4	597.7	618.7	660.5	760.7	1,132.1
Communications	2 245	33.7	43.9	37.3	72.9	103.3	126.8	161.5	210.8
Construction	2 249	....	....	....	....	....	....	....	.6
Insurance	2 253	38.8	31.4	26.6	27.6	32.6	31.4	43.9	55.0
Financial	2 260	140.5	126.6	271.0	292.8	240.0	197.8	273.2	337.9
Computer and information	2 262	....	....	....	....	14.4	11.7	13.8	17.9
Royalties and licence fees	2 266	....	....	....	....	....	....	....	....
Other business services	2 268	138.0	148.0	183.9	167.8	193.0	254.6	225.4	439.2
Personal, cultural, and recreational	2 287	....	....	....	....	....	....	....	....
Government, n.i.e.	2 291	33.0	34.5	36.6	36.6	35.4	38.2	42.9	70.7
Other services, debit	3 200 BA	−344.9	−331.8	−513.8	−480.2	−471.4	−581.2	−503.7	−588.6
Communications	3 245	−14.7	−18.8	−8.2	−21.2	−12.3	−25.1	−33.5	−54.3
Construction	3 249	....	....	....	....	....	....	....	....
Insurance	3 253	−46.4	−53.1	−79.7	−67.4	−81.5	−105.3	−94.2	−72.2
Financial	3 260	−36.4	−59.3	−192.8	−169.1	−138.0	−157.4	−141.9	−220.1
Computer and information	3 262	....	....	....	....	....	....	....	....
Royalties and licence fees	3 266	−42.4	−35.8	−46.7	−42.4	−45.5	−44.6	−42.6	−47.2
Other business services	3 268	−160.2	−114.6	−132.6	−133.6	−149.1	−195.9	−136.3	−138.4
Personal, cultural, and recreational	3 287	....	....	....	....	....	....	....	....
Government, n.i.e.	3 291	−44.8	−50.2	−53.8	−46.5	−45.0	−52.9	−55.2	−56.4

Table 2 (Continued). STANDARD PRESENTATION, 2000–2007

(Millions of U.S. dollars)

	Code	2000	2001	2002	2003	2004	2005	2006	2007
C. INCOME	4 300	**−560.2**	**−590.1**	**−272.3**	**−808.7**	**−1,020.4**	**−1,125.6**	**−1,277.7**	**−1,311.1**
Total credit	2 300	*1,575.3*	*1,384.0*	*953.2*	*805.3*	*790.9*	*1,054.8*	*1,403.0*	*1,875.7*
Total debit	3 300	*−2,135.5*	*−1,974.1*	*−1,225.5*	*−1,614.0*	*−1,811.3*	*−2,180.4*	*−2,680.7*	*−3,186.8*
Compensation of employees, credit	2 310	....	....	....	12.7	3.9	5.2	7.8	7.1
Compensation of employees, debit	3 310	....	....	....	....	....	....	....	....
Investment income, credit	2 320	1,575.3	1,384.0	953.2	792.6	787.0	1,049.6	1,395.2	1,868.6
Direct investment income	2 330	....	....	....	....	....	....	....	....
Dividends and distributed branch profits	2 332	....	....	....	....	....	....	....	....
Reinvested earnings and undistributed branch profits	2 333	....	....	....	....	....	....	....	....
Income on debt (interest)	2 334	....	....	....	....	....	....	....	....
Portfolio investment income	2 339	241.0	282.5	335.5	329.1	358.4	421.4	435.3	588.2
Income on equity	2 340	....	....	....	.9	4.0	1.0	5.6	3.2
Income on bonds and notes	2 350	241.0	282.5	335.5	328.2	354.4	419.9	425.9	583.2
Income on money market instruments	2 360	....	....	....	....	....	.5	3.8	1.8
Other investment income	2 370	1,334.3	1,101.5	617.7	463.5	428.6	628.2	959.9	1,280.4
Investment income, debit	3 320	−2,135.5	−1,974.1	−1,225.5	−1,614.0	−1,811.3	−2,180.4	−2,680.7	−3,186.8
Direct investment income	3 330	−561.9	−568.6	−194.1	−738.7	−967.4	−1,047.8	−1,216.1	−1,540.3
Dividends and distributed branch profits	3 332	−308.9	−482.4	−360.7	−310.6	−403.5	−624.6	−1,011.3	−507.2
Reinvested earnings and undistributed branch profits	3 333	−253.0	−86.2	166.6	−428.1	−563.9	−423.2	−204.8	−1,033.1
Income on debt (interest)	3 334	....	....	....	....	....	....	....	....
Portfolio investment income	3 339	−293.2	−349.1	−369.6	−401.4	−427.4	−504.0	−488.5	−526.1
Income on equity	3 340	....	....	....	....	....	....	....	....
Income on bonds and notes	3 350	−293.2	−349.1	−369.6	−401.4	−427.4	−504.0	−488.5	−526.1
Income on money market instruments	3 360	....	....	....	....	....	....	....	....
Other investment income	3 370	−1,280.4	−1,056.4	−661.8	−473.9	−416.5	−628.6	−976.1	−1,120.4
D. CURRENT TRANSFERS	4 379	**177.0**	**226.1**	**243.8**	**234.4**	**217.1**	**241.7**	**252.5**	**253.2**
Credit	2 379	208.7	277.9	298.8	298.6	297.6	338.2	388.4	416.4
General government	2 380	69.4	85.1	95.6	85.9	82.0	101.8	119.9	114.6
Other sectors	2 390	139.3	192.8	203.2	212.7	215.6	236.4	268.5	301.8
Workers' remittances	2 391	16.4	73.1	84.6	94.1	105.0	124.4	149.3	173.2
Other current transfers	2 392	122.9	119.7	118.6	118.6	110.6	112.0	119.2	128.6
Debit	3 379	−31.7	−51.8	−55.0	−64.2	−80.5	−96.5	−135.9	−163.2
General government	3 380	−5.1	−5.2	−5.2	−2.7	−3.2	−3.9	−10.4	−7.2
Other sectors	3 390	−26.6	−46.6	−49.8	−61.5	−77.3	−92.6	−125.5	−156.0
Workers' remittances	3 391	−22.0	−42.1	−44.7	−56.6	−72.3	−87.6	−120.5	−150.9
Other current transfers	3 392	−4.6	−4.5	−5.1	−4.9	−5.0	−5.0	−5.0	−5.1
CAPITAL AND FINANCIAL ACCOUNT	4 996	**410.0**	**668.9**	**50.3**	**446.6**	**892.8**	**1,379.7**	**218.7**	**2,197.7**
CAPITAL ACCOUNT	4 994	**1.7**	**1.6**	**....**	**10.0**	**9.1**	**15.8**	**15.2**	**43.7**
Total credit	2 994	*1.7*	*1.6*	*....*	*10.0*	*9.1*	*15.8*	*15.2*	*43.7*
Total debit	3 994	....	....	....	....	....	....	....	....
Capital transfers, credit	2 400	1.7	1.6	....	10.0	9.1	15.8	15.2	43.7
General government	2 401	1.7	1.6	....	10.0	9.1	15.8	15.2	43.7
Debt forgiveness	2 402	....	....	....	10.0	9.1	....	....	....
Other capital transfers	2 410	1.7	1.6	....	....	....	15.8	15.2	43.7
Other sectors	2 430	....	....	....	....	....	....	....	....
Migrants' transfers	2 431	....	....	....	....	....	....	....	....
Debt forgiveness	2 432	....	....	....	....	....	....	....	....
Other capital transfers	2 440	....	....	....	....	....	....	....	....
Capital transfers, debit	3 400	....	....	....	....	....	....	....	....
General government	3 401	....	....	....	....	....	....	....	....
Debt forgiveness	3 402	....	....	....	....	....	....	....	....
Other capital transfers	3 410	....	....	....	....	....	....	....	....
Other sectors	3 430	....	....	....	....	....	....	....	....
Migrants' transfers	3 431	....	....	....	....	....	....	....	....
Debt forgiveness	3 432	....	....	....	....	....	....	....	....
Other capital transfers	3 440	....	....	....	....	....	....	....	....
Nonproduced nonfinancial assets, credit	2 480	....	....	....	....	....	....	....	....
Nonproduced nonfinancial assets, debit	3 480	....	....	....	....	....	....	....	....

Table 2 (Continued). STANDARD PRESENTATION, 2000–2007

(Millions of U.S. dollars)

	Code	2000	2001	2002	2003	2004	2005	2006	2007
FINANCIAL ACCOUNT	4 995 ..	**408.3**	**667.3**	**50.3**	**436.6**	**883.7**	**1,363.9**	**203.5**	**2,154.0**
A. DIRECT INVESTMENT	4 500 ..	**623.9**	**467.1**	**98.6**	**817.5**	**1,019.1**	**917.6**	**2,497.9**	**1,907.2**
Direct investment abroad	4 505 ..	....	....	....	....	....	....	....	....
Equity capital	4 510 ..	....	....	....	....	....	....	....	....
Claims on affiliated enterprises	4 515 ..	....	....	....	....	....	....	....	....
Liabilities to affiliated enterprises	4 520 ..	....	....	....	....	....	....	....	....
Reinvested earnings	4 525 ..	....	....	....	....	....	....	....	....
Other capital	4 530 ..	....	....	....	....	....	....	....	....
Claims on affiliated enterprises	4 535 ..	....	....	....	....	....	....	....	....
Liabilities to affiliated enterprises	4 540 ..	....	....	....	....	....	....	....	....
Direct investment in Panama	4 555 ..	623.9	467.1	98.6	817.5	1,019.1	917.6	2,497.9	1,907.2
Equity capital	4 560 ..	193.7	428.6	193.2	331.5	421.0	46.4	1,928.8	622.4
Claims on direct investors	4 565 ..	....	....	....	....	....	....	....	....
Liabilities to direct investors	4 570 ..	193.7	428.6	193.2	331.5	421.0	46.4	1,928.8	622.4
Reinvested earnings	4 575 ..	253.0	86.2	−166.6	428.1	563.9	423.2	204.8	1,033.1
Other capital	4 580 ..	177.2	−47.7	72.0	57.9	34.2	448.0	364.3	251.7
Claims on direct investors	4 585 ..	−203.9	−139.7	−148.5	−233.1	−258.8	−186.8	−321.3	−244.1
Liabilities to direct investors	4 590 ..	381.1	92.0	220.5	291.0	293.0	634.8	685.6	495.8
B. PORTFOLIO INVESTMENT	4 600 ..	**90.5**	**−2.8**	**90.3**	**64.2**	**125.0**	**−700.8**	**−493.1**	**−634.1**
Assets	4 602 ..	**−93.0**	**−752.7**	**−11.9**	**−75.4**	**−650.9**	**−1,102.8**	**−748.0**	**−1,084.1**
Equity securities	4 610 ..	2.0	−1.2	3.0	8.7	6.8	−16.9	−133.1	127.4
Monetary authorities	4 611 ..	....	....	....	....	....	....	....	....
General government	4 612 ..	....	....	....	....	....	....	....	....
Banks	4 613 ..	....	....	....	....	....	....	....	....
Other sectors	4 614 ..	2.0	−1.2	3.0	8.7	6.8	−16.9	−133.1	127.4
Debt securities	4 619 ..	−95.0	−751.5	−14.9	−84.1	−657.7	−1,085.9	−614.9	−1,211.5
Bonds and notes	4 620 ..	−95.0	−751.5	−14.9	−92.1	−657.7	−1,085.1	−541.2	−1,251.9
Monetary authorities	4 621 ..	....	....	....	....	....	....	....	....
General government	4 622 ..	−4.0	−4.4	36.8	5.3	−5.1	....	....	....
Banks	4 623 ..	−93.1	−744.6	−51.7	−36.9	−641.7	−1,087.6	−319.4	−1,450.5
Other sectors	4 624 ..	2.1	−2.5	....	−60.5	−10.9	2.5	−221.8	198.6
Money market instruments	4 630 ..	....	....	....	8.0	....	−.8	−73.7	40.4
Monetary authorities	4 631 ..	....	....	....	....	....	....	....	....
General government	4 632 ..	....	....	....	....	....	....	....	....
Banks	4 633 ..	....	....	....	....	....	....	....	....
Other sectors	4 634 ..	....	....	....	8.0	....	−.8	−73.7	40.4
Liabilities	4 652 ..	**183.5**	**749.9**	**102.2**	**139.6**	**775.9**	**402.0**	**254.9**	**450.0**
Equity securities	4 660 ..	....	....	....	....	....	....	....	....
Banks	4 663 ..	....	....	....	....	....	....	....	....
Other sectors	4 664 ..	....	....	....	....	....	....	....	....
Debt securities	4 669 ..	183.5	749.9	102.2	139.6	775.9	402.0	254.9	450.0
Bonds and notes	4 670 ..	183.5	749.9	102.2	139.6	775.9	402.0	254.9	450.0
Monetary authorities	4 671 ..	....	....	....	....	....	....	....	....
General government	4 672 ..	183.5	749.9	102.2	139.6	775.9	402.0	254.9	450.0
Banks	4 673 ..	....	....	....	....	....	....	....	....
Other sectors	4 674 ..	....	....	....	....	....	....	....	....
Money market instruments	4 680 ..	....	....	....	....	....	....	....	....
Monetary authorities	4 681 ..	....	....	....	....	....	....	....	....
General government	4 682 ..	....	....	....	....	....	....	....	....
Banks	4 683 ..	....	....	....	....	....	....	....	....
Other sectors	4 684 ..	....	....	....	....	....	....	....	....
C. FINANCIAL DERIVATIVES	4 910 ..	....	....	....	....	....	....	....	....
Monetary authorities	4 911 ..	....	....	....	....	....	....	....	....
General government	4 912 ..	....	....	....	....	....	....	....	....
Banks	4 913 ..	....	....	....	....	....	....	....	....
Other sectors	4 914 ..	....	....	....	....	....	....	....	....
Assets	4 900 ..	....	....	....	....	....	....	....	....
Monetary authorities	4 901 ..	....	....	....	....	....	....	....	....
General government	4 902 ..	....	....	....	....	....	....	....	....
Banks	4 903 ..	....	....	....	....	....	....	....	....
Other sectors	4 904 ..	....	....	....	....	....	....	....	....
Liabilities	4 905 ..	....	....	....	....	....	....	....	....
Monetary authorities	4 906 ..	....	....	....	....	....	....	....	....
General government	4 907 ..	....	....	....	....	....	....	....	....
Banks	4 908 ..	....	....	....	....	....	....	....	....
Other sectors	4 909 ..	....	....	....	....	....	....	....	....

Table 2 (Concluded). STANDARD PRESENTATION, 2000–2007

(Millions of U.S. dollars)

	Code	2000	2001	2002	2003	2004	2005	2006	2007
D. OTHER INVESTMENT	4 700	**−414.2**	**826.3**	**−2.7**	**−713.2**	**−657.4**	**1,669.9**	**−1,639.5**	**1,490.5**
Assets	4 703	489.3	818.4	3,270.4	631.2	−1,542.8	−334.4	−3,781.8	−4,998.4
Trade credits	4 706	−20.4	−135.7	100.5	178.5	−133.2	−214.3	−304.4	−167.0
General government	4 707	. . . .	. . . .	. . . .	. . . .	. . . .	. . . .	. . . .	. . . .
of which: Short-term	4 709	. . . .	. . . .	. . . .	. . . .	. . . .	. . . .	. . . .	. . . .
Other sectors	4 710	−20.4	−135.7	100.5	178.5	−133.2	−214.3	−304.4	−167.0
of which: Short-term	4 712	*64.2*	*−93.8*	*98.1*	*123.3*	*−132.6*	*−252.8*	*−301.1*	*−160.8*
Loans	4 714	861.7	117.5	2,568.7	822.0	−886.7	−1,388.1	−1,788.2	−4,521.8
Monetary authorities	4 715	5.0	. . . .	. . . .	. . . .	. . . .	. . . .	. . . .	. . . .
of which: Short-term	4 718	*5.0*	. . . .	. . . .	. . . .	. . . .	. . . .	. . . .	. . . .
General government	4 719	. . . .	. . . .	. . . .	. . . .	. . . .	. . . .	. . . .	. . . .
of which: Short-term	4 721	. . . .	. . . .	. . . .	. . . .	. . . .	. . . .	. . . .	. . . .
Banks	4 722	856.7	117.5	2,568.7	822.0	−886.7	−1,388.1	−1,788.2	−4,521.8
of which: Short-term	4 724	*856.7*	*117.5*	*2,568.7*	*822.0*	*−886.7*	*−1,388.1*	*−1,788.2*	*−4,521.8*
Other sectors	4 725	. . . .	. . . .	. . . .	. . . .	. . . .	. . . .	. . . .	. . . .
of which: Short-term	4 727	. . . .	. . . .	. . . .	. . . .	. . . .	. . . .	. . . .	. . . .
Currency and deposits	4 730	−472.3	696.6	489.7	−318.1	−549.0	2,073.4	−1,508.7	−296.3
Monetary authorities	4 731	. . . .	. . . .	. . . .	. . . .	. . . .	. . . .	. . . .	. . . .
General government	4 732	−4.0	−2.1	−.9	32.1	−598.5	496.7	−309.1	. . . .
Banks	4 733	−468.3	698.7	490.6	−350.2	49.5	1,576.7	−1,199.6	−296.3
Other sectors	4 734	. . . .	. . . .	. . . .	. . . .	. . . .	. . . .	. . . .	. . . .
Other assets	4 736	120.3	140.0	111.5	−51.2	26.1	−805.4	−180.5	−13.3
Monetary authorities	4 737	.2	. . . .	. . . .	. . . .	. . . .	. . . .	. . . .	. . . .
of which: Short-term	4 739	*.2*	. . . .	. . . .	. . . .	. . . .	. . . .	. . . .	. . . .
General government	4 740	. . . .	. . . .	. . . .	. . . .	. . . .	. . . .	. . . .	. . . .
of which: Short-term	4 742	. . . .	. . . .	. . . .	. . . .	. . . .	. . . .	. . . .	. . . .
Banks	4 743	−203.0	200.0	235.2	57.4	126.4	−464.7	139.7	.6
of which: Short-term	4 745	*−203.0*	*200.0*	*235.2*	*57.4*	*126.4*	*−464.7*	*139.7*	*.6*
Other sectors	4 746	323.1	−60.0	−123.7	−108.6	−100.3	−340.7	−320.2	−13.9
of which: Short-term	4 748	*323.1*	*−60.0*	*−123.7*	*−108.6*	*−100.3*	*−340.7*	*−320.2*	*−13.9*
Liabilities	4 753	**−903.5**	**7.9**	**−3,273.1**	**−1,344.4**	**885.4**	**2,004.3**	**2,142.3**	**6,488.9**
Trade credits	4 756	−130.4	−15.1	−36.0	24.1	54.9	107.7	90.7	126.5
General government	4 757	. . . .	. . . .	. . . .	. . . .	. . . .	. . . .	. . . .	. . . .
of which: Short-term	4 759	. . . .	. . . .	. . . .	. . . .	. . . .	. . . .	. . . .	. . . .
Other sectors	4 760	−130.4	−15.1	−36.0	24.1	54.9	107.7	90.7	126.5
of which: Short-term	4 762	*−104.7*	*−13.1*	*−27.5*	*5.7*	*65.1*	*103.7*	*83.1*	*111.5*
Loans	4 764	579.2	287.7	−1,307.6	−701.0	602.8	853.7	780.3	1,648.0
Monetary authorities	4 765	−51.7	−33.3	−8.1	−9.5	−10.0	−9.7	−9.9	−10.3
of which: Use of Fund credit and loans from the Fund.	4 766	*−51.7*	*−33.3*	*−8.1*	*−9.5*	*−10.0*	*−9.7*	*−9.9*	*−10.3*
of which: Short-term	4 768	. . . .	. . . .	. . . .	. . . .	. . . .	. . . .	. . . .	. . . .
General government	4 769	−2.6	3.5	46.1	10.2	−37.0	−54.2	23.7	34.8
of which: Short-term	4 771	. . . .	. . . .	. . . .	. . . .	. . . .	. . . .	. . . .	. . . .
Banks	4 772	584.6	258.5	−1,376.8	−670.7	607.2	838.1	840.5	1,418.8
of which: Short-term	4 774	*213.4*	*153.3*	*−1,461.9*	*−365.1*	*287.2*	*295.6*	*446.0*	*752.0*
Other sectors	4 775	48.9	59.0	31.1	−31.0	42.6	79.5	−74.0	204.7
of which: Short-term	4 777	*56.6*	*73.6*	*38.2*	*−23.1*	*49.4*	*15.6*	*−3.2*	*208.3*
Currency and deposits	4 780	−1,033.5	−311.5	−1,990.8	−433.8	278.7	875.0	1,347.1	4,705.9
Monetary authorities	4 781	−6.4	3.7	−.9	1.6	. . . .	. . . .	2.4	10.1
General government	4 782	. . . .	. . . .	. . . .	. . . .	. . . .	. . . .	. . . .	. . . .
Banks	4 783	−1,027.1	−315.2	−1,989.9	−435.4	278.7	875.0	1,344.7	4,695.8
Other sectors	4 784	. . . .	. . . .	. . . .	. . . .	. . . .	. . . .	. . . .	. . . .
Other liabilities	4 786	−318.8	46.8	61.3	−233.7	−51.0	167.9	−75.8	8.5
Monetary authorities	4 787	. . . .	. . . .	. . . .	. . . .	. . . .	. . . .	. . . .	. . . .
of which: Short-term	4 789	. . . .	. . . .	. . . .	. . . .	. . . .	. . . .	. . . .	. . . .
General government	4 790	.3	.1	. . . .	. . . .	. . . .	. . . .	. . . .	. . . .
of which: Short-term	4 792	*.3*	*.1*	. . . .	. . . .	. . . .	. . . .	. . . .	. . . .
Banks	4 793	17.0	53.4	54.9	−243.2	−65.1	153.3	−84.4	−3.0
of which: Short-term	4 795	*17.0*	*53.4*	*54.9*	*−243.2*	*−65.1*	*153.3*	*−84.4*	*−3.0*
Other sectors	4 796	−336.1	−6.7	6.4	9.5	14.1	14.6	8.6	11.5
of which: Short-term	4 798	*−336.1*	*−6.7*	*6.4*	*9.5*	*14.1*	*14.6*	*8.6*	*11.5*
E. RESERVE ASSETS	4 802	**108.1**	**−623.3**	**−135.9**	**268.2**	**397.0**	**−522.8**	**−161.8**	**−609.6**
Monetary gold	4 812	. . . .	. . . .	. . . .	. . . .	. . . .	. . . .	. . . .	. . . .
Special drawing rights	4 811	1.1	−1.0	.5	.3	. . . .	−.3	−.1	.5
Reserve position in the Fund	4 810	. . . .	. . . .	. . . .	. . . .	. . . .	. . . .	. . . .	. . . .
Foreign exchange	4 803	−41.3	−658.9	−118.9	277.6	421.5	−520.8	−148.5	−620.5
Other claims	4 813	148.3	36.6	−17.5	−9.7	−24.5	−1.7	−13.2	10.4
NET ERRORS AND OMISSIONS	4 998	**262.5**	**−498.6**	**45.2**	**89.9**	**110.4**	**−357.9**	**308.1**	**−775.3**

Table 3. INTERNATIONAL INVESTMENT POSITION (End-period stocks), 2000–2007

(Millions of U.S. dollars)

	Code	2000	2001	2002	2003	2004	2005	2006	2007
ASSETS	8 995 C.	23,880.9	24,395.3	21,341.2	20,515.9	22,345.0	24,303.4	28,996.0	35,711.6
Direct investment abroad	8 505 ..	....	....	....	....	....	....	....	....
Equity capital and reinvested earnings	8 506 ..	....	....	....	....	....	....	....	....
Claims on affiliated enterprises	8 507 ..	....	....	....	....	....	....	....	....
Liabilities to affiliated enterprises	8 508 ..	....	....	....	....	....	....	....	....
Other capital	8 530 ..	....	....	....	....	....	....	....	....
Claims on affiliated enterprises	8 535 ..	....	....	....	....	....	....	....	....
Liabilities to affiliated enterprises	8 540 ..	....	....	....	....	....	....	....	....
Portfolio investment	8 602 ..	2,649.6	3,373.0	3,452.1	3,525.7	4,206.1	5,308.9	6,056.9	7,163.5
Equity securities	8 610 ..	50.4	51.6	53.6	44.9	38.1	55.0	188.1	83.2
Monetary authorities	8 611 ..	....	....	....	....	....	....	....	....
General government	8 612 ..	....	....	....	....	....	....	....	....
Banks	8 613 ..	....	....	....	....	....	....	....	....
Other sectors	8 614 ..	50.4	51.6	53.6	44.9	38.1	55.0	188.1	83.2
Debt securities	8 619 ..	2,599.2	3,321.4	3,398.5	3,480.8	4,168.0	5,253.9	5,868.8	7,080.3
Bonds and notes	8 620 ..	2,599.2	3,321.4	3,390.5	3,480.8	4,168.0	5,253.1	5,794.3	7,046.2
Monetary authorities	8 621 ..	....	....	....	....	....	....	....	....
General government	8 622 ..	52.4	56.8	20.0	12.9	18.0	18.0	18.0	18.0
Banks	8 623 ..	2,521.2	3,236.5	3,288.1	3,325.0	3,996.2	5,083.8	5,403.2	6,853.7
Other sectors	8 624 ..	25.6	28.1	82.4	142.9	153.8	151.3	373.1	174.5
Money market instruments	8 630 ..	....	....	8.0	....	....	.8	74.5	34.1
Monetary authorities	8 631 ..	....	....	....	....	....	....	....	....
General government	8 632 ..	....	....	....	....	....	....	....	....
Banks	8 633 ..	....	....	....	....	....	....	....	....
Other sectors	8 634 ..	....	....	8.0	....	....	.8	74.5	34.1
Financial derivatives	8 900 ..	....	....	....	....	....	....	....	....
Monetary authorities	8 901 ..	....	....	....	....	....	....	....	....
General government	8 902 ..	....	....	....	....	....	....	....	....
Banks	8 903 ..	....	....	....	....	....	....	....	....
Other sectors	8 904 ..	....	....	....	....	....	....	....	....
Other investment	8 703 ..	19,418.2	18,586.4	15,316.0	14,683.7	16,228.6	16,562.9	20,344.7	25,343.1
Trade credits	8 706 ..	2,148.0	2,283.7	2,183.2	2,004.7	2,137.9	2,352.2	2,656.6	2,823.6
General government	8 707 ..	....	....	....	....	....	....	....	....
of which: Short-term	8 709 ..	....	....	....	....	....	....	....	....
Other sectors	8 710 ..	2,148.0	2,283.7	2,183.2	2,004.7	2,137.9	2,352.2	2,656.6	2,823.6
of which: Short-term	8 712 ..	*2,026.1*	*2,119.9*	*2,021.8*	*1,898.5*	*2,031.1*	*2,283.9*	*2,585.0*	*2,745.8*
Loans	8 714 ..	9,942.7	9,810.3	7,241.5	6,419.5	7,312.5	8,700.6	10,488.7	15,010.4
Monetary authorities	8 715 ..	....	....	....	....	....	....	....	....
of which: Short-term	8 718 ..	....	....	....	....	....	....	....	....
General government	8 719 ..	....	....	....	....	....	....	....	....
of which: Short-term	8 721 ..	....	....	....	....	....	....	....	....
Banks	8 722 ..	9,942.7	9,810.3	7,241.5	6,419.5	7,312.5	8,700.6	10,488.7	15,010.4
of which: Short-term	8 724 ..	*9,942.7*	*9,810.3*	*7,241.5*	*6,419.5*	*7,312.5*	*8,700.6*	*10,488.7*	*15,010.4*
Other sectors	8 725 ..	....	....	....	....	....	....	....	....
of which: Short-term	8 727 ..	....	....	....	....	....	....	....	....
Currency and deposits	8 730 ..	6,319.5	5,626.5	5,136.9	5,453.9	6,001.4	3,927.9	5,436.6	5,732.9
Monetary authorities	8 731 ..	....	....	....	....	....	....	....	....
General government	8 732 ..	37.7	39.8	40.7	7.5	606.0	109.3	418.4	418.4
Banks	8 733 ..	6,281.8	5,586.7	5,096.2	5,446.4	5,395.4	3,818.6	5,018.2	5,314.5
Other sectors	8 734 ..	....	....	....	....	....	....	....	....
Other assets	8 736 ..	1,008.0	865.9	754.4	805.6	776.8	1,582.2	1,762.8	1,776.2
Monetary authorities	8 737 ..	....	....	....	....	....	....	....	....
of which: Short-term	8 739 ..	....	....	....	....	....	....	....	....
General government	8 740 ..	29.2	29.2	29.2	29.2	29.2	29.2	29.2	29.2
of which: Short-term	8 742 ..	....	....	....	....	....	....	....	....
Banks	8 743 ..	848.6	646.5	411.3	353.9	224.8	689.5	549.9	549.4
of which: Short-term	8 745 ..	*848.6*	*646.5*	*411.3*	*353.9*	*224.8*	*689.5*	*549.9*	*549.4*
Other sectors	8 746 ..	130.2	190.2	313.9	422.5	522.8	863.5	1,183.7	1,197.6
of which: Short-term	8 748 ..	*130.2*	*190.2*	*313.9*	*422.5*	*522.8*	*863.5*	*1,183.7*	*1,197.6*
Reserve assets	8 802 ..	1,813.1	2,435.9	2,573.2	2,306.5	1,910.4	2,431.6	2,594.4	3,205.0
Monetary gold	8 812 ..	....	....	....	....	....	....	....	....
Special drawing rights	8 811 ..	.3	1.4	1.1	.8	.9	1.1	1.3	.9
Reserve position in the Fund	8 810 ..	15.5	14.9	16.1	17.6	18.4	17.0	17.8	18.7
Foreign exchange	8 803 ..	949.5	2,271.4	2,555.9	2,278.3	1,856.8	2,377.6	2,526.1	3,146.6
Other claims	8 813 ..	847.8	148.2	.1	9.8	34.3	36.0	49.2	38.8

Table 3 (Concluded). INTERNATIONAL INVESTMENT POSITION (End-period stocks), 2000–2007

(Millions of U.S. dollars)

	Code	2000	2001	2002	2003	2004	2005	2006	2007
LIABILITIES	8 995 D.	**32,300.8**	**33,502.2**	**30,382.1**	**29,806.3**	**32,512.5**	**35,795.3**	**40,711.1**	**49,493.8**
Direct investment in Panama	8 555	**6,774.9**	**7,314.3**	**7,412.9**	**8,230.4**	**9,249.5**	**10,167.1**	**12,665.0**	**14,516.3**
Equity capital and reinvested earnings	8 556	5,743.2	6,330.3	6,356.9	7,116.5	8,101.4	8,571.0	10,704.6	12,304.2
Claims on direct investors	8 557	....	....	....	....	....	....	....	....
Liabilities to direct investors	8 558	5,743.2	6,330.3	6,356.9	7,116.5	8,101.4	8,571.0	10,704.6	12,304.2
Other capital	8 580	1,031.7	984.0	1,056.0	1,113.9	1,148.1	1,596.1	1,960.4	2,212.1
Claims on direct investors	8 585	−688.1	−827.8	−976.3	−1,209.4	−1,468.2	−1,655.0	−1,976.3	−2,220.4
Liabilities to direct investors	8 590	1,719.8	1,811.8	2,032.3	2,323.3	2,616.3	3,251.1	3,936.7	4,432.5
Portfolio investment	8 652	**4,097.6**	**4,821.4**	**4,833.7**	**4,956.8**	**5,702.8**	**6,104.8**	**6,359.7**	**6,809.7**
Equity securities	8 660	....	....	....	....	....	....	....	....
Banks	8 663	....	....	....	....	....	....	....	....
Other sectors	8 664	....	....	....	....	....	....	....	....
Debt securities	8 669	4,097.6	4,821.4	4,833.7	4,956.8	5,702.8	6,104.8	6,359.7	6,809.7
Bonds and notes	8 670	4,097.6	4,821.4	4,833.7	4,956.8	5,702.8	6,104.8	6,359.7	6,809.7
Monetary authorities	8 671	....	....	....	....	....	....	....	....
General government	8 672	4,097.6	4,821.4	4,833.7	4,956.8	5,702.8	6,104.8	6,359.7	6,809.7
Banks	8 673	....	....	....	....	....	....	....	....
Other sectors	8 674	....	....	....	....	....	....	....	....
Money market instruments	8 680	....	....	....	....	....	....	....	....
Monetary authorities	8 681	....	....	....	....	....	....	....	....
General government	8 682	....	....	....	....	....	....	....	....
Banks	8 683	....	....	....	....	....	....	....	....
Other sectors	8 684	....	....	....	....	....	....	....	....
Financial derivatives	8 905	....	....	....	....	....	....	....	....
Monetary authorities	8 906	....	....	....	....	....	....	....	....
General government	8 907	....	....	....	....	....	....	....	....
Banks	8 908	....	....	....	....	....	....	....	....
Other sectors	8 909	....	....	....	....	....	....	....	....
Other investment	8 753	**21,428.3**	**21,366.5**	**18,135.5**	**16,619.1**	**17,560.2**	**19,523.4**	**21,686.4**	**28,167.8**
Trade credits	8 756	767.8	752.7	716.7	740.8	795.7	903.4	994.1	1,120.6
General government	8 757	....	....	....	....	....	....	....	....
of which: Short-term	8 759	....	....	....	....	....	....	....	....
Other sectors	8 760	767.8	752.7	716.7	740.8	795.7	903.4	994.1	1,120.6
of which: Short-term	8 762	*726.4*	*713.3*	*685.8*	*691.5*	*756.6*	*860.3*	*943.4*	*1,054.9*
Loans	8 764	6,695.9	6,960.7	5,696.0	5,008.0	5,660.0	6,472.2	7,266.2	8,906.7
Monetary authorities	8 765	172.7	136.6	132.5	127.3	118.9	106.5	97.7	88.0
of which: Use of Fund credit and loans from the Fund	8 766	*90.0*	*53.9*	*49.8*	*44.6*	*36.2*	*23.8*	*15.0*	*5.3*
of which: Short-term	8 768	....	....	....	....	....	....	....	....
General government	8 769	1,350.8	1,332.2	1,415.1	1,433.2	1,440.8	1,349.5	1,385.9	1,412.9
of which: Short-term	8 771	....	....	....	....	....	....	....	....
Banks	8 772	4,656.2	4,914.5	3,537.7	2,867.0	3,474.2	4,312.3	5,152.8	6,571.6
of which: Short-term	8 774	*2,687.7*	*2,841.0*	*1,379.1*	*1,014.0*	*1,301.2*	*1,596.8*	*2,042.8*	*2,794.8*
Other sectors	8 775	516.2	577.4	610.6	580.5	626.0	703.9	629.8	834.3
of which: Short-term	8 777	*444.2*	*517.8*	*556.0*	*532.9*	*582.3*	*597.9*	*594.7*	*803.0*
Currency and deposits	8 780	13,079.9	12,738.3	10,747.5	10,313.7	10,592.8	11,468.1	12,822.3	17,528.2
Monetary authorities	8 781	42.4	46.1	45.2	46.8	46.8	46.8	56.3	66.4
General government	8 782	....	....	....	....	....	....	....	....
Banks	8 783	13,037.5	12,692.2	10,702.3	10,266.9	10,546.0	11,421.3	12,766.0	17,461.8
Other sectors	8 784	....	....	....	....	....	....	....	....
Other liabilities	8 786	884.7	914.8	975.3	556.6	511.7	679.6	603.8	612.3
Monetary authorities	8 787	31.2	31.2	31.2	31.2	31.2	31.2	31.2	31.2
of which: Short-term	8 789	*31.2*	*31.2*	*31.2*	*31.2*	*31.2*	*31.2*	*31.2*	*31.2*
General government	8 790	2.8	2.9	2.1	2.1	2.1	2.1	2.1	2.1
of which: Short-term	8 792	*2.8*	*2.9*	*2.1*	*2.1*	*2.1*	*2.1*	*2.1*	*2.1*
Banks	8 793	826.6	863.3	918.2	490.0	431.0	584.3	499.9	496.9
of which: Short-term	8 795	*826.6*	*863.3*	*918.2*	*490.0*	*431.0*	*584.3*	*499.9*	*496.9*
Other sectors	8 796	24.1	17.4	23.8	33.3	47.4	62.0	70.6	82.1
of which: Short-term	8 798	*24.1*	*17.4*	*23.8*	*33.3*	*47.4*	*62.0*	*70.6*	*82.1*
NET INTERNATIONAL INVESTMENT POSITION	8 995	**−8,419.9**	**−9,106.9**	**−9,040.9**	**−9,290.4**	**−10,167.5**	**−11,491.9**	**−11,715.1**	**−13,782.3**
Conversion rates: balboas per U.S. dollar (end of period)	0 102	**1.0000**	**1.0000**	**1.0000**	**1.0000**	**1.0000**	**1.0000**	**1.0000**	**1.0000**

Table 1. ANALYTIC PRESENTATION, 2000–2007

(Millions of U.S. dollars)

	Code	2000	2001	2002	2003	2004	2005	2006	2007
A. Current Account[1]	4 993 Z.	**345.4**	**282.1**	**−128.7**	**−35.2**	**−81.8**	**422.7**	....	....
Goods: exports f.o.b.	2 100 ..	2,094.1	1,812.9	1,639.9	2,200.8	2,554.8	3,278.0	....	....
Goods: imports f.o.b.	3 100 ..	−998.8	−932.4	−1,077.4	−1,187.3	−1,459.3	−1,525.3	....	....
Balance on Goods	4 100 ..	*1,095.3*	*880.5*	*562.5*	*1,013.5*	*1,095.5*	*1,752.7*	....	....
Services: credit	2 200 ..	242.7	285.1	161.6	232.8	203.2	302.2	....	....
Services: debit	3 200 ..	−772.3	−662.0	−677.8	−867.7	−997.6	−1,167.1	....	....
Balance on Goods and Services	4 991 ..	*565.7*	*503.7*	*46.3*	*378.6*	*301.2*	*887.8*	....	....
Income: credit	2 300 ..	32.0	20.0	27.3	16.2	19.8	26.1	....	....
Income: debit	3 300 ..	−242.1	−250.2	−229.4	−493.0	−456.0	−564.6	....	....
Balance on Goods, Services, and Income	4 992 ..	*355.6*	*273.4*	*−155.9*	*−98.2*	*−135.0*	*349.4*	....	....
Current transfers: credit	2 379 Z.	62.4	75.9	85.8	144.2	130.5	166.9	....	....
Current transfers: debit	3 379 ..	−72.7	−67.3	−58.7	−81.2	−77.3	−93.6	....	....
B. Capital Account[1]	4 994 Z.	....	....	....	....	....	....	....	....
Capital account: credit	2 994 Z.	7.2	5.9	5.1	5.6	6.2	6.4	....	....
Capital account: debit	3 994 ..	−7.2	−5.9	−5.1	−5.6	−6.2	−6.4	....	....
Total, Groups A Plus B	4 981 ..	*345.4*	*282.1*	*−128.7*	*−35.2*	*−81.8*	*422.7*	....	....
C. Financial Account[1]	4 995 W.	**−254.1**	**−151.9**	**56.4**	**−281.9**	**−42.3**	**−752.0**	....	....
Direct investment abroad	4 505 ..	....	....	.7	3.0	....	−6.6	....	....
Direct investment in Papua New Guinea	4 555 Z.	95.9	62.5	18.3	101.0	55.4	33.6	....	....
Portfolio investment assets	4 602 ..	−123.8	−72.7	−1.3	−46.6	−104.0	27.1	....	....
Equity securities	4 610 ..	....	....	16.0	−64.0	−16.0	−17.9	....	....
Debt securities	4 619 ..	−123.8	−72.7	−17.3	17.4	−88.0	44.9	....	....
Portfolio investment liabilities	4 652 Z.	....	....	....	....	....	....	....	....
Equity securities	4 660 ..	....	....	....	....	....	....	....	....
Debt securities	4 669 Z.	....	....	....	....	....	....	....	....
Financial derivatives	4 910 ..	....	....	....	....	....	....	....	....
Financial derivatives assets	4 900 ..	....	....	....	....	....	....	....	....
Financial derivatives liabilities	4 905 ..	....	....	....	....	....	....	....	....
Other investment assets	4 703 ..	−41.0	−66.9	108.8	−221.3	34.2	−639.7	....	....
Monetary authorities	4 701 ..	....	....	....	....	....	....	....	....
General government	4 704 ..	....	....	....	....	....	....	....	....
Banks	4 705 ..	−21.2	−26.7	−46.3	−106.9	−149.9	−141.1	....	....
Other sectors	4 728 ..	−19.8	−40.2	155.1	−114.4	184.2	−498.6	....	....
Other investment liabilities	4 753 W.	−185.2	−74.7	−70.2	−118.0	−27.9	−166.4	....	....
Monetary authorities	4 753 WA	....	....	....	....	−70.8	−112.9	....	....
General government	4 753 ZB	.2	49.0	−86.7	−127.0	−130.4	−117.8	....	....
Banks	4 753 ZC	....	....	....	1.7	5.3	8.7	....	....
Other sectors	4 753 ZD	−185.4	−123.7	16.5	7.2	168.0	55.6	....	....
Total, Groups A Through C	4 983 ..	*91.3*	*130.2*	*−72.4*	*−317.1*	*−124.1*	*−329.3*	....	....
D. Net Errors and Omissions	4 998 ..	**13.1**	**−1.6**	**91.3**	**39.8**	**26.0**	**47.0**	....	....
Total, Groups A Through D	4 984 ..	*104.5*	*128.6*	*18.9*	*−277.3*	*−98.1*	*−282.3*	....	....
E. Reserves and Related Items	4 802 A.	**−104.5**	**−128.6**	**−18.9**	**277.3**	**98.1**	**282.3**	....	....
Reserve assets	4 802 ..	−127.9	−203.6	−55.9	−99.7	−102.3	−82.3	....	....
Use of Fund credit and loans	4 766 ..	18.1	70.9	....	−5.4	−60.0	−62.2	....	....
Exceptional financing	4 920 ..	5.3	4.1	37.0	382.3	260.4	426.8	....	....
Conversion rates: kina per U.S. dollar	0 101 ..	**2.7822**	**3.3887**	**3.8952**	**3.5635**	**3.2225**	**3.1019**	**3.0567**	**2.9653**

[1] Excludes components that have been classified in the categories of Group E.

Table 2. STANDARD PRESENTATION, 2000–2007

(Millions of U.S. dollars)

	Code	2000	2001	2002	2003	2004	2005	2006	2007
CURRENT ACCOUNT	4 993	350.7	286.1	−128.7	139.6	122.2	640.4	....	....
A. GOODS	4 100	1,095.3	880.5	562.5	1,013.5	1,095.5	1,752.7	....	....
Credit	2 100	2,094.1	1,812.9	1,639.9	2,200.8	2,554.8	3,278.0	....	....
General merchandise: exports f.o.b.	2 110	2,094.1	1,812.9	1,639.9	2,200.8	2,554.8	3,278.0		
Goods for processing: exports f.o.b.	2 150	....	....	....	....	....	....		
Repairs on goods	2 160	....	....	....	....	....	....		
Goods procured in ports by carriers	2 170	....	....	....	....	....	....		
Nonmonetary gold	2 180	....	....	....	....	....	....		
Debit	3 100	−998.8	−932.4	−1,077.4	−1,187.3	−1,459.3	−1,525.3	....	....
General merchandise: imports f.o.b.	3 110	−998.8	−932.4	−1,077.4	−1,187.3	−1,459.3	−1,525.3		
Goods for processing: imports f.o.b.	3 150	....	....	....	....	....	....		
Repairs on goods	3 160	....	....	....	....	....	....		
Goods procured in ports by carriers	3 170	....	....	....	....	....	....		
Nonmonetary gold	3 180	....	....	....	....	....	....		
B. SERVICES	4 200	−529.6	−376.9	−516.2	−634.9	−794.3	−864.9	....	....
Total credit	2 200	*242.7*	*285.1*	*161.6*	*232.8*	*203.2*	*302.2*		
Total debit	3 200	*−772.3*	*−662.0*	*−677.8*	*−867.7*	*−997.6*	*−1,167.1*		
Transportation services, credit	2 205	11.8	21.3	4.8	16.7	20.9	31.2	....	....
Passenger	2 850	....	....	....	....	*.1*	*.1*		
Freight	2 851	*11.8*	*21.3*	*4.8*	*16.6*	*20.8*	*31.1*		
Other	2 852	....	....	....	....	....	....		
Sea transport, passenger	2 207	....	....	....	....	....	.1		
Sea transport, freight	2 208	11.8	21.3	4.8	15.7	19.1	19.7		
Sea transport, other	2 209	....	....	....	....	....	....		
Air transport, passenger	2 211	....	....	....	....	....	....		
Air transport, freight	2 212	....	....	....	.9	1.3	5.8		
Air transport, other	2 213	....	....	....	....	....	....		
Other transport, passenger	2 215	....	....	....	....	.1	....		
Other transport, freight	2 216	....	....	....	....	.4	5.6		
Other transport, other	2 217	....	....	....	....	....	....		
Transportation services, debit	3 205	−162.9	−172.9	−170.3	−227.4	−270.8	−278.7	....	....
Passenger	3 850	....	....	....	....	*−.7*	*−.5*		
Freight	3 851	*−162.9*	*−172.9*	*−170.3*	*−187.1*	*−233.4*	*−236.3*		
Other	3 852	....	....	....	*−40.3*	*−36.6*	*−41.8*		
Sea transport, passenger	3 207	....	....	....	....	−.1	−.5		
Sea transport, freight	3 208	−162.9	−172.9	−170.3	−187.1	−233.4	−236.3		
Sea transport, other	3 209	....	....	....	−40.3	−36.6	−41.8		
Air transport, passenger	3 211	....	....	....	....	....	....		
Air transport, freight	3 212	....	....	....	....	....	....		
Air transport, other	3 213	....	....	....	....	....	....		
Other transport, passenger	3 215	....	....	....	....	−.7	....		
Other transport, freight	3 216	....	....	....	−.1	....	....		
Other transport, other	3 217	....	....	....	....	....	....		
Travel, credit	2 236	7.2	5.2	2.8	4.0	5.8	3.6	....	....
Business travel	2 237	6.2	4.4	2.2	3.7	4.3	2.4		
Personal travel	2 240	1.0	.7	.6	.3	1.5	1.2		
Travel, debit	3 236	−50.3	−38.2	−59.5	−51.9	−71.2	−55.6	....	....
Business travel	3 237	−40.6	−29.7	−23.6	−15.6	−20.6	−18.1		
Personal travel	3 240	−9.7	−8.5	−35.9	−36.2	−50.6	−37.5		
Other services, credit	2 200 BA	223.6	258.6	154.0	212.2	176.5	267.4	....	....
Communications	2 245	....	....	....	.4	3.9	5.7		
Construction	2 249	....	....	....	96.3	28.1	15.3		
Insurance	2 253	4.5	5.3	2.4	5.9	8.9	13.0		
Financial	2 260	....	....	....	6.2	5.9	2.5		
Computer and information	2 262	....	....	....	.1	.2	.9		
Royalties and licence fees	2 266	....	....	....	....	....	....		
Other business services	2 268	219.2	253.4	151.6	89.4	107.1	212.6		
Personal, cultural, and recreational	2 287	....	....	....	....	.2	.4		
Government, n.i.e.	2 291	....	....	....	13.8	22.2	17.0		
Other services, debit	3 200 BA	−559.1	−450.9	−448.0	−588.4	−655.6	−832.8	....	....
Communications	3 245	....	....	....	−4.3	−11.1	−7.7		
Construction	3 249	....	....	....	−39.9	−37.9	−58.4		
Insurance	3 253	−40.2	−48.3	−57.4	−64.5	−65.2	−64.6		
Financial	3 260	....	....	....	−16.0	−45.4	−53.4		
Computer and information	3 262	....	....	....	−10.4	−14.5	−11.7		
Royalties and licence fees	3 266	....	....	....	....	....	....		
Other business services	3 268	−518.9	−402.6	−390.6	−448.1	−452.2	−620.8		
Personal, cultural, and recreational	3 287	....	....	....	....	−.2	−.1		
Government, n.i.e.	3 291	....	....	....	−5.3	−29.1	−16.2		

2008, International Monetary Fund: *Balance of Payments Statistics Yearbook*

Table 2 (Continued). STANDARD PRESENTATION, 2000–2007

(Millions of U.S. dollars)

	Code	2000	2001	2002	2003	2004	2005	2006	2007
C. INCOME	4 300	**−210.1**	**−230.3**	**−202.1**	**−476.8**	**−436.2**	**−538.5**	....	....
Total credit	2 300	*32.0*	*20.0*	*27.3*	*16.2*	*19.8*	*26.1*	....	....
Total debit	3 300	*−242.1*	*−250.2*	*−229.4*	*−493.0*	*−456.0*	*−564.6*	....	....
Compensation of employees, credit	2 310	....	....	....	2.9	1.6	1.2	....	....
Compensation of employees, debit	3 310	....	....	−12.0	−50.0	−55.6	−53.7	....	....
Investment income, credit	2 320	**32.0**	**20.0**	**27.3**	**13.3**	**18.2**	**25.0**	....	....
Direct investment income	2 330	1.2	1.6	7.3	6.9	2.2	.9	....	....
Dividends and distributed branch profits	2 332	1.2	1.6	7.3	6.9	2.2	.9	....	....
Reinvested earnings and undistributed branch profits	2 333	....	....	....	....	....	....	....	....
Income on debt (interest)	2 334	....	....	....	....	....	....	....	....
Portfolio investment income	2 339	10.1	5.8	11.5	4.3	14.0	9.7	....	....
Income on equity	2 340	....	....	....	....	....	....	....	....
Income on bonds and notes	2 350	10.1	5.8	11.5	4.3	14.0	9.7	....	....
Income on money market instruments	2 360	....	....	....	....	....	....	....	....
Other investment income	2 370	20.7	12.6	8.5	2.1	2.0	14.4	....	....
Investment income, debit	3 320	**−242.1**	**−250.2**	**−217.5**	**−443.0**	**−400.4**	**−510.9**	....	....
Direct investment income	3 330	−197.7	−205.7	−173.4	−399.7	−361.4	−475.0	....	....
Dividends and distributed branch profits	3 332	−125.9	−154.3	−138.2	−364.0	−328.6	−437.6	....	....
Reinvested earnings and undistributed branch profits	3 333	−21.7	−17.8	−15.4	−16.8	−18.6	−19.3	....	....
Income on debt (interest)	3 334	−50.1	−33.6	−19.8	−18.8	−14.2	−18.1	....	....
Portfolio investment income	3 339	....	....	....	....	....	....	....	....
Income on equity	3 340	....	....	....	....	....	....	....	....
Income on bonds and notes	3 350	....	....	....	....	....	....	....	....
Income on money market instruments	3 360	....	....	....	....	....	....	....	....
Other investment income	3 370	−44.4	−44.6	−44.1	−43.4	−38.9	−35.9	....	....
D. CURRENT TRANSFERS	4 379	**−4.9**	**12.8**	**27.1**	**237.7**	**257.2**	**291.1**	....	....
Credit	2 379	**67.7**	**80.0**	**85.8**	**319.0**	**334.5**	**384.7**	....	....
General government	2 380	5.3	4.1	....	174.7	204.0	217.8	....	....
Other sectors	2 390	62.4	75.9	85.8	144.2	130.5	166.9	....	....
Workers' remittances	2 391	....	....	5.6	4.0	7.9	5.7	....	....
Other current transfers	2 392	62.4	75.9	80.2	140.2	122.5	161.2	....	....
Debit	3 379	**−72.7**	**−67.3**	**−58.7**	**−81.2**	**−77.3**	**−93.6**	....	....
General government	3 380	....	....	....	....	....	....	....	....
Other sectors	3 390	−72.7	−67.3	−58.7	−81.2	−77.3	−93.6	....	....
Workers' remittances	3 391	−11.2	−10.7	−45.4	−41.2	−61.1	−74.5	....	....
Other current transfers	3 392	−61.4	−56.5	−13.2	−40.0	−16.2	−19.1	....	....
CAPITAL AND FINANCIAL ACCOUNT	4 996	**−363.8**	**−284.5**	**37.4**	**−179.4**	**−148.1**	**−687.4**	....	....
CAPITAL ACCOUNT	4 994	....	....	....	....	....	....	....	....
Total credit	2 994	*7.2*	*5.9*	*5.1*	*5.6*	*6.2*	*6.4*	....	....
Total debit	3 994	*−7.2*	*−5.9*	*−5.1*	*−5.6*	*−6.2*	*−6.4*	....	....
Capital transfers, credit	2 400	**7.2**	**5.9**	**5.1**	**5.6**	**6.2**	**6.4**	....	....
General government	2 401	....	....	....	....	....	....	....	....
Debt forgiveness	2 402	....	....	....	....	....	....	....	....
Other capital transfers	2 410	....	....	....	....	....	....	....	....
Other sectors	2 430	7.2	5.9	5.1	5.6	6.2	6.4	....	....
Migrants' transfers	2 431	7.2	5.9	5.1	5.6	6.2	6.4	....	....
Debt forgiveness	2 432	....	....	....	....	....	....	....	....
Other capital transfers	2 440	....	....	....	....	....	....	....	....
Capital transfers, debit	3 400	**−7.2**	**−5.9**	**−5.1**	**−5.6**	**−6.2**	**−6.4**	....	....
General government	3 401	....	....	....	....	....	....	....	....
Debt forgiveness	3 402	....	....	....	....	....	....	....	....
Other capital transfers	3 410	....	....	....	....	....	....	....	....
Other sectors	3 430	−7.2	−5.9	−5.1	−5.6	−6.2	−6.4	....	....
Migrants' transfers	3 431	−7.2	−5.9	−5.1	−5.6	−6.2	−6.4	....	....
Debt forgiveness	3 432	....	....	....	....	....	....	....	....
Other capital transfers	3 440	....	....	....	....	....	....	....	....
Nonproduced nonfinancial assets, credit	2 480	....	....	....	....	....	....	....	....
Nonproduced nonfinancial assets, debit	3 480	....	....	....	....	....	....	....	....

Table 2 (Continued). STANDARD PRESENTATION, 2000–2007

(Millions of U.S. dollars)

	Code	2000	2001	2002	2003	2004	2005	2006	2007
FINANCIAL ACCOUNT.............................	4 995 ..	**−363.8**	**−284.5**	**37.4**	**−179.4**	**−148.1**	**−687.4**	....	....
A. DIRECT INVESTMENT..........................	4 500 ..	**95.9**	**62.5**	**19.0**	**104.1**	**55.4**	**27.0**	....	....
Direct investment abroad.................................	4 505 ..	....	....	.7	3.0	....	−6.6	....	....
Equity capital...	4 510 ..	....	....	....	3.0	−.6	−6.6	....	....
Claims on affiliated enterprises.....................	4 515 ..	....	....	....	....	....	....	....	....
Liabilities to affiliated enterprises.................	4 520 ..	....	....	....	3.0	−.6	−6.6	....	....
Reinvested earnings.......................................	4 525 ..	....	....	....	....	....	....	....	....
Other capital...	4 530 ..	....	....	.7	....	.6	....	....	....
Claims on affiliated enterprises.....................	4 535 ..	....	....	....	....	....	....	....	....
Liabilities to affiliated enterprises.................	4 540 ..	....	....	.7	....	.6	....	....	....
Direct investment in Papua New Guinea............	4 555 ..	**95.9**	**62.5**	**18.3**	**101.0**	**55.4**	**33.6**	....	....
Equity capital...	4 560 ..	74.6	45.3	2.9	84.0	37.5	13.6	....	....
Claims on direct investors.............................	4 565 ..	....	....	−.9	−42.2	−1.0	−1.5	....	....
Liabilities to direct investors.........................	4 570 ..	74.6	45.3	3.8	126.3	38.5	15.0	....	....
Reinvested earnings.......................................	4 575 ..	21.7	17.8	15.4	16.8	18.6	19.3	....	....
Other capital...	4 580 ..	−.4	−.5	....	.1	−.7	.7	....	....
Claims on direct investors.............................	4 585 ..	−.6	−.6	....	....	−.7	−.2	....	....
Liabilities to direct investors.........................	4 590 ..	.2	.1	....	.1	....	.8	....	....
B. PORTFOLIO INVESTMENT........................	4 600 ..	**−123.8**	**−72.7**	**−1.3**	**−46.6**	**−104.0**	**25.5**	....	....
Assets...	4 602 ..	**−123.8**	**−72.7**	**−1.3**	**−46.6**	**−104.0**	**27.1**	....	....
Equity securities..	4 610 ..	....	....	16.0	−64.0	−16.0	−17.9	....	....
Monetary authorities..................................	4 611 ..	....	....	....	....	....	−2.5	....	....
General government....................................	4 612 ..	....	....	....	....	....	....	....	....
Banks...	4 613 ..	....	....	....	....	....	....	....	....
Other sectors..	4 614 ..	....	....	16.0	−64.0	−16.0	−15.3	....	....
Debt securities..	4 619 ..	−123.8	−72.7	−17.3	17.4	−88.0	44.9	....	....
Bonds and notes...	4 620 ..	−10.8	.7	2.9	−2.4	20.2	6.1	....	....
Monetary authorities................................	4 621 ..	....	....	....	....	....	....	....	....
General government..................................	4 622 ..	....	....	....	....	....	6.5	....	....
Banks...	4 623 ..	....	....	....	....	....	....	....	....
Other sectors..	4 624 ..	−10.8	.7	2.9	−2.4	20.2	−.4	....	....
Money market instruments..........................	4 630 ..	−113.0	−73.4	−20.2	19.9	−108.2	38.8	....	....
Monetary authorities................................	4 631 ..	....	....	....	....	....	....	....	....
General government..................................	4 632 ..	....	....	....	....	....	....	....	....
Banks...	4 633 ..	....	....	....	−10.4	....	....	....	....
Other sectors..	4 634 ..	−113.0	−73.4	−20.2	30.3	−108.2	38.8	....	....
Liabilities..	4 652 ..	....	....	....	....	....	**−1.6**	....	....
Equity securities..	4 660 ..	....	....	....	....	....	....	....	....
Banks...	4 663 ..	....	....	....	....	....	....	....	....
Other sectors..	4 664 ..	....	....	....	....	....	....	....	....
Debt securities..	4 669 ..	....	....	....	....	....	−1.6	....	....
Bonds and notes...	4 670 ..	....	....	....	....	....	....	....	....
Monetary authorities................................	4 671 ..	....	....	....	....	....	....	....	....
General government..................................	4 672 ..	....	....	....	....	....	....	....	....
Banks...	4 673 ..	....	....	....	....	....	....	....	....
Other sectors..	4 674 ..	....	....	....	....	....	....	....	....
Money market instruments..........................	4 680 ..	....	....	....	....	....	−1.6	....	....
Monetary authorities................................	4 681 ..	....	....	....	....	....	....	....	....
General government..................................	4 682 ..	....	....	....	....	....	....	....	....
Banks...	4 683 ..	....	....	....	....	....	....	....	....
Other sectors..	4 684 ..	....	....	....	....	....	−1.6	....	....
C. FINANCIAL DERIVATIVES.........................	4 910 ..	....	....	....	....	....	....	....	....
Monetary authorities......................................	4 911 ..	....	....	....	....	....	....	....	....
General government.......................................	4 912 ..	....	....	....	....	....	....	....	....
Banks..	4 913 ..	....	....	....	....	....	....	....	....
Other sectors..	4 914 ..	....	....	....	....	....	....	....	....
Assets...	4 900 ..	....	....	....	....	....	....	....	....
Monetary authorities......................................	4 901 ..	....	....	....	....	....	....	....	....
General government.......................................	4 902 ..	....	....	....	....	....	....	....	....
Banks..	4 903 ..	....	....	....	....	....	....	....	....
Other sectors..	4 904 ..	....	....	....	....	....	....	....	....
Liabilities..	4 905 ..	....	....	....	....	....	....	....	....
Monetary authorities......................................	4 906 ..	....	....	....	....	....	....	....	....
General government.......................................	4 907 ..	....	....	....	....	....	....	....	....
Banks..	4 908 ..	....	....	....	....	....	....	....	....
Other sectors..	4 909 ..	....	....	....	....	....	....	....	....

Table 2 (Concluded). STANDARD PRESENTATION, 2000–2007

(Millions of U.S. dollars)

	Code	2000	2001	2002	2003	2004	2005	2006	2007
D. OTHER INVESTMENT	4 700 ..	−208.1	−70.8	75.7	−137.1	2.8	−657.6	....	....
Assets	4 703 ..	−41.0	−66.9	108.8	−221.3	34.2	−639.7	....	....
Trade credits	4 706 ..	....	....	−29.2	−183.4	−83.8	−203.5	....	....
General government	4 707 ..	....	....	....	....	....	....	....	....
of which: Short-term	4 709 ..	....	....	....	....	....	....	....	....
Other sectors	4 710 ..	....	....	−29.2	−183.4	−83.8	−203.5	....	....
of which: Short-term	4 712 ..	....	....	*−29.2*	*−183.4*	*−83.8*	*−203.5*	....	....
Loans	4 714 ..	....	....	....	....	....	....	....	....
Monetary authorities	4 715 ..	....	....	....	....	....	....	....	....
of which: Short-term	4 718 ..	....	....	....	....	....	....	....	....
General government	4 719 ..	....	....	....	....	....	....	....	....
of which: Short-term	4 721 ..	....	....	....	....	....	....	....	....
Banks	4 722 ..	....	....	....	....	....	....	....	....
of which: Short-term	4 724 ..	....	....	....	....	....	....	....	....
Other sectors	4 725 ..	....	....	....	....	....	....	....	....
of which: Short-term	4 727 ..	....	....	....	....	....	....	....	....
Currency and deposits	4 730 ..	−41.0	−66.9	28.8	−173.4	−107.1	−223.6	....	....
Monetary authorities	4 731 ..	....	....	....	....	....	....	....	....
General government	4 732 ..	....	....	....	....	....	....	....	....
Banks	4 733 ..	−21.2	−26.7	−46.3	−106.9	−149.9	−141.1	....	....
Other sectors	4 734 ..	−19.8	−40.2	75.0	−66.5	42.9	−82.5	....	....
Other assets	4 736 ..	....	....	109.2	135.5	225.0	−212.6	....	....
Monetary authorities	4 737 ..	....	....	....	....	....	....	....	....
of which: Short-term	4 739 ..	....	....	....	....	....	....	....	....
General government	4 740 ..	....	....	....	....	....	....	....	....
of which: Short-term	4 742 ..	....	....	....	....	....	....	....	....
Banks	4 743 ..	....	....	....	....	....	....	....	....
of which: Short-term	4 745 ..	....	....	....	....	....	....	....	....
Other sectors	4 746 ..	....	....	109.2	135.5	225.0	−212.6	....	....
of which: Short-term	4 748 ..	....	....	*109.2*	*135.5*	*225.0*	*−212.6*	....	....
Liabilities	4 753 ..	−167.1	−3.8	−33.1	84.2	−31.4	−17.9	....	....
Trade credits	4 756 ..	....	....	139.0	257.4	258.2	134.7	....	....
General government	4 757 ..	....	....	....	....	....	....	....	....
of which: Short-term	4 759 ..	....	....	....	....	....	....	....	....
Other sectors	4 760 ..	....	....	139.0	257.4	258.2	134.7	....	....
of which: Short-term	4 762 ..	....	....	*139.0*	*257.4*	*258.2*	*134.7*	....	....
Loans	4 764 ..	−159.4	−67.8	−172.1	−174.9	−295.0	−160.4	....	....
Monetary authorities	4 765 ..	18.1	70.9	....	−5.4	−130.8	−175.1	....	....
of which: Use of Fund credit and loans from the Fund..	4 766 ..	*18.1*	*70.9*	....	*−5.4*	*−60.0*	*−62.2*	....	....
of which: Short-term	4 768 ..	....	....	....	....	....	....	....	....
General government	4 769 ..	.2	49.0	−77.2	−118.5	−121.3	−94.5	....	....
of which: Short-term	4 771 ..	....	....	....	....	....	....	....	....
Banks	4 772 ..	....	....	....	....	....	....	....	....
of which: Short-term	4 774 ..	....	....	....	....	....	....	....	....
Other sectors	4 775 ..	−177.7	−187.7	−94.9	−51.0	−42.9	109.2	....	....
of which: Short-term	4 777 ..	....	....	*6.0*	*−15.4*	*−.4*	*−2.8*	....	....
Currency and deposits	4 780 ..	....	....	....	1.7	5.3	7.8	....	....
Monetary authorities	4 781 ..	....	....	....	....	....	....	....	....
General government	4 782 ..	....	....	....	....	....	....	....	....
Banks	4 783 ..	....	....	....	1.7	5.3	8.7	....	....
Other sectors	4 784 ..	....	....	....	....	....	−1.0	....	....
Other liabilities	4 786 ..	−7.7	64.0	....	....	....	....	....	....
Monetary authorities	4 787 ..	....	....	....	....	....	....	....	....
of which: Short-term	4 789 ..	....	....	....	....	....	....	....	....
General government	4 790 ..	....	....	....	....	....	....	....	....
of which: Short-term	4 792 ..	....	....	....	....	....	....	....	....
Banks	4 793 ..	....	....	....	....	....	....	....	....
of which: Short-term	4 795 ..	....	....	....	....	....	....	....	....
Other sectors	4 796 ..	−7.7	64.0	....	....	....	....	....	....
of which: Short-term	4 798 ..	*−7.7*	*64.0*	....	....	....	....	....	....
E. RESERVE ASSETS	4 802 ..	−127.9	−203.6	−55.9	−99.7	−102.3	−82.3	....	....
Monetary gold	4 812 ..	....	....	15.4	.5	....	−2.8	....	....
Special drawing rights	4 811 ..	−11.8	3.1	3.2	2.8	3.0	.7	....	....
Reserve position in the Fund	4 810 ..	−.2	−.2	−.1	−.1	....	....	....	....
Foreign exchange	4 803 ..	−115.9	−209.7	−77.7	−102.9	−105.3	−80.1	....	....
Other claims	4 813 ..	....	3.2	3.2	....	....	....	....	....
NET ERRORS AND OMISSIONS	4 998 ..	13.1	−1.6	91.3	39.8	26.0	47.0	....	....

Table 1. ANALYTIC PRESENTATION, 2000–2007

(Millions of U.S. dollars)

	Code	2000	2001	2002	2003	2004	2005	2006	2007
A. Current Account[1]	4 993 Z.	**−162.8**	**−266.4**	**92.6**	**129.5**	**143.0**	**52.9**	**219.1**	**126.1**
Goods: exports f.o.b.	2 100 ..	2,329.0	1,889.7	1,858.0	2,170.0	2,861.2	3,351.8	4,409.2	5,463.2
Goods: imports f.o.b.	3 100 ..	−2,866.1	−2,503.6	−2,137.9	−2,446.1	−3,105.3	−3,814.3	−5,022.2	−6,008.3
Balance on Goods	4 100 ..	*−537.2*	*−613.9*	*−279.9*	*−276.1*	*−244.1*	*−462.5*	*−613.0*	*−545.0*
Services: credit	2 200 ..	595.3	555.2	568.4	573.8	627.6	692.8	809.0	853.5
Services: debit	3 200 ..	−420.2	−390.0	−354.6	−328.6	−301.0	−343.4	−383.8	−462.9
Balance on Goods and Services	4 991 ..	*−362.0*	*−448.7*	*−66.1*	*−30.8*	*82.5*	*−113.1*	*−187.8*	*−154.5*
Income: credit	2 300 ..	260.5	255.9	195.7	166.3	165.4	205.7	301.0	318.7
Income: debit	3 300 ..	−238.1	−240.1	−152.9	−170.5	−299.1	−263.5	−320.2	−411.4
Balance on Goods, Services, and Income	4 992 ..	*−339.6*	*−432.9*	*−23.3*	*−35.0*	*−51.2*	*−170.9*	*−206.9*	*−247.2*
Current transfers: credit	2 379 Z.	178.3	168.0	117.5	166.0	195.7	225.3	430.0	374.8
Current transfers: debit	3 379 ..	−1.5	−1.5	−1.6	−1.5	−1.5	−1.5	−4.0	−1.5
B. Capital Account[1]	4 994 Z.	**3.0**	**15.0**	**4.0**	**15.0**	**16.0**	**20.0**	**30.0**	**28.0**
Capital account: credit	2 994 Z.	3.0	15.0	4.0	15.0	16.0	20.0	30.0	28.0
Capital account: debit	3 994 ..	....	....	....	....	....	....	....	....
Total, Groups A Plus B	4 981 ..	*−159.8*	*−251.4*	*96.6*	*144.5*	*159.0*	*72.9*	*249.1*	*154.1*
C. Financial Account[1]	4 995 W.	**64.0**	**151.4**	**43.7**	**132.2**	**18.6**	**301.2**	**176.6**	**639.0**
Direct investment abroad	4 505 ..	−5.7	−5.8	−5.5	−5.5	−6.0	−6.4	−4.0	−7.6
Direct investment in Paraguay	4 555 Z.	104.1	84.2	10.0	27.4	37.7	53.5	182.9	196.4
Portfolio investment assets	4 602 ..	2.0	.7	....	....	....	....	....	....
Equity securities	4 610 ..	1.4	.2	....	....	....	....	....	....
Debt securities	4 619 ..	.6	.5	....	....	....	....	....	....
Portfolio investment liabilities	4 652 Z.	.5	−.1	−.1	−.4	−.1	....	....	....
Equity securities	4 660 ..	....	....	....	....	....	....	....	....
Debt securities	4 669 Z.	.5	−.1	−.1	−.4	−.1	....	....	....
Financial derivatives	4 910 ..	....	....	....	....	....	....	....	....
Financial derivatives assets	4 900 ..	....	....	....	....	....	....	....	....
Financial derivatives liabilities	4 905 ..	....	....	....	....	....	....	....	....
Other investment assets	4 703 ..	−212.4	64.4	−16.1	184.0	−39.5	386.5	106.7	483.8
Monetary authorities	4 701 ..	....	....	....	....	....	....	....	....
General government	4 704 ..	−81.2	78.8	−77.7	−52.8	−56.1	−66.7	−36.3	64.4
Banks	4 705 ..	−69.3	68.2	122.5	−109.7	7.4	65.5	−7.8	−55.7
Other sectors	4 728 ..	−61.9	−82.6	−60.9	346.5	9.3	387.7	150.7	475.1
Other investment liabilities	4 753 W.	175.5	8.0	55.4	−73.3	26.5	−132.4	−109.0	−33.6
Monetary authorities	4 753 WA	−3.2	−3.2	−4.4	−4.4	−4.3	−2.5	−2.5	−2.6
General government	4 753 ZB	90.4	41.9	23.0	53.1	5.4	−48.9	−39.1	−61.1
Banks	4 753 ZC	−8.9	−30.5	6.3	−23.9	18.9	−13.8	−12.9	33.8
Other sectors	4 753 ZD	97.2	−.2	30.5	−98.1	6.5	−67.2	−54.5	−3.7
Total, Groups A Through C	4 983 ..	*−95.8*	*−99.9*	*140.3*	*276.7*	*177.6*	*374.1*	*425.6*	*793.1*
D. Net Errors and Omissions	4 998 ..	**−243.5**	**52.9**	**−262.8**	**−40.7**	**95.6**	**−210.8**	**−42.9**	**−168.1**
Total, Groups A Through D	4 984 ..	*−339.3*	*−47.0*	*−122.5*	*236.0*	*273.2*	*163.2*	*382.7*	*625.0*
E. Reserves and Related Items	4 802 A.	**339.3**	**47.0**	**122.5**	**−236.0**	**−273.2**	**−163.2**	**−382.7**	**−625.0**
Reserve assets	4 802 ..	210.1	45.4	85.6	−303.2	−181.2	−149.2	−386.8	−629.5
Use of Fund credit and loans	4 766 ..	....	....	....	....	....	....	....	....
Exceptional financing	4 920 ..	129.2	1.6	36.9	67.2	−92.0	−14.0	4.1	4.5
Conversion rates: guaraníes per U.S. dollar	0 101 ..	**3,486.4**	**4,105.9**	**5,716.3**	**6,424.3**	**5,974.6**	**6,178.0**	**5,635.5**	**5,032.7**

[1] Excludes components that have been classified in the categories of Group E.

Table 2. STANDARD PRESENTATION, 2000–2007

(Millions of U.S. dollars)

	Code	2000	2001	2002	2003	2004	2005	2006	2007
CURRENT ACCOUNT	4 993 ..	−162.8	−266.4	92.6	129.5	143.0	52.9	219.1	126.1
A. GOODS	4 100 ..	−537.2	−613.9	−279.9	−276.1	−244.1	−462.5	−613.0	−545.0
Credit	2 100 ..	2,329.0	1,889.7	1,858.0	2,170.0	2,861.2	3,351.8	4,409.2	5,463.2
General merchandise: exports f.o.b.	2 110 ..	2,322.4	1,882.7	1,851.7	2,163.1	2,854.3	3,315.6	4,345.9	5,381.1
Goods for processing: exports f.o.b.	2 150 ..	....	....	....	....	....	29.3	56.4	75.0
Repairs on goods	2 160 ..	....	.5	.5	.5	.5	.5	.5	.5
Goods procured in ports by carriers	2 170 ..	6.6	6.5	5.8	6.4	6.4	6.4	6.4	6.6
Nonmonetary gold	2 180 ..	....	....	....	....	....	....	....	....
Debit	3 100 ..	−2,866.1	−2,503.6	−2,137.9	−2,446.1	−3,105.3	−3,814.3	−5,022.2	−6,008.3
General merchandise: imports f.o.b.	3 110 ..	−2,863.6	−2,500.4	−2,134.4	−2,442.7	−3,101.9	−3,799.9	−4,995.1	−5,946.0
Goods for processing: imports f.o.b.	3 150 ..	....	....	....	....	....	−11.0	−23.7	−25.8
Repairs on goods	3 160 ..	−.6	−.7	−.7	−.7	−.7	−.7	−.7	−.7
Goods procured in ports by carriers	3 170 ..	−1.9	−2.5	−2.8	−2.7	−2.7	−2.7	−2.7	−35.8
Nonmonetary gold	3 180 ..	....	....	....	....	....	....	....	....
B. SERVICES	4 200 ..	175.2	165.2	213.8	245.2	326.6	349.4	425.2	390.5
Total credit	2 200 ..	*595.3*	*555.2*	*568.4*	*573.8*	*627.6*	*692.8*	*809.0*	*853.5*
Total debit	3 200 ..	*−420.2*	*−390.0*	*−354.6*	*−328.6*	*−301.0*	*−343.4*	*−383.8*	*−462.9*
Transportation services, credit	2 205 ..	69.4	86.6	68.9	84.5	86.7	86.7	97.2	128.4
Passenger	2 850 ..	*14.9*	*21.5*	*14.4*	*16.5*	*16.5*	*18.0*	*20.0*	*18.6*
Freight	2 851 ..	*45.3*	*55.5*	*45.0*	*58.0*	*62.2*	*60.6*	*68.2*	*96.7*
Other	2 852 ..	*9.2*	*9.6*	*9.5*	*10.0*	*8.0*	*8.1*	*9.0*	*13.1*
Sea transport, passenger	2 207 ..	....	....	....	....	....	....	....	....
Sea transport, freight	2 208 ..	....	....	....	....	....	....	....	....
Sea transport, other	2 209 ..	....	....	....	....	....	....	....	....
Air transport, passenger	2 211 ..	9.0	15.0	8.0	10.0	10.0	10.0	12.0	12.0
Air transport, freight	2 212 ..	1.3	....	....	....	....	....	....	....
Air transport, other	2 213 ..	....	....	....	....	....	....	....	....
Other transport, passenger	2 215 ..	5.9	6.5	6.4	6.5	6.5	8.0	8.0	6.6
Other transport, freight	2 216 ..	44.0	55.5	45.0	58.0	62.2	60.6	68.2	96.7
Other transport, other	2 217 ..	9.2	9.6	9.5	10.0	8.0	8.1	9.0	13.1
Transportation services, debit	3 205 ..	−236.5	−213.9	−179.1	−180.4	−164.0	−181.3	−208.8	−261.2
Passenger	3 850 ..	*−72.6*	*−58.3*	*−52.5*	*−48.3*	*−50.3*	*−51.1*	*−52.0*	*−74.6*
Freight	3 851 ..	*−160.4*	*−151.2*	*−121.5*	*−127.2*	*−107.3*	*−122.4*	*−146.5*	*−174.2*
Other	3 852 ..	*−3.5*	*−4.4*	*−5.2*	*−4.9*	*−6.4*	*−7.8*	*−10.3*	*−12.4*
Sea transport, passenger	3 207 ..	....	....	....	....	....	....	....	....
Sea transport, freight	3 208 ..	−32.2	−43.5	−27.0	−22.6	−19.4	−26.3	−35.0	−41.6
Sea transport, other	3 209 ..	....	....	....	....	....	....	....	....
Air transport, passenger	3 211 ..	−64.8	−50.0	−44.0	−40.0	−42.0	−42.8	−42.0	−63.0
Air transport, freight	3 212 ..	−29.7	−21.7	−23.1	−27.4	−22.8	−25.4	−33.7	−40.1
Air transport, other	3 213 ..	....	....	....	....	....	....	....	....
Other transport, passenger	3 215 ..	−7.8	−8.3	−8.5	−8.3	−8.3	−8.3	−10.0	−11.6
Other transport, freight	3 216 ..	−98.5	−86.0	−71.4	−77.2	−65.1	−70.7	−77.8	−92.5
Other transport, other	3 217 ..	−3.5	−4.4	−5.2	−4.9	−6.4	−7.8	−10.3	−12.4
Travel, credit	2 236 ..	72.9	69.2	62.2	63.6	69.7	77.5	91.5	101.8
Business travel	2 237 ..	....	....	....	....	....	....	....	....
Personal travel	2 240 ..	72.9	69.2	62.2	63.6	69.7	77.5	91.5	101.8
Travel, debit	3 236 ..	−80.6	−72.0	−64.8	−66.9	−70.7	−78.6	−92.2	−108.8
Business travel	3 237 ..	....	....	....	....	....	....	....	....
Personal travel	3 240 ..	−80.6	−72.0	−64.8	−66.9	−70.7	−78.6	−92.2	−108.8
Other services, credit	2 200 BA ..	453.0	399.4	437.3	425.7	471.2	528.6	620.3	623.2
Communications	2 245 ..	10.3	11.5	13.0	13.0	16.0	17.0	17.0	14.0
Construction	2 249 ..	....	....	....	....	....	....	....	....
Insurance	2 253 ..	22.0	22.1	19.0	14.2	16.0	16.4	27.0	32.0
Financial	2 260 ..	6.1	4.8	5.1	6.1	10.5	10.2	3.5	1.6
Computer and information	2 262 ..	.4	.3	.4	.2	.4	.4	4.4	4.6
Royalties and licence fees	2 266 ..	202.6	180.1	187.1	193.4	207.9	218.7	236.4	205.6
Other business services	2 268 ..	189.4	150.0	175.3	175.4	190.3	219.7	259.5	286.2
Personal, cultural, and recreational	2 287 ..	....	....	....	....	....	....	....	....
Government, n.i.e.	2 291 ..	22.2	30.6	37.4	23.4	30.1	46.2	72.5	79.2
Other services, debit	3 200 BA ..	−103.0	−104.1	−110.6	−81.3	−66.3	−83.5	−82.8	−92.9
Communications	3 245 ..	−.2	−.2	−.2	−.2	−.2	−6.0	−2.7	−4.0
Construction	3 249 ..	....	....	....	....	....	....	....	....
Insurance	3 253 ..	−51.4	−52.8	−46.7	−40.8	−41.1	−51.2	−46.1	−44.6
Financial	3 260 ..	−5.2	−3.7	−7.1	−4.3	−3.4	−3.6	−3.7	−8.2
Computer and information	3 262 ..	−.2	−4.8	−1.1	−1.2	−.9	−1.8	−1.5	−1.9
Royalties and licence fees	3 266 ..	−8.6	−7.4	−4.6	−4.6	−1.9	−1.7	−3.1	−6.1
Other business services	3 268 ..	−6.9	−7.2	−16.9	−19.2	−4.5	−4.3	−6.5	−7.1
Personal, cultural, and recreational	3 287 ..	....	....	....	....	....	....	....	....
Government, n.i.e.	3 291 ..	−30.5	−28.0	−34.0	−11.0	−14.3	−14.9	−19.2	−21.0

Table 2 (Continued). STANDARD PRESENTATION, 2000–2007

(Millions of U.S. dollars)

	Code	2000	2001	2002	2003	2004	2005	2006	2007
C. INCOME	4 300	**22.4**	**15.8**	**42.8**	**−4.2**	**−133.7**	**−57.8**	**−19.2**	**−92.7**
Total credit	2 300	*260.5*	*255.9*	*195.7*	*166.3*	*165.4*	*205.7*	*301.0*	*318.7*
Total debit	3 300	*−238.1*	*−240.1*	*−152.9*	*−170.5*	*−299.1*	*−263.5*	*−320.2*	*−411.4*
Compensation of employees, credit	2 310	**126.3**	**123.8**	**102.8**	**112.6**	**106.2**	**108.0**	**136.2**	**128.0**
Compensation of employees, debit	3 310	....	....	....	....	....	....	....	....
Investment income, credit	2 320	**134.2**	**132.1**	**92.9**	**53.7**	**59.2**	**97.7**	**164.8**	**190.7**
Direct investment income	2 330	12.4	23.0	31.3	24.0	29.0	25.2	23.9	25.8
Dividends and distributed branch profits	2 332	6.0	17.0	24.5	17.5	18.8	18.6	19.7	18.0
Reinvested earnings and undistributed branch profits	2 333	5.7	5.8	5.5	5.5	6.0	6.4	4.0	7.6
Income on debt (interest)	2 334	.7	.2	1.3	1.0	4.2	.2	.2	.2
Portfolio investment income	2 339	.2	....	2.3	2.3	2.3	2.3	1.1	2.9
Income on equity	2 340	....	....	....	....	....	....	....	....
Income on bonds and notes	2 350	.2	....	2.3	2.3	2.3	2.3	1.1	2.9
Income on money market instruments	2 360	....	....	....	....	....	....	....	....
Other investment income	2 370	121.6	109.1	59.3	27.4	27.9	70.2	139.8	162.0
Investment income, debit	3 320	**−238.1**	**−240.1**	**−152.9**	**−170.5**	**−299.1**	**−263.5**	**−320.2**	**−411.4**
Direct investment income	3 330	−84.3	−88.6	−39.4	−60.0	−192.3	−158.2	−202.6	−284.2
Dividends and distributed branch profits	3 332	−71.0	−87.1	−167.3	−86.1	−101.0	−172.0	−171.3	−228.6
Reinvested earnings and undistributed branch profits	3 333	−7.4	−.1	132.0	32.5	−85.8	15.2	−29.9	−54.2
Income on debt (interest)	3 334	−5.9	−1.4	−4.1	−6.4	−5.5	−1.4	−1.4	−1.4
Portfolio investment income	3 339	....	....	....	....	....	....	....	....
Income on equity	3 340	....	....	....	....	....	....	....	....
Income on bonds and notes	3 350	....	....	....	....	....	....	....	....
Income on money market instruments	3 360	....	....	....	....	....	....	....	....
Other investment income	3 370	−153.8	−151.6	−113.5	−110.5	−106.8	−105.3	−117.6	−127.2
D. CURRENT TRANSFERS	4 379	**176.8**	**166.5**	**115.9**	**164.5**	**194.2**	**223.8**	**426.0**	**373.3**
Credit	2 379	**178.3**	**168.0**	**117.5**	**166.0**	**195.7**	**225.3**	**430.0**	**374.8**
General government	2 380	18.8	20.0	12.0	8.0	11.0	8.0	16.0	8.0
Other sectors	2 390	159.5	148.0	105.5	158.0	184.7	217.3	414.0	366.8
Workers' remittances	2 391	151.7	140.0	98.7	109.5	132.0	161.3	336.0	340.8
Other current transfers	2 392	7.8	8.0	6.8	48.5	52.7	56.0	78.0	26.0
Debit	3 379	**−1.5**	**−1.5**	**−1.6**	**−1.5**	**−1.5**	**−1.5**	**−4.0**	**−1.5**
General government	3 380	−1.5	−1.5	−1.6	−1.5	−1.5	−1.5	−4.0	−1.5
Other sectors	3 390	....	....	....	....	....	....	....	....
Workers' remittances	3 391	....	....	....	....	....	....	....	....
Other current transfers	3 392	....	....	....	....	....	....	....	....
CAPITAL AND FINANCIAL ACCOUNT	4 996	**406.3**	**213.4**	**170.2**	**−88.8**	**−238.6**	**157.9**	**−176.2**	**42.0**
CAPITAL ACCOUNT	4 994	**3.0**	**15.0**	**4.0**	**15.0**	**16.0**	**20.0**	**30.0**	**28.0**
Total credit	2 994	*3.0*	*15.0*	*4.0*	*15.0*	*16.0*	*20.0*	*30.0*	*28.0*
Total debit	3 994	....	....	....	....	....	....	....	....
Capital transfers, credit	2 400	**3.0**	**15.0**	**4.0**	**15.0**	**16.0**	**20.0**	**30.0**	**28.0**
General government	2 401	3.0	15.0	4.0	15.0	16.0	20.0	30.0	28.0
Debt forgiveness	2 402	....	....	....	....	....	....	....	....
Other capital transfers	2 410	3.0	15.0	4.0	15.0	16.0	20.0	30.0	28.0
Other sectors	2 430	....	....	....	....	....	....	....	....
Migrants' transfers	2 431	....	....	....	....	....	....	....	....
Debt forgiveness	2 432	....	....	....	....	....	....	....	....
Other capital transfers	2 440	....	....	....	....	....	....	....	....
Capital transfers, debit	3 400	....	....	....	....	....	....	....	....
General government	3 401	....	....	....	....	....	....	....	....
Debt forgiveness	3 402	....	....	....	....	....	....	....	....
Other capital transfers	3 410	....	....	....	....	....	....	....	....
Other sectors	3 430	....	....	....	....	....	....	....	....
Migrants' transfers	3 431	....	....	....	....	....	....	....	....
Debt forgiveness	3 432	....	....	....	....	....	....	....	....
Other capital transfers	3 440	....	....	....	....	....	....	....	....
Nonproduced nonfinancial assets, credit	2 480	....	....	....	....	....	....	....	....
Nonproduced nonfinancial assets, debit	3 480	....	....	....	....	....	....	....	....

Table 2 (Continued). STANDARD PRESENTATION, 2000–2007

(Millions of U.S. dollars)

	Code	2000	2001	2002	2003	2004	2005	2006	2007
FINANCIAL ACCOUNT......	4 995 ..	**403.3**	**198.4**	**166.2**	**−103.8**	**−254.6**	**137.9**	**−206.2**	**14.0**
A. DIRECT INVESTMENT........	4 500 ..	**98.4**	**78.4**	**4.5**	**21.9**	**31.7**	**47.1**	**178.9**	**188.8**
Direct investment abroad.........	4 505 ..	**−5.7**	**−5.8**	**−5.5**	**−5.5**	**−6.0**	**−6.4**	**−4.0**	**−7.6**
Equity capital........	4 510 ..	....	....	....	....	....	....	....	....
Claims on affiliated enterprises.....	4 515 ..	....	....	....	....	....	....	....	....
Liabilities to affiliated enterprises.....	4 520 ..	....	....	....	....	....	....	....	....
Reinvested earnings....	4 525 ..	−5.7	−5.8	−5.5	−5.5	−6.0	−6.4	−4.0	−7.6
Other capital.........	4 530 ..	....	....	....	....	....	....	....	....
Claims on affiliated enterprises.....	4 535 ..	....	....	....	....	....	....	....	....
Liabilities to affiliated enterprises.....	4 540 ..	....	....	....	....	....	....	....	....
Direct investment in Paraguay........	4 555 ..	**104.1**	**84.2**	**10.0**	**27.4**	**37.7**	**53.5**	**182.9**	**196.4**
Equity capital........	4 560 ..	104.2	130.2	81.3	32.4	10.1	65.3	107.0	87.7
Claims on direct investors......	4 565 ..	....	....	....	....	....	....	....	....
Liabilities to direct investors.....	4 570 ..	104.2	130.2	81.3	32.4	10.1	65.3	107.0	87.7
Reinvested earnings......	4 575 ..	7.4	.1	−132.0	−32.5	85.8	−15.2	29.9	54.2
Other capital........	4 580 ..	−7.5	−46.1	60.7	27.5	−58.2	3.4	46.0	54.5
Claims on direct investors.....	4 585 ..	−9.9	−29.5	−84.5	82.6	−66.3	28.2	−13.7	6.2
Liabilities to direct investors.....	4 590 ..	2.4	−16.6	145.2	−55.1	8.1	−24.8	59.7	48.3
B. PORTFOLIO INVESTMENT............	4 600 ..	**2.5**	**.6**	**−.1**	**−.4**	**−.1**	....	.....	....
Assets........	4 602 ..	**2.0**	**.7**	....	....	....	....	.....	....
Equity securities.........	4 610 ..	1.4	.2	....	....	....	....	....	....
Monetary authorities........	4 611 ..	....	....	....	....	....	....	....	....
General government.....	4 612 ..	....	....	....	....	....	....	....	....
Banks........	4 613 ..	....	....	....	....	....	....	....	....
Other sectors........	4 614 ..	1.4	.2	....	....	....	....	....	....
Debt securities........	4 619 ..	.6	.5	....	....	....	....	....	....
Bonds and notes.........	4 620 ..	.6	.5	....	....	....	....	....	....
Monetary authorities........	4 621 ..	....	....	....	....	....	....	....	....
General government.....	4 622 ..	....	....	....	....	....	....	....	....
Banks........	4 623 ..	2.2	....	....	....	....	....	....	....
Other sectors........	4 624 ..	−1.6	.5	....	....	....	....	....	....
Money market instruments......	4 630 ..	....	....	....	....	....	....	....	....
Monetary authorities........	4 631 ..	....	....	....	....	....	....	....	....
General government.....	4 632 ..	....	....	....	....	....	....	....	....
Banks........	4 633 ..	....	....	....	....	....	....	....	....
Other sectors........	4 634 ..	....	....	....	....	....	....	....	....
Liabilities........	4 652 ..	**.5**	**−.1**	**−.1**	**−.4**	**−.1**	....	.....	....
Equity securities.........	4 660 ..	....	....	....	....	....	....	....	....
Banks........	4 663 ..	....	....	....	....	....	....	....	....
Other sectors........	4 664 ..	....	....	....	....	....	....	....	....
Debt securities........	4 669 ..	.5	−.1	−.1	−.4	−.1	....	....	....
Bonds and notes.........	4 670 ..	.5	−.1	−.1	−.4	−.1	....	....	....
Monetary authorities........	4 671 ..	....	....	....	....	....	....	....	....
General government.....	4 672 ..	....	....	....	....	....	....	....	....
Banks........	4 673 ..	....	....	....	....	....	....	....	....
Other sectors........	4 674 ..	.5	−.1	−.1	−.4	−.1	....	....	....
Money market instruments......	4 680 ..	....	....	....	....	....	....	....	....
Monetary authorities........	4 681 ..	....	....	....	....	....	....	....	....
General government.....	4 682 ..	....	....	....	....	....	....	....	....
Banks........	4 683 ..	....	....	....	....	....	....	....	....
Other sectors........	4 684 ..	....	....	....	....	....	....	....	....
C. FINANCIAL DERIVATIVES............	4 910 ..	....	....	....	....	....	....	....	....
Monetary authorities........	4 911 ..	....	....	....	....	....	....	....	....
General government............	4 912 ..	....	....	....	....	....	....	....	....
Banks........	4 913 ..	....	....	....	....	....	....	....	....
Other sectors........	4 914 ..	....	....	....	....	....	....	....	....
Assets........	4 900 ..	....	....	....	....	....	....	....	....
Monetary authorities........	4 901 ..	....	....	....	....	....	....	....	....
General government.....	4 902 ..	....	....	....	....	....	....	....	....
Banks........	4 903 ..	....	....	....	....	....	....	....	....
Other sectors........	4 904 ..	....	....	....	....	....	....	....	....
Liabilities........	4 905 ..	....	....	....	....	....	....	....	....
Monetary authorities........	4 906 ..	....	....	....	....	....	....	....	....
General government.....	4 907 ..	....	....	....	....	....	....	....	....
Banks........	4 908 ..	....	....	....	....	....	....	....	....
Other sectors........	4 909 ..	....	....	....	....	....	....	....	....

Table 2 (Concluded). STANDARD PRESENTATION, 2000–2007

(Millions of U.S. dollars)

	Code	2000	2001	2002	2003	2004	2005	2006	2007
D. OTHER INVESTMENT	4 700	**92.3**	**74.0**	**76.2**	**177.9**	**−105.0**	**240.1**	**1.8**	**454.7**
Assets	4 703	−212.4	64.4	−16.1	184.0	−39.5	386.5	106.7	483.8
Trade credits	4 706	−25.0	5.8	−8.0	11.4	−7.5	....	−11.5	.1
General government	4 707	....	....	....	....	....	....	....	....
of which: Short-term	4 709	....	....	....	....	....	....	....	....
Other sectors	4 710	−25.0	5.8	−8.0	11.4	−7.5	....	−11.5	.1
of which: Short-term	4 712	−25.0	5.8	−8.0	11.4	−7.5	....	−11.5	.1
Loans	4 714	−235.9	1.2	182.3	−151.6	−28.6	−3.9	2.1	114.4
Monetary authorities	4 715	....	....	....	....	....	....	....	....
of which: Short-term	4 718	....	....	....	....	....	....	....	....
General government	4 719	−34.9	−29.6	−51.1	−46.7	−24.5	−28.0	....	85.7
of which: Short-term	4 721	....	....	....	....	....	....	....	....
Banks	4 722	−176.0	40.2	148.7	−103.5	−1.7	27.9	2.1	25.8
of which: Short-term	4 724	−176.0	40.2	148.7	−103.5	−1.7	27.9	2.1	25.8
Other sectors	4 725	−25.0	−9.4	84.7	−1.4	−2.4	−3.8	....	2.9
of which: Short-term	4 727	−.5	−2.6	3.1	....	....	....	....	....
Currency and deposits	4 730	100.2	−71.3	−161.6	331.9	29.8	430.2	160.1	414.3
Monetary authorities	4 731	....	....	....	....	....	....	....	....
General government	4 732	....	....	....	....	....	....	....	....
Banks	4 733	101.7	14.7	−24.7	−5.9	10.2	36.1	−5.1	−61.1
Other sectors	4 734	−1.5	−86.0	−136.9	337.8	19.6	394.1	165.2	475.4
Other assets	4 736	−51.7	128.7	−28.8	−7.8	−33.2	−39.8	−44.0	−45.0
Monetary authorities	4 737	....	....	....	....	....	....	....	....
of which: Short-term	4 739	....	....	....	....	....	....	....	....
General government	4 740	−46.3	108.4	−26.6	−6.1	−31.6	−38.7	−36.3	−21.3
of which: Short-term	4 742	−46.3	108.4	−26.6	−6.1	−31.6	−38.7	−36.3	−21.3
Banks	4 743	5.0	13.3	−1.5	−.3	−1.1	1.5	−4.8	−20.4
of which: Short-term	4 745	5.0	13.3	−1.5	−.3	−1.1	1.5	−4.8	−20.4
Other sectors	4 746	−10.4	7.0	−.7	−1.4	−.4	−2.7	−2.9	−3.3
of which: Short-term	4 748	−9.6	5.8	−.8	−1.5	−.4	−2.9	−3.0	−3.3
Liabilities	4 753	**304.7**	**9.6**	**92.3**	**−6.1**	**−65.5**	**−146.4**	**−104.9**	**−29.1**
Trade credits	4 756	124.8	12.8	8.0	−22.5	13.3	−19.1	−53.6	16.1
General government	4 757	....	....	....	....	....	....	....	....
of which: Short-term	4 759	....	....	....	....	....	....	....	....
Other sectors	4 760	124.8	12.8	8.0	−22.5	13.3	−19.1	−53.6	16.1
of which: Short-term	4 762	124.8	12.8	8.0	−22.5	13.3	−19.1	−53.6	16.1
Loans	4 764	143.5	11.1	42.2	−19.0	−7.4	−121.4	−54.0	−90.4
Monetary authorities	4 765	−3.3	−3.2	−3.2	−3.2	−3.2	−3.2	−3.2	−3.3
of which: Use of Fund credit and loans from the Fund	4 766	....	....	....	....	....	....	....	....
of which: Short-term	4 768	....	....	....	....	....	....	....	....
General government	4 769	180.4	41.9	23.0	83.1	5.4	−48.9	−39.1	−61.1
of which: Short-term	4 771	....	....	....	....	....	....	....	....
Banks	4 772	−7.2	−10.2	3.7	−17.3	1.1	−4.2	−.4	−2.0
of which: Short-term	4 774	−6.0	−9.0	4.7	−16.3	2.1	−2.9	.7	−1.0
Other sectors	4 775	−26.3	−17.4	18.7	−81.6	−10.7	−65.1	−11.3	−24.0
of which: Short-term	4 777	14.5	−7.4	2.4	−7.6	5.1	2.6	.6	1.0
Currency and deposits	4 780	−12.4	9.9	8.3	3.3	−.5	−7.2	4.6	36.1
Monetary authorities	4 781	....	....	....	....	....	....	....	....
General government	4 782	....	....	....	....	....	....	....	....
Banks	4 783	−12.4	10.0	8.0	2.9	.3	−9.4	2.4	33.9
Other sectors	4 784	....	−.1	.3	.4	−.8	2.2	2.2	2.2
Other liabilities	4 786	48.7	−24.2	33.8	32.2	−70.9	1.3	−1.9	9.1
Monetary authorities	4 787	.1	....	.6	−3.3	−1.1	.7	.7	.7
of which: Short-term	4 789	.1	....	.6	−3.3	−1.1	.7	.7	.7
General government	4 790	33.1	3.3	28.9	40.6	−80.8	−5.1	.2	....
of which: Short-term	4 792	33.1	3.3	28.9	40.6	−80.8	−5.1	.2	....
Banks	4 793	10.9	−30.3	−5.2	−9.3	17.1	−.4	−14.9	1.9
of which: Short-term	4 795	10.9	−30.3	−5.2	−9.3	17.1	−.4	−14.9	1.9
Other sectors	4 796	4.7	2.8	9.5	4.1	−6.1	6.1	12.1	6.5
of which: Short-term	4 798	5.7	1.8	8.3	2.2	−7.3	4.9	10.9	5.3
E. RESERVE ASSETS	4 802	**210.1**	**45.4**	**85.6**	**−303.2**	**−181.2**	**−149.2**	**−386.8**	**−629.5**
Monetary gold	4 812	....	....	....	....	....	....	....	....
Special drawing rights	4 811	−4.8	−3.6	−2.5	−1.9	−2.1	−3.2	−5.0	97.9
Reserve position in the Fund	4 810	....	....	....	....	....	....	....	....
Foreign exchange	4 803	177.4	49.1	87.7	−301.2	−179.1	−152.3	−381.8	−727.4
Other claims	4 813	37.6	−.1	.4	−.1	....	6.3	....	....
NET ERRORS AND OMISSIONS	4 998	**−243.5**	**52.9**	**−262.8**	**−40.7**	**95.6**	**−210.8**	**−42.9**	**−168.1**

Table 3. INTERNATIONAL INVESTMENT POSITION (End-period stocks), 2000–2007

(Millions of U.S. dollars)

	Code	2000	2001	2002	2003	2004	2005	2006	2007
ASSETS	8 995 C.	**2,602.6**	**3,216.3**	**3,133.2**	**2,483.9**	**2,854.8**	**3,471.7**	**4,421.7**	**4,612.7**
Direct investment abroad	8 505 ..	**213.9**	**139.7**	**145.2**	**150.7**	**149.2**	**155.8**	**159.8**	**167.4**
Equity capital and reinvested earnings	8 506 ..	213.9	139.7	145.2	150.7	149.2	155.8	159.8	167.4
Claims on affiliated enterprises	8 507 ..	213.9	139.7	145.2	150.7	149.2	155.8	159.8	167.4
Liabilities to affiliated enterprises	8 508 ..	....	....	....	....	....	....	....	....
Other capital	8 530 ..	....	....	....	....	....	....	....	....
Claims on affiliated enterprises	8 535 ..	....	....	....	....	....	....	....	....
Liabilities to affiliated enterprises	8 540 ..	....	....	....	....	....	....	....	....
Portfolio investment	8 602 ..	**11.9**	**15.0**	**13.3**	**4.0**	**4.0**	**4.0**	**4.0**	**4.0**
Equity securities	8 610 ..	10.3	14.3	12.6	4.0	4.0	4.0	4.0	4.0
Monetary authorities	8 611 ..	9.8	14.1	12.4	3.8	3.8	3.8	3.8	3.8
General government	8 612 ..	....	....	....	....	....	....	....	....
Banks	8 613 ..	....	....	....	....	....	....	....	....
Other sectors	8 614 ..	.5	.2	.2	.2	.2	.2	.2	.2
Debt securities	8 619 ..	1.6	.7	.7	....	....	....	....	....
Bonds and notes	8 620 ..	1.6	.7	.7	....	....	....	....	....
Monetary authorities	8 621 ..	....	....	....	....	....	....	....	....
General government	8 622 ..	....	....	....	....	....	....	....	....
Banks	8 623 ..	....	....	....	....	....	....	....	....
Other sectors	8 624 ..	1.6	.7	.7	....	....	....	....	....
Money market instruments	8 630 ..	....	....	....	....	....	....	....	....
Monetary authorities	8 631 ..	....	....	....	....	....	....	....	....
General government	8 632 ..	....	....	....	....	....	....	....	....
Banks	8 633 ..	....	....	....	....	....	....	....	....
Other sectors	8 634 ..	....	....	....	....	....	....	....	....
Financial derivatives	8 900 ..	....	....	....	....	....	....	....	....
Monetary authorities	8 901 ..	....	....	....	....	....	....	....	....
General government	8 902 ..	....	....	....	....	....	....	....	....
Banks	8 903 ..	....	....	....	....	....	....	....	....
Other sectors	8 904 ..	....	....	....	....	....	....	....	....
Other investment	8 703 ..	**1,605.0**	**2,338.5**	**2,324.5**	**1,336.2**	**1,513.7**	**1,994.8**	**2,533.6**	**2,050.0**
Trade credits	8 706 ..	65.9	74.9	59.3	47.9	55.4	51.5	63.0	62.9
General government	8 707 ..	....	....	....	....	....	....	....	....
of which: Short-term	8 709 ..	....	....	....	....	....	....	....	....
Other sectors	8 710 ..	65.9	74.9	59.3	47.9	55.4	51.5	63.0	62.9
of which: Short-term	8 712 ..	*65.9*	*74.9*	*59.3*	*47.9*	*55.4*	*51.5*	*63.0*	*62.9*
Loans	8 714 ..	732.2	728.2	545.7	693.8	722.4	726.3	724.2	609.8
Monetary authorities	8 715 ..	....	....	....	....	....	....	....	....
of which: Short-term	8 718 ..	....	....	....	....	....	....	....	....
General government	8 719 ..	277.8	307.4	358.5	405.2	429.7	457.7	457.7	372.0
of which: Short-term	8 721 ..	....	....	....	....	....	....	....	....
Banks	8 722 ..	361.3	321.1	172.4	275.9	277.6	249.7	247.6	221.8
of which: Short-term	8 724 ..	*361.3*	*321.1*	*172.4*	*275.9*	*277.6*	*249.7*	*247.6*	*221.8*
Other sectors	8 725 ..	93.1	99.7	14.8	12.7	15.1	18.9	18.9	16.0
of which: Short-term	8 727 ..	*1.3*	*3.9*	*.7*	*.7*	*.7*	*.7*	*.7*	*.7*
Currency and deposits	8 730 ..	676.7	1,502.0	1,661.3	529.2	637.4	1,076.2	1,561.6	1,147.5
Monetary authorities	8 731 ..	....	....	....	....	....	....	....	....
General government	8 732 ..	....	....	....	....	....	....	....	....
Banks	8 733 ..	135.0	120.4	107.4	113.3	102.0	86.9	92.0	153.1
Other sectors	8 734 ..	541.7	1,381.6	1,553.9	415.9	535.4	989.3	1,469.6	994.4
Other assets	8 736 ..	130.2	33.4	58.2	65.3	98.5	140.7	184.8	229.9
Monetary authorities	8 737 ..	....	....	....	....	....	....	....	....
of which: Short-term	8 739 ..	....	....	....	....	....	....	....	....
General government	8 740 ..	99.6	25.3	51.9	58.0	89.7	128.5	164.8	186.2
of which: Short-term	8 742 ..	*99.6*	*25.3*	*51.9*	*58.0*	*89.7*	*128.5*	*164.8*	*186.2*
Banks	8 743 ..	16.5	3.1	.7	1.0	2.1	2.9	7.7	28.1
of which: Short-term	8 745 ..	*16.5*	*3.1*	*.7*	*1.0*	*2.1*	*2.9*	*7.7*	*28.1*
Other sectors	8 746 ..	14.1	5.0	5.6	6.3	6.7	9.3	12.3	15.6
of which: Short-term	8 748 ..	*11.6*	*3.7*	*4.4*	*5.9*	*6.3*	*9.1*	*12.2*	*15.5*
Reserve assets	8 802 ..	**771.9**	**723.1**	**650.2**	**993.1**	**1,187.9**	**1,317.1**	**1,724.4**	**2,391.3**
Monetary gold	8 812 ..	9.6	9.7	12.1	14.1	13.4	....	....	....
Special drawing rights	8 811 ..	102.3	102.2	113.2	125.8	133.6	126.1	137.8	43.6
Reserve position in the Fund	8 810 ..	28.0	27.0	29.2	31.9	33.4	30.7	32.3	33.9
Foreign exchange	8 803 ..	626.9	578.4	490.3	815.0	1,001.3	1,160.3	1,554.2	2,313.6
Other claims	8 813 ..	5.1	5.8	5.4	6.3	6.3	....	....	....

Table 3 (Concluded). INTERNATIONAL INVESTMENT POSITION (End-period stocks), 2000–2007

(Millions of U.S. dollars)

	Code	2000	2001	2002	2003	2004	2005	2006	2007
LIABILITIES	8 995 D.	**4,377.8**	**4,057.4**	**3,939.8**	**4,218.6**	**4,228.0**	**4,111.7**	**4,551.4**	**4,799.7**
Direct investment in Paraguay	8 555	**1,324.5**	**1,135.4**	**901.5**	**1,089.7**	**1,149.5**	**1,281.6**	**1,795.9**	**2,039.7**
Equity capital and reinvested earnings	8 556	1,154.6	1,050.9	755.5	916.2	1,034.3	1,161.5	1,629.8	1,819.1
Claims on direct investors	8 557	....	....	....	....	....	....	....	....
Liabilities to direct investors	8 558	1,154.6	1,050.9	755.5	916.2	1,034.3	1,161.5	1,629.8	1,819.1
Other capital	8 580	169.9	84.5	146.0	173.5	115.2	120.1	166.1	220.6
Claims on direct investors	8 585	−51.3	−67.1	−151.6	−69.0	−136.2	−108.0	−121.7	−115.5
Liabilities to direct investors	8 590	221.2	151.6	297.6	242.5	251.4	228.1	287.8	336.1
Portfolio investment	8 652	**.5**	**.4**	**.3**	**....**	**....**	**.1**	**.2**	**.2**
Equity securities	8 660	....	....	....	....	....	....	....	....
Banks	8 663	....	....	....	....	....	....	....	....
Other sectors	8 664	....	....	....	....	....	....	....	....
Debt securities	8 669	.5	.4	.3	....	....	.1	.2	.2
Bonds and notes	8 670	.5	.4	.3	....	....	.1	.2	.2
Monetary authorities	8 671	....	....	....	....	....	....	....	....
General government	8 672	....	....	....	....	....	....	....	....
Banks	8 673	....	....	....	....	....	....	....	....
Other sectors	8 674	.5	.4	.3	....	....	.1	.2	.2
Money market instruments	8 680	....	....	....	....	....	....	....	....
Monetary authorities	8 681	....	....	....	....	....	....	....	....
General government	8 682	....	....	....	....	....	....	....	....
Banks	8 683	....	....	....	....	....	....	....	....
Other sectors	8 684	....	....	....	....	....	....	....	....
Financial derivatives	8 905	....	....	....	....	....	....	....	....
Monetary authorities	8 906	....	....	....	....	....	....	....	....
General government	8 907	....	....	....	....	....	....	....	....
Banks	8 908	....	....	....	....	....	....	....	....
Other sectors	8 909	....	....	....	....	....	....	....	....
Other investment	8 753	**3,052.8**	**2,921.6**	**3,038.0**	**3,128.9**	**3,078.6**	**2,830.1**	**2,755.4**	**2,759.9**
Trade credits	8 756	437.0	430.7	415.3	392.9	406.3	322.4	268.8	284.9
General government	8 757	....	....	....	....	....	....	....	....
of which: Short-term	8 759	....	....	....	....	....	....	....	....
Other sectors	8 760	437.0	430.7	415.3	392.9	406.3	322.4	268.8	284.9
of which: Short-term	8 762	*437.0*	*430.7*	*415.3*	*392.9*	*406.3*	*322.4*	*268.8*	*284.9*
Loans	8 764	2,393.4	2,304.1	2,438.3	2,524.8	2,530.2	2,355.4	2,330.9	2,274.1
Monetary authorities	8 765	30.5	27.3	24.0	20.7	17.3	13.9	10.6	7.3
of which: Use of Fund credit and loans from the Fund	8 766	....	....	....	....	....	....	....	....
of which: Short-term	8 768	....	....	....	....	....	....	....	....
General government	8 769	1,941.4	1,922.9	2,034.5	2,215.0	2,243.9	2,135.0	2,120.2	2,094.0
of which: Short-term	8 771	....	....	....	....	....	....	....	....
Banks	8 772	40.4	30.2	28.4	11.0	13.9	9.9	7.7	5.6
of which: Short-term	8 774	*27.3*	*18.4*	*17.6*	*1.3*	*3.4*	*.5*	*1.2*	*.2*
Other sectors	8 775	381.2	323.7	351.3	278.0	255.0	196.5	192.3	167.1
of which: Short-term	8 777	*31.0*	*16.2*	*18.6*	*8.9*	*14.0*	*16.6*	*17.3*	*18.3*
Currency and deposits	8 780	23.0	32.8	12.5	15.8	15.3	8.1	12.7	48.8
Monetary authorities	8 781	....	....	....	....	....	....	....	....
General government	8 782	....	....	....	....	....	....	....	....
Banks	8 783	22.6	32.4	11.7	14.6	14.9	5.5	7.9	41.8
Other sectors	8 784	.4	.4	.8	1.2	.4	2.6	4.8	7.0
Other liabilities	8 786	199.3	154.0	172.0	195.5	126.8	144.2	143.0	152.1
Monetary authorities	8 787	2.2	3.9	4.6	1.6	.6	1.3	2.0	2.7
of which: Short-term	8 789	*2.2*	*3.9*	*4.6*	*1.6*	*.6*	*1.3*	*2.0*	*2.7*
General government	8 790	60.4	40.7	55.9	87.8	7.3	7.2	7.4	7.4
of which: Short-term	8 792	*60.4*	*40.7*	*55.9*	*87.8*	*7.3*	*7.2*	*7.4*	*7.4*
Banks	8 793	64.6	34.4	26.3	17.1	34.4	20.9	6.0	7.9
of which: Short-term	8 795	*64.5*	*34.3*	*26.3*	*17.1*	*34.4*	*20.9*	*6.0*	*7.9*
Other sectors	8 796	72.2	75.1	85.2	89.1	84.6	114.9	127.7	134.2
of which: Short-term	8 798	*67.2*	*69.1*	*78.0*	*80.0*	*74.3*	*103.4*	*115.0*	*120.3*
NET INTERNATIONAL INVESTMENT POSITION	8 995	**−1,775.2**	**−841.1**	**−806.6**	**−1,734.7**	**−1,373.2**	**−640.1**	**−129.7**	**−187.0**
Conversion rates: guaraníes per U.S. dollar (end of period)	0 102	**3,526.9**	**4,682.0**	**7,103.6**	**6,115.0**	**6,250.0**	**6,120.0**	**5,190.0**	**4,875.0**

Table 1. ANALYTIC PRESENTATION, 2000–2007

(Millions of U.S. dollars)

	Code	2000	2001	2002	2003	2004	2005	2006	2007
A. Current Account[1]...............................	4 993 Z.	**−1,546**	**−1,203**	**−1,110**	**−949**	**19**	**1,148**	**2,755**	**1,505**
Goods: exports f.o.b..........................	2 100 ..	6,955	7,026	7,714	9,091	12,809	17,368	23,800	27,956
Goods: imports f.o.b..........................	3 100 ..	−7,358	−7,204	−7,393	−8,205	−9,805	−12,082	−14,866	−19,599
Balance on Goods..........................	4 100 ..	*−403*	*−179*	*321*	*886*	*3,004*	*5,286*	*8,934*	*8,356*
Services: credit................................	2 200 ..	1,555	1,437	1,455	1,716	1,993	2,289	2,647	3,343
Services: debit.................................	3 200 ..	−2,290	−2,400	−2,449	−2,616	−2,725	−3,123	−3,428	−4,270
Balance on Goods and Services..........	4 991 ..	*−1,138*	*−1,141*	*−673*	*−14*	*2,273*	*4,452*	*8,153*	*7,429*
Income: credit.................................	2 300 ..	737	670	370	322	332	625	1,033	1,567
Income: debit..................................	3 300 ..	−2,146	−1,771	−1,827	−2,466	−4,017	−5,701	−8,616	−9,985
Balance on Goods, Services, and Income........................	4 992 ..	*−2,547*	*−2,243*	*−2,130*	*−2,158*	*−1,413*	*−624*	*570*	*−989*
Current transfers: credit..................	2 379 Z.	1,010	1,048	1,028	1,215	1,439	1,781	2,194	2,504
Current transfers: debit...................	3 379 ..	−9	−8	−8	−6	−6	−10	−10	−10
B. Capital Account[1]................................	4 994 Z.	**−259**	**−155**	**−112**	**−112**	**−86**	**−123**	**−127**	**−134**
Capital account: credit....................	2 994 Z.	16	20	6	4	27	6	6	3
Capital account: debit.....................	3 994 ..	−275	−175	−118	−116	−113	−129	−133	−137
Total, Groups A Plus B......	4 981 ..	*−1,805*	*−1,358*	*−1,222*	*−1,060*	*−67*	*1,025*	*2,628*	*1,371*
C. Financial Account[1].............................	4 995 W.	**1,015**	**1,534**	**1,983**	**820**	**2,286**	**24**	**1,096**	**9,294**
Direct investment abroad................	4 505 ..	....	−74	....	−60	....	....	....	....
Direct investment in Peru................	4 555 Z.	810	1,144	2,156	1,335	1,599	2,579	3,467	5,343
Portfolio investment assets..............	4 602 ..	−481	−318	−316	−1,287	−425	−817	−1,992	−520
Equity securities..........................	4 610 ..	−478	−341	−388	−1,287	−426	−818	−1,993	−520
Debt securities............................	4 619 ..	−3	23	72	....	1	1	1	1
Portfolio investment liabilities..........	4 652 Z.	75	−54	1,724	1,211	1,244	2,579	155	3,955
Equity securities..........................	4 660 ..	123	43	−9	1	−47	769	182	814
Debt securities............................	4 669 Z.	−48	−97	1,733	1,210	1,291	1,810	−27	3,140
Financial derivatives.......................	4 910 ..	....	....	....	....	....	....	....	....
Financial derivatives assets..............	4 900 ..	....	....	....	....	....	....	....	....
Financial derivatives liabilities..........	4 905 ..	....	....	....	....	....	....	....	....
Other investment assets..................	4 703 ..	191	664	....	127	14	−1,084	8	−30
Monetary authorities.....................	4 701 ..	−31	−16	152	119	86	−162	425	760
General government......................	4 704 ..	−60	−5	−4	−203	−64	−214	−33	−16
Banks..	4 705 ..	233	48	35	186	71	−324	−122	−19
Other sectors..............................	4 728 ..	49	638	−183	25	−79	−384	−262	−754
Other investment liabilities..............	4 753 W.	421	171	−1,581	−506	−146	−3,233	−541	546
Monetary authorities.....................	4 753 WA	24	−11	−4	−8	6	5	32	−24
General government......................	4 753 ZB	666	599	−781	−294	−130	−2,692	−584	−4,568
Banks..	4 753 ZC	−168	−499	−513	−84	53	327	−139	3,596
Other sectors..............................	4 753 ZD	−101	82	−284	−119	−75	−872	149	1,542
Total, Groups A Through C..............	4 983 ..	*−789*	*176*	*761*	*−240*	*2,219*	*1,049*	*3,724*	*10,665*
D. Net Errors and Omissions.................................	4 998 ..	**659**	**255**	**249**	**801**	**236**	**362**	**−503**	**−322**
Total, Groups A Through D..............	4 984 ..	*−130*	*432*	*1,010*	*561*	*2,456*	*1,411*	*3,221*	*10,343*
E. Reserves and Related Items...............................	4 802 A.	**130**	**−432**	**−1,010**	**−561**	**−2,456**	**−1,411**	**−3,221**	**−10,343**
Reserve assets...............................	4 802 ..	329	−276	−851	−515	−2,442	−1,472	−3,209	−10,390
Use of Fund credit and loans............	4 766 ..	−141	−154	−172	−110	−40	−40	−39	−20
Exceptional financing......................	4 920 ..	−58	−1	14	64	26	100	27	67
Conversion rates: nuevos soles per U.S. dollar......	0 101 ..	**3.4900**	**3.5068**	**3.5165**	**3.4785**	**3.4132**	**3.2958**	**3.2740**	**3.1280**

[1] Excludes components that have been classified in the categories of Group E.

Table 2. STANDARD PRESENTATION, 2000–2007

(Millions of U.S. dollars)

	Code	2000	2001	2002	2003	2004	2005	2006	2007
CURRENT ACCOUNT..	4 993 ..	−1,546	−1,203	−1,110	−949	19	1,148	2,755	1,505
A. GOODS..	4 100 ..	−403	−179	321	886	3,004	5,286	8,934	8,356
Credit..	2 100 ..	6,955	7,026	7,714	9,091	12,809	17,368	23,800	27,956
General merchandise: exports f.o.b...............	2 110 ..	5,704	5,747	6,124	6,875	10,253	14,131	19,640	23,624
Goods for processing: exports f.o.b...............	2 150 ..	. . . .	. . . .	. . . .	. . . .	. . . .	. . . .	. . . .	. . . .
Repairs on goods...	2 160 ..	1	. . . .	3	2	2	2	1	2
Goods procured in ports by carriers...............	2 170 ..	106	112	86	112	129	139	155	173
Nonmonetary gold..	2 180 ..	1,145	1,166	1,501	2,102	2,424	3,095	4,004	4,157
Debit...	3 100 ..	−7,358	−7,204	−7,393	−8,205	−9,805	−12,082	−14,866	−19,599
General merchandise: imports f.o.b...............	3 110 ..	−7,030	−6,866	−7,091	−7,986	−9,549	−11,747	−14,451	−19,227
Goods for processing: imports f.o.b...............	3 150 ..	−305	−306	−265	−188	−214	−275	−365	−322
Repairs on goods...	3 160 ..	−5	−4	−11	−6	−9	−24	−11	−10
Goods procured in ports by carriers...............	3 170 ..	−17	−28	−26	−25	−33	−35	−39	−40
Nonmonetary gold..	3 180 ..	. . . .	. . . .	. . . .	. . . .	. . . .	. . . .	. . . .	. . . .
B. SERVICES...	4 200 ..	−735	−963	−994	−900	−732	−834	−781	−928
Total credit...	2 200 ..	*1,555*	*1,437*	*1,455*	*1,716*	*1,993*	*2,289*	*2,647*	*3,343*
Total debit...	3 200 ..	*−2,290*	*−2,400*	*−2,449*	*−2,616*	*−2,725*	*−3,123*	*−3,428*	*−4,270*
Transportation services, credit..........................	2 205 ..	243	257	266	309	373	449	525	634
Passenger..	2 850 ..	*24*	*30*	*49*	*60*	*90*	*130*	*205*	*284*
Freight...	2 851 ..	*10*	*14*	*19*	*26*	*43*	*60*	*64*	*80*
Other...	2 852 ..	*209*	*213*	*198*	*224*	*240*	*259*	*256*	*269*
Sea transport, passenger...............................	2 207 ..	. . . .	. . . .	. . . .	. . . .	. . . .	. . . .	. . . .	. . . .
Sea transport, freight....................................	2 208 ..	6	3	5	2	1	. . . .	. . . .	1
Sea transport, other......................................	2 209 ..	75	74	78	88	100	114	136	144
Air transport, passenger................................	2 211 ..	24	30	49	60	90	130	205	284
Air transport, freight.....................................	2 212 ..	4	10	14	24	42	60	64	79
Air transport, other.......................................	2 213 ..	135	139	120	136	140	144	120	125
Other transport, passenger...........................	2 215 ..	. . . .	. . . .	. . . .	. . . .	. . . .	. . . .	. . . .	. . . .
Other transport, freight................................	2 216 ..	. . . .	. . . .	. . . .	. . . .	. . . .	. . . .	. . . .	. . . .
Other transport, other...................................	2 217 ..	. . . .	. . . .	. . . .	. . . .	. . . .	. . . .	. . . .	. . . .
Transportation services, debit..........................	3 205 ..	−855	−914	−884	−931	−1,087	−1,312	−1,461	−1,889
Passenger..	3 850 ..	*−218*	*−228*	*−200*	*−206*	*−209*	*−218*	*−245*	*−267*
Freight...	3 851 ..	*−565*	*−600*	*−585*	*−615*	*−784*	*−978*	*−1,077*	*−1,447*
Other...	3 852 ..	*−73*	*−86*	*−99*	*−110*	*−94*	*−116*	*−138*	*−176*
Sea transport, passenger...............................	3 207 ..	. . . .	. . . .	. . . .	. . . .	. . . .	. . . .	. . . .	. . . .
Sea transport, freight....................................	3 208 ..	−501	−538	−522	−549	−711	−900	−977	−1,315
Sea transport, other......................................	3 209 ..	−24	−25	−31	−35	−30	−27	−29	−32
Air transport, passenger................................	3 211 ..	−218	−228	−200	−206	−209	−218	−245	−267
Air transport, freight.....................................	3 212 ..	−64	−62	−63	−67	−73	−78	−100	−132
Air transport, other.......................................	3 213 ..	−49	−61	−68	−75	−65	−89	−109	−144
Other transport, passenger...........................	3 215 ..	. . . .	. . . .	. . . .	. . . .	. . . .	. . . .	. . . .	. . . .
Other transport, freight................................	3 216 ..	. . . .	. . . .	. . . .	. . . .	. . . .	. . . .	. . . .	. . . .
Other transport, other...................................	3 217 ..	. . . .	. . . .	. . . .	. . . .	. . . .	. . . .	. . . .	. . . .
Travel, credit..	2 236 ..	837	733	787	963	1,142	1,308	1,577	1,938
Business travel..	2 237 ..	. . . .	. . . .	. . . .	. . . .	. . . .	. . . .	. . . .	. . . .
Personal travel..	2 240 ..	837	733	787	963	1,142	1,308	1,577	1,938
Travel, debit...	3 236 ..	−423	−545	−606	−641	−643	−752	−789	−1,007
Business travel..	3 237 ..	. . . .	. . . .	. . . .	. . . .	. . . .	. . . .	. . . .	. . . .
Personal travel..	3 240 ..	−423	−545	−606	−641	−643	−752	−789	−1,007
Other services, credit.......................................	2 200 BA	476	447	402	443	479	532	546	772
Communications...	2 245 ..	90	67	48	46	60	69	82	88
Construction...	2 249 ..	. . . .	. . . .	. . . .	. . . .	. . . .	. . . .	. . . .	. . . .
Insurance...	2 253 ..	113	116	96	89	82	118	103	297
Financial..	2 260 ..	12	10	12	7	6	6	7	26
Computer and information.............................	2 262 ..	. . . .	. . . .	. . . .	. . . .	. . . .	. . . .	. . . .	. . . .
Royalties and licence fees.............................	2 266 ..	1	1	1	1	. . . .	2	3	2
Other business services.................................	2 268 ..	149	143	132	185	210	212	224	226
Personal, cultural, and recreational................	2 287 ..	. . . .	. . . .	. . . .	. . . .	. . . .	. . . .	. . . .	. . . .
Government, n.i.e..	2 291 ..	110	111	113	116	121	125	128	133
Other services, debit..	3 200 BA	−1,012	−940	−959	−1,043	−995	−1,060	−1,179	−1,374
Communications...	3 245 ..	−70	−72	−66	−80	−81	−96	−109	−110
Construction...	3 249 ..	. . . .	. . . .	. . . .	. . . .	. . . .	. . . .	. . . .	. . . .
Insurance...	3 253 ..	−150	−173	−241	−267	−209	−233	−265	−310
Financial..	3 260 ..	−16	−12	−11	−18	−19	−20	−21	−26
Computer and information.............................	3 262 ..	. . . .	. . . .	. . . .	. . . .	. . . .	. . . .	. . . .	. . . .
Royalties and licence fees.............................	3 266 ..	−74	−65	−71	−74	−78	−82	−86	−90
Other business services.................................	3 268 ..	−576	−491	−446	−481	−485	−501	−567	−701
Personal, cultural, and recreational................	3 287 ..	. . . .	. . . .	. . . .	. . . .	. . . .	. . . .	. . . .	. . . .
Government, n.i.e..	3 291 ..	−126	−126	−123	−122	−122	−128	−131	−138

Table 2 (Continued). STANDARD PRESENTATION, 2000–2007

(Millions of U.S. dollars)

	Code	2000	2001	2002	2003	2004	2005	2006	2007
C. INCOME	4 300 ..	**−1,410**	**−1,101**	**−1,457**	**−2,144**	**−3,686**	**−5,076**	**−7,583**	**−8,418**
Total credit	2 300 ..	*737*	*670*	*370*	*322*	*332*	*625*	*1,033*	*1,567*
Total debit	3 300 ..	*−2,146*	*−1,771*	*−1,827*	*−2,466*	*−4,017*	*−5,701*	*−8,616*	*−9,985*
Compensation of employees, credit	2 310 ..	....	....	....	....	....	....	....	....
Compensation of employees, debit	3 310 ..	....	....	....	....	....	....	....	....
Investment income, credit	2 320 ..	**737**	**670**	**370**	**322**	**332**	**625**	**1,033**	**1,567**
Direct investment income	2 330 ..	....	....	....	....	....	....	....	....
Dividends and distributed branch profits	2 332 ..	....	....	....	....	....	....	....	....
Reinvested earnings and undistributed branch profits	2 333 ..	....	....	....	....	....	....	....	....
Income on debt (interest)	2 334 ..	....	....	....	....	....	....	....	....
Portfolio investment income	2 339 ..	....	....	....	....	....	....	....	....
Income on equity	2 340 ..	....	....	....	....	....	....	....	....
Income on bonds and notes	2 350 ..	....	....	....	....	....	....	....	....
Income on money market instruments	2 360 ..	....	....	....	....	....	....	....	....
Other investment income	2 370 ..	737	670	370	322	332	625	1,033	1,567
Investment income, debit	3 320 ..	**−2,146**	**−1,771**	**−1,827**	**−2,466**	**−4,017**	**−5,701**	**−8,616**	**−9,985**
Direct investment income	3 330 ..	−344	−131	−479	−1,112	−2,567	−4,030	−6,741	−7,865
Dividends and distributed branch profits	3 332 ..	−293	−377	−486	−474	−704	−1,306	−4,387	−3,169
Reinvested earnings and undistributed branch profits	3 333 ..	−51	246	8	−638	−1,864	−2,724	−2,353	−4,696
Income on debt (interest)	3 334 ..	....	....	....	....	....	....	....	....
Portfolio investment income	3 339 ..	−194	−190	−204	−314	−433	−554	−743	−790
Income on equity	3 340 ..	....	....	....	....	....	....	....	....
Income on bonds and notes	3 350 ..	−194	−190	−204	−314	−433	−554	−743	−803
Income on money market instruments	3 360 ..	....	....	....	....	....	....	....	14
Other investment income	3 370 ..	−1,608	−1,450	−1,144	−1,039	−1,018	−1,117	−1,132	−1,330
D. CURRENT TRANSFERS	4 379 ..	**1,001**	**1,040**	**1,019**	**1,209**	**1,433**	**1,772**	**2,185**	**2,495**
Credit	2 379 ..	**1,010**	**1,048**	**1,028**	**1,215**	**1,439**	**1,781**	**2,194**	**2,504**
General government	2 380 ..	8	9	2	1	2	7	8	12
Other sectors	2 390 ..	1,002	1,039	1,026	1,215	1,437	1,774	2,186	2,493
Workers' remittances	2 391 ..	718	753	705	869	1,133	1,440	1,837	2,131
Other current transfers	2 392 ..	284	286	321	346	304	334	349	362
Debit	3 379 ..	**−9**	**−8**	**−8**	**−6**	**−6**	**−10**	**−10**	**−10**
General government	3 380 ..	−9	−8	−8	−6	−6	−10	−10	−10
Other sectors	3 390 ..	....	....	....	....	....	....	....	....
Workers' remittances	3 391 ..	....	....	....	....	....	....	....	....
Other current transfers	3 392 ..	....	....	....	....	....	....	....	....
CAPITAL AND FINANCIAL ACCOUNT	4 996 ..	**887**	**948**	**861**	**147**	**−256**	**−1,510**	**−2,252**	**−1,183**
CAPITAL ACCOUNT	4 994 ..	**−258**	**−154**	**−98**	**−48**	**−59**	**−22**	**−100**	**−67**
Total credit	2 994 ..	*17*	*21*	*20*	*68*	*54*	*106*	*33*	*70*
Total debit	3 994 ..	*−275*	*−175*	*−118*	*−116*	*−113*	*−129*	*−133*	*−137*
Capital transfers, credit	2 400 ..	**17**	**21**	**20**	**68**	**54**	**106**	**33**	**70**
General government	2 401 ..	4	10	14	65	28	103	30	68
Debt forgiveness	2 402 ..	1	1	14	64	26	100	27	67
Other capital transfers	2 410 ..	4	9	....	1	2	3	3	1
Other sectors	2 430 ..	13	11	6	3	26	3	3	2
Migrants' transfers	2 431 ..	....	....	....	....	....	....	....	....
Debt forgiveness	2 432 ..	....	....	....	....	23	....	....	....
Other capital transfers	2 440 ..	13	11	6	3	3	3	3	2
Capital transfers, debit	3 400 ..	**−275**	**−175**	**−118**	**−116**	**−113**	**−129**	**−133**	**−137**
General government	3 401 ..	....	....	....	....	....	....	....	....
Debt forgiveness	3 402 ..	....	....	....	....	....	....	....	....
Other capital transfers	3 410 ..	....	....	....	....	....	....	....	....
Other sectors	3 430 ..	−275	−175	−118	−116	−113	−129	−133	−137
Migrants' transfers	3 431 ..	−275	−175	−118	−116	−113	−129	−133	−137
Debt forgiveness	3 432 ..	....	....	....	....	....	....	....	....
Other capital transfers	3 440 ..	....	....	....	....	....	....	....	....
Nonproduced nonfinancial assets, credit	2 480 ..	....	....	....	....	....	....	....	....
Nonproduced nonfinancial assets, debit	3 480 ..	....	....	....	....	....	....	....	....

Table 2 (Continued). STANDARD PRESENTATION, 2000–2007

(Millions of U.S. dollars)

	Code	2000	2001	2002	2003	2004	2005	2006	2007
FINANCIAL ACCOUNT............................	4 995 ..	**1,145**	**1,102**	**959**	**195**	**−196**	**−1,488**	**−2,152**	**−1,116**
A. DIRECT INVESTMENT..........................	4 500 ..	**810**	**1,070**	**2,156**	**1,275**	**1,599**	**2,579**	**3,467**	**5,343**
Direct investment abroad.................................	4 505 ..	....	−74	....	−60	....	....	....	....
Equity capital..	4 510 ..	....	−74	....	−60	....	....	....	....
Claims on affiliated enterprises.....................	4 515 ..	....	−74	....	−60	....	....	....	....
Liabilities to affiliated enterprises.................	4 520 ..	....	....	....	....	....	....	....	....
Reinvested earnings.......................................	4 525 ..	....	....	....	....	....	....	....	....
Other capital..	4 530 ..	....	....	....	....	....	....	....	....
Claims on affiliated enterprises.....................	4 535 ..	....	....	....	....	....	....	....	....
Liabilities to affiliated enterprises.................	4 540 ..	....	....	....	....	....	....	....	....
Direct investment in Peru.............................	4 555 ..	**810**	**1,144**	**2,156**	**1,335**	**1,599**	**2,579**	**3,467**	**5,343**
Equity capital..	4 560 ..	759	1,390	2,163	697	−265	−145	1,113	646
Claims on direct investors.............................	4 565 ..	....	....	....	....	....	....	....	....
Liabilities to direct investors........................	4 570 ..	759	1,390	2,163	697	−265	−145	1,113	646
Reinvested earnings.......................................	4 575 ..	51	−246	−8	638	1,864	2,724	2,353	4,696
Other capital..	4 580 ..	....	....	....	....	....	....	....	....
Claims on direct investors.............................	4 585 ..	....	....	....	....	....	....	....	....
Liabilities to direct investors........................	4 590 ..	....	....	....	....	....	....	....	....
B. PORTFOLIO INVESTMENT.........................	4 600 ..	**−406**	**−372**	**1,408**	**−76**	**820**	**1,762**	**−1,837**	**3,435**
Assets...	4 602 ..	**−481**	**−318**	**−316**	**−1,287**	**−425**	**−817**	**−1,992**	**−520**
Equity securities..	4 610 ..	−478	−341	−388	−1,287	−426	−818	−1,993	−520
Monetary authorities.......................................	4 611 ..	....	....	....	....	....	....	....	....
General government..	4 612 ..	−69	−54	−42	−56	−58	−60	−56	−2
Banks...	4 613 ..	−157	−117	124	−234	120	56	−399	−55
Other sectors..	4 614 ..	−252	−170	−469	−997	−487	−814	−1,538	−463
Debt securities...	4 619 ..	−3	23	72	....	1	1	1	1
Bonds and notes..	4 620 ..	−3	23	72	....	1	1	1	1
Monetary authorities.......................................	4 621 ..	−3	1	....	....	1	1	1	1
General government..	4 622 ..	....	22	72		....	....	....	....
Banks...	4 623 ..	....	....	....	....	....	....	....	....
Other sectors..	4 624 ..	....	....	....	....	....	....	....	....
Money market instruments..............................	4 630 ..	....	....	....	....	....	....	....	....
Monetary authorities.......................................	4 631 ..	....	....	....	....	....	....	....	....
General government..	4 632 ..	....	....	....	....	....	....	....	....
Banks...	4 633 ..	....	....	....	....	....	....	....	....
Other sectors..	4 634 ..	....	....	....	....	....	....	....	....
Liabilities...	4 652 ..	**75**	**−54**	**1,724**	**1,211**	**1,244**	**2,579**	**155**	**3,955**
Equity securities..	4 660 ..	123	43	−9	1	−47	769	182	814
Banks...	4 663 ..	....	....	....	....	....	....	....	....
Other sectors..	4 664 ..	123	43	−9	1	−47	769	182	814
Debt securities...	4 669 ..	−48	−97	1,733	1,210	1,291	1,810	−27	3,140
Bonds and notes..	4 670 ..	−48	−97	1,733	1,210	1,291	1,810	−27	2,290
Monetary authorities.......................................	4 671 ..	....	....	....	....	....	....	....	....
General government..	4 672 ..	....	....	1,886	1,246	1,295	1,682	....	2,290
Banks...	4 673 ..	....	....	....	....	....	....	....	....
Other sectors..	4 674 ..	−48	−97	−153	−36	−4	127	−27	....
Money market instruments..............................	4 680 ..	....	....	....	....	....	....	....	850
Monetary authorities.......................................	4 681 ..	....	....	....	....	....	....	....	850
General government..	4 682 ..	....	....	....	....	....	....	....	....
Banks...	4 683 ..	....	....	....	....	....	....	....	....
Other sectors..	4 684 ..	....	....	....	....	....	....	....	....
C. FINANCIAL DERIVATIVES...........................	4 910 ..	....	....	....	....	....	....	....	....
Monetary authorities.......................................	4 911 ..	....	....	....	....	....	....	....	....
General government..	4 912 ..	....	....	....	....	....	....	....	....
Banks...	4 913 ..	....	....	....	....	....	....	....	....
Other sectors..	4 914 ..	....	....	....	....	....	....	....	....
Assets...	4 900 ..	....	....	....	....	....	....	....	....
Monetary authorities.......................................	4 901 ..	....	....	....	....	....	....	....	....
General government..	4 902 ..	....	....	....	....	....	....	....	....
Banks...	4 903 ..	....	....	....	....	....	....	....	....
Other sectors..	4 904 ..	....	....	....	....	....	....	....	....
Liabilities...	4 905 ..	....	....	....	....	....	....	....	....
Monetary authorities.......................................	4 906 ..	....	....	....	....	....	....	....	....
General government..	4 907 ..	....	....	....	....	....	....	....	....
Banks...	4 908 ..	....	....	....	....	....	....	....	....
Other sectors..	4 909 ..	....	....	....	....	....	....	....	....

Table 2 (Concluded). STANDARD PRESENTATION, 2000–2007

(Millions of U.S. dollars)

	Code	2000	2001	2002	2003	2004	2005	2006	2007
D. OTHER INVESTMENT	4 700	**412**	**680**	**−1,753**	**−489**	**−172**	**−4,357**	**−573**	**496**
Assets	4 703	**191**	**664**	....	**127**	**14**	**−1,084**	**8**	**−30**
Trade credits	4 706	....	....	....	....	....	....	....	....
General government	4 707	....	....	....	....	....	....	....	....
of which: Short-term	4 709	....	....	....	....	....	....	....	....
Other sectors	4 710	....	....	....	....	....	....	....	....
of which: Short-term	4 712	....	....	....	....	....	....	....	....
Loans	4 714	....	....	....	....	....	....	....	....
Monetary authorities	4 715	....	....	....	....	....	....	....	....
of which: Short-term	4 718	....	....	....	....	....	....	....	....
General government	4 719	....	....	....	....	....	....	....	....
of which: Short-term	4 721	....	....	....	....	....	....	....	....
Banks	4 722	....	....	....	....	....	....	....	....
of which: Short-term	4 724	....	....	....	....	....	....	....	....
Other sectors	4 725	....	....	....	....	....	....	....	....
of which: Short-term	4 727	....	....	....	....	....	....	....	....
Currency and deposits	4 730	221	681	−159	1	−72	−886	−433	−668
Monetary authorities	4 731	....	....	....	....	....	....	....	....
General government	4 732	−60	−5	−4	−203	−64	−214	−33	−16
Banks	4 733	232	48	28	179	71	−288	−138	102
Other sectors	4 734	49	638	−183	25	−79	−384	−262	−754
Other assets	4 736	−30	−16	159	126	86	−198	440	639
Monetary authorities	4 737	−31	−16	152	119	86	−162	425	760
of which: Short-term	4 739	−31	−16	152	119	86	−162	425	760
General government	4 740	....	....	....	....	....	....	....	....
of which: Short-term	4 742	....	....	....	....	....	....	....	....
Banks	4 743	1	....	7	7	....	−36	15	−121
of which: Short-term	4 745	....	....	....	....	....	....	....	....
Other sectors	4 746	....	....	....	....	....	....	....	....
of which: Short-term	4 748	....	....	....	....	....	....	....	....
Liabilities	4 753	**221**	**15**	**−1,753**	**−616**	**−186**	**−3,273**	**−581**	**526**
Trade credits	4 756	....	....	....	....	....	....	....	....
General government	4 757	....	....	....	....	....	....	....	....
of which: Short-term	4 759	....	....	....	....	....	....	....	....
Other sectors	4 760	....	....	....	....	....	....	....	....
of which: Short-term	4 762	....	....	....	....	....	....	....	....
Loans	4 764	280	71	−1,753	−616	−186	−3,258	−581	526
Monetary authorities	4 765	−117	−165	−176	−118	−33	−35	−7	−44
of which: Use of Fund credit and loans from the Fund..	4 766	−141	−154	−172	−110	−40	−40	−39	−20
of which: Short-term..	4 768	24	−11	−4	−8	6	5	32	−24
General government	4 769	666	653	−781	−294	−130	−2,677	−584	−4,568
of which: Short-term	4 771	....	....	....	....	....	....	....	....
Banks	4 772	−168	−499	−513	−84	53	327	−139	3,596
of which: Short-term	4 774	−239	−365	−398	−61	32	352	−265	1,495
Other sectors	4 775	−101	82	−284	−119	−75	−872	149	1,542
of which: Short-term	4 777	−777	−132	−241	5	206	83	102	337
Currency and deposits	4 780	....	....	....	....	....	....	....	....
Monetary authorities	4 781	....	....	....	....	....	....	....	....
General government	4 782	....	....	....	....	....	....	....	....
Banks	4 783	....	....	....	....	....	....	....	....
Other sectors	4 784	....	....	....	....	....	....	....	....
Other liabilities	4 786	−58	−56	....	....	....	−15	....	....
Monetary authorities	4 787	....	....	....	....	....	....	....	....
of which: Short-term	4 789	....	....	....	....	....	....	....	....
General government	4 790	−58	−56	....	....	....	−15	....	....
of which: Short-term	4 792	−58	−56	....	....	....	−15	....	....
Banks	4 793	....	....	....	....	....	....	....	....
of which: Short-term	4 795	....	....	....	....	....	....	....	....
Other sectors	4 796	....	....	....	....	....	....	....	....
of which: Short-term	4 798	....	....	....	....	....	....	....	....
E. RESERVE ASSETS	4 802	**329**	**−276**	**−851**	**−515**	**−2,442**	**−1,472**	**−3,209**	**−10,390**
Monetary gold	4 812	50	−4	−125	−76	−26	−87	−130	−222
Special drawing rights	4 811	−2	....	1	....	....	....	....	−3
Reserve position in the Fund	4 810	....	....	....	....	....	....	....	....
Foreign exchange	4 803	264	−265	−678	−469	−2,406	−1,379	−3,066	−10,164
Other claims	4 813	17	−7	−49	29	−11	−5	−13	−1
NET ERRORS AND OMISSIONS	4 998	**659**	**255**	**249**	**801**	**236**	**362**	**−503**	**−322**

Table 3. INTERNATIONAL INVESTMENT POSITION (End-period stocks), 2000–2007

(Millions of U.S. dollars)

	Code	2000	2001	2002	2003	2004	2005	2006	2007
ASSETS..	8 995 C.	14,370	14,406	15,706	18,029	21,204	24,962	31,977	46,626
Direct investment abroad.....................................	8 505 ..	505	649	666	814	874	1,047	1,476	2,284
Equity capital and reinvested earnings.............................	8 506 ..	505	649	666	814	874	1,047	1,476	2,284
Claims on affiliated enterprises...............................	8 507 ..	505	649	666	814	874	1,047	1,476	2,284
Liabilities to affiliated enterprises...........................	8 508 ..	....	....	....	....	....	....	....	....
Other capital..	8 530 ..	....	....	....	....	....	....	....	....
Claims on affiliated enterprises...............................	8 535 ..	....	....	....	....	....	....	....	....
Liabilities to affiliated enterprises...........................	8 540 ..	....	....	....	....	....	....	....	....
Portfolio investment..	8 602 ..	2,070	2,372	2,702	4,573	5,238	6,643	9,637	12,120
Equity securities..	8 610 ..	1,661	1,948	2,293	3,896	4,346	5,576	8,380	10,739
Monetary authorities...	8 611 ..	....	....	....	....	....	....	....	....
General government..	8 612 ..	....	....	....	....	....	....	....	....
Banks..	8 613 ..	385	502	378	612	492	436	835	915
Other sectors..	8 614 ..	1,276	1,446	1,915	3,284	3,854	5,140	7,545	9,824
Debt securities..	8 619 ..	409	424	409	677	892	1,068	1,257	1,381
Bonds and notes..	8 620 ..	409	424	409	677	892	1,068	1,257	1,381
Monetary authorities.......................................	8 621 ..	....	....	....	....	....	....	....	....
General government...	8 622 ..	409	424	409	677	892	1,068	1,257	1,381
Banks...	8 623 ..	....	....	....	....	....	....	....	....
Other sectors..	8 624 ..	....	....	....	....	....	....	....	....
Money market instruments....................................	8 630 ..	....	....	....	....	....	....	....	....
Monetary authorities.......................................	8 631 ..	....	....	....	....	....	....	....	....
General government...	8 632 ..	....	....	....	....	....	....	....	....
Banks...	8 633 ..	....	....	....	....	....	....	....	....
Other sectors..	8 634 ..	....	....	....	....	....	....	....	....
Financial derivatives...	8 900 ..	....	....	....	....	....	....	....	....
Monetary authorities..	8 901 ..	....	....	....	....	....	....	....	....
General government..	8 902 ..	....	....	....	....	....	....	....	....
Banks..	8 903 ..	....	....	....	....	....	....	....	....
Other sectors..	8 904 ..	....	....	....	....	....	....	....	....
Other investment...	8 703 ..	3,240	2,555	2,656	2,445	2,453	3,161	3,545	4,512
Trade credits..	8 706 ..	....	....	....	....	....	....	....	....
General government..	8 707 ..	....	....	....	....	....	....	....	....
of which: Short-term.......................................	8 709 ..	....	....	....	....	....	....	....	....
Other sectors..	8 710 ..	....	....	....	....	....	....	....	....
of which: Short-term.......................................	8 712 ..	....	....	....	....	....	....	....	....
Loans..	8 714 ..	....	....	....	....	....	....	....	....
Monetary authorities...	8 715 ..	....	....	....	....	....	....	....	....
of which: Short-term.......................................	8 718 ..	....	....	....	....	....	....	....	....
General government..	8 719 ..	....	....	....	....	....	....	....	....
of which: Short-term.......................................	8 721 ..	....	....	....	....	....	....	....	....
Banks..	8 722 ..	....	....	....	....	....	....	....	....
of which: Short-term.......................................	8 724 ..	....	....	....	....	....	....	....	....
Other sectors..	8 725 ..	....	....	....	....	....	....	....	....
of which: Short-term.......................................	8 727 ..	....	....	....	....	....	....	....	....
Currency and deposits..	8 730 ..	3,167	2,481	2,636	2,432	2,440	3,111	3,511	4,356
Monetary authorities...	8 731 ..	....	....	....	....	....	....	....	....
General government..	8 732 ..	....	....	....	....	....	....	....	....
Banks..	8 733 ..	899	851	823	644	573	860	998	896
Other sectors..	8 734 ..	2,268	1,630	1,813	1,788	1,867	2,251	2,513	3,460
Other assets...	8 736 ..	73	74	20	13	13	50	34	155
Monetary authorities...	8 737 ..	46	47	....	....	....	....	....	....
of which: Short-term.......................................	8 739 ..	*46*	*47*						
General government..	8 740 ..	....	....	....	....	....	....	....	....
of which: Short-term.......................................	8 742 ..	....	....	....	....	....	....	....	....
Banks..	8 743 ..	27	27	20	13	13	50	34	155
of which: Short-term.......................................	8 745 ..	....	....	....	....	....	....	....	....
Other sectors..	8 746 ..	....	....	....	....	....	....	....	....
of which: Short-term.......................................	8 748 ..	....	....	....	....	....	....	....	....
Reserve assets..	8 802 ..	8,554	8,830	9,682	10,197	12,639	14,111	17,320	27,710
Monetary gold..	8 812 ..	258	262	387	463	489	576	706	928
Special drawing rights...	8 811 ..	1	2	1	....	....	....	1	4
Reserve position in the Fund.................................	8 810 ..	....	....	....	....	....	....	....	....
Foreign exchange..	8 803 ..	7,975	8,240	8,918	9,387	11,793	13,172	16,238	26,402
Other claims...	8 813 ..	320	327	376	347	358	362	376	377

Table 3 (Concluded). INTERNATIONAL INVESTMENT POSITION (End-period stocks), 2000–2007

(Millions of U.S. dollars)

	Code	2000	2001	2002	2003	2004	2005	2006	2007
LIABILITIES	8 995 D.	**41,321**	**41,456**	**43,411**	**46,308**	**48,483**	**51,250**	**56,794**	**76,388**
Direct investment in Peru	8 555 ..	**11,062**	**11,835**	**12,549**	**12,876**	**13,310**	**15,889**	**19,356**	**24,744**
Equity capital and reinvested earnings	8 556 ..	11,062	11,835	12,549	12,876	13,310	15,889	19,356	24,744
Claims on direct investors	8 557 ..	....	....	....	....	....	....	....	....
Liabilities to direct investors	8 558 ..	11,062	11,835	12,549	12,876	13,310	15,889	19,356	24,744
Other capital	8 580 ..	....	....	....	....	....	....	....	....
Claims on direct investors	8 585 ..	....	....	....	....	....	....	....	....
Liabilities to direct investors	8 590 ..	....	....	....	....	....	....	....	....
Portfolio investment	8 652 ..	**6,384**	**6,436**	**7,544**	**9,570**	**10,963**	**15,316**	**17,626**	**28,421**
Equity securities	8 660 ..	2,278	2,427	2,990	3,845	3,928	6,705	9,043	19,077
Banks	8 663 ..	....	....	....	....	....	....	....	....
Other sectors	8 664 ..	2,278	2,427	2,990	3,845	3,928	6,705	9,043	19,077
Debt securities	8 669 ..	4,106	4,010	4,554	5,724	7,035	8,612	8,583	9,343
Bonds and notes	8 670 ..	4,106	4,010	4,554	5,724	7,035	8,612	8,583	8,453
Monetary authorities	8 671 ..	....	....	....	....	....	....	....	....
General government	8 672 ..	3,727	3,727	4,424	5,630	6,944	8,393	8,392	8,262
Banks	8 673 ..	....	....	....	....	....	....	....	....
Other sectors	8 674 ..	379	283	130	94	91	218	192	192
Money market instruments	8 680 ..	....	....	....	....	....	....	....	890
Monetary authorities	8 681 ..	....	....	....	....	....	....	....	890
General government	8 682 ..	....	....	....	....	....	....	....	....
Banks	8 683 ..	....	....	....	....	....	....	....	....
Other sectors	8 684 ..	....	....	....	....	....	....	....	....
Financial derivatives	8 905 ..	....	....	....	....	....	....	....	....
Monetary authorities	8 906 ..	....	....	....	....	....	....	....	....
General government	8 907 ..	....	....	....	....	....	....	....	....
Banks	8 908 ..	....	....	....	....	....	....	....	....
Other sectors	8 909 ..	....	....	....	....	....	....	....	....
Other investment	8 753 ..	**23,874**	**23,185**	**23,318**	**23,863**	**24,209**	**20,045**	**19,812**	**23,223**
Trade credits	8 756 ..	....	....	....	....	....	....	....	....
General government	8 757 ..	....	....	....	....	....	....	....	....
of which: Short-term	8 759 ..	....	....	....	....	....	....	....	....
Other sectors	8 760 ..	....	....	....	....	....	....	....	....
of which: Short-term	8 762 ..	....	....	....	....	....	....	....	....
Loans	8 764 ..	23,874	23,185	23,318	23,863	24,209	20,045	19,812	23,223
Monetary authorities	8 765 ..	592	410	256	151	122	80	75	31
of which: Use of Fund credit and loans from the Fund	8 766 ..	*558*	*387*	*236*	*139*	*104*	*57*	*20*	....
of which: Short-term	8 768 ..	*34*	*23*	*19*	*12*	*18*	*23*	*54*	*31*
General government	8 769 ..	14,758	14,681	15,754	16,593	16,977	13,415	13,177	11,457
of which: Short-term	8 771 ..	....	....	....	....	....	....	....	....
Banks	8 772 ..	2,005	1,506	993	909	961	1,288	1,149	4,745
of which: Short-term	8 774 ..	*1,526*	*1,161*	*763*	*702*	*733*	*1,085*	*820*	*2,315*
Other sectors	8 775 ..	6,520	6,589	6,315	6,210	6,149	5,262	5,411	6,990
of which: Short-term	8 777 ..	*2,180*	*2,048*	*1,807*	*1,812*	*2,018*	*2,100*	*2,202*	*2,570*
Currency and deposits	8 780 ..	....	....	....	....	....	....	....	....
Monetary authorities	8 781 ..	....	....	....	....	....	....	....	....
General government	8 782 ..	....	....	....	....	....	....	....	....
Banks	8 783 ..	....	....	....	....	....	....	....	....
Other sectors	8 784 ..	....	....	....	....	....	....	....	....
Other liabilities	8 786 ..	....	....	....	....	....	....	....	....
Monetary authorities	8 787 ..	....	....	....	....	....	....	....	....
of which: Short-term	8 789 ..	....	....	....	....	....	....	....	....
General government	8 790 ..	....	....	....	....	....	....	....	....
of which: Short-term	8 792 ..	....	....	....	....	....	....	....	....
Banks	8 793 ..	....	....	....	....	....	....	....	....
of which: Short-term	8 795 ..	....	....	....	....	....	....	....	....
Other sectors	8 796 ..	....	....	....	....	....	....	....	....
of which: Short-term	8 798 ..	....	....	....	....	....	....	....	....
NET INTERNATIONAL INVESTMENT POSITION	8 995 ..	−26,951	−27,050	−27,705	−28,279	−27,278	−26,288	−24,816	−29,762
Conversion rates: nuevos soles per U.S. dollar (end of period)	0 102 ..	3.5270	3.4440	3.5140	3.4630	3.2815	3.4300	3.1955	2.9960

Table 1. ANALYTIC PRESENTATION, 2000–2007

(Millions of U.S. dollars)

	Code	2000	2001	2002	2003	2004	2005	2006	2007
A. Current Account[1]	4 993 Z.	**−2,225**	**−1,744**	**−279**	**288**	**1,633**	**1,984**	**4,830**	**5,766**
Goods: exports f.o.b.	2 100 ..	37,347	31,313	34,403	35,339	38,794	40,263	46,526	49,321
Goods: imports f.o.b.	3 100 ..	−43,318	−37,578	−39,933	−41,190	−44,478	−48,036	−53,258	−57,557
Balance on Goods	4 100 ..	*−5,971*	*−6,265*	*−5,530*	*−5,851*	*−5,684*	*−7,773*	*−6,732*	*−8,236*
Services: credit	2 200 ..	3,377	3,072	3,428	3,389	4,043	4,525	5,927	7,863
Services: debit	3 200 ..	−5,247	−5,360	−5,430	−5,352	−5,815	−5,865	−6,307	−7,371
Balance on Goods and Services	4 991 ..	*−7,841*	*−8,553*	*−7,532*	*−7,814*	*−7,456*	*−9,113*	*−7,112*	*−7,744*
Income: credit	2 300 ..	3,336	3,553	3,306	3,330	3,725	3,937	4,388	5,488
Income: debit	3 300 ..	−3,363	−3,604	−3,733	−3,614	−3,796	−4,231	−5,643	−5,955
Balance on Goods, Services, and Income	4 992 ..	*−7,868*	*−8,604*	*−7,959*	*−8,098*	*−7,527*	*−9,407*	*−8,367*	*−8,211*
Current transfers: credit	2 379 Z.	5,909	7,119	7,948	8,626	9,420	11,711	13,511	14,397
Current transfers: debit	3 379 ..	−266	−259	−268	−240	−260	−320	−314	−420
B. Capital Account[1]	4 994 Z.	**138**	**62**	**27**	**54**	**17**	**40**	**138**	**24**
Capital account: credit	2 994 Z.	168	86	50	82	46	58	181	108
Capital account: debit	3 994 ..	−30	−24	−23	−28	−29	−18	−43	−84
Total, Groups A Plus B	4 981 ..	*−2,087*	*−1,682*	*−252*	*342*	*1,650*	*2,024*	*4,968*	*5,790*
C. Financial Account[1]	4 995 W.	**3,234**	**366**	**394**	**481**	**−1,671**	**1,441**	**1,351**	**4,054**
Direct investment abroad	4 505 ..	−125	140	−65	−303	−579	−189	−103	−3,442
Direct investment in the Philippines	4 555 Z.	2,240	195	1,542	491	688	1,854	2,921	2,928
Portfolio investment assets	4 602 ..	−812	−57	−628	−818	−862	−145	−1,567	−481
Equity securities	4 610 ..	−42	30	−8	−48	−15	−4	1	−29
Debt securities	4 619 ..	−770	−87	−620	−770	−847	−141	−1,568	−452
Portfolio investment liabilities	4 652 Z.	259	97	1,361	1,381	288	3,446	6,144	3,702
Equity securities	4 660 ..	−202	125	227	501	518	1,465	2,525	3,285
Debt securities	4 669 Z.	461	−28	1,134	880	−230	1,981	3,619	417
Financial derivatives	4 910 ..	44	−15	−21	−64	−27	−43	−138	−288
Financial derivatives assets	4 900 ..	166	83	85	54	58	98	159	170
Financial derivatives liabilities	4 905 ..	−122	−98	−106	−118	−85	−141	−297	−458
Other investment assets	4 703 ..	2,454	761	−256	743	−907	−4,791	−3,512	−2,519
Monetary authorities	4 701 ..	....	....	....	....	....	....	....	....
General government	4 704 ..	....	....	....	....	....	....	....	....
Banks	4 705 ..	2,270	908	−241	370	−588	−3,741	−1,391	−1,067
Other sectors	4 728 ..	184	−147	−15	373	−319	−1,050	−2,121	−1,452
Other investment liabilities	4 753 W.	−826	−755	−1,539	−949	−272	1,309	−2,394	4,154
Monetary authorities	4 753 WA	60	620	−662	3	−1,119	−514	−708	−177
General government	4 753 ZB	−184	−65	90	−64	−362	−500	256	397
Banks	4 753 ZC	−325	−752	49	−453	1,233	1,105	−1,229	1,052
Other sectors	4 753 ZD	−377	−558	−1,016	−435	−24	1,218	−713	2,882
Total, Groups A Through C	4 983 ..	*1,147*	*−1,316*	*142*	*823*	*−21*	*3,465*	*6,319*	*9,844*
D. Net Errors and Omissions	4 998 ..	**−1,624**	**629**	**33**	**−902**	**−282**	**−1,803**	**−1,077**	**−1,118**
Total, Groups A Through D	4 984 ..	*−477*	*−687*	*175*	*−79*	*−303*	*1,662*	*5,242*	*8,726*
E. Reserves and Related Items	4 802 A.	**477**	**687**	**−175**	**79**	**303**	**−1,662**	**−5,242**	**−8,726**
Reserve assets	4 802 ..	69	−469	252	356	1,637	−1,622	−2,935	−8,569
Use of Fund credit and loans	4 766 ..	303	−8	−407	−607	−472	−321	−404	....
Exceptional financing	4 920 ..	105	1,164	−21	330	−862	281	−1,902	−157
Conversion rates: Philippine pesos per U.S. dollar	0 101 ..	**44.192**	**50.993**	**51.604**	**54.203**	**56.040**	**55.085**	**51.314**	**46.148**

[1] Excludes components that have been classified in the categories of Group E.

Table 2. STANDARD PRESENTATION, 2000–2007

(Millions of U.S. dollars)

	Code	2000	2001	2002	2003	2004	2005	2006	2007
CURRENT ACCOUNT	4 993	−2,225	−1,744	−279	288	1,633	1,984	4,830	5,766
A. GOODS	4 100	−5,971	−6,265	−5,530	−5,851	−5,684	−7,773	−6,732	−8,236
Credit	2 100	37,347	31,313	34,403	35,339	38,794	40,263	46,526	49,321
General merchandise: exports f.o.b.	2 110	21,533	19,339	21,306	23,345	25,642	25,892	30,968	33,582
Goods for processing: exports f.o.b.	2 150	15,550	11,801	12,956	11,802	12,992	14,231	14,136	15,427
Repairs on goods	2 160	14	38	....	3	....	....	....	....
Goods procured in ports by carriers	2 170	63	41	35	58	91	70	1,148	221
Nonmonetary gold	2 180	187	94	106	131	69	70	274	91
Debit	3 100	−43,318	−37,578	−39,933	−41,190	−44,478	−48,036	−53,258	−57,557
General merchandise: imports f.o.b.	3 110	−30,035	−27,558	−29,022	−31,526	−34,044	−36,049	−40,582	−43,803
Goods for processing: imports f.o.b.	3 150	−13,263	−9,964	−10,787	−9,520	−10,275	−11,694	−11,834	−13,316
Repairs on goods	3 160	....	−50	−53	−55	−45	−42	....	....
Goods procured in ports by carriers	3 170	....	....	−51	−51	−77	−189	−724	−438
Nonmonetary gold	3 180	−20	−6	−20	−38	−37	−62	−118	....
B. SERVICES	4 200	−1,870	−2,288	−2,002	−1,963	−1,772	−1,340	−380	492
Total credit	2 200	*3,377*	*3,072*	*3,428*	*3,389*	*4,043*	*4,525*	*5,927*	*7,863*
Total debit	3 200	*−5,247*	*−5,360*	*−5,430*	*−5,352*	*−5,815*	*−5,865*	*−6,307*	*−7,371*
Transportation services, credit	2 205	464	590	877	951	1,001	962	634	735
Passenger	2 850	*178*	*269*	*257*	*277*	*373*	*490*	*1*	*2*
Freight	2 851	*115*	*98*	*488*	*543*	*499*	*353*	*474*	*503*
Other	2 852	*171*	*223*	*132*	*131*	*129*	*119*	*159*	*230*
Sea transport, passenger	2 207	....	....	....	....	....	....		
Sea transport, freight	2 208	....	....	....	....	....	....	....	....
Sea transport, other	2 209	....	....	....	....	....	....	....	....
Air transport, passenger	2 211	....	....	....	....	....	....	....	....
Air transport, freight	2 212	....	....	....	....	....	....	....	....
Air transport, other	2 213	....	....	....	....	....	....	....	....
Other transport, passenger	2 215	....	....	....	....	....	....	....	....
Other transport, freight	2 216	....	....	....	....	....	....	....	....
Other transport, other	2 217	....	....	....	....	....	....	1	2
Transportation services, debit	3 205	−2,052	−2,019	−2,303	−2,419	−3,095	−3,125	−3,452	−3,815
Passenger	3 850	*−199*	*−207*	*−248*	*−236*	*−251*	*−268*	*−326*	*−392*
Freight	3 851	*−1,553*	*−1,488*	*−1,766*	*−1,940*	*−2,677*	*−2,691*	*−2,966*	*−3,195*
Other	3 852	*−300*	*−324*	*−289*	*−243*	*−167*	*−166*	*−160*	*−228*
Sea transport, passenger	3 207	....	....	....	....	....	....	....	....
Sea transport, freight	3 208	....	....	....	....	....	....	....	....
Sea transport, other	3 209	....	....	....	....	....	....	....	....
Air transport, passenger	3 211	....	....	....	....	....	....	....	....
Air transport, freight	3 212	....	....	....	....	....	....	....	....
Air transport, other	3 213	....	....	....	....	....	....	....	....
Other transport, passenger	3 215	....	....	....	....	....	....	....	....
Other transport, freight	3 216	....	....	....	....	....	....	....	....
Other transport, other	3 217	....	....	....	....	....	....	....	....
Travel, credit	2 236	2,156	1,742	1,761	1,544	2,017	2,265	3,501	4,931
Business travel	2 237	....	....	....	....	....	....		
Personal travel	2 240	....	....	....	....	....	....	3,501	4,931
Travel, debit	3 236	−1,642	−1,711	−1,626	−1,413	−1,275	−1,279	−1,232	−1,615
Business travel	3 237	....	....	....	....	....	....	−36	−48
Personal travel	3 240	....	....	....	....	....	....	−1,196	−1,567
Other services, credit	2 200 BA	757	740	790	894	1,025	1,298	1,792	2,197
Communications	2 245	182	328	378	433	487	522	575	517
Construction	2 249	97	64	30	48	71	66	69	110
Insurance	2 253	12	12	12	12	12	17	21	23
Financial	2 260	80	40	32	38	42	53	101	82
Computer and information	2 262	76	22	37	28	33	89	95	74
Royalties and licence fees	2 266	7	1	1	4	12	6	6	5
Other business services	2 268	285	258	293	322	361	525	898	1,364
Personal, cultural, and recreational	2 287	18	15	7	9	7	20	27	22
Government, n.i.e.	2 291	....	....	....	....	....	....	....	....
Other services, debit	3 200 BA	−1,553	−1,630	−1,501	−1,520	−1,445	−1,461	−1,623	−1,941
Communications	3 245	−61	−72	−85	−81	−128	−115	−98	−97
Construction	3 249	−124	−299	−123	−64	−48	−7	−15	−19
Insurance	3 253	−155	−148	−175	−182	−199	−203	−230	−250
Financial	3 260	−33	−56	−70	−54	−76	−93	−125	−239
Computer and information	3 262	−99	−86	−80	−46	−49	−62	−67	−61
Royalties and licence fees	3 266	−197	−159	−236	−278	−273	−265	−349	−364
Other business services	3 268	−780	−711	−671	−770	−606	−639	−635	−740
Personal, cultural, and recreational	3 287	−32	−37	−17	−15	−15	−9	−8	−45
Government, n.i.e.	3 291	−72	−62	−44	−30	−51	−68	−96	−126

Table 2 (Continued). STANDARD PRESENTATION, 2000–2007

(Millions of U.S. dollars)

	Code	2000	2001	2002	2003	2004	2005	2006	2007
C. INCOME	4 300 ..	**−27**	**−51**	**−427**	**−284**	**−71**	**−294**	**−1,255**	**−467**
Total credit	2 300 ..	*3,336*	*3,553*	*3,306*	*3,330*	*3,725*	*3,937*	*4,388*	*5,488*
Total debit	3 300 ..	*−3,363*	*−3,604*	*−3,733*	*−3,614*	*−3,796*	*−4,231*	*−5,643*	*−5,955*
Compensation of employees, credit	2 310 ..	**1,763**	**2,432**	**2,568**	**2,558**	**2,851**	**2,893**	**2,758**	**3,008**
Compensation of employees, debit	3 310 ..	....	....	....	....	....	....	....	....
Investment income, credit	2 320 ..	**1,573**	**1,121**	**738**	**772**	**874**	**1,044**	**1,630**	**2,480**
Direct investment income	2 330 ..	57	13	19	20	27	19	53	42
Dividends and distributed branch profits	2 332 ..	57	10	19	20	18	17	53	34
Reinvested earnings and undistributed branch profits	2 333 ..	....	....	....	....	....	....	....	....
Income on debt (interest)	2 334 ..	....	3	....	....	9	2	....	8
Portfolio investment income	2 339 ..	605	634	424	532	596	625	802	1,359
Income on equity	2 340 ..	8	6	....	....	....	1	2	7
Income on bonds and notes	2 350 ..	581	584	412	476	487	575	740	1,338
Income on money market instruments	2 360 ..	16	44	12	56	109	49	60	14
Other investment income	2 370 ..	911	474	295	220	251	400	775	1,079
Investment income, debit	3 320 ..	**−3,363**	**−3,604**	**−3,733**	**−3,614**	**−3,796**	**−4,231**	**−5,643**	**−5,955**
Direct investment income	3 330 ..	−230	−683	−1,211	−1,067	−1,373	−1,391	−2,015	−2,068
Dividends and distributed branch profits	3 332 ..	−508	−856	−895	−839	−1,172	−1,158	−1,443	−1,349
Reinvested earnings and undistributed branch profits	3 333 ..	334	258	−235	−168	−141	−140	−485	−567
Income on debt (interest)	3 334 ..	−56	−85	−81	−60	−60	−93	−87	−152
Portfolio investment income	3 339 ..	−1,126	−1,154	−1,144	−1,298	−1,281	−1,549	−1,855	−2,200
Income on equity	3 340 ..	−16	−29	−20	−50	−70	−164	−393	−672
Income on bonds and notes	3 350 ..	−1,091	−1,113	−1,121	−1,248	−1,210	−1,385	−1,462	−1,527
Income on money market instruments	3 360 ..	−19	−12	−3	....	−1	....	....	−1
Other investment income	3 370 ..	−2,007	−1,767	−1,378	−1,249	−1,142	−1,291	−1,773	−1,687
D. CURRENT TRANSFERS	4 379 ..	**5,643**	**6,860**	**7,680**	**8,386**	**9,160**	**11,391**	**13,197**	**13,977**
Credit	2 379 ..	**5,909**	**7,119**	**7,948**	**8,626**	**9,420**	**11,711**	**13,511**	**14,397**
General government	2 380 ..	503	533	563	620	460	530	424	438
Other sectors	2 390 ..	5,406	6,586	7,385	8,006	8,960	11,181	13,087	13,959
Workers' remittances	2 391 ..	5,161	6,328	7,167	7,681	8,617	10,668	12,481	13,266
Other current transfers	2 392 ..	245	258	218	325	343	513	606	693
Debit	3 379 ..	**−266**	**−259**	**−268**	**−240**	**−260**	**−320**	**−314**	**−420**
General government	3 380 ..	−61	−62	−66	−65	−73	−93	−111	−119
Other sectors	3 390 ..	−205	−197	−202	−175	−187	−227	−203	−301
Workers' remittances	3 391 ..	....	....	....	....	....	....	....	....
Other current transfers	3 392 ..	−205	−197	−202	−175	−187	−227	−203	−301
CAPITAL AND FINANCIAL ACCOUNT	4 996 ..	**3,849**	**1,115**	**246**	**614**	**−1,351**	**−181**	**−3,753**	**−4,648**
CAPITAL ACCOUNT	4 994 ..	**138**	**62**	**27**	**54**	**17**	**40**	**138**	**24**
Total credit	2 994 ..	*168*	*86*	*50*	*82*	*46*	*58*	*181*	*108*
Total debit	3 994 ..	*−30*	*−24*	*−23*	*−28*	*−29*	*−18*	*−43*	*−84*
Capital transfers, credit	2 400 ..	**168**	**86**	**50**	**82**	**46**	**58**	**181**	**108**
General government	2 401 ..	122	77	48	41	41	41	61	81
Debt forgiveness	2 402 ..	....	....	....	....	....	....	....	....
Other capital transfers	2 410 ..	122	77	48	41	41	41	61	81
Other sectors	2 430 ..	46	9	2	41	5	17	120	27
Migrants' transfers	2 431 ..	37	9	....	4	3	5	12	17
Debt forgiveness	2 432 ..	....	....	....	....	....	....	91	....
Other capital transfers	2 440 ..	9	....	2	37	2	12	17	10
Capital transfers, debit	3 400 ..	**−30**	**−24**	**−23**	**−28**	**−21**	**−16**	**−43**	**−42**
General government	3 401 ..	....	....	....	....	....	....	....	....
Debt forgiveness	3 402 ..	....	....	....	....	....	....	....	....
Other capital transfers	3 410 ..	....	....	....	....	....	....	....	....
Other sectors	3 430 ..	−30	−24	−23	−28	−21	−16	−43	−42
Migrants' transfers	3 431 ..	−21	−24	−21	−18	−17	−15	−20	−35
Debt forgiveness	3 432 ..	....	....	....	....	....	....	....	....
Other capital transfers	3 440 ..	−9	....	−2	−10	−4	−1	−23	−7
Nonproduced nonfinancial assets, credit	2 480 ..	....	....	....	....	....	....	....	....
Nonproduced nonfinancial assets, debit	3 480 ..	....	....	....	....	−8	−2	....	−42

Table 2 (Continued). STANDARD PRESENTATION, 2000–2007

(Millions of U.S. dollars)

	Code	2000	2001	2002	2003	2004	2005	2006	2007
FINANCIAL ACCOUNT	4 995	**3,711**	**1,053**	**219**	**560**	**−1,368**	**−221**	**−3,891**	**−4,672**
A. DIRECT INVESTMENT	4 500	**2,115**	**335**	**1,477**	**188**	**109**	**1,665**	**2,818**	**−514**
Direct investment abroad	4 505	−125	140	−65	−303	−579	−189	−103	−3,442
Equity capital	4 510	−125	140	−65	−303	−579	−189	−103	−3,442
Claims on affiliated enterprises	4 515	−125	140	−65	−303	−579	−189	−103	−3,442
Liabilities to affiliated enterprises	4 520	....	....	....	....	....	....	....	....
Reinvested earnings	4 525	....	....	....	....	....	....	....	....
Other capital	4 530	....	....	....	....	....	....	....	....
Claims on affiliated enterprises	4 535	....	....	....	....	....	....	....	....
Liabilities to affiliated enterprises	4 540	....	....	....	....	....	....	....	....
Direct investment in the Philippines	4 555	2,240	195	1,542	491	688	1,854	2,921	2,928
Equity capital	4 560	1,333	556	1,607	249	750	1,181	1,324	2,020
Claims on direct investors	4 565	....	....	....	....	....	....	....	....
Liabilities to direct investors	4 570	1,333	556	1,607	249	750	1,181	1,324	2,020
Reinvested earnings	4 575	−334	−258	235	168	141	140	485	567
Other capital	4 580	1,241	−103	−300	74	−203	533	1,112	341
Claims on direct investors	4 585	753	−565	−227	−1	96	190	214	−3
Liabilities to direct investors	4 590	488	462	−73	75	−299	343	898	344
B. PORTFOLIO INVESTMENT	4 600	**−553**	**1,027**	**746**	**563**	**−1,665**	**3,476**	**3,043**	**3,088**
Assets	4 602	−812	−57	−628	−818	−862	−145	−1,567	−481
Equity securities	4 610	−42	30	−8	−48	−15	−4	1	−29
Monetary authorities	4 611	....	....	....	....	....	....	....	....
General government	4 612	....	....	....	....	....	....	....	....
Banks	4 613	....	3	−1	−2	−3	....	2	....
Other sectors	4 614	−42	27	−7	−46	−12	−4	−1	−29
Debt securities	4 619	−770	−87	−620	−770	−847	−141	−1,568	−452
Bonds and notes	4 620	−770	−238	238	−698	−163	−428	−1,272	−722
Monetary authorities	4 621	....	....	....	....	....	....	....	....
General government	4 622	....	....	....	....	....	....	....	....
Banks	4 623	−341	−215	314	−613	−138	353	−1,224	−844
Other sectors	4 624	−429	−23	−76	−85	−25	−781	−48	122
Money market instruments	4 630	....	151	−858	−72	−684	287	−296	270
Monetary authorities	4 631	....	....	....	....	....	....	....	....
General government	4 632	....	....	....	....	....	....	....	....
Banks	4 633	....	76	−661	49	−643	352	−693	....
Other sectors	4 634	....	75	−197	−121	−41	−65	397	270
Liabilities	4 652	259	1,084	1,374	1,381	−803	3,621	4,610	3,569
Equity securities	4 660	−202	125	227	501	518	1,465	2,525	3,285
Banks	4 663	−4	3	−10	4	1	−1	324	127
Other sectors	4 664	−198	122	237	497	517	1,466	2,201	3,158
Debt securities	4 669	461	959	1,147	880	−1,321	2,156	2,085	284
Bonds and notes	4 670	461	959	1,147	880	−1,321	2,145	2,055	302
Monetary authorities	4 671	−195	141	−161	−206	−542	−723	−41	13
General government	4 672	1,394	419	1,193	1,281	−506	2,712	1,272	53
Banks	4 673	−306	−236	−352	5	125	225	122	−66
Other sectors	4 674	−432	635	467	−200	−398	−69	702	302
Money market instruments	4 680	....	....	....	....	....	11	30	−18
Monetary authorities	4 681	....	....	....	....	....	....	....	....
General government	4 682	....	....	....	....	....	....	....	....
Banks	4 683	....	....	....	....	....	....	....	....
Other sectors	4 684	....	....	....	....	....	11	30	−18
C. FINANCIAL DERIVATIVES	4 910	**44**	**−15**	**−21**	**−64**	**−27**	**−43**	**−138**	**−288**
Monetary authorities	4 911	....	....	....	....	....	....	....	....
General government	4 912	....	....	....	....	....	....	....	....
Banks	4 913	44	−15	−21	−64	−27	−43	−138	−288
Other sectors	4 914	....	....	....	....	....	....	....	....
Assets	4 900	**166**	**83**	**85**	**54**	**58**	**98**	**159**	**170**
Monetary authorities	4 901	....	....	....	....	....	....	....	....
General government	4 902	....	....	....	....	....	....	....	....
Banks	4 903	166	83	85	54	58	98	159	170
Other sectors	4 904	....	....	....	....	....	....	....	....
Liabilities	4 905	**−122**	**−98**	**−106**	**−118**	**−85**	**−141**	**−297**	**−458**
Monetary authorities	4 906	....	....	....	....	....	....	....	....
General government	4 907	....	....	....	....	....	....	....	....
Banks	4 908	−122	−98	−106	−118	−85	−141	−297	−458
Other sectors	4 909	....	....	....	....	....	....	....	....

Table 2 (Concluded). STANDARD PRESENTATION, 2000–2007

(Millions of U.S. dollars)

	Code	2000	2001	2002	2003	2004	2005	2006	2007
D. OTHER INVESTMENT	4 700	**2,036**	**175**	**−2,236**	**−483**	**−1,422**	**−3,697**	**−6,678**	**1,611**
Assets	4 703	**2,454**	**761**	**−256**	**743**	**−907**	**−4,791**	**−3,512**	**−2,519**
Trade credits	4 706	....	−3	−3	−9	−3	−17	−3	−29
General government	4 707	....	....	....	....	....	....	....	....
of which: Short-term	4 709	....	....	....	....	....	....	....	....
Other sectors	4 710	....	−3	−3	−9	−3	−17	−3	−29
of which: Short-term	4 712	....	−3	−3	−9	−3	−17	−3	−29
Loans	4 714	1,306	−831	−344	233	156	−1,857	−3,129	−1,154
Monetary authorities	4 715								
of which: Short-term	4 718	....	....	....	....	....	....	....	....
General government	4 719	....	....	....	....	....	....	....	....
of which: Short-term	4 721	....	....	....	....	....	....	....	....
Banks	4 722	1,320	−829	−346	225	351	−1,407	−1,937	−501
of which: Short-term	4 724	*1,311*	*−822*	*−251*	*257*	*294*	*−1,454*	*−1,757*	*−97*
Other sectors	4 725	−14	−2	2	8	−195	−450	−1,192	−653
of which: Short-term	4 727	*−14*	*28*	*15*	*−11*	*−179*	*−457*	*−538*	*−641*
Currency and deposits	4 730	2,294	1,095	1,088	1,286	−944	−3,321	−2,257	−1,605
Monetary authorities	4 731	....	....	....	....	....	....	....	....
General government	4 732	....	....	....	....	....	....	....	....
Banks	4 733	2,187	1,247	1,102	907	−825	−2,750	−1,329	−834
Other sectors	4 734	107	−152	−14	379	−119	−571	−928	−771
Other assets	4 736	−1,146	500	−997	−767	−116	404	1,877	269
Monetary authorities	4 737	....	....	....	....	....	....	....	....
of which: Short-term	4 739	....	....	....	....	....	....	....	....
General government	4 740	....	....	....	....	....	....	....	....
of which: Short-term	4 742	....	....	....	....	....	....	....	....
Banks	4 743	−1,237	490	−997	−762	−114	416	1,875	268
of which: Short-term	4 745	*−1,237*	*491*	*−997*	*−762*	*−114*	*416*	*1,875*	*268*
Other sectors	4 746	91	10	....	−5	−2	−12	2	1
of which: Short-term	4 748	*91*	*10*	....	*−5*	*−2*	*−12*	*2*	*1*
Liabilities	4 753	**−418**	**−586**	**−1,980**	**−1,226**	**−515**	**1,094**	**−3,166**	**4,130**
Trade credits	4 756	−510	−371	−31	125	380	−59	239	586
General government	4 757	....	....	....	....	....	....	....	....
of which: Short-term	4 759	....	....	....	....	....	....	....	....
Other sectors	4 760	−510	−371	−31	125	380	−59	239	586
of which: Short-term	4 762	*−153*	*−128*	*−186*	*311*	*391*	*−112*	*264*	*712*
Loans	4 764	397	−38	−874	−1,012	−1,838	792	−3,141	2,865
Monetary authorities	4 765	468	789	−1,103	−274	−1,362	−729	−1,400	−201
of which: Use of Fund credit and loans from the Fund	4 766	*303*	*−8*	*−407*	*−607*	*−472*	*−321*	*−404*	....
of which: Short-term	4 768	*115*	*681*	*−656*	*138*	*−886*	*−468*	*−433*	*−7*
General government	4 769	−184	−65	90	−64	−362	−500	176	397
of which: Short-term	4 771	....	....	....	....	....	....	....	....
Banks	4 772	−284	−647	920	−79	276	1,099	−1,182	415
of which: Short-term	4 774	*−284*	*−647*	*920*	*−604*	*226*	*1,099*	*−1,410*	*390*
Other sectors	4 775	397	−115	−781	−595	−390	922	−735	2,254
of which: Short-term	4 777	*−175*	*−115*	*32*	*94*	*−103*	*1,024*	*893*	*−598*
Currency and deposits	4 780	−473	775	−1,144	−341	868	147	−339	528
Monetary authorities	4 781	....	....	....	....	....	....	....	....
General government	4 782	....	....	....	....	....	....	....	....
Banks	4 783	−200	826	−933	−373	883	−192	−126	513
Other sectors	4 784	−273	−51	−211	32	−15	339	−213	15
Other liabilities	4 786	168	−952	69	2	75	214	75	151
Monetary authorities	4 787	....	....	....	....	....	....	....	....
of which: Short-term	4 789	....	....	....	....	....	....	....	....
General government	4 790	....	....	....	....	....	....	....	....
of which: Short-term	4 792	....	....	....	....	....	....	....	....
Banks	4 793	159	−931	62	−1	74	198	79	124
of which: Short-term	4 795	*159*	*−931*	*62*	*−1*	*74*	*198*	*79*	*124*
Other sectors	4 796	9	−21	7	3	1	16	−4	27
of which: Short-term	4 798	*9*	*−21*	*7*	*3*	*1*	*16*	*−4*	*27*
E. RESERVE ASSETS	4 802	**69**	**−469**	**252**	**356**	**1,637**	**−1,622**	**−2,935**	**−8,569**
Monetary gold	4 812	−22	1	9	460	955	1,415	944	912
Special drawing rights	4 811	4	−13	4	9	1	....	−1	2
Reserve position in the Fund	4 810	....	....	....	....	....	....	....	....
Foreign exchange	4 803	87	−457	239	−113	681	−3,037	−3,878	−9,483
Other claims	4 813	....	....	....	....	....	....	....	....
NET ERRORS AND OMISSIONS	4 998	**−1,624**	**629**	**33**	**−902**	**−282**	**−1,803**	**−1,077**	**−1,118**

Table 3. INTERNATIONAL INVESTMENT POSITION (End-period stocks), 2000–2007

(Millions of U.S. dollars)

	Code	2000	2001	2002	2003	2004	2005	2006	2007
ASSETS	8 995 C.	....	**29,023**	**30,999**	**32,304**	**33,825**	**40,624**	**50,417**	**67,097**
Direct investment abroad	8 505 ..	....	**892**	**957**	**1,260**	**1,839**	**2,028**	**2,131**	**5,573**
Equity capital and reinvested earnings	8 506 ..	....	892	957	1,260	1,839	2,028	2,131	5,573
Claims on affiliated enterprises	8 507 ..	....	892	957	1,260	1,839	2,028	2,131	5,573
Liabilities to affiliated enterprises	8 508 ..	....	....	....	....	....	....	....	....
Other capital	8 530 ..	....	....	....	....	....	....	....	....
Claims on affiliated enterprises	8 535 ..	....	....	....	....	....	....	....	....
Liabilities to affiliated enterprises	8 540 ..	....	....	....	....	....	....	....	....
Portfolio investment	8 602 ..	....	**2,667**	**3,297**	**4,175**	**5,092**	**5,362**	**6,891**	**6,614**
Equity securities	8 610 ..	....	111	119	167	185	190	119	196
Monetary authorities	8 611 ..	....	....	....	....	....	....	....	....
General government	8 612 ..	....	....	....	....	....	....	....	....
Banks	8 613 ..	....	22	23	25	31	32	30	23
Other sectors	8 614 ..	....	89	96	142	154	158	89	173
Debt securities	8 619 ..	....	2,556	3,178	4,008	4,907	5,172	6,772	6,418
Bonds and notes	8 620 ..	....	2,174	1,938	2,696	2,886	3,438	4,820	4,876
Monetary authorities	8 621 ..	....	29	172	230	237	64	67	83
General government	8 622 ..	....	405	264	264	264	345	83	....
Banks	8 623 ..	....	1,641	1,327	1,940	2,095	1,958	3,182	3,612
Other sectors	8 624 ..	....	99	175	262	290	1,071	1,488	1,181
Money market instruments	8 630 ..	....	382	1,240	1,312	2,021	1,734	1,952	1,542
Monetary authorities	8 631 ..	....	....	....	....	....	....	....	....
General government	8 632 ..	....	....	....	....	....	....	....	....
Banks	8 633 ..	....	63	724	675	1,343	991	1,684	1,342
Other sectors	8 634 ..	....	319	516	637	678	743	268	200
Financial derivatives	8 900 ..	....	....	....	....	....	....	....	....
Monetary authorities	8 901 ..	....	....	....	....	....	....	....	....
General government	8 902 ..	....	....	....	....	....	....	....	....
Banks	8 903 ..	....	....	....	....	....	....	....	....
Other sectors	8 904 ..	....	....	....	....	....	....	....	....
Other investment	8 703 ..	....	**9,771**	**10,379**	**9,806**	**10,665**	**14,740**	**18,428**	**21,157**
Trade credits	8 706 ..	....	3	6	15	18	35	38	67
General government	8 707 ..	....	....	....	....	....	....	....	....
of which: Short-term	8 709 ..	....	....	....	....	....	....	....	....
Other sectors	8 710 ..	....	3	6	15	18	35	38	67
of which: Short-term	8 712 ..	....	*3*	*6*	*15*	*18*	*35*	*38*	*67*
Loans	8 714 ..	....	3,048	3,392	3,159	3,003	4,860	8,273	9,322
Monetary authorities	8 715 ..	....	....	....	....	....	....	....	....
of which: Short-term	8 718 ..	....	....	....	....	....	....	....	....
General government	8 719 ..	....	....	....	....	....	....	....	....
of which: Short-term	8 721 ..	....	....	....	....	....	....	....	....
Banks	8 722 ..	....	2,983	3,329	3,104	2,753	4,160	6,097	6,598
of which: Short-term	8 724 ..	....	*2,925*	*3,176*	*2,919*	*2,625*	*4,079*	*5,836*	*5,933*
Other sectors	8 725 ..	....	65	63	55	250	700	2,176	2,724
of which: Short-term	8 727 ..	....	*31*	*16*	*27*	*206*	*663*	*1,485*	*2,021*
Currency and deposits	8 730 ..	....	6,647	6,297	5,998	6,814	8,192	9,042	9,501
Monetary authorities	8 731 ..	....	....	....	....	....	....	....	....
General government	8 732 ..	....	....	....	....	....	....	....	....
Banks	8 733 ..	....	2,566	2,064	1,974	2,671	3,564	3,571	4,057
Other sectors	8 734 ..	....	4,081	4,233	4,024	4,143	4,628	5,471	5,444
Other assets	8 736 ..	....	73	684	634	830	1,653	1,075	2,267
Monetary authorities	8 737 ..	....	....	....	....	....	....	....	....
of which: Short-term	8 739 ..	....	....	....	....	....	....	....	....
General government	8 740 ..	....	....	....	....	....	....	....	....
of which: Short-term	8 742 ..	....	....	....	....	....	....	....	....
Banks	8 743 ..	....	70	681	626	823	1,634	1,062	2,255
of which: Short-term	8 745 ..	....	*70*	*681*	*626*	*823*	*1,634*	*1,062*	*2,255*
Other sectors	8 746 ..	....	3	3	8	7	19	13	12
of which: Short-term	8 748 ..	....	*3*	*3*	*8*	*7*	*19*	*13*	*12*
Reserve assets	8 802 ..	....	**15,693**	**16,366**	**17,063**	**16,229**	**18,494**	**22,967**	**33,753**
Monetary gold	8 812 ..	....	2,216	3,036	3,408	3,112	2,568	2,941	3,540
Special drawing rights	8 811 ..	2	14	10	2	1	1	2	1
Reserve position in the Fund	8 810 ..	113	110	119	130	136	125	132	138
Foreign exchange	8 803 ..	....	13,353	13,201	13,523	12,980	15,800	19,892	30,074
Other claims	8 813 ..	....	....	....	....	....	....	....	....

Table 3 (Concluded). INTERNATIONAL INVESTMENT POSITION (End-period stocks), 2000–2007

(Millions of U.S. dollars)

	Code	2000	2001	2002	2003	2004	2005	2006	2007
LIABILITIES	8 995 D.	....	65,187	68,600	72,617	72,436	77,406	81,729	94,446
Direct investment in the Philippines	8 555 ..	....	10,385	11,565	11,411	12,737	14,978	16,914	19,950
Equity capital and reinvested earnings	8 556 ..	....	5,876	7,682	8,044	8,920	10,226	12,020	14,568
Claims on direct investors	8 557 ..	....	....	....	....	....	....	....	....
Liabilities to direct investors	8 558 ..	....	5,876	7,682	8,044	8,920	10,226	12,020	14,568
Other capital	8 580 ..	....	4,509	3,883	3,367	3,817	4,752	4,894	5,382
Claims on direct investors	8 585 ..	....	−565	−792	−793	−697	−507	−293	−576
Liabilities to direct investors	8 590 ..	....	5,074	4,675	4,160	4,514	5,259	5,187	5,958
Portfolio investment	8 652 ..	....	15,910	17,843	20,524	19,890	23,923	28,797	33,615
Equity securities	8 660 ..	....	1,636	1,863	2,362	2,880	4,345	6,870	10,155
Banks	8 663 ..	....	23	13	15	16	15	339	466
Other sectors	8 664 ..	....	1,613	1,850	2,347	2,864	4,330	6,531	9,689
Debt securities	8 669 ..	....	14,274	15,980	18,162	17,010	19,578	21,927	23,460
Bonds and notes	8 670 ..	....	14,267	15,980	18,162	17,010	19,521	21,909	23,384
Monetary authorities	8 671 ..	....	1,016	893	777	392	289	248	338
General government	8 672 ..	....	7,198	8,661	10,806	10,143	12,362	13,808	14,287
Banks	8 673 ..	....	637	472	612	639	993	1,457	1,823
Other sectors	8 674 ..	....	5,416	5,954	5,967	5,836	5,877	6,396	6,936
Money market instruments	8 680 ..	....	7	....	....	....	57	18	76
Monetary authorities	8 681 ..	....	....	....	....	....	....	....	....
General government	8 682 ..	....	....	....	....	....	....	....	....
Banks	8 683 ..	....	....	....	....	....	....	....	....
Other sectors	8 684 ..	....	7	....	....	....	57	18	76
Financial derivatives	8 905 ..	....	....	....	....	....	....	....	....
Monetary authorities	8 906 ..	....	....	....	....	....	....	....	....
General government	8 907 ..	....	....	....	....	....	....	....	....
Banks	8 908 ..	....	....	....	....	....	....	....	....
Other sectors	8 909 ..	....	....	....	....	....	....	....	....
Other investment	8 753 ..	....	38,892	39,192	40,682	39,809	38,505	36,018	40,881
Trade credits	8 756 ..	....	1,753	1,632	1,320	1,793	1,717	2,036	2,316
General government	8 757 ..	....	19	15	11	8	4	1	....
of which: Short-term	8 759 ..	....	....	....	....	....	....	....	....
Other sectors	8 760 ..	....	1,734	1,617	1,309	1,785	1,713	2,035	2,316
of which: Short-term	8 762 ..	....	*695*	*506*	*772*	*1,282*	*1,188*	*1,551*	*2,154*
Loans	8 764 ..	....	35,979	36,929	38,547	36,873	35,650	32,830	36,866
Monetary authorities	8 765 ..	....	4,661	3,738	3,648	2,330	1,535	192	....
of which: Use of Fund credit and loans from the Fund	8 766 ..	*2,032*	*1,952*	*1,686*	*1,197*	*756*	*389*	....	....
of which: Short-term	8 768 ..	....	*2,225*	*1,600*	*1,750*	*875*	*375*	....	....
General government	8 769 ..	....	13,101	14,039	15,608	15,752	13,810	14,018	15,033
of which: Short-term	8 771 ..	....	....	....	....	....	....	....	....
Banks	8 772 ..	....	3,943	5,080	5,294	5,020	6,301	5,458	6,291
of which: Short-term	8 774 ..	....	*1,331*	*2,205*	*2,089*	*1,724*	*2,580*	*456*	*2,016*
Other sectors	8 775 ..	....	14,274	14,072	13,997	13,771	14,004	13,162	15,542
of which: Short-term	8 777 ..	....	*810*	*787*	*576*	*640*	*1,696*	*2,466*	*1,908*
Currency and deposits	8 780 ..	....	1,096	560	731	1,066	1,024	1,031	1,532
Monetary authorities	8 781 ..	....	2	....	....	....	41	....	....
General government	8 782 ..	....	....	....	....	....	....	....	....
Banks	8 783 ..	....	1,056	531	705	1,044	965	1,009	1,516
Other sectors	8 784 ..	....	38	29	26	22	18	22	16
Other liabilities	8 786 ..	....	64	71	84	77	114	121	167
Monetary authorities	8 787 ..	....	....	....	....	....	....	....	....
of which: Short-term	8 789 ..	....	....	....	....	....	....	....	....
General government	8 790 ..	....	....	....	....	....	....	....	....
of which: Short-term	8 792 ..	....	....	....	....	....	....	....	....
Banks	8 793 ..	....	61	67	78	73	97	109	120
of which: Short-term	8 795 ..	....	*61*	*67*	*78*	*73*	*97*	*109*	*120*
Other sectors	8 796 ..	....	3	4	6	4	17	12	47
of which: Short-term	8 798 ..	....	*3*	*4*	*6*	*4*	*17*	*12*	*47*
NET INTERNATIONAL INVESTMENT POSITION	8 995 ..	....	−36,164	−37,601	−40,314	−38,611	−36,782	−31,312	−27,349
Conversion rates: Philippine pesos per U.S. dollar (end of period)	0 102 ..	49.998	51.404	53.096	55.569	56.267	53.067	49.132	41.401

Table 1. ANALYTIC PRESENTATION, 2000–2007

(Millions of U.S. dollars)

	Code	2000	2001	2002	2003	2004	2005	2006	2007
A. Current Account[1].............	4 993 Z.	**−10,343**	**−5,945**	**−5,544**	**−5,473**	**−10,067**	**−3,716**	**−9,394**	**−18,595**
Goods: exports f.o.b...........	2 100 ..	35,902	41,663	46,742	61,007	81,862	96,395	117,468	144,609
Goods: imports f.o.b...........	3 100 ..	−48,209	−49,324	−53,991	−66,732	−87,484	−99,161	−124,474	−160,162
Balance on Goods............	4 100 ..	*−12,307*	*−7,661*	*−7,249*	*−5,725*	*−5,622*	*−2,766*	*−7,006*	*−15,553*
Services: credit..............	2 200 ..	10,398	9,753	10,037	11,174	13,471	16,258	20,592	28,790
Services: debit...............	3 200 ..	−8,995	−8,967	−9,262	−10,931	−13,392	−15,520	−19,856	−24,072
Balance on Goods and Services.....	4 991 ..	*−10,904*	*−6,875*	*−6,474*	*−5,482*	*−5,543*	*−2,028*	*−6,270*	*−10,835*
Income: credit..............	2 300 ..	2,978	3,401	2,776	3,284	5,305	6,998	9,040	10,039
Income: debit...............	3 300 ..	−3,709	−4,015	−3,837	−5,745	−13,549	−13,695	−18,768	−26,292
Balance on Goods, Services, and Income........	4 992 ..	*−11,635*	*−7,489*	*−7,535*	*−7,943*	*−13,787*	*−8,725*	*−15,998*	*−27,088*
Current transfers: credit...........	2 379 Z.	2,050	2,529	3,049	3,769	6,878	9,766	11,955	15,241
Current transfers: debit...........	3 379 ..	−758	−985	−1,058	−1,299	−3,158	−4,757	−5,351	−6,748
B. Capital Account[1].............	4 994 Z.	**34**	**76**	**−7**	**−46**	**1,180**	**995**	**2,105**	**4,771**
Capital account: credit..........	2 994 Z.	110	113	46	60	1,326	1,185	2,573	5,410
Capital account: debit...........	3 994 ..	−76	−37	−53	−106	−146	−190	−468	−639
Total, Groups A Plus B........	4 981 ..	*−10,309*	*−5,869*	*−5,551*	*−5,519*	*−8,887*	*−2,721*	*−7,289*	*−13,824*
C. Financial Account[1].............	4 995 W.	**10,221**	**3,173**	**7,180**	**8,686**	**8,038**	**15,228**	**13,101**	**39,832**
Direct investment abroad....	4 505 ..	−16	90	−230	−305	−955	−3,358	−9,149	−4,983
Direct investment in Poland..........	4 555 Z.	9,343	5,714	4,131	4,589	12,716	10,309	19,876	22,959
Portfolio investment assets..........	4 602 ..	−84	48	−1,157	−1,296	−1,331	−2,509	−4,649	−5,962
Equity securities............	4 610 ..	−20	−67	−268	183	−57	−575	−2,996	−5,171
Debt securities.............	4 619 ..	−64	115	−889	−1,479	−1,274	−1,934	−1,653	−791
Portfolio investment liabilities........	4 652 Z.	3,423	1,067	3,051	3,740	10,612	15,109	1,527	930
Equity securities............	4 660 ..	447	−307	−545	−837	1,660	1,333	−2,128	−453
Debt securities.............	4 669 Z.	2,976	1,374	3,596	4,577	8,952	13,776	3,655	1,383
Financial derivatives............	4 910 ..	269	−336	−898	−870	200	193	−689	−2,010
Financial derivatives assets..........	4 900 ..	. . . .	. . . .	. . . .	. . . .	. . . .	. . . .	. . . .	. . . .
Financial derivatives liabilities........	4 905 ..	269	−336	−898	−870	200	193	−689	−2,010
Other investment assets........	4 703 ..	−3,870	−4,072	1,887	−493	−11,999	−2,784	−3,919	−1,443
Monetary authorities..........	4 701 ..	2	3	. . . .	. . . .	−29	−17	9	−225
General government...........	4 704 ..	−48	−38	−37	−47	−39	−160	−30	−323
Banks..........	4 705 ..	−3,015	−3,398	3,107	351	−10,559	−836	−1,937	2,721
Other sectors..........	4 728 ..	−809	−639	−1,183	−797	−1,372	−1,771	−1,961	−3,616
Other investment liabilities.........	4 753 W.	1,156	662	396	3,321	−1,205	−1,732	10,104	30,341
Monetary authorities..........	4 753 WA	−1,393	118	−473	−68	−106	1,910	−765	7,253
General government...........	4 753 ZB	−290	−3,047	−503	−1,236	−2,286	−6,443	−1,192	−1,429
Banks..........	4 753 ZC	−474	283	−550	2,063	1,224	543	5,589	15,427
Other sectors..........	4 753 ZD	3,313	3,308	1,922	2,562	−37	2,258	6,472	9,090
Total, Groups A Through C........	4 983 ..	*−88*	*−2,696*	*1,629*	*3,167*	*−849*	*12,507*	*5,812*	*26,008*
D. Net Errors and Omissions............	4 998 ..	**712**	**2,269**	**−981**	**−1,961**	**1,650**	**−4,361**	**−3,323**	**−12,964**
Total, Groups A Through D........	4 984 ..	*624*	*−427*	*648*	*1,206*	*801*	*8,146*	*2,489*	*13,044*
E. Reserves and Related Items............	4 802 A.	**−624**	**427**	**−648**	**−1,206**	**−801**	**−8,146**	**−2,489**	**−13,044**
Reserve assets............	4 802 ..	−624	427	−648	−1,206	−801	−8,146	−2,489	−13,044
Use of Fund credit and loans.........	4 766 ..	. . . .	. . . .	. . . .	. . . .	. . . .	. . . .	. . . .	. . . .
Exceptional financing........	4 920 ..	. . . .	. . . .	. . . .	. . . .	. . . .	. . . .	. . . .	. . . .
Conversion rates: zlotys per U.S. dollar........	0 101 ..	**4.3461**	**4.0939**	**4.0800**	**3.8891**	**3.6576**	**3.2355**	**3.1032**	**2.7680**

[1] Excludes components that have been classified in the categories of Group E.

Table 2. STANDARD PRESENTATION, 2000–2007

(Millions of U.S. dollars)

	Code	2000	2001	2002	2003	2004	2005	2006	2007
CURRENT ACCOUNT.....................	4 993 ..	**−10,343**	**−5,945**	**−5,544**	**−5,473**	**−10,067**	**−3,716**	**−9,394**	**−18,595**
A. GOODS........................	4 100 ..	**−12,307**	**−7,661**	**−7,249**	**−5,725**	**−5,622**	**−2,766**	**−7,006**	**−15,553**
Credit........................	2 100 ..	**35,902**	**41,663**	**46,742**	**61,007**	**81,862**	**96,395**	**117,468**	**144,609**
General merchandise: exports f.o.b.........	2 110 ..	....	....	....	....	....	....	....	....
Goods for processing: exports f.o.b.......	2 150 ..	....	....	....	....	....	....	....	....
Repairs on goods........................	2 160 ..	....	....	....	....	....	....	....	....
Goods procured in ports by carriers.....	2 170 ..	....	....	....	....	....	....	....	....
Nonmonetary gold......................	2 180 ..	....	....	....	....	....	....	....	....
Debit............................	3 100 ..	**−48,209**	**−49,324**	**−53,991**	**−66,732**	**−87,484**	**−99,161**	**−124,474**	**−160,162**
General merchandise: imports f.o.b........	3 110 ..	....	....	....	....	....	....	....	....
Goods for processing: imports f.o.b......	3 150 ..	....	....	....	....	....	....	....	....
Repairs on goods........................	3 160 ..	....	....	....	....	....	....	....	....
Goods procured in ports by carriers.....	3 170 ..	....	....	....	....	....	....	....	....
Nonmonetary gold......................	3 180 ..	....	....	....	....	....	....	....	....
B. SERVICES........................	4 200 ..	**1,403**	**786**	**775**	**243**	**79**	**738**	**736**	**4,718**
Total credit.........................	2 200 ..	*10,398*	*9,753*	*10,037*	*11,174*	*13,471*	*16,258*	*20,592*	*28,790*
Total debit..........................	3 200 ..	*−8,995*	*−8,967*	*−9,262*	*−10,931*	*−13,392*	*−15,520*	*−19,856*	*−24,072*
Transportation services, credit........	2 205 ..	**2,445**	**2,683**	**3,270**	**3,995**	**4,200**	**5,457**	**6,995**	**9,249**
Passenger............................	2 850 ..	*451*	*475*	*657*	*664*	*666*	*854*	*883*	*1,087*
Freight..............................	2 851 ..	*1,720*	*1,966*	*2,334*	*3,101*	*3,194*	*4,142*	*5,505*	*7,410*
Other...............................	2 852 ..	*274*	*242*	*279*	*230*	*340*	*461*	*607*	*752*
Sea transport, passenger...............	2 207 ..	5	7	8	11	15	18	32	36
Sea transport, freight.................	2 208 ..	799	811	937	1,286	621	680	811	1,046
Sea transport, other...................	2 209 ..	55	53	48	32	135	210	180	146
Air transport, passenger...............	2 211 ..	405	410	587	567	604	773	750	906
Air transport, freight.................	2 212 ..	20	30	42	46	78	67	81	114
Air transport, other...................	2 213 ..	72	43	38	37	48	66	145	186
Other transport, passenger.............	2 215 ..	41	58	62	86	47	63	101	145
Other transport, freight...............	2 216 ..	901	1,125	1,355	1,769	2,495	3,395	4,613	6,250
Other transport, other.................	2 217 ..	147	146	193	161	157	185	282	420
Transportation services, debit.........	3 205 ..	**−1,532**	**−1,581**	**−1,819**	**−2,296**	**−2,948**	**−3,328**	**−4,255**	**−5,667**
Passenger............................	3 850 ..	*−102*	*−99*	*−162*	*−201*	*−316*	*−346*	*−430*	*−588*
Freight..............................	3 851 ..	*−903*	*−950*	*−1,132*	*−1,569*	*−2,076*	*−2,313*	*−3,063*	*−4,002*
Other...............................	3 852 ..	*−527*	*−532*	*−525*	*−526*	*−556*	*−669*	*−762*	*−1,077*
Sea transport, passenger...............	3 207 ..	−4	−4	−4	....	−16	−12	−14	−29
Sea transport, freight.................	3 208 ..	−226	−276	−367	−699	−612	−646	−837	−1,179
Sea transport, other...................	3 209 ..	−173	−156	−145	−24	−122	−134	−116	−149
Air transport, passenger...............	3 211 ..	−79	−75	−139	−160	−277	−313	−390	−534
Air transport, freight.................	3 212 ..	−15	−17	−29	−35	−101	−116	−171	−208
Air transport, other...................	3 213 ..	−280	−291	−281	−320	−289	−303	−334	−382
Other transport, passenger.............	3 215 ..	−19	−20	−19	−41	−23	−21	−26	−25
Other transport, freight...............	3 216 ..	−662	−657	−736	−835	−1,363	−1,551	−2,055	−2,615
Other transport, other.................	3 217 ..	−74	−85	−99	−182	−145	−232	−312	−546
Travel, credit........................	2 236 ..	**5,677**	**4,646**	**4,314**	**4,069**	**5,833**	**6,274**	**7,239**	**10,599**
Business travel........................	2 237 ..	....	....	....	....	....	....	....	....
Personal travel........................	2 240 ..	....	....	....	....	....	....	....	....
Travel, debit.........................	3 236 ..	**−3,315**	**−3,496**	**−3,278**	**−3,085**	**−4,776**	**−5,548**	**−7,224**	**−7,753**
Business travel........................	3 237 ..	....	....	....	....	....	....	....	....
Personal travel........................	3 240 ..	....	....	....	....	....	....	....	....
Other services, credit................	2 200 BA ..	**2,276**	**2,424**	**2,453**	**3,110**	**3,438**	**4,527**	**6,358**	**8,942**
Communications........................	2 245 ..	234	201	164	243	298	308	396	506
Construction...........................	2 249 ..	296	431	550	731	660	862	1,230	1,615
Insurance..............................	2 253 ..	208	185	214	219	65	67	96	20
Financial..............................	2 260 ..	104	173	135	161	159	219	218	328
Computer and information..............	2 262 ..	61	84	99	134	195	196	407	658
Royalties and licence fees.............	2 266 ..	34	48	34	28	30	62	38	108
Other business services...............	2 268 ..	1,286	1,227	1,189	1,532	1,906	2,673	3,763	5,419
Personal, cultural, and recreational....	2 287 ..	50	67	61	58	91	94	148	192
Government, n.i.e......................	2 291 ..	3	8	7	4	34	46	62	96
Other services, debit.................	3 200 BA ..	**−4,148**	**−3,890**	**−4,165**	**−5,550**	**−5,668**	**−6,644**	**−8,377**	**−10,652**
Communications........................	3 245 ..	−423	−279	−188	−245	−313	−364	−469	−703
Construction...........................	3 249 ..	−316	−334	−338	−791	−640	−512	−730	−904
Insurance..............................	3 253 ..	−320	−287	−351	−412	−256	−387	−398	−462
Financial..............................	3 260 ..	−220	−432	−207	−286	−371	−384	−378	−451
Computer and information..............	3 262 ..	−217	−263	−272	−351	−420	−421	−585	−875
Royalties and licence fees.............	3 266 ..	−555	−508	−557	−745	−883	−1,037	−1,313	−1,575
Other business services...............	3 268 ..	−1,825	−1,553	−2,000	−2,471	−2,475	−3,169	−3,852	−5,004
Personal, cultural, and recreational....	3 287 ..	−139	−120	−155	−128	−131	−160	−234	−302
Government, n.i.e......................	3 291 ..	−133	−114	−97	−121	−179	−210	−418	−376

2008, International Monetary Fund: *Balance of Payments Statistics Yearbook*

Table 2 (Continued). STANDARD PRESENTATION, 2000–2007

(Millions of U.S. dollars)

	Code	2000	2001	2002	2003	2004	2005	2006	2007
C. INCOME	4 300	**−731**	**−614**	**−1,061**	**−2,461**	**−8,244**	**−6,697**	**−9,728**	**−16,253**
Total credit	2 300	*2,978*	*3,401*	*2,776*	*3,284*	*5,305*	*6,998*	*9,040*	*10,039*
Total debit	3 300	*−3,709*	*−4,015*	*−3,837*	*−5,745*	*−13,549*	*−13,695*	*−18,768*	*−26,292*
Compensation of employees, credit	2 310	**920**	**969**	**1,092**	**1,543**	**3,600**	**4,649**	**5,531**	**6,226**
Compensation of employees, debit	3 310	**−212**	**−250**	**−267**	**−292**	**−438**	**−571**	**−776**	**−1,238**
Investment income, credit	2 320	**2,058**	**2,432**	**1,684**	**1,741**	**1,705**	**2,349**	**3,509**	**3,813**
Direct investment income	2 330	24	32	−53	3	80	126	670	37
Dividends and distributed branch profits	2 332	17	19	18	14	37	43	62	147
Reinvested earnings and undistributed branch profits	2 333	−12	8	−72	−12	23	56	582	−179
Income on debt (interest)	2 334	19	5	1	1	20	27	26	69
Portfolio investment income	2 339	294	424	277	430	404	413	540	695
Income on equity	2 340	18	8	6	12	8	17	43	92
Income on bonds and notes	2 350	124	414	269	404	390	391	480	583
Income on money market instruments	2 360	152	2	2	14	6	5	17	20
Other investment income	2 370	1,740	1,976	1,460	1,308	1,221	1,810	2,299	3,081
Investment income, debit	3 320	**−3,497**	**−3,765**	**−3,570**	**−5,453**	**−13,111**	**−13,124**	**−17,992**	**−25,054**
Direct investment income	3 330	−700	−714	−770	−2,093	−9,562	−9,283	−13,217	−18,600
Dividends and distributed branch profits	3 332	−558	−982	−1,365	−1,630	−2,683	−5,134	−6,464	−8,012
Reinvested earnings and undistributed branch profits	3 333	400	1,040	1,224	84	−6,211	−3,416	−5,752	−9,137
Income on debt (interest)	3 334	−542	−772	−629	−547	−668	−733	−1,001	−1,451
Portfolio investment income	3 339	−929	−1,053	−1,007	−1,529	−1,851	−2,174	−3,021	−3,589
Income on equity	3 340	−140	−234	−162	−306	−151	−325	−493	−752
Income on bonds and notes	3 350	−692	−817	−841	−1,172	−1,634	−1,747	−2,426	−2,773
Income on money market instruments	3 360	−97	−2	−4	−51	−66	−102	−102	−64
Other investment income	3 370	−1,868	−1,998	−1,793	−1,831	−1,698	−1,667	−1,754	−2,865
D. CURRENT TRANSFERS	4 379	**1,292**	**1,544**	**1,991**	**2,470**	**3,720**	**5,009**	**6,604**	**8,493**
Credit	2 379	**2,050**	**2,529**	**3,049**	**3,769**	**6,878**	**9,766**	**11,955**	**15,241**
General government	2 380	361	406	622	718	2,460	4,231	4,784	5,545
Other sectors	2 390	1,689	2,123	2,427	3,051	4,418	5,535	7,171	9,696
Workers' remittances	2 391	576	594	593	741	1,124	1,822	2,955	4,242
Other current transfers	2 392	1,113	1,529	1,834	2,310	3,294	3,713	4,216	5,454
Debit	3 379	**−758**	**−985**	**−1,058**	**−1,299**	**−3,158**	**−4,757**	**−5,351**	**−6,748**
General government	3 380	−58	−123	−125	−169	−1,818	−3,170	−3,347	−4,169
Other sectors	3 390	−700	−862	−933	−1,130	−1,340	−1,587	−2,004	−2,579
Workers' remittances	3 391	−99	−95	−86	−33	−16	−13	−13	−16
Other current transfers	3 392	−601	−767	−847	−1,097	−1,324	−1,574	−1,991	−2,563
CAPITAL AND FINANCIAL ACCOUNT	4 996	**9,631**	**3,676**	**6,525**	**7,434**	**8,417**	**8,077**	**12,717**	**31,559**
CAPITAL ACCOUNT	4 994	**34**	**76**	**−7**	**−46**	**1,180**	**995**	**2,105**	**4,771**
Total credit	2 994	*110*	*113*	*46*	*60*	*1,326*	*1,185*	*2,573*	*5,410*
Total debit	3 994	*−76*	*−37*	*−53*	*−106*	*−146*	*−190*	*−468*	*−639*
Capital transfers, credit	2 400	**110**	**112**	**44**	**51**	**1,315**	**1,174**	**2,395**	**5,321**
General government	2 401	55	27	37	45	1,256	1,140	2,371	5,282
Debt forgiveness	2 402	32	22	37	43	....	55	....	....
Other capital transfers	2 410	23	5	....	2	1,256	1,085	2,371	5,282
Other sectors	2 430	55	85	7	6	59	34	24	39
Migrants' transfers	2 431	....	....	....	....	4	11	10	28
Debt forgiveness	2 432	22	77	2	2	....	....	....	....
Other capital transfers	2 440	33	8	5	4	55	23	14	11
Capital transfers, debit	3 400	**−60**	**−4**	**−18**	**−8**	**−19**	**−34**	**−115**	**−72**
General government	3 401	−20	....	−2	−4	−10	....	−96	−28
Debt forgiveness	3 402	....	....	−2	−4	−9	....	−95	−15
Other capital transfers	3 410	−20	....	....	....	−1	....	−1	−13
Other sectors	3 430	−40	−4	−16	−4	−9	−34	−19	−44
Migrants' transfers	3 431	....	....	....	....	−6	−18	−13	−24
Debt forgiveness	3 432	−35	−3	−14	....	....	−15	....	−15
Other capital transfers	3 440	−5	−1	−2	−4	−3	−1	−6	−5
Nonproduced nonfinancial assets, credit	2 480	**....**	**1**	**2**	**9**	**11**	**11**	**178**	**89**
Nonproduced nonfinancial assets, debit	3 480	**−16**	**−33**	**−35**	**−98**	**−127**	**−156**	**−353**	**−567**

Table 2 (Continued). STANDARD PRESENTATION, 2000–2007

(Millions of U.S. dollars)

	Code	2000	2001	2002	2003	2004	2005	2006	2007
FINANCIAL ACCOUNT...............................	4 995 ..	**9,597**	**3,600**	**6,532**	**7,480**	**7,237**	**7,082**	**10,612**	**26,788**
A. DIRECT INVESTMENT.................................	4 500 ..	**9,327**	**5,804**	**3,901**	**4,284**	**11,761**	**6,951**	**10,727**	**17,976**
Direct investment abroad.................................	4 505 ..	**−16**	**90**	**−230**	**−305**	**−955**	**−3,358**	**−9,149**	**−4,983**
Equity capital...	4 510 ..	−111	47	−273	−105	−565	−2,700	−7,829	−3,560
Claims on affiliated enterprises..............	4 515 ..	−111	47	−273	−105	−565	−2,700	−7,829	−3,560
Liabilities to affiliated enterprises........	4 520 ..	....	....	....	....	....	....	....	....
Reinvested earnings.....................................	4 525 ..	12	−8	72	12	−22	−55	−582	179
Other capital...	4 530 ..	83	51	−29	−212	−368	−603	−738	−1,602
Claims on affiliated enterprises..............	4 535 ..	73	54	−31	−245	−394	−664	−735	−1,745
Liabilities to affiliated enterprises........	4 540 ..	10	−3	2	33	26	61	−3	143
Direct investment in Poland...........................	4 555 ..	**9,343**	**5,714**	**4,131**	**4,589**	**12,716**	**10,309**	**19,876**	**22,959**
Equity capital...	4 560 ..	8,813	5,301	4,283	4,561	7,321	4,482	7,382	7,743
Claims on direct investors........................	4 565 ..	....	....	....	....	....	....	....	....
Liabilities to direct investors..................	4 570 ..	8,813	5,301	4,283	4,561	7,321	4,482	7,382	7,743
Reinvested earnings.....................................	4 575 ..	−400	−1,040	−1,224	−84	6,210	3,416	5,753	9,137
Other capital...	4 580 ..	930	1,453	1,072	112	−815	2,411	6,741	6,079
Claims on direct investors........................	4 585 ..	18	34	42	−749	−1,162	−681	−1,645	−1,738
Liabilities to direct investors..................	4 590 ..	912	1,419	1,030	861	347	3,092	8,386	7,817
B. PORTFOLIO INVESTMENT...............................	4 600 ..	**3,339**	**1,115**	**1,894**	**2,444**	**9,281**	**12,600**	**−3,122**	**−5,032**
Assets...	4 602 ..	**−84**	**48**	**−1,157**	**−1,296**	**−1,331**	**−2,509**	**−4,649**	**−5,962**
Equity securities...	4 610 ..	−20	−67	−268	183	−57	−575	−2,996	−5,171
Monetary authorities................................	4 611 ..	....	....	....	....	....	....	....	....
General government..................................	4 612 ..	−1	−1	....	....	5	−4	−2	−3
Banks..	4 613 ..	−3	3	−1	11	6	77	−84	−61
Other sectors..	4 614 ..	−16	−69	−267	172	−68	−648	−2,910	−5,107
Debt securities...	4 619 ..	−64	115	−889	−1,479	−1,274	−1,934	−1,653	−791
Bonds and notes......................................	4 620 ..	−8	125	−614	−1,376	−934	−2,175	−1,541	−773
Monetary authorities...........................	4 621 ..	....	....	....	....	....	....	....	....
General government.............................	4 622 ..	11	195	37	−22	−7	−4	4	−21
Banks...	4 623 ..	22	−35	−133	−284	−237	−1,166	59	431
Other sectors......................................	4 624 ..	−41	−35	−518	−1,070	−690	−1,005	−1,604	−1,183
Money market instruments......................	4 630 ..	−56	−10	−275	−103	−340	241	−112	−18
Monetary authorities...........................	4 631 ..	....	....	....	....	....	....	....	....
General government.............................	4 632 ..	−3	....	....	1	....	4	−2	....
Banks...	4 633 ..	−26	−19	−212	26	−293	−36	−187	169
Other sectors......................................	4 634 ..	−27	9	−63	−130	−47	273	77	−187
Liabilities...	4 652 ..	**3,423**	**1,067**	**3,051**	**3,740**	**10,612**	**15,109**	**1,527**	**930**
Equity securities...	4 660 ..	447	−307	−545	−837	1,660	1,333	−2,128	−453
Banks..	4 663 ..	−626	187	14	−181	454	166	−1,096	−775
Other sectors..	4 664 ..	1,073	−494	−559	−656	1,206	1,167	−1,032	322
Debt securities...	4 669 ..	2,976	1,374	3,596	4,577	8,952	13,776	3,655	1,383
Bonds and notes......................................	4 670 ..	2,890	1,365	3,544	4,741	8,950	14,013	4,096	1,409
Monetary authorities...........................	4 671 ..	....	....	....	....	....	....	....	....
General government.............................	4 672 ..	2,206	789	3,433	5,346	8,512	13,314	4,223	3,283
Banks...	4 673 ..	101	60	195	51	356	754	776	−1,732
Other sectors......................................	4 674 ..	583	516	−84	−656	82	−55	−903	−142
Money market instruments......................	4 680 ..	86	9	52	−164	2	−237	−441	−26
Monetary authorities...........................	4 681 ..	....	....	....	....	−1	....	....	....
General government.............................	4 682 ..	12	15	39	−120	27	27	−251	12
Banks...	4 683 ..	....	....	1	−3	−8	−40	5	−18
Other sectors......................................	4 684 ..	74	−6	12	−41	−16	−224	−195	−20
C. FINANCIAL DERIVATIVES...............................	4 910 ..	**269**	**−336**	**−898**	**−870**	**200**	**193**	**−689**	**−2,010**
Monetary authorities...................................	4 911 ..	....	....	....	....	....	....	....	....
General government.....................................	4 912 ..	....	....	−11	....	1	−7	9	−873
Banks...	4 913 ..	378	−185	−685	−192	1,018	230	195	120
Other sectors..	4 914 ..	−109	−151	−202	−678	−819	−30	−893	−1,257
Assets...	4 900 ..	....	....	....	....	....	....	....	....
Monetary authorities...................................	4 901 ..	....	....	....	....	....	....	....	....
General government.....................................	4 902 ..	....	....	....	....	....	....	....	....
Banks...	4 903 ..	....	....	....	....	....	....	....	....
Other sectors..	4 904 ..	....	....	....	....	....	....	....	....
Liabilities...	4 905 ..	**269**	**−336**	**−898**	**−870**	**200**	**193**	**−689**	**−2,010**
Monetary authorities...................................	4 906 ..	....	....	....	....	....	....	....	....
General government.....................................	4 907 ..	....	....	−11	....	1	−7	9	−873
Banks...	4 908 ..	378	−185	−685	−192	1,018	230	195	120
Other sectors..	4 909 ..	−109	−151	−202	−678	−819	−30	−893	−1,257

Table 2 (Concluded). STANDARD PRESENTATION, 2000–2007

(Millions of U.S. dollars)

	Code	2000	2001	2002	2003	2004	2005	2006	2007
D. OTHER INVESTMENT	4 700	**−2,714**	**−3,410**	**2,283**	**2,828**	**−13,204**	**−4,516**	**6,185**	**28,898**
Assets	4 703	**−3,870**	**−4,072**	**1,887**	**−493**	**−11,999**	**−2,784**	**−3,919**	**−1,443**
Trade credits	4 706	−542	−745	−1,216	−777	−1,245	−1,613	−2,073	−2,826
General government	4 707	....	....	....	....	....	....	....	....
of which: Short-term	4 709	....	....	....	....	....	....	....	....
Other sectors	4 710	−542	−745	−1,216	−777	−1,245	−1,613	−2,073	−2,826
of which: Short-term	4 712	*−542*	*−745*	*−1,216*	*−777*	*−1,245*	*−1,613*	*−2,073*	*−2,826*
Loans	4 714	68	82	−77	−438	−59	−308	−347	−984
Monetary authorities	4 715	1	2	....	....	....	....	....	....
of which: Short-term	4 718	....	....	....	....	....	....	....	....
General government	4 719	−14	−18	−21	−28	−50	−36	14	−106
of which: Short-term	4 721	....	....	....	....	....	....	....	....
Banks	4 722	83	95	−41	−261	−92	−226	−241	−720
of which: Short-term	4 724	*47*	*13*	*−2*	*−90*	*58*	*−64*	*−7*	*−44*
Other sectors	4 725	−2	3	−15	−149	83	−46	−120	−158
of which: Short-term	4 727	*−1*	*−1*	....	*−92*	*96*	*−22*	*−23*	*−8*
Currency and deposits	4 730	−3,366	−3,347	3,196	746	−10,646	−731	−1,459	2,799
Monetary authorities	4 731	1	1	....	....	....	....	....	....
General government	4 732	−4	....	....	....	....	1	....	−3
Banks	4 733	−3,098	−3,493	3,148	612	−10,425	−625	−1,691	3,430
Other sectors	4 734	−265	145	48	134	−221	−107	232	−628
Other assets	4 736	−30	−62	−16	−24	−49	−132	−40	−432
Monetary authorities	4 737	....	....	....	....	−29	−17	9	−225
of which: Short-term	4 739	....	....	....	....	....	*−25*	*−9*	*−245*
General government	4 740	−30	−20	−16	−19	11	−125	−44	−214
of which: Short-term	4 742	*−30*	*−20*	*−16*	*−19*	*13*	*−32*	*66*	*5*
Banks	4 743	....	....	....	....	−42	15	−5	11
of which: Short-term	4 745	....	....	....	....	*−42*	*15*	*−5*	*11*
Other sectors	4 746	....	−42	....	−5	11	−5	....	−4
of which: Short-term	4 748	....	*−42*	....	*−5*	*11*	*−5*	....	*−4*
Liabilities	4 753	**1,156**	**662**	**396**	**3,321**	**−1,205**	**−1,732**	**10,104**	**30,341**
Trade credits	4 756	723	479	1,754	1,466	1,250	1,618	1,918	2,237
General government	4 757	....	....	....	....	....	....	....	....
of which: Short-term	4 759	....	....	....	....	....	....	....	....
Other sectors	4 760	723	479	1,754	1,466	1,250	1,618	1,918	2,237
of which: Short-term	4 762	*723*	*479*	*1,754*	*1,466*	*1,250*	*1,618*	*1,918*	*2,237*
Loans	4 764	2,114	−600	−902	69	−2,516	−4,805	7,238	13,841
Monetary authorities	4 765	−6	−7	−2	−4	−2	−1	....	....
of which: Use of Fund credit and loans from the Fund	4 766	....	....	....	....	....	....	....	....
of which: Short-term	4 768	....	....	....	....	*−1*	....	....	....
General government	4 769	−290	−3,047	−503	−1,236	−2,286	−6,443	−1,192	−1,429
of which: Short-term	4 771	....	....	*275*	*−298*	....	....	*1*	*−1*
Banks	4 772	−7	−30	−503	233	1,040	1,038	3,872	8,404
of which: Short-term	4 774	*−143*	*−66*	*−6*	....	*676*	*−691*	*84*	*571*
Other sectors	4 775	2,417	2,484	106	1,076	−1,268	601	4,558	6,866
of which: Short-term	4 777	*−154*	*119*	*83*	*221*	*152*	*−178*	*−24*	*269*
Currency and deposits	4 780	−1,854	438	−518	1,766	80	1,416	952	14,276
Monetary authorities	4 781	−1,387	125	−471	−64	−104	1,911	−765	7,253
General government	4 782	....	....	....	....	....	....	....	....
Banks	4 783	−467	313	−47	1,830	184	−495	1,717	7,023
Other sectors	4 784	....	....	....	....	....	....	....	....
Other liabilities	4 786	173	345	62	20	−19	39	−4	−13
Monetary authorities	4 787	....	....	....	....	....	....	....	....
of which: Short-term	4 789	....	....	....	....	....	....	....	....
General government	4 790	....	....	....	....	....	....	....	....
of which: Short-term	4 792	....	....	....	....	....	....	....	....
Banks	4 793	....	....	....	....	....	....	....	....
of which: Short-term	4 795	....	....	....	....	....	....	....	....
Other sectors	4 796	173	345	62	20	−19	39	−4	−13
of which: Short-term	4 798	*173*	*345*	*62*	*20*	*−19*	*39*	*−4*	*−13*
E. RESERVE ASSETS	4 802	**−624**	**427**	**−648**	**−1,206**	**−801**	**−8,146**	**−2,489**	**−13,044**
Monetary gold	4 812	....	....	....	....	....	....	....	....
Special drawing rights	4 811	−7	−9	−11	−11	−12	−14	−7	−7
Reserve position in the Fund	4 810	....	−247	−148	−80	130	353	134	36
Foreign exchange	4 803	−1,408	1,235	−941	−2,456	−918	−6,831	−3,259	−5,812
Other claims	4 813	791	−552	452	1,341	....	−1,654	643	−7,261
NET ERRORS AND OMISSIONS	4 998	**712**	**2,269**	**−981**	**−1,961**	**1,650**	**−4,361**	**−3,323**	**−12,964**

Table 3. INTERNATIONAL INVESTMENT POSITION (End-period stocks), 2000–2007

(Millions of U.S. dollars)

	Code	2000	2001	2002	2003	2004	2005	2006	2007
ASSETS	8 995 C.	**44,833**	**49,387**	**51,694**	**58,539**	**79,765**	**92,098**	**117,880**	**154,490**
Direct investment abroad	8 505 ..	**1,018**	**1,156**	**1,457**	**2,145**	**3,351**	**6,277**	**14,317**	**19,393**
Equity capital and reinvested earnings	8 506 ..	870	999	1,264	1,621	2,341	4,668	11,758	14,845
Claims on affiliated enterprises	8 507 ..	870	999	1,264	1,621	2,341	4,668	11,758	14,845
Liabilities to affiliated enterprises	8 508 ..	....	....	....	....	....	....	....	....
Other capital	8 530 ..	148	157	193	524	1,010	1,609	2,559	4,548
Claims on affiliated enterprises	8 535 ..	163	169	207	635	1,162	1,813	2,781	4,929
Liabilities to affiliated enterprises	8 540 ..	−15	−12	−14	−111	−152	−204	−222	−381
Portfolio investment	8 602 ..	**1,575**	**1,311**	**2,729**	**4,143**	**6,710**	**8,781**	**13,840**	**21,839**
Equity securities	8 610 ..	47	108	189	229	744	1,681	5,214	11,939
Monetary authorities	8 611 ..	2	10	10	....	....	....	....	....
General government	8 612 ..	....	....	....	....	....	....	....	....
Banks	8 613 ..	31	33	7	7	9	8	9	19
Other sectors	8 614 ..	14	65	172	222	735	1,673	5,205	11,920
Debt securities	8 619 ..	1,528	1,203	2,540	3,914	5,966	7,100	8,626	9,900
Bonds and notes	8 620 ..	1,467	1,185	2,485	3,713	5,580	5,675	5,028	5,007
Monetary authorities	8 621 ..	....	....	....	....	....	....	....	....
General government	8 622 ..	857	415	407	412	465	530	266	268
Banks	8 623 ..	562	548	916	1,107	1,316	1,944	2,360	2,475
Other sectors	8 624 ..	48	222	1,162	2,194	3,799	3,201	2,402	2,264
Money market instruments	8 630 ..	61	18	55	201	386	1,425	3,598	4,893
Monetary authorities	8 631 ..	....	....	....	....	....	....	....	....
General government	8 632 ..	....	....	....	....	....	....	....	....
Banks	8 633 ..	58	16	12	5	5	....	175	6
Other sectors	8 634 ..	3	2	43	196	381	1,425	3,423	4,887
Financial derivatives	8 900 ..	....	....	....	....	**303**	**499**	**551**	**1,279**
Monetary authorities	8 901 ..	....	....	....	....	....	....	....	....
General government	8 902 ..	....	....	....	....	....	....	....	....
Banks	8 903 ..	....	....	....	....	....	316	392	1,023
Other sectors	8 904 ..	....	....	....	....	303	183	159	256
Other investment	8 703 ..	**14,776**	**20,366**	**17,724**	**18,097**	**32,617**	**33,970**	**40,688**	**46,234**
Trade credits	8 706 ..	3,151	4,108	5,312	4,452	6,180	7,100	9,901	13,941
General government	8 707 ..	....	....	....	....	....	....	....	....
of which: Short-term	8 709 ..	....	....	....	....	....	....	....	....
Other sectors	8 710 ..	3,151	4,108	5,312	4,452	6,180	7,100	9,901	13,941
of which: Short-term	8 712 ..	*3,151*	*4,108*	*5,305*	*4,174*	*5,903*	*6,830*	*9,510*	*13,304*
Loans	8 714 ..	621	522	578	1,194	1,299	1,480	1,880	2,960
Monetary authorities	8 715 ..	1	....	....	....	....	....	....	....
of which: Short-term	8 718 ..	....	....	....	....	....	....	....	....
General government	8 719 ..	142	164	92	182	225	262	242	347
of which: Short-term	8 721 ..	....	....	....	....	....	....	....	....
Banks	8 722 ..	458	342	443	800	917	1,071	1,384	2,246
of which: Short-term	8 724 ..	*100*	*109*	*91*	*227*	*170*	*227*	*244*	*305*
Other sectors	8 725 ..	20	16	43	212	157	147	254	367
of which: Short-term	8 727 ..	*1*	*1*	*1*	*102*	*15*	*33*	*41*	*19*
Currency and deposits	8 730 ..	9,913	14,595	10,699	11,201	23,499	23,627	27,046	27,140
Monetary authorities	8 731 ..	....	....	....	....	....	....	....	....
General government	8 732 ..	7	7	7	7	8	8	11	12
Banks	8 733 ..	9,300	14,165	10,145	10,626	22,354	22,061	25,088	24,206
Other sectors	8 734 ..	606	423	547	568	1,137	1,558	1,947	2,922
Other assets	8 736 ..	1,091	1,141	1,135	1,250	1,639	1,763	1,861	2,193
Monetary authorities	8 737 ..	....	....	....	15	129	164	172	183
of which: Short-term	8 739 ..	....	....	....	....	*86*	*126*	*131*	*138*
General government	8 740 ..	1,088	1,093	1,129	1,217	1,455	1,556	1,637	1,961
of which: Short-term	8 742 ..	*1,088*	*1,093*	*1,129*	*1,142*	*1,241*	*1,262*	*1,197*	*1,193*
Banks	8 743 ..	....	....	....	7	53	36	45	38
of which: Short-term	8 745 ..	....	....	....	*7*	*53*	*36*	*45*	*38*
Other sectors	8 746 ..	3	48	6	11	2	7	7	11
of which: Short-term	8 748 ..	*3*	*48*	*6*	*11*	*2*	*7*	*7*	*11*
Reserve assets	8 802 ..	**27,464**	**26,554**	**29,784**	**34,154**	**36,784**	**42,571**	**48,484**	**65,745**
Monetary gold	8 812 ..	901	915	1,134	1,381	1,449	1,697	2,103	2,768
Special drawing rights	8 811 ..	18	26	39	55	70	78	89	101
Reserve position in the Fund	8 810 ..	224	461	651	799	701	299	175	146
Foreign exchange	8 803 ..	25,318	23,631	26,709	31,919	34,539	38,825	45,085	54,636
Other claims	8 813 ..	1,003	1,521	1,250	....	25	1,672	1,032	8,095

Table 3 (Concluded). INTERNATIONAL INVESTMENT POSITION (End-period stocks), 2000–2007

(Millions of U.S. dollars)

	Code	2000	2001	2002	2003	2004	2005	2006	2007
LIABILITIES	8 995 D.	**99,999**	**107,128**	**125,128**	**152,527**	**208,426**	**220,108**	**284,187**	**396,645**
Direct investment in Poland	8 555	**34,227**	**41,247**	**48,320**	**57,877**	**86,756**	**90,876**	**125,782**	**176,095**
Equity capital and reinvested earnings	8 556	25,353	31,011	35,989	41,917	69,284	73,116	98,573	138,913
Claims on direct investors	8 557	....	....	....	....	....	....	....	....
Liabilities to direct investors	8 558	25,353	31,011	35,989	41,917	69,284	73,116	98,573	138,913
Other capital	8 580	8,874	10,236	12,331	15,960	17,472	17,760	27,209	37,182
Claims on direct investors	8 585	−154	−143	−121	−3,257	−4,821	−4,997	−7,170	−9,695
Liabilities to direct investors	8 590	9,028	10,379	12,452	19,217	22,293	22,757	34,379	46,877
Portfolio investment	8 652	**18,057**	**18,895**	**24,042**	**34,392**	**56,676**	**71,441**	**84,658**	**105,678**
Equity securities	8 660	5,350	4,301	4,399	6,705	13,714	18,739	22,753	33,161
Banks	8 663	1,210	1,204	1,417	2,220	5,285	6,666	8,835	14,494
Other sectors	8 664	4,140	3,097	2,982	4,485	8,429	12,073	13,918	18,667
Debt securities	8 669	12,707	14,594	19,643	27,687	42,962	52,702	61,905	72,517
Bonds and notes	8 670	12,448	14,347	19,250	27,333	42,576	52,365	61,769	71,996
Monetary authorities	8 671	....	....	....	....	....	....	....	....
General government	8 672	9,073	10,014	14,680	22,041	36,265	45,517	54,644	66,092
Banks	8 673	110	167	433	682	1,182	2,303	3,545	1,587
Other sectors	8 674	3,265	4,166	4,137	4,610	5,129	4,545	3,580	4,317
Money market instruments	8 680	259	247	393	354	386	337	136	521
Monetary authorities	8 681	....	....	....	....	....	....	....	....
General government	8 682	158	234	277	214	90	84	2	7
Banks	8 683	....	....	....	30	90	92	103	137
Other sectors	8 684	101	13	116	110	206	161	31	377
Financial derivatives	8 905	....	....	....	....	**416**	**524**	**619**	**1,571**
Monetary authorities	8 906	....	....	....	....	....	....	....	....
General government	8 907	....	....	....	....	....	....	....	....
Banks	8 908	....	....	....	....	....	191	243	1,030
Other sectors	8 909	....	....	....	....	416	333	376	541
Other investment	8 753	**47,715**	**46,986**	**52,766**	**60,258**	**64,578**	**57,267**	**73,128**	**113,301**
Trade credits	8 756	5,612	6,530	8,590	7,319	9,256	9,968	12,773	16,344
General government	8 757	....	....	....	....	....	....	....	....
of which: Short-term	8 759	....	....	....	....	....	....	....	....
Other sectors	8 760	5,612	6,530	8,590	7,319	9,256	9,968	12,773	16,344
of which: Short-term	8 762	*5,612*	*6,530*	*8,572*	*7,010*	*8,830*	*9,668*	*12,395*	*15,896*
Loans	8 764	39,241	36,892	40,518	46,924	48,066	38,887	49,764	70,314
Monetary authorities	8 765	15	8	6	3	....	....	....	....
of which: Use of Fund credit and loans from the Fund	8 766	....	....	....	....	....	....	....	....
of which: Short-term	8 768	....	....	....	....	....	....	....	....
General government	8 769	23,747	18,989	20,766	22,805	21,477	13,240	13,130	13,081
of which: Short-term	8 771	....	....	*275*	....	....	....	*1*	....
Banks	8 772	3,595	3,679	3,752	4,855	6,491	6,772	11,431	21,705
of which: Short-term	8 774	*78*	*8*	*7*	*16*	*793*	*67*	*163*	*809*
Other sectors	8 775	11,884	14,216	15,994	19,261	20,098	18,875	25,203	35,528
of which: Short-term	8 777	*243*	*255*	*378*	*542*	*560*	*300*	*292*	*808*
Currency and deposits	8 780	2,638	3,178	3,234	5,662	6,698	7,445	9,047	24,815
Monetary authorities	8 781	421	420	104	196	102	1,973	1,226	8,278
General government	8 782	....	....	....	....	....	....	....	....
Banks	8 783	2,217	2,758	3,130	5,466	6,596	5,472	7,821	16,537
Other sectors	8 784	....	....	....	....	....	....	....	....
Other liabilities	8 786	224	386	424	353	558	967	1,544	1,828
Monetary authorities	8 787	....	....	....	....	6	3	1	2
of which: Short-term	8 789	....	....	....	....	....	....	....	....
General government	8 790	2	17	9	9	....	....	....	....
of which: Short-term	8 792	*2*	*17*	*9*	*9*	....	....	....	....
Banks	8 793	....	....	....	....	....	....	....	....
of which: Short-term	8 795	....	....	....	....	....	....	....	....
Other sectors	8 796	222	369	415	344	552	964	1,543	1,826
of which: Short-term	8 798	*222*	*369*	*415*	*344*	*552*	*964*	*1,543*	*1,826*
NET INTERNATIONAL INVESTMENT POSITION	8 995	**−55,166**	**−57,741**	**−73,434**	**−93,988**	**−128,661**	**−128,010**	**−166,307**	**−242,155**
Conversion rates: zlotys per U.S. dollar (end of period)	0 102	**4.1432**	**3.9863**	**3.8388**	**3.7408**	**2.9904**	**3.2613**	**2.9105**	**2.4350**

Table 1. ANALYTIC PRESENTATION, 2000–2007

(Millions of U.S. dollars)

	Code	2000	2001	2002	2003	2004	2005	2006	2007
A. Current Account[1]	4 993 Z.	−11,595	−11,445	−10,264	−9,593	−13,616	−17,619	−19,640	−21,418
Goods: exports f.o.b.	2 100 ..	24,663	24,456	25,975	32,055	36,986	38,577	43,592	51,746
Goods: imports f.o.b.	3 100 ..	−39,195	−38,362	−39,286	−46,337	−55,386	−58,916	−64,510	−75,853
Balance on Goods	4 100 ..	*−14,532*	*−13,906*	*−13,311*	*−14,282*	*−18,401*	*−20,339*	*−20,918*	*−24,108*
Services: credit	2 200 ..	9,016	9,379	10,357	12,354	14,701	15,193	17,839	23,156
Services: debit	3 200 ..	−7,053	−6,826	−7,146	−8,293	−9,746	−10,456	−11,758	−13,950
Balance on Goods and Services	4 991 ..	*−12,569*	*−11,352*	*−10,101*	*−10,221*	*−13,445*	*−15,603*	*−14,836*	*−14,901*
Income: credit	2 300 ..	4,806	5,669	4,900	6,622	8,040	9,307	13,518	17,332
Income: debit	3 300 ..	−7,177	−9,127	−7,891	−9,260	−11,747	−14,151	−21,492	−27,467
Balance on Goods, Services, and Income	4 992 ..	*−14,939*	*−14,810*	*−13,092*	*−12,859*	*−17,152*	*−20,446*	*−22,810*	*−25,036*
Current transfers: credit	2 379 Z.	5,495	5,677	5,544	6,544	7,297	7,226	8,054	8,709
Current transfers: debit	3 379 ..	−2,150	−2,312	−2,717	−3,278	−3,761	−4,398	−4,884	−5,090
B. Capital Account[1]	4 994 Z.	**1,512**	**1,069**	**1,906**	**2,977**	**2,773**	**2,115**	**1,527**	**2,837**
Capital account: credit	2 994 Z.	1,681	1,278	2,111	3,246	3,130	2,485	2,045	3,290
Capital account: debit	3 994 ..	−169	−209	−205	−269	−358	−371	−518	−453
Total, Groups A Plus B	4 981 ..	*−10,083*	*−10,377*	*−8,359*	*−6,617*	*−10,843*	*−15,504*	*−18,113*	*−18,581*
C. Financial Account[1]	4 995 W.	**10,749**	**10,606**	**8,796**	**−830**	**9,728**	**14,629**	**14,326**	**19,171**
Direct investment abroad	4 505 ..	−8,183	−6,228	210	−6,575	−7,377	−2,252	−7,003	−6,205
Direct investment in Portugal	4 555 Z.	6,682	6,174	1,755	7,255	1,661	4,059	11,344	5,534
Portfolio investment assets	4 602 ..	−4,582	−7,851	−7,034	−21,471	−13,598	−19,659	−9,580	−12,104
Equity securities	4 610 ..	−1,044	−959	−813	−622	−1,708	−1,845	−3,999	−2,412
Debt securities	4 619 ..	−3,538	−6,892	−6,221	−20,849	−11,890	−17,814	−5,581	−9,692
Portfolio investment liabilities	4 652 Z.	2,792	10,661	10,249	14,344	13,882	18,141	13,514	25,117
Equity securities	4 660 ..	415	2,371	3,287	9,863	7,233	5,594	3,829	−664
Debt securities	4 669 Z.	2,376	8,290	6,962	4,481	6,649	12,547	9,685	25,781
Financial derivatives	4 910 ..	322	351	−5	71	−90	−211	−263	930
Financial derivatives assets	4 900 ..	3,673	3,226	3,796	4,590	4,135	4,865	6,790	11,513
Financial derivatives liabilities	4 905 ..	−3,351	−2,875	−3,802	−4,518	−4,226	−5,076	−7,053	−10,583
Other investment assets	4 703 ..	−10,970	−7,403	−6,360	−8,744	777	−1,246	−17,051	−15,881
Monetary authorities	4 701 ..	10	22	−304	345	−954	−717	−1,251	−2,178
General government	4 704 ..	−159	−201	−102	−141	83	−122	139	765
Banks	4 705 ..	−7,201	−1,033	−29	−8,713	−1,453	−1,342	−12,727	−9,408
Other sectors	4 728 ..	−3,619	−6,192	−5,925	−234	3,101	935	−3,213	−5,060
Other investment liabilities	4 753 W.	24,689	14,903	9,981	14,290	14,474	15,797	23,366	21,779
Monetary authorities	4 753 WA	4,861	87	699	−6,725	7,229	5,595	−7,926	−1,095
General government	4 753 ZB	−154	−190	312	5	501	−702	71	1,504
Banks	4 753 ZC	18,231	14,480	8,456	19,391	3,468	9,489	31,114	20,750
Other sectors	4 753 ZD	1,751	526	513	1,619	3,277	1,416	107	620
Total, Groups A Through C	4 983 ..	*666*	*229*	*437*	*−7,447*	*−1,114*	*−875*	*−3,786*	*590*
D. Net Errors and Omissions	4 998 ..	**−295**	**623**	**580**	**991**	**−749**	**−866**	**1,430**	**−1,552**
Total, Groups A Through D	4 984 ..	*371*	*852*	*1,017*	*−6,455*	*−1,863*	*−1,741*	*−2,357*	*−962*
E. Reserves and Related Items	4 802 A.	**−371**	**−852**	**−1,017**	**6,455**	**1,863**	**1,741**	**2,357**	**962**
Reserve assets	4 802 ..	−371	−852	−1,017	6,455	1,863	1,741	2,357	962
Use of Fund credit and loans	4 766 ..	....	....	....	....	....	....	....	....
Exceptional financing	4 920 ..	....	....	....	....	....	....	....	....
Conversion rates: euros per U.S. dollar	0 103 ..	**1.0854**	**1.1175**	**1.0626**	**.8860**	**.8054**	**.8041**	**.7971**	**.7306**

[1] Excludes components that have been classified in the categories of Group E.

Table 2. STANDARD PRESENTATION, 2000–2007

(Millions of U.S. dollars)

	Code	2000	2001	2002	2003	2004	2005	2006	2007
CURRENT ACCOUNT	4 993	−11,595	−11,445	−10,264	−9,593	−13,616	−17,619	−19,640	−21,418
A. GOODS	4 100	−14,532	−13,906	−13,311	−14,282	−18,401	−20,339	−20,918	−24,108
Credit	2 100	24,663	24,456	25,975	32,055	36,986	38,577	43,592	51,746
General merchandise: exports f.o.b.	2 110	24,384	24,143	25,650	31,665	36,469	37,856	42,838	50,976
Goods for processing: exports f.o.b.	2 150	89	82	87	104	113	134	155	113
Repairs on goods	2 160	105	151	166	153	207	237	236	274
Goods procured in ports by carriers	2 170	85	81	72	133	196	349	358	382
Nonmonetary gold	2 180	....	....	....	....	....	....	5	....
Debit	3 100	−39,195	−38,362	−39,286	−46,337	−55,386	−58,916	−64,510	−75,853
General merchandise: imports f.o.b.	3 110	−39,050	−38,160	−39,063	−46,089	−55,137	−58,599	−63,982	−75,213
Goods for processing: imports f.o.b.	3 150	−1	−1	−1	....	−4	−4	−2	−3
Repairs on goods	3 160	−10	−14	−31	−22	−13	−25	−15	−31
Goods procured in ports by carriers	3 170	−65	−93	−128	−175	−180	−241	−473	−594
Nonmonetary gold	3 180	−69	−94	−64	−51	−53	−46	−36	−12
B. SERVICES	4 200	1,963	2,554	3,210	4,061	4,956	4,736	6,082	9,206
Total credit	2 200	*9,016*	*9,379*	*10,357*	*12,354*	*14,701*	*15,193*	*17,839*	*23,156*
Total debit	3 200	*−7,053*	*−6,826*	*−7,146*	*−8,293*	*−9,746*	*−10,456*	*−11,758*	*−13,950*
Transportation services, credit	2 205	1,457	1,580	1,837	2,395	2,883	3,210	4,002	5,885
Passenger	2 850	*784*	*768*	*797*	*1,012*	*1,186*	*1,332*	*1,645*	*2,755*
Freight	2 851	*418*	*466*	*573*	*803*	*1,000*	*1,133*	*1,458*	*1,769*
Other	2 852	*255*	*346*	*467*	*580*	*698*	*745*	*899*	*1,361*
Sea transport, passenger	2 207	....	....	....	1	3	4	3	2
Sea transport, freight	2 208	109	100	108	151	164	224	373	452
Sea transport, other	2 209	76	70	102	121	153	166	233	327
Air transport, passenger	2 211	777	761	787	1,003	1,170	1,317	1,629	2,714
Air transport, freight	2 212	62	85	78	82	114	128	144	170
Air transport, other	2 213	145	223	284	354	418	460	532	826
Other transport, passenger	2 215	7	7	9	8	12	11	13	39
Other transport, freight	2 216	248	281	387	570	722	781	941	1,147
Other transport, other	2 217	33	53	81	106	127	119	134	208
Transportation services, debit	3 205	−1,954	−2,084	−2,119	−2,491	−2,963	−3,186	−3,571	−4,414
Passenger	3 850	*−526*	*−492*	*−506*	*−573*	*−606*	*−694*	*−758*	*−914*
Freight	3 851	*−1,314*	*−1,322*	*−1,310*	*−1,482*	*−1,830*	*−1,998*	*−2,190*	*−2,532*
Other	3 852	*−115*	*−270*	*−303*	*−437*	*−527*	*−494*	*−624*	*−969*
Sea transport, passenger	3 207	−3	−3	....	−1	−6	−6	−10	−9
Sea transport, freight	3 208	−725	−733	−719	−784	−1,035	−1,210	−1,322	−1,528
Sea transport, other	3 209	−36	−51	−52	−67	−73	−54	−68	−103
Air transport, passenger	3 211	−517	−482	−497	−564	−586	−679	−736	−883
Air transport, freight	3 212	−101	−102	−86	−103	−108	−105	−114	−132
Air transport, other	3 213	−69	−206	−239	−362	−444	−418	−541	−844
Other transport, passenger	3 215	−6	−7	−9	−8	−13	−8	−11	−21
Other transport, freight	3 216	−487	−487	−505	−595	−687	−684	−754	−871
Other transport, other	3 217	−10	−13	−12	−8	−10	−22	−15	−23
Travel, credit	2 236	5,243	5,468	5,798	6,622	7,672	7,676	8,416	10,162
Business travel	2 237	....	....	....	....	....	....	....	1,024
Personal travel	2 240	....	....	....	....	....	....	....	9,138
Travel, debit	3 236	−2,228	−2,114	−2,125	−2,409	−2,763	−3,050	−3,340	−3,922
Business travel	3 237	....	....	....	....	....	....	....	−1,440
Personal travel	3 240	....	....	....	....	....	....	....	−2,482
Other services, credit	2 200 BA	2,316	2,331	2,722	3,337	4,146	4,307	5,421	7,109
Communications	2 245	173	201	252	361	485	572	679	846
Construction	2 249	150	192	206	309	434	365	521	819
Insurance	2 253	59	60	74	94	137	101	116	134
Financial	2 260	241	106	151	160	231	212	247	337
Computer and information	2 262	75	61	77	109	145	151	197	270
Royalties and licence fees	2 266	29	25	29	36	41	60	81	105
Other business services	2 268	1,332	1,417	1,679	1,967	2,287	2,475	3,130	4,085
Personal, cultural, and recreational	2 287	136	140	115	135	193	206	255	263
Government, n.i.e.	2 291	121	129	138	166	194	164	196	251
Other services, debit	3 200 BA	−2,871	−2,628	−2,903	−3,393	−4,019	−4,220	−4,846	−5,614
Communications	3 245	−157	−177	−219	−270	−380	−396	−470	−560
Construction	3 249	−59	−78	−109	−160	−159	−109	−135	−166
Insurance	3 253	−101	−96	−143	−173	−244	−210	−233	−257
Financial	3 260	−252	−140	−191	−180	−177	−228	−261	−299
Computer and information	3 262	−162	−154	−192	−231	−220	−257	−305	−381
Royalties and licence fees	3 266	−276	−250	−315	−306	−355	−343	−364	−451
Other business services	3 268	−1,380	−1,295	−1,352	−1,633	−1,950	−2,169	−2,305	−2,733
Personal, cultural, and recreational	3 287	−239	−255	−227	−264	−360	−342	−473	−503
Government, n.i.e.	3 291	−244	−182	−155	−175	−173	−165	−299	−264

Table 2 (Continued). STANDARD PRESENTATION, 2000–2007

(Millions of U.S. dollars)

	Code	2000	2001	2002	2003	2004	2005	2006	2007
C. INCOME............................	4 300 ..	**−2,371**	**−3,458**	**−2,991**	**−2,638**	**−3,707**	**−4,843**	**−7,974**	**−10,135**
Total credit............................	2 300 ..	*4,806*	*5,669*	*4,900*	*6,622*	*8,040*	*9,307*	*13,518*	*17,332*
Total debit............................	3 300 ..	*−7,177*	*−9,127*	*−7,891*	*−9,260*	*−11,747*	*−14,151*	*−21,492*	*−27,467*
Compensation of employees, credit............	2 310 ..	**241**	**221**	**201**	**237**	**230**	**235**	**265**	**343**
Compensation of employees, debit............	3 310 ..	**−203**	**−250**	**−257**	**−259**	**−378**	**−436**	**−445**	**−373**
Investment income, credit....................	2 320 ..	**4,565**	**5,448**	**4,699**	**6,385**	**7,810**	**9,073**	**13,253**	**16,989**
Direct investment income............	2 330 ..	494	646	244	1,309	1,926	2,770	3,356	3,817
Dividends and distributed branch profits..........	2 332 ..	251	266	463	1,210	1,459	2,030	1,951	2,021
Reinvested earnings and undistributed branch profits.....	2 333 ..	191	281	−327	−84	348	606	1,174	1,545
Income on debt (interest)............	2 334 ..	52	99	109	184	119	134	231	251
Portfolio investment income............	2 339 ..	1,678	1,806	1,974	2,308	3,022	3,322	6,010	6,988
Income on equity............	2 340 ..	126	145	156	185	237	370	988	1,524
Income on bonds and notes............	2 350 ..	1,235	1,448	1,623	1,890	2,519	2,649	4,647	5,178
Income on money market instruments............	2 360 ..	317	212	195	232	266	303	376	286
Other investment income............	2 370 ..	2,393	2,997	2,480	2,767	2,862	2,981	3,887	6,184
Investment income, debit....................	3 320 ..	**−6,974**	**−8,877**	**−7,634**	**−9,002**	**−11,369**	**−13,715**	**−21,047**	**−27,094**
Direct investment income............	3 330 ..	−1,717	−1,930	−1,062	−2,126	−2,903	−4,342	−6,204	−7,059
Dividends and distributed branch profits..........	3 332 ..	−923	−1,119	−1,406	−1,537	−2,158	−3,298	−3,248	−4,026
Reinvested earnings and undistributed branch profits.....	3 333 ..	−639	−645	511	−454	−643	−896	−2,797	−2,796
Income on debt (interest)............	3 334 ..	−156	−165	−167	−135	−103	−148	−159	−237
Portfolio investment income............	3 339 ..	−2,114	−2,309	−2,735	−2,979	−3,762	−4,153	−6,986	−8,823
Income on equity............	3 340 ..	−373	−430	−351	−577	−856	−1,271	−1,968	−2,452
Income on bonds and notes............	3 350 ..	−1,626	−1,785	−2,234	−2,206	−2,592	−2,454	−4,455	−5,674
Income on money market instruments............	3 360 ..	−115	−94	−149	−195	−314	−428	−563	−696
Other investment income............	3 370 ..	−3,142	−4,638	−3,837	−3,897	−4,704	−5,220	−7,857	−11,212
D. CURRENT TRANSFERS............	4 379 ..	**3,344**	**3,365**	**2,827**	**3,266**	**3,536**	**2,827**	**3,171**	**3,618**
Credit............................	2 379 ..	**5,495**	**5,677**	**5,544**	**6,544**	**7,297**	**7,226**	**8,054**	**8,709**
General government............	2 380 ..	1,593	1,541	1,930	2,654	2,826	2,813	2,991	2,788
Other sectors............	2 390 ..	3,902	4,136	3,614	3,890	4,471	4,412	5,064	5,921
Workers' remittances............	2 391 ..	3,179	3,340	2,664	2,752	3,032	2,826	3,045	3,552
Other current transfers............	2 392 ..	724	795	950	1,137	1,440	1,587	2,019	2,369
Debit............................	3 379 ..	**−2,150**	**−2,312**	**−2,717**	**−3,278**	**−3,761**	**−4,398**	**−4,884**	**−5,090**
General government............	3 380 ..	−1,365	−1,289	−1,537	−1,900	−2,015	−2,291	−2,646	−2,707
Other sectors............	3 390 ..	−785	−1,024	−1,179	−1,378	−1,745	−2,107	−2,238	−2,384
Workers' remittances............	3 391 ..	−173	−366	−412	−529	−604	−695	−766	−783
Other current transfers............	3 392 ..	−612	−658	−768	−849	−1,142	−1,412	−1,471	−1,601
CAPITAL AND FINANCIAL ACCOUNT............	4 996 ..	**11,890**	**10,822**	**9,684**	**8,602**	**14,364**	**18,484**	**18,210**	**22,970**
CAPITAL ACCOUNT............................	4 994 ..	**1,512**	**1,069**	**1,906**	**2,977**	**2,773**	**2,115**	**1,527**	**2,837**
Total credit............................	2 994 ..	*1,681*	*1,278*	*2,111*	*3,246*	*3,130*	*2,485*	*2,045*	*3,290*
Total debit............................	3 994 ..	*−169*	*−209*	*−205*	*−269*	*−358*	*−371*	*−518*	*−453*
Capital transfers, credit........................	2 400 ..	**1,625**	**1,247**	**2,084**	**3,187**	**2,992**	**2,336**	**1,922**	**3,020**
General government............	2 401 ..	1,513	1,125	1,995	3,116	2,925	2,270	1,876	2,944
Debt forgiveness............	2 402 ..	....	....	....	....	....	....	....	....
Other capital transfers............	2 410 ..	1,513	1,125	1,995	3,116	2,925	2,270	1,876	2,944
Other sectors............	2 430 ..	112	123	89	70	68	66	46	75
Migrants' transfers............	2 431 ..	75	86	66	53	43	41	24	50
Debt forgiveness............	2 432 ..	....	....	2	2	2	1	....	3
Other capital transfers............	2 440 ..	36	36	20	16	23	24	22	22
Capital transfers, debit........................	3 400 ..	**−130**	**−164**	**−181**	**−224**	**−266**	**−282**	**−407**	**−341**
General government............	3 401 ..	−21	−47	−38	−60	−60	−89	−219	−79
Debt forgiveness............	3 402 ..	....	....	....	....	....	....	....	....
Other capital transfers............	3 410 ..	−21	−47	−38	−60	−60	−89	−219	−79
Other sectors............	3 430 ..	−109	−117	−143	−164	−205	−193	−188	−262
Migrants' transfers............	3 431 ..	−78	−90	−123	−148	−182	−175	−166	−155
Debt forgiveness............	3 432 ..	....	....	....	....	....	−1	−1	−87
Other capital transfers............	3 440 ..	−30	−27	−20	−17	−24	−17	−21	−20
Nonproduced nonfinancial assets, credit............	2 480 ..	**56**	**30**	**27**	**59**	**138**	**149**	**123**	**270**
Nonproduced nonfinancial assets, debit............	3 480 ..	**−39**	**−45**	**−25**	**−45**	**−92**	**−89**	**−111**	**−112**

Table 2 (Continued). STANDARD PRESENTATION, 2000–2007

(Millions of U.S. dollars)

	Code	2000	2001	2002	2003	2004	2005	2006	2007
FINANCIAL ACCOUNT	4 995	10,378	9,753	7,778	5,625	11,591	16,370	16,683	20,133
A. DIRECT INVESTMENT	4 500	−1,502	−54	1,965	680	−5,716	1,806	4,341	−671
Direct investment abroad	4 505	−8,183	−6,228	210	−6,575	−7,377	−2,252	−7,003	−6,205
Equity capital	4 510	−7,243	−5,632	1,684	−7,332	−6,483	−62	−5,032	−1,722
Claims on affiliated enterprises	4 515	−7,236	−5,632	1,684	−7,332	−6,484	−62	−5,032	−1,722
Liabilities to affiliated enterprises	4 520	−6	....	1	....	1	....	....	....
Reinvested earnings	4 525	−191	−281	327	84	−348	−606	−1,174	−1,545
Other capital	4 530	−750	−315	−1,801	673	−547	−1,585	−797	−2,937
Claims on affiliated enterprises	4 535	−1,224	−301	−571	478	−242	−1,216	−807	−2,909
Liabilities to affiliated enterprises	4 540	474	−14	−1,230	195	−305	−368	10	−28
Direct investment in Portugal	4 555	6,682	6,174	1,755	7,255	1,661	4,059	11,344	5,534
Equity capital	4 560	5,612	1,465	1,868	7,476	5,311	2,710	7,049	2,702
Claims on direct investors	4 565	−11	−1	....	....	1	....	4	....
Liabilities to direct investors	4 570	5,623	1,466	1,868	7,476	5,310	2,710	7,045	2,702
Reinvested earnings	4 575	639	645	−511	454	643	896	2,797	2,796
Other capital	4 580	431	4,064	397	−675	−4,293	453	1,499	37
Claims on direct investors	4 585	−132	44	−59	−2,041	−1,141	−738	−1,245	−2,960
Liabilities to direct investors	4 590	563	4,020	456	1,366	−3,152	1,191	2,744	2,996
B. PORTFOLIO INVESTMENT	4 600	−1,791	2,810	3,215	−7,127	284	−1,519	3,934	13,013
Assets	4 602	−4,582	−7,851	−7,034	−21,471	−13,598	−19,659	−9,580	−12,104
Equity securities	4 610	−1,044	−959	−813	−622	−1,708	−1,845	−3,999	−2,412
Monetary authorities	4 611	....	....	....	....	....	....	....	....
General government	4 612	−126	40	−76	−202	−299	476	49	−123
Banks	4 613	−30	68	218	252	−283	−677	−726	−235
Other sectors	4 614	−887	−1,067	−954	−673	−1,127	−1,644	−3,323	−2,053
Debt securities	4 619	−3,538	−6,892	−6,221	−20,849	−11,890	−17,814	−5,581	−9,692
Bonds and notes	4 620	−4,088	−6,794	−5,840	−15,445	−14,501	−14,401	−9,423	−12,939
Monetary authorities	4 621	−47	366	149	−885	−1,156	1,479	−4,115	−625
General government	4 622	−295	−475	−271	−115	103	−641	−439	−222
Banks	4 623	1,031	−548	−913	−6,162	−6,135	−3,051	5,690	−6,473
Other sectors	4 624	−4,776	−6,137	−4,805	−8,283	−7,313	−12,189	−10,559	−5,619
Money market instruments	4 630	549	−99	−382	−5,404	2,612	−3,413	3,842	3,247
Monetary authorities	4 631	−488	54	354	−4,749	2,349	−2,696	4,201	1,772
General government	4 632	....	143	−73	−21	24	−2	....	1
Banks	4 633	−13	−198	58	−439	379	−147	−702	470
Other sectors	4 634	1,051	−99	−721	−195	−140	−567	343	1,005
Liabilities	4 652	2,792	10,661	10,249	14,344	13,882	18,141	13,514	25,117
Equity securities	4 660	415	2,371	3,287	9,863	7,233	5,594	3,829	−664
Banks	4 663	52	672	64	−103	−156	805	669	−252
Other sectors	4 664	364	1,699	3,223	9,966	7,389	4,789	3,160	−412
Debt securities	4 669	2,376	8,290	6,962	4,481	6,649	12,547	9,685	25,781
Bonds and notes	4 670	2,151	4,530	5,474	2,624	593	7,320	15,041	23,694
Monetary authorities	4 671	....	....	....	....	....	....	....	....
General government	4 672	2,744	1,848	5,575	934	545	10,054	8,822	2,874
Banks	4 673	−289	1,780	−409	−660	−607	−6,461	1,199	16,152
Other sectors	4 674	−304	903	308	2,351	656	3,727	5,020	4,668
Money market instruments	4 680	225	3,760	1,488	1,857	6,056	5,227	−5,355	2,087
Monetary authorities	4 681	....	....	....	....	....	....	....	....
General government	4 682	−141	1,576	−1,689	2,980	6,092	3,715	−4,426	1,448
Banks	4 683	366	−347	186	602	−663	−1,224	−19	458
Other sectors	4 684	....	2,530	2,991	−1,725	627	2,735	−910	181
C. FINANCIAL DERIVATIVES	4 910	322	351	−5	71	−90	−211	−263	930
Monetary authorities	4 911	1	−2	6	5	1	3	....	....
General government	4 912	185	95	198	−95	−23	−52	−138	307
Banks	4 913	224	270	−143	104	−34	−128	−316	474
Other sectors	4 914	−88	−12	−66	57	−34	−34	191	150
Assets	4 900	3,673	3,226	3,796	4,590	4,135	4,865	6,790	11,513
Monetary authorities	4 901	5	3	7	6	5	6	5	7
General government	4 902	286	672	954	700	555	714	1,420	1,406
Banks	4 903	3,150	2,142	2,343	2,913	2,547	2,860	3,527	7,509
Other sectors	4 904	232	409	492	971	1,029	1,285	1,838	2,591
Liabilities	4 905	−3,351	−2,875	−3,802	−4,518	−4,226	−5,076	−7,053	−10,583
Monetary authorities	4 906	−3	−6	−2	....	−3	−4	−5	−7
General government	4 907	−101	−577	−756	−795	−578	−766	−1,558	−1,100
Banks	4 908	−2,926	−1,871	−2,487	−2,809	−2,581	−2,987	−3,843	−7,035
Other sectors	4 909	−320	−421	−557	−914	−1,063	−1,319	−1,647	−2,441

Table 2 (Concluded). STANDARD PRESENTATION, 2000–2007

(Millions of U.S. dollars)

	Code	2000	2001	2002	2003	2004	2005	2006	2007
D. OTHER INVESTMENT	4 700	**13,719**	**7,499**	**3,621**	**5,547**	**15,251**	**14,552**	**6,315**	**5,898**
Assets	4 703	**–10,970**	**–7,403**	**–6,360**	**–8,744**	**777**	**–1,246**	**–17,051**	**–15,881**
Trade credits	4 706	–874	211	–623	–676	–604	–832	–778	33
General government	4 707	....	....	....	....	....	....	....	....
of which: Short-term	4 709	....	....	....	....	....	....	....	....
Other sectors	4 710	–874	211	–623	–676	–604	–832	–778	33
of which: Short-term	4 712	....	....	....	....	....	....	....	....
Loans	4 714	–2,687	–3,849	–2,359	590	5,106	5,760	175	–5,493
Monetary authorities	4 715	–1	1	–9	–6	16	–7	....	–12
of which: Short-term	4 718	*–1*	*1*	*–9*	*–6*	*16*	*–7*	....	*–12*
General government	4 719	–149	–145	–92	–135	137	–125	148	808
of which: Short-term	4 721	....	....	....	....	....	....	....	....
Banks	4 722	–2,511	–1,002	1,040	–747	569	5,932	–1,508	–6,279
of which: Short-term	4 724	....	....	....	....	....	....	....	....
Other sectors	4 725	–25	–2,703	–3,298	1,479	4,384	–41	1,535	–10
of which: Short-term	4 727	*–13*	*–948*	*296*	*615*	*–91*	*–73*	*–2*	*–125*
Currency and deposits	4 730	–7,405	–3,769	–2,935	–8,142	–2,832	–5,179	–15,260	–8,898
Monetary authorities	4 731	11	21	–295	351	–965	–699	–1,250	–2,165
General government	4 732	–10	–55	–9	–6	–54	2	–5	–42
Banks	4 733	–4,690	–31	–1,069	–7,966	–2,022	–7,274	–11,219	–3,124
Other sectors	4 734	–2,716	–3,703	–1,562	–521	210	2,792	–2,785	–3,566
Other assets	4 736	–3	4	–443	–515	–893	–995	–1,188	–1,524
Monetary authorities	4 737	....	....	....	....	–5	–11	....	–1
of which: Short-term	4 739	....	....	....	....	....	....	....	....
General government	4 740	–1	....	....	....	....	....	–4	....
of which: Short-term	4 742	....	....	....	....	....	....	....	....
Banks	4 743	....	....	....	....	....	....	....	–4
of which: Short-term	4 745	....	....	....	....	....	....	....	*–4*
Other sectors	4 746	–2	4	–443	–515	–888	–983	–1,184	–1,518
of which: Short-term	4 748	*1*	....	*–446*	*–517*	*–881*	*–980*	*–1,179*	*–1,504*
Liabilities	4 753	**24,689**	**14,903**	**9,981**	**14,290**	**14,474**	**15,797**	**23,366**	**21,779**
Trade credits	4 756	829	–353	120	483	1,412	–90	–233	644
General government	4 757	....	....	....	....	....	....	....	....
of which: Short-term	4 759	....	....	....	....	....	....	....	....
Other sectors	4 760	829	–353	120	483	1,412	–90	–233	644
of which: Short-term	4 762	....	....	....	....	....	....	....	....
Loans	4 764	6,402	9,503	9,463	14,731	4,536	8,956	12,562	8,097
Monetary authorities	4 765	7	–53	263	–1,043	–1,635	–123	–856	–125
of which: Use of Fund credit and loans from the Fund	4 766	....	....	....	....	....	....	....	....
of which: Short-term	4 768	*–232*	*300*	*263*	*–2,780*	*–467*	*–72*	*–124*	*–19*
General government	4 769	–154	–190	312	5	501	–702	71	1,504
of which: Short-term	4 771	*–50*	*19*	*–35*	*450*	*445*	*–763*	*1,624*	*1,403*
Banks	4 772	5,620	8,909	8,448	14,666	3,844	8,318	13,075	6,789
of which: Short-term	4 774	....	....	....	....	....	....	....	....
Other sectors	4 775	929	837	440	1,103	1,825	1,463	273	–71
of which: Short-term	4 777	*172*	*–295*	*–137*	*179*	*406*	*493*	*–171*	*–436*
Currency and deposits	4 780	17,470	5,709	442	–957	8,489	6,886	10,970	12,995
Monetary authorities	4 781	4,859	138	433	–5,682	8,866	5,715	–7,069	–966
General government	4 782	....	....	....	....	....	....	....	....
Banks	4 783	12,611	5,571	9	4,725	–377	1,171	18,040	13,961
Other sectors	4 784	....	....	....	....	....	....	....	....
Other liabilities	4 786	–12	44	–43	33	37	45	67	43
Monetary authorities	4 787	–5	2	3	....	–3	3	–1	–4
of which: Short-term	4 789	....	*1*	....	....	*–3*	*3*	*–1*	*–4*
General government	4 790	....	....	....	....	....	....	....	....
of which: Short-term	4 792	....	....	....	....	....	....	....	....
Banks	4 793	....	....	....	....	....	....	....	....
of which: Short-term	4 795	....	....	....	....	....	....	....	....
Other sectors	4 796	–8	42	–47	33	40	43	67	47
of which: Short-term	4 798	....	....	....	....	....	....	....	*3*
E. RESERVE ASSETS	4 802	**–371**	**–852**	**–1,017**	**6,455**	**1,863**	**1,741**	**2,357**	**962**
Monetary gold	4 812	....	....	156	861	727	636	719	....
Special drawing rights	4 811	–12	–10	–8	–7	–8	–8	–5	–4
Reserve position in the Fund	4 810	42	–72	–37	–45	115	205	95	29
Foreign exchange	4 803	–401	–770	–1,128	5,647	1,028	908	1,548	937
Other claims	4 813	....	....	....	....	....	....	....	....
NET ERRORS AND OMISSIONS	4 998	**–295**	**623**	**580**	**991**	**–749**	**–866**	**1,430**	**–1,552**

2008, International Monetary Fund: *Balance of Payments Statistics Yearbook*

Table 3. INTERNATIONAL INVESTMENT POSITION (End-period stocks), 2000–2007

(Millions of U.S. dollars)

	Code	2000	2001	2002	2003	2004	2005	2006	2007
ASSETS	8 995 C.	146,755	159,952	195,759	265,038	307,306	300,672	365,998	440,233
Direct investment abroad	8 505	19,793	22,265	21,325	34,443	43,941	41,965	53,815	69,237
Equity capital and reinvested earnings	8 506	18,012	20,554	17,232	30,499	39,845	37,603	47,860	59,488
Claims on affiliated enterprises	8 507	18,013	20,554	17,232	30,499	39,845	37,603	47,860	59,488
Liabilities to affiliated enterprises	8 508	....	−1	....	....	....	....	....	....
Other capital	8 530	1,781	1,711	4,093	3,944	4,096	4,362	5,954	9,749
Claims on affiliated enterprises	8 535	4,059	3,864	5,285	5,605	5,593	5,515	7,099	11,093
Liabilities to affiliated enterprises	8 540	−2,278	−2,153	−1,192	−1,660	−1,497	−1,153	−1,144	−1,344
Portfolio investment	8 602	40,662	45,915	62,245	97,727	124,949	134,738	160,345	189,762
Equity securities	8 610	7,624	7,556	8,397	11,018	16,556	27,495	39,209	46,858
Monetary authorities	8 611	....	....	....	....	....	....	....	....
General government	8 612	142	293	278	610	1,058	539	658	869
Banks	8 613	1,412	1,144	1,446	1,518	2,544	4,254	6,437	7,386
Other sectors	8 614	6,069	6,119	6,673	8,890	12,953	22,702	32,113	38,604
Debt securities	8 619	33,038	38,359	53,848	86,709	108,394	107,243	121,136	142,904
Bonds and notes	8 620	27,585	32,858	46,754	72,194	96,385	95,209	111,871	136,260
Monetary authorities	8 621	2,236	1,759	1,918	3,477	5,726	3,505	8,212	9,753
General government	8 622	502	940	1,474	1,866	1,960	2,007	2,553	2,998
Banks	8 623	4,476	4,843	6,770	14,403	22,497	22,956	18,823	27,287
Other sectors	8 624	20,371	25,317	36,592	52,448	66,202	66,740	82,283	96,222
Money market instruments	8 630	5,453	5,501	7,094	14,515	12,009	12,034	9,266	6,644
Monetary authorities	8 631	3,925	3,696	4,049	10,175	7,661	9,261	5,869	4,462
General government	8 632	....	65	248	321	322	7	8	9
Banks	8 633	269	457	466	1,046	698	604	1,378	983
Other sectors	8 634	1,258	1,283	2,330	2,973	3,327	2,162	2,011	1,191
Financial derivatives	8 900	2,758	1,929	2,165	2,671	2,097	1,858	1,913	2,521
Monetary authorities	8 901	1	1	8	6	....	....	1	....
General government	8 902	328	378	83	296	....	....		
Banks	8 903	2,428	1,549	2,074	2,370	2,096	1,857	1,912	2,511
Other sectors	8 904	1	2	....	....	....	1	....	9
Other investment	8 703	69,316	74,761	92,323	117,383	124,635	111,747	140,043	167,166
Trade credits	8 706	6,589	6,040	7,923	7,101	8,293	8,036	9,795	10,955
General government	8 707	....	....	....	....	....	....	....	....
of which: Short-term	8 709	....	....	....	....	....	....	....	....
Other sectors	8 710	6,589	6,040	7,923	7,101	8,293	8,036	9,795	10,955
of which: Short-term	8 712	6,589	6,040	7,923	7,101	8,293	8,036	9,795	10,955
Loans	8 714	47,207	50,677	61,268	78,493	80,781	74,169	92,717	107,939
Monetary authorities	8 715	....	....	....	....	....	....	....	....
of which: Short-term	8 718	....	....	....	....	....	....	....	....
General government	8 719	2,105	3,580	3,765	4,052	3,984	3,996	3,933	1,007
of which: Short-term	8 721	1	1	1	1	1	1	1	1
Banks	8 722	44,998	44,412	50,937	68,142	73,363	66,783	86,105	104,082
of which: Short-term	8 724	33,499	32,344	38,300	52,553	56,939	58,256	74,918	85,194
Other sectors	8 725	104	2,685	6,566	6,299	3,434	3,390	2,679	2,850
of which: Short-term	8 727	38	945	685	112	217	450	502	693
Currency and deposits	8 730	15,066	17,611	22,650	27,287	30,429	24,520	31,713	41,424
Monetary authorities	8 731	1,266	1,184	1,692	1,580	2,843	3,138	4,944	8,077
General government	8 732	30	82	105	130	200	160	178	240
Banks	8 733	....	....	....	....	....	....	....	....
Other sectors	8 734	13,770	16,345	20,854	25,578	27,387	21,222	26,591	33,107
Other assets	8 736	455	433	482	4,503	5,132	5,022	5,818	6,848
Monetary authorities	8 737	102	96	114	138	154	143	160	180
of which: Short-term	8 739	....	....	....	....	....	....	....	....
General government	8 740	27	25	30	2,828	2,979	2,701	2,914	3,149
of which: Short-term	8 742	26	25	30	36	39	34	37	42
Banks	8 743	78	76	82	89	94	107	138	152
of which: Short-term	8 745	77	76	81	88	91	85	90	98
Other sectors	8 746	249	235	256	1,449	1,907	2,070	2,607	3,367
of which: Short-term	8 748	240	231	255	1,449	1,899	2,061	2,590	3,333
Reserve assets	8 802	14,227	15,082	17,701	12,813	11,684	10,364	9,883	11,546
Monetary gold	8 812	5,318	5,415	6,522	6,938	6,510	6,885	7,819	10,288
Special drawing rights	8 811	54	62	76	91	103	103	113	123
Reserve position in the Fund	8 810	316	376	447	536	440	202	115	90
Foreign exchange	8 803	8,539	9,228	10,656	5,249	4,631	3,173	1,835	1,044
Other claims	8 813	....	....	....	....	....	....	....	....

Table 3 (Concluded). INTERNATIONAL INVESTMENT POSITION (End-period stocks), 2000–2007

(Millions of U.S. dollars)

	Code	2000	2001	2002	2003	2004	2005	2006	2007
LIABILITIES..	8 995 D.	**191,802**	**213,945**	**275,690**	**368,628**	**432,898**	**424,165**	**529,442**	**655,914**
Direct investment in Portugal..............................	8 555 ..	**32,043**	**36,023**	**44,637**	**60,584**	**66,971**	**63,340**	**87,959**	**114,192**
Equity capital and reinvested earnings...........................	8 556 ..	29,102	29,000	36,013	51,096	62,533	59,730	81,721	107,175
Claims on direct investors.............................	8 557 ..	−1	−1	−2	....	....	....	....	....
Liabilities to direct investors...........................	8 558 ..	29,103	29,001	36,015	51,096	62,533	59,730	81,721	107,175
Other capital..	8 580 ..	2,941	7,024	8,624	9,489	4,438	3,610	6,238	7,017
Claims on direct investors.............................	8 585 ..	−1,845	−1,851	−2,311	−4,985	−5,905	−5,648	−6,284	−10,426
Liabilities to direct investors...........................	8 590 ..	4,786	8,875	10,935	14,473	10,343	9,258	12,521	17,443
Portfolio investment.....................................	8 652 ..	**55,630**	**64,481**	**88,319**	**124,261**	**152,859**	**159,339**	**194,298**	**245,517**
Equity securities...	8 660 ..	18,873	15,605	17,492	34,661	47,722	48,506	64,123	74,162
Banks..	8 663 ..	4,640	3,877	3,464	4,884	5,762	7,105	10,432	11,797
Other sectors..	8 664 ..	14,233	11,728	14,027	29,778	41,959	41,401	53,690	62,365
Debt securities...	8 669 ..	36,757	48,876	70,827	89,600	105,138	110,833	130,175	171,356
Bonds and notes..	8 670 ..	34,820	43,310	62,901	77,368	85,725	88,236	110,619	147,112
Monetary authorities..............................	8 671 ..	....	....	....	....	....	....	....	....
General government...............................	8 672 ..	29,838	34,303	52,278	63,430	70,571	72,107	86,984	98,448
Banks..	8 673 ..	4,038	7,245	8,061	8,363	8,348	4,738	6,333	24,671
Other sectors..	8 674 ..	945	1,762	2,562	5,575	6,805	11,392	17,302	23,993
Money market instruments...........................	8 680 ..	1,936	5,566	7,926	12,232	19,412	22,597	19,556	24,243
Monetary authorities..............................	8 681 ..	....	....	....	....	....	....	....	....
General government...............................	8 682 ..	429	1,978	329	4,213	11,067	12,773	9,584	12,084
Banks..	8 683 ..	1,415	1,049	1,287	2,136	1,466	17	....	484
Other sectors..	8 684 ..	92	2,539	6,310	5,882	6,880	9,807	9,972	11,675
Financial derivatives....................................	8 905 ..	**2,223**	**1,185**	**1,662**	**2,706**	**2,932**	**1,933**	**1,856**	**2,652**
Monetary authorities....................................	8 906 ..	1	3	....	....	....	....	....	....
General government.......................................	8 907 ..	....	....	....	....	357	364	78	84
Banks..	8 908 ..	2,222	1,182	1,662	2,706	2,562	1,495	1,704	2,489
Other sectors...	8 909 ..	....	....	....	....	12	73	75	79
Other investment..	8 753 ..	**101,907**	**112,256**	**141,072**	**181,076**	**210,136**	**199,552**	**245,329**	**293,553**
Trade credits..	8 756 ..	7,127	6,423	7,821	9,182	11,398	9,815	10,744	12,713
General government.......................................	8 757 ..	....	....	....	....	....	....	....	....
of which: Short-term..............................	8 759 ..	....	....	....	....	....	....	....	....
Other sectors..	8 760 ..	7,127	6,423	7,821	9,182	11,398	9,815	10,744	12,713
of which: Short-term..............................	8 762 ..	*7,127*	*6,423*	*7,821*	*9,182*	*11,398*	*9,815*	*10,744*	*12,713*
Loans...	8 764 ..	34,277	42,413	59,020	86,500	98,726	94,831	118,667	139,035
Monetary authorities..................................	8 765 ..	3,447	3,392	3,659	2,714	1,147	928	118	....
of which: Use of Fund credit and loans from the Fund....	8 766 ..	....	....	....	....	....	....	....	....
of which: Short-term..............................	8 768 ..	*3,094*	*3,392*	*3,659*	*902*	*343*	*270*	*51*	....
General government...............................	8 769 ..	1,950	1,672	2,075	2,704	3,507	2,174	2,572	4,263
of which: Short-term..............................	8 771 ..	*33*	*46*	*21*	*523*	*1,090*	*25*	*1,700*	*3,406*
Banks..	8 772 ..	16,616	24,757	38,047	61,819	71,421	70,722	92,447	109,544
of which: Short-term..............................	8 774 ..	....	....	....	....	....	....	....	....
Other sectors..	8 775 ..	12,264	12,593	15,240	19,263	22,650	21,008	23,531	25,228
of which: Short-term..............................	8 777 ..	*831*	*1,126*	*1,172*	*1,600*	*2,167*	*2,388*	*2,454*	*2,253*
Currency and deposits....................................	8 780 ..	60,311	63,191	74,032	85,141	99,706	94,582	115,500	141,299
Monetary authorities..................................	8 781 ..	4,023	3,890	5,366	572	10,504	14,090	8,707	9,148
General government...............................	8 782 ..	....	....	....	....	....	....	....	....
Banks..	8 783 ..	56,288	59,302	68,665	84,569	89,202	80,491	106,792	132,151
Other sectors..	8 784 ..	....	....	....	....	....	....	....	....
Other liabilities...	8 786 ..	191	228	200	254	308	324	419	505
Monetary authorities..................................	8 787 ..	....	....	....	....	....	....	....	....
of which: Short-term..............................	8 789 ..	....	....	....	....	....	....	....	....
General government...............................	8 790 ..	....	....	....	....	....	....	....	....
of which: Short-term..............................	8 792 ..	....	....	....	....	....	....	....	....
Banks..	8 793 ..	105	104	107	110	111	108	110	113
of which: Short-term..............................	8 795 ..	*104*	*104*	*106*	*109*	*110*	*108*	*109*	*112*
Other sectors..	8 796 ..	87	124	93	144	197	216	308	392
of which: Short-term..............................	8 798 ..	*84*	*80*	*90*	*104*	*110*	*100*	*108*	*121*
NET INTERNATIONAL INVESTMENT POSITION........	8 995 ..	**−45,047**	**−53,993**	**−79,931**	**−103,589**	**−125,593**	**−123,492**	**−163,444**	**−215,680**
Conversion rates: euros per U.S. dollar (end of period)..	0 104 ..	**1.0747**	**1.1347**	**.9536**	**.7918**	**.7342**	**.8477**	**.7593**	**.6793**

Table 1. ANALYTIC PRESENTATION, 2000–2007

(Millions of U.S. dollars)

	Code	2000	2001	2002	2003	2004	2005	2006	2007
A. Current Account[1]	4 993 Z.	−1,355	−2,229	−1,525	−3,311	−6,382	−8,621	−12,785	−23,136
Goods: exports f.o.b.	2 100 ..	10,366	11,385	13,876	17,618	23,485	27,730	32,336	40,349
Goods: imports f.o.b.	3 100 ..	−12,050	−14,354	−16,487	−22,155	−30,150	−37,348	−47,172	−64,689
Balance on Goods	4 100 ..	*−1,684*	*−2,969*	*−2,611*	*−4,537*	*−6,665*	*−9,618*	*−14,836*	*−24,340*
Services: credit	2 200 ..	1,747	2,032	2,347	3,028	3,614	5,083	7,032	10,445
Services: debit	3 200 ..	−1,993	−2,153	−2,338	−2,958	−3,879	−5,518	−7,027	−10,169
Balance on Goods and Services	4 991 ..	*−1,930*	*−3,090*	*−2,602*	*−4,467*	*−6,930*	*−10,053*	*−14,831*	*−24,064*
Income: credit	2 300 ..	325	455	413	372	433	1,533	2,176	3,267
Income: debit	3 300 ..	−610	−737	−872	−1,077	−3,582	−4,432	−6,255	−9,055
Balance on Goods, Services, and Income	4 992 ..	*−2,215*	*−3,372*	*−3,061*	*−5,172*	*−10,079*	*−12,952*	*−18,910*	*−29,852*
Current transfers: credit	2 379 Z.	1,079	1,417	1,808	2,200	4,188	4,939	6,995	9,838
Current transfers: debit	3 379 ..	−219	−274	−272	−339	−491	−607	−870	−3,122
B. Capital Account[1]	4 994 Z.	**36**	**95**	**93**	**213**	**643**	**731**	**−34**	**1,126**
Capital account: credit	2 994 Z.	37	108	100	223	669	829	925	1,683
Capital account: debit	3 994 ..	−1	−13	−7	−10	−26	−98	−959	−557
Total, Groups A Plus B	4 981 ..	*−1,319*	*−2,134*	*−1,432*	*−3,098*	*−5,739*	*−7,890*	*−12,819*	*−22,010*
C. Financial Account[1]	4 995 W.	**2,102**	**2,938**	**4,079**	**4,400**	**10,835**	**14,089**	**18,899**	**28,468**
Direct investment abroad	4 505 ..	11	17	−16	−39	−70	30	−422	67
Direct investment in Romania	4 555 Z.	1,037	1,157	1,144	1,844	6,517	6,482	11,393	9,492
Portfolio investment assets	4 602 ..	28	−8	....	9	−559	−140	−828	−215
Equity securities	4 610 ..	31	−7	....	14	−559	−136	−390	−147
Debt securities	4 619 ..	−3	−1	....	−5	....	−3	−438	−68
Portfolio investment liabilities	4 652 Z.	73	583	382	569	28	1,089	589	481
Equity securities	4 660 ..	58	8	21	69	111	229	301	746
Debt securities	4 669 Z.	15	575	361	500	−83	860	289	−265
Financial derivatives	4 910 ..	....	....	....	....	....	−26	−108	−315
Financial derivatives assets	4 900 ..	....	....	....	....	....	36	48	186
Financial derivatives liabilities	4 905 ..	....	....	....	....	....	−62	−156	−501
Other investment assets	4 703 ..	−407	−44	692	72	−212	−1,078	−1,323	−1,343
Monetary authorities	4 701 ..	....	....	....	−1	....	−11	....	−13
General government	4 704 ..	−82	−44	−41	−36	−22	−15	758	188
Banks	4 705 ..	−354	−102	536	229	−43	−198	−433	−50
Other sectors	4 728 ..	29	102	197	−120	−147	−853	−1,648	−1,468
Other investment liabilities	4 753 W.	1,360	1,233	1,877	1,945	5,131	7,731	9,598	20,301
Monetary authorities	4 753 WA	−14	....	−100	....	99	−100	−3	185
General government	4 753 ZB	681	320	465	889	1,015	568	28	114
Banks	4 753 ZC	−107	159	309	918	2,329	3,833	4,879	11,393
Other sectors	4 753 ZD	800	754	1,203	138	1,688	3,430	4,694	8,609
Total, Groups A Through C	4 983 ..	*783*	*804*	*2,647*	*1,302*	*5,096*	*6,199*	*6,080*	*6,458*
D. Net Errors and Omissions	4 998 ..	**125**	**731**	**−856**	**−289**	**1,093**	**612**	**521**	**−164**
Total, Groups A Through D	4 984 ..	*908*	*1,535*	*1,791*	*1,013*	*6,189*	*6,811*	*6,602*	*6,294*
E. Reserves and Related Items	4 802 A.	**−908**	**−1,535**	**−1,791**	**−1,013**	**−6,189**	**−6,811**	**−6,602**	**−6,294**
Reserve assets	4 802 ..	−928	−1,484	−1,802	−1,134	−6,018	−6,777	−6,435	−6,189
Use of Fund credit and loans	4 766 ..	20	−51	11	120	−171	−152	−166	−105
Exceptional financing	4 920 ..	....	....	....	....	....	117	....	....
Conversion rates: Romanian lei per U.S. dollar	0 101 ..	**2.171**	**2.906**	**3.306**	**3.320**	**3.264**	**2.914**	**2.809**	**2.438**

[1] Excludes components that have been classified in the categories of Group E.

Table 2. STANDARD PRESENTATION, 2000–2007

(Millions of U.S. dollars)

	Code	2000	2001	2002	2003	2004	2005	2006	2007
CURRENT ACCOUNT..	4 993 ..	**−1,355**	**−2,229**	**−1,525**	**−3,311**	**−6,382**	**−8,504**	**−12,785**	**−23,136**
A. GOODS..	4 100 ..	**−1,684**	**−2,969**	**−2,611**	**−4,537**	**−6,665**	**−9,618**	**−14,836**	**−24,340**
Credit..	2 100 ..	**10,366**	**11,385**	**13,876**	**17,618**	**23,485**	**27,730**	**32,336**	**40,349**
General merchandise: exports f.o.b...................	2 110 ..	10,127	11,007	13,296	16,819	22,477	14,466	17,830	29,971
Goods for processing: exports f.o.b.................	2 150 ..	202	334	509	716	861	13,243	14,496	10,367
Repairs on goods..	2 160 ..	36	44	71	81	146	....	....	....
Goods procured in ports by carriers...............	2 170 ..	1	....	....	2	1	....	....	....
Nonmonetary gold..	2 180 ..	....	....	....	....	....	20	10	11
Debit..	3 100 ..	**−12,050**	**−14,354**	**−16,487**	**−22,155**	**−30,150**	**−37,348**	**−47,172**	**−64,689**
General merchandise: imports f.o.b.................	3 110 ..	−12,034	−14,339	−16,430	−22,134	−30,128	−28,757	−37,915	−57,990
Goods for processing: imports f.o.b................	3 150 ..	−2	−3	−4	−3	−5	−8,591	−9,256	−6,690
Repairs on goods..	3 160 ..	−5	−4	−7	−10	−7	....	....	....
Goods procured in ports by carriers...............	3 170 ..	−9	−8	−46	−8	−10	....	....	....
Nonmonetary gold..	3 180 ..	....	....	....	....	....	....	−1	−9
B. SERVICES...	4 200 ..	**−246**	**−121**	**9**	**70**	**−265**	**−435**	**5**	**276**
Total credit..	2 200 ..	*1,747*	*2,032*	*2,347*	*3,028*	*3,614*	*5,083*	*7,032*	*10,445*
Total debit...	3 200 ..	*−1,993*	*−2,153*	*−2,338*	*−2,958*	*−3,879*	*−5,518*	*−7,027*	*−10,169*
Transportation services, credit........................	2 205 ..	**632**	**827**	**964**	**1,205**	**1,559**	**1,474**	**1,883**	**2,534**
Passenger..	2 850 ..	*35*	*57*	*65*	*74*	*104*	*273*	*368*	*455*
Freight..	2 851 ..	*419*	*566*	*683*	*842*	*1,076*	*831*	*1,129*	*1,703*
Other..	2 852 ..	*178*	*204*	*216*	*289*	*379*	*370*	*386*	*376*
Sea transport, passenger..............................	2 207 ..	....	....	....	1	1	1	1	20
Sea transport, freight...................................	2 208 ..	40	37	43	51	51	69	106	143
Sea transport, other.....................................	2 209 ..	63	62	56	103	157	186	259	230
Air transport, passenger...............................	2 211 ..	23	35	47	45	70	230	306	371
Air transport, freight....................................	2 212 ..	3	4	3	4	4	37	56	70
Air transport, other......................................	2 213 ..	94	122	146	167	205	151	83	88
Other transport, passenger...........................	2 215 ..	12	22	18	28	33	42	60	64
Other transport, freight................................	2 216 ..	376	525	637	787	1,021	726	968	1,490
Other transport, other..................................	2 217 ..	21	20	14	19	17	33	44	58
Transportation services, debit.........................	3 205 ..	**−627**	**−738**	**−835**	**−1,133**	**−1,500**	**−1,966**	**−2,404**	**−3,274**
Passenger..	3 850 ..	*−22*	*−26*	*−52*	*−93*	*−133*	*−148*	*−149*	*−184*
Freight..	3 851 ..	*−492*	*−654*	*−707*	*−954*	*−1,277*	*−1,683*	*−2,088*	*−2,915*
Other..	3 852 ..	*−113*	*−58*	*−76*	*−86*	*−90*	*−134*	*−167*	*−175*
Sea transport, passenger..............................	3 207 ..	....	....	....	−1	−1	−1	−1	−4
Sea transport, freight...................................	3 208 ..	−79	−136	−137	−183	−287	−469	−551	−795
Sea transport, other.....................................	3 209 ..	−21	−11	−17	−20	−29	−27	−52	−45
Air transport, passenger...............................	3 211 ..	−19	−13	−47	−89	−129	−138	−135	−160
Air transport, freight....................................	3 212 ..	−24	−29	−30	−41	−48	−72	−88	−123
Air transport, other......................................	3 213 ..	−23	−34	−49	−54	−51	−69	−77	−83
Other transport, passenger...........................	3 215 ..	−3	−13	−5	−3	−3	−10	−14	−20
Other transport, freight................................	3 216 ..	−389	−489	−540	−730	−942	−1,143	−1,449	−1,997
Other transport, other..................................	3 217 ..	−69	−13	−10	−12	−10	−37	−38	−47
Travel, credit..	2 236 ..	**359**	**362**	**335**	**449**	**503**	**1,052**	**1,308**	**1,467**
Business travel...	2 237 ..	116	59	23	34	50	514	828	1,015
Personal travel...	2 240 ..	243	303	312	415	453	538	481	452
Travel, debit...	3 236 ..	**−425**	**−449**	**−396**	**−479**	**−539**	**−925**	**−1,310**	**−1,535**
Business travel...	3 237 ..	−241	−245	−215	−282	−320	−640	−937	−1,078
Personal travel...	3 240 ..	−184	−204	−181	−197	−219	−285	−373	−457
Other services, credit.......................................	2 200 BA	**756**	**843**	**1,048**	**1,374**	**1,552**	**2,558**	**3,841**	**6,444**
Communications...	2 245 ..	145	135	167	238	296	674	1,102	1,107
Construction..	2 249 ..	30	59	65	106	120	195	264	285
Insurance..	2 253 ..	21	37	20	48	26	28	24	23
Financial...	2 260 ..	110	94	83	51	74	104	115	1,705
Computer and information.............................	2 262 ..	44	50	78	108	143	332	474	595
Royalties and licence fees.............................	2 266 ..	3	16	3	3	8	48	35	41
Other business services................................	2 268 ..	300	360	513	674	647	1,058	1,716	2,535
Personal, cultural, and recreational................	2 287 ..	76	67	98	118	214	92	83	106
Government, n.i.e...	2 291 ..	27	25	21	28	24	27	27	47
Other services, debit..	3 200 BA	**−941**	**−966**	**−1,107**	**−1,346**	**−1,840**	**−2,627**	**−3,314**	**−5,360**
Communications...	3 245 ..	−82	−91	−59	−86	−203	−361	−487	−578
Construction..	3 249 ..	−28	−24	−15	−32	−84	−197	−232	−509
Insurance..	3 253 ..	−41	−49	−79	−124	−109	−132	−142	−179
Financial...	3 260 ..	−98	−76	−83	−83	−117	−160	−228	−1,609
Computer and information.............................	3 262 ..	−29	−34	−27	−45	−83	−351	−422	−457
Royalties and licence fees.............................	3 266 ..	−45	−60	−85	−80	−108	−173	−236	−242
Other business services................................	3 268 ..	−499	−509	−643	−750	−943	−1,053	−1,346	−1,559
Personal, cultural, and recreational................	3 287 ..	−74	−83	−82	−101	−143	−108	−94	−105
Government, n.i.e...	3 291 ..	−45	−40	−34	−45	−50	−93	−126	−122

Table 2 (Continued). STANDARD PRESENTATION, 2000–2007

(Millions of U.S. dollars)

	Code	2000	2001	2002	2003	2004	2005	2006	2007
C. INCOME	4 300	**−285**	**−282**	**−459**	**−705**	**−3,149**	**−2,900**	**−4,079**	**−5,788**
Total credit	2 300	*325*	*455*	*413*	*372*	*433*	*1,533*	*2,176*	*3,267*
Total debit	3 300	*−610*	*−737*	*−872*	*−1,077*	*−3,582*	*−4,432*	*−6,255*	*−9,055*
Compensation of employees, credit	2 310	**94**	**112**	**136**	**110**	**113**	**954**	**1,165**	**1,618**
Compensation of employees, debit	3 310	**−5**	**−4**	**−6**	**−7**	**−5**	**−24**	**−42**	**−52**
Investment income, credit	2 320	**231**	**343**	**277**	**262**	**320**	**579**	**1,012**	**1,649**
Direct investment income	2 330	8	15	11	11	9	−76	−21	67
Dividends and distributed branch profits	2 332	6	14	11	10	5	....	5	46
Reinvested earnings and undistributed branch profits	2 333	....	....	....	....	....	−78	−33	....
Income on debt (interest)	2 334	2	1	....	1	4	1	7	21
Portfolio investment income	2 339	103	178	184	173	230	488	589	1,131
Income on equity	2 340	5	3	3	....	1	9	21	102
Income on bonds and notes	2 350	....	152	144	103	32	464	563	1,029
Income on money market instruments	2 360	98	23	37	70	197	15	4	....
Other investment income	2 370	120	150	82	78	81	167	444	451
Investment income, debit	3 320	**−605**	**−733**	**−866**	**−1,070**	**−3,577**	**−4,409**	**−6,213**	**−9,003**
Direct investment income	3 330	−72	−117	−197	−254	−2,594	−2,926	−4,164	−6,105
Dividends and distributed branch profits	3 332	−59	−108	−186	−242	−707	−1,369	−733	−2,926
Reinvested earnings and undistributed branch profits	3 333	....	....	....	....	−1,805	−1,447	−3,354	−2,971
Income on debt (interest)	3 334	−13	−9	−11	−12	−82	−110	−77	−208
Portfolio investment income	3 339	−74	−105	−181	−261	−340	−574	−718	−882
Income on equity	3 340	....	−4	−3	−1	−10	−191	−123	−216
Income on bonds and notes	3 350	−69	−101	−178	−260	−327	−384	−595	−666
Income on money market instruments	3 360	−5	....	....	....	−3	....	....	....
Other investment income	3 370	−459	−511	−488	−555	−643	−909	−1,331	−2,016
D. CURRENT TRANSFERS	4 379	**860**	**1,143**	**1,536**	**1,861**	**3,697**	**4,449**	**6,125**	**6,716**
Credit	2 379	**1,079**	**1,417**	**1,808**	**2,200**	**4,188**	**5,056**	**6,995**	**9,838**
General government	2 380	99	252	298	264	213	190	367	1,283
Other sectors	2 390	980	1,165	1,510	1,936	3,975	4,866	6,628	8,555
Workers' remittances	2 391	2	4	7	14	18	3,754	5,509	6,834
Other current transfers	2 392	978	1,161	1,503	1,922	3,957	1,112	1,119	1,721
Debit	3 379	**−219**	**−274**	**−272**	**−339**	**−491**	**−607**	**−870**	**−3,122**
General government	3 380	−29	−31	−17	−41	−56	−107	−102	−1,588
Other sectors	3 390	−190	−243	−255	−298	−435	−500	−767	−1,534
Workers' remittances	3 391	−1	−1	....	−1	−1	−4	−6	−289
Other current transfers	3 392	−189	−242	−255	−297	−434	−496	−761	−1,245
CAPITAL AND FINANCIAL ACCOUNT	4 996	**1,230**	**1,498**	**2,381**	**3,600**	**5,289**	**7,891**	**12,263**	**23,300**
CAPITAL ACCOUNT	4 994	**36**	**95**	**93**	**213**	**643**	**731**	**−34**	**1,126**
Total credit	2 994	*37*	*108*	*100*	*223*	*669*	*829*	*925*	*1,683*
Total debit	3 994	*−1*	*−13*	*−7*	*−10*	*−26*	*−98*	*−959*	*−557*
Capital transfers, credit	2 400	**37**	**108**	**100**	**223**	**669**	**811**	**860**	**1,365**
General government	2 401	35	95	80	115	549	478	569	948
Debt forgiveness	2 402	....	23	....	115	549	....	....	....
Other capital transfers	2 410	35	72	80	....	....	478	569	948
Other sectors	2 430	2	13	20	108	120	333	291	417
Migrants' transfers	2 431	....	....	....	....	1	25	44	81
Debt forgiveness	2 432	....	12	16	95	90	24	18	3
Other capital transfers	2 440	2	1	4	13	29	285	229	333
Capital transfers, debit	3 400	**−1**	**−13**	**−7**	**−10**	**−26**	**−80**	**−897**	**−384**
General government	3 401	....	−11	....	....	....	....	−750	−95
Debt forgiveness	3 402	....	−11	....	....	....	....	−750	−95
Other capital transfers	3 410	....	....	....	....	....	....	....	....
Other sectors	3 430	−1	−2	−7	−10	−26	−80	−147	−289
Migrants' transfers	3 431	....	....	−1	....	−2	−6	−8	−10
Debt forgiveness	3 432	....	....	....	....	....	....	....	....
Other capital transfers	3 440	−1	−2	−6	−10	−24	−74	−139	−279
Nonproduced nonfinancial assets, credit	2 480	....	....	....	....	....	**18**	**65**	**318**
Nonproduced nonfinancial assets, debit	3 480	....	....	....	....	....	**−18**	**−62**	**−173**

Table 2 (Continued). STANDARD PRESENTATION, 2000–2007

(Millions of U.S. dollars)

	Code	2000	2001	2002	2003	2004	2005	2006	2007
FINANCIAL ACCOUNT	4 995	1,194	1,403	2,288	3,387	4,646	7,160	12,297	22,174
A. DIRECT INVESTMENT	4 500	1,048	1,174	1,128	1,805	6,447	6,512	10,971	9,559
Direct investment abroad	4 505	11	17	−16	−39	−70	30	−422	67
Equity capital	4 510	11	17	−16	−39	−70	−8	−269	−41
Claims on affiliated enterprises	4 515	11	17	−16	−39	−70	−8	−269	−135
Liabilities to affiliated enterprises	4 520	....	....	....	....	....			94
Reinvested earnings	4 525	....	....	....	....	....	78	33	....
Other capital	4 530	....	....	....	....	....	−39	−186	108
Claims on affiliated enterprises	4 535	....	....	....	....	....	−39	−186	9
Liabilities to affiliated enterprises	4 540	....	....	....	....	....	....	....	99
Direct investment in Romania	4 555	1,037	1,157	1,144	1,844	6,517	6,482	11,393	9,492
Equity capital	4 560	933	1,023	931	1,366	3,858	3,343	5,245	1,319
Claims on direct investors	4 565	....	....	....	....	....	....	....	−9
Liabilities to direct investors	4 570	933	1,023	931	1,366	3,858	3,343	5,245	1,328
Reinvested earnings	4 575	....	....	....	....	1,805	1,447	3,354	2,971
Other capital	4 580	104	134	213	478	854	1,692	2,795	5,202
Claims on direct investors	4 585	....	....	....	....	....	−384	−58	−395
Liabilities to direct investors	4 590	104	134	213	478	854	2,077	2,852	5,597
B. PORTFOLIO INVESTMENT	4 600	101	575	382	578	−531	949	−239	266
Assets	4 602	28	−8	....	9	−559	−140	−828	−215
Equity securities	4 610	31	−7	....	14	−559	−136	−390	−147
Monetary authorities	4 611	....	....	....	....	....	....	....	....
General government	4 612	....	....	....	....	....	....	....	....
Banks	4 613	6	−2	....	....	−546	....	−18	−32
Other sectors	4 614	25	−5	....	14	−13	−136	−372	−115
Debt securities	4 619	−3	−1	....	−5	....	−3	−438	−68
Bonds and notes	4 620	−3	−1	....	−5	....	−6	−290	14
Monetary authorities	4 621	....	....	....	....	....	....	....	....
General government	4 622	−3	−1	....	....	....	....	....	....
Banks	4 623	....	....	....	−5	....	338	29	27
Other sectors	4 624	....	....	....	....	....	−344	−319	−13
Money market instruments	4 630	....	....	....	....	....	2	−148	−82
Monetary authorities	4 631	....	....	....	....	....	....	....	....
General government	4 632	....	....	....	....	....	....	....	....
Banks	4 633	....	....	....	....	....	....	....	....
Other sectors	4 634	....	....	....	....	....	2	−148	−82
Liabilities	4 652	73	583	382	569	28	1,089	589	481
Equity securities	4 660	58	8	21	69	111	229	301	746
Banks	4 663	....	....	....	....	....	2	−4	59
Other sectors	4 664	58	8	21	69	111	227	304	687
Debt securities	4 669	15	575	361	500	−83	860	289	−265
Bonds and notes	4 670	20	582	358	497	−112	858	303	−371
Monetary authorities	4 671	....	−275	....	....	....	....	....	....
General government	4 672	259	655	352	608	22	240	72	−251
Banks	4 673	−34	−2	−3	−5	40	604	381	−119
Other sectors	4 674	−205	204	9	−106	−174	14	−150	−1
Money market instruments	4 680	−5	−7	3	3	29	2	−15	106
Monetary authorities	4 681	....	....	3	3	29	....	....	....
General government	4 682	....	....	....	....	....	2	....	106
Banks	4 683	....	....	....	....	....	....	....	....
Other sectors	4 684	−5	−7	....	....	....	....	−15	....
C. FINANCIAL DERIVATIVES	4 910	....	....	....	....	....	−26	−108	−315
Monetary authorities	4 911	....	....	....	....	....	....	....	....
General government	4 912	....	....	....	....	....	....	....	....
Banks	4 913	....	....	....	....	....	−34	−103	−300
Other sectors	4 914	....	....	....	....	....	7	−5	−15
Assets	4 900	....	....	....	....	....	36	48	186
Monetary authorities	4 901	....	....	....	....	....	....	....	....
General government	4 902	....	....	....	....	....	....	....	....
Banks	4 903	....	....	....	....	....	28	42	99
Other sectors	4 904	....	....	....	....	....	7	6	87
Liabilities	4 905	....	....	....	....	....	−62	−156	−501
Monetary authorities	4 906	....	....	....	....	....	....	....	....
General government	4 907	....	....	....	....	....	....	....	....
Banks	4 908	....	....	....	....	....	−62	−145	−399
Other sectors	4 909	....	....	....	....	....	....	−11	−102

Table 2 (Concluded). STANDARD PRESENTATION, 2000–2007

(Millions of U.S. dollars)

	Code	2000	2001	2002	2003	2004	2005	2006	2007
D. OTHER INVESTMENT	4 700	**973**	**1,138**	**2,580**	**2,137**	**4,748**	**6,502**	**8,109**	**18,853**
Assets	4 703	−407	−44	692	72	−212	−1,078	−1,323	−1,343
Trade credits	4 706	−67	50	169	−44	−97	101	506	−468
General government	4 707	−81	−50	−43	−46	−37	−3	753	217
of which: Short-term	4 709	....	....	....	....	....	....	....	....
Other sectors	4 710	14	100	212	2	−60	104	−246	−685
of which: Short-term	4 712	20	98	166	−16	−55	109	−311	−781
Loans	4 714	1	−1	28	−31	29	−684	−1,131	−977
Monetary authorities	4 715	....	....	....	....	....	....	....	....
of which: Short-term	4 718	....	....	....	....	....	....	....	....
General government	4 719	....	....	−5	....	....	....	....	....
of which: Short-term	4 721	....	....	....	....	....	....	....	....
Banks	4 722	−14	−3	24	−9	28	29	−27	−132
of which: Short-term	4 724	14	−4	8	1	....	−1	−27	−53
Other sectors	4 725	15	2	9	−22	1	−713	−1,104	−845
of which: Short-term	4 727	....	....	4	....	23	−706	−939	−826
Currency and deposits	4 730	−311	−134	501	134	−148	−480	−659	99
Monetary authorities	4 731	....	....	....	....	....	....	....	....
General government	4 732	....	....	....	....	....	....	....	....
Banks	4 733	−311	−134	525	234	−60	−204	−314	18
Other sectors	4 734	....	....	−24	−100	−88	−276	−345	81
Other assets	4 736	−30	41	−6	13	4	−14	−39	3
Monetary authorities	4 737	....	....	....	−1	....	−11	....	−13
of which: Short-term	4 739	....	....	....	....	....	....	....	....
General government	4 740	−1	6	7	10	15	−12	5	−29
of which: Short-term	4 742	−1	6	7	10	15	2	5	....
Banks	4 743	−29	35	−13	4	−11	−23	−92	64
of which: Short-term	4 745	−29	35	−13	4	−11	−1	−37	21
Other sectors	4 746	....	....	....	....	....	32	47	−19
of which: Short-term	4 748	....	....	....	....	....	34	40	−22
Liabilities	4 753	**1,380**	**1,182**	**1,888**	**2,065**	**4,960**	**7,579**	**9,431**	**20,196**
Trade credits	4 756	−26	73	100	−135	53	620	1,361	1,729
General government	4 757	−12	−16	−14	−14	−27	−1	−46	−29
of which: Short-term	4 759	....	....	....	....	....	....	....	....
Other sectors	4 760	−14	89	114	−121	80	621	1,407	1,758
of which: Short-term	4 762	−6	33	66	−29	118	800	1,660	1,710
Loans	4 764	1,397	970	1,611	1,767	4,041	4,884	7,761	6,900
Monetary authorities	4 765	6	−51	−89	120	−72	−252	−166	−105
of which: Use of Fund credit and loans from the Fund	4 766	20	−51	11	120	−171	−152	−166	−105
of which: Short-term	4 768	−14	....	−100	....	99	−100	....	....
General government	4 769	702	366	569	903	1,042	569	74	−58
of which: Short-term	4 771	....	....	....	....	....	....	....	3
Banks	4 772	−118	−2	54	472	1,445	2,228	3,916	989
of which: Short-term	4 774	−7	3	−2	94	85	396	2,425	−1,753
Other sectors	4 775	807	657	1,077	272	1,626	2,339	3,938	6,074
of which: Short-term	4 777	−11	58	202	381	1,018	471	2,306	2,695
Currency and deposits	4 780	11	143	122	463	616	882	1,063	7,652
Monetary authorities	4 781	....	....	....	....	....	....	....	185
General government	4 782	....	....	....	....	....	....	....	201
Banks	4 783	11	143	122	463	616	882	1,063	7,266
Other sectors	4 784	....	....	....	....	....	....	....	....
Other liabilities	4 786	−2	−4	55	−30	250	1,193	−754	3,915
Monetary authorities	4 787	....	....	....	....	....	....	−3	....
of which: Short-term	4 789	....	....	....	....	....	....	−3	....
General government	4 790	−9	−30	−90	....	....	−1	....	....
of which: Short-term	4 792	−9	....	....	....	....	....	....	....
Banks	4 793	....	18	133	−17	268	724	−100	3,138
of which: Short-term	4 795	....	....	....	....	....	70	−10	−23
Other sectors	4 796	7	8	12	−13	−18	470	−651	777
of which: Short-term	4 798	7	8	12	−13	−18	488	−584	796
E. RESERVE ASSETS	4 802	**−928**	**−1,484**	**−1,802**	**−1,134**	**−6,018**	**−6,777**	**−6,435**	**−6,189**
Monetary gold	4 812	−2	−5	−2	....	....	....	....	....
Special drawing rights	4 811	9	−6	5	2	....	....	....	....
Reserve position in the Fund	4 810	....	....	....	....	....	....	....	....
Foreign exchange	4 803	−935	−1,473	−1,805	−1,136	−6,018	−6,776	−6,436	−6,189
Other claims	4 813	....	....	....	....	....	....	....	....
NET ERRORS AND OMISSIONS	4 998	**125**	**731**	**−856**	**−289**	**1,093**	**612**	**521**	**−164**

Table 3. INTERNATIONAL INVESTMENT POSITION (End-period stocks), 2000–2007

(Millions of U.S. dollars)

	Code	2000	2001	2002	2003	2004	2005	2006	2007
ASSETS	8 995 C.	**9,631**	**11,550**	**13,447**	**15,755**	**24,142**	**30,422**	**42,138**	**54,391**
Direct investment abroad	8 505 ..	**136**	**116**	**144**	**208**	**273**	**214**	**880**	**915**
Equity capital and reinvested earnings	8 506 ..	136	116	144	208	243	150	514	618
Claims on affiliated enterprises	8 507 ..	136	116	144	208	243	150	514	717
Liabilities to affiliated enterprises	8 508 ..	....	....	....	....	....	....	....	−100
Other capital	8 530 ..	....	....	....	....	30	63	365	298
Claims on affiliated enterprises	8 535 ..	....	....	....	... .	34	67	368	403
Liabilities to affiliated enterprises	8 540 ..	....	....	....	....	−4	−4	−3	−105
Portfolio investment	8 602 ..	**6**	**11**	**22**	**13**	**607**	**725**	**1,663**	**2,106**
Equity securities	8 610 ..	....	....	18	10	30	174	594	822
Monetary authorities	8 611 ..	....	....	....	....	....	....	....	....
General government	8 612 ..	....	....	....	....	....	....	....	....
Banks	8 613 ..	....	....	....	3	10	17	38	77
Other sectors	8 614 ..	....	....	18	7	20	157	556	745
Debt securities	8 619 ..	6	11	4	4	577	550	1,069	1,284
Bonds and notes	8 620 ..	6	11	4	4	573	546	910	1,006
Monetary authorities	8 621 ..	....	....	....	....	....	....	....	....
General government	8 622 ..	....	....	....	....	....	....	....	....
Banks	8 623 ..	....	....	1	....	572	189	179	179
Other sectors	8 624 ..	5	10	3	3	1	357	731	826
Money market instruments	8 630 ..	....	....	....	....	4	4	160	278
Monetary authorities	8 631 ..	....	....	....	....	....	....	....	....
General government	8 632 ..	....	....	....	....	....	....	....	....
Banks	8 633 ..	....	....	....	....	....	....	....	....
Other sectors	8 634 ..	....	....	....	....	4	4	160	278
Financial derivatives	8 900 ..	**....**	**....**	**....**	**....**	**....**	**−34**	**−86**	**−295**
Monetary authorities	8 901 ..	....	....	....	....	....	....	....	....
General government	8 902 ..	....	....	....	....	....	....	....	....
Banks	8 903 ..	....	....	....	....	....	−27	−74	−188
Other sectors	8 904 ..	....	....	....	....	....	−7	−12	−107
Other investment	8 703 ..	**6,099**	**6,561**	**5,975**	**6,083**	**6,978**	**7,914**	**9,474**	**11,709**
Trade credits	8 706 ..	3,446	3,403	3,235	3,324	3,785	3,878	3,288	3,718
General government	8 707 ..	2,814	2,872	2,916	2,961	3,402	3,446	2,702	2,585
of which: Short-term	8 709 ..	....	....	....	....	....	....	....	....
Other sectors	8 710 ..	632	531	319	363	383	432	586	1,133
of which: Short-term	8 712 ..	*455*	*359*	*193*	*249*	*333*	*359*	*559*	*1,133*
Loans	8 714 ..	172	173	160	214	201	850	2,131	3,364
Monetary authorities	8 715 ..	....	....	....	....	....	....	....	....
of which: Short-term	8 718 ..	....	....	....	....	....	....	....	....
General government	8 719 ..	....	....	....	....	....	....	....	....
of which: Short-term	8 721 ..	....	....	....	....	....	....	....	....
Banks	8 722 ..	120	123	119	151	135	98	142	257
of which: Short-term	8 724 ..	*15*	*19*	*15*	*15*	*16*	*24*	*57*	*80*
Other sectors	8 725 ..	52	50	41	63	65	752	1,989	3,107
of which: Short-term	8 727 ..	*43*	*43*	*39*	*39*	*19*	*705*	*1,760*	*2,831*
Currency and deposits	8 730 ..	1,425	1,946	1,527	1,475	1,921	2,085	2,841	3,416
Monetary authorities	8 731 ..	....	....	....	....	....	....	....	....
General government	8 732 ..	3	5	5	5	5	5	6	6
Banks	8 733 ..	1,394	1,485	1,042	903	1,074	1,091	1,436	1,742
Other sectors	8 734 ..	27	456	480	567	842	989	1,400	1,668
Other assets	8 736 ..	1,057	1,039	1,054	1,069	1,071	1,101	1,213	1,210
Monetary authorities	8 737 ..	10	10	10	15	15	24	27	42
of which: Short-term	8 739 ..	....	....	....	....	....	....	....	....
General government	8 740 ..	989	995	1,000	1,004	1,007	989	1,039	994
of which: Short-term	8 742 ..	*253*	*247*	*239*	*229*	*217*	*205*	*228*	*152*
Banks	8 743 ..	58	34	44	50	3	24	121	122
of which: Short-term	8 745 ..	*58*	*34*	*44*	*50*	*3*	*2*	*44*	*78*
Other sectors	8 746 ..	....	....	....	....	46	64	26	52
of which: Short-term	8 748 ..	....	....	....	....	*40*	*57*	*25*	*52*
Reserve assets	8 802 ..	**3,390**	**4,861**	**7,306**	**9,450**	**16,284**	**21,604**	**30,207**	**39,957**
Monetary gold	8 812 ..	920	939	1,180	1,410	1,481	1,728	2,140	2,762
Special drawing rights	8 811 ..	1	7	2	....	1	1	....	1
Reserve position in the Fund	8 810 ..	....	....	....	....	....	....	....	....
Foreign exchange	8 803 ..	2,469	3,916	6,123	8,040	14,802	19,875	28,066	37,194
Other claims	8 813 ..	....	....	....	....	....	....	....	....

Table 3 (Concluded). INTERNATIONAL INVESTMENT POSITION (End-period stocks), 2000–2007

(Millions of U.S. dollars)

	Code	2000	2001	2002	2003	2004	2005	2006	2007
LIABILITIES	8 995 D.	**18,022**	**20,883**	**23,093**	**32,168**	**46,594**	**57,785**	**90,384**	**131,857**
Direct investment in Romania	8 555	**6,951**	**8,350**	**7,799**	**12,187**	**20,523**	**25,893**	**45,454**	**60,822**
Equity capital and reinvested earnings	8 556	6,229	7,252	5,764	8,946	16,384	20,693	35,582	44,609
Claims on direct investors	8 557	....	....	....	....	....	....	....	−8
Liabilities to direct investors	8 558	6,229	7,252	5,764	8,946	16,384	20,693	35,582	44,616
Other capital	8 580	722	1,097	2,035	3,241	4,139	5,200	9,872	16,213
Claims on direct investors	8 585	....	....	−124	−16	−46	−444	−581	−1,076
Liabilities to direct investors	8 590	722	1,097	2,159	3,258	4,185	5,644	10,454	17,290
Portfolio investment	8 652	**1,635**	**2,188**	**3,245**	**4,503**	**4,832**	**5,251**	**6,292**	**7,428**
Equity securities	8 660	487	495	516	700	877	984	1,525	2,527
Banks	8 663	....	....	....	....	19	18	23	96
Other sectors	8 664	487	495	516	700	858	966	1,503	2,431
Debt securities	8 669	1,148	1,693	2,729	3,803	3,954	4,267	4,767	4,901
Bonds and notes	8 670	1,135	1,687	2,720	3,787	3,881	4,201	4,709	4,704
Monetary authorities	8 671	286	....	....	....	....	....	....	....
General government	8 672	752	1,391	1,946	3,089	3,304	3,100	3,451	3,585
Banks	8 673	4	2	....	4	128	770	1,166	1,114
Other sectors	8 674	93	294	774	694	449	331	91	5
Money market instruments	8 680	13	7	9	15	74	66	58	198
Monetary authorities	8 681	....	....	....	....	....	....	....	....
General government	8 682	....	....	....	....	25	23	26	162
Banks	8 683	....	....	....	....	....	....	....	....
Other sectors	8 684	13	7	9	15	49	43	32	36
Financial derivatives	8 905	....	....	....	....	....	**−59**	**−203**	**−761**
Monetary authorities	8 906	....	....	....	....	....	....	....	....
General government	8 907	....	....	....	....	....	....	....	....
Banks	8 908	....	....	....	....	....	−58	−192	−640
Other sectors	8 909	....	....	....	....	....	....	−12	−121
Other investment	8 753	**9,436**	**10,345**	**12,049**	**15,478**	**21,240**	**26,700**	**38,841**	**64,368**
Trade credits	8 756	836	846	863	962	1,083	2,108	3,663	5,238
General government	8 757	188	124	77	79	56	82	44	17
of which: Short-term	8 759	....	....	....	....	....	....	....	....
Other sectors	8 760	648	722	785	883	1,027	2,026	3,619	5,221
of which: Short-term	8 762	*358*	*390*	*456*	*518*	*692*	*1,707*	*3,245*	*4,703*
Loans	8 764	8,180	8,914	10,435	13,135	17,907	20,484	29,718	41,559
Monetary authorities	8 765	453	387	428	595	443	261	104	....
of which: Use of Fund credit and loans from the Fund	8 766	*453*	*387*	*428*	*595*	*443*	*261*	*104*	....
of which: Short-term	8 768	....	....	....	....	....	....	....	....
General government	8 769	4,297	4,641	5,474	6,909	8,860	8,776	9,440	10,342
of which: Short-term	8 771	....	....	....	....	....	....	....	....
Banks	8 772	244	240	336	847	2,505	4,367	8,993	11,126
of which: Short-term	8 774	*18*	*21*	*19*	*82*	*212*	*545*	*3,047*	*1,328*
Other sectors	8 775	3,186	3,646	4,196	4,783	6,098	7,080	11,181	20,091
of which: Short-term	8 777	*24*	*74*	*276*	*303*	*1,130*	*1,429*	*3,910*	*7,238*
Currency and deposits	8 780	353	510	664	1,294	2,204	3,546	5,353	16,634
Monetary authorities	8 781	100	100	....	....	100	....	....	213
General government	8 782	....	....	....	....	....	....	....	44
Banks	8 783	253	410	664	1,294	2,104	3,546	5,353	16,377
Other sectors	8 784	....	....	....	....	....	....	....	....
Other liabilities	8 786	67	75	87	87	46	562	108	937
Monetary authorities	8 787	36	36	37	38	38	37	35	39
of which: Short-term	8 789	....	....	....	....	....	....	....	....
General government	8 790	1	1	....	....	1	....	1	1
of which: Short-term	8 792	*1*	*1*	....	....	*1*	....	*1*	*1*
Banks	8 793	....	....	....	....	7	73	72	39
of which: Short-term	8 795	....	....	....	....	*7*	*73*	*72*	*39*
Other sectors	8 796	30	38	50	48	....	450	....	859
of which: Short-term	8 798	*30*	*38*	*50*	*48*	....	*450*	....	*857*
NET INTERNATIONAL INVESTMENT POSITION	8 995	**−8,391**	**−9,333**	**−9,645**	**−16,413**	**−22,452**	**−27,363**	**−48,246**	**−77,465**
Conversion rates: Romanian lei per U.S. dollar (end of period)	0 102	2.593	3.160	3.350	3.260	2.907	3.108	2.568	2.456

Table 1. ANALYTIC PRESENTATION, 2000–2007

(Millions of U.S. dollars)

	Code	2000	2001	2002	2003	2004	2005	2006	2007
A. Current Account[1]	4 993 Z.	**46,839**	**33,935**	**29,280**	**35,410**	**59,512**	**84,409**	**94,340**	**76,241**
Goods: exports f.o.b.	2 100 ..	105,033	101,884	111,204	135,929	183,207	243,798	303,550	354,401
Goods: imports f.o.b.	3 100 ..	−44,862	−53,764	−64,323	−76,070	−97,382	−125,434	−164,281	−223,486
Balance on Goods	4 100 ..	*60,172*	*48,121*	*46,881*	*59,860*	*85,825*	*118,364*	*139,269*	*130,915*
Services: credit	2 200 ..	9,565	11,441	13,987	16,229	20,595	24,970	31,102	39,416
Services: debit	3 200 ..	−16,230	−20,572	−23,937	−27,122	−33,287	−38,865	−44,839	−59,187
Balance on Goods and Services	4 991 ..	*53,506*	*38,990*	*36,931*	*48,966*	*73,133*	*104,470*	*125,533*	*111,144*
Income: credit	2 300 ..	4,753	6,800	5,795	11,057	11,998	17,382	29,504	46,784
Income: debit	3 300 ..	−11,489	−11,038	−12,773	−24,228	−24,769	−36,405	−59,160	−78,180
Balance on Goods, Services, and Income	4 992 ..	*46,770*	*34,752*	*29,953*	*35,795*	*60,361*	*85,446*	*95,877*	*79,748*
Current transfers: credit	2 379 Z.	807	744	1,490	2,537	3,467	4,490	6,403	8,423
Current transfers: debit	3 379 ..	−738	−1,561	−2,164	−2,922	−4,317	−5,528	−7,940	−11,929
B. Capital Account[1]	4 994 Z.	**10,676**	**−9,378**	**−16,579**	**−993**	**−1,624**	**−12,764**	**191**	**−10,224**
Capital account: credit	2 994 Z.	11,543	2,125	2,380	616	862	678	1,023	1,393
Capital account: debit	3 994 ..	−867	−11,503	−18,959	−1,609	−2,486	−13,442	−832	−11,617
Total, Groups A Plus B	4 981 ..	*57,515*	*24,557*	*12,701*	*34,417*	*57,888*	*71,645*	*94,530*	*66,017*
C. Financial Account[1]	4 995 W.	**−34,295**	**−3,732**	**2,101**	**3,024**	**−5,128**	**1,145**	**3,194**	**96,119**
Direct investment abroad	4 505 ..	−3,177	−2,533	−3,966	−9,727	−13,782	−12,767	−23,151	−45,916
Direct investment in the Russian Federation	4 555 Z.	2,714	2,748	3,377	7,958	15,444	12,886	29,701	55,073
Portfolio investment assets	4 602 ..	−411	77	−1,047	−2,180	−3,820	−10,666	6,248	−9,986
Equity securities	4 610 ..	−40	−60	120	−47	−25	−733	116	−3,435
Debt securities	4 619 ..	−371	137	−1,167	−2,133	−3,794	−9,933	6,131	−6,551
Portfolio investment liabilities	4 652 Z.	−12,808	−730	5,996	−2,329	4,443	−713	9,455	16,854
Equity securities	4 660 ..	150	542	3,921	422	270	−100	6,480	18,844
Debt securities	4 669 Z.	−12,959	−1,272	2,074	−2,750	4,173	−613	2,975	−1,990
Financial derivatives	4 910 ..	....	....	26	640	−100	−233	−99	332
Financial derivatives assets	4 900 ..	....	....	98	1,017	758	858	1,242	2,762
Financial derivatives liabilities	4 905 ..	....	....	−72	−377	−857	−1,091	−1,342	−2,430
Other investment assets	4 703 ..	−17,525	149	−4,743	−15,886	−26,644	−33,208	−49,299	−59,637
Monetary authorities	4 701 ..	....	−266	1,034	467	306	205	175	−477
General government	4 704 ..	−1,617	10,099	15,847	−299	−237	11,478	−1,338	7,242
Banks	4 705 ..	−3,332	−1,652	−1,355	−837	−1,964	−9,905	−24,034	−22,678
Other sectors	4 728 ..	−12,577	−8,033	−20,269	−15,216	−24,748	−34,987	−24,102	−43,724
Other investment liabilities	4 753 W.	−3,087	−3,444	2,457	24,547	19,331	45,846	30,340	139,398
Monetary authorities	4 753 WA	155	1,908	−21	1,636	1,909	6,309	−7,331	882
General government	4 753 ZB	−2,875	−7,480	−9,435	−3,705	−5,485	−19,244	−27,053	−3,558
Banks	4 753 ZC	568	1,839	2,520	11,546	6,709	18,087	48,272	51,768
Other sectors	4 753 ZD	−935	289	9,395	15,070	16,197	40,693	16,452	90,306
Total, Groups A Through C	4 983 ..	*23,221*	*20,824*	*14,802*	*37,441*	*52,760*	*72,789*	*97,724*	*162,136*
D. Net Errors and Omissions	4 998 ..	**−9,297**	**−9,558**	**−7,594**	**−9,179**	**−5,870**	**−7,821**	**9,741**	**−13,208**
Total, Groups A Through D	4 984 ..	*13,923*	*11,266*	*7,208*	*28,262*	*46,890*	*64,968*	*107,466*	*148,928*
E. Reserves and Related Items	4 802 A.	**−13,923**	**−11,266**	**−7,208**	**−28,262**	**−46,890**	**−64,968**	**−107,466**	**−148,928**
Reserve assets	4 802 ..	−16,009	−8,211	−6,841	−26,365	−45,236	−61,461	−107,466	−148,928
Use of Fund credit and loans	4 766 ..	−2,899	−3,829	−1,493	−1,897	−1,655	−3,506	....	....
Exceptional financing	4 920 ..	4,985	773	1,126	....	....	....	....	....
Conversion rates: rubles per U.S. dollar	0 101 ..	**28.129**	**29.169**	**31.348**	**30.692**	**28.814**	**28.284**	**27.191**	**25.581**

[1] Excludes components that have been classified in the categories of Group E.

Table 2. STANDARD PRESENTATION, 2000–2007

(Millions of U.S. dollars)

	Code	2000	2001	2002	2003	2004	2005	2006	2007
CURRENT ACCOUNT	4 993 ..	**46,839**	**33,935**	**29,280**	**35,410**	**59,512**	**84,409**	**94,340**	**76,241**
A. GOODS	4 100 ..	**60,172**	**48,121**	**46,881**	**59,860**	**85,825**	**118,364**	**139,269**	**130,915**
Credit	2 100 ..	**105,033**	**101,884**	**111,204**	**135,929**	**183,207**	**243,798**	**303,550**	**354,401**
General merchandise: exports f.o.b.	2 110 ..	99,117	96,452	105,905	128,888	177,556	236,193	294,880	342,059
Goods for processing: exports f.o.b.	2 150 ..	5,460	5,068	4,706	6,478	4,793	5,878	6,492	9,398
Repairs on goods	2 160 ..	148	69	313	205	371	849	673	465
Goods procured in ports by carriers	2 170 ..	308	296	280	358	487	878	1,505	2,480
Nonmonetary gold	2 180 ..	....	....	....	....	....	....	....	....
Debit	3 100 ..	**−44,862**	**−53,764**	**−64,323**	**−76,070**	**−97,382**	**−125,434**	**−164,281**	**−223,486**
General merchandise: imports f.o.b.	3 110 ..	−41,380	−50,374	−60,629	−72,097	−93,312	−120,419	−158,574	−216,280
Goods for processing: imports f.o.b.	3 150 ..	−2,394	−2,384	−2,495	−2,964	−2,790	−3,214	−3,885	−4,797
Repairs on goods	3 160 ..	−169	−191	−344	−312	−426	−609	−262	−271
Goods procured in ports by carriers	3 170 ..	−919	−815	−855	−697	−854	−1,192	−1,559	−2,138
Nonmonetary gold	3 180 ..	....	....	....	....	....	....	....	....
B. SERVICES	4 200 ..	**−6,665**	**−9,131**	**−9,950**	**−10,894**	**−12,693**	**−13,894**	**−13,737**	**−19,771**
Total credit	2 200 ..	*9,565*	*11,441*	*13,987*	*16,229*	*20,595*	*24,970*	*31,102*	*39,416*
Total debit	3 200 ..	*−16,230*	*−20,572*	*−23,937*	*−27,122*	*−33,287*	*−38,865*	*−44,839*	*−59,187*
Transportation services, credit	2 205 ..	**3,555**	**4,654**	**5,597**	**6,119**	**7,792**	**9,113**	**10,081**	**11,829**
Passenger	2 850 ..	....	*1,154*	*1,238*	*1,377*	*1,732*	*1,936*	*2,092*	*2,980*
Freight	2 851 ..	....	*2,016*	*2,470*	*2,660*	*3,598*	*4,256*	*4,669*	*5,156*
Other	2 852 ..	....	*1,483*	*1,889*	*2,082*	*2,462*	*2,921*	*3,320*	*3,693*
Sea transport, passenger	2 207 ..	....	1	1	1	1	1	....	1
Sea transport, freight	2 208 ..	....	746	804	820	1,041	1,171	1,042	1,016
Sea transport, other	2 209 ..	....	831	971	1,112	1,436	1,658	1,742	2,080
Air transport, passenger	2 211 ..	....	1,052	1,115	1,242	1,566	1,737	1,821	2,607
Air transport, freight	2 212 ..	....	410	514	518	718	881	1,093	1,234
Air transport, other	2 213 ..	....	349	612	610	640	880	1,154	1,061
Other transport, passenger	2 215 ..	....	102	122	135	165	198	270	372
Other transport, freight	2 216 ..	....	860	1,152	1,323	1,840	2,204	2,535	2,906
Other transport, other	2 217 ..	....	304	306	361	385	382	424	552
Transportation services, debit	3 205 ..	**−2,330**	**−2,979**	**−2,950**	**−3,103**	**−3,886**	**−5,137**	**−6,722**	**−9,348**
Passenger	3 850 ..	....	*−475*	*−444*	*−547*	*−797*	*−991*	*−1,366*	*−2,031*
Freight	3 851 ..	....	*−1,497*	*−1,489*	*−1,359*	*−1,784*	*−2,683*	*−3,693*	*−5,205*
Other	3 852 ..	....	*−1,007*	*−1,018*	*−1,197*	*−1,305*	*−1,462*	*−1,663*	*−2,111*
Sea transport, passenger	3 207 ..	....	−1	−1	−1	−2	−1	−2	−5
Sea transport, freight	3 208 ..	....	−622	−561	−475	−602	−926	−1,250	−1,774
Sea transport, other	3 209 ..	....	−454	−344	−451	−421	−477	−525	−663
Air transport, passenger	3 211 ..	....	−346	−285	−371	−579	−752	−1,057	−1,596
Air transport, freight	3 212 ..	....	−567	−626	−598	−843	−1,329	−1,880	−2,751
Air transport, other	3 213 ..	....	−342	−430	−494	−582	−704	−916	−1,176
Other transport, passenger	3 215 ..	....	−128	−158	−175	−216	−238	−307	−430
Other transport, freight	3 216 ..	....	−308	−303	−286	−339	−428	−563	−681
Other transport, other	3 217 ..	....	−211	−244	−252	−301	−280	−223	−271
Travel, credit	2 236 ..	**3,429**	**3,572**	**4,040**	**4,502**	**5,530**	**5,870**	**7,628**	**9,607**
Business travel	2 237 ..	1,402	1,402	1,434	1,450	1,936	2,379	3,809	4,929
Personal travel	2 240 ..	2,027	2,169	2,606	3,052	3,595	3,490	3,819	4,678
Travel, debit	3 236 ..	**−8,848**	**−9,285**	**−10,918**	**−12,880**	**−15,285**	**−17,434**	**−18,235**	**−22,259**
Business travel	3 237 ..	−1,824	−1,881	−2,437	−2,458	−2,273	−2,454	−2,405	−2,479
Personal travel	3 240 ..	−7,024	−7,404	−8,482	−10,422	−13,012	−14,980	−15,830	−19,780
Other services, credit	2 200 BA	**2,580**	**3,216**	**4,350**	**5,608**	**7,272**	**9,988**	**13,393**	**17,980**
Communications	2 245 ..	385	437	543	443	471	658	803	1,272
Construction	2 249 ..	170	737	781	1,050	1,577	2,209	3,050	3,450
Insurance	2 253 ..	35	72	114	148	242	323	377	379
Financial	2 260 ..	100	128	154	176	270	390	589	1,174
Computer and information	2 262 ..	59	128	150	175	256	422	632	1,097
Royalties and licence fees	2 266 ..	91	60	159	174	227	260	299	396
Other business services	2 268 ..	1,740	1,343	2,217	3,177	3,940	5,309	7,174	9,624
Personal, cultural, and recreational	2 287 ..	....	85	72	125	164	187	232	291
Government, n.i.e.	2 291 ..	....	227	160	140	126	230	237	297
Other services, debit	3 200 BA	**−5,052**	**−8,308**	**−10,068**	**−11,139**	**−14,117**	**−16,294**	**−19,882**	**−27,581**
Communications	3 245 ..	−288	−498	−550	−555	−691	−746	−917	−1,298
Construction	3 249 ..	−406	−1,801	−1,933	−2,459	−3,047	−4,034	−4,603	−6,454
Insurance	3 253 ..	−412	−384	−593	−774	−1,157	−698	−716	−846
Financial	3 260 ..	−36	−211	−247	−314	−695	−892	−904	−1,472
Computer and information	3 262 ..	−474	−557	−528	−458	−320	−482	−613	−956
Royalties and licence fees	3 266 ..	−69	−343	−374	−711	−1,094	−1,593	−2,002	−2,806
Other business services	3 268 ..	−3,367	−3,594	−5,020	−5,046	−5,732	−6,459	−8,548	−11,618
Personal, cultural, and recreational	3 287 ..	....	−166	−166	−188	−309	−440	−542	−753
Government, n.i.e.	3 291 ..	....	−754	−656	−635	−1,071	−950	−1,036	−1,377

Table 2 (Continued). STANDARD PRESENTATION, 2000–2007

(Millions of U.S. dollars)

	Code	2000	2001	2002	2003	2004	2005	2006	2007
C. INCOME	4 300	**−6,736**	**−4,238**	**−6,978**	**−13,171**	**−12,771**	**−19,023**	**−29,656**	**−31,396**
Total credit	2 300	*4,753*	*6,800*	*5,795*	*11,057*	*11,998*	*17,382*	*29,504*	*46,784*
Total debit	3 300	*−11,489*	*−11,038*	*−12,773*	*−24,228*	*−24,769*	*−36,405*	*−59,160*	*−78,180*
Compensation of employees, credit	2 310	**500**	**624**	**700**	**814**	**1,206**	**1,714**	**1,647**	**2,000**
Compensation of employees, debit	3 310	**−232**	**−493**	**−490**	**−958**	**−1,464**	**−2,921**	**−6,038**	**−9,884**
Investment income, credit	2 320	**4,253**	**6,176**	**5,096**	**10,243**	**10,792**	**15,668**	**27,858**	**44,784**
Direct investment income	2 330	62	599	730	6,338	6,336	8,092	12,357	20,038
Dividends and distributed branch profits	2 332	60	534	705	747	1,264	1,203	1,554	3,033
Reinvested earnings and undistributed branch profits	2 333	1	65	17	5,591	5,071	6,875	10,772	16,677
Income on debt (interest)	2 334	....	....	8	....	....	14	31	328
Portfolio investment income	2 339	120	106	144	430	388	546	777	1,051
Income on equity	2 340	1	3	15	92	102	53	156	242
Income on bonds and notes	2 350	119	104	130	339	286	493	621	809
Income on money market instruments	2 360	....	....	....	....	....	....	....	....
Other investment income	2 370	4,071	5,471	4,221	3,475	4,068	7,030	14,724	23,695
Investment income, debit	3 320	**−11,257**	**−10,544**	**−12,283**	**−23,270**	**−23,305**	**−33,484**	**−53,122**	**−68,296**
Direct investment income	3 330	−887	−1,493	−3,070	−12,521	−10,294	−19,483	−34,601	−43,195
Dividends and distributed branch profits	3 332	−365	−586	−2,007	−5,059	−4,453	−9,874	−19,562	−19,179
Reinvested earnings and undistributed branch profits	3 333	−95	−431	−683	−7,065	−5,330	−9,361	−14,716	−23,389
Income on debt (interest)	3 334	−428	−477	−379	−397	−511	−247	−323	−628
Portfolio investment income	3 339	−3,896	−2,988	−3,705	−4,831	−5,180	−4,472	−5,515	−7,005
Income on equity	3 340	....	−5	−597	−2,330	−2,401	−1,863	−2,712	−4,051
Income on bonds and notes	3 350	−3,896	−2,983	−3,109	−2,501	−2,779	−2,609	−2,804	−2,954
Income on money market instruments	3 360	....	....	....	....	....	....	....	....
Other investment income	3 370	−6,474	−6,063	−5,508	−5,918	−7,831	−9,530	−13,006	−18,096
D. CURRENT TRANSFERS	4 379	**69**	**−817**	**−674**	**−385**	**−850**	**−1,038**	**−1,537**	**−3,506**
Credit	2 379	**807**	**744**	**1,490**	**2,537**	**3,467**	**4,490**	**6,403**	**8,423**
General government	2 380	233	121	477	1,178	1,097	1,609	3,075	4,354
Other sectors	2 390	575	623	1,012	1,359	2,370	2,881	3,328	4,069
Workers' remittances	2 391	....	363	257	300	925	621	766	852
Other current transfers	2 392	575	260	755	1,059	1,445	2,260	2,562	3,217
Debit	3 379	**−738**	**−1,561**	**−2,164**	**−2,922**	**−4,317**	**−5,528**	**−7,940**	**−11,929**
General government	3 380	−284	−361	−255	−279	−351	−689	−1,042	−860
Other sectors	3 390	−454	−1,201	−1,908	−2,644	−3,966	−4,839	−6,899	−11,069
Workers' remittances	3 391	....	−421	−890	−1,306	−2,672	−3,051	−4,587	−6,942
Other current transfers	3 392	−454	−779	−1,018	−1,337	−1,294	−1,788	−2,311	−4,126
CAPITAL AND FINANCIAL ACCOUNT	4 996	**−37,542**	**−24,376**	**−21,686**	**−26,231**	**−53,642**	**−76,587**	**−104,081**	**−63,033**
CAPITAL ACCOUNT	4 994	**10,955**	**−9,356**	**−16,564**	**−993**	**−1,624**	**−12,764**	**191**	**−10,224**
Total credit	2 994	*11,822*	*2,147*	*2,395*	*616*	*862*	*678*	*1,023*	*1,393*
Total debit	3 994	*−867*	*−11,503*	*−18,959*	*−1,609*	*−2,486*	*−13,442*	*−832*	*−11,617*
Capital transfers, credit	2 400	**11,822**	**2,147**	**2,395**	**616**	**862**	**678**	**1,023**	**1,393**
General government	2 401	11,047	1,731	1,983	276	499	95	345	144
Debt forgiveness	2 402	11,035	1,722	1,958	276	499	2	170	....
Other capital transfers	2 410	12	8	26	....	....	94	174	144
Other sectors	2 430	775	416	411	339	364	583	678	1,249
Migrants' transfers	2 431	775	416	411	339	364	583	678	1,249
Debt forgiveness	2 432	....	....	....	....	....	....	....	....
Other capital transfers	2 440	....	....	....	....	....	....	....	....
Capital transfers, debit	3 400	**−867**	**−11,503**	**−18,959**	**−1,609**	**−2,486**	**−13,442**	**−832**	**−11,617**
General government	3 401	....	−10,594	−18,029	−640	−1,434	−12,426	−19	−9,749
Debt forgiveness	3 402	....	−10,594	−18,029	−640	−1,434	−12,426	−19	−9,749
Other capital transfers	3 410	....	....	....	....	....	....	....	....
Other sectors	3 430	−867	−908	−929	−969	−1,052	−1,017	−813	−1,868
Migrants' transfers	3 431	−867	−908	−929	−969	−1,052	−1,017	−813	−890
Debt forgiveness	3 432	....	....	....	....	....	....	....	....
Other capital transfers	3 440	....	....	....	....	....	....	....	−978
Nonproduced nonfinancial assets, credit	2 480	....	....	....	....	....	....	....	....
Nonproduced nonfinancial assets, debit	3 480	....	....	....	....	....	....	....	....

2008, International Monetary Fund: *Balance of Payments Statistics Yearbook*

Table 2 (Continued). STANDARD PRESENTATION, 2000–2007

(Millions of U.S. dollars)

	Code	2000	2001	2002	2003	2004	2005	2006	2007
FINANCIAL ACCOUNT..........................	4 995 ..	−48,497	−15,021	−5,122	−25,238	−52,018	−63,823	−104,272	−52,809
A. DIRECT INVESTMENT........................	4 500 ..	−463	216	−588	−1,769	1,662	118	6,550	9,158
Direct investment abroad................	4 505 ..	−3,177	−2,533	−3,966	−9,727	−13,782	−12,767	−23,151	−45,916
Equity capital..............................	4 510 ..	−2,140	−2,111	−1,430	−3,839	−6,580	−4,575	−10,215	−17,789
Claims on affiliated enterprises.........	4 515 ..	−2,140	−2,111	−1,430	−3,839	−6,580	−4,575	−10,215	−17,789
Liabilities to affiliated enterprises......	4 520 ..	. . . .	. . . .	. . . .	. . . .	. . . .	. . . .	. . . .	. . . .
Reinvested earnings.......................	4 525 ..	−1	−65	−17	−5,591	−5,071	−6,875	−10,772	−16,677
Other capital...............................	4 530 ..	−1,035	−357	−2,519	−297	−2,131	−1,318	−2,164	−11,449
Claims on affiliated enterprises.........	4 535 ..	−1,035	−357	−2,519	−297	−2,131	−1,318	−2,164	−11,449
Liabilities to affiliated enterprises......	4 540 ..	. . . .	. . . .	. . . .	. . . .	. . . .	. . . .	. . . .	. . . .
Direct investment in the Russian Federation.....	4 555 ..	2,714	2,748	3,377	7,958	15,444	12,886	29,701	55,073
Equity capital..............................	4 560 ..	1,580	1,606	2,248	−1,911	8,632	998	6,909	27,119
Claims on direct investors...............	4 565 ..	. . . .	. . . .	. . . .	. . . .	. . . .	. . . .	. . . .	. . . .
Liabilities to direct investors............	4 570 ..	1,580	1,606	2,248	−1,911	8,632	998	6,909	27,119
Reinvested earnings.......................	4 575 ..	95	431	683	7,065	5,330	9,361	14,716	23,389
Other capital...............................	4 580 ..	1,040	712	446	2,804	1,482	2,527	8,076	4,565
Claims on direct investors...............	4 585 ..	. . . .	. . . .	. . . .	. . . .	. . . .	. . . .	. . . .	. . . .
Liabilities to direct investors............	4 590 ..	1,040	712	446	2,804	1,482	2,527	8,076	4,565
B. PORTFOLIO INVESTMENT...................	4 600 ..	−10,334	−653	4,949	−4,509	623	−11,379	15,702	6,868
Assets..	4 602 ..	−411	77	−1,047	−2,180	−3,820	−10,666	6,248	−9,986
Equity securities..........................	4 610 ..	−40	−60	120	−47	−25	−733	116	−3,435
Monetary authorities.....................	4 611 ..	. . . .	−9	. . . .	. . . .	. . . .	10	. . . .	. . . .
General government......................	4 612 ..	. . . .	. . . .	. . . .	. . . .	. . . .	. . . .	. . . .	. . . .
Banks..	4 613 ..	−9	11	. . . .	−21	−5	−272	214	−1,782
Other sectors..............................	4 614 ..	−31	−62	121	−26	−21	−472	−98	−1,653
Debt securities............................	4 619 ..	−371	137	−1,167	−2,133	−3,794	−9,933	6,131	−6,551
Bonds and notes...........	4 620 ..	−371	92	−1,633	−1,773	−3,419	−9,285	5,298	−6,524
Monetary authorities..................	4 621 ..	. . . .	. . . .	−626	−1,497	−1,584	−6,307	7,455	. . . .
General government....................	4 622 ..	. . . .	. . . .	. . . .	. . . .	. . . .	. . . .	. . . .	. . . .
Banks....................................	4 623 ..	151	164	−903	−304	−1,791	−2,634	−1,569	−3,533
Other sectors...........................	4 624 ..	−522	−72	−103	28	−44	−343	−588	−2,990
Money market instruments............	4 630 ..	. . . .	45	465	−361	−375	−649	834	−28
Monetary authorities..................	4 631 ..	. . . .	. . . .	. . . .	. . . .	. . . .	. . . .	. . . .	. . . .
General government....................	4 632 ..	. . . .	. . . .	. . . .	. . . .	. . . .	. . . .	. . . .	. . . .
Banks....................................	4 633 ..	. . . .	45	465	−361	−313	−662	775	806
Other sectors...........................	4 634 ..	. . . .	. . . .	. . . .	. . . .	−63	13	59	−834
Liabilities....................................	4 652 ..	−9,923	−730	5,996	−2,329	4,443	−713	9,455	16,854
Equity securities..........................	4 660 ..	150	542	3,921	422	270	−100	6,480	18,844
Banks..	4 663 ..	2	14	1,144	65	−87	103	266	12,582
Other sectors..............................	4 664 ..	148	529	2,777	357	357	−203	6,214	6,262
Debt securities............................	4 669 ..	−10,073	−1,272	2,074	−2,750	4,173	−613	2,975	−1,990
Bonds and notes...........	4 670 ..	−10,073	−1,963	1,593	−2,453	3,905	−1,061	2,667	−2,871
Monetary authorities..................	4 671 ..	. . . .	−36	. . . .	. . . .	. . . .	. . . .	. . . .	. . . .
General government....................	4 672 ..	−10,761	−2,252	1,400	−1,457	3,093	−1,914	−840	−3,995
Banks....................................	4 673 ..	527	108	−371	−214	363	−311	1,140	888
Other sectors...........................	4 674 ..	160	217	565	−782	449	1,164	2,367	236
Money market instruments............	4 680 ..	. . . .	691	481	−298	268	448	308	881
Monetary authorities..................	4 681 ..	. . . .	. . . .	. . . .	. . . .	. . . .	. . . .	. . . .	. . . .
General government....................	4 682 ..	. . . .	18	34	−31	2	. . . .	. . . .	. . . .
Banks....................................	4 683 ..	. . . .	673	447	−266	265	448	308	881
Other sectors...........................	4 684 ..	. . . .	. . . .	. . . .	. . . .	. . . .	. . . .	. . . .	. . . .
C. FINANCIAL DERIVATIVES...................	4 910 ..	. . . .	. . . .	26	640	−100	−233	−99	332
Monetary authorities.....................	4 911 ..	. . . .	. . . .	. . . .	497	. . . .	. . . .	. . . .	. . . .
General government......................	4 912 ..	. . . .	. . . .	. . . .	. . . .	. . . .	. . . .	. . . .	. . . .
Banks..	4 913 ..	. . . .	. . . .	26	143	−100	−233	−99	332
Other sectors..............................	4 914 ..	. . . .	. . . .	. . . .	. . . .	. . . .	. . . .	. . . .	. . . .
Assets..	4 900 ..	. . . .	. . . .	98	1,017	758	858	1,242	2,762
Monetary authorities...	4 901 ..	. . . .	. . . .	. . . .	497	. . . .	. . . .	. . . .	. . . .
General government......................	4 902 ..	. . . .	. . . .	. . . .	. . . .	. . . .	. . . .	. . . .	. . . .
Banks..	4 903 ..	. . . .	. . . .	98	520	758	858	1,242	2,762
Other sectors..............................	4 904 ..	. . . .	. . . .	. . . .	. . . .	. . . .	. . . .	. . . .	. . . .
Liabilities....................................	4 905 ..	. . . .	. . . .	−72	−377	−857	−1,091	−1,342	−2,430
Monetary authorities.....................	4 906 ..	. . . .	. . . .	. . . .	. . . .	. . . .	. . . .	. . . .	. . . .
General government......................	4 907 ..	. . . .	. . . .	. . . .	. . . .	. . . .	. . . .	. . . .	. . . .
Banks..	4 908 ..	. . . .	. . . .	−72	−377	−857	−1,091	−1,342	−2,430
Other sectors..............................	4 909 ..	. . . .	. . . .	. . . .	. . . .	. . . .	. . . .	. . . .	. . . .

Table 2 (Concluded). STANDARD PRESENTATION, 2000–2007

(Millions of U.S. dollars)

	Code	2000	2001	2002	2003	2004	2005	2006	2007
D. OTHER INVESTMENT	4 700 ..	−21,691	−6,373	−2,668	6,764	−8,968	9,132	−18,960	79,761
Assets	4 703 ..	−17,525	149	−4,743	−15,886	−26,644	−33,208	−49,299	−59,637
Trade credits	4 706 ..	−4,245	827	1,433	−3,926	−546	−7,645	−616	−804
General government	4 707 ..	1	351	3,736	86	110	66	9	100
of which: Short-term	4 709 ..	....	....	....	....	....	....	....	....
Other sectors	4 710 ..	−4,245	475	−2,303	−4,012	−656	−7,711	−626	−904
of which: Short-term	4 712 ..	*−4,245*	*475*	*−2,303*	*−4,012*	*−656*	*−7,711*	*−626*	*−904*
Loans	4 714 ..	5,365	−739	−4,515	4	1,189	−5,538	−27,982	−35,322
Monetary authorities	4 715 ..	....	−80	−65	....	160	....	....	....
of which: Short-term	4 718 ..	....	*−80*	*−18*	*99*	....	....	....	....
General government	4 719 ..	5,806	302	−2,649	2,306	804	931	−4,006	−1,594
of which: Short-term	4 721 ..	....	....	....	....	....	....	....	....
Banks	4 722 ..	−395	−593	−1,600	−684	−1,269	−5,143	−10,053	−11,280
of which: Short-term	4 724 ..	*−221*	*−321*	*−1,267*	*−149*	*−2,025*	*−2,352*	*−6,788*	*−2,988*
Other sectors	4 725 ..	−45	−368	−201	−1,618	1,495	−1,326	−13,923	−22,448
of which: Short-term	4 727 ..	....	*−312*	*−371*	*−1,221*	*1,362*	*142*	*−6,879*	*−7,019*
Currency and deposits	4 730 ..	−5,435	−1,776	−2,955	6,347	−1,470	−5,824	−3,078	3,459
Monetary authorities	4 731 ..	....	−210	1,099	487	140	210	175	−477
General government	4 732 ..	141	229	−18	−41	75	−441	−10	−11
Banks	4 733 ..	−3,182	−671	57	449	−1,255	−4,901	−13,493	−10,409
Other sectors	4 734 ..	−2,395	−1,124	−4,093	5,452	−430	−691	10,249	14,356
Other assets	4 736 ..	−13,210	1,837	1,294	−18,310	−25,818	−14,201	−17,622	−26,970
Monetary authorities	4 737 ..	....	25	....	−20	6	−4	....	....
of which: Short-term	4 739 ..	....	*15*	....	*−20*	*6*	....	....	....
General government	4 740 ..	−7,564	9,217	14,778	−2,650	−1,227	10,923	2,668	8,747
of which: Short-term	4 742 ..	*−7,541*	*9,238*	*14,783*	*−2,621*	*−981*	*10,953*	*2,894*	*8,805*
Banks	4 743 ..	245	−388	188	−602	560	140	−488	−988
of which: Short-term	4 745 ..	*249*	*−392*	*188*	*−594*	*621*	*90*	*−415*	*−707*
Other sectors	4 746 ..	−5,891	−7,016	−13,672	−15,039	−25,157	−25,259	−19,802	−34,728
of which: Short-term	4 748 ..	*−1*	*−414*	*−22*	*−6*	*−16*	*25*	*68*	*51*
Liabilities	4 753 ..	**−4,166**	**−6,521**	**2,075**	**22,650**	**17,676**	**42,340**	**30,340**	**139,398**
Trade credits	4 756 ..	....	....	....	....	....	....	....	....
General government	4 757 ..	....	....	....	....	....	....	....	....
of which: Short-term	4 759 ..	....	....	....	....	....	....	....	....
Other sectors	4 760 ..	....	....	....	....	....	....	....	....
of which: Short-term	4 762 ..	....	....	....	....	....	....	....	....
Loans	4 764 ..	−3,597	−6,332	6,731	18,555	21,842	39,588	18,321	127,392
Monetary authorities	4 765 ..	−2,899	−1,845	−1,483	−380	−109	2,718	−7,395	....
of which: Use of Fund credit and loans from the Fund	4 766 ..	*−2,899*	*−3,829*	*−1,493*	*−1,897*	*−1,655*	*−3,506*	....	....
of which: Short-term	4 768 ..	....	*1,984*	*10*	*1,517*	*1,545*	*6,225*	*−7,395*	....
General government	4 769 ..	634	−5,668	−3,747	−3,707	−1,220	−18,932	−23,880	−2,804
of which: Short-term	4 771 ..	....	....	....	....	....	....	....	....
Banks	4 772 ..	−397	411	2,586	7,513	6,991	14,901	32,756	39,395
of which: Short-term	4 774 ..	*581*	*58*	*631*	*3,978*	*1,729*	*73*	*9,159*	*5,900*
Other sectors	4 775 ..	−935	769	9,374	15,128	16,180	40,900	16,840	90,800
of which: Short-term	4 777 ..	....	*393*	*59*	*1,938*	*698*	*−620*	*3,216*	*29,618*
Currency and deposits	4 780 ..	880	1,529	−38	3,864	−1,220	2,415	14,911	12,445
Monetary authorities	4 781 ..	155	66	−32	119	364	85	63	882
General government	4 782 ..	−2	−1	....	9	−1,426	−533	....	....
Banks	4 783 ..	727	1,464	−6	3,736	−158	2,864	14,847	11,564
Other sectors	4 784 ..	....	....	....	....	....	....	....	....
Other liabilities	4 786 ..	−1,449	−1,718	−4,619	231	−2,946	337	−2,892	−439
Monetary authorities	4 787 ..	....	−142	....	....	....	....	....	....
of which: Short-term	4 789 ..	....	*−142*	....	....	....	....	....	....
General government	4 790 ..	−1,688	−1,060	−4,578	−7	−2,839	222	−3,173	−754
of which: Short-term	4 792 ..	*−1,688*	*−1,060*	*−4,578*	*−1*	*−2,833*	*228*	*−3,166*	*−748*
Banks	4 793 ..	238	−36	−61	297	−123	322	668	809
of which: Short-term	4 795 ..	*173*	*35*	*−48*	*321*	*−160*	*265*	*585*	*606*
Other sectors	4 796 ..	....	−479	20	−58	16	−207	−388	−494
of which: Short-term	4 798 ..	....	*−479*	*20*	*−58*	*16*	*−207*	*−388*	*−494*
E. RESERVE ASSETS	4 802 ..	**−16,009**	**−8,211**	**−6,841**	**−26,365**	**−45,236**	**−61,461**	**−107,466**	**−148,928**
Monetary gold	4 812 ..	....	....	....	....	....	....	....	....
Special drawing rights	4 811 ..	....	−2	2	1	....	−5	−1	7
Reserve position in the Fund	4 810 ..	....	....	....	....	−1	−195	−77	−73
Foreign exchange	4 803 ..	−16,009	−8,208	−6,843	−26,365	−45,235	−61,261	−107,388	−148,861
Other claims	4 813 ..	....	....	....	....	....	....	....	....
NET ERRORS AND OMISSIONS	4 998 ..	**−9,297**	**−9,558**	**−7,594**	**−9,179**	**−5,870**	**−7,821**	**9,741**	**−13,208**

Table 3. INTERNATIONAL INVESTMENT POSITION (End-period stocks), 2000–2007

(Millions of U.S. dollars)

	Code	2000	2001	2002	2003	2004	2005	2006	2007
ASSETS	8 995 C.	**248,752**	**259,498**	**288,480**	**336,825**	**406,635**	**516,292**	**731,347**	**1,098,618**
Direct investment abroad	8 505 ..	**20,141**	**44,219**	**62,350**	**90,873**	**107,291**	**146,679**	**216,488**	**370,161**
Equity capital and reinvested earnings	8 506 ..	18,470	42,167	58,358	86,532	100,402	139,046	213,549	355,745
Claims on affiliated enterprises	8 507 ..	18,470	42,167	58,358	86,532	100,402	139,046	213,549	355,745
Liabilities to affiliated enterprises	8 508 ..	....	....	....	....	....	....	....	....
Other capital	8 530 ..	1,671	2,053	3,992	4,341	6,888	7,633	2,939	14,416
Claims on affiliated enterprises	8 535 ..	1,671	2,053	3,992	4,341	6,888	7,633	2,939	14,416
Liabilities to affiliated enterprises	8 540 ..	....	....	....	....	....	....	....	....
Portfolio investment	8 602 ..	**1,268**	**1,315**	**2,507**	**4,383**	**7,922**	**17,772**	**12,268**	**26,793**
Equity securities	8 610 ..	46	105	53	98	129	334	509	4,082
Monetary authorities	8 611 ..	....	10	11	12	12	....	....	....
General government	8 612 ..	....	....	....	....	....	....	....	....
Banks	8 613 ..	15	1	5	24	33	272	271	2,053
Other sectors	8 614 ..	31	93	36	62	84	61	238	2,029
Debt securities	8 619 ..	1,222	1,210	2,455	4,285	7,793	17,438	11,759	22,711
Bonds and notes	8 620 ..	907	966	2,227	4,024	7,056	16,000	10,421	21,130
Monetary authorities	8 621 ..	....	....	791	2,330	3,923	10,223	2,992	6,900
General government	8 622 ..	....	....	....	....	....	....	....	....
Banks	8 623 ..	354	342	839	1,531	3,015	5,310	6,374	10,384
Other sectors	8 624 ..	553	624	597	163	117	467	1,054	3,846
Money market instruments	8 630 ..	315	244	227	260	738	1,438	1,338	1,581
Monetary authorities	8 631 ..	....	....	....	....	....	....	....	....
General government	8 632 ..	....	....	....	....	....	....	....	....
Banks	8 633 ..	315	244	210	251	665	1,382	1,000	417
Other sectors	8 634 ..	....	....	17	10	72	56	338	1,164
Financial derivatives	8 900 ..	....	....	....	**55**	**153**	**51**	**222**	**1,423**
Monetary authorities	8 901 ..	....	....	....	....	....	....	....	....
General government	8 902 ..	....	....	....	....	....	....	....	....
Banks	8 903 ..	....	....	....	55	153	51	222	1,423
Other sectors	8 904 ..	....	....	....	....	....	....	....	....
Other investment	8 703 ..	**199,371**	**177,342**	**175,830**	**164,576**	**166,728**	**169,551**	**198,637**	**222,350**
Trade credits	8 706 ..	11,711	7,165	5,435	8,338	8,930	16,363	14,839	11,668
General government	8 707 ..	4,454	4,039	1,777	1,746	1,720	1,626	1,636	1,559
of which: Short-term	8 709 ..	....	....	....	....	....	....	....	....
Other sectors	8 710 ..	7,257	3,126	3,659	6,591	7,210	14,737	13,203	10,109
of which: Short-term	8 712 ..	*7,257*	*3,126*	*3,659*	*6,591*	*7,210*	*14,737*	*13,203*	*10,109*
Loans	8 714 ..	22,128	22,570	25,351	24,511	23,831	29,125	57,910	92,929
Monetary authorities	8 715 ..	....	79	142	153	....	....	....	....
of which: Short-term	8 718 ..	....	*79*	*94*	....	....	....	....	....
General government	8 719 ..	18,483	17,966	19,198	15,956	15,402	14,355	18,470	20,353
of which: Short-term	8 721 ..	....	....	....	....	....	....	....	....
Banks	8 722 ..	2,536	3,050	4,521	5,269	6,660	11,706	22,422	34,312
of which: Short-term	8 724 ..	*1,223*	*1,473*	*2,718*	*2,930*	*5,073*	*7,306*	*14,302*	*17,714*
Other sectors	8 725 ..	1,110	1,476	1,491	3,134	1,769	3,064	17,018	38,264
of which: Short-term	8 727 ..	....	*312*	*486*	*1,720*	*482*	*430*	*7,483*	*13,476*
Currency and deposits	8 730 ..	62,393	63,932	65,009	59,182	61,002	66,154	69,976	69,130
Monetary authorities	8 731 ..	1,368	1,541	1,330	895	751	485	353	921
General government	8 732 ..	413	164	120	95	42	474	487	513
Banks	8 733 ..	12,740	13,250	12,480	12,343	13,816	18,271	32,294	43,463
Other sectors	8 734 ..	47,873	48,977	51,079	45,849	46,394	46,924	36,841	24,233
Other assets	8 736 ..	103,138	83,676	80,035	72,545	72,965	57,908	55,913	48,623
Monetary authorities	8 737 ..	68	58	47	47	41	45	46	46
of which: Short-term	8 739 ..	*20*	*19*	*8*	*9*	*3*	*2*	*2*	*2*
General government	8 740 ..	99,177	78,256	74,076	67,231	68,568	55,532	53,096	44,454
of which: Short-term	8 742 ..	*98,942*	*78,005*	*73,792*	*66,901*	*67,982*	*54,941*	*52,276*	*43,571*
Banks	8 743 ..	309	647	796	1,349	828	692	1,198	2,256
of which: Short-term	8 745 ..	*295*	*637*	*787*	*1,335*	*752*	*664*	*1,091*	*1,864*
Other sectors	8 746 ..	3,584	4,715	5,117	3,918	3,528	1,640	1,573	1,866
of which: Short-term	8 748 ..	*3,584*	*4,347*	*4,170*	*3,918*	*3,528*	*1,640*	*1,573*	*1,866*
Reserve assets	8 802 ..	**27,972**	**36,622**	**47,793**	**76,938**	**124,541**	**182,240**	**303,732**	**477,890**
Monetary gold	8 812 ..	3,708	4,080	3,739	3,763	3,732	6,349	8,164	12,012
Special drawing rights	8 811 ..	1	3	1	1	1	6	7	1
Reserve position in the Fund	8 810 ..	1	1	2	2	3	196	283	374
Foreign exchange	8 803 ..	24,263	32,538	44,051	73,172	120,805	175,690	295,277	465,504
Other claims	8 813 ..	....	....	....	....	....	....	....	....

Table 3 (Concluded). INTERNATIONAL INVESTMENT POSITION (End-period stocks), 2000–2007

(Millions of U.S. dollars)

	Code	2000	2001	2002	2003	2004	2005	2006	2007
LIABILITIES..	8 995 D.	**184,207**	**215,587**	**251,301**	**332,901**	**417,270**	**547,860**	**767,508**	**1,225,666**
Direct investment in the Russian Federation.......	8 555 ..	**32,204**	**52,919**	**70,884**	**96,729**	**122,295**	**180,228**	**265,873**	**491,232**
Equity capital and reinvested earnings............................	8 556 ..	27,200	47,228	64,793	87,349	111,269	167,706	244,349	464,344
Claims on direct investors...	8 557 ..	. . . .	. . . .	. . . .	. . . .	. . . .	. . . .	. . . .	. . . .
Liabilities to direct investors.....................................	8 558 ..	27,200	47,228	64,793	87,349	111,269	167,706	244,349	464,344
Other capital..	8 580 ..	5,004	5,690	6,091	9,380	11,026	12,522	21,524	26,888
Claims on direct investors...	8 585 ..	. . . .	. . . .	. . . .	. . . .	. . . .	. . . .	. . . .	. . . .
Liabilities to direct investors.....................................	8 590 ..	5,004	5,690	6,091	9,380	11,026	12,522	21,524	26,888
Portfolio investment.......................................	8 652 ..	**32,132**	**52,317**	**66,911**	**93,358**	**130,822**	**166,340**	**263,175**	**344,754**
Equity securities..	8 660 ..	11,109	27,353	35,762	57,982	89,218	118,297	207,881	292,363
Banks..	8 663 ..	52	53	652	1,108	1,927	5,032	13,870	30,752
Other sectors...	8 664 ..	11,057	27,300	35,110	56,874	87,291	113,264	194,011	261,611
Debt securities...	8 669 ..	21,023	24,964	31,149	35,376	41,605	48,043	55,294	52,390
Bonds and notes..	8 670 ..	20,698	23,953	30,086	34,598	40,573	46,856	53,766	49,927
Monetary authorities..	8 671 ..	36	. . . .	. . . .	. . . .	. . . .	. . . .	. . . .	. . . .
General government...	8 672 ..	19,617	22,601	27,759	30,131	33,877	33,644	32,575	28,635
Banks..	8 673 ..	468	560	732	440	798	638	1,773	3,229
Other sectors...	8 674 ..	577	793	1,595	4,027	5,898	12,574	19,418	18,062
Money market instruments......................................	8 680 ..	325	1,011	1,063	778	1,032	1,188	1,528	2,463
Monetary authorities..	8 681 ..	. . . .	. . . .	. . . .	. . . .	. . . .	. . . .	. . . .	. . . .
General government...	8 682 ..	23	36	27	. . . .	. . . .	. . . .	. . . .	. . . .
Banks..	8 683 ..	302	975	1,036	778	1,032	1,188	1,528	2,463
Other sectors...	8 684 ..	. . . .	. . . .	. . . .	. . . .	. . . .	. . . .	. . . .	. . . .
Financial derivatives.......................................	8 905 ..	. . . .	. . . .	. . . .	**31**	**189**	**52**	**178**	**875**
Monetary authorities...	8 906 ..	. . . .	. . . .	. . . .	. . . .	. . . .	. . . .	. . . .	. . . .
General government..	8 907 ..	. . . .	. . . .	. . . .	. . . .	. . . .	. . . .	. . . .	. . . .
Banks..	8 908 ..	. . . .	. . . .	. . . .	31	189	52	178	875
Other sectors..	8 909 ..	. . . .	. . . .	. . . .	. . . .	. . . .	. . . .	. . . .	. . . .
Other investment...	8 753 ..	**119,871**	**110,351**	**113,507**	**142,783**	**163,964**	**201,240**	**238,283**	**388,805**
Trade credits..	8 756 ..	. . . .	. . . .	. . . .	. . . .	. . . .	. . . .	. . . .	. . . .
General government...	8 757 ..	. . . .	. . . .	. . . .	. . . .	. . . .	. . . .	. . . .	. . . .
of which: Short-term...	8 759 ..	. . . .	. . . .	. . . .	. . . .	. . . .	. . . .	. . . .	. . . .
Other sectors...	8 760 ..	. . . .	. . . .	. . . .	. . . .	. . . .	. . . .	. . . .	. . . .
of which: Short-term...	8 762 ..	. . . .	. . . .	. . . .	. . . .	. . . .	. . . .	. . . .	. . . .
Loans..	8 764 ..	98,345	89,120	93,795	119,575	146,027	180,313	205,195	341,629
Monetary authorities..	8 765 ..	11,714	9,514	7,308	7,459	7,503	10,158	2,985	7,107
of which: Use of Fund credit and loans from the Fund....	8 766 ..	*11,613*	*7,433*	*6,481*	*5,069*	*3,562*	. . . .	. . . .	. . . .
of which: Short-term...	8 768 ..	*102*	*2,080*	*826*	*2,390*	*3,941*	*10,158*	*2,985*	*7,107*
General government...	8 769 ..	67,075	59,237	55,042	57,365	59,127	35,590	14,258	11,579
of which: Short-term...	8 771 ..	. . . .	. . . .	. . . .	. . . .	. . . .	. . . .	. . . .	. . . .
Banks..	8 772 ..	2,561	2,924	5,256	12,946	19,810	34,511	67,757	113,236
of which: Short-term...	8 774 ..	*1,761*	*1,752*	*2,550*	*6,566*	*8,157*	*8,161*	*17,558*	*23,853*
Other sectors...	8 775 ..	16,995	17,446	26,189	41,805	59,586	100,054	120,195	209,706
of which: Short-term...	8 777 ..	*1,835*	*2,228*	*2,498*	*4,486*	*6,274*	*5,542*	*10,439*	*40,772*
Currency and deposits..	8 780 ..	6,083	7,471	7,993	11,801	10,700	13,262	28,760	42,591
Monetary authorities..	8 781 ..	168	220	223	348	741	795	942	1,912
General government...	8 782 ..	1,756	1,755	1,787	1,818	283	24	25	26
Banks..	8 783 ..	4,160	5,495	5,983	9,635	9,676	12,443	27,793	40,653
Other sectors...	8 784 ..	. . . .	. . . .	. . . .	. . . .	. . . .	. . . .	. . . .	. . . .
Other liabilities..	8 786 ..	15,443	13,761	11,719	11,407	7,237	7,665	4,328	4,586
Monetary authorities..	8 787 ..	56	7	. . . .	. . . .	. . . .	. . . .	. . . .	. . . .
of which: Short-term...	8 789 ..	*56*	*7*	. . . .	. . . .	. . . .	. . . .	. . . .	. . . .
General government...	8 790 ..	13,561	12,403	10,554	10,453	6,342	6,485	2,412	1,688
of which: Short-term...	8 792 ..	*13,561*	*12,403*	*10,523*	*10,428*	*6,323*	*6,473*	*2,406*	*1,688*
Banks..	8 793 ..	1,269	1,283	1,086	943	885	1,169	1,901	2,879
of which: Short-term...	8 795 ..	*1,112*	*1,201*	*1,009*	*877*	*760*	*991*	*1,634*	*2,402*
Other sectors...	8 796 ..	557	69	78	11	10	10	14	19
of which: Short-term...	8 798 ..	*557*	*69*	*78*	*11*	*10*	*10*	*14*	*19*
NET INTERNATIONAL INVESTMENT POSITION........	8 995 ..	**64,545**	**43,912**	**37,179**	**3,924**	**−10,635**	**−31,568**	**−36,162**	**−127,048**
Conversion rates: rubles per U.S. dollar (end of period)..............................	0 102 ..	**28.160**	**30.140**	**31.784**	**29.455**	**27.749**	**28.783**	**26.331**	**24.546**

Table 1. ANALYTIC PRESENTATION, 2000–2007

(Millions of U.S. dollars)

	Code	2000	2001	2002	2003	2004	2005	2006	2007
A. Current Account[1]	4 993 Z.	**−94**	**−102**	**−126**	**−121**	**−198**	**−84**	**−180**	**−147**
Goods: exports f.o.b.	2 100 ..	68	93	67	63	98	128	145	184
Goods: imports f.o.b.	3 100 ..	−223	−245	−233	−229	−276	−355	−488	−637
Balance on Goods	4 100 ..	*−155*	*−152*	*−166*	*−166*	*−178*	*−227*	*−343*	*−452*
Services: credit	2 200 ..	59	66	65	76	103	129	131	179
Services: debit	3 200 ..	−200	−189	−202	−204	−240	−304	−243	−272
Balance on Goods and Services	4 991 ..	*−296*	*−275*	*−302*	*−293*	*−315*	*−402*	*−455*	*−545*
Income: credit	2 300 ..	14	14	8	6	6	27	27	48
Income: debit	3 300 ..	−28	−34	−27	−37	−39	−44	−48	−63
Balance on Goods, Services, and Income	4 992 ..	*−310*	*−295*	*−321*	*−324*	*−349*	*−418*	*−476*	*−560*
Current transfers: credit	2 379 Z.	233	210	215	223	169	352	319	435
Current transfers: debit	3 379 ..	−17	−18	−20	−20	−18	−18	−23	−22
B. Capital Account[1]	4 994 Z.	**62**	**50**	**66**	**41**	**61**	**93**	**1,323**	**161**
Capital account: credit	2 994 Z.	62	50	66	41	61	93	1,323	161
Capital account: debit	3 994 ..	....	....	....	....	....	....	....	....
Total, Groups A Plus B	4 981 ..	*−32*	*−52*	*−60*	*−80*	*−138*	*9*	*1,143*	*14*
C. Financial Account[1]	4 995 W.	**11**	**−44**	**81**	**−21**	**−21**	**−59**	**−1,204**	**35**
Direct investment abroad	4 505 ..	....	....	....	....	....	....	14	13
Direct investment in Rwanda	4 555 Z.	8	5	3	5	8	8	11	67
Portfolio investment assets	4 602 ..	....	....	....	....	....	....	....	....
Equity securities	4 610 ..	....	....	....	....	....	....	....	....
Debt securities	4 619 ..	....	....	....	....	....	....	....	....
Portfolio investment liabilities	4 652 Z.	....	....	....	....	....	....	....	....
Equity securities	4 660 Z.	....	....	....	....	....	....	....	....
Debt securities	4 669 Z.	....	....	....	....	....	....	....	....
Financial derivatives	4 910 ..	....	....	....	....	....	....	....	....
Financial derivatives assets	4 900 ..	....	....	....	....	....	....	....	....
Financial derivatives liabilities	4 905 ..	....	....	....	....	....	....	....	....
Other investment assets	4 703 ..	23	....	8	−6	8	−14	−30	−13
Monetary authorities	4 701 ..	....	....	....	....	....	....	....	....
General government	4 704 ..	....	....	....	....	....	....	....	....
Banks	4 705 ..	17	−5	−1	−6	8	−14	−30	−13
Other sectors	4 728 ..	6	4	9	....	....	....	....	....
Other investment liabilities	4 753 W.	−21	−48	70	−19	−37	−52	−1,199	−32
Monetary authorities	4 753 WA	....	....	....	−1	−3	−20	−26	−2
General government	4 753 ZB	−23	−50	58	−27	−32	−36	−1,172	−11
Banks	4 753 ZC	....	....	....	....	....	....	1	....
Other sectors	4 753 ZD	2	2	13	9	−2	4	−3	−19
Total, Groups A Through C	4 983 ..	*−22*	*−96*	*21*	*−101*	*−159*	*−49*	*−60*	*49*
D. Net Errors and Omissions	4 998 ..	**21**	**71**	**−8**	**23**	**−9**	**26**	**87**	**4**
Total, Groups A Through D	4 984 ..	....	*−26*	*13*	*−78*	*−168*	*−23*	*26*	*53*
E. Reserves and Related Items	4 802 A.	....	**26**	**−13**	**78**	**168**	**23**	**−26**	**−53**
Reserve assets	4 802 ..	−53	−34	−14	12	−99	−92	−31	−109
Use of Fund credit and loans	4 766 ..	14	2	−6	−1	−4	−8	−74	3
Exceptional financing	4 920 ..	39	58	7	67	271	123	78	52
Conversion rates: Rwanda francs per U.S. dollar	0 101 ..	**389.696**	**442.992**	**475.365**	**537.655**	**577.449**	**557.823**	**551.710**	**546.955**

[1] Excludes components that have been classified in the categories of Group E.

Table 2. STANDARD PRESENTATION, 2000–2007

(Millions of U.S. dollars)

	Code	2000	2001	2002	2003	2004	2005	2006	2007
CURRENT ACCOUNT.....................................	4 993 ..	**−94**	**−102**	**−126**	**−97**	**−35**	**−52**	**−180**	**−147**
A. GOODS...	4 100 ..	**−155**	**−152**	**−166**	**−166**	**−178**	**−227**	**−343**	**−452**
Credit..	2 100 ..	**68**	**93**	**67**	**63**	**98**	**128**	**145**	**184**
General merchandise: exports f.o.b............	2 110 ..	68	93	67	63	98	128	145	184
Goods for processing: exports f.o.b..........	2 150 ..	....	....	....	....	....	....	....	....
Repairs on goods.....................................	2 160 ..	....	....	....	....	....	....	....	....
Goods procured in ports by carriers..........	2 170 ..	....	....	....	....	....	....	....	....
Nonmonetary gold...................................	2 180 ..	....	....	....	....	....	....	....	....
Debit...	3 100 ..	**−223**	**−245**	**−233**	**−229**	**−276**	**−355**	**−488**	**−637**
General merchandise: imports f.o.b............	3 110 ..	−223	−245	−233	−229	−276	−355	−488	−637
Goods for processing: imports f.o.b..........	3 150 ..	....	....	....	....	....	....	....	....
Repairs on goods.....................................	3 160 ..	....	....	....	....	....	....	....	....
Goods procured in ports by carriers..........	3 170 ..	....	....	....	....	....	....	....	....
Nonmonetary gold...................................	3 180 ..	....	....	....	....	....	....	....	....
B. SERVICES..	4 200 ..	**−141**	**−123**	**−136**	**−127**	**−137**	**−175**	**−112**	**−93**
Total credit..	2 200 ..	*59*	*66*	*65*	*76*	*103*	*129*	*131*	*179*
Total debit...	3 200 ..	*−200*	*−189*	*−202*	*−204*	*−240*	*−304*	*−243*	*−272*
Transportation services, credit...............	2 205 ..	**14**	**16**	**12**	**18**	**21**	**30**	**30**	**36**
Passenger..	2 850 ..	*4*	*4*	....	....	....	....	....	*1*
Freight...	2 851 ..	*6*	*5*	*2*	*4*	*7*	*7*	*4*	*3*
Other...	2 852 ..	*5*	*7*	*10*	*14*	*15*	*23*	*26*	*32*
Sea transport, passenger...........................	2 207 ..	....	....	....	....	....	....	....	....
Sea transport, freight................................	2 208 ..	....	....	....	....	....	....	....	....
Sea transport, other..................................	2 209 ..	....	....	....	....	....	....	....	....
Air transport, passenger............................	2 211 ..	....	....	....	....	....	....	....	....
Air transport, freight.................................	2 212 ..	....	....	....	....	....	....	....	1
Air transport, other...................................	2 213 ..	....	....	....	....	....	....	....	....
Other transport, passenger.......................	2 215 ..	....	....	....	....	....	....	....	....
Other transport, freight.............................	2 216 ..	....	....	....	4	7	7	4	3
Other transport, other...............................	2 217 ..	....	....	....	14	15	23	26	32
Transportation services, debit...............	3 205 ..	**−83**	**−81**	**−89**	**−78**	**−92**	**−135**	**−111**	**−86**
Passenger..	3 850 ..	*−13*	*−13*	....	....	....	....	....	....
Freight...	3 851 ..	*−58*	*−55*	*−60*	*−54*	*−65*	*−84*	*−58*	*−74*
Other...	3 852 ..	*−12*	*−13*	*−29*	*−24*	*−27*	*−51*	*−53*	*−12*
Sea transport, passenger...........................	3 207 ..	....	....	....	....	....	....	....	....
Sea transport, freight................................	3 208 ..	....	....	....	−18	−22	−28	−13	−15
Sea transport, other..................................	3 209 ..	....	....	....	....	....	....	−2	−1
Air transport, passenger............................	3 211 ..	....	....	....	....	....	....	....	....
Air transport, freight.................................	3 212 ..	....	....	....	....	....	....	....	−14
Air transport, other...................................	3 213 ..	....	....	....	....	....	....	−1	−9
Other transport, passenger.......................	3 215 ..	....	....	....	....	....	....	....	....
Other transport, freight.............................	3 216 ..	....	....	....	−36	−44	−56	−44	−44
Other transport, other...............................	3 217 ..	....	....	....	−24	−27	−51	−51	−3
Travel, credit..	2 236 ..	**23**	**25**	**31**	**30**	**44**	**49**	**31**	**65**
Business travel...	2 237 ..	....	....	....	....	....	....	14	....
Personal travel...	2 240 ..	....	....	....	30	44	49	17	65
Travel, debit...	3 236 ..	**−22**	**−20**	**−24**	**−26**	**−31**	**−37**	**−35**	**−69**
Business travel...	3 237 ..	....	....	....	....	....	....	−12	−37
Personal travel...	3 240 ..	....	....	....	−26	−31	−37	−23	−32
Other services, credit...........................	2 200 BA ..	**22**	**25**	**22**	**28**	**38**	**51**	**70**	**78**
Communications......................................	2 245 ..	....	....	....	....	....	4	1	3
Construction..	2 249 ..	....	....	....	....	....	....	....	....
Insurance...	2 253 ..	....	....	....	....	....	....	....	1
Financial..	2 260 ..	....	....	....	....	....	....	....	....
Computer and information.........................	2 262 ..	....	....	....	....	....	....	3	....
Royalties and licence fees.........................	2 266 ..	....	....	....	....	....	....	....	....
Other business services............................	2 268 ..	3	4	4	....	....	....	8	20
Personal, cultural, and recreational............	2 287 ..	....	....	....	....	....	....	....	....
Government, n.i.e.....................................	2 291 ..	19	21	18	28	38	46	57	54
Other services, debit............................	3 200 BA ..	**−96**	**−88**	**−89**	**−99**	**−116**	**−132**	**−97**	**−117**
Communications......................................	3 245 ..	....	....	....	....	....	−4	−2	−3
Construction..	3 249 ..	....	....	....	....	....	....	....	−3
Insurance...	3 253 ..	....	....	....	....	....	....	−6	−2
Financial..	3 260 ..	....	....	....	....	....	....	−9	....
Computer and information.........................	3 262 ..	....	....	....	....	....	....	....	....
Royalties and licence fees.........................	3 266 ..	−1	....	....	....	....	....	−1	....
Other business services............................	3 268 ..	−8	−11	−11	....	....	....	−47	−97
Personal, cultural, and recreational............	3 287 ..	....	....	....	....	....	....	−4	....
Government, n.i.e.....................................	3 291 ..	−87	−76	−78	−99	−116	−128	−29	−13

Table 2 (Continued). STANDARD PRESENTATION, 2000–2007

(Millions of U.S. dollars)

	Code	2000	2001	2002	2003	2004	2005	2006	2007
C. INCOME	4 300	**−15**	**−20**	**−19**	**−31**	**−34**	**−16**	**−21**	**−15**
Total credit	2 300	*14*	*14*	*8*	*6*	*6*	*27*	*27*	*48*
Total debit	3 300	*−28*	*−34*	*−27*	*−37*	*−39*	*−44*	*−48*	*−63*
Compensation of employees, credit	2 310	**3**	**2**	....	....	....	**12**	**4**	**23**
Compensation of employees, debit	3 310	**−12**	**−17**	**−14**	**−14**	**−16**	**−21**	**−30**	**−48**
Investment income, credit	2 320	**11**	**12**	**8**	**6**	**5**	**15**	**23**	**25**
Direct investment income	2 330	....	....	....	....	....	2	1	....
Dividends and distributed branch profits	2 332	....	....	....	....	....	2	1	....
Reinvested earnings and undistributed branch profits	2 333	....	....	....	....	....	....	....	....
Income on debt (interest)	2 334	....	....	....	....	....	....	....	....
Portfolio investment income	2 339	....	....	....	6	5	13	....	....
Income on equity	2 340	....	....	....	6	5	13	....	....
Income on bonds and notes	2 350	....	....	....	....	....	....	....	....
Income on money market instruments	2 360	....	....	....	....	....	....	....	....
Other investment income	2 370	11	12	8	....	....	....	22	25
Investment income, debit	3 320	**−16**	**−17**	**−14**	**−22**	**−23**	**−23**	**−17**	**−15**
Direct investment income	3 330	−3	−3	....	−6	−3	−5	−4	−9
Dividends and distributed branch profits	3 332	−3	−3	....	−6	−3	−5	−4	−8
Reinvested earnings and undistributed branch profits	3 333	....	....	....	....	....	....	....	....
Income on debt (interest)	3 334	....	....	....	....	....	....	....	−1
Portfolio investment income	3 339	....	....	....	−16	−20	−18	....	....
Income on equity	3 340	....	....	....	−16	−20	−18	....	....
Income on bonds and notes	3 350	....	....	....	....	....	....	....	....
Income on money market instruments	3 360	....	....	....	....	....	....	....	....
Other investment income	3 370	−13	−14	−13	....	....	....	−14	−5
D. CURRENT TRANSFERS	4 379	**216**	**193**	**195**	**226**	**314**	**366**	**296**	**413**
Credit	2 379	**233**	**210**	**215**	**246**	**332**	**384**	**319**	**435**
General government	2 380	206	172	172	197	281	322	210	313
Other sectors	2 390	27	38	43	49	51	62	109	122
Workers' remittances	2 391	4	5	7	9	10	9	17	28
Other current transfers	2 392	23	33	36	40	41	53	92	94
Debit	3 379	**−17**	**−18**	**−20**	**−20**	**−18**	**−18**	**−23**	**−22**
General government	3 380	−1	−1	−2	−2	−2	−2	−3	−2
Other sectors	3 390	−16	−16	−19	−18	−16	−15	−21	−20
Workers' remittances	3 391	−16	−16	−18	−15	−15	−14	−17	−20
Other current transfers	3 392	....	....	....	−3	−1	−1	−4	....
CAPITAL AND FINANCIAL ACCOUNT	4 996	**73**	**32**	**134**	**75**	**44**	**26**	**93**	**143**
CAPITAL ACCOUNT	4 994	**63**	**62**	**66**	**41**	**61**	**93**	**1,323**	**161**
Total credit	2 994	*63*	*62*	*67*	*41*	*61*	*93*	*1,323*	*161*
Total debit	3 994	....	....	....	....	....	....	....	....
Capital transfers, credit	2 400	**63**	**62**	**67**	**41**	**61**	**93**	**1,323**	**161**
General government	2 401	63	62	67	41	61	93	1,323	161
Debt forgiveness	2 402	1	12	1	....	....	....	1,150	....
Other capital transfers	2 410	62	50	66	41	61	93	173	161
Other sectors	2 430	....	....	....	....	....	....	....	....
Migrants' transfers	2 431	....	....	....	....	....	....	....	....
Debt forgiveness	2 432	....	....	....	....	....	....	....	....
Other capital transfers	2 440	....	....	....	....	....	....	....	....
Capital transfers, debit	3 400	....	....	....	....	....	....	....	....
General government	3 401	....	....	....	....	....	....	....	....
Debt forgiveness	3 402	....	....	....	....	....	....	....	....
Other capital transfers	3 410	....	....	....	....	....	....	....	....
Other sectors	3 430	....	....	....	....	....	....	....	....
Migrants' transfers	3 431	....	....	....	....	....	....	....	....
Debt forgiveness	3 432	....	....	....	....	....	....	....	....
Other capital transfers	3 440	....	....	....	....	....	....	....	....
Nonproduced nonfinancial assets, credit	2 480	....	....	....	....	....	....	....	....
Nonproduced nonfinancial assets, debit	3 480	....	....	....	....	....	....	....	....

Table 2 (Continued). STANDARD PRESENTATION, 2000–2007

(Millions of U.S. dollars)

	Code	2000	2001	2002	2003	2004	2005	2006	2007
FINANCIAL ACCOUNT..	4 995 ..	10	−31	68	33	−17	−67	−1,230	−18
A. DIRECT INVESTMENT.......................................	4 500 ..	8	5	3	5	8	8	26	80
Direct investment abroad..................................	4 505 ..	....	....	....	....	....	....	14	13
Equity capital...	4 510 ..	....	....	....	....	....	....	14	13
Claims on affiliated enterprises........................	4 515 ..	....	....	....	....	....	....	14	13
Liabilities to affiliated enterprises....................	4 520 ..	....	....	....	....	....	....	....	....
Reinvested earnings.......................................	4 525 ..	....	....	....	....	....	....	....	....
Other capital...	4 530 ..	....	....	....	....	....	....	....	....
Claims on affiliated enterprises........................	4 535 ..	....	....	....	....	....	....	....	....
Liabilities to affiliated enterprises....................	4 540 ..	....	....	....	....	....	....	....	....
Direct investment in Rwanda...........................	4 555 ..	8	5	3	5	8	8	11	67
Equity capital...	4 560 ..	8	5	3	5	8	8	11	67
Claims on direct investors...............................	4 565 ..	....	....	....	....	....	....	....	....
Liabilities to direct investors...........................	4 570 ..	8	5	3	5	8	8	11	67
Reinvested earnings.......................................	4 575 ..	....	....	....	....	....	....	....	....
Other capital...	4 580 ..	....	....	....	....	....	....	....	....
Claims on direct investors...............................	4 585 ..	....	....	....	....	....	....	....	....
Liabilities to direct investors...........................	4 590 ..	....	....	....	....	....	....	....	....
B. PORTFOLIO INVESTMENT...............................	4 600 ..	....	....	....	....	....	....	....	....
Assets...	4 602 ..	....	....	....	....	....	....	....	....
Equity securities..	4 610 ..	....	....	....	....	....	....	....	....
Monetary authorities......................................	4 611 ..	....	....	....	....	....	....	....	....
General government......................................	4 612 ..	....	....	....	....	....	....	....	....
Banks...	4 613 ..	....	....	....	....	....	....	....	....
Other sectors..	4 614 ..	....	....	....	....	....	....	....	....
Debt securities..	4 619 ..	....	....	....	....	....	....	....	....
Bonds and notes...	4 620 ..	....	....	....	....	....	....	....	....
Monetary authorities....................................	4 621 ..	....	....	....	....	....	....	....	....
General government....................................	4 622 ..	....	....	....	....	....	....	....	....
Banks...	4 623 ..	....	....	....	....	....	....	....	....
Other sectors..	4 624 ..	....	....	....	....	....	....	....	....
Money market instruments.............................	4 630 ..	....	....	....	....	....	....	....	....
Monetary authorities....................................	4 631 ..	....	....	....	....	....	....	....	....
General government....................................	4 632 ..	....	....	....	....	....	....	....	....
Banks...	4 633 ..	....	....	....	....	....	....	....	....
Other sectors..	4 634 ..	....	....	....	....	....	....	....	....
Liabilities..	4 652 ..	....	....	....	....	....	....	....	....
Equity securities..	4 660 ..	....	....	....	....	....	....	....	....
Banks...	4 663 ..	....	....	....	....	....	....	....	....
Other sectors..	4 664 ..	....	....	....	....	....	....	....	....
Debt securities..	4 669 ..	....	....	....	....	....	....	....	....
Bonds and notes...	4 670 ..	....	....	....	....	....	....	....	....
Monetary authorities....................................	4 671 ..	....	....	....	....	....	....	....	....
General government....................................	4 672 ..	....	....	....	....	....	....	....	....
Banks...	4 673 ..	....	....	....	....	....	....	....	....
Other sectors..	4 674 ..	....	....	....	....	....	....	....	....
Money market instruments.............................	4 680 ..	....	....	....	....	....	....	....	....
Monetary authorities....................................	4 681 ..	....	....	....	....	....	....	....	....
General government....................................	4 682 ..	....	....	....	....	....	....	....	....
Banks...	4 683 ..	....	....	....	....	....	....	....	....
Other sectors..	4 684 ..	....	....	....	....	....	....	....	....
C. FINANCIAL DERIVATIVES................................	4 910 ..	....	....	....	....	....	....	....	....
Monetary authorities......................................	4 911 ..	....	....	....	....	....	....	....	....
General government......................................	4 912 ..	....	....	....	....	....	....	....	....
Banks...	4 913 ..	....	....	....	....	....	....	....	....
Other sectors..	4 914 ..	....	....	....	....	....	....	....	....
Assets...	4 900 ..	....	....	....	....	....	....	....	....
Monetary authorities......................................	4 901 ..	....	....	....	....	....	....	....	....
General government......................................	4 902 ..	....	....	....	....	....	....	....	....
Banks...	4 903 ..	....	....	....	....	....	....	....	....
Other sectors..	4 904 ..	....	....	....	....	....	....	....	....
Liabilities..	4 905 ..	....	....	....	....	....	....	....	....
Monetary authorities......................................	4 906 ..	....	....	....	....	....	....	....	....
General government......................................	4 907 ..	....	....	....	....	....	....	....	....
Banks...	4 908 ..	....	....	....	....	....	....	....	....
Other sectors..	4 909 ..	....	....	....	....	....	....	....	....

Table 2 (Concluded). STANDARD PRESENTATION, 2000–2007

(Millions of U.S. dollars)

	Code	2000	2001	2002	2003	2004	2005	2006	2007
D. OTHER INVESTMENT	4 700 ..	**54**	**−1**	**79**	**17**	**75**	**16**	**−1,225**	**10**
Assets	4 703 ..	**23**	....	**8**	**−6**	**8**	**−14**	**−30**	**−13**
Trade credits	4 706 ..	6	4	6	....	....	....	....	....
General government	4 707 ..	....	....	....	....	....	....	....	....
of which: Short-term	4 709 ..	....	....	....	....	....	....	....	....
Other sectors	4 710 ..	6	4	6	....	....	....	....	....
of which: Short-term	4 712 ..	6	4	6	....	....	....	....	....
Loans	4 714 ..	17	−5	2	....	....	....	....	....
Monetary authorities	4 715 ..	....	....	....	....	....	....	....	....
of which: Short-term	4 718 ..	....	....	....	....	....	....	....	....
General government	4 719 ..	....	....	....	....	....	....	....	....
of which: Short-term	4 721 ..	....	....	....	....	....	....	....	....
Banks	4 722 ..	17	−5	−1	....	....	....	....	....
of which: Short-term	4 724 ..	17	−5	−1	....	....	....	....	....
Other sectors	4 725 ..	....	....	4	....	....	....	....	....
of which: Short-term	4 727 ..	....	....	4	....	....	....	....	....
Currency and deposits	4 730 ..	....	....	....	−6	8	−14	−30	−13
Monetary authorities	4 731 ..	....	....	....	....	....	....	....	....
General government	4 732 ..	....	....	....	....	....	....	....	....
Banks	4 733 ..	....	....	....	−6	8	−14	−30	−13
Other sectors	4 734 ..	....	....	....	....	....	....	....	....
Other assets	4 736 ..	....	....	....	....	....	....	....	....
Monetary authorities	4 737 ..	....	....	....	....	....	....	....	....
of which: Short-term	4 739 ..	....	....	....	....	....	....	....	....
General government	4 740 ..	....	....	....	....	....	....	....	....
of which: Short-term	4 742 ..	....	....	....	....	....	....	....	....
Banks	4 743 ..	....	....	....	....	....	....	....	....
of which: Short-term	4 745 ..	....	....	....	....	....	....	....	....
Other sectors	4 746 ..	....	....	....	....	....	....	....	....
of which: Short-term	4 748 ..	....	....	....	....	....	....	....	....
Liabilities	4 753 ..	**31**	**−1**	**71**	**24**	**67**	**31**	**−1,195**	**24**
Trade credits	4 756 ..	....	....	....	5	5	9	4	10
General government	4 757 ..	....	....	....	5	5	....	....	....
of which: Short-term	4 759 ..	....	....	....	5	5	....	....	....
Other sectors	4 760 ..	....	....	....	....	....	9	4	10
of which: Short-term	4 762 ..	....	....	....	....	....	9	4	10
Loans	4 764 ..	47	46	64	13	66	41	−1,154	15
Monetary authorities	4 765 ..	14	2	−6	−1	−4	−8	−51	3
of which: Use of Fund credit and loans from the Fund	4 766 ..	14	2	−6	−1	−4	−8	−74	3
of which: Short-term	4 768 ..	....	....	....	....	....	....	23	....
General government	4 769 ..	31	42	58	8	71	54	−1,097	41
of which: Short-term	4 771 ..	....	....	....	....	....	....	....	....
Banks	4 772 ..	....	....	....	....	....	....	....	....
of which: Short-term	4 774 ..	....	....	....	....	....	....	....	....
Other sectors	4 775 ..	2	2	13	6	−2	−5	−7	−29
of which: Short-term	4 777 ..	3	2	10	2	....	....	−1	−33
Currency and deposits	4 780 ..	....	....	....	....	....	....	1	....
Monetary authorities	4 781 ..	....	....	....	....	....	....	....	....
General government	4 782 ..	....	....	....	....	....	....	....	....
Banks	4 783 ..	....	....	....	....	....	....	1	....
Other sectors	4 784 ..	....	....	....	....	....	....	....	....
Other liabilities	4 786 ..	−16	−47	6	5	−4	−19	−46	−2
Monetary authorities	4 787 ..	....	....	....	−1	−3	−20	−49	−2
of which: Short-term	4 789 ..	....	....	....	−1	−3	−20	....	−2
General government	4 790 ..	−16	−47	6	4	−1	1	2	....
of which: Short-term	4 792 ..	−16	−47	6	4	−1	1	2	....
Banks	4 793 ..	....	....	....	....	....	....	....	....
of which: Short-term	4 795 ..	....	....	....	....	....	....	....	....
Other sectors	4 796 ..	....	....	....	2	....	....	....	....
of which: Short-term	4 798 ..	....	....	....	2	....	....	....	....
E. RESERVE ASSETS	4 802 ..	**−53**	**−34**	**−14**	**12**	**−99**	**−92**	**−31**	**−109**
Monetary gold	4 812 ..	....	....	....	....	....	....	....	....
Special drawing rights	4 811 ..	13	−11	3	−17	1	2	4	....
Reserve position in the Fund	4 810 ..	....	....	....	....	....	....	....	....
Foreign exchange	4 803 ..	−65	−22	−17	29	−100	−94	−35	−109
Other claims	4 813 ..	....	....	....	....	....	....	....	....
NET ERRORS AND OMISSIONS	4 998 ..	**21**	**71**	**−8**	**23**	**−9**	**26**	**87**	**4**

Table 3. INTERNATIONAL INVESTMENT POSITION (End-period stocks), 2000–2007

(Millions of U.S. dollars)

	Code	2000	2001	2002	2003	2004	2005	2006	2007
ASSETS...	8 995 C.	**268**	**288**	**335**	**319**	**428**	**502**	**568**	**677**
Direct investment abroad..........................	8 505 ..	....	....	....	....	....	....	....	**13**
Equity capital and reinvested earnings...........................	8 506 ..	....	....	....	....	....	....	....	13
Claims on affiliated enterprises............................	8 507 ..	....	....	....	....	....	....	....	13
Liabilities to affiliated enterprises.......................	8 508 ..	....	....	....	....	....	....	....	....
Other capital...	8 530 ..	....	....	....	....	....	....	....	....
Claims on affiliated enterprises............................	8 535 ..	....	....	....	....	....	....	....	....
Liabilities to affiliated enterprises.......................	8 540 ..	....	....	....	....	....	....	....	....
Portfolio investment..................................	8 602 ..	**1**	**1**	....	....	....	....	....	....
Equity securities..	8 610 ..	1	1	....	....	....	....	....	....
Monetary authorities..	8 611 ..	....	....	....	....	....	....	....	....
General government...	8 612 ..	1	1	....	....	....	....	....	....
Banks...	8 613 ..	....	....	....	....	....	....	....	....
Other sectors...	8 614 ..	....	....	....	....	....	....	....	....
Debt securities..	8 619 ..	....	....	....	....	....	....	....	....
Bonds and notes...	8 620 ..	....	....	....	....	....	....	....	....
Monetary authorities.....................................	8 621 ..	....	....	....	....	....	....	....	....
General government......................................	8 622 ..	....	....	....	....	....	....	....	....
Banks...	8 623 ..	....	....	....	....	....	....	....	....
Other sectors...	8 624 ..	....	....	....	....	....	....	....	....
Money market instruments................................	8 630 ..	....	....	....	....	....	....	....	....
Monetary authorities.....................................	8 631 ..	....	....	....	....	....	....	....	....
General government......................................	8 632 ..	....	....	....	....	....	....	....	....
Banks...	8 633 ..	....	....	....	....	....	....	....	....
Other sectors...	8 634 ..	....	....	....	....	....	....	....	....
Financial derivatives..................................	8 900 ..	....	....	....	....	....	....	....	....
Monetary authorities...	8 901 ..	....	....	....	....	....	....	....	....
General government..	8 902 ..	....	....	....	....	....	....	....	....
Banks..	8 903 ..	....	....	....	....	....	....	....	....
Other sectors..	8 904 ..	....	....	....	....	....	....	....	....
Other investment......................................	8 703 ..	**77**	**74**	**82**	**76**	**84**	**69**	**128**	**115**
Trade credits..	8 706 ..	....	....	....	....	....	....	....	....
General government...	8 707 ..	....	....	....	....	....	....	....	....
of which: Short-term..................................	8 709 ..	....	....	....	....	....	....	....	....
Other sectors...	8 710 ..	....	....	....	....	....	....	....	....
of which: Short-term..................................	8 712 ..	....	....	....	....	....	....	....	....
Loans...	8 714 ..	77	74	....	....	....	....	....	....
Monetary authorities..	8 715 ..	....	....	....	....	....	....	....	....
of which: Short-term..................................	8 718 ..	....	....	....	....	....	....	....	....
General government...	8 719 ..	....	....	....	....	....	....	....	....
of which: Short-term..................................	8 721 ..	....	....	....	....	....	....	....	....
Banks...	8 722 ..	77	74	....	....	....	....	....	....
of which: Short-term..................................	8 724 ..	*77*	*74*	....	....	....	....	....	....
Other sectors...	8 725 ..	....	....	....	....	....	....	....	....
of which: Short-term..................................	8 727 ..	....	....	....	....	....	....	....	....
Currency and deposits......................................	8 730 ..	....	....	82	76	84	69	128	115
Monetary authorities..	8 731 ..	....	....	....	....	....	....	....	....
General government...	8 732 ..	....	....	....	....	....	....	....	....
Banks...	8 733 ..	....	....	82	76	84	69	128	115
Other sectors...	8 734 ..	....	....	....	....	....	....	....	....
Other assets..	8 736 ..	....	....	....	....	....	....	....	....
Monetary authorities..	8 737 ..	....	....	....	....	....	....	....	....
of which: Short-term..................................	8 739 ..	....	....	....	....	....	....	....	....
General government...	8 740 ..	....	....	....	....	....	....	....	....
of which: Short-term..................................	8 742 ..	....	....	....	....	....	....	....	....
Banks...	8 743 ..	....	....	....	....	....	....	....	....
of which: Short-term..................................	8 745 ..	....	....	....	....	....	....	....	....
Other sectors...	8 746 ..	....	....	....	....	....	....	....	....
of which: Short-term..................................	8 748 ..	....	....	....	....	....	....	....	....
Reserve assets...	8 802 ..	**191**	**213**	**253**	**243**	**344**	**433**	**440**	**549**
Monetary gold..	8 812 ..	....	....	....	....	....	....	....	....
Special drawing rights..	8 811 ..	1	12	10	30	30	26	23	24
Reserve position in the Fund................................	8 810 ..	....	....	....	....	....	....	....	....
Foreign exchange..	8 803 ..	190	201	243	213	314	407	417	525
Other claims..	8 813 ..	....	....	....	....	....	....	....	....

Table 3 (Concluded). INTERNATIONAL INVESTMENT POSITION (End-period stocks), 2000–2007

(Millions of U.S. dollars)

	Code	2000	2001	2002	2003	2004	2005	2006	2007
LIABILITIES	8 995 D.	**1,355**	**1,353**	**1,515**	**1,646**	**1,802**	**1,674**	**479**	**568**
Direct investment in Rwanda	8 555 ..	**55**	**57**	**57**	**62**	**69**	**77**	**103**	**170**
Equity capital and reinvested earnings	8 556 ..	55	57	57	62	69	77	103	170
Claims on direct investors	8 557 ..	....	....	....	....	....	....	....	....
Liabilities to direct investors	8 558 ..	55	57	57	62	69	77	103	170
Other capital	8 580 ..	....	....	....	....	....	....	....	....
Claims on direct investors	8 585 ..	....	....	....	....	....	....	....	....
Liabilities to direct investors	8 590 ..	....	....	....	....	....	....	....	....
Portfolio investment	8 652 ..	....	....	....	....	....	....	....	....
Equity securities	8 660 ..	....	....	....	....	....	....	....	....
Banks	8 663 ..	....	....	....	....	....	....	....	....
Other sectors	8 664 ..	....	....	....	....	....	....	....	....
Debt securities	8 669 ..	....	....	....	....	....	....	....	....
Bonds and notes	8 670 ..	....	....	....	....	....	....	....	....
Monetary authorities	8 671 ..	....	....	....	....	....	....	....	....
General government	8 672 ..	....	....	....	....	....	....	....	....
Banks	8 673 ..	....	....	....	....	....	....	....	....
Other sectors	8 674 ..	....	....	....	....	....	....	....	....
Money market instruments	8 680 ..	....	....	....	....	....	....	....	....
Monetary authorities	8 681 ..	....	....	....	....	....	....	....	....
General government	8 682 ..	....	....	....	....	....	....	....	....
Banks	8 683 ..	....	....	....	....	....	....	....	....
Other sectors	8 684 ..	....	....	....	....	....	....	....	....
Financial derivatives	8 905 ..	....	....	....	....	....	....	....	....
Monetary authorities	8 906 ..	....	....	....	....	....	....	....	....
General government	8 907 ..	....	....	....	....	....	....	....	....
Banks	8 908 ..	....	....	....	....	....	....	....	....
Other sectors	8 909 ..	....	....	....	....	....	....	....	....
Other investment	8 753 ..	**1,300**	**1,296**	**1,458**	**1,585**	**1,733**	**1,597**	**376**	**397**
Trade credits	8 756 ..	11	10	12	18	23	32	....	10
General government	8 757 ..	11	10	12	18	23	32	....	....
of which: Short-term	8 759 ..	*11*	*10*	*12*	*18*	*23*	*32*	....	....
Other sectors	8 760 ..	....	....	....	....	....	....	....	10
of which: Short-term	8 762 ..	....	....	....	....	....	....	....	*10*
Loans	8 764 ..	1,271	1,270	1,427	1,540	1,686	1,561	353	372
Monetary authorities	8 765 ..	86	84	85	92	92	77	4	8
of which: Use of Fund credit and loans from the Fund	8 766 ..	*86*	*84*	*85*	*92*	*92*	*77*	*4*	*8*
of which: Short-term	8 768 ..	....	....	....	....	....	....	....	....
General government	8 769 ..	1,165	1,164	1,313	1,430	1,578	1,472	348	390
of which: Short-term	8 771 ..	....	....	....	....	....	....	....	....
Banks	8 772 ..	8	10	17	....	....	....	....	−29
of which: Short-term	8 774 ..	*8*	*10*	*17*	....	....	....	....	*−29*
Other sectors	8 775 ..	13	11	12	18	16	12	....	3
of which: Short-term	8 777 ..	....	....	....	....	....	....	....	*3*
Currency and deposits	8 780 ..	....	....	....	....	....	....	23	17
Monetary authorities	8 781 ..	....	....	....	....	....	....	4	3
General government	8 782 ..	....	....	....	....	....	....	....	....
Banks	8 783 ..	....	....	....	....	....	....	20	14
Other sectors	8 784 ..	....	....	....	....	....	....	....	....
Other liabilities	8 786 ..	18	16	19	27	23	4	....	−2
Monetary authorities	8 787 ..	18	16	19	25	21	2	....	−2
of which: Short-term	8 789 ..	*18*	*16*	*19*	*25*	*21*	*2*	....	*−2*
General government	8 790 ..	....	....	....	....	....	....	....	....
of which: Short-term	8 792 ..	....	....	....	....	....	....	....	....
Banks	8 793 ..	....	....	....	....	....	....	....	....
of which: Short-term	8 795 ..	....	....	....	....	....	....	....	....
Other sectors	8 796 ..	....	....	....	2	2	2	....	....
of which: Short-term	8 798 ..	....	....	....	*2*	*2*	*2*	....	....
NET INTERNATIONAL INVESTMENT POSITION	8 995 ..	**−1,087**	**−1,065**	**−1,180**	**−1,327**	**−1,374**	**−1,172**	**88**	**109**
Conversion rates: Rwanda francs per U.S. dollar (end of period)	0 102 ..	430.486	457.900	511.854	580.280	566.860	553.719	548.650	544.220

Table 1. ANALYTIC PRESENTATION, 2000–2007

(Millions of U.S. dollars)

	Code	2000	2001	2002	2003	2004	2005	2006	2007
A. Current Account[1].....................	4 993 Z.	**−66.21**	**−107.41**	**−124.60**	**−115.79**	**−68.38**	**−64.72**	**−89.77**	**−135.40**
Goods: exports f.o.b.	2 100 ..	51.46	55.02	63.04	57.30	58.79	63.51	58.29	56.77
Goods: imports f.o.b.	3 100 ..	−172.67	−166.58	−177.58	−175.64	−160.82	−185.21	−219.59	−240.39
Balance on Goods	4 100 ..	*−121.21*	*−111.56*	*−114.55*	*−118.34*	*−102.03*	*−121.70*	*−161.30*	*−183.61*
Services: credit	2 200 ..	98.53	97.89	90.27	107.88	135.15	163.15	173.37	160.79
Services: debit	3 200 ..	−76.07	−75.22	−78.70	−80.17	−80.83	−94.92	−101.71	−114.10
Balance on Goods and Services	4 991 ..	*−98.75*	*−88.88*	*−102.98*	*−90.63*	*−47.70*	*−53.47*	*−89.64*	*−136.92*
Income: credit	2 300 ..	5.53	4.67	5.51	5.68	7.57	10.68	13.28	14.13
Income: debit	3 300 ..	−35.63	−39.25	−43.57	−49.44	−46.47	−45.82	−45.62	−45.13
Balance on Goods, Services, and Income ...	4 992 ..	*−128.86*	*−123.47*	*−141.04*	*−134.38*	*−86.60*	*−88.61*	*−121.98*	*−167.91*
Current transfers: credit	2 379 Z.	69.90	26.61	28.33	30.02	31.09	36.79	44.88	46.14
Current transfers: debit	3 379 ..	−7.25	−10.55	−11.89	−11.43	−12.87	−12.90	−12.67	−13.62
B. Capital Account[1].....................	4 994 Z.	**5.99**	**10.91**	**14.58**	**5.37**	**5.38**	**14.72**	**13.16**	**10.36**
Capital account: credit	2 994 Z.	6.17	11.09	14.77	5.57	5.57	14.95	13.38	10.60
Capital account: debit	3 994 ..	−.19	−.19	−.19	−.19	−.19	−.22	−.22	−.24
Total, Groups A Plus B	4 981 ..	*−60.22*	*−96.50*	*−110.01*	*−110.42*	*−63.01*	*−49.99*	*−76.61*	*−125.05*
C. Financial Account[1]...................	4 995 W.	**124.71**	**158.95**	**144.22**	**159.26**	**110.68**	**88.71**	**123.24**	**193.63**
Direct investment abroad	4 505 ..	....	−.12	....	....	....	....	....	....
Direct investment in St. Kitts and Nevis	4 555 Z.	96.21	88.23	79.77	75.61	46.14	92.99	110.42	142.60
Portfolio investment assets	4 602 ..	−.03	−1.09	....	−.01	−.39	....	−1.77	....
Equity securities	4 610 ..	....	....	....	....	....	....	....	....
Debt securities	4 619 ..	....	....	....	....	....	....	....	....
Portfolio investment liabilities	4 652 Z.	5.03	43.77	30.36	48.04	−9.45	−15.02	−19.19	−19.19
Equity securities	4 660 ..	....	....	....	....	....	....	....	....
Debt securities	4 669 Z.	....	....	....	....	....	....	....	....
Financial derivatives	4 910 ..	....	....	....	....	....	....	....	....
Financial derivatives assets	4 900 ..	....	....	....	....	....	....	....	....
Financial derivatives liabilities	4 905 ..	....	....	....	....	....	....	....	....
Other investment assets	4 703 ..	23.50	28.16	34.08	35.63	74.37	10.74	33.79	70.22
Monetary authorities	4 701 ..	....	....	....	....	....	....	....	....
General government	4 704 ..	....	....	....	....	....	....	....	....
Banks	4 705 ..	....	....	....	....	....	....	....	....
Other sectors	4 728 ..	....	....	....	....	....	....	....	....
Other investment liabilities	4 753 W.	....	....	....	....	....	....	....	....
Monetary authorities	4 753 WA	....	....	....	....	....	....	....	....
General government	4 753 ZB	....	....	....	....	....	....	....	....
Banks	4 753 ZC	....	....	....	....	....	....	....	....
Other sectors	4 753 ZD	....	....	....	....	....	....	....	....
Total, Groups A Through C	4 983 ..	*64.49*	*62.45*	*34.20*	*48.84*	*47.67*	*38.72*	*46.62*	*68.58*
D. Net Errors and Omissions...........	4 998 ..	**−68.86**	**−50.84**	**−25.58**	**−49.80**	**−34.03**	**−45.39**	**−29.48**	**−61.50**
Total, Groups A Through D	4 984 ..	*−4.37*	*11.61*	*8.62*	*−.96*	*13.64*	*−6.68*	*17.15*	*7.09*
E. Reserves and Related Items........	4 802 A.	**4.37**	**−11.61**	**−8.62**	**.96**	**−13.64**	**6.68**	**−17.15**	**−7.08**
Reserve assets	4 802 ..	4.37	−11.61	−8.62	.96	−13.64	6.68	−17.15	−7.08
Use of Fund credit and loans	4 766 ..	....	....	....	....	....	....	....	....
Exceptional financing	4 920 ..	....	....	....	....	....	....	....	....
Conversion rates: Eastern Caribbean dollars per U.S. dollar...............	0 101 ..	**2.7000**	**2.7000**	**2.7000**	**2.7000**	**2.7000**	**2.7000**	**2.7000**	**2.7000**

[1] Excludes components that have been classified in the categories of Group E.

Table 2. STANDARD PRESENTATION, 2000–2007

(Millions of U.S. dollars)

	Code	2000	2001	2002	2003	2004	2005	2006	2007
CURRENT ACCOUNT	4 993 ..	−66.21	−107.41	−124.60	−115.79	−68.38	−64.72	−89.77	−135.40
A. GOODS	4 100 ..	−121.21	−111.56	−114.55	−118.34	−102.03	−121.70	−161.30	−183.61
Credit	2 100 ..	51.46	55.02	63.04	57.30	58.79	63.51	58.29	56.77
General merchandise: exports f.o.b.	2 110 ..	49.39	52.50	61.54	54.89	54.65	58.14	53.07	51.70
Goods for processing: exports f.o.b.	2 150 ..	....	....	....	....	....	....	....	....
Repairs on goods	2 160 ..	....	....	....	.02	.04	.07	.07	.07
Goods procured in ports by carriers	2 170 ..	2.07	2.53	1.50	2.39	4.10	5.31	5.14	5.01
Nonmonetary gold	2 180 ..	....	....	....	....	....	....	....	....
Debit	3 100 ..	−172.67	−166.58	−177.58	−175.64	−160.82	−185.21	−219.59	−240.39
General merchandise: imports f.o.b.	3 110 ..	−172.46	−166.40	−177.52	−175.64	−160.82	−185.21	−219.59	−240.39
Goods for processing: imports f.o.b.	3 150 ..	....	....	....	....	....	....	....	....
Repairs on goods	3 160 ..	....	....	....	....	....	....	....	....
Goods procured in ports by carriers	3 170 ..	−.21	−.18	−.07	....	....	....	....	....
Nonmonetary gold	3 180 ..	....	....	....	....	....	....	....	....
B. SERVICES	4 200 ..	22.46	22.67	11.57	27.72	54.32	68.23	71.66	46.69
Total credit	2 200 ..	*98.53*	*97.89*	*90.27*	*107.88*	*135.15*	*163.15*	*173.37*	*160.79*
Total debit	3 200 ..	*−76.07*	*−75.22*	*−78.70*	*−80.17*	*−80.83*	*−94.92*	*−101.71*	*−114.10*
Transportation services, credit	2 205 ..	10.55	11.40	10.03	9.93	9.78	11.16	17.68	19.37
Passenger	2 850 ..	....	....	....	....	....	....	....	....
Freight	2 851 ..	....	....	....	....	....	....	....	....
Other	2 852 ..	....	....	....	....	....	....	....	....
Sea transport, passenger	2 207 ..	....	....	....	....	....	....	....	....
Sea transport, freight	2 208 ..	....	....	....	....	....	....	....	....
Sea transport, other	2 209 ..	....	....	....	....	....	....	....	....
Air transport, passenger	2 211 ..	....	....	....	....	....	....	....	....
Air transport, freight	2 212 ..	....	....	....	....	....	....	....	....
Air transport, other	2 213 ..	....	....	....	....	....	....	....	....
Other transport, passenger	2 215 ..	....	....	....	....	....	....	....	....
Other transport, freight	2 216 ..	....	....	....	....	....	....	....	....
Other transport, other	2 217 ..	....	....	....	....	....	....	....	....
Transportation services, debit	3 205 ..	−31.64	−30.78	−31.90	−32.88	−33.00	−38.16	−43.76	−47.54
Passenger	3 850 ..	....	....	....	....	....	....	....	....
Freight	3 851 ..	....	....	....	....	....	....	....	....
Other	3 852 ..	....	....	....	....	....	....	....	....
Sea transport, passenger	3 207 ..	....	....	....	....	....	....	....	....
Sea transport, freight	3 208 ..	....	....	....	....	....	....	....	....
Sea transport, other	3 209 ..	....	....	....	....	....	....	....	....
Air transport, passenger	3 211 ..	....	....	....	....	....	....	....	....
Air transport, freight	3 212 ..	....	....	....	....	....	....	....	....
Air transport, other	3 213 ..	....	....	....	....	....	....	....	....
Other transport, passenger	3 215 ..	....	....	....	....	....	....	....	....
Other transport, freight	3 216 ..	....	....	....	....	....	....	....	....
Other transport, other	3 217 ..	....	....	....	....	....	....	....	....
Travel, credit	2 236 ..	58.44	61.85	57.14	75.35	102.64	121.16	122.11	106.26
Business travel	2 237 ..	....	....	....	....	....	....	....	....
Personal travel	2 240 ..	....	....	....	....	....	....	....	....
Travel, debit	3 236 ..	−8.85	−8.07	−7.59	−8.14	−9.68	−10.96	−13.53	−14.55
Business travel	3 237 ..	....	....	....	....	....	....	....	....
Personal travel	3 240 ..	....	....	....	....	....	....	....	....
Other services, credit	2 200 BA	29.54	24.64	23.10	22.60	22.74	30.83	33.59	35.16
Communications	2 245 ..	5.37	4.07	3.52	3.66	4.28	4.72	5.28	5.43
Construction	2 249 ..	1.56	1.62	1.85	.06	.25	.38	.19	.20
Insurance	2 253 ..	3.19	2.05	2.24	1.93	1.91	2.77	2.91	3.12
Financial	2 260 ..	....	....	....	....	....	....	....	....
Computer and information	2 262 ..	....	....	....	....	....	....	....	....
Royalties and licence fees	2 266 ..	....	....	....	.11	....	....	....	....
Other business services	2 268 ..	15.97	12.68	11.25	12.76	12.22	18.17	19.48	20.54
Personal, cultural, and recreational	2 287 ..	....	....	....	....	....	....	....	....
Government, n.i.e.	2 291 ..	3.47	4.22	4.24	4.09	4.08	4.78	5.73	5.86
Other services, debit	3 200 BA	−35.58	−36.36	−39.20	−39.15	−38.15	−45.79	−44.42	−52.00
Communications	3 245 ..	−4.33	−2.74	−2.45	−1.78	−2.82	−3.24	−3.56	−3.83
Construction	3 249 ..	−5.12	−3.90	−4.75	−4.75	−1.47	−3.82	−1.89	−6.43
Insurance	3 253 ..	−8.52	−8.36	−9.51	−9.46	−8.66	−10.98	−10.26	−11.13
Financial	3 260 ..	....	....	....	....	....	....	....	....
Computer and information	3 262 ..	....	....	....	....	−.03	−.03	−.03	−.03
Royalties and licence fees	3 266 ..	−.83	−.93	−.89	−1.28	−1.85	−2.02	−1.75	−1.75
Other business services	3 268 ..	−13.10	−16.12	−16.23	−16.25	−18.78	−21.12	−22.28	−23.97
Personal, cultural, and recreational	3 287 ..	....	....	....	....	....	....	....	....
Government, n.i.e.	3 291 ..	−3.68	−4.31	−5.36	−5.63	−4.54	−4.57	−4.65	−4.85

Table 2 (Continued). STANDARD PRESENTATION, 2000–2007

(Millions of U.S. dollars)

	Code	2000	2001	2002	2003	2004	2005	2006	2007
C. INCOME.........	4 300 ..	**−30.11**	**−34.59**	**−38.06**	**−43.76**	**−38.90**	**−35.14**	**−32.34**	**−30.99**
Total credit.................	2 300 ..	*5.53*	*4.67*	*5.51*	*5.68*	*7.57*	*10.68*	*13.28*	*14.13*
Total debit.................	3 300 ..	*−35.63*	*−39.25*	*−43.57*	*−49.44*	*−46.47*	*−45.82*	*−45.62*	*−45.13*
Compensation of employees, credit..........	2 310 ..	**.96**	**.95**	**.45**	**.29**	**.24**	**.29**	**.26**	**.26**
Compensation of employees, debit..........	3 310 ..	**−3.09**	**−3.64**	**−3.20**	**−3.59**	**−3.10**	**−2.63**	**−1.06**	**−1.14**
Investment income, credit.................	2 320 ..	**4.57**	**3.72**	**5.06**	**5.39**	**7.33**	**10.39**	**13.03**	**13.87**
Direct investment income.................	2 330 ..	....	....	.13	.16	.13	.06	.06	.06
Dividends and distributed branch profits..........	2 332 ..	....	....	.13	.16	.13	.06	.06	.06
Reinvested earnings and undistributed branch profits.....	2 333 ..	....	....	....	....	....	....	....	....
Income on debt (interest).................	2 334 ..	....	....	....	....	....	....	....	....
Portfolio investment income.................	2 339 ..	.61	.53	.40	.34	.28	.07	1.21	1.17
Income on equity.................	2 340 ..	.61	.53	.40	.34	.28	.07	1.21	1.17
Income on bonds and notes.................	2 350 ..	....	....	....	....	....	....	....	....
Income on money market instruments..........	2 360 ..	....	....	....	....	....	....	....	....
Other investment income.................	2 370 ..	3.96	3.19	4.52	4.89	6.92	10.26	11.75	12.64
Investment income, debit.................	3 320 ..	**−32.55**	**−35.61**	**−40.38**	**−45.84**	**−43.37**	**−43.19**	**−44.57**	**−43.99**
Direct investment income.................	3 330 ..	−21.22	−23.44	−22.55	−22.98	−19.53	−20.30	−20.18	−21.58
Dividends and distributed branch profits..........	3 332 ..	−13.06	−13.13	−11.29	−12.52	−13.69	−14.88	−15.35	−16.51
Reinvested earnings and undistributed branch profits.....	3 333 ..	−3.66	−3.70	−5.12	−4.22	−3.60	−3.15	−2.36	−2.54
Income on debt (interest).................	3 334 ..	−4.50	−6.61	−6.14	−6.24	−2.24	−2.27	−2.46	−2.53
Portfolio investment income.................	3 339 ..	−3.03	−5.21	−9.52	−11.57	−13.07	−12.39	−12.58	−12.63
Income on equity.................	3 340 ..	−3.03	−5.21	−9.52	−11.57	−13.07	−12.39	−12.58	−12.63
Income on bonds and notes.................	3 350 ..	....	....	....	....	....	....	....	....
Income on money market instruments..........	3 360 ..	....	....	....	....	....	....	....	....
Other investment income.................	3 370 ..	−8.30	−6.96	−8.30	−11.29	−10.76	−10.49	−11.81	−9.78
D. CURRENT TRANSFERS.................	4 379 ..	**62.65**	**16.06**	**16.44**	**18.59**	**18.22**	**23.89**	**32.21**	**32.51**
Credit.................	2 379 ..	**69.90**	**26.61**	**28.33**	**30.02**	**31.09**	**36.79**	**44.88**	**46.14**
General government.................	2 380 ..	1.52	1.87	2.70	2.73	2.13	6.13	11.71	12.04
Other sectors.................	2 390 ..	68.38	24.74	25.63	27.29	28.96	30.66	33.17	34.10
Workers' remittances.................	2 391 ..	23.32	23.81	24.94	26.52	28.21	29.98	32.58	33.49
Other current transfers.................	2 392 ..	45.06	.93	.70	.76	.75	.68	.59	.61
Debit.................	3 379 ..	**−7.25**	**−10.55**	**−11.89**	**−11.43**	**−12.87**	**−12.90**	**−12.67**	**−13.62**
General government.................	3 380 ..	−3.00	−3.04	−3.12	−3.19	−3.47	−3.09	−3.09	−3.32
Other sectors.................	3 390 ..	−4.25	−7.51	−8.77	−8.23	−9.40	−9.80	−9.58	−10.30
Workers' remittances.................	3 391 ..	−4.21	−4.40	−4.57	−3.73	−4.57	−4.88	−4.31	−4.63
Other current transfers.................	3 392 ..	−.04	−3.12	−4.20	−4.50	−4.83	−4.93	−5.27	−5.67
CAPITAL AND FINANCIAL ACCOUNT..........	4 996 ..	**135.07**	**158.25**	**150.18**	**165.60**	**102.41**	**110.11**	**119.25**	**196.90**
CAPITAL ACCOUNT.................	4 994 ..	**5.99**	**10.91**	**14.58**	**5.37**	**5.38**	**14.72**	**13.16**	**10.36**
Total credit.................	2 994 ..	*6.17*	*11.09*	*14.77*	*5.57*	*5.57*	*14.95*	*13.38*	*10.60*
Total debit.................	3 994 ..	*−.19*	*−.19*	*−.19*	*−.19*	*−.19*	*−.22*	*−.22*	*−.24*
Capital transfers, credit.................	2 400 ..	**6.17**	**11.09**	**14.58**	**5.38**	**5.57**	**14.95**	**13.29**	**10.51**
General government.................	2 401 ..	3.35	8.05	11.38	2.26	2.71	11.69	9.89	7.01
Debt forgiveness.................	2 402 ..	....	....	....	....	....	....	....	....
Other capital transfers.................	2 410 ..	3.35	8.05	11.38	2.26	2.71	11.69	9.89	7.01
Other sectors.................	2 430 ..	2.82	3.04	3.21	3.12	2.86	3.26	3.40	3.50
Migrants' transfers.................	2 431 ..	2.82	3.04	3.21	3.12	2.86	3.26	3.40	3.50
Debt forgiveness.................	2 432 ..	....	....	....	....	....	....	....	....
Other capital transfers.................	2 440 ..	....	....	....	....	....	....	....	....
Capital transfers, debit.................	3 400 ..	**−.19**	**−.19**	**−.19**	**−.19**	**−.19**	**−.22**	**−.22**	**−.24**
General government.................	3 401 ..	....	....	....	....	....	....	....	....
Debt forgiveness.................	3 402 ..	....	....	....	....	....	....	....	....
Other capital transfers.................	3 410 ..	....	....	....	....	....	....	....	....
Other sectors.................	3 430 ..	−.19	−.19	−.19	−.19	−.19	−.22	−.22	−.24
Migrants' transfers.................	3 431 ..	−.19	−.19	−.19	−.19	−.19	−.22	−.22	−.24
Debt forgiveness.................	3 432 ..	....	....	....	....	....	....	....	....
Other capital transfers.................	3 440 ..	....	....	....	....	....	....	....	....
Nonproduced nonfinancial assets, credit..........	2 480 ..	....	....	**.19**	**.19**	....	....	**.09**	**.09**
Nonproduced nonfinancial assets, debit..........	3 480 ..	....	....	....	....	....	....	....	....

Table 2 (Continued). STANDARD PRESENTATION, 2000–2007

(Millions of U.S. dollars)

	Code	2000	2001	2002	2003	2004	2005	2006	2007
FINANCIAL ACCOUNT	4 995 ..	**129.08**	**147.34**	**135.59**	**160.22**	**97.03**	**95.39**	**106.09**	**186.54**
A. DIRECT INVESTMENT	4 500 ..	**96.21**	**88.11**	**79.77**	**75.61**	**46.14**	**92.99**	**110.42**	**142.60**
Direct investment abroad	4 505 ..	....	−.12	....	....	....	....	....	....
Equity capital	4 510 ..	....	....	....	....	....	....	....	....
Claims on affiliated enterprises	4 515 ..	....	....	....	....	....	....	....	....
Liabilities to affiliated enterprises	4 520 ..	....	....	....	....	....	....	....	....
Reinvested earnings	4 525 ..	....	....	....	....	....	....	....	....
Other capital	4 530 ..	....	....	....	....	....	....	....	....
Claims on affiliated enterprises	4 535 ..	....	....	....	....	....	....	....	....
Liabilities to affiliated enterprises	4 540 ..	....	....	....	....	....	....	....	....
Direct investment in St. Kitts and Nevis	4 555 ..	96.21	88.23	79.77	75.61	46.14	92.99	110.42	142.60
Equity capital	4 560 ..	64.48	80.31	73.81	68.86	40.51	87.37	104.07	135.69
Claims on direct investors	4 565 ..	....	....	....	....	....	....	....	....
Liabilities to direct investors	4 570 ..	64.48	80.31	73.81	68.86	40.51	87.37	104.07	135.69
Reinvested earnings	4 575 ..	3.66	3.70	5.12	4.22	3.60	3.15	2.36	2.54
Other capital	4 580 ..	28.07	4.21	.84	2.53	2.03	2.47	3.98	4.37
Claims on direct investors	4 585 ..	....	....	....	....	....	....	....	....
Liabilities to direct investors	4 590 ..	28.07	4.21	.84	2.53	2.03	2.47	3.98	4.37
B. PORTFOLIO INVESTMENT	4 600 ..	**5.00**	**42.68**	**30.36**	**48.02**	**−9.84**	**−15.02**	**−20.96**	**−19.19**
Assets	4 602 ..	**−.03**	**−1.09**	....	**−.01**	**−.39**	....	**−1.77**	....
Equity securities	4 610 ..	....	....	....	....	....	....	....	....
Monetary authorities	4 611 ..	....	....	....	....	....	....	....	....
General government	4 612 ..	....	....	....	....	....	....	....	....
Banks	4 613 ..	....	....	....	....	....	....	....	....
Other sectors	4 614 ..	....	....	....	....	....	....	....	....
Debt securities	4 619 ..	....	....	....	....	....	....	....	....
Bonds and notes	4 620 ..	....	....	....	....	....	....	....	....
Monetary authorities	4 621 ..	....	....	....	....	....	....	....	....
General government	4 622 ..	....	....	....	....	....	....	....	....
Banks	4 623 ..	....	....	....	....	....	....	....	....
Other sectors	4 624 ..	....	....	....	....	....	....	....	....
Money market instruments	4 630 ..	....	....	....	....	....	....	....	....
Monetary authorities	4 631 ..	....	....	....	....	....	....	....	....
General government	4 632 ..	....	....	....	....	....	....	....	....
Banks	4 633 ..	....	....	....	....	....	....	....	....
Other sectors	4 634 ..	....	....	....	....	....	....	....	....
Liabilities	4 652 ..	**5.03**	**43.77**	**30.36**	**48.03**	**−9.45**	**−15.02**	**−19.19**	**−19.19**
Equity securities	4 660 ..	....	....	....	....	....	....	....	....
Banks	4 663 ..	....	....	....	....	....	....	....	....
Other sectors	4 664 ..	....	....	....	....	....	....	....	....
Debt securities	4 669 ..	....	....	....	....	....	....	....	....
Bonds and notes	4 670 ..	....	....	....	....	....	....	....	....
Monetary authorities	4 671 ..	....	....	....	....	....	....	....	....
General government	4 672 ..	....	....	....	....	....	....	....	....
Banks	4 673 ..	....	....	....	....	....	....	....	....
Other sectors	4 674 ..	....	....	....	....	....	....	....	....
Money market instruments	4 680 ..	....	....	....	....	....	....	....	....
Monetary authorities	4 681 ..	....	....	....	....	....	....	....	....
General government	4 682 ..	....	....	....	....	....	....	....	....
Banks	4 683 ..	....	....	....	....	....	....	....	....
Other sectors	4 684 ..	....	....	....	....	....	....	....	....
C. FINANCIAL DERIVATIVES	4 910 ..	....	....	....	....	....	....	....	....
Monetary authorities	4 911 ..	....	....	....	....	....	....	....	....
General government	4 912 ..	....	....	....	....	....	....	....	....
Banks	4 913 ..	....	....	....	....	....	....	....	....
Other sectors	4 914 ..	....	....	....	....	....	....	....	....
Assets	4 900 ..	....	....	....	....	....	....	....	....
Monetary authorities	4 901 ..	....	....	....	....	....	....	....	....
General government	4 902 ..	....	....	....	....	....	....	....	....
Banks	4 903 ..	....	....	....	....	....	....	....	....
Other sectors	4 904 ..	....	....	....	....	....	....	....	....
Liabilities	4 905 ..	....	....	....	....	....	....	....	....
Monetary authorities	4 906 ..	....	....	....	....	....	....	....	....
General government	4 907 ..	....	....	....	....	....	....	....	....
Banks	4 908 ..	....	....	....	....	....	....	....	....
Other sectors	4 909 ..	....	....	....	....	....	....	....	....

Table 2 (Concluded). STANDARD PRESENTATION, 2000–2007

(Millions of U.S. dollars)

	Code	2000	2001	2002	2003	2004	2005	2006	2007
D. OTHER INVESTMENT	4 700 ..	23.50	28.16	34.08	35.63	74.37	10.74	33.79	70.22
Assets	4 703 ..	23.50	28.16	34.08	35.63	74.37	10.74	33.79	70.22
Trade credits	4 706 ..	....	....	....	....	....	....	....	....
General government	4 707 ..	....	....	....	....	....	....	....	....
of which: Short-term	4 709 ..	....	....	....	....	....	....	....	....
Other sectors	4 710 ..	....	....	....	....	....	....	....	....
of which: Short-term	4 712 ..	....	....	....	....	....	....	....	....
Loans	4 714 ..	....	....	....	....	....	....	....	....
Monetary authorities	4 715 ..	....	....	....	....	....	....	....	....
of which: Short-term	4 718 ..	....	....	....	....	....	....	....	....
General government	4 719 ..	....	....	....	....	....	....	....	....
of which: Short-term	4 721 ..	....	....	....	....	....	....	....	....
Banks	4 722 ..	....	....	....	....	....	....	....	....
of which: Short-term	4 724 ..	....	....	....	....	....	....	....	....
Other sectors	4 725 ..	....	....	....	....	....	....	....	....
of which: Short-term	4 727 ..	....	....	....	....	....	....	....	....
Currency and deposits	4 730 ..	....	....	....	....	....	....	....	....
Monetary authorities	4 731 ..	....	....	....	....	....	....	....	....
General government	4 732 ..	....	....	....	....	....	....	....	....
Banks	4 733 ..	....	....	....	....	....	....	....	....
Other sectors	4 734 ..	....	....	....	....	....	....	....	....
Other assets	4 736 ..	....	....	....	....	....	....	....	....
Monetary authorities	4 737 ..	....	....	....	....	....	....	....	....
of which: Short-term	4 739 ..	....	....	....	....	....	....	....	....
General government	4 740 ..	....	....	....	....	....	....	....	....
of which: Short-term	4 742 ..	....	....	....	....	....	....	....	....
Banks	4 743 ..	....	....	....	....	....	....	....	....
of which: Short-term	4 745 ..	....	....	....	....	....	....	....	....
Other sectors	4 746 ..	....	....	....	....	....	....	....	....
of which: Short-term	4 748 ..	....	....	....	....	....	....	....	....
Liabilities	4 753 ..	....	....	....	....	....	....	....	....
Trade credits	4 756 ..	....	....	....	....	....	....	....	....
General government	4 757 ..	....	....	....	....	....	....	....	....
of which: Short-term	4 759 ..	....	....	....	....	....	....	....	....
Other sectors	4 760 ..	....	....	....	....	....	....	....	....
of which: Short-term	4 762 ..	....	....	....	....	....	....	....	....
Loans	4 764 ..	....	....	....	....	....	....	....	....
Monetary authorities	4 765 ..	....	....	....	....	....	....	....	....
of which: Use of Fund credit and loans from the Fund..	4 766 ..	....	....	....	....	....	....	....	....
of which: Short-term	4 768 ..	....	....	....	....	....	....	....	....
General government	4 769 ..	....	....	....	....	....	....	....	....
of which: Short-term	4 771 ..	....	....	....	....	....	....	....	....
Banks	4 772 ..	....	....	....	....	....	....	....	....
of which: Short-term	4 774 ..	....	....	....	....	....	....	....	....
Other sectors	4 775 ..	....	....	....	....	....	....	....	....
of which: Short-term	4 777 ..	....	....	....	....	....	....	....	....
Currency and deposits	4 780 ..	....	....	....	....	....	....	....	....
Monetary authorities	4 781 ..	....	....	....	....	....	....	....	....
General government	4 782 ..	....	....	....	....	....	....	....	....
Banks	4 783 ..	....	....	....	....	....	....	....	....
Other sectors	4 784 ..	....	....	....	....	....	....	....	....
Other liabilities	4 786 ..	....	....	....	....	....	....	....	....
Monetary authorities	4 787 ..	....	....	....	....	....	....	....	....
of which: Short-term	4 789 ..	....	....	....	....	....	....	....	....
General government	4 790 ..	....	....	....	....	....	....	....	....
of which: Short-term	4 792 ..	....	....	....	....	....	....	....	....
Banks	4 793 ..	....	....	....	....	....	....	....	....
of which: Short-term	4 795 ..	....	....	....	....	....	....	....	....
Other sectors	4 796 ..	....	....	....	....	....	....	....	....
of which: Short-term	4 798 ..	....	....	....	....	....	....	....	....
E. RESERVE ASSETS	4 802 ..	4.37	−11.61	−8.62	.96	−13.64	6.68	−17.15	−7.08
Monetary gold	4 812 ..	....	....	....	....	....	....	....	....
Special drawing rights	4 811 ..	....	−.01	.01	....	....	....	....	....
Reserve position in the Fund	4 810 ..	−.01	....	....	....	....	....	....	....
Foreign exchange	4 803 ..	4.43	−11.68	−8.86	.96	−13.66	6.85	−17.08	−7.08
Other claims	4 813 ..	−.04	.09	.23	....	.02	−.17	−.07	....
NET ERRORS AND OMISSIONS	4 998 ..	−68.86	−50.84	−25.58	−49.80	−34.03	−45.39	−29.48	−61.50

Table 1. ANALYTIC PRESENTATION, 2000–2007

(Millions of U.S. dollars)

	Code	2000	2001	2002	2003	2004	2005	2006	2007
A. Current Account[1]	4 993 Z.	**−94.80**	**−107.58**	**−106.00**	**−147.27**	**−87.37**	**−150.13**	**−302.69**	**−319.70**
Goods: exports f.o.b.	2 100 ..	52.86	54.28	69.32	71.80	96.31	88.77	96.65	100.34
Goods: imports f.o.b.	3 100 ..	−312.46	−272.07	−271.90	−354.50	−348.01	−418.12	−520.94	−540.94
Balance on Goods	4 100 ..	*−259.60*	*−217.80*	*−202.58*	*−282.70*	*−251.70*	*−329.35*	*−424.29*	*−440.59*
Services: credit	2 200 ..	324.01	273.54	249.87	318.32	367.14	410.46	334.21	347.13
Services: debit	3 200 ..	−133.49	−130.63	−129.06	−144.92	−147.74	−171.71	−168.88	−176.42
Balance on Goods and Services	4 991 ..	*−69.07*	*−74.89*	*−81.77*	*−109.31*	*−32.29*	*−90.60*	*−258.95*	*−269.89*
Income: credit	2 300 ..	3.68	2.62	3.59	4.85	6.20	8.11	10.40	6.24
Income: debit	3 300 ..	−48.28	−49.61	−39.92	−55.69	−75.19	−80.62	−66.12	−68.08
Balance on Goods, Services, and Income	4 992 ..	*−113.67*	*−121.88*	*−118.09*	*−160.14*	*−101.28*	*−163.11*	*−314.67*	*−331.72*
Current transfers: credit	2 379 Z.	28.93	28.88	28.39	28.84	29.87	29.67	31.36	32.24
Current transfers: debit	3 379 ..	−10.06	−14.58	−16.30	−15.97	−15.96	−16.70	−19.38	−20.21
B. Capital Account[1]	4 994 Z.	**14.20**	**25.46**	**19.75**	**17.09**	**3.45**	**5.34**	**11.37**	**5.77**
Capital account: credit	2 994 Z.	16.53	26.20	20.86	18.20	4.56	6.45	12.48	6.88
Capital account: debit	3 994 ..	−2.33	−.74	−1.11	−1.11	−1.11	−1.11	−1.11	−1.11
Total, Groups A Plus B	4 981 ..	*−80.61*	*−82.11*	*−86.26*	*−130.18*	*−83.92*	*−144.80*	*−291.32*	*−313.93*
C. Financial Account[1]	4 995 W.	**86.15**	**86.61**	**93.86**	**135.59**	**106.27**	**122.65**	**309.49**	**326.84**
Direct investment abroad	4 505 ..	....	....	....	....	....	....	....	....
Direct investment in St. Lucia	4 555 Z.	53.75	58.81	51.94	106.43	76.52	78.23	233.93	260.93
Portfolio investment assets	4 602 ..	−.64	−4.29	−16.54	1.01	.90	.19	−7.76	−8.69
Equity securities	4 610 ..	....	....	....	....	....	....	....	....
Debt securities	4 619 ..	....	....	....	....	....	....	....	....
Portfolio investment liabilities	4 652 Z.	29.03	16.03	33.41	61.76	15.39	23.85	4.80	6.10
Equity securities	4 660 ..	....	....	....	....	....	....	....	....
Debt securities	4 669 Z.	....	....	....	....	....	....	....	....
Financial derivatives	4 910 ..	....	....	....	....	....	....	....	....
Financial derivatives assets	4 900 ..	....	....	....	....	....	....	....	....
Financial derivatives liabilities	4 905 ..	....	....	....	....	....	....	....	....
Other investment assets	4 703 ..	40.16	56.34	57.46	65.73	56.06	81.83	116.43	112.47
Monetary authorities	4 701 ..	....	....	....	....	....	....	....	....
General government	4 704 ..	....	....	....	....	....	....	....	....
Banks	4 705 ..	....	....	....	....	....	....	....	....
Other sectors	4 728 ..	....	....	....	....	....	....	....	....
Other investment liabilities	4 753 W.	−36.14	−40.28	−32.40	−99.33	−42.60	−61.46	−37.91	−43.98
Monetary authorities	4 753 WA	....	....	....	....	....	....	....	....
General government	4 753 ZB	....	....	....	....	....	....	....	....
Banks	4 753 ZC	....	....	....	....	....	....	....	....
Other sectors	4 753 ZD	....	....	....	....	....	....	....	....
Total, Groups A Through C	4 983 ..	*5.54*	*4.50*	*7.60*	*5.41*	*22.35*	*−22.15*	*18.17*	*12.91*
D. Net Errors and Omissions	4 998 ..	**7.79**	**8.16**	**−1.80**	**12.92**	**4.47**	**6.92**	**−4.30**	**5.67**
Total, Groups A Through D	4 984 ..	*13.33*	*12.65*	*5.81*	*18.34*	*26.83*	*−15.22*	*13.87*	*18.58*
E. Reserves and Related Items	4 802 A.	**−13.33**	**−12.65**	**−5.81**	**−18.34**	**−26.83**	**15.22**	**−13.87**	**−18.58**
Reserve assets	4 802 ..	−13.33	−12.65	−5.81	−18.34	−26.83	15.22	−13.87	−18.58
Use of Fund credit and loans	4 766 ..	....	....	....	....	....	....	....	....
Exceptional financing	4 920 ..	....	....	....	....	....	....	....	....
Conversion rates: Eastern Caribbean dollars per U.S. dollar	0 101 ..	**2.7000**	**2.7000**	**2.7000**	**2.7000**	**2.7000**	**2.7000**	**2.7000**	**2.7000**

[1] Excludes components that have been classified in the categories of Group E.

Table 2. STANDARD PRESENTATION, 2000–2007

(Millions of U.S. dollars)

	Code	2000	2001	2002	2003	2004	2005	2006	2007
CURRENT ACCOUNT....................................	4 993 ..	−94.80	−107.58	−106.00	−147.27	−87.37	−150.13	−302.69	−319.70
A. GOODS...	4 100 ..	−259.60	−217.80	−202.58	−282.70	−251.70	−329.35	−424.29	−440.59
Credit..	2 100 ..	52.86	54.28	69.32	71.80	96.31	88.77	96.65	100.34
General merchandise: exports f.o.b.............	2 110 ..	43.25	44.30	62.03	62.08	79.78	64.16	72.31	74.76
Goods for processing: exports f.o.b............	2 150 ..	....	....	....	....	....	....	....	....
Repairs on goods.....................................	2 160 ..	.01	.01	....	.01	.01	.01	.01	.01
Goods procured in ports by carriers...........	2 170 ..	9.60	9.97	7.29	9.71	16.53	24.61	24.33	25.58
Nonmonetary gold....................................	2 180 ..	....	....	....	....	....	....	....	....
Debit...	3 100 ..	−312.46	−272.07	−271.90	−354.50	−348.01	−418.12	−520.94	−540.94
General merchandise: imports f.o.b............	3 110 ..	−312.46	−272.07	−271.90	−354.50	−348.01	−418.12	−520.94	−540.94
Goods for processing: imports f.o.b............	3 150 ..	....	....	....	....	....	....	....	....
Repairs on goods.....................................	3 160 ..	....	....	....	....	....	....	....	....
Goods procured in ports by carriers...........	3 170 ..	....	....	....	....	....	....	....	....
Nonmonetary gold....................................	3 180 ..	....	....	....	....	....	....	....	....
B. SERVICES..	4 200 ..	190.53	142.91	120.81	173.39	219.41	238.75	165.34	170.70
Total credit...	2 200 ..	*324.01*	*273.54*	*249.87*	*318.32*	*367.14*	*410.46*	*334.21*	*347.13*
Total debit..	3 200 ..	*−133.49*	*−130.63*	*−129.06*	*−144.92*	*−147.74*	*−171.71*	*−168.88*	*−176.42*
Transportation services, credit...........	2 205 ..	13.29	12.52	11.54	12.27	15.32	21.63	21.70	22.31
Passenger..	2 850 ..	....	....	....	....	....	....	....	....
Freight..	2 851 ..	....	....	....	....	....	....	....	....
Other..	2 852 ..	....	....	....	....	....	....	....	....
Sea transport, passenger...........................	2 207 ..	....	....	....	....	....	....	....	....
Sea transport, freight................................	2 208 ..	....	....	....	....	....	....	....	....
Sea transport, other..................................	2 209 ..	....	....	....	....	....	....	....	....
Air transport, passenger............................	2 211 ..	....	....	....	....	....	....	....	....
Air transport, freight.................................	2 212 ..	....	....	....	....	....	....	....	....
Air transport, other...................................	2 213 ..	....	....	....	....	....	....	....	....
Other transport, passenger........................	2 215 ..	....	....	....	....	....	....	....	....
Other transport, freight.............................	2 216 ..	....	....	....	....	....	....	....	....
Other transport, other...............................	2 217 ..	....	....	....	....	....	....	....	....
Transportation services, debit............	3 205 ..	−53.19	−53.89	−49.98	−63.01	−64.14	−73.48	−80.56	−83.93
Passenger..	3 850 ..	....	....	....	....	....	....	....	....
Freight..	3 851 ..	....	....	....	....	....	....	....	....
Other..	3 852 ..	....	....	....	....	....	....	....	....
Sea transport, passenger...........................	3 207 ..	....	....	....	....	....	....	....	....
Sea transport, freight................................	3 208 ..	....	....	....	....	....	....	....	....
Sea transport, other..................................	3 209 ..	....	....	....	....	....	....	....	....
Air transport, passenger............................	3 211 ..	....	....	....	....	....	....	....	....
Air transport, freight.................................	3 212 ..	....	....	....	....	....	....	....	....
Air transport, other...................................	3 213 ..	....	....	....	....	....	....	....	....
Other transport, passenger........................	3 215 ..	....	....	....	....	....	....	....	....
Other transport, freight.............................	3 216 ..	....	....	....	....	....	....	....	....
Other transport, other...............................	3 217 ..	....	....	....	....	....	....	....	....
Travel, credit......................................	2 236 ..	280.54	232.98	210.01	282.08	325.66	355.98	284.61	295.54
Business travel...	2 237 ..	....	....	....	....	....	....	....	....
Personal travel...	2 240 ..	....	....	....	....	....	....	....	....
Travel, debit..	3 236 ..	−33.30	−31.76	−33.73	−35.67	−36.83	−38.92	−39.34	−41.35
Business travel...	3 237 ..	....	....	....	....	....	....	....	....
Personal travel...	3 240 ..	....	....	....	....	....	....	....	....
Other services, credit..........................	2 200 BA	30.19	28.03	28.33	23.97	26.17	32.85	27.90	29.28
Communications......................................	2 245 ..	8.53	9.29	11.57	7.62	7.89	13.46	8.43	8.87
Construction..	2 249 ..	....	....	....	....	....	....	....	....
Insurance...	2 253 ..	4.09	4.99	4.57	4.73	4.20	5.62	6.06	6.37
Financial...	2 260 ..	....	....	....	....	....	....	....	....
Computer and information........................	2 262 ..	5.00	3.50	2.43	2.43	2.43	3.33	....	....
Royalties and licence fees.........................	2 266 ..	....	....	....	....	....	....	....	....
Other business services............................	2 268 ..	11.21	8.87	8.31	7.73	10.17	8.75	11.64	12.23
Personal, cultural, and recreational............	2 287 ..	....	....	....	....	....	....	....	....
Government, n.i.e.....................................	2 291 ..	1.37	1.39	1.44	1.45	1.47	1.70	1.77	1.81
Other services, debit...........................	3 200 BA	−47.00	−44.98	−45.36	−46.25	−46.77	−59.31	−48.98	−51.14
Communications......................................	3 245 ..	−5.68	−6.05	−6.05	−2.93	−3.91	−13.72	−3.20	−3.29
Construction..	3 249 ..	....	....	....	....	....	....	....	....
Insurance...	3 253 ..	−9.85	−9.29	−9.41	−11.48	−11.19	−13.32	−15.84	−16.42
Financial...	3 260 ..	....	....	....	....	....	....	....	....
Computer and information........................	3 262 ..	....	−.36	−.34	−.50	−.43	....	....	....
Royalties and licence fees.........................	3 266 ..	−1.57	−1.38	−2.18	−2.40	−2.38	−2.38	−2.43	−2.56
Other business services............................	3 268 ..	−22.56	−22.04	−22.22	−24.67	−24.34	−27.21	−24.03	−25.26
Personal, cultural, and recreational............	3 287 ..	....	....	....	....	....	....	....	....
Government, n.i.e.....................................	3 291 ..	−7.34	−5.86	−5.16	−4.26	−4.51	−2.68	−3.48	−3.61

Table 2 (Continued). STANDARD PRESENTATION, 2000–2007

(Millions of U.S. dollars)

	Code	2000	2001	2002	2003	2004	2005	2006	2007
C. INCOME..	4 300	**−44.60**	**−46.98**	**−36.32**	**−50.84**	**−68.99**	**−72.51**	**−55.72**	**−61.84**
Total credit................................	2 300	*3.68*	*2.62*	*3.59*	*4.85*	*6.20*	*8.11*	*10.40*	*6.24*
Total debit.................................	3 300	*−48.28*	*−49.61*	*−39.92*	*−55.69*	*−75.19*	*−80.62*	*−66.12*	*−68.08*
Compensation of employees, credit..............	2 310	**.04**	**.06**	**.06**	**.09**	**.13**	**.17**	**.11**	**.11**
Compensation of employees, debit...............	3 310	....	....	....	....	....	....	....	....
Investment income, credit...............	2 320	**3.64**	**2.56**	**3.54**	**4.76**	**6.07**	**7.94**	**10.29**	**6.13**
Direct investment income.......................	2 330	....	....	....	....	.02	.03	.04	.04
Dividends and distributed branch profits........	2 332	....	....	....	....	.02	.03	.04	.04
Reinvested earnings and undistributed branch profits.....	2 333	....	....	....	....	....	....	....	....
Income on debt (interest).....................	2 334	....	....	....	....	....	....	....	....
Portfolio investment income..................	2 339	1.29	1.23	2.24	2.81	4.22	2.88	4.94	.51
Income on equity........................	2 340	1.29	1.23	2.24	2.81	4.22	2.88	4.94	.51
Income on bonds and notes...............	2 350	....	....	....	....	....	....	....	....
Income on money market instruments.........	2 360	....	....	....	....	....	....	....	....
Other investment income..................	2 370	2.35	1.33	1.30	1.95	1.83	5.03	5.31	5.57
Investment income, debit................	3 320	**−48.28**	**−49.61**	**−39.92**	**−55.69**	**−75.19**	**−80.62**	**−66.12**	**−68.08**
Direct investment income.	3 330	−33.37	−31.10	−22.58	−31.86	−48.85	−51.08	−34.01	−35.74
Dividends and distributed branch profits........	3 332	−14.97	−10.93	−9.66	−12.27	−20.74	−19.31	−18.83	−19.79
Reinvested earnings and undistributed branch profits.....	3 333	−16.00	−16.36	−9.25	−16.20	−22.07	−25.11	−11.00	−11.57
Income on debt (interest).....................	3 334	−2.40	−3.81	−3.66	−3.40	−6.04	−6.66	−4.18	−4.38
Portfolio investment income..................	3 339	−1.05	−2.48	−3.19	−7.70	−9.35	−9.73	−9.46	−9.67
Income on equity........................	3 340	−1.05	−2.48	−3.19	−7.70	−9.35	−9.73	−9.46	−9.67
Income on bonds and notes...............	3 350	....	....	....	....	....	....	....	....
Income on money market instruments.........	3 360	....	....	....	....	....	....	....	....
Other investment income..................	3 370	−13.86	−16.03	−14.15	−16.12	−16.99	−19.81	−22.65	−22.68
D. CURRENT TRANSFERS......................................	4 379	**18.87**	**14.30**	**12.09**	**12.87**	**13.91**	**12.97**	**11.98**	**12.02**
Credit..	2 379	**28.93**	**28.88**	**28.39**	**28.84**	**29.87**	**29.67**	**31.36**	**32.24**
General government................................	2 380	5.14	4.57	3.61	3.57	3.39	2.37	3.20	3.29
Other sectors..	2 390	23.79	24.31	24.78	25.27	26.48	27.30	28.16	28.94
Workers' remittances................................	2 391	23.79	24.07	24.51	25.02	26.18	26.89	27.73	28.50
Other current transfers...........................	2 392	....	.24	.27	.25	.30	.40	.43	.44
Debit..	3 379	**−10.06**	**−14.58**	**−16.30**	**−15.97**	**−15.96**	**−16.70**	**−19.38**	**−20.21**
General government................................	3 380	−1.74	−4.89	−4.59	−3.55	−3.57	−3.61	−3.65	−3.84
Other sectors..	3 390	−8.32	−9.69	−11.71	−12.42	−12.39	−13.09	−15.73	−16.37
Workers' remittances................................	3 391	−2.59	−2.78	−2.78	−2.78	−2.78	−2.99	−3.12	−3.12
Other current transfers...........................	3 392	−5.73	−6.91	−8.93	−9.65	−9.61	−10.09	−12.61	−13.25
CAPITAL AND FINANCIAL ACCOUNT.....................	4 996	**87.02**	**99.42**	**107.80**	**134.35**	**82.90**	**143.21**	**306.99**	**314.03**
CAPITAL ACCOUNT..	4 994	**14.20**	**25.46**	**19.75**	**17.09**	**3.45**	**5.34**	**11.37**	**5.77**
Total credit..	2 994	*16.53*	*26.20*	*20.86*	*18.20*	*4.56*	*6.45*	*12.48*	*6.88*
Total debit...	3 994	*−2.33*	*−.74*	*−1.11*	*−1.11*	*−1.11*	*−1.11*	*−1.11*	*−1.11*
Capital transfers, credit..	2 400	**16.53**	**26.20**	**20.86**	**18.20**	**4.56**	**6.45**	**12.48**	**6.88**
General government................................	2 401	13.92	23.47	18.64	15.94	2.23	4.05	10.01	4.41
Debt forgiveness..............................	2 402	....	....	.49	....	....	....	....	....
Other capital transfers...........................	2 410	13.92	23.47	18.15	15.94	2.23	4.05	10.01	4.41
Other sectors..	2 430	2.61	2.73	2.22	2.26	2.33	2.40	2.47	2.47
Migrants' transfers..............................	2 431	2.61	2.73	2.22	2.26	2.33	2.40	2.47	2.47
Debt forgiveness..............................	2 432	....	....	....	....	....	....	....	....
Other capital transfers...........................	2 440	....	....	....	....	....	....	....	....
Capital transfers, debit..	3 400	**−.74**	**−.74**	**−1.11**	**−1.11**	**−1.11**	**−1.11**	**−1.11**	**−1.11**
General government................................	3 401	....	....	....	....	....	....	....	....
Debt forgiveness..............................	3 402	....	....	....	....	....	....	....	....
Other capital transfers...........................	3 410	....	....	....	....	....	....	....	....
Other sectors..	3 430	−.74	−.74	−1.11	−1.11	−1.11	−1.11	−1.11	−1.11
Migrants' transfers..............................	3 431	−.74	−.74	−1.11	−1.11	−1.11	−1.11	−1.11	−1.11
Debt forgiveness..............................	3 432	....	....	....	....	....	....	....	....
Other capital transfers...........................	3 440	....	....	....	....	....	....	....	....
Nonproduced nonfinancial assets, credit.............	2 480	....	....	....	....	....	....	....	....
Nonproduced nonfinancial assets, debit..............	3 480	**−1.59**	....	....	....	....	....	....	....

Table 2 (Continued). STANDARD PRESENTATION, 2000–2007

(Millions of U.S. dollars)

	Code	2000	2001	2002	2003	2004	2005	2006	2007
FINANCIAL ACCOUNT	4 995	**72.82**	**73.96**	**88.05**	**117.26**	**79.45**	**137.87**	**295.62**	**308.26**
A. DIRECT INVESTMENT	4 500	**53.75**	**58.81**	**51.94**	**106.43**	**76.52**	**78.23**	**233.93**	**260.93**
Direct investment abroad	4 505	....	....	....	....	....	....	....	....
Equity capital	4 510	....	....	....	....	....	....	....	....
Claims on affiliated enterprises	4 515	....	....	....	....	....	....	....	....
Liabilities to affiliated enterprises	4 520	....	....	....	....	....	....	....	....
Reinvested earnings	4 525	....	....	....	....	....	....	....	....
Other capital	4 530	....	....	....	....	....	....	....	....
Claims on affiliated enterprises	4 535	....	....	....	....	....	....	....	....
Liabilities to affiliated enterprises	4 540	....	....	....	....	....	....	....	....
Direct investment in St. Lucia	4 555	**53.75**	**58.81**	**51.94**	**106.43**	**76.52**	**78.23**	**233.93**	**260.93**
Equity capital	4 560	6.76	9.41	11.59	13.78	55.75	52.78	220.18	246.46
Claims on direct investors	4 565	....	....	....	....	....	....	....	....
Liabilities to direct investors	4 570	6.76	9.41	11.59	13.78	55.75	52.78	220.18	246.46
Reinvested earnings	4 575	16.00	16.36	9.25	16.20	22.07	25.11	11.00	11.57
Other capital	4 580	30.99	33.04	31.09	76.45	−1.30	.34	2.75	2.91
Claims on direct investors	4 585	....	....	....	....	....	....	....	....
Liabilities to direct investors	4 590	30.99	33.04	31.09	76.45	−1.30	.34	2.75	2.91
B. PORTFOLIO INVESTMENT	4 600	**28.39**	**11.74**	**16.87**	**62.77**	**16.29**	**24.05**	**−2.96**	**−2.58**
Assets	4 602	−.64	−4.29	−16.54	1.01	.90	.19	−7.76	−8.69
Equity securities	4 610	....	....	....	....	....	....	....	....
Monetary authorities	4 611	....	....	....	....	....	....	....	....
General government	4 612	....	....	....	....	....	....	....	....
Banks	4 613	....	....	....	....	....	....	....	....
Other sectors	4 614	....	....	....	....	....	....	....	....
Debt securities	4 619	....	....	....	....	....	....	....	....
Bonds and notes	4 620	....	....	....	....	....	....	....	....
Monetary authorities	4 621	....	....	....	....	....	....	....	....
General government	4 622	....	....	....	....	....	....	....	....
Banks	4 623	....	....	....	....	....	....	....	....
Other sectors	4 624	....	....	....	....	....	....	....	....
Money market instruments	4 630	....	....	....	....	....	....	....	....
Monetary authorities	4 631	....	....	....	....	....	....	....	....
General government	4 632	....	....	....	....	....	....	....	....
Banks	4 633	....	....	....	....	....	....	....	....
Other sectors	4 634	....	....	....	....	....	....	....	....
Liabilities	4 652	**29.03**	**16.03**	**33.41**	**61.76**	**15.39**	**23.85**	**4.80**	**6.10**
Equity securities	4 660	....	....	....	....	....	....	....	....
Banks	4 663	....	....	....	....	....	....	....	....
Other sectors	4 664	....	....	....	....	....	....	....	....
Debt securities	4 669	....	....	....	....	....	....	....	....
Bonds and notes	4 670	....	....	....	....	....	....	....	....
Monetary authorities	4 671	....	....	....	....	....	....	....	....
General government	4 672	....	....	....	....	....	....	....	....
Banks	4 673	....	....	....	....	....	....	....	....
Other sectors	4 674	....	....	....	....	....	....	....	....
Money market instruments	4 680	....	....	....	....	....	....	....	....
Monetary authorities	4 681	....	....	....	....	....	....	....	....
General government	4 682	....	....	....	....	....	....	....	....
Banks	4 683	....	....	....	....	....	....	....	....
Other sectors	4 684	....	....	....	....	....	....	....	....
C. FINANCIAL DERIVATIVES	4 910	....	....	....	....	....	....	....	....
Monetary authorities	4 911	....	....	....	....	....	....	....	....
General government	4 912	....	....	....	....	....	....	....	....
Banks	4 913	....	....	....	....	....	....	....	....
Other sectors	4 914	....	....	....	....	....	....	....	....
Assets	4 900	....	....	....	....	....	....	....	....
Monetary authorities	4 901	....	....	....	....	....	....	....	....
General government	4 902	....	....	....	....	....	....	....	....
Banks	4 903	....	....	....	....	....	....	....	....
Other sectors	4 904	....	....	....	....	....	....	....	....
Liabilities	4 905	....	....	....	....	....	....	....	....
Monetary authorities	4 906	....	....	....	....	....	....	....	....
General government	4 907	....	....	....	....	....	....	....	....
Banks	4 908	....	....	....	....	....	....	....	....
Other sectors	4 909	....	....	....	....	....	....	....	....

Table 2 (Concluded). STANDARD PRESENTATION, 2000–2007

(Millions of U.S. dollars)

	Code	2000	2001	2002	2003	2004	2005	2006	2007
D. OTHER INVESTMENT	4 700 ..	**4.02**	**16.06**	**25.06**	**−33.60**	**13.46**	**20.37**	**78.52**	**68.49**
Assets	4 703 ..	**40.16**	**56.34**	**57.46**	**65.73**	**56.06**	**81.83**	**116.43**	**112.47**
Trade credits	4 706 ..	....	....	....	....	....	....	....	....
General government	4 707 ..	....	....	....	....	....	....	....	....
of which: Short-term	4 709 ..	....	....	....	....	....	....	....	....
Other sectors	4 710 ..	....	....	....	....	....	....	....	....
of which: Short-term	4 712 ..	....	....	....	....	....	....	....	....
Loans	4 714 ..	....	....	....	....	....	....	....	....
Monetary authorities	4 715 ..	....	....	....	....	....	....	....	....
of which: Short-term	4 718 ..	....	....	....	....	....	....	....	....
General government	4 719 ..	....	....	....	....	....	....	....	....
of which: Short-term	4 721 ..	....	....	....	....	....	....	....	....
Banks	4 722 ..	....	....	....	....	....	....	....	....
of which: Short-term	4 724 ..	....	....	....	....	....	....	....	....
Other sectors	4 725 ..	....	....	....	....	....	....	....	....
of which: Short-term	4 727 ..	....	....	....	....	....	....	....	....
Currency and deposits	4 730 ..	....	....	....	....	....	....	....	....
Monetary authorities	4 731 ..	....	....	....	....	....	....	....	....
General government	4 732 ..	....	....	....	....	....	....	....	....
Banks	4 733 ..	....	....	....	....	....	....	....	....
Other sectors	4 734 ..	....	....	....	....	....	....	....	....
Other assets	4 736 ..	....	....	....	....	....	....	....	....
Monetary authorities	4 737 ..	....	....	....	....	....	....	....	....
of which: Short-term	4 739 ..	....	....	....	....	....	....	....	....
General government	4 740 ..	....	....	....	....	....	....	....	....
of which: Short-term	4 742 ..	....	....	....	....	....	....	....	....
Banks	4 743 ..	....	....	....	....	....	....	....	....
of which: Short-term	4 745 ..	....	....	....	....	....	....	....	....
Other sectors	4 746 ..	....	....	....	....	....	....	....	....
of which: Short-term	4 748 ..	....	....	....	....	....	....	....	....
Liabilities	4 753 ..	**−36.14**	**−40.28**	**−32.40**	**−99.33**	**−42.60**	**−61.46**	**−37.91**	**−43.98**
Trade credits	4 756 ..	....	....	....	....	....	....	....	....
General government	4 757 ..	....	....	....	....	....	....	....	....
of which: Short-term	4 759 ..	....	....	....	....	....	....	....	....
Other sectors	4 760 ..	....	....	....	....	....	....	....	....
of which: Short-term	4 762 ..	....	....	....	....	....	....	....	....
Loans	4 764 ..	....	....	....	....	....	....	....	....
Monetary authorities	4 765 ..	....	....	....	....	....	....	....	....
of which: Use of Fund credit and loans from the Fund	4 766 ..	....	....	....	....	....	....	....	....
of which: Short-term	4 768 ..	....	....	....	....	....	....	....	....
General government	4 769 ..	....	....	....	....	....	....	....	....
of which: Short-term	4 771 ..	....	....	....	....	....	....	....	....
Banks	4 772 ..	....	....	....	....	....	....	....	....
of which: Short-term	4 774 ..	....	....	....	....	....	....	....	....
Other sectors	4 775 ..	....	....	....	....	....	....	....	....
of which: Short-term	4 777 ..	....	....	....	....	....	....	....	....
Currency and deposits	4 780 ..	....	....	....	....	....	....	....	....
Monetary authorities	4 781 ..	....	....	....	....	....	....	....	....
General government	4 782 ..	....	....	....	....	....	....	....	....
Banks	4 783 ..	....	....	....	....	....	....	....	....
Other sectors	4 784 ..	....	....	....	....	....	....	....	....
Other liabilities	4 786 ..	....	....	....	....	....	....	....	....
Monetary authorities	4 787 ..	....	....	....	....	....	....	....	....
of which: Short-term	4 789 ..	....	....	....	....	....	....	....	....
General government	4 790 ..	....	....	....	....	....	....	....	....
of which: Short-term	4 792 ..	....	....	....	....	....	....	....	....
Banks	4 793 ..	....	....	....	....	....	....	....	....
of which: Short-term	4 795 ..	....	....	....	....	....	....	....	....
Other sectors	4 796 ..	....	....	....	....	....	....	....	....
of which: Short-term	4 798 ..	....	....	....	....	....	....	....	....
E. RESERVE ASSETS	4 802 ..	**−13.33**	**−12.65**	**−5.81**	**−18.34**	**−26.83**	**15.22**	**−13.87**	**−18.58**
Monetary gold	4 812 ..	....	....	....	....	....	....	....	....
Special drawing rights	4 811 ..	.09	−.03	−.02	−.02	−.02	−.03	−.04	−.05
Reserve position in the Fund	4 810 ..	....	....	....	−.01	....	....	....	....
Foreign exchange	4 803 ..	−4.51	−10.14	−4.78	−12.79	−25.52	15.99	−18.39	−19.01
Other claims	4 813 ..	−8.91	−2.48	−1.00	−5.51	−1.29	−.74	4.56	.49
NET ERRORS AND OMISSIONS	4 998 ..	**7.79**	**8.16**	**−1.80**	**12.92**	**4.47**	**6.92**	**−4.30**	**5.67**

Table 1. ANALYTIC PRESENTATION, 2000–2007

(Millions of U.S. dollars)

	Code	2000	2001	2002	2003	2004	2005	2006	2007
A. Current Account[1]	4 993 Z.	−23.91	−37.39	−41.97	−79.48	−102.10	−99.37	−120.12	−148.99
Goods: exports f.o.b.	2 100 ..	51.75	42.76	41.24	40.09	39.28	42.57	41.16	50.75
Goods: imports f.o.b.	3 100 ..	−144.36	−151.97	−157.77	−176.81	−198.98	−212.39	−239.65	−276.31
Balance on Goods	4 100 ..	*−92.60*	*−109.21*	*−116.53*	*−136.72*	*−159.70*	*−169.82*	*−198.49*	*−225.56*
Services: credit	2 200 ..	127.66	133.19	137.07	132.76	145.21	157.97	170.84	181.23
Services: debit	3 200 ..	−56.11	−57.49	−57.05	−64.59	−73.22	−78.80	−88.44	−98.46
Balance on Goods and Services	4 991 ..	*−21.06*	*−33.51*	*−36.51*	*−68.54*	*−87.70*	*−90.65*	*−116.09*	*−142.79*
Income: credit	2 300 ..	3.14	2.37	3.37	3.76	4.93	8.40	13.60	14.58
Income: debit	3 300 ..	−22.32	−18.86	−20.98	−27.59	−33.44	−35.17	−37.79	−40.62
Balance on Goods, Services, and Income	4 992 ..	*−40.23*	*−50.00*	*−54.11*	*−92.38*	*−116.21*	*−117.42*	*−140.29*	*−168.83*
Current transfers: credit	2 379 Z.	24.70	23.24	23.74	24.29	25.13	26.40	32.23	33.03
Current transfers: debit	3 379 ..	−8.38	−10.63	−11.59	−11.39	−11.02	−8.35	−12.06	−13.20
B. Capital Account[1]	4 994 Z.	**5.60**	**8.76**	**10.60**	**14.36**	**18.94**	**14.23**	**8.15**	**161.78**
Capital account: credit	2 994 Z.	6.86	10.03	11.87	15.63	20.30	15.66	9.73	163.51
Capital account: debit	3 994 ..	−1.27	−1.27	−1.27	−1.27	−1.37	−1.43	−1.58	−1.73
Total, Groups A Plus B	4 981 ..	*−18.31*	*−28.63*	*−31.36*	*−65.11*	*−83.17*	*−85.13*	*−111.97*	*12.79*
C. Financial Account[1]	4 995 W.	**24.67**	**48.66**	**15.31**	**48.99**	**83.20**	**62.98**	**112.65**	**−23.51**
Direct investment abroad	4 505 ..	....	....	....	....	....	....	....	....
Direct investment in St. Vincent and the Grenadines	4 555 Z.	37.74	21.04	34.05	55.16	65.69	40.09	109.11	91.64
Portfolio investment assets	4 602 ..	−.52	.17	−5.40	−.96	−10.24	−2.21	−1.66	−1.51
Equity securities	4 610 ..	....	....	....	....	....	....	....	....
Debt securities	4 619 ..	....	....	....	....	....	....	....	....
Portfolio investment liabilities	4 652 Z.	1.96	3.31	6.41	21.66	43.41	−5.98	14.17	....
Equity securities	4 660 ..	....	....	....	....	....	....	....	....
Debt securities	4 669 Z.	....	....	....	....	....	....	....	....
Financial derivatives	4 910 ..	....	....	....	....	....	....	....	....
Financial derivatives assets	4 900 ..	....	....	....	....	....	....	....	....
Financial derivatives liabilities	4 905 ..	....	....	....	....	....	....	....	....
Other investment assets	4 703 ..	12.04	41.70	13.15	32.67	59.80	95.70	47.76	59.68
Monetary authorities	4 701 ..	....	....	....	....	....	....	....	....
General government	4 704 ..	....	....	....	....	....	....	....	....
Banks	4 705 ..	....	....	....	....	....	....	....	....
Other sectors	4 728 ..	....	....	....	....	....	....	....	....
Other investment liabilities	4 753 W.	−26.56	−17.56	−32.89	−59.54	−75.45	−64.61	−56.74	−173.33
Monetary authorities	4 753 WA	....	....	....	....	....	....	....	....
General government	4 753 ZB	....	....	....	....	....	....	....	....
Banks	4 753 ZC	....	....	....	....	....	....	....	....
Other sectors	4 753 ZD	....	....	....	....	....	....	....	....
Total, Groups A Through C	4 983 ..	*6.36*	*20.03*	*−16.05*	*−16.12*	*.04*	*−22.15*	*.68*	*−10.73*
D. Net Errors and Omissions	4 998 ..	**7.66**	**−10.98**	**9.43**	**15.62**	**25.37**	**19.27**	**11.43**	**8.88**
Total, Groups A Through D	4 984 ..	*14.02*	*9.06*	*−6.62*	*−.50*	*25.41*	*−2.88*	*12.11*	*−1.85*
E. Reserves and Related Items	4 802 A.	**−14.02**	**−9.06**	**6.63**	**.50**	**−25.41**	**2.88**	**−12.11**	**1.85**
Reserve assets	4 802 ..	−14.02	−9.06	6.63	.50	−25.41	2.88	−12.11	1.85
Use of Fund credit and loans	4 766 ..	....	....	....	....	....	....	....	....
Exceptional financing	4 920 ..	....	....	....	....	....	....	....	....
Conversion rates: Eastern Caribbean dollars per U.S. dollar	0 101 ..	**2.7000**	**2.7000**	**2.7000**	**2.7000**	**2.7000**	**2.7000**	**2.7000**	**2.7000**

[1] Excludes components that have been classified in the categories of Group E.

Table 2. STANDARD PRESENTATION, 2000–2007

(Millions of U.S. dollars)

	Code	2000	2001	2002	2003	2004	2005	2006	2007
CURRENT ACCOUNT	4 993 ..	**−23.91**	**−37.39**	**−41.97**	**−79.48**	**−102.10**	**−99.37**	**−120.12**	**−148.99**
A. GOODS	4 100 ..	**−92.60**	**−109.21**	**−116.53**	**−136.72**	**−159.70**	**−169.82**	**−198.49**	**−225.56**
Credit	2 100 ..	**51.75**	**42.76**	**41.24**	**40.09**	**39.28**	**42.57**	**41.16**	**50.75**
General merchandise: exports f.o.b.	2 110 ..	50.59	41.62	39.30	37.99	36.61	39.88	38.11	47.60
Goods for processing: exports f.o.b.	2 150 ..	....	....	....	....	....	....	....	....
Repairs on goods	2 160 ..	....	.02	.02	....	.01	.01	.01	.01
Goods procured in ports by carriers	2 170 ..	1.16	1.12	1.93	2.10	2.66	2.69	3.05	3.14
Nonmonetary gold	2 180 ..	....	....	....	....	....	....	....	....
Debit	3 100 ..	**−144.36**	**−151.97**	**−157.77**	**−176.81**	**−198.98**	**−212.39**	**−239.65**	**−276.31**
General merchandise: imports f.o.b.	3 110 ..	−143.71	−151.23	−157.09	−176.17	−198.33	−211.67	−238.91	−275.55
Goods for processing: imports f.o.b.	3 150 ..	....	....	....	....	....	....	....	....
Repairs on goods	3 160 ..	....	....	....	....	....	....	....	....
Goods procured in ports by carriers	3 170 ..	−.64	−.74	−.68	−.63	−.65	−.73	−.74	−.76
Nonmonetary gold	3 180 ..	....	....	....	....	....	....	....	....
B. SERVICES	4 200 ..	**71.55**	**75.70**	**80.02**	**68.17**	**71.99**	**79.17**	**82.40**	**82.77**
Total credit	2 200 ..	*127.66*	*133.19*	*137.07*	*132.76*	*145.21*	*157.97*	*170.84*	*181.23*
Total debit	3 200 ..	*−56.11*	*−57.49*	*−57.05*	*−64.59*	*−73.22*	*−78.80*	*−88.44*	*−98.46*
Transportation services, credit	2 205 ..	**10.51**	**9.51**	**9.35**	**9.36**	**10.83**	**10.52**	**11.63**	**13.10**
Passenger	2 850 ..	....	....	....	....	....	....	....	....
Freight	2 851 ..	....	....	....	....	....	....	....	....
Other	2 852 ..	....	....	....	....	....	....	....	....
Sea transport, passenger	2 207 ..	....	....	....	....	....	....	....	....
Sea transport, freight	2 208 ..	....	....	....	....	....	....	....	....
Sea transport, other	2 209 ..	....	....	....	....	....	....	....	....
Air transport, passenger	2 211 ..	....	....	....	....	....	....	....	....
Air transport, freight	2 212 ..	....	....	....	....	....	....	....	....
Air transport, other	2 213 ..	....	....	....	....	....	....	....	....
Other transport, passenger	2 215 ..	....	....	....	....	....	....	....	....
Other transport, freight	2 216 ..	....	....	....	....	....	....	....	....
Other transport, other	2 217 ..	....	....	....	....	....	....	....	....
Transportation services, debit	3 205 ..	**−24.86**	**−25.68**	**−26.25**	**−29.52**	**−32.26**	**−34.24**	**−38.15**	**−43.35**
Passenger	3 850 ..	....	....	....	....	....	....	....	....
Freight	3 851 ..	....	....	....	....	....	....	....	....
Other	3 852 ..	....	....	....	....	....	....	....	....
Sea transport, passenger	3 207 ..	....	....	....	....	....	....	....	....
Sea transport, freight	3 208 ..	....	....	....	....	....	....	....	....
Sea transport, other	3 209 ..	....	....	....	....	....	....	....	....
Air transport, passenger	3 211 ..	....	....	....	....	....	....	....	....
Air transport, freight	3 212 ..	....	....	....	....	....	....	....	....
Air transport, other	3 213 ..	....	....	....	....	....	....	....	....
Other transport, passenger	3 215 ..	....	....	....	....	....	....	....	....
Other transport, freight	3 216 ..	....	....	....	....	....	....	....	....
Other transport, other	3 217 ..	....	....	....	....	....	....	....	....
Travel, credit	2 236 ..	**82.28**	**89.01**	**91.01**	**91.19**	**95.55**	**103.89**	**113.26**	**119.36**
Business travel	2 237 ..	....	....	....	....	....	....	....	....
Personal travel	2 240 ..	....	....	....	....	....	....	....	....
Travel, debit	3 236 ..	**−9.96**	**−11.55**	**−10.18**	**−12.65**	**−14.29**	**−14.91**	**−15.71**	**−17.40**
Business travel	3 237 ..	....	....	....	....	....	....	....	....
Personal travel	3 240 ..	....	....	....	....	....	....	....	....
Other services, credit	2 200 BA ..	**34.87**	**34.67**	**36.71**	**32.21**	**38.84**	**43.56**	**45.94**	**48.77**
Communications	2 245 ..	11.71	11.61	12.24	12.45	12.49	10.14	8.57	9.17
Construction	2 249 ..	....	....	....	....	....	....	....	....
Insurance	2 253 ..	1.53	1.76	1.62	1.90	1.73	2.31	2.87	3.14
Financial	2 260 ..	....	....	....	....	....	....	....	....
Computer and information	2 262 ..	....	....	....	....	....	....	....	....
Royalties and licence fees	2 266 ..	....	....	....	....	....	....	....	....
Other business services	2 268 ..	19.48	19.41	21.00	16.20	22.71	29.08	32.51	34.45
Personal, cultural, and recreational	2 287 ..	....	....	....	....	....	....	....	....
Government, n.i.e.	2 291 ..	2.14	1.89	1.85	1.65	1.90	2.03	1.99	2.01
Other services, debit	3 200 BA ..	**−21.30**	**−20.26**	**−20.62**	**−22.43**	**−26.67**	**−29.65**	**−34.57**	**−37.70**
Communications	3 245 ..	−5.56	−4.04	−5.33	−3.49	−3.87	−1.87	−2.05	−2.24
Construction	3 249 ..	....	....	....	....	....	....	....	−.28
Insurance	3 253 ..	−4.51	−5.19	−5.79	−6.45	−6.89	−7.94	−8.88	−10.03
Financial	3 260 ..	....	....	....	....	....	....	....	....
Computer and information	3 262 ..	....	....	....	−.16	....	−.01	−.01	−.01
Royalties and licence fees	3 266 ..	−.54	−.51	−.32	−.31	−.37	−.43	−.53	−.53
Other business services	3 268 ..	−6.94	−7.28	−5.88	−8.52	−11.67	−12.97	−15.30	−16.74
Personal, cultural, and recreational	3 287 ..	....	....	....	....	....	....	....	....
Government, n.i.e.	3 291 ..	−3.74	−3.25	−3.30	−3.49	−3.88	−6.43	−7.81	−7.86

Table 2 (Continued). STANDARD PRESENTATION, 2000–2007

(Millions of U.S. dollars)

	Code	2000	2001	2002	2003	2004	2005	2006	2007
C. INCOME..	4 300 ..	**−19.17**	**−16.48**	**−17.60**	**−23.83**	**−28.51**	**−26.77**	**−24.19**	**−26.04**
Total credit..	2 300 ..	*3.14*	*2.37*	*3.37*	*3.76*	*4.93*	*8.40*	*13.60*	*14.58*
Total debit...	3 300 ..	*−22.32*	*−18.86*	*−20.98*	*−27.59*	*−33.44*	*−35.17*	*−37.79*	*−40.62*
Compensation of employees, credit...............	2 310 ..	**.13**	**.12**	**.74**	**.60**	**.67**	**1.07**	**3.68**	**3.79**
Compensation of employees, debit...............	3 310 ..	....	....	....	....	....	**−.61**	**−.54**	**−.55**
Investment income, credit.................................	2 320 ..	**3.01**	**2.26**	**2.63**	**3.16**	**4.27**	**7.33**	**9.92**	**10.79**
Direct investment income............................	2 330 ..	....	....	....	....	....	....	....	....
Dividends and distributed branch profits........	2 332 ..	....	....	....	....	....	....	....	....
Reinvested earnings and undistributed branch profits.....	2 333 ..	....	....	....	....	....	....	....	....
Income on debt (interest).........................	2 334 ..	....	....	....	....	....	....	....	....
Portfolio investment income...........................	2 339 ..	1.15	1.29	1.38	1.87	1.72	2.46	4.07	4.39
Income on equity......................................	2 340 ..	1.15	1.29	1.38	1.87	1.72	2.46	4.07	4.39
Income on bonds and notes........................	2 350 ..	....	....	....	....	....	....	....	....
Income on money market instruments..........	2 360 ..	....	....	....	....	....	....	....	....
Other investment income..............................	2 370 ..	1.86	.97	1.25	1.29	2.55	4.87	5.85	6.40
Investment income, debit.................................	3 320 ..	**−22.32**	**−18.86**	**−20.98**	**−27.59**	**−33.44**	**−34.56**	**−37.26**	**−40.07**
Direct investment income............................	3 330 ..	−12.70	−11.15	−15.08	−20.77	−24.91	−22.10	−22.96	−24.85
Dividends and distributed branch profits........	3 332 ..	−3.16	−3.51	−3.39	−5.82	−7.84	−9.27	−8.80	−9.47
Reinvested earnings and undistributed branch profits.....	3 333 ..	−9.32	−7.43	−11.48	−14.57	−16.12	−11.56	−12.90	−14.12
Income on debt (interest).........................	3 334 ..	−.21	−.22	−.22	−.37	−.95	−1.27	−1.27	−1.27
Portfolio investment income...........................	3 339 ..	....	....	....	−.77	−1.08	−2.12	−1.50	−1.09
Income on equity......................................	3 340 ..	....	....	....	−.77	−1.08	−2.12	−1.50	−1.09
Income on bonds and notes........................	3 350 ..	....	....	....	....	....	....	....	....
Income on money market instruments..........	3 360 ..	....	....	....	....	....	....	....	....
Other investment income..............................	3 370 ..	−9.62	−7.70	−5.89	−6.06	−7.46	−10.35	−12.79	−14.13
D. CURRENT TRANSFERS..................................	4 379 ..	**16.32**	**12.61**	**12.14**	**12.90**	**14.11**	**18.05**	**20.17**	**19.83**
Credit..	2 379 ..	**24.70**	**23.24**	**23.74**	**24.29**	**25.13**	**26.40**	**32.23**	**33.03**
General government.....................................	2 380 ..	5.12	3.40	3.07	3.24	3.50	3.32	9.37	9.61
Other sectors..	2 390 ..	19.58	19.84	20.67	21.06	21.63	23.08	22.86	23.43
Workers' remittances.................................	2 391 ..	19.16	19.34	19.69	20.10	20.78	21.35	21.88	22.43
Other current transfers..............................	2 392 ..	.41	.51	.98	.96	.85	1.73	.98	1.00
Debit...	3 379 ..	**−8.38**	**−10.63**	**−11.59**	**−11.39**	**−11.02**	**−8.35**	**−12.06**	**−13.20**
General government.....................................	3 380 ..	−2.35	−3.87	−3.87	−4.24	−3.86	−3.66	−3.54	−3.88
Other sectors..	3 390 ..	−6.03	−6.76	−7.72	−7.15	−7.16	−4.69	−8.52	−9.32
Workers' remittances.................................	3 391 ..	−4.46	−4.55	−3.80	−3.65	−3.94	−4.11	−4.55	−4.98
Other current transfers..............................	3 392 ..	−1.57	−2.21	−3.92	−3.50	−3.22	−.58	−3.97	−4.34
CAPITAL AND FINANCIAL ACCOUNT.....................	4 996 ..	**16.25**	**48.36**	**32.54**	**63.85**	**76.73**	**80.09**	**108.69**	**140.11**
CAPITAL ACCOUNT..	4 994 ..	**5.60**	**8.76**	**10.60**	**14.36**	**18.94**	**14.23**	**8.15**	**161.78**
Total credit..	2 994 ..	*6.86*	*10.03*	*11.87*	*15.63*	*20.30*	*15.66*	*9.73*	*163.51*
Total debit...	3 994 ..	*−1.27*	*−1.27*	*−1.27*	*−1.27*	*−1.37*	*−1.43*	*−1.58*	*−1.73*
Capital transfers, credit...................................	2 400 ..	**6.86**	**10.03**	**11.87**	**15.63**	**20.30**	**15.66**	**9.73**	**163.51**
General government.....................................	2 401 ..	3.67	6.78	9.15	12.81	16.23	11.59	5.56	159.18
Debt forgiveness......................................	2 402 ..	....	.19	3.33	....	....	....	....	150.00
Other capital transfers..............................	2 410 ..	3.67	6.59	5.82	12.81	16.23	11.59	5.56	9.18
Other sectors..	2 430 ..	3.19	3.25	2.72	2.82	4.07	4.07	4.17	4.33
Migrants' transfers...................................	2 431 ..	3.19	3.25	2.72	2.82	4.07	4.07	4.17	4.33
Debt forgiveness......................................	2 432 ..	....	....	....	....	....	....	....	....
Other capital transfers..............................	2 440 ..	....	....	....	....	....	....	....	....
Capital transfers, debit....................................	3 400 ..	**−1.27**	**−1.27**	**−1.27**	**−1.27**	**−1.37**	**−1.43**	**−1.58**	**−1.73**
General government.....................................	3 401 ..	....	....	....	....	....	....	....	....
Debt forgiveness......................................	3 402 ..	....	....	....	....	....	....	....	....
Other capital transfers..............................	3 410 ..	....	....	....	....	....	....	....	....
Other sectors..	3 430 ..	−1.27	−1.27	−1.27	−1.27	−1.37	−1.43	−1.58	−1.73
Migrants' transfers...................................	3 431 ..	−1.27	−1.27	−1.27	−1.27	−1.37	−1.43	−1.58	−1.73
Debt forgiveness......................................	3 432 ..	....	....	....	....	....	....	....	....
Other capital transfers..............................	3 440 ..	....	....	....	....	....	....	....	....
Nonproduced nonfinancial assets, credit.............	2 480 ..	....	....	....	....	....	....	....	....
Nonproduced nonfinancial assets, debit.............	3 480 ..	....	....	....	....	....	....	....	....

Table 2 (Continued). STANDARD PRESENTATION, 2000–2007

(Millions of U.S. dollars)

	Code	2000	2001	2002	2003	2004	2005	2006	2007
FINANCIAL ACCOUNT................................	4 995 ..	**10.65**	**39.60**	**21.93**	**49.49**	**57.79**	**65.86**	**100.54**	**−21.67**
A. DIRECT INVESTMENT..........................	4 500 ..	**37.74**	**21.04**	**34.05**	**55.16**	**65.69**	**40.09**	**109.11**	**91.64**
Direct investment abroad....................	4 505 ..	....	....	....	....	....	....	....	....
Equity capital..........................	4 510 ..	....	....	....	....	....	....	....	....
Claims on affiliated enterprises..........	4 515 ..	....	....	....	....	....	....	....	....
Liabilities to affiliated enterprises.......	4 520 ..	....	....	....	....	....	....	....	....
Reinvested earnings......................	4 525 ..	....	....	....	....	....	....	....	....
Other capital...........................	4 530 ..	....	....	....	....	....	....	....	....
Claims on affiliated enterprises..........	4 535 ..	....	....	....	....	....	....	....	....
Liabilities to affiliated enterprises.......	4 540 ..	....	....	....	....	....	....	....	....
Direct investment in St. Vincent & Grenadines ..	4 555 ..	**37.74**	**21.04**	**34.05**	**55.16**	**65.69**	**40.09**	**109.11**	**91.64**
Equity capital..........................	4 560 ..	13.95	12.44	11.78	19.29	45.96	26.43	94.30	75.38
Claims on direct investors...............	4 565 ..	....	....	....	....	....	....	....	....
Liabilities to direct investors............	4 570 ..	13.95	12.44	11.78	19.29	45.96	26.43	94.30	75.38
Reinvested earnings......................	4 575 ..	9.32	7.43	11.48	14.57	16.12	11.56	12.90	14.12
Other capital...........................	4 580 ..	14.47	1.17	10.78	21.30	3.61	2.10	1.91	2.15
Claims on direct investors...............	4 585 ..	....	....	....	....	....	....	....	....
Liabilities to direct investors............	4 590 ..	14.47	1.17	10.78	21.30	3.61	2.10	1.91	2.15
B. PORTFOLIO INVESTMENT.......................	4 600 ..	**1.44**	**3.48**	**1.00**	**20.69**	**33.17**	**−8.19**	**12.51**	**−1.51**
Assets...................................	4 602 ..	**−.52**	**.17**	**−5.40**	**−.96**	**−10.24**	**−2.21**	**−1.66**	**−1.51**
Equity securities........................	4 610 ..	....	....	....	....	....	....	....	....
Monetary authorities....................	4 611 ..	....	....	....	....	....	....	....	....
General government....................	4 612 ..	....	....	....	....	....	....	....	....
Banks................................	4 613 ..	....	....	....	....	....	....	....	....
Other sectors..........................	4 614 ..	....	....	....	....	....	....	....	....
Debt securities.........................	4 619 ..	....	....	....	....	....	....	....	....
Bonds and notes.......................	4 620 ..	....	....	....	....	....	....	....	....
Monetary authorities..................	4 621 ..	....	....	....	....	....	....	....	....
General government...................	4 622 ..	....	....	....	....	....	....	....	....
Banks..............................	4 623 ..	....	....	....	....	....	....	....	....
Other sectors........................	4 624 ..	....	....	....	....	....	....	....	....
Money market instruments...............	4 630 ..	....	....	....	....	....	....	....	....
Monetary authorities..................	4 631 ..	....	....	....	....	....	....	....	....
General government...................	4 632 ..	....	....	....	....	....	....	....	....
Banks..............................	4 633 ..	....	....	....	....	....	....	....	....
Other sectors........................	4 634 ..	....	....	....	....	....	....	....	....
Liabilities................................	4 652 ..	**1.96**	**3.31**	**6.41**	**21.66**	**43.41**	**−5.98**	**14.17**	....
Equity securities........................	4 660 ..	....	....	....	....	....	....	....	....
Banks................................	4 663 ..	....	....	....	....	....	....	....	....
Other sectors..........................	4 664 ..	....	....	....	....	....	....	....	....
Debt securities.........................	4 669 ..	....	....	....	....	....	....	....	....
Bonds and notes.......................	4 670 ..	....	....	....	....	....	....	....	....
Monetary authorities..................	4 671 ..	....	....	....	....	....	....	....	....
General government...................	4 672 ..	....	....	....	....	....	....	....	....
Banks..............................	4 673 ..	....	....	....	....	....	....	....	....
Other sectors........................	4 674 ..	....	....	....	....	....	....	....	....
Money market instruments...............	4 680 ..	....	....	....	....	....	....	....	....
Monetary authorities..................	4 681 ..	....	....	....	....	....	....	....	....
General government...................	4 682 ..	....	....	....	....	....	....	....	....
Banks..............................	4 683 ..	....	....	....	....	....	....	....	....
Other sectors........................	4 684 ..	....	....	....	....	....	....	....	....
C. FINANCIAL DERIVATIVES.......................	4 910 ..	....	....	....	....	....	....	....	....
Monetary authorities....................	4 911 ..	....	....	....	....	....	....	....	....
General government.....................	4 912 ..	....	....	....	....	....	....	....	....
Banks.................................	4 913 ..	....	....	....	....	....	....	....	....
Other sectors...........................	4 914 ..	....	....	....	....	....	....	....	....
Assets...................................	4 900 ..	....	....	....	....	....	....	....	....
Monetary authorities....................	4 901 ..	....	....	....	....	....	....	....	....
General government.....................	4 902 ..	....	....	....	....	....	....	....	....
Banks.................................	4 903 ..	....	....	....	....	....	....	....	....
Other sectors...........................	4 904 ..	....	....	....	....	....	....	....	....
Liabilities................................	4 905 ..	....	....	....	....	....	....	....	....
Monetary authorities....................	4 906 ..	....	....	....	....	....	....	....	....
General government.....................	4 907 ..	....	....	....	....	....	....	....	....
Banks.................................	4 908 ..	....	....	....	....	....	....	....	....
Other sectors...........................	4 909 ..	....	....	....	....	....	....	....	....

Table 2 (Concluded). STANDARD PRESENTATION, 2000–2007

(Millions of U.S. dollars)

	Code	2000	2001	2002	2003	2004	2005	2006	2007
D. OTHER INVESTMENT	4 700 ..	−14.52	24.14	−19.74	−26.87	−15.65	31.09	−8.98	−113.65
Assets	4 703 ..	12.04	41.70	13.15	32.67	59.80	95.70	47.76	59.68
Trade credits	4 706 ..	....	....	....	....	....	....	....	....
General government	4 707 ..	....	....	....	....	....	....	....	....
of which: Short-term	4 709 ..	....	....	....	....	....	....	....	....
Other sectors	4 710 ..	....	....	....	....	....	....	....	....
of which: Short-term	4 712 ..	....	....	....	....	....	....	....	....
Loans	4 714 ..	....	....	....	....	....	....	....	....
Monetary authorities	4 715 ..	....	....	....	....	....	....	....	....
of which: Short-term	4 718 ..	....	....	....	....	....	....	....	....
General government	4 719 ..	....	....	....	....	....	....	....	....
of which: Short-term	4 721 ..	....	....	....	....	....	....	....	....
Banks	4 722 ..	....	....	....	....	....	....	....	....
of which: Short-term	4 724 ..	....	....	....	....	....	....	....	....
Other sectors	4 725 ..	....	....	....	....	....	....	....	....
of which: Short-term	4 727 ..	....	....	....	....	....	....	....	....
Currency and deposits	4 730 ..	....	....	....	....	....	....	....	....
Monetary authorities	4 731 ..	....	....	....	....	....	....	....	....
General government	4 732 ..	....	....	....	....	....	....	....	....
Banks	4 733 ..	....	....	....	....	....	....	....	....
Other sectors	4 734 ..	....	....	....	....	....	....	....	....
Other assets	4 736 ..	....	....	....	....	....	....	....	....
Monetary authorities	4 737 ..	....	....	....	....	....	....	....	....
of which: Short-term	4 739 ..	....	....	....	....	....	....	....	....
General government	4 740 ..	....	....	....	....	....	....	....	....
of which: Short-term	4 742 ..	....	....	....	....	....	....	....	....
Banks	4 743 ..	....	....	....	....	....	....	....	....
of which: Short-term	4 745 ..	....	....	....	....	....	....	....	....
Other sectors	4 746 ..	....	....	....	....	....	....	....	....
of which: Short-term	4 748 ..	....	....	....	....	....	....	....	....
Liabilities	4 753 ..	−26.56	−17.56	−32.89	−59.54	−75.45	−64.61	−56.74	−173.33
Trade credits	4 756 ..	....	....	....	....	....	....	....	....
General government	4 757 ..	....	....	....	....	....	....	....	....
of which: Short-term	4 759 ..	....	....	....	....	....	....	....	....
Other sectors	4 760 ..	....	....	....	....	....	....	....	....
of which: Short-term	4 762 ..	....	....	....	....	....	....	....	....
Loans	4 764 ..	....	....	....	....	....	....	....	....
Monetary authorities	4 765 ..	....	....	....	....	....	....	....	....
of which: Use of Fund credit and loans from the Fund	4 766 ..	....	....	....	....	....	....	....	....
of which: Short-term	4 768 ..	....	....	....	....	....	....	....	....
General government	4 769 ..	....	....	....	....	....	....	....	....
of which: Short-term	4 771 ..	....	....	....	....	....	....	....	....
Banks	4 772 ..	....	....	....	....	....	....	....	....
of which: Short-term	4 774 ..	....	....	....	....	....	....	....	....
Other sectors	4 775 ..	....	....	....	....	....	....	....	....
of which: Short-term	4 777 ..	....	....	....	....	....	....	....	....
Currency and deposits	4 780 ..	....	....	....	....	....	....	....	....
Monetary authorities	4 781 ..	....	....	....	....	....	....	....	....
General government	4 782 ..	....	....	....	....	....	....	....	....
Banks	4 783 ..	....	....	....	....	....	....	....	....
Other sectors	4 784 ..	....	....	....	....	....	....	....	....
Other liabilities	4 786 ..	....	....	....	....	....	....	....	....
Monetary authorities	4 787 ..	....	....	....	....	....	....	....	....
of which: Short-term	4 789 ..	....	....	....	....	....	....	....	....
General government	4 790 ..	....	....	....	....	....	....	....	....
of which: Short-term	4 792 ..	....	....	....	....	....	....	....	....
Banks	4 793 ..	....	....	....	....	....	....	....	....
of which: Short-term	4 795 ..	....	....	....	....	....	....	....	....
Other sectors	4 796 ..	....	....	....	....	....	....	....	....
of which: Short-term	4 798 ..	....	....	....	....	....	....	....	....
E. RESERVE ASSETS	4 802 ..	−14.02	−9.06	6.63	.50	−25.41	2.88	−12.11	1.85
Monetary gold	4 812 ..	....	....	....	....	....	....	....	....
Special drawing rights	4 811 ..	.01	.03	.02	.02	....	....	....	....
Reserve position in the Fund	4 810 ..	....	....	....	....	....	....	....	....
Foreign exchange	4 803 ..	−12.64	−6.32	8.27	2.05	−23.76	5.41	−9.14	−8.24
Other claims	4 813 ..	−1.39	−2.78	−1.67	−1.57	−1.66	−2.53	−2.97	10.09
NET ERRORS AND OMISSIONS	4 998 ..	7.66	−10.98	9.43	15.62	25.37	19.27	11.43	8.88

Table 1. ANALYTIC PRESENTATION, 2000–2007

(Millions of U.S. dollars)

	Code	2000	2001	2002	2003	2004	2005	2006	2007
A. Current Account[1]	4 993 Z.	....	....	....	....	**−26.16**	**−25.16**	**−49.29**	**−37.54**
Goods: exports f.o.b.	2 100 ..	....	....	....	....	11.90	12.00	10.35	13.89
Goods: imports f.o.b.	3 100 ..	....	....	....	....	−155.38	−187.16	−218.86	−227.10
Balance on Goods	4 100 ..	....	....	....	....	*−143.48*	*−175.17*	*−208.51*	*−213.21*
Services: credit	2 200 ..	....	....	....	....	94.85	113.48	133.39	138.67
Services: debit	3 200 ..	....	....	....	....	−41.96	−56.12	−56.80	−55.46
Balance on Goods and Services	4 991 ..	....	....	....	....	*−90.60*	*−117.81*	*−131.92*	*−130.00*
Income: credit	2 300 ..	....	....	....	....	4.39	5.83	5.98	7.00
Income: debit	3 300 ..	....	....	....	....	−22.22	−19.96	−17.51	−23.73
Balance on Goods, Services, and Income	4 992 ..	....	....	....	....	*−108.43*	*−131.94*	*−143.44*	*−146.73*
Current transfers: credit	2 379 Z.	....	....	....	....	95.84	115.17	107.25	118.96
Current transfers: debit	3 379 ..	....	....	....	....	−13.57	−8.40	−13.09	−9.77
B. Capital Account[1]	4 994 Z.	....	....	....	....	**38.77**	**39.33**	**52.13**	**28.82**
Capital account: credit	2 994 Z.	....	....	....	....	41.95	42.00	54.50	31.09
Capital account: debit	3 994 ..	....	....	....	....	−3.19	−2.67	−2.38	−2.27
Total, Groups A Plus B	4 981 ..	....	....	....	....	*12.61*	*14.16*	*2.84*	*−8.72*
C. Financial Account[1]	4 995 W.	....	....	....	....	**−2.22**	**−8.10**	**−3.09**	**5.55**
Direct investment abroad	4 505 ..	....	....	....	....	−.43	−2.05	....	.03
Direct investment in Samoa	4 555 Z.	....	....	....	....	2.30	−2.98	20.67	2.49
Portfolio investment assets	4 602 ..	....	....	....	....	.02	−.07	−.02	−.09
Equity securities	4 610 ..	....	....	....	....	....	....	−.02	−.09
Debt securities	4 619 ..	....	....	....	....	....	....	....	....
Portfolio investment liabilities	4 652 Z.	....	....	....	....	.39	.12	.34	.90
Equity securities	4 660 ..	....	....	....	....	....	....	....	....
Debt securities	4 669 Z.	....	....	....	....	....	....	....	....
Financial derivatives	4 910 ..	....	....	....	....	....	....	....	....
Financial derivatives assets	4 900 ..	....	....	....	....	....	....	....	....
Financial derivatives liabilities	4 905 ..	....	....	....	....	....	....	....	....
Other investment assets	4 703 ..	....	....	....	....	−9.37	−.85	−1.20	−5.53
Monetary authorities	4 701 ..	....	....	....	....	....	....	....	....
General government	4 704 ..	....	....	....	....	....	....	....	....
Banks	4 705 ..	....	....	....	....	−9.04	−.77	−.17	−5.30
Other sectors	4 728 ..	....	....	....	....	−.33	−.07	−1.03	−.22
Other investment liabilities	4 753 W.	....	....	....	....	4.87	−2.27	−22.86	7.75
Monetary authorities	4 753 WA	....	....	....	....	−.01	1.00	−.45	.04
General government	4 753 ZB	....	....	....	....	5.46	2.13	−17.15	2.63
Banks	4 753 ZC	....	....	....	....	2.35	−1.85	−1.90	6.72
Other sectors	4 753 ZD	....	....	....	....	−2.92	−3.55	−3.37	−1.64
Total, Groups A Through C	4 983 ..	....	....	....	....	*10.39*	*6.06*	*−.24*	*−3.17*
D. Net Errors and Omissions	4 998 ..	....	....	....	....	**−2.58**	**−7.03**	**−4.94**	**11.97**
Total, Groups A Through D	4 984 ..	....	....	....	....	*7.81*	*−.96*	*−5.18*	*8.80*
E. Reserves and Related Items	4 802 A.	....	....	....	....	**−7.81**	**.96**	**5.18**	**−8.80**
Reserve assets	4 802 ..	....	....	....	....	−7.81	.96	3.69	−10.56
Use of Fund credit and loans	4 766 ..	....	....	....	....	....	....	....	....
Exceptional financing	4 920 ..	....	....	....	....	....	....	1.49	1.76
Conversion rates: tala per U.S. dollar	0 101 ..	3.2864	3.4780	3.3763	2.9732	2.7807	2.7103	2.7793	2.6166

[1] Excludes components that have been classified in the categories of Group E.

Table 2. STANDARD PRESENTATION, 2000–2007

(Millions of U.S. dollars)

	Code	2000	2001	2002	2003	2004	2005	2006	2007
CURRENT ACCOUNT..................................	4 993 ..	....	....	....	....	**−26.16**	**−25.16**	**−47.79**	**−35.78**
A. GOODS..	4 100 ..	....	....	....	....	**−143.48**	**−175.17**	**−208.51**	**−213.21**
Credit..	2 100 ..	....	....	....	....	**11.90**	**12.00**	**10.35**	**13.89**
General merchandise: exports f.o.b..............	2 110 ..	....	....	....	....	11.90	12.00	10.35	13.89
Goods for processing: exports f.o.b..............	2 150 ..	....	....	....	....	....	....	....	....
Repairs on goods..	2 160 ..	....	....	....	....	....	....	....	....
Goods procured in ports by carriers..............	2 170 ..	....	....	....	....	....	....	....	....
Nonmonetary gold......................................	2 180 ..	....	....	....	....	....	....	....	....
Debit..	3 100 ..	....	....	....	....	**−155.38**	**−187.16**	**−218.86**	**−227.10**
General merchandise: imports f.o.b..............	3 110 ..	....	....	....	....	−155.38	−187.16	−218.86	−227.10
Goods for processing: imports f.o.b..............	3 150 ..	....	....	....	....	....	....	....	....
Repairs on goods..	3 160 ..	....	....	....	....	....	....	....	....
Goods procured in ports by carriers..............	3 170 ..	....	....	....	....	....	....	....	....
Nonmonetary gold......................................	3 180 ..	....	....	....	....	....	....	....	....
B. SERVICES..	4 200 ..	....	....	....	....	**52.89**	**57.36**	**76.59**	**83.21**
Total credit..	2 200 ..	....	....	....	....	*94.85*	*113.48*	*133.39*	*138.67*
Total debit...	3 200 ..	....	....	....	....	*−41.96*	*−56.12*	*−56.80*	*−55.46*
Transportation services, credit..............	2 205 ..	....	....	....	....	**4.43**	**4.78**	**5.00**	**7.27**
Passenger...	2 850 ..	....	....	....	....	*.99*	*.81*	*1.39*	*.35*
Freight...	2 851 ..	....	....	....	....	*.31*	*.65*	*1.14*	*1.47*
Other...	2 852 ..	....	....	....	....	*3.13*	*3.31*	*2.47*	*5.44*
Sea transport, passenger............................	2 207 ..	....	....	....	....	....	....	....	....
Sea transport, freight.................................	2 208 ..	....	....	....	....	....	....	....	....
Sea transport, other...................................	2 209 ..	....	....	....	....	....	....	....	....
Air transport, passenger.............................	2 211 ..	....	....	....	....	....	....	....	....
Air transport, freight..................................	2 212 ..	....	....	....	....	....	....	....	....
Air transport, other....................................	2 213 ..	....	....	....	....	....	....	....	....
Other transport, passenger.........................	2 215 ..	....	....	....	....	....	....	....	....
Other transport, freight..............................	2 216 ..	....	....	....	....	....	....	....	....
Other transport, other................................	2 217 ..	....	....	....	....	....	....	....	....
Transportation services, debit..............	3 205 ..	....	....	....	....	**−20.13**	**−23.90**	**−30.29**	**−29.42**
Passenger...	3 850 ..	....	....	....	....	*−6.52*	*−7.56*	*−9.50*	*−9.09*
Freight...	3 851 ..	....	....	....	....	*−13.16*	*−15.44*	*−20.19*	*−20.30*
Other...	3 852 ..	....	....	....	....	*−.45*	*−.91*	*−.59*	*−.03*
Sea transport, passenger............................	3 207 ..	....	....	....	....	....	....	....	....
Sea transport, freight.................................	3 208 ..	....	....	....	....	....	....	....	....
Sea transport, other...................................	3 209 ..	....	....	....	....	....	....	....	....
Air transport, passenger.............................	3 211 ..	....	....	....	....	....	....	....	....
Air transport, freight..................................	3 212 ..	....	....	....	....	....	....	....	....
Air transport, other....................................	3 213 ..	....	....	....	....	....	....	....	....
Other transport, passenger.........................	3 215 ..	....	....	....	....	....	....	....	....
Other transport, freight..............................	3 216 ..	....	....	....	....	....	....	....	....
Other transport, other................................	3 217 ..	....	....	....	....	....	....	....	....
Travel, credit..	2 236 ..	....	....	....	....	**69.48**	**78.76**	**89.72**	**106.53**
Business travel...	2 237 ..	....	....	....	....	....	....	....	....
Personal travel...	2 240 ..	....	....	....	....	....	....	....	....
Travel, debit...	3 236 ..	....	....	....	....	**−5.38**	**−9.01**	**−5.55**	**−5.19**
Business travel...	3 237 ..	....	....	....	....	....	....	....	....
Personal travel...	3 240 ..	....	....	....	....	....	....	....	....
Other services, credit...........................	2 200 BA	....	....	....	....	**20.94**	**29.94**	**38.67**	**24.88**
Communications...	2 245 ..	....	....	....	....	2.52	5.84	5.74	.62
Construction..	2 249 ..	....	....	....	....	.52	5.08	2.91	.54
Insurance...	2 253 ..	....	....	....	....	2.17	.67	3.80	1.86
Financial..	2 260 ..	....	....	....	....	....	....	....	....
Computer and information..........................	2 262 ..	....	....	....	....	.08	.22	2.28	.41
Royalties and licence fees...........................	2 266 ..	....	....	....	....	....	....	....	....
Other business services..............................	2 268 ..	....	....	....	....	14.44	16.39	21.87	16.69
Personal, cultural, and recreational.............	2 287 ..	....	....	....	....	.28	1.29	1.57	4.23
Government, n.i.e.......................................	2 291 ..	....	....	....	....	.93	.46	.50	.53
Other services, debit............................	3 200 BA	....	....	....	....	**−16.45**	**−23.21**	**−20.96**	**−20.85**
Communications...	3 245 ..	....	....	....	....	−3.29	−4.13	−3.09	−.84
Construction..	3 249 ..	....	....	....	....	−6.54	−4.62	−5.89	−.49
Insurance...	3 253 ..	....	....	....	....	−2.83	−1.91	−2.58	−2.76
Financial..	3 260 ..	....	....	....	....	....	....	....	....
Computer and information..........................	3 262 ..	....	....	....	....	−.74	−1.25	−1.64	−1.72
Royalties and licence fees...........................	3 266 ..	....	....	....	....	−.17	−.11	....	−.04
Other business services..............................	3 268 ..	....	....	....	....	−1.69	−9.27	−6.62	−14.63
Personal, cultural, and recreational.............	3 287 ..	....	....	....	....	−.14	−.53	−.28	−.13
Government, n.i.e.......................................	3 291 ..	....	....	....	....	−1.05	−1.39	−.87	−.23

Table 2 (Continued). STANDARD PRESENTATION, 2000–2007

(Millions of U.S. dollars)

	Code	2000	2001	2002	2003	2004	2005	2006	2007
C. INCOME	4 300	....	....	....	....	−17.83	−14.13	−11.52	−16.73
Total credit	2 300	....	....	....	....	*4.39*	*5.83*	*5.98*	*7.00*
Total debit	3 300	....	....	....	....	*−22.22*	*−19.96*	*−17.51*	*−23.73*
Compensation of employees, credit	2 310	....	....	....	....	.90	.73	.80	.80
Compensation of employees, debit	3 310	....	....	....	....	−10.86	−10.76	−2.06	−13.08
Investment income, credit	2 320	....	....	....	....	3.49	5.11	5.19	6.20
Direct investment income	2 330	....	....	....	....	....	....	....	....
Dividends and distributed branch profits	2 332	....	....	....	....	....	....	....	....
Reinvested earnings and undistributed branch profits	2 333	....	....	....	....	....	....	....	....
Income on debt (interest)	2 334	....	....	....	....	....	....	....	....
Portfolio investment income	2 339	....	....	....	....	.09	.67	.27	....
Income on equity	2 340	....	....	....	....	.09	.67	.27	....
Income on bonds and notes	2 350	....	....	....	....	....	....	....	....
Income on money market instruments	2 360	....	....	....	....	....	....	....	....
Other investment income	2 370	....	....	....	....	3.40	4.43	4.91	6.20
Investment income, debit	3 320	....	....	....	....	−11.36	−9.20	−15.45	−10.65
Direct investment income	3 330	....	....	....	....	−9.77	−7.70	−13.81	−8.82
Dividends and distributed branch profits	3 332	....	....	....	....	−5.98	−8.13	−5.34	−3.54
Reinvested earnings and undistributed branch profits	3 333	....	....	....	....	−3.79	.43	−8.47	−5.27
Income on debt (interest)	3 334	....	....	....	....	....	....	....	....
Portfolio investment income	3 339	....	....	....	....	....	....	....	....
Income on equity	3 340	....	....	....	....	....	....	....	....
Income on bonds and notes	3 350	....	....	....	....	....	....	....	....
Income on money market instruments	3 360	....	....	....	....	....	....	....	....
Other investment income	3 370	....	....	....	....	−1.59	−1.50	−1.64	−1.84
D. CURRENT TRANSFERS	4 379	....	....	....	....	82.27	106.77	95.64	110.95
Credit	2 379	....	....	....	....	95.84	115.17	108.74	120.72
General government	2 380	....	....	....	....	8.81	5.98	1.49	1.76
Other sectors	2 390	....	....	....	....	87.03	109.20	107.25	118.96
Workers' remittances	2 391	....	....	....	....	....	....	....	....
Other current transfers	2 392	....	....	....	....	....	....	....	....
Debit	3 379	....	....	....	....	−13.57	−8.40	−13.09	−9.77
General government	3 380	....	....	....	....	−3.60	−2.18	....	....
Other sectors	3 390	....	....	....	....	−9.98	−6.22	−13.09	−9.77
Workers' remittances	3 391	....	....	....	....	....	....	....	....
Other current transfers	3 392	....	....	....	....	....	....	....	....
CAPITAL AND FINANCIAL ACCOUNT	4 996	....	....	....	....	28.74	32.19	52.73	23.81
CAPITAL ACCOUNT	4 994	....	....	....	....	38.77	39.33	52.13	28.82
Total credit	2 994	....	....	....	....	*41.95*	*42.00*	*54.50*	*31.09*
Total debit	3 994	....	....	....	....	*−3.19*	*−2.67*	*−2.38*	*−2.27*
Capital transfers, credit	2 400	....	....	....	....	41.95	42.00	54.50	31.09
General government	2 401	....	....	....	....	40.55	38.35	29.78	31.09
Debt forgiveness	2 402	....	....	....	....	....	....	....	....
Other capital transfers	2 410	....	....	....	....	....	....	....	....
Other sectors	2 430	....	....	....	....	1.40	3.65	24.73	....
Migrants' transfers	2 431	....	....	....	....	....	....	....	....
Debt forgiveness	2 432	....	....	....	....	....	....	12.36	....
Other capital transfers	2 440	....	....	....	....	1.40	3.65	12.36	....
Capital transfers, debit	3 400	....	....	....	....	−3.19	−2.67	−2.38	−2.27
General government	3 401	....	....	....	....	....	....	....	....
Debt forgiveness	3 402	....	....	....	....	....	....	....	....
Other capital transfers	3 410	....	....	....	....	....	....	....	....
Other sectors	3 430	....	....	....	....	−3.19	−2.67	−2.38	−2.27
Migrants' transfers	3 431	....	....	....	....	....	....	....	....
Debt forgiveness	3 432	....	....	....	....	....	....	....	....
Other capital transfers	3 440	....	....	....	....	−3.19	−2.67	−2.38	−2.27
Nonproduced nonfinancial assets, credit	2 480	....	....	....	....	....	....	....	....
Nonproduced nonfinancial assets, debit	3 480	....	....	....	....	....	....	....	....

Table 2 (Continued). STANDARD PRESENTATION, 2000–2007

(Millions of U.S. dollars)

	Code	2000	2001	2002	2003	2004	2005	2006	2007
FINANCIAL ACCOUNT	4 995 ..	....	....	....	....	−10.03	−7.14	.61	−5.01
A. DIRECT INVESTMENT	4 500 ..	....	....	....	....	1.87	−5.03	20.67	2.51
Direct investment abroad	4 505 ..	....	....	....	....	−.43	−2.05	....	.03
Equity capital	4 510 ..	....	....	....	....	−.43	−2.05	....	.03
Claims on affiliated enterprises	4 515 ..	....	....	....	....	−.43	−2.05	....	.03
Liabilities to affiliated enterprises	4 520 ..	....	....	....	....	....	....	....	....
Reinvested earnings	4 525 ..	....	....	....	....	....	....	....	....
Other capital	4 530 ..	....	....	....	....	....	....	....	....
Claims on affiliated enterprises	4 535 ..	....	....	....	....	....	....	....	....
Liabilities to affiliated enterprises	4 540 ..	....	....	....	....	....	....	....	....
Direct investment in Samoa	4 555 ..	....	....	....	....	2.30	−2.98	20.67	2.49
Equity capital	4 560 ..	....	....	....	....	−.18	−2.56	12.20	−1.10
Claims on direct investors	4 565 ..	....	....	....	....	−.18	−2.56	12.20	−1.10
Liabilities to direct investors	4 570 ..	....	....	....	....	....	....	....	....
Reinvested earnings	4 575 ..	....	....	....	....	3.79	−.43	8.47	5.27
Other capital	4 580 ..	....	....	....	....	−1.31	.01	−.01	−1.68
Claims on direct investors	4 585 ..	....	....	....	....	....	....	....	....
Liabilities to direct investors	4 590 ..	....	....	....	....	....	....	....	....
B. PORTFOLIO INVESTMENT	4 600 ..	....	....	....	....	.41	.05	.31	.81
Assets	4 602 ..	....	....	....	....	.02	−.07	−.02	−.09
Equity securities	4 610 ..	....	....	....	....	....	....	−.02	−.09
Monetary authorities	4 611 ..	....	....	....	....	....	....	....	....
General government	4 612 ..	....	....	....	....	....	....	....	....
Banks	4 613 ..	....	....	....	....	....	....	....	....
Other sectors	4 614 ..	....	....	....	....	....	....	....	....
Debt securities	4 619 ..	....	....	....	....	....	....	....	....
Bonds and notes	4 620 ..	....	....	....	....	....	....	....	....
Monetary authorities	4 621 ..	....	....	....	....	....	....	....	....
General government	4 622 ..	....	....	....	....	....	....	....	....
Banks	4 623 ..	....	....	....	....	....	....	....	....
Other sectors	4 624 ..	....	....	....	....	....	....	....	....
Money market instruments	4 630 ..	....	....	....	....	....	....	....	....
Monetary authorities	4 631 ..	....	....	....	....	....	....	....	....
General government	4 632 ..	....	....	....	....	....	....	....	....
Banks	4 633 ..	....	....	....	....	....	....	....	....
Other sectors	4 634 ..	....	....	....	....	....	....	....	....
Liabilities	4 652 ..	....	....	....	....	.39	.12	.34	.90
Equity securities	4 660 ..	....	....	....	....	....	....	....	....
Banks	4 663 ..	....	....	....	....	....	....	....	....
Other sectors	4 664 ..	....	....	....	....	....	....	....	....
Debt securities	4 669 ..	....	....	....	....	....	....	....	....
Bonds and notes	4 670 ..	....	....	....	....	....	....	....	....
Monetary authorities	4 671 ..	....	....	....	....	....	....	....	....
General government	4 672 ..	....	....	....	....	....	....	....	....
Banks	4 673 ..	....	....	....	....	....	....	....	....
Other sectors	4 674 ..	....	....	....	....	....	....	....	....
Money market instruments	4 680 ..	....	....	....	....	....	....	....	....
Monetary authorities	4 681 ..	....	....	....	....	....	....	....	....
General government	4 682 ..	....	....	....	....	....	....	....	....
Banks	4 683 ..	....	....	....	....	....	....	....	....
Other sectors	4 684 ..	....	....	....	....	....	....	....	....
C. FINANCIAL DERIVATIVES	4 910 ..	....	....	....	....	....	....	....	....
Monetary authorities	4 911 ..	....	....	....	....	....	....	....	....
General government	4 912 ..	....	....	....	....	....	....	....	....
Banks	4 913 ..	....	....	....	....	....	....	....	....
Other sectors	4 914 ..	....	....	....	....	....	....	....	....
Assets	4 900 ..	....	....	....	....	....	....	....	....
Monetary authorities	4 901 ..	....	....	....	....	....	....	....	....
General government	4 902 ..	....	....	....	....	....	....	....	....
Banks	4 903 ..	....	....	....	....	....	....	....	....
Other sectors	4 904 ..	....	....	....	....	....	....	....	....
Liabilities	4 905 ..	....	....	....	....	....	....	....	....
Monetary authorities	4 906 ..	....	....	....	....	....	....	....	....
General government	4 907 ..	....	....	....	....	....	....	....	....
Banks	4 908 ..	....	....	....	....	....	....	....	....
Other sectors	4 909 ..	....	....	....	....	....	....	....	....

Table 2 (Concluded). STANDARD PRESENTATION, 2000–2007

(Millions of U.S. dollars)

	Code	2000	2001	2002	2003	2004	2005	2006	2007
D. OTHER INVESTMENT................................	4 700 ..	....	....	....	....	**−4.50**	**−3.12**	**−24.07**	**2.22**
Assets...	4 703 ..	....	....	....	....	**−9.37**	**−.85**	**−1.20**	**−5.53**
Trade credits....................................	4 706 ..	....	....	....	....	....	....	....	....
General government......................	4 707 ..	....	....	....	....	....	....	....	....
of which: Short-term..................	4 709 ..	....	....	....	....	....	....	....	....
Other sectors................................	4 710 ..	....	....	....	....	....	....	....	....
of which: Short-term..................	4 712 ..	....	....	....	....	....	....	....	....
Loans..	4 714 ..	....	....	....	....	−8.43	....	....	....
Monetary authorities.....................	4 715 ..	....	....	....	....		....	....	....
of which: Short-term..................	4 718 ..	....	....	....	....	....	....	....	....
General government......................	4 719 ..	....	....	....	....		....	....	....
of which: Short-term..................	4 721 ..	....	....	....	....	....	....	....	....
Banks...	4 722 ..	....	....	....	....	−8.43	....	....	....
of which: Short-term..................	4 724 ..	....	....	....	....	....	....	....	....
Other sectors................................	4 725 ..	....	....	....	....	....	....	....	....
of which: Short-term..................	4 727 ..	....	....	....	....	....	....	....	....
Currency and deposits.......................	4 730 ..	....	....	....	....	−.95	−.85	−1.20	−5.53
Monetary authorities.....................	4 731 ..	....	....	....	....	....	....	....	....
General government......................	4 732 ..	....	....	....	....	....	....	....	....
Banks...	4 733 ..	....	....	....	....	−.62	−.77	−.17	−5.30
Other sectors................................	4 734 ..	....	....	....	....	−.33	−.07	−1.03	−.22
Other assets.......................................	4 736 ..	....	....	....	....	....	....	....	....
Monetary authorities.....................	4 737 ..	....	....	....	....	....	....	....	....
of which: Short-term..................	4 739 ..	....	....	....	....	....	....	....	....
General government......................	4 740 ..	....	....	....	....	....	....	....	....
of which: Short-term..................	4 742 ..	....	....	....	....	....	....	....	....
Banks...	4 743 ..	....	....	....	....	....	....	....	....
of which: Short-term..................	4 745 ..	....	....	....	....	....	....	....	....
Other sectors................................	4 746 ..	....	....	....	....	....	....	....	....
of which: Short-term..................	4 748 ..	....	....	....	....	....	....	....	....
Liabilities..	4 753 ..	....	....	....	....	**4.87**	**−2.27**	**−22.86**	**7.75**
Trade credits....................................	4 756 ..	....	....	....	....	....	....	....	....
General government......................	4 757 ..	....	....	....	....	....	....	....	....
of which: Short-term..................	4 759 ..	....	....	....	....	....	....	....	....
Other sectors................................	4 760 ..	....	....	....	....	....	....	....	....
of which: Short-term..................	4 762 ..	....	....	....	....	....	....	....	....
Loans..	4 764 ..	....	....	....	....	2.53	3.04	−15.81	−1.54
Monetary authorities.....................	4 765 ..	....	....	....	....	....	....	....	....
of which: Use of Fund credit and loans from the Fund..	4 766 ..	....	....	....	....	....	....	....	....
of which: Short-term..................	4 768 ..	....	....	....	....	....	....	....	....
General government......................	4 769 ..	....	....	....	....	5.45	2.18	−17.17	2.63
of which: Short-term..................	4 771 ..	....	....	....	....	....	....	....	....
Banks...	4 772 ..	....	....	....	....		....	−1.07	−2.52
of which: Short-term..................	4 774 ..	....	....	....	....	....	....	....	....
Other sectors................................	4 775 ..	....	....	....	....	−2.92	.86	2.43	−1.64
of which: Short-term..................	4 777 ..	....	....	....	....	....	....	....	....
Currency and deposits.......................	4 780 ..	....	....	....	....	2.34	−.90	−1.26	9.29
Monetary authorities.....................	4 781 ..	....	....	....	....	−.01	1.00	−.45	.04
General government......................	4 782 ..	....	....	....	....	....	−.05	.02	....
Banks...	4 783 ..	....	....	....	....	2.35	−1.85	−.83	9.25
Other sectors................................	4 784 ..	....	....	....	....	....	....	....	....
Other liabilities.................................	4 786 ..	....	....	....	....	....	−4.41	−5.80	....
Monetary authorities.....................	4 787 ..	....	....	....	....	....	....	....	....
of which: Short-term..................	4 789 ..	....	....	....	....	....	....	....	....
General government......................	4 790 ..	....	....	....	....	....	....	....	....
of which: Short-term..................	4 792 ..	....	....	....	....	....	....	....	....
Banks...	4 793 ..	....	....	....	....	....	....	....	....
of which: Short-term..................	4 795 ..	....	....	....	....	....	....	....	....
Other sectors................................	4 796 ..	....	....	....	....	....	−4.41	−5.80	....
of which: Short-term..................	4 798 ..	....	....	....	....	....	....	....	....
E. RESERVE ASSETS................................	4 802 ..	....	....	....	....	**−7.81**	**.96**	**3.69**	**−10.56**
Monetary gold....................................	4 812 ..	....	....	....	....	....	....	....	....
Special drawing rights........................	4 811 ..	....	....	....	....	−.04	−.05	−.08	−.10
Reserve position in the Fund..............	4 810 ..	....	....	....	....	....	....	....	....
Foreign exchange...............................	4 803 ..	....	....	....	....	−7.77	1.02	3.77	−10.46
Other claims......................................	4 813 ..	....	....	....	....	....	....	....	....
NET ERRORS AND OMISSIONS..............	4 998 ..	....	....	....	....	**−2.58**	**−7.03**	**−4.94**	**11.97**

Table 1. ANALYTIC PRESENTATION, 2000–2007

(Millions of U.S. dollars)

	Code	2000	2001	2002	2003	2004	2005	2006	2007
A. Current Account[1]	4 993 Z.	**−19.13**	**−26.99**	**−26.59**	**−28.33**	**−37.68**	**−36.20**	**−57.66**	**−66.85**
Goods: exports f.o.b.	2 100 ..	2.69	3.28	6.18	6.57	5.44	6.79	7.71	6.81
Goods: imports f.o.b.	3 100 ..	−25.13	−26.62	−28.23	−33.57	−38.37	−41.60	−59.24	−64.87
Balance on Goods	4 100 ..	*−22.44*	*−23.33*	*−22.05*	*−27.00*	*−32.93*	*−34.81*	*−51.53*	*−58.06*
Services: credit	2 200 ..	13.56	7.78	8.59	9.22	9.63	9.15	8.40	4.20
Services: debit	3 200 ..	−10.99	−12.47	−12.17	−13.59	−15.51	−11.06	−17.76	−18.67
Balance on Goods and Services	4 991 ..	*−19.87*	*−28.02*	*−25.63*	*−31.37*	*−38.81*	*−36.72*	*−60.89*	*−72.52*
Income: credit	2 300 ..	. . . .	1.30	1.14	1.21	1.19	1.97	6.15	6.76
Income: debit	3 300 ..	−3.62	−4.45	−4.48	−3.73	−4.29	−4.90	−3.12	−2.29
Balance on Goods, Services, and Income	4 992 ..	*−23.49*	*−31.17*	*−28.97*	*−33.89*	*−41.90*	*−39.65*	*−57.86*	*−68.05*
Current transfers: credit	2 379 Z.	4.36	5.28	3.51	6.94	8.29	7.47	5.26	6.47
Current transfers: debit	3 379 ..	. . . .	−1.09	−1.13	−1.38	−4.06	−4.03	−5.06	−5.27
B. Capital Account[1]	4 994 Z.	**12.00**	**17.28**	**14.58**	**18.71**	**18.02**	**65.64**	**23.54**	**62.42**
Capital account: credit	2 994 Z.	12.00	17.28	14.58	18.71	18.02	65.64	23.54	62.42
Capital account: debit	3 994 ..	. . . .	. . . .	. . . .	. . . .	. . . .	. . . .	. . . .	. . . .
Total, Groups A Plus B	4 981 ..	*−7.13*	*−9.71*	*−12.02*	*−9.62*	*−19.66*	*29.44*	*−34.12*	*−4.43*
C. Financial Account[1]	4 995 W.	**3.32**	**9.91**	**6.40**	**8.69**	**16.06**	**12.07**	**36.23**	**−143.67**
Direct investment abroad	4 505 ..	. . . .	. . . .	. . . .	. . . .	. . . .	−14.54	−3.10	−3.10
Direct investment in São Tomé and Príncipe	4 555 Z.	3.80	3.00	3.60	3.40	3.50	15.67	37.51	35.31
Portfolio investment assets	4 602 ..	. . . .	. . . .	. . . .	. . . .	. . . .	. . . .	. . . .	. . . .
Equity securities	4 610 ..	. . . .	. . . .	. . . .	. . . .	. . . .	. . . .	. . . .	. . . .
Debt securities	4 619 ..	. . . .	. . . .	. . . .	. . . .	. . . .	. . . .	. . . .	. . . .
Portfolio investment liabilities	4 652 Z.	. . . .	. . . .	. . . .	. . . .	. . . .	. . . .	. . . .	. . . .
Equity securities	4 660 ..	. . . .	. . . .	. . . .	. . . .	. . . .	. . . .	. . . .	. . . .
Debt securities	4 669 Z.	. . . .	. . . .	. . . .	. . . .	. . . .	. . . .	. . . .	. . . .
Financial derivatives	4 910 ..	. . . .	. . . .	. . . .	. . . .	. . . .	. . . .	. . . .	. . . .
Financial derivatives assets	4 900 ..	. . . .	. . . .	. . . .	. . . .	. . . .	. . . .	. . . .	. . . .
Financial derivatives liabilities	4 905 ..	. . . .	. . . .	. . . .	. . . .	. . . .	. . . .	. . . .	. . . .
Other investment assets	4 703 ..	−4.81	1.46	1.38	.37	2.51	12.93	2.16	5.24
Monetary authorities	4 701 ..	. . . .	. . . .	. . . .	. . . .	. . . .	. . . .	. . . .	. . . .
General government	4 704 ..	. . . .	. . . .	. . . .	. . . .	. . . .	. . . .	. . . .	. . . .
Banks	4 705 ..	−4.81	1.46	1.38	.37	2.51	12.93	2.16	5.24
Other sectors	4 728 ..	. . . .	. . . .	. . . .	. . . .	. . . .	. . . .	. . . .	. . . .
Other investment liabilities	4 753 W.	4.33	5.46	1.42	4.93	10.05	−2.00	−.33	−181.11
Monetary authorities	4 753 WA	. . . .	. . . .	. . . .	. . . .	. . . .	. . . .	. . . .	. . . .
General government	4 753 ZB	4.33	5.46	1.42	4.93	10.05	−2.00	−.33	−181.11
Banks	4 753 ZC	. . . .	. . . .	. . . .	. . . .	. . . .	. . . .	. . . .	. . . .
Other sectors	4 753 ZD	. . . .	. . . .	. . . .	. . . .	. . . .	. . . .	. . . .	. . . .
Total, Groups A Through C	4 983 ..	*−3.81*	*.21*	*−5.62*	*−.93*	*−3.60*	*41.51*	*2.12*	*−148.09*
D. Net Errors and Omissions	4 998 ..	**−1.66**	**1.41**	**2.34**	**3.20**	**−3.75**	**1.59**	**3.90**	**1.69**
Total, Groups A Through D	4 984 ..	*−5.46*	*1.62*	*−3.28*	*2.27*	*−7.35*	*43.10*	*6.01*	*−146.40*
E. Reserves and Related Items	4 802 A.	**5.46**	**−1.62**	**3.28**	**−2.27**	**7.35**	**−43.10**	**−6.01**	**146.40**
Reserve assets	4 802 ..	−1.50	−4.46	−1.78	−6.24	4.01	−48.97	−2.40	−16.64
Use of Fund credit and loans	4 766 ..	2.48	. . . .	. . . .	. . . .	. . . .	.48	.67	−1.67
Exceptional financing	4 920 ..	4.49	2.84	5.06	3.97	3.34	5.38	−4.28	164.71
Conversion rates: dobras per U.S. dollar	0 101 ..	**7,978.2**	**8,842.1**	**9,088.3**	**9,347.6**	**9,902.3**	**10,558.0**	**12,448.6**	**13,536.8**

[1] Excludes components that have been classified in the categories of Group E.

Table 2. STANDARD PRESENTATION, 2000–2007

(Millions of U.S. dollars)

	Code	2000	2001	2002	2003	2004	2005	2006	2007
CURRENT ACCOUNT	4 993 ..	**−19.13**	**−26.99**	**−26.59**	**−28.33**	**−37.68**	**−36.20**	**−57.66**	**−66.85**
A. GOODS	4 100 ..	**−22.44**	**−23.33**	**−22.05**	**−27.00**	**−32.93**	**−34.81**	**−51.53**	**−58.06**
Credit	2 100 ..	**2.69**	**3.28**	**6.18**	**6.57**	**5.44**	**6.79**	**7.71**	**6.81**
General merchandise: exports f.o.b.	2 110 ..	2.69	3.28	6.18	6.57	3.52	3.39	3.82	3.93
Goods for processing: exports f.o.b.	2 150 ..	....	....	....	....	....	....	....	....
Repairs on goods	2 160 ..	....	....	....	....	....	....	....	....
Goods procured in ports by carriers	2 170 ..	....	....	....	....	1.92	3.40	3.89	2.88
Nonmonetary gold	2 180 ..	....	....	....	....	....	....	....	....
Debit	3 100 ..	**−25.13**	**−26.62**	**−28.23**	**−33.57**	**−38.37**	**−41.60**	**−59.24**	**−64.87**
General merchandise: imports f.o.b.	3 110 ..	−25.13	−26.62	−28.23	−33.57	−38.37	−41.60	−59.24	−64.87
Goods for processing: imports f.o.b.	3 150 ..	....	....	....	....	....	....	....	....
Repairs on goods	3 160 ..	....	....	....	....	....	....	....	....
Goods procured in ports by carriers	3 170 ..	....	....	....	....	....	....	....	....
Nonmonetary gold	3 180 ..	....	....	....	....	....	....	....	....
B. SERVICES	4 200 ..	**2.57**	**−4.69**	**−3.58**	**−4.37**	**−5.88**	**−1.91**	**−9.36**	**−14.47**
Total credit	2 200 ..	*13.56*	*7.78*	*8.59*	*9.22*	*9.63*	*9.15*	*8.40*	*4.20*
Total debit	3 200 ..	*−10.99*	*−12.47*	*−12.17*	*−13.59*	*−15.51*	*−11.06*	*−17.76*	*−18.67*
Transportation services, credit	2 205 ..	**.27**	**.12**	**.13**	**.14**	**.15**	**.14**	**.13**	**.07**
Passenger	2 850 ..	....	....	....	....	....	....	....	....
Freight	2 851 ..	....	....	....	....	....	....	....	....
Other	2 852 ..	*.27*	*.12*	*.13*	*.14*	*.15*	*.14*	*.13*	*.07*
Sea transport, passenger	2 207 ..	....	....	....	....	....	....	....	....
Sea transport, freight	2 208 ..	....	....	....	....	....	....	....	....
Sea transport, other	2 209 ..	.14	.06	.07	.07	.08	.07	.07	.03
Air transport, passenger	2 211 ..	....	....	....	....	....	....	....	....
Air transport, freight	2 212 ..	....	....	....	....	....	....	....	....
Air transport, other	2 213 ..	.12	.06	.07	.07	.07	.07	.07	.03
Other transport, passenger	2 215 ..	....	....	....	....	....	....	....	....
Other transport, freight	2 216 ..	....	....	....	....	....	....	....	....
Other transport, other	2 217 ..	....	....	....	....	....	....	....	....
Transportation services, debit	3 205 ..	**−4.64**	**−6.75**	**−6.89**	**−8.03**	**−9.15**	**−8.72**	**−13.60**	**−13.61**
Passenger	3 850 ..	*−1.56*	*−1.43*	*−1.25*	*−1.32*	*−1.48*	*−.40*	*−.87*	*−.64*
Freight	3 851 ..	*−3.08*	*−5.32*	*−5.65*	*−6.71*	*−7.67*	*−8.32*	*−12.72*	*−12.97*
Other	3 852 ..	....	....	....	....	....	....	....	....
Sea transport, passenger	3 207 ..	....	....	....	....	....	....	....	....
Sea transport, freight	3 208 ..	−2.78	−5.22	−5.53	−6.58	−7.52	−8.15	−12.47	−12.71
Sea transport, other	3 209 ..	....	....	....	....	....	....	....	....
Air transport, passenger	3 211 ..	−1.56	−1.43	−1.25	−1.32	−1.48	−.40	−.87	−.64
Air transport, freight	3 212 ..	−.31	−.11	−.11	−.13	−.15	−.17	−.25	−.26
Air transport, other	3 213 ..	....	....	....	....	....	....	....	....
Other transport, passenger	3 215 ..	....	....	....	....	....	....	....	....
Other transport, freight	3 216 ..	....	....	....	....	....	....	....	....
Other transport, other	3 217 ..	....	....	....	....	....	....	....	....
Travel, credit	2 236 ..	**9.89**	**6.22**	**6.88**	**7.37**	**7.70**	**7.32**	**6.72**	**3.36**
Business travel	2 237 ..	1.98	2.49	2.75	2.95	3.08	2.93	2.69	1.34
Personal travel	2 240 ..	7.91	3.73	4.13	4.42	4.62	4.39	4.03	2.02
Travel, debit	3 236 ..	**−.63**	**−.55**	**−.52**	**−.53**	**−.59**	**−.05**	**−.24**	**−.10**
Business travel	3 237 ..	....	....	....	....	....	....	....	....
Personal travel	3 240 ..	−.63	−.55	−.52	−.53	−.59	−.05	−.24	−.10
Other services, credit	2 200 BA	**3.40**	**1.44**	**1.59**	**1.70**	**1.78**	**1.69**	**1.55**	**.78**
Communications	2 245 ..	1.85	.78	.86	.92	.96	.92	.84	.42
Construction	2 249 ..	....	....	....	....	....	....	....	....
Insurance	2 253 ..	.37	....	....	....	....	....	....	....
Financial	2 260 ..	.28	.27	.30	.32	.34	.32	.30	.15
Computer and information	2 262 ..	....	....	....	....	....	....	....	....
Royalties and licence fees	2 266 ..	....	....	....	....	....	....	....	....
Other business services	2 268 ..	.32	.13	.15	.16	.17	.16	.14	.07
Personal, cultural, and recreational	2 287 ..	....	....	....	....	....	....	....	....
Government, n.i.e.	2 291 ..	.59	.25	.28	.29	.31	.29	.27	.13
Other services, debit	3 200 BA	**−5.72**	**−5.16**	**−4.76**	**−5.02**	**−5.77**	**−2.29**	**−3.92**	**−4.95**
Communications	3 245 ..	−.63	−.55	−.52	−.53	−.59	−.05	−.24	−.10
Construction	3 249 ..	....	....	....	....	....	....	....	....
Insurance	3 253 ..	−.77	−.40	−.42	−.50	−.58	−.62	−.95	−.97
Financial	3 260 ..	−.57	−.50	−.47	−.48	−.54	−.05	−.22	−.10
Computer and information	3 262 ..	....	....	....	....	....	....	....	....
Royalties and licence fees	3 266 ..	....	....	....	....	....	....	....	....
Other business services	3 268 ..	−.80	−.74	−.64	−.68	−.76	−.22	−.46	−.34
Personal, cultural, and recreational	3 287 ..	....	....	....	....	....	....	....	....
Government, n.i.e.	3 291 ..	−2.95	−2.97	−2.71	−2.83	−3.30	−1.35	−2.05	−3.44

Table 2 (Continued). STANDARD PRESENTATION, 2000–2007

(Millions of U.S. dollars)

	Code	2000	2001	2002	2003	2004	2005	2006	2007
C. INCOME	4 300	**−3.62**	**−3.15**	**−3.34**	**−2.52**	**−3.10**	**−2.93**	**3.03**	**4.47**
Total credit	2 300	....	*1.30*	*1.14*	*1.21*	*1.19*	*1.97*	*6.15*	*6.76*
Total debit	3 300	*−3.62*	*−4.45*	*−4.48*	*−3.73*	*−4.29*	*−4.90*	*−3.12*	*−2.29*
Compensation of employees, credit	2 310	....	....	....	....	....	....	....	....
Compensation of employees, debit	3 310	**−.62**	**−.65**	**−.47**	**−.55**	**−.61**	**−.48**	**−.67**	**−.69**
Investment income, credit	2 320	....	**1.30**	**1.14**	**1.21**	**1.19**	**1.97**	**6.15**	**6.76**
Direct investment income	2 330	....	....	....	....	....	....	....	....
Dividends and distributed branch profits	2 332	....	....	....	....	....	....	....	....
Reinvested earnings and undistributed branch profits	2 333	....	....	....	....	....	....	....	....
Income on debt (interest)	2 334	....	....	....	....	....	....	....	....
Portfolio investment income	2 339	....	....	.40	.69	.85	.52	....	....
Income on equity	2 340	....	....	.40	.69	.85	.52	....	....
Income on bonds and notes	2 350	....	....	....	....	....	....	....	....
Income on money market instruments	2 360	....	....	....	....	....	....	....	....
Other investment income	2 370	....	1.30	.73	.53	.34	1.45	6.15	6.76
Investment income, debit	3 320	**−3.00**	**−3.80**	**−4.01**	**−3.18**	**−3.68**	**−4.42**	**−2.45**	**−1.60**
Direct investment income	3 330	....	....	....	....	....	....	....	....
Dividends and distributed branch profits	3 332	....	....	....	....	....	....	....	....
Reinvested earnings and undistributed branch profits	3 333	....	....	....	....	....	....	....	....
Income on debt (interest)	3 334	....	....	....	....	....	....	....	....
Portfolio investment income	3 339	....	....	....	....	−.64	....	....	....
Income on equity	3 340	....	....	....	....	−.64	....	....	....
Income on bonds and notes	3 350	....	....	....	....	....	....	....	....
Income on money market instruments	3 360	....	....	....	....	....	....	....	....
Other investment income	3 370	−3.00	−3.80	−4.01	−3.18	−3.04	−4.42	−2.45	−1.60
D. CURRENT TRANSFERS	4 379	**4.36**	**4.19**	**2.37**	**5.56**	**4.23**	**3.45**	**.20**	**1.20**
Credit	2 379	**4.36**	**5.28**	**3.51**	**6.94**	**8.29**	**7.47**	**5.26**	**6.47**
General government	2 380	3.90	4.73	2.71	5.12	7.19	5.97	3.66	4.47
Other sectors	2 390	.46	.55	.80	1.82	1.10	1.50	1.60	2.00
Workers' remittances	2 391	.46	.55	.80	1.82	1.10	1.50	1.60	2.00
Other current transfers	2 392	....	....	....	....	....	....	....	....
Debit	3 379	....	**−1.09**	**−1.13**	**−1.38**	**−4.06**	**−4.03**	**−5.06**	**−5.27**
General government	3 380	....	−.16	−.14	−.21	−2.72	−2.57	−2.84	−3.00
Other sectors	3 390	....	−.93	−.99	−1.18	−1.34	−1.46	−2.23	−2.27
Workers' remittances	3 391	....	....	....	....	....	....	....	....
Other current transfers	3 392	....	−.93	−.99	−1.18	−1.34	−1.46	−2.23	−2.27
CAPITAL AND FINANCIAL ACCOUNT	4 996	**20.79**	**25.57**	**24.26**	**25.14**	**41.43**	**34.61**	**53.76**	**65.16**
CAPITAL ACCOUNT	4 994	**12.00**	**17.28**	**14.58**	**18.71**	**18.02**	**65.64**	**23.54**	**225.12**
Total credit	2 994	*12.00*	*17.28*	*14.58*	*18.71*	*18.02*	*65.64*	*23.54*	*225.12*
Total debit	3 994	....	....	....	....	....	....	....	....
Capital transfers, credit	2 400	**12.00**	**17.28**	**14.58**	**18.71**	**18.02**	**16.44**	**23.54**	**196.52**
General government	2 401	12.00	17.28	14.58	18.71	18.02	16.44	23.54	196.52
Debt forgiveness	2 402	....	2.08	2.29	3.54	3.09	3.10	3.05	165.67
Other capital transfers	2 410	12.00	15.20	12.29	15.17	14.93	13.34	20.49	30.84
Other sectors	2 430	....	....	....	....	....	....	....	....
Migrants' transfers	2 431	....	....	....	....	....	....	....	....
Debt forgiveness	2 432	....	....	....	....	....	....	....	....
Other capital transfers	2 440	....	....	....	....	....	....	....	....
Capital transfers, debit	3 400	....	....	....	....	....	....	....	....
General government	3 401	....	....	....	....	....	....	....	....
Debt forgiveness	3 402	....	....	....	....	....	....	....	....
Other capital transfers	3 410	....	....	....	....	....	....	....	....
Other sectors	3 430	....	....	....	....	....	....	....	....
Migrants' transfers	3 431	....	....	....	....	....	....	....	....
Debt forgiveness	3 432	....	....	....	....	....	....	....	....
Other capital transfers	3 440	....	....	....	....	....	....	....	....
Nonproduced nonfinancial assets, credit	2 480	....	....	....	....	....	49.20	....	28.60
Nonproduced nonfinancial assets, debit	3 480	....	....	....	....	....	....	....	....

Table 2 (Continued). STANDARD PRESENTATION, 2000–2007

(Millions of U.S. dollars)

	Code	2000	2001	2002	2003	2004	2005	2006	2007
FINANCIAL ACCOUNT	4 995	8.79	8.29	9.68	6.43	23.41	−31.03	30.22	−159.96
A. DIRECT INVESTMENT	4 500	3.80	3.00	3.60	3.40	3.50	1.14	34.41	32.21
Direct investment abroad	4 505	....	....	....	....	....	−14.54	−3.10	−3.10
Equity capital	4 510	....	....	....	....	....	−11.44	....	....
Claims on affiliated enterprises	4 515	....	....	....	....	....	−11.44	....	....
Liabilities to affiliated enterprises	4 520	....	....	....	....	....	....	....	....
Reinvested earnings	4 525	....	....	....	....	....	....	....	....
Other capital	4 530	....	....	....	....	....	−3.10	−3.10	−3.10
Claims on affiliated enterprises	4 535	....	....	....	....	....	−3.10	−3.10	−3.10
Liabilities to affiliated enterprises	4 540	....	....	....	....	....	....	....	....
Direct investment in São Tomé and Príncipe	4 555	3.80	3.00	3.60	3.40	3.50	15.67	37.51	35.31
Equity capital	4 560	3.80	3.00	3.60	3.40	3.50	15.67	37.51	35.31
Claims on direct investors	4 565	....	....	....	....	....	....	....	....
Liabilities to direct investors	4 570	3.80	3.00	3.60	3.40	3.50	15.67	37.51	35.31
Reinvested earnings	4 575	....	....	....	....	....	....	....	....
Other capital	4 580	....	....	....	....	....	....	....	....
Claims on direct investors	4 585	....	....	....	....	....	....	....	....
Liabilities to direct investors	4 590	....	....	....	....	....	....	....	....
B. PORTFOLIO INVESTMENT	4 600	....	....	....	....	....	....	....	....
Assets	4 602	....	....	....	....	....	....	....	....
Equity securities	4 610	....	....	....	....	....	....	....	....
Monetary authorities	4 611	....	....	....	....	....	....	....	....
General government	4 612	....	....	....	....	....	....	....	....
Banks	4 613	....	....	....	....	....	....	....	....
Other sectors	4 614	....	....	....	....	....	....	....	....
Debt securities	4 619	....	....	....	....	....	....	....	....
Bonds and notes	4 620	....	....	....	....	....	....	....	....
Monetary authorities	4 621	....	....	....	....	....	....	....	....
General government	4 622	....	....	....	....	....	....	....	....
Banks	4 623	....	....	....	....	....	....	....	....
Other sectors	4 624	....	....	....	....	....	....	....	....
Money market instruments	4 630	....	....	....	....	....	....	....	....
Monetary authorities	4 631	....	....	....	....	....	....	....	....
General government	4 632	....	....	....	....	....	....	....	....
Banks	4 633	....	....	....	....	....	....	....	....
Other sectors	4 634	....	....	....	....	....	....	....	....
Liabilities	4 652	....	....	....	....	....	....	....	....
Equity securities	4 660	....	....	....	....	....	....	....	....
Banks	4 663	....	....	....	....	....	....	....	....
Other sectors	4 664	....	....	....	....	....	....	....	....
Debt securities	4 669	....	....	....	....	....	....	....	....
Bonds and notes	4 670	....	....	....	....	....	....	....	....
Monetary authorities	4 671	....	....	....	....	....	....	....	....
General government	4 672	....	....	....	....	....	....	....	....
Banks	4 673	....	....	....	....	....	....	....	....
Other sectors	4 674	....	....	....	....	....	....	....	....
Money market instruments	4 680	....	....	....	....	....	....	....	....
Monetary authorities	4 681	....	....	....	....	....	....	....	....
General government	4 682	....	....	....	....	....	....	....	....
Banks	4 683	....	....	....	....	....	....	....	....
Other sectors	4 684	....	....	....	....	....	....	....	....
C. FINANCIAL DERIVATIVES	4 910	....	....	....	....	....	....	....	....
Monetary authorities	4 911	....	....	....	....	....	....	....	....
General government	4 912	....	....	....	....	....	....	....	....
Banks	4 913	....	....	....	....	....	....	....	....
Other sectors	4 914	....	....	....	....	....	....	....	....
Assets	4 900	....	....	....	....	....	....	....	....
Monetary authorities	4 901	....	....	....	....	....	....	....	....
General government	4 902	....	....	....	....	....	....	....	....
Banks	4 903	....	....	....	....	....	....	....	....
Other sectors	4 904	....	....	....	....	....	....	....	....
Liabilities	4 905	....	....	....	....	....	....	....	....
Monetary authorities	4 906	....	....	....	....	....	....	....	....
General government	4 907	....	....	....	....	....	....	....	....
Banks	4 908	....	....	....	....	....	....	....	....
Other sectors	4 909	....	....	....	....	....	....	....	....

Table 2 (Concluded). STANDARD PRESENTATION, 2000–2007

(Millions of U.S. dollars)

	Code	2000	2001	2002	2003	2004	2005	2006	2007
D. OTHER INVESTMENT	4 700 ..	**6.49**	**9.75**	**7.86**	**9.27**	**15.90**	**16.80**	**−1.78**	**−175.53**
Assets	4 703 ..	**−4.81**	**1.46**	**1.38**	**.37**	**2.51**	**12.93**	**2.16**	**5.24**
Trade credits	4 706 ..	....	....	....	....	....	....	....	....
General government	4 707 ..	....	....	....	....	....	....	....	....
of which: Short-term	4 709 ..	....	....	....	....	....	....	....	....
Other sectors	4 710 ..	....	....	....	....	....	....	....	....
of which: Short-term	4 712 ..	....	....	....	....	....	....	....	....
Loans	4 714 ..	....	....	....	....	....	....	....	....
Monetary authorities	4 715 ..	....	....	....	....	....	....	....	....
of which: Short-term	4 718 ..	....	....	....	....	....	....	....	....
General government	4 719 ..	....	....	....	....	....	....	....	....
of which: Short-term	4 721 ..	....	....	....	....	....	....	....	....
Banks	4 722 ..	....	....	....	....	....	....	....	....
of which: Short-term	4 724 ..	....	....	....	....	....	....	....	....
Other sectors	4 725 ..	....	....	....	....	....	....	....	....
of which: Short-term	4 727 ..	....	....	....	....	....	....	....	....
Currency and deposits	4 730 ..	−4.81	1.46	1.38	.37	2.51	12.93	2.16	5.24
Monetary authorities	4 731 ..	....	....	....	....	....	....	....	....
General government	4 732 ..	....	....	....	....	....	....	....	....
Banks	4 733 ..	−4.81	1.46	1.38	.37	2.51	12.93	2.16	5.24
Other sectors	4 734 ..	....	....	....	....	....	....	....	....
Other assets	4 736 ..	....	....	....	....	....	....	....	....
Monetary authorities	4 737 ..	....	....	....	....	....	....	....	....
of which: Short-term	4 739 ..	....	....	....	....	....	....	....	....
General government	4 740 ..	....	....	....	....	....	....	....	....
of which: Short-term	4 742 ..	....	....	....	....	....	....	....	....
Banks	4 743 ..	....	....	....	....	....	....	....	....
of which: Short-term	4 745 ..	....	....	....	....	....	....	....	....
Other sectors	4 746 ..	....	....	....	....	....	....	....	....
of which: Short-term	4 748 ..	....	....	....	....	....	....	....	....
Liabilities	4 753 ..	**11.30**	**8.29**	**6.48**	**8.90**	**13.38**	**3.86**	**−3.94**	**−180.77**
Trade credits	4 756 ..	....	....	....	....	....	....	....	....
General government	4 757 ..	....	....	....	....	....	....	....	....
of which: Short-term	4 759 ..	....	....	....	....	....	....	....	....
Other sectors	4 760 ..	....	....	....	....	....	....	....	....
of which: Short-term	4 762 ..	....	....	....	....	....	....	....	....
Loans	4 764 ..	6.81	5.46	1.42	4.93	10.05	−1.52	.34	−182.78
Monetary authorities	4 765 ..	2.48	....	....	....	....	.48	.67	−1.67
of which: Use of Fund credit and loans from the Fund..	4 766 ..	*2.48*	....	....	....	....	*.48*	*.67*	*−1.67*
of which: Short-term	4 768 ..	....	....	....	....	....	....	....	....
General government	4 769 ..	4.33	5.46	1.42	4.93	10.05	−2.00	−.33	−181.11
of which: Short-term	4 771 ..	....	....	....	....	....	....	....	....
Banks	4 772 ..	....	....	....	....	....	....	....	....
of which: Short-term	4 774 ..	....	....	....	....	....	....	....	....
Other sectors	4 775 ..	....	....	....	....	....	....	....	....
of which: Short-term	4 777 ..	....	....	....	....	....	....	....	....
Currency and deposits	4 780 ..	....	....	....	....	....	....	....	....
Monetary authorities	4 781 ..	....	....	....	....	....	....	....	....
General government	4 782 ..	....	....	....	....	....	....	....	....
Banks	4 783 ..	....	....	....	....	....	....	....	....
Other sectors	4 784 ..	....	....	....	....	....	....	....	....
Other liabilities	4 786 ..	4.49	2.84	5.06	3.97	3.34	5.38	−4.28	2.01
Monetary authorities	4 787 ..	....	....	....	....	....	....	....	3.51
of which: Short-term	4 789 ..	....	....	....	....	....	....	....	*3.51*
General government	4 790 ..	4.49	2.84	5.06	3.97	3.34	5.38	−4.28	−1.49
of which: Short-term	4 792 ..	*4.49*	*2.84*	*5.06*	*3.97*	*3.34*	*5.38*	*−4.28*	*−1.49*
Banks	4 793 ..	....	....	....	....	....	....	....	....
of which: Short-term	4 795 ..	....	....	....	....	....	....	....	....
Other sectors	4 796 ..	....	....	....	....	....	....	....	....
of which: Short-term	4 798 ..	....	....	....	....	....	....	....	....
E. RESERVE ASSETS	4 802 ..	**−1.50**	**−4.46**	**−1.78**	**−6.24**	**4.01**	**−48.97**	**−2.40**	**−16.64**
Monetary gold	4 812 ..	....	....	....	....	....	....	....	....
Special drawing rights	4 811 ..	....	....	....	−.01	.02	−.04	....	.06
Reserve position in the Fund	4 810 ..	....	....	....	....	....	....	....	....
Foreign exchange	4 803 ..	−1.50	−4.46	−1.78	−6.23	3.99	−22.77	−1.96	−8.71
Other claims	4 813 ..	....	....	....	....	....	−26.15	−.45	−7.99
NET ERRORS AND OMISSIONS	4 998 ..	**−1.66**	**1.41**	**2.34**	**3.20**	**−3.75**	**1.59**	**3.90**	**1.69**

Table 1. ANALYTIC PRESENTATION, 2000–2007

(Millions of U.S. dollars)

	Code	2000	2001	2002	2003	2004	2005	2006	2007
A. Current Account[1]	4 993 Z.	**14,317**	**9,353**	**11,873**	**28,048**	**51,926**	**90,060**	**99,066**	**95,080**
Goods: exports f.o.b.	2 100 ..	77,481	67,973	72,464	93,244	125,998	180,712	211,305	234,145
Goods: imports f.o.b.	3 100 ..	−27,704	−28,607	−29,624	−33,868	−41,050	−54,595	−63,914	−82,597
Balance on Goods	4 100 ..	*49,777*	*39,366*	*42,840*	*59,376*	*84,947*	*126,117*	*147,391*	*151,547*
Services: credit	2 200 ..	4,779	5,008	5,177	5,713	5,852	6,677	7,297	7,901
Services: debit	3 200 ..	−10,927	−7,155	−7,152	−7,936	−11,057	−14,520	−19,390	−30,798
Balance on Goods and Services	4 991 ..	*43,628*	*37,219*	*40,865*	*57,153*	*79,742*	*118,274*	*135,298*	*128,650*
Income: credit	2 300 ..	3,345	4,125	3,714	2,977	4,278	4,964	10,376	15,014
Income: debit	3 300 ..	−2,865	−4,644	−3,925	−4,277	−3,800	−4,963	−9,734	−14,776
Balance on Goods, Services, and Income	4 992 ..	*44,107*	*36,699*	*40,655*	*55,852*	*80,219*	*118,275*	*135,940*	*128,888*
Current transfers: credit	2 379 Z.	....	....	....	....	....	....	....	....
Current transfers: debit	3 379 ..	−29,791	−27,346	−28,782	−27,804	−28,293	−28,215	−36,874	−33,808
B. Capital Account[1]	4 994 Z.	....	....	....	....	....	....	....	....
Capital account: credit	2 994 Z.	....	....	....	....	....	....	....	....
Capital account: debit	3 994 ..	....	....	....	....	....	....	....	....
Total, Groups A Plus B	4 981 ..	*14,317*	*9,353*	*11,873*	*28,048*	*51,926*	*90,060*	*99,066*	*95,080*
C. Financial Account[1]	4 995 W.	**−11,652**	**−11,262**	**−9,137**	**−26,440**	**−47,428**	**−90,525**	**−98,172**	**−88,912**
Direct investment abroad	4 505 ..	....	....	....	....	....	....	....	....
Direct investment in Saudi Arabia	4 555 Z.	−1,881	20	−614	−587	−334	464	660	−8,069
Portfolio investment assets	4 602 ..	−9,378	−2,797	7,552	−18,738	−26,654	−67,420	−78,567	−81,727
Equity securities	4 610 ..	....	....	....	....	....	....	....	....
Debt securities	4 619 ..	−9,378	−2,797	7,552	−18,738	−26,654	−67,420	−78,567	−81,727
Portfolio investment liabilit es	4 652 Z.	....	....	....	....	....	....	....	....
Equity securities	4 660 ..	....	....	....	....	....	....	....	....
Debt securities	4 669 Z.	....	....	....	....	....	....	....	....
Financial derivatives	4 910 ..	....	....	....	....	....	....	....	....
Financial derivatives assets	4 900 ..	....	....	....	....	....	....	....	....
Financial derivatives liabilities	4 905 ..	....	....	....	....	....	....	....	....
Other investment assets	4 703 ..	−3,937	−7,197	−11,644	−6,333	−21,955	−28,717	−17,664	−11,391
Monetary authorities	4 701 ..	....	....	....	....	....	....	....	....
General government	4 704 ..	....	....	....	....	....	....	....	....
Banks	4 705 ..	−2,591	490	1,033	3,842	−3,124	365	−9,203	−10,411
Other sectors	4 728 ..	−1,346	−7,687	−12,677	−10,175	−18,831	−29,082	−8,461	−980
Other investment liabilities	4 753 W.	3,544	−1,288	−4,431	−783	1,516	5,149	−2,601	12,275
Monetary authorities	4 753 WA	....	....	....	....	....	....	....	....
General government	4 753 ZB	....	....	....	....	....	....	....	....
Banks	4 753 ZC	3,544	−1,288	−4,431	−783	1,516	5,149	−2,601	12,275
Other sectors	4 753 ZD	....	....	....	....	....	....	....	....
Total, Groups A Through C	4 983 ..	*2,665*	*−1,909*	*2,736*	*1,608*	*4,498*	*−465*	*894*	*6,168*
D. Net Errors and Omissions	4 998 ..	....	....	....	....	....	....	....	....
Total, Groups A Through D	4 984 ..	*2,665*	*−1,909*	*2,736*	*1,608*	*4,498*	*−465*	*894*	*6,168*
E. Reserves and Related Items	4 802 A.	**−2,665**	**1,909**	**−2,736**	**−1,608**	**−4,498**	**465**	**−894**	**−6,168**
Reserve assets	4 802 ..	−2,665	1,909	−2,736	−1,608	−4,498	465	−894	−6,168
Use of Fund credit and loans	4 766 ..	....	....	....	....	....	....	....	....
Exceptional financing	4 920 ..	....	....	....	....	....	....	....	....
Conversion rates: riyals per U.S. dollar	0 101 ..	**3.7500**	**3.7500**	**3.7500**	**3.7500**	**3.7500**	**3.7471**	**3.7450**	**3.7475**

[1] Excludes components that have been classified in the categories of Group E.

Table 2. STANDARD PRESENTATION, 2000–2007

(Millions of U.S. dollars)

	Code	2000	2001	2002	2003	2004	2005	2006	2007
CURRENT ACCOUNT	4 993 ..	**14,317**	**9,353**	**11,873**	**28,048**	**51,926**	**90,060**	**99,066**	**95,080**
A. GOODS	4 100 ..	**49,777**	**39,366**	**42,840**	**59,376**	**84,947**	**126,117**	**147,391**	**151,547**
Credit	2 100 ..	**77,481**	**67,973**	**72,464**	**93,244**	**125,998**	**180,712**	**211,305**	**234,145**
General merchandise: exports f.o.b.	2 110 ..	77,268	67,793	72,273	92,997	125,665	180,227	210,740	233,526
Goods for processing: exports f.o.b.	2 150 ..	....	....	....	....	....	....	....	....
Repairs on goods	2 160 ..	....	....	....	....	....	....	....	....
Goods procured in ports by carriers	2 170 ..	212	179	191	247	332	485	566	619
Nonmonetary gold	2 180 ..	....	....	....	....	....	....	....	....
Debit	3 100 ..	**−27,704**	**−28,607**	**−29,624**	**−33,868**	**−41,050**	**−54,595**	**−63,914**	**−82,597**
General merchandise: imports f.o.b.	3 110 ..	−27,704	−28,607	−29,624	−33,868	−41,050	−54,595	−63,914	−82,597
Goods for processing: imports f.o.b.	3 150 ..	....	....	....	....	....	....	....	....
Repairs on goods	3 160 ..	....	....	....	....	....	....	....	....
Goods procured in ports by carriers	3 170 ..	....	....	....	....	....	....	....	....
Nonmonetary gold	3 180 ..	....	....	....	....	....	....	....	....
B. SERVICES	4 200 ..	**−6,149**	**−2,147**	**−1,975**	**−2,223**	**−5,206**	**−7,843**	**−12,093**	**−22,897**
Total credit	2 200 ..	*4,779*	*5,008*	*5,177*	*5,713*	*5,852*	*6,677*	*7,297*	*7,901*
Total debit	3 200 ..	*−10,927*	*−7,155*	*−7,152*	*−7,936*	*−11,057*	*−14,520*	*−19,390*	*−30,798*
Transportation services, credit	2 205 ..	....	....	....	....	....	....	....	....
Passenger	2 850 ..	....	....	....	....	....	....	....	....
Freight	2 851 ..	....	....	....	....	....	....	....	....
Other	2 852 ..	....	....	....	....	....	....	....	....
Sea transport, passenger	2 207 ..	....	....	....	....	....	....	....	....
Sea transport, freight	2 208 ..	....	....	....	....	....	....	....	....
Sea transport, other	2 209 ..	....	....	....	....	....	....	....	....
Air transport, passenger	2 211 ..	....	....	....	....	....	....	....	....
Air transport, freight	2 212 ..	....	....	....	....	....	....	....	....
Air transport, other	2 213 ..	....	....	....	....	....	....	....	....
Other transport, passenger	2 215 ..	....	....	....	....	....	....	....	....
Other transport, freight	2 216 ..	....	....	....	....	....	....	....	....
Other transport, other	2 217 ..	....	....	....	....	....	....	....	....
Transportation services, debit	3 205 ..	**−2,244**	**−2,317**	**−2,400**	**−2,743**	**−3,325**	**−4,422**	**−5,297**	**−8,915**
Passenger	3 850 ..	....	....	....	....	....	....	....	....
Freight	3 851 ..	*−2,244*	*−2,317*	*−2,400*	*−2,743*	*−3,325*	*−4,422*	*−5,297*	*−8,915*
Other	3 852 ..	....	....	....	....	....	....	....	....
Sea transport, passenger	3 207 ..	....	....	....	....	....	....	....	....
Sea transport, freight	3 208 ..	−2,244	−2,317	−2,400	−2,743	−3,325	−4,422	−5,297	−8,915
Sea transport, other	3 209 ..	....	....	....	....	....	....	....	....
Air transport, passenger	3 211 ..	....	....	....	....	....	....	....	....
Air transport, freight	3 212 ..	....	....	....	....	....	....	....	....
Air transport, other	3 213 ..	....	....	....	....	....	....	....	....
Other transport, passenger	3 215 ..	....	....	....	....	....	....	....	....
Other transport, freight	3 216 ..	....	....	....	....	....	....	....	....
Other transport, other	3 217 ..	....	....	....	....	....	....	....	....
Travel, credit	2 236 ..	....	....	....	....	....	....	....	....
Business travel	2 237 ..	....	....	....	....	....	....	....	....
Personal travel	2 240 ..	....	....	....	....	....	....	....	....
Travel, debit	3 236 ..	....	....	....	....	....	....	....	....
Business travel	3 237 ..	....	....	....	....	....	....	....	....
Personal travel	3 240 ..	....	....	....	....	....	....	....	....
Other services, credit	2 200 BA	**4,779**	**5,008**	**5,177**	**5,713**	**5,852**	**6,677**	**7,297**	**7,901**
Communications	2 245 ..	....	....	....	....	....	....	....	....
Construction	2 249 ..	....	....	....	....	....	....	....	....
Insurance	2 253 ..	....	....	....	....	....	....	....	....
Financial	2 260 ..	....	....	....	....	....	....	....	....
Computer and information	2 262 ..	....	....	....	....	....	....	....	....
Royalties and licence fees	2 266 ..	....	....	....	....	....	....	....	....
Other business services	2 268 ..	4,779	5,008	5,177	5,713	5,852	6,677	7,297	7,901
Personal, cultural, and recreational	2 287 ..	....	....	....	....	....	....	....	....
Government, n.i.e.	2 291 ..	....	....	....	....	....	....	....	....
Other services, debit	3 200 BA	**−8,683**	**−4,838**	**−4,752**	**−5,193**	**−7,732**	**−10,098**	**−14,093**	**−21,884**
Communications	3 245 ..	....	....	....	....	....	....	....	....
Construction	3 249 ..	....	....	....	....	....	....	....	....
Insurance	3 253 ..	−249	−257	−267	−305	−369	−491	−589	−991
Financial	3 260 ..	....	....	....	....	....	....	....	....
Computer and information	3 262 ..	....	....	....	....	....	....	....	....
Royalties and licence fees	3 266 ..	....	....	....	....	....	....	....	....
Other business services	3 268 ..	−8,434	−4,580	−4,486	−4,888	−7,363	−9,606	−13,504	−20,893
Personal, cultural, and recreational	3 287 ..	....	....	....	....	....	....	....	....
Government, n.i.e.	3 291 ..	....	....	....	....	....	....	....	....

Table 2 (Continued). STANDARD PRESENTATION, 2000–2007

(Millions of U.S. dollars)

	Code	2000	2001	2002	2003	2004	2005	2006	2007
C. INCOME...........................	4 300	**479**	**−520**	**−211**	**−1,301**	**478**	**1**	**641**	**238**
Total credit............................	2 300	*3,345*	*4,125*	*3,714*	*2,977*	*4,278*	*4,964*	*10,376*	*15,014*
Total debit.............................	3 300	*−2,865*	*−4,644*	*−3,925*	*−4,277*	*−3,800*	*−4,963*	*−9,734*	*−14,776*
Compensation of employees, credit..................	2 310	....	....	....	....	....	....	....	....
Compensation of employees, debit....................	3 310	....	....	....	....	....	....	....	....
Investment income, credit........................	2 320	**3,345**	**4,125**	**3,714**	**2,977**	**4,278**	**4,964**	**10,376**	**15,014**
Direct investment income............................	2 330	....	....	....	....	....	....	....	....
Dividends and distributed branch profits...........	2 332	....	....	....	....	....	....	....	....
Reinvested earnings and undistributed branch profits.....	2 333	....	....	....	....	....	....	....	....
Income on debt (interest)............................	2 334	....	....	....	....	....	....	....	....
Portfolio investment income............................	2 339	....	....	....	....	....	....	....	....
Income on equity............................	2 340	....	....	....	....	....	....	....	....
Income on bonds and notes............................	2 350	....	....	....	....	....	....	....	....
Income on money market instruments........................	2 360	....	....	....	....	....	....	....	....
Other investment income............................	2 370	3,345	4,125	3,714	2,977	4,278	4,964	10,376	15,014
Investment income, debit..................................	3 320	**−2,865**	**−4,644**	**−3,925**	**−4,277**	**−3,800**	**−4,963**	**−9,734**	**−14,776**
Direct investment income............................	3 330	−2,865	−4,644	−3,925	−4,277	−3,800	−4,963	−9,734	−14,776
Dividends and distributed branch profits.............	3 332	−2,865	−4,644	−3,925	−4,277	−3,800	−4,963	−9,734	−14,776
Reinvested earnings and undistributed branch profits.....	3 333	....	....	....	....	....	....	....	....
Income on debt (interest)............................	3 334	....	....	....	....	....	....	....	....
Portfolio investment income............................	3 339	....	....	....	....	....	....	....	....
Income on equity............................	3 340	....	....	....	....	....	....	....	....
Income on bonds and notes............................	3 350	....	....	....	....	....	....	....	....
Income on money market instruments........................	3 360	....	....	....	....	....	....	....	....
Other investment income............................	3 370	....	....	....	....	....	....	....	....
D. CURRENT TRANSFERS..	4 379	**−29,791**	**−27,346**	**−28,782**	**−27,804**	**−28,293**	**−28,215**	**−36,874**	**−33,808**
Credit..	2 379	....	....	....	....	....	....	....	....
General government............................	2 380	....	....	....	....	....	....	....	....
Other sectors............................	2 390	....	....	....	....	....	....	....	....
Workers' remittances............................	2 391	....	....	....	....	....	....	....	....
Other current transfers............................	2 392	....	....	....	....	....	....	....	....
Debit..	3 379	**−29,791**	**−27,346**	**−28,782**	**−27,804**	**−28,293**	**−28,215**	**−36,874**	**−33,808**
General government............................	3 380	−14,401	−12,226	−12,928	−13,021	−14,738	−14,219	−21,262	−17,740
Other sectors............................	3 390	−15,390	−15,120	−15,854	−14,783	−13,555	−13,996	−15,611	−16,068
Workers' remittances............................	3 391	−15,390	−15,120	−15,854	−14,783	−13,555	−13,996	−15,611	−16,068
Other current transfers............................	3 392	....	....	....	....	....	....	....	....
CAPITAL AND FINANCIAL ACCOUNT......................	4 996	**−14,317**	**−9,353**	**−11,873**	**−28,048**	**−51,926**	**−90,060**	**−99,066**	**−95,080**
CAPITAL ACCOUNT..	4 994	....	....	....	....	....	....	....	....
Total credit............................	2 994	....	....	....	....	....	....	....	....
Total debit............................	3 994	....	....	....	....	....	....	....	....
Capital transfers, credit...	2 400	....	....	....	....	....	....	....	....
General government............................	2 401	....	....	....	....	....	....	....	....
Debt forgiveness............................	2 402	....	....	....	....	....	....	....	....
Other capital transfers............................	2 410	....	....	....	....	....	....	....	....
Other sectors............................	2 430	....	....	....	....	....	....	....	....
Migrants' transfers............................	2 431	....	....	....	....	....	....	....	....
Debt forgiveness............................	2 432	....	....	....	....	....	....	....	....
Other capital transfers............................	2 440	....	....	....	....	....	....	....	....
Capital transfers, debit...	3 400	....	....	....	....	....	....	....	....
General government............................	3 401	....	....	....	....	....	....	....	....
Debt forgiveness............................	3 402	....	....	....	....	....	....	....	....
Other capital transfers............................	3 410	....	....	....	....	....	....	....	....
Other sectors............................	3 430	....	....	....	....	....	....	....	....
Migrants' transfers............................	3 431	....	....	....	....	....	....	....	....
Debt forgiveness............................	3 432	....	....	....	....	....	....	....	....
Other capital transfers............................	3 440	....	....	....	....	....	....	....	....
Nonproduced nonfinancial assets, credit.............	2 480	....	....	....	....	....	....	....	....
Nonproduced nonfinancial assets, debit..............	3 480	....	....	....	....	....	....	....	....

Table 2 (Continued). STANDARD PRESENTATION, 2000–2007

(Millions of U.S. dollars)

	Code	2000	2001	2002	2003	2004	2005	2006	2007
FINANCIAL ACCOUNT	4 995 ..	−14,317	−9,353	−11,873	−28,048	−51,926	−90,060	−99,066	−95,080
A. DIRECT INVESTMENT	4 500 ..	−1,881	20	−614	−587	−334	464	660	−8,069
Direct investment abroad	4 505 ..	....	....	....	....	....	....	....	....
Equity capital	4 510 ..	....	....	....	....	....	....	....	....
Claims on affiliated enterprises	4 515 ..	....	....	....	....	....	....	....	....
Liabilities to affiliated enterprises	4 520 ..	....	....	....	....	....	....	....	....
Reinvested earnings	4 525 ..	....	....	....	....	....	....	....	....
Other capital	4 530 ..	....	....	....	....	....	....	....	....
Claims on affiliated enterprises	4 535 ..	....	....	....	....	....	....	....	....
Liabilities to affiliated enterprises	4 540 ..	....	....	....	....	....	....	....	....
Direct investment in Saudi Arabia	4 555 ..	−1,881	20	−614	−587	−334	464	660	−8,069
Equity capital	4 560 ..	....	....	....	....	....	....	....	....
Claims on direct investors	4 565 ..	....	....	....	....	....	....	....	....
Liabilities to direct investors	4 570 ..	....	....	....	....	....	....	....	....
Reinvested earnings	4 575 ..	....	....	....	....	....	....	....	....
Other capital	4 580 ..	−1,881	20	−614	−587	−334	464	660	−8,069
Claims on direct investors	4 585 ..	....	....	....	....	....	....	....	....
Liabilities to direct investors	4 590 ..	....	....	....	....	....	....	....	....
B. PORTFOLIO INVESTMENT	4 600 ..	−9,378	−2,797	7,552	−18,738	−26,654	−67,420	−78,567	−81,727
Assets	4 602 ..	−9,378	−2,797	7,552	−18,738	−26,654	−67,420	−78,567	−81,727
Equity securities	4 610 ..	....	....	....	....	....	....	....	....
Monetary authorities	4 611 ..	....	....	....	....	....	....	....	....
General government	4 612 ..	....	....	....	....	....	....	....	....
Banks	4 613 ..	....	....	....	....	....	....	....	....
Other sectors	4 614 ..	....	....	....	....	....	....	....	....
Debt securities	4 619 ..	−9,378	−2,797	7,552	−18,738	−26,654	−67,420	−78,567	−81,727
Bonds and notes	4 620 ..	−9,378	−2,797	7,552	−18,738	−26,654	−67,420	−78,567	−81,727
Monetary authorities	4 621 ..	....	....	....	....	....	....	....	....
General government	4 622 ..	−9,378	−2,797	7,552	−18,738	−26,654	−67,420	−78,567	−81,727
Banks	4 623 ..	....	....	....	....	....	....	....	....
Other sectors	4 624 ..	....	....	....	....	....	....	....	....
Money market instruments	4 630 ..	....	....	....	....	....	....	....	....
Monetary authorities	4 631 ..	....	....	....	....	....	....	....	....
General government	4 632 ..	....	....	....	....	....	....	....	....
Banks	4 633 ..	....	....	....	....	....	....	....	....
Other sectors	4 634 ..	....	....	....	....	....	....	....	....
Liabilities	4 652 ..	....	....	....	....	....	....	....	....
Equity securities	4 660 ..	....	....	....	....	....	....	....	....
Banks	4 663 ..	....	....	....	....	....	....	....	....
Other sectors	4 664 ..	....	....	....	....	....	....	....	....
Debt securities	4 669 ..	....	....	....	....	....	....	....	....
Bonds and notes	4 670 ..	....	....	....	....	....	....	....	....
Monetary authorities	4 671 ..	....	....	....	....	....	....	....	....
General government	4 672 ..	....	....	....	....	....	....	....	....
Banks	4 673 ..	....	....	....	....	....	....	....	....
Other sectors	4 674 ..	....	....	....	....	....	....	....	....
Money market instruments	4 680 ..	....	....	....	....	....	....	....	....
Monetary authorities	4 681 ..	....	....	....	....	....	....	....	....
General government	4 682 ..	....	....	....	....	....	....	....	....
Banks	4 683 ..	....	....	....	....	....	....	....	....
Other sectors	4 684 ..	....	....	....	....	....	....	....	....
C. FINANCIAL DERIVATIVES	4 910 ..	....	....	....	....	....	....	....	....
Monetary authorities	4 911 ..	....	....	....	....	....	....	....	....
General government	4 912 ..	....	....	....	....	....	....	....	....
Banks	4 913 ..	....	....	....	....	....	....	....	....
Other sectors	4 914 ..	....	....	....	....	....	....	....	....
Assets	4 900 ..	....	....	....	....	....	....	....	....
Monetary authorities	4 901 ..	....	....	....	....	....	....	....	....
General government	4 902 ..	....	....	....	....	....	....	....	....
Banks	4 903 ..	....	....	....	....	....	....	....	....
Other sectors	4 904 ..	....	....	....	....	....	....	....	....
Liabilities	4 905 ..	....	....	....	....	....	....	....	....
Monetary authorities	4 906 ..	....	....	....	....	....	....	....	....
General government	4 907 ..	....	....	....	....	....	....	....	....
Banks	4 908 ..	....	....	....	....	....	....	....	....
Other sectors	4 909 ..	....	....	....	....	....	....	....	....

Table 2 (Concluded). STANDARD PRESENTATION, 2000–2007

(Millions of U.S. dollars)

	Code	2000	2001	2002	2003	2004	2005	2006	2007
D. OTHER INVESTMENT	4 700	**−393**	**−8,485**	**−16,075**	**−7,115**	**−20,440**	**−23,569**	**−20,265**	**884**
Assets	4 703	**−3,937**	**−7,197**	**−11,644**	**−6,333**	**−21,955**	**−28,717**	**−17,664**	**−11,391**
Trade credits	4 706	....	....	....	....	....	....	....	....
General government	4 707	....	....	....	....	....	....	....	....
of which: Short-term	4 709	....	....	....	....	....	....	....	....
Other sectors	4 710	....	....	....	....	....	....	....	....
of which: Short-term	4 712	....	....	....	....	....	....	....	....
Loans	4 714	....	....	....	....	....	....	....	....
Monetary authorities	4 715	....	....	....	....	....	....	....	....
of which: Short-term	4 718	....	....	....	....	....	....	....	....
General government	4 719	....	....	....	....	....	....	....	....
of which: Short-term	4 721	....	....	....	....	....	....	....	....
Banks	4 722	....	....	....	....	....	....	....	....
of which: Short-term	4 724	....	....	....	....	....	....	....	....
Other sectors	4 725	....	....	....	....	....	....	....	....
of which: Short-term	4 727	....	....	....	....	....	....	....	....
Currency and deposits	4 730	−3,938	−7,197	−11,644	−6,333	−21,955	−28,717	−17,664	−11,391
Monetary authorities	4 731	....	....	....	....	....	....	....	....
General government	4 732	....	....	....	....	....	....	....	....
Banks	4 733	−2,591	490	1,033	3,842	−3,124	365	−9,203	−10,411
Other sectors	4 734	−1,346	−7,687	−12,677	−10,175	−18,831	−29,082	−8,461	−980
Other assets	4 736	1	....	....	....	....	....	....	....
Monetary authorities	4 737	....	....	....	....	....	....	....	....
of which: Short-term	4 739	....	....	....	....	....	....	....	....
General government	4 740	....	....	....	....	....	....	....	....
of which: Short-term	4 742	....	....	....	....	....	....	....	....
Banks	4 743	....	....	....	....	....	....	....	....
of which: Short-term	4 745	....	....	....	....	....	....	....	....
Other sectors	4 746	1	....	....	....	....	....	....	....
of which: Short-term	4 748	....	....	....	....	....	....	....	....
Liabilities	4 753	**3,544**	**−1,288**	**−4,431**	**−783**	**1,516**	**5,149**	**−2,601**	**12,275**
Trade credits	4 756	....	....	....	....	....	....	....	....
General government	4 757	....	....	....	....	....	....	....	....
of which: Short-term	4 759	....	....	....	....	....	....	....	....
Other sectors	4 760	....	....	....	....	....	....	....	....
of which: Short-term	4 762	....	....	....	....	....	....	....	....
Loans	4 764	....	....	....	....	....	....	....	....
Monetary authorities	4 765	....	....	....	....	....	....	....	....
of which: Use of Fund credit and loans from the Fund	4 766	....	....	....	....	....	....	....	....
of which: Short-term	4 768	....	....	....	....	....	....	....	....
General government	4 769	....	....	....	....	....	....	....	....
of which: Short-term	4 771	....	....	....	....	....	....	....	....
Banks	4 772	....	....	....	....	....	....	....	....
of which: Short-term	4 774	....	....	....	....	....	....	....	....
Other sectors	4 775	....	....	....	....	....	....	....	....
of which: Short-term	4 777	....	....	....	....	....	....	....	....
Currency and deposits	4 780	3,544	−1,288	−4,431	−783	1,516	5,149	−2,601	12,275
Monetary authorities	4 781	....	....	....	....	....	....	....	....
General government	4 782	....	....	....	....	....	....	....	....
Banks	4 783	3,544	−1,288	−4,431	−783	1,516	5,149	−2,601	12,275
Other sectors	4 784	....	....	....	....	....	....	....	....
Other liabilities	4 786	....	....	....	....	....	....	....	....
Monetary authorities	4 787	....	....	....	....	....	....	....	....
of which: Short-term	4 789	....	....	....	....	....	....	....	....
General government	4 790	....	....	....	....	....	....	....	....
of which: Short-term	4 792	....	....	....	....	....	....	....	....
Banks	4 793	....	....	....	....	....	....	....	....
of which: Short-term	4 795	....	....	....	....	....	....	....	....
Other sectors	4 796	....	....	....	....	....	....	....	....
of which: Short-term	4 798	....	....	....	....	....	....	....	....
E. RESERVE ASSETS	4 802	**−2,665**	**1,909**	**−2,736**	**−1,608**	**−4,498**	**465**	**−894**	**−6,168**
Monetary gold	4 812	....	....	....	....	....	....	....	....
Special drawing rights	4 811	−47	−58	−67	−64	−66	−75	−60	−48
Reserve position in the Fund	4 810	−71	−1,273	−750	−597	1,179	1,340	1,063	220
Foreign exchange	4 803	−2,546	3,240	−1,919	−947	−5,611	−801	−1,897	−6,341
Other claims	4 813	....	....	....	....	....	....	....	....
NET ERRORS AND OMISSIONS	4 998	....	....	....	....	....	....	....	....

Table 1. ANALYTIC PRESENTATION, 2000–2007

(Millions of U.S. dollars)

	Code	2000	2001	2002	2003	2004	2005	2006	2007
A. Current Account[1]........................	4 993 Z.	**−332.4**	**−245.5**	**−316.7**	**−436.4**	**−512.8**	**−677.2**	**−861.3**	....
Goods: exports f.o.b........................	2 100 ..	919.8	1,003.1	1,066.5	1,257.0	1,509.4	1,578.2	1,594.0	....
Goods: imports f.o.b........................	3 100 ..	−1,336.6	−1,428.4	−1,603.9	−2,065.5	−2,495.8	−2,888.8	−3,193.7	....
Balance on Goods........................	4 100 ..	*−416.7*	*−425.3*	*−537.4*	*−808.5*	*−986.4*	*−1,310.6*	*−1,599.7*	....
Services: credit........................	2 200 ..	386.9	398.1	456.2	569.0	670.1	774.2	803.9	....
Services: debit........................	3 200 ..	−405.0	−413.6	−474.2	−591.2	−697.9	−805.0	−838.7	....
Balance on Goods and Services........................	4 991 ..	*−434.8*	*−440.8*	*−555.4*	*−830.7*	*−1,014.1*	*−1,341.4*	*−1,634.5*	....
Income: credit........................	2 300 ..	76.3	61.6	65.1	86.4	95.2	95.5	121.3	....
Income: debit........................	3 300 ..	−187.7	−166.4	−195.1	−222.6	−225.9	−185.0	−184.7	....
Balance on Goods, Services, and Income........................	4 992 ..	*−546.3*	*−545.6*	*−685.4*	*−966.9*	*−1,144.8*	*−1,430.9*	*−1,697.9*	....
Current transfers: credit........................	2 379 Z.	274.9	353.6	414.4	595.6	715.1	859.2	973.7	....
Current transfers: debit........................	3 379 ..	−61.0	−53.4	−45.8	−65.2	−83.1	−105.4	−137.0	....
B. Capital Account[1]........................	4 994 Z.	**83.4**	**146.1**	**126.8**	**150.4**	**750.0**	**199.5**	**2,291.1**	....
Capital account: credit........................	2 994 Z.	83.6	146.1	127.1	150.9	750.4	200.3	2,294.7	....
Capital account: debit........................	3 994 ..	−.3	−.1	−.2	−.6	−.4	−.8	−3.6	....
Total, Groups A Plus B........................	4 981 ..	*−249.0*	*−99.4*	*−189.9*	*−286.0*	*237.2*	*−477.7*	*1,429.8*	....
C. Financial Account[1]........................	4 995 W.	**27.1**	**−102.6**	**−88.2**	**2.5**	**−53.7**	**117.9**	**−1,580.5**	....
Direct investment abroad........................	4 505 ..	−.6	7.0	−34.0	−2.7	−13.1	7.7	−9.9	....
Direct investment in Senegal........................	4 555 Z.	62.9	31.9	78.1	52.5	77.0	44.6	220.3	....
Portfolio investment assets........................	4 602 ..	11.0	15.9	−25.0	−56.3	−47.5	−48.9	−53.3	....
Equity securities........................	4 610 ..	−.2	7.0	.5	−7.9	22.8	4.3	1.7	....
Debt securities........................	4 619 ..	11.3	8.9	−25.5	−48.4	−70.3	−53.2	−55.1	....
Portfolio investment liabilities........................	4 652 Z.	11.9	−8.3	−13.1	10.6	.8	−8.5	−13.6	....
Equity securities........................	4 660 ..	−2.2	−5.2	3.2	3.6	−27.7	−6.1	−.4	....
Debt securities........................	4 669 Z.	14.1	−3.2	−16.4	6.9	28.5	−2.4	−13.3	....
Financial derivatives........................	4 910 ..	....	....	−2.2	2.3	....	−.1	....	....
Financial derivatives assets........................	4 900 ..	....	−.4	−1.9	1.6	.7	....	−.1	....
Financial derivatives liabilities........................	4 905 ..	....	.4	−.4	.7	−.8	−.1	.1	....
Other investment assets........................	4 703 ..	−4.4	−3.9	11.9	58.0	6.0	79.2	−34.3	....
Monetary authorities........................	4 701 ..	....	....	....	....	....	....	....	....
General government........................	4 704 ..	....	....	−1.5	−1.8	3.1	1.0	.4	....
Banks........................	4 705 ..	17.2	−33.0	−16.4	−8.3	−19.4	50.7	−74.8	....
Other sectors........................	4 728 ..	−21.6	29.2	29.8	68.1	22.3	27.5	40.1	....
Other investment liabilities........................	4 753 W.	−53.8	−145.3	−103.8	−61.9	−76.9	43.9	−1,689.7	....
Monetary authorities........................	4 753 WA	8.9	−6.7	10.7	4.3	−20.7	25.9	−44.0	....
General government........................	4 753 ZB	−132.7	−136.1	−161.6	−194.8	−197.3	−149.9	−2,071.1	....
Banks........................	4 753 ZC	−6.1	7.8	−6.5	21.4	15.4	36.3	106.2	....
Other sectors........................	4 753 ZD	76.0	−10.4	53.7	107.1	125.7	131.6	319.1	....
Total, Groups A Through C........................	4 983 ..	*−221.9*	*−202.0*	*−278.1*	*−283.5*	*183.5*	*−359.8*	*−150.7*	....
D. Net Errors and Omissions........................	4 998 ..	**−9.0**	**7.9**	**30.7**	**10.7**	**15.6**	**−1.8**	**28.3**	....
Total, Groups A Through D........................	4 984 ..	*−231.0*	*−194.1*	*−247.3*	*−272.8*	*199.1*	*−361.6*	*−122.4*	....
E. Reserves and Related Items........................	4 802 A.	**231.0**	**194.1**	**247.3**	**272.8**	**−199.1**	**361.6**	**122.4**	....
Reserve assets........................	4 802 ..	−14.1	−90.3	−92.5	−18.1	−155.0	−4.5	−9.9	....
Use of Fund credit and loans........................	4 766 ..	−3.3	3.4	−15.9	−34.5	−44.4	−40.6	−125.1	....
Exceptional financing........................	4 920 ..	248.4	281.0	355.8	325.4	.3	406.7	257.4	....
Conversion rates: CFA francs per U.S. dollar........................	0 101 ..	**711.98**	**733.04**	**696.99**	**581.20**	**528.28**	**527.47**	**522.89**	**479.27**

[1] Excludes components that have been classified in the categories of Group E.

Table 2. STANDARD PRESENTATION, 2000–2007

(Millions of U.S. dollars)

	Code	2000	2001	2002	2003	2004	2005	2006	2007
CURRENT ACCOUNT	4 993 ..	−332.4	−245.5	−316.7	−436.4	−512.8	−677.2	−861.3	....
A. GOODS	4 100 ..	−416.7	−425.3	−537.4	−808.5	−986.4	−1,310.6	−1,599.7	....
Credit	2 100 ..	919.8	1,003.1	1,066.5	1,257.0	1,509.4	1,578.2	1,594.0	....
General merchandise: exports f.o.b.	2 110 ..	892.3	987.7	1,053.0	1,242.8	1,488.2	1,552.7	1,562.6	....
Goods for processing: exports f.o.b.	2 150 ..	....	....	....	....	....	....	....	....
Repairs on goods	2 160 ..	.5	.4	....	.4	.2	.2	....	....
Goods procured in ports by carriers	2 170 ..	27.1	15.1	13.5	13.8	21.1	25.3	31.3	....
Nonmonetary gold	2 180 ..	....	....	....	....	....	....	....	....
Debit	3 100 ..	−1,336.6	−1,428.4	−1,603.9	−2,065.5	−2,495.8	−2,888.8	−3,193.7	....
General merchandise: imports f.o.b.	3 110 ..	−1,336.5	−1,426.7	−1,582.2	−2,051.2	−2,478.7	−2,876.1	−3,182.5	....
Goods for processing: imports f.o.b.	3 150 ..	....	....	....	....	....	....	....	....
Repairs on goods	3 160 ..	....	−1.5	−14.6	−6.0	−7.9	−4.3	−1.1	....
Goods procured in ports by carriers	3 170 ..	−.1	−.2	−7.1	−8.3	−9.2	−8.3	−10.1	....
Nonmonetary gold	3 180 ..	....	....	....	....	....	....	....	....
B. SERVICES	4 200 ..	−18.1	−15.5	−18.0	−22.2	−27.8	−30.8	−34.8	....
Total credit	2 200 ..	*386.9*	*398.1*	*456.2*	*569.0*	*670.1*	*774.2*	*803.9*	....
Total debit	3 200 ..	*−405.0*	*−413.6*	*−474.2*	*−591.2*	*−697.9*	*−805.0*	*−838.7*	....
Transportation services, credit	2 205 ..	31.9	29.2	37.5	76.5	96.3	126.8	113.0	....
Passenger	2 850 ..	*8.3*	*1.0*	*20.3*	*60.4*	*74.7*	*92.0*	*78.9*	....
Freight	2 851 ..	*6.2*	*.6*	*5.0*	*7.1*	*14.0*	*25.3*	*22.8*	....
Other	2 852 ..	*17.5*	*27.6*	*12.2*	*8.9*	*7.6*	*9.4*	*11.3*	....
Sea transport, passenger	2 207 ..	....	....	....	....	....	....	....	....
Sea transport, freight	2 208 ..	....	....	....	....	....	....	....	....
Sea transport, other	2 209 ..	10.0	10.1	1.3	1.5	.1	.2	.6	....
Air transport, passenger	2 211 ..	....	1.0	12.7	51.4	65.7	83.5	70.5	....
Air transport, freight	2 212 ..	....	.6	....	1.1	....	....	....	....
Air transport, other	2 213 ..	6.2	4.9	10.4	6.9	7.5	7.0	10.6	....
Other transport, passenger	2 215 ..	8.3	....	7.6	9.0	9.0	8.5	8.4	....
Other transport, freight	2 216 ..	6.2	....	5.0	6.1	14.0	25.3	22.8	....
Other transport, other	2 217 ..	1.3	12.6	.5	.6	....	....	2.5	....
Transportation services, debit	3 205 ..	−239.8	−236.3	−254.3	−322.3	−380.1	−436.3	−470.9	....
Passenger	3 850 ..	*−78.3*	*−68.8*	*−69.4*	*−73.7*	*−81.0*	*−79.5*	*−84.5*	....
Freight	3 851 ..	*−151.9*	*−161.2*	*−179.8*	*−233.1*	*−281.2*	*−326.9*	*−362.2*	....
Other	3 852 ..	*−9.6*	*−6.4*	*−5.2*	*−15.6*	*−17.8*	*−30.0*	*−24.2*	....
Sea transport, passenger	3 207 ..	....	....	....	....	....	....	....	....
Sea transport, freight	3 208 ..	−95.5	−139.9	−171.4	−224.5	−273.8	−318.0	−355.7	....
Sea transport, other	3 209 ..	....	....	....	−.3	....	....	....	....
Air transport, passenger	3 211 ..	−78.0	−68.8	−68.8	−73.0	−80.3	−79.5	−84.5	....
Air transport, freight	3 212 ..	−55.4	−21.3	−7.3	−7.5	−7.3	−8.7	−4.2	....
Air transport, other	3 213 ..	−9.4	−4.8	−5.0	−15.1	−17.6	−30.0	−24.2	....
Other transport, passenger	3 215 ..	−.4	....	−.6	−.7	−.7	....	....	....
Other transport, freight	3 216 ..	−1.0	....	−1.0	−1.1	−.1	−.1	−2.3	....
Other transport, other	3 217 ..	−.3	−1.6	−.1	−.1	−.2	....	....	....
Travel, credit	2 236 ..	143.9	174.4	189.6	208.6	211.5	242.4	250.3	....
Business travel	2 237 ..	57.9	65.8	71.4	79.1	88.3	97.7	97.7	....
Personal travel	2 240 ..	86.1	108.6	118.2	129.5	123.2	144.7	152.6	....
Travel, debit	3 236 ..	−47.1	−42.9	−43.3	−55.4	−57.0	−64.7	−53.9	....
Business travel	3 237 ..	−6.0	−5.8	−4.4	−8.4	−8.3	−12.7	−10.4	....
Personal travel	3 240 ..	−41.1	−37.1	−38.9	−47.0	−48.7	−52.0	−43.5	....
Other services, credit	2 200 BA	211.1	194.5	229.2	283.9	362.3	405.0	440.6	....
Communications	2 245 ..	52.3	58.3	56.5	78.4	93.3	104.7	141.2	....
Construction	2 249 ..	20.3	10.6	9.4	36.2	72.0	77.4	46.9	....
Insurance	2 253 ..	1.5	3.7	2.0	4.0	3.6	7.7	11.1	....
Financial	2 260 ..	5.3	6.6	4.4	5.6	5.8	6.8	7.2	....
Computer and information	2 262 ..	....	.3	....	.1	....	.8	3.4	....
Royalties and licence fees	2 266 ..	....	....	.2	....	....	....	....	....
Other business services	2 268 ..	74.4	61.5	89.3	78.9	115.9	120.4	139.3	....
Personal, cultural, and recreational	2 287 ..	....	....	....	.1	....	....	....	....
Government, n.i.e.	2 291 ..	57.3	53.5	67.2	80.6	71.7	87.1	91.5	....
Other services, debit	3 200 BA	−118.1	−134.4	−176.6	−213.5	−260.8	−303.9	−313.9	....
Communications	3 245 ..	−8.9	−12.3	−22.7	−19.9	−27.5	−37.5	−37.4	....
Construction	3 249 ..	....	....	−.7	−.5	....	−10.0	−31.3	....
Insurance	3 253 ..	−35.6	−45.7	−44.1	−57.4	−65.6	−75.3	−72.9	....
Financial	3 260 ..	−4.2	−12.8	−7.0	−5.8	−4.1	−3.9	−5.7	....
Computer and information	3 262 ..	−2.6	−1.5	−2.8	−6.6	−7.1	−6.6	−10.2	....
Royalties and licence fees	3 266 ..	−5.5	−2.9	−3.3	−.5	−7.2	−7.4	−5.3	....
Other business services	3 268 ..	−52.6	−48.3	−78.2	−98.7	−132.6	−134.2	−116.9	....
Personal, cultural, and recreational	3 287 ..	....	....	....	....	....	....	....	....
Government, n.i.e.	3 291 ..	−8.8	−11.0	−17.8	−24.0	−16.7	−29.0	−34.2	....

Table 2 (Continued). STANDARD PRESENTATION, 2000–2007

(Millions of U.S. dollars)

	Code	2000	2001	2002	2003	2004	2005	2006	2007
C. INCOME	4 300	**−111.4**	**−104.8**	**−130.0**	**−136.2**	**−130.7**	**−89.6**	**−63.4**	....
Total credit	2 300	*76.3*	*61.6*	*65.1*	*86.4*	*95.2*	*95.5*	*121.3*	....
Total debit	3 300	*−187.7*	*−166.4*	*−195.1*	*−222.6*	*−225.9*	*−185.0*	*−184.7*	....
Compensation of employees, credit	2 310	**54.3**	**45.1**	**47.8**	**62.7**	**69.7**	**71.8**	**74.7**	....
Compensation of employees, debit	3 310	**−7.3**	**−8.6**	**−5.0**	**−8.9**	**−10.3**	**−10.6**	**−9.9**	....
Investment income, credit	2 320	**22.0**	**16.5**	**17.3**	**23.7**	**25.5**	**23.6**	**46.6**	....
Direct investment income	2 330	2.1	1.0	.8	3.5	5.7	.5	18.7	....
Dividends and distributed branch profits	2 332	2.1	.9	.8	.6	.3	.3	18.5	....
Reinvested earnings and undistributed branch profits	2 333	....	....	....	2.9	5.4	.1	.1	....
Income on debt (interest)	2 334	....	.1	....	....	....	....	.1	....
Portfolio investment income	2 339	3.9	2.8	8.0	5.6	8.5	12.3	11.6	....
Income on equity	2 340	.2	.4	.2	.1	.2	.1	.4	....
Income on bonds and notes	2 350	3.7	2.3	7.7	5.3	8.0	9.9	9.8	....
Income on money market instruments	2 360	....	....	.1	.2	.2	2.3	1.5	....
Other investment income	2 370	16.1	12.7	8.5	14.6	11.4	10.9	16.3	....
Investment income, debit	3 320	**−180.4**	**−157.8**	**−190.1**	**−213.7**	**−215.6**	**−174.4**	**−174.8**	....
Direct investment income	3 330	−75.3	−67.1	−90.3	−88.8	−67.6	−61.5	−69.8	....
Dividends and distributed branch profits	3 332	−51.1	−31.4	−48.5	−97.1	−77.3	−115.7	−85.6	....
Reinvested earnings and undistributed branch profits	3 333	−23.6	−35.2	−41.6	8.5	10.2	55.0	17.5	....
Income on debt (interest)	3 334	−.6	−.4	−.2	−.2	−.5	−.8	−1.8	....
Portfolio investment income	3 339	−16.3	−18.1	−24.8	−36.0	−48.2	−43.6	−54.7	....
Income on equity	3 340	−11.1	−10.7	−11.2	−15.0	−26.3	−28.2	−37.3	....
Income on bonds and notes	3 350	−5.2	−7.2	−13.5	−21.0	−21.9	−15.3	−17.3	....
Income on money market instruments	3 360	....	−.2	....	....	....	....	....	....
Other investment income	3 370	−88.8	−72.6	−75.0	−88.9	−99.8	−69.3	−50.4	....
D. CURRENT TRANSFERS	4 379	**213.9**	**300.2**	**368.6**	**530.4**	**632.0**	**753.8**	**836.6**	....
Credit	2 379	**274.9**	**353.6**	**414.4**	**595.6**	**715.1**	**859.2**	**973.7**	....
General government	2 380	80.0	70.0	98.6	124.0	129.8	116.6	96.4	....
Other sectors	2 390	194.9	283.6	315.8	471.6	585.3	742.5	877.3	....
Workers' remittances	2 391	179.2	259.6	296.7	448.2	563.2	717.0	850.6	....
Other current transfers	2 392	15.7	24.0	19.1	23.3	22.1	25.6	26.7	....
Debit	3 379	**−61.0**	**−53.4**	**−45.8**	**−65.2**	**−83.1**	**−105.4**	**−137.0**	....
General government	3 380	−6.7	−5.6	−5.7	−8.3	−8.1	−9.0	−42.5	....
Other sectors	3 390	−54.3	−47.8	−40.1	−56.9	−75.0	−96.4	−94.5	....
Workers' remittances	3 391	−47.6	−42.7	−34.3	−48.2	−66.5	−87.1	−86.5	....
Other current transfers	3 392	−6.7	−5.1	−5.8	−8.7	−8.4	−9.3	−8.0	....
CAPITAL AND FINANCIAL ACCOUNT	4 996	**341.4**	**237.6**	**286.0**	**425.7**	**497.2**	**679.0**	**832.9**	....
CAPITAL ACCOUNT	4 994	**83.4**	**146.1**	**126.8**	**150.4**	**750.0**	**199.5**	**2,291.1**	....
Total credit	2 994	*83.6*	*146.1*	*127.1*	*150.9*	*750.4*	*200.3*	*2,294.7*	....
Total debit	3 994	*−.3*	*−.1*	*−.2*	*−.6*	*−.4*	*−.8*	*−3.6*	....
Capital transfers, credit	2 400	**83.6**	**145.7**	**126.9**	**150.8**	**750.4**	**200.3**	**2,294.7**	....
General government	2 401	80.2	142.9	118.4	139.1	742.0	189.5	2,282.2	....
Debt forgiveness	2 402	5.9	29.4	31.6	35.6	609.7	69.4	2,132.2	....
Other capital transfers	2 410	74.3	113.5	86.8	103.5	132.3	120.1	150.0	....
Other sectors	2 430	3.5	2.8	8.5	11.7	8.4	10.8	12.4	....
Migrants' transfers	2 431	....	....	....	....	....	....	....	....
Debt forgiveness	2 432	....	....	....	....	....	....	....	....
Other capital transfers	2 440	3.5	2.8	8.5	11.7	8.4	10.8	12.4	....
Capital transfers, debit	3 400	....	....	....	....	....	....	....	....
General government	3 401	....	....	....	....	....	....	....	....
Debt forgiveness	3 402	....	....	....	....	....	....	....	....
Other capital transfers	3 410	....	....	....	....	....	....	....	....
Other sectors	3 430	....	....	....	....	....	....	....	....
Migrants' transfers	3 431	....	....	....	....	....	....	....	....
Debt forgiveness	3 432	....	....	....	....	....	....	....	....
Other capital transfers	3 440	....	....	....	....	....	....	....	....
Nonproduced nonfinancial assets, credit	2 480	....	**.4**	**.2**	**.2**	....	....	....	....
Nonproduced nonfinancial assets, debit	3 480	**−.3**	**−.1**	**−.2**	**−.6**	**−.4**	**−.8**	**−3.6**	....

2008, International Monetary Fund: *Balance of Payments Statistics Yearbook*

Table 2 (Continued). STANDARD PRESENTATION, 2000–2007

(Millions of U.S. dollars)

	Code	2000	2001	2002	2003	2004	2005	2006	2007
FINANCIAL ACCOUNT	4 995	**258.0**	**91.5**	**159.2**	**275.3**	**−252.8**	**479.5**	**−1,458.2**	....
A. DIRECT INVESTMENT	4 500	**62.3**	**39.0**	**44.0**	**49.8**	**64.0**	**52.3**	**210.4**	....
Direct investment abroad	4 505	**−.6**	**7.0**	**−34.0**	**−2.7**	**−13.1**	**7.7**	**−9.9**	....
Equity capital	4 510	−1.0	−.2	−33.4	5.6	−1.8	−2.6	−5.2	....
Claims on affiliated enterprises	4 515	....	....	....	....	....	....	....	....
Liabilities to affiliated enterprises	4 520	....	....	....	....	....	....	....	....
Reinvested earnings	4 525	....	....	....	−2.9	−5.4	−.1	−.1	....
Other capital	4 530	.4	7.3	−.6	−5.4	−5.9	10.4	−4.6	....
Claims on affiliated enterprises	4 535	−1.3	−.4	−2.1	−4.2	−5.6	.6	−2.2	....
Liabilities to affiliated enterprises	4 540	1.6	7.7	1.5	−1.2	−.3	9.8	−2.4	....
Direct investment in Senegal	4 555	**62.9**	**31.9**	**78.1**	**52.5**	**77.0**	**44.6**	**220.3**	....
Equity capital	4 560	16.2	−28.7	43.7	72.6	90.2	96.1	288.0	....
Claims on direct investors	4 565	....	....	....	....	....	....	....	....
Liabilities to direct investors	4 570	....	....	....	....	....	....	....	....
Reinvested earnings	4 575	23.6	35.2	41.6	−8.5	−10.2	−55.0	−17.5	....
Other capital	4 580	23.1	25.4	−7.3	−11.5	−3.0	3.5	−50.2	....
Claims on direct investors	4 585	−7.9	.1	−.5	−2.1	1.0	−2.0	−17.6	....
Liabilities to direct investors	4 590	31.0	25.3	−6.7	−9.5	−4.0	5.6	−32.6	....
B. PORTFOLIO INVESTMENT	4 600	**23.0**	**7.6**	**−38.1**	**−45.7**	**−46.7**	**−4.3**	**−67.0**	....
Assets	4 602	**11.0**	**15.9**	**−25.0**	**−56.3**	**−47.5**	**−48.9**	**−53.3**	....
Equity securities	4 610	−.2	7.0	.5	−7.9	22.8	4.3	1.7	....
Monetary authorities	4 611	....	....	....	....	....	....	....	....
General government	4 612	....	....	....	....	....	....	....	....
Banks	4 613	....	....	....	....	.8	.9	.2	....
Other sectors	4 614	−.2	7.0	.5	−7.9	22.1	3.4	1.6	....
Debt securities	4 619	11.3	8.9	−25.5	−48.4	−70.3	−53.2	−55.1	....
Bonds and notes	4 620	18.5	8.0	−41.2	−53.0	−68.0	−53.2	19.7	....
Monetary authorities	4 621	....	....	....	....	....	....	....	....
General government	4 622	11.1	13.6	....	13.8	−10.8	.2	−1.0	....
Banks	4 623	8.6	−5.9	−42.6	−66.2	−41.0	−53.5	21.3	....
Other sectors	4 624	−1.2	.2	1.4	−.5	−16.2	....	−.6	....
Money market instruments	4 630	−7.3	.9	15.8	4.6	−2.4	....	−74.8	....
Monetary authorities	4 631	....	....	....	....	....	....	....	....
General government	4 632	....	....	....	....	....	....	....	....
Banks	4 633	....	....	....	....	−6.6	....	−74.8	....
Other sectors	4 634	−7.3	.9	15.8	4.6	4.3	....	....	....
Liabilities	4 652	**11.9**	**−8.3**	**−13.1**	**10.6**	**.8**	**44.6**	**−13.6**	....
Equity securities	4 660	−2.2	−5.2	3.2	3.6	−27.7	−6.1	−.4	....
Banks	4 663	−.2	−.2	−.4	.3	....	.1	−1.1	....
Other sectors	4 664	−2.0	−4.9	3.6	3.3	−27.7	−6.1	.8	....
Debt securities	4 669	14.1	−3.2	−16.4	6.9	28.5	50.7	−13.3	....
Bonds and notes	4 670	14.1	−3.2	−16.4	6.9	28.4	50.7	−17.0	....
Monetary authorities	4 671	....	....	....	....	....	....	....	....
General government	4 672	−2.7	−2.5	−16.4	−7.7	....	53.1	....	....
Banks	4 673	....	....	....	....	28.0	20.7	−9.8	....
Other sectors	4 674	16.9	−.7	....	14.6	.3	−23.1	−7.2	....
Money market instruments	4 680	....	....	....	....	.1	....	3.7	....
Monetary authorities	4 681	....	....	....	....	....	....	....	....
General government	4 682	....	....	....	....	....	....	....	....
Banks	4 683	....	....	....	....	....	....	3.8	....
Other sectors	4 684	....	....	....	....	.1	....	−.1	....
C. FINANCIAL DERIVATIVES	4 910	....	....	**−2.2**	**2.3**	....	**−.1**	....	....
Monetary authorities	4 911	....	....	....	....	....	....	....	....
General government	4 912	....	....	....	....	....	....	....	....
Banks	4 913	....	−.3	−.3	.4	....	....	....	....
Other sectors	4 914	....	.3	−1.9	1.9	....	−.1	....	....
Assets	4 900	....	**−.4**	**−1.9**	**1.6**	**.7**	....	**−.1**	....
Monetary authorities	4 901	....	....	....	....	....	....	....	....
General government	4 902	....	....	....	....	....	....	....	....
Banks	4 903	....	−.3	−.3	.4	....	....	....	....
Other sectors	4 904	....	−.1	−1.5	1.2	.8	....	−.1	....
Liabilities	4 905	....	**.4**	**−.4**	**.7**	**−.8**	**−.1**	**.1**	....
Monetary authorities	4 906	....	....	....	....	....	....	....	....
General government	4 907	....	....	....	....	....	....	....	....
Banks	4 908	....	....	....	....	....	....	....	....
Other sectors	4 909	....	.4	−.4	.7	−.8	−.1	.1	....

Table 2 (Concluded). STANDARD PRESENTATION, 2000–2007
(Millions of U.S. dollars)

	Code	2000	2001	2002	2003	2004	2005	2006	2007
D. OTHER INVESTMENT	4 700	**186.9**	**135.2**	**248.0**	**287.1**	**−115.0**	**436.1**	**−1,591.8**	....
Assets	4 703	**−4.4**	**−3.9**	**11.9**	**58.0**	**6.0**	**79.2**	**−34.3**	....
Trade credits	4 706	−13.8	−10.7	12.8	11.2	13.9	26.2	8.1	....
General government	4 707	....	....	....	....	....	....	....	....
of which: Short-term	4 709	....	....	....	....	....	....	....	....
Other sectors	4 710	−13.8	−10.7	12.8	11.2	13.9	26.2	8.1	....
of which: Short-term	4 712	....	....	....	....	....	....	....	....
Loans	4 714	2.8	−5.4	−20.8	−19.0	−39.1	42.4	−70.9	....
Monetary authorities	4 715	....	....	....	....	....	....	....	....
of which: Short-term	4 718	....	....	....	....	....	....	....	....
General government	4 719	....	....	....	....	....	....	....	....
of which: Short-term	4 721	....	....	....	....	....	....	....	....
Banks	4 722	2.8	−5.1	−23.7	−19.0	−39.1	42.4	−70.9	....
of which: Short-term	4 724	−2.0	−8.4	−20.7	−4.9	14.8	4.3	−17.5	....
Other sectors	4 725	....	−.3	2.9	....	....	....	....	....
of which: Short-term	4 727	....	−.3	2.9	....	....	....	....	....
Currency and deposits	4 730	6.4	18.4	−23.7	56.6	−4.9	8.5	31.8	....
Monetary authorities	4 731	....	....	....	....	....	....	....	....
General government	4 732	....	....	−1.5	−1.8	3.1	1.0	1.0	....
Banks	4 733	16.1	−29.5	6.0	9.3	20.5	6.4	4.8	....
Other sectors	4 734	−9.7	47.9	−28.3	49.1	−28.6	1.1	26.0	....
Other assets	4 736	.2	−6.2	43.6	9.3	36.1	2.2	−3.3	....
Monetary authorities	4 737	....	....	....	....	....	....	....	....
of which: Short-term	4 739	....	....	....	....	....	....	....	....
General government	4 740	....	....	....	....	....	....	−.6	....
of which: Short-term	4 742	....	....	....	....	....	....	−.6	....
Banks	4 743	−1.7	1.5	1.3	1.4	−.8	1.9	−8.7	....
of which: Short-term	4 745	−1.7	1.5	1.3	1.4	−.8	1.9	−8.7	....
Other sectors	4 746	1.9	−7.7	42.4	7.9	37.0	.3	6.1	....
of which: Short-term	4 748	....	....	....	....	....	....	....	....
Liabilities	4 753	**191.2**	**139.1**	**236.1**	**229.1**	**−121.0**	**356.9**	**−1,557.5**	....
Trade credits	4 756	86.4	−13.6	39.4	90.2	94.0	104.7	185.2	....
General government	4 757	....	....	....	....	....	....	....	....
of which: Short-term	4 759	....	....	....	....	....	....	....	....
Other sectors	4 760	86.4	−13.6	39.4	90.2	94.0	104.7	185.2	....
of which: Short-term	4 762	....	....	....	....	....	....	....	....
Loans	4 764	82.1	121.5	126.8	45.8	−321.1	156.6	−1,873.2	....
Monetary authorities	4 765	−3.3	3.4	−15.9	−34.5	−44.4	−40.6	−125.1	....
of which: Use of Fund credit and loans from the Fund..	4 766	−3.3	3.4	−15.9	−34.5	−44.4	−40.6	−125.1	....
of which: Short-term	4 768	....	....	....	....	....	....	....	....
General government	4 769	57.1	85.6	90.3	68.3	−337.0	203.6	−1,813.7	....
of which: Short-term	4 771	....	....	....	....	....	62.6	....	....
Banks	4 772	−18.0	21.6	−22.1	8.2	42.3	2.3	5.6	....
of which: Short-term	4 774	−4.8	12.4	−25.5	.3	28.6	11.7	−23.1	....
Other sectors	4 775	46.3	10.9	74.6	3.8	18.0	−8.7	60.1	....
of which: Short-term	4 777	45.9	10.4	64.7	−15.7	....	....	53.9	....
Currency and deposits	4 780	10.7	10.1	24.7	33.6	−19.4	85.2	34.6	....
Monetary authorities	4 781	−1.6	1.8	5.5	12.1	−35.5	51.3	−51.2	....
General government	4 782	....	....	....	....	....	....	....	....
Banks	4 783	12.3	8.3	19.2	21.5	16.1	33.8	85.7	....
Other sectors	4 784	....	....	....	....	....	....	....	....
Other liabilities	4 786	12.0	21.2	45.2	59.5	125.6	10.5	95.9	....
Monetary authorities	4 787	10.5	−8.5	5.2	−7.7	14.8	−25.4	7.2	....
of which: Short-term	4 789	....	....	....	....	....	....	....	....
General government	4 790	....	....	....	....	....	....	....	....
of which: Short-term	4 792	....	....	....	....	....	....	....	....
Banks	4 793	....	....	....	.1	−.1	.2	14.9	....
of which: Short-term	4 795	....	....	....	.1	−.1	.2	14.9	....
Other sectors	4 796	1.5	29.6	40.1	67.1	110.9	35.7	73.9	....
of which: Short-term	4 798	....	....	....	....	....	....	....	....
E. RESERVE ASSETS	4 802	**−14.1**	**−90.3**	**−92.5**	**−18.1**	**−155.0**	**−4.5**	**−9.9**	....
Monetary gold	4 812	....	....	....	....	....	....	....	....
Special drawing rights	4 811	1.4	−6.8	−1.1	−1.0	3.3	5.7	1.4	....
Reserve position in the Fund	4 810	....	....	....	....	−.1	−.1	....	....
Foreign exchange	4 803	−15.4	−83.4	−91.4	−17.1	−158.3	−10.1	−11.2	....
Other claims	4 813	....	....	....	....	....	....	....	....
NET ERRORS AND OMISSIONS	4 998	**−9.0**	**7.9**	**30.7**	**10.7**	**15.6**	**−1.8**	**28.3**	....

2008, International Monetary Fund: *Balance of Payments Statistics Yearbook*

Table 3. INTERNATIONAL INVESTMENT POSITION (End-period stocks), 2000–2007

(Millions of U.S. dollars)

	Code	2000	2001	2002	2003	2004	2005	2006	2007
ASSETS	8 995 C.	**830.1**	**906.2**	**1,360.0**	**1,667.8**	**2,803.7**	**2,014.6**	**2,608.9**	....
Direct investment abroad	8 505	**21.9**	**–5.2**	**55.1**	**75.5**	**78.5**	**58.3**	**81.2**	....
Equity capital and reinvested earnings	8 506	20.6	16.4	55.7	55.6	61.9	52.2	63.7	....
Claims on affiliated enterprises	8 507	....	....	....	....	....	....	....	....
Liabilities to affiliated enterprises	8 508	....	....	....	....	....	....	....	....
Other capital	8 530	1.2	–21.6	–.5	19.9	16.6	6.1	17.5	....
Claims on affiliated enterprises	8 535	....	....	....	....	....	....	....	....
Liabilities to affiliated enterprises	8 540	....	....	....	....	....	....	....	....
Portfolio investment	8 602	**95.0**	**90.2**	**133.5**	**226.7**	**331.5**	**260.0**	**329.0**	....
Equity securities	8 610	18.9	13.3	14.9	32.9	20.0	14.5	14.9	....
Monetary authorities	8 611	....	....	....	....	....	....	....	....
General government	8 612	....	....	....	....	....	....	....	....
Banks	8 613	.1	....	.1	....	3.9	3.7	4.6	....
Other sectors	8 614	....	....	....	....	....	....	....	....
Debt securities	8 619	76.1	76.8	118.6	193.8	311.5	245.5	314.1	....
Bonds and notes	8 620	52.8	55.6	104.6	188.5	305.6	238.6	286.3	....
Monetary authorities	8 621	....	....	....	....	....	....	....	....
General government	8 622	....	....	....	....	....	....	....	....
Banks	8 623	52.8	55.6	104.6	188.5	305.6	238.6	286.3	....
Other sectors	8 624	....	....	....	....	....	....	....	....
Money market instruments	8 630	23.3	21.3	14.1	5.3	5.9	6.9	27.8	....
Monetary authorities	8 631	....	....	....	....	....	....	....	....
General government	8 632	....	....	....	....	....	....	....	....
Banks	8 633	23.3	21.3	14.1	5.3	5.9	6.9	27.8	....
Other sectors	8 634	....	....	....	....	....	....	....	....
Financial derivatives	8 900	**.7**	**1.1**	....	**.8**	**.1**	**.1**	**.2**	....
Monetary authorities	8 901	....	....	....	....	....	....	....	....
General government	8 902	....	....	....	....	....	....	....	....
Banks	8 903	.7	1.1	....	.8	.1	.1	.2	....
Other sectors	8 904	....	....	....	....	....	....	....	....
Other investment	8 703	**324.9**	**364.2**	**527.0**	**570.1**	**1,026.1**	**506.9**	**864.3**	....
Trade credits	8 706	115.6	114.7	152.6	181.9	217.4	155.0	205.5	....
General government	8 707	....	....	....	....	....	....	....	....
of which: Short-term	8 709	....	....	....	....	....	....	....	....
Other sectors	8 710	115.6	114.7	152.6	181.9	217.4	155.0	205.5	....
of which: Short-term	8 712	....	....	....	....	....	....	....	....
Loans	8 714	44.5	48.3	82.4	120.6	345.5	109.5	196.6	....
Monetary authorities	8 715	....	....	....	....	....	....	....	....
of which: Short-term	8 718	....	....	....	....	....	....	....	....
General government	8 719	....	....	....	....	....	....	....	....
of which: Short-term	8 721	....	....	....	....	....	....	....	....
Banks	8 722	44.5	47.1	82.4	120.5	345.5	109.5	196.6	....
of which: Short-term	8 724	*26.0*	*33.0*	*61.9*	*80.6*	*140.1*	*56.5*	*81.7*	....
Other sectors	8 725	....	1.2	....	....	....	....	....	....
of which: Short-term	8 727	....	....	....	....	....	....	....	....
Currency and deposits	8 730	139.2	172.4	267.7	262.1	445.7	222.0	209.1	....
Monetary authorities	8 731	....	....	....	....	....	....	....	....
General government	8 732	2.8	3.1	5.4	8.5	5.7	4.0	3.4	....
Banks	8 733	114.2	137.3	156.6	178.3	339.5	141.0	152.3	....
Other sectors	8 734	22.2	32.0	105.7	75.4	100.5	77.0	53.4	....
Other assets	8 736	25.5	28.7	24.3	5.6	17.4	20.4	253.0	....
Monetary authorities	8 737	....	....	....	....	....	....	....	....
of which: Short-term	8 739	....	....	....	....	....	....	....	....
General government	8 740	....	....	....	....	....	....	.7	....
of which: Short-term	8 742	....	....	....	....	....	....	....	....
Banks	8 743	5.3	3.5	2.8	1.8	5.6	.6	9.9	....
of which: Short-term	8 745	*5.3*	*3.5*	*2.8*	*1.8*	*5.6*	*.6*	*9.8*	....
Other sectors	8 746	20.2	25.2	21.5	3.8	11.8	19.8	242.5	....
of which: Short-term	8 748	....	....	....	....	....	....	....	....
Reserve assets	8 802	**387.6**	**455.9**	**644.4**	**794.6**	**1,367.6**	**1,189.3**	**1,334.2**	....
Monetary gold	8 812	....	....	....	....	....	....	....	....
Special drawing rights	8 811	.9	7.5	9.1	10.6	7.3	1.4	.1	.1
Reserve position in the Fund	8 810	1.8	1.8	2.0	2.2	2.4	2.2	2.4	2.6
Foreign exchange	8 803	384.8	446.6	633.3	781.8	1,357.9	1,185.7	1,331.8	....
Other claims	8 813	....	....	....	....	....	....	....	....

Table 3 (Concluded). INTERNATIONAL INVESTMENT POSITION (End-period stocks), 2000–2007

(Millions of U.S. dollars)

	Code	2000	2001	2002	2003	2004	2005	2006	2007
LIABILITIES	8 995 D.	**4,617.4**	**4,523.8**	**5,287.8**	**5,973.0**	**6,603.7**	**5,616.6**	**4,398.2**	....
Direct investment in Senegal	8 555 ..	**294.6**	**194.3**	**241.6**	**346.6**	**441.2**	**358.2**	**477.1**	....
Equity capital and reinvested earnings	8 556 ..	254.7	155.3	196.6	296.6	362.5	272.6	440.8	....
Claims on direct investors	8 557 ..	....	....	....	....	....	....	....	....
Liabilities to direct investors	8 558 ..	....	....	....	....	....	....	....	....
Other capital	8 580 ..	39.9	38.9	45.0	49.9	78.7	85.6	36.4	....
Claims on direct investors	8 585 ..	....	....	....	....	....	....	....	....
Liabilities to direct investors	8 590 ..	....	....	....	....	....	....	....	....
Portfolio investment	8 652 ..	**127.9**	**113.8**	**140.3**	**180.7**	**189.0**	**267.8**	**294.9**	....
Equity securities	8 660 ..	93.7	83.2	107.8	133.7	113.6	91.8	102.0	....
Banks	8 663 ..	1.8	1.8	1.7	2.4	2.6	2.3	1.4	....
Other sectors	8 664 ..	91.9	81.4	106.1	131.3	110.9	89.4	100.6	....
Debt securities	8 669 ..	34.2	30.6	32.6	47.0	75.5	176.0	192.8	....
Bonds and notes	8 670 ..	34.2	30.6	32.6	47.0	75.4	175.9	188.8	....
Monetary authorities	8 671 ..	....	....	....	....	....	....	....	....
General government	8 672 ..	15.0	11.8	11.8	5.6	6.0	50.4	....	....
Banks	8 673 ..	1.4	1.4	1.6	1.0	26.5	20.4	79.0	....
Other sectors	8 674 ..	17.8	17.5	19.2	40.4	42.9	105.1	109.8	....
Money market instruments	8 680 ..	....	....	....	....	.1	.1	4.0	....
Monetary authorities	8 681 ..	....	....	....	....	....	....	....	....
General government	8 682 ..	....	....	....	....	....	....	....	....
Banks	8 683 ..	....	....	....	....	.1	.1	4.0	....
Other sectors	8 684 ..	....	....	....	....	....	....	....	....
Financial derivatives	8 905 ..	....	**.4**	**.1**	**.9**	**.1**	....	**.1**	....
Monetary authorities	8 906 ..	....	....	....	....	....	....	....	....
General government	8 907 ..	....	....	....	....	....	....	....	....
Banks	8 908 ..	....	....	....	....	....	....	....	....
Other sectors	8 909 ..	....	.4	.1	.9	.1	....	.1	....
Other investment	8 753 ..	**4,194.9**	**4,215.3**	**4,905.8**	**5,444.9**	**5,973.4**	**4,990.6**	**3,626.2**	....
Trade credits	8 756 ..	255.1	212.7	265.3	373.2	415.1	445.0	693.9	....
General government	8 757 ..	....	....	....	....	....	....	....	....
of which: Short-term	8 759 ..	....	....	....	....	....	....	....	....
Other sectors	8 760 ..	255.1	212.7	265.3	373.2	415.1	445.0	693.9	....
of which: Short-term	8 762 ..	....	....	....	....	....	....	....	....
Loans	8 764 ..	3,655.1	3,684.5	4,276.2	4,582.7	4,682.7	4,045.4	2,253.8	....
Monetary authorities	8 765 ..	254.6	248.3	252.6	239.7	204.2	148.3	26.1	....
of which: Use of Fund credit and loans from the Fund	8 766 ..	*254.6*	*248.3*	*252.6*	*239.7*	*204.2*	*148.3*	*26.1*	*27.4*
of which: Short-term	8 768 ..	....	....	....	....	....	....	....	....
General government	8 769 ..	3,148.7	3,189.8	3,691.5	3,906.5	3,872.7	3,512.0	1,735.5	....
of which: Short-term	8 771 ..	....	....	....	....	....	....	....	....
Banks	8 772 ..	19.9	40.1	23.1	37.0	183.6	76.9	91.7	....
of which: Short-term	8 774 ..	*12.6*	*24.1*	*.3*	*.7*	*75.2*	*38.9*	*19.1*	....
Other sectors	8 775 ..	231.9	206.2	309.1	399.6	422.3	308.2	400.5	....
of which: Short-term	8 777 ..	....	....	....	....	....	....	....	....
Currency and deposits	8 780 ..	266.3	294.0	341.7	471.1	825.1	488.7	577.4	....
Monetary authorities	8 781 ..	88.4	91.7	108.0	143.4	115.5	148.5	112.1	....
General government	8 782 ..	....	....	....	....	....	....	....	....
Banks	8 783 ..	177.9	202.3	233.7	327.6	709.7	340.1	465.3	....
Other sectors	8 784 ..	....	....	....	....	....	....	....	....
Other liabilities	8 786 ..	18.4	24.1	22.6	18.0	50.4	11.6	101.0	....
Monetary authorities	8 787 ..	10.7	1.8	7.9	.8	17.1	2.2	10.0	....
of which: Short-term	8 789 ..	....	....	....	....	....	....	....	....
General government	8 790 ..	1.3	....	....	....	....	....	....	....
of which: Short-term	8 792 ..	....	....	....	....	....	....	....	....
Banks	8 793 ..	....	....	....	....	....	....	....	....
of which: Short-term	8 795 ..	....	....	....	....	....	....	....	....
Other sectors	8 796 ..	6.4	22.3	14.8	17.1	33.3	9.4	91.0	....
of which: Short-term	8 798 ..	....	....	....	....	....	....	....	....
NET INTERNATIONAL INVESTMENT POSITION	8 995 ..	**−3,787.3**	**−3,617.5**	**−3,927.8**	**−4,305.3**	**−3,800.0**	**−3,602.1**	**−1,789.4**	....
Conversion rates: CFA francs per U.S. dollar (end of period)	0 102 ..	**704.95**	**744.31**	**625.50**	**519.36**	**481.58**	**556.04**	**498.07**	**445.59**

Table 1. ANALYTIC PRESENTATION, 2000–2007

(Millions of U.S. dollars)

	Code	2000	2001	2002	2003	2004	2005	2006	2007
A. Current Account[1]	4 993 Z.	....	....	....	....	....	....	....	**−6,346.2**
Goods: exports f.o.b.	2 100 ..	....	....	....	....	....	....	....	8,776.5
Goods: imports f.o.b.	3 100 ..	....	....	....	....	....	....	....	−17,916.1
Balance on Goods	4 100 ..	....	....	....	....	....	....	....	*−9,139.6*
Services: credit	2 200 ..	....	....	....	....	....	....	....	3,168.3
Services: debit	3 200 ..	....	....	....	....	....	....	....	−3,516.1
Balance on Goods and Services	4 991 ..	....	....	....	....	....	....	....	*−9,487.5*
Income: credit	2 300 ..	....	....	....	....	....	....	....	710.0
Income: debit	3 300 ..	....	....	....	....	....	....	....	−1,539.0
Balance on Goods, Services, and Income	4 992 ..	....	....	....	....	....	....	....	*−10,316.5*
Current transfers: credit	2 379 Z.	....	....	....	....	....	....	....	4,285.4
Current transfers: debit	3 379 ..	....	....	....	....	....	....	....	−315.0
B. Capital Account[1]	4 994 Z.	....	....	....	....	....	....	....	**−407.6**
Capital account: credit	2 994 Z.	....	....	....	....	....	....	....	20.2
Capital account: debit	3 994 ..	....	....	....	....	....	....	....	−427.9
Total, Groups A Plus B	4 981 ..	....	....	....	....	....	....	....	*−6,753.8*
C. Financial Account[1]	4 995 W.	....	....	....	....	....	....	....	**9,319.0**
Direct investment abroad	4 505 ..	....	....	....	....	....	....	....	−943.2
Direct investment in the Republic of Serbia	4 555 Z.	....	....	....	....	....	....	....	3,447.8
Portfolio investment assets	4 602 ..	....	....	....	....	....	....	....	−4.7
Equity securities	4 610 ..	....	....	....	....	....	....	....	−13.2
Debt securities	4 619 ..	....	....	....	....	....	....	....	8.4
Portfolio investment liabilities	4 652 Z.	....	....	....	....	....	....	....	920.5
Equity securities	4 660 ..	....	....	....	....	....	....	....	764.3
Debt securities	4 669 Z.	....	....	....	....	....	....	....	156.2
Financial derivatives	4 910 ..	....	....	....	....	....	....	....	1.6
Financial derivatives assets	4 900 ..	....	....	....	....	....	....	....	....
Financial derivatives liabilities	4 905 ..	....	....	....	....	....	....	....	1.6
Other investment assets	4 703 ..	....	....	....	....	....	....	....	−2,300.8
Monetary authorities	4 701 ..	....	....	....	....	....	....	....	....
General government	4 704 ..	....	....	....	....	....	....	....	−67.8
Banks	4 705 ..	....	....	....	....	....	....	....	−1,069.5
Other sectors	4 728 ..	....	....	....	....	....	....	....	−1,163.5
Other investment liabilities	4 753 W.	....	....	....	....	....	....	....	8,197.8
Monetary authorities	4 753 WA	....	....	....	....	....	....	....	−70.0
General government	4 753 ZB	....	....	....	....	....	....	....	1,789.7
Banks	4 753 ZC	....	....	....	....	....	....	....	425.0
Other sectors	4 753 ZD	....	....	....	....	....	....	....	6,053.0
Total, Groups A Through C	4 983 ..	....	....	....	....	....	....	....	*2,565.2*
D. Net Errors and Omissions	4 998 ..	....	....	....	....	....	....	....	**−1,302.6**
Total, Groups A Through D	4 984 ..	....	....	....	....	....	....	....	*1,262.6*
E. Reserves and Related Items	4 802 A.	....	....	....	....	....	....	....	**−1,262.6**
Reserve assets	4 802 ..	....	....	....	....	....	....	....	−1,017.7
Use of Fund credit and loans	4 766 ..	....	....	....	....	....	....	....	−244.9
Exceptional financing	4 920 ..	....	....	....	....	....	....	....	....
Conversion rates: dinars per U.S. dollar	0 101 ..	**63.1659**	**66.9137**	**64.3983**	**57.5854**	**58.3814**	**66.7138**	**67.1458**	**58.4535**

[1] Excludes components that have been classified in the categories of Group E.

Table 2. STANDARD PRESENTATION, 2000–2007
(Millions of U.S. dollars)

	Code	2000	2001	2002	2003	2004	2005	2006	2007
CURRENT ACCOUNT........................	4 993 ..	....	....	....	....	....	....	....	**−6,346.2**
A. GOODS................................	4 100 ..	....	....	....	....	....	....	....	**−9,139.6**
Credit................................	2 100 ..	....	....	....	....	....	....	Credit	**8,776.5**
General merchandise: exports f.o.b........	2 110 ..	....	....	....	....	....	....	....	8,776.5
Goods for processing: exports f.o.b.......	2 150 ..	....	....	....	....	....	....	....	....
Repairs on goods..........................	2 160 ..	....	....	....	....	....	....	....	....
Goods procured in ports by carriers.......	2 170 ..	....	....	....	....	....	....	....	....
Nonmonetary gold..........................	2 180 ..	....	....	....	....	....	....	....	....
Debit.................................	3 100 ..	....	....	....	....	....	....	....	**−17,916.1**
General merchandise: imports f.o.b........	3 110 ..	....	....	....	....	....	....	....	−17,916.1
Goods for processing: imports f.o.b.......	3 150 ..	....	....	....	....	....	....	....	....
Repairs on goods..........................	3 160 ..	....	....	....	....	....	....	....	....
Goods procured in ports by carriers.......	3 170 ..	....	....	....	....	....	....	....	....
Nonmonetary gold..........................	3 180 ..	....	....	....	....	....	....	....	....
B. SERVICES............................	4 200 ..	....	....	....	....	....	....	....	**−347.8**
Total credit	2 200 ..	....	....	....	....	....	....	....	*3,168.3*
Total debit	3 200 ..	....	....	....	....	....	....	....	*−3,516.1*
Transportation services, credit............	2 205 ..	....	....	....	....	....	....	....	**724.3**
Passenger	2 850 ..	....	....	....	....	....	....	....	*145.0*
Freight	2 851 ..	....	....	....	....	....	....	....	*416.2*
Other	2 852 ..	....	....	....	....	....	....	....	*163.1*
Sea transport, passenger..................	2 207 ..	....	....	....	....	....	....	....	....
Sea transport, freight....................	2 208 ..	....	....	....	....	....	....	....	....
Sea transport, other......................	2 209 ..	....	....	....	....	....	....	....	....
Air transport, passenger..................	2 211 ..	....	....	....	....	....	....	....	128.4
Air transport, freight....................	2 212 ..	....	....	....	....	....	....	....	5.6
Air transport, other......................	2 213 ..	....	....	....	....	....	....	....	25.4
Other transport, passenger................	2 215 ..	....	....	....	....	....	....	....	16.5
Other transport, freight..................	2 216 ..	....	....	....	....	....	....	....	410.6
Other transport, other....................	2 217 ..	....	....	....	....	....	....	....	137.7
Transportation services, debit.............	3 205 ..	....	....	....	....	....	....	....	**−993.5**
Passenger	3 850 ..	....	....	....	....	....	....	....	*−152.3*
Freight	3 851 ..	....	....	....	....	....	....	....	*−491.4*
Other	3 852 ..	....	....	....	....	....	....	....	*−349.8*
Sea transport, passenger..................	3 207 ..	....	....	....	....	....	....	....	−.3
Sea transport, freight....................	3 208 ..	....	....	....	....	....	....	....	−58.6
Sea transport, other......................	3 209 ..	....	....	....	....	....	....	....	−13.8
Air transport, passenger..................	3 211 ..	....	....	....	....	....	....	....	−145.2
Air transport, freight....................	3 212 ..	....	....	....	....	....	....	....	−9.0
Air transport, other......................	3 213 ..	....	....	....	....	....	....	....	−21.6
Other transport, passenger................	3 215 ..	....	....	....	....	....	....	....	−6.7
Other transport, freight..................	3 216 ..	....	....	....	....	....	....	....	−423.9
Other transport, other....................	3 217 ..	....	....	....	....	....	....	....	−314.4
Travel, credit.............................	2 236 ..	....	....	....	....	....	....	....	**865.7**
Business travel...........................	2 237 ..	....	....	....	....	....	....	....	4.8
Personal travel...........................	2 240 ..	....	....	....	....	....	....	....	860.9
Travel, debit..............................	3 236 ..	....	....	....	....	....	....	....	**−1,042.4**
Business travel...........................	3 237 ..	....	....	....	....	....	....	....	−134.7
Personal travel...........................	3 240 ..	....	....	....	....	....	....	....	−907.7
Other services, credit.....................	2 200 BA	....	....	....	....	....	....	....	**1,578.3**
Communications............................	2 245 ..	....	....	....	....	....	....	....	109.0
Construction..............................	2 249 ..	....	....	....	....	....	....	....	199.3
Insurance.................................	2 253 ..	....	....	....	....	....	....	....	29.4
Financial.................................	2 260 ..	....	....	....	....	....	....	....	25.6
Computer and information..................	2 262 ..	....	....	....	....	....	....	....	84.8
Royalties and licence fees................	2 266 ..	....	....	....	....	....	....	....	10.5
Other business services...................	2 268 ..	....	....	....	....	....	....	....	974.9
Personal, cultural, and recreational......	2 287 ..	....	....	....	....	....	....	....	116.2
Government, n.i.e.........................	2 291 ..	....	....	....	....	....	....	....	28.6
Other services, debit......................	3 200 BA	....	....	....	....	....	....	....	**−1,480.2**
Communications............................	3 245 ..	....	....	....	....	....	....	....	−85.2
Construction..............................	3 249 ..	....	....	....	....	....	....	....	−116.7
Insurance.................................	3 253 ..	....	....	....	....	....	....	....	−41.8
Financial.................................	3 260 ..	....	....	....	....	....	....	....	−43.8
Computer and information..................	3 262 ..	....	....	....	....	....	....	....	−161.4
Royalties and licence fees................	3 266 ..	....	....	....	....	....	....	....	−143.9
Other business services...................	3 268 ..	....	....	....	....	....	....	....	−746.9
Personal, cultural, and recreational......	3 287 ..	....	....	....	....	....	....	....	−79.9
Government, n.i.e.........................	3 291 ..	....	....	....	....	....	....	....	−60.6

Table 2 (Continued). STANDARD PRESENTATION, 2000–2007

(Millions of U.S. dollars)

	Code	2000	2001	2002	2003	2004	2005	2006	2007
C. INCOME	4 300	....	....	....	....	....	....	....	**−829.1**
Total credit	2 300	....	....	....	....	....	....	....	*710.0*
Total debit	3 300	....	....	....	....	....	....	....	*−1,539.0*
Compensation of employees, credit	2 310	....	....	....	....	....	....	....	**147.7**
Compensation of employees, debit	3 310	....	....	....	....	....	....	....	**−17.2**
Investment income, credit	2 320	....	....	....	....	....	....	....	**562.3**
Direct investment income	2 330	....	....	....	....	....	....	....	77.6
Dividends and distributed branch profits	2 332	....	....	....	....	....	....	....	54.4
Reinvested earnings and undistributed branch profits	2 333	....	....	....	....	....	....	....	23.2
Income on debt (interest)	2 334	....	....	....	....	....	....	....	....
Portfolio investment income	2 339	....	....	....	....	....	....	....	.4
Income on equity	2 340	....	....	....	....	....	....	....	....
Income on bonds and notes	2 350	....	....	....	....	....	....	....	....
Income on money market instruments	2 360	....	....	....	....	....	....	....	.4
Other investment income	2 370	....	....	....	....	....	....	....	484.4
Investment income, debit	3 320	....	....	....	....	....	....	....	**−1,521.8**
Direct investment income	3 330	....	....	....	....	....	....	....	−603.5
Dividends and distributed branch profits	3 332	....	....	....	....	....	....	....	−264.5
Reinvested earnings and undistributed branch profits	3 333	....	....	....	....	....	....	....	−339.0
Income on debt (interest)	3 334	....	....	....	....	....	....	....	....
Portfolio investment income	3 339	....	....	....	....	....	....	....	−1.1
Income on equity	3 340	....	....	....	....	....	....	....	....
Income on bonds and notes	3 350	....	....	....	....	....	....	....	−.7
Income on money market instruments	3 360	....	....	....	....	....	....	....	−.4
Other investment income	3 370	....	....	....	....	....	....	....	−917.2
D. CURRENT TRANSFERS	4 379	....	....	....	....	....	....	....	**3,970.4**
Credit	2 379	....	....	....	....	....	....	....	**4,285.4**
General government	2 380	....	....	....	....	....	....	....	365.0
Other sectors	2 390	....	....	....	....	....	....	....	3,920.4
Workers' remittances	2 391	....	....	....	....	....	....	....	2,947.6
Other current transfers	2 392	....	....	....	....	....	....	....	972.8
Debit	3 379	....	....	....	....	....	....	....	**−315.0**
General government	3 380	....	....	....	....	....	....	....	−126.6
Other sectors	3 390	....	....	....	....	....	....	....	−188.4
Workers' remittances	3 391	....	....	....	....	....	....	....	−94.9
Other current transfers	3 392	....	....	....	....	....	....	....	−93.4
CAPITAL AND FINANCIAL ACCOUNT	4 996	....	....	....	....	....	....	....	**7,648.8**
CAPITAL ACCOUNT	4 994	....	....	....	....	....	....	....	**−407.6**
Total credit	2 994	....	....	....	....	....	....	....	*20.2*
Total debit	3 994	....	....	....	....	....	....	....	*−427.9*
Capital transfers, credit	2 400	....	....	....	....	....	....	....	**2.3**
General government	2 401	....	....	....	....	....	....	....	.2
Debt forgiveness	2 402	....	....	....	....	....	....	....	....
Other capital transfers	2 410	....	....	....	....	....	....	....	.2
Other sectors	2 430	....	....	....	....	....	....	....	2.1
Migrants' transfers	2 431	....	....	....	....	....	....	....	2.0
Debt forgiveness	2 432	....	....	....	....	....	....	....	....
Other capital transfers	2 440	....	....	....	....	....	....	....	.1
Capital transfers, debit	3 400	....	....	....	....	....	....	....	**−2.1**
General government	3 401	....	....	....	....	....	....	....	....
Debt forgiveness	3 402	....	....	....	....	....	....	....	....
Other capital transfers	3 410	....	....	....	....	....	....	....	....
Other sectors	3 430	....	....	....	....	....	....	....	−2.1
Migrants' transfers	3 431	....	....	....	....	....	....	....	−2.1
Debt forgiveness	3 432	....	....	....	....	....	....	....	....
Other capital transfers	3 440	....	....	....	....	....	....	....	....
Nonproduced nonfinancial assets, credit	2 480	....	....	....	....	....	....	....	**18.0**
Nonproduced nonfinancial assets, debit	3 480	....	....	....	....	....	....	....	**−425.7**

Table 2 (Continued). STANDARD PRESENTATION, 2000–2007

(Millions of U.S. dollars)

	Code	2000	2001	2002	2003	2004	2005	2006	2007
FINANCIAL ACCOUNT	4 995 ..	....	....	....	....	....	....	....	**8,056.4**
A. DIRECT INVESTMENT	4 500 ..	....	....	....	....	....	....	....	**2,504.6**
Direct investment abroad	4 505 ..	....	....	....	....	....	....	....	**−943.2**
Equity capital	4 510 ..	....	....	....	....	....	....	....	−1,109.7
Claims on affiliated enterprises	4 515 ..	....	....	....	....	....	....		....
Liabilities to affiliated enterprises	4 520 ..	....	....	....	....	....	....		
Reinvested earnings	4 525 ..	....	....	....	....	....	....		−23.2
Other capital	4 530 ..	....	....	....	....	....	....		189.7
Claims on affiliated enterprises	4 535 ..	....	....	....	....	....	....		189.7
Liabilities to affiliated enterprises	4 540 ..	....	....	....	....	....	....	....	....
Direct investment in the Republic of Serbia	4 555 ..	....	....	....	....	....	....	....	**3,447.8**
Equity capital	4 560 ..	....	....	....	....	....	....		2,022.8
Claims on direct investors	4 565 ..	....	....	....	....	....	....		2,022.8
Liabilities to direct investors	4 570 ..	....	....	....	....	....	....		
Reinvested earnings	4 575 ..	....	....	....	....	....	....		339.0
Other capital	4 580 ..	....	....	....	....	....	....		1,086.0
Claims on direct investors	4 585 ..	....	....	....	....	....	....		1,086.0
Liabilities to direct investors	4 590 ..	....	....	....	....	....	....		....
B. PORTFOLIO INVESTMENT	4 600 ..	....	....	....	....	....	....	....	**915.8**
Assets	4 602 ..	....	....	....	....	....	....	....	**−4.7**
Equity securities	4 610 ..	....	....	....	....	....	....	....	−13.2
Monetary authorities	4 611 ..	....	....	....	....	....	....	....	....
General government	4 612 ..	....	....	....	....	....	....		....
Banks	4 613 ..	....	....	....	....	....	....		
Other sectors	4 614 ..	....	....	....	....	....	....		−13.2
Debt securities	4 619 ..	....	....	....	....	....	....		8.4
Bonds and notes	4 620 ..	....	....	....	....	....	....		8.4
Monetary authorities	4 621 ..	....	....	....	....	....	....		....
General government	4 622 ..	....	....	....	....	....	....		−.4
Banks	4 623 ..	....	....	....	....	....	....		....
Other sectors	4 624 ..	....	....	....	....	....	....		8.8
Money market instruments	4 630 ..	....	....	....	....	....	....		....
Monetary authorities	4 631 ..	....	....	....	....	....	....		....
General government	4 632 ..	....	....	....	....	....	....		....
Banks	4 633 ..	....	....	....	....	....	....		....
Other sectors	4 634 ..	....	....	....	....	....	....	....	....
Liabilities	4 652 ..	....	....	....	....	....	....	....	**920.5**
Equity securities	4 660 ..	....	....	....	....	....	....	....	764.3
Banks	4 663 ..	....	....	....	....	....	....	....	764.3
Other sectors	4 664 ..	....	....	....	....	....	....		....
Debt securities	4 669 ..	....	....	....	....	....	....		156.2
Bonds and notes	4 670 ..	....	....	....	....	....	....		156.2
Monetary authorities	4 671 ..	....	....	....	....	....	....		....
General government	4 672 ..	....	....	....	....	....	....	....	−13.1
Banks	4 673 ..	....	....	....	....	....	....		116.4
Other sectors	4 674 ..	....	....	....	....	....	....		52.9
Money market instruments	4 680 ..	....	....	....	....	....	....		....
Monetary authorities	4 681 ..	....	....	....	....	....	....		....
General government	4 682 ..	....	....	....	....	....	....		....
Banks	4 683 ..	....	....	....	....	....	....		....
Other sectors	4 684 ..	....	....	....	....	....	....		....
C. FINANCIAL DERIVATIVES	4 910 ..	....	....	....	....	....	....	....	**1.6**
Monetary authorities	4 911 ..	....	....	....	....	....	....	....	....
General government	4 912 ..	....	....	....	....	....	....	....	....
Banks	4 913 ..	....	....	....	....	....	....	....	1.6
Other sectors	4 914 ..	....	....	....	....	....	....	....	....
Assets	4 900 ..	....	....	....	....	....	....	....	....
Monetary authorities	4 901 ..	....	....	....	....	....	....	....	....
General government	4 902 ..	....	....	....	....	....	....	....	....
Banks	4 903 ..	....	....	....	....	....	....	....	....
Other sectors	4 904 ..	....	....	....	....	....	....	....	....
Liabilities	4 905 ..	....	....	....	....	....	....	....	**1.6**
Monetary authorities	4 906 ..	....	....	....	....	....	....	....	....
General government	4 907 ..	....	....	....	....	....	....	....	....
Banks	4 908 ..	....	....	....	....	....	....	....	1.6
Other sectors	4 909 ..	....	....	....	....	....	....	....	....

Table 2 (Concluded). STANDARD PRESENTATION, 2000–2007

(Millions of U.S. dollars)

	Code	2000	2001	2002	2003	2004	2005	2006	2007
D. OTHER INVESTMENT	4 700	....	....	....	....	....	....	....	**5,652.1**
Assets	4 703	....	....	....	....	....	....	....	**−2,300.8**
Trade credits	4 706	....	....	....	....	....	....	....	−1,164.1
General government	4 707	....	....	....	....	....	....	....	....
of which: Short-term	4 709	....	....	....	....	....	....	....	....
Other sectors	4 710	....	....	....	....	....	....	....	−1,164.1
of which: Short-term	4 712	....	....	....	....	....	....	....	*−1,164.1*
Loans	4 714	....	....	....	....	....	....	....	.4
Monetary authorities	4 715	....	....	....	....	....	....	....	....
of which: Short-term	4 718	....	....	....	....	....	....	....	....
General government	4 719	....	....	....	....	....	....	....	....
of which: Short-term	4 721	....	....	....	....	....	....	....	....
Banks	4 722	....	....	....	....	....	....	....	−.2
of which: Short-term	4 724	....	....	....	....	....	....	....	*5.0*
Other sectors	4 725	....	....	....	....	....	....	....	.6
of which: Short-term	4 727	....	....	....	....	....	....	....	....
Currency and deposits	4 730	....	....	....	....	....	....	....	−1,069.3
Monetary authorities	4 731	....	....	....	....	....	....	....	....
General government	4 732	....	....	....	....	....	....	....	....
Banks	4 733	....	....	....	....	....	....	....	−1,069.3
Other sectors	4 734	....	....	....	....	....	....	....	....
Other assets	4 736	....	....	....	....	....	....	....	−67.8
Monetary authorities	4 737	....	....	....	....	....	....	....	....
of which: Short-term	4 739	....	....	....	....	....	....	....	....
General government	4 740	....	....	....	....	....	....	....	−67.8
of which: Short-term	4 742	....	....	....	....	....	....	....	....
Banks	4 743	....	....	....	....	....	....	....	....
of which: Short-term	4 745	....	....	....	....	....	....	....	....
Other sectors	4 746	....	....	....	....	....	....	....	....
of which: Short-term	4 748	....	....	....	....	....	....	....	....
Liabilities	4 753	....	....	....	....	....	....	....	**7,952.9**
Trade credits	4 756	....	....	....	....	....	....	....	3,251.5
General government	4 757	....	....	....	....	....	....	....	1,625.8
of which: Short-term	4 759	....	....	....	....	....	....	....	....
Other sectors	4 760	....	....	....	....	....	....	....	1,625.8
of which: Short-term	4 762	....	....	....	....	....	....	....	*1,625.8*
Loans	4 764	....	....	....	....	....	....	....	4,651.6
Monetary authorities	4 765	....	....	....	....	....	....	....	−244.9
of which: Use of Fund credit and loans from the Fund	4 766	....	....	....	....	....	....	....	*−244.9*
of which: Short-term	4 768	....	....	....	....	....	....	....	....
General government	4 769	....	....	....	....	....	....	....	164.0
of which: Short-term	4 771	....	....	....	....	....	....	....	....
Banks	4 772	....	....	....	....	....	....	....	309.9
of which: Short-term	4 774	....	....	....	....	....	....	....	*472.7*
Other sectors	4 775	....	....	....	....	....	....	....	4,422.6
of which: Short-term	4 777	....	....	....	....	....	....	....	*12.0*
Currency and deposits	4 780	....	....	....	....	....	....	....	115.1
Monetary authorities	4 781	....	....	....	....	....	....	....	....
General government	4 782	....	....	....	....	....	....	....	....
Banks	4 783	....	....	....	....	....	....	....	115.1
Other sectors	4 784	....	....	....	....	....	....	....	....
Other liabilities	4 786	....	....	....	....	....	....	....	−65.4
Monetary authorities	4 787	....	....	....	....	....	....	....	−70.0
of which: Short-term	4 789	....	....	....	....	....	....	....	....
General government	4 790	....	....	....	....	....	....	....	....
of which: Short-term	4 792	....	....	....	....	....	....	....	....
Banks	4 793	....	....	....	....	....	....	....	....
of which: Short-term	4 795	....	....	....	....	....	....	....	....
Other sectors	4 796	....	....	....	....	....	....	....	4.6
of which: Short-term	4 798	....	....	....	....	....	....	....	*4.6*
E. RESERVE ASSETS	4 802	....	....	....	....	....	....	....	**−1,017.7**
Monetary gold	4 812	....	....	....	....	....	....	....	22.1
Special drawing rights	4 811	....	....	....	....	....	....	....	8.0
Reserve position in the Fund	4 810	....	....	....	....	....	....	....	....
Foreign exchange	4 803	....	....	....	....	....	....	....	−1,047.8
Other claims	4 813	....	....	....	....	....	....	....	....
NET ERRORS AND OMISSIONS	4 998	....	....	....	....	....	....	....	**−1,302.6**

Table 1. ANALYTIC PRESENTATION, 2000–2007

(Millions of U.S. dollars)

	Code	2000	2001	2002	2003	2004	2005	2006	2007
A. Current Account[1]	4 993 Z.	**−53.74**	**−158.39**	**−108.35**	**−12.39**	**−63.73**	**−188.16**	**−145.19**	**−274.84**
Goods: exports f.o.b.	2 100 ..	194.78	216.45	236.70	286.42	301.10	350.91	420.08	391.67
Goods: imports f.o.b.	3 100 ..	−311.60	−428.65	−380.06	−375.56	−456.27	−650.21	−710.36	−804.00
Balance on Goods	4 100 ..	*−116.82*	*−212.19*	*−143.35*	*−89.14*	*−155.17*	*−299.31*	*−290.28*	*−412.33*
Services: credit	2 200 ..	286.93	294.15	313.29	330.40	326.60	368.76	430.28	472.22
Services: debit	3 200 ..	−190.23	−215.56	−216.78	−220.23	−215.83	−234.68	−274.15	−302.53
Balance on Goods and Services	4 991 ..	*−20.13*	*−133.60*	*−46.84*	*21.03*	*−44.40*	*−165.22*	*−134.14*	*−242.63*
Income: credit	2 300 ..	10.11	8.25	7.44	11.98	9.44	9.81	10.27	9.62
Income: debit	3 300 ..	−43.41	−37.48	−75.43	−55.18	−43.13	−49.88	−53.89	−80.69
Balance on Goods, Services, and Income	4 992 ..	*−53.42*	*−162.84*	*−114.84*	*−22.16*	*−78.09*	*−205.29*	*−177.77*	*−313.70*
Current transfers: credit	2 379 Z.	7.32	8.17	8.17	12.58	17.26	21.44	42.68	49.50
Current transfers: debit	3 379 ..	−7.64	−3.73	−1.68	−2.82	−2.90	−4.31	−10.10	−10.64
B. Capital Account[1]	4 994 Z.	**.89**	**9.44**	**5.03**	**7.42**	**.99**	**29.88**	**13.24**	**4.61**
Capital account: credit	2 994 Z.	.89	9.44	5.03	7.42	.99	29.88	13.24	4.61
Capital account: debit	3 994 ..	....	....	....	....	....	....	....	....
Total, Groups A Plus B	4 981 ..	*−52.85*	*−148.95*	*−103.32*	*−4.97*	*−62.74*	*−158.28*	*−131.95*	*−270.23*
C. Financial Account[1]	4 995 W.	**75.64**	**93.61**	**130.61**	**−30.91**	**−30.47**	**129.43**	**223.50**	**294.80**
Direct investment abroad	4 505 ..	−10.50	−8.54	−8.73	−8.15	−7.60	−7.45	−8.01	−8.49
Direct investment in Seychelles	4 555 Z.	24.33	64.74	47.72	58.43	38.01	85.88	145.82	249.31
Portfolio investment assets	4 602 ..	−.09	−.07	−.07	−.01	−.04	−.04	−.05	−.04
Equity securities	4 610 ..	....	....	....	....	....	....	....	....
Debt securities	4 619 ..	−.09	−.07	−.07	−.01	−.04	−.04	−.05	−.04
Portfolio investment liabilities	4 652 Z.	1.04	1.09	1.11	1.14	1.11	1.06	198.21	31.33
Equity securities	4 660 ..	....	....	....	....	....	....	....	....
Debt securities	4 669 Z.	1.04	1.09	1.11	1.14	1.11	1.06	198.21	31.33
Financial derivatives	4 910 ..	....	....	....	....	....	....	....	....
Financial derivatives assets	4 900 ..	....	....	....	....	....	....	....	....
Financial derivatives liabilities	4 905 ..	....	....	....	....	....	....	....	....
Other investment assets	4 703 ..	−14.84	−8.76	−10.65	−14.81	−12.25	−9.61	−8.75	−59.03
Monetary authorities	4 701 ..	....	....	....	....	....	....	....	....
General government	4 704 ..	....	....	....	....	....	....	....	....
Banks	4 705 ..	....	....	....	....	....	−3.49	−13.27	−46.49
Other sectors	4 728 ..	−14.84	−8.76	−10.65	−14.81	−12.25	−6.12	4.53	−12.54
Other investment liabilities	4 753 W.	75.70	45.15	101.23	−67.51	−49.71	59.60	−103.72	81.72
Monetary authorities	4 753 WA	41.79	8.46	79.19	−35.51	−33.79	10.82	−75.26	....
General government	4 753 ZB	27.75	−48.21	42.83	−26.13	−24.50	35.66	−45.60	53.94
Banks	4 753 ZC	7.63	−4.30	−5.70	−3.61	8.11	13.57	12.33	37.40
Other sectors	4 753 ZD	−1.46	89.19	−15.08	−2.26	.46	−.45	4.81	−9.62
Total, Groups A Through C	4 983 ..	*22.79*	*−55.34*	*27.29*	*−35.89*	*−93.21*	*−28.85*	*91.55*	*24.57*
D. Net Errors and Omissions	4 998 ..	**3.43**	**1.14**	**−10.10**	**−4.68**	**.68**	**−.52**	**2.19**	**2.03**
Total, Groups A Through D	4 984 ..	*26.22*	*−54.20*	*17.19*	*−40.56*	*−92.53*	*−29.37*	*93.74*	*26.60*
E. Reserves and Related Items	4 802 A.	**−26.22**	**54.20**	**−17.19**	**40.56**	**92.53**	**29.37**	**−93.74**	**−26.60**
Reserve assets	4 802 ..	−19.38	10.32	−25.84	−3.12	32.97	−21.97	−61.97	45.03
Use of Fund credit and loans	4 766 ..	....	....	....	....	....	....	....	....
Exceptional financing	4 920 ..	−6.84	43.89	8.65	43.68	59.56	51.35	−31.77	−71.62
Conversion rates: Seychelles rupees per U.S. dollar	0 101 ..	**5.7138**	**5.8575**	**5.4800**	**5.4007**	**5.5000**	**5.5000**	**5.5197**	**6.7011**

[1] Excludes components that have been classified in the categories of Group E.

Table 2. STANDARD PRESENTATION, 2000–2007

(Millions of U.S. dollars)

	Code	2000	2001	2002	2003	2004	2005	2006	2007
CURRENT ACCOUNT.....................................	4 993 ..	**–42.92**	**–153.06**	**–101.27**	**–9.36**	**–60.32**	**–174.07**	**–133.77**	**–263.81**
A. GOODS...	4 100 ..	**–116.82**	**–212.19**	**–143.35**	**–89.14**	**–155.17**	**–299.31**	**–290.28**	**–412.33**
Credit..	2 100 ..	**194.78**	**216.45**	**236.70**	**286.42**	**301.10**	**350.91**	**420.08**	**391.67**
General merchandise: exports f.o.b.................	2 110 ..	129.65	162.98	181.06	218.55	199.51	211.83	220.10	201.32
Goods for processing: exports f.o.b...............	2 150 ..	....	....	....	....	....	....	....	....
Repairs on goods.....................................	2 160 ..	.68	.70	.77	.81	.74	.80	.88	.82
Goods procured in ports by carriers.............	2 170 ..	64.45	52.77	54.87	67.06	100.85	138.27	199.10	189.54
Nonmonetary gold....................................	2 180 ..	....	....	....	....	....	....	....	....
Debit...	3 100 ..	**–311.60**	**–428.65**	**–380.06**	**–375.56**	**–456.27**	**–650.21**	**–710.36**	**–804.00**
General merchandise: imports f.o.b...............	3 110 ..	–297.77	–416.27	–368.17	–362.41	–431.76	–624.47	–660.16	–749.53
Goods for processing: imports f.o.b.............	3 150 ..	....	....	....	....	....	....	....	....
Repairs on goods.....................................	3 160 ..	–2.67	–1.73	–1.30	–1.35	–4.86	–5.66	–8.59	–14.55
Goods procured in ports by carriers.............	3 170 ..	–11.17	–10.64	–10.59	–11.80	–19.65	–20.08	–41.60	–39.93
Nonmonetary gold....................................	3 180 ..	....	....	....	....	....	....	....	....
B. SERVICES..	4 200 ..	**96.69**	**78.59**	**96.51**	**110.17**	**110.77**	**134.08**	**156.13**	**169.69**
Total credit..	2 200 ..	*286.93*	*294.15*	*313.29*	*330.40*	*326.60*	*368.76*	*430.28*	*472.22*
Total debit..	3 200 ..	*–190.23*	*–215.56*	*–216.78*	*–220.23*	*–215.83*	*–234.68*	*–274.15*	*–302.53*
Transportation services, credit................	2 205 ..	**123.83**	**115.17**	**115.35**	**124.73**	**118.21**	**133.46**	**160.54**	**145.96**
Passenger..	2 850 ..	*86.04*	*74.64*	*83.03*	*87.47*	*84.25*	*77.27*	*95.07*	*87.73*
Freight..	2 851 ..	*15.33*	*19.27*	*5.28*	*6.44*	*6.58*	*25.16*	*30.30*	*27.11*
Other..	2 852 ..	*22.46*	*21.25*	*27.03*	*30.83*	*27.38*	*31.03*	*35.17*	*31.12*
Sea transport, passenger...........................	2 207 ..	....	....	....	....	....	....	....	....
Sea transport, freight................................	2 208 ..	15.33	19.27	5.28	6.44	6.58	22.98	26.62	24.07
Sea transport, other.................................	2 209 ..	14.43	14.03	19.59	21.10	18.87	21.19	22.20	20.35
Air transport, passenger............................	2 211 ..	86.04	74.64	83.03	87.47	84.25	77.27	95.07	87.73
Air transport, freight.................................	2 212 ..	....	....	....	....	....	2.18	3.68	3.04
Air transport, other..................................	2 213 ..	8.03	7.22	7.44	9.72	8.52	9.84	12.97	10.77
Other transport, passenger.........................	2 215 ..	....	....	....	....	....	....	....	....
Other transport, freight..............................	2 216 ..	....	....	....	....	....	....	....	....
Other transport, other...............................	2 217 ..	....	....	....	....	....	....	....	....
Transportation services, debit.................	3 205 ..	**–71.32**	**–75.59**	**–82.75**	**–83.54**	**–93.97**	**–107.84**	**–127.62**	**–146.67**
Passenger..	3 850 ..	*–19.81*	*–17.81*	*–20.13*	*–18.27*	*–18.78*	*–20.22*	*–20.40*	*–30.31*
Freight..	3 851 ..	*–42.64*	*–48.41*	*–52.35*	*–51.63*	*–62.09*	*–73.64*	*–95.25*	*–98.17*
Other..	3 852 ..	*–8.88*	*–9.37*	*–10.27*	*–13.64*	*–13.10*	*–13.98*	*–11.98*	*–18.19*
Sea transport, passenger...........................	3 207 ..	....	....	....	....	....	....	....	....
Sea transport, freight................................	3 208 ..	–42.64	–48.41	–52.35	–51.63	–62.09	–73.64	–95.25	–98.17
Sea transport, other.................................	3 209 ..	–.11	–.02	–.01	–.38	–.23	–.50	–.91	–.83
Air transport, passenger............................	3 211 ..	–19.81	–17.81	–20.13	–18.27	–18.78	–20.22	–20.40	–30.31
Air transport, freight.................................	3 212 ..	....	....	....	....	....	....	....	....
Air transport, other..................................	3 213 ..	–8.77	–9.35	–10.26	–13.26	–12.88	–13.48	–11.07	–17.36
Other transport, passenger.........................	3 215 ..	....	....	....	....	....	....	....	....
Other transport, freight..............................	3 216 ..	....	....	....	....	....	....	....	....
Other transport, other...............................	3 217 ..	....	....	....	....	....	....	....	....
Travel, credit.......................................	2 236 ..	**139.24**	**146.17**	**164.33**	**171.13**	**171.71**	**192.10**	**227.77**	**278.28**
Business travel..	2 237 ..	....	....	....	....	....	....	....	....
Personal travel..	2 240 ..	139.24	146.17	164.33	171.13	171.71	192.10	227.77	278.28
Travel, debit..	3 236 ..	**–23.93**	**–22.68**	**–32.82**	**–36.30**	**–33.52**	**–38.67**	**–35.93**	**–39.95**
Business travel..	3 237 ..	....	....	....	....	....	....	....	....
Personal travel..	3 240 ..	–23.93	–22.68	–32.82	–36.30	–33.52	–38.67	–35.93	–39.95
Other services, credit...........................	2 200 BA	**23.86**	**32.81**	**33.61**	**34.53**	**36.68**	**43.20**	**41.98**	**47.98**
Communications......................................	2 245 ..	8.73	9.36	10.22	10.41	12.14	12.62	12.88	13.21
Construction...	2 249 ..	....	....	....	....	....	....	....	....
Insurance...	2 253 ..	1.15	2.99	2.70	1.56	1.44	3.60	.88	1.75
Financial..	2 260 ..	....	....	....	....	....	....	....	....
Computer and information.........................	2 262 ..	....	....	....	....	....	.16	.16	.13
Royalties and licence fees..........................	2 266 ..	....	....	....	....	....	....	....	....
Other business services............................	2 268 ..	.38	6.46	4.24	3.00	4.90	5.16	6.45	6.47
Personal, cultural, and recreational..............	2 287 ..	....	....	....	....	....	....	....	....
Government, n.i.e.....................................	2 291 ..	13.60	14.00	16.45	19.57	18.20	21.66	21.59	26.42
Other services, debit............................	3 200 BA	**–94.99**	**–117.29**	**–101.22**	**–100.39**	**–88.34**	**–88.17**	**–110.60**	**–115.91**
Communications......................................	3 245 ..	....	....	....	....	....	....	....	....
Construction...	3 249 ..	–34.43	–35.56	–26.13	–17.07	–15.21	–12.83	–23.53	–41.55
Insurance...	3 253 ..	–13.02	–16.85	–17.27	–16.39	–17.84	–20.26	–25.36	–24.43
Financial..	3 260 ..	....	....	....	....	....	....	....	....
Computer and information.........................	3 262 ..	....	....	....	....	....	....	....	....
Royalties and licence fees..........................	3 266 ..	–.44	–.43	–.55	–.56	–.54	–.55	–.54	–.54
Other business services............................	3 268 ..	–42.43	–60.44	–49.93	–58.66	–49.99	–51.09	–52.39	–45.81
Personal, cultural, and recreational..............	3 287 ..	....	....	....	....	....	....	....	....
Government, n.i.e.....................................	3 291 ..	–4.66	–4.02	–7.34	–7.70	–4.76	–3.44	–8.77	–3.58

Table 2 (Continued). STANDARD PRESENTATION, 2000–2007

(Millions of U.S. dollars)

	Code	2000	2001	2002	2003	2004	2005	2006	2007
C. INCOME	4 300 ..	**−33.29**	**−29.23**	**−68.00**	**−43.19**	**−33.69**	**−40.07**	**−43.62**	**−71.07**
Total credit	2 300 ..	*10.11*	*8.25*	*7.44*	*11.98*	*9.44*	*9.81*	*10.27*	*9.62*
Total debit	3 300 ..	*−43.41*	*−37.48*	*−75.43*	*−55.18*	*−43.13*	*−49.88*	*−53.89*	*−80.69*
Compensation of employees, credit	2 310 ..	**.18**	**.17**	**.20**	**.16**	**.16**	**.19**	**.19**	**.30**
Compensation of employees, debit	3 310 ..	**−2.54**	**−2.24**	**−3.40**	**−4.89**	**−5.30**	**−5.96**	**−7.58**	**−10.95**
Investment income, credit	2 320 ..	**9.94**	**8.08**	**7.24**	**11.83**	**9.28**	**9.62**	**10.08**	**9.32**
Direct investment income	2 330 ..	3.50	2.56	2.00	2.89	2.42	2.54	2.67	2.37
Dividends and distributed branch profits	2 332 ..	....	....	....	....	....	....	....	....
Reinvested earnings and undistributed branch profits	2 333 ..	3.50	2.56	2.00	2.89	2.42	2.54	2.67	2.37
Income on debt (interest)	2 334 ..	....	....	....	....	....	....	....	....
Portfolio investment income	2 339 ..	....	....	....	....	....	....	....	....
Income on equity	2 340 ..	....	....	....	....	....	....	....	....
Income on bonds and notes	2 350 ..	....	....	....	....	....	....	....	....
Income on money market instruments	2 360 ..	....	....	....	....	....	....	....	....
Other investment income	2 370 ..	6.44	5.52	5.24	8.93	6.86	7.08	7.41	6.95
Investment income, debit	3 320 ..	**−40.86**	**−35.25**	**−72.03**	**−50.29**	**−37.82**	**−43.91**	**−46.31**	**−69.74**
Direct investment income	3 330 ..	−8.23	−11.74	−49.02	−25.91	−17.21	−20.32	−25.30	−28.73
Dividends and distributed branch profits	3 332 ..	−3.86	−3.62	−38.86	−16.88	−11.19	−9.42	−8.35	−8.89
Reinvested earnings and undistributed branch profits	3 333 ..	−4.38	−8.12	−10.16	−9.03	−6.02	−10.90	−16.95	−19.84
Income on debt (interest)	3 334 ..	....	....	....	....	....	....	....	....
Portfolio investment income	3 339 ..	....	....	....	....	....	....	....	−18.82
Income on equity	3 340 ..	....	....	....	....	....	....	....	....
Income on bonds and notes	3 350 ..	....	....	....	....	....	....	....	−18.82
Income on money market instruments	3 360 ..	....	....	....	....	....	....	....	....
Other investment income	3 370 ..	−32.63	−23.51	−23.02	−24.38	−20.61	−23.60	−21.01	−22.19
D. CURRENT TRANSFERS	4 379 ..	**10.50**	**9.78**	**13.57**	**12.80**	**17.77**	**31.22**	**44.00**	**49.90**
Credit	2 379 ..	**18.14**	**13.51**	**15.24**	**15.62**	**20.68**	**35.53**	**54.10**	**60.53**
General government	2 380 ..	15.16	11.89	13.46	10.92	14.02	23.61	23.43	17.21
Other sectors	2 390 ..	2.98	1.62	1.78	4.70	6.65	11.92	30.67	43.32
Workers' remittances	2 391 ..	2.98	1.62	1.78	4.70	6.65	11.92	13.08	10.89
Other current transfers	2 392 ..	....	....	....	....	....	....	17.59	32.44
Debit	3 379 ..	**−7.64**	**−3.73**	**−1.68**	**−2.82**	**−2.90**	**−4.31**	**−10.10**	**−10.64**
General government	3 380 ..	−.08	−.36	−.18	−.39	−.28	−.31	−.36	−.33
Other sectors	3 390 ..	−7.56	−3.37	−1.50	−2.43	−2.62	−3.99	−9.75	−10.31
Workers' remittances	3 391 ..	−7.56	−3.37	−1.50	−2.43	−2.62	−3.99	−9.75	−10.31
Other current transfers	3 392 ..	....	....	....	....	....	....	....	....
CAPITAL AND FINANCIAL ACCOUNT	4 996 ..	**39.49**	**151.92**	**111.37**	**14.04**	**59.64**	**174.59**	**131.58**	**261.78**
CAPITAL ACCOUNT	4 994 ..	**.89**	**9.44**	**5.03**	**7.42**	**.99**	**29.88**	**13.24**	**4.61**
Total credit	2 994 ..	*.89*	*9.44*	*5.03*	*7.42*	*.99*	*29.88*	*13.24*	*4.61*
Total debit	3 994 ..	....	....	....	....	....	....	....	....
Capital transfers, credit	2 400 ..	**.89**	**9.44**	**5.03**	**7.42**	**.99**	**29.88**	**13.24**	**4.61**
General government	2 401 ..	.89	9.44	5.03	7.42	.99	29.88	13.24	4.61
Debt forgiveness	2 402 ..	....	....	....	....	....	....	....	....
Other capital transfers	2 410 ..	.89	9.44	5.03	7.42	.99	29.88	13.24	4.61
Other sectors	2 430 ..	....	....	....	....	....	....	....	....
Migrants' transfers	2 431 ..	....	....	....	....	....	....	....	....
Debt forgiveness	2 432 ..	....	....	....	....	....	....	....	....
Other capital transfers	2 440 ..	....	....	....	....	....	....	....	....
Capital transfers, debit	3 400 ..	....	....	....	....	....	....	....	....
General government	3 401 ..	....	....	....	....	....	....	....	....
Debt forgiveness	3 402 ..	....	....	....	....	....	....	....	....
Other capital transfers	3 410 ..	....	....	....	....	....	....	....	....
Other sectors	3 430 ..	....	....	....	....	....	....	....	....
Migrants' transfers	3 431 ..	....	....	....	....	....	....	....	....
Debt forgiveness	3 432 ..	....	....	....	....	....	....	....	....
Other capital transfers	3 440 ..	....	....	....	....	....	....	....	....
Nonproduced nonfinancial assets, credit	2 480 ..	....	....	....	....	....	....	....	....
Nonproduced nonfinancial assets, debit	3 480 ..	....	....	....	....	....	....	....	....

Table 2 (Continued). STANDARD PRESENTATION, 2000–2007

(Millions of U.S. dollars)

	Code	2000	2001	2002	2003	2004	2005	2006	2007
FINANCIAL ACCOUNT	4 995 ..	**38.60**	**142.48**	**106.34**	**6.62**	**58.65**	**144.71**	**118.34**	**257.17**
A. DIRECT INVESTMENT	4 500 ..	**13.83**	**56.20**	**38.99**	**50.28**	**30.41**	**78.43**	**137.81**	**240.82**
Direct investment abroad	4 505 ..	**−10.50**	**−8.54**	**−8.73**	**−8.15**	**−7.60**	**−7.45**	**−8.01**	**−8.49**
Equity capital	4 510 ..	−7.00	−5.98	−6.73	−5.25	−5.18	−5.15	−5.26	−6.02
Claims on affiliated enterprises	4 515 ..	−7.00	−5.98	−6.73	−5.25	−5.18	−5.15	−5.26	−6.02
Liabilities to affiliated enterprises	4 520 ..	....	....	....	....	....	....	....	....
Reinvested earnings	4 525 ..	−3.50	−2.56	−2.00	−2.89	−2.42	−2.30	−2.75	−2.47
Other capital	4 530 ..	....	....	....	....	....	....	....	....
Claims on affiliated enterprises	4 535 ..	....	....	....	....	....	....	....	....
Liabilities to affiliated enterprises	4 540 ..	....	....	....	....	....	....	....	....
Direct investment in Seychelles	4 555 ..	**24.33**	**64.74**	**47.72**	**58.43**	**38.01**	**85.88**	**145.82**	**249.31**
Equity capital	4 560 ..	19.95	56.62	37.56	33.65	31.99	74.63	127.96	229.47
Claims on direct investors	4 565 ..	....	....	....	....	....	....	....	....
Liabilities to direct investors	4 570 ..	19.95	56.62	37.56	33.65	31.99	74.63	127.96	229.47
Reinvested earnings	4 575 ..	4.38	8.12	10.16	9.03	6.02	10.90	16.95	19.84
Other capital	4 580 ..	....	....	....	15.74	....	.35	.90	....
Claims on direct investors	4 585 ..	....	....	....	....	....	....	....	....
Liabilities to direct investors	4 590 ..	....	....	....	15.74	....	.35	.90	....
B. PORTFOLIO INVESTMENT	4 600 ..	**.95**	**1.02**	**1.04**	**1.13**	**1.08**	**1.01**	**198.16**	**31.29**
Assets	4 602 ..	**−.09**	**−.07**	**−.07**	**−.01**	**−.04**	**−.04**	**−.05**	**−.04**
Equity securities	4 610 ..	....	....	....	....	....	....	....	....
Monetary authorities	4 611 ..	....	....	....	....	....	....	....	....
General government	4 612 ..	....	....	....	....	....	....	....	....
Banks	4 613 ..	....	....	....	....	....	....	....	....
Other sectors	4 614 ..	....	....	....	....	....	....	....	....
Debt securities	4 619 ..	−.09	−.07	−.07	−.01	−.04	−.04	−.05	−.04
Bonds and notes	4 620 ..	−.09	−.07	−.07	−.01	−.04	−.04	−.05	−.04
Monetary authorities	4 621 ..	....	....	....	....	....	....	....	....
General government	4 622 ..	....	....	....	....	....	....	....	....
Banks	4 623 ..	−.09	−.07	−.07	−.01	−.04	−.04	−.05	−.04
Other sectors	4 624 ..	....	....	....	....	....	....	....	....
Money market instruments	4 630 ..	....	....	....	....	....	....	....	....
Monetary authorities	4 631 ..	....	....	....	....	....	....	....	....
General government	4 632 ..	....	....	....	....	....	....	....	....
Banks	4 633 ..	....	....	....	....	....	....	....	....
Other sectors	4 634 ..	....	....	....	....	....	....	....	....
Liabilities	4 652 ..	**1.04**	**1.09**	**1.11**	**1.14**	**1.11**	**1.06**	**198.21**	**31.33**
Equity securities	4 660 ..	....	....	....	....	....	....	....	....
Banks	4 663 ..	....	....	....	....	....	....	....	....
Other sectors	4 664 ..	....	....	....	....	....	....	....	....
Debt securities	4 669 ..	1.04	1.09	1.11	1.14	1.11	1.06	198.21	31.33
Bonds and notes	4 670 ..	1.04	1.09	1.11	1.14	1.11	1.06	198.21	31.33
Monetary authorities	4 671 ..	....	....	....	....	....	....	....	....
General government	4 672 ..	....	....	....	....	....	....	197.18	30.21
Banks	4 673 ..	1.04	1.09	1.11	1.14	1.11	1.06	1.03	1.12
Other sectors	4 674 ..	....	....	....	....	....	....	....	....
Money market instruments	4 680 ..	....	....	....	....	....	....	....	....
Monetary authorities	4 681 ..	....	....	....	....	....	....	....	....
General government	4 682 ..	....	....	....	....	....	....	....	....
Banks	4 683 ..	....	....	....	....	....	....	....	....
Other sectors	4 684 ..	....	....	....	....	....	....	....	....
C. FINANCIAL DERIVATIVES	4 910 ..	....	....	....	....	....	....	....	....
Monetary authorities	4 911 ..	....	....	....	....	....	....	....	....
General government	4 912 ..	....	....	....	....	....	....	....	....
Banks	4 913 ..	....	....	....	....	....	....	....	....
Other sectors	4 914 ..	....	....	....	....	....	....	....	....
Assets	4 900 ..	....	....	....	....	....	....	....	....
Monetary authorities	4 901 ..	....	....	....	....	....	....	....	....
General government	4 902 ..	....	....	....	....	....	....	....	....
Banks	4 903 ..	....	....	....	....	....	....	....	....
Other sectors	4 904 ..	....	....	....	....	....	....	....	....
Liabilities	4 905 ..	....	....	....	....	....	....	....	....
Monetary authorities	4 906 ..	....	....	....	....	....	....	....	....
General government	4 907 ..	....	....	....	....	....	....	....	....
Banks	4 908 ..	....	....	....	....	....	....	....	....
Other sectors	4 909 ..	....	....	....	....	....	....	....	....

Table 2 (Concluded).　STANDARD PRESENTATION, 2000–2007

(Millions of U.S. dollars)

	Code	2000	2001	2002	2003	2004	2005	2006	2007
D. OTHER INVESTMENT	4 700 ..	**43.21**	**74.94**	**92.16**	**−41.67**	**−5.81**	**87.24**	**−155.66**	**−59.97**
Assets	4 703 ..	**−14.84**	**−8.76**	**−10.65**	**−14.81**	**−12.25**	**−9.61**	**−8.75**	**−59.03**
Trade credits	4 706 ..	....	....	....	....	....	....	....	....
General government	4 707 ..	....	....	....	....	....	....	....	....
of which: Short-term	4 709 ..	....	....	....	....	....	....	....	....
Other sectors	4 710 ..	....	....	....	....	....	....	....	....
of which: Short-term	4 712 ..	....	....	....	....	....	....	....	....
Loans	4 714 ..	....	....	....	....	....	....	....	....
Monetary authorities	4 715 ..	....	....	....	....	....	....	....	....
of which: Short-term	4 718 ..	....	....	....	....	....	....	....	....
General government	4 719 ..	....	....	....	....	....	....	....	....
of which: Short-term	4 721 ..	....	....	....	....	....	....	....	....
Banks	4 722 ..	....	....	....	....	....	....	....	....
of which: Short-term	4 724 ..	....	....	....	....	....	....	....	....
Other sectors	4 725 ..	....	....	....	....	....	....	....	....
of which: Short-term	4 727 ..	....	....	....	....	....	....	....	....
Currency and deposits	4 730 ..	−14.84	−8.76	−10.65	−14.81	−12.25	−9.61	−8.75	−59.03
Monetary authorities	4 731 ..	....	....	....	....	....	....	....	....
General government	4 732 ..	....	....	....	....	....	....	....	....
Banks	4 733 ..	....	....	....	....	....	−3.49	−13.27	−46.49
Other sectors	4 734 ..	−14.84	−8.76	−10.65	−14.81	−12.25	−6.12	4.53	−12.54
Other assets	4 736 ..	....	....	....	....	....	....	....	....
Monetary authorities	4 737 ..	....	....	....	....	....	....	....	....
of which: Short-term	4 739 ..	....	....	....	....	....	....	....	....
General government	4 740 ..	....	....	....	....	....	....	....	....
of which: Short-term	4 742 ..	....	....	....	....	....	....	....	....
Banks	4 743 ..	....	....	....	....	....	....	....	....
of which: Short-term	4 745 ..	....	....	....	....	....	....	....	....
Other sectors	4 746 ..	....	....	....	....	....	....	....	....
of which: Short-term	4 748 ..	....	....	....	....	....	....	....	....
Liabilities	4 753 ..	**58.05**	**83.71**	**102.81**	**−26.86**	**6.44**	**96.85**	**−146.92**	**−.94**
Trade credits	4 756 ..	....	....	4.91	4.82	−5.04	....	....	.06
General government	4 757 ..	....	....	4.91	4.82	−5.04	....	....	.06
of which: Short-term	4 759 ..	....	....	*4.91*	*4.82*	*−5.04*	....	....	....
Other sectors	4 760 ..	....	....	....	....	....	....	....	....
of which: Short-term	4 762 ..	....	....	....	....	....	....	....	....
Loans	4 764 ..	75.70	−36.16	103.78	−63.78	−45.49	54.68	−117.97	97.55
Monetary authorities	4 765 ..	41.79	8.46	79.19	−35.51	−33.79	10.82	−75.26	....
of which: Use of Fund credit and loans from the Fund..	4 766 ..	....	....	....	....	....	....	....	....
of which: Short-term	4 768 ..	....	....	....	....	....	....	....	....
General government	4 769 ..	27.75	−48.21	37.92	−30.95	−19.46	43.89	−37.83	63.29
of which: Short-term	4 771 ..	....	....	....	....	....	....	....	....
Banks	4 772 ..	7.63	−4.30	−5.70	−3.61	−2.35	−.04	−4.88	34.26
of which: Short-term	4 774 ..	*7.63*	*−4.30*	*−5.70*	*−3.61*	*−2.35*	*−.04*	*−4.88*	*34.26*
Other sectors	4 775 ..	−1.46	7.89	−7.63	6.28	10.11	....	....	....
of which: Short-term	4 777 ..	....	....	....	....	....	....	....	....
Currency and deposits	4 780 ..	....	....	....	....	10.46	13.60	17.21	3.15
Monetary authorities	4 781 ..	....	....	....	....	....	....	....	....
General government	4 782 ..	....	....	....	....	....	....	....	....
Banks	4 783 ..	....	....	....	....	10.46	13.60	17.21	3.15
Other sectors	4 784 ..	....	....	....	....	....	....	....	....
Other liabilities	4 786 ..	−17.66	119.86	−5.87	32.11	46.50	28.57	−46.16	−101.69
Monetary authorities	4 787 ..	....	....	....	....	....	....	....	....
of which: Short-term	4 789 ..	....	....	....	....	....	....	....	....
General government	4 790 ..	....	....	....	....	....	31.94	−49.51	42.07
of which: Short-term	4 792 ..	....	....	....	....	....	*40.18*	*−41.74*	*51.48*
Banks	4 793 ..	....	....	....	....	....	....	....	....
of which: Short-term	4 795 ..	....	....	....	....	....	....	....	....
Other sectors	4 796 ..	−17.66	119.86	−5.87	32.11	46.50	−3.37	3.36	−143.76
of which: Short-term	4 798 ..	*−17.66*	*38.56*	*1.58*	*40.65*	*56.15*	*−2.92*	*−1.45*	*−134.14*
E. RESERVE ASSETS	4 802 ..	**−19.38**	**10.32**	**−25.84**	**−3.12**	**32.97**	**−21.97**	**−61.97**	**45.03**
Monetary gold	4 812 ..	....	....	....	....	....	....	....	....
Special drawing rights	4 811 ..	.02	−.01	.01	.01	....	....	....	−.01
Reserve position in the Fund	4 810 ..	....	....	....	....	....	....	....	....
Foreign exchange	4 803 ..	−19.41	10.33	−25.85	−3.13	32.97	−21.97	−61.97	45.04
Other claims	4 813 ..	....	....	....	....	....	....	....	....
NET ERRORS AND OMISSIONS	4 998 ..	**3.43**	**1.14**	**−10.10**	**−4.68**	**.68**	**−.52**	**2.19**	**2.03**

Table 1. ANALYTIC PRESENTATION, 2000–2007

(Millions of U.S. dollars)

	Code	2000	2001	2002	2003	2004	2005	2006	2007
A. Current Account[1]................................	4 993 Z.	**−112.3**	**−97.9**	**−124.6**	**−99.1**	**−140.7**	**−170.6**	**−135.5**	**−237.9**
Goods: exports f.o.b........................	2 100 ..	12.8	29.2	59.8	110.8	154.1	183.6	261.9	292.9
Goods: imports f.o.b........................	3 100 ..	−136.9	−165.1	−254.9	−310.7	−274.3	−361.7	−351.2	−395.4
Balance on Goods........................	4 100 ..	*−124.1*	*−136.0*	*−195.1*	*−199.9*	*−120.2*	*−178.0*	*−89.3*	*−102.6*
Services: credit................................	2 200 ..	42.2	52.0	38.3	66.1	61.5	78.2	42.5	42.1
Services: debit................................	3 200 ..	−112.8	−110.9	−80.8	−93.8	−92.3	−91.4	−85.9	−94.2
Balance on Goods and Services......	4 991 ..	*−194.7*	*−194.9*	*−237.5*	*−227.6*	*−151.1*	*−191.3*	*−132.7*	*−154.6*
Income: credit................................	2 300 ..	7.4	4.3	18.3	1.7	4.1	5.4	12.2	43.3
Income: debit................................	3 300 ..	−12.6	−14.8	−21.1	−16.7	−71.1	−56.3	−52.0	−147.6
Balance on Goods, Services, and Income....	4 992 ..	*−199.9*	*−205.4*	*−240.4*	*−242.6*	*−218.1*	*−242.2*	*−172.5*	*−259.0*
Current transfers: credit................	2 379 Z.	92.3	120.7	119.4	148.5	80.3	73.6	73.5	155.9
Current transfers: debit................	3 379 ..	−4.7	−13.2	−3.6	−5.0	−2.8	−2.0	−36.5	−134.8
B. Capital Account[1]................................	4 994 Z.	....	.2	7.5	16.0	18.4	36.8	224.1	239.5
Capital account: credit..................	2 994 Z.	....	.4	7.5	16.0	18.4	36.8	224.1	239.5
Capital account: debit..................	3 994 ..	....	−.1	....	....	....	....	....	....
Total, Groups A Plus B..................	4 981 ..	*−112.3*	*−97.6*	*−117.1*	*−83.1*	*−122.3*	*−133.8*	*88.6*	*1.6*
C. Financial Account[1]................................	4 995 W.	**124.6**	**30.1**	**18.8**	**33.5**	**76.2**	**62.8**	**35.5**	**108.2**
Direct investment abroad..............	4 505 ..	....	....	....	....	....	7.5	....	....
Direct investment in Sierra Leone....	4 555 Z.	39.0	9.8	10.4	8.6	61.2	83.2	58.6	94.5
Portfolio investment assets............	4 602 ..	....	....	.1	....	....	....	....	....
Equity securities........................	4 610 ..	....	....	.1	....	....	....	....	....
Debt securities..........................	4 619 ..	....	....	....	....	....	....	....	....
Portfolio investment liabilities........	4 652 Z.	....	....	....	....	....	....	....	....
Equity securities........................	4 660 ..	....	....	....	....	....	....	....	....
Debt securities..........................	4 669 Z.	....	....	....	....	....	....	....	....
Financial derivatives......................	4 910 ..	....	....	....	....	....	....	....	....
Financial derivatives assets............	4 900 ..	....	....	....	....	....	....	....	....
Financial derivatives liabilities........	4 905 ..	....	....	....	....	....	....	....	....
Other investment assets................	4 703 ..	44.2	−3.5	8.1	.5	10.1	−1.9	−7.0	13.5
Monetary authorities..................	4 701 ..	....	....	.8	.5	....	−.5	−2.1	1.7
General government..................	4 704 ..	....	....	....	....	....	....	....	....
Banks..	4 705 ..	.1	−3.4	1.9	....	5.7	....	....	−1.4
Other sectors............................	4 728 ..	44.1	−.1	5.4	....	4.3	−1.4	−4.9	13.2
Other investment liabilities	4 753 W.	41.3	23.7	.2	24.4	5.0	−26.1	−16.1	.2
Monetary authorities..................	4 753 WA	....	....	....	....	4.2	....	....	....
General government..................	4 753 ZB	43.4	45.7	.2	24.4	−16.6	−26.1	−15.9	−15.2
Banks..	4 753 ZC	....	....	....	....	....	....	....	....
Other sectors............................	4 753 ZD	−2.1	−22.1	....	....	17.4	....	−.2	15.4
Total, Groups A Through C............	4 983 ..	*12.3*	*−67.6*	*−98.3*	*−49.6*	*−46.1*	*−71.1*	*124.2*	*109.9*
D. Net Errors and Omissions..............	4 998 ..	**−2.5**	**97.2**	**−16.2**	**−50.3**	**−53.6**	**−58.5**	**−63.8**	**−139.8**
Total, Groups A Through D............	4 984 ..	*9.8*	*29.6*	*−114.5*	*−99.9*	*−99.7*	*−129.6*	*60.4*	*−29.9*
E. Reserves and Related Items..............	4 802 A.	**−9.8**	**−29.6**	**114.5**	**99.9**	**99.7**	**129.6**	**−60.4**	**29.9**
Reserve assets................................	4 802 ..	2.0	−13.9	−32.3	24.3	−45.2	−56.4	−11.4	−33.9
Use of Fund credit and loans..........	4 766 ..	−11.8	−15.8	5.0	−14.8	18.5	12.3	−167.8	....
Exceptional financing....................	4 920 ..	....	....	141.8	90.5	126.3	173.7	118.8	63.8
Conversion rates: leones per U.S. dollar..............	0 101 ..	**2,092.13**	**1,986.15**	**2,099.03**	**2,347.94**	**2,701.30**	**2,889.59**	**2,961.91**	**2,985.19**

[1] Excludes components that have been classified in the categories of Group E.

Table 2. STANDARD PRESENTATION, 2000–2007

(Millions of U.S. dollars)

	Code	2000	2001	2002	2003	2004	2005	2006	2007
CURRENT ACCOUNT..	4 993 ..	**−112.3**	**−97.9**	**−73.2**	**−82.8**	**−99.0**	**−104.9**	**−91.5**	**−181.1**
A. GOODS..	4 100 ..	**−124.1**	**−136.0**	**−195.1**	**−199.9**	**−120.2**	**−178.0**	**−89.3**	**−102.6**
Credit..	2 100 ..	**12.8**	**29.2**	**59.8**	**110.8**	**154.1**	**183.6**	**261.9**	**292.9**
General merchandise: exports f.o.b..............	2 110 ..	12.8	29.2	51.0	106.1	144.5	172.5	250.4	281.6
Goods for processing: exports f.o.b.............	2 150 ..	....	....	....	....	....	....	....	....
Repairs on goods..	2 160 ..	....	....	....	....	....	....	....	....
Goods procured in ports by carriers............	2 170 ..	....	....	8.8	4.7	9.5	11.2	11.5	11.3
Nonmonetary gold.......................................	2 180 ..	....	....	....	....	....	....	....	....
Debit..	3 100 ..	**−136.9**	**−165.1**	**−254.9**	**−310.7**	**−274.3**	**−361.7**	**−351.2**	**−395.4**
General merchandise: imports f.o.b..............	3 110 ..	−136.9	−165.1	−254.9	−310.7	−274.3	−361.7	−351.2	−395.4
Goods for processing: imports f.o.b.............	3 150 ..	....	....	....	....	....	....	....	....
Repairs on goods..	3 160 ..	....	....	....	....	....	....	....	....
Goods procured in ports by carriers............	3 170 ..	....	....	....	....	....	....	....	....
Nonmonetary gold.......................................	3 180 ..	....	....	....	....	....	....	....	....
B. SERVICES...	4 200 ..	**−70.6**	**−58.9**	**−42.4**	**−27.7**	**−30.9**	**−13.2**	**−43.4**	**−52.1**
Total credit...	2 200 ..	*42.2*	*52.0*	*38.3*	*66.1*	*61.5*	*78.2*	*42.5*	*42.1*
Total debit..	3 200 ..	*−112.8*	*−110.9*	*−80.8*	*−93.8*	*−92.3*	*−91.4*	*−85.9*	*−94.2*
Transportation services, credit.................	2 205 ..	**17.9**	**19.0**	**....**	**3.0**	**1.4**	**11.6**	**13.6**	**15.4**
Passenger...	2 850 ..	....	....	....	....	*.2*	....	....	....
Freight...	2 851 ..	*.5*	....	....	....	....	....	....	....
Other...	2 852 ..	*17.4*	*19.0*	....	*3.0*	*1.2*	*11.6*	*13.6*	*15.4*
Sea transport, passenger...........................	2 207 ..	....	....	....	....	....	....	....	....
Sea transport, freight................................	2 208 ..	....	....	....	....	....	....	....	....
Sea transport, other..................................	2 209 ..	....	....	....	....	....	9.6	9.6	10.3
Air transport, passenger............................	2 211 ..	....	....	....	....	.2	....	....	....
Air transport, freight.................................	2 212 ..	.5	....	....	....	....	....	....	....
Air transport, other...................................	2 213 ..	17.4	19.0	....	3.0	1.2	2.0	4.0	5.2
Other transport, passenger........................	2 215 ..	....	....	....	....	....	....	....	....
Other transport, freight.............................	2 216 ..	....	....	....	....	....	....	....	....
Other transport, other...............................	2 217 ..	....	....	....	....	....	....	....	....
Transportation services, debit..................	3 205 ..	**−17.4**	**−18.9**	**−29.0**	**−36.1**	**−31.5**	**−42.7**	**−44.0**	**−48.6**
Passenger...	3 850 ..	*−2.5*	*−.2*	*−.1*	*−.8*	*−.3*	*−1.6*	*−3.0*	*−3.3*
Freight...	3 851 ..	*−14.9*	*−18.7*	*−29.0*	*−35.3*	*−31.2*	*−41.1*	*−41.0*	*−45.4*
Other...	3 852 ..	....	....	....	....	....	....	....	....
Sea transport, passenger...........................	3 207 ..	....	....	....	....	....	....	....	....
Sea transport, freight................................	3 208 ..	....	....	−29.0	−35.3	−31.2	−41.1	−39.9	−44.9
Sea transport, other..................................	3 209 ..	....	....	....	....	....	....	....	....
Air transport, passenger............................	3 211 ..	−2.5	−.2	−.1	−.8	−.3	−1.6	−3.0	−3.3
Air transport, freight.................................	3 212 ..	−14.9	−18.7	....	....	....	....	−1.1	−.4
Air transport, other...................................	3 213 ..	....	....	....	....	....	....	....	....
Other transport, passenger........................	3 215 ..	....	....	....	....	....	....	....	....
Other transport, freight.............................	3 216 ..	....	....	....	....	....	....	....	....
Other transport, other...............................	3 217 ..	....	....	....	....	....	....	....	....
Travel, credit..	2 236 ..	**10.5**	**14.2**	**37.9**	**59.9**	**58.2**	**64.0**	**23.0**	**21.9**
Business travel...	2 237 ..	10.5	14.2	18.7	32.4	19.5	21.8	10.4	9.4
Personal travel...	2 240 ..	....	....	19.2	27.5	38.7	42.2	12.6	12.5
Travel, debit...	3 236 ..	**−32.0**	**−41.8**	**−39.0**	**−37.2**	**−29.8**	**−32.2**	**−12.5**	**−14.2**
Business travel...	3 237 ..	−32.0	−41.8	−24.3	−17.5	−10.1	−10.8	−8.1	−6.7
Personal travel...	3 240 ..	....	....	−14.6	−19.6	−19.7	−21.5	−4.4	−7.5
Other services, credit................................	2 200 BA	**13.9**	**18.7**	**.4**	**3.1**	**1.8**	**2.5**	**5.9**	**4.8**
Communications...	2 245 ..	....	....	....	3.0	.1	.1	.7	.1
Construction..	2 249 ..	....	....	....	....	....	....	....	....
Insurance...	2 253 ..	....	....	....	....	....	.8	2.1	.4
Financial..	2 260 ..	....	....	.4	.1	.5	1.5	.3	.5
Computer and information..........................	2 262 ..	....	....	....	....	....	....	....	....
Royalties and licence fees..........................	2 266 ..	....	....	....	....	1.1	....	....	....
Other business services..............................	2 268 ..	10.6	13.4	....	....	.1	.1	2.8	3.8
Personal, cultural, and recreational............	2 287 ..	....	....	....	....	....	....	....	....
Government, n.i.e.......................................	2 291 ..	3.2	5.3	....	....	....	....	....	....
Other services, debit.................................	3 200 BA	**−63.4**	**−50.1**	**−12.8**	**−20.5**	**−31.1**	**−16.5**	**−29.4**	**−31.3**
Communications...	3 245 ..	....	....	−.1	−4.5	−8.3	−.3	−4.3	−5.2
Construction..	3 249 ..	....	....	....	....	....	....	....	....
Insurance...	3 253 ..	−2.9	−3.7	−5.8	−6.6	−5.5	−7.8	−7.5	−8.3
Financial..	3 260 ..	....	....	−.3	−.4	....	−.6	−.1	−.2
Computer and information..........................	3 262 ..	....	....	−.2	−1.0	−.3	−.7	−1.3	−.9
Royalties and licence fees..........................	3 266 ..	....	....	....	−.2	....	....	−1.0	−1.5
Other business services..............................	3 268 ..	−29.3	−28.1	−1.4	−2.7	−11.9	−1.9	−7.0	−7.3
Personal, cultural, and recreational............	3 287 ..	....	....	....	....	....	....	....	....
Government, n.i.e.......................................	3 291 ..	−31.2	−18.3	−5.1	−5.1	−5.1	−5.3	−8.3	−7.8

2008, International Monetary Fund: *Balance of Payments Statistics Yearbook*

Table 2 (Continued). STANDARD PRESENTATION, 2000–2007

(Millions of U.S. dollars)

	Code	2000	2001	2002	2003	2004	2005	2006	2007
C. INCOME	4 300	**−5.2**	**−10.5**	**−2.9**	**−15.0**	**−67.0**	**−50.9**	**−39.8**	**−104.3**
Total credit	2 300	*7.4*	*4.3*	*18.3*	*1.7*	*4.1*	*5.4*	*12.2*	*43.3*
Total debit	3 300	*−12.6*	*−14.8*	*−21.1*	*−16.7*	*−71.1*	*−56.3*	*−52.0*	*−147.6*
Compensation of employees, credit	2 310	....	....	14.4	.1	.1	.1	3.5	2.1
Compensation of employees, debit	3 310	....	....	−2.2	−2.2	−2.2	−2.3	−1.7	−3.2
Investment income, credit	2 320	7.4	4.3	3.9	1.6	4.0	5.3	8.6	41.2
Direct investment income	2 330	.8	1.3	....	....	....	....	1.2	30.8
Dividends and distributed branch profits	2 332	.8	1.3	....	....	....	....	....	....
Reinvested earnings and undistributed branch profits	2 333	....	....	....	....	....	....	....	....
Income on debt (interest)	2 334	....	....	....	....	....	....	1.2	30.8
Portfolio investment income	2 339	....	....	....	....	....	....	....	....
Income on equity	2 340	....	....	....	....	....	....	....	....
Income on bonds and notes	2 350	....	....	....	....	....	....	....	....
Income on money market instruments	2 360	....	....	....	....	....	....	....	....
Other investment income	2 370	6.6	3.0	3.9	1.6	4.0	5.3	7.4	10.4
Investment income, debit	3 320	**−12.6**	**−14.8**	**−19.0**	**−14.5**	**−68.9**	**−54.0**	**−50.3**	**−144.4**
Direct investment income	3 330	−1.8	−.6	−2.0	−9.4	−32.4	−41.2	−27.3	−121.8
Dividends and distributed branch profits	3 332	−.4	−.1	−.4	−6.3	−6.6	....	−1.5	−1.0
Reinvested earnings and undistributed branch profits	3 333	−1.4	−.4	−1.6	−3.1	−9.3	−24.7	−.8	−85.9
Income on debt (interest)	3 334	....	....	....	....	−16.5	−16.5	−25.0	−34.9
Portfolio investment income	3 339	....	....	....	....	....	....	....	....
Income on equity	3 340	....	....	....	....	....	....	....	....
Income on bonds and notes	3 350	....	....	....	....	....	....	....	....
Income on money market instruments	3 360	....	....	....	....	....	....	....	....
Other investment income	3 370	−10.8	−14.2	−17.0	−5.1	−36.6	−12.8	−23.1	−22.6
D. CURRENT TRANSFERS	4 379	**87.6**	**107.5**	**167.2**	**159.8**	**119.1**	**137.2**	**81.0**	**77.8**
Credit	2 379	**92.3**	**120.7**	**170.8**	**164.8**	**122.0**	**139.2**	**117.5**	**212.6**
General government	2 380	78.0	108.3	71.4	61.7	79.7	86.8	45.7	59.4
Other sectors	2 390	14.3	12.4	99.4	103.1	42.3	52.5	71.7	153.3
Workers' remittances	2 391	7.1	6.2	7.5	25.8	24.6	2.3	47.3	146.3
Other current transfers	2 392	7.1	6.2	91.9	77.4	17.6	50.1	24.4	6.9
Debit	3 379	**−4.7**	**−13.2**	**−3.6**	**−5.0**	**−2.8**	**−2.0**	**−36.5**	**−134.8**
General government	3 380	−1.9	−8.0	−2.4	−2.9	−1.5	−.5	−.5	−.5
Other sectors	3 390	−2.8	−5.2	−1.2	−2.0	−1.4	−1.5	−36.0	−134.3
Workers' remittances	3 391	....	−.3	−.4	−1.2	−.4	−.1	−33.8	−132.7
Other current transfers	3 392	−2.8	−4.9	−.8	−.8	−.9	−1.4	−2.2	−1.6
CAPITAL AND FINANCIAL ACCOUNT	4 996	**114.8**	**.7**	**89.5**	**133.1**	**152.6**	**163.4**	**155.3**	**320.9**
CAPITAL ACCOUNT	4 994	....	**.2**	**50.6**	**71.0**	**81.3**	**67.8**	**259.0**	**634.2**
Total credit	2 994	....	*.4*	*50.6*	*71.0*	*81.3*	*67.8*	*259.0*	*634.2*
Total debit	3 994	....	*−.1*	....	....	....	....	....	....
Capital transfers, credit	2 400	....	**.4**	**50.6**	**71.0**	**81.3**	**67.8**	**259.0**	**634.2**
General government	2 401	....	....	48.5	69.7	79.3	66.1	258.9	633.1
Debt forgiveness	2 402	....	....	43.1	55.0	62.9	31.0	34.9	394.7
Other capital transfers	2 410	....	....	5.4	14.7	16.3	35.1	224.0	238.4
Other sectors	2 430	....	.4	2.1	1.3	2.0	1.7	.1	1.1
Migrants' transfers	2 431	....	.4	....	....	....	....	....	....
Debt forgiveness	2 432	....	....	....	....	....	....	....	....
Other capital transfers	2 440	....	....	2.1	1.3	2.0	1.7	.1	1.1
Capital transfers, debit	3 400	....	**−.1**	....	....	....	....	....	....
General government	3 401	....	....	....	....	....	....	....	....
Debt forgiveness	3 402	....	....	....	....	....	....	....	....
Other capital transfers	3 410	....	....	....	....	....	....	....	....
Other sectors	3 430	....	−.1	....	....	....	....	....	....
Migrants' transfers	3 431	....	−.1	....	....	....	....	....	....
Debt forgiveness	3 432	....	....	....	....	....	....	....	....
Other capital transfers	3 440	....	....	....	....	....	....	....	....
Nonproduced nonfinancial assets, credit	2 480	....	....	....	....	....	....	....	....
Nonproduced nonfinancial assets, debit	3 480	....	....	....	....	....	....	....	....

Table 2 (Continued). STANDARD PRESENTATION, 2000–2007

(Millions of U.S. dollars)

	Code	2000	2001	2002	2003	2004	2005	2006	2007
FINANCIAL ACCOUNT	4 995	**114.8**	**.4**	**38.8**	**62.2**	**71.3**	**95.6**	**−103.8**	**−313.3**
A. DIRECT INVESTMENT	4 500	**39.0**	**9.8**	**10.4**	**8.6**	**61.2**	**90.7**	**58.6**	**94.5**
Direct investment abroad	4 505	....	....	....	....	....	7.5	....	....
Equity capital	4 510	....	....	....	....	....	....	....	....
Claims on affiliated enterprises	4 515	....	....	....	....	....	....	....	....
Liabilities to affiliated enterprises	4 520	....	....	....	....	....	....	....	....
Reinvested earnings	4 525	....	....	....	....	....	....	....	....
Other capital	4 530	....	....	....	....	....	7.5	....	....
Claims on affiliated enterprises	4 535	....	....	....	....	....	....	....	....
Liabilities to affiliated enterprises	4 540	....	....	....	....	....	7.5	....	....
Direct investment in Sierra Leone	4 555	**39.0**	**9.8**	**10.4**	**8.6**	**61.2**	**83.2**	**58.6**	**94.5**
Equity capital	4 560	....	....	6.8	13.0	24.5	28.5	66.2	−99.9
Claims on direct investors	4 565	....	....	....	....	....	....	....	....
Liabilities to direct investors	4 570	....	....	6.8	13.0	24.5	28.5	66.2	−99.9
Reinvested earnings	4 575	1.4	.4	1.6	3.1	9.3	24.7	.8	85.9
Other capital	4 580	37.6	9.4	2.1	−7.5	27.4	29.9	−8.4	108.4
Claims on direct investors	4 585	....	....	....	....	....	....	−.1	1.1
Liabilities to direct investors	4 590	37.6	9.4	2.1	−7.5	27.4	29.9	−8.3	107.3
B. PORTFOLIO INVESTMENT	4 600	....	....	.1	....	....	....	....	....
Assets	4 602	....	....	.1	....	....	....	....	....
Equity securities	4 610	....	....	.1	....	....	....	....	....
Monetary authorities	4 611	....	....	....	....	....	....	....	....
General government	4 612	....	....	....	....	....	....	....	....
Banks	4 613	....	....	.1	....	....	....	....	....
Other sectors	4 614	....	....	....	....	....	....	....	....
Debt securities	4 619	....	....	....	....	....	....	....	....
Bonds and notes	4 620	....	....	....	....	....	....	....	....
Monetary authorities	4 621	....	....	....	....	....	....	....	....
General government	4 622	....	....	....	....	....	....	....	....
Banks	4 623	....	....	....	....	....	....	....	....
Other sectors	4 624	....	....	....	....	....	....	....	....
Money market instruments	4 630	....	....	....	....	....	....	....	....
Monetary authorities	4 631	....	....	....	....	....	....	....	....
General government	4 632	....	....	....	....	....	....	....	....
Banks	4 633	....	....	....	....	....	....	....	....
Other sectors	4 634	....	....	....	....	....	....	....	....
Liabilities	4 652	....	....	....	....	....	....	....	....
Equity securities	4 660	....	....	....	....	....	....	....	....
Banks	4 663	....	....	....	....	....	....	....	....
Other sectors	4 664	....	....	....	....	....	....	....	....
Debt securities	4 669	....	....	....	....	....	....	....	....
Bonds and notes	4 670	....	....	....	....	....	....	....	....
Monetary authorities	4 671	....	....	....	....	....	....	....	....
General government	4 672	....	....	....	....	....	....	....	....
Banks	4 673	....	....	....	....	....	....	....	....
Other sectors	4 674	....	....	....	....	....	....	....	....
Money market instruments	4 680	....	....	....	....	....	....	....	....
Monetary authorities	4 681	....	....	....	....	....	....	....	....
General government	4 682	....	....	....	....	....	....	....	....
Banks	4 683	....	....	....	....	....	....	....	....
Other sectors	4 684	....	....	....	....	....	....	....	....
C. FINANCIAL DERIVATIVES	4 910	....	....	....	....	....	....	....	....
Monetary authorities	4 911	....	....	....	....	....	....	....	....
General government	4 912	....	....	....	....	....	....	....	....
Banks	4 913	....	....	....	....	....	....	....	....
Other sectors	4 914	....	....	....	....	....	....	....	....
Assets	4 900	....	....	....	....	....	....	....	....
Monetary authorities	4 901	....	....	....	....	....	....	....	....
General government	4 902	....	....	....	....	....	....	....	....
Banks	4 903	....	....	....	....	....	....	....	....
Other sectors	4 904	....	....	....	....	....	....	....	....
Liabilities	4 905	....	....	....	....	....	....	....	....
Monetary authorities	4 906	....	....	....	....	....	....	....	....
General government	4 907	....	....	....	....	....	....	....	....
Banks	4 908	....	....	....	....	....	....	....	....
Other sectors	4 909	....	....	....	....	....	....	....	....

2008, International Monetary Fund: *Balance of Payments Statistics Yearbook*

Table 2 (Concluded). STANDARD PRESENTATION, 2000–2007
(Millions of U.S. dollars)

	Code	2000	2001	2002	2003	2004	2005	2006	2007
D. OTHER INVESTMENT	4 700	**73.8**	**4.4**	**60.6**	**29.3**	**55.4**	**61.3**	**−151.0**	**−373.9**
Assets	4 703	**44.2**	**−3.5**	**8.1**	**.5**	**10.1**	**−1.9**	**−7.0**	**13.5**
Trade credits	4 706	....	....	....	....	....	....	....	....
General government	4 707	....	....	....	....	....	....	....	....
of which: Short-term	4 709	....	....	....	....	....	....	....	....
Other sectors	4 710	....	....	....	....	....	....	....	....
of which: Short-term	4 712	....	....	....	....	....	....	....	....
Loans	4 714	....	....	....	....	4.3	−1.4	−5.0	11.2
Monetary authorities	4 715	....	....	....	....	....	....	....	....
of which: Short-term	4 718	....	....	....	....	....	....	....	....
General government	4 719	....	....	....	....	....	....	....	....
of which: Short-term	4 721	....	....	....	....	....	....	....	....
Banks	4 722	....	....	....	....	....	....	....	....
of which: Short-term	4 724	....	....	....	....	4.3	−1.4	−5.0	11.2
Other sectors	4 725	....	....	....	....	4.3	−1.4	−5.0	11.2
of which: Short-term	4 727	....	....	....	....	....	−1.4	....	....
Currency and deposits	4 730	44.2	−3.5	7.6	.5	5.7	−.5	−1.6	10.4
Monetary authorities	4 731	....	....	.8	.5	....	−.5	−2.1	1.7
General government	4 732	....	....	....	....	....	....	....	....
Banks	4 733	.1	−3.4	1.4	....	5.7	....	....	−1.4
Other sectors	4 734	44.1	−.1	5.4	....	....	....	.5	10.0
Other assets	4 736	....	....	.5	....	....	....	−.4	−8.0
Monetary authorities	4 737	....	....	....	....	....	....	....	....
of which: Short-term	4 739	....	....	....	....	....	....	....	....
General government	4 740	....	....	....	....	....	....	....	....
of which: Short-term	4 742	....	....	....	....	....	....	....	....
Banks	4 743	....	....	....	.5	....	....	....	....
of which: Short-term	4 745	....	....	....	....	....	....	....	....
Other sectors	4 746	....	....	....	....	....	....	−.4	−8.0
of which: Short-term	4 748	....	....	....	....	....	....	−.4	−8.0
Liabilities	4 753	**29.6**	**7.9**	**52.6**	**28.8**	**45.3**	**63.2**	**−144.0**	**−387.4**
Trade credits	4 756	−1.7	−.2	....	....	....	....	....	....
General government	4 757	....	....	....	....	....	....	....	....
of which: Short-term	4 759	....	....	....	....	....	....	....	....
Other sectors	4 760	−1.7	−.2	....	....	....	....	....	....
of which: Short-term	4 762	−1.7	−.2	....	....	....	....	....	....
Loans	4 764	36.6	26.9	87.3	82.6	90.7	48.2	−144.4	−.1
Monetary authorities	4 765	−11.8	−15.8	5.0	−14.8	18.5	12.3	−167.8	....
of which: Use of Fund credit and loans from the Fund	4 766	−11.8	−15.8	5.0	−14.8	18.5	12.3	−167.8	....
of which: Short-term	4 768	....	....	....	....	....	....	....	....
General government	4 769	48.8	64.5	82.3	97.4	54.7	36.0	23.3	−11.8
of which: Short-term	4 771	−.7	−.8	....	....	....	....	....	....
Banks	4 772	....	....	....	....	....	....	....	....
of which: Short-term	4 774	....	....	....	....	....	....	....	....
Other sectors	4 775	−.4	−21.8	....	....	17.4	....	....	11.7
of which: Short-term	4 777	....	−20.1	....	....	.2	....	....	....
Currency and deposits	4 780	....	....	....	....	....	....	....	....
Monetary authorities	4 781	....	....	....	....	....	....	....	....
General government	4 782	....	....	....	....	....	....	....	....
Banks	4 783	....	....	....	....	....	....	....	....
Other sectors	4 784	....	....	....	....	....	....	....	....
Other liabilities	4 786	−5.3	−18.8	−34.8	−53.8	−45.4	14.9	.4	−387.3
Monetary authorities	4 787	....	....	....	....	5.5	10.5	4.5	−.2
of which: Short-term	4 789	....	....	....	....	2.5	10.5	4.5	−.2
General government	4 790	−5.3	−18.8	−34.8	−53.8	−50.8	4.4	−3.8	−390.8
of which: Short-term	4 792	−5.7	84.9	−44.3	−53.8	−50.8	4.4	−3.8	−390.8
Banks	4 793	....	....	....	....	....	....	....	....
of which: Short-term	4 795	....	....	....	....	....	....	....	3.7
Other sectors	4 796	....	−.1	....	....	....	....	−.2	3.7
of which: Short-term	4 798	....	....	....	....	....	....	....	3.7
E. RESERVE ASSETS	4 802	**2.0**	**−13.9**	**−32.3**	**24.3**	**−45.2**	**−56.4**	**−11.4**	**−33.9**
Monetary gold	4 812	....	....	....	....	....	....	....	....
Special drawing rights	4 811	14.9	4.8	−22.4	−7.8	−14.6	15.0	5.2	....
Reserve position in the Fund	4 810	....	....	....	....	....	....	....	....
Foreign exchange	4 803	−12.9	−18.6	−9.9	32.0	−30.6	−71.4	−16.5	−33.9
Other claims	4 813	....	....	....	....	....	....	....	....
NET ERRORS AND OMISSIONS	4 998	**−2.5**	**97.2**	**−16.2**	**−50.3**	**−53.6**	**−58.5**	**−63.8**	**−139.8**

Table 3. INTERNATIONAL INVESTMENT POSITION (End-period stocks), 2000–2007

(Millions of U.S. dollars)

	Code	2000	2001	2002	2003	2004	2005	2006	2007
ASSETS	8 995 C.	....	50.9	85.8	65.1	131.2	188.5	251.3	365.2
Direct investment abroad	8 505 ..	....	....	....	....	....	....	....	....
Equity capital and reinvested earnings	8 506 ..	....	....	....	....	....	....	....	....
Claims on affiliated enterprises	8 507 ..	....	....	....	....	....	....	....	....
Liabilities to affiliated enterprises	8 508 ..	....	....	....	....	....	....	....	....
Other capital	8 530 ..	....	....	....	....	....	....	....	....
Claims on affiliated enterprises	8 535 ..	....	....	....	....	....	....	....	....
Liabilities to affiliated enterprises	8 540 ..	....	....	....	....	....	....	....	....
Portfolio investment	8 602 ..	....	.2	.9	....	....	....	....	....
Equity securities	8 610 ..	....	....	....	....				
Monetary authorities	8 611 ..	....	....	....	....				
General government	8 612 ..	....	....	....	....				
Banks	8 613 ..	....	....	....	....				
Other sectors	8 614 ..	....	....	....	....				
Debt securities	8 619 ..	....	.2	.9	....	....			
Bonds and notes	8 620 ..	....	.2	.9	....				
Monetary authorities	8 621 ..	....	.2	.9	....				
General government	8 622 ..	....	....	....					
Banks	8 623 ..	....	....	....					
Other sectors	8 624 ..	....	....	....					
Money market instruments	8 630 ..	....	....	....					
Monetary authorities	8 631 ..	....	....	....					
General government	8 632 ..	....	....	....					
Banks	8 633 ..	....	....	....					
Other sectors	8 634 ..	....	....	....					
Financial derivatives	8 900 ..	....	....	....	....	....	....	....	....
Monetary authorities	8 901 ..	....	....	....	....	....	....	....	....
General government	8 902 ..	....	....	....	....	....	....	....	....
Banks	8 903 ..	....	....	....	....	....	....	....	....
Other sectors	8 904 ..	....	....	....	....	....	....	....	....
Other investment	8 703 ..	....	9.4	8.6	8.1	25.0	34.0	78.3	151.3
Trade credits	8 706 ..	....	....	....	....	....	....	....	....
General government	8 707 ..	....	....	....	....	....	....	....	....
of which: Short-term	8 709 ..	....	....	....	....	....	....	....	....
Other sectors	8 710 ..	....	....	....	....	....	....	....	....
of which: Short-term	8 712 ..	....	....	....	....	....	....	....	....
Loans	8 714 ..	....	....	....	....	....	....	....	....
Monetary authorities	8 715 ..	....	....	....	....	....	....	....	....
of which: Short-term	8 718 ..	....	....	....	....	....	....	....	....
General government	8 719 ..	....	....	....	....	....	....	....	....
of which: Short-term	8 721 ..	....	....	....	....	....	....	....	....
Banks	8 722 ..	....	....	....	....	....	....	....	....
of which: Short-term	8 724 ..	....	....	....	....	....	....	....	....
Other sectors	8 725 ..	....	....	....	....	....	....	....	....
of which: Short-term	8 727 ..	....	....	....	....	....	....	....	....
Currency and deposits	8 730 ..	....	9.4	8.6	8.1	25.0	34.0	78.3	151.3
Monetary authorities	8 731 ..	....	9.4	8.6	8.1	8.1	7.7	5.5	3.9
General government	8 732 ..	....	....	....	....	....	....	....	....
Banks	8 733 ..	....	....	....	....	16.9	24.3	70.5	116.4
Other sectors	8 734 ..	....	....	....	....	....	2.0	2.2	31.1
Other assets	8 736 ..	....	....	....	....	....	....	....	....
Monetary authorities	8 737 ..	....	....	....	....	....	....	....	....
of which: Short-term	8 739 ..	....	....	....	....	....	....	....	....
General government	8 740 ..	....	....	....	....	....	....	....	....
of which: Short-term	8 742 ..	....	....	....	....	....	....	....	....
Banks	8 743 ..	....	....	....	....	....	....	....	....
of which: Short-term	8 745 ..	....	....	....	....	....	....	....	....
Other sectors	8 746 ..	....	....	....	....	....	....	....	....
of which: Short-term	8 748 ..	....	....	....	....	....	....	....	....
Reserve assets	8 802 ..	....	41.2	76.3	57.0	106.2	154.6	173.0	213.9
Monetary gold	8 812 ..	....	....	....	....	....	....	....	....
Special drawing rights	8 811 ..	5.2	.4	24.0	34.5	51.0	32.8	29.2	30.7
Reserve position in the Fund	8 810 ..	....	....	....	....	....	....	....	....
Foreign exchange	8 803 ..	....	40.8	52.2	22.5	55.2	121.8	143.8	183.2
Other claims	8 813 ..	....	....	....	....	....	....	....	....

Table 3 (Concluded). INTERNATIONAL INVESTMENT POSITION (End-period stocks), 2000–2007

(Millions of U.S. dollars)

	Code	2000	2001	2002	2003	2004	2005	2006	2007
LIABILITIES	8 995 D.	....	1,265.9	1,420.2	1,656.4	2,098.2	2,033.2	1,905.4	857.1
Direct investment in Sierra Leone	8 555 ..	....	....	36.2	47.7	355.7	299.9	453.0	393.8
Equity capital and reinvested earnings	8 556 ..	....	....	28.2	39.6	167.4	52.6	118.4	−144.3
Claims on direct investors	8 557 ..	....	....	....	....	....	....	....	....
Liabilities to direct investors	8 558 ..	....	....	28.2	39.6	167.4	52.6	118.4	−144.3
Other capital	8 580 ..	....	....	8.0	8.1	188.3	247.3	334.6	538.1
Claims on direct investors	8 585 ..	....	....	....	....	....	....	....	....
Liabilities to direct investors	8 590 ..	....	....	8.0	8.1	188.3	247.3	334.6	538.1
Portfolio investment	8 652 ..	....	....	....	....	....	....	....	....
Equity securities	8 660 ..	....	....	....	....	....	....	....	....
Banks	8 663 ..	....	....	....	....	....	....	....	....
Other sectors	8 664 ..	....	....	....	....	....	....	....	....
Debt securities	8 669 ..	....	....	....	....	....	....	....	....
Bonds and notes	8 670 ..	....	....	....	....	....	....	....	....
Monetary authorities	8 671 ..	....	....	....	....	....	....	....	....
General government	8 672 ..	....	....	....	....	....	....	....	....
Banks	8 673 ..	....	....	....	....	....	....	....	....
Other sectors	8 674 ..	....	....	....	....	....	....	....	....
Money market instruments	8 680 ..	....	....	....	....	....	....	....	....
Monetary authorities	8 681 ..	....	....	....	....	....	....	....	....
General government	8 682 ..	....	....	....	....	....	....	....	....
Banks	8 683 ..	....	....	....	....	....	....	....	....
Other sectors	8 684 ..	....	....	....	....	....	....	....	....
Financial derivatives	8 905 ..	....	....	....	....	....	....	....	....
Monetary authorities	8 906 ..	....	....	....	....	....	....	....	....
General government	8 907 ..	....	....	....	....	....	....	....	....
Banks	8 908 ..	....	....	....	....	....	....	....	....
Other sectors	8 909 ..	....	....	....	....	....	....	....	....
Other investment	8 753 ..	....	1,265.9	1,383.9	1,608.7	1,742.5	1,733.3	1,452.4	463.2
Trade credits	8 756 ..	....	....	....	....	....	....	....	....
General government	8 757 ..	....	....	....	....	....	....	....	....
of which: Short-term	8 759 ..	....	....	....	....	....	....	....	....
Other sectors	8 760 ..	....	....	....	....	....	....	....	....
of which: Short-term	8 762 ..	....	....	....	....	....	....	....	....
Loans	8 764 ..	....	1,265.9	1,383.9	1,511.0	1,654.9	1,604.1	1,372.1	327.2
Monetary authorities	8 765 ..	....	151.8	169.3	169.1	195.8	192.1	34.8	36.5
of which: Use of Fund credit and loans from the Fund	8 766 ..	173.6	151.8	169.3	169.1	195.8	192.1	34.8	36.5
of which: Short-term	8 768 ..	....	....	....	....	....	....	....	....
General government	8 769 ..	....	1,114.1	1,214.6	1,341.9	1,427.1	1,412.0	1,337.3	290.7
of which: Short-term	8 771 ..	....	....	....	....	....	....	....	....
Banks	8 772 ..	....	....	....	....	....	....	....	....
of which: Short-term	8 774 ..	....	....	....	....	....	....	....	....
Other sectors	8 775 ..	....	....	....	....	32.1	....	....	....
of which: Short-term	8 777 ..	....	....	....	....	.7	....	....	....
Currency and deposits	8 780 ..	....	....	....	97.7	87.6	129.2	80.3	136.0
Monetary authorities	8 781 ..	....	....	....	97.7	87.6	129.2	80.3	136.0
General government	8 782 ..	....	....	....	....	....	....	....	....
Banks	8 783 ..	....	....	....	....	....	....	....	....
Other sectors	8 784 ..	....	....	....	....	....	....	....	....
Other liabilities	8 786 ..	....	....	....	....	....	....	....	....
Monetary authorities	8 787 ..	....	....	....	....	....	....	....	....
of which: Short-term	8 789 ..	....	....	....	....	....	....	....	....
General government	8 790 ..	....	....	....	....	....	....	....	....
of which: Short-term	8 792 ..	....	....	....	....	....	....	....	....
Banks	8 793 ..	....	....	....	....	....	....	....	....
of which: Short-term	8 795 ..	....	....	....	....	....	....	....	....
Other sectors	8 796 ..	....	....	....	....	....	....	....	....
of which: Short-term	8 798 ..	....	....	....	....	....	....	....	....
NET INTERNATIONAL INVESTMENT POSITION	8 995 ..	....	−1,215.1	−1,334.4	−1,591.3	−1,966.9	−1,844.6	−1,654.1	−491.8
Conversion rates: leones per U.S. dollar (end of period)	0 102 ..	1,666.67	2,161.27	2,191.73	2,562.18	2,860.49	2,932.52	2,973.94	2,977.60

Table 1. ANALYTIC PRESENTATION, 2000–2007

(Millions of U.S. dollars)

	Code	2000	2001	2002	2003	2004	2005	2006	2007
A. Current Account[1].....................	4 993 Z.	**10,728**	**10,708**	**11,156**	**21,586**	**18,247**	**22,238**	**29,787**	**39,062**
Goods: exports f.o.b..................	2 100 ..	153,095	136,609	140,776	161,702	199,393	232,512	275,288	303,136
Goods: imports f.o.b..................	3 100 ..	−139,138	−119,358	−121,972	−132,266	−168,330	−195,477	−231,855	−254,036
Balance on Goods...................	4 100 ..	*13,956*	*17,252*	*18,804*	*29,436*	*31,063*	*37,036*	*43,433*	*49,099*
Services: credit........................	2 200 ..	28,171	27,405	29,525	36,288	46,804	52,940	61,100	69,829
Services: debit........................	3 200 ..	−29,506	−31,762	−33,436	−40,081	−50,143	−55,630	−63,744	−72,419
Balance on Goods and Services........	4 991 ..	*12,622*	*12,895*	*14,893*	*25,643*	*27,725*	*34,345*	*40,789*	*46,510*
Income: credit........................	2 300 ..	15,623	14,381	14,171	17,419	21,538	27,235	32,220	42,985
Income: debit........................	3 300 ..	−16,357	−14,966	−16,454	−20,069	−29,675	−38,079	−41,814	−48,737
Balance on Goods, Services, and Income........	4 992 ..	*11,888*	*12,310*	*12,609*	*22,993*	*19,588*	*23,502*	*31,195*	*40,757*
Current transfers: credit...........	2 379 Z.	128	124	127	131	136	138	145	152
Current transfers: debit............	3 379 ..	−1,288	−1,727	−1,581	−1,538	−1,477	−1,402	−1,553	−1,847
B. Capital Account[1].....................	4 994 Z.	**−163**	**−161**	**−160**	**−168**	**−184**	**−202**	**−231**	**−259**
Capital account: credit..............	2 994 Z.	....	....	....	....	....	....	....	....
Capital account: debit..............	3 994 ..	....	....	....	....	....	....	....	....
Total, Groups A Plus B...............	4 981 ..	*10,565*	*10,547*	*10,996*	*21,419*	*18,063*	*22,036*	*29,555*	*38,803*
C. Financial Account[1]..................	4 995 W.	**−5,749**	**−11,633**	**−10,226**	**−17,951**	**−8,553**	**−16,962**	**−18,580**	**−18,388**
Direct investment abroad............	4 505 ..	−5,915	−19,965	−2,329	−2,695	−10,803	−6,943	−12,241	−12,300
Direct investment in Singapore......	4 555 Z.	16,484	15,621	7,200	11,664	19,828	13,930	24,743	24,137
Portfolio investment assets.........	4 602 ..	−13,366	−11,065	−13,363	−14,346	−7,050	−8,335	−17,795	−22,600
Equity securities..................	4 610 ..	−8,257	−7,941	−6,069	−7,356	−5,658	−10,467	−9,029	−19,425
Debt securities....................	4 619 ..	−5,109	−3,124	−7,295	−6,990	−1,393	2,132	−8,767	−3,175
Portfolio investment liabilities....	4 652 Z.	−1,224	3,758	219	4,306	1,586	5,040	8,854	6,007
Equity securities..................	4 660 ..	−1,169	−90	−442	2,139	2,383	3,838	6,839	6,743
Debt securities....................	4 669 Z.	−56	3,847	661	2,167	−797	1,202	2,015	−736
Financial derivatives................	4 910 ..	....	....	....	....	....	....	....	....
Financial derivatives assets.........	4 900 ..	....	....	....	....	....	....	....	....
Financial derivatives liabilities....	4 905 ..	....	....	....	....	....	....	....	....
Other investment assets.............	4 703 ..	−15,824	−1,575	−8,373	−21,115	−28,381	−28,380	−49,368	−67,704
Monetary authorities..............	4 701 ..	....	....	....	....	....	....	....	....
General government................	4 704 ..	....	....	....	....	....	....	....	....
Banks..............................	4 705 ..	2,037	−5,875	1,185	10,657	−5,288	−9,233	−28,928	−9,046
Other sectors......................	4 728 ..	−17,692	4,308	−9,724	−31,716	−22,988	−22,988	−24,441	−58,658
Other investment liabilities........	4 753 W.	14,097	1,593	6,420	4,235	16,266	7,725	27,228	54,072
Monetary authorities..............	4 753 WA	....	....	....	....	....	....	....	....
General government................	4 753 ZB	....	....	....	....	....	....	....	....
Banks..............................	4 753 ZC	7,663	8,211	−349	−9,009	4,419	3,014	23,433	20,859
Other sectors......................	4 753 ZD	6,298	−6,765	6,857	13,322	11,781	12,842	12,271	33,212
Total, Groups A Through C...........	4 983 ..	*4,816*	*−1,087*	*770*	*3,468*	*9,510*	*5,074*	*10,975*	*20,414*
D. Net Errors and Omissions............	4 998 ..	**2,006**	**169**	**486**	**3,235**	**2,683**	**7,241**	**6,032**	**−774**
Total, Groups A Through D...........	4 984 ..	*6,822*	*−917*	*1,256*	*6,703*	*12,193*	*12,315*	*17,008*	*19,640*
E. Reserves and Related Items...........	4 802 A.	**−6,822**	**917**	**−1,256**	**−6,703**	**−12,193**	**−12,315**	**−17,008**	**−19,640**
Reserve assets.......................	4 802 ..	−6,822	917	−1,256	−6,703	−12,193	−12,315	−17,008	−19,640
Use of Fund credit and loans........	4 766 ..	....	....	....	....	....	....	....	....
Exceptional financing...............	4 920 ..	....	....	....	....	....	....	....	....
Conversion rates: Singapore dollars per U.S. dollar...............	0 101 ..	**1.7240**	**1.7917**	**1.7906**	**1.7422**	**1.6902**	**1.6644**	**1.5889**	**1.5071**

[1] Excludes components that have been classified in the categories of Group E.

Table 2. STANDARD PRESENTATION, 2000–2007

(Millions of U.S. dollars)

	Code	2000	2001	2002	2003	2004	2005	2006	2007
CURRENT ACCOUNT...	4 993 ..	**10,728**	**10,708**	**11,156**	**21,586**	**18,247**	**22,238**	**29,787**	**39,062**
A. GOODS..	4 100 ..	**13,956**	**17,252**	**18,804**	**29,436**	**31,063**	**37,036**	**43,433**	**49,099**
Credit..	2 100 ..	**153,095**	**136,609**	**140,776**	**161,702**	**199,393**	**232,512**	**275,288**	**303,136**
General merchandise: exports f.o.b...............	2 110 ..	149,662	132,982	137,204	157,486	194,385	225,573	265,867	290,652
Goods for processing: exports f.o.b.............	2 150 ..	. . . .	. . . .	. . . .	. . . .	. . . .	. . . .	. . . .	. . . .
Repairs on goods..	2 160 ..	. . . .	. . . .	. . . .	. . . .	. . . .	. . . .	. . . .	. . . .
Goods procured in ports by carriers............	2 170 ..	3,433	3,628	3,572	4,216	5,008	6,940	9,421	12,483
Nonmonetary gold.......................................	2 180 ..	. . . .	. . . .	. . . .	. . . .	. . . .	. . . .	. . . .	. . . .
Debit...	3 100 ..	**−139,138**	**−119,358**	**−121,972**	**−132,266**	**−168,330**	**−195,477**	**−231,855**	**−254,036**
General merchandise: imports f.o.b..............	3 110 ..	−138,170	−118,515	−121,003	−131,318	−166,809	−193,442	−229,256	−251,184
Goods for processing: imports f.o.b.............	3 150 ..	. . . .	. . . .	. . . .	. . . .	. . . .	. . . .	. . . .	. . . .
Repairs on goods..	3 160 ..	. . . .	. . . .	. . . .	. . . .	. . . .	. . . .	. . . .	. . . .
Goods procured in ports by carriers............	3 170 ..	−969	−842	−969	−948	−1,520	−2,034	−2,599	−2,852
Nonmonetary gold.......................................	3 180 ..	. . . .	. . . .	. . . .	. . . .	. . . .	. . . .	. . . .	. . . .
B. SERVICES...	4 200 ..	**−1,335**	**−4,357**	**−3,911**	**−3,793**	**−3,339**	**−2,690**	**−2,644**	**−2,590**
Total credit..	2 200 ..	*28,171*	*27,405*	*29,525*	*36,288*	*46,804*	*52,940*	*61,100*	*69,829*
Total debit...	3 200 ..	*−29,506*	*−31,762*	*−33,436*	*−40,081*	*−50,143*	*−55,630*	*−63,744*	*−72,419*
Transportation services, credit........................	2 205 ..	**11,670**	**11,334**	**11,852**	**13,368**	**16,873**	**18,918**	**21,037**	**23,210**
Passenger..	2 850 ..	. . . .	. . . .	. . . .	. . . .	. . . .	. . . .	. . . .	. . . .
Freight..	2 851 ..	*6,721*	*6,735*	*6,999*	*8,722*	*11,159*	*12,927*	*14,495*	*15,658*
Other..	2 852 ..	*4,950*	*4,600*	*4,853*	*4,645*	*5,714*	*5,991*	*6,542*	*7,552*
Sea transport, passenger............................	2 207 ..	. . . .	. . . .	. . . .	. . . .	. . . .	. . . .	. . . .	. . . .
Sea transport, freight..................................	2 208 ..	. . . .	. . . .	. . . .	. . . .	. . . .	. . . .	. . . .	. . . .
Sea transport, other....................................	2 209 ..	. . . .	. . . .	. . . .	. . . .	. . . .	. . . .	. . . .	. . . .
Air transport, passenger..............................	2 211 ..	. . . .	. . . .	. . . .	. . . .	. . . .	. . . .	. . . .	. . . .
Air transport, freight....................................	2 212 ..	. . . .	. . . .	. . . .	. . . .	. . . .	. . . .	. . . .	. . . .
Air transport, other.....................................	2 213 ..	. . . .	. . . .	. . . .	. . . .	. . . .	. . . .	. . . .	. . . .
Other transport, passenger.........................	2 215 ..	. . . .	. . . .	. . . .	. . . .	. . . .	. . . .	. . . .	. . . .
Other transport, freight...............................	2 216 ..	. . . .	. . . .	. . . .	. . . .	. . . .	. . . .	. . . .	. . . .
Other transport, other.................................	2 217 ..	. . . .	. . . .	. . . .	. . . .	. . . .	. . . .	. . . .	. . . .
Transportation services, debit.........................	3 205 ..	**−12,521**	**−12,116**	**−10,649**	**−13,053**	**−17,792**	**−20,314**	**−22,131**	**−24,938**
Passenger..	3 850 ..	. . . .	. . . .	. . . .	. . . .	. . . .	. . . .	. . . .	. . . .
Freight..	3 851 ..	*−8,028*	*−7,723*	*−5,895*	*−8,095*	*−11,809*	*−13,671*	*−14,963*	*−16,957*
Other..	3 852 ..	*−4,493*	*−4,393*	*−4,754*	*−4,958*	*−5,983*	*−6,642*	*−7,168*	*−7,981*
Sea transport, passenger............................	3 207 ..	. . . .	. . . .	. . . .	. . . .	. . . .	. . . .	. . . .	. . . .
Sea transport, freight..................................	3 208 ..	. . . .	. . . .	. . . .	. . . .	. . . .	. . . .	. . . .	. . . .
Sea transport, other....................................	3 209 ..	. . . .	. . . .	. . . .	. . . .	. . . .	. . . .	. . . .	. . . .
Air transport, passenger..............................	3 211 ..	. . . .	. . . .	. . . .	. . . .	. . . .	. . . .	. . . .	. . . .
Air transport, freight....................................	3 212 ..	. . . .	. . . .	. . . .	. . . .	. . . .	. . . .	. . . .	. . . .
Air transport, other.....................................	3 213 ..	. . . .	. . . .	. . . .	. . . .	. . . .	. . . .	. . . .	. . . .
Other transport, passenger.........................	3 215 ..	. . . .	. . . .	. . . .	. . . .	. . . .	. . . .	. . . .	. . . .
Other transport, freight...............................	3 216 ..	. . . .	. . . .	. . . .	. . . .	. . . .	. . . .	. . . .	. . . .
Other transport, other.................................	3 217 ..	. . . .	. . . .	. . . .	. . . .	. . . .	. . . .	. . . .	. . . .
Travel, credit...	2 236 ..	**5,142**	**4,619**	**4,428**	**3,783**	**5,229**	**5,909**	**7,204**	**8,680**
Business travel..	2 237 ..	. . . .	. . . .	. . . .	. . . .	. . . .	. . . .	. . . .	. . . .
Personal travel..	2 240 ..	. . . .	. . . .	. . . .	. . . .	. . . .	. . . .	. . . .	. . . .
Travel, debit..	3 236 ..	**−4,535**	**−6,541**	**−8,143**	**−8,260**	**−9,197**	**−10,011**	**−10,989**	**−11,844**
Business travel..	3 237 ..	. . . .	. . . .	. . . .	. . . .	. . . .	. . . .	. . . .	. . . .
Personal travel..	3 240 ..	. . . .	. . . .	. . . .	. . . .	. . . .	. . . .	. . . .	. . . .
Other services, credit......................................	2 200 BA	**11,359**	**11,452**	**13,245**	**19,137**	**24,702**	**28,113**	**32,859**	**37,939**
Communications..	2 245 ..	433	388	377	413	495	560	747	947
Construction..	2 249 ..	134	193	303	426	647	542	600	762
Insurance..	2 253 ..	556	661	798	1,229	1,313	1,208	1,583	1,987
Financial...	2 260 ..	1,471	1,184	1,315	1,838	2,452	3,042	4,170	6,067
Computer and information...........................	2 262 ..	247	312	353	401	527	513	1,077	1,224
Royalties and licence fees...........................	2 266 ..	85	176	204	196	495	623	642	716
Other business services..............................	2 268 ..	8,318	8,405	9,673	14,386	18,484	21,337	23,723	25,896
Personal, cultural, and recreational.............	2 287 ..	19	34	127	154	185	180	203	224
Government, n.i.e..	2 291 ..	95	99	96	92	103	108	113	117
Other services, debit.......................................	3 200 BA	**−12,449**	**−13,105**	**−14,644**	**−18,768**	**−23,154**	**−25,306**	**−30,625**	**−35,637**
Communications..	3 245 ..	−620	−686	−685	−718	−769	−889	−1,030	−1,313
Construction..	3 249 ..	−124	−173	−132	−142	−325	−203	−176	−224
Insurance..	3 253 ..	−1,534	−1,477	−1,540	−1,800	−2,188	−2,553	−2,874	−3,274
Financial...	3 260 ..	−411	−358	−428	−502	−666	−713	−1,150	−1,545
Computer and information...........................	3 262 ..	−226	−276	−272	−330	−315	−384	−676	−769
Royalties and licence fees...........................	3 266 ..	−5,044	−4,829	−4,793	−6,635	−7,918	−9,312	−8,881	−9,905
Other business services..............................	3 268 ..	−4,282	−5,024	−6,405	−8,268	−10,527	−10,787	−15,386	−18,111
Personal, cultural, and recreational.............	3 287 ..	−82	−171	−265	−241	−268	−279	−265	−291
Government, n.i.e..	3 291 ..	−126	−112	−122	−132	−178	−185	−187	−205

Table 2 (Continued). STANDARD PRESENTATION, 2000–2007

(Millions of U.S. dollars)

	Code	2000	2001	2002	2003	2004	2005	2006	2007
C. INCOME	4 300	−734	−585	−2,283	−2,650	−8,137	−10,844	−9,594	−5,752
Total credit	2 300	*15,623*	*14,381*	*14,171*	*17,419*	*21,538*	*27,235*	*32,220*	*42,985*
Total debit	3 300	*−16,357*	*−14,966*	*−16,454*	*−20,069*	*−29,675*	*−38,079*	*−41,814*	*−48,737*
Compensation of employees, credit	2 310	....	....	....	....	....	....	....	....
Compensation of employees, debit	3 310	....	....	....	....	....	....	....	....
Investment income, credit	2 320	....	....	....	....	....	....	....	....
Direct investment income	2 330	....	....	....	....	....	....	....	....
Dividends and distributed branch profits	2 332	....	....	....	....	....	....	....	....
Reinvested earnings and undistributed branch profits	2 333	....	....	....	....	....	....	....	....
Income on debt (interest)	2 334	....	....	....	....	....	....	....	....
Portfolio investment income	2 339	....	....	....	....	....	....	....	....
Income on equity	2 340	....	....	....	....	....	....	....	....
Income on bonds and notes	2 350	....	....	....	....	....	....	....	....
Income on money market instruments	2 360	....	....	....	....	....	....	....	....
Other investment income	2 370	....	....	....	....	....	....	....	....
Investment income, debit	3 320	....	....	....	....	....	....	....	....
Direct investment income	3 330	....	....	....	....	....	....	....	....
Dividends and distributed branch profits	3 332	....	....	....	....	....	....	....	....
Reinvested earnings and undistributed branch profits	3 333	....	....	....	....	....	....	....	....
Income on debt (interest)	3 334	....	....	....	....	....	....	....	....
Portfolio investment income	3 339	....	....	....	....	....	....	....	....
Income on equity	3 340	....	....	....	....	....	....	....	....
Income on bonds and notes	3 350	....	....	....	....	....	....	....	....
Income on money market instruments	3 360	....	....	....	....	....	....	....	....
Other investment income	3 370	....	....	....	....	....	....	....	....
D. CURRENT TRANSFERS	4 379	−1,160	−1,603	−1,453	−1,406	−1,341	−1,264	−1,408	−1,696
Credit	2 379	128	124	127	131	136	138	145	152
General government	2 380	5	5	9	10	10	11	11	11
Other sectors	2 390	123	118	118	122	126	128	134	140
Workers' remittances	2 391	....	....	....	....	....	....	....	....
Other current transfers	2 392	....	....	....	....	....	....	....	....
Debit	3 379	−1,288	−1,727	−1,581	−1,538	−1,477	−1,402	−1,553	−1,847
General government	3 380	−137	−99	−111	−140	−121	−122	−129	−140
Other sectors	3 390	−1,151	−1,627	−1,470	−1,398	−1,356	−1,280	−1,424	−1,708
Workers' remittances	3 391	....	....	....	....	....	....	....	....
Other current transfers	3 392	....	....	....	....	....	....	....	....
CAPITAL AND FINANCIAL ACCOUNT	4 996	−12,734	−10,877	−11,642	−24,822	−20,930	−29,479	−35,819	−38,288
CAPITAL ACCOUNT	4 994	−163	−161	−160	−168	−184	−202	−231	−259
Total credit	2 994	....	....	....	....	....	....	....	....
Total debit	3 994	....	....	....	....	....	....	....	....
Capital transfers, credit	2 400	....	....	....	....	....	....	....	....
General government	2 401	....	....	....	....	....	....	....	....
Debt forgiveness	2 402	....	....	....	....	....	....	....	....
Other capital transfers	2 410	....	....	....	....	....	....	....	....
Other sectors	2 430	....	....	....	....	....	....	....	....
Migrants' transfers	2 431	....	....	....	....	....	....	....	....
Debt forgiveness	2 432	....	....	....	....	....	....	....	....
Other capital transfers	2 440	....	....	....	....	....	....	....	....
Capital transfers, debit	3 400	....	....	....	....	....	....	....	....
General government	3 401	....	....	....	....	....	....	....	....
Debt forgiveness	3 402	....	....	....	....	....	....	....	....
Other capital transfers	3 410	....	....	....	....	....	....	....	....
Other sectors	3 430	....	....	....	....	....	....	....	....
Migrants' transfers	3 431	....	....	....	....	....	....	....	....
Debt forgiveness	3 432	....	....	....	....	....	....	....	....
Other capital transfers	3 440	....	....	....	....	....	....	....	....
Nonproduced nonfinancial assets, credit	2 480	....	....	....	....	....	....	....	....
Nonproduced nonfinancial assets, debit	3 480	....	....	....	....	....	....	....	....

Table 2 (Continued). STANDARD PRESENTATION, 2000–2007

(Millions of U.S. dollars)

	Code	2000	2001	2002	2003	2004	2005	2006	2007
FINANCIAL ACCOUNT	4 995	−12,571	−10,716	−11,482	−24,654	−20,746	−29,277	−35,588	−38,029
A. DIRECT INVESTMENT	4 500	10,569	−4,344	4,871	8,969	9,026	6,987	12,502	11,837
Direct investment abroad	4 505	−5,915	−19,965	−2,329	−2,695	−10,803	−6,943	−12,241	−12,300
Equity capital	4 510	−7,928	−18,184	−2,702	−4,754	−6,939	−6,091	−9,823	−11,191
Claims on affiliated enterprises	4 515	....	....	....	....	....	....	....	....
Liabilities to affiliated enterprises	4 520	....	....	....	....	....	....	....	....
Reinvested earnings	4 525	....	....	....	....	....	....	....	....
Other capital	4 530	2,013	−1,781	374	2,059	−3,863	−852	−2,418	−1,109
Claims on affiliated enterprises	4 535	....	....	....	....	....	....	....	....
Liabilities to affiliated enterprises	4 540	....	....	....	....	....	....	....	....
Direct investment in Singapore	4 555	16,484	15,621	7,200	11,664	19,828	13,930	24,743	24,137
Equity capital	4 560	13,326	14,418	6,228	11,475	19,747	13,767	24,855	25,317
Claims on direct investors	4 565	....	....	....	....	....	....	....	....
Liabilities to direct investors	4 570	....	....	....	....	....	....	....	....
Reinvested earnings	4 575	....	....	....	....	....	....	....	....
Other capital	4 580	3,159	1,203	972	189	82	163	−112	−1,180
Claims on direct investors	4 585	....	....	....	....	....	....	....	....
Liabilities to direct investors	4 590	....	....	....	....	....	....	....	....
B. PORTFOLIO INVESTMENT	4 600	−14,591	−7,307	−13,144	−10,040	−5,465	−3,295	−8,941	−16,593
Assets	4 602	−13,366	−11,065	−13,363	−14,346	−7,050	−8,335	−17,795	−22,600
Equity securities	4 610	−8,257	−7,941	−6,069	−7,356	−5,658	−10,467	−9,029	−19,425
Monetary authorities	4 611	....	....	....	....	....	....	....	....
General government	4 612	....	....	....	....	....	....	....	....
Banks	4 613	....	....	....	....	....	....	....	....
Other sectors	4 614	....	....	....	....	....	....	....	....
Debt securities	4 619	−5,109	−3,124	−7,295	−6,990	−1,393	2,132	−8,767	−3,175
Bonds and notes	4 620	....	....	....	....	....	....	....	....
Monetary authorities	4 621	....	....	....	....	....	....	....	....
General government	4 622	....	....	....	....	....	....	....	....
Banks	4 623	....	....	....	....	....	....	....	....
Other sectors	4 624	....	....	....	....	....	....	....	....
Money market instruments	4 630	....	....	....	....	....	....	....	....
Monetary authorities	4 631	....	....	....	....	....	....	....	....
General government	4 632	....	....	....	....	....	....	....	....
Banks	4 633	....	....	....	....	....	....	....	....
Other sectors	4 634	....	....	....	....	....	....	....	....
Liabilities	4 652	−1,224	3,758	219	4,306	1,586	5,040	8,854	6,007
Equity securities	4 660	−1,169	−90	−442	2,139	2,383	3,838	6,839	6,743
Banks	4 663	....	....	....	....	....	....	....	....
Other sectors	4 664	....	....	....	....	....	....	....	....
Debt securities	4 669	−56	3,847	661	2,167	−797	1,202	2,015	−736
Bonds and notes	4 670	....	....	....	....	....	....	....	....
Monetary authorities	4 671	....	....	....	....	....	....	....	....
General government	4 672	....	....	....	....	....	....	....	....
Banks	4 673	....	....	....	....	....	....	....	....
Other sectors	4 674	....	....	....	....	....	....	....	....
Money market instruments	4 680	....	....	....	....	....	....	....	....
Monetary authorities	4 681	....	....	....	....	....	....	....	....
General government	4 682	....	....	....	....	....	....	....	....
Banks	4 683	....	....	....	....	....	....	....	....
Other sectors	4 684	....	....	....	....	....	....	....	....
C. FINANCIAL DERIVATIVES	4 910	....	....	....	....	....	....	....	....
Monetary authorities	4 911	....	....	....	....	....	....	....	....
General government	4 912	....	....	....	....	....	....	....	....
Banks	4 913	....	....	....	....	....	....	....	....
Other sectors	4 914	....	....	....	....	....	....	....	....
Assets	4 900	....	....	....	....	....	....	....	....
Monetary authorities	4 901	....	....	....	....	....	....	....	....
General government	4 902	....	....	....	....	....	....	....	....
Banks	4 903	....	....	....	....	....	....	....	....
Other sectors	4 904	....	....	....	....	....	....	....	....
Liabilities	4 905	....	....	....	....	....	....	....	....
Monetary authorities	4 906	....	....	....	....	....	....	....	....
General government	4 907	....	....	....	....	....	....	....	....
Banks	4 908	....	....	....	....	....	....	....	....
Other sectors	4 909	....	....	....	....	....	....	....	....

Table 2 (Concluded). STANDARD PRESENTATION, 2000–2007

(Millions of U.S. dollars)

	Code	2000	2001	2002	2003	2004	2005	2006	2007
D. OTHER INVESTMENT	4 700	**−1,727**	**18**	**−1,953**	**−16,880**	**−12,114**	**−20,654**	**−22,141**	**−13,632**
Assets	4 703	**−15,824**	**−1,575**	**−8,373**	**−21,115**	**−28,381**	**−28,380**	**−49,368**	**−67,704**
Trade credits	4 706	−8,501	4,181	−8,751	−14,851	−8,623	2,960	−773	2,022
General government	4 707	....	....	....	....	....	....	....	....
of which: Short-term	4 709	....	....	....	....	....	....	....	....
Other sectors	4 710	−8,501	4,181	−8,751	−14,851	−8,623	2,960	−773	2,022
of which: Short-term	4 712	*−8,501*	*4,181*	*−8,751*	*−14,851*	*−8,623*	*2,960*	*−773*	*2,022*
Loans	4 714	607	−3,196	−1,083	9,549	−5,640	−10,945	−26,000	−5,471
Monetary authorities	4 715	....	....	....	....	....	....	....	....
of which: Short-term	4 718	....	....	....	....	....	....	....	....
General government	4 719	....	....	....	....	....	....	....	....
of which: Short-term	4 721	....	....	....	....	....	....	....	....
Banks	4 722	2,064	−5,252	954	10,627	−3,482	−9,308	−25,340	−3,752
of which: Short-term	4 724	*2,013*	*−5,038*	*1,231*	*11,037*	*−3,197*	*−8,311*	*−24,349*	*−1,552*
Other sectors	4 725	−1,458	2,057	−2,038	−1,078	−2,158	−1,638	−660	−1,718
of which: Short-term	4 727	*−196*	*909*	*−2,055*	*−1,313*	*−2,495*	*−371*	*−252*	*−1,487*
Currency and deposits	4 730	−2,686	−4,475	77	−5,936	−1,180	−13,486	−13,150	−20,533
Monetary authorities	4 731	....	....	....	....	....	....	....	....
General government	4 732	....	....	....	....	....	....	....	....
Banks	4 733	−3	−7	106	31	−9	−1	−1	−8
Other sectors	4 734	−2,682	−4,468	−29	−5,967	−1,172	−13,485	−13,149	−20,525
Other assets	4 736	−5,075	1,922	1,218	−9,821	−12,834	−10,750	−13,447	−43,722
Monetary authorities	4 737	....	....	....	....	....	....	....	....
of which: Short-term	4 739	....	....	....	....	....	....	....	....
General government	4 740	....	....	....	....	....	....	....	....
of which: Short-term	4 742	....	....	....	....	....	....	....	....
Banks	4 743	−24	−615	125	−1	−1,798	75	−3,587	−5,286
of which: Short-term	4 745	*134*	*−257*	*312*	*−278*	*−778*	*−57*	*−172*	*−1,064*
Other sectors	4 746	−5,051	2,537	1,093	−9,820	−11,036	−10,825	−9,859	−38,436
of which: Short-term	4 748	*102*	*448*	*221*	*218*	*40*	*−28*	*−150*	*−312*
Liabilities	4 753	**14,097**	**1,593**	**6,420**	**4,235**	**16,266**	**7,725**	**27,228**	**54,072**
Trade credits	4 756	7,183	−2,136	6,493	9,175	8,167	−617	4,583	−2,494
General government	4 757	....	....	....	....	....	....	....	....
of which: Short-term	4 759	....	....	....	....	....	....	....	....
Other sectors	4 760	7,183	−2,136	6,493	9,175	8,167	−617	4,583	−2,494
of which: Short-term	4 762	*7,183*	*−2,136*	*6,493*	*9,175*	*8,167*	*−617*	*4,583*	*−2,494*
Loans	4 764	6,996	4,018	1,493	−7,614	9,099	15,240	25,106	42,610
Monetary authorities	4 765	....	....	....	....	....	....	....	....
of which: Use of Fund credit and loans from the Fund	4 766	....	....	....	....	....	....	....	....
of which: Short-term	4 768	....	....	....	....	....	....	....	....
General government	4 769	....	....	....	....	....	....	....	....
of which: Short-term	4 771	....	....	....	....	....	....	....	....
Banks	4 772	6,884	4,687	1,392	−8,500	4,660	1,194	18,222	14,512
of which: Short-term	4 774	*6,885*	*4,653*	*1,386*	*−8,730*	*4,621*	*1,185*	*18,068*	*14,390*
Other sectors	4 775	111	−668	100	886	4,439	14,047	6,884	28,098
of which: Short-term	4 777	*−94*	*1,014*	*1,004*	*1,785*	*3,655*	*13,479*	*1,191*	*24,258*
Currency and deposits	4 780	700	1,739	−2,201	−101	875	1,750	4,806	5,778
Monetary authorities	4 781	....	....	....	....	....	....	....	....
General government	4 782	....	....	....	....	....	....	....	....
Banks	4 783	700	1,739	−2,201	−101	875	1,750	4,806	5,778
Other sectors	4 784	....	....	....	....	....	....	....	....
Other liabilities	4 786	−918	−2,176	723	2,853	−1,941	−517	1,208	8,177
Monetary authorities	4 787	....	....	....	....	....	....	....	....
of which: Short-term	4 789	....	....	....	....	....	....	....	....
General government	4 790	....	....	....	....	....	....	....	....
of which: Short-term	4 792	....	....	....	....	....	....	....	....
Banks	4 793	78	1,786	459	−408	−1,116	71	405	569
of which: Short-term	4 795	*2*	*−3*	*−1*	*....*	*4*	*5*	*−8*	*6*
Other sectors	4 796	−997	−3,962	264	3,261	−825	−587	803	7,608
of which: Short-term	4 798	*−1,072*	*−2,624*	*−38*	*1,474*	*4,806*	*−669*	*770*	*7,344*
E. RESERVE ASSETS	4 802	**−6,822**	**917**	**−1,256**	**−6,703**	**−12,193**	**−12,315**	**−17,008**	**−19,640**
Monetary gold	4 812	....	....	....	....	....	....	....	....
Special drawing rights	4 811	−21	−18	−14	−13	−73	−16	−16	−17
Reserve position in the Fund	4 810	87	−75	−71	−39	142	236	51	45
Foreign exchange	4 803	−6,888	1,011	−1,172	−6,652	−12,262	−12,535	−17,043	−19,668
Other claims	4 813	....	....	....	....	....	....	....	....
NET ERRORS AND OMISSIONS	4 998	**2,006**	**169**	**486**	**3,235**	**2,683**	**7,241**	**6,032**	**−774**

Table 3. INTERNATIONAL INVESTMENT POSITION (End-period stocks), 2000–2007

(Millions of U.S. dollars)

	Code	2000	2001	2002	2003	2004	2005	2006	2007
ASSETS	8 995 C.	....	369,819	415,026	472,931	551,616	608,014	753,460	879,864
Direct investment abroad	8 505 ..	....	81,361	90,806	97,140	117,510	126,304	147,931	169,862
Equity capital and reinvested earnings	8 506 ..	....	....	....	....	....	....	....	....
Claims on affiliated enterprises	8 507 ..	....	....	....	....	....	....	....	....
Liabilities to affiliated enterprises	8 508 ..	....	....	....	....	....	....	....	....
Other capital	8 530 ..	....	....	....	....	....	....	....	....
Claims on affiliated enterprises	8 535 ..	....	....	....	....	....	....	....	....
Liabilities to affiliated enterprises	8 540 ..	....	....	....	....	....	....	....	....
Portfolio investment	8 602 ..	....	58,667	69,494	91,109	105,337	130,725	172,780	196,673
Equity securities	8 610 ..	....	30,519	32,635	42,999	53,159	74,321	103,388	120,641
Monetary authorities	8 611 ..	....	....	....	....	....	....	....	....
General government	8 612 ..	....	....	....	....	....	....	....	....
Banks	8 613 ..	....	....	....	....	....	....	....	....
Other sectors	8 614 ..	....	....	....	....	....	....	....	....
Debt securities	8 619 ..	....	28,148	36,859	48,110	52,178	56,404	69,392	76,032
Bonds and notes	8 620 ..	....	....	....	....	....	....	....	....
Monetary authorities	8 621 ..	....	....	....	....	....	....	....	....
General government	8 622 ..	....	....	....	....	....	....	....	....
Banks	8 623 ..	....	....	....	....	....	....	....	....
Other sectors	8 624 ..	....	....	....	....	....	....	....	....
Money market instruments	8 630 ..	....	....	....	....	....	....	....	....
Monetary authorities	8 631 ..	....	....	....	....	....	....	....	....
General government	8 632 ..	....	....	....	....	....	....	....	....
Banks	8 633 ..	....	....	....	....	....	....	....	....
Other sectors	8 634 ..	....	....	....	....	....	....	....	....
Financial derivatives	8 900 ..	....	....	....	....	....	....	....	....
Monetary authorities	8 901 ..	....	....	....	....	....	....	....	....
General government	8 902 ..	....	....	....	....	....	....	....	....
Banks	8 903 ..	....	....	....	....	....	....	....	....
Other sectors	8 904 ..	....	....	....	....	....	....	....	....
Other investment	8 703 ..	....	154,310	172,594	188,813	216,477	235,125	296,474	350,585
Trade credits	8 706 ..	....	....	....	....	....	....	....	....
General government	8 707 ..	....	....	....	....	....	....	....	....
of which: Short-term	8 709 ..	....	....	....	....	....	....	....	....
Other sectors	8 710 ..	....	....	....	....	....	....	....	....
of which: Short-term	8 712 ..	....	....	....	....	....	....	....	....
Loans	8 714 ..	....	....	....	....	....	....	....	....
Monetary authorities	8 715 ..	....	....	....	....	....	....	....	....
of which: Short-term	8 718 ..	....	....	....	....	....	....	....	....
General government	8 719 ..	....	....	....	....	....	....	....	....
of which: Short-term	8 721 ..	....	....	....	....	....	....	....	....
Banks	8 722 ..	....	....	....	....	....	....	....	....
of which: Short-term	8 724 ..	....	....	....	....	....	....	....	....
Other sectors	8 725 ..	....	....	....	....	....	....	....	....
of which: Short-term	8 727 ..	....	....	....	....	....	....	....	....
Currency and deposits	8 730 ..	....	....	....	....	....	....	....	....
Monetary authorities	8 731 ..	....	....	....	....	....	....	....	....
General government	8 732 ..	....	....	....	....	....	....	....	....
Banks	8 733 ..	....	....	....	....	....	....	....	....
Other sectors	8 734 ..	....	....	....	....	....	....	....	....
Other assets	8 736 ..	....	....	....	....	....	....	....	....
Monetary authorities	8 737 ..	....	....	....	....	....	....	....	....
of which: Short-term	8 739 ..	....	....	....	....	....	....	....	....
General government	8 740 ..	....	....	....	....	....	....	....	....
of which: Short-term	8 742 ..	....	....	....	....	....	....	....	....
Banks	8 743 ..	....	....	....	....	....	....	....	....
of which: Short-term	8 745 ..	....	....	....	....	....	....	....	....
Other sectors	8 746 ..	....	....	....	....	....	....	....	....
of which: Short-term	8 748 ..	....	....	....	....	....	....	....	....
Reserve assets	8 802 ..	....	75,480	82,131	95,869	112,293	115,859	136,275	162,743
Monetary gold	8 812 ..								
Special drawing rights	8 811 ..	137	150	177	207	293	285	316	350
Reserve position in the Fund	8 810 ..	310	374	478	564	440	174	130	90
Foreign exchange	8 803 ..	....	....	....	....	....	....	....	....
Other claims	8 813 ..	....	....	....	....	....	....	....	....

Table 3 (Concluded). INTERNATIONAL INVESTMENT POSITION (End-period stocks), 2000–2007

(Millions of U.S. dollars)

	Code	2000	2001	2002	2003	2004	2005	2006	2007
LIABILITIES	8 995 D.	....	308,829	333,278	374,726	439,039	464,787	592,663	725,181
Direct investment in Singapore	8 555 ..	....	126,435	135,720	153,120	182,255	186,948	210,775	232,818
Equity capital and reinvested earnings	8 556 ..	....	....	....	....	....	....	....	....
Claims on direct investors	8 557 ..	....	....	....	....	....	....	....	....
Liabilities to direct investors	8 558 ..	....	....	....	....	....	....	....	....
Other capital	8 580 ..	....	....	....	....	....	....	....	....
Claims on direct investors	8 585 ..	....	....	....	....	....	....	....	....
Liabilities to direct investors	8 590 ..	....	....	....	....	....	....	....	....
Portfolio investment	8 652 ..	....	45,975	45,704	61,059	73,529	86,400	133,094	173,112
Equity securities	8 660 ..	....	36,267	33,854	47,719	59,943	72,715	113,621	153,857
Banks	8 663 ..	....	....	....	....	....	....	....	....
Other sectors	8 664 ..	....	....	....	....	....	....	....	....
Debt securities	8 669 ..	....	9,708	11,850	13,340	13,586	13,686	19,473	19,255
Bonds and notes	8 670 ..	....	....	....	....	....	....	....	....
Monetary authorities	8 671 ..	....	....	....	....	....	....	....	....
General government	8 672 ..	....	....	....	....	....	....	....	....
Banks	8 673 ..	....	....	....	....	....	....	....	....
Other sectors	8 674 ..	....	....	....	....	....	....	....	....
Money market instruments	8 680 ..	....	....	....	....	....	....	....	....
Monetary authorities	8 681 ..	....	....	....	....	....	....	....	....
General government	8 682 ..	....	....	....	....	....	....	....	....
Banks	8 683 ..	....	....	....	....	....	....	....	....
Other sectors	8 684 ..	....	....	....	....	....	....	....	....
Financial derivatives	8 905 ..	....	....	....	....	....	....	....	....
Monetary authorities	8 906 ..	....	....	....	....	....	....	....	....
General government	8 907 ..	....	....	....	....	....	....	....	....
Banks	8 908 ..	....	....	....	....	....	....	....	....
Other sectors	8 909 ..	....	....	....	....	....	....	....	....
Other investment	8 753 ..	....	136,419	151,853	160,546	183,254	191,439	248,794	319,250
Trade credits	8 756 ..	....	....	....	....	....	....	....	....
General government	8 757 ..	....	....	....	....	....	....	....	....
of which: Short-term	8 759 ..	....	....	....	....	....	....	....	....
Other sectors	8 760 ..	....	....	....	....	....	....	....	....
of which: Short-term	8 762 ..	....	....	....	....	....	....	....	....
Loans	8 764 ..	....	....	....	....	....	....	....	....
Monetary authorities	8 765 ..	....	....	....	....	....	....	....	....
of which: Use of Fund credit and loans from the Fund	8 766 ..	....	....	....	....	....	....	....	....
of which: Short-term	8 768 ..	....	....	....	....	....	....	....	....
General government	8 769 ..	....	....	....	....	....	....	....	....
of which: Short-term	8 771 ..	....	....	....	....	....	....	....	....
Banks	8 772 ..	....	....	....	....	....	....	....	....
of which: Short-term	8 774 ..	....	....	....	....	....	....	....	....
Other sectors	8 775 ..	....	....	....	....	....	....	....	....
of which: Short-term	8 777 ..	....	....	....	....	....	....	....	....
Currency and deposits	8 780 ..	....	....	....	....	....	....	....	....
Monetary authorities	8 781 ..	....	....	....	....	....	....	....	....
General government	8 782 ..	....	....	....	....	....	....	....	....
Banks	8 783 ..	....	....	....	....	....	....	....	....
Other sectors	8 784 ..	....	....	....	....	....	....	....	....
Other liabilities	8 786 ..	....	....	....	....	....	....	....	....
Monetary authorities	8 787 ..	....	....	....	....	....	....	....	....
of which: Short-term	8 789 ..	....	....	....	....	....	....	....	....
General government	8 790 ..	....	....	....	....	....	....	....	....
of which: Short-term	8 792 ..	....	....	....	....	....	....	....	....
Banks	8 793 ..	....	....	....	....	....	....	....	....
of which: Short-term	8 795 ..	....	....	....	....	....	....	....	....
Other sectors	8 796 ..	....	....	....	....	....	....	....	....
of which: Short-term	8 798 ..	....	....	....	....	....	....	....	....
NET INTERNATIONAL INVESTMENT POSITION	8 995 ..	....	60,990	81,748	98,206	112,577	143,227	160,796	154,683
Conversion rates: Singapore dollars per U.S. dollar (end of period)	0 102 ..	1.7315	1.8510	1.7365	1.7008	1.6338	1.6642	1.5336	1.4412

2008, International Monetary Fund: *Balance of Payments Statistics Yearbook*

Table 1. ANALYTIC PRESENTATION, 2000–2007

(Millions of U.S. dollars)

	Code	2000	2001	2002	2003	2004	2005	2006	2007
A. Current Account[1]	4 993 Z.	**−694**	....	**−1,955**	**−282**	**−3,296**	**−4,005**	**−3,937**	**−4,103**
Goods: exports f.o.b.	2 100 ..	11,896	....	14,460	21,944	27,663	31,851	41,735	57,806
Goods: imports f.o.b.	3 100 ..	−12,791	....	−16,626	−22,593	−29,220	−34,214	−44,283	−58,715
Balance on Goods	4 100 ..	*−895*	....	*−2,166*	*−649*	*−1,557*	*−2,363*	*−2,549*	*−909*
Services: credit	2 200 ..	2,241	....	2,812	3,297	3,735	4,405	5,436	7,063
Services: debit	3 200 ..	−1,805	....	−2,351	−3,056	−3,466	−4,078	−4,675	−6,531
Balance on Goods and Services	4 991 ..	*−459*	....	*−1,705*	*−408*	*−1,288*	*−2,036*	*−1,787*	*−376*
Income: credit	2 300 ..	268	....	342	907	1,002	1,585	1,959	2,340
Income: debit	3 300 ..	−623	....	−791	−1,026	−3,184	−3,570	−4,051	−5,628
Balance on Goods, Services, and Income	4 992 ..	*−814*	....	*−2,154*	*−527*	*−3,470*	*−4,021*	*−3,880*	*−3,665*
Current transfers: credit	2 379 Z.	344	....	480	537	890	1,403	1,623	2,070
Current transfers: debit	3 379 ..	−224	....	−282	−292	−717	−1,386	−1,681	−2,508
B. Capital Account[1]	4 994 Z.	**91**	....	**110**	**102**	**135**	**−18**	**−42**	**465**
Capital account: credit	2 994 Z.	106	....	130	195	148	16	37	686
Capital account: debit	3 994 ..	−15	....	−20	−93	−14	−33	−79	−221
Total, Groups A Plus B	4 981 ..	*−603*	....	*−1,845*	*−180*	*−3,162*	*−4,022*	*−3,979*	*−3,637*
C. Financial Account[1]	4 995 W.	**1,472**	....	**5,230**	**1,661**	**4,838**	**6,219**	**1,155**	**7,023**
Direct investment abroad	4 505 ..	−22	....	−3	−24	13	−145	−368	−403
Direct investment in Slovak Republic	4 555 Z.	2,052	....	4,104	559	3,037	2,411	4,167	3,363
Portfolio investment assets	4 602 ..	−195	....	265	−742	−829	−691	−186	−1,083
Equity securities	4 610 ..	11	....	1	−347	−40	103	−309	−271
Debt securities	4 619 ..	−206	....	263	−395	−789	−794	123	−811
Portfolio investment liabilities	4 652 Z.	1,016	....	289	168	1,680	−246	1,741	349
Equity securities	4 660 ..	−53	....	10	59	−94	137	36	232
Debt securities	4 669 Z.	1,069	....	279	109	1,774	−382	1,705	117
Financial derivatives	4 910 ..	1	....	3	17	20	−35	−163	52
Financial derivatives assets	4 900 ..	....	....	....	−43	−149	−98	−442	265
Financial derivatives liabilities	4 905 ..	1	....	3	60	169	64	279	−213
Other investment assets	4 703 ..	−973	....	738	−20	−123	−498	−1,020	−1,535
Monetary authorities	4 701 ..	....	....	....	....	....	....	....	....
General government	4 704 ..	1	....	299	58	15	15	12	....
Banks	4 705 ..	−748	....	569	114	170	−349	−610	−1,282
Other sectors	4 728 ..	−226	....	−130	−192	−308	−164	−421	−253
Other investment liabilities	4 753 W.	−407	....	−165	1,703	1,040	5,422	−3,017	6,281
Monetary authorities	4 753 WA	−26	....	−198	618	−928	93	152	−111
General government	4 753 ZB	149	....	−333	−30	9	−992	−115	−39
Banks	4 753 ZC	30	....	390	1,260	2,247	5,369	−4,411	4,892
Other sectors	4 753 ZD	−561	....	−23	−146	−288	952	1,357	1,539
Total, Groups A Through C	4 983 ..	*869*	....	*3,385*	*1,481*	*1,676*	*2,197*	*−2,824*	*3,386*
D. Net Errors and Omissions	4 998 ..	**51**	....	**298**	**27**	**56**	**324**	**167**	**302**
Total, Groups A Through D	4 984 ..	*920*	....	*3,684*	*1,508*	*1,732*	*2,521*	*−2,656*	*3,688*
E. Reserves and Related Items	4 802 A.	**−920**	....	**−3,684**	**−1,508**	**−1,732**	**−2,521**	**2,656**	**−3,688**
Reserve assets	4 802 ..	−794	....	−3,684	−1,508	−1,732	−2,521	2,656	−3,688
Use of Fund credit and loans	4 766 ..	−125	....	....	....	....	....	....	....
Exceptional financing	4 920 ..	....	....	....	....	....	....	....	....
Conversion rates: Slovak koruny per U.S. dollar	0 101 ..	**46.035**	**48.355**	**45.327**	**36.773**	**32.257**	**31.018**	**29.697**	**24.694**

[1] Excludes components that have been classified in the categories of Group E.

Table 2. STANDARD PRESENTATION, 2000–2007

(Millions of U.S. dollars)

	Code	2000	2001	2002	2003	2004	2005	2006	2007
CURRENT ACCOUNT	4 993	**−694**	....	**−1,955**	**−282**	**−3,296**	**−4,005**	**−3,937**	**−4,103**
A. GOODS	4 100	**−895**	....	**−2,166**	**−649**	**−1,557**	**−2,363**	**−2,549**	**−909**
Credit	2 100	**11,896**	....	**14,460**	**21,944**	**27,663**	**31,851**	**41,735**	**57,806**
General merchandise: exports f.o.b.	2 110	....	....	8,119	11,727	....	....	....	....
Goods for processing: exports f.o.b.	2 150	....	....	6,322	10,191	....	....	....	....
Repairs on goods	2 160	....	....	16	21	....	....	....	....
Goods procured in ports by carriers	2 170	....	....	....	....	....	....	....	....
Nonmonetary gold	2 180	....	....	3	5	....	....	....	....
Debit	3 100	**−12,791**	....	**−16,626**	**−22,593**	**−29,220**	**−34,214**	**−44,283**	**−58,715**
General merchandise: imports f.o.b.	3 110	....	....	−12,387	−16,103	....	....	....	....
Goods for processing: imports f.o.b.	3 150	....	....	−4,207	−6,447	....	....	....	....
Repairs on goods	3 160	....	....	−28	−40	....	....	....	....
Goods procured in ports by carriers	3 170	....	....	....	....	....	....	....	....
Nonmonetary gold	3 180	....	....	−3	−3	....	....	....	....
B. SERVICES	4 200	**436**	....	**461**	**241**	**269**	**327**	**761**	**532**
Total credit	2 200	*2,241*	....	*2,812*	*3,297*	*3,735*	*4,405*	*5,436*	*7,063*
Total debit	3 200	*−1,805*	....	*−2,351*	*−3,056*	*−3,466*	*−4,078*	*−4,675*	*−6,531*
Transportation services, credit	2 205	**995**	....	**1,164**	**1,413**	**1,493**	**1,596**	**1,913**	**2,254**
Passenger	2 850	*8*	....	*6*	*11*	*26*	*72*	*134*	*326*
Freight	2 851	*983*	....	*346*	*637*	*1,326*	*1,415*	*1,663*	*1,811*
Other	2 852	*4*	....	*812*	*764*	*141*	*109*	*117*	*117*
Sea transport, passenger	2 207	....	....	....	....	....	....	....	....
Sea transport, freight	2 208	3	....	1	1	1	3	3	5
Sea transport, other	2 209	....	....	....	....	....	....	....	....
Air transport, passenger	2 211	5	....	3	6	21	66	119	313
Air transport, freight	2 212	2	....	2	2	10	18	20	41
Air transport, other	2 213	....	....	....	....	....	....	....	....
Other transport, passenger	2 215	3	....	4	5	5	6	14	14
Other transport, freight	2 216	977	....	343	634	1,316	1,394	1,639	1,765
Other transport, other	2 217	4	....	812	764	141	109	117	117
Transportation services, debit	3 205	**−434**	....	**−604**	**−898**	**−998**	**−1,204**	**−1,192**	**−1,840**
Passenger	3 850	*−45*	....	*−64*	*−89*	*−155*	*−278*	*−170*	*−292*
Freight	3 851	*−387*	....	*−380*	*−659*	*−563*	*−588*	*−685*	*−902*
Other	3 852	*−2*	....	*−160*	*−150*	*−280*	*−337*	*−337*	*−646*
Sea transport, passenger	3 207	....	....	....	....	....	....	....	....
Sea transport, freight	3 208	−22	....	−26	−35	−47	−49	−59	−90
Sea transport, other	3 209	....	....	....	....	....	....	....	....
Air transport, passenger	3 211	−42	....	−62	−84	−151	−274	−161	−280
Air transport, freight	3 212	−4	....	−7	−11	−17	−36	−28	−32
Air transport, other	3 213	....	....	....	....	....	....	....	....
Other transport, passenger	3 215	−2	....	−2	−5	−3	−5	−9	−12
Other transport, freight	3 216	−361	....	−347	−614	−499	−503	−598	−780
Other transport, other	3 217	−2	....	−160	−150	−280	−337	−337	−646
Travel, credit	2 236	**433**	....	**736**	**865**	**905**	**1,210**	**1,521**	**2,026**
Business travel	2 237	....	....	....	....	....	....	....	....
Personal travel	2 240	433	....	736	865	....	....	....	....
Travel, debit	3 236	**−296**	....	**−442**	**−573**	**−744**	**−844**	**−1,060**	**−1,533**
Business travel	3 237	−30	....	−27	−28	....	....	....	....
Personal travel	3 240	−266	....	−415	−544	....	....	....	....
Other services, credit	2 200 BA	**813**	....	**912**	**1,020**	**1,336**	**1,600**	**2,001**	**2,783**
Communications	2 245	51	....	58	76	83	114	259	257
Construction	2 249	68	....	51	86	114	118	86	122
Insurance	2 253	12	....	16	18	19	18	25	63
Financial	2 260	36	....	66	58	87	139	136	272
Computer and information	2 262	52	....	71	84	116	116	170	210
Royalties and licence fees	2 266	16	....	38	50	60	75	90	149
Other business services	2 268	501	....	520	552	715	870	1,054	1,338
Personal, cultural, and recreational	2 287	54	....	67	69	121	123	148	331
Government, n.i.e.	2 291	23	....	25	28	22	25	33	41
Other services, debit	3 200 BA	**−1,076**	....	**−1,305**	**−1,585**	**−1,724**	**−2,030**	**−2,423**	**−3,157**
Communications	3 245	−25	....	−44	−67	−72	−73	−98	−149
Construction	3 249	−77	....	−50	−69	−160	−186	−226	−306
Insurance	3 253	−21	....	−56	−102	−129	−115	−136	−136
Financial	3 260	−66	....	−125	−161	−136	−250	−341	−482
Computer and information	3 262	−57	....	−81	−123	−172	−181	−200	−238
Royalties and licence fees	3 266	−58	....	−63	−91	−99	−94	−107	−124
Other business services	3 268	−693	....	−834	−829	−793	−975	−1,125	−1,501
Personal, cultural, and recreational	3 287	−53	....	−22	−98	−112	−92	−120	−139
Government, n.i.e.	3 291	−26	....	−29	−45	−51	−63	−70	−82

Table 2 (Continued). STANDARD PRESENTATION, 2000–2007

(Millions of U.S. dollars)

	Code	2000	2001	2002	2003	2004	2005	2006	2007
C. INCOME	4 300	**−355**	....	**−449**	**−119**	**−2,181**	**−1,985**	**−2,092**	**−3,288**
Total credit	2 300	*268*	....	*342*	*907*	*1,002*	*1,585*	*1,959*	*2,340*
Total debit	3 300	*−623*	....	*−791*	*−1,026*	*−3,184*	*−3,570*	*−4,051*	*−5,628*
Compensation of employees, credit	2 310	**18**	....	**24**	**425**	**529**	**946**	**1,088**	**1,483**
Compensation of employees, debit	3 310	**−7**	....	**−11**	**−16**	**−22**	**−39**	**−48**	**−73**
Investment income, credit	2 320	**250**	....	**317**	**482**	**473**	**639**	**871**	**857**
Direct investment income	2 330	27	....	10	21	89	31	108	125
Dividends and distributed branch profits	2 332	26	....	10	19	6	21	35	44
Reinvested earnings and undistributed branch profits	2 333	....	....	....	....	78	3	40	49
Income on debt (interest)	2 334	1	....	1	2	4	7	33	33
Portfolio investment income	2 339	139	....	225	404	315	478	637	622
Income on equity	2 340	....	....	....	1	....	....	....	....
Income on bonds and notes	2 350	137	....	222	402	....	....	....	....
Income on money market instruments	2 360	2	....	2	1	....	....	....	....
Other investment income	2 370	84	....	82	56	69	130	126	109
Investment income, debit	3 320	**−616**	....	**−779**	**−1,011**	**−3,162**	**−3,531**	**−4,004**	**−5,555**
Direct investment income	3 330	−43	....	−154	−178	−2,511	−2,715	−3,175	−4,623
Dividends and distributed branch profits	3 332	−36	....	−153	−167	−844	−1,770	−2,179	−3,360
Reinvested earnings and undistributed branch profits	3 333	....	....	....	−2	−1,614	−875	−831	−992
Income on debt (interest)	3 334	−6	....	−1	−9	−53	−70	−165	−270
Portfolio investment income	3 339	−182	....	−312	−529	−345	−406	−384	−361
Income on equity	3 340	....	....	−4	−7	....	....	....	....
Income on bonds and notes	3 350	−177	....	−305	−517	....	....	....	....
Income on money market instruments	3 360	−4	....	−2	−5	....	....	....	....
Other investment income	3 370	−392	....	−314	−304	−306	−410	−444	−571
D. CURRENT TRANSFERS	4 379	**120**	....	**199**	**245**	**174**	**16**	**−58**	**−438**
Credit	2 379	**344**	....	**480**	**537**	**890**	**1,403**	**1,623**	**2,070**
General government	2 380	1	....	1	2	355	706	834	761
Other sectors	2 390	343	....	479	535	535	697	789	1,309
Workers' remittances	2 391	....	....	....	....	....	....	....	....
Other current transfers	2 392	343	....	479	535	....	....	....	....
Debit	3 379	**−224**	....	**−282**	**−292**	**−717**	**−1,386**	**−1,681**	**−2,508**
General government	3 380	−6	....	−8	−15	−291	−496	−558	−737
Other sectors	3 390	−218	....	−274	−277	−426	−891	−1,123	−1,771
Workers' remittances	3 391	....	....	....	....	....	....	....	....
Other current transfers	3 392	−218	....	−274	−277	....	....	....	....
CAPITAL AND FINANCIAL ACCOUNT	4 996	**644**	....	**1,657**	**255**	**3,240**	**3,680**	**3,770**	**3,801**
CAPITAL ACCOUNT	4 994	**91**	....	**110**	**102**	**135**	**−18**	**−42**	**465**
Total credit	2 994	*106*	....	*130*	*195*	*148*	*16*	*37*	*686*
Total debit	3 994	*−15*	....	*−20*	*−93*	*−14*	*−33*	*−79*	*−221*
Capital transfers, credit	2 400	**106**	....	**130**	**195**	**134**	**12**	**27**	**676**
General government	2 401	2	....	12	18	....	....	....	....
Debt forgiveness	2 402	....	....	....	....	....	....	....	....
Other capital transfers	2 410	2	....	12	18	....	....	....	....
Other sectors	2 430	104	....	119	177	....	....	....	....
Migrants' transfers	2 431	....	....	....	−1	....	....	....	....
Debt forgiveness	2 432	....	....	....	....	....	....	....	....
Other capital transfers	2 440	104	....	119	178	....	....	....	....
Capital transfers, debit	3 400	**−15**	....	**−20**	**−93**	**−1**	**−16**	**−45**	**−53**
General government	3 401	−1	....	−6	....	....	....	....	....
Debt forgiveness	3 402	....	....	....	....	....	....	....	....
Other capital transfers	3 410	−1	....	−6	....	....	....	....	....
Other sectors	3 430	−14	....	−14	−93	....	....	....	....
Migrants' transfers	3 431	−1	....	....	....	....	....	....	....
Debt forgiveness	3 432	....	....	....	....	....	....	....	....
Other capital transfers	3 440	−13	....	−14	−92	....	....	....	....
Nonproduced nonfinancial assets, credit	2 480	....	....	....	....	14	4	10	10
Nonproduced nonfinancial assets, debit	3 480	....	....	....	....	−13	−18	−34	−168

Table 2 (Continued). STANDARD PRESENTATION, 2000–2007

(Millions of U.S. dollars)

	Code	2000	2001	2002	2003	2004	2005	2006	2007
FINANCIAL ACCOUNT	4 995	553	....	1,547	153	3,106	3,698	3,812	3,335
A. DIRECT INVESTMENT	4 500	2,031	....	4,101	536	3,051	2,266	3,799	2,960
Direct investment abroad	4 505	−22	....	−3	−24	13	−145	−368	−403
Equity capital	4 510	−15	....	....	−25	−83	−108	−319	−254
Claims on affiliated enterprises	4 515	−15	....	....	−25	−83	−108	−319	−254
Liabilities to affiliated enterprises	4 520	....	....	....	....	....	....	....	....
Reinvested earnings	4 525	....	....	....	....	−78	−3	−40	−49
Other capital	4 530	−7	....	−3	1	175	−33	−9	−101
Claims on affiliated enterprises	4 535	−5	....	−4	1	−62	−102	−33	−76
Liabilities to affiliated enterprises	4 540	−2	....	1	....	237	69	24	−24
Direct investment in Slovak Republic	4 555	2,052	....	4,104	559	3,037	2,411	4,167	3,363
Equity capital	4 560	1,960	....	4,041	871	1,168	700	1,884	1,133
Claims on direct investors	4 565	....	....	....	....	....	....	....	....
Liabilities to direct investors	4 570	1,960	....	4,041	871	1,168	700	1,884	1,133
Reinvested earnings	4 575	....	....	....	2	1,614	875	831	992
Other capital	4 580	92	....	63	−313	255	837	1,452	1,239
Claims on direct investors	4 585	−132	....	−107	−410	40	−519	120	−552
Liabilities to direct investors	4 590	224	....	170	97	215	1,356	1,332	1,790
B. PORTFOLIO INVESTMENT	4 600	821	....	553	−574	850	−937	1,556	−734
Assets	4 602	−195	....	265	−742	−829	−691	−186	−1,083
Equity securities	4 610	11	....	1	−347	−40	103	−309	−271
Monetary authorities	4 611	....	....	....	....	....	....	....	....
General government	4 612	....	....	....	....	....	....	....	....
Banks	4 613	9	....	1	−19	−27	−32	36	−139
Other sectors	4 614	2	....	1	−328	−14	135	−345	−133
Debt securities	4 619	−206	....	263	−395	−789	−794	123	−811
Bonds and notes	4 620	−129	....	266	−356	−910	−798	245	−767
Monetary authorities	4 621	....	....	....	....	....	....	....	....
General government	4 622	....	....	....	....	....	....	....	....
Banks	4 623	−118	....	343	−132	−439	51	224	−153
Other sectors	4 624	−10	....	−77	−223	−471	−849	21	−614
Money market instruments	4 630	−77	....	−2	−39	121	4	−122	−45
Monetary authorities	4 631	....	....	....	....	....	....	....	....
General government	4 632	....	....	....	....	....	....	....	....
Banks	4 633	−5	....	−3	11	−17	16	4	−25
Other sectors	4 634	−72	....	1	−50	138	−12	−126	−20
Liabilities	4 652	1,016	....	289	168	1,680	−246	1,741	349
Equity securities	4 660	−53	....	10	59	−94	137	36	232
Banks	4 663	....	....	....	10	6	....	7	5
Other sectors	4 664	−53	....	10	49	−100	137	29	227
Debt securities	4 669	1,069	....	279	109	1,774	−382	1,705	117
Bonds and notes	4 670	1,071	....	286	115	1,599	−219	1,535	−16
Monetary authorities	4 671	−74	....	....	....	....	....	....	....
General government	4 672	683	....	137	87	1,605	−261	1,309	296
Banks	4 673	−12	....	−1	7	−8	45	245	228
Other sectors	4 674	475	....	151	20	2	−3	−19	−539
Money market instruments	4 680	−2	....	−7	−5	175	−163	170	132
Monetary authorities	4 681	....	....	....	....	....	....	....	....
General government	4 682	....	....	....	....	....	−166	....	....
Banks	4 683	....	....	....	....	....	1	166	128
Other sectors	4 684	−2	....	−7	−5	175	1	4	5
C. FINANCIAL DERIVATIVES	4 910	1	....	3	17	20	−35	−163	52
Monetary authorities	4 911	....	....	....	....	....	....	....	....
General government	4 912	....	....	....	....	....	....	....	....
Banks	4 913	....	....	....	23	17	−34	−137	69
Other sectors	4 914	1	....	3	−6	2	−1	−26	−17
Assets	4 900	....	....	....	−43	−149	−98	−442	265
Monetary authorities	4 901	....	....	....	....	....	....	....	....
General government	4 902	....	....	....	....	....	....	....	....
Banks	4 903	....	....	....	−43	−149	−85	−413	259
Other sectors	4 904	....	....	....	....	....	−14	−30	6
Liabilities	4 905	1	....	3	60	169	64	279	−213
Monetary authorities	4 906	....	....	....	....	....	....	....	....
General government	4 907	....	....	....	....	....	....	....	....
Banks	4 908	....	....	....	66	166	51	276	−190
Other sectors	4 909	1	....	3	−6	3	12	3	−23

Table 2 (Concluded). STANDARD PRESENTATION, 2000–2007

(Millions of U.S. dollars)

	Code	2000	2001	2002	2003	2004	2005	2006	2007
D. OTHER INVESTMENT	4 700	−1,506	....	573	1,683	917	4,924	−4,036	4,746
Assets	4 703	−973	....	738	−20	−123	−498	−1,020	−1,535
Trade credits	4 706	−139	....	−111	−136	−234	−278	−464	−43
General government	4 707	....	....	....	....	....	....	....	....
of which: Short-term	4 709	....	....	....	....	....	....	....	....
Other sectors	4 710	−139	....	−111	−136	−234	−278	−464	−43
of which: Short-term	4 712	*−139*	....	*−112*	*−137*	*−234*	*−281*	*88*	*−38*
Loans	4 714	31	....	267	−181	−197	−252	−39	−919
Monetary authorities	4 715	....	....	....	....	....	....	....	....
of which: Short-term	4 718	....	....	....	....	....	....	....	....
General government	4 719	1	....	299	58	15	15	12	....
of which: Short-term	4 721	....	....	....	....	....	....	....	....
Banks	4 722	120	....	−12	−175	−166	−169	−172	−855
of which: Short-term	4 724	*88*	....	*−13*	*−112*	*−94*	*97*	*−169*	*−640*
Other sectors	4 725	−90	....	−21	−64	−45	−98	121	−64
of which: Short-term	4 727	*1*	....	*−15*	*−17*	*−36*	*11*	*−23*	*−55*
Currency and deposits	4 730	−754	....	338	150	12	29	−508	−565
Monetary authorities	4 731	....	....	....	....	....	....	....	....
General government	4 732	....	....	....	....	....	....	....	....
Banks	4 733	−756	....	336	142	40	−182	−429	−418
Other sectors	4 734	2	....	2	8	−29	211	−79	−147
Other assets	4 736	−112	....	244	147	295	2	−9	−9
Monetary authorities	4 737	....	....	....	....	....	....	....	....
of which: Short-term	4 739	....	....	....	....	....	....	....	....
General government	4 740	....	....	....	....	....	....	....	....
of which: Short-term	4 742	....	....	....	....	....	....	....	....
Banks	4 743	−112	....	244	147	295	2	−9	−9
of which: Short-term	4 745	*−112*	....	*203*	*−76*	*292*	*−48*	*−7*	*−12*
Other sectors	4 746	....	....	....	....	....	....	....	....
of which: Short-term	4 748	....	....	....	....	....	....	....	....
Liabilities	4 753	−533	....	−165	1,703	1,040	5,422	−3,017	6,281
Trade credits	4 756	−5	....	180	104	142	566	1,280	542
General government	4 757	....	....	....	....	....	....	....	....
of which: Short-term	4 759	....	....	....	....	....	....	....	....
Other sectors	4 760	−5	....	180	104	142	566	1,280	542
of which: Short-term	4 762	*6*	....	*175*	*133*	*143*	*583*	*1,289*	*560*
Loans	4 764	−626	....	−721	470	−786	−226	344	220
Monetary authorities	4 765	−134	....	−198	618	−928	93	122	−112
of which: Use of Fund credit and loans from the Fund	4 766	−125	....						
of which: Short-term	4 768	....	....	*−166*	*889*	*−874*	*7*	*−3*	*1*
General government	4 769	149	....	−333	−30	9	−992	−115	−51
of which: Short-term	4 771	....	....	....	....	....	....	....	....
Banks	4 772	−85	....	14	132	563	287	261	−614
of which: Short-term	4 774	*−45*	....	*−8*	*115*	*470*	*195*	*253*	*−894*
Other sectors	4 775	−556	....	−203	−250	−430	386	77	998
of which: Short-term	4 777	*−186*	....	*30*	*46*	*−116*	*111*	*−52*	*−8*
Currency and deposits	4 780	71	....	78	424	2,217	4,382	−4,595	5,526
Monetary authorities	4 781	−17	....	....	....	....	....	30	1
General government	4 782	....	....	....	....	....	....	1	12
Banks	4 783	88	....	78	424	2,217	4,382	−4,627	5,514
Other sectors	4 784	....	....	....	....	....	....	1	....
Other liabilities	4 786	27	....	298	704	−533	700	−45	−7
Monetary authorities	4 787	....	....	....	....	....	....	....	....
of which: Short-term	4 789	....	....	....	....	....	....	....	....
General government	4 790	....	....	....	....	....	....	....	....
of which: Short-term	4 792	....	....	....	....	....	....	....	....
Banks	4 793	27	....	298	704	−533	700	−45	−7
of which: Short-term	4 795	*17*	....	*298*	*763*	*−542*	*583*	*−24*	*−10*
Other sectors	4 796	....	....	....	....	....	....	....	....
of which: Short-term	4 798	....	....	....	....	....	....	....	....
E. RESERVE ASSETS	4 802	−794	....	−3,684	−1,508	−1,732	−2,521	2,656	−3,688
Monetary gold	4 812	....	....	....	....	....	....	....	....
Special drawing rights	4 811	....	....	....	....	....	....	....	....
Reserve position in the Fund	4 810	....	....	....	....	....	....	....	−5
Foreign exchange	4 803	−794	....	−3,683	−1,508	−1,732	−2,521	2,656	−3,683
Other claims	4 813	....	....	....	....	....	....	....	....
NET ERRORS AND OMISSIONS	4 998	51	....	298	27	56	324	167	302

Table 3. INTERNATIONAL INVESTMENT POSITION (End-period stocks), 2000–2007

(Millions of U.S. dollars)

	Code	2000	2001	2002	2003	2004	2005	2006	2007
ASSETS	8 995 C.	**10,089**	**10,594**	**14,739**	**19,712**	**24,150**	**25,160**	**27,097**	**35,905**
Direct investment abroad	8 505	**364**	**507**	**544**	**829**	**842**	**597**	**1,154**	**1,609**
Equity capital and reinvested earnings	8 506	310	446	482	680	981	740	1,250	1,602
Claims on affiliated enterprises	8 507	311	446	482	680	981	740	1,250	1,602
Liabilities to affiliated enterprises	8 508	−1	....	....	....	....	....	....	....
Other capital	8 530	54	61	62	149	−139	−143	−95	6
Claims on affiliated enterprises	8 535	54	62	64	154	147	207	237	343
Liabilities to affiliated enterprises	8 540	....	−1	−1	−5	−287	−350	−333	−337
Portfolio investment	8 602	**336**	**858**	**686**	**1,789**	**2,982**	**3,255**	**4,065**	**6,000**
Equity securities	8 610	15	19	42	447	550	411	879	1,309
Monetary authorities	8 611	....	....	....	....	....	....	....	....
General government	8 612	....	....	....	....	....	....	....	....
Banks	8 613	8	11	5	29	62	86	56	110
Other sectors	8 614	7	8	37	419	488	324	823	1,199
Debt securities	8 619	321	838	644	1,342	2,432	2,844	3,186	4,691
Bonds and notes	8 620	241	531	417	1,076	2,403	2,820	3,030	4,515
Monetary authorities	8 621	....	....	....	....	....	....	....	....
General government	8 622	....	....	....	....	....	....	....	....
Banks	8 623	231	487	274	632	1,219	1,036	983	1,293
Other sectors	8 624	11	44	143	445	1,184	1,784	2,048	3,222
Money market instruments	8 630	80	307	227	265	29	24	156	176
Monetary authorities	8 631	....	....	....	....	....	....	....	....
General government	8 632	....	....	....	....	....	....	....	....
Banks	8 633	5	230	139	....	19	4	....	29
Other sectors	8 634	75	77	88	265	10	21	156	147
Financial derivatives	8 900	....	....	....	**59**	**234**	**294**	**815**	**623**
Monetary authorities	8 901	....	....	....	....	....	....	....	....
General government	8 902	....	....	....	....	....	....	....	....
Banks	8 903	....	....	....	59	233	280	790	585
Other sectors	8 904	....	....	....	....	1	14	25	38
Other investment	8 703	**5,006**	**4,769**	**4,313**	**4,886**	**5,179**	**5,535**	**7,699**	**8,697**
Trade credits	8 706	1,140	1,189	1,404	1,856	2,163	2,348	3,314	3,800
General government	8 707	....	....	....	....	....	....	....	....
of which: Short-term	8 709	....	....	....	....	....	....	....	....
Other sectors	8 710	1,140	1,189	1,404	1,856	2,163	2,348	3,314	3,800
of which: Short-term	8 712	*1,113*	*1,161*	*1,377*	*1,830*	*2,130*	*2,336*	*3,300*	*3,782*
Loans	8 714	1,871	1,720	1,433	1,902	2,196	2,207	2,626	2,734
Monetary authorities	8 715	....	....	....	....	....	....	....	....
of which: Short-term	8 718	....	....	....	....	....	....	....	....
General government	8 719	1,484	1,465	1,101	1,250	1,398	1,208	1,429	452
of which: Short-term	8 721	....	....	....	....	....	....	....	....
Banks	8 722	196	146	186	424	631	722	1,014	2,045
of which: Short-term	8 724	*108*	*67*	*97*	*245*	*359*	*231*	*544*	*1,270*
Other sectors	8 725	191	109	146	229	168	276	183	237
of which: Short-term	8 727	*1*	*7*	*24*	*46*	*92*	*63*	*110*	*183*
Currency and deposits	8 730	1,849	1,680	1,019	728	733	913	1,743	2,140
Monetary authorities	8 731	....	....	....	....	....	....	....	....
General government	8 732	....	....	....	....	....	....	....	....
Banks	8 733	1,845	1,677	1,017	717	685	760	1,445	1,937
Other sectors	8 734	4	3	1	11	48	153	298	203
Other assets	8 736	145	180	457	400	87	67	15	24
Monetary authorities	8 737	....	....	....	....	....	....	....	....
of which: Short-term	8 739	....	....	....	....	....	....	....	....
General government	8 740	....	....	....	....	....	....	....	....
of which: Short-term	8 742	....	....	....	....	....	....	....	....
Banks	8 743	145	180	457	400	87	67	15	24
of which: Short-term	8 745	*145*	*180*	*432*	*315*	*23*	*47*	*12*	*22*
Other sectors	8 746	....	....	....	....	....	....	....	....
of which: Short-term	8 748	....	....	....	....	....	....	....	....
Reserve assets	8 802	**4,384**	**4,461**	**9,196**	**12,149**	**14,913**	**15,480**	**13,364**	**18,976**
Monetary gold	8 812	188	146	387	471	494	579	717	944
Special drawing rights	8 811	....	1	1	1	1	1	1	2
Reserve position in the Fund	8 810	....	....	....	....	....	....	....	5
Foreign exchange	8 803	4,195	4,314	8,808	11,677	14,418	14,899	12,645	18,026
Other claims	8 813	....	....	....	....	....	....	....	....

Table 3 (Concluded). INTERNATIONAL INVESTMENT POSITION (End-period stocks), 2000–2007

(Millions of U.S. dollars)

	Code	2000	2001	2002	2003	2004	2005	2006	2007
LIABILITIES	8 995 D.	**14,368**	**16,105**	**20,907**	**32,122**	**43,110**	**47,735**	**64,890**	**75,947**
Direct investment in Slovak Republic	8 555	**4,504**	**5,731**	**8,924**	**15,776**	**21,876**	**23,656**	**38,335**	**40,702**
Equity capital and reinvested earnings	8 556	3,562	4,836	7,974	14,540	20,035	20,988	33,771	34,197
Claims on direct investors	8 557	....	....	....	....	....	....	....	....
Liabilities to direct investors	8 558	3,562	4,836	7,974	14,540	20,035	20,988	33,771	34,197
Other capital	8 580	942	894	950	1,236	1,841	2,667	4,563	6,505
Claims on direct investors	8 585	−235	−526	−963	−1,897	−2,027	−2,425	−2,847	−4,284
Liabilities to direct investors	8 590	1,177	1,421	1,913	3,133	3,869	5,093	7,410	10,789
Portfolio investment	8 652	**2,830**	**2,878**	**3,323**	**4,172**	**6,742**	**5,787**	**8,722**	**9,844**
Equity securities	8 660	260	401	509	493	460	538	664	684
Banks	8 663	....	....	....	82	102	93	138	31
Other sectors	8 664	260	401	509	411	359	445	526	653
Debt securities	8 669	2,570	2,477	2,814	3,679	6,282	5,249	8,058	9,161
Bonds and notes	8 670	2,555	2,457	2,803	3,676	6,091	5,242	7,878	8,673
Monetary authorities	8 671	....	....	....	....	....	....	....	....
General government	8 672	2,100	2,153	2,361	3,120	5,472	4,656	6,865	7,717
Banks	8 673	....	4	2	8	1	44	351	690
Other sectors	8 674	456	300	440	548	618	543	662	266
Money market instruments	8 680	15	20	11	3	190	6	179	488
Monetary authorities	8 681	....	....	....	....	....	....	....	....
General government	8 682	....	....	....	....	....	4	....	....
Banks	8 683	....	....	....	....	....	....	172	486
Other sectors	8 684	15	20	11	3	190	2	7	2
Financial derivatives	8 905	**....**	**3**	**17**	**108**	**309**	**330**	**672**	**541**
Monetary authorities	8 906	....	....	....	....	....	....	....	....
General government	8 907	....	....	....	....	....	....	....	....
Banks	8 908	....	....	....	97	292	302	652	540
Other sectors	8 909	....	3	17	11	17	28	20	1
Other investment	8 753	**7,034**	**7,493**	**8,644**	**12,066**	**14,183**	**17,962**	**17,161**	**24,859**
Trade credits	8 756	1,600	1,537	2,004	2,545	2,849	3,070	4,557	4,829
General government	8 757	....	....	....	....	....	....	....	....
of which: Short-term	8 759	....	....	....	....	....	....	....	....
Other sectors	8 760	1,600	1,537	2,004	2,545	2,849	3,070	4,557	4,829
of which: Short-term	8 762	*1,515*	*1,466*	*1,917*	*2,474*	*2,774*	*3,026*	*4,513*	*4,799*
Loans	8 764	4,831	5,366	5,243	6,580	6,345	5,700	6,692	7,548
Monetary authorities	8 765	324	266	435	1,146	199	277	421	218
of which: Use of Fund credit and loans from the Fund	8 766	....	....	....	....	....	....	....	....
of which: Short-term	8 768	....	....	....	*901*	....	....	....	....
General government	8 769	788	1,059	944	1,051	1,466	1,125	1,143	1,418
of which: Short-term	8 771	....	....	....	....	....	....	....	....
Banks	8 772	85	286	136	216	886	990	1,376	940
of which: Short-term	8 774	*10*	*217*	*61*	*104*	*658*	*706*	*1,130*	*245*
Other sectors	8 775	3,635	3,754	3,728	4,166	3,793	3,308	3,752	4,972
of which: Short-term	8 777	*97*	*199*	*267*	*390*	*336*	*442*	*449*	*525*
Currency and deposits	8 780	338	543	965	1,567	4,045	7,641	5,759	12,327
Monetary authorities	8 781	....	....	....	....	....	....	67	7
General government	8 782	....	....	....	....	....	....	3	28
Banks	8 783	338	543	965	1,567	4,045	7,641	5,688	12,292
Other sectors	8 784	....	....	....	....	....	....	....	....
Other liabilities	8 786	265	47	432	1,374	944	1,552	154	155
Monetary authorities	8 787	....	....	....	....	....	....	....	....
of which: Short-term	8 789	....	....	....	....	....	....	....	....
General government	8 790	....	....	....	....	....	....	....	....
of which: Short-term	8 792	....	....	....	....	....	....	....	....
Banks	8 793	265	47	432	1,374	944	1,552	154	155
of which: Short-term	8 795	*54*	*30*	*432*	*1,328*	*894*	*1,406*	*99*	*150*
Other sectors	8 796	....	....	....	....	....	....	....	....
of which: Short-term	8 798	....	....	....	....	....	....	....	....
NET INTERNATIONAL INVESTMENT POSITION	8 995	**−4,279**	**−5,511**	**−6,169**	**−12,410**	**−18,960**	**−22,575**	**−37,792**	**−40,042**
Conversion rates: Slovak koruny per U.S. dollar (end of period)	0 102	47.389	48.467	40.036	32.920	28.496	31.948	26.246	22.870

Table 1. ANALYTIC PRESENTATION, 2000–2007

(Millions of U.S. dollars)

	Code	2000	2001	2002	2003	2004	2005	2006	2007
A. Current Account[1]..............................	4 993 Z.	**−548**	**31**	**244**	**−216**	**−893**	**−681**	**−1,088**	**−2,293**
Goods: exports f.o.b..............................	2 100 ..	8,808	9,343	10,471	12,916	16,065	18,146	21,397	27,123
Goods: imports f.o.b..............................	3 100 ..	−9,947	−9,962	−10,719	−13,539	−17,322	−19,404	−22,856	−29,432
Balance on Goods..............................	4 100 ..	*−1,139*	*−620*	*−248*	*−622*	*−1,258*	*−1,258*	*−1,458*	*−2,310*
Services: credit..............................	2 200 ..	1,888	1,961	2,316	2,791	3,455	3,976	4,344	5,650
Services: debit..............................	3 200 ..	−1,438	−1,458	−1,732	−2,183	−2,603	−2,915	−3,254	−4,231
Balance on Goods and Services..............................	4 991 ..	*−689*	*−117*	*336*	*−14*	*−406*	*−198*	*−368*	*−891*
Income: credit..............................	2 300 ..	434	463	468	589	667	781	1,135	1,400
Income: debit..............................	3 300 ..	−408	−444	−617	−821	−1,060	−1,143	−1,642	−2,400
Balance on Goods, Services, and Income..............................	4 992 ..	*−663*	*−98*	*187*	*−246*	*−799*	*−560*	*−874*	*−1,890*
Current transfers: credit..............................	2 379 Z.	341	390	473	538	698	878	988	1,251
Current transfers: debit..............................	3 379 ..	−225	−261	−416	−508	−792	−998	−1,202	−1,654
B. Capital Account[1]..............................	4 994 Z.	**3**	**−3**	**−159**	**−191**	**−123**	**−138**	**−169**	**−72**
Capital account: credit..............................	2 994 Z.	7	4	72	93	191	212	262	443
Capital account: debit..............................	3 994 ..	−3	−7	−230	−284	−314	−350	−432	−515
Total, Groups A Plus B..............................	4 981 ..	*−544*	*28*	*85*	*−406*	*−1,015*	*−818*	*−1,258*	*−2,365*
C. Financial Account[1]..............................	4 995 W.	**680**	**1,204**	**1,987**	**567**	**702**	**844**	**−129**	**2,707**
Direct investment abroad..............................	4 505 ..	−65	−133	−151	−476	−550	−629	−905	−1,574
Direct investment in Slovenia..............................	4 555 Z.	136	503	1,660	302	831	540	649	1,483
Portfolio investment assets..............................	4 602 ..	−59	−108	−94	−220	−809	−2,100	−2,677	−4,493
Equity securities..............................	4 610 ..	−15	−23	−73	−101	−271	−1,022	−929	−1,252
Debt securities..............................	4 619 ..	−44	−84	−21	−119	−539	−1,078	−1,749	−3,241
Portfolio investment liabilities..............................	4 652 Z.	246	189	27	−37	37	102	849	1,379
Equity securities..............................	4 660 ..	25	−2	11	16	−13	98	197	275
Debt securities..............................	4 669 Z.	221	191	16	−53	50	4	652	1,104
Financial derivatives..............................	4 910 ..	....	....	....	....	7	−13	−16	−31
Financial derivatives assets..............................	4 900 ..	....	....	....	....	7	−13	−16	−31
Financial derivatives liabilities..............................	4 905 ..	....	....	....	....	....	....	....	....
Other investment assets..............................	4 703 ..	−519	206	−505	−796	−1,608	−1,899	−2,428	−6,271
Monetary authorities..............................	4 701 ..	−6	−6	−5	....	−11	−2	−1	−1,171
General government..............................	4 704 ..	−1	−1	−1	−1	−13	−11	−13	−24
Banks..............................	4 705 ..	−254	−303	154	17	−323	−939	−576	−3,475
Other sectors..............................	4 728 ..	−259	516	−653	−812	−1,261	−947	−1,839	−1,601
Other investment liabilities..............................	4 753 W.	941	546	1,051	1,794	2,793	4,842	4,399	12,215
Monetary authorities..............................	4 753 WA	....	....	....	....	123	7	9	4,649
General government..............................	4 753 ZB	80	−28	−90	−76	9	−35	−145	−54
Banks..............................	4 753 ZC	291	231	482	1,205	1,517	4,218	3,032	6,297
Other sectors..............................	4 753 ZD	571	343	658	665	1,145	652	1,503	1,322
Total, Groups A Through C..............................	4 983 ..	*136*	*1,232*	*2,072*	*160*	*−313*	*25*	*−1,387*	*342*
D. Net Errors and Omissions..............................	4 998 ..	**42**	**53**	**−255**	**150**	**17**	**181**	**−270**	**−541**
Total, Groups A Through D..............................	4 984 ..	*178*	*1,285*	*1,817*	*310*	*−296*	*206*	*−1,656*	*−199*
E. Reserves and Related Items..............................	4 802 A.	**−178**	**−1,285**	**−1,817**	**−310**	**296**	**−206**	**1,656**	**199**
Reserve assets..............................	4 802 ..	−178	−1,285	−1,817	−310	296	−206	1,656	199
Use of Fund credit and loans..............................	4 766 ..	....	....	....	....	....	....	....	....
Exceptional financing..............................	4 920 ..	....	....	....	....	....	....	....	....
Conversion rates: tolars per U.S. dollar..............................	0 101 ..	**222.66**	**242.75**	**240.25**	**207.11**	**192.38**	**192.71**	**191.03**	**....**
Conversion rates: euros per U.S. dollar..............................	0 103 ..	**1.0854**	**1.1175**	**1.0626**	**.8860**	**.8054**	**.8041**	**.7971**	**.7306**

[1] Excludes components that have been classified in the categories of Group E.

Table 2. STANDARD PRESENTATION, 2000–2007

(Millions of U.S. dollars)

	Code	2000	2001	2002	2003	2004	2005	2006	2007
CURRENT ACCOUNT	4 993	−548	31	244	−216	−893	−681	−1,088	−2,293
A. GOODS	4 100	−1,139	−620	−248	−622	−1,258	−1,258	−1,458	−2,310
Credit	2 100	8,808	9,343	10,471	12,916	16,065	18,146	21,397	27,123
General merchandise: exports f.o.b.	2 110	8,758	9,284	10,414	12,845	16,004	18,073	21,302	26,999
Goods for processing: exports f.o.b.	2 150	47	56	48	66	58	71	85	120
Repairs on goods	2 160	....	....	....	....	....	....	....	....
Goods procured in ports by carriers	2 170	2	2	1	....	....	....	10	3
Nonmonetary gold	2 180	1	1	8	5	2	1	1	1
Debit	3 100	−9,947	−9,962	−10,719	−13,539	−17,322	−19,404	−22,856	−29,432
General merchandise: imports f.o.b.	3 110	−9,885	−9,884	−10,646	−13,445	−17,249	−19,319	−22,747	−29,262
Goods for processing: imports f.o.b.	3 150	−50	−66	−63	−87	−67	−81	−103	−154
Repairs on goods	3 160	....	....	....	....	....	....	....	....
Goods procured in ports by carriers	3 170	....	....	....	....	....	....	....	....
Nonmonetary gold	3 180	−12	−12	−10	−7	−7	−4	−5	−17
B. SERVICES	4 200	450	503	584	608	852	1,061	1,091	1,419
Total credit	2 200	*1,888*	*1,961*	*2,316*	*2,791*	*3,455*	*3,976*	*4,344*	*5,650*
Total debit	3 200	*−1,438*	*−1,458*	*−1,732*	*−2,183*	*−2,603*	*−2,915*	*−3,254*	*−4,231*
Transportation services, credit	2 205	493	500	602	771	1,006	1,145	1,330	1,727
Passenger	2 850	*55*	*58*	*66*	*85*	*101*	*99*	*114*	*182*
Freight	2 851	*282*	*297*	*381*	*500*	*672*	*796*	*926*	*1,179*
Other	2 852	*156*	*145*	*156*	*186*	*234*	*250*	*290*	*366*
Sea transport, passenger	2 207	1	....	....	1	1	1	1	4
Sea transport, freight	2 208	23	22	28	33	65	98	90	141
Sea transport, other	2 209	37	37	39	47	74	93	111	153
Air transport, passenger	2 211	49	53	59	77	92	90	103	163
Air transport, freight	2 212	6	6	7	7	9	10	10	10
Air transport, other	2 213	2	6	5	3	3	6	21	28
Other transport, passenger	2 215	6	5	6	7	8	9	10	14
Other transport, freight	2 216	253	269	346	460	598	689	826	1,029
Other transport, other	2 217	117	103	111	137	157	151	158	185
Transportation services, debit	3 205	−354	−319	−366	−476	−603	−650	−757	−1,005
Passenger	3 850	*−33*	*−32*	*−39*	*−52*	*−69*	*−69*	*−84*	*−116*
Freight	3 851	*−219*	*−192*	*−207*	*−274*	*−326*	*−342*	*−396*	*−499*
Other	3 852	*−102*	*−95*	*−120*	*−150*	*−208*	*−239*	*−277*	*−390*
Sea transport, passenger	3 207	−1	−1	−2	−2	−2	−2	−3	−10
Sea transport, freight	3 208	−30	−33	−36	−47	−69	−90	−116	−205
Sea transport, other	3 209	−8	−6	−7	−6	−15	−18	−20	−30
Air transport, passenger	3 211	−29	−27	−33	−46	−61	−61	−73	−97
Air transport, freight	3 212	−7	−7	−9	−12	−16	−13	−20	−15
Air transport, other	3 213	−3	−2	−4	−7	−9	−11	−19	−36
Other transport, passenger	3 215	−3	−3	−4	−5	−6	−6	−8	−9
Other transport, freight	3 216	−182	−152	−162	−214	−241	−239	−260	−279
Other transport, other	3 217	−92	−86	−109	−137	−184	−210	−237	−324
Travel, credit	2 236	961	1,001	1,086	1,342	1,624	1,795	1,797	2,218
Business travel	2 237	....	....	....	....	....	....	79	99
Personal travel	2 240	961	1,001	1,086	1,342	1,624	1,795	1,718	2,119
Travel, debit	3 236	−511	−528	−608	−753	−868	−950	−974	−1,103
Business travel	3 237	−60	−65	−85	−106	−118	−111	−222	−249
Personal travel	3 240	−452	−463	−523	−647	−750	−838	−752	−854
Other services, credit	2 200 BA	434	460	628	678	824	1,036	1,218	1,704
Communications	2 245	25	34	57	70	90	113	116	145
Construction	2 249	66	70	91	81	90	133	130	211
Insurance	2 253	7	8	8	8	10	14	18	23
Financial	2 260	8	11	48	19	18	22	35	58
Computer and information	2 262	54	64	80	88	98	112	123	149
Royalties and licence fees	2 266	12	14	8	11	12	16	17	18
Other business services	2 268	244	239	318	375	471	591	734	1,056
Personal, cultural, and recreational	2 287	14	16	15	21	30	28	38	38
Government, n.i.e.	2 291	5	3	5	5	6	6	7	7
Other services, debit	3 200 BA	−573	−612	−759	−954	−1,132	−1,316	−1,522	−2,123
Communications	3 245	−51	−60	−84	−107	−120	−136	−135	−177
Construction	3 249	−52	−46	−58	−82	−62	−80	−87	−224
Insurance	3 253	−9	−10	−13	−18	−17	−19	−26	−28
Financial	3 260	−26	−25	−29	−33	−39	−44	−54	−81
Computer and information	3 262	−57	−58	−81	−101	−120	−125	−144	−186
Royalties and licence fees	3 266	−50	−60	−78	−90	−123	−113	−154	−169
Other business services	3 268	−278	−300	−361	−453	−569	−711	−816	−1,113
Personal, cultural, and recreational	3 287	−36	−37	−38	−50	−59	−61	−77	−100
Government, n.i.e.	3 291	−15	−16	−17	−20	−24	−26	−31	−44

Table 2 (Continued). STANDARD PRESENTATION, 2000–2007

(Millions of U.S. dollars)

	Code	2000	2001	2002	2003	2004	2005	2006	2007
C. INCOME..	4 300 ..	**26**	**19**	**−149**	**−232**	**−393**	**−363**	**−506**	**−1,000**
Total credit..	2 300 ..	*434*	*463*	*468*	*589*	*667*	*781*	*1,135*	*1,400*
Total debit...	3 300 ..	*−408*	*−444*	*−617*	*−821*	*−1,060*	*−1,143*	*−1,642*	*−2,400*
Compensation of employees, credit..............	2 310 ..	**188**	**182**	**196**	**217**	**249**	**254**	**274**	**277**
Compensation of employees, debit.................	3 310 ..	**−27**	**−27**	**−45**	**−65**	**−78**	**−90**	**−127**	**−203**
Investment income, credit............................	2 320 ..	**246**	**281**	**272**	**372**	**419**	**526**	**861**	**1,123**
Direct investment income............................	2 330 ..	23	4	−4	24	32	82	257	211
Dividends and distributed branch profits........	2 332 ..	7	9	9	17	18	35	95	152
Reinvested earnings and undistributed branch profits.....	2 333 ..	16	−5	−13	7	14	47	162	−15
Income on debt (interest)............................	2 334 ..	....	....	....	....	....	....	....	73
Portfolio investment income..........................	2 339 ..	119	151	142	232	284	319	379	512
Income on equity......................................	2 340 ..	....	....	....	....	5	17	36	48
Income on bonds and notes........................	2 350 ..	81	104	141	231	279	301	342	454
Income on money market instruments............	2 360 ..	38	47	2	1	....	1	1	9
Other investment income..............................	2 370 ..	105	126	134	117	102	125	226	400
Investment income, debit.............................	3 320 ..	**−381**	**−417**	**−572**	**−756**	**−982**	**−1,054**	**−1,515**	**−2,196**
Direct investment income............................	3 330 ..	−90	−21	−190	−300	−474	−458	−710	−832
Dividends and distributed branch profits........	3 332 ..	−41	−47	−64	−79	−131	−165	−466	−585
Reinvested earnings and undistributed branch profits.....	3 333 ..	−48	26	−126	−221	−343	−293	−244	−71
Income on debt (interest)............................	3 334 ..	....	....	....	....	....	....	....	−177
Portfolio investment income..........................	3 339 ..	−94	−136	−115	−143	−154	−159	−152	−208
Income on equity......................................	3 340 ..	....	....	....	....	−1	−24	−6	−10
Income on bonds and notes........................	3 350 ..	−93	−133	−113	−138	−139	−129	−146	−198
Income on money market instruments............	3 360 ..	−1	−3	−2	−4	−14	−6	....	....
Other investment income..............................	3 370 ..	−198	−260	−268	−314	−355	−437	−653	−1,156
D. CURRENT TRANSFERS.................................	4 379 ..	**116**	**129**	**57**	**30**	**−94**	**−120**	**−214**	**−402**
Credit..	2 379 ..	**341**	**390**	**473**	**538**	**698**	**878**	**988**	**1,251**
General government....................................	2 380 ..	41	55	86	103	262	393	517	531
Other sectors..	2 390 ..	300	335	387	435	437	485	471	721
Workers' remittances................................	2 391 ..	14	17	17	13	12	7	6	5
Other current transfers.............................	2 392 ..	286	318	370	421	425	478	465	716
Debit...	3 379 ..	**−225**	**−261**	**−416**	**−508**	**−792**	**−998**	**−1,202**	**−1,654**
General government....................................	3 380 ..	−102	−122	−139	−153	−372	−534	−647	−830
Other sectors..	3 390 ..	−124	−139	−277	−355	−420	−464	−555	−824
Workers' remittances................................	3 391 ..	....	....	....	....	−1	−1	−1	−1
Other current transfers.............................	3 392 ..	−124	−139	−277	−355	−419	−463	−554	−823
CAPITAL AND FINANCIAL ACCOUNT.....................	4 996 ..	**505**	**−84**	**11**	**66**	**876**	**499**	**1,358**	**2,834**
CAPITAL ACCOUNT...	4 994 ..	**3**	**−3**	**−159**	**−191**	**−123**	**−138**	**−169**	**−72**
Total credit..	2 994 ..	*7*	*4*	*72*	*93*	*191*	*212*	*262*	*443*
Total debit...	3 994 ..	*−3*	*−7*	*−230*	*−284*	*−314*	*−350*	*−432*	*−515*
Capital transfers, credit...............................	2 400 ..	**3**	**2**	**71**	**93**	**190**	**209**	**258**	**439**
General government....................................	2 401 ..	....	....	....	....	24	36	59	180
Debt forgiveness.....................................	2 402 ..	....	....	....	....	....	....	....	....
Other capital transfers.............................	2 410 ..	....	....	....	....	24	36	59	180
Other sectors..	2 430 ..	3	2	71	93	165	174	199	259
Migrants' transfers..................................	2 431 ..	3	2	4	8	5	3	3	2
Debt forgiveness.....................................	2 432 ..	....	....	67	85	161	170	196	257
Other capital transfers.............................	2 440 ..	....	....	....	....	....	....	....	....
Capital transfers, debit................................	3 400 ..	**−3**	**−2**	**−228**	**−281**	**−313**	**−341**	**−421**	**−509**
General government....................................	3 401 ..	....	....	....	....	....	....	....	−1
Debt forgiveness.....................................	3 402 ..	....	....	....	....	....	....	....	....
Other capital transfers.............................	3 410 ..	....	....	....	....	....	....	....	−1
Other sectors..	3 430 ..	−2	−2	−228	−281	−313	−341	−421	−508
Migrants' transfers..................................	3 431 ..	−2	−2	−1	−1	−2	−4	−1	−2
Debt forgiveness.....................................	3 432 ..	....	....	−227	−280	−311	−338	−419	−506
Other capital transfers.............................	3 440 ..	....	....	....	....	....	....	....	....
Nonproduced nonfinancial assets, credit...........	2 480 ..	**4**	**1**	**1**	**....**	**1**	**2**	**4**	**4**
Nonproduced nonfinancial assets, debit...........	3 480 ..	**−1**	**−5**	**−2**	**−2**	**−1**	**−8**	**−11**	**−6**

Table 2 (Continued). STANDARD PRESENTATION, 2000–2007

(Millions of U.S. dollars)

	Code	2000	2001	2002	2003	2004	2005	2006	2007
FINANCIAL ACCOUNT	4 995	**502**	**−81**	**170**	**256**	**998**	**637**	**1,527**	**2,906**
A. DIRECT INVESTMENT	4 500	**71**	**371**	**1,508**	**−174**	**282**	**−89**	**−256**	**−92**
Direct investment abroad	4 505	**−65**	**−133**	**−151**	**−476**	**−550**	**−629**	**−905**	**−1,574**
Equity capital	4 510	−50	−92	−68	−279	−476	−561	−531	−866
Claims on affiliated enterprises	4 515	....	....	....	....	....	....	....	....
Liabilities to affiliated enterprises	4 520	....	....	....	....	....	....	....	....
Reinvested earnings	4 525	−16	5	13	−7	−14	−47	−162	15
Other capital	4 530	....	−46	−97	−191	−60	−21	−212	−724
Claims on affiliated enterprises	4 535	....	−34	−136	−229	9	−58	−245	−856
Liabilities to affiliated enterprises	4 540	....	−11	39	39	−69	37	33	132
Direct investment in Slovenia	4 555	**136**	**503**	**1,660**	**302**	**831**	**540**	**649**	**1,483**
Equity capital	4 560	87	355	1,463	−11	401	321	317	607
Claims on direct investors	4 565	....	....	....	....	....	....	....	....
Liabilities to direct investors	4 570	....	....	....	....	....	....	....	....
Reinvested earnings	4 575	48	−26	126	221	343	293	244	71
Other capital	4 580	....	175	70	92	87	−73	88	804
Claims on direct investors	4 585	....	−9	−151	−196	−1	−393	−7	−230
Liabilities to direct investors	4 590	....	183	221	287	88	320	96	1,034
B. PORTFOLIO INVESTMENT	4 600	**188**	**81**	**−68**	**−257**	**−772**	**−1,998**	**−1,829**	**−3,114**
Assets	4 602	**−59**	**−108**	**−94**	**−220**	**−809**	**−2,100**	**−2,677**	**−4,493**
Equity securities	4 610	−15	−23	−73	−101	−271	−1,022	−929	−1,252
Monetary authorities	4 611	....	....	....	....	....	....	....	....
General government	4 612	....	....	....	....	....	−26	−13	−64
Banks	4 613	−4	−19	−32	−1	−22	−244	−13	−24
Other sectors	4 614	−11	−5	−41	−101	−249	−753	−902	−1,164
Debt securities	4 619	−44	−84	−21	−119	−539	−1,078	−1,749	−3,241
Bonds and notes	4 620	−44	−87	−21	−96	−530	−1,070	−1,571	−1,245
Monetary authorities	4 621	....	....	....	....	....	....	....	1,488
General government	4 622	....	....	....	....	−1	−17	−43	−126
Banks	4 623	−39	−77	21	−56	−216	−760	−1,123	−1,854
Other sectors	4 624	−5	−10	−42	−40	−314	−292	−405	−752
Money market instruments	4 630	....	3	....	−23	−9	−8	−177	−1,996
Monetary authorities	4 631	....	....	....	....	....	....	....	−901
General government	4 632	....	....	....	....	....	....	−1	−2
Banks	4 633	....	....	....	2	−5	−3	−171	−1,071
Other sectors	4 634	....	3	....	−25	−4	−6	−6	−21
Liabilities	4 652	**246**	**189**	**27**	**−37**	**37**	**102**	**849**	**1,379**
Equity securities	4 660	25	−2	11	16	−13	98	197	275
Banks	4 663	....	....	....	....	2	2	−1	77
Other sectors	4 664	25	−2	11	16	−15	96	198	197
Debt securities	4 669	221	191	16	−53	50	4	652	1,104
Bonds and notes	4 670	221	178	−23	−53	19	−63	536	1,104
Monetary authorities	4 671	....	....	....	....	....	....	....	....
General government	4 672	358	165	−15	58	−207	−202	541	1,092
Banks	4 673	−65	−5	−16	−82	249	135	−6	26
Other sectors	4 674	−72	18	8	−29	−24	4	1	−14
Money market instruments	4 680	....	13	39	....	31	67	116	....
Monetary authorities	4 681	....	....	....	....	....	....	....	....
General government	4 682	....	....	24	−21	31	67	116	....
Banks	4 683	....	....	5	16	....	....	....	....
Other sectors	4 684	....	13	10	4	....	....	....	....
C. FINANCIAL DERIVATIVES	4 910	....	....	....	....	**7**	**−13**	**−16**	**−31**
Monetary authorities	4 911	....	....	....	....	....	....	....	....
General government	4 912	....	....	....	....	....	....	....	....
Banks	4 913	....	....	....	....	....	....	....	....
Other sectors	4 914	....	....	....	....	7	−13	−16	−31
Assets	4 900	....	....	....	....	**7**	**−13**	**−16**	**−31**
Monetary authorities	4 901	....	....	....	....	....	....	....	....
General government	4 902	....	....	....	....	....	....	....	....
Banks	4 903	....	....	....	....	....	....	....	....
Other sectors	4 904	....	....	....	....	7	−13	−16	−31
Liabilities	4 905	....	....	....	....	....	....	....	....
Monetary authorities	4 906	....	....	....	....	....	....	....	....
General government	4 907	....	....	....	....	....	....	....	....
Banks	4 908	....	....	....	....	....	....	....	....
Other sectors	4 909	....	....	....	....	....	....	....	....

Table 2 (Concluded). STANDARD PRESENTATION, 2000–2007

(Millions of U.S. dollars)

	Code	2000	2001	2002	2003	2004	2005	2006	2007
D. OTHER INVESTMENT	4 700	**422**	**752**	**546**	**998**	**1,186**	**2,943**	**1,971**	**5,943**
Assets	4 703	**−519**	**206**	**−505**	**−796**	**−1,608**	**−1,899**	**−2,428**	**−6,271**
Trade credits	4 706	−163	−198	−98	−102	−272	−266	−528	−550
General government	4 707	....	....	....	....	....	1	....	....
of which: Short-term	4 709	....	....	....	....	....	*1*	....	....
Other sectors	4 710	−163	−198	−98	−102	−272	−267	−528	−550
of which: Short-term	4 712	*−164*	*−234*	*−117*	*−113*	*−275*	*−265*	*−523*	*−545*
Loans	4 714	−65	11	−163	−260	−347	−503	−924	−2,494
Monetary authorities	4 715	....	....	....	....	....	....	....	....
of which: Short-term	4 718	....	....	....	....	....	....	....	....
General government	4 719	....	....	....	....	....	....	....	....
of which: Short-term	4 721	....	....	....	....	....	....	....	....
Banks	4 722	11	−6	−88	−151	−257	−362	−598	−2,357
of which: Short-term	4 724	*17*	*2*	*−17*	*−37*	*−31*	*−85*	*−121*	*−885*
Other sectors	4 725	−76	17	−76	−109	−90	−141	−325	−137
of which: Short-term	4 727	*−11*	*−5*	*−16*	*−28*	*−45*	*−79*	*−122*	*−82*
Currency and deposits	4 730	−261	423	−177	−356	−902	−1,026	−949	−3,240
Monetary authorities	4 731	....	....	....	....	....	....	....	−1,112
General government	4 732	....	....	....	....	....	....	....	....
Banks	4 733	−241	−276	301	241	−2	−486	39	−1,200
Other sectors	4 734	−20	700	−478	−597	−900	−540	−988	−928
Other assets	4 736	−30	−29	−66	−78	−87	−104	−27	12
Monetary authorities	4 737	−6	−6	−5	....	−11	−2	−1	−59
of which: Short-term	4 739	*−6*	*−6*	*−5*	....	*−11*	*−2*	*−1*	*−11*
General government	4 740	−1	−1	−1	−1	−13	−12	−13	−24
of which: Short-term	4 742	....	....	....	....	....	....	....	....
Banks	4 743	−24	−21	−59	−74	−64	−91	−16	82
of which: Short-term	4 745	*−23*	*−16*	*−29*	*−57*	*−35*	....	*−16*	*81*
Other sectors	4 746	....	−2	−1	−4	1	1	2	13
of which: Short-term	4 748	....	*−2*	*−1*	....	*4*	*1*	*1*	*13*
Liabilities	4 753	**941**	**546**	**1,051**	**1,794**	**2,793**	**4,842**	**4,399**	**12,215**
Trade credits	4 756	−19	−5	78	62	258	292	599	705
General government	4 757	....	....	1	1	4	−2	....	−10
of which: Short-term	4 759	....	....	*1*	*1*	*4*	*−2*	....	*−10*
Other sectors	4 760	−19	−5	77	61	254	293	600	715
of which: Short-term	4 762	....	....	*93*	*68*	*267*	*308*	*605*	*713*
Loans	4 764	944	416	815	1,275	2,077	3,246	2,594	5,225
Monetary authorities	4 765	....	....	....	....	....	....	....	....
of which: Use of Fund credit and loans from the Fund	4 766	....	....	....	....	....	....	....	....
of which: Short-term	4 768	....	....	....	....	....	....	....	....
General government	4 769	79	−28	−91	−77	4	−34	−144	−55
of which: Short-term	4 771	....	−7	....	....	....	....	....	....
Banks	4 772	272	91	325	754	1,184	2,904	1,810	4,673
of which: Short-term	4 774	*−5*	*−1*	*9*	*−6*	*49*	*5*	*−421*	*1,845*
Other sectors	4 775	592	354	581	598	889	376	928	607
of which: Short-term	4 777	*−22*	*−8*	*−13*	*83*	*−68*	*92*	*−1*	*24*
Currency and deposits	4 780	30	136	118	490	421	1,277	1,242	6,328
Monetary authorities	4 781	....	....	....	....	123	7	9	4,649
General government	4 782	....	....	....	....	....	....	....	....
Banks	4 783	30	136	118	490	297	1,269	1,233	1,679
Other sectors	4 784	....	....	....	....	....	....	....	....
Other liabilities	4 786	−13	−2	39	−33	38	28	−36	−43
Monetary authorities	4 787	....	....	....	....	....	....	....	....
of which: Short-term	4 789	....	....	....	....	....	....	....	....
General government	4 790	1	1	....	....	....	1	−1	12
of which: Short-term	4 792	....	....	....	....	....	....	....	....
Banks	4 793	−11	4	39	−40	36	45	−12	−54
of which: Short-term	4 795	*−11*	*4*	*39*	*−40*	*36*	*45*	*−12*	*−54*
Other sectors	4 796	−2	−6	1	7	2	−18	−24	....
of which: Short-term	4 798	....	....	....	....	....	....	....	....
E. RESERVE ASSETS	4 802	**−178**	**−1,285**	**−1,817**	**−310**	**296**	**−206**	**1,656**	**199**
Monetary gold	4 812	....	....	....	....	....	42	....	38
Special drawing rights	4 811	−2	−1	−1	−1	−1	−1	....	....
Reserve position in the Fund	4 810	20	−1	−31	−12	30	60	17	13
Foreign exchange	4 803	−196	−1,282	−1,784	−297	268	−307	1,639	148
Other claims	4 813	....	....	....	....	....	....	....	....
NET ERRORS AND OMISSIONS	4 998	**42**	**53**	**−255**	**150**	**17**	**181**	**−270**	**−541**

Table 3. INTERNATIONAL INVESTMENT POSITION (End-period stocks), 2000–2007

(Millions of U.S. dollars)

	Code	2000	2001	2002	2003	2004	2005	2006	2007
ASSETS	8 995 C.	**8,300**	**10,824**	**15,078**	**19,353**	**23,573**	**26,380**	**33,086**	**51,143**
Direct investment abroad	8 505	**768**	**989**	**1,505**	**2,350**	**3,025**	**3,290**	**4,547**	**7,197**
Equity capital and reinvested earnings	8 506	464	615	956	1,502	2,067	2,759	3,499	4,850
Claims on affiliated enterprises	8 507	464	615	956	1,502	2,067	2,759	3,499	4,850
Liabilities to affiliated enterprises	8 508	....	....	....	....	....	....	....	....
Other capital	8 530	304	374	549	848	959	531	1,048	2,347
Claims on affiliated enterprises	8 535	468	488	719	1,080	1,137	1,042	1,299	2,688
Liabilities to affiliated enterprises	8 540	−164	−115	−170	−232	−179	−511	−252	−341
Portfolio investment	8 602	**175**	**255**	**330**	**689**	**1,730**	**3,253**	**6,759**	**18,636**
Equity securities	8 610	37	26	42	235	642	1,466	2,974	5,560
Monetary authorities	8 611	....	....	....	....	....	....	....	....
General government	8 612	....	....	....	....	....	102	141	217
Banks	8 613	5	4	4	24	50	62	125	324
Other sectors	8 614	32	21	38	211	592	1,301	2,709	5,019
Debt securities	8 619	139	230	288	454	1,088	1,788	3,785	13,076
Bonds and notes	8 620	139	230	288	454	1,076	1,781	3,599	10,558
Monetary authorities	8 621	....	....	....	....	....	....	....	3,721
General government	8 622	....	....	....	2	3	71	120	267
Banks	8 623	131	199	178	244	503	1,071	2,373	4,590
Other sectors	8 624	8	31	110	209	571	639	1,106	1,981
Money market instruments	8 630	....	....	....	....	11	7	186	2,518
Monetary authorities	8 631	....	....	....	....	....	....	....	1,008
General government	8 632	....	....	....	....	....	2	1	5
Banks	8 633	....	....	....	....	7	2	176	1,463
Other sectors	8 634	....	....	....	....	4	4	10	43
Financial derivatives	8 900	....	....	....	....	**2**	**17**	**35**	**79**
Monetary authorities	8 901	....	....	....	....	....	....	....	....
General government	8 902	....	....	....	....	....	....	....	....
Banks	8 903	....	....	....	....	....	....	....	....
Other sectors	8 904	....	....	....	....	2	17	35	78
Other investment	8 703	**4,161**	**5,183**	**6,180**	**7,715**	**9,916**	**11,686**	**14,609**	**24,166**
Trade credits	8 706	2,037	1,701	1,988	2,402	2,886	3,388	4,309	5,480
General government	8 707	....	....	....	....	....	....	....	....
of which: Short-term	8 709	....	....	....	....	....	....	....	....
Other sectors	8 710	2,037	1,701	1,988	2,402	2,886	3,388	4,309	5,480
of which: Short-term	8 712	*1,844*	*1,658*	*1,962*	*2,383*	*2,868*	*3,369*	*4,276*	*5,423*
Loans	8 714	179	150	352	656	1,023	1,422	2,502	5,063
Monetary authorities	8 715	....	....	....	....	....	....	....	....
of which: Short-term	8 718	....	....	....	....	....	....	....	....
General government	8 719	....	....	....	....	....	....	....	....
of which: Short-term	8 721	....	....	....	....	....	....	....	....
Banks	8 722	100	97	208	375	666	989	1,713	4,459
of which: Short-term	8 724	*26*	*12*	*33*	*77*	*104*	*234*	*385*	*1,364*
Other sectors	8 725	79	53	144	281	357	433	789	604
of which: Short-term	8 727	*8*	*3*	*19*	*52*	*69*	*93*	*192*	*344*
Currency and deposits	8 730	1,626	2,041	2,359	2,898	3,892	5,232	6,785	12,589
Monetary authorities	8 731	....	....	....	....	....	....	....	2,382
General government	8 732	....	3	3	3	4	6	4	44
Banks	8 733	1,156	1,379	1,216	1,148	1,232	1,777	1,904	3,286
Other sectors	8 734	470	660	1,141	1,746	2,656	3,449	4,878	6,877
Other assets	8 736	319	1,292	1,481	1,759	2,116	1,644	1,013	1,034
Monetary authorities	8 737	58	76	85	87	230	227	231	302
of which: Short-term	8 739	*58*	*64*	*70*	*70*	*71*	*71*	*73*	*62*
General government	8 740	....	780	908	1,059	1,160	1,019	226	288
of which: Short-term	8 742	....	....	....	....	....	....	....	....
Banks	8 743	261	286	335	444	488	188	225	158
of which: Short-term	8 745	*261*	*286*	*319*	*423*	*463*	*134*	*166*	*93*
Other sectors	8 746	....	150	154	170	238	209	331	286
of which: Short-term	8 748	....	*150*	*154*	*165*	*230*	*202*	*328*	*280*
Reserve assets	8 802	**3,196**	**4,397**	**7,063**	**8,598**	**8,899**	**8,134**	**7,136**	**1,066**
Monetary gold	8 812	....	67	83	101	106	83	103	86
Special drawing rights	8 811	4	5	7	9	11	12	12	13
Reserve position in the Fund	8 810	82	81	121	145	120	52	37	25
Foreign exchange	8 803	3,110	4,244	6,853	8,343	8,662	7,987	6,984	942
Other claims	8 813	....	....	....	....	....	....	....	....

Table 3 (Concluded). INTERNATIONAL INVESTMENT POSITION (End-period stocks), 2000–2007

(Millions of U.S. dollars)

	Code	2000	2001	2002	2003	2004	2005	2006	2007
LIABILITIES..............................	8 995 D.	**10,668**	**11,220**	**15,232**	**21,684**	**27,208**	**30,109**	**40,074**	**61,404**
Direct investment in Slovenia..........................	8 555 ..	**2,893**	**2,594**	**4,112**	**6,308**	**7,590**	**7,236**	**8,985**	**14,048**
Equity capital and reinvested earnings..........................	8 556 ..	1,969	2,196	3,610	5,548	6,630	6,615	8,275	9,662
Claims on direct investors.................	8 557 ..	....	....	....	....	....	....	....	....
Liabilities to direct investors............	8 558 ..	1,969	2,196	3,610	5,548	6,630	6,615	8,275	9,662
Other capital..................................	8 580 ..	924	398	502	760	960	621	710	4,386
Claims on direct investors.................	8 585 ..	−133	−197	−338	−458	−402	−537	−512	−1,137
Liabilities to direct investors............	8 590 ..	1,057	595	839	1,218	1,362	1,157	1,222	5,523
Portfolio investment..........................	8 652 ..	**1,793**	**1,892**	**2,200**	**2,922**	**3,156**	**2,829**	**4,132**	**6,760**
Equity securities..........................	8 660 ..	168	172	111	295	287	362	866	2,062
Banks..........................	8 663 ..	25	10	34	38	47	54	70	282
Other sectors..........................	8 664 ..	143	162	78	257	240	308	796	1,780
Debt securities..........................	8 669 ..	1,626	1,720	2,089	2,627	2,869	2,467	3,266	4,698
Bonds and notes..........................	8 670 ..	1,626	1,707	2,030	2,587	2,851	2,442	3,235	4,698
Monetary authorities.................	8 671 ..	....	....	....	....	....	....	....	....
General government..........................	8 672 ..	1,570	1,684	1,987	2,510	2,537	2,029	2,776	4,169
Banks..........................	8 673 ..	19	....	20	42	301	397	437	519
Other sectors..........................	8 674 ..	37	23	23	35	13	16	22	9
Money market instruments..........................	8 680 ..	....	13	59	39	18	25	31	....
Monetary authorities..........................	8 681 ..	....	....	....	....	....	....	....	....
General government..........................	8 682 ..	....	3	59	39	18	25	31	....
Banks..........................	8 683 ..	....	....	....	....	....	....	....	....
Other sectors..........................	8 684 ..	....	10	....	....	....	....	....	....
Financial derivatives..........................	8 905 ..	....	....	....	....	....	....	....	....
Monetary authorities..........................	8 906 ..	....	....	....	....	....	....	....	....
General government..........................	8 907 ..	....	....	....	....	....	....	....	....
Banks..........................	8 908 ..	....	....	....	....	....	....	....	....
Other sectors..........................	8 909 ..	....	....	....	....	....	....	....	....
Other investment..........................	8 753 ..	**5,982**	**6,734**	**8,920**	**12,453**	**16,462**	**20,044**	**26,957**	**40,596**
Trade credits..........................	8 756 ..	1,787	1,544	1,802	2,117	2,556	3,368	4,395	5,671
General government..........................	8 757 ..	....	....	....	....	....	....	....	....
of which: Short-term..........................	8 759 ..	....	....	....	....	....	....	....	....
Other sectors..........................	8 760 ..	1,787	1,544	1,802	2,117	2,556	3,368	4,395	5,671
of which: Short-term..........................	8 762 ..	*1,706*	*1,491*	*1,763*	*2,079*	*2,533*	*3,360*	*4,392*	*5,658*
Loans..........................	8 764 ..	3,749	4,555	6,179	8,766	11,835	13,699	17,881	22,991
Monetary authorities..........................	8 765 ..	....	....	....	....	....	....	....	....
of which: Use of Fund credit and loans from the Fund....	8 766 ..	....	....	....	....	....	....	....	....
of which: Short-term..........................	8 768 ..	....	....	....	....	....	....	....	....
General government..........................	8 769 ..	753	514	487	478	518	428	318	299
of which: Short-term..........................	8 771 ..	....	....	....	....	....	....	....	....
Banks..........................	8 772 ..	858	1,173	1,701	2,855	4,428	6,995	9,686	16,745
of which: Short-term..........................	8 774 ..	*2*	*1*	*12*	*8*	*67*	*633*	*269*	*2,222*
Other sectors..........................	8 775 ..	2,138	2,868	3,991	5,433	6,888	6,275	7,877	5,946
of which: Short-term..........................	8 777 ..	*42*	*24*	*13*	*101*	*32*	*119*	*90*	*243*
Currency and deposits..........................	8 780 ..	373	492	724	1,367	1,799	2,775	4,387	11,832
Monetary authorities..........................	8 781 ..	....	....	35	38	49	46	59	5,281
General government..........................	8 782 ..	....	....	....	....	....	....	....	....
Banks..........................	8 783 ..	373	492	690	1,329	1,751	2,728	4,328	6,551
Other sectors..........................	8 784 ..	....	....	....	....	....	....	....	....
Other liabilities..........................	8 786 ..	73	144	214	204	273	202	294	102
Monetary authorities..........................	8 787 ..	....	....	....	....	....	....	....	....
of which: Short-term..........................	8 789 ..	....	....	....	....	....	....	....	....
General government..........................	8 790 ..	....	10	10	11	11	11	12	....
of which: Short-term..........................	8 792 ..	....	*10*	*10*	*11*	*11*	*11*	*12*	....
Banks..........................	8 793 ..	67	72	115	80	123	76	61	57
of which: Short-term..........................	8 795 ..	....	*7*	*48*	*11*	*45*	*76*	*61*	*57*
Other sectors..........................	8 796 ..	6	62	89	113	139	115	222	45
of which: Short-term..........................	8 798 ..	....	*57*	*85*	*110*	*125*	*107*	*219*	*31*
NET INTERNATIONAL INVESTMENT POSITION........	8 995 ..	**−2,368**	**−396**	**−154**	**−2,331**	**−3,636**	**−3,729**	**−6,987**	**−10,261**
Conversion rates: tolars per U.S. dollar (end of period)................	0 102 ..	227.38	250.95	221.07	189.37	176.24	202.43	181.93	....
Conversion rates: euros per U.S. dollar (end of period)................	0 104 ..	1.0747	1.1347	.9536	.7918	.7342	.8477	.7593	.6793

Table 1. ANALYTIC PRESENTATION, 2000–2007

(Millions of U.S. dollars)

	Code	2000	2001	2002	2003	2004	2005	2006	2007
A. Current Account[1]	4 993 Z.	**−40.97**	**−64.84**	**−67.58**	**−39.92**	**−18.92**	**−90.20**	**−97.35**	....
Goods: exports f.o.b.	2 100 ..	69.29	40.04	33.47	66.63	85.64	104.76	121.60	....
Goods: imports f.o.b.	3 100 ..	−92.34	−85.34	−69.13	−93.85	−121.41	−185.09	−216.85	....
Balance on Goods	4 100 ..	*−23.05*	*−45.30*	*−35.66*	*−27.22*	*−35.77*	*−80.33*	*−95.25*	....
Services: credit	2 200 ..	52.23	51.61	15.96	25.26	30.80	41.42	59.62	....
Services: debit	3 200 ..	−72.59	−81.20	−48.60	−62.01	−41.30	−57.98	−95.16	....
Balance on Goods and Services	4 991 ..	*−43.41*	*−74.89*	*−68.30*	*−63.97*	*−46.27*	*−96.89*	*−130.79*	....
Income: credit	2 300 ..	7.25	7.11	2.72	3.53	10.51	8.69	18.80	....
Income: debit	3 300 ..	−11.46	−7.01	−10.22	−6.96	−8.32	−7.07	−12.94	....
Balance on Goods, Services, and Income	4 992 ..	*−47.61*	*−74.78*	*−75.81*	*−67.40*	*−44.07*	*−95.27*	*−124.93*	....
Current transfers: credit	2 379 Z.	35.25	30.88	28.53	46.36	50.01	41.06	69.32	....
Current transfers: debit	3 379 ..	−28.61	−20.94	−20.30	−18.88	−24.85	−35.99	−41.73	....
B. Capital Account[1]	4 994 Z.	**7.98**	**4.37**	**7.55**	**12.41**	**1.50**	**27.63**	**29.41**	....
Capital account: credit	2 994 Z.	7.98	4.49	8.99	12.71	1.62	19.68	29.77	....
Capital account: debit	3 994 ..	....	−.12	−1.44	−.30	−.12	7.95	−.36	....
Total, Groups A Plus B	4 981 ..	*−32.99*	*−60.47*	*−60.03*	*−27.51*	*−17.43*	*−62.57*	*−67.94*	....
C. Financial Account[1]	4 995 W.	**40.40**	**14.70**	**−4.24**	**−29.27**	**−19.12**	**−9.37**	**−31.54**	....
Direct investment abroad	4 505 ..	−.06	−.73	−1.12	−.03	−.01	−1.58	.37	....
Direct investment in Solomon Islands	4 555 Z.	13.03	−9.31	−.45	−1.80	6.02	18.58	18.62	....
Portfolio investment assets	4 602 ..	....	.02	....	....	....	....	....	....
Equity securities	4 610 ..	....	....	....	....	....	....	....	....
Debt securities	4 619 ..	....	.02	....	....	....	....	....	....
Portfolio investment liabilities	4 652 Z.	....	−.10	....	....	....	....	....	....
Equity securities	4 660 ..	....	....	....	....	....	....	....	....
Debt securities	4 669 Z.	....	−.10	....	....	....	....	....	....
Financial derivatives	4 910 ..	....	....	....	....	....	....	....	....
Financial derivatives assets	4 900 ..	....	....	....	....	....	....	....	....
Financial derivatives liabilities	4 905 ..	....	....	....	....	....	....	....	....
Other investment assets	4 703 ..	.98	1.89	−4.93	....	....	−11.73	−17.59	....
Monetary authorities	4 701 ..	....	....	....	....	....	....	....	....
General government	4 704 ..	....	....	....	....	....	....	−11.33	....
Banks	4 705 ..	....	....	−4.93	....	....	....	−4.46	....
Other sectors	4 728 ..	.98	1.89	....	....	....	−11.73	−1.81	....
Other investment liabilities	4 753 W.	26.45	22.92	2.26	−27.44	−25.12	−14.63	−32.94	....
Monetary authorities	4 753 WA	....	....	....	....	....	....	....	....
General government	4 753 ZB	14.05	9.13	2.73	−4.48	−2.25	−8.60	−7.30	....
Banks	4 753 ZC	−3.62	....	....	....	....	....	....	....
Other sectors	4 753 ZD	16.02	13.79	−.47	−22.96	−22.87	−6.03	−25.64	....
Total, Groups A Through C	4 983 ..	*7.41*	*−45.78*	*−64.27*	*−56.78*	*−36.54*	*−71.94*	*−99.48*	....
D. Net Errors and Omissions	4 998 ..	**4.75**	**48.77**	**55.26**	**35.19**	**−6.41**	**53.51**	**74.06**	....
Total, Groups A Through D	4 984 ..	*12.16*	*3.00*	*−9.01*	*−21.58*	*−42.95*	*−18.43*	*−25.42*	....
E. Reserves and Related Items	4 802 A.	**−12.16**	**−3.00**	**9.01**	**21.58**	**42.95**	**18.43**	**25.42**	....
Reserve assets	4 802 ..	−19.80	−8.87	4.48	18.43	41.40	17.49	14.33	....
Use of Fund credit and loans	4 766 ..	....	....	....	....	....	....	....	....
Exceptional financing	4 920 ..	7.64	5.87	4.52	3.15	1.55	.94	11.10	....
Conversion rates: Solomon Islands dollars per U.S. dollar	0 101 ..	**5.0889**	**5.2780**	**6.7488**	**7.5059**	**7.4847**	**7.5299**	**7.6095**	**7.6520**

[1] Excludes components that have been classified in the categories of Group E.

Table 2. STANDARD PRESENTATION, 2000–2007

(Millions of U.S. dollars)

	Code	2000	2001	2002	2003	2004	2005	2006	2007
CURRENT ACCOUNT..	4 993 ..	**−40.97**	**−64.84**	**−67.58**	**−39.92**	**−18.92**	**−90.20**	**−97.35**	....
A. GOODS..	4 100 ..	**−23.05**	**−45.30**	**−35.66**	**−27.22**	**−35.77**	**−80.33**	**−95.25**	....
Credit..	2 100 ..	**69.29**	**40.04**	**33.47**	**66.63**	**85.64**	**104.76**	**121.60**	....
General merchandise: exports f.o.b...................	2 110 ..	69.29	40.04	33.47	66.63	85.64	104.76	121.60	....
Goods for processing: exports f.o.b.................	2 150 ..	....	....	....	....	....	....	....	....
Repairs on goods..	2 160 ..	....	....	....	....	....	....	....	....
Goods procured in ports by carriers................	2 170 ..	....	....	....	....	....	....	....	....
Nonmonetary gold...	2 180 ..	....	....	....	....	....	....	....	....
Debit..	3 100 ..	**−92.34**	**−85.34**	**−69.13**	**−93.85**	**−121.41**	**−185.09**	**−216.85**	....
General merchandise: imports f.o.b..................	3 110 ..	−92.34	−85.34	−69.13	−93.85	−121.41	−185.09	−216.85	....
Goods for processing: imports f.o.b.................	3 150 ..	....	....	....	....	....	....	....	....
Repairs on goods..	3 160 ..	....	....	....	....	....	....	....	....
Goods procured in ports by carriers................	3 170 ..	....	....	....	....	....	....	....	....
Nonmonetary gold...	3 180 ..	....	....	....	....	....	....	....	....
B. SERVICES..	4 200 ..	**−20.36**	**−29.59**	**−32.64**	**−36.75**	**−10.50**	**−16.56**	**−35.54**	....
Total credit...	2 200 ..	*52.23*	*51.61*	*15.96*	*25.26*	*30.80*	*41.42*	*59.62*	....
Total debit..	3 200 ..	*−72.59*	*−81.20*	*−48.60*	*−62.01*	*−41.30*	*−57.98*	*−95.16*	....
Transportation services, credit.......................	2 205 ..	**1.14**	**4.41**	**1.04**	**2.01**	**1.11**	**7.97**	**13.89**	....
Passenger...	2 850 ..	*.06*	*3.64*	*.12*	*.13*	*.02*	*4.77*	*6.25*	....
Freight..	2 851 ..	*.67*	*.25*	*.31*	*.42*	*.26*	*.73*	*1.31*	....
Other..	2 852 ..	*.41*	*.53*	*.60*	*1.46*	*.84*	*2.47*	*6.34*	....
Sea transport, passenger.................................	2 207 ..	.02	.02	.02	.10	....	.01	.05	....
Sea transport, freight......................................	2 208 ..	.20	.15	.31	.42	.24	.20	.02	....
Sea transport, other..	2 209 ..	.28	.44	.60	1.44	.80	1.68	6.14	....
Air transport, passenger..................................	2 211 ..	.04	3.62	.11	.03	.02	4.76	6.21	....
Air transport, freight..	2 212 ..	.47	.09			.02	.53	1.28	....
Air transport, other..	2 213 ..	.14	.09		.01	.04	.79	.20	....
Other transport, passenger..............................	2 215 ..	....	....						....
Other transport, freight....................................	2 216 ..	....	....						....
Other transport, other......................................	2 217 ..	....	....	....					....
Transportation services, debit.........................	3 205 ..	**−35.55**	**−34.66**	**−20.95**	**−25.56**	**−18.73**	**−30.66**	**−43.06**	....
Passenger...	3 850 ..	*−2.63*	*−3.87*	*−2.70*	*−1.97*	*−3.25*	*−6.46*	*−6.97*	....
Freight..	3 851 ..	*−24.54*	*−29.55*	*−17.41*	*−23.35*	*−14.91*	*−23.18*	*−31.70*	....
Other..	3 852 ..	*−8.37*	*−1.25*	*−.85*	*−.23*	*−.56*	*−1.02*	*−4.39*	....
Sea transport, passenger.................................	3 207 ..	....	−.02	....	....	....	−.21	....	....
Sea transport, freight......................................	3 208 ..	−24.11	−23.26	−16.18	−23.18	−14.40	−22.40	−30.54	....
Sea transport, other..	3 209 ..	....	−.30	−.53	−.01	−.04	−.34	−.41	....
Air transport, passenger..................................	3 211 ..	−2.63	−3.85	−2.70	−1.97	−3.25	−6.25	−6.97	....
Air transport, freight..	3 212 ..	−.43	−6.29	−1.23	−.17	−.52	−.78	−1.16	....
Air transport, other..	3 213 ..	−8.37	−.95	−.31	−.22	−.52	−.67	−3.98	....
Other transport, passenger..............................	3 215 ..	....	....	....	....	....	....	....	....
Other transport, freight....................................	3 216 ..	....	....	....	....	....	....	....	....
Other transport, other......................................	3 217 ..	....	....	....	....	....	....	....	....
Travel, credit...	2 236 ..	**3.85**	**5.21**	**.72**	**1.54**	**3.52**	**1.55**	**1.60**	....
Business travel..	2 237 ..	3.09	.32	.32	.82	2.23	.27	.54	....
Personal travel..	2 240 ..	.77	4.89	.39	.72	1.28	1.28	1.06	....
Travel, debit..	3 236 ..	**−9.63**	**−6.57**	**−5.82**	**−4.45**	**−8.97**	**−4.73**	**−7.68**	....
Business travel..	3 237 ..	−3.38	−2.50	−2.88	−1.62	−2.54	−1.52	−1.92	....
Personal travel..	3 240 ..	−6.25	−4.07	−2.95	−2.83	−6.43	−3.21	−5.76	....
Other services, credit....................................	2 200 BA	**47.24**	**41.99**	**14.20**	**21.71**	**26.17**	**31.90**	**44.13**	....
Communications..	2 245 ..	1.79	2.08	.12	.05	.15	1.43	.61	....
Construction..	2 249 ..	.20	.28	.02	.05	.18	1.02	.64	....
Insurance..	2 253 ..	....	.04	.04	.10	.11	.04	.01	....
Financial...	2 260 ..	21.73	17.68	2.75	.91	1.21	.68	4.42	....
Computer and information................................	2 262 ..	.04	.02	.02	.02	.13	.09	.44	....
Royalties and licence fees................................	2 266 ..	.24	.06	.08	.11	.29		.03	....
Other business services...................................	2 268 ..	15.23	16.46	10.61	18.13	18.94	22.31	27.48	....
Personal, cultural, and recreational..................	2 287 ..	.63	.27	.09	.64	.73	1.43	1.55	....
Government, n.i.e..	2 291 ..	7.39	5.10	.47	1.69	4.44	4.90	8.95	....
Other services, debit.....................................	3 200 BA	**−27.41**	**−39.96**	**−21.83**	**−32.00**	**−13.60**	**−22.59**	**−44.43**	....
Communications..	3 245 ..	−2.71	−4.95	−1.80	−2.23	−2.33	−1.89	−1.68	....
Construction..	3 249 ..	−.06	−.06	−1.91	....	.01	....	−.01	....
Insurance..	3 253 ..	−.88	−11.31	−1.37	−1.20	−1.83	−1.13	−.67	....
Financial...	3 260 ..	−2.75	−4.76	−3.27	−.82	−2.36	−1.91	−2.96	....
Computer and information................................	3 262 ..	−.83	−1.50	−.84	−.81	−2.45	−1.48	−2.43	....
Royalties and licence fees................................	3 266 ..	−.20	−.06	....	−.01	−.01	−.24	−.52	....
Other business services...................................	3 268 ..	−17.37	−15.78	−12.56	−26.82	−5.82	−14.40	−24.00	....
Personal, cultural, and recreational..................	3 287 ..	−.14	−.19	−.01	−.03	.03	−.11	−.08	....
Government, n.i.e..	3 291 ..	−2.48	−1.36	−.06	−.08	1.15	−1.42	−12.07	....

Table 2 (Continued). STANDARD PRESENTATION, 2000–2007

(Millions of U.S. dollars)

	Code	2000	2001	2002	2003	2004	2005	2006	2007
C. INCOME	4 300 ..	**−4.21**	**.11**	**−7.50**	**−3.43**	**2.20**	**1.62**	**5.86**	....
Total credit	2 300 ..	*7.25*	*7.11*	*2.72*	*3.53*	*10.51*	*8.69*	*18.80*	....
Total debit	3 300 ..	*−11.46*	*−7.01*	*−10.22*	*−6.96*	*−8.32*	*−7.07*	*−12.94*	....
Compensation of employees, credit	2 310 ..	**4.32**	**4.53**	**2.23**	**2.79**	**6.54**	**4.46**	**9.20**	....
Compensation of employees, debit	3 310 ..	**−3.14**	**−1.73**	**−1.13**	**−1.48**	**−1.52**	**−1.74**	**−1.77**	....
Investment income, credit	2 320 ..	**2.93**	**2.59**	**.49**	**.74**	**3.97**	**4.23**	**9.59**	....
Direct investment income	2 330 ..	2.93	.76	....	.05	....	.12	5.14	....
Dividends and distributec branch profits	2 332 ..	.08	.02	....	....	....	....	2.37	....
Reinvested earnings and undistributed branch profits	2 333 ..	....	.38	....	.02	....	.12	2.64	....
Income on debt (interest)	2 334 ..	2.85	.36	....	.03	....	....	.13	....
Portfolio investment income	2 339 ..	....	....	....	....	....	....	.04	....
Income on equity	2 340 ..	....	....	....	....	....	....	.04	....
Income on bonds and notes	2 350 ..	....	....	....	....	....	....	....	....
Income on money market instruments	2 360 ..	....	....	....	....	....	....	....	....
Other investment income	2 370 ..	....	1.82	.49	.69	3.97	4.11	4.42	....
Investment income, debit	3 320 ..	**−8.31**	**−5.28**	**−9.09**	**−5.48**	**−6.80**	**−5.33**	**−11.17**	....
Direct investment income	3 330 ..	−8.31	−2.80	−6.99	−5.48	−6.80	−5.33	−11.02	....
Dividends and distributed branch profits	3 332 ..	−3.03	−1.38	−2.60	−1.87	−3.89	−4.22	−5.02	....
Reinvested earnings and undistributed branch profits	3 333 ..	−.02	....	−1.41	....	−1.75	....	−3.84	....
Income on debt (interest)	3 334 ..	−5.27	−1.41	−2.98	−3.61	−1.16	−1.12	−2.16	....
Portfolio investment income	3 339 ..	....	....	....	....	....	....	−.15	....
Income on equity	3 340 ..	....	....	....	....	....	....	−.15	....
Income on bonds and notes	3 350 ..	....	....	....	....	....	....	....	....
Income on money market instruments	3 360 ..	....	....	....	....	....	....	....	....
Other investment income	3 370 ..	....	−2.48	−2.10	....	....	....	....	....
D. CURRENT TRANSFERS	4 379 ..	**6.64**	**9.94**	**8.23**	**27.48**	**25.15**	**5.07**	**27.59**	....
Credit	2 379 ..	**35.25**	**30.88**	**28.53**	**46.36**	**50.01**	**41.06**	**69.32**	....
General government	2 380 ..	23.09	10.03	16.11	32.15	26.31	13.07	25.78	....
Other sectors	2 390 ..	12.16	20.85	12.42	14.21	23.70	27.99	43.54	....
Workers' remittances	2 391 ..	....	....	.99	1.09	2.15	2.70	9.55	....
Other current transfers	2 392 ..	12.16	20.85	11.42	13.12	21.55	25.29	33.99	....
Debit	3 379 ..	**−28.61**	**−20.94**	**−20.30**	**−18.88**	**−24.85**	**−35.99**	**−41.73**	....
General government	3 380 ..	−.39	−.78	−3.24	−4.58	−1.84	−4.08	−6.14	....
Other sectors	3 390 ..	−28.22	−20.16	−17.06	−14.31	−23.01	−31.91	−35.59	....
Workers' remittances	3 391 ..	−3.32	−.53	−.25	−.10	−.29	−.37	−.80	....
Other current transfers	3 392 ..	−24.90	−19.63	−16.80	−14.21	−22.72	−31.54	−34.79	....
CAPITAL AND FINANCIAL ACCOUNT	4 996 ..	**36.22**	**16.06**	**12.32**	**4.73**	**25.33**	**36.69**	**23.29**	....
CAPITAL ACCOUNT	4 994 ..	**7.98**	**4.37**	**7.55**	**12.41**	**1.50**	**27.63**	**29.41**	....
Total credit	2 994 ..	*7.98*	*4.49*	*8.99*	*12.71*	*1.62*	*19.68*	*29.77*	....
Total debit	3 994 ..	....	*−.12*	*−1.44*	*−.30*	*−.12*	*7.95*	*−.36*	....
Capital transfers, credit	2 400 ..	**7.98**	**4.47**	**8.99**	**12.71**	**1.62**	**19.68**	**29.77**	....
General government	2 401 ..	7.25	4.47	8.47	12.71	1.54	19.68	28.08	....
Debt forgiveness	2 402 ..	....	....	....	....	....	....	....	....
Other capital transfers	2 410 ..	7.25	4.47	8.47	12.71	1.54	19.68	28.08	....
Other sectors	2 430 ..	.73	....	.52	....	.07	....	1.68	....
Migrants' transfers	2 431 ..	....	....	.52	....	....	....	1.68	....
Debt forgiveness	2 432 ..	....	....	....	....	....	....	....	....
Other capital transfers	2 440 ..	.73	....	....	....	.07	....	....	....
Capital transfers, debit	3 400 ..	....	**−.12**	**−1.44**	**−.12**	**−.12**	**7.95**	**−.36**	....
General government	3 401 ..	....	....	−.59	....	....	8.05	....	....
Debt forgiveness	3 402 ..	....	....	....	....	....	8.05	....	....
Other capital transfers	3 410 ..	....	....	−.59	....	....	....	....	....
Other sectors	3 430 ..	....	−.12	−.85	−.12	−.12	−.10	−.36	....
Migrants' transfers	3 431 ..	....	−.12	−.21	−.12	−.12	−.10	−.23	....
Debt forgiveness	3 432 ..	....	....	....	....	....	....	....	....
Other capital transfers	3 440 ..	....	....	−.64	....	....	....	−.13	....
Nonproduced nonfinancial assets, credit	2 480 ..	....	**.02**	....	....	....	....	....	....
Nonproduced nonfinancial assets, debit	3 480 ..	....	....	....	**−.18**	....	....	....	....

Table 2 (Continued). STANDARD PRESENTATION, 2000–2007

(Millions of U.S. dollars)

	Code	2000	2001	2002	2003	2004	2005	2006	2007
FINANCIAL ACCOUNT	4 995	28.25	11.70	4.77	−7.69	23.84	9.06	−6.12	....
A. DIRECT INVESTMENT	4 500	12.97	−10.04	−1.57	−1.83	5.67	17.00	18.99	....
Direct investment abroad	4 505	−.06	−.73	−1.12	−.03	−.01	−1.58	.37	....
Equity capital	4 510	−.02	−.70	−1.12	−.03	−.01	−1.53	.37	....
Claims on affiliated enterprises	4 515	....	−.10	−.90	....	....	.06	.87	....
Liabilities to affiliated enterprises	4 520	−.02	−.60	−.22	−.03	−.01	−1.59	−.49	....
Reinvested earnings	4 525	....	−.38	....	−.02	....	−.12	−2.64	....
Other capital	4 530	−.04	.35	....	.02	....	.07	2.64	....
Claims on affiliated enterprises	4 535	....	....	....	....	....	....	.04	....
Liabilities to affiliated enterprises	4 540	−.04	.35	....	.02	....	.07	2.60	....
Direct investment in Solomon Islands	4 555	13.03	−9.31	−.45	−1.80	5.68	18.58	18.62	....
Equity capital	4 560	2.04	−.41	.96	−.71	8.35	18.40	25.34	....
Claims on direct investors	4 565	....	−.95	−.82	−.80	8.67	16.51	18.08	....
Liabilities to direct investors	4 570	2.04	.54	1.78	.09	−.32	1.88	7.26	....
Reinvested earnings	4 575	.02	....	1.41	....	1.75	....	3.84	....
Other capital	4 580	10.96	−8.90	−2.82	−1.10	−4.42	.18	−10.56	....
Claims on direct investors	4 585	10.96	....	....	....	....	....	....	....
Liabilities to direct investors	4 590	....	−8.90	−2.82	−1.10	−4.42	.18	−10.56	....
B. PORTFOLIO INVESTMENT	4 600	....	−.08	....	....	....	....	....	....
Assets	4 602	....	.02	....	....	....	....	....	....
Equity securities	4 610	....	....	....	....	....	....	....	....
Monetary authorities	4 611	....	....	....	....	....	....	....	....
General government	4 612	....	....	....	....	....	....	....	....
Banks	4 613	....	....	....	....	....	....	....	....
Other sectors	4 614	....	....	....	....	....	....	....	....
Debt securities	4 619	....	.02	....	....	....	....	....	....
Bonds and notes	4 620	....	....	....	....	....	....	....	....
Monetary authorities	4 621	....	....	....	....	....	....	....	....
General government	4 622	....	....	....	....	....	....	....	....
Banks	4 623	....	....	....	....	....	....	....	....
Other sectors	4 624	....	....	....	....	....	....	....	....
Money market instruments	4 630	....	.02	....	....	....	....	....	....
Monetary authorities	4 631	....	....	....	....	....	....	....	....
General government	4 632	....	....	....	....	....	....	....	....
Banks	4 633	....	....	....	....	....	....	....	....
Other sectors	4 634	....	.02	....	....	....	....	....	....
Liabilities	4 652	....	−.10	....	....	....	....	....	....
Equity securities	4 660	....	....	....	....	....	....	....	....
Banks	4 663	....	....	....	....	....	....	....	....
Other sectors	4 664	....	....	....	....	....	....	....	....
Debt securities	4 669	....	−.10	....	....	....	....	....	....
Bonds and notes	4 670	....	−.10	....	....	....	....	....	....
Monetary authorities	4 671	....	....	....	....	....	....	....	....
General government	4 672	....	....	....	....	....	....	....	....
Banks	4 673	....	....	....	....	....	....	....	....
Other sectors	4 674	....	−.10	....	....	....	....	....	....
Money market instruments	4 680	....	....	....	....	....	....	....	....
Monetary authorities	4 681	....	....	....	....	....	....	....	....
General government	4 682	....	....	....	....	....	....	....	....
Banks	4 683	....	....	....	....	....	....	....	....
Other sectors	4 684	....	....	....	....	....	....	....	....
C. FINANCIAL DERIVATIVES	4 910	....	....	....	....	....	....	....	....
Monetary authorities	4 911	....	....	....	....	....	....	....	....
General government	4 912	....	....	....	....	....	....	....	....
Banks	4 913	....	....	....	....	....	....	....	....
Other sectors	4 914	....	....	....	....	....	....	....	....
Assets	4 900	....	....	....	....	....	....	....	....
Monetary authorities	4 901	....	....	....	....	....	....	....	....
General government	4 902	....	....	....	....	....	....	....	....
Banks	4 903	....	....	....	....	....	....	....	....
Other sectors	4 904	....	....	....	....	....	....	....	....
Liabilities	4 905	....	....	....	....	....	....	....	....
Monetary authorities	4 906	....	....	....	....	....	....	....	....
General government	4 907	....	....	....	....	....	....	....	....
Banks	4 908	....	....	....	....	....	....	....	....
Other sectors	4 909	....	....	....	....	....	....	....	....

Table 2 (Concluded). STANDARD PRESENTATION, 2000–2007

(Millions of U.S. dollars)

	Code	2000	2001	2002	2003	2004	2005	2006	2007
D. OTHER INVESTMENT	4 700 ..	**35.08**	**30.69**	**1.85**	**−24.29**	**−23.23**	**−25.43**	**−39.44**	....
Assets	4 703 ..	**.98**	**1.89**	**−4.93**	....	....	**−11.73**	**−17.59**	....
Trade credits	4 706 ..	....	1.89	....	....	....	.05	1.10	....
General government	4 707 ..	....	....	....	....	....	....	....	....
of which: Short-term	4 709 ..	....	....	....	....	....	....	....	....
Other sectors	4 710 ..	....	1.89	....	....	....	.05	1.10	....
of which: Short-term	4 712 ..	....	*1.89*	....	....	....	*.05*	*1.10*	....
Loans	4 714 ..	.29	....	....	....	....	....	.13	....
Monetary authorities	4 715 ..	....	....	....	....	....	....	....	....
of which: Short-term	4 718 ..	....	....	....	....	....	....	....	....
General government	4 719 ..	....	....	....	....	....	....	....	....
of which: Short-term	4 721 ..	....	....	....	....	....	....	....	....
Banks	4 722 ..	....	....	....	....	....	....	....	....
of which: Short-term	4 724 ..	....	....	....	....	....	....	....	....
Other sectors	4 725 ..	.29	....	....	....	....	....	.13	....
of which: Short-term	4 727 ..	....	....	....	....	....	....	*.13*	....
Currency and deposits	4 730 ..	.69	....	−4.93	....	....	....	2.25	....
Monetary authorities	4 731 ..	....	....	....	....	....	....	....	....
General government	4 732 ..	....	....	....	....	....	....	....	....
Banks	4 733 ..	....	....	−4.93	....	....	....	−4.46	....
Other sectors	4 734 ..	.69	....	....	....	....	....	6.70	....
Other assets	4 736 ..	....	....	....	....	....	−11.78	−21.06	....
Monetary authorities	4 737 ..	....	....	....	....	....	....	....	....
of which: Short-term	4 739 ..	....	....	....	....	....	....	....	....
General government	4 740 ..	....	....	....	....	....	....	−11.33	....
of which: Short-term	4 742 ..	....	....	....	....	....	....	....	....
Banks	4 743 ..	....	....	....	....	....	....	....	....
of which: Short-term	4 745 ..	....	....	....	....	....	....	....	....
Other sectors	4 746 ..	....	....	....	....	....	−11.78	−9.73	....
of which: Short-term	4 748 ..	....	....	....	....	....	*−.76*	*−16.88*	....
Liabilities	4 753 ..	**34.09**	**28.79**	**6.79**	**−24.29**	**−23.23**	**−13.69**	**−21.84**	....
Trade credits	4 756 ..	18.47	2.84	−1.04	−22.21	−22.75	−.73	−19.84	....
General government	4 757 ..	....	....	....	....	....	....	....	....
of which: Short-term	4 759 ..	....	....	....	....	....	....	....	....
Other sectors	4 760 ..	18.47	2.84	−1.04	−22.21	−22.75	−.73	−19.84	....
of which: Short-term	4 762 ..	....	*.95*	*−.30*	*−22.21*	*−23.37*	*−.98*	*−20.26*	....
Loans	4 764 ..	11.59	13.82	7.25	−7.82	−1.20	−12.96	−5.03	....
Monetary authorities	4 765 ..	....	....	....	....	....	....	....	....
of which: Use of Fund credit and loans from the Fund	4 766 ..	....	....	....	....	....	....	....	....
of which: Short-term	4 768 ..	....	....	....	....	....	....	....	....
General government	4 769 ..	14.05	12.07	9.23	−1.33	−.39	−8.60	−3.77	....
of which: Short-term	4 771 ..	*19.93*	*2.94*	*6.49*	*3.15*	....	....	*3.52*	....
Banks	4 772 ..	....	....	....	....	....	....	....	....
of which: Short-term	4 774 ..	....	....	....	....	....	....	....	....
Other sectors	4 775 ..	−2.46	1.75	−1.98	−6.49	−.81	−4.35	−1.25	....
of which: Short-term	4 777 ..	*−.67*	*2.94*	*−2.18*	*−6.31*	*−.20*	*−4.55*	*−8.15*	....
Currency and deposits	4 780 ..	−3.62	....	....	....	....	....	....	....
Monetary authorities	4 781 ..	....	....	....	....	....	....	....	....
General government	4 782 ..	....	....	....	....	....	....	....	....
Banks	4 783 ..	−3.62	....	....	....	....	....	....	....
Other sectors	4 784 ..	....	....	....	....	....	....	....	....
Other liabilities	4 786 ..	7.64	12.13	.58	5.74	.72	....	3.03	....
Monetary authorities	4 787 ..	7.64	....	....	....	....	....	....	....
of which: Short-term	4 789 ..	*7.64*	....	....	....	....	....	....	....
General government	4 790 ..	....	....	....	....	....	....	....	....
of which: Short-term	4 792 ..	....	....	....	....	....	....	....	....
Banks	4 793 ..	....	....	....	....	....	....	....	....
of which: Short-term	4 795 ..	....	....	....	....	....	....	....	....
Other sectors	4 796 ..	....	12.13	.58	5.74	.72	....	3.03	....
of which: Short-term	4 798 ..	....	*9.47*	*.58*	*5.74*	*.72*	....	*3.03*	....
E. RESERVE ASSETS	4 802 ..	**−19.80**	**−8.87**	**4.48**	**18.43**	**41.40**	**17.49**	**14.33**	....
Monetary gold	4 812 ..	....	....	....	....	....	....	....	....
Special drawing rights	4 811 ..	.01	....	....	.01	....	....	−.01	....
Reserve position in the Fund	4 810 ..	....	....	−.01	....	....	....	....	....
Foreign exchange	4 803 ..	−19.59	−8.87	4.49	18.43	41.40	17.49	14.34	....
Other claims	4 813 ..	−.22	....	....	....	....	....	....	....
NET ERRORS AND OMISSIONS	4 998 ..	**4.75**	**48.77**	**55.26**	**35.19**	**−6.41**	**53.51**	**74.06**	....

Table 1.　ANALYTIC PRESENTATION, 2000–2007

(Millions of U.S. dollars)

	Code	2000	2001	2002	2003	2004	2005	2006	2007
A. Current Account[1]	4 993 Z.	**−191**	**343**	**884**	**−1,902**	**−7,003**	**−9,723**	**−16,487**	**−20,631**
Goods: exports f.o.b.	2 100 ..	31,950	31,064	31,772	38,700	48,237	55,284	63,841	76,184
Goods: imports f.o.b.	3 100 ..	−27,252	−25,809	−27,016	−35,270	−48,518	−56,279	−69,942	−81,890
Balance on Goods	4 100 ..	*4,698*	*5,255*	*4,756*	*3,431*	*−281*	*−995*	*−6,101*	*−5,705*
Services: credit	2 200 ..	5,046	4,845	4,985	8,298	9,682	11,157	12,014	13,562
Services: debit	3 200 ..	−5,823	−5,232	−5,504	−8,045	−10,328	−12,155	−14,291	−16,612
Balance on Goods and Services	4 991 ..	*3,920*	*4,868*	*4,237*	*3,684*	*−928*	*−1,993*	*−8,377*	*−8,756*
Income: credit	2 300 ..	2,511	2,480	2,179	2,857	3,259	4,640	5,944	6,550
Income: debit	3 300 ..	−5,696	−6,267	−4,975	−7,447	−7,576	−9,569	−11,238	−15,473
Balance on Goods, Services, and Income	4 992 ..	*736*	*1,081*	*1,441*	*−906*	*−5,246*	*−6,922*	*−13,671*	*−17,679*
Current transfers: credit	2 379 Z.	106	126	139	252	257	240	261	265
Current transfers: debit	3 379 ..	−1,033	−865	−695	−1,248	−2,015	−3,041	−3,078	−3,218
B. Capital Account[1]	4 994 Z.	**−52**	**−31**	**−15**	**44**	**52**	**30**	**30**	**28**
Capital account: credit	2 994 Z.	19	16	20	44	55	44	43	41
Capital account: debit	3 994 ..	−71	−47	−35	. . . .	−2	−14	−12	−13
Total, Groups A Plus B	4 981 ..	*−242*	*311*	*869*	*−1,859*	*−6,951*	*−9,692*	*−16,457*	*−20,603*
C. Financial Account[1]	4 995 W.	**73**	**−1,188**	**−707**	**−1,961**	**7,651**	**12,583**	**14,684**	**22,925**
Direct investment abroad	4 505 ..	−277	3,515	402	−553	−1,305	−909	−6,536	−3,757
Direct investment in South Africa	4 555 Z.	969	7,270	1,480	783	701	6,522	−184	5,746
Portfolio investment assets	4 602 ..	−3,672	−5,331	−875	−138	−950	−911	−2,231	−3,458
Equity securities	4 610 ..	−3,019	−4,864	−572	−49	−795	−996	−1,627	−1,827
Debt securities	4 619 ..	−652	−467	−303	−89	−156	85	−605	−1,631
Portfolio investment liabilities	4 652 Z.	1,807	−2,971	457	862	7,357	5,698	21,814	15,074
Equity securities	4 660 ..	4,169	−962	−388	685	6,661	7,230	14,959	8,670
Debt securities	4 669 Z.	−2,361	−2,009	845	176	696	−1,532	6,855	6,404
Financial derivatives	4 910 ..	−142	. . . .	. . . .	. . . .	. . . .	. . . .	. . . .	. . . .
Financial derivatives assets	4 900 ..	−144	. . . .	. . . .	. . . .	. . . .	. . . .	. . . .	. . . .
Financial derivatives liabilities	4 905 ..	2	. . . .	. . . .	. . . .	. . . .	. . . .	. . . .	. . . .
Other investment assets	4 703 ..	34	−3,921	−288	−5,212	−216	−3,503	−7,187	1,270
Monetary authorities	4 701 ..	. . . .	. . . .	. . . .	1	4	−7	. . . .	. . . .
General government	4 704 ..	. . . .	−407	−424	−376	−103	−158	−210	−59
Banks	4 705 ..	−269	−2,695	−2,455	−7,976	−2,297	−3,320	−4,990	159
Other sectors	4 728 ..	303	−819	2,591	3,139	2,180	−18	−1,988	1,170
Other investment liabilities	4 753 W.	1,354	249	−1,884	2,297	2,065	5,686	9,008	8,050
Monetary authorities	4 753 WA	−410	1,582	−1,688	169	510	527	−766	−644
General government	4 753 ZB	6	134	1,944	−277	−285	1,109	504	143
Banks	4 753 ZC	1,196	−787	−1,568	−89	1,128	2,751	4,178	5,816
Other sectors	4 753 ZD	563	−680	−572	2,494	712	1,299	5,092	2,736
Total, Groups A Through C	4 983 ..	*−169*	*−877*	*162*	*−3,820*	*701*	*2,890*	*−1,773*	*2,322*
D. Net Errors and Omissions	4 998 ..	**649**	**855**	**−485**	**3,466**	**5,623**	**2,875**	**5,484**	**3,415**
Total, Groups A Through D	4 984 ..	*480*	*−22*	*−322*	*−354*	*6,324*	*5,766*	*3,711*	*5,737*
E. Reserves and Related Items	4 802 A.	**−480**	**22**	**322**	**354**	**−6,324**	**−5,766**	**−3,711**	**−5,737**
Reserve assets	4 802 ..	−480	22	322	354	−6,324	−5,766	−3,711	−5,737
Use of Fund credit and loans	4 766 ..	. . . .	. . . .	. . . .	. . . .	. . . .	. . . .	. . . .	. . . .
Exceptional financing	4 920 ..	. . . .	. . . .	. . . .	. . . .	. . . .	. . . .	. . . .	. . . .
Conversion rates: rand per U.S. dollar	0 101 ..	**6.940**	**8.609**	**10.541**	**7.565**	**6.460**	**6.359**	**6.772**	**7.045**

[1] Excludes components that have been classified in the categories of Group E.

Table 2. STANDARD PRESENTATION, 2000–2007

(Millions of U.S. dollars)

	Code	2000	2001	2002	2003	2004	2005	2006	2007
CURRENT ACCOUNT	4 993	**−191**	**343**	**884**	**−1,902**	**−7,003**	**−9,723**	**−16,487**	**−20,631**
A. GOODS	4 100	**4,698**	**5,255**	**4,756**	**3,431**	**−281**	**−995**	**−6,101**	**−5,705**
Credit	2 100	**31,950**	**31,064**	**31,772**	**38,700**	**48,237**	**55,284**	**63,841**	**76,184**
General merchandise: exports f.o.b.	2 110	27,345	27,130	27,147	33,999	43,554	50,746	58,344	70,131
Goods for processing: exports f.o.b.	2 150	....	....	....	....	....	....	....	....
Repairs on goods	2 160	....	....	....	....	....	....	....	....
Goods procured in ports by carriers	2 170	552	548	475	439	230	292	276	376
Nonmonetary gold	2 180	4,053	3,386	4,150	4,262	4,453	4,246	5,220	5,677
Debit	3 100	**−27,252**	**−25,809**	**−27,016**	**−35,270**	**−48,518**	**−56,279**	**−69,942**	**−81,890**
General merchandise: imports f.o.b.	3 110	−27,166	−25,736	−26,966	−35,176	−48,418	−56,158	−69,824	−81,780
Goods for processing: imports f.o.b.	3 150	....	....	....	....	....	....	....	....
Repairs on goods	3 160	−27	−10	−6	−20	−24	−30	−37	−40
Goods procured in ports by carriers	3 170	−59	−63	−45	−73	−77	−91	−80	−70
Nonmonetary gold	3 180	....	....	....	....	....	....	....	....
B. SERVICES	4 200	**−777**	**−387**	**−519**	**254**	**−646**	**−998**	**−2,276**	**−3,051**
Total credit	2 200	*5,046*	*4,845*	*4,985*	*8,298*	*9,682*	*11,157*	*12,014*	*13,562*
Total debit	3 200	*−5,823*	*−5,232*	*−5,504*	*−8,045*	*−10,328*	*−12,155*	*−14,291*	*−16,612*
Transportation services, credit	2 205	**1,183**	**1,163**	**1,022**	**1,261**	**1,417**	**1,534**	**1,488**	**1,801**
Passenger	2 850	*661*	*687*	*772*	*962*	*1,058*	*1,114*	*1,091*	*1,447*
Freight	2 851	*255*	*233*	*67*	*99*	*101*	*109*	*76*	*40*
Other	2 852	*267*	*243*	*183*	*200*	*258*	*311*	*321*	*314*
Sea transport, passenger	2 207	....	....	....	....	....	....	....	....
Sea transport, freight	2 208	....	....	....	....	....	....	....	....
Sea transport, other	2 209	....	....	....	....	....	....	....	....
Air transport, passenger	2 211	....	....	....	....	....	....	....	....
Air transport, freight	2 212	....	....	....	....	....	....	....	....
Air transport, other	2 213	....	....	....	....	....	....	....	....
Other transport, passenger	2 215	....	....	....	....	....	....	....	....
Other transport, freight	2 216	....	....	....	....	....	....	....	....
Other transport, other	2 217	....	....	....	....	....	....	....	....
Transportation services, debit	3 205	**−2,441**	**−2,117**	**−2,293**	**−3,174**	**−4,401**	**−5,328**	**−6,628**	**−7,618**
Passenger	3 850	*−599*	*−488*	*−440*	*−765*	*−1,080*	*−1,438*	*−1,845*	*−2,176*
Freight	3 851	*−1,658*	*−1,543*	*−1,795*	*−2,356*	*−3,238*	*−3,761*	*−4,696*	*−5,378*
Other	3 852	*−184*	*−85*	*−57*	*−53*	*−82*	*−129*	*−87*	*−64*
Sea transport, passenger	3 207	....	....	....	....	....	....	....	....
Sea transport, freight	3 208	....	....	....	....	....	....	....	....
Sea transport, other	3 209	....	....	....	....	....	....	....	....
Air transport, passenger	3 211	....	....	....	....	....	....	....	....
Air transport, freight	3 212	....	....	....	....	....	....	....	....
Air transport, other	3 213	....	....	....	....	....	....	....	....
Other transport, passenger	3 215	....	....	....	....	....	....	....	....
Other transport, freight	3 216	....	....	....	....	....	....	....	....
Other transport, other	3 217	....	....	....	....	....	....	....	....
Travel, credit	2 236	**2,677**	**2,569**	**2,923**	**5,571**	**6,322**	**7,335**	**7,876**	**8,443**
Business travel	2 237	584	493	494	776	837	896	889	914
Personal travel	2 240	2,092	2,076	2,429	4,795	5,485	6,440	6,987	7,528
Travel, debit	3 236	**−2,085**	**−1,878**	**−1,811**	**−2,889**	**−3,157**	**−3,373**	**−3,384**	**−3,927**
Business travel	3 237	−738	−685	−701	−1,158	−1,277	−1,374	−1,381	−1,560
Personal travel	3 240	−1,347	−1,193	−1,110	−1,731	−1,880	−1,999	−2,003	−2,368
Other services, credit	2 200 BA	**1,186**	**1,113**	**1,040**	**1,467**	**1,943**	**2,289**	**2,651**	**3,318**
Communications	2 245	57	92	93	136	189	231	305	312
Construction	2 249	....	16	14	21	28	35	40	54
Insurance	2 253	451	53	53	77	106	124	152	214
Financial	2 260	....	240	225	295	426	534	706	876
Computer and information	2 262	....	46	45	66	89	109	129	223
Royalties and licence fees	2 266	49	21	19	27	37	45	46	53
Other business services	2 268	472	489	430	605	742	837	868	1,175
Personal, cultural, and recreational	2 287	....	37	38	60	88	114	103	90
Government, n.i.e.	2 291	158	117	122	179	238	259	302	320
Other services, debit	3 200 BA	**−1,297**	**−1,237**	**−1,400**	**−1,982**	**−2,771**	**−3,454**	**−4,278**	**−5,067**
Communications	3 245	−83	−71	−71	−100	−147	−198	−246	−338
Construction	3 249	....	−3	−3	−4	−5	−6	−6	−7
Insurance	3 253	−380	−204	−225	−297	−391	−478	−587	−638
Financial	3 260	....	−76	−74	−102	−149	−184	−177	−196
Computer and information	3 262	....	−43	−44	−59	−84	−114	−127	−171
Royalties and licence fees	3 266	−246	−330	−447	−617	−891	−1,071	−1,282	−1,596
Other business services	3 268	−421	−384	−405	−603	−833	−1,104	−1,503	−1,758
Personal, cultural, and recreational	3 287	....	−3	−3	−3	−5	−5	−8	−10
Government, n.i.e.	3 291	−166	−124	−129	−198	−265	−292	−342	−354

Table 2 (Continued). STANDARD PRESENTATION, 2000–2007

(Millions of U.S. dollars)

	Code	2000	2001	2002	2003	2004	2005	2006	2007
C. INCOME	4 300	**−3,184**	**−3,787**	**−2,796**	**−4,590**	**−4,318**	**−4,929**	**−5,293**	**−8,923**
Total credit	2 300	*2,511*	*2,480*	*2,179*	*2,857*	*3,259*	*4,640*	*5,944*	*6,550*
Total debit	3 300	*−5,696*	*−6,267*	*−4,975*	*−7,447*	*−7,576*	*−9,569*	*−11,238*	*−15,473*
Compensation of employees, credit	2 310	**325**	**282**	**268**	**391**	**468**	**614**	**692**	**792**
Compensation of employees, debit	3 310	**−614**	**−521**	**−506**	**−706**	**−935**	**−1,041**	**−1,055**	**−1,172**
Investment income, credit	2 320	**2,187**	**2,198**	**1,911**	**2,466**	**2,790**	**4,027**	**5,253**	**5,757**
Direct investment income	2 330	878	679	637	889	1,020	1,459	1,483	1,763
Dividends and distributed branch profits	2 332	756	578	442	631	737	1,061	938	1,088
Reinvested earnings and undistributed branch profits	2 333	....	....	....	....	....	....	....	....
Income on debt (interest)	2 334	121	101	196	258	283	398	545	674
Portfolio investment income	2 339	1,309	1,519	1,273	1,577	1,771	2,568	3,770	3,994
Income on equity	2 340	526	807	633	780	892	1,133	1,622	1,241
Income on bonds and notes	2 350	....	....	....	....	....	....	....	....
Income on money market instruments	2 360	....	....	....	....	....	....	....	....
Other investment income	2 370	....	....	....	....	....	....	....	....
Investment income, debit	3 320	**−5,081**	**−5,746**	**−4,470**	**−6,741**	**−6,642**	**−8,528**	**−10,182**	**−14,300**
Direct investment income	3 330	−2,329	−2,882	−2,025	−3,220	−3,256	−4,320	−4,842	−7,809
Dividends and distributed branch profits	3 332	−2,180	−2,763	−1,947	−3,133	−3,168	−4,216	−4,680	−7,619
Reinvested earnings and undistributed branch profits	3 333	....	....	....	....	....	....	....	....
Income on debt (interest)	3 334	−150	−119	−78	−87	−88	−105	−162	−189
Portfolio investment income	3 339	−2,752	−2,864	−2,445	−3,521	−3,386	−4,208	−5,340	−6,491
Income on equity	3 340	−492	−1,002	−706	−1,432	−1,271	−1,775	−1,960	−2,755
Income on bonds and notes	3 350	....	....	....	....	....	....	....	....
Income on money market instruments	3 360	....	....	....	....	....	....	....	....
Other investment income	3 370	....	....	....	....	....	....	....	....
D. CURRENT TRANSFERS	4 379	**−926**	**−738**	**−556**	**−996**	**−1,758**	**−2,801**	**−2,817**	**−2,953**
Credit	2 379	**106**	**126**	**139**	**252**	**257**	**240**	**261**	**265**
General government	2 380	69	92	103	189	166	146	163	161
Other sectors	2 390	38	34	36	63	92	93	98	104
Workers' remittances	2 391	....	....	....	....	....	....	....	....
Other current transfers	2 392	38	34	36	63	92	93	98	104
Debit	3 379	**−1,033**	**−865**	**−695**	**−1,248**	**−2,015**	**−3,041**	**−3,078**	**−3,218**
General government	3 380	−1,003	−837	−667	−1,195	−1,942	−2,961	−2,996	−3,131
Other sectors	3 390	−30	−28	−28	−53	−73	−80	−82	−87
Workers' remittances	3 391	....	....	....	....	....	....	....	....
Other current transfers	3 392	−30	−28	−28	−53	−73	−80	−82	−87
CAPITAL AND FINANCIAL ACCOUNT	4 996	**−458**	**−1,197**	**−400**	**−1,563**	**1,380**	**6,847**	**11,004**	**17,216**
CAPITAL ACCOUNT	4 994	**−52**	**−31**	**−15**	**44**	**52**	**30**	**30**	**28**
Total credit	2 994	*19*	*16*	*20*	*44*	*55*	*44*	*43*	*41*
Total debit	3 994	*−71*	*−47*	*−35*	*....*	*−2*	*−14*	*−12*	*−13*
Capital transfers, credit	2 400	**19**	**16**	**20**	**44**	**55**	**44**	**43**	**41**
General government	2 401	....	....	....	....	....	....	....	....
Debt forgiveness	2 402	....	....	....	....	....	....	....	....
Other capital transfers	2 410	....	....	....	....	....	....	....	....
Other sectors	2 430	19	16	20	44	55	44	43	41
Migrants' transfers	2 431	19	16	20	44	55	44	43	41
Debt forgiveness	2 432	....	....	....	....	....	....	....	....
Other capital transfers	2 440	....	....	....	....	....	....	....	....
Capital transfers, debit	3 400	**−71**	**−47**	**−35**	**....**	**−2**	**−14**	**−12**	**−13**
General government	3 401	....	....	....	....	....	....	....	....
Debt forgiveness	3 402	....	....	....	....	....	....	....	....
Other capital transfers	3 410	....	....	....	....	....	....	....	....
Other sectors	3 430	−71	−47	−35	....	−2	−14	−12	−13
Migrants' transfers	3 431	−71	−47	−35	....	−2	−14	−12	−13
Debt forgiveness	3 432	....	....	....	....	....	....	....	....
Other capital transfers	3 440	....	....	....	....	....	....	....	....
Nonproduced nonfinancial assets, credit	2 480	....	....	....	....	....	....	....	....
Nonproduced nonfinancial assets, debit	3 480	....	....	....	....	....	....	....	....

Table 2 (Continued). STANDARD PRESENTATION, 2000–2007

(Millions of U.S. dollars)

	Code	2000	2001	2002	2003	2004	2005	2006	2007
FINANCIAL ACCOUNT	4 995	−406	−1,166	−385	−1,607	1,327	6,817	10,974	17,188
A. DIRECT INVESTMENT	4 500	692	10,785	1,882	231	−604	5,613	−6,719	1,989
Direct investment abroad	4 505	−277	3,515	402	−553	−1,305	−909	−6,536	−3,757
Equity capital	4 510	154	4,450	−152	−759	−1,361	−670	−2,716	−3,318
Claims on affiliated enterprises	4 515	154	4,450	−152	−759	−1,361	−670	−2,716	−3,318
Liabilities to affiliated enterprises	4 520	....	....	....	....	....	....	....	....
Reinvested earnings	4 525	....	....	....	....	....	....	....	....
Other capital	4 530	−432	−935	555	206	56	−239	−3,820	−440
Claims on affiliated enterprises	4 535	−432	−935	555	206	56	−239	−3,820	−440
Liabilities to affiliated enterprises	4 540	....	....	....	....	....	....	....	....
Direct investment in South Africa	4 555	969	7,270	1,480	783	701	6,522	−184	5,746
Equity capital	4 560	913	7,032	442	567	125	6,192	−1,556	1,968
Claims on direct investors	4 565	....	....	....	....	....	....	....	....
Liabilities to direct investors	4 570	913	7,032	442	567	125	6,192	−1,556	1,968
Reinvested earnings	4 575	....	....	....	....	....	....	....	....
Other capital	4 580	56	239	1,038	216	577	331	1,373	3,778
Claims on direct investors	4 585	....	....	....	....	....	....	....	....
Liabilities to direct investors	4 590	56	239	1,038	216	577	331	1,373	3,778
B. PORTFOLIO INVESTMENT	4 600	−1,864	−8,302	−417	723	6,407	4,787	19,583	11,616
Assets	4 602	−3,672	−5,331	−875	−138	−950	−911	−2,231	−3,458
Equity securities	4 610	−3,019	−4,864	−572	−49	−795	−996	−1,627	−1,827
Monetary authorities	4 611	....	....	....	....	....	....	....	....
General government	4 612	....	....	....	....	....	....	....	....
Banks	4 613	−84	6	−26	−18	−88	78	27	104
Other sectors	4 614	−2,935	−4,869	−546	−31	−707	−1,073	−1,653	−1,931
Debt securities	4 619	−652	−467	−303	−89	−156	85	−605	−1,631
Bonds and notes	4 620	−652	−467	−303	−89	−156	85	−605	−1,629
Monetary authorities	4 621	....	....	....	....	....	....	....	....
General government	4 622	....	....	....	....	....	....	....	....
Banks	4 623	....	....	....	....	137	402	63	−701
Other sectors	4 624	−652	−467	−303	−89	−292	−317	−667	−928
Money market instruments	4 630	....	....	....	....	....	....	....	−2
Monetary authorities	4 631	....	....	....	....	....	....	....	....
General government	4 632	....	....	....	....	....	....	....	....
Banks	4 633	....	....	....	....	....	....	....	....
Other sectors	4 634	....	....	....	....	....	....	....	....
Liabilities	4 652	1,807	−2,971	457	862	7,357	5,698	21,814	15,074
Equity securities	4 660	4,169	−962	−388	685	6,661	7,230	14,959	8,670
Banks	4 663	274	340	−65	23	578	560	1,250	975
Other sectors	4 664	3,895	−1,302	−323	662	6,083	6,670	13,709	7,695
Debt securities	4 669	−2,361	−2,009	845	176	696	−1,532	6,855	6,404
Bonds and notes	4 670	−2,072	−2,156	946	290	793	−1,557	6,884	6,284
Monetary authorities	4 671	....	....	....	....	....	....	....	....
General government	4 672	−1,958	−1,561	965	398	490	−1,522	4,791	1,069
Banks	4 673	....	....	....	....	....	....	....	1,503
Other sectors	4 674	−114	−595	−19	−107	302	−35	2,093	3,713
Money market instruments	4 680	−289	147	−101	−114	−97	25	−29	120
Monetary authorities	4 681	....	....	....	....	....	....	....	....
General government	4 682	....	....	....	....	....	....	....	....
Banks	4 683	−289	147	−101	−114	−97	25	−29	120
Other sectors	4 684	....	....	....	....	....	....	....	....
C. FINANCIAL DERIVATIVES	4 910	−142	....	....	....	....	....	....	....
Monetary authorities	4 911	....	....	....	....	....	....	....	....
General government	4 912	....	....	....	....	....	....	....	....
Banks	4 913	−142	....	....	....	....	....	....	....
Other sectors	4 914	....	....	....	....	....	....	....	....
Assets	4 900	−144	....	....	....	....	....	....	....
Monetary authorities	4 901	....	....	....	....	....	....	....	....
General government	4 902	....	....	....	....	....	....	....	....
Banks	4 903	−144	....	....	....	....	....	....	....
Other sectors	4 904	....	....	....	....	....	....	....	....
Liabilities	4 905	2	....	....	....	....	....	....	....
Monetary authorities	4 906	....	....	....	....	....	....	....	....
General government	4 907	....	....	....	....	....	....	....	....
Banks	4 908	2	....	....	....	....	....	....	....
Other sectors	4 909	....	....	....	....	....	....	....	....

Table 2 (Concluded). STANDARD PRESENTATION, 2000–2007

(Millions of U.S. dollars)

	Code	2000	2001	2002	2003	2004	2005	2006	2007
D. OTHER INVESTMENT	4 700 ..	**1,388**	**−3,672**	**−2,172**	**−2,915**	**1,849**	**2,183**	**1,821**	**9,321**
Assets	4 703 ..	34	−3,921	−288	−5,212	−216	−3,503	−7,187	1,270
Trade credits	4 706 ..	−622	−858	−394	−288	−213	−694	−214	−106
General government	4 707 ..	....	−407	−424	−376	−103	−158	−210	−59
of which: Short-term	4 709 ..	....	....	....	....	....	....	....	....
Other sectors	4 710 ..	−622	−451	30	88	−110	−537	−4	−47
of which: Short-term	4 712 ..	−622	−451	30	88	−110	−539	−4	−47
Loans	4 714 ..	547	−373	371	325	33	−247	−2,212	160
Monetary authorities	4 715 ..	....	....	....	1	4	−7	....	....
of which: Short-term	4 718 ..	....	....	....	....	....	....	....	....
General government	4 719 ..	....	....	....	....	....	....	....	....
of which: Short-term	4 721 ..	....	....	....	....	....	....	....	....
Banks	4 722 ..	....	....	....	....	−14	−287	−1,852	−17
of which: Short-term	4 724 ..	....	....	....	....	−14	−287	−1,852	−17
Other sectors	4 725 ..	547	−373	371	324	43	47	−360	177
of which: Short-term	4 727 ..	546	−491	486	300	150	51	−346	463
Currency and deposits	4 730 ..	375	−2,370	−484	−7,797	−1,859	−3,013	−3,955	1,730
Monetary authorities	4 731 ..	....	....	....	....	....	....	....	....
General government	4 732 ..	....	....	....	....	....	....	....	....
Banks	4 733 ..	−260	−2,707	−2,363	−8,089	−2,087	−2,984	−3,126	239
Other sectors	4 734 ..	635	336	1,879	291	229	−29	−828	1,492
Other assets	4 736 ..	−267	−320	219	2,548	1,822	451	−806	−515
Monetary authorities	4 737 ..	....	....	....	....	....	....	....	....
of which: Short-term	4 739 ..	....	....	....	....	....	....	....	....
General government	4 740 ..	....	....	....	....	....	....	....	....
of which: Short-term	4 742 ..	....	....	....	....	....	....	....	....
Banks	4 743 ..	−9	12	−92	113	−196	−49	−11	−63
of which: Short-term	4 745 ..	−9	12	−92	113	−196	−49	−11	−63
Other sectors	4 746 ..	−258	−332	311	2,435	2,018	500	−795	−451
of which: Short-term	4 748 ..	−30	−17	550	2,538	2,142	627	−458	144
Liabilities	4 753 ..	1,354	249	−1,884	2,297	2,065	5,686	9,008	8,050
Trade credits	4 756 ..	38	31	67	52	85	269	446	626
General government	4 757 ..	....	....	....	....	....	....	....	....
of which: Short-term	4 759 ..	....	....	....	....	....	....	....	....
Other sectors	4 760 ..	38	31	67	52	85	269	446	626
of which: Short-term	4 762 ..	38	31	67	52	85	269	446	626
Loans	4 764 ..	940	1,207	−1,618	−240	−284	3,588	5,645	5,974
Monetary authorities	4 765 ..	−315	1,584	−1,773	235	402	424	−745	−1,100
of which: Use of Fund credit and loans from the Fund..	4 766 ..	....	....	....	....	....	....	....	....
of which: Short-term	4 768 ..	−315	1,584	−1,773	235	402	424	−745	−1,100
General government	4 769 ..	6	134	1,944	−277	−285	319	226	143
of which: Short-term	4 771 ..	....	....	1,515	....	....	....	....	....
Banks	4 772 ..	382	−186	−1,314	−116	210	1,820	1,061	4,952
of which: Short-term	4 774 ..	434	−110	−1,314	−116	210	1,820	1,061	2,816
Other sectors	4 775 ..	868	−325	−475	−81	−612	1,024	5,104	1,979
of which: Short-term	4 777 ..	682	−19	−234	36	−447	520	1,768	−584
Currency and deposits	4 780 ..	737	−604	−169	−43	1,031	1,040	3,099	1,320
Monetary authorities	4 781 ..	−95	−2	85	−65	108	102	−20	456
General government	4 782 ..	....	....	....	....	....	....	....	....
Banks	4 783 ..	833	−602	−255	23	923	931	3,119	864
Other sectors	4 784 ..	....	....	....	....	....	7	....	....
Other liabilities	4 786 ..	−362	−385	−164	2,527	1,233	788	−182	130
Monetary authorities	4 787 ..	....	....	....	....	....	....	....	....
of which: Short-term	4 789 ..	....	....	....	....	....	....	....	....
General government	4 790 ..	....	....	....	....	....	790	278	....
of which: Short-term	4 792 ..	....	....	....	....	....	790	278	....
Banks	4 793 ..	−19	1	....	3	−5	....	−2	....
of which: Short-term	4 795 ..	−19	1	....	3	−5	....	−2	....
Other sectors	4 796 ..	−343	−386	−164	2,523	1,238	−2	−458	130
of which: Short-term	4 798 ..	−343	−386	−227	2,523	1,238	−2	−458	130
E. RESERVE ASSETS	4 802 ..	**−480**	**22**	**322**	**354**	**−6,324**	**−5,766**	**−3,711**	**−5,737**
Monetary gold	4 812 ..	−534	85	78	764	25	−31	27	23
Special drawing rights	4 811 ..	−17	....	....	....	....	....	....	....
Reserve position in the Fund	4 810 ..	....	....	....	....	....	....	....	....
Foreign exchange	4 803 ..	72	−63	245	−410	−6,349	−5,734	−3,737	−5,760
Other claims	4 813 ..	....	....	....	....	....	....	....	....
NET ERRORS AND OMISSIONS	4 998 ..	**649**	**855**	**−485**	**3,466**	**5,623**	**2,875**	**5,484**	**3,415**

Table 3. INTERNATIONAL INVESTMENT POSITION (End-period stocks), 2000–2007

(Millions of U.S. dollars)

	Code	2000	2001	2002	2003	2004	2005	2006	2007
ASSETS............................	8 995 C.	**93,162**	**64,281**	**74,038**	**100,743**	**130,225**	**154,057**	**182,500**	....
Direct investment abroad................	8 505 ..	**32,325**	**17,580**	**21,980**	**27,185**	**39,083**	**37,706**	**50,826**	....
Equity capital and reinvested earnings...........	8 506 ..	31,424	16,659	20,573	25,170	36,305	34,980	44,281	....
Claims on affiliated enterprises.........	8 507 ..	31,424	16,659	20,573	25,170	36,305	34,980	44,281	....
Liabilities to affiliated enterprises............	8 508 ..	....	....	....	....	....	....	....	....
Other capital................	8 530 ..	901	921	1,408	2,015	2,778	2,726	6,545	....
Claims on affiliated enterprises.........	8 535 ..	901	921	1,408	2,015	2,778	2,726	6,545	....
Liabilities to affiliated enterprises............	8 540 ..	....	....	....	....	....	....	....	....
Portfolio investment......................	8 602 ..	**45,433**	**30,341**	**30,068**	**40,752**	**47,304**	**64,686**	**70,637**	....
Equity securities..................	8 610 ..	41,675	28,500	27,470	38,621	43,984	60,756	66,082	....
Monetary authorities............	8 611 ..	....	....	....	....	....	....	....	....
General government............	8 612 ..	....	....	....	....	....	....	....	....
Banks..................	8 613 ..	92	92	238	332	487	523	439	....
Other sectors..............	8 614 ..	41,584	28,408	27,232	38,289	43,497	60,233	65,642	....
Debt securities..................	8 619 ..	3,758	1,841	2,598	2,131	3,320	3,930	4,555	....
Bonds and notes...............	8 620 ..	3,758	1,841	2,598	2,131	3,320	3,930	4,555	....
Monetary authorities...	8 621 ..	....	....	....	....	....	....	....	....
General government............	8 622 ..	....	....	....	....	....	....	....	....
Banks..................	8 623 ..	169	509	578	808	782	336	244	....
Other sectors..............	8 624 ..	3,589	1,331	2,020	1,323	2,538	3,594	4,312	....
Money market instruments..............	8 630 ..	....	....	....	....	....	....	....	....
Monetary authorities............	8 631 ..	....	....	....	....	....	....	....	....
General government............	8 632 ..	....	....	....	....	....	....	....	....
Banks..................	8 633 ..	....	....	....	....	....	....	....	....
Other sectors..............	8 634 ..	....	....	....	....	....	....	....	....
Financial derivatives........................	8 900 ..	....	....	....	....	....	....	....	....
Monetary authorities................	8 901 ..	....	....	....	....	....	....	....	....
General government................	8 902 ..	....	....	....	....	....	....	....	....
Banks................	8 903 ..	....	....	....	....	....	....	....	....
Other sectors................	8 904 ..	....	....	....	....	....	....	....	....
Other investment......................	8 703 ..	**7,871**	**8,889**	**14,352**	**24,836**	**29,121**	**31,038**	**35,452**	....
Trade credits................	8 706 ..	....	....	....	....	....	....	....	....
General government................	8 707 ..	....	....	....	....	....	....	....	....
of which: Short-term................	8 709 ..	....	....	....	....	....	....	....	....
Other sectors................	8 710 ..	....	....	....	....	....	....	....	....
of which: Short-term................	8 712 ..	....	....	....	....	....	....	....	....
Loans................	8 714 ..	4,838	4,608	6,301	8,201	10,718	10,017	10,473	....
Monetary authorities................	8 715 ..	10	6	8	9	6	12	11	....
of which: Short-term................	8 718 ..	....	....	....	....	....	....	....	....
General government................	8 719 ..	269	703	1,186	1,712	2,086	1,822	2,110	....
of which: Short-term................	8 721 ..	*1*	*1*	*1*	*2*	*2*	*2*	*2*	....
Banks................	8 722 ..	1,049	1,273	1,212	1,341	1,643	1,259	1,418	....
of which: Short-term................	8 724 ..	*1,049*	*1,273*	*1,212*	*1,341*	*1,643*	*1,259*	*1,418*	....
Other sectors................	8 725 ..	3,511	2,626	3,895	5,139	6,984	6,925	6,936	....
of which: Short-term................	8 727 ..	*2,917*	*2,046*	*3,092*	*4,091*	*5,669*	*5,706*	*5,725*	....
Currency and deposits................	8 730 ..	3,033	4,281	8,051	16,635	18,402	21,021	24,979	....
Monetary authorities................	8 731 ..	....	....	....	....	....	....	....	....
General government................	8 732 ..	....	....	....	....	....	....	....	....
Banks................	8 733 ..	3,033	4,281	8,051	16,635	18,402	21,021	24,979	....
Other sectors................	8 734 ..	....	....	....	....	....	....	....	....
Other assets................	8 736 ..	....	....	....	....	....	....	....	....
Monetary authorities................	8 737 ..	....	....	....	....	....	....	....	....
of which: Short-term................	8 739 ..	....	....	....	....	....	....	....	....
General government................	8 740 ..	....	....	....	....	....	....	....	....
of which: Short-term................	8 742 ..	....	....	....	....	....	....	....	....
Banks................	8 743 ..	....	....	....	....	....	....	....	....
of which: Short-term................	8 745 ..	....	....	....	....	....	....	....	....
Other sectors................	8 746 ..	....	....	....	....	....	....	....	....
of which: Short-term................	8 748 ..	....	....	....	....	....	....	....	....
Reserve assets.........................	8 802 ..	**7,532**	**7,471**	**7,638**	**7,970**	**14,718**	**20,628**	**25,585**	....
Monetary gold................	8 812 ..	1,451	1,427	1,735	1,476	1,579	2,051	2,530	....
Special drawing rights................	8 811 ..	290	280	303	331	346	319	335	352
Reserve position in the Fund................	8 810 ..	....	....	1	1	1	1	1	2
Foreign exchange................	8 803 ..	5,791	5,764	5,599	6,162	12,792	18,258	22,718	....
Other claims................	8 813 ..	....	....	....	....	....	....	....	....

Table 3 (Concluded). INTERNATIONAL INVESTMENT POSITION (End-period stocks), 2000–2007

(Millions of U.S. dollars)

	Code	2000	2001	2002	2003	2004	2005	2006	2007
LIABILITIES	8 995 D.	**99,951**	**75,342**	**83,931**	**112,837**	**151,184**	**188,012**	**223,569**	....
Direct investment in South Africa	8 555 ..	**43,451**	**30,569**	**30,604**	**46,869**	**64,451**	**78,986**	**87,765**	....
Equity capital and reinvested earnings	8 556 ..	40,289	27,666	25,973	40,788	56,513	71,461	79,451	....
Claims on direct investors	8 557 ..	....	....	....	....	....	....	....	....
Liabilities to direct investors	8 558 ..	40,289	27,666	25,973	40,788	56,513	71,461	79,451	....
Other capital	8 580 ..	3,162	2,903	4,631	6,081	7,938	7,525	8,314	....
Claims on direct investors	8 585 ..	....	....	....	....	....	....	....	....
Liabilities to direct investors	8 590 ..	3,162	2,903	4,631	6,081	7,938	7,525	8,314	....
Portfolio investment	8 652 ..	**36,564**	**26,402**	**35,677**	**46,257**	**62,853**	**82,837**	**102,750**	....
Equity securities	8 660 ..	22,599	16,577	23,308	32,795	47,448	67,338	84,741	....
Banks	8 663 ..	2,565	2,016	2,474	4,105	8,894	11,572	15,852	....
Other sectors	8 664 ..	20,034	14,561	20,834	28,690	38,555	55,766	68,889	....
Debt securities	8 669 ..	13,965	9,825	12,369	13,462	15,405	15,500	18,009	....
Bonds and notes	8 670 ..	13,873	9,668	12,149	13,305	15,331	15,410	17,961	....
Monetary authorities	8 671 ..	....	....	....	....	....	....	....	....
General government	8 672 ..	8,779	7,357	9,273	10,438	11,919	12,220	13,425	....
Banks	8 673 ..	200	....	....	24	68	25	103	....
Other sectors	8 674 ..	4,894	2,312	2,875	2,842	3,344	3,165	4,432	....
Money market instruments	8 680 ..	92	157	220	157	74	89	49	....
Monetary authorities	8 681 ..	....	....	....	....	....	....	....	....
General government	8 682 ..	....	....	....	....	....	....	....	....
Banks	8 683 ..	92	157	220	157	74	89	49	....
Other sectors	8 684 ..	....	....	....	....	....	....	....	....
Financial derivatives	8 905 ..	....	....	....	....	....	....	....	....
Monetary authorities	8 906 ..	....	....	....	....	....	....	....	....
General government	8 907 ..	....	....	....	....	....	....	....	....
Banks	8 908 ..	....	....	....	....	....	....	....	....
Other sectors	8 909 ..	....	....	....	....	....	....	....	....
Other investment	8 753 ..	**19,936**	**18,370**	**17,650**	**19,711**	**23,880**	**26,189**	**33,054**	....
Trade credits	8 756 ..	....	....	....	....	....	....	....	....
General government	8 757 ..	....	....	....	....	....	....	....	....
of which: Short-term	8 759 ..	....	....	....	....	....	....	....	....
Other sectors	8 760 ..	....	....	....	....	....	....	....	....
of which: Short-term	8 762 ..	....	....	....	....	....	....	....	....
Loans	8 764 ..	14,483	14,438	13,534	15,311	17,818	19,611	24,148	....
Monetary authorities	8 765 ..	2,595	3,976	2,483	3,005	3,501	3,495	2,754	....
of which: Use of Fund credit and loans from the Fund	8 766 ..	....	....	....	....	....	....	....	....
of which: Short-term	8 768 ..	*2,595*	*986*	*956*	*429*	*440*	*696*	*1,073*	....
General government	8 769 ..	589	717	2,805	2,747	2,672	3,523	4,206	....
of which: Short-term	8 771 ..	....	....	....	....	....	*810*	*980*	....
Banks	8 772 ..	3,414	3,266	2,006	1,982	2,347	3,988	4,594	....
of which: Short-term	8 774 ..	*3,328*	*3,265*	*2,006*	*1,982*	*2,347*	*3,988*	*4,594*	....
Other sectors	8 775 ..	7,885	6,480	6,240	7,576	9,298	8,604	12,594	....
of which: Short-term	8 777 ..	*1,878*	*1,651*	*2,353*	*3,125*	*3,967*	*3,911*	*4,787*	....
Currency and deposits	8 780 ..	5,454	3,932	4,117	4,401	6,063	6,578	8,906	....
Monetary authorities	8 781 ..	86	50	163	140	332	404	370	....
General government	8 782 ..	....	....	....	....	....	....	....	....
Banks	8 783 ..	5,368	3,882	3,954	4,261	5,731	6,174	8,536	....
Other sectors	8 784 ..	....	....	....	....	....	....	....	....
Other liabilities	8 786 ..	....	....	....	....	....	....	....	....
Monetary authorities	8 787 ..	....	....	....	....	....	....	....	....
of which: Short-term	8 789 ..	....	....	....	....	....	....	....	....
General government	8 790 ..	....	....	....	....	....	....	....	....
of which: Short-term	8 792 ..	....	....	....	....	....	....	....	....
Banks	8 793 ..	....	....	....	....	....	....	....	....
of which: Short-term	8 795 ..	....	....	....	....	....	....	....	....
Other sectors	8 796 ..	....	....	....	....	....	....	....	....
of which: Short-term	8 798 ..	....	....	....	....	....	....	....	....
NET INTERNATIONAL INVESTMENT POSITION	8 995 ..	**−6,789**	**−11,061**	**−9,893**	**−12,094**	**−20,959**	**−33,955**	**−41,069**	....
Conversion rates: rand per U.S. dollar (end of period)	0 102 ..	7.569	12.127	8.640	6.640	5.630	6.325	6.970	6.810

Table 1. ANALYTIC PRESENTATION, 2000–2007

(Millions of U.S. dollars)

	Code	2000	2001	2002	2003	2004	2005	2006	2007
A. Current Account[1]	4 993 Z.	−23,185	−24,064	−22,239	−30,885	−54,865	−83,388	−110,124	−145,355
Goods: exports f.o.b.	2 100 ..	115,769	117,522	127,162	158,049	185,209	196,580	220,774	256,681
Goods: imports f.o.b.	3 100 ..	−152,856	−152,039	−161,794	−203,205	−251,939	−281,784	−325,444	−380,197
Balance on Goods	4 100 ..	*−37,087*	*−34,518*	*−34,632*	*−45,155*	*−66,730*	*−85,204*	*−104,670*	*−123,515*
Services: credit	2 200 ..	52,453	55,651	60,247	74,308	86,078	94,663	106,628	129,303
Services: debit	3 200 ..	−33,171	−35,182	−38,712	−47,951	−59,188	−67,129	−78,423	−98,900
Balance on Goods and Services	4 991 ..	*−17,805*	*−14,049*	*−13,097*	*−18,798*	*−39,841*	*−57,669*	*−76,465*	*−93,112*
Income: credit	2 300 ..	18,904	20,243	21,536	27,209	33,948	39,445	55,855	72,688
Income: debit	3 300 ..	−25,753	−31,509	−33,194	−38,910	−48,986	−60,701	−81,814	−115,931
Balance on Goods, Services, and Income	4 992 ..	*−24,654*	*−25,315*	*−24,755*	*−30,499*	*−54,879*	*−78,925*	*−102,424*	*−136,355*
Current transfers: credit	2 379 Z.	11,380	12,143	14,575	17,048	20,366	20,194	21,563	26,058
Current transfers: debit	3 379 ..	−9,911	−10,892	−12,059	−17,434	−20,353	−24,656	−29,263	−35,058
B. Capital Account[1]	4 994 Z.	**4,797**	**4,811**	**7,236**	**9,274**	**10,450**	**10,107**	**7,857**	**6,291**
Capital account: credit	2 994 Z.	5,787	5,782	8,118	10,984	11,646	11,225	9,674	8,881
Capital account: debit	3 994 ..	−989	−971	−882	−1,710	−1,197	−1,118	−1,817	−2,590
Total, Groups A Plus B	4 981 ..	*−18,388*	*−19,253*	*−15,003*	*−21,611*	*−44,416*	*−73,281*	*−102,267*	*−139,064*
C. Financial Account[1]	4 995 W.	**15,261**	**18,169**	**17,782**	**4,353**	**36,964**	**73,885**	**104,951**	**134,004**
Direct investment abroad	4 505 ..	−57,411	−32,889	−33,653	−28,759	−61,504	−41,922	−99,492	−127,777
Direct investment in Spain	4 555 Z.	38,835	28,164	39,993	25,607	24,792	24,573	27,250	60,122
Portfolio investment assets	4 602 ..	−59,318	−44,992	−29,089	−90,833	−39,651	−119,356	−11,253	−6,574
Equity securities	4 610 ..	−36,136	−247	123	−13,180	−15,063	−19,370	−25,992	9,779
Debt securities	4 619 ..	−23,183	−44,745	−29,212	−77,653	−24,588	−99,986	14,740	−16,353
Portfolio investment liabilities	4 652 Z.	58,146	27,971	34,105	44,763	141,686	172,713	244,210	124,167
Equity securities	4 660 ..	19,692	7,958	2,810	−3,649	10,918	−9,573	−23,696	15,393
Debt securities	4 669 Z.	38,455	20,013	31,294	48,412	130,768	182,286	267,906	108,774
Financial derivatives	4 910 ..	1,818	−269	−4,720	−3,785	74	273	2,419	−9,529
Financial derivatives assets	4 900 ..	. . . .	. . . .	. . . .	. . . .	. . . .	. . . .	. . . .	. . . .
Financial derivatives liabilities	4 905 ..	1,818	−269	−4,720	−3,785	74	273	2,419	−9,529
Other investment assets	4 703 ..	−18,475	10,690	−23,854	−13,557	−52,659	−42,198	−99,778	−51,347
Monetary authorities	4 701 ..	−7,837	14,992	6,115	5,211	−18,079	17,120	−13,890	26,420
General government	4 704 ..	−242	−69	−1,339	−342	−2,182	−233	−204	−2,383
Banks	4 705 ..	−7,511	−3,742	−17,953	−10,523	−20,402	−50,563	−73,209	−66,840
Other sectors	4 728 ..	−2,884	−492	−10,676	−7,903	−11,995	−8,523	−12,474	−8,545
Other investment liabilities	4 753 W.	51,665	29,494	35,000	70,916	24,226	79,803	41,595	144,942
Monetary authorities	4 753 WA	−141	−185	1,119	−1,331	−89	132	−154	14,649
General government	4 753 ZB	902	575	1,573	−1,026	6,362	193	1,333	593
Banks	4 753 ZC	36,676	15,281	26,982	61,853	17,691	62,843	4,620	103,905
Other sectors	4 753 ZD	14,229	13,824	5,326	11,420	262	16,635	35,795	25,795
Total, Groups A Through C	4 983 ..	*−3,127*	*−1,085*	*2,779*	*−17,259*	*−7,451*	*604*	*2,684*	*−5,060*
D. Net Errors and Omissions	4 998 ..	**247**	**−257**	**912**	**1,769**	**1,039**	**−2,524**	**−2,106**	**5,275**
Total, Groups A Through D	4 984 ..	*−2,880*	*−1,341*	*3,690*	*−15,489*	*−6,412*	*−1,920*	*578*	*215*
E. Reserves and Related Items	4 802 A.	**2,880**	**1,341**	**−3,690**	**15,489**	**6,412**	**1,920**	**−578**	**−215**
Reserve assets	4 802 ..	2,880	1,341	−3,690	15,489	6,412	1,920	−578	−215
Use of Fund credit and loans	4 766 ..	. . . .	. . . .	. . . .	. . . .	. . . .	. . . .	. . . .	. . . .
Exceptional financing	4 920 ..	. . . .	. . . .	. . . .	. . . .	. . . .	. . . .	. . . .	. . . .
Conversion rates: euros per U.S. dollar	0 103 ..	**1.0854**	**1.1175**	**1.0626**	**.8860**	**.8054**	**.8041**	**.7971**	**.7306**

[1] Excludes components that have been classified in the categories of Group E.

Table 2. STANDARD PRESENTATION, 2000–2007

(Millions of U.S. dollars)

	Code	2000	2001	2002	2003	2004	2005	2006	2007
CURRENT ACCOUNT	4 993	−23,185	−24,064	−22,239	−30,885	−54,865	−83,388	−110,124	−145,355
A. GOODS	4 100	−37,087	−34,518	−34,632	−45,155	−66,730	−85,204	−104,670	−123,515
Credit	2 100	115,769	117,522	127,162	158,049	185,209	196,580	220,774	256,681
General merchandise: exports f.o.b.	2 110	113,008	114,521	123,703	153,404	179,287	189,263	212,437	247,200
Goods for processing: exports f.o.b.	2 150	1,015	1,315	1,875	2,749	3,567	3,999	4,580	5,386
Repairs on goods	2 160	193	199	237	273	300	287	400	430
Goods procured in ports by carriers	2 170	1,471	1,418	1,267	1,529	1,984	2,951	3,261	3,594
Nonmonetary gold	2 180	83	69	78	95	71	81	96	71
Debit	3 100	−152,856	−152,039	−161,794	−203,205	−251,939	−281,784	−325,444	−380,197
General merchandise: imports f.o.b.	3 110	−150,200	−148,924	−158,077	−198,732	−246,602	−276,163	−319,337	−372,605
Goods for processing: imports f.o.b.	3 150	−1,219	−1,637	−2,173	−2,901	−3,377	−3,482	−3,650	−4,415
Repairs on goods	3 160	−218	−221	−194	−190	−257	−208	−288	−642
Goods procured in ports by carriers	3 170	−722	−746	−938	−876	−1,149	−1,424	−1,696	−2,099
Nonmonetary gold	3 180	−498	−511	−411	−506	−554	−506	−474	−435
B. SERVICES	4 200	19,282	20,469	21,535	26,358	26,890	27,534	28,206	30,403
Total credit	2 200	*52,453*	*55,651*	*60,247*	*74,308*	*86,078*	*94,663*	*106,628*	*129,303*
Total debit	3 200	*−33,171*	*−35,182*	*−38,712*	*−47,951*	*−59,188*	*−67,129*	*−78,423*	*−98,900*
Transportation services, credit	2 205	8,432	8,825	9,671	11,897	14,321	16,178	18,122	21,538
Passenger	2 850	*2,854*	*3,278*	*3,588*	*4,229*	*4,929*	*5,277*	*6,246*	*7,297*
Freight	2 851	*3,380*	*3,239*	*3,461*	*4,390*	*5,362*	*6,216*	*6,773*	*7,867*
Other	2 852	*2,198*	*2,307*	*2,622*	*3,278*	*4,030*	*4,685*	*5,104*	*6,374*
Sea transport, passenger	2 207	29	30	37	69	100	91	162	267
Sea transport, freight	2 208	623	633	665	823	1,034	1,124	1,290	1,495
Sea transport, other	2 209	452	483	542	744	899	1,062	1,164	1,463
Air transport, passenger	2 211	2,795	3,219	3,522	4,130	4,783	5,130	6,031	6,968
Air transport, freight	2 212	159	152	157	173	174	153	154	178
Air transport, other	2 213	1,657	1,750	2,015	2,445	2,975	3,449	3,692	4,571
Other transport, passenger	2 215	29	30	29	29	46	56	53	61
Other transport, freight	2 216	2,598	2,454	2,639	3,393	4,154	4,939	5,329	6,194
Other transport, other	2 217	89	74	64	88	156	174	247	340
Transportation services, debit	3 205	−10,117	−9,981	−10,793	−13,138	−16,102	−18,523	−20,572	−24,711
Passenger	3 850	*−1,788*	*−1,937*	*−2,071*	*−2,259*	*−2,711*	*−3,395*	*−3,651*	*−4,534*
Freight	3 851	*−6,703*	*−6,259*	*−6,789*	*−8,529*	*−10,673*	*−12,204*	*−13,676*	*−15,948*
Other	3 852	*−1,626*	*−1,785*	*−1,933*	*−2,349*	*−2,719*	*−2,924*	*−3,245*	*−4,229*
Sea transport, passenger	3 207	−60	−47	−18	−24	−34	−63	−86	−112
Sea transport, freight	3 208	−2,268	−2,237	−2,449	−3,077	−3,707	−4,121	−4,936	−5,685
Sea transport, other	3 209	−283	−302	−320	−364	−392	−440	−538	−698
Air transport, passenger	3 211	−1,714	−1,874	−2,047	−2,227	−2,659	−3,307	−3,517	−4,383
Air transport, freight	3 212	−213	−216	−243	−277	−283	−274	−310	−358
Air transport, other	3 213	−1,267	−1,391	−1,484	−1,840	−2,166	−2,239	−2,438	−3,205
Other transport, passenger	3 215	−14	−15	−6	−8	−17	−25	−47	−39
Other transport, freight	3 216	−4,222	−3,806	−4,098	−5,175	−6,682	−7,809	−8,430	−9,906
Other transport, other	3 217	−76	−93	−128	−146	−160	−244	−269	−325
Travel, credit	2 236	29,802	30,550	31,880	39,634	45,067	47,789	51,297	57,882
Business travel	2 237	....	....	....	....	....	....	....	....
Personal travel	2 240	....	....	....	....	....	....	....	....
Travel, debit	3 236	−5,922	−6,529	−7,295	−9,071	−12,153	−15,046	−16,697	−19,724
Business travel	3 237	....	....	....	....	....	....	....	....
Personal travel	3 240	....	....	....	....	....	....	....	....
Other services, credit	2 200 BA	14,219	16,276	18,696	22,778	26,689	30,696	37,209	49,883
Communications	2 245	668	816	934	1,048	1,227	1,475	1,447	1,713
Construction	2 249	588	762	903	1,060	1,327	1,667	2,185	4,255
Insurance	2 253	213	288	364	475	771	803	822	1,617
Financial	2 260	1,394	1,493	1,374	1,902	2,077	2,812	3,972	5,916
Computer and information	2 262	2,043	2,178	2,490	2,913	2,964	3,606	3,955	5,292
Royalties and licence fees	2 266	421	365	370	528	500	565	923	536
Other business services	2 268	8,018	9,385	10,942	13,407	16,081	17,886	21,866	27,927
Personal, cultural, and recreational	2 287	535	630	671	814	966	1,073	1,245	1,663
Government, n.i.e.	2 291	340	359	648	629	775	810	796	963
Other services, debit	3 200 BA	−17,132	−18,672	−20,625	−25,742	−30,933	−33,560	−41,154	−54,465
Communications	3 245	−744	−927	−1,025	−1,239	−1,577	−1,724	−2,352	−3,017
Construction	3 249	−218	−240	−359	−412	−860	−1,073	−1,318	−1,884
Insurance	3 253	−328	−350	−558	−880	−1,197	−1,217	−1,937	−2,667
Financial	3 260	−1,082	−1,197	−1,123	−1,695	−2,015	−2,747	−4,028	−5,303
Computer and information	3 262	−1,227	−1,522	−1,577	−1,672	−1,690	−2,021	−2,107	−2,602
Royalties and licence fees	3 266	−1,681	−1,678	−1,814	−2,520	−3,037	−2,636	−2,516	−3,402
Other business services	3 268	−10,093	−11,203	−12,411	−15,282	−18,286	−20,004	−24,568	−32,706
Personal, cultural, and recreational	3 287	−1,425	−1,277	−1,491	−1,699	−1,905	−1,748	−1,916	−2,415
Government, n.i.e.	3 291	−333	−278	−267	−344	−366	−390	−414	−469

Table 2 (Continued). STANDARD PRESENTATION, 2000–2007

(Millions of U.S. dollars)

	Code	2000	2001	2002	2003	2004	2005	2006	2007
C. INCOME	4 300	−6,849	−11,266	−11,658	−11,701	−15,038	−21,256	−25,959	−43,243
Total credit	2 300	*18,904*	*20,243*	*21,536*	*27,209*	*33,948*	*39,445*	*55,855*	*72,688*
Total debit	3 300	*−25,753*	*−31,509*	*−33,194*	*−38,910*	*−48,986*	*−60,701*	*−81,814*	*−115,931*
Compensation of employees, credit	2 310	697	763	826	1,013	1,157	1,318	1,512	1,965
Compensation of employees, debit	3 310	−842	−836	−841	−925	−1,341	−1,545	−1,866	−2,372
Investment income, credit	2 320	18,206	19,480	20,711	26,197	32,791	38,127	54,343	70,723
Direct investment income	2 330	5,477	4,699	5,940	10,012	12,998	15,938	26,396	32,933
Dividends and distributed branch profits	2 332	1,589	4,295	4,650	7,711	10,069	12,563	15,026	19,560
Reinvested earnings and undistributed branch profits	2 333	3,546	64	461	1,740	2,376	2,608	10,270	12,129
Income on debt (interest)	2 334	343	340	830	561	553	767	1,100	1,244
Portfolio investment income	2 339	4,371	5,818	8,173	9,907	13,295	14,597	16,642	20,156
Income on equity	2 340	750	753	1,103	829	1,420	1,735	2,305	2,980
Income on bonds and notes	2 350	3,470	4,763	6,863	8,763	11,461	12,388	13,496	16,176
Income on money market instruments	2 360	152	302	207	315	413	474	841	1,000
Other investment income	2 370	8,358	8,963	6,598	6,279	6,497	7,591	11,306	17,634
Investment income, debit	3 320	−24,911	−30,673	−32,353	−37,985	−47,645	−59,156	−79,948	−113,559
Direct investment income	3 330	−6,121	−7,118	−8,649	−9,097	−13,109	−15,504	−19,909	−27,660
Dividends and distributed branch profits	3 332	−3,463	−4,619	−5,245	−5,598	−9,235	−12,615	−12,025	−17,382
Reinvested earnings and undistributed branch profits	3 333	−2,057	−1,525	−1,797	−1,523	−1,874	−68	−4,744	−5,615
Income on debt (interest)	3 334	−601	−974	−1,607	−1,976	−2,000	−2,821	−3,141	−4,664
Portfolio investment income	3 339	−8,544	−10,326	−11,836	−15,483	−19,317	−26,396	−38,185	−53,090
Income on equity	3 340	−2,075	−2,645	−2,662	−3,543	−4,149	−5,382	−8,002	−9,529
Income on bonds and notes	3 350	−6,453	−7,668	−9,168	−11,932	−15,117	−20,704	−29,766	−43,061
Income on money market instruments	3 360	−16	−13	−6	−8	−51	−310	−417	−500
Other investment income	3 370	−10,246	−13,229	−11,868	−13,405	−15,218	−17,256	−21,855	−32,808
D. CURRENT TRANSFERS	4 379	1,469	1,250	2,516	−387	14	−4,463	−7,700	−9,000
Credit	2 379	11,380	12,143	14,575	17,048	20,366	20,194	21,563	26,058
General government	2 380	1,304	1,539	2,656	2,913	4,153	4,405	4,267	4,987
Other sectors	2 390	10,076	10,603	11,920	14,135	16,213	15,789	17,296	21,071
Workers' remittances	2 391	3,417	3,665	3,959	4,718	5,196	5,343	6,068	7,281
Other current transfers	2 392	6,659	6,938	7,960	9,417	11,017	10,445	11,228	13,789
Debit	3 379	−9,911	−10,892	−12,059	−17,434	−20,353	−24,656	−29,263	−35,058
General government	3 380	−6,624	−6,596	−7,149	−10,093	−11,216	−13,699	−15,413	−16,898
Other sectors	3 390	−3,287	−4,297	−4,911	−7,341	−9,137	−10,958	−13,850	−18,161
Workers' remittances	3 391	−1,325	−1,987	−2,697	−3,939	−5,211	−6,123	−8,578	−11,166
Other current transfers	3 392	−1,961	−2,310	−2,214	−3,402	−3,926	−4,835	−5,272	−6,995
CAPITAL AND FINANCIAL ACCOUNT	4 996	22,938	24,321	21,328	29,116	53,826	85,912	112,230	140,080
CAPITAL ACCOUNT	4 994	4,797	4,811	7,236	9,274	10,450	10,107	7,857	6,291
Total credit	2 994	*5,787*	*5,782*	*8,118*	*10,984*	*11,646*	*11,225*	*9,674*	*8,881*
Total debit	3 994	*−989*	*−971*	*−882*	*−1,710*	*−1,197*	*−1,118*	*−1,817*	*−2,590*
Capital transfers, credit	2 400	5,489	5,654	7,931	10,893	11,300	10,787	9,522	8,677
General government	2 401	4,607	4,748	7,005	9,948	9,956	9,284	7,990	6,862
Debt forgiveness	2 402	400	391	252	345	331	1,207	2,145	464
Other capital transfers	2 410	4,207	4,358	6,754	9,603	9,625	8,077	5,845	6,398
Other sectors	2 430	882	906	925	945	1,343	1,503	1,532	1,815
Migrants' transfers	2 431	745	666	798	838	1,175	1,299	1,305	1,441
Debt forgiveness	2 432	2	173	19	. . . .	5	. . . .	1	73
Other capital transfers	2 440	136	67	109	108	164	203	226	302
Capital transfers, debit	3 400	−716	−558	−554	−1,295	−675	−733	−1,007	−1,635
General government	3 401	−304	−253	−233	−209	−133	−148	−121	−132
Debt forgiveness	3 402	−297	−252	−230	−205	−98	−102	−53	−42
Other capital transfers	3 410	−8	−1	−4	−5	−35	−47	−68	−90
Other sectors	3 430	−411	−305	−321	−1,085	−543	−585	−886	−1,503
Migrants' transfers	3 431	−319	−252	−251	−275	−425	−468	−571	−1,190
Debt forgiveness	3 432	−2	. . . .	−1	−734	−4	−1	. . . .	. . . .
Other capital transfers	3 440	−90	−54	−69	−76	−114	−116	−315	−314
Nonproduced nonfinancial assets, credit	2 480	297	128	187	91	347	439	152	204
Nonproduced nonfinancial assets, debit	3 480	−274	−413	−327	−415	−522	−385	−810	−955

Table 2 (Continued). STANDARD PRESENTATION, 2000–2007

(Millions of U.S. dollars)

	Code	2000	2001	2002	2003	2004	2005	2006	2007
FINANCIAL ACCOUNT	4 995	**18,141**	**19,510**	**14,092**	**19,842**	**43,376**	**75,804**	**104,373**	**133,789**
A. DIRECT INVESTMENT	4 500	**−18,576**	**−4,726**	**6,340**	**−3,152**	**−36,712**	**−17,349**	**−72,242**	**−67,655**
Direct investment abroad	4 505	**−57,411**	**−32,889**	**−33,653**	**−28,759**	**−61,504**	**−41,922**	**−99,492**	**−127,777**
Equity capital	4 510	−48,031	−26,360	−34,558	−28,455	−54,144	−35,885	−87,515	−109,871
Claims on affiliated enterprises	4 515	−48,031	−26,360	−34,558	−28,455	−54,144	−35,885	−87,515	−109,871
Liabilities to affiliated enterprises	4 520	....	....	....	....	....	....	....	....
Reinvested earnings	4 525	−3,546	−64	−461	−1,740	−2,376	−2,608	−10,270	−12,129
Other capital	4 530	−5,834	−6,465	1,365	1,437	−4,984	−3,429	−1,707	−5,777
Claims on affiliated enterprises	4 535	−6,815	−6,615	1,213	−1,837	−4,056	−5,047	−2,488	−12,312
Liabilities to affiliated enterprises	4 540	981	150	151	3,274	−928	1,618	780	6,535
Direct investment in Spain	4 555	**38,835**	**28,164**	**39,993**	**25,607**	**24,792**	**24,573**	**27,250**	**60,122**
Equity capital	4 560	30,842	17,171	24,872	10,857	15,958	16,371	16,069	39,666
Claims on direct investors	4 565	....	....	....	....	....	....	....	....
Liabilities to direct investors	4 570	30,842	17,171	24,872	10,857	15,958	16,371	16,069	39,666
Reinvested earnings	4 575	2,057	1,525	1,797	1,523	1,874	68	4,744	5,615
Other capital	4 580	5,936	9,468	13,324	13,227	6,960	8,134	6,438	14,841
Claims on direct investors	4 585	−675	−575	733	−1,860	−1,458	−529	−990	−608
Liabilities to direct investors	4 590	6,611	10,042	12,591	15,086	8,417	8,663	7,428	15,450
B. PORTFOLIO INVESTMENT	4 600	**−1,172**	**−17,021**	**5,016**	**−46,070**	**102,035**	**53,357**	**232,957**	**117,593**
Assets	4 602	**−59,318**	**−44,992**	**−29,089**	**−90,833**	**−39,651**	**−119,356**	**−11,253**	**−6,574**
Equity securities	4 610	−36,136	−247	123	−13,180	−15,063	−19,370	−25,992	9,779
Monetary authorities	4 611	....	....	....	....	....	....	....	....
General government	4 612	....	....	....	....	....	....	....	....
Banks	4 613	−291	1,867	−877	78	−2,596	−2,827	−5,712	−4,201
Other sectors	4 614	−35,844	−2,114	1,000	−13,258	−12,466	−16,542	−20,280	13,980
Debt securities	4 619	−23,183	−44,745	−29,212	−77,653	−24,588	−99,986	14,740	−16,353
Bonds and notes	4 620	−18,634	−40,162	−28,584	−65,199	−31,560	−96,227	10,900	−16,924
Monetary authorities	4 621	....	....	−484	−10,022	−11,761	−16,071	−20,759	−16,033
General government	4 622	−1	−5	5	−5	−1,107	−5,758	−13,151	−8,276
Banks	4 623	−3,567	−18,566	−8,445	−31,263	−2,566	−48,523	46,806	124
Other sectors	4 624	−15,066	−21,591	−19,659	−23,910	−16,126	−25,876	−1,995	7,261
Money market instruments	4 630	−4,549	−4,582	−628	−12,453	6,972	−3,759	3,840	571
Monetary authorities	4 631	....	....	....	−7,290	5,459	−5,703	3,184	−3,564
General government	4 632	....	−1	11	5	....	....	−8	9
Banks	4 633	−1,039	−4,710	800	−4,803	−845	1,918	−2,538	836
Other sectors	4 634	−3,510	129	−1,439	−366	2,358	25	3,202	3,290
Liabilities	4 652	**58,146**	**27,971**	**34,105**	**44,763**	**141,686**	**172,713**	**244,210**	**124,167**
Equity securities	4 660	19,692	7,958	2,810	−3,649	10,918	−9,573	−23,696	15,393
Banks	4 663	9,209	3,320	3,154	−698	13,345	−2,264	4,680	−4,321
Other sectors	4 664	10,482	4,638	−344	−2,951	−2,427	−7,309	−28,376	19,714
Debt securities	4 669	38,455	20,013	31,294	48,412	130,768	182,286	267,906	108,774
Bonds and notes	4 670	37,127	21,851	29,678	46,160	130,245	183,073	255,693	101,207
Monetary authorities	4 671	....	....	....	....	....	....	....	....
General government	4 672	31,226	11,024	8,132	−11,536	29,130	3,942	14,320	−22,483
Banks	4 673	4,083	5,496	10,497	31,520	49,381	72,030	89,789	39,915
Other sectors	4 674	1,818	5,331	11,049	26,175	51,733	107,100	151,585	83,776
Money market instruments	4 680	1,328	−1,838	1,616	2,253	524	−787	12,213	7,567
Monetary authorities	4 681	....	....	....	....	....	....	....	....
General government	4 682	1,156	−1,784	431	3,338	−933	−599	2,524	−769
Banks	4 683	1	−22	−2	−166	52	619	7,548	14,425
Other sectors	4 684	170	−31	1,187	−919	1,405	−807	2,141	−6,090
C. FINANCIAL DERIVATIVES	4 910	**1,818**	**−269**	**−4,720**	**−3,785**	**74**	**273**	**2,419**	**−9,529**
Monetary authorities	4 911	....	....	....	....	....	....	....	....
General government	4 912	183	39	113	51	−895	−110	−30	−402
Banks	4 913	3,007	86	−2,578	−2,100	−80	433	3,006	−6,544
Other sectors	4 914	−1,372	−394	−2,255	−1,736	1,049	−51	−557	−2,583
Assets	4 900	....	....	....	....	....	....	....	....
Monetary authorities	4 901	....	....	....	....	....	....	....	....
General government	4 902	....	....	....	....	....	....	....	....
Banks	4 903	....	....	....	....	....	....	....	....
Other sectors	4 904	....	....	....	....	....	....	....	....
Liabilities	4 905	**1,818**	**−269**	**−4,720**	**−3,785**	**74**	**273**	**2,419**	**−9,529**
Monetary authorities	4 906	....	....	....	....	....	....	....	....
General government	4 907	183	39	113	51	−895	−110	−30	−402
Banks	4 908	3,007	86	−2,578	−2,100	−80	433	3,006	−6,544
Other sectors	4 909	−1,372	−394	−2,255	−1,736	1,049	−51	−557	−2,583

Table 2 (Concluded). STANDARD PRESENTATION, 2000–2007

(Millions of U.S. dollars)

	Code	2000	2001	2002	2003	2004	2005	2006	2007
D. OTHER INVESTMENT	4 700 ..	**33,190**	**40,184**	**11,146**	**57,359**	**−28,433**	**37,604**	**−58,183**	**93,595**
Assets	4 703 ..	**−18,475**	**10,690**	**−23,854**	**−13,557**	**−52,659**	**−42,198**	**−99,778**	**−51,347**
Trade credits	4 706 ..	1	1	−4	5	4	18	5	13
General government	4 707 ..	....	....	....	....	....	....	....	....
of which: Short-term	4 709 ..	....	....	....	....	....	....	....	....
Other sectors	4 710 ..	1	1	−4	5	4	18	5	13
of which: Short-term	4 712 ..	....	....	....	....	....	....	....	....
Loans	4 714 ..	−3,031	−4,913	−3,522	−3,805	−6,225	−10,322	−29,440	−20,658
Monetary authorities	4 715 ..	1	4	−3	−1	....	1	−2	−1
of which: Short-term	4 718 ..	....	....	....	....	....	....	−2	−1
General government	4 719 ..	−143	107	−1,068	−377	−989	254	140	−1,354
of which: Short-term	4 721 ..	*11*	*214*	*−884*	*−253*	*−639*	*786*	*407*	*−1,248*
Banks	4 722 ..	−2,844	−5,009	−2,410	−3,257	−5,215	−9,841	−30,185	−20,425
of which: Short-term	4 724 ..	*−859*	*−2,349*	*−233*	*231*	*−608*	*−4,585*	*−15,722*	*−9,619*
Other sectors	4 725 ..	−45	−15	−40	−171	−21	−735	606	1,122
of which: Short-term	4 727 ..	*50*	*95*	*94*	*239*	*439*	*−13*	*820*	*1,384*
Currency and deposits	4 730 ..	−15,086	15,857	−19,846	−9,179	−44,936	−29,889	−67,080	−26,812
Monetary authorities	4 731 ..	−7,838	14,988	6,118	5,212	−18,100	17,119	−13,889	26,428
General government	4 732 ..	−32	−34	70	360	−529	161	398	−131
Banks	4 733 ..	−4,631	1,336	−15,318	−7,253	−15,124	−40,941	−41,275	−44,373
Other sectors	4 734 ..	−2,586	−432	−10,715	−7,497	−11,183	−6,229	−12,313	−8,735
Other assets	4 736 ..	−358	−255	−483	−577	−1,502	−2,005	−3,263	−3,890
Monetary authorities	4 737 ..	....	....	....	....	21	....	....	−7
of which: Short-term	4 739 ..	....	....	....	....	....	....	....	....
General government	4 740 ..	−67	−141	−341	−325	−665	−648	−742	−898
of which: Short-term	4 742 ..	....	....	....	....	....	*−2*	*−2*	*−2*
Banks	4 743 ..	−36	−68	−225	−13	−64	220	−1,749	−2,041
of which: Short-term	4 745 ..	*−36*	*−68*	*−225*	*−13*	*−64*	*220*	*−1,749*	*−2,040*
Other sectors	4 746 ..	−255	−46	83	−239	−795	−1,576	−772	−944
of which: Short-term	4 748 ..	*−107*	*78*	*113*	*−255*	*−694*	*−1,491*	*−414*	*−522*
Liabilities	4 753 ..	**51,665**	**29,494**	**35,000**	**70,916**	**24,226**	**79,803**	**41,595**	**144,942**
Trade credits	4 756 ..	−35	−120	−60	−32	22	−72	−24	−6
General government	4 757 ..	....	....	....	....	....	....	−1	−1
of which: Short-term	4 759 ..	....	....	....	....	....	....	....	....
Other sectors	4 760 ..	−35	−120	−60	−32	22	−72	−23	−6
of which: Short-term	4 762 ..	....	....	....	....	....	....	....	....
Loans	4 764 ..	15,332	14,257	7,163	10,497	5,007	16,810	37,200	26,748
Monetary authorities	4 765 ..	....	....	....	....	....	....	....	....
of which: Use of Fund credit and loans from the Fund	4 766 ..	....	....	....	....	....	....	....	....
of which: Short-term.	4 768 ..	....	....	....	....	....	....	....	....
General government	4 769 ..	902	575	1,573	−1,026	6,362	193	1,334	593
of which: Short-term.	4 771 ..	*917*	*34*	*29*	*−1,288*	*847*	*−1,201*	*1,180*	*−404*
Banks	4 772 ..	....	....	....	....	....	....	....	....
of which: Short-term.	4 774 ..	....	....	....	....	....	....	....	....
Other sectors	4 775 ..	14,430	13,682	5,591	11,522	−1,355	16,617	35,866	26,155
of which: Short-term.	4 777 ..	*3,818*	*1,883*	*−2,846*	*−232*	*−116*	*−1,850*	*5,628*	*−4,232*
Currency and deposits	4 780 ..	36,534	15,096	28,101	60,522	17,602	62,975	4,466	118,554
Monetary authorities	4 781 ..	−141	−185	1,119	−1,331	−89	132	−154	14,649
General government	4 782 ..	....	....	....	....	....	....	....	....
Banks	4 783 ..	36,676	15,281	26,982	61,853	17,691	62,843	4,620	103,905
Other sectors	4 784 ..	....	....	....	....	....	....	....	....
Other liabilities	4 786 ..	−166	262	−204	−70	1,595	90	−47	−354
Monetary authorities	4 787 ..	....	....	....	....	....	....	....	....
of which: Short-term	4 789 ..	....	....	....	....	....	....	....	....
General government	4 790 ..	....	....	....	....	....	....	....	....
of which: Short-term	4 792 ..	....	....	....	....	....	....	....	....
Banks	4 793 ..	....	....	....	....	....	....	....	....
of which: Short-term	4 795 ..	....	....	....	....	....	....	....	....
Other sectors	4 796 ..	−166	262	−204	−70	1,595	90	−47	−354
of which: Short-term	4 798 ..	*−194*	*242*	*−240*	*−110*	*1,511*	*−212*	*−341*	*−604*
E. RESERVE ASSETS	4 802 ..	**2,880**	**1,341**	**−3,690**	**15,489**	**6,412**	**1,920**	**−578**	**−215**
Monetary gold	4 812 ..	....	....	....	....	....	....	....	....
Special drawing rights	4 811 ..	−43	−73	27	−25	100	−27	13	−17
Reserve position in the Fund	4 810 ..	269	−186	−150	−115	356	717	380	96
Foreign exchange	4 803 ..	2,654	1,600	−3,567	15,629	5,956	1,229	−972	−294
Other claims	4 813 ..	....	....	....	....	....	....	....	....
NET ERRORS AND OMISSIONS	4 998 ..	**247**	**−257**	**912**	**1,769**	**1,039**	**−2,524**	**−2,106**	**5,275**

Table 3. INTERNATIONAL INVESTMENT POSITION (End-period stocks), 2000–2007

(Millions of U.S. dollars)

	Code	2000	2001	2002	2003	2004	2005	2006	2007
ASSETS	8 995 C.	**580,931**	**609,047**	**775,294**	**1,024,900**	**1,255,776**	**1,312,652**	**1,718,026**	**2,090,527**
Direct investment abroad	8 505	**167,719**	**191,651**	**233,947**	**292,464**	**370,931**	**375,047**	**517,096**	**687,413**
Equity capital and reinvested earnings	8 506	155,534	173,821	216,313	274,180	346,921	348,937	487,691	650,154
Claims on affiliated enterprises	8 507	....	....	....	....	....	....	....	....
Liabilities to affiliated enterprises	8 508	....	....	....	....	....	....	....	....
Other capital	8 530	12,185	17,830	17,633	18,285	24,010	26,110	29,405	37,259
Claims on affiliated enterprises	8 535	14,023	19,815	20,091	24,632	30,250	33,575	38,175	53,627
Liabilities to affiliated enterprises	8 540	−1,838	−1,986	−2,458	−6,347	−6,240	−7,465	−8,770	−16,369
Portfolio investment	8 602	**180,221**	**205,032**	**269,823**	**424,395**	**517,762**	**581,154**	**666,658**	**747,166**
Equity securities	8 610	78,086	65,741	53,181	79,161	106,316	122,873	175,415	198,384
Monetary authorities	8 611	....	....	....	....	....	....	....	....
General government	8 612	....	....	....	....	....	....	....	....
Banks	8 613	6,184	3,789	3,801	4,028	7,501	9,117	15,269	22,706
Other sectors	8 614	71,903	61,952	49,380	75,134	98,814	113,756	160,146	175,678
Debt securities	8 619	102,135	139,291	216,641	345,234	411,446	458,281	491,243	548,782
Bonds and notes	8 620	94,273	129,379	209,829	323,244	395,191	435,706	471,405	527,336
Monetary authorities	8 621	....	....	510	12,361	25,554	36,672	60,569	83,096
General government	8 622	....	....	8	69	1,219	6,669	21,047	32,397
Banks	8 623	27,926	45,916	69,493	112,044	129,708	160,105	110,243	121,820
Other sectors	8 624	66,347	83,463	139,818	198,770	238,709	232,259	279,546	290,023
Money market instruments	8 630	7,862	9,912	6,812	21,990	16,255	22,575	19,838	21,446
Monetary authorities	8 631	....	....	....	8,135	2,797	8,031	5,951	11,553
General government	8 632	....	....	....	....	....	....	9	....
Banks	8 633	3,509	5,834	3,354	9,063	8,746	9,019	3,700	2,122
Other sectors	8 634	4,353	4,078	3,458	4,791	4,713	5,524	10,178	7,771
Financial derivatives	8 900	....	....	....	....	....	....	**43,426**	**65,718**
Monetary authorities	8 901	....	....	....	....	....	....	....	....
General government	8 902	....	....	....	....	....	....	....	....
Banks	8 903	....	....	....	....	....	....	43,426	65,718
Other sectors	8 904	....	....	....	....	....	....	....	....
Other investment	8 703	**197,414**	**178,110**	**231,221**	**281,232**	**347,324**	**339,224**	**471,506**	**571,176**
Trade credits	8 706	137	129	148	158	164	126	132	133
General government	8 707	....	....	....	....	....	....	....	....
of which: Short-term	8 709	....	....	....	....	....	....	....	....
Other sectors	8 710	137	129	148	158	164	126	132	133
of which: Short-term	8 712	....	....	....	....	....	....	....	....
Loans	8 714	28,570	31,488	36,887	45,096	52,350	54,222	83,242	101,424
Monetary authorities	8 715	....	....	....	....	....	....	....	....
of which: Short-term	8 718	....	....	....	....	....	....	....	....
General government	8 719	8,170	7,907	9,474	10,571	12,562	11,233	11,587	13,192
of which: Short-term	8 721	*2,903*	*2,597*	*3,737*	*4,379*	*5,826*	*4,181*	*3,996*	*5,135*
Banks	8 722	19,690	22,745	26,229	32,658	37,391	41,039	69,476	85,394
of which: Short-term	8 724	*10,239*	*11,827*	*13,639*	*16,982*	*19,443*	*9,659*	*21,363*	*23,270*
Other sectors	8 725	710	837	1,184	1,866	2,398	1,951	2,178	2,837
of which: Short-term	8 727	*179*	*221*	*346*	*513*	*513*	*577*	*490*	*529*
Currency and deposits	8 730	164,289	141,385	187,498	227,128	283,540	273,355	371,914	446,847
Monetary authorities	8 731	42,131	25,696	23,753	23,074	44,064	22,317	39,948	7,056
General government	8 732	240	243	212	17	404	234	242	131
Banks	8 733	68,116	63,932	91,374	110,065	125,888	145,836	202,733	286,667
Other sectors	8 734	53,801	51,515	72,158	93,972	113,185	104,967	128,991	152,992
Other assets	8 736	4,418	5,107	6,688	8,850	11,270	11,521	16,219	22,773
Monetary authorities	8 737	414	392	466	562	589	510	570	644
of which: Short-term	8 739	....	....	....	....	....	....	....	....
General government	8 740	1,274	1,330	1,774	2,292	3,080	3,097	4,005	5,289
of which: Short-term	8 742	....	....	....	....	....	*2*	*4*	*6*
Banks	8 743	30	93	340	405	491	233	2,074	4,536
of which: Short-term	8 745	*30*	*93*	*340*	*405*	*491*	*233*	*2,074*	*4,536*
Other sectors	8 746	2,700	3,292	4,107	5,592	7,110	7,681	9,571	12,303
of which: Short-term	8 748	*120*	*34*	*−71*	*200*	*975*	*2,248*	*2,942*	*3,850*
Reserve assets	8 802	**35,577**	**34,254**	**40,303**	**26,809**	**19,759**	**17,227**	**19,340**	**19,054**
Monetary gold	8 812	4,588	4,672	5,768	7,021	7,370	7,550	8,518	7,574
Special drawing rights	8 811	290	351	354	413	332	332	335	369
Reserve position in the Fund	8 810	1,182	1,326	1,592	1,862	1,575	752	399	319
Foreign exchange	8 803	29,516	27,905	32,590	17,513	10,481	8,593	10,088	10,792
Other claims	8 813	....	....	....	....	....	....	....	....

Table 3 (Concluded). INTERNATIONAL INVESTMENT POSITION (End-period stocks), 2000–2007

(Millions of U.S. dollars)

	Code	2000	2001	2002	2003	2004	2005	2006	2007
LIABILITIES..........	8 995 D.	729,942	774,706	1,022,767	1,400,882	1,750,102	1,825,819	2,468,503	3,171,070
Direct investment in Spain.................	8 555 ..	156,348	177,254	257,106	339,652	395,983	370,997	442,787	570,691
Equity capital and reinvested earnings...........	8 556 ..	132,916	144,850	204,193	261,563	304,040	282,139	337,942	444,252
Claims on direct investors.............	8 557 ..	....	....	....	....	....	....	....	....
Liabilities to direct investors............	8 558 ..	....	....	....	....	....	....	....	....
Other capital.............	8 580 ..	23,432	32,403	52,913	78,089	91,943	88,858	104,845	126,440
Claims on direct investors.............	8 585 ..	−4,241	−4,640	−4,820	−7,749	−10,012	−9,135	−11,203	−13,241
Liabilities to direct investors............	8 590 ..	27,673	37,043	57,732	85,839	101,954	97,992	116,049	139,681
Portfolio investment.............	8 652 ..	289,068	293,540	380,111	533,041	766,167	859,273	1,270,352	1,605,806
Equity securities.............	8 660 ..	137,268	127,040	122,663	186,770	249,551	232,810	323,564	421,325
Banks.............	8 663 ..	45,031	39,968	43,256	65,966	89,314	88,339	126,148	140,304
Other sectors.............	8 664 ..	92,237	87,073	79,407	120,804	160,237	144,472	197,416	281,021
Debt securities.............	8 669 ..	151,800	166,500	257,448	346,271	516,616	626,462	946,788	1,184,481
Bonds and notes.............	8 670 ..	146,966	163,592	252,532	337,513	506,918	618,410	925,881	1,152,819
Monetary authorities.............	8 671 ..	....	....	....	....	....	....	....	....
General government.............	8 672 ..	126,381	133,271	186,925	198,988	247,736	227,443	252,695	255,283
Banks.............	8 673 ..	15,839	20,584	40,658	77,867	142,639	194,010	310,862	390,782
Other sectors.............	8 674 ..	4,746	9,737	24,949	60,658	116,543	196,956	362,324	506,755
Money market instruments.............	8 680 ..	4,834	2,907	4,916	8,758	9,698	8,053	20,906	31,662
Monetary authorities.............	8 681 ..	....	....	....	....	....	....	....	....
General government.............	8 682 ..	3,193	1,408	1,405	5,446	3,781	2,908	6,369	6,631
Banks.............	8 683 ..	143	113	363	412	410	1,157	8,234	24,735
Other sectors.............	8 684 ..	1,499	1,386	3,147	2,901	5,507	3,987	6,304	296
Financial derivatives.............	8 905 ..	....	....	....	....	....	....	56,063	93,459
Monetary authorities.............	8 906 ..	....	....	....	....	....	....	....	....
General government.............	8 907 ..	....	....	....	....	....	....	619	1,064
Banks.............	8 908 ..	....	....	....	....	....	....	55,444	92,396
Other sectors.............	8 909 ..	....	....	....	....	....	....	....	....
Other investment.............	8 753 ..	284,526	303,912	385,550	528,189	587,951	595,549	699,301	901,113
Trade credits.............	8 756 ..	603	468	472	510	564	422	445	485
General government.............	8 757 ..	....	....	....	....	....	....	....	....
of which: Short-term.............	8 759 ..	....	....	....	....	....	....	....	....
Other sectors.............	8 760 ..	603	468	472	510	564	422	445	485
of which: Short-term.............	8 762 ..	....	....	....	....	....	....	....	....
Loans.............	8 764 ..	64,546	77,098	96,686	126,133	140,635	140,822	195,706	243,793
Monetary authorities.............	8 765 ..	....	....	....	....	....	....	....	....
of which: Use of Fund credit and loans from the Fund....	8 766 ..	....	....	....	....	....	....	....	....
of which: Short-term.............	8 768 ..	....	....	....	....	....	....	....	....
General government.............	8 769 ..	10,616	10,807	14,204	16,373	23,930	21,411	24,828	29,171
of which: Short-term.............	8 771 ..	*1,294*	*1,291*	*1,124*	*423*	*960*	*76*	*872*	*1,288*
Banks.............	8 772 ..	....	....	....	....	....	....	....	....
of which: Short-term.............	8 774 ..	....	....	....	....	....	....	....	....
Other sectors.............	8 775 ..	53,930	66,290	82,482	109,760	116,705	119,411	170,878	214,622
of which: Short-term.............	8 777 ..	*17,782*	*20,295*	*20,864*	*24,247*	*25,887*	*21,019*	*29,845*	*29,906*
Currency and deposits.............	8 780 ..	219,207	225,809	287,989	401,049	444,496	452,508	501,506	655,409
Monetary authorities.............	8 781 ..	....	....	1,438	116	21	149	370	5,226
General government.............	8 782 ..	....	....	....	....	....	....	....	....
Banks.............	8 783 ..	219,207	225,809	286,551	400,933	444,475	452,359	501,136	650,182
Other sectors.............	8 784 ..	....	....	....	....	....	....	....	....
Other liabilities.............	8 786 ..	170	537	403	497	2,257	1,798	1,644	1,426
Monetary authorities.............	8 787 ..	....	....	....	....	....	....	....	....
of which: Short-term.............	8 789 ..	....	....	....	....	....	....	....	....
General government.............	8 790 ..	....	....	....	....	....	....	....	....
of which: Short-term.............	8 792 ..	....	....	....	....	....	....	....	....
Banks.............	8 793 ..	....	....	....	....	....	....	....	....
of which: Short-term.............	8 795 ..	....	....	....	....	....	....	....	....
Other sectors.............	8 796 ..	170	537	403	497	2,257	1,798	1,644	1,426
of which: Short-term.............	8 798 ..	*59*	*296*	*82*	....	*1,600*	*1,175*	*914*	*408*
NET INTERNATIONAL INVESTMENT POSITION........	8 995 ..	−149,011	−165,659	−247,473	−375,982	−494,326	−513,166	−750,477	1,080,543
Conversion rates: euros per U.S. dollar (end of period).............	0 104 ..	1.0747	1.1347	.9536	.7918	.7342	.8477	.7593	.6793

Table 1. ANALYTIC PRESENTATION, 2000–2007

(Millions of U.S. dollars)

	Code	2000	2001	2002	2003	2004	2005	2006	2007
A. Current Account[1]	4 993 Z.	**−1,044**	**−237**	**−268**	**−106**	**−677**	**−743**	**−1,599**	**−1,465**
Goods: exports f.o.b.	2 100 ..	5,440	4,817	4,699	5,133	5,757	6,347	6,883	7,741
Goods: imports f.o.b.	3 100 ..	−6,484	−5,377	−5,495	−6,005	−7,200	−7,977	−9,228	−10,170
Balance on Goods	4 100 ..	*−1,044*	*−560*	*−796*	*−872*	*−1,443*	*−1,630*	*−2,345*	*−2,430*
Services: credit	2 200 ..	939	1,355	1,268	1,411	1,527	1,540	1,625	1,712
Services: debit	3 200 ..	−1,621	−1,749	−1,584	−1,679	−1,908	−2,089	−2,394	−2,603
Balance on Goods and Services	4 991 ..	*−1,727*	*−954*	*−1,112*	*−1,140*	*−1,824*	*−2,179*	*−3,114*	*−3,321*
Income: credit	2 300 ..	149	108	75	170	157	76	312	449
Income: debit	3 300 ..	−449	−375	−328	−341	−360	−375	−700	−807
Balance on Goods, Services, and Income	4 992 ..	*−2,027*	*−1,221*	*−1,364*	*−1,312*	*−2,027*	*−2,478*	*−3,502*	*−3,679*
Current transfers: credit	2 379 Z.	1,166	1,155	1,287	1,414	1,564	1,968	2,161	2,502
Current transfers: debit	3 379 ..	−183	−172	−190	−209	−214	−233	−258	−288
B. Capital Account[1]	4 994 Z.	**49**	**50**	**65**	**74**	**64**	**250**	**291**	**269**
Capital account: credit	2 994 Z.	55	55	71	81	71	257	299	278
Capital account: debit	3 994 ..	−6	−5	−6	−6	−7	−8	−8	−10
Total, Groups A Plus B	4 981 ..	*−994*	*−187*	*−203*	*−32*	*−613*	*−493*	*−1,308*	*−1,196*
C. Financial Account[1]	4 995 W.	**447**	**−136**	**−196**	**−219**	**−133**	**67**	**687**	**14**
Direct investment abroad	4 505 ..	....	....	−11	−27	−6	−38	−29	−55
Direct investment in Sri Lanka	4 555 Z.	173	172	197	229	233	272	480	603
Portfolio investment assets	4 602 ..	19	24	78	145	111	276	355	326
Equity securities	4 610 ..	....	24	78	145	111	276	355	423
Debt securities	4 619 ..	19	....	....	....	....	....	....	−97
Portfolio investment liabilities	4 652 Z.	−63	−35	−53	−143	−100	−216	−304	−322
Equity securities	4 660 ..	....	−35	−53	−143	−100	−216	−304	−322
Debt securities	4 669 Z.	−63	....	....	....	....	....	....	....
Financial derivatives	4 910 ..	....	....	....	....	....	....	....	....
Financial derivatives assets	4 900 ..	....	....	....	....	....	....	....	....
Financial derivatives liabilities	4 905 ..	....	....	....	....	....	....	....	....
Other investment assets	4 703 ..	−244	183	104	−94	−354	−223	297	−281
Monetary authorities	4 701 ..	....	....	....	....	....	....	....	....
General government	4 704 ..	−4	....	....	....	....	....	....	....
Banks	4 705 ..	−239	183	104	−94	−354	−223	297	−281
Other sectors	4 728 ..	....	....	....	....	....	....	....	....
Other investment liabilities	4 753 W.	562	−480	−511	−328	−17	−4	−111	−257
Monetary authorities	4 753 WA	76	−33	27	40	179	−80	12	144
General government	4 753 ZB	47	−174	−324	−251	−275	−77	−212	−618
Banks	4 753 ZC	258	71	−145	−2	202	323	293	364
Other sectors	4 753 ZD	182	−343	−69	−115	−123	−170	−203	−148
Total, Groups A Through C	4 983 ..	*−547*	*−323*	*−398*	*−251*	*−746*	*−426*	*−621*	*−1,182*
D. Net Errors and Omissions	4 998 ..	**186**	**15**	**136**	**−114**	**−189**	**−73**	**−96**	**−192**
Total, Groups A Through D	4 984 ..	*−361*	*−308*	*−262*	*−365*	*−935*	*−498*	*−717*	*−1,374*
E. Reserves and Related Items	4 802 A.	**361**	**308**	**262**	**365**	**935**	**498**	**717**	**1,374**
Reserve assets	4 802 ..	447	−241	−444	−627	133	−540	−73	−675
Use of Fund credit and loans	4 766 ..	−86	60	74	50	−112	118	−153	−5
Exceptional financing	4 920 ..	....	489	633	942	913	920	943	2,055
Conversion rates: Sri Lanka rupees per U.S. dollar	0 101 ..	**77.005**	**89.383**	**95.662**	**96.521**	**101.194**	**100.498**	**103.914**	**110.623**

[1] Excludes components that have been classified in the categories of Group E.

Table 2. STANDARD PRESENTATION, 2000–2007

(Millions of U.S. dollars)

	Code	2000	2001	2002	2003	2004	2005	2006	2007
CURRENT ACCOUNT	4 993	**−1,044**	**−215**	**−236**	**−71**	**−648**	**−650**	**−1,498**	**−1,368**
A. GOODS	4 100	**−1,044**	**−560**	**−796**	**−872**	**−1,443**	**−1,630**	**−2,345**	**−2,430**
Credit	2 100	**5,440**	**4,817**	**4,699**	**5,133**	**5,757**	**6,347**	**6,883**	**7,741**
General merchandise: exports f.o.b.	2 110	5,440	4,817	4,699	5,133	5,757	6,347	6,883	7,741
Goods for processing: exports f.o.b.	2 150	....	....	....	....	....	....	....	....
Repairs on goods	2 160	....	....	....	....	....	....	....	....
Goods procured in ports by carriers	2 170	....	....	....	....	....	....	....	....
Nonmonetary gold	2 180	....	....	....	....	....	....	....	....
Debit	3 100	**−6,484**	**−5,377**	**−5,495**	**−6,005**	**−7,200**	**−7,977**	**−9,228**	**−10,170**
General merchandise: imports f.o.b.	3 110	−6,484	−5,377	−5,495	−6,005	−7,200	−7,977	−9,228	−10,170
Goods for processing: imports f.o.b.	3 150	....	....	....	....	....	....	....	....
Repairs on goods	3 160	....	....	....	....	....	....	....	....
Goods procured in ports by carriers	3 170	....	....	....	....	....	....	....	....
Nonmonetary gold	3 180	....	....	....	....	....	....	....	....
B. SERVICES	4 200	**−683**	**−394**	**−316**	**−268**	**−381**	**−549**	**−769**	**−891**
Total credit	2 200	*939*	*1,355*	*1,268*	*1,411*	*1,527*	*1,540*	*1,625*	*1,712*
Total debit	3 200	*−1,621*	*−1,749*	*−1,584*	*−1,679*	*−1,908*	*−2,089*	*−2,394*	*−2,603*
Transportation services, credit	2 205	**400**	**384**	**514**	**562**	**624**	**673**	**751**	**840**
Passenger	2 850	*140*	*134*	*231*	*268*	*295*	*300*	*323*	*365*
Freight	2 851	*42*	*40*	*43*	*45*	*50*	*54*	*63*	*72*
Other	2 852	*218*	*210*	*240*	*249*	*279*	*319*	*365*	*404*
Sea transport, passenger	2 207	....	134	231	268	295	300	323	365
Sea transport, freight	2 208	....	40	43	45	50	54	63	72
Sea transport, other	2 209	....	210	240	249	279	319	365	404
Air transport, passenger	2 211	....	....	....	....	....	....	....	....
Air transport, freight	2 212	....	....	....	....	....	....	....	....
Air transport, other	2 213	....	....	....	....	....	....	....	....
Other transport, passenger	2 215	....	....	....	....	....	....	....	....
Other transport, freight	2 216	....	....	....	....	....	....	....	....
Other transport, other	2 217	....	....	....	....	....	....	....	....
Transportation services, debit	3 205	**−980**	**−845**	**−881**	**−962**	**−1,135**	**−1,267**	**−1,462**	**−1,614**
Passenger	3 850	*−143*	*−152*	*−175*	*−183*	*−203*	*−238*	*−293*	*−316*
Freight	3 851	*−724*	*−600*	*−612*	*−672*	*−805*	*−889*	*−1,028*	*−1,132*
Other	3 852	*−113*	*−93*	*−93*	*−107*	*−127*	*−141*	*−142*	*−166*
Sea transport, passenger	3 207	....	−152	−175	−183	−203	−238	−293	−316
Sea transport, freight	3 208	....	−600	−612	−672	−805	−889	−1,028	−1,132
Sea transport, other	3 209	....	−93	−93	−107	−127	−141	−142	−166
Air transport, passenger	3 211	....	....	....	....	....	....	....	....
Air transport, freight	3 212	....	....	....	....	....	....	....	....
Air transport, other	3 213	....	....	....	....	....	....	....	....
Other transport, passenger	3 215	....	....	....	....	....	....	....	....
Other transport, freight	3 216	....	....	....	....	....	....	....	....
Other transport, other	3 217	....	....	....	....	....	....	....	....
Travel, credit	2 236	**248**	**213**	**363**	**441**	**513**	**429**	**410**	**385**
Business travel	2 237	....	....	....	....	....	....	....	....
Personal travel	2 240	....	213	363	441	513	429	410	385
Travel, debit	3 236	**−240**	**−250**	**−263**	**−279**	**−296**	**−314**	**−373**	**−393**
Business travel	3 237	....	....	....	....	....	....	....	....
Personal travel	3 240	....	−250	−263	−279	−296	−314	−373	−393
Other services, credit	2 200 BA	**291**	**759**	**391**	**407**	**390**	**438**	**464**	**487**
Communications	2 245	45	40	69	53	43	44	68	72
Construction	2 249	....	41	34	38	26	29	29	33
Insurance	2 253	41	423	45	48	50	73	57	55
Financial	2 260	....	....	....	....	....	....	....	....
Computer and information	2 262	....	66	50	65	72	82	98	110
Royalties and licence fees	2 266	....	....	....	....	....	....	....	....
Other business services	2 268	182	168	171	182	178	188	190	196
Personal, cultural, and recreational	2 287	....	....	....	....	....	....	....	....
Government, n.i.e.	2 291	24	22	21	21	20	21	21	20
Other services, debit	3 200 BA	**−401**	**−654**	**−441**	**−439**	**−477**	**−507**	**−558**	**−596**
Communications	3 245	−47	−6	−8	−8	−10	−19	−49	−54
Construction	3 249	....	−10	−8	−4	−6	−6	−6	−6
Insurance	3 253	−94	−377	−88	−96	−110	−123	−140	−153
Financial	3 260	....	....	....	....	....	....	....	....
Computer and information	3 262	....	....	....	....	....	....	....	....
Royalties and licence fees	3 266	....	....	....	....	....	....	....	....
Other business services	3 268	−231	−247	−305	−299	−315	−322	−329	−349
Personal, cultural, and recreational	3 287	....	....	....	....	....	....	....	....
Government, n.i.e.	3 291	−30	−15	−31	−33	−35	−37	−35	−34

Table 2 (Continued). STANDARD PRESENTATION, 2000–2007

(Millions of U.S. dollars)

	Code	2000	2001	2002	2003	2004	2005	2006	2007
C. INCOME	4 300	**−300**	**−267**	**−252**	**−172**	**−204**	**−300**	**−388**	**−358**
Total credit	2 300	*149*	*108*	*75*	*170*	*157*	*76*	*312*	*449*
Total debit	3 300	*−449*	*−375*	*−328*	*−341*	*−360*	*−375*	*−700*	*−807*
Compensation of employees, credit	2 310	**12**	**14**	**9**	**10**	**10**	**7**	**6**	**6**
Compensation of employees, debit	3 310	**−14**	**−17**	**−13**	**−15**	**−16**	**−16**	**−17**	**−17**
Investment income, credit	2 320	**137**	**93**	**66**	**160**	**147**	**69**	**306**	**443**
Direct investment income	2 330	2	3	2	2	3	3	3	3
Dividends and distributed branch profits	2 332	2	3	2	2	3	3	3	3
Reinvested earnings and undistributed branch profits	2 333	....	....	....	....	....	....	....	....
Income on debt (interest)	2 334	....	....	....	....	....	....	....	....
Portfolio investment income	2 339	....	....	....	....	....	....	....	....
Income on equity	2 340	....	....	....	....	....	....	....	....
Income on bonds and notes	2 350	....	....	....	....	....	....	....	....
Income on money market instruments	2 360	....	....	....	....	....	....	....	....
Other investment income	2 370	135	90	64	158	144	66	303	441
Investment income, debit	3 320	**−435**	**−358**	**−314**	**−326**	**−344**	**−359**	**−683**	**−790**
Direct investment income	3 330	−109	−104	−98	−92	−95	−115	−362	−349
Dividends and distributed branch profits	3 332	−98	−104	−98	−92	−95	−115	−362	−126
Reinvested earnings and undistributed branch profits	3 333	−11							−223
Income on debt (interest)	3 334	....	....	....	....	....	....	....	....
Portfolio investment income	3 339	....	....	....	....	....	....	....	....
Income on equity	3 340	....	....	....	....	....	....	....	....
Income on bonds and notes	3 350	....	....	....	....	....	....	....	....
Income on money market instruments	3 360	....	....	....	....	....	....	....	....
Other investment income	3 370	−326	−254	−216	−235	−249	−244	−321	−441
D. CURRENT TRANSFERS	4 379	**983**	**1,005**	**1,128**	**1,241**	**1,380**	**1,828**	**2,004**	**2,311**
Credit	2 379	**1,166**	**1,177**	**1,318**	**1,450**	**1,594**	**2,061**	**2,262**	**2,598**
General government	2 380	23	22	31	36	30	93	101	97
Other sectors	2 390	1,142	1,155	1,287	1,414	1,564	1,968	2,161	2,502
Workers' remittances	2 391	1,142	1,155	1,287	1,414	1,564	1,968	2,161	2,502
Other current transfers	2 392	....	....	....	....	....	....	....	....
Debit	3 379	**−183**	**−172**	**−190**	**−209**	**−214**	**−233**	**−258**	**−288**
General government	3 380	....	....	....	....	....	....	....	....
Other sectors	3 390	−183	−172	−190	−209	−214	−233	−258	−288
Workers' remittances	3 391	....	−172	−190	−209	−214	−233	−258	−288
Other current transfers	3 392	−183	....	....	....	....	....	....	....
CAPITAL AND FINANCIAL ACCOUNT	4 996	**857**	**200**	**100**	**185**	**837**	**723**	**1,594**	**1,560**
CAPITAL ACCOUNT	4 994	**49**	**50**	**65**	**74**	**64**	**250**	**291**	**269**
Total credit	2 994	*55*	*55*	*71*	*81*	*71*	*257*	*299*	*278*
Total debit	3 994	*−6*	*−5*	*−6*	*−6*	*−7*	*−8*	*−8*	*−10*
Capital transfers, credit	2 400	**55**	**55**	**71**	**81**	**71**	**257**	**299**	**278**
General government	2 401	43	40	58	66	55	144	187	180
Debt forgiveness	2 402	....	....	....	....	....	....	....	....
Other capital transfers	2 410	....	40	58	66	55	144	187	180
Other sectors	2 430	12	15	13	14	16	113	112	99
Migrants' transfers	2 431	12	15	13	14	16	15	18	19
Debt forgiveness	2 432	....	....	....	....	....	....	....	....
Other capital transfers	2 440	....	....	....	....	....	98	94	79
Capital transfers, debit	3 400	**−6**	**−5**	**−6**	**−6**	**−7**	**−8**	**−8**	**−10**
General government	3 401	....	....	....	....	....	....	....	....
Debt forgiveness	3 402	....	....	....	....	....	....	....	....
Other capital transfers	3 410	....	....	....	....	....	....	....	....
Other sectors	3 430	−6	−5	−6	−6	−7	−8	−8	−10
Migrants' transfers	3 431	−6	−5	−6	−6	−7	−8	−8	−10
Debt forgiveness	3 432	....	....	....	....	....	....	....	....
Other capital transfers	3 440	....	....	....	....	....	....	....	....
Nonproduced nonfinancial assets, credit	2 480	....	....	....	....	....	....	....	....
Nonproduced nonfinancial assets, debit	3 480	....	....	....	....	....	....	....	....

Table 2 (Continued). STANDARD PRESENTATION, 2000–2007

(Millions of U.S. dollars)

	Code	2000	2001	2002	2003	2004	2005	2006	2007
FINANCIAL ACCOUNT...............................	4 995 ..	**808**	**151**	**35**	**111**	**773**	**473**	**1,304**	**1,292**
A. DIRECT INVESTMENT............................	4 500 ..	**173**	**172**	**185**	**201**	**227**	**234**	**450**	**548**
Direct investment abroad....................	4 505 ..	....	....	−11	−27	−6	−38	−29	−55
Equity capital................................	4 510 ..	....	....	....	....	....	....	....	−55
Claims on affiliated enterprises.............	4 515 ..	....	....	....	....	....	....	....	−55
Liabilities to affiliated enterprises.........	4 520 ..	....	....	....	....	....	....	....	....
Reinvested earnings.........................	4 525 ..	....	....	....	....	....	....	....	....
Other capital...............................	4 530 ..	....	....	−11	−27	−6	−38	−29	....
Claims on affiliated enterprises.............	4 535 ..	....	....	−11	−27	−6	−38	−29	....
Liabilities to affiliated enterprises.........	4 540 ..	....	....	....	....	....	....	....	....
Direct investment in Sri Lanka..............	4 555 ..	**173**	**172**	**197**	**229**	**233**	**272**	**480**	**603**
Equity capital................................	4 560 ..	164	82	192	199	223	272	480	221
Claims on direct investors...................	4 565 ..	....	....	....	....	....	....	....	....
Liabilities to direct investors...............	4 570 ..	....	82	192	199	223	272	480	221
Reinvested earnings.........................	4 575 ..	11	....	....	....	....	....	....	223
Other capital...............................	4 580 ..	−2	90	5	30	10	....	....	159
Claims on direct investors...................	4 585 ..	....	....	....	....	....	....	....	....
Liabilities to direct investors...............	4 590 ..	−2	90	5	30	10	....	....	159
B. PORTFOLIO INVESTMENT......................	4 600 ..	**−44**	**−11**	**25**	**2**	**11**	**60**	**51**	**974**
Assets..	4 602 ..	**19**	**24**	**78**	**145**	**111**	**276**	**355**	**326**
Equity securities............................	4 610 ..	....	24	78	145	111	276	355	423
Monetary authorities......................	4 611 ..	....	....	....	....	....	....	....	....
General government.......................	4 612 ..	....	....	....	....	....	....	....	....
Banks.....................................	4 613 ..	....	....	....	....	....	....	....	....
Other sectors.............................	4 614 ..	....	24	78	145	111	276	355	423
Debt securities..............................	4 619 ..	19	....	....	....	....	....	....	−97
Bonds and notes...........................	4 620 ..	19	....	....	....	....	....	....	....
Monetary authorities......................	4 621 ..	....	....	....	....	....	....	....	....
General government.......................	4 622 ..	....	....	....	....	....	....	....	....
Banks.....................................	4 623 ..	....	....	....	....	....	....	....	....
Other sectors.............................	4 624 ..	....	....	....	....	....	....	....	....
Money market instruments.................	4 630 ..	....	....	....	....	....	....	....	−97
Monetary authorities......................	4 631 ..	....	....	....	....	....	....	....	....
General government.......................	4 632 ..	....	....	....	....	....	....	....	−97
Banks.....................................	4 633 ..	....	....	....	....	....	....	....	....
Other sectors.............................	4 634 ..	....	....	....	....	....	....	....	....
Liabilities.......................................	4 652 ..	**−63**	**−35**	**−53**	**−143**	**−100**	**−216**	**−304**	**648**
Equity securities............................	4 660 ..	....	−35	−53	−143	−100	−216	−304	−322
Banks.....................................	4 663 ..	....	....	....	....	....	....	....	....
Other sectors.............................	4 664 ..	....	−35	−53	−143	−100	−216	−304	−322
Debt securities..............................	4 669 ..	−63	....	....	....	....	....	....	970
Bonds and notes...........................	4 670 ..	−63	....	....	....	....	....	....	500
Monetary authorities......................	4 671 ..	....	....	....	....	....	....	....	....
General government.......................	4 672 ..	....	....	....	....	....	....	....	500
Banks.....................................	4 673 ..	....	....	....	....	....	....	....	....
Other sectors.............................	4 674 ..	....	....	....	....	....	....	....	....
Money market instruments.................	4 680 ..	....	....	....	....	....	....	....	470
Monetary authorities......................	4 681 ..	....	....	....	....	....	....	....	....
General government.......................	4 682 ..	....	....	....	....	....	....	....	470
Banks.....................................	4 683 ..	....	....	....	....	....	....	....	....
Other sectors.............................	4 684 ..	....	....	....	....	....	....	....	....
C. FINANCIAL DERIVATIVES......................	4 910 ..	....	....	....	....	....	....	....	....
Monetary authorities........................	4 911 ..	....	....	....	....	....	....	....	....
General government.........................	4 912 ..	....	....	....	....	....	....	....	....
Banks.......................................	4 913 ..	....	....	....	....	....	....	....	....
Other sectors...............................	4 914 ..	....	....	....	....	....	....	....	....
Assets..	4 900 ..	....	....	....	....	....	....	....	....
Monetary authorities........................	4 901 ..	....	....	....	....	....	....	....	....
General government.........................	4 902 ..	....	....	....	....	....	....	....	....
Banks.......................................	4 903 ..	....	....	....	....	....	....	....	....
Other sectors...............................	4 904 ..	....	....	....	....	....	....	....	....
Liabilities.......................................	4 905 ..	....	....	....	....	....	....	....	....
Monetary authorities........................	4 906 ..	....	....	....	....	....	....	....	....
General government.........................	4 907 ..	....	....	....	....	....	....	....	....
Banks.......................................	4 908 ..	....	....	....	....	....	....	....	....
Other sectors...............................	4 909 ..	....	....	....	....	....	....	....	....

Table 2 (Concluded). STANDARD PRESENTATION, 2000–2007

(Millions of U.S. dollars)

	Code	2000	2001	2002	2003	2004	2005	2006	2007
D. OTHER INVESTMENT	4 700	**233**	**230**	**269**	**535**	**401**	**718**	**875**	**445**
Assets	4 703	**−244**	**183**	**104**	**−94**	**−354**	**−223**	**297**	**−281**
Trade credits	4 706	....	....	....	....	....	....	....	....
General government	4 707	....	....	....	....	....	....	....	....
of which: Short-term	4 709	....	....	....	....	....	....	....	....
Other sectors	4 710	....	....	....	....	....	....	....	....
of which: Short-term	4 712	....	....	....	....	....	....	....	....
Loans	4 714	....	....	....	....	....	....	....	....
Monetary authorities	4 715	....	....	....	....	....	....	....	....
of which: Short-term	4 718	....	....	....	....	....	....	....	....
General government	4 719	....	....	....	....	....	....	....	....
of which: Short-term	4 721	....	....	....	....	....	....	....	....
Banks	4 722	....	....	....	....	....	....	....	....
of which: Short-term	4 724	....	....	....	....	....	....	....	....
Other sectors	4 725	....	....	....	....	....	....	....	....
of which: Short-term	4 727	....	....	....	....	....	....	....	....
Currency and deposits	4 730	−244	183	104	−94	−354	−223	297	−281
Monetary authorities	4 731		....	....	....	....	....	....	....
General government	4 732	−4	....	....	....	....	....	....	....
Banks	4 733	−239	183	104	−94	−354	−223	297	−281
Other sectors	4 734	....	....	....	....	....	....	....	....
Other assets	4 736	....	....	....	....	....	....	....	....
Monetary authorities	4 737	....	....	....	....	....	....	....	....
of which: Short-term	4 739	....	....	....	....	....	....	....	....
General government	4 740	....	....	....	....	....	....	....	....
of which: Short-term	4 742	....	....	....	....	....	....	....	....
Banks	4 743	....	....	....	....	....	....	....	....
of which: Short-term	4 745	....	....	....	....	....	....	....	....
Other sectors	4 746	....	....	....	....	....	....	....	....
of which: Short-term	4 748	....	....	....	....	....	....	....	....
Liabilities	4 753	**477**	**47**	**165**	**628**	**755**	**941**	**578**	**726**
Trade credits	4 756	....	−8	−43	14	37	82	97	20
General government	4 757	....	34	−111	−5	9	65	126	....
of which: Short-term	4 759	....	....	50	....	....	....	....	....
Other sectors	4 760	....	−42	68	19	28	16	−30	20
of which: Short-term	4 762	....	−42	68	19	28	16	−30	20
Loans	4 764	309	18	326	576	336	617	177	197
Monetary authorities	4 765	−86	60	74	50	−112	118	−153	−5
of which: Use of Fund credit and loans from the Fund	4 766	−86	60	74	50	−112	118	−153	−5
of which: Short-term	4 768	....	....	....	....	....	....	....	....
General government	4 769	47	215	273	559	430	488	364	172
of which: Short-term	4 771	....	....	....	....	....	....	....	....
Banks	4 772	....	....	....	....	....	....	....	....
of which: Short-term	4 774	....	....	....	....	....	....	....	....
Other sectors	4 775	348	−257	−21	−33	18	11	−35	31
of which: Short-term	4 777	266	....	....	....	....	....	....	....
Currency and deposits	4 780	334	71	−145	−2	202	323	293	364
Monetary authorities	4 781	76	....	....	....	....	....	....	....
General government	4 782	....	....	....	....	....	....	....	....
Banks	4 783	258	71	−145	−2	202	323	293	364
Other sectors	4 784	....	....	....	....	....	....	....	....
Other liabilities	4 786	−167	−33	27	40	179	−80	12	144
Monetary authorities	4 787	....	−33	27	40	179	−80	12	144
of which: Short-term	4 789	....	−33	27	40	179	−80	12	144
General government	4 790	....	....	....	....	....	....	....	....
of which: Short-term	4 792	....	....	....	....	....	....	....	....
Banks	4 793	....	....	....	....	....	....	....	....
of which: Short-term	4 795	....	....	....	....	....	....	....	....
Other sectors	4 796	−167	....	....	....	....	....	....	....
of which: Short-term	4 798	−167	....	....	....	....	....	....	....
E. RESERVE ASSETS	4 802	**447**	**−241**	**−444**	**−627**	**133**	**−540**	**−73**	**−675**
Monetary gold	4 812	....	....	....	....	....	....	....	....
Special drawing rights	4 811	....	−1	−1	2	....	−1	−1	−4
Reserve position in the Fund	4 810	....	....	....	....	....	....	....	....
Foreign exchange	4 803	446	−234	−426	−620	173	−502	−75	−700
Other claims	4 813	....	−6	−17	−9	−40	−37	3	29
NET ERRORS AND OMISSIONS	4 998	**186**	**15**	**136**	**−114**	**−189**	**−73**	**−96**	**−192**

Table 1. ANALYTIC PRESENTATION, 2000–2007

(Millions of U.S. dollars)

	Code	2000	2001	2002	2003	2004	2005	2006	2007
A. Current Account[1]	4 993 Z.	**−556.8**	**−618.3**	**−1,008.1**	**−955.4**	**−870.9**	**−3,013.1**	**−5,198.7**	**−3,447.1**
Goods: exports f.o.b.	2 100	1,806.7	1,698.7	1,949.1	2,542.2	3,777.8	4,824.3	5,656.6	8,879.2
Goods: imports f.o.b.	3 100	−1,366.3	−1,395.1	−2,293.8	−2,536.1	−3,586.2	−5,946.0	−7,104.7	−7,722.4
Balance on Goods	4 100	*440.4*	*303.6*	*−344.7*	*6.1*	*191.6*	*−1,121.7*	*−1,448.1*	*1,156.8*
Services: credit	2 200	27.4	14.6	132.2	36.5	44.1	113.9	247.1	384.3
Services: debit	3 200	−647.6	−660.3	−818.2	−830.3	−1,064.5	−1,844.4	−2,799.9	−2,938.7
Balance on Goods and Services	4 991	*−179.8*	*−342.1*	*−1,030.7*	*−787.7*	*−828.8*	*−2,852.2*	*−4,000.9*	*−1,397.6*
Income: credit	2 300	4.6	17.8	29.2	10.0	21.8	44.1	89.3	183.7
Income: debit	3 300	−579.6	−571.9	−638.0	−879.2	−1,134.5	−1,405.9	−2,103.3	−2,436.8
Balance on Goods, Services, and Income	4 992	*−754.8*	*−896.2*	*−1,639.5*	*−1,657.0*	*−1,941.5*	*−4,214.0*	*−6,014.9*	*−3,650.7*
Current transfers: credit	2 379 Z.	651.3	730.4	1,085.9	1,218.4	1,580.2	1,680.5	1,899.9	2,321.5
Current transfers: debit	3 379	−453.3	−452.5	−454.5	−516.8	−509.6	−479.6	−1,083.6	−2,117.9
B. Capital Account[1]	4 994 Z.	**−119.3**	**−93.3**	....	....	....	....	....	....
Capital account: credit	2 994 Z.	16.5	11.9	....	....	....	....	....	....
Capital account: debit	3 994	−135.8	−105.2	....	....	....	....	....	....
Total, Groups A Plus B	4 981	*−676.1*	*−711.6*	*−1,008.1*	*−955.4*	*−870.9*	*−3,013.1*	*−5,198.7*	*−3,447.1*
C. Financial Account[1]	4 995 W.	**431.6**	**561.2**	**761.2**	**1,284.4**	**1,427.8**	**2,884.6**	**4,738.7**	**2,996.4**
Direct investment abroad	4 505	....	....	....	....	....	....	....	....
Direct investment in Sudan	4 555 Z.	392.2	574.0	713.2	1,349.2	1,511.1	2,304.6	3,534.1	2,425.6
Portfolio investment assets	4 602	....	.7	14.8	35.3	19.9	50.6	−.1	62.1
Equity securities	4 610	....	....	....	....	....	....	−.1	62.1
Debt securities	4 619	....	.7	14.8	35.3	19.9	50.6	....	....
Portfolio investment liabilities	4 652 Z.	....	....	....	....	....	....	−35.3	−16.6
Equity securities	4 660	....	....	....	....	....	....	−35.3	−16.6
Debt securities	4 669 Z.	....	....	....	....	....	....	....	....
Financial derivatives	4 910	....	....	....	....	....	....	....	....
Financial derivatives assets	4 900	....	....	....	....	....	....	....	....
Financial derivatives liabilities	4 905	....	....	....	....	....	....	....	....
Other investment assets	4 703	−53.4	−55.1	−148.0	381.4	598.8	1,134.7	208.2	−535.3
Monetary authorities	4 701	....	....	....	−.2	−10.2	−13.0	174.3	121.5
General government	4 704	....	....	....	141.7	373.8	358.2	....	....
Banks	4 705	−53.4	−55.1	−145.6	−9.0	−42.0	−198.7	33.9	−124.3
Other sectors	4 728	....	....	−2.4	248.9	277.2	988.3	....	−532.5
Other investment liabilities	4 753 W.	92.8	41.6	181.2	−481.5	−702.0	−605.3	1,031.7	1,060.6
Monetary authorities	4 753 WA	14.0	40.6	64.2	....	....	44.7	156.5	24.8
General government	4 753 ZB	....	....	−87.8	−262.2	−384.5	−275.7	348.5	238.5
Banks	4 753 ZC	78.8	1.0	204.8	4.1	13.0	47.7	2.5	27.7
Other sectors	4 753 ZD	....	....	....	−223.4	−330.6	−422.0	524.3	769.6
Total, Groups A Through C	4 983	*−244.5*	*−150.4*	*−246.9*	*328.9*	*556.9*	*−128.5*	*−460.0*	*−450.7*
D. Net Errors and Omissions	4 998	**338.3**	**−24.1**	**478.7**	**−13.9**	**212.1**	**726.5**	**−130.9**	**26.9**
Total, Groups A Through D	4 984	*93.8*	*−174.5*	*231.8*	*315.1*	*769.0*	*598.0*	*−590.9*	*−423.8*
E. Reserves and Related Items	4 802 A.	**−93.8**	**174.5**	**−231.8**	**−315.1**	**−769.0**	**−598.0**	**590.9**	**423.8**
Reserve assets	4 802	−108.0	127.6	−300.2	−422.7	−729.8	−827.6	208.7	282.0
Use of Fund credit and loans	4 766	−23.9	−28.7	−8.8	−14.8	−18.0	−11.8	−5.3	−36.9
Exceptional financing	4 920	38.1	75.6	77.2	122.4	−21.2	241.4	387.5	178.7
Conversion rates: Sudanese pounds per U.S. dollar	0 101	**2.57**	**2.59**	**2.63**	**2.61**	**2.58**	**2.44**	**2.17**	**2.02**

[1] Excludes components that have been classified in the categories of Group E.

Table 2. STANDARD PRESENTATION, 2000–2007

(Millions of U.S. dollars)

	Code	2000	2001	2002	2003	2004	2005	2006	2007
CURRENT ACCOUNT	4 993	**−517.7**	**−521.9**	**−973.6**	**−938.6**	**−818.2**	**−2,768.0**	**−4,811.2**	**−3,268.4**
A. GOODS	4 100	**440.4**	**303.6**	**−344.7**	**6.1**	**191.6**	**−1,121.7**	**−1,448.1**	**1,156.8**
Credit	2 100	**1,806.7**	**1,698.7**	**1,949.1**	**2,542.2**	**3,777.8**	**4,824.3**	**5,656.6**	**8,879.2**
General merchandise: exports f.o.b.	2 110	1,806.7	1,698.7	1,949.1	2,542.2	3,777.8	4,824.3	5,656.6	8,879.2
Goods for processing: exports f.o.b.	2 150	....	....	....	....	....	....	....	....
Repairs on goods	2 160	....	....	....	....	....	....	....	....
Goods procured in ports by carriers	2 170	....	....	....	....	....	....	....	....
Nonmonetary gold	2 180	....	....	....	....	....	....	....	....
Debit	3 100	**−1,366.3**	**−1,395.1**	**−2,293.8**	**−2,536.1**	**−3,586.2**	**−5,946.0**	**−7,104.7**	**−7,722.4**
General merchandise: imports f.o.b.	3 110	−1,366.3	−1,395.1	−2,293.8	−2,536.1	−3,586.2	−5,946.0	−7,104.7	−7,722.4
Goods for processing: imports f.o.b.	3 150	....	....	....	....	....	....	....	....
Repairs on goods	3 160	....	....	....	....	....	....	....	....
Goods procured in ports by carriers	3 170	....	....	....	....	....	....	....	....
Nonmonetary gold	3 180	....	....	....	....	....	....	....	....
B. SERVICES	4 200	**−620.2**	**−645.7**	**−686.0**	**−793.8**	**−1,020.4**	**−1,730.5**	**−2,552.8**	**−2,554.4**
Total credit	2 200	*27.4*	*14.6*	*132.2*	*36.5*	*44.1*	*113.9*	*247.1*	*384.3*
Total debit	3 200	*−647.6*	*−660.3*	*−818.2*	*−830.3*	*−1,064.5*	*−1,844.4*	*−2,799.9*	*−2,938.7*
Transportation services, credit	2 205	**15.2**	**6.0**	**16.7**	**9.1**	**9.5**	**3.4**	**18.7**	**10.5**
Passenger	2 850	....	....	....	....	....	....	....	....
Freight	2 851	*15.2*	*6.0*	....	....	*9.5*	....	*18.7*	*10.5*
Other	2 852	....	....	*16.7*	*9.1*	....	*3.4*	....	....
Sea transport, passenger	2 207	....	....	....	....	....	....	....	....
Sea transport, freight	2 208	....	....	....	....	....	....	....	....
Sea transport, other	2 209	....	....	....	....	....	....	....	....
Air transport, passenger	2 211	....	....	....	....	....	....	....	....
Air transport, freight	2 212	....	....	....	....	9.5	....	18.7	10.5
Air transport, other	2 213	....	....	16.7	9.1	....	3.4	....	....
Other transport, passenger	2 215	....	....	....	....	....	....	....	....
Other transport, freight	2 216	15.2	6.0	....	....	....	....	....	....
Other transport, other	2 217	....	....	....	....	....	....	....	....
Transportation services, debit	3 205	**−555.3**	**−558.9**	**−686.1**	**−682.4**	**−841.0**	**−1,079.7**	**−1,243.8**	**−1,310.5**
Passenger	3 850	....	....	....	....	....	....	....	....
Freight	3 851	*−555.3*	*−558.9*	*−686.1*	*−682.4*	*−841.0*	*−1,079.7*	*−1,243.8*	*−1,310.5*
Other	3 852	....	....	....	....	....	....	....	....
Sea transport, passenger	3 207	....	....	....	....	....	....	....	....
Sea transport, freight	3 208	....	....	−248.0	−288.2	−407.5	−675.7	−807.4	−877.5
Sea transport, other	3 209	....	....	....	....	....	....	....	....
Air transport, passenger	3 211	....	....	....	....	....	....	....	....
Air transport, freight	3 212	....	....	....	....	....	....	....	....
Air transport, other	3 213	....	....	....	....	....	....	....	....
Other transport, passenger	3 215	....	....	....	....	....	....	....	....
Other transport, freight	3 216	−555.3	−558.9	−438.1	−394.2	−433.5	−404.0	−436.5	−433.0
Other transport, other	3 217	....	....	....	....	....	....	....	....
Travel, credit	2 236	**5.4**	**3.1**	**108.1**	**17.5**	**21.2**	**89.1**	**167.3**	**261.8**
Business travel	2 237	....	....	....	....	....	....	....	....
Personal travel	2 240	5.4	3.1	108.1	17.5	21.2	89.1	167.3	261.8
Travel, debit	3 236	**−55.4**	**−74.2**	**−91.4**	**−119.1**	**−175.6**	**−667.5**	**−1,413.3**	**−1,476.8**
Business travel	3 237	....	....	....	....	....	....	....	....
Personal travel	3 240	−55.4	−74.2	−91.4	−119.1	−175.6	−667.5	−1,413.3	−1,476.8
Other services, credit	2 200 BA	**6.8**	**5.5**	**7.4**	**10.0**	**13.4**	**21.4**	**61.1**	**112.1**
Communications	2 245	2.6	3.2	4.1	2.5	2.4	3.8	7.9	19.9
Construction	2 249	.4	....	....	.5	.9	....	....	3.6
Insurance	2 253	....	1.1	....	....	....	....	....	.1
Financial	2 260	....	....	.4	.8	.9	4.1	25.1	26.9
Computer and information	2 262	....	....	.5	....	....	....	....	1.0
Royalties and licence fees	2 266	....	....	....	....	....	....	....	....
Other business services	2 268	.1	.1	.6	.4	....	.1	.3	13.4
Personal, cultural, and recreational	2 287	.5	....	....	.3	....	....	.2	4.5
Government, n.i.e.	2 291	3.2	1.1	1.7	5.4	9.3	13.4	27.5	42.7
Other services, debit	3 200 BA	**−36.9**	**−27.2**	**−40.6**	**−28.8**	**−47.9**	**−97.3**	**−142.8**	**−151.4**
Communications	3 245	−14.5	−4.4	−5.2	−1.5	−.1	−3.5	−5.7	−22.2
Construction	3 249	....	....	....	−.7	−1.6	....	−.9	−2.8
Insurance	3 253	−.1	....	−.1	....	−.2	−12.1	−2.1	−2.5
Financial	3 260	−.1	....	−.5	−.2	−1.5	−1.2	−7.5	−5.3
Computer and information	3 262	−.5	−.6	−.8	−.8	−2.8	−4.6	−3.5	−2.3
Royalties and licence fees	3 266	−.1	....	....	....	....	....	....	....
Other business services	3 268	−6.0	....	−.2	−.1	−.7	−32.6	−51.1	−45.1
Personal, cultural, and recreational	3 287	....	....	....	....	....	....	....	−5.2
Government, n.i.e.	3 291	−15.6	−22.2	−33.9	−25.5	−41.0	−43.3	−72.0	−66.0

Table 2 (Continued). STANDARD PRESENTATION, 2000–2007

(Millions of U.S. dollars)

	Code	2000	2001	2002	2003	2004	2005	2006	2007
C. INCOME	4 300	**−575.0**	**−554.1**	**−608.8**	**−869.2**	**−1,112.7**	**−1,361.8**	**−2,014.0**	**−2,253.1**
Total credit	2 300	*4.6*	*17.8*	*29.2*	*10.0*	*21.8*	*44.1*	*89.3*	*183.7*
Total debit	3 300	*−579.6*	*−571.9*	*−638.0*	*−879.2*	*−1,134.5*	*−1,405.9*	*−2,103.3*	*−2,436.8*
Compensation of employees, credit	2 310	**2.6**	**9.2**	**7.5**	**5.2**	**1.7**	**1.9**	**1.8**	**2.5**
Compensation of employees, debit	3 310	**−4.4**	**−1.9**	**−3.6**	**−.7**	**−2.1**	**−1.7**	**−2.5**	**−2.0**
Investment income, credit	2 320	**2.0**	**8.6**	**21.7**	**4.8**	**20.1**	**42.2**	**87.4**	**181.2**
Direct investment income	2 330	....	....	....	....	....	....	....	....
Dividends and distributed branch profits	2 332	....	....	....	....	....	....	....	....
Reinvested earnings and undistributed branch profits	2 333	....	....	....	....	....	....	....	....
Income on debt (interest)	2 334	....	....	....	....	....	....	....	....
Portfolio investment income	2 339	....	....	....	....	....	....	....	....
Income on equity	2 340	....	....	....	....	....	....	....	....
Income on bonds and notes	2 350	....	....	....	....	....	....	....	....
Income on money market instruments	2 360	....	....	....	....	....	....	....	....
Other investment income	2 370	2.0	8.6	21.7	4.8	20.1	42.2	87.4	181.2
Investment income, debit	3 320	**−575.2**	**−570.0**	**−634.4**	**−878.6**	**−1,132.4**	**−1,404.2**	**−2,100.8**	**−2,434.8**
Direct investment income	3 330	....	....	−632.8	−878.6	−1,122.2	−1,399.0	−2,093.3	−2,404.1
Dividends and distributed branch profits	3 332	....	....	−632.8	−818.4	−1,037.9	−1,334.8	−2,030.6	−2,319.3
Reinvested earnings and undistributed branch profits	3 333	....	....	....	....	....	....	....	....
Income on debt (interest)	3 334	....	....	....	−60.2	−84.2	−64.2	−62.7	−84.8
Portfolio investment income	3 339	....	....	....	....	−10.2	−5.2	....	....
Income on equity	3 340	....	....	....	....	−10.2	−5.2	....	....
Income on bonds and notes	3 350	....	....	....	....	....	....	....	....
Income on money market instruments	3 360	....	....	....	....	....	....	....	....
Other investment income	3 370	−575.2	−570.0	−1.6	....	....	....	−7.6	−30.7
D. CURRENT TRANSFERS	4 379	**237.1**	**374.3**	**665.9**	**718.4**	**1,123.3**	**1,446.1**	**1,203.7**	**382.3**
Credit	2 379	**690.4**	**826.8**	**1,120.4**	**1,235.2**	**1,632.8**	**1,925.7**	**2,287.4**	**2,500.2**
General government	2 380	52.2	96.4	150.2	16.8	52.7	245.2	387.5	178.7
Other sectors	2 390	638.2	730.4	970.2	1,218.4	1,580.2	1,680.5	1,899.9	2,321.5
Workers' remittances	2 391	638.2	730.4	970.2	1,218.4	1,401.2	1,014.1	1,177.3	1,766.7
Other current transfers	2 392	....	....	....	....	179.0	666.4	722.6	554.8
Debit	3 379	**−453.3**	**−452.5**	**−454.5**	**−516.8**	**−509.6**	**−479.6**	**−1,083.6**	**−2,117.9**
General government	3 380	−10.2	....	−2.2	−6.7	−24.2	−10.7	−22.8	−5.2
Other sectors	3 390	−443.1	−452.5	−452.2	−510.2	−485.4	−468.9	−1,060.9	−2,112.7
Workers' remittances	3 391	....	....	....	....	....	....	....	....
Other current transfers	3 392	−443.1	−452.5	−452.2	−510.2	−485.4	−468.9	−1,060.9	−2,112.7
CAPITAL AND FINANCIAL ACCOUNT	4 996	**179.4**	**546.0**	**494.8**	**952.4**	**606.1**	**2,041.4**	**4,942.1**	**3,241.5**
CAPITAL ACCOUNT	4 994	**−119.3**	**−93.3**	....	....	....	....	....	....
Total credit	2 994	*16.5*	*11.9*	....	....	....	....	....	....
Total debit	3 994	*−135.8*	*−105.2*	....	....	....	....	....	....
Capital transfers, credit	2 400	**16.5**	**11.9**	....	....	....	....	....	....
General government	2 401	16.5	11.9	....	....	....	....	....	....
Debt forgiveness	2 402	....	....	....	....	....	....	....	....
Other capital transfers	2 410	16.5	11.9	....	....	....	....	....	....
Other sectors	2 430	....	....	....	....	....	....	....	....
Migrants' transfers	2 431	....	....	....	....	....	....	....	....
Debt forgiveness	2 432	....	....	....	....	....	....	....	....
Other capital transfers	2 440	....	....	....	....	....	....	....	....
Capital transfers, debit	3 400	**−135.8**	**−105.2**	....	....	....	....	....	....
General government	3 401	−135.8	−105.2	....	....	....	....	....	....
Debt forgiveness	3 402	....	....	....	....	....	....	....	....
Other capital transfers	3 410	−135.8	−105.2	....	....	....	....	....	....
Other sectors	3 430	....	....	....	....	....	....	....	....
Migrants' transfers	3 431	....	....	....	....	....	....	....	....
Debt forgiveness	3 432	....	....	....	....	....	....	....	....
Other capital transfers	3 440	....	....	....	....	....	....	....	....
Nonproduced nonfinancial assets, credit	2 480	....	....	....	....	....	....	....	....
Nonproduced nonfinancial assets, debit	3 480	....	....	....	....	....	....	....	....

Table 2 (Continued). STANDARD PRESENTATION, 2000–2007

(Millions of U.S. dollars)

	Code	2000	2001	2002	2003	2004	2005	2006	2007
FINANCIAL ACCOUNT...	4 995 ..	**298.7**	**639.3**	**494.8**	**952.4**	**606.1**	**2,041.4**	**4,942.1**	**3,241.5**
A. DIRECT INVESTMENT...	4 500 ..	**392.2**	**574.0**	**713.2**	**1,349.2**	**1,511.1**	**2,304.6**	**3,534.1**	**2,425.6**
Direct investment abroad...................................	4 505 ..	....	....	....	....	....	....	....	....
Equity capital...	4 510 ..	....	....	....	....	....	....	....	....
Claims on affiliated enterprises....................	4 515 ..	....	....	....	....	....	....	....	....
Liabilities to affiliated enterprises...............	4 520 ..	....	....	....	....	....	....	....	....
Reinvested earnings.....................................	4 525 ..	....	....	....	....	....	....	....	....
Other capital..	4 530 ..	....	....	....	....	....	....	....	....
Claims on affiliated enterprises....................	4 535 ..	....	....	....	....	....	....	....	....
Liabilities to affiliated enterprises...............	4 540 ..	....	....	....	....	....	....	....	....
Direct investment in Sudan...............................	4 555 ..	392.2	574.0	713.2	1,349.2	1,511.1	2,304.6	3,534.1	2,425.6
Equity capital...	4 560 ..	392.2	574.0	713.2	1,349.2	1,511.1	2,304.6	3,534.1	2,425.6
Claims on direct investors.............................	4 565 ..	....	....	....	....	....	....	....	....
Liabilities to direct investors........................	4 570 ..	392.2	574.0	713.2	1,349.2	1,511.1	2,304.6	3,534.1	2,425.6
Reinvested earnings.....................................	4 575 ..	....	....	....	....	....	....	....	....
Other capital..	4 580 ..	....	....	....	....	....	....	....	....
Claims on direct investors.............................	4 585 ..	....	....	....	....	....	....	....	....
Liabilities to direct investors........................	4 590 ..	....	....	....	....	....	....	....	....
B. PORTFOLIO INVESTMENT.................................	4 600 ..	....	.7	14.8	35.3	19.9	50.6	−35.3	45.5
Assets...	4 602 ..	....	.7	14.8	35.3	19.9	50.6	−.1	62.1
Equity securities...	4 610 ..	....	....	....	....	....	....	−.1	62.1
Monetary authorities..................................	4 611 ..	....	....	....	....	....	....	−.1	.7
General government....................................	4 612 ..	....	....	....	....	....	....	....	....
Banks..	4 613 ..	....	....	....	....	....	....	....	61.4
Other sectors..	4 614 ..	....	....	....	....	....	....	....	....
Debt securities..	4 619 ..	....	.7	14.8	35.3	19.9	50.6	....	....
Bonds and notes...	4 620 ..	....	.7	14.8	35.3	19.9	50.6	....	....
Monetary authorities..............................	4 621 ..	....	....	....	....	....	....	....	....
General government...............................	4 622 ..	....	....	....	....	....	....	....	....
Banks...	4 623 ..	....	....	....	....	....	....	....	....
Other sectors..	4 624 ..	....	.7	14.8	35.3	19.9	50.6	....	....
Money market instruments.........................	4 630 ..	....	....	....	....	....	....	....	....
Monetary authorities..............................	4 631 ..	....	....	....	....	....	....	....	....
General government...............................	4 632 ..	....	....	....	....	....	....	....	....
Banks...	4 633 ..	....	....	....	....	....	....	....	....
Other sectors..	4 634 ..	....	....	....	....	....	....	....	....
Liabilities..	4 652 ..	....	....	....	....	....	....	−35.3	−16.6
Equity securities...	4 660 ..	....	....	....	....	....	....	−35.3	−16.6
Banks..	4 663 ..	....	....	....	....	....	....	−35.3	−16.6
Other sectors..	4 664 ..	....	....	....	....	....	....	....	....
Debt securities..	4 669 ..	....	....	....	....	....	....	....	....
Bonds and notes...	4 670 ..	....	....	....	....	....	....	....	....
Monetary authorities..............................	4 671 ..	....	....	....	....	....	....	....	....
General government...............................	4 672 ..	....	....	....	....	....	....	....	....
Banks...	4 673 ..	....	....	....	....	....	....	....	....
Other sectors..	4 674 ..	....	....	....	....	....	....	....	....
Money market instruments.........................	4 680 ..	....	....	....	....	....	....	....	....
Monetary authorities..............................	4 681 ..	....	....	....	....	....	....	....	....
General government...............................	4 682 ..	....	....	....	....	....	....	....	....
Banks...	4 683 ..	....	....	....	....	....	....	....	....
Other sectors..	4 684 ..	....	....	....	....	....	....	....	....
C. FINANCIAL DERIVATIVES.................................	4 910 ..	....	....	....	....	....	....	....	....
Monetary authorities......................................	4 911 ..	....	....	....	....	....	....	....	....
General government.......................................	4 912 ..	....	....	....	....	....	....	....	....
Banks..	4 913 ..	....	....	....	....	....	....	....	....
Other sectors..	4 914 ..	....	....	....	....	....	....	....	....
Assets...	4 900 ..	....	....	....	....	....	....	....	....
Monetary authorities..................................	4 901 ..	....	....	....	....	....	....	....	....
General government....................................	4 902 ..	....	....	....	....	....	....	....	....
Banks..	4 903 ..	....	....	....	....	....	....	....	....
Other sectors..	4 904 ..	....	....	....	....	....	....	....	....
Liabilities..	4 905 ..	....	....	....	....	....	....	....	....
Monetary authorities..................................	4 906 ..	....	....	....	....	....	....	....	....
General government....................................	4 907 ..	....	....	....	....	....	....	....	....
Banks..	4 908 ..	....	....	....	....	....	....	....	....
Other sectors..	4 909 ..	....	....	....	....	....	....	....	....

2008, International Monetary Fund: *Balance of Payments Statistics Yearbook*

Table 2 (Concluded). STANDARD PRESENTATION, 2000–2007

(Millions of U.S. dollars)

	Code	2000	2001	2002	2003	2004	2005	2006	2007
D. OTHER INVESTMENT	4 700 ..	**14.5**	**−63.0**	**67.0**	**−9.3**	**−195.1**	**513.8**	**1,234.6**	**488.4**
Assets	4 703 ..	**−53.4**	**−55.1**	**−148.0**	**381.4**	**598.8**	**1,134.7**	**208.2**	**−535.3**
Trade credits	4 706 ..	....	....	−2.4	305.7	437.8	1,209.1	....	....
General government	4 707 ..	....	....	....	56.8	160.6	220.8	....	....
of which: Short-term	4 709 ..	....	....	....	*56.8*	*160.6*	*220.8*	....	....
Other sectors	4 710 ..	....	....	−2.4	248.9	277.2	988.3	....	....
of which: Short-term	4 712 ..	....	....	*−2.4*	*248.9*	*277.2*	*988.3*	....	....
Loans	4 714 ..	−17.6	1.9	....	84.9	213.2	222.4	....	....
Monetary authorities	4 715 ..	....	....	....	....	....	....	....	....
of which: Short-term	4 718 ..	....	....	....	....	....	....	....	....
General government	4 719 ..	....	....	....	84.9	213.2	222.4	....	....
of which: Short-term	4 721 ..	....	....	....	....	....	....	....	....
Banks	4 722 ..	−17.6	1.9	....	....	....	....	....	....
of which: Short-term	4 724 ..	*−17.6*	*1.9*	....	....	....	....	....	....
Other sectors	4 725 ..	....	....	....	....	....	....	....	....
of which: Short-term	4 727 ..	....	....	....	....	....	....	....	....
Currency and deposits	4 730 ..	−35.8	−57.0	−145.6	−9.0	−42.0	−198.7	256.0	−583.5
Monetary authorities	4 731 ..	....	....	....	....	....	....	222.0	73.4
General government	4 732 ..	....	....	....	....	....	....	....	....
Banks	4 733 ..	−35.8	−57.0	−145.6	−9.0	−42.0	−198.7	33.9	−124.3
Other sectors	4 734 ..	....	....	....	....	....	....	....	−532.5
Other assets	4 736 ..	....	....	....	−.2	−10.2	−98.0	−47.8	48.2
Monetary authorities	4 737 ..	....	....	....	−.2	−10.2	−13.0	−47.8	48.2
of which: Short-term	4 739 ..	....	....	....	....	....	....	....	....
General government	4 740 ..	....	....	....	....	....	−85.0	....	....
of which: Short-term	4 742 ..	....	....	....	....	....	*−85.0*	....	....
Banks	4 743 ..	....	....	....	....	....	....	....	....
of which: Short-term	4 745 ..	....	....	....	....	....	....	....	....
Other sectors	4 746 ..	....	....	....	....	....	....	....	....
of which: Short-term	4 748 ..	....	....	....	....	....	....	....	....
Liabilities	4 753 ..	**67.9**	**−7.9**	**215.1**	**−390.7**	**−793.9**	**−620.9**	**1,026.4**	**1,023.7**
Trade credits	4 756 ..	....	....	....	−300.4	−495.8	−485.7	724.9	503.5
General government	4 757 ..	....	....	....	−77.0	−165.3	−63.7	200.6	−266.0
of which: Short-term	4 759 ..	....	....	....	....	....	....	*200.6*	*−266.0*
Other sectors	4 760 ..	....	....	....	−223.4	−330.6	−422.0	524.3	769.6
of which: Short-term	4 762 ..	....	....	....	*−223.4*	*−330.6*	*−422.0*	*524.3*	*769.6*
Loans	4 764 ..	62.9	33.0	234.7	−80.2	−306.4	−179.1	239.0	467.7
Monetary authorities	4 765 ..	−9.9	11.9	55.3	105.0	−87.1	32.9	91.0	−36.9
of which: Use of Fund credit and loans from the Fund	4 766 ..	*−23.9*	*−28.7*	*−8.8*	*−14.8*	*−18.0*	*−11.8*	*−5.3*	*−36.9*
of which: Short-term	4 768 ..	*14.0*	*40.6*	*64.2*	....	....	....	*105.1*	....
General government	4 769 ..	....	....	−43.0	−185.2	−219.2	−212.0	147.9	504.6
of which: Short-term	4 771 ..	....	....	....	....	....	....	....	....
Banks	4 772 ..	72.8	21.1	222.4	....	....	....	....	....
of which: Short-term	4 774 ..	*72.8*	*21.1*	*222.4*	....	....	....	....	....
Other sectors	4 775 ..	....	....	....	....	....	....	....	....
of which: Short-term	4 777 ..	....	....	....	....	....	....	....	....
Currency and deposits	4 780 ..	6.0	−20.1	−17.6	4.1	13.0	47.7	1.5	−17.5
Monetary authorities	4 781 ..	....	....	....	....	....	....	−3.0	−1.4
General government	4 782 ..	....	....	....	....	....	....	....	....
Banks	4 783 ..	6.0	−20.1	−17.6	4.1	13.0	47.7	4.4	−16.1
Other sectors	4 784 ..	....	....	....	....	....	....	....	....
Other liabilities	4 786 ..	−1.0	−20.8	−2.1	−14.2	−4.7	−3.8	61.1	70.0
Monetary authorities	4 787 ..	....	....	....	....	....	....	63.1	26.2
of which: Short-term	4 789 ..	....	....	....	....	....	....	*66.1*	*30.9*
General government	4 790 ..	−1.0	−20.8	−2.1	−14.2	−4.7	−3.8	....	....
of which: Short-term	4 792 ..	*−1.0*	*−20.8*	*−2.1*	*−14.2*	*−4.7*	*−3.8*	....	....
Banks	4 793 ..	....	....	....	....	....	....	−2.0	43.9
of which: Short-term	4 795 ..	....	....	....	....	....	....	....	....
Other sectors	4 796 ..	....	....	....	....	....	....	....	....
of which: Short-term	4 798 ..	....	....	....	....	....	....	....	....
E. RESERVE ASSETS	4 802 ..	**−108.0**	**127.6**	**−300.2**	**−422.7**	**−729.8**	**−827.6**	**208.7**	**282.0**
Monetary gold	4 812 ..	....	....	....	....	....	....	....	....
Special drawing rights	4 811 ..	....	....	−.2	−.1	.4	−.1	.1	....
Reserve position in the Fund	4 810 ..	....	....	....	....	....	....	....	....
Foreign exchange	4 803 ..	−108.0	127.6	−300.0	−422.6	−730.2	−827.5	208.6	282.0
Other claims	4 813 ..	....	....	....	....	....	....	....	....
NET ERRORS AND OMISSIONS	4 998 ..	**338.3**	**−24.1**	**478.7**	**−13.9**	**212.1**	**726.5**	**−130.9**	**26.9**

Table 3. INTERNATIONAL INVESTMENT POSITION (End-period stocks), 2000–2007

(Millions of U.S. dollars)

	Code	2000	2001	2002	2003	2004	2005	2006	2007
ASSETS	8 995 C.	....	....	....	....	....	....	....	....
Direct investment abroad	8 505 ..	....	....	....	....	....	....	....	....
Equity capital and reinvested earnings	8 506 ..	....	....	....	....	....	....	....	....
Claims on affiliated enterprises	8 507 ..	....	....	....	....	....	....	....	....
Liabilities to affiliated enterprises	8 508 ..	....	....	....	....	....	....	....	....
Other capital	8 530 ..	....	....	....	....	....	....	....	....
Claims on affiliated enterprises	8 535 ..	....	....	....	....	....	....	....	....
Liabilities to affiliated enterprises	8 540 ..	....	....	....	....	....	....	....	....
Portfolio investment	8 602 ..	....	....	....	19.4	32.3	71.7	63.5	75.1
Equity securities	8 610 ..	....	....	....	19.4	32.3	71.7	63.5	75.1
Monetary authorities	8 611 ..	....	....	....	15.0	25.8	38.7	38.8	39.5
General government	8 612 ..	....	....	....	....	....	....	....	....
Banks	8 613 ..	....	....	....	4.4	6.5	33.0	24.7	35.6
Other sectors	8 614 ..	....	....	....	....	....	....	....	....
Debt securities	8 619 ..	....	....	....	....	....	....	....	....
Bonds and notes	8 620 ..	....	....	....	....	....	....	....	....
Monetary authorities	8 621 ..	....	....	....	....	....	....	....	....
General government	8 622 ..	....	....	....	....	....	....	....	....
Banks	8 623 ..	....	....	....	....	....	....	....	....
Other sectors	8 624 ..	....	....	....	....	....	....	....	....
Money market instruments	8 630 ..	....	....	....	....	....	....	....	....
Monetary authorities	8 631 ..	....	....	....	....	....	....	....	....
General government	8 632 ..	....	....	....	....	....	....	....	....
Banks	8 633 ..	....	....	....	....	....	....	....	....
Other sectors	8 634 ..	....	....	....	....	....	....	....	....
Financial derivatives	8 900 ..	....	....	....	....	....	....	....	....
Monetary authorities	8 901 ..	....	....	....	....	....	....	....	....
General government	8 902 ..	....	....	....	....	....	....	....	....
Banks	8 903 ..	....	....	....	....	....	....	....	....
Other sectors	8 904 ..	....	....	....	....	....	....	....	....
Other investment	8 703 ..	....	....	....	843.2	872.1	1,505.7	1,292.9	1,306.6
Trade credits	8 706 ..	....	....	....	....	....	....	....	....
General government	8 707 ..	....	....	....	....	....	....	....	....
of which: Short-term	8 709 ..	....	....	....	....	....	....	....	....
Other sectors	8 710 ..	....	....	....	....	....	....	....	....
of which: Short-term	8 712 ..	....	....	....	....	....	....	....	....
Loans	8 714 ..	....	....	....	....	....	....	....	....
Monetary authorities	8 715 ..	....	....	....	....	....	....	....	....
of which: Short-term	8 718 ..	....	....	....	....	....	....	....	....
General government	8 719 ..	....	....	....	....	....	....	....	....
of which: Short-term	8 721 ..	....	....	....	....	....	....	....	....
Banks	8 722 ..	....	....	....	....	....	....	....	....
of which: Short-term	8 724 ..	....	....	....	....	....	....	....	....
Other sectors	8 725 ..	....	....	....	....	....	....	....	....
of which: Short-term	8 727 ..	....	....	....	....	....	....	....	....
Currency and deposits	8 730 ..	....	....	....	824.7	849.1	1,478.9	1,218.3	1,280.3
Monetary authorities	8 731 ..	....	....	....	318.1	288.1	581.2	359.2	285.8
General government	8 732 ..	....	....	....	....	....	....	....	....
Banks	8 733 ..	....	....	....	506.6	561.0	897.7	859.1	994.5
Other sectors	8 734 ..	....	....	....	....	....	....	....	....
Other assets	8 736 ..	....	....	....	18.5	23.0	26.8	74.6	26.3
Monetary authorities	8 737 ..	....	....	....	18.5	23.0	26.8	74.6	26.3
of which: Short-term	8 739 ..	....	....	....	*18.5*	*23.0*	*26.8*	*74.6*	*26.3*
General government	8 740 ..	....	....	....	....	....	....	....	....
of which: Short-term	8 742 ..	....	....	....	....	....	....	....	....
Banks	8 743 ..	....	....	....	....	....	....	....	....
of which: Short-term	8 745 ..	....	....	....	....	....	....	....	....
Other sectors	8 746 ..	....	....	....	....	....	....	....	....
of which: Short-term	8 748 ..	....	....	....	....	....	....	....	....
Reserve assets	8 802 ..	....	....	....	529.5	1,338.0	1,868.6	1,659.9	1,377.9
Monetary gold	8 812 ..	....	....	....	....	....	....	....	....
Special drawing rights	8 811 ..	....	....	.2	.3	....	.1	....	....
Reserve position in the Fund	8 810 ..	....	....	....	....	....	....	....	....
Foreign exchange	8 803 ..	....	....	....	529.1	1,338.0	1,868.5	1,659.9	1,377.9
Other claims	8 813 ..	....	....	....	....	....	....	....	....

Table 3 (Concluded). INTERNATIONAL INVESTMENT POSITION (End-period stocks), 2000–2007

(Millions of U.S. dollars)

	Code	2000	2001	2002	2003	2004	2005	2006	2007
LIABILITIES...	8 995 D.	....	....	....	....	....	....	....	....
Direct investment in Sudan.................................	8 555 ..	....	....	....	**3,868.4**	**5,379.4**	**7,684.1**	**11,225.5**	**13,661.8**
Equity capital and reinvested earnings.............................	8 556 ..	....	....	....	3,868.4	5,379.4	7,684.1	11,225.5	13,661.8
Claims on direct investors................................	8 557 ..	....	....	....	....	....	....	....	....
Liabilities to direct investors............................	8 558 ..	....	....	....	3,868.4	5,379.4	7,684.1	11,225.5	13,661.8
Other capital...	8 580 ..	....	....	....	....	....	....	....	....
Claims on direct investors................................	8 585 ..	....	....	....	....	....	....	....	....
Liabilities to direct investors............................	8 590 ..	....	....	....	....	....	....	....	....
Portfolio investment..	8 652 ..	....	....	....	....	....	....	....	....
Equity securities..	8 660 ..	....	....	....	....	....	....	....	....
Banks..	8 663 ..	....	....	....	....	....	....	....	....
Other sectors..	8 664 ..	....	....	....	....	....	....	....	....
Debt securities..	8 669 ..	....	....	....	....	....	....	....	....
Bonds and notes...	8 670 ..	....	....	....	....	....	....	....	....
Monetary authorities.....................................	8 671 ..	....	....	....	....	....	....	....	....
General government.....................................	8 672 ..	....	....	....	....	....	....	....	....
Banks...	8 673 ..	....	....	....	....	....	....	....	....
Other sectors...	8 674 ..	....	....	....	....	....	....	....	....
Money market instruments...............................	8 680 ..	....	....	....	....	....	....	....	....
Monetary authorities.....................................	8 681 ..	....	....	....	....	....	....	....	....
General government.....................................	8 682 ..	....	....	....	....	....	....	....	....
Banks...	8 683 ..	....	....	....	....	....	....	....	....
Other sectors...	8 684 ..	....	....	....	....	....	....	....	....
Financial derivatives...	8 905 ..	....	....	....	....	....	....	....	....
Monetary authorities...	8 906 ..	....	....	....	....	....	....	....	....
General government..	8 907 ..	....	....	....	....	....	....	....	....
Banks...	8 908 ..	....	....	....	....	....	....	....	....
Other sectors..	8 909 ..	....	....	....	....	....	....	....	....
Other investment..	8 753 ..	....	....	....	**27,677.9**	**28,767.6**	**29,176.8**	**30,834.3**	**34,283.3**
Trade credits...	8 756 ..	....	....	....	....	....	....	....	....
General government.......................................	8 757 ..	....	....	....	....	....	....	....	....
of which: Short-term.................................	8 759 ..	....	....	....	....	....	....	....	....
Other sectors..	8 760 ..	....	....	....	....	....	....	....	....
of which: Short-term.................................	8 762 ..	....	....	....	....	....	....	....	....
Loans...	8 764 ..	....	....	....	27,221.6	28,324.0	28,551.4	30,076.9	33,477.4
Monetary authorities.......................................	8 765 ..	....	....	....	3,107.6	3,189.0	3,051.4	3,168.9	3,225.4
of which: Use of Fund credit and loans from the Fund....	8 766 ..	*1,451.4*	*1,371.5*	*1,474.8*	*1,596.4*	*1,649.6*	*1,506.8*	*1,580.4*	*1,621.3*
of which: Short-term.................................	8 768 ..	....	....	....	*182.1*	*166.0*	*119.3*	*139.1*	*129.3*
General government.......................................	8 769 ..	....	....	....	24,114.0	25,135.0	25,500.0	26,908.0	30,252.0
of which: Short-term.................................	8 771 ..	....	....	....	....	....	....	....	....
Banks...	8 772 ..	....	....	....	....	....	....	....	....
of which: Short-term.................................	8 774 ..	....	....	....	....	....	....	....	....
Other sectors..	8 775 ..	....	....	....	....	....	....	....	....
of which: Short-term.................................	8 777 ..	....	....	....	....	....	....	....	....
Currency and deposits......................................	8 780 ..	....	....	....	103.1	121.6	264.9	279.9	330.0
Monetary authorities.......................................	8 781 ..	....	....	....	46.2	49.2	46.4	43.4	42.0
General government.......................................	8 782 ..	....	....	....	....	....	....	....	....
Banks...	8 783 ..	....	....	....	56.9	72.4	218.5	236.5	288.0
Other sectors..	8 784 ..	....	....	....	....	....	....	....	....
Other liabilities..	8 786 ..	....	....	....	353.2	322.0	360.5	477.4	475.9
Monetary authorities.......................................	8 787 ..	....	....	....	353.2	322.0	360.5	477.4	475.9
of which: Short-term.................................	8 789 ..	....	....	....	*294.3*	*265.7*	*308.1*	*428.0*	*432.5*
General government.......................................	8 790 ..	....	....	....	....	....	....	....	....
of which: Short-term.................................	8 792 ..	....	....	....	....	....	....	....	....
Banks...	8 793 ..	....	....	....	....	....	....	....	....
of which: Short-term.................................	8 795 ..	....	....	....	....	....	....	....	....
Other sectors..	8 796 ..	....	....	....	....	....	....	....	....
of which: Short-term.................................	8 798 ..	....	....	....	....	....	....	....	....
NET INTERNATIONAL INVESTMENT POSITION........	8 995 ..	....	....	....	....	....	....	....	....
Conversion rates: Sudanese pounds per U.S. dollar (end of period)...	0 102 ..	**2.57**	**2.61**	**2.62**	**2.60**	**2.51**	**2.31**	**2.01**	**2.05**

Table 1. ANALYTIC PRESENTATION, 2000–2007

(Millions of U.S. dollars)

	Code	2000	2001	2002	2003	2004	2005	2006	2007
A. Current Account[1]...............	4 993 Z.	**32.3**	**−83.6**	**−131.0**	**−159.0**	**−137.7**	**−143.6**	**110.4**	**184.9**
Goods: exports f.o.b.................	2 100 ..	399.1	437.0	369.3	487.8	782.2	1,211.5	1,174.4	1,359.0
Goods: imports f.o.b.................	3 100 ..	−246.1	−297.2	−321.9	−458.0	−740.1	−1,189.1	−1,013.4	−1,185.3
Balance on Goods..................	4 100 ..	*153.0*	*139.8*	*47.4*	*29.8*	*42.1*	*22.4*	*161.0*	*173.7*
Services: credit.....................	2 200 ..	90.9	59.4	38.5	59.0	141.3	204.1	233.6	244.7
Services: debit......................	3 200 ..	−215.5	−174.3	−166.1	−194.6	−271.0	−351.8	−268.5	−317.2
Balance on Goods and Services....	4 991 ..	*28.4*	*24.9*	*−80.2*	*−105.8*	*−87.6*	*−125.3*	*126.1*	*101.2*
Income: credit......................	2 300 ..	13.2	5.4	8.4	11.7	15.6	24.0	28.0	43.6
Income: debit.......................	3 300 ..	−7.2	−113.0	−50.7	−60.2	−78.5	−64.4	−79.6	−35.4
Balance on Goods, Services, and Income........	4 992 ..	*34.4*	*−82.7*	*−122.5*	*−154.3*	*−150.5*	*−165.7*	*74.5*	*109.4*
Current transfers: credit............	2 379 Z.	1.2	2.1	12.9	24.8	75.8	52.3	73.5	137.9
Current transfers: debit.............	3 379 ..	−3.3	−3.0	−21.4	−29.5	−63.0	−30.2	−37.6	−62.4
B. Capital Account[1]..............	4 994 Z.	**2.3**	**1.5**	**5.9**	**9.0**	**18.9**	**14.5**	**19.3**	**8.1**
Capital account: credit..............	2 994 Z.	2.3	1.5	5.9	9.2	18.9	14.5	19.3	8.1
Capital account: debit...............	3 994 ..	....	....	....	−.2	....	....	....	....
Total, Groups A Plus B.............	4 981 ..	*34.6*	*−82.1*	*−125.1*	*−150.0*	*−118.8*	*−129.1*	*129.7*	*193.0*
C. Financial Account[1].............	4 995 W.	**−139.1**	**104.1**	**−38.1**	**−36.5**	**−23.5**	**−20.6**	**−180.5**	**−177.1**
Direct investment abroad............	4 505 ..	....	....	....	....	....	....	....	....
Direct investment in Suriname.......	4 555 Z.	−148.0	−26.8	−73.6	−76.1	−37.3	27.9	−163.4	−246.7
Portfolio investment assets..........	4 602 ..	....	....	....	....	....	....	....	....
Equity securities..................	4 610 ..	....	....	....	....	....	....	....	....
Debt securities....................	4 619 ..	....	....	....	....	....	....	....	....
Portfolio investment liabilities......	4 652 Z.	....	....	....	....	....	−2.0	−.3	−1.3
Equity securities..................	4 660 ..	....	....	....	....	....	....	....	....
Debt securities....................	4 669 Z.	....	....	....	....	....	−2.0	−.3	−1.3
Financial derivatives................	4 910 ..	....	....	....	....	....	....	....	....
Financial derivatives assets.........	4 900 ..	....	....	....	....	....	....	....	....
Financial derivatives liabilities......	4 905 ..	....	....	....	....	....	....	....	....
Other investment assets.............	4 703 ..	24.6	40.7	23.9	46.9	−2.3	−31.9	8.4	83.5
Monetary authorities...............	4 701 ..	....	....	....	....	....	....	....	....
General government................	4 704 ..	....	....	....	....	....	....	....	....
Banks.............................	4 705 ..	....	....	....	....	....	....	....	....
Other sectors......................	4 728 ..	24.6	40.7	23.9	46.9	−2.3	−31.9	8.4	83.5
Other investment liabilities..........	4 753 W.	−15.7	90.2	11.6	−7.3	16.1	−14.6	−25.2	−12.6
Monetary authorities...............	4 753 WA	....	1.6	−.9	4.3	....	....	−.1	....
General government................	4 753 ZB	−21.4	50.7	−30.8	−23.0	−18.5	−14.4	−25.6	−16.8
Banks.............................	4 753 ZC	....	−.8	6.4	−9.1	9.0	.1	....	5.0
Other sectors......................	4 753 ZD	5.7	38.7	36.9	20.5	25.6	−.3	.5	−.8
Total, Groups A Through C.........	4 983 ..	*−104.5*	*22.0*	*−163.2*	*−186.5*	*−142.3*	*−149.7*	*−50.8*	*15.9*
D. Net Errors and Omissions........	4 998 ..	**114.3**	**56.1**	**144.1**	**193.7**	**218.4**	**169.4**	**144.9**	**161.0**
Total, Groups A Through D.........	4 984 ..	*9.8*	*78.1*	*−19.1*	*7.2*	*76.1*	*19.7*	*94.1*	*176.9*
E. Reserves and Related Items.........	4 802 A.	**−9.8**	**−78.1**	**19.1**	**−7.2**	**−76.1**	**−19.7**	**−94.1**	**−176.9**
Reserve assets......................	4 802 ..	−9.8	−78.1	19.1	−7.2	−76.1	−19.7	−94.1	−176.9
Use of Fund credit and loans........	4 766 ..	....	....	....	....	....	....	....	....
Exceptional financing...............	4 920 ..	....	....	....	....	....	....	....	....
Conversion rates: Suriname dollars per U.S. dollar............	0 101 ..	**1.3225**	**2.1782**	**2.3468**	**2.6013**	**2.7336**	**2.7317**	**2.7438**	**2.7450**

[1] Excludes components that have been classified in the categories of Group E.

Table 2. STANDARD PRESENTATION, 2000–2007

(Millions of U.S. dollars)

	Code	2000	2001	2002	2003	2004	2005	2006	2007
CURRENT ACCOUNT	4 993	**32.3**	**−83.6**	**−131.0**	**−159.0**	**−137.7**	**−143.6**	**110.4**	**184.9**
A. GOODS	4 100	**153.0**	**139.8**	**47.4**	**29.8**	**42.1**	**22.4**	**161.0**	**173.7**
Credit	2 100	**399.1**	**437.0**	**369.3**	**487.8**	**782.2**	**1,211.5**	**1,174.4**	**1,359.0**
General merchandise: exports f.o.b.	2 110	399.1	437.0	343.9	400.3	782.2	1,211.5	1,174.4	1,359.0
Goods for processing: exports f.o.b.	2 150	....	....	....	....	....	....	....	....
Repairs on goods	2 160	....	....	....	....	....	....	....	....
Goods procured in ports by carriers	2 170	....	....	....	....	....	....	....	....
Nonmonetary gold	2 180	....	....	25.4	87.5	....	....	....	....
Debit	3 100	**−246.1**	**−297.2**	**−321.9**	**−458.0**	**−740.1**	**−1,189.1**	**−1,013.4**	**−1,185.3**
General merchandise: imports f.o.b.	3 110	−246.1	−297.2	−321.9	−458.0	−740.1	−1,189.1	−1,013.4	−1,185.3
Goods for processing: imports f.o.b.	3 150	....	....	....	....	....	....	....	....
Repairs on goods	3 160	....	....	....	....	....	....	....	....
Goods procured in ports by carriers	3 170	....	....	....	....	....	....	....	....
Nonmonetary gold	3 180	....	....	....	....	....	....	....	....
B. SERVICES	4 200	**−124.6**	**−114.9**	**−127.6**	**−135.6**	**−129.7**	**−147.7**	**−34.9**	**−72.5**
Total credit	2 200	*90.9*	*59.4*	*38.5*	*59.0*	*141.3*	*204.1*	*233.6*	*244.7*
Total debit	3 200	*−215.5*	*−174.3*	*−166.1*	*−194.6*	*−271.0*	*−351.8*	*−268.5*	*−317.2*
Transportation services, credit	2 205	**37.1**	**19.0**	**23.2**	**26.2**	**49.4**	**70.1**	**24.6**	**20.4**
Passenger	2 850	*26.1*	*12.0*	*13.5*	*14.2*	*34.9*	*50.7*	*13.7*	*6.3*
Freight	2 851	*1.8*	*.6*	*3.6*	*.5*	*3.0*	*6.0*	*7.2*	*10.4*
Other	2 852	*9.2*	*6.4*	*6.1*	*11.5*	*11.5*	*13.4*	*3.7*	*3.7*
Sea transport, passenger	2 207	....	....	....	....	....	....	....	....
Sea transport, freight	2 208	....	....	....	....	....	....	....	....
Sea transport, other	2 209	....	....	....	....	....	....	....	....
Air transport, passenger	2 211	26.1	12.0	13.5	14.2	34.9	50.7	13.7	6.3
Air transport, freight	2 212	1.8	.6	3.6	.5	3.0	6.0	7.2	10.4
Air transport, other	2 213	9.2	6.4	6.1	11.5	11.5	13.4	3.7	3.7
Other transport, passenger	2 215	....	....	....	....	....	....	....	....
Other transport, freight	2 216	....	....	....	....	....	....	....	....
Other transport, other	2 217	....	....	....	....	....	....	....	....
Transportation services, debit	3 205	**−88.7**	**−63.8**	**−72.3**	**−109.7**	**−129.1**	**−135.0**	**−63.1**	**−65.6**
Passenger	3 850	*−43.8*	*−39.1*	*−43.9*	*−62.4*	*−71.4*	*−77.4*	*−14.6*	*−5.8*
Freight	3 851	*−13.4*	*−19.6*	*−21.9*	*−36.7*	*−37.4*	*−46.2*	*−39.8*	*−47.4*
Other	3 852	*−31.5*	*−5.1*	*−6.5*	*−10.6*	*−20.3*	*−11.4*	*−8.7*	*−12.4*
Sea transport, passenger	3 207	....	....	....	....	....	....	....	....
Sea transport, freight	3 208	....	....	....	....	....	....	....	....
Sea transport, other	3 209	....	....	....	....	....	....	....	....
Air transport, passenger	3 211	−43.8	−39.1	−43.9	−62.4	−71.4	−77.4	−14.6	−5.8
Air transport, freight	3 212	−13.4	−19.6	−21.9	−36.7	−37.4	−46.2	−39.8	−47.4
Air transport, other	3 213	−31.5	−5.1	−6.5	−10.6	−20.3	−11.4	−8.7	−12.4
Other transport, passenger	3 215	....	....	....	....	....	....	....	....
Other transport, freight	3 216	....	....	....	....	....	....	....	....
Other transport, other	3 217	....	....	....	....	....	....	....	....
Travel, credit	2 236	**15.8**	**14.4**	**3.4**	**3.8**	**17.0**	**44.6**	**94.8**	**66.6**
Business travel	2 237	....	....	....	....	....	....	....	....
Personal travel	2 240	15.8	14.4	3.4	3.8	17.0	44.6	94.8	66.6
Travel, debit	3 236	**−22.9**	**−23.4**	**−9.9**	**−5.6**	**−14.4**	**−16.9**	**−18.3**	**−22.0**
Business travel	3 237	....	....	....	....	....	....	....	....
Personal travel	3 240	−22.9	−23.4	−9.9	−5.6	−14.4	−16.9	−18.3	−22.0
Other services, credit	2 200 BA	**38.0**	**26.0**	**11.9**	**29.1**	**74.9**	**89.4**	**114.2**	**157.8**
Communications	2 245	....	....	....	....	....	....	....	....
Construction	2 249	....	....	....	....	....	....	....	....
Insurance	2 253	.2	....	.4	.1	.3	.7	.8	1.2
Financial	2 260	....	....	....	....	....	....	....	....
Computer and information	2 262	....	....	....	....	....	....	....	....
Royalties and licence fees	2 266	....	....	....	....	....	....	....	.1
Other business services	2 268	32.1	22.8	8.2	21.6	62.3	67.2	90.4	121.8
Personal, cultural, and recreational	2 287	....	....	....	....	....	....	....	....
Government, n.i.e.	2 291	5.7	3.2	3.3	7.4	12.3	21.5	23.0	34.7
Other services, debit	3 200 BA	**−103.9**	**−87.1**	**−83.9**	**−79.3**	**−127.5**	**−199.9**	**−187.1**	**−229.6**
Communications	3 245	....	....	....	....	....	....	....	....
Construction	3 249	....	....	....	....	....	....	....	....
Insurance	3 253	−1.9	−1.8	−2.4	−4.1	−4.2	−5.1	−4.4	−5.3
Financial	3 260	....	....	....	....	....	....	....	....
Computer and information	3 262	....	....	....	....	....	....	....	....
Royalties and licence fees	3 266	....	....	....	....	....	....	....	−2.5
Other business services	3 268	−63.3	−74.9	−67.8	−68.6	−103.2	−182.2	−164.3	−196.8
Personal, cultural, and recreational	3 287	....	....	....	....	....	....	....	....
Government, n.i.e.	3 291	−38.7	−10.4	−13.7	−6.6	−20.1	−12.6	−18.4	−25.0

Table 2 (Continued). STANDARD PRESENTATION, 2000–2007

(Millions of U.S. dollars)

	Code	2000	2001	2002	2003	2004	2005	2006	2007
C. INCOME	4 300	**6.0**	**−107.6**	**−42.3**	**−48.5**	**−62.9**	**−40.4**	**−51.6**	**8.2**
Total credit	2 300	*13.2*	*5.4*	*8.4*	*11.7*	*15.6*	*24.0*	*28.0*	*43.6*
Total debit	3 300	*−7.2*	*−113.0*	*−50.7*	*−60.2*	*−78.5*	*−64.4*	*−79.6*	*−35.4*
Compensation of employees, credit	2 310	....	....	2.2	2.3	2.0	2.4	2.0	2.4
Compensation of employees, debit	3 310	−1.1	−1.2	−1.2	−4.9	−5.3	−4.2	−2.6	−4.4
Investment income, credit	2 320	**13.2**	**5.4**	**6.2**	**9.4**	**13.6**	**21.6**	**26.0**	**41.2**
Direct investment income	2 330	....	....	....	....	....	....	....	....
Dividends and distributed branch profits	2 332	....	....	....	....	....	....	....	....
Reinvested earnings and undistributed branch profits	2 333	....	....	....	....	....	....	....	....
Income on debt (interest)	2 334	....	....	....	....	....	....	....	....
Portfolio investment income	2 339	....	....	....	....	....	....	....	....
Income on equity	2 340	....	....	....	....	....	....	....	....
Income on bonds and notes	2 350	....	....	....	....	....	....	....	....
Income on money market instruments	2 360	....	....	....	....	....	....	....	....
Other investment income	2 370	13.2	5.4	6.2	9.4	13.6	21.6	26.0	41.2
Investment income, debit	3 320	**−6.1**	**−111.8**	**−49.5**	**−55.3**	**−73.2**	**−60.2**	**−77.0**	**−31.0**
Direct investment income	3 330	....	....	....	....	....	−45.0	−45.4	....
Dividends and distributed branch profits	3 332	....	....	....	....	....	−45.0	−45.4	....
Reinvested earnings and undistributed branch profits	3 333	....	....	....	....	....	....	....	....
Income on debt (interest)	3 334	....	....	....	....	....	....	....	....
Portfolio investment income	3 339	....	....	....	....	....	....	....	−15.0
Income on equity	3 340	....	....	....	....	....	....	....	−15.0
Income on bonds and notes	3 350	....	....	....	....	....	....	....	....
Income on money market instruments	3 360	....	....	....	....	....	....	....	....
Other investment income	3 370	−6.1	−111.8	−49.5	−55.3	−73.2	−15.2	−31.6	−16.0
D. CURRENT TRANSFERS	4 379	**−2.1**	**−.9**	**−8.5**	**−4.7**	**12.8**	**22.1**	**35.9**	**75.5**
Credit	2 379	**1.2**	**2.1**	**12.9**	**24.8**	**75.8**	**52.3**	**73.5**	**137.9**
General government	2 380	....	....	....	....	....	....	....	....
Other sectors	2 390	1.2	2.1	12.9	24.8	75.8	52.3	73.5	137.9
Workers' remittances	2 391	....	.2	12.9	21.1	7.1	1.5	.1	137.5
Other current transfers	2 392	1.2	1.9	....	3.7	68.7	50.8	73.4	.4
Debit	3 379	**−3.3**	**−3.0**	**−21.4**	**−29.5**	**−63.0**	**−30.2**	**−37.6**	**−62.4**
General government	3 380	....	....	....	....	....	....	....	....
Other sectors	3 390	−3.3	−3.0	−21.4	−29.5	−63.0	−30.2	−37.6	−62.4
Workers' remittances	3 391	−.7	−.8	−20.9	−23.2	−8.6	−5.3	−1.5	−60.4
Other current transfers	3 392	−2.6	−2.2	−.5	−6.3	−54.4	−24.9	−36.1	−2.0
CAPITAL AND FINANCIAL ACCOUNT	4 996	**−146.6**	**27.5**	**−13.1**	**−34.7**	**−80.7**	**−25.8**	**−255.3**	**−345.9**
CAPITAL ACCOUNT	4 994	**2.3**	**1.5**	**5.9**	**9.0**	**18.9**	**14.5**	**19.3**	**8.1**
Total credit	2 994	*2.3*	*1.5*	*5.9*	*9.2*	*18.9*	*14.5*	*19.3*	*8.1*
Total debit	3 994	....	....	....	*−.2*	....	....	....	....
Capital transfers, credit	2 400	**2.3**	**1.5**	**5.9**	**9.2**	**18.9**	**14.5**	**19.3**	**8.1**
General government	2 401	2.3	1.5	5.9	9.1	18.9	14.5	19.3	8.1
Debt forgiveness	2 402	....	....	....	....	....	....	....	....
Other capital transfers	2 410	2.3	1.5	5.9	9.1	18.9	14.5	19.3	8.1
Other sectors	2 430	....	....	....	.1	....	....	....	....
Migrants' transfers	2 431	....	....	....	.1	....	....	....	....
Debt forgiveness	2 432	....	....	....	....	....	....	....	....
Other capital transfers	2 440	....	....	....	....	....	....	....	....
Capital transfers, debit	3 400	....	....	....	**−.2**	....	....	....	....
General government	3 401	....	....	....	....	....	....	....	....
Debt forgiveness	3 402	....	....	....	....	....	....	....	....
Other capital transfers	3 410	....	....	....	....	....	....	....	....
Other sectors	3 430	....	....	....	−.2	....	....	....	....
Migrants' transfers	3 431	....	....	....	−.2	....	....	....	....
Debt forgiveness	3 432	....	....	....	....	....	....	....	....
Other capital transfers	3 440	....	....	....	....	....	....	....	....
Nonproduced nonfinancial assets, credit	2 480	....	....	....	....	....	....	....	....
Nonproduced nonfinancial assets, debit	3 480	....	....	....	....	....	....	....	....

Table 2 (Continued). STANDARD PRESENTATION, 2000–2007

(Millions of U.S. dollars)

	Code	2000	2001	2002	2003	2004	2005	2006	2007
FINANCIAL ACCOUNT	4 995	−148.9	26.0	−19.0	−43.7	−99.6	−40.3	−274.6	−354.0
A. DIRECT INVESTMENT	4 500	−148.0	−26.8	−73.6	−76.1	−37.3	27.9	−163.4	−246.7
Direct investment abroad	4 505	....	....	....	....	....	....	....	....
Equity capital	4 510	....	....	....	....	....	....	....	....
Claims on affiliated enterprises	4 515	....	....	....	....	....	....	....	....
Liabilities to affiliated enterprises	4 520	....	....	....	....	....	....	....	....
Reinvested earnings	4 525	....	....	....	....	....	....	....	....
Other capital	4 530	....	....	....	....	....	....	....	....
Claims on affiliated enterprises	4 535	....	....	....	....	....	....	....	....
Liabilities to affiliated enterprises	4 540	....	....	....	....	....	....	....	....
Direct investment in Suriname	4 555	−148.0	−26.8	−73.6	−76.1	−37.3	27.9	−163.4	−246.7
Equity capital	4 560	....	....	....	....	.5	....	....	....
Claims on direct investors	4 565	....	....	....	....	....	....	....	....
Liabilities to direct investors	4 570	....	....	....	....	.5	....	....	....
Reinvested earnings	4 575	....	....	....	....	....	....	....	....
Other capital	4 580	−148.0	−26.8	−73.6	−76.1	−37.8	27.9	−163.4	−246.7
Claims on direct investors	4 585	....	....	....	....	....	....	....	....
Liabilities to direct investors	4 590	−148.0	−26.8	−73.6	−76.1	−37.8	27.9	−163.4	−246.7
B. PORTFOLIO INVESTMENT	4 600	....	....	....	....	....	−2.0	−.3	−1.3
Assets	4 602	....	....	....	....	....	....	....	....
Equity securities	4 610	....	....	....	....	....	....	....	....
Monetary authorities	4 611	....	....	....	....	....	....	....	....
General government	4 612	....	....	....	....	....	....	....	....
Banks	4 613	....	....	....	....	....	....	....	....
Other sectors	4 614	....	....	....	....	....	....	....	....
Debt securities	4 619	....	....	....	....	....	....	....	....
Bonds and notes	4 620	....	....	....	....	....	....	....	....
Monetary authorities	4 621	....	....	....	....	....	....	....	....
General government	4 622	....	....	....	....	....	....	....	....
Banks	4 623	....	....	....	....	....	....	....	....
Other sectors	4 624	....	....	....	....	....	....	....	....
Money market instruments	4 630	....	....	....	....	....	....	....	....
Monetary authorities	4 631	....	....	....	....	....	....	....	....
General government	4 632	....	....	....	....	....	....	....	....
Banks	4 633	....	....	....	....	....	....	....	....
Other sectors	4 634	....	....	....	....	....	....	....	....
Liabilities	4 652	....	....	....	....	....	−2.0	−.3	−1.3
Equity securities	4 660	....	....	....	....	....	....	....	....
Banks	4 663	....	....	....	....	....	....	....	....
Other sectors	4 664	....	....	....	....	....	....	....	....
Debt securities	4 669	....	....	....	....	....	−2.0	−.3	−1.3
Bonds and notes	4 670	....	....	....	....	....	−2.0	−.3	−1.3
Monetary authorities	4 671	....	....	....	....	....	....	....	....
General government	4 672	....	....	....	....	....	....	....	....
Banks	4 673	....	....	....	....	....	....	....	....
Other sectors	4 674	....	....	....	....	....	−2.0	−.3	−1.3
Money market instruments	4 680	....	....	....	....	....	....	....	....
Monetary authorities	4 681	....	....	....	....	....	....	....	....
General government	4 682	....	....	....	....	....	....	....	....
Banks	4 683	....	....	....	....	....	....	....	....
Other sectors	4 684	....	....	....	....	....	....	....	....
C. FINANCIAL DERIVATIVES	4 910	....	....	....	....	....	....	....	....
Monetary authorities	4 911	....	....	....	....	....	....	....	....
General government	4 912	....	....	....	....	....	....	....	....
Banks	4 913	....	....	....	....	....	....	....	....
Other sectors	4 914	....	....	....	....	....	....	....	....
Assets	4 900	....	....	....	....	....	....	....	....
Monetary authorities	4 901	....	....	....	....	....	....	....	....
General government	4 902	....	....	....	....	....	....	....	....
Banks	4 903	....	....	....	....	....	....	....	....
Other sectors	4 904	....	....	....	....	....	....	....	....
Liabilities	4 905	....	....	....	....	....	....	....	....
Monetary authorities	4 906	....	....	....	....	....	....	....	....
General government	4 907	....	....	....	....	....	....	....	....
Banks	4 908	....	....	....	....	....	....	....	....
Other sectors	4 909	....	....	....	....	....	....	....	....

Table 2 (Concluded). STANDARD PRESENTATION, 2000–2007

(Millions of U.S. dollars)

	Code	2000	2001	2002	2003	2004	2005	2006	2007
D. OTHER INVESTMENT	4 700 ..	**8.9**	**130.9**	**35.5**	**39.6**	**13.8**	**−46.5**	**−16.8**	**70.9**
Assets	4 703 ..	**24.6**	**40.7**	**23.9**	**46.9**	**−2.3**	**−31.9**	**8.4**	**83.5**
Trade credits	4 706 ..	....	....	....	....	....	....	....	−7.7
General government	4 707 ..	....	....	....	....	....	....	....	....
of which: Short-term	4 709 ..	....	....	....	....	....	....	....	....
Other sectors	4 710 ..	....	....	....	....	....	....	....	−7.7
of which: Short-term	4 712 ..	....	....	....	....	....	....	....	−7.7
Loans	4 714 ..								
Monetary authorities	4 715 ..								
of which: Short-term	4 718 ..								
General government	4 719 ..	....							
of which: Short-term	4 721 ..								
Banks	4 722 ..								
of which: Short-term	4 724 ..								
Other sectors	4 725 ..	....							
of which: Short-term	4 727 ..	....	....	....	....	....	....	....	....
Currency and deposits	4 730 ..	24.6	40.7	23.9	46.9	−2.3	−31.9	8.4	91.2
Monetary authorities	4 731 ..	....	....	....	....	....	....	....	....
General government	4 732 ..	....	....	....	....	....	....	....	....
Banks	4 733 ..	....	....	....	....	....	....	....	....
Other sectors	4 734 ..	24.6	40.7	23.9	46.9	−2.3	−31.9	8.4	91.2
Other assets	4 736 ..	....	....	....	....	....	....	....	....
Monetary authorities	4 737 ..	....	....	....	....	....	....	....	....
of which: Short-term	4 739 ..	....	....	....	....	....	....	....	....
General government	4 740 ..	....	....	....	....	....	....	....	....
of which: Short-term	4 742 ..	....	....	....	....	....	....	....	....
Banks	4 743 ..	....	....	....	....	....	....	....	....
of which: Short-term	4 745 ..	....	....	....	....	....	....	....	....
Other sectors	4 746 ..	....	....	....	....	....	....	....	....
of which: Short-term	4 748 ..	....	....	....	....	....	....	....	....
Liabilities	4 753 ..	**−15.7**	**90.2**	**11.6**	**−7.3**	**16.1**	**−14.6**	**−25.2**	**−12.6**
Trade credits	4 756 ..	....	....	....	....	....	....	.6	.6
General government	4 757 ..	....	....	....	....	....	....	....	....
of which: Short-term	4 759 ..	....	....	....	....	....	....	....	....
Other sectors	4 760 ..	....	....	....	....	....	....	.6	.6
of which: Short-term	4 762 ..	....	....	....	....	....	....	....	....
Loans	4 764 ..	−15.7	89.4	6.1	−2.5	7.1	−14.7	−25.7	−18.2
Monetary authorities	4 765 ..	....	....	....	....	....	....	....	....
of which: Use of Fund credit and loans from the Fund	4 766 ..	....	....	....	....	....	....	....	....
of which: Short-term	4 768 ..	....	....	....	....	....	....	....	....
General government	4 769 ..	−21.4	50.7	−30.8	−23.0	−18.5	−14.4	−25.6	−16.8
of which: Short-term	4 771 ..	....	....	....	....	....	....	....	....
Banks	4 772 ..	....	....	....	....	....	....	....	....
of which: Short-term	4 774 ..	....	....	....	....	....	....	....	....
Other sectors	4 775 ..	5.7	38.7	36.9	20.5	25.6	−.3	−.1	−1.4
of which: Short-term	4 777 ..	....	....	....	....	....	....	....	....
Currency and deposits	4 780 ..	....	....	....	....	....	....	....	....
Monetary authorities	4 781 ..	....	....	....	....	....	....	....	....
General government	4 782 ..	....	....	....	....	....	....	....	....
Banks	4 783 ..	....	....	....	....	....	....	....	....
Other sectors	4 784 ..	....	....	....	....	....	....	....	....
Other liabilities	4 786 ..	....	.8	5.5	−4.8	9.0	.1	−.1	5.0
Monetary authorities	4 787 ..	....	1.6	−.9	4.3	....	....	−.1	....
of which: Short-term	4 789 ..	....	....	....	....	....	....	....	....
General government	4 790 ..	....	....	....	....	....	....	....	....
of which: Short-term	4 792 ..	....	....	....	....	....	....	....	....
Banks	4 793 ..	....	−.8	6.4	−9.1	9.0	.1	....	5.0
of which: Short-term	4 795 ..	....	....	....	....	....	....	....	....
Other sectors	4 796 ..	....	....	....	....	....	....	....	....
of which: Short-term	4 798 ..	....	....	....	....	....	....	....	....
E. RESERVE ASSETS	4 802 ..	**−9.8**	**−78.1**	**19.1**	**−7.2**	**−76.1**	**−19.7**	**−94.1**	**−176.9**
Monetary gold	4 812 ..	−4.4	−2.2	−1.1	−1.3	−.5	−7.1	−7.5	−11.8
Special drawing rights	4 811 ..	.3	.3	.2	.1	.2	.2	.3	.4
Reserve position in the Fund	4 810 ..	....	....	....	....	....	....	....	....
Foreign exchange	4 803 ..	−5.7	−76.2	20.0	−6.0	−75.8	−12.8	−86.9	−165.5
Other claims	4 813 ..	....	....	....	....	....	....	....	....
NET ERRORS AND OMISSIONS	4 998 ..	**114.3**	**56.1**	**144.1**	**193.7**	**218.4**	**169.4**	**144.9**	**161.0**

Table 1. ANALYTIC PRESENTATION, 2000–2007

(Millions of U.S. dollars)

	Code	2000	2001	2002	2003	2004	2005	2006	2007
A. Current Account[1].............................	4 993 Z.	**−45.9**	**9.0**	**33.2**	**89.4**	**71.3**	**−102.6**	**−196.6**	**−65.5**
Goods: exports f.o.b.............................	2 100 ..	967.0	1,039.0	1,078.5	1,666.8	1,806.2	1,636.5	1,662.9	1,744.8
Goods: imports f.o.b.............................	3 100 ..	−1,127.6	−1,120.5	−1,027.0	−1,540.2	−1,715.3	−1,894.6	−1,914.9	−2,015.9
Balance on Goods.............................	4 100 ..	*−160.7*	*−81.5*	*51.5*	*126.6*	*90.9*	*−258.1*	*−252.0*	*−271.1*
Services: credit.................................	2 200 ..	273.2	113.9	93.2	204.8	249.6	282.5	283.3	454.7
Services: debit..................................	3 200 ..	−310.3	−208.3	−209.8	−349.1	−377.6	−402.8	−373.4	−506.8
Balance on Goods and Services............	4 991 ..	*−197.8*	*−175.9*	*−65.1*	*−17.6*	*−37.1*	*−378.4*	*−342.1*	*−323.3*
Income: credit.................................	2 300 ..	136.2	135.7	126.8	61.4	127.5	271.3	241.7	280.8
Income: debit..................................	3 300 ..	−84.9	−42.8	−124.4	−104.6	−124.9	−93.0	−227.7	−217.0
Balance on Goods, Services, and Income......	4 992 ..	*−146.5*	*−83.0*	*−62.7*	*−60.8*	*−34.5*	*−200.1*	*−328.1*	*−259.5*
Current transfers: credit.......................	2 379 Z.	247.5	229.7	216.2	336.6	370.8	339.6	366.3	403.5
Current transfers: debit........................	3 379 ..	−146.9	−137.8	−120.3	−186.4	−265.0	−242.1	−234.8	−209.5
B. Capital Account[1].............................	4 994 Z.	**.1**	**−.2**	**.5**	**. . . .**	**−.6**	**−3.5**	**24.8**	**−30.2**
Capital account: credit.........................	2 994 Z.	.1	.2	.5	. . . .	. . . .	1.0	29.2	11.2
Capital account: debit..........................	3 994 ..	. . . .	−.4	−.1	. . . .	−.6	−4.5	−4.5	−41.4
Total, Groups A Plus B........................	4 981 ..	*−45.8*	*8.8*	*33.7*	*89.4*	*70.7*	*−106.1*	*−171.9*	*−95.7*
C. Financial Account[1]..........................	4 995 W.	**−69.6**	**−143.9**	**−165.8**	**−89.2**	**−204.0**	**148.1**	**260.7**	**431.0**
Direct investment abroad.......................	4 505 ..	−17.1	17.7	.6	−16.4	1.4	22.0	.6	−23.2
Direct investment in Swaziland...............	4 555 Z.	90.7	29.3	92.1	−60.9	69.6	−45.9	121.0	37.5
Portfolio investment assets....................	4 602 ..	−2.0	−5.4	3.9	−.3	−.9	3.7	−9.5	4.2
Equity securities.............................	4 610 ..	−.1	−.1	. . . .	. . . .	.2	. . . .	.2	−.1
Debt securities..............................	4 619 ..	−1.9	−5.3	3.9	−.3	−1.1	3.7	−9.6	4.4
Portfolio investment liabilities.................	4 652 Z.	1.4	−2.5	−2.0	−.1	.3	.8	5.5	1.0
Equity securities.............................	4 660 ..	1.4	−2.5	−2.0	−.1	.3	.8	5.5	1.0
Debt securities..............................	4 669 Z.	. . . .	. . . .	. . . .	. . . .	. . . .	. . . .	. . . .	. . . .
Financial derivatives...........................	4 910 ..	. . . .	. . . .	. . . .	. . . .	. . . .	. . . .	. . . .	. . . .
Financial derivatives assets....................	4 900 ..	. . . .	. . . .	. . . .	. . . .	. . . .	. . . .	. . . .	. . . .
Financial derivatives liabilities.................	4 905 ..	. . . .	. . . .	. . . .	. . . .	. . . .	. . . .	. . . .	. . . .
Other investment assets.......................	4 703 ..	−183.5	−174.8	−218.0	8.1	−231.4	84.3	101.2	357.8
Monetary authorities........................	4 701 ..	. . . .	. . . .	. . . .	. . . .	. . . .	. . . .	. . . .	. . . .
General government........................	4 704 ..	−2.6	−28.9	−33.4	−26.5	−27.3	202.1	427.4	444.0
Banks......................................	4 705 ..	27.7	−27.7	9.6	35.7	−1.6	17.7	−68.5	23.0
Other sectors..............................	4 728 ..	−208.6	−118.2	−194.2	−1.1	−202.5	−135.5	−257.6	−109.2
Other investment liabilities....................	4 753 W.	41.0	−8.1	−42.2	−19.6	−43.0	83.1	41.8	53.7
Monetary authorities........................	4 753 WA	6.2	14.7	−12.1	−2.7	−46.5	−1.2	−.2	4.4
General government........................	4 753 ZB	−1.2	11.7	7.1	−1.7	8.4	27.9	29.5	27.0
Banks......................................	4 753 ZC	6.4	−9.5	4.7	−3.2	−1.7	4.4	7.8	−9.0
Other sectors..............................	4 753 ZD	29.5	−25.1	−42.0	−11.9	−3.3	52.0	4.7	31.3
Total, Groups A Through C....................	4 983 ..	*−115.4*	*−135.1*	*−132.1*	*.2*	*−133.3*	*41.9*	*88.9*	*335.4*
D. Net Errors and Omissions...................	4 998 ..	**161.6**	**210.2**	**62.3**	**−92.1**	**168.2**	**−40.8**	**−237.8**	**−700.8**
Total, Groups A Through D....................	4 984 ..	*46.3*	*75.1*	*−69.8*	*−91.8*	*34.9*	*1.1*	*−148.9*	*−365.5*
E. Reserves and Related Items...............	4 802 A.	**−46.3**	**−75.1**	**69.8**	**91.8**	**−34.9**	**−1.1**	**148.9**	**365.5**
Reserve assets.................................	4 802 ..	−46.3	−75.1	69.8	91.8	−34.4	.6	151.2	365.2
Use of Fund credit and loans...................	4 766 ..	. . . .	. . . .	. . . .	. . . .	. . . .	. . . .	. . . .	. . . .
Exceptional financing..........................	4 920 ..	. . . .	. . . .	. . . .	. . . .	−.5	−1.7	−2.3	.2
Conversion rates: emalangeni per U.S. dollar	0 101 ..	**6.940**	**8.609**	**10.541**	**7.565**	**6.460**	**6.359**	**6.772**	**7.045**

[1] Excludes components that have been classified in the categories of Group E.

Table 2. STANDARD PRESENTATION, 2000–2007

(Millions of U.S. dollars)

	Code	2000	2001	2002	2003	2004	2005	2006	2007
CURRENT ACCOUNT.........................	4 993 ..	**−45.9**	**9.0**	**33.2**	**89.4**	**71.3**	**−102.6**	**−196.6**	**−65.5**
A. GOODS................................	4 100 ..	**−160.7**	**−81.5**	**51.5**	**126.6**	**90.9**	**−258.1**	**−252.0**	**−271.1**
Credit..............................	2 100 ..	**967.0**	**1,039.0**	**1,078.5**	**1,666.8**	**1,806.2**	**1,636.5**	**1,662.9**	**1,744.8**
General merchandise: exports f.o.b............	2 110 ..	965.3	1,026.9	1,067.4	1,636.2	1,791.8	1,585.1	1,560.6	1,625.7
Goods for processing: exports f.o.b...........	2 150 ..	1.4	11.9	11.1	30.6	14.4	35.2	102.3	118.8
Repairs on goods............................	2 160 ..	....	....	....	....	....	....	....	.1
Goods procured in ports by carriers..........	2 170 ..	.3	.2				.1		.1
Nonmonetary gold...........................	2 180 ..	....	....	....	....	....	16.2	....	....
Debit..............................	3 100 ..	**−1,127.6**	**−1,120.5**	**−1,027.0**	**−1,540.2**	**−1,715.3**	**−1,894.6**	**−1,914.9**	**−2,015.9**
General merchandise: imports f.o.b............	3 110 ..	−1,056.2	−1,050.8	−964.4	−1,434.4	−1,640.7	−1,775.0	−1,804.0	−1,934.8
Goods for processing: imports f.o.b...........	3 150 ..	−67.4	−66.1	−61.4	−103.7	−74.1	−114.4	−108.3	−80.6
Repairs on goods............................	3 160 ..	−3.6	−3.2	−.3	−.3	−.3	−.3	−.2	−.7
Goods procured in ports by carriers..........	3 170 ..	−.4	−.3	−.9	−1.8	....	−.5	−.1	.2
Nonmonetary gold...........................	3 180 ..	....	....	....	....	−.2	−4.5	−2.3	....
B. SERVICES............................	4 200 ..	**−37.1**	**−94.4**	**−116.6**	**−144.3**	**−128.0**	**−120.3**	**−90.1**	**−52.2**
Total credit................................	2 200 ..	*273.2*	*113.9*	*93.2*	*204.8*	*249.6*	*282.5*	*283.3*	*454.7*
Total debit.................................	3 200 ..	*−310.3*	*−208.3*	*−209.8*	*−349.1*	*−377.6*	*−402.8*	*−373.4*	*−506.8*
Transportation services, credit...........	2 205 ..	**17.7**	**11.7**	**7.6**	**9.1**	**11.3**	**10.2**	**10.1**	**8.8**
Passenger................................	2 850 ..	*2.6*	*2.1*	*1.7*	*....*	*.1*	*.3*	*.1*	*.2*
Freight...................................	2 851 ..	*15.2*	*9.7*	*6.0*	*9.0*	*10.9*	*9.9*	*10.0*	*8.6*
Other...................................	2 852 ..	*....*	*....*	*....*	*....*	*.2*	*.1*	*....*	*....*
Sea transport, passenger....................	2 207 ..	....	....	....	....	....	....	....	....
Sea transport, freight.......................	2 208 ..	.4	.4	.3	.3	.4	.3	.2	.2
Sea transport, other........................	2 209 ..	....	....	....	....	....	....	....	....
Air transport, passenger.....................	2 211 ..	2.6	2.1	1.7	....	.1	.1	.1	.1
Air transport, freight........................	2 212 ..	.1	.1	....	....	....	....	....	....
Air transport, other.........................	2 213 ..	....	....	....	....	....	....	....	....
Other transport, passenger..................	2 215 ..	....	....	....	....	....	.1	.1	.1
Other transport, freight.....................	2 216 ..	14.7	9.2	5.7	8.7	10.5	9.5	9.8	8.4
Other transport, other......................	2 217 ..	....	....	....	....	.2	.1	....	....
Transportation services, debit...........	3 205 ..	**−34.8**	**−45.0**	**−40.7**	**−58.4**	**−54.8**	**−49.2**	**−44.7**	**−58.0**
Passenger................................	3 850 ..	*−1.3*	*−1.1*	*−1.1*	*−.9*	*−5.8*	*−11.2*	*−4.9*	*−12.3*
Freight...................................	3 851 ..	*−25.6*	*−27.1*	*−21.4*	*−29.8*	*−33.4*	*−28.3*	*−30.3*	*−38.0*
Other...................................	3 852 ..	*−7.8*	*−16.8*	*−19.3*	*−27.6*	*−15.6*	*−9.7*	*−9.6*	*−7.6*
Sea transport, passenger....................	3 207 ..	....	....	....	....	....	....	....	....
Sea transport, freight.......................	3 208 ..	−8.4	−11.4	−8.4	−11.2	−32.6	−25.6	−28.5	−20.0
Sea transport, other........................	3 209 ..	....	....	....	....	....	....	....	....
Air transport, passenger.....................	3 211 ..	−1.3	−1.1	....	−.9	−3.7	−5.6	−2.4	−6.2
Air transport, freight........................	3 212 ..	−.1	−.1	−.1	−.1	−.2	−.1	−.3	−14.9
Air transport, other.........................	3 213 ..	−7.8	−16.8	−19.3	−27.6	....	....	....	....
Other transport, passenger..................	3 215 ..	....	....	....	....	−2.1	−5.6	−2.4	−6.2
Other transport, freight.....................	3 216 ..	−17.1	−15.7	−13.0	−18.5	−.5	−2.6	−1.5	−3.2
Other transport, other......................	3 217 ..	....	....	....	....	−15.6	−9.7	−9.6	−7.6
Travel, credit...........................	2 236 ..	**21.5**	**20.5**	**43.2**	**69.8**	**75.0**	**76.9**	**75.4**	**31.7**
Business travel.............................	2 237 ..	11.8	12.2	20.9	35.5	43.7	44.4	41.7	27.2
Personal travel.............................	2 240 ..	9.7	8.3	22.4	34.3	31.3	32.6	33.7	4.4
Travel, debit............................	3 236 ..	**−30.7**	**−29.6**	**−25.9**	**−21.9**	**−48.2**	**−49.2**	**−48.8**	**−51.4**
Business travel.............................	3 237 ..	−2.5	−2.3	−1.9	−2.6	−1.0	−1.4	−1.7	−2.6
Personal travel.............................	3 240 ..	−28.2	−27.3	−24.1	−19.3	−47.1	−47.9	−47.1	−48.8
Other services, credit....................	2 200 BA	**234.0**	**81.6**	**42.3**	**125.9**	**163.4**	**195.4**	**197.9**	**414.2**
Communications............................	2 245 ..	1.6	1.3	1.3	.1	.6	13.2	1.7	6.4
Construction...............................	2 249 ..	....	....	....	.2	.9	1.1	2.0	.8
Insurance..................................	2 253 ..	....	....	....	.1	4.1	1.2	4.9	5.6
Financial..................................	2 260 ..	....	....	....	97.7	105.3	151.3	32.9	25.4
Computer and information...................	2 262 ..	1.9	1.5	1.1	1.2	....	....	.3	....
Royalties and licence fees...................	2 266 ..	.2	.2	.1	....	....	....	....	....
Other business services.....................	2 268 ..	227.7	76.5	36.4	21.7	37.7	18.4	146.7	368.5
Personal, cultural, and recreational...........	2 287 ..	....	....	....	....	....	.1	.2	.3
Government, n.i.e...........................	2 291 ..	2.6	2.1	3.4	4.8	14.8	10.0	9.2	7.2
Other services, debit.....................	3 200 BA	**−244.8**	**−133.8**	**−143.2**	**−268.8**	**−274.7**	**−304.4**	**−279.9**	**−397.5**
Communications............................	3 245 ..	−2.3	−1.9	−1.5	−2.2	−3.1	−4.3	−1.4	−3.2
Construction...............................	3 249 ..	−.6	−.5	....	−1.2	−3.0	−3.0	−4.7	−17.3
Insurance..................................	3 253 ..	−6.0	−6.0	−5.5	−8.0	−9.3	−7.2	−7.3	−7.6
Financial..................................	3 260 ..	−.1	−.2	−8.4	−35.5	−95.6	−123.1	−56.1	−52.7
Computer and information...................	3 262 ..	−1.8	−1.1	−1.1	−.9	−1.0	−2.3	−2.5	−2.9
Royalties and licence fees...................	3 266 ..	−35.1	−42.8	−54.1	−71.2	−75.6	−105.4	−106.4	−121.0
Other business services.....................	3 268 ..	−188.8	−65.3	−64.8	−142.7	−71.9	−52.5	−93.0	−180.3
Personal, cultural, and recreational...........	3 287 ..	....	....	....	−.1	−.1	−.3	....	....
Government, n.i.e...........................	3 291 ..	−10.1	−16.0	−7.8	−7.0	−15.0	−6.4	−8.5	−12.5

Table 2 (Continued). STANDARD PRESENTATION, 2000–2007

(Millions of U.S. dollars)

	Code	2000	2001	2002	2003	2004	2005	2006	2007
C. INCOME	4 300	**51.3**	**92.9**	**2.4**	**−43.2**	**2.6**	**178.3**	**14.0**	**63.8**
Total credit	2 300	*136.2*	*135.7*	*126.8*	*61.4*	*127.5*	*271.3*	*241.7*	*280.8*
Total debit	3 300	*−84.9*	*−42.8*	*−124.4*	*−104.6*	*−124.9*	*−93.0*	*−227.7*	*−217.0*
Compensation of employees, credit	2 310	**56.8**	**52.7**	**44.1**	**65.2**	**81.7**	**94.1**	**94.3**	**93.6**
Compensation of employees, debit	3 310	....	....	....	**−2.0**	**−3.9**	**−4.9**	**−15.4**	**−6.7**
Investment income, credit	2 320	**79.5**	**83.0**	**82.7**	**−3.8**	**45.8**	**177.2**	**147.3**	**187.2**
Direct investment income	2 330	1.4	1.2	3.4	6.8	1.2	1.6	1.7	6.0
Dividends and distributed branch profits	2 332	.7	.6	2.5	6.1	1.2	1.6	1.7	6.0
Reinvested earnings and undistributed branch profits	2 333	.7	.6	.9	.7	....	....	....	....
Income on debt (interest)	2 334	....	....	....	....	....	....	....	....
Portfolio investment income	2 339	....	....	....	....	.1	.4	.4	.4
Income on equity	2 340	....	....	....	....	.1	.4	.4	.4
Income on bonds and notes	2 350	....	....	....	....	....	....	....	....
Income on money market instruments	2 360	....	....	....	....	....	....	....	....
Other investment income	2 370	78.0	81.8	79.3	−10.6	44.5	175.2	145.3	180.8
Investment income, debit	3 320	**−84.9**	**−42.8**	**−124.4**	**−102.6**	**−121.1**	**−88.0**	**−212.3**	**−210.3**
Direct investment income	3 330	−65.9	−28.9	−123.8	−75.7	−87.4	−44.0	−167.0	−160.0
Dividends and distributed branch profits	3 332	−1.5	−27.6	−50.3	−101.4	−50.3	−64.4	−94.8	−94.7
Reinvested earnings anc undistributed branch profits	3 333	−64.5	−1.3	−73.5	25.7	−37.1	23.0	−72.3	−65.4
Income on debt (interest)	3 334	....	....	....	....	....	−2.6	....	....
Portfolio investment income	3 339	....	....	....	....	−7.3	−19.3	−20.0	−21.1
Income on equity	3 340	....	....	....	....	−7.3	−19.3	−20.0	−21.1
Income on bonds and notes	3 350	....	....	....	....	....	....	....	....
Income on money market instruments	3 360	....	....	....	....	....	....	....	....
Other investment income	3 370	−19.0	−13.9	−.6	−26.8	−26.4	−24.7	−25.3	−29.2
D. CURRENT TRANSFERS	4 379	**100.6**	**92.0**	**95.9**	**150.2**	**105.8**	**97.5**	**131.5**	**194.0**
Credit	2 379	**247.5**	**229.7**	**216.2**	**336.6**	**370.8**	**339.6**	**366.3**	**403.5**
General government	2 380	237.7	223.7	210.9	302.1	348.3	296.4	318.1	338.9
Other sectors	2 390	9.8	6.1	5.3	34.6	22.6	43.2	48.2	64.6
Workers' remittances	2 391	....	....	....	....	1.1	1.3	1.3	1.5
Other current transfers	2 392	9.8	6.1	5.3	34.6	21.5	41.9	46.9	63.1
Debit	3 379	**−146.9**	**−137.8**	**−120.3**	**−186.4**	**−265.0**	**−242.1**	**−234.8**	**−209.5**
General government	3 380	−124.1	−110.4	−96.9	−144.9	−193.6	−164.7	−169.1	−170.8
Other sectors	3 390	−22.8	−27.4	−23.4	−41.5	−71.4	−77.5	−65.7	−38.7
Workers' remittances	3 391	−20.7	−26.5	−21.1	−36.8	−.2	−3.0	−1.2	−1.1
Other current transfers	3 392	−2.0	−.9	−2.2	−4.7	−71.2	−74.4	−64.5	−37.5
CAPITAL AND FINANCIAL ACCOUNT	4 996	**−115.8**	**−219.2**	**−95.5**	**2.7**	**−239.5**	**143.5**	**434.4**	**766.4**
CAPITAL ACCOUNT	4 994	**.1**	**−.2**	**.5**	....	**−.6**	**−3.5**	**24.8**	**−30.2**
Total credit	2 994	*.1*	*.2*	*.5*	....	....	*1.0*	*29.2*	*11.2*
Total debit	3 994	....	*−.4*	*−.1*	....	*−.6*	*−4.5*	*−4.5*	*−41.4*
Capital transfers, credit	2 400	**.1**	**.2**	**.5**	....	....	**1.0**	**29.2**	**11.2**
General government	2 401	....	....	....	....	....	....	25.1	4.0
Debt forgiveness	2 402	....	....	....	....	....	....	....	....
Other capital transfers	2 410	....	....	....	....	....	....	25.1	4.0
Other sectors	2 430	.1	.2	.5	....	....	1.0	4.2	7.2
Migrants' transfers	2 431	.1	.2	.5	....	....	....	3.0	5.3
Debt forgiveness	2 432	....	....	....	....	....	....	....	....
Other capital transfers	2 440	....	....	....	....	....	1.0	1.2	1.9
Capital transfers, debit	3 400	....	**−.4**	**−.1**	....	**−.6**	**−4.5**	**−4.5**	**−41.4**
General government	3 401	....	....	....	....	....	....	....	....
Debt forgiveness	3 402	....	....	....	....	....	....	....	....
Other capital transfers	3 410	....	....	....	....	....	....	....	....
Other sectors	3 430	....	−.4	−.1	....	−.6	−4.5	−4.5	−41.4
Migrants' transfers	3 431	....	−.4	−.1	....	−.6	−.2	−.2	−.3
Debt forgiveness	3 432	....	....	....	....	....	....	....	....
Other capital transfers	3 440	....	....	....	....	....	−4.2	−4.3	−41.0
Nonproduced nonfinancial assets, credit	2 480	....	....	....	....	....	....	....	....
Nonproduced nonfinancial assets, debit	3 480	....	....	....	....	....	....	....	....

Table 2 (Continued). STANDARD PRESENTATION, 2000–2007

(Millions of U.S. dollars)

	Code	2000	2001	2002	2003	2004	2005	2006	2007
FINANCIAL ACCOUNT	4 995	−115.8	−219.0	−95.9	2.7	−238.9	147.0	409.6	796.5
A. DIRECT INVESTMENT	4 500	73.6	47.0	92.6	−77.3	71.0	−23.8	121.6	14.3
Direct investment abroad	4 505	−17.1	17.7	.6	−16.4	1.4	22.0	.6	−23.2
Equity capital	4 510	.7	....	.4	.4	....	−.1	.3	....
Claims on affiliated enterprises	4 515	.7	....	.4	.4	....	−.1	.3	....
Liabilities to affiliated enterprises	4 520	....	....	....	....	....	....	....	....
Reinvested earnings	4 525	−.7	−.6	−.9	−.7	....	....	....	....
Other capital	4 530	−17.0	18.3	1.1	−16.0	1.4	22.1	.3	−23.2
Claims on affiliated enterprises	4 535	−17.0	18.3	.2	−16.7	1.4	22.1	.3	−23.2
Liabilities to affiliated enterprises	4 540	....	....	.9	.7	....	....	....	....
Direct investment in Swaziland	4 555	90.7	29.3	92.1	−60.9	69.6	−45.9	121.0	37.5
Equity capital	4 560	−21.9	37.4	−9.4	−3.8	−4.8	7.2	6.3	5.1
Claims on direct investors	4 565	....	....	....	....	....	....	....	....
Liabilities to direct investors	4 570	−21.9	37.4	−9.4	−3.8	−4.8	7.2	6.3	5.1
Reinvested earnings	4 575	64.5	1.3	73.5	−25.7	37.1	−23.0	72.3	65.4
Other capital	4 580	48.1	−9.4	28.0	−31.4	37.3	−30.0	42.5	−33.0
Claims on direct investors	4 585	....	....	....	....	....	....	....	....
Liabilities to direct investors	4 590	48.1	−9.4	28.0	−31.4	37.3	−30.0	42.5	−33.0
B. PORTFOLIO INVESTMENT	4 600	−.6	−7.9	1.9	−.4	−.6	4.5	−4.0	5.2
Assets	4 602	−2.0	−5.4	3.9	−.3	−.9	3.7	−9.5	4.2
Equity securities	4 610	−.1	−.1	....	....	.2	....	.2	−.1
Monetary authorities	4 611	....	....	....	....	....	....	....	....
General government	4 612	....	....	....	....	....	....	....	....
Banks	4 613	....	....	....	....	....	....	....	....
Other sectors	4 614	−.1	−.1	....	....	.2	....	.2	−.1
Debt securities	4 619	−1.9	−5.3	3.9	−.3	−1.1	3.7	−9.6	4.4
Bonds and notes	4 620	−1.9	−5.3	3.9	−.3	−1.0	3.7	−.3	−4.6
Monetary authorities	4 621	....	....	....	....	....	....	....	....
General government	4 622	....	....	....	....	....	....	....	....
Banks	4 623	....	....	....	....	....	....	....	....
Other sectors	4 624	−1.9	−5.3	3.9	−.3	−1.0	3.7	−.3	−4.6
Money market instruments	4 630	....	....	....	....	−.1	....	−9.3	9.0
Monetary authorities	4 631	....	....	....	....	....	....	....	....
General government	4 632	....	....	....	....	....	....	....	....
Banks	4 633	....	....	....	....	....	....	....	....
Other sectors	4 634	....	....	....	....	−.1	....	−9.3	9.0
Liabilities	4 652	1.4	−2.5	−2.0	−.1	.3	.8	5.5	1.0
Equity securities	4 660	1.4	−2.5	−2.0	−.1	.3	.8	5.5	1.0
Banks	4 663	....	....	....	....	....	....	....	....
Other sectors	4 664	1.4	−2.5	−2.0	−.1	.3	.8	5.5	1.0
Debt securities	4 669	....	....	....	....	....	....	....	....
Bonds and notes	4 670	....	....	....	....	....	....	....	....
Monetary authorities	4 671	....	....	....	....	....	....	....	....
General government	4 672	....	....	....	....	....	....	....	....
Banks	4 673	....	....	....	....	....	....	....	....
Other sectors	4 674	....	....	....	....	....	....	....	....
Money market instruments	4 680	....	....	....	....	....	....	....	....
Monetary authorities	4 681	....	....	....	....	....	....	....	....
General government	4 682	....	....	....	....	....	....	....	....
Banks	4 683	....	....	....	....	....	....	....	....
Other sectors	4 684	....	....	....	....	....	....	....	....
C. FINANCIAL DERIVATIVES	4 910	....	....	....	....	....	....	....	....
Monetary authorities	4 911	....	....	....	....	....	....	....	....
General government	4 912	....	....	....	....	....	....	....	....
Banks	4 913	....	....	....	....	....	....	....	....
Other sectors	4 914	....	....	....	....	....	....	....	....
Assets	4 900	....	....	....	....	....	....	....	....
Monetary authorities	4 901	....	....	....	....	....	....	....	....
General government	4 902	....	....	....	....	....	....	....	....
Banks	4 903	....	....	....	....	....	....	....	....
Other sectors	4 904	....	....	....	....	....	....	....	....
Liabilities	4 905	....	....	....	....	....	....	....	....
Monetary authorities	4 906	....	....	....	....	....	....	....	....
General government	4 907	....	....	....	....	....	....	....	....
Banks	4 908	....	....	....	....	....	....	....	....
Other sectors	4 909	....	....	....	....	....	....	....	....

Table 2 (Concluded). STANDARD PRESENTATION, 2000–2007

(Millions of U.S. dollars)

	Code	2000	2001	2002	2003	2004	2005	2006	2007
D. OTHER INVESTMENT	4 700 ..	**−142.6**	**−183.0**	**−260.3**	**−11.5**	**−274.9**	**165.7**	**140.7**	**411.8**
Assets	4 703 ..	−183.5	−174.8	−218.0	8.1	−231.4	84.3	101.2	357.8
Trade credits	4 706 ..	−.6	−18.6	−23.6	21.3	−2.2	−18.0	−45.9	6.7
General government	4 707 ..	....	....	....	....	....	....	....	....
of which: Short-term	4 709 ..	....	....	....	....	....	....	....	....
Other sectors	4 710 ..	−.6	−18.6	−23.6	21.3	−2.2	−18.0	−45.9	6.7
of which: Short-term	4 712 ..	−.6	−18.6	−23.6	21.3	−2.2	−18.0	−45.9	6.7
Loans	4 714 ..	.2	....	....	−5.3	3.4	−.3	−5.2	−2.9
Monetary authorities	4 715 ..	....	....	....	....	....	....	....	....
of which: Short-term	4 718 ..	....	....	....	....	....	....	....	....
General government	4 719 ..	....	....	....	....	....	....	....	....
of which: Short-term	4 721 ..	....	....	....	....	....	....	....	....
Banks	4 722 ..	....	....	....	....	....	....	....	....
of which: Short-term	4 724 ..	....	....	....	....	....	....	....	....
Other sectors	4 725 ..	.2	....	....	−5.3	3.4	−.3	−5.2	−2.9
of which: Short-term	4 727 ..	....	....	....	....	....	....	....	....
Currency and deposits	4 730 ..	−28.7	−13.0	−16.8	54.7	−18.3	17.1	−130.3	47.4
Monetary authorities	4 731 ..	....	....	....	....	....	....	....	....
General government	4 732 ..	....	....	....	....	....	....	....	....
Banks	4 733 ..	27.7	−27.7	9.6	35.7	−1.6	17.7	−68.5	23.0
Other sectors	4 734 ..	−56.5	14.8	−26.4	19.0	−16.7	−.6	−61.7	24.4
Other assets	4 736 ..	−154.5	−143.3	−177.7	−62.6	−214.4	85.6	282.5	306.6
Monetary authorities	4 737 ..	....	....	....	....	....	....	....	....
of which: Short-term	4 739 ..	....	....	....	....	....	....	....	....
General government	4 740 ..	−2.6	−28.9	−33.4	−26.5	−27.3	202.1	427.4	444.0
of which: Short-term	4 742 ..	−2.6	−28.9	−33.4	−26.5	−27.3	202.1	427.4	444.0
Banks	4 743 ..	....	....	....	....	....	....	....	....
of which: Short-term	4 745 ..	....	....	....	....	....	....	....	....
Other sectors	4 746 ..	−151.8	−114.4	−144.2	−36.1	−187.1	−116.6	−144.8	−137.5
of which: Short-term	4 748 ..	....	....	....	....	....	....	....	....
Liabilities	4 753 ..	**41.0**	**−8.1**	**−42.2**	**−19.6**	**−43.5**	**81.4**	**39.5**	**54.0**
Trade credits	4 756 ..	−3.3	2.0	−6.5	1.9	−1.3	16.9	3.6	−7.4
General government	4 757 ..	....	....	....	....	....	....	....	....
of which: Short-term	4 759 ..	....	....	....	....	....	....	....	....
Other sectors	4 760 ..	−3.3	2.0	−6.5	1.9	−1.3	16.9	3.6	−7.4
of which: Short-term	4 762 ..	−3.3	2.0	−6.5	1.9	−1.3	16.9	3.6	−7.4
Loans	4 764 ..	22.5	−13.3	−21.9	−2.8	6.5	63.0	30.7	65.8
Monetary authorities	4 765 ..	....	....	....	....	....	....	....	....
of which: Use of Fund credit and loans from the Fund..	4 766 ..	....	....	....	....	....	....	....	....
of which: Short-term	4 768 ..	....	....	....	....	....	....	....	....
General government	4 769 ..	−1.2	11.7	7.1	−1.7	8.4	27.9	29.5	27.0
of which: Short-term	4 771 ..	....	....	....	....	....	....	....	....
Banks	4 772 ..	....	....	....	....	....	....	....	....
of which: Short-term	4 774 ..	....	....	....	....	....	....	....	....
Other sectors	4 775 ..	23.7	−25.0	−29.0	−1.0	−1.9	35.1	1.2	38.7
of which: Short-term	4 777 ..	....	....	....	....	....	....	....	....
Currency and deposits	4 780 ..	6.2	14.7	−12.1	−2.7	−46.5	−1.2	−.2	4.4
Monetary authorities	4 781 ..	6.2	14.7	−12.1	−2.7	−46.5	−1.2	−.2	4.4
General government	4 782 ..	....	....	....	....	....	....	....	....
Banks	4 783 ..	....	....	....	....	....	....	....	....
Other sectors	4 784 ..	....	....	....	....	....	....	....	....
Other liabilities	4 786 ..	15.6	−11.6	−1.8	−16.1	−2.2	2.7	5.5	−8.8
Monetary authorities	4 787 ..	....	....	....	....	....	....	....	....
of which: Short-term	4 789 ..	....	....	....	....	....	....	....	....
General government	4 790 ..	....	....	....	....	....	....	....	....
of which: Short-term	4 792 ..	....	....	....	....	....	....	....	....
Banks	4 793 ..	6.4	−9.5	4.7	−3.2	−1.7	4.4	7.8	−9.0
of which: Short-term	4 795 ..	6.4	−9.5	4.7	−3.2	−1.7	4.4	7.8	−9.0
Other sectors	4 796 ..	9.2	−2.1	−6.5	−12.8	−.5	−1.7	−2.3	.2
of which: Short-term	4 798 ..	9.2	−2.1	−6.5	−12.8	−.5	−1.7	−2.3	.2
E. RESERVE ASSETS	4 802 ..	**−46.3**	**−75.1**	**69.8**	**91.8**	**−34.4**	**.6**	**151.2**	**365.2**
Monetary gold	4 812 ..	....	....	....	....	....	.3	....	....
Special drawing rights	4 811 ..	....	....	....	....	....	....	....	....
Reserve position in the Fund	4 810 ..	....	....	....	....	....	....	....	....
Foreign exchange	4 803 ..	−46.2	−75.1	69.8	91.8	−34.4	.3	151.2	365.3
Other claims	4 813 ..	....	....	....	....	....	....	....	....
NET ERRORS AND OMISSIONS	4 998 ..	**161.6**	**210.2**	**62.3**	**−92.1**	**168.2**	**−40.8**	**−237.8**	**−700.8**

Table 3. INTERNATIONAL INVESTMENT POSITION (End-period stocks), 2000–2007

(Millions of U.S. dollars)

	Code	2000	2001	2002	2003	2004	2005	2006	2007
ASSETS	8 995 C.	**1,131.6**	**839.6**	**1,265.6**	**1,486.7**	**1,893.5**	**1,981.5**	**2,693.1**	**3,226.8**
Direct investment abroad	8 505 ..	**88.3**	**42.1**	**58.4**	**94.7**	**110.0**	**75.8**	**68.2**	**92.3**
Equity capital and reinvested earnings	8 506 ..	2.2	1.4	1.4	1.5	1.7	1.6	1.2	21.0
Claims on affiliated enterprises	8 507 ..	2.2	1.4	1.4	1.5	1.7	1.6	1.2	21.0
Liabilities to affiliated enterprises	8 508 ..	....	....	....	....	....	....	....	....
Other capital	8 530 ..	86.1	40.8	57.0	93.2	108.3	74.1	67.0	71.3
Claims on affiliated enterprises	8 535 ..	86.1	40.8	57.0	93.2	108.3	74.1	67.0	71.3
Liabilities to affiliated enterprises	8 540 ..	....	....	....	....	....	....	....	....
Portfolio investment	8 602 ..	**11.5**	**11.0**	**10.7**	**14.2**	**17.8**	**12.1**	**20.2**	**16.2**
Equity securities	8 610 ..	2.4	1.6	2.2	2.9	3.1	2.8	2.4	2.5
Monetary authorities	8 611 ..	....	....	....	....	....	....	....	....
General government	8 612 ..	....	....	....	....	....	....	....	....
Banks	8 613 ..	....	....	....	....	....	....	....	....
Other sectors	8 614 ..	2.4	1.6	2.2	2.9	3.1	2.8	2.4	2.5
Debt securities	8 619 ..	9.1	9.4	8.5	11.3	14.7	9.3	17.8	13.7
Bonds and notes	8 620 ..	9.0	9.4	8.4	11.3	14.5	9.2	8.7	13.6
Monetary authorities	8 621 ..	....	....	....	....	....	....	....	....
General government	8 622 ..	....	....	....	....	....	....	....	....
Banks	8 623 ..	....	....	....	....	....	....	....	....
Other sectors	8 624 ..	9.0	9.4	8.4	11.3	14.5	9.2	8.7	13.6
Money market instruments	8 630 ..	....	....	....	....	.1	.1	9.1	.1
Monetary authorities	8 631 ..	....	....	....	....	....	....	....	....
General government	8 632 ..	....	....	....	....	....	....	....	....
Banks	8 633 ..	....	....	....	....	....	....	....	....
Other sectors	8 634 ..	....	....	....	....	.1	.1	9.1	.1
Financial derivatives	8 900 ..	....	....	....	....	....	....	....	....
Monetary authorities	8 901 ..	....	....	....	....	....	....	....	....
General government	8 902 ..	....	....	....	....	....	....	....	....
Banks	8 903 ..	....	....	....	....	....	....	....	....
Other sectors	8 904 ..	....	....	....	....	....	....	....	....
Other investment	8 703 ..	**685.4**	**510.9**	**901.4**	**1,103.3**	**1,481.9**	**1,641.1**	**2,221.3**	**2,457.1**
Trade credits	8 706 ..	73.2	58.9	111.4	120.6	144.7	146.9	177.9	139.2
General government	8 707 ..	....	....	....	....	....	....	....	....
of which: Short-term	8 709 ..	....	....	....	....	....	....	....	....
Other sectors	8 710 ..	73.2	58.9	111.4	120.6	144.7	146.9	177.9	139.2
of which: Short-term	8 712 ..	*73.2*	*58.9*	*111.4*	*120.6*	*144.7*	*146.9*	*177.9*	*139.2*
Loans	8 714 ..	.4	.3	.4	6.5	3.8	3.7	8.3	3.2
Monetary authorities	8 715 ..	....	....	....	....	....	....	....	....
of which: Short-term	8 718 ..	....	....	....	....	....	....	....	....
General government	8 719 ..	....	....	....	....	....	....	....	....
of which: Short-term	8 721 ..	....	....	....	....	....	....	....	....
Banks	8 722 ..	....	....	....	....	....	....	....	....
of which: Short-term	8 724 ..	....	....	....	....	....	....	....	....
Other sectors	8 725 ..	.4	.3	.4	6.5	3.8	3.7	8.3	3.2
of which: Short-term	8 727 ..	....	....	....	....	....	....	....	....
Currency and deposits	8 730 ..	173.4	117.4	185.3	178.8	231.8	189.1	298.2	295.0
Monetary authorities	8 731 ..	....	....	....	....	....	....	....	....
General government	8 732 ..	....	....	....	....	....	....	....	....
Banks	8 733 ..	86.4	73.6	91.6	78.5	94.4	66.2	126.7	96.4
Other sectors	8 734 ..	87.0	43.8	93.7	100.3	137.4	122.9	171.5	198.5
Other assets	8 736 ..	438.4	334.3	604.4	797.3	1,101.6	1,301.3	1,736.8	2,019.8
Monetary authorities	8 737 ..	....	....	....	....	....	....	....	....
of which: Short-term	8 739 ..	....	....	....	....	....	....	....	....
General government	8 740 ..	29.9	−1.9	−43.4	−86.7	−134.0	84.3	491.7	645.7
of which: Short-term	8 742 ..	*29.3*	*−2.2*	*−43.9*	*−87.3*	*−134.3*	*83.7*	*491.1*	*645.1*
Banks	8 743 ..	....	....	....	....	....	....	....	....
of which: Short-term	8 745 ..	....	....	....	....	....	....	....	....
Other sectors	8 746 ..	408.5	336.2	647.8	884.0	1,235.6	1,217.0	1,245.1	1,374.1
of which: Short-term	8 748 ..	....	....	....	....	....	....	....	....
Reserve assets	8 802 ..	**346.5**	**275.6**	**295.1**	**274.5**	**283.8**	**252.5**	**383.5**	**661.2**
Monetary gold	8 812 ..	....	....	....	....	....	....	....	....
Special drawing rights	8 811 ..	3.2	3.1	3.3	3.7	3.8	3.5	3.7	4.0
Reserve position in the Fund	8 810 ..	8.5	8.2	8.9	9.7	10.2	9.4	9.9	10.4
Foreign exchange	8 803 ..	334.7	264.3	282.8	261.1	269.8	239.6	369.9	646.8
Other claims	8 813 ..	....	....	....	....	....	....	....	....

Table 3 (Concluded). INTERNATIONAL INVESTMENT POSITION (End-period stocks), 2000–2007

(Millions of U.S. dollars)

	Code	2000	2001	2002	2003	2004	2005	2006	2007
LIABILITIES	8 995 D.	**1,039.0**	**716.5**	**1,022.6**	**1,208.5**	**1,442.3**	**1,295.3**	**1,347.4**	**1,380.0**
Direct investment in Swaziland	8 555 ..	**536.8**	**355.8**	**611.7**	**726.6**	**935.0**	**786.2**	**831.0**	**719.5**
Equity capital and reinvested earnings	8 556 ..	327.4	231.8	403.6	491.6	616.8	533.1	560.1	570.3
Claims on direct investors	8 557 ..	327.4	231.8	403.6	491.6	616.8	533.1	560.1	570.3
Liabilities to direct investors	8 558 ..	....	....	....	....	....	....	....	....
Other capital	8 580 ..	209.3	124.0	208.2	235.0	318.2	253.1	270.9	149.2
Claims on direct investors	8 585 ..	209.3	124.0	208.2	235.0	318.2	253.1	270.9	149.2
Liabilities to direct investors	8 590 ..	....	....	....	....	....	....	....	....
Portfolio investment	8 652 ..	**6.8**	**2.4**	**1.0**	**1.2**	**1.1**	**1.7**	**6.9**	**1.9**
Equity securities	8 660 ..	6.8	2.4	1.0	1.2	1.1	1.7	6.9	1.9
Banks	8 663 ..	....	....	....	....	....	....	....	....
Other sectors	8 664 ..	6.8	2.4	1.0	1.2	1.1	1.7	6.9	1.9
Debt securities	8 669 ..	....	....	....	....	....	....	....	....
Bonds and notes	8 670 ..	....	....	....	....	....	....	....	....
Monetary authorities	8 671 ..	....	....	....	....	....	....	....	....
General government	8 672 ..	....	....	....	....	....	....	....	....
Banks	8 673 ..	....	....	....	....	....	....	....	....
Other sectors	8 674 ..	....	....	....	....	....	....	....	....
Money market instruments	8 680 ..	....	....	....	....	....	....	....	....
Monetary authorities	8 681 ..	....	....	....	....	....	....	....	....
General government	8 682 ..	....	....	....	....	....	....	....	....
Banks	8 683 ..	....	....	....	....	....	....	....	....
Other sectors	8 684 ..	....	....	....	....	....	....	....	....
Financial derivatives	8 905 ..	**....**	**....**	**....**	**....**	**....**	**....**	**....**	**....**
Monetary authorities	8 906 ..	....	....	....	....	....	....	....	....
General government	8 907 ..	....	....	....	....	....	....	....	....
Banks	8 908 ..	....	....	....	....	....	....	....	....
Other sectors	8 909 ..	....	....	....	....	....	....	....	....
Other investment	8 753 ..	**495.5**	**358.2**	**410.0**	**480.8**	**506.2**	**507.5**	**509.5**	**658.6**
Trade credits	8 756 ..	36.9	24.5	26.3	36.5	41.5	54.0	52.4	44.9
General government	8 757 ..	....	....	....	....	....	....	....	....
of which: Short-term	8 759 ..	....	....	....	....	....	....	....	....
Other sectors	8 760 ..	36.9	24.5	26.3	36.5	41.5	54.0	52.4	44.9
of which: Short-term	8 762 ..	*36.9*	*24.5*	*26.3*	*36.5*	*41.5*	*54.0*	*52.4*	*44.9*
Loans	8 764 ..	367.5	274.7	317.5	379.7	445.5	434.9	435.1	600.5
Monetary authorities	8 765 ..	....	....	....	....	....	....	....	....
of which: Use of Fund credit and loans from the Fund	8 766 ..	....	....	....	....	....	....	....	....
of which: Short-term	8 768 ..	....	....	....	....	....	....	....	....
General government	8 769 ..	273.5	233.8	295.5	352.2	415.3	372.8	377.5	417.3
of which: Short-term	8 771 ..	....	....	....	....	....	....	....	....
Banks	8 772 ..	....	....	....	....	....	....	....	....
of which: Short-term	8 774 ..	....	....	....	....	....	....	....	....
Other sectors	8 775 ..	93.9	40.9	22.0	27.5	30.2	62.2	57.6	183.2
of which: Short-term	8 777 ..	....	....	....	....	....	....	....	....
Currency and deposits	8 780 ..	60.1	41.2	48.9	56.9	11.8	13.7	19.8	10.7
Monetary authorities	8 781 ..	45.8	39.0	40.1	49.1	4.5	2.8	2.4	2.5
General government	8 782 ..	....	....	....	....	....	....	....	....
Banks	8 783 ..	14.3	2.2	8.8	7.8	7.3	10.9	17.4	8.2
Other sectors	8 784 ..	....	....	....	....	....	....	....	....
Other liabilities	8 786 ..	31.0	17.9	17.2	7.7	7.3	4.8	2.2	2.5
Monetary authorities	8 787 ..	....	....	....	....	....	....	....	....
of which: Short-term	8 789 ..	....	....	....	....	....	....	....	....
General government	8 790 ..	....	....	....	....	....	....	....	....
of which: Short-term	8 792 ..	....	....	....	....	....	....	....	....
Banks	8 793 ..	....	....	....	....	....	....	....	....
of which: Short-term	8 795 ..	....	....	....	....	....	....	....	....
Other sectors	8 796 ..	31.0	17.9	17.2	7.7	7.3	4.8	2.2	2.5
of which: Short-term	8 798 ..	*31.0*	*17.9*	*17.2*	*7.7*	*7.3*	*4.8*	*2.2*	*2.5*
NET INTERNATIONAL INVESTMENT POSITION	8 995 ..	**92.6**	**123.1**	**242.9**	**278.2**	**451.3**	**686.1**	**1,345.7**	**1,846.8**
Conversion rates: emalangeni per U.S. dollar (end of period)	0 102 ..	**7.569**	**12.127**	**8.640**	**6.640**	**5.630**	**6.325**	**6.970**	**6.810**

Table 1. ANALYTIC PRESENTATION, 2000–2007

(Millions of U.S. dollars)

	Code	2000	2001	2002	2003	2004	2005	2006	2007
A. Current Account[1].....	4 993 Z.	**6,617**	**6,696**	**12,784**	**22,844**	**24,127**	**25,526**	**33,159**	**38,416**
Goods: exports f.o.b.....	2 100 ..	87,431	76,200	84,172	102,080	123,187	131,976	148,789	170,462
Goods: imports f.o.b.....	3 100 ..	−72,216	−62,368	−67,541	−83,147	−100,217	−112,274	−128,290	−152,230
Balance on Goods.....	4 100 ..	*15,215*	*13,832*	*16,631*	*18,933*	*22,970*	*19,701*	*20,498*	*18,232*
Services: credit.....	2 200 ..	20,252	21,997	24,009	30,654	39,023	42,887	49,797	63,587
Services: debit.....	3 200 ..	−23,440	−23,020	−23,958	−28,771	−33,138	−35,273	−39,571	−47,953
Balance on Goods and Services.....	4 991 ..	*12,027*	*12,809*	*16,682*	*20,816*	*28,855*	*27,316*	*30,724*	*33,865*
Income: credit.....	2 300 ..	20,074	17,934	18,018	22,934	31,332	38,196	50,619	62,457
Income: debit.....	3 300 ..	−22,137	−20,786	−19,044	−22,637	−31,310	−35,412	−43,241	−52,923
Balance on Goods, Services, and Income.....	4 992 ..	*9,964*	*9,957*	*15,657*	*21,113*	*28,876*	*30,100*	*38,103*	*43,399*
Current transfers: credit.....	2 379 Z.	2,602	2,578	3,345	3,577	4,067	5,027	5,107	4,741
Current transfers: debit.....	3 379 ..	−5,950	−5,839	−6,218	−1,845	−8,817	−9,601	−10,051	−9,724
B. Capital Account[1].....	4 994 Z.	**384**	**509**	**−79**	**−46**	**34**	**308**	**−2,556**	**−441**
Capital account: credit.....	2 994 Z.	1,226	1,111	529	552	526	562	495	942
Capital account: debit.....	3 994 ..	−841	−601	−609	−599	−493	−254	−3,052	−1,384
Total, Groups A Plus B.....	4 981 ..	*7,001*	*7,205*	*12,705*	*22,798*	*24,161*	*25,833*	*30,602*	*37,975*
C. Financial Account[1].....	4 995 W.	**−3,297**	**1,824**	**−10,704**	**−20,163**	**−26,010**	**−28,483**	**−32,016**	**−22,075**
Direct investment abroad.....	4 505 ..	−39,962	−6,959	−10,673	−17,341	−21,318	−26,658	−20,186	−28,568
Direct investment in Sweden.....	4 555 Z.	22,125	13,085	11,709	3,268	10,957	10,018	22,608	12,286
Portfolio investment assets.....	4 602 ..	−12,772	−23,041	−4,038	−13,701	−24,768	−12,942	−33,761	−49,973
Equity securities.....	4 610 ..	758	−22,642	−124	−4,618	−6,210	261	−22,189	−7,870
Debt securities.....	4 619 ..	−13,530	−400	−3,914	−9,083	−18,558	−13,202	−11,571	−42,103
Portfolio investment liabilities.....	4 652 Z.	9,017	10,338	−6,691	4,134	1,586	13,608	13,159	59,636
Equity securities.....	4 660 ..	17,997	−2,336	2,536	452	−83	2,054	242	4,371
Debt securities.....	4 669 Z.	−8,980	12,674	−9,227	3,682	1,669	11,554	12,917	55,265
Financial derivatives.....	4 910 ..	−314	−5,216	−168	1,081	−239	−930	136	−1,173
Financial derivatives assets.....	4 900 ..	31,481	33,678	37,720	40,045	27,730	29,417	54,071	39,239
Financial derivatives liabilities.....	4 905 ..	−31,795	−38,894	−37,888	−38,964	−27,969	−30,347	−53,935	−40,412
Other investment assets.....	4 703 ..	−16,000	929	−998	−8,349	−19,845	−13,301	−50,621	−48,540
Monetary authorities.....	4 701 ..	....	....	....	....	....	....	....	....
General government.....	4 704 ..	−150	37	−1,589	442	−564	228	−15	....
Banks.....	4 705 ..	−13,279	1,672	697	−8,688	−16,915	−13,962	−44,997	....
Other sectors.....	4 728 ..	−2,571	−779	−106	−103	−2,365	434	−5,609	....
Other investment liabilities.....	4 753 W.	34,609	12,689	155	10,744	27,617	1,722	36,649	34,258
Monetary authorities.....	4 753 WA	−556	−812	993	2,605	2,445	2,210	1,166	....
General government.....	4 753 ZB	129	−32	683	−941	−587	525	−627	1,971
Banks.....	4 753 ZC	29,682	10,077	−1,299	1,905	25,940	2,252	38,802	....
Other sectors.....	4 753 ZD	5,354	3,455	−222	7,175	−182	−3,264	−2,691	....
Total, Groups A Through C.....	4 983 ..	*3,704*	*9,030*	*2,001*	*2,634*	*−1,850*	*−2,649*	*−1,413*	*15,900*
D. Net Errors and Omissions.....	4 998 ..	**−3,534**	**−10,078**	**−1,336**	**−558**	**750**	**2,899**	**2,702**	**−16,348**
Total, Groups A Through D.....	4 984 ..	*170*	*−1,048*	*665*	*2,076*	*−1,100*	*250*	*1,289*	*−447*
E. Reserves and Related Items.....	4 802 A.	**−170**	**1,048**	**−665**	**−2,076**	**1,100**	**−250**	**−1,289**	**447**
Reserve assets.....	4 802 ..	−170	1,048	−665	−2,076	1,100	−250	−1,289	447
Use of Fund credit and loans.....	4 766 ..	....	....	....	....	....	....	....	....
Exceptional financing.....	4 920 ..	....	....	....	....	....	....	....	....
Conversion rates: kronor per U.S. dollar.....	0 101 ..	**9.1622**	**10.3291**	**9.7371**	**8.0863**	**7.3489**	**7.4731**	**7.3782**	**6.7588**

[1] Excludes components that have been classified in the categories of Group E.

Table 2. STANDARD PRESENTATION, 2000–2007

(Millions of U.S. dollars)

	Code	2000	2001	2002	2003	2004	2005	2006	2007
CURRENT ACCOUNT	4 993 ..	6,617	6,696	12,784	22,844	24,127	25,526	33,159	38,416
A. GOODS	4 100 ..	15,215	13,832	16,631	18,933	22,970	19,701	20,498	18,232
Credit	2 100 ..	87,431	76,200	84,172	102,080	123,187	131,976	148,789	170,462
General merchandise: exports f.o.b.	2 110 ..	87,139	75,995	....	....	122,771	130,640	147,377	168,947
Goods for processing: exports f.o.b.	2 150 ..	....	....	....	....	....	....	....	....
Repairs on goods	2 160 ..	....	....	....	....	....	685	599	567
Goods procured in ports by carriers	2 170 ..	292	205	....	....	416	651	813	948
Nonmonetary gold	2 180 ..	....	....	....	....	....	....	....	....
Debit	3 100 ..	−72,216	−62,368	−67,541	−83,147	−100,217	−112,274	−128,290	−152,230
General merchandise: imports f.o.b.	3 110 ..	−71,849	−61,970	....	....	−99,359	−110,502	−126,307	−150,136
Goods for processing: imports f.o.b.	3 150 ..	....	....	....	....	....	....	....	....
Repairs on goods	3 160 ..	....	....	....	....	....	−625	−599	−579
Goods procured in ports by carriers	3 170 ..	−367	−399	....	....	−858	−1,147	−1,385	−1,515
Nonmonetary gold	3 180 ..	....	....	....	....	....	....	....	....
B. SERVICES	4 200 ..	−3,188	−1,023	51	1,883	5,885	7,614	10,226	15,633
Total credit	2 200 ..	*20,252*	*21,997*	*24,009*	*30,654*	*39,023*	*42,887*	*49,797*	*63,587*
Total debit	3 200 ..	*−23,440*	*−23,020*	*−23,958*	*−28,771*	*−33,138*	*−35,273*	*−39,571*	*−47,953*
Transportation services, credit	2 205 ..	4,359	5,266	5,158	6,488	8,191	8,668	9,238	11,119
Passenger	2 850 ..	*761*	*947*	*961*	*1,244*	*1,488*	*1,195*	*1,344*	*1,702*
Freight	2 851 ..	*2,992*	*3,696*	*3,512*	*4,143*	*5,341*	*5,840*	*6,127*	*7,084*
Other	2 852 ..	*606*	*623*	*686*	*1,101*	*1,362*	*1,633*	*1,767*	*2,333*
Sea transport, passenger	2 207 ..	77	83	71	31	64	46	51	50
Sea transport, freight	2 208 ..	2,137	2,875	2,463	2,999	3,708	3,957	4,045	4,545
Sea transport, other	2 209 ..	169	163	156	234	282	276	308	354
Air transport, passenger	2 211 ..	652	820	838	1,161	1,370	1,106	1,231	1,581
Air transport, freight	2 212 ..	94	79	98	64	47	107	117	112
Air transport, other	2 213 ..	22	23	26	413	551	573	630	907
Other transport, passenger	2 215 ..	32	44	52	53	54	43	62	71
Other transport, freight	2 216 ..	761	743	950	1,080	1,585	1,775	1,964	2,427
Other transport, other	2 217 ..	415	437	503	454	529	784	829	1,072
Transportation services, debit	3 205 ..	−3,640	−3,593	−3,489	−4,611	−5,047	−5,728	−6,506	−7,608
Passenger	3 850 ..	*−911*	*−995*	*−920*	*−1,079*	*−923*	*−1,073*	*−1,308*	*−1,724*
Freight	3 851 ..	*−1,713*	*−1,677*	*−1,448*	*−1,934*	*−2,226*	*−2,507*	*−2,842*	*−3,327*
Other	3 852 ..	*−1,017*	*−920*	*−1,122*	*−1,599*	*−1,898*	*−2,148*	*−2,356*	*−2,557*
Sea transport, passenger	3 207 ..	−19	−18	−22	−8	−17	−22	−20	−45
Sea transport, freight	3 208 ..	−1,576	−1,547	−1,315	−1,758	−1,988	−2,234	−2,532	−2,936
Sea transport, other	3 209 ..	−540	−455	−665	−825	−996	−997	−1,088	−1,150
Air transport, passenger	3 211 ..	−866	−956	−875	−1,048	−880	−1,030	−1,257	−1,641
Air transport, freight	3 212 ..	−28	−17	−19	−30	−40	−46	−53	−66
Air transport, other	3 213 ..	−123	−109	−111	−331	−319	−464	−646	−665
Other transport, passenger	3 215 ..	−26	−21	−22	−22	−26	−20	−31	−38
Other transport, freight	3 216 ..	−109	−113	−114	−146	−197	−226	−257	−325
Other transport, other	3 217 ..	−354	−356	−346	−443	−583	−687	−622	−742
Travel, credit	2 236 ..	4,064	4,253	4,710	5,304	6,198	7,394	9,141	12,004
Business travel	2 237 ..	....	....	....	....	....	....	....	....
Personal travel	2 240 ..	....	....	....	....	....	....	....	....
Travel, debit	3 236 ..	−8,048	−6,921	−7,301	−8,296	−10,165	−10,771	−11,529	−13,972
Business travel	3 237 ..	−2,695	−2,317	−2,444	−2,777	−3,402	−3,534	−3,646	−4,378
Personal travel	3 240 ..	−5,353	−4,604	−4,858	−5,519	−6,763	−7,238	−7,883	−9,594
Other services, credit	2 200 BA	11,829	12,478	14,140	18,862	24,634	26,826	31,418	40,464
Communications	2 245 ..	644	716	624	815	1,244	1,441	1,604	1,779
Construction	2 249 ..	678	602	482	428	760	662	659	1,035
Insurance	2 253 ..	517	472	509	732	771	866	875	934
Financial	2 260 ..	591	565	513	886	1,272	1,471	1,858	1,863
Computer and information	2 262 ..	1,191	1,433	1,472	1,993	2,537	2,688	3,585	6,529
Royalties and licence fees	2 266 ..	1,275	1,427	1,516	2,336	3,454	3,480	3,992	4,753
Other business services	2 268 ..	6,482	6,912	8,659	11,148	14,019	15,583	18,120	22,708
Personal, cultural, and recreational	2 287 ..	113	111	112	208	178	222	271	329
Government, n.i.e.	2 291 ..	238	239	252	316	398	413	455	533
Other services, debit	3 200 BA	−11,752	−12,506	−13,167	−15,864	−17,926	−18,773	−21,536	−26,374
Communications	3 245 ..	−792	−685	−575	−979	−1,412	−1,579	−1,755	−1,908
Construction	3 249 ..	−322	−298	−286	−608	−512	−480	−628	−842
Insurance	3 253 ..	−311	−260	−324	−311	−325	−371	−312	−374
Financial	3 260 ..	−599	−546	−539	−623	−622	−803	−1,082	−958
Computer and information	3 262 ..	−1,067	−894	−867	−1,179	−1,415	−1,517	−2,257	−3,031
Royalties and licence fees	3 266 ..	−900	−860	−892	−1,277	−1,416	−1,513	−1,673	−1,810
Other business services	3 268 ..	−7,602	−8,777	−9,512	−10,648	−11,918	−12,219	−13,539	−17,048
Personal, cultural, and recreational	3 287 ..	−88	−87	−70	−116	−159	−160	−150	−262
Government, n.i.e.	3 291 ..	−73	−100	−102	−124	−147	−132	−138	−141

Table 2 (Continued). STANDARD PRESENTATION, 2000–2007

(Millions of U.S. dollars)

	Code	2000	2001	2002	2003	2004	2005	2006	2007
C. INCOME..	4 300 ..	**−2,063**	**−2,852**	**−1,025**	**297**	**22**	**2,785**	**7,379**	**9,534**
Total credit..	2 300 ..	*20,074*	*17,934*	*18,018*	*22,934*	*31,332*	*38,196*	*50,619*	*62,457*
Total debit..	3 300 ..	*−22,137*	*−20,786*	*−19,044*	*−22,637*	*−31,310*	*−35,412*	*−43,241*	*−52,923*
Compensation of employees, credit..................	2 310 ..	**304**	**329**	**319**	**336**	**377**	**346**	**372**	**532**
Compensation of employees, debit..................	3 310 ..	**−488**	**−543**	**−537**	**−554**	**−621**	**−534**	**−579**	**−860**
Investment income, credit..................................	2 320 ..	**19,770**	**17,604**	**17,699**	**22,598**	**30,955**	**37,850**	**50,247**	**61,925**
Direct investment income........................	2 330 ..	12,880	10,535	11,800	14,696	20,998	25,613	32,988	38,370
Dividends and distributed branch profits................	2 332 ..	3,001	6,091	5,535	5,209	16,403	12,250	26,692	9,480
Reinvested earnings and undistributed branch profits.....	2 333 ..	7,944	2,632	4,454	7,923	2,724	11,271	3,704	25,327
Income on debt (interest)........................	2 334 ..	1,934	1,812	1,811	1,564	1,872	2,091	2,591	3,562
Portfolio investment income........................	2 339 ..	3,777	4,037	3,626	5,502	6,867	8,337	10,736	14,414
Income on equity........................	2 340 ..	1,495	1,591	1,508	2,598	3,239	4,376	5,775	8,136
Income on bonds and notes........................	2 350 ..	2,140	2,406	2,094	2,816	3,463	3,701	4,653	6,000
Income on money market instruments........................	2 360 ..	143	41	25	87	165	260	308	278
Other investment income........................	2 370 ..	3,113	3,032	2,273	2,400	3,089	3,900	6,523	9,141
Investment income, debit..................................	3 320 ..	**−21,648**	**−20,243**	**−18,507**	**−22,084**	**−30,689**	**−34,878**	**−42,661**	**−52,063**
Direct investment income........................	3 330 ..	−8,867	−6,908	−6,523	−8,547	−15,202	−16,315	−19,218	−23,132
Dividends and distributed branch profits........................	3 332 ..	−4,388	−4,391	−4,077	−3,255	−7,059	−8,351	−12,965	−6,028
Reinvested earnings and undistributed branch profits.....	3 333 ..	−2,728	−939	60	−2,567	−4,874	−4,852	−2,369	−11,746
Income on debt (interest)........................	3 334 ..	−1,750	−1,578	−2,507	−2,725	−3,268	−3,112	−3,884	−5,358
Portfolio investment income........................	3 339 ..	−7,873	−8,257	−7,912	−9,606	−10,855	−12,698	−16,118	−18,794
Income on equity........................	3 340 ..	−1,640	−1,645	−1,273	−1,875	−2,557	−3,637	−5,036	−7,382
Income on bonds and notes........................	3 350 ..	−5,595	−5,631	−5,759	−7,000	−7,617	−8,050	−9,638	−9,225
Income on money market instruments........................	3 360 ..	−639	−981	−880	−731	−682	−1,011	−1,444	−2,187
Other investment income........................	3 370 ..	−4,909	−5,078	−4,072	−3,930	−4,632	−5,864	−7,325	−10,137
D. CURRENT TRANSFERS..	4 379 ..	**−3,348**	**−3,261**	**−2,872**	**1,732**	**−4,750**	**−4,574**	**−4,945**	**−4,983**
Credit..	2 379 ..	**2,602**	**2,578**	**3,345**	**3,577**	**4,067**	**5,027**	**5,107**	**4,741**
General government........................	2 380 ..	462	480	523	459	793	996	1,358	794
Other sectors........................	2 390 ..	2,141	2,098	2,822	3,118	3,275	4,031	3,748	3,947
Workers' remittances........................	2 391 ..	161	185	190	203	....	222	222	242
Other current transfers........................	2 392 ..	1,980	1,913	2,632	2,916	....	3,809	3,526	3,705
Debit..	3 379 ..	**−5,950**	**−5,839**	**−6,218**	**−1,845**	**−8,817**	**−9,601**	**−10,051**	**−9,724**
General government........................	3 380 ..	−3,645	−3,469	−3,743	111	−5,974	−6,361	−6,084	−6,656
Other sectors........................	3 390 ..	−2,305	−2,370	−2,474	−1,957	−2,843	−3,240	−3,967	−3,068
Workers' remittances........................	3 391 ..	−34	−31	−35	−24	....	−255	−258	−282
Other current transfers........................	3 392 ..	−2,271	−2,339	−2,439	−1,933	....	−2,986	−3,709	−2,786
CAPITAL AND FINANCIAL ACCOUNT........................	4 996 ..	**−3,083**	**3,382**	**−11,448**	**−22,286**	**−24,877**	**−28,425**	**−35,861**	**−22,069**
CAPITAL ACCOUNT..	4 994 ..	**384**	**509**	**−79**	**−46**	**34**	**308**	**−2,556**	**−441**
Total credit..	2 994 ..	*1,226*	*1,111*	*529*	*552*	*526*	*562*	*495*	*942*
Total debit..	3 994 ..	*−841*	*−601*	*−609*	*−599*	*−493*	*−254*	*−3,052*	*−1,384*
Capital transfers, credit........................	2 400 ..	**1,057**	**862**	**318**	**416**	**440**	**489**	**419**	**457**
General government........................	2 401 ..	....	....	....	....	....	....	....	....
Debt forgiveness........................	2 402 ..	....	....	....	....	....	....	....	....
Other capital transfers........................	2 410 ..	....	....	....	....	....	....	....	....
Other sectors........................	2 430 ..	1,057	862	318	416	440	489	419	....
Migrants' transfers........................	2 431 ..	46	29	31	39	43	43	....	....
Debt forgiveness........................	2 432 ..	....	....	....	....	....	....	....	....
Other capital transfers........................	2 440 ..	1,012	833	287	376	397	446	....	....
Capital transfers, debit........................	3 400 ..	**−448**	**−412**	**−451**	**−499**	**−392**	**−146**	**−994**	**−992**
General government........................	3 401 ..	−383	−361	−394	−431	−317	−71	−919	....
Debt forgiveness........................	3 402 ..	−54	−58	−62	−74	−10	−47	....	....
Other capital transfers........................	3 410 ..	−329	−303	−333	−357	−307	−25	....	....
Other sectors........................	3 430 ..	−65	−50	−57	−68	−75	−75	−75	....
Migrants' transfers........................	3 431 ..	−23	−16	−18	−22	−25	−25	....	....
Debt forgiveness........................	3 432 ..	−6	....	....	....	....	....	....	....
Other capital transfers........................	3 440 ..	−37	−35	−39	−46	−51	−50	....	....
Nonproduced nonfinancial assets, credit.............	2 480 ..	**168**	**249**	**211**	**137**	**86**	**72**	**76**	**485**
Nonproduced nonfinancial assets, debit..............	3 480 ..	**−393**	**−190**	**−157**	**−99**	**−101**	**−108**	**−2,058**	**−391**

Table 2 (Continued). STANDARD PRESENTATION, 2000–2007

(Millions of U.S. dollars)

	Code	2000	2001	2002	2003	2004	2005	2006	2007
FINANCIAL ACCOUNT	4 995	−3,467	2,872	−11,369	−22,240	−24,910	−28,732	−33,305	−21,627
A. DIRECT INVESTMENT	4 500	−17,837	6,126	1,036	−14,073	−10,362	−16,640	2,422	−16,282
Direct investment abroad	4 505	−39,962	−6,959	−10,673	−17,341	−21,318	−26,658	−20,186	−28,568
Equity capital	4 510	−24,854	−3,566	−13,158	−12,998	−11,598	−17,938	−13,980	−18,475
Claims on affiliated enterprises	4 515	....	....	....	....	....	....	....	....
Liabilities to affiliated enterprises	4 520	....	....	....	....	....	....	....	....
Reinvested earnings	4 525	−7,944	−2,632	−4,454	−7,923	−2,724	−11,271	−3,704	−25,327
Other capital	4 530	−7,164	−761	6,939	3,580	−6,997	2,552	−2,502	15,235
Claims on affiliated enterprises	4 535	....	....	....	....	....	....	....	....
Liabilities to affiliated enterprises	4 540	....	....	....	....	....	....	....	....
Direct investment in Sweden	4 555	22,125	13,085	11,709	3,268	10,957	10,018	22,608	12,286
Equity capital	4 560	11,572	7,896	10,038	−767	5,410	3,800	9,898	1,768
Claims on direct investors	4 565	....	....	....	....	....	....	....	....
Liabilities to direct investors	4 570	....	....	....	....	....	....	....	....
Reinvested earnings	4 575	2,728	939	−60	2,567	4,874	4,852	2,369	11,746
Other capital	4 580	7,825	4,250	1,731	1,468	673	1,365	10,341	−1,228
Claims on direct investors	4 585	....	....	....	....	....	....	....	....
Liabilities to direct investors	4 590	....	....	....	....	....	....	....	....
B. PORTFOLIO INVESTMENT	4 600	−3,754	−12,704	−10,729	−9,567	−23,182	666	−20,602	9,663
Assets	4 602	−12,772	−23,041	−4,038	−13,701	−24,768	−12,942	−33,761	−49,973
Equity securities	4 610	758	−22,642	−124	−4,618	−6,210	261	−22,189	−7,870
Monetary authorities	4 611	....	....	....	....	....	−24	....	....
General government	4 612	....	....	....	....	−2,055	156	−3,245	....
Banks	4 613	....	....	....	....	−831	−1,777	−8,961	....
Other sectors	4 614	....	....	....	....	−3,324	1,905	−9,983	....
Debt securities	4 619	−13,530	−400	−3,914	−9,083	−18,558	−13,202	−11,571	−42,103
Bonds and notes	4 620	−7,786	1,542	4,336	−3,965	−9,559	−4,094	−11,440	−34,646
Monetary authorities	4 621	....	....	....	....	....	....	....	....
General government	4 622	85	−1,503	108	−1,163	−2,287	−4,357	−1,686	....
Banks	4 623	−828	243	4,379	385	−4,726	2,812	−12,172	....
Other sectors	4 624	−7,043	2,802	−151	−3,187	−2,545	−2,548	2,418	....
Money market instruments	4 630	−5,744	−1,942	−8,250	−5,118	−9,000	−9,109	−131	−7,457
Monetary authorities	4 631	....	....	....	....	....	....	....	....
General government	4 632	277	35	47	−4	−35	17	627	....
Banks	4 633	−2,662	720	−480	−769	−3,996	−9,323	−1,927	....
Other sectors	4 634	−3,359	−2,697	−7,816	−4,345	−4,969	198	1,169	....
Liabilities	4 652	9,017	10,338	−6,691	4,134	1,586	13,608	13,159	59,636
Equity securities	4 660	17,997	−2,336	2,536	452	−83	2,054	242	4,371
Banks	4 663	....	....	....	....	....	....	....	....
Other sectors	4 664	17,997	−2,336	2,536	452	....	....	....	....
Debt securities	4 669	−8,980	12,674	−9,227	3,682	1,669	11,554	12,917	55,265
Bonds and notes	4 670	−9,926	6,945	504	12,846	10,911	16,309	8,633	43,826
Monetary authorities	4 671	....	....	....	....	....	....	....	....
General government	4 672	−16,120	645	696	1,010	−2,548	−1,050	−926	....
Banks	4 673	2,398	2,418	54	14,093	17,922	17,873	15,782	....
Other sectors	4 674	3,796	3,882	−247	−2,257	−4,463	−514	−6,222	....
Money market instruments	4 680	946	5,729	−9,731	−9,164	−9,242	−4,756	4,284	11,439
Monetary authorities	4 681	....	....	....	....	....	....	....	....
General government	4 682	−2,439	3,500	−3,378	−3,358	4,378	5,849	9,833	....
Banks	4 683	2,515	4,571	−3,016	−4,022	−12,456	−9,286	−6,482	....
Other sectors	4 684	870	−2,343	−3,337	−1,784	−1,164	−1,318	932	....
C. FINANCIAL DERIVATIVES	4 910	−314	−5,216	−168	1,081	−239	−930	136	−1,173
Monetary authorities	4 911	....	....	....	−15	2	2	....	....
General government	4 912	1,117	−1,633	754	434	353	49	483	....
Banks	4 913	−661	−3,202	−1,942	−1,372	−1,314	864	−233	....
Other sectors	4 914	−770	−381	1,020	2,034	721	−1,844	−114	....
Assets	4 900	31,481	33,678	37,720	40,045	27,730	29,417	54,071	39,239
Monetary authorities	4 901	....	....	....	−15	2	2	....	....
General government	4 902	2,695	2,615	2,942	3,848	2,688	4,211	4,881	....
Banks	4 903	18,863	19,737	18,506	24,975	15,435	15,287	18,944	....
Other sectors	4 904	9,924	11,326	16,272	11,237	9,605	9,917	30,246	....
Liabilities	4 905	−31,795	−38,894	−37,888	−38,964	−27,969	−30,347	−53,935	−40,412
Monetary authorities	4 906	....	....	....	....	....	....	....	....
General government	4 907	−1,578	−4,248	−2,188	−3,414	−2,335	−4,163	−4,397	....
Banks	4 908	−19,524	−22,939	−20,448	−26,347	−16,750	−14,423	−19,177	....
Other sectors	4 909	−10,694	−11,707	−15,251	−9,203	−8,884	−11,761	−30,361	....

Table 2 (Concluded). STANDARD PRESENTATION, 2000–2007

(Millions of U.S. dollars)

	Code	2000	2001	2002	2003	2004	2005	2006	2007
D. OTHER INVESTMENT	4 700	**18,609**	**13,618**	**–843**	**2,396**	**7,772**	**–11,578**	**–13,972**	**–14,282**
Assets	4 703	**–16,000**	**929**	**–998**	**–8,349**	**–19,845**	**–13,301**	**–50,621**	**–48,540**
Trade credits	4 706	–1,612	997	620	–33	–2,933	–48	–2,270	–2,690
General government	4 707	....	....	....	....	....	....	....	....
of which: Short-term	4 709	....	....	....	....	....	....	....	....
Other sectors	4 710	–1,612	997	620	–33	–2,933	–48	–2,270	....
of which: Short-term	4 712	*–1,612*	*997*	*620*	*–33*	*–2,933*	*–48*		
Loans	4 714	–14,139	927	–2,197	–6,521	–19,020	–12,456	–40,507	–33,539
Monetary authorities	4 715	....	....	....	....	....	....	....	....
of which: Short-term	4 718	....	....	....	....	....	....	....	....
General government	4 719	–33	47	–1,269	621	–491	571	118	....
of which: Short-term	4 721	*204*	*502*	*–1,612*	*529*	*–652*	*219*	*–179*	....
Banks	4 722	–13,640	2,437	44	–6,581	–19,060	–13,445	–37,224	....
of which: Short-term	4 724	*–13,483*	*4,101*	*736*	*–4,700*	*–24,051*	*–11,532*	*–33,278*	....
Other sectors	4 725	–466	–1,558	–972	–562	530	419	–3,401	....
of which: Short-term	4 727	*–614*	*–1,691*	*–302*	*–606*	*1,590*	*–750*	*–3,797*	....
Currency and deposits	4 730	....	....	....	....	....	....	....	....
Monetary authorities	4 731	....	....	....	....	....	....	....	....
General government	4 732	....	....	....	....	....	....	....	....
Banks	4 733	....	....	....	....	....	....	....	....
Other sectors	4 734	....	....	....	....	....	....	....	....
Other assets	4 736	–249	–995	580	–1,795	2,108	–797	–7,843	–12,311
Monetary authorities	4 737	....	....	....	....	....	....	....	....
of which: Short-term	4 739	....	....	....	....	....	....	....	....
General government	4 740	–118	–11	–320	–179	–73	–343	–133	....
of which: Short-term	4 742	....	....	....	....	....	....	....	....
Banks	4 743	361	–765	653	–2,107	2,145	–517	–7,772	....
of which: Short-term	4 745	*361*	*–765*	*653*	*–2,107*	*2,145*	*–517*	*–7,772*	....
Other sectors	4 746	–492	–219	247	491	37	63	62	....
of which: Short-term	4 748	....	....	....	....	....	*63*	*62*	....
Liabilities	4 753	**34,609**	**12,689**	**155**	**10,744**	**27,617**	**1,722**	**36,649**	**34,258**
Trade credits	4 756	1,125	13	–731	–860	11	1,210	–761	1,971
General government	4 757	....	....	....	....	....	605	198	1,971
of which: Short-term	4 759	....	....	....	....	....	....	....	....
Other sectors	4 760	1,125	13	–731	–860	11	605	–958	....
of which: Short-term	4 762	*1,125*	*13*	*–731*	*–860*	*11*	*605*	....	....
Loans	4 764	32,278	13,421	464	7,080	30,977	–3,992	30,142	....
Monetary authorities	4 765	–556	–812	993	2,605	2,445	2,210	1,166	....
of which: Use of Fund credit and loans from the Fund	4 766	....	....	....	....	....	....	....	....
of which: Short-term	4 768	*–556*	*–812*	*993*	*2,605*	*2,445*	*2,210*	*1,166*	....
General government	4 769	–18	64	619	–188	–282	–189	–17	....
of which: Short-term	4 771	*–503*	*30*	*101*	*–221*	*–6*	*1*	....	....
Banks	4 772	28,623	10,727	–1,657	–3,373	29,007	–2,742	31,697	....
of which: Short-term	4 774	*28,308*	*9,749*	*–1,589*	*–3,972*	*18,882*	*2,074*	*33,186*	....
Other sectors	4 775	4,229	3,442	510	8,036	–193	–3,270	–2,703	....
of which: Short-term	4 777	*2,878*	*2,602*	*1,355*	*8,352*	*–137*	*–1,521*	*401*	....
Currency and deposits	4 780	....	....	....	....	....	....	....	....
Monetary authorities	4 781	....	....	....	....	....	....	....	....
General government	4 782	....	....	....	....	....	....	....	....
Banks	4 783	....	....	....	....	....	....	....	....
Other sectors	4 784	....	....	....	....	....	....	....	....
Other liabilities	4 786	1,206	–746	422	4,525	–3,371	4,504	7,268	27,313
Monetary authorities	4 787	....	....	....	....	....	....	....	....
of which: Short-term	4 789	....	....	....	....	....	....	....	....
General government	4 790	147	–96	63	–752	–305	109	–808	....
of which: Short-term	4 792	*147*	*–96*	*63*	*–752*	*–305*	*109*	*–808*	....
Banks	4 793	1,059	–650	358	5,277	–3,067	4,994	7,105	....
of which: Short-term	4 795	*1,059*	*–650*	*358*	*5,277*	*–3,067*	*4,994*	*7,105*	....
Other sectors	4 796	....	....	....	....	....	–600	970	....
of which: Short-term	4 798	....	....	....	....	....	*–600*	*970*	....
E. RESERVE ASSETS	4 802	**–170**	**1,048**	**–665**	**–2,076**	**1,100**	**–250**	**–1,289**	**447**
Monetary gold	4 812	....	....	....	....	91	226	104	135
Special drawing rights	4 811	82	10	32	–1	–4	19	–200	....
Reserve position in the Fund	4 810	239	–181	–293	83	218	690	235	73
Foreign exchange	4 803	–491	1,219	–1,721	–2,159	1,163	–1,401	–1,327	–74
Other claims	4 813	....	....	1,317	1	–368	217	–100	313
NET ERRORS AND OMISSIONS	4 998	**–3,534**	**–10,078**	**–1,336**	**–558**	**750**	**2,899**	**2,702**	**–16,348**

Table 3. INTERNATIONAL INVESTMENT POSITION (End-period stocks), 2000–2007

(Millions of U.S. dollars)

	Code	2000	2001	2002	2003	2004	2005	2006	2007
ASSETS	8 995 C.	**365,450**	**368,231**	**412,424**	**556,611**	**692,646**	**703,184**	**933,314**	**1,105,754**
Direct investment abroad	8 505	**115,582**	**123,275**	**144,127**	**181,307**	**216,311**	**208,777**	**262,238**	**306,380**
Equity capital and reinvested earnings	8 506	111,694	101,171	121,657	176,097	197,004	194,223	241,320	280,654
Claims on affiliated enterprises	8 507	....	....	....	....	....	....	....	....
Liabilities to affiliated enterprises	8 508	....	....	....	....	....	....	....	....
Other capital	8 530	3,888	22,105	22,470	5,210	19,307	14,554	20,918	25,727
Claims on affiliated enterprises	8 535	7,723	45,697	51,564	8,960	58,437	....	....	....
Liabilities to affiliated enterprises	8 540	−3,835	−23,592	−29,093	−3,750	−39,130	....	....	....
Portfolio investment	8 602	**133,506**	**144,072**	**139,935**	**210,128**	**272,841**	**298,026**	**393,677**	**439,706**
Equity securities	8 610	89,546	103,990	92,376	141,731	179,243	202,216	259,532	287,854
Monetary authorities	8 611	....	....	....	....	....	....	76	85
General government	8 612	1,030	20,070	17,829	35,078	44,359	48,532	59,648	76,194
Banks	8 613	42,895	9,359	8,314	595	761	4,044	4,047	5,906
Other sectors	8 614	45,621	74,560	66,233	106,057	134,123	149,640	195,761	205,669
Debt securities	8 619	43,960	40,082	47,559	68,397	93,597	95,810	134,144	151,852
Bonds and notes	8 620	40,922	38,395	44,291	62,407	84,720	86,129	126,328	142,089
Monetary authorities	8 621	....	....	....	....	....	....	....	....
General government	8 622	5,879	6,246	9,241	13,190	18,726	20,552	23,172	30,094
Banks	8 623	7,353	7,548	7,746	12,673	20,912	20,305	56,388	53,406
Other sectors	8 624	27,690	24,601	27,304	36,544	45,082	45,273	46,769	58,588
Money market instruments	8 630	3,038	1,687	3,268	5,991	8,877	9,681	7,816	9,763
Monetary authorities	8 631	....	....	....	....	....	....	....	....
General government	8 632	211	28	14	12	41	170	....	112
Banks	8 633	2,201	150	67	116	350	2,125	2,348	5,326
Other sectors	8 634	626	1,509	3,188	5,863	8,485	7,386	5,467	4,325
Financial derivatives	8 900	**18,679**	**15,663**	**24,563**	**29,938**	**33,971**	**26,331**	**25,365**	**34,681**
Monetary authorities	8 901	....	....	....	....	....	....	....	77
General government	8 902	4,772	4,296	4,586	5,928	6,525	4,898	6,802	6,567
Banks	8 903	10,617	8,497	15,910	19,408	20,480	18,928	15,430	20,663
Other sectors	8 904	3,290	2,869	4,067	4,602	6,966	2,504	3,133	7,373
Other investment	8 703	**81,368**	**70,405**	**84,687**	**112,868**	**144,666**	**145,261**	**224,103**	**293,717**
Trade credits	8 706	8,538	7,516	8,254	11,224	14,683	12,010	17,253	20,272
General government	8 707	....	....	....	....	....	....	....	....
of which: Short-term	8 709	....	....	....	....	....	....	....	....
Other sectors	8 710	8,538	7,516	8,254	11,224	14,683	12,010	17,253	20,272
of which: Short-term	8 712	*8,538*	*7,516*	*8,254*	*11,224*	*14,683*	*12,010*	*17,253*	*20,272*
Loans	8 714	64,833	55,251	67,865	89,910	110,783	113,185	174,697	225,749
Monetary authorities	8 715	....	....	....	....	....	....	....	....
of which: Short-term	8 718	....	....	....	....	....	....	....	....
General government	8 719	1,977	2,237	3,476	3,458	4,282	2,719	2,616	2,267
of which: Short-term	8 721	*159*	*281*	*1,503*	*1,240*	*1,990*	*1,172*	....	....
Banks	8 722	55,610	47,101	57,067	77,606	97,646	102,969	156,402	207,698
of which: Short-term	8 724	*40,442*	*31,874*	*38,406*	*52,893*	*77,140*	*78,993*	....	....
Other sectors	8 725	7,246	5,913	-7,321	8,845	8,856	7,498	15,678	15,784
of which: Short-term	8 727	*3,309*	....	*3,724*	*6,150*	*4,926*	*5,333*	....	....
Currency and deposits	8 730 C.	....	....	....	....	....	....	....	....
Monetary authorities	8 731	....	....	....	....	....	....	....	....
General government	8 732	....	....	....	....	....	....	....	....
Banks	8 733	....	....	....	....	....	....	....	....
Other sectors	8 734	....	....	....	....	....	....	....	....
Other assets	8 736	7,997	7,638	8,568	11,735	19,200	20,065	32,153	47,696
Monetary authorities	8 737	....	....	....	....	....	....	....	....
of which: Short-term	8 739	....	....	....	....	....	....	....	....
General government	8 740	4,007	3,619	4,647	5,856	6,496	5,522	6,763	7,691
of which: Short-term	8 742	....	....	....	....	....	....	....	....
Banks	8 743	408	847	604	1,094	7,218	9,614	19,204	33,018
of which: Short-term	8 745	*408*	*847*	*604*	*1,094*	*7,218*	*9,614*	*19,204*	*33,018*
Other sectors	8 746	3,582	3,171	3,317	4,785	5,486	4,929	6,187	6,988
of which: Short-term	8 748	....	....	....	....	....	....	....	....
Reserve assets	8 802	**16,316**	**14,816**	**19,112**	**22,369**	**24,858**	**24,789**	**27,931**	**31,269**
Monetary gold	8 812	1,549	1,446	2,063	2,508	2,629	2,794	3,237	4,027
Special drawing rights	8 811	215	197	179	198	209	176	386	406
Reserve position in the Fund	8 810	890	1,039	1,428	1,468	1,308	532	318	257
Foreign exchange	8 803	13,661	12,132	15,441	18,195	20,286	21,087	23,687	26,579
Other claims	8 813	....	....	....	....	424	200	303	....

Table 3 (Concluded). INTERNATIONAL INVESTMENT POSITION (End-period stocks), 2000–2007

(Millions of U.S. dollars)

	Code	2000	2001	2002	2003	2004	2005	2006	2007
LIABILITIES..	8 995 D.	**424,279**	**421,706**	**476,006**	**629,115**	**788,074**	**775,684**	**990,717**	**1,136,607**
Direct investment in Sweden..........................	8 555 ..	**77,009**	**91,567**	**117,781**	**151,915**	**197,846**	**171,818**	**226,369**	**252,276**
Equity capital and reinvested earnings............................	8 556 ..	77,609	65,993	83,846	152,173	139,476	125,877	153,989	172,602
Claims on direct investors..	8 557 ..	....	....	....	....	....	....	....	....
Liabilities to direct investors.....................................	8 558 ..	....	....	....	....	....	....	....	....
Other capital..	8 580 ..	−600	25,574	33,935	−257	58,369	45,942	72,379	79,674
Claims on direct investors..	8 585 ..	−3,553	−15,474	−21,011	−4,984	−40,912	....	....	....
Liabilities to direct investors.....................................	8 590 ..	2,953	41,048	54,946	4,726	99,281	....	....	....
Portfolio investment.....................................	8 652 ..	**225,025**	**207,798**	**207,123**	**286,014**	**350,813**	**377,293**	**477,736**	**530,613**
Equity securities...	8 660 ..	106,660	76,522	54,043	89,738	124,104	141,280	209,106	204,057
Banks..	8 663 ..	....	....	....	....	....	....	....	....
Other sectors..	8 664 ..	106,660	76,522	54,043	89,738	124,104	141,280	209,106	204,057
Debt securities...	8 669 ..	118,365	131,276	153,080	196,277	226,708	236,013	268,630	326,556
Bonds and notes...	8 670 ..	100,593	105,651	132,513	173,428	191,318	199,357	228,642	266,988
Monetary authorities..	8 671 ..	−12	−10	−12	−16	−17	....	....	....
General government..	8 672 ..	40,002	42,711	55,992	65,850	70,564	67,621	60,888	60,768
Banks..	8 673 ..	46,921	43,534	54,199	82,160	97,302	106,171	140,655	181,034
Other sectors..	8 674 ..	13,681	19,416	22,334	25,433	23,468	25,566	27,099	25,186
Money market instruments.....................................	8 680 ..	17,772	25,625	20,567	22,849	35,391	36,656	39,988	59,568
Monetary authorities..	8 681 ..	....	....	....	....	....	....	....	....
General government..	8 682 ..	3,683	6,806	3,481	6,259	6,541	5,487	5,402	6,731
Banks..	8 683 ..	10,291	15,829	14,333	13,628	24,621	28,428	32,112	49,385
Other sectors..	8 684 ..	3,799	2,990	2,752	2,962	4,228	2,741	2,474	3,452
Financial derivatives.....................................	8 905 ..	**15,276**	**14,225**	**25,453**	**30,545**	**36,136**	**28,284**	**26,515**	**35,610**
Monetary authorities...	8 906 ..	....	....	....	....	....	....	....	3
General government..	8 907 ..	3,893	3,776	4,365	4,701	5,134	4,686	5,264	5,402
Banks..	8 908 ..	7,835	7,074	18,130	22,442	24,660	19,928	18,110	21,299
Other sectors..	8 909 ..	3,548	3,375	2,958	3,402	6,342	3,670	3,141	8,906
Other investment...	8 753 ..	**106,969**	**108,116**	**125,649**	**160,640**	**203,279**	**198,288**	**260,098**	**318,108**
Trade credits...	8 756 ..	6,030	5,684	6,066	7,184	8,689	9,098	12,403	15,693
General government...	8 757 ..	....	....	....	....	....	....	....	....
of which: Short-term..	8 759 ..	....	....	....	....	....	....	....	....
Other sectors..	8 760 ..	6,030	5,684	6,066	7,184	8,689	9,098	12,403	15,693
of which: Short-term..	8 762 ..	*6,030*	*5,684*	*6,066*	*7,184*	*8,689*	*9,098*	*12,403*	*15,693*
Loans...	8 764 ..	99,471	101,308	117,421	150,630	180,685	163,106	211,394	235,792
Monetary authorities...	8 765 ..	....	....	....	....	....	....	....	....
of which: Use of Fund credit and loans from the Fund....	8 766 ..	....	....	....	....	....	....	....	....
of which: Short-term..	8 768 ..	....	....	....	....	....	....	....	....
General government..	8 769 ..	1,321	1,138	1,916	1,788	1,677	1,181	1,067	803
of which: Short-term..	8 771 ..	*253*	*92*	*206*	....	....	....	....	....
Banks..	8 772 ..	79,890	81,063	96,270	114,328	149,842	140,354	185,221	197,853
of which: Short-term..	8 774 ..	*75,244*	*75,633*	*90,024*	*106,081*	*131,107*	*123,160*	....	....
Other sectors..	8 775 ..	18,260	19,107	19,235	34,515	29,166	21,570	25,106	37,136
of which: Short-term..	8 777 ..	*7,060*	*5,285*	*4,451*	*13,943*	*6,339*	*4,712*	....	....
Currency and deposits...	8 780 ..	....	....	....	....	....	....	....	....
Monetary authorities...	8 781 ..	....	....	....	....	....	....	....	....
General government..	8 782 ..	....	....	....	....	....	....	....	....
Banks..	8 783 ..	....	....	....	....	....	....	....	....
Other sectors..	8 784 ..	....	....	....	....	....	....	....	....
Other liabilities...	8 786 ..	1,467	1,125	2,162	2,826	13,905	26,084	36,301	66,623
Monetary authorities...	8 787 ..	....	....	....	....	....	....	....	....
of which: Short-term..	8 789 ..	....	....	....	....	....	....	....	....
General government..	8 790 ..	601	441	823	1,027	885	842	903	1,009
of which: Short-term..	8 792 ..	*601*	*441*	*823*	*1,027*	*885*	*842*	*903*	*1,009*
Banks..	8 793 ..	866	684	1,339	1,800	13,020	25,243	35,398	65,614
of which: Short-term..	8 795 ..	*866*	*684*	*1,339*	*1,800*	*13,020*	*25,243*	*35,398*	*65,614*
Other sectors..	8 796 ..	....	....	....	....	....	....	....	....
of which: Short-term..	8 798 ..	....	....	....	....	....	....	....	....
NET INTERNATIONAL INVESTMENT POSITION........	8 995 ..	−58,829	−53,475	−63,581	−72,504	−95,427	−72,500	−57,404	−30,854
Conversion rates: kronor per U.S. dollar (end of period)...	0 102 ..	9.5350	10.6675	8.8250	7.1892	6.6146	7.9584	6.8644	6.4136

Table 1. ANALYTIC PRESENTATION, 2000–2007

(Millions of U.S. dollars)

	Code	2000	2001	2002	2003	2004	2005	2006	2007
A. Current Account[1]	4 993 Z.	**32,830**	**22,223**	**24,914**	**43,398**	**54,695**	**51,321**	**54,011**	**58,017**
Goods: exports f.o.b.	2 100 ..	94,810	95,897	104,281	118,837	141,874	151,309	167,221	200,490
Goods: imports f.o.b.	3 100 ..	−92,746	−94,264	−97,584	−111,831	−126,089	−145,442	−162,213	−187,740
Balance on Goods	4 100 ..	*2,064*	*1,633*	*6,697*	*7,007*	*15,785*	*5,867*	*5,008*	*12,750*
Services: credit	2 200 ..	30,707	29,568	30,991	36,269	43,941	49,766	55,274	66,374
Services: debit	3 200 ..	−14,646	−15,366	−16,150	−18,533	−23,760	−27,374	−28,261	−33,296
Balance on Goods and Services	4 991 ..	*18,126*	*15,835*	*21,539*	*24,743*	*35,966*	*28,260*	*32,021*	*45,828*
Income: credit	2 300 ..	61,044	52,375	41,594	62,840	71,458	102,307	108,921	130,455
Income: debit	3 300 ..	−41,857	−40,484	−32,288	−38,568	−46,217	−68,285	−77,581	−108,861
Balance on Goods, Services, and Income	4 992 ..	*37,313*	*27,726*	*30,846*	*49,015*	*61,207*	*62,282*	*63,361*	*67,422*
Current transfers: credit	2 379 Z.	6,580	9,721	10,635	13,198	14,300	15,504	17,639	22,883
Current transfers: debit	3 379 ..	−11,063	−15,225	−16,567	−18,815	−20,811	−26,464	−26,989	−32,288
B. Capital Account[1]	4 994 Z.	**−3,541**	**1,523**	**−1,159**	**−667**	**−1,409**	**−665**	**−2,770**	**−2,302**
Capital account: credit	2 994 Z.	490	2,314	274	492	406	470	267	349
Capital account: debit	3 994 ..	−4,031	−791	−1,433	−1,159	−1,815	−1,135	−3,037	−2,650
Total, Groups A Plus B	4 981 ..	*29,289*	*23,746*	*23,754*	*42,731*	*53,286*	*50,657*	*51,241*	*55,716*
C. Financial Account[1]	4 995 W.	**−29,948**	**−36,679**	**−22,789**	**−24,311**	**−63,115**	**−87,172**	**−67,985**	**−37,813**
Direct investment abroad	4 505 ..	−43,989	−18,376	−8,585	−15,674	−26,068	−51,433	−75,919	−48,146
Direct investment in Switzerland	4 555 Z.	19,764	9,392	6,785	17,471	1,856	−925	34,021	39,192
Portfolio investment assets	4 602 ..	−23,169	−43,088	−29,159	−32,903	−42,412	−53,263	−41,700	−20,344
Equity securities	4 610 ..	−20,424	−15,134	−7,454	−2,087	−11,303	−17,729	−13,762	−5,221
Debt securities	4 619 ..	−2,744	−27,954	−21,705	−30,816	−31,109	−35,534	−27,938	−15,123
Portfolio investment liabilities	4 652 Z.	10,247	1,894	7,483	−1,662	2,858	5,636	68	1,626
Equity securities	4 660 ..	8,777	1,840	5,679	−4,428	−2,789	3,951	537	689
Debt securities	4 669 Z.	1,470	54	1,804	2,765	5,647	1,685	−469	937
Financial derivatives	4 910 ..	....	....	....	....	....	....	−2,875	−10,399
Financial derivatives assets	4 900 ..	....	....	....	....	....	....	−2,168	−3,794
Financial derivatives liabilities	4 905 ..	....	....	....	....	....	....	−707	−6,605
Other investment assets	4 703 ..	−101,376	21,393	−38,289	−4,387	−28,124	−70,498	−42,975	−293,599
Monetary authorities	4 701 ..	....	....	....	−18	18	−798	607	−5,338
General government	4 704 ..	31	46	62	113	98	−31	15	2,071
Banks	4 705 ..	−83,538	25,742	−53,922	−11,395	−14,849	−61,664	−24,322	−242,946
Other sectors	4 728 ..	−17,869	−4,395	15,571	6,914	−13,390	−8,005	−19,275	−47,386
Other investment liabilities	4 753 W.	108,575	−7,893	38,975	12,845	28,775	83,312	61,394	293,858
Monetary authorities	4 753 WA	33	840	−860	−24	−223	117	−224	5,218
General government	4 753 ZB	−59	−26	154	−208	184	115	419	243
Banks	4 753 ZC	90,490	−14,861	35,979	6,079	27,840	62,582	41,700	248,245
Other sectors	4 753 ZD	18,111	6,154	3,703	6,998	973	20,498	19,499	40,152
Total, Groups A Through C	4 983 ..	*−659*	*−12,933*	*965*	*18,420*	*−9,828*	*−36,515*	*−16,744*	*17,903*
D. Net Errors and Omissions	4 998 ..	**−3,555**	**13,555**	**1,584**	**−15,016**	**11,446**	**18,300**	**17,114**	**−14,442**
Total, Groups A Through D	4 984 ..	*−4,214*	*622*	*2,549*	*3,405*	*1,618*	*−18,215*	*370*	*3,461*
E. Reserves and Related Items	4 802 A.	**4,214**	**−622**	**−2,549**	**−3,405**	**−1,618**	**18,215**	**−370**	**−3,461**
Reserve assets	4 802 ..	4,214	−622	−2,549	−3,405	−1,618	18,215	−370	−3,461
Use of Fund credit and loans	4 766 ..	....	....	....	....	....	....	....	....
Exceptional financing	4 920 ..	....	....	....	....	....	....	....	....
Conversion rates: Swiss francs per U.S. dollar	0 101 ..	**1.6888**	**1.6876**	**1.5586**	**1.3467**	**1.2435**	**1.2452**	**1.2538**	**1.2004**

[1] Excludes components that have been classified in the categories of Group E.

Table 2. STANDARD PRESENTATION, 2000–2007

(Millions of U.S. dollars)

	Code	2000	2001	2002	2003	2004	2005	2006	2007
CURRENT ACCOUNT	4 993 ..	**32,830**	**22,223**	**24,914**	**43,398**	**54,695**	**51,321**	**54,011**	**58,017**
A. GOODS	4 100 ..	**2,064**	**1,633**	**6,697**	**7,007**	**15,785**	**5,867**	**5,008**	**12,750**
Credit	2 100 ..	94,810	95,897	104,281	118,837	141,874	151,309	167,221	200,490
General merchandise: exports f.o.b.	2 110 ..	81,904	83,242	92,512	105,522	123,677	131,516	148,510	173,151
Goods for processing: exports f.o.b.	2 150 ..	....	....	....	....	....	....	....	....
Repairs on goods	2 160 ..	....	....	....	....	....	....	....	....
Goods procured in ports by carriers	2 170 ..	....	....	....	....	....	....	....	....
Nonmonetary gold	2 180 ..	12,906	12,655	11,768	13,316	18,197	19,793	18,711	27,339
Debit	3 100 ..	−92,746	−94,264	−97,584	−111,831	−126,089	−145,442	−162,213	−187,740
General merchandise: imports f.o.b.	3 110 ..	−81,914	−83,355	−86,459	−99,279	−114,726	−125,179	−139,875	−159,271
Goods for processing: imports f.o.b.	3 150 ..	....	....	....	....	....	....	....	....
Repairs on goods	3 160 ..	....	....	....	....	....	....	....	....
Goods procured in ports by carriers	3 170 ..	....	....	....	....	....	....	....	....
Nonmonetary gold	3 180 ..	−10,832	−10,909	−11,124	−12,551	−11,363	−20,263	−22,338	−28,469
B. SERVICES	4 200 ..	**16,062**	**14,202**	**14,842**	**17,736**	**20,180**	**22,392**	**27,013**	**33,078**
Total credit	2 200 ..	*30,707*	*29,568*	*30,991*	*36,269*	*43,941*	*49,766*	*55,274*	*66,374*
Total debit	3 200 ..	*−14,646*	*−15,366*	*−16,150*	*−18,533*	*−23,760*	*−27,374*	*−28,261*	*−33,296*
Transportation services, credit	2 205 ..	**4,535**	**4,435**	**3,330**	**3,665**	**4,015**	**4,206**	**4,545**	**5,464**
Passenger	2 850 ..	*2,336*	*2,508*	*1,857*	*1,879*	*1,809*	*1,896*	*2,115*	*2,592*
Freight	2 851 ..	*806*	*638*	*482*	*679*	*700*	*809*	*826*	*969*
Other	2 852 ..	*1,393*	*1,288*	*991*	*1,107*	*1,506*	*1,501*	*1,604*	*1,902*
Sea transport, passenger	2 207 ..	....	....	....	....	....	....	....	....
Sea transport, freight	2 208 ..	....	....	....	....	....	....	....	....
Sea transport, other	2 209 ..	....	....	....	....	....	....	....	....
Air transport, passenger	2 211 ..	....	....	....	....	....	....	....	....
Air transport, freight	2 212 ..	....	....	....	....	....	....	....	....
Air transport, other	2 213 ..	....	....	....	....	....	....	....	....
Other transport, passenger	2 215 ..	....	....	....	....	....	....	....	....
Other transport, freight	2 216 ..	....	....	....	....	....	....	....	....
Other transport, other	2 217 ..	1,393	1,288	991	1,107	1,506	1,501	1,604	1,902
Transportation services, debit	3 205 ..	**−5,226**	**−4,987**	**−4,441**	**−4,673**	**−5,263**	**−5,560**	**−6,101**	**−7,069**
Passenger	3 850 ..	*−1,941*	*−1,944*	*−1,673*	*−1,731*	*−1,820*	*−1,797*	*−1,947*	*−2,184*
Freight	3 851 ..	*−1,711*	*−1,739*	*−1,801*	*−2,063*	*−2,327*	*−2,684*	*−2,993*	*−3,464*
Other	3 852 ..	*−1,573*	*−1,304*	*−967*	*−879*	*−1,117*	*−1,079*	*−1,161*	*−1,421*
Sea transport, passenger	3 207 ..	....	....	....	....	....	....	....	....
Sea transport, freight	3 208 ..	....	....	....	....	....	....	....	....
Sea transport, other	3 209 ..	....	....	....	....	....	....	....	....
Air transport, passenger	3 211 ..	....	....	....	....	....	....	....	....
Air transport, freight	3 212 ..	....	....	....	....	....	....	....	....
Air transport, other	3 213 ..	....	....	....	....	....	....	....	....
Other transport, passenger	3 215 ..	....	....	....	....	....	....	....	....
Other transport, freight	3 216 ..	....	....	....	....	....	....	....	....
Other transport, other	3 217 ..	−1,573	−1,304	−967	−879	−1,117	−1,079	−1,161	−1,421
Travel, credit	2 236 ..	**6,652**	**6,782**	**7,260**	**8,614**	**9,595**	**10,041**	**10,808**	**12,185**
Business travel	2 237 ..	....	....	....	....	....	....	....	....
Personal travel	2 240 ..	....	....	....	....	....	....	....	....
Travel, debit	3 236 ..	**−5,419**	**−5,141**	**−5,537**	**−6,883**	**−8,104**	**−8,782**	**−9,252**	**−10,265**
Business travel	3 237 ..	....	....	....	....	....	....	....	....
Personal travel	3 240 ..	....	....	....	....	....	....	....	....
Other services, credit	2 200 BA	**19,520**	**18,351**	**20,401**	**23,991**	**30,330**	**35,519**	**39,922**	**48,726**
Communications	2 245 ..	879	767	839	974	1,223	1,183	1,102	1,068
Construction	2 249 ..	....	....	....	....	....	....	....	....
Insurance	2 253 ..	1,509	1,122	2,759	3,467	3,919	3,326	3,728	4,857
Financial	2 260 ..	10,637	9,512	8,643	10,062	11,469	14,071	16,173	20,517
Computer and information	2 262 ..	....	....	....	....	....	....	....	....
Royalties and licence fees	2 266 ..	....	....	....	....	....	....	....	....
Other business services	2 268 ..	5,224	5,266	6,912	7,744	12,382	15,682	17,571	20,854
Personal, cultural, and recreational	2 287 ..	7	5	4	4	4	5	3	2
Government, n.i.e.	2 291 ..	1,264	1,679	1,244	1,740	1,333	1,253	1,345	1,427
Other services, debit	3 200 BA	**−4,000**	**−5,238**	**−6,172**	**−6,977**	**−10,393**	**−13,032**	**−12,909**	**−15,963**
Communications	3 245 ..	−885	−923	−880	−971	−1,130	−938	−803	−801
Construction	3 249 ..	....	....	....	....	....	....	....	....
Insurance	3 253 ..	−216	−218	−235	−277	−305	−498	−623	−814
Financial	3 260 ..	−783	−651	−593	−668	−856	−1,055	−1,281	−1,790
Computer and information	3 262 ..	....	....	....	....	....	....	....	....
Royalties and licence fees	3 266 ..	....	....	....	....	....	....	....	....
Other business services	3 268 ..	−1,943	−3,270	−4,271	−4,832	−7,856	−10,294	−9,959	−12,301
Personal, cultural, and recreational	3 287 ..	−61	−65	−67	−90	−96	−87	−85	−94
Government, n.i.e.	3 291 ..	−112	−110	−126	−140	−150	−160	−158	−164

Table 2 (Continued). STANDARD PRESENTATION, 2000–2007

(Millions of U.S. dollars)

	Code	2000	2001	2002	2003	2004	2005	2006	2007
C. INCOME	4 300	**19,187**	**11,891**	**9,307**	**24,272**	**25,241**	**34,023**	**31,340**	**21,594**
Total credit	2 300	*61,044*	*52,375*	*41,594*	*62,840*	*71,458*	*102,307*	*108,921*	*130,455*
Total debit	3 300	*−41,857*	*−40,484*	*−32,288*	*−38,568*	*−46,217*	*−68,285*	*−77,581*	*−108,861*
Compensation of employees, credit	2 310	995	1,176	1,225	1,533	1,695	1,626	1,695	1,743
Compensation of employees, debit	3 310	−5,888	−6,561	−7,178	−8,711	−9,782	−9,983	−10,658	−12,114
Investment income, credit	2 320	60,049	51,199	40,369	61,307	69,763	100,681	107,227	128,713
Direct investment income	2 330	26,388	18,636	12,902	32,438	39,353	61,241	54,677	53,331
Dividends and distributed branch profits	2 332	16,411	16,185	18,140	20,463	22,316	28,252	34,078	40,757
Reinvested earnings and undistributed branch profits	2 333	9,976	2,450	−5,238	11,976	17,037	32,989	20,599	12,574
Income on debt (interest)	2 334	....	....	....	....	....	....	....	....
Portfolio investment income	2 339	14,517	14,579	14,732	16,361	18,672	21,249	24,606	30,914
Income on equity	2 340	4,615	5,230	5,280	5,806	6,957	8,646	10,397	13,279
Income on bonds and notes	2 350	....	....	....	....	....	....	....	....
Income on money market instruments	2 360	....	....	....	....	....	....	....	....
Other investment income	2 370	19,144	17,985	12,736	12,507	11,738	18,192	27,944	44,467
Investment income, debit	3 320	−35,969	−33,923	−25,110	−29,857	−36,435	−58,302	−66,923	−96,747
Direct investment income	3 330	−10,616	−7,820	−6,110	−10,743	−15,723	−28,760	−24,155	−33,465
Dividends and distributed branch profits	3 332	−4,140	−7,250	−4,602	−7,915	−8,888	−31,341	−11,066	−14,853
Reinvested earnings and undistributed branch profits	3 333	−6,476	−570	−1,508	−2,828	−6,835	2,581	−13,089	−18,612
Income on debt (interest)	3 334	....	....	....	....	....	....	....	....
Portfolio investment income	3 339	−7,126	−8,134	−7,421	−8,061	−9,548	−11,067	−13,500	−17,158
Income on equity	3 340	−5,540	−6,609	−6,019	−6,568	−7,882	−9,064	−11,085	−14,510
Income on bonds and notes	3 350	....	....	....	....	....	....	....	....
Income on money market instruments	3 360	....	....	....	....	....	....	....	....
Other investment income	3 370	−18,227	−17,969	−11,579	−11,054	−11,164	−18,475	−29,269	−46,124
D. CURRENT TRANSFERS	4 379	**−4,483**	**−5,504**	**−5,932**	**−5,617**	**−6,511**	**−10,961**	**−9,350**	**−9,405**
Credit	2 379	6,580	9,721	10,635	13,198	14,300	15,504	17,639	22,883
General government	2 380	1,414	1,650	1,845	2,309	2,528	2,828	3,149	3,504
Other sectors	2 390	5,166	8,071	8,790	10,889	11,772	12,676	14,491	19,379
Workers' remittances	2 391	125	125	147	173	194	202	209	292
Other current transfers	2 392	5,041	7,947	8,643	10,716	11,577	12,474	14,282	19,087
Debit	3 379	−11,063	−15,225	−16,567	−18,815	−20,811	−26,464	−26,989	−32,288
General government	3 380	−3,308	−3,487	−3,951	−4,710	−5,459	−5,741	−5,834	−6,374
Other sectors	3 390	−7,755	−11,738	−12,615	−14,105	−15,352	−20,724	−21,156	−25,913
Workers' remittances	3 391	−1,704	−1,820	−2,045	−2,740	−3,139	−3,340	−3,718	−4,159
Other current transfers	3 392	−6,052	−9,918	−10,570	−11,365	−12,213	−17,383	−17,437	−21,755
CAPITAL AND FINANCIAL ACCOUNT	4 996	**−29,275**	**−35,778**	**−26,497**	**−28,382**	**−66,141**	**−69,622**	**−71,125**	**−43,575**
CAPITAL ACCOUNT	4 994	**−3,541**	**1,523**	**−1,159**	**−667**	**−1,409**	**−665**	**−2,770**	**−2,302**
Total credit	2 994	*490*	*2,314*	*274*	*492*	*406*	*470*	*267*	*349*
Total debit	3 994	*−4,031*	*−791*	*−1,433*	*−1,159*	*−1,815*	*−1,135*	*−3,037*	*−2,650*
Capital transfers, credit	2 400	....	....	....	....	....	....	....	....
General government	2 401	....	....	....	....	....	....	....	....
Debt forgiveness	2 402	....	....	....	....	....	....	....	....
Other capital transfers	2 410	....	....	....	....	....	....	....	....
Other sectors	2 430	....	....	....	....	....	....	....	....
Migrants' transfers	2 431	....	....	....	....	....	....	....	....
Debt forgiveness	2 432	....	....	....	....	....	....	....	....
Other capital transfers	2 440	....	....	....	....	....	....	....	....
Capital transfers, debit	3 400	−633	−101	−210	−122	−552	−512	−452	−247
General government	3 401	−83	−101	−210	−122	−552	−512	−452	−247
Debt forgiveness	3 402	....	−17	−106	....	−421	−390	−346	−144
Other capital transfers	3 410	−83	−83	−103	−122	−131	−123	−106	−104
Other sectors	3 430	−550	....	....	....	....	....	....	....
Migrants' transfers	3 431	....	....	....	....	....	....	....	....
Debt forgiveness	3 432	....	....	....	....	....	....	....	....
Other capital transfers	3 440	−550	....	....	....	....	....	....	....
Nonproduced nonfinancial assets, credit	2 480	490	2,314	274	492	406	470	267	349
Nonproduced nonfinancial assets, debit	3 480	−3,398	−691	−1,223	−1,037	−1,263	−623	−2,586	−2,403

Table 2 (Continued). STANDARD PRESENTATION, 2000–2007

(Millions of U.S. dollars)

	Code	2000	2001	2002	2003	2004	2005	2006	2007
FINANCIAL ACCOUNT..	4 995 ..	**−25,734**	**−37,301**	**−25,338**	**−27,715**	**−64,733**	**−68,957**	**−68,355**	**−41,273**
A. DIRECT INVESTMENT......................................	4 500 ..	**−24,225**	**−8,984**	**−1,799**	**1,797**	**−24,212**	**−52,359**	**−41,897**	**−8,954**
Direct investment abroad.................................	4 505 ..	**−43,989**	**−18,376**	**−8,585**	**−15,674**	**−26,068**	**−51,433**	**−75,919**	**−48,146**
Equity capital...	4 510 ..	−32,527	−13,129	−16,209	−4,224	−9,330	−18,159	−50,336	−25,252
Claims on affiliated enterprises..................	4 515 ..	−32,527	−13,129	−16,209	−4,224	−9,330	−18,159	−50,336	−25,252
Liabilities to affiliated enterprises...............	4 520 ..	....	....	....	....	....	....	....	....
Reinvested earnings.....................................	4 525 ..	−9,976	−2,450	5,238	−11,976	−17,037	−32,989	−20,599	−12,574
Other capital..	4 530 ..	−1,487	−2,796	2,386	526	299	−285	−4,984	−10,320
Claims on affiliated enterprises..................	4 535 ..	−4,274	−2,774	220	629	−2,123	−4,294	−11,487	−4,305
Liabilities to affiliated enterprises...............	4 540 ..	2,787	−22	2,166	−103	2,422	4,009	6,502	−6,016
Direct investment in Switzerland......................	4 555 ..	**19,764**	**9,392**	**6,785**	**17,471**	**1,856**	**−925**	**34,021**	**39,192**
Equity capital...	4 560 ..	12,267	9,916	3,124	9,605	−1,682	158	18,132	19,813
Claims on direct investors..........................	4 565 ..	....	....	....	....	....	....	....	....
Liabilities to direct investors......................	4 570 ..	12,267	9,916	3,124	9,605	−1,682	158	18,132	19,813
Reinvested earnings.....................................	4 575 ..	6,476	570	1,508	2,828	6,835	−2,581	13,089	18,612
Other capital..	4 580 ..	1,022	−1,093	2,154	5,038	−3,297	1,498	2,800	767
Claims on direct investors..........................	4 585 ..	−529	−395	694	−2,354	−2,824	819	−2,154	−3,379
Liabilities to direct investors......................	4 590 ..	1,551	−698	1,460	7,392	−473	680	4,954	4,146
B. PORTFOLIO INVESTMENT................................	4 600 ..	**−12,922**	**−41,194**	**−21,676**	**−34,565**	**−39,554**	**−47,627**	**−41,631**	**−18,718**
Assets...	4 602 ..	**−23,169**	**−43,088**	**−29,159**	**−32,903**	**−42,412**	**−53,263**	**−41,700**	**−20,344**
Equity securities..	4 610 ..	−20,424	−15,134	−7,454	−2,087	−11,303	−17,729	−13,762	−5,221
Monetary authorities..................................	4 611 ..	....	....	....	....	....	....	....	....
General government..................................	4 612 ..	....	....	....	....	....	....	....	....
Banks..	4 613 ..	....	....	....	....	....	....	....	....
Other sectors..	4 614 ..	....	....	....	....	....	....	....	....
Debt securities..	4 619 ..	−2,744	−27,954	−21,705	−30,816	−31,109	−35,534	−27,938	−15,123
Bonds and notes..	4 620 ..	−1,790	−23,397	−18,001	−24,428	−38,746	−38,864	−36,132	−27,570
Monetary authorities...............................	4 621 ..	....	....	....	....	....	....	....	....
General government...............................	4 622 ..	....	....	....	....	....	....	....	....
Banks...	4 623 ..	....	....	....	....	....	....	....	....
Other sectors...	4 624 ..	....	....	....	....	....	....	....	....
Money market instruments.........................	4 630 ..	−954	−4,557	−3,705	−6,388	7,637	3,330	8,194	12,447
Monetary authorities...............................	4 631 ..	....	....	....	....	....	....	....	....
General government...............................	4 632 ..	....	....	....	....	....	....	....	....
Banks...	4 633 ..	....	....	....	....	....	....	....	....
Other sectors...	4 634 ..	....	....	....	....	....	....	....	....
Liabilities...	4 652 ..	**10,247**	**1,894**	**7,483**	**−1,662**	**2,858**	**5,636**	**68**	**1,626**
Equity securities..	4 660 ..	8,777	1,840	5,679	−4,428	−2,789	3,951	537	689
Banks..	4 663 ..	....	....	....	....	....	....	....	....
Other sectors..	4 664 ..	....	....	....	....	....	....	....	....
Debt securities..	4 669 ..	1,470	54	1,804	2,765	5,647	1,685	−469	937
Bonds and notes..	4 670 ..	1,352	−452	56	1,651	4,231	−1,131	−728	−489
Monetary authorities...............................	4 671 ..	....	....	....	....	....	....	....	....
General government...............................	4 672 ..	....	....	....	....	....	....	....	....
Banks...	4 673 ..	....	....	....	....	....	....	....	....
Other sectors...	4 674 ..	....	....	....	....	....	....	....	....
Money market instruments.........................	4 680 ..	118	505	1,748	1,114	1,415	2,817	259	1,426
Monetary authorities...............................	4 681 ..	....	....	....	....	....	....	....	....
General government...............................	4 682 ..	....	....	....	....	....	....	....	....
Banks...	4 683 ..	....	....	....	....	....	....	....	....
Other sectors...	4 684 ..	....	....	....	....	....	....	....	....
C. FINANCIAL DERIVATIVES................................	4 910 ..	....	....	....	....	....	....	**−2,875**	**−10,399**
Monetary authorities......................................	4 911 ..	....	....	....	....	....	....	....	....
General government.......................................	4 912 ..	....	....	....	....	....	....	....	....
Banks..	4 913 ..	....	....	....	....	....	....	....	....
Other sectors...	4 914 ..	....	....	....	....	....	....	....	....
Assets...	4 900 ..	....	....	....	....	....	....	**−2,168**	**−3,794**
Monetary authorities......................................	4 901 ..	....	....	....	....	....	....	....	....
General government.......................................	4 902 ..	....	....	....	....	....	....	....	....
Banks..	4 903 ..	....	....	....	....	....	....	....	....
Other sectors...	4 904 ..	....	....	....	....	....	....	....	....
Liabilities...	4 905 ..	....	....	....	....	....	....	**−707**	**−6,605**
Monetary authorities......................................	4 906 ..	....	....	....	....	....	....	....	....
General government.......................................	4 907 ..	....	....	....	....	....	....	....	....
Banks..	4 908 ..	....	....	....	....	....	....	....	....
Other sectors...	4 909 ..	....	....	....	....	....	....	....	....

Table 2 (Concluded). STANDARD PRESENTATION, 2000–2007

(Millions of U.S. dollars)

	Code	2000	2001	2002	2003	2004	2005	2006	2007
D. OTHER INVESTMENT	4 700	**7,199**	**13,499**	**686**	**8,458**	**651**	**12,814**	**18,419**	**259**
Assets	4 703	**−101,376**	**21,393**	**−38,289**	**−4,387**	**−28,124**	**−70,498**	**−42,975**	**−293,599**
Trade credits	4 706	....	....	....	....	....	....	....	....
General government	4 707	....	....	....	....	....	....	....	....
of which: Short-term	4 709	....	....	....	....	....	....	....	....
Other sectors	4 710	....	....	....	....	....	....	....	....
of which: Short-term	4 712	....	....	....	....	....	....	....	....
Loans	4 714	−18,276	−4,323	−3,052	−9,068	−40,090	627	−11,473	−76,581
Monetary authorities	4 715	....	....	....	−18	18	−822	607	−5,338
of which: Short-term	4 718	....	....	....	....	18	−822	607	−5,338
General government	4 719	35	50	67	117	102	−27	−25	2,497
of which: Short-term	4 721	....	....	....	....	....	....	....	2,475
Banks	4 722	−9,907	2,370	2,237	−7,059	−29,875	−1,421	−14,939	−41,145
of which: Short-term	4 724	....	....	....	....	....	....	....	....
Other sectors	4 725	−8,403	−6,744	−5,356	−2,108	−10,335	2,897	2,884	−32,595
of which: Short-term	4 727	−7,419	−1,782	−7,197	954	−9,740	4,521	−955	−21,860
Currency and deposits	4 730	−85,181	26,849	−46,724	4,686	11,972	−71,876	−29,237	−216,175
Monetary authorities	4 731	....	....	....	....	....	....	....	....
General government	4 732	....	....	....	....	....	....	....	....
Banks	4 733	−73,631	23,371	−56,160	−4,336	15,026	−60,242	−9,383	−201,802
Other sectors	4 734	−11,551	3,478	9,435	9,022	−3,054	−11,634	−19,854	−14,374
Other assets	4 736	2,081	−1,134	11,487	−5	−5	752	−2,264	−843
Monetary authorities	4 737	....	....	....	....	....	24	....	....
of which: Short-term	4 739	....	....	....	....	....	....	....	....
General government	4 740	−4	−4	−5	−5	−4	−3	40	−426
of which: Short-term	4 742	....	....	....	....	....	....	....	....
Banks	4 743	....	....	....	....	....	....	....	....
of which: Short-term	4 745	....	....	....	....	....	....	....	....
Other sectors	4 746	2,085	−1,129	11,492	....	−1	731	−2,304	−417
of which: Short-term	4 748	2,085	−1,129	11,492	....	−1	731	−2,389	−416
Liabilities	4 753	**108,575**	**−7,893**	**38,975**	**12,845**	**28,775**	**83,312**	**61,394**	**293,858**
Trade credits	4 756	....	....	....	....	....	....	....	....
General government	4 757	....	....	....	....	....	....	....	....
of which: Short-term	4 759	....	....	....	....	....	....	....	....
Other sectors	4 760	....	....	....	....	....	....	....	....
of which: Short-term	4 762	....	....	....	....	....	....	....	....
Loans	4 764	102,700	−14,023	29,275	−2,298	24,375	70,658	49,074	279,425
Monetary authorities	4 765	....	....	....	....	....	....	....	....
of which: Use of Fund credit and loans from the Fund..	4 766	....	....	....	....	....	....	....	....
of which: Short-term	4 768	....	....	....	....	....	....	....	....
General government	4 769	−59	−26	154	−208	184	115	419	243
of which: Short-term	4 771	−59	−26	154	−208	184	115	419	243
Banks	4 772	95,118	−15,647	29,404	−8,663	24,170	59,567	39,217	243,489
of which: Short-term	4 774	96,639	−6,972	29,877	−12,371	24,523	61,958	34,298	244,384
Other sectors	4 775	7,642	1,649	−283	6,573	21	10,976	9,438	35,693
of which: Short-term	4 777	4,665	571	3,342	1,113	2,327	5,716	5,706	30,669
Currency and deposits	4 780	−4,321	1,293	5,514	14,920	3,364	3,123	3,317	11,365
Monetary authorities	4 781	33	840	−860	−24	−223	117	−224	5,218
General government	4 782	....	....	....	....	....	....	....	....
Banks	4 783	−4,628	786	6,574	14,743	3,670	3,015	2,483	4,756
Other sectors	4 784	274	−332	−200	201	−84	−9	1,058	1,391
Other liabilities	4 786	10,196	4,837	4,186	223	1,036	9,532	9,003	3,067
Monetary authorities	4 787	....	....	....	....	....	....	....	....
of which: Short-term	4 789	....	....	....	....	....	....	....	....
General government	4 790	....	....	....	....	....	....	....	....
of which: Short-term	4 792	....	....	....	....	....	....	....	....
Banks	4 793	....	....	....	....	....	....	....	....
of which: Short-term	4 795	....	....	....	....	....	....	....	....
Other sectors	4 796	10,196	4,837	4,186	223	1,036	9,532	9,003	3,067
of which: Short-term	4 798	10,196	4,837	4,186	223	1,036	9,532	9,003	3,067
E. RESERVE ASSETS	4 802	**4,214**	**−622**	**−2,549**	**−3,405**	**−1,618**	**18,215**	**−370**	**−3,461**
Monetary gold	4 812	....	....	....	....	....	....	....	....
Special drawing rights	4 811	295	−124	224	41	−34	9	−215	44
Reserve position in the Fund	4 810	339	−375	−200	41	342	852	392	114
Foreign exchange	4 803	3,552	−123	−2,572	−3,486	−1,925	542	−547	−3,616
Other claims	4 813	28	....	....	....	....	16,812	....	−4
NET ERRORS AND OMISSIONS	4 998	**−3,555**	**13,555**	**1,584**	**−15,016**	**11,446**	**18,300**	**17,114**	**−14,442**

Table 3. INTERNATIONAL INVESTMENT POSITION (End-period stocks), 2000–2007

(Billions of U.S. dollars)

	Code	2000	2001	2002	2003	2004	2005	2006	2007
ASSETS...	8 995 C.	**1,365.91**	**1,322.65**	**1,517.31**	**1,770.53**	**1,997.13**	**2,105.19**	**2,472.29**	**3,164.72**
Direct investment abroad............................	8 505 ..	**232.20**	**252.28**	**292.27**	**341.46**	**400.71**	**428.49**	**519.27**	**595.25**
Equity capital and reinvested earnings...............	8 506 ..	206.27	226.00	263.97	312.49	378.87	407.72	489.41	563.73
Claims on affiliated enterprises......................	8 507 ..	206.27	226.00	263.97	312.49	378.87	407.72	489.41	563.73
Liabilities to affiliated enterprises..................	8 508 ..	....	....	....	....	....	....	....	....
Other capital..	8 530 ..	25.93	26.27	28.30	28.97	21.84	20.77	29.85	31.52
Claims on affiliated enterprises......................	8 535 ..	41.54	39.95	49.14	59.28	57.93	56.60	76.78	89.03
Liabilities to affiliated enterprises..................	8 540 ..	−15.61	−13.67	−20.85	−30.31	−36.09	−35.83	−46.93	−57.51
Portfolio investment................................	8 602 ..	**502.31**	**486.47**	**522.34**	**659.92**	**760.24**	**729.16**	**878.76**	**1,058.03**
Equity securities....................................	8 610 ..	267.27	243.70	218.27	293.66	339.47	357.35	421.50	511.29
Monetary authorities...............................	8 611 ..	....	....	....	....	....	....	....	....
General government...............................	8 612 ..	....	....	....	....	....	....	....	....
Banks..	8 613 ..	....	....	....	....	....	....	....	....
Other sectors......................................	8 614 ..	267.27	243.70	218.27	293.66	339.47	357.35	421.50	511.29
Debt securities......................................	8 619 ..	235.03	242.77	304.07	366.27	420.77	371.81	457.26	546.74
Bonds and notes..................................	8 620 ..	227.54	227.18	282.55	337.80	391.72	339.18	406.86	467.78
Monetary authorities...........................	8 621 ..	.60	1.16	1.73	2.38	2.24	1.52	1.40	1.55
General government...........................	8 622 ..	....	....	....	....	....	....	....	....
Banks..	8 623 ..	11.44	22.11	29.83	35.04	41.44	40.18	47.46	49.04
Other sectors...................................	8 624 ..	215.50	203.90	250.99	300.38	348.04	297.48	358.00	417.19
Money market instruments........................	8 630 ..	7.49	15.60	21.52	28.46	29.04	32.63	50.40	78.96
Monetary authorities...........................	8 631 ..	....	....	....	....	....	....	....	....
General government...........................	8 632 ..	....	....	....	....	....	....	....	....
Banks..	8 633 ..	4.93	7.65	9.94	12.16	15.48	18.97	31.64	47.23
Other sectors...................................	8 634 ..	2.56	7.95	11.59	16.30	13.56	13.66	18.76	31.73
Financial derivatives..............................	8 900 ..	....	....	....	....	....	**60.79**	**93.07**	**123.38**
Monetary authorities................................	8 901 ..	....	....	....	....	....	....	....	....
General government................................	8 902 ..	....	....	....	....	....	....	....	....
Banks..	8 903 ..	....	....	....	....	....	23.18	34.42	50.33
Other sectors.......................................	8 904 ..	....	....	....	....	....	37.61	58.65	73.05
Other investment...................................	8 703 ..	**577.94**	**532.22**	**641.38**	**699.60**	**761.55**	**829.08**	**916.74**	**1,313.89**
Trade credits.......................................	8 706 ..	....	....	....	....	....	....	....	....
General government...............................	8 707 ..	....	....	....	....	....	....	....	....
of which: Short-term..........................	8 709 ..	....	....	....	....	....	....	....	....
Other sectors......................................	8 710 ..	....	....	....	....	....	....	....	....
of which: Short-term..........................	8 712 ..	....	....	....	....	....	....	....	....
Loans..	8 714 ..	140.23	142.98	167.55	189.65	240.17	265.55	296.85	410.14
Monetary authorities...............................	8 715 ..	2.77	6.70	6.55	7.59	8.14	8.04	8.02	13.90
of which: Short-term..........................	8 718 ..	*2.77*	*6.70*	*6.55*	*7.59*	*8.14*	*8.04*	*8.02*	*13.90*
General government...............................	8 719 ..	.48	.31	.36	.39	.42	6.66	7.34	5.48
of which: Short-term..........................	8 721 ..	....	....	....	....	....	*6.30*	*6.95*	*5.08*
Banks..	8 722 ..	69.98	66.24	69.59	80.63	115.63	110.14	129.42	178.07
of which: Short-term..........................	8 724 ..	....	....	....	....	....	....	....	....
Other sectors......................................	8 725 ..	67.00	69.74	91.05	101.04	115.98	140.70	152.07	212.70
of which: Short-term..........................	8 727 ..	*43.31*	*40.71*	*60.92*	*67.22*	*81.06*	*88.01*	*98.41*	*146.09*
Currency and deposits...............................	8 730 ..	406.39	367.12	451.45	476.66	484.29	520.14	564.63	832.33
Monetary authorities...............................	8 731 ..	....	....	....	....	....	....	....	....
General government...............................	8 732 ..	....	....	....	....	....	....	....	....
Banks..	8 733 ..	343.35	309.01	396.29	425.67	426.56	456.22	476.27	722.10
Other sectors......................................	8 734 ..	63.04	58.10	55.16	50.99	57.73	63.92	88.35	110.23
Other assets.......................................	8 736 ..	31.31	22.12	22.37	33.29	37.08	43.39	55.27	71.42
Monetary authorities...............................	8 737 ..	....	.04	.04	.05	.05	.07	.07	.08
of which: Short-term..........................	8 739 ..	....	....	....	....	....	....	....	....
General government...............................	8 740 ..	.28	.28	.34	.39	.43	.37	.36	.85
of which: Short-term..........................	8 742 ..	....	....	....	....	....	....	....	....
Banks..	8 743 ..	....	....	....	....	....	....	....	....
of which: Short-term..........................	8 745 ..	....	....	....	....	....	....	....	....
Other sectors......................................	8 746 ..	31.03	21.81	21.99	32.86	36.61	42.96	54.83	70.49
of which: Short-term..........................	8 748 ..	*31.03*	*21.81*	*21.99*	*32.86*	*36.61*	*42.73*	*54.67*	*70.32*
Reserve assets.....................................	8 802 ..	**53.47**	**51.68**	**61.32**	**69.55**	**74.63**	**57.66**	**64.47**	**74.16**
Monetary gold......................................	8 812 ..	21.22	19.66	21.16	21.93	19.12	21.34	26.40	30.90
Special drawing rights...............................	8 811 ..	.16	.28	.07	.04	.07	.06	.27	.25
Reserve position in the Fund........................	8 810 ..	1.26	1.58	1.92	2.06	1.79	.82	.45	.36
Foreign exchange...................................	8 803 ..	30.83	30.16	38.18	45.53	53.65	35.45	37.33	42.66
Other claims.......................................	8 813 ..	....	....	....	....	....	....	....	....

Table 3 (Concluded). INTERNATIONAL INVESTMENT POSITION (End-period stocks), 2000–2007

(Billions of U.S. dollars)

	Code	2000	2001	2002	2003	2004	2005	2006	2007
LIABILITIES	8 995 D.	**1,080.81**	**1,002.59**	**1,131.92**	**1,340.11**	**1,524.34**	**1,677.83**	**2,020.69**	**2,535.94**
Direct investment in Switzerland	8 555 ..	**101.71**	**103.92**	**143.91**	**184.55**	**223.04**	**193.52**	**243.40**	**305.67**
Equity capital and reinvested earnings	8 556 ..	100.17	103.82	141.09	175.31	218.98	192.03	239.95	301.39
Claims on direct investors	8 557 ..	....	....	....	....	....	....	....	....
Liabilities to direct investors	8 558 ..	100.17	103.82	141.09	175.31	218.98	192.03	239.95	301.39
Other capital	8 580 ..	1.53	.10	2.81	9.23	4.06	1.50	3.45	4.29
Claims on direct investors	8 585 ..	−6.25	−8.27	−8.80	−14.27	−22.18	−21.92	−28.98	−34.76
Liabilities to direct investors	8 590 ..	7.78	8.36	11.61	23.51	26.24	23.41	32.43	39.04
Portfolio investment	8 652 ..	**410.24**	**349.71**	**350.20**	**450.15**	**520.92**	**599.65**	**762.22**	**801.49**
Equity securities	8 660 ..	382.04	321.68	314.77	402.62	456.67	536.49	684.25	725.64
Banks	8 663 ..	....	....	....	....	....	....	....	....
Other sectors	8 664 ..	382.04	321.68	314.77	402.62	456.67	536.49	684.25	725.64
Debt securities	8 669 ..	28.20	28.03	35.43	47.53	64.26	63.16	77.97	75.85
Bonds and notes	8 670 ..	27.63	27.68	34.49	46.63	63.10	62.12	76.55	74.17
Monetary authorities	8 671 ..	....	....	....	....	....	....	....	....
General government	8 672 ..	5.09	6.38	8.99	16.22	26.97	37.40	48.80	42.83
Banks	8 673 ..	....	....	....	....	....	....	....	....
Other sectors	8 674 ..	22.53	21.31	25.50	30.41	36.14	24.71	27.75	31.34
Money market instruments	8 680 ..	.58	.35	.94	.90	1.15	1.05	1.42	1.68
Monetary authorities	8 681 ..	....	....	....	....	....	....	....	....
General government	8 682 ..	....	....	....	....	....	....	....	....
Banks	8 683 ..	....	....	....	....	....	....	....	....
Other sectors	8 684 ..	.58	.35	.94	.90	1.15	1.05	1.42	1.68
Financial derivatives	8 905 ..	....	....	....	....	....	**45.96**	**58.13**	**67.47**
Monetary authorities	8 906 ..	....	....	....	....	....	....	....	....
General government	8 907 ..	....	....	....	....	....	....	....	....
Banks	8 908 ..	....	....	....	....	....	27.80	33.40	49.69
Other sectors	8 909 ..	....	....	....	....	....	18.16	24.73	17.78
Other investment	8 753 ..	**568.87**	**548.96**	**637.81**	**705.41**	**780.38**	**838.69**	**956.93**	**1,361.31**
Trade credits	8 756 ..	....	....	....	....	....	....	....	....
General government	8 757 ..	....	....	....	....	....	....	....	....
of which: Short-term	8 759 ..	....	....	....	....	....	....	....	....
Other sectors	8 760 ..	....	....	....	....	....	....	....	....
of which: Short-term	8 762 ..	....	....	....	....	....	....	....	....
Loans	8 764 ..	430.71	411.45	480.65	518.38	570.21	633.40	712.13	1,060.25
Monetary authorities	8 765 ..	....	....	....	....	....	....	....	....
of which: Use of Fund credit and loans from the Fund	8 766 ..	....	....	....	....	....	....	....	....
of which: Short-term	8 768 ..	....	....	....	....	....	....	....	....
General government	8 769 ..	.41	.38	.62	.46	.71	.72	1.20	1.56
of which: Short-term	8 771 ..	*.41*	*.38*	*.62*	*.46*	*.71*	*.72*	*1.20*	*1.56*
Banks	8 772 ..	375.44	351.11	407.17	433.06	475.98	504.11	564.13	856.28
of which: Short-term	8 774 ..	*357.00*	*342.04*	*396.83*	*417.45*	*459.53*	*491.82*	*545.80*	*837.07*
Other sectors	8 775 ..	54.86	59.95	72.86	84.86	93.52	128.57	146.80	202.42
of which: Short-term	8 777 ..	*24.84*	*25.22*	*33.71*	*35.21*	*41.88*	*64.78*	*75.93*	*122.39*
Currency and deposits	8 780 ..	51.72	53.44	67.10	89.90	99.91	94.04	104.44	125.08
Monetary authorities	8 781 ..	4.13	6.42	6.76	7.75	8.10	7.57	8.21	14.34
General government	8 782 ..	....	....	....	....	....	....	....	....
Banks	8 783 ..	46.76	46.53	60.00	81.56	91.28	85.97	94.61	107.56
Other sectors	8 784 ..	.83	.49	.35	.59	.53	.50	1.62	3.19
Other liabilities	8 786 ..	86.43	84.07	90.06	97.14	110.26	111.26	140.36	175.97
Monetary authorities	8 787 ..	....	....	....	....	....	....	....	....
of which: Short-term	8 789 ..	....	....	....	....	....	....	....	....
General government	8 790 ..	....	....	....	....	....	....	....	....
of which: Short-term	8 792 ..	....	....	....	....	....	....	....	....
Banks	8 793 ..	.90	1.07	1.69	1.47	.85	1.13	2.06	3.00
of which: Short-term	8 795 ..	*.90*	*1.07*	*1.69*	*1.47*	*.85*	*1.13*	*2.06*	*3.00*
Other sectors	8 796 ..	85.53	83.00	88.37	95.67	109.42	110.13	138.30	172.97
of which: Short-term	8 798 ..	*52.91*	*50.20*	*50.11*	*50.39*	*58.51*	*65.08*	*88.47*	*113.68*
NET INTERNATIONAL INVESTMENT POSITION	8 995 ..	**285.10**	**320.07**	**385.40**	**430.42**	**472.79**	**427.36**	**451.61**	**628.78**
Conversion rates: Swiss francs per U.S. dollar (end of period)	0 102 ..	**1.6365**	**1.6773**	**1.3868**	**1.2369**	**1.1316**	**1.3143**	**1.2203**	**1.1255**

Table 1. ANALYTIC PRESENTATION, 2000–2007

(Millions of U.S. dollars)

	Code	2000	2001	2002	2003	2004	2005	2006	2007
A. Current Account[1]............................	4 993 Z.	**1,061**	**1,221**	**1,440**	**728**	**587**	**295**	**890**	....
Goods: exports f.o.b.........................	2 100 ..	5,146	5,706	6,668	5,762	7,220	8,602	10,245	....
Goods: imports f.o.b.........................	3 100 ..	−3,723	−4,282	−4,458	−4,430	−6,957	−8,742	−9,359	....
Balance on Goods..........................	4 100 ..	*1,423*	*1,424*	*2,210*	*1,332*	*263*	*−140*	*886*	....
Services: credit...............................	2 200 ..	1,699	1,781	1,559	1,331	2,613	2,910	2,924	....
Services: debit...............................	3 200 ..	−1,667	−1,694	−1,883	−1,806	−2,235	−2,359	−2,520	....
Balance on Goods and Services.........	4 991 ..	*1,455*	*1,511*	*1,886*	*857*	*642*	*411*	*1,290*	....
Income: credit................................	2 300 ..	345	379	250	282	385	395	428	....
Income: debit................................	3 300 ..	−1,224	−1,162	−1,175	−1,139	−1,114	−1,258	−1,363	....
Balance on Goods, Services, and Income..........	4 992 ..	*576*	*728*	*961*	....	*−88*	*−452*	*355*	....
Current transfers: credit....................	2 379 Z.	495	512	499	743	690	763	770	....
Current transfers: debit....................	3 379 ..	−10	−19	−20	−15	−16	−16	−235	....
B. Capital Account[1].............................	4 994 Z.	**63**	**17**	**20**	**20**	**18**	**18**	**18**	....
Capital account: credit.....................	2 994 Z.	63	17	20	20	20	20	20	....
Capital account: debit.....................	3 994 ..	....	....	....	....	−2	−2	−2	....
Total, Groups A Plus B....................	4 981 ..	*1,124*	*1,238*	*1,460*	*748*	*605*	*313*	*908*	....
C. Financial Account[1]........................	4 995 W.	**−139**	**−244**	**−250**	**−436**	**−97**	**−162**	**−1,052**	....
Direct investment abroad...................	4 505 ..	....	....	....	....	....	....	....	....
Direct investment in Syrian Arab Republic..........	4 555 Z.	270	110	115	160	275	500	600	....
Portfolio investment assets................	4 602 ..	....	....	....	....	....	....	....	....
Equity securities..........................	4 610 ..	....	....	....	....	....	....	....	....
Debt securities...........................	4 619 ..	....	....	....	....	....	....	....	....
Portfolio investment liabilities............	4 652 Z.	....	....	....	....	....	....	....	....
Equity securities..........................	4 660 ..	....	....	....	....	....	....	....	....
Debt securities...........................	4 669 Z.	....	....	....	....	....	....	....	....
Financial derivatives.......................	4 910 ..	....	....	....	....	....	....	....	....
Financial derivatives assets...............	4 900 ..	....	....	....	....	....	....	....	....
Financial derivatives liabilities...........	4 905 ..	....	....	....	....	....	....	....	....
Other investment assets...................	4 703 ..	1,206	1,136	1,180	1,210	−237	−524	−733	....
Monetary authorities.....................	4 701 ..	....	....	....	....	....	....	....	....
General government......................	4 704 ..	....	....	....	....	....	....	....	....
Banks.....................................	4 705 ..	1,206	1,136	1,180	1,210	−237	−524	−733	....
Other sectors.............................	4 728 ..	....	....	....	....	....	....	....	....
Other investment liabilities...............	4 753 W.	−1,615	−1,490	−1,545	−1,806	−135	−138	−919	....
Monetary authorities.....................	4 753 WA	....	....	....	....	....	....	....	....
General government......................	4 753 ZB	....	....	....	2	−235	−388	−479	....
Banks.....................................	4 753 ZC	−1,615	−1,490	−1,545	−1,508	....	....	....	....
Other sectors.............................	4 753 ZD	....	....	....	−300	100	250	−440	....
Total, Groups A Through C................	4 983 ..	*985*	*994*	*1,210*	*312*	*508*	*151*	*−144*	....
D. Net Errors and Omissions..................	4 998 ..	**−171**	**26**	**−160**	**383**	**−256**	**−137**	**−588**	....
Total, Groups A Through D................	4 984 ..	*814*	*1,020*	*1,050*	*695*	*251*	*14*	*−732*	....
E. Reserves and Related Items................	4 802 A.	**−814**	**−1,020**	**−1,050**	**−695**	**−251**	**−14**	**732**	....
Reserve assets..............................	4 802 ..	−814	−1,020	−1,050	−719	−256	−18	702	....
Use of Fund credit and loans.............	4 766 ..	....	....	....	....	....	....	....	....
Exceptional financing......................	4 920 ..	....	....	....	24	5	4	30	....
Conversion rates: Syrian pounds per U.S. dollar....	0 101 ..	**11.225**	**11.225**	**11.225**	**11.225**	**11.225**	**11.225**	**11.225**	....

[1] Excludes components that have been classified in the categories of Group E.

Table 2. STANDARD PRESENTATION, 2000–2007

(Millions of U.S. dollars)

	Code	2000	2001	2002	2003	2004	2005	2006	2007
CURRENT ACCOUNT	4 993	**1,061**	**1,221**	**1,440**	**752**	**592**	**299**	**920**	....
A. GOODS	4 100	**1,423**	**1,424**	**2,210**	**1,332**	**263**	**−140**	**886**	....
Credit	2 100	**5,146**	**5,706**	**6,668**	**5,762**	**7,220**	**8,602**	**10,245**	....
General merchandise: exports f.o.b.	2 110	5,146	5,706	6,668	5,680	7,220	8,602	10,245	....
Goods for processing: exports f.o.b.	2 150	....	....	....	70	....	....	....	....
Repairs on goods	2 160	....	....	....	....	....	....	....	....
Goods procured in ports by carriers	2 170	....	....	....	12	....	....	....	....
Nonmonetary gold	2 180	....	....	....	....	....	....	....	....
Debit	3 100	**−3,723**	**−4,282**	**−4,458**	**−4,430**	**−6,957**	**−8,742**	**−9,359**	....
General merchandise: imports f.o.b.	3 110	−3,723	−4,282	−4,458	−4,363	−6,957	−8,742	−9,359	....
Goods for processing: imports f.o.b.	3 150	....	....	....	−48	....	....	....	....
Repairs on goods	3 160	....	....	....	....	....	....	....	....
Goods procured in ports by carriers	3 170	....	....	....	−19	....	....	....	....
Nonmonetary gold	3 180	....	....	....	....	....	....	....	....
B. SERVICES	4 200	**32**	**87**	**−324**	**−475**	**378**	**551**	**404**	....
Total credit	2 200	*1,699*	*1,781*	*1,559*	*1,331*	*2,613*	*2,910*	*2,924*	....
Total debit	3 200	*−1,667*	*−1,694*	*−1,883*	*−1,806*	*−2,235*	*−2,359*	*−2,520*	....
Transportation services, credit	2 205	**245**	**255**	**250**	**198**	**198**	**218**	**217**	....
Passenger	2 850	....	....	....	*104*	*83*	*91*	*88*	....
Freight	2 851	*245*	*255*	*250*	*66*	*24*	*29*	*35*	....
Other	2 852	....	....	....	*28*	*91*	*98*	*94*	....
Sea transport, passenger	2 207	....	....	....	9	8	9	6	....
Sea transport, freight	2 208	....	....	....	16	....	....	2	....
Sea transport, other	2 209	....	....	....	....	48	53	49	....
Air transport, passenger	2 211	....	....	....	95	70	75	80	....
Air transport, freight	2 212	....	....	....	22	17	20	20	....
Air transport, other	2 213	....	....	....	21	43	45	45	....
Other transport, passenger	2 215	....	....	....	....	5	7	2	....
Other transport, freight	2 216	....	....	....	28	7	9	13	....
Other transport, other	2 217	....	....	....	7	....	....	....	....
Transportation services, debit	3 205	**−698**	**−717**	**−790**	**−813**	**−1,120**	**−1,401**	**−1,255**	....
Passenger	3 850	....	....	....	*−34*	*−38*	*−34*	*−45*	....
Freight	3 851	*−698*	*−717*	*−790*	*−739*	*−1,031*	*−1,264*	*−1,099*	....
Other	3 852	....	....	....	*−40*	*−51*	*−103*	*−111*	....
Sea transport, passenger	3 207	....	....	....	−7	....	....	....	....
Sea transport, freight	3 208	....	....	....	−579	−909	−1,147	−943	....
Sea transport, other	3 209	....	....	....	....	....	−1	−1	....
Air transport, passenger	3 211	....	....	....	−27	−28	−25	−30	....
Air transport, freight	3 212	....	....	....	−123	−120	−115	−150	....
Air transport, other	3 213	....	....	....	−35	−51	−102	−110	....
Other transport, passenger	3 215	....	....	....	....	−10	−9	−15	....
Other transport, freight	3 216	....	....	....	−37	−2	−2	−6	....
Other transport, other	3 217	....	....	....	−5	....	....	....	....
Travel, credit	2 236	**1,082**	**1,150**	**970**	**773**	**1,800**	**1,944**	**2,025**	....
Business travel	2 237	....	....	....	....	....	....	....	....
Personal travel	2 240	....	....	....	773	1,800	1,944	2,025	....
Travel, debit	3 236	**−669**	**−670**	**−760**	**−700**	**−650**	**−550**	**−540**	....
Business travel	3 237	....	....	....	....	....	....	....	....
Personal travel	3 240	....	....	....	−700	−650	−550	−540	....
Other services, credit	2 200 BA	**372**	**376**	**339**	**360**	**615**	**748**	**682**	....
Communications	2 245	....	....	....	40	65	125	120	....
Construction	2 249	....	....	....	2	58	14	....	....
Insurance	2 253	....	....	....	1	....	....	10	....
Financial	2 260	....	....	....	22	26	28	54	....
Computer and information	2 262	....	....	....	50	50	60	50	....
Royalties and licence fees	2 266	....	....	....	....	....	....	....	....
Other business services	2 268	153	161	127	95	84	86	81	....
Personal, cultural, and recreational	2 287	....	....	....	....	62	85	92	....
Government, n.i.e.	2 291	219	215	212	150	270	350	275	....
Other services, debit	3 200 BA	**−300**	**−307**	**−333**	**−293**	**−465**	**−408**	**−725**	....
Communications	3 245	....	....	....	−5	−10	−17	−30	....
Construction	3 249	....	....	....	....	....	....	....	....
Insurance	3 253	....	....	....	−15	−31	−35	−331	....
Financial	3 260	....	....	....	−18	−33	−38	−39	....
Computer and information	3 262	....	....	....	−110	−100	−100	−95	....
Royalties and licence fees	3 266	....	....	....	−10	−10	−12	−20	....
Other business services	3 268	−101	−107	−125	−26	−90	−100	−95	....
Personal, cultural, and recreational	3 287	....	....	....	....	−27	−21	−32	....
Government, n.i.e.	3 291	−199	−200	−208	−109	−164	−85	−83	....

Table 2 (Continued). STANDARD PRESENTATION, 2000–2007

(Millions of U.S. dollars)

	Code	2000	2001	2002	2003	2004	2005	2006	2007
C. INCOME	4 300	**−879**	**−783**	**−925**	**−857**	**−729**	**−863**	**−935**	....
Total credit	2 300	*345*	*379*	*250*	*282*	*385*	*395*	*428*	....
Total debit	3 300	*−1,224*	*−1,162*	*−1,175*	*−1,139*	*−1,114*	*−1,258*	*−1,363*	....
Compensation of employees, credit	2 310	**180**	**170**	**135**	**146**	**165**	**60**	**25**	....
Compensation of employees, debit	3 310	**−29**	**−30**	**−35**	**−40**	**−41**	**−38**	**−75**	....
Investment income, credit	2 320	**165**	**209**	**115**	**136**	**220**	**335**	**403**	....
Direct investment income	2 330	....	....	....	....	220	330	398	....
Dividends and distributed branch profits	2 332	....	....	....	....	....	....	....	....
Reinvested earnings and undistributed branch profits	2 333	....	....	....	....	....	....	....	....
Income on debt (interest)	2 334	....	....	....	....	220	330	398	....
Portfolio investment income	2 339	....	....	....	....	....	5	5	....
Income on equity	2 340	....	....	....	....	....	5	5	....
Income on bonds and notes	2 350	....	....	....	....	....	....	....	....
Income on money market instruments	2 360	....	....	....	....	....	....	....	....
Other investment income	2 370	165	209	115	136	....	....	....	....
Investment income, debit	3 320	**−1,195**	**−1,132**	**−1,140**	**−1,099**	**−1,073**	**−1,220**	**−1,288**	....
Direct investment income	3 330	....	....	....	....	−1,073	−1,220	−1,288	....
Dividends and distributed branch profits	3 332	....	....	....	....	−931	−1,088	−1,165	....
Reinvested earnings and undistributed branch profits	3 333	....	....	....	....	....	....	....	....
Income on debt (interest)	3 334	....	....	....	....	−142	−132	−123	....
Portfolio investment income	3 339	....	....	....	....	....	....	....	....
Income on equity	3 340	....	....	....	....	....	....	....	....
Income on bonds and notes	3 350	....	....	....	....	....	....	....	....
Income on money market instruments	3 360	....	....	....	....	....	....	....	....
Other investment income	3 370	−1,195	−1,132	−1,140	−1,099	....	....	....	....
D. CURRENT TRANSFERS	4 379	**485**	**493**	**479**	**752**	**679**	**751**	**565**	....
Credit	2 379	**495**	**512**	**499**	**767**	**695**	**767**	**800**	....
General government	2 380	19	29	24	24	5	4	30	....
Other sectors	2 390	476	483	475	743	690	763	770	....
Workers' remittances	2 391	....	....	....	743	690	763	770	....
Other current transfers	2 392	476	483	475	....	....	....	....	....
Debit	3 379	**−10**	**−19**	**−20**	**−15**	**−16**	**−16**	**−235**	....
General government	3 380	−10	−19	−20	−15	−15	−14	−75	....
Other sectors	3 390	....	....	....	....	−1	−2	−160	....
Workers' remittances	3 391	....	....	....	....	−1	−2	−160	....
Other current transfers	3 392	....	....	....	....	....	....	....	....
CAPITAL AND FINANCIAL ACCOUNT	4 996	**−890**	**−1,247**	**−1,280**	**−1,135**	**−335**	**−162**	**−332**	....
CAPITAL ACCOUNT	4 994	**63**	**17**	**20**	**20**	**18**	**18**	**18**	....
Total credit	2 994	*63*	*17*	*20*	*20*	*20*	*20*	*20*	....
Total debit	3 994	....	....	....	....	*−2*	*−2*	*−2*	....
Capital transfers, credit	2 400	**63**	**17**	**20**	**20**	**20**	**20**	**20**	....
General government	2 401	....	....	....	20	20	20	20	....
Debt forgiveness	2 402	....	....	....	20	20	....	....	....
Other capital transfers	2 410	....	....	....	....	....	....	....	....
Other sectors	2 430	63	17	20	....	....	....	....	....
Migrants' transfers	2 431	....	....	....	....	....	....	....	....
Debt forgiveness	2 432	....	....	....	....	....	....	....	....
Other capital transfers	2 440	63	17	20	....	....	....	....	....
Capital transfers, debit	3 400	....	....	....	....	**−2**	**−2**	**−2**	....
General government	3 401	....	....	....	....	−2	−2	−2	....
Debt forgiveness	3 402	....	....	....	....	....	....	....	....
Other capital transfers	3 410	....	....	....	....	−2	....	....	....
Other sectors	3 430	....	....	....	....	....	....	....	....
Migrants' transfers	3 431	....	....	....	....	....	....	....	....
Debt forgiveness	3 432	....	....	....	....	....	....	....	....
Other capital transfers	3 440	....	....	....	....	....	....	....	....
Nonproduced nonfinancial assets, credit	2 480	....	....	....	....	....	....	....	....
Nonproduced nonfinancial assets, debit	3 480	....	....	....	....	....	....	....	....

Table 2 (Continued). STANDARD PRESENTATION, 2000–2007

(Millions of U.S. dollars)

	Code	2000	2001	2002	2003	2004	2005	2006	2007
FINANCIAL ACCOUNT...	4 995 ..	**−953**	**−1,264**	**−1,300**	**−1,155**	**−353**	**−180**	**−350**	....
A. DIRECT INVESTMENT..	4 500 ..	**270**	**110**	**115**	**160**	**275**	**500**	**600**	....
Direct investment abroad..................................	4 505 ..	....	....	....	....	....	....	....	....
Equity capital..	4 510 ..	....	....	....	....	....	....	....	....
Claims on affiliated enterprises......................	4 515 ..	....	....	....	....	....	....	....	....
Liabilities to affiliated enterprises.................	4 520 ..	....	....	....	....	....	....	....	....
Reinvested earnings..	4 525 ..	....	....	....	....	....	....	....	....
Other capital..	4 530 ..	....	....	....	....	....	....	....	....
Claims on affiliated enterprises......................	4 535 ..	....	....	....	....	....	....	....	....
Liabilities to affiliated enterprises.................	4 540 ..	....	....	....	....	....	....	....	....
Direct investment in Syrian Arab Republic.........	4 555 ..	**270**	**110**	**115**	**160**	**275**	**500**	**600**	....
Equity capital..	4 560 ..	270	110	115	160	275	500	600	....
Claims on direct investors.............................	4 565 ..	....	....	....	....	275	500	600	....
Liabilities to direct investors........................	4 570 ..	270	110	115	160	....	....	....	....
Reinvested earnings..	4 575 ..	....	....	....	....	....	....	....	....
Other capital..	4 580 ..	....	....	....	....	....	....	....	....
Claims on direct investors.............................	4 585 ..	....	....	....	....	....	....	....	....
Liabilities to direct investors........................	4 590 ..	....	....	....	....	....	....	....	....
B. PORTFOLIO INVESTMENT................................	4 600 ..	....	....	....	....	....	....	....	....
Assets..	4 602 ..	....	....	....	....	....	....	....	....
Equity securities...	4 610 ..	....	....	....	....	....	....	....	....
Monetary authorities.....................................	4 611 ..	....	....	....	....	....	....	....	....
General government......................................	4 612 ..	....	....	....	....	....	....	....	....
Banks..	4 613 ..	....	....	....	....	....	....	....	....
Other sectors..	4 614 ..	....	....	....	....	....	....	....	....
Debt securities...	4 619 ..	....	....	....	....	....	....	....	....
Bonds and notes..	4 620 ..	....	....	....	....	....	....	....	....
Monetary authorities.....................................	4 621 ..	....	....	....	....	....	....	....	....
General government......................................	4 622 ..	....	....	....	....	....	....	....	....
Banks..	4 623 ..	....	....	....	....	....	....	....	....
Other sectors..	4 624 ..	....	....	....	....	....	....	....	....
Money market instruments............................	4 630 ..	....	....	....	....	....	....	....	....
Monetary authorities.....................................	4 631 ..	....	....	....	....	....	....	....	....
General government......................................	4 632 ..	....	....	....	....	....	....	....	....
Banks..	4 633 ..	....	....	....	....	....	....	....	....
Other sectors..	4 634 ..	....	....	....	....	....	....	....	....
Liabilities..	4 652 ..	....	....	....	....	....	....	....	....
Equity securities...	4 660 ..	....	....	....	....	....	....	....	....
Banks..	4 663 ..	....	....	....	....	....	....	....	....
Other sectors..	4 664 ..	....	....	....	....	....	....	....	....
Debt securities...	4 669 ..	....	....	....	....	....	....	....	....
Bonds and notes..	4 670 ..	....	....	....	....	....	....	....	....
Monetary authorities.....................................	4 671 ..	....	....	....	....	....	....	....	....
General government......................................	4 672 ..	....	....	....	....	....	....	....	....
Banks..	4 673 ..	....	....	....	....	....	....	....	....
Other sectors..	4 674 ..	....	....	....	....	....	....	....	....
Money market instruments............................	4 680 ..	....	....	....	....	....	....	....	....
Monetary authorities.....................................	4 681 ..	....	....	....	....	....	....	....	....
General government......................................	4 682 ..	....	....	....	....	....	....	....	....
Banks..	4 683 ..	....	....	....	....	....	....	....	....
Other sectors..	4 684 ..	....	....	....	....	....	....	....	....
C. FINANCIAL DERIVATIVES................................	4 910 ..	....	....	....	....	....	....	....	....
Monetary authorities...	4 911 ..	....	....	....	....	....	....	....	....
General government..	4 912 ..	....	....	....	....	....	....	....	....
Banks..	4 913 ..	....	....	....	....	....	....	....	....
Other sectors..	4 914 ..	....	....	....	....	....	....	....	....
Assets..	4 900 ..	....	....	....	....	....	....	....	....
Monetary authorities.....................................	4 901 ..	....	....	....	....	....	....	....	....
General government......................................	4 902 ..	....	....	....	....	....	....	....	....
Banks..	4 903 ..	....	....	....	....	....	....	....	....
Other sectors..	4 904 ..	....	....	....	....	....	....	....	....
Liabilities..	4 905 ..	....	....	....	....	....	....	....	....
Monetary authorities.....................................	4 906 ..	....	....	....	....	....	....	....	....
General government......................................	4 907 ..	....	....	....	....	....	....	....	....
Banks..	4 908 ..	....	....	....	....	....	....	....	....
Other sectors..	4 909 ..	....	....	....	....	....	....	....	....

Table 2 (Concluded). STANDARD PRESENTATION, 2000–2007

(Millions of U.S. dollars)

	Code	2000	2001	2002	2003	2004	2005	2006	2007
D. OTHER INVESTMENT	4 700	−409	−354	−365	−596	−372	−662	−1,652	....
Assets	4 703	1,206	1,136	1,180	1,210	−237	−524	−733	....
Trade credits	4 706	....	....	....	....	....	....	....	....
General government	4 707	....	....	....	....	....	....	....	....
of which: Short-term	4 709	....	....	....	....	....	....	....	....
Other sectors	4 710	....	....	....	....	....	....	....	....
of which: Short-term	4 712	....	....	....	....	....	....	....	....
Loans	4 714	....	....	....	....	....	....	....	....
Monetary authorities	4 715	....	....	....	....	....	....	....	....
of which: Short-term	4 718	....	....	....	....	....	....	....	....
General government	4 719	....	....	....	....	....	....	....	....
of which: Short-term	4 721	....	....	....	....	....	....	....	....
Banks	4 722	....	....	....	....	....	....	....	....
of which: Short-term	4 724	....	....	....	....	....	....	....	....
Other sectors	4 725	....	....	....	....	....	....	....	....
of which: Short-term	4 727	....	....	....	....	....	....	....	....
Currency and deposits	4 730	....	....	....	....	−237	−524	−733	....
Monetary authorities	4 731	....	....	....	....	....	....	....	....
General government	4 732	....	....	....	....	....	....	....	....
Banks	4 733	....	....	....	....	−237	−524	−733	....
Other sectors	4 734	....	....	....	....	....	....	....	....
Other assets	4 736	1,206	1,136	1,180	1,210	....	....	....	....
Monetary authorities	4 737	....	....	....	....	....	....	....	....
of which: Short-term	4 739	....	....	....	....	....	....	....	....
General government	4 740	....	....	....	....	....	....	....	....
of which: Short-term	4 742	....	....	....	....	....	....	....	....
Banks	4 743	1,206	1,136	1,180	1,210	....	....	....	....
of which: Short-term	4 745	*945*	*970*	*985*	....	....	....	....	....
Other sectors	4 746	....	....	....	....	....	....	....	....
of which: Short-term	4 748	....	....	....	....	....	....	....	....
Liabilities	4 753	−1,615	−1,490	−1,545	−1,806	−135	−138	−919	....
Trade credits	4 756	....	....	....	−300	52	335	−505	....
General government	4 757	....	....	....	....	−48	85	−65	....
of which: Short-term	4 759	....	....	....	....	....	....	....	....
Other sectors	4 760	....	....	....	−300	100	250	−440	....
of which: Short-term	4 762	....	....	....	*−300*	*100*	*250*	*−440*	....
Loans	4 764	....	....	....	2	−187	−473	−414	....
Monetary authorities	4 765	....	....	....	....	....	....	....	....
of which: Use of Fund credit and loans from the Fund	4 766	....	....	....	....	....	....	....	....
of which: Short-term	4 768	....	....	....	....	....	....	....	....
General government	4 769	....	....	....	2	−187	−473	−414	....
of which: Short-term	4 771	....	....	....	....	....	....	....	....
Banks	4 772	....	....	....	....	....	....	....	....
of which: Short-term	4 774	....	....	....	....	....	....	....	....
Other sectors	4 775	....	....	....	....	....	....	....	....
of which: Short-term	4 777	....	....	....	....	....	....	....	....
Currency and deposits	4 780	....	....	....	....	....	....	....	....
Monetary authorities	4 781	....	....	....	....	....	....	....	....
General government	4 782	....	....	....	....	....	....	....	....
Banks	4 783	....	....	....	....	....	....	....	....
Other sectors	4 784	....	....	....	....	....	....	....	....
Other liabilities	4 786	−1,615	−1,490	−1,545	−1,508	....	....	....	....
Monetary authorities	4 787	....	....	....	....	....	....	....	....
of which: Short-term	4 789	....	....	....	....	....	....	....	....
General government	4 790	....	....	....	....	....	....	....	....
of which: Short-term	4 792	....	....	....	....	....	....	....	....
Banks	4 793	−1,615	−1,490	−1,545	−1,508	....	....	....	....
of which: Short-term	4 795	*−1,200*	*−1,150*	*−1,225*	....	....	....	....	....
Other sectors	4 796	....	....	....	....	....	....	....	....
of which: Short-term	4 798	....	....	....	....	....	....	....	....
E. RESERVE ASSETS	4 802	−814	−1,020	−1,050	−719	−256	−18	702	....
Monetary gold	4 812	....	....	....	....	....	....	....	....
Special drawing rights	4 811	....	....	....	....	−54	....	....	....
Reserve position in the Fund	4 810	....	....	....	....	....	....	....	....
Foreign exchange	4 803	−814	−1,020	−1,050	−719	−202	−18	702	....
Other claims	4 813	....	....	....	....	....	....	....	....
NET ERRORS AND OMISSIONS	4 998	−171	26	−160	383	−256	−137	−588	....

Table 1. ANALYTIC PRESENTATION, 2000–2007

(Millions of U.S. dollars)

	Code	2000	2001	2002	2003	2004	2005	2006	2007
A. Current Account[1].........	4 993 Z.	....	....	**−15.1**	**−4.8**	**−57.0**	**−18.9**	**−21.4**	**−495.1**
Goods: exports f.o.b..........	2 100 ..	....	....	699.1	906.2	1,096.9	1,108.1	1,511.8	1,556.9
Goods: imports f.o.b..........	3 100 ..	....	....	−822.9	−1,025.7	−1,232.4	−1,430.9	−1,954.6	−3,115.0
Balance on Goods..........	4 100 ..	....	....	*−123.8*	*−119.5*	*−135.5*	*−322.8*	*−442.8*	*−1,558.1*
Services: credit..........	2 200 ..	....	....	69.0	88.5	122.9	146.3	134.2	148.7
Services: debit..........	3 200 ..	....	....	−104.9	−121.5	−212.5	−251.5	−394.5	−592.1
Balance on Goods and Services..........	4 991 ..	....	....	*−159.6*	*−152.5*	*−225.1*	*−428.0*	*−703.1*	*−2,001.5*
Income: credit..........	2 300 ..	....	....	1.2	.9	1.7	9.6	12.4	22.4
Income: debit..........	3 300 ..	....	....	−42.4	−71.2	−59.2	−50.4	−76.4	−73.2
Balance on Goods, Services, and Income..........	4 992 ..	....	....	*−200.8*	*−222.8*	*−282.7*	*−468.8*	*−767.0*	*−2,052.3*
Current transfers: credit..........	2 379 Z.	....	....	201.7	285.1	348.4	599.9	1,146.0	1,794.3
Current transfers: debit..........	3 379 ..	....	....	−16.1	−67.0	−122.8	−150.0	−400.4	−237.1
B. Capital Account[1].........	4 994 Z.	....	....	....	....	....	....	....	**32.8**
Capital account: credit..........	2 994 Z.	....	....	....	....	....	....	....	32.8
Capital account: debit..........	3 994 ..	....	....	....	....	....	....	....	....
Total, Groups A Plus B..........	4 981 ..	....	....	*−15.1*	*−4.8*	*−57.0*	*−18.9*	*−21.4*	*−462.2*
C. Financial Account[1].........	4 995 W.	....	....	**72.4**	**62.7**	**93.4**	**101.5**	**276.0**	**811.3**
Direct investment abroad..........	4 505 ..	....	....	....	....	....	....	....	....
Direct investment in Tajikistan..........	4 555 Z.	....	....	36.1	31.6	272.0	54.5	338.6	360.0
Portfolio investment assets..........	4 602 ..	....	....	....	....	....	....	....	....
Equity securities..........	4 610 ..	....	....	....	....	....	....	....	....
Debt securities..........	4 619 ..	....	....	....	....	....	....	....	....
Portfolio investment liabilities..........	4 652 Z.	....	....	1.5	.3	5.3	....	....	.2
Equity securities..........	4 660 ..	....	....	1.5	.3	....	....	....	....
Debt securities..........	4 669 Z.	....	....	....	....	5.3	....	....	.2
Financial derivatives..........	4 910 ..	....	....	....	....	....	....	....	....
Financial derivatives assets..........	4 900 ..	....	....	....	....	....	....	....	....
Financial derivatives liabilities..........	4 905 ..	....	....	....	....	....	....	....	....
Other investment assets..........	4 703 ..	....	....	−23.4	−15.6	−28.4	−71.3	−301.9	−386.7
Monetary authorities..........	4 701 ..	....	....	....	....	....	....	....	....
General government..........	4 704 ..	....	....	.2	−.4	−.4	−.5	−.5	−.2
Banks..........	4 705 ..	....	....	−6.6	−14.4	−7.3	−33.7	−233.5	−186.7
Other sectors..........	4 728 ..	....	....	−17.0	−.8	−20.6	−37.1	−67.9	−199.8
Other investment liabilities..........	4 753 W.	....	....	58.2	46.3	−155.5	118.3	239.2	837.8
Monetary authorities..........	4 753 WA	....	....	....	....	....	....	....	....
General government..........	4 753 ZB	....	....	−9.3	−2.1	−151.4	57.1	34.3	251.5
Banks..........	4 753 ZC	....	....	1.2	3.7	1.0	45.0	102.1	240.1
Other sectors..........	4 753 ZD	....	....	66.3	44.7	−5.1	16.1	102.7	346.2
Total, Groups A Through C..........	4 983 ..	....	....	*57.3*	*57.9*	*36.4*	*82.6*	*254.6*	*349.1*
D. Net Errors and Omissions..........	4 998 ..	....	....	**−55.6**	**−30.0**	**−32.5**	**−76.3**	**−264.7**	**−362.9**
Total, Groups A Through D..........	4 984 ..	....	....	*1.7*	*27.9*	*3.9*	*6.3*	*−10.1*	*−13.8*
E. Reserves and Related Items..........	4 802 A.	....	....	**−1.7**	**−27.9**	**−3.9**	**−6.3**	**10.1**	**13.8**
Reserve assets..........	4 802 ..	....	....	.1	−40.5	−46.4	−25.6	−7.1	11.5
Use of Fund credit and loans..........	4 766 ..	....	....	−24.0	−2.7	17.0	15.5	−85.7	....
Exceptional financing..........	4 920 ..	....	....	22.2	15.2	25.5	3.9	103.0	2.3
Conversion rates: somoni per U.S. dollar..........	0 101 ..	**2.0763**	**2.3722**	**2.7641**	**3.0614**	**2.9705**	**3.1166**	**3.2984**	**3.4425**

[1] Excludes components that have been classified in the categories of Group E.

Table 2. STANDARD PRESENTATION, 2000–2007

(Millions of U.S. dollars)

	Code	2000	2001	2002	2003	2004	2005	2006	2007
CURRENT ACCOUNT....................................	4 993 ..	. . . .	. . . .	−15.1	−4.8	−57.0	−18.9	−21.4	−495.1
A. GOODS...	4 100 ..	. . . .	. . . .	−123.8	−119.5	−135.5	−322.8	−442.8	−1,558.1
Credit..	2 100 ..	. . . .	. . . .	699.1	906.2	1,096.9	1,108.1	1,511.8	1,556.9
General merchandise: exports f.o.b..............	2 110 ..	. . . .	. . . .	676.5	881.6	1,073.2	1,086.5	1,490.0	1,533.7
Goods for processing: exports f.o.b..............	2 150 ..	. . . .	. . . .	. . . .	. . . .	. . . .	. . . .	. . . .	. . . .
Repairs on goods....................................	2 160 ..	. . . .	. . . .	. . . .	. . . .	. . . .	. . . .	. . . .	. . . .
Goods procured in ports by carriers..............	2 170 ..	. . . .	. . . .	2.1	.6	.5	. . . .	. . . .	. . . .
Nonmonetary gold..................................	2 180 ..	. . . .	. . . .	20.6	24.0	23.3	21.6	21.8	23.1
Debit..	3 100 ..	. . . .	. . . .	−822.9	−1,025.7	−1,232.4	−1,430.9	−1,954.6	−3,115.0
General merchandise: imports f.o.b..............	3 110 ..	. . . .	. . . .	−817.2	−1,019.2	−1,220.4	−1,415.5	−1,940.2	−3,097.2
Goods for processing: imports f.o.b..............	3 150 ..	. . . .	. . . .	. . . .	. . . .	. . . .	. . . .	. . . .	. . . .
Repairs on goods....................................	3 160 ..	. . . .	. . . .	. . . .	. . . .	. . . .	. . . .	. . . .	. . . .
Goods procured in ports by carriers..............	3 170 ..	. . . .	. . . .	−5.7	−6.6	−12.0	−15.4	−14.4	−17.8
Nonmonetary gold..................................	3 180 ..	. . . .	. . . .	. . . .	. . . .	. . . .	. . . .	. . . .	. . . .
B. SERVICES..	4 200 ..	. . . .	. . . .	−35.9	−33.0	−89.6	−105.2	−260.3	−443.4
Total credit..	2 200 ..	. . . .	. . . .	*69.0*	*88.5*	*122.9*	*146.3*	*134.2*	*148.7*
Total debit...	3 200 ..	. . . .	. . . .	*−104.9*	*−121.5*	*−212.5*	*−251.5*	*−394.5*	*−592.1*
Transportation services, credit....................	2 205 ..	. . . .	. . . .	45.6	49.0	52.3	55.9	61.8	62.8
Passenger...	2 850 ..	. . . .	. . . .	*3.4*	*4.7*	*8.4*	*7.5*	*9.1*	*13.2*
Freight..	2 851 ..	. . . .	. . . .	*41.9*	*43.5*	*43.7*	*48.2*	*52.7*	*49.1*
Other..	2 852 ..	. . . .	. . . .	*.3*	*.7*	*.2*	*.2*	. . . .	*.4*
Sea transport, passenger...........................	2 207 ..	. . . .	. . . .	. . . .	. . . .	. . . .	. . . .	. . . .	. . . .
Sea transport, freight..............................	2 208 ..	. . . .	. . . .	. . . .	. . . .	. . . .	. . . .	. . . .	. . . .
Sea transport, other................................	2 209 ..	. . . .	. . . .	. . . .	. . . .	. . . .	. . . .	. . . .	. . . .
Air transport, passenger...........................	2 211 ..	. . . .	. . . .	2.7	3.2	6.7	5.5	5.2	8.5
Air transport, freight..............................	2 212 ..	. . . .	. . . .	2.7	4.0	4.9	2.1	2.1	1.0
Air transport, other................................	2 213 ..	. . . .	. . . .	.3	.7	.2	.2	. . . .	.4
Other transport, passenger........................	2 215 ..	. . . .	. . . .	.6	1.5	1.8	2.1	3.9	4.7
Other transport, freight............................	2 216 ..	. . . .	. . . .	39.2	39.6	38.8	46.2	50.6	48.1
Other transport, other.............................	2 217 ..	. . . .	. . . .	. . . .	. . . .	. . . .	. . . .	. . . .	. . . .
Transportation services, debit....................	3 205 ..	. . . .	. . . .	−81.5	−95.0	−158.8	−178.6	−241.4	−142.2
Passenger...	3 850 ..	. . . .	. . . .	. . . .	. . . .	. . . .	. . . .	. . . .	. . . .
Freight..	3 851 ..	. . . .	. . . .	*−69.1*	*−85.5*	*−143.1*	*−166.1*	*−227.5*	*−112.5*
Other..	3 852 ..	. . . .	. . . .	*−12.4*	*−9.5*	*−15.7*	*−12.5*	*−13.9*	*−29.8*
Sea transport, passenger...........................	3 207 ..	. . . .	. . . .	. . . .	. . . .	. . . .	. . . .	. . . .	. . . .
Sea transport, freight..............................	3 208 ..	. . . .	. . . .	. . . .	. . . .	. . . .	. . . .	. . . .	. . . .
Sea transport, other................................	3 209 ..	. . . .	. . . .	. . . .	. . . .	. . . .	. . . .	. . . .	. . . .
Air transport, passenger...........................	3 211 ..	. . . .	. . . .	. . . .	. . . .	. . . .	. . . .	. . . .	. . . .
Air transport, freight..............................	3 212 ..	. . . .	. . . .	. . . .	. . . .	. . . .	−.1	. . . .	. . . .
Air transport, other................................	3 213 ..	. . . .	. . . .	−6.5	−6.5	−12.0	−8.7	−10.1	−22.7
Other transport, passenger........................	3 215 ..	. . . .	. . . .	. . . .	. . . .	. . . .	. . . .	. . . .	. . . .
Other transport, freight............................	3 216 ..	. . . .	. . . .	−69.1	−85.5	−143.1	−166.0	−227.5	−112.5
Other transport, other.............................	3 217 ..	. . . .	. . . .	−5.9	−3.0	−3.7	−3.9	−3.8	−7.1
Travel, credit......................................	2 236 ..	. . . .	. . . .	1.6	1.5	1.2	1.6	2.1	3.3
Business travel.......................................	2 237 ..	. . . .	. . . .	1.5	1.2	1.0	1.3	1.6	1.6
Personal travel.......................................	2 240 ..	. . . .	. . . .	.2	.3	.3	.3	.5	1.6
Travel, debit.......................................	3 236 ..	. . . .	. . . .	−1.7	−2.1	−3.4	−3.7	−6.0	−6.6
Business travel.......................................	3 237 ..	. . . .	. . . .	−.8	−1.1	−1.3	−1.7	−2.6	−1.6
Personal travel.......................................	3 240 ..	. . . .	. . . .	−1.0	−1.0	−2.2	−2.1	−3.4	−5.0
Other services, credit............................	2 200 BA	. . . .	. . . .	21.8	38.0	69.4	88.9	70.3	82.7
Communications.....................................	2 245 ..	. . . .	. . . .	6.6	10.4	12.6	13.5	16.2	18.4
Construction..	2 249 ..	. . . .	. . . .	1.0	.1	1.5	7.2	6.4	2.6
Insurance...	2 253 ..	. . . .	. . . .	. . . .	. . . .	. . . .	. . . .	.1	. . . .
Financial...	2 260 ..	. . . .	. . . .	1.2	1.7	4.3	8.3	8.8	12.5
Computer and information.........................	2 262 ..	. . . .	. . . .	. . . .	. . . .	. . . .	.1	.2	.4
Royalties and licence fees..........................	2 266 ..	. . . .	. . . .	.4	.9	1.3	1.2	.7	.9
Other business services............................	2 268 ..	. . . .	. . . .	3.9	2.3	7.6	15.0	13.9	15.7
Personal, cultural, and recreational..............	2 287 ..	. . . .	. . . .	. . . .	. . . .	. . . .	. . . .	. . . .	. . . .
Government, n.i.e..................................	2 291 ..	. . . .	. . . .	8.8	22.6	42.1	43.6	24.0	32.2
Other services, debit.............................	3 200 BA	. . . .	. . . .	−21.7	−24.4	−50.4	−69.2	−147.1	−443.3
Communications.....................................	3 245 ..	. . . .	. . . .	−2.5	−3.7	−4.5	−7.8	−14.0	−20.1
Construction..	3 249 ..	. . . .	. . . .	−4.7	−5.4	−9.8	−30.7	−77.1	−230.4
Insurance...	3 253 ..	. . . .	. . . .	−5.5	−7.1	−11.9	−13.8	−19.0	−16.0
Financial...	3 260 ..	. . . .	. . . .	−1.0	−1.9	−4.7	−4.1	−12.6	−11.5
Computer and information.........................	3 262 ..	. . . .	. . . .	−.1	−.3	−.6	−.9	−1.0	−4.3
Royalties and licence fees..........................	3 266 ..	. . . .	. . . .	−.8	−.2	−.1	−.3	−.1	−.8
Other business services............................	3 268 ..	. . . .	. . . .	−5.4	−4.0	−11.2	−10.3	−21.3	−158.0
Personal, cultural, and recreational..............	3 287 ..	. . . .	. . . .	. . . .	. . . .	. . . .	. . . .	. . . .	. . . .
Government, n.i.e..................................	3 291 ..	. . . .	. . . .	−1.7	−1.8	−7.5	−1.2	−2.0	−2.1

Table 2 (Continued). STANDARD PRESENTATION, 2000–2007

(Millions of U.S. dollars)

	Code	2000	2001	2002	2003	2004	2005	2006	2007
C. INCOME..	4 300 ..	....	....	**−41.1**	**−70.3**	**−57.5**	**−40.8**	**−63.9**	**−50.7**
Total credit..	2 300 ..	....	....	*1.2*	*.9*	*1.7*	*9.6*	*12.4*	*22.4*
Total debit...	3 300 ..	....	....	*−42.4*	*−71.2*	*−59.2*	*−50.4*	*−76.4*	*−73.2*
Compensation of employees, credit...........	2 310 ..	....	....	**.1**	....	....	**1.4**	**3.9**	**5.3**
Compensation of employees, debit...........	3 310 ..	....	....	**−.4**	**−.1**	**−.1**	**−1.3**	**−2.1**	**−3.7**
Investment income, credit......................	2 320 ..	....	....	**1.1**	**.9**	**1.7**	**8.1**	**8.6**	**17.1**
Direct investment income...............	2 330 ..	....	....	....	....	....	....	....	....
Dividends and distributed branch profits..........	2 332 ..	....	....	....	....	....	....	....	....
Reinvested earnings and undistributed branch profits.....	2 333 ..	....	....	....	....	....	....	....	....
Income on debt (interest)...............	2 334 ..	....	....	....	....	....	....	....	....
Portfolio investment income...............	2 339 ..	....	....	....	....	....	....	....	....
Income on equity...............	2 340 ..	....	....	....	....	....	....	....	....
Income on bonds and notes...............	2 350 ..	....	....	....	....	....	....	....	....
Income on money market instruments...............	2 360 ..	....	....	....	....	....	....	....	....
Other investment income...............	2 370 ..	....	....	1.1	.9	1.7	8.1	8.6	17.1
Investment income, debit.......................	3 320 ..	....	....	**−41.9**	**−71.2**	**−59.2**	**−49.1**	**−74.2**	**−69.5**
Direct investment income...............	3 330 ..	....	....	....	−.7	−1.3	−2.2	−46.1	−26.1
Dividends and distributed branch profits..........	3 332 ..	....	....	....	....	....	....	....	....
Reinvested earnings and undistributed branch profits.....	3 333 ..	....	....	....	....	....	....	....	....
Income on debt (interest)...............	3 334 ..	....	....	....	−.7	−1.3	−2.2	−46.1	−26.1
Portfolio investment income...............	3 339 ..	....	....	....	....	....	....	....	....
Income on equity...............	3 340 ..	....	....	....	....	....	....	....	....
Income on bonds and notes...............	3 350 ..	....	....	....	....	....	....	....	....
Income on money market instruments...............	3 360 ..	....	....	....	....	....	....	....	....
Other investment income...............	3 370 ..	....	....	−41.9	−70.5	−57.9	−46.9	−28.1	−43.4
D. CURRENT TRANSFERS...........................	4 379 ..	....	....	**185.6**	**218.1**	**225.6**	**449.9**	**745.6**	**1,557.2**
Credit...	2 379 ..	....	....	**201.7**	**285.1**	**348.4**	**599.9**	**1,146.0**	**1,794.3**
General government...............	2 380 ..	....	....	....	....	....	....	....	....
Other sectors...............	2 390 ..	....	....	201.7	285.1	348.4	599.9	1,146.0	1,794.3
Workers' remittances...............	2 391 ..	....	....	78.4	146.0	252.0	465.2	1,015.0	1,685.4
Other current transfers...............	2 392 ..	....	....	123.3	139.1	96.4	134.7	131.0	108.9
Debit...	3 379 ..	....	....	**−16.1**	**−67.0**	**−122.8**	**−150.0**	**−400.4**	**−237.1**
General government...............	3 380 ..	....	....	....	....	....	....	....	....
Other sectors...............	3 390 ..	....	....	−16.1	−67.0	−122.8	−150.0	−400.4	−237.1
Workers' remittances...............	3 391 ..	....	....	−12.9	−64.4	−118.9	−144.2	−392.8	−180.3
Other current transfers...............	3 392 ..	....	....	−3.2	−2.7	−3.9	−5.8	−7.5	−56.8
CAPITAL AND FINANCIAL ACCOUNT...............	4 996 ..	....	....	**70.7**	**34.8**	**89.5**	**95.2**	**286.1**	**858.0**
CAPITAL ACCOUNT................................	4 994 ..	....	....	**45.4**	**13.9**	**25.5**	....	**99.9**	**32.8**
Total credit..	2 994 ..	....	....	*45.4*	*13.9*	*25.5*	....	*99.9*	*32.8*
Total debit...	3 994 ..	....	....	....	....	....	....	....	....
Capital transfers, credit........................	2 400 ..	....	....	**45.4**	**13.9**	**25.5**	....	**99.9**	**32.8**
General government...............	2 401 ..	....	....	45.4	13.9	25.5	....	99.9	32.8
Debt forgiveness...............	2 402 ..	....	....	45.4	13.9	25.5	....	99.9	32.8
Other capital transfers...............	2 410 ..	....	....	....	....	....	....	....	....
Other sectors...............	2 430 ..	....	....	....	....	....	....	....	....
Migrants' transfers...............	2 431 ..	....	....	....	....	....	....	....	....
Debt forgiveness...............	2 432 ..	....	....	....	....	....	....	....	....
Other capital transfers...............	2 440 ..	....	....	....	....	....	....	....	....
Capital transfers, debit.........................	3 400 ..	....	....	....	....	....	....	....	....
General government...............	3 401 ..	....	....	....	....	....	....	....	....
Debt forgiveness...............	3 402 ..	....	....	....	....	....	....	....	....
Other capital transfers...............	3 410 ..	....	....	....	....	....	....	....	....
Other sectors...............	3 430 ..	....	....	....	....	....	....	....	....
Migrants' transfers...............	3 431 ..	....	....	....	....	....	....	....	....
Debt forgiveness...............	3 432 ..	....	....	....	....	....	....	....	....
Other capital transfers...............	3 440 ..	....	....	....	....	....	....	....	....
Nonproduced nonfinancial assets, credit.............	2 480 ..	....	....	....	....	....	....	....	....
Nonproduced nonfinancial assets, debit.............	3 480 ..	....	....	....	....	....	....	....	....

Table 2 (Continued). STANDARD PRESENTATION, 2000–2007

(Millions of U.S. dollars)

	Code	2000	2001	2002	2003	2004	2005	2006	2007
FINANCIAL ACCOUNT	4 995 ..	....	....	**25.3**	**20.9**	**64.0**	**95.2**	**186.2**	**825.2**
A. DIRECT INVESTMENT	4 500 ..	....	....	**36.1**	**31.6**	**272.0**	**54.5**	**338.6**	**360.0**
Direct investment abroad	4 505 ..	....	....	....	....	....	....	....	....
Equity capital	4 510 ..	....	....	....	....	....	....	....	....
Claims on affiliated enterprises	4 515 ..	....	....	....	....	....	....	....	....
Liabilities to affiliated enterprises	4 520 ..	....	....	....	....	....	....	....	....
Reinvested earnings	4 525 ..	....	....	....	....	....	....	....	....
Other capital	4 530 ..	....	....	....	....	....	....	....	....
Claims on affiliated enterprises	4 535 ..	....	....	....	....	....	....	....	....
Liabilities to affiliated enterprises	4 540 ..	....	....	....	....	....	....	....	....
Direct investment in Tajikistan	4 555 ..	....	....	**36.1**	**31.6**	**272.0**	**54.5**	**338.6**	**360.0**
Equity capital	4 560 ..	....	....	36.1	31.6	272.0	54.5	338.6	360.0
Claims on direct investors	4 565 ..	....	....	....	....	....	....	....	....
Liabilities to direct investors	4 570 ..	....	....	36.1	31.6	272.0	54.5	338.6	360.0
Reinvested earnings	4 575 ..	....	....	....	....	....	....	....	....
Other capital	4 580 ..	....	....	....	....	....	....	....	....
Claims on direct investors	4 585 ..	....	....	....	....	....	....	....	....
Liabilities to direct investors	4 590 ..	....	....	....	....	....	....	....	....
B. PORTFOLIO INVESTMENT	4 600 ..	....	....	**1.5**	**.3**	**5.3**	....	....	**.2**
Assets	4 602 ..	....	....	....	....	....	....	....	....
Equity securities	4 610 ..	....	....	....	....	....	....	....	....
Monetary authorities	4 611 ..	....	....	....	....	....	....	....	....
General government	4 612 ..	....	....	....	....	....	....	....	....
Banks	4 613 ..	....	....	....	....	....	....	....	....
Other sectors	4 614 ..	....	....	....	....	....	....	....	....
Debt securities	4 619 ..	....	....	....	....	....	....	....	....
Bonds and notes	4 620 ..	....	....	....	....	....	....	....	....
Monetary authorities	4 621 ..	....	....	....	....	....	....	....	....
General government	4 622 ..	....	....	....	....	....	....	....	....
Banks	4 623 ..	....	....	....	....	....	....	....	....
Other sectors	4 624 ..	....	....	....	....	....	....	....	....
Money market instruments	4 630 ..	....	....	....	....	....	....	....	....
Monetary authorities	4 631 ..	....	....	....	....	....	....	....	....
General government	4 632 ..	....	....	....	....	....	....	....	....
Banks	4 633 ..	....	....	....	....	....	....	....	....
Other sectors	4 634 ..	....	....	....	....	....	....	....	....
Liabilities	4 652 ..	....	....	**1.5**	**.3**	**5.3**	....	....	**.2**
Equity securities	4 660 ..	....	....	1.5	.3	....	....	....	....
Banks	4 663 ..	....	....	....	....	....	....	....	....
Other sectors	4 664 ..	....	....	1.5	.3	....	....	....	....
Debt securities	4 669 ..	....	....	....	....	5.3	....	....	.2
Bonds and notes	4 670 ..	....	....	....	....	....	....	....	.2
Monetary authorities	4 671 ..	....	....	....	....	....	....	....	....
General government	4 672 ..	....	....	....	....	....	....	....	....
Banks	4 673 ..	....	....	....	....	....	....	....	....
Other sectors	4 674 ..	....	....	....	....	....	....	....	.2
Money market instruments	4 680 ..	....	....	....	....	5.3	....	....	....
Monetary authorities	4 681 ..	....	....	....	....	....	....	....	....
General government	4 682 ..	....	....	....	....	....	....	....	....
Banks	4 683 ..	....	....	....	....	....	....	....	....
Other sectors	4 684 ..	....	....	....	....	5.3	....	....	....
C. FINANCIAL DERIVATIVES	4 910 ..	....	....	....	....	....	....	....	....
Monetary authorities	4 911 ..	....	....	....	....	....	....	....	....
General government	4 912 ..	....	....	....	....	....	....	....	....
Banks	4 913 ..	....	....	....	....	....	....	....	....
Other sectors	4 914 ..	....	....	....	....	....	....	....	....
Assets	4 900 ..	....	....	....	....	....	....	....	....
Monetary authorities	4 901 ..	....	....	....	....	....	....	....	....
General government	4 902 ..	....	....	....	....	....	....	....	....
Banks	4 903 ..	....	....	....	....	....	....	....	....
Other sectors	4 904 ..	....	....	....	....	....	....	....	....
Liabilities	4 905 ..	....	....	....	....	....	....	....	....
Monetary authorities	4 906 ..	....	....	....	....	....	....	....	....
General government	4 907 ..	....	....	....	....	....	....	....	....
Banks	4 908 ..	....	....	....	....	....	....	....	....
Other sectors	4 909 ..	....	....	....	....	....	....	....	....

Table 2 (Concluded). STANDARD PRESENTATION, 2000–2007

(Millions of U.S. dollars)

	Code	2000	2001	2002	2003	2004	2005	2006	2007
D. OTHER INVESTMENT	4 700	....	....	**−12.4**	**29.4**	**−166.9**	**66.3**	**−145.3**	**453.5**
Assets	4 703	....	....	**−23.4**	**−15.6**	**−28.4**	**−71.3**	**−301.9**	**−386.7**
Trade credits	4 706	....	....	−15.7	−2.8	−20.8	−37.1	−67.9	−199.8
General government	4 707	....	....	....	....	....	....	....	....
of which: Short-term	4 709	....	....	....	....	....	....	....	....
Other sectors	4 710	....	....	−15.7	−2.8	−20.8	−37.1	−67.9	−199.8
of which: Short-term	4 712	....	....	*−15.7*	*−2.8*	*−20.8*	*−37.1*	*−67.9*	*−199.8*
Loans	4 714	....	....	.1	....	....	....	....	....
Monetary authorities	4 715	....	....	....	....	....	....	....	....
of which: Short-term	4 718	....	....	....	....	....	....	....	....
General government	4 719	....	....	....	....	....	....	....	....
of which: Short-term	4 721	....	....	....	....	....	....	....	....
Banks	4 722	....	....	.1	....	....	....	....	....
of which: Short-term	4 724	....	....	*.1*	....	....	....	....	....
Other sectors	4 725	....	....	....	....	....	....	....	....
of which: Short-term	4 727	....	....	....	....	....	....	....	....
Currency and deposits	4 730	....	....	−6.7	−14.4	−7.3	−33.7	−233.5	−186.7
Monetary authorities	4 731	....	....	....	....	....	....	....	....
General government	4 732	....	....	....	....	....	....	....	....
Banks	4 733	....	....	−6.7	−14.4	−7.3	−33.7	−233.5	−186.7
Other sectors	4 734	....	....	....	....	....	....	....	....
Other assets	4 736	....	....	−1.2	1.6	−.3	−.5	−.5	−.2
Monetary authorities	4 737	....	....	....	....	....	....	....	....
of which: Short-term	4 739	....	....	....	....	....	....	....	....
General government	4 740	....	....	.2	−.4	−.4	−.5	−.5	−.2
of which: Short-term	4 742	....	....	*.2*	*−.4*	*−.4*	*−.5*	*−.5*	*−.2*
Banks	4 743	....	....	....	....	....	....	....	....
of which: Short-term	4 745	....	....	....	....	....	....	....	....
Other sectors	4 746	....	....	−1.4	2.0	.1	....	....	....
of which: Short-term	4 748	....	....	*−1.4*	*2.0*	*.1*	....	....	....
Liabilities	4 753	....	....	**11.1**	**45.0**	**−138.5**	**137.6**	**156.6**	**840.1**
Trade credits	4 756	....	....	14.9	42.8	−15.9	23.7	15.7	33.9
General government	4 757	....	....	....	....	....	....	....	....
of which: Short-term	4 759	....	....	....	....	....	....	....	....
Other sectors	4 760	....	....	14.9	42.8	−15.9	23.7	15.7	33.9
of which: Short-term	4 762	....	....	*14.9*	*42.8*	*−15.9*	*23.7*	*15.7*	*33.9*
Loans	4 764	....	....	−33.3	−4.8	−134.4	65.3	17.8	570.1
Monetary authorities	4 765	....	....	−24.0	−2.7	17.0	15.5	−85.7	....
of which: Use of Fund credit and loans from the Fund	4 766	....	....	*−24.0*	*−2.7*	*17.0*	*15.5*	*−85.7*	....
of which: Short-term	4 768	....	....	....	....	....	....	....	....
General government	4 769	....	....	−9.3	−2.1	−151.4	57.1	34.3	251.5
of which: Short-term	4 771	....	....	....	....	....	....	....	....
Banks	4 772	....	....	....	....	....	5.8	....	....
of which: Short-term	4 774	....	....	....	....	....	....	....	....
Other sectors	4 775	....	....	....	....	....	−13.2	69.2	318.5
of which: Short-term	4 777	....	....	....	....	....	....	....	....
Currency and deposits	4 780	....	....	1.2	3.7	1.0	39.2	102.1	240.1
Monetary authorities	4 781	....	....	....	....	....	....	....	....
General government	4 782	....	....	....	....	....	....	....	....
Banks	4 783	....	....	1.2	3.7	1.0	39.2	102.1	240.1
Other sectors	4 784	....	....	....	....	....	....	....	....
Other liabilities	4 786	....	....	28.2	3.3	10.8	9.4	20.9	−4.0
Monetary authorities	4 787	....	....	....	....	....	3.9	....	....
of which: Short-term	4 789	....	....	....	....	....	*3.9*	....	....
General government	4 790	....	....	−23.2	1.4	....	....	3.1	....
of which: Short-term	4 792	....	....	*−23.2*	*1.4*	....	....	*3.1*	....
Banks	4 793	....	....	....	....	....	....	....	....
of which: Short-term	4 795	....	....	....	....	....	....	....	....
Other sectors	4 796	....	....	51.4	1.9	10.8	5.6	17.8	−4.0
of which: Short-term	4 798	....	....	*51.4*	*1.9*	*10.8*	*5.6*	*17.8*	*−4.0*
E. RESERVE ASSETS	4 802	....	....	**.1**	**−40.5**	**−46.4**	**−25.6**	**−7.1**	**11.5**
Monetary gold	4 812	....	....	1.7	−5.8	−8.6	−5.1	−6.3	6.5
Special drawing rights	4 811	....	....	3.2	1.0	−.2	−4.9	2.2	.1
Reserve position in the Fund	4 810	....	....	....	....	....	....	....	....
Foreign exchange	4 803	....	....	−4.8	−35.7	−37.6	−15.7	−2.9	−21.0
Other claims	4 813	....	....	....	....	....	....	....	26.0
NET ERRORS AND OMISSIONS	4 998	....	....	**−55.6**	**−30.0**	**−32.5**	**−76.3**	**−264.7**	**−362.9**

Table 1. ANALYTIC PRESENTATION, 2000–2007

(Millions of U.S. dollars)

	Code	2000	2001	2002	2003	2004	2005	2006	2007
A. Current Account[1]......................................	4 993 Z.	−498.6	−395.2	−37.1	−118.1	−361.7	−864.3	−1,171.6	−1,855.8
Goods: exports f.o.b..................................	2 100 ..	663.3	851.3	979.6	1,220.9	1,481.6	1,679.1	1,917.6	2,226.6
Goods: imports f.o.b..................................	3 100 ..	−1,367.6	−1,560.3	−1,511.3	−1,933.5	−2,482.8	−2,997.6	−3,864.1	−4,860.6
Balance on Goods................................	4 100 ..	*−704.3*	*−709.0*	*−531.8*	*−712.6*	*−1,001.2*	*−1,318.5*	*−1,946.5*	*−2,634.1*
Services: credit..	2 200 ..	627.4	915.4	920.1	947.8	1,138.6	1,269.2	1,528.1	1,714.0
Services: debit...	3 200 ..	−682.4	−649.3	−632.5	−725.7	−974.7	−1,207.3	−1,249.4	−1,473.6
Balance on Goods and Services...........	4 991 ..	*−759.3*	*−443.0*	*−244.2*	*−490.5*	*−837.3*	*−1,256.6*	*−1,667.8*	*−2,393.6*
Income: credit..	2 300 ..	50.3	55.3	67.9	87.1	81.8	80.9	53.7	80.8
Income: debit...	3 300 ..	−180.4	−207.6	−156.8	−225.6	−195.3	−185.0	−146.8	−159.8
Balance on Goods, Services, and Income...........	4 992 ..	*−889.4*	*−595.3*	*−333.0*	*−629.1*	*−950.8*	*−1,360.7*	*−1,760.9*	*−2,472.7*
Current transfers: credit..........................	2 379 Z.	463.7	279.6	357.2	574.2	654.1	563.9	655.2	689.4
Current transfers: debit...........................	3 379 ..	−72.9	−79.5	−61.3	−63.3	−65.0	−67.5	−65.9	−72.5
B. Capital Account[1]......................................	4 994 Z.	**420.4**	**1,003.6**	**785.7**	**692.8**	**459.9**	**393.2**	**5,217.7**	**957.8**
Capital account: credit.............................	2 994 Z.	420.4	1,003.6	785.7	692.8	459.9	393.2	5,217.7	957.8
Capital account: debit..............................	3 994 ..	....	....	....	....	....	....	....	....
Total, Groups A Plus B.........................	4 981 ..	*−78.2*	*608.4*	*748.5*	*574.6*	*98.2*	*−471.2*	*4,046.1*	*−897.9*
C. Financial Account[1]..................................	4 995 W.	**493.5**	**−353.0**	**276.9**	**247.5**	**278.8**	**665.3**	**−3,952.2**	**1,030.9**
Direct investment abroad.........................	4 505 ..	....	....	....	....	....	....	....	....
Direct investment in Tanzania..................	4 555 Z.	463.4	388.8	387.6	308.2	330.6	494.1	597.0	647.0
Portfolio investment assets......................	4 602 ..	....	....	....	....	....	....	....	....
Equity securities.....................................	4 610 ..	....	....	....	....	....	....	....	....
Debt securities.......................................	4 619 ..	....	....	....	....	....	....	....	....
Portfolio investment liabilities.................	4 652 Z.	....	8.2	2.2	2.7	2.4	2.5	2.6	2.8
Equity securities.....................................	4 660 ..	....	8.2	2.2	2.7	2.4	2.5	2.6	2.8
Debt securities.......................................	4 669 Z.	....	....	....	....	....	....	....	....
Financial derivatives................................	4 910 ..	....	....	....	....	....	....	....	....
Financial derivatives assets.....................	4 900 ..	....	....	....	....	....	....	....	....
Financial derivatives liabilities.................	4 905 ..	....	....	....	....	....	....	....	....
Other investment assets..........................	4 703 ..	−134.0	−76.7	2.9	−59.0	−11.0	−61.5	−175.0	114.8
Monetary authorities..............................	4 701 ..	....	....	....	....	....	....	....	....
General government...............................	4 704 ..	....	....	....	....	....	....	....	....
Banks...	4 705 ..	−134.0	−76.7	2.9	−59.0	−11.0	−61.5	−175.0	114.8
Other sectors..	4 728 ..	....	....	....	....	....	....	....	....
Other investment liabilities......................	4 753 W.	164.1	−673.3	−115.7	−4.4	−43.2	230.2	−4,376.8	266.4
Monetary authorities..............................	4 753 WA	49.7	−41.3	14.0	115.9	33.7	80.1	−64.0	−135.6
General government...............................	4 753 ZB	145.4	−707.5	−233.7	−27.9	−15.0	196.1	−4,293.0	225.9
Banks...	4 753 ZC	3.9	12.5	18.4	−29.6	11.8	29.1	12.9	188.7
Other sectors..	4 753 ZD	−34.9	63.0	85.6	−62.7	−73.7	−75.1	−32.6	−12.7
Total, Groups A Through C...................	4 983 ..	*415.3*	*255.4*	*1,025.5*	*822.1*	*377.0*	*194.1*	*93.9*	*133.0*
D. Net Errors and Omissions..........................	4 998 ..	**−416.6**	**−304.5**	**−702.1**	**−349.8**	**−173.1**	**−417.7**	**367.2**	**282.6**
Total, Groups A Through D...................	4 984 ..	*−1.3*	*−49.1*	*323.4*	*472.3*	*203.9*	*−223.6*	*461.1*	*415.6*
E. Reserves and Related Items.......................	4 802 A.	**1.3**	**49.1**	**−323.4**	**−472.3**	**−203.9**	**223.6**	**−461.1**	**−415.6**
Reserve assets..	4 802 ..	−199.2	−183.1	−371.3	−507.8	−257.4	246.5	−126.5	−419.7
Use of Fund credit and loans....................	4 766 ..	27.6	29.5	29.1	−.3	−32.6	−48.1	−334.6	4.2
Exceptional financing...............................	4 920 ..	172.9	202.6	18.9	35.7	86.2	25.1	....	....
Conversion rates: Tanzania shillings per U.S. dollar............	0 101 ..	**800.4**	**876.4**	**966.6**	**1,038.4**	**1,089.3**	**1,128.9**	**1,251.9**	**1,245.0**

[1] Excludes components that have been classified in the categories of Group E.

Table 2. STANDARD PRESENTATION, 2000–2007

(Millions of U.S. dollars)

	Code	2000	2001	2002	2003	2004	2005	2006	2007
CURRENT ACCOUNT	4 993	−498.6	−395.2	−37.1	−118.1	−361.7	−864.3	−1,171.6	−1,855.8
A. GOODS	4 100	−704.3	−709.0	−531.8	−712.6	−1,001.2	−1,318.5	−1,946.5	−2,634.1
Credit	2 100	663.3	851.3	979.6	1,220.9	1,481.6	1,679.1	1,917.6	2,226.6
General merchandise: exports f.o.b.	2 110	550.6	597.2	638.5	718.0	852.2	1,024.1	1,144.4	2,226.6
Goods for processing: exports f.o.b.	2 150	....	....	....	....	....	....	....	....
Repairs on goods	2 160	....	....	....	....	....	....	....	....
Goods procured in ports by carriers	2 170	....	....	....	....	....	....	....	....
Nonmonetary gold	2 180	112.7	254.1	341.1	502.8	629.4	655.1	773.2	....
Debit	3 100	−1,367.6	−1,560.3	−1,511.3	−1,933.5	−2,482.8	−2,997.6	−3,864.1	−4,860.6
General merchandise: imports f.o.b.	3 110	−1,367.6	−1,560.3	−1,511.3	−1,933.5	−2,482.8	−2,997.6	−3,864.1	−4,860.6
Goods for processing: imports f.o.b.	3 150	....	....	....	....	....	....	....	....
Repairs on goods	3 160	....	....	....	....	....	....	....	....
Goods procured in ports by carriers	3 170	....	....	....	....	....	....	....	....
Nonmonetary gold	3 180	....	....	....	....	....	....	....	....
B. SERVICES	4 200	−55.0	266.1	287.6	222.1	163.9	61.8	278.7	240.4
Total credit	2 200	*627.4*	*915.4*	*920.1*	*947.8*	*1,138.6*	*1,269.2*	*1,528.1*	*1,714.0*
Total debit	3 200	*−682.4*	*−649.3*	*−632.5*	*−725.7*	*−974.7*	*−1,207.3*	*−1,249.4*	*−1,473.6*
Transportation services, credit	2 205	56.8	105.9	117.1	138.9	183.0	222.9	343.7	331.9
Passenger	2 850	*4.2*	*11.3*	*3.6*	*6.7*	*16.4*	*11.5*	*35.6*	*15.6*
Freight	2 851	*40.7*	*77.2*	*94.6*	*92.8*	*117.5*	*159.6*	*218.5*	*281.8*
Other	2 852	*11.9*	*17.4*	*18.9*	*39.4*	*49.1*	*51.8*	*89.6*	*34.5*
Sea transport, passenger	2 207	....	....	....	....	....	....	....	....
Sea transport, freight	2 208	....	77.2	94.6	92.8	117.5	159.6	218.5	281.8
Sea transport, other	2 209	....	....	....	....	....	....	....	....
Air transport, passenger	2 211	4.2	11.3	3.6	6.7	16.4	11.5	35.6	15.6
Air transport, freight	2 212	....	....	....	....	....	....	....	....
Air transport, other	2 213	....	....	....	....	....	....	....	....
Other transport, passenger	2 215	....	....	....	....	....	....	....	....
Other transport, freight	2 216	40.7	....	....	....	....	....	....	....
Other transport, other	2 217	11.9	17.4	18.9	39.4	49.1	51.8	89.6	34.5
Transportation services, debit	3 205	−205.6	−194.2	−176.9	−214.7	−267.1	−319.5	−418.3	−485.0
Passenger	3 850	*−32.4*	*−36.3*	*−23.9*	*−21.9*	*−24.7*	*−22.7*	*−37.1*	*−21.5*
Freight	3 851	*−167.3*	*−149.7*	*−145.1*	*−185.5*	*−235.2*	*−287.6*	*−371.4*	*−458.6*
Other	3 852	*−5.9*	*−8.3*	*−7.9*	*−7.3*	*−7.2*	*−9.3*	*−9.9*	*−5.0*
Sea transport, passenger	3 207	....	....	....	....	....	....	....	....
Sea transport, freight	3 208	−167.3	−149.7	−145.1	−185.5	−235.2	−287.6	−371.4	−458.6
Sea transport, other	3 209	....	....	....	....	....	....	....	....
Air transport, passenger	3 211	−32.4	−36.3	−23.9	−21.9	−24.7	−22.7	−37.1	−21.5
Air transport, freight	3 212	....	....	....	....	....	....	....	....
Air transport, other	3 213	....	....	....	....	....	....	....	....
Other transport, passenger	3 215	....	....	....	....	....	....	....	....
Other transport, freight	3 216	....	....	....	....	....	....	....	....
Other transport, other	3 217	−5.9	−8.3	−7.9	−7.3	−7.2	−9.3	−9.9	−5.0
Travel, credit	2 236	376.7	615.1	635.0	646.5	746.0	823.6	950.2	1,037.1
Business travel	2 237	....	....	....	....	....	....	....	....
Personal travel	2 240	376.7	615.1	635.0	646.5	746.0	823.6	950.2	1,037.1
Travel, debit	3 236	−337.3	−327.3	−337.5	−353.2	−445.3	−553.8	−534.5	−645.3
Business travel	3 237	....	....	....	....	....	....	....	....
Personal travel	3 240	−337.3	−327.3	−337.5	−353.2	−445.3	−553.8	−534.5	−645.3
Other services, credit	2 200 BA	193.9	194.4	168.0	162.3	209.6	222.7	234.1	345.0
Communications	2 245	26.7	10.5	14.0	20.3	31.6	33.7	37.9	39.6
Construction	2 249	....	....	....	....	....	....	....	....
Insurance	2 253	13.0	15.6	19.2	19.8	25.4	38.0	11.4	22.3
Financial	2 260	4.0	3.8	4.3	4.1	2.5	1.9	4.2	5.1
Computer and information	2 262	.5	.5	.7	.2	5.0	.3	.3	3.4
Royalties and licence fees	2 266	.3	.2	....	....	....	....	....	....
Other business services	2 268	97.3	102.6	68.9	68.8	85.8	94.2	119.1	234.2
Personal, cultural, and recreational	2 287	.1	.1	1.0	1.2	.1	.7	.1	.9
Government, n.i.e.	2 291	52.0	61.2	59.9	48.0	59.3	53.9	61.0	39.4
Other services, debit	3 200 BA	−139.5	−127.8	−118.1	−157.8	−262.3	−334.0	−296.6	−343.2
Communications	3 245	−6.2	−5.1	−7.7	−12.6	−15.4	−15.7	−17.3	−14.6
Construction	3 249	−1.6	−14.5	−10.7	−10.2	−93.0	−143.0	−131.9	−63.9
Insurance	3 253	−18.3	−20.4	−27.4	−34.9	−37.9	−46.1	−52.2	−59.5
Financial	3 260	−3.3	−2.3	−4.5	−6.7	−5.1	−2.6	−4.0	−16.8
Computer and information	3 262	−1.7	−1.0	−3.7	−1.1	−3.1	−4.6	−3.4	−5.1
Royalties and licence fees	3 266	−3.7	−3.6	−.1	−.7	−.6	−.2	−.7	−5.3
Other business services	3 268	−41.8	−66.2	−42.0	−50.2	−55.3	−45.6	−50.0	−126.1
Personal, cultural, and recreational	3 287	−.2	....	....	−.8	....	....	....	−2.0
Government, n.i.e.	3 291	−62.7	−14.7	−21.9	−40.6	−52.0	−76.1	−37.0	−49.8

Table 2 (Continued). STANDARD PRESENTATION, 2000–2007

(Millions of U.S. dollars)

	Code	2000	2001	2002	2003	2004	2005	2006	2007
C. INCOME..	4 300 ..	**−130.1**	**−152.3**	**−88.8**	**−138.5**	**−113.5**	**−104.1**	**−93.1**	**−79.0**
Total credit..	2 300 ..	*50.3*	*55.3*	*67.9*	*87.1*	*81.8*	*80.9*	*53.7*	*80.8*
Total debit...	3 300 ..	*−180.4*	*−207.6*	*−156.8*	*−225.6*	*−195.3*	*−185.0*	*−146.8*	*−159.8*
Compensation of employees, credit..................	2 310 ..	**8.0**	**10.0**	**7.0**	**7.0**	**8.0**	**10.2**	**6.4**	**6.0**
Compensation of employees, debit....................	3 310 ..	**−20.3**	**−22.1**	**−21.1**	**−22.4**	**−28.0**	**−24.9**	**−23.4**	**−46.4**
Investment income, credit................................	2 320 ..	**42.3**	**45.4**	**60.9**	**80.1**	**73.7**	**70.7**	**47.3**	**74.8**
Direct investment income...............................	2 330 ..	....	....	....	....	....	....	....	....
Dividends and distributed branch profits........................	2 332 ..	....	....	....	....	....	....	....	....
Reinvested earnings and undistributed branch profits.....	2 333 ..	....	....	....	....	....	....	....	....
Income on debt (interest)...........................	2 334 ..	....	....	....	....	....	....	....	....
Portfolio investment income..........................	2 339 ..	....	....	....	....	....	....	....	....
Income on equity..............................	2 340 ..	....	....	....	....	....	....	....	....
Income on bonds and notes..................	2 350 ..	....	....	....	....	....	....	....	....
Income on money market instruments..........	2 360 ..	....	....	....	....	....	....	....	....
Other investment income.............................	2 370 ..	42.3	45.4	60.9	80.1	73.7	70.7	47.3	74.8
Investment income, debit................................	3 320 ..	**−160.1**	**−185.5**	**−135.7**	**−203.2**	**−167.3**	**−160.1**	**−123.3**	**−113.4**
Direct investment income...............................	3 330 ..	−13.2	−73.0	−58.7	−59.7	−58.4	−65.6	−66.4	−67.6
Dividends and distributed branch profits........................	3 332 ..	....	−57.4	−37.1	−37.4	−33.3	−35.5	−36.3	−39.0
Reinvested earnings and undistributed branch profits.....	3 333 ..	....	....	....	....	....	....	....	....
Income on debt (interest)...........................	3 334 ..	....	−15.6	−21.6	−22.3	−25.1	−30.1	−30.1	−28.6
Portfolio investment income..........................	3 339 ..	....	−8.5	−17.0	−24.0	−35.4	−35.4	−27.3	−25.4
Income on equity..............................	3 340 ..	....	....	....	....	....	....	....	....
Income on bonds and notes..................	3 350 ..	....	−8.5	−17.0	−24.0	−35.4	−35.4	−27.3	−25.4
Income on money market instruments..........	3 360 ..	....	....	....	....	....	....	....	....
Other investment income.............................	3 370 ..	−146.9	−104.0	−60.0	−119.5	−73.5	−59.0	−29.7	−20.4
D. CURRENT TRANSFERS......................................	4 379 ..	**390.8**	**200.1**	**295.9**	**511.0**	**589.1**	**496.3**	**589.3**	**616.9**
Credit...	2 379 ..	**463.7**	**279.6**	**357.2**	**574.2**	**654.1**	**563.9**	**655.2**	**689.4**
General government....................................	2 380 ..	427.8	223.2	307.0	507.6	582.0	478.5	560.3	595.2
Other sectors..	2 390 ..	35.9	56.4	50.2	66.6	72.1	85.4	94.9	94.2
Workers' remittances............................	2 391 ..	....	5.3	5.0	1.9	5.8	9.1	9.0	8.3
Other current transfers........................	2 392 ..	35.9	51.1	45.2	64.7	66.3	76.3	85.9	85.9
Debit..	3 379 ..	**−72.9**	**−79.5**	**−61.3**	**−63.3**	**−65.0**	**−67.5**	**−65.9**	**−72.5**
General government....................................	3 380 ..	....	−2.0	−3.2	−5.1	−4.6	−3.6	−2.4	−3.7
Other sectors..	3 390 ..	−72.9	−77.5	−58.1	−58.2	−60.5	−64.0	−63.5	−68.8
Workers' remittances............................	3 391 ..	....	−7.6	−5.9	−4.7	−5.9	−8.3	−6.2	....
Other current transfers........................	3 392 ..	−72.9	−69.9	−52.2	−53.5	−54.6	−55.7	−57.3	−68.8
CAPITAL AND FINANCIAL ACCOUNT......................	4 996 ..	**915.2**	**699.7**	**739.2**	**468.0**	**534.8**	**1,282.0**	**804.4**	**1,573.2**
CAPITAL ACCOUNT...	4 994 ..	**420.4**	**1,003.6**	**785.7**	**692.8**	**459.9**	**393.2**	**5,217.7**	**957.8**
Total credit...	2 994 ..	*420.4*	*1,003.6*	*785.7*	*692.8*	*459.9*	*393.2*	*5,217.7*	*957.8*
Total debit...	3 994 ..	....	....	....	....	....	....	....	....
Capital transfers, credit................................	2 400 ..	**420.4**	**1,003.6**	**785.7**	**692.8**	**459.9**	**393.2**	**5,217.7**	**957.8**
General government....................................	2 401 ..	404.7	981.3	755.6	655.5	420.0	350.1	5,169.1	904.6
Debt forgiveness..................................	2 402 ..	90.0	642.1	430.3	334.6	166.3	112.1	4,961.7	523.0
Other capital transfers..........................	2 410 ..	314.7	339.2	325.3	320.9	253.7	238.0	207.4	381.6
Other sectors..	2 430 ..	15.7	22.3	30.1	37.3	39.9	43.1	48.6	53.2
Migrants' transfers...............................	2 431 ..	....	....	....	....	....	....	....	....
Debt forgiveness..................................	2 432 ..	....	....	....	....	....	....	....	....
Other capital transfers..........................	2 440 ..	15.7	22.3	30.1	37.3	39.9	43.1	48.6	53.2
Capital transfers, debit................................	3 400 ..	....	....	....	....	....	....	....	....
General government....................................	3 401 ..	....	....	....	....	....	....	....	....
Debt forgiveness..................................	3 402 ..	....	....	....	....	....	....	....	....
Other capital transfers..........................	3 410 ..	....	....	....	....	....	....	....	....
Other sectors..	3 430 ..	....	....	....	....	....	....	....	....
Migrants' transfers...............................	3 431 ..	....	....	....	....	....	....	....	....
Debt forgiveness..................................	3 432 ..	....	....	....	....	....	....	....	....
Other capital transfers..........................	3 440 ..	....	....	....	....	....	....	....	....
Nonproduced nonfinancial assets, credit.............	2 480 ..	....	....	....	....	....	....	....	....
Nonproduced nonfinancial assets, debit..............	3 480 ..	....	....	....	....	....	....	....	....

Table 2 (Continued). STANDARD PRESENTATION, 2000–2007

(Millions of U.S. dollars)

	Code	2000	2001	2002	2003	2004	2005	2006	2007
FINANCIAL ACCOUNT..	4 995 ..	**494.8**	**−303.9**	**−46.5**	**−224.8**	**74.9**	**888.9**	**−4,413.3**	**615.4**
A. DIRECT INVESTMENT......................................	4 500 ..	**463.4**	**388.8**	**387.6**	**308.2**	**330.6**	**494.1**	**597.0**	**647.0**
Direct investment abroad.................................	4 505 ..	....	....	....	....	....	....	....	....
Equity capital..	4 510 ..	....	....	....	....	....	....	....	....
Claims on affiliated enterprises........................	4 515 ..	....	....	....	....	....	....	....	....
Liabilities to affiliated enterprises....................	4 520 ..	....	....	....	....	....	....	....	....
Reinvested earnings..	4 525 ..	....	....	....	....	....	....	....	....
Other capital...	4 530 ..	....	....	....	....	....	....	....	....
Claims on affiliated enterprises........................	4 535 ..	....	....	....	....	....	....	....	....
Liabilities to affiliated enterprises....................	4 540 ..	....	....	....	....	....	....	....	....
Direct investment in Tanzania..........................	4 555 ..	**463.4**	**388.8**	**387.6**	**308.2**	**330.6**	**494.1**	**597.0**	**647.0**
Equity capital..	4 560 ..	463.4	388.8	387.6	308.2	330.6	494.1	597.0	647.0
Claims on direct investors...............................	4 565 ..	....	....	....	....	....	....	....	....
Liabilities to direct investors...........................	4 570 ..	463.4	388.8	387.6	308.2	330.6	494.1	597.0	647.0
Reinvested earnings..	4 575 ..	....	....	....	....	....	....	....	....
Other capital...	4 580 ..	....	....	....	....	....	....	....	....
Claims on direct investors...............................	4 585 ..	....	....	....	....	....	....	....	....
Liabilities to direct investors...........................	4 590 ..	....	....	....	....	....	....	....	....
B. PORTFOLIO INVESTMENT.................................	4 600 ..	....	**8.2**	**2.2**	**2.7**	**2.4**	**2.5**	**2.6**	**2.8**
Assets..	4 602 ..	....	....	....	....	....	....	....	....
Equity securities...	4 610 ..	....	....	....	....	....	....	....	....
Monetary authorities.......................................	4 611 ..	....	....	....	....	....	....	....	....
General government..	4 612 ..	....	....	....	....	....	....	....	....
Banks..	4 613 ..	....	....	....	....	....	....	....	....
Other sectors..	4 614 ..	....	....	....	....	....	....	....	....
Debt securities..	4 619 ..	....	....	....	....	....	....	....	....
Bonds and notes...	4 620 ..	....	....	....	....	....	....	....	....
Monetary authorities....................................	4 621 ..	....	....	....	....	....	....	....	....
General government.....................................	4 622 ..	....	....	....	....	....	....	....	....
Banks...	4 623 ..	....	....	....	....	....	....	....	....
Other sectors...	4 624 ..	....	....	....	....	....	....	....	....
Money market instruments.............................	4 630 ..	....	....	....	....	....	....	....	....
Monetary authorities....................................	4 631 ..	....	....	....	....	....	....	....	....
General government.....................................	4 632 ..	....	....	....	....	....	....	....	....
Banks...	4 633 ..	....	....	....	....	....	....	....	....
Other sectors...	4 634 ..	....	....	....	....	....	....	....	....
Liabilities..	4 652 ..	....	**8.2**	**2.2**	**2.7**	**2.4**	**2.5**	**2.6**	**2.8**
Equity securities...	4 660 ..	....	8.2	2.2	2.7	2.4	2.5	2.6	2.8
Banks..	4 663 ..	....	....	....	....	....	....	....	....
Other sectors..	4 664 ..	....	8.2	2.2	2.7	2.4	2.5	2.6	2.8
Debt securities..	4 669 ..	....	....	....	....	....	....	....	....
Bonds and notes...	4 670 ..	....	....	....	....	....	....	....	....
Monetary authorities....................................	4 671 ..	....	....	....	....	....	....	....	....
General government.....................................	4 672 ..	....	....	....	....	....	....	....	....
Banks...	4 673 ..	....	....	....	....	....	....	....	....
Other sectors...	4 674 ..	....	....	....	....	....	....	....	....
Money market instruments.............................	4 680 ..	....	....	....	....	....	....	....	....
Monetary authorities.	4 681 ..	....	....	....	....	....	....	....	....
General government.....................................	4 682 ..	....	....	....	....	....	....	....	....
Banks...	4 683 ..	....	....	....	....	....	....	....	....
Other sectors...	4 684 ..	....	....	....	....	....	....	....	....
C. FINANCIAL DERIVATIVES.................................	4 910 ..	....	....	....	....	....	....	....	....
Monetary authorities.......................................	4 911 ..	....	....	....	....	....	....	....	....
General government..	4 912 ..	....	....	....	....	....	....	....	....
Banks..	4 913 ..	....	....	....	....	....	....	....	....
Other sectors..	4 914 ..	....	....	....	....	....	....	....	....
Assets..	4 900 ..	....	....	....	....	....	....	....	....
Monetary authorities.......................................	4 901 ..	....	....	....	....	....	....	....	....
General government..	4 902 ..	....	....	....	....	....	....	....	....
Banks..	4 903 ..	....	....	....	....	....	....	....	....
Other sectors..	4 904 ..	....	....	....	....	....	....	....	....
Liabilities..	4 905 ..	....	....	....	....	....	....	....	....
Monetary authorities.......................................	4 906 ..	....	....	....	....	....	....	....	....
General government..	4 907 ..	....	....	....	....	....	....	....	....
Banks..	4 908 ..	....	....	....	....	....	....	....	....
Other sectors..	4 909 ..	....	....	....	....	....	....	....	....

Table 2 (Concluded). STANDARD PRESENTATION, 2000–2007

(Millions of U.S. dollars)

	Code	2000	2001	2002	2003	2004	2005	2006	2007
D. OTHER INVESTMENT	4 700	**230.6**	**−517.9**	**−64.9**	**−27.9**	**−.7**	**145.8**	**−4,886.3**	**385.4**
Assets	4 703	−134.0	−76.7	2.9	−59.0	−11.0	−61.5	−175.0	114.8
Trade credits	4 706	....	....	....	....	....	....	....	....
General government	4 707	....	....	....	....	....	....	....	....
of which: Short-term	4 709	....	....	....	....	....	....	....	....
Other sectors	4 710	....	....	....	....	....	....	....	....
of which: Short-term	4 712	....	....	....	....	....	....	....	....
Loans	4 714	....	....	....	....	....	....	....	....
Monetary authorities	4 715	....	....	....	....	....	....	....	....
of which: Short-term	4 718	....	....	....	....	....	....	....	....
General government	4 719	....	....	....	....	....	....	....	....
of which: Short-term	4 721	....	....	....	....	....	....	....	....
Banks	4 722	....	....	....	....	....	....	....	....
of which: Short-term	4 724	....	....	....	....	....	....	....	....
Other sectors	4 725	....	....	....	....	....	....	....	....
of which: Short-term	4 727	....	....	....	....	....	....	....	....
Currency and deposits	4 730	−134.0	−76.7	2.9	−59.0	−11.0	−61.5	−175.0	114.8
Monetary authorities	4 731	....	....	....	....	....	....	....	....
General government	4 732	....	....	....	....	....	....	....	....
Banks	4 733	−134.0	−76.7	2.9	−59.0	−11.0	−61.5	−175.0	114.8
Other sectors	4 734	....	....	....	....	....	....	....	....
Other assets	4 736	....	....	....	....	....	....	....	....
Monetary authorities	4 737	....	....	....	....	....	....	....	....
of which: Short-term	4 739	....	....	....	....	....	....	....	....
General government	4 740	....	....	....	....	....	....	....	....
of which: Short-term	4 742	....	....	....	....	....	....	....	....
Banks	4 743	....	....	....	....	....	....	....	....
of which: Short-term	4 745	....	....	....	....	....	....	....	....
Other sectors	4 738	....	....	....	....	....	....	....	....
of which: Short-term	4 748	....	....	....	....	....	....	....	....
Liabilities	4 753	**364.6**	**−441.2**	**−67.8**	**31.1**	**10.3**	**207.2**	**−4,711.3**	**270.6**
Trade credits	4 756	12.8	22.4	25.2	27.2	1.2	1.2	9.9	9.9
General government	4 757	....	....	....	....	....	....	....	....
of which: Short-term	4 759	....	....	....	....	....	....	....	....
Other sectors	4 760	12.8	22.4	25.2	27.2	1.2	1.2	9.9	9.9
of which: Short-term	4 762	*12.8*	*22.4*	*25.2*	*27.2*	*1.2*	*1.2*	*9.9*	*9.9*
Loans	4 764	125.2	−635.4	−145.1	−118.8	−123.0	95.4	−4,684.3	270.7
Monetary authorities	4 765	27.6	29.5	29.1	−.3	−32.6	−48.1	−334.6	4.2
of which: Use of Fund credit and loans from the Fund	4 766	*27.6*	*29.5*	*29.1*	*−.3*	*−32.6*	*−48.1*	*−334.6*	*4.2*
of which: Short-term	4 768	....	....	....	....	....	....	....	....
General government	4 769	145.3	−707.5	−233.7	−27.9	−15.0	196.1	−4,293.0	225.9
of which: Short-term	4 771	....	*−773.5*	*−440.0*	*−421.5*	*−166.3*	*−112.1*	*−4,961.7*	*−523.0*
Banks	4 772	....	2.0	−.8	−.7	−.5	23.7	−14.2	63.2
of which: Short-term	4 774	....	....	....	....	....	....	....	....
Other sectors	4 775	−47.7	40.6	60.4	−89.9	−74.9	−76.3	−42.5	−22.6
of which: Short-term	4 777	....	....	....	....	....	....	....	....
Currency and deposits	4 780	53.6	−30.8	33.2	87.0	46.0	85.5	−36.9	−10.0
Monetary authorities	4 781	49.7	−41.3	14.0	115.9	33.7	80.1	−64.0	−135.6
General government	4 782	....	....	....	....	....	....	....	....
Banks	4 783	3.9	10.5	19.2	−28.9	12.3	5.4	27.1	125.5
Other sectors	4 784	....	....	....	....	....	....	....	....
Other liabilities	4 786	173.0	202.6	18.9	35.7	86.2	25.1	....	....
Monetary authorities	4 787	....	....	....	....	....	....	....	....
of which: Short-term	4 789	....	....	....	....	....	....	....	....
General government	4 790	173.0	202.6	18.9	35.7	86.2	25.1	....	....
of which: Short-term	4 792	*173.0*	*202.6*	*18.9*	*35.7*	*86.2*	*25.1*		....
Banks	4 793	....	....	....	....	....	....	....	....
of which: Short-term	4 795	....	....	....	....	....	....	....	....
Other sectors	4 796	....	....	....	....	....	....	....	....
of which: Short-term	4 798	....	....	....	....	....	....	....	....
E. RESERVE ASSETS	4 802	**−199.2**	**−183.1**	**−371.3**	**−507.8**	**−257.4**	**246.5**	**−126.5**	**−419.7**
Monetary gold	4 812	....	−.1	4.1	27.6	....	....	....	....
Special drawing rights	4 811	.1	−.4	.4	−.4	.4	−.6	.7	−.1
Reserve position in the Fund	4 810	....	....	....	....	....	....	....	....
Foreign exchange	4 803	−199.4	−182.4	−375.9	−535.1	−257.5	247.0	−126.5	−419.8
Other claims	4 813	.1	−.2	.2	.1	−.4	.2	−.7	.1
NET ERRORS AND OMISSIONS	4 998	**−416.6**	**−304.5**	**−702.1**	**−349.8**	**−173.1**	**−417.7**	**367.2**	**282.6**

2008, International Monetary Fund: *Balance of Payments Statistics Yearbook*

Table 3. INTERNATIONAL INVESTMENT POSITION (End-period stocks), 2000–2007

(Millions of U.S. dollars)

	Code	2000	2001	2002	2003	2004	2005	2006	2007
ASSETS	8 995 C.	**1,485.6**	**1,744.5**	**2,114.2**	**2,682.4**	**2,951.1**	**2,765.0**	**3,151.3**	**3,663.6**
Direct investment abroad	8 505 ..	....	....	....	....	....	....	....	....
Equity capital and reinvested earnings	8 506 ..	....	....	....	....	....	....	....	....
Claims on affiliated enterprises	8 507 ..	....	....	....	....	....	....	....	....
Liabilities to affiliated enterprises	8 508 ..	....	....	....	....	....	....	....	....
Other capital	8 530 ..	....	....	....	....	....	....	....	....
Claims on affiliated enterprises	8 535 ..	....	....	....	....	....	....	....	....
Liabilities to affiliated enterprises	8 540 ..	....	....	....	....	....	....	....	....
Portfolio investment	8 602 ..	....	....	....	....	....	....	....	....
Equity securities	8 610 ..	....	....	....	....	....	....	....	....
Monetary authorities	8 611 ..	....	....	....	....	....	....	....	....
General government	8 612 ..	....	....	....	....	....	....	....	....
Banks	8 613 ..	....	....	....	....	....	....	....	....
Other sectors	8 614 ..	....	....	....	....	....	....	....	....
Debt securities	8 619 ..	....	....	....	....	....	....	....	....
Bonds and notes	8 620 ..	....	....	....	....	....	....	....	....
Monetary authorities	8 621 ..	....	....	....	....	....	....	....	....
General government	8 622 ..	....	....	....	....	....	....	....	....
Banks	8 623 ..	....	....	....	....	....	....	....	....
Other sectors	8 624 ..	....	....	....	....	....	....	....	....
Money market instruments	8 630 ..	....	....	....	....	....	....	....	....
Monetary authorities	8 631 ..	....	....	....	....	....	....	....	....
General government	8 632 ..	....	....	....	....	....	....	....	....
Banks	8 633 ..	....	....	....	....	....	....	....	....
Other sectors	8 634 ..	....	....	....	....	....	....	....	....
Financial derivatives	8 900 ..	....	....	....	....	....	....	....	....
Monetary authorities	8 901 ..	....	....	....	....	....	....	....	....
General government	8 902 ..	....	....	....	....	....	....	....	....
Banks	8 903 ..	....	....	....	....	....	....	....	....
Other sectors	8 904 ..	....	....	....	....	....	....	....	....
Other investment	8 703 ..	**511.6**	**588.3**	**585.4**	**644.5**	**655.5**	**717.0**	**892.0**	**777.2**
Trade credits	8 706 ..	....	....	....	....	....	....	....	....
General government	8 707 ..	....	....	....	....	....	....	....	....
of which: Short-term	8 709 ..	....	....	....	....	....	....	....	....
Other sectors	8 710 ..	....	....	....	....	....	....	....	....
of which: Short-term	8 712 ..	....	....	....	....	....	....	....	....
Loans	8 714 ..	....	....	....	....	....	....	....	....
Monetary authorities	8 715 ..	....	....	....	....	....	....	....	....
of which: Short-term	8 718 ..	....	....	....	....	....	....	....	....
General government	8 719 ..	....	....	....	....	....	....	....	....
of which: Short-term	8 721 ..	....	....	....	....	....	....	....	....
Banks	8 722 ..	....	....	....	....	....	....	....	....
of which: Short-term	8 724 ..	....	....	....	....	....	....	....	....
Other sectors	8 725 ..	....	....	....	....	....	....	....	....
of which: Short-term	8 727 ..	....	....	....	....	....	....	....	....
Currency and deposits	8 730 ..	511.6	588.3	585.4	644.5	655.5	717.0	892.0	777.2
Monetary authorities	8 731 ..	....	....	....	....	....	....	....	....
General government	8 732 ..	....	....	....	....	....	....	....	....
Banks	8 733 ..	511.6	588.3	585.4	644.5	655.5	717.0	892.0	777.2
Other sectors	8 734 ..	....	....	....	....	....	....	....	....
Other assets	8 736 ..	....	....	....	....	....	....	....	....
Monetary authorities	8 737 ..	....	....	....	....	....	....	....	....
of which: Short-term	8 739 ..	....	....	....	....	....	....	....	....
General government	8 740 ..	....	....	....	....	....	....	....	....
of which: Short-term	8 742 ..	....	....	....	....	....	....	....	....
Banks	8 743 ..	....	....	....	....	....	....	....	....
of which: Short-term	8 745 ..	....	....	....	....	....	....	....	....
Other sectors	8 738 ..	....	....	....	....	....	....	....	....
of which: Short-term	8 748 ..	....	....	....	....	....	....	....	....
Reserve assets	8 802 ..	**974.0**	**1,156.2**	**1,528.7**	**2,037.9**	**2,295.6**	**2,048.1**	**2,259.3**	**2,886.4**
Monetary gold	8 812 ..	31.6	31.7	27.6	....	....	....	....	....
Special drawing rights	8 811 ..	.1	.5	.1	.5	.1	.7	.1	.2
Reserve position in the Fund	8 810 ..	13.0	12.5	13.6	14.9	15.5	14.3	15.0	15.8
Foreign exchange	8 803 ..	929.1	1,111.5	1,487.5	2,022.6	2,280.0	2,033.1	2,244.2	2,870.4
Other claims	8 813 ..	.2	....	....	....	....	....	....	....

Table 3 (Concluded). INTERNATIONAL INVESTMENT POSITION (End-period stocks), 2000–2007

(Millions of U.S. dollars)

	Code	2000	2001	2002	2003	2004	2005	2006	2007
LIABILITIES...	8 995 D.	**9,540.3**	**9,007.9**	**9,747.2**	**11,398.4**	**12,508.5**	**12,892.2**	**9,430.9**	**10,885.5**
Direct investment in Tanzania.............................	8 555 ..	**1,310.1**	**2,959.7**	**3,242.7**	**4,138.6**	**4,758.5**	**5,135.5**	**5,510.0**	**6,150.5**
Equity capital and reinvested earnings........................	8 556 ..	1,310.1	2,959.7	3,242.7	4,138.6	4,758.5	5,135.5	5,510.0	6,150.5
Claims on direct investors........................	8 557 ..	....	....	....	....	....	....	....	....
Liabilities to direct investors........................	8 558 ..	1,310.1	2,959.7	3,242.7	4,138.6	4,758.5	5,135.5	5,510.0	6,150.5
Other capital........................	8 580 ..	....	....	....	....	....	....	....	....
Claims on direct investors........................	8 585 ..	....	....	....	....	....	....	....	....
Liabilities to direct investors........................	8 590 ..	....	....	....	....	....	....	....	....
Portfolio investment..............................	8 652 ..	....	....	....	....	....	....	....	....
Equity securities........................	8 660 ..	....	....	....	....	....	....	....	....
Banks........................	8 663 ..	....	....	....	....	....	....	....	....
Other sectors........................	8 664 ..	....	....	....	....	....	....	....	....
Debt securities........................	8 669 ..	....	....	....	....	....	....	....	....
Bonds and notes........................	8 670 ..	....	....	....	....	....	....	....	....
Monetary authorities........................	8 671 ..	....	....	....	....	....	....	....	....
General government........................	8 672 ..	....	....	....	....	....	....	....	....
Banks........................	8 673 ..	....	....	....	....	....	....	....	....
Other sectors........................	8 674 ..	....	....	....	....	....	....	....	....
Money market instruments........................	8 680 ..	....	....	....	....	....	....	....	....
Monetary authorities........................	8 681 ..	....	....	....	....	....	....	....	....
General government........................	8 682 ..	....	....	....	....	....	....	....	....
Banks........................	8 683 ..	....	....	....	....	....	....	....	....
Other sectors........................	8 684 ..	....	....	....	....	....	....	....	....
Financial derivatives............................	8 905 ..	....	....	....	....	....	....	....	....
Monetary authorities........................	8 906 ..	....	....	....	....	....	....	....	....
General government........................	8 907 ..	....	....	....	....	....	....	....	....
Banks........................	8 908 ..	....	....	....	....	....	....	....	....
Other sectors........................	8 909 ..	....	....	....	....	....	....	....	....
Other investment..............................	8 753 ..	**8,230.2**	**6,048.2**	**6,504.5**	**7,259.8**	**7,750.0**	**7,756.7**	**3,921.0**	**4,735.0**
Trade credits........................	8 756 ..	28.0	32.0	23.0	25.0	21.0	15.7	24.3	20.3
General government........................	8 757 ..	....	....	....	....	....	....	....	....
of which: Short-term........................	8 759 ..	....	....	....	....	....	....	....	....
Other sectors........................	8 760 ..	28.0	32.0	23.0	25.0	21.0	15.7	24.3	20.3
of which: Short-term........................	8 762 ..	*28.0*	*32.0*	*23.0*	*25.0*	*21.0*	*15.7*	*24.3*	*20.3*
Loans........................	8 764 ..	6,431.1	5,763.7	6,226.9	6,908.2	7,414.2	7,280.7	3,480.8	4,277.4
Monetary authorities........................	8 765 ..	323.6	340.9	399.5	437.3	423.0	342.5	12.6	17.7
of which: Use of Fund credit and loans from the Fund....	8 766 ..	*323.6*	*340.9*	*399.5*	*437.3*	*423.0*	*342.5*	*12.6*	*17.7*
of which: Short-term........................	8 768 ..	....	....	....	....	....	....	....	....
General government........................	8 769 ..	5,742.2	4,659.6	5,029.1	5,756.1	6,331.4	6,277.2	2,712.8	3,515.9
of which: Short-term........................	8 771 ..	....	....	....	....	....	....	....	....
Banks........................	8 772 ..	....	....	....	....	....	....	....	....
of which: Short-term........................	8 774 ..	....	....	....	....	....	....	....	....
Other sectors........................	8 775 ..	365.3	763.2	798.3	714.9	659.9	661.1	755.4	743.7
of which: Short-term........................	8 777 ..	....	....	....	....	....	....	....	....
Currency and deposits........................	8 780 ..	112.9	70.4	103.9	81.8	105.9	333.7	303.4	324.9
Monetary authorities........................	8 781 ..	107.7	54.8	69.0	75.9	87.6	310.0	252.6	148.6
General government........................	8 782 ..	....	....	....	....	....	....	....	....
Banks........................	8 783 ..	5.2	15.7	34.9	5.9	18.3	23.7	50.8	176.3
Other sectors........................	8 784 ..	....	....	....	....	....	....	....	....
Other liabilities........................	8 786 ..	1,658.2	182.1	150.7	244.7	208.9	126.6	112.4	112.4
Monetary authorities........................	8 787 ..	....	....	....	....	....	....	....	....
of which: Short-term........................	8 789 ..	....	....	....	....	....	....	....	....
General government........................	8 790 ..	980.9	150.4	112.2	115.0	117.5	112.0	111.3	111.3
of which: Short-term........................	8 792 ..	*980.9*	*150.4*	*112.2*	*115.0*	*117.5*	*112.0*	*111.3*	*111.3*
Banks........................	8 793 ..	....	....	....	....	....	....	....	....
of which: Short-term........................	8 795 ..	....	....	....	....	....	....	....	....
Other sectors........................	8 796 ..	677.3	31.6	38.5	129.8	91.4	14.5	1.1	1.1
of which: Short-term........................	8 798 ..	....	*31.6*	*38.5*	*129.8*	*91.4*	*14.5*	*1.1*	*1.1*
NET INTERNATIONAL INVESTMENT POSITION........	8 995 ..	**−8,054.6**	**−7,263.4**	**−7,633.0**	**−8,716.0**	**−9,557.4**	**−10,127.1**	**−6,279.6**	**−7,221.9**
Conversion rates: Tanzania shillings per U.S. dollar (end of period)........................	0 102 ..	803.3	916.3	976.3	1,063.6	1,043.0	1,165.5	1,261.6	1,132.1

Table 1. ANALYTIC PRESENTATION, 2000–2007

(Millions of U.S. dollars)

	Code	2000	2001	2002	2003	2004	2005	2006	2007
A. Current Account[1]................................	4 993 Z.	**9,313**	**5,101**	**4,654**	**4,772**	**2,759**	**−7,647**	**2,175**	**15,755**
Goods: exports f.o.b..........................	2 100 ..	67,894	63,082	66,052	78,083	94,979	109,369	127,929	150,026
Goods: imports f.o.b..........................	3 100 ..	−56,193	−54,539	−57,008	−66,909	−84,193	−105,981	−114,085	−124,479
Balance on Goods..........................	4 100 ..	*11,701*	*8,543*	*9,044*	*11,175*	*10,785*	*3,388*	*13,844*	*25,547*
Services: credit..............................	2 200 ..	13,868	13,024	15,391	15,798	19,040	20,163	24,822	30,357
Services: debit..............................	3 200 ..	−15,460	−14,610	−16,720	−18,169	−23,077	−27,027	−33,015	−38,425
Balance on Goods and Services..........	4 991 ..	*10,109*	*6,957*	*7,714*	*8,804*	*6,748*	*−3,477*	*5,651*	*17,478*
Income: credit..............................	2 300 ..	4,235	3,917	3,421	3,150	3,244	3,640	4,659	6,772
Income: debit..............................	3 300 ..	−5,616	−6,375	−7,084	−8,123	−9,364	−10,813	−11,502	−12,433
Balance on Goods, Services, and Income.........	4 992 ..	*8,727*	*4,500*	*4,051*	*3,831*	*628*	*−10,650*	*−1,193*	*11,817*
Current transfers: credit...............	2 379 Z.	952	990	979	1,326	2,479	3,351	3,764	4,395
Current transfers: debit...............	3 379 ..	−366	−389	−375	−385	−348	−348	−396	−457
B. Capital Account[1].............................	4 994 Z.	....	....	....	....	....	....	....	....
Capital account: credit...............	2 994 Z.	....	....	....	....	....	....	....	....
Capital account: debit...............	3 994 ..	....	....	....	....	....	....	....	....
Total, Groups A Plus B.................	4 981 ..	*9,313*	*5,101*	*4,654*	*4,772*	*2,759*	*−7,647*	*2,175*	*15,755*
C. Financial Account[1]..........................	4 995 W.	**−10,434**	**−2,498**	**−540**	**−4,385**	**3,664**	**11,082**	**5,649**	**−3,015**
Direct investment abroad................	4 505 ..	23	−428	−171	−623	−77	−501	−1,033	−2,156
Direct investment in Thailand............	4 555 Z.	3,366	5,067	3,342	5,232	5,860	8,055	9,004	9,498
Portfolio investment assets............	4 602 ..	−153	−360	−913	−939	1,232	−1,522	−2,025	−9,777
Equity securities..........................	4 610 ..	....	....	−9	−149	−244	−47	−589	−1,896
Debt securities..........................	4 619 ..	−153	−360	−905	−790	1,475	−1,475	−1,436	−7,881
Portfolio investment liabilities............	4 652 Z.	−553	−525	−694	851	1,856	7,070	5,714	2,871
Equity securities..........................	4 660 ..	900	352	539	1,786	1,319	5,121	5,242	4,241
Debt securities..........................	4 669 Z.	−1,453	−877	−1,233	−935	537	1,948	472	−1,369
Financial derivatives............	4 910 ..	....	68	24	93	−106	−525	353	....
Financial derivatives assets............	4 900 ..	....	10	7	−1	11	382	−270	....
Financial derivatives liabilities............	4 905 ..	....	58	17	94	−116	−908	623	....
Other investment assets............	4 703 ..	−2,232	262	2,818	−45	−1,695	−1,726	−10,005	−4,663
Monetary authorities............	4 701 ..	....	....	....	....	....	....	....	....
General government............	4 704 ..	−123	−31	−5	−3	162	−29	−21	−22
Banks............	4 705 ..	−2,189	743	4,235	−405	−425	−1,701	−8,765	−1,755
Other sectors............	4 728 ..	81	−450	−1,412	363	−1,432	4	−1,219	−2,886
Other investment liabilities............	4 753 W.	−10,886	−6,583	−4,945	−8,955	−3,406	232	3,641	1,211
Monetary authorities............	4 753 WA	43	894	5,352	3,031	3,022	....	....	....
General government............	4 753 ZB	216	80	−1,361	−609	−1,878	−1,186	−429	−862
Banks............	4 753 ZC	−4,799	−2,534	−1,761	−1,636	−598	−1,052	109	−537
Other sectors............	4 753 ZD	−6,346	−5,023	−7,175	−9,740	−3,951	2,470	3,961	2,610
Total, Groups A Through C............	4 983 ..	*−1,121*	*2,602*	*4,114*	*386*	*6,424*	*3,436*	*7,824*	*12,740*
D. Net Errors and Omissions..................	4 998 ..	**−685**	**−327**	**1,423**	**132**	**−710**	**1,981**	**4,845**	**4,337**
Total, Groups A Through D............	4 984 ..	*−1,806*	*2,276*	*5,537*	*518*	*5,713*	*5,417*	*12,669*	*17,077*
E. Reserves and Related Items...............	4 802 A.	**1,806**	**−2,276**	**−5,537**	**−518**	**−5,713**	**−5,417**	**−12,669**	**−17,077**
Reserve assets..........................	4 802 ..	1,608	−1,307	−4,197	−122	−5,713	−5,417	−12,669	−17,077
Use of Fund credit and loans............	4 766 ..	−192	−1,288	−1,360	−398	....	....	....	....
Exceptional financing.......	4 920 ..	391	320	19	3	....	....	....	....
Conversion rates: baht per U.S. dollar..........	0 101 ..	**40.112**	**44.432**	**42.960**	**41.485**	**40.222**	**40.220**	**37.882**	**34.518**

[1] Excludes components that have been classified in the categories of Group E.

Table 2. STANDARD PRESENTATION, 2000–2007

(Millions of U.S. dollars)

	Code	2000	2001	2002	2003	2004	2005	2006	2007
CURRENT ACCOUNT	4 993	**9,313**	**5,101**	**4,654**	**4,772**	**2,759**	**−7,647**	**2,175**	**15,755**
A. GOODS	4 100	**11,701**	**8,543**	**9,044**	**11,175**	**10,785**	**3,388**	**13,844**	**25,547**
Credit	2 100	**67,894**	**63,082**	**66,052**	**78,083**	**94,979**	**109,369**	**127,929**	**150,026**
General merchandise: exports f.o.b.	2 110	67,871	63,062	65,852	77,680	94,834	109,145	127,414	148,506
Goods for processing: exports f.o.b.	2 150	....	....	....	....	....	....	....	....
Repairs on goods	2 160	....	....	....	....	....	....	....	....
Goods procured in ports by carriers	2 170	....	....	....	....	....	....	....	....
Nonmonetary gold	2 180	23	20	200	403	144	223	515	1,520
Debit	3 100	**−56,193**	**−54,539**	**−57,008**	**−66,909**	**−84,193**	**−105,981**	**−114,085**	**−124,479**
General merchandise: imports f.o.b.	3 110	−55,666	−53,790	−56,314	−66,273	−83,159	−104,203	−112,380	−122,992
Goods for processing: imports f.o.b.	3 150	....	....	....	....	....	....	....	....
Repairs on goods	3 160	....	....	....	....	....	....	....	....
Goods procured in ports by carriers	3 170	....	....	....	....	....	....	....	....
Nonmonetary gold	3 180	−527	−749	−694	−636	−1,034	−1,778	−1,705	−1,486
B. SERVICES	4 200	**−1,592**	**−1,586**	**−1,330**	**−2,370**	**−4,037**	**−6,864**	**−8,193**	**−8,069**
Total credit	2 200	*13,868*	*13,024*	*15,391*	*15,798*	*19,040*	*20,163*	*24,822*	*30,357*
Total debit	3 200	*−15,460*	*−14,610*	*−16,720*	*−18,169*	*−23,077*	*−27,027*	*−33,015*	*−38,425*
Transportation services, credit	2 205	**3,250**	**3,057**	**3,265**	**3,503**	**4,350**	**4,626**	**5,377**	**6,369**
Passenger	2 850	*2,452*	*2,303*	*2,487*	*2,600*	*3,011*	*2,525*	*3,221*	*3,955*
Freight	2 851	*605*	*610*	*679*	*805*	*1,092*	*1,200*	*1,383*	*1,603*
Other	2 852	*193*	*143*	*99*	*98*	*247*	*901*	*774*	*810*
Sea transport, passenger	2 207	....	....	....	....	....	....	....	....
Sea transport, freight	2 208	....	....	....	....	....	....	....	....
Sea transport, other	2 209	....	....	....	....	....	....	....	....
Air transport, passenger	2 211	....	....	....	....	....	....	....	....
Air transport, freight	2 212	....	....	....	....	....	....	....	....
Air transport, other	2 213	....	....	....	....	....	....	....	....
Other transport, passenger	2 215	....	....	....	....	....	....	....	....
Other transport, freight	2 216	....	....	....	....	....	....	....	....
Other transport, other	2 217	....	....	....	....	....	....	....	....
Transportation services, debit	3 205	**−6,760**	**−6,830**	**−7,121**	**−8,484**	**−10,830**	**−14,439**	**−16,309**	**−18,177**
Passenger	3 850	*−446*	*−410*	*−585*	*−617*	*−829*	*−1,117*	*−1,575*	*−1,744*
Freight	3 851	*−6,096*	*−6,152*	*−6,206*	*−7,497*	*−9,536*	*−12,332*	*−13,429*	*−14,774*
Other	3 852	*−218*	*−268*	*−330*	*−369*	*−465*	*−989*	*−1,305*	*−1,659*
Sea transport, passenger	3 207	....	....	....	....	....	....	....	....
Sea transport, freight	3 208	....	....	....	....	....	....	....	....
Sea transport, other	3 209	....	....	....	....	....	....	....	....
Air transport, passenger	3 211	....	....	....	....	....	....	....	....
Air transport, freight	3 212	....	....	....	....	....	....	....	....
Air transport, other	3 213	....	....	....	....	....	....	....	....
Other transport, passenger	3 215	....	....	....	....	....	....	....	....
Other transport, freight	3 216	....	....	....	....	....	....	....	....
Other transport, other	3 217	....	....	....	....	....	....	....	....
Travel, credit	2 236	**7,483**	**7,075**	**7,901**	**7,856**	**10,043**	**9,577**	**13,393**	**16,667**
Business travel	2 237	....	....	....	....	....	....	....	....
Personal travel	2 240	....	....	....	....	....	....	....	....
Travel, debit	3 236	**−2,772**	**−2,924**	**−3,303**	**−2,921**	**−4,514**	**−3,800**	**−4,598**	**−5,143**
Business travel	3 237	....	....	....	....	....	....	....	....
Personal travel	3 240	....	....	....	....	....	....	....	....
Other services, credit	2 200 BA	**3,135**	**2,892**	**4,225**	**4,439**	**4,647**	**5,960**	**6,052**	**7,321**
Communications	2 245	132	109	130	148	201	258	244	232
Construction	2 249	230	296	244	188	236	255	336	518
Insurance	2 253	82	88	92	134	135	280	253	312
Financial	2 260	....	....	....	....	....	....	....	....
Computer and information	2 262	....	....	....	....	....	....	....	....
Royalties and licence fees	2 266	9	9	7	8	14	17	46	54
Other business services	2 268	2,600	2,298	3,665	3,857	3,952	4,998	4,986	5,971
Personal, cultural, and recreational	2 287	....	....	....	....	....	....	....	....
Government, n.i.e.	2 291	83	93	87	104	108	152	186	233
Other services, debit	3 200 BA	**−5,928**	**−4,856**	**−6,297**	**−6,764**	**−7,733**	**−8,788**	**−12,108**	**−15,106**
Communications	3 245	−39	−145	−86	−180	−141	−214	−159	−169
Construction	3 249	−105	−110	−72	−152	−229	−314	−581	−640
Insurance	3 253	−801	−804	−973	−1,125	−1,290	−1,660	−1,791	−1,916
Financial	3 260	....	....	....	....	....	....	....	....
Computer and information	3 262	....	....	....	....	....	....	....	....
Royalties and licence fees	3 266	−710	−823	−1,104	−1,268	−1,584	−1,674	−2,046	−2,287
Other business services	3 268	−4,142	−2,839	−3,913	−3,870	−4,320	−4,779	−7,357	−9,841
Personal, cultural, and recreational	3 287	....	....	....	....	....	....	....	....
Government, n.i.e.	3 291	−131	−135	−149	−170	−169	−146	−174	−253

2008, International Monetary Fund: *Balance of Payments Statistics Yearbook*

Table 2 (Continued). STANDARD PRESENTATION, 2000–2007

(Millions of U.S. dollars)

	Code	2000	2001	2002	2003	2004	2005	2006	2007
C. INCOME	4 300	**−1,381**	**−2,457**	**−3,663**	**−4,973**	**−6,120**	**−7,174**	**−6,844**	**−5,661**
Total credit	2 300	*4,235*	*3,917*	*3,421*	*3,150*	*3,244*	*3,640*	*4,659*	*6,772*
Total debit	3 300	*−5,616*	*−6,375*	*−7,084*	*−8,123*	*−9,364*	*−10,813*	*−11,502*	*−12,433*
Compensation of employees, credit	2 310	**1,697**	**1,252**	**1,380**	**1,607**	**1,622**	**1,187**	**1,333**	**1,635**
Compensation of employees, debit	3 310	....	....	....	....	....	....	....	....
Investment income, credit	2 320	**2,538**	**2,665**	**2,041**	**1,543**	**1,622**	**2,453**	**3,326**	**5,137**
Direct investment income	2 330	....	84	65	135	125	249	163	163
Dividends and distributed branch profits	2 332	....	....	....	....	....	....	....	....
Reinvested earnings and undistributed branch profits	2 333	....	84	65	135	125	249	163	163
Income on debt (interest)	2 334	....	....	....	....	....	....	....	....
Portfolio investment income	2 339	....	....	....	....	....	....	....	....
Income on equity	2 340	....	....	....	....	....	....	....	....
Income on bonds and notes	2 350	....	....	....	....	....	....	....	....
Income on money market instruments	2 360	....	....	....	....	....	....	....	....
Other investment income	2 370	2,538	2,581	1,976	1,408	1,497	2,204	3,163	4,974
Investment income, debit	3 320	**−5,616**	**−6,375**	**−7,084**	**−8,123**	**−9,364**	**−10,813**	**−11,502**	**−12,433**
Direct investment income	3 330	....	−1,175	−2,388	−3,316	−4,223	−4,501	−4,165	−4,165
Dividends and distributed branch profits	3 332	....	....	....	....	....	....	....	....
Reinvested earnings and undistributed branch profits	3 333	....	−1,175	−2,388	−3,316	−4,223	−4,501	−4,165	−4,165
Income on debt (interest)	3 334	....	....	....	....	....	....	....	....
Portfolio investment income	3 339	....	....	....	....	....	....	....	....
Income on equity	3 340	....	....	....	....	....	....	....	....
Income on bonds and notes	3 350	....	....	....	....	....	....	....	....
Income on money market instruments	3 360	....	....	....	....	....	....	....	....
Other investment income	3 370	−5,616	−5,200	−4,696	−4,807	−5,142	−6,312	−7,337	−8,268
D. CURRENT TRANSFERS	4 379	**586**	**601**	**603**	**941**	**2,131**	**3,004**	**3,368**	**3,938**
Credit	2 379	**952**	**990**	**979**	**1,326**	**2,479**	**3,351**	**3,764**	**4,395**
General government	2 380	84	110	55	128	121	159	201	237
Other sectors	2 390	867	880	923	1,198	2,358	3,193	3,563	4,158
Workers' remittances	2 391	....	....	....	....	....	....	....	....
Other current transfers	2 392	....	....	....	....	....	....	....	....
Debit	3 379	**−366**	**−389**	**−375**	**−385**	**−348**	**−348**	**−396**	**−457**
General government	3 380	−7	−6	−8	−19	−35	−34	−25	−30
Other sectors	3 390	−359	−384	−367	−366	−313	−314	−370	−427
Workers' remittances	3 391	....	....	....	....	....	....	....	....
Other current transfers	3 392	....	....	....	....	....	....	....	....
CAPITAL AND FINANCIAL ACCOUNT	4 996	**−8,628**	**−4,774**	**−6,077**	**−4,903**	**−2,049**	**5,666**	**−7,020**	**−20,092**
CAPITAL ACCOUNT	4 994	....	....	....	....	....	....	....	....
Total credit	2 994	....	....	....	....	....	....	....	....
Total debit	3 994	....	....	....	....	....	....	....	....
Capital transfers, credit	2 400	....	....	....	....	....	....	....	....
General government	2 401	....	....	....	....	....	....	....	....
Debt forgiveness	2 402	....	....	....	....	....	....	....	....
Other capital transfers	2 410	....	....	....	....	....	....	....	....
Other sectors	2 430	....	....	....	....	....	....	....	....
Migrants' transfers	2 431	....	....	....	....	....	....	....	....
Debt forgiveness	2 432	....	....	....	....	....	....	....	....
Other capital transfers	2 440	....	....	....	....	....	....	....	....
Capital transfers, debit	3 400	....	....	....	....	....	....	....	....
General government	3 401	....	....	....	....	....	....	....	....
Debt forgiveness	3 402	....	....	....	....	....	....	....	....
Other capital transfers	3 410	....	....	....	....	....	....	....	....
Other sectors	3 430	....	....	....	....	....	....	....	....
Migrants' transfers	3 431	....	....	....	....	....	....	....	....
Debt forgiveness	3 432	....	....	....	....	....	....	....	....
Other capital transfers	3 440	....	....	....	....	....	....	....	....
Nonproduced nonfinancial assets, credit	2 480	....	....	....	....	....	....	....	....
Nonproduced nonfinancial assets, debit	3 480	....	....	....	....	....	....	....	....

Table 2 (Continued). STANDARD PRESENTATION, 2000–2007

(Millions of U.S. dollars)

	Code	2000	2001	2002	2003	2004	2005	2006	2007
FINANCIAL ACCOUNT	4 995	−8,628	−4,774	−6,077	−4,903	−2,049	5,666	−7,020	−20,092
A. DIRECT INVESTMENT	4 500	3,389	4,639	3,171	4,609	5,784	7,554	7,971	7,342
Direct investment abroad	4 505	23	−428	−171	−623	−77	−501	−1,033	−2,156
Equity capital	4 510	37	−126	−77	−295	−340	−465	−866	−1,793
Claims on affiliated enterprises	4 515	....	....	....	....	....	....	....	....
Liabilities to affiliated enterprises	4 520	....	....	....	....	....	....	....	....
Reinvested earnings	4 525	....	−84	−65	−135	−125	−249	−163	−163
Other capital	4 530	−14	−218	−29	−193	388	213	−4	−200
Claims on affiliated enterprises	4 535	....	....	....	....	....	....	....	....
Liabilities to affiliated enterprises	4 540	....	....	....	....	....	....	....	....
Direct investment in Thailand	4 555	3,366	5,067	3,342	5,232	5,860	8,055	9,004	9,498
Equity capital	4 560	3,402	2,698	273	1,383	2,118	2,499	3,377	5,355
Claims on direct investors	4 565	....	....	....	....	....	....	....	....
Liabilities to direct investors	4 570	....	....	....	....	....	....	....	....
Reinvested earnings	4 575	....	1,175	2,388	3,316	4,223	4,501	4,165	4,165
Other capital	4 580	−36	1,194	680	533	−481	1,056	1,461	−22
Claims on direct investors	4 585	....	....	....	....	....	....	....	....
Liabilities to direct investors	4 590	....	....	....	....	....	....	....	....
B. PORTFOLIO INVESTMENT	4 600	−706	−886	−1,608	−88	3,088	5,548	3,689	−6,905
Assets	4 602	−153	−360	−913	−939	1,232	−1,522	−2,025	−9,777
Equity securities	4 610	....	....	−9	−149	−244	−47	−589	−1,896
Monetary authorities	4 611	....	....	....	....	....	....	....	....
General government	4 612	....	....	....	....	....	....	....	−101
Banks	4 613	....	....	....	−146	−164	138	4	87
Other sectors	4 614	....	....	−9	−2	−80	−185	−593	−1,882
Debt securities	4 619	−153	−360	−905	−790	1,475	−1,475	−1,436	−7,881
Bonds and notes	4 620	−153	−361	−947	−815	1,451	−1,129	−1,110	−2,009
Monetary authorities	4 621	....	....	....	....	....	....	....	....
General government	4 622	....	....	....	....	....	....	....	−21
Banks	4 623	−154	−287	−920	−749	1,574	−626	−480	1,101
Other sectors	4 624	1	−73	−27	−67	−122	−503	−630	−3,089
Money market instruments	4 630	....	....	42	25	24	−346	−326	−5,871
Monetary authorities	4 631	....	....	....	....	....	....	....	....
General government	4 632	....	....	....	....	....	....	....	....
Banks	4 633	....	....	....	25	14	−146	5	−641
Other sectors	4 634	....	....	42	....	10	−200	−331	−5,231
Liabilities	4 652	−553	−525	−694	851	1,856	7,070	5,714	2,871
Equity securities	4 660	900	352	539	1,786	1,319	5,121	5,242	4,241
Banks	4 663	....	....	....	593	651	2,536	2,245	187
Other sectors	4 664	900	352	539	1,194	668	2,585	2,997	4,054
Debt securities	4 669	−1,453	−877	−1,233	−935	537	1,948	472	−1,369
Bonds and notes	4 670	−1,062	−1,148	−1,492	−811	641	596	−867	−772
Monetary authorities	4 671	....	....	....	....	....	224	427	136
General government	4 672	−384	−184	−364	−60	297	−521	−1,682	−1,284
Banks	4 673	−87	....	238	−46	15	....	50	−53
Other sectors	4 674	−591	−964	−1,366	−705	328	893	337	429
Money market instruments	4 680	−391	271	258	−125	−104	1,353	1,339	−598
Monetary authorities	4 681	....	....	....	....	....	....	....	−757
General government	4 682	33	138	224	49	−96	793	1,579	134
Banks	4 683	....	....	....	−15	....	....	....	....
Other sectors	4 684	−424	133	34	−159	−9	560	−240	26
C. FINANCIAL DERIVATIVES	4 910	....	68	24	93	−106	−525	353	....
Monetary authorities	4 911	....	....	....	....	....	....	....	....
General government	4 912	....	....	....	....	....	....	....	....
Banks	4 913	....	....	....	....	16	−456	353	....
Other sectors	4 914	....	68	24	93	−122	−70	....	....
Assets	4 900	....	10	7	−1	11	382	−270	....
Monetary authorities	4 901	....	....	....	....	....	....	....	....
General government	4 902	....	....	....	....	....	....	....	....
Banks	4 903	....	....	....	....	10	381	−270	....
Other sectors	4 904	....	10	7	−1	1	1	....	....
Liabilities	4 905	....	58	17	94	−116	−908	623	....
Monetary authorities	4 906	....	....	....	....	....	....	....	....
General government	4 907	....	....	....	....	....	....	....	....
Banks	4 908	....	....	....	....	6	−837	623	....
Other sectors	4 909	....	58	17	94	−123	−70	....	....

Table 2 (Concluded). STANDARD PRESENTATION, 2000–2007

(Millions of U.S. dollars)

	Code	2000	2001	2002	2003	2004	2005	2006	2007
D. OTHER INVESTMENT	4 700	**−12,919**	**−7,289**	**−3,467**	**−9,395**	**−5,101**	**−1,494**	**−6,364**	**−3,452**
Assets	4 703	**−2,232**	**262**	**2,818**	**−45**	**−1,695**	**−1,726**	**−10,005**	**−4,663**
Trade credits	4 706	....	−270	−1,290	548	−463	−1,200	−949	−2,797
General government	4 707	....	....	....	....	....	....	....	....
of which: Short-term	4 709	....	....	....	....	....	....	....	....
Other sectors	4 710	....	−270	−1,290	548	−463	−1,200	−949	−2,797
of which: Short-term	4 712	....	....	....	....	....	....	....	....
Loans	4 714	−214	592	−22	−440	743	−642	−111	87
Monetary authorities	4 715	....	....	....	....	....	....	....	....
of which: Short-term	4 718	....	....	....	....	....	....	....	....
General government	4 719	....	....	....	....	....	−29	−21	−25
of which: Short-term	4 721	....	....	....	....	....	....	....	....
Banks	4 722	−200	575	−63	−322	581	−579	−79	−33
of which: Short-term	4 724	....	....	....	....	....	−363	47	94
Other sectors	4 725	−14	17	40	−117	162	−34	−11	145
of which: Short-term	4 727	....	7	16	−118	....	−21	13	−46
Currency and deposits	4 730	−2,055	−337	4,240	−88	−2,029	28	−8,527	−1,542
Monetary authorities	4 731	....	....	....	....	....	....	....	....
General government	4 732	....	4	....	....	....	....	....	3
Banks	4 733	−2,055	−121	4,322	−75	−1,066	−1,237	−8,336	−1,319
Other sectors	4 734	....	−220	−82	−12	−963	1,265	−191	−226
Other assets	4 736	38	276	−110	−66	54	87	−418	−412
Monetary authorities	4 737	....	....	....	....	....	....	....	....
of which: Short-term	4 739	....	....	....	....	....	....	....	....
General government	4 740	−123	−35	−5	−3	162	....	....	....
of which: Short-term	4 742	....	....	....	....	....	....	....	....
Banks	4 743	66	289	−24	−8	59	114	−350	−403
of which: Short-term	4 745	....	....	....	....	....	....	....	....
Other sectors	4 746	95	23	−80	−55	−167	−27	−68	−8
of which: Short-term	4 748	....	....	....	....	....	....	....	....
Liabilities	4 753	**−10,687**	**−7,551**	**−6,285**	**−9,351**	**−3,406**	**232**	**3,641**	**1,211**
Trade credits	4 756	−837	−508	233	189	461	3,447	635	1,371
General government	4 757	....	....	....	....	....	....	....	....
of which: Short-term	4 759	....	....	....	....	....	....	....	....
Other sectors	4 760	−837	−508	233	189	461	3,447	635	1,371
of which: Short-term	4 762	−694	−423	250	221	482	3,465	669	1,386
Loans	4 764	−9,227	−8,145	−10,340	−10,512	−2,276	−3,339	2,366	−974
Monetary authorities	4 765	−192	−3,119	−3,835	−4,928	....	....	....	....
of which: Use of Fund credit and loans from the Fund	4 766	−192	−1,288	−1,360	−398	....	....	....	....
of which: Short-term	4 768	....	....	....	....	....	....	....	....
General government	4 769	607	400	−1,342	−606	−1,878	−1,182	−429	−862
of which: Short-term	4 771	....	....	....	....	....	....	....	....
Banks	4 772	−4,828	−2,257	−1,683	−1,689	−506	−1,149	−309	−1,275
of which: Short-term	4 774	−4,828	−685	−1,086	−1,147	77	30	−537	−115
Other sectors	4 775	−4,813	−3,168	−3,479	−3,289	108	−1,008	3,103	1,163
of which: Short-term	4 777	−1,053	−302	−740	−466	478	−84	255	1,288
Currency and deposits	4 780	−361	1,766	4,150	1,185	−1,495	50	153	45
Monetary authorities	4 781	43	2,725	7,828	7,560	3,022	....	....	....
General government	4 782	....	....	....	....	....	....	....	....
Banks	4 783	5	−5	6	−10	18	47	145	44
Other sectors	4 784	−409	−954	−3,683	−6,365	−4,534	2	8	1
Other liabilities	4 786	−262	−665	−328	−212	−96	74	488	769
Monetary authorities	4 787	....	....	....	....	....	....	....	....
of which: Short-term	4 789	....	....	....	....	....	....	....	....
General government	4 790	....	....	....	....	....	−4	....	....
of which: Short-term	4 792	....	....	....	....	....	....	....	....
Banks	4 793	23	−272	−83	62	−110	49	273	694
of which: Short-term	4 795	....	....	....	....	....	....	....	....
Other sectors	4 796	−285	−393	−245	−274	14	28	215	75
of which: Short-term	4 798	....	....	....	....	....	....	....	....
E. RESERVE ASSETS	4 802	**1,608**	**−1,307**	**−4,197**	**−122**	**−5,713**	**−5,417**	**−12,669**	**−17,077**
Monetary gold	4 812	31	−31	−6	−24	−43	....	9	−11
Special drawing rights	4 811	163	76	1	4	−1	....	....	1
Reserve position in the Fund	4 810	....	....	....	−107	−47	−37	53	38
Foreign exchange	4 803	1,413	−1,352	−4,192	5	−5,623	−5,380	−12,731	−17,105
Other claims	4 813	....	....	....	....	....	....	....	....
NET ERRORS AND OMISSIONS	4 998	**−685**	**−327**	**1,423**	**132**	**−710**	**1,981**	**4,845**	**4,337**

Table 3. INTERNATIONAL INVESTMENT POSITION (End-period stocks), 2000–2007

(Millions of U.S. dollars)

	Code	2000	2001	2002	2003	2004	2005	2006	2007
ASSETS	8 995 C.	**53,797**	**54,325**	**58,727**	**64,194**	**73,071**	**79,702**	**107,397**	**146,329**
Direct investment abroad	8 505	**2,203**	**2,626**	**2,863**	**3,400**	**3,728**	**5,005**	**6,398**	**8,022**
Equity capital and reinvested earnings	8 506	2,029	2,182	2,446	3,048	3,569	4,383	6,326	8,383
Claims on affiliated enterprises	8 507	2,029	2,182	2,446	3,048	3,569	4,383	6,326	8,383
Liabilities to affiliated enterprises	8 508	....	....	....	....	....	....	....	....
Other capital	8 530	174	444	417	352	159	622	72	−361
Claims on affiliated enterprises	8 535	174	550	779	913	722	1,081	1,248	841
Liabilities to affiliated enterprises	8 540	....	−106	−362	−561	−563	−459	−1,176	−1,202
Portfolio investment	8 602	**488**	**825**	**1,689**	**2,834**	**1,625**	**3,478**	**4,782**	**14,692**
Equity securities	8 610	53	82	84	434	694	1,017	1,775	3,237
Monetary authorities	8 611	....	....	....	....	....	....	....	....
General government	8 612	....	....	....	....	....	....	104	102
Banks	8 613	20	20	27	174	349	193	215	132
Other sectors	8 614	33	62	57	260	345	824	1,457	3,004
Debt securities	8 619	435	743	1,605	2,400	931	2,461	3,007	11,455
Bonds and notes	8 620	124	327	1,344	2,224	780	1,625	2,629	3,867
Monetary authorities	8 621	....	....	....	....	....	....	....	....
General government	8 622	....	....	....	....	....	....	97	116
Banks	8 623	115	224	1,324	2,122	551	1,224	1,872	1,670
Other sectors	8 624	9	103	20	102	229	401	659	2,081
Money market instruments	8 630	311	416	261	176	151	836	378	7,588
Monetary authorities	8 631	....	....	....	....	....	....	....	....
General government	8 632	....	....	....	....	....	....	....	....
Banks	8 633	50	227	39	14	....	142	156	90
Other sectors	8 634	261	189	222	162	151	694	222	7,498
Financial derivatives	8 900	**517**	**141**	**282**	**614**	**643**	**470**	**711**	**1,463**
Monetary authorities	8 901	....	....	....	....	....	....	....	....
General government	8 902	....	....	....	....	....	....	....	....
Banks	8 903	503	133	282	612	642	470	711	1,463
Other sectors	8 904	14	8	....	2	1	....	....	....
Other investment	8 703	**17,928**	**17,684**	**14,968**	**15,197**	**17,244**	**18,684**	**28,522**	**34,696**
Trade credits	8 706	1,158	1,427	2,718	2,168	2,630	3,830	4,836	7,779
General government	8 707	....	....	....	....	....	....	....	....
of which: Short-term	8 709	....	....	....	....	....	....	....	....
Other sectors	8 710	1,158	1,427	2,718	2,168	2,630	3,830	4,836	7,779
of which: Short-term	8 712	*1,157*	*1,418*	*2,694*	*2,156*	*2,619*	*3,814*	*4,812*	*7,738*
Loans	8 714	2,431	1,833	1,882	2,356	1,693	2,179	2,213	2,599
Monetary authorities	8 715	....	....	....	....	....	....	....	....
of which: Short-term	8 718	....	....	....	....	....	....	....	....
General government	8 719	....	....	....	....	....	28	55	89
of which: Short-term	8 721	....	....	....	....	....	....	....	....
Banks	8 722	2,322	1,741	1,829	2,169	1,660	1,804	1,762	1,813
of which: Short-term	8 724	*1,277*	*715*	*871*	*1,276*	*1,162*	*1,083*	*906*	*808*
Other sectors	8 725	109	92	53	187	33	347	396	697
of which: Short-term	8 727	*41*	*34*	*19*	*151*	*7*	*50*	*79*	*167*
Currency and deposits	8 730	13,297	13,557	9,403	9,620	11,856	11,693	20,012	22,388
Monetary authorities	8 731	....	....	....	....	....	....	....	....
General government	8 732	4	....	....	....	....	....	....	24
Banks	8 733	13,125	13,167	8,908	9,105	10,128	11,184	19,435	20,794
Other sectors	8 734	168	390	495	515	1,728	509	577	1,570
Other assets	8 736	1,042	867	965	1,053	1,065	982	1,461	1,929
Monetary authorities	8 737	....	....	....	....	....	....	....	....
of which: Short-term	8 739	....	....	....	....	....	....	....	....
General government	8 740	123	158	166	164	....	....	....	168
of which: Short-term	8 742	....	....	....	....	....	....	....	....
Banks	8 743	895	704	713	746	756	607	1,023	1,433
of which: Short-term	8 745	*885*	*691*	*710*	*690*	*754*	*607*	*1,023*	*1,433*
Other sectors	8 746	24	5	86	143	309	375	438	328
of which: Short-term	8 748	*7*	*4*	*4*	*56*	*36*	*86*	*84*	*83*
Reserve assets	8 802	**32,661**	**33,049**	**38,925**	**42,149**	**49,831**	**52,065**	**66,985**	**87,455**
Monetary gold	8 812	645	686	869	1,071	1,167	1,374	1,693	2,234
Special drawing rights	8 811	83	5	4	....	1	1	1	....
Reserve position in the Fund	8 810	....	....	....	111	165	188	143	111
Foreign exchange	8 803	31,933	32,357	38,051	40,846	48,372	50,149	64,761	84,696
Other claims	8 813	....	....	....	120	126	353	386	414

Table 3 (Concluded). INTERNATIONAL INVESTMENT POSITION (End-period stocks), 2000–2007

(Millions of U.S. dollars)

	Code	2000	2001	2002	2003	2004	2005	2006	2007
LIABILITIES	8 995 D.	**114,241**	**106,169**	**104,468**	**119,885**	**126,552**	**136,986**	**166,766**	**204,008**
Direct investment in Thailand	8 555	**29,915**	**33,268**	**38,449**	**48,944**	**53,187**	**58,195**	**77,163**	**94,759**
Equity capital and reinvested earnings	8 556	25,331	28,256	32,453	44,008	48,536	52,398	70,235	86,543
Claims on direct investors	8 557	....	....	....	....	....	−3	−4	−6
Liabilities to direct investors	8 558	25,331	28,256	32,453	44,008	48,536	52,401	70,239	86,549
Other capital	8 580	4,584	5,012	5,996	4,936	4,651	5,797	6,928	8,216
Claims on direct investors	8 585	−1,203	−1,380	−1,108	−1,671	−1,399	−957	−1,007	−405
Liabilities to direct investors	8 590	5,787	6,392	7,104	6,607	6,050	6,754	7,935	8,621
Portfolio investment	8 652	**16,360**	**17,122**	**17,811**	**29,087**	**32,109**	**40,253**	**46,727**	**63,658**
Equity securities	8 660	8,153	10,240	12,260	24,319	26,618	32,900	38,504	56,568
Banks	8 663	1,435	1,804	2,642	6,483	7,243	10,132	11,990	15,421
Other sectors	8 664	6,718	8,436	9,618	17,836	19,375	22,768	26,514	41,147
Debt securities	8 669	8,207	6,882	5,551	4,768	5,491	7,353	8,223	7,091
Bonds and notes	8 670	7,906	6,409	4,808	4,140	4,969	6,750	7,114	6,669
Monetary authorities	8 671	....	....	....	....	....	....	223	377
General government	8 672	1,513	1,291	935	885	1,199	1,739	1,792	693
Banks	8 673	54	53	45	....	109	93	143	90
Other sectors	8 674	6,339	5,065	3,828	3,255	3,661	4,918	4,956	5,509
Money market instruments	8 680	301	473	743	628	522	603	1,109	422
Monetary authorities	8 681	....	....	....	....	....	....	742	17
General government	8 682	26	147	362	385	288	....	....	3
Banks	8 683	7	7	16	1	....	....	....	....
Other sectors	8 684	268	319	365	242	234	603	367	401
Financial derivatives	8 905	**684**	**507**	**541**	**768**	**843**	**601**	**567**	**765**
Monetary authorities	8 906	....	....	....	....	....	....	....	....
General government	8 907	....	....	....	....	....	....	....	....
Banks	8 908	502	258	266	398	603	599	567	765
Other sectors	8 909	182	249	275	370	240	2	....	....
Other investment	8 753	**67,281**	**55,271**	**47,666**	**41,085**	**40,414**	**37,937**	**42,309**	**44,825**
Trade credits	8 756	3,464	2,885	3,193	3,554	4,661	7,960	8,611	10,064
General government	8 757	....	....	....	....	....	....	....	....
of which: Short-term	8 759	....	....	....	....	....	....	....	....
Other sectors	8 760	3,464	2,885	3,193	3,554	4,661	7,960	8,611	10,064
of which: Short-term	8 762	*3,125*	*2,654*	*2,970*	*3,352*	*4,474*	*7,804*	*8,489*	*9,956*
Loans	8 764	62,361	51,274	43,213	35,992	34,240	28,420	31,417	31,652
Monetary authorities	8 765	12,019	8,327	4,904	....	....	....	....	....
of which: Use of Fund credit and loans from the Fund	8 766	*3,062*	*1,681*	*391*	....	....	....	....	....
of which: Short-term	8 768	....	....	....	....	....	....	....	....
General government	8 769	7,347	7,296	6,315	6,036	4,292	2,779	2,348	1,574
of which: Short-term	8 771	....	....	....	....	....	....	....	....
Banks	8 772	12,200	9,322	8,037	6,743	6,653	4,886	4,568	3,431
of which: Short-term	8 774	*5,324*	*4,909*	*4,038*	*2,937*	*2,317*	*1,881*	*1,143*	*1,124*
Other sectors	8 775	30,795	26,329	23,957	23,213	23,295	20,755	24,501	26,647
of which: Short-term	8 777	*3,496*	*2,462*	*1,802*	*1,753*	*2,240*	*2,063*	*2,381*	*3,690*
Currency and deposits	8 780	694	575	743	804	870	878	1,133	1,231
Monetary authorities	8 781	....	....	....	....	....	....	....	....
General government	8 782	....	....	....	....	....	....	....	....
Banks	8 783	694	575	743	804	870	870	1,117	1,218
Other sectors	8 784	....	....	....	....	....	8	16	14
Other liabilities	8 786	762	537	517	735	643	679	1,148	1,878
Monetary authorities	8 787	....	....	....	....	....	....	....	....
of which: Short-term	8 789	....	....	....	....	....	....	....	....
General government	8 790	....	....	....	....	....	....	....	....
of which: Short-term	8 792	....	....	....	....	....	....	....	....
Banks	8 793	762	537	517	735	643	653	901	1,623
of which: Short-term	8 795	*641*	*446*	*505*	*724*	*629*	*642*	*901*	*1,623*
Other sectors	8 796	....	....	....	....	....	26	247	255
of which: Short-term	8 798	....	....	....	....	....	*26*	*244*	*255*
NET INTERNATIONAL INVESTMENT POSITION	8 995	−60,444	−51,844	−45,741	−55,691	−53,481	−57,284	−59,368	−57,679
Conversion rates: baht per U.S. dollar (end of period)	0 102	43.268	44.222	43.152	39.591	39.061	41.030	36.045	33.718

Table 1. ANALYTIC PRESENTATION, 2000–2007

(Millions of U.S. dollars)

	Code	2000	2001	2002	2003	2004	2005	2006	2007
A. Current Account[1]................................	4 993 Z.	**−139.6**	**−169.1**	**−139.9**	**−161.9**	**−205.7**	**−460.7**	**−340.4**	....
Goods: exports f.o.b................................	2 100 ..	361.8	357.2	424.2	597.7	601.0	660.2	754.5	....
Goods: imports f.o.b................................	3 100 ..	−484.6	−516.1	−575.6	−754.5	−853.3	−1,172.4	−1,218.9	....
Balance on Goods................................	4 100 ..	*−122.8*	*−158.9*	*−151.4*	*−156.8*	*−252.3*	*−512.2*	*−464.4*	....
Services: credit................................	2 200 ..	61.8	71.8	90.0	94.8	150.0	176.8	216.0	....
Services: debit................................	3 200 ..	−117.5	−129.9	−148.1	−204.2	−239.3	−278.5	−297.8	....
Balance on Goods and Services..............	4 991 ..	*−178.5*	*−217.0*	*−209.5*	*−266.3*	*−341.6*	*−613.9*	*−546.2*	....
Income: credit................................	2 300 ..	32.9	25.9	26.2	26.8	39.1	44.2	47.7	....
Income: debit................................	3 300 ..	−62.0	−55.2	−47.8	−50.2	−72.5	−78.7	−85.5	....
Balance on Goods, Services, and Income........	4 992 ..	*−207.6*	*−246.3*	*−231.1*	*−289.6*	*−375.1*	*−648.4*	*−584.0*	....
Current transfers: credit........................	2 379 Z.	73.3	88.3	113.0	161.4	206.8	229.3	284.6	....
Current transfers: debit.........................	3 379 ..	−5.4	−11.1	−21.8	−33.8	−37.4	−41.5	−40.9	....
B. Capital Account[1]................................	4 994 Z.	**8.7**	**21.4**	**13.6**	**20.6**	**40.1**	**51.1**	**64.0**	....
Capital account: credit..........................	2 994 Z.	8.7	21.4	13.6	20.6	40.1	51.1	64.0	....
Capital account: debit...........................	3 994 ..	....	....	....	....	....	....	....	....
Total, Groups A Plus B.........................	4 981 ..	*−131.0*	*−147.8*	*−126.3*	*−141.3*	*−165.6*	*−409.6*	*−276.4*	....
C. Financial Account[1]............................	4 995 W.	**162.8**	**151.2**	**150.8**	**142.9**	**292.0**	**287.4**	**414.2**	....
Direct investment abroad.........................	4 505 ..	−.4	7.3	−2.7	6.3	12.6	14.9	14.4	....
Direct investment in Togo........................	4 555 Z.	41.9	63.6	53.7	33.7	57.3	77.0	77.3	....
Portfolio investment assets......................	4 602 ..	.8	5.3	−1.1	−4.7	−26.5	−26.2	2.0	....
Equity securities................................	4 610 ..	.6	....	−2.0	−.2	−3.9	−18.0	1.0	....
Debt securities.................................	4 619 ..	.2	5.3	.9	−4.5	−22.5	−8.2	1.0	....
Portfolio investment liabilities..................	4 652 Z.	6.1	5.8	13.0	18.6	26.2	28.7	60.6	....
Equity securities................................	4 660 ..	6.1	1.5	6.1	9.8	14.8	16.0	10.4	....
Debt securities.................................	4 669 Z.	....	4.3	6.8	8.8	11.4	12.7	50.3	....
Financial derivatives............................	4 910 ..	−.1	....	....	....	....	.5	....	....
Financial derivatives assets.....................	4 900 ..	....	....	....	....	....	....	....	....
Financial derivatives liabilities.................	4 905 ..	−.1	....	....	....	....	.5	....	....
Other investment assets.........................	4 703 ..	8.8	8.2	−3.8	−28.7	5.7	68.8	42.5	....
Monetary authorities............................	4 701 ..	....	....	....	....	....	....	....	....
General government.............................	4 704 ..	7.5	4.8	−.3	3.1	−2.8	.9	.9	....
Banks..	4 705 ..	−16.8	−8.8	5.5	6.9	−16.7	−11.2	−13.1	....
Other sectors...................................	4 728 ..	18.1	12.3	−9.0	−38.6	25.2	79.0	54.7	....
Other investment liabilities......................	4 753 W.	105.7	61.0	91.7	117.7	216.6	123.7	217.3	....
Monetary authorities............................	4 753 WA	2.5	1.7	10.4	6.7	52.3	−67.2	19.3	....
General government.............................	4 753 ZB	41.6	28.6	19.6	25.8	15.6	25.6	30.0	....
Banks..	4 753 ZC	1.4	.4	−5.7	2.6	−5.5	−7.8	6.7	....
Other sectors...................................	4 753 ZD	60.1	30.3	67.5	82.6	154.1	173.2	161.4	....
Total, Groups A Through C......................	4 983 ..	*31.8*	*3.4*	*24.5*	*1.6*	*126.4*	*−122.3*	*137.9*	....
D. Net Errors and Omissions....................	4 998 ..	**5.0**	**−5.4**	**5.0**	**−10.2**	**14.4**	**8.8**	**20.0**	....
Total, Groups A Through D......................	4 984 ..	*36.8*	*−2.0*	*29.6*	*−8.6*	*140.8*	*−113.5*	*157.8*	....
E. Reserves and Related Items...................	4 802 A.	**−36.8**	**2.0**	**−29.6**	**8.6**	**−140.8**	**113.5**	**−157.8**	....
Reserve assets..................................	4 802 ..	−27.5	7.4	−20.1	22.4	−124.6	124.7	−151.5	....
Use of Fund credit and loans.....................	4 766 ..	−9.3	−10.2	−9.5	−13.8	−16.2	−11.2	−6.4	....
Exceptional financing...........................	4 920 ..	....	4.8	....	....	....	....	....	....
Conversion rates: CFA francs per U.S. dollar..........	0 101 ..	**711.98**	**733.04**	**696.99**	**581.20**	**528.28**	**527.47**	**522.89**	**479.27**

[1] Excludes components that have been classified in the categories of Group E.

Table 2. STANDARD PRESENTATION, 2000–2007

(Millions of U.S. dollars)

	Code	2000	2001	2002	2003	2004	2005	2006	2007
CURRENT ACCOUNT..........................	4 993	**−139.6**	**−169.1**	**−139.9**	**−161.9**	**−205.7**	**−460.7**	**−340.4**	....
A. GOODS..	4 100	**−122.8**	**−158.9**	**−151.4**	**−156.8**	**−252.3**	**−512.2**	**−464.4**	....
Credit...	2 100	**361.8**	**357.2**	**424.2**	**597.7**	**601.0**	**660.2**	**754.5**	....
General merchandise: exports f.o.b.	2 110	354.9	350.9	418.4	588.8	590.9	646.9	737.7	....
Goods for processing: exports f.o.b.	2 150	....	....	....	....	....	....	....	....
Repairs on goods........................	2 160	....	....	....	....	....	....	....	....
Goods procured in ports by carriers	2 170	6.9	6.3	5.9	8.9	10.1	13.3	16.8	....
Nonmonetary gold......................	2 180	....	....	....	....	....	....	....	....
Debit..	3 100	**−484.6**	**−516.1**	**−575.6**	**−754.5**	**−853.3**	**−1,172.4**	**−1,218.9**	....
General merchandise: imports f.o.b.	3 110	−484.3	−515.9	−575.4	−752.7	−851.0	−1,167.7	−1,215.8	....
Goods for processing: imports f.o.b.	3 150	....	....	....	....	....	....	....	....
Repairs on goods........................	3 160	−.2	....	−.1	−.1	−.1	....	....	....
Goods procured in ports by carriers	3 170	−.2	−.2	−.2	−1.8	−2.2	−4.8	−3.1	....
Nonmonetary gold......................	3 180	....	....	....	....	....	....	....	....
B. SERVICES...................................	4 200	**−55.7**	**−58.1**	**−58.1**	**−109.4**	**−89.3**	**−101.7**	**−81.8**	....
Total credit..................................	2 200	*61.8*	*71.8*	*90.0*	*94.8*	*150.0*	*176.8*	*216.0*	....
Total debit...................................	3 200	*−117.5*	*−129.9*	*−148.1*	*−204.2*	*−239.3*	*−278.5*	*−297.8*	....
Transportation services, credit........	2 205	**10.5**	**12.3**	**20.1**	**21.4**	**46.5**	**56.7**	**67.4**	....
Passenger....................................	2 850	*3.3*	*2.5*	*2.8*	*10.9*	*6.4*	*6.9*	*2.1*	....
Freight..	2 851	*1.7*	*2.1*	*1.8*	*2.7*	*23.6*	*25.2*	*36.1*	....
Other..	2 852	*5.6*	*7.6*	*15.4*	*7.8*	*16.5*	*24.6*	*29.3*	....
Sea transport, passenger..............	2 207	....	....	....	....	....	....	....	....
Sea transport, freight...................	2 208	....	....	....	....	....	....	....	....
Sea transport, other.....................	2 209	4.7	6.7	13.4	5.2	12.5	20.2	25.3	....
Air transport, passenger...............	2 211	.9	....	....	7.1	....	....	....	....
Air transport, freight....................	2 212	....	....	....	....	20.3	21.3	29.9	....
Air transport, other......................	2 213	.9	.9	2.0	2.6	4.0	4.4	3.9	....
Other transport, passenger...........	2 215	2.3	2.5	2.8	3.8	6.4	6.9	2.1	....
Other transport, freight................	2 216	1.7	2.1	1.8	2.7	3.3	3.9	6.2	....
Other transport, other..................	2 217	....	....	....	....	....	....	....	....
Transportation services, debit.........	3 205	**−84.0**	**−92.4**	**−103.3**	**−148.5**	**−172.5**	**−213.7**	**−231.6**	....
Passenger....................................	3 850	*−13.4*	*−15.1*	*−21.2*	*−30.4*	*−29.7*	*−34.1*	*−37.0*	....
Freight..	3 851	*−68.9*	*−75.2*	*−80.7*	*−111.6*	*−141.2*	*−175.5*	*−191.2*	....
Other..	3 852	*−1.7*	*−2.0*	*−1.3*	*−6.5*	*−1.6*	*−4.1*	*−3.4*	....
Sea transport, passenger..............	3 207	....	....	....	....	....	....	....	....
Sea transport, freight...................	3 208	−61.9	−67.7	−73.4	−100.3	−115.1	−150.9	−165.5	....
Sea transport, other.....................	3 209	−.4	−.8	....	−4.7	−.2	−.4	−.3	....
Air transport, passenger...............	3 211	−13.4	−15.1	−21.2	−30.4	−29.7	−34.1	−37.0	....
Air transport, freight....................	3 212	−7.0	−7.6	−7.4	−11.3	−26.1	−24.5	−25.7	....
Air transport, other......................	3 213	−1.3	−1.2	−1.2	−1.8	−1.5	−3.7	−3.1	....
Other transport, passenger...........	3 215	....	....	....	....	....	....	....	....
Other transport, freight................	3 216	....	....	....	....	....	....	....	....
Other transport, other..................	3 217	....	....	....	....	....	....	....	....
Travel, credit................................	2 236	**8.0**	**10.9**	**13.2**	**14.7**	**19.1**	**20.4**	**20.5**	....
Business travel............................	2 237	3.9	4.6	6.3	7.8	10.2	9.4	7.9	....
Personal travel............................	2 240	4.2	6.3	6.9	6.9	9.0	11.0	12.7	....
Travel, debit.................................	3 236	**−2.0**	**−4.8**	**−5.0**	**−7.2**	**−8.4**	**−7.7**	**−5.3**	....
Business travel............................	3 237	−2.0	−3.9	−5.0	−6.6	−8.4	−6.7	−4.8	....
Personal travel............................	3 240	....	−.8	....	−.5	−.1	−1.0	−.5	....
Other services, credit....................	2 200 BA	**43.2**	**48.6**	**56.7**	**58.7**	**84.3**	**99.7**	**128.0**	....
Communications..........................	2 245	4.8	8.9	7.1	8.5	10.9	11.7	15.9	....
Construction...............................	2 249	....	4.2	5.4	2.6	.6	1.4	5.0	....
Insurance...................................	2 253	.4	.8	1.1	.5	.9	.9	.8	....
Financial....................................	2 260	3.6	.7	3.6	.4	.9	.6	5.8	....
Computer and information............	2 262	....	.1	....	.5	.9	.4	....	....
Royalties and licence fees............	2 266	....	....	....	....	....	....	....	....
Other business services...............	2 268	18.3	15.4	21.5	23.2	41.9	53.2	59.0	....
Personal, cultural, and recreational	2 287	....	....	....	....	....	....	....	....
Government, n.i.e........................	2 291	16.1	18.6	18.0	22.9	28.2	31.6	41.5	....
Other services, debit.....................	3 200 BA	**−31.5**	**−32.7**	**−39.8**	**−48.5**	**−58.3**	**−57.1**	**−60.9**	....
Communications..........................	3 245	−2.2	−3.1	−4.3	−7.7	−6.3	−6.3	−4.9	....
Construction...............................	3 249	−.6	−1.5	−2.4	−3.9	−.3	−.2	−.2	....
Insurance...................................	3 253	−14.7	−17.9	−17.1	−22.2	−24.2	−31.1	−31.7	....
Financial....................................	3 260	−2.2	−1.8	−2.5	−1.8	−2.9	−2.0	−2.0	....
Computer and information............	3 262	−1.1	−.8	−1.6	−1.4	−1.3	−.5	−1.3	....
Royalties and licence fees............	3 266	−.6	−.8	−.5	−.7	−2.2	−2.7	−7.1	....
Other business services...............	3 268	−9.0	−5.7	−10.4	−10.6	−19.3	−12.2	−10.5	....
Personal, cultural, and recreational	3 287	....	....	....	....	....	....	....	....
Government, n.i.e........................	3 291	−1.1	−1.2	−1.0	−.3	−1.9	−2.1	−3.1	....

Table 2 (Continued). STANDARD PRESENTATION, 2000–2007

(Millions of U.S. dollars)

	Code	2000	2001	2002	2003	2004	2005	2006	2007
C. INCOME	4 300	**−29.1**	**−29.3**	**−21.6**	**−23.3**	**−33.5**	**−34.5**	**−37.8**	....
Total credit	2 300	*32.9*	*25.9*	*26.2*	*26.8*	*39.1*	*44.2*	*47.7*	....
Total debit	3 300	*−62.0*	*−55.2*	*−47.8*	*−50.2*	*−72.5*	*−78.7*	*−85.5*	....
Compensation of employees, credit	2 310	**18.5**	**17.0**	**16.6**	**20.4**	**25.7**	**28.3**	**29.0**	....
Compensation of employees, debit	3 310	**−2.9**	**−.2**	**−.4**	**−1.0**	**−1.1**	**−.7**	**−.7**	....
Investment income, credit	2 320	**14.4**	**9.0**	**9.6**	**6.4**	**13.4**	**15.9**	**18.7**	....
Direct investment income	2 330	2.4	.9	.8	.8	5.4	5.4	6.3	....
Dividends and distributed branch profits	2 332	.3	.8	.1	.4	4.9	4.2	5.8	....
Reinvested earnings and undistributed branch profits	2 333	2.1	....	.3	.2	....	.8	.3	....
Income on debt (interest)	2 334	....	.1	.3	.3	.4	.4	.2	....
Portfolio investment income	2 339	1.1	1.6	1.0	1.6	2.3	2.4	2.2	....
Income on equity	2 340	....	.7	....	.1	....	....	....	....
Income on bonds and notes	2 350	.4	.1	.5	.1	.7	.5	1.3	....
Income on money market instruments	2 360	.7	.8	.5	1.4	1.5	1.9	.9	....
Other investment income	2 370	10.9	6.5	7.8	4.0	5.7	8.1	10.2	....
Investment income, debit	3 320	**−59.2**	**−55.0**	**−47.4**	**−49.2**	**−71.4**	**−78.0**	**−84.8**	....
Direct investment income	3 330	−17.2	−25.2	−18.6	−18.5	−36.7	−45.0	−54.9	....
Dividends and distributed branch profits	3 332	−7.8	−6.7	−8.0	−15.0	−22.2	−18.8	−37.3	....
Reinvested earnings and undistributed branch profits	3 333	−8.4	−17.6	−10.0	−3.3	−14.1	−25.9	−17.0	....
Income on debt (interest)	3 334	−1.0	−1.0	−.7	−.2	−.4	−.4	−.6	....
Portfolio investment income	3 339	−6.2	−3.8	−3.0	−3.1	−3.6	−5.2	−6.8	....
Income on equity	3 340	−1.9	−1.4	−.7	−.8	−1.4	−2.4	−4.5	....
Income on bonds and notes	3 350	−4.2	−2.2	−2.2	−2.3	−2.2	−2.8	−2.4	....
Income on money market instruments	3 360	−.1	−.3	....	....	....	....	....	....
Other investment income	3 370	−35.8	−26.0	−25.8	−27.6	−31.2	−27.8	−23.1	....
D. CURRENT TRANSFERS	4 379	**68.0**	**77.2**	**91.2**	**127.7**	**169.4**	**187.7**	**243.6**	....
Credit	2 379	**73.3**	**88.3**	**113.0**	**161.4**	**206.8**	**229.3**	**284.6**	....
General government	2 380	39.2	20.8	10.8	11.6	19.0	24.0	31.2	....
Other sectors	2 390	34.2	67.5	102.3	149.8	187.9	205.3	253.4	....
Workers' remittances	2 391	15.7	51.5	86.6	128.3	153.3	164.2	199.9	....
Other current transfers	2 392	18.5	15.9	15.7	21.6	34.6	41.1	53.4	....
Debit	3 379	**−5.4**	**−11.1**	**−21.8**	**−33.8**	**−37.4**	**−41.5**	**−40.9**	....
General government	3 380	....	−.6	−.8	−1.5	−.8	−3.4	−3.8	....
Other sectors	3 390	−5.4	−10.5	−21.0	−32.3	−36.7	−38.1	−37.2	....
Workers' remittances	3 391	−3.9	−5.1	−16.6	−27.4	−33.2	−34.8	−34.7	....
Other current transfers	3 392	−1.5	−5.5	−4.4	−4.9	−3.5	−3.3	−2.4	....
CAPITAL AND FINANCIAL ACCOUNT	4 996	**134.7**	**174.5**	**134.9**	**172.1**	**191.3**	**451.9**	**320.4**	....
CAPITAL ACCOUNT	4 994	**8.7**	**21.4**	**13.6**	**20.6**	**40.1**	**51.1**	**64.0**	....
Total credit	2 994	*8.7*	*21.4*	*13.6*	*20.6*	*40.1*	*51.1*	*64.0*	....
Total debit	3 994	....	....	....	....	....	....	....	....
Capital transfers, credit	2 400	**8.7**	**21.4**	**13.6**	**20.6**	**40.1**	**51.1**	**64.0**	....
General government	2 401	6.0	18.3	5.0	7.9	14.9	24.9	30.6	....
Debt forgiveness	2 402	....	12.6	....	....	....	....	....	....
Other capital transfers	2 410	6.0	5.7	5.0	7.9	14.9	24.9	30.6	....
Other sectors	2 430	2.6	3.0	8.6	12.7	25.2	26.2	33.4	....
Migrants' transfers	2 431	....	....	....	....	....	....	....	....
Debt forgiveness	2 432	....	....	....	....	....	....	....	....
Other capital transfers	2 440	2.6	3.0	8.6	12.7	25.2	26.2	33.4	....
Capital transfers, debit	3 400	....	....	....	....	....	....	....	....
General government	3 401	....	....	....	....	....	....	....	....
Debt forgiveness	3 402	....	....	....	....	....	....	....	....
Other capital transfers	3 410	....	....	....	....	....	....	....	....
Other sectors	3 430	....	....	....	....	....	....	....	....
Migrants' transfers	3 431	....	....	....	....	....	....	....	....
Debt forgiveness	3 432	....	....	....	....	....	....	....	....
Other capital transfers	3 440	....	....	....	....	....	....	....	....
Nonproduced nonfinancial assets, credit	2 480	....	....	....	....	....	....	....	....
Nonproduced nonfinancial assets, debit	3 480	....	....	....	....	....	....	....	....

Table 2 (Continued). STANDARD PRESENTATION, 2000–2007

(Millions of U.S. dollars)

	Code	2000	2001	2002	2003	2004	2005	2006	2007
FINANCIAL ACCOUNT	4 995	**126.0**	**153.2**	**121.2**	**151.5**	**151.2**	**400.9**	**256.4**	....
A. DIRECT INVESTMENT	4 500	**41.5**	**70.8**	**51.0**	**40.1**	**69.9**	**91.9**	**91.7**	....
Direct investment abroad	4 505	**−.4**	**7.3**	**−2.7**	**6.3**	**12.6**	**14.9**	**14.4**	....
Equity capital	4 510	2.9	....	−3.1	−.2	−1.1	−.5	....	....
Claims on affiliated enterprises	4 515	2.9	....	−3.4	−.2	−1.1	−.6	....	....
Liabilities to affiliated enterprises	4 520	−.1	....	.3	.1	.1	.1	....	....
Reinvested earnings	4 525	−2.1	....	−.3	−.2	....	−.8	−.3	....
Other capital	4 530	−1.2	7.3	.8	6.7	13.6	16.1	14.7	....
Claims on affiliated enterprises	4 535	−3.9	−2.9	−3.6	−3.9	−.9	.5	2.3	....
Liabilities to affiliated enterprises	4 540	2.7	10.1	4.4	10.6	14.5	15.6	12.4	....
Direct investment in Togo	4 555	**41.9**	**63.6**	**53.7**	**33.7**	**57.3**	**77.0**	**77.3**	....
Equity capital	4 560	19.2	25.8	22.7	31.1	21.7	26.4	25.9	....
Claims on direct investors	4 565	−3.9	1.7	1.4	−1.0	−4.6	−1.9	−.3	....
Liabilities to direct investors	4 570	23.1	24.1	21.3	32.1	26.3	28.4	26.3	....
Reinvested earnings	4 575	8.4	17.6	10.0	3.3	14.1	25.9	17.0	....
Other capital	4 580	14.4	20.2	21.0	−.7	21.6	24.7	34.4	....
Claims on direct investors	4 585	−4.2	−.6	−.9	−.3	−1.2	−1.3	−1.3	....
Liabilities to direct investors	4 590	18.6	20.8	21.9	−.4	22.8	26.0	35.7	....
B. PORTFOLIO INVESTMENT	4 600	**6.9**	**11.1**	**11.9**	**13.8**	**−.3**	**2.5**	**62.7**	....
Assets	4 602	**.8**	**5.3**	**−1.1**	**−4.7**	**−26.5**	**−26.2**	**2.0**	....
Equity securities	4 610	.6	....	−2.0	−.2	−3.9	−18.0	1.0	....
Monetary authorities	4 611	....	....	....	....	....	....	....	....
General government	4 612	....	....	....	....	....	....	....	....
Banks	4 613	−1.0	....	....	−.2	....	....	....	....
Other sectors	4 614	1.6	....	−2.0	....	−3.9	−18.0	1.0	....
Debt securities	4 619	.2	5.3	.9	−4.5	−22.5	−8.2	1.0	....
Bonds and notes	4 620	1.0	7.0	.9	−2.8	−16.8	−8.2	4.2	....
Monetary authorities	4 621	....	....	....	....	....	....	....	....
General government	4 622	....	10.2	4.6	−4.0	6.4	−1.9	....	....
Banks	4 623	....	−1.1	−1.1	−1.7	−24.3	−2.6	5.6	....
Other sectors	4 624	1.0	−2.1	−2.5	2.9	1.1	−3.7	−1.4	....
Money market instruments	4 630	−.7	−1.7	....	−1.7	−5.7	....	−3.2	....
Monetary authorities	4 631	....	....	....	....	....	....	....	....
General government	4 632	....	....	....	....	....	....	....	....
Banks	4 633	....	....	....	−1.7	−5.7	....	−3.2	....
Other sectors	4 634	−.7	−1.7	....	....	....	....	....	....
Liabilities	4 652	**6.1**	**5.8**	**13.0**	**18.6**	**26.2**	**28.7**	**60.6**	....
Equity securities	4 660	6.1	1.5	6.1	9.8	14.8	16.0	10.4	....
Banks	4 663	.1	....	....	.7	....	.1	.1	....
Other sectors	4 664	6.0	1.5	6.1	9.0	14.8	15.9	10.2	....
Debt securities	4 669	....	4.3	6.8	8.8	11.4	12.7	50.3	....
Bonds and notes	4 670	....	2.9	6.8	8.8	11.4	12.7	50.3	....
Monetary authorities	4 671	....	....	....	....	....	....	....	....
General government	4 672	....	....	....	....	....	....	49.2	....
Banks	4 673	....	....	....	....	....	....	2.0	....
Other sectors	4 674	....	2.9	6.8	8.8	11.4	12.7	−.9	....
Money market instruments	4 680	....	1.4	....	....	....	....	....	....
Monetary authorities	4 681	....	....	....	....	....	....	....	....
General government	4 682	....	....	....	....	....	....	....	....
Banks	4 683	....	....	....	....	....	....	....	....
Other sectors	4 684	....	1.4	....	....	....	....	....	....
C. FINANCIAL DERIVATIVES	4 910	**−.1**	....	....	....	....	**.5**	....	....
Monetary authorities	4 911	....	....	....	....	....	....	....	....
General government	4 912	....	....	....	....	....	....	....	....
Banks	4 913	....	....	....	....	....	....	....	....
Other sectors	4 914	−.1	....	....	....	....	.5	....	....
Assets	4 900	....	....	....	....	....	....	....	....
Monetary authorities	4 901	....	....	....	....	....	....	....	....
General government	4 902	....	....	....	....	....	....	....	....
Banks	4 903	....	....	....	....	....	....	....	....
Other sectors	4 904	....	....	....	....	....	....	....	....
Liabilities	4 905	**−.1**	....	....	....	....	**.5**	....	....
Monetary authorities	4 906	....	....	....	....	....	....	....	....
General government	4 907	....	....	....	....	....	....	....	....
Banks	4 908	....	....	....	....	....	....	....	....
Other sectors	4 909	−.1	....	....	....	....	.5	....	....

Table 2 (Concluded). STANDARD PRESENTATION, 2000–2007

(Millions of U.S. dollars)

	Code	2000	2001	2002	2003	2004	2005	2006	2007
D. OTHER INVESTMENT	4 700	**105.2**	**63.9**	**78.5**	**75.2**	**206.2**	**181.3**	**253.5**	....
Assets	4 703	**8.8**	**8.2**	**−3.8**	**−28.7**	**5.7**	**68.8**	**42.5**	....
Trade credits	4 706	9.6	4.3	−8.8	−25.7	−1.7	1.8	7.7	....
General government	4 707	....	....	....	....	....	....	....	....
of which: Short-term	4 709	....	....	....	....	....	....	....	....
Other sectors	4 710	9.6	4.3	−8.8	−25.7	−1.7	1.8	7.7	....
of which: Short-term	4 712	....	*4.3*	*−8.8*	*−25.7*	*−1.7*	*1.8*	*7.7*	....
Loans	4 714	2.9	−6.6	4.3	1.2	−3.6	−21.7	−14.9	....
Monetary authorities	4 715	....	....	....	....	....	....	....	....
of which: Short-term	4 718	....	....	....	....	....	....	....	....
General government	4 719	....	....	....	....	....	....	....	....
of which: Short-term	4 721	....	....	....	....	....	....	....	....
Banks	4 722	2.5	−6.7	4.3	1.2	−3.6	−21.7	−14.9	....
of which: Short-term	4 724	*1.5*	*−8.1*	*2.4*	*5.8*	*−.1*	*−23.2*	*−10.5*	....
Other sectors	4 725	.3	.1	....	....	....	....	....	....
of which: Short-term	4 727	....	....	....	....	....	....	....	....
Currency and deposits	4 730	−11.3	4.7	−3.4	−14.8	−8.9	32.6	33.1	....
Monetary authorities	4 731	....	....	....	....	....	....	....	....
General government	4 732	4.7	....	....	....	−2.8	.9	.9	....
Banks	4 733	−19.3	−2.1	1.3	5.7	−12.7	10.6	1.8	....
Other sectors	4 734	3.3	6.8	−4.7	−20.5	6.6	21.1	30.4	....
Other assets	4 736	7.7	5.8	4.2	10.6	19.9	56.0	16.6	....
Monetary authorities	4 737	....	....	....	....	....	....	....	....
of which: Short-term	4 739	....	....	....	....	....	....	....	....
General government	4 740	2.9	4.8	−.3	3.1	....	....	....	....
of which: Short-term	4 742	....	....	....	....	....	....	....	....
Banks	4 743	....	....	....	....	−.4	....	....	....
of which: Short-term	4 745	....	....	....	....	−.4	....	....	....
Other sectors	4 746	4.9	1.1	4.5	7.5	20.3	56.1	16.6	....
of which: Short-term	4 748	....	....	....	*7.5*	*20.3*	*56.1*	*16.6*	....
Liabilities	4 753	**96.4**	**55.7**	**82.2**	**103.9**	**200.5**	**112.5**	**211.0**	....
Trade credits	4 756	19.3	16.5	17.0	35.4	69.5	103.9	130.5	....
General government	4 757	....	....	....	....	....	....	....	....
of which: Short-term	4 759	....	....	....	....	....	....	....	....
Other sectors	4 760	19.3	16.5	17.0	35.4	69.5	103.9	130.5	....
of which: Short-term	4 762	....	....	....	....	....	....	*130.5*	....
Loans	4 764	57.1	26.4	54.4	46.7	44.3	77.5	40.5	....
Monetary authorities	4 765	−9.3	−10.2	−9.5	−13.8	−16.2	−11.2	−6.4	....
of which: Use of Fund credit and loans from the Fund	4 766	*−9.3*	*−10.2*	*−9.5*	*−13.8*	*−16.2*	*−11.2*	*−6.4*	....
of which: Short-term	4 768	....	....	....	....	....	....	....	....
General government	4 769	41.6	28.6	19.6	25.8	15.6	25.6	30.0	....
of which: Short-term	4 771	*56.6*	*49.2*	*64.4*	*79.3*	*86.0*	*54.9*	*49.3*	....
Banks	4 772	4.9	.7	−2.2	−4.4	−.4	5.0	−4.4	....
of which: Short-term	4 774	*16.9*	*−11.1*	*−.2*	*−8.5*	*.1*	*5.2*	*−6.2*	....
Other sectors	4 775	19.9	7.2	46.4	39.1	45.2	58.2	21.2	....
of which: Short-term	4 777	....	*4.8*	*49.0*	*42.9*	*48.5*	*39.7*	....	....
Currency and deposits	4 780	−3.1	3.8	5.8	11.2	−4.7	−11.8	13.3	....
Monetary authorities	4 781	.4	4.1	9.4	4.1	.3	1.0	2.2	....
General government	4 782	....	....	....	....	....	....	....	....
Banks	4 783	−3.5	−.3	−3.6	7.0	−5.1	−12.8	11.1	....
Other sectors	4 784	....	....	....	....	....	....	....	....
Other liabilities	4 786	23.1	9.1	5.1	10.7	91.4	−57.0	26.7	....
Monetary authorities	4 787	2.1	−2.4	1.0	2.6	52.0	−68.2	17.1	....
of which: Short-term	4 789	....	....	....	....	....	....	....	....
General government	4 790	....	....	....	....	....	....	....	....
of which: Short-term	4 792	....	....	....	....	....	....	....	....
Banks	4 793	....	....	....	....	....	....	....	....
of which: Short-term	4 795	....	....	....	....	....	....	....	....
Other sectors	4 796	21.0	11.5	4.1	8.1	39.4	11.2	9.6	....
of which: Short-term	4 798	....	....	....	....	....	....	....	....
E. RESERVE ASSETS	4 802	**−27.5**	**7.4**	**−20.1**	**22.4**	**−124.6**	**124.7**	**−151.5**	....
Monetary gold	4 812	....	....	....	....	....	....	....	....
Special drawing rights	4 811	.2	−.2	....	.1	.1	....	....	....
Reserve position in the Fund	4 810	....	....	....	....	....	....	....	....
Foreign exchange	4 803	−27.7	7.6	−20.1	22.3	−124.8	124.7	−151.4	....
Other claims	4 813	....	....	....	....	....	....	....	....
NET ERRORS AND OMISSIONS	4 998	**5.0**	**−5.4**	**5.0**	**−10.2**	**14.4**	**8.8**	**20.0**	....

Table 3. INTERNATIONAL INVESTMENT POSITION (End-period stocks), 2000–2007

(Millions of U.S. dollars)

	Code	2000	2001	2002	2003	2004	2005	2006	2007
ASSETS	8 995 C.	**367.7**	**306.2**	**399.9**	**490.5**	**703.8**	**437.4**	**584.7**	....
Direct investment abroad	8 505 ..	**17.4**	**−12.7**	**−12.1**	**2.8**	**−10.5**	**−22.6**	**−41.1**	....
Equity capital and reinvested earnings	8 506 ..	3.8	2.5	6.7	12.3	14.5	13.8	15.1	....
Claims on affiliated enterprises	8 507 ..	3.8	2.5	6.7	12.3	14.5	13.8	15.1	....
Liabilities to affiliated enterprises	8 508 ..	....	....	....	....	....	....	....	....
Other capital	8 530 ..	13.7	−15.1	−18.8	−9.5	−25.0	−36.4	−56.2	....
Claims on affiliated enterprises	8 535 ..	....	....	....	....	....	....	....	....
Liabilities to affiliated enterprises	8 540 ..	13.7	−15.1	−18.8	−9.5	−25.0	−36.4	−56.2	....
Portfolio investment	8 602 ..	**13.8**	**48.4**	**59.5**	**61.5**	**104.7**	**115.6**	**126.9**	....
Equity securities	8 610 ..	7.3	6.6	8.7	5.1	9.7	25.5	27.4	....
Monetary authorities	8 611 ..	....	....	....	....	....	....	....	....
General government	8 612 ..	....	....	....	....	....	....	....	....
Banks	8 613 ..	....	....	....	2.3	2.4	2.0	2.3	....
Other sectors	8 614 ..	7.3	6.6	8.7	2.7	7.3	23.4	25.1	....
Debt securities	8 619 ..	6.5	41.8	50.8	56.5	95.0	90.1	99.5	....
Bonds and notes	8 620 ..	1.7	35.6	42.7	38.6	69.6	68.0	71.6	....
Monetary authorities	8 621 ..	....	....	....	....	....	....	....	....
General government	8 622 ..	....	....	....	....	....	1.8	2.0	....
Banks	8 623 ..	.9	1.9	3.5	1.1	27.9	26.7	23.9	....
Other sectors	8 624 ..	.8	33.7	39.1	37.5	41.6	39.6	45.6	....
Money market instruments	8 630 ..	4.8	6.2	8.1	17.9	25.5	22.1	28.0	....
Monetary authorities	8 631 ..	....	....	....	....	....	....	....	....
General government	8 632 ..	....	....	....	....	....	....	....	....
Banks	8 633 ..	3.9	3.7	8.1	17.9	25.5	22.1	28.0	....
Other sectors	8 634 ..	.9	2.5	....	....	....	....	....	....
Financial derivatives	8 900 ..	**.1**	....	....	**.6**	....	....	....	....
Monetary authorities	8 901 ..	....	....	....	....	....	....	....	....
General government	8 902 ..	....	....	....	....	....	....	....	....
Banks	8 903 ..	....	....	....	.2	....	....	....	....
Other sectors	8 904 ..	.1	....	....	.4	....	....	....	....
Other investment	8 703 ..	**195.5**	**144.3**	**180.2**	**243.0**	**251.9**	**153.0**	**126.1**	....
Trade credits	8 706 ..	63.8	41.1	59.0	99.2	108.8	92.5	95.2	....
General government	8 707 ..	....	....	....	....	....	....	....	....
of which: Short-term	8 709 ..	....	....	....	....	....	....	....	....
Other sectors	8 710 ..	63.8	41.1	59.0	99.2	108.8	92.5	95.2	....
of which: Short-term	8 712 ..	*63.8*	*41.1*	*59.0*	*99.2*	*108.8*	*92.5*	*95.2*	....
Loans	8 714 ..	18.6	24.1	23.0	14.7	19.6	37.5	57.5	....
Monetary authorities	8 715 ..	....	....	....	....	....	....	....	....
of which: Short-term	8 718 ..	....	....	....	....	....	....	....	....
General government	8 719 ..	....	....	....	....	....	....	....	....
of which: Short-term	8 721 ..	....	....	....	....	....	....	....	....
Banks	8 722 ..	17.7	23.3	23.0	14.7	19.6	37.5	57.5	....
of which: Short-term	8 724 ..	*6.8*	*14.4*	*14.4*	*5.8*	*6.1*	*27.3*	*41.5*	....
Other sectors	8 725 ..	.9	.7	....	....	....	....	....	....
of which: Short-term	8 727 ..	*.9*	*.7*	....	....	....	....	....	....
Currency and deposits	8 730 ..	98.1	72.3	89.5	119.9	135.3	86.2	61.6	....
Monetary authorities	8 731 ..	....	....	....	....	....	....	....	....
General government	8 732 ..	17.0	....	....	....	3.0	1.8	1.0	....
Banks	8 733 ..	65.5	64.2	74.9	72.6	88.1	66.2	72.1	....
Other sectors	8 734 ..	15.5	8.2	14.6	47.3	44.2	18.3	−11.5	....
Other assets	8 736 ..	15.1	6.8	8.6	9.3	−11.8	−63.3	−88.2	....
Monetary authorities	8 737 ..	....	....	....	....	....	....	....	....
of which: Short-term	8 739 ..	....	....	....	....	....	....	....	....
General government	8 740 ..	4.3	....	5.8	3.5	3.7	3.2	3.6	....
of which: Short-term	8 742 ..	*4.3*	....	*5.8*	*3.5*	*3.7*	*3.2*	*3.6*	....
Banks	8 743 ..	....	....	....	....	.5	.4	.5	....
of which: Short-term	8 745 ..	....	....	....	....	*.5*	*.4*	*.5*	....
Other sectors	8 746 ..	10.8	6.7	2.8	5.8	−16.0	−67.0	−92.3	....
of which: Short-term	8 748 ..	*10.8*	*6.7*	*2.8*	*5.8*	*−16.0*	*−67.0*	*−92.3*	....
Reserve assets	8 802 ..	**140.9**	**126.2**	**172.4**	**182.5**	**357.7**	**191.5**	**372.8**	....
Monetary gold	8 812 ..	....	....	....	....	....	....	....	....
Special drawing rights	8 811 ..	....	.2	.3	.2	....	....	.1	.1
Reserve position in the Fund	8 810 ..	.4	.4	.4	.5	.5	.5	.5	.5
Foreign exchange	8 803 ..	140.5	125.6	171.8	181.9	357.1	191.0	372.3	....
Other claims	8 813 ..	....	....	....	....	....	....	....	....

Table 3 (Concluded). INTERNATIONAL INVESTMENT POSITION (End-period stocks), 2000–2007

(Millions of U.S. dollars)

	Code	2000	2001	2002	2003	2004	2005	2006	2007
LIABILITIES	8 995 D.	**1,745.3**	**1,802.1**	**2,250.3**	**2,289.4**	**2,675.0**	**2,592.8**	**3,259.2**	....
Direct investment in Togo	8 555	**86.8**	**141.1**	**223.6**	**132.4**	**186.7**	**237.9**	**346.8**	....
Equity capital and reinvested earnings	8 556	62.3	99.0	150.3	118.8	157.0	188.8	255.8	....
Claims on direct investors	8 557	62.3	....	....	....	....	....	....	....
Liabilities to direct investors	8 558	....	99.0	150.3	118.8	157.0	188.8	255.8	....
Other capital	8 580	24.5	42.1	73.3	13.6	29.7	49.1	91.0	....
Claims on direct investors	8 585	....	....	....	....	....	....	....	....
Liabilities to direct investors	8 590	24.5	42.1	73.3	13.6	29.7	49.1	91.0	....
Portfolio investment	8 652	**30.1**	**33.2**	**53.7**	**29.1**	**60.1**	**80.2**	**153.2**	....
Equity securities	8 660	30.1	29.0	41.2	16.7	34.3	45.3	61.4	....
Banks	8 663	.5	.5	.6	.8	.9	.9	1.1	....
Other sectors	8 664	29.5	28.5	40.6	15.8	33.4	44.4	60.3	....
Debt securities	8 669	....	4.2	12.6	12.4	25.8	34.9	91.7	....
Bonds and notes	8 670	....	2.9	11.0	.2	12.7	23.5	79.0	....
Monetary authorities	8 671	....	....	....	....	....	....	....	....
General government	8 672	....	....	....	....	....	....	51.7	....
Banks	8 673	....	....	....	....	....	....	2.1	....
Other sectors	8 674	....	2.9	11.0	.2	12.7	23.5	25.3	....
Money market instruments	8 680	....	1.3	1.6	12.2	13.1	11.4	12.7	....
Monetary authorities	8 681	....	....	....	....	....	....	....	....
General government	8 682	....	....	....	....	....	....	....	....
Banks	8 683	....	1.3	1.6	12.2	13.1	11.4	12.7	....
Other sectors	8 684	....	....	....	....	....	....	....	....
Financial derivatives	8 905	....	....	....	....	....	**.5**	**.6**	....
Monetary authorities	8 906	....	....	....	....	....	....	....	....
General government	8 907	....	....	....	....	....	....	....	....
Banks	8 908	....	....	....	....	....	.5	.6	....
Other sectors	8 909	....	....	....	....	....	....	....	....
Other investment	8 753	**1,628.4**	**1,627.8**	**1,972.9**	**2,127.9**	**2,428.2**	**2,274.3**	**2,758.7**	....
Trade credits	8 756	106.2	118.2	156.9	127.4	207.2	278.0	447.3	....
General government	8 757	....	....	....	....	....	....	....	....
of which: Short-term	8 759	....	....	....	....	....	....	....	....
Other sectors	8 760	106.2	118.2	156.9	127.4	207.2	278.0	447.3	....
of which: Short-term	8 762	*106.2*	*118.2*	*156.9*	*127.4*	*207.2*	*278.0*	*447.3*	....
Loans	8 764	1,437.8	1,417.7	1,698.8	1,893.9	2,012.7	1,881.2	2,140.9	....
Monetary authorities	8 765	69.5	56.9	51.7	42.0	27.0	14.0	8.2	....
of which: Use of Fund credit and loans from the Fund	8 766	*69.5*	*56.9*	*51.7*	*42.0*	*27.0*	*14.0*	*8.2*	*1.7*
of which: Short-term	8 768	....	....	....	....	....	....	....	....
General government	8 769	1,274.6	1,299.2	1,524.3	1,736.5	1,812.1	1,656.9	1,881.6	....
of which: Short-term	8 771	....	*168.0*	*270.6*	*401.0*	*531.4*	*505.4*	*588.4*	....
Banks	8 772	31.2	8.5	7.7	5.1	5.0	9.1	5.5	....
of which: Short-term	8 774	*19.7*	*7.8*	*9.0*	*4.2*	*4.6*	*8.9*	*3.4*	....
Other sectors	8 775	62.5	53.0	115.2	110.4	168.6	201.2	245.6	....
of which: Short-term	8 777	*62.5*	*53.0*	*115.2*	*110.4*	*168.6*	*201.2*	*245.6*	....
Currency and deposits	8 780	55.2	56.8	72.2	93.2	69.5	49.0	68.6	....
Monetary authorities	8 781	9.7	14.1	30.7	27.6	28.9	26.0	31.3	....
General government	8 782	....	....	....	....	....	....	....	....
Banks	8 783	45.4	42.7	41.5	65.6	40.6	23.0	37.4	....
Other sectors	8 784	....	....	....	....	....	....	....	....
Other liabilities	8 786	29.3	35.2	45.0	13.4	138.8	66.1	101.9	....
Monetary authorities	8 787	2.4	−.1	1.0	4.8	88.9	12.4	31.7	....
of which: Short-term	8 789	*2.4*	*−.1*	*1.0*	*4.8*	*88.9*	*12.4*	*31.7*	....
General government	8 790	....	....	....	....	....	....	....	....
of which: Short-term	8 792	....	....	....	....	....	....	....	....
Banks	8 793	....	....	....	....	....	....	....	....
of which: Short-term	8 795	....	....	....	....	....	....	....	....
Other sectors	8 796	26.9	35.3	44.0	8.7	49.8	53.8	70.1	....
of which: Short-term	8 798	....	....	....	....	....	....	....	....
NET INTERNATIONAL INVESTMENT POSITION	8 995	**−1,377.6**	**−1,495.9**	**−1,850.3**	**−1,798.9**	**−1,971.2**	**−2,155.4**	**−2,674.5**	....
Conversion rates: CFA francs per U.S. dollar (end of period)	0 102	**704.95**	**744.31**	**625.50**	**519.36**	**481.58**	**556.04**	**498.07**	**445.59**

Table 1. ANALYTIC PRESENTATION, 2000–2007

(Thousands of U.S. dollars)

	Code	2000	2001	2002	2003	2004	2005	2006	2007
A. Current Account[1]	4 993 Z.	. . . .	**−10,803**	**−3,319**	**−10,493**	**−15,164**	**−13,737**	**−15,423**	**−24,163**
Goods: exports f.o.b.	2 100 ..	. . . .	6,657	18,126	20,741	19,022	18,308	9,589	8,689
Goods: imports f.o.b.	3 100 ..	. . . .	−63,688	−73,373	−75,047	−85,890	−99,998	−86,447	−127,398
Balance on Goods	4 100 ..	. . . .	*−57,031*	*−55,247*	*−54,305*	*−66,868*	*−81,690*	*−76,858*	*−118,709*
Services: credit	2 200 ..	. . . .	19,584	22,628	26,004	26,906	37,288	31,255	32,986
Services: debit	3 200 ..	. . . .	−27,556	−31,937	−44,479	−52,191	−50,163	−58,156	−52,102
Balance on Goods and Services	4 991 ..	. . . .	*−65,004*	*−64,555*	*−72,781*	*−92,154*	*−94,565*	*−103,759*	*−137,825*
Income: credit	2 300 ..	. . . .	5,675	6,611	7,812	5,072	8,226	11,316	11,189
Income: debit	3 300 ..	. . . .	−2,266	−3,791	−4,045	−6,974	−2,205	−3,134	−3,795
Balance on Goods, Services, and Income	4 992 ..	. . . .	*−61,595*	*−61,735*	*−69,014*	*−94,055*	*−88,544*	*−95,577*	*−130,431*
Current transfers: credit	2 379 Z.	. . . .	62,507	74,536	66,960	91,992	87,118	92,697	119,118
Current transfers: debit	3 379 ..	. . . .	−11,716	−16,120	−8,439	−13,101	−12,311	−12,543	−12,850
B. Capital Account[1]	4 994 Z.	. . . .	**9,606**	**13,412**	**10,183**	**11,476**	**13,385**	**6,990**	**18,254**
Capital account: credit	2 994 Z.	. . . .	11,727	14,075	11,642	11,864	13,913	7,785	18,659
Capital account: debit	3 994 ..	. . . .	−2,120	−663	−1,458	−388	−529	−795	−404
Total, Groups A Plus B	4 981 ..	. . . .	*−1,197*	*10,093*	*−309*	*−3,688*	*−353*	*−8,433*	*−5,909*
C. Financial Account[1]	4 995 W.	. . . .	**823**	**−3,174**	**8,471**	**28,042**	**2,835**	**11,645**	**21,826**
Direct investment abroad	4 505 ..	. . . .	. . . .	. . . .	−71	−2,349	−5,058	−1,543	. . . .
Direct investment in Tonga	4 555 Z.	. . . .	. . . .	. . . .	3,446	6,935	12,263	11,600	27,352
Portfolio investment assets	4 602 ..	. . . .	. . . .	. . . .	. . . .	. . . .	. . . .	. . . .	. . . .
Equity securities	4 610 ..	. . . .	. . . .	. . . .	. . . .	. . . .	. . . .	. . . .	. . . .
Debt securities	4 619 ..	. . . .	. . . .	. . . .	. . . .	. . . .	. . . .	. . . .	. . . .
Portfolio investment liabilities	4 652 Z.	. . . .	. . . .	. . . .	. . . .	. . . .	. . . .	. . . .	. . . .
Equity securities	4 660 ..	. . . .	. . . .	. . . .	. . . .	. . . .	. . . .	. . . .	. . . .
Debt securities	4 669 Z.	. . . .	. . . .	. . . .	. . . .	. . . .	. . . .	. . . .	. . . .
Financial derivatives	4 910 ..	. . . .	. . . .	. . . .	. . . .	. . . .	. . . .	. . . .	. . . .
Financial derivatives assets	4 900 ..	. . . .	. . . .	. . . .	. . . .	. . . .	. . . .	. . . .	. . . .
Financial derivatives liabilities	4 905 ..	. . . .	. . . .	. . . .	. . . .	. . . .	. . . .	. . . .	. . . .
Other investment assets	4 703 ..	. . . .	. . . .	. . . .	10,792	33,557	1,550	7,893	466
Monetary authorities	4 701 ..	. . . .	. . . .	. . . .	. . . .	. . . .	. . . .	. . . .	. . . .
General government	4 704 ..	. . . .	. . . .	. . . .	. . . .	. . . .	. . . .	. . . .	257
Banks	4 705 ..	. . . .	. . . .	. . . .	. . . .	. . . .	. . . .	. . . .	. . . .
Other sectors	4 728 ..	. . . .	. . . .	. . . .	. . . .	. . . .	. . . .	. . . .	209
Other investment liabilities	4 753 W.	. . . .	823	−3,174	−5,695	−10,102	−5,919	−6,305	−5,992
Monetary authorities	4 753 WA	. . . .	. . . .	. . . .	. . . .	. . . .	. . . .	. . . .	−233
General government	4 753 ZB	. . . .	. . . .	. . . .	. . . .	. . . .	. . . .	. . . .	−5,096
Banks	4 753 ZC	. . . .	. . . .	. . . .	. . . .	. . . .	. . . .	. . . .	−62
Other sectors	4 753 ZD	. . . .	. . . .	. . . .	. . . .	. . . .	. . . .	. . . .	−601
Total, Groups A Through C	4 983 ..	. . . .	*−375*	*6,919*	*8,162*	*24,354*	*2,483*	*3,212*	*15,918*
D. Net Errors and Omissions	4 998 ..	. . . .	**2,093**	**−47**	**−2,152**	**−5,786**	**−6,008**	**−4,335**	**−324**
Total, Groups A Through D	4 984 ..	. . . .	*1,718*	*6,872*	*6,010*	*18,567*	*−3,525*	*−1,123*	*15,594*
E. Reserves and Related Items	4 802 A.	. . . .	**−1,718**	**−6,872**	**−6,010**	**−18,567**	**3,525**	**1,123**	**−15,594**
Reserve assets	4 802 ..	. . . .	−1,718	−6,872	−6,010	−18,567	3,525	1,123	−15,594
Use of Fund credit and loans	4 766 ..	. . . .	. . . .	. . . .	. . . .	. . . .	. . . .	. . . .	. . . .
Exceptional financing	4 920 ..	. . . .	. . . .	. . . .	. . . .	. . . .	. . . .	. . . .	. . . .
Conversion rates: pa'anga per U.S. dollar	0 101 ..	**1.7585**	**2.1236**	**2.1952**	**2.1459**	**1.9716**	**1.9430**	**2.0259**	**1.9709**

[1] Excludes components that have been classified in the categories of Group E.

Table 2. STANDARD PRESENTATION, 2000–2007

(Thousands of U.S. dollars)

	Code	2000	2001	2002	2003	2004	2005	2006	2007
CURRENT ACCOUNT	4 993	....	−10,803	−3,319	−10,493	−15,164	−13,737	−15,423	−24,163
A. GOODS	4 100	....	−57,031	−55,247	−54,305	−66,868	−81,690	−76,858	−118,709
Credit	2 100	....	6,657	18,126	20,741	19,022	18,308	9,589	8,689
General merchandise: exports f.o.b.	2 110	....	6,640	17,793	20,261	18,573	17,801	9,124	8,199
Goods for processing: exports f.o.b.	2 150	....	....	....	....	....	....	....	....
Repairs on goods	2 160	....	....	6	....	....	....	....	....
Goods procured in ports by carriers	2 170	....	16	327	480	448	507	465	490
Nonmonetary gold	2 180	....	....	....	....	....	....	....	....
Debit	3 100	....	−63,688	−73,373	−75,047	−85,890	−99,998	−86,447	−127,398
General merchandise: imports f.o.b.	3 110	....	−63,688	−72,965	−75,047	−85,890	−99,998	−86,447	−127,398
Goods for processing: imports f.o.b.	3 150	....	....	....	....	....	....	....	....
Repairs on goods	3 160	....	....	−227	....	....	....	....	....
Goods procured in ports by carriers	3 170	....	....	−180	....	....	....	....	....
Nonmonetary gold	3 180	....	....	....	....	....	....	....	....
B. SERVICES	4 200	....	−7,973	−9,309	−18,475	−25,286	−12,876	−26,901	−19,116
Total credit	*2 200*	....	*19,584*	*22,628*	*26,004*	*26,906*	*37,288*	*31,255*	*32,986*
Total debit	*3 200*	....	*−27,556*	*−31,937*	*−44,479*	*−52,191*	*−50,163*	*−58,156*	*−52,102*
Transportation services, credit	2 205	....	4,135	6,353	2,293	2,594	3,123	2,040	3,772
Passenger	*2 850*	....	....	....	....	....	....	....	*807*
Freight	*2 851*	....	....	....	....	....	....	....	*23*
Other	*2 852*	....	....	....	....	....	....	....	*2,942*
Sea transport, passenger	2 207	....	....	....	....	....	....	....	....
Sea transport, freight	2 208	....	....	....	....	....	....	....	....
Sea transport, other	2 209	....	....	....	....	....	....	....	1,241
Air transport, passenger	2 211	....	....	....	....	....	....	....	807
Air transport, freight	2 212	....	....	....	....	....	....	....	23
Air transport, other	2 213	....	....	....	....	....	....	....	1,701
Other transport, passenger	2 215	....	....	....	....	....	....	....	....
Other transport, freight	2 216	....	....	....	....	....	....	....	....
Other transport, other	2 217	....	....	....	....	....	....	....	....
Transportation services, debit	3 205	....	−14,158	−17,602	−28,609	−29,265	−29,821	−34,385	−29,281
Passenger	*3 850*	....	....	....	....	....	....	....	*−58*
Freight	*3 851*	....	....	....	....	....	....	....	*−20,211*
Other	*3 852*	....	....	....	....	....	....	....	*−9,011*
Sea transport, passenger	3 207	....	....	....	....	....	....	....	....
Sea transport, freight	3 208	....	....	....	....	....	....	....	−15,682
Sea transport, other	3 209	....	....	....	....	....	....	....	−1,628
Air transport, passenger	3 211	....	....	....	....	....	....	....	−58
Air transport, freight	3 212	....	....	....	....	....	....	....	−4,529
Air transport, other	3 213	....	....	....	....	....	....	....	−7,383
Other transport, passenger	3 215	....	....	....	....	....	....	....	....
Other transport, freight	3 216	....	....	....	....	....	....	....	....
Other transport, other	3 217	....	....	....	....	....	....	....	....
Travel, credit	2 236	....	6,771	5,898	10,291	12,834	14,877	15,679	14,684
Business travel	2 237	....	....	....	....	....	....	....	4,753
Personal travel	2 240	....	....	....	....	....	....	....	9,931
Travel, debit	3 236	....	−3,147	−3,230	−3,315	−6,113	−3,815	−8,054	−10,025
Business travel	3 237	....	....	....	....	....	....	....	−3,368
Personal travel	3 240	....	....	....	....	....	....	....	−6,657
Other services, credit	2 200 BA	....	8,678	10,377	13,419	11,478	19,288	13,536	14,530
Communications	2 245	....	....	....	....	....	....	....	1,785
Construction	2 249	....	....	....	....	....	....	....	48
Insurance	2 253	....	....	....	....	....	....	....	4,170
Financial	2 260	....	....	....	....	....	....	....	192
Computer and information	2 262	....	....	....	....	....	....	....	32
Royalties and licence fees	2 266	....	....	....	....	....	....	....	....
Other business services	2 268	....	6,787	5,965	8,595	5,528	10,761	4,090	977
Personal, cultural, and recreational	2 287	....	68	95	876	91	1,054	545	561
Government, n.i.e.	2 291	....	1,823	4,318	3,949	5,859	7,473	8,901	6,766
Other services, debit	3 200 BA	....	−10,251	−11,105	−12,555	−16,814	−16,527	−15,718	−12,797
Communications	3 245	....	....	....	....	....	....	....	−1,285
Construction	3 249	....	....	....	....	....	....	....	−49
Insurance	3 253	....	....	....	....	....	....	....	−1,237
Financial	3 260	....	....	....	....	....	....	....	−181
Computer and information	3 262	....	....	....	....	....	....	....	−155
Royalties and licence fees	3 266	....	....	....	....	....	....	....	....
Other business services	3 268	....	−6,455	−6,834	−7,616	−9,561	−10,189	−7,102	−716
Personal, cultural, and recreational	3 287	....	−24	−20	−305	−116	−57	−266	−600
Government, n.i.e.	3 291	....	−3,772	−4,250	−4,634	−7,137	−6,280	−8,351	−8,574

Table 2 (Continued). STANDARD PRESENTATION, 2000–2007

(Thousands of U.S. dollars)

	Code	2000	2001	2002	2003	2004	2005	2006	2007
C. INCOME	4 300	....	**3,409**	**2,820**	**3,767**	**−1,901**	**6,021**	**8,182**	**7,394**
Total credit	2 300	....	*5,675*	*6,611*	*7,812*	*5,072*	*8,226*	*11,316*	*11,189*
Total debit	3 300	....	*−2,266*	*−3,791*	*−4,045*	*−6,974*	*−2,205*	*−3,134*	*−3,795*
Compensation of employees, credit	2 310	....	....	4,178	3,383	3,276	3,548	3,240	3,328
Compensation of employees, debit	3 310	....	....	−752	−910	−108	....	....	−62
Investment income, credit	2 320	....	....	2,433	4,429	1,796	4,678	8,075	7,860
Direct investment income	2 330	....	....	216	835	1,184	2,076	2,630	....
Dividends and distributed branch profits	2 332	....	....	....	....	....	....	....	....
Reinvested earnings and undistributed branch profits	2 333	....	....	....	....	....	....	....	....
Income on debt (interest)	2 334	....	....	....	....	....	....	....	....
Portfolio investment income	2 339	....	....	....	....	....	....	....	....
Income on equity	2 340	....	....	....	....	....	....	....	....
Income on bonds and notes	2 350	....	....	....	....	....	....	....	....
Income on money market instruments	2 360	....	....	....	....	....	....	....	....
Other investment income	2 370	....	....	2,216	3,594	612	2,602	5,446	7,860
Investment income, debit	3 320	....	....	**−3,039**	**−3,135**	**−6,866**	**−2,205**	**−3,134**	**−3,733**
Direct investment income	3 330	....	....	−725	−1,410	−5,478	−1,402	−1,239	9
Dividends and distributed branch profits	3 332	....	....	....	....	....	....	....	....
Reinvested earnings and undistributed branch profits	3 333	....	....	....	....	....	....	....	9
Income on debt (interest)	3 334	....	....	....	....	....	....	....	....
Portfolio investment income	3 339	....	....	....	....	....	....	....	....
Income on equity	3 340	....	....	....	....	....	....	....	....
Income on bonds and notes	3 350	....	....	....	....	....	....	....	....
Income on money market instruments	3 360	....	....	....	....	....	....	....	....
Other investment income	3 370	....	....	−2,314	−1,724	−1,388	−804	−1,895	−3,742
D. CURRENT TRANSFERS	4 379	....	**50,791**	**58,416**	**58,521**	**78,891**	**74,807**	**80,154**	**106,268**
Credit	2 379	....	**62,507**	**74,536**	**66,960**	**91,992**	**87,118**	**92,697**	**119,118**
General government	2 380	....	5,560	3,164	3,451	10,078	7,580	8,807	7,583
Other sectors	2 390	....	56,947	71,372	63,509	81,914	79,538	83,890	111,535
Workers' remittances	2 391	....	52,533	61,893	52,259	64,080	62,160	68,547	95,891
Other current transfers	2 392	....	4,414	9,479	11,251	17,834	17,378	15,342	15,644
Debit	3 379	....	**−11,716**	**−16,120**	**−8,439**	**−13,101**	**−12,311**	**−12,543**	**−12,850**
General government	3 380	....	−735	−707	−148	−565	−251	−323	−39
Other sectors	3 390	....	−10,981	−15,413	−8,291	−12,535	−12,060	−12,220	−12,811
Workers' remittances	3 391	....	−10,674	−14,991	−7,928	−10,280	−11,639	−11,912	−12,079
Other current transfers	3 392	....	−307	−422	−363	−2,255	−421	−308	−732
CAPITAL AND FINANCIAL ACCOUNT	4 996	....	**8,710**	**3,366**	**12,645**	**20,950**	**19,745**	**19,758**	**24,487**
CAPITAL ACCOUNT	4 994	....	**9,606**	**13,412**	**10,183**	**11,476**	**13,385**	**6,990**	**18,254**
Total credit	2 994	....	*11,727*	*14,075*	*11,642*	*11,864*	*13,913*	*7,785*	*18,659*
Total debit	3 994	....	*−2,120*	*−663*	*−1,458*	*−388*	*−529*	*−795*	*−404*
Capital transfers, credit	2 400	....	....	14,075	11,642	11,864	13,913	7,785	18,659
General government	2 401	....	....	9,484	8,721	11,375	13,014	6,670	15,625
Debt forgiveness	2 402	....	....	....	....	....	....	6,670	....
Other capital transfers	2 410	....	....	9,484	8,721	11,375	....	....	15,625
Other sectors	2 430	....	....	4,591	2,921	489	900	1,115	3,033
Migrants' transfers	2 431	....	....	274	184	225	260	216	329
Debt forgiveness	2 432	....	....	....	....	....	....	....	....
Other capital transfers	2 440	....	....	4,317	2,737	264	639	899	2,704
Capital transfers, debit	3 400	....	**−2,120**	**−663**	**−1,458**	**−388**	**−529**	**−795**	**−404**
General government	3 401	....	....	....	....	....	−82	−469	−67
Debt forgiveness	3 402	....	....	....	....	....	....	−469	....
Other capital transfers	3 410	....	....	....	....	....	....	....	−67
Other sectors	3 430	....	−2,120	−663	−1,458	−388	−446	−326	−337
Migrants' transfers	3 431	....	−127	−220	−279	−388	−347	−326	−337
Debt forgiveness	3 432	....	....	....	....	....	....	....	....
Other capital transfers	3 440	....	−1,994	−443	−1,180	....	−99	....	....
Nonproduced nonfinancial assets, credit	2 480	....	....	....	....	....	....	....	....
Nonproduced nonfinancial assets, debit	3 480	....	....	....	....	....	....	....	....

Table 2 (Continued). STANDARD PRESENTATION, 2000–2007

(Thousands of U.S. dollars)

	Code	2000	2001	2002	2003	2004	2005	2006	2007
FINANCIAL ACCOUNT	4 995 ..	....	−896	−10,046	2,461	9,475	6,360	12,767	6,233
A. DIRECT INVESTMENT	4 500 ..	....	....	....	3,375	4,586	7,205	10,057	27,352
Direct investment abroad	4 505 ..	....	....	....	−71	−2,349	−5,058	−1,543	....
Equity capital	4 510 ..	....	....	....	....	....	....	....	....
Claims on affiliated enterprises	4 515 ..	....	....	....	....	....	....	....	....
Liabilities to affiliated enterprises	4 520 ..	....	....	....	....	....	....	....	....
Reinvested earnings	4 525 ..	....	....	....	....	....	....	....	....
Other capital	4 530 ..	....	....	....	....	....	....	....	....
Claims on affiliated enterprises	4 535 ..	....	....	....	....	....	....	....	....
Liabilities to affiliated enterprises	4 540 ..	....	....	....	....	....	....	....	....
Direct investment in Tonga	4 555 ..	....	....	....	3,446	6,935	12,263	11,600	27,352
Equity capital	4 560 ..	....	....	....	....	....	....	....	1,179
Claims on direct investors	4 565 ..	....	....	....	....	....	....	....	1,596
Liabilities to direct investors	4 570 ..	....	....	....	....	....	....	....	−418
Reinvested earnings	4 575 ..	....	....	....	....	....	....	....	−9
Other capital	4 580 ..	....	....	....	....	....	....	....	26,182
Claims on direct investors	4 585 ..	....	....	....	....	....	....	....	27,526
Liabilities to direct investors	4 590 ..	....	....	....	....	....	....	....	−1,344
B. PORTFOLIO INVESTMENT	4 600 ..	....	....	....	....	....	....	....	....
Assets	4 602 ..	....	....	....	....	....	....	....	....
Equity securities	4 610 ..	....	....	....	....	....	....	....	....
Monetary authorities	4 611 ..	....	....	....	....	....	....	....	....
General government	4 612 ..	....	....	....	....	....	....	....	....
Banks	4 613 ..	....	....	....	....	....	....	....	....
Other sectors	4 614 ..	....	....	....	....	....	....	....	....
Debt securities	4 619 ..	....	....	....	....	....	....	....	....
Bonds and notes	4 620 ..	....	....	....	....	....	....	....	....
Monetary authorities	4 621 ..	....	....	....	....	....	....	....	....
General government	4 622 ..	....	....	....	....	....	....	....	....
Banks	4 623 ..	....	....	....	....	....	....	....	....
Other sectors	4 624 ..	....	....	....	....	....	....	....	....
Money market instruments	4 630 ..	....	....	....	....	....	....	....	....
Monetary authorities	4 631 ..	....	....	....	....	....	....	....	....
General government	4 632 ..	....	....	....	....	....	....	....	....
Banks	4 633 ..	....	....	....	....	....	....	....	....
Other sectors	4 634 ..	....	....	....	....	....	....	....	....
Liabilities	4 652 ..	....	....	....	....	....	....	....	....
Equity securities	4 660 ..	....	....	....	....	....	....	....	....
Banks	4 663 ..	....	....	....	....	....	....	....	....
Other sectors	4 664 ..	....	....	....	....	....	....	....	....
Debt securities	4 669 ..	....	....	....	....	....	....	....	....
Bonds and notes	4 670 ..	....	....	....	....	....	....	....	....
Monetary authorities	4 671 ..	....	....	....	....	....	....	....	....
General government	4 672 ..	....	....	....	....	....	....	....	....
Banks	4 673 ..	....	....	....	....	....	....	....	....
Other sectors	4 674 ..	....	....	....	....	....	....	....	....
Money market instruments	4 680 ..	....	....	....	....	....	....	....	....
Monetary authorities	4 681 ..	....	....	....	....	....	....	....	....
General government	4 682 ..	....	....	....	....	....	....	....	....
Banks	4 683 ..	....	....	....	....	....	....	....	....
Other sectors	4 684 ..	....	....	....	....	....	....	....	....
C. FINANCIAL DERIVATIVES	4 910 ..	....	....	....	....	....	....	....	....
Monetary authorities	4 911 ..	....	....	....	....	....	....	....	....
General government	4 912 ..	....	....	....	....	....	....	....	....
Banks	4 913 ..	....	....	....	....	....	....	....	....
Other sectors	4 914 ..	....	....	....	....	....	....	....	....
Assets	4 900 ..	....	....	....	....	....	....	....	....
Monetary authorities	4 901 ..	....	....	....	....	....	....	....	....
General government	4 902 ..	....	....	....	....	....	....	....	....
Banks	4 903 ..	....	....	....	....	....	....	....	....
Other sectors	4 904 ..	....	....	....	....	....	....	....	....
Liabilities	4 905 ..	....	....	....	....	....	....	....	....
Monetary authorities	4 906 ..	....	....	....	....	....	....	....	....
General government	4 907 ..	....	....	....	....	....	....	....	....
Banks	4 908 ..	....	....	....	....	....	....	....	....
Other sectors	4 909 ..	....	....	....	....	....	....	....	....

Table 2 (Concluded). STANDARD PRESENTATION, 2000–2007

(Thousands of U.S. dollars)

	Code	2000	2001	2002	2003	2004	2005	2006	2007
D. OTHER INVESTMENT	4 700 ..	....	822	−3,174	5,096	23,456	−4,369	1,588	−5,525
Assets	4 703 ..	....	....	....	10,792	33,557	1,550	7,893	466
Trade credits	4 706 ..	....	....	....	....	....	....	....	....
General government	4 707 ..	....	....	....	....	....	....	....	....
of which: Short-term	4 709 ..	....	....	....	....	....	....	....	....
Other sectors	4 710 ..	....	....	....	....	....	....	....	....
of which: Short-term	4 712 ..	....	....	....	....	....	....	....	....
Loans	4 714 ..	....	....	....	....	....	....	....	344
Monetary authorities	4 715 ..	....	....	....	....	....	....	....	....
of which: Short-term	4 718 ..	....	....	....	....	....	....	....	....
General government	4 719 ..	....	....	....	....	....	....	....	257
of which: Short-term	4 721 ..	....	....	....	....	....	....	....	....
Banks	4 722 ..	....	....	....	....	....	....	....	....
of which: Short-term	4 724 ..	....	....	....	....	....	....	....	....
Other sectors	4 725 ..	....	....	....	....	....	....	....	87
of which: Short-term	4 727 ..	....	....	....	....	....	....	....	....
Currency and deposits	4 730 ..	....	....	....	....	....	....	....	122
Monetary authorities	4 731 ..	....	....	....	....	....	....	....	....
General government	4 732 ..	....	....	....	....	....	....	....	....
Banks	4 733 ..	....	....	....	....	....	....	....	122
Other sectors	4 734 ..	....	....	....	....	....	....	....	1
Other assets	4 736 ..	....	....	....	....	....	....	....	....
Monetary authorities	4 737 ..	....	....	....	....	....	....	....	1
of which: Short-term	4 739 ..	....	....	....	....	....	....	....	....
General government	4 740 ..	....	....	....	....	....	....	....	1
of which: Short-term	4 742 ..	....	....	....	....	....	....	....	....
Banks	4 743 ..	....	....	....	....	....	....	....	....
of which: Short-term	4 745 ..	....	....	....	....	....	....	....	....
Other sectors	4 746 ..	....	....	....	....	....	....	....	....
of which: Short-term	4 748 ..	....	....	....	....	....	....	....	....
Liabilities	4 753 ..	....	822	−3,174	−5,695	−10,102	−5,919	−6,305	−5,992
Trade credits	4 756 ..	....	....	....	....	....	....	....	−833
General government	4 757 ..	....	....	....	....	....	....	....	−822
of which: Short-term	4 759 ..	....	....	....	....	....	....	....	....
Other sectors	4 760 ..	....	....	....	....	....	....	....	−10
of which: Short-term	4 762 ..	....	....	....	....	....	....	....	....
Loans	4 764 ..	....	....	....	....	....	....	....	−4,375
Monetary authorities	4 765 ..	....	....	....	....	....	....	....	....
of which: Use of Fund credit and loans from the Fund..	4 766 ..	....	....	....	....	....	....	....	....
of which: Short-term	4 768 ..	....	....	....	....	....	....	....	....
General government	4 769 ..	....	....	....	....	....	....	....	−4,273
of which: Short-term	4 771 ..	....	....	....	....	....	....	....	−62
Banks	4 772 ..	....	....	....	....	....	....	....	−39
of which: Short-term	4 774 ..	....	....	....	....	....	....	....	....
Other sectors	4 775 ..	....	....	....	....	....	....	....	−524
of which: Short-term	4 777 ..	....	....	....	....	....	....	....	....
Currency and deposits	4 780 ..	....	....	....	....	....	....	....	....
Monetary authorities	4 781 ..	....	....	....	....	....	....	....	....
General government	4 782 ..	....	....	....	....	....	....	....	....
Banks	4 783 ..	....	....	....	....	....	....	....	−524
Other sectors	4 784 ..	....	....	....	....	....	....	....	−260
Other liabilities	4 786 ..	....	....	....	....	....	....	....	−233
Monetary authorities	4 787 ..	....	....	....	....	....	....	....	....
of which: Short-term	4 789 ..	....	....	....	....	....	....	....	....
General government	4 790 ..	....	....	....	....	....	....	....	....
of which: Short-term	4 792 ..	....	....	....	....	....	....	....	....
Banks	4 793 ..	....	....	....	....	....	....	....	....
of which: Short-term	4 795 ..	....	....	....	....	....	....	....	−27
Other sectors	4 796 ..	....	....	....	....	....	....	....	....
of which: Short-term	4 798 ..	....	....	....	....	....	....	....	....
E. RESERVE ASSETS	4 802 ..	....	−1,718	−6,872	−6,010	−18,567	3,525	1,123	−15,594
Monetary gold	4 812 ..	....							
Special drawing rights	4 811 ..	....	−74	−47	−38	−41	−59	−85	−111
Reserve position in the Fund	4 810 ..	....	....	−2	....	....	....	....	....
Foreign exchange	4 803 ..	....	−1,645	−6,823	−5,972	−18,527	3,584	1,207	−15,483
Other claims	4 813 ..	....	....	....	....	....	....	....	....
NET ERRORS AND OMISSIONS	4 998 ..	....	2,093	−47	−2,152	−5,786	−6,008	−4,335	−324

Table 1. ANALYTIC PRESENTATION, 2000–2007

(Millions of U.S. dollars)

	Code	2000	2001	2002	2003	2004	2005	2006	2007
A. Current Account¹	4 993 Z.	**544**	**416**	**76**	**985**	**1,447**	**3,594**	....	....
Goods: exports f.o.b.	2 100 ..	4,290	4,304	3,920	5,205	6,403	9,672	....	....
Goods: imports f.o.b.	3 100 ..	−3,322	−3,586	−3,682	−3,912	−4,894	−5,725	....	....
Balance on Goods	4 100 ..	*969*	*718*	*238*	*1,293*	*1,509*	*3,948*	....	....
Services: credit	2 200 ..	554	574	637	685	851	897	....	....
Services: debit	3 200 ..	−388	−370	−373	−371	−371	−541	....	....
Balance on Goods and Services	4 991 ..	*1,135*	*922*	*502*	*1,607*	*1,988*	*4,304*	....	....
Income: credit	2 300 ..	81	109	64	78	66	84	....	....
Income: debit	3 300 ..	−709	−648	−544	−759	−664	−844	....	....
Balance on Goods, Services, and Income	4 992 ..	*506*	*383*	*22*	*926*	*1,391*	*3,544*	....	....
Current transfers: credit	2 379 Z.	64	64	96	101	99	102	....	....
Current transfers: debit	3 379 ..	−26	−31	−42	−42	−42	−52	....	....
B. Capital Account¹	4 994 Z.	....	....	....	....	....	....	....	....
Capital account: credit	2 994 Z.	....	....	....	....	....	....		
Capital account: debit	3 994 ..	....	....	....	....	....	....		
Total, Groups A Plus B	4 981 ..	*544*	*416*	*76*	*985*	*1,447*	*3,594*	....	....
C. Financial Account¹	4 995 W.	**174**	**322**	**397**	**34**	**−200**	**−454**	....	....
Direct investment abroad	4 505 ..	−25	−150	−106	225	25	341	....	....
Direct investment in Trinidad and Tobago	4 555 Z.	680	835	791	808	1,098	940	....	....
Portfolio investment assets	4 602 ..	−30	−206	−70	−509	−690	−258	....	....
Equity securities	4 610 ..	....	....	....	....	....	....	....	....
Debt securities	4 619 ..	−30	−206	−70	−509	−690	−258	....	....
Portfolio investment liabilities	4 652 Z.	....	....	....	....	....	....	....	....
Equity securities	4 660 ..	....	....	....	....	....	....	....	....
Debt securities	4 669 Z.	....	....	....	....	....	....	....	....
Financial derivatives	4 910 ..	....	....	....	....	....	....	....	....
Financial derivatives assets	4 900 ..	....	....	....	....	....	....	....	....
Financial derivatives liabilities	4 905 ..	....	....	....	....	....	....	....	....
Other investment assets	4 703 ..	398	285	−316	−257	−389	7	....	....
Monetary authorities	4 701 ..	384	27	18	26	23	22	....	....
General government	4 704 ..	3	....	1	49	100	100	....	....
Banks	4 705 ..	....	257	−335	−332	−513	−115	....	....
Other sectors	4 728 ..	11	1	....	....	....	....	....	....
Other investment liabilities	4 753 W.	−848	−442	99	−233	−245	−1,483	....	....
Monetary authorities	4 753 WA	−269	−61	....	....	....	....	....	....
General government	4 753 ZB	−64	−15	....	....	....	....	....	....
Banks	4 753 ZC	−86	....	256	426	....	213	....	....
Other sectors	4 753 ZD	−430	−366	−157	−659	−245	−1,696	....	....
Total, Groups A Through C	4 983 ..	*718*	*738*	*474*	*1,019*	*1,247*	*3,140*	....	....
D. Net Errors and Omissions	4 998 ..	**−277**	**−235**	**−358**	**−610**	**−537**	**−1,335**	....	....
Total, Groups A Through D	4 984 ..	*441*	*502*	*116*	*409*	*710*	*1,805*	....	....
E. Reserves and Related Items	4 802 A.	**−441**	**−502**	**−116**	**−409**	**−710**	**−1,805**	....	....
Reserve assets	4 802 ..	−441	−502	−116	−409	−710	−1,805	....	....
Use of Fund credit and loans	4 766 ..	....	....	....	....	....	....	....	....
Exceptional financing	4 920 ..	....	....	....	....	....	....	....	....
Conversion rates: Trinidad and Tobago dollars per U.S. dollar	0 101 ..	**6.29980**	**6.23322**	**6.24868**	**6.29510**	**6.29899**	**6.29956**	**6.31228**	**6.32803**

¹ Excludes components that have been classified in the categories of Group E.

Table 2. STANDARD PRESENTATION, 2000–2007

(Millions of U.S. dollars)

	Code	2000	2001	2002	2003	2004	2005	2006	2007
CURRENT ACCOUNT	4 993 ..	544	416	76	985	1,447	3,594	....	....
A. GOODS	4 100 ..	969	718	238	1,293	1,509	3,948	....	....
Credit	2 100 ..	4,290	4,304	3,920	5,205	6,403	9,672	....	....
General merchandise: exports f.o.b.	2 110 ..	4,229	4,234	3,869	5,081	6,341	9,548	....	....
Goods for processing: exports f.o.b.	2 150 ..	15	13	11	9	12	14	....	....
Repairs on goods	2 160 ..	....	....	....	....	....	....	....	....
Goods procured in ports by carriers	2 170 ..	46	57	41	115	50	110	....	....
Nonmonetary gold	2 180 ..	....	....	....	....	....	....	....	....
Debit	3 100 ..	−3,322	−3,586	−3,682	−3,912	−4,894	−5,725	....	....
General merchandise: imports f.o.b.	3 110 ..	−3,306	−3,576	−3,673	−3,899	−4,881	−5,710	....	....
Goods for processing: imports f.o.b.	3 150 ..	−16	−10	−10	−13	−14	−15	....	....
Repairs on goods	3 160 ..	....	....	....	....	....	....	....	....
Goods procured in ports by carriers	3 170 ..	....	....	....	....	....	....	....	....
Nonmonetary gold	3 180 ..	....	....	....	....	....	....	....	....
B. SERVICES	4 200 ..	166	204	264	314	480	356	....	....
Total credit	2 200 ..	*554*	*574*	*637*	*685*	*851*	*897*	....	....
Total debit	3 200 ..	*−388*	*−370*	*−373*	*−371*	*−371*	*−541*	....	....
Transportation services, credit	2 205 ..	208	207	203	247	295	215	....	....
Passenger	2 850 ..	*158*	*160*	*160*	*188*	*227*	*140*	....	....
Freight	2 851 ..	*5*	*5*	*1*	*7*	*9*	*11*	....	....
Other	2 852 ..	*45*	*42*	*41*	*52*	*59*	*64*	....	....
Sea transport, passenger	2 207 ..	....	....	....	....	....	....	....	....
Sea transport, freight	2 208 ..	....	....	....	....	....	....	....	....
Sea transport, other	2 209 ..	....	....	....	....	....	....	....	....
Air transport, passenger	2 211 ..	....	....	....	....	....	....	....	....
Air transport, freight	2 212 ..	....	....	....	....	....	....	....	....
Air transport, other	2 213 ..	....	....	....	....	....	....	....	....
Other transport, passenger	2 215 ..	....	....	....	....	....	....	....	....
Other transport, freight	2 216 ..	....	....	....	....	....	....	....	....
Other transport, other	2 217 ..	....	....	....	....	....	....	....	....
Transportation services, debit	3 205 ..	−173	−117	−117	−161	−162	−191	....	....
Passenger	3 850 ..	*−43*	*−21*	*−22*	*−36*	*−45*	*−54*	....	....
Freight	3 851 ..	*−83*	*−61*	*−61*	*−93*	*−87*	*−90*	....	....
Other	3 852 ..	*−47*	*−35*	*−35*	*−33*	*−30*	*−47*	....	....
Sea transport, passenger	3 207 ..	....	....	....	....	....	....	....	....
Sea transport, freight	3 208 ..	....	....	....	....	....	....	....	....
Sea transport, other	3 209 ..	....	....	....	....	....	....	....	....
Air transport, passenger	3 211 ..	....	....	....	....	....	....	....	....
Air transport, freight	3 212 ..	....	....	....	....	....	....	....	....
Air transport, other	3 213 ..	....	....	....	....	....	....	....	....
Other transport, passenger	3 215 ..	....	....	....	....	....	....	....	....
Other transport, freight	3 216 ..	....	....	....	....	....	....	....	....
Other transport, other	3 217 ..	....	....	....	....	....	....	....	....
Travel, credit	2 236 ..	213	201	242	249	342	453	....	....
Business travel	2 237 ..	50	47	47	68	42	89	....	....
Personal travel	2 240 ..	163	154	195	181	300	364	....	....
Travel, debit	3 236 ..	−147	−151	−186	−107	−96	−180	....	....
Business travel	3 237 ..	....	....	....	....	....	....	....	....
Personal travel	3 240 ..	−147	−151	−186	−107	−96	−180	....	....
Other services, credit	2 200 BA	133	166	193	190	215	229	....	....
Communications	2 245 ..	36	30	30	40	45	38	....	....
Construction	2 249 ..	....	....	....	....	....	....	....	....
Insurance	2 253 ..	46	79	100	108	113	135	....	....
Financial	2 260 ..	....	....	....	....	....	....	....	....
Computer and information	2 262 ..	....	....	....	....	....	....	....	....
Royalties and licence fees	2 266 ..	....	....	....	....	....	....	....	....
Other business services	2 268 ..	41	47	24	29	43	42	....	....
Personal, cultural, and recreational	2 287 ..	....	....	....	....	....	....	....	....
Government, n.i.e.	2 291 ..	11	11	39	13	13	14	....	....
Other services, debit	3 200 BA	−67	−102	−69	−103	−113	−169	....	....
Communications	3 245 ..	−6	−6	−5	−4	−6	−16	....	....
Construction	3 249 ..	....	....	....	....	....	....	....	....
Insurance	3 253 ..	....	−8	....	....	....	−31	....	....
Financial	3 260 ..	....	....	....	....	....	....	....	....
Computer and information	3 262 ..	....	....	....	....	....	....	....	....
Royalties and licence fees	3 266 ..	....	....	....	....	....	....	....	....
Other business services	3 268 ..	−37	−58	−31	−63	−50	−53	....	....
Personal, cultural, and recreational	3 287 ..	....	....	....	....	....	....	....	....
Government, n.i.e.	3 291 ..	−25	−31	−33	−36	−57	−70	....	....

Table 2 (Continued). STANDARD PRESENTATION, 2000–2007

(Millions of U.S. dollars)

	Code	2000	2001	2002	2003	2004	2005	2006	2007
C. INCOME	4 300	−629	−539	−480	−681	−597	−760	....	....
Total credit	2 300	*81*	*109*	*64*	*78*	*66*	*84*	....	....
Total debit	3 300	*−709*	*−648*	*−544*	*−759*	*−664*	*−844*	....	....
Compensation of employees, credit	2 310	....	....	....	....	....	....	....	....
Compensation of employees, debit	3 310	....	....	....	....	....	....	....	....
Investment income, credit	2 320	81	109	64	78	66	84	....	....
Direct investment income	2 330	....	....	....	....	....	....	....	....
Dividends and distributed branch profits	2 332	....	....	....	....	....	....	....	....
Reinvested earnings and undistributed branch profits	2 333	....	....	....	....	....	....	....	....
Income on debt (interest)	2 334	....	....	....	....	....	....	....	....
Portfolio investment income	2 339	....	....	....	....	....	....	....	....
Income on equity	2 340	....	....	....	....	....	....	....	....
Income on bonds and notes	2 350	....	....	....	....	....	....	....	....
Income on money market instruments	2 360	....	....	....	....	....	....	....	....
Other investment income	2 370	....	....	....	....	....	....	....	....
Investment income, debit	3 320	−709	−648	−544	−759	−664	−844	....	....
Direct investment income	3 330	....	....	−165	−366	−253	−292	....	....
Dividends and distributed branch profits	3 332	....	....	....	....	....	....	....	....
Reinvested earnings and undistributed branch profits	3 333	....	....	−165	−366	−253	−292	....	....
Income on debt (interest)	3 334	....	....	....	....	....	....	....	....
Portfolio investment income	3 339	....	....	....	....	....	....	....	....
Income on equity	3 340	....	....	....	....	....	....	....	....
Income on bonds and notes	3 350	....	....	....	....	....	....	....	....
Income on money market instruments	3 360	....	....	....	....	....	....	....	....
Other investment income	3 370	....	....	−379	−393	−411	−552	....	....
D. CURRENT TRANSFERS	4 379	38	33	55	59	56	50	....	....
Credit	2 379	64	64	96	101	99	102	....	....
General government	2 380	23	15	15	12	10	7	....	....
Other sectors	2 390	41	49	81	89	89	95	....	....
Workers' remittances	2 391	38	41	79	87	87	92	....	....
Other current transfers	2 392	3	8	2	2	2	3	....	....
Debit	3 379	−26	−31	−42	−42	−42	−52	....	....
General government	3 380	−4	−5	−5	−4	−5	−5	....	....
Other sectors	3 390	−22	−26	−37	−38	−38	−47	....	....
Workers' remittances	3 391	....	....	....	....	....	....	....	....
Other current transfers	3 392	−22	−26	−37	−38	−38	−47	....	....
CAPITAL AND FINANCIAL ACCOUNT	4 996	−267	−181	282	−374	−910	−2,259	....	....
CAPITAL ACCOUNT	4 994	....	....	....	....	....	....	....	....
Total credit	2 994	....	....	....	....	....	....	....	....
Total debit	3 994	....	....	....	....	....	....	....	....
Capital transfers, credit	2 400	....	....	....	....	....	....	....	....
General government	2 401	....	....	....	....	....	....	....	....
Debt forgiveness	2 402	....	....	....	....	....	....	....	....
Other capital transfers	2 410	....	....	....	....	....	....	....	....
Other sectors	2 430	....	....	....	....	....	....	....	....
Migrants' transfers	2 431	....	....	....	....	....	....	....	....
Debt forgiveness	2 432	....	....	....	....	....	....	....	....
Other capital transfers	2 440	....	....	....	....	....	....	....	....
Capital transfers, debit	3 400	....	....	....	....	....	....	....	....
General government	3 401	....	....	....	....	....	....	....	....
Debt forgiveness	3 402	....	....	....	....	....	....	....	....
Other capital transfers	3 410	....	....	....	....	....	....	....	....
Other sectors	3 430	....	....	....	....	....	....	....	....
Migrants' transfers	3 431	....	....	....	....	....	....	....	....
Debt forgiveness	3 432	....	....	....	....	....	....	....	....
Other capital transfers	3 440	....	....	....	....	....	....	....	....
Nonproduced nonfinancial assets, credit	2 480	....	....	....	....	....	....	....	....
Nonproduced nonfinancial assets, debit	3 480	....	....	....	....	....	....	....	....

Table 2 (Continued). STANDARD PRESENTATION, 2000–2007

(Millions of U.S. dollars)

	Code	2000	2001	2002	2003	2004	2005	2006	2007
FINANCIAL ACCOUNT	4 995	−267	−181	282	−374	−910	−2,259	....	....
A. DIRECT INVESTMENT	4 500	654	685	684	1,034	1,124	1,281	....	....
Direct investment abroad	4 505	−25	−150	−106	225	25	341	....	....
Equity capital	4 510	−25	−150	−106	225	25	341	....	....
Claims on affiliated enterprises	4 515	....	....	....	....	....	....	....	....
Liabilities to affiliated enterprises	4 520	....	....	....	....	....	....	....	....
Reinvested earnings	4 525	....	....	....	....	....	....	....	....
Other capital	4 530	....	....	....	....	....	....	....	....
Claims on affiliated enterprises	4 535	....	....	....	....	....	....	....	....
Liabilities to affiliated enterprises	4 540	....	....	....	....	....	....	....	....
Direct investment in Trinidad and Tobago	4 555	680	835	791	808	1,098	940	....	....
Equity capital	4 560	695	883	640	451	857	664	....	....
Claims on direct investors	4 565	....	....	640	451	857	664	....	....
Liabilities to direct investors	4 570	....	....	....	....	....	....	....	....
Reinvested earnings	4 575	....	....	165	366	253	292	....	....
Other capital	4 580	−16	−48	−14	−9	−12	−16	....	....
Claims on direct investors	4 585	....	....	....	....	....	....	....	....
Liabilities to direct investors	4 590	−16	−48	−14	−9	−12	−16	....	....
B. PORTFOLIO INVESTMENT	4 600	−30	−206	−70	−509	−690	−258	....	....
Assets	4 602	−30	−206	−70	−509	−690	−258	....	....
Equity securities	4 610	....	....	....	....	....	....	....	....
Monetary authorities	4 611	....	....	....	....	....	....	....	....
General government	4 612	....	....	....	....	....	....	....	....
Banks	4 613	....	....	....	....	....	....	....	....
Other sectors	4 614	....	....	....	....	....	....	....	....
Debt securities	4 619	−30	−206	−70	−509	−690	−258	....	....
Bonds and notes	4 620	−30	−206	−70	−509	−690	−258	....	....
Monetary authorities	4 621	....	....	....	....	....	....	....	....
General government	4 622	....	....	....	....	....	....	....	....
Banks	4 623	....	....	....	....	....	....	....	....
Other sectors	4 624	....	....	....	....	....	....	....	....
Money market instruments	4 630	....	....	....	....	....	....	....	....
Monetary authorities	4 631	....	....	....	....	....	....	....	....
General government	4 632	....	....	....	....	....	....	....	....
Banks	4 633	....	....	....	....	....	....	....	....
Other sectors	4 634	....	....	....	....	....	....	....	....
Liabilities	4 652	....	....	....	....	....	....	....	....
Equity securities	4 660	....	....	....	....	....	....	....	....
Banks	4 663	....	....	....	....	....	....	....	....
Other sectors	4 664	....	....	....	....	....	....	....	....
Debt securities	4 669	....	....	....	....	....	....	....	....
Bonds and notes	4 670	....	....	....	....	....	....	....	....
Monetary authorities	4 671	....	....	....	....	....	....	....	....
General government	4 672	....	....	....	....	....	....	....	....
Banks	4 673	....	....	....	....	....	....	....	....
Other sectors	4 674	....	....	....	....	....	....	....	....
Money market instruments	4 680	....	....	....	....	....	....	....	....
Monetary authorities	4 681	....	....	....	....	....	....	....	....
General government	4 682	....	....	....	....	....	....	....	....
Banks	4 683	....	....	....	....	....	....	....	....
Other sectors	4 684	....	....	....	....	....	....	....	....
C. FINANCIAL DERIVATIVES	4 910	....	....	....	....	....	....	....	....
Monetary authorities	4 911	....	....	....	....	....	....	....	....
General government	4 912	....	....	....	....	....	....	....	....
Banks	4 913	....	....	....	....	....	....	....	....
Other sectors	4 914	....	....	....	....	....	....	....	....
Assets	4 900	....	....	....	....	....	....	....	....
Monetary authorities	4 901	....	....	....	....	....	....	....	....
General government	4 902	....	....	....	....	....	....	....	....
Banks	4 903	....	....	....	....	....	....	....	....
Other sectors	4 904	....	....	....	....	....	....	....	....
Liabilities	4 905	....	....	....	....	....	....	....	....
Monetary authorities	4 906	....	....	....	....	....	....	....	....
General government	4 907	....	....	....	....	....	....	....	....
Banks	4 908	....	....	....	....	....	....	....	....
Other sectors	4 909	....	....	....	....	....	....	....	....

Table 2 (Concluded). STANDARD PRESENTATION, 2000–2007

(Millions of U.S. dollars)

	Code	2000	2001	2002	2003	2004	2005	2006	2007
D. OTHER INVESTMENT	4 700 ..	**−451**	**−157**	**−217**	**−490**	**−634**	**−1,476**	....	....
Assets	4 703 ..	**398**	**285**	**−316**	**−257**	**−389**	**7**	....	....
Trade credits	4 706 ..	11	1	1	49	100	100	....	....
General government	4 707 ..	....	....	1	49	100	100	....	....
of which: Short-term	4 709 ..	....	....	*1*	*49*	*100*	*100*	....	....
Other sectors	4 710 ..	11	1	....	....	....	....	....	....
of which: Short-term	4 712 ..	*11*	*1*	....	....	....	....	....	....
Loans	4 714 ..	386	27	−318	−306	−489	−93	....	....
Monetary authorities	4 715 ..	384	27	18	26	23	22	....	....
of which: Short-term	4 718 ..	....	....	....	....	....	....	....	....
General government	4 719 ..	3	....	....	....	....	....	....	....
of which: Short-term	4 721 ..	....	....	....	....	....	....	....	....
Banks	4 722 ..	....	....	−335	−332	−513	−115	....	....
of which: Short-term	4 724 ..	....	....	....	....	....	....	....	....
Other sectors	4 725 ..	....	....	....	....	....	....	....	....
of which: Short-term	4 727 ..	....	....	....	....	....	....	....	....
Currency and deposits	4 730 ..	....	257	....	....	....	....	....	....
Monetary authorities	4 731 ..	....	....	....	....	....	....	....	....
General government	4 732 ..	....	....	....	....	....	....	....	....
Banks	4 733 ..	....	257	....	....	....	....	....	....
Other sectors	4 734 ..	....	....	....	....	....	....	....	....
Other assets	4 736 ..	....	....	....	....	....	....	....	....
Monetary authorities	4 737 ..	....	....	....	....	....	....	....	....
of which: Short-term	4 739 ..	....	....	....	....	....	....	....	....
General government	4 740 ..	....	....	....	....	....	....	....	....
of which: Short-term	4 742 ..	....	....	....	....	....	....	....	....
Banks	4 743 ..	....	....	....	....	....	....	....	....
of which: Short-term	4 745 ..	....	....	....	....	....	....	....	....
Other sectors	4 746 ..	....	....	....	....	....	....	....	....
of which: Short-term	4 748 ..	....	....	....	....	....	....	....	....
Liabilities	4 753 ..	**−848**	**−442**	**99**	**−233**	**−245**	**−1,483**	....	....
Trade credits	4 756 ..	−369	−352	−147	−649	−234	−1,686	....	....
General government	4 757 ..	....	....	....	....	....	....	....	....
of which: Short-term	4 759 ..	....	....	....	....	....	....	....	....
Other sectors	4 760 ..	−369	−352	−147	−649	−234	−1,686	....	....
of which: Short-term	4 762 ..	*−369*	*−352*	*−147*	*−649*	*−234*	*−1,686*	....	....
Loans	4 764 ..	−333	−76	....	....	....	....	....	....
Monetary authorities	4 765 ..	−269	−61	....	....	....	....	....	....
of which: Use of Fund credit and loans from the Fund	4 766 ..	....	....	....	....	....	....	....	....
of which: Short-term	4 768 ..	....	....	....	....	....	....	....	....
General government	4 769 ..	−64	−15	....	....	....	....	....	....
of which: Short-term	4 771 ..	....	....	....	....	....	....	....	....
Banks	4 772 ..	....	....	....	....	....	....	....	....
of which: Short-term	4 774 ..	....	....	....	....	....	....	....	....
Other sectors	4 775 ..	....	....	....	....	....	....	....	....
of which: Short-term	4 777 ..	....	....	....	....	....	....	....	....
Currency and deposits	4 780 ..	−83	....	....	....	....	....	....	....
Monetary authorities	4 781 ..	....	....	....	....	....	....	....	....
General government	4 782 ..	....	....	....	....	....	....	....	....
Banks	4 783 ..	−86	....	....	....	....	....	....	....
Other sectors	4 784 ..	3	....	....	....	....	....	....	....
Other liabilities	4 786 ..	−64	−15	246	416	−11	202	....	....
Monetary authorities	4 787 ..	....	....	....	....	....	....	....	....
of which: Short-term	4 789 ..	....	....	....	....	....	....	....	....
General government	4 790 ..	....	....	....	....	....	....	....	....
of which: Short-term	4 792 ..	....	....	....	....	....	....	....	....
Banks	4 793 ..	....	....	256	426	....	213	....	....
of which: Short-term	4 795 ..	....	....	*256*	*426*	....	*213*	....	....
Other sectors	4 796 ..	−64	−15	−10	−10	−11	−11	....	....
of which: Short-term	4 798 ..	*−64*	*−15*	*−10*	*−10*	*−11*	*−11*	....	....
E. RESERVE ASSETS	4 802 ..	**−441**	**−502**	**−116**	**−409**	**−710**	**−1,805**	....	....
Monetary gold	4 812 ..	....	....	....	....	....	....	....	....
Special drawing rights	4 811 ..	....	....	....	−1	−1	−1	....	....
Reserve position in the Fund	4 810 ..	....	−31	−67	−74	27	89	....	....
Foreign exchange	4 803 ..	−441	−471	−49	−334	−735	−1,893	....	....
Other claims	4 813 ..	....	....	....	....	....	....	....	....
NET ERRORS AND OMISSIONS	4 998 ..	**−277**	**−235**	**−358**	**−610**	**−537**	**−1,335**	....	....

Table 1. ANALYTIC PRESENTATION, 2000–2007

(Millions of U.S. dollars)

	Code	2000	2001	2002	2003	2004	2005	2006	2007
A. Current Account[1]	4 993 Z.	**–821**	**–840**	**–746**	**–730**	**–551**	**–299**	**–619**	**–904**
Goods: exports f.o.b.	2 100 ..	5,840	6,628	6,857	8,027	9,679	10,631	11,689	15,148
Goods: imports f.o.b.	3 100 ..	–8,093	–8,997	–8,981	–10,297	–12,110	–12,594	–14,202	–18,024
Balance on Goods	4 100 ..	*–2,253*	*–2,369*	*–2,123*	*–2,269*	*–2,430*	*–1,963*	*–2,513*	*–2,876*
Services: credit	2 200 ..	2,767	2,912	2,681	2,937	3,629	4,021	4,295	4,909
Services: debit	3 200 ..	–1,218	–1,425	–1,450	–1,612	–1,986	–2,191	–2,454	–2,803
Balance on Goods and Services	4 991 ..	*–705*	*–882*	*–893*	*–945*	*–787*	*–133*	*–673*	*–769*
Income: credit	2 300 ..	94	195	177	224	277	316	367	563
Income: debit	3 300 ..	–1,036	–1,045	–1,061	–1,180	–1,418	–1,794	–1,756	–2,316
Balance on Goods, Services, and Income	4 992 ..	*–1,647*	*–1,732*	*–1,777*	*–1,901*	*–1,928*	*–1,611*	*–2,062*	*–2,523*
Current transfers: credit	2 379 Z.	854	916	1,050	1,200	1,401	1,340	1,470	1,650
Current transfers: debit	3 379 ..	–29	–24	–19	–29	–24	–28	–27	–32
B. Capital Account[1]	4 994 Z.	**3**	**53**	**76**	**59**	**107**	**127**	**145**	**152**
Capital account: credit	2 994 Z.	9	56	83	66	113	129	149	154
Capital account: debit	3 994 ..	–6	–3	–7	–7	–6	–2	–4	–2
Total, Groups A Plus B	4 981 ..	*–819*	*–788*	*–671*	*–671*	*–444*	*–172*	*–474*	*–752*
C. Financial Account[1]	4 995 W.	**646**	**1,058**	**845**	**1,101**	**1,439**	**1,136**	**2,595**	**1,477**
Direct investment abroad	4 505 ..	–1	–35	–32	–48	–50	–72	–71	–104
Direct investment in Tunisia	4 555 Z.	752	487	823	588	642	785	3,311	1,620
Portfolio investment assets	4 602 ..	....	....	....	....	....	....	....	....
Equity securities	4 610 ..	....	....	....	....	....	....	....	....
Debt securities	4 619 ..	....	....	....	....	....	....	....	....
Portfolio investment liabilities	4 652 Z.	–20	–15	6	14	24	12	65	30
Equity securities	4 660 ..	–18	–15	6	14	24	12	65	30
Debt securities	4 669 Z.	–3	....	....	....	....	....	....	....
Financial derivatives	4 910 ..	....	....	....	....	....	....	....	....
Financial derivatives assets	4 900 ..	....	....	....	....	....	....	....	....
Financial derivatives liabilities	4 905 ..	....	....	....	....	....	....	....	....
Other investment assets	4 703 ..	–624	–439	–819	–339	–205	17	19	–178
Monetary authorities	4 701 ..	....	....	....	....	....	....	....	....
General government	4 704 ..	....	....	....	....	....	....	....	....
Banks	4 705 ..	....	....	....	....	....	....	....	....
Other sectors	4 728 ..	–624	–439	–819	–339	–205	17	19	–178
Other investment liabilities	4 753 W.	540	1,059	867	887	1,028	394	–729	109
Monetary authorities	4 753 WA	....	....	....	....	....	....	....	....
General government	4 753 ZB	128	752	392	649	176	219	–672	–155
Banks	4 753 ZC	....	....	....	....	....	....	....	....
Other sectors	4 753 ZD	412	307	475	238	852	175	–57	264
Total, Groups A Through C	4 983 ..	*–172*	*270*	*175*	*430*	*995*	*964*	*2,121*	*725*
D. Net Errors and Omissions	4 998 ..	**–33**	**19**	**–35**	**–47**	**–18**	**–28**	**–38**	**–36**
Total, Groups A Through D	4 984 ..	*–205*	*288*	*140*	*383*	*977*	*936*	*2,082*	*689*
E. Reserves and Related Items	4 802 A.	**205**	**–288**	**–140**	**–383**	**–977**	**–936**	**–2,082**	**–689**
Reserve assets	4 802 ..	245	–257	–140	–383	–977	–936	–2,082	–689
Use of Fund credit and loans	4 766 ..	–40	–31	....	....	....	....	....	....
Exceptional financing	4 920 ..	....	....	....	....	....	....	....	....
Conversion rates: Tunisian dinars per U.S. dollar	0 101 ..	**1.3707**	**1.4387**	**1.4217**	**1.2885**	**1.2455**	**1.2974**	**1.3310**	**1.2814**

[1] Excludes components that have been classified in the categories of Group E.

Table 2. STANDARD PRESENTATION, 2000–2007

(Millions of U.S. dollars)

	Code	2000	2001	2002	2003	2004	2005	2006	2007
CURRENT ACCOUNT	4 993	−821	−840	−746	−730	−551	−299	−619	−904
A. GOODS	4 100	−2,253	−2,369	−2,123	−2,269	−2,430	−1,963	−2,513	−2,876
Credit	2 100	5,840	6,628	6,857	8,027	9,679	10,631	11,689	15,148
General merchandise: exports f.o.b.	2 110	5,840	6,628	6,857	8,027	9,679	10,631	11,689	15,148
Goods for processing: exports f.o.b.	2 150	....	....	....	....	....	....	....	....
Repairs on goods	2 160	....	....	....	....	....	....	....	....
Goods procured in ports by carriers	2 170	....	....	....	....	....	....	....	....
Nonmonetary gold	2 180	....	....	....	....	....	....	....	....
Debit	3 100	−8,093	−8,997	−8,981	−10,297	−12,110	−12,594	−14,202	−18,024
General merchandise: imports f.o.b.	3 110	−8,093	−8,997	−8,981	−10,297	−12,110	−12,594	−14,202	−18,024
Goods for processing: imports f.o.b.	3 150	....	....	....	....	....	....	....	....
Repairs on goods	3 160	....	....	....	....	....	....	....	....
Goods procured in ports by carriers	3 170	....	....	....	....	....	....	....	....
Nonmonetary gold	3 180	....	....	....	....	....	....	....	....
B. SERVICES	4 200	1,548	1,487	1,231	1,325	1,644	1,830	1,840	2,106
Total credit	2 200	*2,767*	*2,912*	*2,681*	*2,937*	*3,629*	*4,021*	*4,295*	*4,909*
Total debit	3 200	*−1,218*	*−1,425*	*−1,450*	*−1,612*	*−1,986*	*−2,191*	*−2,454*	*−2,803*
Transportation services, credit	2 205	595	638	612	727	915	1,136	1,243	1,436
Passenger	2 850	*295*	*310*	*308*	*352*	*462*	*657*	*724*	*798*
Freight	2 851	*179*	*195*	*163*	*195*	*266*	*363*	*363*	*429*
Other	2 852	*120*	*133*	*141*	*181*	*187*	*116*	*157*	*209*
Sea transport, passenger	2 207	36	44	46	54	66	71	74	79
Sea transport, freight	2 208	17	22	14	17	12	11	11	12
Sea transport, other	2 209	7	4	19	11	14	8	17	18
Air transport, passenger	2 211	258	264	260	296	393	584	635	706
Air transport, freight	2 212	33	33	32	38	49	54	47	55
Air transport, other	2 213	89	86	83	130	124	74	132	133
Other transport, passenger	2 215	2	2	1	2	3	2	14	14
Other transport, freight	2 216	130	140	117	140	205	298	305	362
Other transport, other	2 217	23	42	39	40	50	33	8	58
Transportation services, debit	3 205	−548	−654	−653	−766	−989	−1,107	−1,235	−1,459
Passenger	3 850	*−47*	*−49*	*−43*	*−55*	*−87*	*−78*	*−88*	*−93*
Freight	3 851	*−374*	*−452*	*−471*	*−546*	*−634*	*−665*	*−750*	*−944*
Other	3 852	*−127*	*−152*	*−139*	*−165*	*−268*	*−364*	*−397*	*−422*
Sea transport, passenger	3 207	....	....	....	....	....	....	....	....
Sea transport, freight	3 208	−344	−416	−430	−499	−571	−599	−675	−850
Sea transport, other	3 209	−65	−81	−79	−93	−150	−203	−222	−237
Air transport, passenger	3 211	−47	−49	−43	−55	−87	−78	−88	−93
Air transport, freight	3 212	−9	−10	−9	−14	−26	−26	−30	−38
Air transport, other	3 213	−41	−43	−46	−58	−94	−127	−139	−148
Other transport, passenger	3 215	....	....	....	....	....	....	....	....
Other transport, freight	3 216	−22	−27	−31	−33	−38	−40	−45	−57
Other transport, other	3 217	−21	−28	−15	−14	−24	−33	−36	−38
Travel, credit	2 236	1,682	1,751	1,523	1,583	1,970	2,143	2,275	2,575
Business travel	2 237	31	33	28	29	36	40	42	48
Personal travel	2 240	1,652	1,718	1,495	1,553	1,934	2,103	2,233	2,527
Travel, debit	3 236	−263	−273	−260	−300	−340	−374	−410	−437
Business travel	3 237	−23	−24	−26	−31	−36	−40	−44	−51
Personal travel	3 240	−239	−249	−234	−269	−304	−334	−366	−386
Other services, credit	2 200 BA	490	523	546	627	744	743	776	898
Communications	2 245	12	13	11	9	14	18	24	30
Construction	2 249	50	71	89	122	148	143	143	173
Insurance	2 253	15	22	20	20	31	41	47	51
Financial	2 260	34	38	42	55	55	58	66	70
Computer and information	2 262	20	21	18	19	18	19	24	27
Royalties and licence fees	2 266	15	15	16	18	18	14	14	15
Other business services	2 268	255	256	267	283	341	325	323	377
Personal, cultural, and recreational	2 287	3	4	3	5	10	4	3	3
Government, n.i.e.	2 291	87	83	78	95	109	121	133	152
Other services, debit	3 200 BA	−408	−498	−537	−546	−657	−711	−810	−907
Communications	3 245	−10	−13	−14	−14	−22	−28	−31	−28
Construction	3 249	−112	−135	−160	−160	−183	−197	−227	−270
Insurance	3 253	−47	−54	−68	−75	−99	−129	−142	−151
Financial	3 260	−36	−41	−34	−35	−45	−50	−65	−70
Computer and information	3 262	−6	−8	−7	−7	−10	−10	−18	−15
Royalties and licence fees	3 266	−3	−6	−6	−6	−8	−8	−11	−10
Other business services	3 268	−86	−138	−146	−142	−167	−167	−190	−216
Personal, cultural, and recreational	3 287	−9	−10	−5	−4	−6	−6	−10	−7
Government, n.i.e.	3 291	−99	−92	−98	−102	−116	−116	−117	−140

Table 2 (Continued). STANDARD PRESENTATION, 2000–2007

(Millions of U.S. dollars)

	Code	2000	2001	2002	2003	2004	2005	2006	2007
C. INCOME	4 300	−942	−850	−885	−956	−1,141	−1,479	−1,389	−1,754
Total credit	2 300	*94*	*195*	*177*	*224*	*277*	*316*	*367*	*563*
Total debit	3 300	*−1,036*	*−1,045*	*−1,061*	*−1,180*	*−1,418*	*−1,794*	*−1,756*	*−2,316*
Compensation of employees, credit	2 310	....	100	105	143	163	198	206	269
Compensation of employees, debit	3 310	....	−10	−6	−7	−6	−8	−10	−8
Investment income, credit	2 320	94	95	72	81	114	118	160	293
Direct investment income	2 330	3	3	6	9	12	13	7	6
Dividends and distributed branch profits	2 332	3	3	6	9	12	13	7	6
Reinvested earnings and undistributed branch profits	2 333	....	....	....	....	....	....	....	....
Income on debt (interest)	2 334	....	....	....	....	....	....	....	....
Portfolio investment income	2 339	91	92	65	71	102	106	154	287
Income on equity	2 340	2	1	3	6	13	4	2	4
Income on bonds and notes	2 350	89	90	63	65	89	102	151	283
Income on money market instruments	2 360	....	....	....	....	....	....	....	....
Other investment income	2 370	....	....	....	....	....	....	....	....
Investment income, debit	3 320	−1,036	−1,036	−1,056	−1,173	−1,412	−1,786	−1,746	−2,308
Direct investment income	3 330	−468	−480	−473	−537	−678	−962	−930	−1,361
Dividends and distributed branch profits	3 332	−468	−480	−473	−537	−678	−962	−930	−1,361
Reinvested earnings and undistributed branch profits	3 333	....	....	....	....	....	....	....	....
Income on debt (interest)	3 334	....	....	....	....	....	....	....	....
Portfolio investment income	3 339	−568	−556	−583	−636	−734	−824	−817	−948
Income on equity	3 340	−53	−71	−67	−64	−92	−148	−119	−217
Income on bonds and notes	3 350	−516	−485	−516	−573	−642	−676	−698	−731
Income on money market instruments	3 360	....	....	....	....	....	....	....	....
Other investment income	3 370	....	....	....	....	....	....	....	....
D. CURRENT TRANSFERS	4 379	825	892	1,031	1,170	1,377	1,312	1,443	1,619
Credit	2 379	854	916	1,050	1,200	1,401	1,340	1,470	1,650
General government	2 380	29	58	41	41	57	68	82	99
Other sectors	2 390	825	858	1,009	1,159	1,344	1,272	1,388	1,552
Workers' remittances	2 391	796	827	965	1,107	1,268	1,195	1,304	1,446
Other current transfers	2 392	29	31	44	51	75	77	84	106
Debit	3 379	−29	−24	−19	−29	−24	−28	−27	−32
General government	3 380	....	....	....	....	....	....	....	....
Other sectors	3 390	−29	−24	−19	−29	−24	−28	−27	−32
Workers' remittances	3 391	−21	−11	−7	−11	−7	−7	−7	−7
Other current transfers	3 392	−8	−13	−12	−19	−18	−20	−20	−24
CAPITAL AND FINANCIAL ACCOUNT	4 996	854	822	781	778	569	328	658	941
CAPITAL ACCOUNT	4 994	3	53	76	59	107	127	145	152
Total credit	2 994	*9*	*56*	*83*	*66*	*113*	*129*	*149*	*154*
Total debit	3 994	*−6*	*−3*	*−7*	*−7*	*−6*	*−2*	*−4*	*−2*
Capital transfers, credit	2 400	9	56	83	66	113	129	149	154
General government	2 401	9	56	83	66	113	129	149	154
Debt forgiveness	2 402	....	....	....	....	....	....	....	....
Other capital transfers	2 410	9	56	83	66	113	129	149	154
Other sectors	2 430	....	....	....	....	....	....	....	....
Migrants' transfers	2 431	....	....	....	....	....	....	....	....
Debt forgiveness	2 432	....	....	....	....	....	....	....	....
Other capital transfers	2 440	....	....	....	....	....	....	....	....
Capital transfers, debit	3 400	−6	−3	−7	−7	−6	−2	−4	−2
General government	3 401	....	....	....	....	....	....	....	....
Debt forgiveness	3 402	....	....	....	....	....	....	....	....
Other capital transfers	3 410	....	....	....	....	....	....	....	....
Other sectors	3 430	−6	−3	−7	−7	−6	−2	−4	−2
Migrants' transfers	3 431	−6	....	....	....	....	....	....	....
Debt forgiveness	3 432	....	....	....	....	....	....	....	....
Other capital transfers	3 440	....	−3	−7	−7	−6	−2	−4	−2
Nonproduced nonfinancial assets, credit	2 480	....	....	....	....	....	....	....	....
Nonproduced nonfinancial assets, debit	3 480	....	....	....	....	....	....	....	....

Table 2 (Continued). STANDARD PRESENTATION, 2000–2007

(Millions of U.S. dollars)

	Code	2000	2001	2002	2003	2004	2005	2006	2007
FINANCIAL ACCOUNT............................	4 995 ..	851	769	705	719	462	200	513	789
A. DIRECT INVESTMENT........................	4 500 ..	751	452	790	539	592	713	3,240	1,515
Direct investment abroad..........................	4 505 ..	−1	−35	−32	−48	−50	−72	−71	−104
Equity capital..	4 510 ..	−1	−35	−32	−48	−50	−72	−71	−104
Claims on affiliated enterprises...............	4 515 ..	....	....	....	....	....	....	....	....
Liabilities to affiliated enterprises..........	4 520 ..	−1	−35	−32	−48	−50	−72	−71	−104
Reinvested earnings...................................	4 525 ..	....	....	....	....	....	....	....	....
Other capital..	4 530 ..	....	....	....	....	....	....	....	....
Claims on affiliated enterprises...............	4 535 ..	....	....	....	....	....	....	....	....
Liabilities to affiliated enterprises..........	4 540 ..	....	....	....	....	....	....	....	....
Direct investment in Tunisia..............................	4 555 ..	752	487	823	588	642	785	3,311	1,620
Equity capital..	4 560 ..	757	484	818	581	638	782	3,307	1,614
Claims on direct investors........................	4 565 ..	....	....	....	....	....	....	....	....
Liabilities to direct investors....................	4 570 ..	757	484	818	581	638	782	3,307	1,614
Reinvested earnings...................................	4 575 ..	....	....	....	....	....	....	....	....
Other capital..	4 580 ..	−4	3	5	7	4	3	4	5
Claims on direct investors........................	4 585 ..	....	....	....	....	....	....	....	....
Liabilities to direct investors....................	4 590 ..	−4	3	5	7	4	3	4	5
B. PORTFOLIO INVESTMENT....................	4 600 ..	−20	−15	6	14	24	12	65	30
Assets...	4 602 ..	....	....	....	....	....	....	....	....
Equity securities..	4 610 ..	....	....	....	....	....	....	....	....
Monetary authorities.................................	4 611 ..	....	....	....	....	....	....	....	....
General government..................................	4 612 ..	....	....	....	....	....	....	....	....
Banks...	4 613 ..	....	....	....	....	....	....	....	....
Other sectors...	4 614 ..	....	....	....	....	....	....	....	....
Debt securities...	4 619 ..	....	....	....	....	....	....	....	....
Bonds and notes.......................................	4 620 ..	....	....	....	....	....	....	....	....
Monetary authorities.............................	4 621 ..	....	....	....	....	....	....	....	....
General government.............................	4 622 ..	....	....	....	....	....	....	....	....
Banks..	4 623 ..	....	....	....	....	....	....	....	....
Other sectors...	4 624 ..	....	....	....	....	....	....	....	....
Money market instruments.....................	4 630 ..	....	....	....	....	....	....	....	....
Monetary authorities.............................	4 631 ..	....	....	....	....	....	....	....	....
General government.............................	4 632 ..	....	....	....	....	....	....	....	....
Banks..	4 633 ..	....	....	....	....	....	....	....	....
Other sectors...	4 634 ..	....	....	....	....	....	....	....	....
Liabilities...	4 652 ..	−20	−15	6	14	24	12	65	30
Equity securities..	4 660 ..	−18	−15	6	14	24	12	65	30
Banks...	4 663 ..	....	....	....	....	....	....	....	....
Other sectors...	4 664 ..	−18	−15	6	14	24	12	65	30
Debt securities...	4 669 ..	−3	....	....	....	....	....	....	....
Bonds and notes.......................................	4 670 ..	....	....	....	....	....	....	....	....
Monetary authorities.............................	4 671 ..	....	....	....	....	....	....	....	....
General government.............................	4 672 ..	....	....	....	....	....	....	....	....
Banks..	4 673 ..	....	....	....	....	....	....	....	....
Other sectors...	4 674 ..	....	....	....	....	....	....	....	....
Money market instruments.....................	4 680 ..	−3	....	....	....	....	....	....	....
Monetary authorities.............................	4 681 ..	....	....	....	....	....	....	....	....
General government.............................	4 682 ..	....	....	....	....	....	....	....	....
Banks..	4 683 ..	....	....	....	....	....	....	....	....
Other sectors...	4 684 ..	−3	....	....	....	....	....	....	....
C. FINANCIAL DERIVATIVES.....................	4 910 ..	....	....	....	....	....	....	....	....
Monetary authorities.................................	4 911 ..	....	....	....	....	....	....	....	....
General government..................................	4 912 ..	....	....	....	....	....	....	....	....
Banks...	4 913 ..	....	....	....	....	....	....	....	....
Other sectors...	4 914 ..	....	....	....	....	....	....	....	....
Assets...	4 900 ..	....	....	....	....	....	....	....	....
Monetary authorities.................................	4 901 ..	....	....	....	....	....	....	....	....
General government..................................	4 902 ..	....	....	....	....	....	....	....	....
Banks...	4 903 ..	....	....	....	....	....	....	....	....
Other sectors...	4 904 ..	....	....	....	....	....	....	....	....
Liabilities...	4 905 ..	....	....	....	....	....	....	....	....
Monetary authorities.................................	4 906 ..	....	....	....	....	....	....	....	....
General government..................................	4 907 ..	....	....	....	....	....	....	....	....
Banks...	4 908 ..	....	....	....	....	....	....	....	....
Other sectors...	4 909 ..	....	....	....	....	....	....	....	....

Table 2 (Concluded). STANDARD PRESENTATION, 2000–2007

(Millions of U.S. dollars)

	Code	2000	2001	2002	2003	2004	2005	2006	2007
D. OTHER INVESTMENT....................................	4 700 ..	−124	589	49	548	823	412	−710	−68
Assets..	4 703 ..	−624	−439	−819	−339	−205	17	19	−178
Trade credits...............................	4 706 ..	−624	−439	−819	−339	−205	17	19	−178
General government...................	4 707 ..	....	....	....	....	....	....	....	....
of which: Short-term.................	4 709 ..	....	....	....	....	....	....	....	....
Other sectors...........................	4 710 ..	−624	−439	−819	−339	−205	17	19	−178
of which: Short-term.................	4 712 ..	*−624*	*−439*	*−819*	*−339*	*−205*	*17*	*19*	*−178*
Loans..	4 714 ..	....	....	....	....	....	....	....	....
Monetary authorities..................	4 715 ..	....	....	....	....	....	....	....	....
of which: Short-term.................	4 718 ..	....	....	....	....	....	....	....	....
General government...................	4 719 ..	....	....	....	....	....	....	....	....
of which: Short-term.................	4 721 ..	....	....	....	....	....	....	....	....
Banks...	4 722 ..	....	....	....	....	....	....	....	....
of which: Short-term.................	4 724 ..	....	....	....	....	....	....	....	....
Other sectors...........................	4 725 ..	....	....	....	....	....	....	....	....
of which: Short-term.................	4 727 ..	....	....	....	....	....	....	....	....
Currency and deposits..................	4 730 ..	....	....	....	....	....	....	....	....
Monetary authorities..................	4 731 ..	....	....	....	....	....	....	....	....
General government...................	4 732 ..	....	....	....	....	....	....	....	....
Banks...	4 733 ..	....	....	....	....	....	....	....	....
Other sectors...........................	4 734 ..	....	....	....	....	....	....	....	....
Other assets..............................	4 736 ..	....	....	....	....	....	....	....	....
Monetary authorities..................	4 737 ..	....	....	....	....	....	....	....	....
of which: Short-term.................	4 739 ..	....	....	....	....	....	....	....	....
General government...................	4 740 ..	....	....	....	....	....	....	....	....
of which: Short-term.................	4 742 ..	....	....	....	....	....	....	....	....
Banks...	4 743 ..	....	....	....	....	....	....	....	....
of which: Short-term.................	4 745 ..	....	....	....	....	....	....	....	....
Other sectors...........................	4 746 ..	....	....	....	....	....	....	....	....
of which: Short-term.................	4 748 ..	....	....	....	....	....	....	....	....
Liabilities..	4 753 ..	**500**	**1,028**	**867**	**887**	**1,028**	**394**	**−729**	**109**
Trade credits...............................	4 756 ..	277	185	75	47	54	202	61	319
General government...................	4 757 ..	....	....	....	....	....	....	....	....
of which: Short-term.................	4 759 ..	....	....	....	....	....	....	....	....
Other sectors...........................	4 760 ..	277	185	75	47	54	202	61	319
of which: Short-term.................	4 762 ..	*277*	*185*	*75*	*47*	*54*	*202*	*61*	*319*
Loans..	4 764 ..	224	843	793	841	974	192	−790	−209
Monetary authorities..................	4 765 ..	−40	−31	....	....	....	....	....	....
of which: Use of Fund credit and loans from the Fund..	4 766 ..	*−40*	*−31*	....	....	....	....	....	....
of which: Short-term.................	4 768 ..	....	....	....	....	....	....	....	....
General government...................	4 769 ..	128	752	392	649	176	219	−672	−155
of which: Short-term.................	4 771 ..	....	....	....	....	....	....	....	....
Banks...	4 772 ..	....	....	....	....	....	....	....	....
of which: Short-term.................	4 774 ..	....	....	....	....	....	....	....	....
Other sectors...........................	4 775 ..	136	122	400	192	798	−27	−118	−54
of which: Short-term.................	4 777 ..	....	....	....	....	....	....	....	....
Currency and deposits..................	4 780 ..	....	....	....	....	....	....	....	....
Monetary authorities..................	4 781 ..	....	....	....	....	....	....	....	....
General government...................	4 782 ..	....	....	....	....	....	....	....	....
Banks...	4 783 ..	....	....	....	....	....	....	....	....
Other sectors...........................	4 784 ..	....	....	....	....	....	....	....	....
Other liabilities..........................	4 786 ..	....	....	....	....	....	....	....	....
Monetary authorities..................	4 787 ..	....	....	....	....	....	....	....	....
of which: Short-term.................	4 789 ..	....	....	....	....	....	....	....	....
General government...................	4 790 ..	....	....	....	....	....	....	....	....
of which: Short-term.................	4 792 ..	....	....	....	....	....	....	....	....
Banks...	4 793 ..	....	....	....	....	....	....	....	....
of which: Short-term.................	4 795 ..	....	....	....	....	....	....	....	....
Other sectors...........................	4 796 ..	....	....	....	....	....	....	....	....
of which: Short-term.................	4 798 ..	....	....	....	....	....	....	....	....
E. RESERVE ASSETS...............................	4 802 ..	**245**	**−257**	**−140**	**−383**	**−977**	**−936**	**−2,082**	**−689**
Monetary gold.............................	4 812 ..	....	....	....	....	....	....	....	....
Special drawing rights..................	4 811 ..	21	1	−1	1	−6	7	1	....
Reserve position in the Fund..........	4 810 ..	....	....	....	....	....	....	....	....
Foreign exchange........................	4 803 ..	224	−258	−139	−383	−972	−943	−2,083	−688
Other claims...............................	4 813 ..	....	....	....	....	....	....	....	....
NET ERRORS AND OMISSIONS............................	4 998 ..	**−33**	**19**	**−35**	**−47**	**−18**	**−28**	**−38**	**−36**

Table 3. INTERNATIONAL INVESTMENT POSITION (End-period stocks), 2000–2007

(Millions of U.S. dollars)

	Code	2000	2001	2002	2003	2004	2005	2006	2007
ASSETS	8 995 C.	3,276	2,975	4,227	5,411	6,662	6,762	9,255	10,847
Direct investment abroad	8 505 ..	32	32	37	43	47	52	89	118
Equity capital and reinvested earnings	8 506 ..	32	32	37	43	47	52	89	118
Claims on affiliated enterprises	8 507 ..	....	....	....	....	....	....	....	....
Liabilities to affiliated enterprises	8 508 ..	32	32	37	43	47	52	89	118
Other capital	8 530 ..	....	....	....	....	....	....	....	....
Claims on affiliated enterprises	8 535 ..	....	....	....	....	....	....	....	....
Liabilities to affiliated enterprises	8 540 ..	....	....	....	....	....	....	....	....
Portfolio investment	8 602 ..	45	44	50	56	60	54	59	67
Equity securities	8 610 ..	45	44	50	56	60	54	59	67
Monetary authorities	8 611 ..	....	....	....	....	....	....	....	....
General government	8 612 ..	....	....	....	....	....	....	....	....
Banks	8 613 ..	....	....	....	....	....	....	....	....
Other sectors	8 614 ..	45	44	50	56	60	54	59	67
Debt securities	8 619 ..	....	....	....	....	....	....	....	....
Bonds and notes	8 620 ..	....	....	....	....	....	....	....	....
Monetary authorities	8 621 ..	....	....	....	....	....	....	....	....
General government	8 622 ..	....	....	....	....	....	....	....	....
Banks	8 623 ..	....	....	....	....	....	....	....	....
Other sectors	8 624 ..	....	....	....	....	....	....	....	....
Money market instruments	8 630 ..	....	....	....	....	....	....	....	....
Monetary authorities	8 631 ..	....	....	....	....	....	....	....	....
General government	8 632 ..	....	....	....	....	....	....	....	....
Banks	8 633 ..	....	....	....	....	....	....	....	....
Other sectors	8 634 ..	....	....	....	....	....	....	....	....
Financial derivatives	8 900 ..	....	....	....	....	....	....	....	....
Monetary authorities	8 901 ..	....	....	....	....	....	....	....	....
General government	8 902 ..	....	....	....	....	....	....	....	....
Banks	8 903 ..	....	....	....	....	....	....	....	....
Other sectors	8 904 ..	....	....	....	....	....	....	....	....
Other investment	8 703 ..	1,300	924	1,819	2,338	2,543	2,232	2,322	2,729
Trade credits	8 706 ..	505	280	1,050	1,574	1,733	1,271	1,228	1,087
General government	8 707 ..	....	....	....	....	....	....	....	....
of which: Short-term	8 709 ..	....	....	....	....	....	....	....	....
Other sectors	8 710 ..	505	280	1,050	1,574	1,733	1,271	1,228	1,087
of which: Short-term	8 712 ..	*505*	*280*	*1,050*	*1,574*	*1,733*	*1,271*	*1,228*	*1,087*
Loans	8 714 ..	99	98	100	100	100	100	100	100
Monetary authorities	8 715 ..	....	....	....	....	....	....	....	....
of which: Short-term	8 718 ..	....	....	....	....	....	....	....	....
General government	8 719 ..	....	....	....	....	....	....	....	....
of which: Short-term	8 721 ..	....	....	....	....	....	....	....	....
Banks	8 722 ..	....	....	....	....	....	....	....	....
of which: Short-term	8 724 ..	....	....	....	....	....	....	....	....
Other sectors	8 725 ..	99	98	100	100	100	100	100	100
of which: Short-term	8 727 ..	....	....	....	....	....	....	....	....
Currency and deposits	8 730 ..	....	....	....	....	....	....	....	....
Monetary authorities	8 731 ..	....	....	....	....	....	....	....	....
General government	8 732 ..	....	....	....	....	....	....	....	....
Banks	8 733 ..	....	....	....	....	....	....	....	....
Other sectors	8 734 ..	....	....	....	....	....	....	....	....
Other assets	8 736 ..	696	547	669	664	710	861	994	1,542
Monetary authorities	8 737 ..	....	....	....	....	....	....	....	....
of which: Short-term	8 739 ..	....	....	....	....	....	....	....	....
General government	8 740 ..	....	....	....	....	....	....	....	....
of which: Short-term	8 742 ..	....	....	....	....	....	....	....	....
Banks	8 743 ..	696	547	669	664	710	861	994	1,542
of which: Short-term	8 745 ..	....	*547*	*669*	*664*	*710*	*861*	*994*	*1,542*
Other sectors	8 746 ..	....	....	....	....	....	....	....	....
of which: Short-term	8 748 ..	....	....	....	....	....	....	....	....
Reserve assets	8 802 ..	1,898	1,975	2,322	2,974	4,013	4,423	6,786	7,933
Monetary gold	8 812 ..	3	3	3	4	4	3	3	4
Special drawing rights	8 811 ..	4	2	3	2	9	2	1	2
Reserve position in the Fund	8 810 ..	26	25	27	30	31	29	30	32
Foreign exchange	8 803 ..	1,865	1,944	2,288	2,938	3,969	4,389	6,751	7,896
Other claims	8 813 ..	....	....	....	....	....	....	....	....

Table 3 (Concluded). INTERNATIONAL INVESTMENT POSITION (End-period stocks), 2000–2007

(Millions of U.S. dollars)

	Code	2000	2001	2002	2003	2004	2005	2006	2007
LIABILITIES	8 995 D.	**24,043**	**24,875**	**29,615**	**34,878**	**38,442**	**35,922**	**41,764**	**48,158**
Direct investment in Tunisia	8 555	**11,545**	**11,520**	**13,861**	**16,239**	**18,050**	**16,840**	**21,853**	**26,223**
Equity capital and reinvested earnings	8 556	11,545	11,520	13,594	15,971	17,844	16,840	21,853	26,223
Claims on direct investors	8 557	....	....	....	....	....	....	....	....
Liabilities to direct investors	8 558	11,545	11,520	13,594	15,971	17,844	16,840	21,853	26,223
Other capital	8 580	....	....	267	267	207	....	....	....
Claims on direct investors	8 585	....	....	....	....	....	....	....	....
Liabilities to direct investors	8 590	....	....	267	267	207	....	....	....
Portfolio investment	8 652	**993**	**475**	**498**	**618**	**658**	**794**	**1,169**	**1,552**
Equity securities	8 660	993	475	498	618	658	794	1,136	1,498
Banks	8 663	....	....	....	....	....	....	....	....
Other sectors	8 664	993	475	498	618	658	794	1,136	1,498
Debt securities	8 669	....	....	....	....	....	....	33	55
Bonds and notes	8 670	....	....	....	....	....	....	33	55
Monetary authorities	8 671	....	....	....	....	....	....	....	....
General government	8 672	....	....	....	....	....	....	....	....
Banks	8 673	....	....	....	....	....	....	33	55
Other sectors	8 674	....	....	....	....	....	....	....	....
Money market instruments	8 680	....	....	....	....	....	....	....	....
Monetary authorities	8 681	....	....	....	....	....	....	....	....
General government	8 682	....	....	....	....	....	....	....	....
Banks	8 683	....	....	....	....	....	....	....	....
Other sectors	8 684	....	....	....	....	....	....	....	....
Financial derivatives	8 905	....	....	....	....	....	....	....	....
Monetary authorities	8 906	....	....	....	....	....	....	....	....
General government	8 907	....	....	....	....	....	....	....	....
Banks	8 908	....	....	....	....	....	....	....	....
Other sectors	8 909	....	....	....	....	....	....	....	....
Other investment	8 753	**11,506**	**12,880**	**15,256**	**18,021**	**19,733**	**18,288**	**18,742**	**20,383**
Trade credits	8 756	138	1,268	1,424	1,736	1,569	1,167	1,201	1,160
General government	8 757	....	....	....	....	....	....	....	....
of which: Short-term	8 759	....	....	....	....	....	....	....	....
Other sectors	8 760	138	1,268	1,424	1,736	1,569	1,167	1,201	1,160
of which: Short-term	8 762	*138*	*1,268*	*1,424*	*1,736*	*1,569*	*1,167*	*1,201*	*1,160*
Loans	8 764	9,915	10,238	12,354	14,756	16,388	15,153	15,384	16,399
Monetary authorities	8 765	32	....	....	....	....	....	....	....
of which: Use of Fund credit and loans from the Fund	8 766	*32*	....	....	....	....	....	....	....
of which: Short-term	8 768	....	....	....	....	....	....	....	....
General government	8 769	7,334	7,671	8,822	10,542	11,158	10,440	10,385	11,067
of which: Short-term	8 771	....	....	....	....	....	....	....	....
Banks	8 772	....	....	....	....	....	....	....	....
of which: Short-term	8 774	....	....	....	....	....	....	....	....
Other sectors	8 775	2,549	2,567	3,532	4,214	5,230	4,714	4,999	5,333
of which: Short-term	8 777	....	....	....	....	....	....	....	....
Currency and deposits	8 780	1,452	1,374	1,478	1,529	1,776	1,968	2,156	2,824
Monetary authorities	8 781	....	....	....	....	....	....	....	....
General government	8 782	....	....	....	....	....	....	....	....
Banks	8 783	1,452	1,374	1,478	1,529	1,776	1,968	2,156	2,824
Other sectors	8 784	....	....	....	....	....	....	....	....
Other liabilities	8 786	....	....	....	....	....	....	....	....
Monetary authorities	8 787	....	....	....	....	....	....	....	....
of which: Short-term	8 789	....	....	....	....	....	....	....	....
General government	8 790	....	....	....	....	....	....	....	....
of which: Short-term	8 792	....	....	....	....	....	....	....	....
Banks	8 793	....	....	....	....	....	....	....	....
of which: Short-term	8 795	....	....	....	....	....	....	....	....
Other sectors	8 796	....	....	....	....	....	....	....	....
of which: Short-term	8 798	....	....	....	....	....	....	....	....
NET INTERNATIONAL INVESTMENT POSITION	8 995	**−20,767**	**−21,900**	**−25,388**	**−29,467**	**−31,779**	**−29,161**	**−32,509**	**−37,312**
Conversion rates: Tunisian dinars per U.S. dollar (end of period)	0 102	**1.3853**	**1.4683**	**1.3341**	**1.2083**	**1.1994**	**1.3634**	**1.2971**	**1.2207**

Table 1. ANALYTIC PRESENTATION, 2000–2007

(Millions of U.S. dollars)

	Code	2000	2001	2002	2003	2004	2005	2006	2007
A. Current Account[1]	4 993 Z.	−9,920	3,760	−626	−7,515	−14,431	−22,137	−31,893	−37,697
Goods: exports f.o.b.	2 100 ..	30,825	34,729	40,719	52,394	68,535	78,365	93,611	115,356
Goods: imports f.o.b.	3 100 ..	−52,882	−38,092	−47,109	−65,883	−91,271	−111,353	−134,552	−162,025
Balance on Goods	4 100 ..	*−22,057*	*−3,363*	*−6,390*	*−13,489*	*−22,736*	*−32,988*	*−40,941*	*−46,669*
Services: credit	2 200 ..	19,528	15,234	14,046	18,013	22,960	26,648	25,312	28,853
Services: debit	3 200 ..	−8,153	−6,098	−6,161	−7,502	−10,163	−11,376	−11,481	−14,974
Balance on Goods and Services	4 991 ..	*−10,682*	*5,773*	*1,495*	*−2,978*	*−9,939*	*−17,716*	*−27,110*	*−32,790*
Income: credit	2 300 ..	2,836	2,753	2,486	2,246	2,651	3,608	4,383	6,384
Income: debit	3 300 ..	−6,838	−7,753	−7,040	−7,803	−8,260	−9,483	−11,074	−13,527
Balance on Goods, Services, and Income	4 992 ..	*−14,684*	*773*	*−3,059*	*−8,535*	*−15,548*	*−23,591*	*−33,801*	*−39,933*
Current transfers: credit	2 379 Z.	4,856	3,045	2,477	1,081	1,155	1,475	2,244	2,778
Current transfers: debit	3 379 ..	−92	−58	−44	−61	−38	−21	−336	−542
B. Capital Account[1]	4 994 Z.	....	....	....	....	....	....	....	....
Capital account: credit	2 994 Z.	....	....	....	....	....	....	....	....
Capital account: debit	3 994 ..	....	....	....	....	....	....	....	....
Total, Groups A Plus B	4 981 ..	*−9,920*	*3,760*	*−626*	*−7,515*	*−14,431*	*−22,137*	*−31,893*	*−37,697*
C. Financial Account[1]	4 995 W.	8,584	−14,558	1,190	7,192	17,730	43,502	42,691	48,567
Direct investment abroad	4 505 ..	−870	−498	−176	−499	−780	−1,064	−924	−2,106
Direct investment in Turkey	4 555 Z.	982	3,352	1,133	1,751	2,785	10,031	19,989	22,195
Portfolio investment assets	4 602 ..	−593	−788	−2,096	−1,386	−1,388	−1,233	−4,029	−2,063
Equity securities	4 610 ..	−33	−36	−42	−33	−25	−20	−42	−116
Debt securities	4 619 ..	−560	−752	−2,054	−1,353	−1,363	−1,213	−3,987	−1,947
Portfolio investment liabilities	4 652 Z.	1,615	−3,727	1,503	3,851	9,411	14,670	11,402	2,780
Equity securities	4 660 ..	489	−79	−16	905	1,427	5,669	1,939	5,138
Debt securities	4 669 Z.	1,126	−3,648	1,519	2,946	7,984	9,001	9,463	−2,358
Financial derivatives	4 910 ..	....	....	....	....	....	....	....	....
Financial derivatives assets	4 900 ..	....	....	....	....	....	....	....	....
Financial derivatives liabilities	4 905 ..	....	....	....	....	....	....	....	....
Other investment assets	4 703 ..	−1,939	−601	−777	−986	−6,955	259	−13,437	−4,852
Monetary authorities	4 701 ..	1	−39	−30	−28	−24	−16	....	2
General government	4 704 ..	....	....	....	....	....	....	....	....
Banks	4 705 ..	−1,574	233	643	348	−5,324	−149	−11,018	−3,386
Other sectors	4 728 ..	−366	−795	−1,390	−1,306	−1,607	424	−2,419	−1,468
Other investment liabilities	4 753 W.	9,389	−12,296	1,603	4,461	14,657	20,839	29,690	32,613
Monetary authorities	4 753 WA	706	817	1,433	605	−51	−474	−986	−1,096
General government	4 753 ZB	−883	−1,977	−669	−2,194	−1,163	−2,165	−712	82
Banks	4 753 ZC	3,736	−9,644	−2,016	2,846	6,564	10,524	11,704	3,735
Other sectors	4 753 ZD	5,830	−1,492	2,855	3,204	9,307	12,954	19,684	29,892
Total, Groups A Through C	4 983 ..	*−1,336*	*−10,798*	*564*	*−323*	*3,299*	*21,365*	*10,798*	*10,870*
D. Net Errors and Omissions	4 998 ..	−2,598	−2,090	−778	4,410	961	1,811	−177	1,182
Total, Groups A Through D	4 984 ..	*−3,934*	*−12,888*	*−214*	*4,087*	*4,260*	*23,176*	*10,621*	*12,052*
E. Reserves and Related Items	4 802 A.	3,934	12,888	214	−4,087	−4,260	−23,176	−10,621	−12,052
Reserve assets	4 802 ..	−383	2,718	−6,177	−4,030	−787	−17,854	−6,102	−8,065
Use of Fund credit and loans	4 766 ..	3,316	10,169	6,390	−57	−3,520	−5,322	−4,519	−3,987
Exceptional financing	4 920 ..	1,000	....	....	....	47	....	....	....
Conversion rates: new liras per U.S. dollar	0 101 ..	.6252	1.2256	1.5072	1.5009	1.4255	1.3436	1.4285	1.3033

[1] Excludes components that have been classified in the categories of Group E.

Table 2. STANDARD PRESENTATION, 2000–2007

(Millions of U.S. dollars)

	Code	2000	2001	2002	2003	2004	2005	2006	2007
CURRENT ACCOUNT	4 993	**−9,920**	**3,760**	**−626**	**−7,515**	**−14,431**	**−22,137**	**−31,893**	**−37,697**
A. GOODS	4 100	**−22,057**	**−3,363**	**−6,390**	**−13,489**	**−22,736**	**−32,988**	**−40,941**	**−46,669**
Credit	2 100	**30,825**	**34,729**	**40,719**	**52,394**	**68,535**	**78,365**	**93,611**	**115,356**
General merchandise: exports f.o.b.	2 110	30,825	34,703	40,666	52,318	68,444	78,174	92,915	114,324
Goods for processing: exports f.o.b.	2 150	....	....	....	....	....	....	....	....
Repairs on goods	2 160	....	....	....	....	....	....	....	....
Goods procured in ports by carriers	2 170	....	....	....	....	....	59	59	60
Nonmonetary gold	2 180	....	26	53	76	91	132	637	972
Debit	3 100	**−52,882**	**−38,092**	**−47,109**	**−65,883**	**−91,271**	**−111,353**	**−134,552**	**−162,025**
General merchandise: imports f.o.b.	3 110	−50,982	−37,103	−45,701	−63,285	−87,773	−107,061	−130,086	−156,142
Goods for processing: imports f.o.b.	3 150	....	....	....	....	....	....	....	....
Repairs on goods	3 160	....	....	....	....	....	....	....	....
Goods procured in ports by carriers	3 170	....	....	....	....	....	−406	−484	−557
Nonmonetary gold	3 180	−1,900	−989	−1,408	−2,598	−3,498	−3,886	−3,982	−5,326
B. SERVICES	4 200	**11,375**	**9,136**	**7,885**	**10,511**	**12,797**	**15,272**	**13,831**	**13,879**
Total credit	2 200	*19,528*	*15,234*	*14,046*	*18,013*	*22,960*	*26,648*	*25,312*	*28,853*
Total debit	3 200	*−8,153*	*−6,098*	*−6,161*	*−7,502*	*−10,163*	*−11,376*	*−11,481*	*−14,974*
Transportation services, credit	2 205	**2,955**	**2,854**	**2,795**	**2,184**	**3,267**	**4,797**	**4,695**	**6,181**
Passenger	2 850	....	....	....	....	....	*1,568*	*1,667*	*2,162*
Freight	2 851	*1,653*	*1,796*	*1,859*	*1,322*	*1,765*	*2,048*	*1,823*	*2,424*
Other	2 852	*1,302*	*1,058*	*936*	*862*	*1,502*	*1,181*	*1,205*	*1,595*
Sea transport, passenger	2 207	....	....	....	....	....	....	....	....
Sea transport, freight	2 208	....	....	....	619	823	946	418	748
Sea transport, other	2 209	....	....	....	....	....	....	....	....
Air transport, passenger	2 211	....	....	....	....	....	1,568	1,667	2,162
Air transport, freight	2 212	....	....	....	113	152	175	246	284
Air transport, other	2 213	....	....	....	....	....	1,181	1,205	1,595
Other transport, passenger	2 215	....	....	....	....	....	....	....	....
Other transport, freight	2 216	1,653	1,796	1,859	590	790	927	1,159	1,392
Other transport, other	2 217	1,302	1,058	936	862	1,502	....	....	....
Transportation services, debit	3 205	**−2,463**	**−2,021**	**−1,934**	**−2,707**	**−4,331**	**−4,732**	**−4,309**	**−6,520**
Passenger	3 850	....	....	....	....	....	*−338*	*−412*	*−460*
Freight	3 851	*−1,407*	*−1,065*	*−1,328*	*−2,034*	*−2,907*	*−3,548*	*−3,141*	*−5,214*
Other	3 852	*−1,056*	*−956*	*−606*	*−673*	*−1,424*	*−846*	*−756*	*−846*
Sea transport, passenger	3 207	....	....	....	....	....	....	....	....
Sea transport, freight	3 208	....	....	....	−1,685	−2,420	−3,009	−2,571	−4,640
Sea transport, other	3 209	....	....	....	....	....	....	....	....
Air transport, passenger	3 211	....	....	....	....	....	−338	−412	−460
Air transport, freight	3 212	....	....	....	−181	−237	−251	−332	−302
Air transport, other	3 213	....	....	....	....	....	−846	−756	−846
Other transport, passenger	3 215	....	....	....	....	....	....	....	....
Other transport, freight	3 216	−1,407	−1,065	−1,328	−168	−250	−288	−238	−272
Other transport, other	3 217	−1,056	−956	−606	−673	−1,424	....	....	....
Travel, credit	2 236	**7,636**	**8,090**	**8,479**	**13,203**	**15,888**	**18,152**	**16,853**	**18,487**
Business travel	2 237	1,488	1,575	1,496	1,148	1,463	2,914	2,703	2,970
Personal travel	2 240	6,148	6,515	6,983	12,055	14,425	15,238	14,150	15,517
Travel, debit	3 236	**−1,713**	**−1,738**	**−1,880**	**−2,113**	**−2,524**	**−2,872**	**−2,743**	**−3,260**
Business travel	3 237	−393	−685	−700	−693	−846	−1,063	−1,017	−1,207
Personal travel	3 240	−1,320	−1,053	−1,180	−1,420	−1,678	−1,809	−1,726	−2,053
Other services, credit	2 200 BA	**8,937**	**4,290**	**2,772**	**2,626**	**3,805**	**3,699**	**3,764**	**4,185**
Communications	2 245	....	....	....	224	346	412	416	506
Construction	2 249	1,033	685	847	743	743	882	936	856
Insurance	2 253	32	25	28	211	274	323	522	645
Financial	2 260	368	331	221	291	288	345	277	395
Computer and information	2 262	....	....	....	....	....	....	12	15
Royalties and licence fees	2 266	....	....	....	....	....	....	....	....
Other business services	2 268	4,652	2,025	254	272	482	338	289	197
Personal, cultural, and recreational	2 287	2,591	1,074	1,355	781	1,418	1,079	998	971
Government, n.i.e.	2 291	261	150	67	104	254	320	314	600
Other services, debit	3 200 BA	**−3,977**	**−2,339**	**−2,347**	**−2,682**	**−3,308**	**−3,772**	**−4,429**	**−5,194**
Communications	3 245	−84	−102	−72	−231	−207	−228	−299	−305
Construction	3 249	−65	−31	−15	−61	−19	−8	−57	−97
Insurance	3 253	−342	−282	−372	−622	−839	−891	−1,140	−1,542
Financial	3 260	−671	−722	−621	−374	−377	−386	−524	−623
Computer and information	3 262	....	....	....	....	....	....	−15	−26
Royalties and licence fees	3 266	−173	−119	−107	−167	−362	−439	−531	−647
Other business services	3 268	−572	−330	−322	−298	−353	−538	−723	−1,029
Personal, cultural, and recreational	3 287	−1,541	−288	−205	−117	−176	−88	−106	−111
Government, n.i.e.	3 291	−529	−465	−633	−812	−975	−1,194	−1,034	−814

Table 2 (Continued). STANDARD PRESENTATION, 2000–2007

(Millions of U.S. dollars)

	Code	2000	2001	2002	2003	2004	2005	2006	2007
C. INCOME................	4 300 ..	**−4,002**	**−5,000**	**−4,554**	**−5,557**	**−5,609**	**−5,875**	**−6,691**	**−7,143**
Total credit..........	2 300 ..	*2,836*	*2,753*	*2,486*	*2,246*	*2,651*	*3,608*	*4,383*	*6,384*
Total debit...........	3 300 ..	*−6,838*	*−7,753*	*−7,040*	*−7,803*	*−8,260*	*−9,483*	*−11,074*	*−13,527*
Compensation of employees, credit..........	2 310 ..	....	....	....	....	....	....	....	....
Compensation of employees, debit..........	3 310 ..	....	....	....	....	....	−96	−107	−106
Investment income, credit................	2 320 ..	**2,836**	**2,753**	**2,486**	**2,246**	**2,651**	**3,608**	**4,383**	**6,384**
Direct investment income..........	2 330 ..	368	361	293	203	244	201	129	108
Dividends and distributed branch profits..........	2 332 ..	343	324	262	193	237	200	111	33
Reinvested earnings and undistributed branch profits.....	2 333 ..	25	37	31	10	7	1	18	75
Income on debt (interest)..........	2 334 ..	....	....	....	....	....	....	....	....
Portfolio investment income..........	2 339 ..	1,300	1,253	1,409	1,409	1,710	2,402	2,801	4,118
Income on equity..........	2 340 ..	....	....	....	....	....	....	....	....
Income on bonds and notes..........	2 350 ..	1,300	1,253	1,409	1,409	1,710	2,402	2,801	4,118
Income on money market instruments..........	2 360 ..	....	....	....	....	....	....	....	....
Other investment income..........	2 370 ..	1,168	1,139	784	634	697	1,005	1,453	2,158
Investment income, debit................	3 320 ..	**−6,838**	**−7,753**	**−7,040**	**−7,803**	**−8,260**	**−9,387**	**−10,967**	**−13,421**
Direct investment income..........	3 330 ..	−279	−309	−401	−643	−1,043	−1,051	−1,168	−2,193
Dividends and distributed branch profits..........	3 332 ..	−277	−303	−379	−469	−802	−890	−1,017	−1,804
Reinvested earnings and undistributed branch profits.....	3 333 ..	−2	−6	....	−132	−204	−84	−108	−300
Income on debt (interest)..........	3 334 ..	....	....	−22	−42	−37	−77	−43	−89
Portfolio investment income..........	3 339 ..	−1,734	−1,947	−2,244	−2,616	−2,905	−3,326	−3,463	−3,735
Income on equity..........	3 340 ..	−58	−124	−25	−14	....	−2	....	−1
Income on bonds and notes..........	3 350 ..	−1,676	−1,823	−2,219	−2,602	−2,905	−3,324	−3,463	−3,734
Income on money market instruments..........	3 360 ..	....	....	....	....	....	....	....	....
Other investment income..........	3 370 ..	−4,825	−5,497	−4,395	−4,544	−4,312	−5,010	−6,336	−7,493
D. CURRENT TRANSFERS................	4 379 ..	**4,764**	**2,987**	**2,433**	**1,020**	**1,117**	**1,454**	**1,908**	**2,236**
Credit..........	2 379 ..	**4,856**	**3,045**	**2,477**	**1,081**	**1,155**	**1,475**	**2,244**	**2,778**
General government..........	2 380 ..	296	259	541	352	351	624	653	848
Other sectors..........	2 390 ..	4,560	2,786	1,936	729	804	851	1,591	1,930
Workers' remittances..........	2 391 ..	4,560	2,786	1,936	729	804	851	1,111	1,209
Other current transfers..........	2 392 ..	....	....	....	....	....	....	480	721
Debit..........	3 379 ..	**−92**	**−58**	**−44**	**−61**	**−38**	**−21**	**−336**	**−542**
General government..........	3 380 ..	−92	−58	−44	−61	−38	−21	−77	−39
Other sectors..........	3 390 ..	....	....	....	....	....	....	−259	−503
Workers' remittances..........	3 391 ..	....	....	....	....	....	....	....	....
Other current transfers..........	3 392 ..	....	....	....	....	....	....	−259	−503
CAPITAL AND FINANCIAL ACCOUNT..........	4 996 ..	**12,518**	**−1,670**	**1,404**	**3,105**	**13,470**	**20,326**	**32,070**	**36,515**
CAPITAL ACCOUNT..........	4 994 ..	....	....	....	....	....	....	....	....
Total credit..........	2 994 ..	....	....	....	....	....	....	....	....
Total debit..........	3 994 ..	....	....	....	....	....	....	....	....
Capital transfers, credit..........	2 400 ..	....	....	....	....	....	....	....	....
General government..........	2 401 ..	....	....	....	....	....	....	....	....
Debt forgiveness..........	2 402 ..	....	....	....	....	....	....	....	....
Other capital transfers..........	2 410 ..	....	....	....	....	....	....	....	....
Other sectors..........	2 430 ..	....	....	....	....	....	....	....	....
Migrants' transfers..........	2 431 ..	....	....	....	....	....	....	....	....
Debt forgiveness..........	2 432 ..	....	....	....	....	....	....	....	....
Other capital transfers..........	2 440 ..	....	....	....	....	....	....	....	....
Capital transfers, debit..........	3 400 ..	....	....	....	....	....	....	....	....
General government..........	3 401 ..	....	....	....	....	....	....	....	....
Debt forgiveness..........	3 402 ..	....	....	....	....	....	....	....	....
Other capital transfers..........	3 410 ..	....	....	....	....	....	....	....	....
Other sectors..........	3 430 ..	....	....	....	....	....	....	....	....
Migrants' transfers..........	3 431 ..	....	....	....	....	....	....	....	....
Debt forgiveness..........	3 432 ..	....	....	....	....	....	....	....	....
Other capital transfers..........	3 440 ..	....	....	....	....	....	....	....	....
Nonproduced nonfinancial assets, credit..........	2 480 ..	....	....	....	....	....	....	....	....
Nonproduced nonfinancial assets, debit..........	3 480 ..	....	....	....	....	....	....	....	....

Table 2 (Continued). STANDARD PRESENTATION, 2000–2007

(Millions of U.S. dollars)

	Code	2000	2001	2002	2003	2004	2005	2006	2007
FINANCIAL ACCOUNT	4 995	12,518	−1,670	1,404	3,105	13,470	20,326	32,070	36,515
A. DIRECT INVESTMENT	4 500	112	2,854	957	1,252	2,005	8,967	19,065	20,089
Direct investment abroad	4 505	−870	−498	−176	−499	−780	−1,064	−924	−2,106
Equity capital	4 510	−845	−461	−145	−489	−773	−1,063	−906	−2,031
Claims on affiliated enterprises	4 515	−845	−461	−145	−489	−773	−1,063	−906	−2,031
Liabilities to affiliated enterprises	4 520	....	....	....	....	....	....	....	....
Reinvested earnings	4 525	−25	−37	−31	−10	−7	−1	−18	−75
Other capital	4 530	....	....	....	....	....	....	....	....
Claims on affiliated enterprises	4 535	....	....	....	....	....	....	....	....
Liabilities to affiliated enterprises	4 540	....	....	....	....	....	....	....	....
Direct investment in Turkey	4 555	982	3,352	1,133	1,751	2,785	10,031	19,989	22,195
Equity capital	4 560	980	3,346	617	1,603	2,231	9,891	19,796	21,344
Claims on direct investors	4 565	....	....	....	....	....	....	....	....
Liabilities to direct investors	4 570	980	3,346	617	1,603	2,231	9,891	19,796	21,344
Reinvested earnings	4 575	2	6	....	132	204	84	108	300
Other capital	4 580	....	....	516	16	350	56	85	551
Claims on direct investors	4 585	....	....	....	....	....	....	....	....
Liabilities to direct investors	4 590	....	....	516	16	350	56	85	551
B. PORTFOLIO INVESTMENT	4 600	1,022	−4,515	−593	2,465	8,023	13,437	7,373	717
Assets	4 602	−593	−788	−2,096	−1,386	−1,388	−1,233	−4,029	−2,063
Equity securities	4 610	−33	−36	−42	−33	−25	−20	−42	−116
Monetary authorities	4 611	....	....	....	....	....	....	....	....
General government	4 612	−33	−36	−42	−33	−25	−20	−42	−116
Banks	4 613	....	....	....	....	....	....	....	....
Other sectors	4 614	....	....	....	....	....	....	....	....
Debt securities	4 619	−560	−752	−2,054	−1,353	−1,363	−1,213	−3,987	−1,947
Bonds and notes	4 620	−560	−752	−2,054	−1,353	−1,363	−1,213	−3,987	−1,947
Monetary authorities	4 621	....	....	....	....	....	....	....	....
General government	4 622	....	....	....	....	....	....	....	....
Banks	4 623	−680	−281	−1,437	−932	−666	−1,285	−3,754	−1,844
Other sectors	4 624	120	−471	−617	−421	−697	72	−233	−103
Money market instruments	4 630	....	....	....	....	....	....	....	....
Monetary authorities	4 631	....	....	....	....	....	....	....	....
General government	4 632	....	....	....	....	....	....	....	....
Banks	4 633	....	....	....	....	....	....	....	....
Other sectors	4 634	....	....	....	....	....	....	....	....
Liabilities	4 652	1,615	−3,727	1,503	3,851	9,411	14,670	11,402	2,780
Equity securities	4 660	489	−79	−16	905	1,427	5,669	1,939	5,138
Banks	4 663	....	....	....	....	....	....	....	....
Other sectors	4 664	489	−79	−16	905	1,427	5,669	1,939	5,138
Debt securities	4 669	1,126	−3,648	1,519	2,946	7,984	9,001	9,463	−2,358
Bonds and notes	4 670	1,126	−3,648	1,519	2,946	7,984	9,001	9,463	−2,358
Monetary authorities	4 671	....	....	....	....	....	....	....	....
General government	4 672	984	−3,645	1,958	3,123	7,984	9,351	9,463	−2,358
Banks	4 673	142	−3	−439	−177	....	−350	....	....
Other sectors	4 674	....	....	....	....	....	....	....	....
Money market instruments	4 680	....	....	....	....	....	....	....	....
Monetary authorities	4 681	....	....	....	....	....	....	....	....
General government	4 682	....	....	....	....	....	....	....	....
Banks	4 683	....	....	....	....	....	....	....	....
Other sectors	4 684	....	....	....	....	....	....	....	....
C. FINANCIAL DERIVATIVES	4 910	....	....	....	....	....	....	....	....
Monetary authorities	4 911	....	....	....	....	....	....	....	....
General government	4 912	....	....	....	....	....	....	....	....
Banks	4 913	....	....	....	....	....	....	....	....
Other sectors	4 914	....	....	....	....	....	....	....	....
Assets	4 900	....	....	....	....	....	....	....	....
Monetary authorities	4 901	....	....	....	....	....	....	....	....
General government	4 902	....	....	....	....	....	....	....	....
Banks	4 903	....	....	....	....	....	....	....	....
Other sectors	4 904	....	....	....	....	....	....	....	....
Liabilities	4 905	....	....	....	....	....	....	....	....
Monetary authorities	4 906	....	....	....	....	....	....	....	....
General government	4 907	....	....	....	....	....	....	....	....
Banks	4 908	....	....	....	....	....	....	....	....
Other sectors	4 909	....	....	....	....	....	....	....	....

Table 2 (Concluded). STANDARD PRESENTATION, 2000–2007

(Millions of U.S. dollars)

	Code	2000	2001	2002	2003	2004	2005	2006	2007
D. OTHER INVESTMENT	4 700	**11,766**	**−2,728**	**7,216**	**3,418**	**4,229**	**15,776**	**11,734**	**23,774**
Assets	4 703	**−1,939**	**−601**	**−777**	**−986**	**−6,955**	**259**	**−13,437**	**−4,852**
Trade credits	4 706	−26	−445	−921	−910	−1,607	424	−2,419	−1,468
General government	4 707	....	....	....	....	....	....	....	....
of which: Short-term	4 709	....	....	....	....	....	....	....	....
Other sectors	4 710	−26	−445	−921	−910	−1,607	424	−2,419	−1,468
of which: Short-term	4 712	−26	−445	−921	−910	−1,607	424	−2,419	−1,468
Loans	4 714	116	−734	19	−404	617	177	−725	139
Monetary authorities	4 715	....	−40	−30	−28	−24	−16	....	2
of which: Short-term	4 718								
General government	4 719	....	....	....	....	....	....	....	....
of which: Short-term	4 721	....	....	....	....	....	....	....	....
Banks	4 722	116	−694	49	−376	641	193	−725	137
of which: Short-term	4 724	212	−632	−41	67	−82	−168	−497	−306
Other sectors	4 725	....	....	....	....	....	....	....	....
of which: Short-term	4 727	....	....	....	....	....	....	....	....
Currency and deposits	4 730	−1,690	927	594	724	−5,965	−342	−10,293	−3,523
Monetary authorities	4 731	....	....	....	....	....	....	....	....
General government	4 732	....	....	....	....	....	....	....	....
Banks	4 733	−1,690	927	594	724	−5,965	−342	−10,293	−3,523
Other sectors	4 734	....	....	....	....	....	....	....	....
Other assets	4 736	−339	−349	−469	−396	....	....	....	....
Monetary authorities	4 737	1	1	....	....	....	....	....	....
of which: Short-term	4 739	1	1	....	....	....	....	....	....
General government	4 740	....	....	....	....	....	....	....	....
of which: Short-term	4 742	....	....	....	....	....	....	....	....
Banks	4 743	....	....	....	....	....	....	....	....
of which: Short-term	4 745	....	....	....	....	....	....	....	....
Other sectors	4 746	−340	−350	−469	−396	....	....	....	....
of which: Short-term	4 748	−340	−350	−469	−396	....	....	....	....
Liabilities	4 753	**13,705**	**−2,127**	**7,993**	**4,404**	**11,184**	**15,517**	**25,171**	**28,626**
Trade credits	4 756	805	−1,930	2,483	2,181	4,201	3,074	674	4,230
General government	4 757	....	....	....	....	....	....	....	....
of which: Short-term	4 759	....	....	....	....	....	....	....	....
Other sectors	4 760	805	−1,930	2,483	2,181	4,201	3,074	674	4,230
of which: Short-term	4 762	797	−1,941	1,130	1,215	3,715	3,014	618	4,112
Loans	4 764	12,833	553	5,065	747	6,178	11,641	19,593	27,367
Monetary authorities	4 765	3,313	10,168	6,390	−57	−3,520	−5,322	−4,519	−3,987
of which: Use of Fund credit and loans from the Fund	4 766	3,316	10,169	6,390	−57	−3,520	−5,322	−4,519	−3,987
of which: Short-term	4 768	....	....	....	....	....	....	....	....
General government	4 769	117	−1,977	−669	−2,194	−1,163	−2,165	−712	82
of which: Short-term	4 771	1,000	−1,000	....	....	....	....	....	....
Banks	4 772	4,378	−8,076	−1,028	1,975	5,708	9,248	5,814	5,608
of which: Short-term	4 774	4,741	−7,052	−731	2,015	3,347	2,704	−3,952	−1,663
Other sectors	4 775	5,025	438	372	1,023	5,153	9,880	19,010	25,664
of which: Short-term	4 777	128	183	−728	288	388	367	495	244
Currency and deposits	4 780	−20	−832	348	1,368	647	489	4,622	−3,323
Monetary authorities	4 781	622	736	1,336	497	−209	−787	−1,268	−1,450
General government	4 782	....	....	....	....	....	....	....	....
Banks	4 783	−642	−1,568	−988	871	856	1,276	5,890	−1,873
Other sectors	4 784	....	....	....	....	....	....	....	....
Other liabilities	4 786	87	82	97	108	158	313	282	352
Monetary authorities	4 787	87	82	97	108	158	313	282	354
of which: Short-term	4 789	87	82	97	108	158	313	282	354
General government	4 790	....	....	....	....	....	....	....	....
of which: Short-term	4 792	....	....	....	....	....	....	....	....
Banks	4 793	....	....	....	....	....	....	....	....
of which: Short-term	4 795	....	....	....	....	....	....	....	....
Other sectors	4 796	....	....	....	....	....	....	....	−2
of which: Short-term	4 798	....	....	....	....	....	....	....	....
E. RESERVE ASSETS	4 802	**−383**	**2,718**	**−6,177**	**−4,030**	**−787**	**−17,854**	**−6,102**	**−8,065**
Monetary gold	4 812	....	....	....	....	....	....	....	....
Special drawing rights	4 811	−29	24	−24	9	21	−7	12	−33
Reserve position in the Fund	4 810	....	....	....	....	....	....	....	....
Foreign exchange	4 803	−354	2,694	−6,153	−4,039	−808	−17,847	−6,114	−8,032
Other claims	4 813	....	....	....	....	....	....	....	....
NET ERRORS AND OMISSIONS	4 998	**−2,598**	**−2,090**	**−778**	**4,410**	**961**	**1,811**	**−177**	**1,182**

2008, International Monetary Fund: *Balance of Payments Statistics Yearbook*

Table 3. INTERNATIONAL INVESTMENT POSITION (End-period stocks), 2000–2007

(Millions of U.S. dollars)

	Code	2000	2001	2002	2003	2004	2005	2006	2007
ASSETS	8 995 C.	**53,192**	**52,778**	**62,772**	**74,492**	**87,001**	**106,161**	**143,208**	**169,096**
Direct investment abroad	8 505 ..	**3,668**	**4,581**	**5,847**	**6,138**	**7,060**	**8,315**	**8,866**	**12,210**
Equity capital and reinvested earnings	8 506 ..	3,668	4,581	5,847	6,138	7,060	8,315	8,866	12,210
Claims on affiliated enterprises	8 507 ..	3,668	4,581	5,847	6,138	7,060	8,315	8,866	12,210
Liabilities to affiliated enterprises	8 508 ..	....	....	....	....	....	....	....	....
Other capital	8 530 ..	....	....	....	....	....	....	....	....
Claims on affiliated enterprises	8 535 ..	....	....	....	....	....	....	....	....
Liabilities to affiliated enterprises	8 540 ..	....	....	....	....	....	....	....	....
Portfolio investment	8 602 ..	**4**	**550**	**809**	**1,963**	**936**	**732**	**3,126**	**2,023**
Equity securities	8 610 ..	4	53	45	68	124	103	165	93
Monetary authorities	8 611 ..	4	4	5	15	16	14	15	16
General government	8 612 ..	....	....	....	....	....	....	....	....
Banks	8 613 ..	....	....	....	7	59	50	80	47
Other sectors	8 614 ..	....	49	40	46	49	39	70	30
Debt securities	8 619 ..	....	497	764	1,895	812	629	2,961	1,930
Bonds and notes	8 620 ..	....	464	730	1,882	800	611	2,898	1,893
Monetary authorities	8 621 ..	....	....	....	....	....	....	....	....
General government	8 622 ..	....	....	....	....	....	....	....	....
Banks	8 623 ..	....	373	627	1,739	662	276	2,481	1,384
Other sectors	8 624 ..	....	91	103	143	138	335	417	509
Money market instruments	8 630 ..	....	33	34	13	12	18	63	37
Monetary authorities	8 631 ..	....	....	....	....	....	....	....	....
General government	8 632 ..	....	....	....	....	....	....	....	....
Banks	8 633 ..	....	2	4	....	....	....	....	19
Other sectors	8 634 ..	....	31	30	13	12	18	63	18
Financial derivatives	8 900 ..	....	....	....	....	....	....	....	....
Monetary authorities	8 901 ..	....	....	....	....	....	....	....	....
General government	8 902 ..	....	....	....	....	....	....	....	....
Banks	8 903 ..	....	....	....	....	....	....	....	....
Other sectors	8 904 ..	....	....	....	....	....	....	....	....
Other investment	8 703 ..	**26,196**	**27,687**	**28,030**	**31,217**	**41,362**	**44,685**	**67,931**	**78,424**
Trade credits	8 706 ..	2,697	3,089	3,972	5,158	7,005	6,721	9,584	12,009
General government	8 707 ..								
of which: Short-term	8 709 ..	....	....	....	....	....	....	....	....
Other sectors	8 710 ..	2,697	3,089	3,972	5,158	7,005	6,721	9,584	12,009
of which: Short-term	8 712 ..	*2,697*	*3,089*	*3,972*	*5,158*	*7,005*	*6,721*	*9,584*	*12,009*
Loans	8 714 ..	2,063	2,950	2,370	2,816	2,189	1,348	1,946	1,843
Monetary authorities	8 715 ..	208	183	154	119	84	34	31	28
of which: Short-term	8 718 ..	....	....	....	....	....	....	....	....
General government	8 719 ..	....	....	....	....	....	....	....	....
of which: Short-term	8 721 ..	....	....	....	....	....	....	....	....
Banks	8 722 ..	1,855	2,767	2,216	2,697	2,105	1,314	1,915	1,815
of which: Short-term	8 724 ..	*331*	*1,200*	*760*	*493*	*567*	*349*	*733*	*1,088*
Other sectors	8 725 ..	....	....	....	....	....	....	....	....
of which: Short-term	8 727 ..	....	....	....	....	....	....	....	....
Currency and deposits	8 730 ..	19,654	19,829	19,788	21,209	30,143	34,610	54,275	62,319
Monetary authorities	8 731 ..	....	....	....	....	....	....	....	....
General government	8 732 ..	....	....	....	....	....	....	....	....
Banks	8 733 ..	11,007	10,392	9,980	9,795	16,143	16,314	27,536	31,812
Other sectors	8 734 ..	8,647	9,437	9,808	11,414	14,000	18,296	26,739	30,507
Other assets	8 736 ..	1,782	1,819	1,900	2,034	2,025	2,006	2,125	2,253
Monetary authorities	8 737 ..	1,184	1,235	1,257	1,272	1,288	1,326	1,395	1,468
of which: Short-term	8 739 ..	....	....	....	....	....	....	....	....
General government	8 740 ..	598	584	643	762	737	680	730	785
of which: Short-term	8 742 ..	....	....	....	....	....	....	....	....
Banks	8 743 ..	....	....	....	....	....	....	....	....
of which: Short-term	8 745 ..	....	....	....	....	....	....	....	....
Other sectors	8 746 ..	....	....	....	....	....	....	....	....
of which: Short-term	8 748 ..	....	....	....	....	....	....	....	....
Reserve assets	8 802 ..	**23,324**	**19,960**	**28,086**	**35,174**	**37,643**	**52,429**	**63,286**	**76,439**
Monetary gold	8 812 ..	1,006	1,032	1,279	1,558	1,635	1,915	2,373	3,123
Special drawing rights	8 811 ..	29	4	31	30	14	16	12	50
Reserve position in the Fund	8 810 ..	147	142	153	168	175	161	170	178
Foreign exchange	8 803 ..	22,143	18,782	26,622	33,418	35,819	50,337	60,731	73,088
Other claims	8 813 ..	....	....	....	....	....	....	....	....

Table 3 (Concluded). INTERNATIONAL INVESTMENT POSITION (End-period stocks), 2000–2007

(Millions of U.S. dollars)

	Code	2000	2001	2002	2003	2004	2005	2006	2007
LIABILITIES	8 995 D.	**151,844**	**136,948**	**147,780**	**179,630**	**213,492**	**279,436**	**346,176**	**482,564**
Direct investment in Turkey	8 555	**19,209**	**19,677**	**18,795**	**33,537**	**38,523**	**71,297**	**94,561**	**156,078**
Equity capital and reinvested earnings	8 556	19,209	18,047	16,259	30,936	37,169	69,927	92,872	153,491
Claims on direct investors	8 557	....	....	....	....	....	....	....	....
Liabilities to direct investors	8 558	19,209	18,047	16,259	30,936	37,169	69,927	92,872	153,491
Other capital	8 580	....	1,630	2,536	2,601	1,354	1,370	1,689	2,587
Claims on direct investors	8 585	....	....	....	....	....	....	....	....
Liabilities to direct investors	8 590	....	1,630	2,536	2,601	1,354	1,370	1,689	2,587
Portfolio investment	8 652	**35,862**	**24,710**	**23,883**	**30,024**	**45,751**	**72,606**	**84,410**	**120,629**
Equity securities	8 660	7,404	5,635	3,450	8,954	16,141	33,387	33,816	64,201
Banks	8 663	....	....	....	....	....	....	....	....
Other sectors	8 664	7,404	5,635	3,450	8,954	16,141	33,387	33,816	64,201
Debt securities	8 669	28,458	19,075	20,433	21,070	29,610	39,219	50,594	56,428
Bonds and notes	8 670	28,458	19,075	20,433	21,070	29,610	39,219	50,594	56,428
Monetary authorities	8 671	....	....	....	....	....	....	....	....
General government	8 672	27,509	18,149	19,912	20,720	29,260	39,219	50,594	56,428
Banks	8 673	949	926	521	350	350	....	....	....
Other sectors	8 674	....	....	....	....	....	....	....	....
Money market instruments	8 680	....	....	....	....	....	....	....	....
Monetary authorities	8 681	....	....	....	....	....	....	....	....
General government	8 682	....	....	....	....	....	....	....	....
Banks	8 683	....	....	....	....	....	....	....	....
Other sectors	8 684	....	....	....	....	....	....	....	....
Financial derivatives	8 905	....	....	....	....	....	....	....	....
Monetary authorities	8 906	....	....	....	....	....	....	....	....
General government	8 907	....	....	....	....	....	....	....	....
Banks	8 908	....	....	....	....	....	....	....	....
Other sectors	8 909	....	....	....	....	....	....	....	....
Other investment	8 753	**96,773**	**92,561**	**105,102**	**116,069**	**129,218**	**135,533**	**167,205**	**205,857**
Trade credits	8 756	7,863	5,677	7,356	9,123	12,908	15,365	16,794	21,584
General government	8 757	....	....	....	....	....	....	....	....
of which: Short-term	8 759	....	....	....	....	....	....	....	....
Other sectors	8 760	7,863	5,677	7,356	9,123	12,908	15,365	16,794	21,584
of which: Short-term	8 762	*7,863*	*5,677*	*7,144*	*8,866*	*12,593*	*15,011*	*16,383*	*21,084*
Loans	8 764	72,799	72,212	80,685	85,493	92,092	98,261	122,424	157,675
Monetary authorities	8 765	4,210	14,145	22,109	24,112	21,517	14,655	10,772	7,168
of which: Use of Fund credit and loans from the Fund	8 766	*4,176*	*14,117*	*22,086*	*24,092*	*21,507*	*14,646*	*10,762*	*7,158*
of which: Short-term	8 768	*26*	*20*	*15*	*11*	*1*	*1*	*1*	*1*
General government	8 769	21,836	20,382	21,763	21,579	21,873	19,716	20,741	22,845
of which: Short-term	8 771	*1,000*	....	....	....	....	....	....	....
Banks	8 772	16,452	7,785	6,681	8,870	14,782	23,719	29,886	37,108
of which: Short-term	8 774	*11,140*	*4,005*	*3,195*	*5,320*	*8,716*	*11,250*	*7,511*	*6,013*
Other sectors	8 775	30,301	29,900	30,132	30,932	33,920	40,171	61,025	90,554
of which: Short-term	8 777	*1,885*	*1,977*	*1,281*	*1,595*	*1,471*	*1,588*	*1,578*	*1,626*
Currency and deposits	8 780	16,111	14,672	17,061	21,453	24,218	21,907	27,987	26,598
Monetary authorities	8 781	10,351	10,680	13,912	17,081	18,405	15,416	15,668	15,791
General government	8 782	....	....	....	....	....	....	....	....
Banks	8 783	5,760	3,992	3,149	4,372	5,813	6,491	12,319	10,807
Other sectors	8 784	....	....	....	....	....	....	....	....
Other liabilities	8 786	....	....	....	....	....	....	....	....
Monetary authorities	8 787	....	....	....	....	....	....	....	....
of which: Short-term	8 789	....	....	....	....	....	....	....	....
General government	8 790	....	....	....	....	....	....	....	....
of which: Short-term	8 792	....	....	....	....	....	....	....	....
Banks	8 793	....	....	....	....	....	....	....	....
of which: Short-term	8 795	....	....	....	....	....	....	....	....
Other sectors	8 796	....	....	....	....	....	....	....	....
of which: Short-term	8 798	....	....	....	....	....	....	....	....
NET INTERNATIONAL INVESTMENT POSITION	8 995	**−98,652**	**−84,170**	**−85,008**	**−105,138**	**−126,491**	**−173,275**	**−202,968**	**−313,467**
Conversion rates: new liras per U.S. dollar (end of period)	0 102	.6734	1.4501	1.6437	1.3966	1.3395	1.3451	1.4090	1.1621

Table 1. ANALYTIC PRESENTATION, 2000–2007

(Millions of U.S. dollars)

	Code	2000	2001	2002	2003	2004	2005	2006	2007
A. Current Account[1]	4 993 Z.	−825.4	−369.5	−362.0	−353.7	−316.5	−413.9	−323.1	−744.7
Goods: exports f.o.b.	2 100 ..	449.9	475.6	480.7	563.0	759.1	1,017.0	1,187.6	1,686.2
Goods: imports f.o.b.	3 100 ..	−949.7	−975.4	−1,052.0	−1,245.6	−1,426.8	−1,745.6	−2,215.6	−2,982.5
Balance on Goods	4 100 ..	*−499.8*	*−499.9*	*−571.3*	*−682.6*	*−667.6*	*−728.6*	*−1,027.9*	*−1,296.4*
Services: credit	2 200 ..	213.2	216.9	224.7	265.7	369.5	507.4	452.3	499.3
Services: debit	3 200 ..	−458.8	−505.6	−557.9	−502.4	−626.8	−777.1	−949.9	−1,178.0
Balance on Goods and Services	4 991 ..	*−745.4*	*−788.6*	*−904.5*	*−919.3*	*−924.9*	*−998.2*	*−1,525.6*	*−1,975.1*
Income: credit	2 300 ..	53.1	37.5	24.2	27.6	35.7	49.8	71.9	98.4
Income: debit	3 300 ..	−165.5	−202.7	−148.0	−170.8	−328.8	−298.9	−298.0	−377.2
Balance on Goods, Services, and Income	4 992 ..	*−857.8*	*−953.8*	*−1,028.3*	*−1,062.5*	*−1,218.0*	*−1,247.2*	*−1,751.7*	*−2,253.9*
Current transfers: credit	2 379 Z.	340.0	888.5	1,023.4	923.2	1,143.5	1,184.3	1,762.8	1,816.2
Current transfers: debit	3 379 ..	−307.6	−304.2	−357.1	−214.4	−241.9	−350.9	−334.2	−307.0
B. Capital Account[1]	4 994 Z.	....	....	....	....	....	....	3,428.1	....
Capital account: credit	2 994 Z.	....	....	....	....	....	....	3,428.1	....
Capital account: debit	3 994 ..	....	....	....	....	....	....	....	....
Total, Groups A Plus B	4 981 ..	*−825.4*	*−369.5*	*−362.0*	*−353.7*	*−316.5*	*−413.9*	*3,105.0*	*−744.7*
C. Financial Account[1]	4 995 W.	320.5	441.2	177.5	358.6	442.9	493.7	628.0	1,328.5
Direct investment abroad	4 505 ..	....	....	....	....	....	....	....	....
Direct investment in Uganda	4 555 Z.	160.7	151.5	184.6	202.2	295.4	379.8	393.2	484.0
Portfolio investment assets	4 602 ..	....	....	1.5	−4.3	....	....	....	....
Equity securities	4 610 ..	....	....	1.5	−4.3	....	....	....	....
Debt securities	4 619 ..	....	....	....	....	....	....	....	....
Portfolio investment liabilities	4 652 Z.	....	....	.4	20.3	6.2	−13.4	21.7	14.3
Equity securities	4 660 ..	....	....	.4	....	24.0	....	19.1	−47.8
Debt securities	4 669 Z.	....	....	....	20.3	−17.8	−13.4	2.5	62.2
Financial derivatives	4 910 ..	....	....	....	....	....	....	....	....
Financial derivatives assets	4 900 ..	....	....	....	....	....	....	....	....
Financial derivatives liabilities	4 905 ..	....	....	....	....	....	....	....	....
Other investment assets	4 703 ..	−.9	29.4	−59.1	−124.9	.1	−7.1	76.1	282.2
Monetary authorities	4 701 ..	....	....	....	22.9	11.8	....	....	15.4
General government	4 704 ..	....	....	5.3	−12.0	−12.3	1.9	16.3	83.1
Banks	4 705 ..	−65.8	17.0	8.5	−109.7	−3.8	43.1	−106.4	−58.8
Other sectors	4 728 ..	64.9	12.4	−73.0	−26.1	4.4	−52.2	166.2	242.6
Other investment liabilities	4 753 W.	160.7	260.4	50.1	265.3	141.2	134.4	137.1	547.9
Monetary authorities	4 753 WA	....	....	....	....	....	....	....	....
General government	4 753 ZB	154.9	284.0	55.7	268.5	126.0	96.1	61.1	308.5
Banks	4 753 ZC	....	−6.7	9.0	2.2	−4.6	7.0	37.7	84.8
Other sectors	4 753 ZD	5.8	−16.9	−14.6	−5.4	19.8	31.3	38.3	154.6
Total, Groups A Through C	4 983 ..	*−504.9*	*71.7*	*−184.4*	*4.8*	*126.5*	*79.8*	*3,733.0*	*583.8*
D. Net Errors and Omissions	4 998 ..	40.6	19.3	9.3	−7.7	−3.9	1.9	41.5	62.1
Total, Groups A Through D	4 984 ..	*−464.3*	*91.0*	*−175.1*	*−2.8*	*122.5*	*81.7*	*3,774.5*	*645.9*
E. Reserves and Related Items	4 802 A.	464.3	−91.0	175.1	2.8	−122.5	−81.7	−3,774.5	−645.9
Reserve assets	4 802 ..	−45.1	−160.0	100.4	−77.1	−162.0	−92.5	−403.0	−700.7
Use of Fund credit and loans	4 766 ..	−37.4	−29.6	−39.4	−42.6	−52.7	−46.2	−124.0	....
Exceptional financing	4 920 ..	546.8	98.7	114.2	122.5	92.2	56.9	−3,247.5	54.8
Conversion rates: Uganda shillings per U.S. dollar	0 101 ..	1,644.5	1,755.7	1,797.6	1,963.7	1,810.3	1,780.7	1,831.5	1,723.5

[1] Excludes components that have been classified in the categories of Group E.

Table 2. STANDARD PRESENTATION, 2000–2007

(Millions of U.S. dollars)

	Code	2000	2001	2002	2003	2004	2005	2006	2007
CURRENT ACCOUNT	4 993	−358.8	−369.5	−362.0	−353.7	−316.5	−413.9	−323.1	−744.7
A. GOODS	4 100	−499.8	−499.9	−571.3	−682.6	−667.6	−728.6	−1,027.9	−1,296.4
Credit	2 100	449.9	475.6	480.7	563.0	759.1	1,017.0	1,187.6	1,686.2
General merchandise: exports f.o.b.	2 110	384.8	414.2	415.3	486.8	657.2	912.5	1,028.5	1,583.4
Goods for processing: exports f.o.b.	2 150	. . . .	. . . .	. . . .	. . . .	. . . .	. . . .	. . . .	. . . .
Repairs on goods	2 160	. . . .	. . . .	. . . .	. . . .	. . . .	. . . .	. . . .	. . . .
Goods procured in ports by carriers	2 170	9.4	11.0	5.5	30.4	28.1	31.5	36.2	37.0
Nonmonetary gold	2 180	55.7	50.4	59.9	45.8	73.8	73.0	122.9	65.8
Debit	3 100	−949.7	−975.4	−1,052.0	−1,245.6	−1,426.8	−1,745.6	−2,215.6	−2,982.5
General merchandise: imports f.o.b.	3 110	−949.7	−975.4	−1,052.0	−1,245.6	−1,426.8	−1,745.6	−2,215.6	−2,982.5
Goods for processing: imports f.o.b.	3 150	. . . .	. . . .	. . . .	. . . .	. . . .	. . . .	. . . .	. . . .
Repairs on goods	3 160	. . . .	. . . .	. . . .	. . . .	. . . .	. . . .	. . . .	. . . .
Goods procured in ports by carriers	3 170	. . . .	. . . .	. . . .	. . . .	. . . .	. . . .	. . . .	. . . .
Nonmonetary gold	3 180	. . . .	. . . .	. . . .	. . . .	. . . .	. . . .	. . . .	. . . .
B. SERVICES	4 200	−245.6	−288.7	−333.2	−236.8	−257.3	−269.6	−497.6	−678.7
Total credit	2 200	*213.2*	*216.9*	*224.7*	*265.7*	*369.5*	*507.4*	*452.3*	*499.3*
Total debit	3 200	*−458.8*	*−505.6*	*−557.9*	*−502.4*	*−626.8*	*−777.1*	*−949.9*	*−1,178.0*
Transportation services, credit	2 205	31.5	29.2	31.0	8.9	9.6	11.0	11.6	14.7
Passenger	2 850	. . . .	*22.0*	*23.3*	*1.0*	*1.4*	*1.9*	*1.4*	*3.4*
Freight	2 851	. . . .	. . . .	. . . .	. . . .	. . . .	. . . .	. . . .	. . . .
Other	2 852	. . . .	*7.2*	*7.7*	*7.9*	*8.2*	*9.2*	*10.2*	*11.3*
Sea transport, passenger	2 207	. . . .	. . . .	. . . .	. . . .	. . . .	. . . .	. . . .	. . . .
Sea transport, freight	2 208	. . . .	. . . .	. . . .	. . . .	. . . .	. . . .	. . . .	. . . .
Sea transport, other	2 209	. . . .	. . . .	. . . .	. . . .	. . . .	. . . .	. . . .	. . . .
Air transport, passenger	2 211	. . . .	21.2	22.4	. . . .	. . . .	. . . .	. . . .	. . . .
Air transport, freight	2 212	. . . .	. . . .	. . . .	. . . .	. . . .	. . . .	. . . .	. . . .
Air transport, other	2 213	. . . .	. . . .	. . . .	. . . .	. . . .	. . . .	. . . .	. . . .
Other transport, passenger	2 215	. . . .	.9	.9	1.0	1.4	1.9	1.4	3.4
Other transport, freight	2 216	. . . .	. . . .	. . . .	. . . .	. . . .	. . . .	. . . .	. . . .
Other transport, other	2 217	. . . .	7.2	7.7	7.9	8.2	9.2	10.2	11.3
Transportation services, debit	3 205	−149.2	−177.1	−191.0	−225.8	−259.5	−317.4	−468.1	−623.6
Passenger	3 850	. . . .	*−1.9*	*−2.0*	*−2.1*	*−3.2*	*−3.8*	*−72.9*	*−87.9*
Freight	3 851	*−149.2*	*−175.2*	*−189.0*	*−223.8*	*−256.3*	*−313.6*	*−395.2*	*−535.8*
Other	3 852	. . . .	. . . .	. . . .	. . . .	. . . .	. . . .	. . . .	. . . .
Sea transport, passenger	3 207	. . . .	. . . .	. . . .	. . . .	. . . .	. . . .	. . . .	. . . .
Sea transport, freight	3 208	. . . .	. . . .	. . . .	. . . .	. . . .	. . . .	. . . .	. . . .
Sea transport, other	3 209	. . . .	. . . .	. . . .	. . . .	. . . .	. . . .	. . . .	. . . .
Air transport, passenger	3 211	. . . .	. . . .	. . . .	. . . .	. . . .	. . . .	−70.1	−84.1
Air transport, freight	3 212	. . . .	. . . .	. . . .	. . . .	. . . .	−24.0	−63.0	−101.1
Air transport, other	3 213	. . . .	. . . .	. . . .	. . . .	. . . .	. . . .	. . . .	. . . .
Other transport, passenger	3 215	. . . .	−1.9	−2.0	−2.1	−3.2	−3.8	−2.9	−3.7
Other transport, freight	3 216	−149.2	−175.2	−189.0	−223.8	−256.3	−289.6	−332.2	−434.7
Other transport, other	3 217	. . . .	. . . .	. . . .	. . . .	. . . .	. . . .	. . . .	. . . .
Travel, credit	2 236	165.2	165.4	171.5	184.2	267.0	379.9	308.7	355.5
Business travel	2 237	67.7	67.8	70.3	51.6	74.8	106.4	86.4	99.5
Personal travel	2 240	97.5	97.6	101.2	132.6	192.2	273.5	222.3	256.0
Travel, debit	3 236	. . . .	. . . .	. . . .	. . . .	−108.1	−124.4	−95.1	−111.8
Business travel	3 237	. . . .	. . . .	. . . .	. . . .	−63.8	−73.4	−56.1	−65.4
Personal travel	3 240	. . . .	. . . .	. . . .	. . . .	−44.3	−51.0	−39.0	−46.4
Other services, credit	2 200 BA	16.5	22.3	22.2	72.6	92.9	116.5	132.0	129.0
Communications	2 245	8.1	12.1	9.1	16.6	18.7	17.9	24.2	29.2
Construction	2 249	. . . .	. . . .	. . . .	. . . .	. . . .	. . . .	. . . .	. . . .
Insurance	2 253	. . . .	1.7	1.9	3.2	4.1	7.4	8.8	10.9
Financial	2 260	. . . .	. . . .	. . . .	12.8	16.4	16.9	17.9	25.2
Computer and information	2 262	. . . .	. . . .	. . . .	.1	.7	7.9	32.8	31.5	8.8
Royalties and licence fees	2 266	. . . .	. . . .	. . . .	.6	. . . .	7.4	2.4	.5
Other business services	2 268	. . . .	. . . .	2.3	28.4	33.9	20.8	32.4	38.0
Personal, cultural, and recreational	2 287	. . . .	. . . .	. . . .	. . . .	. . . .	. . . .	. . . .	. . . .
Government, n.i.e.	2 291	8.4	8.4	8.7	10.3	11.9	13.3	14.8	16.4
Other services, debit	3 200 BA	−309.6	−328.5	−366.9	−276.6	−259.3	−335.3	−386.7	−442.5
Communications	3 245	−5.3	−6.1	−6.1	−10.1	−11.4	−10.9	−14.7	−18.5
Construction	3 249	. . . .	. . . .	. . . .	. . . .	. . . .	. . . .	. . . .	. . . .
Insurance	3 253	−14.9	−21.8	−23.6	−30.4	−39.2	−47.9	−56.9	−72.5
Financial	3 260	. . . .	. . . .	−5.5	−4.4	−5.0	−5.8	−6.0	−7.2
Computer and information	3 262	. . . .	. . . .	−1.4	−3.2	−10.8	−22.2	−17.6	−10.3
Royalties and licence fees	3 266	. . . .	. . . .	−6.9	−7.9	−1.4	−1.5	−10.6	−4.8
Other business services	3 268	−289.4	−300.6	−315.3	−205.6	−174.5	−231.5	−266.2	−309.8
Personal, cultural, and recreational	3 287	. . . .	. . . .	. . . .	. . . .	. . . .	. . . .	. . . .	. . . .
Government, n.i.e.	3 291	. . . .	. . . .	−8.2	−14.8	−16.9	−15.5	−14.6	−19.4

Table 2 (Continued). STANDARD PRESENTATION, 2000–2007

(Millions of U.S. dollars)

	Code	2000	2001	2002	2003	2004	2005	2006	2007
C. INCOME	4 300	**−112.4**	**−165.3**	**−123.8**	**−143.2**	**−293.1**	**−249.0**	**−226.1**	**−278.8**
Total credit	2 300	*53.1*	*37.5*	*24.2*	*27.6*	*35.7*	*49.8*	*71.9*	*98.4*
Total debit	3 300	*−165.5*	*−202.7*	*−148.0*	*−170.8*	*−328.8*	*−298.9*	*−298.0*	*−377.2*
Compensation of employees, credit	2 310	....	....	....	....	....	....	....	....
Compensation of employees, debit	3 310	**−45.4**	**−50.5**	**−46.4**	**−47.4**	**−54.4**	**−52.2**	**−21.1**	**−56.6**
Investment income, credit	2 320	**53.1**	**37.5**	**24.2**	**27.6**	**35.7**	**49.8**	**71.9**	**98.4**
Direct investment income	2 330	....	....	....	....	....	....	....	....
Dividends and distributed branch profits	2 332	....	....	....	....	....	....	....	....
Reinvested earnings and undistributed branch profits	2 333	....	....	....	....	....	....	....	....
Income on debt (interest)	2 334	....	....	....	....	....	....	....	....
Portfolio investment income	2 339	....	....	....	....	....	....	....	....
Income on equity	2 340	....	....	....	....	....	....	....	....
Income on bonds and notes	2 350	....	....	....	....	....	....	....	....
Income on money market instruments	2 360	....	....	....	....	....	....	....	....
Other investment income	2 370	53.1	37.5	24.2	27.6	35.7	49.8	71.9	98.4
Investment income, debit	3 320	**−120.1**	**−152.2**	**−101.6**	**−123.4**	**−274.4**	**−246.7**	**−276.9**	**−320.5**
Direct investment income	3 330	−19.1	−65.7	−62.5	−82.6	−218.6	−201.7	−236.0	−265.6
Dividends and distributed branch profits	3 332	....	−23.6	−17.5	−29.2	−77.8	−71.6	−83.8	−94.3
Reinvested earnings and undistributed branch profits	3 333	−19.1	−42.1	−42.1	−51.9	−139.0	−128.0	−149.0	−167.6
Income on debt (interest)	3 334	....	....	−2.9	−1.5	−1.8	−2.1	−3.2	−3.7
Portfolio investment income	3 339	....	....	....	−1.0	−2.9	−2.8	−3.2	−7.2
Income on equity	3 340	....	....	....	−.1	−.1	−1.8	−2.1	−3.3
Income on bonds and notes	3 350	....	....	....	....	....	−.2	−.3	−.2
Income on money market instruments	3 360	....	....	....	−.9	−2.8	−.8	−.8	−3.7
Other investment income	3 370	−101.0	−86.5	−39.0	−39.9	−53.0	−42.2	−37.6	−47.8
D. CURRENT TRANSFERS	4 379	**499.0**	**584.3**	**666.3**	**708.8**	**901.6**	**833.3**	**1,428.6**	**1,509.2**
Credit	2 379	**806.6**	**888.5**	**1,023.4**	**923.2**	**1,143.5**	**1,184.3**	**1,762.8**	**1,816.2**
General government	2 380	466.6	425.8	426.3	473.5	680.8	598.5	557.7	278.9
Other sectors	2 390	340.0	462.7	597.2	449.7	462.7	585.8	1,205.1	1,537.3
Workers' remittances	2 391	238.1	342.4	420.8	306.1	310.5	323.4	665.2	848.6
Other current transfers	2 392	101.9	120.3	176.4	143.6	152.2	262.4	539.9	688.7
Debit	3 379	**−307.6**	**−304.2**	**−357.1**	**−214.4**	**−241.9**	**−350.9**	**−334.2**	**−307.0**
General government	3 380	....	....	−1.8	−2.4	−1.9	....	−.5	....
Other sectors	3 390	−307.6	−304.2	−355.3	−212.0	−240.0	−350.9	−333.7	−307.0
Workers' remittances	3 391	−307.6	−304.2	−355.3	−212.0	−240.0	−350.9	−333.7	−307.0
Other current transfers	3 392	....	....	....	....	....	....	....	....
CAPITAL AND FINANCIAL ACCOUNT	4 996	**318.2**	**350.2**	**352.6**	**361.4**	**320.4**	**411.9**	**281.7**	**682.6**
CAPITAL ACCOUNT	4 994	**69.7**	**55.2**	**63.6**	**61.0**	**63.8**	**64.3**	**3,612.9**	**45.1**
Total credit	2 994	*69.7*	*55.2*	*63.6*	*61.0*	*63.8*	*64.3*	*3,612.9*	*45.1*
Total debit	3 994	....	....	....	....	....	....	....	....
Capital transfers, credit	2 400	**69.7**	**55.2**	**63.6**	**61.0**	**63.8**	**64.3**	**3,612.9**	**45.1**
General government	2 401	69.7	55.2	63.6	61.0	63.8	64.3	3,612.9	45.1
Debt forgiveness	2 402	69.7	55.2	63.6	61.0	63.8	64.3	3,612.9	45.1
Other capital transfers	2 410	....	....	....	....	....	....	....	....
Other sectors	2 430	....	....	....	....	....	....	....	....
Migrants' transfers	2 431	....	....	....	....	....	....	....	....
Debt forgiveness	2 432	....	....	....	....	....	....	....	....
Other capital transfers	2 440	....	....	....	....	....	....	....	....
Capital transfers, debit	3 400	....	....	....	....	....	....	....	....
General government	3 401	....	....	....	....	....	....	....	....
Debt forgiveness	3 402	....	....	....	....	....	....	....	....
Other capital transfers	3 410	....	....	....	....	....	....	....	....
Other sectors	3 430	....	....	....	....	....	....	....	....
Migrants' transfers	3 431	....	....	....	....	....	....	....	....
Debt forgiveness	3 432	....	....	....	....	....	....	....	....
Other capital transfers	3 440	....	....	....	....	....	....	....	....
Nonproduced nonfinancial assets, credit	2 480	....	....	....	....	....	....	....	....
Nonproduced nonfinancial assets, debit	3 480	....	....	....	....	....	....	....	....

Table 2 (Continued). STANDARD PRESENTATION, 2000–2007

(Millions of U.S. dollars)

	Code	2000	2001	2002	2003	2004	2005	2006	2007
FINANCIAL ACCOUNT...............................	4 995 ..	**248.5**	**295.1**	**289.1**	**300.5**	**256.6**	**347.6**	**−3,331.2**	**637.6**
A. DIRECT INVESTMENT..........................	4 500 ..	**160.7**	**151.5**	**184.6**	**202.2**	**295.4**	**379.8**	**393.2**	**484.0**
Direct investment abroad......................	4 505 ..	....	....	....	....	....	....	....	....
Equity capital...................................	4 510 ..	....	....	....	....	....	....	....	....
Claims on affiliated enterprises.........	4 515 ..	....	....	....	....	....	....	....	....
Liabilities to affiliated enterprises......	4 520 ..	....	....	....	....	....	....	....	....
Reinvested earnings..........................	4 525 ..	....	....	....	....	....	....	....	....
Other capital...................................	4 530 ..	....	....	....	....	....	....	....	....
Claims on affiliated enterprises.........	4 535 ..	....	....	....	....	....	....	....	....
Liabilities to affiliated enterprises......	4 540 ..	....	....	....	....	....	....	....	....
Direct investment in Uganda..............	4 555 ..	**160.7**	**151.5**	**184.6**	**202.2**	**295.4**	**379.8**	**393.2**	**484.0**
Equity capital...................................	4 560 ..	82.4	86.5	99.6	102.1	166.9	253.2	249.5	321.2
Claims on direct investors...............	4 565 ..	....	....	....	....	....	....	....	....
Liabilities to direct investors...........	4 570 ..	82.4	86.5	99.6	102.1	166.9	253.2	249.5	321.2
Reinvested earnings..........................	4 575 ..	19.1	42.1	42.1	51.9	139.0	128.0	149.0	167.6
Other capital...................................	4 580 ..	59.2	22.9	42.9	48.2	−10.4	−1.4	−5.4	−4.8
Claims on direct investors...............	4 585 ..	....	....	....	....	....	....	....	....
Liabilities to direct investors...........	4 590 ..	59.2	22.9	42.9	48.2	−10.4	−1.4	−5.4	−4.8
B. PORTFOLIO INVESTMENT..................	4 600 ..	....	....	**1.9**	**16.0**	**6.2**	**−13.4**	**21.7**	**14.3**
Assets...	4 602 ..	....	....	**1.5**	**−4.3**	....	....	....	....
Equity securities...............................	4 610 ..	....	....	1.5	−4.3	....	....	....	....
Monetary authorities......................	4 611 ..	....	....	....	....	....	....	....	....
General government........................	4 612 ..	....	....	....	....	....	....	....	....
Banks...	4 613 ..	....	....	....	....	....	....	....	....
Other sectors.................................	4 614 ..	....	....	1.5	−4.3	....	....	....	....
Debt securities................................	4 619 ..	....	....	....	....	....	....	....	....
Bonds and notes............................	4 620 ..	....	....	....	....	....	....	....	....
Monetary authorities....................	4 621 ..	....	....	....	....	....	....	....	....
General government......................	4 622 ..	....	....	....	....	....	....	....	....
Banks...	4 623 ..	....	....	....	....	....	....	....	....
Other sectors...............................	4 624 ..	....	....	....	....	....	....	....	....
Money market instruments...............	4 630 ..	....	....	....	....	....	....	....	....
Monetary authorities....................	4 631 ..	....	....	....	....	....	....	....	....
General government......................	4 632 ..	....	....	....	....	....	....	....	....
Banks...	4 633 ..	....	....	....	....	....	....	....	....
Other sectors...............................	4 634 ..	....	....	....	....	....	....	....	....
Liabilities..	4 652 ..	....	....	**.4**	**20.3**	**6.2**	**−13.4**	**21.7**	**14.3**
Equity securities...............................	4 660 ..	....	....	.4	....	24.0	....	19.1	−47.8
Banks...	4 663 ..	....	....	.4	....	24.0	....	19.1	−47.8
Other sectors.................................	4 664 ..	....	....	....	....	....	....	....	....
Debt securities................................	4 669 ..	....	....	....	20.3	−17.8	−13.4	2.5	62.2
Bonds and notes............................	4 670 ..	....	....	....	....	.7	1.9	3.1	11.7
Monetary authorities....................	4 671 ..	....	....	....	....	....	....	....	....
General government......................	4 672 ..	....	....	....	....	.7	1.9	3.1	11.7
Banks...	4 673 ..	....	....	....	....	....	....	....	....
Other sectors...............................	4 674 ..	....	....	....	....	....	....	....	....
Money market instruments...............	4 680 ..	....	....	....	20.3	−18.5	−15.2	−.6	50.5
Monetary authorities....................	4 681 ..	....	....	....	....	....	....	....	....
General government......................	4 682 ..	....	....	....	20.3	−18.5	−15.2	−.6	50.5
Banks...	4 683 ..	....	....	....	....	....	....	....	....
Other sectors...............................	4 684 ..	....	....	....	....	....	....	....	....
C. FINANCIAL DERIVATIVES..................	4 910 ..	....	....	....	....	....	....	....	....
Monetary authorities..........................	4 911 ..	....	....	....	....	....	....	....	....
General government...........................	4 912 ..	....	....	....	....	....	....	....	....
Banks...	4 913 ..	....	....	....	....	....	....	....	....
Other sectors....................................	4 914 ..	....	....	....	....	....	....	....	....
Assets...	4 900 ..	....	....	....	....	....	....	....	....
Monetary authorities......................	4 901 ..	....	....	....	....	....	....	....	....
General government........................	4 902 ..	....	....	....	....	....	....	....	....
Banks...	4 903 ..	....	....	....	....	....	....	....	....
Other sectors.................................	4 904 ..	....	....	....	....	....	....	....	....
Liabilities..	4 905 ..	....	....	....	....	....	....	....	....
Monetary authorities......................	4 906 ..	....	....	....	....	....	....	....	....
General government........................	4 907 ..	....	....	....	....	....	....	....	....
Banks...	4 908 ..	....	....	....	....	....	....	....	....
Other sectors.................................	4 909 ..	....	....	....	....	....	....	....	....

Table 2 (Concluded). STANDARD PRESENTATION, 2000–2007

(Millions of U.S. dollars)

	Code	2000	2001	2002	2003	2004	2005	2006	2007
D. OTHER INVESTMENT	4 700 ..	**132.9**	**303.6**	**2.1**	**159.3**	**117.0**	**73.7**	**−3,343.1**	**839.9**
Assets	4 703 ..	**−.9**	**29.4**	**−59.1**	**−124.9**	**.1**	**−7.1**	**76.1**	**282.2**
Trade credits	4 706 ..	....	....	....	....	....	....	....	....
General government	4 707 ..	....	....	....	....	....	....	....	....
of which: Short-term	4 709 ..	....	....	....	....	....	....	....	....
Other sectors	4 710 ..	....	....	....	....	....	....	....	....
of which: Short-term	4 712 ..	....	....	....	....	....	....	....	....
Loans	4 714 ..	....	....	....	....	−.4	−8.8	4.2	−.6
Monetary authorities	4 715 ..	....	....	....	....	....	....	....	....
of which: Short-term	4 718 ..	....	....	....	....	....	....	....	....
General government	4 719 ..	....	....	....	....	....	....	....	....
of which: Short-term	4 721 ..	....	....	....	....	....	....	....	....
Banks	4 722 ..	....	....	....	....	−.4	−8.8	4.2	−.6
of which: Short-term	4 724 ..	....	....	....	....	−.4	−8.8	4.2	−.6
Other sectors	4 725 ..	....	....	....	....	....	....	....	....
of which: Short-term	4 727 ..	....	....	....	....	....	....	....	....
Currency and deposits	4 730 ..	−.9	29.4	−59.1	−124.9	1.6	1.7	−35.6	90.6
Monetary authorities	4 731 ..	....	....	....	22.9	12.5	....	....	....
General government	4 732 ..	....	....	5.3	−12.0	−11.9	1.9	16.3	83.1
Banks	4 733 ..	−65.8	17.0	8.5	−109.7	−3.4	52.0	−110.6	−58.2
Other sectors	4 734 ..	64.9	12.4	−73.0	−26.1	4.4	−52.2	58.7	65.7
Other assets	4 736 ..	....	....	....	....	−1.1	....	107.5	192.3
Monetary authorities	4 737 ..	....	....	....	....	−.7	....	....	15.4
of which: Short-term	4 739 ..	....	....	....	....	....	....	....	....
General government	4 740 ..	....	....	....	....	−.4	....	....	....
of which: Short-term	4 742 ..	....	....	....	....	....	....	....	....
Banks	4 743 ..	....	....	....	....	....	....	....	....
of which: Short-term	4 745 ..	....	....	....	....	....	....	....	....
Other sectors	4 746 ..	....	....	....	....	....	....	107.5	176.9
of which: Short-term	4 748 ..	....	....	....	....	....	....	....	....
Liabilities	4 753 ..	**133.8**	**274.2**	**61.2**	**284.2**	**116.8**	**80.8**	**−3,419.2**	**557.6**
Trade credits	4 756 ..	....	−10.7	−10.5	3.3	13.0	16.5	17.4	21.8
General government	4 757 ..	....	....	....	....	....	....	....	....
of which: Short-term	4 759 ..	....	....	....	....	....	....	....	....
Other sectors	4 760 ..	....	−10.7	−10.5	3.3	13.0	16.5	17.4	21.8
of which: Short-term	4 762 ..	....	−10.7	−10.5	3.3	13.0	16.5	17.4	21.8
Loans	4 764 ..	123.3	260.3	49.4	272.2	101.1	61.0	−3,469.1	449.6
Monetary authorities	4 765 ..	−37.4	−29.6	−39.4	−42.6	−52.7	−46.2	−124.0	....
of which: Use of Fund credit and loans from the Fund	4 766 ..	−37.4	−29.6	−39.4	−42.6	−52.7	−46.2	−124.0	....
of which: Short-term	4 768 ..	....	....	....	....	....	....	....	....
General government	4 769 ..	154.9	285.7	59.6	271.9	129.0	71.9	−3,390.0	294.8
of which: Short-term	4 771 ..	....	....	....	....	....	....	....	....
Banks	4 772 ..	....	....	....	....	....	....	....	....
of which: Short-term	4 774 ..	....	....	....	....	....	....	....	....
Other sectors	4 775 ..	5.8	4.2	29.2	42.9	24.8	35.3	45.0	154.7
of which: Short-term	4 777 ..	....	6.8	3.6	10.6	9.9	10.2	13.2	7.2
Currency and deposits	4 780 ..	....	−6.7	9.0	−5.9	11.9	−13.9	25.5	68.5
Monetary authorities	4 781 ..	....	....	....	....	....	....	....	....
General government	4 782 ..	....	....	....	....	....	....	....	....
Banks	4 783 ..	....	−6.7	9.0	−5.9	11.9	−13.9	25.5	68.5
Other sectors	4 784 ..	....	....	....	....	....	....	....	....
Other liabilities	4 786 ..	10.5	31.5	13.4	14.6	−9.2	17.1	7.0	17.7
Monetary authorities	4 787 ..	....	....	....	....	....	....	....	....
of which: Short-term	4 789 ..	....	....	....	....	....	....	....	....
General government	4 790 ..	10.5	31.5	13.4	6.5	7.4	−3.8	−5.2	1.4
of which: Short-term	4 792 ..	10.5	31.5	13.4	6.5	7.4	−3.8	−5.2	1.4
Banks	4 793 ..	....	....	....	8.1	−16.6	20.9	12.2	16.3
of which: Short-term	4 795 ..	....	....	....	8.1	−16.6	20.9	12.2	16.3
Other sectors	4 796 ..	....	....	....	....	....	....	....	....
of which: Short-term	4 798 ..	....	....	....	....	....	....	....	....
E. RESERVE ASSETS	4 802 ..	**−45.1**	**−160.0**	**100.4**	**−77.1**	**−162.0**	**−92.5**	**−403.0**	**−700.7**
Monetary gold	4 812 ..	....	....	....	....	....	....	....	....
Special drawing rights	4 811 ..	−1.4	1.6	−.8	−1.4	4.2	−.9	1.1	−.2
Reserve position in the Fund	4 810 ..	....	....	....	....	....	....	....	....
Foreign exchange	4 803 ..	−43.7	−161.6	101.2	−75.7	−166.3	−91.6	−404.1	−700.5
Other claims	4 813 ..	....	....	....	....	....	....	....	....
NET ERRORS AND OMISSIONS	4 998 ..	**40.6**	**19.3**	**9.3**	**−7.7**	**−3.9**	**1.9**	**41.5**	**62.1**

Table 3. INTERNATIONAL INVESTMENT POSITION (End-period stocks), 2000–2007

(Millions of U.S. dollars)

	Code	2000	2001	2002	2003	2004	2005	2006	2007
ASSETS	8 995 C.	**1,073.7**	**1,231.9**	**1,174.1**	**1,469.0**	**1,732.8**	**1,703.6**	**2,303.8**	**3,121.6**
Direct investment abroad	8 505 ..	....	....	....	....	....	....	....	....
Equity capital and reinvested earnings	8 506 ..	....	....	....	....	....	....	....	....
Claims on affiliated enterprises	8 507 ..	....	....	....	....	....	....	....	....
Liabilities to affiliated enterprises	8 508 ..	....	....	....	....	....	....	....	....
Other capital	8 530 ..	....	....	....	....	....	....	....	....
Claims on affiliated enterprises	8 535 ..	....	....	....	....	....	....	....	....
Liabilities to affiliated enterprises	8 540 ..	....	....	....	....	....	....	....	....
Portfolio investment	8 602 ..	....	....	....	....	....	....	....	....
Equity securities	8 610 ..	....	....	....	....	....	....	....	....
Monetary authorities	8 611 ..	....	....	....	....	....	....	....	....
General government	8 612 ..	....	....	....	....	....	....	....	....
Banks	8 613 ..	....	....	....	....	....	....	....	....
Other sectors	8 614 ..	....	....	....	....	....	....	....	....
Debt securities	8 619 ..	....	....	....	....	....	....	....	....
Bonds and notes	8 620 ..	....	....	....	....	....	....	....	....
Monetary authorities	8 621 ..	....	....	....	....	....	....	....	....
General government	8 622 ..	....	....	....	....	....	....	....	....
Banks	8 623 ..	....	....	....	....	....	....	....	....
Other sectors	8 624 ..	....	....	....	....	....	....	....	....
Money market instruments	8 630 ..	....	....	....	....	....	....	....	....
Monetary authorities	8 631 ..	....	....	....	....	....	....	....	....
General government	8 632 ..	....	....	....	....	....	....	....	....
Banks	8 633 ..	....	....	....	....	....	....	....	....
Other sectors	8 634 ..	....	....	....	....	....	....	....	....
Financial derivatives	8 900 ..	....	....	....	....	....	....	....	....
Monetary authorities	8 901 ..	....	....	....	....	....	....	....	....
General government	8 902 ..	....	....	....	....	....	....	....	....
Banks	8 903 ..	....	....	....	....	....	....	....	....
Other sectors	8 904 ..	....	....	....	....	....	....	....	....
Other investment	8 703 ..	**265.6**	**248.6**	**240.1**	**388.7**	**424.7**	**359.4**	**492.9**	**561.8**
Trade credits	8 706 ..	....	....	....	....	....	....	....	....
General government	8 707 ..	....	....	....	....	....	....	....	....
of which: Short-term	8 709 ..	....	....	....	....	....	....	....	....
Other sectors	8 710 ..	....	....	....	....	....	....	....	....
of which: Short-term	8 712 ..	....	....	....	....	....	....	....	....
Loans	8 714 ..	....	....	....	.5	1.0	10.0	6.0	6.8
Monetary authorities	8 715 ..	....	....	....	....	....	....	....	....
of which: Short-term	8 718 ..	....	....	....	....	....	....	....	....
General government	8 719 ..	....	....	....	....	....	....	....	....
of which: Short-term	8 721 ..	....	....	....	....	....	....	....	....
Banks	8 722 ..	....	....	....	.5	1.0	10.0	6.0	6.8
of which: Short-term	8 724 ..	....	....	....	....	....	....	....	....
Other sectors	8 725 ..	....	....	....	....	....	....	....	....
of which: Short-term	8 727 ..	....	....	....	....	....	....	....	....
Currency and deposits	8 730 ..	265.6	248.6	240.1	388.2	423.7	349.4	486.9	555.1
Monetary authorities	8 731 ..	....	....	....	26.0	13.5	9.8	16.9	11.1
General government	8 732 ..	....	....	....	....	....	....	....	....
Banks	8 733 ..	265.6	248.6	240.1	362.2	410.2	339.6	470.1	544.0
Other sectors	8 734 ..	....	....	....	....	....	....	....	....
Other assets	8 736 ..	....	....	....	....	....	....	....	....
Monetary authorities	8 737 ..	....	....	....	....	....	....	....	....
of which: Short-term	8 739 ..	....	....	....	....	....	....	....	....
General government	8 740 ..	....	....	....	....	....	....	....	....
of which: Short-term	8 742 ..	....	....	....	....	....	....	....	....
Banks	8 743 ..	....	....	....	....	....	....	....	....
of which: Short-term	8 745 ..	....	....	....	....	....	....	....	....
Other sectors	8 746 ..	....	....	....	....	....	....	....	....
of which: Short-term	8 748 ..	....	....	....	....	....	....	....	....
Reserve assets	8 802 ..	**808.1**	**983.3**	**934.0**	**1,080.3**	**1,308.1**	**1,344.2**	**1,810.9**	**2,559.8**
Monetary gold	8 812 ..	....	....	....	....	....	....	....	....
Special drawing rights	8 811 ..	3.5	1.9	3.0	4.8	.7	1.1	.1	.3
Reserve position in the Fund	8 810 ..	....	....	....	....	....	....	....	....
Foreign exchange	8 803 ..	804.5	981.5	931.1	1,075.5	1,307.4	1,343.1	1,810.8	2,559.5
Other claims	8 813 ..	....	....	....	....	....	....	....	....

Table 3 (Concluded). INTERNATIONAL INVESTMENT POSITION (End-period stocks), 2000–2007

(Millions of U.S. dollars)

	Code	2000	2001	2002	2003	2004	2005	2006	2007
LIABILITIES	8 995 D.	**4,394.8**	**4,783.8**	**5,296.1**	**6,124.6**	**6,900.6**	**6,857.3**	**4,507.3**	**5,311.9**
Direct investment in Uganda	8 555 ..	**807.1**	**962.3**	**1,146.9**	**1,349.1**	**1,644.6**	**2,024.4**	**2,417.5**	**2,901.6**
Equity capital and reinvested earnings	8 556 ..	539.9	700.3	842.0	996.0	1,301.9	1,683.1	2,081.7	2,570.5
Claims on direct investors	8 557 ..	....	....	....	....	....	....	....	....
Liabilities to direct investors	8 558 ..	539.9	700.3	842.0	996.0	1,301.9	1,683.1	2,081.7	2,570.5
Other capital	8 580 ..	267.2	262.0	304.9	353.1	342.7	341.2	335.9	331.1
Claims on direct investors	8 585 ..	....	....	....	....	....	....	....	....
Liabilities to direct investors	8 590 ..	267.2	262.0	304.9	353.1	342.7	341.2	335.9	331.1
Portfolio investment	8 652 ..	**.2**	**.2**	**.7**	**22.8**	**29.3**	**33.7**	**54.1**	**161.4**
Equity securities	8 660 ..	.2	.2	.7	.7	24.6	24.6	43.8	66.0
Banks	8 663 ..	....	....	.4	.4	24.4	24.4	43.5	65.8
Other sectors	8 664 ..	.2	.2	.2	.2	.3	.3	.3	.2
Debt securities	8 669 ..	....	....	....	22.1	4.6	9.1	10.3	95.3
Bonds and notes	8 670 ..	....	....	....	....	.7	2.5	5.8	23.4
Monetary authorities	8 671 ..	....	....	....	....	....	....	....	....
General government	8 672 ..	....	....	....	....	.7	2.5	5.8	23.4
Banks	8 673 ..	....	....	....	....	....	....	....	....
Other sectors	8 674 ..	....	....	....	....	....	....	....	....
Money market instruments	8 680 ..	....	....	....	22.1	3.9	6.6	4.5	72.0
Monetary authorities	8 681 ..	....	....	....	....	....	....	....	....
General government	8 682 ..	....	....	....	22.1	3.9	6.6	4.5	72.0
Banks	8 683 ..	....	....	....	....	....	....	....	....
Other sectors	8 684 ..	....	....	....	....	....	....	....	....
Financial derivatives	8 905 ..	....	....	....	....	....	....	....	....
Monetary authorities	8 906 ..	....	....	....	....	....	....	....	....
General government	8 907 ..	....	....	....	....	....	....	....	....
Banks	8 908 ..	....	....	....	....	....	....	....	....
Other sectors	8 909 ..	....	....	....	....	....	....	....	....
Other investment	8 753 ..	**3,587.5**	**3,821.2**	**4,148.4**	**4,752.7**	**5,226.8**	**4,799.1**	**2,035.6**	**2,249.0**
Trade credits	8 756 ..	....	....	....	....	....	....	....	....
General government	8 757 ..	....	....	....	....	....	....	....	....
of which: Short-term	8 759 ..	....	....	....	....	....	....	....	....
Other sectors	8 760 ..	....	....	....	....	....	....	....	....
of which: Short-term	8 762 ..	....	....	....	....	....	....	....	....
Loans	8 764 ..	3,529.0	3,769.5	4,087.8	4,673.7	5,157.4	4,725.6	1,918.8	2,046.9
Monetary authorities	8 765 ..	316.1	275.4	256.8	236.0	191.5	131.1	9.0	9.5
of which: Use of Fund credit and loans from the Fund	8 766 ..	*316.1*	*275.4*	*256.8*	*236.0*	*191.5*	*131.1*	*9.0*	*9.5*
of which: Short-term	8 768 ..	....	....	....	....	....	....	....	....
General government	8 769 ..	3,088.7	3,378.9	3,686.5	4,250.5	4,753.8	4,347.1	1,617.4	1,590.3
of which: Short-term	8 771 ..	....	....	....	....	....	....	....	....
Banks	8 772 ..	....	....	....	....	....	....	....	....
of which: Short-term	8 774 ..	....	....	....	....	....	....	....	....
Other sectors	8 775 ..	124.2	115.2	144.4	187.3	212.1	247.4	292.4	447.1
of which: Short-term	8 777 ..	*.8*	*.9*	*4.5*	*15.1*	*25.0*	*35.2*	*48.5*	*55.7*
Currency and deposits	8 780 ..	58.5	51.7	60.7	64.9	65.1	49.4	79.0	148.1
Monetary authorities	8 781 ..	....	....	....	....	....	....	....	....
General government	8 782 ..	....	....	....	....	....	....	....	....
Banks	8 783 ..	58.5	51.7	60.7	64.9	65.1	49.4	· 79.0	148.1
Other sectors	8 784 ..	....	....	....	....	....	....	....	....
Other liabilities	8 786 ..	....	....	....	14.1	4.3	24.1	37.9	54.0
Monetary authorities	8 787 ..	....	....	....	....	2.4	1.7	1.8	1.4
of which: Short-term	8 789 ..	....	....	....	....	*2.4*	*1.7*	*1.8*	*1.4*
General government	8 790 ..	....	....	....	....	....	....	....	....
of which: Short-term	8 792 ..	....	....	....	....	....	....	....	....
Banks	8 793 ..	....	....	....	14.1	1.9	22.5	36.1	52.6
of which: Short-term	8 795 ..	....	....	....	....	....	....	....	....
Other sectors	8 796 ..	....	....	....	....	....	....	....	....
of which: Short-term	8 798 ..	....	....	....	....	....	....	....	....
NET INTERNATIONAL INVESTMENT POSITION	8 995 ..	**−3,321.2**	**−3,551.9**	**−4,122.0**	**−4,655.6**	**−5,167.9**	**−5,153.7**	**−2,203.5**	**−2,190.3**
Conversion rates: Uganda shillings per U.S. dollar (end of period)	0 102 ..	1,766.7	1,727.4	1,852.6	1,935.3	1,738.6	1,816.9	1,741.4	1,697.3

Table 1. ANALYTIC PRESENTATION, 2000–2007

(Millions of U.S. dollars)

	Code	2000	2001	2002	2003	2004	2005	2006	2007
A. Current Account[1]	4 993 Z.	**1,481**	**1,402**	**3,174**	**2,891**	**6,909**	**2,531**	**−1,617**	**−5,272**
Goods: exports f.o.b.	2 100 ..	15,722	17,091	18,669	23,739	33,432	35,024	38,949	49,840
Goods: imports f.o.b.	3 100 ..	−14,943	−16,893	−17,959	−23,221	−29,691	−36,159	−44,143	−60,412
Balance on Goods	4 100 ..	*779*	*198*	*710*	*518*	*3,741*	*−1,135*	*−5,194*	*−10,572*
Services: credit	2 200 ..	3,800	3,995	4,682	5,214	7,859	9,354	11,290	14,161
Services: debit	3 200 ..	−3,004	−3,580	−3,535	−4,444	−6,622	−7,548	−9,164	−11,741
Balance on Goods and Services	4 991 ..	*1,575*	*613*	*1,857*	*1,288*	*4,978*	*671*	*−3,068*	*−8,152*
Income: credit	2 300 ..	143	167	165	254	389	758	1,332	3,656
Income: debit	3 300 ..	−1,085	−834	−769	−835	−1,034	−1,743	−3,054	−4,315
Balance on Goods, Services, and Income	4 992 ..	*633*	*−54*	*1,253*	*707*	*4,333*	*−314*	*−4,790*	*−8,811*
Current transfers: credit	2 379 Z.	967	1,516	1,967	2,270	2,671	3,111	3,533	4,147
Current transfers: debit	3 379 ..	−119	−60	−46	−86	−95	−266	−360	−608
B. Capital Account[1]	4 994 Z.	**−8**	**3**	**17**	**−17**	**7**	**−65**	**3**	**3**
Capital account: credit	2 994 Z.	....	8	28	11	21	14	22	27
Capital account: debit	3 994 ..	−8	−5	−11	−28	−14	−79	−19	−24
Total, Groups A Plus B	4 981 ..	*1,473*	*1,405*	*3,191*	*2,874*	*6,916*	*2,466*	*−1,614*	*−5,269*
C. Financial Account[1]	4 995 W.	**−847**	**−260**	**−1,071**	**133**	**−4,521**	**8,126**	**3,929**	**15,127**
Direct investment abroad	4 505 ..	−1	−23	5	−13	−4	−275	133	−673
Direct investment in Ukraine	4 555 Z.	595	792	693	1,424	1,715	7,808	5,604	9,891
Portfolio investment assets	4 602 ..	−4	1	2	1	−6	....	−3	−29
Equity securities	4 610 ..	−2	−1	....	−4	−6	....	−2	−21
Debt securities	4 619 ..	−2	2	2	5	....	....	−1	−8
Portfolio investment liabilities	4 652 Z.	142	−46	335	866	2,073	2,757	3,586	5,782
Equity securities	4 660 ..	146	87	95	84	−61	82	322	715
Debt securities	4 669 Z.	−4	−133	240	782	2,134	2,675	3,264	5,067
Financial derivatives	4 910 ..	....	....	....	....	....	....	....	....
Financial derivatives assets	4 900 ..	....	....	....	....	....	....	....	....
Financial derivatives liabilities	4 905 ..	....	....	....	....	....	....	....	....
Other investment assets	4 703 ..	−883	−1,905	−2,840	−2,860	−12,495	−7,913	−15,580	−22,838
Monetary authorities	4 701 ..	−15	1	−23	−30	−266	267	−111	52
General government	4 704 ..	1,002	....	....	....	....	−5	−3	....
Banks	4 705 ..	−64	137	−86	−455	−906	−601	−1,098	−2,440
Other sectors	4 728 ..	−1,806	−2,043	−2,731	−2,375	−11,323	−7,574	−14,368	−20,450
Other investment liabilities	4 753 W.	−696	921	734	715	4,196	5,749	10,189	22,994
Monetary authorities	4 753 WA	....	....	−4	16	7	−18	−16	−20
General government	4 753 ZB	−1,457	−537	−384	−379	922	93	−152	502
Banks	4 753 ZC	113	180	76	779	579	2,663	5,706	13,011
Other sectors	4 753 ZD	648	1,278	1,046	299	2,688	3,011	4,651	9,501
Total, Groups A Through C	4 983 ..	*626*	*1,145*	*2,120*	*3,007*	*2,395*	*10,592*	*2,315*	*9,858*
D. Net Errors and Omissions	4 998 ..	**−53**	**−152**	**−889**	**−834**	**128**	**133**	**94**	**−452**
Total, Groups A Through D	4 984 ..	*573*	*993*	*1,231*	*2,173*	*2,523*	*10,725*	*2,409*	*9,406*
E. Reserves and Related Items	4 802 A.	**−573**	**−993**	**−1,231**	**−2,173**	**−2,523**	**−10,725**	**−2,409**	**−9,406**
Reserve assets	4 802 ..	−401	−1,609	−1,047	−2,045	−2,226	−10,425	−1,999	−8,979
Use of Fund credit and loans	4 766 ..	−603	−86	−181	−203	−298	−299	−410	−427
Exceptional financing	4 920 ..	431	702	−2	75	....	....	....	....
Conversion rates: hryvnias per U.S. dollar	0 101 ..	**5.4402**	**5.3722**	**5.3266**	**5.3327**	**5.3192**	**5.1247**	**5.0500**	**5.0500**

[1] Excludes components that have been classified in the categories of Group E.

Table 2. STANDARD PRESENTATION, 2000–2007

(Millions of U.S. dollars)

	Code	2000	2001	2002	2003	2004	2005	2006	2007
CURRENT ACCOUNT	4 993	1,481	1,402	3,174	2,891	6,909	2,531	−1,617	−5,272
A. GOODS	4 100	779	198	710	518	3,741	−1,135	−5,194	−10,572
Credit	2 100	15,722	17,091	18,669	23,739	33,432	35,024	38,949	49,840
General merchandise: exports f.o.b.	2 110	13,775	15,116	16,509	21,430	30,572	32,164	36,146	46,126
Goods for processing: exports f.o.b.	2 150	1,806	1,823	1,999	2,123	2,525	2,511	2,496	3,346
Repairs on goods	2 160	135	146	156	179	326	332	279	326
Goods procured in ports by carriers	2 170	6	6	5	7	9	17	28	42
Nonmonetary gold	2 180	....	....	....	....	....	....	....	....
Debit	3 100	−14,943	−16,893	−17,959	−23,221	−29,691	−36,159	−44,143	−60,412
General merchandise: imports f.o.b.	3 110	−13,788	−15,697	−16,522	−21,451	−27,699	−34,164	−41,952	−57,428
Goods for processing: imports f.o.b.	3 150	−1,025	−1,091	−1,331	−1,635	−1,832	−1,761	−1,891	−2,623
Repairs on goods	3 160	−11	−13	−12	−31	−20	−21	−32	−37
Goods procured in ports by carriers	3 170	−119	−92	−94	−104	−140	−213	−268	−324
Nonmonetary gold	3 180	....	....	....	....	....	....	....	....
B. SERVICES	4 200	796	415	1,147	770	1,237	1,806	2,126	2,420
Total credit	2 200	*3,800*	*3,995*	*4,682*	*5,214*	*7,859*	*9,354*	*11,290*	*14,161*
Total debit	3 200	*−3,004*	*−3,580*	*−3,535*	*−4,444*	*−6,622*	*−7,548*	*−9,164*	*−11,741*
Transportation services, credit	2 205	2,920	2,961	3,384	3,514	4,041	4,481	5,351	6,114
Passenger	2 850	*169*	*186*	*213*	*269*	*371*	*417*	*533*	*723*
Freight	2 851	*2,179*	*2,117*	*2,413*	*2,426*	*2,556*	*2,635*	*3,261*	*3,376*
Other	2 852	*572*	*658*	*758*	*819*	*1,114*	*1,429*	*1,557*	*2,015*
Sea transport, passenger	2 207	3	....	1	1	4	5	4	3
Sea transport, freight	2 208	80	43	60	71	64	60	60	67
Sea transport, other	2 209	352	380	419	414	585	716	743	848
Air transport, passenger	2 211	91	102	113	155	227	268	355	467
Air transport, freight	2 212	46	47	58	91	85	93	125	160
Air transport, other	2 213	82	99	94	123	147	201	241	293
Other transport, passenger	2 215	75	84	99	113	140	144	174	253
Other transport, freight	2 216	2,053	2,027	2,295	2,264	2,407	2,482	3,076	3,149
Other transport, other	2 217	138	179	245	282	382	512	573	874
Transportation services, debit	3 205	−390	−409	−487	−1,358	−1,627	−2,051	−3,208	−3,902
Passenger	3 850	*−91*	*−110*	*−137*	*−164*	*−197*	*−273*	*−368*	*−453*
Freight	3 851	*−91*	*−88*	*−102*	*−916*	*−1,049*	*−1,276*	*−2,257*	*−2,667*
Other	3 852	*−208*	*−211*	*−248*	*−278*	*−381*	*−502*	*−583*	*−782*
Sea transport, passenger	3 207	....	....	....	....	....	....	....	−3
Sea transport, freight	3 208	−36	−35	−46	−70	−77	−143	−133	−256
Sea transport, other	3 209	−75	−94	−104	−92	−113	−155	−177	−177
Air transport, passenger	3 211	−46	−53	−73	−90	−112	−168	−239	−278
Air transport, freight	3 212	−5	−5	−6	−18	−21	−23	−33	−63
Air transport, other	3 213	−51	−52	−60	−78	−123	−158	−208	−282
Other transport, passenger	3 215	−45	−57	−64	−74	−85	−105	−129	−172
Other transport, freight	3 216	−50	−48	−50	−828	−951	−1,110	−2,091	−2,348
Other transport, other	3 217	−82	−65	−84	−108	−145	−189	−198	−323
Travel, credit	2 236	394	573	788	935	2,560	3,125	3,485	4,597
Business travel	2 237	....	....	....	....	240	288	324	306
Personal travel	2 240	....	....	....	....	2,320	2,837	3,161	4,291
Travel, debit	3 236	−470	−566	−657	−789	−2,463	−2,805	−2,834	−3,569
Business travel	3 237	....	....	....	....	−574	−600	−415	−668
Personal travel	3 240	....	....	....	....	−1,889	−2,205	−2,419	−2,901
Other services, credit	2 200 BA	486	461	510	765	1,258	1,748	2,454	3,450
Communications	2 245	89	93	89	83	125	203	283	313
Construction	2 249	38	27	29	51	73	115	189	145
Insurance	2 253	4	6	6	14	18	25	70	86
Financial	2 260	22	18	19	20	24	36	80	322
Computer and information	2 262	6	7	10	17	30	44	97	191
Royalties and licence fees	2 266	1	5	4	14	40	22	32	53
Other business services	2 268	323	204	251	361	538	846	1,161	1,672
Personal, cultural, and recreational	2 287	3	3	3	4	11	16	74	158
Government, n.i.e.	2 291	....	98	99	201	399	441	468	510
Other services, debit	3 200 BA	−2,144	−2,605	−2,391	−2,297	−2,532	−2,692	−3,122	−4,270
Communications	3 245	−99	−101	−100	−79	−105	−91	−91	−89
Construction	3 249	−171	−463	−216	−124	−201	−125	−126	−102
Insurance	3 253	−85	−116	−200	−579	−417	−119	−134	−160
Financial	3 260	−74	−35	−56	−62	−125	−256	−406	−887
Computer and information	3 262	−51	−96	−75	−67	−79	−128	−137	−160
Royalties and licence fees	3 266	−663	−183	−110	−292	−268	−421	−428	−577
Other business services	3 268	−576	−1,168	−1,222	−611	−829	−857	−1,056	−1,384
Personal, cultural, and recreational	3 287	−11	−30	−20	−18	−48	−109	−162	−225
Government, n.i.e.	3 291	−414	−413	−392	−465	−460	−586	−582	−686

Table 2 (Continued). STANDARD PRESENTATION, 2000–2007

(Millions of U.S. dollars)

	Code	2000	2001	2002	2003	2004	2005	2006	2007
C. INCOME	4 300	**−942**	**−667**	**−604**	**−581**	**−645**	**−985**	**−1,722**	**−659**
Total credit	2 300	*143*	*167*	*165*	*254*	*389*	*758*	*1,332*	*3,656*
Total debit	3 300	*−1,085*	*−834*	*−769*	*−835*	*−1,034*	*−1,743*	*−3,054*	*−4,315*
Compensation of employees, credit	2 310	33	56	74	145	218	359	540	2,210
Compensation of employees, debit	3 310	−2	....	−4	−4	−6	−10	−9	−11
Investment income, credit	2 320	110	111	91	109	171	399	792	1,446
Direct investment income	2 330	....	....	....	....	2	5	8	19
Dividends and distributed branch profits	2 332	....	....	....	....	2	4	2	11
Reinvested earnings and undistributed branch profits	2 333	....	....	....	....	....	....	....	....
Income on debt (interest)	2 334	....	....	....	....	....	1	6	8
Portfolio investment income	2 339	3	2	5	....	21	39	198	522
Income on equity	2 340	....	2	2	....	....	....	2	1
Income on bonds and notes	2 350	3	....	3	....	21	39	196	521
Income on money market instruments	2 360	....	....	....	....	....	....	....	....
Other investment income	2 370	107	109	86	109	148	355	586	905
Investment income, debit	3 320	**−1,083**	**−834**	**−765**	**−831**	**−1,028**	**−1,733**	**−3,045**	**−4,304**
Direct investment income	3 330	−43	−79	−105	−90	−180	−268	−996	−1,178
Dividends and distributed branch profits	3 332	....	−79	−103	−62	−141	−197	−856	−1,019
Reinvested earnings and undistributed branch profits	3 333	....	....	−2	−12	−5	−4	−35	−17
Income on debt (interest)	3 334	....	....	....	−16	−34	−67	−105	−142
Portfolio investment income	3 339	−461	−256	−237	−300	−341	−544	−672	−975
Income on equity	3 340	....	−14	−7	−3	−1	−10	−27	−33
Income on bonds and notes	3 350	−461	−242	−230	−297	−340	−534	−645	−942
Income on money market instruments	3 360	....	....	....	....	....	....	....	....
Other investment income	3 370	−579	−499	−423	−441	−507	−921	−1,377	−2,151
D. CURRENT TRANSFERS	4 379	**848**	**1,456**	**1,921**	**2,184**	**2,576**	**2,845**	**3,173**	**3,539**
Credit	2 379	**967**	**1,516**	**1,967**	**2,270**	**2,671**	**3,111**	**3,533**	**4,147**
General government	2 380	414	432	371	464	452	555	537	622
Other sectors	2 390	553	1,084	1,596	1,806	2,219	2,556	2,996	3,525
Workers' remittances	2 391	....	84	133	185	193	236	289	2,292
Other current transfers	2 392	553	1,000	1,463	1,621	2,026	2,320	2,707	1,233
Debit	3 379	**−119**	**−60**	**−46**	**−86**	**−95**	**−266**	**−360**	**−608**
General government	3 380	....	−32	−10	−38	−29	−27	−36	−66
Other sectors	3 390	....	−28	−36	−48	−66	−239	−324	−542
Workers' remittances	3 391	....	....	....	....	....	−2	−2	−7
Other current transfers	3 392	....	−28	−36	−48	−66	−237	−322	−535
CAPITAL AND FINANCIAL ACCOUNT	4 996	**−1,428**	**−1,250**	**−2,285**	**−2,057**	**−7,037**	**−2,664**	**1,523**	**5,724**
CAPITAL ACCOUNT	4 994	**−8**	**3**	**17**	**−17**	**7**	**−65**	**3**	**3**
Total credit	2 994	....	*8*	*28*	*11*	*21*	*14*	*22*	*27*
Total debit	3 994	*−8*	*−5*	*−11*	*−28*	*−14*	*−79*	*−19*	*−24*
Capital transfers, credit	2 400	....	8	23	11	19	14	20	27
General government	2 401	....	....	....	....	....	....	....	....
Debt forgiveness	2 402	....	....	....	....	....	....	....	....
Other capital transfers	2 410	....	....	....	....	....	....	....	....
Other sectors	2 430	....	8	23	11	19	14	20	27
Migrants' transfers	2 431	....	1	2	....	....	....	....	1
Debt forgiveness	2 432	....	....	....	....	....	....	....	....
Other capital transfers	2 440	....	7	21	11	19	14	20	26
Capital transfers, debit	3 400	**−8**	**−5**	**−11**	**−25**	**−14**	**−22**	**−19**	**−24**
General government	3 401	....	....	....	....	....	....	....	....
Debt forgiveness	3 402	....	....	....	....	....	....	....	....
Other capital transfers	3 410	....	....	....	....	....	....	....	....
Other sectors	3 430	−8	−5	−11	−25	−14	−22	−19	−24
Migrants' transfers	3 431	−8	−5	−11	−25	−14	−22	−19	−24
Debt forgiveness	3 432	....	....	....	....	....	....	....	....
Other capital transfers	3 440	....	....	....	....	....	....	....	....
Nonproduced nonfinancial assets, credit	2 480	....	....	5	....	2	....	2	....
Nonproduced nonfinancial assets, debit	3 480	....	....	....	−3	....	−57	....	....

Table 2 (Continued). STANDARD PRESENTATION, 2000–2007

(Millions of U.S. dollars)

	Code	2000	2001	2002	2003	2004	2005	2006	2007
FINANCIAL ACCOUNT	4 995	**−1,420**	**−1,253**	**−2,302**	**−2,040**	**−7,044**	**−2,599**	**1,520**	**5,721**
A. DIRECT INVESTMENT	4 500	**594**	**769**	**698**	**1,411**	**1,711**	**7,533**	**5,737**	**9,218**
Direct investment abroad	4 505	−1	−23	5	−13	−4	−275	133	−673
Equity capital	4 510	....	−23	5	−13	−4	−275	8	−975
Claims on affiliated enterprises	4 515	....	....	....	....	....	....	....	−975
Liabilities to affiliated enterprises	4 520	....	....	....	....	....	....	....	....
Reinvested earnings	4 525	....	....	....	....	....	....	....	....
Other capital	4 530	....	....	....	....	....	....	125	302
Claims on affiliated enterprises	4 535	....	....	....	....	....	....	125	....
Liabilities to affiliated enterprises	4 540	....	....	....	....	....	....	....	302
Direct investment in Ukraine	4 555	**595**	**792**	**693**	**1,424**	**1,715**	**7,808**	**5,604**	**9,891**
Equity capital	4 560	....	....	691	1,267	1,490	7,489	4,504	8,364
Claims on direct investors	4 565	....	....	....	....	....	....	....	....
Liabilities to direct investors	4 570	....	....	....	....	....	....	....	8,364
Reinvested earnings	4 575	....	....	2	12	6	4	35	17
Other capital	4 580	....	....	....	145	219	315	1,065	1,510
Claims on direct investors	4 585	....	....	....	....	....	....	....	....
Liabilities to direct investors	4 590	....	....	....	....	219	315	1,065	1,510
B. PORTFOLIO INVESTMENT	4 600	**138**	**−45**	**337**	**867**	**2,067**	**2,757**	**3,583**	**5,753**
Assets	4 602	**−4**	**1**	**2**	**1**	**−6**	**....**	**−3**	**−29**
Equity securities	4 610	−2	−1	....	−4	−6	....	−2	−21
Monetary authorities	4 611	....	....	....	....	....	....	....	....
General government	4 612	....	....	....	−4	−3	....	....	....
Banks	4 613	−2	−1	....	....	−1	....	....	....
Other sectors	4 614	....	....	....	....	−2	....	−2	−21
Debt securities	4 619	−2	2	2	5	....	....	−1	−8
Bonds and notes	4 620	−2	2	2	5	....	....	−1	−8
Monetary authorities	4 621	....	....	....	....	....	....	....	....
General government	4 622	....	....	....	....	....	....	....	....
Banks	4 623	−2	3	....	5	1	....	−1	−8
Other sectors	4 624	....	−1	....	....	−1	....	....	....
Money market instruments	4 630	....	....	....	....	....	....	....	....
Monetary authorities	4 631	....	....	....	....	....	....	....	....
General government	4 632	....	....	....	....	....	....	....	....
Banks	4 633	....	....	....	....	....	....	....	....
Other sectors	4 634	....	....	....	....	....	....	....	....
Liabilities	4 652	**142**	**−46**	**335**	**866**	**2,073**	**2,757**	**3,586**	**5,782**
Equity securities	4 660	146	87	95	84	−61	82	322	715
Banks	4 663	....	....	....	....	....	....	....	....
Other sectors	4 664	146	87	95	84	−61	82	322	715
Debt securities	4 669	−4	−133	240	782	2,134	2,675	3,264	5,067
Bonds and notes	4 670	−4	−133	240	785	2,134	2,663	3,190	5,143
Monetary authorities	4 671	....	....	−8	−4	−5	....	....	....
General government	4 672	−4	−133	128	610	1,211	1,320	761	1,330
Banks	4 673	....	....	....	103	253	873	1,853	3,695
Other sectors	4 674	....	....	120	76	675	470	576	118
Money market instruments	4 680	....	....	....	−3	....	12	74	−76
Monetary authorities	4 681	....	....	....	....	....	....	....	....
General government	4 682	....	....	....	....	....	....	....	....
Banks	4 683	....	....	....	−3	....	12	74	−76
Other sectors	4 684	....	....	....	....	....	....	....	....
C. FINANCIAL DERIVATIVES	4 910	**....**	**....**	**....**	**....**	**....**	**....**	**....**	**....**
Monetary authorities	4 911	....	....	....	....	....	....	....	....
General government	4 912	....	....	....	....	....	....	....	....
Banks	4 913	....	....	....	....	....	....	....	....
Other sectors	4 914	....	....	....	....	....	....	....	....
Assets	4 900	**....**	**....**	**....**	**....**	**....**	**....**	**....**	**....**
Monetary authorities	4 901	....	....	....	....	....	....	....	....
General government	4 902	....	....	....	....	....	....	....	....
Banks	4 903	....	....	....	....	....	....	....	....
Other sectors	4 904	....	....	....	....	....	....	....	....
Liabilities	4 905	**....**	**....**	**....**	**....**	**....**	**....**	**....**	**....**
Monetary authorities	4 906	....	....	....	....	....	....	....	....
General government	4 907	....	....	....	....	....	....	....	....
Banks	4 908	....	....	....	....	....	....	....	....
Other sectors	4 909	....	....	....	....	....	....	....	....

Table 2 (Concluded). STANDARD PRESENTATION, 2000–2007

(Millions of U.S. dollars)

	Code	2000	2001	2002	2003	2004	2005	2006	2007
D. OTHER INVESTMENT	4 700	**−1,751**	**−368**	**−2,289**	**−2,273**	**−8,597**	**−2,463**	**−5,801**	**−271**
Assets	4 703	**−883**	**−1,905**	**−2,840**	**−2,860**	**−12,495**	**−7,913**	**−15,580**	**−22,838**
Trade credits	4 706	....	....	−90	−187	−792	−218	−1,317	−1,446
General government	4 707	....	....	....	....	....	....	....	....
of which: Short-term	4 709	....	....	....	....	....	....	....	....
Other sectors	4 710	....	....	−90	−187	−792	−218	−1,317	−1,446
of which: Short-term	4 712	....	....	*−90*	*−187*	*−792*	*−218*	*−1,319*	*−1,440*
Loans	4 714	12	−4	13	−10	−182	−200	−221	−612
Monetary authorities	4 715	....	....	....	....	....	....	....	....
of which: Short-term	4 718	....	....	....	....	....	....	....	....
General government	4 719	....	....	....	....	....	....	....	....
of which: Short-term	4 721	....	....	....	....	....	....	....	....
Banks	4 722	12	−4	13	−10	−182	−200	−221	−612
of which: Short-term	4 724	*9*	*−11*	*3*	*−12*	*−181*	*−146*	*−143*	*−427*
Other sectors	4 725	....	....	....	....	....	....	....	....
of which: Short-term	4 727	....	....	....	....	....	....	....	....
Currency and deposits	4 730	−1,546	−559	−808	−658	−4,521	−3,925	−9,559	−15,385
Monetary authorities	4 731	−15	1	−23	−30	−266	267	−111	52
General government	4 732	....	....	....	....	....	....	....	....
Banks	4 733	−76	141	−99	−445	−724	−401	−877	−1,828
Other sectors	4 734	−1,455	−701	−686	−183	−3,531	−3,791	−8,571	−13,609
Other assets	4 736	651	−1,342	−1,955	−2,005	−7,000	−3,570	−4,483	−5,395
Monetary authorities	4 737	....	....	....	....	....	....	....	....
of which: Short-term	4 739	....	....	....	....	....	....	....	....
General government	4 740	1,002	....	....	....	....	−5	−3	....
of which: Short-term	4 742	*1,002*	....	....	....	....	....	....	....
Banks	4 743	....	....	....	....	....	....	....	....
of which: Short-term	4 745	....	....	....	....	....	....	....	....
Other sectors	4 746	−351	−1,342	−1,955	−2,005	−7,000	−3,565	−4,480	−5,395
of which: Short-term	4 748	*−351*	*−1,342*	*−1,955*	*−2,005*	*−7,000*	*−3,565*	*−4,480*	*−5,395*
Liabilities	4 753	**−868**	**1,537**	**551**	**587**	**3,898**	**5,450**	**9,779**	**22,567**
Trade credits	4 756	....	....	38	69	2,124	−636	1,228	3,288
General government	4 757	....	....	....	....	....	....	....	....
of which: Short-term	4 759	....	....	....	....	....	....	....	....
Other sectors	4 760	....	....	38	69	2,124	−636	1,228	3,288
of which: Short-term	4 762	....	....	*38*	*69*	*2,124*	*−636*	*1,146*	*1,739*
Loans	4 764	−1,672	392	728	1,073	2,959	4,588	8,911	17,515
Monetary authorities	4 765	−603	−86	−185	−187	−291	−317	−426	−447
of which: Use of Fund credit and loans from the Fund	4 766	*−603*	*−86*	*−181*	*−203*	*−298*	*−299*	*−410*	*−427*
of which: Short-term	4 768	....	....	....	....	....	*−5*	....	....
General government	4 769	−1,356	16	−30	−22	922	93	−152	502
of which: Short-term	4 771	....	....	....	....	....	....	....	....
Banks	4 772	18	148	106	502	251	1,781	5,690	11,328
of which: Short-term	4 774	*18*	*148*	*106*	*319*	*128*	*1,029*	*3,464*	*4,497*
Other sectors	4 775	269	314	837	780	2,077	3,031	3,799	6,132
of which: Short-term	4 777	*−1*	*82*	*346*	*182*	*241*	*393*	*218*	*370*
Currency and deposits	4 780	95	32	−30	277	328	882	16	1,683
Monetary authorities	4 781	....	....	....	....	....	....	....	....
General government	4 782	....	....	....	....	....	....	....	....
Banks	4 783	95	32	−30	277	328	882	16	1,683
Other sectors	4 784	....	....	....	....	....	....	....	....
Other liabilities	4 786	709	1,113	−185	−832	−1,513	616	−376	81
Monetary authorities	4 787	....	....	....	....	....	....	....	....
of which: Short-term	4 789	....	....	....	....	....	....	....	....
General government	4 790	330	149	−356	−282	....	....	....	....
of which: Short-term	4 792	*330*	*149*	*−356*	*−282*	....	....	....	....
Banks	4 793	....	....	....	....	....	....	....	....
of which: Short-term	4 795	....	....	....	....	....	....	....	....
Other sectors	4 796	379	964	171	−550	−1,513	616	−376	81
of which: Short-term	4 798	*379*	*964*	*171*	*−550*	*−1,513*	*616*	*−376*	*81*
E. RESERVE ASSETS	4 802	**−401**	**−1,609**	**−1,047**	**−2,045**	**−2,226**	**−10,425**	**−1,999**	**−8,979**
Monetary gold	4 812	−87	−5	1	3	−5	−10	−19	−20
Special drawing rights	4 811	−187	−12	231	8	20	....	....	−1
Reserve position in the Fund	4 810	....	....	....	....	....	....	....	....
Foreign exchange	4 803	−127	−1,592	−1,279	−2,056	−2,241	−10,415	−1,980	−8,958
Other claims	4 813	....	....	....	....	....	....	....	....
NET ERRORS AND OMISSIONS	4 998	**−53**	**−152**	**−889**	**−834**	**128**	**133**	**94**	**−452**

Table 3. INTERNATIONAL INVESTMENT POSITION (End-period stocks), 2000–2007

(Millions of U.S. dollars)

	Code	2000	2001	2002	2003	2004	2005	2006	2007
ASSETS	8 995 C.	. . . .	**13,728**	**15,884**	**19,705**	**28,164**	**42,712**	**57,023**	**90,188**
Direct investment abroad	8 505 ..	. . . .	**156**	**144**	**166**	**198**	**468**	**344**	**6,077**
Equity capital and reinvested earnings	8 506 ..	. . . .	156	144	166	198	219	221	6,256
Claims on affiliated enterprises	8 507 ..	. . . .	156	144	166	198	219	221	6,256
Liabilities to affiliated enterprises	8 508 ..	. . . .	. . . .	. . . .	. . . .	. . . .	. . . .	. . . .	. . . .
Other capital	8 530 ..	. . . .	. . . .	. . . .	. . . .	. . . .	249	123	−179
Claims on affiliated enterprises	8 535 ..	. . . .	. . . .	. . . .	. . . .	. . . .	249	123	−179
Liabilities to affiliated enterprises	8 540 ..	. . . .	. . . .	. . . .	. . . .	. . . .	. . . .	. . . .	. . . .
Portfolio investment	8 602 ..	. . . .	**30**	**28**	**26**	**36**	**56**	**63**	**91**
Equity securities	8 610 ..	. . . .	20	19	23	33	50	56	76
Monetary authorities	8 611 ..	. . . .	. . . .	. . . .	. . . .	. . . .	. . . .	. . . .	. . . .
General government	8 612 ..	. . . .	. . . .	. . . .	4	. . . .	. . . .	. . . .	. . . .
Banks	8 613 ..	. . . .	2	1	1	2	1	1	1
Other sectors	8 614 ..	. . . .	18	18	18	31	49	55	75
Debt securities	8 619 ..	. . . .	10	9	3	3	6	7	15
Bonds and notes	8 620 ..	. . . .	10	9	3	3	6	7	15
Monetary authorities	8 621 ..	. . . .	. . . .	. . . .	. . . .	. . . .	. . . .	. . . .	. . . .
General government	8 622 ..	. . . .	. . . .	. . . .	. . . .	. . . .	. . . .	. . . .	. . . .
Banks	8 623 ..	. . . .	7	7	2	1	5	6	14
Other sectors	8 624 ..	. . . .	3	2	1	2	1	1	1
Money market instruments	8 630 ..	. . . .	. . . .	. . . .	. . . .	. . . .	. . . .	. . . .	. . . .
Monetary authorities	8 631 ..	. . . .	. . . .	. . . .	. . . .	. . . .	. . . .	. . . .	. . . .
General government	8 632 ..	. . . .	. . . .	. . . .	. . . .	. . . .	. . . .	. . . .	. . . .
Banks	8 633 ..	. . . .	. . . .	. . . .	. . . .	. . . .	. . . .	. . . .	. . . .
Other sectors	8 634 ..	. . . .	. . . .	. . . .	. . . .	. . . .	. . . .	. . . .	. . . .
Financial derivatives	8 900 ..	. . . .	. . . .	. . . .	. . . .	. . . .	. . . .	. . . .	. . . .
Monetary authorities	8 901 ..	. . . .	. . . .	. . . .	. . . .	. . . .	. . . .	. . . .	. . . .
General government	8 902 ..	. . . .	. . . .	. . . .	. . . .	. . . .	. . . .	. . . .	. . . .
Banks	8 903 ..	. . . .	. . . .	. . . .	. . . .	. . . .	. . . .	. . . .	. . . .
Other sectors	8 904 ..	. . . .	. . . .	. . . .	. . . .	. . . .	. . . .	. . . .	. . . .
Other investment	8 703 ..	. . . .	**10,453**	**11,295**	**12,576**	**18,405**	**22,797**	**34,360**	**51,557**
Trade credits	8 706 ..	. . . .	1,613	1,694	1,937	2,780	3,038	4,433	6,013
General government	8 707 ..	. . . .	. . . .	. . . .	. . . .	. . . .	. . . .	. . . .	. . . .
of which: Short-term	8 709 ..	. . . .	. . . .	. . . .	. . . .	. . . .	. . . .	. . . .	. . . .
Other sectors	8 710 ..	. . . .	1,613	1,694	1,937	2,780	3,038	4,433	6,013
of which: Short-term	8 712 ..	. . . .	*1,613*	*1,694*	*1,937*	*2,780*	*3,030*	*4,427*	*6,001*
Loans	8 714 ..	. . . .	33	21	34	221	406	680	1,328
Monetary authorities	8 715 ..	. . . .	. . . .	. . . .	. . . .	. . . .	. . . .	. . . .	. . . .
of which: Short-term	8 718 ..	. . . .	. . . .	. . . .	. . . .	. . . .	. . . .	. . . .	. . . .
General government	8 719 ..	. . . .	. . . .	. . . .	. . . .	. . . .	. . . .	. . . .	. . . .
of which: Short-term	8 721 ..	. . . .	. . . .	. . . .	. . . .	. . . .	. . . .	. . . .	. . . .
Banks	8 722 ..	. . . .	33	21	34	221	406	680	1,328
of which: Short-term	8 724 ..	. . . .	*18*	*16*	*31*	*217*	*346*	*515*	*976*
Other sectors	8 725 ..	. . . .	. . . .	. . . .	. . . .	. . . .	. . . .	. . . .	. . . .
of which: Short-term	8 727 ..	. . . .	. . . .	. . . .	. . . .	. . . .	. . . .	. . . .	. . . .
Currency and deposits	8 730 ..	. . . .	8,379	9,255	10,053	14,659	18,501	28,259	43,113
Monetary authorities	8 731 ..	. . . .	157	197	261	538	300	444	505
General government	8 732 ..	. . . .	. . . .	. . . .	. . . .	. . . .	. . . .	. . . .	. . . .
Banks	8 733 ..	. . . .	698	819	1,321	2,082	2,417	3,387	5,399
Other sectors	8 734 ..	. . . .	7,524	8,239	8,471	12,039	15,784	24,428	37,209
Other assets	8 736 ..	. . . .	428	325	552	745	852	988	1,103
Monetary authorities	8 737 ..	. . . .	. . . .	. . . .	. . . .	37	34	36	37
of which: Short-term	8 739 ..	. . . .	. . . .	. . . .	. . . .	. . . .	. . . .	. . . .	. . . .
General government	8 740 ..	. . . .	. . . .	. . . .	. . . .	90	99	104	106
of which: Short-term	8 742 ..	. . . .	. . . .	. . . .	. . . .	. . . .	. . . .	. . . .	. . . .
Banks	8 743 ..	. . . .	. . . .	. . . .	. . . .	. . . .	. . . .	. . . .	. . . .
of which: Short-term	8 745 ..	. . . .	. . . .	. . . .	. . . .	. . . .	. . . .	. . . .	. . . .
Other sectors	8 746 ..	. . . .	428	325	552	618	719	848	960
of which: Short-term	8 748 ..	. . . .	*428*	*325*	*552*	*618*	*719*	*848*	*960*
Reserve assets	8 802 ..	. . . .	**3,089**	**4,417**	**6,937**	**9,525**	**19,391**	**22,256**	**32,463**
Monetary gold	8 812 ..	. . . .	134	175	206	222	276	358	490
Special drawing rights	8 811 ..	249	251	28	21	1	1	1	3
Reserve position in the Fund	8 810 ..	. . . .	. . . .	. . . .	. . . .	. . . .	. . . .	. . . .	. . . .
Foreign exchange	8 803 ..	. . . .	2,704	4,214	6,710	9,302	19,114	21,897	31,970
Other claims	8 813 ..	. . . .	. . . .	. . . .	. . . .	. . . .	. . . .	. . . .	. . . .

Table 3 (Concluded). INTERNATIONAL INVESTMENT POSITION (End-period stocks), 2000–2007

(Millions of U.S. dollars)

	Code	2000	2001	2002	2003	2004	2005	2006	2007
LIABILITIES	8 995 D.	. . . .	**25,968**	**28,003**	**31,427**	**40,283**	**56,870**	**76,942**	**121,585**
Direct investment in Ukraine	8 555 ..	. . . .	**4,801**	**5,924**	**7,566**	**9,606**	**17,209**	**23,125**	**38,059**
Equity capital and reinvested earnings	8 556 ..	. . . .	4,801	5,648	7,152	9,047	16,375	21,182	34,980
Claims on direct investors	8 557 ..	. . . .	. . . .	. . . .	. . . .	. . . .	. . . .	. . . .	. . . .
Liabilities to direct investors	8 558 ..	. . . .	4,801	5,648	7,152	9,047	16,375	21,182	34,980
Other capital	8 580 ..	. . . .	. . . .	276	414	559	834	1,943	3,079
Claims on direct investors	8 585 ..	. . . .	. . . .	. . . .	. . . .	. . . .	. . . .	. . . .	. . . .
Liabilities to direct investors	8 590 ..	. . . .	. . . .	276	414	559	834	1,943	3,079
Portfolio investment	8 652 ..	. . . .	**2,980**	**3,293**	**4,065**	**6,391**	**9,011**	**12,861**	**18,596**
Equity securities	8 660 ..	. . . .	763	668	464	589	876	1,248	2,083
Banks	8 663 ..	. . . .	. . . .	. . . .	. . . .	. . . .	. . . .	. . . .	. . . .
Other sectors	8 664 ..	. . . .	763	668	464	589	876	1,248	2,083
Debt securities	8 669 ..	. . . .	2,217	2,625	3,601	5,802	8,135	11,613	16,513
Bonds and notes	8 670 ..	. . . .	2,217	2,625	3,590	5,791	8,111	11,515	16,492
Monetary authorities	8 671 ..	. . . .	21	14	10	5	. . . .	. . . .	. . . .
General government	8 672 ..	. . . .	2,196	2,491	3,280	4,548	5,604	6,356	7,522
Banks	8 673 ..	. . . .	. . . .	. . . .	103	356	1,232	3,304	6,999
Other sectors	8 674 ..	. . . .	. . . .	120	197	882	1,275	1,855	1,971
Money market instruments	8 680 ..	. . . .	. . . .	. . . .	11	11	24	98	21
Monetary authorities	8 681 ..	. . . .	. . . .	. . . .	. . . .	. . . .	. . . .	. . . .	. . . .
General government	8 682 ..	. . . .	. . . .	. . . .	. . . .	. . . .	. . . .	. . . .	. . . .
Banks	8 683 ..	. . . .	. . . .	. . . .	11	11	24	98	21
Other sectors	8 684 ..	. . . .	. . . .	. . . .	. . . .	. . . .	. . . .	. . . .	. . . .
Financial derivatives	8 905 ..	. . . .	. . . .	. . . .	. . . .	. . . .	. . . .	. . . .	. . . .
Monetary authorities	8 906 ..	. . . .	. . . .	. . . .	. . . .	. . . .	. . . .	. . . .	. . . .
General government	8 907 ..	. . . .	. . . .	. . . .	. . . .	. . . .	. . . .	. . . .	. . . .
Banks	8 908 ..	. . . .	. . . .	. . . .	. . . .	. . . .	. . . .	. . . .	. . . .
Other sectors	8 909 ..	. . . .	. . . .	. . . .	. . . .	. . . .	. . . .	. . . .	. . . .
Other investment	8 753 ..	. . . .	**18,187**	**18,786**	**19,796**	**24,286**	**30,650**	**40,956**	**64,930**
Trade credits	8 756 ..	. . . .	5,059	5,068	5,290	7,565	8,262	9,668	13,243
General government	8 757 ..	. . . .	. . . .	. . . .	. . . .	. . . .	. . . .	. . . .	. . . .
of which: Short-term	8 759 ..	. . . .	. . . .	. . . .	. . . .	. . . .	. . . .	. . . .	. . . .
Other sectors	8 760 ..	. . . .	5,059	5,068	5,290	7,565	8,262	9,668	13,243
of which: Short-term	8 762 ..	. . . .	*5,059*	*5,068*	*5,290*	*7,565*	*5,976*	*7,277*	*9,247*
Loans	8 764 ..	. . . .	9,367	10,096	11,692	15,103	19,373	28,763	47,489
Monetary authorities	8 765 ..	. . . .	1,972	1,933	1,909	1,685	1,254	880	462
of which: Use of Fund credit and loans from the Fund	8 766 ..	*2,073*	*1,911*	*1,876*	*1,836*	*1,605*	*1,188*	*830*	*431*
of which: Short-term	8 768 ..	. . . .	. . . .	. . . .	. . . .	. . . .	. . . .	. . . .	. . . .
General government	8 769 ..	. . . .	5,360	5,477	5,647	6,656	6,610	6,538	7,151
of which: Short-term	8 771 ..	. . . .	. . . .	. . . .	. . . .	. . . .	. . . .	. . . .	. . . .
Banks	8 772 ..	. . . .	275	612	1,095	1,424	3,091	8,896	20,448
of which: Short-term	8 774 ..	. . . .	*275*	*387*	*720*	*858*	*1,861*	*5,381*	*9,815*
Other sectors	8 775 ..	. . . .	1,760	2,074	3,041	5,338	8,418	12,449	19,428
of which: Short-term	8 777 ..	. . . .	*149*	*401*	*363*	*471*	*634*	*736*	*838*
Currency and deposits	8 780 ..	. . . .	264	247	537	871	1,765	1,791	3,503
Monetary authorities	8 781 ..	. . . .	. . . .	. . . .	. . . .	. . . .	. . . .	. . . .	. . . .
General government	8 782 ..	. . . .	. . . .	. . . .	. . . .	. . . .	. . . .	. . . .	. . . .
Banks	8 783 ..	. . . .	264	247	537	871	1,765	1,791	3,503
Other sectors	8 784 ..	. . . .	. . . .	. . . .	. . . .	. . . .	. . . .	. . . .	. . . .
Other liabilities	8 786 ..	. . . .	3,497	3,375	2,277	747	1,250	734	695
Monetary authorities	8 787 ..	. . . .	. . . .	. . . .	. . . .	. . . .	. . . .	. . . .	. . . .
of which: Short-term	8 789 ..	. . . .	. . . .	. . . .	. . . .	. . . .	. . . .	. . . .	. . . .
General government	8 790 ..	. . . .	626	285	2	. . . .	. . . .	. . . .	. . . .
of which: Short-term	8 792 ..	. . . .	*66*	*1*	*2*	. . . .	. . . .	. . . .	. . . .
Banks	8 793 ..	. . . .	. . . .	. . . .	. . . .	. . . .	. . . .	. . . .	. . . .
of which: Short-term	8 795 ..	. . . .	. . . .	. . . .	. . . .	. . . .	. . . .	. . . .	. . . .
Other sectors	8 796 ..	. . . .	2,871	3,090	2,275	747	1,250	734	695
of which: Short-term	8 798 ..	. . . .	*2,595*	*2,821*	*2,052*	*747*	*1,250*	*734*	*695*
NET INTERNATIONAL INVESTMENT POSITION	8 995 ..	. . . .	**−12,240**	**−12,119**	**−11,722**	**−12,119**	**−14,158**	**−19,919**	**−31,397**
Conversion rates: hryvnias per U.S. dollar (end of period)	0 102 ..	5.4345	5.2985	5.3324	5.3315	5.3054	5.0500	5.0500	5.0500

Table 1. ANALYTIC PRESENTATION, 2000–2007

(Billions of U.S. dollars)

	Code	2000	2001	2002	2003	2004	2005	2006	2007
A. Current Account[1]	4 993 Z.	**−37.36**	**−31.42**	**−24.61**	**−24.47**	**−35.18**	**−55.00**	**−93.62**	**−119.16**
Goods: exports f.o.b.	2 100 ..	284.38	272.28	279.87	307.80	349.66	384.32	447.58	442.15
Goods: imports f.o.b.	3 100 ..	−334.23	−331.57	−351.64	−387.25	−461.13	−509.39	−590.47	−621.41
Balance on Goods	4 100 ..	*−49.85*	*−59.29*	*−71.77*	*−79.45*	*−111.48*	*−125.08*	*−142.89*	*−179.26*
Services: credit	2 200 ..	120.40	120.98	135.31	158.61	197.43	209.43	234.45	278.67
Services: debit	3 200 ..	−99.75	−100.19	−110.02	−127.25	−149.92	−164.58	−177.26	−201.95
Balance on Goods and Services	4 991 ..	*−29.20*	*−38.50*	*−46.48*	*−48.09*	*−63.96*	*−80.23*	*−85.70*	*−102.54*
Income: credit	2 300 ..	204.24	202.93	187.29	205.80	260.54	340.53	434.21	571.18
Income: debit	3 300 ..	−197.29	−186.11	−151.84	−165.70	−211.71	−293.37	−420.18	−560.18
Balance on Goods, Services, and Income	4 992 ..	*−22.25*	*−21.69*	*−11.03*	*−7.99*	*−15.13*	*−33.07*	*−71.66*	*−91.54*
Current transfers: credit	2 379 Z.	16.03	20.79	18.41	19.95	23.66	31.38	33.77	31.33
Current transfers: debit	3 379 ..	−31.14	−30.52	−31.99	−36.43	−43.72	−53.31	−55.72	−58.95
B. Capital Account[1]	4 994 Z.	**2.57**	**1.89**	**1.42**	**2.42**	**3.78**	**2.80**	**1.58**	**5.09**
Capital account: credit	2 994 Z.	3.94	4.79	3.51	4.59	6.60	7.85	7.18	8.95
Capital account: debit	3 994 ..	−1.37	−2.90	−2.09	−2.17	−2.82	−5.05	−5.60	−3.85
Total, Groups A Plus B	4 981 ..	*−34.79*	*−29.53*	*−23.19*	*−22.04*	*−31.41*	*−52.20*	*−92.03*	*−114.07*
C. Financial Account[1]	4 995 W.	**24.39**	**20.63**	**12.05**	**31.75**	**10.44**	**73.80**	**82.11**	**120.43**
Direct investment abroad	4 505 ..	−246.26	−61.82	−50.33	−65.64	−98.19	−91.71	−89.53	−269.10
Direct investment in United Kingdom	4 555 Z.	122.16	53.84	25.53	27.61	77.95	195.55	146.12	224.95
Portfolio investment assets	4 602 ..	−97.19	−124.73	1.22	−58.42	−259.16	−291.52	−366.89	−255.57
Equity securities	4 610 ..	−28.46	−63.63	7.41	−29.79	−102.96	−113.67	−35.01	−79.18
Debt securities	4 619 ..	−68.73	−61.10	−6.19	−28.63	−156.20	−177.86	−331.88	−176.39
Portfolio investment liabilities	4 652 Z.	255.65	69.57	76.24	155.62	159.88	240.34	292.41	420.86
Equity securities	4 660 ..	179.17	33.11	4.22	15.56	−15.22	15.21	−9.09	39.36
Debt securities	4 669 Z.	76.48	36.47	72.02	140.05	175.10	225.13	301.50	381.50
Financial derivatives	4 910 ..	2.26	12.18	1.35	−8.49	−14.27	16.53	14.48	−35.00
Financial derivatives assets	4 900 ..	. . . .	. . . .	. . . .	. . . .	. . . .	. . . .	. . . .	. . . .
Financial derivatives liabilities	4 905 ..	2.26	12.18	1.35	−8.49	−14.27	16.53	14.48	−35.00
Other investment assets	4 703 ..	−426.81	−255.47	−151.03	−415.62	−596.92	−931.59	−776.70	−1,519.95
Monetary authorities	4 701 ..	. . . .	. . . .	. . . .	. . . .	. . . .	. . . .	. . . .	. . . .
General government	4 704 ..	−.40	.01	−1.05	−.31	−.58	−1.23	−1.96	−1.70
Banks	4 705 ..	−289.04	−124.85	−111.14	−258.76	−400.47	−541.14	−533.13	−1,197.70
Other sectors	4 728 ..	−137.37	−130.63	−38.84	−156.54	−195.88	−389.22	−241.60	−320.55
Other investment liabilities	4 753 W.	414.59	327.05	109.07	396.69	741.16	936.20	862.22	1,554.23
Monetary authorities	4 753 WA	. . . .	. . . .	. . . .	. . . .	. . . .	. . . .	. . . .	. . . .
General government	4 753 ZB	. . . .	.40	−1.01	.83	−.80	.26	1.53	−.08
Banks	4 753 ZC	308.95	182.41	141.42	276.67	566.53	517.36	598.42	1,371.34
Other sectors	4 753 ZD	105.63	144.24	−31.35	119.20	175.42	418.58	262.27	182.97
Total, Groups A Through C	4 983 ..	*−10.40*	*−8.90*	*−11.13*	*9.71*	*−20.97*	*21.61*	*−9.92*	*6.36*
D. Net Errors and Omissions	4 998 ..	**15.70**	**4.44**	**10.50**	**−12.30**	**21.37**	**−19.88**	**8.62**	**−3.79**
Total, Groups A Through D	4 984 ..	*5.30*	*−4.46*	*−.63*	*−2.59*	*.41*	*1.73*	*−1.30*	*2.57*
E. Reserves and Related Items	4 802 A.	**−5.30**	**4.46**	**.63**	**2.59**	**−.41**	**−1.73**	**1.30**	**−2.57**
Reserve assets	4 802 ..	−5.30	4.46	.63	2.59	−.41	−1.73	1.30	−2.57
Use of Fund credit and loans	4 766 ..	. . . .	. . . .	. . . .	. . . .	. . . .	. . . .	. . . .	. . . .
Exceptional financing	4 920 ..	. . . .	. . . .	. . . .	. . . .	. . . .	. . . .	. . . .	. . . .
Conversion rates: pound sterling per U.S. dollar	0 101 ..	**.66093**	**.69466**	**.66722**	**.61247**	**.54618**	**.55000**	**.54349**	**.49977**

[1] Excludes components that have been classified in the categories of Group E.

Table 2. STANDARD PRESENTATION, 2000–2007

(Billions of U.S. dollars)

	Code	2000	2001	2002	2003	2004	2005	2006	2007
CURRENT ACCOUNT	4 993 ..	**−37.36**	**−31.42**	**−24.61**	**−24.47**	**−35.18**	**−55.00**	**−93.62**	**−119.16**
A. GOODS	4 100 ..	**−49.85**	**−59.29**	**−71.77**	**−79.45**	**−111.48**	**−125.08**	**−142.89**	**−179.26**
Credit	2 100 ..	**284.38**	**272.28**	**279.87**	**307.80**	**349.66**	**384.32**	**447.58**	**442.15**
General merchandise: exports f.o.b.	2 110 ..	284.38	272.28	279.87	307.80	349.66	384.32	447.58	442.15
Goods for processing: exports f.o.b.	2 150 ..	....	....	....	....	....	....	....	....
Repairs on goods	2 160 ..	....	....	....	....	....	....	....	....
Goods procured in ports by carriers	2 170 ..	....	....	....	....	....	....	....	....
Nonmonetary gold	2 180 ..	....	....	....	....	....	....	....	....
Debit	3 100 ..	**−334.23**	**−331.57**	**−351.64**	**−387.25**	**−461.13**	**−509.39**	**−590.47**	**−621.41**
General merchandise: imports f.o.b.	3 110 ..	−334.23	−331.57	−351.64	−387.25	−461.13	−509.39	−590.47	−621.41
Goods for processing: imports f.o.b.	3 150 ..	....	....	....	....	....	....	....	....
Repairs on goods	3 160 ..	....	....	....	....	....	....	....	....
Goods procured in ports by carriers	3 170 ..	....	....	....	....	....	....	....	....
Nonmonetary gold	3 180 ..	....	....	....	....	....	....	....	....
B. SERVICES	4 200 ..	**20.65**	**20.78**	**25.29**	**31.36**	**47.51**	**44.85**	**57.19**	**76.72**
Total credit	2 200 ..	*120.40*	*120.98*	*135.31*	*158.61*	*197.43*	*209.43*	*234.45*	*278.67*
Total debit	3 200 ..	*−99.75*	*−100.19*	*−110.02*	*−127.25*	*−149.92*	*−164.58*	*−177.26*	*−201.95*
Transportation services, credit	2 205 ..	**19.15**	**18.37**	**18.84**	**22.28**	**29.97**	**33.01**	**30.05**	**32.58**
Passenger	2 850 ..	*8.21*	*7.27*	*7.27*	*8.07*	*8.96*	*9.00*	*9.00*	*9.42*
Freight	2 851 ..	*5.90*	*6.05*	*6.69*	*8.81*	*14.84*	*17.67*	*13.49*	*14.40*
Other	2 852 ..	*5.04*	*5.05*	*4.89*	*5.39*	*6.17*	*6.34*	*7.56*	*8.76*
Sea transport, passenger	2 207 ..	.96	.70	.88	1.62	1.61	1.36	.88	.95
Sea transport, freight	2 208 ..	4.01	4.37	4.70	6.39	11.75	14.57	10.18	11.22
Sea transport, other	2 209 ..	1.57	1.56	1.51	1.55	1.47	1.46	1.73	1.79
Air transport, passenger	2 211 ..	7.08	6.41	6.25	6.30	7.15	7.40	7.86	8.13
Air transport, freight	2 212 ..	.65	.53	.53	.60	.72	.72	.72	.66
Air transport, other	2 213 ..	3.47	3.49	3.37	3.84	4.70	4.88	5.83	6.97
Other transport, passenger	2 215 ..	.16	.16	.14	.15	.20	.24	.25	.35
Other transport, freight	2 216 ..	1.24	1.15	1.46	1.82	2.37	2.38	2.59	2.51
Other transport, other	2 217 ..	....	....	....	....	....	....	....	....
Transportation services, debit	3 205 ..	**−24.13**	**−23.44**	**−25.42**	**−28.47**	**−34.19**	**−36.95**	**−35.91**	**−37.64**
Passenger	3 850 ..	*−8.75*	*−8.48*	*−9.38*	*−10.77*	*−13.02*	*−14.14*	*−15.03*	*−16.04*
Freight	3 851 ..	*−7.76*	*−8.12*	*−8.93*	*−10.34*	*−12.48*	*−12.87*	*−12.88*	*−13.90*
Other	3 852 ..	*−7.62*	*−6.84*	*−7.11*	*−7.36*	*−8.69*	*−9.95*	*−8.00*	*−7.70*
Sea transport, passenger	3 207 ..	−.65	−.67	−.76	−.80	−.92	−.87	−1.06	−1.33
Sea transport, freight	3 208 ..	−5.00	−5.11	−5.41	−6.50	−8.19	−8.39	−8.37	−8.78
Sea transport, other	3 209 ..	−1.65	−1.85	−2.43	−2.65	−3.76	−4.87	−2.48	−1.94
Air transport, passenger	3 211 ..	−7.84	−7.56	−8.36	−9.73	−11.80	−12.96	−13.63	−14.33
Air transport, freight	3 212 ..	−1.11	−1.18	−1.23	−1.26	−1.25	−1.25	−1.23	−1.30
Air transport, other	3 213 ..	−5.97	−4.99	−4.68	−4.70	−4.93	−5.08	−5.51	−5.76
Other transport, passenger	3 215 ..	−.25	−.24	−.26	−.25	−.31	−.31	−.35	−.39
Other transport, freight	3 216 ..	−1.65	−1.82	−2.29	−2.58	−3.04	−3.22	−3.28	−3.82
Other transport, other	3 217 ..	....	....	....	....	....	....	....	....
Travel, credit	2 236 ..	**21.77**	**18.86**	**20.55**	**22.67**	**28.20**	**30.57**	**33.89**	**37.69**
Business travel	2 237 ..	6.39	5.44	5.77	5.98	7.21	7.88	9.28	9.88
Personal travel	2 240 ..	15.38	13.43	14.78	16.69	20.99	22.69	24.61	27.81
Travel, debit	3 236 ..	**−38.26**	**−37.93**	**−41.74**	**−47.85**	**−56.44**	**−59.53**	**−63.32**	**−72.44**
Business travel	3 237 ..	−7.55	−6.76	−6.66	−7.13	−8.07	−8.91	−9.55	−10.90
Personal travel	3 240 ..	−30.71	−31.18	−35.09	−40.72	−48.37	−50.62	−53.77	−61.53
Other services, credit	2 200 BA	**79.48**	**83.74**	**95.92**	**113.67**	**139.25**	**145.86**	**170.52**	**208.41**
Communications	2 245 ..	2.81	2.93	3.31	4.05	5.38	6.87	7.90	8.38
Construction	2 249 ..	.33	.25	.30	.40	.56	1.14	1.50	2.16
Insurance	2 253 ..	4.06	5.28	8.39	8.81	9.06	2.98	6.97	10.47
Financial	2 260 ..	22.12	22.52	23.89	28.61	37.14	42.55	52.88	70.89
Computer and information	2 262 ..	4.32	4.68	5.93	8.16	11.68	11.23	12.99	14.08
Royalties and licence fees	2 266 ..	8.15	8.17	8.68	10.10	12.28	13.80	14.25	16.03
Other business services	2 268 ..	33.88	35.77	40.64	47.30	55.53	59.60	66.31	77.96
Personal, cultural, and recreational	2 287 ..	1.97	1.95	2.41	3.09	3.93	4.08	3.94	4.23
Government, n.i.e.	2 291 ..	1.83	2.19	2.37	3.16	3.70	3.61	3.78	4.20
Other services, debit	3 200 BA	**−37.35**	**−38.82**	**−42.86**	**−50.93**	**−59.29**	**−68.10**	**−78.03**	**−91.88**
Communications	3 245 ..	−2.82	−2.87	−3.06	−3.53	−4.34	−6.42	−7.39	−8.92
Construction	3 249 ..	−.08	−.15	−.16	−.19	−.26	−1.03	−1.15	−1.52
Insurance	3 253 ..	−1.09	−1.10	−1.14	−1.27	−1.52	−1.62	−1.80	−2.00
Financial	3 260 ..	−4.47	−4.77	−5.33	−6.66	−7.30	−9.26	−10.80	−11.97
Computer and information	3 262 ..	−1.27	−1.69	−1.99	−2.94	−3.69	−4.30	−4.99	−6.01
Royalties and licence fees	3 266 ..	−6.64	−6.47	−6.93	−7.86	−9.17	−9.46	−9.52	−11.13
Other business services	3 268 ..	−16.95	−17.89	−20.21	−22.78	−26.66	−29.96	−35.86	−42.40
Personal, cultural, and recreational	3 287 ..	−1.18	−1.04	−1.20	−1.40	−1.66	−1.55	−1.58	−1.86
Government, n.i.e.	3 291 ..	−2.85	−2.84	−2.85	−4.30	−4.69	−4.49	−4.94	−6.08

Table 2 (Continued). STANDARD PRESENTATION, 2000–2007

(Billions of U.S. dollars)

	Code	2000	2001	2002	2003	2004	2005	2006	2007
C. INCOME	4 300	**6.95**	**16.82**	**35.46**	**40.10**	**48.83**	**47.16**	**14.04**	**11.00**
Total credit	2 300	*204.24*	*202.93*	*187.29*	*205.80*	*260.54*	*340.53*	*434.21*	*571.18*
Total debit	3 300	*−197.29*	*−186.11*	*−151.84*	*−165.70*	*−211.71*	*−293.37*	*−420.18*	*−560.18*
Compensation of employees, credit	2 310	**1.55**	**1.56**	**1.69**	**1.83**	**2.14**	**1.77**	**1.95**	**2.32**
Compensation of employees, debit	3 310	**−1.34**	**−1.47**	**−1.58**	**−1.73**	**−2.01**	**−2.88**	**−3.33**	**−3.65**
Investment income, credit	2 320	**202.69**	**201.37**	**185.60**	**203.98**	**258.40**	**338.76**	**432.26**	**568.86**
Direct investment income	2 330	68.17	67.31	77.48	90.01	118.11	144.41	155.80	172.72
Dividends and distributed branch profits	2 332	25.96	25.09	27.58	53.41	58.13	67.71	69.36	64.10
Reinvested earnings and undistributed branch profits	2 333	38.29	39.17	48.01	34.89	59.42	77.22	87.79	111.70
Income on debt (interest)	2 334	3.92	3.05	1.89	1.71	.56	−.51	−1.35	−3.07
Portfolio investment income	2 339	49.85	50.22	48.71	53.17	67.21	82.54	101.57	132.55
Income on equity	2 340	14.91	14.18	15.77	16.94	20.52	24.00	28.57	35.88
Income on bonds and notes	2 350	31.09	31.93	30.55	33.66	42.75	54.04	67.24	90.03
Income on money market instruments	2 360	3.85	4.11	2.39	2.57	3.94	4.50	5.76	6.63
Other investment income	2 370	84.66	83.84	59.41	60.80	73.08	111.81	174.89	263.58
Investment income, debit	3 320	**−195.95**	**−184.64**	**−150.26**	**−163.98**	**−209.69**	**−290.49**	**−416.85**	**−556.52**
Direct investment income	3 330	−41.53	−30.91	−24.01	−35.85	−51.19	−64.89	−96.22	−102.32
Dividends and distributed branch profits	3 332	−20.17	−26.04	−12.27	−16.28	−25.36	−34.97	−43.08	−23.64
Reinvested earnings and undistributed branch profits	3 333	−16.53	1.40	−5.26	−11.98	−17.02	−18.48	−42.13	−66.25
Income on debt (interest)	3 334	−4.82	−6.28	−6.48	−7.59	−8.80	−11.44	−11.00	−12.43
Portfolio investment income	3 339	−46.79	−49.57	−48.12	−51.73	−66.54	−85.36	−105.01	−132.20
Income on equity	3 340	−14.90	−18.92	−21.10	−22.40	−25.54	−32.24	−38.78	−44.94
Income on bonds and notes	3 350	−21.12	−19.36	−20.03	−23.87	−33.80	−41.62	−50.44	−67.90
Income on money market instruments	3 360	−10.77	−11.29	−7.00	−5.46	−7.20	−11.50	−15.80	−19.36
Other investment income	3 370	−107.63	−104.16	−78.13	−76.39	−91.97	−140.24	−215.62	−322.01
D. CURRENT TRANSFERS	4 379	**−15.11**	**−9.73**	**−13.58**	**−16.48**	**−20.05**	**−21.93**	**−21.96**	**−27.62**
Credit	2 379	**16.03**	**20.79**	**18.41**	**19.95**	**23.66**	**31.38**	**33.77**	**31.33**
General government	2 380	3.75	7.18	5.52	6.50	7.34	7.72	7.97	8.45
Other sectors	2 390	12.28	13.61	12.90	13.45	16.32	23.66	25.80	22.88
Workers' remittances	2 391	....	....	....	....	....	....	....	....
Other current transfers	2 392	....	....	....	....	....	....	....	....
Debit	3 379	**−31.14**	**−30.52**	**−31.99**	**−36.43**	**−43.72**	**−53.31**	**−55.72**	**−58.95**
General government	3 380	−12.16	−10.92	−14.01	−17.86	−22.54	−24.96	−25.48	−28.34
Other sectors	3 390	−18.98	−19.60	−17.98	−18.57	−21.17	−28.35	−30.24	−30.61
Workers' remittances	3 391	....	....	....	....	....	....	....	....
Other current transfers	3 392	....	....	....	....	....	....	....	....
CAPITAL AND FINANCIAL ACCOUNT	4 996	**21.66**	**26.97**	**14.11**	**36.77**	**13.81**	**74.87**	**84.99**	**122.95**
CAPITAL ACCOUNT	4 994	**2.57**	**1.89**	**1.42**	**2.42**	**3.78**	**2.80**	**1.58**	**5.09**
Total credit	2 994	*3.94*	*4.79*	*3.51*	*4.59*	*6.60*	*7.85*	*7.18*	*8.95*
Total debit	3 994	*−1.37*	*−2.90*	*−2.09*	*−2.17*	*−2.82*	*−5.05*	*−5.60*	*−3.85*
Capital transfers, credit	2 400	**3.69**	**4.54**	**3.25**	**4.23**	**6.24**	**7.24**	**6.24**	**7.38**
General government	2 401	....	....	....	....	....	....	....	....
Debt forgiveness	2 402	....	....	....	....	....	....	....	....
Other capital transfers	2 410	....	....	....	....	....	....	....	....
Other sectors	2 430	3.69	4.54	3.25	4.23	6.24	7.24	6.24	7.38
Migrants' transfers	2 431	2.06	3.26	2.79	3.20	4.21	4.53	5.02	5.91
Debt forgiveness	2 432	....	....	....	....	....	....	....	....
Other capital transfers	2 440	1.63	1.28	.46	1.03	2.03	2.71	1.22	1.47
Capital transfers, debit	3 400	**−1.17**	**−2.51**	**−1.63**	**−1.70**	**−1.88**	**−3.96**	**−4.45**	**−2.42**
General government	3 401	−.37	−.37	−.42	−.59	−.74	−.77	−.73	−.88
Debt forgiveness	3 402	−.03	−.03	−.02	−.03	−.02	−.03	−.02	−.02
Other capital transfers	3 410	−.34	−.34	−.40	−.56	−.72	−.74	−.71	−.85
Other sectors	3 430	−.79	−2.14	−1.21	−1.11	−1.14	−3.19	−3.71	−1.54
Migrants' transfers	3 431	−.71	−1.87	−.86	−.90	−.94	−1.00	−1.23	−1.39
Debt forgiveness	3 432	−.08	−.27	−.35	−.21	−.20	−2.19	−2.48	−.15
Other capital transfers	3 440	....	....	....	....	....	....	....	....
Nonproduced nonfinancial assets, credit	2 480	**.25**	**.26**	**.26**	**.36**	**.35**	**.62**	**.94**	**1.56**
Nonproduced nonfinancial assets, debit	3 480	**−.21**	**−.39**	**−.46**	**−.47**	**−.94**	**−1.09**	**−1.15**	**−1.44**

Table 2 (Continued). STANDARD PRESENTATION, 2000–2007

(Billions of U.S. dollars)

	Code	2000	2001	2002	2003	2004	2005	2006	2007
FINANCIAL ACCOUNT..	4 995 ..	**19.09**	**25.08**	**12.69**	**34.35**	**10.03**	**72.07**	**83.41**	**117.86**
A. DIRECT INVESTMENT......................................	4 500 ..	**−124.11**	**−7.97**	**−24.80**	**−38.02**	**−20.24**	**103.85**	**56.59**	**−44.15**
Direct investment abroad.................................	4 505 ..	**−246.26**	**−61.82**	**−50.33**	**−65.64**	**−98.19**	**−91.71**	**−89.53**	**−269.10**
Equity capital...	4 510 ..	−233.74	−24.22	−39.75	−33.26	−33.60	−28.65	−47.69	−114.96
Claims on affiliated enterprises............	4 515 ..	−233.74	−24.22	−39.75	−33.26	−33.60	−28.65	−47.69	−114.96
Liabilities to affiliated enterprises.........	4 520 ..	....	....	....	....	....	....	....	....
Reinvested earnings.................................	4 525 ..	−38.29	−39.17	−48.01	−34.89	−59.42	−77.22	−87.79	−111.70
Other capital...	4 530 ..	25.77	1.57	37.43	2.51	−5.16	14.16	45.95	−42.44
Claims on affiliated enterprises............	4 535 ..	−19.89	−17.88	−22.51	−17.71	−37.85	−38.22	−1.25	−89.82
Liabilities to affiliated enterprises.........	4 540 ..	45.66	19.46	59.95	20.22	32.68	52.39	47.20	47.38
Direct investment in United Kingdom...............	4 555 ..	**122.16**	**53.84**	**25.53**	**27.61**	**77.95**	**195.55**	**146.12**	**224.95**
Equity capital...	4 560 ..	89.53	30.21	18.11	7.35	44.87	151.79	101.24	155.93
Claims on direct investors...................	4 565 ..	....	....	....	....	....	....	....	....
Liabilities to direct investors...............	4 570 ..	89.53	30.21	18.11	7.35	44.87	151.79	101.24	155.93
Reinvested earnings.................................	4 575 ..	16.53	−1.40	5.26	11.98	17.02	18.48	42.13	66.25
Other capital...	4 580 ..	16.09	25.04	2.16	8.28	16.05	25.28	2.74	2.77
Claims on direct investors...................	4 585 ..	−3.44	−1.48	−15.12	5.23	10.20	−13.91	−23.28	−14.27
Liabilities to direct investors...............	4 590 ..	19.53	26.52	17.28	3.06	5.86	39.20	26.02	17.04
B. PORTFOLIO INVESTMENT.................................	4 600 ..	**158.46**	**−55.16**	**77.46**	**97.20**	**−99.28**	**−51.18**	**−74.48**	**165.29**
Assets..	4 602 ..	**−97.19**	**−124.73**	**1.22**	**−58.42**	**−259.16**	**−291.52**	**−366.89**	**−255.57**
Equity securities.......................................	4 610 ..	−28.46	−63.63	7.41	−29.79	−102.96	−113.67	−35.01	−79.18
Monetary authorities.............................	4 611 ..	....	....	....	....	....			
General government.............................	4 612 ..	....	....	....	....	....	−.08	−.05	−.05
Banks..	4 613 ..	−10.61	1.99	18.15	−30.72	−58.23	−64.02	−40.22	−22.60
Other sectors.......................................	4 614 ..	−17.86	−65.62	−10.75	.93	−44.73	−49.57	5.27	−56.53
Debt securities...	4 619 ..	−68.73	−61.10	−6.19	−28.63	−156.20	−177.86	−331.88	−176.39
Bonds and notes...................................	4 620 ..	−71.90	−44.40	−12.07	−9.03	−160.85	−169.84	−307.76	−177.18
Monetary authorities.........................	4 621 ..	....	....	....	....	....	....	....	....
General government.........................	4 622 ..	....	....	....	....	....	....	....	....
Banks..	4 623 ..	−56.42	−55.62	−3.57	21.53	−105.91	−116.65	−190.37	−83.23
Other sectors...................................	4 624 ..	−15.49	11.22	−8.50	−30.56	−54.94	−53.20	−117.39	−93.95
Money market instruments....................	4 630 ..	3.18	−16.69	5.88	−19.60	4.66	−8.01	−24.12	.79
Monetary authorities.........................	4 631 ..	....	....	....	....	....	....	....	....
General government.........................	4 632 ..	....	−.64	−.69	1.48	−.01	....	.01	−4.79
Banks..	4 633 ..	−1.74	−10.61	5.70	−11.77	8.29	−4.21	−9.30	−16.70
Other sectors...................................	4 634 ..	4.92	−5.44	.87	−9.32	−3.62	−3.80	−14.83	22.27
Liabilities...	4 652 ..	**255.65**	**69.57**	**76.24**	**155.62**	**159.88**	**240.34**	**292.41**	**420.86**
Equity securities.......................................	4 660 ..	179.17	33.11	4.22	15.56	−15.22	15.21	−9.09	39.36
Banks..	4 663 ..	−4.38	.19	−1.72	.95	−.60	.13	1.33	7.23
Other sectors.......................................	4 664 ..	183.55	32.92	5.94	14.61	−14.62	15.09	−10.42	32.13
Debt securities...	4 669 ..	76.48	36.47	72.02	140.05	175.10	225.13	301.50	381.50
Bonds and notes...................................	4 670 ..	16.38	7.77	27.82	142.91	156.19	238.86	224.63	341.65
Monetary authorities.........................	4 671 ..	....	....	....	....	....	....	....	....
General government.........................	4 672 ..	−.58	−1.15	−5.35	18.46	22.97	55.82	46.31	50.70
Banks..	4 673 ..	7.41	6.58	10.17	47.34	58.64	75.98	79.58	125.53
Other sectors...................................	4 674 ..	9.55	2.34	23.00	77.11	74.58	107.07	98.75	165.42
Money market instruments....................	4 680 ..	60.09	28.69	44.20	−2.85	18.91	−13.74	76.87	39.85
Monetary authorities.........................	4 681 ..	....	....	....	....	....	....	....	....
General government.........................	4 682 ..	−.44	.44	−.33	3.56	3.62	−1.91	1.44	7.13
Banks..	4 683 ..	56.67	27.87	28.44	.62	14.81	−7.04	82.11	26.68
Other sectors...................................	4 684 ..	3.87	.39	16.08	−7.04	.49	−4.79	−6.68	6.04
C. FINANCIAL DERIVATIVES.................................	4 910 ..	**2.26**	**12.18**	**1.35**	**−8.49**	**−14.27**	**16.53**	**14.48**	**−35.00**
Monetary authorities..................................	4 911 ..	....	....	....	....	....	....	....	....
General government...................................	4 912 ..	....	....	....	....	....	....	....	....
Banks..	4 913 ..	....	....	....	....	....	....	....	....
Other sectors..	4 914 ..	....	....	....	....	....	....	....	....
Assets..	4 900 ..	....	....	....	....	....	....	....	....
Monetary authorities..............................	4 901 ..	....	....	....	....	....	....	....	....
General government.............................	4 902 ..	....	....	....	....	....	....	....	....
Banks..	4 903 ..	....	....	....	....	....	....	....	....
Other sectors.......................................	4 904 ..	....	....	....	....	....	....	....	....
Liabilities...	4 905 ..	**2.26**	**12.18**	**1.35**	**−8.49**	**−14.27**	**16.53**	**14.48**	**−35.00**
Monetary authorities..............................	4 906 ..	....	....	....	....	....	....	....	....
General government.............................	4 907 ..	....	....	....	....	....	....	....	....
Banks..	4 908 ..	....	....	....	....	....	....	....	....
Other sectors.......................................	4 909 ..	....	....	....	....	....	....	....	....

Table 2 (Concluded). STANDARD PRESENTATION, 2000–2007

(Billions of U.S. dollars)

	Code	2000	2001	2002	2003	2004	2005	2006	2007
D. OTHER INVESTMENT	4 700	−12.23	71.58	−41.96	−18.92	144.23	4.61	85.52	34.28
Assets	4 703	−426.81	−255.47	−151.03	−415.62	−596.92	−931.59	−776.70	−1,519.95
Trade credits	4 706	.06	.45	−.45	−.93	.61	2.54	−2.54	1.04
General government	4 707	....	....	....	....	....	....	....	....
of which: Short-term	4 709	....	....	....	....	....	....	....	....
Other sectors	4 710	.06	.45	−.45	−.93	.61	2.54	−2.54	1.04
of which: Short-term	4 712	*.06*	*.45*	*−.45*	*−.93*	*.61*	*2.54*	*−2.54*	*1.04*
Loans	4 714	−86.50	−70.66	−22.77	−112.86	−205.72	−248.38	−213.15	−448.65
Monetary authorities	4 715	....	....	....	....	....	....	....	....
of which: Short-term	4 718	....	....	....	....	....	....	....	....
General government	4 719	.04	.03	.03	.03	.03	.03	.02	.02
of which: Short-term	4 721	....	....	....	....	....	....	....	....
Banks	4 722	−86.44	−70.62	−23.08	−113.31	−206.16	−249.55	−215.94	−449.58
of which: Short-term	4 724	*−86.44*	*−70.62*	*−23.08*	*−113.31*	*−206.16*	*−249.55*	*−215.94*	*−449.58*
Other sectors	4 725	−.10	−.07	.29	.43	.42	1.14	2.77	.91
of which: Short-term	4 727	....	....	....	....	....	....	....	....
Currency and deposits	4 730	−340.02	−185.51	−127.09	−301.69	−391.42	−686.68	−561.50	−1,070.78
Monetary authorities	4 731	....	....	....	....	....	....	....	....
General government	4 732	....	....	....	....	....	....	....	....
Banks	4 733	−202.60	−54.23	−88.06	−145.45	−194.31	−291.59	−317.19	−748.12
Other sectors	4 734	−137.42	−131.28	−39.03	−156.24	−197.11	−395.09	−244.31	−322.66
Other assets	4 736	−.36	.25	−.73	−.14	−.40	.93	.50	−1.58
Monetary authorities	4 737	....	....	....	....	....	....	....	....
of which: Short-term	4 739	....	....	....	....	....	....	....	....
General government	4 740	−.44	−.02	−1.08	−.34	−.60	−1.26	−1.99	−1.72
of which: Short-term	4 742	*−.36*	*.06*	*−.95*	*−.14*	*−.42*	*−.40*	*−.53*	*−.33*
Banks	4 743	....	....	....	....	....	....	....	....
of which: Short-term	4 745	....	....	....	....	....	....	....	....
Other sectors	4 746	.08	.27	.35	.21	.20	2.19	2.48	.15
of which: Short-term	4 748	*.08*	*.27*	*.35*	*.21*	*.20*	*2.19*	*2.48*	*.15*
Liabilities	4 753	**414.59**	**327.05**	**109.07**	**396.69**	**741.16**	**936.20**	**862.22**	**1,554.23**
Trade credits	4 756	....	....	....	....	....	....	....	....
General government	4 757	....	....	....	....	....	....	....	....
of which: Short-term	4 759	....	....	....	....	....	....	....	....
Other sectors	4 760	....	....	....	....	....	....	....	....
of which: Short-term	4 762	....	....	....	....	....	....	....	....
Loans	4 764	103.73	144.39	−31.98	121.81	176.27	417.50	260.62	183.08
Monetary authorities	4 765	....	....	....	....	....	....	....	....
of which: Use of Fund credit and loans from the Fund	4 766	....	....	....	....	....	....	....	....
of which: Short-term	4 768	....	....	....	....	....	....	....	....
General government	4 769	−.45	−.03	−.05	.26	1.08	.12	.44	−.06
of which: Short-term	4 771	....	....	....	....	....	....	....	....
Banks	4 772	....	....	....	....	....	....	....	....
of which: Short-term	4 774	....	....	....	....	....	....	....	....
Other sectors	4 775	104.18	144.43	−31.93	121.55	175.19	417.37	260.18	183.14
of which: Short-term	4 777	*104.18*	*144.43*	*−31.93*	*121.55*	*175.19*	*417.37*	*260.20*	*183.14*
Currency and deposits	4 780	308.95	182.41	141.42	276.67	566.53	517.36	598.42	1,371.34
Monetary authorities	4 781	....	....	....	....	....	....	....	....
General government	4 782	....	....	....	....	....	....	....	....
Banks	4 783	308.95	182.41	141.42	276.67	566.53	517.36	598.42	1,371.34
Other sectors	4 784	....	....	....	....	....	....	....	....
Other liabilities	4 786	1.90	.24	−.37	−1.79	−1.64	1.35	3.18	−.19
Monetary authorities	4 787	....	....	....	....	....	....	....	....
of which: Short-term	4 789	....	....	....	....	....	....	....	....
General government	4 790	.46	.43	−.96	.57	−1.88	.14	1.09	−.02
of which: Short-term	4 792	*.46*	*.43*	*−.96*	*.57*	*−1.88*	*.14*	*1.09*	*−.02*
Banks	4 793	....	....	....	....	....	....	....	....
of which: Short-term	4 795	....	....	....	....	....	....	....	....
Other sectors	4 796	1.45	−.19	.58	−2.36	.23	1.20	2.09	−.17
of which: Short-term	4 798	*1.45*	*−.19*	*.58*	*−2.36*	*.23*	*1.20*	*2.09*	*−.17*
E. RESERVE ASSETS	4 802	**−5.30**	**4.46**	**.63**	**2.59**	**−.41**	**−1.73**	**1.30**	**−2.57**
Monetary gold	4 812	1.34	1.13	.38	....	....	....	.01	....
Special drawing rights	4 811	.17	.02	−.04	.02	.06	.02	−.09	.05
Reserve position in the Fund	4 810	.75	−.93	−.74	.46	1.03	2.82	1.01	.37
Foreign exchange	4 803	−7.49	4.24	.79	1.80	−1.53	−3.97	−.16	−3.04
Other claims	4 813	−.07	−.01	.24	.32	.03	−.59	.54	.04
NET ERRORS AND OMISSIONS	4 998	**15.70**	**4.44**	**10.50**	**−12.30**	**21.37**	**−19.88**	**8.62**	**−3.79**

Table 3. INTERNATIONAL INVESTMENT POSITION (End-period stocks), 2000–2007

(Billions of U.S. dollars)

	Code	2000	2001	2002	2003	2004	2005	2006	2007
ASSETS	8 995 C.	**4,448.52**	**4,573.30**	**5,064.98**	**6,310.42**	**7,649.70**	**8,432.69**	**10,411.05**	**12,995.02**
Direct investment abroad	8 505 ..	**923.37**	**894.81**	**1,026.99**	**1,233.44**	**1,330.66**	**1,295.99**	**1,439.98**	**1,705.12**
Equity capital and reinvested earnings	8 506 ..	874.93	844.38	998.19	1,196.93	1,282.90	1,287.77	1,491.21	1,714.19
Claims on affiliated enterprises	8 507 ..	....	....	....	....	....	....	....	....
Liabilities to affiliated enterprises	8 508 ..	....	....	....	....	....	....	....	....
Other capital	8 530 ..	48.43	50.43	28.80	36.51	47.76	8.22	−51.23	−9.07
Claims on affiliated enterprises	8 535 ..	....	....	....	....	....	....	....	....
Liabilities to affiliated enterprises	8 540 ..	....	....	....	....	....	....	....	....
Portfolio investment	8 602 ..	**1,352.04**	**1,359.63**	**1,360.38**	**1,670.20**	**2,109.70**	**2,366.34**	**3,140.51**	**3,654.40**
Equity securities	8 610 ..	640.63	586.88	493.04	663.87	879.34	1,068.41	1,366.48	1,584.70
Monetary authorities	8 611 ..	....	....	....	....	....	....	....	....
General government	8 612 ..	....	....	....	....	....	....	....	....
Banks	8 613 ..	29.36	20.74	4.40	37.13	102.32	148.36	214.43	254.51
Other sectors	8 614 ..	611.27	566.14	488.64	626.75	777.02	920.05	1,152.06	1,330.19
Debt securities	8 619 ..	711.41	772.75	867.35	1,006.33	1,230.36	1,297.93	1,774.03	2,069.70
Bonds and notes	8 620 ..	647.30	693.75	789.20	895.92	1,117.94	1,189.14	1,629.93	1,916.11
Monetary authorities	8 621 ..	....	....	....	....	....	....	....	....
General government	8 622 ..	....	....	....	....	....	....	....	....
Banks	8 623 ..	430.73	463.59	535.62	576.61	685.79	704.46	931.39	1,100.78
Other sectors	8 624 ..	216.57	230.17	253.58	319.31	432.15	484.68	698.55	815.34
Money market instruments	8 630 ..	64.11	79.00	78.15	110.41	112.42	108.79	144.10	153.59
Monetary authorities	8 631 ..	....	....	....	....	....	....	....	....
General government	8 632 ..	....	.66	1.49	....	....	....	....	4.79
Banks	8 633 ..	52.10	61.01	55.79	76.33	71.86	68.62	83.98	107.84
Other sectors	8 634 ..	12.00	17.32	20.87	34.08	40.56	40.17	60.11	40.96
Financial derivatives	8 900 ..	....	....	....	....	....	....	....	....
Monetary authorities	8 901 ..	....	....	....	....	....	....	....	....
General government	8 902 ..	....	....	....	....	....	....	....	....
Banks	8 903 ..	....	....	....	....	....	....	....	....
Other sectors	8 904 ..	....	....	....	....	....	....	....	....
Other investment	8 703 ..	**2,130.14**	**2,281.63**	**2,636.51**	**3,364.29**	**4,164.47**	**4,727.20**	**5,785.55**	**7,582.04**
Trade credits	8 706 ..	.65	.17	.66	1.76	1.25	−1.29	1.21	.21
General government	8 707 ..	....	....	....	....	....	....	....	....
of which: Short-term	8 709 ..	....	....	....	....	....	....	....	....
Other sectors	8 710 ..	.65	.17	.66	1.76	1.25	−1.29	1.21	.21
of which: Short-term	8 712 ..	*.65*	*.17*	*.66*	*1.76*	*1.25*	*−1.29*	*1.21*	*.21*
Loans	8 714 ..	430.67	481.65	541.38	723.92	972.72	1,118.78	1,403.94	1,926.49
Monetary authorities	8 715 ..	....	....	....	....	....	....	....	....
of which: Short-term	8 718 ..	....	....	....	....	....	....	....	....
General government	8 719 ..	.37	.33	.34	.34	.34	.27	.29	.27
of which: Short-term	8 721 ..	....	....	....	....	....	....	....	....
Banks	8 722 ..	425.13	476.20	535.71	717.66	965.80	1,113.36	1,398.52	1,921.60
of which: Short-term	8 724 ..	*417.90*	*468.82*	*529.61*	*711.12*	*958.62*	*1,106.24*	*1,392.06*	*1,915.20*
Other sectors	8 725 ..	5.17	5.12	5.32	5.92	6.58	5.14	5.13	4.62
of which: Short-term	8 727 ..	*.79*	*.77*	*.86*	*.95*	*1.03*	*.91*	*1.04*	*1.06*
Currency and deposits	8 730 ..	1,691.74	1,792.87	2,085.33	2,628.07	3,178.87	3,589.79	4,356.74	5,629.23
Monetary authorities	8 731 ..	....	....	....	....	....	....	....	....
General government	8 732 ..	....	....	....	....	....	....	....	....
Banks	8 733 ..	1,154.55	1,165.01	1,355.81	1,641.30	1,941.69	2,062.33	2,522.88	3,433.63
Other sectors	8 734 ..	537.19	627.85	729.51	986.77	1,237.18	1,527.46	1,833.86	2,195.59
Other assets	8 736 ..	7.08	6.94	9.14	10.55	11.63	19.92	23.67	26.12
Monetary authorities	8 737 ..	....	....	....	....	....	....	....	....
of which: Short-term	8 739 ..	....	....	....	....	....	....	....	....
General government	8 740 ..	5.42	5.33	6.92	8.29	9.58	17.99	22.52	24.68
of which: Short-term	8 742 ..	....	....	....	....	....	....	....	....
Banks	8 743 ..	....	....	....	....	....	....	....	....
of which: Short-term	8 745 ..	....	....	....	....	....	....	....	....
Other sectors	8 746 ..	1.66	1.61	2.22	2.25	2.04	1.93	1.14	1.44
of which: Short-term	8 748 ..	*1.66*	*1.61*	*2.22*	*2.25*	*2.04*	*1.93*	*1.14*	*1.44*
Reserve assets	8 802 ..	**42.97**	**37.24**	**41.10**	**42.48**	**44.87**	**43.15**	**45.01**	**53.46**
Monetary gold	8 812 ..	4.26	3.15	3.46	4.19	4.42	5.14	6.35	8.34
Special drawing rights	8 811 ..	.33	.29	.36	.38	.33	.29	.40	.36
Reserve position in the Fund	8 810 ..	4.28	5.05	6.21	6.32	5.53	2.33	1.41	1.10
Foreign exchange	8 803 ..	33.91	28.18	30.78	31.63	34.43	34.77	36.89	43.55
Other claims	8 813 ..	.19	.57	.29	−.04	.16	.63	−.04	.11

Table 3 (Concluded). INTERNATIONAL INVESTMENT POSITION (End-period stocks), 2000–2007

(Billions of U.S. dollars)

	Code	2000	2001	2002	2003	2004	2005	2006	2007
LIABILITIES	8 995 D.	**4,484.12**	**4,658.03**	**5,123.46**	**6,389.11**	**7,863.87**	**8,679.29**	**11,086.00**	**13,697.08**
Direct investment in United Kingdom	8 555 ..	**463.13**	**527.18**	**548.95**	**634.53**	**742.35**	**863.00**	**1,133.41**	**1,347.60**
Equity capital and reinvested earnings	8 556 ..	359.05	376.73	369.45	438.45	537.31	626.60	849.07	1,062.58
Claims on direct investors	8 557 ..	....	....	....	....	....	....	....	....
Liabilities to direct investors	8 558 ..	....	....	....	....	....	....	....	....
Other capital	8 580 ..	104.08	150.45	179.51	196.09	205.05	236.40	284.35	285.03
Claims on direct investors	8 585 ..	....	....	....	....	....	....	....	....
Liabilities to direct investors	8 590 ..	....	....	....	....	....	....	....	....
Portfolio investment	8 652 ..	**1,489.58**	**1,390.22**	**1,438.28**	**1,869.12**	**2,274.83**	**2,464.55**	**3,339.25**	**3,806.73**
Equity securities	8 660 ..	901.93	767.90	660.48	877.20	1,012.83	1,082.29	1,527.14	1,605.09
Banks	8 663 ..	8.85	7.37	4.81	7.48	8.10	8.67	13.71	21.19
Other sectors	8 664 ..	893.07	760.53	655.67	869.72	1,004.73	1,073.62	1,513.44	1,583.89
Debt securities	8 669 ..	587.65	622.31	777.80	991.92	1,262.00	1,382.26	1,812.11	2,201.65
Bonds and notes	8 670 ..	389.60	396.50	502.08	712.96	958.17	1,104.98	1,455.26	1,784.00
Monetary authorities	8 671 ..	....	....	....	....	....	....	....	....
General government	8 672 ..	93.08	86.83	90.88	117.99	161.87	190.59	265.90	316.92
Banks	8 673 ..	115.48	121.94	153.18	217.18	297.41	346.83	459.80	609.83
Other sectors	8 674 ..	181.03	187.73	258.02	377.79	498.89	567.56	729.56	857.25
Money market instruments	8 680 ..	198.05	225.81	275.72	278.96	303.83	277.28	356.84	417.65
Monetary authorities	8 681 ..	....	....	....	....	....	....	....	....
General government	8 682 ..	.04	.13	.26	3.44	7.63	4.69	6.95	14.41
Banks	8 683 ..	165.58	193.00	226.12	233.14	252.52	234.40	317.91	364.94
Other sectors	8 684 ..	32.43	32.69	49.34	42.37	43.68	38.20	31.99	38.31
Financial derivatives	8 905 ..	....	....	....	....	....	....	....	....
Monetary authorities	8 906 ..	....	....	....	....	....	....	....	....
General government	8 907 ..	....	....	....	....	....	....	....	....
Banks	8 908 ..	....	....	....	....	....	....	....	....
Other sectors	8 909 ..	....	....	....	....	....	....	....	....
Other investment	8 753 ..	**2,531.40**	**2,740.63**	**3,136.23**	**3,885.46**	**4,846.68**	**5,351.74**	**6,613.34**	**8,542.74**
Trade credits	8 756 ..	1.63	1.63	1.64	1.63	1.65	1.64	1.64	1.64
General government	8 757 ..	....	....	....	....	....	....	....	....
of which: Short-term	8 759 ..	....	....	....	....	....	....	....	....
Other sectors	8 760 ..	1.63	1.63	1.64	1.63	1.65	1.64	1.64	1.64
of which: Short-term	8 762 ..	*1.63*	*1.63*	*1.64*	*1.63*	*1.65*	*1.64*	*1.64*	*1.64*
Loans	8 764 ..	620.40	725.47	787.58	993.27	1,234.83	1,531.62	1,914.02	2,198.77
Monetary authorities	8 765 ..	....	....	....	....	....	....	....	....
of which: Use of Fund credit and loans from the Fund	8 766 ..	....	....	....	....	....	....	....	....
of which: Short-term	8 768 ..	....	....	....	....	....	....	....	....
General government	8 769 ..	2.02	1.90	1.96	2.37	3.62	3.31	4.12	4.14
of which: Short-term	8 771 ..	....	....	....	....	....	....	....	....
Banks	8 772 ..	....	....	....	....	....	....	....	....
of which: Short-term	8 774 ..	....	....	....	....	....	....	....	....
Other sectors	8 775 ..	618.38	723.57	785.63	990.90	1,231.22	1,528.31	1,909.91	2,194.63
of which: Short-term	8 777 ..	*618.38*	*723.57*	*785.63*	*990.90*	*1,231.22*	*1,528.31*	*1,909.08*	*2,193.80*
Currency and deposits	8 780 ..	1,888.52	1,992.89	2,321.90	2,866.58	3,585.88	3,790.02	4,656.39	6,300.35
Monetary authorities	8 781 ..	....	....	....	....	....	....	....	....
General government	8 782 ..	....	....	....	....	....	....	....	....
Banks	8 783 ..	1,888.52	1,992.89	2,321.90	2,866.58	3,585.88	3,790.02	4,656.39	6,300.35
Other sectors	8 784 ..	....	....	....	....	....	....	....	....
Other liabilities	8 786 ..	20.85	20.64	25.11	23.98	24.33	28.46	41.29	41.97
Monetary authorities	8 787 ..	....	....	....	....	....	....	....	....
of which: Short-term	8 789 ..	....	....	....	....	....	....	....	....
General government	8 790 ..	3.88	4.23	3.62	4.64	3.08	2.95	4.43	4.45
of which: Short-term	8 792 ..	*3.88*	*4.23*	*3.62*	*4.64*	*3.08*	*2.95*	*4.43*	*4.45*
Banks	8 793 ..	....	....	....	....	....	....	....	....
of which: Short-term	8 795 ..	....	....	....	....	....	....	....	....
Other sectors	8 796 ..	16.98	16.41	21.49	19.34	21.25	25.52	36.86	37.52
of which: Short-term	8 798 ..	*16.98*	*16.41*	*21.49*	*19.34*	*21.25*	*25.52*	*36.86*	*37.52*
NET INTERNATIONAL INVESTMENT POSITION	8 995 ..	**−35.60**	**−84.72**	**−58.48**	**−78.70**	**−214.17**	**−246.60**	**−674.95**	**−702.06**
Conversion rates: pound sterling per U.S. dollar (end of period)	0 102 ..	**.67015**	**.68946**	**.62042**	**.56032**	**.51776**	**.58075**	**.50942**	**.49915**

Table 1. ANALYTIC PRESENTATION, 2000–2007

(Billions of U.S. dollars)

	Code	2000	2001	2002	2003	2004	2005	2006	2007
A. Current Account[1]	4 993 Z.	**−417.42**	**−384.70**	**−461.28**	**−523.40**	**−624.99**	**−728.99**	**−788.11**	**−731.21**
Goods: exports f.o.b.	2 100 ..	774.63	721.84	685.93	716.70	811.01	898.46	1,026.85	1,152.57
Goods: imports f.o.b.	3 100 ..	−1,226.69	−1,148.26	−1,167.40	−1,264.34	−1,477.13	−1,681.81	−1,861.41	−1,967.87
Balance on Goods	4 100 ..	*−452.06*	*−426.42*	*−481.46*	*−547.64*	*−666.12*	*−783.35*	*−834.55*	*−815.30*
Services: credit	2 200 ..	295.97	283.05	288.79	301.05	349.58	385.30	430.16	493.16
Services: debit	3 200 ..	−223.74	−221.76	−231.05	−250.33	−291.19	−313.51	−348.89	−378.11
Balance on Goods and Services	4 991 ..	*−379.84*	*−365.13*	*−423.73*	*−496.92*	*−607.73*	*−711.57*	*−753.28*	*−700.26*
Income: credit	2 300 ..	350.92	290.80	280.94	320.46	413.74	535.26	685.15	817.78
Income: debit	3 300 ..	−329.86	−259.08	−253.54	−275.15	−346.52	−462.91	−627.95	−736.03
Balance on Goods, Services, and Income	4 992 ..	*−358.78*	*−333.40*	*−396.33*	*−451.61*	*−540.51*	*−639.21*	*−696.09*	*−618.50*
Current transfers: credit	2 379 Z.	10.83	9.01	12.30	14.99	20.28	18.96	25.17	22.33
Current transfers: debit	3 379 ..	−69.47	−60.31	−77.24	−86.79	−104.76	−108.75	−117.20	−135.03
B. Capital Account[1]	4 994 Z.	**−1.01**	**−1.27**	**−1.47**	**−3.48**	**−2.37**	**−4.04**	**−3.88**	**−1.84**
Capital account: credit	2 994 Z.	1.00	.99	.97	.98	1.04	1.22	1.24	1.80
Capital account: debit	3 994 ..	−2.01	−2.27	−2.44	−4.46	−3.41	−5.25	−5.12	−3.65
Total, Groups A Plus B	4 981 ..	*−418.43*	*−385.97*	*−462.75*	*−526.88*	*−627.36*	*−733.03*	*−791.99*	*−733.05*
C. Financial Account[1]	4 995 W.	**477.99**	**405.16**	**504.20**	**531.36**	**529.53**	**686.62**	**836.70**	**774.47**
Direct investment abroad	4 505 ..	−159.21	−142.35	−154.46	−149.56	−316.22	−36.24	−241.25	−333.27
Direct investment in United States	4 555 Z.	321.27	167.02	84.37	63.75	145.97	112.64	241.96	237.54
Portfolio investment assets	4 602 ..	−127.91	−90.64	−48.57	−123.13	−177.36	−257.54	−498.98	−294.57
Equity securities	4 610 ..	−106.71	−109.12	−16.95	−118.00	−84.76	−186.69	−137.41	−118.02
Debt securities	4 619 ..	−21.19	18.48	−31.61	−5.13	−92.61	−70.85	−361.57	−176.55
Portfolio investment liabilities	4 652 Z.	436.57	428.34	427.61	550.16	867.34	832.04	1,126.88	1,145.14
Equity securities	4 660 ..	193.60	121.46	54.07	33.98	61.79	89.26	145.57	197.52
Debt securities	4 669 Z.	242.97	306.88	373.54	516.18	805.55	742.78	981.31	947.63
Financial derivatives	4 910 ..	....	....	....	....	....	....	29.71	6.50
Financial derivatives assets	4 900 ..	....	....	....	....	....	....	....	....
Financial derivatives liabilities	4 905 ..	....	....	....	....	....	....	29.71	6.50
Other investment assets	4 703 ..	−273.11	−144.71	−87.94	−54.26	−510.09	−266.96	−513.90	−661.89
Monetary authorities	4 701 ..	....	....	....	....	....	....	....	....
General government	4 704 ..	−.94	−.49	.35	.54	1.71	5.54	5.35	−22.27
Banks	4 705 ..	−133.38	−135.71	−38.26	−25.72	−359.04	−151.08	−329.34	−515.83
Other sectors	4 728 ..	−138.79	−8.52	−50.02	−29.08	−152.76	−121.42	−189.91	−123.79
Other investment liabilities	4 753 W.	280.38	187.51	283.18	244.39	519.90	302.67	692.27	675.02
Monetary authorities	4 753 WA	−11.19	35.30	69.54	10.59	13.30	8.45	2.23	−10.68
General government	4 753 ZB	−1.83	−2.31	.14	−.72	−.13	−.42	2.82	5.34
Banks	4 753 ZC	122.72	88.40	117.63	136.06	346.70	232.42	343.39	476.55
Other sectors	4 753 ZD	170.67	66.11	95.87	98.46	160.03	62.23	343.84	203.80
Total, Groups A Through C	4 983 ..	*59.56*	*19.19*	*41.45*	*4.47*	*−97.84*	*−46.41*	*44.70*	*41.42*
D. Net Errors and Omissions	4 998 ..	**−59.26**	**−14.27**	**−37.76**	**−6.00**	**95.03**	**32.31**	**−47.10**	**−41.29**
Total, Groups A Through D	4 984 ..	*.29*	*4.93*	*3.69*	*−1.53*	*−2.80*	*−14.10*	*−2.39*	*.13*
E. Reserves and Related Items	4 802 A.	**−.29**	**−4.93**	**−3.69**	**1.53**	**2.80**	**14.10**	**2.39**	**−.13**
Reserve assets	4 802 ..	−.29	−4.93	−3.69	1.53	2.80	14.10	2.39	−.13
Use of Fund credit and loans	4 766 ..	....	....	....	....	....	....	....	....
Exceptional financing	4 920 ..	....	....	....	....	....	....	....	....

[1] Excludes components that have been classified in the categories of Group E.

Table 2. STANDARD PRESENTATION, 2000–2007

(Billions of U.S. dollars)

	Code	2000	2001	2002	2003	2004	2005	2006	2007
CURRENT ACCOUNT	4 993	**−417.42**	**−384.70**	**−461.28**	**−523.40**	**−624.99**	**−728.99**	**−788.11**	**−731.21**
A. GOODS	4 100	**−452.06**	**−426.42**	**−481.46**	**−547.64**	**−666.12**	**−783.35**	**−834.55**	**−815.30**
Credit	2 100	**774.63**	**721.84**	**685.93**	**716.70**	**811.01**	**898.46**	**1,026.85**	**1,152.57**
General merchandise: exports f.o.b.	2 110	771.99	718.71	682.42	713.42	807.52	894.63	1,023.11	1,148.48
Goods for processing: exports f.o.b.	2 150	. . . .	. . . .	. . . .	. . . .	. . . .	. . . .	. . . .	. . . .
Repairs on goods	2 160	2.64	3.13	3.51	3.29	3.49	3.83	3.75	4.09
Goods procured in ports by carriers	2 170	. . . .	. . . .	. . . .	. . . .	. . . .	. . . .	. . . .	. . . .
Nonmonetary gold	2 180	. . . .	. . . .	. . . .	. . . .	. . . .	. . . .	. . . .	. . . .
Debit	3 100	**−1,226.69**	**−1,148.26**	**−1,167.40**	**−1,264.34**	**−1,477.13**	**−1,681.81**	**−1,861.41**	**−1,967.87**
General merchandise: imports f.o.b.	3 110	−1,223.47	−1,146.01	−1,166.98	−1,263.68	−1,477.05	−1,681.78	−1,861.38	−1,963.71
Goods for processing: imports f.o.b.	3 150	. . . .	. . . .	. . . .	. . . .	. . . .	. . . .	. . . .	. . . .
Repairs on goods	3 160	−.01	−.03	−.02	−.04	−.03	−.03	−.03	−.02
Goods procured in ports by carriers	3 170	. . . .	. . . .	. . . .	. . . .	. . . .	. . . .	. . . .	. . . .
Nonmonetary gold	3 180	−3.21	−2.22	−.40	−.63	−.04			−4.15
B. SERVICES	4 200	**72.23**	**61.29**	**57.74**	**50.73**	**58.39**	**71.78**	**81.27**	**115.04**
Total credit	2 200	*295.97*	*283.05*	*288.79*	*301.05*	*349.58*	*385.30*	*430.16*	*493.16*
Total debit	3 200	*−223.74*	*−221.76*	*−231.05*	*−250.33*	*−291.19*	*−313.51*	*−348.89*	*−378.11*
Transportation services, credit	2 205	**50.49**	**46.37**	**46.24**	**47.31**	**55.81**	**62.25**	**68.36**	**77.17**
Passenger	2 850	*20.69*	*17.93*	*17.05*	*15.89*	*18.85*	*20.97*	*22.04*	*25.59*
Freight	2 851	*12.55*	*11.73*	*12.29*	*13.94*	*15.48*	*16.47*	*17.41*	*19.60*
Other	2 852	*17.26*	*16.71*	*16.91*	*17.48*	*21.48*	*24.81*	*28.92*	*31.99*
Sea transport, passenger	2 207	.49	.75	.76	.80	.92	.36	.40	.41
Sea transport, freight	2 208	4.29	3.77	3.72	4.30	4.53	3.94	3.88	5.06
Sea transport, other	2 209	. . . .	. . . .	. . . .	. . . .	. . . .	. . . .	. . . .	. . . .
Air transport, passenger	2 211	20.20	17.18	16.29	15.09	17.93	20.61	21.64	25.17
Air transport, freight	2 212	5.78	5.43	5.79	6.87	7.73	9.33	10.08	11.08
Air transport, other	2 213	. . . .	. . . .	. . . .	. . . .	. . . .	. . . .	. . . .	. . . .
Other transport, passenger	2 215	. . . .	. . . .	. . . .	. . . .	. . . .	. . . .	. . . .	. . . .
Other transport, freight	2 216	2.48	2.53	2.78	2.78	3.22	3.20	3.45	3.46
Other transport, other	2 217	17.26	16.71	16.91	17.48	21.48	24.81	28.92	31.99
Transportation services, debit	3 205	**−65.70**	**−61.32**	**−58.38**	**−65.69**	**−78.88**	**−88.09**	**−92.76**	**−95.54**
Passenger	3 850	*−24.27*	*−22.63*	*−19.97*	*−20.99*	*−24.72*	*−26.15*	*−27.50*	*−28.49*
Freight	3 851	*−27.39*	*−25.74*	*−25.97*	*−31.77*	*−39.23*	*−43.92*	*−45.70*	*−45.58*
Other	3 852	*−14.04*	*−12.95*	*−12.43*	*−12.93*	*−14.94*	*−18.02*	*−19.56*	*−21.47*
Sea transport, passenger	3 207	−.66	−.71	−.78	−.86	−.99	−.96	−.86	−.82
Sea transport, freight	3 208	−20.07	−19.40	−18.62	−24.17	−30.49	−34.65	−36.10	−35.77
Sea transport, other	3 209	. . . .	. . . .	. . . .	. . . .	. . . .	. . . .	. . . .	. . . .
Air transport, passenger	3 211	−23.61	−21.92	−19.19	−20.13	−23.73	−25.19	−26.65	−27.67
Air transport, freight	3 212	−4.74	−3.96	−4.88	−5.02	−5.98	−6.11	−6.27	−6.38
Air transport, other	3 213	. . . .	. . . .	. . . .	. . . .	. . . .	. . . .	. . . .	. . . .
Other transport, passenger	3 215	. . . .	. . . .	. . . .	. . . .	. . . .	. . . .	. . . .	. . . .
Other transport, freight	3 216	−2.58	−2.38	−2.47	−2.58	−2.76	−3.16	−3.34	−3.43
Other transport, other	3 217	−14.04	−12.95	−12.43	−12.93	−14.94	−18.02	−19.56	−21.47
Travel, credit	2 236	**97.94**	**88.78**	**84.75**	**83.32**	**94.11**	**102.07**	**106.84**	**119.22**
Business travel	2 237	3.69	3.93	4.06	4.07	4.27	4.29	4.30	4.47
Personal travel	2 240	94.25	84.85	80.69	79.24	89.84	97.78	102.53	114.75
Travel, debit	3 236	**−67.04**	**−62.82**	**−61.74**	**−60.94**	**−69.63**	**−73.32**	**−76.95**	**−81.09**
Business travel	3 237	−.31	−.32	−.32	−.34	−.33	−.36	−.38	−.40
Personal travel	3 240	−66.74	−62.50	−61.42	−60.60	−69.29	−72.96	−76.57	−80.69
Other services, credit	2 200 BA	**147.53**	**147.91**	**157.80**	**170.43**	**199.66**	**220.98**	**254.96**	**296.76**
Communications	2 245	4.13	4.59	4.13	4.69	4.91	5.06	7.60	8.61
Construction	2 249	2.42	2.95	2.35	2.65	3.29	3.79	5.37	6.47
Insurance	2 253	3.63	3.42	4.42	5.97	7.31	7.57	10.10	10.29
Financial	2 260	16.03	15.50	17.75	19.70	27.77	31.00	47.44	58.27
Computer and information	2 262	5.62	5.42	5.39	5.39	6.25	6.70	7.32	10.34	12.73
Royalties and licence fees	2 266	43.23	40.70	44.51	46.99	56.72	64.40	72.19	82.61
Other business services	2 268	48.22	52.31	57.15	60.16	66.02	71.73	68.25	82.27
Personal, cultural, and recreational	2 287	6.38	6.62	6.53	7.14	7.55	6.96	12.18	15.04
Government, n.i.e.	2 291	17.88	16.39	15.58	16.88	19.39	23.16	21.50	20.48
Other services, debit	3 200 BA	**−91.00**	**−97.63**	**−110.93**	**−123.70**	**−142.69**	**−152.11**	**−179.18**	**−201.49**
Communications	3 245	−5.93	−5.20	−4.60	−4.70	−5.16	−5.15	−6.97	−7.90
Construction	3 249	−.50	−.59	−.58	−.65	−.58	−.43	−1.75	−1.85
Insurance	3 253	−11.28	−16.71	−21.93	−25.23	−29.09	−28.71	−37.37	−42.76
Financial	3 260	−4.84	−4.49	−4.16	−4.00	−5.49	−6.42	−14.24	−18.93
Computer and information	3 262	−1.63	−1.80	−1.51	−1.94	−2.15	−2.35	−13.60	−14.82
Royalties and licence fees	3 266	−16.47	−16.54	−19.35	−19.03	−23.27	−24.61	−23.78	−25.05
Other business services	3 268	−34.35	−34.90	−37.01	−39.96	−44.03	−50.05	−45.92	−52.31
Personal, cultural, and recreational	3 287	−.13	−.12	−.14	−.21	−.41	−.96	−1.09	−1.44
Government, n.i.e.	3 291	−15.86	−17.29	−21.66	−27.98	−32.52	−33.42	−34.45	−36.44

Table 2 (Continued). STANDARD PRESENTATION, 2000–2007

(Billions of U.S. dollars)

	Code	2000	2001	2002	2003	2004	2005	2006	2007
C. INCOME	4 300	**21.06**	**31.72**	**27.40**	**45.31**	**67.22**	**72.36**	**57.20**	**81.75**
Total credit	2 300	*350.92*	*290.80*	*280.94*	*320.46*	*413.74*	*535.26*	*685.15*	*817.78*
Total debit	3 300	*−329.86*	*−259.08*	*−253.54*	*−275.15*	*−346.52*	*−462.91*	*−627.95*	*−736.03*
Compensation of employees, credit	2 310	**2.84**	**2.88**	**2.81**	**2.81**	**2.82**	**2.89**	**2.88**	**2.97**
Compensation of employees, debit	3 310	**−7.52**	**−8.09**	**−8.38**	**−8.51**	**−8.96**	**−9.29**	**−9.49**	**−10.00**
Investment income, credit	2 320	**348.08**	**287.92**	**278.13**	**317.64**	**410.92**	**532.37**	**682.27**	**814.81**
Direct investment income	2 330	151.84	128.67	145.59	186.42	250.61	294.54	328.54	368.28
Dividends and distributed branch profits	2 332	52.86	53.24	54.60	59.46	81.56	298.71	91.11	98.56
Reinvested earnings and undistributed branch profits	2 333	93.60	69.78	85.27	120.69	162.91	−10.32	231.57	263.31
Income on debt (interest)	2 334	5.37	5.65	5.72	6.27	6.14	6.14	5.87	6.41
Portfolio investment income	2 339	71.42	68.71	79.14	90.61	108.56	129.33	165.72	216.38
Income on equity	2 340	33.47	34.17	38.23	41.55	54.09	64.63	84.33	114.62
Income on bonds and notes	2 350	37.94	34.54	40.91	46.45	50.47	55.39	63.87	79.34
Income on money market instruments	2 360	....	....	....	2.60	4.00	9.31	17.52	22.42
Other investment income	2 370	124.83	90.55	53.40	40.62	51.75	108.51	188.01	230.15
Investment income, debit	3 320	**−322.34**	**−250.99**	**−245.16**	**−266.64**	**−337.56**	**−453.62**	**−618.47**	**−726.03**
Direct investment income	3 330	−56.91	−12.78	−43.24	−73.75	−99.75	−121.33	−144.40	−134.42
Dividends and distributed branch profits	3 332	−37.27	−25.41	−21.19	−43.26	−36.29	−64.40	−57.28	−41.26
Reinvested earnings and undistributed branch profits	3 333	.26	33.85	−1.58	−14.29	−49.53	−41.73	−68.84	−68.53
Income on debt (interest)	3 334	−19.90	−21.22	−20.47	−16.21	−13.94	−15.20	−18.28	−24.63
Portfolio investment income	3 339	−145.18	−146.51	−149.39	−163.13	−195.54	−238.34	−304.52	−381.98
Income on equity	3 340	−19.65	−21.13	−23.56	−25.66	−37.04	−38.08	−44.89	−54.34
Income on bonds and notes	3 350	−125.53	−125.38	−125.83	−131.48	−150.42	−181.46	−230.01	−292.16
Income on money market instruments	3 360	....	....	....	−5.99	−8.08	−18.80	−29.62	−35.48
Other investment income	3 370	−120.26	−91.70	−52.54	−29.76	−42.26	−93.95	−169.55	−209.63
D. CURRENT TRANSFERS	4 379	**−58.64**	**−51.29**	**−64.95**	**−71.80**	**−84.48**	**−89.78**	**−92.03**	**−112.70**
Credit	2 379	**10.83**	**9.01**	**12.30**	**14.99**	**20.28**	**18.96**	**25.17**	**22.33**
General government	2 380	....	....	....	....	....	....	....	....
Other sectors	2 390	10.83	9.01	12.30	14.99	20.28	18.96	25.17	22.33
Workers' remittances	2 391	....	....	....	....	....	....	....	....
Other current transfers	2 392	....	....	....	....	....	....	....	....
Debit	3 379	**−69.47**	**−60.31**	**−77.24**	**−86.79**	**−104.76**	**−108.75**	**−117.20**	**−135.03**
General government	3 380	−21.42	−17.32	−22.22	−27.51	−29.90	−39.34	−33.65	−40.56
Other sectors	3 390	−48.05	−42.99	−55.02	−59.27	−74.87	−69.41	−83.55	−94.47
Workers' remittances	3 391	−23.44	−26.51	−27.75	−28.03	−30.38	−31.34	−34.43	−35.64
Other current transfers	3 392	−24.61	−16.48	−27.28	−31.24	−44.48	−38.06	−49.12	−58.83
CAPITAL AND FINANCIAL ACCOUNT	4 996	**476.69**	**398.97**	**499.03**	**529.40**	**529.96**	**696.69**	**835.21**	**772.50**
CAPITAL ACCOUNT	4 994	**−1.01**	**−1.27**	**−1.47**	**−3.48**	**−2.37**	**−4.04**	**−3.88**	**−1.84**
Total credit	2 994	*1.00*	*.99*	*.97*	*.98*	*1.04*	*1.22*	*1.24*	*1.80*
Total debit	3 994	*−2.01*	*−2.27*	*−2.44*	*−4.46*	*−3.41*	*−5.25*	*−5.12*	*−3.65*
Capital transfers, credit	2 400	**1.00**	**.99**	**.97**	**.98**	**1.04**	**1.22**	**1.24**	**1.80**
General government	2 401	....	....	....	....	....	....	....	....
Debt forgiveness	2 402	....	....	....	....	....	....	....	....
Other capital transfers	2 410	....	....	....	....	....	....	....	....
Other sectors	2 430	....	....	....	....	....	....	....	....
Migrants' transfers	2 431	....	....	....	....	....	....	....	....
Debt forgiveness	2 432	....	....	....	....	....	....	....	....
Other capital transfers	2 440	....	....	....	....	....	....	....	....
Capital transfers, debit	3 400	**−2.01**	**−2.27**	**−2.44**	**−4.46**	**−3.41**	**−5.25**	**−5.12**	**−3.65**
General government	3 401	....	....	....	....	....	....	....	....
Debt forgiveness	3 402	....	....	....	....	....	....	....	....
Other capital transfers	3 410	....	....	....	....	....	....	....	....
Other sectors	3 430	....	....	....	....	....	....	....	....
Migrants' transfers	3 431	....	....	....	....	....	....	....	....
Debt forgiveness	3 432	....	....	....	....	....	....	....	....
Other capital transfers	3 440	....	....	....	....	....	....	....	....
Nonproduced nonfinancial assets, credit	2 480	....	....	....	....	....	....	....	....
Nonproduced nonfinancial assets, debit	3 480	....	....	....	....	....	....	....	....

Table 2 (Continued). STANDARD PRESENTATION, 2000–2007

(Billions of U.S. dollars)

	Code	2000	2001	2002	2003	2004	2005	2006	2007
FINANCIAL ACCOUNT	4 995	**477.70**	**400.24**	**500.50**	**532.89**	**532.33**	**700.72**	**839.09**	**774.34**
A. DIRECT INVESTMENT	4 500	**162.06**	**24.67**	**−70.09**	**−85.81**	**−170.26**	**76.40**	**.72**	**−95.73**
Direct investment abroad	4 505	**−159.21**	**−142.35**	**−154.46**	**−149.56**	**−316.22**	**−36.24**	**−241.25**	**−333.27**
Equity capital	4 510	−78.04	−60.94	−42.71	−35.48	−133.28	−61.94	−32.31	−87.97
Claims on affiliated enterprises	4 515	....	....	....	....	....	....	....	....
Liabilities to affiliated enterprises	4 520	....	....	....	....	....	....	....	....
Reinvested earnings	4 525	−93.60	−69.78	−85.27	−120.69	−162.91	10.32	−231.57	−263.31
Other capital	4 530	12.43	−11.63	−26.48	6.61	−20.04	15.38	22.63	18.01
Claims on affiliated enterprises	4 535	5.54	−23.40	−39.50	−18.02	−56.96	4.37	−9.61	−11.64
Liabilities to affiliated enterprises	4 540	6.90	11.77	13.02	24.63	36.92	11.02	32.23	29.64
Direct investment in United States	4 555	**321.27**	**167.02**	**84.37**	**63.75**	**145.97**	**112.64**	**241.96**	**237.54**
Equity capital	4 560	259.64	140.90	105.34	93.42	92.90	70.73	117.77	147.43
Claims on direct investors	4 565	....	....	....	....	....	....	....	....
Liabilities to direct investors	4 570	....	....	....	....	....	....	....	....
Reinvested earnings	4 575	−.26	−33.85	1.58	14.29	49.53	41.73	68.84	68.53
Other capital	4 580	61.89	59.97	−22.56	−43.96	3.53	.18	55.35	21.58
Claims on direct investors	4 585	−21.90	7.32	−12.08	−22.97	−25.00	−14.67	−18.61	−57.84
Liabilities to direct investors	4 590	83.79	52.65	−10.48	−20.99	28.53	14.85	73.95	79.42
B. PORTFOLIO INVESTMENT	4 600	**308.67**	**337.70**	**379.04**	**427.03**	**689.97**	**574.50**	**627.90**	**850.57**
Assets	4 602	**−127.91**	**−90.64**	**−48.57**	**−123.13**	**−177.36**	**−257.54**	**−498.98**	**−294.57**
Equity securities	4 610	−106.71	−109.12	−16.95	−118.00	−84.76	−186.69	−137.41	−118.02
Monetary authorities	4 611	....	....	....	....	....	....	....	....
General government	4 612	....	....	....	....	....	....	....	....
Banks	4 613	....	....	....	....	....	....	....	....
Other sectors	4 614	....	....	....	....	....	....	....	....
Debt securities	4 619	−21.19	18.48	−31.61	−5.13	−92.61	−70.85	−361.57	−176.55
Bonds and notes	4 620	−21.19	18.48	−31.61	−28.72	−85.79	−64.51	−227.80	−170.71
Monetary authorities	4 621	....	....	....	....	....	....	....	....
General government	4 622	....	....	....	....	....	....	....	....
Banks	4 623	....	....	....	....	....	....	....	....
Other sectors	4 624	....	....	....	....	....	....	....	....
Money market instruments	4 630	....	....	....	23.59	−6.81	−6.34	−133.77	−5.84
Monetary authorities	4 631	....	....	....	....	....	....	....	....
General government	4 632	....	....	....	....	....	....	....	....
Banks	4 633	....	....	....	18.61	−2.15	−1.88	−5.77	−7.47
Other sectors	4 634	....	....	....	4.98	−4.66	−4.46	−128.00	1.63
Liabilities	4 652	**436.57**	**428.34**	**427.61**	**550.16**	**867.34**	**832.04**	**1,126.88**	**1,145.14**
Equity securities	4 660	193.60	121.46	54.07	33.98	61.79	89.26	145.57	197.52
Banks	4 663	....	....	....	....	....	....	....	....
Other sectors	4 664	....	....	....	....	....	....	....	....
Debt securities	4 669	242.97	306.88	373.54	516.18	805.55	742.78	981.31	947.63
Bonds and notes	4 670	242.97	306.88	373.54	486.33	705.00	785.80	953.74	781.66
Monetary authorities	4 671	....	....	....	....	....	....	....	....
General government	4 672	74.55	111.50	222.53	257.53	438.97	454.34	407.38	357.99
Banks	4 673	....	....	....	....	....	....	....	....
Other sectors	4 674	168.42	195.38	151.02	228.80	266.03	331.46	546.36	423.67
Money market instruments	4 680	....	....	....	29.85	100.55	−43.02	27.57	165.96
Monetary authorities	4 681	....	....	....	....	....	....	....	....
General government	4 682	....	....	....	22.00	36.96	−58.94	−11.40	48.52
Banks	4 683	....	....	....	....	....	....	....	....
Other sectors	4 684	....	....	....	7.85	63.59	15.92	38.96	117.45
C. FINANCIAL DERIVATIVES	4 910	....	....	....	....	....	....	**29.71**	**6.50**
Monetary authorities	4 911	....	....	....	....	....	....	....	....
General government	4 912	....	....	....	....	....	....	....	....
Banks	4 913	....	....	....	....	....	....	....	....
Other sectors	4 914	....	....	....	....	....	....	....	....
Assets	4 900	....	....	....	....	....	....	....	....
Monetary authorities	4 901	....	....	....	....	....	....	....	....
General government	4 902	....	....	....	....	....	....	....	....
Banks	4 903	....	....	....	....	....	....	....	....
Other sectors	4 904	....	....	....	....	....	....	....	....
Liabilities	4 905	....	....	....	....	....	....	**29.71**	**6.50**
Monetary authorities	4 906	....	....	....	....	....	....	....	....
General government	4 907	....	....	....	....	....	....	....	....
Banks	4 908	....	....	....	....	....	....	....	....
Other sectors	4 909	....	....	....	....	....	....	....	....

Table 2 (Concluded). STANDARD PRESENTATION, 2000–2007

(Billions of U.S. dollars)

	Code	2000	2001	2002	2003	2004	2005	2006	2007
D. OTHER INVESTMENT........................	4 700 ..	**7.26**	**42.79**	**195.24**	**190.14**	**9.81**	**35.72**	**178.37**	**13.13**
Assets..	4 703 ..	**−273.11**	**−144.71**	**−87.94**	**−54.26**	**−510.09**	**−266.96**	**−513.90**	**−661.89**
Trade credits..................................	4 706 ..	−.48	5.52	1.13	−2.23	−.41	−.36	−3.34	−8.35
General government..................	4 707 ..	....	....	....	....	....	....	....	....
of which: Short-term............	4 709 ..	....	....	....	....	....	....	....	....
Other sectors............................	4 710 ..	−.48	5.52	1.13	−2.23	−.41	−.36	−3.34	−8.35
of which: Short-term............	4 712 ..	....	....	....	....	....	....	....	....
Loans..	4 714 ..	−.94	−.49	.35	14.94	−209.91	−100.42	−138.38	−470.05
Monetary authorities................	4 715 ..	....	....	....	....	....	....	....	....
of which: Short-term............	4 718 ..	....	....	....	....	....	....	....	....
General government..................	4 719 ..	−.94	−.49	.35	.54	1.71	5.54	5.35	−22.27
of which: Short-term............	4 721 ..	....	....	....	....	....	....	....	....
Banks.......................................	4 722 ..	....	....	....	1.49	−193.23	−93.32	−137.86	−458.87
of which: Short-term............	4 724 ..	....	....	....	....	....	....	....	....
Other sectors............................	4 725 ..	....	....	....	12.92	−18.40	−12.64	−5.87	11.09
of which: Short-term............	4 727 ..	....	....	....	....	....	....	....	....
Currency and deposits....................	4 730 ..	−133.38	−135.71	−38.26	−70.00	−251.94	−93.13	−277.14	−272.14
Monetary authorities................	4 731 ..	....	....	....	....	....	....	....	....
General government..................	4 732 ..	....	....	....	....	....	....	....	....
Banks.......................................	4 733 ..	−133.38	−135.71	−38.26	−27.20	−165.81	−57.75	−191.48	−56.96
Other sectors............................	4 734 ..	....	....	....	−42.80	−86.13	−35.38	−85.66	−215.18
Other assets..................................	4 736 ..	−138.32	−14.04	−51.16	3.03	−47.84	−73.05	−95.04	88.64
Monetary authorities................	4 737 ..	....	....	....	....	....	....	....	....
of which: Short-term............	4 739 ..	....	....	....	....	....	....	....	....
General government..................	4 740 ..	....	....	....	....	....	....	....	....
of which: Short-term............	4 742 ..	....	....	....	....	....	....	....	....
Banks.......................................	4 743 ..	....	....	....	....	....	....	....	....
of which: Short-term............	4 745 ..	....	....	....	....	....	....	....	....
Other sectors............................	4 746 ..	−138.32	−14.04	−51.16	3.03	−47.84	−73.05	−95.04	88.64
of which: Short-term............	4 748 ..	....	....	....	....	....	....	....	....
Liabilities..	4 753 ..	**280.38**	**187.51**	**283.18**	**244.39**	**519.90**	**302.67**	**692.27**	**675.02**
Trade credits..................................	4 756 ..	1.44	−2.47	2.52	2.50	.92	7.01	2.55	2.04
General government..................	4 757 ..	....	....	....	....	....	....	....	....
of which: Short-term............	4 759 ..	....	....	....	....	....	....	....	....
Other sectors............................	4 760 ..	1.44	−2.47	2.52	2.50	.92	7.01	2.55	2.04
of which: Short-term............	4 762 ..	....	....	....	....	....	....	....	....
Loans..	4 764 ..	....	....	....	113.90	252.05	96.05	185.05	268.94
Monetary authorities................	4 765 ..	....	....	....	....	....	....	....	....
of which: Use of Fund credit and loans from the Fund..	4 766 ..	....	....	....	....	....	....	....	....
of which: Short-term............	4 768 ..	....	....	....	....	....	....	....	....
General government..................	4 769 ..	....	....	....	....	....	....	....	....
of which: Short-term............	4 771 ..	....	....	....	....	....	....	....	....
Banks.......................................	4 772 ..	....	....	....	113.77	241.30	121.81	83.96	239.92
of which: Short-term............	4 774 ..	....	....	....	....	....	....	....	....
Other sectors............................	4 775 ..	....	....	....	.13	10.75	−25.76	101.09	29.01
of which: Short-term............	4 777 ..	....	....	....	....	....	....	....	....
Currency and deposits....................	4 780 ..	119.36	112.20	136.49	32.88	118.70	119.05	261.66	225.96
Monetary authorities................	4 781 ..	−3.36	23.79	18.86	10.59	13.30	8.45	2.23	−10.68
General government..................	4 782 ..	....	....	....	....	....	....	....	....
Banks.......................................	4 783 ..	122.72	88.40	117.63	22.29	105.40	110.61	259.43	236.63
Other sectors............................	4 784 ..	....	....	....	....	....	....	....	....
Other liabilities..............................	4 786 ..	159.58	77.78	144.17	95.11	148.23	80.57	243.02	178.09
Monetary authorities................	4 787 ..	−7.83	11.51	50.68	....	....	....	....	....
of which: Short-term............	4 789 ..	*−7.83*	*11.51*	*50.68*	....	....	....	....	....
General government..................	4 790 ..	−1.83	−2.31	.14	−.72	−.13	−.42	2.82	5.34
of which: Short-term............	4 792 ..	....	....	....	....	....	....	....	....
Banks.......................................	4 793 ..	....	....	....	....	....	....	....	....
of which: Short-term............	4 795 ..	....	....	....	....	....	....	....	....
Other sectors............................	4 796 ..	169.24	68.58	93.35	95.83	148.36	80.99	240.21	172.75
of which: Short-term............	4 798 ..	....	....	....	....	....	....	....	....
E. RESERVE ASSETS.............................	4 802 ..	**−.29**	**−4.93**	**−3.69**	**1.53**	**2.80**	**14.10**	**2.39**	**−.13**
Monetary gold...................................	4 812 ..	....	....	....	....	....	....	....	....
Special drawing rights......................	4 811 ..	−.72	−.63	−.48	.60	−.40	4.50	−.22	−.15
Reserve position in the fund.............	4 810 ..	2.30	−3.62	−2.64	1.50	3.83	10.21	3.35	1.02
Foreign exchange.............................	4 803 ..	−1.88	−.68	−.57	−.57	−.62	−.62	−.73	−.99
Other claims....................................	4 813 ..	....	....	....	....	....	....	....	....
NET ERRORS AND OMISSIONS.............	4 998 ..	**−59.26**	**−14.27**	**−37.76**	**−6.00**	**95.03**	**32.31**	**−47.10**	**−41.29**

2008, International Monetary Fund: *Balance of Payments Statistics Yearbook*

Table 3. INTERNATIONAL INVESTMENT POSITION (End-period stocks), 2000–2007

(Billions of U.S. dollars)

	Code	2000	2001	2002	2003	2004	2005	2006	2007
ASSETS	8 995 C.	**6,238.78**	**6,308.68**	**6,649.08**	**7,638.09**	**9,340.63**	**11,961.55**	**14,381.30**	**17,639.95**
Direct investment abroad	8 505 ..	**1,531.61**	**1,693.13**	**1,867.04**	**2,054.46**	**2,498.49**	**2,651.72**	**2,935.98**	**3,332.83**
Equity capital and reinvested earnings	8 506 ..	....	....	....	....	....	....	....	....
Claims on affiliated enterprises	8 507 ..	....	....	....	....	....	....	....	....
Liabilities to affiliated enterprises	8 508 ..	....	....	....	....	....	....	....	....
Other capital	8 530 ..	....	....	....	....	....	....	....	....
Claims on affiliated enterprises	8 535 ..	....	....	....	....	....	....	....	....
Liabilities to affiliated enterprises	8 540 ..	....	....	....	....	....	....	....	....
Portfolio investment	8 602 ..	**2,425.53**	**2,169.74**	**2,076.72**	**3,169.52**	**3,808.03**	**4,598.68**	**5,988.38**	**7,048.45**
Equity securities	8 610 ..	1,852.84	1,612.67	1,373.98	2,079.42	2,560.42	3,317.71	4,328.96	5,170.60
Monetary authorities	8 611 ..	....	....	....	....	....	....	....	....
General government	8 612 ..	....	....	....	....	....	....	....	....
Banks	8 613 ..	....	....	....	....	....	....	....	....
Other sectors	8 614 ..	....	....	....	....	....	....	....	....
Debt securities	8 619 ..	572.69	557.06	702.74	1,090.10	1,247.61	1,280.98	1,659.42	1,877.85
Bonds and notes	8 620 ..	572.69	557.06	702.74	868.95	984.98	1,011.55	1,275.52	1,478.09
Monetary authorities	8 621 ..	....	....	....	....	....	....	....	....
General government	8 622 ..	....	....	....	....	....	....	....	....
Banks	8 623 ..	....	....	....	....	....	....	....	....
Other sectors	8 624 ..	....	....	....	....	....	....	....	....
Money market instruments	8 630 ..	....	....	....	221.15	262.63	269.42	383.91	399.76
Monetary authorities	8 631 ..	....	....	....	....	....	....	....	....
General government	8 632 ..	....	....	....	....	....	....	....	....
Banks	8 633 ..	....	....	....	5.70	7.86	9.74	15.51	22.98
Other sectors	8 634 ..	....	....	....	215.44	254.78	259.69	368.40	376.79
Financial derivatives	8 900 ..	....	....	....	....	....	**1,190.03**	**1,239.00**	**2,284.58**
Monetary authorities	8 901 ..	....	....	....	....	....	....	....	....
General government	8 902 ..	....	....	....	....	....	....	....	....
Banks	8 903 ..	....	....	....	....	....	....	....	....
Other sectors	8 904 ..	....	....	....	....	....	....	....	....
Other investment	8 703 ..	**2,153.24**	**2,315.85**	**2,546.71**	**2,230.53**	**2,844.52**	**3,333.08**	**3,998.09**	**4,696.89**
Trade credits	8 706 ..	33.10	27.59	26.45	28.65	29.23	29.23	32.80	41.44
General government	8 707 ..	....	....	....	....	....	....	....	....
of which: Short-term	8 709 ..	....	....	....	....	....	....	....	....
Other sectors	8 710 ..	33.10	27.59	26.45	28.65	29.23	29.23	32.80	41.44
of which: Short-term	8 712 ..	....	....	....	....	....	....	....	....
Loans	8 714 ..	2,120.14	2,288.27	2,520.26	961.23	1,192.49	1,291.72	1,559.83	2,045.23
Monetary authorities	8 715 ..	....	....	....	....	....	....	....	....
of which: Short-term	8 718 ..	....	....	....	....	....	....	....	....
General government	8 719 ..	85.17	85.65	85.31	84.77	83.06	77.52	72.19	94.47
of which: Short-term	8 721 ..	....	....	....	....	....	....	....	....
Banks	8 722 ..	1,231.52	1,390.90	1,559.46	848.77	1,059.79	1,154.65	1,418.18	1,889.96
of which: Short-term	8 724 ..	....	....	....	....	....	....	....	....
Other sectors	8 725 ..	803.46	811.72	875.49	27.69	49.64	59.55	69.46	60.80
of which: Short-term	8 727 ..	....	....	....	....	....	....	....	....
Currency and deposits	8 730 ..	....	....	....	1,146.16	1,451.72	1,607.33	1,898.54	2,190.21
Monetary authorities	8 731 ..	....	....	....	....	....	....	....	....
General government	8 732 ..	....	....	....	....	....	....	....	....
Banks	8 733 ..	....	....	....	538.19	719.28	792.26	983.11	1,045.03
Other sectors	8 734 ..	....	....	....	607.98	732.44	815.07	915.43	1,145.18
Other assets	8 736 ..	....	....	....	94.48	171.07	404.80	506.92	420.01
Monetary authorities	8 737 ..	....	....	....	....	....	....	....	....
of which: Short-term	8 739 ..	....	....	....	....	....	....	....	....
General government	8 740 ..	....	....	....	....	....	....	....	....
of which: Short-term	8 742 ..	....	....	....	....	....	....	....	....
Banks	8 743 ..	....	....	....	....	....	....	....	....
of which: Short-term	8 745 ..	....	....	....	....	....	....	....	....
Other sectors	8 746 ..	....	....	....	94.48	171.07	404.80	506.92	420.01
of which: Short-term	8 748 ..	....	....	....	....	....	....	....	....
Reserve assets	8 802 ..	**128.40**	**129.96**	**158.60**	**183.58**	**189.59**	**188.04**	**219.85**	**277.21**
Monetary gold	8 812 ..	71.80	72.33	90.81	108.87	113.95	134.18	165.27	218.03
Special drawing rights	8 811 ..	10.54	10.78	12.17	12.64	13.63	8.21	8.87	9.48
Reserve position in the Fund	8 810 ..	14.82	17.87	21.98	22.53	19.54	8.04	5.04	4.24
Foreign exchange	8 803 ..	31.24	28.98	33.65	39.54	42.47	37.62	40.68	45.47
Other claims	8 813 ..	....	....	....	....	....	....	....	....

Table 3 (Concluded). INTERNATIONAL INVESTMENT POSITION (End-period stocks), 2000–2007

(Billions of U.S. dollars)

	Code	2000	2001	2002	2003	2004	2005	2006	2007
LIABILITIES	8 995 D.	**7,569.42**	**8,177.56**	**8,687.05**	**9,724.60**	**11,586.05**	**13,886.70**	**16,607.10**	**20,081.78**
Direct investment in United States	8 555	**1,421.02**	**1,518.47**	**1,499.95**	**1,580.99**	**1,742.72**	**1,905.98**	**2,151.62**	**2,422.80**
Equity capital and reinvested earnings	8 556	....	....	....	....	....	....	....	....
Claims on direct investors	8 557	....	....	....	....	....	....	....	....
Liabilities to direct investors	8 558	....	....	....	....	....	....	....	....
Other capital	8 580	....	....	....	....	....	....	....	....
Claims on direct investors	8 585	....	....	....	....	....	....	....	....
Liabilities to direct investors	8 590	....	....	....	....	....	....	....	....
Portfolio investment	8 652	**3,862.63**	**4,153.84**	**4,330.53**	**5,546.32**	**6,621.23**	**7,337.84**	**8,843.57**	**10,298.23**
Equity securities	8 660	1,643.21	1,572.68	1,335.79	1,839.51	2,123.26	2,304.01	2,791.91	3,107.84
Banks	8 663	....	....	....	....	....	....	....	....
Other sectors	8 664	....	....	....	....	....	....	....	....
Debt securities	8 669	2,219.43	2,581.16	2,994.74	3,706.81	4,497.97	5,033.82	6,051.66	7,190.39
Bonds and notes	8 670	2,219.43	2,581.16	2,994.74	3,164.74	3,835.42	4,421.83	5,404.94	6,364.83
Monetary authorities	8 671	....	....	....	....	....	....	....	....
General government	8 672	1,391.11	1,546.51	1,848.46	1,800.08	2,198.77	2,589.02	3,017.25	3,522.84
Banks	8 673	....	....	....	....	....	....	....	....
Other sectors	8 674	828.31	1,034.65	1,146.27	1,364.66	1,636.64	1,832.81	2,387.70	2,842.00
Money market instruments	8 680	....	....	....	542.07	662.55	611.99	646.72	825.56
Monetary authorities	8 681	....	....	....	....	....	....	....	....
General government	8 682	....	....	....	290.92	323.67	264.73	253.33	301.85
Banks	8 683	....	....	....	....	....	....	....	....
Other sectors	8 684	....	....	....	251.15	338.88	347.27	393.39	523.71
Financial derivatives	8 905	....	....	....	....	....	**1,132.11**	**1,179.16**	**2,201.05**
Monetary authorities	8 906	....	....	....	....	....	....	....	....
General government	8 907	....	....	....	....	....	....	....	....
Banks	8 908	....	....	....	....	....	....	....	....
Other sectors	8 909	....	....	....	....	....	....	....	....
Other investment	8 753	**2,285.77**	**2,505.24**	**2,856.57**	**2,597.29**	**3,222.11**	**3,510.77**	**4,432.76**	**5,159.71**
Trade credits	8 756	14.29	11.82	14.34	17.17	18.18	23.05	25.67	27.87
General government	8 757	....	....	....	....	....	....	....	....
of which: Short-term	8 759	....	....	....	....	....	....	....	....
Other sectors	8 760	14.29	11.82	14.34	17.17	18.18	23.05	25.67	27.87
of which: Short-term	8 762	....	....	....	....	....	....	....	....
Loans	8 764	....	....	....	1,013.24	1,375.79	1,482.90	1,951.72	2,260.14
Monetary authorities	8 765	....	....	....	....	....	....	....	....
of which: Use of Fund credit and loans from the Fund	8 766	....	....	....	....	....	....	....	....
of which: Short-term	8 768	....	....	....	....	....	....	....	....
General government	8 769	....	....	....	....	....	....	....	....
of which: Short-term	8 771	....	....	....	....	....	....	....	....
Banks	8 772	....	....	....	818.70	1,143.20	1,260.23	1,620.76	1,899.39
of which: Short-term	8 774	....	....	....	....	....	....	....	....
Other sectors	8 775	....	....	....	194.54	232.59	222.67	330.96	360.75
of which: Short-term	8 777	....	....	....	....	....	....	....	....
Currency and deposits	8 780	205.41	229.20	248.06	1,148.13	1,279.44	1,383.44	1,695.05	1,928.55
Monetary authorities	8 781	205.41	229.20	248.06	258.65	271.95	280.40	282.63	271.95
General government	8 782	....	....	....	....	....	....	....	....
Banks	8 783	....	....	....	889.48	1,007.48	1,103.04	1,412.43	1,656.59
Other sectors	8 784	....	....	....	....	....	....	....	....
Other liabilities	8 786	2,066.07	2,264.22	2,594.17	418.74	548.71	621.38	760.31	943.15
Monetary authorities	8 787	....	....	....	....	....	....	....	....
of which: Short-term	8 789	....	....	....	....	....	....	....	....
General government	8 790	19.32	17.01	17.14	16.42	16.29	15.87	18.68	24.02
of which: Short-term	8 792	....	....	....	....	....	....	....	....
Banks	8 793	1,322.14	1,460.72	1,694.03	....	....	....	....	....
of which: Short-term	8 795	....	....	....	....	....	....	....	....
Other sectors	8 796	724.61	786.49	883.00	402.32	532.42	605.51	741.63	919.13
of which: Short-term	8 798	....	....	....	....	....	....	....	....
NET INTERNATIONAL INVESTMENT POSITION	8 995	**−1,330.63**	**−1,868.87**	**−2,037.97**	**−2,086.51**	**−2,245.42**	**−1,925.15**	**−2,225.80**	**−2,441.83**

Table 1. ANALYTIC PRESENTATION, 2000–2007

(Millions of U.S. dollars)

	Code	2000	2001	2002	2003	2004	2005	2006	2007
A. Current Account[1]	4 993 Z.	−566.3	−497.6	381.9	−87.3	3.1	24.3	−369.2	−185.7
Goods: exports f.o.b.	2 100 ..	2,383.8	2,139.5	1,922.1	2,281.2	3,145.0	3,774.1	4,407.1	5,063.0
Goods: imports f.o.b.	3 100 ..	−3,311.1	−2,914.8	−1,873.8	−2,097.8	−2,992.2	−3,753.3	−4,867.0	−5,554.3
Balance on Goods	4 100 ..	*−927.3*	*−775.3*	*48.3*	*183.4*	*152.8*	*20.8*	*−459.9*	*−491.3*
Services: credit	2 200 ..	1,275.8	1,122.5	771.3	771.3	1,111.6	1,311.3	1,392.2	1,761.8
Services: debit	3 200 ..	−881.6	−806.7	−618.1	−636.3	−786.1	−939.5	−986.7	−1,248.9
Balance on Goods and Services	4 991 ..	*−533.1*	*−459.5*	*201.5*	*318.5*	*478.3*	*392.6*	*−54.3*	*21.6*
Income: credit	2 300 ..	781.5	832.8	453.1	241.9	372.4	563.1	734.0	878.5
Income: debit	3 300 ..	−842.2	−900.7	−344.4	−730.3	−960.4	−1,057.3	−1,175.2	−1,220.0
Balance on Goods, Services, and Income	4 992 ..	*−593.8*	*−527.3*	*310.2*	*−169.9*	*−109.7*	*−101.5*	*−495.5*	*−319.9*
Current transfers: credit	2 379 Z.	48.0	48.0	83.7	95.0	127.2	143.1	150.0	159.4
Current transfers: debit	3 379 ..	−20.5	−18.3	−11.9	−12.3	−14.3	−17.3	−23.7	−25.1
B. Capital Account[1]	4 994 Z.	....	....	....	4.3	5.3	3.8	6.5	3.7
Capital account: credit	2 994 Z.	....	....	....	4.3	5.3	3.8	6.5	3.7
Capital account: debit	3 994 ..	....	....	....	....	....	....	....	....
Total, Groups A Plus B	4 981 ..	*−566.3*	*−497.6*	*381.9*	*−82.9*	*8.4*	*28.1*	*−362.7*	*−181.9*
C. Financial Account[1]	4 995 W.	765.4	490.1	−1,884.6	6.7	−81.9	923.6	2,840.4	1,226.0
Direct investment abroad	4 505 ..	−.8	−6.2	−13.7	−15.1	−17.7	−36.3	1.0	−3.6
Direct investment in Uruguay	4 555 Z.	268.6	296.8	193.7	416.4	332.4	847.4	1,398.8	879.2
Portfolio investment assets	4 602 ..	−1.9	236.5	280.0	−512.6	−695.7	577.7	−97.2	176.7
Equity securities	4 610 ..	−3.4	10.2	15.3	8.9	.9	.3	−.2	−.2
Debt securities	4 619 ..	1.5	226.3	264.8	−521.6	−696.6	577.4	−96.9	176.9
Portfolio investment liabilities	4 652 Z.	193.3	271.2	48.6	201.6	273.4	228.2	1,783.5	995.3
Equity securities	4 660 ..	5.1	34.9	−9.5	−6.4	20.1	−2.4	−26.6	−26.6
Debt securities	4 669 Z.	188.2	236.3	58.1	208.0	253.3	230.6	1,810.2	1,021.9
Financial derivatives	4 910 ..	....	....	....	....	....	....	....	....
Financial derivatives assets	4 900 ..	....	....	....	....	....	....	....	....
Financial derivatives liabilities	4 905 ..	....	....	....	....	....	....	....	....
Other investment assets	4 703 ..	−690.3	−2,275.3	1,781.3	−1,254.9	−259.7	−1,112.7	1,414.9	−1,853.1
Monetary authorities	4 701 ..	.9	−5.4	−522.6	270.4	218.0	−324.8	334.1	−1,004.7
General government	4 704 ..	....	....	1.8	−14.9	−1.0	−1.1	−.8	....
Banks	4 705 ..	−549.2	−2,210.6	2,967.3	−1,399.6	−397.6	−843.6	1,109.6	−483.4
Other sectors	4 728 ..	−142.0	−59.2	−665.3	−110.8	−79.1	56.7	−28.0	−365.0
Other investment liabilities	4 753 W.	996.4	1,967.0	−4,174.4	1,171.3	285.4	419.4	−1,660.7	1,031.5
Monetary authorities	4 753 WA	−46.6	−52.4	−14.5	−63.9	−25.8	−31.5	−33.7	110.0
General government	4 753 ZB	200.7	144.5	667.3	328.9	39.5	49.9	−575.1	5.8
Banks	4 753 ZC	862.6	1,781.6	−4,693.6	963.9	366.3	405.2	−1,197.1	124.0
Other sectors	4 753 ZD	−20.2	93.4	−133.7	−57.6	−94.6	−4.3	145.1	791.7
Total, Groups A Through C	4 983 ..	*199.1*	*−7.5*	*−1,502.6*	*−76.3*	*−73.5*	*951.8*	*2,477.7*	*1,044.1*
D. Net Errors and Omissions	4 998 ..	25.8	286.8	−2,394.5	1,034.2	377.9	−173.4	−110.3	−38.7
Total, Groups A Through D	4 984 ..	*224.9*	*279.2*	*−3,897.1*	*957.9*	*304.4*	*778.4*	*2,367.4*	*1,005.4*
E. Reserves and Related Items	4 802 A.	−224.9	−279.2	3,897.1	−957.9	−304.4	−778.4	−2,367.4	−1,005.4
Reserve assets	4 802 ..	−224.9	−279.2	2,331.1	−1,380.4	−454.2	−620.9	15.8	−1,005.4
Use of Fund credit and loans	4 766 ..	....	....	1,565.9	422.5	149.8	−175.5	−2,383.2	....
Exceptional financing	4 920 ..	....	....	....	....	....	18.0	....	....
Conversion rates: Uruguayan pesos per U.S. dollar	0 101 ..	12.0996	13.3191	21.2570	28.2087	28.7037	24.4786	24.0734	23.4710

[1] Excludes components that have been classified in the categories of Group E.

Table 2. STANDARD PRESENTATION, 2000–2007

(Millions of U.S. dollars)

	Code	2000	2001	2002	2003	2004	2005	2006	2007
CURRENT ACCOUNT	4 993 ..	**−566.3**	**−497.6**	**381.9**	**−87.3**	**3.1**	**42.3**	**−369.2**	**−185.7**
A. GOODS	4 100 ..	**−927.3**	**−775.3**	**48.3**	**183.4**	**152.8**	**20.8**	**−459.9**	**−491.3**
Credit	2 100 ..	**2,383.8**	**2,139.5**	**1,922.1**	**2,281.2**	**3,145.0**	**3,774.1**	**4,407.1**	**5,063.0**
General merchandise: exports f.o.b.	2 110 ..	2,299.5	2,057.6	1,861.0	2,205.9	3,041.7	3,622.2	4,263.8	4,876.7
Goods for processing: exports f.o.b.	2 150 ..	....	....	....	....	....	....	....	....
Repairs on goods	2 160 ..	....	....	....	....	....	....	....	....
Goods procured in ports by carriers	2 170 ..	84.3	81.9	61.0	75.3	103.3	151.9	143.3	186.3
Nonmonetary gold	2 180 ..	....	....	....	....	....	....	....	....
Debit	3 100 ..	**−3,311.1**	**−2,914.8**	**−1,873.8**	**−2,097.8**	**−2,992.2**	**−3,753.3**	**−4,867.0**	**−5,554.3**
General merchandise: imports f.o.b.	3 110 ..	−3,276.4	−2,883.8	−1,849.5	−2,064.6	−2,963.2	−3,696.2	−4,805.6	−5,479.8
Goods for processing: imports f.o.b.	3 150 ..	....	....	....	....	....	....	....	....
Repairs on goods	3 160 ..	....	....	....	....	....	....	....	....
Goods procured in ports by carriers	3 170 ..	−34.7	−31.0	−24.3	−33.2	−29.0	−57.0	−61.4	−74.5
Nonmonetary gold	3 180 ..	....	....	....	....	....	....	....	....
B. SERVICES	4 200 ..	**394.2**	**315.8**	**153.3**	**135.0**	**325.5**	**371.8**	**405.5**	**512.9**
Total credit	2 200 ..	*1,275.8*	*1,122.5*	*771.3*	*771.3*	*1,111.6*	*1,311.3*	*1,392.2*	*1,761.8*
Total debit	3 200 ..	*−881.6*	*−806.7*	*−618.1*	*−636.3*	*−786.1*	*−939.5*	*−986.7*	*−1,248.9*
Transportation services, credit	2 205 ..	**374.3**	**312.4**	**265.1**	**258.8**	**379.0**	**464.8**	**478.2**	**608.4**
Passenger	2 850 ..	*114.0*	*88.8*	*57.5*	*74.4*	*97.1*	*105.0*	*112.1*	*118.2*
Freight	2 851 ..	*165.7*	*141.5*	*132.9*	*111.7*	*215.4*	*286.9*	*284.9*	*392.7*
Other	2 852 ..	*94.6*	*82.1*	*74.7*	*72.7*	*66.5*	*73.0*	*81.1*	*97.5*
Sea transport, passenger	2 207 ..	....	....	....	....	....	....	....	....
Sea transport, freight	2 208 ..	....	....	....	....	....	....	....	....
Sea transport, other	2 209 ..	....	....	....	....	....	....	....	....
Air transport, passenger	2 211 ..	....	....	....	....	....	....	....	....
Air transport, freight	2 212 ..	....	....	....	....	....	....	....	....
Air transport, other	2 213 ..	....	....	....	....	....	....	....	....
Other transport, passenger	2 215 ..	114.0	88.8	57.5	74.4	97.1	105.0	112.1	118.2
Other transport, freight	2 216 ..	165.7	141.5	132.9	111.7	215.4	286.9	284.9	392.7
Other transport, other	2 217 ..	94.6	82.1	74.7	72.7	66.5	73.0	81.1	97.5
Transportation services, debit	3 205 ..	**−399.5**	**−354.9**	**−259.8**	**−264.6**	**−353.0**	**−419.0**	**−457.5**	**−620.4**
Passenger	3 850 ..	*−99.8*	*−81.2*	*−65.2*	*−66.7*	*−73.4*	*−79.3*	*−91.7*	*−109.5*
Freight	3 851 ..	*−151.5*	*−141.6*	*−91.9*	*−100.6*	*−135.0*	*−168.6*	*−180.2*	*−240.0*
Other	3 852 ..	*−148.2*	*−132.0*	*−102.8*	*−97.4*	*−144.6*	*−171.1*	*−185.6*	*−271.0*
Sea transport, passenger	3 207 ..	....	....	....	....	....	....	....	....
Sea transport, freight	3 208 ..	....	....	....	....	....	....	....	....
Sea transport, other	3 209 ..	....	....	....	....	....	....	....	....
Air transport, passenger	3 211 ..	....	....	....	....	....	....	....	....
Air transport, freight	3 212 ..	....	....	....	....	....	....	....	....
Air transport, other	3 213 ..	....	....	....	....	....	....	....	....
Other transport, passenger	3 215 ..	−99.8	−81.2	−65.2	−66.7	−73.4	−79.3	−91.7	−109.5
Other transport, freight	3 216 ..	−151.5	−141.6	−91.9	−100.6	−135.0	−168.6	−180.2	−240.0
Other transport, other	3 217 ..	−148.2	−132.0	−102.8	−97.4	−144.6	−171.1	−185.6	−271.0
Travel, credit	2 236 ..	**712.8**	**610.5**	**350.9**	**344.7**	**493.9**	**594.4**	**597.8**	**808.8**
Business travel	2 237 ..	....	....	....	....	....	....	....	....
Personal travel	2 240 ..	712.8	610.5	350.9	344.7	493.9	594.4	597.8	808.8
Travel, debit	3 236 ..	**−281.4**	**−257.0**	**−177.6**	**−168.8**	**−193.6**	**−251.7**	**−213.2**	**−239.3**
Business travel	3 237 ..	....	....	....	....	....	....	....	....
Personal travel	3 240 ..	−281.4	−257.0	−177.6	−168.8	−193.6	−251.7	−213.2	−239.3
Other services, credit	2 200 BA	**188.7**	**199.6**	**155.3**	**167.9**	**238.6**	**252.0**	**316.3**	**344.7**
Communications	2 245 ..	27.4	41.5	29.9	23.0	24.4	21.6	22.0	24.4
Construction	2 249 ..	....	....	....	....	....	....	....	....
Insurance	2 253 ..	32.8	22.1	17.1	2.1	9.7	4.2	3.6	3.4
Financial	2 260 ..	62.0	71.9	54.2	58.0	53.4	65.7	63.5	76.8
Computer and information	2 262 ..	10.0	14.6	13.8	11.7	72.1	82.5	121.6	130.0
Royalties and licence fees	2 266 ..	.1	.1	....	....	....	.1	....	....
Other business services	2 268 ..	24.4	22.7	13.6	47.1	52.2	51.5	76.7	81.2
Personal, cultural, and recreational	2 287 ..	4.7	3.7	.2	.4	.9	.4	2.2	2.2
Government, n.i.e.	2 291 ..	27.2	23.2	26.6	25.7	25.9	26.1	26.6	26.6
Other services, debit	3 200 BA	**−200.7**	**−194.8**	**−180.7**	**−202.9**	**−239.4**	**−268.7**	**−316.0**	**−389.1**
Communications	3 245 ..	−22.8	−29.5	−26.5	−18.3	−19.2	−20.0	−16.6	−17.3
Construction	3 249 ..	....	....	....	....	....	....	....	....
Insurance	3 253 ..	−33.9	−29.2	−27.7	−19.0	−27.0	−24.9	−28.8	−35.3
Financial	3 260 ..	−18.8	−12.4	−9.4	−17.5	−10.8	−11.3	−15.4	−28.9
Computer and information	3 262 ..	−1.9	−1.3	−2.8	−1.7	−3.8	−3.9	−4.2	−4.2
Royalties and licence fees	3 266 ..	−6.5	−9.8	−6.8	−14.0	−4.3	−6.9	−7.3	−7.3
Other business services	3 268 ..	−65.0	−62.8	−64.0	−87.3	−128.6	−153.1	−192.9	−245.3
Personal, cultural, and recreational	3 287 ..	−12.6	−16.2	−18.0	−10.5	−7.2	−10.0	−9.5	−9.5
Government, n.i.e.	3 291 ..	−39.4	−33.6	−25.5	−34.5	−38.4	−38.7	−41.3	−41.3

2008, International Monetary Fund: *Balance of Payments Statistics Yearbook*

Table 2 (Continued). STANDARD PRESENTATION, 2000–2007

(Millions of U.S. dollars)

	Code	2000	2001	2002	2003	2004	2005	2006	2007
C. INCOME	4 300	**−60.7**	**−67.8**	**108.6**	**−488.4**	**−588.0**	**−494.2**	**−441.2**	**−341.5**
Total credit	2 300	*781.5*	*832.8*	*453.1*	*241.9*	*372.4*	*563.1*	*734.0*	*878.5*
Total debit	3 300	*−842.2*	*−900.7*	*−344.4*	*−730.3*	*−960.4*	*−1,057.3*	*−1,175.2*	*−1,220.0*
Compensation of employees, credit	2 310	....	....	.4	....	....	....	....	....
Compensation of employees, debit	3 310	....	....	....	....	....	....	....	....
Investment income, credit	2 320	781.5	832.8	452.7	241.9	372.4	563.1	734.0	878.5
Direct investment income	2 330	1.3	.6	7.6	3.2	8.0	5.4	10.9	11.0
Dividends and distributed branch profits	2 332	....	.3	7.4	3.2	7.5	3.2	10.1	10.1
Reinvested earnings and undistributed branch profits	2 333	1.3	....	....	....	....	....	....	....
Income on debt (interest)	2 334	....	.3	.2	....	.5	2.1	.9	.9
Portfolio investment income	2 339	70.6	79.7	.3	5.7	128.3	168.5	195.6	196.8
Income on equity	2 340	....	....	.1	....	1.3	.4	.9	3.0
Income on bonds and notes	2 350	70.6	79.7	.1	5.7	127.0	168.1	194.7	193.8
Income on money market instruments	2 360	....	....	....	....	....	....	....	....
Other investment income	2 370	709.6	752.5	444.8	232.9	236.0	389.2	527.5	670.7
Investment income, debit	3 320	**−842.2**	**−900.7**	**−344.4**	**−730.3**	**−960.4**	**−1,057.3**	**−1,175.2**	**−1,220.0**
Direct investment income	3 330	−99.0	−107.9	264.2	−127.4	−229.0	−227.6	−266.3	−349.0
Dividends and distributed branch profits	3 332	73.9	138.0	337.3	54.5	−79.3	−85.9	−35.6	−91.8
Reinvested earnings and undistributed branch profits	3 333	−163.2	−240.4	−62.8	−172.9	−142.1	−132.6	−223.9	−250.4
Income on debt (interest)	3 334	−9.6	−5.4	−10.3	−9.0	−7.6	−9.0	−6.8	−6.8
Portfolio investment income	3 339	−158.4	−181.9	−186.2	−220.5	−267.4	−295.5	−456.0	−492.1
Income on equity	3 340	....	....	−.4	−21.7	−9.1	−5.6	−.8	....
Income on bonds and notes	3 350	−158.4	−181.9	−185.8	−198.8	−258.3	−290.0	−455.1	−492.1
Income on money market instruments	3 360	....	....	....	....	....	....	....	....
Other investment income	3 370	−584.9	−610.9	−422.4	−382.4	−464.0	−534.2	−452.9	−378.9
D. CURRENT TRANSFERS	4 379	**27.5**	**29.7**	**71.8**	**82.7**	**112.8**	**143.8**	**126.3**	**134.2**
Credit	2 379	48.0	48.0	83.7	95.0	127.2	161.1	150.0	159.4
General government	2 380	18.0	18.0	18.0	18.2	20.1	40.6	19.3	20.4
Other sectors	2 390	30.0	30.0	65.7	76.8	107.1	120.5	130.7	139.0
Workers' remittances	2 391	....	....	35.7	61.8	69.9	76.7	88.9	96.6
Other current transfers	2 392	30.0	30.0	30.0	15.0	37.2	43.8	41.8	42.4
Debit	3 379	**−20.5**	**−18.3**	**−11.9**	**−12.3**	**−14.3**	**−17.3**	**−23.7**	**−25.1**
General government	3 380	−14.5	−14.3	−10.7	−8.1	−8.7	−11.2	−12.7	−13.4
Other sectors	3 390	−6.0	−4.0	−1.2	−4.2	−5.7	−6.1	−11.0	−11.7
Workers' remittances	3 391	....	....	....	−1.4	−1.8	−2.2	−2.8	−3.5
Other current transfers	3 392	−6.0	−4.0	−1.2	−2.8	−3.9	−3.9	−8.2	−8.2
CAPITAL AND FINANCIAL ACCOUNT	4 996	**540.5**	**210.9**	**2,012.5**	**−946.9**	**−381.0**	**131.1**	**479.5**	**224.3**
CAPITAL ACCOUNT	4 994	....	....	....	**4.3**	**5.3**	**3.8**	**6.5**	**3.7**
Total credit	2 994	....	....	....	*4.3*	*5.3*	*3.8*	*6.5*	*3.7*
Total debit	3 994	....	....	....	....	....	....	....	....
Capital transfers, credit	2 400	....	....	....	4.3	5.3	3.8	6.5	3.7
General government	2 401	....	....	....	4.3	5.3	3.8	6.5	3.7
Debt forgiveness	2 402	....	....	....	4.3	5.3	3.8	6.5	3.7
Other capital transfers	2 410	....	....	....	....	....	....	....	....
Other sectors	2 430	....	....	....	....	....	....	....	....
Migrants' transfers	2 431	....	....	....	....	....	....	....	....
Debt forgiveness	2 432	....	....	....	....	....	....	....	....
Other capital transfers	2 440	....	....	....	....	....	....	....	....
Capital transfers, debit	3 400	....	....	....	....	....	....	....	....
General government	3 401	....	....	....	....	....	....	....	....
Debt forgiveness	3 402	....	....	....	....	....	....	....	....
Other capital transfers	3 410	....	....	....	....	....	....	....	....
Other sectors	3 430	....	....	....	....	....	....	....	....
Migrants' transfers	3 431	....	....	....	....	....	....	....	....
Debt forgiveness	3 432	....	....	....	....	....	....	....	....
Other capital transfers	3 440	....	....	....	....	....	....	....	....
Nonproduced nonfinancial assets, credit	2 480	....	....	....	....	....	....	....	....
Nonproduced nonfinancial assets, debit	3 480	....	....	....	....	....	....	....	....

Table 2 (Continued). STANDARD PRESENTATION, 2000–2007

(Millions of U.S. dollars)

	Code	2000	2001	2002	2003	2004	2005	2006	2007
FINANCIAL ACCOUNT	4 995 ..	**540.5**	**210.9**	**2,012.5**	**−951.3**	**−386.3**	**127.3**	**473.0**	**220.6**
A. DIRECT INVESTMENT	4 500 ..	**267.8**	**290.6**	**180.0**	**401.3**	**314.7**	**811.1**	**1,399.8**	**875.6**
Direct investment abroad	4 505 ..	**−.8**	**−6.2**	**−13.7**	**−15.1**	**−17.7**	**−36.3**	**1.0**	**−3.6**
Equity capital	4 510 ..	.6	−6.2	−12.7	−10.0	−24.2	−39.9	−1.7	−6.3
Claims on affiliated enterprises	4 515 ..	.6	−6.2	−12.7	−10.0	−24.2	−39.9	−1.7	−6.3
Liabilities to affiliated enterprises	4 520 ..	....	....	....	....	....	....	....	....
Reinvested earnings	4 525 ..	−1.3	....	....	....	....	....	....	....
Other capital	4 530 ..	....	....	−1.0	−5.0	6.5	3.6	2.7	2.7
Claims on affiliated enterprises	4 535 ..	....	....	.1	−6.3	1.9	−4.0	8.2	8.2
Liabilities to affiliated enterprises	4 540 ..	....	....	−1.1	1.2	4.6	7.6	−5.5	−5.5
Direct investment in Uruguay	4 555 ..	**268.6**	**296.8**	**193.7**	**416.4**	**332.4**	**847.4**	**1,398.8**	**879.2**
Equity capital	4 560 ..	77.2	36.4	27.2	222.8	138.7	231.0	475.7	377.4
Claims on direct investors	4 565 ..	....	....	....	....	....	....	....	....
Liabilities to direct investors	4 570 ..	77.2	36.4	27.2	222.8	138.7	231.0	475.7	377.4
Reinvested earnings	4 575 ..	163.2	240.4	62.8	172.9	142.1	132.6	223.9	250.4
Other capital	4 580 ..	28.2	20.0	103.8	20.7	51.6	483.8	699.2	251.4
Claims on direct investors	4 585 ..	5.8	−13.6	12.8	14.9	−15.8	28.4	−20.4	−20.4
Liabilities to direct investors	4 590 ..	22.5	33.6	91.0	5.7	67.4	455.4	719.6	271.8
B. PORTFOLIO INVESTMENT	4 600 ..	**191.4**	**507.7**	**328.6**	**−311.0**	**−422.2**	**805.9**	**1,686.4**	**1,172.0**
Assets	4 602 ..	**−1.9**	**236.5**	**280.0**	**−512.6**	**−695.7**	**577.7**	**−97.2**	**176.7**
Equity securities	4 610 ..	−3.4	10.2	15.3	8.9	.9	.3	−.2	−.2
Monetary authorities	4 611 ..	....	....	....	....	....	....	....	....
General government	4 612 ..	....	....	....	....	....	....	....	....
Banks	4 613 ..	....	....	....	....	....	....	....	....
Other sectors	4 614 ..	−3.4	10.2	15.3	8.9	.9	.3	−.2	−.2
Debt securities	4 619 ..	1.5	226.3	264.8	−521.6	−696.6	577.4	−96.9	176.9
Bonds and notes	4 620 ..	1.5	226.3	264.8	−521.6	−696.6	577.4	−96.9	176.9
Monetary authorities	4 621 ..	−4.3	−5.0	−5.5	59.8	−2.5	38.3	5.6	....
General government	4 622 ..	....	....	....	....	....	....	....	....
Banks	4 623 ..	5.8	231.3	270.4	−582.0	−692.4	225.1	−76.5	176.7
Other sectors	4 624 ..	....	....	−.1	.6	−1.7	314.0	−26.0	.2
Money market instruments	4 630 ..	....	....	....	....	....	....	....	....
Monetary authorities	4 631 ..	....	....	....	....	....	....	....	....
General government	4 632 ..	....	....	....	....	....	....	....	....
Banks	4 633 ..	....	....	....	....	....	....	....	....
Other sectors	4 634 ..	....	....	....	....	....	....	....	....
Liabilities	4 652 ..	**193.3**	**271.2**	**48.6**	**201.6**	**273.4**	**228.2**	**1,783.5**	**995.3**
Equity securities	4 660 ..	5.1	34.9	−9.5	−6.4	20.1	−2.4	−26.6	−26.6
Banks	4 663 ..	....	....	....	....	....	....	....	....
Other sectors	4 664 ..	5.1	34.9	−9.5	−6.4	20.1	−2.4	−26.6	−26.6
Debt securities	4 669 ..	188.2	236.3	58.1	208.0	253.3	230.6	1,810.2	1,021.9
Bonds and notes	4 670 ..	188.2	236.3	58.1	208.0	253.3	230.6	1,810.2	1,021.9
Monetary authorities	4 671 ..	−51.8	−160.5	−31.5	−242.2	−31.4	−116.5	−23.6	−3.3
General government	4 672 ..	345.8	449.0	147.0	450.3	271.8	403.1	1,854.8	1,023.8
Banks	4 673 ..	−105.8	−52.2	−57.5	−.1	12.9	−56.1	−21.0	1.5
Other sectors	4 674 ..	....	....	....	....	....	....	....	....
Money market instruments	4 680 ..	....	....	....	....	....	....	....	....
Monetary authorities	4 681 ..	....	....	....	....	....	....	....	....
General government	4 682 ..	....	....	....	....	....	....	....	....
Banks	4 683 ..	....	....	....	....	....	....	....	....
Other sectors	4 684 ..	....	....	....	....	....	....	....	....
C. FINANCIAL DERIVATIVES	4 910 ..	....	....	....	....	....	....	....	....
Monetary authorities	4 911 ..	....	....	....	....	....	....	....	....
General government	4 912 ..	....	....	....	....	....	....	....	....
Banks	4 913 ..	....	....	....	....	....	....	....	....
Other sectors	4 914 ..	....	....	....	....	....	....	....	....
Assets	4 900 ..	....	....	....	....	....	....	....	....
Monetary authorities	4 901 ..	....	....	....	....	....	....	....	....
General government	4 902 ..	....	....	....	....	....	....	....	....
Banks	4 903 ..	....	....	....	....	....	....	....	....
Other sectors	4 904 ..	....	....	....	....	....	....	....	....
Liabilities	4 905 ..	....	....	....	....	....	....	....	....
Monetary authorities	4 906 ..	....	....	....	....	....	....	....	....
General government	4 907 ..	....	....	....	....	....	....	....	....
Banks	4 908 ..	....	....	....	....	....	....	....	....
Other sectors	4 909 ..	....	....	....	....	....	....	....	....

Table 2 (Concluded). STANDARD PRESENTATION, 2000–2007

(Millions of U.S. dollars)

	Code	2000	2001	2002	2003	2004	2005	2006	2007
D. OTHER INVESTMENT	4 700	**306.2**	**−308.3**	**−827.2**	**338.8**	**175.5**	**−868.9**	**−2,629.0**	**−821.6**
Assets	4 703	−690.3	−2,275.3	1,781.3	−1,254.9	−259.7	−1,112.7	1,414.9	−1,853.1
Trade credits	4 706	−8.9	27.6	7.0	−1.8	−7.3	−110.0	48.9	−13.1
General government	4 707	....	....	....	....	....	....	....	....
of which: Short-term	4 709	....	....	....	....	....	....	....	....
Other sectors	4 710	−8.9	27.6	7.0	−1.8	−7.3	−110.0	48.9	−13.1
of which: Short-term	4 712	−8.9	27.6	7.0	−1.8	−7.3	−110.0	48.9	−13.1
Loans	4 714	113.2	−1,173.3	275.7	−9.7	29.0	38.6	−6.0	−10.2
Monetary authorities	4 715	....	....	....	....	....	....	....	....
of which: Short-term	4 718	....	....	....	....	....	....	....	....
General government	4 719	....	....	....	....	....	....	....	....
of which: Short-term	4 721	....	....	....	....	....	....	....	....
Banks	4 722	113.3	−1,173.3	276.2	3.4	20.4	41.1	−6.6	−9.4
of which: Short-term	4 724	113.3	−1,173.3	276.2	3.4	20.4	41.1	−6.6	−9.4
Other sectors	4 725	−.1	....	−.5	−13.1	8.6	−2.5	.6	−.7
of which: Short-term	4 727	−.1	....	−.5	−13.1	8.6	−2.5	.6	−.7
Currency and deposits	4 730	−850.9	−715.1	1,785.1	−574.5	−297.2	−405.7	112.4	−1,674.6
Monetary authorities	4 731	1.7	....	−507.5	283.2	224.1	−330.5	329.3	−896.3
General government	4 732	....	....	1.8	−14.9	−1.0	−1.1	−.8	....
Banks	4 733	−719.6	−634.1	2,961.6	−556.7	−448.4	−248.3	−114.9	−403.6
Other sectors	4 734	−133.0	−81.0	−670.8	−286.1	−72.0	174.1	−101.2	−374.7
Other assets	4 736	56.4	−414.5	−286.5	−669.0	15.9	−635.6	1,259.5	−155.3
Monetary authorities	4 737	−.8	−5.4	−15.1	−12.8	−6.1	5.7	4.8	−108.4
of which: Short-term	4 739	....	....	....	....	....	....	....	....
General government	4 740	....	....	....	....	....	....	....	....
of which: Short-term	4 742	....	....	....	....	....	....	....	....
Banks	4 743	57.1	−403.3	−270.5	−846.3	30.4	−636.4	1,231.1	−70.4
of which: Short-term	4 745	57.1	−403.3	−270.5	−846.3	30.4	−636.4	1,231.1	−70.4
Other sectors	4 746	....	−5.8	−.9	190.1	−8.4	−4.9	23.7	23.5
of which: Short-term	4 748	....	−5.8	−.9	190.1	−8.4	−4.9	23.7	23.5
Liabilities	4 753	**996.4**	**1,967.0**	**−2,608.5**	**1,593.7**	**435.2**	**243.9**	**−4,043.9**	**1,031.5**
Trade credits	4 756	−3.9	−4.2	−.3	1.8	12.2	82.6	112.4	336.5
General government	4 757	....	....	....	....	....	....	....	....
of which: Short-term	4 759	....	....	....	....	....	....	....	....
Other sectors	4 760	−3.9	−4.2	−.3	1.8	12.2	82.6	112.4	336.5
of which: Short-term	4 762	−3.9	−4.2	−.3	1.8	12.2	82.6	112.4	336.5
Loans	4 764	339.8	118.4	1,545.1	54.1	−175.7	−358.4	−2,926.2	403.8
Monetary authorities	4 765	−44.7	−49.0	1,561.5	349.6	113.0	−192.1	−2,400.2	−10.9
of which: Use of Fund credit and loans from the Fund	4 766	....	....	1,565.9	422.5	149.8	−175.5	−2,383.2	....
of which: Short-term	4 768	....	....	....	....	....	....	....	....
General government	4 769	200.7	144.5	667.3	328.9	39.5	49.9	−575.1	5.8
of which: Short-term	4 771	....	....	....	....	....	....	....	....
Banks	4 772	200.1	5.7	−550.1	−557.5	−228.2	−127.1	18.3	−44.4
of which: Short-term	4 774	202.2	8.9	−547.5	−554.5	−225.0	−124.2	21.7	−40.1
Other sectors	4 775	−16.3	17.2	−133.6	−66.9	−100.0	−89.0	30.9	453.3
of which: Short-term	4 777	−5.8	−10.7	−76.6	23.9	−24.7	−49.5	−1.5	−1.3
Currency and deposits	4 780	685.9	1,275.5	−4,196.5	734.1	628.4	−180.0	109.1	216.5
Monetary authorities	4 781	....	....	....	....	....	....	....	....
General government	4 782	....	....	....	....	....	....	....	....
Banks	4 783	685.9	1,275.5	−4,196.5	734.1	628.4	−180.0	109.1	216.5
Other sectors	4 784	....	....	....	....	....	....	....	....
Other liabilities	4 786	−25.4	577.3	43.2	803.7	−29.6	699.6	−1,339.2	74.7
Monetary authorities	4 787	−1.9	−3.4	−10.1	8.9	11.0	−14.9	−16.7	120.9
of which: Short-term	4 789	....	....	....	....	....	....	....	....
General government	4 790	....	....	....	....	....	....	....	....
of which: Short-term	4 792	....	....	....	....	....	....	....	....
Banks	4 793	−23.5	500.3	53.0	787.3	−33.8	712.3	−1,324.4	−48.0
of which: Short-term	4 795	−23.5	500.3	53.0	787.3	−33.8	712.3	−1,324.4	−48.0
Other sectors	4 796	....	80.4	.2	7.4	−6.8	2.2	1.9	1.9
of which: Short-term	4 798	....	80.4	.2	7.4	−6.8	2.2	1.9	1.9
E. RESERVE ASSETS	4 802	**−224.9**	**−279.2**	**2,331.1**	**−1,380.4**	**−454.2**	**−620.9**	**15.8**	**−1,005.4**
Monetary gold	4 812	230.3	292.2	−.6	....	....	−.1	....	−.1
Special drawing rights	4 811	.3	−1.4	−3.0	2.8	3.1	−5.8	6.2	.7
Reserve position in the Fund	4 810	....	....	47.1	....	....	....	....	....
Foreign exchange	4 803	−392.1	−629.4	2,289.7	−1,327.9	−452.0	−615.7	10.8	−1,008.3
Other claims	4 813	−63.4	59.4	−2.0	−55.3	−5.4	.6	−1.2	2.3
NET ERRORS AND OMISSIONS	4 998	**25.8**	**286.8**	**−2,394.5**	**1,034.2**	**377.9**	**−173.4**	**−110.3**	**−38.7**

Table 3. INTERNATIONAL INVESTMENT POSITION (End-period stocks), 2000–2007

(Millions of U.S. dollars)

	Code	2000	2001	2002	2003	2004	2005	2006	2007
ASSETS	8 995 C.	**13,789.1**	**16,986.1**	**10,276.7**	**14,223.5**	**15,383.2**	**17,137.3**	**16,640.6**	**19,850.5**
Direct investment abroad	8 505 ..	**54.0**	**132.0**	**108.0**	**111.6**	**122.8**	**158.8**	**218.4**	**306.9**
Equity capital and reinvested earnings	8 506 ..	....	....	....	....	....	....	....	....
Claims on affiliated enterprises	8 507 ..	....	....	....	....	....	....	....	....
Liabilities to affiliated enterprises	8 508 ..	....	....	....	....	....	....	....	....
Other capital	8 530 ..	54.0	132.0	108.0	111.6	122.8	158.8	218.4	306.9
Claims on affiliated enterprises	8 535 ..	54.0	132.0	108.0	111.6	122.8	158.8	218.4	306.9
Liabilities to affiliated enterprises	8 540 ..	....	....	....	....	....	....	....	....
Portfolio investment	8 602 ..	**799.0**	**1,203.4**	**999.3**	**1,753.6**	**2,448.7**	**1,858.3**	**1,935.8**	**1,754.5**
Equity securities	8 610 ..	....	....	....	....	....	....	....	....
Monetary authorities	8 611 ..	....	....	....	....	....	....	....	....
General government	8 612 ..	....	....	....	....	....	....	....	....
Banks	8 613 ..	....	....	....	....	....	....	....	....
Other sectors	8 614 ..	....	....	....	....	....	....	....	....
Debt securities	8 619 ..	799.0	1,203.4	999.3	1,753.6	2,448.7	1,858.3	1,935.8	1,754.5
Bonds and notes	8 620 ..	799.0	1,203.4	999.3	1,753.6	2,448.7	1,858.3	1,935.8	1,754.5
Monetary authorities	8 621 ..	59.8	64.9	101.1	41.2	43.9	5.5	....	....
General government	8 622 ..	....	....	....	....	....	....	....	....
Banks	8 623 ..	739.2	621.0	898.2	655.2	1,515.4	1,287.5	1,364.1	1,182.8
Other sectors	8 624 ..	....	517.5	....	1,057.1	889.4	565.2	571.7	571.7
Money market instruments	8 630 ..	....	....	....	....	....	....	....	....
Monetary authorities	8 631 ..	....	....	....	....	....	....	....	....
General government	8 632 ..	....	....	....	....	....	....	....	....
Banks	8 633 ..	....	....	....	....	....	....	....	....
Other sectors	8 634 ..	....	....	....	....	....	....	....	....
Financial derivatives	8 900 ..	....	....	....	....	....	....	....	....
Monetary authorities	8 901 ..	....	....	....	....	....	....	....	....
General government	8 902 ..	....	....	....	....	....	....	....	....
Banks	8 903 ..	....	....	....	....	....	....	....	....
Other sectors	8 904 ..	....	....	....	....	....	....	....	....
Other investment	8 703 ..	**10,158.3**	**12,550.7**	**8,392.1**	**10,324.4**	**10,299.8**	**12,048.8**	**11,389.1**	**13,667.6**
Trade credits	8 706 ..	....	46.1	67.4	67.4	67.4	177.4	190.5	203.6
General government	8 707 ..	....	....	....	....	....	....	....	....
of which: Short-term	8 709 ..	....	....	....	....	....	....	....	....
Other sectors	8 710 ..	....	46.1	67.4	67.4	67.4	177.4	190.5	203.6
of which: Short-term	8 712 ..	....	*46.1*	*67.4*	*67.4*	*67.4*	*177.4*	*190.5*	*203.6*
Loans	8 714 ..	1,450.6	2,621.8	244.1	561.2	209.0	158.9	180.0	189.2
Monetary authorities	8 715 ..	....	....	....	....	....	....	....	....
of which: Short-term	8 718 ..	....	....	....	....	....	....	....	....
General government	8 719 ..	....	....	....	....	....	....	....	....
of which: Short-term	8 721 ..	....	....	....	....	....	....	....	....
Banks	8 722 ..	1,450.6	2,604.2	230.3	534.3	182.1	134.8	145.1	154.5
of which: Short-term	8 724 ..	*1,450.6*	*2,604.2*	*230.3*	*534.3*	*182.1*	*134.8*	*145.1*	*154.5*
Other sectors	8 725 ..	....	17.5	13.8	26.9	26.9	24.1	34.9	34.7
of which: Short-term	8 727 ..	....	*17.5*	*13.8*	*26.9*	*26.9*	*24.1*	*34.9*	*34.7*
Currency and deposits	8 730 ..	8,444.2	9,094.8	6,905.7	8,005.0	8,359.9	9,415.1	9,945.1	12,046.2
Monetary authorities	8 731 ..	....	9.3	507.4	224.2	....	327.9	11.9	896.3
General government	8 732 ..	....	....	....	....	....	5.1	8.0	8.0
Banks	8 733 ..	4,996.5	5,589.5	2,084.3	3,165.8	3,477.9	3,726.2	3,794.2	4,197.9
Other sectors	8 734 ..	3,447.7	3,496.0	4,314.0	4,615.0	4,882.0	5,355.9	6,131.0	6,944.0
Other assets	8 736 ..	263.5	788.0	1,174.9	1,690.8	1,663.5	2,297.4	1,073.5	1,228.6
Monetary authorities	8 737 ..	103.4	167.7	93.0	166.7	172.8	159.6	164.4	272.8
of which: Short-term	8 739 ..	....	....	*93.0*	*166.7*	*172.8*	*159.6*	*164.4*	*272.8*
General government	8 740 ..	....	....	....	....	....	....	....	....
of which: Short-term	8 742 ..	....	....	....	....	....	....	....	....
Banks	8 743 ..	160.1	611.1	883.0	1,514.9	1,480.0	2,116.4	885.3	955.6
of which: Short-term	8 745 ..	*160.1*	*611.1*	*883.0*	*1,514.9*	*1,480.0*	*2,116.4*	*885.3*	*955.6*
Other sectors	8 746 ..	....	9.2	198.9	9.2	10.7	21.4	23.8	.2
of which: Short-term	8 748 ..	....	*9.2*	*198.9*	*9.2*	*10.7*	*21.4*	*23.8*	*.2*
Reserve assets	8 802 ..	**2,777.8**	**3,100.0**	**777.3**	**2,033.9**	**2,511.9**	**3,071.5**	**3,097.3**	**4,121.5**
Monetary gold	8 812 ..	294.5	2.3	2.9	3.5	3.6	4.4	5.3	7.1
Special drawing rights	8 811 ..	.5	1.8	5.7	3.7	1.2	6.3	1.1	.4
Reserve position in the Fund	8 810 ..	46.5	44.8	....	....	....	....	....	....
Foreign exchange	8 803 ..	2,430.9	3,047.4	702.1	2,026.7	2,507.4	3,061.8	3,090.7	4,116.0
Other claims	8 813 ..	5.4	3.6	66.6	....	−.3	−1.0	.2	−2.0

Table 3 (Concluded). INTERNATIONAL INVESTMENT POSITION (End-period stocks), 2000–2007

(Millions of U.S. dollars)

	Code	2000	2001	2002	2003	2004	2005	2006	2007
LIABILITIES	8 995 D.	**15,583.1**	**18,800.6**	**12,134.0**	**15,479.8**	**16,902.5**	**18,438.2**	**17,725.3**	**21,146.2**
Direct investment in Uruguay	8 555 ..	**2,088.0**	**2,406.2**	**1,402.5**	**1,799.6**	**2,110.3**	**2,843.7**	**3,898.7**	**5,443.2**
Equity capital and reinvested earnings	8 556 ..	2,088.0	2,406.2	1,402.5	1,799.6	2,110.3	2,843.7	3,898.7	5,443.2
Claims on direct investors	8 557 ..	....	....	....	....	....	....	....	....
Liabilities to direct investors	8 558 ..	2,088.0	2,406.2	1,402.5	1,799.6	2,110.3	2,843.7	3,898.7	5,443.2
Other capital	8 580 ..	....	....	....	....	....	....	....	....
Claims on direct investors	8 585 ..	....	....	....	....	....	....	....	....
Liabilities to direct investors	8 590 ..	....	....	....	....	....	....	....	....
Portfolio investment	8 652 ..	**2,721.1**	**3,053.0**	**2,433.9**	**2,738.9**	**3,830.7**	**4,409.9**	**6,435.8**	**7,857.8**
Equity securities	8 660 ..	....	....	....	....	....	....	....	....
Banks	8 663 ..	....	....	....	....	....	....	....	....
Other sectors	8 664 ..	....	....	....	....	....	....	....	....
Debt securities	8 669 ..	2,721.1	3,053.0	2,433.9	2,738.9	3,830.7	4,409.9	6,435.8	7,857.8
Bonds and notes	8 670 ..	2,721.1	3,053.0	2,433.9	2,738.9	3,830.7	4,409.9	6,435.8	7,857.8
Monetary authorities	8 671 ..	....	....	440.3	157.0	144.4	26.8	3.3	....
General government	8 672 ..	2,721.1	3,053.0	1,993.6	2,581.9	3,686.3	4,383.1	6,432.5	7,857.8
Banks	8 673 ..	....	....	....	....	....	....	....	....
Other sectors	8 674 ..	....	....	....	....	....	....	....	....
Money market instruments	8 680 ..	....	....	....	....	....	....	....	....
Monetary authorities	8 681 ..	....	....	....	....	....	....	....	....
General government	8 682 ..	....	....	....	....	....	....	....	....
Banks	8 683 ..	....	....	....	....	....	....	....	....
Other sectors	8 684 ..	....	....	....	....	....	....	....	....
Financial derivatives	8 905 ..	....	....	....	....	....	....	....	....
Monetary authorities	8 906 ..	....	....	....	....	....	....	....	....
General government	8 907 ..	....	....	....	....	....	....	....	....
Banks	8 908 ..	....	....	....	....	....	....	....	....
Other sectors	8 909 ..	....	....	....	....	....	....	....	....
Other investment	8 753 ..	**10,774.0**	**13,341.4**	**8,297.6**	**10,941.3**	**10,961.5**	**11,184.6**	**7,390.8**	**7,845.2**
Trade credits	8 756 ..	22.6	87.3	19.2	144.0	51.3	355.3	709.4	1,093.0
General government	8 757 ..	....	....	....	....	....	....	....	....
of which: Short-term	8 759 ..	....	....	....	....	....	....	....	....
Other sectors	8 760 ..	22.6	87.3	19.2	144.0	51.3	355.3	709.4	1,093.0
of which: Short-term	8 762 ..	*22.6*	*87.3*	*19.2*	*144.0*	*51.3*	*355.3*	*709.4*	*1,093.0*
Loans	8 764 ..	4,858.7	5,363.6	6,283.5	6,895.7	6,830.4	6,228.5	3,302.3	3,082.1
Monetary authorities	8 765 ..	509.3	545.0	2,185.4	2,795.7	3,032.2	2,443.3	51.4	41.7
of which: Use of Fund credit and loans from the Fund	8 766 ..	*148.8*	*143.5*	*1,792.9*	*2,416.0*	*2,684.2*	*2,304.2*	....	....
of which: Short-term	8 768 ..	....	....	....	....	....	....	....	....
General government	8 769 ..	1,904.1	2,077.6	2,493.8	2,836.0	2,892.9	2,978.7	2,418.1	2,426.4
of which: Short-term	8 771 ..	....	....	....	....	....	....	....	....
Banks	8 772 ..	1,870.4	1,876.6	1,093.1	768.8	495.7	373.2	396.8	352.4
of which: Short-term	8 774 ..	*1,870.4*	*1,876.6*	*1,093.1*	*768.8*	*495.7*	*373.2*	*396.8*	*352.4*
Other sectors	8 775 ..	574.9	864.4	511.2	495.2	409.6	433.3	436.0	261.6
of which: Short-term	8 777 ..	*574.9*	*864.4*	*511.2*	*495.2*	*409.6*	*433.3*	*436.0*	*261.6*
Currency and deposits	8 780 ..	5,734.6	7,014.6	1,254.1	2,359.2	2,619.3	2,439.3	2,546.3	2,762.8
Monetary authorities	8 781 ..	....	....	....	....	....	....	....	....
General government	8 782 ..	....	....	....	....	....	....	....	....
Banks	8 783 ..	5,734.6	7,014.6	1,254.1	2,359.2	2,619.3	2,439.3	2,546.3	2,762.8
Other sectors	8 784 ..	....	....	....	....	....	....	....	....
Other liabilities	8 786 ..	158.1	875.9	740.8	1,542.4	1,460.5	2,161.5	832.8	907.3
Monetary authorities	8 787 ..	9.2	5.8	6.8	15.7	26.7	13.1	9.6	130.5
of which: Short-term	8 789 ..	*9.2*	*5.8*	....	....	....	....	....	....
General government	8 790 ..	....	....	....	....	....	....	....	....
of which: Short-term	8 792 ..	....	....	....	....	....	....	....	....
Banks	8 793 ..	148.9	788.4	652.3	1,444.7	1,401.6	2,114.0	789.4	741.4
of which: Short-term	8 795 ..	*148.9*	*788.4*	*652.3*	*1,444.7*	*1,401.6*	*2,114.0*	*789.4*	*741.4*
Other sectors	8 796 ..	....	81.7	81.7	82.0	32.2	34.4	33.8	35.4
of which: Short-term	8 798 ..	....	*81.7*	*81.7*	*82.0*	*32.2*	*34.4*	*33.8*	*35.4*
NET INTERNATIONAL INVESTMENT POSITION	8 995 ..	**−1,794.0**	**−1,814.6**	**−1,857.3**	**−1,256.3**	**−1,519.2**	**−1,300.9**	**−1,084.7**	**−1,295.7**
Conversion rates: Uruguayan pesos per U.S. dollar (end of period)	0 102 ..	12.5150	14.7680	27.2000	29.3000	26.3500	24.1000	24.4000	21.5000

Table 1. ANALYTIC PRESENTATION, 2000–2007

(Millions of U.S. dollars)

	Code	2000	2001	2002	2003	2004	2005	2006	2007
A. Current Account¹	4 993 Z.	−13.65	−14.53	−30.57	−34.43	−41.61	−52.71	−50.35	−53.78
Goods: exports f.o.b.	2 100 ..	27.19	19.89	20.20	26.84	38.14	38.11	37.69	33.55
Goods: imports f.o.b.	3 100 ..	−76.94	−77.96	−78.44	−91.80	−113.00	−131.15	−147.55	−176.48
Balance on Goods	4 100 ..	*−49.74*	*−58.07*	*−58.24*	*−64.96*	*−74.85*	*−93.03*	*−109.86*	*−142.93*
Services: credit	2 200 ..	129.81	119.26	93.61	110.66	122.28	138.85	145.82	185.94
Services: debit	3 200 ..	−70.15	−72.99	−51.56	−60.65	−65.58	−73.76	−71.24	−75.68
Balance on Goods and Services	4 991 ..	*9.91*	*−11.80*	*−16.19*	*−14.95*	*−18.15*	*−27.95*	*−35.29*	*−32.67*
Income: credit	2 300 ..	18.74	17.23	22.46	24.21	27.15	27.65	31.82	36.26
Income: debit	3 300 ..	−31.71	−21.23	−33.99	−38.60	−45.86	−53.66	−51.93	−61.01
Balance on Goods, Services, and Income	4 992 ..	*−3.06*	*−15.80*	*−27.72*	*−29.34*	*−36.87*	*−53.96*	*−55.40*	*−57.41*
Current transfers: credit	2 379 Z.	27.41	39.53	5.92	4.82	5.27	7.39	10.06	6.65
Current transfers: debit	3 379 ..	−38.00	−38.26	−8.77	−9.90	−10.00	−6.15	−5.00	−3.02
B. Capital Account¹	4 994 Z.	−23.58	−16.03	7.77	7.41	12.76	20.10	33.74	29.96
Capital account: credit	2 994 Z.	31.88	46.07	7.77	7.41	12.76	20.10	33.74	29.96
Capital account: debit	3 994 ..	−55.46	−62.10	....	....	....	....	....	....
Total, Groups A Plus B	4 981 ..	*−37.22*	*−30.57*	*−22.80*	*−27.02*	*−28.85*	*−32.61*	*−16.61*	*−23.82*
C. Financial Account¹	4 995 W.	19.33	12.75	25.91	37.57	48.36	37.92	33.44	14.97
Direct investment abroad	4 505 ..	....	....	−.57	−.67	−.76	−.77	−.73	−.63
Direct investment in Vanuatu	4 555 Z.	20.26	18.00	14.16	18.01	19.84	13.25	43.45	34.16
Portfolio investment assets	4 602 ..	.69	−4.33	−.33	2.11	.21	−1.06	−.26	1.68
Equity securities	4 610 ..	....	....	....	....	....	....	....	....
Debt securities	4 619 ..	....	....	−.33	2.11	.21	−1.06	−.26	1.68
Portfolio investment liabilities	4 652 Z.	....	....	....	....	....	....	....	....
Equity securities	4 660 ..	....	....	....	....	....	....	....	....
Debt securities	4 669 Z.	....	....	....	....	....	....	....	....
Financial derivatives	4 910 ..	....	....	....	....	....	....	....	....
Financial derivatives assets	4 900 ..	....	....	....	....	....	....	....	....
Financial derivatives liabilities	4 905 ..	....	....	....	....	....	....	....	....
Other investment assets	4 703 ..	−13.55	−11.41	−5.60	48.16	−14.77	26.60	−27.47	51.25
Monetary authorities	4 701 ..	....	....	....	....	....	....	....	....
General government	4 704 ..	....	....	....	....	....	....	....	....
Banks	4 705 ..	−13.10	−14.81	−22.39	11.55	−7.18	−12.28	−12.80	−36.44
Other sectors	4 728 ..	−.45	3.40	16.80	36.61	−7.59	38.88	−14.67	87.69
Other investment liabilities	4 753 W.	11.93	10.48	18.24	−30.04	43.84	−.10	18.45	−71.48
Monetary authorities	4 753 WA	−.03	.53	−.17	−.32	−.14	.40	−.13	.82
General government	4 753 ZB	16.36	3.20	−.35	−.91	−2.61	−3.00	−1.59	−1.79
Banks	4 753 ZC	−4.79	3.05	34.11	−8.69	−6.76	12.17	11.72	−2.47
Other sectors	4 753 ZD	.39	3.70	−15.35	−20.12	53.34	−9.67	8.44	−68.03
Total, Groups A Through C	4 983 ..	*−17.89*	*−17.82*	*3.10*	*10.55*	*19.51*	*5.31*	*16.83*	*−8.85*
D. Net Errors and Omissions	4 998 ..	−.88	7.55	−21.28	−21.79	−24.50	−16.65	−3.94	−4.31
Total, Groups A Through D	4 984 ..	*−18.77*	*−10.27*	*−18.18*	*−11.24*	*−4.99*	*−11.33*	*12.88*	*−13.16*
E. Reserves and Related Items	4 802 A.	18.77	10.27	18.18	11.24	4.99	11.33	−12.88	13.16
Reserve assets	4 802 ..	.87	.62	4.66	−1.03	−14.86	−8.97	−32.56	−9.04
Use of Fund credit and loans	4 766 ..	....	....	....	....	....	....	....	....
Exceptional financing	4 920 ..	17.90	9.64	13.52	12.27	19.85	20.30	19.68	22.20
Conversion rates: vatu per U.S. dollar	0 101 ..	137.64	145.31	139.20	122.19	111.79	109.25	110.64	102.44

¹ Excludes components that have been classified in the categories of Group E.

Table 2. STANDARD PRESENTATION, 2000–2007

(Millions of U.S. dollars)

	Code	2000	2001	2002	2003	2004	2005	2006	2007
CURRENT ACCOUNT	4 993	4.99	1.82	−17.06	−22.15	−22.44	−34.05	−30.13	−34.41
A. GOODS	4 100	−49.74	−58.07	−58.24	−64.96	−74.85	−93.03	−109.86	−142.93
Credit	2 100	27.19	19.89	20.20	26.84	38.14	38.11	37.69	33.55
General merchandise: exports f.o.b.	2 110	27.19	19.89	20.20	26.84	38.14	38.11	37.69	33.55
Goods for processing: exports f.o.b.	2 150	....	....	....	....	....	....	....	....
Repairs on goods	2 160	....	....	....	....	....	....	....	....
Goods procured in ports by carriers	2 170	....	....	....	....	....	....	....	....
Nonmonetary gold	2 180	....	....	....	....	....	....	....	....
Debit	3 100	−76.94	−77.96	−78.44	−91.80	−113.00	−131.15	−147.55	−176.48
General merchandise: imports f.o.b.	3 110	−74.11	−75.30	−74.85	−87.25	−106.89	−124.55	−140.91	−168.72
Goods for processing: imports f.o.b.	3 150	....	....	....	....	....	....	....	....
Repairs on goods	3 160	....	....	....	....	....	....	....	....
Goods procured in ports by carriers	3 170	−2.82	−2.66	−3.59	−4.55	−6.10	−6.60	−6.65	−7.76
Nonmonetary gold	3 180	....	....	....	....	....	....	....	....
B. SERVICES	4 200	59.65	46.27	42.05	50.01	56.70	65.09	74.57	110.26
Total credit	2 200	*129.81*	*119.26*	*93.61*	*110.66*	*122.28*	*138.85*	*145.82*	*185.94*
Total debit	3 200	*−70.15*	*−72.99*	*−51.56*	*−60.65*	*−65.58*	*−73.76*	*−71.24*	*−75.68*
Transportation services, credit	2 205	28.73	26.47	22.51	26.03	24.05	25.57	23.54	31.81
Passenger	2 850	*12.72*	*11.73*	*17.67*	*18.66*	*18.16*	*18.91*	*16.99*	*23.40*
Freight	2 851	*2.31*	*2.31*	*.53*	*.95*	*1.13*	*1.26*	*1.55*	*2.41*
Other	2 852	*13.70*	*12.44*	*4.31*	*6.42*	*4.76*	*5.39*	*5.01*	*6.00*
Sea transport, passenger	2 207	....	....	....	....	....	....	....	....
Sea transport, freight	2 208	.23	.23	....	....	....	....	....	....
Sea transport, other	2 209	2.74	2.49	2.16	3.21	2.38	2.69	2.50	3.00
Air transport, passenger	2 211	12.72	11.73	17.67	18.66	18.16	18.91	16.99	23.40
Air transport, freight	2 212	2.08	2.08	.53	.95	1.13	1.26	1.55	2.41
Air transport, other	2 213	10.96	9.95	2.16	3.21	2.38	2.69	2.50	3.00
Other transport, passenger	2 215	....	....	....	....	....	....	....	....
Other transport, freight	2 216	....	....	....	....	....	....	....	....
Other transport, other	2 217	....	....	....	....	....	....	....	....
Transportation services, debit	3 205	−23.98	−23.63	−27.17	−31.71	−34.87	−42.87	−43.73	−45.62
Passenger	3 850	....	....	*−1.62*	*−2.04*	*−2.25*	*−2.35*	*−2.11*	*−1.87*
Freight	3 851	*−14.76*	*−15.41*	*−14.05*	*−16.39*	*−17.16*	*−21.54*	*−25.62*	*−31.15*
Other	3 852	*−9.22*	*−8.22*	*−11.49*	*−13.28*	*−15.46*	*−18.97*	*−16.00*	*−12.60*
Sea transport, passenger	3 207	....	....	....	....	....	....	....	....
Sea transport, freight	3 208	−11.07	−11.55	−13.35	−15.57	−16.30	−20.47	−24.34	−29.59
Sea transport, other	3 209	−.92	−.82	−2.30	−2.66	−3.09	−3.79	−3.20	−2.52
Air transport, passenger	3 211	....	....	−1.62	−2.04	−2.25	−2.35	−2.11	−1.87
Air transport, freight	3 212	−3.69	−3.85	−.70	−.82	−.86	−1.08	−1.28	−1.56
Air transport, other	3 213	−8.30	−7.40	−9.20	−10.62	−12.37	−15.17	−12.80	−10.08
Other transport, passenger	3 215	....	....	....	....	....	....	....	....
Other transport, freight	3 216	....	....	....	....	....	....	....	....
Other transport, other	3 217	....	....	....	....	....	....	....	....
Travel, credit	2 236	56.11	46.12	54.16	63.91	74.96	85.47	92.44	118.69
Business travel	2 237	5.61	4.61	53.50	63.12	74.05	84.49	91.48	117.47
Personal travel	2 240	50.50	41.51	.66	.79	.92	.98	.96	1.22
Travel, debit	3 236	−8.90	−7.88	−9.11	−11.53	−12.94	−11.19	−8.55	−10.62
Business travel	3 237	−6.67	−5.91	−7.95	−9.90	−10.76	−9.28	−7.32	−8.95
Personal travel	3 240	−2.22	−1.97	−1.16	−1.62	−2.19	−1.91	−1.22	−1.67
Other services, credit	2 200 BA	44.97	46.67	16.94	20.72	23.27	27.82	29.84	35.43
Communications	2 245	3.37	2.06	1.99	2.67	2.79	3.25	4.17	4.55
Construction	2 249	.73	.69	....	....	....	....	....	....
Insurance	2 253	1.66	1.02	....	....	.18	.20	.05	....
Financial	2 260	6.30	6.95	6.87	8.76	11.64	14.12	15.10	17.22
Computer and information	2 262	....	....	....	....	....	....	....	....
Royalties and licence fees	2 266	....	....	....	....	....	....	.18	.27
Other business services	2 268	21.41	28.90	4.83	6.62	4.15	6.15	4.51	4.37
Personal, cultural, and recreational	2 287	....	....	....	....	....	....	....	....
Government, n.i.e.	2 291	11.49	7.06	3.26	2.67	4.51	4.10	5.83	9.02
Other services, debit	3 200 BA	−37.27	−41.49	−15.29	−17.41	−17.77	−19.70	−18.97	−19.44
Communications	3 245	−1.03	−.88	−1.07	−1.49	−1.41	−1.47	−1.61	−1.65
Construction	3 249	−.72	−.40	....	....	−.01	−.01	....	....
Insurance	3 253	−2.83	−1.14	−.84	−.96	−1.19	−1.42	−1.72	−2.22
Financial	3 260	−4.63	−6.95	−.55	−.89	−1.19	−2.20	−2.12	−2.74
Computer and information	3 262	....	....	−1.00	−1.45	−1.64	−.76	−1.09	−1.19
Royalties and licence fees	3 266	....	....	−.20	−.26	−.36	−.47	−.20	....
Other business services	3 268	−20.39	−25.70	−6.45	−7.36	−7.29	−8.17	−7.17	−6.43
Personal, cultural, and recreational	3 287	....	....	−1.05	....	....	....	....	....
Government, n.i.e.	3 291	−7.68	−6.41	−4.13	−5.00	−4.69	−5.20	−5.05	−5.20

Table 2 (Continued). STANDARD PRESENTATION, 2000–2007

(Millions of U.S. dollars)

	Code	2000	2001	2002	2003	2004	2005	2006	2007
C. INCOME	4 300 ..	**−12.97**	**−4.00**	**−11.53**	**−14.39**	**−18.72**	**−26.01**	**−20.11**	**−24.74**
Total credit	2 300 ..	*18.74*	*17.23*	*22.46*	*24.21*	*27.15*	*27.65*	*31.82*	*36.26*
Total debit	3 300 ..	*−31.71*	*−21.23*	*−33.99*	*−38.60*	*−45.86*	*−53.66*	*−51.93*	*−61.01*
Compensation of employees, credit	2 310 ..	**2.54**	**2.62**	**4.04**	**3.93**	**4.86**	**5.02**	**4.92**	**4.33**
Compensation of employees, debit	3 310 ..	**−2.53**	**−1.95**	**−2.00**	**−2.56**	**−2.80**	**−2.82**	**−2.93**	**−2.29**
Investment income, credit	2 320 ..	**16.20**	**14.61**	**18.42**	**20.28**	**22.29**	**22.63**	**26.90**	**31.94**
Direct investment income	2 330 ..	....	....	.58	.71	.81	.81	.79	.67
Dividends and distributed branch profits	2 332 ..	....	....	....	....	....	....	....	....
Reinvested earnings and undistributed branch profits	2 333 ..	....	....	.29	.35	.38	.37	.37	.34
Income on debt (interest)	2 334 ..	....	....	.29	.35	.43	.44	.42	.33
Portfolio investment income	2 339 ..	1.05	.30	.69	.33	.30	.37	.47	.52
Income on equity	2 340 ..	....	....	....	....	....	....	....	....
Income on bonds and notes	2 350 ..	....	....	.69	.33	.30	.37	.47	.52
Income on money market instruments	2 360 ..	....	....	....	....	....	....	....	....
Other investment income	2 370 ..	15.15	14.31	17.15	19.24	21.19	21.44	25.64	30.75
Investment income, debit	3 320 ..	**−29.18**	**−19.28**	**−31.98**	**−36.04**	**−43.06**	**−50.84**	**−49.00**	**−58.71**
Direct investment income	3 330 ..	−21.93	−13.97	−18.07	−20.83	−27.09	−35.34	−34.20	−45.61
Dividends and distributed branch profits	3 332 ..	−3.53	−2.15	....	....	....	....	....	−18.08
Reinvested earnings and undistributed branch profits	3 333 ..	−18.40	−11.82	−12.44	−17.87	−22.32	−27.86	−25.32	−29.11
Income on debt (interest)	3 334 ..	....	....	−5.63	−2.96	−4.77	−7.48	−8.87	1.58
Portfolio investment income	3 339 ..	....	....	....	....	....	....	....	....
Income on equity	3 340 ..	....	....	....	....	....	....	....	....
Income on bonds and notes	3 350 ..	....	....	....	....	....	....	....	....
Income on money market instruments	3 360 ..	....	....	....	....	....	....	....	....
Other investment income	3 370 ..	−7.25	−5.31	−13.92	−15.22	−15.97	−15.50	−14.80	−13.11
D. CURRENT TRANSFERS	4 379 ..	**8.05**	**17.62**	**10.67**	**7.19**	**14.43**	**19.91**	**25.27**	**23.00**
Credit	2 379 ..	**46.05**	**55.88**	**19.44**	**17.09**	**24.44**	**26.06**	**30.27**	**26.02**
General government	2 380 ..	18.64	16.35	15.98	14.66	21.33	21.18	22.51	22.78
Other sectors	2 390 ..	27.41	39.53	3.46	2.43	3.10	4.88	7.76	3.24
Workers' remittances	2 391 ..	10.96	15.81	.06	.07	.07	.07	.07	1.22
Other current transfers	2 392 ..	16.45	23.72	3.40	2.37	3.03	4.81	7.68	2.02
Debit	3 379 ..	**−38.00**	**−38.26**	**−8.77**	**−9.90**	**−10.00**	**−6.15**	**−5.00**	**−3.02**
General government	3 380 ..	−1.34	−2.87	−.07	....	−.65	−1.35	−.46	−.84
Other sectors	3 390 ..	−36.67	−35.39	−8.70	−9.90	−9.36	−4.80	−4.54	−2.18
Workers' remittances	3 391 ..	−14.67	−14.16	−.14	−.16	−.18	−.18	−.21	−.33
Other current transfers	3 392 ..	−22.00	−21.23	−8.56	−9.74	−9.18	−4.61	−4.34	−1.85
CAPITAL AND FINANCIAL ACCOUNT	4 996 ..	**−4.12**	**−9.37**	**38.34**	**43.94**	**46.94**	**50.69**	**34.08**	**38.72**
CAPITAL ACCOUNT	4 994 ..	**−23.58**	**−16.03**	**7.77**	**7.41**	**12.76**	**22.07**	**33.74**	**29.96**
Total credit	2 994 ..	*31.88*	*46.07*	*7.77*	*7.41*	*12.76*	*22.07*	*33.74*	*29.96*
Total debit	3 994 ..	*−55.46*	*−62.10*	....	....	....	....	....	....
Capital transfers, credit	2 400 ..	**31.88**	**46.07**	**6.34**	**5.59**	**7.22**	**7.78**	**5.96**	**6.45**
General government	2 401 ..	10.72	11.80	6.34	5.59	7.22	7.78	5.96	6.45
Debt forgiveness	2 402 ..	....	....	....	....	....	1.96	....	....
Other capital transfers	2 410 ..	....	....	6.34	5.59	7.22	5.82	5.96	6.45
Other sectors	2 430 ..	21.16	34.27	....	....	....	....	....	....
Migrants' transfers	2 431 ..	21.16	34.27	....	....	....	....	....	....
Debt forgiveness	2 432 ..	....	....	....	....	....	....	....	....
Other capital transfers	2 440 ..	....	....	....	....	....	....	....	....
Capital transfers, debit	3 400 ..	**−55.46**	**−62.10**	....	....	....	....	....	....
General government	3 401 ..	....	....	....	....	....	....	....	....
Debt forgiveness	3 402 ..	....	....	....	....	....	....	....	....
Other capital transfers	3 410 ..	....	....	....	....	....	....	....	....
Other sectors	3 430 ..	−55.46	−62.10	....	....	....	....	....	....
Migrants' transfers	3 431 ..	−55.46	−62.10	....	....	....	....	....	....
Debt forgiveness	3 432 ..	....	....	....	....	....	....	....	....
Other capital transfers	3 440 ..	....	....	....	....	....	....	....	....
Nonproduced nonfinancial assets, credit	2 480 ..	....	....	1.44	1.82	5.55	14.28	27.77	23.51
Nonproduced nonfinancial assets, debit	3 480 ..	....	....	....	....	....	....	....	....

Table 2 (Continued). STANDARD PRESENTATION, 2000–2007

(Millions of U.S. dollars)

	Code	2000	2001	2002	2003	2004	2005	2006	2007
FINANCIAL ACCOUNT...............................	4 995 ..	**19.46**	**6.67**	**30.57**	**36.53**	**34.18**	**28.63**	**.34**	**8.77**
A. DIRECT INVESTMENT..............................	4 500 ..	**20.26**	**18.00**	**13.59**	**17.34**	**19.08**	**12.48**	**42.72**	**33.52**
Direct investment abroad........................	4 505 ..	....	....	−.57	−.67	−.76	−.77	−.73	−.63
Equity capital...................................	4 510 ..	....	....	−.20	−.25	−.31	−.33	−.31	−.25
Claims on affiliated enterprises............	4 515 ..	....	....	−.20	−.25	−.31	−.33	−.31	−.25
Liabilities to affiliated enterprises.........	4 520 ..	....	....	....	....	....	....	....	....
Reinvested earnings...........................	4 525 ..	....	....	−.29	−.35	−.38	−.37	−.37	−.34
Other capital...................................	4 530 ..	....	....	−.08	−.07	−.07	−.07	−.05	−.04
Claims on affiliated enterprises............	4 535 ..	....	....	−.08	−.07	−.07	−.07	−.05	−.04
Liabilities to affiliated enterprises.........	4 540 ..	....	....	....	....	....	....	....	....
Direct investment in Vanuatu....................	4 555 ..	**20.26**	**18.00**	**14.16**	**18.01**	**19.84**	**13.25**	**43.45**	**34.16**
Equity capital...................................	4 560 ..	....	....	.43	.98	−4.46	−14.31	17.84	2.83
Claims on direct investors..................	4 565 ..	....	....	....	....	....	....	....	....
Liabilities to direct investors..............	4 570 ..	....	....	.43	.98	−4.46	−14.31	17.84	2.83
Reinvested earnings...........................	4 575 ..	18.40	11.82	12.44	17.87	22.32	27.86	25.32	29.11
Other capital...................................	4 580 ..	1.85	6.19	1.29	−.84	1.99	−.29	.29	2.22
Claims on direct investors..................	4 585 ..	....	....	....	....	....	....	....	....
Liabilities to direct investors..............	4 590 ..	1.85	6.19	1.29	−.84	1.99	−.29	.29	2.22
B. PORTFOLIO INVESTMENT........................	4 600 ..	**.69**	**−4.33**	**−.33**	**2.11**	**.90**	**−1.39**	**−.80**	**1.68**
Assets..	4 602 ..	**.69**	**−4.33**	**−.33**	**2.11**	**.21**	**−1.06**	**−.26**	**1.68**
Equity securities...............................	4 610 ..	....	....	....	....	....	....	....	....
Monetary authorities........................	4 611 ..	....	....	....	....	....	....	....	....
General government........................	4 612 ..	....	....	....	....	....	....	....	....
Banks...	4 613 ..	....	....	....	....	....	....	....	....
Other sectors.................................	4 614 ..	....	....	....	....	....	....	....	....
Debt securities.................................	4 619 ..	....	....	−.33	2.11	.21	−1.06	−.26	1.68
Bonds and notes.............................	4 620 ..	....	....	−.33	2.11	.21	−1.06	−.26	1.68
Monetary authorities......................	4 621 ..	....	....	....	....	....	....	....	....
General government......................	4 622 ..	....	....	....	....	....	....	....	....
Banks.......................................	4 623 ..	....	....	....	....	....	....	....	....
Other sectors...............................	4 624 ..	....	....	−.33	2.11	.21	−1.06	−.26	1.68
Money market instruments..................	4 630 ..	....	....	....	....	....	....	....	....
Monetary authorities......................	4 631 ..	....	....	....	....	....	....	....	....
General government......................	4 632 ..	....	....	....	....	....	....	....	....
Banks.......................................	4 633 ..	....	....	....	....	....	....	....	....
Other sectors...............................	4 634 ..	....	....	....	....	....	....	....	....
Liabilities......................................	4 652 ..	....	....	....	....	**.68**	**−.32**	**−.54**	....
Equity securities...............................	4 660 ..	....	....	....	....	....	....	....	....
Banks...	4 663 ..	....	....	....	....	....	....	....	....
Other sectors.................................	4 664 ..	....	....	....	....	....	....	....	....
Debt securities.................................	4 669 ..	....	....	....	....	.68	−.32	−.54	....
Bonds and notes.............................	4 670 ..	....	....	....	....	.68	−.32	−.54	....
Monetary authorities......................	4 671 ..	....	....	....	....	....	....	....	....
General government......................	4 672 ..	....	....	....	....	....	....	....	....
Banks.......................................	4 673 ..	....	....	....	....	....	....	....	....
Other sectors...............................	4 674 ..	....	....	....	....	.68	−.32	−.54	....
Money market instruments..................	4 680 ..	....	....	....	....	....	....	....	....
Monetary authorities......................	4 681 ..	....	....	....	....	....	....	....	....
General government......................	4 682 ..	....	....	....	....	....	....	....	....
Banks.......................................	4 683 ..	....	....	....	....	....	....	....	....
Other sectors...............................	4 684 ..	....	....	....	....	....	....	....	....
C. FINANCIAL DERIVATIVES.........................	4 910 ..	....	....	....	....	....	....	....	....
Monetary authorities...........................	4 911 ..	....	....	....	....	....	....	....	....
General government...........................	4 912 ..	....	....	....	....	....	....	....	....
Banks..	4 913 ..	....	....	....	....	....	....	....	....
Other sectors...................................	4 914 ..	....	....	....	....	....	....	....	....
Assets..	4 900 ..	....	....	....	....	....	....	....	....
Monetary authorities...........................	4 901 ..	....	....	....	....	....	....	....	....
General government...........................	4 902 ..	....	....	....	....	....	....	....	....
Banks..	4 903 ..	....	....	....	....	....	....	....	....
Other sectors...................................	4 904 ..	....	....	....	....	....	....	....	....
Liabilities......................................	4 905 ..	....	....	....	....	....	....	....	....
Monetary authorities...........................	4 906 ..	....	....	....	....	....	....	....	....
General government...........................	4 907 ..	....	....	....	....	....	....	....	....
Banks..	4 908 ..	....	....	....	....	....	....	....	....
Other sectors...................................	4 909 ..	....	....	....	....	....	....	....	....

Table 2 (Concluded). STANDARD PRESENTATION, 2000–2007

(Millions of U.S. dollars)

	Code	2000	2001	2002	2003	2004	2005	2006	2007
D. OTHER INVESTMENT	4 700	−2.36	−7.64	12.65	18.12	29.07	26.50	−9.02	−17.39
Assets	4 703	−13.55	−11.41	−5.60	48.16	−14.77	26.60	−27.47	51.25
Trade credits	4 706	....	....	....	....	....	....	....	....
General government	4 707	....	....	....	....	....	....	....	....
of which: Short-term	4 709	....	....	....	....	....	....	....	....
Other sectors	4 710	....	....	....	....	....	....	....	....
of which: Short-term	4 712	....	....	....	....	....	....	....	....
Loans	4 714	....	....	24.26	8.13	29.28	11.91	21.99	18.95
Monetary authorities	4 715	....	....	....	....	....	....	....	....
of which: Short-term	4 718	....	....	....	....	....	....	....	....
General government	4 719	....	....	....	....	....	....	....	....
of which: Short-term	4 721	....	....	....	....	....	....	....	....
Banks	4 722	....	....	....	....	....	−1.38	−1.48	−3.57
of which: Short-term	4 724	....	....	....	....	....	....	....	....
Other sectors	4 725	....	....	24.26	8.13	29.28	13.29	23.47	22.51
of which: Short-term	4 727	....	....	....	....	....	....	....	....
Currency and deposits	4 730	−13.55	−11.41	−24.03	10.81	−35.22	33.38	−16.09	−9.16
Monetary authorities	4 731	....	....	....	....	....	....	....	....
General government	4 732	....	....	....	....	....	....	....	....
Banks	4 733	−13.10	−14.81	−22.39	11.55	−7.18	−10.89	−11.31	−32.87
Other sectors	4 734	−.45	3.40	−1.64	−.74	−28.04	44.27	−4.78	23.71
Other assets	4 736	....	....	−5.82	29.22	−8.83	−18.69	−33.37	41.47
Monetary authorities	4 737	....	....	....	....	....	....	....	....
of which: Short-term	4 739	....	....	....	....	....	....	....	....
General government	4 740	....	....	....	....	....	....	....	....
of which: Short-term	4 742	....	....	....	....	....	....	....	....
Banks	4 743	....	....	....	....	....	....	....	....
of which: Short-term	4 745	....	....	....	....	....	....	....	....
Other sectors	4 746	....	....	−5.82	29.22	−8.83	−18.69	−33.37	41.47
of which: Short-term	4 748	....	....	....	....	....	....	....	....
Liabilities	4 753	11.19	3.78	18.24	−30.04	43.84	−.10	18.45	−68.65
Trade credits	4 756	....	....	....	....	....	....	....	....
General government	4 757	....	....	....	....	....	....	....	....
of which: Short-term	4 759	....	....	....	....	....	....	....	....
Other sectors	4 760	....	....	....	....	....	....	....	....
of which: Short-term	4 762	....	....	....	....	....	....	....	....
Loans	4 764	16.01	.20	1.65	3.32	23.34	−10.92	14.45	−18.90
Monetary authorities	4 765	....	....	....	....	....	....	....	....
of which: Use of Fund credit and loans from the Fund	4 766	....	....	....	....	....	....	....	....
of which: Short-term	4 768	....	....	....	....	....	....	....	....
General government	4 769	15.62	−3.50	−.35	−.91	−2.61	−3.00	−1.59	−1.89
of which: Short-term	4 771	....	....	....	....	....	....	....	....
Banks	4 772	....	....	....	....	....	....	....	2.83
of which: Short-term	4 774	....	....	....	....	....	....	....	*2.83*
Other sectors	4 775	.39	3.70	1.99	4.24	25.95	−7.92	16.04	−19.84
of which: Short-term	4 777	....	....	....	....	....	....	....	....
Currency and deposits	4 780	−4.82	3.58	43.72	−7.80	3.17	19.74	18.04	21.75
Monetary authorities	4 781	−.03	.53	−.17	−.32	−.14	.40	−.13	.82
General government	4 782	....	....	....	....	....	....	....	.10
Banks	4 783	−4.79	3.05	34.11	−8.69	−6.76	12.17	11.72	−2.47
Other sectors	4 784	....	....	9.77	1.20	10.07	7.17	6.45	23.31
Other liabilities	4 786	....	....	−27.12	−25.56	17.32	−8.91	−14.05	−71.49
Monetary authorities	4 787	....	....	....	....	....	....	....	....
of which: Short-term	4 789	....	....	....	....	....	....	....	....
General government	4 790	....	....	....	....	....	....	....	....
of which: Short-term	4 792	....	....	....	....	....	....	....	....
Banks	4 793	....	....	....	....	....	....	....	....
of which: Short-term	4 795	....	....	....	....	....	....	....	....
Other sectors	4 796	....	....	−27.12	−25.56	17.32	−8.91	−14.05	−71.49
of which: Short-term	4 798	....	....	....	....	....	....	....	....
E. RESERVE ASSETS	4 802	.87	.62	4.66	−1.03	−14.86	−8.97	−32.56	−9.04
Monetary gold	4 812	....	....	....	....	....	....	....	....
Special drawing rights	4 811	−.13	−.11	−.07	−.06	−.06	−.09	−.13	−.17
Reserve position in the Fund	4 810	....	....	....	....	....	....	....	....
Foreign exchange	4 803	1.00	.74	4.73	−.98	−14.80	−8.88	−32.43	−8.87
Other claims	4 813	....	....	....	....	....	....	....	....
NET ERRORS AND OMISSIONS	4 998	−.88	7.55	−21.28	−21.79	−24.50	−16.65	−3.94	−4.31

2008, International Monetary Fund: *Balance of Payments Statistics Yearbook*

Table 3. INTERNATIONAL INVESTMENT POSITION (End-period stocks), 2000–2007

(Millions of U.S. dollars)

	Code	2000	2001	2002	2003	2004	2005	2006	2007
ASSETS..	8 995 C.	....	....	458.94	503.20	471.00	510.23	594.32	....
Direct investment abroad..................	8 505 ..	....	....	9.33	11.84	13.22	13.28	14.77	....
Equity capital and reinvested earnings............	8 506 ..	....	....	....	....	....	....	....	....
Claims on affiliated enterprises................	8 507 ..	....	....	....	....	....	....	....	....
Liabilities to affiliated enterprises............	8 508 ..	....	....	....	....	....	....	....	....
Other capital..	8 530 ..	....	....	....	....	....	....	....	....
Claims on affiliated enterprises................	8 535 ..	....	....	....	....	....	....	....	....
Liabilities to affiliated enterprises............	8 540 ..	....	....	....	....	....	....	....	....
Portfolio investment...........................	8 602 ..	....	....	11.79	12.19	13.47	13.96	14.86	....
Equity securities...................................	8 610 ..	....	....	....	....	....	....	....	....
Monetary authorities...........................	8 611 ..	....	....	....	....	....	....	....	....
General government............................	8 612 ..	....	....	....	....	....	....	....	....
Banks...	8 613 ..	....	....	....	....	....	....	....	....
Other sectors....................................	8 614 ..	....	....	....	....	....	....	....	....
Debt securities.....................................	8 619 ..	....	....	11.79	12.19	13.47	13.96	14.86	....
Bonds and notes................................	8 620 ..	....	....	11.79	12.19	13.47	13.96	14.86	....
Monetary authorities........................	8 621 ..	....	....	....	....	....	....	....	....
General government.........................	8 622 ..	....	....	....	....	....	....	....	....
Banks..	8 623 ..	....	....	....	....	....	....	....	....
Other sectors..................................	8 624 ..	....	....	....	....	13.47	13.96	14.86	....
Money market instruments.....................	8 630 ..	....	....	....	....	....	....	....	....
Monetary authorities........................	8 631 ..	....	....	....	....	....	....	....	....
General government.........................	8 632 ..	....	....	....	....	....	....	....	....
Banks..	8 633 ..	....	....	....	....	....	....	....	....
Other sectors..................................	8 634 ..	....	....	....	....	....	....	....	....
Financial derivatives..........................	8 900 ..	....	....	....	....	....	....	....	....
Monetary authorities.............................	8 901 ..	....	....	....	....	....	....	....	....
General government..............................	8 902 ..	....	....	....	....	....	....	....	....
Banks...	8 903 ..	....	....	....	....	....	....	....	....
Other sectors......................................	8 904 ..	....	....	....	....	....	....	....	....
Other investment...............................	8 703 ..	....	....	401.30	435.10	382.50	415.78	460.02	....
Trade credits.......................................	8 706 ..	....	....	....	....	....	....	....	....
General government............................	8 707 ..	....	....	....	....	....	....	....	....
of which: Short-term.......................	8 709 ..	....	....	....	....	....	....	....	....
Other sectors....................................	8 710 ..	....	....	....	....	....	....	....	....
of which: Short-term.......................	8 712 ..	....	....	....	....	....	....	....	....
Loans...	8 714 ..	....	....	105.95	126.47	95.68	85.20	65.58	....
Monetary authorities...........................	8 715 ..	....	....	....	....	....	....	....	....
of which: Short-term.......................	8 718 ..	....	....	....	....	....	....	....	....
General government............................	8 719 ..	....	....	....	....	....	....	....	....
of which: Short-term.......................	8 721 ..	....	....	....	....	....	....	....	....
Banks...	8 722 ..	....	....	....	....	....	10.26	12.32	....
of which: Short-term.......................	8 724 ..	....	....	....	....	....	....	....	....
Other sectors....................................	8 725 ..	....	....	....	....	95.68	74.95	53.26	....
of which: Short-term.......................	8 727 ..	....	....	....	....	....	....	....	....
Currency and deposits...........................	8 730 ..	....	....	258.13	296.67	262.74	289.30	316.71	....
Monetary authorities...........................	8 731 ..	....	....	....	....	....	....	....	....
General government............................	8 732 ..	....	....	....	....	....	....	....	....
Banks...	8 733 ..	....	....	....	....	262.74	268.59	291.18	....
Other sectors....................................	8 734 ..	....	....	....	....	....	20.71	25.53	....
Other assets..	8 736 ..	....	....	37.22	11.96	24.08	41.28	77.73	....
Monetary authorities...........................	8 737 ..	....	....	....	....	....	....	....	....
of which: Short-term.......................	8 739 ..	....	....	....	....	....	....	....	....
General government............................	8 740 ..	....	....	....	....	....	....	....	....
of which: Short-term.......................	8 742 ..	....	....	....	....	....	....	....	....
Banks...	8 743 ..	....	....	....	....	....	....	....	....
of which: Short-term.......................	8 745 ..	....	....	....	....	....	....	....	....
Other sectors....................................	8 746 ..	....	....	....	....	24.08	41.28	77.73	....
of which: Short-term.......................	8 748 ..	....	....	....	....	....	....	....	....
Reserve assets..................................	8 802 ..	....	....	36.52	44.07	61.81	67.20	104.67	....
Monetary gold.....................................	8 812 ..	....	....	....	....	....	....	....	....
Special drawing rights...........................	8 811 ..	.91	.99	1.15	1.32	1.44	1.42	1.63	1.89
Reserve position in the Fund...................	8 810 ..	3.25	3.14	3.39	3.71	3.88	3.57	3.75	3.94
Foreign exchange..................................	8 803 ..	....	....	31.98	39.04	56.49	62.22	99.29	....
Other claims..	8 813 ..	....	....	....	....	....	....	....	....

Table 3 (Concluded). INTERNATIONAL INVESTMENT POSITION (End-period stocks), 2000–2007

(Millions of U.S. dollars)

	Code	2000	2001	2002	2003	2004	2005	2006	2007
LIABILITIES	8 995 D.	....	....	483.14	578.92	607.27	562.07	651.78	....
Direct investment in Vanuatu	8 555 ..	....	....	108.88	149.45	148.77	148.62	196.47	....
Equity capital and reinvested earnings	8 556 ..	....	....	....	....	128.33	127.83	172.25	....
Claims on direct investors	8 557 ..	....	....	....	....	....	....	....	....
Liabilities to direct investors	8 558 ..	....	....	....	....	128.33	127.83	172.25	....
Other capital	8 580 ..	....	....	....	....	20.44	20.79	24.22	....
Claims on direct investors	8 585 ..	....	....	....	....	....	....	....	....
Liabilities to direct investors	8 590 ..	....	....	....	....	20.44	20.79	24.22	....
Portfolio investment	8 652 ..	....	....	....	....	....	....	....	....
Equity securities	8 660 ..	....	....	....	....	....	....	....	....
Banks	8 663 ..	....	....	....	....	....	....	....	....
Other sectors	8 664 ..	....	....	....	....	....	....	....	....
Debt securities	8 669 ..	....	....	....	....	....	....	....	....
Bonds and notes	8 670 ..	....	....	....	....	....	....	....	....
Monetary authorities	8 671 ..	....	....	....	....	....	....	....	....
General government	8 672 ..	....	....	....	....	....	....	....	....
Banks	8 673 ..	....	....	....	....	....	....	....	....
Other sectors	8 674 ..	....	....	....	....	....	....	....	....
Money market instruments	8 680 ..	....	....	....	....	....	....	....	....
Monetary authorities	8 681 ..	....	....	....	....	....	....	....	....
General government	8 682 ..	....	....	....	....	....	....	....	....
Banks	8 683 ..	....	....	....	....	....	....	....	....
Other sectors	8 684 ..	....	....	....	....	....	....	....	....
Financial derivatives	8 905 ..	....	....	....	....	....	....	....	....
Monetary authorities	8 906 ..	....	....	....	....	....	....	....	....
General government	8 907 ..	....	....	....	....	....	....	....	....
Banks	8 908 ..	....	....	....	....	....	....	....	....
Other sectors	8 909 ..	....	....	....	....	....	....	....	....
Other investment	8 753 ..	....	....	374.27	429.47	458.51	413.45	455.32	....
Trade credits	8 756 ..	....	....	....	....	....	....	....	....
General government	8 757 ..	....	....	....	....	....	....	....	....
of which: Short-term	8 759 ..	....	....	....	....	....	....	....	....
Other sectors	8 760 ..	....	....	....	....	....	....	....	....
of which: Short-term	8 762 ..	....	....	....	....	....	....	....	....
Loans	8 764 ..	....	....	113.83	136.26	167.26	130.21	151.71	....
Monetary authorities	8 765 ..	....	....	....	....	....	....	....	....
of which: Use of Fund credit and loans from the Fund	8 766 ..	....	....	....	....	....	....	....	....
of which: Short-term	8 768 ..	....	....	....	....	....	....	....	....
General government	8 769 ..	....	....	....	....	82.73	75.53	78.03	....
of which: Short-term	8 771 ..	....	....	....	....	....	....	....	....
Banks	8 772 ..	....	....	....	....	....	....	....	....
of which: Short-term	8 774 ..	....	....	....	....	....	....	....	....
Other sectors	8 775 ..	....	....	....	....	84.53	54.68	73.68	....
of which: Short-term	8 777 ..	....	....	....	....	....	....	....	....
Currency and deposits	8 780 ..	....	....	113.48	123.35	126.30	136.59	162.16	....
Monetary authorities	8 781 ..	....	....	....	....	1.90	2.18	2.17	....
General government	8 782 ..	....	....	....	....	....	....	....	....
Banks	8 783 ..	....	....	....	....	61.14	69.69	85.96	....
Other sectors	8 784 ..	....	....	....	....	63.27	64.72	74.03	....
Other liabilities	8 786 ..	....	....	146.96	169.86	164.95	146.66	141.44	....
Monetary authorities	8 787 ..	....	....	....	....	....	....	....	....
of which: Short-term	8 789 ..	....	....	....	....	....	....	....	....
General government	8 790 ..	....	....	....	....	....	....	....	....
of which: Short-term	8 792 ..	....	....	....	....	....	....	....	....
Banks	8 793 ..	....	....	....	....	....	....	....	....
of which: Short-term	8 795 ..	....	....	....	....	....	....	....	....
Other sectors	8 796 ..	....	....	....	....	164.95	146.66	141.44	....
of which: Short-term	8 798 ..	....	....	....	....	....	....	....	....
NET INTERNATIONAL INVESTMENT POSITION	8 995 ..	....	....	−24.20	−75.72	−136.27	−51.84	−57.47	....
Conversion rates: vatu per U.S. dollar (end of period)	0 102 ..	142.81	146.74	133.17	111.81	106.53	112.33	106.48	99.86

Table 1. ANALYTIC PRESENTATION, 2000–2007

(Millions of U.S. dollars)

	Code	2000	2001	2002	2003	2004	2005	2006	2007
A. Current Account[1]	4 993 Z.	**11,853**	**1,983**	**7,599**	**11,796**	**15,519**	**25,110**	**27,149**	**20,001**
Goods: exports f.o.b.	2 100 ..	33,529	26,667	26,781	27,230	39,668	55,647	65,210	69,165
Goods: imports f.o.b.	3 100 ..	−16,865	−19,211	−13,360	−10,483	−17,021	−24,195	−32,498	−45,463
Balance on Goods	4 100 ..	*16,664*	*7,456*	*13,421*	*16,747*	*22,647*	*31,452*	*32,712*	*23,702*
Services: credit	2 200 ..	1,182	1,376	1,013	878	1,114	1,341	1,572	1,673
Services: debit	3 200 ..	−4,435	−4,681	−3,922	−3,512	−4,497	−5,349	−6,005	−7,524
Balance on Goods and Services	4 991 ..	*13,411*	*4,151*	*10,512*	*14,113*	*19,264*	*27,444*	*28,279*	*17,851*
Income: credit	2 300 ..	3,049	2,603	1,474	1,729	2,050	4,146	7,934	10,114
Income: debit	3 300 ..	−4,437	−4,623	−4,230	−4,066	−5,723	−6,411	−9,026	−7,549
Balance on Goods, Services, and Income	4 992 ..	*12,023*	*2,131*	*7,756*	*11,776*	*15,591*	*25,179*	*27,187*	*20,416*
Current transfers: credit	2 379 Z.	261	356	288	257	227	249	296	285
Current transfers: debit	3 379 ..	−431	−504	−445	−237	−299	−318	−334	−700
B. Capital Account[1]	4 994 Z.	....	....	....	....	....	....	....	....
Capital account: credit	2 994 Z.	....	....	....	....	....	....	....	....
Capital account: debit	3 994 ..	....	....	....	....	....	....	....	....
Total, Groups A Plus B	4 981 ..	*11,853*	*1,983*	*7,599*	*11,796*	*15,519*	*25,110*	*27,149*	*20,001*
C. Financial Account[1]	4 995 W.	**−2,969**	**−211**	**−9,246**	**−5,547**	**−10,861**	**−16,480**	**−19,244**	**−22,919**
Direct investment abroad	4 505 ..	−521	−204	−1,026	−1,318	−619	−1,167	−2,076	−2,237
Direct investment in Venezuela	4 555 Z.	4,701	3,683	782	2,040	1,483	2,602	−590	646
Portfolio investment assets	4 602 ..	−954	397	−1,354	−823	−813	−2,297	−5,382	−37
Equity securities	4 610 ..	13	138	−164	−233	27	−204	3	28
Debt securities	4 619 ..	−967	259	−1,190	−590	−840	−2,093	−5,385	−65
Portfolio investment liabilities	4 652 Z.	−2,180	710	−956	−143	−1,271	3,225	−3,982	4,129
Equity securities	4 660 ..	−574	31	−5	97	−170	28	41	66
Debt securities	4 669 Z.	−1,606	679	−951	−240	−1,101	3,197	−4,023	4,063
Financial derivatives	4 910 ..	....	....	....	....	....	....	....	....
Financial derivatives assets	4 900 ..	....	....	....	....	....	....	....	....
Financial derivatives liabilities	4 905 ..	....	....	....	....	....	....	....	....
Other investment assets	4 703 ..	−4,839	−3,919	−7,169	−4,030	−8,233	−18,425	−7,020	−30,029
Monetary authorities	4 701 ..	18	42	22	11	10	−21	16	−5,783
General government	4 704 ..	−228	−1,016	65	−718	−2,594	−7,011	2,385	−1,527
Banks	4 705 ..	−50	267	−32	46	−552	−103	−288	−322
Other sectors	4 728 ..	−4,579	−3,212	−7,224	−3,369	−5,097	−11,290	−9,133	−22,397
Other investment liabilities	4 753 W.	824	−878	477	−1,273	−1,408	−418	−194	4,609
Monetary authorities	4 753 WA	8	18	−4	19	250	−23	−51	384
General government	4 753 ZB	36	−1	170	298	−586	−358	−74	−984
Banks	4 753 ZC	197	122	−257	−141	1	82	610	−132
Other sectors	4 753 ZD	583	−1,017	568	−1,449	−1,073	−119	−679	5,341
Total, Groups A Through C	4 983 ..	*8,884*	*1,772*	*−1,647*	*6,249*	*4,658*	*8,630*	*7,905*	*−2,918*
D. Net Errors and Omissions	4 998 ..	**−2,926**	**−3,601**	**−2,781**	**−795**	**−2,503**	**−3,205**	**−2,828**	**−2,439**
Total, Groups A Through D	4 984 ..	*5,958*	*−1,829*	*−4,428*	*5,454*	*2,155*	*5,425*	*5,077*	*−5,357*
E. Reserves and Related Items	4 802 A.	**−5,958**	**1,829**	**4,428**	**−5,454**	**−2,155**	**−5,425**	**−5,077**	**5,357**
Reserve assets	4 802 ..	−5,449	2,027	4,428	−5,454	−2,155	−5,425	−5,077	5,357
Use of Fund credit and loans	4 766 ..	−508	−198	....	....	....	....	....	....
Exceptional financing	4 920 ..	....	....	....	....	....	....	....	....
Conversion rates: bolívares per U.S. dollar	0 101 ..	**.6800**	**.7237**	**1.1610**	**1.6070**	**1.8913**	**2.0898**	**2.1470**	**2.1470**

[1] Excludes components that have been classified in the categories of Group E.

Table 2. STANDARD PRESENTATION, 2000–2007

(Millions of U.S. dollars)

	Code	2000	2001	2002	2003	2004	2005	2006	2007
CURRENT ACCOUNT...	4 993 ..	**11,853**	**1,983**	**7,599**	**11,796**	**15,519**	**25,110**	**27,149**	**20,001**
A. GOODS..	4 100 ..	**16,664**	**7,456**	**13,421**	**16,747**	**22,647**	**31,452**	**32,712**	**23,702**
Credit..	2 100 ..	**33,529**	**26,667**	**26,781**	**27,230**	**39,668**	**55,647**	**65,210**	**69,165**
General merchandise: exports f.o.b.................	2 110 ..	32,908	26,201	26,366	27,109	39,468	55,244	64,916	68,843
Goods for processing: exports f.o.b................	2 150 ..	....	....	....	....	....	....	....	....
Repairs on goods..	2 160 ..	4	4	4	4	4	4	4	4
Goods procured in ports by carriers..............	2 170 ..	340	290	277	8	8	8	8	8
Nonmonetary gold.......................................	2 180 ..	277	172	134	109	188	391	282	310
Debit...	3 100 ..	**−16,865**	**−19,211**	**−13,360**	**−10,483**	**−17,021**	**−24,195**	**−32,498**	**−45,463**
General merchandise: imports f.o.b................	3 110 ..	−16,817	−19,182	−13,331	−10,454	−16,997	−24,173	−32,403	−45,388
Goods for processing: imports f.o.b...............	3 150 ..	....	....	....	....	....	....	....	....
Repairs on goods..	3 160 ..	−28	−8	−8	−8	−8	−6	−36	−25
Goods procured in ports by carriers..............	3 170 ..	−20	−21	−21	−21	−16	−16	−59	−50
Nonmonetary gold.......................................	3 180 ..	....	....	....	....	....	....	....	....
B. SERVICES...	4 200 ..	**−3,253**	**−3,305**	**−2,909**	**−2,634**	**−3,383**	**−4,008**	**−4,433**	**−5,851**
Total credit	2 200 ..	*1,182*	*1,376*	*1,013*	*878*	*1,114*	*1,341*	*1,572*	*1,673*
Total debit	3 200 ..	*−4,435*	*−4,681*	*−3,922*	*−3,512*	*−4,497*	*−5,349*	*−6,005*	*−7,524*
Transportation services, credit...................	2 205 ..	**374**	**386**	**304**	**307**	**346**	**383**	**409**	**404**
Passenger	2 850 ..	*46*	*62*	*50*	*47*	*52*	*72*	*75*	*77*
Freight	2 851 ..	*100*	*105*	*99*	*89*	*101*	*104*	*106*	*103*
Other	2 852 ..	*228*	*219*	*155*	*171*	*193*	*207*	*228*	*224*
Sea transport, passenger..............................	2 207 ..	....	....	....	....	....	....	....	....
Sea transport, freight...................................	2 208 ..	94	102	95	88	99	102	105	103
Sea transport, other....................................	2 209 ..	209	197	134	151	168	175	199	188
Air transport, passenger..............................	2 211 ..	46	62	50	47	52	72	75	77
Air transport, freight...................................	2 212 ..	6	3	4	1	2	2	1	....
Air transport, other.....................................	2 213 ..	19	22	21	20	25	32	29	36
Other transport, passenger..........................	2 215 ..	....	....	....	....	....	....	....	....
Other transport, freight...............................	2 216 ..	....	....	....	....	....	....	....	....
Other transport, other.................................	2 217 ..	....	....	....	....	....	....	....	....
Transportation services, debit....................	3 205 ..	**−1,808**	**−1,967**	**−1,545**	**−1,261**	**−1,730**	**−2,214**	**−2,769**	**−3,719**
Passenger	3 850 ..	*−589*	*−610*	*−565*	*−452*	*−527*	*−567*	*−578*	*−707*
Freight	3 851 ..	*−1,013*	*−1,143*	*−804*	*−659*	*−1,038*	*−1,463*	*−1,999*	*−2,815*
Other	3 852 ..	*−206*	*−214*	*−176*	*−150*	*−165*	*−184*	*−192*	*−197*
Sea transport, passenger..............................	3 207 ..	....	....	....	....	....	....	....	....
Sea transport, freight...................................	3 208 ..	−798	−892	−615	−507	−768	−1,100	−1,469	−2,079
Sea transport, other....................................	3 209 ..	−133	−122	−99	−87	−104	−118	−122	−120
Air transport, passenger..............................	3 211 ..	−589	−610	−565	−452	−527	−567	−578	−707
Air transport, freight...................................	3 212 ..	−148	−162	−123	−98	−143	−207	−278	−394
Air transport, other.....................................	3 213 ..	−73	−92	−77	−63	−61	−66	−70	−77
Other transport, passenger..........................	3 215 ..	....	....	....	....	....	....	....	....
Other transport, freight...............................	3 216 ..	−67	−89	−66	−54	−127	−156	−252	−342
Other transport, other.................................	3 217 ..	....	....	....	....	....	....	....	....
Travel, credit..	2 236 ..	**423**	**615**	**434**	**331**	**502**	**650**	**768**	**817**
Business travel..	2 237 ..	230	342	243	186	199	275	270	258
Personal travel..	2 240 ..	193	273	191	145	303	375	498	559
Travel, debit...	3 236 ..	**−1,058**	**−1,108**	**−981**	**−859**	**−1,077**	**−1,276**	**−1,229**	**−1,394**
Business travel..	3 237 ..	−386	−354	−219	−241	−316	−419	−390	−370
Personal travel..	3 240 ..	−672	−754	−762	−618	−761	−857	−839	−1,024
Other services, credit................................	2 200 BA	**385**	**375**	**275**	**240**	**266**	**308**	**395**	**452**
Communications..	2 245 ..	106	80	52	48	55	83	154	176
Construction...	2 249 ..	....	....	....	....	....	....	....	....
Insurance...	2 253 ..	3	2	1	2	2	1	2	2
Financial..	2 260 ..	....	....	....	....	....	....	....	....
Computer and information............................	2 262 ..	7	7	7	6	6	8	8	9
Royalties and licence fees............................	2 266 ..	....	....	....	....	....	....	....	....
Other business services...............................	2 268 ..	138	146	110	92	109	117	123	139
Personal, cultural, and recreational................	2 287 ..	6	6	5	5	4	5	5	5
Government, n.i.e..	2 291 ..	125	134	100	87	90	94	103	121
Other services, debit.................................	3 200 BA	**−1,569**	**−1,606**	**−1,396**	**−1,392**	**−1,690**	**−1,859**	**−2,007**	**−2,411**
Communications..	3 245 ..	−84	−78	−62	−58	−68	−76	−98	−115
Construction...	3 249 ..	....	....	....	....	....	....	....	....
Insurance...	3 253 ..	−181	−193	−156	−115	−165	−228	−297	−417
Financial..	3 260 ..	−46	−70	−125	−157	−110	−243	−197	−292
Computer and information............................	3 262 ..	−67	−71	−65	−58	−69	−85	−94	−101
Royalties and licence fees............................	3 266 ..	−184	−260	−211	−183	−219	−239	−257	−276
Other business services...............................	3 268 ..	−736	−691	−634	−508	−662	−641	−602	−617
Personal, cultural, and recreational................	3 287 ..	−72	−71	−58	−52	−165	−181	−254	−312
Government, n.i.e..	3 291 ..	−199	−172	−85	−261	−232	−166	−208	−281

Table 2 (Continued). STANDARD PRESENTATION, 2000–2007

(Millions of U.S. dollars)

	Code	2000	2001	2002	2003	2004	2005	2006	2007
C. INCOME	4 300 ..	**−1,388**	**−2,020**	**−2,756**	**−2,337**	**−3,673**	**−2,265**	**−1,092**	**2,565**
Total credit	2 300 ..	*3,049*	*2,603*	*1,474*	*1,729*	*2,050*	*4,146*	*7,934*	*10,114*
Total debit	3 300 ..	*−4,437*	*−4,623*	*−4,230*	*−4,066*	*−5,723*	*−6,411*	*−9,026*	*−7,549*
Compensation of employees, credit	2 310 ..	**17**	**19**	**19**	**21**	**20**	**20**	**20**	**20**
Compensation of employees, debit	3 310 ..	**−29**	**−27**	**−23**	**−30**	**−28**	**−28**	**−28**	**−27**
Investment income, credit	2 320 ..	**3,032**	**2,584**	**1,455**	**1,708**	**2,030**	**4,126**	**7,914**	**10,094**
Direct investment income	2 330 ..	296	767	286	791	725	1,349	2,984	3,751
Dividends and distributed branch profits	2 332 ..	328	622	38	585	570	1,061	1,729	3,281
Reinvested earnings anc undistributed branch profits	2 333 ..	−32	145	248	206	155	288	1,255	470
Income on debt (interest)	2 334 ..	....	....	....	....	....	....	....	....
Portfolio investment income	2 339 ..	666	454	299	332	367	535	1,449	1,874
Income on equity	2 340 ..	18	18	14	10	7	3	9	17
Income on bonds and notes	2 350 ..	223	202	202	264	289	308	711	991
Income on money market instruments	2 360 ..	425	234	83	58	71	224	729	866
Other investment income	2 370 ..	2,070	1,363	870	585	938	2,242	3,481	4,469
Investment income, debit	3 320 ..	**−4,408**	**−4,596**	**−4,207**	**−4,036**	**−5,695**	**−6,383**	**−8,998**	**−7,522**
Direct investment income	3 330 ..	−1,424	−1,884	−1,915	−1,802	−3,498	−3,953	−6,302	−4,753
Dividends and distributed branch profits	3 332 ..	−1,014	−1,047	−1,098	−726	−1,786	−1,823	−4,308	−2,964
Reinvested earnings anc undistributed branch profits	3 333 ..	−354	−800	−797	−1,045	−1,673	−2,086	−1,950	−1,738
Income on debt (interest)	3 334 ..	−56	−37	−20	−31	−39	−44	−44	−51
Portfolio investment income	3 339 ..	−1,788	−1,808	−1,611	−1,678	−1,677	−1,824	−2,016	−1,839
Income on equity	3 340 ..	−139	−232	−118	−161	−176	−85	−213	−172
Income on bonds and notes	3 350 ..	−1,649	−1,576	−1,493	−1,517	−1,501	−1,739	−1,803	−1,667
Income on money market instruments	3 360 ..	....	....	....	....	....	....	....	....
Other investment income	3 370 ..	−1,196	−904	−681	−556	−520	−606	−680	−930
D. CURRENT TRANSFERS	4 379 ..	**−170**	**−148**	**−157**	**20**	**−72**	**−69**	**−38**	**−415**
Credit	2 379 ..	**261**	**356**	**288**	**257**	**227**	**249**	**296**	**285**
General government	2 380 ..	44	8	8	25	61	74	112	128
Other sectors	2 390 ..	217	348	280	232	166	175	184	157
Workers' remittances	2 391 ..	....	....	....	187	123	128	145	116
Other current transfers	2 392 ..	217	348	280	45	43	47	39	41
Debit	3 379 ..	**−431**	**−504**	**−445**	**−237**	**−299**	**−318**	**−334**	**−700**
General government	3 380 ..	−51	−47	−32	−14	−70	−86	−42	−35
Other sectors	3 390 ..	−380	−457	−413	−223	−229	−232	−292	−665
Workers' remittances	3 391 ..	−302	−379	−360	−179	−186	−183	−225	−571
Other current transfers	3 392 ..	−78	−78	−53	−44	−43	−49	−67	−94
CAPITAL AND FINANCIAL ACCOUNT	4 996 ..	**−8,927**	**1,618**	**−4,818**	**−11,001**	**−13,016**	**−21,905**	**−24,321**	**−17,562**
CAPITAL ACCOUNT	4 994 ..	....	....	....	....	....	....	....	....
Total credit	2 994 ..	....	....	....	....	....	....	....	....
Total debit	3 994 ..	....	....	....	....	....	....	....	....
Capital transfers, credit	2 400 ..	....	....	....	....	....	....	....	....
General government	2 401 ..	....	....	....	....	....	....	....	....
Debt forgiveness	2 402 ..	....	....	....	....	....	....	....	....
Other capital transfers	2 410 ..	....	....	....	....	....	....	....	....
Other sectors	2 430 ..	....	....	....	....	....	....	....	....
Migrants' transfers	2 431 ..	....	....	....	....	....	....	....	....
Debt forgiveness	2 432 ..	....	....	....	....	....	....	....	....
Other capital transfers	2 440 ..	....	....	....	....	....	....	....	....
Capital transfers, debit	3 400 ..	....	....	....	....	....	....	....	....
General government	3 401 ..	....	....	....	....	....	....	....	....
Debt forgiveness	3 402 ..	....	....	....	....	....	....	....	....
Other capital transfers	3 410 ..	....	....	....	....	....	....	....	....
Other sectors	3 430 ..	....	....	....	....	....	....	....	....
Migrants' transfers	3 431 ..	....	....	....	....	....	....	....	....
Debt forgiveness	3 432 ..	....	....	....	....	....	....	....	....
Other capital transfers	3 440 ..	....	....	....	....	....	....	....	....
Nonproduced nonfinancial assets, credit	2 480 ..	....	....	....	....	....	....	....	....
Nonproduced nonfinancial assets, debit	3 480 ..	....	....	....	....	....	....	....	....

Table 2 (Continued). STANDARD PRESENTATION, 2000–2007

(Millions of U.S. dollars)

	Code	2000	2001	2002	2003	2004	2005	2006	2007
FINANCIAL ACCOUNT	4 995	−8,927	1,618	−4,818	−11,001	−13,016	−21,905	−24,321	−17,562
A. DIRECT INVESTMENT	4 500	4,180	3,479	−244	722	864	1,435	−2,666	−1,591
Direct investment abroad	4 505	−521	−204	−1,026	−1,318	−619	−1,167	−2,076	−2,237
Equity capital	4 510	−416	−198	−295	−94	−91	−21	824	−111
Claims on affiliated enterprises	4 515	−416	−198	−295	−94	−91	−21	824	−111
Liabilities to affiliated enterprises	4 520	....	....	....	....	....	....	....	....
Reinvested earnings	4 525	32	−145	−248	−206	−155	−288	−1,255	−470
Other capital	4 530	−137	139	−483	−1,018	−373	−858	−1,645	−1,656
Claims on affiliated enterprises	4 535	−139	165	−480	−527	−373	−632	−2,241	−2,684
Liabilities to affiliated enterprises	4 540	2	−26	−3	−491	....	−226	596	1,028
Direct investment in Venezuela	4 555	4,701	3,683	782	2,040	1,483	2,602	−590	646
Equity capital	4 560	2,615	1,115	577	565	654	502	−173	−1,030
Claims on direct investors	4 565	....	....	....	....	....	....	....	....
Liabilities to direct investors	4 570	2,615	1,115	577	565	654	502	−173	−1,030
Reinvested earnings	4 575	354	800	797	1,045	1,673	2,086	1,950	1,738
Other capital	4 580	1,732	1,768	−592	430	−844	14	−2,367	−62
Claims on direct investors	4 585	....	−47	18	−24	−6	−87	−14	−15
Liabilities to direct investors	4 590	1,732	1,815	−610	454	−838	101	−2,353	−47
B. PORTFOLIO INVESTMENT	4 600	−3,134	1,107	−2,310	−966	−2,084	928	−9,364	4,092
Assets	4 602	−954	397	−1,354	−823	−813	−2,297	−5,382	−37
Equity securities	4 610	13	138	−164	−233	27	−204	3	28
Monetary authorities	4 611	....	....	....	....	....	....	....	....
General government	4 612	....	....	....	....	....	....	....	....
Banks	4 613	−2	−6	9	−148	3	41	63	72
Other sectors	4 614	15	144	−173	−85	24	−245	−60	−44
Debt securities	4 619	−967	259	−1,190	−590	−840	−2,093	−5,385	−65
Bonds and notes	4 620	−333	−221	−778	−602	−875	−2,026	−4,979	18
Monetary authorities	4 621	1	1	....	....	....	....	−2,052	
General government	4 622	−66	−71	−77	−85	−92	−2,371	−1,422	1,519
Banks	4 623	−25	−23	−56	68	−271	−1,192	−855	−1,021
Other sectors	4 624	−243	−128	−645	−585	−512	1,537	−650	−480
Money market instruments	4 630	−634	480	−412	12	35	−67	−406	−83
Monetary authorities	4 631	....	....	....	....	....	....	....	....
General government	4 632	....	....	....	....	....	....	....	....
Banks	4 633	25	62	38	−241	61	−3	−73	−125
Other sectors	4 634	−659	418	−450	253	−26	−64	−333	42
Liabilities	4 652	−2,180	710	−956	−143	−1,271	3,225	−3,982	4,129
Equity securities	4 660	−574	31	−5	97	−170	28	41	66
Banks	4 663	−9	−9	....	....	−3	−2	3	27
Other sectors	4 664	−565	40	−5	97	−167	30	38	39
Debt securities	4 669	−1,606	679	−951	−240	−1,101	3,197	−4,023	4,063
Bonds and notes	4 670	−1,486	679	−951	−240	−1,101	3,197	−4,023	4,063
Monetary authorities	4 671	−12	−13	−11	−17	−13	−15		
General government	4 672	−1,060	297	−409	172	1,591	3,254	−3,961	183
Banks	4 673	....	....	....	....	....	....	....	....
Other sectors	4 674	−414	395	−531	−395	−2,679	−42	−62	3,880
Money market instruments	4 680	−120	....	....	....	....	....	....	....
Monetary authorities	4 681	....	....	....	....	....	....	....	....
General government	4 682	....	....	....	....	....	....	....	....
Banks	4 683	....	....	....	....	....	....	....	....
Other sectors	4 684	−120	....	....	....	....	....	....	....
C. FINANCIAL DERIVATIVES	4 910	....	....	....	....	....	....	....	....
Monetary authorities	4 911	....	....	....	....	....	....	....	....
General government	4 912	....	....	....	....	....	....	....	....
Banks	4 913	....	....	....	....	....	....	....	....
Other sectors	4 914	....	....	....	....	....	....	....	....
Assets	4 900	....	....	....	....	....	....	....	....
Monetary authorities	4 901	....	....	....	....	....	....	....	....
General government	4 902	....	....	....	....	....	....	....	....
Banks	4 903	....	....	....	....	....	....	....	....
Other sectors	4 904	....	....	....	....	....	....	....	....
Liabilities	4 905	....	....	....	....	....	....	....	....
Monetary authorities	4 906	....	....	....	....	....	....	....	....
General government	4 907	....	....	....	....	....	....	....	....
Banks	4 908	....	....	....	....	....	....	....	....
Other sectors	4 909	....	....	....	....	....	....	....	....

Table 2 (Concluded). STANDARD PRESENTATION, 2000–2007

(Millions of U.S. dollars)

	Code	2000	2001	2002	2003	2004	2005	2006	2007
D. OTHER INVESTMENT	4 700	**−4,523**	**−4,995**	**−6,692**	**−5,303**	**−9,641**	**−18,843**	**−7,214**	**−25,420**
Assets	4 703	**−4,839**	**−3,919**	**−7,169**	**−4,030**	**−8,233**	**−18,425**	**−7,020**	**−30,029**
Trade credits	4 706	−448	1,223	−815	−907	−431	−2,825	−4,957	−6,148
General government	4 707	....	−52	50	2	....	....	−122	....
of which: Short-term	4 709	....	*−52*	*50*	*2*	....	....	....	....
Other sectors	4 710	−448	1,275	−865	−909	−431	−2,825	−4,835	−6,148
of which: Short-term	4 712	*−447*	*1,280*	*−877*	*−872*	*−418*	*−2,825*	*−4,835*	*−6,148*
Loans	4 714	649	139	33	43	47	28	−191	30
Monetary authorities	4 715	6	−48	13	9	18	12	1	2
of which: Short-term	4 718	*−2*	*1*	*1*	....	....	....	....	....
General government	4 719	....	....	....	....	....	....	....	....
of which: Short-term	4 721	....	....	....	....	....	....	....	....
Banks	4 722	....	....	....	....	....	....	....	....
of which: Short-term	4 724	....	....	....	....	....	....	....	....
Other sectors	4 725	643	187	20	34	29	16	−192	28
of which: Short-term	4 727	*599*	*134*	....	....	....	....	....	....
Currency and deposits	4 730	−5,057	−5,351	−6,370	−3,086	−7,725	−15,542	−1,879	−23,797
Monetary authorities	4 731	....	....	....	....	....	....	....	−5,797
General government	4 732	−187	−937	22	−698	−2,570	−6,993	2,508	−1,527
Banks	4 733	−50	267	−32	46	−552	−103	−288	−322
Other sectors	4 734	−4,820	−4,681	−6,360	−2,434	−4,603	−8,446	−4,099	−16,151
Other assets	4 736	17	70	−17	−80	−124	−86	7	−114
Monetary authorities	4 737	12	90	9	2	−8	−33	15	12
of which: Short-term	4 739	*12*	*90*	*9*	*2*	*−8*	*−33*	*15*	*12*
General government	4 740	−41	−27	−7	−22	−24	−18	−1	....
of which: Short-term	4 742	....	....	....	....	....	....	....	....
Banks	4 743	....	....	....	....	....	....	....	....
of which: Short-term	4 745	....	....	....	....	....	....	....	....
Other sectors	4 746	46	7	−19	−60	−92	−35	−7	−126
of which: Short-term	4 748	*55*	*−9*	*6*	*−75*	*−92*	*−35*	*3*	*−126*
Liabilities	4 753	**316**	**−1,076**	**477**	**−1,273**	**−1,408**	**−418**	**−194**	**4,609**
Trade credits	4 756	5	−354	−162	390	139	1,096	265	1,659
General government	4 757	49	65	−33	−19	−58	−19	−50	−18
of which: Short-term	4 759	....	....	....	....	....	....	....	....
Other sectors	4 760	−44	−419	−129	409	197	1,115	315	1,677
of which: Short-term	4 762	*15*	*−361*	*−94*	*445*	*240*	*1,144*	*320*	*1,677*
Loans	4 764	280	−604	789	−1,765	−1,713	−1,268	−905	2,927
Monetary authorities	4 765	−501	−203	....	....	....	....	....	....
of which: Use of Fund credit and loans from the Fund	4 766	*−508*	*−198*	....	....	....	....	....	....
of which: Short-term	4 768	*7*	*−5*	....	....	....	....	....	....
General government	4 769	−25	−39	261	325	−523	−346	−24	−966
of which: Short-term	4 771	....	....	....	....	....	....	....	....
Banks	4 772	129	193	−257	−222	59	106	130	301
of which: Short-term	4 774	*114*	*192*	*−255*	*−206*	*61*	*108*	*152*	*283*
Other sectors	4 775	677	−555	785	−1,868	−1,249	−1,028	−1,011	3,592
of which: Short-term	4 777	*59*	*−74*	*320*	*−619*	*−149*	*−19*	*−4*	*−117*
Currency and deposits	4 780	65	−69	6	80	−63	−30	196	−148
Monetary authorities	4 781	−3	2	6	−1	−5	−6	1	....
General government	4 782	....	....	....	....	....	....	....	....
Banks	4 783	68	−71	....	81	−58	−24	195	−148
Other sectors	4 784	....	....	....	....	....	....	....	....
Other liabilities	4 786	−34	−49	−156	22	229	−216	250	171
Monetary authorities	4 787	4	21	−10	20	255	−17	−52	384
of which: Short-term	4 789	*4*	*21*	*−10*	*20*	*255*	*−17*	*−52*	*384*
General government	4 790	12	−27	−58	−8	−5	7	....	....
of which: Short-term	4 792	*12*	*−27*	*−58*	*−8*	*−5*	*7*	....	....
Banks	4 793	....	....	....	....	....	....	285	−285
of which: Short-term	4 795	....	....	....	....	....	....	*285*	*−285*
Other sectors	4 796	−50	−43	−88	10	−21	−206	17	72
of which: Short-term	4 798	*−50*	*−43*	*−88*	*10*	*−21*	*−206*	*17*	*72*
E. RESERVE ASSETS	4 802	**−5,449**	**2,027**	**4,428**	**−5,454**	**−2,155**	**−5,425**	**−5,077**	**5,357**
Monetary gold	4 812	−145	−207	112	−271	....	....	....	....
Special drawing rights	4 811	89	25	−1	2	2	3	5	−1
Reserve position in the Fund	4 810	....	....	....	....	....	....	....	....
Foreign exchange	4 803	−5,375	2,232	4,330	−5,176	−2,149	−5,426	−5,074	5,377
Other claims	4 813	−18	−23	−13	−9	−8	−2	−8	−19
NET ERRORS AND OMISSIONS	4 998	**−2,926**	**−3,601**	**−2,781**	**−795**	**−2,503**	**−3,205**	**−2,828**	**−2,439**

Table 3. INTERNATIONAL INVESTMENT POSITION (End-period stocks), 2000–2007

(Millions of U.S. dollars)

	Code	2000	2001	2002	2003	2004	2005	2006	2007
ASSETS	8 995 C.	**67,931**	**70,064**	**75,513**	**88,329**	**99,146**	**122,309**	**144,851**	**174,592**
Direct investment abroad	8 505 ..	**7,676**	**7,894**	**8,732**	**9,548**	**9,175**	**9,429**	**11,524**	**13,814**
Equity capital and reinvested earnings	8 506 ..	6,604	6,955	7,696	7,997	8,260	8,569	9,019	9,653
Claims on affiliated enterprises	8 507 ..	6,604	6,955	7,696	7,997	8,260	8,569	9,019	9,653
Liabilities to affiliated enterprises	8 508 ..	....	....	....	....	....	....	....	....
Other capital	8 530 ..	1,072	939	1,036	1,551	915	860	2,505	4,161
Claims on affiliated enterprises	8 535 ..	1,118	963	1,071	1,595	1,968	1,687	3,928	6,612
Liabilities to affiliated enterprises	8 540 ..	−46	−24	−35	−44	−1,053	−827	−1,423	−2,451
Portfolio investment	8 602 ..	**4,057**	**3,836**	**5,405**	**6,607**	**6,740**	**9,070**	**14,966**	**15,354**
Equity securities	8 610 ..	245	101	262	549	519	745	754	749
Monetary authorities	8 611 ..	....	....	....	....	....	....	....	....
General government	8 612 ..	....	....	....	....	....	....	....	....
Banks	8 613 ..	9	13	4	182	176	153	93	24
Other sectors	8 614 ..	236	88	258	367	343	592	661	725
Debt securities	8 619 ..	3,812	3,735	5,143	6,058	6,221	8,325	14,212	14,605
Bonds and notes	8 620 ..	2,076	2,482	3,478	4,406	4,794	6,810	12,230	12,609
Monetary authorities	8 621 ..	28	25	25	25	29	35	2,198	2,393
General government	8 622 ..	1,309	1,301	1,604	1,708	1,910	4,236	5,790	4,271
Banks	8 623 ..	84	108	162	91	350	1,549	2,517	3,661
Other sectors	8 624 ..	655	1,048	1,687	2,582	2,505	990	1,725	2,284
Money market instruments	8 630 ..	1,736	1,253	1,665	1,652	1,427	1,515	1,982	1,996
Monetary authorities	8 631 ..	....	....	....	....	....	....	....	....
General government	8 632 ..	....	....	....	....	....	....	....	....
Banks	8 633 ..	138	74	36	277	25	25	92	217
Other sectors	8 634 ..	1,598	1,179	1,629	1,375	1,402	1,490	1,890	1,779
Financial derivatives	8 900 ..	....	....	....	....	....	....	....	....
Monetary authorities	8 901 ..	....	....	....	....	....	....	....	....
General government	8 902 ..	....	....	....	....	....	....	....	....
Banks	8 903 ..	....	....	....	....	....	....	....	....
Other sectors	8 904 ..	....	....	....	....	....	....	....	....
Other investment	8 703 ..	**34,707**	**39,812**	**46,516**	**50,807**	**59,024**	**73,442**	**80,921**	**111,138**
Trade credits	8 706 ..	2,702	1,484	1,968	2,861	3,289	3,925	8,891	15,039
General government	8 707 ..	....	52	2	....	....	....	122	122
of which: Short-term	8 709 ..	....	52	2	....	....	....	....	....
Other sectors	8 710 ..	2,702	1,432	1,966	2,861	3,289	3,925	8,769	14,917
of which: Short-term	8 712 ..	*2,666*	*1,389*	*1,940*	*2,813*	*3,238*	*3,925*	*8,769*	*14,917*
Loans	8 714 ..	439	294	262	231	185	156	347	317
Monetary authorities	8 715 ..	54	102	90	82	65	53	52	50
of which: Short-term	8 718 ..	*3*	*2*	....	....	....	....	....	....
General government	8 719 ..	....	....	....	....	....	....	....	....
of which: Short-term	8 721 ..	....	....	....	....	....	....	....	....
Banks	8 722 ..	....	....	....	....	....	....	....	....
of which: Short-term	8 724 ..	....	....	....	....	....	....	....	....
Other sectors	8 725 ..	385	192	172	149	120	103	295	267
of which: Short-term	8 727 ..	*134*	....	....	....	....	....	....	....
Currency and deposits	8 730 ..	30,685	37,225	43,557	46,901	54,612	68,238	70,169	94,145
Monetary authorities	8 731 ..	....	....	....	....	....	....	....	5,797
General government	8 732 ..	735	1,675	1,647	2,285	4,857	10,134	7,686	9,213
Banks	8 733 ..	753	485	517	471	1,022	1,071	1,348	1,670
Other sectors	8 734 ..	29,197	35,065	41,393	44,145	48,733	57,033	61,135	77,465
Other assets	8 736 ..	881	809	729	814	938	1,123	1,514	1,637
Monetary authorities	8 737 ..	113	23	16	14	22	58	38	27
of which: Short-term	8 739 ..	*113*	*23*	*16*	*14*	*22*	*58*	*38*	*27*
General government	8 740 ..	695	722	636	682	706	746	770	778
of which: Short-term	8 742 ..	....	....	....	....	....	....	....	....
Banks	8 743 ..	....	....	....	....	....	....	....	....
of which: Short-term	8 745 ..	....	....	....	....	....	....	....	....
Other sectors	8 746 ..	73	64	77	118	210	319	706	832
of which: Short-term	8 748 ..	*47*	*54*	*42*	*115*	*207*	*316*	*703*	*829*
Reserve assets	8 802 ..	**21,491**	**18,522**	**14,860**	**21,367**	**24,207**	**30,368**	**37,440**	**34,286**
Monetary gold	8 812 ..	2,794	3,056	3,516	4,632	5,122	5,718	7,255	9,281
Special drawing rights	8 811 ..	36	10	11	10	9	5	....	1
Reserve position in the Fund	8 810 ..	419	405	438	478	500	460	484	509
Foreign exchange	8 803 ..	17,951	14,739	10,570	15,912	18,236	23,842	29,350	24,125
Other claims	8 813 ..	291	313	325	334	341	343	351	370

Table 3 (Concluded). INTERNATIONAL INVESTMENT POSITION (End-period stocks), 2000–2007

(Millions of U.S. dollars)

	Code	2000	2001	2002	2003	2004	2005	2006	2007
LIABILITIES..	8 995 D.	**69,595**	**71,885**	**72,471**	**79,459**	**82,230**	**86,129**	**85,215**	**87,741**
Direct investment in Venezuela..........................	8 555 ..	**35,480**	**39,074**	**39,007**	**41,373**	**42,359**	**44,518**	**45,445**	**43,957**
Equity capital and reinvested earnings............................	8 556 ..	22,582	24,460	24,714	26,414	28,522	30,590	34,008	31,925
Claims on direct investors............................	8 557 ..	....	....	....	....	....	....	....	....
Liabilities to direct investors........................	8 558 ..	22,582	24,460	24,714	26,414	28,522	30,590	34,008	31,925
Other capital..	8 580 ..	12,898	14,614	14,293	14,959	13,837	13,928	11,437	12,032
Claims on direct investors............................	8 585 ..	....	−47	−29	−53	−59	−146	−160	−175
Liabilities to direct investors........................	8 590 ..	12,898	14,661	14,322	15,012	13,896	14,074	11,597	12,207
Portfolio investment............................	8 652 ..	**16,557**	**16,322**	**15,850**	**19,175**	**22,129**	**24,577**	**22,773**	**22,061**
Equity securities..	8 660 ..	1,706	1,301	948	1,713	1,812	1,173	2,259	843
Banks..	8 663 ..	54	19	12	17	17	7	23	12
Other sectors..	8 664 ..	1,652	1,282	936	1,696	1,795	1,166	2,236	831
Debt securities..	8 669 ..	14,851	15,021	14,902	17,462	20,317	23,404	20,514	21,218
Bonds and notes....................................	8 670 ..	14,851	15,021	14,902	17,462	20,317	23,404	20,514	21,218
Monetary authorities............................	8 671 ..	82	68	56	38	24	7	7	7
General government............................	8 672 ..	10,088	9,919	10,474	13,136	19,307	22,430	19,615	16,819
Banks..	8 673 ..	....	....	....	....	....	....	....	....
Other sectors..................................	8 674 ..	4,681	5,034	4,372	4,288	986	967	892	4,392
Money market instruments........................	8 680 ..	....	....	....	....	....	....	....	....
Monetary authorities............................	8 681 ..	....	....	....	....	....	....	....	....
General government............................	8 682 ..	....	....	....	....	....	....	....	....
Banks..	8 683 ..	....	....	....	....	....	....	....	....
Other sectors..................................	8 684 ..	....	....	....	....	....	....	....	....
Financial derivatives............................	8 905 ..	....	....	....	....	....	**22**	**59**	**59**
Monetary authorities................................	8 906 ..	....	....	....	....	....	....	....	....
General government................................	8 907 ..	....	....	....	....	....	....	....	....
Banks..	8 908 ..	....	....	....	....	....	....	....	....
Other sectors..	8 909 ..	....	....	....	....	....	22	59	59
Other investment............................	8 753 ..	**17,558**	**16,489**	**17,614**	**18,911**	**17,742**	**17,012**	**16,938**	**21,664**
Trade credits..	8 756 ..	2,773	2,471	2,482	2,878	3,056	4,282	4,532	6,195
General government....................................	8 757 ..	104	183	112	99	73	80	29	14
of which: Short-term..............................	8 759 ..	....	....	....	....	....	....	....	....
Other sectors..	8 760 ..	2,669	2,288	2,370	2,779	2,983	4,202	4,503	6,181
of which: Short-term..............................	8 762 ..	*2,480*	*2,150*	*2,268*	*2,712*	*2,952*	*4,190*	*4,496*	*6,181*
Loans..	8 764 ..	13,384	12,725	14,127	14,901	13,423	11,684	10,923	13,968
Monetary authorities................................	8 765 ..	228	20	20	20	20	20	20	20
of which: Use of Fund credit and loans from the Fund....	8 766 ..	*203*	....	....	....	....	....	....	....
of which: Short-term..............................	8 768 ..	*5*	....	....	....	....	....	....	....
General government....................................	8 769 ..	4,454	4,375	4,976	5,675	5,370	5,618	5,814	4,975
of which: Short-term..............................	8 771 ..	....	....	....	....	....	....	....	....
Banks..	8 772 ..	347	540	285	63	122	227	357	658
of which: Short-term..............................	8 774 ..	*297*	*489*	*236*	*30*	*91*	*199*	*351*	*634*
Other sectors..	8 775 ..	8,355	7,790	8,846	9,143	7,911	5,819	4,732	8,315
of which: Short-term..............................	8 777 ..	*885*	*811*	*1,127*	*303*	*154*	*163*	*105*	*102*
Currency and deposits................................	8 780 ..	98	28	20	98	36	7	203	55
Monetary authorities................................	8 781 ..	22	23	15	12	8	3	4	4
General government....................................	8 782 ..	....	....	....	....	....	....	....	....
Banks..	8 783 ..	76	5	5	86	28	4	199	51
Other sectors..	8 784 ..	....	....	....	....	....	....	....	....
Other liabilities..	8 786 ..	1,303	1,265	985	1,034	1,227	1,039	1,280	1,446
Monetary authorities................................	8 787 ..	28	50	40	54	310	292	240	626
of which: Short-term..............................	8 789 ..	*28*	*50*	*40*	*54*	*310*	*292*	*240*	*626*
General government....................................	8 790 ..	809	794	610	635	594	632	623	616
of which: Short-term..............................	8 792 ..	*809*	*794*	*610*	*635*	*594*	*632*	*623*	*616*
Banks..	8 793 ..	....	....	....	....	....	....	285	....
of which: Short-term..............................	8 795 ..	....	....	....	....	....	....	*285*	....
Other sectors..	8 796 ..	466	421	335	345	323	115	132	204
of which: Short-term..............................	8 798 ..	*466*	*421*	*335*	*345*	*323*	*115*	*132*	*204*
NET INTERNATIONAL INVESTMENT POSITION........	8 995 ..	**−1,663**	**−1,821**	**3,042**	**8,870**	**16,916**	**36,180**	**59,636**	**86,851**
Conversion rates: bolívares per U.S. dollar (end of period)..	0 102 ..	.6998	.7630	1.4013	1.5980	1.9180	2.1470	2.1470	2.1470

Table 1. ANALYTIC PRESENTATION, 2000–2007

(Millions of U.S. dollars)

	Code	2000	2001	2002	2003	2004	2005	2006	2007
A. Current Account[1]	4 993 Z.	1,106	682	−604	−1,931	−957	−560	−164	−6,992
Goods: exports f.o.b.	2 100 ..	14,448	15,027	16,706	20,149	26,485	32,447	39,826	48,561
Goods: imports f.o.b.	3 100 ..	−14,073	−14,546	−17,760	−22,730	−28,772	−34,886	−42,602	−58,921
Balance on Goods	4 100 ..	*375*	*481*	*−1,054*	*−2,581*	*−2,287*	*−2,439*	*−2,776*	*−10,360*
Services: credit	2 200 ..	2,702	2,810	2,948	3,272	3,867	4,176	5,100	6,030
Services: debit	3 200 ..	−3,252	−3,382	−3,698	−4,050	−4,739	−4,472	−5,108	−6,924
Balance on Goods and Services	4 991 ..	*−175*	*−91*	*−1,804*	*−3,359*	*−3,159*	*−2,735*	*−2,784*	*−11,254*
Income: credit	2 300 ..	331	318	167	125	188	364	668	1,093
Income: debit	3 300 ..	−782	−795	−888	−936	−1,079	−1,569	−2,097	−3,261
Balance on Goods, Services, and Income	4 992 ..	*−626*	*−568*	*−2,525*	*−4,170*	*−4,050*	*−3,940*	*−4,213*	*−13,422*
Current transfers: credit	2 379 Z.	1,732	1,250	1,921	2,239	3,093	3,380	4,049	6,430
Current transfers: debit	3 379 ..	....	....	....	....	....	....	....	....
B. Capital Account[1]	4 994 Z.	....	....	....	....	....	....	....	....
Capital account: credit	2 994 Z.	....	....	....	....	....	....	....	....
Capital account: debit	3 994 ..	....	....	....	....	....	....	....	....
Total, Groups A Plus B	4 981 ..	*1,106*	*682*	*−604*	*−1,931*	*−957*	*−560*	*−164*	*−6,992*
C. Financial Account[1]	4 995 W.	−316	371	2,090	3,279	2,807	3,087	3,088	17,540
Direct investment abroad	4 505 ..	....	....	....	....	....	−65	−85	−150
Direct investment in Vietnam	4 555 Z.	1,298	1,300	1,400	1,450	1,610	1,954	2,400	6,700
Portfolio investment assets	4 602 ..	....	....	....	....	....	....	....	....
Equity securities	4 610 ..	....	....	....	....	....	....	....	....
Debt securities	4 619 ..	....	....	....	....	....	....	....	....
Portfolio investment liabilities	4 652 Z.	....	....	....	....	....	865	1,313	6,243
Equity securities	4 660 ..	....	....	....	....	....	115	1,313	6,243
Debt securities	4 669 Z.	....	....	....	....	....	750	....	....
Financial derivatives	4 910 ..	....	....	....	....	....	....	....	....
Financial derivatives assets	4 900 ..	....	....	....	....	....	....	....	....
Financial derivatives liabilities	4 905 ..	....	....	....	....	....	....	....	....
Other investment assets	4 703 ..	−2,089	−1,197	624	1,372	35	−634	−1,535	2,623
Monetary authorities	4 701 ..	....	....	....	....	....	....	....	....
General government	4 704 ..	....	....	....	....	....	....	....	....
Banks	4 705 ..	−2,089	−1,197	624	1,372	35	−634	−1,535	2,623
Other sectors	4 728 ..	....	....	....	....	....	....	....	....
Other investment liabilities	4 753 W.	475	268	66	457	1,162	967	995	2,124
Monetary authorities	4 753 WA	....	....	....	....	....	....	....	....
General government	4 753 ZB	....	....	....	....	....	....	....	....
Banks	4 753 ZC	....	....	....	....	....	....	....	....
Other sectors	4 753 ZD	475	268	66	457	1,162	967	995	2,124
Total, Groups A Through C	4 983 ..	*790*	*1,053*	*1,486*	*1,348*	*1,850*	*2,527*	*2,924*	*10,548*
D. Net Errors and Omissions	4 998 ..	−680	−847	−1,038	798	−915	−397	1,400	−342
Total, Groups A Through D	4 984 ..	*110*	*206*	*448*	*2,146*	*935*	*2,130*	*4,324*	*10,206*
E. Reserves and Related Items	4 802 A.	−110	−206	−448	−2,146	−935	−2,130	−4,324	−10,206
Reserve assets	4 802 ..	−89	−267	−435	−2,099	−808	−2,077	−4,292	−10,180
Use of Fund credit and loans	4 766 ..	−21	61	−13	−74	−73	−54	−33	−26
Exceptional financing	4 920 ..	....	....	....	26	−54	....	....	....
Conversion rates: dong per U.S. dollar	0 101 ..	14,168	14,725	15,280	15,510	15,746	15,859	15,994	16,096

[1] Excludes components that have been classified in the categories of Group E.

Table 2. STANDARD PRESENTATION, 2000–2007

(Millions of U.S. dollars)

	Code	2000	2001	2002	2003	2004	2005	2006	2007
CURRENT ACCOUNT	4 993 ..	**1,106**	**682**	**−604**	**−1,931**	**−957**	**−560**	**−164**	**−6,992**
A. GOODS	4 100 ..	**375**	**481**	**−1,054**	**−2,581**	**−2,287**	**−2,439**	**−2,776**	**−10,360**
Credit	2 100 ..	**14,448**	**15,027**	**16,706**	**20,149**	**26,485**	**32,447**	**39,826**	**48,561**
General merchandise: exports f.o.b.	2 110 ..	14,448	15,027	16,706	20,149	26,485	32,447	39,826	48,561
Goods for processing: exports f.o.b.	2 150 ..	....	....	....	....	....	....	....	....
Repairs on goods	2 160 ..	....	....	....	....	....	....	....	....
Goods procured in ports by carriers	2 170 ..	....	....	....	....	....	....	....	....
Nonmonetary gold	2 180 ..	....	....	....	....	....	....	....	....
Debit	3 100 ..	**−14,073**	**−14,546**	**−17,760**	**−22,730**	**−28,772**	**−34,886**	**−42,602**	**−58,921**
General merchandise: imports f.o.b.	3 110 ..	−14,073	−14,546	−17,760	−22,730	−28,772	−34,886	−42,602	−58,921
Goods for processing: imports f.o.b.	3 150 ..	....	....	....	....	....	....	....	....
Repairs on goods	3 160 ..	....	....	....	....	....	....	....	....
Goods procured in ports by carriers	3 170 ..	....	....	....	....	....	....	....	....
Nonmonetary gold	3 180 ..	....	....	....	....	....	....	....	....
B. SERVICES	4 200 ..	**−550**	**−572**	**−750**	**−778**	**−872**	**−296**	**−8**	**−894**
Total credit	2 200 ..	*2,702*	*2,810*	*2,948*	*3,272*	*3,867*	*4,176*	*5,100*	*6,030*
Total debit	3 200 ..	*−3,252*	*−3,382*	*−3,698*	*−4,050*	*−4,739*	*−4,472*	*−5,108*	*−6,924*
Transportation services, credit	2 205 ..	....	....	....	....	....	....	....	....
Passenger	2 850 ..	....	....	....	....	....	....	....	....
Freight	2 851 ..	....	....	....	....	....	....	....	....
Other	2 852 ..	....	....	....	....	....	....	....	....
Sea transport, passenger	2 207 ..	....	....	....	....	....	....	....	....
Sea transport, freight	2 208 ..	....	....	....	....	....	....	....	....
Sea transport, other	2 209 ..	....	....	....	....	....	....	....	....
Air transport, passenger	2 211 ..	....	....	....	....	....	....	....	....
Air transport, freight	2 212 ..	....	....	....	....	....	....	....	....
Air transport, other	2 213 ..	....	....	....	....	....	....	....	....
Other transport, passenger	2 215 ..	....	....	....	....	....	....	....	....
Other transport, freight	2 216 ..	....	....	....	....	....	....	....	....
Other transport, other	2 217 ..	....	....	....	....	....	....	....	....
Transportation services, debit	3 205 ..	....	....	....	....	....	....	....	....
Passenger	3 850 ..	....	....	....	....	....	....	....	....
Freight	3 851 ..	....	....	....	....	....	....	....	....
Other	3 852 ..	....	....	....	....	....	....	....	....
Sea transport, passenger	3 207 ..	....	....	....	....	....	....	....	....
Sea transport, freight	3 208 ..	....	....	....	....	....	....	....	....
Sea transport, other	3 209 ..	....	....	....	....	....	....	....	....
Air transport, passenger	3 211 ..	....	....	....	....	....	....	....	....
Air transport, freight	3 212 ..	....	....	....	....	....	....	....	....
Air transport, other	3 213 ..	....	....	....	....	....	....	....	....
Other transport, passenger	3 215 ..	....	....	....	....	....	....	....	....
Other transport, freight	3 216 ..	....	....	....	....	....	....	....	....
Other transport, other	3 217 ..	....	....	....	....	....	....	....	....
Travel, credit	2 236 ..	....	....	....	....	....	....	....	....
Business travel	2 237 ..	....	....	....	....	....	....	....	....
Personal travel	2 240 ..	....	....	....	....	....	....	....	....
Travel, debit	3 236 ..	....	....	....	....	....	....	....	....
Business travel	3 237 ..	....	....	....	....	....	....	....	....
Personal travel	3 240 ..	....	....	....	....	....	....	....	....
Other services, credit	2 200 BA	....	....	....	....	....	....	....	....
Communications	2 245 ..	....	....	....	....	....	....	....	....
Construction	2 249 ..	....	....	....	....	....	....	....	....
Insurance	2 253 ..	....	....	....	....	....	....	....	....
Financial	2 260 ..	....	....	....	....	....	....	....	....
Computer and information	2 262 ..	....	....	....	....	....	....	....	....
Royalties and licence fees	2 266 ..	....	....	....	....	....	....	....	....
Other business services	2 268 ..	....	....	....	....	....	....	....	....
Personal, cultural, and recreational	2 287 ..	....	....	....	....	....	....	....	....
Government, n.i.e.	2 291 ..	....	....	....	....	....	....	....	....
Other services, debit	3 200 BA	....	....	....	....	....	....	....	....
Communications	3 245 ..	....	....	....	....	....	....	....	....
Construction	3 249 ..	....	....	....	....	....	....	....	....
Insurance	3 253 ..	....	....	....	....	....	....	....	....
Financial	3 260 ..	....	....	....	....	....	....	....	....
Computer and information	3 262 ..	....	....	....	....	....	....	....	....
Royalties and licence fees	3 266 ..	....	....	....	....	....	....	....	....
Other business services	3 268 ..	....	....	....	....	....	....	....	....
Personal, cultural, and recreational	3 287 ..	....	....	....	....	....	....	....	....
Government, n.i.e.	3 291 ..	....	....	....	....	....	....	....	....

Table 2 (Continued). STANDARD PRESENTATION, 2000–2007

(Millions of U.S. dollars)

	Code	2000	2001	2002	2003	2004	2005	2006	2007
C. INCOME	4 300	**−451**	**−477**	**−721**	**−811**	**−891**	**−1,205**	**−1,429**	**−2,168**
Total credit	2 300	*331*	*318*	*167*	*125*	*188*	*364*	*668*	*1,093*
Total debit	3 300	*−782*	*−795*	*−888*	*−936*	*−1,079*	*−1,569*	*−2,097*	*−3,261*
Compensation of employees, credit	2 310	....	....	....	....	....	....	....	....
Compensation of employees, debit	3 310	....	....	....	....	....	....	....	....
Investment income, credit	2 320	....	....	....	....	....	....	....	....
Direct investment income	2 330	....	....	....	....	....	....	....	....
Dividends and distributed branch profits	2 332	....	....	....	....	....	....	....	....
Reinvested earnings and undistributed branch profits	2 333	....	....	....	....	....	....	....	....
Income on debt (interest)	2 334	....	....	....	....	....	....	....	....
Portfolio investment income	2 339	....	....	....	....	....	....	....	....
Income on equity	2 340	....	....	....	....	....	....	....	....
Income on bonds and notes	2 350	....	....	....	....	....	....	....	....
Income on money market instruments	2 360	....	....	....	....	....	....	....	....
Other investment income	2 370	....	....	....	....	....	....	....	....
Investment income, debit	3 320	....	....	....	....	....	....	....	....
Direct investment income	3 330	....	....	....	....	....	....	....	....
Dividends and distributed branch profits	3 332	....	....	....	....	....	....	....	....
Reinvested earnings and undistributed branch profits	3 333	....	....	....	....	....	....	....	....
Income on debt (interest)	3 334	....	....	....	....	....	....	....	....
Portfolio investment income	3 339	....	....	....	....	....	....	....	....
Income on equity	3 340	....	....	....	....	....	....	....	....
Income on bonds and notes	3 350	....	....	....	....	....	....	....	....
Income on money market instruments	3 360	....	....	....	....	....	....	....	....
Other investment income	3 370	....	....	....	....	....	....	....	....
D. CURRENT TRANSFERS	4 379	**1,732**	**1,250**	**1,921**	**2,239**	**3,093**	**3,380**	**4,049**	**6,430**
Credit	2 379	**1,732**	**1,250**	**1,921**	**2,239**	**3,093**	**3,380**	**4,049**	**6,430**
General government	2 380	147	150	154	139	174	230	249	250
Other sectors	2 390	1,585	1,100	1,767	2,100	2,919	3,150	3,800	6,180
Workers' remittances	2 391	....	....	....	....	....	....	....	....
Other current transfers	2 392	....	....	....	....	....	....	....	....
Debit	3 379	....	....	....	....	....	....	....	....
General government	3 380	....	....	....	....	....	....	....	....
Other sectors	3 390	....	....	....	....	....	....	....	....
Workers' remittances	3 391	....	....	....	....	....	....	....	....
Other current transfers	3 392	....	....	....	....	....	....	....	....
CAPITAL AND FINANCIAL ACCOUNT	4 996	**−426**	**165**	**1,642**	**1,133**	**1,872**	**957**	**−1,236**	**7,334**
CAPITAL ACCOUNT	4 994	....	....	....	....	....	....	....	....
Total credit	2 994	....	....	....	....	....	....	....	....
Total debit	3 994	....	....	....	....	....	....	....	....
Capital transfers, credit	2 400	....	....	....	....	....	....	....	....
General government	2 401	....	....	....	....	....	....	....	....
Debt forgiveness	2 402	....	....	....	....	....	....	....	....
Other capital transfers	2 410	....	....	....	....	....	....	....	....
Other sectors	2 430	....	....	....	....	....	....	....	....
Migrants' transfers	2 431	....	....	....	....	....	....	....	....
Debt forgiveness	2 432	....	....	....	....	....	....	....	....
Other capital transfers	2 440	....	....	....	....	....	....	....	....
Capital transfers, debit	3 400	....	....	....	....	....	....	....	....
General government	3 401	....	....	....	....	....	....	....	....
Debt forgiveness	3 402	....	....	....	....	....	....	....	....
Other capital transfers	3 410	....	....	....	....	....	....	....	....
Other sectors	3 430	....	....	....	....	....	....	....	....
Migrants' transfers	3 431	....	....	....	....	....	....	....	....
Debt forgiveness	3 432	....	....	....	....	....	....	....	....
Other capital transfers	3 440	....	....	....	....	....	....	....	....
Nonproduced nonfinancial assets, credit	2 480	....	....	....	....	....	....	....	....
Nonproduced nonfinancial assets, debit	3 480	....	....	....	....	....	....	....	....

Table 2 (Continued). STANDARD PRESENTATION, 2000–2007

(Millions of U.S. dollars)

	Code	2000	2001	2002	2003	2004	2005	2006	2007
FINANCIAL ACCOUNT	4 995 ..	−426	165	1,642	1,133	1,872	957	−1,236	7,334
A. DIRECT INVESTMENT	4 500 ..	1,298	1,300	1,400	1,450	1,610	1,889	2,315	6,550
Direct investment abroad	4 505 ..	....	....	....	....	....	−65	−85	−150
Equity capital	4 510 ..	....	....	....	....	....	....	....	....
Claims on affiliated enterprises	4 515 ..	....	....	....	....	....	....	....	....
Liabilities to affiliated enterprises	4 520 ..	....	....	....	....	....	....	....	....
Reinvested earnings	4 525 ..	....	....	....	....	....	....	....	....
Other capital	4 530 ..	....	....	....	....	....	....	....	....
Claims on affiliated enterprises	4 535 ..	....	....	....	....	....	....	....	....
Liabilities to affiliated enterprises	4 540 ..	....	....	....	....	....	....	....	....
Direct investment in Vietnam	4 555 ..	1,298	1,300	1,400	1,450	1,610	1,954	2,400	6,700
Equity capital	4 560 ..	....	....	....	....	....	1,204	1,605	6,190
Claims on direct investors	4 565 ..	....	....	....	....	....	....	....	....
Liabilities to direct investors	4 570 ..	....	....	....	....	....	....	....	....
Reinvested earnings	4 575 ..	....	....	....	....	....	....	....	....
Other capital	4 580 ..	....	....	....	....	....	750	795	510
Claims on direct investors	4 585 ..	....	....	....	....	....	....	....	....
Liabilities to direct investors	4 590 ..	....	....	....	....	....	750	795	510
B. PORTFOLIO INVESTMENT	4 600 ..	....	....	....	....	....	865	1,313	6,243
Assets	4 602 ..	....	....	....	....	....	....	....	....
Equity securities	4 610 ..	....	....	....	....	....	....	....	....
Monetary authorities	4 611 ..	....	....	....	....	....	....	....	....
General government	4 612 ..	....	....	....	....	....	....	....	....
Banks	4 613 ..	....	....	....	....	....	....	....	....
Other sectors	4 614 ..	....	....	....	....	....	....	....	....
Debt securities	4 619 ..	....	....	....	....	....	....	....	....
Bonds and notes	4 620 ..	....	....	....	....	....	....	....	....
Monetary authorities	4 621 ..	....	....	....	....	....	....	....	....
General government	4 622 ..	....	....	....	....	....	....	....	....
Banks	4 623 ..	....	....	....	....	....	....	....	....
Other sectors	4 624 ..	....	....	....	....	....	....	....	....
Money market instruments	4 630 ..	....	....	....	....	....	....	....	....
Monetary authorities	4 631 ..	....	....	....	....	....	....	....	....
General government	4 632 ..	....	....	....	....	....	....	....	....
Banks	4 633 ..	....	....	....	....	....	....	....	....
Other sectors	4 634 ..	....	....	....	....	....	....	....	....
Liabilities	4 652 ..	....	....	....	....	....	865	1,313	6,243
Equity securities	4 660 ..	....	....	....	....	....	115	1,313	6,243
Banks	4 663 ..	....	....	....	....	....	....	....	....
Other sectors	4 664 ..	....	....	....	....	....	....	1,313	6,243
Debt securities	4 669 ..	....	....	....	....	....	750	....	....
Bonds and notes	4 670 ..	....	....	....	....	....	750	....	....
Monetary authorities	4 671 ..	....	....	....	....	....	....	....	....
General government	4 672 ..	....	....	....	....	....	750	....	....
Banks	4 673 ..	....	....	....	....	....	....	....	....
Other sectors	4 674 ..	....	....	....	....	....	....	....	....
Money market instruments	4 680 ..	....	....	....	....	....	....	....	....
Monetary authorities	4 681 ..	....	....	....	....	....	....	....	....
General government	4 682 ..	....	....	....	....	....	....	....	....
Banks	4 683 ..	....	....	....	....	....	....	....	....
Other sectors	4 684 ..	....	....	....	....	....	....	....	....
C. FINANCIAL DERIVATIVES	4 910 ..	....	....	....	....	....	....	....	....
Monetary authorities	4 911 ..	....	....	....	....	....	....	....	....
General government	4 912 ..	....	....	....	....	....	....	....	....
Banks	4 913 ..	....	....	....	....	....	....	....	....
Other sectors	4 914 ..	....	....	....	....	....	....	....	....
Assets	4 900 ..	....	....	....	....	....	....	....	....
Monetary authorities	4 901 ..	....	....	....	....	....	....	....	....
General government	4 902 ..	....	....	....	....	....	....	....	....
Banks	4 903 ..	....	....	....	....	....	....	....	....
Other sectors	4 904 ..	....	....	....	....	....	....	....	....
Liabilities	4 905 ..	....	....	....	....	....	....	....	....
Monetary authorities	4 906 ..	....	....	....	....	....	....	....	....
General government	4 907 ..	....	....	....	....	....	....	....	....
Banks	4 908 ..	....	....	....	....	....	....	....	....
Other sectors	4 909 ..	....	....	....	....	....	....	....	....

Table 2 (Concluded). STANDARD PRESENTATION, 2000–2007

(Millions of U.S. dollars)

	Code	2000	2001	2002	2003	2004	2005	2006	2007
D. OTHER INVESTMENT............................	4 700 ..	−1,635	−868	677	1,782	1,070	279	−573	4,721
Assets..	4 703 ..	−2,089	−1,197	624	1,372	35	−634	−1,535	2,623
Trade credits...	4 706 ..	....	....	....	....	....	....	....	....
General government...............................	4 707 ..	....	....	....	....	....	....	....	....
of which: Short-term............................	4 709 ..	....	....	....	....	....	....	....	....
Other sectors...............................	4 710 ..	....	....	....	....	....	....	....	....
of which: Short-term............................	4 712 ..	....	....	....	....	....	....	....	....
Loans...	4 714 ..	....	....	....	....	....	....	....	....
Monetary authorities...............................	4 715 ..	....	....	....	....	....	....	....	....
of which: Short-term............................	4 718 ..	....	....	....	....	....	....	....	....
General government...............................	4 719 ..	....	....	....	....	....	....	....	....
of which: Short-term............................	4 721 ..	....	....	....	....	....	....	....	....
Banks...	4 722 ..	....	....	....	....	....	....	....	....
of which: Short-term............................	4 724 ..	....	....	....	....	....	....	....	....
Other sectors...............................	4 725 ..	....	....	....	....	....	....	....	....
of which: Short-term............................	4 727 ..	....	....	....	....	....	....	....	....
Currency and deposits.............................	4 730 ..	−2,089	−1,197	624	1,372	35	−634	−1,535	2,623
Monetary authorities...............................	4 731 ..	....	....	....	....	....	....	....	....
General government...............................	4 732 ..	....	....	....	....	....	....	....	....
Banks...	4 733 ..	−2,089	−1,197	624	1,372	35	−634	−1,535	2,623
Other sectors...............................	4 734 ..	....	....	....	....	....	....	....	....
Other assets...	4 736 ..	....	....	....	....	....	....	....	....
Monetary authorities...............................	4 737 ..	....	....	....	....	....	....	....	....
of which: Short-term............................	4 739 ..	....	....	....	....	....	....	....	....
General government...............................	4 740 ..	....	....	....	....	....	....	....	....
of which: Short-term............................	4 742 ..	....	....	....	....	....	....	....	....
Banks...	4 743 ..	....	....	....	....	....	....	....	....
of which: Short-term............................	4 745 ..	....	....	....	....	....	....	....	....
Other sectors...............................	4 746 ..	....	....	....	....	....	....	....	....
of which: Short-term............................	4 748 ..	....	....	....	....	....	....	....	....
Liabilities..	4 753 ..	**454**	**329**	**53**	**410**	**1,035**	**913**	**962**	**2,098**
Trade credits...	4 756 ..	....	....	....	....	....	46	−30	79
General government...............................	4 757 ..	....	....	....	....	....	....	....	....
of which: Short-term............................	4 759 ..	....	....	....	....	....	....	....	....
Other sectors...............................	4 760 ..	....	....	....	....	....	46	−30	79
of which: Short-term............................	4 762 ..	....	....	....	....	....	*46*	*−30*	*79*
Loans...	4 764 ..	15	178	−57	410	1,035	867	992	2,019
Monetary authorities...............................	4 765 ..	−21	61	−13	−74	−73	−54	−33	−26
of which: Use of Fund credit and loans from the Fund..	4 766 ..	*−21*	*61*	*−13*	*−74*	*−73*	*−54*	*−33*	*−26*
of which: Short-term............................	4 768 ..	....	....	....	....	....	....	....	....
General government...............................	4 769 ..	....	....	....	....	....	....	....	....
of which: Short-term............................	4 771 ..	....	....	....	....	....	....	....	....
Banks...	4 772 ..	....	....	....	....	....	....	....	....
of which: Short-term............................	4 774 ..	....	....	....	....	....	....	....	....
Other sectors...............................	4 775 ..	36	117	−44	483	1,108	921	1,025	2,045
of which: Short-term............................	4 777 ..	....	....	....	*26*	*−54*	....	....	....
Currency and deposits.............................	4 780 ..	....	....	....	....	....	....	....	....
Monetary authorities...............................	4 781 ..	....	....	....	....	....	....	....	....
General government...............................	4 782 ..	....	....	....	....	....	....	....	....
Banks...	4 783 ..	....	....	....	....	....	....	....	....
Other sectors...............................	4 784 ..	....	....	....	....	....	....	....	....
Other liabilities...	4 786 ..	439	151	110	....	....	....	....	....
Monetary authorities...............................	4 787 ..	....	....	....	....	....	....	....	....
of which: Short-term............................	4 789 ..	....	....	....	....	....	....	....	....
General government...............................	4 790 ..	....	....	....	....	....	....	....	....
of which: Short-term............................	4 792 ..	....	....	....	....	....	....	....	....
Banks...	4 793 ..	....	....	....	....	....	....	....	....
of which: Short-term............................	4 795 ..	....	....	....	....	....	....	....	....
Other sectors...............................	4 796 ..	439	151	110	....	....	....	....	....
of which: Short-term............................	4 798 ..	....	....	....	....	....	....	....	....
E. RESERVE ASSETS..............................	4 802 ..	**−89**	**−267**	**−435**	**−2,099**	**−808**	**−2,077**	**−4,292**	**−10,180**
Monetary gold...	4 812 ..	....	....	....	....	....	....	....	....
Special drawing rights.................................	4 811 ..	1	−14	15	−2	2	−1	−1	−6
Reserve position in the Fund......................	4 810 ..	....	....	....	....	....	....	....	....
Foreign exchange..	4 803 ..	−90	−253	−450	−2,097	−810	−2,076	−4,291	−10,174
Other claims...	4 813 ..	....	....	....	....	....	....	....	....
NET ERRORS AND OMISSIONS............................	4 998 ..	**−680**	**−847**	**−1,038**	**798**	**−915**	**−397**	**1,400**	**−342**

Table 1. ANALYTIC PRESENTATION, 2000–2007

(Millions of U.S. dollars)

	Code	2000	2001	2002	2003	2004	2005	2006	2007
A. Current Account[1]	4 993 Z.	**−1,047.0**	**−741.3**	**−457.8**	**−978.6**	**−1,417.0**	**−1,107.1**	. . . .	. . . .
Goods: exports f.o.b.	2 100 ..	526.4	448.0	365.1	383.6	410.3	411.6	. . . .	. . . .
Goods: imports f.o.b.	3 100 ..	−2,933.8	−2,117.1	−1,835.9	−2,279.9	−2,710.1	−3,049.5	. . . .	. . . .
Balance on Goods	4 100 ..	*−2,407.4*	*−1,669.1*	*−1,470.8*	*−1,896.4*	*−2,299.9*	*−2,638.0*	. . . .	. . . .
Services: credit	2 200 ..	462.1	177.8	191.9	213.6	181.4	265.3	. . . .	. . . .
Services: debit	3 200 ..	−566.2	−702.2	−650.7	−516.0	−489.1	−487.4	. . . .	. . . .
Balance on Goods and Services	4 991 ..	*−2,511.5*	*−2,193.5*	*−1,929.6*	*−2,198.8*	*−2,607.6*	*−2,860.1*	. . . .	. . . .
Income: credit	2 300 ..	866.6	503.9	392.1	457.8	459.3	609.5	. . . .	. . . .
Income: debit	3 300 ..	−42.4	−18.6	−11.1	−2.2	−33.3	−36.3	. . . .	. . . .
Balance on Goods, Services, and Income	4 992 ..	*−1,687.3*	*−1,708.2*	*−1,548.5*	*−1,743.1*	*−2,181.6*	*−2,286.8*	. . . .	. . . .
Current transfers: credit	2 379 Z.	763.7	1,067.6	1,187.3	917.4	903.6	1,308.5	. . . .	. . . .
Current transfers: debit	3 379 ..	−123.3	−100.6	−96.5	−152.9	−139.0	−128.8	. . . .	. . . .
B. Capital Account[1]	4 994 Z.	**198.1**	**225.5**	**300.5**	**304.7**	**670.3**	**422.2**	. . . .	. . . .
Capital account: credit	2 994 Z.	198.1	225.5	300.5	304.7	670.3	422.2	. . . .	. . . .
Capital account: debit	3 994 ..	. . . .	. . . .	. . . .	. . . .	. . . .	. . . .	. . . .	. . . .
Total, Groups A Plus B	4 981 ..	*−848.9*	*−515.8*	*−157.2*	*−674.0*	*−746.7*	*−684.8*	. . . .	. . . .
C. Financial Account[1]	4 995 W.	**890.1**	**366.9**	**10.6**	**887.6**	**727.6**	**656.6**	. . . .	. . . .
Direct investment abroad	4 505 ..	−213.2	−377.3	−359.7	−48.5	50.8	−8.8	. . . .	. . . .
Direct investment in West Bank and Gaza	4 555 Z.	62.0	19.2	9.4	18.0	48.9	46.5	. . . .	. . . .
Portfolio investment assets	4 602 ..	−113.2	−150.3	−160.9	−37.9	54.1	−11.3	. . . .	. . . .
Equity securities	4 610 ..	−1.2	3.5	2.1	−22.9	−11.5	8.7	. . . .	. . . .
Debt securities	4 619 ..	−112.1	−153.8	−163.0	−15.0	65.6	−20.0	. . . .	. . . .
Portfolio investment liabilities	4 652 Z.	12.2	13.9	8.2	13.2	7.8	13.7	. . . .	. . . .
Equity securities	4 660 ..	12.2	13.9	8.2	13.2	7.8	13.7	. . . .	. . . .
Debt securities	4 669 Z.	. . . .	. . . .	. . . .	. . . .	. . . .	. . . .	. . . .	. . . .
Financial derivatives	4 910 ..	. . . .	. . . .	. . . .	. . . .	. . . .	. . . .	. . . .	. . . .
Financial derivatives assets	4 900 ..	. . . .	. . . .	. . . .	. . . .	. . . .	. . . .	. . . .	. . . .
Financial derivatives liabilities	4 905 ..	. . . .	. . . .	. . . .	. . . .	. . . .	. . . .	. . . .	. . . .
Other investment assets	4 703 ..	1,084.1	865.3	551.6	1,020.5	495.3	504.3	. . . .	. . . .
Monetary authorities	4 701 ..	. . . .	. . . .	. . . .	. . . .	. . . .	. . . .	. . . .	. . . .
General government	4 704 ..	. . . .	. . . .	. . . .	. . . .	. . . .	. . . .	. . . .	. . . .
Banks	4 705 ..	795.5	422.2	−53.3	528.7	−75.6	−3.1	. . . .	. . . .
Other sectors	4 728 ..	288.6	443.2	604.8	491.8	570.9	507.4	. . . .	. . . .
Other investment liabilities	4 753 W.	58.2	−3.9	−38.1	−77.6	70.7	112.1	. . . .	. . . .
Monetary authorities	4 753 WA	. . . .	. . . .	. . . .	. . . .	. . . .	. . . .	. . . .	. . . .
General government	4 753 ZB	120.5	42.4	43.3	26.8	55.3	51.5	. . . .	. . . .
Banks	4 753 ZC	−55.9	−53.7	−187.2	−15.4	−7.2	64.3	. . . .	. . . .
Other sectors	4 753 ZD	−6.4	7.4	105.7	−89.0	22.7	−3.6	. . . .	. . . .
Total, Groups A Through C	4 983 ..	*41.3*	*−148.9*	*−146.7*	*213.6*	*−19.1*	*−28.2*	. . . .	. . . .
D. Net Errors and Omissions	4 998 ..	**49.7**	**132.6**	**161.2**	**−113.2**	**46.4**	**2.6**	. . . .	. . . .
Total, Groups A Through D	4 984 ..	*91.0*	*−16.3*	*14.5*	*100.5*	*27.4*	*−25.7*	. . . .	. . . .
E. Reserves and Related Items	4 802 A.	**−91.0**	**16.3**	**−14.5**	**−100.5**	**−27.4**	**25.7**	. . . .	. . . .
Reserve assets	4 802 ..	−91.0	16.3	−14.5	−100.5	−27.4	25.7	. . . .	. . . .
Use of Fund credit and loans	4 766 ..	. . . .	. . . .	. . . .	. . . .	. . . .	. . . .	. . . .	. . . .
Exceptional financing	4 920 ..	. . . .	. . . .	. . . .	. . . .	. . . .	. . . .	. . . .	. . . .

[1] Excludes components that have been classified in the categories of Group E.

Table 2. STANDARD PRESENTATION, 2000–2007

(Millions of U.S. dollars)

	Code	2000	2001	2002	2003	2004	2005	2006	2007
CURRENT ACCOUNT	4 993	−1,047.0	−741.3	−457.8	−978.6	−1,417.0	−1,107.1	....	....
A. GOODS	4 100	−2,407.4	−1,669.1	−1,470.8	−1,896.4	−2,299.9	−2,638.0	....	....
Credit	2 100	526.4	448.0	365.1	383.6	410.3	411.6	....	....
General merchandise: exports f.o.b.	2 110	455.2	407.6	335.8	349.4	375.0	381.6		
Goods for processing: exports f.o.b.	2 150	68.7	38.9	28.8	33.8	34.5	22.2		
Repairs on goods	2 160	2.5	1.6	.5	.4	.7	1.9		
Goods procured in ports by carriers	2 170	....	....	....	....	....	....		
Nonmonetary gold	2 180	....	....	....	....	....	5.9		
Debit	3 100	−2,933.8	−2,117.1	−1,835.9	−2,279.9	−2,710.1	−3,049.5	....	....
General merchandise: imports f.o.b.	3 110	−2,933.7	−2,116.4	−1,835.8	−2,279.8	−2,710.0	−3,025.9		
Goods for processing: imports f.o.b.	3 150	....	....	....	....	....	....		
Repairs on goods	3 160	−.1	−.1	−.1	−.2	−.1	−.4		
Goods procured in ports by carriers	3 170	....	....	....	....	....	....		
Nonmonetary gold	3 180	−.1	−.5	....	....	....	−23.3		
B. SERVICES	4 200	−104.1	−524.5	−458.8	−302.4	−307.7	−222.1	....	....
Total credit	2 200	*462.1*	*177.8*	*191.9*	*213.6*	*181.4*	*265.3*		
Total debit	3 200	*−566.2*	*−702.2*	*−650.7*	*−516.0*	*−489.1*	*−487.4*		
Transportation services, credit	2 205	37.9	34.3	55.4	8.2	8.7	6.5	....	....
Passenger	2 850	....	....	....	....	....	....		
Freight	2 851	....	....	....	....	....	....		
Other	2 852	....	....	....	....	....	....		
Sea transport, passenger	2 207	....	....	....	....	....	....		
Sea transport, freight	2 208	....	....	....	....	....	....		
Sea transport, other	2 209	....	....	....	....	....	....		
Air transport, passenger	2 211	....	....	....	....	....	....		
Air transport, freight	2 212	....	....	....	....	....	....		
Air transport, other	2 213	....	....	....	....	....	....		
Other transport, passenger	2 215	....	....	....	....	....	....		
Other transport, freight	2 216	....	....	....	....	....	....		
Other transport, other	2 217	....	....	....	....	....	....		
Transportation services, debit	3 205	−57.1	−66.9	−38.7	−47.8	−57.4	−72.4	....	....
Passenger	3 850	....	....	....	....	....	....		
Freight	3 851	....	....	....	....	....	....		
Other	3 852	....	....	....	....	....	....		
Sea transport, passenger	3 207	....	....	....	....	....	....		
Sea transport, freight	3 208	....	....	....	....	....	....		
Sea transport, other	3 209	....	....	....	....	....	....		
Air transport, passenger	3 211	....	....	....	....	....	....		
Air transport, freight	3 212	....	....	....	....	....	....		
Air transport, other	3 213	....	....	....	....	....	....		
Other transport, passenger	3 215	....	....	....	....	....	....		
Other transport, freight	3 216	....	....	....	....	....	....		
Other transport, other	3 217	....	....	....	....	....	....		
Travel, credit	2 236	282.5	34.6	32.9	107.0	55.6	120.7	....	....
Business travel	2 237	....	....	....	....	....	....		
Personal travel	2 240	....	....	....	....	....	....		
Travel, debit	3 236	−309.1	−423.9	−387.7	−316.7	−286.4	−264.6	....	....
Business travel	3 237	....	....	....	....	....	....		
Personal travel	3 240	....	....	....	....	....	....		
Other services, credit	2 200 BA	141.7	108.8	103.7	98.3	117.1	138.1	....	....
Communications	2 245	1.2	3.7	3.9	8.2	14.7	25.0		
Construction	2 249	46.0	24.0	15.0	13.8	18.2	18.7		
Insurance	2 253	....	....	....	....	....	....		
Financial	2 260	....	....	....	....	....	....		
Computer and information	2 262	.6	.7	1.0	1.1	.4	.4		
Royalties and licence fees	2 266	....	....	....	....	....	....		
Other business services	2 268	65.3	58.0	45.7	50.0	59.1	60.7		
Personal, cultural, and recreational	2 287	8.9	2.0	.6	2.7	1.3	4.9		
Government, n.i.e.	2 291	19.8	20.4	37.5	22.5	23.3	28.4		
Other services, debit	3 200 BA	−200.0	−211.4	−224.3	−151.4	−145.3	−150.5	....	....
Communications	3 245	−36.0	−20.2	−15.9	−16.3	−41.0	−42.3		
Construction	3 249	−2.8	−.8	−13.7	−.9	−1.7	−1.7		
Insurance	3 253	−9.3	−9.4	−12.7	−6.3	−10.9	−6.5		
Financial	3 260	−.5	−.3	....	−.1	−.3	−.4		
Computer and information	3 262	−.7	−3.3	−.3	−1.4	−.7	−.8		
Royalties and licence fees	3 266	−.1	−.1	−2.1	−.3	−1.9	−1.9		
Other business services	3 268	−47.9	−40.0	−30.1	−36.2	−44.6	−56.2		
Personal, cultural, and recreational	3 287	−13.3	−21.8	−38.5	−36.0	−15.9	−6.8		
Government, n.i.e.	3 291	−89.5	−115.5	−111.2	−54.0	−28.3	−33.9		

Table 2 (Continued). STANDARD PRESENTATION, 2000–2007

(Millions of U.S. dollars)

	Code	2000	2001	2002	2003	2004	2005	2006	2007
C. INCOME	4 300	**824.2**	**485.3**	**381.1**	**455.6**	**426.0**	**573.2**	....	....
Total credit	2 300	*866.6*	*503.9*	*392.1*	*457.8*	*459.3*	*609.5*	....	....
Total debit	3 300	*–42.4*	*–18.6*	*–11.1*	*–2.2*	*–33.3*	*–36.3*	....	....
Compensation of employees, credit	2 310	**777.1**	**362.2**	**301.1**	**402.9**	**401.0**	**486.4**	....	....
Compensation of employees, debit	3 310	**–.8**	**–.8**	**–.8**	**–.8**	**–.9**	**–1.0**	....	....
Investment income, credit	2 320	**89.6**	**141.7**	**91.0**	**54.9**	**58.3**	**123.1**	....	....
Direct investment income	2 330	27.7	37.3	40.8	5.9	20.1	40.0	....	....
Dividends and distributed branch profits	2 332	27.7	37.2	40.8	5.9	20.1	40.0	....	....
Reinvested earnings and undistributed branch profits	2 333	....	....	....	....	....	....	....	....
Income on debt (interest)	2 334	....	....	....	....	....	....	....	....
Portfolio investment income	2 339	1.0	.9	4.1	.7	1.0	2.3	....	....
Income on equity	2 340	.6	.3	3.5	.7	1.0	2.0	....	....
Income on bonds and notes	2 350	....	....	....	....	....	....	....	....
Income on money market instruments	2 360	....	....	....	....	....	....	....	....
Other investment income	2 370	60.9	103.5	46.1	48.2	37.2	80.8	....	....
Investment income, debit	3 320	**–41.6**	**–17.8**	**–10.2**	**–1.3**	**–32.4**	**–35.3**	....	....
Direct investment income	3 330	–33.5	–6.2	–6.4	....	–17.7	–15.8	....	....
Dividends and distributed branch profits	3 332	–33.5	–6.2	–6.4	....	–17.7	–15.8	....	....
Reinvested earnings and undistributed branch profits	3 333	....	....	....	....	....	....	....	....
Income on debt (interest)	3 334	....	....	....	....	....	....	....	....
Portfolio investment income	3 339	–.3	–.1	....	–.1	....	–.1	....	....
Income on equity	3 340	–.3	–.1	....	–.1	....	....	....	....
Income on bonds and notes	3 350	....	....	....	....	....	....	....	....
Income on money market instruments	3 360	....	....	....	....	....	....	....	....
Other investment income	3 370	–7.8	–11.5	–3.8	–1.2	–14.8	–19.4	....	....
D. CURRENT TRANSFERS	4 379	**640.3**	**966.9**	**1,090.8**	**764.5**	**764.6**	**1,179.8**	....	....
Credit	2 379	**763.7**	**1,067.6**	**1,187.3**	**917.4**	**903.6**	**1,308.5**	....	....
General government	2 380	243.8	328.8	418.4	666.3	535.1	957.3	....	....
Other sectors	2 390	519.9	738.8	768.9	251.1	368.5	351.2	....	....
Workers' remittances	2 391	64.8	28.5	25.1	39.5	35.3	45.1	....	....
Other current transfers	2 392	455.1	710.3	743.7	211.5	333.2	306.1	....	....
Debit	3 379	**–123.3**	**–100.6**	**–96.5**	**–152.9**	**–139.0**	**–128.8**	....	....
General government	3 380	–.1	–.1	–.1	–.1	–.1	–.1	....	....
Other sectors	3 390	–123.2	–100.5	–96.4	–152.8	–138.9	–128.6	....	....
Workers' remittances	3 391	–21.8	–8.9	–7.9	–12.6	–11.8	–14.7	....	....
Other current transfers	3 392	–101.4	–91.6	–88.5	–140.2	–127.0	–113.9	....	....
CAPITAL AND FINANCIAL ACCOUNT	4 996	**997.3**	**608.7**	**296.6**	**1,091.8**	**1,370.6**	**1,104.5**	....	....
CAPITAL ACCOUNT	4 994	**198.1**	**225.5**	**300.5**	**304.7**	**670.3**	**422.2**	....	....
Total credit	2 994	*198.1*	*225.5*	*300.5*	*304.7*	*670.3*	*422.2*	....	....
Total debit	3 994	....	....	....	....	....	....	....	....
Capital transfers, credit	2 400	**196.8**	**224.2**	**299.3**	**303.4**	**669.0**	**420.9**	....	....
General government	2 401	139.9	158.3	244.0	222.5	568.4	238.5	....	....
Debt forgiveness	2 402	....	....	....	....	....	....	....	....
Other capital transfers	2 410	139.9	158.3	244.0	222.5	568.4	238.5	....	....
Other sectors	2 430	56.9	65.9	55.2	80.9	100.6	182.5	....	....
Migrants' transfers	2 431	16.9	18.2	17.5	29.4	18.5	66.4	....	....
Debt forgiveness	2 432	....	....	....	....	....	....	....	....
Other capital transfers	2 440	40.0	47.7	37.8	51.5	82.1	116.0	....	....
Capital transfers, debit	3 400	....	....	....	....	....	....	....	....
General government	3 401	....	....	....	....	....	....	....	....
Debt forgiveness	3 402	....	....	....	....	....	....	....	....
Other capital transfers	3 410	....	....	....	....	....	....	....	....
Other sectors	3 430	....	....	....	....	....	....	....	....
Migrants' transfers	3 431	....	....	....	....	....	....	....	....
Debt forgiveness	3 432	....	....	....	....	....	....	....	....
Other capital transfers	3 440	....	....	....	....	....	....	....	....
Nonproduced nonfinancial assets, credit	2 480	**1.3**	**1.3**	**1.3**	**1.3**	**1.3**	**1.3**	....	....
Nonproduced nonfinancial assets, debit	3 480	....	....	....	....	....	....	....	....

Table 2 (Continued). STANDARD PRESENTATION, 2000–2007

(Millions of U.S. dollars)

	Code	2000	2001	2002	2003	2004	2005	2006	2007
FINANCIAL ACCOUNT	4 995	**799.1**	**383.2**	**−3.9**	**787.2**	**700.3**	**682.3**	....	....
A. DIRECT INVESTMENT	4 500	**−151.2**	**−358.2**	**−350.2**	**−30.5**	**99.7**	**37.8**	....	....
Direct investment abroad	4 505	**−213.2**	**−377.3**	**−359.7**	**−48.5**	**50.8**	**−8.8**	....	....
Equity capital	4 510	−213.2	−377.3	−359.6	−48.5	50.8	−8.8	....	....
Claims on affiliated enterprises	4 515	−213.2	−377.3	−359.6	−48.5	50.8	−8.8	....	....
Liabilities to affiliated enterprises	4 520	....	....	....	....	....	....	....	....
Reinvested earnings	4 525	....	....	....	....	....	....	....	....
Other capital	4 530	....	....	....	....	....	....	....	....
Claims on affiliated enterprises	4 535	....	....	....	....	....	....	....	....
Liabilities to affiliated enterprises	4 540	....	....	....	....	....	....	....	....
Direct investment in West Bank and Gaza	4 555	**62.0**	**19.2**	**9.4**	**18.0**	**48.9**	**46.5**	....	....
Equity capital	4 560	62.0	19.2	9.4	18.0	48.9	39.3	....	....
Claims on direct investors	4 565	....	....	....	5.1	28.4	10.3	....	....
Liabilities to direct investors	4 570	62.0	19.2	9.4	12.9	20.5	29.0	....	....
Reinvested earnings	4 575	....	....	....	....	....	....	....	....
Other capital	4 580	....	....	....	....	....	7.2	....	....
Claims on direct investors	4 585	....	....	....	....	....	....	....	....
Liabilities to direct investors	4 590	....	....	....	....	....	7.2	....	....
B. PORTFOLIO INVESTMENT	4 600	**−101.0**	**−136.4**	**−152.6**	**−24.7**	**61.9**	**2.4**	....	....
Assets	4 602	**−113.2**	**−150.3**	**−160.9**	**−37.9**	**54.1**	**−11.3**	....	....
Equity securities	4 610	−1.2	3.5	2.1	−22.9	−11.5	8.7	....	....
Monetary authorities	4 611	....	....	....	....	....	....	....	....
General government	4 612	....	....	....	....	....	....	....	....
Banks	4 613	....	....	....	....	....	....	....	....
Other sectors	4 614	....	....	....	....	....	....	....	....
Debt securities	4 619	−112.1	−153.8	−163.0	−15.0	65.6	−20.0	....	....
Bonds and notes	4 620	−112.1	−153.8	−163.0	−15.0	65.6	−20.0	....	....
Monetary authorities	4 621	....	....	....	....	....	....	....	....
General government	4 622	....	....	....	....	....	....	....	....
Banks	4 623	....	....	....	....	....	....	....	....
Other sectors	4 624	....	....	....	....	....	....	....	....
Money market instruments	4 630	....	....	....	....	....	....	....	....
Monetary authorities	4 631	....	....	....	....	....	....	....	....
General government	4 632	....	....	....	....	....	....	....	....
Banks	4 633	....	....	....	....	....	....	....	....
Other sectors	4 634	....	....	....	....	....	....	....	....
Liabilities	4 652	**12.2**	**13.9**	**8.2**	**13.2**	**7.8**	**13.7**	....	....
Equity securities	4 660	12.2	13.9	8.2	13.2	7.8	13.7	....	....
Banks	4 663	....	....	....	....	....	....	....	....
Other sectors	4 664	....	....	....	....	....	....	....	....
Debt securities	4 669	....	....	....	....	....	....	....	....
Bonds and notes	4 670	....	....	....	....	....	....	....	....
Monetary authorities	4 671	....	....	....	....	....	....	....	....
General government	4 672	....	....	....	....	....	....	....	....
Banks	4 673	....	....	....	....	....	....	....	....
Other sectors	4 674	....	....	....	....	....	....	....	....
Money market instruments	4 680	....	....	....	....	....	....	....	....
Monetary authorities	4 681	....	....	....	....	....	....	....	....
General government	4 682	....	....	....	....	....	....	....	....
Banks	4 683	....	....	....	....	....	....	....	....
Other sectors	4 684	....	....	....	....	....	....	....	....
C. FINANCIAL DERIVATIVES	4 910	....	....	....	....	....	....	....	....
Monetary authorities	4 911	....	....	....	....	....	....	....	....
General government	4 912	....	....	....	....	....	....	....	....
Banks	4 913	....	....	....	....	....	....	....	....
Other sectors	4 914	....	....	....	....	....	....	....	....
Assets	4 900	....	....	....	....	....	....	....	....
Monetary authorities	4 901	....	....	....	....	....	....	....	....
General government	4 902	....	....	....	....	....	....	....	....
Banks	4 903	....	....	....	....	....	....	....	....
Other sectors	4 904	....	....	....	....	....	....	....	....
Liabilities	4 905	....	....	....	....	....	....	....	....
Monetary authorities	4 906	....	....	....	....	....	....	....	....
General government	4 907	....	....	....	....	....	....	....	....
Banks	4 908	....	....	....	....	....	....	....	....
Other sectors	4 909	....	....	....	....	....	....	....	....

Table 2 (Concluded). STANDARD PRESENTATION, 2000–2007

(Millions of U.S. dollars)

	Code	2000	2001	2002	2003	2004	2005	2006	2007
D. OTHER INVESTMENT	4 700 ..	**1,142.3**	**861.5**	**513.4**	**942.9**	**566.0**	**616.5**	....	....
Assets	4 703 ..	**1,084.1**	**865.3**	**551.6**	**1,020.5**	**495.3**	**504.3**	....	....
Trade credits	4 706 ..	132.7	112.4	209.6	181.1	113.6	−12.0	....	....
General government	4 707 ..	....	....	....	....	....	....	....	....
of which: Short-term	4 709 ..	....	....	....	....	....	....	....	....
Other sectors	4 710 ..	132.7	112.4	209.6	181.1	113.6	−12.0	....	....
of which: Short-term	4 712 ..	....	....	....	....	....	....	....	....
Loans	4 714 ..	.9	−3.9	1.7	−10.5	−13.0	−21.5	....	....
Monetary authorities	4 715 ..	....	....	....	....	....	....	....	....
of which: Short-term	4 718 ..	....	....	....	....	....	....	....	....
General government	4 719 ..	....	....	....	....	....	....	....	....
of which: Short-term	4 721 ..	....	....	....	....	....	....	....	....
Banks	4 722 ..	.9	−3.9	1.7	−10.5	−13.0	−21.5	....	....
of which: Short-term	4 724 ..	*.9*	*−3.9*	*1.7*	*−10.5*	*−13.0*	*−21.5*	....	....
Other sectors	4 725 ..	....	....	....	....	....	....	....	....
of which: Short-term	4 727 ..	....	....	....	....	....	....	....	....
Currency and deposits	4 730 ..	967.8	732.9	339.4	843.4	397.6	536.3	....	....
Monetary authorities	4 731 ..	....	....	....	....	....	....	....	....
General government	4 732 ..	....	....	....	....	....	....	....	....
Banks	4 733 ..	812.0	402.1	−55.9	532.7	−59.7	16.9	....	....
Other sectors	4 734 ..	155.8	330.8	395.3	310.7	457.2	519.4	....	....
Other assets	4 736 ..	−17.3	23.9	.9	6.4	−3.0	1.5	....	....
Monetary authorities	4 737 ..	....	....	....	....	....	....	....	....
of which: Short-term	4 739 ..	....	....	....	....	....	....	....	....
General government	4 740 ..	....	....	....	....	....	....	....	....
of which: Short-term	4 742 ..	....	....	....	....	....	....	....	....
Banks	4 743 ..	−17.3	23.9	.9	6.4	−3.0	1.5	....	....
of which: Short-term	4 745 ..	....	....	....	....	....	....	....	....
Other sectors	4 746 ..	....	....	....	....	....	....	....	....
of which: Short-term	4 748 ..	....	....	....	....	....	....	....	....
Liabilities	4 753 ..	**58.2**	**−3.9**	**−38.1**	**−77.6**	**70.7**	**112.1**	....	....
Trade credits	4 756 ..	....	....	....	....	....	....	....	....
General government	4 757 ..	....	....	....	....	....	....	....	....
of which: Short-term	4 759 ..	....	....	....	....	....	....	....	....
Other sectors	4 760 ..	....	....	....	....	....	....	....	....
of which: Short-term	4 762 ..	....	....	....	....	....	....	....	....
Loans	4 764 ..	120.5	42.4	43.3	26.8	55.3	51.5	....	....
Monetary authorities	4 765 ..	....	....	....	....	....	....	....	....
of which: Use of Fund credit and loans from the Fund	4 766 ..	....	....	....	....	....	....	....	....
of which: Short-term	4 768 ..	....	....	....	....	....	....	....	....
General government	4 769 ..	120.5	42.4	43.3	26.8	55.3	51.5	....	....
of which: Short-term	4 771 ..	....	....	....	....	....	....	....	....
Banks	4 772 ..	....	....	....	....	....	....	....	....
of which: Short-term	4 774 ..	....	....	....	....	....	....	....	....
Other sectors	4 775 ..	....	....	....	....	....	....	....	....
of which: Short-term	4 777 ..	....	....	....	....	....	....	....	....
Currency and deposits	4 780 ..	−61.0	−40.9	−80.4	−104.5	15.5	60.7	....	....
Monetary authorities	4 781 ..	....	....	....	....	....	....	....	....
General government	4 782 ..	....	....	....	....	....	....	....	....
Banks	4 783 ..	−54.6	−48.3	−186.2	−15.4	−7.2	64.3	....	....
Other sectors	4 784 ..	−6.4	7.4	105.7	−89.0	22.7	−3.6	....	....
Other liabilities	4 786 ..	−1.3	−5.4	−1.0	....	....	....	....	....
Monetary authorities	4 787 ..	....	....	....	....	....	....	....	....
of which: Short-term	4 789 ..	....	....	....	....	....	....	....	....
General government	4 790 ..	....	....	....	....	....	....	....	....
of which: Short-term	4 792 ..	....	....	....	....	....	....	....	....
Banks	4 793 ..	−1.3	−5.4	−1.0	....	....	....	....	....
of which: Short-term	4 795 ..	....	....	....	....	....	....	....	....
Other sectors	4 796 ..	....	....	....	....	....	....	....	....
of which: Short-term	4 798 ..	....	....	....	....	....	....	....	....
E. RESERVE ASSETS	4 802 ..	**−91.0**	**16.3**	**−14.5**	**−100.5**	**−27.4**	**25.7**	....	.....
Monetary gold	4 812 ..	....	....	....	....	....	....	....	....
Special drawing rights	4 811 ..	....	....	....	....	....	....	....	....
Reserve position in the Fund	4 810 ..	....	....	....	....	....	....	....	....
Foreign exchange	4 803 ..	−91.0	16.3	−14.5	−100.5	−27.4	25.7	....	....
Other claims	4 813 ..	....	....	....	....	....	....	....	....
NET ERRORS AND OMISSIONS	4 998 ..	**49.7**	**132.6**	**161.2**	**−113.2**	**46.4**	**2.6**	....	....

Table 1. ANALYTIC PRESENTATION, 2000–2007

(Millions of U.S. dollars)

	Code	2000	2001	2002	2003	2004	2005	2006	2007
A. Current Account[1]................................	4 993 Z.	**1,336.6**	**667.1**	**538.2**	**148.7**	**224.6**	**624.1**	**205.7**	**−1,327.7**
Goods: exports f.o.b..................................	2 100 ..	3,797.2	3,366.9	3,620.7	3,934.3	4,675.7	6,413.2	7,316.4	7,131.0
Goods: imports f.o.b..................................	3 100 ..	−2,484.4	−2,600.4	−2,932.0	−3,557.4	−3,858.6	−4,712.9	−5,926.1	−7,212.3
Balance on Goods..................................	4 100 ..	*1,312.8*	*766.4*	*688.7*	*376.9*	*817.1*	*1,700.3*	*1,390.3*	*−81.3*
Services: credit..	2 200 ..	210.9	166.4	166.2	317.7	369.7	372.1	548.8	643.1
Services: debit..	3 200 ..	−809.4	−847.8	−934.8	−1,003.6	−1,059.4	−1,241.4	−1,855.0	−2,124.6
Balance on Goods and Services................	4 991 ..	*714.2*	*85.1*	*−79.9*	*−308.9*	*127.3*	*830.9*	*84.0*	*−1,562.8*
Income: credit..	2 300 ..	149.6	178.5	135.0	98.9	103.6	178.2	316.2	384.9
Income: debit..	3 300 ..	−926.7	−869.4	−900.6	−1,008.3	−1,450.1	−1,790.7	−1,550.5	−1,536.9
Balance on Goods, Services, and Income........	4 992 ..	*−62.9*	*−605.8*	*−845.6*	*−1,218.3*	*−1,219.1*	*−781.5*	*−1,150.3*	*−2,714.7*
Current transfers: credit............................	2 379 Z.	1,471.9	1,344.4	1,456.8	1,442.1	1,493.1	1,458.4	1,401.7	1,435.6
Current transfers: debit............................	3 379 ..	−72.4	−71.4	−73.1	−75.0	−49.4	−52.8	−45.7	−48.6
B. Capital Account[1]................................	4 994 Z.	**338.9**	**49.5**	....	**5.5**	**163.3**	**202.3**	**94.4**	**94.2**
Capital account: credit............................	2 994 Z.	338.9	49.5	....	5.5	163.3	202.3	94.4	94.2
Capital account: debit............................	3 994 ..	....	....	....	....	....	....	....	....
Total, Groups A Plus B..........................	4 981 ..	*1,675.5*	*716.7*	*538.2*	*154.2*	*387.9*	*826.4*	*300.1*	*−1,233.5*
C. Financial Account[1]..............................	4 995 W.	**−376.2**	**−53.5**	**−156.8**	**19.7**	**−68.6**	**−605.9**	**631.8**	**747.4**
Direct investment abroad..........................	4 505 ..	....	....	....	....	....	....	....	....
Direct investment in the Republic of Yemen........	4 555 Z.	6.4	155.1	114.3	−89.1	143.6	−302.1	1,121.0	917.3
Portfolio investment assets........................	4 602 ..	.1	−1.4	−5.8	−.4	−6.4	−14.2	−34.0	−8.5
Equity securities..................................	4 610 ..	.1	−1.4	−5.8	−.4	−6.4	−14.2	−34.0	−8.5
Debt securities..................................	4 619 ..	....	....	....	....	....	....	....	....
Portfolio investment liabilities....................	4 652 Z.	....	....	....	....	....	....	....	....
Equity securities..................................	4 660 ..	....	....	....	....	....	....	....	....
Debt securities..................................	4 669 Z.	....	....	....	....	....	....	....	....
Financial derivatives................................	4 910 ..	....	....	....	....	....	....	....	....
Financial derivatives assets........................	4 900 ..	....	....	....	....	....	....	....	....
Financial derivatives liabilities....................	4 905 ..	....	....	....	....	....	....	....	....
Other investment assets............................	4 703 ..	−177.9	5.6	−124.5	49.1	−25.4	−81.6	−387.1	−87.8
Monetary authorities............................	4 701 ..	....	....	....	....	....	....	....	....
General government............................	4 704 ..	....	75.6	−57.6	....	−5.7	−109.0	91.1	−89.1
Banks..	4 705 ..	−177.9	−70.0	−147.7	−12.8	−19.7	27.4	−478.1	1.4
Other sectors..................................	4 728 ..	....	....	80.8	61.9	....	....	....	....
Other investment liabilities........................	4 753 W.	−204.8	−212.8	−140.8	60.2	−180.4	−208.0	−68.2	−73.7
Monetary authorities............................	4 753 WA	−8.1	−11.5	−22.4	−10.9	−45.7	5.4	5.7	9.0
General government............................	4 753 ZB	−207.7	−171.6	−110.3	68.1	−165.6	−222.3	−110.7	−123.0
Banks..	4 753 ZC	11.0	−29.7	−8.1	2.9	30.9	8.9	36.8	40.3
Other sectors..................................	4 753 ZD	....	....	....	....	....	....	....	....
Total, Groups A Through C......................	4 983 ..	*1,299.3*	*663.2*	*381.4*	*173.9*	*319.3*	*220.6*	*931.9*	*−486.1*
D. Net Errors and Omissions....................	4 998 ..	**295.1**	**−110.0**	**43.3**	**156.4**	**53.3**	**213.3**	**179.8**	**132.4**
Total, Groups A Through D......................	4 984 ..	*1,594.4*	*553.2*	*424.7*	*330.3*	*372.5*	*433.8*	*1,111.7*	*−353.7*
E. Reserves and Related Items..................	4 802 A.	**−1,594.4**	**−553.2**	**−424.7**	**−330.3**	**−372.5**	**−433.8**	**−1,111.7**	**353.7**
Reserve assets..	4 802 ..	−1,429.4	−761.3	−556.9	−326.3	−532.3	−713.4	−1,401.2	83.5
Use of Fund credit and loans......................	4 766 ..	−71.0	69.0	−17.2	−19.3	−41.2	−55.8	−60.1	−86.8
Exceptional financing................................	4 920 ..	−94.0	139.1	149.4	15.3	201.0	335.4	349.6	357.0
Conversion rates: Yemeni rials per U.S. dollar.......	0 101 ..	**161.718**	**168.672**	**175.625**	**183.448**	**184.776**	**191.509**	**197.049**	**198.953**

[1] Excludes components that have been classified in the categories of Group E.

Table 2. STANDARD PRESENTATION, 2000–2007

(Millions of U.S. dollars)

	Code	2000	2001	2002	2003	2004	2005	2006	2007
CURRENT ACCOUNT	4 993	**1,336.6**	**667.1**	**538.2**	**148.7**	**224.6**	**624.1**	**205.7**	**−1,327.7**
A. GOODS	4 100	**1,312.8**	**766.4**	**688.7**	**376.9**	**817.1**	**1,700.3**	**1,390.3**	**−81.3**
Credit	2 100	**3,797.2**	**3,366.9**	**3,620.7**	**3,934.3**	**4,675.7**	**6,413.2**	**7,316.4**	**7,131.0**
General merchandise: exports f.o.b.	2 110	3,780.9	3,349.2	3,601.7	3,912.8	4,657.6	6,395.1	7,296.5	7,111.1
Goods for processing: exports f.o.b.	2 150	....	....	....	....	....	....	....	....
Repairs on goods	2 160	....	....	....	....	....	....	....	....
Goods procured in ports by carriers	2 170	16.3	17.7	19.0	21.5	18.1	18.1	19.9	19.9
Nonmonetary gold	2 180	....	....	....	....	....	....	....	....
Debit	3 100	**−2,484.4**	**−2,600.4**	**−2,932.0**	**−3,557.4**	**−3,858.6**	**−4,712.9**	**−5,926.1**	**−7,212.3**
General merchandise: imports f.o.b.	3 110	−2,484.4	−2,600.4	−2,932.0	−3,557.4	−3,858.6	−4,712.9	−5,926.1	−7,212.3
Goods for processing: imports f.o.b.	3 150	....	....	....	....	....	....	....	....
Repairs on goods	3 160	....	....	....	....	....	....	....	....
Goods procured in ports by carriers	3 170	....	....	....	....	....	....	....	....
Nonmonetary gold	3 180	....	....	....	....	....	....	....	....
B. SERVICES	4 200	**−598.6**	**−681.3**	**−768.6**	**−685.8**	**−689.8**	**−869.4**	**−1,306.2**	**−1,481.5**
Total credit	2 200	*210.9*	*166.4*	*166.2*	*317.7*	*369.7*	*372.1*	*548.8*	*643.1*
Total debit	3 200	*−809.4*	*−847.8*	*−934.8*	*−1,003.6*	*−1,059.4*	*−1,241.4*	*−1,855.0*	*−2,124.6*
Transportation services, credit	2 205	**21.5**	**23.9**	**20.3**	**51.9**	**46.0**	**46.0**	**31.2**	**31.2**
Passenger	2 850	....	....	....	....	....	....	....	....
Freight	2 851	....	....	....	....	....	....	....	....
Other	2 852	*21.5*	*23.9*	*20.3*	*51.9*	*46.0*	*46.0*	*31.2*	*31.2*
Sea transport, passenger	2 207	....	....	....	....	....	....	....	....
Sea transport, freight	2 208	....	....	....	....	....	....	....	....
Sea transport, other	2 209	19.9	18.6	19.5	38.9	42.4	42.4	27.6	27.6
Air transport, passenger	2 211	....	....	....	....	....	....	....	....
Air transport, freight	2 212	....	....	....	....	....	....	....	....
Air transport, other	2 213	1.6	5.3	.8	13.0	3.6	3.6	3.6	3.6
Other transport, passenger	2 215	....	....	....	....	....	....	....	....
Other transport, freight	2 216	....	....	....	....	....	....	....	....
Other transport, other	2 217	....	....	....	....	....	....	....	....
Transportation services, debit	3 205	**−339.9**	**−353.1**	**−390.7**	**−461.8**	**−496.0**	**−593.1**	**−736.6**	**−882.8**
Passenger	3 850	*−57.0*	*−57.0*	*−57.0*	*−57.0*	*−57.0*	*−57.0*	*−62.7*	*−62.7*
Freight	3 851	*−282.9*	*−296.1*	*−333.7*	*−404.8*	*−439.0*	*−536.1*	*−673.9*	*−820.1*
Other	3 852	....	....	....	....	....	....	....	....
Sea transport, passenger	3 207	....	....	....	....	....	....	....	....
Sea transport, freight	3 208	−282.3	−295.5	−333.1	−404.2	−438.4	−535.5	−673.3	−819.5
Sea transport, other	3 209	....	....	....	....	....	....	....	....
Air transport, passenger	3 211	−57.0	−57.0	−57.0	−57.0	−57.0	−57.0	−62.7	−62.7
Air transport, freight	3 212	−.6	−.6	−.6	−.6	−.6	−.6	−.6	−.6
Air transport, other	3 213	....	....	....	....	....	....	....	....
Other transport, passenger	3 215	....	....	....	....	....	....	....	....
Other transport, freight	3 216	....	....	....	....	....	....	....	....
Other transport, other	3 217	....	....	....	....	....	....	....	....
Travel, credit	2 236	**72.7**	**38.0**	**38.0**	**139.0**	**139.0**	**180.7**	**180.7**	**425.0**
Business travel	2 237	....	....	....	....	....	....	....	....
Personal travel	2 240	72.7	38.0	38.0	139.0	139.0	180.7	180.7	425.0
Travel, debit	3 236	**−69.8**	**−78.7**	**−77.5**	**−77.1**	**−125.7**	**−167.2**	**−162.1**	**−183.6**
Business travel	3 237	....	....	....	....	....	....	....	....
Personal travel	3 240	−69.8	−78.7	−77.5	−77.1	−125.7	−167.2	−162.1	−183.6
Other services, credit	2 200 BA	**116.7**	**104.5**	**107.9**	**126.9**	**184.7**	**145.4**	**336.9**	**186.9**
Communications	2 245	59.2	47.0	50.6	43.2	98.8	41.4	103.7	103.7
Construction	2 249	....	....	....	....	....	....	....	....
Insurance	2 253	....	....	....	....	....	....	....	....
Financial	2 260	....	....	....	....	....	....	....	....
Computer and information	2 262	....	....	....	....	....	....	....	....
Royalties and licence fees	2 266	....	....	....	....	....	....	149.0	....
Other business services	2 268	21.0	20.7	20.6	10.4	8.4	17.3	3.1	2.4
Personal, cultural, and recreational	2 287	....	....	....	....	....	....	....	....
Government, n.i.e.	2 291	36.5	36.9	36.7	73.2	77.6	86.7	81.1	80.8
Other services, debit	3 200 BA	**−399.8**	**−416.0**	**−466.5**	**−464.7**	**−437.7**	**−481.2**	**−956.3**	**−1,058.2**
Communications	3 245	−14.0	−10.5	−10.4	−7.2	−57.6	−9.2	−60.5	−60.5
Construction	3 249	−51.0	−38.7	−29.9	−34.3	−107.8	−107.8	−106.2	−115.2
Insurance	3 253	−56.5	−59.1	−66.7	−80.9	−87.8	−107.2	−134.8	−164.0
Financial	3 260	....	....	....	....	−.8	−.8	−1.2	−1.2
Computer and information	3 262	....	....	....	....	−9.2	−9.2	−9.2	−9.2
Royalties and licence fees	3 266	....	....	....	....	....	....	....	....
Other business services	3 268	−226.0	−254.3	−308.1	−285.9	−119.6	−188.4	−589.8	−652.1
Personal, cultural, and recreational	3 287	....	....	....	....	....	....	....	....
Government, n.i.e.	3 291	−52.2	−53.4	−51.5	−56.4	−55.0	−58.6	−54.6	−56.0

Table 2 (Continued). STANDARD PRESENTATION, 2000–2007

(Millions of U.S. dollars)

	Code	2000	2001	2002	2003	2004	2005	2006	2007
C. INCOME	4 300 ..	**−777.1**	**−690.9**	**−765.6**	**−909.4**	**−1,346.5**	**−1,612.5**	**−1,234.3**	**−1,151.9**
Total credit	2 300 ..	*149.6*	*178.5*	*135.0*	*98.9*	*103.6*	*178.2*	*316.2*	*384.9*
Total debit	3 300 ..	*−926.7*	*−869.4*	*−900.6*	*−1,008.3*	*−1,450.1*	*−1,790.7*	*−1,550.5*	*−1,536.9*
Compensation of employees, credit	2 310 ..	....	....	....	....	....	....	....	....
Compensation of employees, debit	3 310 ..	....	....	....	....	−72.4	−72.4	−79.6	−79.6
Investment income, credit	2 320 ..	**149.6**	**178.5**	**135.0**	**98.9**	**103.6**	**178.2**	**316.2**	**384.9**
Direct investment income	2 330 ..	....	....	....	....	....	....	....	....
Dividends and distributed branch profits	2 332 ..	....	....	....	....	....	....	....	....
Reinvested earnings and undistributed branch profits	2 333 ..	....	....	....	....	....	....	....	....
Income on debt (interest)	2 334 ..	....	....	....	....	....	....	....	....
Portfolio investment income	2 339 ..	....	....	....	98.9	103.6	....	....	....
Income on equity	2 340 ..	....	....	....	98.9	103.6	....	....	....
Income on bonds and notes	2 350 ..	....	....	....	....	....	....	....	....
Income on money market instruments	2 360 ..	....	....	....	....	....	....	....	....
Other investment income	2 370 ..	149.6	178.5	135.0	....	....	178.2	316.2	384.9
Investment income, debit	3 320 ..	**−926.7**	**−869.4**	**−900.6**	**−1,008.3**	**−1,377.7**	**−1,718.3**	**−1,470.9**	**−1,457.2**
Direct investment income	3 330 ..	−855.4	−799.9	−839.7	−944.7	−1,289.4	−1,602.7	−1,402.8	−1,390.4
Dividends and distributed branch profits	3 332 ..	−855.4	−799.9	−839.7	−944.7	−1,289.4	−1,602.7	−1,402.8	−1,390.4
Reinvested earnings and undistributed branch profits	3 333 ..	....	....	....	....	....	....	....	....
Income on debt (interest)	3 334 ..	....	....	....	....	....	....	....	....
Portfolio investment income	3 339 ..	....	....	....	−63.6	−88.2	....	....	....
Income on equity	3 340 ..	....	....	....	−63.6	−88.2	....	....	....
Income on bonds and notes	3 350 ..	....	....	....	....	....	....	....	....
Income on money market instruments	3 360 ..	....	....	....	....	....	....	....	....
Other investment income	3 370 ..	−71.3	−69.5	−60.9	....	....	−115.5	−68.1	−66.8
D. CURRENT TRANSFERS	4 379 ..	**1,399.5**	**1,273.0**	**1,383.7**	**1,367.1**	**1,443.7**	**1,405.7**	**1,356.0**	**1,387.0**
Credit	2 379 ..	**1,471.9**	**1,344.4**	**1,456.8**	**1,442.1**	**1,493.1**	**1,458.4**	**1,401.7**	**1,435.6**
General government	2 380 ..	83.8	49.6	156.5	151.6	184.7	169.4	117.6	152.2
Other sectors	2 390 ..	1,388.1	1,294.7	1,300.3	1,290.5	1,308.4	1,289.0	1,284.1	1,283.4
Workers' remittances	2 391 ..	1,288.0	1,294.6	1,294.0	1,269.9	1,282.6	1,282.6	1,282.6	1,282.6
Other current transfers	2 392 ..	100.1	.1	6.3	20.6	25.8	6.4	1.5	.8
Debit	3 379 ..	**−72.4**	**−71.4**	**−73.1**	**−75.0**	**−49.4**	**−52.8**	**−45.7**	**−48.6**
General government	3 380 ..	−11.9	−7.8	−8.8	−15.0	−13.5	−15.7	−4.9	−7.8
Other sectors	3 390 ..	−60.5	−63.6	−64.3	−60.0	−35.9	−37.1	−40.8	−40.8
Workers' remittances	3 391 ..	−60.5	−63.6	−64.3	−60.0	−35.9	−37.1	−40.8	−40.8
Other current transfers	3 392 ..	....	....	....	....	....	....	....	....
CAPITAL AND FINANCIAL ACCOUNT	4 996 ..	**−1,631.7**	**−557.1**	**−581.5**	**−305.1**	**−277.9**	**−837.4**	**−385.5**	**1,195.3**
CAPITAL ACCOUNT	4 994 ..	**338.9**	**49.5**	....	**5.5**	**163.3**	**202.3**	**94.4**	**94.2**
Total credit	2 994 ..	*338.9*	*49.5*	....	*5.5*	*163.3*	*202.3*	*94.4*	*94.2*
Total debit	3 994 ..	....	....	....	....	....	....	....	....
Capital transfers, credit	2 400 ..	**338.9**	**49.5**	....	**5.5**	**163.3**	**202.3**	**94.4**	**94.2**
General government	2 401 ..	338.9	49.5	....	5.5	76.8	115.8	7.8	7.6
Debt forgiveness	2 402 ..	338.9	49.5	....	5.5	76.8	115.8	7.8	7.6
Other capital transfers	2 410 ..	....	....	....	....	....	....	....	....
Other sectors	2 430 ..	....	....	....	....	86.5	86.5	86.6	86.6
Migrants' transfers	2 431 ..	....	....	....	....	....	....	....	....
Debt forgiveness	2 432 ..	....	....	....	....	....	....	....	....
Other capital transfers	2 440 ..	....	....	....	....	86.5	86.5	86.6	86.6
Capital transfers, debit	3 400 ..	....	....	....	....	....	....	....	....
General government	3 401 ..	....	....	....	....	....	....	....	....
Debt forgiveness	3 402 ..	....	....	....	....	....	....	....	....
Other capital transfers	3 410 ..	....	....	....	....	....	....	....	....
Other sectors	3 430 ..	....	....	....	....	....	....	....	....
Migrants' transfers	3 431 ..	....	....	....	....	....	....	....	....
Debt forgiveness	3 432 ..	....	....	....	....	....	....	....	....
Other capital transfers	3 440 ..	....	....	....	....	....	....	....	....
Nonproduced nonfinancial assets, credit	2 480 ..	....	....	....	....	....	....	....	....
Nonproduced nonfinancial assets, debit	3 480 ..	....	....	....	....	....	....	....	....

Table 2 (Continued). STANDARD PRESENTATION, 2000–2007

(Millions of U.S. dollars)

	Code	2000	2001	2002	2003	2004	2005	2006	2007
FINANCIAL ACCOUNT	4 995 ..	−1,970.6	−606.7	−581.5	−310.6	−441.2	−1,039.7	−479.9	1,101.1
A. DIRECT INVESTMENT	4 500 ..	6.4	155.1	114.3	−89.1	143.6	−302.1	1,121.0	917.3
Direct investment abroad	4 505 ..	....	....	....	....	....	....	....	....
Equity capital	4 510 ..	....	....	....	....	....	....	....	....
Claims on affiliated enterprises	4 515 ..	....	....	....	....	....	....	....	....
Liabilities to affiliated enterprises	4 520 ..	....	....	....	....	....	....	....	....
Reinvested earnings	4 525 ..	....	....	....	....	....	....	....	....
Other capital	4 530 ..	....	....	....	....	....	....	....	....
Claims on affiliated enterprises	4 535 ..	....	....	....	....	....	....	....	....
Liabilities to affiliated enterprises	4 540 ..	....	....	....	....	....	....	....	....
Direct investment in the Republic of Yemen	4 555 ..	6.4	155.1	114.3	−89.1	143.6	−302.1	1,121.0	917.3
Equity capital	4 560 ..	6.4	135.5	....	−200.0	....	....	....	40.4
Claims on direct investors	4 565 ..	....	....	....	....	....	....	....	....
Liabilities to direct investors	4 570 ..	6.4	135.5	....	−200.0	....	....	....	40.4
Reinvested earnings	4 575 ..	....	....	....	....	....	....	....	....
Other capital	4 580 ..	....	19.7	114.3	110.9	143.6	−302.1	1,121.0	876.9
Claims on direct investors	4 585 ..	....	....	....	....	....	....	....	....
Liabilities to direct investors	4 590 ..	....	19.7	114.3	110.9	143.6	−302.1	1,121.0	876.9
B. PORTFOLIO INVESTMENT	4 600 ..	.1	−1.4	−5.8	−.4	−6.4	−14.2	−34.0	−8.5
Assets	4 602 ..	.1	−1.4	−5.8	−.4	−6.4	−14.2	−34.0	−8.5
Equity securities	4 610 ..	.1	−1.4	−5.8	−.4	−6.4	−14.2	−34.0	−8.5
Monetary authorities	4 611 ..	....	....	....	....	....	....	....	....
General government	4 612 ..	....	....	....	....	....	....	....	....
Banks	4 613 ..	.1	−1.4	−5.8	−.4	−6.4	−14.2	−34.0	−8.5
Other sectors	4 614 ..	....	....	....	....	....	....	....	....
Debt securities	4 619 ..	....	....	....	....	....	....	....	....
Bonds and notes	4 620 ..	....	....	....	....	....	....	....	....
Monetary authorities	4 621 ..	....	....	....	....	....	....	....	....
General government	4 622 ..	....	....	....	....	....	....	....	....
Banks	4 623 ..	....	....	....	....	....	....	....	....
Other sectors	4 624 ..	....	....	....	....	....	....	....	....
Money market instruments	4 630 ..	....	....	....	....	....	....	....	....
Monetary authorities	4 631 ..	....	....	....	....	....	....	....	....
General government	4 632 ..	....	....	....	....	....	....	....	....
Banks	4 633 ..	....	....	....	....	....	....	....	....
Other sectors	4 634 ..	....	....	....	....	....	....	....	....
Liabilities	4 652 ..	....	....	....	....	....	....	....	....
Equity securities	4 660 ..	....	....	....	....	....	....	....	....
Banks	4 663 ..	....	....	....	....	....	....	....	....
Other sectors	4 664 ..	....	....	....	....	....	....	....	....
Debt securities	4 669 ..	....	....	....	....	....	....	....	....
Bonds and notes	4 670 ..	....	....	....	....	....	....	....	....
Monetary authorities	4 671 ..	....	....	....	....	....	....	....	....
General government	4 672 ..	....	....	....	....	....	....	....	....
Banks	4 673 ..	....	....	....	....	....	....	....	....
Other sectors	4 674 ..	....	....	....	....	....	....	....	....
Money market instruments	4 680 ..	....	....	....	....	....	....	....	....
Monetary authorities	4 681 ..	....	....	....	....	....	....	....	....
General government	4 682 ..	....	....	....	....	....	....	....	....
Banks	4 683 ..	....	....	....	....	....	....	....	....
Other sectors	4 684 ..	....	....	....	....	....	....	....	....
C. FINANCIAL DERIVATIVES	4 910 ..	....	....	....	....	....	....	....	....
Monetary authorities	4 911 ..	....	....	....	....	....	....	....	....
General government	4 912 ..	....	....	....	....	....	....	....	....
Banks	4 913 ..	....	....	....	....	....	....	....	....
Other sectors	4 914 ..	....	....	....	....	....	....	....	....
Assets	4 900 ..	....	....	....	....	....	....	....	....
Monetary authorities	4 901 ..	....	....	....	....	....	....	....	....
General government	4 902 ..	....	....	....	....	....	....	....	....
Banks	4 903 ..	....	....	....	....	....	....	....	....
Other sectors	4 904 ..	....	....	....	....	....	....	....	....
Liabilities	4 905 ..	....	....	....	....	....	....	....	....
Monetary authorities	4 906 ..	....	....	....	....	....	....	....	....
General government	4 907 ..	....	....	....	....	....	....	....	....
Banks	4 908 ..	....	....	....	....	....	....	....	....
Other sectors	4 909 ..	....	....	....	....	....	....	....	....

Table 2 (Concluded). STANDARD PRESENTATION, 2000–2007

(Millions of U.S. dollars)

	Code	2000	2001	2002	2003	2004	2005	2006	2007
D. OTHER INVESTMENT	4 700 ..	**−547.7**	**.9**	**−133.2**	**105.3**	**−46.0**	**−10.1**	**−165.8**	**108.7**
Assets	4 703 ..	**−177.9**	**5.6**	**−124.5**	**49.1**	**−25.4**	**−81.6**	**−387.1**	**−87.8**
Trade credits	4 706 ..	....	75.6	−57.6	−18.9	−5.7	−109.0	91.1	−89.1
General government	4 707 ..	....	75.6	−57.6		−5.7	−109.0	91.1	−89.1
of which: Short-term	4 709 ..	....	*75.6*	*−57.6*	....	*−5.7*	*−109.0*	*91.1*	*−89.1*
Other sectors	4 710 ..	....	....	....	−18.9	....	....	....	....
of which: Short-term	4 712 ..	....	....	....	*−18.9*	....	....	....	....
Loans	4 714 ..		....	....	....	....	....	....	....
Monetary authorities	4 715 ..	....		....	....	....	....	....	....
of which: Short-term	4 718 ..	....	....	....	....	....	....	....	....
General government	4 719 ..	....	....	....	....	....	....	....	....
of which: Short-term	4 721 ..	....	....	....	....	....	....	....	....
Banks	4 722 ..	....	....	....	....	....	....	....	....
of which: Short-term	4 724 ..	....	....	....	....	....	....	....	....
Other sectors	4 725 ..	....	....	....	....	....	....	....	....
of which: Short-term	4 727 ..	....	....	....	....	....	....	....	....
Currency and deposits	4 730 ..	−177.9	−70.0	−66.9	68.0	−19.7	27.4	−478.1	1.4
Monetary authorities	4 731 ..	....	....	....	....	....	....	....	....
General government	4 732 ..	....	....	....	....	....	....	....	....
Banks	4 733 ..	−177.9	−70.0	−147.7	−12.8	−19.7	27.4	−478.1	1.4
Other sectors	4 734 ..	....	....	80.8	80.8	....	....	....	....
Other assets	4 736 ..	....	....	....	....	....	....	....	....
Monetary authorities	4 737 ..	....	....	....	....	....	....	....	....
of which: Short-term	4 739 ..	....	....	....	....	....	....	....	....
General government	4 740 ..	....	....	....	....	....	....	....	....
of which: Short-term	4 742 ..	....	....	....	....	....	....	....	....
Banks	4 743 ..	....	....	....	....	....	....	....	....
of which: Short-term	4 745 ..	....	....	....	....	....	....	....	....
Other sectors	4 746 ..	....	....	....	....	....	....	....	....
of which: Short-term	4 748 ..	....	....	....	....	....	....	....	....
Liabilities	4 753 ..	**−369.7**	**−4.7**	**−8.6**	**56.2**	**−20.6**	**71.5**	**221.3**	**196.5**
Trade credits	4 756 ..	−17.7	....	....	....	....	....	....	....
General government	4 757 ..	−17.7	....	....	....	....	....	....	....
of which: Short-term	4 759 ..	....	....	....	....	....	....	....	....
Other sectors	4 760 ..	....	....	....	....	....	....	....	....
of which: Short-term	4 762 ..	....	....	....	....	....	....	....	....
Loans	4 764 ..	−2.8	49.7	−8.6	40.9	−30.2	69.1	218.8	194.3
Monetary authorities	4 765 ..	−79.0	57.5	−39.6	−30.2	−86.9	−50.4	−54.3	−77.8
of which: Use of Fund credit and loans from the Fund	4 766 ..	*−71.0*	*69.0*	*−17.2*	*−19.3*	*−41.2*	*−55.8*	*−60.1*	*−86.8*
of which: Short-term	4 768 ..	*3.7*	*4.4*	*−8.6*	*5.5*	*4.7*	*5.4*	*5.7*	*9.0*
General government	4 769 ..	65.3	21.9	39.1	68.1	25.8	110.6	236.4	231.9
of which: Short-term	4 771 ..	....	....	....	....	....	....	....	....
Banks	4 772 ..	11.0	−29.7	−8.1	2.9	30.9	8.9	36.8	40.3
of which: Short-term	4 774 ..	*22.7*	*−17.2*	*2.4*	*2.9*	*30.9*	*8.9*	*36.8*	*40.3*
Other sectors	4 775 ..	....	....	....	....	....	....	....	....
of which: Short-term	4 777 ..	....	....	....	....	....	....	....	....
Currency and deposits	4 780 ..	....	....	....	....	....	....	....	....
Monetary authorities	4 781 ..	....	....	....	....	....	....	....	....
General government	4 782 ..	....	....	....	....	....	....	....	....
Banks	4 783 ..	....	....	....	....	....	....	....	....
Other sectors	4 784 ..	....	....	....	....	....	....	....	....
Other liabilities	4 786 ..	−349.2	−54.4	....	15.3	9.5	2.5	2.5	2.2
Monetary authorities	4 787 ..	....	....	....	....	....	....	....	....
of which: Short-term	4 789 ..	....	....	....	....	....	....	....	....
General government	4 790 ..	−349.2	−54.4	....	15.3	9.5	2.5	2.5	2.2
of which: Short-term	4 792 ..	*−349.2*	*−54.4*	....	*15.3*	*9.5*	*2.5*	*2.5*	*2.2*
Banks	4 793 ..	....	....	....	....	....	....	....	....
of which: Short-term	4 795 ..	....	....	....	....	....	....	....	....
Other sectors	4 796 ..	....	....	....	....	....	....	....	....
of which: Short-term	4 798 ..	....	....	....	....	....	....	....	....
E. RESERVE ASSETS	4 802 ..	**−1,429.4**	**−761.3**	**−556.9**	**−326.3**	**−532.3**	**−713.4**	**−1,401.2**	**83.5**
Monetary gold	4 812 ..	....	....	....	....	....	....	....	....
Special drawing rights	4 811 ..	83.1	63.9	−22.6	42.2	−45.2	29.6	12.3	7.3
Reserve position in the Fund	4 810 ..	....	....	....	....	....	....	....	....
Foreign exchange	4 803 ..	−1,512.5	−825.2	−534.3	−368.4	−487.1	−742.9	−1,413.5	76.2
Other claims	4 813 ..	....	....	....	....	....	....	....	....
NET ERRORS AND OMISSIONS	4 998 ..	**295.1**	**−110.0**	**43.3**	**156.4**	**53.3**	**213.3**	**179.8**	**132.4**

Table 3. INTERNATIONAL INVESTMENT POSITION (End-period stocks), 2000–2007

(Millions of U.S. dollars)

	Code	2000	2001	2002	2003	2004	2005	2006	2007
ASSETS	8 995 C.	**3,686.8**	**4,441.7**	**5,405.6**	**6,020.7**	**6,744.8**	**7,290.4**	**9,121.0**	....
Direct investment abroad	8 505 ..	....	....	....	....	....	....	....	....
Equity capital and reinvested earnings	8 506 ..	....	....	....	....	....	....	....	....
Claims on affiliated enterprises	8 507 ..	....	....	....	....	....	....	....	....
Liabilities to affiliated enterprises	8 508 ..	....	....	....	....	....	....	....	....
Other capital	8 530 ..	....	....	....	....	....	....	....	....
Claims on affiliated enterprises	8 535 ..	....	....	....	....	....	....	....	....
Liabilities to affiliated enterprises	8 540 ..	....	....	....	....	....	....	....	....
Portfolio investment	8 602 ..	**.3**	**1.7**	**7.5**	**7.9**	**14.4**	**28.5**	**62.5**	....
Equity securities	8 610 ..	.3	1.7	7.5	7.9	14.4	28.5	62.5	....
Monetary authorities	8 611 ..	....	....	....	....	....	....	....	....
General government	8 612 ..	....	....	....	....	....	....	....	....
Banks	8 613 ..	.3	1.7	7.5	7.9	14.4	28.5	62.5	....
Other sectors	8 614 ..	....	....	....	....	....	....	....	....
Debt securities	8 619 ..	....	....	....	....	....	....	....	....
Bonds and notes	8 620 ..	....	....	....	....	....	....	....	....
Monetary authorities	8 621 ..	....	....	....	....	....	....	....	....
General government	8 622 ..	....	....	....	....	....	....	....	....
Banks	8 623 ..	....	....	....	....	....	....	....	....
Other sectors	8 624 ..	....	....	....	....	....	....	....	....
Money market instruments	8 630 ..	....	....	....	....	....	....	....	....
Monetary authorities	8 631 ..	....	....	....	....	....	....	....	....
General government	8 632 ..	....	....	....	....	....	....	....	....
Banks	8 633 ..	....	....	....	....	....	....	....	....
Other sectors	8 634 ..	....	....	....	....	....	....	....	....
Financial derivatives	8 900 ..	....	....	....	....	....	....	....	....
Monetary authorities	8 901 ..	....	....	....	....	....	....	....	....
General government	8 902 ..	....	....	....	....	....	....	....	....
Banks	8 903 ..	....	....	....	....	....	....	....	....
Other sectors	8 904 ..	....	....	....	....	....	....	....	....
Other investment	8 703 ..	**772.9**	**767.3**	**972.5**	**1,004.3**	**1,043.2**	**1,119.2**	**1,514.2**	....
Trade credits	8 706 ..	149.1	73.5	131.0	149.9	155.6	258.9	175.7	....
General government	8 707 ..	149.1	73.5	131.0	149.9	155.6	258.9	167.8	....
of which: Short-term	8 709 ..	*149.1*	*73.5*	*131.0*	*149.9*	*155.6*	*258.9*	*167.8*	....
Other sectors	8 710 ..	....	....	....	....	....	....	7.9	....
of which: Short-term	8 712 ..	....	....	....	....	....	....	*7.9*	....
Loans	8 714 ..	....	....	....	....	7.9	7.9	7.9	....
Monetary authorities	8 715 ..	....	....	....	....	....	....	....	....
of which: Short-term	8 718 ..	....	....	....	....	....	....	....	....
General government	8 719 ..	....	....	....	....	....	....	....	....
of which: Short-term	8 721 ..	....	....	....	....	....	....	....	....
Banks	8 722 ..	....	....	....	....	....	....	....	....
of which: Short-term	8 724 ..	....	....	....	....	....	....	....	....
Other sectors	8 725 ..	....	....	....	....	7.9	7.9	7.9	....
of which: Short-term	8 727 ..	....	....	....	....	*7.9*	*7.9*	*7.9*	....
Currency and deposits	8 730 ..	623.8	693.8	841.5	854.4	874.4	847.1	1,325.2	....
Monetary authorities	8 731 ..	....	....	....	....	....	....	....	....
General government	8 732 ..	....	....	....	....	....	....	....	....
Banks	8 733 ..	623.8	693.8	841.5	854.4	874.1	846.8	1,324.9	....
Other sectors	8 734 ..	....	....	....	....	.3	.3	.3	....
Other assets	8 736 ..	....	....	....	....	5.3	5.3	5.3	....
Monetary authorities	8 737 ..	....	....	....	....	....	....	....	....
of which: Short-term	8 739 ..	....	....	....	....	....	....	....	....
General government	8 740 ..	....	....	....	....	....	....	....	....
of which: Short-term	8 742 ..	....	....	....	....	....	....	....	....
Banks	8 743 ..	....	....	....	....	....	....	....	....
of which: Short-term	8 745 ..	....	....	....	....	5.3	5.3	5.3	....
Other sectors	8 746 ..	....	....	....	....	5.3	5.3	5.3	....
of which: Short-term	8 748 ..	....	....	....	....	*5.3*	*5.3*	*5.3*	....
Reserve assets	8 802 ..	**2,913.6**	**3,672.7**	**4,425.6**	**5,008.5**	**5,687.2**	**6,142.6**	**7,544.4**	....
Monetary gold	8 812 ..	....	....	....	....	....	....	....	....
Special drawing rights	8 811 ..	84.6	18.5	44.9	4.9	51.3	18.8	7.1	....
Reserve position in the Fund	8 810 ..	....	....	....	....	....	....	....	....
Foreign exchange	8 803 ..	2,829.0	3,654.2	4,380.7	5,003.6	5,635.9	6,123.8	7,537.3	....
Other claims	8 813 ..	....	....	....	....	....	....	....	....

Table 3 (Concluded). INTERNATIONAL INVESTMENT POSITION (End-period stocks), 2000–2007

(Millions of U.S. dollars)

	Code	2000	2001	2002	2003	2004	2005	2006	2007
LIABILITIES	8 995 D.	**6,372.9**	**6,006.5**	**6,092.8**	**6,543.6**	**6,825.2**	**6,180.0**	**7,646.2**	....
Direct investment in the Republic of Yemen	8 555	**843.0**	**998.1**	**1,112.4**	**1,010.7**	**1,248.9**	**803.3**	**1,924.3**	....
Equity capital and reinvested earnings	8 556	....	....	....	....	....	....	....	....
Claims on direct investors	8 557	....	....	....	....	....	....	....	....
Liabilities to direct investors	8 558	....	....	....	....	....	....	....	....
Other capital	8 580	843.0	998.1	1,112.4	1,010.7	1,248.9	803.3	1,924.3	....
Claims on direct investors	8 585	....	....	....	....	....	....	....	....
Liabilities to direct investors	8 590	843.0	998.1	1,112.4	1,010.7	1,248.9	803.3	1,924.3	....
Portfolio investment	8 652	....	....	....	....	....	....	....	....
Equity securities	8 660	....	....	....	....	....	....	....	....
Banks	8 663	....	....	....	....	....	....	....	....
Other sectors	8 664	....	....	....	....	....	....	....	....
Debt securities	8 669	....	....	....	....	....	....	....	....
Bonds and notes	8 670	....	....	....	....	....	....	....	....
Monetary authorities	8 671	....	....	....	....	....	....	....	....
General government	8 672	....	....	....	....	....	....	....	....
Banks	8 673	....	....	....	....	....	....	....	....
Other sectors	8 674	....	....	....	....	....	....	....	....
Money market instruments	8 680	....	....	....	....	....	....	....	....
Monetary authorities	8 681	....	....	....	....	....	....	....	....
General government	8 682	....	....	....	....	....	....	....	....
Banks	8 683	....	....	....	....	....	....	....	....
Other sectors	8 684	....	....	....	....	....	....	....	....
Financial derivatives	8 905	....	....	....	....	....	....	....	....
Monetary authorities	8 906	....	....	....	....	....	....	....	....
General government	8 907	....	....	....	....	....	....	....	....
Banks	8 908	....	....	....	....	....	....	....	....
Other sectors	8 909	....	....	....	....	....	....	....	....
Other investment	8 753	**5,529.9**	**5,008.4**	**4,980.3**	**5,532.9**	**5,576.3**	**5,376.7**	**5,721.9**	....
Trade credits	8 756	55.6	....	....	....	....	....	....	....
General government	8 757	55.6	....	....	....	....	....	....	....
of which: Short-term	8 759	....	....	....	....	....	....	....	....
Other sectors	8 760	....	....	....	....	....	....	....	....
of which: Short-term	8 762	....	....	....	....	....	....	....	....
Loans	8 764	5,474.3	5,008.4	4,980.3	5,532.9	5,576.3	5,376.7	5,721.9	....
Monetary authorities	8 765	538.0	596.3	576.4	586.5	515.4	436.9	396.5	....
of which: Use of Fund credit and loans from the Fund	8 766	317.3	373.7	385.8	401.4	376.2	292.3	246.2	169.2
of which: Short-term	8 768	133.2	137.5	129.0	134.5	139.2	144.6	150.3	....
General government	8 769	4,879.7	4,385.2	4,385.2	4,924.8	5,006.4	4,876.5	5,225.2	....
of which: Short-term	8 771	....	....	....	....	....	....	....	....
Banks	8 772	56.5	26.9	18.7	21.7	52.6	61.5	98.3	....
of which: Short-term	8 774	33.5	16.3	18.7	21.7	52.6	61.5	98.3	....
Other sectors	8 775	....	....	....	....	1.9	1.9	1.9	....
of which: Short-term	8 777	....	....	....	....	1.6	1.6	1.6	....
Currency and deposits	8 780	....	....	....	....	....	....	....	....
Monetary authorities	8 781	....	....	....	....	....	....	....	....
General government	8 782	....	....	....	....	....	....	....	....
Banks	8 783	....	....	....	....	....	....	....	....
Other sectors	8 784	....	....	....	....	....	....	....	....
Other liabilities	8 786	....	....	....	....	....	....	....	....
Monetary authorities	8 787	....	....	....	....	....	....	....	....
of which: Short-term	8 789	....	....	....	....	....	....	....	....
General government	8 790	....	....	....	....	....	....	....	....
of which: Short-term	8 792	....	....	....	....	....	....	....	....
Banks	8 793	....	....	....	....	....	....	....	....
of which: Short-term	8 795	....	....	....	....	....	....	....	....
Other sectors	8 796	....	....	....	....	....	....	....	....
of which: Short-term	8 798	....	....	....	....	....	....	....	....
NET INTERNATIONAL INVESTMENT POSITION	8 995	−2,686.1	−1,564.8	−687.2	−522.9	−80.4	1,110.4	1,474.8	....
Conversion rates: Yemeni rials per U.S. dollar (end of period)	0 102	165.590	173.270	179.010	184.310	185.870	195.080	198.500	199.540

Table 1. ANALYTIC PRESENTATION, 2000–2007

(Millions of U.S. dollars)

	Code	2000	2001	2002	2003	2004	2005	2006	2007
A. Current Account[1]	4 993 Z.	**−622.6**	**−724.4**	**−642.5**	**−707.2**	**−463.2**	**−730.7**	**−78.5**	**−780.3**
Goods: exports f.o.b.	2 100 ..	757.0	910.8	989.1	1,086.5	1,844.5	2,246.8	3,928.9	4,593.7
Goods: imports f.o.b.	3 100 ..	−977.7	−1,252.9	−1,204.0	−1,392.5	−1,726.9	−2,160.8	−2,635.8	−3,610.6
Balance on Goods	4 100 ..	*−220.7*	*−342.1*	*−214.8*	*−306.0*	*117.6*	*86.1*	*1,293.1*	*983.1*
Services: credit	2 200 ..	115.0	144.0	115.3	165.0	231.8	273.3	228.1	278.6
Services: debit	3 200 ..	−334.6	−366.6	−374.8	−403.4	−447.3	−470.8	−586.9	−913.9
Balance on Goods and Services	4 991 ..	*−440.3*	*−564.7*	*−474.3*	*−544.4*	*−97.9*	*−111.4*	*934.3*	*347.9*
Income: credit	2 300 ..	19.4	21.4	41.6	32.0	32.0	12.6	18.4	35.2
Income: debit	3 300 ..	−183.7	−161.1	−189.8	−176.6	−381.8	−607.8	−1,186.7	−1,418.6
Balance on Goods, Services, and Income	4 992 ..	*−604.6*	*−704.4*	*−622.5*	*−689.0*	*−447.7*	*−706.6*	*−234.0*	*−1,035.5*
Current transfers: credit	2 379 Z.	....	....	....	36.3	48.4	52.9	248.2	351.1
Current transfers: debit	3 379 ..	−18.0	−20.0	−20.0	−54.5	−63.9	−77.0	−92.7	−95.9
B. Capital Account[1]	4 994 Z.	**152.7**	**222.0**	**236.0**	**240.0**	**239.0**	**287.0**	**197.0**	**222.8**
Capital account: credit	2 994 Z.	152.7	222.0	236.0	240.0	239.0	287.0	197.0	222.8
Capital account: debit	3 994 ..	....	....	....	....	....	....	....	....
Total, Groups A Plus B	4 981 ..	*−469.9*	*−502.4*	*−406.5*	*−467.2*	*−224.2*	*−443.7*	*118.5*	*−557.5*
C. Financial Account[1]	4 995 W.	**134.5**	**287.2**	**204.1**	**406.5**	**77.6**	**−1,567.3**	**−1,606.0**	**728.8**
Direct investment abroad	4 505 ..	....	....	....	....	....	....	....	....
Direct investment in Zambia	4 555 Z.	121.7	71.7	303.4	347.0	363.4	357.0	615.8	983.9
Portfolio investment assets	4 602 ..	....	....	....	....	....	....	....	....
Equity securities	4 610 ..	....	....	....	....	....	....	....	....
Debt securities	4 619 ..	....	....	....	....	....	....	....	....
Portfolio investment liabilties	4 652 Z.	5.6	7.5	−.3	2.3	−.1	122.4	50.4	41.8
Equity securities	4 660 ..	5.6	7.5	−.3	2.3	−.1	5.3	2.0	3.8
Debt securities	4 669 Z.	....	....	....	....	....	117.1	48.5	38.0
Financial derivatives	4 910 ..	....	....	....	....	....	....	....	....
Financial derivatives assets	4 900 ..	....	....	....	....	....	....	....	....
Financial derivatives liabilties	4 905 ..	....	....	....	....	....	....	....	....
Other investment assets	4 703 ..	−85.5	19.3	−26.7	45.8	−199.7	−225.6	−508.0	−647.7
Monetary authorities	4 701 ..	....	....	....	....	....	....	....	....
General government	4 704 ..	....	....	....	....	....	....	....	....
Banks	4 705 ..	−85.5	19.3	−26.7	45.8	−96.3	−15.4	−94.4	−164.1
Other sectors	4 728 ..	....	....	....	....	−103.4	−210.3	−413.6	−483.6
Other investment liabilities	4 753 W.	92.7	188.8	−72.3	11.5	−86.2	−1,821.1	−1,764.2	350.9
Monetary authorities	4 753 WA	−7.4	−5.1	−5.1	−6.4	−6.0	−6.3	....	....
General government	4 753 ZB	−53.2	−23.9	−41.0	−82.5	−200.3	−1,857.8	−1,779.3	33.9
Banks	4 753 ZC	6.4	−3.0	20.8	2.1	6.2	102.9	32.7	114.2
Other sectors	4 753 ZD	146.9	220.7	−47.0	98.2	114.0	−59.9	−17.6	202.8
Total, Groups A Through C	4 983 ..	*−335.5*	*−215.2*	*−202.4*	*−60.7*	*−146.7*	*−2,011.0*	*−1,487.4*	*171.3*
D. Net Errors and Omissions	4 998 ..	**316.1**	**−470.0**	**−417.6**	**−398.5**	**−90.2**	**−75.1**	**−303.2**	**−139.8**
Total, Groups A Through D	4 984 ..	*−19.3*	*−685.2*	*−620.0*	*−459.2*	*−236.8*	*−2,086.1*	*−1,790.6*	*31.5*
E. Reserves and Related Items	4 802 A.	**19.3**	**685.2**	**620.0**	**459.2**	**236.8**	**2,086.1**	**1,790.6**	**−31.5**
Reserve assets	4 802 ..	−245.3	105.8	−163.6	−20.4	−64.4	−86.6	−260.7	−348.2
Use of Fund credit and loans	4 766 ..	26.0	−114.6	−45.5	−243.0	−6.8	−231.4	−558.4	41.8
Exceptional financing	4 920 ..	238.6	694.0	829.1	722.6	308.1	2,404.1	2,609.8	274.9
Conversion rates: Zambian kwacha per U.S. dollar	0 101 ..	**3,110.8**	**3,610.9**	**4,398.6**	**4,733.3**	**4,778.9**	**4,463.5**	**3,603.1**	**4,002.5**

[1] Excludes components that have been classified in the categories of Group E.

Table 2. STANDARD PRESENTATION, 2000–2007

(Millions of U.S. dollars)

	Code	2000	2001	2002	2003	2004	2005	2006	2007
CURRENT ACCOUNT	4 993	−591.0	−693.4	−546.4	−642.2	−419.1	−599.6	127.9	−505.4
A. GOODS	4 100	−220.7	−342.1	−214.8	−306.0	117.6	86.1	1,293.1	983.1
Credit	2 100	757.0	910.8	989.1	1,086.5	1,844.5	2,246.8	3,928.9	4,593.7
General merchandise: exports f.o.b.	2 110	746.3	884.1	965.2	1,065.0	1,824.7	2,208.1	3,876.8	4,537.3
Goods for processing: exports f.o.b.	2 150	....	....	....	....	....	....	....	....
Repairs on goods	2 160	....	....	....	....	....	....	....	....
Goods procured in ports by carriers	2 170	10.7	26.7	23.9	21.5	19.8	32.0	33.6	35.3
Nonmonetary gold	2 180	....	....	....	....	....	6.7	18.5	21.1
Debit	3 100	−977.7	−1,252.9	−1,204.0	−1,392.5	−1,726.9	−2,160.8	−2,635.8	−3,610.6
General merchandise: imports f.o.b.	3 110	−977.7	−1,252.9	−1,204.0	−1,392.5	−1,726.9	−2,160.8	−2,635.8	−3,610.6
Goods for processing: imports f.o.b.	3 150	....	....	....	....	....	....	....	....
Repairs on goods	3 160	....	....	....	....	....	....	....	....
Goods procured in ports by carriers	3 170	....	....	....	....	....	....	....	....
Nonmonetary gold	3 180	....	....	....	....	....	....	....	....
B. SERVICES	4 200	−219.6	−222.6	−259.5	−238.4	−215.5	−197.5	−358.8	−635.3
Total credit	2 200	*115.0*	*144.0*	*115.3*	*165.0*	*231.8*	*273.3*	*228.1*	*278.6*
Total debit	3 200	*−334.6*	*−366.6*	*−374.8*	*−403.4*	*−447.3*	*−470.8*	*−586.9*	*−913.9*
Transportation services, credit	2 205	**42.6**	**53.7**	**40.1**	**42.6**	**48.2**	**85.9**	**86.3**	**96.2**
Passenger	2 850	....	....	....	....	....	....	....	....
Freight	2 851	*42.6*	*53.7*	*40.1*	*42.6*	*48.2*	*85.9*	*86.3*	*96.2*
Other	2 852	....	....	....	....	....	....	....	....
Sea transport, passenger	2 207	....	....	....	....	....	....	....	....
Sea transport, freight	2 208	....	....	....	....	....	....	....	....
Sea transport, other	2 209	....	....	....	....	....	....	....	....
Air transport, passenger	2 211	....	....	....	....	....	....	....	....
Air transport, freight	2 212	....	....	....	....	....	....	....	....
Air transport, other	2 213	....	....	....	....	....	....	....	....
Other transport, passenger	2 215	....	....	....	....	....	....	....	....
Other transport, freight	2 216	42.6	53.7	40.1	42.6	48.2	85.9	86.3	96.2
Other transport, other	2 217	....	....	....	....	....	....	....	....
Transportation services, debit	3 205	**−202.3**	**−227.3**	**−229.1**	**−234.9**	**−230.9**	**−272.9**	**−315.2**	**−411.7**
Passenger	3 850	*−58.4*	*−58.4*	*−61.6*	*−66.3*	*−30.9*	*−30.0*	*−29.1*	*−41.9*
Freight	3 851	*−88.9*	*−113.9*	*−109.5*	*−126.6*	*−157.0*	*−196.4*	*−239.6*	*−328.3*
Other	3 852	*−55.0*	*−55.0*	*−58.0*	*−42.0*	*−43.0*	*−46.5*	*−46.5*	*−41.5*
Sea transport, passenger	3 207	....	....	....	....	....	....	....	....
Sea transport, freight	3 208	....	....	....	....	....	....	....	....
Sea transport, other	3 209	....	....	....	....	....	....	....	....
Air transport, passenger	3 211	....	....	....	....	....	....	....	....
Air transport, freight	3 212	....	....	....	....	....	....	....	....
Air transport, other	3 213	....	....	....	....	....	....	....	....
Other transport, passenger	3 215	−58.4	−58.4	−61.6	−66.3	−30.9	−30.0	−29.1	−41.9
Other transport, freight	3 216	−88.9	−113.9	−109.5	−126.6	−157.0	−196.4	−239.6	−328.3
Other transport, other	3 217	−55.0	−55.0	−58.0	−42.0	−43.0	−46.5	−46.5	−41.5
Travel, credit	2 236	**66.5**	**79.8**	**63.8**	**87.7**	**91.7**	**98.4**	**110.0**	**137.8**
Business travel	2 237	66.5	79.8	63.8	87.7	91.7	98.4	110.0	137.8
Personal travel	2 240	....	....	....	....	....	....	....	....
Travel, debit	3 236	**−43.6**	**−43.6**	**−47.1**	**−48.6**	**−54.9**	**−58.0**	**−68.0**	**−55.7**
Business travel	3 237	−39.7	−39.7	−43.0	−44.0	−50.0	−53.0	−63.0	−50.7
Personal travel	3 240	−3.9	−3.9	−4.1	−4.6	−4.9	−5.0	−5.0	−5.0
Other services, credit	2 200 BA	**5.9**	**10.5**	**11.4**	**34.7**	**91.9**	**89.0**	**31.8**	**44.6**
Communications	2 245	.1	4.1	4.3	4.5	10.3	12.0	13.2	14.7
Construction	2 249	....	....	....	....	....	....	....	....
Insurance	2 253	5.1	5.6	6.2	6.8	10.5	8.0	8.5	9.5
Financial	2 260	....	....	....	....	....	....	....	8.5
Computer and information	2 262	....	....	....	....	....	....	8.0	8.9
Royalties and licence fees	2 266	....	....	....	....	....	....	....	....
Other business services	2 268	....	....	....	....	....	3.0	2.1	3.0
Personal, cultural, and recreational	2 287	....	....	....	....	....	....	....	....
Government, n.i.e.	2 291	.8	.8	.9	23.4	71.1	66.0	....	....
Other services, debit	3 200 BA	**−88.7**	**−95.7**	**−98.6**	**−119.9**	**−161.5**	**−139.9**	**−203.7**	**−446.5**
Communications	3 245	−5.0	−5.5	−5.8	−6.4	−6.7	−6.7	−6.7	−8.2
Construction	3 249	−34.7	−33.7	−35.6	−39.9	−23.4	−35.4	−82.2	−282.4
Insurance	3 253	−19.8	−25.3	−24.3	−28.1	−34.9	−43.7	−53.2	−72.9
Financial	3 260	....	....	....	....	....	−2.6	−3.1	−3.8
Computer and information	3 262	....	....	....	....	....	....	....	−3.6
Royalties and licence fees	3 266	−.4	−.4	−.4	−.4	....	−.4	−.4	−1.2
Other business services	3 268	−16.5	−17.3	−18.3	−29.5	−67.0	−26.0	−31.6	−46.3
Personal, cultural, and recreational	3 287	....	....	....	....	....	....	....	....
Government, n.i.e.	3 291	−12.3	−13.5	−14.2	−15.6	−29.5	−25.1	−26.5	−28.1

Table 2 (Continued). STANDARD PRESENTATION, 2000–2007

(Millions of U.S. dollars)

	Code	2000	2001	2002	2003	2004	2005	2006	2007
C. INCOME	4 300	**−164.3**	**−139.7**	**−148.2**	**−144.6**	**−349.8**	**−595.2**	**−1,168.3**	**−1,383.4**
Total credit	2 300	*19.4*	*21.4*	*41.6*	*32.0*	*32.0*	*12.6*	*18.4*	*35.2*
Total debit	3 300	*−183.7*	*−161.1*	*−189.8*	*−176.6*	*−381.8*	*−607.8*	*−1,186.7*	*−1,418.6*
Compensation of employees, credit	2 310	....	....	....	....	....	....	....	....
Compensation of employees, debit	3 310	**−6.1**	**−8.4**	**−17.5**	**−17.0**	**−12.2**	**−16.7**	**−22.7**	**−28.0**
Investment income, credit	2 320	**19.4**	**21.4**	**41.6**	**32.0**	**32.0**	**12.6**	**18.4**	**35.2**
Direct investment income	2 330	....	....	....	....	....	....	....	....
Dividends and distributed branch profits	2 332	....	....	....	....	....	....	....	....
Reinvested earnings and undistributed branch profits	2 333	....	....	....	....	....	....	....	....
Income on debt (interest)	2 334	....	....	....	....	....	....	....	....
Portfolio investment income	2 339	11.4	12.3	13.0	9.4	9.4	2.9	....	....
Income on equity	2 340	....	....	....	....	....	....	....	....
Income on bonds and notes	2 350	11.4	12.3	13.0	9.4	9.4	2.9	....	....
Income on money market instruments	2 360	....	....	....	....	....	....	....	....
Other investment income	2 370	8.0	9.1	28.6	22.6	22.6	9.7	18.4	35.2
Investment income, debit	3 320	**−177.6**	**−152.7**	**−172.3**	**−159.6**	**−369.6**	**−591.1**	**−1,164.0**	**−1,390.6**
Direct investment income	3 330	....	....	....	−23.9	−238.4	−461.1	−1,107.0	−1,362.0
Dividends and distributed branch profits	3 332	....	....	....	....	−198.4	−400.8	−722.6	−792.7
Reinvested earnings and undistributed branch profits	3 333	....	....	....	−23.9	−40.0	−60.3	−384.4	−569.3
Income on debt (interest)	3 334	....	....	....	....	....	....	....	....
Portfolio investment income	3 339	....	....	....	....	....	....	....	....
Income on equity	3 340	....	....	....	....	....	....	....	....
Income on bonds and notes	3 350	....	....	....	....	....	....	....	....
Income on money market instruments	3 360	....	....	....	....	....	....	....	....
Other investment income	3 370	−177.6	−152.7	−172.3	−135.7	−131.2	−130.0	−57.0	−28.6
D. CURRENT TRANSFERS	4 379	**13.6**	**11.0**	**76.1**	**46.8**	**28.6**	**107.0**	**361.9**	**530.1**
Credit	2 379	**31.6**	**31.0**	**96.1**	**101.3**	**92.5**	**184.0**	**454.6**	**626.0**
General government	2 380	31.6	31.0	96.1	65.0	44.1	131.1	208.5	302.2
Other sectors	2 390	....	....	....	36.3	48.4	52.9	246.1	323.8
Workers' remittances	2 391	....	....	....	36.3	48.4	52.9	57.7	59.3
Other current transfers	2 392	....	....	....	....	....	....	188.4	264.5
Debit	3 379	**−18.0**	**−20.0**	**−20.0**	**−54.5**	**−63.9**	**−77.0**	**−92.7**	**−95.9**
General government	3 380	....	....	....	....	....	....	....	....
Other sectors	3 390	−18.0	−20.0	−20.0	−54.5	−63.9	−77.0	−92.7	−95.9
Workers' remittances	3 391	−18.0	−20.0	−20.0	−54.5	−63.9	−77.0	−92.7	−95.9
Other current transfers	3 392	....	....	....	....	....	....	....	....
CAPITAL AND FINANCIAL ACCOUNT	4 996	**274.9**	**1,163.5**	**964.0**	**1,040.7**	**509.3**	**674.7**	**175.3**	**645.2**
CAPITAL ACCOUNT	4 994	**152.7**	**568.0**	**673.0**	**629.0**	**503.0**	**2,560.0**	**2,600.4**	**222.8**
Total credit	2 994	*152.7*	*568.0*	*673.0*	*629.0*	*503.0*	*2,560.0*	*2,600.4*	*222.8*
Total debit	3 994	....	....	....	....	....	....	....	....
Capital transfers, credit	2 400	**152.7**	**568.0**	**673.0**	**629.0**	**503.0**	**2,560.0**	**2,600.4**	**222.8**
General government	2 401	152.7	568.0	673.0	629.0	503.0	2,560.0	2,600.4	222.8
Debt forgiveness	2 402	152.7	568.0	673.0	629.0	503.0	2,560.0	2,600.4	222.8
Other capital transfers	2 410	....	....	....	....	....	....	....	....
Other sectors	2 430	....	....	....	....	....	....	....	....
Migrants' transfers	2 431	....	....	....	....	....	....	....	....
Debt forgiveness	2 432	....	....	....	....	....	....	....	....
Other capital transfers	2 440	....	....	....	....	....	....	....	....
Capital transfers, debit	3 400	....	....	....	....	....	....	....	....
General government	3 401	....	....	....	....	....	....	....	....
Debt forgiveness	3 402	....	....	....	....	....	....	....	....
Other capital transfers	3 410	....	....	....	....	....	....	....	....
Other sectors	3 430	....	....	....	....	....	....	....	....
Migrants' transfers	3 431	....	....	....	....	....	....	....	....
Debt forgiveness	3 432	....	....	....	....	....	....	....	....
Other capital transfers	3 440	....	....	....	....	....	....	....	....
Nonproduced nonfinancial assets, credit	2 480	....	....	....	....	....	....	....	....
Nonproduced nonfinancial assets, debit	3 480	....	....	....	....	....	....	....	....

Table 2 (Continued). STANDARD PRESENTATION, 2000–2007

(Millions of U.S. dollars)

	Code	2000	2001	2002	2003	2004	2005	2006	2007
FINANCIAL ACCOUNT	4 995 ..	**122.2**	**595.5**	**291.0**	**411.7**	**6.3**	**−1,885.3**	**−2,425.1**	**422.4**
A. DIRECT INVESTMENT	4 500 ..	**121.7**	**71.7**	**303.4**	**347.0**	**363.4**	**357.0**	**615.8**	**983.9**
Direct investment abroad	4 505 ..	....	....	....	....	....	....	....	....
Equity capital	4 510 ..	....	....	....	....	....	....	....	....
Claims on affiliated enterprises	4 515 ..	....	....	....	....	....	....	....	....
Liabilities to affiliated enterprises	4 520 ..	....	....	....	....	....	....	....	....
Reinvested earnings	4 525 ..	....	....	....	....	....	....	....	....
Other capital	4 530 ..	....	....	....	....	....	....	....	....
Claims on affiliated enterprises	4 535 ..	....	....	....	....	....	....	....	....
Liabilities to affiliated enterprises	4 540 ..	....	....	....	....	....	....	....	....
Direct investment in Zambia	4 555 ..	**121.7**	**71.7**	**303.4**	**347.0**	**363.4**	**357.0**	**615.8**	**983.9**
Equity capital	4 560 ..	121.7	71.7	303.4	323.1	323.4	296.7	231.4	414.6
Claims on direct investors	4 565 ..	....	....	....	....	25.0	....	....	....
Liabilities to direct investors	4 570 ..	121.7	71.7	303.4	323.1	298.4	296.7	231.4	414.6
Reinvested earnings	4 575 ..	....	....	....	23.9	40.0	60.3	384.4	569.3
Other capital	4 580 ..	....	....	....	....	....	....	....	....
Claims on direct investors	4 585 ..	....	....	....	....	....	....	....	....
Liabilities to direct investors	4 590 ..	....	....	....	....	....	....	....	....
B. PORTFOLIO INVESTMENT	4 600 ..	**5.6**	**7.5**	**−.3**	**2.3**	**−.1**	**122.4**	**50.4**	**41.8**
Assets	4 602 ..	....	....	....	....	....	....	....	....
Equity securities	4 610 ..	....	....	....	....	....	....	....	....
Monetary authorities	4 611 ..	....	....	....	....	....	....	....	....
General government	4 612 ..	....	....	....	....	....	....	....	....
Banks	4 613 ..	....	....	....	....	....	....	....	....
Other sectors	4 614 ..	....	....	....	....	....	....	....	....
Debt securities	4 619 ..								
Bonds and notes	4 620 ..								
Monetary authorities	4 621 ..	....	....	....	....	....	....	....	....
General government	4 622 ..	....	....	....	....	....	....	....	....
Banks	4 623 ..	....	....	....	....	....	....	....	....
Other sectors	4 624 ..	....	....	....	....	....	....	....	....
Money market instruments	4 630 ..	....	....	....	....	....	....	....	....
Monetary authorities	4 631 ..	....	....	....	....	....	....	....	....
General government	4 632 ..	....	....	....	....	....	....	....	....
Banks	4 633 ..	....	....	....	....	....	....	....	....
Other sectors	4 634 ..	....	....	....	....	....	....	....	....
Liabilities	4 652 ..	**5.6**	**7.5**	**−.3**	**2.3**	**−.1**	**122.4**	**50.4**	**41.8**
Equity securities	4 660 ..	5.6	7.5	−.3	2.3	−.1	5.3	2.0	3.8
Banks	4 663 ..	....	....	....	....	....	....	....	....
Other sectors	4 664 ..	5.6	7.5	−.3	2.3	−.1	5.3	2.0	3.8
Debt securities	4 669 ..	....	....	....	....	....	117.1	48.5	38.0
Bonds and notes	4 670 ..	....	....	....	....	....	28.6	15.6	23.1
Monetary authorities	4 671 ..	....	....	....	....	....	28.6	15.6	23.1
General government	4 672 ..	....	....	....	....	....	....	....	....
Banks	4 673 ..	....	....	....	....	....	....	....	....
Other sectors	4 674 ..	....	....	....	....	....	....	....	....
Money market instruments	4 680 ..	....	....	....	....	....	88.5	32.8	14.9
Monetary authorities	4 681 ..	....	....	....	....	....	88.5	32.8	14.9
General government	4 682 ..	....	....	....	....	....	....	....	....
Banks	4 683 ..	....	....	....	....	....	....	....	....
Other sectors	4 684 ..	....	....	....	....	....	....	....	....
C. FINANCIAL DERIVATIVES	4 910 ..	....	....	....	....	....	....	....	....
Monetary authorities	4 911 ..	....	....	....	....	....	....	....	....
General government	4 912 ..	....	....	....	....	....	....	....	....
Banks	4 913 ..	....	....	....	....	....	....	....	....
Other sectors	4 914 ..	....	....	....	....	....	....	....	....
Assets	4 900 ..	....	....	....	....	....	....	....	....
Monetary authorities	4 901 ..	....	....	....	....	....	....	....	....
General government	4 902 ..	....	....	....	....	....	....	....	....
Banks	4 903 ..	....	....	....	....	....	....	....	....
Other sectors	4 904 ..	....	....	....	....	....	....	....	....
Liabilities	4 905 ..	....	....	....	....	....	....	....	....
Monetary authorities	4 906 ..	....	....	....	....	....	....	....	....
General government	4 907 ..	....	....	....	....	....	....	....	....
Banks	4 908 ..	....	....	....	....	....	....	....	....
Other sectors	4 909 ..	....	....	....	....	....	....	....	....

Table 2 (Concluded). STANDARD PRESENTATION, 2000–2007

(Millions of U.S. dollars)

	Code	2000	2001	2002	2003	2004	2005	2006	2007
D. OTHER INVESTMENT	4 700 ..	**240.2**	**410.5**	**151.4**	**82.8**	**−292.6**	**−2,278.1**	**−2,830.6**	**−255.1**
Assets	4 703 ..	**−85.5**	**19.3**	**−26.7**	**45.8**	**−199.7**	**−225.6**	**−508.0**	**−647.7**
Trade credits	4 706 ..	....	....	....	....	....	....	....	....
General government	4 707 ..	....	....	....	....	....	....	....	....
of which: Short-term	4 709 ..	....	....	....	....	....	....	....	....
Other sectors	4 710 ..	....	....	....	....	....	....	....	....
of which: Short-term	4 712 ..	....	....	....	....	....	....	....	....
Loans	4 714 ..	−.2	.3	....	....	....	....	....	....
Monetary authorities	4 715 ..	....	....	....	....	....	....	....	....
of which: Short-term	4 718 ..	....	....	....	....	....	....	....	....
General government	4 719 ..	....	....	....	....	....	....	....	....
of which: Short-term	4 721 ..	....	....	....	....	....	....	....	....
Banks	4 722 ..	−.2	.3	....	....	....	....	....	....
of which: Short-term	4 724 ..	*−.2*	*.3*	....	....	....	....	....	....
Other sectors	4 725 ..	....	....	....	....	....	....	....	....
of which: Short-term	4 727 ..	....	....	....	....	....	....	....	....
Currency and deposits	4 730 ..	−85.2	19.0	−26.7	45.8	−199.7	−225.6	−508.0	−647.7
Monetary authorities	4 731 ..	....	....	....	....	....	....	....	....
General government	4 732 ..	....	....	....	....	....	....	....	....
Banks	4 733 ..	−85.2	19.0	−26.7	45.8	−96.3	−15.4	−94.4	−164.1
Other sectors	4 734 ..	....	....	....	....	−103.4	−210.3	−413.6	−483.6
Other assets	4 736 ..	....	....	....	....	....	....	....	....
Monetary authorities	4 737 ..	....	....	....	....	....	....	....	....
of which: Short-term	4 739 ..	....	....	....	....	....	....	....	....
General government	4 740 ..	....	....	....	....	....	....	....	....
of which: Short-term	4 742 ..	....	....	....	....	....	....	....	....
Banks	4 743 ..	....	....	....	....	....	....	....	....
of which: Short-term	4 745 ..	....	....	....	....	....	....	....	....
Other sectors	4 746 ..	....	....	....	....	....	....	....	....
of which: Short-term	4 748 ..	....	....	....	....	....	....	....	....
Liabilities	4 753 ..	**325.7**	**391.2**	**178.2**	**37.1**	**−93.0**	**−2,052.4**	**−2,322.6**	**392.6**
Trade credits	4 756 ..	....	....	....	.5	.5	2.1	74.0	243.7
General government	4 757 ..	....	....	....	....	....	....	....	....
of which: Short-term	4 759 ..	....	....	....	....	....	....	....	....
Other sectors	4 760 ..	....	....	....	.5	.5	2.1	74.0	243.7
of which: Short-term	4 762 ..	....	....	....	....	....	....	....	....
Loans	4 764 ..	325.8	369.8	145.4	−14.5	−99.7	−2,157.5	−2,429.3	34.7
Monetary authorities	4 765 ..	18.6	−119.7	−50.6	−249.4	−12.8	−237.7	−558.4	41.8
of which: Use of Fund credit and loans from the Fund	4 766 ..	*26.0*	*−114.6*	*−45.5*	*−243.0*	*−6.8*	*−231.4*	*−558.4*	*41.8*
of which: Short-term	4 768 ..	*−7.4*	*−5.1*	*−5.1*	*−6.4*	*−6.0*	*−6.3*	....	....
General government	4 769 ..	163.8	262.1	243.0	137.1	−200.3	−1,857.8	−1,779.3	33.9
of which: Short-term	4 771 ..	*−10.0*	*31.0*	*12.0*	*49.0*	....	....	....	....
Banks	4 772 ..	−3.5	6.7	....	....	....	....	....	....
of which: Short-term	4 774 ..	....	....	....	....	....	....	....	....
Other sectors	4 775 ..	146.9	220.7	−47.0	97.7	113.5	−62.0	−91.6	−40.9
of which: Short-term	4 777 ..	....	....	....	....	....	....	....	....
Currency and deposits	4 780 ..	9.9	−9.6	20.8	2.1	6.2	102.9	32.7	114.2
Monetary authorities	4 781 ..	....	....	....	....	....	....	....	....
General government	4 782 ..	....	....	....	....	....	....	....	....
Banks	4 783 ..	9.9	−9.6	20.8	2.1	6.2	102.9	32.7	114.2
Other sectors	4 784 ..	....	....	....	....	....	....	....	....
Other liabilities	4 786 ..	−10.0	31.0	12.0	49.0	....	....	....	....
Monetary authorities	4 787 ..	....	....	....	....	....	....	....	....
of which: Short-term	4 789 ..	....	....	....	....	....	....	....	....
General government	4 790 ..	−10.0	31.0	12.0	49.0	....	....	....	....
of which: Short-term	4 792 ..	*−10.0*	*31.0*	*12.0*	*49.0*	....	....	....	....
Banks	4 793 ..	....	....	....	....	....	....	....	....
of which: Short-term	4 795 ..	....	....	....	....	....	....	....	....
Other sectors	4 796 ..	....	....	....	....	....	....	....	....
of which: Short-term	4 798 ..	....	....	....	....	....	....	....	....
E. RESERVE ASSETS	4 802 ..	**−245.3**	**105.8**	**−163.6**	**−20.4**	**−64.4**	**−86.6**	**−260.7**	**−348.2**
Monetary gold	4 812 ..	....	....	....	....	....	....	....	....
Special drawing rights	4 811 ..	−22.3	−46.1	3.0	74.0	−23.0	6.7	3.2	4.1
Reserve position in the Fund	4 810 ..	....	....	....	....	....	....	....	....
Foreign exchange	4 803 ..	−223.0	151.9	−166.6	−94.4	−41.4	−93.3	−263.9	−352.3
Other claims	4 813 ..	....	....	....	....	....	....	....	....
NET ERRORS AND OMISSIONS	4 998 ..	**316.1**	**−470.0**	**−417.6**	**−398.5**	**−90.2**	**−75.1**	**−303.2**	**−139.8**